German Dictionary of Business, Commerce and Finance

Wörterbuch für Wirtschaft, Handel und Finanzen Englisch

Routledge

German Dictionary of Business, Commerce and Finance

Wörterbuch für Wirtschaft, Handel und Finanzen Englisch

German–English/English–German
Deutsch–Englisch/Englisch–Deutsch

London and New York

First published 1997
by Routledge
11 New Fetter Lane, London EC4P 4EE

Simultaneously published in the USA and Canada
by Routledge
29 West 35th Street, New York, NY 10001

© 1997 Routledge

Typeset in Monotype Times, Helvetica Neue and Bauer Bodoni
by Routledge

Printed in England by T.J. International Ltd, Padstow, Cornwall

Printed on acid-free paper

British Library Cataloguing-in-Publication Data
A catalogue record for this book is available from the British Library

Library of Congress Cataloging-in-Publication Data
Applied for

ISBN 0–415–09391–0

1001 189 69 X

German Dictionary of Business, Commerce and Finance
Wörterbuch für Wirtschaft, Handel und Finanzen Englisch

Project Managers/Projektleitung

Sabine Bohnacker-Bruce   Rebecca Moy

Managing Editor/Redaktionsleitung

Sinda López

Editorial/Lektorat

Martin Barr   Justine Bird   Lisa Carden
Cécile Guinard   Gemma Marren   Janice McNeillie
Jessica Ramage   Robert Timms

Programme Manager/Programmleitung

Elizabeth White

Marketing

Vanessa Markey
Rachel Miller

Systems/Datenbanksystem

Omar Raman
Simon Thompson

Administration/Verwaltung

Amanda Brindley

Production/Herstellung

Michelle Draycott   Nigel Marsh   Joanne Tinson

Contributors/Mitarbeit

Therese Apweiler
Charlotte Crawford-Ameler
Brigitte Geddes
Claudia Gehricke
Vicky Jeunhomme
Rila Lingemann
Marion Meunier-Geske

Hannelore Schatz
Brigitte Scott
Ute Scholl
Reinhard Stollberg
Ursula Wappler
Lieselotte Wlachopulos

Lexicographers & Proofreaders/Lexikographie & Korrekturlesen

Nicola Cooke
Hazel Curties
Stephen Curtis
Petra Kopp
Anke Kornmüller

Gunhild Prowe
Gillian Schneider
Martin Stark
Jill Williams

Specialist Consultants/Fachliche Beratung

Gerta Badde

Norman Bartlett
The Institute of European Trade and Technology

Peter Bond
The Chartered Institute of Bankers

Brian Clifford
Manchester Business School

Walter Chromik

Ursula Cullum

Elke Davies

Prof. Dr. Hans-Dieter Feser
Universität Kaiserlautern

Norman Hart
The Chartered Institute of Marketing

Manfred Herrmann

Lutz Höppner

Dr. Friedrich Horlacher
Universität Erlangen-Nürnberg

Susanne Kirchmeyer
Friedrich-Schiller-Universität Jena

Michael Knepper

David Mackie

Ludwig Merz

Margarete Rasch-Hönny

Robert Robin

Margit Röntgen-Bick

Rainer Schwalb

Keyboarders/Datenerfassung

Emmanuelle Bels, Beatriz Fernández, Antonio Fernández Entrena, Rosa Gálvez López,
Christiane Grosskopf, Michael Jopling, Ute Krebs, Ilona Lehmann, Géraldine Monnereau,
David Morgan, Geir Moulson, Roger Pena Muiño, Nathalie Pernstich, Fabienne Rangeard,
Beate Schmitt, Deborah Thomas

Acknowledgements

We also wish to acknowledge the valuable contribution of Flavia Hodges and Wendy Morris during the early stages of the project.

We are particularly grateful to Frank Abate and his team for checking American coverage during the compilation of this dictionary.

Danksagung

Wir möchten ebenfalls Flavia Hodges und Wendy Morris unseren Dank für ihren wertvollen Beitrag in der Frühphase des Projektes ausdrücken.

Wir bedanken uns besonders bei Frank Abate und seinem Team für das Prüfen der amerikanischen Einträge während der Zusammenstellung dieses Wörterbuches.

Contents/Inhalt

Preface/Vorwort

The *German Dictionary of Business, Commerce and Finance* is the second dictionary to be published in Routledge's programme of bilingual business dictionaries. The series was launched in December 1995 with the *French Dictionary of Business, Commerce and Finance.*

It would not have been possible to compile this dictionary within a relatively short timescale, and to the standard achieved, without the use of a highly sophisticated, custom-designed database. The database's most significant feature is that it is designed as a relational database: term records for each language are held in separate files, with further files consisting only of link records. Links between terms in different language files represent translations, enabling us to handle various types of one-to-many and many-to-one equivalences. Links between terms within a single language file represent cross-references between geographical variants and abbreviations.

The content of the database for this dictionary was created in three principal phases. A considerable proportion of the English term list was already available following the publication of the *French Dictionary of Business, Commerce and Finance.* The term list was then sent out to specialist translators – with current practical experience of business translation – who supplied German equivalences and expanded the English and German term lists to include the main relevant terminology in their particular spheres of work.

The terms in each language were then vetted by native-speaker subject specialists, working at the leading edge of their respective fields, in order to ensure the currency of the terminology, the accuracy of translations and the comprehensiveness of coverage. Finally, all the entries were reviewed by regional editors to ensure coverage of geographical variants so that this information could be incorporated into the dictionary.

The creation and editing of the database of terms was, however, only the first stage in the making of

Dieses *Wörterbuch für Wirtschaft, Handel und Finanzen Englisch* ist das zweite Wörterbuch, das im Rahmen des Programms zweisprachiger Wirtschaftswörterbücher von Routledge veröffentlicht wird. Die Reihe wurde im Dezember 1995 mit dem *French Dictionary of Business, Commerce and Finance* begonnen.

Es wäre ohne den Einsatz einer hochkomplexen, und speziell auf uns zugeschnittenen Datenbank unmöglich gewesen, dieses Wörterbuch innerhalb eines verhältnismäßig kurzen Zeitraums und in der vorliegenden Qualität zusammenzustellen. Die herausragendste Eigenschaft der Datenbank ist, daß sie als relationale Datenbank konzipiert wurde: die Datensätze zu den einzelnen Stichwörtern sind für jede Sprache in einer separaten Datei untergebracht, während weitere Dateien nur Datensätze enthalten, die die Verbindungen zwischen Ausgangs- und Zielsprache herstellen. Diese Verbindungen zwischen den Sprachen stellen die Übersetzungen dar, sie schaffen die Möglichkeit, komplexe und sehr unterschiedliche Verknüpfungen herzustellen: von einem Ausgangswort zu mehreren Übersetzungen und von mehreren Ausgangswörtern zu einer gemeinsamen Übersetzung. Innerhalb der einsprachigen Dateien lassen sich ebenfalls Verknüpfungen schaffen, nämlich Querverweise unterschiedlichster Art: abweichende Schreibweisen, geographische Varianten und Abkürzungen.

Der Inhalt der Datenbank für dieses Wörterbuch wurde in drei Stufen zusammengestellt. Nach der Veröffentlichung des *French Dictionary of Business, Commerce and Finance* konnten wir bereits auf eine erhebliche Anzahl englischer Stichwörter zurückgreifen. Diese Stichwortliste wurde dann von Fachübersetzern mit aktueller praktischer Erfahrung im Übersetzen von Wirtschafts- und Handelstexten ins Deutsche übertragen, und mit relevanter Terminologie aus ihrem jeweiligen Spezialgebiet erweitert.

Die Wortlisten in den einzelnen Sprachen wurden dann von Muttersprachlern überprüft, die als

the dictionary. Within the database the distinction between source and target languages is not overt, so a software module was used to process the data and produce two alphabetic sequences of German headwords with English translations and vice versa, each displaying the nesting of compounds, ordering of translations, style of cross-references and other features according to a complex algorithm.

At this stage the formatted text was edited by a team of experienced German and English lexicographers whose task it was to eliminate duplication or inconsistency; edit the entries to ensure that all relevant information was present, correct and easily interpreted; and remove terms that were on the one hand too general, or, on the other, too specialized for inclusion in a business dictionary covering a broad range of areas. This phased method of working has enabled us to set very high standards of quality control throughout the compilation and editing stages of the dictionary.

The editorial team

Fachleute in den jeweiligen Gebieten arbeiten. So wurde sichergestellt, daß die Wortliste höchste Aktualität hat, daß die Übersetzungen präzise sind und daß wirklich das in Fachkreisen geläufige Vokabular behandelt wird. Schließlich wurden noch alle Einträge von Redakteuren überprüft, um eine internationale Terminologieabdeckung zu gewährleisten.

Die Erstellung und Bearbeitung der Datenbankgrundlage war jedoch nur der erste Schritt bei der Herstellung dieses Wörterbuches. Innerhalb der Datenbank ist der Unterschied zwischen Ausgangs- und Zielsprache nicht offensichtlich und so wurden mit Hilfe eines Softwaremoduls die Daten formatiert und zwei alphabetische Listen erstellt, eine deutsche Stichwortliste mit englischen Übersetzungen und umgekehrt. In jeder dieser Listen wurden einem komplexen Algorithmus entsprechend Komposita in Nestern dargestellt, Übersetzungen in sinnvoller Reihenfolge angeordnet und verschiedene Arten von Querverweisen typographisch unterschiedlich gestaltet.

Dann wurde der formatierte Text von einem Team erfahrener deutscher und englischer Lexikographen redigiert; ihre Aufgabe war es, Doppelnennungen und Unstimmigkeiten auszumerzen, die zum Wortzusammenhang gehörigen Informationen zu bearbeiten und all die Stichwörter zu streichen, die einerseits zu allgemeinsprachlich oder andererseits zu spezialisiert für ein Wirtschaftswörterbuch waren, das eine Vielzahl von Gebieten abdeckt. Diese stufenweise Arbeitsmethode gab uns die Möglichkeit, während der gesamten Zusammenstellung und Bearbeitung des Wörterbuches hohe Qualitätsmaßstäbe zu setzen.

Das Redaktionsteam

Features of the dictionary/
Aufbau und Anordnung der Einträge

The following text extracts illustrate the principal features of the dictionary. For a more detailed explanation of each of these features, and a full guide to using the dictionary, see pages xv–xviii

Die folgenden Textbeispiele illustrieren Aufbau und Anordnung der Einträge. Weitere Erläuterungen und Hinweise zur Benutzung des Wörterbuches befinden sich auf den Seiten xix–xxii

Base form of adjective is replaced by a swung dash in adjective–noun combinations

beschäftigungsorientiert: **~e Kostenrechnung** *f* RECHNUNG activity-based costing (*BrE*)

— Die Grundform des Adjektivs wird in flektierten Formen durch eine Tilde ersetzt

Beschäftigung: **Beschäftigungspolitik** *f* PERSON manpower policy, employment policy; **Beschäftigungsprognose** *f* GESCHÄFT manpower forecasting; **Beschäftigungsprogramm** *nt* VW job creation program (*AmE*), job creation programme (*BrE*), job creation scheme; **Beschäftigungsreserve** *f* VW reserve of potential labor (*AmE*), reserve of potential labour (*BrE*); **Beschäftigungssicherheit** *f* PERSON security of employment; **Beschäftigungssituation** *f* GESCHÄFT employment situation, labor market situation (*AmE*), labour market situation (*BrE*); **Beschäftigungsstand** *m* VW level of employment

British English and American English variants are given in full and labelled accordingly

— Britische und amerikanische Varianten werden voll ausgeschrieben und entsprechend gekennzeichnet

beschäftigungsunfähig *adj* PERSON unemployable

Beschäftigung: **Beschäftigungsverbot** *nt* PERSON prohibition notice; **Beschäftigungsverhältnis** *nt* PERSON employment relationship

Definitions are provided where no direct translation exists

beschäftigungswirksam *adj* VW having a positive influence on employment

— Wenn ein Stichwort keine äquivalente Übersetzung hat, wird es durch eine Definition erklärt

Beschäftigung: **Beschäftigungszahlen** *f pl* VW employment figures

Bescheid *m* RECHT administrative decision

bescheiden *adj* GESCHÄFT modest; **~es Einkommen** *nt* FINANZ moderate income

Cross-references between abbreviations and full forms are shown at both entries and translations

Bescheinigung *f* (*Besch.*) GESCHÄFT certificate (*cert.*), KOMM certificate (*cert.*), advice, RECHT certification; **~ über große Havarie** VERSICH general average certificate (*GAC*); **~ über Ordungsmäßigkeit** VERWALT certificate of compliance; ◆ **eine ~ beibringen** VERWALT furnish a certificate, submit a certificate

— Querverweise zwischen Abkürzungen und Vollformen werden sowohl beim Eintrag als auch bei der Übersetzung angegeben

Contexts give supplementary information to help locate the right translation

Beschlagnahme *f* GRUND distraint, IMP/EXP confiscation, seizure, RECHT arrest, sequestration, *von Besitz* levy, *von Grundbesitz* distraint, TRANSP detention, VERSICH attachment; **~ von Eigentum** RECHT distraint of property

— Die Angabe von Zusammenhängen ergänzt die gegebenen Informationen und unterstützt die Suche nach dem passenden Übersetzungsäquivalent

beschlagnahmen *vt* IMP/EXP confiscate, seize, impound, RECHT sequester, sequestrate, impound, TRANSP detain; ◆ **etw von jdm ~** GESCHÄFT confiscate sth from sb

beschlagnahmt: **~es Konto** *nt* FINANZ impound account

Subject area labels given in alphabetical order show appropriate translations

Beschlagnahmung *f* GRUND distraint, IMP/EXP confiscation, seizure, RECHT sequestration, *von Besitz* levy, *von Grundbesitz* distraint, TRANSP detention, VERSICH attachment

— Sachgebietskürzel in alphabetischer Reihenfolge helfen beim Finden der korrekten Übersetzung

beschlagnehmen *vt* GESCHÄFT confiscate, seize, RECHT impound

Numbered sections indicate different grammatical categories

beschleunigen 1. *vt* GESCHÄFT accelerate, expedite, speed up; **2.** *vi* GESCHÄFT speed up; **3. sich ~** *v refl* GESCHÄFT accelerate, speed up

— Numerierte Abschnitte zeigen unterschiedliche grammatische Kategorien an

Beschleunigerkarte *f* COMP *Graphik, Bildschirmaufbau* accelerator card

beschleunigt 1. *adj* GESCHÄFT accelerated; **2.** *adv* ◆ **~ abfertigen** GESCHÄFT expedite

Headword in bold italics indicates the continuation of an earlier entry

beschleunigt: **~e Abschreibung** *f* FINANZ, RECHNUNG accelerated depreciation; **~e Amortisation** *f* RECHNUNG accelerated amortization; **~e Bewegung** *f* V&M accelerated motion; **~e Mittelbereitstellung** *f* BANK expedited funds availability; **~er Rückkauf** *m* GESCHÄFT accelerated redemption; **~e Umwandlung** *f* BANK accelerated conversion; **~es Wachstum** *nt* VW accelerated growth

— Ein fett und kursiv gedrucktes Basiswort zeigt die Fortsetzung eines vorhergehenden Eintrags an

Definitionen und
Äquivalente geben
kulturelle Informationen

Sachgebietskürzel in
alphabetischer Reihenfolge
helfen beim Finden der
korrekten Übersetzung

Numerierte Abschnitte
zeigen unterschiedliche
grammatische Kategorien
an

Veranschaulichende
Phrasen folgen unmittelbar
auf das Stichwort und sind
durch eine Raute
gekennzeichnet

Britische und
amerikanische Varianten
werden voll
ausgeschrieben und
entsprechend
gekennzeichnet

Ein fett und kursiv
gedrucktes Basiswort zeigt
die Fortsetzung eines
vorhergehenden Eintrags
an

Zusammengesetzte Begriffe
werden alphabetisch hinter
dem ersten Element
angeordnet

Die Angabe von
Zusammenhängen ergänzt
die gegebenen
Informationen und
unterstützt die Suche nach
dem passenden
Übersetzungsäquivalent

B/Dft *abbr* (*bank draft*) BANK Bankscheck *m*, Banktratte *m*, Bankwechsel *m*

bdi *abbr* (*both dates inclusive*) GEN COMM beide Daten eingeschlossen

BE *abbr* (*Bank of England*) BANK, ECON englische Zentralbank, ≈ BBk (*Deutsche Bundesbank*)

B/E *abbr* BANK, FIN (*bill of exchange*) Tratte *f*, Wechsel *m*, IMP/EXP (*bill of entry*) Deklarationsschein *m*, Einfuhrdeklaration *f*, Einfuhrerklärung *f*, Zolldeklaration *f*, Zolleinfuhrerklärung *f*, Zolleingangsschein *m*, Zollerklärung *f*

BEA *abbr* (*Bureau of Economic Analysis*) ECON Amt für Wirtschaftsanalyse

beancounter *n* *infrml* ACC Erbsenzähler *m* (*infrml*), Pfennigfuchser *m* (*infrml*)

bear 1. *n* FIN, STOCK Baissespekulant *m*, Baissier *m*, Contremineur *m*; **2.** *vt* GEN COMM *costs* bestreiten, tragen; ◆ **~ a date** GEN COMM das Datum tragen, datiert sein; **~ in mind** GEN COMM berücksichtigen; **~ interest** BANK Zinsen bringen; **~ an interest of** ACC Zinsen tragen in Höhe von; **~ the market** STOCK Leerverkäufe als Baissemanöver tätigen; **~ the risk** STOCK das Risiko tragen; **3.** *vi* STOCK auf Baisse spekulieren

bear: **~ account** *n* STOCK Baisseposition *f*; **~ call spread** *n* STOCK *options* Baissespread *m* mit Kaufoptionen; **~ covering** *n* STOCK Deckungskauf *m* des Baissiers

bearer *n* BANK *of negotiable instrument* Inhaber, in *m,f*, Überbringer, in *m,f*; **~ bond** *n* FIN Inhaberobligation *f*, Inhaberschuldverschreibung *f*; **~ check** *AmE*, **~ cheque** *BrE n* BANK Inhaberscheck *m*, Überbringerscheck *m*; **~ clause** *n* STOCK Inhaberklausel *f*, Überbringerklausel *f*; **~ debenture** *n* STOCK Inhaberobligation *f*, Inhaberschuldverschreibung *f*; **~ form** *n* STOCK Inhaberformular *nt*; **~ marketable bond** *n* STOCK börsengängige Industrieobligation *f*, börsengängige Industrieschuldverschreibung *f*; **~ share** *n* STOCK Inhaberaktie *f*; **~ stock** *n* STOCK Inhaberaktie *f*; **~ warrant** *n* STOCK Inhaberoptionsschein *m*

bear: **~ hug takeover** *n* FIN Übernahme *f* nach Vorverhandlung

bearing: **~ surface** *n* TRANSP *shipping* Ladefläche *f*

bearish: **~ downward movement** *n* STOCK Baissebewegung *f*

bearishness *n* STOCK Baissestimmung *f*, Baisseströmung *f*, Baissetendenz *f*

bearish: **~ signal formation** *n* STOCK *in point and figure analysis* Baissesignal *nt*; **~ tone** *n* STOCK *of market* Baissestimmung *f*, Baisseströmung *f*, Baissetendenz *f*

bear: **~ market** *n* STOCK Baissemarkt *m*; **~ operation** *n* STOCK Baissespekulation *f*; **~ position** *n* STOCK Baisseengagement *nt*; **~ put spread** *n* STOCK *options* Baisseverkaufsspanne *f*; **~ raiding** *n* STOCK Leerverkäufe *m pl* der Baissespekulation; **~ sale** *n* STOCK Leerverkauf *m*, Verkauf *m* auf Baisse; **~ speculation** *n* STOCK Baissespekulation *f*; **~ transaction** *n* STOCK Baissegeschäft *nt*, Baissespekulation *f*

beat down *vt* GEN COMM *price* herunterhandeln auf [+acc]

— Definitions and equivalents
provide cultural information

— Subject area labels given in
alphabetical order show
appropriate translations

— Numbered sections indicate
different grammatical
categories

— Illustrative phrases are
grouped together at the
relevant entry after a
diamond

— British English and American
English variants are given in
full and labelled accordingly

Headword in bold italics
indicates the continuation of
— an earlier entry

Compound forms are nested
alphabetically at the first
— element

Contexts give supplementary
information to help locate the
— right translation

Using the dictionary

Range & selection of terms

This is a single-volume general business dictionary which covers a broad range of terminology drawn from all the main fields of business and commercial language. As such, we have aimed to include the essential vocabulary of each subject area, as well as including more specialized references such as organizations, legal acts and financial and accounting systems. Overlap with a general bilingual dictionary has been kept to a minimum by only including terms which can be applied in a business context. All the material has been checked by leading subject experts to ensure that both the English and the German terms are accurate and current and that the translations are valid equivalents. Although other variant translations may sometimes be permissible in a particular subject area, we have given the terms and spellings most widely preferred by specialists working in that area.

Coverage of the subject areas is weighted representatively so that a core and wide-ranging field such as Economics has a count of around 5000 terms, whereas a more specialized area such as Environment has fewer terms.

Placement & ordering of entries

All terms are entered at their first element except where that element is an article, preposition, conjunction, pronoun or other delexicalized word. In such cases, the term is entered at the next valid element. For example:

red: **in the** ~ *phr* BANK, GEN COMM in den roten Zahlen, in den Roten (*infrml*)

English compound forms are listed at the first word, with the headword replaced by a swung dash at each entry:

franchise *n* INS Franchise *f*, POL Stimmrecht *nt*, S&M Franchise *nt*, Franchising *nt*, Alleinverkaufsrecht *nt*, Konzession *f*; ~ **agreement** *n* LAW Konzessionsvertrag *m*, Lizenzvertrag *m*; ~ **clause** *n* INS Selbstbehaltsklausel *f*, Franchiseklausel *f*

If the first word of the compound has no business sense of its own it is untranslated and a colon precedes the compounds:

lightning: ~ **rise** *n* HRM, MGMNT rasanter Aufstieg *m*; ~ **strike** *n* HRM Blitzstreik *m*

In the case of German noun nests, open forms are listed first with the headword replaced by a swung dash. Solid and hyphenated forms then follow, spelt out in full:

Erteilung *f* GESCHÄFT award, MGMNT *Vollmacht* delegation, PATENT, RECHT grant, conferral; ~ **von Importlizenzen** IMP/EXP import licensing; ~ **von Zeichnungsvollmacht** GESCHÄFT delegation of signing authority; **Erteilungsdatum** *nt* PATENT date of grant

Where the first element of German noun compounds has no business sense of its own, but modifies a number of business-related compounds, it is entered as a headword and is translated. The nest of compounds follows:

Mutter- *in cpds* GESCHÄFT mother, parent; **Muttergesellschaft** *f* GESCHÄFT, RECHNUNG parent company, RECHT holding company; **Mutterkarte** *f* COMP motherboard, mothercard; **Mutterland** *nt* FINANZ, GESCHÄFT home country; **Mutterplatte** *f* COMP motherboard

Compounds are entered in alphabetical sequence. When a nest is interrupted by other entries, the run of compounds is picked up again later in the correct alphabetical order. A headword in bold italics indicates the continuation of a sequence of compounds. For example:

option *n* FIN Option *f*, GEN COMM *ability to choose* Entscheidungsfreiheit *f*, freie Wahl *f*, *alternative* Alternative *f*, Wahlmöglichkeit *f*, *right to buy* Vorkaufsrecht *nt*, STOCK Option *f*; ~ **account** *n* FIN *credit card* Abrechnung *f* für Optionsgeschäfte
optional: ~ **character** *n* COMP beliebiges Zeichen *nt*; ~ **modes of settlement** *n pl* INS *life insurance* Regulierung *f* nach Wahl; ~ **retirement** *n* HRM freiwillige Pensionierung *f*

option: ~ **demand** *n* STOCK Optionsnachfrage *f*; ~ **fee** *n* FIN *hire purchase* Optionsgebühr *f*; ~ **forward** *n* STOCK Optionsgeschäft *nt* mit Termindevisen; ~ **holder** *n* STOCK Optionsinhaber, in *m,f*; ~ **on actuals** *n* STOCK Option *f* auf Kassakontrakte; ~ **on futures** *n* STOCK Option *f* auf Terminkontrakte; ~ **price model** *n* (*OPM*) STOCK Optionspreismodell *nt*

German adjective–noun combinations are entered at the base form of the adjective. Within the nest, the base form is replaced by a swung dash and followed by the relevant inflection. Adjective inflections are ignored for the purposes of alphabetical ordering:

dynamisch *adj* GESCHÄFT dynamic; **~es Absichern** *nt* FINANZ dynamic hedging; **~e Absicherung** *f* FINANZ dynamic hedging; **~e Analyse** *f* vw dynamic analysis; **~e Bewertung** *f* GESCHÄFT dynamic evaluation; **~er Datenaustausch** *m* COMP dynamic data exchange (*DDE*); **~e Lebensversicherung** *f* VERSICH indexed life insurance; **~es Managementmodell** *nt* MGMNT dynamic management model; **~e Planung** *f* GESCHÄFT dynamic programming; **~e Positionierung** *f* GESCHÄFT, V&M dynamic positioning (*DP*); **~es Programmieren** *nt* COMP, MATH dynamic programming

Illustrative phrases, preceded by a ♦ symbol, are grouped together at the relevant entry. Any compounds of the base form then follow on at a bold italics headword. For example:

Presse *f* MEDIEN, POL, V&M press; ♦ **der ~ zuspielen** MEDIEN, POL leak to the press
Presse: **Presseagentur** *f* MEDIEN press agency; **Presseamt** *nt* MEDIEN, POL press office; **Presseausweis** *m* MEDIEN press card; **Pressebericht** *m* MEDIEN press report, write-up

Within nests, articles, pronouns, prepositions and conjunctions are ignored in determining the sequence of nested forms and phrases. For example:

exclusion: ~ **clause** *n* INS, LAW Haftungsausschlußklausel *f*; ~ **of liability** *n* INS Haftungsausschluß *m*, LAW *contracts* Ausschluß *m* der Gewährleistung, Haftungsausschluß *m*; ~ **principle** *n* ECON Ausschlußprinzip *nt*, Ausschlußprinzip *nt* des Preises, Preisausschlußprinzip *nt*; ~ **of risk** *n* LAW *transactions* Risikoausschluß *m*

Terms starting with numbers are alphabetized according to the number as written out in full:

one: **~-price law** *n* ECON Einheitspreisgesetz *nt*, Einpreisgesetz *nt*
1Q *abbr* (*first quarter*) GEN COMM erstes Quartal *nt*
one: **~-shot deal** *n* GEN COMM einmaliges Geschäft *nt*

Parts of speech

Part of speech labels are given at all entries except illustrative phrases. At translations, genders are given for all German nouns. For a complete list of the part of speech labels, see page xxiii.

For entries which can have more than one part of speech, numbered sections show the relevant grammatical category. Compounds then follow in a new nest headed by the headword in bold italics. For example:

complete 1. *adj* GEN COMM komplett, vollständig, total, voll; **2.** *vt* FIN abwickeln, GEN COMM vollenden, vervollständigen, ergänzen, *sale, order* abschließen, beenden, PROP *sale* abschließen, LAW *contract* erfüllen, abschließen
complete: ~ **audit** *n* ACC Jahresrevision *f*, lückenlose Prüfung *f*

Illustrative phrases follow a diamond at the end of the numbered section to which they refer. For example:

return 1. *n* ACC Ertrag *m*, FIN Rendite *f*, GEN COMM Herausgabe *f*, *on investment* Rendite *f*, Rentabilität *f*, *arrival* Wiederkehr *f*, Rückkehr *f*, *giving back* Rückgabe *f*, *journey* Rückfahrt *f*, Rückreise *f*, *yield* Ertrag *m*, Verzinsung *f*, *report* Bericht *m*, STOCK Rentabilität *f*, *yield* Verzinsung *f*, Rendite *f*, Ertrag *m*, Gewinn *m*, TAX Steuererklärung *f*; ♦ **by ~ of post** COMMS postwendend; **in ~ for** LAW als Gegenleistung; **2.** *vt* COMMS *package* rückliefern, FIN *interest* abwerfen, GEN COMM *borrowed article* zurückgeben, zurückbringen, S&M *goods sold to supplier* zurücksenden; ♦ **~ sb's call** COMMS *telephone* zurückrufen; **~ to sender** COMMS zurück an Absender; **~ to source** ACC auflösen; **3.** *vi* GEN COMM zurückkehren, zurückkommen

On the English–German side of the dictionary, phrasal verbs are entered as separate headwords immediately after the base entry from which they are formed. Transitivity is shown and any phrases are given following a diamond. For example:

draw 1. *n* BANK Kreditinanspruchnahme *f*; **2.** *vt* BANK *money* abheben, entnehmen, ECON, FIN, GEN COMM *money* abheben, STOCK zeichnen, ziehen, LAW *legal document* aufsetzen; ♦ **~ a check** *AmE*, **~ a cheque** *BrE* BANK einen Scheck ausstellen; **~ a conclusion** GEN COMM einen Schluß ziehen; **~ a distinction between** GEN COMM eine Unterscheidung machen zwischen; **~ sickness payments** HRM Krankengeld beziehen
draw from *vt* HRM rekrutieren
draw on *vt* GEN COMM angreifen; ♦ **~ one's savings** FIN auf seine Ersparnisse zurückgreifen
draw up *vt* ACC aufstellen, GEN COMM aufstellen, *plan, will* ausarbeiten, anfertigen, ausstellen, *report* erstellen, INS *marine insurance* aufmachen, LAW aufsetzen, ausfertigen, verfassen; ♦ **~ an agenda** ADMIN, MGMNT eine Tagesordnung aufstellen; **~ a shortlist** HRM eine Auswahlliste aufstellen; **~ a statement of account** BANK einen Kontoauszug machen

Ordering of translations

Every term is accompanied by one or more subject labels indicating the area in which it is used. For a complete list of these labels and their expansions, see pages xxiv–xxv.

Where the same term is used in more than one subject area, multiple labels are given as appropriate. These labels are listed in alphabetical order. If a term has the same translation in more than one subject area, the translation is given after the sequence of labels. For example:

Planrevision *f* FINANZ, RECHNUNG, VW budget review, budgetary adjustment

If a term has different translations according to the subject area in which it is used, the appropriate translation is given after each label or set of labels. For example:

unrecoverable *adj* COMP *data, file* nicht wiederherstellbar, FIN, GEN COMM *debt* nicht eintreibbar, uneinbringlich

Supplementary information

In many cases, additional information is given about a term in order to show how it is used. This includes:

1. the typical subject or object of a verb, for example:

flourish *vi* GEN COMM *business, competition* florieren

2. typical nouns used with an adjective, for example:

schnurlos *adj* KOMM *Telefon* cordless

3. words indicating the reference of a noun, for example:

Waschzettel *m* MEDIEN, V&M *eines Buches* blurb

4. information which supplements the subject area label, for example:

absolute: ~ **deviation** *n* MATH *statistics* absolute Abweichung *f*

When various different translations apply within the same subject area, contextual information is also used to show which translation is appropriate in different circumstances. For example:

justice *n* LAW *fairness* Gerechtigkeit *f*, *judicial system* Gerichtsbarkeit *f*, Justiz *f*, *judge* Richter, in *m,f*

Where no real equivalent of a headword exists in the target language, an explanatory translation is given and is distinguished by a change in typeface. For example:

Big: ~ **Bang** *n* STOCK *on London Stock Exchange* Deregulierung des britischen Wertpapiermarktes am 27. Oktober 1986

In the case of organizations and institutions, an explanatory translation is given as well as an equivalent body where it exists. For example:

House: ~ **of Lords** *n* BrE (*H of L*) POL britisches Oberhaus, ≈ Bundesrat *m*

Where the feminine form of an occupation or profession can be formed by adding **in** to a German masculine stem, the noun entry has part of speech *m,f* with the inflection indicated at the headword:

Werksleiter, in *m,f* IND, MGMNT, PERSON plant manager, works manager

Where the feminine and masculine forms have different English translations, both entries are provided in full:

Polizist *m* POL policeman
Polizistin *f* POL policewoman

Case information is given following certain German prepositions and verbs, for example:

succeed 1. *vt* GEN COMM *follow* folgen [+dat], folgen auf [+acc], nachfolgen [+dat]; **2.** *vi* GEN COMM *achieve success* erfolgreich sein, Erfolg haben, gelingen, LAW erben

German nouns whose forms vary according to gender and case are given part of speech *mf* and followed by the label [decl. as adj] to show that they decline as adjectives. For example:

Bezogene(r) *mf* [decl. as adj] BANK acceptor, drawee

Cross-references

Spelling variants are cross-referred to the preferred spelling, where full information is given. For example:

gram *n* (*g*) GEN COMM Gramm *nt* (*g*)
gramme *see gram*

In the case of geographical spellings, the American English form is cross-referred to the British English form:

salable *AmE see saleable BrE*

saleable *adj* BrE LAW, PROP veräußerlich, S&M *fit for selling* verkäuflich, *marketable* marktfähig

Geographical lexical variants are cross-referred, with full translations given at each entry:

earthing *n* BrE (*cf grounding AmE*) COMP, IND *electricity* Erdung *f*

grounding *n* AmE (*cf earthing BrE*) COMP, IND *electricity* Erdung *f*

Both spelling and lexical variants are given in full when they are translations:

Erdung *f* COMP, IND *Elektrizität* earthing (*BrE*), grounding (*AmE*)

Herkunftsbezeichnung *f* V&M informative labeling (*AmE*), informative labelling (*BrE*)

Abbreviations are cross-referred to their full forms and vice versa, with the appropriate translations given at each entry. For example:

Sonderziehungsrechte *nt pl* (*SZR*) BANK special drawing rights (*SDR*)

SZR *abbr* (*Sonderziehungsrechte*) BANK SDR (*special drawing rights*)

If a source language abbreviation does not have a target language equivalent, the translation of the expanded form is given. For example:

OID *abbr* (*original issue discount*) FIN, STOCK Abzinsungsbetrag *m*, Emissionsdisagio *nt*

Where an abbreviation has different full forms according to subject areas, the relevant expanded forms appear after each label or set of labels:

AI *abbr* COMP (*artificial intelligence*) KI (*künstliche Intelligenz*), FIN (*accrued interest*) aufgelaufene Zinsen *m pl*

Hinweise zur Benutzung des Wörterbuches

Auswahl der Stichwörter

Dieses Werk ist ein einbändiges allgemeines Wirtschaftswörterbuch, das den gebräuchlichen Wortschatz in allen Bereichen der Wirtschaft und des Handels abdeckt. Wir haben uns zum Ziel gesetzt, sowohl aus jedem Fachgebiet das Basisvokabular, als auch etwas speziellere Einträge wie Organisationen, Gesetze, Finanz- und Buchführungssysteme aufzunehmen. Überschneidungen mit einem allgemeinen zweisprachigen Wörterbuch wurden auf ein Minimum beschränkt und nur Stichwörter aufgenommen, die in einem Wirtschaftskontext verwendet werden können. Das gesamte Material wurde von Fachleuten überprüft, um sicherzustellen, daß sowohl die englischen als auch die deutschen Stichwörter richtig und aktuell sind und die Übersetzungen gültige Entsprechungen darstellen. Gelegentlich mögen Übersetzungsvarianten zwar in einem bestimmten Fachgebiet zulässig sein, doch haben wir die Stichwörter und Schreibweisen aufgenommen, die von Spezialisten in dem jeweiligen Bereich bevorzugt verwenden werden.

Die einzelnen Fachgebiete sind ihrer Anwendungshäufigkeit entsprechend vertreten, so daß also ein etabliertes und umfangreiches Gebiet wie die Volkswirtschaft rund 5000 Stichwörter umfaßt, während ein Spezialgebiet wie etwa die Umwelt entsprechend weniger Stichwörter aufweist.

Anordnung & Reihenfolge der Einträge

Alle Stichwörter sind nach ihrem ersten Element, dem Basiswort, angeordnet, es sei denn, dieses Element ist ein Artikel, eine Präposition, eine Konjunktion, ein Pronomen oder ein anderes ausgegliedertes Wort. In solchen Fällen erscheint das Stichwort als erstes gültiges Element, zum Beispiel:

red: **in the ~** *phr* BANK, GEN COMM in den roten Zahlen, in den Roten (*infrml*)

Englische Zusammensetzungen werden unter dem ersten Wort angeführt, wobei das Stichwort in jedem Eintrag durch eine Tilde wiedergegeben wird:

franchise *n* INS Franchise *f*, POL Stimmrecht *nt*, S&M Franchise *nt*, Franchising *nt*, Alleinverkaufsrecht *nt*, Konzession *f*; **~ agreement** *n* LAW Konzessionsvertrag *m*, Lizenzvertrag *m*; **~ clause** *n* INS Selbstbehaltsklausel *f*, Franchiseklausel *f*

Wenn das erste Wort der Zusammensetzung selbst keine wirtschaftliche Bedeutung hat, wird es nicht übersetzt, und den Zusammensetzungen geht ein Doppelpunkt voraus:

lightning: **~ rise** *n* HRM, MGMNT rasanter Aufstieg *m*; **~ strike** *n* HRM Blitzstreik *m*

Bei deutschen Substantivnestern werden offene Formen zuerst angeführt, wobei das Stichwort durch eine Tilde ersetzt wird. Danach folgen feste Formen und solche mit Bindestrich; diese werden voll ausgeschrieben:

Erteilung *f* GESCHÄFT award, MGMNT *Vollmacht* delegation, PATENT, RECHT grant, conferral; **~ von Importlizenzen** IMP/EXP import licensing; **~ von Zeichnungsvollmacht** GESCHÄFT delegation of signing authority; **Erteilungsdatum** *nt* PATENT date of grant

Wenn das Basiswort eines deutschen Substantivkompositums selbst keine wirtschaftliche Bedeutung hat, aber eine Reihe von wirtschaftsbezogenen Zusammensetzungen modifiziert, wird es als eigenes Stichwort mit vollständiger Übersetzung angeführt, gefolgt vom Kompositanest:

Mutter- *in cpds* GESCHÄFT mother, parent; **Muttergesellschaft** *f* GESCHÄFT, RECHNUNG parent company, RECHT holding company; **Mutterkarte** *f* COMP motherboard, mothercard; **Mutterland** *nt* FINANZ, GESCHÄFT home country; **Mutterplatte** *f* COMP motherboard

Komposita sind in alphabetischer Reihenfolge angeordnet. Nester, die durch andere Stichwörter unterbrochen werden, werden bei der nächsten alphabetisch adäquaten Gelegenheit wieder aufgenommen. Ein fett und kursiv gedrucktes

Basiswort weist auf die Fortführung einer Kompositafolge hin, zum Beispiel:

option *n* FIN Option *f*, GEN COMM *ability to choose* Entscheidungsfreiheit *f*, freie Wahl *f*, *alternative* Alternative *f*, Wahlmöglichkeit *f*, *right to buy* Vorkaufsrecht *nt*, STOCK Option *f*; ~ **account** *n* FIN *credit card* Abrechnung *f* für Optionsgeschäfte

optional: ~ **character** *n* COMP beliebiges Zeichen *nt*; ~ **modes of settlement** *n pl* INS *life insurance* Regulierung *f* nach Wahl; ~ **retirement** *n* HRM freiwillige Pensionierung *f*

option: ~ **demand** *n* STOCK Optionsnachfrage *f*; ~ **fee** *n* FIN *hire purchase* Optionsgebühr *f*; ~ **forward** *n* STOCK Optionsgeschäft *nt* mit Termindevisen; ~ **holder** *n* STOCK Optionsinhaber, in *m,f*; ~ **on actuals** *n* STOCK Option *f* auf Kassakontrakte; ~ **on futures** *n* STOCK Option *f* auf Terminkontrakte; ~ **price model** *n* (*OPM*) STOCK Optionspreismodell *nt*

Deutsche Zusammensetzungen aus Adjektiv und Substantiv sind unter der Grundform des Adjektivs angeführt. Innerhalb des Nests wird die Grundform durch eine Tilde ersetzt, gefolgt von der entsprechenden Flexionsendung. Bei der alphabetischen Anordnung werden die Adjektivendungen ignoriert:

dynamisch *adj* GESCHÄFT dynamic; ~**es Absichern** *nt* FINANZ dynamic hedging; ~**e Absicherung** *f* FINANZ dynamic hedging; ~**e Analyse** *f* vw dynamic analysis; ~**e Bewertung** *f* GESCHÄFT dynamic evaluation; ~**er Datenaustausch** *m* COMP dynamic data exchange (*DDE*); ~**e Lebensversicherung** *f* VERSICH indexed life insurance; ~**es Managementmodell** *nt* MGMNT dynamic management model; ~**e Planung** *f* GESCHÄFT dynamic programming; ~**e Positionierung** *f* GESCHÄFT, V&M dynamic positioning (*DP*); ~**es Programmieren** *nt* COMP, MATH dynamic programming

Veranschaulichende Phrasen folgen unmittelbar auf das Stichwort und sind durch eine Raute gekennzeichnet. Zusammensetzungen mit dem Stichwort schließen sich danach an das kursiv gedruckte Stichwort an, zum Beispiel:

Presse *f* MEDIEN, POL, V&M press; ♦ **der ~ zuspielen** MEDIEN, POL leak to the press

Presse: **Presseagentur** *f* MEDIEN press agency; **Presseamt** *nt* MEDIEN, POL press office; **Presseausweis** *m* MEDIEN press card; **Pressebericht** *m* MEDIEN press report, write-up

Innerhalb eines Nests werden Artikel, Pronomen, Präpositionen und Konjunktionen bei der Reihenfolge der eingenesteten Formen und Phrasen ignoriert, zum Beispiel:

exclusion: ~ **clause** *n* INS, LAW Haftungsausschlußklausel *f*; ~ **of liability** *n* INS Haftungsausschluß *m*, LAW *contracts* Ausschluß *m* der Gewährleistung, Haftungsausschluß *m*; ~ **principle** *n* ECON Ausschlußprinzip *nt*, Ausschlußprinzip *nt* des Preises, Preisausschlußprinzip *nt*; ~ **of risk** *n* LAW *transactions* Risikoausschluß *m*

Stichwörter, die mit Zahlen beginnen, werden an der Stelle angeführt, an der die ausgeschriebene Form der entsprechenden Zahlen erscheinen würde, zum Beispiel:

one: ~~**price law** *n* ECON Einheitspreisgesetz *nt*, Einpreisgesetz *nt*

1Q *abbr* (*first quarter*) GEN COMM erstes Quartal *nt*

one: ~~**shot deal** *n* GEN COMM einmaliges Geschäft *nt*

Wortarten

Alle Einträge, ausgenommen die veranschaulichenden Phrasen, sind mit einem Kürzel versehen, das die Wortart angibt. Bei Übersetzungen wird für alle deutschen Substantive das Geschlecht angegeben. Eine vollständige Liste der Wortartkürzel finden Sie auf Seite xxiii.

Einträge, die mehr als einer Wortart angehören können, erhalten numerierte Abschnitte mit der entsprechenden grammatischen Kategorie. Dann folgen Komposita in einem neuen Nest, das mit dem kursiv und fett gedruckten Stichwort beginnt, zum Beispiel:

complete 1. *adj* GEN COMM komplett, vollständig, total, voll; **2.** *vt* FIN abwickeln, GEN COMM vollenden, vervollständigen, ergänzen, *sale, order* abschließen, beenden, PROP *sale* abschließen, LAW *contract* erfüllen, abschließen

complete: ~ **audit** *n* ACC Jahresrevision *f*, lückenlose Prüfung *f*

Veranschaulichende Phrasen stehen nach einer Raute am Ende des numerierten Abschnitts, auf den sie sich beziehen, zum Beispiel:

return 1. *n* ACC Ertrag *m*, FIN Rendite *f*, GEN COMM Herausgabe *f*, *on investment* Rendite *f*, Rentabilität *f*, *arrival* Wiederkehr *f*, Rückkehr *f*, *giving back* Rückgabe *f*, *journey* Rückfahrt *f*, Rückreise *f*, *yield* Ertrag *m*, Verzinsung *f*, *report* Bericht *m*, STOCK Rentabilität *f*, *yield* Verzinsung *f*, Rendite *f*, Ertrag *m*, Gewinn *m*, TAX Steuererklärung *f*; ♦ **by ~ of post** COMMS postwendend; **in ~ for** LAW als Gegenleistung; **2.** *vt* COMMS *package* rückliefern, FIN *interest* abwerfen, GEN COMM *borrowed article* zurückgeben, zurückbringen, S&M *goods sold to supplier* zurücksenden; ♦ ~ **sb's call** COMMS *telephone* zurückrufen; ~ **to sender** COMMS zurück an Absender; ~ **to source** ACC auflösen; **3.** *vi* GEN COMM zurückkehren, zurückkommen

Im englisch–deutschen Abschnitt des Wörterbuches stehen Zusammensetzungen aus Verb und Präposition als eigene Stichwörter unmittelbar nach der Grundform des Verbs, aus dem sie gebildet werden. Der auf die Präposition folgende Fall wird angegeben und veranschaulichende Phrasen nach einer Raute aufgeführt, zum Beispiel:

draw 1. *n* BANK Kreditinanspruchnahme *f*; **2.** *vt* BANK *money* abheben, entnehmen, ECON, FIN, GEN COMM *money* abheben, STOCK zeichnen, ziehen, LAW *legal document* aufsetzen; ♦ ~ **a check** *AmE*, ~ **a cheque** *BrE* BANK einen Scheck ausstellen; ~ **a conclusion** GEN COMM einen Schluß ziehen; ~ **a distinction between** GEN COMM eine Unterscheidung machen zwischen; ~ **sickness payments** HRM Krankengeld beziehen

draw from *vt* HRM rekrutieren

draw on *vt* GEN COMM angreifen; ♦ ~ **one's savings** FIN auf seine Ersparnisse zurückgreifen

draw up *vt* ACC aufstellen, GEN COMM aufstellen, *plan, will* ausarbeiten, anfertigen, ausstellen, *report* erstellen, INS *marine insurance* aufmachen, LAW aufsetzen, ausfertigen, verfassen; ♦ ~ **an agenda** ADMIN, MGMNT eine Tagesordnung aufstellen; ~ **a shortlist** HRM eine Auswahlliste aufstellen; ~ **a statement of account** BANK einen Kontoauszug machen

Reihenfolge der Übersetzungen

Auf jedes Stichwort folgen ein oder mehrere Kürzel, die das Fachgebiet angeben, in dem das Wort benutzt wird. Eine vollständige Liste dieser Kürzel und ihrer Erweiterungen finden Sie auf Seite xxiv–xxv.

Wird dasselbe Stichwort in mehreren Fachgebieten verwendet, so werden entsprechend mehrere Kürzel angegeben, immer in alphabetischer Reihenfolge. Falls die Übersetzung in mehr als einem Fachgebiet benutzt wird, so folgt sie jeweils im Anschluß an die entsprechenden Kürzel, zum Beispiel:

Planrevision *f* FINANZ, RECHNUNG, VW budget review, budgetary adjustment

Hat ein Stichwort verschiedene, vom jeweiligen Fachgebiet abhängige Übersetzungen, so steht die zutreffende Übersetzung nach dem oder den jeweiligen Kürzeln, zum Beispiel:

unrecoverable *adj* COMP *data, file* nicht wiederherstellbar, FIN, GEN COMM *debt* nicht eintreibbar, uneinbringlich

Zusatzinformationen

In vielen Fällen werden zum Stichwort noch zusätzliche Hinweise gegeben, die zeigen, wie es verwendet wird. Diese können folgende Formen annehmen:

1. bei einem Verb ein typisches Subjekt oder Objekt, zum Beispiel:

flourish *vi* GEN COMM *business, competition* florieren

2. bei einem Adjektiv typische Substantive, die damit verwendet werden, zum Beispiel:

schnurlos *adj* KOMM *Telefon* cordless

3. bei Substantiven Wörter, die einen typischen Bezug anzeigen, zum Beispiel:

Waschzettel *m* MEDIEN, V&M *eines Buches* blurb

4. Informationen, die das Fachgebietskürzel näher definieren, zum Beispiel:

absolute: ~ **deviation** *n* MATH *statistics* absolute Abweichung *f*

Wenn in einem Fachgebiet verschiedene Übersetzungen für ein Stichwort möglich sind, dienen Kontextangaben dazu, anzuzeigen, welche im jeweiligen Zusammenhang die zutreffendste ist. Zum Beispiel:

justice *n* LAW *fairness* Gerechtigkeit *f*, *judicial system* Gerichtsbarkeit *f*, Justiz *f*, *judge* Richter, in *m,f*

Existiert in der Zielsprache kein wirkliches Gegenstück zum Stichwort, so wird, hervorgehoben durch eine andere Schriftart, eine erklärende Übersetzung gegeben. Zum Beispiel:

Big: ~ **Bang** *n* STOCK *on London Stock Exchange* Deregulierung des britischen Wertpapiermarktes am 27. Oktober 1986

Bei Organisationen und Institutionen wird eine beschreibende Übersetzung gegeben und, wo vorhanden, die äquivalente Körperschaft. Zum Beispiel:

House: ~ **of Lords** *n* *BrE* (*H of L*) POL britisches Oberhaus, ≈ Bundesrat *m*

In Fällen, in denen die weibliche Form einer Beschäftigung oder eines Berufs durch Anhängen von **in** an den deutschen maskulinen Stamm gebildet wird, erhält das Substantiv das Wortartkürzel *m,f* und die Endung wird am Stichwort angezeigt:

Werksleiter, in *m,f* IND, MGMNT, PERSON plant manager, works manager

In Fällen, in denen die weibliche und die männliche Form unterschiedlich ins Englische übersetzt werden, sind beide Einträge vollständig angeführt:

Polizist *m* POL policeman
Polizistin *f* POL policewoman

Angaben zum Fall, der auf bestimmte deutsche Präpositionen oder Verben folgt, stehen in eckigen Klammern, zum Beispiel:

succeed 1. *vt* GEN COMM *follow* folgen [+dat], folgen auf [+acc], nachfolgen [+dat]; **2.** *vi* GEN COMM *achieve success* erfolgreich sein, Erfolg haben, gelingen, LAW erben

Deutsche Substantive, deren Endung sich je nach

Geschlecht und Fall ändert, erhalten das Wortartkürzel *mf*, gefolgt vom Kürzel [decl. as adj] um anzuzeigen, daß sie wie Adjektive dekliniert werden. Zum Beispiel:

Bezogene(r) *mf* [decl. as adj] BANK acceptor, drawee

Querverweise

Abweichende Schreibweisen enthalten einen Querverweis auf die bevorzugte Schreibweise, unter der die vollständigen Angaben zu finden sind.

gram *n* (*g*) GEN COMM Gramm *nt* (*g*)
gramme *see gram*

Bei geographischen Abweichungen in der Schreibweise enthält die Form in amerikanischem Englisch einen Querverweis auf die Form in britischem Englisch:

salable *AmE see saleable BrE*

saleable *adj BrE* LAW, PROP veräußerlich, S&M *fit for selling* verkäuflich, *marketable* marktfähig

Geographische Varianten lexikalischer Art enthalten einen Querverweis und werden an jedem Eintrag übersetzt:

earthing *n BrE* (*cf grounding AmE*) COMP, IND *electricity* Erdung *f*

grounding *n AmE* (*cf earthing BrE*) COMP, IND *electricity* Erdung *f*

Abweichende Schreibweisen und lexikalische

Varianten werden vollständig angeführt, wenn es sich um Übersetzungen handelt:

Erdung *f* COMP, IND *Elektrizität* earthing (*BrE*), grounding (*AmE*)

Herkunftsbezeichnung *f* V&M informative labeling (*AmE*), informative labelling (*BrE*)

Abkürzungen enthalten einen Querverweis auf die ausgeschriebene Form und umgekehrt. In beiden Einträgen wird die entsprechende Übersetzung gegeben.

Sonderziehungsrechte *nt pl* (*SZR*) BANK special drawing rights (*SDR*)

SZR *abbr* (*Sonderziehungsrechte*) BANK SDR (*special drawing rights*)

Wenn einer Abkürzung in der Quellsprache keine äquivalente Abkürzung in der Zielsprache gegenübersteht, wird die Übersetzung der ausgeschriebenen Form gegeben, zum Beispiel:

OID *abbr* (*original issue discount*) FIN, STOCK Abzinsungsbetrag *m*, Emissionsdisagio *nt*

Wenn eine Abkürzung je nach Fachgebiet unterschiedliche ausgeschriebene Formen haben kann, dann erscheinen die ausgeschriebenen Formen jeweils nach dem oder den Fachgebietskürzeln:

AI *abbr* COMP (*artificial intelligence*) KI (*künstliche Intelligenz*), FIN (*accrued interest*) aufgelaufene Zinsen *m pl*

Abbreviations used in this dictionary/
Im Wörterbuch verwendete Abkürzungen

Parts of speech/Wortarten

abbr	abbreviation	Abkürzung
adj	adjective	Adjektiv
adv	adverb	Adverb
f	feminine	Femininum
f pl	feminine plural	Femininum Plural
in cpds	base form of compounds	Bestimmungswort bei Komposita
m	masculine	Maskulinum
mf	masculine or feminine	Maskulinum oder Femininum
m,f	masculine, feminine	Maskulinum, Femininum
m pl	masculine plural	Maskulinum Plural
n	noun	Substantiv
n pl	noun plural	Substantiv Plural
nt	neuter	Neutrum
nt pl	neuter plural	Neutrum Plural
phr	phrase	Satzglied
pl	plural	Plural
pref	prefix	Vorsilbe
prep	preposition	Präposition
vi	intransitive verb	Intransitives Verb
v refl	reflexive verb	Reflexives Verb
vt	transitive verb	Transitives Verb

Geographic codes/Geographische Angaben

AmE	American English	Amerikanisches Englisch
BrE	British English	Britisches Englisch
Öst	Austrian German	Österreichisches Deutsch
Sch	Swiss German	Schweizerisches Deutsch

Level codes/Stilangaben und Sprachgebrauch

frml	formal	förmlich
infrml	informal	umgangssprachlich
jarg	jargon	Jargon
obs	obsolete	veraltet

Grammatical codes/Grammatische Angaben

[+acc]	followed by the accusative case	mit Akkusativobjekt
[+dat]	followed by the dative case	mit Dativobjekt
[+gen]	followed by the genitive case	mit Genitivobjekt
[decl. as adj]	declines as adjective	wird wie ein Adjektiv dekliniert

Other abbreviations/Weitere Abkürzungen

sb	somebody, someone
sth	something
jd, jdn, jdm, jds	jemand, jemanden, jemandem, jemandes
etw	etwas

Subject area labels/Fachgebietskürzel

ACC	Accountancy	Rechnungswesen
ADMIN	Business Administration	Verwaltung
BANK	Banking	Bankwesen
COMMS	Communications	Kommunikation
COMP	Computing	Computerwesen
ECON	Economics	Volkswirtschaft
ENVIR	Environment	Umwelt
FIN	Finance	Finanzwesen
GEN COMM	General Commerce	Geschäftswesen
HRM	Human Resource Management	Personalführung
IMP/EXP	Import & Export	Import & Export
IND	Industry	Industrie
INS	Insurance	Versicherungswesen
LAW	Law	Recht
LEIS	Leisure & Tourism	Freizeit & Tourismus
MATH	Mathematics	Mathematik
MEDIA	Media	Medien
MGMNT	Management	Management
PATENTS	Patents	Patentwesen
POL	Politics	Politik
PROP	Property	Grundbesitz
S&M	Sales & Marketing	Verkauf & Marketing
STOCK	Stock Market	Börsen- & Wertpapierwesen
TAX	Taxation	Steuerwesen
TRANSP	Transport	Transportwesen
WEL	Welfare & Safety	Soziale Wohlfahrt & Sicherheit
BANK	Bankwesen	Banking
BÖRSE	Börsen- & Wertpapierwesen	Stock Market
COMP	Computerwesen	Computing
FINANZ	Finanzwesen	Finance
FREI	Freizeit & Tourismus	Leisure & Tourism
GESCHÄFT	Geschäftswesen	General Commerce
GRUND	Grundbesitz	Property
IMP/EXP	Import & Export	Import & Export
IND	Industrie	Industry
KOMM	Kommunikation	Communications
MATH	Mathematik	Mathematics
MEDIEN	Medien	Media

MGMNT	Management	Management
PATENT	Patentwesen	Patents
PERSON	Personalführung	Human Resource Management
POL	Politik	Politics
RECHNUNG	Rechnungswesen	Accountancy
RECHT	Recht	Law
SOZIAL	Soziale Wohlfahrt & Sicherheit	Welfare & Safety
STEUER	Steuerwesen	Taxation
TRANSP	Transportwesen	Transport
UMWELT	Umwelt	Environment
VERSICH	Versicherungswesen	Insurance
VERWALT	Verwaltung	Business Administration
V&M	Verkauf & Marketing	Sales & Marketing
VW	Volkswirtschaft	Economics

Registered trademarks®

Warenzeichen®

WÖRTERBUCH DEUTSCH–ENGLISCH

GERMAN–ENGLISH DICTIONARY

A

ab *prep* TRANSP ex

abänderbar *adj* RECHT commutable

abändern *vt* COMP *Text* amend, GESCHÄFT *Bedingungen* amend, *verbessern* correct, rectify, *Produkt* modify, change, RECHT *Urteil* commute, *Entscheidung* revise, *Gesetz* amend

Abänderung *f* GESCHÄFT change, rectification, POL, RECHT amendment, revision; ◆ **eine ~ einreichen** RECHT propose an amendment, table an amendment; **eine ~ vorlegen** RECHT propose an amendment, table an amendment

Abänderung: **Abänderungsantrag** *m* POL, RECHT proposed amendment, proposed revision

Abandon *m* RECHT, VERSICH abandonment; **Abandonerklärung** *f* VERSICH abandonment clause, notice of abandonment; **Abandonfrist** *f* VERSICH notice of abandonment

Abandonist *m* RECHT, VERSICH abandoner

Abandonnement *nt* RECHT, VERSICH abandonment

abandonnieren *vt* BÖRSE, VERSICH *Optionsaufgabe* abandon; ◆ **etw ~** BÖRSE, VERSICH give up all claims to sth

Abandon: **Abandonrecht** *nt* RECHT right of abandonment; **Abandonrevers** *m* VERSICH declaration of abandonment

abarbeiten *vt* COMP execute, process, FINANZ *Schuld* work off, GESCHÄFT *Liste* work down, *Schuld, Vorschuß* work off

Abarbeiten *nt* COMP execution

Abbau *m* GESCHÄFT scaling-down, MGMNT, PERSON scaling-down, *von Personal* downsizing, VW *von Personal* downsizing, UMWELT *von Regenwäldern, natürlichen Ressourcen* exploitation, degradation, VW *von Mineralien, Kohle* exploitation, *von Restriktionen* dismantling; **~ des Lohngefälles** PERSON tapering

abbaubar: **~er Rohstoff** *m* VW depletable resource

abbauen *vt* FINANZ *Schulden* repay, GESCHÄFT abolish gradually, *System* dismantle, cut down, reduce, *Schulden* work off, abolish, MGMNT, PERSON *Personalstand, Belegschaft* cut down, downsize, slim, UMWELT *natürliche Resourcen* exploit, V&M reduce, VW cut down, run down, *Handelsschranken* remove, dismantle, abolish

Abbau: **Abbauland** *nt* VW wasting assets; **Abbaurecht** *nt* GRUND, RECHT mineral right, mining right

abbauwürdig: **~e Vorräte** *m pl* UMWELT *Bodenschätze* recoverable reserves

Abbild *nt* COMP map

abbilden *vt* MATH transform

Abbildung *f* COMP map, MATH *von Koordinaten, Variablen* transformation, *Logik* mapping, function, PATENT figure

abbrechen *vt* COMP *Programm* abort, truncate, cancel, GESCHÄFT *Versuch, Kampagne* abort, *Verhandlungen, Gespräche* break off, GRUND *Gebäude* demolish, pull down

Abbruch *m* COMP *Programm* abort, truncation, GRUND *eines Gebäudes* demolition; **Abbruchanordnung** *f* GRUND *Gebäude* condemnation; **Abbruchkosten** *pl*

GESCHÄFT cost of demolition, cost of dismantling, demolition cost; **Abbruchtaste** *f* COMP Escape key *(Esc)*; **Abbruchwert** *m* RECHNUNG break-up value

abbuchen *vt* BANK debit, GESCHÄFT debit, charge off, RECHNUNG close out, write off, charge off, debit

Abbuchung *f* BANK payment by standing order, RECHNUNG charge off; **~ durch Einzugsermächtigung** BANK, FINANZ direct debit *(DD)*

ABC-Verfahren *nt* VERWALT ABC method

Abdeckung *f* COMP cover; **~ von Haftpflichtschäden des Arbeitgebers** VERSICH employer's liability coverage

Abdruck *m* GESCHÄFT copy, reprint, reproduction, V&M imprint, *eines Siegels* stamp

Abend- *in cpds* GESCHÄFT evening; **Abendkurs** *m* GESCHÄFT evening class; **Abendschicht** *f* PERSON evening shift, twilight shift *(BrE)*; **Abendsendezeit** *f* MEDIEN early fringe

aberkennen *vt* PERSON deprive, disallow

Aberkennung *f* PERSON *von Titel, Recht* deprivation, disallowance

Abfahrt *f* TRANSP departure, start; **Abfahrtsdatum** *nt* TRANSP sailing date *(S/D)*; **Abfahrtsort** *m* IMP/EXP, TRANSP point of departure

Abfall *m* GESCHÄFT garbage *(AmE)*, refuse, rubbish *(BrE)*, trash *(AmE)*, waste, POL *von Partei* break, breaking away, VW *Kurs* drop, fall; **Abfallaufbereitung** *f* UMWELT waste recycling; **Abfallbeseitigung** *f* GESCHÄFT, UMWELT waste disposal; **Abfalleimer** *f* UMWELT *auf öffentlichen Plätzen* litter bin *(BrE)*, trashcan *(AmE)*, *in einem Haus* garbage can *(AmE)*, rubbish bin *(BrE)*, trashcan *(AmE)*, waste bin

abfallen *vi* POL *von Partei* break, VW *Kurs* drop, fall

Abfall: **Abfallentsorgung** *f* GESCHÄFT, UMWELT waste disposal; **Abfallprodukt** *nt* UMWELT waste product; **Abfallrecycling** *nt* UMWELT waste recycling; **Abfallvermeidung** *f* UMWELT waste prevention; **Abfallwiederaufbereitung** *f* UMWELT recycling of waste; **Abfallwirtschaft** *f* GESCHÄFT waste disposal industry, UMWELT waste disposal industry, waste management

abfangen *vt* GESCHÄFT absorb

abfassen *vt* GESCHÄFT, RECHT, V&M *Reklametext* draft

Abfassung *f* PATENT drawing up; **~ eines Reklametextes** V&M copy writing

abfertigen *vt* COMP dispatch, process, GESCHÄFT attend to, process, serve, IMP/EXP, TRANSP clear through customs

Abfertigung *f* KOMM dispatch, PERSON *Gläubiger* compensation, settlement, TRANSP dispatch; **Abfertigungsagent** *m* IMP/EXP clearing agent; **Abfertigungsbucht** *f* TRANSP dispatch bay; **Abfertigungsvermerk** *m* IMP/EXP out of charge note

abfinden 1. *vt* FINANZ buy out, pay off, *Aktionäre* indemnify, GESCHÄFT compensate, indemnify, PERSON compensate; **2. sich ~ mit** *v refl* GESCHÄFT *Entscheidung* abide by

Abfindung *f* FINANZ money compensation, GESCHÄFT,

PATENT damages, PERSON *Arbeit* ex gratia payment, *Entlassung* payoff, RECHT indemnity, STEUER termination payments; **Abfindungskonto** *nt* **für Investoren** BANK investors' indemnity account; **Abfindungszahlung** *f* PERSON redundancy pay (*BrE*), severance pay, severance payment, termination pay; **Abfindungszahlung** *f* **bei Stillegungen** PERSON *Arbeit* redundancy payment

abflachen *vt* GESCHÄFT level off, MATH *Kurve* flatten

Abflachen *nt* GESCHÄFT leveling-off (*AmE*), levelling-off (*BrE*); **~ der Unternehmenshierarchien** PERSON, VERWALT flattening of hierarchies

abflauen *vi* GESCHÄFT, VW ease off, flag, slacken, *Wachstum* slow down, tail away

Abflauen *nt* VW slackening

abflauend *adj* VW flagging

Abflug *m* TRANSP departure; **Abflughalle** *f* TRANSP departure lounge; **Abflugkontrollsystem** *nt* TRANSP departure control system (*DCS*)

Abfluß *m* FINANZ outflow, TRANSP outlet, UMWELT effluent, efflux, VW *Geldabfluß* drain

Abfrage *f* COMP enquiry, query; **Abfragedatei** *f* COMP enquiry file; **Abfrageeinheit** *f* COMP enquiry unit; **Abfrageergebnis** *nt* COMP search result

abfragen *vt* COMP enquire

Abfrage: **Abfrageprogramm** *nt* COMP enquiry program; **Abfragesprache** *f* COMP *Datenbank* query language (*QL*); **Abfragesystem** *nt* COMP enquiry system

Abführung *f* STEUER transfer (*tr.*, *tfr*)

Abg. *abbr* (*Abgeordnete(r)*) POL delegate, deputy, MP (*BrE*) (*Member of Parliament*), Rep. (*AmE*) (*Representative*)

Abgabe *f* FINANZ levy, GESCHÄFT royalty, charge, tax, IMP/EXP levy, STEUER imposition, VW charge, tax, *Förderungsabgabe* royalty; **~ von Angeboten** GESCHÄFT bidding, submission of bids, MGMNT submission of bids, VW bidding technique; **~ von Geboten** GESCHÄFT bidding; ♦ **zur ~ von Angeboten auffordern** GESCHÄFT invite tenders

Abgabe: **Abgabefrist** *f* GESCHÄFT closing date, due date, filing date, *Annahmeschluß* final date for acceptance; **Abgabefristverlängerung** *f* STEUER extension of time for filing; **Abgabekurs** *m* BÖRSE issue price

abgabenpflichtig *adj* IMP/EXP, STEUER dutiable, RECHT, STEUER chargeable, liable to pay tax, liable to pay taxes, liable to tax, taxable; **~e Waren** *f pl* IMP/EXP, STEUER chargeable goods, dutiable goods

Abgabe: **Abgabesatz** *m* **der Bank** BÖRSE, FINANZ bank selling rate; **Abgabetermin** *m* RECHT final deadline

Abgang *m* TRANSP *eines Zuges, eines Schiffes* departure; **~ von flüssigen Mitteln** FINANZ cash drain; **Abgangsalter** *nt* VERSICH age at expiry; **Abgangsgespräch** *nt* VERWALT exit interview; **Abgangsursache** *f* VERSICH cause of cancellation; **Abgangszeugnis** *nt* SOZIAL school leaving certificate

Abgas *nt* UMWELT *von Fahrzeugen* car exhaust emissions, exhaust gas; **Abgasemission** *f* UMWELT exhaust emission

abgeändert *adj* GESCHÄFT amended; **~e Lebensversicherung** *f* VERSICH modified life insurance

abgeben *vt* GESCHÄFT *Angebot* submit, VERSICH cede

abgebend: **~e Gesellschaft** *f* VERSICH ceding company

abgedunkelt *adj* COMP *Bildschirm* dimmed

abgeführt: **~e Mehrwertsteuer** *f* STEUER value-added tax paid (*BrE*), VAT paid (*BrE*)

abgegrenzt: **~er Gewinnbeteiligungsplan** *m* STEUER deferred profit-sharing plan

abgehend: **~e Fracht** *f* TRANSP cargo outward

abgeholt: **nicht ~er Brief** *m* KOMM unclaimed letter

abgekürzt *adj* VERSICH deferred; **~e Lebensversicherung** *f* VERSICH deferred annuity; **~e Todesfallversicherung** *f* VERSICH term insurance, term life insurance; **~es Verfahren** *nt* GESCHÄFT, RECHT expedited procedure, summary judgment, summary proceedings

abgelaufen *adj* BANK mature, BÖRSE lapsed, FINANZ mature, GESCHÄFT expired, no longer valid; **~e Option** *f* BÖRSE lapsed option

abgeleitet: **~e Nachfrage** *f* VW derived demand, indirect demand

abgelten *vt* GESCHÄFT compensate, pay in settlement, satisfy, PATENT reimburse

Abgeltung *f* FINANZ payment, GESCHÄFT compensation, PATENT reimbursement

abgemacht *adj* GESCHÄFT agreed; **~er Preis** *m* GESCHÄFT agreed price; **~e Summe** *f* GESCHÄFT agreed sum

Abgeordnete(r) *mf* [decl. as adj] (*Abg.*) POL delegate, deputy, Member of Parliament (*BrE*) (*MP*), Representative (*AmE*) (*Rep.*); **~ des Europaparlaments** POL European Member of Parliament (*Euro MP*), Member of the European Parliament (*MEP*)

abgerechnet *adj* BANK, FINANZ cleared (*cld*); **~er Scheck** *m* BANK cleared check (*AmE*), cleared cheque (*BrE*)

abgerufen: **~e Ware** *f* TRANSP goods called forward

Abgesandte(r) *mf* [decl. as adj] POL ambassador, delegate, emissary

abgeschaltet *adj* COMP disabled

abgeschirmt *adj* GESCHÄFT screened; **nicht ~** *adj* GESCHÄFT unscreened

abgeschlossen *adj* GESCHÄFT completed, closed, RECHT completed; **~es Bilanzjahr** *nt* RECHNUNG accounting year ended; **~es Geschäftsjahr** *nt* RECHNUNG accounting year ended, STEUER accounting year ended, fiscal year ended; **~es Haushaltsjahr** *nt* RECHNUNG accounting year ended, STEUER accounting year ended, fiscal year ended; **~e Hypothek** *f* BANK closed-end mortgage; **~es Konto** *nt* BANK, FINANZ, RECHNUNG closed account; **~es Rechnungsjahr** *nt* RECHNUNG accounting year ended; **~es Wirtschaftsjahr** *nt* STEUER accounting year ended, fiscal year ended

abgeschrieben *adj* RECHNUNG written off; **nicht ~** *adj* RECHNUNG undepreciated, unamortized; **nicht ~es Agio** *nt* **auf Investitionen** BÖRSE unamortized premiums on investments; **~er Betrag** *m* RECHNUNG depreciated amount; **nicht ~es Disagio** *nt* BÖRSE unamortized bond discount; **nicht ~es Disagio** *nt* **von Schatzwechseln** BÖRSE unamortized discount on Treasury bills; **~e Forderungen** *f pl* FINANZ written-off receivables; **nicht ~e Kosten** *pl* RECHNUNG undepreciated cost

abgesehen: **~ von** *prep* GESCHÄFT apart from

abgesetzt: **~es Manuskript** *nt* V&M dead matter

abgesichert: **~er Kredit** *m* FINANZ secured credit; **~e Verbindlichkeit** *f* RECHNUNG hedged liability; **~es Vermögen** *nt* RECHNUNG hedged asset

abgesondert: **~e Fracht** *f* TRANSP cargo in isolation

abgestimmt: **aufeinander ~** *adj* GESCHÄFT coordinated, synchronized; **aufeinander ~e Formulare** *nt pl* VERWALT aligned forms; **aufeinander ~e Hersteller** *m pl* IND *Einzelhandelskette* quasi-manufacturer; **~e Vergleichsstichprobe** *f* V&M matched sample; **~e Weltzeit** *f* GESCHÄFT universal time (*UT*), universal time coordinated (*UTC*); **aufeinander ~e Werbung** *f* V&M tie-in promotion

abgestuft: **nicht ~** *adj* GESCHÄFT ungraded; **~es Sozialrentensystem** *nt* PERSON graduated pension scheme

abgetakelt *adj infrml* GESCHÄFT clapped out (*BrE*) (*infrml*)

abgeteilt: **~e Menge** *f* IND batch

abgewickelt *adj* BÖRSE closed-out

abgeworben: **~ werden** *vi* PERSON *Suche nach Führungskräften* be headhunted

abgezeichnet *adj* GESCHÄFT acknowledged

abgezielt: **~ sein auf** *phr* GESCHÄFT be aimed at, cater for

abgezinst: **~er Cash-Flow** *m* FINANZ, RECHNUNG discounted cash flow (*DCF*)

Abgleich *m* FINANZ, RECHNUNG balancing

abgrenzen *vt* RECHNUNG adjust, accrue

Abgrenzung *f* RECHNUNG adjustment

abhaken *vt* GESCHÄFT tick (*BrE*), check (*AmE*), *in einer Liste* tick off (*BrE*), check off (*AmE*)

abhalten *vt* GESCHÄFT *Referendum*, MGMNT *Konferenz, Tagung* hold; ♦ **~ von** GESCHÄFT deter from

abhandeln *vt* GESCHÄFT *Thema* treat

abhängen *vi*: **~ von** GESCHÄFT *Ereignis* depend on

abhängig: **~e Beschäftigung** *f* VW dependent economy; **~e Deckung** *f* VERSICH dependent coverage; **~e Gesellschaft** *f* BÖRSE, VW controlled company; **~es Patent** *nt* PATENT dependent patent; **~ sein von** *phr* PATENT be dependent on; **~er Versicherungsschutz** *m* VERSICH dependent coverage; **~e Volkswirtschaft** *f* VW dependent economy

Abhängigkeit *f* GESCHÄFT dependence, dependency; **~ von Einnahmen** FINANZ revenue dependency; **Abhängigkeitsanspruch** *m* PATENT dependent claim

abheben *vt* BANK *Geld*, FINANZ, GESCHÄFT, VW *Geld* draw, withdraw

Abhebung *f* BANK, FINANZ, GESCHÄFT, VW withdrawal

abhelfen *vt* GESCHÄFT remedy, RECHT redress

Abhilfe *f* GESCHÄFT remedy, RECHT redress

abholen *vt* TRANSP *Ladung* pick up

Abholung *f* TRANSP pick-up; **Abholungskosten** *pl* TRANSP pick-up cost; **Abholungsservice** *m* TRANSP pick-up service

Abholzung *f* UMWELT, VW exploitation

abhören *vt* KOMM *Telefon* tap, tap into

Abhören *nt* COMP, GESCHÄFT, KOMM telephone tapping, wiretapping

Abitur *nt* GESCHÄFT, SOZIAL (*cf Matura, cf Maturitätsprüfung*) ≈ Advanced level (*BrE*) (*A level*), ≈ High School Diploma (*AmE*)

abkippen *vt* UMWELT dump

abklappern *vt infrml* POL *Gemeinden, Wahlkampf* whistle-stop, do the rounds (*infrml*)

Abkommen *nt* GESCHÄFT agreement; **~ mit Erstversicherer** VERSICH leading underwriter agreement; **~ über Nichtbeteiligung an Streiks** PERSON strike-free agreement (*BrE*); **~ zwischen Regionalbanken** BANK regional banking pacts; **~ zur Stabilisierung der Rohstoffpreise** VW *Außenwirtschaft* commodity stabilization schemes; **~ zur Stabilisierung der Wechselkurse** VW currency stabilization scheme; ♦ **sich einem ~ anschließen** POL accede to a treaty

Abkömmling *m* RECHT *Erben* descendant, issue

Abkühlungszeit *f* BÖRSE, PERSON, VERSICH cooling-off period

Abkunft *f* V&M lineage

abkürzen *vt* GESCHÄFT abbreviate, shorten, KOMM *Inhalt* abridge, VERSICH abbreviate, shorten

Abkürzung *f* GESCHÄFT abbreviation, KOMM *Inhalt* abridgement, VERSICH abbreviation

ABl. *abbr* (*Amtsblatt, Amtsblatt der Europäischen Union*) POL, VERWALT OJ (*Official Journal*)

abladen 1. *vt* GESCHÄFT, IND, TRANSP offload, unload; **2.** *vi* GESCHÄFT, IND, TRANSP offload, unload

Abladen *nt* GESCHÄFT, IND, TRANSP offloading, unloading

Ablage *f* VERWALT filing; **~ für Eingänge** VERWALT in-tray; **~ nach Sachgebieten** subject filing; **Ablagefach** *nt* VERWALT filing drawer; **Ablagekopie** *f* VERWALT file copy

Ablagekorb *m* VERWALT filing basket, letter tray; **~ für abgehende Sendungen** VERWALT out-tray; **~ für unerledigte Arbeiten** VERWALT pending tray

Ablagerung *f* UMWELT dumping

Ablage: **Ablagesystem** *nt* VERWALT filing system

Ablauf *m* COMP flow, *Programm* procedure, GESCHÄFT procedure, expiry, expiration, VERWALT procedure, *Funktionieren* functioning; ♦ **nach ~ wertlos sein** BÖRSE expire worthless

Ablauf: **Ablaufbahn** *f* TRANSP *Schiff* runway; **Ablaufdatum** *nt* **der Exportlizenz** IMP/EXP export licence expiry date (*BrE*), export license expiry date (*AmE*); **Ablaufdiagramm** *nt* COMP process chart, GESCHÄFT flowchart

ablaufen *vi* GESCHÄFT *Ereignis* come to an end, *Frist* expire, VERSICH lapse

Ablauf: **Ablaufkontrolle** *f* MGMNT progress control; **Ablaufkonzept** *nt* BÖRSE flow concept; **Ablauflinie** *f* BÖRSE flow line; **Ablaufplan** *m* TRANSP operating schedule; **Ablaufplanung** *f* GESCHÄFT scheduling, MGMNT operational planning; **Ablauftag** *m* **der Ausfuhrgenehmigung** IMP/EXP export licence expiry date (*BrE*), export license expiry date (*AmE*); **Ablauftermin** *m* BANK date of maturity (*DOM*), GESCHÄFT expiry date; **Ablauftermin** *m* **für Ausfuhrgenehmigung** IMP/EXP export licence expiry date (*BrE*), export license expiry date (*AmE*)

ablegen *vt* VERWALT *Dokumente* file

Ableger *m* GESCHÄFT *Firma* spin-off

ablehnen *vt* GESCHÄFT decline, turn away, oppose, *Vorschlag* object to, PERSON *Streik* repudiate, RECHT decline, reject

Ablehnung *f* GESCHÄFT refusal, PATENT refusal, rejection, RECHT repudiation; **Ablehnungsbereich** *m* MATH critical region

ablesen *vt* GESCHÄFT take a reading

Ablichtung *f* GESCHÄFT photostat

ablösbar *adj* GESCHÄFT commutable; **~e Schuldverschreibungen** *f pl* RECHNUNG redeemable bonds

ablösen vt GESCHÄFT relieve, *Verpflichtung* commute, *Vorgänger* supersede; ♦ **jdn** ~ GESCHÄFT take over from sb

Ablösung f BÖRSE *Verbindlichkeiten* liquidation, anticipated redemption, FINANZ anticipated redemption; **Ablösungsrecht** nt BANK equity of redemption

ABM abbr (*Arbeitsbeschaffungsmaßnahmen*) PERSON job-creating measures, community programme (*BrE*), community program (*AmE*), special employment measures (*SEM*)

abmachen vi GESCHÄFT make arrangements

abmelden: sich ~ v refl COMP *Benutzer* log off, log out, FREI check out

Abmeldung f FREI, V&M *Hotel* checkout

abmessen vt GESCHÄFT gage (*AmE*), gauge (*BrE*)

Abnahme f BÖRSE taking delivery, MEDIEN *von Manuskripten*, TRANSP, V&M, VERSICH acceptance, VW decline; ~ **aus Devisengeschäft** RECHT *Vertragsrecht* commitment to accept delivery of foreign exchange in forward transaction; ~ **der Gewinnspanne** RECHNUNG margin shrinkage; **Abnahmebescheinigung** f TRANSP acceptance certificate; **Abnahmeprüfung** f IND, TRANSP acceptance trial; **Abnahmetest** m V&M acceptance trial; **Abnahmeverpflichtung** f RECHT *Vertragsrecht* guarantee to purchase, purchase commitment; **Abnahmezeugnis** nt TRANSP acceptance certificate

abnehmen 1. vt GESCHÄFT take away, accept, *Waren* buy, take; **2.** vi GESCHÄFT *Nachfrage* dwindle, tail away, VW contract, decline, shrink

abnehmend: ~**er Anteil** m VW declining share; ~**e Erträge** m pl VW diminishing returns; ~**e Grenzrate** f **der Substitution** VW diminishing marginal rate of substitution; **nach** ~**er Liquidität** phr RECHNUNG in decreasing liquidity order; ~**e Skalenerträge** m pl VW diminishing returns to scale

abnorm adj GESCHÄFT abnormal

abnutzbar: ~**es unbewegliches Vermögen** nt GRUND depreciable real estate; ~**es Vermögen** nt RECHNUNG depreciable asset, depreciable property

abnutzen vt VW erode

Abnutzung f GESCHÄFT wear and tear, VW erosion; ~ **durch Gebrauch** GESCHÄFT wear and tear; **Abnutzungsfaktor** m V&M wearout factor; **Abnutzungsgrad** m GESCHÄFT attrition rate

Abo nt infrml (*Abonnement*) BÖRSE, MEDIEN sub (*infrml*) (*BrE*) (*subscription*)

Abonnement nt (*Abo*) BÖRSE, MEDIEN subscription (*sub*); **Abonnementsfahrkarte** f TRANSP commutation ticket (*AmE*), season ticket (*BrE*); **Abonnementspreis** m GESCHÄFT subscription price

Abonnent, in m,f MEDIEN, V&M subscriber; **Abonnentenfernsehen** nt MEDIEN pay TV

abonnieren vt GESCHÄFT *Zeitungen, Bücher* subscribe to, MEDIEN, V&M take out a subscription

abonniert: ~**e Auflage** f V&M subscribed circulation

Abraumbau m IND opencast mining (*BrE*)

Abreaktionskanäle m pl KOMM, PERSON abreaction channels

abrechnen 1. vt BANK clear, account for; **2.** vi GESCHÄFT cash up, RECHNUNG make up one's accounts

Abrechnung f BANK clearing, FINANZ make-up, clearance, GESCHÄFT billing, RECHNUNG reckoning, invoicing; ~ **für Optionsgeschäfte** FINANZ option account; ♦ ~ **verlegen** RECHNUNG render an accounting for sth

Abrechnung: **Abrechnungsabteilung** f BANK settlements department; **Abrechnungsbank** f BANK, FINANZ clearing bank; **Abrechnungskurse** m pl BÖRSE strike price; **Abrechnungskurszeiträume** m pl BÖRSE strike price intervals; **Abrechnungspaket** nt COMP accounting package; **Abrechnungsperiode** f; BÖRSE settlement period, RECHNUNG accounting period, accounting year, fiscal period, STEUER fiscal period; **Abrechnungsstelle** f FINANZ, TRANSP clearing house; **Abrechnungstag** m BÖRSE name day, settlement day, GESCHÄFT account day; **Abrechnungsverfahren** m BANK clearing; **Abrechnungsverkehr** m BANK clearing; **Abrechnungszeitraum** m BÖRSE account (*BrE*)

abreisen vi FREI check out

Abreiß- in cpds GESCHÄFT tear-off; **Abreißkalender** m GESCHÄFT tear-off calendar; **Abreißkupon** m GESCHÄFT tear-off coupon

Abriß m GESCHÄFT summary, synopsis, GRUND demolition, MEDIEN, V&M synopsis

abrollen vt COMP *Bildschirm* scroll down

Abruf m FINANZ call; ♦ **auf** ~ **borgen** BANK borrow at call

Abruf: **Abrufauftrag** m GESCHÄFT blanket order

abrufen vt COMP retrieve

Abruf: **Abrufprogramm** nt COMP calling program; **Abrufzeit** f COMP retrieval time

abrunden vt MATH *Zahl* round down

Absage f GESCHÄFT refusal, cancellation; ~ **mangels Eignung** PERSON *Stellengesuch* application turned down on the grounds of unsuitability

absahnen vt infrml GESCHÄFT *Geld, Markt* cream off (*infrml*)

Absatz m V&M sales, VERWALT paragraph; ~ **festverzinslicher Wertpapiere** BÖRSE bond sales; ~ **über Händlernetz** V&M network marketing; **Absatzaktivität** f V&M sales activity; **Absatzanalyse** f V&M marketing research; **Absatzanalytiker** m V&M sales analyst; **Absatzanteil** m V&M market coverage; **Absatzbelebung** f VW revival of sales; **Absatzbereich** m V&M market coverage; **Absatzeinbruch** m V&M slump in sales; **Absatzerwartungen** f pl V&M market prospects; **Absatzexperte** m, **Absatzexpertin** f PERSON, V&M marketeer; **Absatzfachkraft** f PERSON, V&M marketeer; **Absatzfeld** nt V&M outlet; **Absatzförderung** f **von Lockartikeln** V&M leader merchandising; **Absatzforschung** f V&M field survey; **Absatzgebiet** nt GESCHÄFT trading area, distribution area, V&M sales territory, outlet, market area; **Absatzgremium** nt V&M sales conference; **Absatzkanal** m GESCHÄFT distribution channel, V&M channel of sales, channel of distribution, marketing channel; **Absatzkette** f V&M marketing chain; **Absatzkonferenz** f V&M marketing conference; **Absatzleiter, in** m,f MGMNT distribution manager, PERSON marketing manager, distribution manager, TRANSP distribution manager; **Absatzleitung** f MGMNT sales management; **Absatzmagnet** m V&M anchor tenant; **Absatzmanagement** nt V&M market management; **Absatzmarktberatungsdienst** m V&M market prospects service; **Absatzmaximierung** f V&M sales maximization; **Absatzmix** m V&M sales mix; **Absatzmodalitäten** f pl IMP/EXP terms of sale;

Absatzmodelle *nt pl* V&M marketing models; **Absatzmöglichkeit** *f* V&M sales opportunity, market opportunity; **Absatznetz** *nt* V&M sales network; **Absatzorganisation** *f* V&M sales force

absatzorienterte: Verflechtung *f* VW forward linkage

Absatz: **Absatzorientierung** *f* V&M marketing orientation; **Absatzphase** *f* BÖRSE *nach Neuemission* period of digestion; **Absatzplan** *m* V&M market plan, sales projection; **Absatzplanung** *f* V&M marketing plan; **Absatzpolitik** *f* GESCHÄFT, TRANSP distribution policy, V&M marketing policy, sales policy, distribution policy; **Absatzprognose** *f* V&M sales forecast; **Absatzprogramm** *nt* V&M sales mix; **Absatzprüfung** *f* V&M marketing audit; **Absatzrückgang** *m* V&M slump in sales; **Absatzstrategie** *f* V&M marketing strategy; **Absatzvereinbarung** *f* V&M marketing agreement; **Absatzweg** *m* V&M trade channel, distribution channel; **Absatzwerkzeuge** *nt pl* V&M marketing tools; **Absatzwirtschaft** *f* V&M distributive trades; **Absatzzahlen** *f pl* V&M sales figures; **Absatzzentrum** *nt* TRANSP distribution center (*AmE*), distribution centre (*BrE*); **Absatzziel** *nt* V&M sales goal, sales target, marketing objective

abschaffen *vt* GESCHÄFT abolish, supersede

Abschaffung *f* GESCHÄFT abolishment, abolition; **~ von Zöllen** VW abolition of tariffs

abschalten *vt* COMP turn off, GESCHÄFT shut off, KOMM turn off

Abschalten *nt* COMP turning-off, GESCHÄFT shutting off, KOMM turning-off

abschätzbar *adj* GESCHÄFT appreciable

abschätzen *vt* GESCHÄFT size up (*infrml*)

abschicken *vt* GESCHÄFT post

abschieben *vt* POL deport

Abschiebung *f* POL deportation

Abschied: ohne ~ weggehen *phr* GESCHÄFT take French leave

abschirmen *vt* GESCHÄFT insulate, screen, shield

Abschlag: auf ~ *phr* PERSON in part payment

abschlägig: ~e Antwort *f* GESCHÄFT refusal

Abschlag: **Abschlagsdividende** *f* RECHNUNG interim dividend; **Abschlagszahlung** *f* BANK payment on account, FINANZ part payment; **Abschlagszahlungen** *f pl* FINANZ progress payments

Abschlepp- *in cpds* TRANSP breakdown-, tow, towaway, towing

abschleppen *vt* TRANSP tow

Abschlepp-: Abschleppen *nt* TRANSP towing; **Abschleppseil** *nt* TRANSP towrope; **Abschleppwagen** *m* TRANSP breakdown van (*BrE*), recovery vehicle, tow truck (*AmE*), towing ambulance; **Abschleppzone** *f* TRANSP towaway zone (*AmE*)

abschließen *vt* BANK make up, take out, balance, FINANZ balance, GESCHÄFT complete, top up (*BrE*), *Vertrag* finalize, transact, *beenden* conclude, *Meeting* round off, GRUND complete, RECHNUNG transact, balance, *Bücher* close, RECHT complete, conclude, VERSICH take out, VERWALT conclude; ◆ **Konto ~** BANK post up an account, FINANZ settle an account, RECHNUNG rule off

Abschluß *m* BANK making up, BÖRSE *einzelner Abschluß an Londoner Börse*, FINANZ bargain, GESCHÄFT bargain, *Vertrag* completion, deal, conclusion, transaction, RECHNUNG transaction, financial statement, RECHT *Vertrag* conclusion, SOZIAL qualification, VERWALT *Vertrag* conclusion, V&M sale; **~ auf Basis von Marktpreisen** GESCHÄFT, STEUER, V&M arm's-length transaction; **~ mit Bestätigungsvermerk** RECHNUNG certified financial statement; **~ von Leistungsverträgen** GESCHÄFT incentive contracting; **~ von Nebenverträgen** GESCHÄFT subcontracting; ◆ **zum ~ bringen** PATENT carry out; **einen ~ erreichen** GESCHÄFT reach a deal; **einen ~ tätigen** GESCHÄFT reach a deal

Abschluß: **Abschlußalter** *nt* VERSICH age at entry; **Abschlußbesprechung** *f* MGMNT debriefing; **eine Abschlußbesprechung durchführen** *phr* MGMNT debrief; **Abschlußbestätigung** *f* BÖRSE transaction slip; **Abschlußbewertung** *f* RECHNUNG accounts appraisal; **Abschlußbilanz** *f* BANK, FINANZ, RECHNUNG ending balance; **Abschlußblatt** *nt* BÖRSE, COMP, FINANZ, RECHNUNG, VERWALT balance sheet, spreadsheet, work sheet; **Abschlußbuchung** *f* RECHNUNG closing entry; **Abschlußdividende** *f* BÖRSE final dividend; **Abschlüsse** *m pl* BÖRSE dealings; **Abschlußgebühr** *f* BÖRSE, V&M sales charge; **Abschlußinventar** *nt* RECHNUNG ending inventory; **Abschlußkauf** *m* BÖRSE closing purchase (*BrE*); **Abschlußkosten** *pl* FINANZ closing costs; **Abschlußprovision** *f* VERSICH acquisition commission; **Abschlußprovision** *f* **des Generalvertreters** VERSICH overriding commission; **Abschlußprüferrichtlinie** *f* RECHNUNG Auditor's Operational Standard; **Abschlußprüfung** *f* RECHNUNG audit, SOZIAL *Hochschule* finals, final examination, *Schule* leaving examination; **Abschlußrechnung** *f* RECHNUNG accounting report; **Abschlußrede** *f* GESCHÄFT *Konferenz* closing address, closing speech, POL closing address, closing speech, wrap-up (*AmE*); **Abschlußspanne** *f* BÖRSE trading variation; **Abschlußtest** *m* V&M post test; **Abschlußverlust** *m* RECHNUNG terminal loss; **Abschlußvermittler, in** *m,f* VERSICH acquisition agent; **Abschlußwert** *m* RECHNUNG winding-up value; **Abschlußzahlen** *f pl* RECHNUNG accounting data; **Abschlußzahlung** *f* FINANZ final instalment (*BrE*), final installment (*AmE*); **Abschlußzeugnis** *nt* SOZIAL *Gymnasium, Fachoberschule, Realschule* high-school diploma (*AmE*), leaving certificate (*BrE*)

abschneiden *vt* COMP *Dezimalstellen* truncate

Abschnitt *m* BÖRSE apron, GESCHÄFT chapter, section, MEDIEN leg, VERWALT paragraph; ◆ **~ aufheben** BÖRSE lift a leg

abschöpfen *vt* GESCHÄFT cream off, siphon off, VW absorb; ◆ **einen Gebrauchtwagenüberschuß ~** GESCHÄFT absorb a used car surplus

Abschöpfung *f* GESCHÄFT skimming, VW *Liquidität* absorption, drain; **~ im Rahmen der gemeinsamen Agrarpolitik** VW CAP levy, Common Agricultural Policy levy; **Abschöpfungspolitik** *f* V&M skimming policy

abschotten *vt* GESCHÄFT compartmentalize, insulate

Abschottung *f* GESCHÄFT, VW compartmentation

Abschreckung: als ~ *phr* GESCHÄFT in terrorem; **Abschreckungsmittel** *nt* GESCHÄFT deterrent

abschreibbar *adj* RECHNUNG amortizable

abschreiben *vt* BANK *Vermögenswerte, Aktiva* amortize, FINANZ write off, GESCHÄFT *Forderung, Verlust* write off, *Text* transcribe, RECHNUNG write down, *Vermögenswerte, Aktiva* amortize, depreciate, VERSICH write off, vw *Vermögenswerte, Aktiva* depreciate; ◆ **über zehn Jahre ~ lassen** RECHNUNG write off over ten years

Abschreibepolice *f* SOZIAL floating policy, VERSICH floater (*AmE*), floating policy; **~ über persönliches Eigentum/bewegliche Sachwerte** VERSICH personal property floater

Abschreibung *f* GESCHÄFT write-off, transcription, GRUND depreciation, RECHNUNG amortizement, capital allowance (*BrE*), writing-off, allowance for depreciation (*AmE*), amortization, vw capital consumption, capital consumption allowance; **~ auf Anlagevermögen** BANK depreciation of fixed assets; **~ durch Wertminderung** GESCHÄFT, VW wear and tear; **Abschreibungsanpassung** *f* RECHNUNG depreciation adjustment; **Abschreibungsarten** *f pl* vw methods of depreciation; **Abschreibungsbasis** *f* RECHNUNG depreciable basis; **Abschreibungsbetrag** *m* RECHNUNG allowance for depreciation (*AmE*), capital allowance (*BrE*), depreciable amount, STEUER writing-down allowance

abschreibungsfähig *adj* RECHNUNG amortizable; **~e Kosten** *pl* RECHNUNG depreciable cost

Abschreibung: **Abschreibungsmethoden** *f pl* vw methods of depreciation; **Abschreibungsrücklage** *f* RECHNUNG depreciation reserve; **Abschreibungssatz** *m* RECHNUNG rate of depreciation; **Abschreibungstabellen** *f pl* STEUER guideline lives; **Abschreibungszeitraum** *m* STEUER, vw depreciable life

Abschrift *f* GESCHÄFT copy; **~ vom Original** GESCHÄFT copy from the original

Abschußliste *f infrml* GESCHÄFT hit list (*infrml*)

abschütteln *vt* GESCHÄFT shake off

abschwächen 1. *vt* BANK, BÖRSE sag, GESCHÄFT *Idee, Politik, Aussage* water down, weaken, V&M sag; **2.** *vi* BÖRSE sag, vw *Kurse, Andrang* level off, weaken; **3. sich ~** *v refl* GESCHÄFT tail away, vw slow down

Abschwächung *f* vw slowdown; **Abschwächungsoption** *f* MGMNT fallback option

Abschwung *m* GESCHÄFT downturn, vw contraction, downswing, downturn

abseits *adv* GESCHÄFT aloof

absenden *vt* KOMM, TRANSP dispatch

Absender, in *m,f* IMP/EXP, KOMM, TRANSP consignor, forwarder (*fwdr*), sender

Absentismus *m* PERSON absenteeism

absetzbar *adj* STEUER allowable

absetzen *vt* GESCHÄFT sell

Absetzung *f* STEUER *Einkommenssteuer* deduction; **~ für Abnutzung** (*AfA*) RECHNUNG allowance for depreciation

absichern *vt* BÖRSE secure, GESCHÄFT shield; ◆ **sich ~ gegen** GESCHÄFT *Risiko* guard against

Absicherung *f* BÖRSE safe hedge; **~ gegen Inflation** VERSICH hedge against inflation; **~ eines Wertpapierportefeuilles gegen Kursverlust** BÖRSE portfolio insurance; **Absicherungsklausel** *f* BÖRSE hedge clause

Absicht *f* RECHT intention, intent; ◆ **in der ~, etw zu tun** GESCHÄFT with a view to doing sth

absichtlich: **~ falsche Angaben machen** *phr* RECHT *bei Vertragsschluß* wilfully misrepresent the facts

Absicht: **Absichtserklärung** *f* BÖRSE letter of intent,

purposes statement, GESCHÄFT memorandum of intent, RECHT *Vertragsrecht* declaration of intent

absolut 1. *adj* GESCHÄFT absolute; ◆ **in ~en Größen** vw in absolute terms; **2.** *adv* vw in absolute terms

absolut: **~e Abweichung** *f* MATH absolute deviation; **~e Adresse** *f* COMP machine address, KOMM absolute address; **~e Adressierung** *f* COMP *Programme*, KOMM absolute addressing; **~ Arme** *pl* vw absolute poor; **~e Armut** *f* vw absolute poverty; **~e Einkommenshypothese** *f* vw absolute income hypothesis; **~er Fehler** *m* MATH absolute error; **~e Häufigkeit** *f* MATH absolute frequency; **~er Höchststand** *m* BÖRSE, GESCHÄFT all-time high; **~e Klassenhäufigkeit** *f* MATH absolute class frequency; **~e Konzentration** *f* vw absolute concentration; **~es Limit** *nt* GESCHÄFT absolute limit; **~er Mangel** *m* vw absolute scarcity; **~er Mehrwert** *m* vw absolute surplus value; **~e Mittellosigkeit** *f* vw absolute poverty; **~er Steuereffekt** *m* STEUER absolute tax incidence; **~e Steuerinzidenz** *f* STEUER absolute tax incidence; **~e Steuerwirkung** *f* STEUER absolute tax incidence

absorbieren *vt* GESCHÄFT absorb

Absorption *f* GESCHÄFT absorption, vw absorption, total domestic expenditure; **Absorptionskapazität** *f* GESCHÄFT, vw absorptive capacity; **Absorptionstheorie** *f* vw absorption approach

Abspaltung *f* GESCHÄFT *von Muttergesellschaft* spin-off

abspanen *vt* IND machine

abspecken *vt* MGMNT, PERSON *Arbeiterschaft* slim down

abspeisen: **jdn mit etw ~** *phr infrml* V&M fob sb off with sth (*infrml*)

abspielen *vt* COMP *Band* replay

Absprache *f* GESCHÄFT accord; **~ unter Ehrenmännern** RECHT gentleman's agreement; ◆ **nur nach ~** GESCHÄFT by appointment only; **~ treffen** GESCHÄFT agree

absprechen: **sich ~** *v refl* GESCHÄFT agree

Abstand *m* COMP *Schriftzeichen* pitch, *Zeilen* space; ◆ **~ halten von** PERSON stand off

Abstand: **Abstandsgeld** *nt* vw compensation

absteigend: **~e Folge** *f* COMP decreasing order

abstellen *vt* GESCHÄFT shut off, PERSON second, UMWELT abate

Abstellgleis *nt* TRANSP side track (*AmE*), siding

Abstellung *f* PERSON secondment, temporary transfer

abstempeln 1. *vt* GESCHÄFT stamp; **2.** *vi* IND, PERSON clock off

abstimmen 1. *vt* GESCHÄFT agree, RECHNUNG agree, balance, reconcile, square; ◆ **aufeinander ~** GESCHÄFT coordinate; **~ mit** GESCHÄFT tailor to; **2.** *vi* PERSON, POL vote

Abstimmung *f* FINANZ reconciliation, GESCHÄFT *Maßnahmen, Listen* tuning, coordination, MGMNT voting, *von Plänen* coordination, PERSON, POL voting, vote, RECHNUNG reconciliation, vw *zwischen Arbeitslosigkeit und Inflation* trade-off; **~ durch Handaufheben** PERSON, POL vote by show of hands; **~ über Investitionen** POL capital expenditure vote; **~ von Konten** RECHNUNG account matching, account reconciliation; **~ laufender Einnahmen und Ausgaben** MGMNT cash management; **~ per Telefon** KOMM, MEDIEN, POL phone-in poll

Abstinenz *f* vw abstinence; **Abstinenztheorie** *f* vw agio theory of interest; **Abstinenztheorie** *f* **des Zinses** VW abstinence theory of interest

abstoßen *vt* BÖRSE sell off, FINANZ divest, unload, GESCHÄFT sell off, shed, RECHT divest, TRANSP offload, vw *Beteiligung* hive off

Abstoßen *nt* BÖRSE bailing out, dumping, unloading; **~ einer Tochtergesellschaft** FINANZ, RECHT divestiture

Abstrakt *nt* vw abstract

abstrakt: **~e Arbeitskräfte** *f pl* PERSON abstract labor (*AmE*), abstract labour (*BrE*)

Absturz *m* COMP system crash, abnormal system end, *Programme* breakdown, crash, TRANSP *Flugzeug* crash

abstürzen *vi* COMP *Programm, Computer*, TRANSP *Flugzeug* crash

Abtastbereich *m* COMP scan area

abtasten *vt* COMP scan

Abtasten *nt* COMP scanning

Abtastgerät *nt* COMP scanner

Abtastung *f* COMP scanning

Abteilung *f* GESCHÄFT department (*dept.*), division, section, vw department (*dept.*); **~ für Aktionärspflege** BÖRSE investor relations department; **~ für Börsenzulassung** VERWALT linking department, quotation department; **~ für Einkauf** GESCHÄFT purchasing department; **~ für Einschußzahlungen** BÖRSE margin department; **~ mit Kundenkontakt** VERWALT front office; **~ für Öffentlichkeitsarbeit** PERSON, V&M public relations department (*PRD*); **~ zur Registrierung von Staats- und anderen Anleihen** BANK registrar's department; **~ für Sonderangebote** V&M *Warenhaus* bargain basement; **~ für Steueraufkommen** STEUER revenue department; **~ Wohnraumlenkung** SOZIAL accommodation bureau (*AmE*); ♦ **zwischen Abteilungen** GESCHÄFT, VERWALT interdepartmental

Abteilung: **Abteilungsbildung** *f* VERWALT departmentation; **Abteilungserfolgsrechnung** *f* RECHNUNG accounting by functions, activity accounting, profit center accounting (*AmE*), profit centre accounting (*BrE*); **Abteilungsfranchise** *f* V&M mini franchise; **Abteilungsführung** *f* GESCHÄFT departmental management; **Abteilungsgemeinkosten** *pl* RECHNUNG departmental burden, departmental expenses, departmental overheads; **Abteilungsgewinn** *m* RECHNUNG departmental profit; **Abteilungsgliederung** *f* VERWALT departmental structure; **Abteilungshandbuch** *nt* VERWALT departmental manual; **Abteilungshierarchie** *f* VERWALT departmental hierarchy

abteilungsintern *adj* VERWALT intradepartmental

Abteilung: **Abteilungskalkulation** *f* RECHNUNG departmental cost estimation; **Abteilungskostenrechnung** *f* RECHNUNG departmental costing; **Abteilungsleiter, in** *m,f* GESCHÄFT departmental head, departmental manager, PERSON department head, departmental manager, division head; **Abteilungsorganisation** *f* RECHNUNG departmental organization; **Abteilungsplan** *m* GESCHÄFT, MGMNT departmental plan; **Abteilungsprogramm** *nt* VERWALT departmental program (*AmE*), departmental programme (*BrE*); **Abteilungsrechnung** *f* RECHNUNG departmental costing; **Abteilungsspanne** *f* RECHNUNG departmental profit

abteilungsübergreifend *adj* VERWALT interdepartmental; **~e Flexibilität** *f* PERSON interdepartmental flexibility (*IDF*)

Abteilung: **Abteilungsvermögen** *nt* FINANZ departmental assets

abtragen *vt* BANK *Schulden, Hypothek* repay, amortize, pay off, pay back, FINANZ divest, RECHNUNG *Schulden, Hypothek* amortize, pay back, pay off, repay

abtrennbar *adj* GESCHÄFT *Kupon* detachable

Abtrennung *f* GESCHÄFT separation, RECHT severance

abtretbar *adj* BÖRSE transferable, RECHT *Vertragsrecht* assignable

Abtretbarkeit *f* BÖRSE transferability, RECHT assignability

abtreten *vt* RECHT, RECHNUNG, VERSICH assign, cede, make over, set over, transfer

Abtretende(r) *mf* [decl. as adj] GESCHÄFT assignor, RECHT, VERSICH assignor, transferor, transferrer, *Zedent* cedent

Abtretung *f* GESCHÄFT cession, RECHNUNG assignment, RECHT, VERSICH assignment, cession, transfer (*tr., tfr*); **Abtretungsakt** *m* GESCHÄFT, RECHT act of cession; **Abtretungsanzeige** *f* RECHNUNG notice of assignment; **Abtretungsempfänger, in** *m,f* RECHT assignee, transferee; **Abtretungserklärung** *f* KOMM letter of subrogation (*BrE*), RECHT *Vertragsrecht* assignment document, declaration of assignment; **Abtretungsformular** *nt* **für Bezugsrechte** BÖRSE letter of renunciation; **Abtretungshandlung** *f* GESCHÄFT, RECHT act of cession; **Abtretungstermin** *m* BÖRSE assignment day; **Abtretungsurkunde** *f* GESCHÄFT deed of assignation; **Abtretungsverbotsklausel** *f* GESCHÄFT non-assignment clause; **Abtretungsvertrag** *m* GRUND bargain and sale, RECHT *Vertragsrecht* contract of assignment

abtrünnig: **~e Gewerkschaft** *f* PERSON breakaway union

Abverkauf *m* V&M sale, selling-off; **~ zu Schleuderpreisen** V&M blowout (*AmE*)

abwägen *vt* GESCHÄFT *Vorschlag* weigh up

Abwägen *nt* FINANZ weighting

abwählen *vt* COMP *Option* deselect, POL *Person* vote out of office

abwälzen *vt* FINANZ, VW pass along, pass on; ♦ **~ auf** [+acc] GESCHÄFT *Verantwortlichkeit* shift on to, VW *Kosten* pass on to

Abwanderung *f* PERSON drift, outward migration; **~ von Wissenschaftlern** PERSON brain drain (*infrml*); **~ von Kapital** FINANZ exodus of capital, flight of capital

abwartend: **~e Haltung** *f* VW wait-and-see policy

abwärts 1. *adj* GESCHÄFT downward; **2.** *adv* GESCHÄFT downward

Abwärts- *in* *cpds* GESCHÄFT downward; **Abwärtsbewegung** *f* GESCHÄFT downstream float, downward movement; **Abwärtskompatibilität** *f* COMP downward compatibility; **Abwärtstrend** *m* FINANZ downside trend, vw downtrend, down-market

Abwasser *nt* UMWELT effluent, wastewater; **Abwasserabgabe** *f* UMWELT sewage levy; **Abwasserabgabengesetz** *nt* RECHT, UMWELT water pollution control levy; **Abwasseraufbereitung** *f* UMWELT wastewater treatment; **Abwasserbehandlung** *f* UMWELT wastewater treatment; **Abwasserbeseitigung** *f* UMWELT sewage disposal, wastewater disposal; **Abwasserreinigungskläranlage** *f* UMWELT sewage treatment works

abwechseln: **sich ~** *v refl* GESCHÄFT alternate

abwechselnd *adj* GESCHÄFT alternate

Abwehr *f* GESCHÄFT defence (*BrE*), defense (*AmE*),

protection; **Abwehranspruch** *m* RECHT claim to protection against abridgment of legal rights

abwehren *vt* GESCHÄFT *Frage* fend off, *Gefahr* stave off

Abwehr: **Abwehrklage** *f* RECHT action brought to repel unlawful interference; **Abwehrklausel** *f* RECHT clause inserted to defend unlawful interference; **Abwehrkonditionen** *f pl* GESCHÄFT defensive conditions; **Abwehrmaßnahmen** *f pl* GESCHÄFT insulating measures; **Abwehrpreis** *m* V&M keep-out price; **Abwehrquote** *f* VW protective quota; **Abwehrwerbung** *f* V&M counteradvertising; **Abwehrzoll** *m* VW protective tariff

abweichen *vi* GESCHÄFT *Wechselkurs* depart from sth, diverge

abweichend *adj* GESCHÄFT differing; **~e Meinung** *f* MGMNT dissenting opinion, dissenting view, divergent thinking, RECHT dissenting opinon, dissenting vote, dissent

Abweichung *f* FINANZ variance, GESCHÄFT anomaly, discrepancy, *Variation* variance, variation, MATH azimuth, polar angle, RECHNUNG variance, RECHT *vom Gesetz* deviation, nonconformity; **~ zweiten Grades** RECHNUNG composite variation, incidental variation; **Abweichungsanalyse** *f* RECHNUNG cost variance analysis; **Abweichungsindikator** *m* VW divergence indicator; **Abweichungsklausel** *f* VERSICH deviation clause (*D/C*); **Abweichungskoeffizient** *m* RECHNUNG coefficient of variation; **Abweichungspolitik** *f* MGMNT deviation policy; **Abweichungsschwelle** *f* FINANZ, VW divergence threshold

abwenden *vt* GESCHÄFT *Unheil* stave off

abwerben *vt* PERSON bid away, contract away, entice away, *Arbeitskräfte* poach, *Führungskräfte* headhunt, RECHT alienate, contract away, divert custom, V&M divert custom, VW *Kunden* poach

Abwerber, in *m,f* PERSON *Führungskräfte* headhunter

Abwerbung *f* PERSON labor piracy (*AmE*), labour piracy (*BrE*), poaching, *von Führungskräften* headhunting, RECHT diverting custom, V&M alienation, contracting away, diverting custom, poaching; **Abwerbungswirkung** *f* V&M alienation effect

abwerfen *vt* BÖRSE *Ertrag, Gewinn* yield, FINANZ return, GESCHÄFT *Ertrag, Gewinn* yield, VW produce

abwerten *vt* RECHNUNG depreciate, VW depreciate, *Währung* devaluate, devalue

Abwertung *f* GRUND depreciation, VW currency devaluation, devalorization, devaluation; **~ auf Fertigerzeugnisse** RECHNUNG inventory adjustments; **~ auf Roh-, Hilfs- und Betriebsstoffe** RECHNUNG inventory adjustments; **~ auf Roh-, Hilfs- und Betriebswaren** RECHNUNG inventory adjustments; **~ auf unfertige Erzeugnisse** RECHNUNG inventory adjustments; **~ aus Wettbewerbsgründen** VW competitive devaluation

abwesend *adj* GESCHÄFT absent

Abwesende(r) *mf* [decl. as adj] GESCHÄFT absentee

Abwesenheit *f* GESCHÄFT absence; ♦ **in jds ~** GESCHÄFT in sb's absence

Abwesenheit: **Abwesenheitsprotest** *f* BÖRSE protest for absence; **Abwesenheitsrate** *f* GESCHÄFT absentee rate; **Abwesenheitszeit** *f* PERSON absence time

abwickeln *vt* FINANZ complete, settle, GESCHÄFT carry out, handle, process, RECHNUNG liquidate, wind up

Abwickler *m* RECHNUNG, RECHT liquidating authority, liquidator

Abwicklung *f* GESCHÄFT processing, *einer Firma* winding up, handling, liquidation, MGMNT winding up, liquidation, VERSICH runoff; **~ aller Kauf- und Verkaufsaufträge** BÖRSE clearing the market; **mit der ~ betraute(r) Angestellte(r)** *mf* [decl. as adj] BÖRSE red button (*BrE*); **~ von Investitionen** FINANZ investment management; **Abwicklungsendvermögen** *nt* FINANZ net worth at end of winding-up; **Abwicklungseröffnungsbilanz** *f* RECHT opening balance sheet; **Abwicklungsgebühr** *f* BANK agency fee; **Abwicklungsstelle** *f* BÖRSE cage (*AmE*); **Abwicklungstermin** *m* BÖRSE settlement date; **Abwicklungsverfahren** *nt* RECHT liquidation procedure, winding-up procedure; **Abwicklungszeit** *f* GESCHÄFT handling time, processing time; **Abwicklungszeitraum** *m* RECHT liquidation period, winding up period

abzahlen *vt* FINANZ pay off in installments (*AmE*), pay off in instalments (*BrE*)

abzählen *vt* GESCHÄFT have a headcount

Abzahlung: **auf ~ kaufen** *phr* V&M buy on hire purchase (*BrE*), buy on the installment plan (*AmE*); **auf Abzahlungsbasis** *phr* FINANZ on hire purchase (*BrE*), on the installment plan (*AmE*); **auf Abzahlungsbasis kaufen** *phr* FINANZ buy on hire purchase (*BrE*), buy on the installment plan (*AmE*); **Abzahlungsgeschäft** *nt* GESCHÄFT hire-purchase transaction (*BrE*), tally trade (*BrE*); **Abzahlungshypothek** *f* FINANZ constant payment mortgage, installment mortgage (*AmE*), instalment mortgage (*BrE*); **Abzahlungskauf** *m* RECHT *Vertragsrecht* hire purchase (*BrE*), installment sale (*AmE*), instalment sale (*BrE*); **Abzahlungskauf** *m* **ohne Eigentumsvorbehalt** RECHT *Vertragsrecht* credit sale (*BrE*); **Abzahlungskonto** *nt* BANK charge account; **Abzahlungskredit** *m* FINANZ installment credit (*AmE*), instalment credit (*BrE*); **Abzahlungsperiode** *f* FINANZ repayment period; **Abzahlungspreis** *m* GESCHÄFT hire-purchase price (*BrE*), installment price (*AmE*), instalment price (*BrE*); **Abzahlungsverkauf** *m* GESCHÄFT, V&M hire-purchase sale (*BrE*), installment sale (*AmE*), instalment sale (*BrE*); **Abzahlungsvertrag** *m* FINANZ hire-purchase contract (*BrE*), installment contract (*AmE*), instalment contract (*BrE*); **Abzahlungswechsel** *m* FINANZ installment bill of exchange (*AmE*), instalment bill of exchange (*BrE*); **Abzahlungszeitraum** *m* FINANZ, V&M hire-purchase period (*BrE*), installment sale period (*AmE*), instalment sale period (*BrE*)

abzeichnen *vt* GESCHÄFT acknowledge

Abzeichnung *f* KOMM acknowledgement

abziehen *vt* FINANZ *Kapital* alienate, MATH deduct, RECHT alienate, VERSICH deduct; **~ von** MATH, STEUER, VERSICH deduct from

abzielen *vt*: **~ auf** [+acc] GESCHÄFT, V&M target at

Abzielen *nt* GESCHÄFT, V&M targeting

abzinsen *vt* FINANZ, RECHNUNG discount

Abzinsung *f* FINANZ, RECHNUNG discounting; **Abzinsungsbetrag** *m* BÖRSE, FINANZ original issue discount (*OID*); **Abzinsungsfaktor** *m* FINANZ discount factor; **Abzinsungsmechanismus** *m* FINANZ discount mechanism; **Abzinsungsobligation** *f* BÖRSE, FINANZ original issue discount bond; **Abzinsungspapier** *nt* FINANZ discounted paper; **Abzinsungstabelle** *f* FINANZ discount table

Abzug *m* BÖRSE withholding, discount (*dis, disc.*), FINANZ *Kapital* alienation, GESCHÄFT deduction, STEUER *Gehalt*, VERSICH deduction, V&M allowance; ~ **vom Lohn** STEUER deduction from wages; ~ **an der Quelle** STEUER deduction at source; ~ **vom Rückkaufswert** VERSICH surrender charge; ♦ **nach** ~ GESCHÄFT less; **nach** ~ **von Steuern** RECHNUNG, STEUER after-tax basis; **in** ~ **bringen** FINANZ deduct; **vor** ~ **der Steuern** RECHNUNG, STEUER before tax, pre-tax

Abzüge *m pl* STEUER deductions from salary, statutory deductions; ~ **von Lohn oder Gehalt** STEUER pay-as-you-earn (*BrE*) (*PAYE*), payroll deduction scheme; ~ **neu für alt** VERSICH deduction new for old; ~ **nach Steuern** RECHNUNG, STEUER after tax

abzüglich *prep* [+gen] GESCHÄFT less

Abzug: **Abzugsbetrag** *m* **vom Versicherungswert** VERSICH excess franchise

abzugsfähig *adj* FINANZ deductible, STEUER allowable, deductible, tax-deductible; ~ **er Betrag** *m* STEUER deduction

Abzug: **Abzugsfähigkeit** *f* **des Arbeitgeberanteils** STEUER deductibility of employer contributions; **Abzugsfranchise** *f* VERSICH deductible (*AmE*), excess (*BrE*), excess franchise; **Abzugssteuer** *f* STEUER withholding tax

Abzuschiebende(r) *mf* [decl. as adj] POL deportee

Account-Manager, in *m,f* V&M account manager (*AM*)

Achse *f* MATH, TRANSP axis; ♦ **auf** ~ TRANSP on track

Achsgewicht *nt* TRANSP axle weight

achten *vt* GESCHÄFT respect

ächten *vt* RECHT *die Rechtsgültigkeit entziehen* outlaw

Achtung *f* RECHT *vor dem Gesetz* respect

Ächtung *f* RECHT, VW boycott

Ackerland *nt* VW farmland

actus reus *m* RECHT *objektiver Tatbestand, äußere Tatbestandsmerkmale* actus reus

ADAC *abbr* (*Allgemeiner Deutscher Automobil-Club*) TRANSP ≈ AA (*Automobile Association*), ≈ AAA (*American Automobile Association*)

Adapter *m* COMP adaptor

Adaption *f* GESCHÄFT adaptation

adaptiv *adj* COMP, GESCHÄFT, VW adaptive; ~ **e Erwartungen** *f pl* VW adaptive expectations; ~ **es Filtern** *nt* GESCHÄFT adaptive filtering; ~ **e Regelung** *f* COMP adaptive control; ~ **e Regelung** *f* **mit Rückführung** COMP closed-loop adaptation

adäquat *adj* GESCHÄFT, RECHT adequate; ~ **er Kausalzusammenhang** *m* RECHT adequate causal nexus; ~ **er Schadensersatz** *m* RECHT compensatory damages

Addier- *in cpds* GESCHÄFT add, adding; **Addierbefehl** *m* COMP add instruction

addieren *vt* GESCHÄFT add up, foot up (*AmE*), tot up (*BrE*), MATH cast up, RECHNUNG cast up

Addieren *nt* GESCHÄFT adding, footing (*AmE*)

Addier-: **Addiermaschine** *f* COMP, FINANZ adding machine, GESCHÄFT add lister; **Addierwerk** *nt* COMP adding counter

Addition *f* COMP addition, GESCHÄFT addition, footing (*AmE*), summation, MATH addition, footing (*AmE*); **Additionsanweisung** *f* COMP add statement; **Additionsmaschine** *f* COMP, FINANZ adding machine, GESCHÄFT add listing machine; **Additionssätze** *m pl* **der Wahrscheinlichkeit** MATH addition theorems of probability; **Additionsstreifen** *m* GESCHÄFT addition slip; **Additionstabelle** *f* COMP addition table; **Additionstheorem** *nt* MATH addition theorem; **Additionsübertrag** *m* COMP add-carry

additiv: ~ **e Grenzkosten** *pl* VERWALT, VW additive marginal costs; ~ **er Zufallsprozeß** *m* MATH additive random walk process

Additivität *f* MATH additive property

ad hoc *phr* GESCHÄFT ad hoc; ~ **Ausschuß** *m* GESCHÄFT ad hoc committee; ~ **Verband** *m* RECHT single-purpose association

ad idem *phr* GESCHÄFT *in vollem Einvernehmen* ad idem

ad interim *phr* GESCHÄFT ad interim

adjungiert *adj* MATH adjoint; ~ **e Matrix** *f* MATH adjoint of a matrix, adjugate of a matrix

Administration *f* POL administration

administrativ *adj* GESCHÄFT, IMP/EXP, RECHNUNG administrative; ~ **e Abwicklung** *f* GESCHÄFT administrative handling; ~ **e Handelshemmnisse** *nt pl* IMP/EXP administrative barriers to trade; ~ **e und organisatorische Kontrollen** *f pl* RECHNUNG administrative and organizational controls (*BrE*); ~ **er Protektionismus** *m* IMP/EXP administrative protectionism

administriert *adj* POL, VERWALT, VW administered; ~ **e Inflation** *f* VW administered inflation; ~ **e Preisfestsetzung** *f* VW administered pricing

Adreß- *in cpds* COMP, KOMM address

Adressat, in *m,f* KOMM addressee; ♦ ~ **unbekannt** KOMM unknown at this address

Adreß-: **Adreßaufkleber** *m* KOMM address label; **Adreßbuch** *nt* GESCHÄFT directory, KOMM address book; **Adreßbus** *m* COMP address bus; **Adreßdatei** *f* COMP address file

Adresse *f* GESCHÄFT address; ~ **des Absenders** KOMM return address; ♦ **ohne** ~ TRANSP free of address

Adresse: **Adressenänderung** *f* KOMM change of address; **Adressenangaben** *f pl* COMP, KOMM address information; **Adressenauswahl** *f* COMP address selection; **Adressendatei** *f* COMP address file; **Adressenerzeugung** *f* COMP address generation; **Adressenfeld** *nt* COMP address field; **Adressenkapazität** *f* COMP address capacity; **Adressenliste** *f* KOMM mailing list, PERSON list of addresses; **Adressenverlag** *m* GESCHÄFT list broker; **Adressenzeile** *f* V&M address line

Adreß-: **Adreßetikett** *nt* KOMM address label; **Adreßfeld** *nt* COMP address field

Adressier- *in cpds* GESCHÄFT address, addressing

adressierbar *adj* GESCHÄFT addressable

adressieren *vt* GESCHÄFT address

Adressier-: **Adressierkarte** *f* COMP address card; **Adressiermaschine** *f* KOMM addressing machine, Addressograph®; **Adressiermethode** *f* COMP addressing; **Adressiersystem** *nt* COMP addressing system; **Adressierverfahren** *nt* COMP addressing

Adressierung *f* GESCHÄFT addressing; **Adressierungsart** *f* COMP addressing mode

Adreß-: **Adreßindex** *m* COMP address index; **Adreßkonstante** *f* COMP address constant; **Adreßmarke** *f* COMP address marker; **Adreßmodifikation** *f* COMP address modification; **Adreßraum** *m* COMP address space;

Adreßraumverwaltung *f* COMP address space administration; **Adreßregister** *nt* COMP address register; **Adreßschlüssel** *m* COMP actual key; **Adreßspediteur** *m* GESCHÄFT receiving forwarding agent

ADV *abbr* (*automatisierte Datenverarbeitung*) COMP ADP (*automatic data processing*)

ad valorem: **~ Frachtbrief** *m* IMP/EXP ad valorem bill of lading; **~ Ladebrief** *m* IMP/EXP ad valorem bill of lading; **~ Zoll** *m* IMP/EXP *Berechnungsgrundlage bei der Zollbemessung*, STEUER ad valorem customs duty

AEB *abbr* (*Afrikanische Entwicklungsbank*) BANK, FINANZ ADB (*African Development Bank*), AfDB (*African Development Bank*)

Aerogramm *nt* KOMM *Brief* aerogramme, air letter

Aerosol *nt* UMWELT aerosol

AfA *abbr* (*Absetzung für Abnutzung*) RECHNUNG allowance for depreciation

Affektionswert *m* GESCHÄFT fancy value, VERSICH affection value

affektiv: **~es Verhalten** *nt* GESCHÄFT affective behavior (*AmE*), affective behaviour (*BrE*)

AFRASEC *abbr* (*Afro-asiatische Organisation für wirtschaftliche Zusammenarbeit*) POL, VW AFRASEC (*Afro-Asian Organization for Economic Cooperation*)

Afrikanisch: **~e Entwicklungsbank** *f* (*AEB*) BANK, FINANZ African Development Bank (*ADB, AfDB*)

Afro-asiatisch: **~e Organisation** *f* **für wirtschaftliche Zusammenarbeit** (*AFRASEC*) POL, VW Afro-Asian Organization for Economic Cooperation (*AFRASEC*)

AG *abbr* (*Aktiengesellschaft*) GESCHÄFT Inc. (*Incorporated AmE*), plc (*public limited company BrE*), PLC (*public limited company BrE*) joint-stock company, stock corporation (*AmE*)

AGB *abbr* (*allgemeine Geschäftsbedingungen*) GESCHÄFT, RECHT general terms and conditions

Agenda *f* MGMNT agenda; ♦ **auf der ~ stehen** MGMNT, VERWALT be on the agenda

Agens *nt* IND agent

Agent, in *m,f* GESCHÄFT commercial agent, IMP/EXP, TRANSP distributor, V&M representative selling agent; **~ im Fachhandel** PERSON stockist agent; **~ des Fachhandels** PERSON stockist agent; **~ des Vermögensverwalters** PERSON receiver's agent; ♦ **vom Agenten bezahlt** TRANSP *Schiffahrt* paid by agent (*PBA*)

Agentur *f* GESCHÄFT agency (*agcy*); **~ mit Allround-Service** MEDIEN, V&M full-service agency; **~ mit komplettem Serviceangebot** MEDIEN, V&M agency with full service; **~ mit umfassendem Service** MEDIEN, V&M agency with full service, full-service agency; **Agenturfonds** *m* MEDIEN agency fund; **Agenturgeschäft** *nt* GESCHÄFT agency business; **Agenturhandel** *m* GESCHÄFT agency trade; **Agenturkosten** *pl* GESCHÄFT agency fee; **Agenturvergütung** *f* GESCHÄFT agency commission; **Agenturvertrag** *m* V&M agency agreement; **Agenturvertreter** *m* V&M agency representative; **Agenturwerbung** *f* MEDIEN agency billing

Agglomeration *f* VW agglomeration; **Agglomerationsvorteil** *m* VW agglomeration economy

Aggregat *nt* IND apparatus, set of machines, MATH, VW aggregate

Aggregation *f* FINANZ, MATH, VW aggregation;

Aggregationsmethode *f* FINANZ *beim Investieren*, MATH bottom-up approach, bottom-up method; **Aggregationsproblem** *nt* VW aggregation problem

Aggregat: **Aggregattafel** *f* VERSICH aggregate table

aggregiert: **~e Zahlen** *f pl* VW aggregate data; **~es Zahlenmaterial** *f pl* VW aggregate data

aggressiv *adj* V&M aggressive; **nicht ~ durchgeführtes Streikpostenstehen** *nt* PERSON, POL *Arbeitskonflikt* peaceful picketing; **~er Käufer** *m* FINANZ gunslinger (*jarg*); **~es Marketing** *nt* V&M aggressive marketing; **~e Preispolitik** *f* V&M aggressive pricing; **~es Überraschungsmanöver** *nt* BÖRSE, FINANZ dawn raid (*jarg*); **~e Verkaufspolitik** *f* V&M high-pressure selling; **~e Werbung** *f* V&M aggressive advertising

agieren *vi* GESCHÄFT act

Agio *nt* BÖRSE, FINANZ agio, premium; **~ aus Aktienemission** BÖRSE, FINANZ, RECHNUNG share premium; ♦ **mit einem ~** BÖRSE, FINANZ at a premium; **mit einem ~ notiert werden** BÖRSE stand at a premium

Agio: **Agioanleihe** *f* BÖRSE premium bond; **Agioerlös** *m* RECHNUNG paid-in surplus (*AmE*); **Agiorücklage** *f* RECHNUNG capital paid in excess of par value, capital surplus, share premium reserve

Agiotage *f* BÖRSE, FINANZ agiotage

Agrar- *in cpds* VW agricultural; **Agrarabschöpfung** *f* VW agricultural levy; **Agrarbank** *f* BANK, VW agricultural bank; **Agrardarlehen** *nt* BANK agricultural job; **Agrareinkommen** *nt* VW farm income; **Agrarerzeugnis** *nt* VW agricultural product, farm produce; **Agrarexportbeihilfe** *f* VW agricultural export subsidy; **Agrarfonds** *m* VW European Agricultural Guidance and Guarantee Fund; **Agrargenossenschaft** *f* VW agricultural cooperative

agrarisch *adj* VW agricultural; **~er Rohstoff** *m* VW agricultural commodity

Agrar-: **Agrarkredit** *m* GESCHÄFT agricultural credit, VW farm loan; **Agrarkreditsystem** *nt* VW Farm Credit System (*AmE*); **Agrarlobby** *f* POL farm lobby; **Agrarmarkt** *m* VW agricultural commodities market; **Agrarmesse** *f* IND, V&M, VW agricultural show; **Agrarministerrat** *m* VW *EU* European Community of Agricultural Ministers; **Agrarpolitik** *f* VW agricultural policy, farm policy; **Agrarpreisstützung** *f* VW agricultural price support; **Agrarpreissubvention** *f* VW deficiency payment; **Agrarprodukt** *nt* VW agricultural product, farm produce; **Agrarprodukt** *nt* **für den Export** VW cash crop; **Agrarproduktion** *f* VW agricultural production; **Agrarsektor** *m* VW agricultural sector; **Agrarstruktur** *f* VW farm structure; **Agrarsubventionen** *f pl* VW agricultural subsidy, farm subsidy; **Agrarüberschuß** *m* VW farm surplus; **Agrarwirtschaft** *f* VW farming

agrarwirtschaftlich *adj* GESCHÄFT, POL, UMWELT, VERSICH agricultural

Agrar-: **Agrarzölle** *m pl* IMP/EXP customs duties levied on exported and imported products; **Agrarzuschüsse** *f pl* VW agricultural subsidy

Agrochemikalie *f* UMWELT agrochemical

Agroindustrie *f* IND agroindustry

Agronom, in *m,f* UMWELT agronomist

Agronomie *f* UMWELT agronomy

ähnlich *adj* GESCHÄFT analogous, similar; **~e Kriterien** *nt pl* GESCHÄFT criteria of a similar nature; ♦ **~er Art** GESCHÄFT ejusdem generis, of a similar kind; **bei ~er**

Gelegenheit GESCHÄFT on a similar occasion; **einer ~en Kurve folgen** MATH follow a similar curve; **einem ~en Muster folgen** GESCHÄFT follow a similar pattern

Ähnlichkeit *f* PATENT similarity

Aide-mémoire *nt* V&M aide-mémoire

Airbrushtechnik *f* V&M airbrush technique

Airbus *m* TRANSP air bus

Airflex-Kupplung *f* TRANSP airflex clutch (*AFC*)

AK *abbr* (*Anschaffungskosten*) RECHNUNG historical cost

Akademiker, in *m,f* PERSON graduate

akademisch *adj* SOZIAL academic

AK/HK *abbr* (*Anschaffungs- oder Herstellungskosten*) RECHNUNG costs of acquisition or production

akkommodierend: ~e Geldpolitik *f* POL, VW accommodative policy; **~e Politik** *f* POL, VW accommodative policy

Akkord *m* GESCHÄFT amicable settlement of dispute, IND breakeven quantity, *Arbeit* piecework, RECHT composition proceedings; **im ~ arbeitende Belegschaft** *f* PERSON task force; ♦ **nach ~ bezahlt** PERSON paid piece rate

Akkord: **Akkordarbeit** *f* GESCHÄFT piecework, IND jobbing, PERSON piecework; **Akkordarbeit** *f* **einer Kolonne** PERSON gang piecework; **Akkordlohn** *m* IND piecework rate, piecework wage; **Akkordprämie** *f* PERSON production incentive; **Akkordrichtsatz** *m* IND basic piece rate; **Akkordsystem** *nt* PERSON piecework system; **Akkordzuschlag** *m* IND bonus increment

akkreditieren *vt* GESCHÄFT, SOZIAL, V&M accredit

akkreditiert *adj* V&M accredited

Akkreditierung *f* SOZIAL *Institutionen, Personen* accreditation

Akkreditiv *nt* BANK letter of credit (*L/C*) **~ bei einer definierten Bank** FINANZ straight credit; **Akkreditivbank** *f* BANK issuing bank, opening bank; **Akkreditivbevorschussung** *f* BANK advance against a document credit, anticipatory packing credit, packaging credit, IMP/EXP advance against a document credit; **Akkreditive** *nt pl* BÖRSE credits

akkreditiveröffnend: ~e Bank *f* BANK issuing bank, opening bank

Akkreditiv: **Akkreditivverpflichtung** *f* FINANZ liability under a letter of credit; **Akkreditivwährung** *f* FINANZ currency of the credit; **Akkreditivwährungsdeckungskonto** *nt* FINANZ foreign currency credit cover account

Akkumulation *f* GESCHÄFT, VW accumulation

Akkumulator *m* COMP *Rechner* accumulator, IND battery

akkumulieren *vt* GESCHÄFT, VW accumulate

akkumuliert *adj* RECHNUNG accumulated; **~e Abschreibung** *f* RECHNUNG accumulated depreciation

Akontozahlung *f* BANK payment on account

AKP-Staaten *m pl* (*Staaten in Afrika, im karibischen Raum und im Pazifischen Ozean*) VW ACP states (*African, Caribbean and Pacific states*)

Akquisiteur *m* GESCHÄFT canvasser

Akquisition *f* FINANZ, RECHNUNG, V&M, VERSICH, VW *Tochtergesellschaft durch Übernahme* acquisition; **Akquisitionskosten** *pl* GESCHÄFT, RECHNUNG, V&M, VERSICH acquisition costs, canvassing costs, sales development costs

Akt *m* GESCHÄFT act

Akte *f* GESCHÄFT case papers, PATENT, VERWALT file, POL act; ♦ **etw in die Akten eintragen** GESCHÄFT put sth on record; **zu den Akten geben** PATENT file; **zu den Akten legen** GESCHÄFT file away, PATENT file; **die Akten auf dem neuesten Stand halten** VERWALT keep the filing up-to-date; **eine ~ prüfen** COMP search a file; **eine ~ überprüfen** COMP search a file

Akte: **Aktenablage** *f* **in offenen Regalen** VERWALT open-shelf filing; **Aktenkopie** *f* VERWALT file copy; **Aktenmappe** *f* GESCHÄFT portfolio; **Aktenprüfung** *f* PATENT inspection of files; **Aktenschrank** *m* VERWALT *Kartothek* filing cabinet; **Aktenstück** *nt* VERWALT file; **Aktentasche** *f* GESCHÄFT briefcase; **Aktentaschencomputer** *m obs* COMP pocket computer, portable computer, laptop, laptop computer; **Aktenvernichter** *m* VERWALT shredder; **Aktenverwaltung** *f* MGMNT records management; **Aktenzeichen** *nt* GESCHÄFT file number, reference (*ref.*)

Aktie *f* BÖRSE, FINANZ, RECHNUNG share (*BrE*), stock (*AmE*); **~ drittbester Klassifizierung** BÖRSE A-share (*BrE*); **~ mit leicht steigender Tendenz** BÖRSE uptick; ♦ **eine ~ unter dem Nennwert emittieren** BÖRSE issue a share at a discount; **~ sperren** BÖRSE stop a stock

Aktien *f pl* BÖRSE, FINANZ, RECHNUNG shares (*BrE*), stock (*AmE*); **~ im Aufwärtstrend** BÖRSE shares moved ahead; **~ des Boardmitglieds** BÖRSE director's shares; **~ mit einer drittbesten Anleiheklassifizierung** BÖRSE A-share (*BrE*); **~ mit geringem Umsatzvolumen** BÖRSE inactive stock; **~ der Kategorie A** BÖRSE Class A shares (*AmE*); **~ der Kategorie B** BÖRSE Class B shares (*AmE*); **~ konjunkturreagibler Unternehmen** BÖRSE cyclical shares, vw cyclical stock; **~ von Rüstungsunternehmen** BÖRSE war babies (*jarg*); **~ mit sehr niedrigen Nennbeträgen und Kursen** BÖRSE penny shares (*BrE*), penny stock (*AmE*); ♦ **~ und Anleihen kaufen und verkaufen** BÖRSE trade in stocks and bonds; **~ hereinnehmen** BÖRSE take in stock; **in ~ investieren** BÖRSE invest in shares; **~ auf dem Markt abstoßen** BÖRSE unload stocks on the market; **~ auf dem offenen Markt kaufen** BÖRSE buy shares on the open market; **~ vom Publikum zurückkaufen** BÖRSE go private; **~ übernehmen** BÖRSE take up stocks; **~ verkaufen** BÖRSE *in der Erwartung eines Preisrückgangs* sell shares; **~ zeichnen** BÖRSE apply for shares, subscribe for shares; **~ zur Zeichnung auflegen** BÖRSE invite subscriptions to shares; **~ zuteilen** BÖRSE allot shares

Aktien: **Aktienagio** *nt* BÖRSE, FINANZ, RECHNUNG share premium (*BrE*)

aktienähnlich: ~e Obligationen *f pl* BÖRSE equity-related bonds; **~e Termingeschäfte** *nt pl* BÖRSE equity-related futures; **~e Terminkontrakte** *m pl* BÖRSE equity-related futures

Aktien: **Aktienanpassungsprinzip** *nt* BÖRSE stock adjustment principle; **Aktienarten** *f pl* BÖRSE types of shares; **Aktienaufteilung** *f* BÖRSE stock split (*AmE*); **Aktienaustausch** *m* FINANZ exchange of shares, exchange of stock; **Aktienbank** *f* BANK joint-stock bank; **Aktienbesitz** *m* BÖRSE equity holding, shareholding; **Aktienbestand** *m* BÖRSE, FINANZ share portfolio, stock portfolio, stockholding; **Aktienbesteuerung** *f* STEUER equity taxation; **Aktienbeteiligung** *f* BÖRSE equity interest, equity stake, shareholding, FINANZ stockholding; **Aktienbeteiligungsplan** *m* BÖRSE share scheme; **Aktienbezugsplan** *m* BÖRSE stock purchase plan;

Aktienbezugsrecht *nt* BÖRSE share option right, share purchase warrant, stock option right, stock purchase warrant; **Aktienbezugsrechtsplan** *m* BÖRSE, STEUER share option scheme; **Aktienbezugsrechtsschein** *m* BÖRSE equity warrant; **Aktienbörse** *f* BÖRSE, FINANZ, VW stock exchange (*stk exch*), stock market; **Aktienbruchteil** *m* BÖRSE subshare; **Aktienbuch** *nt* BÖRSE stock register, RECHT *Verzeichnis der Aktionäre einer Gesellschaft* Register of Members; **Aktiendividende** *f* BÖRSE share dividend; **Aktienemission** *f* BÖRSE, FINANZ, RECHNUNG equity issue, share issue, stock issue; **Aktienemissionsagio** *nt* BÖRSE, FINANZ, RECHNUNG share premium (*BrE*), stock issue premium (*AmE*), capital surplus (*AmE*); **Aktienemissionsaufgeld** *f* RECHNUNG stock issue bonus; **Aktienerwerb** *m* **durch leitende Angestellte** BÖRSE share incentive scheme; **Aktienerwerbsplan** *m* **für Arbeitnehmer** BÖRSE employee share ownership plan (*BrE*) (*ESOP*), employee stock ownership plan (*AmE*) (*ESOP*); **Aktienfinanzierung** *f* FINANZ equity financing; **Aktienfluktuation mittragen** *phr* BÖRSE roundtrip; **Aktienfonds** *m* BÖRSE equity fund, investment fund for shares, RECHNUNG equity fund

aktiengebunden: ~e Politik *f* BÖRSE equity-linked policy

Aktien: **Aktiengesellschaft** *f* (*AG*) GESCHÄFT public company, Incorporated (*AmE*) (*Inc.*), limited company (*BrE*) (*Ltd*), limited liability company (*BrE*); **Aktiengesetz** *nt* RECHT the Companies Act (*BrE*); **Aktienhandel** *m* BÖRSE, FINANZ stockbroking; **Aktien- und Kursindizes** *m pl* BÖRSE stock indexes and averages; **Aktienindex** *m* BÖRSE share index; **Aktienindex** *m* **der Financial Times** *m* BÖRSE Financial Times Stock Exchange Index (*FT-SE*); **Aktienindex** *m* **der Frankfurter Allgemeinen Zeitung** (*FAZ Index*) BÖRSE Financial Times Actuaries All Shares Index (*All Share Index*); **Aktieninhaber, in** *m,f* BÖRSE shareholder, stockholder; **Aktieninvestmentfonds** *m* BÖRSE, FINANZ common stock fund; **Aktienkapital** *nt* BÖRSE, FINANZ share capital, stockholders' equity, RECHNUNG capital, equity, VW share capital; **Aktienkapitalübertragung** *f* FINANZ spin-off (*AmE*); **Aktienkurse** *m pl* BÖRSE share prices, stock market prices; **die Aktienkurse erreichten einen historischen Höchststand** *phr* BÖRSE share prices reached an all-time high (*BrE*), stock prices reached an all-time high; **Aktienkursentwicklung** *f* BÖRSE, FINANZ share price performance; **Aktienkursleistung** *f* BÖRSE, FINANZ share price performance; **Aktienmakler, in** *m,f* BÖRSE, FINANZ stockbroker; **Aktienmarkt** *m* BÖRSE share market, equity market; **Aktiennotierung** *f* BÖRSE stock quotation

Aktienoption *f* BÖRSE stock option; ~, **die zur Wahrnehmung bestimmter Rechte berechtigt** BÖRSE qualifying stock option; ♦ **eine ~ verkaufen** BÖRSE write a stock option

Aktienoption: **Aktienoptionsplan** *m* BÖRSE stock option plan, stock purchase plan

Aktien: **Aktienpaket** *nt* BÖRSE block, chunk of stock (*infrml*), line, parcel; **Aktienportefeuille** *nt* BÖRSE, FINANZ share portfolio, stock portfolio; **Aktienprämie** *f* RECHNUNG share premium; **Aktienpreisindex** *m* BÖRSE share price index; **Aktienquittung** *f* BÖRSE stock receipt; **Aktienrecht** *nt* RECHT stock corporation law; **Aktienregister** *nt* BÖRSE share register, stock record; **Aktienrendite** *f* BÖRSE stock yield; **Aktien-**

Reportnehmer *m* BÖRSE giver on stock; **Aktienrückkauf** *m* BÖRSE share buyback; **Aktienrückkaufplan** *m* BÖRSE share repurchase plan; **Aktienscheck** *m* BANK stock check (*AmE*), stock cheque (*BrE*); **Aktienschwindel** *m* BÖRSE share pushing; **Aktiensplit** *m* BÖRSE share split, stock split (*AmE*), FINANZ share bonus (*BrE*), RECHNUNG stock split (*AmE*); **Aktiensplitting** *nt* **fünf zu eins** BÖRSE five-for-one split (*BrE*); **Aktienstützungsaktion** *f* BÖRSE share support operation; **Aktienübernahme** *f* BÖRSE, FINANZ share acquisition, stock takeover

Aktienübertragung *f* BÖRSE share transfer; **Aktienübertragungs-Broker** *m* BÖRSE stock transfer agent; **Aktienübertragungsformular** *nt* BÖRSE stock transfer form

Aktien: **Aktienurkunde** *f* BÖRSE share certificate (*BrE*), stock certificate (*AmE*); **Aktienverhältnis** *nt* RECHNUNG stock ratio; **Aktienverkehrswert** *m* BÖRSE value share; **Aktienverzeichnis** *nt* BÖRSE stock register; **Aktien-Warrant** *m* FINANZ equity warrant; **Aktienzeichner, in** *m,f* BÖRSE, FINANZ applicant, applicant for shares; **Aktienzeichnung** *f* BÖRSE application for shares, subscription for shares; **Aktienzertifikat** *nt* BÖRSE share certificate (*BrE*), stock certificate (*AmE*); **Aktienzusammenlegung** *f* FINANZ reverse split, share consolidation, GESCHÄFT stock splitdown; **Aktienzuteilung** *f* BÖRSE share allotment, stock allotment

Aktion *f* COMP, GESCHÄFT, VERWALT, VW action

Aktionär, in *m,f* PERSON member, equity holder, shareholder, stockholder; **als ~ vorgeschobener Strohmann** *m* BÖRSE nominee shareholder; **Aktionärsausschüttung** *f* BÖRSE stockholder diffusion; **Aktionärsbindungsvertrag** *m* RECHT *Innominatsvertrag* shareholder commitment contract; **Aktionärsbuch** *nt* BÖRSE share register; **Aktionärsdarlehen** *nt* FINANZ shareholder loan; **Aktionärsgruppe** *f* VW shareholder group; **Aktionärshauptversammlung** *f* BÖRSE shareholders' general meeting; **Aktionärsinformation** *f* RECHT proxy statement; **Aktionärsregister** *m* RECHT Register of Members; **Aktionärsversammlung** *f* BÖRSE shareholders' meeting, GESCHÄFT company meeting, PERSON shareholders' meeting; **Aktionärsverzeichnis** *nt* BÖRSE stock record; **Aktionärswirtschaft** *f* VW share economy

Aktion: **Aktionen** *f pl* **zur Unterstützung von Währungen** FINANZ monetary support operations; **Aktionscode** *m* COMP action code; **Aktionsforschung** *f* MGMNT action research; **Aktionsliste** *f* POL hit list (*infrml*); **Aktionsnachricht** *f* COMP action message; **Aktionsparameter** *m* VERWALT action parameter; **Aktionsprogramm** *nt* GESCHÄFT, VW action program (*AmE*), action programme (*BrE*), program of action (*AmE*), programme of action (*BrE*); **Aktionswerbung** *f* V&M direct-action advertising

aktiv *adj* GESCHÄFT active, VW buoyant; **nicht ~** *adj* COMP inactive; **~er Betrieb** *m* GESCHÄFT going concern; **~e Bevölkerung** *f* PERSON *Arbeit* active population; **~e Bilanzgestaltung** *f* RECHNUNG creative accounting; **~er Börsenticker** *m* BÖRSE broad tape (*AmE*); **~e Datei** *f* COMP active file; **~es Fenster** *nt* COMP active window; **~e Fiskalpolitik** *f* VW active fiscal policy; **Förderungsmaßnahmen** *f pl* PERSON, POL, VERWALT, VW *zugunsten von Minderheiten* affirmative action (*AmE*), positive discrimination (*BrE*); **~er**

Gesellschafter *m*, **~e Gesellschafterin** *f* MGMNT acting partner, active partner; **~e Handelsbilanz** *f* IMP/EXP, VW active trade balance, favorable balance of trade (*AmE*), favourable trade balance (*AmE*), favourable balance of trade (*BrE*), favourable trade balance (*BrE*); **~e Leistungsbilanz** *f* FINANZ, IMP/EXP surplus on current account; **~es Management** *nt* GESCHÄFT active management; **~e Rechnungsabgrenzung** *f* RECHNUNG accruals; **~e Rechnungsabgrenzungposten** *m pl* RECHT accrued income, accrued revenue; **~e Rückversicherung** *f* VERSICH active reinsurance; **~ tätig** *adj* PERSON in active employment; **~e Treuhand** *f* RECHT living trust (*AmE*); **~es Unternehmen** *nt* GESCHÄFT active business; **~e Veredelung** *f* IMP/EXP *Zoll* inward processing; **~e Zahlungsbilanz** *f* FINANZ, VW active balance of payments

Aktiv- *in cpds* BANK, FINANZ asset, GESCHÄFT active, RECHNUNG asset

Aktiva *nt pl* RECHNUNG assets

Aktiv-: **Aktivgeschäft** *nt* FINANZ lending business; **Aktivhandel** *m* IMP/EXP foreign trade; **Aktivhypotheken** *f pl* FINANZ mortgage lendings

aktivieren *vt* GESCHÄFT activate, RECHNUNG capitalize, charge to capital

Aktivierung *f* COMP enablement, FINANZ, RECHNUNG capitalization, carrying as assets, VW heading into surplus, moving into surplus

aktivierungspflichtig: **~er Aufwand** *m* FINANZ, RECHNUNG capital expenditure (*capex*); **~er Leasingvertrag** *m* FINANZ, GESCHÄFT capital lease

Aktivierung: **Aktivierungsrecht** *nt* RECHNUNG right to capitalize; **Aktivierungsverbot** *nt* RECHNUNG legal prohibition to capitalize

aktivisch: **~ abgegrenzt** *adj* RECHNUNG deferred

Aktivist, in *m,f* POL, VW activist

Aktivität *f* GESCHÄFT activity; **Aktivitätsanalyse** *f* GESCHÄFT activity analysis; **Aktivitätskennzahl** *f* FINANZ activity ratio; **Aktivitätsordnung** *f* VERSICH active life table

Aktiv-: **Aktivkonto** *nt* RECHNUNG asset account; **Aktivkredit** *m* FINANZ business lending to outside parties; **Aktiv-Management** *nt* FINANZ asset management; **Aktiv-Passiv-Management** *nt* BANK, FINANZ asset and liability management, assets and liabilities management; **Aktiv- und Passivsteuerung** *f* BANK, FINANZ asset and liability management, assets and liabilities management; **Aktivposten** *m* GESCHÄFT asset, RECHNUNG asset item; **Aktivseite** *f* RECHNUNG asset side; **Aktivtausch** *m* RECHNUNG accounting exchange on the assets side, asset swap, VERWALT asset swap

Aktivum *nt* RECHNUNG asset

Aktiv-: **Aktivvermögen** *nt* FINANZ actual assets

aktualisieren *vt* COMP actualize, FINANZ actualize, bring sth up to date, GESCHÄFT actualize, update

Aktualisierung *f* COMP update, GESCHÄFT updating

aktuell *adj* FINANZ actual, GESCHÄFT current, up-to-date, up-to-the-minute, VW current; **~e Arbeitslosigkeit** *f* VW actual unemployment; **~er Betriebsgewinn** *m* RECHNUNG current operating profit; **~e Bewertungsgrundlagen** *f pl* **für die Kostenrechnung** RECHNUNG current cost basis; **~er Einstandspreis** *m* FINANZ current entry price; **~e Ereignisse** *nt pl* GESCHÄFT current events; **~e Ertragslage** *f* FINANZ

current profitability; **~er Gesamtbetrag** *m* FINANZ total to date; **~e Information** *f* GESCHÄFT up-to-date information; **~er Inlandswert** *m* IMP/EXP *einer Ware* current domestic value (*CDV*); **~er Kontostand** *m* GESCHÄFT current account balance (*BrE*); **~er Marktwert** *m* V&M current market value; **~es politisches Geschehen** *nt* POL current affairs; **~es Programm** *nt* COMP active program, current program; **~er Satz** *m* GESCHÄFT current rate; **~ verfügbar** *adj* GESCHÄFT available on a current basis; **~es Vermögen** *nt* RECHNUNG current asset; **~es Zeitgeschehen** *nt* GESCHÄFT current affairs

akustisch: **~er Speicher** *m* COMP acoustic memory, acoustic storage, acoustic store

akut *adj* GESCHÄFT urgent; **~e Gefahr** *f* VERSICH imminent danger, imminent peril

AKV *abbr* (*Allgemeine Kreditvereinbarungen*) FINANZ, VW *IWF GAB* (*general arrangement to borrow*)

Akzeleration *f* VW acceleration; **Akzelerationskoeffizient** *m* VW acceleration coefficient; **Akzelerationsprinzip** *nt* VW acceleration principle

Akzelerator *m* VW accelerator

Akzent: **den ~ verschieben** *phr* GESCHÄFT shift the emphasis

Akzenttaste *f* COMP *Tastatur* dead key

Akzept *nt* BANK, FINANZ acceptance; **zum ~ vorgelegter Wechsel** *m* BANK acceptance bill; ♦ **mit ~ versehen** GESCHÄFT accepted

akzeptabel *adj* GESCHÄFT acceptable

Akzept: **Akzept-Akkreditiv** *nt* FINANZ, IMP/EXP acceptance credit

Akzeptant *m* BANK drawee, *eines Wechsels* acceptor, RECHT *Vertrag* acceptor; ♦ **an ~** GESCHÄFT refer to acceptor (*R/A*)

Akzeptant: **Akzeptantenwechsel** *m* FINANZ acceptor's bill

Akzeptanz *f* FINANZ approval, POL acceptance, V&M *Annahme auf dem Markt* acceptance, consumer acceptance, market acceptance; **Akzeptanztest** *m* **einer Produktidee** V&M concept test

Akzept: **Akzeptbank** *f* BANK, FINANZ acceptance bank, accepting banker, accepting house; **Akzeptebuch** *nt* BANK, FINANZ acceptance ledger, RECHNUNG register of bills payable; **Akzeptfazilität** *f* BANK acceptance facility

akzeptgebend *adj* BANK, FINANZ accepting; **~e Bank** *f* BANK, FINANZ accepting bank

Akzept: **Akzeptgebühr** *f* BANK acceptance fee, FINANZ acceptance charge; **Akzepthaus** *nt* BANK acceptance house, accepting house; **Akzeptkredit** *nt* BANK acceptance facility; **Akzeptkreditrahmen** *m* BANK acceptance line (*AmE*)

akzeptieren *vt* BANK *Kreditkarte*, FINANZ, KOMM *Gespräch* accept; ♦ **~ bei Vorlage** GESCHÄFT accept on presentation

akzeptierend *adj* BANK, FINANZ accepting; **~e Bank** *f* BANK, FINANZ acceptance bank, accepting banker, accepting house

akzeptiert *adj* BANK, COMP accepted, GESCHÄFT accepted, approved of; **nicht ~** *adj* BANK dishonored (*AmE*), dishonoured (*BrE*), *Rechnung* unaccepted, GESCHÄFT *Rechnung* unaccepted; **~er Anteil** *m* VERSICH written line; **allgemein ~es Tausch- und Zahlungsmittel** *nt* VW generalized medium; **~er Wechsel** *m* BANK accepted draft, acceptance

Akzeptierung *f* FINANZ acceptance

Akzeptierverweigerung *f* BANK dishonor (*AmE*), dishonour (*BrE*)

Akzept: **Akzeptkonto** *nt* BANK acceptance account; **Akzeptkredit** *m* BANK acceptance credit; **Akzeptlinie** *f* BANK acceptance liability, acceptance line (*AmE*); **Akzeptmarkt** *m* BANK acceptance market; **Akzeptmeldung** *f* FINANZ notification of acceptance; **Akzeptobligo** *nt* RECHNUNG bills payable; **Akzeptpreis** *m* BANK acceptance price; **Akzeptprovision** *f* BANK acceptance commission; **Akzepttausch** *m* FINANZ exchange of acceptances; **Akzeptumlauf** *m* FINANZ acceptances outstanding; **Akzeptverbindlichkeiten** *f pl* FINANZ acceptance commitments, acceptance liabilities

Akzession *f* GESCHÄFT accession

akzessorisch *adj* RECHT accessory; **~e Besicherung** *f* FINANZ; **~e Sicherheit** *f* RECHNUNG asset coverage, RECHT collateral security; **~e Verpflichtung** *f* RECHT accessory undertaking

Akzidenzarbeit *f* IND jobbing

Akzisen *f pl* FINANZ excise taxes

al *abbr* (*alias*) GESCHÄFT aka (*also known as*)

A-la-carte-Vergütungssystem *nt* PERSON cafeteria benefit plan (*AmE*)

A-Länder *nt pl* IMP/EXP A countries

Alarm *m* GESCHÄFT alarm; ♦ **~ geben** GESCHÄFT raise the alarm; **~ schlagen** GESCHÄFT give the alert, raise the alarm

Alarm: **Alarmanlage** *f* GESCHÄFT burglar alarm; **Alarmbereitschaft** *f* GESCHÄFT alert; **Alarmeinrichtung** *f* COMP alarm equipment; **Alarmsignal** *nt* GESCHÄFT alarm signal; **Alarmzeichen** *nt* GESCHÄFT alarm signal; **Alarmzustand** *m* GESCHÄFT alert

aleatorisch *adj* RECHT, V&M aleatory, VERSICH aleatory, aleatoric; **~er Vertrag** *m* RECHT aleatory contract, hazardous contract; VERSICH aleatory contract; **~e Werbung** *f* V&M aleatory advertising

Algebra *f* MATH algebra; **~ der Logik** MATH Boolean algebra, Boolean logic

algorithmisch *adj* COMP, MATH algorithmic

Algorithmisierung *f* COMP, MATH algorithmization

Algorithmus *m* COMP, MATH algorithm

alias *adv* (*al*) GESCHÄFT also known as (*aka*)

aliquot *adj* MATH aliquot; **~e Teile** *f pl* MATH aliquot parts

Allbranchenversicherung *f* VERSICH all-lines insurance

allein: **für sich ~** *phr* GESCHÄFT per se

Allein- *in cpds* GESCHÄFT exclusive, sole; **Alleinabnehmer** *m*, **Alleinabnehmerin** *f* GRUND sole buyer; **Alleinauftrag** *m* GESCHÄFT exclusive contract

alleinberechtigt: **~er Mieter** *m*, **~e Mieterin** *f* GRUND, RECHT tenant in severalty; **~er Pächter** *m*, **~e Pächterin** *f* GRUND, RECHT tenant in severalty

Allein-: **Alleinbesitzer, in** *m,f* GRUND sole owner; **Alleinbetrieb** *m* GESCHÄFT one-man business, sole trader; **Alleineigentümer, in** *m,f* GESCHÄFT sole proprietor, GRUND, RECHT sole owner; **Alleinerbe** *m*, **Alleinerbin** *f* RECHT sole heir, sole legatee; **Alleinerfinder, in** *m,f* PATENT sole inventor; **Alleinherstellungsrecht** *nt* IND monopoly

alleinig: **~er Eigentümer** *m*, **~e Eigentümerin** *f* MGMNT sole proprietor; **~es Eigentumsrecht** *nt* RECHT sole ownership, sole proprietorship; **~er Erfinder** *m*, **~e Erfinderin** *f* PATENT sole inventor; **~er Inhaber** *m*, **~e Inhaberin** *f* GESCHÄFT sole trader; **~es Patentrecht** *nt* PATENT sole right to a patent; **~es Vertriebsrecht** *nt* V&M sole selling right; **~e Zuständigkeit** *f* RECHT exclusive jurisdiction; **mit dem alleinigen Ziel, daß** *phr* GESCHÄFT with the sole object of

Allein-: **Alleininhaber** *m* GESCHÄFT sole proprietor, sole trader; **Alleinkonzessionär** *m,f* GESCHÄFT sole concessionaire; **Alleinlizenz** *f* PATENT exclusive licence (*BrE*), exclusive license (*AmE*); **Alleinrecht** *nt* PATENT exclusive right

alleinstehend *adj* V&M solus position

Allein-: **Alleinstellung** *f* PATENT unique position; **Alleinverhandlungspartner, in** *m,f* **für Tarifverhandlungen** PERSON sole bargaining agent (*BrE*); **Alleinverhandlungsrechte** *nt pl* PERSON sole bargaining rights (*BrE*); **Alleinverkaufsrecht** *nt* GRUND exclusive agency listing, exclusive right-to-sell listing (*AmE*), PATENT exclusive licence (*BrE*), exclusive license (*AmE*), V&M franchise; **Alleinvertreter, in** *m,f* V&M, VW sole agent

Alleinvertretung *f* GESCHÄFT sole agency, exclusive agency; ♦ **die ~ haben für** GESCHÄFT *eine Firma* have exclusive agency for

Alleinvertretung: **Alleinvertretungsrecht** *nt* RECHT *Vertragsrecht* exclusive representation; **Alleinvertretungsvertrag** *m* RECHT *Handelsrecht* exclusive agency agreement

Allein-: **Alleinvertrieb** *m* V&M exclusive marketing; **Alleinvertriebsabkommen** *nt* RECHT exclusive sales contract; **Alleinvertriebsvertrag** *m* RECHT agreement for exclusiveness; **Alleinwerbung** *f* V&M individual advertising

Alles-oder-Nichts-Klausel *f* BÖRSE all or nothing clause (*AON clause*)

alle vor allem *phr* GESCHÄFT primarily

Allgefahrendeckung *f* VERSICH all-risks cover

allgemein 1. *adj* GESCHÄFT across-the-board, general, MGMNT general, STEUER broad-based; **2.** *adv* GESCHÄFT generally, widely; ♦ **~ anerkannt** GESCHÄFT widely recognized

allgemein: **~ anerkannte Buchprüfungsnormen** *f pl* RECHNUNG Generally Accepted Auditing Standards (*AmE*) (*GAAS*); **~ anerkannte Grundsätze** *m pl* **der Rechnungslegung** RECHNUNG Generally Accepted Accounting Principles (*AmE*) (*GAAP*), Statement of Standard Accounting Practice (*BrE*) (*SSAP*); **~e Arbeitslosigkeit** *f* VW general unemployment; **~e Ausgaben** *f pl* **der öffentlichen Hand** VW general government expenditure (*BrE*); **~e Aussage** *f* GESCHÄFT blanket statement; **~e Ausschlußklausel** *f* VERSICH general exclusions clause; **~er Ausweis** *m* GESCHÄFT, RECHNUNG general statement; **~e Bemessungsgrundlage** *f* SOZIAL general basis of assessment; **~e Berufsausbildung** *f* PERSON *Arbeit* general training; **~e Betriebskosten** *pl* RECHNUNG general operating costs; **~e Bevölkerungswachstumsrate** *f* VW crude population rate

Allgemein: **~er Deutscher Automobil-Club** *m* (*ADAC*) TRANSP ≈ Automobile Association (*AA*), ≈ American Automobile Association (*AAA*); **~e Deutsche Binnentransportbedingungen** *f pl* TRANSP General

Domestic Transport Conditions; **~e Deutsche Seeversicherungsbedingungen** *f pl* VERSICH General German Marine Insurance; **~e Deutsche Spediteurbedingungen** *f pl* IMP/EXP General German Forwarders' Conditions

allgemein: **~er Dienstvertrag** *m* TRANSP general service contract (*BrE*); **~e Einnahmen** *f pl* FINANZ common revenue; **~e Empfehlung** *f* BÖRSE blanket recommendation; **~e Erhöhung** *f* MGMNT, PERSON across-the-board increase; **~er Feiertag** *m* GESCHÄFT, PERSON, RECHT bank holiday (*BrE*), legal holiday (*AmE*), statutory holiday (*AmE*); **~e Geschäftsbedingungen** *f pl* (*AGB*) RECHT *Vertragsrecht* general terms and conditions, standard terms and conditions; **~e Geschäftskosten** *pl* FINANZ indirect expenses; **~er Geschäftsplan** *m* GESCHÄFT generic business plan; **~e Gesetzesvorschrift** *f* GESCHÄFT blanket statute; **~e Gewerkschaft** *f* PERSON general union; **~es Gleichgewicht** *nt* VW general equilibrium (*GE*); **~e Haftpflichtversicherung** *f* VERSICH general liability insurance; **~es Handelsschiff** *nt* TRANSP general trader; **~e Haushaltserhebung** *f* VW General Household Survey (*GHS*); **~e Hilfskostenstelle** *f* RECHNUNG general indirect cost center (*AmE*), general indirect cost centre (*BrE*), general service department; **~e Importgenehmigung** *f* IMP/EXP open general import licence (*BrE*) (*OGIL*), open general import license (*AmE*) (*OGIL*); **~e Kapitalgesellschaft** *f* GESCHÄFT public corporation, publicly held company; **~e kaufmännisch orientierte Programmiersprache** *f* (*COBOL*) COMP common business-oriented language (*COBOL*)

Allgemein: **~e Kreditvereinbarungen** *f pl* (*AKV*) FINANZ, VW *IWF* general arrangement to borrow (*GAB*)

allgemein: **~e Lebensversicherung** *f* VERSICH composite life insurance; **~e Lebensversicherungspolice** *f* VERSICH composite life policy; **~e Lieferbedingungen** *f pl* GESCHÄFT general terms and conditions of delivery; **~es Lohnniveau** *nt* VW general wage level; **~es Marktgleichgewicht** *nt* VW general market equilibrium; **~e Nutzereinrichtung** *f* GESCHÄFT common user facility; **~er Partner** *m* RECHNUNG general service partner; **~es Präferenzsystem** *nt* VW generalized system of preferences (*GSP*); **~e Rahmeneinfuhrgenehmigung** *f* IMP/EXP open general import licence (*BrE*) (*OGIL*), open general import license (*AmE*) (*OGIL*); **~e Rahmengenerallizenz** *f* IMP/EXP open general import licence (*BrE*) (*OGIL*), open general import license (*AmE*) (*OGIL*); **~e Rauferei** *f infrml* RECHNUNG free-for-all (*infrml*); **~es Rechnungswesen** *nt* RECHNUNG general accounting; **~e Regeln** *f pl* GESCHÄFT standard code; **~e Richtung** *f* GESCHÄFT tendency; **~er Rohstoffkurs** *m* BÖRSE general commodity rate (*GCR*); **~e Rücklage** *f* GESCHÄFT unappropriated surplus; **~e Rückstellungen** *f pl* RECHNUNG general provisions; **~e Steuerermäßigung** *f* **bei Restbeständen** STEUER general holdover relief (*BrE*); **~e Steuermittel** *nt pl* STEUER general revenue (*AmE*); **~er Steuernachlaß** *m* **bei Restbeträgen** STEUER general holdover relief (*BrE*); **~er Steuersatz** *m* STEUER composite rate tax; **~e Umsatzsteuer** *f* STEUER general sales tax; **~e Veränderungen** *f pl* GESCHÄFT, MGMNT across-the-board changes; **~es Verbot** *nt* GESCHÄFT blanket ban; **~e Verbrauchssteuer** *f* STEUER general consumption tax; **~er Verhaltenskodex** *m*

GESCHÄFT common code of practice; **~e Verwaltung** *f* MGMNT general management; **~e Verwaltungskosten** *pl* VERWALT administrative expenses; **~e Vorschrift** *f* GESCHÄFT blanket statute; **~es Wahlrecht** *nt* POL universal suffrage; **~er Warenkurs** *m* BÖRSE general commodity rate (*GCR*); **~e Wirtschaftsdaten** *pl* GESCHÄFT general business statistics; **~es Wissen** *nt* SOZIAL common learnings; **~e Zinstendenz** *f* VW general interest tendency; **~er Zollbegleitschein** *m* IMP/EXP general transire

Allgemein: **~es Zoll- und Handelsabkommen** *nt* (*GATT*) POL, VW General Agreement on Tariffs and Trade (*GATT*); **~e Zollordnung** *f* (*AZO*) IMP/EXP General Customs Regulations

allgemein: **~es Zoll- und Präferenzsystem** *nt* IMP/EXP generalized system of tariffs and preferences (*GSTP*); **~es Zurückbehaltungsrecht** *nt* GRUND general lien; **~er Zweck** *m* GESCHÄFT general purpose (*GP*)

Allgemeinheit *f* GESCHÄFT, RECHT general public, public, public at large; ◆ **nicht für die ~ bestimmt** POL *Dokumente* restricted

allgemeinverständlich: **~ machen** *phr* GESCHÄFT vulgarize

Allianz *f* POL alliance

allmählich 1. *adj* GESCHÄFT gradual; **2.** *adv* GESCHÄFT gradually

allmählich: **~e Abschaffung** *f* GESCHÄFT phasing out

Allmenderessourcen *f pl* VW common access resources

Allokation *f* VERWALT, VW allocation; **~ externer Kosten** VW allocation of social costs; **~ von Ressourcen** VW allocation of resources; **Allokationseffizienz** *f* VW allocative efficiency; **Allokationsmechanismus** *m* VERWALT, VW allocative mechanism

Allonge *f* BANK allonge, BÖRSE apron

Allround- *in cpds* GESCHÄFT all-round; **Allround-Geschäftsfrau** *f* GESCHÄFT business generalist; **Allround-Geschäftsmann** *m* GESCHÄFT business generalist

alltäglich: **~er Vertrag** *m* RECHT simple contract

Allzweck- *in cpds* GESCHÄFT all-purpose, general-purpose (*GP*); **Allzweckfrachter** *m* TRANSP omnicarrier; **Allzweckliegeplatz** *m* TRANSP general-purpose berth

Alpenländer *nt pl* GESCHÄFT Alpine countries

Alpha *nt* BÖRSE alpha; **Alpha-Aktie** *f* BÖRSE alpha stock; **Alpha-Beta-Testverfahren** *nt* V&M Alpha/Beta testing

alphabetisch *adj* GESCHÄFT alphabetical; ◆ **in ~er Reihenfolge** GESCHÄFT in alphabetical order

alphanumerisch *adj* COMP alphanumeric (*A/N*), MATH numeric alphabetic; **~e Daten** *pl* COMP alphanumeric data, alphanumerics; **~e Tastatur** *f* COMP alphanumeric keyboard

Alpha: **Alpha-Stadium** *nt* FINANZ alpha stage; **Alphatest** *m* COMP *Programme* alpha test; **Alpha-Wert** *m* BÖRSE alpha stock

alt: **~e Aktie** *f* BÖRSE old share; **~e Ausgabe** *f* MEDIEN back issue, back number; **~e Charter** *f* TRANSP old charter; **~er Hase** *m* infrml GESCHÄFT grey-hair (*infrml*); **~es Industriegebiet** *nt* IND rustbelt (*AmE*); **~e Konzession** *f* TRANSP old charter; **~e Nummer** *f* MEDIEN *von Zeitungen, Zeitschriften* back issue, back number

Altbausanierung *f* GESCHÄFT area rehabilitation, modernizing and refitting older buildings

älter *adj* GESCHÄFT, RECHT senior (*Snr*); **~es Patent** *nt* PATENT prior patent

Alter *nt* GESCHÄFT age; **Alter/Einkommensprofil** *nt* PERSON age-earnings profile; **Alter/Einkommensübersicht** *f* PERSON age-earnings profile

altern *vi* GESCHÄFT age

Alternativ- *in cpds* GESCHÄFT alternative

alternativ *adj* GESCHÄFT alternative; **~e Energie** *f* UMWELT alternative energy; **~e Kosten** *pl* VW opportunity costs; **~e Nutzung** *f* GRUND alternative use; **~e Presse** *f* MEDIEN alternate press; **~e Substitution** *f* GESCHÄFT, VERWALT alternative substitution; **~e Technologie** *f* IND, UMWELT alternative technology; **~e Wirtschaftsstrategie** *f* VW alternative economic strategy

Alternative *f* GESCHÄFT alternative, option; ◆ **es gibt keine ~** VW there is no alternative (*TINA*)

Alternativ-: **Alternativfrage** *f* GESCHÄFT, V&M closed question, dichotomous question; **Alternativhypothese** *f* MATH alternative hypothesis; **Alternativkosten** *pl* FINANZ alternative costs, RECHNUNG accounting costs, opportunity costs, VW alternative costs; **Alternativlösung** *f* GESCHÄFT alternative solution; **Alternativplan** *m* GESCHÄFT contingency plan; **Alternativplanung** *f* GESCHÄFT contingency planning; **Alternativsanierung** *f* FINANZ alternative reorganization; **Alternativvereinbarungen** *f pl* GESCHÄFT contingency arrangements; **Alternativvorschlag** *m* MGMNT alternative proposal; **Alternativweg** *m* COMP alternative route

alternd: **~e Bevölkerung** *f* VW ageing population

alternieren *vi* GESCHÄFT alternate

alternierend *adj* GESCHÄFT alternate

Alter: **Altersaufbau** *m* PERSON, POL, VW *der Bevölkerung* age distribution; **Altersaufbau** *m* **des Anlagevermögens** FINANZ age ranking of fixed assets; **Altersdiskriminierung** *f* VW ageism; **Altersfreibetrag** *m* STEUER old-age allowance (*BrE*); **Altersgliederung** *f* PERSON, POL, VW age distribution; **Altersgrenze** *f* GESCHÄFT age limit; **die Altersgrenze erreichen** *phr* GESCHÄFT reach the age limit; **Altersgruppe** *f* GESCHÄFT age group, MEDIEN age bracket, V&M *Marktforschung* age bracket, age group; **Alters-, Behinderten- und Hinterbliebenenversorgung** *f* PERSON old-age, disabled and survivors' social security system; **Altersklasse** *f* GESCHÄFT age group; **Alterspyramide** *f* VW age pyramid; **Altersrente** *f* FINANZ old-age pension, retirement pension, retiring allowance; **Altersrentensystem** *nt* FINANZ old-age pension scheme; **Altersruhegeld** *nt* PERSON retirement benefit

altersspezifisch *adj* VERWALT age-specific

Alter: **Altersstruktur** *f* PERSON, POL, VW *der Bevölkerung* age distribution; **Altersversicherungsbeitrag** *m* PERSON *Ruhestand* superannuation contribution; **Altersversorgung** *f* FINANZ retirement pension, retiring allowance; **Altersversorgungsanwartschaften** *f pl* FINANZ retirement pension rights; **Altersverteilung** *f* PERSON, POL, VW age distribution; **Alterszuschlag** *m* VERSICH addition to age

Altindustrie *f* IND sunset industry

Altlasten *f pl* FINANZ pre-currency reform claims, UMWELT contaminated site, VW inherited burdens; **Altlastensanierung** *f* UMWELT cleanup operation

Altmetall *nt* IND *Schrott* scrap metal

altmodisch *adj* GESCHÄFT old-fashioned, out of fashion

Altöl *nt* UMWELT waste oils

Altpapier *nt* IND scrap paper, UMWELT wastepaper, scrap paper

Altruismus *m* VW altruism

altruistisch *adj* VW altruistic

Altschulden *f pl* FINANZ prior debt

Alt-Taste *f* COMP Alt key (*Alternate key*)

Altwarenhändler, in *m,f* GESCHÄFT scrap dealer

Alt: **~e Welt** *f* VW First World

Altwert *m* FINANZ residual value

Alu *abbr* (*Aluminium*) UMWELT, IND Alu. (*aluminium BrE, aluminum AmE*)

Aluminium *nt* (*Alu*) UMWELT, IND aluminium (*BrE*) (*Alu.*), aluminum (*AmE*) (*Alu.*); **Aluminium-abdeckungen** *f pl* TRANSP aluminium covers (*BrE*), aluminum covers (*AmE*); **Aluminiumindustrie** *f* GESCHÄFT aluminium industry (*BrE*), aluminum industry (*AmE*)

Amateur *m* FREI amateur

Ambition *f* GESCHÄFT ambition

Ambivalenzkonflikt *m* GESCHÄFT plus-minus conflict

ambulant: **~er Handel** *m* V&M itinerant selling; **~er Verkauf** *m* V&M door-to-door selling; **~e Versorgung** *f* SOZIAL medical care to out-patients

Ambulanz *f* SOZIAL *Klinik* outpatients' department

amendiert: **~e Steuererklärung** *f* STEUER amended tax return

Amerika-Klausel *f* VERSICH American clause

amerikanisch: **~e Bedingungen** *f pl* VW *Getreidehandel* American terms; **zu ~en Bedingungen** *phr* VW in American terms; **~e Buchführung** *f* RECHNUNG columnar bookkeeping, tabular bookkeeping; **~e flüssige Viertelgallone** *f* GESCHÄFT American liquid quart; **~e Klausel** *f* VERSICH American clause; **~e Option** *f* BÖRSE American option; **~e Parität** *f* VW American parity, American terms; **~e Tonne** *f* GESCHÄFT American short ton; **~e Viertelgallone** *f* GESCHÄFT American dry quart; **~e Wertpapiere** *nt pl* BÖRSE Yankees (*jarg*); **~er Zinstender** *m* FINANZ US-style variable tender

Amex: **~ Warenbörse** *f* BÖRSE, FINANZ Amex Commodities Exchange (*ACE*)

Amoroso-Robinson-Relation *f* VW Amoroso-Robinson relation

Amortisation *f* FINANZ payback, payout, RECHNUNG amortization, amortizement, V&M payback, payout; **Amortisationsanleihe** *f* BÖRSE redemption bond, FINANZ amortization loan; **Amortisationsanpassung** *f* RECHNUNG amortization adjustment; **Amortisationsfonds** *m* FINANZ amortization fund, sinking fund; **Amortisationshypothek** *f* BANK amortized mortgage loan; **Amortisationsplan** *m* RECHNUNG amortization schedule; **Amortisationsverhältnis** *nt* V&M payout ratio; **Amortisationszeit** *f* FINANZ period of redemption, PERSON *Finanzwesen* payback period

amortisierbar *adj* BANK, FINANZ amortizable

amortisieren *vt* BANK amortize, GESCHÄFT pay off, RECHNUNG *Vermögenswerte, Aktiva* amortize

amortisiert: **~er Wert** *m* RECHNUNG amortized value

Amortisierung *f* BANK, RECHNUNG amortization

Amsterdam: **~er Interbankenangebotssatz** *m* BANK Amsterdam Interbank Offered Rate (*AIBOR*)

Amt *nt* GESCHÄFT office, PATENT authority, PERSON

position, RECHT agency (*agcy*), VERWALT bureau (*AmE*); **~ für Management und Haushaltsplanung** POL Office of Management and Budget (*AmE*) (*OMB*); **~ für öffentliche Arbeiten** GESCHÄFT, SOZIAL Public Works Department (*PWD*); ♦ **im ~ sein** PERSON be in office, POL hold office; **ein ~ antreten** POL accede to an office; **ein ~ bekleiden** POL hold office; **das ~ des PA ausüben** PERSON perform the office of PA; **von Amts wegen** PERSON *Arbeit* ex officio

Amt: **Amthaftungsanklage** *f* RECHT suit to establish liability of public authorities

amtierend *adj* GESCHÄFT, MGMNT acting, POL incumbent; **~er Direktor** *m* MGMNT acting director; **~e Direktorin** *f* MGMNT acting director

amtlich 1. *adj* GESCHÄFT official; **nicht ~** MEDIEN, POL off-the-record; **2.** *adv* GESCHÄFT officially; **nicht ~** GESCHÄFT unofficially; ♦ **~ als AG eingetragen** BÖRSE incorporated (*AmE*) (*Inc.*); **~ notieren** BÖRSE quote in the official list; **~ versiegeln** RECHT put under seal

amtlich: **~ beglaubigt** *adj* RECHT, VERWALT certified, legalized, officially attested, officially authenticated; **~ beglaubigte Kopie** *f* VERWALT certified copy; **~e Bekanntmachung** *f* RECHT official announcement; **~ bestellter Schiffssachverständiger** *m* [decl. as adj], **~ bestellte Schiffssachverständige** *f* [decl. as adj] PERSON surveyor; **~es Börsenkursblatt** *nt* BÖRSE Stock Exchange Daily Official List (*BrE*) (*SEDOL*); **~e Börsennotiz** *f* BÖRSE official quotation; **~er Börsenschluß** *m* BÖRSE close; **~er Devisenkurs** *m* FINANZ official foreign exchange quotation; **nicht ~ eingetragene Urkunde** *f* GRUND, RECHT unrecorded deed; **~e Genehmigung** *f* RECHT official approval; **~ geprüfter Buchhalter** *m*, **~ geprüfte Buchhalterin** *f* RECHNUNG qualified accountant; **~ geprüfter Buchprüfer** *m*, **~ geprüfte Buchprüferin** *f* RECHNUNG qualified auditor; **~er Kurs** *m* BANK official rate; **~er Kursmakler** *m*, **~e Kursmaklerin** *f* BÖRSE official broker; **~er Markt** *m* VW official market; **~e Nachrichtenverlautbarung** *f* KOMM news bulletin; **~ notierte Aktien** *f pl* BÖRSE shares quoted officially (*BrE*), stock quoted officially (*AmE*); **~ nicht notierte Aktien** *f pl* BÖRSE unquoted shares; **~ notierte Firma** *f* FINANZ publicly listed company; **~ nicht notierter Wert** *m* BÖRSE, FINANZ unlisted security; **nicht zur ~en Notierung zugelassene Aktie** *f* BÖRSE unlisted share; **~es Register** *nt* VERWALT registry office; **~e Registrierungsbescheinigung** *f* RECHT certificate of incorporation; **~er Schätzer** *m*, **~e Schätzerin** *f* GRUND appraiser, RECHT official valuer; **~e Systematik** *f* **der Betriebsstätten** IND standard industrial classification (*SIC*); **~e Vorprüfung** *f* PATENT preliminary research; **~e Währungsreserven** *f pl* FINANZ official reserves; **~er Wechselkurs** *m* FINANZ official exchange rate; **~e Zahlen** *f pl* GESCHÄFT official figures; **~ zugelassen** *adj* BÖRSE officially listed, officially quoted; **~ zugelassener Finanzierungsplaner** *m*, **~ zugelassene Finanzierungsplanerin** *f* FINANZ certified financial planner; **~ zugelassener Sondervergütungsexperte** *m*, **~ zugelassene Sondervergütungsexpertin** *f* PERSON *Unternehmen, Industrie* certified employee benefit specialist (*AmE*); **~ zugelassener Wirtschaftsprüfer** *m*, **~ zugelassene Wirtschaftsprüferin** *f* RECHNUNG Accredited Chartered Accountant (*ACA*)

Amt: **Amtmann** *m* RECHT head clerk; **Amtsarzt** *m*, **Amtsärztin** *f* PERSON medical officer of health

(*MOH*), SOZIAL health officer; **Amtsblatt** *nt* POL, VERWALT Official Journal (*OJ*); **Amtsblatt** *nt* **der Europäischen Union** POL, VERWALT Official Journal (*OJ*); **Amtsbonus** *m* GESCHÄFT advantage of incumbency; **Amtsfonds** *m* RECHT *Sondervermögen, zweckgebundene Mittel* agency fund; **Amtsgericht** *nt* RECHT county court, district court (*AmE*), small-claims court, VERWALT registrar of companies; **Amtsgericht** *nt* **in Strafsachen** RECHT court of petty session; **Amtsgewalt** *f* GESCHÄFT authority; **Amtsinhaber, in** *m,f* PERSON holder of an office; **Amtsmißbrauch** *m* GESCHÄFT abuse of administrative authority; **Amtsperiode** *f* GESCHÄFT term of office, POL administration, term; **Amtsrichter, in** *m,f* RECHT magistrate; **urteilsbefugte Amtsrichter** *m pl* RECHT magistrates entitled to adjudicate; **Amtssitz** *m* POL seat; **Amtsvergütung** *f* MGMNT executive compensation; **Amtszeit** *f* GESCHÄFT term of office, PERSON tenure; **Amtszimmer** *nt* VERWALT *Geschäftszimmer* bureau

an: **~ sich** *phr* GESCHÄFT per se

analog 1. *adj* COMP analog, GESCHÄFT analogical, analogous; **2.** *adv* RECHT mutatis mutandis

analog: **~e Darstellung** *f* GESCHÄFT analog representation

Analog- *in cpds* COMP analog; **Analogbildschirm** *m* COMP analog monitor; **Analog-Digital-Rechner** *m* COMP hybrid computer; **Analog-Digital-Wandler** *m* COMP analog-to-digital converter (*ADC*); **Analogkanal** *m* COMP analog channel; **Analogrechner** *m* COMP analog computer; **Analog-Repräsentation** *f* GESCHÄFT analog representation

Analyse *f* GESCHÄFT analysis; **~ der Anforderungen an das Ausbildungsprogramm** PERSON *Fachausbildung/ Grundausbildung* training needs analysis; **~ des Ausbildungsbedarfs** GESCHÄFT training needs analysis; **~ des betriebswirtschaftlichen Risikos** FINANZ commercial risk analysis; **~ der Geschäftsabschlüsse** FINANZ, MGMNT transactional analysis (*TA*); **~ von Kapitalanlagen** BÖRSE, FINANZ investment analysis; **~ konkurrierender Produkte** V&M competitor analysis; **~ von Stärken, Schwächen, Chancen und Risiken** V&M strengths, weaknesses, opportunities and threats analysis (*SWOT*); **~ der Umweltwirkungen** UMWELT environmental impact analysis; **~ der Wachstumsdeterminanten** VW growth accounting; **Analysenbuch** *nt* RECHNUNG analysis book; **Analysenzertifikat** *nt* TRANSP certificate of analysis; **Analyseprogramm** *nt* COMP analyser (*BrE*), analyzer (*AmE*); **Analyseverfahren** *nt* MGMNT analytic process

analysieren *vt* GESCHÄFT analyse (*BrE*), analyze (*AmE*)

Analytiker, in *m,f* MGMNT analyst

analytisch *adj* GESCHÄFT analytic, analytical; **~e Arbeitsbewertung** *f* IND analytic job evaluation; **~er Bericht** *m* RECHNUNG analytical review; **~e Prüfung** *f* RECHNUNG analytical audit, analytical auditing; **~es Rechnungswesen** *nt* RECHNUNG analytic accounting

Anamnese *f* SOZIAL health record

Anarchie *f* POL anarchy; **~ der Produktion** POL *Marxismus* anarchy of production; **Anarchielehre** *f* POL anarchism

Anarchismus *m* POL anarchism

Anarcho-Kommunismus *m* jarg POL anarcho-communism (*jarg*)

Anarcho-Syndikalismus *m jarg* POL anarcho-syndicalism (*jarg*)

Anbau *m* GESCHÄFT annex (*AmE*), annexe (*BrE*), VW *production of a crop* cultivation

anbauen *vt* VW *Landwirtschaft* cultivate

anbei *frml adv* KOMM enclosed; ◆ ~ **schicken wir Ihnen** KOMM please find enclosed

anberaumt: ~ **sein für** *phr* GESCHÄFT be arranged for, be scheduled for

Anbetracht: in ~ *phr* [+gen] GESCHÄFT in consideration of

anbieten 1. *vt* FREI tout, GESCHÄFT bid on (*AmE*), bid for, offer, tender, PERSON *Stellung* offer; **2. sich** ~ *v refl* GESCHÄFT volunteer

Anbieter, in *m,f* GESCHÄFT bidder, offerer, tenderer, *Lieferant* supplier; ~ **von Dienstleistungen** GESCHÄFT purveyor of services; **Anbieterabsprache** *f* VW collusive bidding, collusive tendering; **Anbietergemeinschaft** *f* V&M bidding association

Anbordgehen *nt* TRANSP embarkation

anbringen *vt* KOMM affix

andauern *vi* GESCHÄFT last

andauernd *adj* GESCHÄFT ongoing

An-Deck-Konnossement *nt* TRANSP on-deck bill of lading

Andenmarkt *m* VW Andean Common Market (*ACM, ANCOM*)

Andenpakt *m* VW Andean Pact

andere: ~ **Verbindlichkeiten** *f pl* RECHNUNG other liabilities

Anderkonto *nt* BANK escrow account, FINANZ escrow account, third-party account, RECHNUNG client account

ändern 1. *vt* GESCHÄFT alter, change, vary, POL switch, VERSICH adjust; **2. sich** ~ *v refl* GESCHÄFT vary

andersartig: ~ **als** *adj* GESCHÄFT alien from

Änderung *f* GESCHÄFT alteration, altering, change, *von Daten* modification, GRUND *an Gebäuden* modification, PATENT amendment, POL amendment, switch, RECHT amendment, VW *Angebot und Nachfrage* change; ~ **der Anschrift** KOMM change of address; ~ **der Begünstigungsklausel** VERSICH change of beneficiary provision; ~ **des Bezugsteils** TRANSP *Luftfahrt* master change (*MC*), specification change notice (*SCN*); ~ **in der Buchführung** RECHNUNG accounting change; ~ **des Grundkapitals** GESCHÄFT alteration of capital; ~ **der Originalvorlage** specification change notice (*SCN*); ~ **der Rechtsfrom des Unternehmens** RECHT transformation of legal form of business organization; ~ **der Technologie** IND technological change; ~ **einer Transportstrecke** TRANSP rerouting; ◆ **Änderungen vorbehalten** GESCHÄFT subject to change without notice

Änderung: **Änderungen** *f pl* RECHT *im Vertrag* different terms; **Änderungen** *f pl* **und Verbesserungen** RECHNUNG alterations and improvements; **Änderungsanfrage** *f* TRANSP change request; **Änderungsantrag** *m* POL, RECHT application for amendment, TRANSP request for change, change request; **Änderungsbitte** *f* TRANSP change request; **Änderungsdatei** *f* COMP change file; **Änderungsentwurf** *m* RECHT draft amendments; **Änderungsgesetz** *nt* RECHT amending statute;

Änderungsgesuch *nt* TRANSP change request, request for change

anderweitig: nicht ~ **spezifiziert** *adj* GESCHÄFT not elsewhere specified (*NES*), not otherwise specified; ~**e Verabredung** *f* GESCHÄFT other engagement

Andeutung *f* GESCHÄFT hint, pointer

Andrang *m* GESCHÄFT *auf dem Markt* congestion, V&M rush

andrehen *vt* GESCHÄFT palm off (*infrml*); ◆ **jdm etw** ~ *infrml* GESCHÄFT palm sth off on sb (*infrml*), fob sth off on sb (*infrml*)

Andruck *m* GESCHÄFT, MEDIEN test print

Andruckbögen *m pl* GESCHÄFT, MEDIEN proof sheets

aneignen: sich ~ *v refl* GESCHÄFT acquire, RECHT appropriate

Aneignung *f* RECHT acquisition of ownership by occupancy

aneinandergrenzend *adj* GESCHÄFT adjoining

anekdotisch *adj* SOZIAL *Beweis* anecdotal

anerkannt *adj* GESCHÄFT accepted, acknowledged, recognized, V&M accredited; **nicht** ~ *adj* GESCHÄFT unacknowledged, unrecognized; ~**er Beleg** *m* RECHNUNG approved voucher; ~**er Berufsverband** *m* FINANZ recognized professional body (*RPB*); ~**e Beteiligungsfirmen** *f pl* **der Dritten Welt** FINANZ recognized third-world investment firms; ~**e Clearingstelle** *f* BANK recognized clearing house (*RCH*); ~**e Finanzlage** *f* STEUER approved status (*BrE*); ~**e Gewerkschaft** *f* PERSON recognized trade union; ~**es Gewerkschaftsstatut** *nt* PERSON union rule book; ~**er Gewinn** *m* STEUER recognized gain; ~**e Investmentbörse** *f* BÖRSE recognized investment exchange (*RIE*); ~**er Kontokorrentauszug** *m* RECHNUNG account stated; ~**e Lieferstelle** *f* BÖRSE approved delivery facility; ~**er Praxiscode** *m* GESCHÄFT approved code of practice (*ACOP*); ~**er Rechnungsabschluß** *m* RECHNUNG account stated; ~**er Verhaltenskodex** *m* GESCHÄFT approved code of practice (*ACOP*); ~**e Werbeagentur** *f* V&M accredited advertising agency

anerkennen *vt* GESCHÄFT recognize, accept, acknowledge, *Rechte* establish, *Forderung* allow, admit, PERSON *Gewerkschaft*, POL, RECHT recognize, VERSICH *Schadensanspruch* allow

Anerkenntnis *f* BANK, FINANZ, GESCHÄFT acknowledgement, RECHT acknowledgement, acknowledgement of debt

Anerkennung *f* GESCHÄFT acceptance, acknowledgement (*ack*), recognition, reward, RECHT *eines Anspruchs* recognition, V&M reward; ~ **einer Gewerkschaft** PERSON *durch einen Arbeitgeber* trade union recognition (*BrE*), *für Tarifverhandlungen* certification mark; **Anerkennungsklausel** *f* PERSON recognition-only clause

anfallen *vi* GESCHÄFT come to hand

anfällig *adj* PERSON vulnerable

Anfang *m* GESCHÄFT outset, start, start-up; **von** ~ **an** **finanziell abgesichertes Programm** *nt* POL hard money; ◆ **zu** ~ GESCHÄFT at the outset

anfangen 1. *vt* GESCHÄFT begin, start, start up; **2.** *vi* GESCHÄFT begin, start, start up; ◆ **schon angefangen haben** GESCHÄFT be under way

anfänglich *adj* GESCHÄFT initial, start-up; ~**e Provisionsbelastung** *f* FINANZ front-end loading; ~**e**

Unmöglichkeit f RECHT *Verträge* impossibility ab initio, impossibility at the time of making, original impossibility

Anfang: **Anfangsausgaben** f pl FINANZ initial expenditure; **Anfangsauszahlung** f FINANZ initial investment; **Anfangsbestand** m RECHNUNG beginning inventory, opening balance, opening inventory; **Anfangsbilanz** f RECHNUNG opening balance sheet; **Anfangsdividende** f FINANZ initial dividend; **Anfangseinschuß** m BÖRSE original margin; **Anfangsgehalt** nt PERSON starting salary; **Anfangsindustrie** f IND sunrise industry; **Anfangsinventar** f RECHNUNG initial inventory, opening inventory; **Anfangskapital** nt FINANZ front money, initial capital, original capital, start-up capital; **Anfangslohn** m PERSON starting wage; **Anfangsstellung** f PERSON *Arbeit* entry-level job; **Anfangstemperatur** f IND *Siedebeginn* initial boiling point; **Anfangstermin** m RECHNUNG dies a quo; **Anfangswert** m GESCHÄFT initial value

anfechtbar adj MATH refutable, RECHT, VERSICH contestable, voidable; **~e Behauptung** f MATH refutable assertion; **~e Klausel** f VERSICH contestable clause; **~e Police** f VERSICH voidable policy; **~e Rechtshandlung** f RECHT voidable transaction

anfechten vt PATENT avoid, rescind, RECHT rescind, avoid, *Testament* dispute, contest, challenge, *Urteil* appeal against

Anfechtung f RECHT appeal, avoidance, challenge, contestation, opposition, rescission, VERSICH avoidance; **Anfechtungsklage** f RECHT action for rescission; **Anfechtungsklausel** f RECHT avoidance clause; **Anfechtungsrecht** nt RECHT right of avoidance

anfertigen vt GESCHÄFT *Liste* draw up, make up

Anflug m GESCHÄFT, VW hint

anfordern vt COMP, GESCHÄFT, KOMM ask for, request

Anforderung f COMP request, GESCHÄFT requirement, request, KOMM request; **~ des Verbrauchers** V&M consumer requirement; ◆ **den Anforderungen entsprechen** GESCHÄFT be able to meet the demands, fulfil the expectations (*BrE*), fulfill the expectations (*AmE*); **den Anforderungen genügen** PERSON *Arbeit* be up to standard

Anforderung: **Anforderungsprofil** nt PERSON job spec (*infrml*), job specification

Anfrage f COMP enquiry, PATENT request

anfragen vi COMP, GESCHÄFT enquire

anfügen vt GESCHÄFT, KOMM add

Anführer m GESCHÄFT leader

Angabe f GESCHÄFT, PERSON statement; **~ von Ankauf- und Verkaufskurs** BÖRSE double-barreled quotation (*AmE*), double-barrelled quotation (*BrE*); **~ der Bedingungen** PERSON statement of terms and conditions; **~ des Familienstandes** GESCHÄFT status information; **~ risikoerheblicher Tatbestände** VERSICH material representation; **Angaben** f pl GESCHÄFT details, particulars; **Angaben** f pl **zur Börsenzulassung** BÖRSE listing particulars; **Angabepflicht** f RECHNUNG disclosure requirement

angeben vt GESCHÄFT indicate, state

angeblich adj GESCHÄFT alleged, so-called, RECHT *behauptet, mutmaßlich* alleged

Angebot nt BÖRSE offer, GESCHÄFT tender, proposition, offer, proposal, quotation, quote, bid, RECHT offer, VW supply; **~ und Annahme** f RECHT offer and acceptance;

~ und Nachfrage f GESCHÄFT, VW supply and demand; **~ an Privatkunden** BÖRSE retail offer; **~ der vollständigen Rückerstattung** V&M complete refund offer; **~ von Wertpapieren im Sekundärmarkt** BÖRSE secondary offering; ◆ **im ~** GRUND *Haus* under offer (*BrE*), V&M on offer; **ein ~ abgeben** MGMNT *für ein Projekt* tender; **das ~ ablehnen** RECHT *Vertragsrecht* decline the offer; **~ und Annahme stimmen überein** RECHT *Vertragsrecht* offer and acceptance correspond; **das ~ erhöhen** VW increase the supply; **um Angebote ersuchen** GESCHÄFT appeal for tenders; **~ geht ein** GESCHÄFT bid is received; **~ liegt vor** GESCHÄFT bid is received; **~ machen** GESCHÄFT bid; **oder ~** V&M at or near offer, or nearest offer (*ono*); **~ unterbreiten** GESCHÄFT make an offer, tender; **~ verbessern** FREI upgrade

Angebot: **Angebotsabgabe** f GESCHÄFT, MGMNT submission of bids, tendering; **Angebotsanalyse** f GESCHÄFT comparative evaluation sheet; **Angebotselastizität** f VW elasticity of supply; **Angebotsempfänger, in** m,f GESCHÄFT offeree; **Angebotseröffnung** f GESCHÄFT opening of tenders; **Angebotsfunktion** f VW supply function

angebotsinduziert: **~e Rezession** f VW supply-induced recession

Angebot: **Angebotskontrolle** f VW supply control; **Angebotskurs** m BANK bid rate, BÖRSE asked price; **Angebotskurve** f VW supply curve

angebotsorientiert: **~e Wirtschaftspolitik** f VW supply-oriented economic policy, supply-side economics

Angebot: **Angebotspreis** m GESCHÄFT tender price, GRUND asked, price, VW bid price, offer price, quoted price, supply price; **Angebotsrückgang** m VW fall in supplies; **Angebotsschock** m VW supply shock, supply-side shock; **Angebotsüberhang** m BÖRSE sellers over, surplus of selling orders, GESCHÄFT, IND work backlog; **Angebotsüberschuß** m VW excess supply, surplus offers; **Angebotsunterlagen** f pl BANK tender documents, GESCHÄFT offer document; **Angebotszeichnungen** f pl VW proposal drawings

angebracht adj GESCHÄFT advisable

angefallen: **~er Verlust** m RECHNUNG historical loss

angegeben adj RECHNUNG stated; **alles ~** phr GESCHÄFT all told; **den ~en Börsenkurs akzeptieren** phr BÖRSE take the rate; **~e Investitionsbörsen** f pl BÖRSE designated investment exchanges (*BrE*); **zum ~en Kurs oder besser** phr BÖRSE at or better; **~er Preis** m VW displayed price; **~e Rendite** f BÖRSE indicated yield; **~e Verzinsung** f BÖRSE indicated yield; **~er Wert** m RECHNUNG stated value; **zu einer ~en Zeit** phr GESCHÄFT at a given time

angeglichen: **~e Formulare** f pl VERWALT aligned forms; **~ an [+acc]** phr GESCHÄFT affiliated to

angegliedert adj BANK, GESCHÄFT, PERSON affiliated; **~e Gesellschaft** f GESCHÄFT associated company

angehäuft: **~es Einkommen** nt STEUER rolled-up income

angehen vt GESCHÄFT affect, *Problem* address, concern; ◆ **jdn um etw ~** GESCHÄFT ask sb for sth

angehoben adj GESCHÄFT advanced

angekündigt adj GESCHÄFT *Kontrolle, Veranstaltung* advertised

Angelegenheit f GESCHÄFT affair, business, matter; ◆ **die ~ ist rechtsabhängig** RECHT the matter is sub judice; **die ~ offen lassen** GESCHÄFT leave the matter open;

seine Angelegenheiten in Ordnung bringen GESCHÄFT put one's affairs in order

angelegt: **~er Betrag** *m* RECHNUNG amount invested

angelernt *adj* PERSON semi-skilled; **~er Arbeiter** *m*, **~e Arbeiterin** *f* PERSON semi-skilled worker; **~e Arbeitskraft** *f* PERSON, VW semi-skilled labor (*AmE*), semi-skilled labour (*BrE*)

Angelpunkt *m* GESCHÄFT fulcrum

angemeldet: **nicht ~** *adj* RECHT *geistiges Eigentum* unregistered

angemessen *adj* GESCHÄFT fair, reasonable, proportionate, *entsprechend* commensurate, adequate, PERSON, RECHNUNG *entsprechend* commensurate, fair, adequate, reasonable, RECHT just; **~er Anteil** *m* GESCHÄFT fair share; **~e Auslagen** *f pl* GESCHÄFT reasonable expense; **~e Entschädigung** *f* GESCHÄFT reasonable compensation, RECHT just compensation; **~e Finanzierung** *f* GESCHÄFT adequate funding; **~e Frist** *f* RECHNUNG reasonable time; **~e Gebühr** *f* GESCHÄFT commensurate charge; **~e Geschäftspraktiken** *f pl* GESCHÄFT fair business practices; **~e Kapitalausstattung** *f* BANK capital adequacy, FINANZ capitalization, VW capital resources, capitalization; **~e Kosten** *pl* GESCHÄFT reasonable expense; **~es Muster** *nt* GESCHÄFT fair sample; **~er Preis** *m* GESCHÄFT bona fide price, reasonable price; **~e Tagesleistung** *f* PERSON fair day's work; **~er Tageslohn** *m* PERSON fair day's pay; **~e Vergütung** *f* GESCHÄFT quantum merit, reasonable compensation; **~e Verzinsung** *f* FINANZ, RECHNUNG fair rate of return, fair return; **~er Wert** *m* RECHNUNG fair value; ♦ **in ~er Entfernung** GESCHÄFT at an appropriate distance

Angemessenheit *f* GESCHÄFT adequacy; **~ von Preisen** GESCHÄFT appropriate nature of prices

angenehm: **~es Arbeitsumfeld** *nt* PERSON *Arbeitszufriedenheit* pleasant working environment

angenommen *adj* GESCHÄFT accepted, *Name* assumed; **~e Lieferung** *f* GESCHÄFT accepted lot; **~er Name** *m* GESCHÄFT alias; **~er Totalverlust** *m* VERSICH constructive total loss (*CTL*), constructive total loss only (*CTLO*)

angepaßt *adj* BÖRSE, RECHNUNG adjusted, V&M *an höheres Niveau* upgraded; **~er Basispreis** *m* BÖRSE adjusted exercise price (*BrE*); **~e Bewertungsgrundlagen** *f pl* **für die Aufwandsrechnung** RECHNUNG adjusted cost base (*AmE*) (*ACB*), adjusted cost basis; **~e Technik** *f* VERWALT, VW adapted technology; **~er Verkaufspreis** *m* RECHNUNG adjusted selling price; ♦ **~ an** [+acc] GESCHÄFT affiliated to

angerechnet *adj* GESCHÄFT accounted for

angeschaltet *adj* GESCHÄFT switched on

angeschlossen *adj* BANK, GESCHÄFT, PERSON affiliated; ♦ **~ an** [+acc] GESCHÄFT affiliated to

angeschlossen: **~e Bank** *f* BANK affiliated bank; **~e Gewerkschaft** *f* PERSON affiliated trade union

angesehen *adj* GESCHÄFT renowned, prestigious

angesichts *prep* GESCHÄFT in the face of

angespannt: **~er Arbeitsmarkt** *m* VW tight labor market (*AmE*), tight labour market (*BrE*); **~er Geldmarkt** *m* FINANZ stringent money market; **~e Liquiditätslage** *f* FINANZ tight liquidity position

Angestellte(r) *mf* [decl. as adj] GESCHÄFT, PERSON employee, *Gehaltsempfänger* salaried employee, *in*

einem Büro clerical worker, clerk, office worker, white-collar worker; **~ im Front Office** PERSON, VERWALT front-office clerk; **~ in leitender Position** VERWALT business manager; **~ in der Zentrale** VERWALT front-office clerk; **Angestellte** *pl* [decl. as adj] PERSON personnel, staff, *in einem Büro* clerical staff, office personnel, office staff; **Angestelltengewerkschaft** *f* PERSON nonmanual union, white-collar union; **Angestelltenstatus** *m* PERSON staff status

angestrebt: **~e Kapitalverzinsung** *f* FINANZ adequate target rate, target rate of return; **~e Mindestverzinsung** *f* FINANZ *Investitionsrechnung* required rate of return; **~er Preis** *m* GESCHÄFT, V&M target price; **~er Termin** *m* GESCHÄFT target date; **~er Zinssatz** *m* BÖRSE target rate

angetrieben: **~ von** *phr* GESCHÄFT driven by

angewandt *adj* GESCHÄFT applied; **~e Forschung** *f* MGMT applied research; **~e Kosten** *pl* RECHNUNG applied cost; **~e Wirtschaftsforschung** *f* VW applied economic research

angleichen *vt* GESCHÄFT align, harmonize, PERSON harmonize, RECHT, RECHNUNG assimilate, VERSICH adjust, VW align, harmonize; ♦ **~ an** [+acc] GESCHÄFT, MATH *Zahlen*, VERSICH adjust to, VW *Preise, Zeitplan* adjust to, align with; **aneinander ~** GESCHÄFT coordinate; **nach oben ~** VW *Preise* adjust upwards; **nach unten ~** MATH, VW adjust downwards

Angleichung *f* GESCHÄFT adaptation, adjustment, alignment, shakedown (*infrml*) (*AmE*), RECHNUNG *des EG-Rechts durch die Mitgliedsstaaten* assimilation, RECHT *des EG-Rechts durch die Mitgliedsstaaten* assimilation, approximation; **~ der Gesetze** RECHT *EG* legal harmonization; **~ von Zollsätzen** IMP/EXP adjustment of tariff rates, alignment of tariff rates

Angleichungsprozeß *m* GESCHÄFT harmonization process

angliedern *vt* GESCHÄFT affiliate

Angliederung *f* GESCHÄFT affiliation; **Angliederungsfinanzierung** *f* FINANZ procurement of funds to finance a holding in, or the acquisition of, another company

anglo *prep* GESCHÄFT Anglo-; **anglo-französisch** *adj* GESCHÄFT Anglo-French

angreifen *vt* GESCHÄFT *Reserven* affect, attack, break into, draw on

angrenzend *adj* GESCHÄFT adjoining, neighboring (*AmE*), neighbouring (*BrE*)

Angriff *m* GESCHÄFT, IND attack; ♦ **in ~ nehmen** MGMT *Problem* tackle

Angriff: **Angriffslinie** *f* GESCHÄFT line of attack; **Angriffsspitze** *f* GESCHÄFT spearhead

Angst: **~ vor Computern** COMP computer phobia; **Angstkäufe** *m pl* GESCHÄFT panic buying, V&M scare buying

Anhalten *nt* TRANSP stoppage

anhaltend *adj* GESCHÄFT continuing; **~er Erfolg** *m* GESCHÄFT continued success; **~e Kurserholung** *f* BÖRSE sustained rally; **~e Nachfrage** *f* V&M persistent demand

Anhang *m* GESCHÄFT annex (*AmE*), annexe (*BrE*), appendix, RECHT annex (*AmE*), annexe (*BrE*); **~ zur Bilanz** RECHNUNG notes to the financial statements

Anhängadresse *f* KOMM address label

anhängen *vt* COMP *Daten, Datei* add, append, attach

Anhänger *m* GESCHÄFT tie-on label, *einer Bewegung*

supporter, TRANSP trailer; **~ zur rückwärtigen Verladung an Rampen** TRANSP rear-ramp loading trailer

Anhänger: **Anhängerausnutzung** *f* TRANSP trailer utilization; **Anhängerleergewicht** *nt* GESCHÄFT trailer unladen weight; **Anhängernutzung** *f* TRANSP trailer utilization; **Anhängerzughaken** *m* TRANSP tow hook

Anhängezettel *m* GESCHÄFT tie-on label

anhängig: **~er Rechtsstreit** *m* RECHT lis pendens, proceeding pending before a court

anhäufen 1. *vt* FINANZ accrue, accumulate, GESCHÄFT *Besitz, Waren, Geld* accumulate, amass; **2. sich ~** *v refl* GESCHÄFT accumulate

Anhäufung *f*: **~ von Gewinnen durch Spekulation** FINANZ pyramiding (*BrE*)

anhebbar *adj* GESCHÄFT upgradable

anheben *vt* BÖRSE mark up, GESCHÄFT increase, raise, TRANSP lift

Anheben *nt* BÖRSE marking up, GESCHÄFT increasing, raising, TRANSP lifting

anheften *vt* GESCHÄFT *Etikett* affix

anheizen *vt* GESCHÄFT, V&M *Interesse, Zuhörer* whip up, VW *Inflation* fuel

Anhörung *f* GESCHÄFT consultation, RECHT *mündliche Verhandlung* hearing; **~ der Gegenpartei** GESCHÄFT audita altera parte procedure; **~ der Gegenseite** GESCHÄFT audita altera parte procedure; **Anhörungsrecht** *nt* RECHT right to be heard

Ankauf *m* GESCHÄFT acquisition, purchase; **Ankaufgebühren** *f pl* BÖRSE sales charge; **Ankaufkurs** *m* FINANZ buying rate; **Ankaufsermächtigung** *f* FINANZ order to negotiate, GESCHÄFT authority to buy, authority to purchase; **Ankaufskurs** *m* BANK buying rate of exchange; **Ankaufsmethode** *f* RECHNUNG purchase method; **Ankaufssatz** *m* BANK buying rate of exchange, BÖRSE *für rediskontfähiges Wechselmaterial* buyer's rate, check price

anketten *vt* COMP chain

Anklage *f* RECHT accusation, charge; **Anklagejury** *f* RECHT grand jury (*AmE*)

anklagen *vt* RECHT accuse, charge

Anklang *m* GESCHÄFT appeal; ♦ **~ finden bei** GESCHÄFT appeal to

ankleben *vt* GESCHÄFT affix

anklicken *vt* COMP *Maustaste* click

ankommend: **~er Ruf** *m* KOMM incoming call

Ankommende(r) *mf* [decl. as adj] GESCHÄFT, TRANSP arrival

ankündigen *vt* GESCHÄFT announce, MEDIEN *Programm* trail

Ankündigung *f* GESCHÄFT announcement, notice; **~ von Neuigkeiten** MEDIEN *Public Relations* news advisory; **~ eines Zwangserwerbs** GRUND blight notice; **Ankündigungseffekt** *m* POL announcement effect; **Ankündigungsschreiben** *nt* GESCHÄFT announcement letter, KOMM letter of advice

Ankunft *f* GESCHÄFT, TRANSP arrival; ♦ **bei ~ erreichbar** TRANSP reachable on arrival; **bei ~ immer zugänglich** TRANSP always accessible on arrival, always reachable on arrival

Ankunft: **Ankunftsanzeige** *f* TRANSP arrival notification form (*ANF*); **Ankunftsdatum** *nt* TRANSP arrival date; **Ankunftshafen** *m* IMP/EXP, TRANSP port of arrival; **Ankunftstag** *m* TRANSP arrival date

ankurbeln *vt* GESCHÄFT *Nachfrage* stimulate, IMP/EXP boost, VW boost, pep up (*infrml*)

Ankurbelung *f* GESCHÄFT, POL, VW reflation, **Ankurbelungspolitik** *f* VW reflationary policy

Anl. *abbr* (*Anlage*) GESCHÄFT encl. (*enclosure*)

Anlage *f* (*Anl.*) BANK, BÖRSE investment, COMP system, E-Mail attachment, FINANZ investment, GESCHÄFT appendix, enclosure (*encl.*), *am Ende eines Schreibens* enclosed, IND plant, RECHT annex (*AmE*), annexe (*BrE*), VW investment; **~ in Staatspapieren** FINANZ funding; ♦ **als ~** KOMM enclosed

Anlage: **Anlageberater, in** *m,f* BÖRSE, FINANZ investment consultant, investment counsellor (*BrE*), investment counselor (*AmE*); **Anlageberatung** *f* BÖRSE, FINANZ investment counseling (*AmE*), investment counselling (*BrE*); **Anlageberatungsservice** *m* BÖRSE Investment Advisory Service (*AmE*)

anlagebereite: **~ Mittel** *nt pl* FINANZ, VW idle balance

Anlage: **Anlagedevisen** *nt pl* FINANZ investment currency; **Anlageerneuerung** *f* GESCHÄFT replacement; **Anlageerträge** *m pl* FINANZ investment income; **Anlagefinanzierung** *f pl* BANK, FINANZ investment financing; **Anlagegegenstand** *m* RECHNUNG fixed asset; **Anlagegut** *nt* FINANZ capital asset; **Anlagegüter** *nt pl* GESCHÄFT capital assets, capital goods, STEUER capital assets; **Anlageinvestitionen** *f pl* RECHNUNG business capital spending, fixed asset investment, VW business capital spending, new plant and equipment; **Anlagekapital** *nt* FINANZ fixed capital, capital employed, RECHNUNG capital employed, STEUER capital assets; **Anlagekonto** *nt* **mit eingeschränkter Zahlungsverkehrsmöglichkeit** BANK money market deposit account (*AmE*); **Anlagekosten** *pl* FINANZ, RECHNUNG capital expenditure (*capex*)

Anlagen *f pl* BANK, BÖRSE investments, FINANZ assets, investments, VW investments; **Anlagenausschlachtung** *f* FINANZ asset stripping (*infrml*); **Anlagenauswahl** *f* FINANZ portfolio selection, PATENT plant varieties; **Anlagenbewertung** *f* RECHNUNG asset valuation; **Anlagenerhaltung** *f* GESCHÄFT plant location; **Anlagenherstellung** *f* IND plant manufacturing; **Anlagenintensität** *f* GESCHÄFT capitalization ratio

anlagenintensiv *adj* VW capital-intensive

Anlagen: **Anlageninvestition** *f* VW capital investment; **Anlagenkonto** *nt* RECHNUNG fixed asset account, investment account, VW property account; **Anlagenplanung** *f* IND plant layout study; **Anlagenproduktion** *f* IND plant manufacturing; **Anlagenrendite** *f* FINANZ return on assets (*ROA*); **Anlagenstreuung** *f* FINANZ asset diversification; **Anlagen-Umsatzrendite** *f* RECHNUNG net resource income; **Anlagenunterbrechung** *f* GESCHÄFT plant interruption; **Anlagenverkauf** *m* RECHNUNG, VERWALT asset sale; **Anlagenverpachtung** *f* GESCHÄFT plant hire; **Anlagenverwaltung** *f* FINANZ, MGMNT, RECHNUNG asset management; **Anlagenverwaltungsgesellschaft** *f* FINANZ, VERWALT asset management company; **Anlagenverwaltungskonto** *nt* FINANZ asset management account (*AMA*); **Anlagenverzinsung** *f* BANK investment yield, BÖRSE asset return; **Anlagenwertverlust** *m* RECHNUNG loss in value of assets; **Anlagenwirtschaft** *f* FINANZ, MGMNT, RECHNUNG asset management; **Anlagenzugang** *m* RECHNUNG addition, addition of fixed asset units, addition to plant and equipment

Anlage: **Anlageobjekt** *nt* V&M property; **Anlageoption** *f* FINANZ lock-up option; **Anlagepolitik** *f* FINANZ, POL, VW investment policy; **Anlageprogramm** *nt* COMP, FINANZ investment software; **Anlagerisiko** *nt* FINANZ investment risk; **Anlagevermögen** *nt* RECHNUNG fixed assets, noncurrent asset, STEUER capital assets, VW fixed capital; **das Anlagevermögen betreffende Grundsätze** *m pl* RECHNUNG fixed asset policies; **Anlagevermögenspolitik** *f* RECHNUNG fixed asset policy; **Anlageverwalter, in** *m,f* BÖRSE asset manager; **Anlageverwaltung** *f* FINANZ investment management; **Anlagewährung** *f* FINANZ investment currency; **Anlageziel** *nt* FINANZ investment goal, investment objective; **Anlagezinsfuß** *m* FINANZ investment rate of interest

Anlaß: ~ **geben** *phr* GESCHÄFT give rise to; ~ **zu einer Vermutung geben** *phr* GESCHÄFT raise a presumption

Anlauf *m* GESCHÄFT *Betriebsgründung* start-up; **Anlaufkosten** *pl* FINANZ, RECHNUNG launching costs, pre-operating expenses, start-up costs, starting-load costs, front-end costs; **Anlaufphase** *f* GESCHÄFT start-up phase, VW phase-in period

anlegen *vt* BANK, BÖRSE *Kapital*, FINANZ, VW invest, *Geld* sink, GESCHÄFT *Zeit* invest; ♦ ~ **für** GESCHÄFT spend on; ~ **in** [+dat] GESCHÄFT *Geld* invest in

Anlegen *nt* GESCHÄFT *von Geld* placement; ~ **von Vorräten** GESCHÄFT stockpiling

Anleger, in *m,f* BÖRSE, FINANZ investor; **Anlegerdienstleistungsbüro** *nt* FINANZ investors' service bureau; **Anlegerschutz** *m* BÖRSE investor protection

Anleihe *f* FINANZ, VW bond, loan; ~ **mit beigehefteten Optionsscheinen** BÖRSE bond with warrants attached; ~ **eines Bundesstaates** BÖRSE moral obligation bond, state bond; ~ **mit Endfälligkeit** BANK bullet loan; ~ **für ein Kleinunternehmen** GESCHÄFT small business bond; ~ **der öffentlichen Wohnungsbaubehörde** BÖRSE public housing authority bond; ~ **mit Optionsschein** BÖRSE bond cum warrant; ~ **ohne laufende Tilgung** BANK bullet; ~ **ohne Optionsscheine** BÖRSE bond ex warrants; ~ **für private Zwecke** BÖRSE private-purpose bond; ~ **mit Sicherung durch eine Gesamthypothek** BÖRSE general mortgage bond; ~ **mit Staffelzinsen** FINANZ compound interest bond; ~ **mit variablem Zinssatz** BANK floating-rate loan; ~ **mit Zinshöchstsatz** BÖRSE cap rate loan; ♦ **eine** ~ **auflegen** FINANZ launch a bond offering; BÖRSE float a loan, float an issue; **eine** ~ **aufnehmen** FINANZ contract a loan, raise a loan, take up a loan; **eine** ~ **finanzieren** BANK fund a loan; **eine** ~ **konsolidieren** BANK fund a loan; **in Anleihen investieren** BÖRSE invest in bonds; **eine** ~ **neu auflegen** BANK refloat a loan; ~ **zeichnen** BANK subscribe for a loan

Anleihe: **Anleiheausstattung** *f* BÖRSE bond features, bond terms; **Anleiheberechtigung** *f* BÖRSE bond power; **Anleihebesitzer, in** *m,f* FINANZ loan holder; **Anleihebewertung** *f* BÖRSE bond rating, bond valuation; **Anleihebewertungsvertretung** *f* BÖRSE bond-rating agency; **Anleiheemission** *f* BÖRSE bond flotation, bond issue, FINANZ loan issue; **eine Anleiheemission auflegen** *phr* BÖRSE launch a bond coupon, launch a bond issue; **Anleiheemissionsagio** *nt* BÖRSE bond premium; **Anleiheerlös** *m* BÖRSE bond proceeds; **Anleihefinanzierung** *f* BÖRSE bond financing; **Anleihegeschäft** *nt* BÖRSE bond issue operation;

Anleihegläubiger, in *m,f* BÖRSE bond creditor, FINANZ loan holder; **Anleihekapital** *nt* BÖRSE bond capital, bond principal; **Anleihekonversion** *f* BÖRSE bond conversion; **Anleihekosten** *pl* BÖRSE bond costs, bonding cost, issue costs; **Anleihekündigung** *f* FINANZ call-in of a loan; **Anleihekupon** *m* BÖRSE bond coupon; **Anleihelaufzeit** *f* FINANZ term of a loan; **Anleihemarkt** *m* **für ausländische Emittenten** BÖRSE Yankee bond market (*AmE*); **Anleihemodalitäten** *f pl* BÖRSE bond terms; **Anleiheportefeuille** *nt* BANK bond portfolio, loan portfolio; **Anleiherendite** *f* BÖRSE bond yield, loan yield; **Anleiherendite** *f* **nach Steuern** RECHNUNG, STEUER after-tax bond yield; **Anleiheschein** *m* BÖRSE bond certificate; **Anleiheschuld** *f* BÖRSE bond debt, bonded debt, funded debt, FINANZ obligation bond; **Anleihestückelung** *f* BÖRSE bond denomination; **Anleihetilgungsfonds** *m* BÖRSE bond sinking fund; **Anleihetilgungsprämie** *f* RECHNUNG bond redemption premium; **Anleiheumlauf** *m* BÖRSE bonds outstanding; **Anleiheverbindlichkeit** *f* BÖRSE bonded debt, bonded indebtedness; **Anleiheverbindlichkeiten** *f pl* BÖRSE bonds payable; **Anleihevertrag** *m* BÖRSE bond indenture, indenture, loan agreement; **Anleihevolumen** *nt* FINANZ bond volume; **Anleihezins** *m* GESCHÄFT coupon

Anleitung *f*: ~ **für Geschäftsvorhaben** GESCHÄFT business plan guide

Anlernling *m* PERSON threshold worker (*AmE*), trainee

Anliegen: **einem** ~ **dienen** *phr* GESCHÄFT serve a purpose

Anliegerstaat *m* RECHT bordering state

Anliegerweg *m* TRANSP accommodation road

Anmahnung *f* FINANZ, RECHNUNG reminder

Anmelde- *in cpds* GESCHÄFT receiving, registering; **Anmeldeamt** *nt* GESCHÄFT, PATENT receiving office (*RO*); **Anmeldeformular** *nt* GESCHÄFT application form; **Anmeldegebühr** *f* GESCHÄFT registration fee

anmelden 1. *vt* GESCHÄFT register, PATENT apply for; **2. sich** ~ *v refl* COMP *Benutzer* log in, log on, FREI book in, *Hotel* check in, GESCHÄFT register, TRANSP *Flughafen* check in

Anmelder, in *m,f* GESCHÄFT, PATENT applicant

Anmelde-: **Anmeldeschluß** *m* GESCHÄFT closing date, deadline; **Anmeldesystem** *nt* PATENT registration system; **Anmeldeverfahren** *nt* GESCHÄFT application procedure, PATENT patent application proceedings

Anmeldung *f* GESCHÄFT, PATENT application, RECHT *Kraftfahrzeug* registration; **automatische** ~ COMP auto-login, auto-logon; **Anmeldungsschwelle** *f* STEUER registration threshold

Anmerkungen *f pl* RECHNUNG notes to the accounts

annähern *vt* GESCHÄFT, MATH approximate

annähernd 1. *adj* GESCHÄFT, MATH approximate; **2.** *adv* GESCHÄFT, MATH approximately (*approx.*)

annähernd: ~**e Gleichheit** *f* GESCHÄFT, MATH approximation; ~ **richtiges Ergebnis** *nt* GESCHÄFT, MATH approximation

Annäherung *f* GESCHÄFT, MATH, POL *Standpunkte* approximation; **Annäherungskurs** *m* BÖRSE approximate price; **Annäherungsverfahren** *nt* GESCHÄFT, POL approximation

Annahme *f* BANK acceptance, FINANZ *eines Vorschlags* approval, GESCHÄFT *Vermutung* assumption, *von Waren, Vertrag* acceptance, presumption, *von Waren* receipt (*rcpt, recpt*), IND, MEDIEN acceptance, PATENT presumption, RECHT *Vertrag* acceptance, passage, V&M *von Waren* receipt (*rcpt, recpt*), VERSICH acceptance, VW adoption; ~ **einer Abfindung** FINANZ acceptance of lump sum settlement; ~ **einer nicht geschuldeten Leistung** RECHT substituted mode of performance; ~ **einer Pauschalentschädigung** FINANZ acceptance of lump sum settlement; ~ **unter Vorbehalt** RECHNUNG qualified report; ◆ **die ~ einer Tratte verweigern** BANK refuse acceptance of a draft; ~ **durch Willenserklärung nach außen bekanntgeben** RECHT *Vertrag* signify acceptance by conduct

Annahme: **Annahmebedingungen** *f pl* FINANZ terms of acceptance; **Annahmebereich** *m* IND acceptance region; **Annahmebestätigung** *f* GESCHÄFT acknowledgement of receipt; **Annahmepflicht** *f* BANK acceptance duty, RECHT *Vertrag* obligation to accept; **Annahmerichtlinien** *f pl* **der Erstversicherer für Schiffskaskogeschäfte** VERSICH leading underwriters' agreement for marine hull business (*LUAMH*); **Annahmerichtlinien** *f pl* **der Erstversicherer für Seefrachtgeschäfte** VERSICH leading underwriters' agreement for marine cargo business (*LUAMC*); **Annahmeschein** *m* VERSICH acceptance slip; **Annahmestelle** *f* GESCHÄFT receiving office (*RO*), point of acceptance, PATENT receiving office (*RO*); **Annahmeunterlassung** *f* GESCHÄFT failure to accept; **Annahmeverweigerung** *f* BANK *Wechsel* dishonor (*AmE*), dishonour (*BrE*), GESCHÄFT nonacceptance, RECHT *Vertrag* refusal to accept, nonacceptance of delivery; **Annahmeverzug** *m* RECHT default in acceptance, default in accepting the delivery of goods

annehmbar *adj* GESCHÄFT, TRANSP, VW acceptable; **~er Container-Zustand** *m* TRANSP acceptable container condition (*ACC*); **~er Preis** *m* GESCHÄFT acceptable price; **~e Qualität** *f* GESCHÄFT acceptable quality

Annehmbarkeit *f* GESCHÄFT, VW acceptability

annehmen *vt* BANK *Kreditkarte* accept, GESCHÄFT presume, suppose, proceed on the assumption, *Herausforderung* take up, *Aufgabe* agree to, assume, KOMM *Anruf* accept, MEDIEN presume, RECHT pass

annektieren *vt* GESCHÄFT annex (*AmE*), annexe (*BrE*)

Annonce *f* MEDIEN, V&M ad (*infrml*), advert (*infrml*), advertisement, classified advertisement; ◆ **per ~ zum Verkauf anbieten** MEDIEN, V&M advertise, for sale

annoncieren *vt* V&M advertise

annualisieren *vt* FINANZ, GESCHÄFT annualize

annualisiert *adj* FINANZ, GESCHÄFT annualized

Annuität *f* FINANZ annual installment (*AmE*), annual instalment (*BrE*), annuity, regular annual payment, RECHNUNG debt service; **Annuitätenhypothek** *f* BANK amortized mortgage loan, FINANZ level-payment mortgage (*AmE*), redemption mortgage

annullierbar *adj* BANK, GESCHÄFT, RECHT voidable, rescindable

annullieren *vt* BANK, GESCHÄFT cancel, annul, RECHT declare null and void, avoid, *Vertrag* rescind, annul, *Urteil* set aside

annullierend *adj* BANK, GESCHÄFT, RECHT annulling

annulliert: **~er Scheck** *m* BANK canceled check (*AmE*), cancelled cheque (*BrE*)

Annullierung *f* BANK, GESCHÄFT annulment, cancellation, RECHT avoidance, *Urteil* setting aside, *Vertrag* rescission, annulment; ~ **einer Registereintragung** STEUER cancellation of registration; **Annullierungsgrund** *m* VERSICH cause of cancellation

annum: **per ~** *phr* GESCHÄFT per annum (*p.a.*)

anomal: **~e Angebotskurve** *f* VW backward-bending supply curve; **~e Kurve** *f* **des Arbeitskräfteangebots** VW backward-bending labor supply curve (*AmE*), backward-bending labour supply curve (*BrE*)

Anomalie *f* GESCHÄFT anomaly

Anomie *f* PERSON *Sozialwesen* anomie

anonym *adj* GESCHÄFT anonymous, anonymously; **~er Aktienbesitz** *m* FINANZ nominal holdings; **~er Brief** *m* GESCHÄFT poison-pen letter; **~er Produkttest** *m* V&M anonymous product testing; **~er Test** *m* V&M blind test

Anonymität *f* GESCHÄFT anonymity

anordnen *vt* GESCHÄFT command, *arrangieren* arrange

Anordnung *f* GESCHÄFT arrangement, structuring, structure, MATH array, RECHT order (*ord.*); ~ **des endgültigen Pfandverkaufs** RECHT *nach Ausschlußfrist* strict foreclosure; ~ **des Fraktionsführers** POL whip (*BrE*); ~ **der Nachlaßverwaltung** RECHT administration order; ~ **der Vermögensverwaltung** VERWALT administration order; ~ **zur Zwangsenteignung** GRUND compulsory purchase order (*BrE*); ◆ **einer ~ zuwiderhandeln** RECHT fail to comply with an order

anormal *adj* GESCHÄFT abnormal; **~es Risiko** *nt* VERSICH abnormal risk; **~e unteilbare Last** *f* TRANSP abnormal indivisible load

ANOVA *abbr* (*Varianzanalyse*) MATH ANOVA (*analysis of variance*)

anpacken *vt* MGMNT tackle

anpassen 1. *vt* GESCHÄFT align, modify, RECHNUNG assimilate, VERSICH adjust, VW align; ◆ **~ an** [+acc] GESCHÄFT adjust to, gear to, RECHT align with, VERSICH adjust to, VW *Preis, Zeitplan* adjust to; **~ an Kundenspezifikationen** COMP *Hardware, Software* customize; **nach oben ~** VW *Preise* adjust upwards; **nach unten ~** VW *Preise* adjust downwards; **2. sich ~** *v refl* GESCHÄFT adapt; ◆ **sich ~ an** [+acc] GESCHÄFT adapt to

anpassend: **~e Geldpolitik** *f* POL, VW accommodative policy; **~e Politik** *f* POL, VW accommodative policy

Anpassung *f* GESCHÄFT accommodation, adaptation, adjustment, alignment, shakedown (*infrml*) (*AmE*), RECHNUNG assimilation, VERSICH, VW adjustment; ~ **zwischen Fremd- und Eigenkapital** FINANZ gearing adjustment (*BrE*), leverage adjustment (*AmE*); ~ **nach oben** GESCHÄFT *Preise* upward revision; ~ **der Versicherungssumme** VERSICH adjustment of sum insured; **Anpassungsdarlehen** *nt* **für den Agrarsektor** FINANZ agricultural sector adjustment loan (*ASAL*)

anpassungsfähig *adj* GESCHÄFT adaptable, flexible, tailorable

Anpassung: **Anpassungsfähigkeit** *f* GESCHÄFT, PERSON adaptability, flexibility; **Anpassungsgeschwindigkeit** *f* VW adjustment speed; **Anpassungsinvestition** *f* FINANZ rationalization investment; **Anpassungslücke** *f* VW adjustment gap; **Anpassungsmaßnahme** *f* GESCHÄFT adjustment measure; **Anpassungsprozeß** *m* GESCHÄFT, VW process of adjustment; **Anpassungssubvention** *f* FINANZ, VW sector adjustment lending

anpeilen *vt* GESCHÄFT target

anrechenbar *adj* GESCHÄFT chargeable; ◆ **~ auf** GESCHÄFT *Dienstjahre* counting towards, STEUER creditable against *anrechenbar*: ~er **Betrag** *m* STEUER creditable amount; ~e **Vermögenswerte** *m pl* STEUER chargeable assets, creditable assets; ~e **Vorsteuer** *f* STEUER recoverable input tax

anrechnen *vt* GESCHÄFT charge, count, take into account

Anrechnung *f* GESCHÄFT *Belastung* charge, debit, *Abzug* deduction, allowance, *Kreditposten* credit, vw imputation

anrechnungsfähig *adj* GESCHÄFT eligible; ♦ **für etw ~ sein** GESCHÄFT be eligible for sth

anrechnungsfähig: ~e **Versicherungsjahre** *nt pl* PERSON eligible insured years

Anrecht *nt* GESCHÄFT entitlement, claim, RECHT title; **~ auf Information** POL *Presse* right to know

anreden *vt* GESCHÄFT address

anregen *vt* GESCHÄFT *Nachfrage* stimulate

Anreiz *m* GESCHÄFT stimulus, inducement, spur, appeal, incentive, V&M incentive, vw stimulation; **~ für den Reiseverkehr** V&M travel incentive; **~ für Verkaufsanstrengungen** V&M push incentive; **Anreizeffekt** *m* VW incentive effect

anreizorientiert: ~e **Wirtschaftsplanung** *f* POL, VW incitative planning

Anreiz: **Anreizplan** *m* PERSON incentive plan; **Anreizprodukt** *nt* GESCHÄFT, V&M appeal product; **Anreizrate** *f* FINANZ teaser rate

Anreizsystem *nt* PERSON incentive scheme, VW incentive system; **~ auf Betriebsebene** PERSON factory incentive scheme, plant incentive scheme; **~ auf Gruppenebene** PERSON group incentive scheme; **~ für Mitarbeiter** PERSON *Arbeit, Produktivität, Motivation* staff incentives

Anruf *m* KOMM *Telefon* call, incoming call; ♦ **einen ~ verfolgen** KOMM *Fangschaltung, Telefon* trace a call

Anruf: **Anrufbeantworter** *m* COMP, GESCHÄFT, KOMM answering machine, answerphone; **Anrufbeantwortungsdienst** *m* COMP, GESCHÄFT, KOMM, V&M telephone answering service

anrufen *vt* GESCHÄFT, KOMM call, call up, phone, ring (*BrE*), telephone

Anruf: **Anrufhäufigkeit** *f* V&M call frequency

ansammeln *vt* GESCHÄFT contract

Ansammlung *f* BANK *Zinsen* accrual, GESCHÄFT concentration, build-up, congestion, accumulation, vw *Zinsen* accrual

ansässig *adj* GESCHÄFT based, resident; ♦ **~ sein in** [+dat] GESCHÄFT be based in

ansässig: ~e **Industrie** *f* IND local industry; ~er **Verwalter** *m,f* GRUND resident manager

Ansatz *m* GESCHÄFT, MGMNT, VERWALT, VW approach; **Ansatzpunkt** *m* GESCHÄFT starting point; **Ansatzstück** *nt* BANK allonge, GESCHÄFT attachment

anschaffen *vt* FINANZ procure, *Deckung* provide, *einzahlen* remit, GESCHÄFT, RECHNUNG acquire, purchase, vw buy

Anschaffung *f* FINANZ procurement, GESCHÄFT purchasing, acquisition, RECHNUNG acquisition, purchasing, RECHT acquisition; **Anschaffungskosten** *pl* (*AK*) GESCHÄFT acquisition costs, RECHNUNG acquisition costs, historical cost, initial outlay, original cost, VERSICH, V&M acquisition costs, vw cost; **Anschaffungs- oder Herstellungskosten** *pl* (*AK/HK*) RECHNUNG costs of acquisition or production;

Anschaffungswert *m* FINANZ net cash outflow, GESCHÄFT, RECHNUNG, RECHT acquisition value; **Anschaffungswertprinzip** *nt* RECHNUNG acquisition accounting, historical cost concept

anschalten *vt* GESCHÄFT switch on

Anschauung *f* GESCHÄFT opinion, view; **Anschauungsmaterial** *nt* GESCHÄFT visuals, MEDIEN visual aid, V&M visual aid, visual demonstration material, visuals; **Anschauungsmodell** *nt* V&M mock-up

Anscheinsvollmacht *f* RECHT *Vertragsrecht* apparent authority

Anschlag *m* GESCHÄFT bill, plot, *Plakat* placard, poster, IND backstop, V&M poster; **Anschlagbogen** *m* V&M bill; **Anschlagbrett** *nt* KOMM bulletin board (*BB*), notice board (*BrE*); **Anschlagdrucker** *m* COMP impact printer

anschlagen *vt* GESCHÄFT put up, VERWALT post

Anschlag: **Anschlaggeschirr** *nt* TRANSP sling; **Anschlagstelle** *f* V&M poster site; **Anschlagstellenklassifizierung** *f* V&M poster site classification; **Anschlagtafel** *f* V&M hoarding; **Anschlagwerbung** *f* V&M billboard advertising, billsticking

anschließen 1. *vt* COMP, KOMM connect; ♦ **~ an** [+acc] COMP connect with, hook up to (*infrml*), plug into, KOMM connect with; **2. sich ~** *v refl* GESCHÄFT affiliate oneself, RECHT contract in; **sich nicht ~** RECHT contract out

anschließend 1. *adj* GESCHÄFT subsequent; **2.** *adv* GESCHÄFT subsequently

Anschluß *m* COMP port, GESCHÄFT follow-up, KOMM phone number, *Nebenstelle* extension, TRANSP connection; ♦ **im ~ an** GESCHÄFT in the aftermath of, subsequent to, further to

Anschluß: **Anschlußaufträge** *m pl* BÖRSE backup support, GESCHÄFT follow-up orders, renewal orders, sequence orders, V&M add-on sales (*BrE*); **Anschlußbahn** *f* TRANSP branch line; **Anschlüsse** *m pl* und unbewegliches Inventar *nt* RECHNUNG fixtures and fittings; **Anschlußflug** *m* TRANSP connecting flight, onward flight; **Anschlußgleis** *nt* TRANSP sidetrack (*AmE*), siding (*BrE*); **Anschlußlinie** *f* TRANSP branch line; **Anschlußmarkt** *m* V&M after-market; **Anschlußnorm** *f* IND follow-up standard specification; **Anschlußnummer** *f* GESCHÄFT, KOMM phone number, telephone number (*tel. no.*); **Anschlußquellensteuer** *f* STEUER backup withholding tax (*AmE*); **Anschlußspediteur** *m* TRANSP connecting carrier; **Anschlußteilnehmer, in** *m,f* KOMM telephone subscriber; **Anschlußwerbung** *f* V&M follow-up advertising

Anschreiben *nt* VERWALT *Begleitschreiben* letter of transmittal

Anschrift *f* GESCHÄFT, KOMM address; ♦ **~ wie oben** GESCHÄFT address as above

Anschrift: **Anschriftfeld** *nt* COMP address field

Anschubfinanzierung *f* FINANZ knock-on financing

Ansehen *nt* GESCHÄFT standing, reputation, V&M established image

ansetzen *vt* GESCHÄFT *Kosten* calculate, estimate, *Preis* fix, *Treffen* arrange, RECHNUNG report, show, state

Ansicht *f* GESCHÄFT view, V&M belief; **~ der Geschäftsführung** MGMNT administrative point of view (*APV*); ♦ **zur ~** GESCHÄFT on approval (*on appro.*), on inspection; **seine Ansichten äußern** GESCHÄFT air one's views, state one's opinions; **seine Ansichten kundtun** GESCHÄFT air one's views

Ansicht: **Ansichtsexemplar** *nt* GESCHÄFT inspection specimen; **Ansichtssache** *f* GESCHÄFT matter of opinion

Ansiedlung *f* GESCHÄFT location; **~ für Firmen** IND technology park

Anspannungsindex *m* VW employment index

Ansporn *m* GESCHÄFT stimulus

Ansprache *f* KOMM address

ansprechen *vt* GESCHÄFT address

ansprechend: **~e Werbung** *f* V&M advertising appeal

Anspruch *m* GESCHÄFT *auf Sachen* title, PATENT claim, PERSON entitlement, SOZIAL *Sozialfürsorge*, STEUER, VERSICH claim; **~ eines Dritten** RECHT third-party claim; **nicht in ~ genommene Entlastung** *f* STEUER unused relief; **~ aus einem Recht** RECHT title under a right; ♦ **seinen ~ aufrechterhalten** RECHT sustain one's claim; **einen ~ begründen** RECHT substantiate a claim; **jds Dienste in ~ nehmen** GESCHÄFT retain sb's services; **einen ~ durchsetzen** RECHT *Vertragsrecht* enforce a claim; **einen ~ einreichen** RECHT file a claim; **~ erheben auf** RECHT lay claim to; **einen ~ erheben** RECHT put in a claim, set up a claim; **einen ~ gegen jdn erheben** RECHT, VERSICH claim against sb, make a claim against sb; **einen ~ geltend machen** RECHT *Vertragsrecht* advance a claim, assert a claim, bring forward a claim, put forth a claim; **nicht in ~ genommen** GESCHÄFT nonutilized; **jeglichen ~ fallenlassen** RECHT abandon any claim; **einen ~ regulieren** VERSICH adjust a claim; **~ auf Urlaubsgeld haben** PERSON qualify for holiday pay; **~ zurückweisen** RECHT reject a claim

Ansprüche *m pl* PATENT set of claims; **~ derselben Kategorie** PATENT claims of the same category; **~ derselben Klasse** PATENT claims of the same category; **~ unterschiedlicher Kategorien** PATENT claims of different categories; **~ unterschiedlicher Klassen** PATENT claims of different categories; **~ verschiedener Klassen** PATENT claims of different categories; ♦ **~ geltend machen** VERSICH claim against sb

anspruchmindernd: **~es Mitverschulden** *nt* RECHT comparative negligence

anspruchsberechtigt: **für etw ~ sein** *phr* GESCHÄFT be eligible for sth

Anspruch: **Anspruchsberechtigte(r)** *mf* [decl. as adj] RECHT, VERSICH beneficiary, claimant; **Anspruchsgrenze** *f* VERSICH claims limit; **Anspruchsniveau** *nt* V&M, VW aspiration level; **Anspruchsteller, in** *m,f* VERSICH claimant; **Anspruchsverzicht** *m* RECHT quitclaim

anspruchsvoll *adj* GESCHÄFT critical, demanding, exacting, V&M up-market; **~e Zeitschrift** *f* V&M class magazine; **~e Zeitung** *f* MEDIEN quality newspaper

Anstalt *f* GESCHÄFT institution, institute; **~ des öffentlichen Rechts** GESCHÄFT public body, MEDIEN institution incorporated under public law, VERWALT public body

Ansteckungseffekt *m* VW ripple effect

anstehen *vi* GESCHÄFT wait in line (*AmE*)

ansteigen *vi* VW *Arbeitslosigkeit, Zinsen, Gewinne* increase, rise, climb

anstellen **1.** *vt* GESCHÄFT employ; **2. sich ~** *v refl*

GESCHÄFT queue (*BrE*), stand in line (*AmE*), queue up (*BrE*)

Anstellung *f* PERSON employment, appointment; **~ auf Lebenszeit** PERSON life tenure, permanent tenure; **Anstellungsbedingungen** *f pl* PERSON terms and conditions of employment; **Anstellungsschreiben** *nt* PERSON letter of appointment

anstempeln *vt* IND clock in

Anstieg *m* BANK, BÖRSE advance, GESCHÄFT increase, rise, RECHNUNG advance, VW *der Preise* takeoff; **~ des Ölpreises** VW oil price increase

Anstoß *m* GESCHÄFT impetus, stimulus, impact; **Anstoßwirkung** *f* GESCHÄFT knock-on effect, VW impact effect

anstreben *vt* V&M aim, aspire to, target

Ansturm *m* BANK run, V&M rush; **~ auf eine Bank** BANK run on a bank; **~ auf die Banken** BANK run on the banks

antagonistisch: **~e Produktionsbedingungen** *f pl* POL antagonistic conditions of production; **~es Wachstum** *nt* VW antagonistic growth

Anteil *m* BÖRSE, FINANZ share (*BrE*), stock (*AmE*), GESCHÄFT *an einem Unternehmen* stake, interest, share, MATH proportion, quantity (*qnty, qty*), RECHNUNG stock (*AmE*), share (*BrE*); **~ an einer Bank** BANK holding in a bank, interest in a bank; **~ des gehaltenen Kapitals** RECHNUNG percentage of capital held; **~ investiver Ausgaben** VW capital-outlay ratio; **~ des Warenhandels am Außenhandel** IMP/EXP commodity concentration; **~ der Wertpapiergattungen am Gesamtnominalkapital** FINANZ capitalization ratio; ♦ **als ein ~ von** GESCHÄFT as a proportion of; **dem ~ entsprechend** GESCHÄFT, PERSON pro rata; **~ an etw erwerben** GESCHÄFT acquire an interest in sth

anteilig *adj* GESCHÄFT pro rata, proportionate, PERSON pro rata, VW rateable; **~er Bilanzverlust** *m* RECHNUNG proportionate share in loss; **~er Bundeszuschuß** *m* SOZIAL *zur Gewährleistung von öffentlichen Dienstleistungen* percentage grant; **~e Finanzierung** *f* FINANZ pro rata financing; **~e Konsolidierung** *f* RECHNUNG proportional consolidation; **~e Kosten** *pl* RECHNUNG prorated cost; **~er Zuschuß** *m* VW proportionate grant

anteilmäßig: **~e Aufteilung** *f* **auf der Grundlage der Kilometerzahl** TRANSP proration mileage (*AmE*); **~e Verrechnung** *f* TRANSP proration; ♦ **~ aufteilen** GESCHÄFT prorate

Anteil: **Anteilsbesitz** *m* FINANZ investment holdings; **Anteilsbruchteil** *m* BÖRSE fractional share; **Anteilseigner, in** *m,f* MGMNT, PERSON shareholder (*BrE*), stockholder (*AmE*); **Anteilsmiete** *f* FINANZ leverage lease; **Anteilsschein** *m* BÖRSE certificate (*cert.*), share certificate (*BrE*), stock certificate (*AmE*); **Anteilszeichner, in** *m,f* FINANZ applicant for shares; **Anteilszoll** *m* IMP/EXP compensatory levy

Anthropometrie *f* VERWALT *Ergonomie* anthropometry

Antidumping *nt* POL antidumping; **Antidumpingabkommen** *nt* POL antidumping agreement; **Antidumpinggesetzgebung** *f* POL antidumping legislation; **Antidumpingvereinbarung** *f* POL antidumping agreement

Antifouling-System *nt* TRANSP antifouling system

antigewerkschaftlich: **~e Gesetzgebung** *f* PERSON anti-union legislation anti-inflationär *adj* VW anti-inflationary; ~e Haltung *f* VW anti-inflation stance

Antimarketing *nt* V&M demarketing

Antiselektion *f* VERSICH adverse selection

Antitrustrecht *nt* RECHT antitrust acts, antitrust laws, antitrust law

Anti-Übernahme-Strategie *f* VW poison pill

Antiviren-Software *f* COMP antivirus software

Antizipation *f* IMP/EXP anticipation; Antizipationsäquivalenz *f* IMP/EXP anticipation equivalence; Antizipationsaufwand *m* RECHNUNG anticipated cost

antizipativ *adj* BANK, RECHNUNG accrued; ~e Aktiva *nt pl* RECHNUNG accrued income; ~er Aktivposten *m* RECHNUNG accrued asset, accrued revenue; ~e Passiva *pl* BANK accrued charges, RECHNUNG accruals, accrued expense, accrued expenses; ~es Sicherungsgeschäft *nt* BÖRSE anticipatory hedge; ~e Zinsabgrenzung *f* RECHNUNG deferred interest

antizipieren *vt* GESCHÄFT anticipate

antizipiert: ~e Inflation *f* VW steady-state inflation; ~er Vertragsbruch *m* RECHT anticipatory breach of contract

antizyklisch *adj* VW anticyclical; ~e Finanzierung *f* FINANZ functional financing; ~e Finanzpolitik *f* VW compensatory finance, countercyclical fiscal policy; ~e Fiskalpolitik *f* VW anticyclical policy; ~e Politik *f* VW anticyclical policy, contracyclical policy, countercyclical policy; ~e Werbung *f* V&M anticyclic advertising

Antrag *m* GESCHÄFT application, PATENT request; ~ auf Abänderung POL, RECHT application for amendment; ~ auf Ausfuhrgenehmigung IMP/EXP application for export licence (*BrE*), application for export license (*AmE*); ~ auf Bereitstellung von Mitteln POL application for the supply of funding; ~ auf Börsennotierung BÖRSE application for quotation; ~ auf Börsenzulassung BÖRSE application for listing; ~ auf Reisekostenerstattung GESCHÄFT travel claim, travel expense claim; ~ auf Zuschüsse GESCHÄFT application for subsidies; ◆ auf ~ GESCHÄFT upon application, upon request, RECHT upon the initiative; einen ~ ablehnen GESCHÄFT reject a request, RECHT dismiss a notion; einen ~ einbringen POL table a motion (*BrE*) (*frml*); einen ~ stellen POL table a motion (*BrE*) (*frml*), VERSICH file a claim; einen ~ stellen auf [+acc] GESCHÄFT make an application for; einen ~ bei der zuständigen Behörde stellen GESCHÄFT make a request to the appropriate authority

Antrag: Antragsannahme *f* VERSICH acceptance of proposal; Antragsdatum *nt* GESCHÄFT date of application, PATENT date of filing; Antragsformular *nt* IMP/EXP application form; Antragsteller, in *m,f* GESCHÄFT applicant, proposer, PATENT applicant, PERSON claimant, RECHT *Bittsteller* applicant, VERSICH proposer; Antragsteller, in *m,f* für Unternehmensgründung GESCHÄFT applicant entrepreneur

antreiben *vt* GESCHÄFT whip up, *Inflation* drive, fuel, V&M whip up

antreten *vt* GESCHÄFT begin, RECHT *Beweis* adduce, prove

Antrieb *m* GESCHÄFT drive, incentive, VW stimulation; Antriebskraft *f* GESCHÄFT driving force; Antriebskräfte *f pl* VW propellant forces, stimulating forces

Antritt *m* POL accession; Antrittstransit *m* TRANSP inaugural transit; Antrittszeitplan *m* TRANSP inaugural schedule

Antwort *f* COMP answer, GESCHÄFT response, RECHT *Bescheid* answer; ◆ ~ erhalten GESCHÄFT get an answer; sich mit der ~ Zeit lassen GESCHÄFT be slow to respond; als ~ auf GESCHÄFT in response to; die ~ hinausschieben GESCHÄFT be slow to respond; um ~ wird gebeten (*u.A.w.g.*) KOMM répondez s'il vous plaît (*RSVP*)

Antwort: Antwortcode *m* KOMM, VERWALT answerback code

antworten *vi* GESCHÄFT answer, respond, reply; ◆ ~ auf [+acc] GESCHÄFT answer, respond to; jdm ~ GESCHÄFT answer sb, answer to sb

Antwort: Antwortkarte *f* V&M answer print; Antwortmodus *m* COMP answer mode; Antwortpostkarte *f* KOMM reply-paid card; Antwortvordruck *m* V&M answer print

anvertrauen *vt* GESCHÄFT entrust

anvisieren *vt* GESCHÄFT target

Anwachsen *nt* GESCHÄFT increasing

anwachsend *adj* COMP incremental, GESCHÄFT growing, increasing; ~e Steuer *f* STEUER buoyant tax

Anwachsung *f* RECHT accrual; Anwachsungsrecht *nt* des Überlebenden RECHT right of survivorship

Anwalt *m* GESCHÄFT advocate, RECHT *Bevollmächtigter* attorney (*AmE*), barrister (*BrE*), legal counsel, practicing lawyer (*AmE*), practising lawyer (*BrE*), solicitor (*BrE*); ~ der Krone RECHT Queen's Counsel (*BrE*) (*QC*); ◆ jdn als ~ zulassen RECHT admit sb to the Bar (*AmE*), call sb to the Bar (*BrE*)

Anwältin *f* RECHT attorney (*AmE*), barrister (*BrE*), legal counsel, practicing lawyer (*AmE*), practising lawyer (*BrE*), solicitor (*BrE*); ~ der Krone RECHT Queen's Counsel (*BrE*) (*QC*)

Anwaltsberuf *m* RECHT bar

Anwaltschaft *f* RECHT bar: die ~ *f* RECHT the legal profession

anwaltschaftlich: sich ~ beraten lassen *phr* RECHT seek legal advice

Anwalt: Anwaltsgebühren *f pl* RECHT legal fees; Anwaltskammer *f* RECHT ≈ Law Society (*BrE*); Anwaltskanzlei *f* RECHT law firm; Anwaltsreferendar, in *m,f* RECHT articled clerk (*BrE*); Anwaltstätigkeit *f* RECHT law practice

Anwartschaft *f* PERSON legal right to future pension payments, RECHT right in course of acquisition; Anwartschaftsberechtigte(r) *mf* [decl. as adj] FINANZ remainderman, PERSON *allgemein Recht* eligible person, RECHT *Vertragsrecht* person entitled in expectancy; Anwartschaftsrecht *nt* PERSON reversionary interest, RECHT *Vertragsrecht* contingent right, expectancy; Anwartschaftsrente *f* VERSICH annuity in reversion

anweisen *vt* GESCHÄFT instruct

Anweisung *f* COMP statement, GESCHÄFT instruction, IMP/EXP transit; Anweisungen *f pl* GESCHÄFT briefing

anwendbar: ~ auf *adj* GESCHÄFT applicable to; ~ sein *phr* GESCHÄFT apply

anwenden *vt* GESCHÄFT apply, exert, *legal* exercise, *Methode* employ, RECHT *Gesetz* apply; ◆ ~ auf [+acc] COMP apply to; ~ gegen GESCHÄFT, RECHT bring to bear against

Anwender, in *m,f* COMP end-user, GESCHÄFT user

anwendereigen: ~e **Software** *f* COMP proprietary software

anwenderfeindlich *adj* COMP user-unfriendly

anwenderfreundlich *adj* COMP easy to use, user-friendly, V&M user-friendly

Anwender: **Anwendergruppe** *f* COMP user group

anwenderorientiert *adj* COMP user-oriented

anwenderunfreundlich *adj* COMP user-unfriendly

Anwendung *f* COMP *Programme* application, GESCHÄFT application, appliance, exercise, MGMNT *einer Methode* adoption; ~ **der Buchhaltungsvorschriften in gutem Glauben** RECHNUNG application of accounting rules in good faith; ~ **der Quotenregelung** GESCHÄFT application of the quota system, use of the quota system; ~ **unterschiedlicher Stichprobenverfahren** V&M differential sampling; ♦ ~ **finden** GESCHÄFT apply

Anwendung: **Anwendungsbereich** *m* GESCHÄFT area of application, scope of application

anwendungsbezogen: ~e **Forschung** *f* MGMNT action research, applied research

Anwendung: **Anwendungsentwurf** *m* IND application design; **Anwendungskontrolle** *f* RECHNUNG application control; **Anwendungspaket** *nt* COMP *Programme* applications package; **Anwendungsprogramm** *nt* COMP applications program; **Anwendungsprogrammierer, in** *m,f* COMP applications programmer; **Anwendungssoftware** *f* COMP applications software; **Anwendungstechnik** *f* IND applications engineering; **Anwendungsterminal** *nt* COMP applications terminal

Anwerbeland *nt* PERSON recruitment country

Anwerbung *f* PERSON recruitment; ~ **und Auswahl** PERSON recruitment and selection; **Anwerbungsbüro** *nt* PERSON recruiting office; **Anwerbungsprämie** *f* PERSON recruitment bonus

Anwesen *nt* GRUND premises

anwesend *adj* GESCHÄFT present; ~ **sein** *phr* GESCHÄFT be present

Anwesende: **unter den Anwesenden** *phr* GESCHÄFT among those present, inter praesentes

Anwesenheit *f* GESCHÄFT presence; **Anwesenheitsprämie** *f* PERSON attendance bonus

Anz. *abbr* (*Anzahl*) GESCHÄFT, MATH no. (*number*)

Anzahl *f* GESCHÄFT amount (*amt*), number (*no.*), MATH number (*no.*); ~ **der Angestellten** RECHNUNG number of employees; ~ **der Bezieher** GESCHÄFT number of subscribers

anzahlen *vt* GESCHÄFT prepay

Anzahlung *f* BANK advance, payment on account, GESCHÄFT prepayment, deposit, GRUND earnest money, PATENT deposit, RECHNUNG advance, deposit, down payment, V&M cash deposit, down payment, VERWALT down payment; ♦ ~ **leisten** BANK make a down payment, make an advance payment, VW make a down payment

Anzahlung: **Anzahlungen** *f pl* FINANZ progress payments; **Anzahlungsgarantie** *f* BÖRSE advance guaranty (*BrE*), advance payment bond, advance security, security bond for down payment, GESCHÄFT advance guaranty (*BrE*), IMP/EXP advance payment guarantee

anzapfen *vt* GESCHÄFT *Ressourcen*, UMWELT *Ölressourcen* tap

Anzapfen *nt* GESCHÄFT *Ressourcen*, UMWELT *Ölressourcen* tapping; ~ **von Leitungen** KOMM wiretapping; ~ **der Telefonleitung** KOMM telephone tapping

Anzeichen *nt* GESCHÄFT sign, *einer möglichen Lösung* pointer

Anzeige *f* COMP display, indicator, GESCHÄFT, KOMM advice, MEDIEN advertisement (*ad*), PATENT notification, V&M advertisement (*ad*), VERSICH advice, VW advertisement (*ad*); ~ **über abgeschlossene Versicherung** VERSICH advice card (*BrE*); ~ **der Dauer und/oder Belastung** GESCHÄFT, KOMM advice of duration and/or charge (*ADC*); ~ **der Nichterfüllung** FINANZ notice of default; **Anzeigebildschirm** *m* COMP display monitor; **Anzeigedatei** *f* COMP display file; **Anzeigeeinheit** *f* COMP display device, display unit; **Anzeigeeinstellung** *f* COMP display setting

anzeigen *vt* COMP display, GESCHÄFT indicate, show

Anzeige: **Anzeigenabteilung** *f* V&M advertising department; **Anzeigenbearbeiter** *m* PERSON advertising copywriter, advertising man (*adman*); **Anzeigenbearbeiterin** *f* PERSON advertising copywriter; **Anzeigenblatt** *nt* GESCHÄFT advertising journal, freesheet; **Anzeigenbrett** *nt* KOMM bulletin board (*BB*), notice board (*BrE*); **Anzeigenerinnerungstest** *m* V&M blind product test; **Anzeigengrundpreis** *m* V&M basic rate; **Anzeigenkauf** *m* V&M space buying; **Anzeigenkäufer, in** *m,f* V&M space buyer; **Anzeigepflicht** *f* **bei Fusionen** RECHT premerger notification duty; **Anzeigenplazierung** *f* V&M positioning of advertising

Anzeigenpreis *m* V&M adrate; ~ **für eine Schwarzweißseite** V&M page rate; **Anzeigenpreisliste** *f* V&M rate card, rate list

Anzeige: **Anzeigenraum** *m* V&M advertising space; **Anzeigenschluß** *m* GESCHÄFT copy deadline, V&M copy date; **Anzeigensplit** *m* V&M split run; **Anzeigentarife** *m pl* V&M advertising rates, space rates; **Anzeigentext** *m* **für Probetest** V&M pre-testing copy; **Anzeigenuntersuchung** *f* V&M copy test; **Anzeigenwerbezweck** *m* V&M advertising program objectives (*AmE*), advertising programme objectives (*BrE*); **Anzeigenwerbung** *f* V&M press advertising

anziehen *vi* BÖRSE firm, rally, advance, FINANZ *Einkünfte, Gewinne* rise, GESCHÄFT rise, *Preise* advance

anziehend *adj* BÖRSE advancing, firming, moving up, GESCHÄFT advancing, rising, VW rising

Anziehungskraft *f* V&M *Signalreiz* appeal

ANZUS-Pakt *m* VW ANZUS (*Australia, New Zealand and United States*)

AP *abbr* (*Assoziierte Presse*) MEDIEN Associated Press (*AmE*)

APEC-Staaten *m pl* VW APEC (*Asia Pacific Economic Cooperation*)

Aphorismus *m* GESCHÄFT aphorism

Apparat *m* GESCHÄFT gadget, IND apparatus, RECHT *Gesetze*, VW *Verwaltung* machinery; ~ **zur Durchführung von** PATENT apparatus for carrying out

Apparatschik *m* *infrml* POL *Bürokratie* apparatchik (*infrml*), mandarin

Appartementhaus *nt* GRUND apartment building (*AmE*), block of flats (*BrE*)

Appell *m* GESCHÄFT appeal

a priori *phr frml* GESCHÄFT a priori

Apriori-Erklärung *f* GESCHÄFT a priori statement

AQL-System *nt* IND acceptable quality level system (*AQL system*)

äquivalent *adj* GESCHÄFT equivalent; **~er steuerlicher Ertrag** *m* STEUER equivalent taxable yield

Äquivalenz *f* GESCHÄFT equivalence; **Äquivalenzprinzip** *nt* FINANZ compensatory principle of taxation, cost-of-service principle, STEUER benefit principle, benefit-received principle, VERSICH principle of equivalence, vw benefit principle, benefit-received principle; **Äquivalenzverkehr** *m* IMP/EXP setting off with equivalent goods

arabisch: ~e Zahlen *f pl* MATH Arabic numerals

Arbeit *f* GESCHÄFT task, work, workmanship, PERSON, VW labor (*AmE*), labour (*BrE*); **ohne ~ erzieltes Einkommen** *nt* FINANZ, RECHNUNG, STEUER unearned income; **~ nach Vorschrift** *nt* PERSON, VW go-slow; ♦ **in ~ sein** GESCHÄFT be in process; **~ aufnehmen** PERSON take a job; **mit ~ eingedeckt sein** PERSON be up to one's neck in work (*infrml*); **an der ~ hindern** PERSON ratten (*AmE*); **die ~ beenden** GESCHÄFT finish work; **die ~ einstellen** GESCHÄFT finish work; **die ~ im Griff haben** PERSON *Arbeitslast* be on top of one's job; **sich an die ~ machen** GESCHÄFT get down to work; **die ~ niederlegen** PERSON down tools

arbeiten *vi* GESCHÄFT work; ♦ **~ an** [+dat] MGMNT be engaged in; **~ in** [+dat] GESCHÄFT be based in; **nicht ~** BANK *Geld* lie idle (*infrml*); **jedes zweite Wochenende ~** GESCHÄFT work alternate weekends

Arbeiten *f pl* GESCHÄFT working

arbeitend *adj* COMP, FINANZ active, GESCHÄFT active, working; **nicht ~er Ehegatte** *m*, **nicht ~e Ehegattin** *f* PERSON nonworking spouse; **~es Kapital** *nt* FINANZ active capital; **~e Rechneranlage** *f* COMP active computer; **~es Unternehmen** *nt* GESCHÄFT going concern; **~er Zins** *m* FINANZ working interest

Arbeiter, in *m,f* PERSON working man, workman, manual worker, *Arbeiterverhältnis* worker, vw blue-collar worker; **~ auf der Höhe seiner/ihrer Schaffenskraft** PERSON prime-age worker; **~ am Rande des Existenzminimums** PERSON marginal worker, peripheral worker; **~ am Rande des Produktionsprozesses** PERSON peripheral worker; **Arbeiterbeteiligung** *f* PERSON shop-floor participation, worker involvement; **Arbeiterbewegung** *f* PERSON labor movement (*AmE*), labour movement (*BrE*), vw movement of labor (*AmE*), movement of labour (*BrE*); **Arbeitergenossenschaft** *f* PERSON, VW workers' cooperative; **Arbeitergewerkschaft** *f* PERSON manual union (*BrE*); **Arbeiterklasse** *f* PERSON laboring class (*AmE*), working class, *Sozialpolitik* labouring class (*BrE*); **Arbeiterkollektiv** *nt* PERSON workers' collective; **Arbeiterrentenversicherung** *f* VERSICH invalidity and old-age insurance for wage earners; **Arbeiterschaft** *f* GESCHÄFT workforce, IND, PERSON commonality, workforce; **Arbeiterselbstbestimmung** *f* PERSON *Arbeitspartizipation, Mitarbeiterbeteiligung* worker control, workers' control; **Arbeiterselbstverwaltung** *f* MGMNT, PERSON *Geschäftsführung* autogestion, self-management; **Arbeiterunruhen** *f pl* PERSON labor unrest (*AmE*), labour unrest (*BrE*), labor troubles (*AmE*), labour troubles (*BrE*)

Arbeitgeber *m* FINANZ, GESCHÄFT, PERSON, STEUER employer; **vom ~ vorgeschriebene, ausdrückliche Vertragsvereinbarung** *f* PERSON employer express term; **Arbeitgeberanteil** *m* FINANZ, PERSON employer's contribution, STEUER employer rate (*BrE*), employer's contribution; **Arbeitgeber-Arbeitnehmer-Beziehungen** *f pl* PERSON, vw industrial relations, labor relations (*AmE*), labour relations (*BrE*); **Arbeitgeberbeitrag** *m* FINANZ, PERSON employer's contribution, STEUER employer rate (*BrE*), employer's contribution

arbeitgeberfreundlich: ~e Gewerkschaft *f* PERSON scab union (*BrE*) (*infrml*)

Arbeitgeber: Arbeitgeberhaftpflicht *f* STEUER employer's liabilities; **Arbeitgeberrückerstattung** *f* STEUER employer's return; **Arbeitgeberrückzahlung** *f* STEUER employer's return; **Arbeitgeberverband** *m* GESCHÄFT, PERSON employers' association

Arbeitnehmer, in *m,f* GESCHÄFT, PERSON employee; **Arbeitnehmeranteil** *m* PERSON employee's contribution, STEUER employee rate (*BrE*), employee contribution; **Arbeitnehmerbeitrag** *m* PERSON employee's contribution, STEUER employee rate (*BrE*), employee's contribution; **Arbeitnehmerbeteiligung** *f* PERSON employee participation scheme, employee shareholding scheme; **Arbeitnehmerkommunikation** *f* PERSON employee communications; **von den Arbeitnehmern geführte Firma** *f* MGMNT labor-managed firm (*AmE*), labour-managed firm (*BrE*); **von den Arbeitnehmern geleitete Firma** *f* MGMNT labor-managed firm (*AmE*), labour-managed firm (*BrE*); **Arbeitnehmer-Sparzulage** *f* PERSON employee's savings premium; **Arbeitnehmerverband** *m* PERSON employee association; **Arbeitnehmerversicherung** *f* **durch den Arbeitgeber** VERSICH split dollar life insurance (*AmE*); **Arbeitnehmervertretung** *f* PERSON employee-elected representation; **Arbeitnehmervertretungsausschuß** *m* PERSON Labour Representation Committee (*BrE*) (*LRC*)

Arbeitsablauf *m* GESCHÄFT work flow, PERSON operational sequence, process, sequence of operations; **Arbeitsablaufbogen** *m* MATH flow process chart, MGMNT flow process chart, *Algorithmus* flowchart; **Arbeitsablaufplanung** *f* GESCHÄFT task scheduling, work flow planning, MGMNT work flow planning; **Arbeitsablaufschaubild** *nt* IND outline process chart

arbeitsadditiv: ~er technischer Fortschritt *m* vw labor-augmenting technical progress (*AmE*), labour-augmenting technical progress (*BrE*)

Arbeit: Arbeitsamt *nt* PERSON, SOZIAL, VERWALT employment office (*BrE*), employment service (*AmE*), Jobcentre (*BrE*), labour exchange (*dat*) (*BrE*); **Arbeitsanalyse** *f* PERSON job analysis, job study; **Arbeitsanfang registrieren** *phr* IND clock in; **Arbeitsanweisung** *f* PERSON *vom Vorgesetzten an den Arbeitnehmer* job instruction, work assignment, work order; **Arbeitsaufgabe** *f* PERSON job; **Arbeitsauftrag** *m* GESCHÄFT IND job order, labor voucher (*AmE*), labour voucher (*BrE*), operation ticket, work order; **Arbeitsaufwand** *m* vw labor cost (*AmE*), labour cost (*BrE*), labor costs (*AmE*), labour costs (*BrE*); **Arbeitsaufwand** *m* **je Produkteinheit** vw unit labor cost (*AmE*), unit labour cost (*BrE*); **Arbeitsausschuß** *m* GESCHÄFT study group, PERSON working party; **Arbeitsbedarf** *m* vw labor demand (*AmE*), labour demand (*BrE*); **Arbeitsbedingungen** *f pl* PERSON conditions of employment, working conditions; **Arbeitsbelastung** *f* GESCHÄFT, MGMNT, PERSON *Berufsleben, Streß* workload; **Arbeitsbereich** *m* COMP *Notizblock* scratch area, IND work area, work space,

PERSON area of operations, working area; **Arbeitsbereicherung** *f* PERSON job enrichment; **Arbeitsbereitschaft** *f* vw propensity to work **Arbeitsbeschaffung** *f* vw make-work (*AmE*); **Arbeitsbeschaffungsmaßnahmen** *f pl* (*ABM*) PERSON, vw job-creating measures, community programme (*BrE*), community program (*AmE*), special employment measures (*SEM*); **Arbeitsbeschaffungspraktiken** *f pl* PERSON job-creating measures; **Arbeitsbeschaffungsprogramm** *nt* GESCHÄFT, SOZIAL public works program (*AmE*), public works programme (*BrE*), vw job creation program (*AmE*), job creation programme (*BrE*), job creation scheme

Arbeit: **Arbeitsbesessene(r)** *mf* [decl. as adj] PERSON workaholic; **Arbeitsbeziehungen** *f pl* PERSON, vw industrial relations (*IR*), labor relations (*AmE*), labour relations (*BrE*); **Arbeitsblatt** *nt* BÖRSE, COMP, FINANZ, RECHNUNG, VERWALT spreadsheet, *Tabellenkalkulation* work sheet; VERWALT *Tabellenkalkulation* spreadsheet; **Arbeitsbuch** *nt* PERSON *Personalwirtschaft, Lohnabrechnung* time book; **Arbeitsdatei** *f* COMP scratch file, VERWALT work file; **Arbeitsdirektor, in** *m,f* PERSON *Arbeitspartizipation* worker director; **Arbeitsdokument** *nt* GESCHÄFT work-in-process document (*AmE*), work-in-progress document (*BrE*), RECHNUNG working paper; **Arbeitsdruck** *m* IND working pressure (*WP*); **Arbeitseinkommen** *nt* PERSON earnings, vw service income; **Arbeitseinteilung** *f* MGMNT, PERSON work management; **Arbeitsende registrieren** *phr* IND, PERSON clock off; **Arbeitsentfremdung** *f* VERWALT alienation; **Arbeitsentgelt** *nt* PERSON compensation, remuneration; **Arbeitsentgelt** *nt* **für Bereitschaftsdienst** PERSON standby rate; **Arbeitsentgelt** *nt* **zum Zeitlohnsatz** PERSON *EG-Richtlinien* pay for work at time rates; **Arbeitserfahrung** *f* GESCHÄFT, MGMNT, PERSON work experience; **Arbeitserlaubnis** *f* PERSON work permit, VERWALT working visa; **Arbeitsertragsrückgangstheorie** *f* vw labor disutility theory (*AmE*), labour disutility theory (*BrE*); **Arbeitsessen** *nt* GESCHÄFT working dinner, *Mittagessen* working lunch; **Arbeitsethos** *nt* MGMNT, PERSON work ethic

arbeitsfähig *adj* PERSON able to work, employable, fit for work, vw able to work

Arbeit: **Arbeitsfähigkeit** *f* GESCHÄFT capacity to work, PERSON, vw ability to work; **Arbeitsflußdiagramm** *nt* IND operation flow chart, MGMNT flow process chart; **Arbeitsförderung** *f* vw promotion; **Arbeitsfortschrittsbericht** *m* GESCHÄFT progress report

arbeitsfrei: ~**er Tag** *m* PERSON day off

Arbeit: **Arbeitsfreude** *f* PERSON, vw propensity to work; **Arbeitsfrühstück** *nt* GESCHÄFT working breakfast; **Arbeitsgang** *m* PERSON *Produktionstechnik* work cycle; **Arbeits- und Gehaltsbedingungen** *f pl* PERSON *Arbeitsvertrag* pay and conditions; **Arbeitsgemeinschaft** *f* GESCHÄFT study group, PERSON consortium, joint venture, RECHT de facto corporation, special partnership, vw de facto corporation; **Arbeitsgemeinschaft** *f* **der öffentlich-rechtlichen Rundfunkanstalten der Bundesrepublik Deutschland** (*ARD*) MEDIEN ≈ Australian Broadcasting Corporation (*ABC*), ≈ American Broadcasting Corporation (*ABC*), ≈ British Broadcasting Corporation (*BBC*); **Arbeitsgericht** *nt* PERSON, RECHT industrial tribunal

(*BrE*) (*IT*), labor court (*AmE*); **Arbeitsgesetz** *nt* PERSON, RECHT employment law (*BrE*), labor law (*AmE*), labour law (*BrE*); **Arbeitsgesetzgebung** *f* RECHT job legislation; **Arbeitsgestaltung** *f* GESCHÄFT work design, work structuring, PERSON optimum combination of labor, equipment and materials (*AmE*), optimum combination of labour, equipment and materials (*BrE*), *Ergonomik, Synergie* work structuring; **Arbeitsgruppe** *f* GESCHÄFT, POL study group, working group, working party (*W/P*); **Arbeitshygiene** *f* PERSON industrial health, industrial hygiene, SOZIAL industrial hygiene; **Arbeitshypothese** *f* GESCHÄFT working hypothesis; **Arbeitsinhalt** *m* GESCHÄFT work content, PERSON job content

arbeitsintensiv *adj* IND, PERSON, vw labor-intensive (*AmE*), labour-intensive (*BrE*); ~**e Industrie** *f* PERSON labor-intensive industry (*AmE*), labour-intensive industry (*BrE*)

Arbeit: **Arbeitskamerad, in** *m,f obs* GESCHÄFT colleague, workmate; **Arbeitskampf** *m* IND, PERSON, vw industrial action, industrial dispute, labor dispute (*AmE*), labour dispute (*BrE*); **Arbeitskampfmaßnahmen** *f pl* PERSON job action (*jarg*); **Arbeitskampfmaßnahmen ergreifen** *phr* PERSON take industrial action; **Arbeitskenngrößen** *f pl* IND performance characteristics; **Arbeitsklausel** *f* PERSON labor clause (*AmE*), labour clause (*BrE*); **Arbeitsklima** *nt* PERSON, POL working atmosphere; **Arbeitskodex** *m* PERSON labor code (*AmE*), labour code (*BrE*); **Arbeitskollege** *m*, **Arbeitskollegin** *f* GESCHÄFT colleague, workmate; **Arbeitskonflikt** *m* PERSON industrial conflict, industrial dispute, industrial strife; **von Arbeitskonflikten geprägter Zeitraum** *m* PERSON strife-ridden period; **Arbeitskontrolle** *f* GESCHÄFT progress control, IND process control, production control; **Arbeitskosten** *pl* VERWALT cost of labor (*AmE*), cost of labour (*BrE*), vw labor costs (*AmE*), labour costs (*BrE*); **Arbeitskraft** *f* IND labor force (*AmE*), labour force (*BrE*), *Arbeiter* worker, *Arbeiterschaft* workforce

Arbeitskräfte *f pl* GESCHÄFT, IND workforce, PERSON, VERWALT human resources, vw labor force (*AmE*), labour force (*BrE*); ~**, die der Bauherr selbst stellt** FINANZ direct labor organization (*AmE*), direct labour organization (*BrE*); ~ **ohne Papiere** RECHT undocumented workers; ~ **auf Zeit** PERSON contract labor (*AmE*), contract labour (*BrE*); **Arbeitskräfteabgang** *m* PERSON attrition, labor wastage (*AmE*), labour wastage (*BrE*); **Arbeitskräfteangebot** *nt* vw labor supply (*AmE*), labour supply (*BrE*); **Arbeitskräfteeinsatz** *m* MGMNT manpower management; **Arbeitskräftefluktuation** *f* GESCHÄFT, PERSON, vw employee turnover, labor turnover (*AmE*), labour turnover (*BrE*), staff turnover; **Arbeitskräftelenkung** *f* MGMNT manpower management; **Arbeitskräftemangel** *m* PERSON labor shortage (*AmE*), labour shortage (*BrE*); **Arbeitskräftenachfrage** *f* vw labor demand (*AmE*), labour demand (*BrE*); **Arbeitskräfteplanung** *f* MGMNT manpower planning; **Arbeitskräftereserven** *f pl* IND labor force (*AmE*), labour force (*BrE*), manpower reserve; **Arbeitskräftereservoir** *nt* PERSON, vw labor shed (*AmE*), labour shed (*BrE*)

Arbeit: **Arbeitslaufzettel** *nt* PERSON job ticket; **Arbeitsleistung** *f* PERSON job performance, VERWALT output; **Arbeitslohn** *m* BÖRSE compensating income (*BrE*), IND employment compensation, STEUER employment income, VW wage, wage rate; **Arbeitslöhne** *m pl* PERSON, VW wages, labor costs (*AmE*), labour costs (*BrE*)

arbeitslos *adj* PERSON, SOZIAL, VW unemployed, jobless, off the payroll, out of work, workless, at liberty (*AmE*); ◆ **~ sein** PERSON be out of work; **als ~ gemeldet** GESCHÄFT registered unemployed; **sich ~ melden** PERSON register as unemployed, sign on (*BrE*)

arbeitslos: **~e Arbeitskräfte** *f pl* PERSON unemployed labour force (*BrE*), unemployed labor force (*AmE*), unemployed workforce

Arbeitslose(r) *mf* [decl. as adj] PERSON, VW unemployed person, jobless person; **die Arbeitslosen** *pl* PERSON, SOZIAL, VW the jobless, the unemployed, the job queue (*BrE*); **Arbeitslosengeld** *nt* GESCHÄFT, SOZIAL, VW unemployment benefit (*BrE*), unemployment compensation (*AmE*); **Arbeitslosenquote** *f* PERSON, VW unemployment rate, jobless rate; **Arbeitslosenstatistik** *f* PERSON, VW unemployment statistics; **Arbeitslosenversicherung** *f* PERSON, VERSICH, VW unemployment insurance; **Arbeitslosenversicherungskonto** *nt* PERSON, VERSICH, VW *Rechnungswesen* unemployment insurance account; **Arbeitslosenzahl** *f* PERSON, SOZIAL, VW unemployment rate; **Arbeitslosenzahlen** *nt* PERSON, SOZIAL, VW unemployment figures

Arbeitslosenunterstützung *f* GESCHÄFT, PERSON, SOZIAL, VW unemployment benefit (*BrE*), dole (*infrml*) (*BrE*), unemployment compensation (*AmE*), unemployment pay; **~ empfangen** PERSON, SOZIAL receive unemployment benefit (*BrE*), receive unemployment compensation (*AmE*), be on the dole (*infrml*) (*BrE*), be on welfare (*AmE*)

Arbeitslosigkeit *f* PERSON, SOZIAL, VW unemployment, unemployment rate; ◆ **die ~ bekämpfen** GESCHÄFT fight unemployment

Arbeitslosigkeit: **Arbeitslosigkeitsfalle** *f* PERSON, SOZIAL, VW *Sozialwesen* unemployment trap

Arbeit: **Arbeitsluke** *f* TRANSP workable hatch (*WH*); **Arbeitsmangel** *m* PERSON shortage

Arbeitsmarkt *m* GESCHÄFT, PERSON, VW job market, labor market (*AmE*), labour market (*BrE*); ◆ **in den ~ eintreten** PERSON, VW enter the labor market (*AmE*), enter the labour market (*BrE*); **auf den ~ treten** PERSON, VW enter the labor market (*AmE*), enter the labour market (*BrE*); **was den ~ angeht** PERSON, POL, VW on the employment front

Arbeitsmarkt: **Arbeitsmarktabgabe** *f* VW labor-market levy (*AmE*), labour-market levy (*BrE*); **Arbeitsmarktpolitik** *f* POL, VW labor-market policy (*AmE*), labour-market policy (*BrE*); **Arbeitsmarkttheorie** *f* VW labor economics (*AmE*), labor-market theory (*AmE*), labour economics (*BrE*), labour-market theory (*BrE*)

Arbeit: **Arbeitsministerium** *nt* VW Department of Employment (*DE*); **Arbeitsmobilität** *f* PERSON, VW mobility, mobility of labor (*AmE*), mobility of labour (*BrE*), labor mobility (*AmE*), labour mobility (*BrE*); **Arbeitsmöglichkeit** *f* PERSON job prospect, job opportunity; **Arbeitsmoral** *f* PERSON morale, work attitude; **Arbeitsniederlegung** *f* GESCHÄFT walkout (*infrml*), PERSON stoppage of work (*BrE*), walkout (*infrml*); **Arbeitsniederlegung organisieren** *phr* PERSON stage a walkout; **Arbeitsnorm** *f* VW labor standard (*AmE*), labour standard (*BrE*); **Arbeitsökonomik** *f* VW labor

economics (*AmE*), labour economics (*BrE*); **Arbeitsordnung** *f* GESCHÄFT rule book; **Arbeitsorganisation** *f* GESCHÄFT work organization; **Arbeitspapier** *nt* POL exposure draft, working paper, RECHNUNG exposure draft, VERWALT working paper; **Arbeitspartizipation** *f* MGMNT involvement of employees, PERSON employee involvement (*EI*), employee involvement and participation (*BrE*), involvement of employees, worker involvement, worker participation; **Arbeitspensum** *nt* GESCHÄFT task work, workload, MGMNT, PERSON workload, amount of work; **Arbeitsplan** *m* GESCHÄFT working program (*AmE*), working programme (*BrE*), work schedule, IND schedule of job operations, MGMNT work schedule, TRANSP operating schedule, VERWALT work schedule; **Arbeitsplanung** *f* GESCHÄFT task scheduling, IND work scheduling; **Arbeitsplanungsbogen** *m* COMP multiple activity chart, MGMNT activity chart; **Arbeitsplanzertifikat** *nt* TRANSP routing certificate; **Arbeitsplatte** *f* COMP scratch disk

Arbeitsplatz *m* GESCHÄFT *Platz* duty station, work station, post, work center (*AmE*), work centre (*BrE*), place of work, workplace, job site, position, *Arbeit* job, IND work area, works, PERSON *Stelle* working area, work location, workplace, place of work, *Arbeit* job, VERWALT workplace; ◆ **den ~ verlieren** PERSON be made redundant, lose one's job; **jdn für einen ~ empfehlen** PERSON put sb in for a job

Arbeitsplatz: **Arbeitsplatzanalyse** *f* PERSON job analysis, job description, occupational analysis, VERWALT ergonomics; **Arbeitsplatzangebot** *nt* PERSON job offer, VW availability of jobs, supply of jobs; **Arbeitsplatzannahmebereitschaft** *f* VW job acceptance schedule; **Arbeitsplatzbeschreibung** *f* PERSON job description; **Arbeitsplatzbewertung** *f* PERSON job appraisal, job evaluation, labor grading (*AmE*), labour grading (*BrE*)

arbeitsplatzbezogen: **~e Verletzungen** *f pl* PERSON job-related injuries

Arbeitsplatz: **Arbeitsplatz-Datenbank** *f* PERSON job bank, job database

Arbeitsplätze *m pl* VW *innerhalb der EG* community jobs; ◆ **~ einsparen** GESCHÄFT shed jobs; **~ erhalten** GESCHÄFT preserve jobs; **~ gefährden** PERSON endanger jobs; **~ schaffen** VERWALT create jobs

Arbeitsplatz: **Arbeitsplatzeinweisung** *f* GESCHÄFT orientation; **Arbeitsplatzerwartungen** *f pl* PERSON job expectations; **Arbeitsplatzflexibilität** *f* PERSON job flexibility; **Arbeitsplatzgestaltung** *f* PERSON job engineering, workplace layout, VERWALT *Ergonomie* human engineering; **Arbeitsplatzmerkmale** *nt pl* PERSON job characteristics; **Arbeitsplatzrisiko** *nt* PERSON occupational hazard; **Arbeitsplatzsicherheit** *f* PERSON employment security, job security; **Arbeitsplatzsicherung** *f* PERSON safeguarding of jobs; **Arbeitsplatzstudie** *f* GESCHÄFT time and motion study; **Arbeitsplatzteilung** *f* PERSON job share, job sharing, job splitting; **Arbeitsplatzverbesserung** *f* PERSON job improvement; **Arbeitsplatzwechsel** *m* PERSON job change, job shift, VW labor turnover (*AmE*), labour turnover (*BrE*)

Arbeit: **Arbeitspraxis** *f* GESCHÄFT working practice; **Arbeitsproduktivität** *f* PERSON labor efficiency (*AmE*), labour efficiency (*BrE*), VW efficiency of labor (*AmE*), efficiency of labour (*BrE*), efficiency ratio;

Arbeitsprogramm *nt* COMP working program, GESCHÄFT, MGMNT work schedule; **Arbeitsprozeßtheorie** *f* PERSON labor-process theory (*AmE*), labour-process theory (*BrE*); **Arbeitspsychologie** *f* IND, MGMNT, PERSON industrial psychology, organizational psychology, personnel psychology; **Arbeitspuffer** *m* COMP scratch pad; **Arbeitsqualität** *f* GESCHÄFT workmanship; **Arbeitsraum** *m* PERSON working area, work space; **Arbeitsrecht** *nt* PERSON industrial law (*BrE*), labor law (*AmE*), labour law (*BrE*), RECHT industrial law (*BrE*), job legislation, labor law (*AmE*), labour law (*BrE*)

arbeitsrechtlich: **~e Streitfrage** *f* VW labor dispute (*AmE*), labour dispute (*BrE*); **~e Vorschriften** *f pl* PERSON, RECHT labor legislation (*AmE*), labour legislation (*BrE*), labor rules (*AmE*), labour rules (*BrE*)

Arbeit: **Arbeitsregulierung** *f* PERSON job regulation; **Arbeitsreserve** *f* PERSON, VW labor shed (*AmE*), labour shed (*BrE*); **Arbeitsrhythmus** *m* PERSON working patterns; **Arbeitsrückstand** *m* GESCHÄFT backlog, backlog of work; **Arbeitsschluß** *m* PERSON, VERWALT end of work, knocking-off time (*infrml*)

Arbeitsschutz *m* PERSON industrial safety; **Arbeitsschutzbestimmungen** *f pl* IND industrial safety regulations; **Arbeitsschutzkomitee** *nt* SOZIAL *privat* Safety Committee (*AmE*), *staatlich* Safety Commission (*AmE*); **Arbeitsschutzrechte** *nt pl* PERSON *des Arbeitnehmers* employment protection rights

Arbeit: **Arbeitssicherheit** *f* PERSON on-the-job safety, VERWALT industrial safety; **Arbeitssitzung** *f* COMP session, GESCHÄFT working session, RECHNUNG working meeting

arbeitssparend *adj* PERSON labor-saving (*AmE*), labour-saving (*BrE*)

Arbeit: **Arbeitsspeicher** *m* COMP main memory, working storage; **Arbeitsstätte** *f* IND place of work; **Arbeitsstreit** *m* VW labor dispute (*AmE*), labour dispute (*BrE*); **Arbeitsstreß** *m* MGMNT, PERSON work stress; **Arbeitsstudie** *f* GESCHÄFT, MGMNT, PERSON work study

Arbeitsstunde *f* MGMNT man-hour; **Arbeitsstundenanpassung** *f* PERSON spreadover; **Arbeitsstundenanpassung** *f* **durch Gleitzeit oder Wechselschicht** PERSON spreadover working; **Arbeitsstundensystem** *nt* **auf Jahresbasis** PERSON *Lohnstreifen* annualized hours system

Arbeit: **Arbeitssuchende(r)** *mf* [decl. as adj] PERSON jobseeker; **Arbeitssystem** *nt* **des Managements** MGMNT management operating system; **Arbeitstag** *m* GESCHÄFT, IND, PERSON workday (*AmE*), working day (*BrE*); **Arbeitstakt** *m* GESCHÄFT work cycle; **Arbeitsteilung** *f* PERSON work-sharing, vw division of labor (*AmE*), division of labour (*BrE*); **Arbeitstrennung** *f* PERSON job segregation; **Arbeitsüberwachung** *f* IND job control; **Arbeitsumwelt** *f* PERSON working environment; **Arbeitsunfähigkeit** *f* PERSON disability, inability to work; **Arbeitsunfall** *m* IND industrial injury, PERSON industrial accident; **Arbeitsunfallrente** *f* FINANZ disablement pension; **Arbeitsunterbrechung** *f* PERSON interruption of work, work stoppage; **Arbeitsunterlage** *f* POL, VERWALT working paper; **Arbeitsunterteilung** *f* PERSON job breakdown; **Arbeitsurlaub** *m* GESCHÄFT working holiday; **Arbeitsvereinfachung** *f* MGMNT, PERSON work simpli-

fication; **Arbeitsverhältnis** *nt* PERSON employment relationship, employment

arbeitsvermehrend: **~er technischer Fortschritt** *m* VW labor-augmenting technical progress (*AmE*), labour-augmenting technical progress (*BrE*)

Arbeit: **Arbeitsvermittlung** *f* PERSON job placement, placement of employees, *Stelle* employment agency, *staatlich* Jobcentre (*BrE*), employment service (*AmE*), SOZIAL, VERWALT *staatlich* Jobcentre (*BrE*), employment service (*AmE*), employment agency; **Arbeitsvermögen** *nt* PERSON labor power (*AmE*), labour power (*BrE*), VERWALT, VW human capital; **Arbeitsverteilung** *f* PERSON *Arbeitsvorbereitung, Produktionsplanung* allocation of work, assignment of activities

Arbeitsvertrag *m* PERSON contract of employment, employment contract, labor contract (*AmE*), labour contract (*BrE*); **~ mit Gewerkschaftsbeitrittsverbot** PERSON, RECHT yellow-dog contract (*AmE*)

Arbeit: **Arbeitsvolumen** *nt* GESCHÄFT work content, VW total number of man-hours worked; **Arbeitsvorbereitung** *f* IND planning of process layout, process planning, work scheduling, *Einteilung* production scheduling, MGMNT production scheduling, process planning, work scheduling, planning of process layout; **Arbeitsvorgang** *m* GESCHÄFT operation; **Arbeitsvorrat** *m* GESCHÄFT unfilled orders, workload, IND, MGMNT, PERSON workload; **Arbeitsweise** *f* IND process, MGMNT method, VERWALT procedure

Arbeitswert *m* GESCHÄFT job value; **Arbeitswertlehre** *f* vw labor theory of value (*AmE*), labour theory of value (*BrE*); **Arbeitswertlehre** *f* **vom negativen Nutzen** VW labor disutility theory (*AmE*), labour disutility theory (*BrE*); **Arbeitswerttheorie** *f* VW labor theory of value (*AmE*), labour theory of value (*BrE*)

Arbeit: **Arbeitswissenschaft** *f* COMP ergonomics; **Arbeitswoche** *f* PERSON workweek (*AmE*), working week (*BrE*); **Arbeitzeichen** *nt* PATENT work mark

Arbeitszeit *f* GESCHÄFT, PERSON hours of work, working hours, working time; ◆ **außerhalb der normalen Arbeitszeiten** PERSON *Arbeit, Überstunden* unsocial hours; **~ registrieren** IND clock in

Arbeitszeit: **Arbeitszeiteinteilung** *f* GESCHÄFT work schedule, work time study, PERSON, IND work time study, MGMNT work schedule, work time study, PERSON work time study; **Arbeitszeitermittlung** *f* GESCHÄFT, PERSON, IND, PERSON work time study; **Arbeitszeitkontrolleur, in** *m* VERWALT timekeeper; **Arbeitszeitnachweis** *m* PERSON time sheet; **Arbeitszeitplan** *m* GESCHÄFT working timetable; **Arbeitszeitstudie** *f* GESCHÄFT time study, work time study, PERSON, IND, PERSON work time study; **Arbeitszeitstudien** *f pl* MGMNT stopwatch studies; **Arbeitszeitverkürzung** *f* PERSON reduction in working hours, shorter working hours; **Arbeitsziele festsetzen** *phr* GESCHÄFT, PERSON set objectives

Arbeit: **Arbeitszufriedenheit** *f* PERSON job satisfaction; **Arbeitszwischenfall** *m* PERSON, SOZIAL industrial incident; **Arbeitszyklus** *m* COMP operation cycle, IND job cycle

Arbitrage *f* BANK arbitrage, BÖRSE spread trading, RECHT arbitration; **~ bei unternormalen Kursdifferenzen** BÖRSE backspread; **~ bei unternormalen Preisdifferenzen** BÖRSE backspread; **~ zwischen zwei Parallelmärkten** BÖRSE, FINANZ, PERSON shunting (*BrE*); **Arbitragecode** *m* BÖRSE code of arbitration;

Arbitragefirma *f* BÖRSE arbitrage house; **Arbitragegeschäft** *nt* BÖRSE arbitrage dealing, arbitrage transaction, GESCHÄFT arbitraging; **Arbitragegeschäfte machen** *phr* BÖRSE, FINANZ *Ausnutzung von Kursunterschieden im Börsengeschäft* arbitrate; **Arbitragehandel** *mf* BÖRSE arbitrage trading; **Arbitragehändler, in** *m,f* BÖRSE arbitrage dealer, arbitrage trader, arbitrager, arbitrageur; **Arbitrage-Interventionspunkte** *m pl* FINANZ arbitrage support points; **Arbitrageklausel** *f* GESCHÄFT arbitration clause, IMP/EXP arbitrage clause, RECHT clause of arbitration; **Arbitragepreis-Theorie** *f* BÖRSE arbitrage pricing theory (*APT*); **Arbitragerechnung** *f* FINANZ arbitrage calculation, arbitration of exchange; **Arbitrageschuldverschreibungen** *f pl* BÖRSE arbitrage bonds (*AmE*); **Arbitragespanne** *f* BÖRSE arbitrage margin (*BrE*); **Arbitrage-Transaktion** *f* BÖRSE arbitrage dealing, arbitrage operation, arbitrage transaction

Arbitrageur *m* BÖRSE, FINANZ, PERSON arbitrager, arbitrageur, shunter (*BrE*)

Arbitrage: **Arbitragewerte** *m pl* BÖRSE arbitrage stocks

Arbitration *f* IND, PERSON arbitration

arbitrieren *vt* BÖRSE, FINANZ arbitrate

Arbitriumwert *m* PERSON value of an enterprise as a whole

Architekt, in *m,f* GRUND architect; **Architektenhaftung** *f* VERSICH architect's liability

Architektur *f* COMP, GRUND architecture

Archiv *nt* COMP *Daten* archive, MEDIEN morgue (*infrml*), VERWALT *Dokumentensammlung* archive storage

Archivar, in *m,f* VERWALT archivist, record keeper

Archiv: **Archivbestände** *m pl* VERWALT *Registratur* archive; **Archivdatei** *f* COMP archive file

archivieren *vt* COMP store, archive, VERWALT archive

Archivierung *f* COMP *Daten* archival storage, computer storage, VERWALT filing

Archiv: **Archivkopie** *f* COMP archive copy

ARD *abbr* (*Arbeitsgemeinschaft der öffentlich-rechtlichen Rundfunkanstalten der Bundesrepublik Deutschland*) MEDIEN ≈ ABC (*American Broadcasting Company, Australian Broadcasting Corporation*), ≈ BBC (*British Broadcasting Corporation*)

Ärgernis *nt* GESCHÄFT nuisance

Arglist *f* GESCHÄFT, RECHNUNG *Betrug* fraudulence, RECHT *Betrug* fraudulence, intention to deceive

arglistig *adj* RECHT *betrügerisch, böswillig* fraudulent; **~e Täuschung** *f* GESCHÄFT fraud, RECHT fraud, intention to deceive, misrepresentation intended to deceive

arithmetisch: **~e degressive Abschreibung** *f* RECHNUNG sum-of-the-year's-digit method of depreciation; **~e Folge** *f* MATH arithmetic progression sequence; **~es Mittel** *nt* MATH arithmetic mean

arm *adj* PERSON, SOZIAL, VW poor

Ärmelkanal *m* TRANSP the English Channel

Armen: **die ~** *pl* SOZIAL the poor; **Armenrecht** *f* RECHT *Rechtshilfe* right to cost exemption, legal aid

Armut *f* SOZIAL poverty; **Armutsfalle** *f* SOZIAL poverty trap; **Armutsgrenze** *f* SOZIAL poverty line

Arrangeur *m* FINANZ *Kreditsyndizierungen und Emissionen* arranger

arrangieren: **sich ~** *v refl* GESCHÄFT, VW make a deal, come to an arrangement; ♦ **sich mit jdm ~** GESCHÄFT come to an arrangement with sb

Arrest: **Arrestbefehl** *m* RECHT *Vorführungsbefehl* writ of attachment; **Arrestverfahren** *nt* RECHT attachment procedure

Arrondierungskauf *m* GESCHÄFT rounding-off buying

Art. *abbr* (*Artikel*) PATENT gds (*goods*)

Art *f* GESCHÄFT nature, type, PATENT nature; **~ der Erfindung** PATENT nature of the invention

artengerecht: **aus ~er Tierhaltung** *phr* UMWELT *Fleisch* organic

Art: **Artenschutzabkommen** *nt* RECHT, UMWELT biodiversity treaty

Artikel *m* GESCHÄFT article, product, PATENT goods (*BrE*) (*gds*), gds (*BrE*) (*goods*), RECHT *Teil des Gesetzes* article, section, V&M item; **~ des persönlichen Bedarfs** *m* GESCHÄFT article for personal use; **~ im Sonderangebot** V&M flash item; **Artikelaufschlag** *m* V&M item mark-up; **Artikelinhalt** *m* GESCHÄFT copy; **Artikelnummer** *f* V&M item number; **Artikelstatus** *m* V&M item status

Arzneimittel *nt* GESCHÄFT drug; **nicht rezeptpflichtiges ~** SOZIAL, V&M over-the-counter medicine; **Arzneimittelhandel** *m* GESCHÄFT drug trade; **Arzneimittelindustrie** *f* GESCHÄFT pharmaceutical industry; **Arzneimittelschäden** *m pl* VERSICH damage by pharmaceutical products

Ärzte- *in cpds* SOZIAL health; **Ärztekammer** *f* GESCHÄFT ≈ General Medical Council (*BrE*), ≈ State Medical Board of Registration (*AmE*); **Ärztezentrum** *nt* SOZIAL health center (*AmE*), health centre (*BrE*)

ärztlich: **~e Untersuchung** *f* SOZIAL *eines Patienten* medical examination, physical examination

ASCII *abbr* (*ASCII-Code*) COMP ASCII (*American Standard Code for Information Interchange*); **in ~** *phr* COMP in ASCII; **ASCII-Code** *m* (*ASCII*) COMP ASCII (*American Standard Code for Information Interchange*); **im ASCII-Code** *phr* COMP in ASCII; **ASCII-Datei** *f* COMP ASCII file

asiatisch: **~e Produktionsweise** *f* VW Asiatic mode of production

Asiatisch: **~e Freihandelszone** *f* POL, VW Asian Free Trade Area (*AFTA*)

a similibus ad similia *phr* GESCHÄFT a similibus ad similia

Aspekt *m* GESCHÄFT aspect

Assekurant *m* VERSICH insurance company, insurer

Assekuranz *f* VERSICH insurance industry

Assembler *m* COMP assembler, assembly program

Assemblierprogramm *nt* COMP assembler, assembly program

assertorisch: **~er Eid** *m* RECHT assertory oath

Assessment Center *nt* PERSON assessment center (*AmE*), assessment centre (*BrE*)

Asset: **~ Swap** *m* BANK asset swap

Assimilation *f* GESCHÄFT adjustment, assimilation, RECHNUNG assimilation

assimiliert: **~ werden** *phr* POL *ethnischen Minderheiten* be absorbed

Assistent, in *m,f* GESCHÄFT, PERSON assistant (*asst*); **~ der Geschäftsleitung** PERSON executive assistent; **~ im Rechnungswesen** MGMNT assistant controller

assoziieren *vt* V&M assort

assoziieren: **sich ~ mit** *v refl* GESCHÄFT, MGMNT work in partnership with

assoziiert: ~**er Arbeitgeber** *m*, ~**e Arbeitgeberin** *f* PERSON associated employer; ~**es Land** *nt* VW associated country; ~**es Unternehmen** *nt* GESCHÄFT associated company, associated enterprise; ~**es Warenzeichen** *nt* PATENT associated mark

AStV *abbr* (*Ausschuß der Ständigen Vertreter*) VW *EU* COREPER (*Committee of Permanent Representatives of the EC*)

Asyl *nt* POL, RECHT asylum

Asylant, in *m,f* POL, RECHT asylum seeker

Asyl: **Asylantrag** *m* POL, RECHT asylum application; **Asylbewerber** *m*, **Asylbewerberin** *f* POL, RECHT asylum seeker; **Asylrecht** *nt* POL, RECHT right to asylum, right to seek asylum; **Asylstaat** *m* POL, RECHT asylum

Asymmetrie *f* GESCHÄFT asymmetry

asymmetrisch: ~**e Auskunft** *f* VERSICH asymmetric information; ~**e Information** *f* VERSICH asymmetric information

asynchron *adj* COMP asynchronous; ~**e Kommunikation** *f* COMP asynchronous communication

Atelier *nt* GESCHÄFT studio; **Atelierleiter, in** *m,f* V&M *einer Werbeagentur* art manager

Atmosphäre *f* GESCHÄFT, UMWELT atmosphere

Atom- *in cpds* GESCHÄFT, IND, RECHT nuclear

atomistisch: ~**e Konkurrenz** *f* VW atomistic competition

Atom-: **Atomkraftwerk** *nt* IND nuclear power station; **Atommeiler** *m* IND nuclear reactor (*NR*); **Atommüll** *m* IND, UMWELT nuclear waste; **Atomprogramm** *nt* VW nuclear energy program (*AmE*), nuclear energy programme (*BrE*); **Atomrisiko-Versicherung** *f* RECHT nuclear risk insurance; **Atomwirtschaft** *f* GESCHÄFT nuclear-based industry

Attest *nt* GESCHÄFT bill of health; ~ **ohne gesundheitliche Einschränkungen** GESCHÄFT clean bill of health

attraktiv *adj* BÖRSE attractive, GESCHÄFT attractive, favorable (*AmE*), favourable (*BrE*); ~**es Angebot** *nt* GESCHÄFT attractive offer; ~**e Ausstattung** *f* GESCHÄFT *Schuldverschreibungen* attractive terms; ~**e Bedingungen** *f pl* GESCHÄFT attractive terms; ~**es Risiko** *nt* VERSICH target risk

Attraktivität *f* V&M appeal, attractiveness, sell; ~ **der Anzeigenaussage** V&M copy appeal

Attribut *nt* COMP attribute, IND attribute, qualitative characteristic; **Attributenkontrolle** *f* IND go-and-not-go gage (*AmE*), go-and-not-go gauge (*BrE*), sampling by attributes, MATH, MEDIEN attribute sampling

audio-visuell *adj* GESCHÄFT, KOMM, MEDIEN, V&M *Verkaufshilfen* audiovisual; ~**e Anzeige** *f* V&M audiovisual display; ~**e Ausrüstung** *f* V&M audiovisual equipment; ~**e Hilfen** *f pl* KOMM audiovisual aids; ~**es Hilfsmittel** *nt* COMP audiovisual aids; ~**e Unterstützung** *f* MEDIEN audiovisual aids

Audit *nt* FINANZ, RECHNUNG audit

Auditor *m* RECHNUNG auditor

aufaddieren *vt* MATH, RECHNUNG cast up

aufarbeiten *vt* GESCHÄFT recondition

Aufbau *m* GESCHÄFT structure; ~ **eines Netzwerks** GESCHÄFT network building; ~ **eines Unternehmens** GESCHÄFT company structure; **Aufbauanleihe** *f* FINANZ economic recovery loan (*ERL*)

aufbauen *vt* GESCHÄFT *Firma* build up, IND erect

aufbereiten *vt* COMP edit, GESCHÄFT recycle, IND process, VW organize

aufbereitet: ~**es Papier** *nt* GESCHÄFT recycled paper

Aufbereitung *f*: ~ **von Daten** COMP data editing, VW data organization; **Aufbereitungsanlage** *f* IND processing plant

aufbessern *vt* GESCHÄFT brush up, PERSON raise

Aufbewahrung *f* BANK safekeeping, BÖRSE custody, retention, RECHT safekeeping; ~ **von Aktien** BÖRSE custody of shares; **Aufbewahrungsfrist** *f* BÖRSE retention period; **Aufbewahrungsgebühr** *f* FINANZ safe deposit fee; **Aufbewahrungsstelle** *f* VERWALT repository; **Aufbewahrungsstelle** *f* **für postlagernde Sendungen** KOMM poste restante

aufbieten *vt* GESCHÄFT bring into play, call into play

aufblähen *vt* VW inflate

aufbrauchen *vt* GESCHÄFT finish completely, use up

aufbringen *vt* FINANZ cough up (*infrml*), put up, raise, stump up (*infrml*) (*BrE*)

Aufbringen *nt* VERSICH arrest

Aufdruck *m* V&M imprint

aufdrücken *vt* GESCHÄFT *Stempel* affix

Aufeinanderfolge *f* GESCHÄFT sequence

aufeinanderfolgend *adj* GESCHÄFT alternate, consecutive, successive, sequential; ~**e Einzahlungsaufforderungen** *f pl* FINANZ successive calls; ~**e Tage** *m pl* GESCHÄFT consecutive days

aufeinanderzubewegen: **sich** ~ *v refl* VW move together

Aufenthalt *m* GESCHÄFT stay, *Wohnsitz* domicile, residence; **Aufenthaltsgenehmigung** *f* POL green card (*AmE*), VERWALT residence permit, right of residence; **Aufenthaltsort** *m* RECHT *Wohnort* place of abode, place of residence; **Aufenthaltsräume** *m pl* GESCHÄFT rest rooms (*AmE*); **Aufenthaltsvisum** *nt* VERWALT residence visa

auferlegen *vt* GESCHÄFT *Restriktionen* impose, RECHT *Beschränkungen, Gesetze, Vorschriften, Geldstrafe, Steuer* impose, levy; ◆ **jdm etw** ~ GESCHÄFT, POL, VW impose sth on sb, inflict sth on sb

Auferlegung *f* GESCHÄFT imposition, RECHT levy

auffällig *adj* V&M eye-catching; ~**er Konsum** *m* VW conspicuous consumption

Auffang- *in cpds* BANK, FINANZ backing, backup

auffangen *vt* GESCHÄFT absorb, cushion, VW counterbalance

Auffang-: **Auffanggesellschaft** *f* PERSON rescue company; **Auffangkonsortium** *nt* FINANZ backing syndicate; **Auffang-Kreditlinie** *f* BANK backup credit line (*AmE*); **Auffanglinie** *f* BANK backup line

Auffassung *f* GESCHÄFT perception

aufflackern *vi* GESCHÄFT flare up; ◆ **jdn** ~ **lassen** *infrml* RECHT blow the whistle on sb (*infrml*)

auffordern: **jdn** ~, **etw zu tun** *phr* GESCHÄFT require sb to do sth

Aufforderung *f* GESCHÄFT calling, demand, request, RECHT invitation; ~ **zur Abgabe eines Angebots** RECHT invitation to treat; ~ **zur Angebotsabgabe** FINANZ appeal for tenders, request for proposals, RECHT *Vertragsrecht* invitation to make an offer, VERWALT call for tender; ~ **zur Einlösung von Wertpapieren** RECHNUNG call for redemption of securities; ~ **zur Nachbesserung** RECHT *Vertragsrecht* request for subsequent improvement

auffrischen *vt* COMP refresh, GESCHÄFT *Kenntnisse* brush up

auffrischend: ~e **Ausbildung** f COMP refresher training, PERSON booster training

aufführen vt COMP list

Aufführungsrechte nt pl RECHT performing rights

Auffüllung f GESCHÄFT build-up, replenishment; ~ **von Lagerbeständen** RECHNUNG *Material* inventory build-up, replenishment of inventories, stockbuilding; ~ **der Lagervorräte** VERWALT addition to stock

Aufgabe f COMP task, GESCHÄFT job, task, PATENT abandonment, PERSON *Arbeit, Pflicht* duty, job, abandonment, task, RECHT disclaimer, discontinuance; ~ **eines Anspruchs** VERSICH disclaimer; ~ **zur Post** COMP mailing; ~ **eines Rechts** GESCHÄFT remise; ~ **einer Stellung** PERSON abandonment of a position; ♦ **sich etw zur ~ machen** GESCHÄFT make sth one's business, make sth one's job

Aufgabe: **Aufgabenbereich** m GESCHÄFT area of responsibility, line of duty, sphere of activity, *eines Komitees* terms of reference; **Aufgabenerteilung** f GESCHÄFT task setting; **Aufgabengebiet** nt GESCHÄFT activity; **Aufgabeninitiierung** f COMP task initiation; **Aufgabenkreis** m GESCHÄFT scope of application, PERSON *Arbeitsplatzbeschreibung* scope of employment; **Aufgabenmanagement** nt COMP, MGMNT task management

aufgabenorientiert: ~e **Budgets** nt pl V&M mission budgets; ~e **Kostenerfassung** f V&M mission costing

Aufgabe: **Aufgabenstellung** f GESCHÄFT task setting, terms of reference; **Aufgabentrennung** f GESCHÄFT, MGMNT, PERSON segregation of duties; **Aufgabenverteilung** f GESCHÄFT, MGMNT, PERSON allocation, job assignment, *Arbeitsvorbereitung, Produktionsplanung* allocation of responsibilities, assignment of activities; **Aufgabenverwaltung** f COMP, MGMNT task management; **Aufgabenzuweisung** f GESCHÄFT, PERSON allocation of responsibilities; **Aufgabetag** m BÖRSE name day, ticket day (*BrE*), GESCHÄFT day of posting

aufgearbeitet adj GESCHÄFT reconditioned

aufgeben vt BÖRSE *Option* abandon, GESCHÄFT *Plan* abandon, relinquish, renounce, post, GRUND *Besitz* part with, PATENT waive, RECHT *Gebühr* waive, *Besitz* part with, *Anspruch* renounce, give up, abandon, disclaim, STEUER waive, VERSICH sacrifice

Aufgeben nt PATENT waiving, RECHT *Gebühr* waiving, disclaiming, giving up, renouncing, STEUER waiving

aufgebläht: ~e **Bilanz** f RECHNUNG blown-up balance sheet; ~e **Verpackung** f V&M slack fill

aufgegeben: ~er **Besitz** m RECHT *Herrenlosigkeit* vacant possession; ~es **Gepäck** nt TRANSP baggage checked, registered baggage, registered luggage

aufgegliedert adj GESCHÄFT *Rechnung* itemized

aufgehen vi GESCHÄFT, MATH *Zahlen, Ergebnisse* add up

aufgehoben adj GESCHÄFT closed, lifted, terminated, RECHT repealed, disaffirmed, VW lifted; **nicht ~** adj RECHT unrepealed

aufgelaufen adj BANK accrued, BÖRSE, FINANZ, RECHNUNG accrued, accumulated, TRANSP aground; ~e**, aber noch nicht ausgeschüttete Dividende** f BÖRSE accrued dividend; ~er **Betriebsgewinn** m RECHNUNG accumulated profits; ~e **Dividende** f BANK accrued dividend, BÖRSE accrued dividend, dividend in arrears, RECHNUNG accrued dividend; ~es **Einkommen** nt RECHNUNG accrued income; ~er **Gewinn** m RECHNUNG accumulated surplus; ~er **Verlust** m RECHNUNG accumulated deficit; ~e **Zinsen** m pl FINANZ accrued interest (*AI*), RECHNUNG accrual, accumulated interest; ~e **Zinseszinsen** m pl BANK accrued compound interest; ~e **Zinsforderungen** f pl RECHNUNG accrued interest receivable; ~e **Zinsverbindlichkeiten** f pl RECHNUNG accrued interest payable

Aufgeld nt BÖRSE agio, premium, *einer Kaufoption* time value, FINANZ agio, GESCHÄFT surcharge, extra charge, VW agio; **Aufgeldkonto** nt VW agio account

aufgelegt adj FINANZ issued for subscription, open for subscription

aufgelöst: ~e **Darstellung** f V&M exploded view

aufgenommen: ~es **Darlehen** nt RECHNUNG outstanding advance; ~e **Gelder** nt pl FINANZ creditor's account; ~es **Kapital** nt BANK borrowed capital; ~e **Kredite** m pl BANK borrowings; ~e **Mittel** nt pl FINANZ borrowed funds; ~ **sein in** phr [+acc] GESCHÄFT be integrated into

aufgerechnet adj FINANZ, RECHNUNG offset

aufgeschlüsselt adj GESCHÄFT broken down

aufgeschoben adj GESCHÄFT, PERSON, RECHNUNG, VERSICH deferred (*def.*); ~e **Ausgaben** f pl RECHNUNG deferred charge; ~e **Besteuerung** f FINANZ, STEUER deferred taxation; ~e **Gewinnbeteiligung** f PERSON deferred profit sharing; ~er **Gewinnverteilungsplan** m PERSON deferred contribution plan; ~e **Lohnerhöhung** f PERSON *Arbeit, Industrie* deferred wage increase; ~e **Pensionierung** f PERSON *Arbeit, Sozialwesen, Spätrente* deferred retirement; ~e **Rente** f VERSICH deferred annuity; ~e **Steuer** f FINANZ, STEUER deferred tax; ~e **Versicherungsleistungen und Zahlungen** f pl VERSICH deferred benefits and payments; ~e **Zahlungen** f pl FINANZ deferred payments; ~e **Zahlung** f **der Jahresrente** VERSICH deferred payment annuity

aufgestaut: ~e **Nachfrage** f VW pent-up demand; ~e **Penetrationspolitik** f V&M penetration pricing

aufgeteilt: ~er **Chartervertrag** m TRANSP split charter; ~er **Markt** m GESCHÄFT fragmented market

aufgezeichnet adj FREI, MEDIEN recorded

aufgliedern vt GESCHÄFT break down, classify, itemize, RECHNUNG break down

Aufgliederung f BÖRSE *eines Gesamtbetrages* break-out, GESCHÄFT break-out, breakdown, classification, itemization, RECHNUNG breakdown; ~ **in Abteilungen** GESCHÄFT departmentalization; ~ **der Bilanz** RECHNUNG account format; ~ **eines Gesamtbetrages** BÖRSE, GESCHÄFT breakout

aufgreifen: **etw ~** phr GESCHÄFT *Thema, Problem* address oneself to sth

aufgrund: ~ **von** prep GESCHÄFT on the strength of, PERSON on the basis of; ♦ ~ **von schlechten Nachrichten kaufen** BÖRSE buy on the bad news

aufhängen vt KOMM hang up

aufheben 1. vt FINANZ revoke, GESCHÄFT abolish, *Restriktionen* remove, *Urteil* annul, *Entscheidung* overrule, make void, *Embargo, Sanktionen* lift, override, raise, MATH cancel, POL *Entscheidung* overrule, override, RECHNUNG lift, abolish, cancel, RECHT *Vertrag* abrogate, disaffirm, nullify, rescind, terminate, *Gesetz* annul, repeal, reverse, strike down, *Beschränkungen* lift, *Urteil* supersede, *Vorschriften* avoid, cancel, VERWALT abolish, abrogate, VW abolish; **2. sich ~** v refl MATH, RECHNUNG cancel out

aufhebend adj RECHT *Klausel* annulling

Aufhebung f GESCHÄFT removal, abolition, annulment, avoidance, von Beschränkungen lifting, RECHNUNG abolition, RECHT eines Vertrags abrogation, disaffirmance, disaffirmation, nullification, rescission, termination, eines Gesetzes annulment, repeal, reversal, striking down, Beschränkungen lifting, eines Urteils supersedence, Vorschriften avoidance, cancellation VERWALT cancellation, abrogation, vw abolishment, abolition; **~ der Börsennotierung** BÖRSE delisting; **~ von Zöllen** vw abolition of tariffs; **Aufhebungserklärung** f RECHT declaration of avoidance; **Aufhebungsklage** f RECHT action for cancellation, action for rescission; **Aufhebungsrecht** nt RECHT Vertrag right of rescission; **Aufhebungsverfahren** nt RECHT Vertrag action for cancellation

aufholen vt BÖRSE rally, GESCHÄFT catch up, gain ground, pick up, verlorene Zeit make up, vw catch up

Aufholprozeß m vw catching-up process

aufhören vi GESCHÄFT cease

Aufkauf m BÖRSE, FINANZ buyout, Tochtergesellschaft durch Übernahme acquisition, GESCHÄFT buying-up, takeover, RECHNUNG durch Übernahme, vw acquisition; **~ durch die Belegschaft** FINANZ, PERSON Unternehmensschließung worker buyout

aufkaufen vt FINANZ corner, Unternehmen acquire, buy out, buy up, buy off

Aufkäufer m FINANZ cornerer, GESCHÄFT buyer, purchaser, speculative buyer, V&M purchaser

aufklären vt GESCHÄFT solve, investigate

Aufklärung f RECHT investigation; **Aufklärungspflicht** f RECHT duty to warn; **Aufklärungswerbung** f V&M educational advertising

aufkleben vt GESCHÄFT, KOMM, V&M affix

Aufkleber m GESCHÄFT adhesive label, sticker, KOMM, V&M sticker, stick-on label

Aufklebezettel m GESCHÄFT adhesive label, V&M facing

Aufkommen nt FINANZ, STEUER yield, revenue, proceeds; **~ an Steuern** FINANZ, STEUER revenue from taxes

Auflage f GESCHÄFT circulation, MEDIEN Druck print run, von Zeitungen oder Zeitschriften circulation, RECHT Bedingung burden, condition, requirement, modus, VERWALT print run, vw burden; **♦ mit der ~, daß** GESCHÄFT on condition that, on the stipulation that, with the stipulation that

Auflage: **Auflageneinbruch** m GESCHÄFT circulation breakdown; **Auflagenhöhe** f GESCHÄFT, MEDIEN von Zeitungen oder Zeitschriften circulation; **Auflagenüberwachungsstelle** m V&M Audit Bureau of Circulation

Auflassung f GRUND mit Eigentumsübertragung beim Grunderwerb closing, RECHT conveyance by agreement; **Auflassungsdatum** nt GRUND closing date; **Auflassungsklausel** f RECHT dingliche Übertragungsklausel habendum; **Auflassungskosten** pl GRUND bei Eigentumsübertragung von Grundstücken closing costs; **Auflassungsurkunde** f GRUND closing statement

auflaufen vi BANK, BÖRSE, FINANZ Schulden, RECHNUNG Zinsen accrue, accumulate, run on, TRANSP Schiff run aground, run ashore

Auflaufen nt BANK, BÖRSE, FINANZ, RECHNUNG accrual, accumulation; **~ von Zinsen** BANK, RECHNUNG accrual of interest

auflaufend adj FINANZ accruing

aufleben vi GESCHÄFT buck up (infrml), revive

auflegen **1.** vt BANK issue, FINANZ float, invite subscriptions, issue, launch, offer for subscription, GESCHÄFT announce, KOMM Telefonhörer put down, replace, hang up; **2.** vi KOMM on telephone hang up

Auflegung f BANK, FINANZ issue

auflisten vt COMP list, GESCHÄFT schedule

Auflistung f COMP listing, GESCHÄFT scheduling (AmE)

auflösen vt FINANZ close, unlock, GESCHÄFT break up, Parlament, Partnerschaft, POL dissolve, RECHNUNG release, withdraw, return to source, retransfer, write back, RECHT cancel, dissolve; **♦ jds Arbeitsvertrag ~** PERSON terminate sb's employment

auflösend: **~e Bedingung** f RECHT Vertrag condition subsequent (AmE), suspensive condition (BrE)

Auflösung f COMP Bildschirm, Drucker resolution, FINANZ absorption, closing, GESCHÄFT break-up, disintegration, dissolution, winding-up, PERSON eines Vertrags termination, dissolution, POL dissolution, RECHNUNG liquidation, retransfer, return to source, writing back, release, reversal (AmE), withdrawal, RECHT Gesellschaftsrecht dissolution, VERWALT break-up, vw disintegration; **~ der Aufteilung in Abteilungen** BÖRSE decompartmentalization; **Auflösungsgründe** m pl RECHT statutory grounds for dissolution; **Auflösungspreis** m BÖRSE exit price

aufmachen vt GESCHÄFT Firma start, VERSICH draw up

Aufmacher m MEDIEN splash, Druck lead

Aufmerksamkeit f GESCHÄFT, V&M die einem Produkt geschenkt wird attention; **~, Interesse, Wunsch, Aktion** GESCHÄFT attention, interest, desire, action (AIDA); **~ und Kontrolle** SOZIAL care and control; **♦ jds ~ erregen** GESCHÄFT attract sb's attention; **jds ~ erwecken** GESCHÄFT attract sb's attention; **jds ~ auf sich lenken** GESCHÄFT attract sb's attention; **seine ~ richten auf** [+acc] GESCHÄFT turn one's attention to; **jds ~ auf sich ziehen** GESCHÄFT attract sb's attention

Aufmerksamkeit: **Aufmerksamkeitsfaktor** m V&M attention factor

Aufnahme f BÖRSE einer neuen Emission take-up, von Wertpapieren assimilation, FINANZ von Schatzwechseln take-up, GESCHÄFT absorption, admission, MEDIEN von Sendungen außerhalb des Senders pick-up (jarg), pre-recorded broadcast, vw absorption; **zur ~ bewilligte Sache** POL item approved for inclusion; **~ von Fremdmitteln** GESCHÄFT borrowing external funds; **~ von Geldern** BANK borrowing; **~ in der Presse** V&M press reception; **Aufnahmeantrag** m BÖRSE application for admission (BrE); **Aufnahmebogen** m GESCHÄFT checklist

aufnahmefähig: **~er Markt** m BÖRSE Wertpapiere und Waren broad market, ready market

Aufnahme: **Aufnahmefähigkeit** f BÖRSE des Marktes absorbing capacity, GESCHÄFT absorptive capacity, des Marktes absorption capacity, vw absorption capacity, des Marktes absorptive capacity; **Aufnahmegebühr** m GESCHÄFT admission fee; **Aufnahmeland** nt VW receiving country; **Aufnahmeprüfung** f GESCHÄFT entrance examination

aufnehmen vt BANK Kredit, Darlehen obtain, borrow, take out, take up, BÖRSE Wertpapiere assimilate, Kredit borrow, FINANZ Geld obtain, put up, raise, GESCHÄFT Warenbestand absorb, Betrieb start up, Sitzung record,

MEDIEN record, PERSON *neue Geschäftspartner* admit, SOZIAL *Geld* take up, TRANSP *Inhalt* accommodate; ♦ **in sich ~** GESCHÄFT absorb

aufnehmend: ~e Bank *f* BANK borrowing bank

Aufpasser *m* BÖRSE, GESCHÄFT watchdog; **Aufpasser-Komitee** *nt* GESCHÄFT watchdog committee

aufpolieren *vt infrml* GESCHÄFT, V&M *Produkt, Image* revamp (*infrml*)

Aufprall *m* BÖRSE, GESCHÄFT crash, TRANSP crash, collision

Aufpreis *m* RECHNUNG extra charge

Aufräumungskosten *pl* VERSICH costs of clearance of debris

aufrechnen *vt* FINANZ offset, GESCHÄFT counterbalance, RECHNUNG counterbalance, offset, set against, RECHT set off; ♦ **etw gegen etw ~** RECHNUNG balance sth against sth

aufrechnend *adj* FINANZ, RECHNUNG offsetting

Aufrechnung *f* BANK settlement per contra, FINANZ offset, offsetting, RECHNUNG balancing against, counterbalancing, offset, offsetting, set-off, RECHT set-off; **Aufrechnungsdifferenz** *f* RECHNUNG set-off difference

aufrecht *adj* TRANSP upright

aufrechthalten *vt* GESCHÄFT preserve, RECHT uphold, VW sustain

aufrichtig *adj* GESCHÄFT honest, sincere

Aufrichtigkeit *f* GESCHÄFT honesty, sincerity

Aufriß *m* IND elevation

aufrollen *vt* COMP *Bildschirm* scroll up

Aufruf *m* COMP call, GESCHÄFT appeal; ♦ **~ richten an** GESCHÄFT appeal to

aufrufen *vt* [+acc] COMP call, FINANZ call in, call up, GESCHÄFT *Öffentlichkeit, Streik* appeal, VW call in

Aufruhr *m* POL civil commotion (*CC*), revolt, tumult, turmoil, uprising, VERSICH civil commotion (*CC*)

Aufrührer, in *m,f* GESCHÄFT insurgent

aufrunden *vt* GESCHÄFT even up, MATH *Zahl* round up

aufsaugen *vt* GESCHÄFT *Unternehmen* absorb

aufschieben *vt* GESCHÄFT *Entscheidung* put off, defer, *Plan* delay, *Projekt* shelve, *Treffen* postpone, MGMNT adjourn, PERSON, RECHNUNG defer

aufschiebend: ~e bedingte Lasten *f pl* STEUER conditional liabilities and burdens; **~e Bedingung** *f* RECHT condition precedent (*AmE*), suspensive condition (*BrE*); **~e Voraussetzung** *f* RECHT condition precedent (*AmE*), suspensive condition (*BrE*)

Aufschiebung *f* GESCHÄFT delay, deferral, postponement, MGMNT *einer Entscheidung* adjournment

Aufschlag *m* BÖRSE mark-up, FINANZ load, GESCHÄFT *Fracht, Gebühren, Preis, Tarif* surcharge, extra charge, recargo, premium, V&M mark-up; **Aufschlagskalkulation** *f* V&M mark-up pricing; **Aufschlagswert** *m* TRANSP surcharge value

aufschließen *vt* IND develop

aufschlüsseln *vt* GESCHÄFT allocate, apportion, break down, subdivide, *Klassifizierung* classify, subclassify, RECHNUNG break down, RECHT allocate

Aufschlüsselung *f* GESCHÄFT allocation, apportionment, breaking down, subdivision, *Klassifizierung* classification, subclassification, MGMNT *Zwecks Analyse*, PERSON breakdown; **~ der Forderungen nach Fälligkeit** RECHNUNG ageing of receivables

aufschreiben *vt* GESCHÄFT jot down, write down

Aufschrift *f* GESCHÄFT address, *Etikett* label, *auf Laden* name of business, MEDIEN lettering

Aufschub *m* GESCHÄFT deferment, delay, postponement, PATENT period of grace; ♦ **ohne ~** KOMM without respite; **~ gewähren** RECHT *internationales Vertragsrecht* grant a delay, grant respite

aufschwatzen: jdm etw ~ *phr infrml* GESCHÄFT talk sb into sth (*infrml*)

Aufschwung *m* GESCHÄFT boom, upturn, VW *der Wirtschaft* upswing, upturn; ♦ **der ~ ist im Gang** VW the recovery is under way

Aufseher, in *m,f* FINANZ comptroller, controller, MGMNT, PERSON supervisor, overseer

aufsetzen *vt* RECHT *Urkunde, Vertrag* draw, draw up

Aufsicht *f* GESCHÄFT care, supervision, MGMNT, PERSON supervision, VW control; ♦ **unter ~ der Behörden** POL government-regulated

Aufsicht: Aufsichtsamt *f* RECHT supervisory office, SOZIAL inspectorate; **Aufsichtsausschuß** *m* POL *EU* regulatory committee, watchdog committee; **Aufsichtsbeamte(r)** *m* [decl. as adj], **Aufsichtsbeamtin** *f* PERSON, V&M checker (*AmE*), supervisor (*BrE*)

Aufsichtsbehörde *f* GESCHÄFT *Durchführung* regulatory agency, watchdog, *Aufsichtsamt* inspectorate, *zuständig* regulatory authority, RECHT regulatory authority; **~ für Anlagenberatung** FINANZ Investment Management Regulatory Organization (*BrE*); **~ für Effektenverwaltung** FINANZ Investment Management Regulatory Organization (*BrE*)

aufsichtsführend: ~e Börse *f* **für Kommunalanleihen** BÖRSE municipal securities rulemaking board

Aufsicht: Aufsichtsgenehmigung *f* IMP/EXP surveillance licence (*BrE*) (*SL*), surveillance license (*AmE*) (*SL*); **Aufsichtspersonal** *nt* PERSON supervisory personnel; **Aufsichtsrat** *m* GESCHÄFT supervisory board, MGMNT board of directors, supervisory board, PERSON, RECHNUNG supervisory board; **Aufsichtsratmitglied** *nt* MGMNT top executive; **Aufsichtsratssitzung** *f* MGMNT board meeting; **Aufsichtsratssteuer** *f* STEUER directors' tax; **Aufsichtsratsvorsitzende(r)** *mf* [decl. as adj] MGMNT chairman of the board, chairman of the supervisory board; **Aufsichtsverwaltung** *f* MGMNT, PERSON supervisory management

aufspalten *vt* BANK split

Aufstand *m* POL insurrection

aufständisch *adj* POL insurgent

Aufständische(r) *mf* [decl. as adj] POL insurgent

aufsteigen *vi* PERSON be promoted, rise

aufstellen *vt* BANK *Konto* make up, GESCHÄFT *Bedingungen* set out, draw up, prepare, *Liste* make up, IND install, erect, PERSON post, RECHNUNG draw up, prepare, RECHT *Grundsätze, Regeln, Norm* lay down

Aufstellen *nt* RECHT *von Verbotsschildern* posting

Aufstellplakat *nt* V&M show card

Aufstellung *f* BANK making up, COMP tabulation, GESCHÄFT *Aufschlüsslung* breakdown, list, schedule (*AmE*), IND siting, installation, RECHNUNG drawing-up, preparation; **~ der Aktiven und Passiven** RECHNUNG statement of assets and liabilities; **~ einer Bilanz** RECHNUNG drawing up of a balance sheet, making-up of a balance sheet; **~ eines**

Haushaltsplanes RECHNUNG budgeting; ♦ **eine ~ anfertigen von** GESCHÄFT make a list of

Aufstellung: **Aufstellungsort** m COMP Gerät site licence (BrE), site license (AmE)

Aufstieg m PERSON advancement, ascendancy, career development, VW takeoff; **~ in der Leitungshierarchie** MGMNT executive advancement; **Aufstiegschancen** f pl PERSON career development prospects, scope for advancement; **mit Aufstiegschancen** phr GESCHÄFT Stellung upgradable

aufstockbar: **~e Hypothek** f BANK, FINANZ open mortgage, open-end mortgage, open-ended mortgage

aufstocken vt GESCHÄFT Ersparnisse top up (BrE), increase, scale up, build up

Aufstockung f GESCHÄFT increase, scaling-up; **Aufstockungsaktie** f FINANZ bonus share; **Aufstockungsklausel** f BANK Erhöhung eines Kredits oder einer Sicherheit topping-up clause (BrE)

aufstrebend adj GESCHÄFT sozial up-and-coming, upwardly mobile; **~e Wirtschaftsnationen** f pl VW Südostasien newly industrializing economies (NIEs)

aufsuchen vt GESCHÄFT call on

aufsummieren vt MATH add, add up

Auftabellierung f GESCHÄFT tabulation

Auftanken nt TRANSP refueling (AmE), refuelling (BrE)

auftauchen vi GESCHÄFT arise, emerge

aufteilen vt BANK split, FINANZ apportion, GESCHÄFT Bereiche, Unternehmen split up, anteilig festlegen apportion, zuteilen allocate, GRUND anteilig festlegen apportion, PATENT apportion, RECHNUNG divide, V&M partition, divide, VERWALT apportion, Bereiche, Unternehmen split up, VW Mittel, Gelder allocate; ♦ **Kosten ~** RECHNUNG assign costs

Aufteilung f BANK split, FINANZ apportionment, GESCHÄFT break-up, anteilige Festlegung apportionment, Zuteilung allocation, GRUND apportionment, MGMNT subdivision, PATENT apportionment, RECHNUNG apportionment, division, RECHT Grundbesitz distribution, V&M partition, carving-up, division, VERWALT break-up, partition, VW eines Marktes fragmentation; **~ von Immobilien in handelsfähige Einheiten** VW unitization; **~ der Kosten** RECHNUNG allocation of costs; **~ des Marktes in Schichten** V&M stratifying the market; **~ von Schäden auf mehrere Versicherer** VERSICH adjustment; **Aufteilungsplan erstellen** phr GRUND für Land plat; **Aufteilungssatz** m TRANSP proration rate

Auftrag m BÖRSE order, COMP job, GESCHÄFT Aufgabe task, order, Bestellung sales order, purchase order, Anweisung brief, contract, RECHNUNG purchase order, RECHT mandate, V&M order, mission; **~ mit Festpreisen** PERSON lump sum contract; **~ gültig bis zur Annullierung** BÖRSE good-till-canceled order (AmE) (GTC order), good-till-cancelled order (BrE) (GTC order); **~ zur sofortigen Ausführung** BÖRSE immediate-or-cancel order; **~ mit verschiedenen Frachtraten** IMP/EXP miscellaneous charges order (MCO); ♦ **im ~ von** (i.A.) GESCHÄFT order of (O/o); **einen ~ bearbeiten** VERWALT process an order; **im ~ Dritter handeln** RECHT act on sb's behalf; **für Aufträge** GESCHÄFT for orders (fo); **Aufträge ausführen** BÖRSE execute orders; **Aufträge beschaffen** GESCHÄFT solicit new business, secure new orders, VW attract new business; **Aufträge hereinholen** GESCHÄFT solicit new

business, secure new orders, VW attract new business; **in ~ geben** VW commission; **im ~ von jdm handeln** RECHT act on sb's behalf; **bei Aufträgen** GESCHÄFT for orders (fo); **an jdn einen ~ vergeben** GESCHÄFT let out a contract to sb

auftragen vt MATH Graph plot

Auftrag: **Auftraggeber, in** m,f BANK originator, COMP user, FINANZ principal, GESCHÄFT customer, client, RECHNUNG mandant, principal; **Auftragnehmer,in** m,f PERSON contractor; **Auftragsabwicklung** f COMP job handling, GESCHÄFT order filling, order handling, order processing; **Auftragsangebot** nt RECHT tender to contract (TTC); **Auftragsbericht** m MGMNT mission statement; **Auftragsbestand** m GESCHÄFT backlog of orders, backlog order books, backlogged orders, orders on hand, unfilled orders, V&M level of orders; **Auftragsbestätigung** f GESCHÄFT, KOMM acknowledgement of order, confirmation of order; **Auftragsboom** m GESCHÄFT boom in orders; **Auftragsbuch** nt GESCHÄFT order book; **Auftragsdurchführungsverordnung** f GESCHÄFT order regulation; **Auftragseingabe** f COMP job entry; **Auftragseingang** m GESCHÄFT booking of new orders, incoming business, inflow of orders, new orders, orders received, orders taken, rate of new orders, order intake, V&M order entry, vw new orders; **Auftragserteilung** f MGMNT award; **Auftragsfluß** m GESCHÄFT flow of orders; **Auftragsformular** nt V&M order form

auftragsgebunden: **~es Material** nt GESCHÄFT allocated material, apportioned material, assigned material, obligated material (AmE), reserved material

auftragsgemäß adj GESCHÄFT as per order

Auftrag: **Auftragskarte** f V&M order card; **Auftragsmißverhältnis** nt BÖRSE imbalance of orders; **Auftragsnummer** f FINANZ trade number, V&M order number; **Auftragsplanung** f IND job order planning; **Auftragsrückgang** m VW drop in orders; **Auftragsrückstand** m GESCHÄFT backlog, backlog of orders, unfilled orders; **Auftragssteuerung** f COMP job control; **Auftragssystem** nt V&M booking system; **Auftragsüberhang** m GESCHÄFT dead load; **Auftragsüberwachung** f GESCHÄFT order control; **Auftragsumfang** m GESCHÄFT volume of orders; **Auftragsvergabe** f GESCHÄFT allocation, contract award process, placing of orders; **Auftragswarteschlange** f COMP job queue; **Auftragsweg** m V&M channel for orders; **keine Auftragswerbung, sondern nur zur Information** phr BÖRSE not a solicitation, for information only; **Auftragswert** m BÖRSE contract value; **Auftragszugangsmuster** nt V&M order flow pattern

Auftrieb m GESCHÄFT, VW boost; **Auftriebskräfte** f pl VW buoyant forces

Aufwand m FINANZ Finanzbuchhaltung, GESCHÄFT, RECHNUNG, STEUER expense, VW cost, expenditure; **~ für wissenschaftliche Forschung** RECHNUNG, STEUER scientific research expenditure (BrE); ♦ **als ~ verbucht** RECHNUNG expensed; **als ~ verrechnen** RECHNUNG charge against the operations of an accounting period, charge as present operating cost, charge as an expense

Aufwand: **Aufwandsentschädigung** f GESCHÄFT expense allowance, reimbursement, representation allowance, PERSON Direktor benefits, VERWALT entertainment allowance; **Aufwands- und Ertragsrechnung** f

RECHNUNG income statement; **Aufwandskonto** *nt* RECHNUNG expense account; **Aufwandsposten** *m* RECHNUNG expense item

aufwärts 1. *adj* GESCHÄFT upwards; **2.** *adv* GESCHÄFT upward, upwards

Aufwärts- *in cpds* GESCHÄFT upward; **Aufwärtsbewegung** *f* BÖRSE rise, GESCHÄFT rise, upturn, upward movement, VW upside trend, uptrend; **Aufwärtsentwicklung** *f* VW upside trend, uptrend; **Aufwärtskompatibilität** *f* COMP upward compatibility; **Aufwärtsspirale** *f* GESCHÄFT upward spiral; **Aufwärtstrend** *m* VW upside trend, uptrend

aufwenden *vt* GESCHÄFT expend

Aufwendung *f* RECHNUNG expenses; **Aufwendungen** *f pl* FINANZ expenditure, outgoings, GESCHÄFT expenditure, RECHNUNG charges, VW expenditure; ◆ **Aufwendungen machen** RECHNUNG incur expenses

aufwerfen *vt* GESCHÄFT *Frage, Problem* pose

aufwerten *vt* GESCHÄFT upgrade, *Waren* valorize, RECHNUNG revalue, VW revalue, *Währung* appreciate

Aufwertung *f* FINANZ revaluation, GESCHÄFT valorization, *Währung* revaluation, upward revaluation, upvaluation, VW revalorization; **~ des Vermögens** RECHNUNG revaluation of assets; **~ der Währung** VW appreciation of currency, revaluation of exchange rate; **Aufwertungsdruck** *m* VW upward pressure; **Aufwertungsreserve** *f* RECHNUNG revaluation reserves; **Aufwertungssatz** *m* VW revaluation rate

aufzählen *vt* GESCHÄFT enumerate

Aufzählung *f* GESCHÄFT enumeration

aufzeichnen *vt* COMP record, GESCHÄFT *Geschäfte* record, transcribe, *notieren* note, take down, put down, MEDIEN, RECHNUNG record

Aufzeichnung *f* COMP recording, GESCHÄFT transcription, record, note, MEDIEN pick-up (*jarg*), prerecorded broadcast; **Aufzeichnungen** *f pl* RECHNUNG *Rechnungsprüfung*, VERWALT records

aufziehen *vi* COMP, MEDIEN *Bildschirmausschnitt* zoom out

Aufzinsung *f* FINANZ accumulation, act of recording, MATH accumulation; **Aufzinsungsfaktor** *m* MATH accumulation factor

Auge: in den Augen des Gesetzes *phr* RECHT in the eyes of the law; **jdm ins ~ sehen** *phr* GESCHÄFT face up to sb

Augenblick *m* GESCHÄFT moment; ◆ **aus dem ~ heraus** GESCHÄFT ad hoc

augenblicklich *adj* GESCHÄFT current, immediate, present

Augenblick: Augenblicksverband *m* RECHT single-purpose association

augenscheinlich: ~ guter Zustand *m* **der Waren** TRANSP apparent good order of the goods

Augenwischerei *f* infrml V&M eyewash

Augenzeuge *m* RECHT eye witness

Auktion *f* GESCHÄFT, RECHNUNG auction, sale at auction, V&M *öffentliche Versteigerung* public sale (*P/S*), auction, sale at auction, VW auction; **Auktionshammer** *m* GESCHÄFT gavel; **Auktionslokal** *nt* GESCHÄFT auction room; **Auktionsmarkt** *m* VW auction market; **Auktionspreis** *m* GESCHÄFT hammer price

aus *adv* COMP off

ausarbeiten *vt* GESCHÄFT draw up, prepare, PERSON *Kündigungsfrist* work out

Ausarbeitung *f* GESCHÄFT draft, memo (*infrml*), memor-

andum, paper, *Erstellung* preparation; **~ der Politik** GESCHÄFT, MGMNT *für bestimmtes Gebiet* policy formulation; **~ einer Strategie** GESCHÄFT, MGMNT strategy formulation

Ausbau *m* COMP *System* upgrade, upgrading

ausbaubar *adj* COMP *System* upgradeable

ausbauen *vt* COMP *System* upgrade

ausbaufähig *adj* COMP open-ended, MGMNT extensible

ausbedingen: sich ~ *v refl* GESCHÄFT, RECHT stipulate

ausbessern: nicht mehr auszubessern *phr* GESCHÄFT beyond repair

Ausbesserungen *f pl* GESCHÄFT maintenance and repair work

ausbeuten *vt* GESCHÄFT exploit, *Ressourcen* tap, PERSON *jarg* exploit, UMWELT exploit, *Ressourcen* tap, V&M milk, VW exploit

Ausbeutung *f* GESCHÄFT, UMWELT *von Ressourcen* exploitation, V&M *eines Unternehmens* milking strategy, VW *von Ressourcen* exploitation; **~ auf Wettbewerbsbasis** GESCHÄFT, UMWELT, VW competitive exploitation; **Ausbeutungsbetrieb** *m* PERSON sweatshop; **Ausbeutungsgrad** *m* FINANZ rate of exploitation

ausbilden: sich ~ lassen *v refl* PERSON train

Ausbildende(r) *mf* [decl. as adj] PERSON training officer

Ausbilder, in *m,f* PERSON *von Berufsanfängern* trainer

Ausbildung *f* GESCHÄFT training, PERSON education, instruction, training, SOZIAL education, educational background, schooling; **~ der Ausbilder** PERSON training of trainers; **~ von Führungskräften** GESCHÄFT, MGMNT, PERSON executive development, executive training; **Ausbildungsbedarf** *m* GESCHÄFT, V&M training needs; **Ausbildungsbedarfsanalyse** *f* V&M training needs analysis; **Ausbildungsbeihilfe** *f* PERSON training allowance, VERSICH educational endowment; **Ausbildungsentwicklung** *f* SOZIAL educational development; **Ausbildungslehrgang** *m* PERSON training course; **Ausbildungsleiter, in** *m,f* GESCHÄFT training officer, MGMNT training manager, PERSON training officer; **Ausbildungsmängel** *m pl* PERSON training needs; **Ausbildungspaket** *nt* MGMNT training pack; **Ausbildungsprogramm** *nt* IND, MGMNT training package, PERSON training package, training program (*AmE*), training programme (*BrE*), training scheme (*BrE*); **Ausbildungsstand** *m* PERSON level of training; **Ausbildungsstätte** *f* PERSON training center (*AmE*), training centre (*BrE*), teaching company; **Ausbildungszeitraum** *m* SOZIAL qualification period

Ausblick *m* GESCHÄFT perspective

ausbooten *vt* infrml GESCHÄFT boot out (*infrml*), kick out (*infrml*), get rid of

ausbreiten 1. *vt* GESCHÄFT spread; **2. sich ~** *v refl* GESCHÄFT spill over

Ausbreitungseffekt *m* VW spread effect

ausbuchen *vt* FINANZ balance, GESCHÄFT charge off, debit, enter a debit against, write off, RECHNUNG close out, write off, charge off, VERSICH write off

Ausbuchung *f* FINANZ balancing, write-off, debit, RECHNUNG charge off, closing out, write-off, balancing, debit

ausdehnen *vt* FINANZ expand, extend, GESCHÄFT *Befugnisse* expand, extend, widen

Ausdehnung *f* FINANZ, GESCHÄFT widening, expansion, extension

ausdiskutieren *vt* GESCHÄFT *Problem* discuss fully, thrash out (*infrml*)

Ausdruck *m* COMP *Programmiersprachen* expression, *Datenausgabe* hard copy, *Drucker* printout, VERWALT printout; ♦ **zum ~ bringen** GESCHÄFT express, signify

ausdrucken *vt* COMP print out

ausdrücken *vt* GESCHÄFT express

ausdrücklich: **~e Bedingungen** *f pl* GESCHÄFT express terms, express conditions, RECHT express conditions, express terms; **~es Beschreiben** *nt* **bei zugesicherten Eigenschaften** RECHT *Kaufvertrag* description of warranted qualities; **~e Garantie** *f* GESCHÄFT, RECHT express warranty; **~e Genehmigung** *f* RECHT express authority; **~er Vertrag** *m* RECHT explicit contract, express contract; **~e Vertragsvereinbarung** *f* PERSON express term; **~e Vollmacht** *f* RECHT *für ein Geschäft* express authority

ausdünnen *vt* GESCHÄFT reduce

auseinanderbrechen *vi* GESCHÄFT fall apart

auseinandergezogen: **~e Darstellung** *f* V&M exploded view

auseinandernehmen *vt* GESCHÄFT dismantle, take apart

auseinandersetzen: **sich mit jdm ~** *phr* GESCHÄFT have it out with sb

Auseinandersetzung *f* PERSON dispute; **~ mit der Gewerkschaft** PERSON *Arbeitskonflikt* trade dispute; **Auseinandersetzungsbilanz** *f* RECHNUNG balance sheet for settlement purposes

auseinanderziehen *vt* COMP *Graphikdarstellung* explode

auserlesen *adj* GESCHÄFT select, selected

auserwählt *adj* GESCHÄFT select, selected

Ausf. *abbr* (*Ausfuhr*) IMP/EXP, VW exp. (*export*)

Ausfall *m* COMP breakdown, FINANZ deficiency, financial loss, GESCHÄFT failure, TRANSP breakdown; **Ausfallbürgschaft** *f* RECHT, VERWALT indemnity bond

ausfallen *vi* COMP break down

Ausfall: **Ausfallquote** *f* GESCHÄFT failure rate, RECHNUNG delinquency ratio; **Ausfallrisiko** *nt* VW payment risk; **Ausfallurteil** *nt* RECHT deficiency judgment; **Ausfallverhalten** *nt* IND failure behavior (*AmE*), failure behaviour (*BrE*); **Ausfallzeit** *f* COMP *System*, IND downtime, outage time, VW downtime

ausfertigen *vt* BANK, FINANZ *Scheck* issue, GESCHÄFT copy, RECHT *Urkunde* draw up, write out, execute

Ausfertigung *f* BANK, FINANZ *Scheck* issue, GESCHÄFT copy, counterpart, RECHT execution; **Ausfertigungsdatum** *nt* VERSICH date of issue

ausfindig: **~ machen** *vt* PERSON scout out, search out

Ausflugsfahrkarte *f* FREI, TRANSP excursion ticket

Ausfluß *m* UMWELT effluent, efflux, leaking

ausfragen *vt* GESCHÄFT interrogate, quiz, sound out

Ausfuhr *f* (*Ausf.*) IMP/EXP, VW exporting, exporting, export (*exp.*); **Ausfuhrabteilung** *f* IMP/EXP outward freight department; **Ausfuhragent, in** *m,f* PERSON export agent; **Ausfuhranpassungskredit** *m* FINANZ export adjustment loan (*EAL*); **Ausfuhrbeihilfe** *f* IMP/EXP export subsidy; **Ausfuhrbewilligung** *f* IMP/EXP export licence (*BrE*), export license (*AmE*), export permit; **Ausfuhr-Einfuhr-Bank** *f* FINANZ, IMP/EXP export-import bank (*EXIM bank*)

ausführen *vt* BÖRSE execute, COMP *Befehl* execute, GESCHÄFT carry out, *entscheidung* put into execution, accomplish, execute, implement, IMP/EXP export, PATENT *Erfindung* carry out, VW export

ausführend *adj* POL, RECHT executive; **~e Gewalt** *f* POL, RECHT executive

Ausfuhr: **Ausfuhrerklärung** *f* GESCHÄFT export declaration, IMP/EXP clearance outwards; **Ausfuhrerstattung** *f* IMP/EXP refund; **Ausfuhrgenehmigung** *f* GESCHÄFT export authorization, IMP/EXP export licence (*BrE*), export license (*AmE*); **Ausfuhrgenehmigungskennzeichen** *nt* IMP/EXP export licence number (*BrE*), export license number (*AmE*)

ausfuhrgerecht *adj* IMP/EXP export-oriented

Ausfuhr: **Ausfuhrhandel** *m* IMP/EXP export trade, export business; **Ausfuhrkontingent** *nt* VW export quota; **Ausfuhrkredit** *m* IMP/EXP export credit; **Ausfuhrkreditversicherung** *f* IMP/EXP, VERSICH export credit insurance; **Ausfuhrkreditversicherungsanstalt** *f* IMP/EXP Export Credit Guarantees Department (*BrE*) (*ECGD*)

ausführlich 1. *adj* GESCHÄFT in depth, detailed; **2.** *adv* GESCHÄFT in depth; ♦ **~ beschreiben** GESCHÄFT describe in full detail, detail, VERWALT write out

ausführlich: **~e Berichterstattung** *f* MEDIEN *Rundfunk, Fernsehen, Presse* full coverage

Ausfuhr: **Ausfuhrmarkt** *m* IMP/EXP, VW export market; **Ausfuhrnachrichtendienst** *m* IMP/EXP export intelligence service (*BrE*) (*EIS*); **Ausfuhrpapiere** *nt pl* IMP/EXP export documentation; **Ausfuhrpolitik** *f* IMP/EXP export policy; **Ausfuhrquote** *f* VW export quota; **Ausfuhrregelung** *f* IMP/EXP export regulation; **Ausfuhrsendung** *f* IMP/EXP export consignment, outshipment, TRANSP outshipment; **Ausfuhrsperre** *f* IMP/EXP ban on export, embargo on exports; **Ausfuhrstopp** *m* IMP/EXP ban on export; **Ausfuhrüberschuß** *m* VW export surplus; **Ausfuhrüberwachung** *f* IMP/EXP export control

Ausführung *f* BÖRSE execution, COMP execution, GESCHÄFT *einer Aufgabe* undertaking, carrying out, accomplishment, achievement, *einer Anordnung* execution, implementation, performance, *Qualität* quality, PATENT carrying out, design, RECHT, VW *des Gemeinschaftsrechts* implementation; **~ der Politik** GESCHÄFT policy execution; **Ausführungsanzeige** *f* BÖRSE contract note, *bei Wertpapiergeschäften* advice of deal; **Ausführungsbestimmungen** *f pl* RECHT implementing regulations; **Ausführungsgrenzen** *f pl* GESCHÄFT scope of tender; **Ausführungsprogramm** *nt* UMWELT *Öl-, Gasförderung* completion program (*AmE*), completion programme (*BrE*); **Ausführungsverordnung** *f* GESCHÄFT regulation, RECHT implementing ordinance; **Ausführungszeit** *f* COMP execution time

Ausfuhr: **Ausfuhrverbot** *nt* IMP/EXP ban, export ban, export prohibition; **Ausfuhrvergütung** *f* STEUER export rebate; **Ausfuhrvertrag** *m* IMP/EXP export contract; **Ausfuhrvolumen** *nt* IMP/EXP, VW volume of exports; **Ausfuhrvorschriften** *f pl* IMP/EXP export regulations; **Ausfuhrzahlen** *f pl* IMP/EXP export figures

ausfüllen *vt* GESCHÄFT *Formular* fill in

Ausg. *abbr* BANK *Geld*, BÖRSE *Aktien* (*Ausgabe*) issue, COMP (*Ausgabe*) ed. (*edition*), *Daten* output, computer output, output data, FINANZ (*Ausgaben*) outgoings, *Kosten* issue, GESCHÄFT (*Ausgabe*) ed. (*edition*),

(*Ausgaben*) *Kosten* outlay, expenditure, expense, MEDIEN (*Ausgabe*) ed. (*edition*), copy number, issue
Ausgabe *f* (*Ausg.*) BANK *Geld*, BÖRSE *Aktien* issue, COMP *edition* (*ed.*), *Daten* output, computer output, FINANZ *money* issue, GESCHÄFT edition (*ed.*), *Kosten* outlay, number, expense, expenditure, MEDIEN copy number, edition (*ed.*), issue; ~ **von Gratisaktien** BÖRSE capitalization issue (*cap issue*), FINANZ bonus issue (*BrE*); ~ **von Wertpapieren** VW capitalization; ~ **einer Zeitung** GESCHÄFT copy, V&M run of paper (*ROP*); ♦ **die ~ auf sich nehmen** GESCHÄFT go to the expense of
Ausgabe: **Ausgabebudget** *nt* FINANZ appropriation act, appropriation bill, VW appropriation bill; **Ausgabedatei** *f* COMP output file; **Ausgabedaten** *nt pl* COMP output data; **Ausgabeermächtigung** *f* FINANZ spending authority, budget authority (*AmE*), total obligational authority (*BrE*) (*TOA*); **Ausgabegerät** *nt* COMP output device; **Ausgabekarte** *f* IND issue card; **Ausgabekurs** *m* BÖRSE bond issuing price; **Ausgabemarke** *f* GESCHÄFT issue voucher
Ausgaben *f pl* (*Ausg.*) FINANZ expenditure, outflows, outgoings, outlays, GESCHÄFT, VERWALT expenditure, VW expenditure, high-street spending (*BrE*), outlay; ~ **für Kapitalzuschüsse** FINANZ grants expenditures; ~ **der öffentlichen Hand** FINANZ, VW government expenditure, public expenditure; ~ **für Subventionen** FINANZ grants expenditures; ~ **für Werbung** V&M advertising expenditure, advertising expense; ♦ ~ **auf einen bestimmten Zeitraum abgrenzen** RECHNUNG apply expenses to a period; ~ **decken** GESCHÄFT cover expenses; ~ **kontrollieren** VW control spending, control the purse strings; ~ **kürzen** VW cut spending, make cuts in spending
Ausgaben: **Ausgabenansätze** *m pl* FINANZ *im Haushalt* estimates, expenditure estimates; **Ausgabenbefugnis** *f* POL spending authority; **Ausgabenbegrenzung** *f* BANK, PERSON, VW cash limit, spending limitation; **Ausgabenbeschränkung** *f* BANK, PERSON cash limit, VW cash limit, economic austerity; **Ausgabenbewilligung** *f* FINANZ budgetary appropriation, budget appropriation, RECHNUNG appropriation, authorization for expenditure; **Ausgabenetat** *m* FINANZ, GESCHÄFT, VW expenditure budget; **Ausgabenfunktion** *f* VW expenditure function; **Ausgabengrenze** *f* GESCHÄFT spending level, VW budget ceiling, spending target; **eine Ausgabengrenze überschreiten** *phr* FINANZ overspend a target; **Ausgabenhöhe** *f* GESCHÄFT spending level, VW level of expenditure; **Ausgabenkompetenz** *f* GESCHÄFT spending power; **Ausgabenkurve** *f* VW outlay curve; **Ausgabenmodelle** *nt pl* GESCHÄFT spending patterns; **Ausgabenmultiplikator** *m* VW expenditure multiplier; **Ausgabenplanung** *f* **des Ministeriums** VERWALT departmental expenditure plan; **Ausgabenreste** *m pl* VW unspent budget balances; **Ausgabenschema** *nt* GESCHÄFT spending patterns; **Ausgabensteuer** *f* STEUER, VW expenditure tax
Ausgabe: **Ausgabepreis** *m* FINANZ issue price, RECHNUNG asked price; **Ausgabeschalter** *m* VW delivery counter; **Ausgabetag** *m* VERSICH date of issue; **Ausgabewert** *m* FINANZ issue price
Ausgang *m* FINANZ outgoings, GESCHÄFT exit, *Ergebnis* outcome, result; **Ausgangsabgaben** *f pl* STEUER export duties and taxes; **Ausgangsdaten** *pl* COMP raw data; **Ausgangsdeklarierung** *f* IMP/EXP clearance outwards;

Ausgangskapital *nt* FINANZ initial capital; **Ausgangskasse** *f* V&M checkout, checkout lane; **Ausgangsland** *nt* IMP/EXP country of departure; **Ausgangsmaterial** *nt* IND raw material; **Ausgangspreis** *m* GESCHÄFT, STEUER base price; **Ausgangspunkt** *m* GESCHÄFT starting point; **Ausgangssprache** *f* KOMM source language; **Ausgangsversand** *m* TRANSP outward transit; **Ausgangszahl** *f* GESCHÄFT benchmark figure
ausgeben *vt* BANK, BÖRSE issue, COMP *Daten, Anweisungen* output, *Speicherinhalt* dump, FINANZ issue, GESCHÄFT expend, spend, lay out, pay out, disburse, V&M *Geld* spend; ♦ **sich ~ als** GESCHÄFT pass oneself off as; **zuviel ~** FINANZ, RECHNUNG, VW overspend; **zu wenig ~** FINANZ, POL, VW underspend
ausgebeutet *adj* PERSON exploited; ~**e Arbeiter** *m pl* GESCHÄFT, PERSON exploited workers, sweatshop labor (*AmE*), sweatshop labour (*BrE*)
ausgebildet *adj* PERSON *Arbeit, Lebenslauf* educated
ausgebucht *adj* FREI, GESCHÄFT, TRANSP *Hotel* booked up, RECHNUNG charged off, expensed (*AmE*), written off, VERSICH written off
ausgedehnt *adj* FINANZ extended, GESCHÄFT extended, widened
ausgedient *adj* GESCHÄFT worn out, clapped out (*infrml*) (*BrE*), PERSON retired
ausgefallen: ~**e Dividende** *f* RECHNUNG omitted dividend; ~**e Größen** *f pl* IND *Produktion* odd sizes
ausgeflossen: ~**es Öl** *nt* UMWELT oil spillage
ausgeführt *adj* GESCHÄFT executed (*ex*)
ausgegeben *adj* BANK, BÖRSE, FINANZ issued; **nicht ~** *adj* FINANZ unexpended; ~**e Aktien** *f pl* BÖRSE outstanding shares, issued shares; ~**es Aktienkapital** *nt* BÖRSE outstanding capital stock, issued share capital, FINANZ, RECHNUNG issued share capital; **nicht ~es Aktienkapital** *nt* BÖRSE unissued capital stock; ~ **und ausstehend** *phr* BÖRSE issued and outstanding; ~**es Kapital** *nt* BÖRSE capital stock issued, outstanding capital stock, GESCHÄFT subscribed capital
ausgeglichen *adj* FINANZ offset, GESCHÄFT in-balance, in-line, on an even keel, PERSON level-headed, RECHNUNG balanced, offset; **nicht ~** *adj* FINANZ, GESCHÄFT undischarged; ~**es Budget** *nt* FINANZ balanced budget, in-balance budget, in-line budget, POL neutral budget; ~**er Haushalt** *m* FINANZ balanced budget, in-balance budget, in-line budget, VW balanced budget; ~**es Konto** *nt* RECHNUNG account in balance, closed account
ausgehandelt: ~**er Marktpreis** *m* VW negotiated market price; ~**er Preis** *m* V&M, VW negotiated price; ~**e Risikoübernahme** *f* BÖRSE negotiated underwriting
ausgehängt: ~**er Preis** *m* VW displayed price
ausgehend: ~**e Ladung** *f* IMP/EXP outward cargo; ~**e Post** *f* KOMM outgoing mail
ausgelaufen *adj* GESCHÄFT expired
ausgeleiert *adj* GESCHÄFT clapped out (*BrE*) (*infrml*)
ausgeliehen: ~**e Mittel** *nt pl* BANK borrowed reserves
ausgelöst *adj* GESCHÄFT expunged
ausgelost: ~**e Anleihe** *f* BÖRSE drawn bond; ~**e Obligation** *f* BÖRSE drawn bond
ausgenommen *prep* GESCHÄFT apart from, except, excepted, with the exception of, exclusive of (*ex*)
ausgepreist: **nicht ~** *adj* GESCHÄFT *Ware* unpriced

ausgerichtet *adj* COMP *Text* justified, GESCHÄFT directed at, tailored, V&M tailored; **nicht ~** *adj* COMP *Text* unjustified; ◆ **~ auf [+acc]** GESCHÄFT directed at

ausgeschaltet *adj* COMP disabled, GESCHÄFT switched off, eliminated

ausgeschieden: **~es Wirtschaftsgut** *nt* STEUER retired asset

ausgeschlossen *adj* GESCHÄFT eliminated; **~er Aktionär** *m*, **~e Aktionärin** *f* GESCHÄFT expelled shareholder; **~er Bereich** *m* IND excluded sector

ausgeschrieben: **nicht ~** *adj* GESCHÄFT unadvertised; **nicht ~e Stelle** *f* GESCHÄFT unadvertised job

ausgeschüttet: **~e, aber noch nicht ausgezahlte Dividende** *f* FINANZ unpaid dividend; **~e Dividende** *f* FINANZ cash dividend; **~er Gewinn** *m* FINANZ, RECHNUNG distributed profit; **nicht ~er Gewinn** *m* FINANZ undistributed profit; **nicht ~e Gewinne** *m pl* FINANZ retained profits, RECHNUNG retained income; **nicht ~er Zins** *m* FINANZ undivided interest

ausgesetzt: **~er Handel** *m* BÖRSE suspended trading; **~e Steuerfestsetzung** *f* STEUER suspended tax assessment; **~e Strafe** *f* RECHT suspended sentence

ausgesperrt *adj* PERSON locked-out

ausgesprochen: **~ bedürftig** *adj* SOZIAL categorically needy

Ausgestaltungsform *f* RECHT form

ausgestellt: **~ in** *phr* BANK made out in; **~e Rechnung** *f* BANK account rendered

ausgestrichen *adj* GESCHÄFT expunged

ausgesucht: **~e Häfen** *m pl* TRANSP picked ports (*pp*)

ausgeweitet *adj* VW expanded

ausgewiesen *adj* GESCHÄFT accounted for, *Gewinn* reported, stated, POL *Person* expelled; **nicht ~** *adj* GESCHÄFT unaccounted for; **~e Dividende** *f* FINANZ declared dividend; **~e eigene Mittel** *nt pl* RECHNUNG reported equity; **~es Eigenkapital** *nt* RECHNUNG reported equity capital; **~e Flächen** *f pl* **mit besonderem Entwicklungsstatus** VW enterprise zone (*EZ*); **~er Gewinn** *m* RECHNUNG reported earnings, reported income, recognized profit; **~es Kapital** *nt* RECHNUNG stated capital; **~e Kosten** *pl* VW explicit cost; **~e Marktinformationen** *f pl* BÖRSE recorded market information; **~er Wert** *m* RECHNUNG stated value

ausgewogen: **~e Mischung** *f* IND blending; **~er Wertpapierbestand** *m* BÖRSE balanced portfolio

ausgezahlt: **~er Betrag** *m* RECHNUNG amount paid out; **~e Geldmittel** *nt pl* FINANZ money paid out

ausgezeichnet *adj* PERSON excellent; ◆ **über ~e Referenzen verfügen** PERSON have excellent references; **über ~e Zeugnisse verfügen** PERSON have excellent references

Ausgleich *m* FINANZ offset, offsetting, GESCHÄFT adjustment, *eines Kontos* balance, *von Mangel* compensation, equalization, *einer Summe* settlement, squaring, RECHNUNG offset, offsetting, *eines Kontos* reconciliation, VW compensation, *zwischen Wachstum und Rentabilität* trade-off; **~ von Einnahmen und Ausgaben** FINANZ equalization of revenue and expenditure; **~ der Grenznutzen** VW consumer equilibrium; **zum ~ des Lohngefälles** PERSON compensating wage differential; ◆ **zum ~ verkaufen** BÖRSE evening up, selling for the settlement

ausgleichen 1. *vt* BANK *Konto* balance, settle, balance out, FINANZ average out, offset, *Konto* balance, balance out, settle, GESCHÄFT *Summe, Zahlen* balance, balance out, cancel out, compensate, equalize, even out, level out, make up, recoup, settle, RECHNUNG *Konto* balance, balance out, offset, reconcile, VW *Fluktuationen* make up, trade off, smooth out; ◆ **etw mit etw ~** GESCHÄFT balance sth with sth, balance sth against sth; **2. sich ~** *v refl* GESCHÄFT level up RECHNUNG balance out

ausgleichend *adj* BÖRSE compensating, GESCHÄFT balancing, compensating, equalizing, RECHNUNG offsetting; **~er Fehler** *m* RECHNUNG offsetting error; **~e Lohnerhöhung** *f* PERSON catch-up increase; **~e Lohnzulage** *f* VW equalizing wage differential

Ausgleich: **Ausgleichsabgabe** *f* IMP/EXP compensatory levy, equalization levy, STEUER compensatory tax, compensation tax; **Ausgleichsanleihe** *f* **für Industrie- und Handelspolitik** FINANZ industrial and trade policy adjustment loan (*ITPAL*); **Ausgleichsanspruch** *m* RECHT claim for adjustment; **Ausgleichsarbitrage** *f* FINANZ foreign exchange arbitrage; **Ausgleichsbehörde** *f* STEUER board of equalization; **Ausgleichsbilanz** *f* BANK compensating balance; **Ausgleichsbuchung** *f* BANK charge back, RECHNUNG offsetting entry; **Ausgleichseffekt** *m* PERSON catch-up effect; **Ausgleichsfinanzierung** *f* GESCHÄFT, KOMM compensatory financing, POL compensatory finance, compensatory financing, VW *Mechanismen für Zahlungsbilanzungleichgewichte* compensatory financing; **Ausgleichsfonds** *m* BÖRSE compensation fund (*BrE*), IMP/EXP Exchange Stabilization Fund, VERSICH equalization fund; **Ausgleichslager** *nt* VW buffer stock, buffer store, equalization store; **Ausgleichsplan** *m* **der Anleger** BÖRSE investors' compensation scheme (*BrE*); **Ausgleichsposten** *m* RECHNUNG per contra item, offsetting item, VW balancing item; **Ausgleichsstandard** *m* GESCHÄFT standard of equalization; **Ausgleichsstelle** *f* STEUER board of equalization; **Ausgleichssteuer** *f* POL corrective tax, STEUER turnover equalization tax; **Ausgleichstabelle** *f* RECHNUNG reconciliation table; **Ausgleichstransaktionen** *f pl* VW accommodating transactions; **Ausgleichsverlust** *m* BÖRSE compensating loss (*BrE*); **Ausgleichsvorrat** *m* TRANSP buffer stock; **Ausgleichszahlung** *f* FINANZ deficiency payment, equalization payment, IMP/EXP *EG, Export* compensatory levy, STEUER compensatory payment; **Ausgleichszoll** *m* IMP/EXP compensating tariff, contingent duty, countervailing duties, matching duty; **Ausgleichszugeständnisse** *nt pl* IMP/EXP compensatory concessions; **Ausgleichszuschuß** *m* FINANZ matching grant, POL, VW corrective subsidy

Ausgleichung *f* FINANZ reconciliation

ausgliedern *vt* GESCHÄFT hive off

Ausgliederung *f* GESCHÄFT, VW *eines Unternehmensbereichs* spin-off; **~ von Betriebsteilen** GESCHÄFT hive-off; **~ eines Unternehmensbereiches** FINANZ spin-off

ausgründen *vt* VW hive off

aushandelbar: **~er Punkt** *m* PERSON negotiable issue

aushandeln *vt* BANK *Kredit* arrange, negotiate, BÖRSE, GESCHÄFT, PERSON negotiate, RECHT plea-bargain

Aushändigung *f* GESCHÄFT delivery, handing over

Aushilfe *f* PERSON fill-in, transient worker, temporary worker, temp (*infrml*)

Aushilfs- *in cpds* GESCHÄFT, PERSON temporary; **Aushilfsarbeit** *f* GESCHÄFT, PERSON temporary employment, temporary work; **Aushilfskraft** *f*

GESCHÄFT, PERSON casual worker, fill-in, temporary worker, temp (*infrml*), casual laborer (*AmE*), casual labourer (*BrE*); **Aushilfssekretär, in** *m,f* PERSON temp (*infrml*), temporary secretary; **als Aushilfssekretär arbeiten** *phr* PERSON, GESCHÄFT temp (*infrml*), work as a temp (*infrml*)

aushöhlen *vt* BÖRSE, GESCHÄFT, RECHT, VW *Kaufkraft* erode

Aushöhlung *f* BÖRSE GESCHÄFT, RECHT, VW erosion; **~ eines Gesetzes** RECHT dismantling of a law; **~ der Steuerbasis** VW tax erosion; **Aushöhlungseffekt** *m* VW backwash effect

auskalkulieren *vt* GESCHÄFT make a complete estimate of

auskämmen *vt* GESCHÄFT weed out

auskaufen *vt* FINANZ buy out

Ausklinkprinzip *nt* RECHT release principle

auskömmlich *adj* GESCHÄFT adequate, comfortable, sufficient

Auskunft *f* KOMM *Telefonvermittlungsstelle* directory assistance, directory enquiries (*BrE*), directory information (*AmE*), telephone operator

Auskunftei *f* FINANZ credit reference agency, GESCHÄFT commercial agency, V&M mercantile agency, VERWALT *Auskunftsbüro* enquiry office

Auskunft: **Auskunftsersuchen** *nt* RECHT request for information; **Auskunftspflicht** *f* GESCHÄFT duty to disclose information; **Auskunftsrecht** *nt* POL right to information, right to know; **Auskunftsschalter** *m* GESCHÄFT enquiry desk; **Auskunftssperre** *f* FINANZ Chinese walls; **Auskunftsstelle** *f* GESCHÄFT information bureau, information office; **Auskunftsstellen** *f pl* **für den Außenhandel** IMP/EXP foreign trade information agencies

ausladen *vt* GESCHÄFT discharge, unload, IND offload, TRANSP offload, unload

Ausladen *nt* GESCHÄFT, IND offloading, discharging, unloading, TRANSP offloading, stripping, unloading

Ausladung *f* GESCHÄFT, IND unloading, offloading, TRANSP offloading, unshipment

Auslage *f* GESCHÄFT window display, KOMM display, V&M shop front, window display; **Auslagen** *f pl* GESCHÄFT, RECHNUNG expenses, outlays, VW outlay; **Auslagendekoration** *f* GESCHÄFT, V&M window-dressing; **Auslagenersatz** *m* GESCHÄFT reimbursement

Auslagerungsvermerk *m* IMP/EXP removal note

Ausland *nt* GESCHÄFT foreign country; **im ~ getätigte Übernahme** *f* FINANZ offshore takeover; **im ~ tätige Führungskraft** *f* GESCHÄFT expatriate executive; **im ~ tätiger Mitarbeiter** *m*, **im ~ tätige Mitarbeiterin** *f* GESCHÄFT expatriate employee; **im ~ verdientes Einkommen** *nt* STEUER income earned overseas; ♦ **im ~** GESCHÄFT abroad; **im In- und ~** GESCHÄFT at home and abroad

Ausländer, in *m,f* GESCHÄFT foreigner, RECHT *Fremder* alien; **~ mit Aufenthaltsgenehmigung** VERWALT *Fremdarbeiter* resident alien; **Ausländeranmeldeschein** *m* VERWALT alien registration card (*AmE*); **Ausländerkonto** *nt* VW external account; **Ausländerrecht** *nt* RECHT law relating to nonresidents

ausländisch *adj* BANK, FINANZ offshore, GESCHÄFT foreign, from abroad, overseas; ♦ **in ~em Besitz** BANK, GESCHÄFT, TRANSP foreign-owned

ausländisch: **~er Arbeitnehmer** *m*, **~e Arbeitnehmerin** *f* PERSON, VW foreign employee, foreign worker, guest-worker, immigrant worker, migrant worker, migratory worker; **~er Arbeitsmarkt** *m* VW external labor market (*AmE*), external labour market (*BrE*); **~er Bankplatz** *m* BANK offshore place; **~e Betriebsstätte** *f* STEUER permanent establishment abroad; **~e Direktinvestition** *f* FINANZ, VW direct foreign investment (*DFI*), direct outward investment, foreign direct investment (*FDI*); **~er Direktinvestor** *m* FINANZ inward investor; **~es Einkaufshaus** *nt* IMP/EXP foreign buying house; **~e Einkünfte** *pl* STEUER foreign-source income; **~er Emittent** *m*, **~e Emittentin** *f* FINANZ nonresident issuer; **~e Erzeugnis** *nt* GESCHÄFT foreign product; **~e Erzeugnisse** *nt pl* GESCHÄFT goods of foreign origin; **~es Fabrikat** *nt* GESCHÄFT foreign product; **~e Gesellschaft** *f* RECHT foreign corporation, out-of-state corporation, alien corporation; **~e große Havarie** *f* GESCHÄFT foreign general average (*f.g.a.*); **~er Investor** *m* VW overseas investor; **~e Regierungen** *f pl* GESCHÄFT overseas governments; **~e(r) Staatsangehörige(r)** *mf* [decl. as adj] PERSON foreign national; **~e Tochtergesellschaft** *f* GESCHÄFT, RECHT, STEUER foreign subsidiary; **~es Unternehmen** *nt* GESCHÄFT foreign company; **~es Vermögen** *nt* GESCHÄFT assets held abroad; **~e Währungseinheit** *f* VW foreign currency unit

Ausland: **Auslandsabsatz** *m* GESCHÄFT, V&M foreign sales; **Auslandsabteilung** *f* BÖRSE foreign section, FINANZ, PERSON foreign operations department, international department; **Auslandsaktiva** *nt pl* GESCHÄFT assets held abroad, VW overseas assets; **Auslandsanleihe** *f* FINANZ external loan, foreign bond, foreign loan; **Auslandsauftrag** *m* GESCHÄFT order from abroad; **Auslandsbank** *f* BANK foreign bank; **Auslandsbankgeschäfte** *nt pl* BANK foreign banking; **Auslandsbesitz** *m* VW nonresident's holding; **in Auslandsbesitz befindliches Unternehmen** *nt* GESCHÄFT foreign-controlled enterprise; **Auslandsbeteiligung** *f* FINANZ, GESCHÄFT associated company abroad, foreign participation; **Auslandsbeziehungen** *f pl* GESCHÄFT external relations; **Auslandsdelegation** *f* V&M inwards mission; **Auslandsdividenden** *f pl* BÖRSE foreign dividends; **Auslandseinkünfte** *pl* STEUER income earned overseas; **Auslandseinlage** *f* FINANZ nonresident deposit; **Auslandsfiliale** *f* BANK foreign branch; **Auslandsgeldanweisung** *f* BANK international money draft; **Auslandsgelder** *nt pl* FINANZ, VW external funds; **Auslandsgeschäft** *nt* GESCHÄFT international business; **Auslandgespräch** *nt* KOMM international call; **Auslandsguthaben** *nt pl* BANK balances abroad, foreign assets, funds abroad, nonresident deposits; **Auslandshilfe** *f* VW external economic aid, foreign aid, overseas aid; **Auslandsinvestition** *f* VW foreign investment; **Auslandskonkurrent** *m* VW foreign competitor; **Auslandskonto** *nt* BANK foreign account, VW external account; **Auslandskorrespondent, in** *m,f* MEDIEN foreign correspondent; **Auslandskredit** *m* VW foreign loan; **Auslandslagebericht** *m* IMP/EXP overseas status report; **Auslandsliefervertrag** *m* RECHT international sales contract; **Auslandsmarkt** *m* GESCHÄFT, VW foreign market, external market; **Auslandsnachfrage** *f* VW foreign demand; **Auslandsniederlassung** *f* BANK foreign branch, overseas branch, GESCHÄFT foreign branch, IMP/EXP foreign branch, overseas branch; **Auslandsporto** *nt* KOMM overseas postage; **Auslandspostanweisung** *f* BANK, KOMM *Vertragsrecht* international money order (*IMO*);

Auslandsscheckausgabe *f* BANK foreign check issue (*AmE*), foreign cheque issue (*BrE*); **Auslandsschulden** *f pl* FINANZ, RECHNUNG, VW external borrowings, external debts, external liabilities; **Auslandsschuldner**, in *m,f* FINANZ, RECHNUNG, VW external debtor; **Auslandstarifbestimmung** *f* IMP/EXP overseas tariff regulation; **Auslandstarife** *m pl* **und -bestimmungen** *f pl* IMP/EXP overseas tariff and regulations (*OTAR*); **Auslandstourismus** *m* FREI overseas tourism; **Auslandstrust** *m* RECHT offshore trust; **Auslandsumsatz** *m* IMP/EXP export turnover; **Auslandsunternehmen** *nt* GESCHÄFT foreign firm; **Auslandsunternehmung** *f* GESCHÄFT foreign venture; **Auslandsventure** *nt* GESCHÄFT foreign venture; **Auslandsvermögen** *nt* GESCHÄFT assets held abroad; **Auslandsverschuldung** *f* FINANZ, VW external debt, external borrowings; **Auslandsverschuldungsgrad** *m* FINANZ, VW external debt ratio; **Auslandsvertreter, in** *m,f* GESCHÄFT foreign agent, foreign representative, overseas agent; **Auslandswechsel** *m* BANK external bill, foreign bill; **Auslandswerte** *m pl* VW foreign assets; **Auslandszahlung** *f* FINANZ outward payment; **Auslandszulage** *f* PERSON foreign service pay

auslassen *vt* GESCHÄFT omit

Auslassen *nt* GESCHÄFT omission

Auslassung *f* GESCHÄFT omission

auslasten *vt* GESCHÄFT *Maschinen* make full use of, use to capacity, TRANSP load; ♦ **nicht ~** GESCHÄFT *Maschinen* underuse

Auslastung *f* IND operating rate, TRANSP load factor; **~ des Fuhrparks** TRANSP fleet utilization; **Auslastungsfaktor** *m* MATH, TRANSP, VW load factor; **Auslastungsgrad** *m* **von Arbeitskräften** PERSON overall performance

auslastungsorientiert: **~e Kostenrechnung** *f* RECHNUNG activity-based costing (*BrE*)

Auslauf *m* VERSICH run off; **Auslaufeffekt** *m* GESCHÄFT spill-off effect

auslaufen *vi* GESCHÄFT die, expire, run out, STEUER *Steuervergünstigung* taper, VW taper off; ♦ **~ lassen** COMP *Modell* phase out, GESCHÄFT *Produktion* phase out, wind up

Auslaufen *nt* GESCHÄFT phase-out, TRANSP sailing

Auslauf: **Auslaufhafen** *m* GESCHÄFT embarkation port; **Auslaufmonat** *m* BÖRSE expiration month; **Auslaufrhythmus** *m* BÖRSE expiration cycle; **Auslaufsphase** *f* VW phase-out period; **Auslaufware** *f* V&M end-of-line goods

auslegen *vt* GESCHÄFT, GRUND, IND construct, KOMM, RECHT interpret

Auslegung *f* GESCHÄFT, GRUND, IND construction, KOMM, RECHT *eines Gesetzes* interpretation; **Auslegungsrichtlinien** *f pl* RECHT interpretative regulations, interpretive regulations

ausleihen *vt* BÖRSE, FINANZ lend; ♦ **~ an** [+acc] BANK lend to

Ausleihung *f* BANK lending; **Ausleihungen** *f pl* BANK asset exposure, bank lending, FINANZ assets, lendings, total amount loaned

ausleihungsfähig: **~e Mittel** *nt pl* BANK, FINANZ lendable funds

Auslese *f* GESCHÄFT selection

Auslieferung *f* GESCHÄFT, TRANSP delivery; **Auslieferungsanpruch** *m* TRANSP claim to delivery, right to delivery; **Auslieferungsauftrag** *m* TRANSP delivery order (*D/O*); **Auslieferungskosten** *pl*, **-fracht** *f* **und -versicherung** *f* TRANSP cost insurance freight landed; **Auslieferungsspediteur** *m* TRANSP delivering carrier; **Auslieferungsversprechen** *nt* TRANSP promise to deliver

Auslösemechanismus *m* GESCHÄFT trigger mechanism

auslösen *vt* COMP *Vorgang* initiate, GESCHÄFT *Panik, Streit* ignite, set off, trigger, spark off, *Reaktion* set off, trigger, expunge

auslösend: **~er Impuls** *m* GESCHÄFT adjustment trigger

Auslosung *f* VW prize competition

Auslösung *f* BANK redemption, PERSON severance payment, termination payment, RECHT bail; **Auslösungsrecht** *nt* BANK equity of redemption

ausmachen *vt* GESCHÄFT arrange

ausmachend: **~er Betrag** *m* FINANZ actual amount

ausmisten *vt infrml* GESCHÄFT muck out (*infrml*)

Ausnahme *f* GESCHÄFT exception; ♦ **mit ~ von** GESCHÄFT with the exception of; **eine ~ machen** GESCHÄFT make an exception

Ausnahme: **Ausnahmebescheinigung** *f* IND certificate of occupancy; **Ausnahmeklausel** *f* TRANSP exceptions clause

ausnehmen *vt* GESCHÄFT milk (*infrml*), raid, make an exception of

ausnutzen *vt* GESCHÄFT exploit, utilize, take advantage of, PATENT work, PERSON exploit

Ausnutzung *f* FINANZ, GESCHÄFT exploitation

Ausnutzungsgrad *m* GESCHÄFT utilization percent, IND operating rate, plant utilization rate, rate of capacity utilization

auspacken *vt* GESCHÄFT unpack, unwrap, RECHT denounce, TRANSP unload, unwrap

ausprägen *vt* VW coin, mint

auspressen *vt infrml* GESCHÄFT bleed (*infrml*), squeeze dry

ausprobieren *vt* GESCHÄFT test, try out

Auspuffemissionen *f pl* UMWELT car exhaust emissions

ausquetschen *vt infrml* GESCHÄFT bleed (*infrml*)

ausradieren *vt* GESCHÄFT erase, rub out, wipe out

ausräumen *vt* GESCHÄFT smooth out

ausrechnen *vt* GESCHÄFT calculate, work out

ausreichen *vi*: **~ an** [+acc] BANK lend to

ausreichend 1. *adj* FINANZ adequate, GESCHÄFT adequate, sufficient, RECHT, VERSICH adequate; **2.** *adv* FINANZ, GESCHÄFT, RECHT, VERSICH adequately, sufficiently; ♦ **~ finanziert** FINANZ adequately funded; **~ versichert** VERSICH adequately insured, held covered

ausreichend: **keine ~e Deckung** *f* BANK *Scheckvermerk* not provided for, GESCHÄFT not sufficient funds (*nsf*); **nicht ~ gedeckter Scheck** *m* BANK not sufficient funds check (*AmE*), not sufficient funds cheque (*BrE*); **nicht ~e Kapazität** *f* IND undercapacity; **~e Kapitalausstattung** *f* FINANZ capital adequacy; **~e Sorgfalt** *f* RECHT adequate care

Ausreifungszeit *f* VW *des Kapitals* gestation period

Ausreise *f* TRANSP outward voyage; **Ausreisebeschränkung** *f* POL exit barrier; **Ausreisefracht** *f* IMP/EXP outward cargo; **Ausreisehalle** *f* TRANSP departure lounge; **Ausreisesteuer** *f* STEUER departure tax

Ausreißer *m* MATH outlier

ausrichten *vt* COMP *Text* align, justify, GESCHÄFT align, [+acc] aim; ◆ **~ auf** [+acc] GESCHÄFT *anpassen* gear towards, tailor to

Ausrichtung *f* COMP *Textverarbeitung* alignment, flush, justification, GESCHÄFT alignment, orientation, tailoring

Ausrollen *nt* TRANSP roll-out

ausrotten *vt* GESCHÄFT destroy, eradicate, wipe out, POL, SOZIAL stamp

Ausrottung *f* GESCHÄFT eradication

ausrufen *vt* GESCHÄFT call out, KOMM page

ausrüsten *vt* GESCHÄFT equip, TRANSP fit out

Ausrüstung *f* GESCHÄFT equipment, TRANSP fitting out; **Ausrüstungsgegenstände** *m pl* VW equipment goods; **Ausrüstungsindustrie** *f* GESCHÄFT supply industry; **Ausrüstungssicherheitszeugnis** *nt* **für Frachtschiffe** TRANSP cargo ship safety equipment certificate; **Ausrüstungsvermietung** *f* FINANZ equipment leasing, operation lease, operating leasing

Aussage *f* GESCHÄFT statement; **~ der Staatsanwaltschaft** RECHT statement of prosecution; ◆ **eine ~ machen** RECHT *Erklärung abgeben* make a statement

aussagenlogisch *adj* COMP Boolean

ausschalten *vt* COMP power off, turn off, GESCHÄFT *Fehlerquelle* eliminate, *Gerät* switch off, turn off, shut off; KOMM turn off

Ausschalten *nt* GESCHÄFT *Fehlerquelle* elimination, *Gerät* switching off, turning off, shutting off

auschecken *vt infrml* VERWALT book sb out

ausscheiden *vi* GESCHÄFT, PERSON retire

Ausscheiden *nt* GESCHÄFT, PERSON retirement

Ausscheidung *f* PERSON retirement, GESCHÄFT elimination; **Ausscheidungsrate** *f* VW cutoff point; **Ausscheidungsverfahren** *nt* RECHNUNG cutoff procedure; **Ausscheidungswettbewerb** *m* PERSON competitive examination

Ausschiffung *f* TRANSP disembarkation

ausschl. *abbr* (*ausschließlich*) GESCHÄFT ex (*exclusive of*), excl. (*excluding*)

Ausschlachten *nt*: **~ von Unternehmen** *infrml* RECHNUNG, VW asset-stripping (*infrml*)

Ausschlag *m* GESCHÄFT decisive factor; ◆ **den ~ geben** GESCHÄFT tip the scales

ausschlagbar: **~e Anzeigenseite** *f* MEDIEN, V&M gatefold

ausschlagen *vt* GESCHÄFT *Angebot* renounce

ausschlaggebend: **~er Aktienanteil** *m* BÖRSE control stock; **~e Stimme** *f* PERSON decisive vote, tiebreaking vote

ausschließen *vt* BÖRSE lock out, GESCHÄFT bar, boot off (*infrml*), exclude, expel, preclude, wall out (*AmE*), crowd out, eliminate, rule out, RECHT bar

ausschließlich 1. *adj* (*ausschl.*) GESCHÄFT exclusive; **2.** *adv* GESCHÄFT exclusively; **3.** *prep* BÖRSE exclusive of (*ex*), GESCHÄFT excluding (*excl.*), exclusive of (*ex*); ◆ **~ Be- und Entladung** IMP/EXP, TRANSP exclusive of loading and unloading (*xl & ul*); **~ Dividende** FINANZ ex dividend (*ex div.*); **~ Laden und Löschen** IMP/EXP, TRANSP exclusive of loading and unloading (*xl & ul*)

ausschließlich: **~e Benutzung** *f* PATENT exclusive use; **~e Gewerbeberechtigung** *f* IND monopoly; **~e Nutzung** *f*

PATENT exclusive use; **~e Zuständigkeit** *f* RECHT exclusive jurisdiction

Ausschließlichkeitsvertrag *m* PATENT exclusive licensing arrangement, V&M exclusive dealer arrangement

Ausschließung *f* GESCHÄFT exclusion, TRANSP shut-out

Ausschluß *m* BANK *Kreditgewährung* red lining (*jarg*), bar, FINANZ *Markt* foreclosure, GESCHÄFT elimination, exclusion; **~ der Gewährleistung** RECHT *Vertragsrecht* exclusion of liability; **~ laut Satzung oder Gesetz** VERSICH statutory exclusion; ◆ **unter ~ von** GESCHÄFT to the exclusion of, with the exception of; **unter ~ der Öffentlichkeit** RECHT closed to the public, in camera

Ausschluß: **Ausschlußfrist** *f* GESCHÄFT term of limitation, RECHT time bar, time limit; **Ausschlußkauf** *m* V&M preclusive buying; **Ausschlußklausel** *f* VERSICH red-line clause; **Ausschlußprinzip** *nt* VW exclusion principle; **Ausschlußprinzip** *nt* **des Preises** VW exclusion principle; **Ausschlußrecht** *nt* PATENT, RECHT exclusive right

ausschneiden *vt* COMP cut; ◆ **~ und einfügen** COMP *Textverarbeitung, Graphik* cut and paste

Ausschnitt *m* MEDIEN *aus einer Zeitung* clipping (*AmE*), cutting (*BrE*)

ausschreiben *vt* BÖRSE, GESCHÄFT, V&M advertise for bids for, invite tenders for, put out for tender

Ausschreibung *f* GESCHÄFT advertised bidding, tender to contract (*TTC*), RECHT invitation to bid, V&M competitive tendering; **~ von Angeboten** GESCHÄFT opening of tenders; ◆ **durch ~** V&M by tender; **sich an einer ~ beteiligen** GESCHÄFT tender; **~ vornehmen** GESCHÄFT invite tenders

Ausschreibung: **Ausschreibungsbeteiligte(r)** *mf* [decl. as adj] GESCHÄFT bidder; **Ausschreibungsbedingungen** *f pl* GESCHÄFT bidding requirements, conditions of tender, terms of tender, RECHT contract specifications; **Ausschreibungsfrist** *f* GESCHÄFT bidding period; **Ausschreibungsverfahren** *nt* FINANZ tender, GESCHÄFT bidding procedure, tendering procedure

Ausschreitung *f* SOZIAL riot; **Ausschreitungen** *f pl* **und politische Unruhen** SOZIAL riots and civil commotions (*R&CC*); **Ausschreitungen** *f pl*, **politische Unruhen und Streiks** SOZIAL riots, civil commotions and strikes (*RCC&S*)

Ausschuß *m* GESCHÄFT commission (*comm*), committee (*comm*), industriell wastage, spoilage, *fehlerhafte Arbeit* bad work, IND *fehlerhafte Arbeit* rejects, defective units, lost units; **~ für allgemeine Richtlinien** VERWALT *des GCBS* General Policy Committee (*GPC*); **~ der Aufsichtsbehörde** POL *EU* regulatory committee, watchdog committee; **~ zur Beilegung von Streitigkeiten** PERSON Disputes Committee (*BrE*); **~ zur Bekämpfung des unlauteren Wettbewerbs** POL, VW Federal Trade Commission (*AmE*) (*FTC*); **~ für Entwicklungshilfe** VW Development Assistance Committee (*DAC*); **~ für die Koordinierung des europäischen Luftraums** IND Committee for European Airspace Coordination (*CEAC*); **~ für Marketing** V&M marketing board; **~ der Regionen** RECHT *EU* Committee of the Regions; **~ für die Schiffseigner der Europäischen Gemeinschaft** VERWALT Committee of Shipowners Associations of the European Community; **~ für Standardisierungsfragen** RECHT Committee on Standardization Principles; **~ der Ständigen Vertreter** (*AStV*) VW Committee of Permanent Representatives of the EC (*COREPER*); ~ **zur Untersuchung der Staatsausgaben** vw Public Expenditure Survey Committee (*PESC*); ~ **für Verbraucherpolitik** RECHT Committee on Consumer Policy; ~ **für wirtschaftliche Entwicklung** vw Committee for Economic Development (*CED*); ~ **für Wirtschaftsentwicklung** vw Economic Development Committee (*EDC*); ◆ **einem ~ einen Antrag vorlegen** GESCHÄFT lay a proposal before a committee

Ausschuß: **Ausschußmitglied** *nt* GESCHÄFT committee member; **Ausschußsitzung** *f* GESCHÄFT committee meeting; **Ausschußvorsitzende** *f* [decl. as adj] GESCHÄFT committee chairwoman; **Ausschußvorsitzende(r)** *m* [decl. as adj] GESCHÄFT committee chairman

ausschüttbar: **nicht ~es Kapital** *nt* FINANZ undistributable capital

ausschütteln *vt* GESCHÄFT shake out

ausschütten *vt* FINANZ distribute; **nicht ~** *vt* GESCHÄFT plough back (*BrE*), plow back (*AmE*)

Ausschüttung *f* BÖRSE **der Dividenden** distribution; ~ **von Kapitalgewinnen** BÖRSE capital gains distribution; ~ **realisierter Kursgewinne** BÖRSE capital gains distribution; ~ **in einer Summe** BÖRSE lump sum distribution; ◆ **bei ~** BÖRSE when distributed

Ausschüttung: **Ausschüttungsbereich** *m* BÖRSE distribution area; **Ausschüttungsbeschluß** *m* FINANZ dividend resolution

ausschüttungsfähig: **~er Gewinn** *m* FINANZ, RECHNUNG distributable profit; **nicht ~er Gewinn** *m* RECHNUNG restricted surplus (*AmE*)

Ausschüttung: **Ausschüttungskosten** *pl* FINANZ distribution costs; **Ausschüttungspolitik** *f* BÖRSE, FINANZ dividend policy; **Ausschüttungssatz** *m* FINANZ payout rate, RECHNUNG dividend payout ratio; **Ausschüttungssperre** *f* RECHT limitation on profit distribution

Aussehen *nt* COMP appearance, GESCHÄFT appearance, aspect, looks

außen: **nach ~ blickend** *adj* GESCHÄFT outward-looking

Außen- *in cpds* GESCHÄFT, MGMNT, PERSON, POL, VW outer, external, foreign; **Außenanlagen** *f pl* GRUND external improvements, IND outside facilities; **Außenbereich** *m* GRUND white land; **Außenbeziehungen** *f pl* MGMNT external relations, POL foreign relations; **Außenbezirke** *m pl* GESCHÄFT outer suburbs, outlying district; **Außenbilanz** *f* VW external balance

Außendienst *m* GESCHÄFT field service, field organization, V&M field sales force; **Außendienstarbeiter, in** *m,f* VERSICH agency worker; **Außendienstleiter, in** *m,f* PERSON *Arbeit* field sales manager; **Außendienstmitarbeiter** *m pl* GESCHÄFT, PERSON, V&M field workers, field operators, field force, field staff, vw outdoor staff; **Außendienstmitarbeiter, in** *m,f* GESCHÄFT, PERSON field worker, field operator; **Außendienstorganisation** *f* VERWALT field organization, V&M field sales force; **Außendienstverkauf** *m* V&M field selling, field sales

Außen-: **Außenfinanzbeamte(r)** *m* [decl. as adj], **Außenfinanzbeamtin** *f* VERWALT financial officer; **Außenfinanzierung** *f* FINANZ, RECHNUNG external financing, outside finance; **Außenfinanzierungsplafond** *m* FINANZ external finan-

cing limit (*EFL*); **Außengrenze** *f* GESCHÄFT external border, external frontier

Außenhandel *m* GESCHÄFT external trade, international trade, vw foreign trade; **Außenhandelsakzept** *nt* IMP/EXP trade acceptance; **Außenhandelsbilanzdefizit** *nt* IMP/EXP, POL, vw trade deficit, trade gap; **Außenhandelsdefizit** *nt* IMP/EXP, POL, vw trade deficit, trade gap; **Außenhandelsgarantie** *f* VERSICH external trade guarantee; **Außenhandelsgewinne** *m pl* vw gains from trade, gains from exchange; **Außenhandelsindikator** *m* vw external trade indicator; **Außenhandelsmultiplikator** *m* vw foreign trade multiplier; **Außenhandelsorganisation** *f* FINANZ, IMP/EXP foreign trade organization (*FTO*); **Außenhandelspolitik** *f* IMP/EXP, POL, vw foreign trade policy, trade policy, trade regime; **Außenhandelsstatistik** *f* vw external trade statistics, foreign trade statistics, Overseas Trade Statistics (*BrE*) (*OTS*); **Außenhandelstheorie** *f* vw international trade theory; **Außenhandelsüberschuß** *m* vw foreign trade surplus, trade surplus; **Außenhandelsunternehmen** *nt* IMP/EXP export management company (*AmE*), import/export merchant (*BrE*), vw foreign trade firm; **Außenhandelsvereinigung** *f* FINANZ, IMP/EXP foreign trade organization (*FTO*); **Außenhandelsvertrag** *m* RECHT foreign trade contract; **Außenhandelsvolumen** *nt* IMP/EXP, vw volume of foreign trade

Außen-: **Außenminister, in** *m,f* POL foreign minister, Secretary of State (*AmE*), Foreign Secretary (*BrE*); **Außenministerium** *nt* POL foreign ministry, Foreign and Commonwealth Office (*FCO*) (*BrE*), State Department (*AmE*); **Außenpolitik** *f* POL foreign affairs, foreign policy, vw foreign policy; **Außenprüfer, in** *m,f* VERWALT financial officer; **Außenseiter, in** *m,f* GESCHÄFT outsider, VERSICH independent; **Außensouveränität** *f* vw external sovereignty; **Außenstände** *m pl* RECHNUNG outstanding, accounts receivable, *Schulden* uncollected receivables, outstanding debts; **Außenstehende(r)** *mf* [decl. as adj] GESCHÄFT outside party, outside person, MGMNT outsider, RECHT bystander; **Außentarif** *m* IMP/EXP external tariff; **Außenwerbung** *f* V&M outdoor advertising

Außenwirtschaft *f* GESCHÄFT external economy; **Außenwirtschaftspolitik** *f* **der Regierung** vw external government policy; **Außenwirtschaftszahlen** *f pl* GESCHÄFT, POL, vw trade figures

Außen-: **Außenzoll** *m* IMP/EXP, vw external tariff

außer *prep* GESCHÄFT apart from, except, excluding (*excl.*)

außerbetrieblich: **~e Kosten** *pl* RECHNUNG external cost; **~e Lohnfestsetzung** *f* PERSON outsider wage setting; **~er Revisor** *m*, **~e Revisorin** *f* RECHNUNG independent auditor; **~e Weiterbildung** *f* PERSON *Bildung, Ausbildung* off-the-job training (*BrE*); **~er Wirtschaftsprüfer** *m*, **~e Wirtschaftsprüferin** *f* RECHNUNG independent auditor

außerbörslich: **~er Handel** *m* BÖRSE off-board trading; **~er Handel** *m* **mit börsennotierten Aktien** vw third market; **~es Handelspapier** *nt* BÖRSE, FINANZ off-exchange instrument; **~er Kurs** *m* BÖRSE off-the-board price; **~es sekundäres Handelspapier** *nt* BÖRSE over-the-counter derivative instrument (*AmE*)

äußere: **~ Umstände** *m pl* GESCHÄFT external facts; **~ Verpackung** *f* V&M outer pack; **~ Verschuldung** *f*

GESCHÄFT borrowing abroad; ~ **Verzögerung** *f* POL outside lag

außergerichtlich: ~e **Entscheidung** *f* RECHT award; ~er **Vergleich** *m* RECHT out-of-court settlement, amicable settlement, *freiwillig* voluntary settlement

außergewöhnlich *adj* GESCHÄFT abnormal, exceptional, *Ereignis* unique; ~e **Aufwendungen** *f pl* RECHNUNG extraordinary expenditure; ~e **Ausgaben** *f pl* RECHNUNG exceptional expenses; ~er **Preisnachlaß** *m* GESCHÄFT abnormal discount; ~er **Test** *m* V&M stand-out test

außerhalb 1. *adv* GESCHÄFT outside; **2.** *prep* GESCHÄFT outside; ♦ ~ **der Hauptzeiten** KOMM, TRANSP off-peak; ~ **der Hochsaison** GESCHÄFT off-season; ~ **der Saison** GESCHÄFT off-season

außerhalb: ~ **der Stadt gelegenes Zentrum** *nt* V&M out-of-town center (*AmE*), out-of-town centre (*BrE*)

Außerkraftsetzung *f* RECHT *eines Gesetzes*, VERWALT abrogation

außerordentlich: ~e **Abschreibung** *f* RECHNUNG extraordinary depreciation; ~e **Anwaltsgebühr** *f* RECHT refresher; ~er **Aufwand** *m* FINANZ, RECHNUNG extraordinary charge, nonrecurring charge; ~er **Aufwands- oder Ertragsposition** *m* FINANZ extraordinary item; ~e **Aufwendungen** *f pl* RECHNUNG extraordinary expenditure, extraordinary expenses; ~e **Dividende** *f* BÖRSE extraordinary dividend, FINANZ superdividend, surplus dividend; ~er **Ertrag** *m* FINANZ extraordinary item, RECHNUNG extraordinary gain, extraordinary income, nonrecurrent income; ~es **Geschworenengericht** *nt* RECHT special jury; ~e **Hauptversammlung** *f* FINANZ, MGMNT special meeting of shareholders, extraordinary general meeting (*EGM*); ~er **Posten** *m* RECHNUNG, VERWALT extraordinary item; ~er **Professor** *m* PERSON *Akademiker* adjunct professor (*AmE*), visiting professor; ~e **Reserven** *f pl* BANK excess reserves; ~er **Rücklagenfonds** *m* FINANZ contingency fund; ~er **Verlust** *m* RECHNUNG extraordinary loss; ~e **Vollversammlung** *f* MGMNT extraordinary general meeting (*EGM*); ~e **Zuwendungen** *f pl* RECHNUNG extraordinary benefits

außerplanmäßig *adj* GESCHÄFT *Sitzung* unscheduled, PERSON nonscheduled; ~e **Ausgaben** *f pl* GESCHÄFT extra-budgetary outlay, unbudgeted expenditure; ~e **Sitzung** *f* MGMNT extraordinary meeting, special meeting; ~e **Tagung** *f* MGMNT extraordinary meeting, special meeting; ~es **Treffen** *nt* MGMNT extraordinary meeting, special meeting; ~e **Versammlung** *f* MGMNT extraordinary meeting, special meeting; ~e **Zusammenkunft** *f* MGMNT extraordinary meeting, special meeting

außerpreislich: ~er **Wettbewerb** *m* V&M, VW nonprice competition

außerrechtlich *adj* RECHT ex-legal

äußerst: ~e **Frist** *f* GESCHÄFT absolute limit; ~er **kalkulierter Preis** *m* GESCHÄFT rock-bottom price; ~er **Kurs** *m* VW ceiling price; ~er **Preis** *m* GESCHÄFT bottom price, knockdown price, lowest price, VW bottom price

Äußersten: jdn bis zum ~ treiben *phr* GESCHÄFT push sb to the limit

aussetzen *vt* BÖRSE, GESCHÄFT, RECHT, STEUER suspend; ♦ **an jdn etw ~** GESCHÄFT find fault with sb; **etw an jdm auszusetzen haben** GESCHÄFT find fault with sb

Aussetzen *nt* TRANSP launching; ~ **der Notierung** BÖRSE trading halt

Aussetzung *f* BÖRSE, GESCHÄFT, STEUER suspension

Aussicht *f* GESCHÄFT prospect

aussieben *vt* PERSON screen out

Aussiedler, in *m,f* GESCHÄFT refugee

aussöhnen *vt* FINANZ conciliate, reconcile

aussondern *vt* GESCHÄFT *Unerwünschtes* weed out, RECHT segregate

Aussonderungsrecht *nt* RECHT *Vertragsrecht* right of segregation

aussortieren *vt* GESCHÄFT sort out

Aussperrung *f* GESCHÄFT, PERSON *der Arbeitnehmer durch Arbeitgeber* lock-out

ausspielen: jdn ~ gegen *phr* GESCHÄFT play sb off against

aussprechen *vt* GESCHÄFT express, pronounce

Ausstand *m* GESCHÄFT, IND, PERSON strike, walkout (*infrml*)

ausstanzen *vt* IND stamp out

ausstatten *vt* COMP equip, GESCHÄFT fit out, equip; ~ **mit** GESCHÄFT *Befugnissen* vest with, POL *Vollmacht* invest with, vest with

Ausstattung *f* BANK *eines Kredits* terms, COMP equipment, FINANZ provision of funds, structure, terms of issue, GESCHÄFT equipment; ~ **mit Barmitteln** FINANZ cash resources; **Ausstattungseffekt** *m* BANK endowment effect

ausstehend *adj* GESCHÄFT outstanding, RECHNUNG active; ~e **Aktien** *f pl* BÖRSE outstanding capital stock; ~er **Betrag** *m* GESCHÄFT, RECHNUNG amount outstanding, outstanding amount; ~e **Buchung** *f* RECHNUNG outstanding entry; ~e **Einlagen** *f pl* BÖRSE outstanding capital stock, outstanding contributions, unpaid call on capital (*BrE*); ~er **Posten** *m* RECHNUNG outstanding item; ~e **Rechnungen** *f pl* RECHNUNG invoices not yet received; ~e **Restzahlung** *f* RECHNUNG outstanding balance; ~er **Schuldschein** *m* FINANZ note receivable

aussteigen *vi* COMP abort, GESCHÄFT back out, drop out, bail out, bale out, VW opt out

Aussteigen *nt infrml* BÖRSE bailing out

ausstellen *vt* BANK, FINANZ *Scheck* issue, GESCHÄFT *Rechnung* make out, *Scheck, Quittung* write out, issue, *Garantie* accredit, *Ware* exhibit, *Vertrag* draw up, exhibit, *Dokumente, Zeugnisse* issue, PATENT, V&M exhibit, VERSICH close out; ♦ ~ **auf** [+acc] BANK make payable to

Ausstellen *nt* BANK, FINANZ issue, RECHNUNG billing; ~ **einer Vorausrechnung** RECHNUNG advance billing; ~ **und Zusenden** *nt* **von Rechnungen** RECHNUNG billing of customers

ausstellend: ~e **Behörde** *f* VERWALT issuing authority; ~e **Dienststelle** *f* VERWALT issuing office; ~er **Frachtführer** *m* TRANSP issuing carrier

Aussteller, in *m,f* BANK drawer, FINANZ issuer, KOMM addresser, RECHT *einer Urkunde* maker

Ausstellung *f* BANK *Scheck* issue, BÖRSE exposition, FINANZ issue, GESCHÄFT exhibition, fair, show, *Dokumente, Zeugnisse* issue, KOMM display, PATENT exhibition, V&M exhibition, show; ~ **eines Auslandsschecks** BANK foreign check issue (*AmE*), foreign cheque issue (*BrE*); ~ **vor Beginn einer Werbekampagne** V&M pre-campaign exposure; ~ **eines noch nicht gedeckten Schecks** BANK check kiting (*AmE*), cheque kiting (*BrE*); ~ **des Unabhängig-keitszertifikats für eine Gewerkschaft** PERSON union certification; **Ausstellungsbeamte(r)** *m* [decl. as adj], **Ausstellungsbeamtin** *f* BANK drawing officer; **ab Ausstellungsdatum** *phr* GESCHÄFT after date (*a*/*d*); **nach Ausstellungsdatum** *phr* GESCHÄFT after date (*a*/*d*); **Ausstellungsfläche** *f* V&M retail floorspace; **Ausstellungsraum** *m* GESCHÄFT exhibition room; **Ausstellungsspedition** *f* IMP/EXP exhibition forwarding; **Ausstellungsstand** *m* MEDIEN display stand, exhibition stand; **Ausstellungsstück** *nt* GESCHÄFT display article, exhibit, showpiece, PATENT, V&M exhibit; **Ausstellungstag** *m* GESCHÄFT issuing date, date of issue; **Ausstellungsversicherung** *f* VERSICH exhibition risks insurance, trade fair insurance; **Ausstellungszentrum** *nt* GESCHÄFT exhibition center (*AmE*), exhibition centre (*BrE*)

Aussterben *nt* UMWELT extinction

Aussteuer *f* GRUND *Mitgift* dowry

Ausstiegskurs *m* BÖRSE takeout price

Ausstoß *m* VW output

ausstreichen *vt* GESCHÄFT expunge

aussuchen *vt* GESCHÄFT select

austarieren *vt* FINANZ average out

Austausch *m* GESCHÄFT exchange (*exch.*), interchange, IND replacement, KOMM *Informationen, Meinungen* exchange (*exch.*), VW exchange (*exch.*); ~ **von Fachwissen** GESCHÄFT exchange of know-how; ~ **von Handelsdaten** VW Trade Data Interchange (*TDI*)

austauschbar *adj* GESCHÄFT exchangeable, interchangeable, replaceable, KOMM, VW exchangeable, replaceable; **nicht ~** *adj* GESCHÄFT, KOMM, VW unexchangeable, irreplaceable

Austausch: **Austauschbarkeit** *f* COMP compatibility; **Austauschbeziehung** *f* VW trade-off; **Austausch-Container** *m* TRANSP interchange container

austauschen *vt* GESCHÄFT exchange, interchange, replace, trade, KOMM exchange, VW trade

Austausch: **Austauschmotor** *m* GESCHÄFT replacement engine

austesten *vt* COMP debug, GESCHÄFT test

Australisch: **~e Zentralbank** *f* BANK Reserve Bank of Australia

austreten *vi* GESCHÄFT leave, opt out, *kündigen* resign, withdraw, RECHT withdraw, contract out, VERSICH withdraw; ◆ ~ **aus** GESCHÄFT leave, opt out of, *kündigen* retire from, withdraw from, RECHT withdraw from

Austritt *m* RECHT, VERSICH withdrawal; **Austrittsalter** *nt* VERSICH age at withdrawal; **Austrittsgebühren** *f pl* STEUER contracted-out rates

ausübbar *adj* BÖRSE exercisable

ausüben 1. *vt* BÖRSE exercise, GESCHÄFT, RECHT exercise, practice (*AmE*), practise (*BrE*), STEUER perform, V&M *Privileg* exercise; **2.** *vi* BÖRSE tender notice

Ausübung *f* BÖRSE, GESCHÄFT, RECHT exercise, STEUER performance; **durch ~ des Vorkaufsrechtes erworbener Werbespot** *m* V&M pre-empt spot; ~ **von Rechten** BÖRSE exercise of rights; ~ **nicht zustehender Rechte** GESCHÄFT exercise of undue authority; **Ausübungsfrist** *f* BÖRSE exercise deadline; **Ausübungspreis** *m* BÖRSE striking price; **Ausübungsverfahren** *nt* BÖRSE exercise procedure

Ausverkauf *m* GESCHÄFT, V&M sale; ~ **anläßlich der Inventur** GESCHÄFT stocktaking sale; ~ **wegen Geschäftsaufgabe** GESCHÄFT closing-down sale, winding-up sale

ausverkaufen *vt* FINANZ, GESCHÄFT, V&M sell out

Ausverkauf: **Ausverkaufspreis** *m* V&M bargain price, sale price

ausverkauft *adj* FREI, GESCHÄFT, TRANSP *Theater* booked up, sold out, V&M, VW *Waren* out of stock (*o.s.*); ~**es Haus** *nt* FREI *Theater* sellout (*infrml*); ~**er Markt** *m* BÖRSE sold-out market

Ausverkauf: **Ausverkaufwaren** *f pl* GESCHÄFT bunches (*infrml*) (*BrE*), clearing items

Auswahl *f* GESCHÄFT assortment, choice, range of goods, selection, PERSON *unter Stellenbewerbern* screening; ◆ **in die engere ~ kommen** GESCHÄFT, PERSON *Bewerbung* be shortlisted; **in die engere ~ nehmen** GESCHÄFT, PERSON shortlist; **seine ~ treffen** GESCHÄFT take one's pick (*infrml*)

Auswahl: **Auswahlanforderungen** *f pl* GESCHÄFT eligibility requirement; **Auswahleinheit** *f* **der ersten Stufe** V&M sampling point

auswählen *vt* GESCHÄFT select, single out

Auswahl: **Auswahlfeld** *nt* COMP, GESCHÄFT check box (*AmE*), tick box (*BrE*); **Auswahlkommission** *f* PERSON selection board; **Auswahlliste** *f* GESCHÄFT, PERSON shortlist; **eine Auswahlliste aufstellen** *phr* PERSON *Selektion* draw up a shortlist; **Auswahlverfahren** *nt* PERSON screening technique

auswalzen *vt* GESCHÄFT roll out

auswärtig *adj* BANK, FINANZ offshore, POL foreign; ~**e Angelegenheiten** *f pl* POL foreign affairs; ~**e Beziehungen** *f pl* MGMNT external relations

auswärts: ~ **in Arbeit geben** *phr* MGMNT *Auftrag* book out

Auswärts- *in cpds* IMP/EXP outward; **Auswärtsmission** *f* IMP/EXP outward mission; **Auswärtsvergabe** *f* VW subcontracting

auswechseln *vt* GESCHÄFT replace

Auswechselrate *f* GESCHÄFT switching-out rate

Auswechslungskosten *pl* VERSICH replacement costs

Ausweich- *in cpds* GESCHÄFT alternative, *ausweichend* evasive

Ausweichen *nt* GESCHÄFT evasion

ausweichend *adj* GESCHÄFT *Antwort* evasive

Ausweich-: **Ausweichgleis** *nt* TRANSP siding (*BrE*), sidetrack (*AmE*); **Ausweichklausel** *f* RECHT *Vertrag* escape clause, opt-out clause; **Ausweichkurs** *m* BÖRSE fictitious security price; **Ausweichplan** *m* MGMNT contingency plan

Ausweis *m* BANK, RECHNUNG statement of account, VERWALT identity card, identification card, proof of identity, permit, pass; ~ **der ausgegebenen Instrumente** BANK statement of instruments issued; ~ **über die Verwendung des Kapitals** RECHNUNG application of funds statement

ausweisen 1. *vt* RECHNUNG post, report, show on the books, recognize; **2. sich ~** *v refl* RECHT prove one's identity

Ausweis: **Ausweiskarte** *f* VERWALT identity card (*ID card*)

Ausweisung *f* POL expulsion

ausweiten *vt* GESCHÄFT, VW expand

Ausweitung f FINANZ expansion, GESCHÄFT expansion, *Tätigkeit* enrichment, vw *Produktionsausweitung* expansion

auswerfen vt COMP eject

auswerten vt COMP interpret, GESCHÄFT appraise, evaluate, interpret, MGMNT *Daten* analyse (*BrE*), analyze (*AmE*), PATENT exploit, work

Auswertung f COMP interpretation, GESCHÄFT appraisal, evaluation, IND working, MGMNT *von Daten* analysis, PATENT exploitation, working; ~ **von Anrufen** V&M call analysis; ~ **der Rechnungslegung** RECHNUNG accounting analysis; ~ **von Vertreterbesuchen** V&M call analysis

auswickeln vt TRANSP unwrap

auswirken: sich ~ auf [+acc] v refl GESCHÄFT have an impact on

Auswirkung f GESCHÄFT consequence, effect, impact, repercussion; ~ **auf den Gewinn** GESCHÄFT profit implication; **Auswirkungen** f pl GESCHÄFT implications

Ausz. abbr (*Auszahlung*) GESCHÄFT PYT (*payment*)

auszahlbar adj FINANZ disbursable

auszahlen vt BÖRSE *Teilhaber, Aktionär* buy out, FINANZ buy out, disburse, pay off, pay out, GESCHÄFT *Teilhaber, Aktionär* buy out, PERSON *Arbeitnehmer* pay off

auszahlend: ~e Bank f BANK paying banker

Auszahler m FINANZ disburser

Auszahlung f (*Ausz.*) FINANZ payback, GESCHÄFT payment (*PYT*), PERSON *Entlassung* payoff, RECHNUNG *Kreditbetrag* amount paid out, disbursement, vw payoff; ~ **in bar** BANK cash payment; **Auszahlungsermächtigung** f BANK withdrawal warrant; **Auszahlungsprovision** f GESCHÄFT disbursement commission; **Auszahlungssperre** f BANK stop-payment order; **Auszahlungsvolumen** nt FINANZ volume of loans granted

auszeichnen vt GESCHÄFT, V&M price, label

Auszeichnung f GESCHÄFT *für Leistung* honor (*AmE*), honour (*BrE*), V&M labeling (*AmE*), labelling (*BrE*), price marking

Auszubildende(r) mf [decl. as adj] (*Azubi*) PERSON, vw apprentice, trainee, threshold worker (*AmE*)

Auszug m BANK statement of account, GESCHÄFT abstract, *aus Dokument* extract, PATENT abstract, RECHT *Exzerpt* abstract, extract; ~ **aus dem Register** PATENT extract from the register; ♦ ~ **anfertigen über** [+acc] GESCHÄFT *Informationen* extract

auszuschüttend: ~e Dividenden f pl RECHNUNG dividends payable

autark adj GESCHÄFT, vw autarchic, self-reliant, self-sufficient; ~**e Wirtschaft** f vw self-sufficient economy

Autarkie f GESCHÄFT, vw autarky, self-sufficiency

Authority to Purchase f FINANZ, IMP/EXP authority to purchase

Auto- in cpds GESCHÄFT self-, automatic, IND automotive, auto-, TRANSP self-, automatic, automotive; **Autoarbeitergewerkschaft** f PERSON United Automobile Workers (*AmE*) (*UAW*); **Autobahn** f TRANSP motorway (*BrE*), expressway (*AmE*), superhighway (*AmE*); **Autodidakt, in** m,f SOZIAL autodidact, self-educated person, self-taught person; **Autofähre** f TRANSP car ferry; **Autohersteller** m IND, TRANSP car manufacturer; **keine Autoimporte zulassen** phr IMP/EXP wall out car imports; **Autoindustrie** f IND

automotive industry; **Autokomplettreise** f FREI motorist inclusive tour; **Autokorrelation** f vw autocorrelation

Automat m GESCHÄFT automatic vending machine, slot machine, vending machine; **Automatenverkauf** m V&M automatic merchandising; **Automatenversicherung** f VERSICH coin-machine insurance

Automation f COMP automation

automatisch 1. adj GESCHÄFT, IND automatic; **2.** adv GESCHÄFT, IND automatically; ♦ **sich ~ abdeckend** FINANZ self-liquidating; ~ **fertigen** IND automate; **sich ~ liquidierend** FINANZ self-liquidating

automatisch: ~**e Abhebung** f BÖRSE automatic withdrawal; ~**e Aktualisierung** f COMP automatic updating; ~**er Anlasser** m PERSON self-starter; ~**e Anmeldung** f COMP *in einem System* auto-login, auto-logon; ~**e Ausfertigung** f **der Scheckunterschrift** VERWALT check signer (*AmE*), cheque signer (*BrE*); ~**es Banken-Verrechnungssystem** nt BANK Banks Automated Clearing Services (*BACS*); ~**er Bankschalter** m BANK, FINANZ automated teller machine (*ATM*), automatic telling machine (*ATM*), automatic teller; ~**es Booten** nt COMP autoboot; ~**es Clearinghaus** nt FINANZ Automated Clearing House (*ACH*); ~**es Clearingsystem** nt BANK Automated Clearing System Settlement (*ACSS*); ~**e Duplikation** f COMP autoduplication; ~**er Einzug** m COMP *Drucker* autofeed; ~**er Fahrpreiseinzug** m TRANSP automatic fare collection; ~**er fiskalpolitischer Konjunkturstabilisator** m vw automatic fiscal stabilizer, built-in stabilizer; ~**e Gehaltsregulierung** f PERSON *Angestelltenverhältnis* automatic adjustment point; ~**e Geräteprüfung** f COMP built-in check, built-in test; ~**er Inflationsverstärker** m vw built-in inflator; ~**er Konjunkturstabilisator** m vw built-in flexibility; ~**es Laden** nt COMP *Programme* autoloading; ~**er Neustart** m COMP autorestart; ~**es Parken** nt COMP *Lese-/Schreibköpfe* autopark; ~**er Regelmechanismus** m vw built-in stabilizer; ~**es Rücksetzen** nt COMP automatic reset; ~**er Seefunk-Telex-Dienst** m TRANSP automatic maritime radio telex service; ~**es Sichern** nt COMP autosave; ~**er Stabilisator** m vw automatic stabilizer, vw automatic stabilizer, built-in stabilizer; ~**er Start** m COMP autostart; ~**e Überweisung** f BANK automatic transfer; ~**er Überweisungsverkehr** m BANK automatic transfer service (*BrE*) (*ATS*); ~**es Urladen** nt COMP autoboot; ~**er Verrechnungsdienst** m BANK *Gelder von Scheck- und Sparkonten* automatic transfer service (*BrE*) (*ATS*); ~**es Verrechnungssystem** nt BANK Automated Clearing Settlement System (*ACSS*); ~**e Wahlwiederholung** f KOMM *Telefon* automatic redialing (*AmE*), automatic redialling (*BrE*); ~**e Wiederanlage** f BÖRSE automatic reinvestment; ~**er Zahlungsverkehr** m BANK, FINANZ, RECHNUNG automatic funds transfer (*AFT*)

automatisieren vt COMP automate, IND automate, robotize

automatisiert: ~**e Abrechnungsstelle** f FINANZ Automated Clearing House (*ACH*); ~**er Banken-Abrechnungsdienst** m BANK Banks Automated Clearing Services (*BACS*); ~**es Banken-Clearing-System** nt BANK Banks Automated Clearing Services (*BACS*); ~**es Banküberweisungssystem** nt BANK bank giro credit system (*BrE*); ~**e Datenverarbeitung** (*ADV*) f COMP automatic data processing (*ADP*); ~**es Übergangsticket** nt TRANSP transitional automated ticket (*TAT*); ~**er Überweisungsverkehr** m BANK,

FINANZ, RECHNUNG automatic funds transfer (*AFT*)

Automatisiert: **~es Zahlungssystem** *nt* **der Clearinghouses** BANK Clearing House Automated Payments System (*BrE*) (*CHAPS*)

Automatisierung *f* COMP automation

Automobil *nt* GESCHÄFT, IND, TRANSP automobile; **Automobilarbeiter, in** *m,f* IND, TRANSP car worker; **Automobilindustrie** *f* IND, TRANSP car industry, motor industry; **Automobilkran** *m* TRANSP lorry-mounted crane (*BrE*), truck-mounted crane (*AmE*); **Automobilwerte** *m pl* BÖRSE automotive stock, VW motors; **Automobilwirtschaft** *f* VW autoeconomy

autonom *adj* COMP stand-alone, GESCHÄFT autonomous, MGMNT self-managed, PERSON self-managed, autonomous, POL self-governing; **~e Arbeitsgruppen** *f pl* PERSON autonomous work groups (*BrE*); **~e Ausgaben** *f pl* VW autonomous expenditure; **~er Hafen** *m* TRANSP self-governing port; **~e Investition** *f* VW autonomous investment; **~er Konsum** *m* VW autonomous consumption; **~es System** *nt* COMP stand-alone system

Autonomie *f* GESCHÄFT autonomy

Auto-: **Autopalette** *f* TRANSP car pallet; **Autopauschalreise** *f* FREI motorist inclusive tour

>**Autorisation** *f* BANK, GESCHÄFT authorization

autorisieren *vt* BANK, GESCHÄFT authorize

autorisiert: **~e Aktien** *f pl* BÖRSE shares authorized; **~es Aktienkapital** *nt* FINANZ, RECHNUNG authorized share capital, VW authorized capital; **~es Grundkapital** *nt* VW authorized capital; **nicht ~e Untersuchung** *f* POL warrantless investigation

Autorisierungszentrale *f* BANK authorization center (*AmE*), authorization centre (*BrE*)

autoritär: **~er Führungsstil** *m* POL directive style of leadership; **~e Gesellschaft** *f* VW authoritarian society; **~es Management** *nt* PERSON authoritarian management; **~es System** *nt* VW authoritarian society

Autorität *f* GESCHÄFT authority, expert, PERSON von *Führungskräften* authority; **Autoritätsbefugnis** *f* BANK discretionary authority; **Autoritätsstruktur** *f* GESCHÄFT, VERWALT authority structure

Auto-: **Autosteuer** *f* STEUER car tax; **Autostraße** *f* TRANSP motorway (*BrE*), expressway (*AmE*), superhighway (*AmE*); **Autotelefon** *nt* KOMM car phone; **Autotransporter** *m* TRANSP car transporter; **Autotransportschiff** *nt* TRANSP car carrier; **Autovermietung** *f* FREI, TRANSP car hire (*BrE*), car rental (*AmE*), car-hire service (*BrE*), car-rental service (*AmE*), self-drive hire; **Autoversicherung** *f* VERSICH motor insurance (*BrE*), automobile insurance (*AmE*); **Autoversicherung** *f* **für Personenschäden ohne Prüfung** VERSICH no-fault motor insurance (*BrE*), no-fault automobile insurance (*AmE*)

Aval *m* BANK credit by way of bank guaranty; ♦ **per ~** BANK guaranteed by

Aval: **Avalakzept** *nt* FINANZ collateral acceptance

avaliert: **~es Akkreditiv** *nt* BANK guaranteed letter of credit; **~er Wechsel** *m* BÖRSE backed bill of exchange, guaranteed bill of exchange

Aval: **Avalprovision** *f* FINANZ commission on guaranty

avantgardistisch *adj* IND at the forefront

Avis *m or nt* GESCHÄFT advice, notice, notification; ♦ **kein ~** GESCHÄFT no advice (*N/A*); **ohne ~** GESCHÄFT no advice (*N/A*)

avisieren *vt* GESCHÄFT advise, advise on, give advice to, inform, notify

avisierend: **~e Bank** *f* BANK advising bank

avisiert: **~er Wechsel** *m* BANK advised bill

Avoirdupois *nt* GESCHÄFT avoirdupois (*avdp.*)

axial: **~e Komposition** *f* GESCHÄFT, V&M axial composition

AZO *abbr* (*Allgemeine Zollordnung*) IMP/EXP General Customs Regulations

Azubi *abbr* (*Auszubildende(r)*) PERSON, VW apprentice, trainee, threshold worker (*AmE*)

B

Babybond *m* BÖRSE baby bond

Babyboom *m* VW baby boom

Bach: **den ~ hinuntergehen** *phr infrml* GESCHÄFT go downhill

Back-Data-Informationen *f pl* V&M back data information

Backslash *m jarg* COMP backslash; **Backslash-Taste** *f jarg* COMP backslash key

Backspace-Taste *f* COMP back arrow, backspace

Backup *nt* COMP *Datenarchivierung* backup; **Backup-Dienstprogramm** *nt* COMP backup utility program; **Backup-Einrichtung** *f* COMP backup facility

baden: **~ gehen** *phr infrml* BÖRSE *Aktien, Kurse* take a bath (*jarg*)

Baden-Württembergisch: **~e Wertpapierbörse** *f* **zu Stuttgart** BÖRSE Stuttagrt Securities Exchange

Badewannentheorem *nt* VW bathtub theorem

Bagatell- in cpds FINANZ, RECHT petty, trifling; **Bagatellbetrag** *m* FINANZ, VW trifle, trifling amount, piddling sum (*infrml*); **Bagatellbeträge** *m pl* RECHNUNG petty cash; **Bagatellfall** *m* FINANZ de minimis case

Bagatelle *f* FINANZ, RECHT trifle

Bahn *f* TRANSP rail, railway (*BrE*), railroad (*AmE*); ♦ **mit der ~ verschicken** TRANSP ship by rail

Bahn: **Bahnanlage** *f* TRANSP rail network; **Bahnbeförderung** *f* TRANSP rail transport

bahnbrechend *adj* GESCHÄFT, IND epoch-making, pioneering, trailblazing (*infrml*), at the forefront; ♦ **~ wirken** GESCHÄFT, IND pioneer

Bahn: **Bahnbrecher, in** *m,f* GESCHÄFT, IND pioneer; **Bahncard** *f* FREI Railrover (*BrE*); **Bahn-Flug-Verbindung** *f* TRANSP rail-air link

Bahnfracht *f* TRANSP rail freight; **Bahnfrachtbrief** *m* TRANSP railway consignment note (*BrE*), railway bill (*BrE*); **Bahnfrachtgeschäft** *nt* TRANSP rail transport; **Bahnfrachtkosten** *pl* TRANSP rail charges

Bahn: **Bahnhof** *m* TRANSP railroad station (*AmE*), railway station (*BrE*), station (*stn*), train station (*BrE*); **Bahnhofsvorsteher** *m* TRANSP stationmaster; **Bahnreise** *f* FREI rail tour; **Bahnreise** *f* **mit Führung** FREI rail guided tour; **Bahnreisende(r)** *mf* [decl. as adj] TRANSP rail traveler (*AmE*), rail traveller (*BrE*); **Bahnstation** *f* TRANSP railroad station (*AmE*), railway station (*BrE*), train station (*BrE*); **Bahntransport** *m* TRANSP rail transport; **Bahnverbindung** *f* TRANSP rail link; **Bahnversand** *m* TRANSP forwarding by rail, rail shipment

Baisse *f* BÖRSE falling prices, sharp drop, stock market slump, FINANZ downturn phase; ♦ **auf ~ spekulieren** BÖRSE bear, speculate for a fall in prices

Baisse: **Baissebewegung** *f* BÖRSE bearish downward movement; **Baisseengagement** *nt* BÖRSE bear position, engagement to sell short, short account, short interest, short position; **Baisseengagement-Theorie** *f* BÖRSE short interest theory; **Baissegeschäft** *nt* BÖRSE bear transaction, short selling; **Baisse-Kauf-**

Optionsposition *f* BÖRSE short call position; **Baissemarkt** *m* BÖRSE bear market; **auf einem Baisse-markt kaufen** *phr* BÖRSE buy on a falling market; **Baisseposition** *f* BÖRSE bear account, short, short position, short account; **Baissepositions-Theorie** *f* BÖRSE short interest theory; **Baissesignal** *nt* BÖRSE bearish signal formation; **Baissespekulant, in** *m,f* BÖRSE, FINANZ bear; **Baissespekulation** *f* BÖRSE bear operation, bear speculation, bear transaction, going short; **Baissespread** *m* **mit Kaufoptionen** BÖRSE bear call spread; **Baissestimmung** *f* BÖRSE bearish tone, bearishness; **Baisseströmung** *f* BÖRSE bearish tone, bearishness; **Baissetendenz** *f* BÖRSE bearish tone, bearishness; **Baisseverkaufsspanne** *f* BÖRSE bear put spread

Baissier *m* BÖRSE, FINANZ bear; ♦ **die Baissiers zu Deckungskäufen zwingen** BÖRSE squeeze the shorts; **die Baissiers unter Druck setzen** BÖRSE squeeze the bears

Bakkalaureus *m* PERSON *Inhaber des niedrigsten akademischen Grades* Bachelor; **~ für Industriedesign** PERSON Bachelor of Industrial Design (*BID*); **~ für industrielles Design** PERSON Bachelor of Industrial Design (*BID*); **~ der Naturwissenschaften** PERSON Bachelor of Science (*BSc*); **~ des Rechts** PERSON, RECHT, SOZIAL Bachelor of Laws (*BLL, LLB*); **~ der Rechtswissenschaft** PERSON, RECHT, SOZIAL Bachelor of Laws (*BLL, LLB*)

bald: **so ~ wie möglich** *phr* GESCHÄFT, KOMM as soon as possible (*a.s.a.p.*)

baldmöglichst *adv* GESCHÄFT, KOMM as soon as possible (*a.s.a.p.*)

Bale *nt* IND, TRANSP *Masseneinheit* bale (*B*)

Balken- *in cpds* COMP pop-up, MEDIEN banner; **Balkendiagramm** *nt* MATH bar chart, bar graph, histogram; **Balkenmenü** *nt* COMP pop-down menu, pop-up menu, pull-down menu; **Balkenschlagzeile** *f* MEDIEN streamer; **Balkenüberschrift** *f* MEDIEN banner headline; **in Balkenüberschriften** *phr* MEDIEN *in Zeitungen* in banner headlines

Ballast *m* IND ballast

Ballen *m* IND, TRANSP bale (*B*); **Ballenkubikmeter** *m pl* IND bale cubic meters (*AmE*) (*BC*), bale cubic metres (*BrE*) (*BC*); **Ballenware** *f* IND bale (*B*)

Ballon-Elastikreifen *m* TRANSP cushion tire (*AmE*), cushion tyre (*BrE*)

Ballungsraum *m* VW agglomeration

Ballungszentrum *nt* VW agglomeration

Baltisch: **~e Terminbörse** *f* BÖRSE Baltic Futures Exchange

Bambusvorhang *m* POL bamboo curtain

Bancomat *m Sch* BANK automated cash dispenser (*ACD*), automatic cash dispenser (*ACD*), cash dispenser, cash-dispensing machine

Band 1. *m* MEDIEN *Buch* volume; **2.** *nt* COMP tape, *Datenträger* reel, GESCHÄFT *der Freundschaft, Familienbande* tie, IND assembly line, KOMM, MEDIEN tape, PERSON assembly line; **auf ~ aufgenommene**

Präsentation *f* V&M *Kassette, Video* canned presentation; ◆ **auf ~** MEDIEN on tape; **auf ~ aufnehmen** MEDIEN tape; **etw vom ~ löschen** GESCHÄFT wipe sth from a tape

Band: **Bandarchiv** *nt* GESCHÄFT tape library; **Bandbreite** *f* COMP *Datenübertragung* bandwidth, FINANZ currency band, exchange margins, margin of fluctuation, official spread, MEDIEN bandwidth, STEUER band, VW spread, *für Kursschwankungen* fluctuation band, band; **Bandbreite** *f* **zwischen An- und Verkaufskurs** VW franchise gap; **Bandbreite** *f* **der Arbeitszeit** PERSON *bei Gleitzeitsystemen* bandwidth; **Banddatei** *f* COMP tape file; **Bandfabrikation** *f* IND flow production; **Bandfertigung** *f* IND synchronous assembly-line production; **Bandkassette** *f* COMP tape cartridge; **Bandlaufwerk** *nt* COMP *Magnetband* streamer, tape drive; **Bandmaß** *nt* GESCHÄFT tape measure; **Bandproduktion** *f* IND synchronous assembly-line production, flow production; **Bandsäge** *f* IND band saw; **Bandspule** *f* COMP spool, *Datenträger* reel

Bank *f* BANK bank (*bk*), banking establishment, banking house; **~ im ausländischen Besitz** BANK foreign-owned bank; **zur ~ bringen** BANK bank; **von einer ~ garantierter Scheck** *m* BANK certified check (*AmE*), certified cheque (*BrE*); **~ für Internationalen Zahlungsausgleich** (*BIZ*) BANK, VW Bank for International Settlements (*BIS*); **~ unter ausländischer Kontrolle** BANK foreign-controlled bank; **Bankabrechnungsbeleg** *m* BANK bank settlement voucher; **Bankabrechnungsverkehr** *m* BANK bank settlement system; **Bankabrufverfahren** *nt* FINANZ automatic debit transfer system; **Bankabsprachen** *f pl* BANK banking arrangements; **Bankadresse** *f* BANK bank address

bankähnlich: **~es Institut** *nt* VW near bank

Bank: **Bankaktien** *f pl* BANK bank shares; **Bankakzept** *nt* BANK bank acceptance, bank bill, bank draft, banker's acceptance; **Bankangestellte(r)** *mf* [decl. as adj] BANK bank clerk, bank officer, banker; **Bankanleihe** *f* BANK bank bond; **Bankanweisung** *f* BANK banker's order; **Bankanzeige** *f* BANK bank advice; **Bankauskunft** *f* BANK banker's reference; **Bankauswahlverfahren** *nt* COMP *Computerspeicher* bank switching; **Bankausweis** *m* BANK bank return (*BrE*); **Bankauszug** *m* BANK bank statement; **Bankautomat** *m* BANK, FINANZ automatic teller; **Bankautomaten-Kontoauszug** *m* BANK, FINANZ automated teller machine statement; **Bankavis** *nt* BANK bank advice; **Bank-an-Bank-Ausleihungen** *f pl* BANK, FINANZ interbank lendings; **Bank-an-Bank-Kredit** *m* BANK, FINANZ interbank loan; **Bankbeamte(r)** *m* [decl. as adj], **Bankbeamtin** *f* BANK bank officer

bankbestätigt: **~er Scheck** *m* VW certified check (*AmE*), certified cheque (*BrE*)

Bank: **Bankbeteiligung** *f* BANK banking interest; **Bankbetrieb** *m* BANK banking business, banking operations; **Bankbetrug** *m* GESCHÄFT racket, ramp (*BrE*); **Bankbote** *m*, **Bankbotin** *f* BANK bank messenger, bank runner; **Bankbriefkurs** *m* BANK bank selling rate; **Bankbuch** *nt* BANK, FINANZ bankbook; **Bankbürgschaft** *f* BANK bank guarantee; **Bankdarlehen** *nt* BANK bank advance, bank loan, bank accommodation; **Bankdienstleistungen** *f pl* BANK banking services; **Bankdirektor, in** *m,f* FINANZ bank manager; **Bankdiskont** *m* BANK bank discount, bank

discount rate; **Bankdiskontsatz** *m* BANK bank discount rate; **Bankeffizienz** *f* BANK bank efficiency

Bankeinlage *f* BANK bank deposit; ◆ **eine ~ hinterlegen** BÖRSE take a deposit

Bankeinlage: **Bankeinlagen** *f pl* BANK bank deposit monies; **Bankeinlagenversicherung** *f* VERSICH bank deposit insurance

Bank: **Bankenabrechnung** *f* BANK bank clearings, settling of inter-bank transactions; **Bankenapparat** *m* BANK, FINANZ banking system; **Banken-Clearing** *nt* BANK bank clearings, settling of inter-bank transactions

bankenfinanziert *adj* BANK bank-financed

Bank: **Bankenfreiheit** *f* BANK free banking; **Bankengruppe** *f* BANK bank group (*AmE*), banking group (*BrE*)

bankenindossiert *adj* BANK bank-endorsed

Bank: **Bankenkette** *f* BANK bank group (*AmE*), banking group (*BrE*); **Bankenkonsortium** *nt* BANK bank group (*AmE*), banking group (*BrE*), consortium of banks, syndicate; **Bankenkrach** *m* BANK bank crash; **Bankenliquidität** *f* BANK bank liquidity; **Bankensektor** *m* BANK banking sector; **Bankensystem** *nt* BANK, FINANZ banking system; **Bankenzusammenschluß** *m* BANK alternative mortgage instrument

Banker, in *m,f infrml* BANK banker

bankfähig *adj* BANK bankable, BÖRSE negotiable; **nicht ~** *adj* BANK unbankable; **~es Papier** *nt* BANK paper eligible for discount; **~er Vermögenswert** *m* BANK bankable asset; **~e Vermögenswerte** *m pl* RECHNUNG bank assets; **~er Wechsel** *m* BANK bankable bill

Bank: **Bankfazilitäten** *f pl* RECHNUNG bank facilities, credit facilities; **Bankfeiertag** *m* GESCHÄFT, PERSON, RECHT bank holiday (*BrE*), legal holiday (*AmE*), statutory holiday (*AmE*); **Bankfiliale** *f* BANK bank branch, high-street bank (*BrE*); **Bankfinanzierung** *f* BANK bank financing; **Bankfloat** *m* BANK bank float

bankfremd: **~er Sektor** *m* FINANZ nonbank sector

Bank: **Bankgarantie** *f* BANK bank guarantee; **Bankgebühr** *f* BANK bank service charge; **Bankgebühren** *f pl* BANK banking charges, bank charges, charges on banking transactions; **Bankgebührenfreiheit** *f* BANK free banking; **Bankgeschäft** *nt* BANK *Betrieb* banking, banking business, banking operation, *Abschluß* bank transaction, banking transaction; **Bankgewerbe** *nt* BANK banking, banking industry

bankgiriert *adj* BANK bank-endorsed

Bank: **Bankgiro** *nt* BANK bank giro (*BrE*); **Bankguthaben** *nt* BANK balance in bank, bank balance, cash in bank, cash balance; **Bankhaus** *nt* BANK banking establishment, banking house; **Bank-Holding** *nt* BANK, GESCHÄFT bank holding company; **Bank-Holdinggesellschaft** *f* BANK, GESCHÄFT bank holding company

Bankier *m* BANK banker

Bank: **Bankinstitut** *nt* BANK bank (*bk*), banking establishment, banking house; **Bankkapital** *nt* BANK bank capital; **Bankkarte** *f* BANK bank card; **Bankkassierer, in** *m,f* BANK bank teller; **Bankkauffrau** *f*, **Bankkaufmann** *m* BANK banker

Bankkonto *nt* BANK account (*a/c*), bank account, bank accommodation; **~ des Ministeriums** RECHNUNG departmental bank account; ♦ ~ **überziehen** BANK overdraw

Bank: **Bankkontrolle** f BANK bank audit; **Bankkonzern** m BANK bank group (AmE), banking group (BrE); **Bankkosten** pl BANK bank charges; **Bankkredit** m BANK bank advance, bank credit, bank loan; **Bankkredit** m **aufnehmen** BANK arrange a loan, borrow from a bank, FINANZ arrange a loan; **Bankkredite** m pl BANK bank lending; **Bankkreise** m pl BANK banking circles, banking community; **Bankleitzahl** f (BLZ) BANK bank code, sort code (BrE), bank routing number, FINANZ routing symbol, transit number; **Banklombardgeschäft** nt FINANZ collateral loan business; **Banknetz** nt BANK banking network

Banknote f BANK, FINANZ bank bill (AmE), banknote (BrE), bill (AmE), note (BrE); **Banknoten** f pl BANK, FINANZ paper money; **Banknotenausgabe** f vw note issue; **Banknotenbündel** nt BANK bankroll (AmE), wad (infrml); **Banknotenhandel** m BANK banknote trading; **Banknotenumlauf** m vw active circulation of bank notes

Bank: **Bankobligation** f BANK bank bond, bank credit transfer; **Banköffnungszeiten** f pl BANK banking hours; **Bankpapier** nt BANK bank paper, securities issued by a bank; **Bankplatz** m BANK banking centre (BrE), banking center (AmE); **Bankprovision** f BANK bank commission; **Bankreferenz** f BANK banker's reference; **Bankreserve** f BANK bank reserve; **Bankrevision** f BANK bank examination (AmE), banking audit, bank audit; **Bankrevisor, in** m,f BANK bank examiner (AmE), banking auditor

bankrott adj BANK, FINANZ, GESCHÄFT bankrupt, broke (infrml), bust (infrml); ♦ ~ **sein** GESCHÄFT be bankrupt, be on the rocks (infrml); ~ **gehen** GESCHÄFT go bankrupt, go toes up (infrml); **jdn gerichtlich für** ~ **erklären** RECHNUNG, RECHT adjudge sb bankrupt, adjudicate sb bankrupt; ~ **machen** GESCHÄFT go bankrupt, go broke (infrml), go bust (infrml), go toes up (infrml); **jdn offiziell für** ~ **erklären** RECHNUNG, RECHT adjudge sb bankrupt, adjudicate sb bankrupt

Bank: **Bankrücklage** f BANK bank reserve; **Bankrun** m BANK run on a bank; **Banksaldo** m BANK bank balance; **Bankscheck** m BANK bank check (AmE), bank cheque (BrE), bank draft (B/D, B/Dft), banker's check (AmE), banker's cheque (BrE), banker's draft, cashier's check (AmE), cashier's cheque (BrE), registered check (AmE), registered cheque (BrE), treasurer check (AmE), treasurer cheque (BrE); **Bankschließfach** nt BANK safety deposit box; **Banktag** m RECHNUNG banking day; **Banktochter** f BANK banking subsidiary; **Banktransaktion** f BANK, RECHNUNG banking transaction; **Banktratte** f BANK bank draft (B/D, B/Dft), banker's draft; **Banküberweisung** f BANK bank credit transfer, bank giro (BrE), bank remittance, credit transfer, bank transfer; **Bankumsätze** m pl FINANZ bank turnovers; **Bankvalutierungsgewinn** m BANK bank float; **Bankverbindlichkeiten** f pl BANK bank debts, indebtedness to banks; **Bankvermögen** nt BANK bank assets; **Bankvorschriften** f pl BANK bank requirements; **Bankwechsel** m BANK bank acceptance, bank bill, bank draft (B/D, B/Dft), bank paper, banker's bill, banker's draft; **Bankwerte** m pl BANK bank shares; **Bankwertpapiere** nt pl BANK bank security; **Bankwesen** nt BANK banking; **Bankzertifikat** nt BANK

bank certificate; **Bankzinsen** m pl BANK bank interest; **Bankzinssatz** m **für erste Adressen** FINANZ prime lending rate; **Bankzusammenbruch** m BANK bank crash

bar 1. adj FINANZ, GESCHÄFT cash, for cash (flc), in cash; ♦ **für ~e Münze nehmen** GESCHÄFT take at face value; **in ~er Münze zahlen** GESCHÄFT pay in specie; **gegen** ~ **verkaufen** BÖRSE cash in; **2.** adv GESCHÄFT cash, in cash; ♦ **in** ~ GESCHÄFT for cash (flc), in cash, in specie; ~ **abgerechnet** GESCHÄFT cash-settled; ~ **abrechnen** GESCHÄFT settle in cash; **in** ~ **bezahlt** GESCHÄFT paid in cash; ~ **zahlen** GESCHÄFT pay cash, pay in cash

Bar- in cpds GESCHÄFT cash; **Barabfindung** f BÖRSE, FINANZ cash settlement; **Barabhebung** f BANK, RECHNUNG cash drawdown, cash withdrawal; **Barablösungswert** m VERSICH cash surrender value, cash value life insurance (AmE); **Barabzug** m GESCHÄFT cash deduction; **Baranforderung** f RECHNUNG cash requirement; **Barausgaben** f pl FINANZ expenditure, outlay; **Barausschüttung** f FINANZ cash distribution, cash dividend; **Barauszahlung** f FINANZ cash payment; **Barbestand** m GESCHÄFT, RECHNUNG cash on hand

Barclays: ~ **Index** m BÖRSE Barclays Index

Bar-: **Bardividende** f FINANZ cash dividend, cash payout, VERSICH bonus in cash, cash benefit, cash bonus; **Bareinkauf** m BÖRSE, FINANZ cash purchase; **Bareinlage** f RECHNUNG cash contribution, cash deposit; **Bareinnahmen** f pl FINANZ cash earnings, RECHNUNG cash receipts; **Barentnahme** f BANK, RECHNUNG cash drawdown, cash withdrawal; **Barerlös** m GESCHÄFT proceeds in cash; **Barerstattungsdatum** nt BÖRSE cash refunding date; **Bargegenwerte** m pl FINANZ cash equivalents

Bargaining: ~-**Theorie** f **des Lohns** vw bargaining theorie of wages

Bargeld nt GESCHÄFT cash, hard money, cash in hand, ready cash (BrE); ~ **einer Bank für den täglichen Bedarf** BANK vault cash, vault reserve (AmE); ~ **auf die Klaue** infrml GESCHÄFT cash on the barrel head (infrml) (AmE), cash on the nail (infrml) (BrE); ♦ **mit** ~ **überschwemmt** GESCHÄFT awash with cash (infrml); **über** ~ **verfügen** GESCHÄFT have cash in hand, have cash on hand

Bargeld: **Bargeldanweisung** f FINANZ cash acknowledgement; **Bargeldbedarf** m FINANZ cash needs; **Bargeldbestände** m pl RECHNUNG cash holdings; **Bargeldeinzug** m FINANZ cash collection; **Bargeldkarte** f BANK cash card; **Bargeldknappheit** f FINANZ cash shortage, cash squeeze

bargeldlos: ~**e Gesellschaft** f vw cashless society; ~**e Lohn- und Gehaltzahlung** f FINANZ cashless pay; ~**e Vergütungen** f pl PERSON noncash rewards; ~**e Zahlung** f BANK bank giro (BrE), cashless payment, noncash payment; ~**er Zahlungsverkehr** m BANK bank giro credit system (BrE), banking transfer system, cashless payment system, noncash payment system

Bargeld: **Bargeldreserve** f GESCHÄFT spare cash; **Bargeldüberschuß** m BANK, FINANZ excess cash; **Bargeldumlauf** m vw currency in circulation; **Bargeldvolumen** nt vw volume of notes and coins in circulation; **Bargeldzertifikat** nt FINANZ cash certificate; **Bargeldzyklus** m FINANZ cash conversion cycle

Bar-: **Bargeschäft** nt RECHNUNG cash deal, cash transaction; **Barguthaben** nt RECHNUNG cash balance, cash in hand; **Barkäufer, in** *m,f* V&M cash buyer; **Barkredit** *m* GESCHÄFT cash credit (*C/C*); **Barliquidität** *f* FINANZ available cash, cash position, cash ratio, liquid cash resources, RECHNUNG available cash

Barmittel *nt pl* FINANZ cash, liquid funds; **Barmittelbegrenzung** *f* BANK, PERSON, VW cash limit; **Barmittelproblem** *nt* FINANZ, RECHNUNG cash flow problem; **Barmittelrisiko** *nt* BÖRSE cash risk; **Barmittelrücklage** *f* BANK, RECHNUNG cash reserve; **Barmittelstrom** *m* FINANZ, RECHNUNG cash flow; **Barmittelzufluß** *m* FINANZ cash inflow

Barometer *nt* VW *Trends* barometer; **Barometer-Aktie** *f* BÖRSE barometer stock

Bar-: **Barposition** *f* RECHNUNG cash position; **Barpreis** *m* GESCHÄFT cash price; **Barregulierung** *f* BÖRSE *von Wertpapiertransaktionen* cash settlement

Barrel *nt* TRANSP, UMWELT barrel; ◆ **~ pro Tag** VW barrels per day (*b/d*)

Barren *m* BANK, BÖRSE ingot

Bar-: **Barreserve** *f* BANK cash reserve, vault cash, vault reserve (*AmE*), RECHNUNG legal reserves, cash reserve; **Barreservesatz** *m* BANK cash deposits ratio

Barriere *f* GESCHÄFT barrier

Barron: **~ Aktiengruppendurchschnittswerte** *m pl* BÖRSE Barron's Group Stock Averages (*AmE*)

Bar-: **Barschaden** *m* VERSICH cash loss; **Barscheck** *m* BANK cashier's check (*AmE*), cashier's cheque (*BrE*), cashable check (*AmE*), cashable cheque (*BrE*), open check (*AmE*), open cheque (*BrE*); **Barsicherheit** *f* RECHNUNG cash deposit

Bartergeschäft *nt* GESCHÄFT *Abschluß* barter transaction, vw *Handel* barter economy, barter

Bar-: **Bartransaktion** *f* FINANZ cash operation, cash transaction; **Barüberweisung** *f* BANK, FINANZ cash transfer; **Barverdienst** *m* FINANZ cash earnings; **Barverkauf** *m* GESCHÄFT, RECHNUNG cash transaction; **Barvermögen** *nt* FINANZ cash assets; **Barwert** *m* FINANZ actual cash value, cash value, net present value (*NPV*), RECHNUNG cash value, net present value (*NPV*), present value, V&M cash equivalence, present value, vw net present value (*NPV*); **Barwertanwartschaft** *f* VERSICH present value of an expectancy; **Barwertfaktor** *m* FINANZ present value factor; **Barwert** *m* **einer Lebensversicherung** VERSICH cash surrender value, cash value life insurance (*AmE*)

Barytpapier *nt* VERWALT baryta paper

Barzahlung *f* BANK cash payment; **~ bei Lieferung** (*c.o.d.*) GESCHÄFT, IMP/EXP cash on delivery (*COD*); **~ vor Lieferung** GESCHÄFT, IMP/EXP cash before delivery (*CBD*); **~ ohne Abzug** RECHNUNG net cash; ◆ **gegen ~** GESCHÄFT for cash (*f/c*), on a cash basis

Barzahlung: **Barzahlungsbeleg** *m* RECHNUNG petty cash voucher; **Barzahlungsrabatt** *m* FINANZ, GESCHÄFT, V&M *Skonto* cash discount

Baseler: **~ Konkordat** *nt* BANK Basle Concordat on Banking Supervision

Baseline *f* V&M baseline

BASIC *abbr* (*Beginner's All-Purpose Symbolic Instruction Code*) COMP BASIC (*beginner's all-purpose symbolic instruction code*)

Basis *f* BÖRSE *Terminkontrakthandel* basis, COMP *Transistoren* base, radix, GESCHÄFT base, POL *Parteien* grass roots, STEUER basis; ◆ **auf der ~ von** GESCHÄFT on the

basis of; **auf ~ von Barzahlung** GESCHÄFT on a cash basis; **auf ~ von Marktpreis** GESCHÄFT, STEUER, V&M arm's length

Basis: **Basisadresse** *f* COMP base address; **Basisband** *nt* COMP baseband; **Basisbudget** *nt* RECHNUNG base budget; **Basisdatum** *nt* BÖRSE base date; **Basisdollar** *m pl* vw constant dollars (*AmE*); **Basiseingabe/ Ausgabesystem** *nt* COMP basic input/output operating system (*BIOS*); **Basiseinkommen** *nt* **des Haushalts** vw breakeven level of income; **Basisforschung** *f* V&M basic research; **Basisforschungskosten** *pl* V&M basic research cost; **Basisgeldreserven** *f pl* BANK reserve base; **Basisgewicht** *nt* GESCHÄFT base load, IND base load, MATH base weight; **Basisgewichtstabellen** *f pl* GESCHÄFT basic weight scales; **Basisinstrument** *nt* BÖRSE actuals; **Basisjahr** *nt* FINANZ, VW base year; **Basisjahranalyse** *f* vw base year analysis; **Basismedien** *nt pl* MEDIEN basic media; **Basismodell** *nt* COMP bare-bones version, vw plain vanilla model (*infrml*); **Basispreis** *m* BÖRSE exercise price, strike price, striking price, GESCHÄFT basic price; **Basispreis** *m* **einer Kaufoption** BÖRSE call exercise price, call's strike; **Basispreis** *m* **einer Verkaufsoption** BÖRSE put strike, put's strike; **Basispunkt** *m* BÖRSE, FINANZ; **Basispunkt-Wertverhältnis** *nt* BÖRSE basis point value ratio; **Basisrisiko** *nt* FINANZ basis risk; **Basisswap** *m* FINANZ basis swap; **Basiswert** *m* FINANZ underlying instrument, underlying security, BÖRSE actuals; **Basiszins** *m* BANK, FINANZ, vw base lending rate

Batch *m* COMP batch

Batterie *f* COMP, IND battery; **Batterienotstromversorgung** *f* COMP battery backup

Bau *m* GESCHÄFT site, GRUND, IND *Gebäude* building, construction, structure, *Bauen* construction, *Baustelle* building site, construction site; **im ~ befindliche Anlagen** *f pl* RECHNUNG assets under construction; ◆ **im ~** IND under construction

Bau: **Bau- und Anwendungsbestimmungen** *f pl* IND construction and use regulations (*C&U regulations*); **Bauarbeiter, in** *m,f* IND construction worker; **Bauart** *f* VERSICH class of construction; **Bauartenkategorien** *f pl* VERSICH categories of construction types; **Bauartenklassen** *f pl* VERSICH categories of construction types; **Bauauflagen** *f pl* GRUND planning restrictions; **Bauaufwand** *m* GRUND cost of construction; **Bauausnahmegenehmigung** *f* **für die Errichtung von Geschäftshäusern** GRUND spot zoning; **Baubedarf** *m* GRUND, IND building materials; **Baubeginn** *m* GRUND start of building work

Baud *nt* COMP *Datenübertragung* baud, data transfer rate

Bau: **Baudarlehen** *nt* BANK construction loan, house-building loan; **Baudarlehensvertrag** *m* BANK building loan agreement

Baud: **Baud-Rate** *f* COMP baud rate

bauen 1. *vt* GRUND, IND build, construct, erect; **2.** *vi* GRUND, IND build

Bauer *m* POL, VW farmer; **Bauernhof** *m* GRUND farmstead (*BrE*), homestead (*AmE*); **Bauerninteressenverband** *m* POL farm lobby; **Bauernlobby** *f* POL farm lobby; **Bauernverband** *m* GESCHÄFT farmers' association

Bäuerin *f* POL, VW farmer

Bau: **Baufälligkeit** *f* GRUND dilapidation; **Baugenehmigung** *f* GRUND planning approval, building permit (*AmE*), planning permission (*BrE*),

RECHT, VERWALT planning permission (*BrE*); **Baugewerbe** *nt* GRUND, IND construction industry; **Baugrundstück** *nt* GRUND building lot, plot; **Baugruppe** *f* IND assembly; **Bauherrenhaftpflichtversicherung** *f* VERSICH owners' and contractors' protective liability insurance (*AmE*); **Bauholz** *nt* IND lumber (*AmE*), timber (*BrE*); **Bauhypothek** *f* FINANZ building mortgage; **Bauindustrie** *f* GRUND, IND construction industry, building industry; **Baukastenprinzip** *nt* IND building block concept, concept of modular assembly, modular concept, MATH modularity; **Bauklasse** *f* VERSICH class of construction; **Baukonjunktur** *f* VW overall construction activity; **Baukostenindex** *m* BÖRSE construction cost index (*BrE*); **Baukostenkalkulation** *f* GRUND, IND quantity surveying; **Baulandbeschaffung** *f* RECHT provision of land for building sites; **Bauleistungsversicherung** *f* VERSICH contractor's all risks insurance; **Bauleiter, in** *m,f* GRUND, IND site manager; **Baulinie** *f* GRUND *Fluchtlinie* building line; **Baumaterial** *nt* IND building materials

Baumstruktur *f* COMP hierarchical menu, tree structure

Baumwollbörse *f* BÖRSE cotton exchange

Bau: **Bauordnung** *f* GRUND building code; **Bauplatz** *m* GESCHÄFT site, GRUND, IND building site, construction site; **Baurate** *f* IND construction rate; **Baurezession** *f* VW construction slump; **Bausachverständige(r)** *mf* [decl. as adj] GRUND, IND building expert, quantity surveyor; **Bausatz** *m* IND assembly; **Bausparer, in** *m,f* FINANZ member of building society (*BrE*), member of savings and loan association (*AmE*); **Bausparkasse** *f* BANK, FINANZ benefit society, friendly society (*BrE*), building and loan association (*AmE*), building society (*BrE*), ≈ savings and loan association (*AmE*) (*S&L*); **Bausparkassenzentralbanksystem** *nt* FINANZ Federal Home Loan Bank System (*AmE*)

bausteinartig: **~e Produktion** *f* IND modular production

Bau: **Baustelle** *f* GESCHÄFT site, GRUND, IND building site, construction site; **Baustellenleiter** *m* PERSON site foreman; **Baustoff** *m* IND building materials; **Bausubventionen** *f pl* IND construction subsidies; **Bautechnik** *f* IND structural engineering; **Bauteil** *nt* COMP component part, IND component; **Bauträgerfirma** *f* GRUND property developer; **Bauunternehmer, in** *m,f* GRUND construction firm, *Grundstückserschließung* commercial developer; **Bauvertrag** *m* **mit schlüsselfertiger Übergabe** VW turnkey contract; **Bau- und Verwendungsbestimmungen** *f pl* IND construction and use regulations (*C&U regulations*); **Bauvorhaben** *nt* GRUND construction project, SOZIAL *Wohnanlage, Wohnsiedlung* housing project (*AmE*), housing scheme (*BrE*); **Bauvorschriften** *f pl* GRUND, RECHT building code, building regulations; **Bauwerk** *nt* GRUND, IND structure; **Bauwesen** *nt* GRUND, IND construction industry, building industry, structural engineering; **im Bauzustand** *phr* IND under construction

b. a. W. *abbr* (*bis auf Widerruf*) GESCHÄFT till countermanded (*T/C*), V&M *Werbung* till canceled (*AmE*) (*TC*), till cancelled (*BrE*) (*TC*), till forbid (*TF*)

Bayerisch: **~e Börse** *f* BÖRSE Bavarian Stock Exchange

Bayes- *in cpds* MATH, MGMNT, V&M Bayesian; **Bayesianische Entscheidungstheorie** *f* MGMNT, V&M, VW Bayesian decision theory; **Bayes-Regel** *f* MGMNT, V&M, VW Bayesian method; **Bayes-Regel** *f* der

Entscheidungsfindung MGMNT, V&M, VW Bayesian approach to decision-making

BBC *abbr* (*British Broadcasting Corporation*) MEDIEN BBC (*British Broadcasting Corporation*), the Beeb (*infrml*) (*British Broadcasting Corporation*)

BBS *abbr* KOMM BBS (*Bulletin Board Service*)

BDI *abbr* (*Bundesverband der Deutschen Industrie*) IND ≈ CBI (*Confederation of British Industry*)

BDW *abbr* (*Bund Deutscher Werbeberater und Werbeleiter*) V&M ≈ Advertising Association (*BrE*)

beabsichtigen *vt* RECHT contemplate

beabsichtigt: **~e Leistungsverwendung** *f* PERSON projected benefit application

Beachtung *f* GESCHÄFT attention

Beamte(r) *m* [decl. as adj] PERSON, VERWALT civil servant, official, officer; **~ der Einwanderungsbehörde** PERSON immigration officer (*IO*); **~ des Gesundheitsamtes** PERSON health officer; **~ auf Zeit** PERSON civil servant on limited appointment; **Beamtendeutsch** *nt* infrml VERWALT officialese (*infrml*)

Beamtin *f* PERSON, VERWALT civil servant, official, officer; **~ der Einwanderungsbehörde** PERSON immigration officer (*IO*); **~ des Gesundheitsamtes** PERSON health officer; **~ auf Zeit** PERSON civil servant on limited appointment

beanspruchen *vt* GESCHÄFT, PATENT, RECHT claim, lay claim to

beansprucht: **nicht ~** *adj* GESCHÄFT *Kredit* unused; **nicht ~e Dividende** *f* RECHNUNG unrequired dividend; **nicht ~es Recht** *nt* RECHT unclaimed right

Beanspruchung *f* GESCHÄFT, PATENT, RECHT pressure, claim

beantragen *vt* GESCHÄFT *Lizenz, Paß* apply for, MGMNT *Vorschlag* put forward, SOZIAL *Arbeitslosenunterstützung* claim

beantragt: **selbst ~e Konkurserklärung** *f* FINANZ voluntary bankruptcy

Beantragung *f* GESCHÄFT application, MGMNT *Vorschlag* proposal, SOZIAL claim; **~ von Arbeitslosenunterstützung** SOZIAL signing on (*BrE*)

beantworten *vt* GESCHÄFT answer

Beantwortung *f* GESCHÄFT answer, reply; ♦ **in ~ Ihres Schreibens** *frml* KOMM in answer to your letter, in reply to your letter

bearbeiten *vt* BANK process, COMP edit, GESCHÄFT handle, *Eingänge* process, *Text* adapt, IND process, *Material* treat, PATENT process, VW *Land* cultivate

Bearbeitung *f* BANK processing, GESCHÄFT handling, *von Eingängen* processing, *eines Textes* adapting, IND processing, *von Materialien* treating, PATENT processing, VW *des Landes* cultivation; ♦ **in ~** GESCHÄFT under examination; **in ~ sein** GESCHÄFT be in the pipeline

Bearbeitung: **Bearbeitungsgebühr** *f* BANK bank service charge, GESCHÄFT handling charge, service fee, V&M handling charge, VERWALT service charge; **Bearbeitungsstempel** *m* VERWALT date stamp; **Bearbeitungsverfahren** *nt* IND manufacturing method, machining procedure; **Bearbeitungszeit** *f* COMP, IND processing time, VERWALT lead time, processing time

Beaufort: **~ Skala** *f* UMWELT Beaufort scale

beaufsichtigen *vt* GESCHÄFT, MGMNT, PERSON *Produktion, Arbeitsgang* supervise, oversee

beaufsichtigend *adj* COMP, GESCHÄFT, MGMNT, PERSON supervisory

Beaufsichtigung *f* GESCHÄFT, MGMNT, PERSON *Arbeit, Arbeitsablauf* supervision; ~ **der Kreditinstitute** FINANZ supervision of credit institutions

beauftragen *vt* GESCHÄFT charge with, commission, instruct, RECHT authorize, empower

beauftragt: ~**e Bank** *f* BANK paying bank

Beauftragte(r) *mf* [decl. as adj] GESCHÄFT agent, representative (*rep.*), PATENT assignee, representative (*rep.*), RECHNUNG assignee, RECHT attorney-in-fact (*AmE*), mandatory, private attorney, VERWALT commissary (*AmE*), commissioner; ~ **für Umwelthygiene** UMWELT Environmental Health Officer (*BrE*); ◆ **etw durch einen Beauftragten schicken** GESCHÄFT send sth via an agent

Beauftragung *f* RECHT *eines Maklers* listing

bebauen *vt* GRUND build up

bebaut: ~**e Fläche** *f* GRUND built-up area, improved area; ~**es Gebiet** *nt* GRUND built-up area

Bebauung *f* GRUND, IND building, VW *des Landes* cultivation; **Bebauungsgrenze** *f* RECHT building line (*AmE*); **Bebauungsplan** *m* GRUND building plan, zoning ordinance

Bedachte(r) *mf* [decl. as adj] GRUND beneficiary

bedanken: wir ~ uns sehr *phr* KOMM we should like to express our thanks

Bedarf *m* GESCHÄFT need, requirement, demand, VW demand, taste; ~ **an liquiden Mitteln** RECHNUNG cash requirements; ◆ **den ~ an etw decken** GESCHÄFT meet the needs of, satisfy the demand for sth; ~ **haben an** GESCHÄFT require

Bedarf: Bedarfsanalyse *f* V&M demand analysis, needs analysis; **Bedarfsartikelgeschäft** *nt* V&M convenience shop (*BrE*), convenience store (*AmE*); **Bedarfs-Kreditlinie** *f* FINANZ demand line of credit, swing line; **Bedarfsprämie** *f* VERSICH burning cost, net rate, premium rate; **Bedarfsstandard** *m* VW needs standard; **Bedarfsstruktur** *f* VW order of preference, preference system; **Bedarfsvorwegnahme** *f* VW anticipated demand; **Bedarfswirtschaft** *f* VW needs economy

bedauern *vt* GESCHÄFT regret

Bedauern *nt* GESCHÄFT regret; ◆ **mit ~** GESCHÄFT regretfully

bedenkenlos *adj* GESCHÄFT unhesitating, unscrupulous

Bedenkzeit *f* GESCHÄFT cooling-off period

bedeuten *vt* GESCHÄFT signify, *Initialen* stand for

bedeutend *adj* GESCHÄFT significant, powerful, considerable; ◆ ~**er sein als** GESCHÄFT rank above; **weniger ~ sein als** GESCHÄFT rank below

bedeutend: ~**e Persönlichkeit** *f* (*VIP*) GESCHÄFT very important person (*VIP*)

bedeutsam *adj* GESCHÄFT significant

Bedeutung *f* GESCHÄFT importance, meaning, significance; ◆ **nach ~** GESCHÄFT in order of importance; **etw ~ beimessen** GESCHÄFT attach importance to

bedienen *vt* GESCHÄFT *Markt* service, *Kunden* serve, attend to, V&M serve

Bediener, in *m,f* IND plant operator, operator

Bedienung *f* GESCHÄFT servicing, service, IND operation; ~ **von Hypothekenkrediten** FINANZ mortgage servicing, *von Schulden* servicing; ~ **der Rücklage** RECHNUNG appropriation to a reserve; **Bedienungsanleitung** *f*

GESCHÄFT instruction book, instructions for use, IND operating instructions; **Bedienungsaufschlag** *m* GESCHÄFT service charge; **Bedienungsfeld** *nt* COMP *Gerät* operator control panel; **Bedienungsgelder** *nt pl* GESCHÄFT, RECHNUNG tips and gratuities; **Bedienungshandbuch** *nt* GESCHÄFT instruction manual, service manual; **Bedienungskraft** *f* MGMNT, PERSON *einer Maschine* machine operator, operative; **Bedienungstheorie** *f* MATH, VW queueing theory

bedingt *adj* RECHT conditional; ~**es Angebot** *nt* RECHT *Vertragsrecht* conditional offer; ~**e Annahme** *f* RECHT *Vertragsrecht* conditional acceptance; ~**er Arbeitsvertrag** *m* PERSON conditional employment contract; ~**e Betriebsstillstandsversicherung** *f* VERSICH contingent business interruption insurance; ~**e Betriebsunterbrechungsversicherung** *f* VERSICH contingent business interruption insurance; ~**es Fremdkapital** *nt* RECHNUNG contingent asset; ~**es Kapital** *nt* FINANZ authorized capital; ~**er Markt** *m* VERSICH contingent market; ~**er Programmstopp** *m* COMP breakpoint, breakpoint instruction, checkpoint; ~**er Schutz** *m* PATENT conditional protection; ~**e Verbindlichkeiten** *f pl* RECHT contingent liabilities; ~**er Vertrag** *m* RECHT conditional contract; ~**e Verzweigung** *f* COMP conditional branch

Bedingung *f* COMP condition, GESCHÄFT condition, precondition, prerequisite, RECHT condition, stipulation; ◆ **unter der ~, daß** GESCHÄFT on the condition that, on the stipulation that, with the stipulation that; **zur ~ machen** GESCHÄFT stipulate

Bedingung: Bedingungen *f pl* BANK terms, RECHT *eines Vertrag* conditions, terms; **an Bedingungen geknüpfter Vertrag** *m* RECHT conditional contract; **zu den üblichen Bedingungen** *f pl* GESCHÄFT on usual terms; **Bedingungsdifferenzversicherung** *f* VERSICH difference in conditions insurance

bedingungslos *adj* COMP unconditional, FINANZ unconditional, RECHNUNG without qualification, RECHT *uneingeschränkt, absolut* absolute, without qualification, without stipulation, *vorbehaltslos* unconditional; ~**e Annahme** *f* BANK general acceptance, GESCHÄFT unconditional acceptance; ~**e Schenkung** *f* RECHT absolute gift, STEUER outright gift

Bedrohung: eine ~ darstellen *phr* GESCHÄFT pose a threat

bedruckt: ~**es Schreibpapier** *nt* KOMM printed writing paper

Bedürfnis *nt* GESCHÄFT need, requirement, want, VW taste; **Bedürfnisbefriedigung** *f* MGMNT need satisfaction, satisfaction of wants; **Bedürfnishierarchie** *f* PERSON hierarchy of needs

Bedürftige(r) *mf* [decl. as adj] GESCHÄFT, SOZIAL pauper, poor person; **die Bedürftigen** *pl* SOZIAL the needy

Bedürftigkeitsprüfung *f* SOZIAL means test

beeindruckend *adj* GESCHÄFT impressive; **wenig ~** *adj* GESCHÄFT unimpressive

beeinflußbar *adj* GESCHÄFT *Mensch* impressionable, susceptible; **nicht ~** *adj* FINANZ, GESCHÄFT, VW uncontrollable; ~**e Kosten** *pl* RECHNUNG controllable cost

beeinflussen *vt* GESCHÄFT affect, influence, RECHT affect, prejudice

Beeinflussung *f* GESCHÄFT influence; ~ **des Verfahrens** RECHT prejudicing the outcome of a trial

beeinträchtigen *vt* GESCHÄFT spoil, impair, affect, RECHT *Vertrag* interfere with, encroach, encroach on, *Rechte* restrict, curtail, VW *Kaufkraft* impair

Beeinträchtigung *f* GESCHÄFT abridgement, encroachment, interference, RECHT *eines Vorrechts* derogation, encroachment; **~ des Besitzes durch den Verpächter** GRUND constructive eviction

beenden *vt* COMP *Programm* exit, quit, terminate, GESCHÄFT cease, complete, terminate, MGMNT *Sitzung* wind up, RECHT *Vertrag* terminate

Beenden *nt* COMP *eines Programms* termination, GESCHÄFT completion, termination, MGMNT *einer Sitzung* winding-up, RECHT *eines Vertrags* termination

beendet *adj* COMP, PERSON *arbeit*, RECHT *vertrag* terminated

Beendigung *f* COMP *eines Programms* termination, GESCHÄFT completion, termination, PERSON *des Beschäftigungsverhältnisses*, RECHT *eines Vertrags* termination

Be- und Entladeschaden *m* VERSICH damage whilst loading and unloading

Be- und Entladungszeit *f* **im Hafen** TRANSP port turnaround time (*AmE*), port turnround time (*BrE*)

befähigen *vt* GESCHÄFT, PERSON enable, qualify; ◆ **jdn ~, etw zu tun** PERSON qualify sb to do sth

Befähigung *f* GESCHÄFT, PERSON ability, aptitude, capacity, enablement, *nach Ausbildung* qualification; **Befähigungsnachweis** *m* GESCHÄFT evidence of formal qualification, proof of ability, RECHT certificate of qualification, SOZIAL paper qualifications, qualification, TRANSP certificate of competency

Befangenheit *f* GESCHÄFT bias, prejudice

befassen: sich ~ mit *v refl* GESCHÄFT deal with, handle

Befehl *m* COMP command, instruction, GESCHÄFT, PERSON *Arbeit* command; **~ in Maschinensprache** COMP computer instruction; **Befehlsdatei** *f* COMP command file; **Befehlshandbuch** *nt* GESCHÄFT instruction manual; **Befehlstaste** *f* COMP command key; **Befehlswirtschaft** *f* POL, VW command economy; **Befehlszeile** *f* COMP command line

befestigen 1. *vt* GESCHÄFT fasten, secure; ◆ **~ an** [+dat] GESCHÄFT *Etikett* affix; **2. sich ~** *vi* BÖRSE advance, firm

Befestigung *f* BÖRSE advance, GESCHÄFT fastening, securing

befolgen *vt* GESCHÄFT *Regelung, Anweisung* abide by, adhere to, follow, obey, RECHT *beachten* obey, *Gesetz* comply with

Befolgung *f* GESCHÄFT, RECHT adherence

Beförderer *m* IMP/EXP, KOMM, TRANSP carrier, forwarder (*fwdr*)

befördern *vt* GESCHÄFT advance, *Waren* convey, carry, transport, forward (*fwd*), KOMM dispatch, ship, PERSON *Arbeitnehmer* promote, TRANSP convey, *abschicken* dispatch, *Waren, Lasten* carry, VERWALT advance

befördert: ~ **werden** *phr* PERSON be promoted, be upgraded

Beförderung *f* GESCHÄFT advancement, *Beschäftigungspolitik* upgrading, IMP/EXP freighting, shipment, KOMM shipment, PERSON *Aufstieg* advancement, upgrading, vertical promotion, promotion, TRANSP transport, transportation, carriage, haulage; **~ von Führungskräften** MGMNT, PERSON executive promotion; **~ in großen Mengen** TRANSP forwarding in bulk;

~ auf dem Landweg TRANSP land carriage, land transport; **~ auf dem Luftweg** TRANSP air transport; **~ im Straßenverkehr** TRANSP road haulage; **Beförderungsbedingungen** *f pl* TRANSP conditions of carriage, conditions of transport; **Beförderungsbescheinigung** *f* TRANSP routing certificate; **Beförderungseinheit** *f* TRANSP transport unit; **Beförderungsgut** *nt* TRANSP cargo; **Beförderungskosten** *pl* TRANSP carriage expenses, cost of transport, cost of transportation, freight, transport expenses, trucking charges (*AmE*); **Beförderungsmittel** *nt* TRANSP transport facilities, means of conveyance, means of transport, mode of transport; **Beförderungsrisiko** *nt* RECHT, TRANSP *Vertragsrecht* risk of transportation; **Beförderungsunternehmen** *nt* TRANSP carrier, private carrier, transport company; **Beförderungsunternehmer** *m* TRANSP carrier; **Beförderungsvertrag** *m* RECHT contract of carriage, transportation contract; **Beförderungszertifikat** *nt* TRANSP routing certificate; **Beförderungszulage** *f* PERSON seniority pay

befrachten *vt* IMP/EXP, TRANSP affreight, forward freight, freight, load, *Fahrzeug* charter

Befrachter *m* IMP/EXP, TRANSP charterer, freighter, shipper; **~ und Beförderer** *m* IMP/EXP, TRANSP shipper and carrier (*s&c*); ◆ **~ zahlt Abgaben** IMP/EXP, TRANSP charterer pays dues (*cpd*)

Befrachter: **Befrachteranweisungen** *f pl* IMP/EXP, TRANSP shipper's letter of instruction

Befrachtung *f* IMP/EXP, TRANSP freighting; **Befrachtungsmakler, in** *m,f* IMP/EXP, TRANSP charter broker, chartering broker

befragen *vt* GESCHÄFT *ausfragen* examine, question, *Öffentlichkeit* survey, *zu Rate ziehen* consult

Befragte(r) *mf* [decl. as adj] PERSON interviewee, V&M *Meinungsumfrage* respondent

befreien *vt* FINANZ *Schulden* discharge, GESCHÄFT discharge, dispense, exempt, exonerate, free, relieve, RECHT excuse, insulate against, insulate from, relieve

befreit *adj* GESCHÄFT exempt, STEUER exempt; **nicht ~** *adj* STEUER nonexempt; ◆ **~ von** RECHT relieved of, immune from

Befreiung *f* GESCHÄFT exemption, STEUER tax exemption; **~ von der Mehrwertsteuer** GESCHÄFT, STEUER zerorating; **~ von Verbindlichkeiten** RECHT acquittal, discharge, release from obligations; **Befreiungsklausel** *f* GESCHÄFT escape clause

befreundet: ~**e Firma** *f* GESCHÄFT business connection

befrieden *vt* GESCHÄFT, POL pacify

befriedigen *vt* GESCHÄFT gratify, satisfy, RECHT pay off, VW *Nachfrage* meet

befriedigend *adj* GESCHÄFT satisfactory

Befriedigung *f* GESCHÄFT gratification, satisfaction; **~ im Beruf** MGMNT job satisfaction

befristet *adj* RECHT *Vertrag* limited in time, terminable; ~**e Einlage** *f* BANK time deposit; ~**e Einstellung** *f* PERSON *Arbeitsvertrag* contingency claims contracting; ~**e Genehmigung** *f* IMP/EXP limited authorization; ~**e Police** *f* VERSICH time policy; ~**e Zulassung** *f* IMP/EXP limited authorization

Befugnis *f* BANK authorization, GESCHÄFT authority, competence, power, POL warrant

befürworten *vt* GESCHÄFT advocate, back up, *Projekt* back, POL sponsor, VW back up

Befürworter, in *m,f* GESCHÄFT supporter, backer, POL sponsor; **~ des Goldstandards** VW goldbug; **~ des Intervenierens** POL, VW *EU* interventionist; **~ einer unnachgiebigen Politik** POL hardliner

Befürwortung *f* GESCHÄFT backing, POL sponsorship

begabt *adj* SOZIAL *Student, Trainee* gifted

Begabungsstufe *f* SOZIAL ability level

begebbar *adj* BANK, BÖRSE, FINANZ negotiable, RECHT *Vertragsrecht* assignable; **nicht ~** *adj* GESCHÄFT unnegotiable, non-negotiable; **~es Instrument** *nt* VW negotiable instrument; **nicht ~er Namensfrachtbrief** *m* IMP/EXP direct bill of lading; **nicht ~er Namensfrachtschein** *m* TRANSP direct bill of lading

begeben *vt* BANK, BÖRSE negotiate, FINANZ negotiate, *Anleihe* float, issue, launch, sell; ♦ **sich ~** MGMNT adjourn to

begeben: **~e Wertpapiere** *nt pl* BÖRSE floating securities

Begebung *f* BÖRSE, FINANZ flotation, issue; **~ einer Anleihe** BÖRSE flotation, FINANZ issue of a loan, launching of a loan; **~ eines Auslandsschecks** BANK foreign check issue *(AmE)*, foreign cheque issue *(BrE)*; **~ eines Schuldtitels** BÖRSE flotation; **Begebungszeit** *f* BÖRSE, FINANZ *von Aktien* issue, IMP/EXP float time

Beggar-my-neighbour-Politik *f* VW beggar-my-neighbour-policy *(BrE)*, beggar-my-neighbor-policy *(AmE)*

Begierde *f* GESCHÄFT ambition, desire

Beginn *m* GESCHÄFT beginning, comencement, onset, start, outset; BÖRSE *der Börsensitzung* opening; **~ der Deckung** VERSICH commencement of coverage; **~ der Rechtsfähigkeit** RECHT beginning of the legal capacity; **~ des Versicherungsschutzes** VERSICH commencement of coverage; ♦ **zu ~** GESCHÄFT at the outset

beginnen *vt* GESCHÄFT begin, commence, start, PERSON launch

Beginner: **~'s All-Purpose Symbolic Instruction Code** *m (BASIC)* COMP beginner's all-purpose symbolic instruction code *(BASIC)*

beglaubigen *vt* BÖRSE authenticate, GESCHÄFT, RECHNUNG verify, RECHT attest to, authenticate, certify, legalize

beglaubigend: **~e(r) Beamte(r)** *m* [decl. as adj], **~e Beamtin** *f* VERWALT certifying officer

beglaubigt: **~e Abschrift** *f* RECHT, VERWALT certified copy, certified true copy; **~e Buchhaltung** *f* RECHNUNG certified accounts; **~e Kopie** *f* RECHT, VERWALT certified copy, certified true copy; **~e schriftliche Zeugenaussage** *f* RECHT *Beweisführung* deposition; **~e Urkunde** *f* RECHT authenticated document

Beglaubigung *f* BÖRSE, GESCHÄFT, RECHT authentication, certification, verification

begleichen *vt* BANK *Rechnung* settle, balance, FINANZ *Kosten* meet, balance, GESCHÄFT *Kosten* square, *Rechnung* settle, pay, defray, discharge, PATENT pay; ♦ **alte Rechnungen ~** GESCHÄFT settle old scores

Begleichung *f* BANK, FINANZ settlement; **~ von Schulden** BANK settlement of debts; **Begleichungstermin** *m* FINANZ settlement date

Begleit- *in cpds* GESCHÄFT, KOMM, VERWALT accompanying; **Begleitbrief** *m* KOMM, VERWALT accompanying letter, covering letter; **Begleitdokument** *nt* KOMM, VERWALT accompanying document

begleiten *vt* GESCHÄFT accompany, escort

begleitend *adj* GESCHÄFT accompanying, collateral; **~e Werbeaktion** *f* V&M accessory advertising

begleitet *adj* GESCHÄFT accompanied; **~es Gepäck** *nt* FREI, TRANSP accompanied baggage

Begleit-: **Begleitpapier** *nt* KOMM, TRANSP, VERWALT accompanying document; **Begleitschein** *m* KOMM, TRANSP, VERWALT accompanying document; **Begleitschreiben** *nt* GESCHÄFT, KOMM, VERWALT covering letter, accompanying letter

beglichen *adj* BANK, FINANZ, GESCHÄFT settled, paid, discharged; **nicht ~** *adj* FINANZ, GESCHÄFT undischarged; **~e Schulden** *f pl* RECHNUNG liquidated debt

begreifen *vt* GESCHÄFT *Konzept, Problematik* understand

begrenzen *vt* BÖRSE *Risiko* limit, narrow, GESCHÄFT restrict, set limits on, limit, put a cap on *(infrml)*, KOMM frame, delimit, RECHT limit

begrenzt *adj* BÖRSE narrow, thin, tight, GESCHÄFT restricted, limited, UMWELT *Ressourcen* finite; ♦ **in einem ~en Bereich** GESCHÄFT in a limited sphere; **mit nicht ~er Zahl auszugebender Anteile** GESCHÄFT *Finanzierung* open-ended

begrenzt: **~er Abrechnungsaufschub** *m* IMP/EXP limited-postponed accounting; **~e Bedingungen** *f pl* VERSICH limited terms; **~e Entscheidungsfreiheit** *f* BÖRSE limited discretion; **~e Frist** *f* VERSICH binder *(AmE)*; **~e Handlungsbevollmächtigung** *f* BÖRSE limited-trading authorization; **~er Jahresbericht** *m* RECHNUNG limited annual statements; **~er Markt** *m* BÖRSE, VW narrow market, thin market, tight market, limited market; **~es Risiko** *nt* BÖRSE limited risk; **~e Verteilung** *f* TRANSP limited distribution; **~e Zuständigkeit** *f* RECHT limited jurisdiction

Begrenzung *f* GESCHÄFT containment, limitation, restriction, *Grenze* boundary, POL containment, VW cap; **~ der Kapitalbeschaffungsmöglichkeiten** FINANZ capital rationing; **~ des räumlichen Nutzens** VW *Thiebout-Theorem* spatial benefit limitation; **Begrenzungsanschlag** *m* IND backstop

Begriff *m* GESCHÄFT concept, term

begründet: **ein ~es Anrecht auf etw besitzen** *phr* GESCHÄFT have a vested interest in sth

Begründung *f* GESCHÄFT rationale, reason, substantiation, PATENT *Einspruchsbegründung* grounds; **Begründungsfrist** *f* STEUER time limit set for stating reasons for an administrative appeal

begrüßen *vt* GESCHÄFT welcome

Begrüßung *f* COMP welcome message, GESCHÄFT welcome; **Begrüßungsfeier** *f* GESCHÄFT welcoming party; **Begrüßungsmeldung** *f* COMP welcome message

begünstigen *vt* GESCHÄFT benefit, favor *(AmE)*, favour *(BrE)*, foster, promote, *unterstützen* support, RECHT benefit

begünstigt: **~es Ausfuhrland** *f* IMP/EXP exporting beneficiary country; **~e Einfuhr** *f* IMP/EXP preferential import

Begünstigte(r) *mf* [decl. as adj] FINANZ, GESCHÄFT, GRUND beneficiary, RECHT beneficiary, cestui que trust, VERSICH beneficiary, creditor beneficiary; ♦ **gegen den eigentlich Begünstigten** GESCHÄFT contra preferentem

Begünstigungsklausel *f* VERSICH beneficiary clause, benefit of insurance clause

begutachten *vt* GESCHÄFT appraise, assess, evaluate, *Experte* give an expert opinion on, survey

Begutachtung *f* GESCHÄFT appraisal, valuation, expert valuation

begütert: **~e Klasse** *f* GESCHÄFT the rich, GRUND propertied class

behaftet *adj* GESCHÄFT afflicted, surrounded

Behälter *m* TRANSP container, tank (*ta*), VERWALT repository; **~ für staubförmige Güter** TRANSP bulk container; **Behälterdruck** *m* TRANSP tank pressure; **Behältertransport** *m* TRANSP container transport; **Behälterwagen** *m* TRANSP container car (*AmE*), container wagon (*BrE*); **Behälterwaggon** *m* TRANSP container car (*AmE*), container wagon (*BrE*)

behandeln *vt* GESCHÄFT *Problem* deal with, tackle, treat, IND, UMWELT *Abwasser* treat

behandelt: **~er Gegenstand** *m* GESCHÄFT, PATENT subject matter

Behandlung *f* IND, UMWELT treating; **~ von Ansprüchen** VERSICH claims procedure; **~ gemäß EG-Richtlinien** IMP/EXP Community treatment; **Behandlungskosten** *pl* VERSICH cost of treatment

beharrlich *adj* GESCHÄFT persistent

behaupten 1. *vt* GESCHÄFT assert, claim, maintain; **2. sich ~** *v refl* GESCHÄFT hold one's ground, stand one's ground

Behauptung *f* GESCHÄFT allegation, assertion, claim, contention, RECHT allegation, statement; ◆ **eine ~ beweisen** GESCHÄFT prove an assertion

Behausung *f* GRUND, SOZIAL accommodation

beheben *vt* GESCHÄFT remove, *Meinungsverschiedenheiten* rectify, resolve

Behebung *f* GESCHÄFT clearing, rectification, removal, *Lösung* solution

behelfsmäßig *adj* GESCHÄFT makeshift, temporary

beherbergen *vt* SOZIAL *durch Hotels und Gaststätten* accommodate

beherrschen *vt* GESCHÄFT *Markt* dominate, control

beherrschend *adj* GESCHÄFT dominant; **~e Gesellschaft** *f* BÖRSE, VW controlling company; **~e Stellung** *f* VW dominant position

beherrscht: **~e Gesellschaft** *f* BÖRSE, VW controlled company

Beherrschung *f* GESCHÄFT, POL containment, control, dominance

behindern *vt* GESCHÄFT inhibit, obstruct, *in Gefahr bringen* jeopardize, *Wachstum* hamper, hinder, impede

behindert *adj* PERSON disabled

Behinderte(r) *mf* [decl. as adj] PERSON disabled person; **Behindertenquote** *f* PERSON disabled quota

Behinderung *f* GESCHÄFT hindrance, obstruction, PERSON disability

Behörde *f* GESCHÄFT board, public authority, PATENT authority, RECHT agency (*agcy*), VERWALT bureau (*AmE*), *Amt* administrative agency, government agency, VW agency (*agcy*); **~ zur Festsetzung von Landarbeiterlöhnen** PERSON agricultural wages board (*BrE*); **Behörden** *f pl* VW public authorities; **Behördendeutsch** *nt infrml* VERWALT officialese (*infrml*); **Behörden** *f pl* **für nicht verbrauchte Haushaltsteile** FINANZ continuing appropriation authorities; **Behördenvertrag** *m* RECHT government contract

behördlich: **~es Dokument** *nt* VERWALT official docu-ment; **~e Verwaltung** *f* VERWALT public administration; **~e Zulassung** *f* STEUER concession

bei *prep* GESCHÄFT, IMP/EXP, KOMM care of (*c/o*)

Beiakte *f* RECHT related files, VERWALT subfile

beiderseitig *adj* GESCHÄFT mutual; **~ ausgeschlossen** *adj* GESCHÄFT mutually exclusive; **~er Vorteil** *m* GESCHÄFT mutual benefit; **~ zugängliches Warenauslageregal** *nt* V&M gondola (*jarg*)

beiderseits: **~ schuldig** *phr* RECHT in pari delicto (*frml*)

beidrücken *vt* KOMM *Siegel* affix

beidseitig *adj* COMP duplex; **~es Drucken** *nt* COMP duplex printing

beifügen *vt* GESCHÄFT, KOMM add, append, enclose

Beigabe *f* GESCHÄFT addition, adjunct

beigefügt: **~es Dokument** *nt* KOMM enclosed document; **~e Kopie** *f* **des Schreibens** KOMM subjoined copy of letter; **~es Zeugnis** *nt* RECHT *Bescheinigung* enclosed testimonial

beigeheftet *adj* GESCHÄFT enclosed

beigelegt: **~er Zugabeartikel** *m* V&M in-pack premium

Beigeordnete(r) *mf* [decl. as adj] GESCHÄFT adjunct

beiheften *vt* GESCHÄFT enclose

Beihilfe *f* BANK *Entwicklungsländer* aid, GESCHÄFT, PERSON benefit, RECHT aid, SOZIAL government aid, government benefit, VERWALT grant; ◆ **~ leisten** FINANZ *an Entwicklungsländer, Unternehmen, Industrie* aid, RECHT aid and abet, VW *an Entwicklungsländer* aid

Beilage *f* V&M supplement; **Beilagen** *f pl* V&M loose inserts

beiläufig: **~e Bemerkung** *f* GESCHÄFT obiter dictum

beilegen *vt* GESCHÄFT *Meinungsverschiedenheiten* resolve, settle, V&M supplement

Beilegung *f* GESCHÄFT *eines Streites* adjustment, settlement; **~ eines Streitfalls** PERSON dispute resolution, RECHT settlement of disputes

beimessen *vt* GESCHÄFT ascribe, attribute; ◆ **jdm etw ~** GESCHÄFT ascribe sth to sb, attribute sth to sb

beinahe: **~ Schönschrift** *f obs* COMP near letter quality (*NLQ*)

Beinahgeld *nt* GESCHÄFT, VW near money, quasi-money

beinhalten *vt* GESCHÄFT comprise, imply

beipflichten *vi* [+dat] GESCHÄFT *Vorschlag* agree

Beipflichten *nt* GESCHÄFT agreement, assent

Beirat *m* GESCHÄFT prudential committee (*AmE*), POL advisory committee, board, council, VERWALT *einer Gesellschaft* advisory board

Bei-Sicht-Anleihe *f* BANK on demand bond

Beispiel *nt* (*Bsp.*) GESCHÄFT example (*ex.*), illustration; ◆ **zum ~** (*z.B.*) GESCHÄFT exempli gratia (*e.g.*), for example (*e.g.*)

beispiellos *adj* GESCHÄFT unparalleled, unprecedented

Beistand *m* GESCHÄFT aid, assistance, support, RECHT legal advisor; **Beistandskredit** *m* BANK, FINANZ stand-by credit; **Beistandspakt** *m* VW mutual aid pact; **Beistandspflicht** *f* RECHT, STEUER duty to assist

beistehen *vt* GESCHÄFT, VW back up

beisteuern *vt* GESCHÄFT contribute

Beistrich *m* VERWALT comma

Beitrag *m* FINANZ subscription, financial contribution, GESCHÄFT, STEUER, VW contribution, tax; **~ für große Havarie** VERSICH general average contribution (*G/A con*); ◆ **einen ~ leisten** GESCHÄFT make a contribution

Beitrag: **Beiträge** *m pl* **zur Altersversorgung** STEUER pension contributions; **Beitragsabrechnung** *f* FINANZ premium statement; **Beitragsanalyse** *f* FINANZ contribution analysis; **Beitragsbefreiung** *f* SOZIAL exemption from contributions, VERSICH waiver of premium; **Beitragseinzug** *m* VERSICH collection of premiums, premium income

beitragen *vt* GESCHÄFT contribute; ♦ **zu etw ~** GESCHÄFT take a share in sth

beitragend *adj* RECHT contributory

beitragsfrei: **~e Betriebspension** *f* FINANZ noncontributory pension plan, noncontributory pension scheme; **~er Pensionsplan** *m* FINANZ noncontributory pension plan, noncontributory pension scheme; **~e Versicherung** *f* VERSICH fully paid-up policy

Beitrag: **Beitragsfreistellung** *f* VERSICH exemption from payment of premium; **Beitragsnachverrechnung** *f* VERSICH adjustment premium

beitragspflichtig: **~e Pensionskasse** *f* FINANZ contributory pension plan, contributory pension scheme; **~er Pensionsplan** *m* FINANZ contributory pension plan, contributory pension scheme; **~es Pensionssystem** *nt* FINANZ contributory pension plan, contributory pension scheme; **nicht ~er Rentenplan** *m* FINANZ noncontributory pension plan, noncontributory pension scheme

Beitrag: **Beitragsrückerstattung** *f* VERSICH refund of premium; **Beitragssatz** *m* GESCHÄFT membership fee, SOZIAL rate of contribution; **Beitragsstaffelung** *f* GESCHÄFT premium grading; **Beitragsstandard** *m* VW contribution standard; **Beitragsübertrag** *m* VERSICH premium transfer; **Beitragswert** *m* VERSICH contributory value

beitreibbar: **~e Forderung** *f* RECHNUNG recoverable debt

beitreten *vt* [+dat] FINANZ contract in, PERSON *einer Gewerkschaft* join, POL accede to, enter, VERSICH contract in; **nicht ~** *vt* FINANZ, VERSICH contract out

Beitreten *nt* POL *einem Abkommen* accession, entry

Beitritt *m* POL accession, entry; **Beitrittsalter** *nt* VERSICH age at entry; **Beitrittserklärung** *f* POL declaration of accession; **Beitrittsgebühren** *f pl* STEUER contracted-in rates (*BrE*)

beizulegend: **~er Wert** *m* RECHNUNG current value accounting

bejahend *adj* GESCHÄFT affirmative, approving

bekämpfen *vt* GESCHÄFT *Arbeitslosigkeit, Kriminalität* combat, fight, UMWELT *Lärm* abate

bekannt *adj* GESCHÄFT big-name, well-known, V&M well-known; ♦ **~ sein mit** GESCHÄFT be acquainted with; **auch ~ als** GESCHÄFT, KOMM also known as (*aka*); **auch ~ unter** GESCHÄFT, KOMM also known as (*aka*)

bekannt: **~e Marke** *f* V&M established brand; **~es Produkt** *nt* V&M established product; **~er Verlust** *m* VERSICH known loss

Bekanntenkreis *m* GESCHÄFT acquaintance, circle of acquaintances

Bekannte(r) *mf* [decl. as adj] GESCHÄFT acquaintance

Bekanntgabe *f* GESCHÄFT announcement; **~ eines Abkommens** GESCHÄFT announcement of an engagement; **~ einer Erfindung** PATENT disclosure of an invention; **~ einer Vereinbarung** GESCHÄFT announcement of an engagement

bekanntgeben *vt* GESCHÄFT air, announce, disclose, *Veröffentlichung* publish, PATENT publish

Bekanntheit *f* GESCHÄFT *Kenntnis* knowledge, V&M familiarity; **~ auf dem Markt** V&M market awareness; **Bekanntheitsebene** *f* V&M awareness level; **Bekanntheitsgrad** *m* V&M *von Werbung beim Verbraucher* customer awareness

bekanntmachen *vt* GESCHÄFT announce, disclose, make public

Bekanntmachung *f* GESCHÄFT announcement, RECHT public notice; **~ von Aufzeichnungen** GESCHÄFT note disclosure; **~ der Börsenorgane** BÖRSE notification by stock exchange authorities

Bekanntschaft *f* GESCHÄFT acquaintance; ♦ **jds ~ machen** GESCHÄFT make sb's acquaintance

bekanntwerden *vi* GESCHÄFT become known, leak out, KOMM *Nachrichten* break, MEDIEN, POL leak out

Beklagte(r) *mf* [decl. as adj] RECHT *Antragsgegner* defendant

Bekleidung *f* IND clothing; **Bekleidungsbranche** *f* IND apparel and wool industry (*AmE*), clothing trade (*BrE*); **Bekleidungsindustrie** *f* IND apparel industry (*AmE*), clothing industry (*BrE*)

Bekräftigung *f* RECHT affirmation (*BrE*), confirmation, corroboration, substantiation

bekunden *vt* GESCHÄFT express, show, state, RECHT *aussagen* attest to, testify

bekundet: **~e Präferenz** *f* GESCHÄFT revealed preference

Beladen *nt* TRANSP loading (*ldg*), stowage

Beladungsgrenze *f* TRANSP maximum load

Belagerungswirtschaft *f* VW siege economy

Belang *m* GESCHÄFT importance, significance; ♦ **ohne ~** GESCHÄFT irrelevant

belangbar *adj* GESCHÄFT actionable

belangen *vt* RECHT sue

belanglos *adj* GESCHÄFT irrelevant, trifling

belasten *vt* BANK charge, *Konto* debit, GESCHÄFT charge against, RECHNUNG charge, debit to, *Konto* debit, RECHT burden, charge, encumber, UMWELT pollute

belastet *adj* BANK charged, *Konto* debited, GESCHÄFT charged against, RECHNUNG charged, debited to, UMWELT polluted

Belastung *f* GESCHÄFT burden, *Last* load, pressure, FINANZ debit, RECHNUNG debit, charge, RECHT burden, charge, encumbrance, STEUER burden, VW charge, burden, UMWELT pollution; ♦ **ohne ~ der Bilanzstruktur** RECHNUNG off-balance-sheet

Belastung: **Belastungen** *f pl* **im Rahmen der gemeinsamen Agrarpolitik** VW *EG* CAP charges; **Belastungsanzeige** *f* BANK debit memorandum (*AmE*), GESCHÄFT debit note (*D/N*); **Belastungsgebiet** *nt* UMWELT high-pollution area; **Belastungszeuge** *m*, **Belastungszeugin** *f* RECHT witness for the prosecution

belaufen: **sich ~ auf** *v refl* [+acc] GESCHÄFT add up to, amount to, come to, *Angebot, Preis, Gebot* stand at, MATH aggregate

beleben 1. *vt* GESCHÄFT, VW reinvigorate, revitalize, revive, stimulate; **2. sich ~** *v refl* GESCHÄFT, VW revive

belebt *adj* GESCHÄFT busy, VW stimulated, *Preise* buoyant

Belebung *f* VW recovery, upturn

Beleg *m* GESCHÄFT voucher, STEUER document, record, *Gutschein* voucher, *Zettel* slip; **~ über Frachtraumgebühren** IMP/EXP, TRANSP tonnage dues slip; **~ für kombinierten Transport** TRANSP combined transport document (*CTD*); **Belegbuchhaltung** *f* RECHNUNG ledgerless accounting, V&M voucher system; **Belegdokumente** *nt pl* RECHT supporting documents; **Belegdurchlauf** *m* COMP document rate; **Belege** *m pl* MATH supporting data

belegen *vt* GESCHÄFT prove, RECHT situate

Beleg: **Belegexemplar** *nt* GESCHÄFT author's specimen copy; **Beleggrundbuch** *nt* BANK, FINANZ acceptance ledger; **Belegkopie** *f* V&M voucher; **Belegleser** *m* COMP document reader

beleglos *adj* BÖRSE dematerialized; **~e Abwicklung** *f* **von Börsentransaktionen** BÖRSE, VW dematerialization; **~e Buchung** *f* BANK paperless entry; **~er Handel** *m* COMP paperless trading; **~er Überweisungsverkehr** *m* FINANZ electronic funds transfer (*EFT*); **~er Zahlungsverkehr** *m* FINANZ electronic funds transfer (*EFT*)

Belegschaft *f* GESCHÄFT employees, personnel, staff, workforce, IND commonality, workforce, shop floor, PERSON labor force (*AmE*), labour force (*BrE*), *Betrieb, Unternehmen* rank-and-file, VW labor force (*AmE*), labour force (*BrE*), workforce; **Belegschaftsaktien-Beteiligungsplan** *m* PERSON employee shareholding scheme; **Belegschaftsaktienfonds** *m* BÖRSE employee share ownership plan (*BrE*) (*ESOP*), employee stock ownership plan (*AmE*) (*ESOP*), employee share ownership trust (*BrE*); **Belegschaftsaktionär, in** *m,f* BÖRSE shareholder employee; **Belegschaftsangehörige(r)** *mf* [decl. as adj] PERSON company employee; ♦ **zur ~ gehörend** PERSON on the payroll

Beleg: **Belegstreifen** *m* GESCHÄFT tear strip, RECHNUNG detail strip

belegt *adj* COMP assigned, busy, GESCHÄFT occupied

Belegung *f* COMP assignment, GRUND occupancy, occupancy rate; **Belegungsarbitrage** *f* GESCHÄFT space arbitrage; **Belegungsstufe** *f* GRUND occupancy level

Beleg: **Belegvorschub** *m* COMP *Drucker* document feeder, form feed (*FF*)

belehren *vt* RECHT instruct

belehrend: **~e Werbung** *f* V&M educational advertising

Belehrung *f* RECHT instruction

beleidigend *adj* RECHT defamatory, *mündlich* slanderous, *schriftlich* libellous

Beleidigung *f* RECHT defamation, *mündlich* slander, *schriftlich* libel; **Beleidgungsklage** *f* RECHT action for libel

beleihbar *adj* BANK *acceptable*, FINANZ eligible as collateral

Beleihung: **~ von Lagerbeständen** BANK floor planning, flooring; **~ einer Versicherungspolice** BANK premium loan, VERSICH policy loan; **Beleihungsgrenze** *f* GESCHÄFT lending ceiling, lending limit; **Beleihungskredit** *m* GESCHÄFT advance on collateral; **Beleihungsquote** *f* FINANZ loan-to-value ratio (*LTV*); **Beleihungssatz** *m* FINANZ loan-to-value ratio (*LTV*); **Beleihungswert** *m* **einer Lebensversicherung** VERSICH loan value

Belfast: **~er Börse** *f* BÖRSE Belfast Stock Exchange

belgisch-luxemburgisch: **~e Wirtschaftsunion** *f* VW Belgium-Luxembourg Economic Union (*BLEU*)

beliebig: **aus ~em Grund** *phr* GESCHÄFT for any reason; **~es Zeichen** *nt* COMP optional character

beliebt: **~er Preis** *m* V&M popular price

Beliebtheitsgrad *m* MEDIEN, POL popularity rating

beliefern *vt* GESCHÄFT supply

Belohnung *f* GESCHÄFT, V&M reward; ♦ **als ~ für** GESCHÄFT as a reward for; **~ erhalten** GESCHÄFT reap rewards; **Belohnungen realisieren** BÖRSE reap rewards

bemannen *vt* PERSON man

Bemannung *f* PERSON manning, TRANSP manning level

bemerken *vt* GESCHÄFT comment, remark, *wahrnehmen* notice

bemerkenswert *adj* GESCHÄFT remarkable

Bemerkung *f* GESCHÄFT remark; **Bemerkungsfeld** *nt* COMP comments field

bemessen *vt* GESCHÄFT assess, determine, RECHT award to

Bemessung *f* GESCHÄFT assessment; **Bemessungsgrundlage** *f* GESCHÄFT basis for assessment, RECHT measure, STEUER measure, taxable base; **Bemessungsverhältnis** *nt* GRUND *zwischen Marktwert und geschätztem Wert* assessment ratio

bemühen: **sich ~** *v refl* GESCHÄFT endeavor (*AmE*), endeavour (*BrE*), try hard; ♦ **sich ~ um** GESCHÄFT solicit, PERSON *Arbeitsstelle, Beförderung* put in for

benachbart *adj* COMP *Speicherplatz, Datenfeld* contiguous, GESCHÄFT adjoining, neighboring (*AmE*), neighbouring (*BrE*)

benachrichtigen *vt* GESCHÄFT advise, give notice of, inform, notify; ♦ **jdn von etw ~** KOMM advise sb of sth; **jdn über eine Entscheidung ~** RECHT notify sb of a decision

Benachrichtigung *f* GESCHÄFT advice, information (*inf., info*), notice, PATENT communication, RECHT notification; **~ über einen Fristablauf** VERSICH expiration notice; ♦ **~ beigefügt** KOMM advice enclosed

Benachrichtigung: **Benachrichtigungsadresse** *f* TRANSP notify address, notify party; **Benachrichtigungsnotiz** *f* KOMM advice note; **Benachrichtigungsschreiben** *nt* KOMM letter of advice

benachteiligt *adj* GESCHÄFT *gesellschaftlich, wirtschaftlich* underprivileged, disadvantaged, VW *Gebiet, Menschen* less-favored (*AmE*), less-favoured (*BrE*)

Benachteiligung *f* RECHT discrimination, unfavorable treatment (*AmE*), unfavourable treatment (*BrE*)

Benchmark *f* COMP *Tests* benchmark; **Benchmarkreserve** *f* BANK benchmark reserve (*AmE*); **Benchmarktest** *m* COMP benchmark test

Benelux-Wirtschaftsunion *f* VW Benelux

Benennung *f* RECHNUNG *von Konten* coding of accounts

benötigen: **wir ~ dringend Ihre Unterstützung** *phr* GESCHÄFT your support is vital to us

benutzen *vt* GESCHÄFT make use of, use

Benutzer, in *m,f* COMP end-user, user, GESCHÄFT user; **Benutzer-EDV** *f* COMP end-user computing

benutzerfeindlich *adj* COMP, V&M user-unfriendly

benutzerfreundlich *adj* COMP user-friendly, easy to use, V&M user-friendly

Benutzer: **Benutzerfreundlichkeit** *f* COMP, V&M user-friendliness; **Benutzergruppe** *f* COMP user group; **Benutzerhandbuch** *nt* COMP user manual; **Benutzerklasse** *f* COMP user class

benutzerorientiert *adj* COMP user-oriented, V&M consumer-oriented

Benutzer: **Benutzerprofil** *nt* V&M user profile;

Benutzerschnittstelle *f* COMP user interface; **Benutzerstrategie** *f* V&M user strategy

benutzerunfreundlich *adj* COMP, V&M user-unfriendly

Benutzer: **Benutzerverhalten** *nt* V&M user attitude

benutzt: ~e **Kapazität** *f* IND utilized capacity

Benutzung *f* GESCHÄFT use; **Benutzungsanleitung** *f* GESCHÄFT directions for use; **Benutzungs-berechtigte(r)** *mf* [decl. as adj] RECHT licensee; **Benutzungsgebühr** *f* RECHNUNG user charge; **Benutzungskosten** *pl* FINANZ, GESCHÄFT user cost

Benzin *nt* TRANSP, UMWELT gas (*AmE*), gasoline (*AmE*), petrol (*BrE*)

beobachten *vt* BÖRSE, FINANZ watch, GESCHÄFT observe, waste

Beobachter, in *m,f* GESCHÄFT observer

Beobachtung *f* GESCHÄFT observation; **Beobachtungsliste** *f* GESCHÄFT observation list; **Beobachtungstest** *m* RECHNUNG observation test

berappen 1. *vt infrml* GESCHÄFT *Geld* fork out (*infrml*), stump up (*infrml*) (*BrE*); 2. *vi infrml* GESCHÄFT stump up (*infrml*) (*BrE*)

beraten 1. *vt* GESCHÄFT, MGMNT advise, RECHT counsel; 2. *vi* RECHT deliberate; 3. **sich ~** *v refl* GESCHÄFT, MGMNT consult, confer, RECHT deliberate

beratend *adj* GESCHÄFT advisory, consultative, in an advisory capacity, prudential (*AmE*); ~e **Aufgabe** *f* GESCHÄFT advisory capacity, PERSON advisory function; ~er **Ausschuß** *m* BANK, FINANZ, POL advisory committee, consultative committee; ~e **Funktion** *f* PERSON advisory function, *bei Verhandlungen, Konferenzen* advisory capacity; ~es **Gremium** *nt* GESCHÄFT advisory body, advisory committee, consultative body, advisory board; ~er **Ingenieur** *m*, ~e **Ingenieurin** *f* IND consultant engineer; ~er **Verkäufer** *m*, ~e **Verkäuferin** *f* PERSON merchandiser

Berater, in *m,f* GESCHÄFT advisor, aide, consultant, counsellor (*BrE*), counselor (*AmE*), MGMNT consultant, PERSON advisor, consultant, POL aide; ♦ **als ~** GESCHÄFT in an advisory capacity

Berater: **Beratergruppe** *f* GESCHÄFT advisory group; **Beraterstab** *m* **Finanzen** BANK, FINANZ financial support staff; **Beratervertrag** *m* GESCHÄFT advisory contract, consultancy agreement, consulting contract

Beratung *f* GESCHÄFT advice, counseling (*AmE*), counselling (*BrE*), *Konsultation* consultation, consulting, MGMNT meeting, RECHT deliberation; ~ **auf allen Gebieten** MEDIEN, V&M full-service agency; ~ **beim Positionswechsel** PERSON outplacement; ~ **zur Realisierung von Geschäftsvorhaben** GESCHÄFT business plan consulting; ♦ **in ~ mit** GESCHÄFT in consultation with

Beratung: **Beratungsarbeit** *f* PERSON advisory work; **Beratungsausschuß** *m* GESCHÄFT advisory committee, prudential committee (*AmE*), POL *der Europäischen Gemeinschaft* Consultative Committee; **Beratungsdienst** *m* GESCHÄFT advisory service consultancy service; **Beratungsfirma** *f* GESCHÄFT consultancy, consulting firm; **Beratungsfonds** *m* FINANZ advisory funds (*AmE*); **Beratungsgegenstand** *m* GESCHÄFT subject of discussion; **Beratungsgremium** *nt* **des staatlichen Marktes** BÖRSE national market advisory board; **Beratungsgruppe** *f* **Finanzen** BANK, FINANZ financial support staff; **Beratungsingenieur, in** *m,f* IND consulting engineer; **Beratungsservice** *m*

GESCHÄFT consulting service; **Beratungsstelle** *f* FINANZ advisory service, GESCHÄFT advisory body, advisory service, VERWALT consulting agency; **Beratungstätigkeit** *f* GESCHÄFT advisory activity, consultancy work, consulting activity; **Beratungsunternehmen** *nt* GESCHÄFT consulting firm

berechenbar *adj* GESCHÄFT predictable, MATH calculable

berechnen *vt* COMP compute, FINANZ price, GESCHÄFT *Gebühr* calculate, charge, estimate, work out, MATH calculate, V&M *Preis, Gebühr* charge; ♦ **zu ~** GESCHÄFT chargeable

Berechnen *nt* COMP computing, GESCHÄFT, MATH calculation

berechnet: ~e **Menge** *f* GESCHÄFT amount charged; ~e **Summe** *f* GESCHÄFT amount charged

Berechnung *f* COMP calculation, computation, GESCHÄFT calculation, estimate; ~ **der Fristen** RECHT computation of time limits; ~ **der Produktionskosten** IND process costing; **Berechnungsgrundlage** *f* FINANZ basis of calculation; **Berechnungsgrundlage** *f* **für die zweite Rate** STEUER second installment base (*AmE*), second instalment base (*BrE*); **Berechnungsmethode** *f* GESCHÄFT method of calculation

berechtigen *vt* RECHT entitle; ♦ **jdn ~, etw zu tun** PERSON qualify sb to do sth

berechtigt *adj* RECHT *gesetzlich* entitled, legitimate, justifiable, rightful; ♦ **für etw ~ sein** GESCHÄFT be eligible for

berechtigt: ~er **Anspruch** *m* RECHT legitimate claim, rightful claim, valid claim; ~er **Erbe** *m* RECHT *des Grundvermögens* rightful heir; ~e **Erbin** *f* RECHT *des Grundvermögens* rightful heiress; ~es **Interesse** *nt* RECHT vital interest

Berechtigte(r) *mf* [decl. as adj] GRUND beneficiary, RECHT beneficiary, obligee, promisee, VERSICH beneficiary

Berechtigung *f* COMP *Zugriff* permission, GESCHÄFT validity, POL amendment, warrant, RECHT *Anrecht*, SOZIAL entitlement, VERSICH warrant

Bereich *m* COMP area, array, region, GESCHÄFT *Gebiet* domain, region, sector, *Umfang* area, range, sphere, zone, PATENT scope, V&M *eines Marktes* segment, VW domain; ~, **der nicht betreten werden darf** GESCHÄFT off-limits area; ♦ **im ~ von** GESCHÄFT in the region of; **Bereiche bilden** MGMNT compartmentalize; **in den ~ fallen von** PATENT fall within the scope of; **im ~ des Möglichen** GESCHÄFT within the bounds of possibility

Bereicherung *f* RECHT enrichment; ~ **des Aufgabengebietes** MGMNT job enrichment; ~ **des Tätigkeitsbereiches** MGMNT job enrichment; ~ **des Tätigkeitsspektrums** MGMNT job enrichment; **Bereicherungsabsicht** RECHT intent to enrich oneself

Bereich: **Bereichsanpassungsanleihe** *f* FINANZ sector adjustment loan (*SECAL*); **Bereichsinvestitions- und Erhaltungsanleihe** *f* FINANZ sector investment and maintenance loan (*SIM*); **Bereichsleiter, in** *m,f* MGMNT, PERSON area manager, division head, division manager, divisional director (*BrE*); **Bereichsleitung** *f* MGMNT, PERSON divisional management

bereichsübergreifende: ~ **Flexibilität** *f* PERSON interdepartmental flexibility

Bereich: **Bereichsvorstand** *m* MGMNT, PERSON divisional board of management

bereinigen *vt* BANK adjust, account for, GESCHÄFT correct, redress, settle, RECHNUNG, VW adjust

bereinigt *adj* BANK adjusted, GESCHÄFT adjusted, corrected, settled, RECHNUNG, VW adjusted; **~er Index** *m* RECHNUNG adjusted index; **~es Kapitalverhältnis** *nt* BANK adjusted capital ratio; **~es Kassenbudget** *nt* FINANZ consolidated cash budget; **~e Wahrscheinlichkeit** *f* MATH corrected probability; **~e Zahlen** *f pl* GESCHÄFT revised figures

Bereinigung *f* GESCHÄFT adjustment, correction, settlement, IND streamlining

bereit: **~ zur Aussprache** *phr* GESCHÄFT open to debate; **sich ~ erklären, etw zu tun** *phr* GESCHÄFT agree to do sth, volunteer for sth

Bereitschafts- *in cpds* COMP standby; **Bereitschaftsdarlehen** *nt* FINANZ standby loan; **Bereitschaftsdienst** *m* SOZIAL emergency service; **Bereitschaftskredit** *m* BANK, FINANZ standby credit; **Bereitschaftskreditabkommen** *nt* FINANZ standby agreement

bereitstellen *vt* FINANZ *Mittel, Gelder* allocate, appropriate, provide, earmark, GESCHÄFT make ready for use, make available, furnish, provide, supply, RECHNUNG appropriate

Bereitstellung *f* FINANZ earmarking, allocation, appropriation, GESCHÄFT supply, allocation, provision, RECHNUNG appropriation; **~ bewilligter Mittel durch die Regierung für Verteidigungszwecke** POL government defence appropriations (*BrE*), government defense appropriations (*AmE*); **~ von Dienstleistungen** GESCHÄFT provision of services, service delivery; **Bereitstellungsantrag** *m* POL, VW supply bill; **Bereitstellungsantrag** *m* **für das Ausgabenbudget** POL supply bill; **Bereitstellungsdarlehen** *nt* FINANZ standby loan; **Bereitstellungsermächtigung** *f* FINANZ commitment authority; **Bereitstellungsgebühren** *f pl* FINANZ standby fees; **Bereitstellungskonto** *nt* RECHNUNG appropriation account; **Bereitstellungsplanung** *f* IND procurement budgeting; **Bereitstellungsprovision** *f* BANK commitment fee; **Bereitstellungszins** *m* FINANZ commitment interest

Berg *m* VERWALT *von Papieren* mountain; ♦ **über den ~ sein** GESCHÄFT be out of the woods

bergab: **~ gehen** *vi* GESCHÄFT go downhill

Bergbau *m* IND mining, mining industry; **Bergbauaktien** *f pl* BÖRSE mining shares (*BrE*), mining stocks (*AmE*); **Bergbaugesellschaft** *f* IND mining company; **Bergbauunternehmen** *nt* IND mining company

Bergen *nt* TRANSP salvage

Berger *m* TRANSP salvor

bergrechtliche: **~ Gesellschaft** *f* IND mining company

Berg: **Bergschäden** *m pl* IND coal mining subsidence, subsidence damage

Bergung *f* TRANSP salvage; **Bergungsfahrzeug** *nt* TRANSP recovery vehicle, breakdown van (*BrE*), tow truck (*AmE*); **Bergungskosten** *pl* TRANSP salvage charges (*sc*); **Bergungsverlust** *m* VERSICH salvage loss; **Bergungsvertrag** *m* TRANSP salvage agreement

Berg: **Bergwerk** *nt* IND coal mine

Bericht *m* COMP report, GESCHÄFT report, account, return, MEDIEN write-up; **~ einer Auskunftei** GESCHÄFT, MGMNT status report; **~ mit begrenzter Geltungsdauer** POL sunset report; **~ der Brundtland-Kommission** VW Brundtland Report; **~ des Finanzdirektors** FINANZ treasurer's report; **~ des Geschäftsführers** GESCHÄFT director's report; **~ über Unregelmäßigkeiten** IND irregularity report; **~ über die Vermögenslage** FINANZ financial report, financial statement, VERWALT financial report; **~ mit zeitlich begrenzter Aktualität** POL sunset report; ♦ **Berichten zufolge** KOMM *in einem Dokument, in den Medien* as reported; **~ erstatten** GESCHÄFT report; **einen ~ über die Vermögenslage vorlegen** FINANZ submit a statement of one's affairs; **einen ~ vorlegen** GESCHÄFT issue a report, present a report, submit a report

berichten 1. *vt* GESCHÄFT, MEDIEN report; **2.** *vi* GESCHÄFT, MEDIEN report

berichtend: **~e Gesellschaft** *f* GESCHÄFT reporting company, reporting corporation

berichterstattend: **~er Händler** *m*, **~e Händlerin** *f* BÖRSE reporting dealer

Berichterstattung *f* MEDIEN commentary, news coverage, reporting, RECHNUNG disclosure; **~ über einzelne Geschäftsbereiche** RECHNUNG business segment reporting; **~ durch die Medien** MEDIEN V&M media coverage; **~ in den Medien** MEDIEN V&M media coverage; **~ an Ort und Stelle** MEDIEN spot coverage; **Berichterstattungsgrundsatz** *m* RECHNUNG basic standard of reporting; **Berichterstattungsnormen** *f pl* GESCHÄFT reporting standards

berichtigen *vt* BANK adjust, GESCHÄFT adjust, rectify, *Fehler* correct, *Text* amend, MATH *Fehler* adjust, RECHNUNG adjust, *Konto* reconcile, VW *Preis, Zeitplan* adjust

berichtigt *adj* BANK adjusted, GESCHÄFT adjusted, rectified, *Fehler* corrected, *Text* amended, MATH *Fehler* adjusted, RECHNUNG adjusted, *Konto* reconciled, VW *Preis, Zeitplan* adjusted; **nicht ~** *adj* GESCHÄFT, MEDIEN uncorrected; **~e Bilanz** *f* RECHNUNG adjusted balance sheet; **~e Probebilanz** *f* RECHNUNG adjusted trial balance, postclosing trial balance; **~e Rechnung** *f* FINANZ corrected invoice; **~e Rohbilanz** *f* RECHNUNG adjusted trial balance; **~e Saldenbilanz** *f* RECHNUNG adjusted trial balance; **~er Verkaufspreis** *m* V&M adjusted selling price; **~e Wahrscheinlichkeit** *f* FINANZ, MATH corrected probability; **~e Zahlen** *f pl* GESCHÄFT revised figures

Berichtigung *f* BANK, GESCHÄFT adjustment, rectification, correction, PATENT correction, RECHNUNG adjustment, reconciliation; **~ des Inventarwerts** RECHNUNG inventory valuation adjustment; **~ der Planungsrechnung** FINANZ, RECHNUNG, VW budget review; **Berichtigungsbuchung** *f* RECHNUNG adjusted trial balance, adjusting entry, correcting entry, VERWALT correcting entry; **Berichtigungseintrag** *m* GESCHÄFT adjusting entry; **Berichtigungseintragung** *f* RECHNUNG correcting entry; **Berichtigungsfeststellung** *f* RECHT, STEUER adjusting assessment; **Berichtigungskonto** *nt* BANK reconciliation account, RECHNUNG adjustment account; **Berichtigungsschein** *m* GESCHÄFT survey certificate; **Berichtigungstabelle** *f* RECHNUNG reconciliation table

Bericht: **Berichtsdatei** *f* COMP report file; **Berichtserzeugung** *f* COMP report generation; **Berichtsjahr** *nt* GESCHÄFT, RECHNUNG trading year, year under review; **Berichtsnormen** *f pl* RECHNUNG reporting standards; **Berichtsobjekt** *nt* GESCHÄFT reporting object; **Berichtssystem** *nt* FINANZ reporting system; **Berichtssystem** *nt* **der Ministerien** VERWALT departmental reporting system; **Berichtsterminal** *m*

COMP report terminal; **Berichtswesen** *nt* GESCHÄFT reporting; **Berichtszeitpunkt** *m* GESCHÄFT reporting date, reporting day; **Berichtszeitraum** *m* GESCHÄFT, VW period under review, reporting period

Berlin: **~er Wertpapierbörse** *f* BÖRSE Berlin Securities Exchange

Bern: **~er Union** *f* VERSICH Berne Union

Bertrand: **~sches Duopol-Modell** *nt* VW Bertrand duopoly model

berücksichtigen *vt* GESCHÄFT take into consideration, take into account, take account of, make allowance for, allow for, account for, bear in mind

Berücksichtigung *f* GESCHÄFT, VERSICH consideration; **~ des billigsten Angebots** V&M allocation to the lowest tenderer; **~ der Verluste** *f* STEUER allowance for loss; ♦ **unter ~ von** GESCHÄFT *Versandkosten* making allowance for; **nach ~ der Steuern** RECHNUNG, STEUER after-tax basis; **unter ~ der Umstände** GESCHÄFT in view of the circumstances

Beruf *m* GESCHÄFT occupation, vocation, profession, *Laufbahn* career, *Stellung* job, PERSON occupation, vocation, profession, *Laufbahn* career, *Stellung* job, *Geschäftszweig* trade; **~ ohne Aufstiegsmöglichkeiten** PERSON blind-alley job (*AmE*), dead-end job (*BrE*); **~ des Buchhalters, Steuerberaters, Wirtschaftsprüfers oder Buchprüfers** RECHNUNG accountancy profession

berufen: **sich ~ auf** *v refl* [+acc] RECHT *Gesetz, Strafe* invoke

beruflich *adj* GESCHÄFT, PERSON professional; **~er Aufstieg** *m* PERSON career advancement; **~e Bildung** *f* SOZIAL vocational training; **~e Dienstleistungen** *f pl* GESCHÄFT professional services; **~e Entwicklung** *f* PERSON career development; **~er Erfolg** *m* GESCHÄFT professional achievements, professional success; **~e Fähigkeiten** *f pl* PERSON job skills; **~es Fortkommen** *nt* PERSON career advancement; **~e Herausforderung** *f* MGMNT job challenge; **~e Kompetenz** *f* PERSON job competence; **~e Laufbahn** *f* PERSON career; **~e Mobilität** *f* PERSON job mobility, occupational mobility; **~e Qualifikationen** *f pl* PERSON professional qualifications, vocational qualifications; **~e Rehabilitation** *f* PERSON vocational rehabilitation; **~e Sackgasse** *f* PERSON dead-end job (*BrE*), blind-alley job (*AmE*); **~e Spezialisierung** *f* PERSON job specialization; **~e Trennung** *f* VW occupational segregation; **~es Weiterkommen** *nt* PERSON career advancement; **~er Werdegang** *m* PERSON career path, work history

Beruf: **Berufsausbildung** *f* PERSON, SOZIAL apprenticeship, vocational training; **Berufsausbildungsplatz** *m* PERSON apprenticeship; **Berufsausbildungszuschuß** *m* FINANZ, PERSON vocational training grant; **Berufsausrüstung** *f* GESCHÄFT occupational outfit, tools of the trade; **Berufsaussichten** *f pl* PERSON work prospects; **Berufsausübung** *f* GESCHÄFT, PERSON exercise of occupation, exercise of profession, exercise of trade; **Berufsbeamtenausschuß** *m* VERWALT Civil Service Commission (*BrE*) (*CSC*); **Berufsberater, in** *m,f* PERSON, SOZIAL career adviser, vocational counsellor (*BrE*), vocational counselor (*AmE*), vocational guide; **Berufsberatung** *f* PERSON, SOZIAL vocational counseling (*AmE*), vocational counselling (*BrE*), vocational guidance, career counseling (*AmE*), career counselling (*BrE*), career guidance; **Berufsbezeichnung** *f* MGMNT, PERSON job title

berufsbezogen: **~e Ausbildung** *f* PERSON, SOZIAL vocational training; **~e Aus- und Weiterbildung** *f* PERSON career-oriented training

berufsbildend: **~e Schule** *f* SOZIAL vocational school

Beruf: **Berufserfahrung** *f* PERSON professional experience, vocational experience; **Berufsethos** *nt* GESCHÄFT professional ethics, RECHT ethics of the profession; **Berufsfachschule** *f* SOZIAL college of further education (*CFE*) (*BrE*); **Berufsgeheimnis** *nt* GESCHÄFT professional secrecy, trade secret; **Berufsgenossenschaft** *f* GESCHÄFT trade association; **Berufsgewerkschaft** *f* PERSON occupational union (*BrE*); **Berufsgruppenklassifikation** *f* VERSICH classification of occupations; **Berufshaftpflichtversicherung** *f* VERSICH professional indemnity insurance; **Berufshaftung** *f* RECHT professional liability; **Berufshändler, in** *m,f* VW professional trader; **Berufsinteresse** *nt* PERSON job interest; **Berufsklassifizierung** *f* PERSON job classification; **Berufskrankheit** *f* PERSON, SOZIAL industrial disease, occupational disease, occupational illness; **Berufsleben** *nt* PERSON working life

berufsmäßig: **nicht ~es Verhalten** *nt* PERSON unprofessional behavior (*AmE*), unprofessional behaviour (*BrE*)

Beruf: **Berufsrente** *f* FINANZ, PERSON occupational pension; **Berufsrisiko** *nt* GESCHÄFT, PERSON occupational hazard; **Berufsschule** *f* SOZIAL vocational school, college of further education (*CFE*) (*BrE*)

berufsstandswidrig: **~es Verhalten** *nt* GESCHÄFT unprofessional conduct

berufstätig: **~e Frau** *f* PERSON working woman; **~er Mann** *m* PERSON working man

Beruf: **Berufsunfähigkeitsrente** *f* SOZIAL pension for occupational invalidity, VERSICH disability insurance income (*AmE*); **Berufsunfähigkeitsrentenversicherung** *f* VERSICH disability replacement insurance (*AmE*); **Berufsunfall** *m* IND industrial injury, SOZIAL occupational accident; **Berufsunfall- und Krankenversicherung** *f* PERSON, VERSICH worker compensation insurance; **Berufsunfallpflichtversicherung** *f* VERSICH workers' compensation and employers' liability insuring agreement; **Berufsverband** *m* GESCHÄFT professional association, professional body; **Berufsvereinigung** *f* GESCHÄFT trade association; **Berufsverkehrsteilnehmer, in** *m,f* TRANSP commuter; **Berufsvorbereitung** *f* PERSON training; **Berufszugehörigkeit** *f* PERSON work classification; **Berufszweig** *m* PERSON line of occupation

Berufung *f* PATENT appeal, PERSON appointment, RECHT appeal; ♦ **~ einlegen** RECHT appeal against; **in ~ gehen** RECHT enter an appeal

Berufung: **Berufungseinlegung** *f* PATENT notice of appeal; **Berufungsfrist** *f* RECHT period set aside for appeal; **Berufungsgericht** *nt* RECHT *Appellationsgericht* appeal court, appeals court, court of appeal, *Revisionsgericht* appellate court; **Berufungsgericht** *nt* **für Beschäftigungskonflikte** PERSON Employment Appeal Tribunal (*BrE*) (*EAT*); **Berufungsinstanz** *f* **in Steuersachen** STEUER General Commissioners (*BrE*); **Berufungsverfahren** *nt* RECHT appeal proceedings

berühmt *adj* GESCHÄFT famous, prominent

berühren *vt* RECHT affect

Besatzartikel *m pl* GESCHÄFT trimmings

Besch. *abbr* (*Bescheinigung*) GESCHÄFT, KOMM cert. (*certificate*)

beschädigt: ~**er Buchstabe** *m* MEDIEN, V&M battered letter; ~**er Geldschein** *m* BANK mutilated note; ~**es Wertpapier** *nt* BÖRSE mutilated security

Beschädigung *f* COMP, IND damage; ~ **auf der Festplatte** COMP hard error

beschaffen *vt* BÖRSE *Kapital*, FINANZ *Geld* raise, GESCHÄFT procure, provide, collect

Beschaffenheit *f* RECHT composition; **Beschaffenheitsbestätigung** *f* GESCHÄFT certificate of conditioning; **Beschaffenheitsschaden** *m* GESCHÄFT inherent defect; **Beschaffenheitszeugnis** *nt* TRANSP certificate of inspection

Beschaffung *f* GESCHÄFT collection, *Besorgung* procurement, V&M *Besorgung* procurement; ~ **von Barmitteln** FINANZ cash generation; ~ **öffentlicher Mittel** GESCHÄFT, FINANZ collection of public money; **Beschaffungsabteilung** *f* GESCHÄFT procurement department; **Beschaffungsbeamte(r)** *m* [decl. as adj], **Beschaffungsbeamtin** *f* GESCHÄFT procurement officer; **Beschaffungskosten** *pl* GESCHÄFT procurement costs, purchasing costs; **Beschaffungskredit** *m* BANK buyer credit

Beschaffung: **Beschaffungsplanung** *f* GESCHÄFT procurement planning

beschaffungsseitig: ~**e Verflechtung** *f* VW backward linkage

Beschaffung: **Beschaffungsvertrag** *m* FINANZ procurement contract; **Beschaffungsvertreter, in** *m,f* GESCHÄFT procurement agent; **Beschaffungsweg** *m* GESCHÄFT trade channel; **Beschaffungswesen** *f* FINANZ government procurement, VERWALT buying; **Beschaffungszeit** *f* GESCHÄFT purchasing time, V&M lead time

beschäftigen 1. *vt* GESCHÄFT engage, occupy, PERSON employ; **2. sich ~ mit** *v refl* GESCHÄFT deal with, MGMNT be engaged in

beschäftigt *adj* GESCHÄFT busy, engaged, preoccupied, PERSON employed; ◆ ~ **sein mit** GESCHÄFT be busy doing sth

Beschäftigte *pl* GESCHÄFT, IND workforce, MGMNT, PERSON workforce, employees; **Beschäftigte(r)** *mf* [decl. as adj] PERSON, MGMNT employee; **Beschäftigtenanzahl** *f* PERSON labor force (*AmE*), labour force (*BrE*), number of employees; **Beschäftigtenzahlen** *f pl* GESCHÄFT employment figures, jobs data

Beschäftigung *f* PERSON employment, VW activity; ~ **in beschützenden Werkstätten** PERSON *für Behinderte* sheltered employment; ~ **auf Lebenszeit** PERSON, VW lifetime employment; ~ **im öffentlichen Dienst** PERSON public service employment (*PSE*); **Beschäftigungschance** *f* PERSON job opportunity; **Beschäftigungsdauer** *f* PERSON length of employment, length of service; **Beschäftigungsfunktion** *f* VW employment function; **Beschäftigungsgrad** *m* RECHNUNG, VERWALT, VW activity level; **Beschäftigungskontinuität** *f* PERSON continuity of employment; **Beschäftigungslosigkeit** *f* PERSON *Statistik, Steuerwesen* nonemployment; **Beschäftigungsmöglichkeit** *f* PERSON job opportunity, job prospect; **Beschäftigungsmultiplikator** *m* VW employment multiplier; **Beschäftigungsnachweis** *m* PERSON *beruflicher Werdegang* employment record

beschäftigungsorientiert: ~**e Kostenrechnung** *f* RECHNUNG activity-based costing (*BrE*)

Beschäftigung: **Beschäftigungspolitik** *f* PERSON manpower policy, employment policy; **Beschäftigungsprognose** *f* GESCHÄFT manpower forecasting; **Beschäftigungsprogramm** *nt* VW job creation program (*AmE*), job creation programme (*BrE*), job creation scheme; **Beschäftigungsreserve** *f* VW reserve of potential labor (*AmE*), reserve of potential labour (*BrE*); **Beschäftigungssicherheit** *f* PERSON security of employment; **Beschäftigungssituation** *f* GESCHÄFT employment situation, labor market situation (*AmE*), labour market situation (*BrE*); **Beschäftigungsstand** *m* VW level of employment

beschäftigungsunfähig *adj* PERSON unemployable

Beschäftigung: **Beschäftigungsverbot** *nt* PERSON prohibition notice; **Beschäftigungsverhältnis** *nt* PERSON employment relationship

beschäftigungswirksam *adj* VW having a positive influence on employment

Beschäftigung: **Beschäftigungszahlen** *f pl* VW employment figures

Bescheid *m* RECHT administrative decision

bescheiden *adj* GESCHÄFT modest; ~**es Einkommen** *nt* FINANZ moderate income

Bescheinigung *f* (*Besch.*) GESCHÄFT certificate (*cert.*), KOMM certificate (*cert.*), advice, RECHT certification; ~ **über große Havarie** VERSICH general average certificate (*GAC*); ~ **über Ordungsmäßigkeit** VERWALT certificate of compliance; ◆ **eine ~ beibringen** VERWALT furnish a certificate, submit a certificate

Beschlagnahme *f* GRUND distraint, IMP/EXP confiscation, seizure, RECHT arrest, sequestration, *von Besitz* levy, *von Grundbesitz* distraint, TRANSP detention, VERSICH attachment; ~ **von Eigentum** RECHT distraint of property

beschlagnahmen *vt* IMP/EXP confiscate, seize, impound, RECHT sequester, sequestrate, impound, TRANSP detain; ◆ **etw von jdm ~** GESCHÄFT confiscate sth from sb

beschlagnahmt: ~**es Konto** *nt* FINANZ impound account

Beschlagnahmung *f* GRUND distraint, IMP/EXP confiscation, seizure, RECHT sequestration, *von Besitz* levy, *von Grundbesitz* distraint, TRANSP detention, VERSICH attachment

beschlagnehmen *vt* GESCHÄFT confiscate, seize, RECHT impound

beschleunigen 1. *vt* GESCHÄFT accelerate, expedite, speed up; **2.** *vi* GESCHÄFT speed up; **3. sich ~** *v refl* GESCHÄFT accelerate, speed up

Beschleunigerkarte *f* COMP *Graphik, Bildschirmaufbau* accelerator card

beschleunigt 1. *adj* GESCHÄFT accelerated; **2.** *adv* ◆ ~ **abfertigen** GESCHÄFT expedite

beschleunigt: ~**e Abschreibung** *f* FINANZ, RECHNUNG accelerated depreciation; ~**e Amortisation** *f* RECHNUNG accelerated amortization; ~**e Bewegung** *f* V&M accelerated motion; ~**e Mittelbereitstellung** *f* BANK expedited funds availability; ~**er Rückkauf** *m* GESCHÄFT accelerated redemption; ~**e Umwandlung** *f* BANK accelerated conversion; ~**es Wachstum** *nt* VW accelerated growth

Beschleunigung *f* GESCHÄFT speed-up, acceleration, VW *Wirtschaftswachstum* acceleration; **Beschleunigungsgebühr** *f* KOMM, TRANSP dispatch money

beschließen *vt* FINANZ declare, GESCHÄFT adopt, decide on, *Meeting* round off, POL adopt, RECHT *Gesetz* adopt, pass, VERWALT adopt, VW *Budget* pass; ◆ ~, **etw zu tun** GESCHÄFT resolve to do sth

beschlossen *adj* GESCHÄFT agreed, decided, RECHT completed; **~e Dividende** *f* FINANZ declared dividend

Beschluß *m* GESCHÄFT, MGMNT *des Vorstands* decision, resolution, POL act, RECHT *des Gerichts* order (*ord.*)

beschlußfähig: **~ sein** *phr* MGMNT be quorate, form a quorum, have a quorum

Beschluß: **Beschlußfähigkeit** *f* MGMNT quorum; **Beschlußfassung** *f* GESCHÄFT resolution, MGMNT, PERSON voting; **Beschlußunfähigkeit** *f* MGMNT absence of a quorum

beschneiden *vt* GESCHÄFT *Rechte* truncate, cut back, *Kosten* whittle down, pare down

Beschneidung *f* GESCHÄFT truncation, whittling down, VW paring down

beschränken *vt* BÖRSE *Risiko* limit, GESCHÄFT constrain, limit, restrict

beschränkend *adj* GESCHÄFT limiting, restrictive

beschränkt: **mit ~em Aktionärskreis** *phr* BÖRSE closely-held; **~er Artikel** *m* TRANSP restricted article; **~e Disposition** *f* BÖRSE limited discretion; **~es Eigentumsrecht** *nt* VERSICH short tail; **~es Erbrecht** *nt* VERSICH short tail; **~es Giro** *nt* FINANZ conditional endorsement; **~ haftender Gesellschafter** *m*, **~ haftende Gesellschafterin** *f* RECHT limited partner; **~er Handel** *m* BÖRSE restricted trading; **nur ~ lieferbar sein** *phr* GESCHÄFT be in short supply; **~er Markt** *m* VW restricted market; **~e Prüfung** *f* RECHNUNG limited audit; **~ steuerpflichtig** *adj* RECHT, STEUER subject to limited tax liability; **~e Verteilung** *f* TRANSP limited distribution; **~e Vollmacht** *f* RECHT limited authority

Beschränkung *f* GESCHÄFT curtailment, limitation, restriction, *Hindernis* barrier; **~ der Gerichtsberichterstattung** RECHT gag order; **~ des Kapitalverkehrs** IMP/EXP restrictions on capital movements; **~ der Kreditaufnahme** BANK, FINANZ, VW credit squeeze

beschreiben *vt* GESCHÄFT, PATENT describe, specify

beschreibend *adj* GESCHÄFT, PATENT descriptive

Beschreibung *f* GESCHÄFT description, PATENT description, patent specification

Beschriftung *f* GESCHÄFT marking, MEDIEN lettering; **Beschriftungs-Bescheinigung** *f* TRANSP carving note (*BrE*)

Beschwerde *f* GESCHÄFT complaint, PATENT appeal, PERSON *Arbeit* grievance, RECHT appeal; ◆ **~ bei jdm einlegen** GESCHÄFT lodge a complaint with sb; **~ führen** RECHT appeal against a decision, take an appeal to court

beschwerdeführend: **~e Partei** *f* RECHT *Vertragsrecht* complaining party

Beschwerde: **Beschwerdeverfahren** *nt* PERSON grievance procedure, RECHT complaint proceedings

beschweren: **sich ~** *v refl* GESCHÄFT complain

beschwichtigen *vt* GESCHÄFT, POL pacify

beschwindeln *vt* GESCHÄFT cheat, swindle, RECHNUNG, RECHT defraud

beseitigen *vt* GESCHÄFT remove, *Meinungsverschiedenheiten, Unstimmigkeiten* resolve, eliminate, *abschaffen* abolish, RECHT redress, VERWALT abolish, VW *Inflation* stamp out, abolish

beseitigt *adj* GESCHÄFT eliminated

Beseitigung *f* GESCHÄFT abolition, removal, RECHNUNG, RECHT, VERWALT, VW abolition; **~ von Handelsschranken** VW abolition of trade barriers; **~ von Steuerverzerrungen** STEUER removal of tax distortions

besetzen *vt* PERSON fill

besetzt *adj* COMP busy, KOMM *Telefon, Fax* busy (*AmE*), engaged (*BrE*)

Besetztzeichen *nt* KOMM busy signal (*AmE*), engaged signal (*BrE*), engaged tone (*BrE*)

Besetzung *f* GRUND occupation, PERSON staffing, *eines Betriebs als Arbeitskampfmaßnahme* occupation (*BrE*); **Besetzungsebenen** *f pl* PERSON staffing levels

besichern *vt* BANK, BÖRSE secure, FINANZ collateralize, *Anleihe* supply security for

besichert: **~es Darlehen** *nt* BANK secured advance, collateral loan; **~er Kredit** *m* **mit fester Laufzeit** BANK secured fixed-term loan; **~en Kredit gewähren** *phr* BÖRSE lend on security; **~er Personalkredit** *m* BANK secured personal loan; **~er Schuldschein** *m* FINANZ secured debenture

Besichtigung *f* FREI tour, sight-seeing tour, GRUND *von Haus* viewing, IND *von Maschinen, Waren* inspection, survey; ◆ **~ nur nach Voranmeldung** GRUND viewing by appointment only

Besichtigung: **Besichtigungsbericht** *m* VERSICH survey report; **Besichtigungsgebühr** *f* GESCHÄFT survey fee; **Besichtigungsschein** *m* TRANSP *eines Schiffes* certificate of survey

besiegeln *vt* GESCHÄFT seal

Besitz *m* BÖRSE holding, GESCHÄFT property, ownership, GRUND occupancy, RECHT possession, *Innehaben* occupation; ◆ **~ entziehen** GRUND dispossess (*AmE*); **~ ergreifen von** GRUND take possession of, RECHT, VW appropriate

Besitz: **Besitzanspruch** *m* RECHT possessory claim; **Besitzdauer** *f* BÖRSE holding period; **Besitzeinkommen** *nt* FINANZ, RECHNUNG, STEUER unearned income

besitzen *vt* GESCHÄFT *gekaufte Waren* own, GRUND occupy

Besitzen *nt* GRUND occupancy, RECHT holding

Besitz: **Besitzentziehung** *f* FINANZ, RECHT divestment

Besitzer, in *m,f* GESCHÄFT owner, proprietor, RECHT possessor; ◆ **den Besitzer wechseln** V&M change hands

Besitzlose(r) *mf* [decl. as adj] GRUND, RECHT, VW nonproperty owner

Besitz: **Besitzstand** *m* GESCHÄFT acquired rights, vested rights, RECHT status of possession; **Besitzstandsklausel** *f* POL grandfather clause (*AmE*); **Besitzsteuern** *f pl* FINANZ, STEUER taxes from income and property

besitzstörend: **~e Tätigkeit** *f* RECHT nuisance

Besitz: **Besitzstörer, in** *m,f* RECHT *Rechtsverletzung* trespasser; **Besitzstörer werden gerichtlich verfolgt** *phr* RECHT trespassers will be prosecuted; **Besitzübersicht** *f* RECHT summary possession; **Besitzurkunde** *f* RECHT title deed; **Besitzverflechtung** *f* GESCHÄFT cross-ownership; **Besitzwechsel** *m pl* RECHNUNG bills receivable

Besoldungsgruppe *f* VW salary grade

Besoldungssatz *m* PERSON salary rate

besondere: ~ **Havarie** *f* VERSICH particular average (*p.a.*); ~ **Kennziffer** *f* VERWALT unique reference number (*URN*); ~ **Lage** *f* GESCHÄFT special situation; ~**s Merkmal** *nt* GESCHÄFT speciality, specialty (*AmE*); ~ **Position** *f* V&M special position; ~ **Rücklage** *f* RECHNUNG special reserve; **der ~n Schadenbeteiligungsklausel unterworfen** *phr* VERSICH subject to particular average (*SPA*); **der ~n Schadenbeteiligung unterworfen** *phr* VERSICH subject to particular average (*SPA*); ~ **Umstände** *m pl* GESCHÄFT special circumstances; ~ **Vollmachten** *f pl* POL special warrant

Besonderheit *f* GESCHÄFT exceptional quality, speciality, specialty (*AmE*), unusual quality, V&M special feature

besonders *adv* GESCHÄFT especially (*esp.*), specially; ♦ ~ **kreuzen** BANK cross specially

besonders: ~ **benachteiligte Region** *f* VW least-favored region (*AmE*), least-favoured region (*BrE*); ~ **lukrativer Geschäftsbereich** *m* VW crown jewels (*infrml*)

besonnen *adj* GESCHÄFT prudent; ~**er Mensch** *m* GESCHÄFT reasonable person

Besorgnis *f* GESCHÄFT doubt, worry; ~ **der Befangenheit** RECHT doubt as to impartiality, fear of prejudice

besprechen *vt* GESCHÄFT discuss, MEDIEN *Film, Theaterstück* review; ♦ **etw mit jdm ~** GESCHÄFT have a word with sb about sth

Besprechung *f* GESCHÄFT discussion, MEDIEN *Film, Theaterstück* review; **Besprechungsexemplar** *nt* MEDIEN review copy

besser *adv* GESCHÄFT better; ♦ ~ **als der Durchschnitt** GESCHÄFT better than average; ~ **als erwartet** GESCHÄFT better than expected; ~ **als vorhergesagt** GESCHÄFT better than predicted

bessergestellt *adj* GESCHÄFT better-off

Besserung *f* VW upturn; **Besserungsanstalt** *f obs* SOZIAL reformatory (*obs*), adjustment center (*AmE*), adjustment centre (*BrE*)

Best. *abbr* (*Bestätigung*) KOMM cert. (*certificate*)

Bestand *m* BANK position, BÖRSE portfolio, V&M *eines Geschäfts* stock, VERSICH portfolio; ~ **an Anlagewerten** BÖRSE, FINANZ asset portfolio; ~ **an festen Aufträgen** GESCHÄFT backlog of final orders; ~ **an liquiden Mitteln** RECHNUNG cash position; ~ **an Wertpapieren** BANK, FINANZ, VW portfolio; ♦ **den ~ aufnehmen** GESCHÄFT take stock

Bestände *m pl* GESCHÄFT, VW supplies; ~ **an Handelswaren** RECHNUNG merchandise inventory; ♦ ~ **aufnehmen** RECHNUNG take inventory, take stock

Bestände: Beständeschwund *m* VW inventory shrinkage

beständig *adj* GESCHÄFT *stabil* stable, standing, consistent, steady, *dauerhaft* permanent, VW steady

Bestand: Bestandsaufnahme *f* GESCHÄFT, RECHNUNG, V&M stocktaking, inventory, stock inventory; **Bestandsberechnung** *f* RECHNUNG inventory valuation, inventory computation; **Bestandsberichtigungen** *f pl* RECHNUNG inventory adjustments; **Bestandsbuch** *nt* TRANSP warehouse book (*WB*); **Bestandsdatei** *f* COMP main file; **Bestandsfehlbetrag** *m* VW inventory shortage; **Bestandsführung** *f* FINANZ inventory management, RECHNUNG stock control; **Bestandshaltekosten** *pl* BÖRSE cost of carry; **Bestandskartei** *f* VERWALT inventory file; **Bestandskonto** *nt* RECHNUNG asset account;

Bestandskontrolle *f* RECHNUNG inventory control; **Bestandskontrolleur, in** *m,f* RECHNUNG inventory controller; **Bestandsliste** *f* GESCHÄFT stock list, stock sheet; **Bestandsnachweis** *m* IND inventory; **Bestandsposten** *m* RECHNUNG inventory item; **Bestandsübertragung** *f* GESCHÄFT transfer of stock, VERSICH portfolio transfer; **Bestandsüberwachung** *f* VW stock control; **Bestandsversicherung** *f* VERSICH portfolio insurance; **Bestandsverwaltung** *f* FINANZ inventory management, RECHNUNG stock control; **Bestandsverzeichnis** *nt* VERSICH inventory; **Bestandteil** *m* GESCHÄFT, IND component part, component

bestätigen *vt* COMP *Befehl* acknowledge, GESCHÄFT acknowledge, confirm, accredit, *Anspruch* validate, verify, vindicate, *Zeuge* witness, KOMM acknowledge, RECHNUNG verify, RECHT acknowledge, V&M endorse, indorse

bestätigt *adj* GESCHÄFT approved, acknowledged, confirmed; ~**e Kopie** *f* RECHT confirmed copy; ~**er Kredit** *m* BANK confirmed credit; ~**er Scheck** *m* BANK certified check (*AmE*), certified cheque (*BrE*), marked check (*AmE*), marked cheque (*BrE*), VW marked check (*AmE*), marked cheque (*BrE*); ~**er unwiderruflicher Kredit** *m* BANK confirmed irrevocable credit; ~**es unwiderrufliches Akkreditiv** *nt* BANK confirmed irrevocable letter of credit

Bestätigung *f* (*Best.*) BANK approval, GESCHÄFT acknowledgement (*ack*), certification, *Echtheit* verification, *Termin* confirmation, *Anspruch* validation, vindication, KOMM *Unterschrift, Initialen auf Dokumenten* acknowledgement (*ack*), *Dokument* certificate (*cert.*), RECHNUNG, RECHT confirmation, attestation, V&M endorsement; ~ **durch eine amtliche Stelle** BÖRSE authentication; ~ **der Barhinterlegung** FINANZ cash deposit acknowledgement; ~ **einer Bestimmung** GESCHÄFT allocation to a provision; ~ **der Echtheit einer Unterschrift** BANK guarantee of signature; ~ **der Erneuerung** VERSICH confirmation of renewal; ~ **der Richtigkeit der Buchführung** RECHNUNG verification of accounts; ~ **der Verlängerung** VERSICH confirmation of renewal; ♦ **zur ~ einreichen** GESCHÄFT submit for approval; **zur ~ vorlegen** GESCHÄFT submit for approval

Bestätigung: Bestätigungsmitteilung *f* GESCHÄFT confirmation notice; **Bestätigungsschein** *m* RECHT record of acknowledgement; **Bestätigungsvermerk** *m* RECHNUNG accounts certification, audit certificate, auditor's certificate, auditor's opinion, *Bericht* auditor's report, auditor's statement, audit report

beste *adj* GESCHÄFT best; ♦ **sich nach dem ~n Preis umsehen** V&M shop around for the best price

beste: ~ **Alternative** *f* GESCHÄFT best alternative; ~**r Anbieter** *m* GESCHÄFT best profferer; ~**s Angebot** *nt* GESCHÄFT best bid; ~ **angewandte Mittel** *nt pl* GESCHÄFT best practical means (*bpm*); ~**s Gebot** *nt* GESCHÄFT best bid; ~ **Möglichkeit** *f* GESCHÄFT best option; ~**r Preis** *m* GESCHÄFT rock-bottom price; ~ **Qualität** *f* GESCHÄFT top quality; ~ **Wahl** *f* GESCHÄFT best choice

bestechen 1. *vt* GESCHÄFT bribe; ♦ **jdn ~** GESCHÄFT bribe sb, give sb bribes, grease sb's palm (*infrml*), oil sb's palm (*infrml*); **2. sich ~ lassen** *v refl* GESCHÄFT, POL take bribes

Bestechung *f* FINANZ fix (*AmE*), GESCHÄFT bribe,

bribery, payoff; **Bestechungsfonds** *m* FINANZ, POL slush fund; **Bestechungsgeld** *nt* FINANZ bribe, sweetener (*infrml*), GESCHÄFT bribe, bribe money, hush money (*infrml*), boodle (*infrml*), *Abzahlung* bribery, payoff, POL graft (*infrml*); **Bestechungsgelder** *nt pl* GESCHÄFT bribe, V&M *Schmiergelder* payola (*infrml*) (*AmE*); **Bestechungsgeschenk** *nt* GESCHÄFT bribe

bestehen: ~ **aus** *vt* GESCHÄFT comprise

bestellen *vt* GESCHÄFT order, *Eintrittskarte, Platz* book, reserve, RECHT *Buchprüfer* appoint, nominate, *Hypothek* create, VW commission

Bestellpunktsystem *nt* TRANSP order point system

bestellt *adj* RECHT appointed, nominated, V&M *Person, Unternehmen* appointed, *Waren* on order; ~**er Fachhändler** *m*, ~**e Fachhändlerin** *f* V&M appointed stockist; ~**er Vertreter** *m*, ~**e Vertreterin** *f* RECHT appointed representative

Bestelltätigkeit *f* GESCHÄFT booking orders

Bestellung *f* GESCHÄFT *für ein Amt* appointment, RECHNUNG purchase order, RECHT *für ein Amt* appointment; ~ **mit vereinbarter Barzahlung** V&M cash order (*co*); ◆ **Bestellungen annehmen** GESCHÄFT take orders

Bestellverfahren *nt* V&M ordering procedure

bestens *adj* BÖRSE at best

Bestens-Auftrag *m* BÖRSE discretionary order

Besteuerung *f* STEUER, VW imposition, taxation; **Besteuerungseinheit** *f* STEUER, VW tax unit; **Besteuerungsgegenstand** *m* RECHT, STEUER taxable event; **Besteuerungsgrundsätze** *m pl* STEUER canons of taxation

bestimmen *vt* FINANZ ring-fence, GESCHÄFT *Wert* value, PERSON *Komitee, Ausschuß* appoint, VW *Preis* determine, earmark, ring-fence

bestimmt *adj* GESCHÄFT particular, *Artikel* specific, *festgesetzter Preis oder Tag* fixed, *genau genannt* definite; ◆ ~ **für** TRANSP bound for; **jdn mit einer** ~**en Aufgabe betrauen** GESCHÄFT entrust sb with a specific task, task sb with sth (*jarg*) (*AmE*); **einen** ~**en Preis fordern** VW command a certain price; **zu einer** ~**en Zeit** GESCHÄFT at a given time; **zu einem** ~**en Zeitpunkt** GESCHÄFT at a certain time; **an einen** ~**en Zweck binden** GESCHÄFT earmark

bestimmt: ~**es Amt** *nt* PATENT designated office; ~**e Bedingungen** *f pl* GESCHÄFT certain conditions; ~**er Betrag** *m* GESCHÄFT specific amount; ~**e Menge** *f* GESCHÄFT specific amount; ~**er Punkt** *m* GESCHÄFT certain point

Bestimmtheit *f* GESCHÄFT certainty; **Bestimmtheitsmaß** *nt* MATH coefficient of determination

Bestimmung *f* GESCHÄFT allocation, RECHNUNG *von Geldern* appropriation, RECHT *Vorschrift* stipulation, provision, VERSICH *Klausel* clause, VW appropriation, regulation; ~ **des richtigen Zeitpunktes** GESCHÄFT timing; ~ **über die Vertragsdauer** RECHT termination clause; **Bestimmungen** *f pl* **für den Aktienhandel** BÖRSE trading rules; **Bestimmungsflughafen** *m* IMP/EXP, TRANSP destination airport

bestimmungsgemäß: ~**er Gebrauch** *m* RECHT contractual use

Bestimmung: **Bestimmungshafen** *m* IMP/EXP, TRANSP destination port, port of destination; **Bestimmungsland** *nt* IMP/EXP, TRANSP country of destination, VW receiving country; **Bestimmungsort** *m* GESCHÄFT place of destination, destination

bestmöglich *adj* GESCHÄFT best possible; ~**e Zeit** *f* V&M best time available

Bestochene(r) *mf* [decl. as adj] FINANZ recipient of bribe, bagman (*infrml*) (*AmE*)

Bestpreis *m* GESCHÄFT highest price, best price

Bestreben *nt* GESCHÄFT aim

bestreiken *vt* [+dat] PERSON go on strike against

bestreikt *adj* PERSON strikebound

bestreitbar *adj* GESCHÄFT contestable, disputable, RECHT traversable; ~**er Markt** *m* VW contestable market

bestreiten *vt* GESCHÄFT *Kosten* bear, meet, RECHT *Forderung* dispute, *Anrecht* deny; ◆ **die Kosten** ~ GESCHÄFT bear the costs, defray the costs, meet costs

Bestreiten *nt* GESCHÄFT contestation, RECHT *Einwendung* traverse; **Nicht-Bestreiten** *nt* RECHT nolo contendere (*frml*)

bestritten: ~**er Anspruch** *m* FINANZ contested claim

Bestseller *m* MEDIEN *Buch, Schallplatte*, V&M best seller

bestücken *vt* IND equip, tool up

Bestückung *f* IND capacity utilization; **Bestückungsausbau** *m* IND capacity utilization rate; **Bestückungsbetrieb** *m* COMP circuit board assembly, IND component factory

Besuch *m* GESCHÄFT visit; ◆ **jdm einen** ~ **abstatten** GESCHÄFT pay sb a visit

besuchen *vt* GESCHÄFT visit, pay a visit to

Besucher, in *m,f* GESCHÄFT visitor; ~ **aus Übersee** GESCHÄFT overseas visitor; **Besucherzahlen** *f pl* GESCHÄFT attendance figures

besucht *adj* GESCHÄFT attended

Beta *nt* BÖRSE beta (*AmE*); **Beta-Aktie** *f* BÖRSE beta stock; **Beta-Fehler** *m* MATH beta error, *Statistik* type-II error; **Beta-Koeffizient** *m* BÖRSE beta coefficient (*AmE*), beta factor (*BrE*); **Beta-Standort** *m* COMP *Programmtest* beta site; **Beta-Stand** *m* **des Portefeuilles** BÖRSE portfolio beta score; **Betatest** *m* COMP *Programmtest* beta test; ~**-Version** *f* COMP *Software* beta version

betätigen *vt* IND activate

beteiligen: sich an etw ~ *phr* GESCHÄFT acquire an interest in sth, take part in sth

beteiligt: ~**e Partei** *f* GESCHÄFT interested party

Beteiligte(r) *mf* [decl. as adj] GESCHÄFT partner, RECHT interested party, involved party, privy

Beteiligung *f* BÖRSE stake, FINANZ equity holding, interest (*int.*), GESCHÄFT *an einem Unternehmen* stake, involvement, POL *Wahl* turnout, RECHNUNG participation, share, VW trade investments; ~ **an einer Bank** BANK stake in a bank; ~ **am Gewinn** *f* FINANZ profit share; ◆ **eine** ~ **an etw erwerben** GESCHÄFT acquire an interest in sth

Beteiligung: **Beteiligungen** *f pl* BANK, BÖRSE, FINANZ investments, RECHNUNG long-term financial investments, VW investments; **Beteiligungen** *f pl* **an anderen Gesellschaften** RECHNUNG share investments in other companies; **Beteiligungsausgaben** *f pl* STEUER investment interest expense (*AmE*); **Beteiligungserträge** *m pl* BÖRSE income from investments; **Beteiligungserwerb** *m* BÖRSE acquisition of stock, FINANZ acquisition of participations; **Beteiligungsfinanzierung** *f* FINANZ equity financing; **Beteiligungs- und Fremdfinanzierung** *f* FINANZ, RECHNUNG external financing; **Beteiligungs- und**

Fusionsberatungsservice *m* BÖRSE *einer Bank* mergers and acquisitions (*M&A*); **Beteiligungsgeschäft** *nt* BÖRSE, GESCHÄFT, MGMNT, RECHNUNG, VW joint venture (*JV*); **Beteiligungsgesellschaft** *f* BÖRSE joint-venture company, GESCHÄFT associated company, affiliate, affiliate company; **Beteiligungskapital** *nt* BANK, FINANZ, GESCHÄFT, VW venture capital; **Beteiligungskäufe** *m pl* BÖRSE acquisition of shareholdings; **Beteiligungsportefeuille** *nt* BANK, BÖRSE, FINANZ investment portfolio; **Beteiligungsvertrag** *m* RECHT participation agreement; **Beteiligungswert** *m* RECHNUNG book value of investment; **Beteiligungszusage** *f* **der Versicherung bei Klageerhebung** RECHT sue and labor clause (*AmE*) (*S/LC*), sue and labour clause (*BrE*) (*S/LC*)

betonen *vt* GESCHÄFT emphasize, lay the emphasis on, place emphasis on

Betonung *f* GESCHÄFT emphasis

Betracht: **in ~ ziehen** *phr* GESCHÄFT take into account, take into consideration, take account of

Betrachter, in *m,f* GRUND looker

beträchtlich 1. *adj* GESCHÄFT appreciable, considerable, substantial, VW sizeable; **2.** *adv* GESCHÄFT substantially; ◆ **~ diversifiziert** GESCHÄFT broadly diversified

Betrachtungsweise *f* GESCHÄFT, MGMNT, VERWALT, VW approach

Betrag *m* FINANZ, GESCHÄFT amount (*amt*); ◆ **einen ~ von einem Bankkonto abheben** BANK withdraw a sum from a bank account; **dieser ~ erscheint nicht in den Büchern** RECHNUNG this sum does not appear in the accounts; **den ~ feststellen** RECHT *Schadensersatz* settle the figure; **einen ~ hinterlegen** BÖRSE place a deposit

Beträge *m pl* FINANZ, RECHNUNG amounts, dividends; **~ im Falle eines unvorhergesehenen Ereignisses** RECHNUNG contingency payments

betragen *vi* GESCHÄFT amount to, come to, work out at, RECHNUNG add up to

Betrag: **Betragsleitende(r)** *mf* [decl. as adj] VW contributor; **Betragszahl** *f* GESCHÄFT figure number

betreffen *vt* GESCHÄFT concern, refer to

betreffend *adj* GESCHÄFT *Person* in question, *Schriftstück* pertaining to; **die ~en Personen** *f pl* GESCHÄFT the persons concerned

Betreffende *pl* [decl. as adj] GESCHÄFT the persons concerned

betreffs *prep frml* KOMM regarding, re, concerning

betreibbar: **~e Forderung** *f* RECHNUNG recoverable debt

betreiben *vt* COMP power, GESCHÄFT *Unternehmen* run, operate, *Gewerbe* conduct, IND operate, power, SOZIAL *Studium* pursue

Betreiben *nt* IND operation; **~ einer Deponie** UMWELT site operation

Betreten: **~ verboten** *phr* RECHT no trespassing

Betreuung *f* GESCHÄFT care; **Betreuungsmaßnahmen** *f pl* COMP support activities

Betrieb *m* COMP mode, GESCHÄFT *Firma* concern, business, workplace, operation, IND *Fabrik* factory, works, *von Maschine* operation, PERSON *Arbeitsstelle* workplace, place of work, establishment, workplace, VERWALT workplace; **~ mit Kundenauftragsfertigung** PERSON *Arbeit* job shop; **~ mit modifizierter Gewerkschaftsbindung** PERSON modified union shop

(*AmE*); ◆ **außer ~** GESCHÄFT out of order, out of action; **außer ~ sein** VW be down; **im ~** IND, PERSON on the shop floor; **im ~ sein** GESCHÄFT be at work; **in ~ COMP** *Maschine* busy; **in ~ gehen** IND come on stream; **in ~ sein** IND be on stream; **in ~ nehmen** IND start up; **in ~ setzen** IND activate

betrieblich *adj* GESCHÄFT operational, MGMNT managerial; **~e Altersversorgung** *f* VERWALT company pension plan; **~es Anreizsystem** *nt* PERSON factory incentive scheme, plant incentive scheme; **~e Aufwendungen** *f pl* RECHNUNG operating costs, operating expenditure, operating expenses; **~e Ausbildung** *f* PERSON in-plant training; **~e Ausgaben** *f pl* STEUER corporate spending; **~er Bruttoertrag** *m* RECHNUNG gross operating revenue; **~e Durchlaufzeit** *f* RECHNUNG operating cycle; **~e Ermüdung** *f* PERSON industrial fatigue; **~e Erträge** *m pl* RECHNUNG operating income, operating revenue; **~e Instanzen** *f pl* VW organizational lines; **~e Kosten** *pl* RECHNUNG overheads; **~e Leistungsfähigkeit** *f* IND operating capacity, plant capacity, operating efficiency; **~e Mitbestimmung** *f* PERSON *der Arbeitnehmer* codetermination at plant level, involvement of employees; **~es Netz** *nt* COMP corporate network; **~e Nutzung** *f* GRUND industrial occupancy; **~e Pensionskasse** *f* FINANZ, PERSON employer's occupational pension scheme (*BrE*), occupational pension plan, occupational pension scheme (*BrE*); **~e Pensionsregelung** *f* FINANZ, PERSON occupational pension plan, occupational pension scheme (*BrE*); **~e Planung** *f* GESCHÄFT, MGMNT company planning, operational planning; **~es Planungswesen** *nt* RECHNUNG budget system; **~er Rechner** *m* COMP business computer; **~es Rechnerwesen** *nt* COMP business computing; **~er Rechnungsprüfer** *m*, **~e Rechnungsprüferin** *f* RECHNUNG management accountant; **~es Rechnungswesen** *nt* FINANZ corporate finance; **~e Sozialleistungen** *f pl* PERSON *Sozialversorgung* company benefits; **~es Tarifwesen** *nt* GESCHÄFT, PERSON plant bargaining; **~es Transportunternehmen** *nt* TRANSP industrial carrier; **~es Umfeld** *nt* GESCHÄFT business environment; **~er Vergleich** *m* GESCHÄFT interfirm comparison; **~es Vorschlagswesen** *nt* GESCHÄFT, PERSON suggestion scheme; **~e vorzeitige Abschreibung** *f* STEUER accelerated company tax depreciation; **~e Wohlfahrtseinrichtungen** *f pl* PERSON, SOZIAL plant welfare facilities; **~e Zusatzrente** *f* FINANZ supplementary company pension scheme

Betrieb: **Betriebsablauf** *m* PERSON sequence of operations; **Betriebsanalyse** *f* MGMNT operations breakdown, PERSON, RECHNUNG operational analysis, operations analysis; **Betriebsanlage** *f* IND plant, operating plant, fixed plant; **Betriebsanleitung** *f* GESCHÄFT instruction book; **Betriebsassistent, in** *m,f* MGMNT assistant to manager; **Betriebsaufwand** *m* RECHNUNG operating costs, operating expenditure, operating expenses; **Betriebsausgaben** *f pl* GESCHÄFT business expenses, business charges; **Betriebsauswahl** *f* PATENT plant varieties

betriebsbedingt: **~er Aufwand** *m* RECHNUNG operating costs, operating expenditure, operating expenses

Betrieb: **Betriebsberatung** *f* GESCHÄFT management consulting; **Betriebsbewilligung** *f* RECHNUNG operating grant

betriebsbezogen: ~**e Investitionen** *f pl* RECHNUNG operational investment

Betrieb: **Betriebsbüro** *nt* GESCHÄFT, MGMNT, VERWALT planning department; **Betriebsdatenbank** *f* COMP corporate database; **Betriebsdatenzentrum** *nt* COMP corporate data center (*AmE*), corporate data centre (*BrE*); **Betriebsdruck** *m* IND working pressure (*WP*); **Betriebseinstellung** *f* GESCHÄFT shutdown; **Betriebsergebnis** *nt* FINANZ, GESCHÄFT trading results, RECHNUNG operating results; **Betriebsergebnisrechnung** *f* RECHNUNG operating statement; **Betriebseröffnung** *f* GESCHÄFT, RECHT, STEUER opening of a business; **Betriebsferien** *pl* PERSON general holiday

betriebsfertig *adj* IMP/EXP *Lieferklausel* turnkey, IND ready to operate

betriebsfremd: ~**e Erträge** *m pl* RECHNUNG other income, other revenue

Betrieb: **Betriebsführer, in** *m,f* IND, MGMNT plant manager, VERWALT financial officer; **Betriebsführung** *f* MGMNT, VW business management; **Betriebsgelände** *nt* IND industrial site; **Betriebsgelegenheit** *f* IND plant location; **Betriebs- und Geschäftsausstattung** *f* GESCHÄFT fixtures and fittings, furniture and fittings; **Betriebs- und Geschäftseinrichtung** *f* GESCHÄFT fixtures and fittings, furniture and fittings, business equipment and furnishing; **Betriebsgewährung** *f* RECHNUNG operating grant; **Betriebsgewerkschaft** *f* PERSON company union, enterprise union; **Betriebsgewinn** *m* RECHNUNG operating profit; **Betriebsgewinn** *m* **pro Aktie** FINANZ basic earnings per share

betriebsgewöhnlich: ~**e Nutzungsdauer** *f* GESCHÄFT average life, RECHNUNG, RECHT asset depreciation range (*ADR*)

Betrieb: **Betriebshaftpflichtversicherung** *f* VERSICH business liability insurance, general liability insurance; **Betriebshandelsspanne** *f* RECHNUNG gross profit margin; **Betriebshygiene** *f* PERSON, SOZIAL industrial hygiene; **Betriebsingenieur, in** *m,f* IND industrial plant engineer

betriebsintern: ~**er Größenvorteil** *m* VW internal economy of scale; ~**e Investitionen** *f pl* RECHNUNG operational investment

Betrieb: **Betriebsjahr** *nt* IND working year, *Maschine, Fabrik* operating year; **Betriebskalkulation** *f* RECHNUNG cost accounting; **Betriebskantine** *f* PERSON staff canteen, works canteen; **Betriebskapazität** *f* GESCHÄFT, IND plant capacity, VW operating capacity; **Betriebskapital** *nt* FINANZ net current assets, working capital, GESCHÄFT working capital, RECHNUNG net quick assets, VW circulating capital, share capital, operating capital; **Betriebskapitalvorschuß** *m* FINANZ, GESCHÄFT working capital advance; **Betriebsklima** *nt* PERSON staff relations; **Betriebskonto** *nt* BANK operating account; **Betriebskontrolle** *f* IND manufacturing control, performance monitoring (*PM*); **Betriebskosten** *pl* FINANZ current expenditure, running costs, running expense, GESCHÄFT operating expenses, running expense, RECHNUNG operating expenses, running expense, operating costs, TRANSP operating expenses, VW running expense; **Betriebskrankenkasse** *f* PERSON, VERSICH company's health insurance scheme; **Betriebsleiter, in** *m,f* IND, MGMNT, PERSON plant manager, works

manager, production manager, operations manager; **Betriebsleitung** *f* IND, MGMNT, PERSON factory management, plant management, operating management, operations management, VERWALT business management

Betriebsmittel *nt* GESCHÄFT, IND resource, working capital, PERSON working area; **Betriebsmittelindustrie** *f* IND resource industry; **Betriebsmittelverwaltung** *f* GESCHÄFT, MGMNT resource management; **Betriebsmittelvorschuß** *m* FINANZ, GESCHÄFT working capital advance; **Betriebsmittelzuteilung** *f* COMP resource allocation

betriebsnotwendig: ~**er Kapitalbedarf** *m* FINANZ operating capital requirements

Betrieb: **Betriebsoptimum** *nt* VW ideal capacity, maximum practical capacity, practical capacity; **Betriebsordnung** *f* PERSON, SOZIAL works regulations; **Betriebspachtvertrag** *m* RECHT company lease agreement, TRANSP operation lease; **Betriebspaß** *m* IND issue card; **Betriebsplan** *m* TRANSP operating plan; **Betriebsplanstudie** *f* IND plant layout study; **Betriebsplanung** *f* GESCHÄFT, MGMNT operational planning, business planning; **Betriebs- und Produkthaftpflichtversicherung** *f* VERSICH comprehensive general liability insurance; **Betriebspsychologie** *f* IND, MGMNT, PERSON industrial psychology; **Betriebsrat** *m* PERSON employees' committee, works council (*BrE*), *Arbeitspartizipation* works committee (*BrE*); **Betriebsratsvorsitzende** *f* [decl. as adj] PERSON mother of chapel (*BrE*) (*MoC*); **Betriebsratsvorsitzende(r)** *m* [decl. as adj] PERSON chairman of works council, father of chapel (*BrE*) (*FoC*); **Betriebsrentenfinanzierung** *f* FINANZ pension plan funding; **Betriebsrentenkasse** *f* FINANZ occupational pension plan, occupational pension scheme (*BrE*); **Betriebsrentensystem** *nt* VERWALT company pension plan, group annuity contract; **Betriebsrisikobeschreibung** *f* VERSICH description of operational risk; **Betriebsschließung** *f* GESCHÄFT shutdown, IND plant closure; **Betriebssicherheit** *f* IND, PERSON industrial safety, industrial security; **Betriebssparen** *nt* FINANZ contractual savings; **Betriebsspionage** *f* GESCHÄFT industrial espionage; **Betriebsstillegung** *f* GESCHÄFT shutdown, IND plant closure; **Betriebsstillstand** *m* IND operations breakdown; **Betriebsstillstandsversicherung** *f* VERSICH business interruption insurance; **Betriebsstoffe** *m pl* GESCHÄFT expendable goods, IND factory supplies, supplies, VW supplies; **Betriebsstrategie** *f* MGMNT operating strategy; **Betriebsstruktur** *f* GESCHÄFT business organization, PERSON corporate structure; **Betriebssubvention** *f* FINANZ operating subsidy; **Betriebssystem** *nt* COMP operating system (*OS*); **Betriebstechnik** *f* IND industrial engineering, *Produktion* production engineering; **Betriebsübernahme** *f* **durch Arbeitnehmer** FINANZ, PERSON worker buyout; **Betriebsumfeld** *nt* VW organizational environment; **Betriebsunfall** *m* PERSON, VERSICH industrial accident, industrial injury, occupational accident, job-related injury; **Betriebsunterbrechung** *f* TRANSP breakdown; **Betriebsunterbrechungspolice** *f* VERSICH business interruption policy; **Betriebsunterbrechungsversicherung** *f* VERSICH business closure insurance, business interruption insurance; **Betriebsunterlagen** *f pl* GESCHÄFT play book (*AmE*),

PERSON, RECHNUNG operational data; **Betriebsurlaub** *m* PERSON general holiday; **Betriebsvereinbarung** *f* PERSON plant agreement, shop floor agreement (*BrE*); **Betriebsvereinbarungsbestimmungen** *f pl* PERSON shop's articles; **Betriebsverlegung** *f* VW movement of operations; **Betriebsverlust** *m* RECHNUNG operating loss; **Betriebsvermögen** *nt* FINANZ, GESCHÄFT, RECHNUNG business assets; **Betriebsvermögen** *nt* **abzüglich immaterieller Anlagewerte** BÖRSE tangible net worth; **Betriebsversicherung** *f* VERSICH commercial insurance; **Betriebsvoranschlag** *m* RECHNUNG operating budget; **Betriebsvorschriften** *f pl* GESCHÄFT business regulations; **Betriebswirt, in** *m,f* GESCHÄFT business economist, PERSON Bachelor of Business Administration, Bachelor of Science in Business Administration, VERWALT business administrator; **Betriebswirtschaft** *f* MGMNT science of business management, VERWALT business administration, VW business studies

betriebswirtschaftlich: ~**e Kennziffer** *f* FINANZ activity ratio, MGMNT management ratio

Betrieb: **Betriebswirtschaftslehre** *f* MGMNT science of business management, VERWALT business administration, VW business studies; **Betriebswissenschaft** *f* MGMNT scientific management; **Betriebswohnung** *f* GRUND factory-owned apartment, factory-owned flat (*BrE*), job-related accommodation; **Betriebszeitschrift** *f* V&M house magazine; **Betriebszusammenbruch** *m* IND operations breakdown; **Betriebszusatzrente** *f* FINANZ supplementary company pension scheme; **Betriebszuschuß** *m* FINANZ operating subsidy; **Betriebszyklus** *m* RECHNUNG operating cycle

betrifft *adv* GESCHÄFT concerning, regarding

Betrug *m* GESCHÄFT fraud, swindle, ramp (*infrml*) (*BrE*), RECHNUNG, RECHT *arglistige Täuschung* fraud

betrügen *vt* GESCHÄFT cheat, swindle, RECHNUNG, RECHT defraud

Betrüger *m* GESCHÄFT confidence trickster, con artist (*infrml*), con man (*infrml*), embezzler, swindler, RECHNUNG, RECHT defrauder

Betrügerin *f* GESCHÄFT confidence trickster, con artist (*infrml*), embezzler, swindler, RECHNUNG, RECHT defrauder

betrügerisch 1. *adj* GESCHÄFT, RECHNUNG, RECHT fraudulent; **2.** *adv* GESCHÄFT, RECHNUNG, RECHT fraudulently; ♦ **etw ~ erlangen** RECHT obtain sth by fraud

betrügerisch: ~**er Bankrott** *m* GESCHÄFT, RECHNUNG, RECHT fraudulent bankruptcy; ~**e Buchung** *f* GESCHÄFT, RECHNUNG, RECHT fraudulent entry; ~**er Eintrag** *m* GESCHÄFT, RECHNUNG, RECHT fraudulent entry; **mit ~en Mitteln arbeitende Maklerfirma** *f* BÖRSE bucket shop; ~**es Unternehmen** *nt* GESCHÄFT racket; ~**er Verkauf** *m* **wertloser Aktien** BÖRSE share pushing

Betrug: **Betrugskommando** *nt* GESCHÄFT fraud squad (*BrE*); **Betrugsspiel** *nt* GESCHÄFT confidence game

beunruhigen *vt* GESCHÄFT unsettle, worry

beunruhigt *adj* GESCHÄFT unsettled, worried

beurkunden *vt* GESCHÄFT authenticate, place on record, register, verify, *Vertrag* record, RECHNUNG verify, RECHT acknowledge, attest to

Beurkundung *f* GESCHÄFT document, RECHNUNG authentication, verification, RECHT acknowledgement (*ack*), act of acknowledgement

Beurlaubung *f* PERSON *Arbeitsmarkt* furlough (*AmE*), leave of absence, *Suspendierung* suspension from office

beurteilen *vt* GESCHÄFT judge, *Wert, Leistung* assess, appraise, MGMNT *Projekt* appraise

Beurteilung *f* GESCHÄFT appraisal, assessment, judgment, MGMNT appraisal; RECHT judgment; ~ **von Personal** PERSON, RECHNUNG *Rechnungsprüfung* manpower audit; ~ **nach Schlüsselbereichen** MGMNT key-area evaluation; **Beurteilungsgespräch** *nt* PERSON appraisal interview; **Beurteilungsskala** *f* GESCHÄFT rating scale

Beute: auf ~ aus sein *phr infrml* GESCHÄFT be on the take (*infrml*)

Bevölkerung *f* VW population; **Bevölkerungsaufbau** *m* VW population structure; **Bevölkerungsdichte** *f* VW population density; **Bevölkerungsexplosion** *f* VW population explosion; **Bevölkerungsoptimum** *nt* VW optimum population; **Bevölkerungspolitik** *f* VW population policy; **Bevölkerungspyramide** *f* VW age pyramid; **Bevölkerungsrückgang** *m* VW fall in population; **Bevölkerungsstatistik** *f* MATH, VW population statistics, census of population, demographic statistics; **Bevölkerungsstatistiken** *f pl* MATH, VW demographics; **Bevölkerungszählung** *f* VW population count

bevollmächtigen *vt* GESCHÄFT authorize, empower, RECHNUNG, RECHT appoint as attorney-in-fact

bevollmächtigt *adj* GESCHÄFT authorized, empowered, RECHNUNG, RECHT invested with power of attorney, V&M accredited; ~**e Instanz** *f* **für Steuersachen** STEUER General Commissioners (*BrE*); ~**er Vertreter** *m*, ~**e Vertreterin** *f* GESCHÄFT, PERSON authorized agent, authorized representative

Bevollmächtigte(r) *mf* [decl. as adj] GESCHÄFT authorized agent, representative (*rep.*), agent (*agt*), RECHNUNG, RECHT attorney-in-fact; **durch einen Bevollmächtigten abgegebene Stimme** *f* POL proxy vote; ♦ **etw durch einen Bevollmächtigten schicken** GESCHÄFT send sth via an agent

Bevollmächtigung *f* GESCHÄFT agency (*agcy*), authorization, RECHT authorization, power of attorney (*PA*); ~ **nach Gegenleistung** GESCHÄFT authorization under consideration (*AC*); **Bevollmächtigungsbeamte(r)** *m*, **Bevollmächtigungsbeamtin** *f* PERSON, VERWALT Certification Officer (*BrE*) (*CO*)

Bevormundungsstaat *m* POL, SOZIAL welfare state, VW welfare state, nanny state (*infrml*)

Bevorratung *f* GESCHÄFT stockpiling

bevorrechtigt *adj* FINANZ, GESCHÄFT privileged, RECHT entitled to priority; ~**er Gläubiger** *m*, ~**e Gläubigerin** *f* FINANZ, RECHNUNG, VW secured creditor, senior creditor; **nicht ~er Gläubiger** *m*, **nicht ~e Gläubigerin** *f* RECHNUNG general creditor; **nicht ~e Konkursforderung** *f* FINANZ unsecured debt; **nicht ~er Konkursgläubiger** *m*, **nicht ~e Konkursgläubigerin** *f* RECHNUNG general creditor; ~**e Umfinanzierung** *f* BÖRSE senior refunding

Bevorschussung *f* BANK, GESCHÄFT advance

bevorstehend *adj* GESCHÄFT forthcoming; ~**es Steuerjahr** *nt* STEUER upcoming fiscal year

bevorzugen *vt* FINANZ, GESCHÄFT, RECHNUNG, V&M favor (*AmE*), favour (*BrE*), prefer

bevorzugt 1. *adj* FINANZ, GESCHÄFT, RECHNUNG, V&M preferred; **2.** *adv* ♦ ~ **behandeln** GESCHÄFT prioritize

bevorzugt: ~**e Dividendendeckung** *f* RECHNUNG preferred dividend coverage; ~**e Einstellung** *f* GESCHÄFT preferential hiring (*AmE*); **~e Position** *f* V&M preferred position; **~es Risiko** *nt* VERSICH preferred risk; **am wenigsten ~es Gebiet** *nt* VW least-favored region (*AmE*), least-favoured region (*BrE*); **~e Wiedereinstellung** *f* RECHT preferential rehiring

Bevorzugung *f* FINANZ, GESCHÄFT, RECHNUNG, V&M preference (*pref.*), preferential treatment

bewahren *vt* GESCHÄFT preserve, *Vertrauen* sustain

bewährt *adj* GESCHÄFT proven, tried and tested, well-tried

bewandert *adj* GESCHÄFT knowledgeable

bewegend: **~e Kraft** *f* MGMNT mover and shaker (*infrml*)

Beweggrund *m* GESCHÄFT motive, rationale, reason

beweglich *adj* GESCHÄFT moveable, mobile, flexible; **~es Eigentum** *nt* RECHT moveable property; **~e Gegenstände** *m pl* RECHT moveable objects; **~e Güter** *nt pl* RECHT moveable goods, chattels; **~e Habe** *f* GRUND personal estate; **~er Maschinenpark** *m* VW flexible plant; **~e Preisskala** *f* FINANZ sliding scale; **~es Privateigentum** *nt* GRUND personal property; **~e Sachen** *f pl* RECHT moveables, set of chattels; **~e Skala** *f* GESCHÄFT *Löhne, Preise* sliding scale; **~es Telefon** *nt* KOMM mobile phone, mobile telephone, mobile; **~es Unternehmen** *nt* GESCHÄFT flexible firm; **~es Vermögen** *nt* GRUND chattels personal, moveable property, personal estate, RECHT moveable property, STEUER personalty

Bewegung *f* GESCHÄFT movement, *Markt* swing, POL movement; ♦ **in ~ setzen** GESCHÄFT set in motion

Bewegung: **Bewegungsablauf** *m* IND sequence of movements; **Bewegungsbilanz** *f* FINANZ, RECHNUNG source and application of funds statement, funds statement; **Bewegungsdatei** *f* COMP change file, transaction file; **Bewegungsfreiheit** *f* GESCHÄFT freedom of movement, freedom of action; **Bewegungsökonomie** *f* VW motion economy; **Bewegungsstudie** *f* MATH, MGMNT, VW motion study; **Bewegungs-Zeit-Studie** *f* MATH, MGMNT, VW time and motion study

Beweis *m* RECHT *Gerichtsverfahren* evidence, *Nachweis* proof; ♦ **~ für** GESCHÄFT evidence of; **~ erbringen** GESCHÄFT prove

Beweis: **Beweisaufnahme** *f* **unter Ausschluß der Öffentlichkeit** RECHT private hearing

beweisen *vt* GESCHÄFT, RECHT prove

beweiserheblich *adj* RECHT evidentiary

Beweis: **Beweisermittlungsverfahren** *nt* RECHT discovery; **Beweisfragen** *f pl* RECHT *schriftlich und unter Eid zu beantworten* interrogatories; **Beweislast** *f* RECHT *in Gerichtsverfahren* burden of proof; **als Beweismittel geltend** *phr* RECHT evidentiary; **Beweisstück** *nt* RECHT exhibit

beweisunerheblich *adj* RECHT immaterial

bewerben: **sich ~** *v refl* GESCHÄFT, MGMNT *Projekte, Verträge* bid; ♦ **sich ~ um** GESCHÄFT solicit, tender for, *Arbeitsstelle* apply for, seek, MGMNT *Auftrag* tender, PERSON *Arbeitsstelle* apply for; **sich erneut ~ um** PERSON *Arbeitsstelle* reapply for

Bewerber, in *m,f* FINANZ, GESCHÄFT bidder, PERSON *für eine Arbeitstelle* applicant, job candidate

Bewerbung *f* GESCHÄFT application, PERSON *Arbeitsmarkt* application, job application; ♦ **eine ~ unterbreiten** PERSON put in an application

Bewerbung: **Bewerbungsformular** *nt* VERWALT application form; **Bewerbungsschreiben** *nt* KOMM, PERSON application, letter of application

bewerkstelligen *vt* GESCHÄFT manage

bewertbar *adj* GESCHÄFT appreciable

bewerten *vt* GESCHÄFT make a valuation of, assess, *schätzen* evaluate, value, MGMNT *Projekt* appraise, PERSON appraise

bewertet: **~ sein mit** *phr* BÖRSE be valued at

Bewertung *f* FINANZ rating, GESCHÄFT assessment, evaluation, valuation, MGMNT appraisal, PERSON appraisal, report card; **~ als Werbeträger** MEDIEN, V&M media evaluation; **~ von Aktien** RECHNUNG stock valuation; **~ des Anlagevermögens** RECHNUNG fixed asset assessment; **~ nach Baufortschritt** RECHNUNG percentage-of-completion method; **~ bestimmter Personen nach deren Beliebtheit** GESCHÄFT, MEDIEN, POL popularity ratings; **~ von Büroarbeiten** PERSON *Unternehmen, Industrie* clerical work measurement (*CWM*); **~ von Fernsehsendungen durch Zuschauer** MEDIEN, V&M television rating (*TVR*); **~ eines Investitionsprojekts** VW capital project evaluation; **~ einer Kapitalanlage** BÖRSE, FINANZ investment appraisal; **~ der Umweltbelastung** UMWELT environmental impact assessment; **Bewertungsabschlag** *m* RECHT, STEUER downward valuation adjustment, VW import allowance; **Bewertungsbeschränkungen** *f pl* VW valuation restrictions; **Bewertungsdurchschnitt** *m* GESCHÄFT weighted average; **Bewertungsfragebogen** *m* GESCHÄFT evaluation questionnaire; **Bewertungsgrundlagen** *f pl* GESCHÄFT valuation basis, RECHNUNG valuation criteria, valuation principles; **Bewertungsgrundsatz** *m* RECHNUNG standard of valuation, RECHT, STEUER standard of value; **Bewertungsklausel** *f* VERSICH valuation clause (*VC*); **Bewertungsmethode** *f* FINANZ cost method, RECHNUNG method of valuation; **Bewertungsrecht** *nt* GRUND, RECHT, STEUER law regulating the valuation of property; **Bewertungsrechte** *nt pl* BÖRSE appraisal rights (*AmE*); **Bewertungsskala** *f* GESCHÄFT rating scale; **Bewertungsunterlagen** *f pl* GESCHÄFT valuation data; **Bewertungsverbesserung** *f* GESCHÄFT appraisal increment; **Bewertungszuschreibung** *f* RECHNUNG appraisal increment

bewilligen *vt* FINANZ *Kredit* grant, GESCHÄFT allow, authorize, PATENT *Lizenz* grant, VW *Gelder für einen Zweck* appropriate

bewilligt *adj* FINANZ granted, GESCHÄFT allowed, authorized, PATENT granted, VW appropriated; **~e Ausgaben** *f pl* RECHNUNG authorized expenditure; **~er Etat** *m* POL supply; **~e Haushaltsmittel** *nt pl* FINANZ budgetary appropriation; **~er Verteidigungshaushalt** *m* POL government defence appropriations (*BrE*), government defense appropriations (*AmE*)

Bewilligung *f* PATENT, RECHT grant; **~ durch Abstimmung** PERSON, POL vote; **~ von betrieblichen Aufwendugen** RECHNUNG operating expenditure vote; **~ des Feuerwehrfonds** POL, VW Treasury Board contingencies vote; **~ von Geldern** RECHNUNG fund appropiation, appropriation bill; **~ von Haushaltsmitteln** FINANZ, POL budget appropiation; **Bewilligungsausschuß** *m* FINANZ appropiations committee; **Bewilligungsdatum** *nt* PATENT date of grant; **Bewilligungsgesetz** *nt* POL appropriation bill, RECHNUNG appropiations bill (*AmE*)

bewirken *vt* GESCHÄFT bring about

bewirten vt GESCHÄFT accommodate, entertain

Bewirtschaftung f MGMNT management, VERWALT administration, vw control, *des Landes* farming, cultivation; **Bewirtschaftungsmethode** f vw farming method

Bewirtung f FREI catering, GESCHÄFT entertainment; **Bewirtungspauschale** f GESCHÄFT entertainment allowance

bewohnen vt GRUND occupy

Bewohner, in m,f GRUND occupant, occupier, *Eigentümer* owner

Bewußtseinsklasse f POL class

Bez. abbr (*Bezahlung*) GESCHÄFT PYT (*payment*)

bezahlbar adj GESCHÄFT affordable

bezahlen vt BANK *Scheck* honor (*AmE*), honour (*BrE*), GESCHÄFT pay, pay for; ♦ **die Kosten ~** GESCHÄFT defray the cost, defray the expenses, pay out

bezahlt adj BANK *Scheck* honored (*AmE*), honoured (*BrE*), GESCHÄFT paid, paid for, settled, received; **nicht ~** adj BANK dishonored (*AmE*), dishonoured (*BrE*), GESCHÄFT unpaid; ♦ **~ bei Lieferung** TRANSP paid on delivery (*POD*); **sich ~ machen** GESCHÄFT be profitable

bezahlt: **~e Rückantwort** f KOMM reply paid; **~er Schaden** m VERSICH claim paid; **~er Urlaub** m PERSON paid leave (*BrE*), paid vacation (*AmE*); **nicht ~er Wechsel** m BANK dishonored bill of exchange (*AmE*), dishonoured bill of exchange (*BrE*)

Bezahlung f GESCHÄFT payment (*PYT*), remuneration, settlement; **~ im öffentlichen Dienst** vw public sector pay; **~ für Platznutzung** GESCHÄFT yardage; **~ pro Stück** PERSON paid by the piece; ♦ **gegen ~** GESCHÄFT against payment

bezeichnen vt GESCHÄFT designate, *kennzeichnen* mark

bezeichnend 1. adj GESCHÄFT characteristic, typical; **2.** adv GESCHÄFT typically

Bezeichner m COMP identifier

bezeichnet adj GESCHÄFT named

Bezeichnung f GESCHÄFT *Wort* term, PATENT designation, vw denomination (*denom.*)

bezeugen vt GESCHÄFT attest to, RECHT attest to, *aussagen* testify

beziehen 1. vt GESCHÄFT *Position* take up, vw buy; **2.** **sich ~ auf** v refl [+acc] GESCHÄFT refer to; ♦ **sich beziehend auf** [+acc] GESCHÄFT referring to

Bezieher, in m,f MEDIEN *einer Zeitung* subscriber; **~ eines festen Einkommens** FINANZ, PERSON person on fixed income; **~ eines hohen Einkommens** FINANZ, PERSON big income earner

Beziehung f FINANZ, GESCHÄFT relationship, MATH interrelation; **~ innerhalb des Fachgebiets** MGMNT line relationship; **~ innerhalb der Linie** MGMNT *Produktionsprozeß* line relationship

Beziehungen f pl GESCHÄFT relations; **~ zu den Medien** MEDIEN, V&M media relations; **~ zur Presse** MEDIEN press relations; **~ zwischen Regierungen** POL government relations; ♦ **~ spielen lassen** GESCHÄFT pull strings (*BrE*), pull wires (*AmE*)

Beziehung: **Beziehungsanalyse** f PERSON *Psychologie, Betriebswirtschaft* relations analysis; **Beziehungskauf** m GESCHÄFT direct purchase

beziehungsweise adv GESCHÄFT respectively

beziffert: **~er Schadensersatz** m RECHT liquidated damages

Bezirk m GESCHÄFT territory, *Verwaltungseinheit* district, POL borough; **Bezirksbüro** nt VERWALT area office; **Bezirksdirektor, in** m,f VERSICH agency superintendent (*AmE*), district manager; **Bezirkskrankenhaus** nt SOZIAL district hospital; **Bezirksleiter, in** m,f PERSON district manager, territory manager; **Bezirksreferent, in** m,f PERSON district officer (*DO*)

bezogen: **aufeinander ~e Ereignisse** nt pl PERSON related events

Bezogene(r) mf [decl. as adj] BANK acceptor, drawee

bezug: **in ~ auf** phr GESCHÄFT concerning, regarding, with reference to, with regard to; **in ~ auf Ihren Anruf vom** phr KOMM further to your telephone call of; **in ~ auf Ihr Schreiben vom** phr KOMM further to your letter of

Bezug m BÖRSE subscription, GESCHÄFT *Waren* procurement, *Zeitungen, Zeitschriften* subscription; ♦ **~ nehmen auf** [+acc] GESCHÄFT, PATENT refer to

Bezüge m pl GESCHÄFT emolument

bezüglich 1. adj GESCHÄFT relative; **2.** prep KOMM regarding

Bezugnahme f KOMM reference; ♦ **~ auf** [+acc] PATENT reference to; **unter ~ auf** [+acc] GESCHÄFT with reference to, referring to; **außerhalb der ~ auf** GESCHÄFT outside the reference of

bezugnehmend: **~ auf** phr [+acc] GESCHÄFT referring to, KOMM with reference to; **~ auf Ihre Anfrage** phr KOMM with reference to your enquiry; **~ auf Ihr Schreiben** phr KOMM with reference to your letter

Bezug: **Bezugsberechtigte(r)** mf [decl. as adj] BÖRSE allottee, FINANZ remainderman, VERSICH beneficiary; **Bezugsberechtigungsklausel** f VERSICH benefit of insurance clause

bezugsfertig adj GRUND *Haus* ready to move into, turnkey

Bezug: **Bezugsforderung** f BÖRSE subscription receivable; **Bezugsgröße** f *des Währungssystems* vw numeraire; **Bezugsgruppe** f GESCHÄFT reference group; **Bezugskategorie** f PATENT *Warengattung* reference line; **Bezugskosten** pl GESCHÄFT purchasing costs, RECHNUNG delivery costs; **Bezugslinie** f COMP, MATH baseline, PATENT reference line; **Bezugsmarke** f COMP, GESCHÄFT benchmark; **Bezugsmaß** nt GESCHÄFT, IND basic size; **Bezugsniveau** nt FINANZ reference level; **Bezugspreis** m FINANZ subscription price, GESCHÄFT price of delivery; **Bezugspunkt** m COMP benchmark, GESCHÄFT reference point, vw benchmark; **Bezugsquelle** f GESCHÄFT supply source, VERWALT resource

Bezugsrecht nt BÖRSE share purchase warrant, stock purchase warrant, subscription right, VERSICH right to life insurance benefits; ♦ **mit ~** BÖRSE cum warrant

Bezugsrecht: **Bezugsrechte** nt pl RECHT rights; **Bezugsrechtsausgabe** f BÖRSE, FINANZ, RECHNUNG rights issue; **Bezugsrechtsemission** f BÖRSE, FINANZ, RECHNUNG rights issue; **Bezugsrechtsstichtag** m FINANZ record date

Bezug: **Bezugstermin** m BÖRSE base date; **Bezugsverhältnis** nt BÖRSE exchange ratio, subscription ratio; **Bezugswährung** f vw base currency; **Bezugswert** m vw reference value; **Bezugszeichen** nt PATENT reference sign

bezuschußt: ~e **Reise** f FREI subsidized travel

Bezuschussung f GESCHÄFT subsidizing, *Betrag* subsidy

bezweifeln vt GESCHÄFT doubt, question

BFS abbr (*Bundesanstalt für Flugsicherung*) TRANSP BAA (*British Airports Authority*)

Bibliothek f GESCHÄFT library; **Bibliotheksdienst** m GESCHÄFT library service

bidirektional: ~er **Drucker** m COMP bidirectional printer

Bienenwabenschein m FINANZ honeycomb slip

bieten 1. vt GESCHÄFT *Geld, Dienstleistung* tender, *Möglichkeit* offer; **2.** vi GESCHÄFT *auf Auktion* bid, make a bid

Bietende(r) mf [decl. as adj] GESCHÄFT bidder

Bieten: ~ **eines neuen Anreizes zum Kauf** phr GESCHÄFT bounce-back; ~ **eines neuen Kaufanreizes** phr GESCHÄFT bounce-back

Bieter, in m,f GESCHÄFT bidder; **Bieterraum** m BÖRSE pit

Bietungsgarantie f BANK tender bond, GRUND earnest money, vw provisional deposit

Bilanz f RECHNUNG annual accounts, asset and liability statement, balance, balance sheet (*B/S*), statement of financial position; ~ **des öffentlichen Sektors** vw public sector balance sheet; ~ **der unsichtbaren Leistungen** FINANZ, vw invisible balance; ~ **des Warenhandels** vw visible trade balance; ♦ **außerhalb der** ~ FINANZ off-balance; **die** ~ **kippen** GESCHÄFT tilt the balance; **in der** ~ **ungeklärt geblieben sein** RECHNUNG be unaccounted for in the balance sheet; **die** ~ **ziehen** GESCHÄFT strike a balance, RECHNUNG balance the books

Bilanz: **Bilanzanalyse** f RECHNUNG statement analysis; **Bilanzanlage** f RECHNUNG balance sheet supplement; **Bilanzauffassungen** f pl RECHNUNG, VERWALT accounting doctrines; **Bilanzaufstellung** f BANK, FINANZ statement of condition, RECHNUNG preparation of a balance sheet; **Bilanzbericht** m **über Abschlüsse** RECHNUNG transaction balance report; **Bilanzbuchhalter, in** m,f RECHNUNG Accountant General (*AG*), chief accountant; **Bilanzdelikt** nt RECHNUNG accounting fraud; **Bilanzformblatt** nt RECHNUNG account form, balance sheet format; **Bilanzfrisur** f RECHNUNG window-dressing; **Bilanzgerade** f vw budget line; **Bilanzgewinn** m GESCHÄFT unappropriated surplus, RECHNUNG net profit for the year, unappropriated retained earnings, accumulated profits; **Bilanzgleichung** f RECHNUNG accounting equation, accounting identity, vw *für den Haushalt* budget equation; **Bilanzgliederung** f RECHNUNG account format, accounting plan; **Bilanzidentität** f RECHNUNG accounting identity

bilanziell: ~e **Abschreibung** f RECHNUNG book depreciation

Bilanzierung f FINANZ, RECHNUNG balancing, balancing of an account, financial accounting; ~ **auf der Basis des Wiederbeschaffungswertes** RECHNUNG current cost accounting (*CCA*); ~ **langfristiger Beteiligungen** RECHNUNG equity method of accounting; **Bilanzierungs- und Bewertungsverfahren** nt RECHNUNG accounting policy; **Bilanzierungsgrundsätze** m pl RECHNUNG accounting principles, accounting rules; **Bilanzierungsgrundsatz** f **der Wesentlichkeit** RECHNUNG materiality; **Bilanzierungsperiode** f FINANZ accounting period

Bilanz: **Bilanzjahr** nt FINANZ, RECHNUNG, STEUER accounting year, financial year, fiscal year (*FY*); **Bilanzkennzahl** f RECHNUNG accounting ratio, balance sheet ratio; **Bilanzkosmetik** f RECHNUNG window-dressing; **Bilanzposten** m RECHNUNG balance item, balance sheet item; **Bilanzprüfer, in** m,f RECHNUNG auditor, balance sheet auditor; **Bilanzrichtliniengesetz** nt RECHNUNG, RECHT accounting and reporting law, accounting directives law, accounting law; **Bilanzstatus** m RECHNUNG statement of assets and liabilities

bilanzunwirksam adj FINANZ, RECHNUNG, VW off the balance sheet, off-balance-sheet; ~e **Finanzierung** f FINANZ, RECHNUNG off-balance-sheet financing, off-balance-sheet finance; ~e **Verbindlichkeiten** f pl RECHNUNG off-balance-sheet commitments

Bilanz: **Bilanzwahrheit** f VERWALT accuracy; **Bilanzwert** m RECHNUNG carrying value, value of a balance sheet item; **Bilanzziehung** f GESCHÄFT balancing

bilateral adj POL, VW bilateral; ~e **Anleihe** f BANK bilateral loan; ~e **Auszahlung** f vw bilateral disbursement; ~e **Entwicklungshilfe** f vw bilateral aid; ~er **Fehler** m GESCHÄFT bilateral mistake; ~e **Geberinstitutionen** f pl vw bilateral donors; ~es **Handelsabkommen** nt vw bilateral trade agreement; ~er **Handelsvertrag** m vw bilateral trade treaty; ~es **Monopol** nt vw bilateral monopoly; ~es **Verkehrsabkommen** nt TRANSP bilateral road agreement

Bilateralismus m POL, VW bilateralism

Bild nt COMP image, GESCHÄFT picture; ♦ **jdn ins** ~ **setzen** GESCHÄFT put sb in the picture

Bild: **Bilddatei** f COMP *Grafik* display file, image file; **Bildelement** nt COMP *Bildschirm* pixel

bilden vt GESCHÄFT *Ausschuß* form, MEDIEN *öffentliche Meinung* mold (*AmE*), mould (*BrE*)

bildend: ~e **Künste** f pl MEDIEN visual arts

Bildertext m MEDIEN caption

Bild: **Bildhintergrund** m COMP background picture; **Bildkantenverhältnis** nt COMP aspect ratio; **Bildmaterial** f MEDIEN visual material, pictorial material, V&M visual material; **Bildmontage** f MEDIEN paste-up, montage

Bildschirm m COMP screen, terminal screen, computer screen, display, monitor; **Bildschirmaufteilung** f COMP split screen; **Bildschirmausgabe** f COMP soft copy; **Bildschirmauszug** m COMP screen dump, screen copy; **Bildschirmeditor** m COMP screen editor; **Bildschirmformat** nt COMP computer map, map, aspect ratio; **Bildschirmgerät** nt COMP, KOMM, MEDIEN, V&M video display, video terminal, visual display terminal (*AmE*) (*VDT*), visual display unit (*BrE*) (*VDU*); **Bildschirmoperator** m COMP terminal operator

bildschirmorientiert: ~es **Textsystem** nt COMP, KOMM screen-based text system, videotext

Bildschirm: **Bildschirmtext** m (*Btx*) COMP, KOMM Videotex®, Viewdata®, Teletext®, teletex; **Bildschirmtextsystem** nt COMP, KOMM videotext, videotext system, Viewdata®; **Bildschirmtreiber** m COMP screen driver; **Bildschirmwerbung** f V&M screen advertising

Bild: **Bildtelefon** nt KOMM visual telephone; **Bildtext** m MEDIEN, V&M picture caption; **Bildüberschrift** f MEDIEN, V&M caption

Bildung f GESCHÄFT accumulation, PERSON, SOZIAL education; ~ **von Seilschaften** infrml backscratching (*infrml*) (*BrE*), log-rolling (*AmE*); ~ **von Sondervermögen** FINANZ funding; **Bildungsanstalt** *f* SOZIAL educational establishment; **Bildungsentwicklung** *f* SOZIAL educational development; **Bildungsökonomie** *f* VW economics of education; **Bildungsweg** *m* SOZIAL educational background; **Bildungswesen** *nt* PERSON training and education system

Bild: **Bildunterschrift** *f* MEDIEN, V&M caption; **Bildverschiebung** *f* COMP *vertikal, horizontal* scrolling; **Bildvorlage** *f* COMP *Grafikprogramme* clip art; **Bildzeichen** *nt* PATENT device mark, figurative device

billig *adj* GESCHÄFT cheap, inexpensive, low-cost, low-priced; **~e Flagge** *f* TRANSP convenience flag, flag of convenience; **~es Geld** *nt* BANK cheap money; **~e Handelsflagge** *f* TRANSP convenience flag, flag of convenience; **~e Imitation** *f* IND cheap imitation, knock-off (*infrml*); **~e Ware** *f* GESCHÄFT bargain

billigen *vt* GESCHÄFT approve, RECHT endorse, indorse

Billigerzeugnissen: **mit ~ handeln** *phr* GESCHÄFT trade down

Billigkeit *f* RECHT, VW equity

billigkeitsrechtlich *adj* RECHT, VW equitable

Billigreisen *f pl* FREI discount travel

billigst *adj* BÖRSE at best

Billigung *f* GESCHÄFT acceptance, approval (*appro*), assent, *Bestätigung* confirmation, sanction, POL assent, RECHT approval (*appro*), VW sanction

bimetallisch *adj* IND, UMWELT bimetallic

Bimetallismus *m* VW bimetallism

bimodal: **~e Verteilung** *f* MATH bimodal distribution; **~e Verteilungskurve** *f* MATH bimodal frequency curve

binär *adj* COMP, MATH binary; **~ codierte Dezimalziffer** *f* COMP binary-coded decimal

Binär- *in cpds* COMP, MATH binary; **Binäraddition** *f* COMP binary addition; **Binärdatei** *f* COMP binary file; **Binär-Dezimal-Umwandlung** *f* COMP binary-to-decimal conversion; **Binärkodierung** *f* COMP binary coding; **Binäroperator** *m* COMP binary operator; **Binärsuche** *f* COMP binary search; **Binärzahl** *f* COMP, MATH binary number; **Binärziffer** *f* COMP, MATH *Zahlensysteme* binary digit, bit

Bindefristklausel *f* VERSICH attestation clause

binden *vt* FINANZ *Kapital* lock up, tie up, IND bind; ♦ **sich an etw ~** GESCHÄFT commit oneself to sth

bindend *adj* RECHT *verpflichtende Verträge* binding; **~es Angebot** *nt* GESCHÄFT binding bid, binding offer, binding tender; **~es Versprechen** *nt* RECHT affirmation (*BrE*), promise; **~e Wirkung** *f* RECHT binding effect; **~e Zusage** *f* GESCHÄFT binding promise

Binder *m* COMP binder

Bindung *f* GESCHÄFT absorption, **~ von Währungen** VW linking of currencies; **Bindungswille** *m* RECHT *Vertragsparteien* intention to undergo commitments

Binnen- *in cpds* IMP/EXP domestic, inland, POL home, domestic, TRANSP domestic, inland, VW *Handel* domestic, home, internal; **Binnenabkommen** *nt* PERSON domestic agreement (*BrE*); **Binnenbeförderungsunternehmen** *nt* TRANSP inland carrier; **Binnenfrachtführer** *m* IMP/EXP inland carrier; **Binnenhafen** *m* TRANSP inner harbor (*AmE*), inner harbour (*BrE*); **Binnenhandel** *m* VW domestic trade, home trade, internal trade, intra-EU trade, trade within the EU;

Binnenmarkt *m* VW domestic market, home market, internal market, *gemeinsam* single market; **Binnennachfrage** *f* VW domestic demand; **Binnenschiff** *nt* TRANSP inland waterway vessel; **Binnenschiffahrtsbeihilfe** *f* TRANSP fresh water allowance; **Binnenschiffahrtsweg** *m* TRANSP inland waterway; **Binnenstaat** *m* POL landlocked country, landlocked state; **Binnentransport** *m* IMP/EXP, TRANSP inland haulage; **Binnentransportfirma** *f* IMP/EXP, TRANSP inland carrier; **Binnentransportversicherung** *f* VERSICH inland marine insurance; **Binnenumschlagplatz** *m* UMWELT onshore terminal; **Binnenwirtschaft** *f* VW internal economy, domestic economy

binnenwirtschaftlich: **~es Gleichgewicht** *nt* VW internal balance; **~e Lage** *f* VW domestic situation

binomisch *adj* VW binomial; **~e Belastung** *f* VW binomial charge

Bio- *pref* IND, UMWELT, VW bio-, biological; **Biochip** *m* COMP biochip

biographisch: **~e Daten** *pl* PERSON biographical data

Bio-: **Biokontrolle** *m* UMWELT biocontrol; **Biokost** *f* SOZIAL health foods; **Bioladen** *m* V&M health-food shop

biologisch *adj* IND biological, UMWELT, VW organic, biological; **~ abbaubar** *adj* UMWELT biodegradable; **~e Abbaubarkeit** *f* UMWELT biodegradability; **aus ~em Anbau** *phr* UMWELT *Gemüse, Lebensmittel* organic

Bio-: **Bioökonomie** *f* VW bioeconomics; **Biotechnik** *f* IND bioengineering; **Biotechnologie** *f* IND biotechnology

Biotop *nt* UMWELT biotope

BIP *abbr* (*Bruttoinlandsprodukt*) VW GDP (*gross domestic product*); **~ pro Kopf der Bevölkerung** VW GDP per capita, GDP per head

bipolar *adj* COMP bipolar; **~er Transistor** *m* COMP bipolar transistor

bis *prep* GESCHÄFT until; ♦ **~ zu** GESCHÄFT not exceeding; **~ dato** *frml* GESCHÄFT to date; **~ zum Ende führen** MGMNT *Projekt* follow through; **~ höchstens** GESCHÄFT up to a maximum of; **~ auf den letzten Rest gefüllt** IND at full capacity; **~ zur Stornierung** V&M *Werbung* till canceled (*AmE*) (*TC*), till cancelled (*BrE*) (*TC*), till forbid (*TF*); **~ auf weitere Nachricht** GESCHÄFT until further notice; **~ auf weiteres** GESCHÄFT until further notice; **~ auf Widerruf** (*b. a. W.*) GESCHÄFT till countermanded (*T/C*), V&M *Werbung* till canceled (*AmE*) (*TC*), till cancelled (*BrE*) (*TC*), till forbid (*TF*)

bisher *adv* GESCHÄFT to date

bisherig: **~ gezeigte Leistungen** *f pl* GESCHÄFT track record

bislang *adv* GESCHÄFT to date

Bit *nt* COMP, MATH bit, binary digit; **Bitabbildung** *f* COMP bit, bit-mapped graphics; **Bitabbildungszeichen** *nt* COMP *Drucker* bit-mapped character; **Bitdichte** *f* COMP bit density; **Bitfolge** *f* COMP bit string; **Bitkonfiguration** *f* COMP bit configuration; **Bitposition** *f* COMP bit location; **Bitrate** *f* COMP bit rate

Bits: **~ pro Sekunde** *phr* (*BPS*) COMP *Datenübertragung* bits per second (*bps*); **~ pro Zoll** *phr* (*BPI*) COMP *Speicherdichte* bits per inch (*bpi*)

bitte: **~ beachten** *phr* GESCHÄFT nota bene (*NB*), please note; **~ weiterleiten** *phr* KOMM please forward; **~ wenden** *phr* (*b.w.*) KOMM please turn over (*pto*)

Bitte *f* GESCHÄFT request; ◆ **auf ~ von** GESCHÄFT at the request of; **~ vorbringen** GESCHÄFT make a request

bitten: **um etw ~** *phr* GESCHÄFT ask for sth; **jdn um etw ~** *phr* GESCHÄFT ask sb for sth

Bittschrift *f* GESCHÄFT petition

bituminiert: **~es Papier** *nt* IND, KOMM waterproof paper

BIZ *abbr* (*Bank für Internationalen Zahlungsausgleich*) BANK, VW BIS (*Bank for International Settlements*)

Black-Box *f* COMP *Denkmodell* black box

Blackout *m jarg* COMP blackout

Black-Scholes: **~ Optionspreismodell** *nt* BÖRSE Black-Scholes option pricing model

blank *adj* COMP blank

Blankett *nt* GESCHÄFT blank form, document signed in blank

Blanko- *in cpds* GESCHÄFT blank; **Blankoauftrag** *m* GESCHÄFT blank order, blanket order; **Blankobankscheck** *m* BANK counter check (*AmE*), counter cheque (*BrE*); **Blankobeleg** *m* GESCHÄFT blank receipt; **Blankodarlehen** *nt* BÖRSE uncovered advance; **Blankoformular** *nt* GESCHÄFT blank form, document signed in blank; **Blankoindossament** *nt* BÖRSE blank endorsement; **Blankokredit** *m* **mit fester Laufzeit** BANK unsecured fixed-term loan; **Blankoquittung** *f* GESCHÄFT blank receipt; **Blankoscheck** *m* BANK blank check (*AmE*), blank cheque (*BrE*); **Blankoüberziehungskredit** *m* BANK unsecured overdraft; **Blankounterschrift** *f* BANK blank signature; **Blankoverkäufer, in** *m,f* BÖRSE short seller

Blase *f* VW fad; **Blasenpolitik** *f* UMWELT, VW bubble policy

Blatt *nt* KOMM, MEDIEN sheet, leaf, *Seite* page, *Zeitung* paper, newspaper

blättern *vi* COMP *Bildschirm* browse, scroll

Blaubuch *nt* POL, RECHNUNG, VW bluebook (*BrE*)

blaumachen *vi infrml* PERSON skip work (*infrml*)

Blechdose *f* IND, V&M can

Blechwaren *f pl* IND tinware

bleiben: **~ Sie bitte am Apparat** *phr* KOMM *Telefon* hold the line

Bleierz *nt* UMWELT lead ore

bleifrei *adj* TRANSP, UMWELT *Benzin* lead-free, unleaded; **~es Benzin** *nt* UMWELT lead-free gas (*AmE*), lead-free petrol (*BrE*), unleaded gas (*AmE*), unleaded petrol (*BrE*); **~er Kraftstoff** *m* UMWELT lead-free fuel

Bleisatz *m* MEDIEN *Typographie* hot type, hot-metal setting

blendfrei *adj* COMP *Bildschirm* antiglare, glare-free

Blickfang *m* V&M attention getter, guttersnipe, stopper

Blickkontakt *m* V&M eye contact

blind *adj* V&M blind; **~er Glaube** *m* GESCHÄFT blind faith; **~es Vertrauen** *nt* GESCHÄFT blind faith

Blindenfreibetrag *m* STEUER blind person's allowance (*BrE*)

blindschreiben *vi* COMP, VERWALT touch-type

Blindschreiben *nt* COMP, VERWALT touch-typing

Blindtest *m* V&M blind test

blinken *vi* COMP *Cursor* blink, GESCHÄFT *Signal* flash

Blisterpackung *f* V&M blister pack

Blitzbesuch *m* GESCHÄFT flying visit

Blitzstreik *m* PERSON lightning strike

Block *m* COMP *Text, Daten* block, *Vordrucke* pad,

GESCHÄFT pad, POL bloc; **Blockabstimmung** *f* PERSON block voting

Blockade *f* PERSON blockade

Block: **Blockbetrieb** *m* COMP burst mode; **Blockbusting** *nt* GRUND blockbusting (*infrml*) (*AmE*); **Blockdiagramm** *nt* COMP block diagram

blocken *vt* COMP block

Block: **Blockfinanzierung** *f* RECHNUNG block funding; **Blockhandel** *m* BÖRSE block trading

blockieren *vt* RECHT *Gesetzentwurf*, VW block

blockiert *adj* COMP deadlocked, GESCHÄFT, VW blocked

Block: **Blockkoeffizient** *m* TRANSP block coefficient; **Blockmodus** *m* COMP *Textverarbeitung* block mode; **Blockparzellierung** *f* GRUND lot and block (*AmE*); **Blockpolice** *f* VERSICH ticket policy; **Blockreihe** *f* TRANSP row; **Blockstichprobe** *f* RECHNUNG block sampling; **Blocktransfer** *m* COMP *Datenübertragung* block transfer; **Blockverschiebung** *f* COMP *Daten, Text* block move; **Blockzeit** *f* TRANSP block time

bloß: **~e Übernahme** *f* **des Vertriebs einer Neuemission** BÖRSE best efforts

blühend *adj* GESCHÄFT, VW thriving

BLZ *abbr* (*Bankleitzahl*) BANK bank code, sort code (*BrE*), bank routing number

Boden *m* UMWELT land; ◆ **an ~ gewinnen** GESCHÄFT gain ground; **an ~ verlieren** GESCHÄFT lose ground

Boden: **Bodenabschwemmung** *f* UMWELT soil erosion; **Bodenabtrag** *m* UMWELT soil erosion; **Bodenauswaschung** *f* UMWELT soil erosion; **Bodenbeschaffungsplan** *m* VW land acquisition program (*AmE*), land acquisition programme (*BrE*); **Bodendegradierung** *f* UMWELT soil degradation; **Bodenkontrolle** *f* KOMM, TRANSP *Flughafen* ground control; **Bodenkreditanstalt** *f* BANK land bank, land mortgage bank; **Bodennutzung** *f* UMWELT land use; **Bodennutzungsintensität** *f* UMWELT land-use intensity; **Bodenpersonal** *nt* TRANSP *Flughafen* ground crew; **Bodenreform** *f* VW land reform; **Bodenrente** *f* VERWALT ground rent; **Bodenschätze** *m pl* UMWELT natural resources, mineral resources; **auf Bodenschätzen basierende Wirtschaft** *f* VW mineral-based economy; **nach Bodenschätzen suchen** *phr* IND prospect; **Bodentransport** *m* TRANSP ground transportation, surface transport; **Bodenverschlechterung** *f* UMWELT soil degradation; **Bodenvorratspolitik** *f* GESCHÄFT resource-of-land policy; **Bodenwertzuwachssteuer** *f* STEUER land value tax

Bodmerei *f* TRANSP bottomry; **Bodmereibrief** *m* IMP/EXP, TRANSP, VERSICH bottomry bond; **Bodmereidarlehen** *nt* FINANZ maritime loan

Bogen *m* FINANZ coupon sheet, GESCHÄFT *Papier* sheet, KOMM sheet, MATH arc, curve, MEDIEN sheet; **~ mit Personalangaben** VERWALT personal data sheet; **Bogenelastizität** *f* MATH arc elasticity

Bohr- *in cpds* UMWELT *Erdöl* drilling; **Bohrinsel** *f* IND mobile offshore drilling unit (*MODU*), oil platform, oil rig, UMWELT drilling platform, platform; **Bohrlochkosten** *pl* FINANZ, IND wellhead cost; **Bohrplattform** *f* IND mobile offshore drilling unit (*MODU*), oil platform, oil rig, UMWELT drilling platform, platform; **Bohrprogramm** *nt* UMWELT drilling program (*AmE*), drilling programme (*BrE*); **Bohrturm** *m* UMWELT oil rig; **Bohrversuchsprogramm** *nt* VW developmental drilling program (*AmE*), developmental drilling programme (*BrE*)

Bombendrohung *f* POL bomb scare

Bon *m* FINANZ credit slip, GESCHÄFT cash register slip, issue voucher, coupon (*c., cp.*), *Gutschein* voucher, *Quittung* receipt

bona fide: ~ **Klausel** *f* GESCHÄFT bona fide clause

Bond *m*: ~ **bester Bonitätseinstufung** BÖRSE AAA Bond; ~ **mit kurzer Restlaufzeit** BÖRSE short coupon; **Bond-Analyse** *f* FINANZ fixed-interest research; **Bond-Zertifikat** *nt* BÖRSE bond certificate

Bonifikation *f* BANK agency commission, BÖRSE concession, FINANZ selling commission, GESCHÄFT bonus, premium, V&M selling commission

Bonität *f* BANK credit standing, FINANZ creditworthiness, financial standing, GESCHÄFT *Kredit* reliability, standing, VW *Agrarwirtschaft* quality of farm land

bonitätsmäßig: ~**e Einstufung** *f* **einer Anleihe** BÖRSE bond rating; ~**e Klassifizierung** *f* **einer Anleihe** BÖRSE bond rating

Bonität: **Bonitätsprüfer, in** *m,f* BANK credit analyst; **Bonitätsrisiko** *nt* RECHT, VERSICH *Vertragsrecht* risk of financial reliability; **Bonitätsverbesserung** *f* BANK credit enhancement

Bonus *m* BÖRSE bounty, extra dividend, FINANZ bonus, VERSICH extra dividend; **Bonuszuteilung** *f* VERSICH allotment of bonus

Bonze *m* infrml POL *Partei* bigwig (*infrml*), mandarin

boolesch *adj* COMP Boolean; ~**e Algebra** *f* MATH Boolean algebra; ~**e Variable** *f* COMP Boolean variable

Boom *m* GESCHÄFT, VW boom

Bootdiskette *f jarg* COMP boot disk

booten *vt* COMP bootstrap, boot up

Booten *nt jarg* COMP boot-up

Bord: **an** ~ *phr* IMP/EXP, TRANSP *Schiff, Flugzeug* aboard; **an** ~ **gebracht** *phr* IMP/EXP, TRANSP shipped on board; **an** ~ **nehmen** *phr* IMP/EXP, TRANSP *Fracht, Leute* take aboard; **an** ~ **verschifft** *phr* IMP/EXP, TRANSP shipped on board

Bord- *in cpds* TRANSP *Flugzeug* in-flight, *Schiff* on-board; **Bordbuch** *nt* VERWALT log book; **Bordempfangsschein** *m* IMP/EXP, TRANSP mate's receipt; **Bordinformationen** *f pl* TRANSP in-flight information; **Bordkarte** *f* TRANSP embarkation card, boarding card, boarding pass; **Bordkino** *nt* TRANSP in-flight film; **Bordkonnossement** *nt* IMP/EXP, TRANSP ocean bill of lading, shipped bill, shipped bill of lading; **Bordmusik** *f* TRANSP in-flight music; **Bordpersonal** *nt* TRANSP cabin staff; **Bordservice** *m* TRANSP in-flight service; **Bordunterhaltung** *f* TRANSP in-flight entertainment; **Bordverpflegung** *f* TRANSP in-flight catering, in-flight meal; **Bordzeitschrift** *f* TRANSP in-flight magazine

Börse *f* BÖRSE market, exchange, stock market, FINANZ, VW stock market; ~ **mit ausreichenden Umsätzen** BÖRSE liquid market; ♦ **außerhalb der** ~ BÖRSE away from the market; **an der** ~ **kaufen** BÖRSE buy at market; **an der** ~ **notiert** BÖRSE, RECHNUNG listed on the stock exchange, quoted on the stock exchange; **an der** ~ **spekulieren** BÖRSE gamble on the stock exchange

Börse: **Börsenangestellte(r)** *mf* [decl. as adj] BÖRSE floor official; **Börsenaufsichtsbehörde** *f* BÖRSE Securities and Exchange Commission (*AmE*) (*SEC*), stock market supervisory authority, Council to the Stock Exchange (*BrE*); **Börsenbericht** *m* BÖRSE market report, stock exchange report, FINANZ financial news; **Börsenbeteiligung** *f* BÖRSE market holding; **Börsenbrief** *m* BÖRSE market letter (*AmE*); **Börsendiener** *m* BÖRSE waiter (*BrE*); **Börsendrittmarkt** *m* FINANZ, VW third market; **Börseneinführung** *f* BÖRSE admission to listing; **Börseneinführungskosten** *pl* BÖRSE flotation cost, stock exchange admission fee; **Börsenetage** *f* BÖRSE dealing floor

börsenfähig *adj* BÖRSE listable, marketable, negotiable

börsengängig: ~**e Dividendenwerte** *m pl* BÖRSE marketable equities; ~**e Industrieobligation** *f* BÖRSE bearer marketable bond; ~**e Industrieschuldverschreibung** *f* BÖRSE bearer marketable bond; ~**e Obligation** *f* BÖRSE marketable bond; ~**e Schuldverschreibung** *f* BÖRSE marketable bond

börsengehandelt: **nicht** ~ *adj* BÖRSE over-the-counter (*AmE*) (*OTC*)

Börse: **Börsengeschäft** *nt* BÖRSE stock exchange transaction, FINANZ bargain

Börsenhandel *m* BÖRSE stock exchange dealings, FINANZ market dealing; **Börsenhandelsbuch** *nt* FINANZ trading book; **Börsenhandelsperiode** *f* BÖRSE accounting period; **Börsenhandelsprogramm** *nt* FINANZ trading program (*AmE*), trading programme (*BrE*)

Börse: **Börsenhändler, in** *m,f* BÖRSE stock exchange trader, FINANZ broker; **Börsenindex** *m* BÖRSE market index; **Börsenkapitalisierung** *f* BÖRSE market capitalization, capitalization

Börsenkurs *m* BÖRSE list price, stock exchange price, stock exchange quotation; ♦ **unter dem** ~ BÖRSE below-market; **zum** ~ BÖRSE at the market price; **zum letzen** ~ **bewertet** BÖRSE, VW marked-to-market; **Börsenkurse manipulieren** BÖRSE manipulate the market

Börsenkurs: **Börsenkursindex** *m* BÖRSE stock exchange price index; **Börsenkursnotierung** *f* BÖRSE stock market listing; **zur Börsenkursnotierung** *phr* BÖRSE at the market call

Börse: **Börsenmakler, in** *m,f* BÖRSE board broker, floor broker, stockbroker

börsenmäßig *adj* BÖRSE under the rule (*jarg*)

Börse: **Börsenmitglied** *nt* BÖRSE member corporation; **Börsenmitglieder** *nt pl* FINANZ members of the House; **Börsennachrichten** *f pl* FINANZ financial news

börsennotiert *adj* BÖRSE, RECHNUNG listed on the stock exchange, quoted on the stock exchange; ~**e Aktie** *f* BÖRSE listed share, quoted share; ~**e Bank** *f* BANK listed bank; ~**e Gesellschaft** *f* BÖRSE, GESCHÄFT, VW listed company, quoted company; **nicht** ~**e Gesellschaft** *f* BÖRSE, GESCHÄFT, VW unlisted company; ~**er Gesellschaftsanteil** *m* BÖRSE listed share; ~**e Option** *f* BÖRSE listed option; ~**es Unternehmen** *nt* BÖRSE, GESCHÄFT, VW listed company, quoted company; ~**e Wertpapiere** *nt pl* BÖRSE, VW listed securities, quoted securities

Börse: **Börsenpanik** *f* BÖRSE, FINANZ panic; **Börsenparkett** *nt* BÖRSE dealing floor; **Börsenpreise** *m pl* BÖRSE stock market prices; **Börsenpreisindex** *m* BÖRSE stock market price index; **Börsenrat** *m* BÖRSE Council to the Stock Exchange (*BrE*); **Börsensaal** *m* BÖRSE boardroom

Börsenschluß *m* BÖRSE close; ♦ **zum** ~ **kaufen** BÖRSE buy on close; **zum** ~ **verkaufen** BÖRSE sell on close

Börsenschluß: **Börsenschlußeinheit** *f* BÖRSE trading unit

Börse: **Börsenspekulant, in** *m,f* BÖRSE punter (*infrml*), stock exchange speculator; **Börsenspiel** *nt* VW agiotage; **Börsenstimmung** *f* BÖRSE market tone; **Börsentag** *m* BÖRSE market day; **Börsenticker** *m* BÖRSE ticker; **den Börsenticker ablesen** *phr* BÖRSE read the tape; **Börsentickersymbol** *nt* BÖRSE ticker symbol; **Börsentips** *m pl* BÖRSE stock tips; **Börsenumsatzsteuer** *f* STEUER stock exchange transfer tax; **Börsenweltverband** *m* BÖRSE World Federation of Stock Exchanges (*WFSE*); **Börsenwert** *m* BÖRSE, FINANZ exchange value, market value

Börsenzulassung *f* BÖRSE admission to listing (*BrE*), listing; ♦ **die ~ aufgeben** BÖRSE go private

Börsenzulassung: **Börsenzulassungsausschuß** *m* BÖRSE Council to the Stock Exchange (*BrE*), listing committee; **Börsenzulassungsverfahren** *nt* BÖRSE listing procedure

böse: **in ~r Absicht** *phr* RECHT *unredlich* mala fide (*frml*); **~r Wille** *m* GESCHÄFT ill will

bösgläubig *adj* RECHT *unredlich* mala fide (*frml*)

Boß *m infrml* GESCHÄFT boss (*infrml*)

Boston: **~er Börse** *f* BÖRSE Boston Stock Exchange (*AmE*)

böswillig *adv* RECHT maliciously

Bote *m* GESCHÄFT, KOMM runner, messenger, messenger boy; **Botenberaubungsversicherung** *f* VERSICH cash messenger insurance, messenger robbery insurance; **Botengang** *m* BANK bank run, GESCHÄFT errand; **einen Botengang machen** *phr* GESCHÄFT run an errand; **Botenjunge** *m* GESCHÄFT, KOMM messenger boy

Botin *f* GESCHÄFT, KOMM runner, messenger

Botschaft *f* POL embassy, V&M *Werbebotschaft* message

Botschafter, in *m,f* POL ambassador

Boulevard- *in cpds* MEDIEN tabloid; **Boulevardpresse** *f* MEDIEN gutter press, tabloid press; **Boulevardzeitung** *f* MEDIEN tabloid

Boutique *f* V&M boutique

Box- *in cpds* TRANSP box; **Box-Container** *m* TRANSP box container; **Boxpalette** *f* TRANSP box pallet

Boykott *m* PERSON, RECHT, VW boycott; **~ gegen einen nicht direkt am Arbeitskonflikt beteiligten Betrieb** PERSON secondary boycott

boykottieren *vt* PERSON, RECHT, VW boycott

BPI *abbr* (*Bits pro Zoll*) COMP *Speicherdichte* bpi (*bits per inch*)

BPS *abbr* (*Bits pro Sekunde*) COMP *Datenübertragung* bps (*bits per second*)

brachliegend *adj* GESCHÄFT *Kapital* unused; **~es Geld** *nt* vw idle money; **~e Guthaben** *nt pl* FINANZ, VW idle balance

Brachzeit *f* IND dead time, downtime, lost time, *ablaufbedingt* machine idle time, *störungsbedingt* machine downtime, *überlappend* machine interference time, PERSON dead time, downtime

Brady: **~ Ausschuß** *m* BÖRSE Brady Commission (*AmE*)

Brainstorming *nt* MGMNT brainstorming

Branche *f* GESCHÄFT trade, industry, IND industry, VERWALT branch, VW sector; ♦ **in welcher ~ sind Sie tätig?** GESCHÄFT what line of business are you in?

Branche: **Branchenanalyse** *f* FINANZ, GESCHÄFT sector analysis; **Brancheneinfuhrabfertigungssystem** *nt* IMP/

EXP Departmental Entry Processing System (*BrE*) (*DEPS*); **Branchenführer** *m* V&M industry leader; **Branchenführerprogramm** *nt* MGMNT industry leadership program (*AmE*), industry leadership programme (*BrE*)

branchenintern: **~er Handel** *m* IND intra-industry trade

Branche: **Branchenkenntnisse** *f pl* GESCHÄFT tricks of the trade (*infrml*)

branchenspezifisch *adj* VW sector-specific; **~e Hilfe** *f* VW sector-specific aid

Branche: **Branchenstrategie** *f* MGMNT sectoral strategy; **Branchentarifverhandlungen** *f pl* PERSON pattern bargaining; **Branchentarifvertrag** *m* PERSON industry-wide wage agreement; **Branchenverbindungen** *f pl* GESCHÄFT line relations; **Branchenverzeichnis** *nt* GESCHÄFT trade directory, vw Trade Data Elements Directory (*TDED*)

branchenweit: **~e Vereinbarung** *f* PERSON industry-wide agreement

Brand *m* VERSICH hostile fire; **Brandlegung** *f* VERSICH arson; **Brandmauer** *f* SOZIAL, VERSICH fire wall; **Brandrisiko** *nt* SOZIAL fire hazard; **Brandschutzvorschriften** *f pl* RECHT fire regulations; **Brandstiftung** *f* VERSICH arson, incendiarism; **Brandverhütung** *f* SOZIAL fire prevention

brandmarken *vt* GESCHÄFT brand

Brauchbarkeit *f* GESCHÄFT acceptability, PATENT usefulness, vw acceptability

brauchen *vt* GESCHÄFT need, require

braun: **~e Ware** *f* V&M *Radio, Fernsehgerät, Heimvideogerät* brown goods

Break-Even- *in cpds* BÖRSE, FINANZ, VW breakeven; **Break-Even-Analyse** *f* FINANZ, VW breakeven analysis; **Break-Even-Punkt** *m* BÖRSE, FINANZ, VW breakeven point; **Break-Even-Punkt** *m* **nach unten** BÖRSE downside breakeven point; **Break-Even-Stückzahl** *f* VERWALT, VW breakeven quantity

Breakpunkt-Verkauf *m* FINANZ breakpoint sale

brechen *vt* GESCHÄFT *Vertrag, Versprechen*, PERSON *Streik*, RECHT *Vertrag, Gesetz* break, violate, VW *Monopol* break

breit 1. *adj* GESCHÄFT wide; ♦ **auf ~er Bemessungsgrundlage** STEUER broad-based; **2.** *adv* GESCHÄFT broadly, widely; ♦ **~ fundiert** STEUER broad-based; **~ gestreut** GESCHÄFT broadly diversified

breit: **~e Antiquaschrift** *f* MEDIEN expanded type; **~e Masse** *f* POL broad masses; **~e Öffentlichkeit** *f* GESCHÄFT public at large; **~es Sortiment** *nt* GESCHÄFT, V&M *an Waren* wide range; **~es Warensortiment** *nt* GESCHÄFT, V&M wide range of goods

Breitband *nt* COMP broadband

breiteste: **auf ~r Basis** *phr* GESCHÄFT on a mammoth scale

breitgefächert: **~es Unternehmen** *nt* VW diversified company

Bremseffekt *m*: **~ der Steuerprogression** FINANZ, STEUER, VW fiscal drag

bremsen *vt* VW *Wachstum* dampen

Brennpunkt *m* GESCHÄFT focus

Brennstoff *m* STEUER, TRANSP, UMWELT fuel; **Brennstoffersparnis** *f* UMWELT fuel efficiency; **Brennstoffgebührenordnung** *f* STEUER fuel scale charges; **Brennstoffgebührentabelle** *f* STEUER fuel scale charges; **Brennstoffsteuer** *f* STEUER fuel tax; **Brennstoff-Steuerrabatt** *m* STEUER fuel duty rebate (*BrE*)

Bretton Woods: Bretton Woods-Abkommen *nt* VW Bretton Woods Agreement; **Bretton Woods-Konferenz** *f* VW Bretton Woods Conference

Bridge-Programm *nt* COMP bridgeware, bridging software

Bridgeware *f* COMP *jarg* bridgeware, bridging software

Brief *m* BÖRSE asked, offer price, price offered, KOMM letter; ~ **und Geld** *nt* BÖRSE asked and bid; ♦ ~ **vom** KOMM letter dated the

Brief: **Briefeinwurf** *m* KOMM *im Haus*, VERWALT mailbox (*AmE*), postbox (*BrE*); **Briefende** *nt* KOMM letterfoot; **Briefentwurf** *m* KOMM draft letter; **Briefkasten** *m* KOMM, VERWALT mailbox (*AmE*), postbox (*BrE*), letter box (*BrE*); **Briefkastengesellschaft** *f* BÖRSE nominee company; **Briefkopf** *m* KOMM letterhead; **Briefkurs** *m* BÖRSE asked price, offer, offer price, price (*pr.*), price offered, sellers' rate

brieflich: ~e **Anfrage** *f* KOMM letter of enquiry; ~e **Auszahlung** *f* BANK, KOMM mail transfer (*MT*); ~e **Befragung** *f* V&M, VW mail interview, mail survey; ~ **bestätigen** *phr* KOMM acknowledge receipt by letter

Brief: **Briefmarke** *f* KOMM postage stamp, stamp; **Briefpost** *f* KOMM first-class mail; **Briefqualität** *f* COMP letter quality (*LQ*); **Brieftelegramm** *nt* KOMM night letter (*AmE*); **Briefträger** *m* KOMM mail carrier (*AmE*), mailman (*AmE*), postman (*BrE*); **Briefträgerin** *f* KOMM mail carrier (*AmE*); **Briefwahl** *f* PERSON, POL postal ballot, postal vote; **Briefwechsel** *m* KOMM correspondence, interchange of letters

bringen *vt* BANK, FINANZ earn

Bringschuld *f* RECHT *Verträge* obligation which debtor has to perform at the creditor's address

brisant *adj* POL volatile

Britisch: ~es **Institut für Normung** *nt* VERWALT British Standards Institute (*BSI*); ~e **Klassifikation** *f* **für Zoll und Übersehandel** VW *internationaler Handel* United Kingdom tariff and overseas trade classification (*UKTOTC*)

britisch: ~e **Norm** *f* IND British Standard (*BS*); ~e **Normalzeit** *f* GESCHÄFT British Standard Time; ~es **Patentamt** *nt* PATENT UK Patent Office; ~e **Sommerzeit** *f* GESCHÄFT British Summer Time; ~e **Staatsanleihen** *f pl* BÖRSE UK government stocks; ~e **Staatsanleihepapiere** *nt pl* BÖRSE UK gilt-edged stocks; ~e **Steuerinländertreuhand** *f* RECHT UK resident trust; ~e **Viertelgallone** *f* GESCHÄFT *1,14 l*. British quart; ~e **Wertpapierbörsen** *f pl* BÖRSE UK stock exchanges

British: ~ **Broadcasting Corporation** *f* (*BBC*) MEDIEN British Broadcasting Corporation (*BBC, the Beeb*)

Broker *m* BÖRSE broker-dealer, FINANZ broker; **Brokerauftrag** *m* BÖRSE broker's order; **Brokerfonds** *m* BÖRSE broker fund (*BrE*); **Brokerkonto** *nt* BÖRSE brokerage account

Brookings-Institut *nt* VW Brookings Institution (*AmE*)

broschiert: ~es **Buch** *nt* MEDIEN paperback

Broschüre *f* FREI, GESCHÄFT brochure, V&M hand-out

Brötchen *nt* *infrml* GESCHÄFT bread (*infrml*); **Brötchengeber, in** *m,f infrml* VW employer

Bruch *m* GESCHÄFT breakage, KOMM break, MATH fraction, RECHT *von Vertragsbestimmungen* violation; ~ **der Geheimhaltung** GESCHÄFT breach of secrecy; **Bruchbelastung** *f* TRANSP breaking load; **Bruchklausel** *f* VERSICH breakage clause; **Bruchlast** *f* TRANSP breaking load; **Bruchschluß** *m* BÖRSE odd lot; **Bruchteileigentümer, in** *m,f* RECHT owner of a fractional share of property

Brücke *f* TRANSP bridge; **Brückengeld** *nt* TRANSP toll; **Brückenwaage** *f* TRANSP scale platform, weighbridge

Brundtland-Bericht *m* VW Brundtland Report

Brüssel: ~er **Zollrat** *m* (*BZR*) IMP/EXP Customs Co-operation Council (*CCC*)

Brust: Brust- und Rückenplakat *nt* V&M sandwich board

brutto **1.** *adj* GESCHÄFT gross; **2.** *adv* GESCHÄFT gross

Brutto- *in cpds* GESCHÄFT gross; **Bruttoallphasenumsatzsteuer** *f* STEUER all-stage gross turnover tax; **Bruttoanlageinvestitionen** *f pl* RECHNUNG gross fixed capital formation; **Bruttoanlagenkapitalbildung** *f* GESCHÄFT gross fixed capital formation; **Bruttoarbeitseinkommen** *nt* PERSON, STEUER earned income before deductions; **Bruttoauflagenhöhe** *f* V&M gross circulation; **Bruttoaufschlag** *m* VW mark-on; **Bruttoberechnung** *f* RECHNUNG, V&M grossing-up; **Bruttobetrag** *m* RECHNUNG gross amount; **Bruttobuchwert** *m* RECHNUNG book value before adjustment, gross book value; **Bruttocashflow** *m* FINANZ gross cash flow; **Bruttodividende** *f* FINANZ, vw gross dividend yield; **Bruttodividendenertrag** *m* VW gross dividend yield; **Bruttodividendenrendite** *f* BÖRSE gross dividend yield; **Bruttoeinkommen** *nt* PERSON gross earnings, RECHNUNG gross income; **Bruttoeinnahmen-Pool** *m* TRANSP gross receipts pool; **Bruttoeinzelhandelspreis** *m* V&M gross retail price (*GRP*); **Bruttoerlös** *m* PERSON gross earnings, RECHNUNG gross sales; **Bruttoersparnisse** *f pl* FINANZ gross savings; **Bruttoetat** *m* FINANZ gross budget; **Bruttoexzedentenrückversicherung** *f* VERSICH gross excess reinsurance policy; **Bruttofakturierung** *f* V&M gross billing (*AmE*); **Bruttoform** *f* **des Chartervertrages** TRANSP gross form of charter; **Bruttogewicht** *nt* GESCHÄFT gross weight (*gr.wt.*); **Bruttogewinn** *m* FINANZ gross margin (*GM*), profit, RECHNUNG contribution margin, gross margin (*GM*), gross profit, VERWALT, VW gross margin (*GM*), gross profit; **Bruttogewinnspanne** *f* RECHNUNG gross profit margin; **Bruttogewinnverhältnis** *nt* RECHNUNG gross profit ratio; **Bruttohandelsspanne** *f* FINANZ, VW gross margin (*GM*); **Bruttoinlandsprodukt** *nt* (*BIP*) VW gross domestic product (*GDP*); **Bruttoinvestitionen** *f pl* RECHNUNG gross investment; **Bruttolohn** *m* PERSON *Arbeitsentgelt* gross pay, gross wage; **Bruttomarge** *f* FINANZ, VW gross margin (*GM*); **Bruttomasse** *f* GESCHÄFT gross mass (*G*); **Bruttomehrwertsteuer** *f* STEUER output tax; **Bruttomiete** *f* GRUND gross lease; **Bruttomietemultiplikator** *m* GRUND gross rent multiplier (*GRM*); **Bruttomietfläche** *f* GRUND gross leasable area (*AmE*); **Bruttonachlaß** *m* STEUER gross estate; **Bruttopacht** *f* GRUND gross lease; **Bruttoregistertonne** *f* GESCHÄFT gross register ton (*GRT*), gross register tonne (*GRT*), gross registered tonnage; **Bruttoreichweite** *f* V&M gross reach; **Bruttorendite** *f* VERWALT gross return; **Bruttosatz** *m* TRANSP gross rate; **Bruttosozialprodukt** *nt* (*BSP*) VW gross national product (*GNP*), gross social product;

Bruttospanne *f* BÖRSE gross spread, FINANZ gross margin (*GM*), gross spread, RECHNUNG, VW gross margin (*GM*); **Bruttotonnage** *f* GESCHÄFT gross tonnage (*GT*); **Bruttotonne** *f* GESCHÄFT long ton, long tonne, gross ton, gross tonne; **Bruttoumsatz** *m* RECHNUNG gross sales, gross turnover; **Bruttoumsatzerlöse** *m pl* RECHNUNG gross sales revenue; **Bruttoverdienst** *m* PERSON gross earnings; **Bruttoverlust** *m* **an Einlagegeldern** BANK, VW disintermediation; **Bruttovermögen** *nt* STEUER gross estate; **Bruttoverpackungsgewicht** *nt* TRANSP gross tare weight; **Bruttovolkseinkommen** *nt* VW gross national income (*GNI*); **Bruttowarengewinn** *m* RECHNUNG gross trading profit; **Bruttozuggewicht** *nt* TRANSP gross train weight (*GTW*)

BSP *abbr* (*Bruttosozialprodukt*) VW GNP (*gross national product*), gross social product

Bsp. *abbr* (*Beispiel*) GESCHÄFT ex (*example*)

Btx *abbr* (*Bildschirmtext*) COMP, KOMM (*Btx*) Teletext®, teletex

Bubblesort *nt* COMP bubble sort

Buch *nt* BÖRSE, MEDIEN, RECHNUNG book; **~ mit den begehrenswertesten Stellen** VERWALT plum book (*AmE*); **~ mit festem Einband** MEDIEN casebound book, hardback; ♦ **~ führen über** [+acc] GESCHÄFT keep track of, RECHNUNG keep accounts for

Buch: **Buchdruck** *m* MEDIEN backstrip; **Bucheintrag** *m* RECHNUNG book entry

buchen *vt* GESCHÄFT *reservieren* book, reserve, RECHNUNG enter on the books, make an entry in the accounts, post

Bücher *nt pl* RECHNUNG books; ♦ **die ~ abschließen** RECHNUNG balance the books, rule off; **die ~ frisieren** *infrml* RECHNUNG fiddle accounts *infrml*, manipulate accounts; **in den Büchern** RECHNUNG in the books; **~ prüfen** RECHNUNG audit; **~ revidieren** RECHNUNG audit

Bücher: **Büchergutschein** *m* V&M book token; **Bücherrezensent, in** *m,f* MEDIEN book reviewer

Buch: **Buchforderung** *f* RECHNUNG book debt, book receivables; **Buchforderungen** *f pl* RECHNUNG outstanding amounts

Buchführung *f* PERSON, RECHNUNG, VERWALT accountancy (*acc., accy*), accounting, book-keeping; **~ mit Bewertung zum Zeitwert** RECHNUNG present value method; **~ auf Einnahmen- und Ausgabenbasis** RECHNUNG cash basis of accounting; **~ eines gemeinnützigen Vereins** RECHNUNG fund accounting; **~ per Computer** RECHNUNG computer accounting; **~ zum Tageswert** RECHNUNG current cost accounting (*CCA*); **~ zu Wiederbeschaffungskosten** RECHNUNG replacement cost accounting, replacement costing; **Buchführungsgrundsätze** *m pl* RECHNUNG accounting principles, accounting rules; **Buchführungsmodell** *nt* FINANZ, RECHNUNG accounting model; **Buchführungsrichtlinien** *f pl* RECHNUNG, VERWALT accounting doctrines; **Buchführungssystem** *nt* RECHNUNG accounting system; **Buchführungsunterlagen** *f pl* RECHNUNG accounting records

Buch: **Buchgeld** *nt* BANK deposit currency, deposit money, bank money, FINANZ credit money (*BrE*), VW deposit money; **Buchgewinn** *m* RECHNUNG accounting profit, book profit

Buchhalter, in *m,f* PERSON, RECHNUNG, VERWALT accountant, accounting officer (*AO*), accounting clerk, bookkeeper; **Buchhalterberuf** *m* RECHNUNG accountancy (*acc., accy*), accountancy profession

Buchhaltung *f* PERSON, RECHNUNG, VERWALT accountancy (*acc., accy*), accounting, book-keeping, *Abteilung* accounts department, accounting department, accounting office; **~ per Computer** RECHNUNG computer accounting; **~ des Profitzentrums** FINANZ profit center accounting (*AmE*), profit centre accounting (*BrE*); **Buchhaltungsabteilung** *f* RECHNUNG accounting department, accounting office, accounts department; **Buchhaltungs- und Bilanzierungsrichtlinien** *f pl* RECHNUNG, VERWALT accounting conventions; **Buchhaltungsbüro** *nt* RECHNUNG accounting practice; **Buchhaltungsgebühren** *f pl* RECHNUNG accounting fees; **Buchhaltungskreislauf** *m* RECHNUNG accounting cycle; **Buchhaltungsmethode** *f* RECHNUNG accounting method, method of preparation; **Buchhaltungspraxis** *f* RECHNUNG accounting practice; **Buchhaltungssoftware** *f* COMP, RECHNUNG accounting software; **Buchhaltungsumstellung** *f* RECHNUNG accounting change

Buch: **Buchhandel** *m* MEDIEN book trade; **Buchhonorar** *nt* MEDIEN book royalty; **Buchinventur** *f* FINANZ perpetual inventory, RECHNUNG book inventory, perpetual inventory; **Buchkritiker, in** *m,f* MEDIEN book reviewer; **Buchmacher** *m* FREI bookmaker, bookie (*infrml*), turf accountant (*frml*)

buchmäßig: **~er Gewinn** *m* RECHNUNG book profit; **~e Gewinnverteilung** *f* RECHNUNG, VERWALT appropriation of earnings; **~er Verlust** *m* RECHNUNG book loss; **~ verwaltete Wertpapiere** *nt pl* BÖRSE book entry securities

Buch: **Buchprüfer, in** *m,f* FINANZ, RECHNUNG auditor; **Buchprüfertätigkeit** *f* RECHNUNG accounting practice; **Buchprüfung** *f* FINANZ, RECHNUNG audit, auditing; **Buchprüfungsabteilung** *f* RECHNUNG auditing department; **Buchrücken** *m* MEDIEN backstrip

Buchstabe *m* COMP, MEDIEN letter; **Buchstabenabstand** *m* MEDIEN letter spacing; **Buchstaben-Ziffern-Umschaltung** *f* COMP case shift

buchtechnisch: **~e Behandlung** *f* RECHNUNG accounting treatment

Buchung *f* GESCHÄFT *Reservierung* reservation, booking, RECHNUNG accounting entry; ♦ **~ aufgeben** GESCHÄFT book in; **eine ~ stornieren** RECHNUNG reverse an entry; **eine ~ vornehmen** RECHNUNG pass an entry

Buchung: **Buchungsanzeige** *f* TRANSP booking note; **Buchungsbeleg** *m* RECHNUNG journal voucher, supporting book entry, vouch mark, voucher, accountable receipt; **Buchungsdaten** *pl* RECHNUNG accounting data, accounting information; **Buchungsfehler** *m* RECHNUNG accounting error; **Buchungsgebühr** *f* FINANZ transaction charge, GESCHÄFT booking fee

buchungspflichtig *adj* RECHNUNG accountable; **~er Beleg** *m* RECHNUNG accountable receipt; **~e Vorauszahlung** *f* PERSON, RECHNUNG accountable advance; **~er Vorschuß** *m* PERSON, RECHNUNG accountable advance

Buchung: **Buchungsplan** *m* RECHNUNG conceptual framework; **Buchungspreis** *m* BÖRSE entry price; **Buchungsrichtlinien** *f pl* RECHNUNG conceptual framework; **Buchungssystem** *nt* FREI booking system; **Buchungsverfahren** *f pl* RECHNUNG accounting procedure, RECHT posting; **Buchungsvorfälle** *m pl*

RECHNUNG internal transactions; **Buchungszahlen** *f pl* RECHNUNG accounting data; **Buchungszeitraum** *m* STEUER fiscal period

Buch: **Buchverlust** *m* RECHNUNG book loss

Buchwert *m* FINANZ book value, GESCHÄFT written-down value, RECHNUNG accounting value, book cost, carrying value, VW cost; **~ nach Abschreibungen** FINANZ net book value; **~ vor Abschreibungen** RECHNUNG gross book value; **~ des Anlagevermögens** RECHNUNG net investment in property, plant and equipment; **Buchwertabschreibung** *f* FINANZ declining-balance depreciation, RECHNUNG book depreciation

buddhistisch: **~e Wirtschaftsform** *f* VW Buddhist economics

Budget *nt* FINANZ, GESCHÄFT, RECHNUNG, POL, VW budget, estimates; ◆ **ein ~ aufstellen** FINANZ, MGMNT, RECHNUNG, VW prepare a budget; **das ~ nicht voll ausschöpfen** RECHNUNG underspend the budget

Budget: **Budgetausarbeitung** *f* FINANZ, MGMNT, RECHNUNG, VW budget preparation; **Budgetberichtigung** *f* FINANZ, RECHNUNG, VW budgetary adjustment; **Budgeteinsparungen** *f pl* FINANZ budget cuts; **Budgeterstellung** *f* FINANZ, MGMNT, RECHNUNG, VW budget preparation

budgetiert: **~e Kosten** *pl* RECHNUNG budgeted cost

Budgetierung *f* FINANZ, GESCHÄFT, RECHNUNG budgeting; **~ der Investitionen** RECHNUNG capital budgeting; **~ auf Nullbasis** FINANZ, RECHNUNG zero-base budgeting *(ZBB)*; **~ nach Verantwortungsbereichen** RECHNUNG responsibility budgeting; **Budgetierungssystem** *nt* RECHNUNG, VERWALT budget system

Budget: **Budgetinzidenz** *f* VW budget incidence; **Budgetkontrolle** *f* FINANZ, RECHNUNG budgetary control *(BC)*, budgeting control; **Budgetkosten** *pl* FINANZ, VW budgetary costs; **Budgetperiode** *f* FINANZ, RECHNUNG, VW budget period; **Budgetrestriktion** *f* FINANZ, RECHNUNG, VW budget constraint; **Budgetrevision** *f* FINANZ, RECHNUNG, VW budget review; **Budgetstandard** *m* FINANZ, GESCHÄFT budget standard; **Budgetwesen** *nt* RECHNUNG budget system

Bugsier- *in cpds* TRANSP tow, towage; **Bugsiergebühr** *f* TRANSP towage charges, towage dues; **Bugsierschiff** *nt* TRANSP towboat, towing boat; **Bugsierschlepper** *m* TRANSP towboat, towing boat

Bulk- *in cpds* IMP/EXP, TRANSP bulk

Bulkfracht *f* TRANSP break bulk; ◆ **~ abladen** TRANSP break bulk; **~ aufteilen** TRANSP break bulk; **~ ausladen** TRANSP break bulk; **~ entladen** TRANSP break bulk; **~ teilen** TRANSP break bulk

Bulkfracht: **Bulkfrachtmakler, in** *m,f* TRANSP break bulk agent; **Bulkfrachtumsatzplatz** *m* TRANSP break bulk center *(AmE)*, break bulk centre *(BrE)*; **Bulkfrachtumschlagplatz** *m* TRANSP break bulk center *(AmE)*, break bulk centre *(BrE)*

Bulk-: **Bulkhandel** *m* TRANSP bulk cargo trade; **Bulklizenz** *f* IMP/EXP bulk licence *(BrE)*, bulk license *(AmE)*

Bullet *nt jarg* COMP bullet

Bulletin *nt* KOMM news bulletin

Bullock: **~ Report** *m* PERSON Bullock report *(BrE)*

Bummelstreik *m* PERSON, VW go-slow *(BrE)*, slowdown *(AmE)*; ◆ **einen ~ machen** PERSON *Arbeitskonflikt* stage a go-slow *(BrE)*, stage a slowdown *(AmE)*

Bummelzug *m* TRANSP accommodation train *(AmE)*, stopping train

Bund *m* GESCHÄFT alliance, association, POL alliance, confederation; **~ Deutscher Werbeberater und Werbeleiter** *n (BDW)* V&M ≈ Advertising Association *(BrE)*

Bündel *nt* KOMM parcel, package *(pkg.)*, MEDIEN batch, TRANSP bundle, V&M package; **~ finanzpolitischer Maßnahmen** FINANZ financing package; **~ von Reformen** POL reform package; ◆ **im ~ mit** COMP *Softwarehandel* bundled with; **ein ~ Banknoten** BANK, GESCHÄFT wad of banknotes

bündeln *vt* COMP, V&M bundle

Bündeln *nt* COMP, V&M bundling

Bündelung *f* STEUER bunching

Bundes- *in cpds* GESCHÄFT federal *(fed.)*, national *(nat.)*; **Bundesamt** *nt* **für Grundstücke der öffentlichen Hand** VERWALT land office; **Bundesanstalt** *f* **für Flugsicherung** *(BFS)* TRANSP British Airports Authority *(BAA)*; **Bundesarbeitsamt** *nt* PERSON ≈ national employment agency; **Bundesaufsichtsamt** *nt* **für Bausparkassen** BANK Federal Savings and Loan Insurance Corporation *(AmE) (FSLIC)*; **Bundesaufsichtsbehörde** *f* **für das Bausparkassenwesen** VW Federal Home Loan Bank Board *(AmE)*; **auf Bundesebene** *phr* POL, VW federal-level; **Bundesgerichtshof** *m* RECHT federal tribunal; **Bundesgesetz** *nt* RECHT national legislation; **Bundeshaushaltsplanung** *f* **und -budgetierung** *f* VW federal financial program *(AmE)*, federal financial programme *(BrE)*; **Bundeshypothekenanstalt** *m* GRUND ≈ Federal Home Loan Mortgage Corporation *(AmE)*, ≈ Federal National Mortgage Association *(AmE) (FNMA, Fannie Mae)*; **Bundeskartellamt** *nt* VW Federal Cartel Office *(AmE) (FCO)*; **Bundeskartellbehörde** *f* POL, VW Federal Trade Commission *(AmE) (FTC)*, VW Federal Cartel Office *(AmE) (FCO)*; **Bundeslandwirtschaftsbank** *f* BANK Federal Land Bank *(AmE)*; **Bundesluftfahrtbehörde** *f* TRANSP Federal Aviation Administration *(AmE) (FAA)*; **Bundesrat** *m* POL upper house of German parliament, ≈ House of Lords *(BrE) (H of L)*, ≈ Senate *(AmE)*; **Bundesrechnungshof** *m* RECHNUNG General Accounting Office *(AmE) (GAO)*

bundesstaatlich *adj* POL, VW federal; **~es Finanzprogramm** *nt* VW federal financial program *(AmE)*, federal financial programme *(BrE)*; **~es Finanzwesen** *nt* FINANZ federal finance *(AmE)*; **~e Hypothekenkreditanstalt** *f* FINANZ Government National Mortgage Association *(AmE) (Ginnie Mae, GNMA)*; **~ regulierte Börse** *f* BÖRSE federally regulated exchange *(AmE)*

Bundes-: **Bundesstaatsanleihe** *f* BÖRSE federal government bond *(AmE)*; **Bundessteuerbehörde** *f* STEUER Internal Revenue Service *(IRS) (AmE)*; **Bundessteuerpfandrecht** *nt* STEUER federal tax lien *(AmE)*; **Bundesstraße** *f* TRANSP highway *(AmE)*, trunk road *(BrE)*; **Bundestag** *m* POL lower house of German parliament, ≈ House of Commons *(BrE) (H of C)*, ≈ House of Representatives *(AmE)*; **Bundesverband** *m* **der Deutschen Industrie** *(BDI)* IND ≈ Confederation of British Industry *(CBI)*; **Bundesversicherungsanstalt** *f* **für Bauspareinlagen** BANK Federal Savings and Loan Insurance Corporation *(AmE) (FSLIC)*; **Bundeswahl** *f* POL federal election

bundesweit: ~e **Tageszeitung** *f* GESCHÄFT national newpaper

Bundes-: **Bundeswirtschaftsrat** *m* (*BWR*) VW American Economic Association (*AEA*), National Economic Development Council (*BrE*) (*Neddy*); **Bundeswohnbauverwaltung** *f* GRUND ≈ Federal Housing Administration (*AmE*) (*FHA*); **Bundeszuschuß** *m* SOZIAL flat grant

Bundling *nt* COMP, V&M bundling

Bündnis *nt* POL alliance

Bundsteg *m* MEDIEN *Typographie* gutter

Bunker *m* TRANSP bin container

Bürge *m* BANK, FINANZ guarantor; ◆ **als ~ für jdn agieren** FINANZ stand as guarantor for sb

Bürgenhaftung *f* BANK surety liability

Bürger, in *m,f* POL citizen; **Bürgeranleihen** *f pl* BÖRSE citizen bonds; **Bürgercharta** *f* POL Citizen's Charter (*BrE*); **Bürgerkrieg** *m* POL civil war

bürgerlich: ~**er Beruf** *m* PERSON civilian employment

Bürger: **Bürgerrechte** *nt pl* RECHT *Verfassung* civil rights; **Bürgerunruhen** *f pl* POL, VERSICH civil commotion (*CC*)

Bürgin *f* BANK, FINANZ guarantor

Bürgschaft *f* BANK guarantee, guaranty, FINANZ security, RECHT bail, suretyship; ◆ ~ **für jdn leisten** BANK stand surety for sb; **mit ~ gesichert** GESCHÄFT guaranteed (*guar*)

Bürgschaft: **Bürgschaftsleistung** *f* FINANZ surety; **Bürgschaftsleistung** *f* **in bar** RECHT surety in cash; **Bürgschaftsurkunde** *f* RECHT bail bond; **Bürgschaftsverpflichtung** *f* RECHNUNG guarantee liability

Büro *nt* GESCHÄFT office; ~ **für gegenseitige Sicherheit** VERWALT Mutual Security Agency (*AmE*) (*MSA*); ~ **des Geschäftsführers** VERWALT manager's office; ~ **für Überseehandel** VW Overseas Trade Board (*BrE*); ◆ **im ~ vorstellig werden** GESCHÄFT apply at the office

Büro: **Büroalltag** *m* GESCHÄFT office routine; **Büroangestellte** *pl* [decl. as adj] PERSON clerical staff; **Büroangestellte(r)** *mf* [decl. as adj] PERSON clerk, clerical worker, office worker; **Büroarbeit** *f* PERSON clerical work, office work; **Büroausstattung** *f* VERWALT office equipment; **Büroautomation** *f* COMP, IND, VERWALT office automation (*OA*); **Büroautomatisierung** *f* COMP, IND, VERWALT office automation (*OA*); **Bürobedarf** *m* VERWALT office requisites, office stationery; **Bürobedarfsartikel** *m pl* VERWALT office supplies; **Bürobote** *m* PERSON office boy; **Bürochef, in** *m,f* MGMNT chief clerk, head clerk, office manager, senior clerk; **Büroeinbruchdiebstahl- und Raubversicherung** *f* VERSICH office burglary and robbery insurance; **Bürofläche** *f* GRUND office space; **Bürogebäude** *nt* GRUND office block, office building; **Bürogehilfe** *m*,

Bürogehilfin *f* PERSON staff assistant; **Bürohaus** *nt* GRUND office block; **Bürohilfe** *f* GESCHÄFT office aid; **Bürokommunikation** *f* GESCHÄFT office communication; **Bürokosten** *pl* RECHNUNG office expenses

Bürokrat *m* PERSON, VERWALT bureaucrat

Bürokratie *f* PERSON, VERWALT bureaucracy; ◆ **die ~ auf Trab bringen** VERWALT spin red tape

bürokratisch *adj* PERSON, VERWALT bureaucratic

Bürokratisierung *f* PERSON, VERWALT bureaucratization

Bürokratismus *m* PERSON, VERWALT bureaucracy, red tape

Büro: **Bürolandschaft entwerfen** *phr* VERWALT landscape (*jarg*); **Büroleiter, in** *m,f* MGMNT chief clerk, head clerk, office manager, senior clerk; **Büroleitung** *f* MGMNT office management; **Büromaschine** *f* GESCHÄFT business machine; **Büromaschinen** *f pl* VERWALT office equipment; **Büromaterial** *nt* GESCHÄFT stationery; **Büroorganisation** *f* MGMNT office management; **Büropersonal** *nt* PERSON clerical personnel, clerical staff, office staff; **Büropersonal** *nt* **im front Office** PERSON, VERWALT front-office personnel; **Büroplanung** *f* GESCHÄFT office planning; **Büroräume** *m pl* GRUND office accommodation, office space, office premises; **Bürostunden** *f pl* VERWALT office hours; **Bürotätigkeit** *f* PERSON white-collar job, office job; **Bürotechnik** *f* VERWALT office technology; **Büroverwaltung** *f* MGMNT office management; **Bürovorsteher, in** *m,f* MGMNT, PERSON senior clerk, office manager

Burstmodus *m* COMP burst mode

Bus *m* COMP bus

Büschelkarte *f* MATH bunch graph, bunch map

Businessgrafik *f* MGMNT management chart

Businessklasse *f* FREI, TRANSP business class, executive class

Bus: **Busklasse** *f* TRANSP coach class; **Busmailing** *nt jarg* COMP bus mailing; **Buspendelverkehr** *m* TRANSP bus shuttle

Buße *f* RECHT, VERSICH punitive damages

Bußgeld *nt* RECHT, VERSICH *zivilrechtliche Geldstrafe* administrative fine, civil penalty (*AmE*), monetary fine, punitive damages; **Bußgeldbescheid** *m* RECHT penalty notice

Butan *nt* IND butane; **Butangas** *nt* IND butane gas

Butterberg *m* VW butter mountain

Butterfly-Spread *m* BÖRSE butterfly spread

Buy-out *nt* BÖRSE, FINANZ buyout; ~ **von Arbeitskräften** FINANZ, PERSON worker buyout

b.w. *abbr* (*bitte wenden*) KOMM pto (*please turn over*)

BWR *abbr* (*Bundeswirtschaftsrat*) VW ≈ AEA (*American Economic Association*)

Byte *nt* COMP byte

BZR *abbr* (*Brüsseler Zollrat*) IMP/EXP CCC (*Customs Cooperation Council*)

C

ca. *abbr* (*zirka*) GESCHÄFT about, approximately (*approx.*), ca. (*circa*)

Cache *m* COMP *Speicher* cache; **Cache-Speicher** *m* COMP cache memory, cache storage, cache store

CAD *abbr* (*computerunterstützte Entwicklung, computerunterstützter Entwurf*) COMP, IND CAD (*computer-aided design, computer-assisted design*)

CAD/CAM *abbr* (*computerunterstützter Entwurf und Fertigung*) COMP, IND CAD/CAM (*computer-aided design and computer-aided manufacturing, computer-assisted design and computer-assisted manufacturing*)

CADD *abbr* (*computerunterstütztes Konstruieren und technisches Zeichnen*) COMP, IND CADD (*computer-aided design and drafting, computer-assisted design and drafting*)

CAE *abbr* (*computerunterstütztes Ingenieurwesen*) COMP, IND CAE (*computer-aided engineering, computer-assisted engineering*)

CAI *abbr* (*computerunterstützter Unterricht*) IND, COMP CAI (*computer-aided instruction, computer-assisted instruction*)

Cairns-Gruppe *f* VW Cairn's Group

CAL *abbr* (*computerunterstütztes Lernen*) COMP CAL (*computer-aided learning, computer-assisted learning*)

CALL *abbr* (*computerunterstütztes Lernen von Sprachen*) COMP CALL (*computer-aided language learning, computer-assisted language learning*)

Call *m*: ~ **aus dem Geld** *jarg* BÖRSE out-of-the-money call; ~ **out of the money** *jarg* BÖRSE out-of-the-money call

CAM *abbr* (*computerunterstützte Fertigung*) COMP, IND CAM (*computer-aided manufacturing, computer-assisted manufacturing*)

Cambridge: ~ **Schule** *f* VW Cambridge school; **Cambridge-Kontroversen** *f pl* VW Cambridge controversies; **Cambridge-Ökonomen** *m pl* VW *die 1974 eine expansionäre Fiskalpolitik forderten* Cambridge Economic Policy Group

Cap *m* FINANZ cap

Carnet *nt* IMP/EXP carnet; ~ **TIR** *nt* IMP/EXP TIR carnet; **Carnetsystem** *nt* IMP/EXP *EG* carnet system

Carrykosten *pl* BÖRSE cost of carry

CASE *abbr* (*computerunterstützte Software-Erstellung*) COMP CASE (*computer-aided software engineering, computer-assisted software engineering*)

Cash-Cow-Produkte *nt pl* GESCHÄFT cash cow products

Cash-Crop *nt* VW cash crop

Cashflow *m* FINANZ cash flow; ~ **vor Steuern** FINANZ before-tax cash flow, gross cash flow, RECHNUNG, STEUER before-tax cash flow; **Cashflow-Bericht** *m* FINANZ cash flow statement; **Cashflow-Problem** *nt* RECHNUNG cash flow problem; **Cashflow-Prognose** *f* RECHNUNG cash flow forecast

cbm *abbr* (*Kubikmeter*) GESCHÄFT cbm (*cubic meter AmE, cubic metre BrE*), m^3 (*cubic meter AmE, cubic metre BrE*)

CBS-Tendenzindex *m* BÖRSE CBS Tendency index

cc *abbr* GESCHÄFT *Motorhubraum* cc (*cubic capacity*), (*Kubikzentimeter*) cc (*cubic centimeter AmE, cubic centimetre BrE*), cm^3 (*cubic centimeter AmE, cubic centimetre BrE*)

CD *abbr* COMP (*Compact Disc*) CD (*compact disc*), GESCHÄFT (*Compact Disc*) CD (*compact disc*), (*Depositenzertifikat*) certificate of deposit, MEDIEN (*Compact Disc*) CD (*compact disc*); **CD-Markt** *m* BANK certificate of deposit market; **CD-ROM** *abbr* (*Compact-Disc-Festwertspeicher*) COMP, MEDIEN *Speicher* CD-ROM (*compact disc read-only memory*)

CEN *abbr* (*Europäisches Komitee für Normung*) VW CEN (European Committee for Standardization)

CENELEC *abbr* (*Europäisches Komitee für elektrotechnische Normung*) VW CEN (European Committee for Electrotecnical Standardization)

Central: ~**e Marketing-Gesellschaft** *f* **der deutschen Agrarwirtschaft mbH** (*CMA*) VW ≈ Agricultural Marketing Board (*BrE*)

Centronics®**-Schnittstelle** *f* COMP *Drucker* Centronics® interface

CES-Produktionsfunktion *f* (*Produktionsfunktion der konstanten Substitutionselastizität*) VW CES production function (*constant elasticity of substitution production function*)

ceteris paribus *phr* GESCHÄFT ceteris paribus, all else being equal; ~**-Klausel** *f* GESCHÄFT ceteris paribus

CGA-Karte *f* COMP color graphics adapter (*AmE*), colour graphics adapter (*BrE*) (*CGA*)

Chance *f* GESCHÄFT opportunity, break (*infrml*), *Wetten* chance, FINANZ, POL, VW opportunity; ♦ **eine ~ ergreifen, etw zu tun** GESCHÄFT take advantage of an opportunity to do sth; **eine gute ~ haben für** GESCHÄFT stand a good chance of

Chance: **Chancengleichheit** *f* PERSON *Arbeit* equal opportunity (*BrE*), affirmative action (*AmE*); **Chancengleichheit** *f* **am Arbeitsmarkt** PERSON equal employment opportunity

Chaosforschung *f* IND chaos research

Character-String *m* *jarg* COMP character string

Charakter *m* V&M character

charakteristisch: ~**es Merkmal** *nt* PATENT characterizing portion

charakterlich: ~**e Zuverlässigkeit** *f* PERSON character firmness

Charge *f* IND batch; **Chargengröße** *f* IND batch size

Charter *f* TRANSP charter; **ohne ~** TRANSP off hire; **Charteragent** *m* TRANSP chartering agent

Charterer *m* IMP/EXP, TRANSP charterer

Charter: **Charterflug** *m* TRANSP charter flight, chartered flight; **Charterflugzeug** *nt* TRANSP charter plane, chartered plane; **Chartermaschine** *f* TRANSP charter plane, chartered plane

chartern *vt* GESCHÄFT, PERSON hire, IMP/EXP, TRANSP *Flugzeug oder Schiff* charter

Chartern *nt* TRANSP chartering

Charter: **Charterpartie** *f* TRANSP charter party (*C/P*);

Charter- und Vergütungs-Unternehmer *m* TRANSP hire and reward operator; **Chartervertrag** *m* TRANSP charter party (*C*/*P*), charter contract; **Chartervertrag-Konnossement** *nt* TRANSP C/P bill of lading, charter party bill of lading; **Chartervertragsbetrug** *m* TRANSP charter party fraud; **Chartervertragsfracht** *f* TRANSP charter party freight

checken *vt* GESCHÄFT check

Checkliste *f* GESCHÄFT checklist; **~ für Exportaufträge** IMP/EXP export order check list

Chef, in *m,f* GESCHÄFT *Manager* superior, boss (*infrml*), *einer Abteilung* head, MGMNT chief operating officer; **~ der Prüfungsgruppe** RECHNUNG head of the audit group; **~ des Rechnungswesens** MGMNT controller, comptroller; **Chefbuchhalter, in** *m,f* RECHNUNG head accountant; **Chefgespräche** *nt pl* VW bilaterals; **Chefkonstrukteur, in** *m,f* MGMNT chief designer; **Chefredakteur, in** *m,f* MEDIEN chief editor, chief subeditor (*BrE*) (*chief sub*); **Chefredaktion** *f* MEDIEN editorship; **Chefsekretär, in** *m,f* MGMNT, PERSON, VERWALT personal assistant (*PA*), personal secretary (*P*/*Sec*, *PS*); **Chefsteward** *m* PERSON *Schiffahrt, Fluggesellschaften* chief steward; **Chefstewardess** *f* PERSON *Schiffahrt, Fluggesellschaften* chief stewardess; **Chefsuite** *m* PERSON executive suite; **Chefunterhändler, in** *m,f* GESCHÄFT chief negotiator

Chemie *f* GESCHÄFT *infrml* chemistry, IND, UMWELT chemicals, chemistry; **Chemiefaser** *f* IND, UMWELT man-made fiber (*AmE*), man-made fibre (*BrE*); **Chemieindustrie** *f* IND chemical industry; **Chemiewerke** *nt pl* IND chemical works

Chemikalien *f pl* IND, TRANSP, UMWELT chemicals; **Chemikalientanker** *m* TRANSP chemical tanker

chemisch: **~er Eintrag** *m* UMWELT chemical input; **~e Industrie** *f* IND chemical industry

Chicago: **~er Schule** *f* VW Chicago School

Chief-Executive-Officer *m* PERSON *Unternehmensleitung* chief executive officer (*AmE*) (*CEO*)

Chiffre *f* KOMM cipher; **Chiffreanzeige** *f* V&M blind advertisement, keyed advertisement; **Chiffrenummer** *f* PERSON box number, reference number

Chip *m* COMP chip; **Chipkarte** *f* BANK smart card, COMP chip card, chip-based card, smart card

Chi-Quadrat *nt* MATH chi square; **Chi-Quadrat-Test** *m* MATH chi-square test; **Chi-Quadrat-Verteilung** *f* MATH chi-squared distribution

chronologisch: **~es Akzeptverzeichnis** *nt* BANK acceptance register

CI *abbr* (*Corporate Identity*) V&M corporate identity

cif: **~ einschließlich Löschen** *phr* IMP/EXP *Lieferklausel* CIF landed; **~ nach Londoner Bestimmungen** *phr* IMP/EXP *Lieferklausel* cost, insurance and freight London terms; **cif-Vertrag** *m* IMP/EXP CIF contract

CIM *abbr* (*computerintegrierte Fertigung, computerintegrierte Herstellung*) COMP, IND CIM (*computer-integrated manufacture, computer-integrated manufacturing*)

CIO *abbr* (*Industriegewerkschaftsverband*) PERSON CIO (*Congress of Industrial Organizations*)

cl *abbr* (*Zentiliter*) GESCHÄFT cl (*centiliter AmE, centilitre BrE*)

Clearing *nt* BANK clearing; **~ von hohen Beträgen** BANK high-value clearings (*BrE*); **Clearingabkommen** *nt* BANK agreement of clearing; **Clearingbank** *f* BANK,

FINANZ clearing bank; **Clearinggesellschaft** *f* BANK clearing corporation (*AmE*); **Clearinghaus** *nt* FINANZ clearing house; **Clearingstelle** *f* BANK clearing center (*AmE*), clearing centre (*BrE*), TRANSP clearing house; **Clearingsystem** *nt* **für den Massenwertpapierverkehr** BANK high-volume paper clearings; **Clearingverkehr** *m* BANK clearing transactions; **Clearingzentrale** *f* BANK clearing center (*AmE*), clearing centre (*BrE*)

Client/Server *m jarg* COMP client/server

Clipart *nt jarg* COMP clip art

Clipboard *nt jarg* COMP clipboard

Club *m*: **~ of Rome** VW Club of Rome; **Club-Gut** *nt* VW club good; **Club-Klasse** *f* FREI club class

Cluster *m* COMP *Speichersektoren*, GESCHÄFT *Datensätze* cluster; **Clusteranalyse** *f* MATH cluster sampling, V&M cluster sampling, cluster analysis; **Clustereinheit** *f* V&M cluster sample; **Clustering** *nt* V&M clustering; **Clustersteuereinheit** *f* COMP cluster controller

cm *abbr* (*Zentimeter*) GESCHÄFT cm (*centimeter AmE, centimetre BrE*)

cm³ *abbr* (*Kubikzentimeter*) GESCHÄFT cc (*cubic centimeter AmE, cubic centimetre BrE*), cm³ (*cubic centimeter AmE, cubic centimetre BrE*)

CMA *abbr* (*Centrale Marketing-Gesellschaft der deutschen Agrarwirtschaft mbH*) VW ≈ Agricultural Marketing Board (*BrE*)

c/o *abbr* (*Post*) GESCHÄFT *Post*, IMP/EXP c/o (*care of*)

Co.: **und ~** *phr* GESCHÄFT and Co

Coase *nt* VW Coase; **Coase-Theorem** *nt* VW Coase theorem

Cobb-Douglas-Funktion *f* VW *makroökonomische Produktionsfunktion* Cobb Douglas production function; **Cobb-Douglas-Produktionsfunktion** *f* VW *makroökonomische Produktionsfunktion* Cobb Douglas production function

COBOL *abbr* (*allgemeine kaufmännisch orientierte Programmiersprache*) COMP COBOL (*common business-oriented language*)

Cobweb-Theorem *nt* VW *Modell der Preisbildung* cobweb theorem

c.o.d. *abbr* (*Barzahlung bei Lieferung*) GESCHÄFT, IMP/EXP COD (*cash on delivery*)

Code *m* COMP code, KOMM cipher; **Codebezeichnung** *f* COMP code name

Codec *m* (*Codierer-Decodierer*) COMP codec (*coder-decoder*)

Code: **Codeelement** *nt* COMP code element; **Codeliste** *f* COMP code set; **Codename** *m* COMP code name; **Codeprüfung** *f* COMP code check; **Codeseite** *f* COMP code sheet; **Codetabelle** *f* COMP code table; **Codewandler** *m* KOMM *Nachrichtenverarbeitung, Übermittlungstechnik* transcoder

Codieren *nt* COMP coding

Codierer-Decodierer *m* (*Codec*) COMP coder-decoder (*codec*)

Codierlinie *f* COMP code line

Codierzeile *f* COMP code line

Comeback: **ein ~ erleben** *phr* GESCHÄFT make a comeback

COMECON *abbr* VW COMECON (*obs*) (*Council for Mutual Economic Aid*)

COMET-Modell *nt* VW Common Market Medium Term Model (*COMET*)

Comit-Index *m* BÖRSE Comit Index

Common: ~ **Law** *nt* PERSON, RECHT common law

Commonwealth *nt* VW commonwealth; **Commonwealthpräferenz** *f* IMP/EXP Commonwealth preference

Compact Disc *f* (*CD*) COMP, GESCHÄFT, MEDIEN compact disc (*CD*); **~-Festwertspeicher** *m* (*CD-ROM*) COMP compact disc read-only memory (*CD-ROM*)

Compiler *m* COMP compiler

Computer *m* COMP computer; ~ **der zweiten Generation** COMP second-generation computer; **Computeranimation** *f* V&M computer animation; **Computerausdruck** *m* COMP computer print-out; **Computerbank** *f* BANK computer bank; **Computerbediener, in** *m,f* COMP computer operator; **Computerbetrug** *m* RECHT computer fraud; **Computerbörse** *f* BÖRSE screen trading system; **Computercenter** *nt* COMP *Verkauf* computer center (*AmE*), computer centre (*BrE*); **Computercode** *m* COMP computer code; **Computerdesign** *nt* COMP *Hardware* computer design; **Computerexperte** *m*, **Computerexpertin** *f* COMP computer expert; **Computerfachkenntnis** *f* COMP computer literacy; **Computergenie** *nt* COMP wizard, computer wizard; **Computergesetz** *nt* COMP computer law

computergesteuert *adj* COMP computer-driven, computer-controlled, computer-operated

computergestützt *adj* COMP computer-aided, computer-assisted, computer-based, PC-based; **~e Ausbildung** *f* COMP computer-based training (*CBT*); **~es Buchungssystem** *nt* RECHNUNG computerized accounting system; **~e Clearingstelle** *f* FINANZ Automated Clearing House (*ACH*); **~er Interbankenmarkt** *m* **für Wertpapiere** BÖRSE fourth market; **~e Verwaltung** *f* COMP *Daten, Systeme* computerized management; **~e Werbung** *f* V&M computer-aided advertising system (*CAAS*); **~e Wertpapiertransaktionen** *f pl* BÖRSE, COMP program trading

Computer: **Computergrafik** *f* COMP computer graphics; **Computerhersteller** *m* COMP computer company

computerintegriert *adj* COMP computer-integrated; **~e Fertigung** *f* (*CIM*) COMP, IND computer-integrated manufacturing (*CIM*); **~e Herstellung** *f* (*CIM*) COMP, IND computer-integrated manufacturing (*CIM*)

computerisieren *vt* COMP computerize

computerisiert *adj* COMP computerized; **~es Bankwesen** *nt* BANK computerized banking

Computerisierung *f* COMP computerization

Computer: **Computerkarte** *f* BANK, COMP smart card; **Computerkasse** *f* COMP electronic till; **Computerkommunikation** *f* COMP *Datenübertragung* computer communication; **Computerkonferenz** *f* COMP *Datenübertragung* computer conferencing; **Computerkreise** *m pl* COMP computer circles; **Computerkriminalitäts-Versicherung** *f* VERSICH computer crime insurance; **Computerlauf** *m* COMP computer run; **Computerleasingfirma** *f* COMP computer-leasing firm; **Computerleasinggeschäft** *nt* COMP computer-leasing business; **Computermesse** *f* COMP computing show; **Computermißbrauch-Versicherung** *f* VERSICH computer crime insurance; **Computernetzwerk** *nt* COMP computer network; **Computerpaket** *nt* COMP *Verkauf* computer package; **Computerpapier** *nt* COMP computer paper; **Computerprogramm** *nt* COMP computer program; **Computerprotokoll** *nt* COMP computer log; **Computerraum** *m* COMP computer room; **Computerservice** *m* COMP computer services, computer services bureau; **Computersimulation** *f* COMP computer simulation; **Computersoftware** *f* COMP computer software; **Computerspeicher** *m* COMP computer memory; **Computersteuererklärung** *f* STEUER computer return; **Computersteuerung** *f* COMP computer control; **Computersystem** *nt* COMP computer system; **Computertechnik** *f* COMP computer engineering, computer technology; **Computertechniker, in** *m,f* COMP computer engineer; **Computerumgebung** *f* COMP computer environment

computerunterstützt *adj* COMP computer-aided, computer-assisted, computer-based, PC-based; **~es Ausbildungsprogramm** *nt* COMP computer-aided learning program, computer-assisted learning program; **~e Entwicklung** *f* (*CAD*) COMP, IND computer-aided design, computer-assisted design (*CAD*); **~e Entwicklung und Fertigung** *f* (*CAD/CAM*) COMP, IND computer-aided design and manufacturing (*CAD/CAM*), computer-assisted design and manufacturing (*CAD/CAM*); **~er Entwurf** *m* (*CAD*) COMP, IND computer-aided design, computer-assisted design (*CAD*); **~e Fertigung** *f* (*CAM*) IND, COMP computer-aided manufacturing (*CAM*), computer-assisted manufacturing (*CAM*); **~es Ingenieurwesen** *nt* (*CAE*) COMP, IND computer-aided engineering (*CAE*), computer-assisted engineering (*CAE*); **~es Konstruieren** *nt* (*CAD*) COMP, IND computer-aided design, computer-assisted design (*CAD*); **~es Konstruieren** *nt* **und technisches Zeichnen** (*CADD*) COMP, IND computer-aided design and drafting, computer-assisted design and drafting (*CADD*); **~e Konstruktion** *f* (*CAD*) COMP, IND computer-aided design, computer-assisted design (*CAD*); **~es Lernen** *nt* (*CAL*) COMP computer-aided learning (*CAL*), computer-assisted learning (*CAL*); **~es Lernen** *nt* **von Sprachen** (*CALL*) COMP computer-aided language learning (*CALL*), computer-assisted language learning (*CALL*); **~es Prüfen** *nt* COMP computer-aided testing (*CAT*), computer-assisted testing (*CAT*); **~e Qualitätssicherung** *f* COMP, IND computer-aided quality assurance (*CAQ*); **~e Software-Erstellung** *f* (*CASE*) COMP computer-aided software engineering (*CASE*), computer-assisted software engineering (*CASE*); **~es Testen** *nt* COMP computer-aided testing (*CAT*), computer-assisted testing (*CAT*); **~e Übersetzung** *f* COMP computer-aided translation (*CAT*), computer-assisted translation (*CAT*); **~er Unterricht** *m* (*CAI*) COMP computer-aided instruction (*CAI*), computer-assisted instruction (*CAI*), computer-aided teaching (*CAT*), computer-assisted teaching (*CAT*)

Computer: **Computerverbindung** *f* COMP computer line; **Computervirus** *nt* COMP computer virus; **Computerwissenschaft** *f* COMP computing; **Computerwissenschaftler, in** *m,f* COMP computer scientist; **Computerwunderkind** *nt* infrml COMP computer whiz-kid (*infrml*); **Computerzeitalter** *nt* COMP computer age

Container *m* TRANSP container; ~ **für flüssiges Massengut** TRANSP bulk liquid container; ~ **für kombinierten Transport** TRANSP intermodal container; ~ **auf Plattformwagen** TRANSP container on flat car

(*AmE*), container on flat wagon (*BrE*); ♦ **in ~ laden** TRANSP containerize; **auf ~ umgestellt** TRANSP containerized; **in ~ verladen** TRANSP containerized; **in ~ verpacken** TRANSP containerize

Container: **Containeranwenderanalyse** *f* TRANSP container user analysis; **Containerbefestigungs-vorrichtung** *f* TRANSP tie-down; **Containerblock** *m* TRANSP container block; **Containerboden** *m* TRANSP container base (*CB*); **Containerdepot** *nt* TRANSP container depot, container yard (*CY*); **Containerdienst** *m* TRANSP container service; **Containerdienst-Tarif** *m* TRANSP container service tariff (*CST*); **Containerentladung** *f* TRANSP container unstuffing

containerfähig: **nicht ~e Güter** *nt pl* TRANSP uncontainerable goods

Container: **Containerfrachtbrief** *m* TRANSP container bill of lading; **Containerfrachtstation** *f* TRANSP container freight station (*CFS*); **Containerfüllung** *f* TRANSP container stuffing; **Containergebühren** *f pl* TRANSP container dues; **Containerhafen** *m* TRANSP container port; **Containerimportfracht-Manifest** *nt* TRANSP container import cargo manifest

containerisieren *vt* TRANSP containerize

Container: **Containerkai** *m* TRANSP container dock; **Containerkonnossement** *nt* IMP/EXP, TRANSP container bill; **Containerkontrolle** *f* TRANSP container control (*CC*); **Containerkopf** *m* TRANSP container head; **Containerkran** *m* TRANSP container crane; **Containerladung** *f* TRANSP container load; **Containerleasing** *nt* TRANSP container leasing; **Containermarkt** *m* TRANSP container market; **Containernutzung** *f* TRANSP container utilization; **Containerpackstation** *f* TRANSP container freight station (*CFS*); **Containerpark** *m* TRANSP container park; **Containerplatz** *m* TRANSP container berth; **Containerplatzzuteilung** *f* TRANSP container space allocation; **Containerpool** *m* TRANSP container pool; **Containerrahmen** *m* TRANSP container frame; **Containerreihe** *f* TRANSP container line; **Containerschiff** *nt* TRANSP container ship; **Containerspediteur** *m* TRANSP container operator; **Containerspedition** *f* TRANSP containerized shipping, container operation; **Containerstapel** *m* TRANSP container stack, unit load (*U*); **Containerstaugerüst** *nt* TRANSP *Laderaum* cell guide; **Containerstückgut** *nt* TRANSP container partload; **Containerterminal** *nt* TRANSP container terminal; **Containertransport** *m* TRANSP container transport; **Containerunternehmer** *m* TRANSP container operator; **Containerverkehr** *m* TRANSP container traffic, trunking; **Containerverladung** *f* TRANSP containerized shipping; **Containerverpackungs-Zertifikat** *nt* TRANSP container packing certificate; **Containerversand** *m* TRANSP containerized shipping; **Containerverschiffung** *f* TRANSP

containerized shipping; **Containerverwendung** *f* TRANSP container use; **Containerwagen** *m* TRANSP container car (*AmE*), container wagon (*BrE*); **Containerwaggon** *m* TRANSP container car (*AmE*), container wagon (*BrE*); **Containerzelle** *f* TRANSP *Laderaum* cell

Contango *m* BÖRSE contango

Contracts: **~ Manager** *m* PERSON *Arbeit* contracts manager

Contremineur *m* BÖRSE bear

Controller *m* FINANZ, RECHNUNG comptroller, controller, financial controller

Coprozessor *m* COMP coprocessor

Copyright *nt* COMP, RECHT copyright

Copytesten *nt* V&M copytesting

Corporate Identity *f* (*CI*) V&M corporate identity

Coup: **einen ~ landen** *phr infrml* GESCHÄFT make a scoop (*infrml*)

Cournot: **~sches Dyopol** *nt* VW Cournot's duopoly model

Courtage *f* BANK commission rate, BÖRSE broker's commission, brokerage; **Courtagekonto** *nt* BÖRSE brokerage account; **Courtagerechnung** *f* BÖRSE brokerage statement, broker's statement

Cowboy-Wirtschaft *f* VW cowboy economy (*infrml*) (*AmE*)

Cowles-Kommission *f* GESCHÄFT Cowles Commission (*AmE*)

CO₂-Steuer *f* (*Kohlendioxydsteuer*) STEUER CO_2 tax (*carbon dioxide tax*)

CPM: **CPM-Methode** *f* MATH *Netzplantechnik* critical path method (*CPM*); **CPM-Theorie** *f* VW critical path theory

Cross: **~ Hedge** *m* BÖRSE cross hedge; **~ Rate** *f* VW cross rate

Crowding-Out *nt* VW crowding out

CRT *abbr* (*Kathodenstrahlröhre*) COMP CRT (*cathode ray tube*)

CTRL-Taste *f* (*Steuerungstaste*) COMP CTRL key (*control key*)

C&F *abbr* (*Kosten und Fracht*) IMP/EXP, TRANSP *Lieferklausel* C&F (*cost and freight*), CAF (*cost and freight*)

C&I *abbr* (*Kosten und Versicherung*) IMP/EXP, TRANSP C&I (*cost and insurance*)

Currency-Theorie *f* VW Currency School (*BrE*)

Curriculum *nt* SOZIAL curriculum

Cursor *m* COMP *Bildschirm* cursor; **Cursortastenblock** *m* COMP *Cursorbewegung* cursor control pad

Cutoff-Verfahren *nt* RECHNUNG cutoff method

Cymogen *nt* IND *Gefahrgut* cymogene

D

d/a *abbr* GESCHÄFT (*Dokumente gegen Akzept*) DA (*documents against acceptance*)

DA *abbr* GESCHÄFT (*Dokumente gegen Akzept*) DA (*documents against acceptance*)

D/A *abbr* COMP (*digital-analog*) D/A (*digital-to-analog*), GESCHÄFT (*Dokumente gegen Akzept*) DA (*documents against acceptance*)

Dach- *in cpds* GESCHÄFT, GRUND, TRANSP umbrella, parent, roof; **Dachgesellschaft** *f* GESCHÄFT parent company, proprietary company, RECHNUNG holding company, parent company; **Dachkomitee** *nt* GESCHÄFT umbrella committee; **Dachkonzern** *f* FINANZ umbrella group; **Dachlast** *f* TRANSP roof load; **Dachmarke** *f* PATENT umbrella brand name, V&M family brands; **Dachpolice** *f* VERSICH umbrella policy; **Dachrahmen** *m* TRANSP roof rail; **Dachsteuer** *f* STEUER roof tax

damit: ~ **verbundene Gewerbe** *nt pl* IND allied industries

Damnum *nt* BANK debt discount, loan discount

Dampf *m* IND, TRANSP steam

dämpfen *vt* GESCHÄFT slow down, curb, soft-pedal (*infrml*), *Begeisterung* dampen, VW *Wachstum* dampen, slow down

Dämpfer: **einen ~ aufsetzen** *phr* GESCHÄFT put a damper on (*infrml*), soft-pedal (*infrml*)

Dampf: **Dampfwalze** *f obs* IND steamroller

daneben *adv* TRANSP alongside

Dank: **jdm zu ~ verpflichtet sein** [+dat] *phr* GESCHÄFT be indebted to sb; **vielen ~ für Ihr Schreiben** *phr* KOMM thank you for your letter; **vielen ~ im voraus** *phr* KOMM thanking you in advance, thanking you in anticipation

dankbar *adj* GESCHÄFT grateful, obliged

Dankschreiben *nt* GESCHÄFT thank-you letter, bread-and-butter letter (*infrml*)

darbieten *vt* GESCHÄFT perform

Darbietung *f* V&M exposure

darlegen *vt* GESCHÄFT spell out, set forth, *Bedingungen* set out

Darlegung *f* TRANSP *Zoll* presentation of goods ready for inspection, presentation of goods to be cleared

Darlehen *nt* BANK advance, loan, GESCHÄFT, RECHNUNG *Verbindlichkeit* advance; ~ **für eine erste Hypothek** BANK first mortgage loan; ~ **mit festem Rückzahlungstermin** FINANZ loan with fixed date for repayment; ~, **Investitionen** *f pl* **und Vorschußzahlungen** *f pl* RECHNUNG loans, investments and advances; ~ **mit konstanten Raten** BANK constant payment loan (*BrE*); ~ **mit konstanten Ratenzahlungen** BANK constant payment loan (*BrE*); ~ **mit Regreß** FINANZ recourse loan; ~ **für technische Hilfe** FINANZ technical assistance loan (*TAL*); ~ **der Tochtergesellschaft an die Muttergesellschaft** FINANZ upstream loan; ~ **in verschiedenen Währungen** BANK multicurrency loan; ◆ ~ **auf Abruf aufnehmen** BANK borrow at call; **ein ~ aufnehmen** BANK raise a loan, obtain a loan, FINANZ contract a loan; **ein ~ aushandeln** BANK arrange a loan, negotiate a loan; **ein ~ beantragen** BANK, FINANZ apply for a loan; **ein ~ bedienen** FINANZ service a loan; **ein**

~ **geben** *vt* BANK grant a loan; **ein ~ gewähren** BANK extend a loan, make a loan; **ein ~ herauslegen an** [+acc] BANK extend a loan

Darlehen: **Darlehensantrag** *m* BANK loan application; **Darlehensaufnahme** *f* BANK borrowing; **Darlehensbank** *f* BANK lending banker; **Darlehensbefugnis** *f* BANK loan authorization; **Darlehensbestand** *m* BANK loan portfolio; **Darlehensempfänger, in** *m,f* BANK borrower, loan recipient; **Darlehensgeber, in** *m,f* BANK lender; **Darlehensgesellschaft** *f* FINANZ loan company; **Darlehensgewährung** *f* BANK loan grant; **Darlehensgewährung** *f* **über Pari** FINANZ lending at a premium; **Darlehenskasse** *f* FINANZ loan bank; **Darlehenskonto** *nt* BANK loan account; **Darlehenskosten** *pl* BANK cost of a loan, loan charges; **Darlehensnehmer, in** *m,f* BANK advance holder, borrower; **Darlehensrückzahlung** *f* GESCHÄFT amortization of a loan; **Darlehensrückzahlungsplan** *m* BANK loan repayment schedule; **Darlehenstilgung** *f* BANK, FINANZ loan repayment; **Darlehensverbindlichkeiten** *f pl* BANK loan liabilities; **Darlehensvergabe** *f* BANK lending; **Darlehensverlängerung** *f* **für steuerfreies Rentensparkonto** STEUER individual retirement account rollover (*IRA rollover*); **Darlehensvertrag** *m* BANK loan agreement; **Darlehenszinssatz** *m* BANK borrowing rate; **Darlehenszusage** *f* BANK loan commitment

darnieder: ~ **liegen** *phr* VW be down

darstellen *vt* GESCHÄFT represent, *beschreiben* describe, *ein Bild entwerfen* portray, PATENT *Beeinträchtigung* constitute

Darstellung *f* GESCHÄFT description, representation, *Bericht* account, MGMNT *der Unternehmenspläne* presentation; **Darstellungsart** *f* COMP, GESCHÄFT appearance

darüber: ~ **hinaus** *adv* GESCHÄFT, KOMM above

dasselbe: ~ **tun** *phr* GESCHÄFT follow suit

Datei *f* COMP computer file, *Modem* file; ◆ ~ **nicht gefunden** COMP file not found

Datei: **Dateiabschnitt** *m* COMP file section; **Dateianfang** *m* COMP beginning of file (*BOF*); **Dateiende** *nt* COMP end of file (*EOF*); **Dateiendemarke** *f* COMP end-of-file mark; **Dateikennsatz** *m* COMP file identifier; **Dateikomprimierung** *f* COMP *Speicherplatz* file compression; **Dateikonvertierung** *f* COMP file conversion; **Dateimenü** *nt* COMP file menu; **Dateischutz** *m* COMP *Magnetbänder* file protection; **Dateiserver** *m* COMP file server; **Dateiverwaltung** *f* COMP file management; **Dateiverzeichnis** *nt* COMP file directory; **Dateizuordnungstabelle** *f* (*FAT*) COMP file allocation table (*FAT*)

Daten *pl* COMP data, GESCHÄFT facts and figures, RECHNUNG aggregate data, VERWALT, VW data; ◆ ~ **in ein Register eintragen** GESCHÄFT enter information onto a register

Daten: **Datenart** *f* COMP data type; **Datenaufbereitung** *f*

COMP *Datenerfassung*, VERWALT data preparation; **Datenausgabe** *f* COMP data output; **Datenaustauschbarkeit** *f* COMP portability; **Datenautobahn** *f jarg* COMP information highway

Datenbank *f* COMP data bank, database; **Datenbank-Abfragesprache** *f* COMP query language (*QL*); **Datenbankverwaltung** *f* COMP database management; **Datenbankverwaltungssystem** *nt* (*DMS*) COMP database management system (*DBMS*)

Daten: **Datenbit** *nt* COMP data bit, information bit; **Datenbus** *m* COMP data bus; **Datenbusleitung** *f* COMP data bus; **Datenbusschiene** *f* COMP data bus; **Datendatei** *f* COMP data file; **Dateneingabe** *f* COMP data entry, data input; **Dateneingabestation** *f* COMP data entry terminal; **Datenendeinrichtung** *f* COMP *Datenübertragung* data terminal equipment (*DTE*); **Datenerfasser** *m* COMP data entry operator

Datenerfassung *f* COMP data acquisition, data capture, *Sammeln* data collection, data gathering, VW data acquisition; **~ für ein einzelnes Land** VERWALT single-country data capture; **Datenerfassungskasse** *f* V&M POS machine; **Datenerfassungswerbung** *f* V&M POS advertising, point-of-sale advertising

Daten: **Datenerhebung** *f* VW data acquisition, data collection; **Datenfeld** *nt* COMP data field, IND field; **Datenfernverarbeitung** *f* VERWALT remote data processing, teleprocessing; **Datenfluß** *m* COMP data flow, GESCHÄFT data stream; **Datenflußplan** *m* MATH data flow chart, flow chart; **Datenfrachtempfang** *m* TRANSP data freight receipt (*DFR*); **Datenfunk** *m* KOMM data broadcasting; **Datenintegrität** *f* COMP data integrity; **Datenkarte** *f* COMP data card; **Datenkommunikation** *f* KOMM data communications; **Datenkomprimierung** *f* COMP data compression; **Datenkonvertierung** *f* COMP data conversion; **Datenmüll** *m* COMP garbage (*AmE*); **Datennetz** *nt* COMP data network, information network; **Datenpaket** *nt* COMP data packet

Datenpost *f* KOMM data post (*BrE*); **~ auf Abruf** KOMM data post on demand (*BrE*); **~ auf Verlangen** KOMM data post on demand (*BrE*)

Daten: **Datenreihe** *f* GESCHÄFT array; **Datenrundfunk** *m* KOMM data broadcasting

Datensatz *m* COMP data record, data set; **Datensatzformat** *nt* COMP record format; **Datensatzschlüssel** *m* COMP record key; **Datensatzsperre** *f* COMP record locking

Daten: **Datenschild** *nt* TRANSP data plate; **Datenschutz** *m* COMP data protection; **Datenschutzgesetz** *nt* RECHT in 1984 Data Protection Act (*BrE*); **Datensicherheit** *f* COMP computer security, data privacy (*BrE*), data security (*AmE*); **Datensichtgerät** *nt* (*DSG*) COMP visual display terminal (*VDT*), visual display unit (*VDU*); **Datensichtgerät** *nt* **mit Ganzseitenbildschirm** COMP *Hardware* full-screen terminal; **Datenspeicher** *m* COMP data storage; **Datenstation** *f* COMP, PERSON work station; **Datenstationsrechner** *m* COMP terminal computer; **Datenstruktur** *f* COMP data structure; **Datenträger** *m* COMP *Speicher* data carrier; **Datentransfer** *m* COMP data transfer; **Datentypist, in** *m,f* COMP, VERWALT keyboarder; **Datenübermittlung** *f* KOMM data communications

Datenübertragung *f* COMP data communication, data transfer; **Datenübertragungseinrichtung** *f* COMP data communications equipment (*DCE*), data transmission facility; **Datenübertragungsnetz** *nt* COMP communica-

tions network; **Datenübertragungsrate** *f* COMP data transfer rate, *Datenverarbeitung* data rate

Daten: **Datenverarbeitung** *f* (*DV*) COMP, VERWALT data processing (*DP*); **Datenverarbeitungsversicherung** *f* VERSICH data processing insurance; **Datenverbiegung** *f* vw data mining; **Datenverbindungsabschnitt** *m* COMP data link; **Datenverwaltung** *f* COMP data management; **Datenwiedergewinnung** *f* COMP data retrieval; **Datenwort** *nt* COMP data word; **Datenzentrum** *nt* eines Unternehmens COMP corporate data center (*AmE*), corporate data centre (*BrE*)

datiert *adj* GESCHÄFT dated; ◆ **~ sein** GESCHÄFT be dated, bear a date

dato: **~ nach heute** *phr* GESCHÄFT after date (*a/d*)

Datum *nt* GESCHÄFT date; **~ der Abschrift** GESCHÄFT copy date; **~ des Angebots** GESCHÄFT date of quotation; **~ des Erlöschens** PERSON *eines Vertrags* expiry date; **~ für die Festsetzung des Anleihezinssatzes** BÖRSE loan-pricing date; **~ des Inkrafttretens** RECHT effective date; **~ des Poststempels** KOMM date as postmarked; ◆ **ab ~** GESCHÄFT after date (*a/d*); **nach ~** COMP *Sortieren* by date; **ein ~ festsetzen** GESCHÄFT set a date; **das ~ auf ein Formular stempeln** VERWALT stamp the date on a form; **das ~ tragen** GESCHÄFT bear the date; **beide Daten eingeschlossen** GESCHÄFT both dates inclusive (*bdi*)

Datum: **Datumsangabe** *f* V&M *auf vorgepackten Waren* date marking; **Datumsstempel** *m* KOMM postmark

Dauer *f* GESCHÄFT duration, POL term, VW period; **~ der provisorischen Deckung** VERSICH time on risk; **~ der Versicherungsleistungen** VERSICH duration of benefits; **~ eines Werbefeldzugs** V&M drive time; ◆ **für die ~ von** GESCHÄFT for the duration of

Dauer: **Dauerauftrag** *m* BANK money transfer order, banker's order, standing order (*S.O.*), FINANZ banker's order; **Dauerbeschäftigung** *f* PERSON permanent employment; **Dauerbeteiligung** *f* RECHNUNG permanent participation; **Dauereinlage** *f* IMP/EXP standing deposit; **Daueremission** *f* BANK tap, tap issue, BÖRSE tap issue, constant issue, tap; **Dauerfinanzierung** *f* FINANZ continuous funding, permanent financing; **Dauergebrauchstest** *m* V&M extended use test; **Dauergenehmigung** *f* IMP/EXP standing authorization

dauerhaft *adj* GESCHÄFT durable, long-lasting, stable, permanent; **~e Haushaltskonsumgüter** *nt pl* V&M household durables; **~e Konsumgüter** *nt pl* vw consumer durables; **~e Wiederkehr** *f* vw *des Wachstums* sustained resurgence

Dauer: **Dauerinflation** *f* VW persistent inflation; **Dauerkarte** *f* GESCHÄFT season ticket; **Dauerkarteninhaber, in** *m,f* GESCHÄFT season ticket holder; **Dauerkonto** *nt* RECHNUNG permanent account; **Dauermarktanalyse** *f* V&M continuous survey; **Dauerposten** *m* PERSON permanent job, permanent position; **Dauerprüfung** *f* RECHNUNG continuing audit, TRANSP continuous survey (*CS*); **Dauerreisekostenvorschuß** *m* GESCHÄFT standing travel advance

Daumenindex *m* GESCHÄFT *Buch* thumb index

Daumenschätzung *f* infrml GESCHÄFT guesstimate (*infrml*)

D/A: **D/A-Wandler** *m* (*Digital-Analog-Wandler*) COMP DAC (*digital-to-analog converter*)

DAX *abbr* (*Deutscher Aktienindex*) BÖRSE German stock index

dazugehörig: **~e Gebäudeteile** *m pl* VERSICH appurtenant structures

dB *abbr* (*Dezibel*) GESCHÄFT dB (*decibel*)

DB *abbr* TRANSP (*Deutsche Bahn AG*) privatized German railway company, formerly Deutsche Bundesbahn, *obs* (*Deutsche Bundesbahn*) *vor Privatisierung* German national railway company, ≈ BR (*obs*) (*British Rail*)

DD *abbr* (*doppelte Dichte*) COMP DD (*double density*)

Deadweight *nt* TRANSP deadweight (*dw*)

Dealer, in *m,f* GESCHÄFT *Drogen* trafficker

Debet *nt obs* FINANZ debit; **Debetsaldo** *obs m* FINANZ debit balance; **Debetspalte** *f* FINANZ debit column

Debitoren *m pl* RECHNUNG accounts receivable (*A/R*); **Debitorenaufstellung** *f* RECHNUNG accounts receivable statement; **Debitorenausfall** *m* BANK loan write-off; **Debitorenbuch** *nt* RECHNUNG accounts receivable ledger, sales ledger (*BrE*); **Debitorenbuchhaltung** *f* RECHNUNG accounts receivable accounting; **Debitorenkonto** *nt* RECHNUNG accounts receivable account; **Debitorenkontoauszug** *m* RECHNUNG accounts receivable statement; **Debitorenumschlag** *m* FINANZ accounts receivable collection period, receivables turnover, RECHNUNG accounts receivable turnover; **Debitorenziehung** *f* FINANZ bill drawn by a bank on a debtor

Debt-Equity-Swap *m* FINANZ debt equity swap

Debugger *m jarg* COMP debugger

Deck *nt* TRANSP deck; **auf ~ befindlich** *phr* TRANSP above deck (*AD*); **Deckadresse** *f* KOMM accommodation address (*BrE*)

decken 1. *vt* BANK, BÖRSE, FINANZ cover, VW *Fehlbetrag* make up, *Kosten* cover; **2. sich ~ mit** *v refl* GESCHÄFT coincide with

deckend *adj* BÖRSE compensating

Deckung *f* BÖRSE covering purchase, short covering, cover, FINANZ cover, GESCHÄFT coverage, VERSICH cover, insurance cover (*BrE*), insurance coverage (*AmE*), VERWALT cover, VW *Währung* backing; **~ bei Auslandsinvestitionen** VERSICH overseas investment cover; **~ gegen Insolvenz der Projektteilnehmer** VERSICH project participants insolvency cover; **~ gegen Strandung** VERSICH cover against stranding; ♦ **keine ~** BANK no-account (*n/a*), GESCHÄFT no funds (*N/F, NF*), no effects (*NE*); **ohne ~** GESCHÄFT no funds (*N/F, NF*)

Deckung: **Deckungsbeitrag** *m* RECHNUNG contribution margin, variable gross margin; **Deckungsbeitragsanalyse** *f* FINANZ contribution analysis; **Deckungsbeitragsrechnung** *f* FINANZ breakeven analysis, direct costing, RECHNUNG contribution costing, direct costing, marginal costing, VW breakeven analysis, direct costing; **Deckungsbereich** *m* VERSICH scope of coverage; **Deckungsbestätigung** *f* VERSICH cover note (*BrE*) (*C/N, CN*); **Deckungserfordernisse** *nt pl* BANK margin requirements; **Deckungsfazilität** *f* FINANZ backup line; **Deckungsgewicht** *nt* TRANSP breakeven weight

deckungsgleich: **~ mit** *phr* GESCHÄFT congruent with

Deckung: **Deckungsgleichheit** *f* GESCHÄFT congruence; **Deckungsgrad** *m* FINANZ cash ratio, cover ratio; **Deckungsgrundlage** *f* VERSICH cover note (*BrE*) (*C/N, CN*); **Deckungskapital** *nt* BANK guaranty fund, VERSICH cover of assurance (*BrE*), premium reserve,

reimbursement fund, unearned premium reserve; **Deckungskauf** *m* GESCHÄFT covering purchase, RECHT *Vertragsrecht* buying in, covering purchase; **Deckungskauf** *m* **zum Ausgleich eines Leerverkaufs** BÖRSE short covering; **Deckungskauf** *m* **des Baissiers** BÖRSE bear covering; **Deckungskäufe vornehmen** *phr* BÖRSE, GESCHÄFT buy in; **Deckungslinie** *f* BANK, FINANZ backup line, GESCHÄFT backup facilities; **Deckungslücke** *f* GESCHÄFT budgetary deficit, shortfall; **Deckungspunkt** *m* FINANZ breakeven point; **Deckungspunktanalyse** *f* FINANZ, VW breakeven analysis; **Deckungsquote** *f* FINANZ cover ratio; **Deckungsrückstellung** *f* FINANZ premium reserve, VERSICH cover of assurance (*BrE*), pro rata unearned premium reserve; **Deckungssatz** *m* BANK reserve ratio, VERSICH cover ratio; **Deckungssumme** *f* BÖRSE margin maintenance; **Deckungssummen innehaben** *phr* FINANZ hold margins; **Deckungsumfang** *m* VERSICH insurance cover (*BrE*), insurance coverage (*AmE*), scope of coverage; **Deckungszusage** *f* VERSICH cover note (*BrE*) (*C/N, CN*); **Deckungszusage** *f* **des Erstversicherers** VERSICH lead slip; **Deckungszusage** *f* **mit vielen Ausschlußklauseln** BÖRSE honeycomb slip

Decoder *m jarg* COMP decoder

Decodierung *f* KOMM decryption

Decodierwerk *nt* COMP decoder

de facto *adj* RECHT *faktisch, tatsächlich, den Tatsachen entsprechend* de facto

De-facto-Bevölkerung *f* VW de facto population

De-facto-Manager *m* MGMNT de facto manager

defensiv: **~e Strategie** *f* GESCHÄFT defensive strategy; **~e Werbung** *f* V&M advocacy advertising

Definition *f* GESCHÄFT, VERSICH definition; **~ der Deckungssumme** VERSICH definition of limits; **~ der Einzelposten** VERSICH definition of items; **~ der Haftungssumme** VERSICH definition of limits; **~ der Posten** VERSICH definition of items; **Definitionsbereich** *m* MATH domain

Defizit *nt* FINANZ deficit, GESCHÄFT shortage, *Mangel* deficiency, VW deficit; **~ der öffentlichen Haushalte** VW public sector deficit; **~ der Zahlungsbilanz** VW balance of payments deficit (*BOP deficit*); ♦ **ein ~ auflaufen lassen** FINANZ run up a deficit

defizitär: **~e Bewegung** *f* BÖRSE adverse movement

Defizit: **Defizitfinanzierung** *f* VW deficit spending; **Defizitpolitik** *f* FINANZ deficit spending policy

Deflation *f* VW deflation

deflationär *adj* VW deflationary

Deflation: **Deflationsdruck** *m* VW contractionary pressure

Deflator *m* MATH, VW deflator

deflatorisch: **~er Druck** *m* VW deflationary pressures; **~e Lücke** *f* VW contractionary national income gap, deflationary gap

Defragmentierung *f* COMP defragmentation

Degenerationsphase *f* GESCHÄFT *Produktlebenszyklus* shoulder period, V&M decline stage

Degression *f* MATH degression; **Degressionsgewinn** *m* VW economy of scale

degressiv: **~e Abschreibung** *f* FINANZ declining-balance depreciation, reducing balance, double-declining balance, RECHNUNG declining-balance method, diminishing-balance method, reducing balance, reducing-balance method, VW reducing-installment system (*AmE*), reducing-instalment system (*BrE*); **~e Steuer** *f* STEUER degressive tax

Deindustrialisierung *f* IND, VW deindustrialization

deintensiviert: **~e Landwirtschaft** *f* UMWELT deintensified farming

de jure *phr* RECHT *rechtlich, von Rechts wegen, legitim* de jure

De-jure-Bevölkerung *f* VW de jure population

Dekade *f* GESCHÄFT decade

Dekartellierung *f* GESCHÄFT decartelization

Dekartellisierung *f* BANK deconcentration, GESCHÄFT decartelization

Deklaration *f* IMP/EXP declaration, entry; **~ zur Einlagerung unter Zollverschluß** IMP/EXP warehouse entry; **Deklarationsschein** *m* BANK, IMP/EXP bill of entry (*B/E*)

deklarieren *vt* COMP *Programmiersprachen*, IMP/EXP, STEUER declare

deklarierend: **zu ~er Artikel** *m* TRANSP restricted article

dekontaminieren *vt* UMWELT clean

Delegation *f* GESCHÄFT delegation (*del.*); **~ von Kompetenzen** GESCHÄFT delegation of authority

delegieren *vt* MGMNT *Befugnis* delegate

Delegierte(r) *mf* [decl. as adj] MGMNT conference delegate, convention participant

Delikt *nt* RECHT unlawful act, *unerlaubte Handlung* delict, tort; **Deliktshaftung** *f* GESCHÄFT liability in tort, respondeat superior

Delkredere *nt* GESCHÄFT del credere; **Delkredere-Agent** *m* GESCHÄFT del credere agent; **Delkredere-Fonds** *m* FINANZ contingency fund; **Delkredererückstellung** *f* RECHNUNG provision for contingent losses; **Delkredereschutz** *m* FINANZ credit protection; **Delkredere-Vereinbarung** *f* RECHT *Vertragsrecht* del credere guarantee

Delors-Plan *m* VW Delors Plan

Delphi-Methode *f* MGMNT Delphi technique

Delta *nt* BÖRSE, FINANZ delta; **Delta-Aktie** *f* BÖRSE delta stock; **Delta-Faktor** *m* BÖRSE delta factor

deltaneutral *adj* BÖRSE delta-neutral; **~e Geldverknappung** *f* BÖRSE delta-neutral strangle; **~e Optionsposition** *f* BÖRSE delta-neutral straddle; **~er Straddle** *m* BÖRSE delta-neutral straddle

DEL-Taste *f* COMP delete key (*DEL*)

demeritorisch: **~es Gut** *nt* VW demerit good

demgemäß *adv* GESCHÄFT accordingly

Demigrossist, in *m,f* V&M semi-wholesaler

De-minimis-Regelung *f* RECHT de minimis rule

Demographie *f* VW demography

demographisch: **~er Übergang** *m* VW demographic transition; **~er Wandel** *m* VW demographic transition

Demokratie *f* GESCHÄFT, POL democracy

demokratisch *adj* GESCHÄFT, POL democratic; **~er Führungsstil** *m* PERSON democratic style of leadership; **~er Industriestaat** *m* POL industrial democracy; **~es Management** *nt* PERSON *Geschäftsleitung* democratic management; **~er Zentralismus** *m* POL democratic centralism

Demometrie *f* VW demometrics

Demonetisierung *f* VW demonetization

demonstrieren *vt* GESCHÄFT demonstrate

Demontagekosten *pl* GESCHÄFT cost of demolition, cost of dismantling

demontierbar: **~es System** *nt* TRANSP demountable system; **~e Vorderseite** *f* TRANSP detachable front end

demontiert *adj* GESCHÄFT, TRANSP dismantled

demoralisieren *vt* PERSON demoralize

Demotivation *f* PERSON demotivation

demotivieren *vt* PERSON demotivate

Denison: **~scher Rest** *m* VW Denison residual

Denkansatz *m* GESCHÄFT, MGMNT, VERWALT, VW approach

Denken *nt* GESCHÄFT thinking

Denkfabrik *f* *infrml* GESCHÄFT think-tank (*infrml*)

Denkmodell *nt* VERWALT conceptual model

Denkpause *f* GESCHÄFT cooling-off period

Denkungsart: **jdn zur eigenen ~ bekehren** *phr* GESCHÄFT win sb over to one's way of thinking

Dennison: **~sches Gesetz** *nt* VW Dennison's law

Denomination *f* FINANZ form of capital reduction of a German stock corporation

denominieren *vt* VW denominate

de novo *adv* RECHT *von neuem* de novo

Denunziant, in *m,f* GESCHÄFT informer, whistle-blower (*infrml*)

Dep. *abbr* (*Depot*) GESCHÄFT, IMP/EXP, TRANSP, V&M dpt (*depot*), storehouse, whse (*warehouse*)

Dependencia-Theorie *f* VW dependency theory

Deponie *f* UMWELT dumping ground; **Deponiebetrieb** *m* UMWELT site operation; **Deponiegelände** *nt* UMWELT landfill site

Deport *m* BÖRSE backwardation; **Deportgeschäft** *nt* BÖRSE backwardation business; **Deportsatz** *m* FINANZ backwardation rate

Depositbank *f* BANK deposit bank

Depositen *pl* BANK deposits; **Depositenbuch** *nt* BANK deposit passbook; **Depositengelder** *nt pl* BANK deposits; **Depositengeschäft** *nt* BANK deposit banking; **Depositeninhaberversicherung** *f* **gegen Fälschung** VERSICH depositors forgery insurance; **Depositenkonto** *nt* BANK deposit account (*BrE*) (*D/A*); **Depositen- und Treuhandkonten** *nt pl* BANK deposit and trust accounts; **Depositenzertifikat** *nt* (*CD*) GESCHÄFT certificate of deposit

Depositum *nt* PATENT deposit

Depot *nt* (*Dep.*) BANK securities account, GESCHÄFT, IMP/EXP, TRANSP, VW depot (*dpt*), storehouse, warehouse (*whse*); **im ~ gehaltenes Gold für Rechnung** VW earmarked gold; **Depotbescheinigung** *f* FINANZ deposit certificate, GESCHÄFT trust receipt; **Depotgebühr** *f* BANK custodian fee, custody charge, IMP/EXP depot charge; **Depotkonto** *nt* BANK custodial account, custodianship account, custody account, *Wertpapiere* securities account; **Depotkontogebühr** *f* BANK custody account charge; **Depotschein** *m* BANK deposit receipt (*DR*), deposit slip; **Depot-Treuhandgesellschaft** *f* BÖRSE Depository Trust Company (*AmE*) (*DTC*); **Depotversicherung** *f* BANK bank deposit insurance (*AmE*), VERSICH deposit insurance; **Depotverwahrung** *f* BANK safe custody department; **Depotverwahrung** *f* **von Vermögenswerten** BANK safekeeping of assets; **Depotzahlung** *f* VERSICH lump sum (*ls*)

Depression *f* VW depression

Deputat *nt* PERSON payment in kind

deregulieren *vt* GESCHÄFT, VW deregulate

Deregulierung *f* GESCHÄFT, VW deregulation

Derivat *nt* FINANZ derivative instrument, V&M derivative product

derivativ *adj* BÖRSE derivative; **~es Instrument** *nt* FINANZ derivative instrument; **~e Nachfrage** *f* VW derived demand

derzeitig: bei ~er Lage der Dinge *phr* GESCHÄFT in the present state of affairs; **~er Satz** *m* GESCHÄFT current rate

Design *nt* PATENT design; **~ und Layout** V&M design and layout; **Designentwurf** *m* V&M scamp

Designerprodukt *nt* V&M designer product

designiert: ~es Amt *nt* PATENT designated office

Desinflation *f* VW disinflation

Desinformation *f* GESCHÄFT, POL disinformation

Desintegration *f* GESCHÄFT, VW disintegration

Desinvestition *f* FINANZ disinvestment

Desk *nt* BÖRSE desk

deskriptiv: ~e Statistik *f* MATH descriptive statistics

Desktop-Publishing *nt* (*DTP*) COMP *Publikationsherstellung*, MEDIEN desktop publishing (*DTP*)

Detail *nt* GESCHÄFT detail

detailliert: ~e Berichterstattung *f* RECHNUNG segmental reporting; **~es Formular** *nt* IMP/EXP long form, TRANSP short form, VERWALT long form; **~er Geschäftsplan** *m* GESCHÄFT in-depth business plan

Detail: Detailplanung *f* MGMNT detailed planning

DEUPRO *abbr* TRANSP German freight trade facilitation organization

deutlich *adj* GESCHÄFT clear-cut, *offensichtlich* appreciable, evident, explicit, specific; ♦ **~ in Erscheinung treten** GESCHÄFT evident; **eine ~e Sprache sprechen** GESCHÄFT be plain; **mit ~en Worten** GESCHÄFT in plain language

deutlich: ~e Krise *f* POL manifest crisis

Deutsch: ~er Aktienindex *m* (*DAX*) BÖRSE German stock index; **~e Bahn AG** *f* (*DB*) TRANSP privatized German railway company, formerly Deutsche Bundesbahn; **~e Börse** *f* BÖRSE German Stock Exchange, ≈ American Stock Exchange (*ASE*), ≈ London Stock Exchange (*obs*); **~e Bundesbahn** *f obs* (*DB*) TRANSP *vor Privatisierung* German national railway company, ≈ British Rail (*obs*) (*BR*); **~e Bundesbank** *f* (*BBk*) BANK, VW German central bank, ≈ Bank of England (*B E, B of E*), ≈ Federal Reserve Bank (*AmE*) (*FRB*); **~e Bundespost** *f obs* KOMM *vor Privatisierung* German national post office, ≈ Royal Mail (*BrE*); **~er Gewerkschaftsbund** *m* (*DGB*) PERSON Trades Union Congress (*BrE*) (*TUC*), ≈ Australian Council of Trade Unions (*ACTU*), ≈ American Federation of Labor-Congress of Industrial Organizations (*AFL-CIO*), ≈ Congress of Industrial Organizations (*CIO*), ≈ Trades Union Congress (*BrE*) (*TUC*); **~e Handelskammer** *f* GESCHÄFT German Chamber of Commerce (*GCC*); **~e Handelskammer** *f* **für das Vereinigte Königreich** GESCHÄFT German Chamber of Commerce for the UK (*GCCUK*); **~e Industrie- und Handelskammer** *f* GESCHÄFT German Chamber of Industry and Commerce (*GCIC*); **~er Industrie- und Handelstag** *m* (*DIHT*) IND ≈ Association of British Chambers of Commerce (*ABCC*), ≈ American Board

of Trade (*ABT*), ≈ British Chamber of Commerce (*BCC*); **~e Industrienorm** *f* (*DIN*) IND, RECHT German industrial standard, ≈ British Standard (*BS*); **~es Institut** *nt* **für Normung** (*DIN*) IND, RECHT German national standards institution, ≈ American National Standards Institute (*ANSI*), ≈ American Standards Authority, ≈ British Standards Institution (*BSI*); **~er Luftfahrverband** *m* (*DLV*) TRANSP German air transport association, ≈ Transport Association of America (*ATA*); **~er Normenausschuß** *m* (*DNA*) GESCHÄFT *German committee for standards*, ≈ American Society for Testing and Materials (*ASTM*); **~e Post AG** *f* KOMM privatized German post office, formerly Deutsche Bundespost; **~er Reisebüro-Verband** *m* (*DRV*) FREI German association of travel agents, ≈ Association of British Travel Agents (*ABTA*); **~es Rotes Kreuz** *nt* (*DRK*) SOZIAL German Red Cross; **~e Statistische Gesellschaft** *f* (*DStG*) MATH German statistical association, ≈ American Statistical Association (*ASA*); **~e Terminbörse** *f* BÖRSE German Futures Exchange; **~er Werbeausschuß** *m* V&M German advertising committee, ≈ Advertising Standards Authority (*ASA*); **~e Wirtschaftsforschungsinstitute** *nt pl* VW German economic institutes

deutsch: ~es Wirtschaftswunder *nt* VW German economic miracle

Dev. *abbr* (*Devisen*) VW exch. (*exchange*)

devaluieren *vt* VW *Währung* devalue

Deviationsbetrag *m* TRANSP deviation fraud

Devisen *f pl* BANK, BÖRSE, FINANZ, FREI, GESCHÄFT, RECHNUNG foreign exchange (*forex*), VW exchange (*exch.*), foreign exchange (*forex*); **auf ~ entfallenes Aufgeld** *nt* BANK currency at a discount; ♦ **mit ~ versorgt sein** VW be long in a currency

Devisen: Devisenabfluß *m* VW foreign currency outflow, outflow of foreign exchange; **Devisenabrechnung** *f* FINANZ foreign exchange note; **Devisenabsicherung** *f* RECHNUNG foreign exchange hedge; **Devisenabteilung** *f* BANK foreign exchange department, BÖRSE exchange department; **Devisenarbitrage** *f* BÖRSE currency arbitrage, exchange arbitrage, FINANZ arbitration of exchange; **Devisenaufgeld** *nt* FINANZ premium on exchange; **Devisenaufsichtsabteilung** *f* BÖRSE surveillance department of exchanges; **Devisenausländer, in** *m,f* GESCHÄFT nonresident; **Devisenbank** *f* BANK authorized bank; **Devisenberatung** *f* BANK foreign exchange advisory service; **Devisenbeschränkungen** *f pl* VW currency restrictions, foreign exchange restrictions; **Devisenbestände** *m pl* BANK foreign exchange holdings, VW currency holdings; **Devisenbewirtschaftung** *f* VW exchange control; **Devisenbilanz** *f* VW balance for official financing (*BOF*); **Devisenbörse** *f* VW currency market, foreign exchange market; **Devisenbringer, in** *m,f* GESCHÄFT foreign exchange earner; **Devisendiskont** *m* BÖRSE exchange discount

devisenfrei: ~er Außenhandel *m* GESCHÄFT switch trading

Devisen: Devisenhandel *m* BANK forex trading, VW agiotage; **Devisenhändler, in** *m,f* BÖRSE foreign exchange trader, FINANZ foreign exchange dealer; **Devisenkassakurs** *m* BÖRSE, VW spot exchange rate; **Devisenkassamarkt** *m* VW spot currency market; **Devisenkonto** *nt* BANK foreign exchange account, FINANZ, VW currency account; **Devisenkontrakt** *m*

BANK forward exchange contract; **Devisenkontrollreferent, in** *m,f* PERSON *Bankwesen* exchange control officer; **Devisenkurs** *m* VW foreign exchange rate, rate of exchange; **Devisenkursarbitrage** *f* FINANZ foreign exchange arbitrage; **Devisenkurse verbinden** *phr* BÖRSE link rates of exchange; **Devisenmakler, in** *m,f* FINANZ foreign exchange broker; **Devisenmarkt** *m* BÖRSE, VW currency market, foreign exchange market; **Devisenmarktintervention** *f* VW exchange of intervention; **Devisenmittelkurs** *m* FINANZ, VW middle rate; **Devisenreserven** *f pl* BANK foreign exchange holdings; **Devisenrücklage** *f* RECHNUNG foreign currency translation reserve; **Devisenschutz** *m* RECHNUNG foreign exchange hedge; **Devisenspekulation** *f* FINANZ foreign exchange speculation, vw currency speculation; **Devisenstandard** *m* BÖRSE currency standard; **Devisentauschvertrag** *m* RECHT swap contract; **Devisentermingeschäft** *nt* BÖRSE forward exchange dealing, vw forward exchange, forward-forward currency deal; **Devisenterminhandel** *m* BÖRSE forward exchange trading, forward exchange dealing vw forward exchange; **Devisenterminkurs** *m* BÖRSE forward exchange rate, FINANZ forward rate, VW forward exchange rate; **Devisenterminmarkt** *m* BÖRSE forward exchange market; **Devisentransaktion** *f* IMP/EXP, VW foreign currency transaction; **Devisenumrechnungskurs** *m* FINANZ foreign exchange conversion rate; **Devisenumtauschvertrag** *m* RECHT exchange contract; **Devisenvertrag** *m* BÖRSE currency contract

dezentral: ~**e Leitung** *f* MGMNT decentralized management; ~**e Marktwirtschaft** *f* POL, VW decentralized market economy (*DME*); ~**e Planung** *f* MGMNT decentralized planning

dezentralisieren *vt* MGMNT, POL decentralize

dezentralisiert *adj* MGMNT, POL decentralized; ~**es Management** *nt* MGMNT decentralized management; ~**es Rechnungswesen** *nt* VERWALT departmental account

Dezentralisierung *f* MGMNT, POL decentralization

Dezernat *nt* MGMNT department

Dezernent, in *m,f* MGMNT head of department

Dezibel *nt* (*dB*) GESCHÄFT decibel (*dB*)

dezimal *adj* MATH decimal; ~~**binäre Umwandlung** *f* COMP, MATH decimal to binary conversion

Dezimal- *in cpds* COMP, MATH decimal; **Dezimaldarstellung** *f* MATH decimal notation; **Dezimalpunkt** *m* COMP, MATH decimal point; **Dezimalstelle** *f* COMP, MATH decimal digit; **Dezimalzahl** *f* COMP, MATH decimal number; **Dezimalzeichen** *nt* COMP, MATH decimal point

dezimieren *vt* GESCHÄFT decimate

d.h. *abbr* (*das heißt*) GESCHÄFT i.e. (*id est*), that is to say

DGB *abbr* (*Deutscher Gewerkschaftsbund*) PERSON ≈ ACTU (*Australian Council of Trade Unions*), ≈ AFL-CIO (*American Federation of Labor-Congress of Industrial Organizations*), ≈ CIO (*Congress of Industrial Organizations*), ≈ TUC *BrE* (*Trades Union Congress*)

Diagnose *f* COMP, GESCHÄFT diagnosis; **Diagnosemeldung** *f* COMP diagnostic message

diagnostisch *adj* COMP, GESCHÄFT diagnostic; ~**e Routine** *f* GESCHÄFT diagnostic routine

diagonal: ~**es Wachstum** *nt* VW diagonal expansion

Diagramm *nt* COMP chart, GESCHÄFT chart, diagram, MATH chart

Dialog *m* COMP, GESCHÄFT dialog (*AmE*), dialogue (*BrE*); ◆ **in** ~ COMP in conversational mode

Dialog: **in Dialogbetrieb** *phr* COMP conversationally; **Dialogbox** *f* COMP dialog box (*AmE*), dialogue box (*BrE*); **Dialogeingabe** *f* COMP conversational entry

dialogfähig: **nicht ~es Videotextsystem** *nt* COMP, MEDIEN Teletext®, teletex

Dialog: **Dialogmodus** *m* COMP *Programme* conversational mode, interactive mode; **Dialogsystem** *nt* COMP conversational system, interactive system; **Dialogverarbeitung** *f* COMP interactive processing

Diamantinvestmentgesellschaft *f* BÖRSE diamond investment trust

Diaprojektor *m* MEDIEN slide projector

dichotomisch: ~**es Suchen** *nt* COMP binary search

dicht: ~**er Behälter** *m* TRANSP siftproof receptacle; ~ **besiedelt** *adj* VW densely populated; ~ **besiedeltes Gebiet** *nt* VW densely populated area; ~**e Verpackung** *f* TRANSP siftproof packaging

dichtbevölkert *adj* VW densely populated; ~**es Gebiet** *nt* vw densely populated area

Dichte *f* GRUND *der Bebauung* density; ~ **der Gewerkschaftsangehörigkeit** PERSON *Unternehmen oder Industrie* union density

dickköpfig *adj* V&M hard-headed

Diebstahl *m* GESCHÄFT, TRANSP, VERSICH theft; **Diebstahlrisiko** *nt* VERSICH theft risk; **Diebstahlsicherung** *f* GESCHÄFT, TRANSP antitheft device

dienen *vi* [+dat] GESCHÄFT serve

dienlich *adj* GESCHÄFT instrumental, conducive to

Dienst *m* GESCHÄFT duty, service; ~ **am Kunden vor dem Verkauf** V&M presale service; ◆ **seine Dienste anbieten** GESCHÄFT offer one's services; **zu Diensten Ihrer Majestät** POL, VERWALT On Her Majesty's Service (*OHMS*) (*BrE*); **wieder in ~ gestellt** GESCHÄFT recommissioned (*recmd*)

Dienst: **Dienstalter** *nt* PERSON length of service, seniority; **Dienstaltersplan** *m* PERSON seniority system; **Dienstaltersprinzip** *nt* PERSON seniority principle; **Dienstalterszulage** *f* PERSON seniority allowance, seniority bonus, seniority premium; **Dienstälteste(r)** *mf* [decl. as adj] GESCHÄFT longest-serving employee; **Dienstaufsichtsbeschwerde** *f* RECHT remonstration of an official; **Dienstbereitschaft** *f* **rund um die Uhr** GESCHÄFT round-the-clock service; **Dienstbezüge** *m pl* GESCHÄFT, PERSON remuneration; **Dienste** *m pl* **der Nebenstelle** FINANZ extension services

dienstfrei: ~**er Tag** *m* PERSON day off

Dienst: **nur für den Dienstgebrauch** *phr* GESCHÄFT *Applikation* for official use only, restricted; **zum Dienstgebrauch** *m* VERWALT for office use only; **Dienstgeheimnis** *nt* PERSON business secret, POL official secret; **Dienstgespräch** *nt* GESCHÄFT, KOMM business call, official call

diensthabend *adj* GESCHÄFT on duty

Dienstleistung *f* GESCHÄFT business service, service, VERWALT business service, vw tertiary product; ~ **gegen Gebühr** BANK fee-based service; **Dienstleistungen** *f pl* GESCHÄFT, PATENT, PERSON, V&M, VW services; **Dienstleistungen** *f pl* **der gehobenen Preisklasse**

GESCHÄFT up-market service; **Dienstleistungen** *f pl* **eines rückläufigen Marktes** V&M down-market service; **Dienstleistungsabend** *m* GESCHÄFT late-night opening; **Dienstleistungsabkommen** *nt* GESCHÄFT service agreement; **Dienstleistungsbetrieb** *m* GESCHÄFT service company, service enterprise; **Dienstleistungsbilanz** *f* FINANZ invisible balance, VW invisible trade balance, balance on services, services account, balance of invisible trade, invisible balance; **Dienstleistungsexporte** *m pl* IMP/EXP, VW invisible exports; **Dienstleistungsgebührenpolitik** *f* VERWALT fee-for-service policy; **Dienstleistungsgesellschaft** *f* RECHT nontrading partnership, VW service economy; **Dienstleistungsgewerbe** *nt* IND service industry, PERSON service company, VW service industry; **Dienstleistungsimporte** *m pl* IMP/EXP, VW invisible imports; **Dienstleistungsindustrie** *f* IND, VW service industry; **Dienstleistungsmarke** *f* PATENT, RECHT service mark; **Dienstleistungspalette** *f* VERWALT range of services; **Dienstleistungssektor** *m* IND service industry, PERSON public services, VW service industry, tertiary sector, service sector; **Dienstleistungsunternehmen** *nt* GESCHÄFT service company, service enterprise; **Dienstleistungsvereinbarung** *f* GESCHÄFT service agreement; **Dienstleistungsverkehr** *m* VW invisible trade, service transactions; **Dienstleistungsvertrag** *m* GESCHÄFT service contract, RECHT contract for services, agreement of service; **Dienstleistungsverzeichnis** *nt* PATENT specification of services

dienstlich: nur für ~e Zwecke *phr* VERWALT for office use only

Dienst: Dienstort *m* PERSON duty station, VERWALT work station; **Dienstplan** *m* GESCHÄFT duty rota, roster, PERSON *Schichtwechsel* roster; **Dienstprogramm** *nt* COMP utility, utility program; **Dienstreise** *f* GESCHÄFT business trip, POL *von Bürokraten* facility trip; **Dienststelle** *f* RECHT agency (*agcy*), VERWALT administrative office, bureau (*AmE*), official agency, VW agency (*agcy*)

diensttuend *adj* GESCHÄFT on duty

Dienst: Dienstvereinbarung *f* GESCHÄFT service agreement; **Dienstverhältnis** *nt* PERSON employment, RECHT master-servant rule; **Dienstvertrag** *m* GESCHÄFT service agreement, service contract, PERSON contract of service (*BrE*), RECHT agreement of service; **Dienstweg** *m* GESCHÄFT official channels, MGMNT *Antragstellung* chain of command; **den Dienstweg nehmen** *phr* GESCHÄFT go through the proper channels; **Dienstzeit** *f* PERSON length of service, period of service, term of office

Diesel *m* TRANSP diesel; **Dieselkraftstoff** *m* TRANSP diesel fuel, Derv (*BrE*); **Dieselöl** *nt* TRANSP, UMWELT diesel oil (*DO*); **Dieseltreibstoff** *m* TRANSP diesel fuel, Derv (*BrE*)

dieses: ~ Monats *phr* (*d. M.*) KOMM instant (*inst.*)

Differential *nt* TRANSP differential; **Differentialanalyse** *f* MGMNT differential analysis; **Differentialinzidenz** *f* **der Besteuerung** STEUER differential tax incidence; **Differentialsperre** *f* TRANSP differential lock

Differenz *f* GESCHÄFT difference; **~ zwischen Anleihenennwert und Beleihungswert** RECHNUNG safety margin; **~ zwischen Zinssätzen** VW margin between the rates of interest; ♦ **die ~ finanzieren** VW finance the

difference; **sich in die ~ teilen** GESCHÄFT split the difference

Differenz: Differenzengleichung *f* VW difference equation

differenzieren *vt* GESCHÄFT differentiate

differenziert: ~es Marketing *nt* V&M differentiated marketing; **~es Produkt** *nt* V&M differentiated product; **~e Produktanforderungen** *f pl* V&M demand for sophisticated products; **~e Ware** *f* V&M differentiated goods

Differenziertheit *f* GESCHÄFT sophistication

Differenzierung *f* V&M *des Marktes* differentiation, sophistication; **Differenzierungsstrategie** *f* V&M differentiation strategy (*BrE*)

Differenz: Differenzkosten *pl* GESCHÄFT avoidable costs, VW differential cost; **Differenzkostenmethode** *f* MGMNT relevant cost approach

differieren *vi* GESCHÄFT differ

Diffusion *f* IND, V&M, VW diffusion; **Diffusionsgeschwindigkeit** *f* IND diffusion rate; **Diffusionsindex** *m* VW diffusion index; **Diffusionskurve** *f* V&M diffusion curve

Digital- *in cpds* COMP digital

digital *adj* COMP, KOMM *Kommunikationstechnik* digital; **~e Abschreibung** *f* **zur privaten Ausgabenbegrenzung** RECHNUNG sum-of-the-year's digit method of depreciation; **~-analog** *adj* (*D/A*) COMP digital-to-analog (*D/A*); **~ darstellen** *phr* COMP, KOMM digitize; **~e Daten** *pl* COMP digital data; **~e Datenverarbeitung** *f* COMP digital data processing; **~er Selektivruf** *m* KOMM digital selective calling (*DSC*); **~e Sortierung** *f* COMP digital sort

Digital-: Digital-Analog-Wandler *m* (*D/A-Wandler*) COMP digital-to-analog converter (*DAC*); **Digitalrechner** *m* COMP digital computer

DIHT *abbr* (*Deutscher Industrie- und Handelstag*) IND ≈ ABCC (*Association of British Chambers of Commerce*), ≈ ABT (*American Board of Trade*), ≈ BCC (*British Chamber of Commerce*)

Diktat *nt* VERWALT shorthand dictation

diktieren *vt* GESCHÄFT, VERWALT dictate

Dillon-Runde *f* VW Dillon Round

dimensionslos: ~e Maßzahl *f* MATH absolute measure

DIN *abbr* IND, RECHT, VERWALT (*Deutsches Institut für Normung*) German national standards institution, ≈ BSI (*British Standards Institution*), ≈ ANSI (*American National Standards Institution*), ≈ American Standards Authority, (*Deutsche Industrie-Norm*) German industrial standard, ≈ BS (*British Standard*); **~ A4 Hochformat** GESCHÄFT, KOMM *Papiergröße* A4 letter; **~ B5 Format** GESCHÄFT, KOMM *Papiergröße* B5 Letter; **DIN-Format** GESCHÄFT, KOMM *Papiergröße* German standard paper size

dinglich *adj frml* RECHT in rem; **~er Anspruch** *m* RECHT *Vertragsrecht* claim in rem (*frml*) *m*; **~er Arrest** *m* RECHT attachment, distraint (*BrE*); **~e Belastung** *f* RECHT *Grundstück* encumbrance; **~ mit dem Grundstück verbunden sein** *adj* RECHT *Grundbesitz* run with the land; **~e Klage** *f jarg* RECHT actio in rem (*jarg*); **~es Recht** *nt* **auf Lebenszeit** RECHT lebenslanges Nießbrauchrecht life interest; **~e Sicherheit** *f* FINANZ collateral security, RECHT real security; **~er Vertrag** *m* RECHT real agreement (*AmE*); **~es Vorkaufsrecht** *nt* RECHT real right of preemption

Diode *f* COMP diode

Diplom *nt* GESCHÄFT diploma; **Diplomabschluß** *m* SOZIAL Higher National Certificate (*BrE*) (*HNC*), Higher National Diploma (*BrE*) (*HND*)

Diplomatenpost *f* KOMM, POL diplomatic bag (*BrE*), diplomatic pouch (*AmE*)

Diplomatie *f* MGMNT diplomacy

diplomatisch: ~**er Auftrag** *f* POL diplomatic mission; ~**er Dienst** *m* POL diplomatic service; ~**e Dienststelle** *f* POL diplomatic service post; ~**e Mission** *f* POL diplomatic mission; ~**e Vertretung** *f* POL diplomatic mission

Diplom: **Diplombetriebswirt, in** *m,f* PERSON ≈ Master of Commerce (*MCom*); **Diplomökonom, in** *m,f* GESCHÄFT Master of Economics (*MEcon*); **Diplomvolkswirt, in** *m,f* GESCHÄFT Master of Economics (*MEcon*)

DIP-Schalter *m* COMP *Hardware* DIP switch

Dir. *abbr* (*Direktor*) PERSON dir. (*director*)

Direct Costing *nt* FINANZ, RECHNUNG, VW direct costing

Direkt- *in cpds* GESCHÄFT direct, TRANSP *Flug* nonstop, direct, *Zug, Weg* through, direct

direkt 1. *adj* FREI *Radio- oder Fernsehübertragung* live, GESCHÄFT direct (*dir.*), plain-spoken, TRANSP direct (*dir.*); ♦ **auf** ~**em oder indirektem Wege versichert** VERSICH direct or held covered; **2.** *adv* MATH directly; ♦ ~ **bezogen auf** GESCHÄFT directly related to; ~ **finanzieren** FINANZ finance directly; ~ **transportiert** IMP/EXP, TRANSP *EU* directly transported; **jdm** ~ **unterstellt sein** [+dat] GESCHÄFT be directly responsible to sb

direkt: ~**e Arbeiter** *m pl* PERSON direct workers; ~**er Ausgabenumschlag** *m* FINANZ direct spending envelope; ~**es Beteilungsprogramm** *nt* FINANZ direct participation program (*AmE*), direct participation programme (*BrE*); ~**er Bus** *m* TRANSP through coach; ~**e Busverbindung** *f* TRANSP through coach; ~**e Dateneingabe** *f* COMP direct data entry (*DDE*); ~**es Exportgeschäft** *nt* IMP/EXP direct export trading; ~**er Exporthandel** *m* IMP/EXP direct export trading; ~**e Familie** *f* BÖRSE immediate family; ~**e finanzielle Verpflichtung** *f* BANK direct obligation; ~**es Finanzierungs-Leasing** *nt* VW direct financial leasing; ~**e Handelseingabe** *f* IMP/EXP direct trader input (*DTI*); ~**er Handelsinput** *m* IMP/EXP direct trader input (*DTI*); ~**e und indirekte Besteuerung** *f* STEUER, VW direct and indirect taxation; ~**e und indirekte Gemeinkosten** *pl* FINANZ supplementary cost; ~**es Kapitalbeteiligungsprogramm** *nt* FINANZ direct participation program (*AmE*), direct participation programme (*BrE*); ~**e Kosten** *pl* FINANZ, RECHNUNG, VW direct costs; ~**e Lohnkosten** *pl* RECHNUNG direct labor costs (*AmE*), direct labour costs (*BrE*); ~**e Produktion** *f* VW direct production; ~**e Produktrentabilität** *f* V&M direct product profitability (*DPP*); ~**e Steuer** *f* STEUER direct tax; ~**e Umsatzaufwendungen** *f pl* GESCHÄFT direct cost of sales; ~ **unproduktive auf Gewinn gerichtete Aktivitäten** *f pl* VW directly unproductive profit-seeking activities (*DUP*); ~**er Warentausch** *m* VW direct exchange; ~**e Zahlungsverpflichtung** *f* BANK direct obligation; ~**er Zugriff** *m* COMP direct access; ~**e Zugverbindung** *f* TRANSP through train

Direkt-: **Direktabrechnung** *f* SOZIAL *Arzt* bulk billing; **Direktanschlußmodem** *nt* COMP *Datenübertragung* direct-connect modem; **Direktantwort** *f* GESCHÄFT,

V&M direct response; **Direktbuchung** *f* FREI direct booking; **Direktclearingstelle** *f* BANK direct clearer; **Direkteinkauf** *m* GESCHÄFT direct purchase; **Direkteinlage** *f* BANK direct deposit; **Direktertrag** *m* BANK, BÖRSE direct yield; **Direktexport** *m* IMP/EXP direct export trading; **Direktflug** *m* TRANSP nonstop flight, through flight; **Direktgespräch** *nt* KOMM direct call; **Direkthafen** *m* TRANSP direct port (*dp*); **Direktinvestition** *f* **aus dem Ausland** FINANZ, VW direct foreign investment (*DFI*); **Direktinvestition** *f* **im Ausland** FINANZ, VW direct foreign investment (*DFI*); **Direktinvestitionen** *f pl* BÖRSE portfolio investment; **Direktinvestitionen** *f pl* **im Ausland** FINANZ, VW direct outward investment; **Direktkonnossement** *nt* IMP/EXP, TRANSP direct bill of lading; **Direktkredite** *m pl* BANK borrowings; **Direktlieferung** *f* TRANSP direct delivery; **Direktmarketing** *nt* V&M direct marketing

Direktor, in *m,f* (*Dir.*) GESCHÄFT manager, PERSON director (*dir.*), *Unternehmensleitung* development director; ~ **für Aus- und Weiterbildung** MGMNT training manager; ~ **einer Niederlassung** GESCHÄFT, MGMNT, PERSON branch office manager; ~ **ohne Geschäftsbereich** MGMNT non-executive director, outside director; ~ **der Produktionsabteilung** IND production director, production manager, MGMNT, PERSON production director; ~ **der technischen Abteilung** PERSON technical director; ~ **der Werbeabteilung** PERSON, V&M advertising director

Direktorat *nt* PERSON directorate, directorship

Direktorium *nt* GESCHÄFT board of management, MGMNT board of directors, board of management; ~ **des Zentralbankensystems** *nt* VW Board of Governors of the Federal Reserve System (*AmE*)

Direkt-: **Direktplazierung** *f* BANK direct placement; **Direktrendite** *f* BANK, BÖRSE direct yield; **Direktroute** *f* TRANSP direct route, through route; **Direktumladung** *f* TRANSP direct transhipment; **Direktverbindung** *f* KOMM direct call, TRANSP *Zug* through train; **eine Direktverbindung herstellen mit** *phr* KOMM establish a direct link with

Direktverkauf *m* V&M *ohne Zwischenhändler* direct sales, direct selling; ~ **durch Grossisten** V&M *ohne eigenes Lager* drop shipping (*AmE*); ~ **durch Vertreter** V&M *Haustürverkauf* personal selling, door-to-door selling

Direkt-: **Direktversand** *m* IMP/EXP direct transportation, V&M direct mail; **Direktversicherer** *m* VERSICH direct insurer, original insurer; **Direktversicherung** *f* VERSICH direct insurance; **Direktweg** *m* COMP primary route, TRANSP direct route; **Direktwerbung** *f* V&M direct advertising; **Direktzugriff** *m* COMP direct access, immediate access, random access; **Direktzugriffsspeicher** *m* (*RAM*) COMP random access memory (*RAM*); **Direktzusage** *f* PERSON employer's pension commitment

dirigieren *vt* GESCHÄFT lead, *Autoverkehr* direct

Dirigismus *m* POL, VW dirigism

Disagio *nt* BANK discount, debt discount, loan discount, GESCHÄFT disagio; ♦ **mit einem** ~ **von** BÖRSE at a discount of; **mit einem** ~ **notiert werden** BÖRSE stand at a discount

Disagio: **Disagioanteil** *m* **versicherungstechnischer Verlängerungen** FINANZ unamortized portion of actuarial deficiencies

Discounter *m* V&M discount house, discounter

Disincentive-Effekt *m* VW disincentive effect

Diskette *f* COMP diskette, floppy, *Datenträger* floppy disk, *Speicher* disk; **~ mit doppelter Speicherdichte** COMP double-density disk, double-density diskette; **~ mit hoher Speicherdichte** COMP high-density disk (*HDD*); **~ mit Kopierschutz** COMP copy-protected disk; **Diskettenlaufwerk** *nt* COMP diskette drive, floppy disk drive; **Diskettenspeicher** *m* COMP diskette storage

Diskont *m* BANK, BÖRSE discount (*dis, disc.*), FINANZ hard discount, settlement discount, discount (*dis, disc.*), V&M, VW discount (*dis, disc.*); **Diskontbank** *f* BANK acceptance house, discounting bank, FINANZ discount house, discounting bank; **Diskontbanker** *m* BANK discounting banker; **Diskontbankier** *m* BANK discounting banker; **Diskontdividenden-Reinvestitionsplan** *m* FINANZ discount dividend reinvestment plan; **Diskontertrag** *m* BÖRSE discount yield; **Diskonterträge** *m pl* BANK income from discounting

diskontfähig *adj* BANK bankable, discountable, eligible for discount, RECHNUNG available for discounting; **nicht ~** *adj* BANK indiscountable, unbankable; **nicht ~es Papier** *nt* BANK ineligible paper; **~er Wechsel** *m* BANK bankable paper, FINANZ discountable bill; **nicht ~er Wechsel** *m* BANK unbankable paper

Diskont: **Diskontfähigkeitstest** *m* BANK eligibility test; **Diskontfenster** *nt jarg* BANK, FINANZ discount window; **Diskontgeber, in** *m,f* FINANZ discounter; **Diskontgefälle** *nt* FINANZ discount rate differential; **Diskontgeschäft** *nt* FINANZ discount business, discounting, RECHNUNG discounting; **Diskonthaus** *nt* FINANZ discount centre (*BrE*), discount center (*AmE*), discount house

diskontierbar *adj* BANK, BÖRSE, FINANZ discountable; **~er Wechsel** *m* BANK bankable bill

diskontieren *vt* BANK, BÖRSE, FINANZ discount

Diskontierer, in *m,f* FINANZ discounter

diskontiert: **~er Aktienpreis** *m* BÖRSE discounted share price; **~e Anleihe** *f* BANK discounted loan; **~er Bargeldfluß** *m* FINANZ, RECHNUNG discounted cash flow (*DCF*); **~er Barwert** *m* FINANZ discounted present value; **~er Einnahmeüberschuß** *m* FINANZ, RECHNUNG discounted cash flow (*DCF*); **~er Wechsel** *m* BANK discounted bill; **~er Zeitwert** *m* FINANZ discounted present value

Diskontierung *f* FINANZ, RECHNUNG discounting; **Diskontierungsinstrument** *nt* BÖRSE discount instrument

Diskont: **Diskontinstrument** *nt* BÖRSE discount instrument; **Diskontladen** *m* V&M discount house, discount shop (*BrE*), discount store (*AmE*); **Diskontmarkt** *m* FINANZ discount market; **Diskontmarktdarlehen** *nt* FINANZ discount market loan; **Diskontpunkte** *m pl* BANK discount points; **Diskontsatz** *m* BANK bank rate, discount rate; **Diskontsatz** *m* **der Geschäftsbanken** BANK private rate of discount; **Diskontsatz** *m* **der Notenbank** FINANZ bank rate; **Diskontsenkung** *f* BANK fall in the bank rate; **Diskontspesen** *pl* RECHNUNG discount charges; **Diskontwechsel** *m* BANK bill discounted, bill for discount, discounted bill, RECHNUNG discount bill; **Diskontzentrale** *f* FINANZ discount center (*AmE*), discount centre (*BrE*)

Diskrepanz *f* GESCHÄFT discrepancy

diskret: **~e Variable** *f* MATH discontinuous variable

diskretionär *adj* GESCHÄFT, STEUER, VW discretionary; **~e Ausgabenkompetenz** *f* VW discretionary spending power; **~e Fiskalpolitik** *f* VW discretionary fiscal policy; **~e Kosten** *pl* VW discretionary cost; **~e Politik** *f* VW discretionary economic policy

diskriminieren *vt* GESCHÄFT discriminate, discriminate against, RECHT discriminate, discriminate against, treat unfavorably (*AmE*), treat unfavourably (*BrE*), VW discriminate, discriminate against

diskriminierend: **~e Besteuerung** *f* STEUER discriminatory taxation; **~es Monopol** *nt* VW discriminating monopoly

Diskriminierung *f* GESCHÄFT, VW discrimination; **~ am Arbeitsplatz** PERSON discrimination in the workplace; **~ aufgrund des Alters** VW ageism; **~ nach Einstellung** PERSON post-entry discrimination; **~ vor der Einstellung** pre-entry closed shop (*BrE*), pre-entry discrimination; **kein Diskriminierungsfaktor** *phr* GESCHÄFT no discrimination factor

Diskussion *f* GESCHÄFT discussion; ♦ **das zur ~ stehende Problem** GESCHÄFT the issue at stake

Diskussion: **Diskussionsbasis** *f* GESCHÄFT basis for discussion; **Diskussionsgrundlage** *f* GESCHÄFT basis for discussion; **Diskussionsgruppe** *f* V&M discussion group; **Diskussionspapier** *nt* RECHNUNG exposure draft

diskutieren *vt* GESCHÄFT discuss

Dispache *f* VERSICH average statement, average adjustment, *Schadensberechnung* statement of average, claims adjustment

Dispacheur *m* VERSICH average adjuster (*AA*), claims adjuster, general average adjuster, average stater

Disparität *f* GESCHÄFT, VW disparity

Dispens *m* RECHT *Befreiung* dispensation

Display *nt* V&M display; **Displaymaterial** *nt* V&M display material; **Displaynachlaß** *m* **im Einzelhandel** V&M retail display allowance

Dispokredit *m* BANK current account loan (*BrE*), overdraft facility, personal credit line, *Einzelhandel* retail customer credit

Disponent, in *m,f* FINANZ fund manager, GESCHÄFT, MGMNT procurement manager

Disponibilität *f* VW *Geld* availability

Dispositionskredit *m* BANK personal credit line, current account loan (*BrE*), overdraft facility, *Einzelhandel* retail customer credit

Dissens *m* RECHT *Vertragsrecht* dissent

Distanzfracht *f* TRANSP distance freight, pro rata freight

distanziert *adj* GESCHÄFT distant

Distribution *f* V&M distribution, VW income distribution; **Distributionskette** *f* IND chain of distribution; **Distributionskontrolle** *f* V&M distribution check; **Distributionsplanung** *f* TRANSP distribution planning; **Distributionsservice** *m* TRANSP distribution service

Disziplin *f* GESCHÄFT, PERSON discipline

Disziplinar- *in cpds* PERSON, RECHT disciplinary; **Disziplinarbestimmung** *f* PERSON disciplinary rule; **Disziplinarentlassung** *f* PERSON *Arbeit, Konflikt* disciplinary layoff; **Disziplinarmaßnahmen** *f pl* RECHT disciplinary measures; **Disziplinarordnung** *f* PERSON disciplinary rule; **Disziplinarverfahren** *nt* PERSON disciplinary procedure, RECHT disciplinary proceedings

diszipliniert: **~e Beförderung** *f* TRANSP disciplined movement

Div. *abbr* (*Dividende*) BÖRSE, VERSICH div. (*dividend*)

divergent: **~es Marketing** *nt* V&M divergent marketing

Divergenz *f* GESCHÄFT divergence; **Divergenzschwelle** *f* VW divergence threshold

divergierend: **~e Fertigung** *f* IND divergent manufacturing; **~e Laufzeiten** *f pl* BANK maturity mismatch, mismatched maturity

divers: **~e Artikel** *m pl* RECHNUNG sundry articles

Diversifikation *f* V&M diversification; **Diversifikationsstrategie** *f* V&M diversification strategy; **Diversifikationsvorteil** *m* VW economy of scale

diversifizieren *vt* GESCHÄFT, MGMNT, PERSON diversify

Diversifizierung *f* GESCHÄFT, MGMNT, PERSON diversification

Dividende *f* (*Div.*) BÖRSE, VERSICH dividend (*div.*); **~ pro Aktie** FINANZ dividend per share (*BrE*) (*DPS*); **~ in Form von Schuldurkunden** RECHNUNG liability dividend; **~ einer Muttergesellschaft** RECHNUNG parent company dividend; **~ nach Steuern** RECHNUNG, STEUER after-tax dividend; ♦ **ohne ~** FINANZ ex dividend (*ex div.*); **eine ~ ausfallen lassen** FINANZ pass a dividend; **eine ~ ausschütten** FINANZ distribute a dividend, pay a dividend

Dividenden *f pl* BÖRSE, FINANZ, RECHNUNG dividends; **~ einer Tochtergesellschaft** BÖRSE subsidiary dividends; **auf ~ zu zahlende Kapitalertragsteuer** *f* STEUER dividend withholding tax; **Dividendenanteilschein** *m* FINANZ dividend warrant; **Dividendenbedarf** *m* RECHNUNG dividend requirement; **Dividendenbeleg** *m* BÖRSE dividend voucher; **Dividendenberechtigungsschein** *m* FINANZ dividend warrant; **Dividendeneinkommen** *nt* BÖRSE dividend income; **Dividendeneinnahme** *f* BÖRSE dividend income; **Dividendenertrag** *m* BÖRSE dividend yield; **Dividendenfreibetrag** *m* STEUER dividend exclusion (*AmE*); **Dividendenpolitik** *f* BÖRSE dividend policy, FINANZ dividend payout policy; **Dividendenquellensteuer** *f* STEUER dividend withholding tax; **Dividendenquittung** *f* BÖRSE dividend voucher; **Dividendenrendite** *f* BÖRSE dividend yield; **Dividendenrolloverplan** *m* BÖRSE dividend rollover plan; **Dividendenrücklage** *f* GESCHÄFT bonus reserve, RECHNUNG dividend reserve fund; **Dividendenschein** *m* FINANZ dividend coupon, dividend warrant; **Dividendensteuer** *f* STEUER dividend tax; **Dividendensteuerbefreiung** *f* STEUER dividend exclusion; **Dividendenstichtag** *m* VW record; **Dividenden-Stripping** *nt* FINANZ dividend stripping; **Dividendenzahlungsanweisung** *f* FINANZ dividend warrant

dividieren *vt* COMP, MATH divide

Divisia-Geldindex *m* VW Divisia money index

Divisionalisierung *f* GESCHÄFT divisionalization

Divisionskakulation *f* RECHNUNG process costing

DLV *abbr* (*Deutscher Luftfahrverband*) TRANSP German air transport association, ≈ ATA (*Air Transport Association of America*)

d.M. *abbr* (*dieses Monats*) KOMM inst. (*instant*)

DMS *abbr* (*Datenbankverwaltungssystem*) COMP *Datenbanken* DBMS (*database management system*)

DNA *abbr* (*Deutscher Normenausschuß*) GESCHÄFT German committee for standards, ≈ ASTM (*American Society for Testing and Materials*)

Dock *nt* TRANSP dock; **Dockempfangsschein** *m* IMP/EXP, TRANSP dock warrant (*D/W*)

Docken *nt* TRANSP dry docking (*DD*)

Dock: **Dockgebühren** *f pl* TRANSP dock charges, dock dues; **Dockhafen** *m* TRANSP wet dock; **Docklagerschein** *m* IMP/EXP, TRANSP dock warrant (*D/W*); **Dockprüfung** *f* TRANSP docking survey; **Docktätigkeiten** *f pl* TRANSP dock operations (*DO*)

Doktor *m* (*Dr.*) GESCHÄFT, SOZIAL Doctor (*Dr.*); **~ der Betriebswirtschaft** GESCHÄFT Doctor of Commerce (*DCom*); **~ des Handelsrechts** GESCHÄFT Doctor of Commercial Law (*DComL*); **~ der Medizin** (*Dr. med.*) SOZIAL Doctor of Medicine (*MD*); **~ der Philosophie** (*Dr. phil.*) GESCHÄFT, SOZIAL Doctor of Philosophy (*DPhil, PhD*); **~ der Rechte** (*Dr. jur.*) PERSON, RECHT, SOZIAL Doctor of Laws (*LLD*); **~ des Wirtschaftsrechts** GESCHÄFT Doctor of Commercial Law (*DComL*); **~ der Wirtschaftswissenschaften** GESCHÄFT Doctor of Economics (*DEcon*)

Doktorand, in *m,f* GESCHÄFT postgraduate

Doktor: **Doktorgrad** *m* PERSON, SOZIAL Doctor of Philosophy (*DPhil, PhD*), doctor's degree, doctorate

Doktrin *f* POL, VW doctrine; **~ der realen Wechsel** VW real bills doctrine

Dokument *nt* COMP *Textverarbeitung* document, FINANZ instrument, GESCHÄFT, RECHT document; ♦ **gegen Dokumente** GESCHÄFT against documents

Dokumentar- *in cpds* MEDIEN, V&M documentary

dokumentär: **~er Nachweis** *m* GESCHÄFT documentary evidence; **nicht ~e Zahlung** *f* FINANZ clean payment

Dokumentar-: **Dokumentarbericht** *m* MEDIEN *Druck* feature article, V&M documentary; **Dokumentarfilm** *m* V&M documentary

dokumentarisch *adj* GESCHÄFT documentary

Dokumentar-: **Dokumentarsendung** *f* V&M documentary

Dokumentation *f* COMP, GESCHÄFT documentation

Dokument: **Dokumente** *f pl* **gegen Akzept** (*DA, D/A, d/a*) GESCHÄFT documents against acceptance (*DA*); **Dokumente** *f pl* **gegen Zahlung** (*DZ*) GESCHÄFT documents against payment (*DAP*); **Dokumentenakkreditiv** *nt* BANK documentary letter of credit, FINANZ documentary credit; **ein Dokumentenakkreditiv ausstellen** *phr* BÖRSE issue a letter of credit; **Dokumentencode** *m* COMP *Textverarbeitung* document code; **Dokumenteninhaber, in** *m,f* GESCHÄFT document holder; **Dokumenteninkasso** *nt* RECHT *Vertragsrecht* collection of commercial documents; **Dokumentenmodus** *m* COMP document mode; **Dokumentenname** *m* COMP document name; **Dokumentenrimesse** *f* BANK documentary remittance; **Dokumententratte** *f* BANK *Außenhandel* acceptance bill, GESCHÄFT, IMP/EXP, VERWALT documentary draft; **Dokumentenvernichter** *m* VERWALT shredder; **Dokumentenvorlage** *f* IMP/EXP *Zollabfertigung* presentation of documents; **Dokumentenwiedergewinnungssystem** *nt* COMP document retrieval system

Dollar *m* BÖRSE dollar-for-dollar offset, GESCHÄFT dollar, buck (*infrml*); **~ im Bezugsjahr** VW constant dollars (*AmE*); **~ zum Tageskurs** FINANZ current dollars; **Dollarabfluß** *m* VW dollar drain; **Dollaraufgeld** *nt* BÖRSE dollar premium; **Dollarausgleich** *m* VW dollar balance; **Dollarblock** *m* VW dollar area; **Dollardurchschnittskostenmethode** *f* BÖRSE dollar cost averaging; **Dollargeschäft** *nt* BANK dollar transaction

Dollarisierung *f* BÖRSE, FINANZ, VW dollarization

Dollar: **Dollarkurs** *m* BÖRSE dollar bid, dollar rate, dollar price; **Dollarlücke** *f* VW dollar gap; **Dollarmangel** *m* BÖRSE dollar shortage; **Dollarprämie** *f* BÖRSE dollar premium; **Dollarpreis** *m* BÖRSE dollar rate, GESCHÄFT dollar price; **Dollarraum** *m* VW dollar area; **Dollarschein** *m* VW dollar bill (*AmE*), greenback (*infrml*) (*AmE*); **Dollarstandard** *m* VW dollar standard; **Dollarsubmissionsangebot** *nt* BÖRSE dollar bid; **Dollartitel** *m* *pl* FINANZ dollar securities; **Dollarüberschuß** *m* VW dollar surplus; **Dollarverknappung** *f* BÖRSE dollar shortage; **Dollarwert** *m* BÖRSE dollar value; **Dollarzinsspanne** *f* VW dollar gap

dolmetschen 1. *vt* KOMM interpret; 2. *vi* KOMM interpret

Dolmetschen *nt* KOMM interpreting

Dolmetscher, in *m,f* KOMM interpreter

Domei *nt* PERSON Domei

Domestizierung *f* VW domestication

dominant *adj* GESCHÄFT dominant; **~e Werbung** *f* V&M dominant advertising

Dominanz *f* GESCHÄFT dominance

Dongle *m* *jarg* COMP dongle

Donoghues-Geldfondsdurchschnitt *m* BÖRSE Donoghue's Money Fund Average (*AmE*)

Donovan-Kommission *f* IND, PERSON Donovan Commission (*BrE*)

Doppel: **Doppelakquisition** *f* GESCHÄFT dual sourcing; **Doppelbelastung** *f* RECHT, STEUER double economic burden; **Doppelbesetzung** *f* PERSON *Arbeitsplatz* double staffing; **Doppelfunktion** *f* BÖRSE dual capacity; **Doppelhaushälfte** *f* GRUND duplex (*AmE*), semidetached house (*BrE*); **Doppelklick** *m* COMP *Maus* double-click; **Doppelklickgeschwindigkeit** *f* COMP double-click speed; **Doppelseite** *f* MEDIEN *Druck* center spread (*AmE*), centerfold (*AmE*), centre spread (*BrE*), centrefold (*BrE*)

doppelseitig *adj* COMP two-sided, double-sided; **~e Anzeige** *f* MEDIEN *Druck*, V&M double spread advertising, double-page spread; **~e Diskette** *f* COMP double-sided disk, double-sided diskette

Doppel: **Doppelsenkung** *f* GESCHÄFT double reduction (*DR*); **Doppelspalte** *f* MEDIEN, V&M double column; **Doppelstatus** *m* GESCHÄFT dual status; **Doppelsteuerungsabkommen** *nt* STEUER double tax agreement

doppelt: **~e Ansässigkeit** *f* RECHT, STEUER double residency; **~er Anschlag** *m* COMP *Drucker* double strike; **~e Besteuerung** *f* **von Spareinlagen** STEUER double taxation of savings; **~e Buchführung** *f* RECHNUNG double-entry accounting, double-entry bookkeeping; **~e Dichte** *f (DD)* COMP *Disketten* double density (*DD*); **~es Einreisevisum** *nt* VERWALT double-entry visa; **~e Fahrbahn** *f* TRANSP double decking; **~ faktorales Austauschverhältnis** *nt* VW double factorial terms of trade; **~e Genauigkeit** *f* COMP *Gleitkommazahlen* double precision; **~es Konto** *nt* RECHNUNG double account; **~er Satz** *m* COMP duplicated record; **~er Schadensersatz** *m* RECHT double damages; **~e Typenbreite** *f* VERWALT dual pitch; **~e Umschichtung** *f* VW double switching; **~er**

Usowechsel *m* GESCHÄFT bill at double usance; **~er Zeilenabstand** *m* COMP double spacing

doppeltwirkend *adj* IND double acting

Doppelung *f* GESCHÄFT doubling

Doppel: **Doppelusowechsel** *m* GESCHÄFT bill at double usance; **Doppelverdienen** *nt* PERSON dual job holding, moonlighting (*infrml*); **Doppelverdiener, in** *m,f* PERSON dual job holder, moonlighter; **Doppelverdienerhaushalt** *m* VW double income household; **Doppelversicherung** *f* VERSICH double insurance; **Doppelwohnsitz** *m* RECHT, STEUER double residency; **Doppelzählung** *f* FINANZ double counting; **Doppelzahlung** *f* **der Versicherungsleistungen** VERSICH duplication of benefits; **Doppelzentner** *m* GESCHÄFT quintal; **Doppelzimmer** *nt* FREI double room

DOS *abbr* (*Plattenbetriebssystem*) COMP DOS (*disk operating system*)

Dose *f* V&M can, jar

DOS: **DOS-Eingabeaufforderung** *f* COMP DOS prompt; **DOS-Prompt** *m* *jarg* COMP DOS prompt

Dossier *nt* VERWALT dossier

Dotierung *f* FINANZ provision of funds

Dow-Jones: **Dow-Jones-Durchschnitt** *m* BÖRSE Dow Jones average; **Dow-Jones-Index** *m* FINANZ Dow Jones Index; **Dow-Jones-Industrieaktienindex** *m* BÖRSE Dow Jones Industrial Average (*DJIA*)

Download *m* COMP *Dateitransfer* download

downloaden *vt* *jarg* COMP download

dpi *abbr* (*Punkte pro Zoll*) COMP *Drucker, Bildschirm* dpi (*dots per inch*)

Dr. *abbr* (*Doktor*) GESCHÄFT, SOZIAL *Titel* Dr. (*Doctor*)

drahtlos: **~es Hochfrequenzfernsprechwesen** *nt* TRANSP high-frequency radiotelephony; **~e Hochfrequenztelefonie** *f* TRANSP high-frequency radiotelephony; **~es Mittelfrequenzfernsprechwesen** *nt* TRANSP medium-frequency radiotelephony; **~e Telefonie** *nt* KOMM radiotelephony (*RT*)

Drain *m* COMP *eines Feldeffekttransistors* drain

DRAM *abbr* (*dynamischer Speicher*) COMP DRAM (*dynamic random access memory*)

drastisch *adj* GESCHÄFT, POL *Änderungen* sweeping; **~er Anstieg** *m* VW sharp rise; **~e Maßnahmen** *f* *pl* VW drastic measures; **~er Rückgang** *m* VW *der Preise* sharp drop

Draufgabe *f* GRUND *Handgeld* earnest money

Draufgeld *nt* BANK token payment

Dreh- *in cpds* MEDIEN shooting; **Drehbuch** *nt* MEDIEN scenario; **Drehgestell** *nt* TRANSP bogie; **Drehplan** *m* MEDIEN, V&M shooting script; **Drehpunkt** *m* GESCHÄFT fulcrum

Dreieck *nt* GESCHÄFT, MATH triangle

dreieckig *adj* GESCHÄFT, MATH triangular

Dreieck: **Dreiecksfusion** *f* GESCHÄFT triangular merger; **Dreiecksgeschäft** *nt* IMP/EXP three-way switch deal, VW triangular operation; **Dreieckshandel** *m* IMP/EXP triangulation; **Dreieckskompensation** *f* VW triangular compensation; **Dreiecksverkehr** *m* TRANSP triangle service

Dreierpack *m* GESCHÄFT tripack

dreifach *adj* GESCHÄFT treble, triple, triplicate, in triplicate; **~e Senkung** *f* GESCHÄFT triple reduction (*TR*) (*AmE*)

Dreifach- *in cpds* GESCHÄFT, TRANSP three-way, triple; **Dreifachsplitting** *nt* GESCHÄFT three-way split

Dreifelderwirtschaft *f* VW three-course rotation

dreimonatig: ~e **Abzinsungsrendite** *f* BÖRSE three-month discount yield; ~e **Kündigungsfrist** *f* BÖRSE three-month call; ~e **Zusatzrendite** *f* BÖRSE three-month add-on yield

Dreimonats- *in cpds* BÖRSE, FINANZ three-month; **Dreimonats-Eurodollar-Festgelder** *nt pl* BÖRSE three-month Eurodollar time deposits; **Dreimonatsgeld** *nt* FINANZ three-month funds; **Dreimonatspapiere** *nt pl* FINANZ three-month maturities; **Dreimonatsrate** *f* FINANZ three-month rate; **Dreimonats-US-Schatzwechsel** *m pl* BÖRSE three-month US Treasury bills

Dreiseitigkeit *f* PERSON tripartism

dreistellig *adj* GESCHÄFT *Zahl* three-digit; ~e **Branchengliederung** *f* **einer Industrie** VW three-digit industry

dreistufig: ~e **Methode** *f* **der kleinsten Quadrate** VW three-stage least squares methods

dreiteilig: ~e **Organisation** *f* GESCHÄFT three-ply organisation *(jarg)*; ~es **Wertpapiergeschäft** *nt* BÖRSE reverse conversion

dringend 1. *adj* GESCHÄFT urgent; **2.** *adv* GESCHÄFT urgently; ◆ **jdn** ~ **bitten, etw zu tun** GESCHÄFT urge sb to do sth; ~ **brauchen** GESCHÄFT be in urgent need of; ~ **nötig haben** GESCHÄFT be in urgent need of

dringend: ~e **Angelegenheit** *f* GESCHÄFT matter of urgency; ~er **Kapitalbedarf** *nt* VW pressing financial needs

Dringlichkeit *f* GESCHÄFT priority; **Dringlichkeitsstufe** *f* VW precedence rating, priority level

Dritt- *in cpds* GESCHÄFT, RECHT, VERSICH three, third, third party; **Drittbegünstigte(r)** *mf* [decl. as adj] FINANZ, RECHT third-party beneficiary

dritte *adj* GESCHÄFT third; ~r **Frachtführer** *m* TRANSP third carrier; ~r **Lebensabschnitt** *m* VW third age; ~r **Markt** *m* BÖRSE, VW over-the-counter market *(AmE)* *(OTCM)*, Third Market *(BrE)*; ~ **Person** *f* PATENT third party; ~s **Quartal** *nt* GESCHÄFT third quarter *(3Q)*; ~r **Weg** *m* VW third way

Dritte: ~ **Welt** *f* GESCHÄFT *Entwicklungsländer* Third World; **Dritte-Welt-Land** *nt* VW Third World country

Dritte(r) *mf* [decl. as adj] GESCHÄFT third person, PATENT, RECHT, VERSICH third party

drittens *adv* GESCHÄFT thirdly

drittklassig *adj* GESCHÄFT third-rate, TRANSP third-class; ~e **Sache** *f* GESCHÄFT third-class matter *(AmE)*

Dritt-: **Drittland** *nt* VW third country; **Drittmarkt** *m* BÖRSE third market

drittrangig *adj* GESCHÄFT third-rate

Dritt-: **Drittschaden** *m* RECHT *Vertragsrecht* third-party damage; **Drittschadenhaftpflichtrisiko** *nt* VERSICH third-party risk; **Drittschuldner** *m* RECHT garnishee; **Drittschuldnerpfändung vornehmen** *phr* RECHT *Forderungspfändungsverfahren* garnish; **Drittvergleichsgrundsatz** *m* RECHT, STEUER arm's-length principle; **Drittverzug** *m* BANK, FINANZ cross default; **Drittwährung** *f* GESCHÄFT third currency, IMP/EXP third-party currency

Dr. jur. *abbr* (*Doktor der Rechte*) PERSON, RECHT, SOZIAL LLD (*Doctor of Laws*)

DRK *abbr* (*Deutsches Rotes Kreuz*) SOZIAL German Red Cross

Dr. med. *abbr* (*Doktor der Medizin*) SOZIAL MD (*Doctor of Medicine*)

Droge *f* GESCHÄFT drug; **Drogengeld** *nt* VW narcodollars; **Drogenhandel** *m* GESCHÄFT, IMP/EXP drug trafficking; **Drogenwirtschaft** *f* VW drug economy

Droheffekt *m* VW threat effect

drohend: ~e **Gefahr** *f* VERSICH imminent peril, imminent danger

drosseln *vt* VW curb, restrict

Drosselung: ~ **der Kreditgewährung** *f* BANK credit rationing

Dr. Phil. *abbr* (*Doktor der Philosophie*) PERSON, SOZIAL DPhil (*Doctor of Philosophy*), PhD (*Doctor of Philosophy*)

Druck *m* COMP compression, printing, GESCHÄFT pressure, MEDIEN print, printing, POL leverage, TRANSP compression, V&M letterpress, VW *Preisdruck, Kursdruck* downward pressure; ◆ **auf jdn** ~ **ausüben** GESCHÄFT bring pressure to bear on sb, put pressure on sb; **in** ~ **gehen** MEDIEN go to press, go to the printers; **unter** ~ **geraten** GESCHÄFT come under pressure; **unter** ~ **handeln** GESCHÄFT act under pressure; **unter** ~ **setzen** PERSON, VW pressurize, *Preise* squeeze

Druck: **Druckaggregat** *nt* GESCHÄFT printing unit; **Druckauflage** *f* MEDIEN print run; **Druckausübung** *f* RECHT *Vertragsrecht* oppression

Drückeberger *m* PERSON shirker *(infrml)*

drucken *vt* COMP, MEDIEN print

Drucken *nt* COMP printing; ~ **im Hintergrundmodus** COMP *Multitasking* background printing

drücken 1. *vt* COMP *Taste* press, IND *Schalter* activate, VW *Preis, Zinsen* drive down, force down; ◆ **den Kurs durch Leerverkäufe nach unten** ~ BÖRSE hammer the market; **2. sich** ~ *v refl* PERSON goldbrick *(infrml)* *(AmE)*, malinger, shirk *(infrml)*

Drucker *m* COMP *Gerät*, GESCHÄFT, MEDIEN *Person* printer; **Druckeranschluß** *m* COMP printer port

Druckerei *f* MEDIEN printing works

Drucker: **Druckerport** *m* *jarg* COMP printer port; **Druckerpresse** *f* V&M letterpress; **Druckerschnittstelle** *f* COMP printer port; **Druckerschrift** *f* COMP printer font; **Druckertreiber** *m* COMP printer driver

Druck: **Druckfahnen** *f pl* MEDIEN proof sheets, proofs; **Druckfehler** *m* COMP, GESCHÄFT typing error, typographical error *(typo)*, MEDIEN literal, literal error, typing error, typographical error *(typo)*, VERWALT typing error, typographical error *(typo)*, misprint; **Druckgerät** *f* GESCHÄFT printing unit; **Druckgeschwindigkeit** *f* COMP printing speed; **Druckknopf** *m* COMP printing push button; **Druckmaschine** *f* MEDIEN printing press; **Druckmedien** *nt pl* MEDIEN print media; **Druckpresse** *f* MEDIEN printing press; **Drucksache** *f* GESCHÄFT printed matter, KOMM third-class mail *(AmE)*, MEDIEN printed matter; **Druckspalte** *f* COMP, MEDIEN print column; **Druckvorschau** *f* COMP *Textverarbeitung* print preview; **Druckwalze** *f* COMP *Drucker* drum; **Druckzeile** *f* COMP print line

DRV *abbr* (*Deutscher Reisebüro-Verband*) FREI German association of travel agents, ≈ ABTA (*Association of British Travel Agents*)

DSG *abbr* (*Datensichtgerät*) COMP VDT (*AmE*) (*visual display terminal*), VDU (*BrE*) (*visual display unit*)

DStG *abbr* (*Deutsche Statistische Gesellschaft*) MATH German statistical association, ≈ ASA (*American Statistical Association*)

DTP *abbr* (*Desktop-Publishing*) COMP, MEDIEN DTP (*desktop publishing*)

Dtz. *abbr* (*Dutzend*) GESCHÄFT doz. (*dozen*)

Dtzd. *abbr* (*Dutzend*) GESCHÄFT doz. (*dozen*)

dual: ~er **Arbeitsmarkt** *m* VW dual labor market (*AmE*), dual labour market (*BrE*); ~es **Bankensystem** *nt* BANK dual banking (*AmE*); ~er **Föderalismus** *m* POL dual federalism; ~e **Volkswirtschaft** *f* VW dual economy; ~er **Wechselkurs** *m* VW dual exchange rate

Dualzahl *f* MATH binary number

dubios: ~es **Papier** *nt* FINANZ unsafe paper

Dukatenesel *m* *infrml* GESCHÄFT money-spinner (*infrml*)

Duldungsmuster *nt* MGMNT indulgency pattern

Dumping *nt* BÖRSE, GESCHÄFT dumping

Düngemittel *nt* UMWELT fertilizer

düngen *vt* UMWELT fertilize

Dünger *m* UMWELT fertilizer

dünn: ~ **besiedelt** *adj* VW sparsely populated; ~ **besiedeltes Gebiet** *nt* VW sparsely populated area

Duopol *nt* VW duopoly

Duplex *nt* COMP duplex, full duplex; **Duplexbetrieb** *m* COMP duplex operation; **Duplexsystem** *nt* COMP duplex computer

duplikatorisch *adj* GESCHÄFT duplicatory

duplizieren *vt* COMP duplicate

Du-Pont-Formel *f* FINANZ Du Pont formula

Durationsanalyse *f* FINANZ duration analysis

Durbin-Watson: **Durbin-Watson-Statistik** *f* MATH Durbin-Watson statistic (*DW statistic*)

durcharbeiten *vi* PERSON work through

Durchbruch *m* VERWALT, VW breakthrough

durchchecken *vt* GESCHÄFT *Dokument, Maschine* check thoroughly

durchdringen *vt* V&M penetrate

Durchfahrt *f* TRANSP passage

Durchfracht *f* GESCHÄFT through rate, TRANSP through freight; **Durchfrachtkonnossement** *nt* IMP/EXP, TRANSP through bill of lading

durchführbar *adj* GESCHÄFT feasible

Durchführbarkeit *f* GESCHÄFT feasibility, viability; **Durchführbarkeitsbericht** *m* COMP feasibility report; **Durchführbarkeitsuntersuchung** *f* GESCHÄFT feasibility study

durchführen *vt* GESCHÄFT carry out, transact, *Einigung* effect, *Untersuchung* hold, execute, *Aktienverkauf* conduct, MGMNT execute, *Konferenz, Tagung* hold, PATENT carry out, *Anmeldung* prosecute, RECHT execute

Durchführen *nt*: ~ **von Meinungsumfragen** V&M opinion polling

Durchführung *f* GESCHÄFT performance, transaction, MGMNT *einer Politik* execution, *einer Reorganisation* implementation, PATENT implementation, TRANSP carrying charge; ~ **eines Markttests** V&M test marketing; ~ **einer politischen Maßnahme** POL policy execution; **Durchführungsbeleg** *m* V&M voucher; **Durchführungsbestimmungen** *f pl* RECHT rules and regulations, implementing regulations; **Durchführungskosten** *pl*

von Verwaltungsvorschriften VERWALT administrative costs of regulation; **Durchführungsverordnung** *f* GESCHÄFT regulation, implementing ordinance; **Durchführungsverzögerung** *f* VW administration lag, implementation lag

Durchgang *m* GESCHÄFT *zwischen Ladentischen, Sitzreihen* aisle, IND run; **Durchgangsfahrpreis** *m* TRANSP through fare; **Durchgangsfrachtsatz** *m* IMP/EXP through rate; **Durchgangsgebühr** *f* TRANSP through charge; **Durchgangskonto** *nt* **zur Aufnahme des Gewinnvortrags** RECHNUNG appropriation account; **Durchgangskosten** *pl* IMP/EXP through charge; **Durchgangsladung** *f* TRANSP through shipment; **Durchgangstarif** *m* GESCHÄFT, TRANSP through rate; **Durchgangsverkehr** *m* V&M corridor traffic

durchgeben *vt* GESCHÄFT *Ankündigung, Ergebnis* broadcast

durchgehend *adj* GESCHÄFT continuous, round-the-clock; ~ **geöffnet** *adj* GESCHÄFT open all day; ~er **Zug** *m* TRANSP through train

durchgesetzt *adj* RECHT enforced

durchgestrichen *adj* GESCHÄFT expunged

durchgezogen: ~e **Linie** *f* MATH solid line

Durchhandeln *nt* BÖRSE round trip, round-trip trade

Durchkonnossement *nt* IMP/EXP, TRANSP through bill of lading

Durchlauf *m* FINANZ throughput, thruput (*AmE*), IND run; **Durchlaufaktie** *f* BÖRSE flow-through share; **Durchlaufdarlehen** *nt* FINANZ pass-through loan

durchlaufend: ~e **Einnahmen** *f pl* VW transitory income; ~e **Kredite** *m pl* BANK, FINANZ flow-through credits, loans in transit; ~e **Zahlungsmittel** *nt pl* RECHNUNG cash in transit

Durchlauf: **Durchlaufkredit** *m* FINANZ transmitted credit; **Durchlaufzeit** *f* IND time from receipt of order till dispatch

Durchluftfrachtbrief *m* IMP/EXP, TRANSP through air waybill (*TAWB*)

durchmachen *vt* GESCHÄFT undergo

durchpeitschen *vt* *infrml* GESCHÄFT *Projekt* steamroller through (*infrml*)

durchrechnen *vt* GESCHÄFT calculate

Durchreise *f* TRANSP passage; **Durchreisevisum** *nt* VERWALT transit visa

durchrutschen *vi* GESCHÄFT scrape through

durchsagen *vt* GESCHÄFT *Ergebnis* announce, broadcast

Durchsatz *m* COMP, FINANZ, IND throughput, thruput (*AmE*); **Durchsatzleistung** *f* IND throughput rate, thruput rate (*AmE*)

Durchschlag *m* KOMM carbon copy (*cc*), TRANSP puncturing; **Durchschlagpapier** *nt* GESCHÄFT manifold, KOMM carbon paper

Durchschnitt *m* GESCHÄFT, MATH, RECHNUNG average (*av.*); ~ **aller Sektoren** VW all-sector average; ♦ **über dem** ~ GESCHÄFT, VW above-average; **im** ~ GESCHÄFT at an average; **unter dem** ~ GESCHÄFT below-average; **den** ~ **ermitteln von** FINANZ *Kosten, Gewinn* average out, average; **den** ~ **nehmen** MATH take an average

durchschnittlich *adj* GESCHÄFT average, at an average, run-of-the-mill; ~er **Absatz** *m* MEDIEN average sold circulation; ~e **Arbeitswoche** *f* PERSON average working week (*BrE*), average workweek (*AmE*); ~e **Auslastung** *f* IND average utilization; ~e **Bindungsdauer** *f* FINANZ duration; ~e **Einzahlung** *f*

FINANZ average deposit; ~e **Fixkosten** *pl* RECHNUNG average fixed cost; ~e **Gesamtkosten** *pl* RECHNUNG average total cost; ~es **Guthaben** *nt* BANK average balance; ~e **Konsumquote** *f* VW average propensity to consume (*APC*); ~e **Kosten** *pl* RECHNUNG, VERWALT average costs; ~e **Laufzeit** *f* BÖRSE average maturity; ~er **LIBOR-Satz** *m* BANK average interest rate; ~e **Liegezeit** *f* TRANSP average laytime; ~er **Preisaufschlag** *f* GESCHÄFT average mark-up; ~e **Schadenkosten** *pl* VERSICH average cost of claims; ~e **Schadenshöhe** *f* VERSICH average size of loss; ~e **Sparneigung** *f* VW average propensity to save (*APS*); ~er **Steuersatz** *m* STEUER average tax rate; ~e **Stückkosten** *pl* RECHNUNG average unit cost; ~er **Stundenlohn** *m* PERSON average hourly earnings; ~er **Zinssatz** *m* BANK average interest rate; ♦ ~ **befragen** FINANZ average out

Durchschnitt: **Durchschnittsbesteuerung** *f* FINANZ, STEUER *Verteilung von Einkommen auf mehrere Jahre* income averaging; **Durchschnittsbetrag** *m* GESCHÄFT average amount; **Durchschnittsbildung** *f* BÖRSE, GESCHÄFT, STEUER averaging; **Durchschnittsdauer** *f* **der Außenstände** RECHNUNG average collection period; **Durchschnittseinkommen** *nt* PERSON average income, RECHNUNG average pay; **Durchschnittsentgelt** *nt* PERSON average pay, RECHNUNG average compensation, average pay; **Durchschnittserlös** *m* FINANZ, RECHNUNG average revenue (*AR*); **Durchschnittsertrag** *m* FINANZ, RECHNUNG average revenue (*AR*), average yield; **Durchschnittsfirma** *f* VW representative firm; **Durchschnittskosten** *pl* RECHNUNG average costs, mean cost, VERWALT, VW average costs; **Durchschnittskosten** *pl* **eines Schadens** VERSICH average cost of claims; **Durchschnittskurs** *m* BÖRSE average, average market price, average rate, FINANZ average market price, GESCHÄFT average market price, RECHNUNG average rate; **Durchschnittsleser, in** *m,f* MEDIEN, V&M average reader; **Durchschnitts-LIBOR** *m* BANK average LIBOR; **Durchschnittslohn** *m* PERSON average wage; **Durchschnittsmarktpreis** *m* FINANZ average market price; **Durchschnittsmethode** *f* BANK averaging formula, FINANZ averaging; **Durchschnittsprämie** *f* VERSICH average premium, flat rate; **Durchschnittsprämiensystem** *nt* VERSICH average premium system; **Durchschnittsqualität** *f* GESCHÄFT, IMP/EXP fair average quality (*f.a.q.*); **Durchschnittsrendite** *f* BÖRSE mean return, FINANZ, RECHNUNG average yield; **Durchschnittssatz** *m* BANK blended rate, BÖRSE, RECHNUNG average rate; **Durchschnittsschaden** *m* VERSICH average claim, average size of loss; **Durchschnittssteuersatz** *m* STEUER average tax rate; **Durchschnitts-Stundenverdienst** *m* PERSON average hourly earnings; **Durchschnittsverdienst** *m* PERSON average earning; **Durchschnittsverzinsung** *f* BANK average interest rate; **Durchschnittswerte** *m pl* BÖRSE market averages

Durchschrift *f* GESCHÄFT carbon copy

Durchschuß *m* MEDIEN *Textverarbeitung* line space

durchsehen *vt* GESCHÄFT, MGMNT review

durchsetzbar *adj* RECHT enforceable

durchsetzen 1. *vt* BÖRSE put through, GESCHÄFT force, *Anspruch* enforce; **2. sich ~** *v refl* GESCHÄFT stand one's ground; ♦ **sich ~ gegen** GESCHÄFT prevail against

Durchsetzung *f* RECHT enforcement; ~ **einer Strategie** GESCHÄFT, MGMNT strategy implementation; **Durchsetzungsvermögen** *nt* PERSON assertiveness

Durchsicht *f* GESCHÄFT revision, MGMNT review

durchsickern *vi* GESCHÄFT leak out, MEDIEN, POL leak, leak out

Durchsickern *nt* MEDIEN, POL leakage

Durchstehvermögen *nt* MGMNT staying power

durchstellen *vt* KOMM put through

durchstreichen *vt* GESCHÄFT delete, expunge

durchsuchen *vt* COMP browse, GESCHÄFT search

Durchsuchen *nt* COMP *Dateien, Datenbank* browsing

Durchsuchung *f* GESCHÄFT search

Durchwahl *f* KOMM direct dialing (*AmE*), direct dialling (*BrE*)

durchziehen *vt infrml* GESCHÄFT *Projekt* follow through, *Deal* pull (*infrml*)

Dürre *f* UMWELT drought

Duty-Free-Laden *m* FREI, IMP/EXP, STEUER duty-free shop (*BrE*), tax-free shop (*AmE*)

Duty-Free-Shop *m* FREI, IMP/EXP, STEUER duty-free shop (*BrE*), tax-free shop (*AmE*)

Dutzend *nt* (*Dtz., Dtzd.*) GESCHÄFT dozen (*doz.*)

DV *abbr* (*Datenverarbeitung*) COMP, VERWALT DP (*data processing*)

DWA *abbr* (*Deutscher Werbeausschuß*) V&M ≈ ASA (*Advertising Standards Authority*)

Dynamik *f* GESCHÄFT dynamism

dynamisch *adj* GESCHÄFT dynamic; ~es **Absichern** *nt* FINANZ dynamic hedging; ~e **Absicherung** *f* FINANZ dynamic hedging; ~e **Analyse** *f* VW dynamic analysis; ~e **Bewertung** *f* GESCHÄFT dynamic evaluation; ~er **Datenaustausch** *m* COMP dynamic data exchange (*DDE*); ~e **Lebensversicherung** *f* VERSICH indexed life insurance; ~es **Managementmodell** *nt* MGMNT dynamic management model; ~e **Planung** *f* GESCHÄFT dynamic programming; ~e **Positionierung** *f* GESCHÄFT, V&M dynamic positioning (*DP*); ~es **Programmieren** *nt* COMP, MATH dynamic programming; ~e **Programmierung** *f* COMP, MATH dynamic programming; ~er **Prozeß** *m* VW continuous process; ~er **Speicher** *m* (*DRAM*) COMP dynamic random access memory (*DRAM*); ~ **unvereinbare Politik** *f* POL dynamically inconsistent policy; ~e **Veralterung** *f* V&M dynamic obsolescence

DZ *abbr* (*Dokumente gegen Zahlung*) GESCHÄFT DAP (*documents against payment*)

E

E *abbr* IND (*Energie*) energy, TRANSP (*Europastraße*) Euro-route

E/A *abbr* (*Eingabe-Ausgabe*) COMP I/O (*input/output*)

EAG *abbr* (*Europäische Atomgemeinschaft*) IND EURATOM (*European Atomic Energy Community*), EAEC (*European Atomic Energy Community*)

EAGFL *abbr* (*Europäischer Ausrichtungs- und Garantiefonds*) BANK, VW EAGGF (*European Agricultural Guidance and Guarantee Fund*)

EAN *abbr* (*Europäische Artikelnummer*) COMP, V&M EAN (*European Article Number*)

East: ~ **European Trade Council** *m* GESCHÄFT East European Trade Council

ebd. *abbr* (*ebenda*) GESCHÄFT ibid. (*ibidem*)

ebenda *adv* (*ebd.*) GESCHÄFT ibidem (*ibid.*)

Ebene *f* COMP level

EBWE *abbr* (*Europäische Bank für Wiederaufbau und Entwicklung*) VW EBRD (*European Bank for Reconstruction and Development*)

EC *abbr* (*Eurocheque*) FINANZ eurocheque

ECDC *abbr* (*Wirtschaftliche Zusammenarbeit zwischen den Entwicklungsländern*) VW ECDC (*economic co-operation among developing countries*)

ECE *abbr* (*Europäische Wirtschaftskommission*) VW ECE (*Economic Commission for Europe*)

echt *adj* COMP actual; **~e Adresse** *f* COMP *Programme* absolute address, actual address; **~es Angebotsmonopol** *nt* VW absolute monopoly, pure monopoly; **~er Befehl** *m* COMP *Programmiersprachen* actual instruction; **~e Berufsqualifikation** *f* PERSON genuine occupational qualification (*BrE*) (*GOQ*); **~e Berufsqualifizierung** *f* PERSON genuine occupational qualification (*BrE*) (*GOQ*); **~er Ermessensspielraum** *m* VERWALT pure discretion

Echt/365 *jarg* BANK exact interest

echt: **~es Geld** *nt* BANK, VW good money; **~es Konnossement** *nt* IMP/EXP clean bill of lading; **~e Kunden** *m pl* V&M live customers

Echtheitsbescheinigung *f* BÖRSE authentication

Echtzeit *f* COMP, RECHNUNG, VW real time

Eck- *in cpds* FINANZ, GESCHÄFT, PERSON basic

eckig: **~e Klammern** *f pl* COMP, MEDIEN *Typographie* square brackets

Eck-: **Ecklohn** *m* PERSON base pay rate, VW basic pay (*BrE*); **Ecklohntarif** *m* PERSON base pay rate, basic rate; **Ecklösung** *f* VW corner solution; **Eckpunkt** *m* **einer Matrix** GESCHÄFT corner; **Ecktermin** *m* GESCHÄFT basic time limit; **Eckwertmethode** *f* FINANZ benchmark method; **Eckzins** *m* FINANZ base lending rate, base rate (*BrE*); **Eckzins** *m* **der Londoner Clearing-Banken für Ausleihungen** FINANZ base lending rate, base rate (*BrE*)

ECP *abbr* (*Euro-Commercial Paper*) FINANZ ECP (*euro commercial paper*)

ECU *abbr* (*Europäische Währungseinheit*) FINANZ, VW ECU (*European Currency Unit*); **ECU-Leitkurs** *m* FINANZ ECU central rate

Edelmetall *nt* GESCHÄFT precious metal; **Edelmetallbarren** *m* BANK bullion; **Edelmetallbestand** *m* GESCHÄFT bullion stock; **Edelmetallgewicht** *nt* GESCHÄFT troy weight; **Edelmetallkonto** *nt* BANK precious metal account; **Edelmetallvorräte** *m pl* GESCHÄFT stock of bullion

Edelstahl *m* IND stainless steel

Edelsteine *m pl* GESCHÄFT, IND precious stones

Edgeworth-Box *f* VW *bilateraler Tausch* Edgeworth Box

EDI *abbr* (*elektronischer Datenaustausch*) COMP, KOMM EDI (*electronic data interchange*)

editieren *vt* COMP *Textverarbeitung* edit

Editiermodus *m* COMP *Textverarbeitung* edit mode

Edit-Menu *nt* COMP edit menu

Editor *m* COMP *Programm* line editor, *Textverarbeitung* editor

EDV *abbr* (*elektronische Datenverarbeitung*) COMP EDP (*electronic data processing*), IT (*information technology*); **EDV-Abteilung** *f* COMP computer department, IT department; **EDV-Berater, in** *m,f* COMP computer consultant; **EDV-Händler, in** *m,f* COMP computer vendor; **EDV-Strategie** *f* COMP computer strategy, IT strategy; **EDV-System** *nt* COMP computer system, IT system

EEA *abbr* (*Einheitliche Europäische Akte*) RECHT SEA (*Single European Act*)

EEB *abbr* (*Europäisches Umweltbüro*) UMWELT EEB (*European Environmental Bureau*)

EEF *abbr* (*Europäischer Entwicklungsfonds*) VW EDF (*European Development Fund*)

Effekten *pl* BÖRSE stock exchange securities, stocks and bonds, FINANZ stocks and bonds; **Effektenabrechnung** *f* FINANZ contract note; **Effektenabteilung** *f* FINANZ investment department; **Effektenarbitrage** *f* BÖRSE arbitrage in securities (*BrE*), stock arbitrage, securities arbitrage; **Effektenberatungstätigkeit** *f* BÖRSE investment consultancy, investment services; **Effektenbestand** *m* FINANZ security holding; **Effektenbestandsguthaben** *nt* BÖRSE, FINANZ security balance; **Effektenbörse** *f* BÖRSE, FINANZ, VW bourse, stock exchange (*stk exch*); **Effektenbroker, in** *m,f* BÖRSE agency broker; **Effektendarlehen** *nt* BÖRSE securities loan; **Effektendifferenzgeschäft** *nt* BÖRSE margin trading; **Effektenemission** *f* **auf fremde Rechnung** BANK, BÖRSE agency selling (*AmE*); **Effektenemissionsgeschäft** *nt* BÖRSE, FINANZ underwriting business; **Effektenfinanzierung** *f* FINANZ financing through securities; **Effektenhandel** *m* BÖRSE securities trade, FINANZ stock trading; **Effektenhandel** *m* **mit Contangos** BÖRSE jobbing in contangos (*BrE*); **Effekteninvestmentabteilung** *f* FINANZ investment department; **Effektenkaufabrechnung** *f* BÖRSE bought note; **Effektenkauf** *m* **mit Einschuß** BÖRSE buying on margin; **Effektenkredit** *m* FINANZ security loan; **Effektenkreditkonto** *nt* BÖRSE margin account; **Effektenleihe** *f* BÖRSE stock borrowing; **Effektenlombard** *m* BÖRSE advance on securities; **Effektenmakler, in** *m,f* BÖRSE, FINANZ stockbroker; **Effektennotierung** *f* BÖRSE stock market prices;

Effektenportefeuille *nt* BANK, BÖRSE, FINANZ investment portfolio; **Effektensammeldepot** *nt* FINANZ collective securities deposit; **Effektenverkaufsabrechnung** *f* BÖRSE sold note; **Effektenverwalter, in** *m,f* BÖRSE portfolio management theory; **Effektenverwaltung** *f* FINANZ, MGMNT portfolio management

Effektiv- *in cpds* GESCHÄFT actual, effective

effektiv 1. *adj* GESCHÄFT actual, effective; **2.** *adv* GESCHÄFT effectively; ◆ ~ **geschlossen** TRANSP effectively closed

effektiv: ~e **Bestandsaufnahme** *f* RECHNUNG physical inventory; ~er **Diskontsatz** *m* GESCHÄFT market rate of discount; ~e **Hilfsrate** *f* vw effective rate of assistance (*ERA*); ~er **Jahreszins** *m* FINANZ annual percentage rate (*APR*), annualized percentage rate (*APR*); ~e **Kreditgebühr** *f* BANK effective loan charges; ~es **Management** *nt* MGMNT effective management; ~e **Nachfrage** *f* vw effective demand, effectual demand; ~e **Pferdestärke** *f* IND effective horsepower (*ehp*), TRANSP brake horsepower (*bhp*); ~e **Protektionsrate** *f* vw effective rate of protection; ~e **Rendite** *f* BANK, FINANZ real rate of return (*RRR*), true rate of return; ~er **Wechselkurs** *m* vw effective exchange rate; ~er **Wertpapierkurs** *m* BÖRSE actual quotation; ~er **Wettbewerb** *m* vw workable competition; ~er **Zins** *m* BANK effective interest rate, RECHNUNG effective rate; ~er **Zahlungsausgang** *m* RECHNUNG actual cash disbursement; ~er **Zinssatz** *m* vw effective rate of interest

Effektiv-: **Effektivfinanzierungsrate** *f* BÖRSE effective funding rate; **Effektivgeschäft** *nt* BÖRSE spot market transaction

Effektivität *f* GESCHÄFT effectiveness; ~ **der Organisationsstruktur** MGMNT organizational effectiveness

Effektiv-: **Effektivklausel** *f* FINANZ currency clause; **Effektivkontrolle** *f* FINANZ effective control; **Effektivleistung** *f* TRANSP brake horsepower (*bhp*); **Effektivlohn** *m* PERSON *Arbeitsentgelt*, RECHNUNG actual earnings, actual wage; **Effektivrendite** *f* BÖRSE dividend yield; **Effektivverdienst** *m* PERSON, RECHNUNG actual earnings; **Effektivverzinsung** *f* BANK true rate of return, effective rate, effective yield, redemption yield, BÖRSE market rate, redemption yield, GESCHÄFT redemption yield; **Effektivware** *f* BÖRSE spot commodity, *Terminbörse* physical commodity; **Effektivzins** *m* BANK true rate of return, effective rate, effective yield, effective interest rate, BÖRSE market rate

effizient *adj* GESCHÄFT efficient; ~e **Allokation** *f* vw efficient allocation; ~e **Arbeitsmobilität** *f* vw efficient job mobility; ~es **Portefeuille** *nt* BÖRSE efficient portfolio; ~e **Schätzfunktion** *f* vw *Statistik* efficient estimator

Effizienz *f* GESCHÄFT efficiency

EFRE *abbr* (*Europäischer Fonds für regionale Entwicklung*) vw ERDF (*European Regional Development Fund*)

EFTA *abbr* (*Europäische Freihandelszone*) vw EFTA (*European Free Trade Association*)

EFTPOS *abbr* (*elektronische Geldüberweisung am Verkaufsort*) BANK, COMP, V&M EFTPOS (*electronic funds transfer at point of sale*)

EFWZ *abbr* (*Europäischer Fonds für währungspolitische Zusammenarbeit*) BANK, vw EMCF (*European Monetary Cooperation Fund*)

EG *abbr* (*Europäische Gemeinschaft*) POL EC (*European Community*); **EG-Kommission** *f obs* vw Commission of the European Community (*CEC*)

EGA *abbr* (*verbesserter Grafikadapter*) COMP EGA (*enhanced graphics adapter*)

Egalitarismus *m* POL egalitarianism

EGB *abbr* (*Europäischer Gewerkschaftsbund*) PERSON ETUC (*European Trade Union Confederation*)

EG: **EG-Binnenmarkt** *m* vw European Single Market; **EG-Durchfuhr** *f* IMP/EXP, TRANSP Community transit (*CT*); **EG-Haushalt** *m* vw European Community Budget; **EG-Importe** *m pl* IMP/EXP Community imports; **EG-Kommission** *f obs* vw Commission of the European Community (*obs*) (*CEC*); **EG-Transit** *m* IMP/EXP, TRANSP Community transit (*CT*); **EG-Transitformular** *nt* TRANSP EC transit form; **EG-Waren** *f pl* IMP/EXP Community goods

EGKS *abbr* (*Europäische Gemeinschaft für Kohle und Stahl*) vw ECSC (*European Caol and Steel Community*)

Ehefrau: **und** ~ *phr* RECHT *alte Rechtsdokumente* et ux.

Ehegattenabzug *m* STEUER marriage deduction

Ehegattenfreibetrag *m* STEUER marriage allowance, married couples' allowance (*BrE*)

ehelich: ~e **Gemeinschaft** *f* RECHT *Gemeinschaftsvertrag* consortium

ehemalig *adj* GESCHÄFT former, quondam, ex-; ~er **Käufer** *m* V&M, ~e **Käuferin** *f* V&M former buyer; ~er **Mitarbeiter** *m*, ~e **Mitarbeiterin** *f* PERSON *Arbeit* ex-employee

eher: **was auch immer** ~ **eintritt** *phr* GESCHÄFT whichever is sooner

ehern: ~es **Lohngesetz** *nt* vw iron law of wages

Ehevertrag *m* RECHT prenuptial agreement, prenuptial contract

EHR *abbr* (*Europäisches Handelsregister*) GESCHÄFT ERC (*European Registry of Commerce*)

Ehre *f* GESCHÄFT kudos; **Ehrenakzept** *nt* GESCHÄFT acceptance for honor (*AmE*), acceptance for honour (*BrE*), acceptance supra protest

ehrenamtlich 1. *adj* PERSON honorary, lay; **2.** *adv* PERSON in an honorary capacity

ehrenamtlich: ~er **Präsident** *m*, ~e **Präsidentin** *f* PERSON honorary president; ~e **Tätigkeit** *f* PERSON *Arbeit* voluntary work; ~er **Vertreter** *m*, ~e **Vertreterin** *f* PERSON *Gewerkschaft* lay official

Ehre: **Ehrenannahme** *f* GESCHÄFT acceptance for honor (*AmE*), acceptance for honour (*BrE*), acceptance supra protest; **Ehrenannahme** *f* **eines Wechsels** RECHT act of honor (*AmE*), act of honour (*BrE*); **Ehrenkodex** *m* GESCHÄFT code of ethics; **Ehrenmitgliedschaft** *f* PERSON honorary membership; **Ehrenpräsident, in** *m,f* PERSON honorary president; **Ehrenvorsitzende(r)** *mf* [decl. as adj] PERSON honorary chairman; **Ehrenvorsitzende(r)** *mf* [decl. as adj] **des Verwaltungsrats** MGMNT honorary chairman of the board of directors; **Ehrenvorstand** *m* **der Geschäftsleitung** MGMNT honorary chairman of the board of directors; **Sehr Ehrenwerte(r)** *adj* POL *Titel eines Geheimrats* Right Honourable (*BrE*) (*Rt Hon*); **Ehrenwort** *nt* RECHT word of honour

Ehrgeiz *m* GESCHÄFT, MGMNT ambition

ehrgeizig adj GESCHÄFT, MGMNT ambitious

Ehrgeizling m infrml GESCHÄFT, MGMNT pusher (infrml), high flier

ehrlich adj GESCHÄFT Geschäft above board; **~es Geschäftsgebaren** nt GESCHÄFT clean hands; **~er Makler** m POL honest broker; **~er Unterhändler** m POL honest broker

Ehrverletzung f RECHT Verleumdung, üble Nachrede defamation

EIB abbr (Europäische Investitionsbank) BANK EIB (European Investment Bank)

EIC abbr (Euro Info Center) GESCHÄFT EIC (Euro Info Centre)

Eichmaß nt GESCHÄFT gauge

Eichung f GESCHÄFT, TRANSP calibration

Eid m RECHT oath; ♦ **unter ~** RECHT Aussage under oath; **unter ~ aussagen** RECHT vor Gericht give evidence on oath, give evidence under oath

eidesstattlich: **eine ~e Erklärung abgeben, daß** phr RECHT swear an affidavit that; **~e Versicherung** f RECHT ohne die Ausübung des Grundpfandrechts no-lien affidavit

Eid: **Eidgenossenschaft** f Sch POL confederation

eidlich: **~ erklären** vt RECHT declare on oath; **~e Versicherung** f RECHT assertory oath

Eigen- in cpds GESCHÄFT self-, own, personal

eigen adj GESCHÄFT own; ♦ **aus ~em Anbau** GESCHÄFT home-grown; **aus ~em Antrieb** MGMNT, PERSON self-motivating; **nach ~em Eingeständnis** GESCHÄFT by one's own admission; **nach ~em Ermessen** GESCHÄFT in one's own estimation; **auf ~e Gefahr** GESCHÄFT at one's own peril, VERSICH at owner's risk; **auf ~e Kosten** GESCHÄFT at one's own expense; **auf ~e Rechnung** GESCHÄFT on one's own account, at one's own expense; **auf ~e Rechnung handeln** BÖRSE trade for one's account; **auf ~e Rechnung kaufen** BÖRSE position; **in ~em Recht** GESCHÄFT in its own right; **auf ~es Risiko** GESCHÄFT at owner's risk; **~e Verluste reduzieren** FINANZ cut one's losses

eigen: **~e Aktien** f pl RECHNUNG own shares (BrE), treasury stock (AmE); **~e Akzepte** nt pl RECHNUNG acceptances outstanding; **~e Finanzierung** f FINANZ, RECHNUNG internal funding; **~er Luftfrachtbrief** m IMP/EXP, TRANSP house air waybill (HAWB); **~e Marke** f V&M own label

Eigen-: **Eigenbedarf** m RECHNUNG personal requirements; **Eigenbedarfsmarkt** m V&M captive market; **Eigenbetreiber, in** m,f TRANSP own account operator; **Eigenbetrieb** m GESCHÄFT owner-operator; **Eigenbeurteilung** f PERSON Arbeit self-appraisal; **Eigenentwicklung** f VW me-too-product

eigenerwirtschaftet adj FINANZ, RECHNUNG self-generated; **~e Mittel** nt pl FINANZ, RECHNUNG internally generated funds

Eigen-: **Eigenfinanzierung** f FINANZ autofinancing, self-financing, equity financing, RECHNUNG self-financing; **Eigenfinanzierungsquote** f BÖRSE, FINANZ self-financing ratio; **Eigen- und Fremdkapital** nt RECHT equity and debt capital

eigengenutzt: **~e landwirtschaftliche Fläche** f GRUND owner-occupied farmland

Eigen-: **Eigengewicht** nt TRANSP unladen weight, tare weight; **Eigengewichtsfracht** f GESCHÄFT deadweight cargo; **Eigenhandel** m VW own account trading

eigenhändig adj KOMM to addressee only

Eigen-: **Eigenhändler, in** m,f in Aktien BÖRSE stockjobber (obs) (BrE)

Eigenheim nt GRUND one's own home; **auf dem ~ gesichertes Hypothekendarlehen** nt BANK home mortgage loan; **Eigenheimbesitz** m GRUND home ownership; **Eigenheimbesitzer, in** m,f GRUND, STEUER owner-occupier; **Eigenheimerwerbsdarlehen** nt BANK home purchase loan; **Eigenheimhypothek** f BANK home mortgage; **Eigenheiminvestitionen** f pl GRUND home improvement

Eigenkapital nt BÖRSE equity ownership, stockholders' equity, FINANZ equity capital, GESCHÄFT personal capital, RECHNUNG capital and reserves, equity, net worth, stockholders' equity, VW equity, net total assets, net worth; **an das ~ gebundene Hypothek** f FINANZ equity-linked mortgage; **~ je Aktie** FINANZ net assets per share; **~ minus Firmenwert** BÖRSE tangible net worth; **Eigenkapitalausstattung** f FINANZ equity position; **Eigenkapitalbasis** f FINANZ equity capital base; **Eigenkapitalbewertung** f RECHNUNG net worth assessment; **Eigenkapitaldecke** f FINANZ equity position; **Eigenkapitalentwicklung** f RECHNUNG movements on shareholders' equity

eigenkapitalgebunden: **~e Hypothek** f FINANZ equity-linked mortgage

Eigenkapital: **Eigenkapitalhypothek** f FINANZ equity-linked mortgage; **Eigenkapitalmethode** f RECHNUNG equity accounting; **Eigenkapitalquote** f BANK capital ratio, RECHNUNG capital-to-asset ratio; **Eigenkapitalrendite** f BÖRSE, FINANZ return on equity (ROE), RECHNUNG return on equity (ROE), return on net assets, return on net assets employed, VW return on equity (ROE), net income to net worth ratio; **Eigenkapitalrentabilität** f BÖRSE return on equity (ROE), (EKR) equity return, FINANZ, RECHNUNG, VW return on equity (ROE); **Eigenkapitalwert** m BANK equity value

Eigen-: **Eigenleistung** f FINANZ borrower's own funding

eigenmächtig adj GESCHÄFT arbitrary; **~e Abwesenheit** f PERSON absence without leave

Eigen-: **Eigenmarke** f V&M own brand, store brand; **Eigenmittel** nt pl FINANZ own funds, self-generated funds, RECHNUNG capital and reserves, self-generated funds, VW capital resources; **Eigennutzung** f GRUND owner occupation; **Eigenpreise** m pl VW eigenprices; **aus Eigenproduktion** phr GESCHÄFT home-made, Obst und Gemüse home-grown

Eigenschaft f GESCHÄFT attribute, PATENT feature; **Eigenschaften** f pl einer Marke V&M brand properties; **Eigenschaftskontrolle** f durch Stichproben RECHNUNG attribute sampling

Eigentum nt GESCHÄFT ownership, GRUND Liegenschaft property; ♦ **in ~ investieren** GRUND invest in property; **das ~ einer Sache übertragen** GRUND transfer ownership of sth

Eigentümer, in m,f GESCHÄFT owner, proprietor; **Eigentümer-Unternehmer** m MGMNT owner-manager; **Eigentümerverband** m GRUND homeowners' association

Eigentum: **Eigentumsbescheinigung** f GRUND certificate of ownership; **Eigentumsbildung** f FINANZ acquisition of assets; **Eigentumsdelikt** nt RECHT criminal damage, offence against property (BrE);

Eigentumsfeststellungsverfahren *nt* GRUND, RECHT *Grundbesitz* quiet title suit; **Eigentumsgrenze** *f* GRUND property line; **Eigentumsnachweis** *m* BÖRSE proof of ownership, GRUND certificate of ownership, *Grundbuchauszug* certificate of title, RECHT proof of title, *Besitz* evidence of title; **Eigentumsrecht** *nt* GRUND marketable title, merchantable title, vw right of ownership; **Eigentumsrechte** *nt pl* BÖRSE proprietary rights, GRUND property rights; **Eigentumsrecht an den Waren** RECHT entitlement to the goods; **Eigentumsübertragung** *f* GRUND bargain and sale, vw alienation; **Eigentumsübertragungsurkunde** *f* **der Unterzeichner** GESCHÄFT assurance of subscribers; **Eigentumsübertragung** *f* **der Unterzeichner der Urkunde** GESCHÄFT assurance of subscribers; **Eigentumsurkunde** *f* BÖRSE proof of ownership, GESCHÄFT certificate of ownership, GRUND certificate of ownership, RECHT document of title, title deed; **Eigentumsvermutung** *f* GESCHÄFT presumption of ownership; **Eigentumsvorbehalt** *m* RECHT *Vertragsrecht* conditional sale, reservation of title, V&M conditional sale; **Eigentumszeichen** *nt* PATENT mark

Eigen-: **Eigenverbrauch** *m* GESCHÄFT private consumption; **Eigenwechsel** *m* BANK, FINANZ promissory note (*P/N, PN*); **Eigenwirtschaftlichkeit** *f* vw economic viability; **Eigenzinssatz** *m* vw own rate of interest

Eigeständis *nt* GESCHÄFT acknowledgement

Eigner *m* TRANSP owner; **vom ~ eingesetzter Schiffsführer** TRANSP managing owner

Eignung *f* GESCHÄFT qualification, PERSON *Arbeitsmarkt* aptitude, SOZIAL qualification; **Eignungsprüfung** *f* IND performance testing, PERSON, V&M aptitude test, occupational test; **Eignungsregeln** *f pl* FINANZ suitability rules; **Eignungstest** *m* PERSON, V&M *Arbeitsmarkt* aptitude test

Eil- *in cpds* GESCHÄFT, KOMM, TRANSP express, urgent; **Eilauftrag** *m* GESCHÄFT rush job, express order, rush order, urgent order, vw rush order; **Eilbestellung** *f* GESCHÄFT urgent order

eilen *vi* GESCHÄFT rush

Eil-: **Eilfracht** *f* TRANSP express freight (*BrE*), fast freight (*AmE*); **Eilgeld** *nt* KOMM, TRANSP dispatch money; **Eilpost** *f* KOMM express delivery, priority mail (*AmE*); **Eilzustellung** *f* **auf dem Landweg** KOMM accelerated surface post; **Eilzustellungsdienst** *m* GESCHÄFT express mail service, KOMM special delivery

einarbeiten: sich ~ *v refl* PERSON learn the ropes; ♦ **sich in etw ~** GESCHÄFT acquaint oneself with sth

Einarbeitung *f* GESCHÄFT induction, training

einbauen *vt* GESCHÄFT build in, install, *Möbel* fit, MEDIEN incorporate, insert

einbehalten 1. *adj* FINANZ, GESCHÄFT, GRUND, RECHT, STEUER retained, undistributed, withheld; **2.** *vt* BÖRSE retain, withhold, GESCHÄFT plough back (*BrE*), plow back (*AmE*), STEUER retain

einbehalten: **~e Garantiesumme** *f* GESCHÄFT, GRUND retention money; **~er Gewinn** *m* RECHNUNG undistributed income, retained earnings, retained profits, accumulated profits; **~e Gewinne** *m pl* FINANZ retained profits, vw reinvested earnings; **~es Kapital** *nt* FINANZ undistributable capital; **~e Kapitalertragssteuer** *f* STEUER withholding tax; **~e Steuern** *f pl* RECHNUNG taxes withheld; **~er Teil** *m* **der Vertragssumme** GRUND holdback

Einbehaltung *f* BÖRSE retention, withholding, GRUND holdback, STEUER retention; **Einbehaltungserfordernis** *f* STEUER retention requirement; **Einbehaltungszeitraum** *m* BÖRSE retention period

einberufen *vt* MGMNT *Sitzung* convene

Einberufer, in *m,f* GESCHÄFT, PERSON convenor

Einberufung *f* GESCHÄFT *einer Versammlung* calling, POL *Parlament* summoning

einbetten *vt* COMP embed

Einbettkabine *f* TRANSP single-berth cabin

einbeziehen *vt* GESCHÄFT include

Einbeziehung *f* GESCHÄFT inclusion, integration; **~ von Drittländern** vw third-country cooperation

Einbezug: unter ~ aller Faktoren *phr* GESCHÄFT taking all factors into account

Einbootung *f* TRANSP *Personen* embarkation

einbringen *vt* FINANZ yield, GESCHÄFT *Gewinn, Bestellungen* bring in, MGMNT *Vorschlag* submit, put forward, POL *Parlamentsantrag* introduce, RECHT *Gesetz* bring in, vw earn, *Kapital* contribute

einbringend: ~e Gesellschaft *f* GESCHÄFT *Fusion* vendor company

Einbruch *m* BÖRSE slump, GESCHÄFT setback, RECHT burglary, vw slump; **Einbruchdiebstahl** *m* RECHT burglary; **Einbruch- und Diebstahlversicherung** *f* VERSICH interior robbery policy

Einbuße: ~ erleiden *phr* GESCHÄFT suffer a loss

einchecken: sich ~ *v refl* FREI, TRANSP book in, *Flughafen* check in

eindämmen *vt* GESCHÄFT stem, *Nachfrage, Inflation* contain

Eindämmung *f* vw containment

eindecken: sich ~ *v refl* BÖRSE buy in; ♦ **sich ~ mit** GESCHÄFT buy in

Eindecker *m* TRANSP *Flugzeug* single-deck plane, *Schiff* single-deck ship

eindeutig: ~e Neutralität *f* POL positive neutrality

eindringen *vi*: **~ in** [+acc] GESCHÄFT *Markt* penetrate

Eindruck *m* GESCHÄFT impression; ♦ **einen ~ machen** GESCHÄFT make an impression

Einf. *abbr* (*Einfuhr*) IMP/EXP, vw imp. (*importation*)

einfach *adj* GESCHÄFT simple, POL rank-and-file; **~es Akkreditiv** *nt* FINANZ clean credit (*C/C*); **~e Arbeit** *f* GESCHÄFT, IND simple task; **~er Aufschub** *m* FINANZ simple deferment; **~er Bruch** *m* MATH simple fraction; **~e Buchführung** *f* RECHNUNG single-entry bookkeeping; **~e Devisenabfrage** *f* FINANZ direct arbitrage; **~e Dichte** *f* COMP *Diskette* single density (*SD*); **~er Ertrag** *m* BÖRSE simple yield; **~e Fahrkarte** *f* TRANSP one-way fare, single fare (*BrE*), single ticket; **~er Fahrpreis** *m* TRANSP one-way fare, single fare (*BrE*); **~e Fahrt** *f* TRANSP one-way fare, single fare (*BrE*); **~ faktorales Austauschverhältnis** *nt* vw single factorial terms of trade; **~e Genauigkeit** *f* COMP *Gleitkommazahlen* single precision; **~e lineare Regression** *f* RECHNUNG simple linear regression; **~-logarithmischer Maßstab** *m* MATH ratio scale; **~e Mehrheit** *f* POL qualified majority, simple majority; **~e Mitglieder** *nt pl* PERSON rank-and-file; **~e Option** *f* BÖRSE single option; **~e Pacht** *f* GRUND one-way lease; **~e Rendite** *f* BÖRSE simple yield; **~e Speicherdichte** *f* COMP *Diskette* single density (*SD*); **~es Termingeschäft** *nt* BÖRSE outright forward transaction; **~es Transportdokument** *nt* VERWALT *im EU-Verkehr* single transport document; **~er Vertrag** *m* RECHT bare contract, simple contract; **~e Zinsen** *m pl* BANK simple interest; **~er Zinsswap** *m* FINANZ plain vanilla swap (*infrml*)

Einfachbesetzung *f* TRANSP single staffing

Einfachfertigung *f* IND single-process production

Einfahrtshafen *m* IMP/EXP port of entry

Einfahrzeit *f* GESCHÄFT running-in period

Einfallsreichtum *m* GESCHÄFT ingenuity

Einfamilienhaus *nt* GRUND, STEUER one-family home, single-family dwelling, single-family house

Einfluß *m* GESCHÄFT influence; **~ auf den Gewinn** GESCHÄFT profit impact; ◆ **~ geltend machen** GESCHÄFT pull strings (*BrE*), pull wires (*AmE*)

Einfluß: **Einflußbereich** *m* V&M reach, halo

einflußreich *adj* GESCHÄFT influential, powerful, prestigious

Einforderung *f* FINANZ call

einfressen *vt* IND corrode

Einfressen *nt* IND corrosion

einfrieren *vt* BANK block, FINANZ *Konto*, STEUER freeze

Einfrieren *nt* FINANZ *eines Kontos*, STEUER freezing; **~ der Preise** GESCHÄFT price freeze

einfügen *vt* COMP *Textverarbeitung, Grafik* insert, GESCHÄFT add in, put in, MEDIEN add

Einfügung *f* COMP *Textverarbeitung, Grafik* insertion, MEDIEN addition

Einfuhr *f* (*Einf.*) IMP/EXP, VW *Zoll* import (*imp.*), importation (*imp.*); **Einfuhrabfertigungsstelle** *f* IMP/EXP entry processing unit (*EPU*); **Einfuhrbewilligung** *f* IMP/EXP import licence (*BrE*) (*I/L*), import license (*AmE*) (*I/L*); **Einfuhrdeklaration** *f* BANK, IMP/EXP bill of entry (*B/E*)

einführen *vt* COMP *Technik, Service, System* feed, GESCHÄFT introduce, IMP/EXP import, RECHT *Gesetz* bring in, SOZIAL induct, V&M launch

einführend *adj* GESCHÄFT pioneering; **~er Bericht** *m* MEDIEN standfirst

Einfuhr: **Einfuhrerklärung** *f* BANK bill of entry (*B/E*), IMP/EXP clearance inwards, bill of entry (*B/E*); **Einfuhrerlaubnis** *f* IMP/EXP import admission; **Einfuhrgenehmigung** *f* IMP/EXP import licence (*BrE*) (*I/L*), import license (*AmE*) (*I/L*); **Einfuhrgenehmigungsverfahren** *nt* IMP/EXP import licensing; **Einfuhrhandel** *m* VW passive trade; **Einfuhrkontingent** *nt* IMP/EXP import quota; **Einfuhrkontingente** *nt pl* VW limitation on imports; **Einfuhrpreis** *m* IMP/EXP entry price; **Einfuhrsperre** *f* IMP/EXP ban on imports, embargo; **Einfuhrstopp** *m* IMP/EXP ban on imports, embargo; **Einfuhrtätigkeit** *f* IMP/EXP importing

Einführung *f* COMP introduction, IMP/EXP importation (*imp.*), PERSON *in ein Amt* induction, SOZIAL induction course, V&M *auf dem Markt* launching; **Einführungskurs** *m* SOZIAL induction course, introductory course; **Einführungspreis** *m* V&M introductory price, *Werbepreis* advertising price; **Einführungsseminar** *nt* SOZIAL induction course, introductory course; **Einführungsstadium** *nt* V&M introductory stage; **Einführungsvorlesung** *f* SOZIAL *Universität* introductory course; **Einführungswerbung** *f* V&M announcement advertising, pioneering advertise-

ment, VW pioneering advertising; **Einführungszeit** *f* V&M lead time

Einfuhr: **Einfuhrverbot** *nt* IMP/EXP, STEUER ban on imports; **Einfuhrzoll** *m* IMP/EXP, STEUER import duty (*ID*), import tariff; **Einfuhrzölle** *m pl* STEUER customs

Eingabe *f* COMP input, GESCHÄFT *Gesuch* input, petition; ◆ **eine ~ machen** VERWALT hand in a petition

Eingabe: **Eingabeaufforderung** *f* COMP prompt

Eingabe-Ausgabe *f* (*E/A*) COMP input/output (*I/O*); **Eingabe-Ausgabe-Analyse** *f* COMP, FINANZ, MATH, VW input-output analysis; **Eingabe-Ausgabe-Prozessor** *m* COMP input/output processor; **Eingabe-Ausgabe-Steuersystem** *nt* COMP input-output control system (*IOCS*); **Eingabe-Ausgabe-Tabelle** *f* COMP, FINANZ, MATH, VW input-output table

Eingabe: **Eingabedaten** *pl* COMP input data; **Eingabeformat** *nt* COMP input format; **Eingabegerät** *nt* COMP input device; **Eingabekosten** *pl* RECHNUNG input cost; **Eingabemaske** *f* COMP input form; **Eingabemeldung** *f* COMP input message; **Eingabestift** *m* COMP *bleistiftähnliches Eingabegerät* pen, stylus; **Eingabetastatur** *f* COMP keyboard

Eingang *m* GESCHÄFT entrance, intake, *Brief* arrival, TRANSP *Brief* arrival; **~ und Ausgang** GESCHÄFT ingress and egress; **~ von bereits als Verlust abgebuchten Forderungen** RECHNUNG bad debt recovery; ◆ **~ vorbehalten** BANK subject to collection

Eingang: **Eingangsbeleg** *m* der Handkasse RECHNUNG petty cash voucher; **Eingangsbenachrichtigung** *f* TRANSP arrived notification form; **Eingangsdaten** *pl* COMP incoming data; **Eingangsdatum** *nt* GESCHÄFT date of receipt; **Eingangsdeklarierung** *f* IMP/EXP clearance inwards; **Eingangsfracht** *f* GESCHÄFT, TRANSP carriage inward, freight inward; **Eingangshafen** *m* IMP/EXP port of entry; **Eingangspreis** *m* GESCHÄFT threshold price; **Eingangsrechnung** *f* GESCHÄFT purchase invoice; **Eingangssatz** *m* STEUER basic rate; **Eingangsschein** *m* TRANSP goods received note; **Eingangsstempel** *m* KOMM receipt stamp

eingearbeitet: **~ sein in** [+acc] *phr* GESCHÄFT be familiar with

eingebaut *adj* COMP built-in, on-board, GESCHÄFT installed (*inst.*), vw built-in

eingeben *vt* COMP *Daten* enter, input, key in, type in

eingebettet *adj* COMP embedded; **~er Befehl** *m* COMP embedded command

eingebunden *adj* MEDIEN casebound; **~es Buch** *nt* MEDIEN casebound book

eingefleischt: **~er Demokrat** *m*, **~e Demokratin** *f* POL dyed-in-the-wool democrat (*BrE*), yellow-dog democrat (*AmE*)

eingefordert: **~es Kapital** *nt* FINANZ, RECHNUNG called-up share capital; **nicht ~es Kapital** *nt* FINANZ uncalled capital

eingefroren *adj* BANK blocked; vw *Löhne* frozen; **~e Guthaben** *nt pl* FINANZ frozen assets; **~es Konto** *nt* BANK frozen account, eingreforenes Konto; **~e Kredite** *m pl* FINANZ frozen credits; **~e Vermögenswerte** *m pl* FINANZ frozen assets

eingeführt: **~e Marke** *f* V&M established brand; **~es Produkt** *nt* V&M established product

eingegangen: **durch jdn ~e Verbindlichkeiten** *f pl* BANK debt incurred by sb

eingegliedert *adj* BANK, GESCHÄFT, PERSON affiliated; **nicht ~** *adj* BANK, GESCHÄFT *Gesellschaft*, PERSON unaffiliated; **~e Person** *f* GESCHÄFT affiliated person

eingehen 1. *vt* GESCHÄFT *Risiko* undertake, *Vertrag* enter into; **2.** *vi* KOMM *Post* arrive

eingehend: ~ untersuchen *phr* GESCHÄFT examine carefully

eingelöst: nicht ~er Scheck *m* BANK dishonored check (*AmE*), dishonoured cheque (*BrE*)

eingemacht *adj* GESCHÄFT preserved

eingereicht: nicht ~er Scheck *m* BANK unpresented check (*AmE*), unpresented cheque (*BrE*)

eingeschaltet *adj* GESCHÄFT switched on

eingeschlagen *adj* GESCHÄFT *mit Papier, Folie* wrapped

eingeschlossen: alles ~ *phr* GESCHÄFT all-in, all-inclusive

eingeschränkt *adj* GESCHÄFT limited, restricted; **~e Bedingungen** *f pl* VERSICH limited terms; **~er Bestätigungsvermerk** *m* RECHNUNG qualified opinion, qualifed report; **~er Bestensauftrag** *m* BÖRSE conditional market order (*BrE*); **~e Genehmigung** *f* GESCHÄFT qualified approval; **~es Indossament** *nt* BANK qualified endorsement; **~e Mehrheit** *f* POL qualified majority, simple majority; **~e Rationalität** *f* VW bounded rationality

eingeschrieben *adj* KOMM *Post, Brief* registered (*regd.*); **~er Brief** *m* KOMM registered letter

eingesetzt: ~es Kapital *nt* FINANZ, RECHNUNG capital employed; **~e Mittel** *nt pl* FINANZ total funds applied

eingespart: ~e Arbeitszeit *f* TRANSP working time saved; **~e Gesamtarbeitszeit** *f* TRANSP all working time saved

Eingeständnis *nt* GESCHÄFT admission, acknowledgement

eingestehen *vt* GESCHÄFT *Irrtum* acknowledge

eingestellt *adj* IND discontinued, PERSON hired; **~er Betrieb** *m* IND discontinued operations

eingetragen *adj* GESCHÄFT, PATENT, VERSICH, VERWALT recorded, registered; **nicht ~** *adj* GESCHÄFT unrecorded

eingetragen: **~er Aktienmarktmacher** *m* BÖRSE registered equity market maker; **~er Aktionär** *m*, **~e Aktionärin** *f* BÖRSE registered shareholder, registered stockholder; **~er Alters-Versorgungsfonds** *m* VERSICH registered retirement income fund (*RRIF*); **~er Eigentümer, ~e Eigentümerin** *f* GRUND *im Grundbuch* registered proprietor; **~es Firmenzeichen** *nt* PATENT registered mark, registered trademark; **nicht ~es Firmenzeichen** *nt* PATENT unregistered mark, unregistered trademark; **~es Gebrauchsmuster** *nt* RECHT registered design; **~er einer Gesellschaft** *f* RECHT registered office, VERWALT registered company; **~er Lizenznehmer** *m* PATENT *Warenzeichenbenutzer* registered user; **~er Marktmacher** *m* BÖRSE registered market maker; **~er Optionshändler** *m* BÖRSE registered options trader; **~er Pensionsfonds** *m* VERSICH registered retirement income fund (*RRIF*); **~e Pensionskasse** *f* VERSICH registered retirement income fund (*RRIF*); **~er Pensionssparplan** *m* VERSICH registered retirement savings plan (*RRSP*); **~er Rechtsanspruch** *m* VERWALT registered title; **~er Sitz** *m* RECHT registered office; **~er Sparplan** *m* **für den Ruhestand** VERSICH registered retirement savings plan (*RRSP*); **~er Verein** *m* BÖRSE, GESCHÄFT, POL registered society; **~es Warenzeichen** *nt* GESCHÄFT registered trademark, PATENT registered mark, registered trade-

mark, RECHT registered trademark; **nicht ~es Warenzeichen** *nt* GESCHÄFT unregistered trademark, PATENT unregistered mark; **~er Wertpapierhändler** *m* BÖRSE registered trader; **~er Wertpapierinhaber** *m*, **~e Wertpapierinhaberin** *f* BÖRSE holder of record

eingetretenen: ~e Kapitalbeschaffungskosten *pl* BÖRSE realized cost of funds; **~e Substanzverringerung** *f* RECHNUNG accumulated depletion

eingetrieben: ~e Forderung *f* RECHNUNG recovered bad debt

eingewickelt *adj* GESCHÄFT wrapped

eingezahlt: ~es Grundkapital *nt* FINANZ paid-up capital

eingezogen *adj* BÖRSE called-in, redeemed, GESCHÄFT collected; ♦ **~ und ausgeliefert** GESCHÄFT collected and delivered (*C&D*)

eingezogen: **~e Aktie** *f* BÖRSE called-in share, redeemed share; **nicht ~e Gelder** *nt pl* BANK uncollected funds

eingipflig: ~e Verteilung *f* MATH unimodal distribution

eingleisig: ~e Strecke *f* TRANSP single track

eingliedern *vt* GESCHÄFT classify, absorb, incorporate, integrate

eingreifen *vi* FINANZ intervene, GESCHÄFT step in, PERSON, POL, VW intervene

Eingreifen *nt* GESCHÄFT intervention; **~ des Staates** VW state intervention

eingrenzen *vt* GESCHÄFT, POL contain, restrict

Eingrenzung *f* GESCHÄFT, POL containment, restriction

Eingriff *m* GESCHÄFT infringement

Eingruppierung *f* GESCHÄFT grouping; **~ nach Leistung** *f* SOZIAL *Schüler* ability grouping

Einhalt: ~ gebieten *phr* GESCHÄFT stem

einhalten *vt* GESCHÄFT meet, *Verabredung* keep, *Vertrag* adhere to, *Regeln* abide by, RECHT *Klausel* comply with, *Vorschriften, Gesetze* observe

Einhaltung *f* GESCHÄFT, RECHT *der Vorschriften* adherence, compliance, observance

Ein-Haus-Veto *nt* POL one-house veto (*AmE*)

einheimisch *adj* PERSON, VW domestic, local; **~e Arbeitskräfte** *f pl* PERSON, VW local labor (*AmE*), local labour (*BrE*), local workers; **~er Arbeitsmarkt** *m* VW internal labor market (*AmE*), internal labour market (*BrE*); **~e Erzeugnisse** *nt pl* VW home production; **~e Industrie** *f* IND native industry

Einheit *f* COMP, GESCHÄFT, PATENT, VW unity; **~ der Erfindung** PATENT unity of invention; **~ des europäischen Patents** PATENT unity of European patent; **~ bei Kursschwankungen** BÖRSE point; ♦ **um eine ~ vermindern** COMP decrement

einheitlich *adj* GESCHÄFT coherent, standard, uniform; **~es Betriebsverfahren** *nt* GESCHÄFT standard operating procedure (*s.o.p., SOP*); **~er Binnenmarkt** *m* GESCHÄFT, VW single European market; **~e Buchführung** *f* RECHNUNG uniform accounting

Einheitlich: ~e Europäische Akte *f* (*EEA*) RECHT Single European Act (*SEA*)

einheitlich: **~e europäische Währung** *f* VW Single European Currency; **~es Handelsrecht** *nt* RECHT ≈ Uniform Commercial Code (*AmE*); **~e Inkassorichtlinien** *f pl* BANK uniform rules for collections; **~er Markt** *m* BÖRSE, V&M single market; **~e Projektleitung** *f* MGMNT integrated project management (*IPM*); **~e Richtlinien** *f pl* **für Inkassi** BANK uniform rules for collections; **~e Richtlinien** *f pl*

und Praktiken *f pl* **für Dokumenten-Akkreditive** (*ERA*) vw *Dokumenten-Akkreditierung* Uniform Customs and Practice for Documentary Credits (*UC&P*)
Einheitlichkeit *f* GESCHÄFT uniformity, coherence; **~ der Erfindung** PATENT unity of invention
Einheit: **Einheitsbedingungen** *f pl* RECHT standard conditions; **Einheitsformular** *nt* IMP/EXP, TRANSP, VERWALT single administrative document (*SAD*); **Einheitskurs** *m* BÖRSE middle price; **Einheitsladung** *f* TRANSP *Verteilung* unit load (*U*); **Einheitsluftfrachtbrief** *m* IMP/EXP, TRANSP universal air waybill (*UAWB*); **Einheitspolice** *f* **der Feuerversicherung** VERSICH standard fire policy; **Einheitsprämie** *f* PERSON *Produktivität* flat-rate bonus; **Einheitspreis** *m* FINANZ standard price, uniform price; **Einheitssatz** *m* STEUER standard rate; **zum Einheitssatz** *phr* STEUER standard-rated; **Einheitssorte** *f* GESCHÄFT standard grade; **Einheitssteuerbewegung** *f obs* STEUER single tax movement; **Einheitssteuersatz** *m* STEUER standard rate; **zum Einheitssteuersatz** *phr* STEUER standard-rated; **Einheitstarif** *m* FINANZ flat fee, V&M flat rate; **Einheitsvertrag** *m* GESCHÄFT, RECHT standard agreement, standard contract, standard-form contract; **Einheitswährung** *f* GESCHÄFT single currency; **Einheitswarenbegleitschein** *m* IMP/EXP, TRANSP national standard shipping note (*NSSN*); **Einheitswert** *m* GESCHÄFT unit value, GRUND, STEUER rateable value (*obs*) (*BrE*), vw unit value; **Einheitswertindex** *m* vw unit value index (*UVI*); **Einheitszeit** *f* GESCHÄFT standard time
einhergehen *vi*: **~ mit** GESCHÄFT accompany
einholen *vt* GESCHÄFT *Forderungen* recover
einigen 1. *vt* GESCHÄFT unify; **2. sich ~** *v refl* GESCHÄFT come to an understanding, come to terms, agree; ♦ **sich ~ auf** [+acc] GESCHÄFT *Preis, Bedingungen, Lösung* agree on, agree upon, *Vorschlag* agree; **sich ~ über** [+acc] GESCHÄFT *Preis, Bedingungen, Lösung* agree on, agree upon, *Vorschlag* agree; **sich gütlich ~** PERSON settle amicably; **sich mit jdm ~** GESCHÄFT come to an understanding with sb, RECHT come to terms with sb
Einigkeit *f* GESCHÄFT agreement, RECHT accord
Einigung *f* GESCHÄFT agreement; ♦ **keine ~ erzielen** GESCHÄFT fail to reach an agreement; **zu einer ~ gelangen mit** GESCHÄFT *Lieferanten* come to an arrangement with
Einigung: **Einigungsamt** *nt* GESCHÄFT arbitration board
einkalkulieren *vt* GESCHÄFT take account of, take into account
einkassierbar *adj* BANK encashable
Einkassierung *f* BANK encashment
Einkauf *m* GESCHÄFT, V&M buying, purchasing; **~ im Versandhandel** V&M catalog buying (*AmE*), catalogue buying (*BrE*); **~ im Versandhaus** V&M catalog buying (*AmE*), catalogue buying (*BrE*); **Einkaufbuch** *nt* RECHNUNG bought ledger
Einkäufe *m pl* GESCHÄFT shopping; ♦ **~ machen** V&M shop
einkaufen *vt* GESCHÄFT buy in, vw buy, shop
Einkaufen *nt* GESCHÄFT shopping; **~ außerhalb der Stadt** V&M out-of-town shopping
Einkäufer, in *m,f* GESCHÄFT buyer, MGMNT purchasing executive, PERSON purchasing officer, procurement manager

Einkauf: **Einkaufsabteilung** *f* GESCHÄFT purchasing department; *Einzelhändler* open-to-buy (*AmE*); **Einkaufschef, in** *m,f* MGMNT chief buyer, purchasing executive; **Einkaufsexperte** *m*, **Einkaufsexpertin** *f* V&M sourcing expert; **Einkaufsgalerie** *f* V&M *Einkaufszentrum* mall; **Einkaufsgenossenschaft** *f* **des Einzelhandels** V&M retail cooperative; **Einkaufsjournal** *nt* RECHNUNG bought book, bought journal; **Einkaufskontenbuch** *nt* RECHNUNG purchases journal; **Einkaufsleiter, in** *m,f* GESCHÄFT head buyer, MGMNT, PERSON purchasing manager; **Einkaufspassage** *f* GESCHÄFT shopping arcade; **Einkaufspolitik** *f* V&M sourcing; **Einkaufspreis** *m* VW buying-in price, purchase price; **Einkaufspreisbewertungsmethode** *f* BÖRSE purchase price method; **Einkaufsprovision** *f* V&M buying commission; **Einkaufsrechnung** *f* GESCHÄFT purchase invoice; **Einkaufssyndikat** *nt* V&M buying syndicate; **Einkaufstagesjournal** *nt* RECHNUNG bought day book; **Einkaufsvereinigung** *f* V&M voluntary group; **Einkaufsverhalten** *nt* V&M buying pattern, purchasing pattern; **Einkaufsvollmacht** *f* GESCHÄFT authority to purchase; **Einkaufszentrum** *nt* GESCHÄFT, V&M shopping center (*AmE*), shopping centre (*BrE*), shopping mall (*AmE*), shopping precinct (*BrE*), *Einzelhandel* retail center (*AmE*), retail centre (*BrE*), retail park
einklagbar *adj* GESCHÄFT, RECHT actionable, enforceable; **nicht ~er Vertrag** *m* RECHT unenforceable contract
Einklang: **im ~ mit** *phr* GESCHÄFT in accordance with; **miteinander in ~ bringen** *phr* GESCHÄFT reconcile
Einklarierung *f* IMP/EXP clearance inwards
einkleben *vt* COMP *Textverarbeitung* paste
Einklebung *f* COMP pasting, MEDIEN *Druck* tip-in
Einkommen *nt* FINANZ, RECHNUNG, STEUER, VW income; **~ im Hinblick auf einen Verstorbenen** STEUER income in respect of a decedent (*AmE*); **~-Splitting** *nt* RECHNUNG income splitting; **~-Splitting-System** *nt* RECHNUNG income-splitting system; **~ unter Berücksichtigung eines Verstorbenen** STEUER income in respect of a decedent; **~ aus Unternehmenstätigkeit und Vermögen** RECHNUNG, STEUER property and entrepreneurship; **~ aus Vermögen** FINANZ, RECHNUNG, STEUER unearned income; **Einkommensaufteilungssystem** *nt* STEUER income-splitting system; **Einkommensausfall** *m* FINANZ loss of income; **Einkommensdifferenz** *f* VW income differential; **Einkommenseffekt** *m* VERWALT, VW income effect
einkommensabhängige: **~ Zulage** *f* RECHNUNG income-tested supplement
einkommenselastisch *adj* VW income-elastic (*jarg*)
Einkommen: **Einkommenselastizität** *f* **der Nachfrage** VW income-elasticity of demand (*jarg*); **Einkommensersatz** *m* VERSICH income replacement; **Einkommensersatzrate** *f* SOZIAL replacement ratio; **Einkommensgefälle** *nt* PERSON *Arbeit* earnings differential; **Einkommensgruppe** *f* V&M *Marktforschung* income group, VERWALT income bracket; **Einkommensinvestmentgesellschaft** *f* FINANZ income investment company; **Einkommenskonsumkurve** *f* VW income-consumption curve (*ICC*); **Einkommens- und Körperschaftsteuergesetz** *nt* STEUER Income and Corporation Taxes Act (*BrE*); **Einkommenskreislaufgeschwindigkeit** *f* **des Geldes** VW income velocity of money; **Einkommensmaximum** *nt* PERSON

zu Berechnungszwecken earnings ceiling; **Einkommensniveau** *nt* VERWALT income level; **Einkommenspolitik** *f* PERSON, POL, VERWALT, VW incomes policy; **Einkommensschwache** *pl* [decl. as adj] PERSON, POL, SOZIAL, VW the low-paid; **Einkommensspanne** *f* FINANZ income spread

Einkommenssteuer *f* RECHNUNG, STEUER income tax; ♦ **~ von x %** STEUER income tax thereon at x %

einkommensteuerbefreit *adj* RECHNUNG, STEUER exempt from income tax

Einkommenssteuer: **Einkommenssteuererklärung** *f* RECHNUNG income tax return

einkommensteuerfrei *adj* RECHNUNG, STEUER free of income tax (*f.i.t.*)

Einkommenssteuer: **Einkommenssteuergewinn** *m* STEUER income tax gain; **Einkommenssteuergrenzsatz** *m* STEUER marginal income tax rates; **Einkommenssteuergrundtabelle** *f* STEUER income tax scale; **Einkommenssteuerrückzahlung** *f* STEUER income tax refund; **Einkommenssteuerrückzahlungsanspruch** *m* STEUER income tax repayment claim; **Einkommenssteuersatzspannweite** *f* STEUER income tax rate band (*BrE*); **Einkommenssteuerschuld** *f* STEUER income tax liability; **Einkommenssteuerstattung** *f* STEUER tax refund; **für Einkommenssteuerzwecke** *phr* STEUER for income tax purposes

Einkommen: **Einkommens- und Substitutionseffekt** *m* VW *Slutsky-Gleichung* income and substitution effects; **Einkommensumverteilung** *f* VW income redistribution; **Einkommens- und Verbrauchsstichprobe** *f* VW *Wirtschaftsrechnungen/amtliche Statistik* New Earnings Survey (*BrE*); **Einkommensverschiebung** *f* STEUER assignment of income; **Einkommensverteilung** *f* FINANZ income distribution; **Einkommensverteilung** *f* **zwischen Generationen** VW intergenerational distribution of income

Einkünfte *pl* FINANZ, GESCHÄFT earnings, income, revenue, emolument; **~ aus Gewerbebetrieb** STEUER income from trades and professions; **~ aus Kapitalvermögen** STEUER passive income; **~ aus unsichtbaren Leistungen** FINANZ, VW invisible earnings

Einladung *f* GESCHÄFT invitation

Einlagen *f pl* BANK deposits; ♦ **~ abziehen** BANK, GESCHÄFT disintermediate

Einlagen: **Einlagenbestand** *m* BANK volume of deposits; **Einlagenbuch** *nt* BANK deposit book; **Einlagenentwicklung** *f* VW movement of deposits; **Einlagengarantie** *f* BANK bank guarantee; **Einlagengeschäft** *nt* BANK deposit-taking business; **Einlagenkapital** *nt* FINANZ initial capital; **Einlagenkonto** *nt* BANK deposit account (*BrE*) (*D/A*); **Einlagenschein** *m* BANK deposit certificate; **Einlagensicherungsfonds** *m* BANK deposit guarantee fund; **Einlagenumschichtung** *f* FINANZ shift in deposits; **Einlagenverbindlichkeiten** *f pl* BANK deposit liabilities; **Einlagenversicherung** *f* BANK bank deposit insurance (*AmE*); **Einlagenzertifikat** *nt* BANK deposit certificate, FINANZ certificate of deposit; **Einlagenzins** *m* BANK bank deposit rate, deposit interest, deposit rate

Einlagerung *f* IND storage, warehousing, TRANSP storage; **Einlagerungskredit** *m* FINANZ stockpiling loan;

Einlagerungsschein *m* IMP/EXP, IND, RECHT, TRANSP warehouse receipt

Einlaß: **~ ab neun Uhr** *phr* GESCHÄFT doors open at nine

einlassen: **sich ~ auf** *v refl* [+acc] GESCHÄFT *Projekt* venture on

einlaufen: **~ lassen** *phr* GESCHÄFT phase in

Einlaufstempel *m* IMP/EXP entry stamp

Einlaufzeit *f* GESCHÄFT running-in period

Einleger, in *m,f* BANK, GESCHÄFT bailor, depositor

einleitend: **~e Floskeln** *f pl* GESCHÄFT, PATENT introduction, preamble

Einleitung *f* GESCHÄFT, PATENT introduction, preamble; **Einleitungsformel** *f* KOMM *einer Urkunde* caption; **Einleitungsformeln** *f pl* GESCHÄFT preamble

einlesen *vt* COMP read

einlösbar *adj* BANK cashable, payable, BÖRSE encashable

einlösen *vt* BANK *Schecks* honour (*BrE*), honor (*AmE*), BÖRSE collect, encash, FINANZ, GESCHÄFT repay; **nicht ~** *vt* BANK dishonour (*AmE*), dishonour (*BrE*)

einlösend: **~e Bank** *f* BANK *Akkreditiv* negotiating bank, *Scheck* paying bank

Einlösung *f* BÖRSE collection, encashment, FINANZ, GESCHÄFT payment, redemption; **~ von Zinsscheinen** FINANZ coupon collection; **Einlösungsfrist** *f* FINANZ redemption period; **Einlösungsstelle** *f* FINANZ paying agent; **Einlösungstermin** *m* BÖRSE redemption date, RECHNUNG encashment schedule

Einmal- *in cpds* BÖRSE, VW one-off; **Einmalemission** *f* BÖRSE one-off issue; **Einmalfertigung** *f* IND one-off production

einmalig *adj* GESCHÄFT *Chance* unique; **~e Aufwendungen** *f pl* BÖRSE nonrecurring expenditure, RECHNUNG exceptional expenditure; **~e Ausgabe** *f* BÖRSE nonrecurring expenditure; **~e Beeinträchtigung** *f* VERSICH unique impairment; **~e Erträge** *f pl* VW nonrecurrent income; **~es Geldgeschenk** *nt* STEUER one-off cash gift; **~e Gelegenheit** *f* V&M unique opportunity; **~es Geschäft** *nt* GESCHÄFT one-shot deal; **~er Produktionskostentrugschluß** *m* FINANZ sunk cost fallacy; **~e Schädigung** *f* VERSICH unique impairement; **~es Verkaufsargument** *nt* V&M unique selling point (*USP*), unique selling proposition (*USP*); **~e Zahlung** *f* FINANZ one-off payment

Einmal-: **Einmalkäufer** *m* V&M one-time buyer; **Einmalprämie** *f* PERSON *Versicherung* single premium; **Einmaltarif** *m* V&M one-time rate; **Einmalzahlung** *f* FINANZ single payment, VERSICH lump sum (*ls*)

Einmannbetrieb *m* GESCHÄFT one-man business

Einmütigkeit *f* GESCHÄFT, POL unanimity

Einnahme *f* RECHNUNG, VW revenue; **Einnahmebuch** *nt* GESCHÄFT, RECHNUNG receipt book; **Einnahmebudget** *nt* RECHNUNG revenue budget; **Einnahmegenerator** *m* VW revenue earner; **Einnahmen** *f pl* BÖRSE receipts, FINANZ revenue, FREI box-office takings, gate, GESCHÄFT revenue, accruals, VW income; **Einnahmen und Ausgaben** *f pl* RECHNUNG income and expenses (*AmE*), revenue and expenses; **Einnahmen-Ausgaben-Planung** *f* RECHNUNG cash budget, cash budgeting, VW cash budgeting; **Einnahmen-Ausgaben-Rechnung** *f* RECHNUNG statement of revenue and expense, cash basis of accounting, receipts and payments account, *ohne Periodenabgrenzung* cash accounting; **Einnahmen**

f pl **aus Dienstleistungen** RECHNUNG income from services

einnahmeneutral *adj* STEUER revenue-neutral

Einnahme: **Einnahmenkurve** *f* VW revenue curve; **Einnahmenmaximierung** *f* VW revenue maximization; **Einnahmenmethode** *f* GRUND income approach; **Einnahmenverteilung** *f* TRANSP revenue allocation; **Einnahmequelle** *f* GESCHÄFT source of revenue

einnehmen *vt* GESCHÄFT *Geld* take, *Haltung* take up, PERSON fill; ◆ **jds Stelle ~** GESCHÄFT take on sb's job

einordnen *vt* GESCHÄFT classify

Einordnung *f* GESCHÄFT classification; **~ nach Objekt** GESCHÄFT classification by object

einpacken *vt* GESCHÄFT pack

Einpacken *nt* GESCHÄFT packing

einpendeln: **sich ~** *v refl* VW *Löhne* adjust, *Preise, Zeitpläne* even out

Einpersonenhaushalt *m* V&M single-person household

einplanen *vi* FINANZ, GESCHÄFT, VW budget

Einplatzhafen *m* TRANSP single-user port

einprägsam *adj* MEDIEN, V&M catchy

Einpreisgesetz *nt* VW one-price law

einräumen *vt* GESCHÄFT admit, allow

Einräumung *f* RECHT granting, concession; **~ von Exklusivrechten** RECHT granting of exclusive rights

Einrede *f* RECHT defence (*BrE*), defense (*AmE*); ◆ **eine ~ vorbringen** RECHT *Gesuch einreichen* put in a plea

einreichen *vt* BANK present, BÖRSE tender, GESCHÄFT *Anfrage* send in, *Antrag, Bewerbung* file, PATENT submit, PERSON *Beschwerde* lodge, *Kündigung* tender, POL, RECHT *Forderung, Antrag* submit

Einreichung *f* BANK presentation, PATENT, POL, RECHT, VW submission; **~ der Dokumente** IMP/EXP *Zollabfertigung* presentation of documents; **Einreichungsfristverlängerung** *f* STEUER extension of time for filing; **Einreichungsschluß** *m* BÖRSE bid closing, bid closing date

einreihen *vt* GESCHÄFT categorize

Einreihung *f* GESCHÄFT categorization

Einreise *f* IMP/EXP, VERWALT, VW entry; **Einreisebeschränkung** *f* IMP/EXP, VW entry restriction; **Einreisegenehmigung** *f* VERWALT entry permit; **Einreisestempel** *m* IMP/EXP entry stamp; **Einreisevisum** *nt* VERWALT entry visa

einrichten *vt* COMP *Programm* set up, GESCHÄFT arrange, facilitate, organize

Einrichtung *f* COMP, GESCHÄFT facility, IND apparatus, plant; **~ zur Durchführung von** PATENT apparatus for carrying out; **Einrichtungen** *f pl* PERSON facilities

einrücken *vt* COMP *Textverarbeitung* ident

Einrückung *f* COMP *Textverarbeitung* indentation, indent

einsacken *vt* TRANSP *Frachtgut* bag

Einsacken *nt* TRANSP *von Frachtgut* bagging

Einsatz *m* FINANZ stake, GESCHÄFT input, stake, *von Arbeitskräften* deployment, *von Dingen* utilization; **~ an anderem Arbeitsplatz** GESCHÄFT redeployment; **~ der moralischen Autorität** BANK *Kontrolle der Geschäftsbanken* moral suasion; **~ unlauterer Arbeitskampfmethoden seitens Arbeitgeber** PERSON *Arbeit* employer interference; ◆ **der ~ ist hoch** GESCHÄFT the stakes are high

Einsatz: **Einsatzbesprechung** *f* GESCHÄFT briefing session; **Einsatzfaktorenübersicht** *f* VW summary of input factors; **Einsatzflexibilität** *f* PERSON task flexibility; **Einsatzgüter** *nt pl* VW inputs; **Einsatzmaterial** *nt* IND, VW feedstocks; **Einsatzpreis** *m* BÖRSE starting price

einschalten 1. *vt* COMP power on, power up, turn on, enable, GESCHÄFT switch on, IND, KOMM turn on; **2. sich ~** *v refl* GESCHÄFT step in

Einschalten *nt* COMP enablement, powering up, turning-on, GESCHÄFT, KOMM turning-on

Einschaltplan *m* V&M *Werbung* advertising schedule

Einschaltung *f* MEDIEN, V&M *einer Anzeige* insertion, putting in; **~ eines Immobilienmaklers** GRUND listing

Einschaltzeichen *nt* MEDIEN, V&M caret

Einschaltzeit *f* MEDIEN viewing time

einschätzen *vt* GESCHÄFT assess, size up (*infrml*), MGMNT appraise

Einschätzung *f* GESCHÄFT assessment, sizing up (*infrml*) MGMNT appraisal; ◆ **nach meiner ~** GESCHÄFT in my estimation

einschieben *vt* GESCHÄFT *Klausel* put in

Einschienenbahn *f* TRANSP monorail

einschiffen: **sich ~** *v refl* TRANSP embark

Einschiffung *f* TRANSP embarkation

einschl. *abbr* (*einschließlich*) GESCHÄFT incl. (*included, including, inclusive*)

einschlagen 1. *vt* GESCHÄFT *Richtung* embark on; **2.** *vi* V&M *Produkt* hit the market

einschlägig: **~es Geschäft** *nt* BÖRSE stockist (*BrE*); **~e Technologie** *f* UMWELT appropriate technology

Einschleusungspreis *m* VW *EG* sluicegate price

einschließen *vt* GESCHÄFT comprise, include, enshrine, *Betrieb* incorporate, VERSICH comprise

einschließlich *prep* (*einschl.*) GESCHÄFT included (*incl.*), inclusive (*incl.*); ◆ **~ und ausschließlich** BÖRSE cum and ex; **~ aller Rechte** RECHT all-in; **~ besonderer Havarieschäden** VERSICH *Seeversicherung* with particular average (*WPA*); **~ Dividende** BÖRSE cum dividend (*c.div., cd*); **~ Havarie** VERSICH with average (*W.A.*); **~ Sonn- und Feiertage** GESCHÄFT Sundays and holidays included (*SHINC*); **~ Totalverlust** VERSICH comprised total loss

Einschluß *m* GESCHÄFT inclusion

einschmelzen *vt* IND smelt

einschneidend *adj* GESCHÄFT radical

Einschnitt *m* MEDIEN slot

einschränken *vt* FINANZ cut back, GESCHÄFT restrict

einschränkend *adj* GESCHÄFT restrictive; **~es Konnossement** *nt* IMP/EXP claused bill of lading

Einschränkung *f* FINANZ cutback, GESCHÄFT restriction, RECHNUNG qualification, SOZIAL qualification period; **~ des Gutachtens** FINANZ qualification of opinion; **Einschränkungen** *f pl* **bei der Berichterstattung** MEDIEN reporting restrictions

einschreiben: **sich ~** *v refl* GESCHÄFT register

Einschreiben *nt* KOMM certified mail (*AmE*), registered mail (*AmE*), registered post (*BrE*), registered letter; ◆ **per ~** KOMM by registered mail (*AmE*), by registered post (*BrE*), registered (*regd.*)

Einschreibung *f* GESCHÄFT enrollment (*AmE*), enrolment (*BrE*)

einschreiten *vi* GESCHÄFT step in

einschüchtern *vt* PERSON intimidate

Einschüchterung *f* PERSON intimidation

Einschuß *m* BÖRSE initial deposit, VERSICH general average deposit (*G/A dep*); **Einschußbedarf** *m* BÖRSE margin requirement; **Einschußeinzahlung** *f* BÖRSE margin deposit; **Einschußkonto** *nt* BANK marginal account, BÖRSE margin account; **Einschußniveau** *nt* BÖRSE initial margin level; **Einschußpflicht** *f* BÖRSE margin requirement; **Einschußsätze** *m pl* BANK margin requirements; **Einschußsicherheit** *f* BÖRSE margin security; **Einschußzahlung** *f* BÖRSE deposit, margin

einseitig 1. *adj* COMP single-sided, GESCHÄFT ex parte, *Urteil* one-sided, subjective, PERSON, POL unilateral, V&M *Urteil* subjective, vw unilateral; ◆ **~ mit doppelter Speicherdichte** COMP single-sided double-density (*SSDD*); **~ mit einfacher Speicherdichte** COMP single-sided single-density (*SSSD*); **2.** *adv* GESCHÄFT unilaterally

einseitig: **~es Abkommen** *nt* VW unilateral agreement; **~ bindendes Abkommen** *nt* VW unilateral agreement; **~e Hinterbliebenenrente** *f* FINANZ survivorship annuity; **~e Lohnkürzung** *f* PERSON rate cutting (*BrE*); **~e Magnetplatte** *f* COMP *Diskette* single-sided disk (*SSD*); **~e Maßnahme** *f* POL, UMWELT unilateral measure; **~e Referenz** *f* PERSON unilateral reference; **~er Test** *m* MATH one-tailed test; **~ verpflichtende Vorschrift** *f* PERSON unilateral regulation

einsenden *vt* GESCHÄFT send in

Einsendeschluß *m* MEDIEN, V&M closing date

einsetzen *vt* GESCHÄFT bring into play, call into play, *Fähigkeiten, Mittel* utilize, *Details, Zahlen* add in, *Arbeitskräfte* deploy, IND, UMWELT utilize

einsparen *vt* GESCHÄFT *Material, Kosten* save

Einsparung *f* GESCHÄFT *von Materialen, Kosten* saving, economy; **~ von Arbeitskräften** PERSON labor-saving (*AmE*), labour-saving (*BrE*); **Einsparungen** *f pl* VERWALT economies

einspringen: **für jdn ~** *phr* PERSON stand in for sb, fill in for sb

Einspruch *m* PATENT appeal, caveat, RECHT objection; ◆ **~ erheben** GESCHÄFT *Veto einlegen* put a veto on; **~ erheben gegen** GESCHÄFT oppose; **~ gegen einen Steuerbescheid** STEUER tax appeal; **dem ~ wird stattgegeben** RECHT objection sustained; **dem ~ wird nicht stattgegeben** RECHT objection overruled

Einspruch: **Einspruchseinlegung** *f* PATENT notice of opposition; **Einspruchsverfahren** *nt* PATENT opposition proceedings

einstampfen *vt* GESCHÄFT *Papier* pulp

Einstandspreis *m* RECHNUNG cost price, acquisition cost; **~ der verkauften Ware** VW cost of sales

einstanzen *vt* IND punch a hole in

einstecken *vt* COMP plug, plug in, GESCHÄFT post

einstellbar *adj* GESCHÄFT adjustable

einstellen *vt* BANK suspend, COMP set up, GESCHÄFT take on, *beenden* cease, appoint, *Arbeitskräfte* sign up, *Verfahren* focus, employ, supersede, IND discontinue, PERSON *Arbeitskräfte* engage, recruit, *Mitarbeiter* hire, take on, appoint, RECHT *Konkursverfahren* stop, *gerichtliche Anordnung* abate, V&M *Verkauf* close, VERSICH adjust; **~ und entlassen** *vt* PERSON hire and fire; ◆ **~ in** [+acc] *vt* RECHNUNG allocate to; **jds finanzielle Unterstützung ~** GESCHÄFT stop sb's allowance

einstellig *adj* MATH single digit, V&M monadic

Einstellung *f* BANK suspension, COMP set-up, setting, GESCHÄFT cessation, closure, stoppage, frame of mind, *eines Geräts* adjustment, *Haltung* stance, MGMNT attitude, PERSON recruitment, V&M attitude; **~ des Handels** GESCHÄFT stoppage of trade; **~ der Prämienzahlung** VERSICH cessation of payment of premiums; **~ in die Rücklage** RECHNUNG appropriation to a reserve; **~ in die Rücklagen** RECHNUNG allocation to reserves; **~ des Unternehmens** GESCHÄFT spirit of enterprise; **~ von Zinszahlungen** BANK cessation of interest (*BrE*); ◆ **welche ~ haben Sie zu dieser Frage?** GESCHÄFT what is your stance on this issue?

Einstellung: **Einstellungen** *f pl* COMP settings; **Einstellungsgespräch** *nt* PERSON interview; **Einstellungsprämie** *f* PERSON *Arbeit, Headhunting* golden hello (*infrml*); **Einstellungssachbearbeiter, in** *m,f* PERSON recruiting officer; **Einstellungsstopp** *m* PERSON job freeze; **Einstellungstest** *m* PERSON *Arbeit* employment test

Einstich *m* TRANSP puncturing

einstimmig 1. *adj* GESCHÄFT, POL unanimous; **2.** *adv* GESCHÄFT by common consent, unanimously, POL unanimously; ◆ **~ angenommen** GESCHÄFT *Vorschlag* unanimously accepted

einstimmig: **~er Beschluß** *m* GESCHÄFT unanimous resolution

Einstimmigkeit *f* GESCHÄFT, POL unanimity

einstmalig *adj* GESCHÄFT quondam

einstöckig: **~er Bus** *m* TRANSP single-decker (*BrE*)

einstufen *vt* GESCHÄFT categorize, grade, classify, pigeonhole, PERSON, POL, VERWALT classify

Einstufung *f* GESCHÄFT classification, categorization, PERSON *Arbeit* classification, POL class, VERWALT classification; **Einstufungsskala** *f* GESCHÄFT rating scale; **Einstufungstest** *m* PERSON *Arbeit* placement test

einstürzen *vi* GESCHÄFT *Gebäude* fall down

einstweilig 1. *adj* GESCHÄFT, RECHT ad interim (*frml*), interim, provisional, temporary; **2.** *adv* GESCHÄFT, RECHT ad interim (*frml*), in the interim

einstweilig: **~e Annahme** *f* GESCHÄFT provisional acceptance; **~e Verfügung** *f* PATENT interim injunction, RECHT temporary injunction

eintasten *vt* COMP type in

eintauschen *vt* BÖRSE, GESCHÄFT trade in, VW exchange, trade off; ◆ **etw gegen etw ~** GESCHÄFT barter sth for sth

einteilen *vt* GESCHÄFT classify, compartmentalize, grade

Einteilung *f* GESCHÄFT *Arbeit* classification, planning, MGMNT subdivision

Eintrag *m* RECHNUNG item; ◆ **einen ~ verbuchen** RECHNUNG post an entry; **einen ~ vornehmen** RECHNUNG pass an entry

eintragen 1. *vt* BÖRSE post, GESCHÄFT *Datum, Name* fill in, RECHNUNG record, post, RECHT *Firmennamen*, VERWALT register; ◆ **~ in** [+acc] GESCHÄFT *Datum, Name* fill in; **~ lassen** GESCHÄFT register; **2. sich ~** *v refl* GESCHÄFT register, FREI *Hotel* book in

einträglich *adj* GESCHÄFT gainful, rewarding; **nicht ~** *adj* GESCHÄFT unremunerative

Eintragung *f* GESCHÄFT booking, enrollment (*AmE*), enrolment (*BrE*), registration, PATENT *amtliche* registration, VERWALT entry, registration; **durch ~ einer höheren Summe gefälschter Scheck** *m* BANK raised check (*AmE*), raised cheque (*BrE*); ~ **in der Patentrolle** PATENT record in the register; ~ **im Register** PATENT record in the register; ◆ **eine** ~ **löschen** GESCHÄFT, RECHT, VERWALT cancel an entry

Eintragung: **Eintragungsbescheinigung** *f* RECHT *geistiges Eigentum* certificate of registration; **Eintragungsdatum** *nt* PATENT date of registration; **Eintragungsnummer** *f* FINANZ minute number; **Eintragungsverfahren** *nt* RECHT posting

eintreibbar: nicht ~ *adj* FINANZ, GESCHÄFT, STEUER unrecoverable

eintreiben *vt* FINANZ, GESCHÄFT collect, exact, *Schulden* recover, STEUER levy, VW *Geld* recover

Eintreibung *f* FINANZ *Kosten*, GESCHÄFT collection, recovery, STEUER levy

eintreten: ~ **für** *vi* GESCHÄFT *Politik* advocate

Eintritt *m* BÖRSE entry, GESCHÄFT admission, admittance, entrance, entrance fee; ◆ ~ **frei** FREI, GESCHÄFT admission free; ~ **verboten** GESCHÄFT no admittance

Eintritt: **Eintrittsalter** *nt* VERSICH age at entry; **Eintrittserlaubnis** *f* GESCHÄFT entry permit; **Eintrittsgebühr** *f* GESCHÄFT admission fee, entrance, entrance fee; **Eintrittsgeld** *nt* GESCHÄFT admission fee, entrance, entrance fee; **Eintrittskarte** *f* FREI, GESCHÄFT ticket; **Eintrittsperrenpreis** *m* VW limit price; **Eintrittspreis** *m* GESCHÄFT admission fee; **Eintreittspreis** *m* **für Erwachsene** GESCHÄFT adult price

Einvernehmen: zu einem ~ **kommen** *phr* GESCHÄFT come to an understanding

einvernehmlich 1. *adj* GESCHÄFT amicable; **2.** *adv* GESCHÄFT, RECHT amicably

einverstanden: ~ **sein** *phr* GESCHÄFT be agreed, agree; **nicht** ~ **sein** *phr* GESCHÄFT disagree; ~ **sein mit** *phr* GESCHÄFT agree to, agree with, be in favor of (*AmE*), be in favour of (*BrE*); **sich** ~ **erklären mit** *phr* GESCHÄFT agree to; **sich** ~ **erklären, etw zu tun** *phr* GESCHÄFT agree to do sth

Einverstandensein *nt* POL assent

einverständlich *adj* RECHT *Verträge* by stipulation

Einverständnis *nt* RECHT consent; **Einverständnisschreiben** *nt* **des Kunden** FINANZ client agreement letter (*BrE*)

Einwaage *f* GESCHÄFT contents

Einwand *m* GESCHÄFT objection; ◆ **einen** ~ **anmelden** RECHT enter a plea; **einen** ~ **erheben** GESCHÄFT make an objection, raise an objection; **keinen** ~ **haben** GESCHÄFT have no objection

Einwanderer, in *m,f* VERWALT, VW immigrant

Einwanderung *f* VERWALT, VW immigration; **Einwanderungsbeamte(r)** *m* [decl. as adj.], **Einwanderungsbeamtin** *f* GESCHÄFT immigration officer (*IO*), VERWALT immigration official; **Einwanderungskontrolle** *f* VERWALT immigration control; **Einwanderungspolitik** *f* RECHT immigration policy

einwandfrei *adj* GESCHÄFT accurate, sound, *Plan, Argument* watertight; ~**er äußerer Zustand** *m* **der Waren** TRANSP apparent good order of the goods; ~**er Erhalt** *m* **als Voraussetzung für Verkauf** V&M sale subject to safe arrival; **nicht ganz** ~**er Gesundheitspaß** *m* GESCHÄFT touched bill of health; ~**e Übergabe** *f* BÖRSE good delivery

einwechseln *vt* GESCHÄFT, VW *Geld* change, switch

Einwechselrate *f* GESCHÄFT, VW change in rate, switching in rate

Einweg- *in cpds* UMWELT *Verpackung* nonreusable, disposable, non-returnable; **Einwegpalette** *f* TRANSP expendable pallet; **Einwegverpackung** *f* V&M disposable packaging, nonreturnable packaging

einweisen *vt* PERSON assign

Einweisung *f* MGMNT briefing

einwenden *vt:* ~ **gegen** RECHT object to

einwerfen *vt* GESCHÄFT post

einwickeln *vt* GESCHÄFT wrap up (*infrml*)

einwilligen *vi* GESCHÄFT consent; ◆ ~ **in** [+acc] GESCHÄFT agree to

Einwilligung *f* GESCHÄFT assent, acceptance; **Einwilligungsbescheinigung** *f* GESCHÄFT certificate of compliance

einwirken *vi:* ~ **auf** [+acc] GESCHÄFT affect, influence

Einwohner, in *m,f* GESCHÄFT inhabitant; **Einwohnermeldeamt** *nt* VERWALT registration office

einzahlen *vt* BANK pay in, bank

Einzahler, in *m,f* BANK depositor; **Einzahlerversicherung** *f* **gegen Fälschung** VERSICH depositor's forgery insurance

Einzahlung *f* RECHNUNG deposit; **zur** ~ **aufgerufenes Aktienkapital** *nt* BÖRSE called-up share capital; ◆ **eine** ~ **machen** BÖRSE place a deposit

Einzahlung: **Einzahlungsbeleg** *m* BANK pay-in slip (*AmE*), paying-in form (*BrE*), deposit receipt (*DR*), FINANZ credit memorandum, credit slip; **Einzahlungsbuch** *nt* BANK paying-in book; **Einzahlungsheft** *nt* BANK paying-in book; **Einzahlungsschein** *m* BANK deposit slip, pay-in slip (*AmE*), paying-in form (*BrE*), FINANZ credit slip

einzeilig: ~**er Abstand** *m* COMP *Textverarbeitung* single spacing

Einzel- *in cpds* COMP *Gerät* free-standing, stand-alone, GESCHÄFT individual, single, sole; **Einzelanleger, in** *m,f* BÖRSE individual investor; **Einzelauftrag** *m* GESCHÄFT individual order; **Einzelaufzählung** *f* GESCHÄFT itemization; **Einzelbankensystem** *nt* BANK unit banking; **Einzelbewertung** *f* VERWALT individual assessment; **Einzelbilanz** *f* RECHNUNG individual company accounts; **Einzelblatt** *nt* COMP *Drucker* cut paper, single sheet; **Einzelblatteinzug** *m* COMP sheet feeder, single-sheet feeder, sheet feeding; **Einzelblattzuführung** *f* COMP sheet feeder, single-sheet feeder, sheet feeding; **Einzelebene** *f* TRANSP single plane; **Einzeleinfuhrgenehmigung** *f* IMP/EXP individual import licence (*BrE*), individual import license (*AmE*); **Einzelfahrkarte** *f* TRANSP single, single ticket; **Einzelfahrt** *f* TRANSP single fare; **Einzelfirma** *f* GESCHÄFT individual firm, sole proprietorship, sole trader; **Einzelfrachttarif** *m* TRANSP commodity rate; **Einzelgenehmigung** *f* IMP/EXP individual licence (*BrE*), individual license (*AmE*)

einzelgewerkschaftlich: ~**es Streikverbotsabkommen** *nt* PERSON single union no-strike agreement (*BrE*)

Einzelhandel *m* IND retail trade, retailing, V&M retail business; ~ **ohne Ladengeschäft** V&M nonstore retailing; **Einzelhandelsbesitz** *m* GRUND retail property; **Einzelhandelsbetrieb** *m* VW retail business; **Einzelhandelsgenossenschaft** *f* V&M retail cooperative, retailers' cooperative; **Einzelhandelsgeschäft** *nt* V&M retail store; **Einzelhandelsgewerbe** *nt* IND retail trade; **Einzelhandelsgewinnspanne** *f* V&M retail margin; **Einzelhandelskette** *f* V&M store group; **Einzelhandelsladen** *m* **mit Rabattsystem** V&M discount house, discount shop (*BrE*), discount store (*AmE*); **Einzelhandelsleitung** *f* IND, MGMNT, V&M retail management; **Einzelhandelsmakler, in** *m,f* FINANZ retail house; **Einzelhandelsmanagement** *nt* IND, MGMNT retail management; **Einzelhandelsmarketing** *nt* V&M retail marketing; **Einzelhandelsnetz** *nt* V&M retail network; **Einzelhandelspreisindex** *m* GESCHÄFT, V&M, VW retail price index (*RPI*); **Einzelhandelsrichtpreis** *m* V&M recommended retail price (*RRP*); **Einzelhandelsstatistik** *f* VW census of retail trade (*AmE*); **Einzelhandelsübernahme** *f* FINANZ retail takeover; **Einzelhandelsumsätze** *m pl* FINANZ retail sales; **Einzelhandelsunternehmen** *nt* V&M retail business, retailing; **Einzelhandelsvertrieb** *m* V&M retail marketing; **Einzelhandelszentrum** *nt* GRUND retail center (*AmE*), retail centre (*BrE*)

Einzel-: **Einzelhändler, in** *m,f* V&M retail trader, retailer

Einzelheit *f* GESCHÄFT detail, particular

Einzelheiten *f pl* GESCHÄFT details, particulars, minutiae; **~ zum Verkauf** GRUND particulars of sale; ♦ **die ~ auslassen** GESCHÄFT skip the details; **die ~ bekanntgeben** GESCHÄFT announce the details; **die ~ übergehen** GESCHÄFT skip the details

Einzel-: **Einzelimportlizenz** *f* IMP/EXP individual import licence (*BrE*), individual import license (*AmE*); **Einzelkaufmann** *m* GESCHÄFT sole trader, MGMNT sole proprietor; **Einzelkosten** *pl* RECHNUNG direct expenses; **Einzellebensversicherung** *f* VERSICH individual life insurance; **Einzellizenz** *f* IMP/EXP individual licence (*BrE*), individual license (*AmE*)

einzeln 1. *adj* GESCHÄFT single, individual; **2.** *adv* GESCHÄFT individually, singly; ♦ **~ angefertigt** GESCHÄFT one-off; **~ aufgeführt** GESCHÄFT specified; **~ nennen** GESCHÄFT itemize

einzeln: **~ aufgeführte Abzüge** *f pl* STEUER itemized deductions

Einzel-: **Einzelnachweis aufführen** *phr* GESCHÄFT *Rechnung* itemize; **Einzelpackung** *f* V&M unit pack; **Einzelperson** *f* GESCHÄFT, PERSON individual; **Einzelpolice** *f* VERSICH insurance certificate, voyage policy; **Einzelpreis** *m* V&M unit price; **Einzelrentenpolice** *f* VERSICH individual annuity policy; **Einzelschiedsrichter, in** *m,f* VERSICH sole arbitrator; **Einzelspaltenzentimeter** *m* MEDIEN single column centimeter (*AmE*), single column centimetre (*BrE*) (*SCC*); **Einzelspaltenzoll** *m* MEDIEN single column inch (*SCI*)

einzelstaatlich *adj* GESCHÄFT national (*nat.*)

Einzel-: **Einzelsteuer** *f* STEUER unit tax; **Einzelsystem** *nt* COMP stand-alone system; **Einzeltarifverhandlung** *f* PERSON *zwischen Arbeitgeber und Arbeitnehmer* individual bargaining; **Einzelteil** *nt* IND component part; **Einzelunternehmen** *nt* GESCHÄFT individual firm; **Einzelunternehmer, in** *m,f* GESCHÄFT proprietor; **Einzelunterricht** *m* SOZIAL private tuition; **Einzelverbraucher, in** *m,f* GESCHÄFT, V&M individual consumer; **Einzelverwaltungsdokument** *nt* IMP/EXP, TRANSP, VERWALT single administrative document (*SAD*); **Einzelzeichendrucker** *m* COMP character-at-a-time printer; **Einzelzelle** *f* SOZIAL adjustment center (*AmE*), adjustment centre (*BrE*); **Einzelzimmer** *nt* FREI single room; **Einzelzimmerzuschlag** *m* FREI single-room supplement

einziehen *vt* BÖRSE, GESCHÄFT collect

einziehend: **~e Bank** *f* FINANZ collecting bank

Einziehung *f* BANK, FINANZ, BÖRSE collection, STEUER *öffentlicher Gelder* collection of public money; **~ der Gewerkschaftsbeiträge durch Arbeitgeber** PERSON check-off (*AmE*); **~ eines Rechnungsbetrages** RECHNUNG collection of a bill

einzig *adj* GESCHÄFT single; ♦ **aus einer ~en Bezugsquelle** GESCHÄFT single-sourced

einzigartig *adj* GESCHÄFT unique

einzig: **~er Schiedsrichter** *m* PERSON single arbitrator (*BrE*)

Einzug *m* BANK, RECHNUNG collection; **Einzugsbereich** *m* V&M catchment area; **Einzugsermächtigung** *f* BANK, FINANZ direct debit authorization; **Einzugsgebiet** *nt* GESCHÄFT commuter belt; **Einzugsgebühr** *f* GESCHÄFT collection charge; **Einzugskosten** *pl* GESCHÄFT collection costs; **Einzugsschacht** *m* COMP *Drucker* feed bin; **Einzugsspesen** *pl* GESCHÄFT collection costs; **Einzugstermin** *m* GRUND completion date; **Einzugsverfahren** *nt* BANK direct debit (*DD*), FINANZ automatic debit transfer system, direct debit (*DD*); **Einzugswechsel** *m* BANK bill for collection

Eis: **etw auf ~ legen** *phr* GESCHÄFT put sth off

Eisberg-Gesellschaft *f* GESCHÄFT iceberg company (*jarg*)

Eisen *nt* IND iron (*IRN*)

Eisenbahn *f* TRANSP railroad (*AmE*), railway (*BrE*) (*rly*), rail; **Eisenbahnabonnement** *nt* GESCHÄFT commutation ticket (*AmE*), season ticket (*BrE*); **Eisenbahnaktien** *f pl* BÖRSE rail shares; **Eisenbahner** *m* PERSON railman (*AmE*), railwayman (*BrE*); **Eisenbahnfähre** *f* TRANSP train ferry; **Eisenbahnfährschiff** *nt* TRANSP train ferry; **Eisenbahnfrachtbrief** *m* FINANZ, TRANSP railroad bill of lading (*AmE*), railway bill of lading (*BrE*); **Eisenbahngüterverkehr** *m* TRANSP rail freight traffic; **Eisenbahnnetz** *nt* TRANSP rail network, railroad network (*AmE*), railroad system (*AmE*), railway network (*BrE*), railway system (*BrE*); **Eisenbahnstreik** *m* PERSON, TRANSP rail strike; **Eisenbahntarif** *m* TRANSP train fare; **Eisenbahnterminal** *m* TRANSP rail terminal; **Eisenbahntransport** *m* TRANSP truckage; **Eisenbahnverbindung** *f* TRANSP railroad service (*AmE*), railway service (*BrE*); **Eisenbahnwagen** *m* TRANSP railcar, railroad car (*AmE*), railway coach (*BrE*); **Eisenbahnwertpapiere** *nt pl* BÖRSE railway securities (*BrE*); **Eisenbahnwesen** *f* TRANSP railroad (*AmE*), railway (*BrE*) (*rly*)

Eisenerz *nt* IND iron ore; **Eisenerzfrachter** *m* TRANSP iron ore carrier; **Eisenerztransportschiff** *nt* TRANSP iron ore carrier

eisenhaltig *adj* UMWELT ferrous

Eisen: **Eisenhütte** *f* IND ironworks, smelting works

eisern: **~ durchgreifen** *phr* MGMNT, POL take drastic action; **~es Lohngesetz** *nt* VW iron law of wages

EKR *abbr* (*Eigenkapitalrentabilität*) BÖRSE equity return

EKV *abbr* (*Europäische Kooperationsvereinigung*) RECHT ECG (*European Cooperation Grouping*)

elastisch: **~es Angebot** *nt* VW elastic supply; **~e Nachfrage** *f* VW elastic demand

Elastizität *f* VW elasticity; **~ der Nachfrage** VW elasticity of demand; **Elastizitätskoeffizient** *m* VW elasticity coefficient

Elektrifizierung *f* TRANSP electrification

elektrisch: **~e Schreibmaschine** *f* VERWALT electric typewriter; **~e Zentrale** *f* IND power station; **~er Zug** *m* TRANSP electric train

Elektrizität *f* GESCHÄFT, IND electricity; **Elektrizitätserzeugung** *f* IND electricity generation; **Elektrizitäts-Freistellungsklausel** *f* VERSICH electrical exemption clause; **Elektrizitäts-Freizeichnungsklausel** *f* VERSICH electrical exemption clause; **Elektrizitäts-Haftungsausschlußklausel** *f* VERSICH electrical exemption clause; **Elektrizitätsindustrie** *f* IND electricity industry; **Elektrizitätslieferung** *f* IND electricity generation; **Elektrizitätssektor** *m* IND electricity sector; **Elektrizitätsversorgung** *f* IND electricity supply; **Elektrizitätswerk** *nt* (*E-Werk*) IND power station, UMWELT generating station; **Elektrizitätswirtschaft** *f* IND, VW electricity industry; **Elektrizitätszulieferungsindustrie** *f* IND electricity support industry

Elektro- *in cpds* GESCHÄFT electric, electrical; **Elektroantrieb** *m* TRANSP electrical propulsion; **Elektrobranche** *f* IND electrical engineering; **Elektrofahrzeug** *nt* TRANSP electric vehicle; **Elektrogerät** *nt* GESCHÄFT electrical appliance; **Elektroingenieur, in** *m,f* IND electrical engineer; **Elektroisolieranstrich** *m* IND electrically insulated coating (*EIC*); **Elektroisolierüberzug** *m* IND electrically insulated coating (*EIC*)

Elektronik *f* IND electronics; **Elektronikindustrie** *f* IND electronics industry

elektronisch *adj* GESCHÄFT electronic; **~e Abwicklung** *f* **von Bankgeschäften** BANK electronic banking; **~e Anschlagstafel** *f* BÖRSE electronic posting board; **~e Bank** *f* BANK electronic bank; **~e Bankdienstleistung** *f* BANK electronic banking service; **~e Bankgeschäfte** *nt pl* **zu Hause** BANK electronic home banking; **~e Bankleistung** *f* BANK electronic banking service; **~es Bauelement** *nt* COMP electronic component; **~er Belegleser** *m* COMP scanner; **~e Bestellung** *f* COMP, V&M teleordering; **~e Börseninformation** *f* BÖRSE SEAQ Automated Execution Facility (*BrE*) (*SAEF*), Stock Exchange Automated Quotation System (*SEAQ*); **~es Buchhaltungssystem** *nt* RECHNUNG electronic accounting system; **~es Büro** *nt* GESCHÄFT, VERWALT electronic office; **~er Datenaustausch** *m* (*EDI*) COMP, KOMM electronic data interchange (*EDI*); **~e Datenübermittlung** *f* VERWALT electronic mail (*e-mail*); **~e Datenverarbeitung** *f* (*EDV*) COMP electronic data processing (*EDP*), information technology (*IT*); **~er Dokumentenaustausch** *m* KOMM electronic document interchange; **~e Geldüberweisung** *f* **am Verkaufsort** (*EFTPOS*) BANK, COMP, V&M electronic funds transfer at point of sale (*EFTPOS*); **~e Kommunikation** *f* COMP mailbox; **~e Medien** *nt pl* V&M electronic media; **~es Notizbuch** *nt* GESCHÄFT organizer; **~e Panne** *f* COMP glitch; **~er POS** *m* GESCHÄFT electronic point of sale (*EPOS*); **~e Post** *f* (*E-Mail*) COMP, VERWALT electronic mail (*e-mail*); **~es Publizieren** *nt* COMP electronic publishing; **~e Rechenmaschine** *f* COMP electronic calculator; **~e Überweisung** *f* BANK automatic transfer service (*ATS*) (*BrE*); **~er Überweisungsverkehr** *m* **der Kreditinstitute** BANK direct fund transfer (*DFT*); **~es**

Zahlungsterminal *nt* FINANZ electronic payment terminal (*EPT*); **~er Zahlungsverkehr** *m* BANK, FINANZ, VERWALT automatic funds transfer (*AFT*), electronic funds transfer (*EFT*); **~es Zahlungsverkehrssystem** *nt* BANK electronic funds transfer system (*EFTS*); **~es Zahlungsverkehrsterminal** *nt* FINANZ electronic payment terminal (*EPT*); **~er Zahlungsverkehr** *m* **für Überweisungen** (*EZÜ*) BANK automatic transfer service (*ATS*) (*BrE*)

elektrostatisch: **~er Drucker** *m* COMP electrostatic printer

Elektro-: **Elektrotechnik** *f* IND electrical engineering

Element *nt* COMP *Daten, Liste* item, GESCHÄFT element

elementar: **~er Arbeitsmarkt** *m* PERSON single labor market (*AmE*), single labour market (*BrE*)

Elementarschaden *m* VERSICH elementary loss

Elend *nt* SOZIAL hardship; **Elendsindex** *m* VW discomfort index, misery index

Eleve *m* PERSON apprentice

Elfenbeinturmliberale(r) *mf* [decl. as adj] *infrml* POL limousine liberal (*infrml*)

Elfenbeinturmliberalismus *m* POL limousine liberalism

Elite *f* GESCHÄFT elite, PERSON *Kandidaten, Mitarbeiter* cream of the crop (*infrml*)

Elternschaftsurlaub *m* PERSON parental leave

E-Mail *f* (*elektronische Post*) COMP Datenübertragung e-mail (*electronic mail*)

Emanzipation *f* RECHT emancipation

Emballagen *f pl* TRANSP packaging

Embargo *nt* GESCHÄFT, IMP/EXP, MEDIEN *Pressemitteilung*, TRANSP embargo; ♦ **ein ~ verhängen über** [+acc] GESCHÄFT, MEDIEN *Pressemitteilung* lay an embargo on

Emigrant, in *m,f* PERSON, POL refugee

Emission *f* BANK *Geld*, BÖRSE *Aktien*, FINANZ issue, UMWELT *von Gasen* emission; **~ einer Aktiengesellschaft** FINANZ corporate issue; **~ von Berichtigungsaktien** BÖRSE, FINANZ scrip issue; **~ von Bezugsrechtsscheinen** FINANZ warrant issue; **~ der Bundesbehörde** FINANZ Federal Agency Issue (*AmE*); **~en** *f pl* **mit Devisenoptionen** BÖRSE issues with currency options; **~ von Gratisaktien** BÖRSE capitalization issue (*cap issue*); **~ von Kommunalobligationen** BANK municipal bond offering; **~ von Kommunalschuldverschreibungen** BANK municipal bond offering; **~ eines Schuldtitels** BANK note issue; **~ von Stammaktien** BÖRSE equity issue; **~ mit variablem Zinssatz** BÖRSE floating-rate notes; ♦ **eine ~ begeben** BÖRSE launch an issue; **eine ~ durchsetzen** BÖRSE force an issue; **eine ~ übernehmen** BÖRSE take over an issue; **eine ~ unterbringen** BÖRSE place an issue; **die ~ war unterzeichnet** BÖRSE the issue was undersubscribed; **eine ~ zeichnen** FINANZ subscribe to an issue

Emission: **Emissionsabgabe** *f* UMWELT emission charges, VW effluent fee; **Emissionsagio** *nt* BÖRSE issue premium; **Emissionsagiorücklage** *f* FINANZ share premium account (*BrE*); **auf das Emissions- und Akzeptgeschäft spezialisierte Bank** *f* BANK merchant bank (*BrE*); **Emissionsanzeige** *f* FINANZ tombstone ad; **Emissionsbank** *f* BANK bank of issue, issuing bank, investment bank; **Emissionsdatum** *nt* BÖRSE *Neuemission* issue date, offering date; **Emissionsdisagio** *nt* BÖRSE, FINANZ original issue discount (*OID*); **Emissionserlös** *m* FINANZ proceeds of an issue; **Emissionsfazilität** *f* FINANZ issuance facility; **Emissionsfirma** *f* FINANZ underwriting house; **Emissionsgebühr** *f* UMWELT *Verunreinigung* emission fee; **Emissionsgewinn** *m* FINANZ underwriting profit; **Emissionsgrenze** *f* UMWELT emission limit; **Emissionshaus** *nt* BÖRSE issuing house; **Emissionshöchstwert** *m* UMWELT primary standard; **Emissionsjahr** *nt* BÖRSE year of issue; **Emissionskonditionen** *f pl* FINANZ terms of issue; **Emissionskonsortium** *nt* BÖRSE distributing syndicate, FINANZ underwriting syndicate; **Emissionskosten** *pl* BÖRSE flotation cost, FINANZ cost of issue; **Emissionskurs** *m* BÖRSE issue price, offering price; **Emissionsmarkt** *m* BÖRSE issue market; **Emissionsprospekt** *m* BÖRSE prospectus, FINANZ prospectus, underwriting prospectus; **Emissionssatz** *m* FINANZ tender rate; **Emissionsschutzwall** *m* UMWELT emission reductions banking; **Emissionsstandard** *m* UMWELT emission standard; **Emissionssteuer** *f* BÖRSE, STEUER security issue tax; **Emissionsstoß** *m* BÖRSE flurry of new issue activity; **Emissionsübernahmekonsortium** *nt* FINANZ underwriting syndicate; **Emissionsvertrag** *m* BANK agreement among underwriters

Emittent *m* BANK, BÖRSE, FINANZ issuer, issuing company; **~ von Verbindlichkeiten** BÖRSE liability issuer

emittieren *vt* BANK, BÖRSE, FINANZ *Wertpapiere* issue

emittierend: **~e Gesellschaft** *f* BÖRSE issuing company

emittiert *adj* BANK, BÖRSE issued; **~e Aktien** *f pl* BÖRSE issued and floating shares

emotional: **~e Aufmachung** *f* V&M emotional appeal

Empfang *m* FREI, GESCHÄFT reception, reception area, TRANSP, VERWALT reception; ♦ **den ~ bescheinigen** GESCHÄFT receipt; **~ bestätigen** GESCHÄFT receipt; **den ~ von etw bestätigen** GESCHÄFT, KOMM acknowledge receipt of sth; **den ~ durch Brief bestätigen** KOMM acknowledge receipt by letter

empfangen **1.** *adj* GESCHÄFT received (*recd*); **2.** *vt* GESCHÄFT receive

Empfänger, in *m,f* IMP/EXP consignee, KOMM addressee, PERSON receiver, TRANSP consignee; **~ eines Zuschusses** PERSON recipient of an allowance

Empfang: **Empfangsberechtigte(r)** *mf* [decl. as adj] GRUND beneficiary; **Empfangsbereich** *m* FREI reception point; **Empfangsbescheinigung** *f* GESCHÄFT receipt, KOMM advice of delivery; **Empfangsbestätigung** *f* GESCHÄFT, KOMM acknowledgement (*ack*), acknowledgement of receipt; **Empfangsbestätigung** *f* **für Dokumentation** PATENT receipt for documents; **Empfangsbestätigung** *f* **für Dokumente** PATENT receipt for documents; **Empfangschef, in** *m,f* PERSON receptionist, V&M floorwalker; **Empfangsdatum** *nt* GESCHÄFT date of receipt, TRANSP delivery date; **Empfangsdepot** *nt* TRANSP reception depot; **Empfangshalle** *f* VERWALT reception area; **Empfangskomitee** *nt* GESCHÄFT welcoming party; **Empfangsschein** *m* KOMM advice of delivery; **Empfangssekretär, in** *m,f* PERSON receptionist; **Empfangsspediteur** *m* TRANSP receiving carrier; **Empfangsstelle** *f* **der Wareneingangsabteilung** TRANSP receiving station; **Empfangstransporter** *m* TRANSP receiving carrier

empfehlen *vt* GESCHÄFT advise, recommend

empfehlenswert *adj* GESCHÄFT advisable; **nicht ~** *adj* GESCHÄFT unadvisable

Empfehlung *f* GESCHÄFT recommendation; **Empfehlungsschreiben** *nt* KOMM letter of introduction, PERSON letter of recommendation; **Empfehlungszettel** *m* KOMM compliment slip

empfindlich *adj* BÖRSE sensitive; **~ reagierende Börse** *f* BÖRSE sensitive market

emphatisch *adj* GESCHÄFT emphatic

Empirie *f* VW empirics

empirisch *adj* GESCHÄFT, MATH empirical

emporschnellen *vi* GESCHÄFT rocket (*infrml*), shoot up, *Preise* soar

Emulation *f* COMP *Systeme* emulation; **Emulationskarte** *f* COMP emulation card; **Emulationsplatine** *f* COMP emulation board; **Emulationssoftware** *f* COMP emulation software

Emulator *m* COMP *Systeme* emulator

emulieren *vt* COMP *Systeme* emulate

EN *abbr* (*europäische Normen*) GESCHÄFT European standard specifications

End- *in cpds* GESCHÄFT end, final; **Endabnahme** *f* GESCHÄFT *von Waren* final acceptance; **Endabnehmer, in** *m,f* VW end consumer, end-user; **Endabrechnung** *f* RECHNUNG final accounts; **Endalter** *nt* VERSICH age at expiry; **Endanwender** *m* VW end-user; **Endaufnahme** *f* V&M pack shot; **Endbearbeitung** *f* IND finishing; **Endbestand** *m* RECHNUNG closing inventory, ending inventory, final balance

Ende *nt* GESCHÄFT *der Liste* end, tail, expiration, V&M final; **~ des Finanzjahres** RECHNUNG end of financial year; **~ der Mitteilung** COMP end of message (*EOM*); **~ der Versuchsperiode** V&M trial close; **das dann zu ~ gegangene Geschäftsjahr** *nt* RECHNUNG financial year then ended (*BrE*), fiscal year then ended (*AmE*); ♦ **zu ~ bringen** GESCHÄFT bring to an end, wrap up, *Produktion* wind up; **zu ~ gehen** GESCHÄFT run out, VW taper off; **zu einem ~ kommen** GESCHÄFT come to an end; **am oberen ~** GESCHÄFT at the top end; **am ~ des Tages** GESCHÄFT at the end of the day; **zu ~ verfolgen** MGMNT *Projekt* follow through

endemisch *adj* GESCHÄFT endemic

enden *vi* GESCHÄFT cease

End-: **Endergebnis** *nt* FINANZ, GESCHÄFT, VW bottom line (*infrml*), end result, net result; **Endgewinn** *m* FINANZ, RECHNUNG bottom line (*infrml*)

endfällig: **~e Anleihe** *f* BANK bullet

endgültig *adj* GESCHÄFT absolute, conclusive, final RECHT absolute; **~er Bescheid** *m* GESCHÄFT final notice; **~er Bestimmungsort** *m* GESCHÄFT, IMP/EXP final destination; **~e Präsidentschaftsvorwahl** *f* POL run-off primary (*AmE*); **~er Untersuchungsbericht** *m* GESCHÄFT non-negotiable report of findings (*NNRF*); **~er Untersuchungsergebnis** *nt* GESCHÄFT non-negotiable report of findings (*NNRF*); **~e Vereinbarung** *f* STEUER closing agreement (*AmE*); **~er Vertragsabrechnungspreis** *m* BÖRSE final contract settlement price; **~e Zahlung** *f* VW direct payment

End-: **Endkorrektur** *f* MEDIEN final proof

endlich: **~er Rohstoff** *m* UMWELT, VW depletable resource

End-: **Endloseinzug** *m* COMP *Drucker* continuous form feed; **Endlosformulare** *nt pl* GESCHÄFT continuous forms; **Endlospapier** *nt* COMP *Drucker* continuous stationery; **Endmontage** *f* GESCHÄFT final assembly; **Endnachfrage** *f* VW final demand

endogen: **~e Variable** *f* VW endogenous variable

Endogenisierung *f*: **~ exogener Variablen** VW endogenizing the exogenous

End-: **Endprodukt** *nt* GESCHÄFT end product, final product, VW final good; **Endsaldo** *m* BANK closing balance, RECHNUNG final balance; **Endtermin** *m* GESCHÄFT target date, RECHT final deadline; **Endterminverschiebung** *f* RECHT *Vertragsrecht* extension of original term; **Endverbrauch** *m* IMP/EXP end use; **Endverbraucher, in** *m,f* GESCHÄFT, V&M ultimate consumer, VW end consumer, end-user; **Endverbrauchsgüter** *nt pl* IMP/EXP end use goods; **Endverbrauchshändler, in** *m,f* IMP/EXP end use trader; **Endverlust** *m* FINANZ, RECHNUNG bottom line (*infrml*); **Endwertmodell** *nt* FINANZ final value model

Energie *f* (*E*) IND energy, power; ♦ **~ sparen** UMWELT save energy

Energie: **Energiebedarf** *m* VW energy demand; **Energieeinsparung** *f* GESCHÄFT, UMWELT energy efficiency; **Energieerhaltung** *f* UMWELT energy conservation; **Energieerzeugung** *f* IND power generation; **Energiekrise** *f* UMWELT energy crisis; **Energienachfrage** *f* VW energy demand; **Energienutzungsgrad** *m* GESCHÄFT, UMWELT energy efficiency; **Energiepolitik** *f* GESCHÄFT energy policy; **Energiequelle** *f* GESCHÄFT energy source; **Energiequellen** *f pl* UMWELT energy resources; **Energiereserven** *f pl* UMWELT energy reserves; **Energieressourcen** *f pl* UMWELT energy reserves, energy resources; **Energierückgewinnung** *f* UMWELT energy recovery

energiesparend: **~e Maschine** *f* UMWELT energy-efficient machine

Energie: **Energiesystem** *nt* GESCHÄFT energy system

energieverschwendend *adj* IND, UMWELT energy-wasting

Energie: **Energieversorguna** *f* GESCHÄFT energy supply; **Energievorräte** *m pl* IND, UMWELT energy reserves; **Energiewerte** *m pl* BÖRSE utilities; **Energiewirtschaft** *f* IND power industries, MGMNT energy management

energisch *adj* GESCHÄFT *Maßnahme, Programm* stringent, *Protest, Maßnahme* vigorous; **~e Verkaufstechnik** *f* V&M hard sell, hard selling

eng 1. *adj* GESCHÄFT close; ♦ **in die ~ere Auswahl kommen** GESCHÄFT, PERSON *Bewerbung* be shortlisted; **in die ~ere Auswahl nehmen** GESCHÄFT, PERSON shortlist; **~er fassen** GESCHÄFT *Vorschriften* stiffen; **in ~em Kontakt** GESCHÄFT in close touch; **2.** *adv* ♦ **~ mit jdm zusammenarbeiten** GESCHÄFT work closely with sb

eng: **~es Band** *nt* VW *des Wechselkursmechanismus der EU* narrow band; **~ definierte Geldmenge** *f* VW narrowly defined money supply; **~e Korrelation** *f* MATH close correlation; **~er Markt** *m* BÖRSE narrow market, tight market; **~er Raum** *m* TRANSP slot

Engagement *nt* FREI commitment, GESCHÄFT booking, *Handelsposition an Börse* engagement; **~ des Personals** PERSON *Arbeit* staff commitment

engagiert: **sich ~ einsetzen für** *phr* POL be a strong supporter of

Engel: **~sches Gesetz** *nt* VW Engel's law; **Engel-Koeffizient** *m* VW Engel coefficient

Engineering *nt* IND engineering

englisch: **~e Küstenverkehrszone** *f* TRANSP English Inshore Traffic Zone (*EITZ*); **~e Zinsrechnung** *f* BANK exact interest

Engpaß *m* GESCHÄFT, VW bottleneck

Engpässe: **die~ beseitigen in** *phr* VERWALT, VW debottleneck

Engpaßfaktor *m* VW constraining factor

en gros: **~ verkaufen** *phr* V&M sell in bulk

Engrosverkauf *m* GESCHÄFT wholesale business

engstirnig: **~e Bestimmungen** *f pl* FINANZ petty regulations

entbehrlich *adj* GESCHÄFT expendable

Entdeckungsstichprobe *f* MATH discovery sampling

enteignen *vt* RECHT, VERWALT expropriate

Enteignung *f* RECHT, VERWALT expropriation

enteignungsgleich: **~er Eingriff** *m* GRUND, RECHT inverse condemnation

Enteignung: **Enteignungsrecht** *nt* **des Staates** POL condemnation, eminent domain

Enteiser *m* TRANSP de-icing fluid

Enteisungsflüssigkeit *f* TRANSP de-icing fluid

Enter-Taste *f* COMP enter key

entfachen *vt* GESCHÄFT spark off

Entfaltung *f* GESCHÄFT development, growth; **~ der Persönlichkeit** PERSON personal growth

entfernen *vt* COMP *Textverarbeitung* remove, GESCHÄFT eliminate

entfernt *adj* GESCHÄFT aloof, remote, eliminated; **~e Möglichkeit** *f* GESCHÄFT remote possibility

Entfernung *f* GESCHÄFT removal, elimination, TRANSP distance

entflechten *vt* GESCHÄFT *Konzern* unscramble, *Preise* unbundle

Entflechtung *f* GESCHÄFT *Preise* unbundling, *Trusts* trustbusting (*infrml*) (*AmE*), VW demerger

entfremden *vt* PERSON, VW alienate, distance

entfremdet: **~er Funktionär** *m* POL mandarin

Entfremdung *f* PERSON, VW alienation

ENTF-Taste *f* COMP delete character (*DEL*), delete key (*DEL*)

Entführungsversicherung *f* VERSICH kidnap insurance

entfusionieren *vt* GESCHÄFT, VW demerger

Entfusionierung *f* GESCHÄFT, VW demerger

entgangen: **~e Steuereinnahmen** *f pl* VW *des Staates* lost tax revenue

entgegenhalten *vt* PATENT cite

Entgegenhaltung *f* PATENT citation

Entgegenkommen *nt* GESCHÄFT *Zugeständnis* accommodation

entgegenkommend: **~e Schuldenkonsolidierung** *f* FINANZ, VERWALT soft funding

entgegennehmen *vt* GESCHÄFT, KOMM *Gespräch* accept

entgegenwirkend *adj* GESCHÄFT adverse

Entgelt *nt* BÖRSE financial reward, VW compensation; **~ für die Unternehmensführung** PERSON *volkswirtschaftliche Gesamtrechnung* executive remuneration; ♦ **als ~ für** GESCHÄFT as a reward for

entgeltlich: ~**er Inhaber** *m*, ~**e Inhaberin** *f* BANK holder for value

Entgelt: **Entgeltvereinbarung** *f* VW compensation agreement

enthalten: **sich ~** *v refl* GESCHÄFT, POL abstain

Enthaltung *f* GESCHÄFT, POL abstention

enthüllen *vt* GESCHÄFT bring to light, *Plan* unveil

Entlade- *in cpds* TRANSP *Fracht* unloading, offloading, discharging; **Entladeantrag** *m* TRANSP request to offload; **Entladehafen** *m* TRANSP discharge port, port of discharge; **Entladekai** *m* TRANSP discharging berth, discharging wharf; **Entladekran** *m* TRANSP unloader crane

entladen *vt* IND offload, TRANSP unload

Entladen *nt* IND, TRANSP offloading, unloading

entladen: **nicht ~** *adj* TRANSP undischarged

Entladung *f* TRANSP unloading, unshipment, *eines Lieferwagens* devanning

entlassen *vt* GESCHÄFT *Arbeitskräfte* shed, PERSON make redundant (*BrE*), *Arbeitskräfte* lay off, dismiss, fire (*infrml*), sack (*BrE*) (*infrml*), discharge; ◆ **jdn ~** PERSON give sb his cards (*BrE*) (*infrml*), give sb the sack (*BrE*) (*infrml*)

Entlassung *f* PERSON *Arbeit* dismissal, firing (*infrml*), sack (*BrE*) (*infrml*), *nach spezifischen gesetzlichen Bestimmungen* (*EPCA 1978*) redundancy (*BrE*); ~ **aus triftigem Grund** PERSON fair dismissal, just cause dismissal; ~ **aus einer Verpflichtung vor Gericht** RECHT release of recognizance; **Entlassungsabfindung** *f* GESCHÄFT redundancy payment, termination benefits, severance pay, severance wage; **Entlassungsgehalt** *nt* PERSON dismissal wage; **Entlassungsgrund** *m* PERSON grounds for dismissal; **Entlassungsgründe** *m pl* RECHT *Verträge* case of relief; **Entlassungspapiere** *f pl* PERSON pink slip (*infrml*) (*AmE*), cards (*infrml*) (*BrE*) *Kündigung durch den Arbeitgeber* termination papers; **Entlassungsrücksprache** *f* PERSON redundancy consultation; **Entlassungsschreiben** *nt* VW pink slip (*infrml*) (*AmE*); **Entlassungsverfahren** *nt* PERSON redundancy procedure; **Entlassungszahlung** *f* PERSON lay-off pay

entlasten *vt* BANK, RECHT exculpate, STEUER relieve; ◆ ~ **von** RECHT *Verpflichtungen* discharge, extinguish

entlastend *adj* BANK, RECHT *Treuhänder* exculpatory

Entlastung *f* STEUER relief; ~ **der Binnenzollbehandlung** IMP/EXP inward process relief; ~ **des Gemeinschuldners** RECHT discharge of a bankrupt; ~ **des Treuhänders** RECHT discharge of the trustee; **Entlastungsgründe** *m pl* RECHT *Verträge* case of relief

Entlohnung *f* GESCHÄFT remuneration, payment (*PYT*); ~ **in Sachwerten** GESCHÄFT payment in kind

entmutigen *vt* GESCHÄFT, PERSON discourage

Entnahmemaximierung *f* VW maximization of annual withdrawals

Entnahmeplan *m* BÖRSE *bei Vermögensbildungsmaßnahmen* withdrawal plan

entnehmen *vt* BANK draw

Entrichtung *f* FINANZ payment

entschädigen *vt* GESCHÄFT, PATENT reimburse, PERSON compensate, RECHT, VERSICH compensate, indemnify, VW compensate; ◆ ~ **für** PATENT compensate for; **jdn für etw ~** GESCHÄFT compensate sb for sth

Entschädigung *f* GESCHÄFT, PATENT damages, reimbursement, PERSON compensation, RECHT compensation, indemnity, redress, VERSICH compensation, indemnity, VW compensation; ~ **mit Strafcharakter** VERSICH punitive damages; ~ **für Verlust und Schaden** VERSICH compensation for loss or damage; **Entschädigungsanspruch** *m* RECHT *Regreßanspruch* claim of compensation, indemnity claim, right of recovery; **Entschädigungsbetrag** *m* PERSON *Schadensabfindung* compensation money; **Entschädigungsfonds** *m* BÖRSE compensation fund (*BrE*); **Entschädigungsleistung** *f* VERSICH adjustment; **Entschädigungssumme** *f* VERSICH compensatory amount; **Entschädigungsvertrag** *m* VERSICH contract of indemnity; **Entschädigungszahlung** *f* VW compensatory amount

entschärfen *vt* PERSON defuse

entscheiden 1. *vt* GESCHÄFT adjudicate, decide, RECHT find; ◆ **gerichtlich ~** RECHT adjudicate to; **2. sich ~** *v refl* MGMNT opt; ◆ **sich ~ für** MGMNT opt for

Entscheiden *nt* GESCHÄFT, MGMNT decision making

entscheidend *adj* GESCHÄFT, MGMNT, PERSON decisive

Entscheidung *f* GESCHÄFT decision, RECHT *eines Verfahrens vor Gericht* determination, *Entscheid* ruling; ~ **über Eigenfertigung oder Kauf** GESCHÄFT make-or-buy decision; ~ **auf höchster Ebene** GESCHÄFT high-level decision; ~ **in letzter Minute** GESCHÄFT last-minute decision; ◆ **eine ~ anfechten** RECHT appeal against a decision; **eine ~ aufschieben** GESCHÄFT shelve a decision; **über seine ~ berichten** GESCHÄFT report one's conclusions; **eine ~ fällen** GESCHÄFT, MGMNT make a decision; **eine ~ treffen** GESCHÄFT, MGMNT make a decision; **eine ~ zugunsten von jdm fällen** GESCHÄFT give a ruling in favor of sb (*AmE*), give a ruling in favour of sb (*BrE*)

Entscheidung: **Entscheidungsanalyse** *f* MGMNT decision analysis; **Entscheidungsbaum** *m* MGMNT, PERSON decision tree

entscheidungsfindend: ~**e Einheit** *f* MGMNT decision-making unit

Entscheidungsfindung *f* MGMNT decision making; **Entscheidungsfindungsprozeß** *m* MGMNT decision-making process; **Entscheidungsfindungssystem** *nt* MGMNT decision support system (*DSS*)

Entscheidung: **Entscheidungsfreiheit** *f* GESCHÄFT, POL, V&M freedom of choice, option; **Entscheidungsgrund** *m* GESCHÄFT ratio decidendi; **Entscheidungshilfen** *f pl* GESCHÄFT decision-making aids; **Entscheidungshorizont** *m* VW *Arbeitsbewertung* time span; **Entscheidungsmodell** *nt* MGMNT decision model

entscheidungsorientiert: ~**e Buchführung** *f* RECHNUNG management accounting; ~**er Buchhalter** *m*, ~**e Buchhalterin** *f* RECHNUNG management accountant; ~**es Rechnungswesen** *nt* RECHNUNG managerial accounting, management accountancy, management accounting

Entscheidung: **Entscheidungspaket** *nt* FINANZ, MGMNT decision package; **Entscheidungsprozeß** *m* MGMNT decision process, decision-making process; **Entscheidungstabelle** *f* COMP decision table; **Entscheidungstheorie** *f* MGMNT decision theory; **Entscheidungsträger, in** *m,f* GESCHÄFT, MGMNT *in Behörden* decision maker, decision-making unit; **Entscheidungsunterstützungssystem** *nt* MGMNT

decision support system (*DSS*); **Entscheidungsvariable** *f* VW choice variable
entschieden *adj* GESCHÄFT decided
Entschließungsentwurf *m* RECHT draft resolution
Entschluß *m* GESCHÄFT resolution, resolve
entschlüsseln *vt* COMP decrypt, GESCHÄFT unscramble
Entschlüsselung *f* COMP *Programmiersprachen*, KOMM decryption
entschlußfreudig *adj* GESCHÄFT decisive
entschuldigen: sich ~ *v refl* GESCHÄFT apologize; ◆ **sich ~ bei** GESCHÄFT apologize to; **sich ~ für** GESCHÄFT apologize for; **sich gegenüber jdm für etwas ~** GESCHÄFT apologize to sb for sth
Entschuldigung *f* GESCHÄFT apology; **Entschuldigungsschreiben** *nt* KOMM letter of apology
Entsorgung *f* GESCHÄFT *Müll* refuse disposal, UMWELT disposal, *Müll* refuse disposal; **Entsorgungseinrichtung** *f* UMWELT *Müll, Abfall* disposal unit
entspannen: sich ~ *v refl* FREI relax
Entsparen *nt* VW dissaving, negative saving
entsperren *vt* COMP *Tastatur* unlock, FINANZ *Konto* unblock
entsprechen *vi* [+dat] GESCHÄFT correspond to, *Erfordernissen* fit, *Normen* comply with, *Vorjahreszahlen* match, conform
entsprechend 1. *adj* GESCHÄFT commensurate, corresponding, *Erwartungen* in line with, analogous; **2.** *adv* GESCHÄFT accordingly
entsprechend: ~es Stück *nt* GESCHÄFT analog
entspricht: es ~ der üblichen Praxis, so zu handeln *phr* GESCHÄFT it is standard practice to do so
entstaatlichen *vt* GESCHÄFT, VW privatize
Entstaatlichung *f* GESCHÄFT, VW privatization
entstanden *adj* RECHNUNG accrued, incurred; **~e Aufwendungen** *f pl* RECHNUNG incurred expenses; **~e Ausgaben** *f pl* RECHNUNG incurred costs; **~e Kosten** *pl* RECHNUNG incurred costs; **~e Refinanzierungskosten** *pl* BÖRSE realized cost of funds; **~e Verbindlichkeit** *f* RECHNUNG accrued liability
entstehen *vi* FINANZ, GESCHÄFT *Kosten*, RECHNUNG accrue
entstehend *adj* FINANZ accruing
Entstehung: Entstehungs- und Verteilungsrechnung *f* VW National Income and Product Accounts (*NIPA*)
enttäuschend *adj* GESCHÄFT disappointing
entvölkern *vt* GESCHÄFT depopulate
Entvölkerung *f* GESCHÄFT depopulation
Entweder-Oder *nt* GESCHÄFT alternative, either/or
entwerfen *vt* COMP draft, GESCHÄFT plan, sketch, design, outline, RECHT draft
entwerten *vt* RECHNUNG, VW depreciate
Entwertung *f* VW debasement, depreciation
entwickeln 1. *vt* COMP *System, Software*, GESCHÄFT, IND, TRANSP, V&M develop; **2. sich ~** *v refl* GESCHÄFT shape up; ◆ **sich sehr schnell ~** VW boom
entwickelt: ~er Markt *m* V&M developed market; **~e Volkswirtschaft** *f* VW developed economy
Entwicklung *f* COMP development, GESCHÄFT advancement, *Ertrag* evolution, IND development, V&M *eines Produkts*, VW development; **~ des Managements** MGMNT management development; **~ eines neuen Produktes** V&M new product development;

Entwicklungsausschuß *m* RECHT development committee; **Entwicklungsbank** *f* BANK development bank
entwicklungsbedingt: ~es Überholtsein *nt* IND *Produktion* technological obsolescence
Entwicklung: Entwicklungsbohrprogramm *nt* VW developmental drilling program (*AmE*), developmental drilling programme (*BrE*)
entwicklungsfähig *adj* FINANZ viable, GESCHÄFT capable of development, viable
Entwicklung: Entwicklungsgebiet *nt* VW development region; **Entwicklungshelfer, in** *m,f* GESCHÄFT volunteer development worker
Entwicklungshilfe *f* BANK aid, VW budget payment, development aid, development assistance, donor aid, program aid (*AmE*), programme aid (*BrE*), *wirtschaftlich* economic aid; ◆ **~ leisten** FINANZ, VW aid
Entwicklungshilfe: Entwicklungshilfekredit *m* BANK aid development loan (*BrE*), aid loan, development loan; **Entwicklungshilfeorganisation** *f* FINANZ, VW *Entwicklungsländer* aid donor; **Entwicklungshilfeprojekt** *nt* FINANZ aid-financed project, VW Overseas Service Aid Scheme (*OSAS*), aid-financed project
Entwicklung: Entwicklungskontrolle *f* IND progress control; **Entwicklungskosten** *pl* FINANZ development expenditure; **Entwicklungslabor** *nt* IND research laboratory; **Entwicklungsland** *nt* VW less-developed country (*LDC*), developing country, Third World country; **Entwicklungsmanagement** *nt* MGMNT development management; **Entwicklungsmodell, das zwei Lücken berücksichtigt** *phr* VW two-gap development model; **Entwicklungsökonomie** *f* VW development economics; **Entwicklungsplanung** *f* VW development planning; **Entwicklungspolitik** *f* POL development policy; **Entwicklungspotential** *nt* GESCHÄFT development potential; **Entwicklungsprogramm** *nt* FINANZ, MGMNT development program (*AmE*), development programme (*BrE*), PERSON training program (*AmE*), training programme (*BrE*); **Entwicklungsprogramm nt der Vereinten Nationen** (*UNDP*) VW United Nations Development Programme (*UNDP*); **Entwicklungsprojekt** *nt* VW development project; **Entwicklungsrichtung** *f* GESCHÄFT tendency, VW *des Zinsniveaus* direction; **Entwicklungsstrategie** *f* MGMNT development strategy; **Entwicklungstendenz** *f* GESCHÄFT tendency; **Entwicklungstendenz** *f* einer Strategie GESCHÄFT, MGMNT strategy formulation; **Entwicklungs-zyklus** *m* eines Produktes V&M product life cycle; **Entwicklungszyklus** *m* des Wohnwesens GRUND housing development
entworfen *adj* COMP drafted, GESCHÄFT sketched, designed, RECHT drafted
Entwurf *m* COMP *Drucker* draft, GESCHÄFT sketch, design, outline, RECHNUNG layout, RECHT draft; **~ des Haushaltsplans** RECHNUNG draft budget; ◆ **als ~** RECHT in draft form
Entwurf: Entwurfsautomatisierung *f* COMP design automation (*DA*); **Entwurfsdruck** *m* COMP draft printing; **Entwurfshilfen** *f pl* GESCHÄFT design aids; **Entwurfsskizze** *f* einer Werbesendung V&M storyboard; **Entwurfsmodus** *m* COMP *Drucker* draft mode; **Entwurfsphase** *f* RECHT draft stage; **im Entwurfsstadium** *phr* MGMNT on the drawing board
entzerren *vt* GESCHÄFT *Preiszinsstruktur* correct a distorted pattern in, rectify

Entzerrung *f* GESCHÄFT correction, rectification
entziehen 1. *vt* GESCHÄFT, FINANZ, VW withdraw; **2. sich ~** *v refl* RECHT *zahlungssäumiger Gläubiger* abscond
Entziehung *f* FINANZ, GESCHÄFT, VW withdrawal
entziffern *vt* GESCHÄFT decipher
Entzug *m* VW *Kaufkraftentzug* drain
EP *abbr* (*Europaparlament*) POL EP (*European Parliament*)
EPA *abbr* (*Europäisches Patentamt*) PATENT EPO (*European Patent Organization*)
Ephemeralisierung *f* VW ephemeralization
EPO *abbr* (*Europäische Patentorganisation*) PATENT EPO (*European Patent Organization*)
EPÜ *abbr* (*Europäisches Patentübereinkommen*) PATENT, RECHT EPC (*European Patent Convention*)
ERA *abbr* (*Einheitliche Richtlinien und Praktiken für Dokumenten-Akkreditierung*) VW UC&P (*Uniform Customs and Practice for Documentary Credits*)
erarbeiten *vt* MGMNT prepare
Erarbeitung *f* MGMNT *Bericht* preparation
Erb- *in cpds* GRUND, RECHT inheritance; **Erbanspruch** *m* RECHT claim to an inheritance; **Erbanteil** *m* RECHT share of the inheritance; **Erbbaurecht** *nt* RECHT rental right; **Erbbaurechtsvertrag** *m* GRUND *Grundstückspacht* ground lease; **Erbbauzins** *m* GRUND ground rent
Erbe 1. *m* RECHT heir; **2.** *nt* RECHT *Nachlaß* inheritance
erben 1. *vt* RECHT inherit; **2.** *vi* RECHT succeed
Erbe: **Erbengemeinschaft** *f* RECHT joint heirs
erbenlos: **~er Nachlaß** *m* RECHT absence of next of kin, bona vacantia
Erb-: **Erbfall** *m* RECHT *Vermögen* devolution, inheritance; **Erbfolge** *f* GESCHÄFT, RECHT succession
Erbin *f* RECHT heiress
erbitten *vt* GESCHÄFT solicit, *Bestätigung* seek
erbittert: **~er Wettbewerb** *m* GESCHÄFT bitter competition
Erb-: **Erbpacht** *f* GRUND hereditary lease, RECHT rental right
erbracht: **für ~e Leistungen** *phr* GESCHÄFT for services rendered
Erb-: **Erbrecht** *nt* RECHT succession law
Erbringung *f*: **~ von Dienstleistungen** GESCHÄFT performance of services, rendering of services, service delivery, VW supply of services
Erbschaft *f* FINANZ inheritance; ♦ **eine ~ ausschlagen** RECHT renounce an inheritance
Erbschaft: **Erbschafts- und Schenkungssteuer** *f* STEUER capital transfer tax (*BrE*) (*CTT*); **Erbschaftssteuer** *f* FINANZ inheritance tax, RECHT *bei Testamentserbfolge* probate duty, STEUER inheritance tax (*AmE*), death duty (*obs*) (*BrE*), legacy duty (*BrE*), legacy tax (*AmE*), estate tax (*AmE*); **Erbschaftssteuererklärung** *f* STEUER inheritance tax return; **Erbschaftssteuer** *f pl* STEUER death duty (*dat*) (*BrE*), death tax (*AmE*); **Erbschaftssteuerpreis** *m* BÖRSE probate price
Erbsenzähler *m* *infrml* RECHNUNG beancounter (*infrml*)
Erb-: **Erbzins** *m* SOZIAL rent charge
Erdarbeiten *f pl* GRUND earthworks
Erdbebenversicherung *f* VERSICH earthquake insurance
Erdgas *nt* UMWELT natural gas

erdgebunden *adj* GESCHÄFT, MEDIEN *Übertragungstechnik, Funk, Fernsehen* terrestrial
Erdöl *nt* IND, UMWELT oil, petroleum; **Erdölfeld** *nt* IND, UMWELT oilfield
erdölführend *adj* IND, UMWELT oil-bearing
erdölhaltig *adj* IND, UMWELT oil-bearing, petroliferous
Erdöl: **Erdölindustrie** *f* IND, UMWELT oil industry, petroleum industry; **Erdöllagerstätte** *f* UMWELT oil deposit; **Erdöllistenpreis** *m* GESCHÄFT, VW posted price
erdölproduzierend: **~es Land** *nt* IND, UMWELT, VW oil-producing country
Erdöl: **Erdölraffinerie** *f* IND oil refinery; **Erdölwerte** *m pl* BÖRSE oils
Erdrutsch *m* POL landslide
Erdung *f* COMP, IND *Elektrizität* earthing (*BrE*), grounding (*AmE*)
ERE *abbr* (*Europäische Rechnungseinheit*) FINANZ, VW EUA (*European Unit of Account*)
Ereignis *nt* COMP, GESCHÄFT event; **~ nach dem Bilanzstichtag** RECHNUNG post-balance-sheet event; **Ereignisse** *nt pl* **nach dem Bilanzstichtag** RECHNUNG events subsequent to the closing date
erfahren 1. *adj* GESCHÄFT seasoned, experienced, PERSON *Arbeit, Laufbahn* experienced, expert; **2.** *vt* GESCHÄFT experience
erfahren: **~e Mitarbeiter** *m pl* PERSON experienced workforce
Erfahrung *f* GESCHÄFT experience, PERSON background, expertise, VW experience good; **Erfahrungsaustausch** *m* GESCHÄFT exchange of know-how, interchange of know-how; **Erfahrungsbericht** *m* MEDIEN report; **Erfahrungskurve** *f* VW experience curve; **Erfahrungsmangel** *m* PERSON lack of experience; **Erfahrungstarifierung** *f* VERSICH experience rating; **Erfahrungsverlust** *m* FINANZ, VERSICH experience loss; **Erfahrungswerte** *m pl* GESCHÄFT experience figures
erfassen *vt* GESCHÄFT *Daten* record, collect
erfaßt *adj* GESCHÄFT recorded, V&M cumulative; **nicht ~** *adj* GESCHÄFT unrecorded; **~e Gesamthörerzahl** *f* V&M cumulative audience
Erfassung *f* GESCHÄFT collection, VERWALT coverage; **~ von Geschäftsvorfällen** VW recording of business transactions; **Erfassungsbereich** *m* GESCHÄFT scope of coverage; **Erfassungsbreite** *f* GESCHÄFT scope of coverage
erfinden *vt* IND, PATENT invent
Erfinder, in *m,f* IND, PATENT inventor
erfinderisch *adj* IND, PATENT inventive
Erfinder: **Erfinderrecht** *nt* PATENT title of the invention
Erfindung *f* GESCHÄFT brainchild, IND, PATENT, VW invention; **Erfindungshöhe** *f* PATENT inventive step; **Erfindungspatent** *nt* RECHT patent of invention; **Erfindungsübereinstimmung** *f* PATENT unity of invention
Erfolg *m* GESCHÄFT success; ♦ **mit ~ geprüft** GESCHÄFT passed; **~ haben** GESCHÄFT succeed
erfolglos *adj* GESCHÄFT unsuccessful; **~e Bewerbung** *f* PERSON *Stellensuche* unsuccessful job application; **~e Werbung** *f* V&M burst advertising
erfolgreich *adj* GESCHÄFT, V&M successful; ♦ **~ sein** GESCHÄFT succeed
erfolgreich: **~es Ergebnis** *nt* GESCHÄFT *von Verhandlungen* successful outcome; **~es Jahr** *nt*

GESCHÄFT banner year; **wenig ~es Produkt** *nt* V&M dog; **~es Unternehmen** *nt* VW going business, going concern, *Projekt* successful venture

Erfolg: **Erfolgsaussicht** *f* GESCHÄFT viability; **Erfolgsbereich** *f* MGMNT *eines Unternehmens* profit center (*AmE*), profit centre (*BrE*); **Erfolgsbeteiligung** *f* FINANZ, PERSON, RECHNUNG profit-sharing; **Erfolgsbeteiligungsplan** *m* GESCHÄFT profit-sharing plan (*AmE*), profit-sharing scheme (*BrE*); **Erfolgsgeschichte** *f* V&M success story; **Erfolgshonorar** *nt* GESCHÄFT contingent fee, VERWALT incentive fee; **Erfolgskennzahl** *f* FINANZ profitability ratio; **Erfolgskonto** *nt* BANK operating account, trading account, working account; **Erfolgskriterium** *nt* VW measure of performance; **Erfolgsmensch** *m* PERSON high flier; **Erfolgsplanung** *f* FINANZ, GESCHÄFT profit planning; **Erfolgsquotient** *m* GESCHÄFT achievement quotient; **Erfolgsstrategie** *f* FINANZ profit strategy; **Erfolgstest** *m* GESCHÄFT achievement test; **Erfolgsvergleichsrechnung** *f* FINANZ comparative earnings analysis

erfolgswirksam: nicht ~e Kosten *pl* VW unexpired cost

Erfolg: **Erfolgszurechnung** *f* PERSON *Gewinn- und Verlustrechnung, Bilanz, Steuern* allocation of earnings, income statement

erforderlich: ~e Arbeitskräfte *f pl* PERSON necessary labor (*AmE*), necessary labour (*BrE*); **~es Handeln** *nt* GESCHÄFT required action; **~e Investitionsrendite** *f* FINANZ hurdle rate of return; **~e Kapitaldecke** *f* BANK capital adequacy

erfordern *vt* GESCHÄFT require, necessitate

Erfordernis *nt* GESCHÄFT requirement, prerequisite

erfreuen: sich ~ *v refl* [+gen] GESCHÄFT enjoy

erfüllen *vt* GESCHÄFT *Anforderungen* meet, *Formalitäten, Bedingungen* comply with, *Pflicht, Aufgabe* perform, *seine Verpflichtungen* honour (*BrE*), honor (*AmE*), *Verpflichtungen* fulfill (*AmE*), fulfil (*BrE*), RECHT complete, execute, VERWALT execute; **nicht ~** *vt* GESCHÄFT *Erwartungen* fall short of

erfüllt *adj* RECHT *Vertrag* completed, executed; **~er Vertrag** *m* RECHT executed contract

Erfüllung *f* GESCHÄFT compliance, performance, RECHT execution, performance, V&M fulfilment (*BrE*), fulfillment (*AmE*); **~ von Warenterminkontrakten vor Fälligkeit** BÖRSE ringing out; **bei ~ zahlbarer Betrag** *m* RECHNUNG amount payable on settlement; ♦ **zur ~ von** RECHNUNG in satisfaction of; **~ durchsetzen** GESCHÄFT force performance

Erfüllung: **Erfüllungsannahme** *f* RECHT *Vertrag* acceptance as performance; **Erfüllungsfrist** *f* RECHT *Vertragsrecht* completion deadline; **Erfüllungsgarantie** *f* GESCHÄFT contract bond, performance bond, RECHT *Vertragsrecht* indemnity obligation; **Erfüllungsgehilfe** *m* RECHT *Vertragsrecht* person employed by the debtor in the performance of his or her obligations; **Erfüllungshindernis** *nt* VW obstacle of performance; **Erfüllungsklage** *f* RECHT *Vertragsrecht* action for specific performance; **Erfüllungskosten** *pl* RECHNUNG, UMWELT compliance costs; **Erfüllungsmethode** *f* STEUER compliance system; **Erfüllungsort** *m* RECHT *Vertragsrecht* place of performance, TRANSP place of delivery (*POD*); **Erfüllungsprüfung** *f* RECHNUNG compliance audit; **Erfüllungssystem** *nt* STEUER compliance system; **Erfüllungstag** *m* BÖRSE settlement day;

Erfüllungstest *m* GESCHÄFT compliance test; **Erfüllungsverweigerung** *f* RECHT refusal to fulfil an obligation (*BrE*), refusal to fulfill an obligation (*AmE*)

ergänzen *vt* GESCHÄFT supplement, complement, complete, RECHT supplement

ergänzend *adj* GESCHÄFT complementary, ancillary, PATENT supplementary; **~es Buchhaltungssytem** *nt* RECHNUNG supplementary accounting system; **~es Sondereinlageprogramm** *nt* BANK Supplementary Special Deposit Scheme (*BrE*); **~e Tätigkeiten** *f pl* GESCHÄFT ancillary operations

Ergänzendes *nt* FINANZ supplementaries

ergänzt *adj* GESCHÄFT completed, supplemented

Ergänzung *f* BÖRSE add-on, GESCHÄFT add-on, addition, supplement, PATENT amendment; ♦ **ohne ~, ohne Korrektur** GESCHÄFT no addition, no correction

Ergänzung: **Ergänzungsabgabe** *f* GESCHÄFT surcharge; **Ergänzungsgrundlage** *f* GESCHÄFT add-on basis; **Ergänzungsinlandseinlagenzertifikate** *nt pl* BÖRSE add-on domestic certificates of deposit (*BrE*) (*add-on CDs*); **Ergänzungsrendite** *f* BÖRSE add-on yield; **Ergänzungsverzinsungswert** *m* BÖRSE add-on yield equivalent

ergattern *vt* GESCHÄFT snatch

ergaunern *vt* GESCHÄFT hustle (*infrml*) (*AmE*)

Ergebnis *nt* FINANZ profit performance, GESCHÄFT outcome, result; ♦ **als ~** GESCHÄFT as a result; **mit dem ~, daß** GESCHÄFT with the result that; **das ~ abwarten** GESCHÄFT sit on the fence; **über seine Ergebnisse berichten** GESCHÄFT report one's findings; **Ergebnisse erzielen** GESCHÄFT, PERSON get results

Ergebnis: **Ergebnisanalyse** *f* VW performance analysis; **Ergebniseinheit** *f* FINANZ, MGMNT, VW profit center (*AmE*), profit centre (*BrE*); **Ergebnisplanung** *f* FINANZ profit planning; **Ergebnisrechnung** *f* RECHNUNG operating statement

Ergiebigkeit *f* GESCHÄFT abundance, plentifulness, IND productivity

Ergonom, in *m,f* GESCHÄFT ergonomist

Ergonomie *f* COMP ergonomics, PERSON *Arbeit* ergonomics, human engineering, VERWALT ergonomics

ergonomisch 1. *adj* COMP, GESCHÄFT ergonomic; **2.** *adv* COMP ergonomically; ♦ **~ konstruiert** *adj* COMP *Arbeitsplatz* ergonomically designed

Erhalt *m* GESCHÄFT receipt (*rcpt, recpt*); **~ und Verladen** *nt* **von Fracht** TRANSP receiving and loading of cargo; ♦ **bei ~ von** GESCHÄFT on receipt of

erhalten *vt* GESCHÄFT gain, obtain, receive, PATENT obtain, RECHT recover, *Genehmigung* obtain, UMWELT *bewahren* preserve; **nicht ~** *vt* BÖRSE fail to receive; ♦ **~ haben** GESCHÄFT *Brief, Zahlung* be in receipt of

erhältlich *adj* GESCHÄFT available, obtainable; **nicht ~** *adj* GESCHÄFT not available, unavailable

Erhaltung *f* UMWELT conservation, *von Lebensräumen* preservation; **auf ~ der Bodenschätze ausgerichtete Politik** GESCHÄFT, MGMNT resource management policy; **Erhaltungsaufwand** *m* STEUER maintenance expenditures; **Erhaltungscamp** *nt* UMWELT conservation camp

erheben *vt* GESCHÄFT survey, *Steuern, Gebühren* levy, MATH ascertain, RECHT *Klage* bring, *Anspruch, Forderung* submit, STEUER *Steuern* levy, VW ascertain

erheblich *adj* BÖRSE substantial, GESCHÄFT considerable, substantial, VW sizeable; **~es Risiko** *nt* BÖRSE substantial risk; **~e Strafe** f **für Falschangaben** STEUER serious misdeclaration penalty (*BrE*)

Erheblichkeit f RECHNUNG materiality

Erhebung f FINANZ levy, GESCHÄFT survey, collection, IMP/EXP *Abgaben, Zollgebühren* levy, V&M survey; **Erhebungsgebühr** FINANZ survey fee

erhöhen vt GESCHÄFT advance, *Produktion* step up, *Preis, Produktion* increase, *Preise* jack up (*infrml*), *Wert* raise, *Wirkung* heighten, STEUER enrich, V&M advance, *Produktion* step up, *Preis, Produktion* increase, *Preise* jack up (*infrml*), *Wert* raise, *Wirkung* heighten, VW *Kaufkraft* enhance

erhöhend: sich ~e Steuer f STEUER buoyant tax

erhöht adj GESCHÄFT advanced; **~e Grundlage** f STEUER stepped-up basis; **~es Risiko** nt VERSICH abnormal risk; **~er Wert** m GESCHÄFT increased value (*iv*)

Erhöhung f FINANZ raise (*AmE*), rise (*BrE*), GESCHÄFT boost, increase, advance, PERSON raise (*AmE*), rise (*BrE*), V&M advance; **~ des Kapitals** VW capital increase

erholen: sich ~ v refl BÖRSE rally, GESCHÄFT revive, VW pick up, *Wirtschaft* recover

Erholung f BÖRSE rallying, VW pick-up (*infrml*); **~ im nachbörslichen Verkehr** BÖRSE after-hours rally; **~ am Rentenmarkt** BÖRSE bond market rally; ◆ **die ~ ist im Gang** VW the recovery is under way

Erholung: **Erholungseinrichtungen** f pl FREI recreational facilities

Erinnerung f GESCHÄFT reminder; **Erinnerungsbrief** m V&M follow-up letter; **Erinnerungsschreiben** nt KOMM follow-up letter; **Erinnerungstest** m V&M aided recall test; **Erinnerungswerbung** f V&M reminder advertising

erkannt: ~er Verlust m VERSICH known loss

erkennbar: ~er Mangel m RECHT *Vertragsrecht* apparent defect

erkennen: ~ lassen vt GESCHÄFT signify

Erkenntnis f MGMNT cognition; **Erkenntnistätigkeit** f MGMNT cognition

Erkennungsmelodie f MEDIEN, V&M signature tune, theme tune jingle

Erkennungsverzögerung f VW recognition lag

erklären vt GESCHÄFT explain, IMP/EXP, STEUER *bekanntgeben* declare; ◆ **jdn für etw ~** RECHT adjudge sb to do sth

erklärt: ~er Zollwert m IMP/EXP declared value for customs

Erklärung f GESCHÄFT declaration, statement, explanation, MEDIEN, POL statement; **~ der eingeschätzten Steuereingänge** STEUER declaration of estimated tax (*AmE*); **~ über geschätzte Steuereingänge** STEUER declaration of estimated tax (*AmE*); **~ der Lieferbereitschaft** TRANSP notice of shipment; ◆ **eine ~ abgeben** MEDIEN put out a statement

Erklärung: **Erklärungsfrist** f BÖRSE exercise deadline

erkundigen vt V&M enquire

Erkundigung f V&M enquiry; **Erkundigungstest** m V&M enquiry test

Erkundungen: ~ einziehen phr MGMNT, V&M make enquiries

erlangen vt GESCHÄFT acquire, obtain, gain

erlangt adj GESCHÄFT acquired, obtained

Erlangung f GESCHÄFT obtainment

Erlaß m POL decree, RECHT remission, enactment, *einer Strafe, von Schulden* release, remittal

erlaßbar: ~e Anleihe f FINANZ forgivable loan

erlassen vt FINANZ waive, release RECHT *Gesetz* enact, legislate, *Strafe* abate

Erlassung f FINANZ waiving; **~ einer Schuld** FINANZ waiving of a debt

erlauben vt BANK, GESCHÄFT, PATENT allow, RECHT allow, permit

Erlaubnis f BANK, GESCHÄFT, PATENT authorization, RECHT licence (*BrE*), license (*AmE*), permit

erlaubt adj GESCHÄFT admissible, allowable, authorized, licensed, RECHT permitted; **~e Fangquote** f VW allowable catch

erläutern vt GESCHÄFT explain

Erläuterung f GESCHÄFT commentary, explanation

erleben vt GESCHÄFT experience, undergo

erledigen vt GESCHÄFT dispatch; ◆ **etw ~** GESCHÄFT arrange for sth to be done

Erledigung f GESCHÄFT dispatch, *Pflicht* discharge, dispatch

erleichtern vt GESCHÄFT, TRANSP facilitate, VW *Kreditbedingungen* ease

Erleichterung f GESCHÄFT, TRANSP facilitation, VW *Bestimmungen* easing

erleiden vt GESCHÄFT, PATENT suffer, RECHNUNG sustain, VW *Schaden* suffer

Erliegen: zum ~ kommen phr IND come to a standstill

erlitten: ~er Verlust m RECHT loss suffered

Erlös m GESCHÄFT proceeds, revenue; **~ vom Wiederverkauf** GESCHÄFT proceeds from resale

erloschen: ~e Gesellschaft f VW defunct company

erlöschen vi GESCHÄFT, RECHNUNG lapse, RECHT discharge

Erlöschen nt GESCHÄFT discharge, lapse, RECHNUNG lapse; **~ eines Eigentumsrechtes** BÖRSE defeasance; **~ eines Pfandrechts** RECHT discharge of lien

Erlös: **Erlösmaximierung** f VW revenue maximization

ermächtigen vt GESCHÄFT authorize, entitle; ◆ **jdn ~, etw zu tun** GESCHÄFT empower sb to do sth, confer the right on sb to do sth

Ermächtigung f BANK authorization, GESCHÄFT authorization, power; **~ zur Anwendung außerordentlicher Maßnahmen** PERSON emergency powers; ◆ **~ unter Vorbehalt** GESCHÄFT authorization under consideration (*AC*)

Ermächtigung: **Ermächtigungsklausel** f RECHT enabling clause; **Ermächtigungsschreiben** nt GESCHÄFT letter of authority (*L/A*)

Ermangelung: in ~ eines Gegenbeweises phr RECHT in the absence of evidence to the contrary

ermäßigen vt GESCHÄFT *Preise, Inflationsrate* bring down, abate, reduce

ermäßigt: ~er Beitrag m POL, VW abated contribution (*BrE*); **~er Fahrpreis** m FREI reduced fare; **~er Fahrpreis** m **für Ehepartner** FREI spouse fare; **~er Gruppenfrachttarif** m TRANSP *Luftfrachtklassifizierung* reduced class rate (*R*); **~es Porto** nt **für Büchersendungen** KOMM library rate (*AmE*), printed paper rate (*BrE*); **~e Reise** f FREI discount travel; **~er Satz** m STEUER reduced rate; **~e Steuer** f STEUER reduced tax

Ermäßigung f GESCHÄFT abatement, reduction

Ermessen *nt* GESCHÄFT discretion; ◆ **nach ~ von** GESCHÄFT at the discretion of; **in das ~ gestellt** GESCHÄFT in one's own estimation

Ermessen: **Ermessensauswahl** *f* V&M convenience sampling; **Ermessensgrenze** *f* BANK discretionary limit; **Ermessenszeitraum** *m* GESCHÄFT time span of discretion

ermitteln *vt* GESCHÄFT *Preis* ascertain, establish, investigate, MATH ascertain, VW ascertain; ◆ **die Kosten ~ von** [+dat] VERWALT cost out

Ermittlung *f* GESCHÄFT ascertainment; **~ des Bruttobetrags** RECHNUNG grossing-up; **Ermittlungsausschuß** *m* PERSON commission of inquiry; **Ermittlungsbeamte(r)** *m* [decl. as adj], **Ermittlungsbeamtin** *f* PERSON *Zoll, Polizei* investigating officer; **Ermittlungsbefugnisse** *f pl* RECHT investigatory powers

ermutigen *vt* GESCHÄFT encourage

ermutigend *adj* GESCHÄFT encouraging

Ermutigung *f* GESCHÄFT encouragement

Ernährer, in *m,f* vw breadwinner

ernannt *adj* GESCHÄFT appointed, RECHT *Treuhänder* constituted

Ernannte(r) *mf* [decl. as adj] GESCHÄFT *auf Geschäftsleitungsebene* appointee

ernennen *vt* GESCHÄFT, RECHT appoint, nominate

Ernennung *f* GESCHÄFT appointment, nomination; **Ernennungsbefugnis** *f* RECHT power of appointment; **Ernennungsrecht** *nt* GESCHÄFT power of appointment; **Ernennungsschreiben** *nt* GESCHÄFT letter of assignment

erneuerbar: **nicht ~e Bodenschätze** *m pl* UMWELT nonrenewable natural resources; **nicht ~e Ressourcen** *f pl* UMWELT nonrenewable resources; **~er Rohstoff** *m* UMWELT, VW renewable resource; **nicht ~er Rohstoff** *m* vw nonrenewable resource

erneuern *vt* GESCHÄFT renew, revive

Erneuerung *f* GESCHÄFT renovation, PATENT *Urheberrechtserneuerung* innovation, renewal, SOZIAL *Stadtteile* renewal; **Erneuerungsbestätigung** *f* VERSICH confirmation of renewal; **Erneuerungsgebühr** *f* PATENT renewal fee; **Erneuerungsschein** *m* BÖRSE talon

erneut 1. *adj* COMP, GESCHÄFT renewed; **2.** *adv* COMP, GESCHÄFT once again; ◆ **~ bestätigen** GESCHÄFT reaffirm; **~ einführen** V&M relaunch; **~ kaufen** V&M rebuy; **~ überprüfen** GESCHÄFT re-examine; **~ verhandeln** GESCHÄFT renegotiate

erneut: **~es Booten** *nt jarg* COMP rebooting; **~e Fokussierung** *f* GESCHÄFT refocusing; **~er Geldzufluß** *m* FINANZ reinfusion; **~es Urladen** *nt* COMP rebooting; **~e Verhandlung** *f* GESCHÄFT renegotiation

ernst: **~es Anzeichen** *nt* GESCHÄFT warning sign

Ernte *f* GESCHÄFT crop, UMWELT harvest, VERSICH crop, vw yield, crop; **~ zur Eigenbedarfsdeckung** vw subsistence crops; **~ auf dem Halm** RECHT *Landwirtschaft* emblements; **Erntehagelversicherung** *f* VERSICH crop hail insurance

erodieren *vt* UMWELT erode

eröffnen *vt* BANK *Konto* open, GESCHÄFT *Geschäft* start up; ◆ **ein Konto ~ bei** [+dat] BANK open an account with

Eröffnung *f* BANK, BÖRSE opening; **~ des Konkurs-**

verfahrens FINANZ, RECHNUNG, RECHT adjudication in bankruptcy; ◆ **bei ~** BÖRSE at the opening

Eröffnung: **Eröffnungsangebot** *nt* GESCHÄFT *Auktion* opening bid; **Eröffnungsbestand** *m* RECHNUNG opening balance; **Eröffnungsbilanz** *f* BANK, RECHNUNG opening balance

erörtern *vt* GESCHÄFT debate, discuss

Erörterung *f* GESCHÄFT debate, discussion

Erosion *f* UMWELT erosion

ERP *abbr* (*Europäisches Wiederaufbauprogramm*) VW ERP (*European Recovery Program AmE, European Recovery Programme BrE*)

erpressen *vt* GESCHÄFT blackmail, extort

erpresserisch: **~er Kauf** *m* **eines Aktienpakets** BÖRSE greenmail (*AmE*)

Erpressung *f* GESCHÄFT blackmail, extortion

erprobt *adj* GESCHÄFT well-tried, seasoned

Erprobung *f* COMP, GESCHÄFT, V&M test, tryout

erratisch *adj* BÖRSE erratic

errechnen *vt* MATH calculate

Errechnung *f* MATH calculation, computation; **~ des Bruttobetrages** RECHNUNG grossing-up

erregen *vt* GESCHÄFT give rise to

erreichbar *adj* GESCHÄFT accessible, *Ziel* achievable, obtainable; **nicht ~** *adj* GESCHÄFT not available, unavailable, *Waren* unobtainable

Erreichbarkeit *f* COMP, GESCHÄFT accessibility

erreichen *vt* GESCHÄFT *Ziel, Wachstum* achieve, meet, MGMNT *Ziel* meet; ◆ **nicht zu ~** GESCHÄFT *Person* not available, unavailable

erreicht: **~es Alter** *nt* VERSICH attained age

Erreichung *f* GESCHÄFT attainment; **~ des Höchststandes** BÖRSE topping out (*jarg*)

errichten *vt* GESCHÄFT build up, construct, *gründen* set up, *Zollschranken* erect

Errichtung *f* RECHT establishment

Errungenschaft *f* GESCHÄFT achievement

Ersatz *m* GESCHÄFT replacement, RECHT, V&M substitute; **Ersatzanlage** *f* IND standby power plant; **Ersatzanspruch** *m* VERSICH claim for indemnification; **Ersatzbelegschaft** *f* PERSON *Arbeit* replacement labor force (*AmE*), replacement labour force (*BrE*); **Ersatzbeschaffung** *f* GESCHÄFT replacement; **Ersatzfrau** *f* GESCHÄFT alternate member (*AmE*); **Ersatzgeld** *nt* FINANZ token money; **Ersatzgüter** *nt pl* V&M substitute goods; **Ersatzinvestition** *f* STEUER replaced asset, replacement capital, reinvestment; **Ersatzkosten** *pl* VERSICH substituted expenses; **Ersatzlieferung** *f* GESCHÄFT replacement, RECHT *Vertragsrecht* substitute delivery; **Ersatzmann** *m* GESCHÄFT alternate member (*AmE*), replacement (*BrE*); **Ersatzstoff** *m* vw substitute; **Ersatzteil** *nt* GESCHÄFT replacement part, IND spare, VW spare part

erscheinen *vi* GESCHÄFT appear, MEDIEN *Buch, Zeitschrift* come out, appear

erscheint: **~ monatlich** *phr* MEDIEN published monthly

Erscheinung *f* GESCHÄFT aspect; **Erscheinungsbild** *nt* COMP appearance, GESCHÄFT appearance, picture; **Erscheinungsdatum** *nt* MEDIEN publication date

erschließen *vt* GESCHÄFT tap, *Markt, Gebiet* open up

Erschließung *f* GRUND, IND, UMWELT, VW development, opening-up; **~ von Bauland** GRUND, IND, SOZIAL, UMWELT land development, site development, land improvement; **~ durch die öffentliche Hand** VW public development; **~ von Überseemärkten** VW market selection overseas; **Erschließungsunternehmen** *nt* GRUND developer; **Erschließungsvorhaben** *nt* **zur Erdgas- und Erdölförderung** VW developmental drilling program (*AmE*), developmental drilling programme (*BrE*)

erschlossen: ~es Gebiet *nt* GESCHÄFT improved land; **~es Gelände** *nt* GRUND, UMWELT improved land

erschöpfbar: ~e Ressourcen *f pl* UMWELT, VW depletable resources

erschöpfen *vt* GESCHÄFT *Vorrat, Möglichkeiten* exhaust, UMWELT *Rohstoff* deplete

erschöpfend *adj* GESCHÄFT exhaustive; **sich ~e Externalität** *f* VW depletable externality

erschöpft *adj* PERSON worn out

erschütternd *adj* FINANZ staggering (*infrml*); **~es Haushaltsdefizit** *nt* FINANZ staggering budget deficit (*infrml*)

erschüttert *adj* GESCHÄFT staggered (*infrml*)

Erschwernis *f* SOZIAL, VW hardship; **Erschwerniszulage** *f* PERSON bonus for especially hard work

erschwinglich *adj* GESCHÄFT affordable; **~er Preis** *m* V&M affordable price

ersessen: ~es Recht *nt* GRUND prescriptive right

ersetzen *vt* GESCHÄFT supersede, replace

ersetzt: ~es Wirtschaftsgut *nt* STEUER replaced asset

Ersetzung *f* VW replacement, substitution; **Ersetzungsprinzip** *nt* PERSON substitution principle

Ersitzung *f* GRUND *Art der Landerwerbung* prescription (*AmE*), RECHT acquisition of ownership by occupancy; **Ersitzungsrecht** *nt* GRUND, RECHT squatter's rights

Ersparnis *nt* BANK saving; ♦ **Ersparnisse angreifen** GESCHÄFT dip into savings; **mit Ersparnissen verbunden** GESCHÄFT savings-linked; **auf seine Ersparnisse zurückgreifen** FINANZ draw on one's savings

Ersparnis: Ersparnisbildung *f* **der privaten Haushalte** BANK personal saving

Erst- *in cpds* BÖRSE, GESCHÄFT initial, issuing, first, original; **Erstabsatz** *m* BÖRSE *Wertpapiere* initial sales of newly issued securities

erstatten *vt* GESCHÄFT refund, reimburse, STEUER reimburse

Erstattung *f* GESCHÄFT reimbursement; **Erstattungsanspruch** *m* STEUER claim for refund

erstattungsfähig *adj* GESCHÄFT, STEUER, V&M refundable; **nicht ~** *adj* STEUER nonrefundable; **nicht ~e Einlage** *f* V&M nonrefundable deposit; **nicht ~e Gebühr** *f* V&M nonrefundable fee; **~e Kosten** *pl* GESCHÄFT refundable expenses; **nicht ~e Steuern** *f pl* STEUER nonrefundable taxes

Erst-: Erstauftrag *m* GESCHÄFT original order, initial order, pilot order; **Erstausfertigung** *f* GESCHÄFT original; **Erstausgabepreis** *m* BÖRSE initial offering price, issuing price; **Erstausstattung** *f* GESCHÄFT initial supply

erste *adj* GESCHÄFT first, prime; ♦ **nach dem ~n Anschein** GESCHÄFT prima facie; **bei der ~n Gelegenheit** GESCHÄFT, POL, VW at the first opportunity; **der ~n Generation** IND first-generation; **in ~r Linie** GESCHÄFT primarily; **den ~n Schritt tun** GESCHÄFT make the first move; **an ~r Stelle** GESCHÄFT

in the first instance; **an ~r Stelle stehen** GESCHÄFT top the list

erste: **~ Adresse** *f* BÖRSE first-class, GESCHÄFT blue-chip customer; **~r Ankündigungstag** *m* FINANZ first notice day; **~ Anlage** *f* FINANZ prime investment; **~r Benachrichtigungstag** *m* FINANZ first notice day; **~s Bestimmungsland** *nt* IMP/EXP, TRANSP first country of destination; **~r Buchhalter** *m*, **~ Buchhalterin** *f* RECHNUNG chief accountant; **~r Entwurf** *m* RECHT rough draft; **~ Etappe** *f* FREI outward leg; **~s Gebot** *nt* GESCHÄFT opening bid; **~s Gossensches Gesetz** *nt* VW law of satiable wants; **~s Haus** *nt* GRUND starter home; **~ Hypothek** *f* BANK first mortgage; **~ Jahreshälfte** *f* GESCHÄFT first half of the year; **~ Klasse** *f* FREI, TRANSP first class; **~r Kurs** *m* BÖRSE initial quotation; **~ Mahnung** *f* RECHNUNG first reminder; **~r Maschinist** *m*, **~ Maschinistin** *f* PERSON *Schiffahrt* chief engineer; **~ Monatshälfte** *f* GESCHÄFT first half of the month (*fh*); **~s öffentliches Zeichnungsangebot** *nt* BÖRSE initial public offering (*AmE*) (*IPO*); **~r Offizier** *m* PERSON *Schiffahrt* chief officer; **~ Qualität** *f* GESCHÄFT distinction; **~s Quartal** *nt* GESCHÄFT first quarter (*1Q*); **~r Spediteur** *m* TRANSP first carrier; **~ Umschlagseite** *f* V&M front cover; **~r Urheberrechtsinhaber**, **~ Urheberrechtsinhaberin** *f* RECHT *geistiges Eigentum* first owner of copyright; **~s verfügbares Schiff** *nt* TRANSP first available vessel (*firavv*); **~r Vizepräsident** *m*, **~ Vizepräsidentin** *f* PERSON first vice president; **~ Wahl** *f* GESCHÄFT prime quality, top quality

Erste: **jeden ~n** *phr* GESCHÄFT every first day of the month; **an jeden ~n** *phr* GESCHÄFT every first day of the month; **~ Welt** *f* VW First World; **~r Weltkrieg** *m* POL World War I, First World War

Erste-Hilfe-Ausrüstung *f* SOZIAL first-aid kit

ersteigern: selbst ~ *phr* GESCHÄFT *Auktion* buy in

Erst-: Ersteintragung *f* RECHNUNG prime entry

erstellen *vt* COMP create, prepare, GESCHÄFT *Bericht* draw up, MGMNT prepare

Erstellung *f* GESCHÄFT, MGMNT *Plan* preparation; **~ eines Finanzierungskonzeptes** FINANZ financial engineering; **~ eines flexiblen Modells** VW soft modeling (*AmE*), soft modelling (*BrE*); **~ eines konsolidierten Abschlusses** RECHNUNG consolidation; **~ eines Modells** MATH modeling (*AmE*), modelling (*BrE*); **~ eines Simulationsmodells** VW simulation modeling (*AmE*), simulation modelling (*BrE*); **~ eines statistischen Modells** MATH statistical modeling (*AmE*), statistical modelling (*BrE*); **Erstellungskosten** *pl* GESCHÄFT cost of construction

Erst-: Erstfinanzierung *f* FINANZ initial funding; **Erstgebot** *nt* GESCHÄFT first bid

erstklassig *adj* BÖRSE top-grade, blue-chip, prime, GESCHÄFT first-rate, first-class, top-flight, *Güter* A1, high-class, TRANSP *Güter* A1; **~e Aktie** *f* BÖRSE blue-chip stock; **~ bewertet** *adj* BÖRSE triple-A rated; **~es Erzeugnis** *nt* GESCHÄFT top-rank product; **~es Handelspapier** *nt* BÖRSE prime paper; **~er Kunde** *m* GESCHÄFT blue-chip customer; **~e Schuldverschreibung** *f* BÖRSE high-grade bond; **~e Vermögenswerte** *m pl* BÖRSE Tier One assets (*BrE*); **~er Wechsel** *m* BÖRSE approved bill of exchange, prime bill; **~es Wertpapier** *nt* FINANZ, VW blue chip; **~e Wertpapiere** *nt pl* BÖRSE top-grade securities

erstmalig: ~es Auslaufen *nt* TRANSP inaugural sailing

Erst-: **Erstmeldung** *f* MEDIEN scoop; **Erstpfandrechtsanleihe** *f* BÖRSE prior-lien bond; **Erstplazierung** *f* BÖRSE initial placing of securities

erstrangig: ~e **Hypothek** *f* BANK, FINANZ, GRUND senior mortgage; ~es **Pfandrecht** *nt* GRUND first lien; ~ **Vorzugsaktie** *f* BÖRSE first preference share; ~ **Vorzugsaktien** *f pl* BÖRSE first preference stock

erstrebt: ~e **Mindestverzinsung** *f* FINANZ minimum acceptable rate of return

erststellig: ~es **Darlehen** *nt* BANK senior loan; ~e **Hypothek** *f* BANK, FINANZ, GRUND senior mortgage; ~e **Schuldverschreibung** *f* FINANZ senior bond; ~e **Vorzugsaktien** *f pl* BÖRSE prior-preferred stock

Erst-: **Erstverkauf** *m* V&M initial sale; **Erstverpflichtete(r)** *mf* [decl. as adj] BANK *Wechsel* principal; **Erstversicherer** *m* BANK, FINANZ leading underwriter, VERSICH direct insurer, original insurer, leader; **Erstversicherung** *f* VERSICH direct insurance; **Erstverwahrer, in** *m,f* FINANZ original custodian; **Erstzeichner, in** *m,f* BÖRSE original subscriber

ersuchen: ~ **um** *vt* GESCHÄFT appeal for; **jdn ersuchen, etw zu tun** *phr* GESCHÄFT urge sb to do sth

Ersuchen *nt* GESCHÄFT application, petition, appeal

ersuchend: ~e **Stelle** *f* RECHT applicant

erteilen *vt* FINANZ *Kredit* grant, GESCHÄFT award, *Auftrag* place, MGMNT *Vollmacht* delegate, PATENT *Lizenz* grant, RECHT confer

erteilt *adj* FINANZ granted, GESCHÄFT awarded, *Auftrag* placed, MGMNT delegated, PATENT granted, RECHT conferred; ~e **Rechnung** *f* BANK account rendered

Erteilung *f* GESCHÄFT award, MGMNT *Vollmacht* delegation, PATENT, RECHT grant, conferral; ~ **von Importlizenzen** IMP/EXP import licensing; ~ **von Zeichnungsvollmacht** GESCHÄFT delegation of signing authority; **Erteilungsdatum** *nt* PATENT date of grant

Ertrag *m* BÖRSE return, GESCHÄFT avails, return, yield, income, RECHNUNG output, return, VERWALT earnings, vw yield; ~ **aus Beteiligungen** RECHNUNG income from investments; ~ **aus Immobilien** GRUND return on real estate; ~ **des investierten Kapitals** FINANZ, RECHNUNG, vw return on invested capital (*ROIC*), return on investment (*ROI*); ~ **aus investiertem Nettovermögen** RECHNUNG return on net assets employed; ~ **aus Kapitalanlage** FINANZ, RECHNUNG, vw return on capital employed (*ROCE*); ~ **aus der Normalverzinsung** FINANZ nominal yield; ~ **nach Steuern** RECHNUNG, STEUER after-tax income

Erträge *m pl* GESCHÄFT income; ~ **und Aufwendungen** *f pl* RECHNUNG income and expenses; ~ **aus Beteiligungen an Tochtergesellschaften** FINANZ income from subsidiaries; ~ **aus dem Diskontgeschäft** BANK income from discounting; ~ **aus Wertpapieranlagen** RECHNUNG income from securities; ◆ ~ **einer Periode abgrenzen** RECHNUNG apply income to a period

ertragen *vt* RECHT *Schaden, Verletzung* sustain, VERWALT earn, vw yield

ertragreich *adj* GESCHÄFT productive, high-yield, gainful; **nicht** ~ *adj* BÖRSE unproductive; ~e **Anbausorten** *f pl* GESCHÄFT high-yield crops

Ertrag: **Ertragsabweichung** *f* GESCHÄFT yield variance; **Ertragsanpassung** *f* RECHNUNG yield adjustment; **Ertragsausfall** *m* FINANZ loss of earnings; **Ertragsbasis** *f* FINANZ earnings base; **Ertragseinbußen** *f pl* FINANZ reductions in profit;

Ertragsentwicklung *f* FINANZ trend of profits; **Ertragserwirtschaftung** *f* GESCHÄFT revenue production; **Ertragsfähigkeit** *f* IND productivity; **Ertragsfähigkeit** *f* **eines Unternehmens** vw corporate earning power; **Ertragsfaktoranalyse** *f* FINANZ profit factor analysis; **Ertragsfunktion** *f* vw production function; **Ertragsgesetz** *nt* vw law of diminishing returns, law of variable proportions; **Ertragskampagne** *f* IND productivity campaign; **Ertragskapazität** *f* GESCHÄFT earning capacity; **Ertragskraft** *f* GESCHÄFT, RECHNUNG earning power; **Ertragskraft** *f* **eines Unternehmens** vw corporate earning power; **die Ertragskraft verbessern** *phr* FINANZ improve profitability; **Ertragskurve** *f* BANK yield curve; **Ertragslage** *f* FINANZ earnings position, profit situation, profitability; **Ertragsleistung** *f* GESCHÄFT earning performance; **Ertragsminderung** *f* FINANZ reduction of profit

ertragsorientiert: ~es **Budget erstellen** *phr* PERSON *Finanzwesen* performance budgeting

Ertrag: **Ertragsprojekt** *nt* GESCHÄFT revenue project; **Ertragsrückgang** *m* FINANZ drop in earnings, vw diminishing returns; **Ertragsschwelle** *f* RECHNUNG, vw breakeven point

ertragsstark: ~e **Produkte** *nt pl* GESCHÄFT cash cow products

Ertrag: **Ertragsstrategie** *f* GESCHÄFT profit strategy; **Ertragstest** *m* RECHNUNG revenue test; **Ertragssteuer** *f* RECHNUNG, STEUER profits tax; **Ertragsverwässerung** *f* GESCHÄFT revenue dilution; **Ertragswirtschaft** *f* vw revenue economy; **Ertragszentrum** *nt* GESCHÄFT revenue center (*AmE*), revenue centre (*BrE*); **Ertragsziel** *nt* vw performance target; **Ertragszinsen** *m pl* BANK, RECHNUNG interest received, interest earned

erwachsen: ~e **Bevölkerung** *f* GESCHÄFT adult population

Erwachsene(r) *mf* [decl. as adj] GESCHÄFT, PERSON adult

Erwägung: **in** ~ **ziehen** *phr* GESCHÄFT take into consideration

erwähnen *vt* GESCHÄFT mention, refer to

erwähnt *adj* GESCHÄFT stated

Erwähnung: ~ *f* **im Leitartikel** V&M mention in leader column; **Erwähnungen** *f pl* **in der Presse** V&M press mentions

erwarten *vt* GESCHÄFT *Problem, Verzögerung* anticipate; ◆ **von jdm etw** ~ GESCHÄFT expect sth from sb

erwartet *adj* GESCHÄFT expected, anticipated; ~e **Besitzdauer** *f* BÖRSE anticipated holding period; ~e **Gefahren** *f pl* VERSICH expected perils; ~er **Gewinn** *m* RECHNUNG anticipated profit; ~e **Istkapazität** *f* vw expected actual capacity; ~e **Mindestrendite** *f* FINANZ hurdle rate of return, vw hurdle rate; ~e **Nutzungsdauer** *f* GESCHÄFT life expectancy; ~e **Risiken** *nt pl* VERSICH expected perils; ~er **Verfall** *m* RECHNUNG estimated lapse

Erwartung *f* GESCHÄFT, MATH, vw expectation, anticipation; ◆ **in** ~ **von** GESCHÄFT in expectation of; **den Erwartungen entsprechen** GESCHÄFT come up to scratch (*infrml*); **die Erwartungen erfüllen** GESCHÄFT fulfil the expectations (*BrE*), fulfill the expectations (*AmE*); **hinter den Erwartungen zurückbleiben** *phr* GESCHÄFT underperform; **die Erwartungen zurücknehmen** GESCHÄFT scale back expectations

Erwartung: **Erwartungselastizität** *f* vw elasticity of expectations, elasticity of anticipation

erwartungsfrei: ~e **Schätzfunktion** *f* VW unbiased estimator

Erwartung: **Erwartungswert** *m* MATH expected value, expectancy

erweiterbar *adj* COMP expandable, IND modular; ~e **Produktion** *f* IND modular production

erweitern *vt* BANK extend, COMP extend, enhance, *Speicher* upgrade, GESCHÄFT expand, widen, KOMM enrich, RECHT extend, STEUER widen, VW expand

erweitert *adj* BANK extended, COMP extended, enhanced, advanced, upgraded, GESCHÄFT expanded, widened, RECHT extended, STEUER widened, VW expanded; ♦ **einen ~en Kredit gewähren** FINANZ grant extended credit

erweitert: ~e **Ausgabe** *f* GESCHÄFT enlarged edition; ~e **Bedingungen** *f pl* BANK extended terms; ~er **Cashflow** *m* RECHNUNG incremental cash flow; ~e **Deckung** *f* VERSICH extended coverage, extended cover; ~e **Fondsfazilität** *f* FINANZ extended fund facility (*EFF*); ~e **Kreditfazilität** *f* FINANZ extended fund facility (*EFF*); ~es **Programm** *nt* GESCHÄFT enriched program (*AmE*), enriched programme (*BrE*), extended program (*AmE*), extended programme (*BrE*); ~e **Strukturanpassungsfazilität** *f* FINANZ *IWF* Enhanced Structural Adjustment Facility (*ESAF*); ~er **Versicherungsschutz** *m* VERSICH additional extended coverage

Erweiterung *f* BANK extension, COMP enhancement, upgrade, upgrading, *Dateinamen* extension, FINANZ expansion, GESCHÄFT enlargement, widening, expansion, RECHT extension, STEUER widening, VW *Betriebserweiterung* expansion; ~ **des Aufgabengebietes** MGMNT job enlargement; ~ **des Tätigkeitsbereiches** MGMNT job enlargement; ~ **des Tätigkeitsspektrums** MGMNT job enlargement

erweiterungsfähig *adj* COMP upgradeable

Erweiterung: **Erweiterungsinvestition** *f* VW capital widening; **Erweiterungskarte** *f* COMP expansion card; **Erweiterungsplatine** *f* COMP expansion board; **Erweiterungsspeicher** *m* COMP expanded memory, *Betriebssysteme* extended memory

Erwerb *m* BÖRSE, FINANZ, GESCHÄFT, RECHT *bei Ehegatten*, STEUER acquisition, VW purchase; ~ **von Options- oder Terminkontrakten** BÖRSE going long

erwerben *vt* BÖRSE gain, *Option* acquire, FINANZ, GESCHÄFT *Ruf* earn, acquire, GRUND *Grundstück, Gebäude* acquire, VW buy

erwerbend: ~e **Behörde** *f* GRUND *im Zwangsverfahren* acquiring authority; ~e **Gesellschaft** *f* GESCHÄFT acquiring company

Erwerber, in *m,f* BANK transferee, GESCHÄFT buyer, purchaser, vendee (*AmE*), RECHT grantee, V&M purchaser; ~ **auf Grund eines Vorkaufsrechts** RECHT preemptor (*AmE*); ~ **einer Kaufoption** BÖRSE giver for a call; ~ **einer Kauf- und Verkaufsoption** BÖRSE giver for a put and call; ~ **eines Nochgeschäfts** BÖRSE giver for a call of more

Erwerb: **Erwerbsbevölkerung** *f* PERSON working population, VW labor force (*AmE*), labour force (*BrE*); **Erwerbseinkommen** *nt* VERWALT earned income

erwerbsfähig *adj* PERSON, VW able to work

Erwerb: **Erwerbsfähigkeit** *f* PERSON ability to work, *Arbeit* earning power, VW ability to work; **Erwerbsgartenbau** *m* VW market gardening (*BrE*),

truck farming (*AmE*); **Erwerbsgeschäft** *nt* GESCHÄFT profit-making enterprise; **Erwerbskurs** *m* BÖRSE basic price, flat price

erwerbsorientiert *adj* GESCHÄFT acquisitive

Erwerbsquote *f* PERSON participation rate, labor force participation rate (*AmE*), labour force participation rate (*BrE*) (*LFPR*), VW activity rate, labor force participation rate (*AmE*), labour force participation rate (*BrE*) (*LFPR*)

erwerbssüchtig *adj* GESCHÄFT acquisitive

Erwerb: **Erwerbstätige** *pl* VW labor force (*AmE*), labour force (*BrE*); **Erwerbsunfähigkeit** *f* VERSICH disability; **Erwerbsunfähigkeitsrente** *f* VERSICH disability annuity, disability benefit

erwidern *vt* GESCHÄFT answer; ♦ ~ **auf** [+acc] GESCHÄFT answer

Erwiderung *f* RECHT *des Klägers, Staatsanwaltes* answer, reply; **Erwiderungsrecht** *nt* RECHT *des Antragstellers bei Debatte* right of reply

erwirtschaften *vt* VW generate

erworben *adj* GESCHÄFT acquired; ~e **Aktie** *f* BÖRSE acquired share; ~es **Eigentum** *nt* GRUND property acquired

Erz *nt* UMWELT *Kupfer, Zink* ore

erzeugen *vt* COMP *Werte*, GESCHÄFT *Energie, Gewinn, Abfall* generate, IND *herstellen* manufacture, VW produce

Erzeuger, in *m,f* IND maker, manufacturer (*mfr*), VW producer; **Erzeugerbeihilfe-Äquivalent** *nt* VW producer subsidy equivalent; **Erzeugerhandel** *m* V&M direct selling; **Erzeugerindustrie** *f* IND manufacturing industry; **Erzeugerpreis** *m* V&M manufacturer's price; **Erzeugerpreisindex** *m* VW producer price index (*PPI*); **Erzeugerstatistik** *f* IND, MATH census of manufacturers (*AmE*)

Erzeugnis *nt* GESCHÄFT, IND product

Erzeugung *f* GESCHÄFT generation, production, IND manufacture, production; **Erzeugungsgebiet** *nt* GESCHÄFT production area, manufacturing area; **Erzeugungskosten** *pl* IND production costs, manufacturing costs

Erz: **Erzfrachter** *m* TRANSP ore carrier; **Erzhütte** *f* IND smelting works

erziehen *vt* PERSON educate, RECHT discipline

Erziehung *f* PERSON, SOZIAL education; **Erziehungsheim** *nt* SOZIAL adjustment center (*AmE*), adjustment centre (*BrE*); **Erziehungsministerium** *nt* SOZIAL Ministry of Education; **Erziehungsrente** *f* VERSICH educational endowment; **Erziehungszentrum** *nt* **für Kinder im Vorschulalter** SOZIAL preschool center (*AmE*), preschool centre (*BrE*); **Erziehungszoll-Argument** *nt* IND, VW infant industry argument

erzielen *vt* GESCHÄFT effect, *Preis* fetch, *Einigung* reach, *Ergebnis* obtain, *Gewinn* make, *Wachstum, Niveau* achieve, RECHT *Einigung* reach

erzielt: ~e **Bruttodividende** *f* FINANZ grossed-up dividend

erzwingen *vt* GESCHÄFT, RECHT enforce

erzwingbar: **nicht** ~er **Vertrag** *m* RECHT unenforceable contract

erzwungen *adj* RECHT enforced

Escape-Folge *f* COMP escape sequence

ESCAPE-Taste *f* COMP Escape key (*Esc*)

Escape-Zeichen *nt* COMP escape character

ESF *abbr* (*Europäischer Sozialfonds*) VW ESF (*European Social Fund*)

eskalieren 1. *vt* GESCHÄFT *Kosten* escalate; **2.** *vi* GESCHÄFT *Kosten* escalate

eskomptieren *vt* BÖRSE anticipate

Eskorte *f* GESCHÄFT escort

ESRO *abbr* (*Europäische Organisation für Weltraumforschung*) GESCHÄFT ESRO (*European Space Research Organization*)

Essen: ~ auf Rädern *phr* SOZIAL *Wohlfahrt* meals on wheels (*BrE*); **Essensbon** *m* PERSON luncheon voucher (*BrE*) (*LV*); **Essensmarke** *f* PERSON *Arbeit* luncheon voucher (*BrE*) (*LV*); **Essenszuschuß** *m* PERSON meal allowance

Establishment: das ~ *nt* GESCHÄFT the Establishment (*BrE*)

etablieren: sich ~ *v refl* GESCHÄFT establish oneself

etabliert: ~er Markt *m* V&M established market

Etagengestell *nt* TRANSP tier

et al. *phr* GESCHÄFT *und andere* et al.

Etappe *f* GESCHÄFT phase, stage; **Etappenzahlung** *f* FINANZ stage payment; **Etappenziel** *nt* POL intermediate target

Etat *m* FINANZ estimates, RECHNUNG budget, expense budget, V&M account; **im ~ veranschlagte Ausgaben** *f pl* POL budgetary spending; **im ~ veranschlagte Einnahmen** *f pl* POL budgetary revenue; ♦ **~ aufstellen** FINANZ, GESCHÄFT, VW budget

Etat: Etatabweichung *f* RECHNUNG budget variance; **Etatansatz** *m* FINANZ budget appropriation; **Etateinschränkung** *f* RECHNUNG budgetary constraint

etatisieren *vt* FINANZ, GESCHÄFT budget, RECHNUNG budget for, vw budget

Etatisierung *f* FINANZ, GESCHÄFT, RECHNUNG budgeting; **~ vom Ausgangspunkt** FINANZ, RECHNUNG zero-base budget

Etat: Etatkontrolle *f* FINANZ, RECHNUNG budgetary control (*BC*), budget control; **Etatkürzung** *f* FINANZ, RECHNUNG budget reduction

Ethik *f* MGMNT *Geschäftsführung* ethics; **Ethikfonds** *m* FINANZ ethical unit trust

ethisch *adj* MGMNT ethical; **~e Investition** *f* BÖRSE ethical investment; **~ motivierter Investmentfonds** *m* FINANZ ethical unit trust

ethnisch: ~e Statistik *f* PERSON *zwecks Einhaltung der Diskriminierungsverbote* ethnic monitoring

Etikett *nt* COMP, TRANSP, V&M label, tag

Etikettierung *f* V&M *Auszeichnung* labeling (*AmE*), labelling (*BrE*); **Etikettierungsgesetze** *nt pl* RECHT labeling laws (*AmE*), labelling laws (*BrE*)

ETO *abbr* (*Europäische Transportorganisation*) TRANSP ETO (*European Transport Organization*)

Etui *nt* FREI case

etwa *adv* GESCHÄFT about, approximately (*approx.*); ♦ **~ gleichwertig** GESCHÄFT roughly equivalent

Et-Zeichen *nt* COMP, MEDIEN ampersand

EU *abbr* (*Europäische Union*) POL, VW EU (*European Union*); **EU-Beitritt** *m* VW accession to the EU, joining of the EU; **EU-Beratungsstelle** *f* **für kleine und mittlere Unternehmen** GESCHÄFT Euro Info Centre (*EIC*)

EuGH *abbr* (*Europäischer Gerichtshof*) RECHT ECJ (*European Court of Justice*)

EU: EU-Handel *m* GESCHÄFT trade within the EU

EuK *abbr* (*Europäische Kommission*) POL EC (*European Commission*)

EU: EU-Kennzeichung *f* IND EU-mark

Euler: ~sches Theorem *nt* MATH, VW Euler's theorem

EU: EU-Markierung *f* IND EU-mark

EURATOM *abbr* (*Europäische Atomgemeinschaft*) IND EURATOM (*European Atomic Energy Community*), EAEC (*European Atomic Energy Community*)

EU: EU-Richtlinie *f* RECHT EU directive

Euro- *pref* GESCHÄFT, POL Euro-; **Euroanleihe** *f* BANK eurobond, eurocurrency loan, BÖRSE eurobond, Eurocapital market issue; **Eurobank** *f* BANK Eurobank, **Eurobankgeschäfte** *nt pl* BANK Eurobanking; **Eurobanking** *nt* BANK Eurobanking; **Eurobond** *m* BÖRSE eurobond; **Eurocheque** *m* (*EC*) FINANZ, VW eurocheque; **Euro-Clear** *nt* BANK Euro-clear; **Euro-Commercial Paper** *nt* (*ECP*) FINANZ euro commercial paper (*ECP*)

EURO COOP *abbr* (*Europäische Gemeinschaft der Konsumgenossenschaften*) GESCHÄFT Euro Co-op (*European Community of Consumer Cooperatives*)

Eurodollar *m* VW Eurodollar; **Eurodollaranleihe** *f* VW Eurodollar bond; **Eurodollar-CDs** *nt pl* BANK Eurodollar certificates of deposit; **Eurodollar-Depositenzertifikate** *nt pl* BANK Eurodollar certificates of deposit; **Eurodollareinlage** *f* BANK, VW Eurodollar deposit; **Eurodollar-Index** *m* BÖRSE Eurodollar index; **Eurodollarmarkt** *m* VW Eurodollar market; **Eurodollar-Termineinlage** *f* BÖRSE Eurodollar time deposit; **Eurodollar-Termineinlagenfonds** *m* BÖRSE Eurodollar time deposit funds; **Eurodollar-Termineinlagen-Terminkontrakt** *m* BÖRSE Eurodollar time deposit futures contract; **Eurodollar-Termingeschäft** *nt* BÖRSE Eurodollar future; **Eurodollar-Terminkontrakt** *m* BÖRSE Eurodollar future; **Eurodollarzins** *m* BÖRSE, VW Eurodollar rate

Euro-: Euroequities *pl* VW Euroequity; **Eurofranc** *m* VW Eurofranc; **Eurogeld** *nt* BANK Euromoney; **Eurogeldmarkt** *m* BÖRSE, VW eurocurrency market

Euro: ~ Info Center *nt* (*EIC*) GESCHÄFT Euro Info Centre (*EIC*)

Euro-: Eurokapitalmarktanleihe *f* BÖRSE Eurocapital market issue; **Eurokapitalmarkt-Emission** *f* BÖRSE Eurocapital market issue; **Eurokredit aufnehmen** *phr* GESCHÄFT borrow in the Euromarket; **Eurokreditgeschäft** *nt* FINANZ Euromarket lending business; **Eurokurse** *m pl* BANK Euro-rates; **Euromarkt** *m* VW Euromarket, eurocurrency market; **am Euromarkt begebener Schuldtitel** *m* FINANZ eurobond; **im Euromarkt Kredit aufnehmen** *phr* GESCHÄFT borrow in the Euromarket; **Euronet** *nt* KOMM Euronet

Europa *nt* GESCHÄFT Europe; **~ Bahnseniorenkarte** *f* FREI Rail Europe Senior Card; **~ betreffende Angelegenheiten** *f pl* GESCHÄFT European affairs; **Europahandel** *m* V&M, VW continental trade

europäisch *adj* GESCHÄFT European

Europäisch *adj* GESCHÄFT European; **~er Agrarfonds** *m* VW European Agricultural Fund

europäisch: ~e Angelegenheiten *f pl* GESCHÄFT European affairs

Europäisch: ~e **Artikelnummer** *f* (*EAN*) COMP, V&M European Article Number (*EAN*); ~e **Atomenergiebehörde** *f* GESCHÄFT European Nuclear Energy Authority (*ENEA*); ~e **Atomgemeinschaft** *f* (*EAG, EURATOM*) IND, VW European Atomic Energy Community (*EAEC, EURATOM*); ~er **Ausrichtungs- und Garantiefonds für die Landwirtschaft** *m* (*EAGFL*) BANK European Agricultural Guidance and Guarantee Fund (*EAGGF*); ~er **Ausschuß** *m* **für Zusammenarbeit in Rechtsfragen** RECHT European Committee of Legal Cooperation

europäisch: ~es **Austauschverhältnis** *nt* VW *Devisenhandel* European terms

Europäisch: ~e **Bank** *f* **für Wiederaufbau und Entwicklung** (*EBWE*) VW European Bank for Reconstruction and Development (*EBRD*)

europäisch: ~er **Binnenmarkt** *m* GESCHÄFT, VW single European market

Europäisch: ~e **Energiecharta** *f* GESCHÄFT European Energy Charter; ~er **Entwicklungsfonds** *m* (*EEF*) VW European Development Fund (*EDF*)

europäisch: das ~e **Festland** *nt* GESCHÄFT the Continent (*BrE*)

Europäisch: ~er **Fonds** *m* **für regionale Entwicklung** (*EFRE*) VW European Regional Development Fund (*ERDF*); ~er **Fonds** *m* **für währungspolitische Zusammenarbeit** (*EFWZ*) BANK, VW *EG* European Monetary Cooperation Fund (*EMCF*); ~e **Freihandelszone** *f* (*EFTA*) VW European Free Trade Association (*EFTA*); ~e **Gemeinschaft** *f* (*EG*) POL European Community (*EC*); ~e **Gemeinschaft** *f* **für Kohle und Stahl** (*EGKS*) VW European Coal and Steel Community (*ECSC*); ~e **Gemeinschaft** *f* **der Konsumgenossenschaften** (*EURO COOP*) GESCHÄFT European Community of Consumer Cooperatives (*Euro Co-op*); ~er **Gerichtshof** *m* (*EuGH*) RECHT *EG* European Court of Justice (*ECJ*); ~e **Gesetzesvorlage** *f* RECHT Commission White Paper; ~er **Gewerkschaftsbund** *m* (*EGB*) PERSON European Trade Union Confederation (*ETUC*); ~er **Handelsausschuß** *m* GESCHÄFT European Trade Committee (*ETC*); ~e **Handelsbörse** *f* FINANZ European Mercantile Exchange

europäisch: ~e **Handelsgesellschaft** *f* GESCHÄFT European trading company

Europäisch: ~es **Handelsregister** *nt* (*EHR*) GESCHÄFT European Registry of Commerce (*ERC*); ~e **Investitionsbank** *f* (*EIB*) BANK European Investment Bank (*EIB*); ~es **Jahr** *nt* **der Umwelt** UMWELT European Year of the Environment (*EYE*); ~er **Kernforschungsrat** *m* IND European Council for Nuclear Research (*ECNR*); ~es **Komitee** *m* **für Normung** (*CEN*) VW European Committee for Standardization (*CEN*); ~es **Komitee** *m* **für elektrotechnische Normung** (*CENELEC*) VW European Committee for Electrotechnical Standardization (*CENELEC*); ~ **Kommission** *f* (*EuK*) POL European Commission (*EC*)

europäisch: ~er **Kontinent** *m* GESCHÄFT continent of Europe

Europäisch: ~e **Kooperationsvereinigung** *f* (*EKV*) RECHT European Cooperation Grouping (*CGA*); ~e **Liga** *f* **für wirtschaftliche Zusammenarbeit** VW European League for Economic Cooperation (*ELEC*); ~e

Menschenrechtskonvention *f* SOZIAL European Convention on Human Rights

europäisch: ~e **Normen** *f pl* (*EN*) GESCHÄFT European standard specifications

Europäisch: ~er **Optionsmarkt** *m* BÖRSE European Options Market (*EOM*); ~e **Organisation** *f* **zur Förderung des Handels** GESCHÄFT European Trade Promotion Organization (*ETPO*); ~e **Organisation** *f* **für Weltraumforschung** GESCHÄFT (*ESRO*) European Space Research Organization (*ESRO*)

europäisch: ~er **Paletten-Pool** *m* TRANSP European pallet pool

Europäisch: ~es **Parlament** *nt* POL European Parliament (*EP*)

europäisch: ~es **Patent** *nt* PATENT European patent

Europäisch: ~es **Patentamt** *nt* (*EPA*) PATENT European Patent Office, European Patent Organization (*EPO*)

europäisch: ~e **Patentanmeldung** *f* PATENT European patent application

Europäisch: ~e **Patentorganisation** *f* (*EPO*) PATENT European Patent Organization (*EPO*); ~es **Patentübereinkommen** *nt* (*EPÜ*) RECHT *EU, geistiges Eigentum* European Patent Convention (*EPC*); ~er **Rat** *m* VW European Council; ~e **Rechnungseinheit** *f* (*ERE*) FINANZ European Unit of Account (*EUA*); ~e **Sozialcharta** *f* VW European Social Charter; ~er **Sozialfonds** *m* (*ESF*) VW *EU* European Social Fund (*ESF*); ~e **Stiftung** *f* GESCHÄFT European Foundation (*EF*); ~e **Transportorganisation** *f* (*ETO*) TRANSP European Transport Organization (*ETO*); ~es **Umweltbüro** *nt* (*EEB*) UMWELT European Environmental Bureau (*EEB*); ~e **Union** *f* (*EU*) POL, VW European Union (*EU*); ~er **Verband** *m* **der Werbeagenturen** V&M European Association of Advertising Agencies (*EAAA*); ~e **Vereinigung** *f* **für Schiffahrtsinformatik** GESCHÄFT European Association for Shipping Informatics (*EASI*); ~es **Währungsabkommen** *nt* GESCHÄFT European Monetary Agreement (*EMA*); ~e **Währungseinheit** *f* (*ECU*) FINANZ, VW European Currency Unit (*ECU*); ~er **Währungsfonds** *m* (*EWF*) VW *EG* European Monetary Fund (*EMF*); ~es **Währungsinstitut** *nt* POL, VW *EG* European Monetary Institute (*EMI*)

europäisch: ~e **währungspolitische Zusammenarbeit** *f* VW European monetary cooperation

Europäisch: ~es **Währungssystem** *nt* (*EWS*) VW European Monetary System (*EMS*); ~e **Währungsunion** *f* (*EWU*) VW European Monetary Union (*EMU*); ~e **Weltraumorganisation** *f* (*EWO*) GESCHÄFT European Space Agency (*ESA*); ~es **Wiederaufbauprogramm** *nt* (*ERP*) VW European Recovery Program (*AmE*) (*ERP*), European Recovery Programme (*BrE*) (*ERP*); ~e **Wirtschaftliche Interessenvereinigung** *f* (*EWIV*) VW European Economic Interest Grouping (*EEIG*); ~e **Wirtschaftsgemeinschaft** *f obs* (*EWG*) VW European Economic Community (*obs*) (*EEC*); ~e **Wirtschaftskommission** *f* (*ECE*) VW Economic Commission for Europe (*ECE*); ~es **Wirtschaftsraum** *nt obs* (*EWR*) VW European Economic Area (*obs*); ~e **Zahlungsunion** *f* (*EZU*) GESCHÄFT, VW European Payments Union (*EPU*); ~e **Zentralbank** *f* (*EZB*) VW European Central Bank (*ECB*)

europäisch: ~e **Zonengebühr** *f* TRANSP *Rollgeld* European zone charge (*EZC*)

Euro-: **Europalette** *f* GESCHÄFT Europallet

Europa: **Europaparlament** *nt* POL European Parliament (*EP*); **Europapatent** *nt* PATENT European patent; **Europarat** *m* POL Council of Europe; **Europastraße** *f* (*E*) TRANSP Euro-route

europhil *adj* GESCHÄFT europhile

europhobisch *adj* GESCHÄFT europhobic

Eurorebell *m* POL Eurorebel (*BrE*)

Euro-: **Euroscheck** *m* BANK, FINANZ eurocheque

Euroskeptiker, in *m,f* POL Eurosceptic (*BrE*)

euroskeptisch *adj* POL eurosceptical (*BrE*)

Euro-: **Eurotagesgeld** *nt* BANK Euromoney

Eurovision *f* VERWALT Eurovision

Eurowährung *f* BANK, BÖRSE, VW eurocurrency; **Eurowährungsanleihe** *f* BANK eurocurrency loan; **Eurowährungskredit** *m* BANK eurocurrency loan; **Eurowährungskurse** *m pl* VW eurocurrency rates; **Eurowährungsmarkt** *m* BÖRSE eurocurrency market

eurozentrisch *adj* GESCHÄFT eurocentric

EU: **EU-Sicherheitskennzeichnung** *f* IND EU-mark

Eventual- *in cpds* GESCHÄFT, RECHNUNG, RECHT contingent; **Eventualforderung** *f* RECHNUNG contingent asset, contingent claim; **Eventualhaushalt** *m* FINANZ contingency budget

Eventualität *f* GESCHÄFT eventuality

Eventual-: **Eventualverbindlichkeit** *f* FINANZ contingent liability, GESCHÄFT contingency, RECHNUNG, RECHT contingent liability; **Eventualvergütung** *f* GESCHÄFT contingent consideration; **Eventualverpflichtung** *f* RECHT *Finanzwesen* contingent liability

eventuell: **~er Markt** *m* VERSICH contingent market

evident *adj* GESCHÄFT evident

Evidenzkonto *nt* VW evidence accounts

Evidenzzentrale *f* FINANZ Central Risk Service

Evolution *f* GESCHÄFT evolution

evolutorisch: **~e Unternehmenstheorie** *f* VW evolutionary theory of the firm

EWA *abbr* (*Europäisches Währungsabkommen*) GESCHÄFT EMA (*European Monetary Agreement*)

E-Werk *nt* (*Elektrizitätswerk*) UMWELT generating station

EWF *abbr* (*Europäischer Währungsfonds*) VW EMF (*European Monetary Fund*)

EWG *abbr obs* VW (*Europäische Wirtschaftsgemeinschaft*), EEC (*obs*) (*European Economic Community*)

EWI *abbr* (*Europäisches Währungsinstitut*) POL, VW EMI (*European Monetary Institute*)

ewig: **~e Rente** *f* BÖRSE perpetuity

EWIV *abbr* (*Europäische Wirtschaftliche Interessenvereinigung*) VW EEIG (*European Economic Interest Grouping*)

EWO *abbr* (*Europäische Weltraumorganisation*) GESCHÄFT ESA (*European Space Agency*)

EWR *abbr obs* (*Europäischer Wirtschaftsraum*) VW EEA (*European Economic Area*) (*obs*)

EWS *abbr* (*Europäisches Währungssystem*) VW EMS (*European Monetary System*)

EWU *abbr* (*Europäische Währungsunion*) VW EMU (*European Monetary Union*)

exakt *adj* GESCHÄFT accurate, MATH exact

exB *abbr* (*ex Bezugsrecht*) FINANZ ex allotment

ex: **~ Anspruch** *phr* RECHT ex claim; **~ ante-Variablen** *f pl* VW ex ante variables; **~ Bezugsrecht** *phr* (*exB*)

FINANZ ex allotment; **~ Dividende** *f* FINANZ ex dividend (*ex div.*, *x-d.*); **~ Schiff** *phr* (*x-Schiff*) IMP/EXP, TRANSP ex ship (*x-ship*)

Exekutivausschuß *m* MGMNT *Entscheidungsfindung* executive committee, PERSON executive committee (*BrE*), principal executive committee (*BrE*), RECHT executive committee

Exekutive *f* POL administration, executive, RECHT executive

Exemplar *nt* GESCHÄFT copy

Exequatur *nt* RECHT exequature

Exequaturverfahren *nt* RECHT *Vertragsrecht* exequature

ex: **~ Gratisaktien** *phr* BÖRSE, GESCHÄFT ex scrip, ex coupon (*ex cp*, *x-c.*)

Existenzminimum *nt* PERSON minimum living wage; **Existenzminimumtheorie** *f* **des Lohnes** VW subsistence theory of wages, iron law of wages

exkl. *abbr* (*exklusiv*) GESCHÄFT excl. (*excluding, exclusive*)

Exklusiv- *in cpds* GESCHÄFT, MEDIEN, PATENT exclusive; **Exklusivhandelsvertrag** *m* BÖRSE selected dealer agreement

exklusiv *adj* (*exkl.*) GESCHÄFT *sophisticated* select, *sole* exclusive (*excl.*), V&M exclusive (*excl.*), up-market; **~es Monopol** *nt* VW exclusive monopoly; **~e Zirkulation** *f* POL exclusive distribution

exklusive *prep* GESCHÄFT without

Exklusivität *f* V&M exclusivity

Exklusiv-: **Exklusivmeldung** *f* MEDIEN scoop; **Exklusivrecht** *nt* GESCHÄFT exclusive dealing right, PATENT, RECHT exclusive right

ex: **~ Kupon** *phr* BÖRSE, GESCHÄFT ex coupon (*ex cp*, *x-c.*)

Exkursion *f* FREI, GESCHÄFT tour, SOZIAL field trip

exogen: **~e Erwartungen** *f pl* VW exogenous expectations; **~er Schock** *m* VW external shock; **~e Variable** *f* VW exogenous variable

exorbitant *adj* GESCHÄFT exorbitant

exotisch: **~e Papiere** *nt pl* BÖRSE exotics; **~e Währung** *f* VW exotic currency; **~e Währungen** *f pl* BÖRSE exotics

Exp. *abbr* (*Export*) IMP/EXP, VW exp. (*export*)

expandieren *vt* VW expand

expandiert *adj* VW expanded

Expansion *f* FINANZ, GESCHÄFT, VW expansion; **Expansionsrate** *f* VW rate of increase; **Expansionsstrategie** *f* GESCHÄFT, VW expansion strategy

expansiv *adj* VW *Fiskalpolitik* expansionary

Expedient *m* KOMM dispatcher, PERSON *Versandabteilung, Spedition* forwarding clerk, TRANSP dispatcher, shipping clerk

Experiment *nt* GESCHÄFT experiment

Experte *m* GESCHÄFT, PERSON *Arbeit, Gutachten* expert; **Expertengewalt** *f* MGMNT expert power; **Expertengruppe** *f* MGMNT panel of experts; **Expertennetz** *nt* COMP expert network; **Expertensystem** *nt* COMP knowledge-based system (*KBS*), *künstliche Intelligenz* expert system (*ES*), GESCHÄFT expert system (*ES*)

Expertin *f* GESCHÄFT, PERSON expert

Expertise *f* VERSICH survey report

explizit *adj* GESCHÄFT explicit

explosiv: **~e, korrodierende, gefährliche Fracht** *f*

TRANSP toxic, explosive, corrosive, hazardous cargo (*TECH cargo*)

Explosivstoff *m* TRANSP explosive substance

Exponent *m* MATH exponent

Exponential- *in cpds* COMP, MATH exponential; **Exponentialfunktion** *f* COMP, MATH exponential function; **Exponentialschreibweise** *f* COMP, MATH exponential notation; **Exponentialtrend** *m* VW exponential trend

exponentiell *adj* MATH exponential; **~e Glättung** *f* FINANZ, MATH exponential smoothing

exponiert: **~er Bereich** *m* GESCHÄFT exposed sector; **~e Nettovermögensposition** *f* GESCHÄFT exposed net asset position; **an ~er Stelle** *phr* GESCHÄFT in an exposed position

Export *m* (*Exp.*) IMP/EXP, VW export (*exp.*), exportation; **~ von Arbeitslosigkeit** GESCHÄFT beggar-my-neighbor policy (*AmE*), beggar-my-neighbour policy (*BrE*); ♦ **~ per Post** IMP/EXP postal export

Export: **Exportabfall** *m* IMP/EXP export reject; **Exportabteilung** *f* IMP/EXP export department; **Exportakkreditiv** *nt* FINANZ export letter of credit; **Exportakzeptkredit** *m* BANK exporter's acceptance credit; **Exportangleichungskredit** *m* FINANZ export adjustment loan (*EAL*); **Exportauftrag** *m* IMP/EXP, IND export order; **Exportbasis** *f* VW economic base; **Exportbestimmungen** *f pl* IMP/EXP export regulations; **Exportbewilligung** *f* IMP/EXP export licence (*BrE*), export license (*AmE*); **Exportbewilligungsverfallsdatum** *nt* IMP/EXP export licence expiry date (*BrE*), export license expiry date (*AmE*); **Exportbüro** *nt* IMP/EXP export office; **Exportdatenmappe** *f* IMP/EXP export data folder; **Exportdirektor, in** *m,f* PERSON export director; **Exportdokumente** *nt pl* IMP/EXP export documentation; **Exportergebnis** *nt* IMP/EXP export performance; **Exporterlöse** *m pl* VW export earnings

Exporteur, in *m,f* IMP/EXP, PERSON exporter

Export: **Exportfactoring** *nt* IMP/EXP export factoring; **Exportfinanzierung** *f* FINANZ export financing, IMP/EXP export finance; **Exportfinanzierungshaus** *nt* FINANZ, IMP/EXP export finance house; **Exportfirma** *f* IMP/EXP export house; **Exportförderung** *f* IMP/EXP export promotion (*EP*); **Exportgenehmigung** *f* IMP/EXP export permit

exportgerecht *adj* IMP/EXP export-oriented

Export: **Exportgeschäft** *nt* IMP/EXP export business, export transactions; **ein Exportgeschäft abwickeln** *phr* IMP/EXP process an export transaction; **ein Exportgeschäft finanzieren** *phr* IMP/EXP finance an export transaction; **Exporthalle** *f* IMP/EXP export shed; **Exporthandel** *m* IMP/EXP export trade

exportieren *vt* IMP/EXP, VW export

exportiert *adj* IMP/EXP, VW exported

exportinduziert *adj* VW *Wachstum* export-led; **~er Aufschwung** *m* VW export-led economic recovery; **~es Wachstum** *nt* IMP/EXP export-led growth

exportintensiv: **~e Industrie** *f* VW export-intensive industry

Export: **Exportkatalog** *m* V&M export catalog (*AmE*), export catalogue (*BrE*); **Exportkauffrau** *f*, **Exportkaufmann** *m* IMP/EXP, PERSON export merchant; **Exportklub** *m* IMP/EXP export club; **Exportkommissär, in** *m,f* IMP/EXP export commission agent; **Exportkonnossement** *nt* IMP/EXP outward bill of lading; **Exportkontrolle** *f* IMP/EXP export control; **Exportkredit** *m* BANK export loan, exporter credit, IMP/EXP export credit; **Exportkunde** *m*, **Exportkundin** *f* V&M export customer; **Exportlagergebühren** *f pl* IMP/EXP export depot charges; **Exportleistung** *f* IMP/EXP export performance; **Exportleiter, in** *m,f* MGMNT, V&M export sales manager, export manager; **Exportliegeplatz** *m* TRANSP export berth; **Exportlizenz** *f* IMP/EXP export licence (*BrE*), export license (*AmE*); **Exportlizenznummer** *f* IMP/EXP export licence number (*BrE*), export license number (*AmE*); **Exportmarketing** *nt* IMP/EXP, V&M export marketing; **Exportmarkt** *m* IMP/EXP, VW export market; **Exportmarktforschung** *f* IMP/EXP, V&M export market research; **Exportmesse** *f* IMP/EXP, V&M export fair; **Exportnachrichtendienst** *m* IMP/EXP export intelligence service (*BrE*) (*EIS*)

exportorientiert *adj* IMP/EXP export-oriented

Export: **Exportort** *m* IMP/EXP point of export; **Exportpacker** *m* IMP/EXP export packer; **Exportpreise** *m pl* IMP/EXP, VW export prices; **Exportquote** *f* VW export quota; **Exportrechnung** *f* IMP/EXP export invoice; **Export-Rembourskredit** *m* BANK exporter's acceptance credit; **Exportsachbearbeiter, in** *m,f* PERSON *Arbeit* export clerk, export coordinator; **Exportschutzversicherung** *f* IMP/EXP, VERSICH export credit insurance; **Exportsendungsidentifizierungsnummer** *f* IMP/EXP export consignment identifying number; **Exportsendungskennummer** *f* IMP/EXP export consignment identifying number; **Exportsendungskennzeichen** *nt* IMP/EXP export consignment identifying number

exportstimulierend: **~ wirken** *phr* IMP/EXP *Maßnahme* be a stimulus for exports

Export: **Exportsubvention** *f* IMP/EXP export subsidy; **Exporttätigkeit** *f* IMP/EXP exporting; **Exportüberhang** *m* IMP/EXP, VW export surplus; **Exportumsatz** *m* IMP/EXP export turnover; **Exportunterlagen** *f pl* IMP/EXP export documentation; **Exportunternehmen** *nt* IMP/EXP export house; **Exportverkäufe** *m pl* IMP/EXP, V&M export sales; **Exportverkaufsbedingungen** *f pl* IMP/EXP terms of export sale; **Exportverpackung** *f* **ab Werk** IMP/EXP, TRANSP ex works export packing; **Exportversandanweisung** *f* IMP/EXP export cargo shipping instruction (*ECSI*); **Exportversandliste** *f* IMP/EXP export cargo packing declaration (*ECPD*); **Exportvertrag** *m* IMP/EXP, RECHT agreement on export; **Exportvertreter, in** *m,f* IMP/EXP manufacturer's export agent, VW confirming house (*BrE*); **Exportvolumen** *nt* IMP/EXP, VW volume of exports; **Exportwelle** *f* IMP/EXP, V&M surge of export orders; **Exportwirtschaft** *f* IMP/EXP export sector, export business; **Exportziffern** *f pl* IMP/EXP export figures

ex: **~ post** *adv* VW ex post; **~ post-Variablen** *f pl* VW ex post variables

Expreß- *in cpds* GESCHÄFT express; **Expreßbeförderung** *f* GESCHÄFT express delivery; **Expreßgut** *nt* GESCHÄFT express consignment; **Expreßpost** *f* KOMM express mail (*BrE*), priority mail (*AmE*)

extensiv: **~e Bewirtschaftung** *f* VW extensive farming; **~er Verkauf** *m* V&M extensive selling

extern: **~er Arbeitsmarkt** *m* VW external labor market (*AmE*), external labour market (*BrE*); **~er Bericht** *m* GESCHÄFT external report; **~es Berichtswesen** *nt* VERWALT external reporting; **~er Bilanzvergleich** *m*

RECHNUNG external balance sheet comparison; ~er **Buchprüfer** *m*, **~e Buchprüferin** *f* RECHNUNG independent auditor; **~ datierte Rentenbezüge** *m pl* FINANZ externally funded pensions (*BrE*); **~e Effekte** *m pl* VW externality, neighborhood effect (*AmE*), neighbourhood effect (*BrE*); **~e Effekte** *m pl* **des Konsums** VW external effects of consumption; **~e Festplatte** *f* COMP *Speicher* external hard disk; **~ finanzierte Pensionsanteile** *f pl* **des Arbeitnehmers** FINANZ externally funded pensions (*BrE*); **~er gemeinschaftlicher Versandschein** *m* IMP/EXP external community transit document; **~e Konsumeffekte** *m* VW external effects of consumption; **~e Nutzen** *m pl* VW external economy of scale; **~e Skalenerträge** *m pl* VW external economy of scale; **~es Verfahren** *nt* TRANSP external procedure; **~e Verschuldung** *f* GESCHÄFT borrowing abroad

externalisieren *vt* VW externalize

Externalität *f* VW externality, neighborhood effect (*AmE*), neighbourhood effect (*BrE*)

exterritorial *adj* BANK, FINANZ offshore; **~e Vollstreckung** *f* RECHT extraterritorial enforcement

Extra *nt* GESCHÄFT extra (*ex.*); ◆ **ohne Extras** GESCHÄFT with no trimmings

Extra: **Extradividende** *f* FINANZ bonus; **Extrapolation** *f* MATH *von Werten* extrapolation

extrapolierend: **~e Erwartungen** *f pl* VW extrapolative expectations

Extra: **Extras** *nt pl* GESCHÄFT trimmings; **Extra-Tara** *f* GESCHÄFT extra tare

Extrem- *in cpds* VERSICH, VW extreme

extrem: **~er Anwender** *m* COMP heavy user; **~ niedriger Preis** *m* V&M keen price

Extrem-: **Extremschadensdeckung** *f* VERSICH catastrophe cover; **Extremwert** *m* VW extremum

extrinsisch: **~e Motivation** *f* PERSON extrinsic motivation

Exzedent *m* VERSICH excess (*BrE*)

Exzeß *m* MATH *Statistik* kurtosis

EZB *abbr* (*Europäische Zentralbank*) VW ECB (*European Central Bank*)

EZU *abbr* (*Europäische Zahlungsunion*) GESCHÄFT, VW EPU (*European Payments Union*)

EZÜ *abbr* (*elektronischer Zahlungsverkehr für Überweisung*) BANK ATS (*automatic transfer service*)

F

Fa. *abbr* (*Firma*) GESCHÄFT Co. (*company*), corp. (*AmE*) (*corporation*)

Fabrik *f* IND factory, manufacturing plant; **~ auf dem neuesten Stand** IND advanced factory; ◆ **ab ~** (*x-Fabrik*) GESCHÄFT, IMP/EXP, TRANSP ex factory, ex mill (*x-mill*), ex works (*EXW*); **vor einer ~ Streikposten aufstellen** PERSON picket a factory

Fabrik: **Fabrikanlage** *f* IND factory, industrial plant

Fabrikant, in *m,f* IND maker, manufacturer (*mfr*)

Fabrik: **Fabrikarbeiter** *m* GESCHÄFT factory hand, IND shop floor

Fabrikat *nt* GESCHÄFT brand, make, product, V&M, VERSICH make, VW manufactured product

Fabrikation *f* IND manufacturing, production, making; **Fabrikationsauftrag** *m* IND production order; **Fabrikationskapazität** *f* IND manufacturing capacity; **Fabrikationsleiter, in** *m,f* IND production manager; **Fabrikationsnummer** *f* GESCHÄFT serial number; **Fabrikationstätigkeit** *f* IND manufacturing activity

Fabrik: **Fabrikbesitzer, in** *m,f* IND factory owner; **Fabrikgebäude** *nt* IND factory; **Fabrikgrundstück** *nt* IND factory site, plant; **Fabrikinspektor, in** *m,f* IND factory inspector; **Fabrikklausel** *f* GESCHÄFT ex factory clause; **Fabriklage** *f* IND plant location; **Fabrikleiter, in** *m,f* IND, MGMNT plant manager; **Fabrikmarke** *f* PATENT mark

fabrikmäßig: **~ herstellen** *phr* IND mass-produce, manufacture; **~e Herstellung** *f* GESCHÄFT, IND manufacturing, mass production, manufacture

fabrikneu *adj* GESCHÄFT brand-new

Fabrik: **Fabrikzeichen** *nt* PATENT mark

fabrizieren *vt* IND manufacture

Fach- *in cpds* GESCHÄFT, IND, PERSON skilled, specialist, specialized, professional; **Facharbeiter** *m pl* PERSON, VW skilled labor (*AmE*), skilled labour (*BrE*); **Facharbeiter, in** *m,f* PERSON, VW *manuelle Arbeit* skilled worker; **Fachausbildung** *f* IND training within industry (*TWI*); **Fachausstellung** *f* V&M *Messe* trade exhibition, trade show; **Fachblatt** *nt* MEDIEN professional journal, trade journal, trade magazine; **Facheinzelhändler, in** *m,f* V&M speciality retailer, specialty retailer (*AmE*); **Fachgebiet** *nt* GESCHÄFT area of expertise, specialist field, specialization; **Fachgeschäft** *nt* V&M specialist shop (*BrE*), speciality store (*AmE*), stockist (*BrE*); **Fachgewerkschaft** *f* PERSON craft union, skilled union (*BrE*); **Fachgremium** *nt* GESCHÄFT expert body, professional body; **Fachhandelsagent, in** *m,f* PERSON stockist agent; **Fachhochschulabschluß** *m* SOZIAL Higher National Diploma (*BrE*) (*HND*); **Fachhochschule** *f* SOZIAL specialized institution of higher education, technical college (*BrE*); **Fachhochschulreife** *f* SOZIAL Higher National Certificate (*BrE*) (*HNC*); **Fachkenntnisse** *f pl* GESCHÄFT expert knowledge, specialist knowledge, technical knowledge, know-how (*infrml*)

fachkundig *adj* GESCHÄFT informed

fachlich 1. *adj* GESCHÄFT technical; 2. *adv* GESCHÄFT technically; ◆ **sich ~ beraten lassen** GESCHÄFT take expert advice

fachlich: **~e Eignung** *f* PERSON professional qualifications; **~e Perfektion** *f* GESCHÄFT technical mastery

Fachmann *m* GESCHÄFT expert, specialist; ◆ **einen ~ zu Rate ziehen** GESCHÄFT take expert advice

fachmännisch *adj* GESCHÄFT expert, specialist, technical; **~e Auskunft** *f* GESCHÄFT specialist information

Fach-: **Fachmesse** *f* V&M trade fair, trade show; **Fachorgan** *nt* MEDIEN trade journal; **Fachorganisation** *f* GESCHÄFT trade organization; **Fachpresse** *f* MEDIEN trade press, technical press; **Fachschulabschluß** *m* SOZIAL Higher National Certificate (*BrE*) (*HNC*); **Fachschule** *f* SOZIAL technical education institution

Fachsimpelei *f infrml* GESCHÄFT shop talk (*infrml*)

fachsimpeln *vi infrml* GESCHÄFT talk shop

fachspezifisch *adj* GESCHÄFT technical

Fach-: **Fachsprache** *f* GESCHÄFT jargon, technical language, terminology; **Fachverband** *m* VW professional association, trade association; **Fachverkäufer, in** *m,f* V&M speciality salesperson; **Fachwissen** *nt* GESCHÄFT, PERSON expert knowledge; **Fachzeitschrift** *f* MEDIEN professional journal, trade journal, trade magazine

Facing *nt* V&M facing

Factoring *nt* FINANZ factoring, debt factoring, RECHNUNG factoring, accounts receivable financing; **Factoring-Institut** *nt* FINANZ factoring company; **Factoring-Unternehmen** *nt* FINANZ factoring company; **Factoring-Vertrag** *m* RECHT factoring contract

fähig *adj* GESCHÄFT able, capable, competent, efficient; ◆ **~ zu** GESCHÄFT capable of

Fähigkeit *f* GESCHÄFT ability, capability, *Kompetenz* competence, skill, *Leistungsfähigkeit* efficiency, PERSON competency; **Fähigkeitsniveau** *nt* SOZIAL ability level

Fahndungsabteilung *f* STEUER Investigation Division (*BrE*)

Fähranleger *m* TRANSP ferry berth

Fahrbahn *f* TRANSP carriageway, roadway, traffic lane

Fährbetriebsleiter, in *m,f* PERSON, TRANSP ferry line manager

Fahrcharter *f* TRANSP trip charter

Fahrdienstleiter, in *m,f* PERSON *öffentliche Verkehrsmittel* traffic superintendent (*TS*)

Fähre *f* TRANSP ferry boat; **~ für Personenwagen** TRANSP passenger vehicle ferry

Fahrenheit *nt* (*F*) GESCHÄFT Fahrenheit (*F*)

Fahrer, in *m,f* PERSON, TRANSP driver; **Fahrerhaftpflichtversicherung** *f* VERSICH *für Fahrzeuge von Dritten* Drive Other Car insurance (*AmE*) (*DOC*); **Fahrerhaus** *nt* TRANSP *Fahrzeug* driver's cab

Fahrgastschiff *nt* TRANSP passenger ship

Fahrkarte *f* FREI, GESCHÄFT, TRANSP ticket; **~ außerhalb der Hauptzeiten** TRANSP off-peak ticket; **~ zum verbilligten Tarif** TRANSP cheap fare; **Fahrkartenausgabe** *f* TRANSP ticket office, booking office;

Fahrkartenkontrolleur, in *m,f* GESCHÄFT, TRANSP ticket collector; **Fahrkartenschalter** *m* TRANSP ticket office, booking office; **Fahrkartenverkaufsstelle** *f* TRANSP ticket agency

fahrlässig *adj* RECHT negligent

Fahrlässigkeit *f* RECHT negligence; **Fahrlässigkeitsklausel** *f* RECHT, VERSICH neglect clause, negligence clause

Fahrplan *m* FREI schedule, timetable, TRANSP sailing schedule, schedule, timetable; **Fahrplangestaltung** *f* TRANSP timetable planning

fahrplanmäßig *adj* TRANSP according to schedule

Fahrpreis *m* TRANSP fare, passenger fare; **~ für Hin- und Rückfahrt** TRANSP return fare (*BrE*), round-trip fare (*AmE*)

Fahrrad *nt* GESCHÄFT bicycle, TRANSP, VERSICH bicycle, cycle; **Fahrraddiebstahlversicherung** *f* VERSICH cycle theft insurance; **Fahrradversicherung** *f* VERSICH cycle insurance

Fährrampe *f* TRANSP ferry ramp

Fahrschein *m* TRANSP ticket; **Fahrscheininhaber, in** *m,f* TRANSP ticket holder

Fährschiff *nt* TRANSP ferry boat

Fahrspur *f* TRANSP traffic lane

Fahrstrecke *f* TRANSP itinerary

Fahrstuhlhaftpflichtversicherung *f* VERSICH elevator liability insurance (*AmE*)

Fahrt *f* GESCHÄFT, TRANSP journey, trip; ♦ **~ aufnehmen** GESCHÄFT gather speed

Facht: Fahrtchartervertrag *m* TRANSP trip charter; **Fahrtenschreiber** *m* TRANSP tachograph

Fahrzeug *nt* GESCHÄFT, TRANSP vehicle; **~ mit Aufbauten** TRANSP built-up vehicle; **~ im Straßentransport** TRANSP road haulage vehicle (*RHV*); **Fahrzeug-Eigengewicht** *nt* TRANSP vehicle unladen weight; **Fahrzeugfähre** *f* TRANSP vehicular ferry; **Fahrzeuggesamtgewicht** *nt* TRANSP gross vehicle weight (*GVW*); **Fahrzeug-Leasing** *nt* TRANSP vehicle leasing; **Fahrzeugpark** *m* TRANSP fleet, pool of vehicles; **Fahrzeugpauschale** *f* GESCHÄFT car allowance; **Fahrzeugumladung** *f* IMP/EXP, TRANSP vehicle transhipment; **Fahrzeugumlaufzeit** *f* TRANSP vehicle turnaround time (*AmE*), vehicle turnround time (*BrE*); **Fahrzeugwendezeit** *f* TRANSP vehicle turnaround time (*AmE*), vehicle turnround time (*BrE*)

fair: ~e Beschäftigung *f* PERSON fair employment

Faksimile *nt* (*Fax*) GESCHÄFT, KOMM facsimile (*fax*); **Faksimileunterschrift** *f* GESCHÄFT facsimile signature

Fakt. *abbr obs* (*Faktur*) GESCHÄFT inv. (*invoice*)

Fakten *m pl* GESCHÄFT facts; **~ und Zahlen** *f pl* GESCHÄFT facts and figures

Faktor *m* FINANZ factoring company, GESCHÄFT factor; **~ der täglichen Schwankungsbreite** BÖRSE, FINANZ Daily Range Factor (*DRF*); ♦ **ein ~ sein bei** GESCHÄFT be a factor in

Faktor: Faktoranalyse *f* MATH factor analysis; **Faktorausstattung** *f* VW factor endowment; **Faktoreinkommen** *nt* VW factor income

faktoriell: ~es Austauschverhältnis *nt* VW factorial terms of trade

Faktorielle *f* MATH factorial

Faktoring: Faktoringentgelt *nt* FINANZ factorage; **Faktoringgebühr** *f* FINANZ factorage

Faktor: Faktorkosten *pl* IND, VW *Produktion* factor costs; **zu Faktorkosten** *phr* IND, VW at factor cost; **Faktormarkt** *m* VW factor market, input market, resource market; **Faktorpreisausgleichstheorem** *nt* VW factor price equalization theorem; **Faktorproduktivität** *f* VW factor productivity

Faktum *nt* GESCHÄFT material fact

Faktur *f obs* (*Fakt.*) GESCHÄFT invoice (*inv.*)

Faktura *f obs* GESCHÄFT account, bill (*BrE*), check (*AmE*), invoice (*inv.*), RECHNUNG commercial invoice; **Fakturawert** *m obs* GESCHÄFT invoice value (*iv*)

Fakturen- in *cpds* GESCHÄFT billing (*AmE*), invoicing (*BrE*); **Fakturendatum** *nt obs* GESCHÄFT billing date (*AmE*), date of invoice (*BrE*)

Fakturier-: Fakturierabteilung *f* GESCHÄFT billing department (*AmE*), invoicing department (*BrE*); **Fakturierzyklus** *m* GESCHÄFT billing cycle

Fakturiermaschine *f* GESCHÄFT automatic billing machine, biller

Fakturierung *f* GESCHÄFT billing, invoicing

Fakturist, in *m,f* GESCHÄFT invoice clerk

Fakultät *f* GESCHÄFT *Universität* faculty, MATH factorial

fakultativ *adj* GESCHÄFT facultative; **fakultativ/ obligatorisch** *adj* VERSICH facultative/obligatory (*factoblig*)

Fall *m* BÖRSE, FINANZ *von Kurs* drop, fall, GESCHÄFT *Umstand* case, instance, occasion, POL *einer Regierung* downfall, RECHT *gerichtlich* case, VW *von Kurs* drop, fall; ♦ **in diesem ~** GESCHÄFT in this case, in this instance; **auf keinen ~** GESCHÄFT on no account

Fall: Fallbeispiel *nt* GESCHÄFT case history

Falle *f* GESCHÄFT pitfall

fallen *vi* BÖRSE, FINANZ *Kurse* fall, drop, slip, GESCHÄFT slip back, VW *Absatz, Inflation, Preise* drop, fall

fallend: ~e Preise *m pl* VW falling prices; **~e Spitzenwerte** *m pl* BÖRSE descending tops; **~e Tendenz** *f* BÖRSE falling trend

fallenlassen *vt* GESCHÄFT *Plan, Projekt* abandon, *Plan, Projekt, Idee* scrap, PATENT abandon

Fall: Fallgeschichte *f* GESCHÄFT case history

fällig *adj* BANK, BÖRSE, FINANZ matured, GESCHÄFT due, due and payable, payable, *Schulden* mature, VW payable; ♦ **~e Beträge einziehen** FINANZ collect sums due; **~e Forderung von** RECHNUNG debt due from; **~ werden** BANK become due, *Schulden* mature, FINANZ *Schulden* mature

fällig: ~e Auszahlung *f* VERSICH *der Lebensversicherung* matured endowment; **~er Betrag** *m* FINANZ amount due; **~es Kapital** *nt* FINANZ due capital; **~e Obligationen** *f pl* BÖRSE matured bonds; **~e Rechnung** *f* GESCHÄFT invoice outstanding; **noch nicht ~e Schuld** *f* BÖRSE unmatured debt; **~e Schuldverschreibungen** *f pl* BÖRSE matured bonds; **~e Steuern** *f pl* RECHNUNG taxes due; **täglich ~es Geld** *nt* BANK day loan; **~er Wechsel** *m* BANK expired bill, FINANZ due bill (*AmE*), RECHNUNG bill payable; **~e Zahlung** *f* FINANZ payment due

Fälligkeit *f* BANK maturity, BÖRSE expiration (*AmE*), FINANZ due date, maturity; **nach ~ aufgeschlüsselte Saldenbilanz** *f* RECHNUNG aged trial balance; **~ der Prämie** VERSICH due date of premium; **~ der Verlängerung** VERSICH due date of renewal; ♦ **bei ~** BÖRSE, FINANZ at maturity, on maturity, when due; **vor**

~ FINANZ ahead of schedule, GESCHÄFT anticipated; **nach ihrer ~ aufschlüsseln** RECHNUNG age

Fälligkeit: **Fälligkeitsbasis** *f* RECHNUNG accrual basis of accounting; **Fälligkeitsdatum** *nt* BÖRSE, GESCHÄFT date of maturity (*DOM*), due date; **Fälligkeitsstruktur** *f* **der Schulden** vw maturity structure of debt; **Fälligkeitstag** *m* RECHNUNG day of maturity, due date; **Fälligkeitstermin** *m* BANK date of maturity (*DOM*), BÖRSE delivery date (*d.d.*), PERSON date of delivery, VERWALT due date; **zum Fälligkeitstermin** *phr* BÖRSE at maturity, GESCHÄFT at due date; **Fälligkeit-bei-Verkauf-Klausel** *f* BANK due-on-sale clause (*AmE*); **Fälligkeitswert** *m* BANK, VW maturity value; **Fälligkeitszeitpunkt** *m* RECHT *Vertragsrecht* due date

Fall: **Fallmethode** *f* GESCHÄFT case method, MGMNT case study method; **Fallnotizen** *f pl* GESCHÄFT case notes; **Fallordner** *m* GESCHÄFT case file; **Fallrecht** *nt* RECHT case law; **Fallstrick** *m* GESCHÄFT pitfall; **Fallstudie** *f* GESCHÄFT, MGMNT, V&M case study; **Fallstudienmethode** *f* GESCHÄFT *Strategiefestlegung* case study method

falls: **~ unzustellbar, an Absender zurück** *phr* KOMM if undelivered please return to sender

Fall: **Fallunterlagen** *f pl* GESCHÄFT case papers

fallweise *adj* GESCHÄFT ad hoc

falsch 1. *adj* GESCHÄFT false, incorrect, wrong, *fehlerhaft* erroneous, *künstlich* artificial; ♦ **eine ~e Beschreibung macht den Gegenstand nicht ungültig** GESCHÄFT falsa demonstratio non nocet; **auf der ~en Fährte sein** GESCHÄFT be on the wrong track; **im ~en Job sein** PERSON be in the wrong job; **auf der ~en Spur sein** GESCHÄFT be on the wrong track; **~e Zahlen ermitteln** GESCHÄFT get the figures wrong; **2.** *adv* GESCHÄFT falsely, wrongly; ♦ **~ ablegen** GESCHÄFT misfile; **~ darstellen** GESCHÄFT misrepresent; **~ berechnen** GESCHÄFT miscalculate

falsch: **~e Altersangabe** *f* VERSICH misstatement of age; **~e Angaben** *f pl* RECHT misrepresentation, VERWALT false statement; **~ angesetztes Kursverhältnis** *nt* VW misaligned rate of exchange; **~e Erklärung** *f* STEUER misdeclaration; **~e Handhabung** *f* GESCHÄFT mishandling; **~e oder irreführende Information** *f* RECHT false or misleading information; **~e Sparsamkeit** *f* VW false economy; **~e Verbindung** *f* KOMM *Telefon, Fax* wrong connection, TRANSP misconnection; **~er Zeuge** *m*, **~e Zeugin** *f* RECHT *Person* false witness; **~es Zeugnis** *nt* RECHT *Aussage* false witness

fälschen *vt* GESCHÄFT forge, RECHT *Original* falsify

Falschinformation *f*: **~ zu Täuschungszwecken** GESCHÄFT, POL disinformation

fälschlicherweise *adv* GESCHÄFT wrongly

Fälschung *f* GESCHÄFT forgery, RECHNUNG falsification, RECHT *Dokumente* falsification, *Münzen* counterfeit

fälschungssicher *adj* GESCHÄFT *Dokument* tamper-proof

faltbar: **~e Seite** *f* MEDIEN, V&M gatefold

Faltblatt *nt* GESCHÄFT folder

familiär: **~er Lebensstil** *m* V&M family life-style

Familien- *in cpds* GESCHÄFT family; **Familienbeihilfe** *f* SOZIAL family allowance (*BrE*); **Familienbeihilfen** *f pl* SOZIAL family benefits; **Familienbericht** *m* VW ≈ Family Expenditure Survey (*BrE*) (*FES*); **Familienbetrieb** *m* GESCHÄFT family business, family-owned business; **Familienbudget** *nt* V&M family budget; **Familienfahrpreis** *m* TRANSP family fare;

Familiengesellschaft *f* VW closed corporation (*AmE*), family-owned company; **Familienlebensversicherung** *f* VERSICH family life insurance; **Familienpackung** *f* V&M family-size pack

familienpolitisch *adj* SOZIAL child-centered (*AmE*), child-centred (*BrE*)

Familien-: **Familienprogramm** *nt* MEDIEN family hour; **Familienschutzpolice** *f* VERSICH family protection policy; **Familienschutzversicherung** *f* VERSICH family protection policy; **Familienunternehmen** *nt* GESCHÄFT family business; **Familienverhältnisse** *nt pl* RECHT *Arbeit, Rechtsverfahren* family circumstances; **Familienvorsorgeversicherung** *f* VERSICH family income benefit policy (*AmE*)

Fang: **auf ~ gehen** *phr infrml* GESCHÄFT be on the take (*infrml*); **Fanggebiete** *nt pl* VW fishing grounds; **Fanggründe** *m pl* VW fishing grounds

Fanzeitung *f* MEDIEN fanzine

Farb- *in cpds* COMP, MEDIEN color (*AmE*), colour (*BrE*); **Farbanzeige** *f* COMP color display (*AmE*), colour display (*BrE*); **Farbband** *nt* COMP, MEDIEN *Drucker* ribbon; **Farbbandkassette** *f* COMP *Drucker* ribbon cartridge; **Farbbeilage** *f* MEDIEN *Zeitung, Zeitschrift* color supplement (*AmE*), colour supplement (*BrE*); **Farbbildschirm** *m* COMP color display (*AmE*), colour display (*BrE*); **Farbdisplay** *nt jarg* COMP color display (*AmE*), colour display (*BrE*)

Farbe *f* COMP, MEDIEN color (*AmE*), colour (*BrE*)

farbecht *adj* IND guaranteed not to fade

färben *vt* IND dye

Farb-: **Farbgrafikadapter** *m* COMP color graphics adapter (*AmE*) (*CGA*), colour graphics adapter (*BrE*) (*CGA*); **Farbgrafikanordnung** *f* COMP color graphics array (*AmE*) (*CGA*), colour graphics array (*BrE*) (*CGA*); **Farbtrennung** *f* V&M color separation (*AmE*), colour separation (*BrE*)

Faschismus *m* POL fascism

Faseroptik *f* COMP, IND fiber optics (*AmE*), fibre optics (*BrE*)

Faserplatte *f* IND fiberboard (*AmE*), fibreboard (*BrE*)

Faß *nt* TRANSP keg, barrel, cask (*ck*)

Fassade *f* GRUND *eines Gebäudes* facade

Faß: **Faßfabrik** *f* IND cooperage; **Faßöl** *nt* IND case oil (*co*)

Fassung *f* GESCHÄFT version; ♦ **in der ~ von** RECHT as amended

Fassungsvermögen: **das ganze ~ gefüllt** *phr* IND at full capacity

fast: **~ fertig** *phr* GESCHÄFT *Fertigstellung* near completion

FAT *abbr* (*Dateizuordnungstabelle*) COMP *Magnetplatte* FAT (*file allocation table*)

faul: **~er Scheck** *m infrml* BANK dud check (*AmE*) (*infrml*), dud cheque (*BrE*) (*infrml*); **~er Wechsel** *m infrml* BANK bad paper (*infrml*); **~er Zauber** *m infrml* V&M eyewash (*infrml*)

Faustregel *f* GESCHÄFT rough guide, rule of thumb

Fautfracht *f* TRANSP deadfreight (*df*)

Fauxpas *m* GESCHÄFT faux pas, bad break (*infrml*)

Favorit *m* POL *Präsidentschaftswahl* point, favorite (*AmE*), favourite (*BrE*)

Fax *nt* (*Faksimile*) KOMM fax (*facsimile*); ♦ **per ~ übermitteln** KOMM send by fax

faxen *vt* KOMM fax, send by fax

Fax: **Faxgerät** *nt* KOMM fax machine; **Faxübermittlung** *f* KOMM fax transmission; **Faxübertragung** *f* KOMM fax transmission

Fazilitäten *f pl* BANK facilities

FAZ Index *m* (*Aktienindex der Frankfurter Allgemeinen Zeitung*) BÖRSE All Share Index (*Financial Times Actuaries All Shares Index*)

FB *abbr* (*Frachtbrief*) IMP/EXP, TRANSP b.l. (*bill of lading*), B/L (*bill of lading*)

FCKWs *abbr* (*Fluorchlorkohlenwasserstoffe*) UMWELT CFCs (*chlorofluorocarbons*)

Feature *nt* MEDIEN feature

Fed: **die ~** *f jarg* BANK, FINANZ, VW the Fed (*Federal Reserve System*) (*AmE*)

Federführung *f* FINANZ lead management

Federzeichnung *f* MEDIEN, V&M line drawing

Fed: **Fed-Schuldverschreibung** *f jarg* BANK federal reserve note (*AmE*)

Feedback *nt* GESCHÄFT feedback

Fehl- *in cpds* GESCHÄFT false, mis-; **Fehlalarm** *m* GESCHÄFT false alarm; **Fehlallokation** *f* VW misallocation

fehlbar *adj* GESCHÄFT fallible

Fehlbarkeit *f* GESCHÄFT fallibility

Fehl-: **Fehlbearbeitung** *f* GESCHÄFT mishandling; **Fehlberechnung** *f* GESCHÄFT miscalculation; **Fehlbestand** *m* GESCHÄFT deficiency; **Fehlbetrag** *m* FINANZ deficit, GESCHÄFT shortage, shortfall, RECHNUNG shortfall, STEUER deficiency; **Fehlbuchung** *f* RECHNUNG posting error; **Fehlcodierung** *f* COMP miscoding

Fehlen *nt* FINANZ, GESCHÄFT absence, lack; **~ der Gegenleistung** FINANZ, GESCHÄFT absence of consideration; ◆ **bei ~ von** GESCHÄFT in the absence of

fehlen *vt*: **~ an** [+dat] GESCHÄFT be short of, lack

fehlend: **~e Fracht** *f* TRANSP missing cargo (*msca*); **~es Konnossement** *nt* IMP/EXP, TRANSP missing bill of lading (*msbl*); **~er Markt** *m* VW missing market; **~e Steuerrate** *f* STEUER deficient tax installment (*AmE*), deficient tax instalment (*BrE*)

Fehler *m* COMP error, *Software* fault, GESCHÄFT flaw, mistake, *Irrtum* erratum, fault, MATH error; **~ zweiter Ordnung** MATH beta error; ◆ **einen ~ machen** GESCHÄFT make an error; **~ einkalkulieren** RECHNUNG allow for a margin of error

Fehler: **Fehlerbaumanalyse** *f* GESCHÄFT fault tree analysis; **Fehlerbericht** *m* COMP error report; **Fehlerbeseitigung** *f* COMP debugging, error recovery

fehlerfrei *adj* COMP error-free, GESCHÄFT faultless, free from defects, sound, without fault

Fehler: **Fehlerfreiheit** *f* RECHT *Vertragsrecht* faultlessness; **Fehlergrenze** *f* VERWALT margin of error

fehlerhaft *adj* GESCHÄFT deficient, faulty, flawed, less-than-perfect, RECHT defective; **~e Arbeit** *f* GESCHÄFT bad work; **~e Installation** *f* VERSICH faulty installation; **~e Montage** *f* VERSICH faulty installation; **~er Sektor** *m* COMP *Disketten, Festplatten* bad sector; **~e Waren** *f pl* V&M faulty goods

Fehler: **Fehlerhäufigkeit** *f* COMP error rate; **Fehlerkennzeichen** *nt* COMP flag; **Fehlerkontrolle** *f* **mit Rückwärtsübertragung** COMP message feedback; **Fehlermeldung** *f* COMP error message; **Fehlersektor** *m*

COMP *Disketten, Festplatten* bad sector; **Fehlersuche** *f* COMP, GESCHÄFT troubleshooting; **Fehlersucher** *m* COMP, GESCHÄFT troubleshooter; **Fehlersuchprogramm** *nt* COMP debugger; **Fehlersuchseminar** *nt* MGMNT faults diagnosis clinic

fehlertolerant *adj* COMP fault-tolerant; **~es System** *nt* COMP fault-tolerant system

Fehler: **Fehlertoleranz** *f* **des Kassierers** GESCHÄFT cashier's error allowance; **Fehlerüberwachung** *f* COMP error control

Fehl-: **Fehlfracht** *f* TRANSP deadfreight (*df*), missing cargo (*msca*); **Fehlinvestition** *f* BANK, FINANZ bad investment, unprofitable investment; **Fehlinvestition** *f* **aufgrund falscher Umsatzprognosen** BANK unintended investment; **Fehlleitung** *f* VW misallocation; **Fehlmenge** *f* GESCHÄFT, RECHNUNG shortfall; **Fehlmengenkosten** *pl* GESCHÄFT out-of-stock cost, stockout cost; **einen Fehlschlag erleiden** *phr* GESCHÄFT suffer a setback; **sich als Fehlschlag herausstellen** *phr* GESCHÄFT go sour *infrml*; **Fehlstreuung** *f* V&M waste circulation; **Fehlurteil** *nt* RECHT miscarriage of justice, misjudgment; **Fehlverhalten** *nt* GESCHÄFT faux pas

Feierabendverkehr *m* TRANSP rush hour

Feierlichkeit *f* FREI function

feilschen: **~ um** *vt* GESCHÄFT, V&M bargain about, haggle over

fein *adj* IND refined

Fein- *in cpds* IND, VW precision, fine-tuned

feinabstimmen *vt* VW fine-tune

Feinabstimmung *f* IND *eines Geräts*, VW *der Wirtschaft* fine tuning

feindlich: **~e Übernahmeofferte** *f* FINANZ, GESCHÄFT hostile takeover bid, unfriendly takeover attempt

Fein-: **Feineinstellung** *f* COMP fine tuning; **Feingehalt** *m* BANK standard; **den Feingehalt feststellen** *phr* GESCHÄFT assay; **Feingehaltsstempel** *m* BANK hallmark, hallmark stamp, plate mark; **Feinhöhenmesser** *m* IND variometer; **Feinmechanik** *f* IND light engineering, precision engineering; **Feinplanung** *f* MGMNT detailed planning; **Feinsteuerung** *f* VW *der Wirtschaft* fine tuning; **Feintechnik** *f* IND precision engineering; **Feinwerktechnik** *f* IND light engineering

Feld *nt* COMP *Textverarbeitung*, IND *Fachgebiet*, V&M *Marktforschung* field; **Feldforschung** *f* V&M field research; **Feldfrüchte** *f pl* RECHT emblements; **Feldlinie** *f* MATH flow line; **Feldmarkung** *f* GRUND *Grenzstein* landmark; **Feldname** *m* COMP identifier; **Feldrechner** *m* COMP array processor; **Feldtheorie** *f* **der Motivation** PERSON *Arbeitspsychologie* field theory of motivation; **Feldversuch** *m* V&M field testing

felizifisch: **~e Berechnung** *f* VW *Utilitarismus* felicific calculus

Fenster *nt* COMP, GESCHÄFT window; **Fensteraufkleber** *m* V&M *Werbung* window sticker; **Fensterbriefumschlag** *m* VERWALT panel envelope, window envelope; **Fensterglasversicherung** *f* VERSICH glass insurance

Ferien *pl* FREI, GESCHÄFT, PERSON holiday (*BrE*), vacation (*AmE*), leave; ◆ **in die ~ gehen** FREI, GESCHÄFT, PERSON go on holiday (*BrE*), go on vacation (*AmE*), take a holiday (*BrE*), take a vacation (*AmE*), take leave; **~ machen** FREI, GESCHÄFT, PERSON go on holiday

(*BrE*), go on vacation (*AmE*), take a holiday (*BrE*), take a vacation (*AmE*), take leave

Ferien: **Ferien- und Freizeitversicherung** *f* VERSICH holiday and leisure insurance; **Feriengast** *m* FREI, GESCHÄFT holiday guest (*BrE*), paying guest (*BrE*) (*PG*), vacation guest (*AmE*); **Ferienunterkunft** *f* GRUND holiday accommodation; **Ferienzeit** *f* FREI holiday period

Fern- *in cpds* COMP, KOMM, TRANSP remote, long-distance

fern *adj* GESCHÄFT absent, aloof, remote, PERSON absent

Fern-: **Fernakademie** *f* SOZIAL correspondence college, correspondence school; **Fernbleiben** *nt* GESCHÄFT absence; **Fernfahrer, in** *m,f* TRANSP long-distance lorry driver (*BrE*), long-distance truck driver (*AmE*); **Ferngespräch** *nt* KOMM long-distance call, trunk call (*BrE*), toll call (*AmE*)

ferngesteuert *adj* COMP remote-controlled

Fern-: **Fernkauf** *m* V&M catalog buying (*AmE*), catalogue buying (*BrE*); **Fernkopie** *f* dat KOMM fax (*facsimile*); **Fernkopierer** *m* dat GESCHÄFT, KOMM fax (*facsimile*), fax machine; **Fernlastfahrer, in** *m,f* TRANSP long-distance lorry driver (*BrE*), long-distance truck driver (*AmE*); **Fernleitung** *f* KOMM trunk line

Fernmelde- *in cpds* KOMM telecommunications; **Fernmeldeamt** *nt* KOMM office of telecommunications (*BrE*), telephone exchange, trunk exchange (*AmE*); **Fernmeldenetz** *nt* KOMM telecommunication network; **Fernmeldesatellit** *m* KOMM telecommunications satellite; **Fernmeldetechnik** *f* KOMM telecommunication technology, telecommunications; **Fernmeldewesen** *nt* KOMM telecommunication, telecommunications

fernmündlich: **~ mitteilen** *phr* KOMM telecommunicate

Fern-: **Fernschreiben** *nt* KOMM, VERWALT *Nachricht* teleprinter message (*BrE*), teletype message (*AmE*), telex (*tx.*); **Fernschreiber** *m* KOMM, VERWALT *Gerät* telex (*tx.*), teleprinter (*BrE*), teletyper (*AmE*), teletypewriter (*AmE*), telewriter (*AmE*), *Person* teletype operator (*AmE*), teletypist (*AmE*), telex operator; **Fernschreibgerät** *nt* KOMM, VERWALT teleprinter (*BrE*), teletyper (*AmE*), teletypewriter (*AmE*)

Fernseh- *in cpds* KOMM, MEDIEN television, TV; **Fernsehbildschirm** *m* KOMM, MEDIEN television screen

Fernsehen *nt* (*FS*) KOMM, MEDIEN television (*TV*); ◆ **im ~ senden** MEDIEN broadcast

Fernseh-: **Fernsehnetz** *nt* MEDIEN television network, TV network; **Fernsehschirm** *m* KOMM, MEDIEN television screen; **Fernsehsendung** *f* MEDIEN broadcast, telecast (*AmE*); **Fernsehunterstützung** *f* V&M television support; **Fernsehwerbezeit** *f* MEDIEN, V&M airtime; **Fernsehwerbezeit kaufen** *phr* V&M buy airtime; **Fernsehwerbung** *f* MEDIEN, V&M television advertising

Fern-: **Fernspediteur** *m* TRANSP haulage contractor

Fernsprech- *in cpds* KOMM telephone; **Fernsprechadresse** *f* KOMM telephone address (*tel. add.*); **Fernsprechauftragsdienst** *m* KOMM answering service

Fernsprecher *m* frml GESCHÄFT, KOMM telephone (*tel.*)

Fernsprech-: **Fernsprechgebühren** *f pl* KOMM telephone charges, telephone rates (*AmE*); **Fernsprechkonferenz** *f* COMP teleconference, KOMM audio conference, teleconference, V&M teleconference; **Fernsprechteilnehmer, in** *m,f* KOMM telephone subscriber; **Fernsprechteilnehmerverzeichnis** *nt* KOMM phone book, telephone book, telephone directory;

Fernsprechvermittlung *f* KOMM telephone exchange; **Fernsprechwesen** *nt* KOMM telephony

Fern-: **Fernsteuerung** *f* KOMM *Geräte* remote control; **Fernstraße** *f* TRANSP highway (*AmE*), trunk road (*BrE*); **Fernstrecke** *f* TRANSP trunk line; **Fernstudium** *nt* SOZIAL correspondence course, distance learning, home study course; **Fernuniversität** *f* SOZIAL correspondence school, open university; **Fernunterricht** *m* SOZIAL distance learning; **Fernunterstützung** *f* COMP remote support; **Fernverarbeitung** *f* COMP remote processing, teleprocessing; **Fernwartung** *f* COMP remote maintenance; **Fernzugriff** *m* COMP remote access

Fertig- *in cpds* GESCHÄFT, IND *vollendet* ready, finished, *vorgefertigt* prefabricated (*prefab*), ready-made; **Fertiggericht** *nt* V&M ready-made meal; **Fertighaus** *nt* GRUND manufactured home, prefabricated house, prefab house

Fertigkeit *f* GESCHÄFT, PERSON skill; **Fertigkeitenanalyse** *f* PERSON skills analysis

Fertig-: **Fertiglebensmittel** *nt pl* IND processed foods; **Fertigprodukt** *nt* GESCHÄFT finished product; **Fertigprogamm** *nt* COMP canned program

fertigstellen *vt* IND turn around

Fertigstellung *f* GESCHÄFT completion; **Fertigstellungsbasis** *f* RECHNUNG completion basis; **Fertigstellungsgarantie** *f* GRUND, RECHT completion bond (*AmE*); **Fertigstellungsprogramm** *nt* UMWELT completion program (*AmE*), completion programme (*BrE*); **Fertigstellungstermin** *m* GESCHÄFT target date, completion date

Fertigung *f* IND manufacture, production; **Fertigungsabteilung** *f* IND production department; **Fertigungsanlage** *f* IND factory; **Fertigungsarbeitskräfte** *f pl* PERSON manufacturing; **Fertigungsauftrag** *m* IND manufacturing order; **Fertigungsaufwand** *m* IND production costs; **Fertigungsbereich** *m* VW manufacturing sector; **Fertigungsbetrieb** *m* IND component factory; **Fertigungseinzelkosten** *pl* VW prime costs; **Fertigungsgemeinkosten** *pl* RECHNUNG factory overheads, manufacturing overheads, VW indirect labor costs (*AmE*), indirect labour costs (*BrE*); **Fertigungsindustrie** *f* IND manufacturing industry; **Fertigungskapazität** *f* IND manufacturing capacity; **Fertigungskontrolle** *f* GESCHÄFT process control, progress control, IND process control, production control; **Fertigungskosten** *pl* RECHNUNG manufacturing cost, manufacturing costs, manufacturing overheads, production costs; **Fertigungsleiter, in** *m,f* PERSON production manager; **Fertigungslohn** *m* FINANZ, IND, VW *Kostenrechnung* direct labor (*AmE*), direct labour (*BrE*); **Fertigungslöhne** *m pl* FINANZ, IND, PERSON, VW *Kostenrechnung* direct labor (*AmE*), direct labour (*BrE*); **Fertigungslohnkosten** *pl* FINANZ, IND, PERSON, VW direct labor cost (*AmE*), direct labour cost (*BrE*); **Fertigungsmaterial** *nt* VW direct and indirect material; **Fertigungsorganisation** *f* IND industrial engineering; **Fertigungsphase** *f* IND processing stage; **Fertigungsplan** *m* IND, MGMNT production schedule; **Fertigungsplanung** *f* IND, MGMNT process engineering, production scheduling; **Fertigungsplanung und -kontrolle** *f* GESCHÄFT, IND, MGMNT production planning and control; **Fertigungssektor** *m* VW secondary sector; **Fertigungssteuerung** *f* IND manufacturing control

fertigungssynchron: ~**e Materialwirtschaft** *f* IND just-in-time purchasing

Fertigung: **Fertigungssystem** *nt* IND manufacturing system; **Fertigungstechnik** *f* IND production technology, production engineering, product engineering; **Fertigungsüberwachung** *f* IND performance monitoring (*PM*); **Fertigungsvorbereitung** *f* IND production scheduling

Fertig-: **Fertigwaren** *f pl* GESCHÄFT finished goods

Fesselballonwerbung *f* V&M balloon advertising

fest 1. *adj* BANK fixed, nonvariable, GESCHÄFT stable, steady, permanent, pegged, VW firm, pegged; ♦ **ein ~es Angebot machen** GESCHÄFT make a firm offer; **in ~er Decke gebunden** MEDIEN *Buch* casebound; **ohne ~e Grenze** GESCHÄFT open-ended; **ohne ~en Termin** FINANZ, GESCHÄFT sine die (*frml*); **ohne ~en Wohnsitz** RECHT without permanent residence, of no fixed abode; **in ~em Zustand befindlich** GESCHÄFT solid-state; **2.** *adv* GESCHÄFT steadily, firmly, permanently; ♦ **~ angelegt** BANK, FINANZ illiquid, tied up; **~ bleiben** GESCHÄFT stand firm; **~ daran glauben, daß** GESCHÄFT be convinced that, stand firm in the belief that; **~ tendieren** BÖRSE firm; **~ umrissen** GESCHÄFT *Ziel* specific

Fest- *in cpds* GESCHÄFT binding, firm

fest: ~**er Abschluß** *m* GESCHÄFT firm deal; ~**es Angebot** *nt* GESCHÄFT binding offer, firm offer; ~**e Arbeitskräfte** *f pl* PERSON permanent labor (*AmE*), permanent labour (*BrE*); ~**e Belastung** *f* VW fixed charge; ~**es Disagio** *nt* FINANZ hard discount; ~**e Einkünfte** *pl* BÖRSE fixed income; ~**e Fahrtroute** *f* TRANSP fixed route; ~**er Fristablauf** *m* GESCHÄFT strict time limit; ~**e Gebühr** *f* GESCHÄFT fixed fee; ~**e Haltung** *f* GESCHÄFT tough stance; ~**e Kosten** *pl* FINANZ standing expenses; ~**er Kundenkreis** *m* GESCHÄFT established clientele; ~**er Kurs** *m* BÖRSE firm price; ~**e Laufzeit** *f* BANK fixed maturity; ~**e Leistungen** *f pl* GESCHÄFT fixed benefits; ~**e Notierung** *f* BÖRSE firm price; ~**e Plankostenrechnung** *f* VERWALT fixed budgeting; ~**er Schlußtermin** *m* GESCHÄFT strict time limit; ~**er Seitenumbruch** *m* COMP *Textverarbeitung* hard page break; ~**e Übernahme** *f* **einer Anleihe durch eine Emissionsbank** BÖRSE firm commitment underwriting; ~**e Übernahmeverpflichtung** *f* BÖRSE firm commitment; ~**e Überzeugung** *f* GESCHÄFT firm belief; ~**er Verrechnungspreis** *m* FINANZ standard price; ~**e Versorgungsleistungen** *f pl* GESCHÄFT fixed benefits; ~**er Wechselkurs** *m* VW fixed exchange rate, pegged exchange rate

Fest-: **Festangebot** *nt* GESCHÄFT binding offer, firm offer; **Festanlage** *f* BANK fixed-term deposit; **Festanlage-Effekt** *m* BÖRSE locked-in effect; **Festanstellung** *f* PERSON *Arbeit* permanent appointment; **Festgebot** *nt* VERWALT firm bid

festgefahren *adj* GESCHÄFT *Verhandlungen* stalemated

Fest-: **Festgehalt** *nt* PERSON fixed salary; **Festgeld** *nt* BANK fixed deposit, fixed-period deposit, time deposit (*AmE*), term deposit; **Festgeldkonto** *nt* BANK investment account, time deposit account (*AmE*), FINANZ term account; **Festgeldkonto-Wertpapier** *nt* BANK investment account security

festgelegt *adj* BÖRSE, GESCHÄFT, MGMNT locked-in, tied up; ♦ **in der ~en Reihenfolge** GESCHÄFT in the order specified

festgelegt: ~**e Geldbuße** *f* STEUER fixed penalty; ~**es Kapital** *nt* RECHNUNG tied-up capital; ~**e Ratenzahlung** *f* FINANZ fixed installment (*AmE*), fixed instalment (*BrE*); ~**e Regeln** *f pl* GESCHÄFT set rules; ~**er Satz** *m* TRANSP fixture rate; ~**er Verfalltag** *m* BÖRSE fixed expiration date

festgeschrieben *adj* BÖRSE locked-in; ~**er Wert** *m* BÖRSE locked-in value

festgesetzt *adj* GESCHÄFT arranged, set, specified; ♦ **in der ~en Reihenfolge** GESCHÄFT in the order specified; **zum ~en Zeitpunkt** GESCHÄFT at the appointed time

festgesetzt: ~**e Geldstrafe** *f* STEUER fixed penalty; ~**er Preis** *m* BÖRSE predetermined price; ~**er Tag** *m* GESCHÄFT term day; ~**er Termin** *m* GESCHÄFT appointed day

festgestellt: ~**es Gewicht** *nt* GESCHÄFT weight ascertained; ~**er Sachverhalt** *m* RECHT findings; ~**e Tatsache** *f* GESCHÄFT ascertained fact

festhalten *vt*: **~ an** [+dat] GESCHÄFT *Entscheidung, Regelung* abide by, *Grundsatz* adhere to

festigen *vt* GESCHÄFT strengthen, VW stabilize

Festigung *f* GESCHÄFT strengthening

Fest-: **Festkommazahl** *f* MATH fixed-point number; **Festkonditionen** *f pl* VERWALT fixed terms; **Festkörper** *m* GESCHÄFT solid-state; **Festlandumschlagplatz** *m* UMWELT onshore terminal

festlegen *vt* BÖRSE lock in, *Wertpapiere* lock away (*jarg*), FINANZ tie up, GESCHÄFT schedule, *Datum, Ort* appoint, *Termin, Details* establish, work out, fix, RECHT *in einem Vertrag, Verfassung* lay down, *Regeln, Richtlinien, Bedingungen* formulate, VW *Wert* set, *Preis* determine

Festlegung *f* BANK capping, BÖRSE fixation; **~ von Akkordsätzen** PERSON rate fixing; **~ der Kosten** BÖRSE fixing of costs; **~ des Leitwegs** TRANSP routing; **~ einer Obergrenze** BANK capping; **~ der Rechnungslegungsgrundsätze** RECHNUNG accounting standard setting; **~ der Route** TRANSP routing

Festplatte *f* COMP *Speichermedium* fixed disk, hard disk (*HD*); **Festplatteneinheit** *f* COMP hard disk unit; **Festplattenfehler** *m* COMP hard disk error; **Festplattenlaufwerk** *nt* COMP hard disk drive (*HDD*); **Festplattenverwaltung** *f* COMP hard disk management

Fest-: **Festprämie** *f* VERSICH fixed premium; **Festpreis** *m* BÖRSE, RECHNUNG fixed price; **Festpreisauftrag** *m* V&M fixed-price contract; **Festrente** *f* VERSICH fixed annuity; **Festsatzbond** *m* BÖRSE straight bond; **Festsatzhypothek** *f* BANK fixed-rate mortgage

festschnallen *vt* GESCHÄFT fasten

festschreiben *vt* BÖRSE lock in

festsetzen *vt* BÖRSE declare, GESCHÄFT arrange, set, specify, VW *Wert* set

Festsetzen *nt*: **~ eines hohen Preises** V&M pricing up

Festsetzung *f* BÖRSE declaration, GESCHÄFT setting; **~ eines Fehlbetrages** STEUER assessment of deficiency; **~ der Laufzeit** GESCHÄFT dating; **~ von Prestigepreisen** V&M prestige pricing; **~ des Verrechnungspreises** GESCHÄFT transfer pricing; **Festsetzungsdatum** *nt* **für die Kreditkonditionen** BÖRSE loan-pricing date

Fest-: **Festspeicher** *m* (*ROM*) COMP read-only memory (*ROM*)

feststehend: ~**e Adresse** *f* GESCHÄFT registered address; ~**es Verfahren** *nt* GESCHÄFT standing procedure

feststellen vt GESCHÄFT adopt, *Preis* ascertain, establish, POL, RECHT adopt, VERWALT adopt, ascertain

Feststellung f GESCHÄFT ascertainment; ~ **der Höhe des Schadensersatzes** RECHT assessment of compensation; ~ **der Jahresrente** RECHT *Rentenzahlungen* settling of an annuity; **Feststellungen** f pl RECHT *bei einer Untersuchung, vor Gericht* findings

festverzinslich: ~**es Darlehen** nt FINANZ fixed-interest loan; ~**e Kapitalanlage** f BÖRSE fixed-income investment; ~**er Schuldtitel** m BÖRSE loan stock; ~**e Wertpapiere** nt pl FINANZ, RECHNUNG, VW loan capital, loan stock

Fest-: **Festwert** m VERSICH agreed value; **Festwertversicherung** f VERSICH agreed value insurance

Festzins- in cpds BANK, FINANZ fixed-rate interest; **Festzinsanleihe** f BÖRSE straight bond; **Festzinsanleihenmarkt** m FINANZ straight market; **Festzinsbondsmarkt** m FINANZ straight market; **Festzinshypothek** f BANK fixed-rate mortgage; **Festzinskredit** m BANK fixed-rate loan, FINANZ straight loan; **Festzinsmittel** nt pl BANK stable-rate funds

fett adj COMP, MEDIEN *Schriftzeichen* bold; ~**er Buchstabe** m MEDIEN *Druck* bold type; ~**er Satz** m COMP, MEDIEN bold face; ~**e Schrift** f COMP, MEDIEN bold type

Fettdruck m COMP, MEDIEN bold printing

fettgedruckt adj COMP, MEDIEN printed in bold type; ~**e Schrift** f COMP, MEDIEN bold face; ~**es Zeichen** nt COMP, MEDIEN boldface character

Fettnäpfchencheck nt jarg POL *bei einer öffentlichen Rede* snakecheck (jarg)

feuchtigkeitsfest adj GESCHÄFT damp-proof, TRANSP moisture-proof

Feudalismus m POL feudalism

Feuer nt GESCHÄFT, VERSICH fire; ♦ **jdn gegen ~ versichern** VERSICH insure sb against fire

Feuer: **Feuerbestattungsversicherung** f VERSICH cremation expenses insurance

feuerfest adj GESCHÄFT fire-resistant, fireproof

Feuer: **Feuergefahr** f SOZIAL, VERSICH fire hazard; **Feuerhaftpflichtversicherung** f VERSICH fire legal liability insurance (AmE); **Feuerleiter** f PERSON *an Gebäude, Schiff* fire escape

feuern vt infrml PERSON fire, sack (infrml) (BrE)

Feuer: **Feuerschutzmauer** f SOZIAL, VERSICH fire wall; **Feuerschutztür** f PERSON fire door

feuersicher adj GESCHÄFT fireproof; ~**e Bauart** f VERSICH fire-resistant construction, fireproof construction

Feuer: **Feuerverhütung** f SOZIAL fire prevention; **Feuerversicherungsvertrag** m VERSICH fire insuring agreement (AmE), fire insurance agreement (BrE); **Feuerwehr** f GESCHÄFT fire brigade (BrE), fire service; **Feuerwehrfonds** m RECHNUNG firefighting fund; **Feuerwehrübung** f PERSON fire drill

ff. abbr (fortgesetzt) GESCHÄFT cont. (continued), contd (continued)

Fiberglas nt IND fiberglass (AmE), fibreglass (BrE)

Fire: ~~**Wall-Abschottung** f COMP firewall

fiduziär: ~**er Notenumlauf** m BANK fiduciary currency, fiduciary issue

fiduziarisch adv RECHT *treuhänderisch* fiduciary; ~**es Bankgeschäft** nt BANK fiduciary banking

Fifo-Methode f RECHNUNG first in first out (FIFO)

fiktiv adj FINANZ notional, GESCHÄFT fictitious; ~**e Buchung** f VW imputation; ~**e Dividende** f FINANZ sham dividend; ~**es Einkommen** nt RECHNUNG imputed income; ~**e Miete** f GRUND *eigengenutzte Wohnung im Einfamilienhaus* notional rent; ~**er Wert** m RECHNUNG imputed value; ~**e Zinsen** m pl STEUER imputed interest

Filial- in cpds BANK branch; **Filialbank** f BANK branch bank; **Filialbanksystem** nt BANK branch banking system; **Filialbankwesen** nt BANK branch banking, chain banking (AmE); **Filialbetrieb** m GESCHÄFT branch operation

Filiale f BANK area office, branch, GESCHÄFT branch, branch office, branch operation, suboffice, V&M chain store

Filial-: **Fillialkette** f V&M chain store; **Filialleiter, in** m,f BANK branch manager, GESCHÄFT, MGMNT, PERSON branch office manager; **Filialnetz** nt BANK branch network; **Filialnummer** f BANK branch number; **Filialvorsteher, in** m,f GESCHÄFT, MGMNT, PERSON branch office manager

Film m FREI, MEDIEN film, motion picture (AmE); **Filmaufnahme** f MEDIEN, V&M shoot; **Filmbranche** f MEDIEN film industry, motion picture industry (AmE); **Filmdrehbuch** nt MEDIEN film script; **Filmemachen** nt MEDIEN film-making; **Filmemacher** m MEDIEN filmmaker; **Filmfestspiele** f pl FREI, MEDIEN film festival; **Filmindustrie** f MEDIEN film industry, motion picture industry (AmE); **Filmlänge** f MEDIEN footage; **Filmmeter** m MEDIEN footage; **Filmprobe** f MEDIEN film test; **Filmproduktionskosten** pl STEUER film production costs; **Filmrohfassung** f MEDIEN film rush; **Filmtest** m MEDIEN screen test; **Filmwerbung** f V&M cinema advertising (BrE), film advertising, motion picture advertising (AmE)

Filter m or nt COMP filter

Finanz- in cpds FINANZ, STEUER financial, fiscal; **Finanzamt** nt POL the Exchequer (BrE) (Exch.), STEUER Inland Revenue Office (BrE), Internal Revenue Service (IRS) (AmE), revenue office, *Person* taxation office, tax collector, taxman; **Finanzamtsleiter, in** m,f STEUER head of local tax office; **Finanzanlageinvestition** f VW trade investments; **Finanzanlagen** f pl BANK, BÖRSE, FINANZ investments, VW financial assets, investments; **Finanzanzeige** f VW *bereits vollzogene Aktienemission oder Fusion* tombstone; **Finanzausweis** m RECHNUNG financial statement; **Finanzbedarf** m FINANZ financial requirements; **Finanzbehörde** f BANK, FINANZ, STEUER fiscal authority, revenue authority, tax authority; **Finanzbehörden** f pl BANK, FINANZ, STEUER fiscal authorities; **Finanzbereich** m FINANZ financial field; **Finanzbericht** m FINANZ financial management report, RECHNUNG statement of financial position; **Finanzbewertung** f FINANZ financial appraisal; **Finanzbuchhaltung** f FINANZ, RECHNUNG financial accounting; **Finanzbudget** nt VERWALT financial budget, VW capital budget; **Finanzchef, in** m,f MGMNT chief financial officer; **Finanz-Controller** m RECHNUNG financial controller; **Finanzdefizit** nt RECHNUNG fiscal deficit; **Finanzdienstleistungen** f pl FINANZ financial services; **Finanzdirektor, in** m,f PERSON chief financial officer (CFO), MGMNT financial director, finance director, treasurer AmE; **Finanz-Disposystem** nt BANK cash management system; **Finanzexperte** m,

Finanzexpertin *f* BANK financier; **Finanzföderalismus** *m* STEUER fiscal federalism; **Finanzgebiet** *nt* FINANZ financial field; **Finanzgenie** *nt infrml* GESCHÄFT financial wizard (*infrml*); **Finanzgericht** *nt* STEUER first-instance fiscal court, tax court; **Finanzgesetz** *nt* RECHT finance act; **Finanzgruppe** *f* GESCHÄFT syndicate; **Finanzgutachten** *nt* FINANZ financial appraisal; **Finanzhilfe** *f* VW financial aid, financial assistance; **Finanzhöhepunkte** *m pl* RECHNUNG financial highlights; **Finanzholding** *f* FINANZ financial holding company

finanziell 1. *adj* GESCHÄFT financial, pecuniary; ♦ **in ~en Schwierigkeiten** FINANZ cash-strapped; **sich in ~en Schwierigkeiten befinden** FINANZ be in financial straits; **einen ~en Zuschuß geben** GESCHÄFT make an allowance on; **2.** *adv* GESCHÄFT financially; ♦ **~ gesund** GESCHÄFT financially sound; **~ im Plus** *infrml* VW in financial surplus; **~ schwach** FINANZ cash-strapped; **sich ~ übernehmen** FINANZ overstretch oneself; **~ unterstützt durch** FINANZ backed by

finanziell: **~e Abfindung** *f* GESCHÄFT, KOMM, POL compensatory financing; **~er Anreiz** *m* FINANZ financial incentive; **~er Anspruch** *m* RECHNUNG financial claim; **~e Belastung** *f* FINANZ financial burden, financial encumbrance; **~e Beratungsgruppe** *f* BANK, FINANZ financial support staff; **~e Beteiligung** *f* FINANZ financial involvement; **~e Dienstleistungen** *f pl* FINANZ financial services; **~es Engagement** *nt* RECHNUNG capital commitment; **~er Engpaß** *m* VERWALT financial straits; **~e Entschädigung** *f* POL compensatory finance; **~er Gewinn** *m* **oder Verlust** *m* RECHNUNG financial profit or loss; **~es Gleichgewicht** *nt* VW financial balance; **~e Informations- und Budgetierungssysteme** *nt pl* FINANZ financial information and budgeting systems (*FIBS*); **~e Informations- und Haushaltsysteme** *nt pl* FINANZ financial information and budgeting systems (*FIBS*); **~e Lage** *f* FINANZ financial standing, VW financial climate; **~e Leistungsfähigkeit** *f* FINANZ viability; **~e Macht** *f* VERWALT, V&M financial muscle; **~e Mittel** *nt pl* FINANZ financial means, financing; **~e Offenlegung** *f* FINANZ financial disclosure; **~e Reserven** *f pl* GESCHÄFT bottom-up; **~es Risiko** *nt* BÖRSE financial risk; **~e Stabilität** *f* FINANZ financial stability; **~er Standard** *m* FINANZ financial standard; **~er Überblick** *m* FINANZ financial review, financial summary; **~ Unabhängige(r)** *mf* [decl. as adj] GESCHÄFT person of independent means; **~e Unterstützung** *f* FINANZ financial backing, financial aid, financial assistance, financial support; **~er Verlust** *m* FINANZ financial loss; **~er Vermögenswert** *m* FINANZ financial asset; **~e Zeichnungsberechtigung** *f* FINANZ financial signing authority; **~e Zwischenanleihe** *f* FINANZ financial intermediary loan (*FIL*)

Finanzier *m* BANK, FINANZ financier

finanzieren *vt* FINANZ finance, fund

Finanzierung *f* FINANZ finance, financing, *Projekt* funding; **~ mit eingeschränktem Rückgriffsrecht** BANK limited-recourse financing; **~ etablierter Programme** FINANZ established programmes financing (*BrE*), established programs financing (*AmE*); **~ durch Forderungsabtretung** RECHNUNG accounts receivable financing; **~ aus einer Hand** FINANZ, VW one-stop financing, financing package, single finance; **~ durch die Hintertür** POL, VW *unter Umgehung der Legislative* backdoor financing; **~ nach Plan** FINANZ formula funding; **~ durch Staatsverschuldung** FINANZ, VW deficit financing; **~ eines Warenlagers** BANK floor planning, flooring; ♦ **~ besorgen** FINANZ raise finance

Finanzierung: **Finanzierungsanpassung** *f* FINANZ financing adjustment; **Finanzierungsbedarf** *m* BANK borrowing requirement, FINANZ capital requirements; **Finanzierungsfiliale** *f* FINANZ funding agency; **Finanzierungsgebühr** *f* FINANZ factoring charge; **Finanzierungsgesellschaft** *f* FINANZ finance house (*BrE*); **Finanzierungsgesellschaft** *f* **für Kleinkredite** FINANZ consumer loan institute; **Finanzierungsinstitut** *nt* FINANZ financial enterprise, finance house (*BrE*); **Finanzierungskonglomerat** *nt* FINANZ financial conglomerate; **Finanzierungskosten** *pl* BANK finance charge, VERWALT financial expenses, VW capital costs; **Finanzierungs-Leasing** *nt* FINANZ capital lease, finance lease; **Finanzierungs-Leasingvertrag** *m* FINANZ capital lease agreement; **Finanzierungslücke** *f* FINANZ funding gap; **Finanzierungsmittel** *nt* BÖRSE credit instrument, FINANZ financial means; **Finanzierungsspezialist, in** *m,f* BANK, FINANZ loan officer; **Finanzierungsplan** *m* FINANZ financing plan, RECHNUNG financial planning; **Finanzierungsprogramm** *nt* VERWALT funding scheme; **Finanzierungsprogramm** *nt* **der Bundesregierung** VW federal financial program (*AmE*), federal financial programme (*BrE*); **Finanzierungsquelle** *f* FINANZ funding source; **Finanzierungssatz** *m* BÖRSE financing rate; **Finanzierungsstandard** *m* GESCHÄFT financial standard; **Finanzierungsstrategie** *f* FINANZ financial strategy; **Finanzierungsströme** *m pl* VW financial flow; **Fianzierungsstruktur** *f* FINANZ, VW financial structure; **Finanzierungstechnik** *f* FINANZ financial engineering; **Finanzierungs- und Teilzahlungskreditinstitut** *nt* BANK secondary bank

Finanz-: **Finanzinstitut** *nt* FINANZ financial institution; **Finanzinvestition** *f* FINANZ financial investment; **Finanzjahr** *nt* FINANZ, RECHNUNG, STEUER fiscal year (*FY*), financial year; **Finanzjournalismus** *m* FINANZ financial journalism; **Finanzkapital** *nt* FINANZ financial capital; **Finanzkonglomerat** *nt* FINANZ financial conglomerate; **Finanzkontrolle** *f* FINANZ, RECHNUNG budgetary control (*BC*), budgeting control, financial control; **Finanzkraft** *f* BANK financial strength, VERWALT, V&M financial muscle; **Finanzkreise** *m pl* FINANZ financial circles; **Finanzkrise** *f* FINANZ financial crisis, STEUER fiscal crisis; **Finanzlage** *f* RECHNUNG financial position, financial situation, position; **Finanzlage** *f* **des Gläubigers** FINANZ creditor position; **Finanzlage** *f* **des Projektes** FINANZ project finance; **Finanzleiter, in** *m,f* MGMNT financial manager, PERSON chief financial officer (*CFO*); **Finanzmagnat, in** *m,f* FINANZ financial magnate; **Finanzmakler, in** *m,f* BANK, FINANZ money broker; **Finanzmanagement** *nt* FINANZ, RECHNUNG financial management, cash management; **Finanzmanagement-System** *nt* FINANZ financial management system; **Finanzmarkt** *m* FINANZ financial market; **Finanzminister** *m* FINANZ, POL, VW finance minister, Chancellor of the Exchequer (*BrE*), Secretary of the Treasury (*AmE*); **Finanzministerium** *nt* FINANZ, POL, VW finance ministry, Department of the Treasury (*AmE*), Her Majesty's Treasury (*BrE*), Treasury (*BrE*), the Exchequer (*BrE*) (*Exch.*); **Finanzneutralität** *f* STEUER fiscal neutrality; **Finanzperiode** *f* FINANZ budgetary period; **Finanzperspektive** *f* VW financial perspective; **Finanzplan** *m* FINANZ, MGMNT, RECHNUNG, VERWALT budget; **Finanzplanung** *f* FINANZ, MGMNT, RECHNUNG, VERWALT budgeting, budgetary planning, financial management, financial planning; **Finanzplanungsbericht** *m* FINANZ financial management report; **Finanzpolitik** *f* FINANZ financial policy

finanzpolitisch: ~e **Ausgleichsregelung** *f* GESCHÄFT, POL compensatory finance

Finanz-: **Finanzprognosen** *f pl* FINANZ financial forecasts; **Finanzpyramide** *f* FINANZ financial pyramid; **Finanzsektor** *m* FINANZ finance sector; **Finanzsimulationssoftware** *f* FINANZ financial simulation software; **Finanzstatus** *m* BANK, FINANZ statement of condition (*AmE*), *Liquidität* financial statement, RECHNUNG asset and liability statement, financial position; **Finanzstrategie** *f* GESCHÄFT financial strategy; **Finanz-Supermarkt** *m* FINANZ financial supermarket; **Finanzsystem** *nt* FINANZ financial system; **Finanzterminbörse** *f* **New York** BÖRSE New York Futures Exchange (*NYFE*); **Finanzterminmarkt** *f* BÖRSE, FINANZ financial futures market; **Finanztreuhandkonto** *nt* FINANZ revenue trust account; **Finanzüberblick** *m* GESCHÄFT financial review; **Finanzverwaltung** *f* FINANZ, MGMNT financial administration, financial management, STEUER revenue department, VERWALT financial administration, financial management; **Finanzverwaltungsgesetz** *nt* RECHT Financial Administration Act; **Finanzverwaltungssystem** *nt* FINANZ, MGMNT, VERWALT system of financial administration; **Finanzvorlage** *f* VW Finance Bill (*BrE*), financial proposal; **Finanzvorstand** *m* PERSON financial director, finance director, financial executive, financial manager, vice president finance (*AmE*); **Finanzwechsel** *m* BANK finance bill, FINANZ accommodation bill, finance bill; **Finanzwelt** *f* FINANZ world of finance; **Finanzwesen** *nt* FINANZ finance, MGMNT financial management; **Finanzwirtschaft** *f* FINANZ, MGMNT *eines Unternehmens* business finance, financial management, VW public finances

finanzwirtschaftlich: ~ **gebildete Person** *f* PERSON financial sophisticate; ~e **Kennzahl** *f* FINANZ financial ratio, accounting ratio

Finanz-: **Finanzzentrum** *nt* FINANZ revenue center (*AmE*), revenue centre (*BrE*), financial center (*AmE*), financial centre (*BrE*)

Fingerzeig *m* GESCHÄFT hint, pointer

fingiert: ~e **Empfangsbestätigung** *f* STEUER constructive receipt; ~e **Rechnung** *f* GESCHÄFT fictitious invoice

Firma *f* (*Fa.*) GESCHÄFT business, business enterprise, company (*Co. BrE*), corporation (*corp. AmE*), establishment, firm; ♦ **diese** ~ **ist erstklassig bewertet worden** BÖRSE the company is rated triple-A

Firmen- *in* *cpds* GESCHÄFT corporate; **Firmenangelegenheiten** *f pl* GESCHÄFT company's affairs; **Firmenanwalt** *m*, **Firmenanwältin** *f* RECHT company's solicitor (*BrE*), corporate lawyer

firmeneigen *adj* GESCHÄFT company-owned, in-house; ~er **Außendienst** *m* IMP/EXP company's own field organization; ~er **Stil** *m* MEDIEN house style; ~e **Versicherung** *f* VERSICH self-insurance; ~e **Werbung** *f* V&M *Repräsentationswerbung* institutional advertising

Firmen-: **Firmeneinkauf** *m* V&M corporate purchasing; **Firmenfahrzeug** *nt* TRANSP company vehicle;

Firmenförderung *f* V&M corporate sponsorship; **Firmenfusionen und Übernahmen** *f pl* BÖRSE mergers and acquisitions (*M&A*); **Firmenimage** *nt* GESCHÄFT, V&M corporate image; **Firmenkampagne** *f* V&M corporate campaign; **Firmenkredite** *m pl* BANK corporate lending; **Firmenkreditkarte** *f* FINANZ corporate credit card, STEUER company credit card; **Firmenkreditmarkt** *m* BANK corporate lending market

Firmenkunde *m* BANK corporate client, corporate customer; **Firmenkundeneinlage** *f* BANK corporate account deposit; **Firmenkundengeschäft** *nt* BANK corporate banking; **Firmenkundenkredit** *m* BANK corporate credit; **Firmenkundenkreditmanager, in** *m,f* BANK corporate credit manager

Firmen-: **Firmenkundin** *f* BANK corporate client, corporate customer; **Firmenleitung** *f* MGMNT corporate management; **Firmenlogo** *nt* GESCHÄFT, V&M company logo, organizational symbol; **Firmenmantel** *m* GESCHÄFT shell company, shell corporation; **Firmenmodell** *nt* GESCHÄFT company model; **Firmenname** *m* GESCHÄFT corporate name, trade name, name of business; **Firmenorganisation** *f* GESCHÄFT business organization; **Firmenregister** *nt* VERWALT register of companies; **Firmenschild** *nt* V&M facia; **Firmenschriftzug** *m* GESCHÄFT, V&M logotype (*logo*); **Firmensiegel** *nt* RECHT company seal

firmenspezifisch: ~e **Karte** *f* FINANZ company-specific card

Firmen-: **Firmenstruktur** *f* GESCHÄFT corporate structure; **Firmenvertretung** *f* MGMNT company's representative; **Firmenverzeichnis** *nt* GESCHÄFT, trade directory; **Firmenvorstand** *m* GESCHÄFT, RECHNUNG, VERWALT board of directors; **Firmenwagen** *m* TRANSP company car; **Firmenwartungsvertrag** *m* GESCHÄFT company service contract; **Firmenwerbung** *f* V&M corporate advertising; **Firmenwert** *m* GESCHÄFT, RECHNUNG goodwill; **Firmenwert-Abschreibung** *f* RECHNUNG goodwill amortization; **Firmenzeichen** *nt* GESCHÄFT, V&M logotype (*logo*), motif, trade sign; **Firmenzusammenschluß** *m* RECHNUNG business combination, RECHT combine

Firmware *f* COMP *Programme* firmware

Fisch- *in cpds* IND, TRANSP, VW fishing

Fischerei *f* IND, VW fishing, fishing industry; **Fischereihafen** *m* IND fishing port; **Fischereiwirtschaft** *f* VW fishery

Fisch-: **Fischindustrie** *f* IND fishing industry; **Fischzucht** *f* VW fish farming

Fisher: ~-**Effekt** *m* VW Fisher effect; ~-**Theorem** *nt* VW Fisher theorem

Fiscal Drag-Effekt *m* FINANZ, STEUER, VW fiscal incidence

Fiskal- *in cpds* FINANZ, POL, STEUER, VW fiscal

fiskalisch *adj* FINANZ, POL, STEUER, VW fiscal; ~e **Bremse** *f* STEUER, VW fiscal drag; ~er **Indikator** *m* STEUER fiscal indicator; ~e **Planung** *f* STEUER fiscal projections; ~e **Schranke** *f* VW fiscal barrier; ~er **Standpunkt** *m* VW fiscal stance; ~e **Vorhersage** *f* STEUER fiscal projections

Fiskal-: **Fiskalist** *m* STEUER fiscalist; **Fiskalmultiplikator** *m* VW fiscal multiplier; **Fiskalpolitik** *f* VW fiscal policy

fiskalpolitisch: ~e **Sparmaßnahmen** *f pl* VW fiscal austerity

Fiskus *m* BANK fiscal authorities, the Exchequer (*BrE*) (*Exch.*), treasury, FINANZ, STEUER fiscal authorities

fit: ~ **sein** *phr* FREI, SOZIAL be fit

Fitneß *f* FREI, SOZIAL fitness; **Fitneß-Club** *m* FREI health club

fix *adj* BANK nonvariable; **~e Anlagen** *f pl* STEUER capital assets; **~e Gemeinkosten** *pl* RECHNUNG fixed overheads; **~e Kosten** *pl* RECHNUNG fixed costs, committed costs, VERWALT constant cost, VW fixed costs; **~e Rate** *f* FINANZ fixed installment (*AmE*), fixed instalment (*BrE*)

Fix- *in cpds* GESCHÄFT firm, fixed **Fixauftrag** *m* V&M firm order; **Fixgeschäft** *nt* BÖRSE time bargain, RECHT *Vertragsrecht* contract where time is of the essence, V&M transaction for delivery by a fixed date

fixieren *vt* GESCHÄFT, VW peg

fixiert *adj* GESCHÄFT, VW fixed, pegged, pre-arranged, VW pegged

Fixierung *f* BÖRSE fixation

Fix-: **Fixkosten** *pl* RECHNUNG, VW fixed charge, fixed costs, fixed expenses; **Fixkostendeckung** *f* RECHNUNG fixed-charge coverage; **Fixpunkt** *m* COMP, GESCHÄFT benchmark

Fixum *nt* GESCHÄFT fixed allowance, PERSON fixed salary

flach *adj* COMP slimline; **~er Markt** *m* BÖRSE shallow market; **~e Organisation** *f* MGMNT flat organization

Flach- *in cpds* TRANSP flat

flachfalten *vt* GESCHÄFT, TRANSP collapse

Flach-: **Flachcontainer** *m* TRANSP flat container

Fläche *f* VW area, surface area; **Flächenaufteilung** *f* GRUND zoning; **Flächenmaß** *nt* GESCHÄFT square measure; **Flächennutzung** *f* UMWELT land use; **Flächennutzungsplanung** *f* GRUND, VW land-use planning; **Flächenstichprobe** *f* V&M area sample

Flach-: **Flachgestell** *nt* TRANSP flat rack

flachgipflig: **~e Verteilungskurve** *f* MATH *Statistik* platykurtic frequency distribution

Flach-: **Flachgipfligkeit** *f* MATH *Statistik* platykurtosis; **Flachwagen** *m* TRANSP flat car (*AmE*), flat wagon (*BrE*); **Flachwagenanhänger** *m* TRANSP trailer on flat car (*AmE*), trailer on flat wagon (*BrE*); **Flachwagencontainer** *m* TRANSP container on flat car (*AmE*), container on flat wagon (*BrE*)

flackern *vi* COMP *Bildschirm* flicker

Flag *nt jarg* COMP flag

Flagge *f* TRANSP flag; **Flaggenrecht** *nt* RECHT law of the flag

flankierend *adj* GESCHÄFT collateral

Flaschenhals *m* GESCHÄFT, VW bottleneck

Flattersatz: **im ~** *phr* COMP, MEDIEN *Text* unjustified

flau *adj* BÖRSE lifeless, GESCHÄFT flat, slack, quiet, VW *Geschäft* slack; **~er Markt** *m* BÖRSE narrow market, GESCHÄFT stale market

Flaute *f* GESCHÄFT slack period, lull, stalemate

Fleischberg *m* VW *EG* meat mountain

flexibel *adj* GESCHÄFT flexible; **flexibler Akzelerator** *m* VW flexible accelerator; **flexible Arbeitszeit** *f* PERSON flexible time, flexible working hours, flexitime, flextime, flexible schedule; **flexibles Arbeitszeitprogramm** *nt* PERSON flexible schedule; **flexibles Budget** *nt* VW flexible budget, variable budget; **flexibler Investmentfonds** *m* VW management company; **flexible Lebensversicherung** *f* VERSICH modified life insurance; **flexible Normalkosten** *pl* VW normal standard cost; **flexible Planung** *f* MGMNT contingency planning; **flexibler Preis** *m* VW flexible price, flexprice; **flexibles Unternehmen** *nt* VW flexible firm; **flexibler Wechselkurs** *m* VW flexible exchange rate, floating exchange rate

Flexibilität *f* GESCHÄFT flexibility

Flexodruck *m* V&M flexography

Flickzeug *nt* GESCHÄFT repair kit

fliegend: **~er Arzt** *m* SOZIAL *in dünn besiedelten Gebieten* flying doctor; **~er Händler** *m*, **~e Händlerin** *f* GESCHÄFT pedlar, street trader (*BrE*), street vendor (*AmE*)

Fließ- *in cpds* IND assembly, flow; **Fließarbeit** *f* IND continuous flow production, flow production; **Fließbandarbeit** *f* IND assembly line work, flow production; **Fließbandarbeiter, in** *m,f* IND, PERSON assembly line worker; **Fließdruck** *m* TRANSP yield load

fließen *vi* GESCHÄFT, IND flow

Fließ-: **Fließfabrikation** *f* IND continuous flow production, flow production; **Fließfertigung** *f* IND continuous flow production, flow production; **Fließprozeß** *m* VW continuous process; **Fließtext** *m* V&M body copy

flimmerfrei *adj* COMP *Bildschirm* flicker-free

Flimmern *nt* COMP *Bildschirm* flicker

Flip-Chart *f* GESCHÄFT flipchart

Flip-Flop *nt* TRANSP flip-flop

Float *m* BANK float

Floaten *nt* FINANZ *Währung* floating

Floating *nt* FINANZ *Währung* floating

Flop *m infrml* GESCHÄFT flop (*infrml*)

Floppy *f jarg* COMP *Datenträger* diskette, floppy, floppy disk; **Floppy-Laufwerk** *nt jarg* COMP disk drive, diskette drive

florieren *vi* GESCHÄFT *Handel* flourish, thrive

florierend *adj* GESCHÄFT *Handel* flourishing, thriving, vw thriving

flott: **~ gehend** *adj* GESCHÄFT *Handel* flourishing, thriving, vw thriving

Flottenleiter, in *m,f* PERSON, TRANSP fleet manager

Flottenplanung *f* TRANSP fleet planning

Flow-Größe *f jarg* VW flow

Flower Bond *m* BÖRSE flower bond

Flucht *f* GESCHÄFT flight

Fluchtgelder *nt pl* GESCHÄFT, VERWALT hot money

flüchtig *adj* COMP *Speicher* volatile, GESCHÄFT slapdash

Flüchtling *m* GESCHÄFT, POL refugee

Flug *m* FREI, TRANSP flight; **~ mit Umsteigen** TRANSP interchange flight; **Flugbegleiter** *m* FREI, TRANSP air steward, flight attendant, steward; **Flugbegleiterin** *f* FREI, TRANSP air hostess, flight attendant, air stewardess; **Flugbenzin** *nt* TRANSP aviation fuel, aviation spirit; **Flugbeschränkungsgebiet** *nt* TRANSP restricted area; **Flugbetriebsregelung** *f* KOMM, TRANSP dispatching; **Flugbetriebsregler, in** *m,f* KOMM, TRANSP dispatcher; **Flugblatt** *nt* GESCHÄFT pamphlet, KOMM flyer, MEDIEN flyer, *Zeitung* broadsheet, broadsheet newspaper, pamphlet, V&M flyer

Flügel *m* TRANSP wing; **Flügeltank** *m* TRANSP wing tank

Flug: **Fluggast** *m* FREI, TRANSP air passenger, air traveler (*AmE*), air traveller (*BrE*); **Fluggastbrücke** *f* TRANSP jetway; **Fluggastversicherung** *f* VERSICH aircraft passenger insurance; **Fluggesellschaft** *f* TRANSP airline, carrier

Flughafen *m* TRANSP airport, aerodrome (*BrE*), airdrome (*AmE*); **Flughafenabfertigungsgebäude** *nt* TRANSP air terminal; **Flughafengebühr** *f* STEUER airport tax; **Flughafenhotel** *nt* FREI airport hotel; **Flughafenwerbung** *f* V&M airport advertising

Flug: **Fluginformation** *f* TRANSP flight information; **Flugkapitän** *m* PERSON, TRANSP pilot-in-command; **Flugkartenverkaufsstelle** *f* TRANSP ticket agency; **Flugkilometer** *m pl* TRANSP aircraft kilometers (*AmE*), aircraft kilometres (*BrE*); **Flugkorridor** *m* TRANSP airway, air corridor; **Flugkraftstoff** *m* TRANSP aviation fuel, aviation spirit; **Flug-Kupon** *m* TRANSP flight coupon; **Fluglinie** *f* TRANSP *Route* airway, *Unternehmen* airline, carrier; **Fluglotse** *m* PERSON, TRANSP air-traffic controller; **Flugnummer** *f* TRANSP flight number; **Flugplan** *m* FREI, TRANSP flight plan, flight schedule, timetable; **Flugplaner, in** *m,f* TRANSP flight scheduler; **Flugplatz** *m* TRANSP airfield, airport, aerodrome (*BrE*), airdrome (*AmE*); **Flugpreis** *m* FREI, TRANSP air fare; **Flugreise** *f* FREI, TRANSP air travel; **Flugreiselebensversicherung** *f* VERSICH aviation trip life insurance; **Flugreisende(r)** *mf* [decl. as adj] FREI, TRANSP air passenger, air traveler (*AmE*), air traveller (*BrE*); **Flugrisiko** *nt* VERSICH aviation risk; **Flugroute** *f* TRANSP airway; **Flugschau** *f* TRANSP airshow; **Flugschein** *m* TRANSP ticket, flight coupon; **Flugsicherung** *f* (*FS*) TRANSP air-traffic control (*ATC*); **Flugsicherungssystem** *nt* TRANSP air-traffic control system; **Flugsicherungszentrale** *f* TRANSP air-traffic control (*ATC*); **Flugsteig** *m* TRANSP boarding gate, gate; **Flugstraße** *f* TRANSP airway; **Flugstrategie** *f* TRANSP flight strategy; **Flugstrecke** *f* TRANSP *Route* airway

flugtauglich *adj* TRANSP airworthy

Flug: **Flugtauglichkeitsbescheinigung** *f* TRANSP airworthiness certification, certificate of airworthiness; **Flugticket** *nt* TRANSP ticket; **Flugtüchtigkeitszeugnis** *nt* TRANSP airworthiness certification, certificate of airworthiness; **Flugturbinenkraftstoff** *m* TRANSP aviation turbine fuel; **Flugverkehr** *m* TRANSP air traffic; **Flugwesen** *nt* TRANSP aviation; **Flugzeit** *f* TRANSP airborne time, flight time

Flugzeug *nt* TRANSP aircraft, aeroplane (*BrE*), airplane (*AmE*); ♦ **per ~** KOMM, TRANSP *Beförderungsart* by air; **per ~ transportieren** TRANSP transport by air; **von ~ gezogenes Werbespruchband** *m* V&M aeroplane banner (*BrE*), airplane banner (*AmE*)

Flugzeug: **Flugzeugbesatzung** *f* FREI, PERSON aircrew; **Flugzeugbetreiber** *m* TRANSP aircraft operator; **Flugzeugbewegungsmeldung** *f* TRANSP aircraft movement message; **Flugzeugindustrie** *f* TRANSP aircraft industry; **Flugzeuginsassenversicherung** *f* VERSICH aircraft passenger insurance; **Flugzeugkilometer** *m pl* TRANSP aircraft kilometers (*AmE*), aircraft kilometres (*BrE*); **Flugzeugmonteur** *m* PERSON, TRANSP rigger; **Flugzeugumschlagzeit** *f* TRANSP aircraft turnaround time (*AmE*), aircraft turnround time (*BrE*); **Flugzeugversicherung** *f* VERSICH aircraft hull insurance

Fluktuation *f* GESCHÄFT fluctuation, PERSON *Personalbestand* turnover, VW *Währung* swing; **Fluktuationsbegrenzung** *f* BÖRSE fluctuation limit; **Fluktuationsrate** *f* PERSON staff turnover

Fluorchlorkohlenwasserstoff *m* (*FCKW*) UMWELT chlorofluorocarbon (*CFC*)

Fluß *m* COMP flow, GESCHÄFT *Verlauf* flow, flux, *Gewässer* river; **Flußanliegerrechte** *nt pl* RECHT riparian rights; **Flußdiagramm** *nt* COMP flowchart, MATH flow diagram

flüssig *adj* BANK, FINANZ liquid, **nicht ~** *adj* BANK, FINANZ illiquid; ♦ **~ machen** IND smelt, VW mobilize

Flüssig- *in cpds* TRANSP, UMWELT liquefied, liquid

flüssig: **~e Gelder** *nt pl* FINANZ, RECHNUNG liquid funds; **~e Massengutladung** *f* TRANSP wet bulk cargo; **~e Mittel** *nt pl* BÖRSE liquidity, FINANZ cash resources, liquid assets, liquid funds, RECHNUNG available funds, liquid assets, liquid funds; **~e Mittel** *nt pl* **und Forderungen** *f pl* FINANZ, RECHNUNG quick assets, realizable assets; **~es Propangas** *nt* IND, UMWELT liquid petroleum gas (*LPG*)

Flüssig-: **Flüssigerdgas** *nt* IND, UMWELT liquefied natural gas (*LNG*); **Flüssigerdgastanker** *m* TRANSP LNG carrier; **Flüssiggas** *nt* IND, UMWELT liquid petroleum gas (*LPG*); **Flüssiggastanker** *m* TRANSP LPG carrier

flüssig: **~e Ware** *f* BÖRSE wet goods

Flüssigkeit *f* GESCHÄFT liquid; **Flüssigkeitsmaß** *nt* GESCHÄFT liquid measure

Flüssig-: **Flüssigmassenfrachtgut** *nt* TRANSP liquid bulk cargo; **Flüssigmethantanker** *m* TRANSP LNG carrier; **Flüssigpropangastanker** *m* TRANSP LPG carrier; **Flüssigunze** *f* GESCHÄFT *Maßeinheit* fluid ounce (*fl.oz.*)

Fluß: **Flußmündung** *f* TRANSP estuary; **Flußprinzip** *nt* TRANSP flow line; **Flußsteuerung** *f* COMP flow control; **Flußtonnagegebühren** *f pl* TRANSP river tonnage dues; **Flußverschmutzung** *f* UMWELT river pollution; **Flußverunreinigung** *f* UMWELT river pollution

Flut *f* GESCHÄFT spate, flood

föderal *adj* POL, VW federal

Föderalismus *m* POL, VW federalism; **~ mit bundesstaatlichem Übergewicht** POL, VW top-sided federalism

Föderation *f* POL federation

fokussieren *vt* GESCHÄFT focus

Folge *f* COMP *Aufeinanderfolge* sequence, GESCHÄFT *Aufeinanderfolge* sequence, *Ergebnis* consequence, outcome; ♦ **mit der ~, daß** GESCHÄFT with the result that; **zur ~ haben** GESCHÄFT result in; **die ~n tragen** GESCHÄFT suffer the consequences

Folge: **Folgeanalyse** *f* V&M sequential analysis; **Folgebrief** *m* V&M follow-up letter; **Folgeerscheinung** *f* GESCHÄFT aftereffect; **Folgefehler** *m* COMP sequence error; **Folgekonto** *nt* FINANZ succeeding account

folgen *vi* [+dat] GESCHÄFT follow, succeed; ♦ **~ auf** [+acc] GESCHÄFT follow, succeed

folgend *adj* GESCHÄFT subsequent, succeeding

Folge: **Folgenummer** *f* COMP sequence number, MATH sequential number; **Folgeprovision** *f* VERSICH installment commission (*AmE*), instalment commission (*BrE*); **Folgeprüfung** *f* MATH sequential analysis; **Folgeschaden** *m* VERSICH consequential damage, consequential loss; **Folgeschaden-Police** *f* VERSICH consequential loss policy; **Folgewirkung** *f* **eines Gerichtverfahrens** RECHT consequential effect of a court action

folglich *adv* GESCHÄFT accordingly

Foliant *m* V&M *Druck* folio

Folie *f* MEDIEN foil; **Foliendruck** *m* MEDIEN foil stamping

Folioblatt *nt* V&M *Druck* folio

Fonds *m* FINANZ fund; **dem ~ gutgeschriebene Eingänge** *m pl* FINANZ receipts credited to the fund; **~ für Investitionen in abgewirtschaftete Unternehmen** FINANZ vulture fund; **~ für Überseeprojekte** VW Overseas Project Fund; **Fondsanteil** *m* **einer Unternehmung für gemeinsame Kapitalanlagen** FINANZ unit of a collective investment undertaking

fondsgebunden: ~e Lebensversicherung *f* VERSICH fund-linked life insurance, unit-linked assurance (*BrE*)

Fonds: **Fondsmakler, in** *m,f* BÖRSE bond broker; **Fondsverwaltung** *f* BANK fund management

forcieren *vt* GESCHÄFT accelerate

forciert: ~es Wirtschaftswachstum *nt* VW accelerated growth

Förder- *in cpds* GESCHÄFT, IND assisted, promoted, conveyor; **Förderband** *nt* IND production line, conveyor belt; **Förderbeihilfe** *f* FINANZ enterprise allowance (*BrE*); **Förderer** *m* GESCHÄFT sponsor; **Fördergebiet** *nt* VW assisted area, development area (*BrE*), enterprise zone (*EZ*); **Förderin** *f* GESCHÄFT sponsor

förderlich *adj* GESCHÄFT instrumental

fordern *vt* GESCHÄFT claim, demand, exact, require

fördern *vt* GESCHÄFT benefit, encourage, promote, sponsor, IND *Mineralien, Bodenschätze* extract, V&M promote, sponsor, VW *Entwicklungsländer, Verständigung* aid

fördernd *adj* GESCHÄFT, V&M promotional

Förder-: **Förderprämie** *f* FINANZ enterprise allowance (*BrE*); **Förderprogramm** *nt* MGMNT development program (*AmE*), development programme (*BrE*); **Fördertätigkeit** *f* V&M sponsorship

Forderung *f* GESCHÄFT requirement, VERSICH claim; ◆ **~ an** RECHNUNG debt owed by; **eine ~ einreichen** RECHT file a claim; **eine ~ einziehen** FINANZ collect a debt; **eine ~ erlassen** VW release a debt; **eine ~ liquidieren** FINANZ collect a debt; **eine ~ regulieren** VERSICH adjust a claim; **eine ~ stellen** RECHT set up a claim

Förderung *f* GESCHÄFT boost, advancement, encouragement, sponsorship, IND *Mineralien, Bodenschätze* extraction, TRANSP facilitation, V&M promotion, VERWALT *berufliche Laufbahn* advancement; **~ der Kunst** V&M arts sponsorship

Forderungen *f pl* PATENT set of claims, RECHNUNG accounts receivable (*A/R*), receivables; **~ aus Anleihezeichnungen** RECHNUNG subscriptions receivable; **~ gegen verbundene Gesellschaften** RECHNUNG loans to related companies; **~ aus Lieferungen und Leistungen** RECHNUNG trade account receivables (*AmE*), trade debtors; **~ und Verbindlichkeiten** FINANZ claims and liabilities (*BrE*); **~ aus Warenlieferungen** RECHNUNG trade receivables; ◆ **~ erfüllen** MGMNT meet demands

Forderung: **Forderungsabtretung** *f* RECHNUNG assignment of claims, assignment of debts; **Forderungsberechtigte(r)** *mf* [decl. as adj] RECHT *Antragsteller* claimant; **Forderungseinziehung** *f* RECHNUNG collection of accounts; **auf Forderungseinzug verzichten** *phr* RECHNUNG forego collection of a debt; **auf Forderungsinkasso verzichten** *phr* RECHNUNG forego collection of a debt; **Forderungsnachweis** *m* FINANZ proof of debt (*POD*); **Forderungsrecht** *nt* RECHT chose in action;

Forderungsübernehmer, in *m,f* PATENT, RECHNUNG assignee; **Forderungsumschlag** *m* FINANZ receivables turnover, RECHNUNG collection period, collection ratio; **Forderungsverkauf** *m* FINANZ, RECHNUNG factoring

förderwürdig: ~e Reserve *f* UMWELT *Bodenschätze* recoverable reserves

Förder-: **Förderzuschuß** *m* FINANZ enterprise allowance (*BrE*)

Fordismus *m* VW Fordism

Forfaitierung *f* VW forfaiting; **Forfaitierung-System** *nt* STEUER forfait system

Form *f* MATH shape, PATENT embodiment, form; ◆ **in ~ von** GESCHÄFT in the form of; **in ~ einer Subvention** FINANZ in grant form

formal *adj* GESCHÄFT formal; **~e Handelsverbindungen** *f pl* GESCHÄFT formal trade links; **~e Vereinbarung** *f* GESCHÄFT formal agreement

formalisieren *vt* GESCHÄFT formalize

Formalisierung *f* GESCHÄFT formalization

Formalität *f* GESCHÄFT formality

Format *nt* COMP *Papier, Speicherung* format, PERSON calibre (*BrE*), caliber (*AmE*), VERWALT format

formatieren *vt* COMP *Diskette, Dokument* format

Formatierung *f* COMP *Textverarbeitung* formatting

formbedürftig: ~er Vertrag *m* RECHT contract requiring specific form

Form: **Formblatt** *nt* GESCHÄFT blank form, business form, PATENT form

Formel *f* GESCHÄFT *Vertrag* wording, MATH formula

formell: ~e Empfangsbestätigung *f* GESCHÄFT formal receipt; **~e Mitteilung** *f* GESCHÄFT formal notice; **~e Weiterentwicklung** *f* **des Management** MGMNT formal management development

formen *vt* MEDIEN *öffentliche Meinung* mold (*AmE*), mould (*BrE*)

Form: **Formfreiheit** *f* RECHT *Verträge* absence of formal requirements; **Formgebungsverfahren** *nt* IND production process; **Formgestalter, in** *m,f* GESCHÄFT stylist

förmlich *adj* GESCHÄFT formal; **nicht ~** *adj* GESCHÄFT informal; **~e Mitteilung** *f* GESCHÄFT formal notice; **~es rechtsverbindliches Versprechen** *nt* RECHT *Gewährleistungsversprechen, Nebenvereinbarung* covenant

formlos *adj* GESCHÄFT *gestaltos* formless, *zwanglos* informal; **~e Befragung** *f* PERSON informal interview; **~e Organisation** *f* MGMNT informal organization

Formlosigkeit *f* GESCHÄFT *Gestaltlosigkeit* formlessness, *Zwanglosigkeit* informality

Form: **Formsache** *f* GESCHÄFT technicality, routine

Formular *nt* PATENT form; **Formularvorschub** *m* COMP form feed (*FF*)

formulieren *vt* GESCHÄFT formulate

Formulierung *f* GESCHÄFT *Vertrag* wording, MGMNT *einer Politik* formulation, RECHT wording

forschen *vi* GESCHÄFT research, search

Forschung *f* GESCHÄFT research; **~ und Entwicklung** *f* (*F&E*) IND research and development (*R&D*); **Forschungsabteilung** *f* IND, V&M research department; **Forschungsansatz** *m* GESCHÄFT, MGMNT, VERWALT, VW approach; **Forschungsanstalt** *nt* IND research laboratory; **Forschungsaufwand** *m* RECHNUNG, STEUER scientific research expenditure (*BrE*); **Forschungsberichte** *m pl* MATH published research; **Forschungsbudget** *nt* RECHNUNG research budget;

Forschungsdirektor, in *m,f* PERSON research director; **Forschungsinstitut** *nt* **der Vereinten Nationen für soziale Entwicklung** SOZIAL United Nations Research Institute for Social Development (*UNRISD*)

forschungsintensiv *adj* IND research-intensive

Forschung: **Forschungslabor** *nt* IND research laboratory

forschungsorientiert *adj* IND research-oriented

Forschung: **Forschungsprogramm** *nt* IND research program (*AmE*), research programme (*BrE*); **Forschungsstudent, in** *m,f* SOZIAL research student; **Forschungsteam** *nt* V&M research team; **Forschungsziel** *nt* GESCHÄFT research objective

Forstwirtschaft *f* UMWELT agroforestry; **Forstwirtschaftsindustrie** *f* IND forestry industry

fortbestehend *adj* GESCHÄFT ongoing

Fortbildung *f* PERSON advancement, further education, SOZIAL further education; **Fortbildungsprogramm** *nt* PERSON employee development program (*AmE*), employee development programme (*BrE*), training program (*AmE*), training programme (*BrE*)

Fortdruck *m* IND production run

Fortfall *m* GESCHÄFT discontinuance

fortführen *vt* GESCHÄFT continue

fortg. *abbr* (*fortgesetzt*) GESCHÄFT cont. (*continued*), contd (*continued*)

fortgeschrieben: **~e Bevölkerungsstatistik** *f* VW current population survey (*CPS*)

fortgeschritten *adj* COMP, VW advanced; **~e biologische Agrarwirtschaft** *f* VW advanced organic economy; **~e Ausbildung** *f* PERSON *Berufsausbildung* advanced training

fortgesetzt *adj* (*fortg.*) GESCHÄFT continued (*cont.*, *contd*)

fortlaufend 1. *adj* GESCHÄFT continuous, permanent; **2.** *adv* MEDIEN, PATENT consecutively; ♦ **~ numerieren** MEDIEN, PATENT number consecutively

fortlaufend: **~e Abrechnung** *f* BÖRSE rolling settlement; **~e Nettoabrechnung** *f* BÖRSE continuous net settlement (*BrE*) (*CNS*); **~e Verpflichtung** *f* GESCHÄFT continuing commitment

Fortschreibung *f* COMP, RECHNUNG updating, STEUER adjustment of assessed value

fortschreiten *vi* GESCHÄFT advance, progress

fortschreitend *adj* GESCHÄFT progressive

Fortschritt *m* GESCHÄFT advance, progress; ♦ **Fortschritte machen** GESCHÄFT take shape

fortschrittlich *adj* GESCHÄFT advanced; **~er Betrieb** *m* IND advanced factory; **~e Technik** *f* IND advanced engineering

Fortschritt: **Fortschrittsüberwachung** *f* IND progress control; **Fortschrittsveraltung** *f* V&M progress obsolescence

fortsetzen *vt* GESCHÄFT continue

Fortsetzung *f* GESCHÄFT continuation; **~ des Pachtvertrags** RECHT *mit neuem Eigentümer* attornment (*AmE*)

fortwährend *adj* GESCHÄFT in perpetuity

Forum *nt* POL forum

fossil: **~er Brennstoff** *m* UMWELT fossil fuel

Foto *nt* MEDIEN photo, photograph; **Fotogravur** *f* V&M photogravure; **Fotokopie** *f* VERWALT photocopy, Xerox®, photostat; **Fotokopierautomat** *m* VERWALT photocopier

fotokopieren *vt* VERWALT photocopy, Xerox®

Foto: **Fotomontage** *f* MEDIEN montage; **Fotosatz** *m* MEDIEN *Druck* filmsetting (*BrE*), photosetting (*AmE*), cold type; **Fotosatzgerät** *nt* MEDIEN *Druck* filmsetter (*BrE*), photosetter (*AmE*); **Fototermin** *m* MEDIEN, V&M visual, photocall, photograph session; **Fotozelle** *f* V&M photocell

fr. *abbr* IMP/EXP, TRANSP (*franko*) fco. (*franco*), (*frei*) free

Fr. *abbr* (*Fracht*) TRANSP gds (*goods*), frt (*freight*)

Fracht *f* (*Fr.*) TRANSP cargo, freight (*frt*), goods (*BrE*) (*gds*), load; **~ gegen Nachnahme** IMP/EXP, TRANSP freight collect, freight forward (*frt fwd*); **~ mit geringer Dichte** TRANSP low-density cargo; **~ unter Zollverschluß** IMP/EXP, TRANSP bonded cargo; ♦ **~ nach Abmessung bezahlen** TRANSP pay for cargo by measurement; **~ aller Art** TRANSP freight all kinds; **~ bezahlt** IMP/EXP, TRANSP carriage paid (*carr pd*); **~ bezahlt Empfänger** IMP/EXP, TRANSP freight forward (*frt fwd*), freight prepaid (*frt ppd*); **~ gezahlt an** TRANSP freight paid to; **~ und Versicherung bezahlt** IMP/EXP, TRANSP, VERSICH freight and insurance paid, carriage and insurance paid (*CIP*); **~ im voraus bezahlt** IMP/EXP, TRANSP freight prepaid (*frt ppd*); **als ~ zahlen** IMP/EXP, TRANSP, VERSICH pay as cargo

Fracht: **Frachtabfertigung** *f* IMP/EXP *Zoll* cargo clearance; **Frachtabrechnungsvorrichtung** *f* TRANSP cargo accounting device; **Frachtagent, in** *m,f* TRANSP cargo agent; **Frachtanforderung** *f* TRANSP reclaiming; **Frachtanhänger** *m* TRANSP cargo tag; **Frachtanspruch** *m* TRANSP cargo claim; **Frachtaufseher, in** *m,f* PERSON cargo superintendent; **ohne Frachtauftrag** *phr* TRANSP off hire; **Frachtausschluß** *m* TRANSP cargo shut-out; **Frachtbörse** *f* BÖRSE freight market

Frachtbrief *m* (*FB*) IMP/EXP, TRANSP, VERSICH shipping bill, waybill, bill of lading (*b.l.*, *B/L*), bill of freight, trucking bill of lading (*AmE*), consignment note (*C/N, CN*), letter of contract, bill; **~ ohne Vorbehalt** IMP/EXP clean bill of lading; **~ für Transportbehälter** IMP/EXP container bill; **Frachtbrieftonne** *f* IMP/EXP, TRANSP bill of lading ton, bill of lading tonne; **bei Frachtbriefvorlage** *phr* IMP/EXP, TRANSP on surrender of the bill of lading

Fracht: **Frachtderrick** *m* TRANSP cargo derrick

Frachter *m* TRANSP cargo boat, cargo vessel, freighter; ♦ **jeder ~** VERSICH any one steamer (*AOS*)

Fracht: **Frachterklärung** *f* TRANSP cargo declaration; **Frachterlaß** *m* IMP/EXP freight release (*F/R*); **Frachtfeuergefahr** *f* TRANSP fire risk on freight; **Frachtflugzeug** *nt* TRANSP freight aircraft, cargo plane, freighter

frachtfrei 1. *adj* IMP/EXP, TRANSP carriage free, carriage paid (*carr pd*), freight prepaid (*frt ppd*); **2.** *adv* ♦ **~ versichert** IMP/EXP *Vertragsrecht* carriage and insurance paid (*CIP*)

Fracht: **Frachtfreigabe-Bescheinigung** *f* IMP/EXP freight release (*F/R*); **Frachtführer** *m* TRANSP carrier, common carrier; **Frachtführer-Haftpflicht** *f* VERSICH carrier's liability; **Frachtführer** *m* **mit Vertrag zwischen Fluglinien** TRANSP interline carrier; **Frachtgebühren** *f pl* TRANSP cargo dues; **Frachtgeld** *nt* TRANSP carriage, carriage charge, freight (*frt*); **Frachtgewicht** *nt* TRANSP weight of cargo; **Frachtgut** *nt* TRANSP cargo; **als Frachtgut zahlen** *phr* VERSICH pay as cargo;

Frachtkapazität *f* TRANSP cargo capacity (*CC*); **Frachtkonfiguration** *f* TRANSP cargo configuration; **Frachtkontrolleur, in** *m,f* PERSON tally clerk; **Frachtkosten** *pl* TRANSP carriage expenses, cost of freight, freight (*frt*), truckage; **Frachtkosten** *pl* **für durchgehende Ladungen** IMP/EXP through charge; **Frachtkosten** *pl* **per Nachnahme** IMP/EXP, TRANSP carriage forward (*carr fwd, CF*); **Frachtladekosten** *pl* TRANSP cargo handling charge (*CHC*); **Frachtladeraum** *m* TRANSP cargo stowage; **Frachtlieferbedingungen** *f pl* TRANSP cargo delivery terms; **Frachtmanifest** *nt* TRANSP cargo manifest, freight manifest; **Frachtmanifest** *nt* **des Luftfahrzeugs** TRANSP aircraft manifest; **Frachtmarkierungssymbol** *nt* TRANSP cargo marking symbol; **Frachtmarkt** *m* BÖRSE freight market; **Frachtmischung** *f* TRANSP cargo mix; **Frachtöl** *nt* TRANSP cargo oil (*co*); **Frachtplan** *m* TRANSP cargo plan; **Frachtpolice** *f* VERSICH freight policy; **Frachtratenunterbietung** *f* TRANSP rate cutting; **Frachtraum** *m* TRANSP cargo tonnage; **Frachtraumgebühren** *f pl* TRANSP tonnage dues; **Frachtsachverständige(r)** *mf* [decl. as adj] PERSON *Arbeit* cargo surveyor; **Frachtsatz** *m* **für Ladungen unter einem Zentner** IMP/EXP through rate; **Frachtsatzverringerung** *f* TRANSP rate dilution; **Frachtschiff** *nt* **für Sammelladung** TRANSP general cargo ship; **Frachtschiff** *nt* **für Stückgut** TRANSP general cargo ship; **Frachtspediteur** *m* IMP/EXP forwarder (*fwdr*); **Frachtstrategie** *f* TRANSP freight strategy; **Frachttarif** *m* TRANSP freight tariff; **Frachttarif** *m* **unter Kosten** TRANSP under-cost freight rate; **Frachtterminal** *nt* TRANSP freight terminal; **Frachttermingeschäftsmarkt** *m* BÖRSE freight futures market; **Frachtterminkontrakt** *m* BÖRSE, FINANZ freight futures contract; **Frachttonne** *f* TRANSP freight ton (*F/T*), freight tonne (*F/T*); **Frachttonnenkilometerzahl** *f* TRANSP cargo tonne kilometers used (*AmE*), cargo tonne kilometres used (*BrE*); **Frachttransfer** *m* TRANSP cargo transfer; **Frachttransit** *m* TRANSP cargo transit; **Frachttransportunternehmen** *nt* TRANSP freight forwarder; **Frachtumschlagausrüstung** *f* TRANSP cargo handling equipment; **Frachtumschlagkosten** *pl* TRANSP cargo handling charge (*CHC*); **Frachtumschlagplatz** *m* TRANSP cargo center (*AmE*), cargo centre (*BrE*); **Frachtunternehmen** *nt* TRANSP carrier haulage, *Schiffahrt* ocean carrier; **Frachtverkehr** *m* TRANSP movement of freight, freight traffic; **Frachtversicherung** *f* VERSICH consignment insurance, freight insurance; **Frachtversicherungspolice** *f* VERSICH freight policy; **Frachtvorauszahlung** *f* TRANSP advance of freight, advance freight (*AF*); **Fracht-, Versicherungs- und Transportgebühren** *f pl* IMP/EXP freight, insurance and shipping charges (*FIS*); **Fracht-, Versicherungs- und Transportkosten** *pl* IMP/EXP freight, insurance and shipping charges (*FIS*); **Fracht-, Versicherungs- und Versandkosten** *pl* IMP/EXP freight, insurance and shipping charges (*FIS*); **Frachtvorschuß** *m* TRANSP advance freight (*AF*); **Frachtzerlegung** *f* TRANSP cargo disassembly; **Frachtzettel** *m* KOMM, TRANSP dispatch note; **Frachtzusammenstellung** *f* TRANSP cargo assembly, cargo configuration; **Frachtzuschlag** *m* TRANSP extra freight

Frage *f* GESCHÄFT question; ~ **mit Mehrfachwahlmöglichkeit** V&M multiple-choice question; ~ **stellen** GESCHÄFT ask; ♦ **in** ~ **stellen** GESCHÄFT query; **Fragen präsent haben** MEDIEN have one's questions ready; **eine** ~ **auf die Tagesordnung setzen** MGMNT place a question on the agenda

Frage: **Fragebogen** *m* GESCHÄFT enquiry form, questionnaire, STEUER *zur Überprüfung von Steuerangaben* information return, V&M questionnaire; **Fragebogen** *m* **mit offenen Fragen** V&M open-ended questionnaire

fragen *vt* GESCHÄFT ask; ♦ ~ **um** GESCHÄFT *Rat* seek

Frage: **Fragestunde** *f* POL *Parlament* question time (*BrE*)

fraglich *adj* GESCHÄFT doubtful, questionable

fragmentierter: ~ **Market** *m* GESCHÄFT fragmented market

Fragmentierung *f* COMP *Datenspeicherung*, VW *eines Marktes* fragmentation

fragwürdig *adj* GESCHÄFT dubious, questionable

Fraktion *f* POL *innerhalb des Parlaments* congressional party (*AmE*), parliamentary group, parliamentary party, *innerhalb einer Partei* faction

fraktionieren *f* MATH fractionalize

Fraktion: **Fraktionseinpeitscher** *m* POL whip (*BrE*); **Fraktionsführer** *m* POL whip (*BrE*); **Fraktionslose(r)** *mf* [decl. as adj] POL independent, *Oberhaus* cross-bencher (*BrE*); **Fraktionszwang** *m* POL three-line whip (*BrE*)

Frame *m* jarg COMP *Datenübertragung* frame

Franchise 1. *f* VERSICH excess insurance; **2.** *nt* V&M franchise

Franchise: **Franchisegeber, in** *m,f* GESCHÄFT, V&M franchisor; **Franchiseklausel** *f* VERSICH franchise clause; **Franchisenehmer, in** *m,f* V&M franchisee

Franchising *nt* V&M franchising, franchise

Frankiermaschine *f* KOMM postage meter, franking machine (*BrE*), stamping machine

frankiert: ~**er Rückumschlag** *m* KOMM stamped addressed envelope (*BrE*) (*s.a.e.*), self-addressed stamped envelope (*s.a.s.e.*)

Frankierung *f* KOMM postage

franko *adv* (*fro.*) GESCHÄFT, KOMM delivered free, postage paid, postage-free; ♦ ~ **Löschung** IMP/EXP, TRANSP landed terms

Free-rider-Verhalten *nt* VW easy rider

frei 1. *adj* COMP, GESCHÄFT free, IMP/EXP (*fr.*) free, franco (*fco.*), PERSON idle, TRANSP (*fr.*) free, franco (*fco.*), VERWALT idle; ♦ ~ **aus** IMP/EXP, TRANSP free out terms, free out (*FO*); ~ **in** TRANSP free in (*fi*); **einen ~en Beruf ausüben** VW practice a profession (*AmE*), practise a profession (*BrE*); ~**er Eintritt** FREI, GESCHÄFT admission free; ~ **Haus** IMP/EXP carriage free; ~ **von Havarie** GESCHÄFT, TRANSP, VERSICH free of all average (*f.a.a.*); ~ **Kai** IMP/EXP, TRANSP ex quay (*x quay*); ~ **von Rechten Dritter** RECHT free and clear (*AmE*); ~ **von Schäden** VERSICH free of damage (*fod*); ~ **von Schadensansprüchen aus dem übermittelten Unfall** VERSICH free of claim for accident reported (*FCAR*); ~ **Werk** IMP/EXP ex mill (*x-mill*); **2.** *adv* TRANSP ex

Frei- *in cpds* GESCHÄFT free, complimentary

frei: ~ **beantwortbare Frage** *f* V&M open-ended question; ~ **begebbares Akkreditiv** *nt* VW freely negotiable credit; ~ **begebbare Wertpapiere** *nt pl* BÖRSE negotiable securities; ~ **benutzbare Software** *f* COMP public domain software; ~**es Faßvermögen** *nt* IND excess capacity; ~**e Fläche** *f* GRUND open space; ~**es Format** *nt* COMP free format; ~**es Grundeigentum** *nt* GRUND freehold, freehold estate, freehold property (*BrE*); **~er Grundeigentümer** *m*, **~e Grundeigentümerin** *f* GRUND freeholder; **~es Gut** *nt* VW free good; **im ~en Handel erhältliches Arzneimittel** *nt* SOZIAL, V&M over-the-counter medicine; **~e Kapazität** *f* IND, TRANSP, VW excess capacity, idle capacity, spare capacity; **nicht ~e konvertierbare Währung** *f* POL, VW inconvertible money; **~e Lieferung** *f* TRANSP free delivery; **~es Löschen** *nt* TRANSP free discharge (*fd*); **~er Markt** *m* VW open market; **~er Marktpreis** *m* VW competitive price; **~e Marktwirtschaft** *f* VW free enterprise economy, free market economy; **~e Rücklage** *f* RECHNUNG unappropriated profit; **~ schwankender Wechselkurs** *m* VW flexible exchange rate, floating exchange rate, fluctuating exchange rate, fluctuating currency; **~e Stelle** *f* PERSON *Arbeitsmarkt* appointment vacant, unfilled vacancy, vacancy; **~ transferierbares Wertpapier** *nt* FINANZ transferable security; **~es Umtauschrecht** *nt* BÖRSE free right of exchange; **~es Unternehmertum** *nt* VW free enterprise; **~ vereinbarte Schiedsgerichtsbarkeit** *f* PERSON voluntary arbitration; **~ vereinbarte Übernahme** *f* VW agreed takeover; **~ verfügbares Einkommen** *nt* VW discretionary income; **~ verfügbare Kaufkraft** *f* V&M discretionary buying power; **~er Versand** *m* TRANSP free dispatch (*fd*); **~e Wahl** *f* GESCHÄFT option; **~e Wahl** *f* **des Arbeitsplatzes** RECHT free choice of employment; **~er Waren- und Dienstleistungsverkehr** *m* VW *EU* free movement of goods and services; **~er Warenverkehr** *m* VW *EU* free movement of goods; **~er Wechselkurs** *m* VW flexible exchange rate, floating exchange rate, fluctuating exchange rate, floating rate; **~er Wettbewerb** *m* GESCHÄFT, STEUER, V&M arm's length bargaining, VW free competition; **~e Zeit** *f* FREI leisure time; **~e Zirkulation** *f* UMWELT free circulation; **~er Zugang und freie Wahl** *f* GESCHÄFT free access and choice; **~e Zustellung** *f* **in ländlichen Gebieten** KOMM rural delivery service (*AmE*) (*RDS*)

Frei-: **Freiberufler, in** *m,f* PERSON freelance, freelance worker, self-employed person

freiberuflich *adj* PERSON, PERSON, STEUER self-employed; **~e Dienstleistungen** *f pl* GESCHÄFT professional services; **~er Journalist** *m*, **~e Journalistin** *f* MEDIEN freelance writer; **~er Korrespondent** *m*, **~e Korrespondentin** *f* MEDIEN freelance correspondent

Freibetrag *m* STEUER allowance (*BrE*), tax credit (*AmE*), tax exemption, tax relief, tax-free amount; **~ für Einkünfte aus selbständiger Tätigkeit** PERSON earned income allowance; **~ für Haushaltsenergie** UMWELT residential energy credit; **Freibetragsatz** *m* STEUER rate of relief

freibleibend *adj* GESCHÄFT *Angebot* not binding, subject to confirmation, without engagement

Frei-: **Freibrief** *m* PATENT patent (*pat.*); **Freiexemplar** *nt* MEDIEN *Buch* presentation copy, complimentary copy; **Freifläche** *f* GRUND open space

Freigabe *f* COMP release, FINANZ unblocking, unfreezing, GESCHÄFT release, TRANSP release note (*RN*); **~ von Gehaltsschecks** BANK release of pay checks (*AmE*), release of pay cheques (*BrE*); **~ von Lohnschecks** BANK release of pay checks (*AmE*), release of pay cheques (*BrE*); **~ von Nachrichten** MEDIEN news release; **Freigabedatum** *nt* BÖRSE release date, COMP purge date; **Freigabemitteilung** *f* TRANSP release note

(*RN*); **Freigabeschein** *m* TRANSP release note (*RN*); **Freigabezeugnis** *nt* IMP/EXP certificate of pratique

freigeben *vt* COMP *Softwareversion, Produkt* release, FINANZ *Konto* unblock, GESCHÄFT release

freigebig *adj* STEUER generous

freigegeben *adj* BÖRSE freed up; **~es Pressematerial** *nt* MEDIEN press release; **~e Pressemitteilung** *f* MEDIEN press release; **~e Presseverlautbarung** *f* MEDIEN press release; **~er Wechselkurs** *m* VW floating exchange rate

freigemacht: **~er Rückumschlag** *m* KOMM stamped addressed envelope (*BrE*) (*s.a.e.*), self-addressed stamped envelope (*s.a.s.e.*)

Frei-: **Freigepäck** *nt* FREI, IMP/EXP, TRANSP free allowance of luggage, free baggage allowance, baggage allowance; **Freigepäckgrenze** *f* IMP/EXP free baggage limit

freigestempelt *adj* KOMM metered; **~e Post** *f* KOMM metered mail

Frei-: **Freigrenze** *f* IMP/EXP, STEUER *Zoll* duty-free allowance (*BrE*); **Freihafen** *m* IMP/EXP free port, VW free zone; **Freihafengebiet** *nt* VW free zone; **Freihafenniederlage** *f* TRANSP sufferance wharf; **Freihafenzone** *f* TRANSP free port zone (*FPZ*)

Freihandel *m* VW free trade; **Freihandelsabkommen** *nt* VW Free Trade Agreement (*FTA*); **Freihandelszone** *f* IMP/EXP, VW free-trade zone (*FTZ*), free-trade area

freihändig *adj* GESCHÄFT by private contract; **~e Angebotsabgabe** *f* V&M tender by private contract; **~er Verkauf** *m* GRUND private treaty

Freiheit *f* RECHT *Unabhängigkeit* freedom; **Freiheitszone** *f* TRANSP zone of freedom

Freijahr *nt* FINANZ, TRANSP redemption-free year, year of grace; **Freijahrbesichtigung** *f* TRANSP year of grace survey (*YGS*); **Freijahrinspektion** *f* TRANSP year of grace survey (*YGS*)

Frei-: **Freikarte** *f* FREI complimentary ticket, free ticket, punched paper (*AmE*), *Bahn* free pass; **Freilager** *nt* IMP/EXP bonded warehouse; **Freiliste** *f* **für Importwaren** IMP/EXP open general import licence (*BrE*) (*OGIL*); **Freiraum** *m* IND excess capacity; **Freischaffende(r)** *mf* [decl. as adj] PERSON freelance worker

freisprechen *vt* RECHT acquit; ♦ **jdn** ~ RECHT declare sb not guilty

Frei-: **Freispruch** *m* RECHT *eines Angeklagten* acquittal

freistehend *adj* COMP free-standing

freistellen *vt* GESCHÄFT exempt, RECHT excuse

Frei-: **Freistellung** *f* **von Mitteln** RECHNUNG decommitment; **Freistellungsklausel** *f* VERWALT exemption clause; **Freistellungsverpflichtung** *f* RECHT, VERWALT indemnity bond; **Freistempler** *m* GESCHÄFT franking machine, postage meter (*AmE*); **Freiumschlag** *m* KOMM, VERWALT business reply envelope (*BRE*), business reply mail (*BRM*), reply-paid envelope; **Freiverkaufsvereinbarung** *f* TRANSP free sale agreement

Freiverkehr *m* BÖRSE, VW kerb market, unlisted market, over-the-counter market (*AmE*) (*OTCM*), open market; ♦ **im ~** BÖRSE over-the-counter (*OTC*)

Freiverkehr: **Freiverkehrsbörse** *f* BÖRSE Unlisted Securities Market (*BrE*) (*USM*) over-the-counter market (*AmE*) (*OTCM*); **Freiverkehrshandel** *m* FINANZ over-the-counter trading; **Freiverkehrswert** *m* BÖRSE unlisted security

freiwillig 1. *adj* GESCHÄFT voluntary, noncompulsory, unsolicited, SOZIAL voluntary, VERSICH, VW noncompulsory; **2.** *adv* GESCHÄFT voluntarily; ◆ **~ geben** GESCHÄFT *Informationen* volunteer; **~ in Liquidation gehen** GESCHÄFT go into voluntary liquidation; **sich ~ melden** GESCHÄFT volunteer; **sich ~ für etw zur Verfügung stellen** GESCHÄFT volunteer for sth

freiwillig: **~e Abwicklung** *f* GESCHÄFT voluntary winding-up; **~e Ausfuhrbeschränkung** *f* IMP/EXP voluntary export restraint (*VER*); **~e Beiträge** *m pl* STEUER voluntary contributions (*BrE*); **~e Entlassung** *f* PERSON voluntary redundancy (*BrE*); **~e Exportbeschränkung** *f* IMP/EXP voluntary export restraint (*VER*); **~e Großhandelskette** *f* GESCHÄFT voluntary chain; **~e Handelskette** *f* GESCHÄFT voluntary chain; **~er Kapitalansammlungsplan** *m* FINANZ voluntary accumulation plan; **~er Konkurs** *m* FINANZ voluntary bankruptcy; **~e Konkurserklärung** *f* FINANZ voluntary bankruptcy; **~e Kontrollen** *f pl* V&M voluntary controls; **~e Körperschaft** *f* SOZIAL voluntary body; **~e Ladenkette** *f* GESCHÄFT voluntary chain; **~e Leistung** *f* VERSICH ex gratia payment, noncompulsory contribution; **~e Liquidation** *f* FINANZ voluntary liquidation, GESCHÄFT voluntary winding-up; **~e Pensionierung** *f* PERSON optional retirement; **~e Selbstkontrolle** *f* VW self-regulation; **~e Versicherung** *f* VERSICH voluntary insurance; **~e Zahlung** *f* FINANZ ex gratia payment; **~e Zusatzleistung** *f* STEUER additional voluntary contribution (*AVC*); **~e Zuzahlung** *f* RECHNUNG, STEUER additional voluntary contribution (*AVC*)

Freiwillige(r) *mf* [decl. as adj] PERSON volunteer

Freiwilligkeitsprinzip *nt* PERSON voluntarism

freizeichnen *vt* BANK exculpate, RECHT contract out, disclaim, exculpate

freizeichnend *adj* RECHT exculpatory

Frei-: **Freizeichnung** *f* RECHT contracting out; **Freizeichnungsklausel** *f* RECHT contracting out clause, exemption clause, nonwarranty clause, VERSICH average clause

Freizeit *f* FREI leisure time, spare time, time off, time off work, PERSON *Arbeit* time off, time off work; **Freizeitanlage** *f* FREI leisure center (*AmE*), leisure centre (*BrE*); **Freizeitausgleich** *m* PERSON lieu days; **Freizeitausgleichstage** *m pl* PERSON lieu days; **Freizeitcenter** *nt* FREI leisure center (*AmE*), leisure centre (*BrE*); **Freizeiteinrichtung** *f* FREI leisure center (*AmE*), leisure centre (*BrE*), SOZIAL *für Ruheständler* leisure development; **Freizeiteinrichtungen** *f pl* FREI recreational facilities; **Freizeitindustrie** *f* FREI leisure industry; **Freizeitpark** *m* FREI leisure center (*AmE*), leisure centre (*BrE*)

Frei-: **Freizone** *f* IMP/EXP free zone

freizügig *adj* VW liberal

Freizügigkeit *f* POL, VW freedom of movement; **~ der Arbeitnehmer** *m pl* RECHT, VW *EU* free movement of labor (*AmE*), free movement of labour (*BrE*)

Fremd- *in cpds* GESCHÄFT external, foreign

fremd *adj* GESCHÄFT alien; ◆ **in ~em Namen handeln** RECHT act on sb's behalf

fremd: **~e Flagge** *f* TRANSP foreign flag

Fremd-: **Fremdarbeiter, in** *m,f* PERSON foreign worker, guestworker

Fremdenverkehr *m* FREI tourism, tourist trade;

Fremdenverkehrsamt *nt* FREI tourist office; **Fremdenverkehrsbüro** *nt* FREI tourist information bureau, tourist information office; **Fremdenverkehrsgewerbe** *nt* FREI tourist trade

fremdfinanziert: **~es Management Buy-In** *nt* (*LMBI*) FINANZ, MGMNT leveraged management buy-in (*LMBI*); **~es Management Buy-Out** *nt* (*LMBO*) FINANZ, MGMNT leveraged management buyout (*LMBO*); **~es Submissionsangebot** *nt* BÖRSE leveraged bid; **~es Übernahmeangebot** *nt* FINANZ leveraged buyout; **~e Übernahme** *f* **durch das Management** (*LMBO*) FINANZ, MGMNT leveraged management buyout (*LMBO*)

Fremdfinanzierung *f* BANK borrowing, FINANZ, RECHNUNG debt financing, VW trading on the equity; **Fremdfinanzierungsgrenze** *f* FINANZ external financing limit (*EFL*); **Fremdfinanzierungsquote** *f* RECHNUNG borrowing ratio

Fremdkapital *nt* BANK borrowed capital, borrowings, outside capital, FINANZ outside capital, RECHNUNG loan capital, VW loan capital, outside capital; ◆ **~ aufnehmen** GESCHÄFT raise external funds

Fremdkapital: **den Fremdkapitalanteil erhöhen** *phr* FINANZ leverage up; **Fremdkapitalanteil** *nt* **beim Einschuß** BÖRSE margin leverage (*AmE*); **Fremdkapitalaufnahme** *f* BÖRSE gearing (*BrE*), FINANZ procurement of outside capital

Fremdmittel *nt pl* BANK, FINANZ borrowed capital, borrowed funds, outside capital; ◆ **~ aufnehmen** BANK borrow funds

Fremdmittel: **Fremdmittelbedarf** *m* BANK borrowing requirement; **Fremdmittelbedarf** *m* **der öffentlichen Hand** FINANZ, VW public sector borrowing requirement (*BrE*) (*PSBR*)

Fremd-: **Fremdproduktion** *f* VW outside production; **Fremdsprache** *f* GESCHÄFT foreign language

Fremdwährung *f* BANK, FINANZ, RECHT, VW foreign currency; **Fremdwährungsanleihe** *f* FINANZ foreign currency loan, foreign currency loan issue; **Fremdwährungsfreibetrag** *m* FINANZ foreign currency allowance; **Fremdwährungskonto** *nt* BANK foreign exchange account; **Fremdwährungskredit** *m* VW foreign currency loan; **Fremdwährungskreditaufnahme** *f* BANK foreign currency borrowing; **Fremdwährungsmarkt** *m* VW eurocurrency market; **Fremdwährungsposition** *f* VW foreign currency position; **Fremdwährungsumrechnung** *f* **zu Stichtagskursen** RECHNUNG closing rate method (*BrE*), current rate method (*AmE*)

Frequenz *f* KOMM, MEDIEN frequency; **Frequenzmodulation** *f* KOMM, MEDIEN frequency modulation

freundlich: **Mit ~en Grüßen** *phr* KOMM *Grußformel an Briefende* Sincerely yours, Yours faithfully, Yours sincerely, Yours truly

freundschaftlich *adj* GESCHÄFT amicable; **~e Vereinbarung** *f* RECHT friendly agreement

frfr. *abbr* (*frachtfrei*) IMP/EXP, TRANSP carriage free, carr pd (*carriage paid*), frt ppd (*freight prepaid*)

Friedensdividende *f* POL peace dividend

Friedensrichter *m* PERSON Justice of the Peace (*BrE*) (*JP*)

Friedman-Theorie *f* VW Friedman theory

friktionell: ~e **Arbeitslosigkeit** *f* vw frictional unemployment

Friktionsantrieb *m* COMP friction feed, *Einzelblatteinzug* tractor feed; ◆ **mit** ~ COMP tractor-fed

Friktionsführung *f* COMP friction feed

Friktionsvorschubdrucker *m* COMP friction-feed printer

Frisch- *in cpds* GESCHÄFT fresh

frisch: ~es **Geld** *nt jarg* GESCHÄFT fresh money; ~ **privatisiert** *adj* vw newly privatized

Frisch-: **Frischkost** *f* IND live food; **Frischnahrung** *f* IND live food; **Frischwasser** *nt* UMWELT fresh water; **Frischwasserbeihilfe** *f* TRANSP fresh water allowance (*FWA*)

frisieren *vt infrml* RECHNUNG *Zahlen* dress up, massage, fiddle (*infrml*)

Frisieren *nt infrml* RECHNUNG doctoring (*infrml*), window-dressing; ~ **der Bilanz** *infrml* RECHNUNG window-dressing

Frist *f* GESCHÄFT time limit, time span, period; ◆ **die** ~ **für etw verlängern** GESCHÄFT extend the time limit for sth; **mit einer** ~ **von zwei Tagen** GESCHÄFT at two days' notice

Frist: **Fristablauf** *m* GESCHÄFT expiration of time, lapse of time; **Fristablaufsbenachrichtigung** *f* VERSICH expiration notice; **Fristaufschub** *m* **für Steuererklärungen** STEUER extension for returns; **Fristeinhaltung ist Vertragsgrundlage** *phr* RECHT *beim Fixgeschäft* time is of the essence; **Fristenbeginn** *m* VERSICH attachment date

fristenkongruent: ~ **finanziert** *phr* RECHNUNG adequately funded

Frist: **Fristeninkongruenz** *f* BANK maturity mismatch, mismatched maturity, vw mismatched maturity; **Fristentransformation** *f* FINANZ maturity transformation

fristgemäß *adj* GESCHÄFT timely; ~er **Widerspruch** *m* RECHT *Vertragsrecht* timely objection

fristgerecht: ~ **finanziert** *adj* RECHNUNG adequately funded; ~e **Kündigung** *f* PERSON dismissal with due notice, dismissal with timely notice

Fristigkeitsstruktur *f*: ~ **der Zinssätze** vw term structure of interest rates

fristlos 1. *adj* GESCHÄFT instant, without notice; **2.** *adv* ◆ **jdn** ~ **entlassen** PERSON dismiss sb without notice

fristlos: ~e **Entlassung** *f* PERSON dismissal without notice, instant dismissal, summary dismissal

Frist: **Fristsetzung** *f* RECHT *Vertragsrecht* fixing of a time limit; **Fristverlängerung** *f* PATENT extension of time limits, RECHT extension of time, *Vertragsrecht* extension of original term, *Zahlungen* extension of time for payment; **Fristverlängerung** *f* **für Steuererklärungen** STEUER extension for returns

Front: ~ **Office** *nt* VERWALT front office; ~-**end-Prozessor** *m* COMP front-end computer; ~-**end-Rechner** *m* COMP front-end computer; ~-**running** *nt* BÖRSE front running

Frontlänge *f* GRUND frontage

Frontlinie *f* GESCHÄFT front line

fro. *abbr obs.* (*franko*) IMP/EXP, TRANSP fco (*franco*)

Frostgürtel *m* IND frostbelt (*AmE*)

Frucht *f* UMWELT, vw crop; **Fruchtanbau** *m* vw fruit farming; **Fruchtbauer** *m*, **Fruchtbäuerin** *f* vw fruit farmer; **Fruchtfolge** *f* UMWELT crop rotation; **Fruchtlos**

adj GESCHÄFT fruitless; **Fruchttransportschiff** *nt* TRANSP fruit carrier; **Fruchtumschlagplatz** *m* TRANSP fruit terminal; **Fruchtumschlagterminal** *nt* TRANSP fruit terminal; **Fruchtwechsel** *m* UMWELT crop rotation

früh: ~e **Mehrheit** *f* V&M *bei der Einführung eines Produktes* early majority (*jarg*); ~e **Veröffentlichung** *f* MEDIEN early publication

Frühausgabe *f* MEDIEN *einer Zeitung* early edition, bulldog edition (*AmE*)

früher 1. *adj* GESCHÄFT prior; **2.** *adv* GESCHÄFT earlier; ◆ ~ **als geplant** GESCHÄFT with time to spare, KOMM ahead of schedule

früher: ~e **Anmeldung** *f* PATENT earlier application; ~e **Nutzung** *f* GRUND pre-existing use; ~e **Priorität** *f* PATENT earlier priority

Frühindikator *m* vw forward indicator, leading indicator

Frührente *f* PERSON early-retirement benefit

Frühvorstellung *f* FREI matinée

frühzeitig: ~ **buchen** *phr* GESCHÄFT book early; ~ **reservieren** *phr* GESCHÄFT book early; ~e **Veröffentlichung** *f* PATENT early publication

FS *abbr abbr* MEDIEN (*Fernsehen*) TV (*television*), TRANSP (*Flugsicherung*) ATC (*air-traffic control*)

F-Statistik *f* MATH F statistic

F-Test *m* vw *Signifikanztest* F test

führen *vt* COMP *Akten, Aufzeichnungen* keep, GESCHÄFT *leiten* lead, *Akten, Aufzeichnungen* keep, MGMNT manage, RECHNUNG *Akten, Aufzeichnungen* keep

führend *adj* GESCHÄFT top-flight, leading, major, V&M leading; ◆ **eine** ~e **Position in der Welt haben** IND be a world leader

führend: ~e **Aktie** *f* BÖRSE leading share; ~e **Bank** *f* BANK lead bank; ~er **Broker** *m* BÖRSE running broker; ~e **Industrien** *f pl* IND leading industries; ~e **Industriewerte** *m pl* BÖRSE blue-chip industrials; ~e **Marke** *f* V&M leading line; ~e **Persönlichkeit** *f* **des Wirtschaftslebens** GESCHÄFT policy maker; ~e **Position** *f* GESCHÄFT top of the range; ~er **Versicherer** *m* VERSICH leader; ~e **Volkswirtschaft** *f* vw core economy; ~er **Wert** *m* BÖRSE bellwether; ~e **Zeile** *f* PATENT leading line

Führer, in *m,f* GESCHÄFT leader, head, TRANSP driver, *von Flugzeug* pilot; ~ **des Handelsregisters beim Amtsgericht** VERWALT registrar of companies; **Führerschein** *m* PERSON driving licence (*BrE*), driving license (*AmE*), driver's licence (*BrE*), driver's license (*AmE*)

Fuhrpark *m* TRANSP car pool, fleet, pool of vehicles; **Fuhrparkleiter, in** *m,f* MGMNT motor transport officer; PERSON fleet manager; **Fuhrparkpolice** *f* VERSICH fleet policy

Führung *f* GESCHÄFT *Leitung* guidance, leadership, MGMNT *Leitung* management, *Vorstand* directors, leadership, PERSON *Verhalten* conduct, *Leitung* leadership; ◆ **die** ~ **übernehmen** GESCHÄFT take the lead

Führung: **Führungsausschuß** *m* MGMNT management committee; **Führungseffektivität** *f* MGMNT managerial effectiveness; **Führungsetage** *f* MGMNT boardroom; **Führungsfunktion** *f* MGMNT managerial function; **Führungsgruppe** *f* MGMNT, PERSON management team; **Führungshierarchie** *f* MGMNT line of command; **Führungsinformation** *f* COMP, MGMNT management information; **Führungsinformationssystem** *nt* COMP, MGMNT management information system (*MIS*);

Führungsinstrument *nt* MGMNT management technique; **Führungskaderqualifizierung** *f* MGMNT management development; **Führungskontrolle** *f* RECHNUNG management control

Führungskraft *f* MGMNT, PERSON *Unternehmensleitung* executive (*exec.*), executive manager, sales executive, VERWALT company executive, V&M sales executive; ~ **mit Linienfunktion** MGMNT line executive; ~ **auf unterster Leitungsebene** MGMNT, PERSON first-line manager; **Führungskräfte** *f pl* MGMNT, PERSON management staff, managerial staff, senior management; **Führungskräfte-Marketing** *nt* MGMNT executive search; **nach Führungskräften suchen** *phr* PERSON headhunt; **Führungskräftestrategie** *f* MGMNT executive manpower strategy

Führung: **Führungslehre** *f* MGMNT management science, management theory; **Führungslinie** *f* V&M leading line; **Führungsloch** *nt* COMP *Endlospapier* feed hole; **Führungsmannschaft** *f* MGMNT management team; **Führungsmethode** *f* MGMNT management method; **Führungsmodell** *nt* MGMNT managerial model; **Führungsnachwuchs** *m* MGMNT junior management; **Führungspersonal** *nt* MGMNT, PERSON management staff; **Führungspersonal** *nt* **mit Aufsichtsfunktionen** MGMNT, PERSON supervisory management; **Führungsposition** *f* MGMNT, PERSON managerial position; **Führungspotential** *nt* MGMNT management potential; **Führungsprovision** *f* BANK management fee; **Führungsqualitäten** *f pl* MGMNT management skills; **Führungsstil** *m* MGMNT management style, managerial style; **Führungsstruktur** *f* MGMNT management structure, managerial structure; **Führungstheorie** *f* MGMNT management theory

Fuhrunternehmen *nt* TRANSP haulage company, hauler (*AmE*), haulier (*BrE*), road haulage company, trucking contractor (*AmE*)

Fuhrunternehmer *m* TRANSP haulage company, hauler (*AmE*), haulier (*BrE*), road haulage company, trucking contractor (*AmE*)

Füllanzeige *f* V&M filler

Fülle *f* GESCHÄFT abundance; ~ **von Möglichkeiten** GESCHÄFT, PERSON wealth of opportunities

Füllfederhalter *m* GESCHÄFT fountain pen

Füllmaterial *nt* GESCHÄFT padding, TRANSP stuffing

Füllsel *nt* MEDIEN fills

fundamental *adj* GESCHÄFT fundamental; ~**e Aktienanalyse** *f* FINANZ fundamental analysis; ~**es Gleichgewicht** *nt* VW fundamental equilibrium

Fundamentalanalyse *f* FINANZ fundamental analysis

F&E *abbr* (*Forschung und Entwicklung*) IND R&D (*research and development*)

fundiert *adj* BÖRSE, FINANZ funded, GESCHÄFT sound, well-established; ~**e Schuld** *f* BÖRSE funded debt, FINANZ funded debt, long-term liability; ~**e Staatsanleihe** *f* FINANZ, GESCHÄFT consols

Fundierung *f* TRANSP foundation

Fünf- *in cpds* GESCHÄFT five; **Fünfer-Gruppe** *f* (*G5*) VW Group of Five (*G5*); **Fünfhundert-Dollar-Regel** *f* BÖRSE five hundred dollar rule; **Fünfjahresformel** *f* BANK five-year formula; **Fünfjahresplan** *m* RECHNUNG, VW five-year plan; **Fünf-Prozent-Regel** *f* BÖRSE five percent rule

fungibel *adj* RECHT fungible; **fungible Vermögenswerte** *m pl* FINANZ fungible assets; **fungible Waren** *f pl* VW fungibles

Fungibilien *pl* VW fungibles

Fungibilität *f* RECHT fungibility

Funk *m* KOMM, MEDIEN radio

funkelnagelneu *adj* *infrml* GESCHÄFT spanking new (*infrml*)

Funk: **Funk-Logbuch** *nt* TRANSP wireless log book; **Funkpeilanlage** *f* TRANSP direction finder (*DF*); **Funkpeiler** *m* TRANSP direction finder (*DF*), radio direction finder; **Funkpeilgerät** *nt* TRANSP direction finder (*DF*), radio direction finder; **Funkrufzeichen** *nt* TRANSP call sign; **Funksprechgerät** *nt* KOMM radiotelephone; **Funkspruch** *m* KOMM radio message; **Funktelegramm** *nt* KOMM radiotelegram; **Funktelegraphie** *m* KOMM radiotelephony (*RT*)

Funktion *f* COMP, GESCHÄFT, MATH function; ♦ **als ~ von** GESCHÄFT as a function of

funktional *adj* GESCHÄFT functional; ~**e Autorität** *f* PERSON functional authority; ~**e Beziehungen** *f pl* GESCHÄFT functional relations; ~**e Obsoleszenz** *f* V&M functional obsolescence; ~**e Organisation** *f* GESCHÄFT functional organization; ~**e Veralterung** *f* V&M functional obsolescence; ~**e Verantwortung** *f* GESCHÄFT functional responsibility; ~**es Weisungsrecht** *nt* PERSON functional authority

Funktionär, in *m,f* PERSON functionary, official, *Gewerkschaftsbewegung* officer

funktionell *adj* GESCHÄFT functional; ~**e Einkommensverteilung** *f* VW functional income distribution; ~**e Finanzierung** *f* FINANZ functional financing; ~**e Kostenbewertung** *f* RECHNUNG functional costing; ~**e Methode** *f* GESCHÄFT functional approach; ~**e Struktur** *f* GESCHÄFT functional layout; ~**e Unternehmensführung** *f* MGMNT functional management

funktionieren *vi* GESCHÄFT act, function, operate, work

Funktion: **Funktionsanalyse** *f* GESCHÄFT functional analysis; **Funktionsbeziehungen** *f pl* MGMNT functional relations

funktionsbezogen: ~**e Organisation** *f* MGMNT *eines Unternehmens* functional organization; ~**e Verantwortung** *f* MGMNT functional responsibility

funktionsfähig *adj* GESCHÄFT workable; **nicht ~** *adj* GESCHÄFT unworkable; ~**er Wettbewerb** *m* VW workable competition

Funktion: **Funktionsflexibilität** *f* PERSON functional flexibility

funktionsgestört *adj* MGMNT disfunctional

Funktion: **Funktionsmeistersystem** *f* IND functional management; **Funktionsprüfung** *f* IND performance testing; **Funktionsstörung** *f* GESCHÄFT malfunction; **Funktionstaste** *f* COMP function key (*F key*)

funktionstüchtig *adj* GESCHÄFT in running order, in working order, IND in working order; **nicht ~** *adj* GESCHÄFT out of order

Funk: **Funkwerbungsmengenrabatt** *m* V&M time discount; **Funk-Zertifikat** *nt* TRANSP wireless certificate

Für *nt*: ~ **und Wider** *nt* GESCHÄFT advantages and disadvantages, pros and cons

Fürsorger, in *m,f* PERSON, SOZIAL welfare worker

Fürsprecher, in *m,f* GESCHÄFT advocate

fürstlich: ~**es Gehalt** *nt* VW princely salary

Fusion *f* BÖRSE, FINANZ *von Unternehmen* amalgamation, fusion, merger, VERWALT amalgamation, VW outright consolidation; **Fusionen und Akquisitionen** *f pl* BÖRSE, VW mergers and acquisitions (*M&A*); **Fusionen und Übernahmen** *f pl* BÖRSEVW mergers and acquisitions (*M&A*)

fusionieren 1. *vt* BÖRSE, FINANZ, VW *Unternehmen, Bereiche* amalgamate, merge; **2.** *vi* BÖRSE, FINANZ, VW *Unternehmen, Bereiche* amalgamate, merge

fusionierend: ~**e Gesellschaft** *f* BANK amalgamating corporation, FINANZ merger company

fusioniert: ~**e Bank** *f* BANK amalgamated bank

Fusion: **Fusionsarbitrage** *f* BÖRSE merger arbitrage; **Fusionsbuchführung** *f* RECHNUNG merger accounting (*BrE*); **Fusionswelle** *f* VW merger wave

Fuß *m* GESCHÄFT *Maßeinheit* foot (*ft*); ♦ ~ **fassen auf** [+dat] GESCHÄFT breach, gain a toehold in, get a toehold in

Fußgänger, in *m,f* GESCHÄFT pedestrian

Fuß: **Fußnote** *f* COMP *Textverarbeitung* footnote; **Fußvolk** *nt* GESCHÄFT rank and file; **Fußzeile** *f* COMP *Textverarbeitung* footer

Futterkrippensystem *nt* POL spoils system (*AmE*)

Futuregeschäfte *nt pl* FINANZ dealings in futures

G

g *abbr* (*Gramm*) GESCHÄFT g (*gram, gramme*)

G. *abbr* (*Güter*) TRANSP frt (*freight*), gds (*goods*)

GAA *abbr* (*Geldaugsgabeautomat*) BANK ACD (*automated cash dispenser, automatic cash dispenser*)

Gabelstapler *m* TRANSP fork-lift truck

Galionsfigur *f* GESCHÄFT figurehead, MGMNT, PERSON titular head of an organization

Gallone *f* GESCHÄFT gallon (*gal*)

Gallup-Umfrage *f* V&M Gallup poll

galoppierend: **~e Inflation** *f* VW galloping inflation, runaway inflation

Gamma *nt* BÖRSE gamma; **Gamma-Aktie** *f* BÖRSE gamma stock

Gang *m* GESCHÄFT *zwischen Ladentischen, Sitzreihen* aisle; ◆ **im ~ sein** GESCHÄFT be at work, *schon angefangen haben* be under way; **im ~ befindlich** GESCHÄFT ongoing; **in ~ bringen** GESCHÄFT get off the ground (*infrml*); **in ~ kommen** GESCHÄFT get off the ground (*infrml*), rise; **in ~ setzen** IND actuate, V&M *Kampagne* launch

gängeln *vt* GESCHÄFT spoon feed

gängig *adj* BÖRSE active, GESCHÄFT *Ware* tradeable, prevailing, vendible, VW tradeable; **~e Aktie** *f* BÖRSE active share; **nicht ~e Aktie** *f* BÖRSE wallflower (*jarg*); **nicht ~e Größen** *f pl* IND odd sizes

Gangway *f* TRANSP gangway

Gantt-Karte *f* COMP Gantt chart

ganz 1. *adj* GESCHÄFT whole, full, entire, *unversehrt* intact; **2.** *adv* GESCHÄFT completely, reasonably; ◆ **~ neu** GESCHÄFT brand-new; **~ neu beginnen** GESCHÄFT start from scratch; **~ oben auf der Liste stehen** GESCHÄFT top the list; **~ unzutreffend** GESCHÄFT wide of the mark (*infrml*)

ganzheitlich: **~e Betrachtungsweise** *f* SOZIAL unitary approach; **~es Modell** *nt* SOZIAL unitary model

Ganzseiteneditor *m* COMP *Textverarbeitung* full-screen editor

ganztägig *adj* PERSON full-time; **~er Handel** *m* BÖRSE all-day trading

Ganztags- *in cpds* PERSON full-time; **Ganztagsbeschäftigung** *f* PERSON full-time employment

ganzzahlig *adj* MATH even-numbered

ganzzeitlich: **~ arbeiten** *phr* PERSON, SOZIAL work full-time

GAP *abbr* (*gemeinsame Agrarpolitik*) POL, VW CAP (*Common Agricultural Policy*)

gar. *abbr* (*garantiert*) GESCHÄFT guar (*guaranteed*)

Garant *m* FINANZ warrant, GESCHÄFT guarantor

Garantie *f* BANK guarantee, FINANZ security, GESCHÄFT guarantee, guaranty, warranty; ◆ **unter ~** GESCHÄFT under guarantee

Garantie: **Garantieabkommen** *nt* BANK guarantee agreement; **Garantiedauer** *f* GESCHÄFT duration of guaranty; **Garantieerklärung** *f* BÖRSE guaranty bond, GESCHÄFT letter of indemnity (*L/I*), RECHT, VERWALT indemnity bond; **Garantiefonds** *m* BANK *Versicherungen* guaranty

fund; **Garantiehaftung** *f* RECHT, VERSICH liability under a guarantee; **Garantieinhaber, in** *m,f* GESCHÄFT, RECHT warrantee; **Garantiekarte** *f* BANK warranty card; **Garantiekonsortium** *nt* VERSICH underwriting syndicate; **Garantiekonzept** *nt* **für den Einstieg in einen Markt** V&M market entry guarantee scheme; **Garantielohn** *m* PERSON guaranteed minimum wage, *Arbeitsentgelt* guaranteed wage; **Garantiepreis** *m* FINANZ guaranteed price; **Garantieprogramm** *nt* **für Hauseigentümer** VERSICH homeowner warranty program (*AmE*), homeowner warranty programme (*BrE*)

garantieren 1. *vt* GESCHÄFT guarantee; **2.** *vi* GESCHÄFT guarantee; ◆ **~ für** GESCHÄFT guarantee, *Verantwortung übernehmen* answer for

garantiert *adj* (*gar.*) GESCHÄFT guaranteed (*guar*), VERSICH warranted (*W/d*); **~es Einkommen** *nt* FINANZ guaranteed income; **~es Gewicht** *nt* TRANSP guaranteed weight; **~es Investmentzertifikat** *nt* FINANZ guaranteed investment certificate; **~es Jahreseinkommen** *nt* PERSON guaranteed annual wage (*GAW*); **~er Jahreslohn** *m* PERSON *Arbeitsverhältnis* annual wage; **~es jährlicher Mindestlohn** *m* PERSON guaranteed annual wage (*GAW*); **~er Kredit** *m* FINANZ guaranteed facility; **~er Mindestlohn** *m* PERSON guaranteed minimum wage, VW minimum wage; **~e Mindestzahlung** *f* PERSON guaranteed pay; **~e Versicherbarkeit** *f* VERSICH guaranteed insurability; **~er Wochenlohn** *m* PERSON guaranteed week

Garantie: **Garantierücksendung** *f* GESCHÄFT return of guarantee; **Garantieschreiben** *nt* BÖRSE guarantee letter; **Garantie-Standardsatz** *m* VERSICH institute warranty; **Garantieurkunde** *f* BANK guarantee deed; **Garantieverletzung** *f* RECHT breach of warranty; **Garantieverpflichtung** *f* RECHNUNG guarantee liability; **Garantieversprechen** *nt* RECHT maintenance bond, *Vertragsrecht* guarantee for fulfilment of contract (*BrE*), guarantee for fulfillment of contract (*AmE*); **Garantiezurückbehaltung** *f* VW retention bond

Garderobe *f* TRANSP checkroom (*AmE*), left-luggage office (*BrE*)

Garten: **Gartenappartement** *nt* GRUND garden apartment (*AmE*), garden flat (*BrE*); **Gartenbaubetrieb** *m* VW market gardening (*BrE*), truck farming (*AmE*); **Gartenwohnung** *f* GRUND garden apartment (*AmE*), garden flat (*BrE*)

Gas *nt* GESCHÄFT gas; **Gasanstalt** *f* IND, UMWELT gasworks; **Gasauswertung** *f* IND gas exploitation; **Gaserkundungskonzession** *f* UMWELT gas exploration licence (*BrE*), gas exploration license (*AmE*); **Gasgesellschaft** *f* UMWELT gas company; **Gasgewinnung** *f* IND gas exploitation; **Gasindustrie** *f* UMWELT gas industry; **Gasöl** *nt* UMWELT gas oil; **Gasstrom** *m* IND flow

Gast *m* GESCHÄFT visitor; **Gastarbeiter, in** *m,f* PERSON, VW guestworker, foreign worker; **Gastarbeiter** *m pl* PERSON, VW migrant labour (*BrE*), migrant labor (*AmE*)

Gästehaus *nt* FREI guest-house, boarding house

Gast: **Gastgeberstadt** *f* GESCHÄFT host city; **Gastland** *nt* FREI, GESCHÄFT, VW host country

Gastronomie f FREI catering, catering trade

Gast: **Gastspielensemble** nt FREI touring company; **Gaststätte** f GESCHÄFT restaurant; **Gaststättenwesen** nt GESCHÄFT catering

Gas: **Gasturbine** f TRANSP gas turbine; **Gas-Turboelektrik-Schiff** nt TRANSP gas turbo-electric ship (*GT-E*)

Gast: **Gastwirt, in** m,f PERSON restaurateur

Gas: **Gaswerk** nt IND, UMWELT gasworks; **Gaswirtschaft** f UMWELT gas industry

Gateway m COMP *Vernetzung*, TRANSP gateway

GATT abbr (*Allgemeines Zoll- und Handelsabkommen*) POL, VW GATT (*General Agreement on Tariffs and Trade*)

Gatter nt FREI gate

gattungsbedingt adj GESCHÄFT generic

Gattungsname m V&M generic brand

Gattungssache f RECHT *Kaufvertrag* fungible item

Gattungsschuld f RECHT indeterminate obligation, *Vertragsrecht* obligation to supply unascertained goods

Gauner m infrml RECHT criminal, small-time crook (*infrml*)

Gaunerei f FINANZ churning, twisting

Gauß: **~sche Normalverteilung** f MATH *Statistik* normal distribution

GB abbr (*Gigabyte*) COMP Gb (*gigabyte*)

GD abbr (*geschäftsführender Direktor*) MGMNT, PERSON executive director, MD (*managing director BrE*), (*Generaldirektor*) MD (*managing director BrE*)

geändert adj GESCHÄFT altered (*alt.*); **~e Steuererklärung** f STEUER amended tax return

Gebäude nt GESCHÄFT, GRUND building; **Gebäudenachversicherung** f **gegen zusätzliche Risiken** VERSICH additional extended coverage; **Gebäudereparatur** f GRUND building repair

geben vt GESCHÄFT award, give

Geber m SOZIAL, VW donor; **Gebereinrichtung** f SOZIAL *Hilfe für Land/Gebiet/Region* donor agency; **Geberland** nt FINANZ aid donor, VW *Außenwirtschaft* donor country, aid donor; **Geberregierung** f SOZIAL *Hilfe für Land/Gebiet/Region* donor government

Gebiet nt GESCHÄFT area, *Region* region, territory, IND field, VW area; **in ~e aufgeteilte Kampagne** f V&M zoned campaign; **in ~e aufgeteilte Werbung** f V&M zoned advertising; **Gebietsfremde(r)** mf [decl. as adj] RECHT nonresident; **Gebietskörperschaft** f FINANZ subdivision, VERWALT local government; **Gebietsleiter, in** m,f MGMNT area manager, regional manager, territory manager; **Gebietsverkäufer** m GESCHÄFT, PERSON area salesman; **Gebietsverkäuferin** f GESCHÄFT, PERSON area saleswoman; **Gebietszentrum** nt GESCHÄFT regional center (*AmE*), regional centre (*BrE*)

gebildet adj GESCHÄFT knowledgeable, PERSON *Allgemeinbildung* educated

Gebirgsort m FREI mountain resort

geboren: **~er Führer** m, **~e Führerin** f GESCHÄFT, MGMNT, PERSON born leader; **~er Leiter** m, **~e Leiterin** f GESCHÄFT, MGMNT, PERSON born leader

Gebot nt GESCHÄFT bid; ♦ **das ~ beenden** GESCHÄFT stop bidding

geboten: **~e Miete** f GRUND bid rent

Gebrauch m GESCHÄFT, PATENT, V&M use; ♦ **~ machen von** GESCHÄFT *von einem Angebot* take up

gebrauchen vt GESCHÄFT apply

Gebrauch: **Gebrauchsabschreibung** f RECHNUNG physical depreciation; **Gebrauchsanweisung** f GESCHÄFT directions for use; **Gebrauchsartikel** m GESCHÄFT commodity, V&M nonluxury item; **Gebrauchsbescheinigung** f PATENT utility certificate; **Gebrauchsgegenstand** m GESCHÄFT article of consumption; **Gebrauchsgüter** nt pl GESCHÄFT consumer hardgoods, V&M consumer durables; **Gebrauchsmodell** nt PATENT utility model; **Gebrauchsnachweis** m PATENT evidence of use; **Gebrauchswert** m VW use value, value in use; **Gebrauchszeichen** nt PATENT service mark; **Gebrauchszertifikat** nt PATENT utility certificate

Gebraucht- in cpds GESCHÄFT second-hand, used

gebraucht adj GESCHÄFT second-hand; **~e Vermögenswerte** m pl STEUER used assets

Gebraucht-: **Gebrauchttonnage** f TRANSP second-hand tonnage; **Gebrauchtwagen** m TRANSP used car; **Gebrauchtwarengeschäft** nt GESCHÄFT second-hand shop (*BrE*), thrift shop (*AmE*); **Gebrauchtwarenmarkt** m GESCHÄFT second-hand market

Gebühr f FINANZ charge, GESCHÄFT, PATENT fee, STEUER benefit tax, VW charge, tax; **~ nach Gebührenordnung** RECHT scale fee; **~ für Gewerbezulassung** VW occupation tax; **~ gleicher Höhe** GESCHÄFT commensurate charge; **~ für heimwärts laufendes Boot** TRANSP inward charges; **~ für Mehrgepäck** FREI, TRANSP excess baggage charge; **~ nach Tarif** STEUER scale charge; **~ für Übergepäck** FREI, TRANSP excess baggage charge; ♦ **~ bezahlt** GESCHÄFT postage paid; **~ bezahlt Empfänger** KOMM ≈ Freepost (*BrE*)

Gebühren f pl BANK charges, FINANZ, VW charges, rates; **~ bei Austritt** STEUER contracted-out rates; **~ für Bankgeschäfte** BANK charges on banking transactions; **~ für Bereitschaftskredit** BANK standby charges; **~ bei Eintritt** STEUER contracted-in rates; ♦ **die ~ überweisen** KOMM transfer the charges

gebührend: **~e Sorgfalt** f FINANZ due diligence

Gebühren: **Gebührenerlaß** m STEUER remission of charges

gebührenfrei 1. adj GESCHÄFT free of charge (*foc*), without charge (*w.c.*), IMP/EXP charges prepaid, KOMM *Brief* Freepost (*BrE*), postage paid, *Anruf* Freefone® (*BrE*), toll-free (*AmE*), TRANSP toll-free; **2.** adv GESCHÄFT at no charge, free of charge (*foc*), without charge (*w.c.*), KOMM *Brief* post-free; ♦ **jdn ~ anrufen** KOMM call sb toll-free (*AmE*)

gebührenfrei: **~er Anruf** m KOMM, V&M Freefone® call (*BrE*), toll-free call (*AmE*); **~e Rufnummer** f KOMM, V&M Freefone® number (*BrE*), toll-free number (*AmE*)

Gebühren: **Gebührenmodell** nt VW toll model; **Gebührenordnung** f GESCHÄFT scale of charges

gebührenpflichtig: **~e Ansprüche** m pl PATENT claims incurring fees; **~es Ausleihungsrecht** nt MEDIEN public lending right (*PLR*); **~e Autobahn** f TRANSP toll motorway (*BrE*), turnpike (*AmE*); **~e Brücke** f TRANSP tollbridge

Gebühren: **Gebührenrechnung** f FINANZ bill of costs, RECHNUNG bill of charges; **Gebührentabelle** f GESCHÄFT scale of charges

gebündelt: **~es Angebot** nt V&M banded offer; **~e Versicherung** f VERSICH comprehensive policy

gebunden *adj* MEDIEN casebound, *Buch* hardback, hardcover; ◆ ~ **sein an** [+acc] GESCHÄFT be tied to

gebunden: ~**es Buch** *nt* MEDIEN casebound book, hardback, hardcover; ~**e Entwicklungshilfe** *f* VW tied aid; ~**es Fachwissen** *nt* VW locked-in knowledge; **nicht** ~**e finanzielle Mittel** *nt pl* FINANZ uncommitted funds; ~**e Frage** *f* V&M closed question; ~**e Gaststätte** *f* GESCHÄFT tied house

geburtenstark: ~**e Jahrgänge** *m pl* V&M *als Zielgruppe* baby boomers

Geburtsurkunde *f* GESCHÄFT birth certificate

gechartert: ~**es Flugzeug** *m* TRANSP charter plane, chartered plane

Gedächtnis *nt* GESCHÄFT memory: **Gedächtnisschwäche** *f* V&M memory lapse; **Gedächtnisstütze** *f* GESCHÄFT aide-mémoire; **Gedächtnistest** *m* GESCHÄFT recall test, V&M aided recall test

Gedanken- *in cpds* GESCHÄFT cognitive; **Gedankenaustausch** *m* GESCHÄFT communication, MGMNT division of thought, POL exchange of ideas; **Gedankenblitz** *m* GESCHÄFT flash of inspiration, brainwave (*infrml*); **Gedankengang** *m* GESCHÄFT thinking; **Gedankengleichheit** *f* MGMNT cognitive consonance; **Gedankensplitter** *m* GESCHÄFT aphorism; **Gedankenstrich** *m* MEDIEN *Schriftzeichen* dash; **Gedankenverschiedenheit** *f* MGMNT cognitive dissonance

gedeckt: ~**e Baisseposition** *f* BÖRSE covered long; ~**e Kaufoption** *f* BÖRSE covered call (*BrE*); **nicht** ~**er Kredit** *m* BANK uncovered advance; ~**e Option** *f* BÖRSE covered option; ~**er Optionsverkäufer** *m* BÖRSE covered writer; ~**e Position** *f* BÖRSE covered position (*BrE*), matched book; ~**er Scheck** *m* BANK certified check (*AmE*), certified cheque (*BrE*); ~**e Short-Position** *f* BÖRSE covered short; ~**e Verkaufsoption** *f* BÖRSE covered put

gedeihen *vi* GESCHÄFT thrive

Gedenkfeier *f* GESCHÄFT anniversary

gedrückt *adj* BÖRSE heavy

gedruckt: **das** ~**e Wort** *nt* KOMM the printed word

geehrt: **Sehr** ~**e Damen und Herren** *phr* GESCHÄFT Ladies and Gentlemen

geeignet *adj* GESCHÄFT applicable, *qualifiziert* qualified, suitable, RECHT *Person* fit and proper; ◆ **für etw** ~ **sein** GESCHÄFT be eligible for sth

geeignet: ~**e Geschwindigkeit** *f* TRANSP convenient speed; ~**e Investition** *f* BÖRSE fit investment; ~**e Person** *f* **für die Stelle** PERSON suitable person for the job; ~**e Technologie** *f* UMWELT appropriate technology

geerbt: ~**e Zuschauer** *m pl* MEDIEN *Fernsehen* inherited audience (*jarg*)

Gefahr *f* GESCHÄFT hazard, PERSON *Arbeit* danger, VERSICH peril; ~ **des Meeres** TRANSP, VERSICH sea risks; ◆ **in** ~ GESCHÄFT at risk; **auf** ~ **des Eigentümers** VERSICH at owner's risk; **auf** ~ **des Empfängers** GESCHÄFT at receiver's risk; **alle Gefahren** VERSICH all peril, all risks (*A/R*); **gegen alle Gefahren** VERSICH against all risks (*AAR*); ~ **laufen** GESCHÄFT run the risk of

gefährden *vt* GESCHÄFT endanger, jeopardize

gefährdet *adj* GESCHÄFT at risk, UMWELT endangered; ~**e Art** *f* UMWELT endangered species

Gefahr: **Gefahrenausgleich** *m* VERSICH balancing of portfolio; **Gefahrenelement** *nt* GESCHÄFT element of risk; **Gefahrengutskommission** *f* GESCHÄFT Dangerous Good Board; **Gefahrenherd** *m* GESCHÄFT, POL trouble spot; **Gefahrenklasse** *f* VERSICH class of risk; **Gefahrenklassifikation** *f* VERSICH classification of risks; **Gefahrenpunkt** *m* GESCHÄFT danger point; **Gefahrenumfang** *m* GESCHÄFT degree of risk; **Gefahrenzulage** *f* PERSON danger money; **Gefahrgut** *nt* TRANSP dangerous cargo, hazardous cargo, igniter; **Gefahrgüter** *nt pl* RECHT dangerous goods; **Gefahrgüteranzeige** *f* TRANSP dangerous goods note (*DGN*); **Gefahrgutsatz** *m* TRANSP dangerous goods rate; **Gefahrgutvorschriften** *f pl* TRANSP dangerous goods regulations; **Gefahrgutzusammensetzung** *f* TRANSP dangerous cargo compound

gefährlich *adj* GESCHÄFT dangerous, hazardous, VW touch-and-go; ~**e Abfälle** *m pl* UMWELT dangerous waste; ~**e Chemikalie** *f* TRANSP hazardous chemical (*hazchem*); ~**er Stoff** *m* UMWELT hazardous substance; ~**e Substanz** *f* UMWELT hazardous substance

Gefahr: **Gefahrübergang** *m* VERSICH passing of risk; **Gefahrübernahme** *f* RECHT *Vertragsrecht* assumption of the risk; **Gefahrverminderung** *f* VERSICH decrease of risk

Gefälle *nt* GESCHÄFT slope

gefallen *vi* [+dat] GESCHÄFT appeal to

gefallen: ~**e Kosten** *pl* RECHNUNG sunk costs; ~ **sein** *phr* VW *Preise* be down

Gefälligkeit *f* BANK, FINANZ, GESCHÄFT accommodation; ◆ **eine** ~ **erweisen** GESCHÄFT accommodate

Gefälligkeit: **Gefälligkeitsadresse** *f* FINANZ accommodation party; **Gefälligkeitsakzept** *nt* GESCHÄFT accommodation acceptance; **Gefälligkeitsbeteiligte(r)** *mf* [decl. as adj] FINANZ accommodation party; **Gefälligkeitsdarlehen** *nt* FINANZ accommodation loan; **Gefälligkeitsindossament** *nt* FINANZ, GESCHÄFT accommodation endorsement; **Gefälligkeitspapier** *nt* GESCHÄFT accommodation paper; **Gefälligkeitstratte** *f* GESCHÄFT accommodation draft; **Gefälligkeitsvereinbarung** *f* RECHT *Vertragsrecht* noncontractual agreement; **Gefälligkeitswechsel** *m* BANK accommodation note, BÖRSE kite, FINANZ accommodation bill, accommodation draft, kite, GESCHÄFT accommodation bill; **Gefälligkeitszahlung** *f* BANK accommodation payment

gefälscht: ~**er Scheck** *m* BANK forged check (*AmE*), forged cheque (*BrE*)

gefaltet: ~**e Seite** *f* MEDIEN, V&M gatefold

Gefangenen-Dilemma *nt* VW prisoner's dilemma

Gefängnisstrafe *f* RECHT imprisonment

Gefäß *nt* GESCHÄFT vessel

gefestigt *adj* GESCHÄFT strengthened; ~**e Stellung** *f* **für den taktischen Rückzug** PERSON fallback position

gefolgert: ~**e Autorität** *f* PERSON inferred authority

gefördert: ~**es Buch** *nt* V&M sponsored book; ~**e Ereignisse** *nt pl* FREI, V&M sponsored events

gefordert: ~**e Kapitalverzinsung** *f* VW required rental on capital

gefragt *adj* GESCHÄFT, PERSON sought-after, in demand

Gefüge *nt* GESCHÄFT structure

Gefühlsverarmung *m* MGMNT sensory deprivation

geg. *abbr* (*gegen*) GESCHÄFT against, v (*versus*), vs (*versus*)

gegebenenfalls *adv* GESCHÄFT should the occasion arise

gegeben: **unter den ~en Umständen** *phr* GESCHÄFT given the circumstances

Gegen- *in cpds* GESCHÄFT counter, reverse, opposite, against

gegen *prep* (*geg.*) GESCHÄFT against, versus (*v*, *vs*); ◆ **etw ~ jdn richten** GESCHÄFT aim sth at sb; **~ Vorlage** RECHNUNG on demand (*O/D*)

Gegen-: **Gegenakkreditiv** *nt* BANK back-to-back credit; **Gegenangebot** *nt* V&M competitive bid, counteroffer, contra deal; **Gegenanspruch** *m* RECHT counterclaim; **Gegenauslese** *f* VERSICH adverse selection; **Gegenbroker** *m* BÖRSE contra broker; **Gegenbuchung** *f* RECHNUNG contra entry, offsetting entry, reversing entry; **Gegendarstellung** *f* V&M against text; **Gegendiskriminierung** *f* SOZIAL *Benachteiligung von Angehörigen privilegierter gesellschaftlicher Gruppen* reverse discrimination; **Gegeneintrag** *m* RECHNUNG reversing entry

gegengerichtet: **ein ~es Swapgeschäft abschließen** *phr* BÖRSE reverse a swap

Gegen-: **Gegengeschäft** *nt* BANK back-to-back transaction, counter deal, GESCHÄFT opposite transaction, vw mirror contract

gegengewichtig: **~e Marktmacht** *f* VW countervailing power

Gegen-: **Gegenhalter** *m* IND backstop; **eine Gegenklage zustellen** *phr* RECHT serve a counter-notice; **Gegenkonto** *nt* RECHNUNG contra account; **Gegenkredit** *m* BANK back-to-back credit

gegenläufig: **~e Fusion** *f* FINANZ reverse takeover, GESCHÄFT reverse triangular merger, vw reverse takeover

Gegenleistung *f* BÖRSE consideration, GESCHÄFT quid pro quo, RECHT *Vertragsrecht* consideration, counter-performance, quid pro quo, VERWALT consideration; ◆ **als ~** RECHT in return for

Gegen-: **Gegenlieferungsgeschäft** *nt* VW counter purchase; **Gegenmacht** *f* VW countervailing power; **Gegenmaßnahme** *f* GESCHÄFT countermeasure; **Gegenposten** *m* RECHNUNG contra; **Gegenprüfung** *f* BANK crosscheck; **Gegenreaktion** *f* GESCHÄFT reactive response; **Gegenrechnung** *f* RECHNUNG contra account, *als Kontrollrechnung* controlling account

gegenseitig 1. *adj* GESCHÄFT reciprocal; ◆ **in ~em Einvernehmen** GESCHÄFT, RECHT by mutual agreement, by mutual consent; **in ~em Einverständnis** GESCHÄFT, RECHT by mutual agreement, by mutual consent; **2.** *adv* GESCHÄFT reciprocally; ◆ **~ abhängig** GESCHÄFT interdependent

gegenseitig: **~e Abhängigkeit** *f* vw interdependence; **~e Anerkennung** *f* RECHT mutual recognition; **sich ~ aufhebende Buchungsfehler** *m pl* RECHNUNG compensating errors; **~er Austausch** *m* **von Lizenzen** COMP, GESCHÄFT, RECHT cross-licensing; **~e Benutzbarkeit** *f* FINANZ interoperability; **~er Fonds** *m* **für soziales Bewußtsein** FINANZ social consciousness mutual fund; **~e Haftpflicht** *f* VERSICH cross-liability; **~e Haftung** *f* VERSICH cross-liability; **~e Kapitalbeteiligung** *f* **zwischen Unternehmen** BÖRSE cross-holdings between companies; **~e Lizenz** *f* RECHT *Vertragsrecht* cross-licence; **~er Regreßverzicht** *m* VERSICH knock-for-knock; **~e Regreßverzichtserklärung** *f* VERSICH knock-for-knock; **~e Verbindung** *f* GESCHÄFT interconnection; **~es Verrechnungssystem** *nt* BÖRSE

Mutual Offset System; **~er Vertrag** *m* RECHT bilateral contract, mutual contract, *geistiges Eigentum* reciprocal agreement; **~e Verträglichkeit** *f* IND compatibility

Gegenseitigkeit *f* BANK mutuality, reciprocity; **~ des Vertrags** RECHT mutuality of contract; **Gegenseitigkeitsabkommen** *nt* PERSON mutuality agreement, reciprocal agreement; **Gegenseitigkeitsgesellschaft** *f* FINANZ mutual company; **Gegenseitigkeitsprinzip** *nt* GESCHÄFT reciprocal principle; **Gegenseitigkeitsverband** *m* FINANZ mutual association; **Gegenseitigkeitsversicherung** *f* VERSICH joint insurance

Gegenspieler, in *m,f* PERSON opposite number

Gegenstand *m* GESCHÄFT article, *Vereinbarung, Rede* subject; **~ einer Abteilung** VERWALT departmental object, *Abteilungszweck* departmental line object; **~ des Anlagevermögens** RECHNUNG fixed asset; **~ der Auseinandersetzung** GESCHÄFT issue; **~ des beweglichen Vermögens** RECHT chose; **~ der Erfindung** PATENT subject matter; **~ des Interesses** GESCHÄFT issue; **~ des persönlichen Bedarfs** GESCHÄFT article for personal use **~ des Verfahrens** RECHT corpus; ◆ **~ nicht verkauft** GESCHÄFT subject unsold

Gegen-: **Gegenstimme** *f* RECHT dissenting vote; **Gegenstimmen** *f pl* POL opposing votes; **Gegenstrategie** *f* GESCHÄFT reactive strategy; **Gegenstück** *nt* GESCHÄFT analog

gegenteilig *adv* GESCHÄFT conversely

gegenüber *prep* GESCHÄFT against, vis-à-vis; ◆ **sich ~ dem Verlust einer Wette absichern** GESCHÄFT hedge one's bets against

gegenwärtig *adj* GESCHÄFT current, VW actual; ◆ **zu ~en Börsenkursen** BÖRSE at current prices, at ruling prices, FINANZ at ruling prices; **zu ~en Preisen** BÖRSE at current prices, at ruling prices, FINANZ at ruling prices

gegenwärtig: **beim ~en Rechtsstand** RECHT as the law stands at present; **~e Risiken** *nt pl* vw current risks; **der ~e Stand** *m* **der Technik** GESCHÄFT the state of the art; **~er Wirtschaftstrend** *m* vw current economic trend

Gegenwartswert *m* FINANZ present value; **~ der Kaufkraft** vw current purchasing power (*CPP*)

Gegen-: **Gegenwert** *m* GESCHÄFT equivalent amount; **Gegenzeichnung** *f* KOMM *Unterschrift, Initialen auf Dokumenten* acknowledgement (*ack*)

gegliedert *adj* GESCHÄFT structured

gegr. *abbr* (*gegründet*) BÖRSE, GESCHÄFT constituted, est. (*established*)

gegründet *adj* (*gegr.*) BÖRSE, GESCHÄFT constituted, established (*est.*)

Gehalt *nt* GESCHÄFT, PERSON *monatlich* salary; **~ nach Vereinbarung** PERSON *Stellenangebot in Kleinanzeigen* salary to be negotiated; ◆ **den ~ von etw bestimmen** GESCHÄFT assay sth; **ein ~ in Höhe von DM 6.000 beziehen** PERSON earn a salary of DM6,000

gehalten: **~ für** *adj* GESCHÄFT deemed

Gehälterliste *f* PERSON pay sheet

Gehalt: **Gehaltsabrechnung** *f* PERSON wage and salary administration; **Gehaltsabzug** *m* PERSON salary deduction, *vom Bruttolohn* payroll deduction, RECHNUNG salary deduction; **Gehaltsabzüge** *m pl* RECHNUNG payroll deductions; **Gehaltsangleichung** *f* vw adjustment; **Gehaltsanpassung** *f* PERSON, RECHNUNG salary adjustment; **Gehaltsempfänger, in** *m,f* PERSON salaried employee, salaried person, *Jahresgehalt* salary earner; **Gehaltsempfänger** *m pl* PERSON salaried staff; **Gehaltsentwicklungskurve** *f* PERSON salary progression curve

Gehaltserhöhung *f* PERSON salary increase, raise (*AmE*), rise (*BrE*); **~ nach Dauer der Betriebszugehörigkeit** PERSON longevity pay; ◆ **eine ~ bekommen** PERSON *Tarifverträge, firmeneigene Gehälterrevision, Beförderung* receive a pay rise

Gehalt: **Gehaltsforderung** *f* PERSON salary demands

gehaltsgebunden: **~es Rentensystem** *nt* VERSICH benefit-based pension plan

Gehalt: **Gehaltsgrundlage** *f* PERSON salary base; **Gehaltsgruppe** *f* PERSON salary bracket; **Gehaltsklasse** *f* PERSON salary grade; **Gehaltsliste** *f* PERSON, RECHNUNG payroll, pay bill (*AmE*); **Gehaltsrevision** *f* PERSON salary review; **Gehaltsscheck** *m* BANK, PERSON pay check (*AmE*), pay cheque (*BrE*); **Gehaltssenkungsplan** *m* PERSON salary reduction plan; **Gehaltsskala** *f* PERSON salary scale; **Gehaltssteigerung** *f* PERSON raise (*AmE*), rise (*BrE*); **Gehaltsstruktur** *f* PERSON, VW salary structure; **Gehaltsstruktur** *f* **mit wenigen Stufen** PERSON broadband; salary structure; **Gehaltsstufe** *f* PERSON salary grade; **Gehaltssystem** *nt* PERSON salary scheme; **Gehaltsüberprüfung** *f* PERSON salary review; **Gehaltsverzichtplan** *m* STEUER salary sacrifice scheme (*BrE*); **Gehaltsvorschuß** *m* PERSON salary advance, *Angestelltenverhältnis* advance on salary; **Gehaltszahlung** *f* PERSON salary payment; **Gehaltszulage** *f* PERSON extra pay; **Gehaltszuwachs** *m* PERSON incremental payment; **Gehaltszuwachstabelle** *f* PERSON incremental scale

gehandelt: **~e Monate** *m pl* BÖRSE months traded; **~es Volumen** *nt* BÖRSE amount of business

geheim *adj* GESCHÄFT secret, POL *Dokumente* restricted; **~e Abstimmung** *f* PERSON *Gewerkschaftsbewegung*, POL secret ballot; **~e Bilanzprüfung** *f* RECHNUNG undercover audit; **~e Entscheidung** *f* GESCHÄFT hidden decision; **~er Kanal** *m* POL back channel (*AmE*); **~e Provision** *f* RECHT *Staats- und Privatverträge*, *Schmiergeld* kickback; **~e Rücklage** *f* FINANZ, RECHNUNG secret reserve

Geheim: **~er Staatsrat** *m* GESCHÄFT Privy Council (*BrE*)

geheim: **~e Tagesordnung** *f* MGMNT hidden agenda; **~e Verführer** *m pl* V&M hidden persuaders; **~er Vorbehalt** *m* RECHT *Vertragsrecht* mental reservation; **~e Wahl** *f* PERSON *Gewerkschaften*, POL secret ballot; **~e Zahlung** *f* PERSON secret payment

Geheimfonds *m* FINANZ, POL slush fund

Geheimhaltung *f* GESCHÄFT secrecy; ◆ **jdn auf ~ einschwören** GESCHÄFT swear sb to secrecy

Geheimhaltung: **Geheimhaltungsvertrag** *m* RECHT *Verschwiegenheitsvereinbarung* confidentiality agreement

gehemmt: **~e Marktpreisbildung** *f* VW constrained market pricing

gehen *vi* FINANZ go

Gehilfe *m* GESCHÄFT, PERSON assistant (*asst*)

Gehilfin *f* GESCHÄFT, PERSON assistant (*asst*)

Gehirn *nt* MGMNT nerve center (*AmE*), nerve centre (*BrE*)

gehoben: **~e Führungskraft** *f* MGMNT, PERSON senior executive; **~e Preisklasse** *f* GESCHÄFT up-market segment

Gehöft *nt* GRUND homestead (*AmE*), farmstead (*BrE*)

Gei *f* TRANSP guy

Geistesprodukt *nt* GESCHÄFT brainchild (*infrml*)

geistig: **~er Diebstahl** *m* RECHT pirating; **~es Eigentum** *nt* PATENT, RECHT intellectual property; **~e Fähigkeit** *f* GESCHÄFT, PERSON skill

geistlich *adj* PERSON *kirchlich* clerical

Geitenhöhe *f* TRANSP depth

geizen: **~ und sparen** *phr* GESCHÄFT scrimp and save

gekauft: **~er Wechsel** *m* **mit Wiederverkaufsvereinbarung** RECHNUNG note purchased under resale agreement

gekennzeichnet: **~e Datei** *f* COMP labeled file (*AmE*), labelled file (*BrE*)

geklebt: **~er Karton** *m* IND pasteboard

geknickt: **~e Preis-Absatz-Kurve** *f* VW kinked demand curve

gekoppelt: **~ mit** *phr* COMP, GESCHÄFT coupled with; **~er Wertpapierauftrag** *m* BÖRSE contingent order

gekreuzt *adj* BANK *Scheck* crossed

gekündigt *adj* PERSON dismissed; ◆ **~ werden** GESCHÄFT be dismissed, get one's cards (*BrE*) (*infrml*), get the pink slip (*AmE*) (*infrml*), get the sack (*BrE*) (*infrml*)

gekünstelt *adj* GESCHÄFT *Gespräch* strained

gel. *abbr* (*geliefert*) GESCHÄFT D (*delivered*), dd (*delivered*)

Gelände *nt* GESCHÄFT plot, GRUND premises; **Geländefahrt** *f* GESCHÄFT field trip

geläutert *adj* IND refined

gelb: **~e Gewerkschaft** *f* PERSON company union, enterprise union

Gelb: **~e Seiten**® *f pl* KOMM, V&M *Branchenverzeichnis* Yellow Pages®

Gelbguß *m* IND yellow metal

Geld *nt* BÖRSE buyer's rate, FINANZ, GESCHÄFT, VW money, bread (*infrml*), dough (*infrml*), dosh (*infrml*) (*BrE*), wampum (*infrml*) (*AmE*); **~ auf Abruf** BANK, FINANZ money at call; **~ anderer Leute** FINANZ other people's money (*OPM*); **~ mit kleinem Geldschöpfungsmultiplikator** VW low-powered money; ◆ **~ abführen** STEUER pay over, transfer; **~ anlegen** GESCHÄFT invest money, put money down; **~ aufnehmen** BANK borrow funds, borrow money; **~ auf etw aufnehmen** GESCHÄFT raise money on sth; **~ ausgeben** GESCHÄFT spend; **etw für sein ~ bekommen** VW get good value for money; **~ von jdm borgen** GESCHÄFT borrow money off sb; **um ~ ersuchen** GESCHÄFT appeal for funds; **~ großzügiger ausgeben** FINANZ loosen one's belt; **~ auf eine Hypothek aufnehmen** GESCHÄFT raise money on a mortgage; **~ investieren** FINANZ invest money, put money down; **zu ~ kommen** *infrml* GESCHÄFT come into money; **~ leihen** FINANZ lend money, BANK borrow money; **~ von jdm leihen** GESCHÄFT borrow money off sb; **~ scheffeln** *infrml* GESCHÄFT rake it in (*infrml*); **im ~ schwimmen** *infrml* GESCHÄFT awash with cash (*infrml*); **~ sparen** BANK save; **~ spielt keine Rolle** GESCHÄFT money is no object; **~ vorübergehend anlegen** BÖRSE park money; **~ wie Heu haben** *infrml* GESCHÄFT have money to burn (*infrml*)

Geld: **Geldabfindung** *f* BÖRSE, FINANZ cash settlement

geldähnlich: **~e Forderungen** *f pl* VW near money

Geld: **Geldangebot** *nt* VW money supply; **Geldangelegenheiten** *f pl* GESCHÄFT money matters;

Geldanlage *f* **über Banken und Finanzinstitute** FINANZ intermediation; **Geldanlage** *f* **im Interbankgeschäft** BANK, FINANZ wholesale deposits; **Geldanreiz** *m* FINANZ monetary inducement; **Geldausgabeautomat** *m* BANK automated cash dispenser (*ACD*), automatic cash dispenser (*ACD*), cash dispenser, cash dispensing machine; **Geldausgänge** *m pl* RECHNUNG monies paid in; **Geldautomat** *m* BANK, FINANZ automated cash dispenser (*ACD*), automatic cash dispenser (*ACD*), cash dispenser, cash-dispensing machine, automatic teller; **Geldautomatenkarte** *f* BANK autobank card, automated teller card, cash card; **Geldbasis** *f* vw high-powered money; **Geldbedarf** *m* RECHNUNG cash requirements, vw money supply; **Geldbeschaffung** *f* FINANZ fund-raising; **Geldbeschaffungsausschuß** *m* FINANZ Ways and Means Committee (*AmE*); **Geldbestand** *m* RECHNUNG cash balance; **Geldbetrag** *m* vw money; **Geldbeutel** *m* vw pocket; **über den Geldbeutel verfügen** *phr* vw hold the purse strings; **Geldbewilligung** *f* **der Finanzbehörde für unvorhergesehene Ausgaben** POL, VW Treasury Board contingencies vote; **Geldbörse** *f* FINANZ purse (*BrE*); **Geld- und Briefkurse** *m pl* BÖRSE bid and asked quotations; **Geld- und Briefkurse stellen** *phr* BÖRSE make a market; **Geldbuße** *f* PERSON *Gewerkschaftsmitglied* fine; **Gelddisposition** *f* BANK, PERSON, VW cash management; **Gelddispositionskonto** *nt* FINANZ cash management account (*CMA*); **Gelddispositionsmethode** *f* MGMNT cash management technique; **Gelddreher** *m* GESCHÄFT money-spinner (*infrml*); **Geldeinheit** *f* FINANZ monetary unit; **Geldeingänge** *m pl* FINANZ monies in, monies received; **Geldeinkommen** *nt* vw money income; **Geldentwertung** *f* vw inflation; **Geldersatz** *m* FINANZ token money; **Geldgeber, in** *m,f* BANK financier, FINANZ money lender, backer, financial backer, FREI sponsor, GESCHÄFT *Theater* angel (*infrml*), backer, V&M sponsor; **Geldgeber** *m* **der letzten Zuflucht** BANK lender of last resort; **Geldhandel** *m* vw money dealing; **Geldhandelsabteilung** *f* BANK money desk; **Geldillusion** *f* vw inflation illusion, money illusion; **Geldinflation** *f* vw monetary inflation; **Geldinstitut** *nt* BANK bank (*bk*), FINANZ financial institution; **Geldknappheit** *f* FINANZ tight money, vw monetary tightness; **Geldkurs** *m* BANK bid rate, buying rate of exchange, BÖRSE demand price, bid price, price bid, bid, *für Devisen, Sorten* buyer's rate, FINANZ buying rate, vw demand price; **einen Geldkurs akzeptieren** *phr* BÖRSE hit the bid; **Geldleistung** *f* GESCHÄFT, VERSICH, VERWALT cash benefit

geldlich *adj* GESCHÄFT pecuniary; **~e Hilfe** *f* GESCHÄFT accommodation

Geld: **Geldmakler, in** *m,f* BANK, FINANZ money broker; **Geldmarkt** *m* BANK money market, BÖRSE money mart; **Geldmarktanlagen** *f pl* BANK, FINANZ wholesale deposits; **Geldmarktdokument** *nt* BÖRSE money market instrument; **Geldmarkteinlagenkonto** *nt* FINANZ money market deposit account (*MMDA*); **Geldmarkterträge** *m pl* BÖRSE money market returns

geldmarktfähig: **~e Aktiva** *nt pl* BANK, FINANZ assets eligible for the money market

Geld: **Geldmarktfonds** *m* FINANZ money market mutual fund (*MMMF*) (*AmE*); **Geldmarkt-Investmentfonds** *m* BÖRSE money market fund (*MMF*); **Geldmarktkapital** *nt* BÖRSE money market fund;

Geldmarktpapier *nt* BÖRSE money market paper; **Geldmarktsatz** *m* BÖRSE money market rate; **Geldmarkt** *m* **für sehr kurzfristige Kredite** FINANZ loan market; **Geldmarkturkunde** *f* BÖRSE money market instrument; **Geldmarktzertifikat** *nt* FINANZ money market certificate (*MMC*) (*AmE*)

Geldmenge *f* vw money supply; **Geldmenge** *f* **in der engen Definition** vw narrowly-defined money supply; **Geldmenge** *f* **in ihrer weitesten Abgrenzung** BANK broad money; **Geldmenge** *f* **M3** BANK broad money; **Geldmenge** *f* **M3 für Sterling** FINANZ sterling M3; **Geldmengenaggregat** *nt* vw monetary aggregate (*BrE*); **Geldmengenziel** *nt* vw monetary target

Geldmittel *nt pl* BANK, FINANZ cash, financial means, funds, exchequer; ♦ **~ beschaffen** FINANZ raise funds; **um ~ dringend ersuchen** FINANZ appeal for funds; **~ leihen** BANK borrow funds

Geldmittel: **Geldmittelbewegung** *f* RECHNUNG, VW flow of funds, funds flow

Geld: **Geldmultiplikator** *m* vw money multiplier; **Geldnachfrage** *f* vw demand for money; **Geldneutralität** *f* vw neutrality of money; **Geld- oder Kapitalanlage** *f* FINANZ financial investment; **Geldpolitik** *f* vw monetary policy

geldpolitisch: **~e Maßnahmen** *f pl* vw measures of monetary policy; **~e Restriktion** *f* vw monetary restriction; **~es Ziel** *nt* FINANZ monetary target

Geld: **Geldposten** *m* RECHNUNG monetary item; **Geldrente** *f* GESCHÄFT regular payment; **Geldreserve** *f* BANK money reserve; **Geldschein** *m* BANK bank bill (*AmE*), banknote (*BrE*); **Geldschleier** *m* vw monetary veil; **Geldschneiderei** *f* infrml FINANZ extortion; **Geldschöpfungsmultiplikator** *m* vw deposit multiplier; **Geldschwemme** *f* GESCHÄFT glut of money; **Geldsorte** *f* vw money

Geldstrafe *f* RECHT *Buße* fine; ♦ **zu einer ~ verurteilen** RECHT impose a fine on

Geld: **Geldstrom** *m* RECHNUNG, VW flow of funds, funds flow; **Geldstromanalyse** *f* vw flow-of-funds analysis; **Geldstromtabelle** *f* FINANZ flow-of-funds table; **Geldstück** *nt* GESCHÄFT coin; **Geldsurrogat** *nt* FINANZ token money; **Geldüberhang** *m* vw monetary overhang; **Geldüberweisung** *f* **durch die Post** BANK, FINANZ, GESCHÄFT postal money order (*AmE*), postal order (*PO*) (*BrE*); **Geldumlaufgeschwindigkeit** *f* vw velocity of circulation of money; **Geldungleichgewicht** *nt* vw disequilibrium money; **Geldverdiener** *m* GESCHÄFT moneymaker; **Geldverknappung** *f* vw contraction of money supply, money squeeze; **Geldvermögen** *nt* RECHNUNG monetary assets; **Geldvolumen** *nt* **M1** (*M1*) vw money 1 (*M1*); **Geldvolumen** *nt* **M2** (*M2*) vw money 2 (*M2*); **Geldvolumen** *nt* **M3** (*M3*) vw money 3 (*M3*); **Geldvorrat** *m* vw money supply; **Geldwäsche** *f* BANK money laundering; **Geldwäscherei** *f* FINANZ money laundering; **Geldwert** *m* GESCHÄFT value for money, vw value of money

geldwert: **~er Ausgleichsbetrag** *m* FINANZ monetary compensatory amount

Geld: **Geldwert-Index** *m* BÖRSE golds index; **Geldwirtschaft** *f* vw monetary economics; **Geldzuschuß** *m* vw injection; **Geldzuweisung** *f* GESCHÄFT gratuity, vw appropriation

geleast *adj* GESCHÄFT leased

gelegen *adj* GESCHÄFT located

Gelegenheit *f* GESCHÄFT opportunity, window, POL, VW opportunity; ♦ **jdm ~ geben, etw zu tun** GESCHÄFT give sb the opportunity to do sth; **die ~ haben, etw zu tun** GESCHÄFT have the opportunity to do sth; **eine ~ wahrnehmen, etw zu tun** GESCHÄFT take advantage of an opportunity to do sth

Gelegenheit: **Gelegenheitsarbeit** *f* GESCHÄFT jobbing, PERSON casual work, odd jobs, casual labor (*AmE*), casual labour (*BrE*); **Gelegenheitsarbeiter, in** *m,f* PERSON casual laborer (*AmE*), casual labourer (*BrE*), casual worker, occasional worker, odd job person; **Gelegenheitspreis** *m* GESCHÄFT bargain price; **Gelegenheitsspediteur** *m* V&M private carrier

gelegentlich *adj* GESCHÄFT occasional; **~er Kunde** *m*, **~e Kundin** *f* VW occasional customer

geleiten *vt* GESCHÄFT accompany

Geleitschutz *m* GESCHÄFT escort

gelenkt: **~es Interview** *nt* V&M directed interview; **~e Kosten** *pl* VW managed costs; **~er Markt** *m* VW controlled market; **~e Wirtschaft** *f* VW controlled economy

gelernt *adj* PERSON, VW *Arbeiter* skilled; **~e Arbeitskräfte** *f pl* PERSON, VW skilled labor (*AmE*), skilled labour (*BrE*)

geliefert *adj* (*gel.*) GESCHÄFT delivered (*D, dd*); ♦ **~ ab Kai** IMP/EXP delivered ex quay (*DEQ*); **~ ab Schiff** IMP/EXP delivered ex ship (*DES*); **~ Grenze** IMP/EXP delivered at frontier (*DAF*); **~ unverzollt** IMP/EXP delivered duty unpaid (*DDU*); **~ verzollt** IMP/EXP delivered duty paid (*DDP*)

geliefert: **~e Menge** *f* VW quantity supplied

geliehen: **~e Aktien** *f pl* BÖRSE borrowed stock; **~e Währungsreserven** *f pl* VW borrowed reserves

gelingen *vi* GESCHÄFT succeed

gelöscht: **~e Börsenumsätze** *m pl* BÖRSE volume deleted; **~e Dezimalstellen** *f pl* **auf dem Börsenticker** BÖRSE digits deleted

geltend *adj* GESCHÄFT prevailing; ♦ **~ machen** GESCHÄFT set up; **zu ~en Preisen** BÖRSE, FINANZ at ruling prices

geltend: **~er Preis** *m* V&M *handelsüblicher Preis* ruling price; **~e Rückkaufrate** *f* FINANZ implied repo rate (*infrml*)

Geltendmachung *f* RECHT enforcement

Geltung *f* GESCHÄFT validity; **Geltungsbereich** *m* GESCHÄFT scope of application, VERWALT coverage; **Geltungskonsum** *m* VW conspicuous consumption; **Geltungssüchtige(r)** *mf* [decl. as adj] GESCHÄFT, PERSON status seeker

gelungen *adj* GESCHÄFT, V&M successful

gemäß *prep* GESCHÄFT, RECHT according to, in accordance with, in conformity with; ♦ **~ Artikel** RECHT pursuant to article; **~ Ihren Anweisungen** GESCHÄFT in accordance with your instructions; **~ spezifiziertem Inhalt** GESCHÄFT at the specified tenor; **~ den vertraglichen Bedingungen** RECHT under the terms of the contract

gemäßigt *adj* VW modest

gemein: **~es Recht** *nt* PERSON, RECHT common law

Gemeinde *f* GESCHÄFT community, POL borough; **~ im ländlichen Raum** VW rural community; **Gemeindebesteuerung** *f* **von Pendlern** STEUER commuter tax (*AmE*); **Gemeindedirektor, in** *m,f* MGMNT chief executive; **Gemeindegrundsteuern** *f pl* STEUER rates (*BrE*); **Gemeindeland** *nt* GRUND common area; **Gemeinderat** *m* POL, VERWALT borough council (*BrE*); **Gemeindeschule** *f* GESCHÄFT village school; **Gemeindesteuerbescheid** *m* STEUER rate bill (*BrE*); **Gemeindesteuereinnehmer, in** *m,f* VERWALT rate collector (*BrE*); **Gemeindesteuer** *f* **auf Grundbesitz** STEUER rates (*BrE*); **Gemeindeverband** *m* GRUND community association

Gemeineigentum *nt* POL, VW public ownership, collective ownership; ♦ **in ~ überführen** POL, VW nationalize, bring under public ownership, communize

Gemeinkosten *pl* FINANZ overheads, IND on costs, RECHNUNG fixed charge, fixed costs, overheads, overhead charge, overhead costs, general cost, general expenses, VERWALT burden, general cost, VW burden, common costs; ♦ **~ verrechnen** RECHNUNG absorb overheads

Gemeinkosten: **Gemeinkostendeckung** *f* FINANZ overheads recovery; **Gemeinkostenlöhne** *m pl* VW indirect labor costs (*AmE*), indirect labour costs (*BrE*); **Gemeinkostenumlage** *f* VERWALT allocation of overheads; **Gemeinkostenunterdeckung** *f* RECHNUNG underapplied overhead, underrecovery of overhead costs; **Gemeinkostenverrechnung** *f* RECHNUNG allocation of overheads

gemeinnützig *adj* FINANZ, GESCHÄFT, RECHNUNG, STEUER non-profit-making, not-for-profit; **~e Gesellschaft** *f* GESCHÄFT non-profit-making company, nonprofit corporation (*AmE*); **~e Organisation** *f* VW non-profit-making organization, nonprofit organization (*AmE*); **~es Unternehmen** *nt* VW nonprofit enterprise (*NPE*)

gemeinsam 1. *adj* GESCHÄFT collective, common, joint, *Gemeinschaftsaktivitäten* collaborative, PERSON *Projekt* collaborative; ♦ **~e Haltung einnehmen** GESCHÄFT adopt a joint stance; **2.** *adv* GESCHÄFT collectively; ♦ **~ mit** GESCHÄFT in association with; **~ arbeiten mit** GESCHÄFT work in tandem with; **~ benutzen** COMP share

gemeinsam: **~e Agrarpolitik** *f* (*GAP*) POL, VW *EG* Common Agricultural Policy (*CAP*); **~e Anleihe** *f* BANK joint loan; **~er Anmelder** *m*, **~e Anmelderin** *f* PATENT joint applicant; **~er Antrag** *m* KOMM round robin; **~er Arabischer Markt** *m* VW *arabische Liga* Arab Common Market; **~e Arbeitsgruppe** *f* PERSON joint working party (*JWP*); **~e Aufgabe** *f* GESCHÄFT joint assignment; **~er Ausgleichszoll** *m* VW compensating common tariff; **~e Auslieferung** *f* TRANSP consolidated delivery; **~er Ausschuß** *m* PERSON joint committee; **~er Außenzoll** *m* VW *EG* common external tariff (*CET*); **~es Bankkonto** *nt* BANK joint bank account; **~e Befugnis** *f* BANK joint authorization; **~e Bekanntgabe** *f* **von Interesse** BANK joint declaration of interest (*JDI*); **~e Bemühung** *f* GESCHÄFT concerted effort; **~e Beratung** *f* MGMNT, PERSON joint consultation; **~er Beratungsausschuß** *m* PERSON joint consultative committee; **~e Bezeichnung** *f* PATENT joint designation; **~e Dateinutzung** *f* COMP *Zugriff* file sharing; **~e Datenbank** *f* COMP shared database; **~es Eigentum** *nt* GRUND property held in joint names; **~er Eigentümer** *m*, **~e Eigentümerin** *f* GRUND joint owner; **~er Einsatz** *m* TRANSP joint service; **~ emittierte Schuldverschreibung** *f* BÖRSE joint bond; **~er**

Energiefonds *m* UMWELT energy mutual fund; **~e Erklärung** *f* GESCHÄFT joint statement; **~er Fahrpreis** *m* TRANSP joint fare; **~er Fonds** *m* FINANZ, GESCHÄFT pool; **~e Garantie** *f* FINANZ joint guarantee; **~e Gebühr** *f* TRANSP joint charge; **~ genutzte Datenbank** *f* COMP shared database; **~e Grenze** *f* IMP/EXP mutual border; **~ haftbar sein** *phr* RECHT be jointly liable; **~ haften** GESCHÄFT be jointly liable; **~e Haftung** *f* BANK, RECHT joint liability; **~e Handelsbank** *f* BANK joint-venture merchant bank; **~e Investitionsbank** *f* BANK joint-venture investment bank; **~es Konto** *nt* BANK joint account (*J/A*); **~er Ladetank** *m* TRANSP common cargo tank; **~er Markt** *m* VW *EG* common market (*CM*); **~er Markt** *m* **der Anden** VW Andean Common Market (*ACM, ANCOM*); **unter die ~e Marktordnung** *f* **fallende Agra** VW CAP goods; **~e Negoziierung** *f* BÖRSE joint negotiation; **~er Nenner** *m* GESCHÄFT *Entscheidungsfindung* common denominator, PERSON *Abstimmung, Gewerkschaftsbewegung* common distinguishing factor; **~e Petition** *f* KOMM *Unterschriften sind kreisförmig angeordnet.* round robin; **~e Politik** *f* GESCHÄFT, POL common policy; **~er Preis** *m* TRANSP joint rate; **~er Produktionsausschuß** *m* PERSON joint production committee; **~e Prüfer** *m pl* RECHNUNG joint auditors; **~e Richtlinie** *f* RECHT *EG* common directive; **~es Sorgerecht** *nt* BANK joint custody; **~e Sprache** *f* GESCHÄFT common language; **~e Steuererklärung** *f* STEUER consolidated tax return, joint return; **~es System** *nt* STEUER common system; **~e Verbindlichkeit** *f* BANK joint liability; **~es Verhandeln** *nt* BÖRSE, MGMNT joint negotiation; **~e Verhandlung** *f* BÖRSE, MGMNT joint negotiation; **~e Verhandlungen** *pl* GESCHÄFT, PERSON joint negotiations; **~e Werbung** *f* **von Hersteller und Einzelhändler** V&M tie-in promotion

Gemeinsam: ~er Zolltarif *m* (*GZT*) IMP/EXP *EG* common customs tariff (*CCT*)

gemeinsam: **~er Zugriff** *m* **auf Daten** COMP data sharing

Gemeinschaft *f* GESCHÄFT community, KOMM community network; **~ Unabhängiger Staaten** (*GUS*) POL Commonwealth of Independent States (*CIS*)

gemeinschaftlich *adj* GESCHÄFT collective; **~es Eigentum** *nt* PERSON social ownership; **~e Leitung** *f* MGMNT joint management

Gemeinschaft: **Gemeinschaftsaktion** *f* GESCHÄFT Community action; **Gemeinschaftsausschuß** *m* KOMM party line; **Gemeinschaftsbehandlung** *f* IMP/EXP *EG* Community treatment; **Gemeinschaftsberatung** *f* GESCHÄFT joint consultations; **Gemeinschaftsbesitz** *m* GRUND communal ownership; **Gemeinschaftsbetrieb** *m* COMP time-sharing; **Gemeinschaftsbilanz** *f* RECHNUNG consolidated balance sheet; **Gemeinschaftsbudget** *nt* VW Community budget; **Gemeinschaftsschulsystem** *nt* SOZIAL cooperative education; **Gemeinschaftsdarlehen** *nt* FINANZ participation loan; **Gemeinschaftseigentum** *nt* GRUND communal ownership, res communis, RECHT res communis; **in Gemeinschaftseigentum überführen** *phr* GRUND communize; **Gemeinschaftseinfuhren** *f pl* IMP/EXP *EG* Community imports; **Gemeinschaftsfirma** *f* MGMNT joint-venture company; **Gemeinschaftsfläche** *f* GRUND common elements; **Gemeinschaftsgeist** *m* GESCHÄFT community spirit, esprit de corps; **Gemeinschaftsgut** *nt* RECHT community property; **Gemeinschaftshaushalt** *m* VW Community budget;

Gemeinschaftshilfe *f* VW Community aid; **Gemeinschaftskonto** *nt* BANK joint account (*J/A*), tandem account; **Gemeinschaftskontovertrag** *m* BANK joint account agreement; **Gemeinschaftskredit** *m* FINANZ syndicated loan; **Gemeinschaftsmarke** *f* V&M distributors' brand; **Gemeinschaftsmarkt** *m* VW single market; **Gemeinschaftsmaßnahme** *f* GESCHÄFT *EG* Community action; **Gemeinschaftspraxis** *f* SOZIAL health center (*AmE*), health centre (*BrE*); **Gemeinschaftsprogramm** *nt* PERSON community program (*CP*) (*AmE*), community programme (*CP*) (*BrE*); **Gemeinschaftsroute** *f* TRANSP multi-user route; **Gemeinschaftssatzung** *f* **zu grundlegenden Sozialrechten der Arbeiter** PERSON Community Charter of Fundamental Social Rights of Workers; **Gemeinschaftssinn** *m* GESCHÄFT community spirit, PERSON *gute Zusammenarbeit* team spirit; **Gemeinschafts-Solawechsel** *m* FINANZ joint promissory note; **Gemeinschaftsunternehmen** *nt* BÖRSE, GESCHÄFT, MGMNT, RECHNUNG, VW joint venture (*JV*); **Gemeinschaftsunternehmung** *f* GESCHÄFT equity joint venture; **Gemeinschaftsverhandlung** *f* GESCHÄFT joint negotiations, MGMNT joint negotiation, PERSON joint negotiations; **Gemeinschaftsvermögen** *nt* GRUND, RECHT res communis; **Gemeinschaftsvertretung** *f* GESCHÄFT, MGMNT, PERSON joint representation; **Gemeinschaftswährung** *f* VW common currency; **Gemeinschaftswaren** *f pl* IMP/EXP Community goods; **Gemeinschaftswerbung** *f* V&M cooperative advertising

Gemeinwesen *nt* GESCHÄFT community

gemeldet: **~e Arbeitslosigkeit** *f* PERSON registered unemployment

gemessen: **~e Zeitlohnarbeit** *f* PERSON measured day-work (*MDW*)

gemietet: **~es Grundstück** *nt* GESCHÄFT leasehold estate

gemischt *adj* GESCHÄFT composite, SOZIAL *Schule* coeducational (*co-ed*); **~e Auktion** *f* BÖRSE hybrid auction; **~e Dachgesellschaft** *f* FINANZ mixed-activity holding company; **~e Ergebnisse** *nt pl* GESCHÄFT mixed results; **~es Gymnasium** *nt* SOZIAL coeducational high school; **~e Ladung** *f* TRANSP mixed consignment; **~e Lebensversicherung** *f* VERSICH endowment assurance, endowment insurance, endowment life assurance, endowment life insurance; **~e Oberschule** *f* SOZIAL coeducational high school; **~es Risiko** *nt* VERSICH mixed perils (*AmE*); **~er Wertzoll** *m* IMP/EXP compound duty; **~e Wirtschaftsform** *f* VW mixed economic system

Gemischtwaren *f pl* GESCHÄFT general merchandise, V&M *Auswahl von Waren bei einem Einzelhändler* mix

gemischtwirtschaftlich: **~es System** *nt* VW mixed economic system

Gemüseanbau *m* VW market gardening (*BrE*), truck farming (*AmE*); **Gemüseanbauer** *m* VW market gardener (*BrE*), truck farmer (*AmE*)

Gemütsverfassung *f* GESCHÄFT frame of mind

genannt: **~es Amt** *nt* PATENT designated office

genau 1. *adj* GESCHÄFT accurate, MATH exact; ♦ **mit ~en Angaben versehen** GESCHÄFT specified; **einer ~en Prüfung unterzogen werden** GESCHÄFT come under scrutiny; **2.** *adv* GESCHÄFT accurately, exactly; ♦ **~ um sieben Uhr** GESCHÄFT at seven o'clock sharp

genau: **~es Einhalten** *nt* **des Vertrags** RECHT strict adherence to the contract; **~e Prüfung** *f* GESCHÄFT close examination

genauestens: ~ überprüfen *phr* GESCHÄFT vet

Genauigkeit *f* GESCHÄFT, RECHNUNG accuracy

genehmigen *vt* BANK *Kredit, Darlehen* approve, GESCHÄFT approve, allow, ratify, authorize, RECHNUNG *Gelder* appropriate for, RECHT permit

genehmigend *adj* GESCHÄFT approving

genehmigt *adj* COMP, VERSICH approved, VW appropriated; **nicht ~** *adj* BÖRSE nonapproved; **~e Aktien** *f pl* BÖRSE authorized shares; **nicht ~e Aktien** *f pl* BÖRSE unauthorized shares; **~es Aktienkapital** *nt* BÖRSE authorized stock; **nicht ~e finanzielle Mittel** *nt pl* FINANZ unapproved funds; **~er Gewinnbeteiligungsplan** *m* PERSON *Arbeitnehmerbeteiligung* approved profit-sharing scheme (*BrE*); **~es Kapital** *nt* FINANZ authorized share capital, VW authorized capital; **~er Kredit** *m* BANK authorized credit; **~er Marketingfonds** *m* V&M marketing appropriation; **~er Ort** *m* VERWALT *Stelle* approved place; **nicht ~er Pensionsplan** *m* FINANZ nonapproved pension scheme; **~er Preis** *m* GESCHÄFT, POL approved price; **nicht ~er Streik** *m* PERSON unofficial strike; **~er Werbeetat** *m* V&M appropriation of advertising

Genehmigung *f* BANK, GESCHÄFT approval, authorization, IMP/EXP *Produkteinfuhr* homologation, licence (*BrE*), license (*AmE*), PATENT authorization, RECHT permit; **~ durch Dritte** V&M third-party endorsement; **~ zur Erdölsuche** UMWELT oil exploration licence (*BrE*), oil exploration license (*AmE*); **~ zur Gasexploration** UMWELT gas exploration licence (*BrE*), gas exploration license (*AmE*); **~ für Gefahrgütertransport** TRANSP dangerous goods authority form; **~ unter Vorbehalt** GESCHÄFT authorization under consideration (*AC*); **~ eines Vertreters** RECHT agent by ratification; **~ einer Vertretung** RECHT agency by ratification; ♦ **zur ~** GESCHÄFT for approval; **jds ~ einholen** GESCHÄFT seek sb's approval; **die ~ haben von** GESCHÄFT have the approval of

Genehmigung: **Genehmigungs-Code** *m* BANK authorization code

genehmigungsfrei *adj* RECHT permit-free

Genehmigung: **Genehmigungsnummer** *f* BANK authorization number

genehmigungspflichtig *adj* GESCHÄFT subject to approval, IMP/EXP licensable, V&M subject to approval

Genehmigung: **Genehmigungsprozess** *m* BANK approval process; **Genehmigungsschreiben** *nt* GESCHÄFT letter of authority (*L/A*); **Genehmigungsstelle** *f* BANK authorization center (*AmE*), authorization centre (*BrE*); **Genehmigungsverfahren** *nt* VW licensing procedure; **Genehmigungszeichen** *nt* TRANSP approval mark

General- *in cpds* GESCHÄFT general; **Generalbevollmächtigte(r)** *mf* [decl. as adj] MGMNT *eines Unternehmens* chief executive, PERSON agent general (*AG*), Accountant General (*AG*), RECHT general agent, VERWALT agent general (*AG*), Accountant General (*AG*); **Generaldirektor, in** *m,f* (*GD*) MGMNT *eines Unternehmens* general executive, general manager, executive director, president, chief executive, PERSON managing director (*BrE*) (*MD*), *Unternehmensleitung* director general; **Generalgouverneur** *m* POL Governor General

Generalist, in *m,f* PERSON generalist

General-: **Generalkonsul** *m* GESCHÄFT, POL Consul-General; **Generalpolice** *f* SOZIAL floating policy, TRANSP floating marine policy (*FP*), VERSICH floating marine policy (*FP*), blanket contract, block policy, floater (*AmE*), floating policy; **Generalsekretär, in** *m,f* PERSON General Secretary; **Generalstaatsanwalt** *m*, **Generalstaatsanwältin** *f* RECHT Attorney General (*BrE*) (*Atty Gen*); **Generalstabschef** *m* PERSON chief of staff; **Generalstreik** *m* PERSON general strike; **Generalunternehmer** *m* GESCHÄFT general contractor, VW main contractor; **Generalvertrag** *m* GESCHÄFT, PERSON blanket agreement, RECHT blanket agreement, blanket contract; **Generalvertreter, in** *m,f* GESCHÄFT universal agent, PERSON agent general (*AG*), RECHT *Generalbevollmächtigter* universal agent, VERWALT agent general (*AG*); **Generalvollmacht** *f* GESCHÄFT general authorization (*GA*)

Generation *f* IND generation; **Generationenkonflikt** *m* SOZIAL generation conflict; **Generationenproblem** *nt* SOZIAL generation gap; **Generationenvertrag** *m* VW intergenerational equity; **Generationskonflikt** *m* SOZIAL generation conflict; **Generationsproblem** *nt* SOZIAL generation gap

Generator *m* GESCHÄFT generator (*gen*)

generell *adj* GESCHÄFT across-the-board; **~e Erhöhung** *f* MGMNT across-the-board increase; **~e Exportförderung** *f* VW across-the-board export promotion; **~e Prüfung** *f* RECHNUNG across-the-board investigation

Generierung *f* COMP generation

generisch: ~e Bezeichnungen *f pl* **für Arbeitsplätze** PERSON generic job grades, generic job titles

genetisch *adj* GESCHÄFT genetic

Genf: ~er Börse *f* BÖRSE Geneva Stock Exchange

Genie *nt* GESCHÄFT child prodigy, whiz kid (*infrml*)

genießen *vt* GESCHÄFT *Ruf* enjoy

genormt *adj* GESCHÄFT standardized; **~e Größe** *f* GESCHÄFT basic size

Genossenschaft *f* GESCHÄFT association, cooperative society, cooperative (*co-op*)

genossenschaftlich: ~es Absatzwesen *nt* V&M cooperative marketing; **~er Ein- und Verkauf** *m* **in der Landwirtschaft** VW cooperative farming

genossenschaftsähnlich: ~e Bank *f* BANK, VW mutual savings bank; **~e Sparkasse** *f* BANK mutual savings bank

Genossenschaft: **auf Genossenschaftsbasis** *phr* IND, MGMNT, PERSON, VW cooperative; **Genossenschaftswohnung** *f* GRUND cooperative (*co-op*)

Gentechnik *f* GESCHÄFT genetic engineering

Gentleman's-Agreement *nt* RECHT gentleman's agreement

Gentrifizierung *f jarg* SOZIAL, UMWELT, VW gentrification (*jarg*)

genug *adv* GESCHÄFT sufficient

genügend 1. *adj* GESCHÄFT sufficient; **2.** *adv* ♦ **nicht ~ kapitalisiert** IND undercapitalized; **nicht ~ produzieren** IND underproduce; **nicht ~ Wechselgeld herausgeben** GESCHÄFT short-change

genutzt: ~e Ressource *f* UMWELT exploited resource

geöffnet: ab neun Uhr ~ *phr* GESCHÄFT doors open at nine

geographisch *adj* GESCHÄFT geographic; **~e Breite** *f*

GESCHÄFT latitude (*lat.*); **~es Gebiet** *nt* GESCHÄFT geographical area; **~e Handelsstruktur** *f* VW geographical trade structure

geometrisch: ~e Folge *f* MATH geometric progression; **~es Mittel** *nt* MATH geometric mean (*GM*); **~er Mittelwert** *m* MATH geometric mean (*GM*)

geopolitisch *adj* POL geopolitical

Gepäck *nt* FREI, TRANSP baggage, luggage; **Gepäckabfertigung** *f* FREI, TRANSP baggage handling; **Gepäckanforderung** *f* TRANSP reclaiming; **Gepäckanhänger** *m* FREI, TRANSP baggage tag; **Gepäckaufbewahrung** *f* TRANSP checkroom (*AmE*), left-luggage office (*BrE*); **Gepäckaufbewahrungsstelle** *f* GESCHÄFT checkroom (*AmE*), luggage lockers (*BrE*); **Gepäckaufkleber** *m* FREI, TRANSP baggage tag; **Gepäckausgabe** *f* FREI, TRANSP baggage reclaim area, reclaim area; **Gepäckbeförderung** *f* FREI, TRANSP baggage handling; **Gepäckkontrolle** *f* FREI, TRANSP baggage check; **Gepäckschein** *m* FREI, TRANSP baggage check; **Gepäckübergewichtsgebühr** *f* FREI, TRANSP excess baggage charge; **Gepäckwagen** *m* FREI, TRANSP baggage vehicle

gepfändet: ~es Eigentum *nt* GRUND distressed property

gepfeffert *adj infrml* GESCHÄFT, VW *Preis* steep (*infrml*)

Gepflogenheiten *f pl* PERSON custom and practice, RECHT *Vertragsrecht* standard practice

geplant: ~es Grundstückserschließungsprojekt *nt* GRUND planned unit development (*PUD*); **~e Kapazität** *f* VW planned capacity; **~e Kosten** *pl* **über Ist-Kosten** RECHNUNG favorable variance (*AmE*), favourable variance (*BrE*), favorable difference (*AmE*), favourable difference (*BrE*); **~e Umsätze** *m pl* V&M anticipated sales; **~es Veralten** *nt* V&M, VW built-in obsolescence, planned obsolescence; **~er Verkauf** *m* V&M planned selling; **~er Verschleiß** *m* V&M, VW built-in obsolescence, planned obsolescence

geplatzt: ~e Kampagne *f* V&M burst campaign; **~er Scheck** *m* BANK, GESCHÄFT bounced check (*AmE*), bounced cheque (*BrE*)

geprüft *adj* GESCHÄFT examined (*ex*); **nicht ~** *adj* RECHNUNG unaudited; **~er Abschluß** *m* RECHNUNG audited accounts; **~e Auflagenmeldung** *f* V&M publisher's statement; **~er Finanzberater** *m*, **~e Finanzberaterin** *f* FINANZ chartered financial consultant; **~er Konzernabschluß** *m* RECHNUNG consolidated audited accounts; **nicht auf Programmfehler ~** *phr* COMP nondebugged; **~es Unternehmen** *nt* RECHNUNG auditee; **wird noch ~** *phr* GESCHÄFT under examination

gepunktet: ~e Linie *f* COMP, MATH, VERWALT dotted line

Gequassel *nt infrml* GESCHÄFT jabbering, spiel (*infrml*)

gerade 1. *adj* COMP even; **2.** *adv* ◆ **~ privatisiert** VW newly privatized

gerade: ~ Bitzahl *f* COMP even parity; **~ feststellbarer Unterschied** *m* VERWALT just noticeable difference; **~ Parität** *f* COMP even parity; **~r Lift** *m* TRANSP straight lift

geradzahlig *adj* GESCHÄFT even-numbered

Gerät *nt* COMP device, hardware device, GESCHÄFT appliance, device, gadget; ◆ **es wurde zu wenig in neue Geräte investiert** FINANZ there was an underspend on new equipment

Gerät: Geräteeinbau und -abnahme *f* IND equipment installation and checkout (*EIC*); **Gerätefehler** *m* GESCHÄFT equipment failure; **Geräteleasing** *nt*

GRUND, IND equipment leasing; **Geräteselbstprüfung** *f* COMP built-in check, built-in test

gerätespezifisch *adj* COMP device-specific

Gerät: Gerätetreiber *m* COMP device driver; **Geräteübergabevertrag** *m* IND equipment handover agreement

geräteunabhängig *adj* COMP device-independent

Gerät: Geräteverleih *m* IND equipment leasing

Geratewohl: aufs ~ *phr* GESCHÄFT at random, randomly, hit-or-miss (*infrml*)

geräumt *adj* GESCHÄFT *Lager* unstocked

Geräusch *nt* COMP noise; **~e** *nt pl* MEDIEN sound effects; **Geräuschpegel** *m* UMWELT noise level

gerecht *adj* GESCHÄFT equitable, RECHT *angemessen, anständig* fair, just; **~er Lohn** *m* VW just wage; **~er Preis** *m* VW just price; **~e Verteilung** *f* GESCHÄFT equitable distribution

gerechtfertigt *adj* GESCHÄFT justified, VERSICH warranted (*Wld*); **~er Preis** *m* BÖRSE justified price

Gerechtigkeit: ~ erlangen *phr* RECHT get justice

Gerede *nt* GESCHÄFT rumor (*AmE*), rumour (*BrE*)

geregelt: ~er Freiverkehr *m* BÖRSE Unlisted Securities Market (*BrE*) (*USM*); **~er Markt** *m* BÖRSE Unlisted Securities Market (*BrE*) (*USM*); **~er Wertpapiermarkt** *m* VW organized stock market

gereinigt *adj* IND refined

Gericht *nt* RECHT court; **~ erster Instanz** RECHT Court of First Instance; **~ des Lordkanzlers** RECHT court of chancery; **~ zuständig für Wettbewerbsbeschränkungen** RECHT Restrictive Practices Court (*BrE*); ◆ **vor ~ aussagen** RECHT give evidence; **vor ~ erscheinen** RECHT appear in court, come before court; **zu ~ sitzen** RECHT sit in judgment; **das ~ tagt** RECHT court is now in session

gerichtlich 1. *adj* RECHT *richterlich* judicial; **2.** *adv* RECHT *gerichtlich* judicially; ◆ **~ entscheiden** RECHT adjudge to

gerichtlich: ~e Angelegenheiten *f pl* RECHT judicial affairs; **~e Einsetzung** *f* **eines Zwangsverwalters** RECHT writ of sequestration; **~e einstweilige Verfügung** *f* RECHT temporary injunction; **~er Liquidationsbeschluß** *m* RECHT *Gesellschaftsrecht* winding-up order; **~e Position** *f* RECHT juridical position; **~er Schiedsrichter** *m* RECHT judicial arbitrator; **~e Schritte** *m pl* RECHT legal action; **~es Verfahren** *nt* RECHT court proceedings; **~e Vollstreckung** *f* **aus einem Grundpfandrecht** RECHT judicial foreclosure

Gerichtsbarkeit *f* RECHT *Befugnis, Recht zu sprechen und einen Fall zu verhandeln* jurisdiction; ◆ **es fällt unter unsere ~** RECHT it comes under our jurisdiction

Gerichtsbefehl *m* RECHT warrant; ◆ **jdm einen ~ zustellen** RECHT serve sb with a warrant

Gericht: Gerichtsbekanntmachung *f* RECHT legal notice; **Gerichtsbezirk** *m* RECHT circuit, jurisdiction; **Gerichtsdiener** *m* GRUND, RECHT bailiff; **Gerichtshof** *m* GESCHÄFT forum, RECHT court; **Gerichtshof der Europäischen Union** RECHT EG European Court of Justice; **Gerichtskosten** *pl* RECHT *Anwaltsgebühren* legal charges, VW costs; **Gerichtssaal** *m* RECHT courtroom, court; **Gerichtsstandsvereinbarung** *f* RECHT *Vertragsrecht* stipulation as to venue; **Gerichtsurteil** *nt* RECHT *Urteilsfindung* finding; **Gerichtsverfahren** *nt pl* RECHT court procedures, judicial proceedings, legal proceedings; **Gerichtsvollzieher** *m* GRUND, RECHT bailiff; **Gerichtswesen** *nt* RECHT judiciary

gering *adj* GESCHÄFT small, minor, light; ♦ **bei ~em Angebot** GESCHÄFT in scarce supply; **in ~em Maße** GESCHÄFT on a small scale

gering: **~e Deckung** *f* MEDIEN scant coverage; **~e Ersparnisse** *f pl* FINANZ small savings; **zu ~e Investition** *f* BANK underinvestment; **~er Schaden** *m* VERSICH small damage (*s/d*); **~e Spanne** *f* RECHNUNG narrow margin; **~ belastetes Konto** *nt* BANK undercharged account

geringer: **in ~em Maße** *phr* GESCHÄFT to a lesser extent

geringfügig 1. *adj* GESCHÄFT trifling, slight; **2.** *adv* GESCHÄFT modestly; ♦ **~ umweltverschmutzend** UMWELT low-polluting

geringfügig: **~ Beschäftigte(r)** *m,f* [decl. as adj] PERSON peripheral worker; **~e Entlohnung** *f* GESCHÄFT pin money; **~er Ladendiebstahl** *m* GESCHÄFT grazing (*jarg*); **~er Mangel** *m* RECHT *Vertragsrecht* minor defect; **~er Schaden** *m* VERSICH small damage (*s/d*)

Geringverdiener *m pl* PERSON the low-paid

gerissen: **~er Geschäftemacher** *m* *infrml* GESCHÄFT wheeler-dealer (*infrml*)

Germanisch: **~er Lloyd** *m* (*GL*) TRANSP Germanischer Lloyd (*GL*)

Gerschenkron-Effekt *m* vw Gerschenkron effect

Gerücht *nt* GESCHÄFT rumor (*AmE*), rumour (*BrE*), hearsay; **Gerüchteküche** *f* GESCHÄFT grapevine

gesammelt: **~e Richtlinien** *f pl* GESCHÄFT set of rules

Gesamt- *in cpds* GESCHÄFT, VERSICH, VW aggregate, all-in, all-round, collective, overall

gesamt *adj* GESCHÄFT all-in, all-inclusive, all-out, overall (*oa*), whole, RECHNUNG gross, VW aggregate; **~e gesparte Zeit** *f* TRANSP all time saved; **~e Konsequenzen** *f pl* GESCHÄFT full implications; **~e Löhne** *m pl* **und Gehälter** *nt pl* RECHNUNG total wages and salaries; **~er Nettofluß** *m* VW total net flow; **~er Nicht-Haushalt** *m* FINANZ total non-budget; **~e öffentliche Ausgaben** *f pl* VW total public spending; **~e Soziallasten** *f pl* RECHNUNG total social charges; **~e Staatsverschuldung** *f* VW total public debt; **~e zur Verfügung gestellte Mittel** *nt pl* FINANZ total funds provided

Gesamt-: **Gesamtabrechnung** *f* RECHNUNG aggregate statement; **Gesamtabschreibung** *f* vw aggregate depreciation; **Gesamtaktivitäten** *f pl* GESCHÄFT activity total; **Gesamtangebotskurve** *f* VW aggregate supply curve; **Gesamtanlagenwartung** *f* GESCHÄFT, IND total plant maintenance; **Gesamtauftrag** *m* FREI, V&M block booking; **Gesamtausfall** *m* **der Stromversorgung** COMP blackout; **Gesamtausgabenansätze** *m pl* FINANZ *im Haushalt* total estimates; **Gesamtausleihungen** *f pl* FINANZ loan exposure; **Gesamtbasenzahl** *f* (*TBN*) IND total base number (*TBN*); **Gesamtbasispreis** *m* BÖRSE aggregate exercise price; **Gesamtbetrag** *m* FINANZ total, GESCHÄFT full lot, RECHNUNG gross amount; **Gesamtbetrag** *m* **der Staatsausgaben** VW total public spending; **Gesamtbilanz** *f* GESCHÄFT general statement, RECHNUNG consolidated balance sheet, general statement; **Gesamtbreite** *f* TRANSP overall width; **Gesamtbuchwert** *m* RECHNUNG aggregate book value; **Gesamtbudget** *nt* FINANZ total budget, RECHNUNG master budget; **Gesamtdarlehen** *nt* FINANZ whole loan;

Gesamtdeadweight *nt* TRANSP deadweight all told (*dwat*); **Gesamtdurchschnitt** *m* MATH, VERSICH general average (*G/A, GA*); **Gesamteigentum** *nt* RECHT joint tenancy; **Gesamteinnahmen** *f pl* vw total revenue; **Gesamteintrag** *m* RECHNUNG compound entry; **Gesamtentwicklung** *f* VW overall development; **Gesamtetat** *m* V&M billing; **Gesamtfertilitätsrate** *f* vw total fertility rate (*TRF*); **Gesamtfinanzierung** *f* FINANZ financing package; **Gesamtfrachtcharter** *f* TRANSP whole cargo charter; **Gesamtfrühindikator** *m* BÖRSE composite leading indicator; **Gesamtgeschäftsführung** *f* MGMNT general management, joint management; **Gesamtgewicht** *nt* GESCHÄFT full weight; **Gesamthauseigentümer** *m pl* **mit Überlebensfallrecht** RECHT joint tenants with right of survivorship; **Gesamthaushalt** *m* FINANZ comprehensive budget; **Gesamthaushaltsberichtigungsgesetz** *nt* FINANZ, STEUER Omnibus Budget Reconciliation Act (*OBRA*)

Gesamtheit *f* GESCHÄFT entirety; **~ der Gläubiger** RECHNUNG body of creditors; ♦ **als ~** GESCHÄFT collectively

Gesamt-: **Gesamthypothek** *f* BANK blanket mortgage, general mortgage; **durch Gesamthypothek besicherte Schuldverschreibung** *f* BÖRSE blanket bond; **Gesamtjahresabschluß** *m* vw comprehensive annual financial report (*CAFR*); **Gesamtjahreswachstum** *nt* VW compound annual growth; **Gesamtkapitalausstattung** *f* **einer Unternehmung** FINANZ capital fund; **Gesamtkapitalisierung** *f* FINANZ total capitalization; **Gesamtkapitalrentabilität** *f* FINANZ, RECHNUNG asset turnover, return on assets (*ROA*); **Gesamtkosten** *pl* GESCHÄFT, VW total costs; **Gesamtkostenmethode** *f* RECHNUNG overall expenses method; **Gesamtkreditkosten** *pl* **für den Verbraucher** FINANZ total cost of the credit to the consumer; **Gesamtlänge** *f* MEDIEN footage; **Gesamtleistung** *f* VW overall performance; **Gesamtnachfrage** *f* VW market demand; **Gesamtnachfrage-Gesamtangebot** *phr* VW aggregate demand-aggregate supply (*AD-AS*); **Gesamtnachfragekurve** *f* vw aggregate demand curve; **Gesamtplan** *m* MGMNT, VW master plan; **Gesamtpreis** *m* GESCHÄFT all-round price; **Gesamtproduktion** *f* VW aggregate production; **Gesamtqualitätskontrolle** *f* IND, MGMNT total quality control (*TQC*); **Gesamtqualitätsleitung** *f* MGMNT total quality management (*TQM*); **Gesamtqualitätssicherung** *f* MGMNT total quality management (*TQM*); **Gesamtqualitätsüberwachung** *f* MGMNT total quality management (*TQM*); **Gesamtreichweite** *f* V&M cumulative reach; **Gesamtrendite** *f* VW total yield; **Gesamtrentabilität** *f* VW operating efficiency; **Gesamtrisiko** *nt* GESCHÄFT aggregate risk; **Gesamtsaldo** *m* RECHNUNG aggregate balance; **Gesamtschaden** *m* VERSICH total loss (*T/L*); **Gesamtschaden-Exzedenten-Rückversicherung** *f* VERSICH stop loss insurance; **Gesamtschulbildung** *f* SOZIAL comprehensive school education; **Gesamtschulden** *f pl* FINANZ gross debt

gesamtschuldnerisch *adv* RECHT jointly and severally; ♦ **~ haftbar** RECHT jointly liable

gesamtschuldnerisch: **~e Haftung** *f* RECHT joint and several liability

Gesamt-: **Gesamtsteueraufkommen** *nt* STEUER, VW total revenue; **Gesamtsumme** *f* FINANZ principal sum, GESCHÄFT grand total, full lot; **Gesamttragfähigkeit** *f* TRANSP deadweight all told (*dwat*); **Gesamtumsatz** *m* BÖRSE book inventory; **Gesamtumsatz** *m* **eines Wertpapierhändlers** BÖRSE book; **Gesamtverantwortung** *f* GESCHÄFT comprehensive responsibility

gesamtverbindlich: **~e Verpflichtung** *f* RECHT joint and several obligation

Gesamt-: **Gesamtvergleich** *m* **mit Gläubigern** RECHT composition; **Gesamtverkaufseinnahmen** *f pl* V&M sales revenue; **Gesamtvermögen** *nt* RECHNUNG total assets; **Gesamtverschuldung** *f* **des Staates** VW total public debt; **Gesamtversicherung** *f* VERSICH all-loss insurance, all-risk insurance, all-risks insurance; **Gesamtvertrag** *m* PERSON comprehensive agreement; **Gesamtwachstumsrate** *f* VW compound growth rate; **Gesamtwerbeaufwand** *m* V&M media weight; **Gesamtwert** *m* STEUER aggregate value; **Gesamtwertindex** *m* BÖRSE Value Line Composite Index (*AmE*); **Gesamtwirtschaft** *f* VW national economy

gesamtwirtschaftlich *adj* VW aggregate; **~e Bedarfsliste** *f* VW macroeconomic demand schedule; **~e Konzentration** *f* VW aggregate concentration; **~e Produktion** *f* VW aggregate production; **~er Rahmenplan** *m* VW overall economic plan; **~es Rechnungswesen** *nt* RECHNUNG System of National Accounts (*SNA*); **~e Vermögensbildung** *f* VW aggregate wealth formation; **~e Wertminderung** *f* VW aggregate depreciation; **~e Wertschöpfung** *f* VW aggregate value added

Gesamt-: **Gesamtwirtschaftspolitik** *f* VW macroeconomic policy; **Gesamtzahl** *f* **der Werbeträger** V&M *Werbemittel* total effective exposure; **Gesamtziele** *nt pl* **des Unternehmens** GESCHÄFT overall company objectives; **Gesamtzuladungsgewicht** *nt* GESCHÄFT, TRANSP deadweight tonnage (*dwt*)

Gesandte(r) *mf* [decl. as adj] POL ambassador

gesättigt: **~er Markt** *m* V&M mature market

geschädigt: **~e Partei** *f* RECHT aggrieved party

Geschädigte(r) *mf* [decl. as adj] RECHT aggrieved party, injured party, wronged party, VERSICH claimant

Geschäft *nt* GESCHÄFT *Handel, Kommerz* business, trade, dealing, *Abschluß* deal, transaction, bargain, *Firma* business, concern, enterprise, operation, *Laden* shop (*BrE*), store (*AmE*), *infrml Büro* office, V&M sale; **~ mit Artikeln des täglichen Bedarfs** V&M corner shop (*BrE*), neighborhood store (*AmE*), mom-and-pop store (*AmE*); **~ mit aufgeschobener Erfüllung** BÖRSE, RECHNUNG account transaction; **~ für zollfreie Waren** FREI, IMP/EXP, STEUER duty-free shop (*BrE*), tax-free shop (*AmE*); ◆ **ein ~ abschließen** GESCHÄFT strike a deal, strike a bargain; **ein ~ zum Abschluß führen** GESCHÄFT task closure; **ein ~ aufmachen** GESCHÄFT start in business, open a business; **aus einem ~ aussteigen** BÖRSE cash in; **ein ~ betreiben** GESCHÄFT run a business; **ein ~ durchführen** GESCHÄFT make a transaction; **von ~ zu ~** GESCHÄFT business to business; **das ~ hat einen Tiefststand erreicht** GESCHÄFT business is at a low ebb; **das ~ ist ruhig** GESCHÄFT business is slack; **das ~ perfekt machen** GESCHÄFT swing the deal; **über das ~ reden** GESCHÄFT talk business; **das ~ schließen** GESCHÄFT shut up shop; **ein ~ unter Dach und Fach bringen** GESCHÄFT swing

the deal; **sich vom ~ zurückziehen** GESCHÄFT retire from business

Geschäfte *nt pl* GESCHÄFT operations, business, MGMNT dealings; ◆ **jds ~ führen** MGMNT manage sb's affairs; **~ tätigen** GESCHÄFT do business

Geschäfte: **Geschäftemacher** *m infrml* GESCHÄFT profiteer, wheeler-dealer (*infrml*)

geschäftlich 1. *adj* GESCHÄFT on business, MGMNT managerial; **2.** *adv* GESCHÄFT commercially; ◆ **~ ausgerichtet** GESCHÄFT business-oriented; **~ unterwegs sein** GESCHÄFT be on the road

geschäftlich: **~e Angelegenheiten** *f pl* GESCHÄFT business affairs, mercantile affairs; **~e Beziehungen** *f pl* MGMNT business relations; **~e Entwicklung** *f* GESCHÄFT, MGMNT business development; **~e Haftung** *f* RECHT business liability; **~e Nutzung** *f* GRUND commercial occupancy; **~es Treffen** *nt* GESCHÄFT business meeting; **~e Verbindung** *f* GESCHÄFT affiliation; **~er Vorschlag** *m* GESCHÄFT business proposition; **~er Zusammenbruch** *m* GESCHÄFT business failure

Geschäft: **Geschäftsabschluß** *m* GESCHÄFT deal; **Geschäftsadresse** *f* GESCHÄFT business address; **Geschäftsanteil** *m* MGMNT trust share; **einen Geschäftsanteil an einem Unternehmen besitzen** *phr* GESCHÄFT have a share in a business; **Geschäftsanteile an einem Unternehmen halten** *phr* GESCHÄFT have holdings in a company; **Geschäftsauftrag** *m* MGMNT corporate mission; **Geschäftsausdehnung** *f* MGMNT business expansion; **Geschäftsausgaben** *f pl* RECHNUNG expenses; **Geschäftsaussichten** *f pl* VW business outlook; **Geschäftsbank** *f* BANK commercial bank, money center bank (*AmE*), money centre bank (*BrE*), business bank, retail bank, FINANZ, VW commercial bank; **Geschäftsbedingungen** *f pl* GESCHÄFT business conditions; **Geschäftsbekanntschaft** *f* GESCHÄFT, MGMNT business acquaintance; **Geschäftsbereich** *m* GESCHÄFT area of responsibility, sphere of activity, POL portfolio; **Geschäftsbericht** *m* RECHNUNG annual report; **Geschäftsbeschränkungen** *f pl* VW dealing restrictions; **Geschäftsbetrieb** *m* GESCHÄFT business concern, business operations; **Geschäftsbeziehungen** *f pl* GESCHÄFT business relations, MGMNT business relations, dealings, VW business relations; **Geschäftsbibliothek** *f* GESCHÄFT business library; **Geschäftsbrief** *m* GESCHÄFT business letter; **Geschäftsbuch** *nt* BANK book; **Geschäftsbücher** *nt pl* RECHNUNG accounting records, accounts; **Geschäftsbuchhaltung** *f* FINANZ financial accounting; **Geschäftschance** *f* GESCHÄFT business opportunity; **Geschäftscomputer** *m* COMP business computer; **Geschäftsdiversifizierung** *f* MGMNT business diversification; **Geschäftseigentümerpolice** *f* VERSICH business owner's policy; **Geschäftseinheit** *f* GESCHÄFT business unit, V&M shop unit (*BrE*); **Geschäftsentscheidung** *f* GESCHÄFT business decision; **Geschäftsentwicklung** *f* GESCHÄFT, MGMNT business development; **Geschäftserfahrung** *f* GESCHÄFT business experience; **Geschäftsergebnisse** *f pl* GESCHÄFT company results; **Geschäftserholung** *f* GESCHÄFT business recovery; **Geschäftserweiterung** *f* MGMNT business expansion; **Geschäftsessen** *nt* GESCHÄFT business lunch; **Geschäftsethik** *f* GESCHÄFT business ethics; **Geschäftsetikette** *f* GESCHÄFT business etiquette; **Geschäftsfähige(r)** *mf* [decl. as adj] RECHT person with full capacity to contract; **Geschäftsfeld-**

Berichterstattung *f* VERWALT business segment reporting; **Geschäftsfelder-Portfolio** *nt* VW business portfolio; **Geschäftsfluß** *m* VW business stream; **Geschäftsformular** *nt* GESCHÄFT business form; **Geschäftsfrau** *f* GESCHÄFT businesswoman, entrepreneur; **Geschäftsfreund, in** *m,f* GESCHÄFT, MGMNT business acquaintance

geschäftsführend *adj* GESCHÄFT acting, MGMNT active, PERSON, VERWALT managing; **~er Ausschuß** *m* GESCHÄFT, MGMNT management committee, POL management committee, National Executive Committee *(BrE) (NEC)*, VW management committee; **~er Direktor** *m*, **~e Direktorin** *f (GD)* MGMNT acting director, executive director, managing director *(BrE) (MD)*; **~er Gesellschafter** *m*, **~e Gesellschafterin** *f* PERSON managing partner; **~er Partner** *m*, **~e Partnerin** *f* MGMNT acting partner, active partner; **~er Vizepräsident** *m*, **~e Vizepräsidentin** *f* MGMNT executive vice-president; **~er Vorstand** *m* MGMNT executive committee

Geschäft: **Geschäftsführer, in** *m,f* GESCHÄFT leader, managing director, topper, runner, MEDIEN business manager, MGMNT manager, managing agent, business manager, PERSON business manager, director *(dir.)*, vw economic agent

Geschäftsführung *f* MGMNT, VW business management; ◆ **jdn mit der ~ beauftragen** VERWALT entrust sb with the management; **nicht an der ~ beteiligt** PERSON nonexecutive

Geschäftsführung: **Geschäftsführungsassistent, in** *m,f* VERWALT executive assistant; **Geschäftsführungsausschuß** *m* MGMNT management committee; **Geschäftsführungs- und Personalbüro** *nt* VERWALT management and personnel office *(MPO)*

Geschäft: **Geschäftsgang** *m* GESCHÄFT errand; **Geschäftsgebäude** *nt* GESCHÄFT business premises, GRUND commercial property; **Geschäftsgeheimnis** *nt* GESCHÄFT trade secret, PERSON business secret; **Geschäftsgrafik** *f* COMP, MEDIEN business graphics; **Geschäftsgrundlage** *f* RECHT *Vertragsrecht* implicit basis of contract; **Geschäftsgrundstücks- und Haftpflichtversicherungspaket** *nt* VERSICH business property and liability insurance package; **Geschäftsgründung** *f* GESCHÄFT business creation, establishment; **Geschäftshaftpflichtversicherung** *f* VERSICH business liability insurance; **Geschäftsinhaberpolice** *f* VERSICH business owner's policy; **Geschäftsinteresse** *nt* GESCHÄFT business interest, vw commercial interest; **Geschäftsjahr** *nt* FINANZ fiscal year *(FY)*, GESCHÄFT business year, trading year, RECHNUNG accounting year, financial period, fiscal year *(FY)*, trading year, STEUER accounting year, fiscal year *(FY)*; **Geschäftskapital** *nt* FINANZ capital stock *(AmE)*, share capital *(BrE)*; **Geschäftskarte** *f* GESCHÄFT, MGMNT business card; **Geschäftskonto** *nt* BANK business account, RECHNUNG commercial account; **Geschäftskonvention** *f* GESCHÄFT business convention; **auf Geschäftskosten** *phr* GESCHÄFT all expenses paid; **Geschäftskreise** *m pl* GESCHÄFT business circles; **Geschäftslage** *f* GESCHÄFT business outlook, transaction status, IND, V&M transaction status; **Geschäftslage** *f* **des Unternehmens** GESCHÄFT the company's affairs; **Geschäftsleiter, in** *m,f* **für Commerce** GESCHÄFT commercial officer; **Geschäftsleiter, in** *m,f* **eines Gerichts** RECHT head

clerk; **Geschäftsleitung** *f* MGMNT, VERWALT business management; **Geschäftsleitungskosten** *pl* RECHNUNG management accounts, management expenses; **Geschäftsleute** *pl* GESCHÄFT business people, tradespeople; **Geschäftslokal** *nt* GESCHÄFT business premises, RECHT, VERWALT business office; **Geschäftsmann** *m* GESCHÄFT businessman, entrepreneur

geschäftsmäßig: **~e Lagerung** *f* TRANSP commercial storage

Geschäft: **Geschäftsmethoden** *f pl* GESCHÄFT business policy; **Geschäftsmittelpunkt** *m* GESCHÄFT hub of activity; **Geschäftsmoral** *f* GESCHÄFT corporate morality; **den Geschäftsnamen Schmidt führen** *phr* GESCHÄFT trade under the name of Schmidt; **Geschäftsordnung** *f* BANK bylaw, POL procedure

geschäftsorientiert *adj* GESCHÄFT business-oriented

Geschäft: **Geschäftspaket** *nt* COMP *Software*, GESCHÄFT business package; **Geschäftsperiode** *f* STEUER fiscal period; **Geschäftsplan** *m* MGMNT business plan; **Geschäftsplanung** *f* MGMNT *Unternehmensplanung* corporate planning; **Geschäftspolitik** *f* GESCHÄFT, VW business policy; **Geschäftspraxis** *f* GESCHÄFT business practice; **Geschäftsprognose** *f* GESCHÄFT business outlook; **Geschäftsprogramm** *nt* FINANZ trading program *(AmE)*, trading programme *(BrE)*; **Geschäftsräume** *m pl* GESCHÄFT business premises, GRUND office premises; **Geschäftsreise** *f* FREI business travel, GESCHÄFT business trip; **Geschäftsreisende(r)** *mf* [decl. as adj] GESCHÄFT business canvasser, commercial traveler *(AmE)*, commercial traveller *(BrE)*; **Geschäftsreisende(r)** *m* [decl. as adj] GESCHÄFT traveling salesman *(AmE)*, travelling salesman *(BrE)*; **Geschäftsreisenmarkt** *m* FREI business travel market; **Geschäftsrichtung** *f* GESCHÄFT business stream; **Geschäftsroutine** *f* GESCHÄFT business routine; **Geschäftsschulden** *f pl* FINANZ trading debts; **Geschäftssinn** *m* GESCHÄFT business sense, commercial acumen; **Geschäftssitzverlagerung** *f* GESCHÄFT dedomiciling; **Geschäftsstelle** *f* BÖRSE, GESCHÄFT, VERWALT agency *(agcy)*, branch, VERWALT agency *(agcy)*; **Geschäftsstellennetz** *nt* BANK branch network; **Geschäftsstrategie** *f* GESCHÄFT, MGMNT, VW business strategy; **Geschäftssystem** *nt* GESCHÄFT business system, portfolio, vw business system; **Geschäftstätigkeit** *f* GESCHÄFT business activity, business operations; **die Geschäftstätigkeit einstellen** *phr* GESCHÄFT go out of business; **Geschäftstrend** *m* GESCHÄFT business trend, economic trend; **Geschäftstresor-Einbruchdiebstahlversicherung** *f* VERSICH mercantile safe burglary insurance; **Geschäftstüchtigkeit** *f* GESCHÄFT commercial acumen; **Geschäftsübernahme** *f* GESCHÄFT takeover, MGMNT under new management; **Geschäftsübertragung auf** *phr* GESCHÄFT business transferred to; **Geschäftsumfang** *m* GESCHÄFT business volume, volume of trading, amount of business; **Geschäftsumschlagperiode** *f* RECHNUNG operating cycle; **Geschäftsumschwung** *m* **eines Unternehmens** GESCHÄFT corporate turnaround; **Geschäftsunterbrechung** *f* GESCHÄFT business interruption; **Geschäftsverbindungen** *f pl* GESCHÄFT business, business dealings, vw business relations; **Geschäftsverkehr** *m* GESCHÄFT business connections; **Geschäftsverlust** *m* RECHNUNG operating loss, business loss; **Geschäftsverluste** *m pl* FINANZ trading losses; **Geschäftsvermögen** *nt* FINANZ, GESCHÄFT, RECHNUNG business assets; **Geschäftsversicherung** *f* **des Lagerbestands gegen Diebstahl** VERSICH mercantile open-stock burglary insurance; **Geschäftsverstand** *m* MGMNT business acumen; **Geschäftsverteilungsplan** *m* MGMNT organization chart, organizational chart; **Geschäftsvertreter, in** *m,f* GESCHÄFT business canvasser; **Geschäftsviertel** *nt* GESCHÄFT business quarter, business center (*AmE*), business centre (*BrE*); **Geschäftsvolumen** *nt* GESCHÄFT business volume, amount of business; **Geschäftsvorgänge** *m pl* GESCHÄFT operations; **Geschäftsvorschlag** *m* GESCHÄFT, VW business proposition; **Geschäftswaren** *f pl* GESCHÄFT business goods; **Geschäftswelt** *f* GESCHÄFT business community, business world, commercial world; **Geschäftswerber, in** *m,f* GESCHÄFT *im Sinne aufdringlich* business tout; **Geschäftswert** *m* RECHNUNG goodwill; **Geschäftszeichen** *nt* GESCHÄFT reference (*ref.*); **ein Geschäftszeichen angeben** *phr* KOMM quote a reference number; **Geschäftszeiten** *f pl* (*GeschZ*) GESCHÄFT, V&M hours of business (*h.b.*), office hours; **Geschäftszentrum** *nt* GESCHÄFT shopping center (*AmE*), shopping centre (*BrE*), business center (*AmE*), business centre (*BrE*), shopping mall (*AmE*); **Geschäftszusammenschluß** *m* RECHNUNG payment, business combination; **Geschäftszuweisung** *f* GESCHÄFT transfers to business; **Geschäftszweig** *m* GESCHÄFT branch of a business

geschärft: **~es Bewußtsein** *nt* GESCHÄFT, POL acute awareness

geschätzt: **~es Einkommen** *nt* RECHNUNG estimated revenue; **~e Leserzahl** *f* **einer Publikation** V&M page traffic; **~er Veräußerungswert** *m* BANK estimated realizable value; **~er Wert** *m* GRUND appraised value, VERSICH estimated value; **~er Wert** *m* **von Grundstücken** GRUND estimated value of real estate (*BrE*), plottage value

gescheitert: **~e Fracht** *f* TRANSP frustrated cargo (*jarg*); **~e Übernahme** *f* FINANZ failed takeover bid; **~es Übernahmeangebot** *nt* FINANZ failed takeover bid

Geschenkgutschein *m* GESCHÄFT gift token, gift voucher

geschichtet: **~es Stichprobenverfahren** *nt* MATH stratified sampling; **~es Zufallsstichprobenverfahren** *nt* MATH stratified random sampling

Geschick *nt* GESCHÄFT, PERSON ability

Geschicklichkeit *f* GESCHÄFT, PERSON skill

geschickt *adj* PERSON expert

geschlechtsbezogen: **~e Diskriminierung** *f* RECHT gender discrimination, sexual discrimination, sex discrimination

geschlossen *adj* GESCHÄFT closed; **~es Bild** *nt* GESCHÄFT complete picture; **~er Container** *m* TRANSP closed box container, closed container; **~es Dock** *nt* TRANSP enclosed dock; **~es Fahrzeugdeck** *nt* TRANSP closed vehicle deck; **~e Filmvorstellung** *f* V&M trade show; **~e Gangway** *f* TRANSP covered gangway; **~er Investmentfonds** *m* BÖRSE closed-end mutual fund, FINANZ closed-end fund; **~e Investmentgesellschaft** *f* FINANZ closed-end management company (*BrE*); **~e Ladung** *f* GESCHÄFT bulk commodity; **~e Ortschaft** *f* GESCHÄFT built-up area, urban area; **~e Position** *f* FINANZ closed position; **~er Stromkreis** *m* COMP closed

circuit; **~er Trockencontainer** *m* TRANSP covered dry container; **~e Volkswirtschaft** *f* VW closed economy

Geschmacksmusterrolle *f* RECHT *geistiges Eigentum* Designs Registry (*BrE*)

geschrieben: **~es Recht** *nt* GESCHÄFT codified law, lex scripta

geschuldet: **~er Betrag** *m* FINANZ amount due

geschützt *adj* GESCHÄFT screened, RECHT licensed, *unter Naturschutz* protected; **nicht ~** PATENT generic; ♦ **~ vor unbefugtem Eindringen durch Hacker** COMP *Computersystem* hacker-proof (*infrml*)

Geschwätz *nt* GESCHÄFT spiel (*infrml*), V&M eyewash (*infrml*)

Geschwindigkeit *f* COMP *Datenübertragung, Bitübertragung* rate, GESCHÄFT speed, velocity, VW rate

Geschworene(r) *mf* [decl. as adj] RECHT juror, member of the jury; **die Geschworenen** *pl* RECHT the jury, *in der Hauptverhandlung* the trial jury; **die Geschworenen auswählen** *phr* RECHT *durch Eliminierung* strike a jury; **Geschworenengericht** *nt* RECHT jury; **Geschworenengerichtsentscheidung** *f* RECHT *aufgrund von bindender richterlicher Anweisung* directed verdict; **Geschworenenprozeß** *m* RECHT jury trial

GeschZ *abbr* (*Geschäftszeiten*) GESCHÄFT h.b. (*hours of business*)

Geselle *m* PERSON journeyman

Gesellschaft *f* GESCHÄFT association, company (*Co*), society, RECHT *Vertragsrecht*, VW company (*Co*); **~ mit beschränktem Aktionärskreis** GESCHÄFT, VW closed corporation (*AmE*), closely-held corporation (*AmE*); **~ mit beschränkter Haftung** (*GmbH, Ges.m.b.H. Öst*) GESCHÄFT Incorporated (*AmE*) (*Inc.*), limited company (*BrE*) (*Ltd*), limited liability company (*BrE*), private limited company, proprietary company (*Pty*); **~ mit beschränkter Mitgliederzahl** GESCHÄFT, VW close company (*BrE*), closed corporation (*AmE*), closely-held corporation (*AmE*); **~ bürgerlichen Rechts** GESCHÄFT partnership; **~ mit geringer Mitgliederzahl** GESCHÄFT, VW close company (*BrE*), closed corporation (*AmE*), closely-held corporation (*AmE*); **~ für Stadtentwicklung** VW Urban Development Corporation (*BrE*); ♦ **eine ~ gründen** GESCHÄFT form a partnership; **eine ~ auf Matrixmanagement umstellen** GESCHÄFT go matrix

Gesellschafter, in *m,f* GESCHÄFT, PERSON partner, associate

gesellschaftlich *adj* GESCHÄFT corporate, social; **~es Ansehen** *nt* SOZIAL social standing; **~ erforderliche Arbeitszeit** *f* PERSON socially necessary labor time (*AmE*), socially necessary labour time (*BrE*); **~er Gewinn** *m* VW social profit; **~e Organisation** *f* POL social organization; **~er Rang** *m* POL class, SOZIAL social standing; **~e Verwaltung** *f* VERWALT *körperschaftlich* corporate governance; **~e Wohlfahrtsfunktion** *f* VW social welfare function

Gesellschaft: **Gesellschaftsanalyse** *f* SOZIAL, V&M social analysis; **Gesellschaftsgründung** *f* GESCHÄFT company formation; **Gesellschaftskapital** *nt* GESCHÄFT company capital; **Gesellschaftsklasse** *f* POL class; **Gesellschaftskunde** *f* SOZIAL social studies; **Gesellschaftslehre** *f* *obs* SOZIAL social studies; **Gesellschaftsmittel** *nt pl* VERWALT corporate funds; **Gesellschaftspolitik** *f* SOZIAL social policy; **Gesellschaftsrecht** *nt* RECHT Companies Code, company law, corporate law, stock corporation law; **Gesellschaftsregister** *nt* RECHT Companies Registration Office; **Gesellschafts-Registeramt** *nt* GESCHÄFT Companies Registration Office (*BrE*) (*CRO*); **Gesellschaftsregisterstelle** *f* GESCHÄFT Companies Registration Office (*BrE*) (*CRO*); **Gesellschaftssatzung** *f* RECHT charter; **Gesellschaftsschicht** *f* POL, SOZIAL class; **Gesellschaftssiegel** *nt* BANK corporate seal; **Gesellschaftssitz** *m* RECHT, STEUER domicile; **Gesellschaftssitz** *m* **nehmen** GESCHÄFT, VERWALT take up legal residence; **Gesellschaftsstruktur** *f* GESCHÄFT company structure; **Gesellschaftssystem** *nt* SOZIAL social system; **Gesellschaftsvermögen** *nt* FINANZ, VERWALT corporate assets; **Gesellschaftsvertrag** *m* PERSON company agreement, RECHT articles of incorporation, deed of partnership, vw partnership, partnership agreement

Gesetz *nt* POL Act of Parliament (*BrE*), RECHT law, act, statute; **~ vom abnehmenden Ertrag** vw law of diminishing returns; **~ der abnehmenden Erträge** vw law of diminishing returns; **~ vom abnehmenden Ertragszuwachs** vw law of variable proportions; **~ vom abnehmenden Grenznutzen** vw law of diminishing marginal utility; **~ von Angebot und Nachfrage** vw law of supply and demand; **~ zur Aufrechterhaltung von Ruhe und Ordnung** PERSON Public Order Act (*BrE*); **~ vom Ausgleich der Grenznutzen** vw law of equi-marginal returns; **~ über Bank-Holdinggesellschaften** BANK Bank Holding Company Act (*AmE*); **~ der Bedürfnissättigung** vw law of satiable wants; **~ mit begrenzter Geltungsdauer** POL sunset act (*AmE*), RECHT sunset law; **~ zur Bewilligung von Geldern** POL appropriation bill; **~ zur einstweiligen Steuereinziehung** STEUER Provisional Collection of Taxes Act; **~ gegen geschlechtsbezogene Diskriminierung** PERSON, RECHT Sex Discrimination Act (*BrE*) (*SDA*); **~ gegen Investitionsbetrug** RECHT Prevention of Fraud Act (*BrE*); **~ gegen sexuelle Diskriminierung** PERSON, RECHT Sex Discrimination Act (*BrE*) (*SDA*); **~ gegen Wettbewerbsbeschränkungen** (*UWG*), RECHT, vw Fair Trading Act; **~ der großen Zahl** MATH law of large numbers; **~ zum Güterkraftverkehr** RECHT *1965* Carriage of Goods by Road Act (*BrE*); **~ zur Informationspflicht von Behörden** RECHT Freedom of Information Act (*AmE*) (*FOIA*); **~ über Kapitalgesellschaften** RECHT Business Corporation Law (*AmE*); **~ zum kombinierten Verkehr** RECHT multimodal transport law, intermodal transport law, TRANSP intermodal transport law; **~ des komparativen Vorteils** vw law of comparative advantage; **~ von Pareto** vw *Einkommensverteilung* Pareto's Law; **~ über Planung und Entschädigung** RECHT Planning and Compensation Act (*BrE*); **~ der reziproken Nachfrage** vw law of reciprocal demand; **~ des Rückflusses** BANK law of reflux; **~ zum Schutz des Persönlichkeitsrechts** RECHT privacy law; **~ zum Schutz des Verbrauchers beim Kauf** RECHT consumer protection legislation of sale; **~ zur Seefrachtbeförderung** RECHT *1924, 1971* Carriage of Goods by Sea Act (*BrE*) (*COGSA*); **~ der steigenden Kosten** vw law of increasing costs; **~ der steigenden Opportunitätskosten** vw increasing opportunity costs law; **~ der Unterschiedslosigkeit der Preise** vw law of price indifference; **~ mit zeitlich begrenzter Gültigkeit** POL sunset act (*AmE*); ◆ **durch ~** RECHT *geschriebenes Recht, Statut, Satzung* by statute; **vor dem ~** RECHT in

the eyes of the law; **ein ~ abschaffen** RECHT repeal a law; **ein ~ aufheben** RECHT repeal a law; **das ~ einhalten** RECHT respect the law; **nicht nach dem ~ handeln** RECHT fail to observe the law; **ein ~ verletzen** RECHT fall foul of the law; **dem ~ zuwiderhandeln** RECHT fail to observe the law; **das ~ zwingt niemanden, Unmögliches zu tun** RECHT lex non cogit ad impossibilia

gesetzähnlich: **~e Bestimmung** *f* RECHT *Zuteilung* quasi-statutory allocation

Gesetz: **Gesetzbuch** *nt* RECHT *Gesetzessammlung* statute book (*BrE*); **Gesetze** *nt pl* **über Aktiengesellschaften** RECHT Companies Act (*BrE*); **Gesetze** *nt pl* **gegen Luxus** RECHT sumptuary laws

gesetzesgemäß: **~e Stimmenabgabe** *f* RECHT statutory voting

Gesetz: **Gesetzesgrundlage** *f* RECHT statutory basis; **Gesetzeskraft haben** *phr* RECHT have statutory effect; **Gesetzeslücke** *f* RECHT loophole; **Gesetzesprogramm** *nt* POL statutory program (*AmE*), statutory programme (*BrE*); **Gesetzesrecht** *nt* RECHT statutory right (*BrE*); **Gesetzessammlung** *f* RECHT corpus; **Gesetzesübertreter, in** *m,f* RECHT tort feasor; **Gesetzesübertretung** *f* RECHT violation of the law; **Gesetzesvorlage** *f* RECHT *Gesetzgebungsverfahren* bill

gesetzgebend *adj* RECHT *legislativ* legislative; **~e Gewalt** *f* RECHT legislative power

Gesetzgebung *f* RECHT legislation, law; **~ im Interesse der örtichen Wähle** RECHT pork barrel legislations (*AmE*) (*infrml*); **~ zur Sicherung des Renteneinkommens** PERSON retirement income security act

gesetzlich 1. *adj* GESCHÄFT, POL statutory, RECHT by statute, statutory, VERSICH statutory; **2.** *adv* RECHT legally, by statute; ◆ **~ verbieten** RECHT *untersagen* prohibit

gesetzlich: **~e Anerkennung** *f* RECHT legal recognition; **~e Aufwertung** *f* RECHNUNG legal revaluation; **~e Ausnahme** *f* RECHT statutory exemption; **~e Autorität** *f* POL statutory authority; **~e Bereitstellung** *f* POL statutory appropriation; **~e Buchprüfung** *f* RECHNUNG statutory audit; **~er Eigentumserwerb** *m* RECHT statutory appropriation; **~er Erbe** *m* RECHT legal heir; **~er Feiertag** *m* GESCHÄFT, PERSON, RECHT bank holiday (*BrE*), legal holiday (*AmE*), public holiday, statutory holiday (*AmE*); **~ festgelegte Ausgaben** *f pl* POL statutory expenditure; **~ festgelegter Posten** *m* POL statutory item; **~ festgesetztes Krankengeld** *nt* VERSICH statutory sick pay (*BrE*) (*SSP*); **~e Formvorschriften** *f pl* RECHT *Vertragsrecht* statutory forms; **~e Fusion** *f* RECHT *Unternehmenszusammenschluß* statutory merger; **~ geschütztes Arzneimittel** *nt* GESCHÄFT proprietary drug; **~e Gewährleistung** *f* RECHT implied warranty; **~e Haftpflicht** *f* RECHT legal liability, *Versicherung* third-party liability; **~es Handwerkerpfandrecht** *nt* GRUND tradesman's lien; **~e Immunität** *f* RECHT legal immunity, statutory immunity; **~e Inzidenz** *f* STEUER statutory incidence; **~er Jahresabschluß** *m* RECHNUNG statutory accounts; **~es Krankengeld** *nt* VERSICH statutory sick pay (*BrE*) (*SSP*); **~e Kündigungsfrist** *f* RECHT legal notice, statutory notice; **~er Mindestlohn** *m* PERSON minimum wage; **~es Monopol** *nt* vw legal monopoly; **~e Neubewertung** *f* RECHNUNG legal revaluation; **~e Privilegien** *nt pl* PERSON, RECHT *Gewerkschaftsgesetz* statutory immunities; **~e Rücklagen** *f pl* RECHNUNG capital reserves, legal reserves, RECHT legal reserves; **~es Treuhandverhältnis** *nt* RECHT involuntary trust *(AmE)*; **~e Verjährungsvorschriften** *f pl* RECHT statute of limitations; **~e Verpflichtung** *f* RECHT legal requirement, statutory obligation; **~e Verpflichtung** *f* **des Arbeitgebers zur Finanzierung** PERSON *der Altersversicherung* employer's legal obligation to fund; **~e Vollmacht** *f* POL statutory authority; **~e Voraussetzungen** *f pl* POL statutory requirement; **~ vorgeschriebene Aufwendungen** *f pl* POL statutory expenditure; **~ vorgeschriebene Bücher und Verzeichnisse** *nt pl* RECHT *einer Kapitalgesellschaft* statutory books; **~ vorgeschriebene Gründungsversammlung** *f* RECHT *einer Gesellschaft* statutory meeting; **~ vorgeschriebene Investition** *f* FINANZ statutory investment; **~ vorgeschriebene Zuweisung** *f* POL statutory allocation; **~ vorgeschriebener Bereitstellungsfonds** *m* POL statutory appropriation; **~ vorgeschriebener Haushaltsposten** *m* POL statutory item; **~ vorgeschriebenes Programm** *nt* POL statutory program *(AmE)*, statutory programme *(BrE)*; **~e Vorschrift** *f* POL statutory requirement; **~e Vorschriften** *f pl* **über die Klageausschlußfrist** RECHT *Verjährung* statutes of limitation of action; **~er Wohnsitz** *m* RECHT legal residence; **~es Zahlungsmittel** *nt* BANK currency, FINANZ legal tender, currency, GESCHÄFT legal tender, VW currency, functional currency; **~er Zinsfuß** *m* VW legal rate of interest; **~ zugelassener Pfandverkauf** *m* RECHT statutory foreclosure; **~ zulässige Übertragung** *f* BÖRSE legal transfer; **~e Zuweisung** *f* POL statutory allocation

gesetzmäßig *adj* RECHT lawful, legal

gesetzwidrig *adj* RECHT illegal, unlawful

gesichert *adj* VW secure; **~es Angebot** *nt* BÖRSE hedged tender; **~er Arbeitsplatz** *m* PERSON secure job; **~e Ausschreibung** *f* BÖRSE hedged tender; **nicht ~es Darlehen** *nt* RECHNUNG unsecured loan; **~er Gläubiger** *m* FINANZ, RECHNUNG, VW secured creditor; **nicht ~er Gläubiger** *m* RECHNUNG unsecured creditor; **~e Gläubigerin** *f* FINANZ, RECHNUNG, VW secured creditor; **nicht ~e Gläubigerin** *f* RECHNUNG unsecured creditor; **~e Industrieobligationen** *f pl* VW secured bonds; **~e oder ungesicherte Anleihe** *f* **in gleicher Stückelung** BÖRSE debenture bond; **~es Recht** *nt* GESCHÄFT vested interest; **~e Schuldverschreibung** *f* FINANZ secured debenture; **~e Verbindlichkeit** *f* FINANZ secured debt

Gesichtsfeld *nt* IND field

Gesichtspunkt *m* GESCHÄFT aspect, point of view

gesiegelt: ~e Schuldurkunde *f* VERSICH sealed instrument of debt; **~er Vertrag** *m* RECHT special contract

Gesinnung *f* GESCHÄFT thinking; **Gesinnungsgenosse** *m*, **Gesinnungsgenossin** *f* POL fellow traveler *(AmE)*, fellow traveller *(BrE)*

Ges.m.b.H. *abbr (Öst) (Gesellschaft mit beschränkter Haftung)* GESCHÄFT limited liability company *(BrE)*, Ltd *(limited company BrE)*, private limited company, Inc. *(Incorporated AmE)*, Pty *(proprietary company)*

gesondert: ~er Ausweis *m* **als Anmerkung zur Bilanz** RECHNUNG footnote disclosure

gespalten: ~e Einstufung *f* FINANZ split rating; **~e Lohnstruktur** *f* PERSON *Arbeitsentgelt* two-tier wage structure; **~es Steuersystem** *nt* STEUER two-rate system; **~er Wechselkurs** *m* VW multicurrency rate

gespannt *adj* GESCHÄFT *Lage* strained

gesperrt *adj* VW *Konto* frozen; **~e Aktien** *f pl* BÖRSE stopped stock; **~e Anleihen** *f pl* FINANZ stopped bonds; **~es Konto** *nt* BANK frozen account, blocked account; **~e Schuldverschreibungen** *f pl* FINANZ stopped bonds

gesponsert: ~es Buch *nt* V&M sponsored book; **~e Veranstaltungen** *f pl* FREI, V&M sponsored events

Gespräch *nt* GESCHÄFT *Telefon* call; ♦ **im ~** GESCHÄFT under discussion; **ein ~ durchstellen** GESCHÄFT, KOMM, VERWALT put a call through

Gespräch: **Gespräche** *nt pl* GESCHÄFT, KOMM talks, MGMNT negotiations, POL talks; **Gespräche** *nt pl* **auf höchster Ebene** MGMNT top-level talks; **Gesprächsgebühr** *f* KOMM call charge; **Gesprächsleiter, in** *m,f* GESCHÄFT chair, MEDIEN talking head

Gespür *nt* GESCHÄFT feel; **~ für den Markt** GESCHÄFT, V&M feel of the market

gestaffelt *adj* BÖRSE, FINANZ, GESCHÄFT, PERSON staggered; **~e Anleihe** *f* BÖRSE stepped bond; **~e Arbeitszeiten** *f pl* PERSON staggered working hours; **~e Fälligkeiten** *f pl* BÖRSE staggering maturities; **~e Kosten** *pl* FINANZ stepped cost; **~e Schuldverschreibung** *f* BÖRSE stepped bond

Gestalt *f* PATENT embodiment, form; **die ~ künftiger Dinge** GESCHÄFT the shape of things to come; ♦ **~ annehmen** GESCHÄFT take shape

Geständnis *nt* GESCHÄFT *Eingeständnis* admission, RECHT *Eingeständnis* admission, confession

gestatten *vt* GESCHÄFT allow

Gestehungskosten *pl* GESCHÄFT prime costs, RECHNUNG original cost, replacement costs, replacement, VW prime costs

gesteigert: ~es Durchdringungsvermögen *nt* V&M cumulative penetration

Gestell *nt* COMP rack, TRANSP stillage

gestörtes: ~ Gleichgewicht *nt* FINANZ imbalance

gestrichelt: ~e Linie *f* COMP, MATH, VERWALT dashed line; **auf der ~en Linie unterschreiben** *phr* VERWALT sign on the dotted line

gestundet *adj* GESCHÄFT prolonged; **~e Steuerverbindlichkeiten** *f pl* FINANZ, STEUER deferred tax liabilities

gestützt *adj* GESCHÄFT, VW pegged; **~e Erinnerung** *f* V&M aided recall; **~er Kurs** *m* FINANZ, VW pegged price; **~er Preis** *m* GESCHÄFT subsidized price, supported price

Gesuch *nt* GESCHÄFT petition

gesucht *adj* GESCHÄFT sought-after

gesund *adj* BANK sound, GESCHÄFT *Wettbewerb, Markt* healthy; ♦ **als ~ entlassen werden** SOZIAL be given a clean bill of health; **~ an Leib und Seele sein** SOZIAL be given a clean bill of health; **für völlig ~ erklärt werden** SOZIAL be given a clean bill of health

gesund: **~er Menschenverstand** *m* GESCHÄFT common sense, law 29 *(jarg)*; **~e Währung** *f* GESCHÄFT *sichere Valuta* sound currency

Gesundheit *f* GESCHÄFT health; **~ am Arbeitsplatz** SOZIAL occupational health; **~ und Sicherheit** PERSON health and safety

gesundheitlich: ~e Gründe *m pl* PERSON health grounds, medical grounds

Gesundheit: **Gesundheitsbehörde** *f* GESCHÄFT Health Authority; **Gesundheitserziehung** *f* GESCHÄFT health education; **Gesundheitsfarm** *f* SOZIAL health farm; **Gesundheitsfürsorgegesamtplan** *m* SOZIAL comprehensive health-care system; **Gesundheitsgefährdung** *f* SOZIAL health risk; **aus Gesundheitsgründen** *phr* PERSON on the grounds of ill health; **Gesundheitsindustrie** *f* VERSICH health care industry; **Gesundheitsökonomik** *f* VW health economics; **Gesundheitspaß** *m* **mit Einschränkungen** SOZIAL foul bill of health; **Gesundheitspaß** *m* **mit dem Vermerk ansteckungsverdächtig** SOZIAL suspect bill of health; **Gesundheitsrisiko** *nt* SOZIAL health hazard, health risk; **Gesundheitsschaden** *m* VERSICH damage to health; **Gesundheitsschädigung** *f* VERSICH damage to health; **Gesundheitsversicherung** *f* VERSICH health insurance; **Gesundheitsvorschriften** *f pl* RECHT health regulations; **Gesundheitswesen** *nt* IND health care industry, VW health sector; **Gesundheitszentrum** *nt* SOZIAL health center (*AmE*), health centre (*BrE*); **Gesundheitszertifikat** *nt* VERWALT health benefit certificate; **Gesundheitszeugnis** *nt* SOZIAL bill of health (*BH*), certificate of health

Gesundschrumpfen *nt* GESCHÄFT shake-out

Gesundschrumpfung *f* GESCHÄFT shake-out

getäuscht: **~ werden** *phr* GESCHÄFT be taken in

geteilt: **~e Provision** *f* VW split commission

getilgt *adj* FINANZ liquidated; **~e Schulden** *f pl* RECHNUNG liquidated debt

getippt *adj infrml* GESCHÄFT, PATENT, VERWALT typewritten

Getreide *nt* BÖRSE cereal, grain; **Getreidebörse** *f* BÖRSE corn exchange (*BrE*), grain exchange (*AmE*); **Getreidebörse** *f* **in Minneapolis** BÖRSE Minneapolis Grain Exchange; **Getreideernte** *f* VW grain crop, grain harvest; **Getreide- und Freihandelsassoziation** *f* VW Grain and Free Trade Association (*GAFTA*); **Getreidehandel** *m* IND, VW grain trade; **Getreidesilo** *m* TRANSP granary; **Getreidespeicher** *m* GESCHÄFT grain silo, granary; **Getreideterminal** *m* TRANSP grain terminal; **Getreidezertifikat** *nt* TRANSP grain certificate

getrennt *adj* GESCHÄFT segregated; ♦ **mit ~er Post** KOMM under separate cover

getrennt: **~e Veranlagung** *f* STEUER separate tax return

Getriebe *nt* TRANSP gears

Geviert *nt* MEDIEN *Typographie* em space; **Geviertstrich** *m* MEDIEN em dash

Gew. *abbr* (*Gewerkschaft*) GESCHÄFT, PERSON, POL labor union (*AmE*), TU (*trade union*) (*BrE*), union

gewagt *adj* GESCHÄFT risky; **~e Sache** *f* GESCHÄFT wildcat venture

Gewähr: **ohne ~** *phr* BANK without recourse, GESCHÄFT unwarranted, not binding, subject to confirmation, without engagement

gewähren *vt* BANK *Kredit* accommodate, FINANZ *Kredit* grant, GESCHÄFT award, grant, allow, VERSICH allow

Gewährleistung *f* GESCHÄFT guarantee, guaranty, VERSICH warranty; **~ der Durchschnittsqualität** GESCHÄFT warranty of merchantability; **Gewährleistungsgarantie** *f* BANK performance bond; **Gewährleistungshaftung** *f* GESCHÄFT liability for breach of warranty; **Gewährleistungshaftung** *f* **des Abnehmers** RECHT caveat subscriptor; **Gewährleistungshaftung** *f* **des Verkäufers** RECHT caveat venditor; **Gewährleistungspflicht** *f* GESCHÄFT

warranty obligation; **Gewährleistungs-Standardsatz** *m* VERSICH institute warranty

Gewährsmangel *m* RECHT *Vertragsrecht* redhibition

Gewährung *f* PATENT grant; **~ der Meistbegünstigung** VW most favored nation treatment (*AmE*) (*MFN*), most favoured nation treatment (*BrE*) (*MFN*)

gewaltsam: **~es Eindringen** *nt* RECHT *der Polizei* forcible entry; **~ eingreifen** *phr* GESCHÄFT use strong-arm tactics

gewalttätig: **~e Streikbrecher** *m pl* PERSON blacklegs (*BrE*) (*infrml*), goon squad (*AmE*) (*infrml*)

Gewand *nt* GESCHÄFT apparel (*AmE*), clothing (*BrE*)

gewandelt: **nicht ~** *adj* BANK unconverted

gewandt *adj* GESCHÄFT nimble, quick

Gewässerverschmutzung *f* IND, UMWELT water pollution

Gewässerverunreinigung *f* IND, UMWELT water pollution

Gewerbe *nt* IND industry; ♦ **ein ~ betreiben als** GESCHÄFT trade as; **ein ~ treiben als** GESCHÄFT trade as

Gewerbe: **Gewerbeaufseher, in** *m,f* SOZIAL labor inspector (*AmE*), labour inspector (*BrE*); **Gewerbeaufsichtsamt** *nt* IND Factory Inspectorate (*BrE*), SOZIAL labor inspectorate (*AmE*), labour inspectorate (*BrE*), Factory Inspectorate (*BrE*), VW Trading Standards Office (*AmE*); **Gewerbeausstellung** *f* V&M *Handelsmesse* trade fair; **Gewerbebetrieb** *m* GESCHÄFT business enterprise; **Gewerbeerlaubnis** *f* GESCHÄFT trading authorization, V&M *für Kleinbetrieb oder Verkaufsautomat in einem größeren Etablissement* concession; **Gewerbefläche** *f* GRUND trade park (*AmE*), industrial estate; **Gewerbefläche** *f* **für den Einzelhandel** V&M retail floorspace; **Gewerbefreiheit** *f* POL, VW economic freedom; **Gewerbegebiet** *nt* GRUND industrial estate (*BrE*), trade park (*AmE*), trading estate, IND, UMWELT industrial park, VW enterprise zone (*EZ*); **Gewerbepark** *m* GRUND industrial estate (*BrE*), trade park (*AmE*), trading estate; **Gewerbepolizei** *f* IND, SOZIAL factory inspectorate, industrial inspection; **Gewerbetreibende** *pl* [decl. as adj] GESCHÄFT tradespeople; **Gewerbeverband** *m* GESCHÄFT trade association; **Gewerbezeichen** *nt* GESCHÄFT trade sign

gewerblich *adj* GESCHÄFT commercial, trade, industrial; **~e Abfälle** *m pl* IND industrial waste; **~e Anmeldung** *f* PATENT industrial application; **~er Arbeitnehmer** *m*, **~e Arbeitnehmerin** *f* VW blue-collar worker; **~e Ausleihungen** *f pl* BANK commercial lending; **~es Eigentum** *nt* GESCHÄFT, GRUND, PATENT industrial property; **~e Einbauten** *m pl* GRUND trade fixtures; **~es Erzeugnis** *nt* IND industrial product; **~e Genossenschaft** *f* IND industrial cooperative; **~ genutzter Brunnen** *m* UMWELT commercial well; **~es Grundstück** *nt* IND industrial site; **~e Hedger** *m pl* BÖRSE commercial hedgers; **~-industrielle Unternehmen** *nt pl* VW industrial and commercial companies (*ICCs*); **~e Kooperation** *f* IND industrial cooperation; **~er Kredit** *m* BANK business loan, commercial loan; **~er Lagerhalter** *m*, **Lagerhalterin** *f* IMP/EXP warehouse officer; **~e Lagerung** *f* TRANSP commercial storage; **~e Nutzung** *f* GESCHÄFT commercial use, GRUND commercial use, industrial occupancy; **~e Pacht** *f* GRUND industrial rent; **~e Räume** *m pl* GESCHÄFT business premises; **~er Rechtsschutz** *m* PATENT, RECHT industrial property protection, intellectual property rights; **~es**

Schiedsgericht *nt* PERSON, RECHT industrial tribunal (*BrE*) (*IT*), labor court (*AmE*); **~e Schiedsgerichtsbarkeit** *f* PERSON industrial arbitration; **~e Schutz- und Urheberrechte** *nt pl* PATENT, RECHT intellectual property rights; **~e Schutzrechte** *nt pl* PATENT industrial property; **~e Tätigkeit** *f* IND commercial activity, industrial activity; **~es Unternehmen** *nt* GESCHÄFT business enterprise, trading company; **~e Wirtschaft** *f* VW industrial economics, trade and industry; **~e Zusammenarbeit** *f* IND industrial cooperation

gewerbsmäßig: **~er Schwindler** *m*, **~e Schwindlerin** *f* GESCHÄFT confidence trickster

Gewerkschaft *f* (*Gew.*) GESCHÄFT, PERSON, POL labor union (*AmE*), trade union (*BrE*) (*TU*), union; **~ mit Mitgliedersperre** PERSON *Gewerkschaftsbewegung* closed union; ♦ **einer ~ angehören** PERSON belong to a union; **einer ~ beitreten** PERSON join a union

Gewerkschaft: **Gewerkschaften** *f pl* **und Unternehmensleitung** *f* PERSON unions and management

Gewerkschafter, in *m,f* GESCHÄFT, PERSON, POL labor unionist (*AmE*), trade unionist (*BrE*)

gewerkschaftlich: **~en Einfluß beseitigen** *phr* PERSON *aus einem Betrieb* de-unionization; **~ nicht genehmigte Arbeitskampfmaßnahmen** *f pl* PERSON *Streik, Bummelstreik* unofficial industrial action; **~er Obmann** *m* IND, MGMNT, PERSON shop steward; **~ organisiert** *phr* PERSON unionized; **~ organisierte Mitarbeiter** *m pl* PERSON organized labor (*AmE*), organized labour (*BrE*); **~e Tarifpolitik** *f* PERSON union wage policy; **~e Verhandlungsgruppe** *f* PERSON bargaining unit; **~er Vertrauensmann** *m* IND, MGMNT, PERSON shop steward; **~e Vorschriften** *f pl* PERSON *Gewerkschaftsbewegung* union rules; **~e Zusammenfassung** *f* PERSON unionization

Gewerkschaft: **Gewerkschaftsanwerbung** *f* PERSON union recruitment; **Gewerkschaftsbeitrag** *m* PERSON trade union subscription (*BrE*); **Gewerkschaftsbeiträge** *f pl* PERSON trade union dues (*BrE*), trade union contributions (*BrE*), union fees; **Gewerkschaftsbewegung** *f* PERSON labor movement (*AmE*), labour movement (*BrE*), trade unionism (*BrE*), union movement; **Gewerkschaftsetikett** *nt* PERSON union label

gewerkschaftsfrei: **~es Unternehmen** *nt* PERSON non-union firm

Gewerkschaft: **Gewerkschaftsführer** *m* PERSON union leader; **Gewerkschaftsfunktionär, in** *m,f* PERSON union officer, union official; **Gewerkschaftsmitglied** *nt* PERSON member of a union; **Gewerkschaftsmitgliedschaft** *f* PERSON union membership; **Gewerkschaftspflichten** *f pl* PERSON union liability

gewerkschaftspflichtig: **~er Betrieb** *m* PERSON *Gewerkschaftsbewegung*, VW closed shop; **nicht ~er Betrieb** *m* PERSON *Gewerkschaftsbewegung* open shop

Gewerkschaft: **Gewerkschaftsprivilegien** *nt pl* PERSON, RECHT *Gewerkschaftsgesetz* statutory immunities, union immunities; **Gewerkschaftsrechte** *nt pl* PERSON union rights, RECHT *gesetzliche Privilegien* union immunities; **Gewerkschaftsstruktur** *f* PERSON union structure; **Gewerkschaftsverband** *m* PERSON union national unit (*AmE*); **Gewerkschaftsvertreter, in** *m,f* GESCHÄFT, IND business agent (*AmE*), PERSON union representative; **Gewerkschaftsverwaltung** *f* PERSON union

government; **Gewerkschaftszugehörigkeit** *f* PERSON union affiliation

Gewicht *nt* (*Gw.*) GESCHÄFT, MATH, TRANSP weight (*wgt, wt*); **~ der Fracht** TRANSP weight of cargo

gewichten *vt* BÖRSE weight

gewichtet *adj* STEUER weighted; **~er Index** *m* GESCHÄFT weighted index; **~es Mittel** *nt* MATH weighted average; **~er Preisindex** *m* BÖRSE price-weighted index

Gewicht: **Gewicht/Maß** *nt* TRANSP weight/measurement; **Gewichtsbescheinigung** *f* TRANSP certificate of weight; **Gewichtsfracht** *f* TRANSP deadweight cargo; **Gewichtsgrenze** *f* GESCHÄFT, TRANSP weight limit; **Gewichtskosten** *pl* TRANSP weight charge; **Gewichtsnota** *f* TRANSP certificate of weight; **Gewichtstonne** *f* GESCHÄFT weight ton

Gewichtung *f* FINANZ weighting, PERSON loading, V&M weighting

Gewinn *m* BÖRSE return, FINANZ assets, earnings, surplus, FREI benefit, GESCHÄFT advantage, surplus, income, RECHNUNG book profit, surplus, STEUER emolument, VERWALT earnings, VW surplus; **~ und Abschreibungen** *f pl* FINANZ cash flow; **~ vor Akquisition** RECHNUNG pre-acquisition profits; **~ im Geschäftsjahr** RECHNUNG profit for the financial year; **~ je Aktie** FINANZ, RECHNUNG earnings per share (*EPS*); **~ je Stammaktie nach Steuern zu Kurs der Stammaktie** BÖRSE earnings yield; **~ aus Kapitalvermögen** FINANZ, GESCHÄFT capital profit; **~ aus langfristigem Geschäft** STEUER long-term gain; **~ des Produzenten** FREI producer's profits; **~ nach Steuern** RECHNUNG, STEUER after-tax income, after-tax profit; **~ vor Steuern** RECHNUNG profit before taxes, STEUER pre-tax earnings; **~ aus der Veräußerung von Kapitalanlagegütern** RECHNUNG capital gains; **~ und Verlust** RECHNUNG profit and loss (*P&L*); **~ und Verlustrechnung** *f* RECHNUNG asset and liability statement; **~ vom Wiederverkauf** GESCHÄFT proceeds from resale; ♦ **~ erwirtschaften** VW run a surplus; **~ erzielen** BÖRSE move into the money, RECHNUNG make a profit; **~ machen** RECHNUNG make a profit, make profits, VW make a turn, run a surplus; **einen ~ melden** RECHNUNG report a profit; **Gewinne abziehen** VW milk profits (*infrml*); **Gewinne einheimsen** *infrml* GESCHÄFT rake in profits (*infrml*); **Gewinne erzielen** BÖRSE make gains; **Gewinne übertrafen die Vorhersagen im ersten Quartal** FINANZ profits surpassed forecasts in the first quarter

Gewinn: **Gewinnabsicht** *f* FINANZ profit goal; **Gewinnanteil** *m* BÖRSE dividend (*div.*), MEDIEN royalty; **Gewinnanteile** *m pl* **aus einer Kommanditgesellschaft** RECHNUNG income from a limited partnership; **Gewinnausfall** *m* GESCHÄFT shortfall in earnings; **Gewinnausschüttung** *f* BÖRSE capital gains distribution; **Gewinnaussichten** *f pl* FINANZ, GESCHÄFT, VW profit outlook; **Gewinnauswirkungen** *f pl* FINANZ profit impact; **Gewinnbegleiterscheinung** *f* FINANZ profit implication

gewinnberechtigt: **nicht ~e Police** *f* VW nonparticipating policy

Gewinn: **im Gewinnbereich** *phr* VW in financial surplus; **Gewinnbeteiligung** *f* FINANZ, PERSON, RECHNUNG profit-sharing, VW *der Arbeitnehmer* revenue sharing (*AmE*), profit-sharing; **Gewinnbeteiligung** *f* **der Arbeitnehmer** PERSON employee profit-sharing; **Gewinnbeteiligungsplan** *m* RECHNUNG, STEUER profit-sharing plan (*AmE*), profit-sharing scheme (*BrE*); **Gewinnbeteiligungssteuer** *f* STEUER fringe benefits tax; **Gewinnbeteiligungssystem** *nt* PERSON financial participation scheme (*BrE*), RECHNUNG profit-sharing plan (*AmE*), profit-sharing scheme (*BrE*)

gewinnbezogen: ~**es Arbeitsentgelt** *nt* PERSON incentive wage, performance-related pay (*PRP*), profit-related pay (*PRP*), wage incentive; ~**es Entgelt** *nt* PERSON incentive wage, performance-related pay (*PRP*), profit-related pay (*PRP*), wage incentive

gewinnbringend *adj* GESCHÄFT advantageous, beneficial, gainful, RECHNUNG profitable, VW productive; ~**e Firma** *f* RECHNUNG profitable firm; ~**es Unternehmen** *nt* GESCHÄFT profit-making enterprise

Gewinn: **Gewinndefizit** *nt* GESCHÄFT shortfall in earnings; **Gewinndiagramm** *nt* FINANZ profit graph; **Gewinndruck** *m* VW profit squeeze; **Gewinneffekt** *m* FINANZ profit impact; **Gewinnempfindlichkeitsanalyse** *f* RECHNUNG profit sensitivity analysis

gewinnen *vt* BÖRSE gain, GESCHÄFT extract, *Kenntnisse* gather; ♦ **für sich ~** GESCHÄFT win over; **jdn für sich ~** GESCHÄFT win sb's favor (*AmE*), win sb's favour (*BrE*)

Gewinn: **Gewinnentwicklung** *f* FINANZ, GESCHÄFT, RECHNUNG earnings performance; **Gewinnentwicklung** *f* **einer Aktie** FINANZ earnings performance of a stock; **Gewinne** *m pl* ~ **und Verluste** *m pl* VW rises and falls (*BrE*), gains and losses (*AmE*); **Gewinnfaktoranalyse** *f* FINANZ profit factor analysis; **Gewinnfolgen** *f pl* FINANZ profit implication; **Gewinnkennzahl** *f* **einer Unternehmung** BÖRSE earnings ratio; **Gewinnkennziffer** *f* GESCHÄFT, VERWALT earnings ratio; **Gewinn- und Leistungsplanung** *f* MGMNT profit and performance planning (*PPP*)

gewinnlos: ~**e Konkurrenz** *f* VW no-profit competition

Gewinn: **Gewinnmarge** *f* FINANZ, VW profit margin; **Gewinnmaximierung** *f* FINANZ, GESCHÄFT, VW profit maximization; **Gewinnmitnahme** *f* VW profit taking; **Gewinnmitnahmestrategie** *f* BÖRSE, MGMNT profit-taking strategy; **Gewinnmotiv** *nt* FINANZ, GESCHÄFT, VW profit motive; **Gewinnobligation** *f* BÖRSE income bond; **Gewinnoptimierung** *f* FINANZ, GESCHÄFT, VW profit optimization

gewinnorientiert: nicht ~**e Buchführung** *f* RECHNUNG nonprofit accounting

Gewinn: **Gewinnplafond** *m* VW profit ceiling; **Gewinnplanung** *f* GESCHÄFT, MGMNT profit planning; **Gewinnplanziel** *nt* FINANZ profit target; **Gewinnpoolungsvertrag** *m* GESCHÄFT pooling arrangements; **Gewinnpotential** *nt* BÖRSE profit potential; **Gewinnpotential** *nt* **nach oben** BÖRSE upside profit potential; **Gewinnprofil** *nt* BÖRSE profit profile; **Gewinnprognose** *f* FINANZ profit projection, earnings forecast; **Gewinnprojektierung** *f* GESCHÄFT profit projection; **Gewinnprüfung** *f* RECHNUNG profit test; **Gewinnrealisierung** *f* VW profit taking; **Gewinnrealisierungsstrategie** *f* MGMNT profit-taking strategy; **Gewinnrendite** *f* BÖRSE, FINANZ earnings yield; **Gewinnrückführung** *f* VW repatriation of profits; **Gewinnrücklage** *f* RECHNUNG income available for fixed charges, capital reserves, surplus reserve; **Gewinnrücklagen** *f pl* RECHNUNG earning reserves; **Gewinnrückstellung** *f* FINANZ surplus reserves, VERSICH cleanup fund; **Gewinnschaubild** *nt* FINANZ profit graph; **Gewinnschuldverschreibung** *f* BÖRSE adjustment bond (*AmE*), income bond, income debenture,

STEUER income bond; **Gewinnschwelle** *f* BÖRSE, FINANZ, GESCHÄFT, GRUND, RECHNUNG, VW breakeven point; **die Gewinnschwelle erreichen** *phr* VERWALT, VW break even; **Gewinnschwellenanalyse** *f* FINANZ, VW breakeven analysis; **Gewinnspanne** *f* FINANZ profit margin, RECHNUNG margin of profit, margin, V&M return on sales, margin, VW profit margin; **Gewinnsteigerung** *f* GESCHÄFT profit improvement; **Gewinnsteuer** *f* RECHNUNG, STEUER profits tax; **Gewinnstrategie** *f* FINANZ profit strategy; **Gewinnströme** *m pl* FINANZ earning streams; **Gewinnsucht** *f* GESCHÄFT acquisitiveness

gewinnsüchtig *adj* GESCHÄFT acquisitive

Gewinnung *f* GESCHÄFT *Rohstoffe* extraction, IND *Mineralstoffe* production, VW exploitation

Gewinn: **Gewinnverbesserung** *f* FINANZ, GESCHÄFT profit improvement; **Gewinn- und Verlustrechnung** *f* (*GuV-Rechnung*) FINANZ earnings report, RECHNUNG income statement (*BrE*), operating statement, profit and loss account, profit and loss statement, statement of income, income accounts, income and expenditure account, statement of earnings; **Gewinn- und Verlustrechnung** *f* **in Staffelform** RECHNUNG vertical profit and loss account format; **Gewinnverteilungskonto** *nt* RECHNUNG appropriation account; **Gewinnverwendung** *f* VERWALT appropriation of earnings, appropriation of income; **Gewinn-Volumen-Verhältnis** *nt* RECHNUNG profit-volume ratio (*P/V*); **Gewinnvortrag** *m* FINANZ retained profits, undistributed profit, accumulation, RECHNUNG profit carried forward, accumulated profits, accumulated surplus; **Gewinnziel** *nt* FINANZ profit goal, RECHNUNG profit target; **Gewinnzone** *f* VW profit wedge; **in der Gewinnzone** VW in financial surplus

gewiß: gewisse Grenze *f* GESCHÄFT sticking point; **gewisse Verbindungen** *f pl* GESCHÄFT wheels within wheels

gewissenhaft 1. *adj* GESCHÄFT faithful, painstaking; **2.** *adv* GESCHÄFT painstakingly

gewissenlos *adj* GESCHÄFT unscrupulous

gewissermaßen *adv* GESCHÄFT quasi

Gewißheit *f* VW certainty

gewogen *adj* MATH, VW weighted; ~**er Außenwert** *m* VW *einer Währung* trade-weighted external value; ~**er Außenwert** *m* **einer Währung** VW trade-weighted exchange rate; ~**e Durchschnittskosten** *pl* RECHNUNG weighted average cost; ~**er Index** *m* GESCHÄFT weighted index; ~**es Mittel** *nt* GESCHÄFT, MATH weighted average; ~**er Mittelwert** *m* VW weighted average

Gewohnheit *f* GESCHÄFT routine

gewohnheitsmäßig 1. *adj* GESCHÄFT routine; **2.** *adv* GESCHÄFT as a matter of routine

gewöhnlich: ~**e Abnutzung** *f* RECHNUNG normal wear and tear; ~**e und notwendige Geschäftsausgaben** *f pl* STEUER ordinary and necessary business expenses; ~**e Steuer** *f* STEUER noncumulative tax; ~**er Zins** *m* FINANZ ordinary interest

gewohnt *adj* GESCHÄFT customary

gewonnen: ~**e Rechnung** *f* GESCHÄFT won invoice

gez. *abbr* (*gezeichnet*) GESCHÄFT sgd (*signed*)

gezahlt: ~**er Betrag** *m* GESCHÄFT amount paid

gezeichnet *adj* (*gez.*) GESCHÄFT signed (*sgd*); ~**es Kapital** *nt* GESCHÄFT subscribed capital; **nicht** ~**es Kapital** *nt* BÖRSE unissued capital

Gezeitenenergie *f* UMWELT tidal power

Gezeitenhub *m* TRANSP tidal range

gezielt *adj* V&M targeted; **~ Aktien einer Unternehmung aufkaufen** *phr* BÖRSE raid a company; **~er Einsatz** *m* VW targeting; **~er Hinweis** *m* GESCHÄFT tip-off; **~e Kampagne** *f* V&M targeted campaign

gezogen: ~er Wechsel *m* BANK draft (*dft*), VW drawn bill

gezont: ~es Dezimalformat *nt* COMP zoned decimal format

gezwungen *adj* GESCHÄFT *Atmosphäre* strained

GFK *abbr* IND (*glasfaserverstärkter Kunststoff*) GRP (*glass fiber-reinforced plastic AmE, glass fibre-reinforced plastic BrE*)

G5 *abbr* (*Fünfer-Gruppe, Gruppe der Fünf*) VW G5 (*Group of Five*)

Ghostwriter *m* V&M ghost writer

GICC *abbr* TRANSP GICC (*German International Chamber of Commerce*)

Giffengut *nt* VW *Giffen-Effekt* Giffen good

Giffen-Paradoxon *nt* VW Giffen paradox

Gift *nt* UMWELT poison, toxin

giftig *adj* UMWELT poisonous, toxic

Giftigkeit *f* UMWELT toxicity

Gift: Giftmüll *m* UMWELT toxic waste

Gigabyte *nt* (*GB*) COMP gigabyte (*Gb*)

Gigantomanie *f* jarg PERSON gigantomania (*jarg*)

gigantomanisch *adj* jarg PERSON gigantomaniac (*jarg*)

GIGO *abbr* jarg (*Müll rein, Müll raus*) COMP GIGO (*jarg*) (*garbage-in/garbage-out*)

Gilde *f* PERSON guild

Gini-Koeffizient *m* VW Gini coefficient

Gipfel *m* POL summit; **Gipfelkonferenz** *f* GESCHÄFT, POL summit conference; **Gipfeltreffen** *nt* GESCHÄFT, POL summit conference, summit meeting; **Gipfeltreffen von Maastricht** GESCHÄFT *EU* Maastricht Summit

Giralgeld *nt* BANK bank money, FINANZ fiat money, credit money (*BrE*); **Giralgeldschöpfungsmultiplikator** *m* FINANZ credit multiplier

Giro *nt* BANK giro; **Girobank** *f* BANK clearing bank, deposit bank, FINANZ clearing bank; **Giroeinlage** *f* BANK sight deposit; **Girokonto** *nt* BANK transfer account, checking account (*AmE*) (*C/A*), cheque account (*BrE*) (*C/A*), current account (*BrE*) (*C/A*), credit account (*C/A*), drawing account; **Giroverkehr** *m* BANK banking transfer system, clearing

Gitterstruktur *f* FINANZ grid structure

Gl. *abbr* (*Gläubiger*) FINANZ, GESCHÄFT Cr (*creditor*), RECHT *Berechtigter* obligee, VERWALT Cr (*creditor*)

GL *abbr* (*Germanischer Lloyd*) TRANSP GL (*Germanischer Lloyd*)

Glanz *m* MEDIEN *Fotografie* gloss; **Glanzabzug** *m* MEDIEN *Fotografie* gloss print

glänzend *adj* PERSON *Laufbahn* distinguished

Glanz: Glanzlichter *nt pl* GESCHÄFT highlights; **Glanzpapier** *nt* GESCHÄFT, MEDIEN *Druck* glossy paper; **Glanzstück** *nt* GESCHÄFT showpiece

Glas *nt* IND glass; **Glasballon** *m* IND, TRANSP carboy; **Glasbruchrisiko** *nt* VERSICH breakage of glass risk; **Glasfaserkabel** *f* IND fiberoptic cable (*AmE*), fibreoptic cable (*BrE*); **Glasfasern** *f pl* IND fiberglass (*AmE*), fibreglass (*BrE*); **Glasfaseroptik** *f* KOMM fiberoptics (*AmE*), fibreoptics (*BrE*)

glasfaserverstärkt: ~er Kunststoff *m* (*GFK*) IND glassfiber-reinforced plastic (*AmE*) (*GRP*), glassfibre-reinforced plastic (*BrE*) (*GRP*)

Glasgow: ~er Wertpapierbörse *f* BÖRSE Glasgow Stock Exchange

Glas: Glasseide *f* IND fiberglass (*AmE*), fibreglass (*BrE*); **Glasversicherung** *f* VERSICH glass insurance

glasverstärkt: ~e Plattierung *f* TRANSP glass-reinforced cladding

Glas: Glaswolle *f* TRANSP glass wool

glatt *adj* GESCHÄFT slick, smooth, UMWELT slick; **~es Geschäft** *nt* GESCHÄFT swimming market

glätten *vt* GESCHÄFT smooth out

glattgestellt: ~e Position *f* BANK evened-out position, BÖRSE closed position, evened-out position

glattstellen *vt* BANK *Transaktionen* settle, BÖRSE *Wertpapierpositionen* sell off, sell out

Glattstellung *f* BÖRSE liquidization, offset; **Glattstellungsbereich** *m* BÖRSE closing range; **Glattstellungsverkauf** *m* BÖRSE sell-off

Glauben: in gutem ~ *phr* VERWALT, GESCHÄFT in good faith; **in gutem ~ handeln** *phr* RECHT act in good faith

glaubhaft *adj* GESCHÄFT convincing, probable

Glaubhaftmachung *f* RECHT *von Ansprüchen* authentication

Gläubiger, in *m,f* (*Gl.*) FINANZ, GESCHÄFT creditor (*Cr*), RECHT *Berechtigter* obligee, VERWALT creditor (*Cr*); **~ aus Lieferungen und Leistungen** GESCHÄFT trade creditor; **Gläubigerabteilung** *f* VERWALT creditor department; **Gläubigerausschuß** *m* FINANZ creditor's committee, RECHT committee of inspection; **Gläubigerbuch** *nt* RECHNUNG creditors' ledger; **Gläubigergemeinschaft** *f* RECHNUNG body of creditors; **Gläubigernummer** *f* FINANZ Dun's Market Identifier; **Gläubigerstellung** *f* FINANZ creditor position; **Gläubigerverzug** *m* RECHT *Vertragsrecht* creditor's fault of acception, delay of the creditor

glaubwürdig *adj* GESCHÄFT trustworthy; **~er Eigentumsanspruch** *m* GRUND color of title (*AmE*), colour of title (*BrE*)

Glaubwürdigkeit *f* GESCHÄFT trustworthiness, V&M credibility; **~ der Informationsquelle** V&M source credibility; **Glaubwürdigkeitslücke** *f* V&M credibility gap

gleich *adj* MATH equal; ◆ **~ sein** MATH equal; **alles andere bleibt ~** GESCHÄFT all else being equal; **auf ~er Basis** GESCHÄFT on the same footing; **zu den ~en Bedingungen** GESCHÄFT on the same terms, on equal terms; **~ und gegensätzlich** GESCHÄFT equal and opposite; **auf ~e Höhe bringen** COMP align; **~er Lohn für gleiche Arbeit** PERSON equal pay for work of equal value (*BrE*); **~er Meinung sein** GESCHÄFT be agreed; **mit ~er Post** GESCHÄFT by the same post; **zu ~en Teilen** GESCHÄFT in equal proportions; **unter sonst ~en Umständen** VW all else being equal

gleich: ~e Basis *f* GESCHÄFT equal footing; **~er Geldwert** *m* GESCHÄFT level money; **~e Größe** *f* V&M same size; **~ große Gebühr** *f* GESCHÄFT commensurate charge; **~er Lohn** *m* PERSON equal pay; **~e Produktivität** *f* PERSON comparable worth (*CW*); **~es Stimmrecht** *nt* RECHT *für Partner einer Gesellschaft* equal voting rights

Gleich: ~es mit Gleichem vergleichen *phr* GESCHÄFT compare like with like *gleich*: **die ~e Wellenlänge haben wie** *jarg phr* GESCHÄFT be on the same wavelength as

gleichartig *adj* GESCHÄFT similar; **~es Vermögen** *nt* STEUER like-kind property (*AmE*); **~e Vermögenswerte** *m pl* STEUER like-kind property (*AmE*)

Gleichartigkeit *f* PATENT similarity

gleichberechtigt *adj* GESCHÄFT of equal rank, pari passu

Gleichberechtigungsergänzungsgesetz *nt* PERSON, RECHT Equal Rights Amendment (*ERA*)

gleichbleibend: **~e Abschreibungsmethode** *f* RECHNUNG straight-line method; **~es Geld** *nt* GESCHÄFT level money; **~e Prämie** *f* VERSICH level premium; **~es Risiko** *nt* VERSICH constant risk

gleichgerichtet: **~e Preisgestaltung** *f* VW parallel pricing

Gleichgestellte(r) *mf* [decl. as adj] PERSON equal

gleichgewichtig: **~es Wachstum** *nt* VW balanced growth

Gleichgewicht *nt* VW equilibrium; **~ der Kräfte** GESCHÄFT balance of power; ♦ **ins ~ bringen** GESCHÄFT redress; **das ~ finden** BÖRSE find the balance; **das ~ wiederherstellen** RECHNUNG redress the balance

Gleichgewicht: **Gleichgewichtsbasis** *f* BÖRSE equilibrium basis; **Gleichgewichtslage** *f* TRANSP trim; **Gleichgewichtsmarkt** *m* VW clearing market; **Gleichgewichtsmenge** *f* VW equilibrium output; **Gleichgewichtspreis** *m* VW equilibrium price, market clearing price; **Gleichgewichtsproduktion** *f* VW equilibrium output; **Gleichgewichtswachstum** *nt* VW balanced growth; **Gleichgewichtswachstumsrate** *f* VW warranted rate of growth

gleichgültig *adj* GESCHÄFT *Markt* unresponsive

Gleichheit *f* PERSON *Chancengleichheit, Gleichberechtigung* equality; **~ vor dem Gesetz** RECHT *Garantie in der Verfassung* Equal Protection of the Laws (*AmE*), equality before the law; **~ bei den Raten** TRANSP parity on rates; **Gleichheitsstandard** *m* POL equality standard

gleichkommen *vi* [+dat] GESCHÄFT correspond

Gleichlauf *m* GESCHÄFT synchronization (*sync*)

gleichlaufen *vi* GESCHÄFT coincide, synchronize

gleichlautend: **~e Abschrift** *f* RECHT confirmed copy

Gleichmacherei *f* *infml* POL egalitarianism

gleichmäßig 1. *adj* COMP even, GESCHÄFT synchronized; **2.** *adv* ♦ **~ verteilt** GESCHÄFT evenly spread

Gleichmäßigkeitsannahme *f* VW uniformity assumption

gleichordnen *vt* GESCHÄFT coordinate

gleichrangig *adj* GESCHÄFT of equal rank, pari passu; **~er Föderalismus** *m* POL dual federalism; **~er Mitarbeiter** *m*, **~e Mitarbeiterin** *f* VW pecuniary peer

gleichsam *adv* GESCHÄFT quasi

gleichschalten *vt* GESCHÄFT coordinate

Gleichschritt: **sich im ~ bewegen** *phr* BÖRSE move in tandem

gleichsetzen *vt* GESCHÄFT equalize

gleichsetzend *adj* GESCHÄFT equalizing

Gleichsetzung *f* GESCHÄFT equalization

Gleichung *f* MATH equation

gleichwertig *adj* GESCHÄFT equivalent

Gleichwertigkeit *f* BÖRSE equal value

Gleichzeit *f* PERSON *Arbeitszeit* flexible schedule

gleichzeitig *adj* GESCHÄFT simultaneous; **~e Ausübung** *f* **von Marketmaker- und Brokerfunktionen** BÖRSE dual capacity; **~e Eröffnung** *f* **von Kauf- und Verkaufspositionen** BÖRSE spread trading

Gleis *nt* TRANSP track; **Gleisverbindung** *f* TRANSP track connection; **Gleiswaage** *f* TRANSP track scales

Gleit- *in cpds* GESCHÄFT sliding, flexible, gliding

gleitend: **~e Arbeitszeit** *f* PERSON flexible time, flexible working hours, flexitime; **~e Jahressumme** *f* MATH moving annual total (*MAT*); **~e Lebensversicherung** *f* VERSICH indexed life insurance; **~e Lohnskala** *f* PERSON *Lohnbuchhaltung* sliding wage scale; **~er Lohntarif** *m* PERSON sliding wage scale; **~e Prognose** *f* VW moving projection; **~e Skala** *f* FINANZ sliding scale; **~e Wechselkursanpassung** *f* BÖRSE crawling peg

Gleit-: **Gleitkommazahl** *f* COMP, MATH floating-point number; **Gleitkufe** *f* TRANSP skid; **Gleitparität** *f* VW crawling peg; **Gleitschicht** *f* PERSON gliding shift; **Gleitzeit** *f* PERSON flexitime, flexible time, flexible working hours, staggered working hours, VERWALT flexible working hours; **Gleitzoll** *m* BÖRSE gliding rate, IMP/EXP sliding-scale tariff

Glied: **aus dem ~ treten** *phr* PERSON *Gewerkschaften* break ranks

gliedern *vt* GESCHÄFT structure

Gliedertaxe *f* VERSICH disability percentage table

Gliederung *f* GESCHÄFT arrangement, classification, structure; **~ in Geschäftsbereiche** GESCHÄFT divisionalization; **Gliederungsbogen** *m* BÖRSE, COMP, FINANZ, RECHNUNG, VERWALT spread sheet; **Gliederungstiefe** *f* RECHNUNG materiality level

Global- *in cpds* GESCHÄFT global

global *adj* GESCHÄFT worldwide, all-in, all-inclusive, global; **~e Aufbewahrung** *f* FINANZ global custody; **~e Bank** *f* BANK global bank; **~e Bankgarantie** *f* BANK comprehensive bank guarantee; **~e Deregulierung** *f* VW global deregulation; **~es Finanzzentrum** *nt* VW global financial center (*AmE*), global financial centre (*BrE*); **~es Gleichgewicht** *nt* UMWELT global balance; **~e Harmonisierung** *f* RECHNUNG global harmonization; **~es Image** *nt* V&M global image; **~er Monetarismus** *m* VW global monetarism; **~es Netz** *nt* COMP global network

Global-: **Globales Positionsbestimmungssystem** *nt* TRANSP Global Positioning System (*GPS*); **Globales Seenot- und Sicherheitssystem** *nt* TRANSP Global Maritime Distress and Safety System (*GMDSS*)

global: **~er Speicher** *m* COMP global memory; **~e Strategie** *f* GESCHÄFT global strategy; **~e Suchen** *nt* COMP *Daten* global search; **~es Suchen** *nt* **und Ersetzen** *nt* COMP global search and replace; **~e Variable** *f* COMP global variable

Global-: **Globaldepot** *nt* FINANZ global custody

globalisieren *vt* GESCHÄFT globalize

Globalisierung *f* GESCHÄFT globalization

Global-: **Globalkauf** *m* FINANZ lump sum purchase; **Globalkürzung** *f* MGMNT, PERSON across-the-board cut; **Globalpolice** *f* VERSICH blanket contract; **Globalstreik** *m* PERSON all-out strike; **Globalversicherung** *f* VERSICH all-loss insurance, all-risk insurance, all-risk cover; **Globalzeichen** *nt* COMP wild card

Glockenkurve *f* MATH bell-shaped curve

Glockenpolitik *f* UMWELT, VW bubble policy

Glück: **sein ~ versuchen** *phr* FREI have a flutter (*infrml*) (*BrE*)

glücklich: ~**e Gelegenheit** *f* GESCHÄFT break (*infrml*)

Glücksfall *m* GESCHÄFT lucky break

GmbH *abbr* (*Gesellschaft mit beschränkter Haftung*) GESCHÄFT Inc. (*Incorporated AmE*), limited liability company (*BrE*), Ltd (*BrE*) (*limited company*), private limited company, Pty (*proprietary company*)

GMT *abbr* (*Greenwich Mean Time*) GESCHÄFT GMT (*Greenwich Mean Time*)

Gnadenfrist *f* PATENT period of grace, RECHNUNG grace days, RECHT period of grace

GoB *abbr* (*Grundsätze ordnungsgemäßer Buchführung*) RECHNUNG GAAP (*Generally Accepted Accounting Principles AmE*), SSAP (*Statement of Standard Accounting Practice BrE*)

Goethe-Institut *nt* VERWALT ≈ British Council (*BC*)

Gold *nt* BÖRSE gold; ~ **Card** *f* BANK gold card; **Goldabbau** *m* IND gold mining; **Goldausfuhrpunkt** *m* FINANZ, IMP/EXP, VW gold export point, gold exporting point; **Goldbarrenmarkt** *m* BÖRSE bullion market; **Goldbergbau** *m* IND gold mining; **Goldbergwerksgesellschaft** *f* UMWELT gold-mining company; **Golddeckung** *f* VW gold cover; **Golddemonetisierung** *f* VW gold demonetization; **Golddevisenwährung** *f* VW gold exchange standard; **Goldeinfuhr** *f* IMP/EXP gold import; **Goldeinfuhrpunkt** *m* FINANZ, IMP/EXP, VW gold import point

Golden: ~ **Age-Wachstumspfad** *nt* VW golden age path; ~**es Dreieck** *nt* VW Golden Triangle

golden: ~**e Handschellen** *f pl infrml* VW golden rule; ~**e Regel** *f* VW golden rule

Gold: **Golderz** *nt* UMWELT gold ore; **Goldfixing** *nt* BANK gold fixing

goldgerändert: ~**e Aktie** *f infrml* BÖRSE blue-chip stock; ~**es Papier** *nt* FINANZ, VW blue chip

Gold: **Goldgewinner** *m* IND gold producer; **Goldgewinnung** *f* IND gold mining

Goldgrube *f infrml* GESCHÄFT bonanza; ♦ **eine** ~ **entdecken** *infrml* GESCHÄFT strike it rich (*infrml*)

Gold: **Goldkernwährung** *f* VW gold bullion standard; **Goldknappheit** *f* VW gold shortage; **Goldkredit** *m* BÖRSE gold credit; **Goldmarkt** *m* VW gold market; **Goldmünze** *f* BANK gold coin; **Goldpreis** *m* BÖRSE gold price; **Goldproduzent** *m* IND gold producer; **Goldpunkt** *m* GESCHÄFT specie point, IMP/EXP gold point; **Goldrausch** *m* GESCHÄFT gold rush; **Goldreserven** *f pl* VW gold reserves

Goldsmith-Banksystem *nt* BANK Goldsmith banking system

Gold: **Goldstandard** *m* VW gold standard; **Goldumlauf** *m* BANK gold currency; **Goldwährung** *f* BANK gold currency

Goodhart-Gesetz *nt* VW Goodhart's law

Goodwill *m* RECHNUNG goodwill; **Goodwill-Abschreibung** *f* RECHNUNG goodwill amortization

Gouverneur *m* GESCHÄFT governor; ~ **der Bank von England** VW Governor of the Bank of England

G-Prädikat *nt* V&M G-spool

Grad *m* GESCHÄFT degree; ~ **der Beschädigung** VERSICH degree of damage; ~ *m pl* **Celsius** GESCHÄFT degrees Centigrade; ~ **an Devisenengagement** BÖRSE degree of exposure; ~ *m pl* **Fahrenheit** GESCHÄFT degrees Fahrenheit; ~ **an Kreditengagement** BÖRSE degree of exposure; ~ **an Kursschwankungen** BÖRSE degree of

fluctuation; ~ **an Preisschwankungen** BÖRSE degree of fluctuation; ~ **an Wertpapierengagement** BÖRSE degree of exposure; **Gradmaß** *nt* MATH *Winkelmessung* degree measure

graduell *adj* GESCHÄFT gradual

Graduierte(r) *mf* [decl. as adj] PERSON graduate

Grafik *f* COMP graphics, MATH chart; **Grafikbrett** *nt* COMP graphics board; **Grafikdatei** *f* COMP graphics file, *Grafikprogramm* drawing file; **Grafikdatenbank** *f* COMP graphics database; **Grafikdatenverarbeitung** *f* COMP graphic data processing; **Grafikdrucker** *m* COMP graphics printer

grafikfähig: ~**er Bildschirm** *m* COMP graphics display terminal

Grafik: **Grafikkarte** *f* COMP graphics card; **Grafikmodus** *m* COMP graphics mode; **Grafiksoftware** *f* COMP graphics software, *Grafikprogramm* drawing software; **Grafiktafel** *f* COMP graphics board

grafisch *adj* COMP graphic; ~**e Benutzerschnittstelle** *f* (*GUI*) COMP graphical user interface (*GUI*); ~**e Darstellung** *f* COMP graph; ~**es Editieren** *nt* MEDIEN graphical editing; ~**er Ideengestalter** *m*, ~**e Ideengestalterin** *f* V&M visualizer; ~ **illustriert** *adj* GESCHÄFT graphically illustrated

Grafschaft *f* GESCHÄFT county (*BrE*)

Graham-und-Dodd: ~-**Investitionsmethode** *f* BÖRSE Graham and Dodd method of investing

Gramm *nt* (*g*) GESCHÄFT gram (*g*), gramme (*g*)

Grammy *m* MEDIEN *Preis* Grammy

Graph *m* COMP, MATH graph

Grassroots *pl jarg* POL *Parteien, soziale Bewegungen* grass roots

gratis 1. *adj* GESCHÄFT free, gratis, free of charge (*foc*); 2. *adv* GESCHÄFT gratis

Gratisaktie *f* FINANZ bonus issue; **Gratisaktien** *f pl* RECHNUNG free issue of new shares

Gratiswerbesendung *f* V&M plug (*infrml*)

Grau- *in cpds* GESCHÄFT grey (*BrE*), gray (*AmE*)

grau: ~**e Gesellschaft** *f* VW grey society (*BrE*), gray society (*AmE*); ~**er Gürtel** *m* VW grey belt (*jarg*) (*BrE*); ~**er Markt** *m* BÖRSE *Wertpapieremissionen* grey market (*BrE*), gray market (*AmE*), VW grey market (*BrE*), gray market (*AmE*), semi-black market; ~**er Montag** *m* BÖRSE grey Monday (*BrE*), gray Monday (*AmE*)

Grau-: **Graupappe** *f* GESCHÄFT chipboard; **Grauskala** *f* COMP greyscale (*BrE*), grayscale (*AmE*); **Grauzone** *f* VW Intermediate Area

gravierend: ~**er Fehler** *m* GESCHÄFT fatal error

Greenwich: ~ **Mean Time** *f* (*GMT*) GESCHÄFT Greenwich Mean Time (*GMT*)

Greif- *in cpds* TRANSP grabbing

greifbar: ~**es Anlagenkapital** *nt* RECHNUNG tangible fixed assets; ~**e Vermögenswerte** *m pl* FINANZ tangible fixed assets

greifen *vt* GESCHÄFT snatch

Greifer *m* TRANSP grab

Greif-: **Greifhaken** *m* TRANSP dog hook

Gremium *nt* GESCHÄFT body, POL commission (*comm*), committee (*comm*); ~ **zur Feststellung der Übereinstimmung mit Agenturvorschriften** TRANSP Agency Compliance Board

Grenz- *in cpds* GESCHÄFT, VW marginal; **Grenzausgaben** *f pl* V&M incremental spending; **Grenzausgleich** *m* VW

Monetary Compensation Amount (*MCA*); **Grenzausgleichzahlungen** *f pl* VW Monetary Compensation Amount (*MCA*); **Grenzbetrachtung** *f* FINANZ marginal analysis; **Grenzbetrieb** *m* VW marginal firm

Grenze *f* GESCHÄFT frontier, GRUND boundary, VW cap, limit

Grenz-: **Grenzerlös** *m* VW marginal profit, marginal revenue; **Grenzerlösprodukt** *nt* VW marginal revenue product (*MRP*); **Grenzertrag** *m* **des investierten Kapitals** FINANZ marginal return on capital; **Grenzfall** *m* GESCHÄFT borderline case; **Grenzgänger, in** *m,f* PERSON frontier worker; **Grenzhandel** *m* IMP/EXP border trade; **Grenzkontrolle** *f* IMP/EXP, VW border control, *von Waren* frontier control; **Grenzkosten** *pl* FINANZ, RECHNUNG marginal costs, alternative costs, VW incremental cost, marginal costs; **Grenzkostenkurve** *f* VW marginal cost curve; **Grenzkostenrechnung** *f* FINANZ marginal costing, RECHNUNG marginal costing, marginal pricing; **Grenzleistungsfähigkeit** *f* **der Investition** VW marginal efficiency of investment; **Grenzleistungsfähigkeit** *f* **des Kapitals** VW marginal efficiency of capital; **Grenznutzen** *m* VW marginal utility; **Grenzplankostenkalkulation** *f* VW marginal cost pricing; **Grenzplankostenrechnung** *f* FINANZ direct costing, RECHNUNG accounting by functions, direct costing, VW accounting by functions, activity accounting, direct costing, marginal costing; **Grenzpostenveto** *nt* POL line item veto (*AmE*); **Grenzpreisbildung** *f* VW marginal pricing; **Grenzprodukt** *nt* IND marginal product; **Grenzprodukt** *nt* **der Arbeit** VW marginal product of labor (*AmE*), marginal product of labour (*BrE*); **Grenzproduktivität** *f* VW marginal productivity; **Grenzproduktivitätstheorie** *f* VW marginal productivity theory; **Grenzproduzent** *m* VW marginal firm, marginal producer; **Grenzrate** *f* **der Substitution** VW marginal rate of substitution (*MRS*); **Grenzrate** *f* **der Transformation** VW marginal rate of transformation; **Grenzsteuersatz** *m* STEUER marginal tax rate; **Grenzübergang** *m* TRANSP border crossing-point, checkpoint; **Grenzübergangsstelle** *f* GESCHÄFT point of entry

grenzüberschreitend *adj* GESCHÄFT cross-border, transnational, V&M transfrontier; **~e Entflechtung** *f* VW cross-border demerger; **~es Finanzgeschäft** *nt* FINANZ cross-border financial transaction; **~e Firmenzusammenschlüsse** *m pl* BÖRSE, GESCHÄFT cross-border merger; **~e Fusion** *f* BÖRSE, GESCHÄFT, VW cross-border merger; **~es Gemeinschaftsunternehmen** *nt* MGMNT cross-border joint venture; **~er Handel** *m* IMP/EXP, VW cross-border trade; **~er Handelsverkehr** *m* IMP/EXP, VW cross-border trading; **~es Joint-Venture** *nt* MGMNT cross-border joint venture; **~e Transaktion** *f* VW cross-border transaction; **~er Transfer** *m* TRANSP, UMWELT cross-border transfer

Grenz-: **Grenzumsatz** *m* VW marginal profit; **Grenzumsatzprodukt** *nt* VW marginal revenue product (*MRP*); **Grenzverkehr** *m* GESCHÄFT border traffic; **Grenzwert** *m* UMWELT *Luftverschmutzung* ambient standard; **Grenzwertanalyse** *f* GESCHÄFT incremental analysis, RECHNUNG, VW marginal analysis; **Grenzwerte für eine Neubewertung sammeln** *phr* BÖRSE gather in the stops; **Grenzzollstelle** *f* IMP/EXP frontier customs post

Gresham: **~sches Gesetz** *nt* VW Gresham's Law

Griff *m* COMP handle

grob: **~er Ansatz** *m* GESCHÄFT, POL approximation; **~ fahrlässige Unkenntnis** *f* RECHT *Vertragsrecht* gross ignorance; **~ fahrlässig handeln** *phr* RECHT be guilty of gross negligence; **~e Schätzung** *f* GESCHÄFT rough estimate; **~ umreißen** *phr* GESCHÄFT outline, sketch; **~ umrissen** *adj* POL *Plan, Vorhaben* broad-brush; **~es Verschulden** *nt* RECHT *Vertragsrecht* gross fault

Grobraster *nt* V&M coarse screen

Gros *nt obs* MATH gross

Groß- *in cpds* GESCHÄFT, IND, V&M, VW large, bulk, heavy, large-scale

groß 1. *adj* GESCHÄFT great, massive, *Großeinkauf* large; ◆ **das ~e Geld machen** *infrml* GESCHÄFT strike it rich (*infrml*); **ohne ~e Havarie** GESCHÄFT, VERSICH free of general average (*fga*); **in ~em Maße** GESCHÄFT on a large scale; **in ~en Mengen** GESCHÄFT in large quantities; **in ~en Mengen kaufen** GESCHÄFT buy in large quantities; **in ~em Umfang** GESCHÄFT to a large extent; **sich in ~e Unkosten stürzen** GESCHÄFT go to great expense; **im ~en verkaufen** V&M sell in bulk; **2.** *adv* ◆ **~ abkassieren** *infrml* GESCHÄFT strike it rich (*infrml*); **~ angelegt** GESCHÄFT, VW *Projekte* large-scale

groß: **~e Aufmachung** *f* **in der Presse** MEDIEN splash; **~e Gefahr** *f* VERSICH large risk; **die ~e Gesellschaft** *f* VW Great Society (*AmE*), **~ Havarie** *f* VERSICH general average (*GA, G/A*); **sehr ~e Kursspanne** *f* BÖRSE alligator spread; **~e Küstenfahrt** *f* TRANSP short sea shipping; **~er Küstenhandel** *m* TRANSP short sea trade; **~er Name** *m* GESCHÄFT big name; **~es Risiko** *nt* VERSICH large risk; **sehr ~er Rohöltanker** *m* TRANSP ultra-large crude carrier, very large crude carrier (*VLCC*); **~er Verbrauchermarkt** *m* V&M superstore

Groß-: **Großabnehmer** *m* GESCHÄFT bulk buyer, bulk purchaser, quantity buyer, big industrial user; **Großaktionär, in** *m,f* BÖRSE principal stockholder; **Großanlage** *f* IND heavy industrial plant; **Großanleger, in** *m,f* FINANZ big investor; **Großanzeige** *f* V&M display advertising; **Großauftrag** *m* GESCHÄFT bulk order, large order; **Großbank** *f* BANK big bank; **Großbetrieb** *m* GESCHÄFT big business; **Großbrandbereich** *m* VERSICH conflagration area; **Großbuchstabe** *m* COMP, MEDIEN capital letter (*cap.*), upper case letter; **Großbuchstaben** *m pl* COMP, MEDIEN capital letters (*caps*), upper case letters, upper case

Größe *f* COMP size, VW size, bulk; ◆ **nach ~ geordnet** GESCHÄFT graded by size

Groß-: **Großeinkauf** *m* GESCHÄFT bulk purchase, spending spree (*infrml*); **Großeinkäufer, in** *m,f* GESCHÄFT bulk purchaser; **Großeinkaufszentrum** *nt* VW hypermarket

Größe: **Größennachteile** *m pl* VW diseconomies of scale; **Größenordnung** *f* MATH order of magnitude; **Größenverteilung** *f* MATH size distribution; **Größenvorteil** *m* VW economy of size; **Größenvorteile** *m pl* VW scale economies; **Größenwahn** *m* PERSON megalomania; **Größenwahnsinnige(r)** *mf* [*decl. as adj*] PERSON megalomaniac

größer: **~e Geldbeträge verwalten** *phr* FINANZ handle large sums of money; **in ~e Geschäftsgebäude umziehen** *phr* VERWALT move to larger premises

Groß-: **Großexporteur** *m* IMP/EXP, VW large-scale exporter

großflächig: ~**es Netz** *nt* (*WAN*) COMP, KOMM, MGMNT wide-area network (*WAN*)

großformatig: ~**e Anzeige** *f* V&M sheet; ~**es Flugblatt** *nt* MEDIEN *Werbung* broadsheet; ~**e Zeitung** *f obs* MEDIEN broadsheet, broadsheet newspaper

Großhandel *m* BÖRSE jobbing, GESCHÄFT wholesale, wholesale business, wholesale trade, V&M, VW wholesale trade; ◆ **im** ~ GESCHÄFT by wholesale

Großhandel: **Großhandelsartikel** *m pl* GESCHÄFT, IND, VW wholesale goods; **Großhandelsbetrieb** *m* GESCHÄFT, VW wholesale dealer, wholesale merchant, wholesale trader, wholesaler; **Großhandelserzeugnisse** *nt pl* GESCHÄFT, IND, VW wholesale goods; **Großhandelsgeschäft** *nt* GESCHÄFT wholesale business; **Großhandelsgewerbe** *nt* V&M, VW wholesaling; **Großhandelskauf** *m* V&M wholesale purchasing; **Großhandelskauffrau** *f* GESCHÄFT, VW wholesale dealer, wholesale merchant, wholesale trader, wholesaler; **Großhandelskaufmann** *m* GESCHÄFT, VW wholesale dealer, wholesale merchant, wholesale trader, wholesaler; **Großhandelslieferung** *f* GESCHÄFT, V&M wholesale delivery; **Großhandelsmarkt** *m* GESCHÄFT wholesale market; **Großhandelsperson** *f* GESCHÄFT, VW wholesale dealer, wholesale merchant, wholesale trader, wholesaler; **Großhandelspreis** *m* GESCHÄFT, V&M wholesale price; **zum Großhandelspreis** *phr* GESCHÄFT by wholesale; **Großhandelspreisindex** *m* VW wholesale price index; **Großhandelspreisinflation** *f* VW wholesale price inflation; **Großhandelsrabatt** *m* GESCHÄFT trade allowance

Groß-: **Großhändler, in** *m,f* GESCHÄFT, V&M jobber, wholesale dealer, wholesale merchant, wholesale trader, wholesaler; **Großindustrie** *f* GESCHÄFT big business, IND large-scale industry; **Großindustrielle(r)** *mf* [decl. as adj] FINANZ business magnate, GESCHÄFT tycoon, PERSON captain of industry, tycoon

Grossist, in *m,f* GESCHÄFT, V&M wholesale dealer, wholesale merchant, wholesale trader, wholesaler

Groß-: **Großkredit** *m* BANK jumbo loan, FINANZ large exposure; **Großkunde** *m*, **Großkundin** *f* GESCHÄFT big customer, major customer; **auf das Großkundengeschäft ausgerichtete Bank** *f* BANK merchant bank, wholesale bank; **Großkundengeschäft** *nt* **der Banken** BANK merchant banking; **Großkundensachbearbeiter, in** *m,f* PERSON *Unternehmen* national accounts manager; **Großlager** *nt* GESCHÄFT bulk storage; **Großmarkt** *m* GESCHÄFT wholesale market; **Großmaschinenbau** *m* IND heavy engineering; **Großpackung** *f* GESCHÄFT bulk package, economy-sized packet, V&M economy-sized packet; **Großpalette** *f* GESCHÄFT flat; **Großproduktion** *f* IND large-scale production; **Großprospekt** *m* MEDIEN broadsheet; **Großraumbüro** *nt* VERWALT open-plan office; **Großraumflugzeug** *nt* TRANSP heavy jet, wide-body aircraft; **Großraum-Jet** *m* TRANSP jumbo (*infrml*), jumbo jet (*infrml*); **Großrechner** *m* COMP supercomputer

großschreiben *vt* GESCHÄFT capitalize

Groß-: **Großschreibung** *f* COMP, GESCHÄFT, MEDIEN capitalization; **Großstadt** *f* GESCHÄFT metropolitan town; **Großstadtgebiet** *nt* VW metropolitan area

großstädtisch *adj* GESCHÄFT metropolitan; **nicht** ~ *adj* GESCHÄFT nonmetropolitan

Groß-: **Großtat** *f* GESCHÄFT achievement

größte: ~ **Bundessteuerbehörde** *f* STEUER Inland Revenue (*BrE*); ~**r Teil** *m* GESCHÄFT bulk; ~**r Teil** *m* **des Geschäftes** GESCHÄFT bulk of the business

Groß-: **Großteil** *m* VW bulk; **Großunfall** *m* TRANSP multi-accident; **Großunternehmen** *nt* GESCHÄFT big company; **Großverdiener, in** *m,f* FINANZ, PERSON big income earner; **Großverladung** *f* IMP/EXP, TRANSP volume shipping; **Großzählung** *f* GESCHÄFT census

großzügig *adj* GESCHÄFT, STEUER generous; ~**e Abfindung** *f* FINANZ golden parachute (*infrml*); ~**er Haushaltsplan** *m* FINANZ soft budget

Grubenbetrieb *m* IND mining

grün *adj* UMWELT green; ~**es Benzin** *nt* UMWELT green petrol; ~**e Energie** *f* UMWELT green energy; ~**es Licht** *nt* GESCHÄFT *Erlaubnis* green light; ~**e Lobby** *f* UMWELT green lobby; ~**es Pfund** *nt* VW *EG* green pound; ~**e Revolution** *f* VW green revolution; ~**e Versicherungskarte** *f* VERSICH green card

Grund *m* GESCHÄFT rationale; ~ **und Boden** *m* IND premises; ◆ **auf** ~ TRANSP aground; **auf** ~ **gelaufen** TRANSP aground; **auf** ~ **laufen** TRANSP run aground, run ashore; **aus diesem** ~ GESCHÄFT for that reason

Grund: **Grundanliegen** *nt* POL *eine die Grundbedürfnisse betreffende Frage* bread-and-butter issue (*infrml*) (*BrE*); **Grundaussage** *f* V&M *Botschaft* basic message; **Grundausstattung** *f* COMP *Rechner* base configuration; **Grundbedürfnisse** *nt pl* VW basic needs, basics, bare necessities; **Grundbegriff** *m* GESCHÄFT basic concept; **Grundbesitz** *m* GRUND freehold property, landed property, VW land ownership, domain; **Grundbesitz** *m* **mit beschränkten Rechten** GRUND nonmerchantable title (*AmE*); **Grundbetrag** *m* GESCHÄFT basic amount; **Grundbilanz** *f* VW basic balance; **Grundbuch** *nt* GRUND, VERWALT land register (*BrE*), plat book (*AmE*), FINANZ, RECHNUNG book of first entry, book of original entry, book of prime entry; **Grundbuchamt** *nt* GRUND, RECHT registry of deeds, VERWALT land office (*AmE*), land registry; **Grundbuchauszug** *m* GRUND extract from the land register, land certificate; **Grundbucheintragung** *f* GRUND land registration; **Grundbuchung** *f* RECHNUNG original entry; **Grunddefinition** *f* GESCHÄFT basic definition; **Grunddienstbarkeit** *f* GRUND easement; **Grundeigentum** *nt* GRUND, VERWALT freehold, freehold property; **Grundeigentumsurkunden** *f pl* RECHT muniments, muniments of title; **Grundeinheit** *f* GESCHÄFT basic unit; **Grundeinkommen** *nt* FINANZ basic income

gründen *vt* GESCHÄFT *Firma* form, found, start, *Unternehmen* incorporate, set up, RECHT *Unternehmen* incorporate, VW *Unternehmen* start up; ◆ ~ **auf** [+acc] GESCHÄFT base on

Grund: **Grundetat** *m* RECHNUNG base budget; **Grundfläche** *f* GRUND floor space; **Grundfreibetrag** *m* STEUER basic relief; **Grundgebühr** *f* FINANZ flat fee, GESCHÄFT service fee; **Grundgehalt** *nt* PERSON basic pay (*BrE*), base salary (*AmE*), VERWALT flat pay; **Grundgesamtheit** *f* POL *Statistik* parent population, V&M universe; **Grundgeschäft** *nt* FINANZ bottom line (*infrml*), GESCHÄFT bread-and-butter line (*infrml*); **Grundhaftungsgrenzen** *f pl* VERSICH basic limits of liability; **Grundindustrie** *f* IND, VW basic industry; **Grundinflation** *f* VW underlying inflation; **Grundinflationsrate** *f* VW underlying inflation rate; **Grundinformationen** *f pl* GESCHÄFT basics; **Grundkapital** *nt* FINANZ authorized capital, authorized capital stock, capital fund, original capital, capital stock, RECHNUNG capital, stated capital, vw share capital, base capital; **Grundkenntnisse von etw haben** *phr* GESCHÄFT, PERSON have a working knowledge of sth; **Grundkonfiguration** *f* COMP base configuration

Grundlage *f* GESCHÄFT substructure, STEUER basis; ♦ **die ~ für etw bilden** BANK provide the base for sth; **die ~ für etwas schaffen** GESCHÄFT lay the ground for sth

Grundlagen *f pl* GESCHÄFT basics; **Grundlagenarbeit** *f* GESCHÄFT groundwork; **Grundlagenforschung** *f* GESCHÄFT basic research, basics

Grund: **Grundlastkraftwerk** *nt* IND base load power station

grundlegend *adj* GESCHÄFT *Veränderungen* sweeping, POL sweeping; **~er Fall** *m* RECHT *Fall von grundsätzlicher Bedeutung* landmark case; **~e Haftungsgrenzen** *f pl* VERSICH basic limits of liability; **~e Rate** *f* vw underlying rate; **~er Tarif** *m* vw underlying rate

gründlich *adj* GESCHÄFT in-depth; ♦ **jdn einer ~en Prüfung unterziehen** PERSON screen sb for a job; **gründlich überprüfen** GESCHÄFT check thoroughly

gründlich: **~e Analyse** *f* GESCHÄFT in-depth analysis; **~e Überprüfung** *f* MGMNT *eines Systems* overhaul; **~e Untersuchung** *f* GESCHÄFT in-depth study

Grund: **Grundlinie** *f* COMP *Schriftzeichen*, MATH baseline; **Grundlohn** *m* PERSON basic pay (*BrE*), base pay (*AmE*), basic wage, wage floor, basic rate, vw basic pay (*BrE*), base pay (*AmE*)

grundlos: **~e Entlassung** *f* PERSON wrongful dismissal, *Arbeitsrecht, Kündigungsschutzklage* unfair dismissal, RECHT wrongful dismissal

Grund: **Grundmiete** *f* GRUND base rent; **Grundnahrungsmittel** *nt pl* GESCHÄFT basic foodstuffs, essential foodstuffs; **Grundpfandrecht** *nt* GRUND, RECHT mortgage lien; **Grundpfandrecht** *nt* **auf Pachtgrundstück** GRUND, RECHT leasehold mortgage; **Grundplatine** *f* COMP motherboard; **Grundprämie** *f* VERSICH basic premium; **Grundpreis** *m* FINANZ basis price, GESCHÄFT base price, basic price, STEUER base price; **Grundprinzip** *nt* GESCHÄFT guiding principle; **Grundprodukt** *nt* IND base product; **Grundrechenarten** *f pl* MATH basic arithmetical operations; **Grundrechnungsarten** *f pl* MATH basic arithmetical operations; **Grundregeln** *f pl* GESCHÄFT ground rules; **Grundrente** *f* GRUND ground rent, SOZIAL rent charge; **Grundriß** *m* GESCHÄFT ground plan, plot, outline, GRUND floor plan

Grundsatz *m* GESCHÄFT convention, principle; **~ der Gewinnrealisierung** RECHNUNG completed contract method; **~ der Periodenabgrenzung** RECHNUNG matching principle (*AmE*), accrual concept, accrual principle; **~ der strikten Bedingungserfüllung** BANK doctrine of strict compliance; **~ der Unabhängigkeit** GESCHÄFT, STEUER, V&M arm's-length principle; **~ der Vorsicht** GESCHÄFT conservatism, RECHNUNG conservatism principle; **Grundsatzentscheidung** *f* GESCHÄFT policy decision; **Grundsätze des finanziellen Berichtwesens** RECHNUNG Financial Reporting Standard (*FRS*); **Grundsätze** *m pl* **ordnungsgemäßer Buchführung** (*GoB*) RECHNUNG Generally Accepted Accounting Principles (*AmE*) (*GAAP*), Statement of Standard Accounting Practice (*BrE*) (*SSAP*); **Grundsatzerklärung** *f* GESCHÄFT rationale, policy statement; **Grundsätze** *m pl* **der Unternehmenspolitik** VERWALT, VW business policy

grundsätzlich *adv* GESCHÄFT a priori, principally, in principle, on principle

Grundsatz: **Grundsatzpapier** *nt* POL position paper; **Grundsatzprogramm** *nt* GESCHÄFT policy statement

Grund: **Grundschuld** *f* BÖRSE, FINANZ, GRUND underlying debt; **Grundservice** *m* TRANSP parent service; **Grundstein** *m* GESCHÄFT cornerstone; **Grundsteuer** *f* STEUER land tax, real property tax; **Grundsteuerzahler, in** *m,f* STEUER ratepayer

Grundstoff *m* BÖRSE primary commodity, GESCHÄFT primary product, vw basic commodity, basic material, primary commodity, primary product; **Grundstoffindustrie** *f* IND basic industry, *Bergbau, Öl- und Gasförderung* extractive industry, vw basic industry, extractive industry, primary industry; **Grundstoffsektor** *nt* GESCHÄFT basic goods sector

Grundstück *nt* GESCHÄFT plot, GRUND parcel, plot, premises; **am ~ Berechtigte(r)** *mf* [decl. as adj] RECHT party to an estate; **~, Lehensbesitz** *m* **am Grundstück und dingliche Rechte** *nt pl* RECHT land, tenements and hereditaments; **Grundstücksbelastung** *f* RECHT encumbrance; **Grundstücksbenutzung** *f* UMWELT land use; **Grundstücksbestandteile** *m pl* GRUND fixtures; **Grundstückseigentum** *nt* GRUND fee simple; **Grundstückseigentümer, in** *m,f* GRUND freehold owner; **Grundstückseinrichtungen** *f pl* GRUND land improvements; **Grundstücksentschädigungsgesetz** *nt* RECHT *Enteignung* Land Compensation Act (*BrE*); **Grundstückserschließung** *f* GRUND land improvement, property development; **Grundstückserschließungsprojekt** *nt* GRUND property development project; **Grundstücksgrenze** *f* GRUND lot line; **Grundstücksmakler, in** *m,f* GRUND estate agent (*BrE*), listing agent (*AmE*), listing broker (*AmE*); **Grundstücksmaklervertrag** *m* **mit Nettoangebot** GRUND net listing; **Grundstücksmarkt** *m* GRUND property market; **Grundstücksmiete** *f* GRUND land rent; **Grundstücksnebenrechte** *nt pl* GRUND, RECHT incorporeal hereditaments; **Grundstücksnießbrauch** *m* GRUND life estate; **Grundstücksnullgrenze** *f* GRUND zero lot line; **Grundstücksnutzungsvorschrift** *f* GRUND land-use regulation; **Grundstücksnutzungswechsel** *m* GRUND land-use succession; **Grundstückspacht** *f* GRUND land rent; **Grundstücksparzellenlinie** *f* GRUND lot line; **Grundstückspekulant, in** *m,f* GRUND property speculator; **Grundstücksplan** *m* GRUND plot plan; **den Grundstückspreis nachträglich erhöhen** *phr* GRUND gazump (*jarg*) (*BrE*); **Grundstücksteilung** *f* RECHT partition; **Grundstücksübereignung** *f* **anstatt der Vollstreckung** GRUND, RECHT deed in lieu of foreclosure; **Grundstücksüberlassungsvertrag** *m* GRUND land contract; **Grundstücksübertragung** *f* RECHT *Eigentum* conveyance; **Grundstücksübertragungsmethode** *f* GRUND avulsion; **Grundstücksurkunde** *f* GRUND, RECHT title deed; **Grundstücksvertrag** *m* GRUND land certificate, land contract; **Grundstücksverwaltung** *f* GRUND property management; **Grundstückswertregister** *nt* STEUER cadastre; **Grundstückswertschätzung** *f* GRUND estimated value of real estate

Grund: **Grundtarif** *m* GESCHÄFT base rate (*BrE*); **Grundtarifsteuer** *m* STEUER base-rate tax; **Grundtechnik** *f* GESCHÄFT basic technique, bread-and-butter technique (*infrml*); **Grundtendenz** *f*

GESCHÄFT basic trend, underlying tendency, vw underlying tendency

Gründung *f* RECHT *einer Gesellschaft* incorporation, the Establishment; **Gründungsaufwand** *m* RECHNUNG organization cost, organization expense, original cost; **Gründungsbericht** *m* GESCHÄFT statutory report; **Gründungsgesellschaft** *f* GESCHÄFT founding company; **Gründungskapital** *nt* FINANZ initial capital, original capital, seed capital, seed money, start-up capital; **Gründungskosten** *pl* FINANZ setting-up costs, organization expense, promotion cost, RECHNUNG organization cost, preliminary expenses, setting-up costs; **Gründungsmitglied** *nt* GESCHÄFT founder member; **Gründungsprospekt** *m* BÖRSE, FINANZ prospectus; **Gründungsurkunde** *f* RECHT *Gesellschaftsrecht* charter, *Satzung* articles of association (*BrE*), articles of incorporation (*AmE*), *Vertragsrecht* certificate of incorporation; **Gründungsversammlung** *f* MGMNT organization meeting; **Gründungsvertrag** *m* RECHT *Gründungssatzung* memorandum of association

Grund: **Grundverdienst** *m* FINANZ basic income; **Grundverpackung** *f* GESCHÄFT primary package; **Grundzuschuß** *m* GESCHÄFT, POL sustaining grant

Grüne: **die Grünen** *pl* POL, UMWELT *Partei* Greens; **~ Partei** *f* POL, UMWELT Green Party; **~ Währung** *f* vw green currency

Grüngürtel *m* UMWELT green belt

Gruppe *f* GESCHÄFT body, group of companies, RECHNUNG group; **~ von Bankern** BANK Banking School (*BrE*); **~ mit besonderen Interessen** GESCHÄFT special interest group (*SIG*); **~ der Fünf** (*G5*) vw Group of Five; **~ von Gleichrangigen** V&M peer group; **~ der 7 führenden Weltwirtschaftsnationen** (*G7*) vw Group of Seven (*G7*); **~ verbundener Kunden** FINANZ group of connected clients; **Gruppenabschluß** *m* RECHNUNG group accounts; **Gruppenabschreibung** *f* FINANZ composite depreciation; **Gruppenabstimmung** *f* COMP batch control; **Gruppenakkord** *m* PERSON group piecework; **Gruppenakkordsystem** *nt* VERWALT group incentive payment system; **Gruppenanreiz** *m* PERSON group incentive; **Gruppenanreizsystem** *nt* PERSON group incentive scheme; **Gruppenarbeit** *f* PERSON group working; **Gruppenarbeitssystem** *nt* PERSON group working; **Gruppenbanking** *nt* BANK group banking; **Gruppenbesprechung** *f* MGMNT team briefing; **Gruppenbuchung** *f* FREI, V&M block booking; **Gruppendiskussion** *f* V&M group discussion; **Gruppendynamik** *f* PERSON group dynamics; **Gruppeneinweisung** *f* MGMNT team briefing; **Gruppenerwerbsunfähigkeitsversicherung** *f* VERSICH group disability insurance; **Gruppenfinanzierung** *f* STEUER block funding; **Gruppengespräch** *nt* GESCHÄFT group discussion, PERSON group interview; **Gruppenklage** *f* RECHT class action; **Gruppenkonnossement** *nt* IMP/EXP, TRANSP groupage bill of lading; **Gruppenkrankenversicherung** *f* GESCHÄFT contributory sickness fund, VERSICH group health insurance; **Gruppenlebensversicherung** *f* VERSICH group life insurance; **Gruppenleiter, in** *m,f* MGMNT team leader, PERSON group leader, team leader; **Gruppenliegeplatz** *m* TRANSP nesting berth; **Gruppenprämie** *f* PERSON group bonus; **Gruppenreise** *f* FREI group travel; **Gruppenreiseticket** *nt* FREI party ticket; **Gruppenstruktur** *f* GESCHÄFT group structure; **Gruppentarif** *m* GESCHÄFT blanket rate; **Gruppen-**

theorie *f* vw team theory; **Gruppentraining** *nt* PERSON group training; **Gruppenunfallversicherung** *f* VERSICH collective accident insurance; **Gruppenversicherung** *f* PERSON *Rentenversicherung* deferred group annuity, contributory pension fund, *private Altersversicherung* contributory pension scheme, VERSICH collective insurance; **Gruppenvertrag** *m* GESCHÄFT group contract

gruppieren *vt* GESCHÄFT align

Gruppierung *f* GESCHÄFT alignment, grouping, MATH grouping; **Gruppierungskonnossement** *nt* IMP/EXP, TRANSP groupage bill of lading; **Gruppierungsspediteur** *m* IMP/EXP, TRANSP groupage operator

Grüße *m pl* KOMM greetings

Grußformel *f* KOMM *am Ende eines Briefes* complimentary close

G7 *abbr* (*Gruppe der 7 führenden Weltwirtschaftsnationen, Siebener-Gruppe*) vw Group of Seven

GUI *abbr* (*grafische Benutzerschnittstelle*) COMP GUI (*graphical user interface*)

gültig *adj* VERWALT *Reisepaß* valid; ♦ **für ~ erklären** GESCHÄFT *Dokument* validate

gültig: **~e Rechnung** *f* GESCHÄFT valid invoice; **~er Rechtsanspruch** *m* GRUND good title; **~er Rechtstitel** *m* GRUND good title; **~er Reisepaß** *m* VERWALT valid passport

Gültigkeit *f* PATENT validity, RECHNUNG currency; **Gültigkeitsbereich** *m* PATENT scope; **Gültigkeitsdauer** *f* GESCHÄFT validity period, time limit, PATENT validity; **Gültigkeitsprüfung** *f* COMP validation

Gummi *m* BÖRSE rubber

gummibereift: **~er Verkehr** *m* TRANSP rubber-tired traffic (*AmE*), rubber-tyred traffic (*BrE*)

gummiert: **~er Briefumschlag** *m* VERWALT adhesive envelope; **~es Etikett** *nt* VERWALT adhesive label

Gummi: **Gummilinse** *f* MEDIEN zoom; **Gummistempel** *m* GESCHÄFT rubber stamp

Gunst: **jds ~ erringen** *phr* GESCHÄFT win sb's favor (*AmE*), win sb's favour (*BrE*)

günstig *adj* BÖRSE attractive, favorable (*AmE*), favourable (*BrE*), GESCHÄFT advantageous, attractive, favorable (*AmE*), favourable (*BrE*), *preiswert* good value; ♦ **zu ~en Bedingungen** GESCHÄFT concessional; **~ ein- und teuer verkaufen** BÖRSE buy low and sell high; **bei ~em Wetter** GESCHÄFT, TRANSP weather permitting (*WP*)

günstig: **~er Kauf** *m* V&M bargain, snip; **~e Konditionen** *f pl* GESCHÄFT concessional terms; **~es Konjunkturklima** *nt* vw favorable economic climate (*AmE*), favourable economic climate (*BrE*); **~e Konjunkturlage** *f* vw favorable economic conditions (*AmE*), favourable economic conditions (*BrE*); **~er Tarif** *m* vw favorable rate (*AmE*), favourable rate (*BrE*); **~er Wechselkurs** *m* BÖRSE favorable exchange rate (*AmE*), favourable exchange rate (*BrE*); **~e Wirtschaftslage** *f* vw favorable economic conditions (*AmE*), favourable economic conditions (*BrE*); **~es Wirtschaftsklima** *nt* vw favorable economic climate (*AmE*), favourable economic climate (*BrE*)

günstiger: **~es Angebot** *nt* GESCHÄFT attractive offer, bargain offer, better offer, V&M bargain offer; **ein ~es Angebot machen als jd** *phr* GESCHÄFT underbid sb

günstigst *adj* GESCHÄFT optimal, optimum; **~e Situation** *f* GESCHÄFT, vw best-case scenario

GUS abbr (*Gemeinschaft Unabhängiger Staaten*) POL CIS (*Commonwealth of Independent States*)

gut 1. *adj* GESCHÄFT good, strong; ◆ **mit ~en EDV-Kenntnissen** COMP computer-literate; **~ in Form** *infrml* GESCHÄFT good in trim; **in ~er Geschäftslage** GESCHÄFT well situated for business; **etw auf ~ Glück kaufen** *infrml* GESCHÄFT buy sth on spec (*infrml*); **~e Leistungen vorzuweisen haben** PERSON *Bewerbung, Lebenslauf, Zeugnisse* show a proven track record; **in ~er Position** GESCHÄFT well-placed; **eine ~e Presse haben** GESCHÄFT have a good press; **in ~er Verfassung** GESCHÄFT in good trim (*infrml*); **mit einer ~en Vorbildung** PERSON well-grounded; **in ~em Wartungszustand** GESCHÄFT in good repair; **2.** *adv* GESCHÄFT well; ◆ **~ ausgebildet** PERSON well-grounded, *schulisch* well-educated; **~ ausgewogen** *adj* GESCHÄFT well-balanced; **~ beraten sein** GESCHÄFT be well advised; **~ dotiert** PERSON well-paid; **~ eingeführt** GESCHÄFT *Firma* well-established; **sich ~ entwickeln** GESCHÄFT thrive; **~ erhalten sein** GESCHÄFT be well preserved; **~ in Form sein** FREI, SOZIAL be in good form; **~ gehend** GESCHÄFT, VW thriving; **~ informiert** GESCHÄFT, POL well-informed; **~ marktgängig** GESCHÄFT good sound merchantable (*BrE*) (*gsm*); **~ motiviert** PERSON *Betriebsklima, Arbeitszufriedenheit* well-motivated; **~ im Rennen liegen** GESCHÄFT be well placed, be in the running for; **~ präsentiert** V&M well-packaged; **~ situiert** GESCHÄFT well-off; **~ in Stand sein** *jarg* FREI, SOZIAL be in good shape; **~ auf Streß reagieren** PERSON react well under stress; **~ unterrichtet** GESCHÄFT, POL well-informed; **~ verpackt** TRANSP well-packaged; **~ versorgt** GESCHÄFT well-off

gut: **~e Durchschnittsqualität** *f* GESCHÄFT fair average quality (*f.a.q.*), good fair average (*gfa*), IMP/EXP fair average quality (*f.a.q.*); **~er Kauf** *m* GESCHÄFT bargain; **~er Leumund** *m* GESCHÄFT renown; **~e Nachrichten** *f pl* GESCHÄFT good news; **~er Name** *m* GESCHÄFT renown, reputation; **~es Preis-/Leistungsverhältnis** *nt* GESCHÄFT good value for money; **~e Rendite** *f* RECHNUNG good return; **~es Risiko** *nt* VERSICH good risk; **~er Ruf** *m* GESCHÄFT renown, V&M established image

Gutachten *nt* GESCHÄFT survey, appraisal, appraisal report, opinion, valuation report; ◆ **ein ~ einholen** GESCHÄFT ask for an expert opinion

Gutachter, in *m,f* GESCHÄFT adjudicator, MGMNT consultant, *Ziviltechniker* surveyor; **Gutachtergebühr** *f* GESCHÄFT survey fee; **Gutachterkommission** *f* GESCHÄFT, POL advisory committee; **Gutachterstimme** *f* GESCHÄFT advisory voice; **Gutachtertätigkeit** *f* GESCHÄFT advisory service

Gut: **Gutbefund** *m* FINANZ approval

gutbestückt *adj* GESCHÄFT well-stocked

Gutdünken: **nach ~ von** *phr* GESCHÄFT at the discretion of

Gute: **alles ~ hat seinen Preis** *phr* GESCHÄFT there's no such thing as a free lunch

Güte *f* V&M quality; ◆ **der ~ nach** GESCHÄFT qualitative, qualitatively

Güte: **Gütebestätigung** *f* GESCHÄFT, IND, MGMNT, V&M quality assessment; **Gütekontrolle** *f* GESCHÄFT, IND, V&M quality control (*QC*); **Gütemarke** *f* GESCHÄFT, RECHT certification mark; **Gütepaß** *m* IMP/EXP quality certificate

Güter *nt pl* (*G.*) TRANSP freight (*frt*), goods (*BrE*) (*gds*); **~ des täglichen Bedarfs** GESCHÄFT, V&M convenience goods, essential commodities; **~ unter Zollverschluß** GESCHÄFT, IMP/EXP, VW bonded goods (*B/G, b/g*); **Güterangebot** *nt* VW supply of goods; **Güteraustausch** *m* GESCHÄFT trade

güterbezogen: **~er Ansatz** *m* **des Marketing** V&M commodity approach

Güter: **Güterbündel** *nt* VW composite commodity; **Güterempfangsbestätigung** *f* IMP/EXP goods received note; **Güterfreigabe** *f* IMP/EXP freight release; **Gütergemeinschaft** *f* GRUND, RECHT tenancy by the entirety; **Güterkraftverkehr** *m* TRANSP road haulage; **Güterkraftverkehrkonnossement** *nt* TRANSP trucking bill of lading (*AmE*); **Güterkraftverkehrsunternehmen** *nt* TRANSP trucking company (*AmE*), road haulage company (*BrE*); **Gütermarkt** *m* VW commodity market; **Güternachfrage** *f* VW demand for goods; **Gütertonne** *f* GESCHÄFT freight ton (*F/T*), freight tonne (*F/T*); **Gütertransport** *m* TRANSP freight transport, conveyance of goods; **Gütertransportversicherung** *f* VERSICH cargo insurance, freight insurance; **Güterverkehr** *m* TRANSP movement of freight, freight traffic; **Güterverladungsanlagen** *f pl* TRANSP cargo handling equipment; **Güterverladungskosten** *pl* TRANSP cargo handling charge (*CHC*); **Güterverzeichnissätze** *m pl* IMP/EXP commodity classification rates (*CCR*); **Güterwagen** *m* TRANSP *Zug* boxcar (*AmE*), freight car (*AmE*), goods wagon (*BrE*), truck (*BrE*)

güterwirtschaftlich: **~es Gleichgewicht** *nt* VW equilibrium GNP

Güter: **Güterzug** *m* TRANSP freight train (*AmE*), goods train (*BrE*)

Güte: **Gütesicherung** *f* GESCHÄFT, IND, MGMNT, V&M quality assessment; **Gütezeichen** *nt* BANK hallmark, GESCHÄFT quality label, certification mark, PATENT, RECHT certification mark, V&M brand name

gutgeschrieben: **~ auf** *phr* FINANZ credited to

gutgläubig: **~es Angebot** *nt* GESCHÄFT bona fide offer; **~e Einlage** *f* BÖRSE good-faith deposit; **~er Erwerber** *m* GESCHÄFT bona fide purchaser; **~er Inhaber** *m* BÖRSE bona fide holder

Guthaben *nt* BANK credit balance, credit; ◆ **~ der Geschäftsbanken bei der Bank von England** BANK bankers' deposits (*BrE*)

Guthaben: **Guthabensaldo** *m* BANK bank balance, deposit balance, FINANZ, RECHNUNG bank balance

gütlich 1. *adj* GESCHÄFT *Einigung, Vergleich, Beilegung* amicable; **2.** *adv* RECHT *einverständliche Durchführung eines Rechtsstreits* amicably

gütlich: **~e Beilegung** *f* GESCHÄFT, RECHT *Rechtsstreit* amicable settlement; **~e Einigung** *f* GESCHÄFT arrangement, private arrangement

Gutschein *m* FINANZ credit note (*C/N, CN*), GESCHÄFT issue voucher, coupon (*c., cp.*), voucher, credit note (*C/N, CN*)

gutschreiben *vt* [+dat] RECHNUNG credit

Gutschrift *f* FINANZ credit memorandum, GESCHÄFT credit note (*C/N, CN*), RECHNUNG credit entry; ◆ **zur ~ auf** RECHNUNG credited to

Gutschrift: **Gutschriftsanzeige** *f* FINANZ credit memorandum, credit note (*C/N, CN*), GESCHÄFT credit note (*C/N, CN*); **Gutschriftzettel** *f* FINANZ credit slip

Gutsverwalter, in *m,f* GRUND, RECHT bailiff

guttun *vi* [+dat] GESCHÄFT benefit

GuV *abbr* (*Gewinn und Verlust*) RECHNUNG P&L (*profit and loss*); **GuV-Rechnung** *f* (*Gewinn- und Verlustrechnung*) RECHNUNG P & L account

Gw. *abbr* (*Gewicht*) GESCHÄFT, MATH, TRANSP wgt, wt (*weight*)

G10 *abbr* (*Zehnergruppe*) VW G10 (*Group of Ten*)

GZT *abbr* (*Gemeinsamer Zolltarif*) IMP/EXP CCT (*common customs tariff*)

H

H *abbr* (*Wasserstoff*) IND, UMWELT H (*hydrogen*)

ha *abbr* (*hektar*) GESCHÄFT ha (*hectare*)

Haag: ~**er Protokoll** *nt* RECHT Hague Protocol; ~**er Regeln** *f pl* TRANSP Hague Rules; ~**er Vorschriften** *f pl* TRANSP Hague Rules

Haarstilist, in *m,f* MEDIEN stylist

Habeas: ~ **Corpus** *phr* RECHT habeas corpus

Haben: **im** ~ FINANZ, RECHNUNG above the line; **Habenbuchung** *f* RECHNUNG credit entry; **Habensaldo** *m* BANK, FINANZ, RECHNUNG balance in bank; **Habenseite** *f* FINANZ credit side, right column, RECHNUNG credit side, right column, right-hand column; **Habenzinsen** *m pl* BANK, RECHNUNG interest earned, interest received

hacken *vt infrml* COMP hack (*infrml*)

Hacken *nt infrml* COMP hacking (*infrml*)

Hacker, in *m,f infrml* COMP hacker (*infrml*), computer hacker

hackersicher *adj infrml* COMP hacker-proof (*infrml*)

Hafen *m* TRANSP harbor (*AmE*), harbour (*BrE*), port; ~ **für Luftkissenboote** *m* TRANSP hoverport; ♦ **ab** ~ (*x-Hafendamm*) IMP/EXP, TRANSP ex wharf (*x-wharf*); **einen** ~ **anlaufen** TRANSP make port; **von** ~ **zu Hafen** IMP/EXP, TRANSP port to port (*P to P*); **Hafen-Hafen** IMP/EXP, TRANSP port to port (*P to P*)

Hafen: **Hafenabgabe** *f* STEUER, TRANSP port liner terms charge (*PLTC*), port tax; **Hafenagent, in** *m,f* TRANSP port agent; **Hafenamt** *nt* TRANSP harbor authority (*AmE*), harbour authority (*BrE*); **Hafenanlagen** *f pl* TRANSP harbor facilities (*AmE*), harbour facilities (*BrE*), port facilities; **Hafenanordnung** *f* TRANSP port layout; **Hafenarbeiter** *m* PERSON, TRANSP docker (*BrE*), longshoreman (*AmE*); **Hafenauslagen** *f pl* TRANSP port disbursements; **Hafenaustausch** *m* TRANSP port interchange; **Hafenbahnhof** *m* TRANSP maritime terminal; **Hafenbecken** *nt* TRANSP inner harbor (*AmE*), inner harbour (*BrE*); **Hafenbehörde** *f* TRANSP harbor authority (*AmE*), harbour authority (*BrE*); **Hafenbetrieb** *m* TRANSP port operation; **Hafendirektor, in** *m,f* PERSON, TRANSP port director; **Hafendurchsatzleistung** *f* TRANSP port throughput, port thruput (*AmE*); **Hafeneinrichtungen** *f pl* TRANSP port facilities, harbor facilities (*AmE*), harbour facilities (*BrE*); **Hafengebühr** *f* IMP/EXP, TRANSP port liner terms charge (*PLTC*), port tax; **Hafengebühren** *f pl* STEUER, TRANSP harbor dues (*AmE*), harbour dues (*BrE*), port charges, port dues (*PD*); **Hafengeld** *nt* STEUER, TRANSP harbor dues (*AmE*), harbour dues (*BrE*), port liner terms charge (*PLTC*); **Hafengesundheitsbehörde** *f* TRANSP port health authority; **Hafenkontrolle** *f* TRANSP port control; **Hafenkosten** *pl* STEUER, TRANSP port liner terms charge (*PLTC*); **Hafenmeister** *m* PERSON harbormaster (*AmE*), harbourmaster (*BrE*); **Hafenoperationsbeamte(r)** *m* [decl. as adj], **Hafenoperationsbeamtin** *f* PERSON, TRANSP Port Operations Officer (*POO*); **Hafenstatistik** *f* TRANSP port statistics; **Hafensteuer** *f* STEUER, TRANSP port tax; **Hafentarif** *m* STEUER, TRANSP port tariffs;

Hafenumschlagszeit *f* TRANSP port turnaround time (*AmE*), port turnround time (*BrE*); **Hafenusance** *f* TRANSP custom of port (*C/P*); **Hafenverkehr** *m* TRANSP port traffic; **Hafenverkehrskontrolle** *f* TRANSP port traffic control; **Hafenverwalter, in** *m,f* PERSON, TRANSP port manager; **Hafenverwaltung** *f* TRANSP port management; **Hafenzollwache** *f* IMP/EXP, TRANSP Waterguard Service (*BrE*); **Hafenzugang** *m* TRANSP port access; **Hafenzuschlag** *m* STEUER, TRANSP port surcharge

Haft *f* RECHT *vor das Gerichtsverhalten* custody, *Strafe* imprisonment

haftbar *adj* GESCHÄFT answerable, accountable, RECHT, VERSICH liable, responsible; ♦ **jdn für etw ~ machen** RECHT hold sb liable for sth

Haftbarkeit *f* RECHT, VERSICH liability, responsibility

Haftbefehl *m* RECHT warrant

haften *vi*: ~ **für etw** GESCHÄFT answer for sth, RECHT, VERSICH accept liability for sth, be liable for sth, be responsible for sth

haftend: ~**es Eigenkapital** *nt* FINANZ, RECHNUNG actual net worth

Haft: **Haftentlassung** *f* **gegen Sicherheitsleistung** RECHT bailment; **Haftkaution** *f* RECHT bail bond

Haftpflicht *f* RECHT, VERSICH liability, responsibility; **Haftpflichtdeckung** *f* VERSICH third-party insurance cover

haftpflichtig *adj* RECHT, VERSICH liable

Haftpflicht: **Haftpflichtrisiko** *nt* VERSICH third-party risk

Haftpflichtversicherung *f* VERSICH errors and omissions insurance, liability insurance; ~ **des Arbeitgebers für Arbeitsunfälle** VERSICH workers' compensation and employers' liability insuring agreement; ~ **des Buchhalters** RECHNUNG, VERSICH accountant's professional liability insurance; ~ **für Geschäftsführung** VERSICH directors' and officers' liability insurance; ~ **mit Vollkaskoversicherung** VERSICH fully comprehensive insurance policy; **Haftpflichtversicherungspolice** *f* VERSICH third-party insurance policy; **Haftpflichtversicherungsschutz** *m* VERSICH third-party insurance cover; **Haftpflichtversicherungsvertrag** *m* VERSICH liability insuring agreement

Haft: **Haftprüfung** *f* RECHT remand

Haftung *f* RECHT, VERSICH liability, responsibility; ~ **des Dienstherren für Gehilfen** RECHT respondeat superior; ~ **für Dritte** RECHT vicarious liability; ~ **für den Erfüllungsgehilfen** RECHT respondeat superior; ~ **für Geschäftsrisiken** RECHT business exposures liability; ~ **des Kaibesitzers** RECHT wharfowner's liability (*WOL*); ~ **mit Selbstbeteiligung** VERSICH excess liabilities; ~ **aus unerlaubter Handlung** RECHT *zivilrechtlich* tort liability; ~ **aus vorsätzlichen Straftaten** RECHT, VERSICH criminal liability; ♦ ~ **für etw anerkennen** RECHT accept liability for sth; **ohne jegliche** ~ **unsererseits** RECHT without any liability on our part; **die** ~ **für etw übernehmen** RECHT take responsibility for sth, accept liability for sth

Haftung: **Haftungsausschluß** *m* RECHT, VERSICH *Vertragsrecht* exclusion of liability, indemnity against liability, nonliability; **Haftungsausschlußklausel** *f* RECHT, VERSICH *Vertragsrecht* disclaimer clause, exclusion clause, exemption from liability clause; **Haftungsbeschränkung** *f* GESCHÄFT corporate veil, RECHT, VERSICH *Vertragsrecht* limitation of liability; **Haftungsbeschränkungsklausel** *f* RECHT, VERSICH *Vertragsrecht* liability limitation clause; **Haftungsdauer** *f* RECHT, VERSICH indemnity period; **Haftungsfreistellung** *f* RECHT, VERSICH *Vertragsrecht* indemnity, release from liability; **Haftungsgrund** *m* RECHT, VERSICH cause of liability; **Haftungsklage** *f* RECHT, VERSICH action based on liability; **Haftungsklausel** *f* **für finanzielle Verantwortung** RECHT, VERSICH financial responsibility clause (*AmE*); **Haftungsminderung** *f* RECHT, VERSICH reduction of liability; **Haftungsrisiko** *nt* RECHT, VERSICH *Vertragsrecht* risk of liability; **Haftungsübernahme** *f* RECHT, VERSICH *Vertragsrecht* assumption of liability; **Haftungsvereinbarung** *f* **zwischen Tankereignern in Bezug auf Umweltverschmutzung** RECHT, TRANSP, UMWELT, Pollution Liability Agreement Among Tanker Owners (*PLATO*)

Haig-Simons-Einkommensdefinition *f* vw Haig Simons definition of income

Häkchen *nt* GESCHÄFT check mark (*AmE*), tick mark (*BrE*)

Haken *m* GESCHÄFT check mark (*AmE*), tick mark (*BrE*), *Problem* snag (*infrml*)

Halb- in cpds GESCHÄFT half, semi-

halb: **~e Basispreisabstufung** *f* BÖRSE half a strike price interval; **ein ~es Dutzend** *nt* GESCHÄFT half a dozen; **~e-halbe machen** *vi infrml* GESCHÄFT go halves with sb; **~es Jahr** *nt* GESCHÄFT half year; **über ein ~es Jahr hinaus gewährter Exportkredit** *m* V&M extended credit; **~er Preis** *m* GESCHÄFT half fare; **zum ~en Preis** *phr* GESCHÄFT at half-price; **~er Quartilsabstand** *m* MATH semi-interquartile range, vw quartile deviation; **sich auf ~em Wege entgegenkommen** *phr* GESCHÄFT split the difference

Halb-: **Halbaddierwerk** *nt* COMP half adder; **Halbduplexbetrieb** *m* COMP *Datenübertragung* half-duplex (*HDX*); **Halberzeugnis** *nt* IND semi-finished product; **Halbfabrikat** *nt* IND semi-finished product; **Halbfabrikate** *nt pl* IND partly finished goods, semi-finished goods; **Halbfertig- und Fertiggerichte** *nt pl* V&M convenience foods; **Halbfertigprodukt** *nt* IND semi-finished product; **Halbfertigwaren** *f pl* IND semi-finished goods; **Halbgeviertstrich** *m* MEDIEN en dash; **Halbgrossist, in** *m,f* V&M semi-wholesaler

halbindustrialisiert *adj* IND, VW semi-industrialized

halbintelligent: **~es Terminal** *nt* COMP smart terminal

Halb-: **Halbjahresfrist** *f* GESCHÄFT six-monthly period; **Halbjahresperiode** *f* GESCHÄFT six-monthly period

halbjährlich *adj* GESCHÄFT half-yearly, biannual

Halb-: **Halbleiter** *m* COMP, IND semiconductor

halbmonatlich *adj* GESCHÄFT half-monthly

Halb-: **Halbpension** *f* FREI half-board

halbprivat: **~e Bank** *f* BANK semi-private bank

halbstrukturiert *adj* GESCHÄFT semi-structured

halbtags: **~ arbeiten** *phr* GESCHÄFT be on half-time, work half-time

Halb-: **Halbton** *m* MEDIEN *Drucker, Kopierer* halftone

halbveredelt: **~es Produkt** *nt* IND semi-processed product

Halb-: **Halbzeitstudie** *f* TRANSP half-time survey (*HT*); **Halbzeitübersicht** *f* TRANSP half-time survey (*HT*)

haltbar *adj* GESCHÄFT stable, IND durable, hardwearing; ♦ **~ machen** IND *Lebensmittel* preserve, *Produkt* process; **~ sein** IND stand up to wear, *Lebensmittel* keep well

haltbar: **~es Lebensmittel** *nt* IND preserved food

Haltbarkeit *f* IND, V&M shelf life; **Haltbarkeitsangabe** *f* V&M open dating (*AmE*); **Haltbarkeitsdatum** *nt* GESCHÄFT, V&M use-by date

halten: **~ sich** *v refl* IND keep

Haltung *f* GESCHÄFT, MGMNT attitude, stance, frame of mind

Hamburg: **~er Kaffeebörse** *f* BÖRSE Hamburg Coffee Exchange

Hand *f* GESCHÄFT hand; ♦ **bei der ~** GESCHÄFT ready to hand; **unter der ~** GESCHÄFT by private contract; **zur ~** GESCHÄFT ready to hand; **in der ~ zu halten** V&M hand-held; **in den Händen von** GESCHÄFT in the hands of; **zu Händen von** (*z. Hd. v.*) GESCHÄFT care of (*c/o*), IMP/EXP, KOMM care of (*c/o*), for the attention of (*FAO*); **in den Händen Dritter** GESCHÄFT in the hands of a third party; **in den Händen eines Konkursverwalters sein** RECHT be in the hands of a receiver; **etw unter der ~ verkaufen** GESCHÄFT sell sth by private treaty

Hand: **Handbuch** *nt* GESCHÄFT guide, handbook, manual

Handel *m* GESCHÄFT *Gewerbe* commerce, trade, trading, *Abschluß* bargain, deal, transaction, *von illegaler Waren* traffic, V&M distributive trades; **~ in Freiverkehrswerten** BÖRSE unlisted trading; **~ mit Industriewaren** IND trade in industrial goods; **~ innerhalb der EU** vw intra-EU trade; **~ mit dem Kauf und späteren Verkauf eines Wertpapiers** BÖRSE in and out trading; **~ an der Nachbörse** BÖRSE after-hours trading; **~ auf Reziprozitätsbasis** vw reciprocal trading; **~ rund um die Uhr** BÖRSE twenty-four-hour trading; **~ an der Tafel** BÖRSE blackboard trading; ♦ **den ~ aussetzen** BÖRSE suspend trading; **~ betreiben** VW trade; **auf den ~ bezogen** vw trade-related; **einen ~ erfolgreich abschließen** GESCHÄFT pull off a deal; **~ treiben** VW trade

handelbar *adj* BÖRSE, FINANZ, VW tradeable; **~es Emissionszertifikat** *nt* UMWELT, VW tradeable discharge permit (*TDP*), tradeable emission permit; **~e Option** *f* BÖRSE traded option; **~es Wertpapier** *nt* FINANZ convertible security

handeln 1. *vt* GESCHÄFT barter, transact; **2.** *vi* GESCHÄFT trade, traffic; ♦ **~ an** [+dat] BÖRSE trade at; **~ mit** GESCHÄFT *illegale Waren* traffic in, vw *Waren, Produktion* trade; **~ um** GESCHÄFT bargain, haggle about, haggle over; **im Namen von jdm ~** RECHT act on sb's behalf

Handeln *nt* GESCHÄFT *Feilschen* bargaining, haggling, *Gewerbe* trade, trading

Handel: **Handelsabkommen** *nt* GESCHÄFT commercial agreement, trade agreement; **Handelsablenkung** *f* vw trade diversion; **Handelsadreßbuch** *nt* GESCHÄFT trade directory; **Handelsakademie** *f* PERSON business college; **Handelsakzept** *nt* GESCHÄFT trade acceptance; **Handelsanforderungen** *f pl* BANK needs of trade; **Handelsangelegenheit** *f* GESCHÄFT commercial concern; **Handelsauskunft** *f* RECHT commercial agency report; **Handelsbank** *f* BANK, FINANZ, VW commercial bank, mercantile bank; **Handelsbanker** *m* BANK, FINANZ, VW mercantile banker; **Handelsbedingungen** *f pl* GESCHÄFT trade terms; **Handelsbeschränkung** *f* IMP/EXP, VW trade restriction; **Handelsbestand** *m* BANK trading portfolio, GESCHÄFT commercial stock; **Handelsbezeichnung** *f* GESCHÄFT trade name, V&M brand name; **Handelsbeziehungen** *f pl* GESCHÄFT trading links; **Handelsbeziehungen** *f pl* **und Exporte** *m pl* IMP/EXP Commercial Relations and Exports (*BrE*) (*CRE*)

Handelsbilanz *f* IMP/EXP, POL, VW balance of trade, merchandise balance of trade, trade balance, visible balance; **Handelsbilanzdefizit** *nt* IMP/EXP, POL, VW trade gap; **Handelsbilanzüberschuß** *m* IMP/EXP, POL, VW trade surplus; **Handelsbilanzungleichgewicht** *nt* IMP/EXP, POL, VW imbalance of trade

Handel: **Handelsblock** *m* POL, VW trading bloc; **Handelsbrauch** *m* GESCHÄFT trade custom, commercial usage, RECHT *Vertragsrecht* commercial usage; **Handelsbulletin** *nt* VW trade brief; **Handelsdefizit** *nt* IMP/EXP, POL, VW trade deficit; **Handelsdesk** *nt* BÖRSE desk; **Handelsdiplom** *nt* GESCHÄFT Diploma of Commerce (*DipCOM*); **Handelsdividende** *f* BÖRSE trading dividend; **Handelseinheit** *f* BÖRSE full lot

handelseinig: ~ **werden** *phr* RECHT *Vertragsrecht* strike a bargain; **mit jdm ~ werden** *phr* RECHT *Vertragsrecht* come to terms with sb

Handel: **Handelseinkommen** *nt* FINANZ trading income; **Handelseinrichtung** *f* GESCHÄFT commercial establishment; **Handelsergebnis** *nt* FINANZ trading results; **Handelserlaubnis** *f* GESCHÄFT trading authorization; **Handelserleichterung** *f* VW trade facilitation

handelsfähig *adj* VW merchantable, tradeable; **nicht ~e Güter** *nt pl* VW nontradeables

Handel: **Handelsfähigkeit** *f* VW tradeability; **Handelsförderung** *f* V&M trade promotion; **Handelsfracht** *f* TRANSP commercial cargo

handelsfrei: **~es Gleichgewicht** *nt* VW no-trade equilibrium

Handel: **Handelsgeist** *m* VW commercialism; **Handelsgepflogenheiten** *f pl* PERSON custom and trade practices; **Handelsgeschäft** *nt* BANK trading operation, GESCHÄFT commercial business; **Handelsgesellschaft** *f* GESCHÄFT association, trading company

Handelsgesetz *nt* GESCHÄFT commercial law, RECHT lex mercatoria, mercantile law; **Handelsgesetzbuch** *nt* (*HGB*) RECHT Commercial Code

Handel: **Handelsgespräche** *nt pl* VW trade talks; **Handelsgewicht** *nt* GESCHÄFT avoirdupois (*avdp.*); **Handelsgläubiger, in** *m,f* RECHNUNG trade creditor; **Handelsgrenze** *f* VW trading limit; **Handelsgröße** *f* BÖRSE unit of trading; **Handelsgut** *nt* GESCHÄFT commodity; **Handelshafen** *m* TRANSP commercial port, trading port; **Handelshemmnis** *nt* IMP/EXP, VW barrier to trade, trade barrier; **Handelshindernis** *nt* IMP/EXP, VW barrier to trade; **Handelskai** *m* TRANSP commercial dock (*CD*); **Handelskammer** *f* (*HK*) GESCHÄFT board of trade (*AmE*), chamber of commerce (*CC*), Chamber of Trade, trade chamber; **Handelskapitalismus** *m* VW merchant capitalism; **Handelskniffe** *m pl* GESCHÄFT tricks of the trade (*infrml*); **Handelskredit** *m* RECHNUNG trade credit; **Handelskreditversicherung** *f* VERSICH commercial credit insurance (*AmE*); **Handelskrieg** *m* VW trade war; **Handelslaufzeit** *f*

BÖRSE trading life; **Handelsleute** *pl* GESCHÄFT tradespeople; **Handelsliberalisierung** *f* RECHT, VW liberalization of trade, trade liberalization; **Handelsmakler, in** *m,f* GRUND commercial broker (*AmE*), RECHT mercantile broker; **Handelsmaklerstand** *m* BÖRSE trading pit; **Handelsmarine** *f* TRANSP commercial marine, mercantile marine, merchant marine, merchant navy; **Handelsmarke** *f* PATENT mark, V&M trademark, brand; **Handelsmetropole** *nt* V&M commercial center (*AmE*), commercial centre (*BrE*); **Handelsministerium** *nt* POL Ministry of International Trade and Industry, Board of Trade (*BrE*) (*BOT*); **Handelsmuster** *nt* BÖRSE trading pattern, GESCHÄFT sample; **Handelsname** *m* GESCHÄFT proprietary brand, PATENT trading name; **Handelsniederlassung** *f* GESCHÄFT commercial establishment; **Handelsnormen** *f pl* GESCHÄFT trading standards; **Handelsorganisation** *f* GESCHÄFT trade organization; **Handelspanel** *nt* V&M retail audit; **Handelspapier** *nt* BANK, BÖRSE, FINANZ commercial paper (*CP*), instrument; **Handelspartner** *m* GESCHÄFT, POL commercial partner, VW trading partner; **Handelspolitik** *f* IMP/EXP, VW commercial policy, trade policy; **Handelspraktik** *f* VERWALT trade practice; **Handelspraktiken** *f pl* PERSON custom and trade practices; **Handelsprogramm** *nt* GESCHÄFT trading program (*AmE*), trading programme (*BrE*); **Handelsprotektionismus** *m* IMP/EXP, VW trade protectionism; **Handelsrechnung** *f* RECHNUNG, RECHT commercial invoice; **Handelsrecht** *nt* RECHT commercial law, lex mercatoria; **Handelsregister** *nt* GESCHÄFT Companies Registration Office (*CRO*), trade register; **Handelsregister-Eintragung** *f* (*HR-Eintragung*) GESCHÄFT commercial registration; **Handelsreisende** *f* [decl. as adj] PERSON commercial traveler (*AmE*), commercial traveller (*BrE*), traveling saleswoman (*AmE*), travelling saleswoman (*BrE*); **Handelsreisende(r)** *m* [decl. as adj] PERSON commercial traveler (*AmE*), commercial traveller (*BrE*), traveling salesman (*AmE*), travelling salesman (*BrE*); **Handelsrestriktion** *f* IMP/EXP, VW barrier to trade, trade restriction; **Handelsrisikoversicherung** *f* VERSICH commercial insurance; **Handelsroute** *f* TRANSP, VW trade route

handelsschaffend: **~e Wirkungen** *f pl* VW trade creation

Handelsschiff *nt* TRANSP merchant ship, merchant vessel, trading vessel; **Handelsschiffahrt** *f* IMP/EXP, TRANSP merchant service, merchant shipping, merchant haulage (*MH*); **Handelsschiffahrtsgesetz** *nt* TRANSP Merchant Shipping Act (*MSA*)

Handel: **Handelsschranke** *f* IMP/EXP, VW barrier to trade, trade barrier; **Handelsschuldner** *m* RECHNUNG trade debtor; **Handelsschule** *f* SOZIAL business school, college of further education (*BrE*) (*CFE*); **Handelsspanne** *f* RECHNUNG, V&M margin; **Handelsspekulation** *f* MGMNT commercial venture; **Handelssperre** *f* GESCHÄFT stoppage of trade; **Handelsstatistik** *f* GESCHÄFT trade returns; **Handelsstrategie** *f* GESCHÄFT commercial strategy, trade strategy; **Handelsstrom** *m* VW trade flow; **Handelstransport** *m* IMP/EXP, TRANSP merchant haulage (*MH*)

handelsüblich *adj* GESCHÄFT prevailing; **~er Computer** *m* COMP commercial computer; **~e Qualität** *f* VW merchantable quality; **~er Versand** *m* TRANSP customary despatch; **~e Vertragsformeln** *f pl* GESCHÄFT trade terms

Handel: **Handelsumfang** *m* GESCHÄFT amount of business, trading volume; **Handelsungleichgewicht** *nt* VW disequilibrium in the balance of trade; **Handelsunternehmen** *nt* GESCHÄFT business concern, business enterprise; **Handelsverband** *m* GESCHÄFT trade association; **Handelsvereinbarung** *f* VW trade agreement; **Handelsverkehr** *m* GESCHÄFT commerce, trade, traffic; **Handelsverlagerung** *f* IMP/EXP trade diversion; **Handelsvertrag** *m* RECHT commercial contract

Handelsvertreter, in *m,f* PERSON agent (*agt*), commercial agent, commercial representative, V&M sales agent, sales rep (*infrml*) (*sales representative*), rep (*infrml*); **Handelsvertreter und Eigenhändler** *m* RECHT *Vertragsrecht* agent; **~ mit Festgehalt** PERSON salaried agent

Handel: **Handelsvertretung** *f* GESCHÄFT commercial representation; **Handelsvertretung** *f* **der Vereinigten Staaten** POL US Trade Representative; **Handelsverzerrung** *f* VW trade distortion; **Handelsvolumen** *nt* GESCHÄFT trade volume, volume of trading; **nach Handelsvolumen gewichteter Umrechnungskurs** *m* GESCHÄFT trade-weighted exchange rate; **Handelsvorschriften** *f pl* GESCHÄFT business regulations; **Handelsvorteil** *m* GESCHÄFT commercial advantage; **Handelswagen** *m* TRANSP trade car; **Handelsware** *f* GESCHÄFT commodity; **Handelswechsel** *m* BANK, BÖRSE business paper, trade bill, commercial bill, GESCHÄFT trade acceptance; **Handelsweg** *m* TRANSP, VW trade route; **Handelswert** *m* GESCHÄFT market value, commercial value; **ohne Handelswert** *phr* GESCHÄFT no commercial value (*n.c.v.*); **Handelswirt** *m* PERSON Bachelor of Commerce (*BCom*); **Handelswoche** *f* GESCHÄFT trade week; **Handels- und Zahlungsabkommen** *nt* RECHT trade and payment agreement; **Handelszeichen** *nt* GESCHÄFT trademark, PATENT mark; **Handelszentrum** *nt* GESCHÄFT business center (*AmE*), business centre (*BrE*), commercial center (*AmE*), commercial centre (*BrE*), V&M emporium, mart, trade mart; **Handelsziel** *nt* GESCHÄFT commercial target; **Handelszielstellung** *f* GESCHÄFT commercial target; **Handelsziffern** *f pl* POL, VW trade figures; **Handelszone** *f* GESCHÄFT trading area

handgemacht *adj* IND *Produktion* handmade

Hand: **Handgepäck** *nt* GESCHÄFT hand luggage, TRANSP unchecked baggage; **Handgepäckaufbewahrungsstelle** *f* TRANSP checkroom (*AmE*), left-luggage office (*BrE*)

handgeschrieben *adj* GESCHÄFT handwritten

handgewebt *adj* IND *Produktion* hand-woven

Hand: **Handkasse** *f* RECHNUNG petty cash; **Handlanger** *m* FINANZ jockey, GESCHÄFT dogsbody (*infrml*)

Händler, in *m,f* BÖRSE trading member, dealer, broker-dealer, GESCHÄFT dealer, trader, agent, V&M vendor; **Händlerbefragung** *f* V&M shop audit; **Händlermarke** *f* V&M dealer brand, distributors' brand; **Händlernetz** *nt* BÖRSE dealer network; **Händlerorganisation** *f* BÖRSE dealer network; **Händlerprüfung** *f* V&M dealer audit; **Händlerwerbung** *f* V&M trade advertising; **Händlerwettbewerb** *m* V&M dealer incentive

Handling *nt* TRANSP handling (*hdlg*)

Handlung *f* GESCHÄFT act, action; **Handlungen** *f pl* **in Überschreitung der satzungsmäßigen Befugnisse** RECHT ultra vires activities; **Handlungsbefugnis** *f* GESCHÄFT acting allowance

handlungsbereit: **~ und verfügungsberechtigt** *adj* GESCHÄFT ready, willing and able

Handlung: **Handlungsbevollmächtigte(r)** *mf* [decl. as adj] MGMNT registered manager, PERSON, VERWALT agent general (*AG*); **Handlungserlaubnis** *f* GESCHÄFT acting allowance; **Handlungsfreiheit** *f* GESCHÄFT freedom of action; **Handlungsgehilfe** *m*, **Handlungsgehilfin** *f* PERSON commercial employee

handlungsorientiert *adj* GESCHÄFT action-oriented

Handlung: **Handlungsprogramm** *nt* GESCHÄFT action program (*AmE*), action programme (*BrE*), program of action (*AmE*), programme of action (*BrE*); **Handlungsspielraum** *m* MGMNT, VW action scope; **Handlungsweise** *f* MGMNT course of action

Hand: **Handschrift** *f* GESCHÄFT, KOMM handwriting

handschriftlich *adj* GESCHÄFT, KOMM handwritten

Hand: **Handsystem** *m* TRANSP manual system (*MS*); **Handwerker, in** *m,f* PERSON handyman, craftsman; **Handwerkszeug** *nt* GESCHÄFT tools of the trade

Handy *nt* *infrml* KOMM mobile phone, mobile telphone, mobile, cellphone

Hand: **Handzettel** *m* KOMM handbill

Hänger *m* TRANSP trailer

Hängeregistraturmappe *f* VERWALT lateral suspension file

Hang-Seng-Index *m* BÖRSE Hang Seng Index

Hanseatisch: **~e Wertpapierbörse** *f* BÖRSE Hanseatic Securities Exchange

happig *adj* *infrml* GESCHÄFT *Preis* pricey (*infrml*), steep (*infrml*)

Hardliner *m* POL hardliner

Hardware *f* COMP hardware; **Hardware-Anforderungen** *f pl* COMP hardware requirements; **Hardware-Erweiterung** *f* COMP hardware upgrade; **Hardware-Fehler** *m* COMP hardware error; **Hardware-Hersteller** *m* COMP hardware firm; **Hardware-Interrupt** *m* COMP hardware interrupt; **Hardware-Kompatibilität** *f* COMP hardware compatibility; **Hardware-Konfiguration** *f* COMP hardware configuration; **Hardware-Sicherheit** *f* COMP hardware security; **Hardware-Spezialist** *m* COMP hardware specialist; **Hardware-Unterbrechung** *f* COMP hardware interrupt; **Hardware-Upgrade** *m* *jarg* COMP hardware upgrade; **Hardware-Versagen** *nt* COMP hardware failure

harmonisch: **~es Mittel** *nt* MATH harmonic mean; **~er Mittelwert** *m* MATH harmonic mean

harmonisieren *vt* GESCHÄFT harmonize

Harmonisierung *f* GESCHÄFT harmonization, POL *der Wirtschaftspolitik* approximation; **Harmonisierungsprozeß** *m* GESCHÄFT harmonization process

Harrod-Domar-Modell *nt* VW *Wachstumstheorie* Harrod Domar model

hart 1. *adj* GESCHÄFT *Bedingungen* tough, *Fakten* hard; ♦ **den ~en Konkurrenztest bestehen** GESCHÄFT stand the acid test of competition; **2.** *adv* STEUER harshly; ♦ **~ verhandeln** GESCHÄFT drive a hard bargain

hart: **~es Darlehen** *nt* BANK hard loan; **~er Konkurrent** *m* GESCHÄFT tough competitor; **~er Konkurrenzkampf** *m* GESCHÄFT harsh competition, tough competition; **~e**

Kosten *pl* FINANZ hard cost; **~e Landung** *f* *infrml* GESCHÄFT, VW hard landing (*infrml*); **~er Seitenumbruch** *m* COMP hard page break; **~e Währung** *f* POL, VW hard currency, hard money; **~er Wettbewerb** *m* GESCHÄFT harsh competition, tough competition; **~er Zeilenvorschub** *m* COMP *Textverarbeitung* hard return

Härte *f* SOZIAL, VW hardship; **Härteklausel** *f* RECHT *Vertragsrecht* hardship clause

Hartfaserplatte *f* IND chipboard

Hartgeld *nt* GESCHÄFT coins, coinage, specie, hard cash, hard money; **Hartgeldfluß-Mechanismus** *m* BANK specie flow mechanism; **Hartgeldsystem** *nt* VW coinage system

hartnäckig *adj* GESCHÄFT persistent, PERSON hard-headed

häufig: ~er Stellenwechsel *m* PERSON *Arbeitsmarkt* job hopping

Häufigkeit *f* MATH frequency, STEUER incidence, V&M frequency; **~ von Vertreterbesuchen** V&M call frequency; **Häufigkeitskurve** *f* MATH frequency curve; **Häufigkeitspolygon** *nt* MATH frequency polygon; **Häufigkeitstabelle** *f* MATH frequency table; **Häufigkeitsverteilung** *f* MATH frequency distribution

häufigste: häufigster Wert *m* MATH mode

Häufung *f* VERSICH accumulation

Haupt- *in cpds* GESCHÄFT, VW main, chief, principal, primary, prime; **Hauptabsatzmarkt** *m* VW prime market; **Hauptabteilungsleiter, in** *m,f* VERWALT business manager; **Hauptagent** *m* TRANSP umbrella agent; **Hauptaktionär, in** *m,f* BÖRSE principal stockholder

hauptamtlich: ~er Geschäftsführer *m*, **~e Geschäftsführerin** *f* MGMNT executive director

Haupt-: **Hauptanbieter, in** *m,f* GESCHÄFT principal bidder, main bidder; **Hauptanspruch** *m* PATENT independent claim; **Hauptanteil** *m* GESCHÄFT the lion's share; **Hauptarbeitsmarkt** *m* VW primary labor market (*AmE*), primary labour market (*BrE*); **Hauptarbeitsstunden** *f pl* IND core hours; **Hauptartikel** *m* VW staple commodity; **die Hauptattraktion sein** *phr* FREI get top billing; **Hauptbeförderer** *m* TRANSP principal carrier; **Hauptbelastungszeit** *f* MEDIEN peak hour

hauptberuflich: ~er Direktor, ~e Direktorin *f* VERWALT executive director

Haupt-: **Hauptbildschirm** *m* COMP main screen

Hauptbuch *nt* FINANZ, RECHNUNG book of final entry, book of secondary entry, general ledger, ledger; **Hauptbuchführungssytem** *nt* FINANZ, RECHNUNG principal accounting system; **Hauptbuchhalter, in** *m,f* RECHNUNG chief accountant, FINANZ chief accounting officer; **Hauptbuchkontenstand** *m* FINANZ, RECHNUNG ledger balance; **Hauptbuchkonto** *nt* FINANZ, RECHNUNG ledger account; **Hauptbuchsammelkonto** *nt* RECHNUNG controlling account

Haupt-: **Hauptbüro** *nt* GESCHÄFT head office (*HO*), headquarters (*HQ*); **Hauptcontroller** *m* RECHNUNG Comptroller General (*AmE*); **Hauptdatei** *f* COMP main file, master file; **Haupteinfahrt** *f* TRANSP gateway; **Haupteinfuhrzeiten** *f pl* IMP/EXP peak importing season; **Haupteinkäufer, in** *m,f* V&M chief buyer, head buyer; **Haupteinkaufsstraße** *f* V&M high street (*BrE*), main street (*AmE*); **Haupteinschaltzeit** *f* MEDIEN prime

listening time, prime time; **Hauptfernsehzeit** *f* MEDIEN prime viewing time; **Hauptfilm** *m* FREI feature film

Hauptgeschäft *nt* GESCHÄFT *Büro* head office (*HO*), headquarters (*HQ*), *Dienstleistungen* main business, V&M flagship store; **Hauptgeschäftsbereich** *m* GESCHÄFT core business, flagship site; **Hauptgeschäftsführer, in** *m,f* MGMNT *eines Unternehmens* chief executive, chief operating officer, general manager, managing director; **Hauptgeschäftssitz** *m* GESCHÄFT head office (*HO*), headquarters (*HQ*)

Haupt-: **Haupthandelspartner, in** *m,f* VW main trading partner, major trading partner; **Hauptinhalt** *m* GESCHÄFT gist; **Hauptkarte** *f* COMP master card; **Hauptkunde** *m*, **Hauptkundin** *f* GESCHÄFT principal customer, MGMNT chief buyer; **Hauptleitung** *f* IND, TRANSP pipeline; **Hauptlieferant** *m* GESCHÄFT prime contractor, prime supplier; **Hauptlinie** *f* TRANSP trunk line; **Hauptmenü** *nt* COMP main menu; **Hauptmerkmal** *nt* GESCHÄFT key feature; **Hauptniederlassung** *f* GESCHÄFT principal establishment, principal place of business; **Hauptpacht** *f* GRUND master lease; **Hauptpalette** *f* TRANSP master pallet; **Hauptpolice** *f* VERSICH master policy (*AmE*); **Hauptpreis** *m* GESCHÄFT chief value (*CV*); **Hauptproblem** *nt* GESCHÄFT key issue; **Hauptprodukt** *nt* V&M staple product, base product; **Hauptproduzent** *m* VW major producer; **Hauptpunkt** *m* GESCHÄFT key point; **Hauptpunkt** *m* **eines Vertrages** GESCHÄFT head of an agreement

hauptrechnergesteuert *adj* COMP host-driven

Haupt-: **Hauptrohrleitung** *f* IND, TRANSP pipeline; **in der Hauptsache** *phr* GESCHÄFT primarily

hauptsächlich 1. *adj* GESCHÄFT primary, principal; **2.** *adv* GESCHÄFT primarily, principally; ♦ **sich ~ auf etw stützen** GESCHÄFT rest heavily on

hauptsächlich: **~er Leserstamm** *m* V&M primary readership

Haupt-: **Hauptsaison** *f* GESCHÄFT peak season; **Hauptschuldner, in** *m,f* FINANZ, V&M principal debtor; **Hauptsendezeit** *f* MEDIEN peak hour, prime time; **Hauptsitz** *m* GESCHÄFT head office (*HO*), headquarters (*HQ*), principal place of business; **Hauptsparte** *f* FINANZ bottom line (*infrml*); **Hauptspediteur** *m* TRANSP principal carrier; **Hauptstelle** *f* GESCHÄFT main branch; **Hauptstraße** *f* TRANSP major road, main line (*AmE*), main road (*BrE*), V&M high street (*BrE*), main street (*AmE*); **Hauptstrecke** *f* TRANSP main line, trunk line; **an der Hauptstrecke** *phr* TRANSP on the main line; **Hauptteil** *m* GESCHÄFT bulk; **Haupttermin** *m* VW main deadline; **Hauptursache** *f* RECHT main cause, procuring cause; **Hauptverbindung** *f* TRANSP main line; **Hauptvermögen** *nt* BÖRSE, RECHNUNG principal assets; **Hauptvermögenswerte** *m pl* BÖRSE, RECHNUNG chief assets; **Hauptversammlung** *f* MGMNT annual general meeting (*AGM*), shareholders' annual meeting; **Hauptversammlung** *f* **der Aktionäre** BÖRSE general meeting of shareholders; **Hauptvertrag** *m* RECHT prime contract; **Hauptverwaltung** *f* (*HV*) GESCHÄFT head office (*HO*), headquarters (*HQ*), VERWALT administrative center (*AmE*), adminstrative centre (*BrE*); **Hauptwert** *m* GESCHÄFT chief value (*CV*); **Hauptwirtschaftsbranche** *f* IND leading industry; **Hauptwohnsitz** *m* GRUND main residence; **Hauptziel** *nt* GESCHÄFT priority; **Hauptzollanmeldung** *f* IMP/EXP prime entry

Haus *nt* POL *Parlament* house; **von einem ~ eingelegtes**

Veto *nt* POL one-house veto (*AmE*); ♦ **von ~ zu Haus** IMP/EXP house-to-house, TRANSP *Lieferung* door-to-door; **Haus-Haus** TRANSP *Lieferung* house-to-house; **Haus-Lager** TRANSP *Lieferung* door-to-depot, house-to-depot; **ein ~ auf den Markt bringen** GRUND put a house on the market

Haus: **Hausbesitz** *m* GRUND home ownership; **Hausdurchsuchung** *f* RECHT *bei Verdacht* house search; **Hausdurchsuchungsbefehl** *m* RECHT search warrant

hauseigen *adj* COMP, MEDIEN in-house; **~e Software** *f* COMP in-house software; **~es System** *nt* COMP *Software-Entwicklung* in-house system

Haus: **Hausfrau** *f* GESCHÄFT housewife; **Haus- und Grundbesitzerhaftpflichtpolice** *f* VERSICH owners', landlords' and tenants' liability policy (*AmE*)

Haushalt *m* FINANZ budget, GESCHÄFT household, POL, RECHNUNG budget, VW interfund; **~ mit geringem Einkommen** V&M low-income household; ♦ **den ~ ausgleichen** FINANZ balance the budget; **im ~ veranschlagen** RECHNUNG budget for; **im ~ vorgesehen** RECHNUNG budgeted; **im ~ vorsehen** RECHNUNG budget for

haushälterisch *adj* GESCHÄFT prudent

Haushalt: **Haushaltsabschluß** *m* POL budgetary statement; **Haushaltsanalyse** FINANZ, RECHNUNG budget analysis; **Haushaltsanpassung** *f* FINANZ, RECHNUNG, VW budgetary adjustment; **Haushaltsansatz** *m* FINANZ estimate; **Haushaltsaufstellung** *f* FINANZ, MGMNT, RECHNUNG, VW budget preparation; **Haushaltsausgabe** *f* FINANZ, POL, VW budget expenditure; **Haushaltsausgaben** *f pl* FINANZ, POL, VW budgetary spending, budgetary expenditure; **Haushaltsausgabenansatz** *m* VERWALT estimate; **Haushaltsbefugnisse** *f pl* POL budgetary powers; **Haushaltsbehörde** *f* POL budget authority (*AmE*); **Haushaltsbeschluß** *m* POL budget resolution (*AmE*); **Haushaltsbewilligung** *f* POL budgetary appropriation; **Haushalts- und Bewilligungsausschuß** *m* POL supply and demand; **Haushaltsdefizit** *nt* FINANZ, GESCHÄFT, POL budget deficit, budgetary deficit, RECHNUNG fiscal deficit, VW budget deficit, budgetary deficit; **Haushaltseinnahmen** *f pl* FINANZ budgetary revenue; **Haushaltsentscheidungen** *f pl* VW household decision-making; **Haushaltsentwurf** *m* RECHNUNG draft budget; **Haushaltsgerät** *nt* GESCHÄFT household appliance; **Haushaltsgeräte** *nt pl* GESCHÄFT white goods; **Haushaltsgesetz** *nt* FINANZ appropriation act, appropriation bill; **Haushaltshöhe** *f* RECHNUNG budget level; **Haushaltsjahr** *nt* FINANZ, POL, RECHNUNG, STEUER accounting year, budget year, financial year, fiscal year (*FY*), tax year, budget period, budgetary period; **Haushaltskonto** *nt* FINANZ, RECHNUNG, VW budgetary account; **Haushaltskontrolle** *f* FINANZ, RECHNUNG audit, budgetary control (*BC*), budgeting control; **Haushaltskrise** *f* STEUER fiscal deficit; **Haushaltskürzung** *f* FINANZ, RECHNUNG, VW budget cut, budgetary cut, budget cutting

haushaltsmäßig *adj* FINANZ, POL, RECHNUNG, VW budgetary

Haushalt: **Haushaltsnachtrag** *m* FINANZ, POL Supplementary Estimates (*BrE*); **Haushaltsname** *m* V&M household name; **Haushaltsperiode** *f* FINANZ, POL, RECHNUNG, VW budget period, budgetary period; **Haushaltsplafond** *m* RECHNUNG budget ceiling

Haushaltsplan *m* FINANZ, POL, RECHNUNG, VW budget

Haushalt: **Haushaltsplanung** *f* FINANZ, POL, RECHNUNG budgetary planning, budgeting; **Haushaltspolitik** *f* POL budgetary policy; **Haushaltsposition** *f* RECHNUNG budgetary position; **Haushaltsrechnung** *f* FINANZ, RECHNUNG, VW budgetary account; **Haushaltsrede** *f* **des Finanzministers** POL, VW Budget speech (*BrE*); **die Haushaltsrede halten** *phr* VW deliver the Budget speech (*BrE*); **Haushaltsrede** *f* **des Schatzkanzlers** POL, VW Budget speech (*BrE*)

Haushaltsreisende *f* [decl. as adj] V&M door-to-door saleswoman; **Haushaltsreisende(r)** *m* [decl. as adj] V&M door-to-door salesman

Haushalt: **Haushaltssektor** *m* VW personal sector; **Haushaltsstandard** *m* FINANZ budget standard; **Haushaltsüberschreitung** *f* RECHNUNG overspend; **Haushaltsüberschuß** *m* FINANZ, GESCHÄFT, POL, VW budget surplus, budgetary surplus; **Haushaltsübersicht** *f* POL budgetary statement; **Haushaltsverabschiedung** *f* POL budget resolution (*AmE*); **Haushaltsverhalten** *nt* VW household behavior (*AmE*), household behaviour (*BrE*); **Haushaltsvoranschlag** *m* FINANZ estimate; **Haushaltsvorlage** *f* FINANZ budget proposal, budgetary submission, POL budget paper, RECHNUNG budget proposal, budgetary submission, VW budget proposal, budgetary submission, Finance Bill (*BrE*); **Haushaltsvorstand** *m* STEUER head of household; **Haushaltswaren** *f pl* GESCHÄFT household commodities, household goods; **Haushaltszuweisung** *f* FINANZ budget allotment

Haushaltungsschule *f* SOZIAL college of further education (*BrE*) (*CFE*)

Hausierer *m* GESCHÄFT, V&M hawker, huckster (*AmE*) (*infrml*), pedlar

Haus: **Hauskauf** *m* GRUND house purchase; **Hausluftfrachtbrief** *m* IMP/EXP, TRANSP house air waybill (*HAWB*); **Hausmarke** *f* V&M own brand, own funds, private brand; **Hausmüll** *m* UMWELT domestic waste; **Hauspreise** *m pl* GRUND house prices; **Hausrat** *m* VERSICH household effects; **Hausratversicherung** *f* VERSICH home contents insurance; **Hausrevision** *f* V&M home audit

Hausse *f* BÖRSE, FINANZ, VW boom, bullish movement, rise; ♦ **auf ~ spekulieren** BÖRSE go a bull

Hausse: **Hausseengagement** *nt* BÖRSE bull account; **Haussegeschäft** *nt* BÖRSE bull transaction; **Haussekauf** *m* BÖRSE bull buying; **Haussekündigungsspread** *f* BÖRSE bull call spread; **Hausseposition** *f* BÖRSE, FINANZ bull account, long position; **Haussespekulant** *m* BÖRSE, FINANZ bull; **Haussespekulation** *f* BÖRSE going long, bull speculation; **Hausseverkaufsspread** *m* BÖRSE bull put spread

Haussier *m* BÖRSE, FINANZ bull

Haus: **Haustürverkauf** *m* V&M door-to-door sales, door-to-door selling; **Hausversand** *m* V&M house mailing; **Hauswirtschaft** *f* VW home economics; **Haus-zu-Haus-Betreiber** *m* TRANSP through transport operator; **von-Haus-zu-Haus-Klausel** *f* VERSICH door-to-door clause; **Haus-zu-Haus-System** *nt* TRANSP through transport system

Havanna-Charta *f* VW Havana Charter

Havarie *f* TRANSP *Schiffahrt* accident at sea, sea damage (*SD*), VERSICH average, *Schiffahrt* accident at sea, sea damage (*SD*); ♦ **~ aufteilen** VERSICH apportion the average

Havarie: **Havarieagent** *m* VERSICH average agent; **Havariebond** *m* BÖRSE average bond; **Havarieeinschuß** *m* VERSICH average contribution

havariefrei *adj* VERSICH free of all average (*f.a.a.*)

Havarie: **Havariegeld** *nt* VERSICH average charges; **Havarieklausel** *f* VERSICH average clause; **Havariekommissar** *m* VERSICH average adjuster (*AA*), average agent; **Havariekosten** *pl* VERSICH average expenses; **Havarieregulierung** *f* VERSICH adjustment of average; **Havarieverpflichtungsschein** *m* BÖRSE average bond

HD *abbr* (*hohe Speicherdichte*) COMP *Disketten* HD (*high density*)

Hebelwirkung *f* FINANZ gearing (*BrE*), leverage (*AmE*), VW leverage effect

Heben *nt* TRANSP lifting

Heckscher-Ohlin-Theorem *nt* VW Heckscher-Ohlin theorem, Heckscher-Ohlin trade theorem

Hedge-Manager *m* BÖRSE hedge manager

Hedger *m* BÖRSE hedger

Hedge-Verwaltung *f* BÖRSE hedge management

hedonisch: ~e **Löhne** *m pl* VW hedonic wages; ~**er Preis** *m* VW hedonic price; ~e **Produktion** *f* VW hedonic output

heftig *adj* BÖRSE *Kursbewegungen* erratic, GESCHÄFT erratic, fierce

Hegemonie *f* POL hegemony

heikel *adj* GESCHÄFT sticky, tricky

Heim- *in cpds* GESCHÄFT home, homeward, return; **Heimarbeit** *f* IND domestic industry, PERSON homework, outwork, VW domestic system; **Heimarbeiter, in** *m,f* PERSON homeworker, outworker

Heimathafen *m* TRANSP port of registry

Heim-: **Heimcomputer** *m* COMP home computer; **Heimfahrt** *f* TRANSP homeward voyage; **Heimfall** *m* RECHT escheat; **Heimfallanspruch** *m* RECHT estate in reversion; **Heimfallrecht** *nt* GRUND, RECHT estate in reversion; **Heimindustrie** *f* IND cottage industry, domestic industry

heimisch: ~**er Arbeitsmarkt** *m* PERSON, VW local labor market (*AmE*), local labour market (*BrE*); ~**es Erzeugnis** *nt* GESCHÄFT local produce; ~**e Exportfinanzierung** *f* IMP/EXP domestic export financing; ~**es Gericht** *nt* RECHT domestic court; ~**er Wirtschaftszweig** *m* IND domestic industry

heimlich: ~e **Absprache** *f* VW collusion; ~**es Oligopol** *nt* VW collusive oligopoly; ~e **Steuererhöhung** *f* FINANZ, STEUER, VW tax-bracket creep; ~e **Steuerprogression** *f* FINANZ, STEUER, VW fiscal drag, tax-bracket creep; ~e **Zahlung** *f* GESCHÄFT undercover payment

Heim-: **Heimwerken** *nt* GESCHÄFT do-it-yourself (*DIY*)

Heirat: **Heiratsabzug** *m* STEUER marriage deduction; **Heiratszulage** *f* STEUER marriage allowance

heiß: ~**er Draht** *m* KOMM, POL hotline; ~**es Geld** *nt jarg* FINANZ hot money (*jarg*), refugee capital, GESCHÄFT, VW hot money; ~e **Ware** *f infrml* GESCHÄFT hot stock (*infrml*), hot property (*infrml*)

heißt: **das** ~ *phr* (*d.h.*) GESCHÄFT id est (*i.e.*), that is to say

Heiz- *in cpds* IND, TRANSP, UMWELT heating; **Heizgerät** *nt* GESCHÄFT heater (*htr*); **Heizoberfläche** *f* IND heating surface (*HS*); **Heizöl** *nt* TRANSP fuel oil; **Heizöltankfarm** *f* TRANSP fuel oil tank farm;

Heizöltanklager *nt* TRANSP fuel oil tank farm; **Heizstoffsteuerrabatt** *m* STEUER fuel duty rebate (*BrE*)

Heizungsindustrie *f* IND heating industry

Hektar *m* GESCHÄFT hectare (*ha*); **Hektarertrag** *m* VW yield per acre

Helfershelfer, in *m,f* RECHT accessory

Heliport *m* TRANSP heliport

hellerleuchtet *adj* COMP highlighted

Helligkeit *f* COMP *Bildschirm* brightness

hemmen *vt* GESCHÄFT block, inhibit

herabgesetzt *adj* V&M, VW reduced; ~**er Preis** *m* V&M reduced price

herabsetzen *vt* GESCHÄFT *Person* belittle, disparage, RECHT abate, V&M *Preise* reduce, VW *Inflationsrate* bring down, lower

herabsetzend: ~e **Aussage** *f* PATENT disparaging statement; ~**er Werbetext** *m* V&M disparaging copy; ~e **Werbung** *f* V&M knocking copy

Herabsetzung *f* GESCHÄFT *von einer Person* belittling, disparagement, RECHT abatement, V&M *Preise* cut, cutting, reduction, VW *Inflationsrate* lowering

Herabstufung *f* PERSON downgrading; ~ **von Arbeitsplätzen** PERSON deskilling

herabwürdigen *vt* GESCHÄFT vulgarize

Herabzonung *f* GRUND downzoning

heranwachsend: ~**er Straftäter** *m* RECHT status offender (*AmE*)

heranziehen: **jdn zu etw** ~ *phr* POL, GESCHÄFT, VW task sb with sth (*jarg*) (*AmE*)

heraufsetzen *vt* GESCHÄFT advance

herausbringen *vt* MEDIEN *Buch* put out, V&M *Produkt* launch

herausfinden *vt* GESCHÄFT sound out

herausfordern *vt* GESCHÄFT challenge

Herausforderung *f* GESCHÄFT challenge; ~ **durch den Arbeitsplatz** PERSON job challenge

Herausgabe *f* GESCHÄFT *Rückgabe* return, MEDIEN publication, issue; **Herausgabeklage** *f* RECHT *wegen widerrechtlicher Besitzentziehung* replevin; **Herausgabemanagement** *nt* V&M *Werbung* issue management (*BrE*)

herausgeben *vt* MEDIEN *Zeitschrift, Zeitung* issue, publish

Herausgeber, in *m,f* MEDIEN publisher, *Redakteur* editor; ~ **von Modezeitschriften** MEDIEN fashion editor

herausgegeben *adj* GESCHÄFT, MEDIEN published

herauskristallisieren: **sich** ~ *v refl* GESCHÄFT take shape

herausnehmen *vt* MEDIEN edit out

herausragend *adj* GESCHÄFT pre-eminent

herausrücken *vt infrml* FINANZ cough up (*infrml*)

herausschütteln *vt* GESCHÄFT shake out

herausziehen *vt* GESCHÄFT extract

herbeiführen *vt* GESCHÄFT *Einigung* work out

hereinbringen *vt* GESCHÄFT *Aufträge, Einkommen* bring in

hereinfallen *vi* GESCHÄFT be taken in

hereinholen *vt* GESCHÄFT *Aufträge* attract, VW *Kosten* recapture

hereinkommend: ~**er Auftrag** *m* V&M incoming order

hereinlassen *vt* GESCHÄFT admit

Herfindahl-Hirschman-Index *m* vw Herfindahl-Hirschman index

Herfracht *f* IMP/EXP inward cargo; **Herfrachtabteilung** *f* IMP/EXP inward freight department

hergestellt *adj* GESCHÄFT manufactured (*mfd*)

herkömmlich *adj* GESCHÄFT conventional, traditional; **~e Fracht** *f* TRANSP conventional cargo

Herkunft *f* FINANZ, GESCHÄFT source; **Herkunftsbescheinigung** *f* IMP/EXP certificate of origin (*c/o, co*); **Herkunftsbezeichnung** *f* V&M informative labeling (*AmE*), informative labelling (*BrE*); **Herkunftsdokument** *nt* FINANZ source document; **Herkunftsland** *nt* IMP/EXP country of origin (*COO*), TRANSP place of origin, point of origin; **Herkunftsort** *m* TRANSP place of origin, point of origin

Hermes-Modell *nt* vw Hermes Model

hermetisch: **~ abgeschlossen** *phr* IND airtight

Herr *m* GESCHÄFT esquire (*Esq.*); ◆ **sein eigener ~ sein** PERSON be one's own boss

Herr: **Herrenabteilung** *f* V&M men's department

herrenlos: **~es Anwesen** *nt* RECHT estate in abeyance; **~es Gut** *nt* RECHT bona vacantia; **~e Sache** *f* GRUND, RECHT res nullius

Herrichtungskosten *pl* GRUND fixing-up expense

Herrschaft *f* GESCHÄFT reign

herrschend *adj* GESCHÄFT prevailing, POL *Partei* ruling; **~es Grundstück** *nt* GRUND dominant tenement; **~e Klasse** *f* GESCHÄFT ruling class; **~er Lohnsatz** *m* PERSON going rate, rate for the job; **~e Stellung** *f* vw dominant position

Herrscher, in *m,f* POL ruler, sovereign

herrühren *vi*: **~ von** GESCHÄFT stem from

Herst. *abbr* (*Hersteller*) GESCHÄFT, IND, V&M mfr (*manufacturer*), maker, producer

herstammen *vi* GESCHÄFT originate

herstellen *vt* GESCHÄFT *Kontakt, Beziehung* build up, IND *Produkt* fabricate, manufacture, produce

Hersteller, in *m,f* (*Herst.*) GESCHÄFT, IND, V&M maker, manufacturer (*mfr*), producer; **~ von Wollwaren** IND woollen manufacturer; **Herstellereinkäufer** *m* IND producer buyer; **Herstellerfirma** *f* IND manufacturer (*mfr*); **Herstellermarke** *f* V&M manufacturer's brand, producer's brand; **Herstellerrichtpreis** *m* V&M manufacturer's recommended price (*MRP*); **Herstellerwerbung** *f* V&M producer advertising

Herstellkosten *pl* IND production costs

Herstellung *f* IND manufacture, manufacturing, production; **~ falschen Beweismaterials** RECHT forgery; **~ nach Kundenbestellung** IND intermittent production; **~ unter Zollverschluß** IMP/EXP in-bond manufacturing; ◆ **in der ~ sein** GESCHÄFT be in process

Herstellung: **Herstellungsabteilung** *f* IND production department; **Herstellungsaufwand** *m* V&M product costing; **Herstellungsgemeinkosten** *pl* vw manufacturing overheads; **Herstellungskosten** *pl* (*HK*) RECHNUNG cost of goods manufactured, historical cost, manufacturing expenses, manufacturing overheads, production costs, vw mill cost of sales; **Herstellungsleiter, in** *m,f* IND production manager; **Herstellungspreis** *m* V&M manufacturer's price; **Herstellungsprozess** *m* IND manufacturing process; **Herstellungsrechte** *nt pl* RECHT manufacturing rights; **Herstellungssystem** *nt* IND manufacturing system;

Herstellungstechnik *f* IND production technology; **Herstellungswert** *m* RECHNUNG value at cost

herumführen *vt* GESCHÄFT show round

herumkriegen *vt jarg* GESCHÄFT win over

Herumraterei *f* GESCHÄFT guesstimate (*infrml*)

herunterdrücken *vt* FINANZ *Gewinn* pull down

heruntergekommen: **~es Wohnviertel** *nt* GRUND blighted area

herunterhandeln: **~ auf** *vt* [+acc] GESCHÄFT bargain down, beat down, knock down

herunterladen *vt* COMP download, load

herunterschrauben *vt* POL *Problem* play down, soft-pedal (*infrml*)

herunterspielen *vt* POL *Problem* play down, soft-pedal (*infrml*)

herunterstufen *vt* PERSON downgrade

hervorbringen *vt* GESCHÄFT *Ideen* generate

hervorgehoben *adj* COMP highlighted

hervorheben *vt* COMP highlight, GESCHÄFT emphasize, highlight, stress, underscore

Hervorhebung *f* COMP highlighting, GESCHÄFT emphasis, highlighting, stress, underscoring

hervorragend *adj* GESCHÄFT excellent, pre-eminent; **~e Agentur** *f* V&M hot shop

Herz: **auf ~ und Nieren prüfen** *phr* GESCHÄFT vet

Heteroskedastizität *f* MATH heteroscedasticity

heuer *adj* Öst, Sch (*cf dieses Jahrs*) GESCHÄFT this year

Heuer *f* TRANSP *Schiffahrt* pay, wage; **Heuerbedingungen** *f pl* TRANSP articles of agreement, signed articles

heuern und feuern *phr infrml* PERSON hire and fire

Heuer: **Heuervertrag** *m* TRANSP articles of agreement, ship's articles, signed articles

Heuristik *f* COMP, GESCHÄFT, MGMNT *Problemlösung* heuristics

heuristisch *adj* COMP, GESCHÄFT, MGMNT *Problemlösung* heuristic

heute: **ab ~** *phr* GESCHÄFT after date (*a/d*)

heutig: **~er Wert** *m* **in Dollar** vw current dollars

H-Form *f* vw H-form

HGB *abbr* (*Handelsgesetzbuch*) RECHT Commercial Code

Hicks: **Hicks-Einkommensbestimmung** *f* vw Hicksian income measure; **Hicks-Einkommensbewertung** *f* vw Hicksian income measure; **Hicks-Pläne** *m pl* vw Hicks Charts

hieb: **hieb- und stichfest** *adj* GESCHÄFT *Argument* watertight

Hierarchie *f* MGMNT, PERSON hierarchy; **~ des Führungspersonals** MGMNT, PERSON management hierarchy, gorilla scale (*infrml*)

hierarchisch: **~e Aufgabenanalyse** *f* MGMNT hierarchical task analysis (*HTA*); **~es Dekompositionsprinzip** *nt* MGMNT hierarchical decomposition principle; **~es Menü** *nt* COMP hierarchical menu

hieraus *adv* KOMM hereof

hierunter *adv* KOMM hereunder

hierzu *adv* KOMM hereto

hiesig: **~e Industrie** *f* IND local industry

Highlights *nt pl* GESCHÄFT highlights

High-Tech- *in cpds* COMP, GESCHÄFT high-tech; **High-Tech-Aktien** *f pl* BÖRSE high-tech stock

Hilfe *f* COMP *Programme* help, FINANZ, VW assistance, *Entwicklungsländer* aid; ~ **der Gemeinschaft** *f* VW Community aid; ◆ ~ **suchen bei** GESCHÄFT fall back on

Hilfe: **Hilfebildschirm** *m* COMP help screen; **Hilfemodus** *m* COMP help mode; **Hilfetaste** *f* COMP help key

Hilfs- *in cpds* COMP *Speicher, Programm* auxiliary (*aux.*), GESCHÄFT auxiliary (*aux.*), subsidiary; **Hilfsarbeiter, in** *m,f* GESCHÄFT low-wage worker, PERSON laborer (*AmE*), labourer (*BrE*), supernumerary, unskilled worker, daily paid worker

hilfsbereit *adj* GESCHÄFT cooperative

Hilfs-: **Hilfs- und Betriebsstoffe** *m pl* IND factory supplies, manufacturing supplies; **Hilfsbücher** *nt pl* RECHNUNG subsidiary accounting record; **Hilfsdienst** *m* GESCHÄFT ancillary service, backup service; **Hilfsgelder** *nt pl* FINANZ, VW *Entwicklungsländer* aid money; **Hilfsgüter** *nt pl* IMP/EXP relief goods; **Hilfskassierer, in** *m,f* BANK assistant cashier (*BrE*), assistant teller (*AmE*); **Hilfskostenumlagesystem** *nt* RECHNUNG common service cost distribution system; **Hilfskraft** *f* GESCHÄFT, PERSON assistant; **Hilfskraft** *f* **mit kurzfristigem Vertrag** PERSON short-term worker; **Hilfsoperation** *f* MGMNT ancillary operation; **Hilfsprogramm** *nt* COMP utility program, FINANZ, VW *Entwicklungsländer* aid program (*AmE*), aid programme (*BrE*), aid scheme, VW aid scheme; **Hilfsprojekt** *nt* FINANZ, VW *Entwicklungsländer* aid scheme; **Hilfsquelle** *f* GESCHÄFT potential; **Hilfsrevisor** *m* PERSON assistant controller (*AC*); **Hilfsspeicher** *m* COMP *Hardware* auxiliary memory, auxiliary storage

Hinaufschnellen *nt* GESCHÄFT upsurge

hinaufsetzen *vt* GESCHÄFT advance, *Angebot, Preis* raise up

hinaus *adv* KOMM, GESCHÄFT above

hinausdrängen *vt* VW crowd out

hinausrollen *vt* GESCHÄFT roll out; ◆ **über etw** ~ GESCHÄFT overshoot

hinausschicken *vt* GESCHÄFT send out

hinausschießen: ~ **über** *vt* [+acc] GESCHÄFT overshoot

hinauswerfen *vt infml* GESCHÄFT evict, *Geld* splash out (*infml*), PERSON sack (*infml*) (*BrE*), RECHT evict, SOZIAL *Mieter* eject, evict

Hinblick: **im** ~ **auf** *phr* GESCHÄFT with a view to; **im** ~ **darauf** *phr* GESCHÄFT with this in view; **im** ~ **darauf, daß** *phr* RECHT *Präambelformel* in view of the fact that

hindern *vt* GESCHÄFT obstruct

Hindernis *nt* GESCHÄFT obstacle, obstruction, VW *Handel* barrier

Hinderung *f* RECHT estoppel

hindeuten *vt*: ~ **auf** [+acc] GESCHÄFT be indicative of

hineinlassen *vt* GESCHÄFT admit

Hinfracht *f* IMP/EXP, TRANSP outward cargo

hinhalten *vt* GESCHÄFT stave off, *Pläne* stall

Hinnehmen *nt* GESCHÄFT assent

hinreichend *adj* GESCHÄFT sufficient, VW adequate

Hin-: ~ **und Rückreise** *f* TRANSP round trip; ~ **und Rückreisekosten** *pl* TRANSP round-trip cost; ~ **und Rückreisetarif** *m* TRANSP round-trip rate; ~ **und Rückreisezeit** *f* TRANSP round-trip time

Hinsicht: **in dieser** ~ *phr* GESCHÄFT in this respect

hinsichtlich *prep* GESCHÄFT in terms of, in respect of

Hinter- *in cpds* GESCHÄFT back, rear

hinter: ~**er Anschlag** *m* IND backstop; ~**er Buchdeckel** *m* MEDIEN back cover; ~**er Klappentext** *m* MEDIEN inside back cover; ~**er Rand** *m* MEDIEN back margin

Hinter-: **Hinterbänkler** *m* POL backbench MP (*BrE*), backbencher (*BrE*)

Hinterbliebenen- *in cpds* BANK, VERSICH survivor, survivorship; **Hinterbliebenenkonto** *nt* BANK survivorship account; **Hinterbliebenenrente** *f* VERSICH death benefit; **Hinterbliebenenversicherung** *f* VERSICH survivorship insurance; **Hinterbliebenenversicherungsklausel** *f* VERSICH common disaster clause (*AmE*), survivorship clause (*AmE*); **Hinterbliebenenversicherungspolice** *f* VERSICH survivor policy

Hintergrund *m* COMP *des Bildschirms* background, GESCHÄFT backdrop, background; **Hintergrundbericht** *m* MEDIEN background story; **Hintergrundfarbe** *f* COMP *des Bildschirms* background color (*AmE*), background colour (*BrE*); **Hintergrundfeld** *nt* COMP background field; **Hintergrundinformation** *f* GESCHÄFT background information; **Hintergrundkenntnisse** *f pl* PATENT background art; **Hintergrundpapier** *nt* FINANZ background paper

Hinterland *nt* TRANSP, VW hinterland

Hinterlassung: **ohne** ~ **eines Testaments sterben** *phr* BANK, RECHT die intestate

hinterlegen *vt* BANK, GESCHÄFT, RECHT deposit

Hinterleger, in *m,f* BANK, GESCHÄFT, RECHT bailor, depositor

Hinterlegung *f* BANK, GESCHÄFT bailment, deposit, RECHT deposit, deposition; ~ **von Geld oder Wertpapieren** BANK special deposit; **Hinterlegungsschein** *m* GESCHÄFT deposit slip, trust receipt; **Hinterlegungsstelle** *f* VERWALT deposit facility, deposit institution, depositary; **Hinterlegungsvereinbarung** *f* RECHT deposit agreement; **Hinterlegungsvertrag** *m* GESCHÄFT, RECHT bailment

Hinter-: **Hintermann** *m* FINANZ backer; **Hintertürchen** *nt* GESCHÄFT loophole; **Hintertürchen-Paragraph** *m* RECHT joker (*AmE*)

hinterziehen *vt* STEUER evade

hinwegsetzen: **sich** ~ **über** *v refl* [+acc] GESCHÄFT override

Hinweis *m* GESCHÄFT, MGMNT hint, pointer, word of advice, V&M cue; **Hinweise** *m pl* **für Exporteure** IMP/EXP hints to exporters; **Hinweisfenster** *nt* COMP alert box

hinweisen: **jdn auf etw** ~ *phr* GESCHÄFT refer sb to sth

hinziehen: **sich** ~ *v refl* GESCHÄFT *Sitzung* spill over

hinzufügen *vt* COMP *Datei* attach, GESCHÄFT *Einzelheiten, Zahlen* add in, MATH *Zahlen*, MEDIEN *Text* add

Hinzufügung *f* COMP *Datei*, GESCHÄFT *Einzelheiten, Zahlen*, MATH *Zahlen*, MEDIEN *Text* addition

hinzukommend *adj* GESCHÄFT accessory

hinzurechnen *vt* MATH add

hinzuzählen *vt* MATH add

Histogramm *nt* MATH histogram

historisch 1. *adj* GESCHÄFT historical; **2.** *adv* GESCHÄFT historically

historisch: ~**es Gebäude** *nt* GRUND historic building, historic structure; ~**er Handel** *m* TRANSP historical trade; ~**er Höchststand** *m* VW record high; ~**er Rekord** *m* GESCHÄFT all-time record, all-time high; ~**e Schule** *f* VW Historical School

Hitliste *f infrml* GESCHÄFT hit list (*infrml*)

hitzebeständig *adj* IND heat-resistant

HK *abbr* (*Handelskammer*) GESCHÄFT CC (*Chamber of Commerce*), board of trade (*AmE*); (*Herstellungskosten*) RECHNUNG historical cost

hoch 1. *adj* GESCHÄFT *Preis, Schätzung, Steuer* high, *Anspruch, Standard* exacting; ♦ **mit hohen Ansprüchen an handwerkliches Geschick** PERSON *Aufgabe, Arbeit* skill-intensive; **einen hohen finanziellen Verlust erleiden** FINANZ take a cleaning (*infrml*); **in hohem Maße** GESCHÄFT substantially, to a large extent, heavily, STEUER heavily; **auf hohem Niveau stehend** GESCHÄFT sophisticated; **einen zu hohen Preis fordern** FINANZ overprice; **hohen Schadensersatz zusprechen** RECHT adjudge heavy damages; **2.** *adv* GESCHÄFT highly, heavily; ♦ **~ belastet** BANK, RECHNUNG, VW heavily mortgaged; **~ differenziert** GESCHÄFT sophisticated

Hoch- *in cpds* GESCHÄFT high, peak

hoch: **hohe Abfindung** *f* PERSON *Führungskraft* golden handshake (*infrml*); **hohe Abschlußzahlung** *f* BANK balloon payment, balloon repayment; **hohes Amt** *nt* PERSON high office, important office; **hohe Anfangskosten** *pl* BÖRSE front-end load, VW front-end costs; **hohe Belastung** *f* BANK, RECHNUNG, VW heavy mortgaging; **hoher Beschäftigungsüberschuß** *m* VW high employment surplus; **~ bewertete Aktien** *f pl* BÖRSE high-flying stock; **hohe Einkommensgruppe** *f* VW higher income bracket; **hohe Einkommensstufe** *f* VW higher income bracket; **hoher Ertrag** *m* BÖRSE high return; **hohe Investitionsrate** *f* VW high rate of investment; **etw auf die hohe Kante legen** *infrml* GESCHÄFT save for a rainy day; **hoher Lebensstandard** *m* SOZIAL high standard of living; **hoher Leistungsbereich** *m* COMP high-end; **hohe Normwerte** *m pl* GESCHÄFT high standards; **hoher Preis** *m* GESCHÄFT high price; **hohe Rendite** *f* BÖRSE high return; **hohe Speicherdichte** *f* (*HD*) COMP *Disketten* high density (*HD*); **hoher Staufaktor** *m* TRANSP high stowage factor; **hohe Steuern** *f pl* STEUER heavy duties; **hohes Tier** *nt infrml* GESCHÄFT big cheese (*infrml*) (*BrE*), brass (*infrml*), very important person (*VIP*); **~ verschuldet** *adj* BANK badly in debt; **hohe Verzinsung** *f* BÖRSE high return; **hoher Vorschluß** *m* FINANZ front-end money; **hoher Zins** *m* BÖRSE balloon interest

Hoch: **Hoher Ausschuß** *m* POL High Commission (*BrE*); **Hohe Kommission** *f* POL High Commission (*BrE*)

Hochachtungsvoll *adv frml* KOMM *Grußformel am Briefende* Yours faithfully, Yours sincerely, Yours truly

hochangesehen: **~e Marke** *f* PATENT mark with high reputation

hochauflösend *adj* COMP *Bildschirm, Scanner* high-resolution

Hoch-: **Hochbegabte(r)** *mf* [decl. as adj] PERSON high flier

hochbelastet: **~es Gebiet** *nt* UMWELT high-pollution area

Hoch-: **Hochdruckverkauf** *m* V&M sales drive

hochentwickelt *adj* GESCHÄFT advanced, sophisticated, IND high-stream; ♦ **mit ~er Technologie** IND technologically advanced

hochentwickelt: **~es Land** *nt* POL, VW advanced country (*AC*); **~er Markt** *m* BÖRSE sophisticated market; **~e**

Technologie *f* IND advanced technology; **~e Volkswirtschaft** *f* GESCHÄFT, VW advanced economy

Hoch-: **Hochfestigkeit** *f* IND extra high strength (*EHS*); **Hochfinanz** *f* FINANZ high finance; **Hochformat** *nt* COMP, MEDIEN *Drucker* portrait; **Hochfrequenzsprechfunk** *m* KOMM high-frequency radiotelephony; **Hochgeschwindigkeitszug** *m* TRANSP high-speed train (*HST*)

hochgestellt *adj* COMP *Typographie* superscript, GESCHÄFT *Persönlichkeit* top-ranking, MEDIEN *Typographie* superscript; **~es Zeichen** *adj* COMP, MEDIEN *Typographie* superscript

hochgipflig: **~e Verteilungskurve** *f* MATH *Statistik* leptokurtic frequency distribution

Hochgipfligkeit *f* MATH *Statistik* leptokurtosis

Hoch-: **Hochglanzmagazin** *nt* MEDIEN glossy (*infrml*), glossy magazine; **Hochglanzpapier** *nt* KOMM glossy paper; **Hochhaus** *nt* GRUND, SOZIAL high-rise, multistorey (*BrE*), multistory (*AmE*), tower block; **Hochheben** *nt* TRANSP *Fracht* lifting

hochintelligent *adj* GESCHÄFT sophisticated

hochkarätig *adj* GESCHÄFT top-flight, PERSON high-caliber (*AmE*), high-calibre (*BrE*)

hochklappbar: **~e Reklame** *f* V&M pop-up

Hoch-: **Hochkommissariat** *nt* **der Vereinten Nationen für Flüchtlinge** (*UNHCR*) VW United Nations High Commission for Refugees (*UNHCR*); **Hochkonjunktur** *f* GESCHÄFT bonanza, VW boom; **Hochlader** *m* TRANSP high loader; **Hochleistungscomputer** *m* COMP front-end, high-end computer; **Hochleistungstechnik** *f* COMP advanced technology; **Hochlohn-Arbeitskräfte** *f pl* PERSON high-cost labor (*AmE*), high-cost labour (*BrE*)

hochmodisch *adj* GESCHÄFT in fashion, trendy (*infrml*) (*BrE*)

Hoch-: **Hochprämien-Wandelschuldverschreibung** *f* BÖRSE high-premium convertible debenture

hochprofiliert *adj* V&M high-profile

hochqualifiziert *adj* PERSON highly skilled

hochrangig *adj* GESCHÄFT high-powered, top-ranking

Hoch-: **Hochrechnung** *f* MATH *Statistik* extrapolation

hochregeln *vt* MATH adjust upwards

Hoch-: **Hochsaisonpreis** *m* FREI high-season fare

Hochschul- *in cpds* SOZIAL A level (*BrE*), High School (*AmE*), tertiary, academic; **Hochschulabschluß** *m* PERSON university degree; **Hochschulabsolvent, in** *m,f* SOZIAL graduate, postgraduate (*AmE*); **Hochschulbildung** *f* SOZIAL tertiary education; **Hochschulforschung** *f* SOZIAL academic research; **Hochschulreife** *f* SOZIAL ≈ Advanced level (*BrE*) (*A level*), ≈ High School Diploma (*AmE*)

Hochsee *f* TRANSP open sea; **Hochseefischerei** *f* VW seafarming; **Hochseeroute** *f* TRANSP deep-sea shipping lane, deepwater route; **Hochseeschiff** *nt* TRANSP ocean-going ship

hochspekulativ: **~e Anlage** *f* FINANZ aggressive investment

Höchst- *in cpds* BÖRSE, GESCHÄFT premium, highest, maximum; **Höchstanspruch** *m* VERSICH claims limit

Hochstapler *m* GESCHÄFT con artist (*infrml*), con man (*infrml*), confidence trickster, crook (*infrml*)

Hochstaplerin *f* GESCHÄFT con artist (*infrml*), confidence trickster, crook (*infrml*)

Höchst-: **Höchstaufkäufe** *m pl* BÖRSE premium raid; **Höchstaufnahmefähigkeit** *f* IND optimum capacity; **Höchstbelastung** *f* TRANSP maximum load; **Höchstbelastungssatz** *m* VW psychological breaking point; **Höchstbetrag** *m* FINANZ ceiling; **Höchstbietende(r)** *mf* [decl. as adj] GESCHÄFT best bidder; **Höchstdruck** *m* IND extreme pressure (*EP*)

höchste: **~(r) Beamte(r)** *m* [decl. as adj], **~ Beamtin** *f* VERWALT top-ranking official; **am ~n belastet sein mit** *phr* STEUER be charged on top of; **~r Break-Even-Punkt** *m* BÖRSE upside break-even; **~ und beste Nutzung** *f* GRUND highest and best use; **~ Gutgläubigkeit** *f* RECHT, VERSICH utmost good faith; **~ Gutgläubigkeit** *f* **und Redlichkeit** *f* RECHT, VERSICH uberrimae fidei; **~ Priorität** *f* GESCHÄFT number one priority; **~ Redlichkeit** *f* RECHT, VERSICH utmost good faith; **nach ~r Schätzung** *phr* GESCHÄFT at the highest estimate

hochstehend: **~e Führungskraft** *f* MGMNT, PERSON high executive; **~e(r) Angestellte(r)** *mf* [decl. as adj] MGMNT, PERSON senior manager

höchstens *adj* GESCHÄFT not exceeding

Höchst-: **Höchstgebot** *nt* BÖRSE highest bid, best bid, GESCHÄFT closing bid, highest tender

Höchstgrenze *f* GESCHÄFT upper limit, RECHNUNG ceiling; **~ des Selbstbehalts** VERSICH net line

Höchst-: **Höchstkapazität** *f* IND *Produktion* maximum capacity; **Höchstkredit** *m* FINANZ high credit; **Höchstkurs** *m* BÖRSE, GESCHÄFT all-time high, high, highest price, top price; **Höchstlast** *f* IND optimum capacity, safe working load; **Höchstlohn** *m* PERSON *Arbeitsentgelt* wage ceiling

Höchstpreis *m* BÖRSE highest price, GESCHÄFT chief value (*CV*), top price, V&M maximum price, premium price, VW ceiling price, price ceiling; **♦ zum ~** BÖRSE at best; **zu Höchstpreisen kaufen** V&M buy at the top of the market

Höchstpreis: **Höchstpreisfestlegung** *f* V&M premium pricing

Höchst-: **Höchstrisiko** *nt* BÖRSE maximum risk; **Höchstsatz** *m* BANK maximum rate

Höchststand *m* BÖRSE high, GESCHÄFT high, VW peak; **~ am Abend** BÖRSE evening peak; **♦ einen historischen ~ erreichen** BÖRSE reach an all-time high, GESCHÄFT top out, VW peak

Höchst-: **Höchstwert** *m* GESCHÄFT chief value (*CV*); **Höchstzins** *m* BANK interest rate ceiling, capitalization rate, cap rate; **Höchstzinssatz** *m* **bei Cap-Floatern** FINANZ cap

höchstzulässig *adj* GESCHÄFT maximum, maximum permissible

Hoch-: **Hochtarif** *m* GESCHÄFT peak rate

hochtechnisiert *adj* COMP, IND sophisticated

Hoch-: **Hochtechnologie** *f* COMP, IND high technology, high-tech; **Hochtechnologieindustrie** *f* IND technology-based industry

hochtechnologisch *adj* COMP, IND high-tech

Hoch-: **auf Hochtouren arbeiten** *phr infrml* GESCHÄFT work flat out (*infrml*)

hochtreiben *vt* VW *Preise* inflate

Hoch-: **Hochwasserversicherung** *f* VERSICH flood insurance

hochwertig: **~es Produkt** *nt* GESCHÄFT high-quality product (*BrE*), upscale product (*AmE*)

Hoch-: **Hochzahl** *f* MATH exponent; **Hochzinsfinanzierung** *f* FINANZ high-yield financing

Hoffnungen: **seine ~ auf etw setzen** *phr* GESCHÄFT pin one's hopes on

höflich: **~e Begleitnotiz** *f* V&M compliment slip

Hoflieferant *m* GESCHÄFT purveyor to the Royal Household (*BrE*)

Höhe *f* GESCHÄFT height (*hgt*), *Preise* level; **~ der finanziellen Unterstützung** VW level of support; **♦ in die ~ schießen** GESCHÄFT *Preise* rocket (*infrml*), shoot up; **in die ~ schnellen** GESCHÄFT soar, *Preise* escalate

Hoheit *f* POL sovereignty; **Hoheitsgebiet** *nt* GESCHÄFT territory; **Hoheitsgewässer** *nt pl* RECHT territorial waters

höher *adj* COMP, SOZIAL advanced; **♦ ~ auszeichnen** V&M *Ware* mark up; **auf ein ~es Niveau bringen** VW level up; **einen ~en Rang einnehmen als** GESCHÄFT rank above

höher: **~er Aktienkurs** *m* **als vorher notiert** BÖRSE uptick; **~e(r) Beamte(r)** *m* [decl. as adj], **~e Beamtin** *f* PERSON senior officer (*SO*); **~ bewerteter Überschuß** *m* RECHNUNG appreciated surplus; **~e Bildung** *f* SOZIAL higher education, advanced education; **~er Fachschulabschluß** *m* SOZIAL Higher National Diploma (*BrE*) (*HND*); **~e Gewalt** *f* RECHT, VERSICH force majeure; **~e Handelsschule** *f* SOZIAL college of further education (*BrE*) (*CFE*); **~e Programmiersprache** *f* COMP high-order language, high-level language (*HLL*), advanced language; **~e Schulbildung** *f* SOZIAL secondary education; **~e(r) Staatsbeamte(r)** *m* [decl. as adj], **~e Staatsbeamtin** *f* PERSON senior civil servant; **~e Version** *f* COMP advanced version

Höherbewertung *f* GESCHÄFT upvaluation, write-up

Höhere-Gewalt-Klausel *f* RECHT, VERSICH force majeure clause

Höherstufung *f* PERSON upgrading

höherverzinslich: **~es Kontokorrentkonto** *nt* BANK super NOW account (*AmE*)

Holding *f* BANK, BÖRSE, FINANZ, RECHNUNG, RECHT holding company; **~ mit eigener Bank als 100%-iger Tochter** BANK, BÖRSE, FINANZ, RECHNUNG one-bank holding company (*AmE*); **Holdingbankwesen** *nt* BANK group banking; **Holdinggesellschaft** *f* BANK, BÖRSE, FINANZ, RECHNUNG, RECHT holding company; **Holdinggesellschaft** *f* **mit verschiedenen Tätigkeitsbereichen** BANK, BÖRSE, FINANZ, RECHNUNG mixed-activity holding company

Holschuld *f* RECHT *Vertragsrecht* liability to be discharged at the domicile of the debtor

Holz *nt* IND wood (*w*); **Holzbelag** *m* IND wood cover; **Holzfaserplatte** *f* IND fiberboard (*AmE*), fibreboard (*BrE*); **Holzindustrie** *f* IND lumber industry (*AmE*), timber industry (*BrE*); **Holzpalette** *f* IND wooden pallet; **Holzspanplatte** *f* IND chipboard

holzverarbeitend: **~e Gewerbe** *nt pl* IND wood-processing industry

Home: **~ Banking** *nt* BANK home banking

homogen *adj* GESCHÄFT homogeneous; **~es Gut** *nt* VW homogeneous good; **~er Markt** *m* V&M homogeneous market; **~es Oligopol** *nt* VW homogeneous oligopoly

Homologation *f* IMP/EXP homologation

Homoskedastizität *f* MATH homoscedasticity

Honorar *nt* GESCHÄFT honorarium, professional fee, remuneration; **Honoraraufteilung** *f* RECHNUNG fee split; **Honorareinkommen** *nt* RECHNUNG fee income; **Honorarvertrag** *m* PERSON freelance contract; **Honorarvorschuß** *m* RECHT retainer

honorieren *vt* BANK *Scheck* honor (*AmE*), honour (*BrE*); **nicht ~** *vt* BANK dishonor (*AmE*), dishonour (*BrE*)

honoriert: nicht ~ *adj* BANK *Scheck* dishonored (*AmE*), dishonoured (*BrE*)

Hörensagen *nt* RECHT hearsay

Hörfunk *m* KOMM radio

Horizont: am ~ *phr* GESCHÄFT on the horizon

horizontal *adj* GESCHÄFT horizontal; **~e Analyse** *f* RECHNUNG horizontal analysis; **~e Arbeitsfeldvergrößerung** *f* PERSON job enlargement; **~e Arbeitsteilung** *f* MGMNT horizontal specialization; **~e Bilanz** *f* RECHNUNG horizontal balance sheet; **~e Diskriminierung** *f* VW *Arbeitsplatz* horizontal discrimination; **~e Fachgewerkschaft** *f* PERSON horizontal union; **~e Fusion** *f* VW horizontal amalgamation; **~e Integration** *f* MGMNT horizontal channel integration, VW horizontal integration, lateral integration; **~e Kommunikation** *f* GESCHÄFT horizontal communication; **~e Publikation** *f* MEDIEN horizontal publication; **~e Spezialisierung** *f* MGMNT horizontal specialization; **~e Steuergerechtigkeit** *f* STEUER horizontal equity; **~es Wachstum** *nt* VW horizontal expansion; **~er Zusammenschluß** *m* VW horizontal amalgamation, horizontal combination, horizontal merger

Horizontanalyse *f* FINANZ horizon analysis

Host *m* COMP host; **Host-Computer** *m* COMP host computer

Hotel *nt* FREI, GRUND hotel; **~ mit internationalem Standard** FREI international-standard hotel; **Hotelbesitzer** *m* FREI, GRUND hotel proprietor; **Hotel- und Gaststättengewerbe** *nt* FREI catering trade

Hotelier *m* FREI, GRUND hotelier

Hotel: Hotelmanager *m* FREI, GRUND hotel manager; **Hotelregister** *nt* FREI hotel register; **Hotelunterbringung** *f* FREI hotel accommodation; **Hotelunterkunft** *f* FREI hotel accommodation; **Hotelverzeichnis** *nt* FREI hotel register

Hotkey *m jarg* COMP *Funktionstasten* hot key; **Hotkey-Taste** *f jarg* COMP hot key

Hotline *f* COMP *Produktberatung* support hotline, hotline

HR-Eintragung *f* (*Handelsregister-Eintragung*) GESCHÄFT, RECHT commercial registration

Hub *m* TRANSP lifting

Hubschrauber *m* TRANSP helicopter; **Hubschrauberflugplatz** *m* TRANSP heliport, helistop; **Hubschraubergeld** *nt* VW helicopter money; **Hubschrauberlandplatz** *m* TRANSP heliport, helistop

Huckepack- *in cpds* BÖRSE, FINANZ, RECHT, TRANSP, V&M piggyback, pickaback

huckepack: ~ befördern *vt* TRANSP carry on piggyback

Huckepack-: Huckepackanleihe *f* FINANZ piggyback loan; **Huckepackausfuhrsystem** *nt* V&M piggyback export scheme; **Huckepackgesetzgebung** *f* RECHT piggyback legislation; **Huckepackregistrierung** *f* BÖRSE piggyback registration; **Huckepackverkauf** *m* V&M piggyback selling; **Huckepackverkaufsförderung** *f* V&M piggyback promotion; **Huckepackverkehr** *m* TRANSP piggyback traffic (*AmE*), road-rail transport (*BrE*); **im Huckepackverkehr** *m* TRANSP carry on piggyback

Hulbert-Klassifizierung *f* FINANZ Hulbert rating

Hülle *f* COMP, MEDIEN *Disketten* jacket, *Compact Disc* sleeve

Hüllkurve *f* MATH envelope curve

Human: ~ Relations *pl* GESCHÄFT, PERSON human relations

Human- *in cpds* PERSON, VERWALT, VW human; **Humanfaktoren** *m pl* PERSON human factors; **Humankapital** *nt* PERSON, VERWALT human resources, VW human capital; **Humankapitalrechnung** *f* PERSON, VERWALT human resource accounting (*HRA*); **Humanvermögen** *nt* PERSON, VERWALT human resources; **Humanvermögensrechnung** *f* PERSON, VERWALT human resource accounting (*HRA*), human asset accounting

human: ~e Skaleneffekte *m pl* VW human-scale economics

Hundert *nt* MATH hundred; ◆ **vom ~** (*v. H.*) GESCHÄFT per cent (*P/C, pc*)

hundertprozentig: ~e Rücklagenbildung *f* BANK one-hundred-percent reserve banking; **~er Standort** *m* V&M one-hundred-percent location

Hungerlohn *m* GESCHÄFT pittance, starvation wage

Hürde *f* GESCHÄFT hurdle, barrier

Hut: auf der ~ sein *phr* GESCHÄFT be on one's guard; **den ~ herumgehen lassen** *phr infrml* PERSON *für einen Kollegen* have a whip-round (*infrml*) (*BrE*)

Hüttenwerk *nt* IND smelting works

HV *abbr* GESCHÄFT (*Hauptverwaltung*) HO (*head office*), HQ (*headquarters*), (*Hauptversammlung*) AGM (*annual general meeting*), shareholders' annual meeting

hybrid: ~e Einkommenssteuer *f* STEUER hybrid income tax

Hybridcomputer *m* COMP hybrid computer

Hybridrechner *m* COMP hybrid computer

Hydraulik- *in cpds* IND hydraulic; **Hydraulikkupplung** *f* IND hydraulic coupling (*HC*)

hydraulisch *adj* IND hydraulic

Hydro- *in cpds* IND hydro-; **Hydrocharter** *f* TRANSP hydrocharter

hydrodynamisch *adj* IND hydrodynamic

hydroelektrisch *adj* IND, UMWELT hydroelectric

Hydro-: Hydrometer *nt* UMWELT hydrometer; **Hydrostatik** *f* IND hydrostatics

Hygienestandard *m* SOZIAL standard of hygiene

hygroskopisch: ~e Substanz *f* UMWELT hygroscopic substance

Hyp. *abbr* (*Hypothek*) BANK, GRUND, VW mortg. (*mortgage*)

Hyperinflation *f* VW hyperinflation

Hypothek *f* BANK, GRUND, VW home loan, mortgage (*mortg.*); **~ mit Gewinnbeteiligung des Gläubigers** BANK, GRUND shared appreciation mortgage; **~ mit Zins- und Tilgungszahlungsgarantie eines Dritten** BANK guaranteed mortgage; ◆ **aus einer ~ die Zwangsvollstreckung betreiben** FINANZ, RECHT, VW foreclose a mortgage

hypothekarisch: ~ belasten *phr* BANK, GRUND, VW mortgage; **nicht ~ belastet** *adj* BANK, GRUND, VW unmortgaged; ~ **gesichertes Wertpapier** *nt* FINANZ mortgage-backed security (*AmE*)

Hypothek: **Hypothekenabschlußzahlung** *f* FINANZ final mortgage payment; **Hypothekenbank** *f* BANK mortgage bank, mortgage loan company

Hypothekendarlehen *nt* BANK mortgage loan; ~ **mit regelmäßig neu ausgehandeltem Zinssatz** BANK rollover mortgage

hypothekengebunden *adj* BANK, GRUND subject to mortgage

Hypothek: **Hypothekengeldgeber** *m* BANK mortgage lender; **Hypothekengesellschaft** *f* BANK mortgage loan company

hypothekengesichert: **~er Anteilsschein** *m* FINANZ mortgage-backed certificate; **~er Pfandbrief** *m* FINANZ mortgage-backed security

Hypothek: **Hypothekengläubiger, in** *m,f* BANK lender, mortgagee; **Hypothekenkonditionen** *f pl* BANK mortgage rate; **Hypothekenkonto** *nt* BANK mortgage account; **Hypothekenkreditverband** *m* FINANZ mortgage credit association; **Hypothekenkreditzusage** *f* FINANZ mortgage commitment; **Hypothekenmakler, in** *m,f* FINANZ mortgage broker (*AmE*); **Hypothekennachlaß** *m* FINANZ mortgage discount; **Hypothekenobergrenze** *f* GRUND mortgage ceiling; **Hypothekenrückzahlung** *f* BANK mortgage repayment;

Hypothekensanierungsplan *m* GRUND mortgage rescue scheme (*BrE*); **Hypothekenschuld** *f* BANK mortgage debt; **Hypothekenschuldner, in** *m,f* BANK borrower, mortgager; **Hypothekentilgung** *f* BANK mortgage redemption, mortgage repayment; **Hypothekentilgungsversicherung** *f* VERSICH endowment policy (*BrE*), mortgage life insurance (*AmE*); **Hypothekenübernahme** *f* BANK assumption of mortgage; **Hypothekenversicherung** *f* VERSICH mortgage insurance; **Hypothekenversicherungspolice** *f* VERSICH mortgage insurance policy; **Hypothekenzins** *m* BANK mortgage rate

Hypothese *f* GESCHÄFT hypothesis; ~ **der dualen Entscheidung** VW dual decision hypothesis; ~ **von der Kapitalmarkteffizienz** VW efficient market hypothesis; ~ **der Wertdiskrepanz** VW value-discrepancy hypothesis; ~ **zusätzlicher Arbeitnehmer** PERSON additional worker hypothesis; **Hypothesentest** *m* MATH hypothesis testing

hypothetisch *adj* GESCHÄFT academic, hypothetical; **~e Bedingungen** *f pl* GESCHÄFT hypothetical conditions; **~e Frage** *f* GESCHÄFT academic question, hypothetical question; **~e Lage** *f* GESCHÄFT hypothetical situation; **~er Punkt** *m* GESCHÄFT hypothetical point; **~e Umstände** *m pl* GESCHÄFT hypothetical circumstances

Hysterese *f* VW hysteresis

I

i.A. *abbr* (*im Auftrag von*) GESCHÄFT O/o (*order of*)

IAA *abbr* (*Internationales Arbeitsamt*) PERSON ILO (*International Labour Office*)

IAO *abbr* (*Internationale Arbeitsorganisation*) IND ILO (*International Labour Organization*)

IAS *abbr* (*internationaler Antwortschein für Postsendungen*) KOMM IRC (*international reply coupon*)

IATA *abbr* (*Internationaler Lufttransportverband*) TRANSP IATA (*International Air Transport Association*)

IBFG *abbr* (*Internationaler Bund Freier Gewerkschaften*) PERSON, RECHT ICFTU (*International Confederation of Free Trade Unions*)

IBWE *abbr* (*Internationale Bank für Wiederaufbau und Entwicklung*) BANK IBRD (*International Bank for Reconstruction and Development*)

ICEM *abbr* (*Zwischenstaatliches Komitee für europäische Auswanderung*) SOZIAL ICEM (*Intergovernmental Committee for European Migration*)

Icon *nt* COMP icon

ICS *abbr* (*Internationale Schiffahrtskammer*) TRANSP ICS (*International Chamber of Shipping*)

id. *abbr* (*idem*) GESCHÄFT id. (*idem*)

ID *abbr* (*Identifikation*) COMP ID (*identification*)

IDA *abbr* (*Internationale Entwicklungsorganisation*) VW IDA (*International Development Agency, International Development Association*)

ideal *adj* GESCHÄFT ideal

Idealgrenze *f* VW ideal limit

Idee: **Ideenblitz** *m* GESCHÄFT flash of inspiration; **Ideenfindung** *f* MGMNT brainstorming

ideenreich *adj* GESCHÄFT enterprising

Idee: **Ideensitzung** *f* MGMNT brainstorming

idem *adj* (*id.*) GESCHÄFT idem (*id.*)

Identifikation *f* (*ID*) COMP identification (*ID*); **Identifikationsnummer** *f* (*ID-Nummer*) COMP identification number (*ID-Number*); **Identifikationsproblem** *nt* VW identification problem

ID: **~-Nummer** *f* (*Identifikationsnummer*) COMP ID number (*identification number*)

IdW *abbr* (*Institut der Wirtschaftsprüfer*) RECHNUNG ≈ ICA (*Institute of Chartered Accountants*)

IEA *abbr* (*Internationale Energie-Agentur*) UMWELT IEA (*International Energy Agency*)

IFAD *abbr* (*International Fund for Agricultural Development*) BANK IFAD (*Internationaler Agrarentwicklungsfonds*)

IFC *abbr* (*Internationale Finanzcorporation*) FINANZ IFC (*International Finance Corporation*)

IFO *abbr* (*Institut für Wirtschaftsforschung*) VW economic research institute in Munich

IGB *abbr* (*Internationaler Gewerkschaftsbund*) PERSON IFTU (*International Federation of Trade Unions*), WFTU (*World Federation of Trade Unions*)

IGH *abbr* (*Internationaler Gerichtshof*) RECHT ICJ (*International Court of Justice*)

IHK *abbr* (*Industrie- und Handelskammer*) IND, VW CCI (*Chamber of Commerce and Industry*), ACC (*American Chamber of Commerce*)

Ihr: **~ Kabeltelegramm** *phr* KOMM your cable (*y/c*); **~ Kontostand** *phr* BANK the amount standing to your account; **~ Zeichen** *phr* KOMM your reference (*your ref.*)

IKRK *abbr* (*Internationales Komitee vom Roten Kreuz*) SOZIAL ICRC (*International Committee of the Red Cross*)

illegal 1. *adj* RECHT illegal; **2.** *adv* RECHT illegally; ♦ **~ kopieren** COMP, MEDIEN, RECHT pirate

illegal: **~-er Einwanderer** *m* RECHT illegal alien, VERWALT illegal immigrant; **~e Einwanderung** *f* RECHT, VERWALT illegal immigration; **~e Kopie** *f* COMP, GESCHÄFT, RECHT pirate copy; **~e Preisabsprache** *f* RECHT price-fixing; **~er Streik** *m* PERSON snap strike

illiquid *adj* BANK, FINANZ illiquid; **~es Aktivvermögen** *nt* FINANZ illiquid assets

Illustration *f* MEDIEN, PATENT figure, illustration

illustrieren *vt* MEDIEN illustrate

illustriert: **~e Präsentation** *f* V&M pictorial presentation

Image *nt* V&M image; **Imageanzeige** *f* V&M imaging; **Imageprojektion** *f* V&M image projection; **Imageprüfung** *f* V&M image audit; **Imagewerbung** *f* V&M image advertising

imaginär *adj* FINANZ notional

Imitation *f* IND counterfeit

immanent: **~es Wachstum** *nt* VW organic growth

immateriell *adj* FINANZ intangible, GESCHÄFT incorporeal, RECHNUNG intangible, RECHT incorporeal, intangible, VW intangible; **~e Aktiva** *pl* FINANZ, RECHNUNG intangible assets; **~es Anlagevermögen** *nt* FINANZ, RECHNUNG intangible fixed assets; **~er Beitrag** *m* GESCHÄFT intangible contribution; **~e Belohnung** *f* PERSON intangible reward; **~es Eigentum** *nt* RECHT incorporeal property; **~e Entlohnung** *f* VW intangible reward; **~e Gegenstände** *m pl* RECHT incorporeal property; **~es Vermögen** *nt* FINANZ intangible assets, RECHNUNG intangible assets, intangible property; **~e Vermögensgegenstände** *m pl* RECHT incorporeal hereditaments; **~er Vermögenswert** *m* FINANZ, RECHNUNG intangible asset worth; **~e Vermögenswerte** *m pl* FINANZ, RECHNUNG intangible assets; **~er Wert** *m* RECHNUNG intangible value

Immigration *f* POL, VW immigration

Immobilie *f* GRUND, VW property; **~ als Bruchteilseigentum** GRUND estate in severalty, tenancy in common

Immobilien *f pl* GRUND, VW property, real estate (*AmE*); **Immobilienbranche** *f* GRUND real-estate industry; **Immobilienbüro** *nt* GRUND estate agency (*BrE*), real-estate agency (*AmE*), real-estate bureau (*AmE*), real-estate office (*AmE*); **Immobilieneigentümer, in** *m,f* GRUND *Grundstückseigentümer* property owner; **Immobilienfonds** *m* BANK, GRUND, RECHNUNG real-estate investment trust (*AmE*) (*REIT*), real-estate fund; **Immobilienfondszertifikat** *nt* GRUND property bonds; **Immobiliengesellschaft** *f* GESCHÄFT, GRUND property company, real-estate company; **Immobilieninvest-**

mentgesellschaft *f* FINANZ real-estate investment trust (*AmE*); **Immobilienmakler, in** *m,f* GRUND estate agent (*BrE*), real-estate agent (*AmE*), realtor (*AmE*); **Immobilienmarkt** *m* GRUND real-estate market; **Immobilienprovision** *f* GRUND real-estate commission; **Immobilienwirtschaft** *f* vw land economy

Immunisierungsstrategie *f* FINANZ immunization

Immunität *f* PERSON, RECHT immunity

Imp. *abbr* (*Import*) IMP/EXP, VW imp. (*import, importation*)

Impaktmultiplikator *m* VW impact multiplier

Impfung *f* SOZIAL vaccination

implementieren *vt* COMP *System* implement

Implementierung *f* COMP *eines Systems* implementation; ~ **einer bestimmten Politik** POL policy execution

implizieren *vt* GESCHÄFT imply

implizit *adj* GESCHÄFT implicit; ~**er Deflator** *m* VW implicit price deflator; ~**es Marginaleinkommen** *nt* VW implicit marginal income; ~**er Preisindex** *m* VW implied price index; ~**e Repo-Rate** *f* FINANZ implied repo-rate

Import *m* (*Imp.*) IMP/EXP, VW import (*imp.*), importation (*imp.*); **Importabgabe** *f* IMP/EXP, STEUER import duty (*ID*), import tariff; **Importakkreditiv** *nt* FINANZ, IMP/EXP import letter of credit; **Importanteil** *m* IMP/EXP import penetration ratio; **Importbewilligung** *f* IMP/EXP import licence (*BrE*) (*I/L*), import license (*AmE*) (*I/L*); **Importdirektor, in** *m,f* IMP/EXP, MGMNT, PERSON import director; **Importerlaubnis** *f* IMP/EXP import permit

Importeur, in *m,f* IMP/EXP importer

Import: **Import-Export** *m* COMP *Daten*, IMP/EXP import-export; **Importfirma** *f* IMP/EXP importer; **Importfreigabebescheinigung** *f* IMP/EXP import release note (*IRN*); **Importgenehmigung** *f* IMP/EXP import licence (*BrE*) (*I/L*), import license (*AmE*) (*I/L*); **Importgeschäft** *nt* IMP/EXP import trade; **Importgüter** *nt pl* IMP/EXP imported goods; **Importhalle** *f* IMP/EXP import shed; **Importhandel** *m* IMP/EXP import trade; **Importhändler, in** *m,f* IMP/EXP importer

importieren *vt* COMP *Daten*, IMP/EXP, STEUER, VW import

importiert *adj* COMP *Daten*, IMP/EXP, STEUER, VW imported; ~**e Dienstleistungen** *f pl* STEUER imported services; ~**e Inflation** *f* VW imported inflation

Import: **Importkonnossement** *nt* IMP/EXP, TRANSP inward bill of lading; **Importlagergebühren** *f pl* IMP/EXP import depot charges; **Importleiter, in** *m,f* PERSON import manager; **Importliegeplatz** *m* TRANSP import berth; **Importlizenz** *f* IMP/EXP import licence (*BrE*) (*I/L*), import license (*AmE*) (*I/L*); **Importpreis** *m* VW import price; **Importquote** *f* IMP/EXP, VW import quota, import penetration ratio; **Importsachbearbeiter, in** *m,f* PERSON import clerk; **Importsanierungsanleihe** *f* FINANZ rehabilitation import loan (*RIL*); **Importsanierungskredit** *m* FINANZ rehabilitation import credit (*RIC*); **Importschuppen** *m* IMP/EXP import shed; **Importsubstitution** *f* IMP/EXP import substitution; **Importtätigkeit** *f* IMP/EXP importing; **Importüberschuß** *m* IMP/EXP, VW import surplus; **Importverkaufsleiter, in** *m,f* PERSON import sales executive; **Importwaren** *f pl* IMP/EXP, VW imported goods; **Importzoll** *m* IMP/EXP, STEUER import duty (*ID*), import tariff; **Importzollgesetz** *nt* IMP/EXP, STEUER Import Duty Act (*IDA*)

Impressum *nt* MEDIEN imprint, *Zeitung, Zeitschrift* masthead

Imprimatur: **das ~ geben** *phr* MEDIEN pass for press

improvisieren *vi* GESCHÄFT improvise, play it by ear (*infrml*)

Impuls *m* COMP pulse, GESCHÄFT *Konjunktur* stimulus, impetus; **Impulskauf** *m* GESCHÄFT, V&M impulse buying; **Impulskäufer, in** *m,f* GESCHÄFT, V&M impulse buyer; **Impulswahl** *f* KOMM pulse dialing (*AmE*), pulse dialling (*BrE*)

inaktiv *adj* GESCHÄFT inactive

Inanspruchnahme *f* BANK drawdown, SOZIAL *Sozialleistungen* take-up; ~ **des Geldmarktes** BÖRSE borrowing in the money market

inbegriffen: **alles ~** *phr* GESCHÄFT all-in, all-inclusive

Inbetriebnahme *f* GESCHÄFT start-up, TRANSP commissioning, VW start-up

Inch *m* GESCHÄFT inch (*in*)

Incoterms *abbr* (*internationale Regeln für die Auslegung von Handelsklauseln*) VW Incoterms (*international commercial terms*)

Indenthaus *nt* GESCHÄFT indent house

Index *m* BÖRSE, COMP, VW index; ~ **der Frühindikatoren** FINANZ index of leading indicators; ~ **führender Indikatoren** FINANZ index of leading indicators; ~ **kürzer führender Indikatoren** FINANZ index of shorter leading indicators; ~ **länger führender Indikatoren** FINANZ index of longer leading indicators; ~ **der physischen Lebensqualität** VW physical quality of life index (*PQLI*); ~ **der Spätindikatoren** FINANZ index of lagging indicators; ~ **übereinstimmender Indikatoren** FINANZ index of coincident indicators; ~ **der Verbraucherpreise** VW consumer price index (*CPI*); **Indexaktie** *f* FINANZ index-linked stock; **Indexanleihe** *f* BANK indexed bond, indexed loan; **Indexbasis** *f* MATH index basis; **Indexbindung** *f* PERSON index linking, indexation, VW index linking, indexing; **Indexdatei** *f* COMP, VERWALT index file; **Index-Fonds** *m* BÖRSE index fund

indexgebunden: ~**es Darlehen** *nt* FINANZ index-linked loan; ~**e Entlastung** *f* STEUER indexation relief

indexieren *vi* BÖRSE, COMP, FINANZ, STEUER, VW index

indexiert *adj* VERSICH index-linked; ~**e Lebensversicherung** *f* VERSICH indexed life insurance; ~**e Staatsanleihe** *f* BÖRSE index-linked gilt; ~**er Wertpapierinvestitionsplan** *m* BÖRSE indexed security investment plan

Indexierung *f* BÖRSE indexing, VW indexation

Index: **Indexklausel** *f* VERSICH escalation clause; **Indexliste** *f* COMP subscript list; **Indexmiete** *f* GRUND index lease; **Indexoption** *f* BÖRSE index option

indexorientiert: ~**er Fonds** *m* FINANZ index-tracking fund

Index: **Indexpacht** *f* GRUND index lease; **Indexpreis** *m* BÖRSE index price; **Indexpunkt** *m* BÖRSE index point; **Indexterminkontrakt** *m* BÖRSE index futures contract; **Indexverbindung** *f* VW index linkage

indexwachstumsgebunden: ~**e Fondsanteile** *m pl* BÖRSE index growth linked units (*IGLU*)

Index: **Indexzahl** *f* MATH, VW index number; **Indexziffer** *f* VW index number

Indifferenzkurve *f* VW indifference curve

indikativ: ~**e Planung** *f* MGMNT, VW indicative planning

Indikator *m* VW indicator; **Indikatorenanalyse** *f* MATH item analysis; **Indikatorvariable** *f* VW indicator variable

indirekt 1. *adj* GESCHÄFT indirect; **2.** *adv* GESCHÄFT indirectly; ◆ **~ bezogen auf** GESCHÄFT indirectly related to; **~ verbunden mit** GESCHÄFT indirectly related to

indirekt: **~e Adressierung** *f* COMP indirect addressing, vw multi-level addressing; **~e Besteuerung** *f* STEUER indirect taxation; **~e Diskriminierung** *f* PERSON indirect discrimination; **~er Exporthandel** *m* IMP/EXP indirect export trading; **~e Investition** *f* FINANZ portfolio investment; **~e Kosten** *pl* FINANZ, RECHNUNG, VW indirect costs, overhead charge; **~e Lohnkosten** *pl* RECHNUNG indirect labor costs (*AmE*), indirect labour costs (*BrE*); **~e Parität** *f* vw cross rate, exchange cross rate; **~e Steuer** *f* STEUER duty, vw outlay tax; **~e Vollmacht** *f* BANK indirect authorization; **~er Wechselkurs** *m* FINANZ cross-rate of exchange

Individual- *in cpds* GESCHÄFT, VERSICH, VERWALT, VW individual, private; **Individualeinkommen** *nt* VERWALT individual income; **Individualgut** *nt* vw private good

individualisieren *vt* SOZIAL individualize

individualisiert: **~e Absatzpolitik** *f* V&M direct marketing

Individualisierung *f* SOZIAL individualization

Individual-: **Individuallebensversicherung** *f* VERSICH individual life insurance; **Individualrentenpolice** *f* VERSICH individual annuity policy; **Individualverkehr** *m* GESCHÄFT, TRANSP private transport (*BrE*), private transportation (*AmE*)

individuell *adj* GESCHÄFT individual; **~e Arbeitsschutzrechte** *nt pl* PERSON legislation protective of workers and employees; **~e Kosten** *pl* vw private cost; **~e Rentenpolice** *f* VERSICH individual annuity policy; **~e Schlichtung** *f* PERSON individual conciliation; **~es Schlichtungsverfahren** *nt* PERSON individual grievance procedure

Indizienbeweis *m* RECHT circumstantial evidence

indizieren *vt* COMP, MATH index

indiziert *adj* COMP, MATH indexed; **~e Abrechnung** *f* RECHNUNG price level accounting

Indossament *nt* BANK endorsement, indorsement, RECHT endorsement, backing, indorsement; **~ ohne Obligo** BANK qualified endorsement; **~ und Übergabe** *f* BANK, RECHT endorsement and delivery; ◆ **durch ~ rückübertragen** BANK endorse back; **durch ~ übertragen** BANK transfer by endorsement

Indossament: **Indossamentstempel** *m* BANK endorsement stamp

Indossant, in *m,f* BANK endorser, endorsor, indorser, indorsor, GESCHÄFT backer, RECHT, V&M endorser, endorsor, indorser, indorsor

Indossatar *m* BANK endorsee, indorsee

indossierbar: **~e Anweisung** *f* BANK money order (*AmE*)

indossieren *vt* BANK, GESCHÄFT endorse, indorse, RECHT back

Induktion *f* GESCHÄFT induction

induktiv: **~es Denken** *nt* MGMNT inductive reasoning; **~e Statistik** *f* MATH inferential statistics

Industrial Engineering *nt* IND industrial engineering

industrialisieren *vt* IND, vw industrialize

industrialisiert *adj* IND, vw industrialized

Industrialisierung *f* IND, vw industrialization

Industrie *f* IND, VW industry; **~ im Niedergang** IND ailing industry, declining industry; **Industrieabfälle** *m pl* IND, UMWELT industrial waste; **Industrieaktie** *f* BÖRSE

industrial share; **Industriealkohol** *m* IND industrial spirits; **Industrieanlage** *f* IND industrial plant, science park, technology park; **Industrieareal** *nt* IND industrial site; **Industriebetriebslehre** *f* IND industrial engineering; **Industriedienstleistungen** *f pl* IND industrial services; **Industrieeinrichtungen** *f pl* IND industrial equipment; **Industrieerzeugnis** *nt* IND industrial product; **Industriefahrzeug** *nt* TRANSP industrial vehicle; **Industriefördergebiet** *nt* vw enterprise zone (*EZ*); **Industrieführer** *m* PERSON captain of industry; **Industriegebiet** *nt* GRUND, IND industrial estate, trading estate (*AmE*), vw enterprise zone (*EZ*); **Industriegelände** *nt* IND industrial estate, industrial site, trading estate (*AmE*); **Industriegesellschaft** *f* vw industrial society, manufacturing-based economy; **Industriegewerkschaft** *f* PERSON industrial union; **Industriegewerkschaftsverband** *m* PERSON *amerikanische Gewerkschaftsbewegung* Congress of Industrial Organizations (*AmE*) (*CIO*); **Industriegüter** *nt pl* vw manufactured goods, manufactures; **Industrie- und Handelskammer** *f* (*IHK*) IND, vw Chamber of Commerce and Industry (*CCI*), American Chamber of Commerce (*ACC*); **Industriekapitalismus** *m* IND industrial capitalism; **Industriekapitän** *m* GESCHÄFT captain of industry; **Industrieland** *nt* IND, vw developed country (*DC*), industrial country, industrialized country

industriell *adj* GESCHÄFT, IND industrial; ◆ **~er Anwendung unterliegend** PATENT susceptible to industrial application

industriell: **~e Absatzforschung** *f* V&M industrial research; **~es Ballungsgebiet** *nt* vw area of industrial concentration; **~e Basis** *f* IND industrial base; **~er Bereich** *m* IND industrial sector; **~ betriebene Landwirtschaft** *f* vw factory farming; **~e Demokratie** *f* POL industrial democracy; **~e Ermüdung** *f* PERSON industrial fatigue; **~e Flaute** *f* IND industrial inertia; **~e Forschung** *f* V&M industrial research; **~e Kapazitätsnutzung** *f* IND industrial capacity utilization; **~er Kapitalismus** *m* IND industrial capitalism; **~e und kommerzielle Unternehmen** *nt pl* vw industrial and commercial companies (*ICCs*); **~e Nachfrage** *f* IND industrial demand; **~e Nutzung** *f* GRUND industrial occupancy, PATENT exploitation in industry; **~ Organisation** *f* IND industrial organization (*IO*); **~e Planung** *f* IND engineering; **~e Reservearmee** *f* PERSON *marxistische Wirtschaftslehre* reserve army of labor (*AmE*), reserve army of labour (*BrE*); **~e Revolution** *f* vw industrial revolution; **~er Schadstoffausstoß** *m* IND, UMWELT industrial discharge; **~er Sektor** *m* IND industrial sector; **~e Sicherheit** *f* IND industrial security; **~es System** *nt* IND industrial system; **~er Ursprung** *m* UMWELT *von Verschmutzung* industrial source; **~e Verwertung** *f* IND exploitation in industry; **~e Zusammenballung** *f* IND concentration of industry

Industrielle(r) *mf* [decl. as adj] IND, vw industrialist, manufacturer (*mfr*)

Industrie: **Industrieminister** *m,f* POL industry minister; **Industriemüll** *m* IND, UMWELT, vw industrial waste; **Industrienation** *f* GESCHÄFT, vw advanced economy, industrial nation; **Industrienorm** *f* IND, vw industry standard; **Industrieökonomik** *f* vw industrial organization; **Industriepark** *m* GRUND industrial estate, trading estate (*AmE*), IND, UMWELT industrial park; **Industriepolitik** *f* IND industrial policy;

Industrieprodukte *nt pl* IND industrial goods; **Industrieproduktion** *f* VW industrial production; **Industrierat** *m* **für Fortbildungstechnologie** SOZIAL Industrial Council for Educational & Training Technology *BrE* (*ICETT*); **Industrieregion** *f* **im Abwärtstrend** VW declining industrial area; **Industrierückgang** *m* IND ailing industry, declining industry; **Industrieschutzbeauftragte(r)** *mf* [decl. as adj] PERSON *Arbeitsschutzgesetz, EG Direktive 1989* safety representative; **Industrieschutzhelm** *m* IND industrial safety helmet; **Industriespionage** *f* IND industrial espionage; **Industriestaat** *m* IND, VW developed country (*DC*), industrialized country; **Industriewert** *m* FINANZ industrial security; **Industriezentrum** *nt* IND industrial center (*AmE*), industrial centre (*BrE*); **Industriezone** *f* IND industrial estate (*BrE*), trading estate (*AmE*); **Industriezweig** *m* IND branch of industry

induzieren *vt* FINANZ, VW induce

induzierend: **~es Gut** *nt* VW inducement good

induziert: **~er technischer Fortschritt** *m* VW induced technical progress; **~er Wechsel** *m* FINANZ induced draft

ineffizient *adj* GESCHÄFT, VW inefficient

Ineffizienz *f* GESCHÄFT, VW inefficiency

Inelastizität *f* VW inelasticity

Inertialinflation *f* VW inertial inflation

Inferenzstatistik *f* MATH inferential statistics

inferior: **~e Güter** *nt pl* VW inferior goods

infiziert *adj* COMP infected by a virus; **nicht ~** *adj* COMP virus-free

Inflation *f* VW inflation; **~ bei gleichzeitiger Rezession** VW slumpflation; **~ durch Nachfragestruktur-veränderungen** VW demand-shift inflation; ♦ **die ~ anheizen** VW refuel inflation; **~ drücken** VW pull inflation down; **mit der ~ mitgehen** VW *Preis, Beihilfe* rise in line with inflation; **die ~ niedrig halten** VW keep inflation down; **mit der ~ steigen** VW *Preis, Beihilfe* rise in line with inflation; **~ untergräbt Kaufkraft** VW inflation undercuts purchasing power; **gegen ~ sichern** VW safeguard against inflation

inflationär *adj* VW inflationary

inflationieren *vt* VW inflate

Inflationist, in *m,f* VW inflationist

inflationsbereinigt *adj* VW adjusted for inflation; **~es Defizit** *nt* VW inflation-adjusted deficit; **~es Einkommen** *nt* VW inflation-adjusted income; **~e Rechnungslegung** *f* RECHNUNG general price level accounting (*GPLA*)

Inflation: **Inflationsbereinigung** *f* VW accounting for inflation; **Inflationsdruck** *m* VW inflationary pressure; **Inflationserwartungen** *f pl* VW inflationary expectations; **Inflationslücke** *f* VW inflationary gap; **Inflationsnachtrag** *m* VERSICH inflation endorsement

inflationsneutral: **~e Buchführung** *f* RECHNUNG inflation accounting

Inflation: **Inflationsrate** *f* VW inflation rate, rate of inflation; **Inflationssicherung** *f* VERSICH hedge against inflation; **Inflationsspirale** *f* VW inflationary spiral; **Inflationssteuer** *f* STEUER inflation tax; **Inflationsverstärkung** *f* **durch Gewinnspannenerhöhung** VW mark-up inflation; **Inflationszusatz** *m* VERSICH inflation endorsement

inflatorisch: **~e Lücke** *f* VW inflationary gap; **~e Tendenzen** *f pl* VW inflationary trends

Info *abbr* *infrml* (*Information*) GESCHÄFT inf. (*information*), info (*infrml*) (*information*)

Infobahn *f* COMP (*jarg*) information highway

infolge *prep* GESCHÄFT as a consequence of

infolgedessen *adv* GESCHÄFT as a result

Informant, in *m,f* GESCHÄFT informer

Informatik *f* COMP computer science, informatics

Informatiker, in *m,f* COMP computer scientist

Information *f* (*Info*) GESCHÄFT information (*inf.*, *info*); **eine ~** GESCHÄFT piece of information; ♦ **~ vertraulich behandeln** RECHT treat information confidentially; **~ zurückhalten** RECHT withhold information

Informationen *f pl* (*Infos*) GESCHÄFT information (*info*); **~ aus erster Hand** GESCHÄFT inside information; **~ über Fernsehzuschauerschaft** MEDIEN, V&M televisual audience data; **~ durch Firmen auf einer regelmäßigen Basis** FINANZ information on a regular basis by companies; **~ über die Geschäftslage** GESCHÄFT, MGMNT status report

Information: **Informationsaustausch** *m* GESCHÄFT exchange of information; **Informationsbarriere** *f* BANK, BÖRSE Chinese walls; **Informationsbearbeitung** *f* COMP, GESCHÄFT information handling, information processing; **Informationsbehandlung** *f* COMP, GESCHÄFT information handling; **Informationsbericht** *m* RECHT Green Paper (*BrE*); **Informationsbit** *nt* COMP information bit; **Informationsdefizit** *nt* GESCHÄFT paucity of information; **Informations- und Dokumentationswissenschaft** *f* COMP informatics; **Informationsfluß** *m* COMP, GESCHÄFT information flow; **Informationsfluß** *m* **von oben nach unten** MGMNT downward communication; **Informationskomitee** *nt* GESCHÄFT committee on information; **Informationsnetz** *nt* COMP information network; **Informationsschalter** *m* FREI information desk; **Informationsspeicherkapazität** *f* COMP information storage capacity; **Informationsspeicherung** *f* COMP information storage; **Informationssystem** *nt* COMP information system; **Informationstechnik** *f* (*IT*) COMP information technology (*IT*); **Informationstechnologie** *f* (*IT*) COMP information technology (*IT*); **Informationstheorie** *f* COMP, MATH, MGMNT information theory; **Informationsübertragung** *f* COMP information transfer; **Informationsverarbeitung** *f* COMP information processing; **Informationsvereinbarung** *f* GESCHÄFT information agreement; **Informationsvorsprung** *m* GESCHÄFT superior knowledge; **Informationswerbung** *f* V&M informative advertising; **Informationswiedergewinnung** *f* COMP information retrieval

informell *adj* GESCHÄFT informal; **~e Organisation** *f* MGMNT informal organization; **~e Vereinbarung** *f* GESCHÄFT informal arrangement; **~e Wirtschaft** *f* VW informal economy

informieren *vt* GESCHÄFT inform, notify, brief, KOMM brief; ♦ **jdn über etw ~** KOMM acquaint sb of sth, acquaint sb with sth; **jdn von etw ~** KOMM acquaint sb of sth, acquaint sb with sth

informiert *adj* GESCHÄFT informed; **~e Öffentlichkeit** *f* GESCHÄFT informed public

Infos *abbr* (*Informationen*) GESCHÄFT info (*infrml*) (*information*)

Infrastruktur *f* GESCHÄFT substructure, infrastructure, TRANSP infrastructure, VW infrastructure, overhead capital

infrastrukturell *adj* TRANSP, VW infrastructural

Ingenieur, in *m,f* IND, PERSON engineer; **Ingenieurwesen** *nt* IND engineering

Inhaber, in *m,f* BANK bearer, GESCHÄFT proprietor, PATENT owner, proprietor, RECHT *Besitzer* occupant, *geistiges Eigentum* proprietor; **~ eines akademischen Grades** GESCHÄFT honors graduate (*AmE*), honours graduate (*BrE*); **auf der ~ lautend** RECHT unregistered; **Inhaberaktie** *f* BÖRSE bearer share, bearer stock, unregistered stock; **Inhaberformular** *nt* BÖRSE bearer form; **Inhaberklausel** *f* BÖRSE bearer clause; **Inhaberobligation** *f* BÖRSE bearer debenture, FINANZ bearer bond; **Inhaberoptionsschein** *m* BÖRSE bearer warrant; **Inhaberpapier** *nt* VW made-to-bearer instrument; **Inhaberpolice** *f* STEUER policy to bearer; **Inhaberschaft** *f* **an Rechten** GESCHÄFT ownership; **Inhaberscheck** *m* BANK bearer check (*AmE*), bearer cheque (*BrE*); **Inhaberschuldverschreibung** *f* BÖRSE bearer debenture, FINANZ bearer bond; **Inhaberschuldverschreibung** *f* **cum Kupon** BÖRSE full coupon bond; **Inhaberschuldverschreibung** *f* **mit Kupon** BÖRSE full coupon bond

inhaftieren *vt* RECHT detain, imprison

Inhaftierung *f* RECHT *Gefängnisstrafe* detention, imprisonment

Inhalt *m* COMP contents, GESCHÄFT *Gespräch* subject matter, *Paket* contents, PATENT content; ◆ **~ vor Form** RECHNUNG substance over form

Inhalt: **Inhaltsausgabe** *f* GESCHÄFT *Produkt* contents

inhaltsreich *adj* GESCHÄFT comprehensive

Inhalt: **Inhaltsvermerk** *m* GESCHÄFT bordereau; **Inhaltsverzeichnis** *nt* GESCHÄFT, MEDIEN table of contents

Initial *nt* KOMM, MEDIEN initial, initial letter

Initiale *f* KOMM, MEDIEN initial, initial letter

initialisieren *vt* COMP *Vorgang* initialize

Initialisierung *f* COMP initialization

initiativ *adj* GESCHÄFT aggressive

Initiative *f* GESCHÄFT enterprise, *Aktion* campaign, MGMNT initiative; ◆ **die ~ ergreifen** MGMNT take the initiative

Initiator, in *m,f* POL initiator

initiieren *vt* COMP *Vorgang* initiate

Injektion *f* VW injection

Inkassi *nt pl* BANK float

Inkasso *nt* BANK collection, encashment, FINANZ collection, RECHNUNG collection, encashment, VERSICH collection; **Inkassoabteilung** *f* FINANZ collection department; **Inkassoanzeige** *f* BANK advice of collection; **Inkassoauftrag** *m* FINANZ debt collection order (*DCO*); **Inkassobank** *f* FINANZ collecting bank; **Inkassobeauftragte** *f* [decl. as adj] GESCHÄFT debt collector, repo woman (*infrml*); **Inkassobeauftragte(r)** *m* [decl. as adj] GESCHÄFT debt collector, repo man (*infrml*); **Inkassobenachrichtigung** *f* BANK advice of collection; **Inkassobüro** *nt* FINANZ debt collection agency (*DCA*), IMP/EXP collector's office; **Inkassogebühr** *f* GESCHÄFT, TRANSP collection charge; **Inkassokosten** *pl* VERSICH collection costs; **Inkassoprovision** *f* VERSICH collecting commission;

Inkassotarif *m* IMP/EXP collection tariff; **Inkassotermin** *m* RECHNUNG encashment schedule; **Inkassoüberweisung** *f* BANK remittance for collection; **Inkassowechsel** *m* BANK bill for collection, draft for collection; **Inkassowert** *m* RECHNUNG value for collection

Ink-Jet-Printer *m jarg* COMP ink-jet printer

inkl. *abbr* (*inklusive*) GESCHÄFT incl. (*included, including, inclusive*)

Inklusivangebot *nt* FREI package deal

inklusive 1. *adj* (*inkl.*) GESCHÄFT included (*incl.*), inclusive (*incl.*); **2.** *prep* [+gen] (*inkl.*) GESCHÄFT including (*incl.*), inclusive of

inklusive: **~ Sonn- und Feiertage** *phr* GESCHÄFT Sundays and holidays included (*SHINC*)

Inklusivpreise *m pl* GESCHÄFT inclusive terms

inkompatibel *adj* COMP, GESCHÄFT incompatible

Inkompatibilität *f* COMP, GESCHÄFT incompatibility

Inkrafttreten *nt* PATENT entry into force, VERSICH *einer Police* commencement

inkremental *adj* COMP, GESCHÄFT, STEUER incremental; **~e Analyse** *f* STEUER incremental analysis; **~e Ölsteuer** *f* STEUER incremental oil revenue tax (*IORT*)

Inkrementaltechnologie *f* GESCHÄFT incremental technology

Inland- *in cpds* GESCHÄFT domestic, home, internal, national, IMP/EXP inland, POL domestic, home, internal, TRANSP *Flug* domestic, internal, *Schiffahrt* inland, VW domestic, home

inländisch *adj* TRANSP, VW domestic, inland, national (*nat.*); **~e Absorption** *f* VW domestic absorption; **~es Bankensystem** *nt* BANK domestic banking system; **~es Erzeugnis** *nt* GESCHÄFT domestic product; **~e Faktorkosten** *pl* VW domestic resource cost (*DRC*); **~es Filialnetz** *nt* GESCHÄFT *Einzelhandel* national branch network; **~e Filialstruktur** *f* GESCHÄFT national subsidiary structure; **~er Geldmarkt** *m* VW domestic money market; **~e Gesamtnachfrage** *f* VW absorption; **~e Guthaben** *nt pl* BANK domestic assets; **~e Industrie** *f* IND domestic industry; **~er Investor** *m* VW inbound investor; **~e Kapitalgesellschaft** *f* VW domestic corporation; **~e Kreditausweitung** *f* FINANZ domestic credit expansion (*DCE*); **~e Produktion** *f* VW domestic output; **~e Tochter** *f jarg* VW domestic subsidiary; **~e Tochtergesellschaft** *f* VW domestic subsidiary; **~er Zuwachs** *m* **des Kreditvolumens** VW domestic credit expansion (*DCE*)

Inland-: **Inlandsabfertigungslager** *nt* IMP/EXP *Zoll* inland clearance depot (*ICD*); **Inlandsabsatz** *m* V&M domestic sales; **Inlandsangelegenheiten** *f pl* POL home affairs; **Inlandsarbeitsmarkt** *m* VW internal labor market (*AmE*), internal labour market (*BrE*); **Inlandsbahndepot** *nt* IMP/EXP TRANSP *Zollabfertigung von internationaler Bahnfracht* inland rail depot (*IRD*); **Inlandsbank** *f* BANK domestic bank; **Inlandscontainer** *m* TRANSP inland container (*IC*); **Inlandsemission** *f* BÖRSE domestic issue; **Inlandsexportfinanzierung** *f* IMP/EXP domestic export financing

Inlandsflug *m* FREI, TRANSP internal flight, domestic flight; **Inlandsfluglinie** *f* FREI, TRANSP domestic airline, national airline; **Inlandsflugpreis** *m* FREI, TRANSP internal fare

Inland-: **Inlandsfracht** *f* IMP/EXP, TRANSP inland haulage; **Inlandsgeschäft** *nt* GESCHÄFT domestic business;

Inlandsguthaben *nt pl* BANK domestic assets; **Inlandshafen** *m* TRANSP domestic port; **Inlandsinvestition** *f* VW domestic investment; **Inlandsmarkt** *m* VW domestic market, home market; **Inlandsnachfrage** *f* VW domestic demand; **Inlandspatent** *nt* PATENT national patent; **Inlandsporto** *nt* KOMM inland postage; **Inlandsprodukt** *nt* GESCHÄFT home product, VW domestic product; **Inlandsproduktion** *f* VW home production; **Inlandsrisiko** *nt* VERSICH domestic risks; **Inlandssatz** *m* BÖRSE, GESCHÄFT, TRANSP domestic rate; **Inlandsschuld** *f* VW internal debt; **Inlandstransport** *m* IMP/EXP, TRANSP inland haulage; **Inlandstransportunternehmen** *nt* IMP/EXP, TRANSP inland carrier; **Inlandstrend** *m* VW national trend; **Inlandsumsatz** *m* VERWALT home sales; **Inlandsverbindlichkeiten** *f pl* BANK domestic liabilities; **Inlandsverbrauch** *m* UMWELT domestic consumption; **Inlandsverkäufe** *m pl* V&M home sales; **Inlandswert** *m* IMP/EXP *einer Ware* current domestic value (*CDV*); **Inlandszahlung** *f* FINANZ inward payment

inmateriell: **~er Wohlstand** *m* VW intangible wealth

in natura *phr* GESCHÄFT in kind

innehaben *vt* GESCHÄFT *Stellung* occupy, PERSON fill, POL hold

innehabend *adj* PERSON, POL incumbent

Innen- *in cpds* GESCHÄFT, RECHNUNG, VERWALT, VW interior, internal, in-house; **Innenausstattung** *f* GESCHÄFT, V&M *Geschäft* decoration and furnishings; **Innendienstverkaufsleiter, in** *m,f* PERSON indoor sales manager; **Innenfinanzierung** *f* FINANZ internal financing; **Innengeld** *nt* VW inside money; **Innenministerium** *nt* POL Department of the Interior (*AmE*), Home Office (*BrE*); **Innenpolitik** *f* POL home affairs (*BrE*), internal affairs, domestic affairs; **Innenpolitik** *f* **der Regierung** POL, VW internal government policy

innenpolitisch: **~e Fragen** *f pl* POL home affairs (*BrE*), domestic affairs, internal affairs

Innen-: **Innenrevision** *f* MGMNT operational control, operational audit, operations audit, RECHNUNG administrative audit, internal audit, VERWALT in-house audit; **Innenstadt** *f* GESCHÄFT, GRUND, UMWELT, VW city center (*AmE*), city centre (*BrE*), inner city; **Innenstadtsanierung** *f* **und Begrünung** *f* UMWELT greenlining

innerbetrieblich *adj* IND, PERSON in-house, in-service, internal; **~e Beziehungen** *f pl* PERSON employee relations; **~e Kommunikationswege** *m pl* MGMNT internal lines of communication; **~e Prüfung** *f* PERSON *durch Innenrevisor* staff audit; **~e Schulung** *f* IND, PERSON in-house training, in-service training, industrial training; **~e Weiterbildung** *f* PERSON employment training (*BrE*) (*ET*), on-the-job training, training within industry (*TWI*); ◆ **eine ~e Schulung abhalten** PERSON hold in-service training

innere: **~ Abschottung** *f* BANK, BÖRSE Chinese walls; **~ Angelegenheiten** *f pl* POL home affairs; **~s Gefühl** *nt* V&M hunch; **~r Mangel** *m* RECHT *Vertragswesen* inherent defect, interior defect; **~ Motivation** *f* PERSON intrinsic motivation; **~ Unruhe** *f* POL, VERSICH civil commotion (*CC*); **~r Wert** *m* FINANZ, VW intrinsic value; **~ Wirkungsverzögerung** *f* POL, VW inside lag

innergemeinschaftlich: **~er Handel** *m* VW intracommunity trade, intra-EU trade

innergewerblich: **~er Handel** *m* IND, VW inter-industry trade

innerhalb *prep* [+gen] GESCHÄFT *einer Organisation* inside, within; ◆ **~ einer Frist von** GESCHÄFT within a period of; **~ der rechtlichen Befugnisse** RECHT intra vires; **~ der vorgeschriebenen Zeit** GESCHÄFT within the prescribed time; **~ vorgeschriebener Grenzen** RECHT within prescribed limits

innerstaatlich *adj* POL interstate

innerstädtisch: **~er Bereich** *m* UMWELT inner-city area; **~es Geschäft** *nt* V&M in-town store

Innominatvertrag *m* RECHT innominate contract

Innovation *f* IND *Produktion* innovation; **Innovationszentrum** *nt* IND innovation center (*AmE*), innovation centre (*BrE*)

innovativ *adj* GESCHÄFT, PATENT, V&M innovative

Innovator, in *m,f* V&M innovator

Innung *f* PERSON guild

inoffiziell *adj* GESCHÄFT informal, *Erklärung, Aussage* unofficial, MEDIEN off-the-record, POL, VERWALT *Erklärung, Aussage* off-the-record, unofficial; **~er Leiter** *m*, **~e Leiterin** *f* PERSON unofficial leader

Input *m* GESCHÄFT input; **Input-Faktor** *m* FINANZ input factor; **Input-Output-Analyse** *f jarg* COMP, FINANZ, MATH, VW input/output analysis

Insasse *m* FREI passenger, RECHT *Gefängnis* inmate, TRANSP passenger

Insassin *f* FREI passenger, RECHT *Gefängnis* inmate, TRANSP passenger

insb. *abbr* (*insbesondere*) GESCHÄFT esp. (*especially*)

insbesondere *adv* (*insb.*) GESCHÄFT especially (*esp.*)

Inselplazierung *f* V&M *Werbung* island display, island site

Inserat *nt* GESCHÄFT, MEDIEN, V&M ad (*infrml*), advertisement, classified advertisement, classified ad

Inserent, in *m,f* V&M advertiser, advertising space buyer

inserieren 1. *vt* MEDIEN, V&M advertise; **2.** *vi* MEDIEN, V&M advertise

insg. *abbr* (*insgesamt*) GESCHÄFT oa (*overall*)

insgesamt *adv* (*insg.*) FINANZ total funds applied, GESCHÄFT collectively, overall (*oa*), in the aggregate; ◆ **~ ergeben** GESCHÄFT reach a total of

Insichgeschäft *nt* FINANZ, RECHT self-dealing

Insider: **Insidergeschäfte** *nt pl* BÖRSE, FINANZ insider dealing; **Insiderhandel** *m* BÖRSE, FINANZ insider dealing; **Insiderinformation** *f* GESCHÄFT inside information; **Insiderlohnabschluß** *m* PERSON insider wage setting

insofern *adv* GESCHÄFT pro tanto

insolvent *adj* BANK, FINANZ, GESCHÄFT bankrupt, insolvent; ◆ **für ~ erklärt** GESCHÄFT declared insolvent

Insolvenz *f* BANK, GESCHÄFT failure, business failure, insolvency; **Insolvenzklausel** *f* VERSICH insolvency clause

insoweit *adv* GESCHÄFT pro tanto

Inspektion *f* GESCHÄFT inspection, *Behörde* inspectorate, IMP/EXP turnout; **~ vor Lieferung** TRANSP preshipment inspection, predelivery inspection (*PDI*); **~ vor Verladung** TRANSP preloading inspection; **~ nach Versand** TRANSP post-shipment inspection

Inspektor, in *m,f* GESCHÄFT inspector

instabil: **~e Regierung** *f* POL unstable government

Installation *f* COMP, GESCHÄFT installation, IND *Anlage* plant; **Installationsdiskette** *f* COMP installation diskette

installieren *vt* COMP, GESCHÄFT install

installiert *adj* GESCHÄFT installed (*inst.*)

Installierung *f* COMP *Gerät, Programm*, GESCHÄFT installation

Instandhaltungskosten *pl* GRUND maintenance fee

Instandsetzung *f* GESCHÄFT, IND correction maintenance; **~ von Eigentum** GRUND reconditioning property; **Instandsetzungsabteilung** *f* GESCHÄFT, IND maintenance department; **Instandsetzungszeit** *f* VW repair time

Instanz *f* VW organizational unit

instinktiv: ~es Gefühl *nt* V&M gut feeling (*infrml*)

Institut *nt* GESCHÄFT institute (*inst.*); **~ für Öffentlichkeitsarbeit** V&M Institute of Public Relations (*IPR*); **~ für Tropenprodukte** VW Tropical Products Institute (*TPI*); **~ der Vereinten Nationen für Ausbildung und Forschung** PERSON United Nations Institute for Training and Research (*UNITAR*); **~ für Wirtschaftsforschung** (*IFO*) VW economic research institute in Munich; **~ der Wirtschaftsprüfer** (*IdW*) RECHNUNG ≈ Institute of Chartered Accountants (*BrE*) (*ICA*)

Institution *f* GESCHÄFT institution

institutionell: ~er Anleger *m*, **~e Anlegerin** *f* BÖRSE institutional investor

Institution: Institutionenökonomik *f* VW institutional economics

instruieren *vt* GESCHÄFT brief, instruct, RECHT instruct

Instruktion *f* GESCHÄFT, RECHT instruction; **Instruktionen** *f pl* GESCHÄFT brief

Instrument *nt* GESCHÄFT, IND apparatus, instrument, tool

instrumental *adj* GESCHÄFT instrumental

Instrument: Instrumentenvariable *f* VW instrument variable

int. *abbr* (*international*) GESCHÄFT intl (*international*)

intakt *adj* GESCHÄFT intact

Integration *f* GESCHÄFT integration; **~ in die Sozialversicherung** PERSON, SOZIAL integration with social security

integrativ: ~e Verhandlungen *f pl* PERSON integrative bargaining

integrieren *vt* GESCHÄFT integrate

integriert *adj* GESCHÄFT integrated; ◆ **~ sein in** [+acc] GESCHÄFT be integrated into

integriert: ~es Dienstleistungsdatennetz *nt* (*ISDN*) COMP, KOMM Integrated Services Digital Network (*ISDN*); **~es Führungssystem** *nt* MGMNT integrated management system; **~es Managementsystem** *nt* MGMNT integrated management system; **~e Projektleitung** *f* MGMNT integrated project management (*IPM*); **~es Projektmanagement** *nt* MGMNT integrated project management (*IPM*); **~e Projektverwaltung** *f* MGMNT integrated project management (*IPM*); **~e Schadstoffkontrolle** *f* UMWELT integrated pollution control (*IPC*); **~er Schaltkreis** *m* (*IS*) COMP integrated circuit (*IC*); **~e Software** *f* COMP integrated software; **~er Umweltschutz** *m* UMWELT integrated pollution control (*IPC*)

Integrität *f* GESCHÄFT integrity

intelligent: ~e Datenstation *f* COMP intelligent terminal; **~es Dokument** *nt* COMP *Informationswiedergewinnung* intelligent document; **~e Informationswieder-** **gewinnung** *f* COMP intelligent information retrieval; **~e Kreditkarte** *f* BANK, COMP smart card

Intelligenzstufe *f* SOZIAL ability level

Intensiv- *in cpds* IND, V&M intensive

intensiv *adj* GESCHÄFT intensive, PERSON hands-on, VW intensive; **~e Bewirtschaftung** *f* VW intensive farming; **~e Produktion** *f* IND, VW intensive production; **~es Verhandeln** *nt* GESCHÄFT intensive negotiating, wheeling and dealing (*infrml*); **~e Verhandlung** *f* BÖRSE intensive negotiation, wheeling and dealing (*infrml*); **~e Viehwirtschaft** *f* VW intensive livestock farming

Intensiv-: Intensivbewirtschaftung *f* UMWELT factory farming

intensivieren *vt* GESCHÄFT intensify

Intensivierung *f* GESCHÄFT intensification

Intensiv-: Intensivproduktion *f* IND, VW intensive production; **Intensivverkauf** *m* V&M intensive selling

Interaktionsmatrix *f* MGMNT interaction matrix

interaktiv *adj* COMP, GESCHÄFT interactive

Interbank; ~-Kreditgeschäft *nt* BANK bank-to-bank lending

Interbank: Interbankmittel *nt pl* BANK, FINANZ interbank funds

Interbanken- *in cpds* BANK, FINANZ, VW interbank; **Interbankenangebotssatz** *m* BANK interbank offered rate (*IBOR*); **Interbanken-Clearing** *nt* BANK settling of inter-bank transactions; **Interbankeneinlagen** *f pl* BANK interbank deposits; **Interbankengeldmarkt** *m* FINANZ wholesale money market; **Interbankengeschäft** *nt* BANK, FINANZ, VW interbank business, interbank transactions; **Interbankenmarkt** *m* BANK, VW interbank market; **am Interbankenmarkt gehandelte Geschäftsbankenguthaben** *nt pl* BANK, VW clearing house funds; **Interbankenrate** *f* BANK, VW interbank rate; **Interbankenwechselkurs** *m* BANK, VW interbank exchange rate

Inter-Branchen-Konkurrenz *f* IND, VW interindustry competition

Intercity *m* TRANSP *Zug* InterCity (*BrE*)

interdependent: ~e Volkswirtschaft *f* VW interdependent economy

Interdependenz *f* GESCHÄFT interdependence

Interesse *nt* GESCHÄFT, RECHT interest (*int.*); ◆ **im ~ einer abwesenden Person handeln** RECHT *Vorträge* act in the interest of an absent person; **jds Interessen schützen** GESCHÄFT protect sb's interests; **jds Interessen wahrnehmen** GESCHÄFT protect sb's interests

Interesse: Interessengemeinschaft *f* GESCHÄFT consortium, syndicate, community of interests, RECHNUNG pooling of interests (*AmE*), VERSICH pool; **Interessengruppe** *f* GESCHÄFT interest group, reference group, stakeholders, POL lobby, lobby group, pressure group; **Interessengruppe** *f* **für Umweltfragen** POL environmental lobby; **Interessenkonflikt** *m* GESCHÄFT conflict of interest

Interessent, in *m,f* GESCHÄFT prospective customer, VW potential customer; **Interessentenkreis** *m* GESCHÄFT target audience

Interesse: Interessenverband *m* POL association, pressure group; **Interessenvereinigung** *f* POL lobby, lobby group, pressure group, RECHNUNG pooling of interests (*AmE*); **Interessenvertretung** *f* POL lobby, lobby group, pressure group; **Interessenwerbung** *f* V&M advocacy advertising

interessewahrend: ~**er Auftrag** *m* BÖRSE discretionary order

Interface *nt* COMP, GESCHÄFT interface

Interferenz *f* GESCHÄFT interference

Interfunktionsfähigkeit *f* IND *Produktion* interoperability

intergenerativ: ~**e Einkommensverteilung** *f* VW intergenerational distribution of income

Interim *nt* GESCHÄFT, POL interim; **Interimsbilanz** *f* RECHNUNG interim balance; **Interimsdividende** *f* BÖRSE interim dividend, RECHNUNG interim audit; **Interimskonten** *nt pl* RECHNUNG interim accounts; **Interimspolice** *f* VERSICH provisional policy; **Interimsschein** *m* BÖRSE, FINANZ scrip

Interkontenhandel *m* FINANZ inter-account dealing

interkontinental *adj* TRANSP intercontinental

interkulturell: ~**es Marketing** *nt* V&M intercultural marketing

Inter-Lieferungs-Spread *m* BÖRSE intercommodity spread, interdelivery spread

intermedial: ~**er Vergleich** *m* MEDIEN, V&M intermediate comparison

intermediär: ~**es Finanzinstitut** *nt* FINANZ, VW nonbank financial institution

Intermediärkredit *m* FINANZ financial intermediary loan (*FIL*)

interministeriell: ~**e Regelung** *f* RECHT interdepartmental settlement

intermodal: ~**er Verkehr** *m* TRANSP intermodal transport; ~**es Verkehrssystem** *nt* TRANSP intermodal transport system

intern *adj* COMP in-house, GESCHÄFT, VW in-house, internal; ~**e Arbeitsmarktbeteiligung** *f* VW internal labor market contracting (*AmE*), internal labour market contracting (*BrE*); ~**es Berichtswesen** *nt* MGMNT internal reporting; ~**e Bewertung** *f* GRUND in-house valuation; ~ **erwirtschaftete Geldmittel** *nt pl* FINANZ, RECHNUNG internally generated funds; ~**e Finanzierung** *f* FINANZ internal financing; ~**e Geschäftsinformation** *f* FINANZ inside information; ~**e Grenze** *f* GESCHÄFT internal frontier; ~**e Kommunikation** *f* KOMM internal communications; ~**e Kontrolle** *f* RECHNUNG internal control; ~**e Kostendegression** *f* VW internal economy of scale; ~**er Machtkampf** *m* MGMNT internal feud, internal power struggle; ~**e Prüfung** *f* GESCHÄFT internal check; ~**es Rechnungswesen** *nt* RECHNUNG management accounting; ~**e Revision** *f* RECHNUNG administrative audit, internal audit; ~**e Schuld** *f* VW internal debt; ~**er Speicher** *m* COMP internal storage; ~**es Stellenangebot** *nt* PERSON *interner Arbeitsmarkt* internal search; ~**er Verbrauch** *m* UMWELT, VW internal consumption; ~**es Wachstum** *nt* VW internal expansion, internal growth; ~**er Zinsfuß** *m* FINANZ adequate target rate, internal rate of return (*IRR*), RECHNUNG, VW internal rate of return (*IRR*)

Interna *pl* GESCHÄFT inside information

internalisieren *vt* VW internalize

Internalisierung *f* VW internalization; ~ **externer Effekte** VW internalizing an externality; ~ **sozialer Kosten** VW internalizing an externality; ~ **von Sozialkosten** VERWALT allocation of social costs

international *adj* (*int.*) GESCHÄFT international (*intl*); ◆ **auf ~er Ebene** GESCHÄFT at an international level, on an international scale

international, International: **internationales Abkommen** *nt* RECHT international agreement; **internationale Agentur** *f* VERWALT international agency; **internationaler Agrarentwicklungsfonds** *m* (*IFAD*) BANK International Fund for Agricultural Development (*IFAD*); **internationale Angelegenheiten** *f pl* POL international affairs; **internationale Anmeldung** *f* PATENT international application; **internationaler Antwortschein** *m* **für Postsendungen** (*IAS*) KOMM international reply coupon (*IRC*); **Internationaler Arbeitgeberverband** *m* PERSON International Organization of Employers (*IOE*); **Internationales Arbeitsamt** *nt* (*IAA*) PERSON International Labour Office (*ILO*); **Internationale Arbeitsorganisation** *f* (*IAO*) IND International Labour Organization (*ILO*); **Internationaler Ausschuß** *m* **für Buchprüfungspraktiken** RECHNUNG International Auditing Practices Committee (*IAPC*); **Internationaler Ausschuß** *m* **für Rechnungslegungsgrundsätze** RECHNUNG International Accounting Standards Committee (*IASC*); **internationale Außenhandelsorganisation** *f* GESCHÄFT international trade organization (*ITO*); **internationales Bankengesetz** *nt* BANK, RECHT International banking act; **internationale Bankfazilität** *f* BANK international banking facility (*IBF*); **internationales Bankgeschäft** *nt* BANK international banking; **internationale Banktätigkeit** *f* BANK international banking; **Internationale Bank** *f* **für Wiederaufbau und Entwicklung** (*IBWE*) BANK International Bank for Reconstruction and Development (*IBRD*); **Internationale Bank** *f* **für wirtschaftliche Zusammenarbeit** BANK, VW International Bank for Economic Cooperation (*IBEC*); **internationale Beförderung** *f* TRANSP international carriage; **internationale Behörde** *f* VERWALT international agency; **Internationaler Beratungsausschuß** *m* **für Telegramm und Telefon** KOMM International Telegraph and Telephone Consultative Committee; **internationale Beziehungen** *f pl* POL international affairs, international relations; **Internationaler Bund** *m* **Freier Gewerkschaften** (*IBFG*) PERSON, RECHT International Confederation of Free Trade Unions (*ICFTU*); **Internationale Clearingstelle** *f* **für Terminkontrakte** BÖRSE International Commodities Clearing House (*ICCH*); **Internationale Clearingunion** *f* VW International Clearing Union (*ICU*); **Internationaler Code** *m* **für Seegefahrgüter** IND International Maritime Dangerous Goods Code (*IMDG Code*); **Internationale Deutsche Handelskammer** *f* GESCHÄFT German International Chamber of Commerce (*GICC*); **Internationaler Dienst** *m* **für nationale Agrarforschung** VW International Service for National Agricultural Research (*ISNAR*); **internationale Eintragung** *f* PATENT international registration; **internationale elektronische Börseninformation** *f* BÖRSE Stock Exchange Automated Quotation International (*BrE*) (*SEAQI, SEAQ International*); **Internationale Energie-Agentur** *f* (*IEA*) UMWELT International Energy Agency (*IEA*); **internationales Entwicklungsforschungszentrum** *nt* GESCHÄFT International Development Research Centre (*BrE*) (*IDRC*); **internationales Entwicklungshilfe- und Kreditbulletin** *nt* BANK International Aid and Loan Bulletin; **Internationale Entwicklungsorganisation** *f* (*IDA*) VW *UN*

International Development Association (*IDA*); **internationaler Fernfahrerverband** *m* (*IRU*) TRANSP International Road Transport Union (*IRU*); **internationale Fernmeldeunion** *f* KOMM International Telecommunications Union (*ITU*); **internationaler Fernmeldeverein** *m* KOMM International Telecommunications Union (*ITU*); **Internationale Finanzkorporation** *f* FINANZ International Finance Corporation (*IFC*); **internationales Finanzmanagement** *nt* FINANZ international financial management; **internationale Finanzplanung** *f* FINANZ international financial management; **internationale Fluggesellschaft** *f* FREI, TRANSP international airline; **internationaler Flughafen** *m* FREI, TRANSP international airport; **Internationaler Fonds** *m* **zur Entschädigung für Ölverschmutzung** BANK, UMWELT International Oil Pollution Compensation Fund (*IOPC Fund*); **internationaler Führerschein** *m* TRANSP, VERWALT international driving permit, international driver's license (*AmE*), international driving licence (*BrE*); **internationale Geldanweisung** *f* BANK foreign money order; **internationaler Geldmarkt** *m* BÖRSE, VW International Monetary Market (*IMM*); **internationaler Geldmarkt-Dreimonats-Diskont-Index** *m* BÖRSE International Monetary Market Three-month Discount index; **Internationaler Geldmarkt-Einlagenzertifikat-Index** *m* BÖRSE International Monetary Market Certificate of Deposit index (*IMM CD index*); **Internationaler Geldmarkt-Schatzwechsel-Index** *m* BÖRSE International Monetary Market Treasury bill index (*IMM T-bill index*); **internationaler Geldstrom** *m* VW international money flow; **Internationaler Gerichtshof** *m* (*IGH*) RECHT International Court of Justice (*ICJ*); **internationales Geschäft** *nt* GESCHÄFT international trade, vw cross-border transaction; **Internationaler Gewerkschaftsbund** *m* (*IGB*) PERSON International Federation of Trade Unions (*IFTU*), World Federation of Trade Unions (*WFTU*); **Internationale Gläubigerliga** *f* BANK International League for Creditors; **internationale Gleichheit** *f* IND, VW international parity; **internationale Grundsätze** *m pl* **der betriebsinternen Revision** RECHNUNG international auditing standards; **internationale Güterkraftverkehrsgenehmigung** *f* TRANSP, VERWALT international road haulage permit; **Internationaler Hafenverband** *m* IMP/EXP International Association of Ports and Harbours (*IAPH*); **internationale Handelsbescheinigung** *f* IMP/EXP international trading certificate (*ITC*); **internationale Handelserlaubnis** *f* IMP/EXP international trading certificate (*ITC*); **internationales Handelsgesetz** *nt* RECHT international trade law; **Internationale Handelskammer** *f* GESCHÄFT International Chamber of Commerce (*ICC*); **internationale Handelsorganisation** *f* GESCHÄFT international trade organization (*ITO*); **internationale Handelspolitik** *f* VW international trade policy; **internationales Handelszentrum** *nt* GESCHÄFT international trade center (*AmE*), international trade centre (*BrE*); **Internationaler Hotelverband** *m* FREI International Hotel Association; **Internationales Institut** *nt* **für tropische Landwirtschaft** VW International Institute for Tropical Agriculture (*IITA*); **Internationales Institut** *nt* **für die Vereinheitlichung des Privatrechts** RECHT International Institute for Unification of Private Law; **internationale Investitionsbank** *f* (*IIB*) BANK international investment

bank (*IIB*); **internationale Investmentbank** *f* BANK international investment bank (*IIB*)

internationalisieren *vt* POL, VW internationalize

Internationalisierung *f* POL, VW internationalization

Internationalismus *m* POL, VW internationalism

international, International: **internationaler Kapitalmarkt** *m* BÖRSE international capital market; **internationales Kartell** *nt* VW international cartel; **Internationales Komitee** *nt* **vom Roten Kreuz** (*IKRK*) SOZIAL International Committee of the Red Cross (*ICRC*); **internationale Konferenz** *f* GESCHÄFT international conference; **internationales Kongreßzentrum** *nt* GESCHÄFT international conference center (*AmE*), international conference centre (*BrE*), international convention center (*AmE*), international convention centre (*BrE*); **internationales Konsortium** *nt* BANK international consortium, international syndicate; **internationale Konvention** *f* **über Schienentransport** TRANSP international convention on carriage of goods by rail; **internationaler Kredit** *m* BANK, FINANZ international credit; **internationaler Kreditverband** *m* FINANZ international credit club; **internationales Leasinggeschäft** *nt* RECHT *Vertragsrecht* international leasing transaction; **internationale Liquidität** *f* VW international liquidity; **internationale Liquiditätskennzahlen** *f pl* BANK international liquidity ratios; **internationales Lohnniveau** *nt* VW international wage level; **internationale Luftfahrtsprache** *f* TRANSP international language for aviation (*ILA*); **Internationaler Lufttransportverband** *f* (*IATA*) TRANSP International Air Transport Association (*IATA*); **internationales Management** *nt* MGMNT international management; **internationales Marketing** *nt* IMP/EXP export marketing, V&M export marketing, international marketing; **internationale Norm** *f* GESCHÄFT, IND, UMWELT international standard; **internationale Organisation** *f* GESCHÄFT international organization; **Internationale Organisation** *f* **der Bergarbeiter** IND International Miners' Organization (*IMO*); **Internationale Organisation** *f* **für Eichung** IND, RECHT International Organization for Legal Metrology (*OIML*); **Internationale Organisation** *f* **für Normung** (*ISO*) GESCHÄFT International Standards Organization (*ISO*); **Internationale Organisation** *f* **für Wertpapieraufsicht** BÖRSE International Organization of Securities Commissioners (*IOSCO*); **Internationales Presseinstitut** *nt* MEDIEN International Press Institute (*IPI*); **internationales Prüfamt** *nt* PATENT international preliminary examining authority; **internationale Prüfungsrichtlinien** *f pl* RECHNUNG international auditing standards; **internationaler Reederverein** *m* TRANSP International Shipping Federation (*ISP*); **internationale Regeln** *f pl* **für die Auslegung von Handelsklauseln** (*Incoterms*) VW international commercial terms (*Incoterms*); **internationale Reisetätigkeit** *f* FREI, TRANSP international travel; **internationale Reserve** *f* VW international reserve; **Internationale Rohölbörse** *f* BÖRSE International Petroleum Exchange (*IPE*); **internationales Rohstoffabkommen** *nt* BÖRSE International Commodity Agreement (*ICA*); **internationaler Schiffahrtsinformationsdienst** *m* TRANSP International Shipping Information Service (*ISIS*); **Internationale Schiffahrtskammer** *f* (*ICS*) TRANSP International Chamber of Shipping (*ICS*); **internatio-**

nales Seefahrtsbüro *nt* TRANSP International Maritime Bureau (*IMB*); **internationales Seerechtskomitee** *nt* TRANSP International Maritime Committee (*IMC*); **Internationaler Sozialdienst** *m* (*ISD*) SOZIAL International Social Service (*ISS*); **internationaler Spediteur** *m* TRANSP international freight forwarder, international hauler (*AmE*), international haulier (*BrE*); **internationale Standardbedingungen** *f pl* RECHT *Vertragsrecht* international standard conditions; **internationale Standardbuchnummer** *f* (*ISBN*) MEDIEN International Standard Book Number (*ISBN*); **internationale Standardklassifikation** *f* **der Berufe** (*ISCO*) VW international standard classification of occupations (*ISCO*); **internationale Standardseriennummer** *f* (*ISSN*) MEDIEN International Standard Serial Number (*ISSN*); **internationales Statistikinstitut** *nt* GESCHÄFT International Statistical Institute (*ISI*); **internationale Streuung** *f* **des Portefeuilles** BÖRSE overseas portfolio diversification; **Internationale Systematik** *f* **der Wirtschaftszweige** IND International Standard Industrial Classification of all Economic Activities (*AmE*) (*ISIC*); **internationales Tagungszentrum** *nt* GESCHÄFT international conference center (*AmE*), international conference centre (*BrE*), international convention center (*AmE*), international convention centre (*BrE*); **internationales Telegramm** *nt* KOMM international telegram; **internationales Tor** *nt* TRANSP international gateway; **internationaler Transport** *m* TRANSP international carriage; **internationale Transportarbeiter-Föderation** *f* (*ITF*) TRANSP International Transport Workers' Federation (*ITF*); **internationale Unternehmensführung** *f* MGMNT international management; **internationale Untersuchungsbehörde** *f* PATENT international searching authority; **Internationaler Verband** *m* **amtlicher Fremdenverkehrsorganisationen** (*IUOTO*) PERSON International Union of Official Travel Organizations (*IUOTO*); **Internationaler Verband** *m* **für Dokumentation** GESCHÄFT International Federation for Documentation (*FID*); **Internationaler Verband** *m* **für Entwicklung** VW International Development Association (*IDA*); **Internationaler Verband** *m* **für gewerbliche Schutzrechte** RECHT International Association for the Protection of Industrial Property (*IAPIP*); **Internationaler Verband** *m* **der Klassifizierungsgesellschaften** GESCHÄFT International Association of Classification Societies (*IACS*); **Internationaler Verband** *m* **für die Koordinierung von Frachtangelegenheiten** TRANSP International Cargo-Handling Coordination Association (*ICHCA*); **Internationaler Verband** *m* **der Produzenten landwirtschaftlicher Erzeugnisse** IND International Federation of Agricultural Producers (*IFAP*); **Internationaler Verband** *m* **der Spediteur-Vereinigungen** TRANSP International Federation of Freight Forwarders Associations; **Internationaler Verband** *m* **für Speditionsvereinigungen** TRANSP International Federation of Forwarding Agents Associations; **Internationale Vereinigung** *f* **der Seeversicherer** VERSICH International Union of Marine Insurance; **Internationale Vereinigung** *f* **der Umweltkoordinatoren** UMWELT International Association of Environmental Coordinators (*IAEC*); **internationaler Vergleich** *m* VW international comparison; **internationaler Vergleich** *m* **der Lebenshaltungskosten** VW international comparisons of the cost of living; **Inter-**

nationale Verrechnungsinstitution *f* VW International Clearing Union (*ICU*); **internationale Verrechnungsstelle** *f* BANK international clearing house; **internationale Vertretung** *f* GESCHÄFT international representation, VERWALT international agency; **internationale Voruntersuchungsbehörde** *f* PATENT international preliminary examining authority; **internationale Währungsbehörde** *f* FINANZ international monetary organization; **Internationaler Währungsfonds** *m* (*IWF*) VW International Monetary Fund (*IMF*); **internationaler Währungskorb** *m* BÖRSE, FINANZ, VW basket of currencies; **internationale Warenbestimmungen** *f pl* TRANSP international goods regulations; **internationaler Warenverkehr** *m* VW cross-border trade; **internationales Warenverzeichnis** *nt* **für den Außenhandel** GESCHÄFT standard international trade classification (*SITC*); **internationale Warenvorschriften** *f pl* TRANSP international goods regulations; **Internationaler Weizenrat** *m* VW International Wheat Council; **Internationale Weizenübereinkunft** *f* (*IWÜ*) VW International Wheat Agreement (*IWA*); **Internationaler Welt-Kapital-Index** *m* BÖRSE International Capital World Index; **Internationale Wertpapieraufsichtsbehörde** *f* BÖRSE International Securities Regulatory Organization (*ISRO*); **Internationale Wertpapierbörse** *f* BÖRSE International Stock Exchange (*ISE*); **internationale Wettbewerbsfähigkeit** *f* VW international competitiveness; **internationale wirtschaftliche Zusammenarbeit** *f* VW international economic cooperation; **Internationales Wollsekretariat** *nt* IND International Wool Secretariat; **internationaler Zahlungsauftrag** *m* BANK international payment order (*IPO*); **internationaler Zahlungsverkehr** *m* BANK, VW international payments; **internationales Zentrum** *nt* **für Industrie und Umwelt** IND, UMWELT International Center for Industry and the Environment (*AmE*) (*ICIE*), International Centre for Industry and the Environment (*BrE*) (*ICIE*); **internationales Zinsgefälle** *nt* BÖRSE arbitrage margin (*BrE*); **Internationale Zivilluftfahrtorganisation** *f* (*IZLO*) TRANSP International Civil Aviation Organization (*ICAO*); **Internationales Zolltarifbüro** *nt* IMP/EXP International Customs Tariffs Bureau (*ICTB*); **Internationale Zuckerorganisation** *f* IND International Sugar Organization; **Internationaler Zuckerrat** *m* IND International Sugar Council (*ISC*); **Internationales Zuckerübereinkommen** *nt* (*ISA*) VW *internationales Rohstoffabkommen* International Sugar Agreement (*ISA*)

Interoperabilität *f* COMP interoperability

interparlamentarisch: **~e Union** *f* POL Interparliamentary Union (*IPU*)

interpersonell: **~e Fertigkeiten** *f pl* PERSON interpersonal skills; **~er Nutzenvergleich** *m* VW interpersonal utility comparison

Interpolation *f* MATH interpolation

Interpret *m* COMP *Programm* interpreter

Interpretation *f* GESCHÄFT interpretation

Interpreterprogramm *nt* COMP *Softwarepaket* interpreter

interpretieren *vt* KOMM interpret; ◆ **etw breit ~** GESCHÄFT give a loose interpretation of sth

interregional: **~es Aggregationsmodell einer Volkswirtschaft** *nt* VW bottom-up linkage model

Intervall *nt* GESCHÄFT bracket, MATH *Statistik* interval; **Intervallschätzung** *f* MATH interval estimate;

Intervallservice *m* TRANSP interval service; **Intervallskala** *f* MATH interval scale

intervenieren *vi* FINANZ, PERSON, POL, VW intervene

Intervention *f* FINANZ, GESCHÄFT, PERSON, POL, VW intervention; **~ am Devisenmarkt** VW exchange intervention; **~ durch Dritte** PERSON third-party intervention

interventionistisch *adj* POL interventionist, VW hands-on, interventionist

Intervention: **Interventionsakzept** *nt* GESCHÄFT acceptance by intervention; **Interventionsannahme** *f* GESCHÄFT acceptance by intervention

interventionsfrei: **~e Politik** *f* VW hands-off policy

Intervention: **Interventionskurs** *m* FINANZ, VW intervention rate; **Interventionspreis** *m* FINANZ, VW intervention price; **Interventionspunkt** *m* MATH chart point, VW peg point; **Interventionspunkte** *m pl* FINANZ support points; **Interventionssystem** *nt* VW pegging system; **Interventionswährung** *f* FINANZ, VW intervention currency

Interview *nt* PERSON interview; ◆ **ein ~ arrangieren** PERSON set up an interview

Interview: **Interview-Führer, in** *m,f* PERSON interview guide; **Interview-Hilfe** *f* PERSON interview guide

Intrige *f* GESCHÄFT plot

intuitiv: **~e Handlungsweise** *f* MGMNT intuitive management; **~es Management** *nt* MGMNT intuitive management

Invalidenrente *f* VERSICH disability annuity, disability insurance income (*AmE*); **Invalidenrentenversicherung** *f* VERSICH disability replacement insurance (*AmE*)

Invalidität *f* FINANZ, VERSICH *Behinderung* invalidity; **Invaliditätsgrad** *m* VERSICH degree of disablement; **Invaliditätsrente** *f* FINANZ, VERSICH disability pension; **Invaliditätsskala** *f* VERSICH disability percentage table; **Invaliditätsübernahmeversicherung** *f* VERSICH disability buy-out insurance (*AmE*); **Invaliditätsversicherung** *f* VERSICH disability insurance

Inventar *f* GESCHÄFT, IND, RECHNUNG, VERSICH inventory, stock list; ◆ **~ nach Alter aufstellen** RECHNUNG age inventories

Inventar: **Inventarbuch** *nt* RECHNUNG inventory book

inventarisieren *vt* GESCHÄFT, IND, RECHNUNG, VERSICH take stock

Inventar: **Inventarliste** *f* GESCHÄFT, IND, RECHNUNG, VERSICH inventory; **Inventarumschlag** *m* RECHNUNG inventory turnover; **Inventarverwaltung** *f* RECHNUNG management of inventories; **Inventarverzeichnis** *nt* IND inventory; **Inventarwert** *m* FINANZ, RECHNUNG net asset value (*NAV*)

Inventur *f* GESCHÄFT stocktaking, IND, RECHNUNG inventory, VW stocktaking; ◆ **~ machen** GESCHÄFT, IND take stock, RECHNUNG mark stock, take inventory

Inventur: **Inventurwert** *m* RECHNUNG stocktaking value

invers *adj* COMP reverse, MATH inverse; **~e Elastizitätsregel** *f* VW inverse elasticity rule; **~es Renditengefälle** *nt* BÖRSE reverse yield gap; **~er Schrägstrich** *m* COMP *Schriftzeichen* backslash; **~e Schrift** *f* COMP *Druck* reverse printing; **~e Zinsstrukturkurve** *f* VW inverted yield curve

invertieren *vt* MATH *Schriftzeichen* invert

Inverzugsetzung *f* FINANZ notice of default, RECHT *Vertragsrecht* formal notice of default

investierbar *adj* BANK, BÖRSE, FINANZ, VW investible

investieren 1. *vt* BANK, BÖRSE, FINANZ, GESCHÄFT *Zeit*, VW *Kapital* invest, lay out; **2.** *vi* FINANZ, VW invest; ◆ **~ in** [+acc] FINANZ invest in, VW invest in, pour money into

investiert: **nicht ~** *adj* BANK uninvested; **~es Kapital** *nt* FINANZ, RECHNUNG employed capital

Investition *f* BANK, BÖRSE, FINANZ investment, VW capital investment, investment; **Investitionen** *f pl* **der Unternehmen** FINANZ corporate investment; **Investitionsanreiz** *m* BANK investment incentive; **Investitionsaufwand** *m* FINANZ, RECHNUNG capital expenditure (*capex*), VW capital outlay, capital spending; **Investitionsausgaben** *f pl* POL capital expenditure vote, VW capital outlay, capital spending; **Investitionsausschuß** *m* FINANZ investment committee (*BrE*) (*IC*), GESCHÄFT board of investment; **Investitionsbanker** *m* BANK investment banker; **Investitionsbasis** *f* BANK investment base; **Investitionsbeihilfe** *f* RECHNUNG investment subsidy; **Investitionsbeschränkung** *f* VW investment restriction; **Investitionsbeurteilung** *f* BÖRSE, FINANZ investment appraisal; **Investitionsbewilligung** *f* RECHNUNG investment grant; **Investitionsbudget** *nt* FINANZ investment budget, RECHNUNG capital expenditure budget, investment budget; **Investitionsdrosselung** *f* FINANZ investment curb; **Investitionseinstufung** *f* BÖRSE investment grade (*AmE*); **Investitionsempfänger, in** *m,f* BANK, BÖRSE, FINANZ, VW investee; **Investitionsentscheidung** *f* FINANZ investment decision; **Investitionsfinanzierung** *f* BANK, FINANZ investment financing; **Investitionsfonds** *m* BANK, FINANZ investment fund; **Investitionsfonds** *m* **für aufstrebende Märkte** FINANZ Emerging Markets Investment Fund (*EMIF*); **Investitionsfonds** *m* **für Schwellenländer** FINANZ Emerging Markets Investment Fund (*EMIF*)

investitionsgebunden: **~er technischer Fortschritt** *m* VW *Produktion* embodied technical progress

Investition: **Investitionsgeschichte** *f* FINANZ investment history; **Investitionsgesellschaft** *f* BÖRSE, FINANZ investment company; **Investitions-Girokonto-Kombination** *f* FINANZ cash management account (*CMA*); **Investitionsgoldmünze** *f* FINANZ investment gold coin; **Investitionsgrundstück** *nt* GRUND investment property; **Investitionsgüter** *nt pl* FINANZ investment goods, GESCHÄFT capital goods, IND industrial goods, VW equipment goods, industrial goods; **Investitionsgüter-Leasing** *nt* VW equipment leasing; **Investitionsgüter-Marketing** *nt* V&M industrial marketing; **Investitionsgüterverkauf** *m* V&M industrial selling; **Investitionshaushalt** *m* RECHNUNG capital budget; **Investitionskapital** *nt* BÖRSE, FINANZ, VW investment capital; **Investitionsklima** *nt* VW investment climate; **Investitionskosten** *pl* GESCHÄFT up-front cost, VW capital costs; **Investitionskredit** *m* BANK development loan; **Investitionskredit** *m* **für kleine und mittlere Betriebe** GESCHÄFT small business development bond (*SBDB*); **Investitionskriterien** *f pl* FINANZ investment criteria; **Investitionslebenszyklus** *m* BÖRSE investment life cycle; **Investitionslücke** *f* FINANZ investment deficit; **Investitionsmix** *m* FINANZ investment mix; **Investitionsmöglichkeit** *f* BANK investment opportunity; **Investitionsmultiplikator** *m* VW investment multiplier, Keynesian multiplier; **Investitionsneigung** *f* VW propensity to invest; **Investitionsplan** *m* FINANZ investment budget, RECHNUNG investment budget, capital expenditure budget, capital budget, VERWALT capital budget; **Investitionsplanung** *f* VW capital budget; **Investitionspolitik** *f* FINANZ, POL, VW investment policy; **Investitionsprogramm** *nt* FINANZ capital program (*AmE*), capital programme (*BrE*), investment program (*AmE*), investment programme (*BrE*); **das Investitionsprogramm kürzen** *phr* FINANZ trim the investment program (*AmE*), trim the investment programme (*BrE*); **Investitionsprojekt** *nt* FINANZ investment project, capital project, RECHNUNG capital project; **Investitionsprojektsbewertung** *f* FINANZ capital project evaluation; **Investitionsprüfung** *f* FINANZ investment review; **Investitionsquote** *f* FINANZ, VW capital-outlay ratio; **Investitionsrechnung** *f* BÖRSE investment analysis, FINANZ capital investment appraisal, capital project evaluation, investment analysis, RECHNUNG capital budgeting, VW capital budget, capital budgeting, capital expenditure appraisal; **Investitionsrentabilität** *f* FINANZ, RECHNUNG, VW return on investment (*ROI*); **Investitionsservice** *m* FINANZ investment service; **Investitionssoftware** *f* COMP, FINANZ investment software; **Investitionssparkonto** *nt* BANK investment savings account; **Investitionsstrategie** *f* BÖRSE investment strategy, FINANZ investment strategy, capital investment strategy, capital strategy; **Investitionsstrategieausschuß** *m* FINANZ investment strategy committee; **Investitionssumme** *f* FINANZ amount to be invested; **Investitionstätigkeit** *f* VW investment activity

investitionsunabhängig: **~er technischer Fortschritt** *m* VW disembodied technical progress

Investition: **Investitionsuntersuchung** *f* **zur Wertlinie** FINANZ value line investment survey; **Investitionsvolumen** *nt* FINANZ, RECHNUNG capital commitment; **Investitionsvorhaben** *nt* FINANZ, RECHNUNG capital project; **Investitionswert** *m* **eines wandlungsfähigen Wertpapiers** BÖRSE investment value of a convertible security; **Investitionszentrale** *f* FINANZ investment center (*AmE*), investment centre (*BrE*)

Investment *nt* BANK, BÖRSE, FINANZ, VW investment; **Investmentbank** *f* BANK investment bank

Investmentfonds *m* FINANZ mutual fund (*AmE*), VW managed fund, leverage fund; **~ für Aktien** BÖRSE investment fund for shares; **~ mit begrenzter Emissionshöhe** FINANZ closed-end fund, closed-end investment fund; **~ des sozialen Gewissens** VW social conscience fund; **~ mit unveränderlichem Portefeuille** BÖRSE fixed-investment trust (*AmE*), nondiscretionary trust (*BrE*); ♦ **einen ~ kündigen** FINANZ terminate a fund

Investmentgesellschaft *f* BÖRSE investment company, unit trust (*BrE*), FINANZ investment budget, investment firm, investment trust (*BrE*), unit trust; **~ mit begrenztes Emissionshöhe** FINANZ closed-end investment trust

Investment: **Investment-Hedger** *m* BÖRSE investment hedger; **Investmentzentrum** *nt* FINANZ investment center (*AmE*), investment centre (*BrE*)

Investor, in *m,f* BANK, FINANZ, VW investor;

Investorengruppe *f* BANK, FINANZ investor group; **Investorenprämienkonto** *nt* BANK, FINANZ investors' indemnity account

Inzahlungnahme *f* GESCHÄFT trade-in; **~ einer gebrauchten Sache** GESCHÄFT trade-in allowance

I/O *abbr* (*Input-Output*) COMP I/O (*input/output*); **I/O-Fehlermeldung** *f* COMP I/O error message

ipso facto *phr* GESCHÄFT ipso facto

irreführen *vt* GESCHÄFT, PATENT, RECHT, V&M mislead, deceive

irgendwann: **~ in der Zukunft** *phr* GESCHÄFT at some time in the future

irreführend *adj* GESCHÄFT, PATENT, RECHT, V&M misleading, deceptive; **~e Verpackung** *f* V&M deceptive packaging; **~e Werbepost** *f* V&M mail fraud; **~e Werbung** *f* GESCHÄFT, V&M deceptive advertising, false advertising, misleading advertising

irrelevant *adj* GESCHÄFT irrelevant

irren: **sich ~** *v refl* GESCHÄFT *in einem Urteil* err

irreparabel *adj* GESCHÄFT irreparable, beyond repair

irreversibel *adj* GESCHÄFT irreversible

Irrfahrttheorie: *f* BÖRSE, VW random walk theory

Irrtum *m* GESCHÄFT mistake, RECHT, VERSICH error; ♦ **~ vorbehalten** GESCHÄFT (*I. v.*) errors and omissions excepted (*E&OE*)

irrtümlich *adj* GESCHÄFT mistaken, erroneous, VERSICH mistaken

Irrtum: **Irrtums- und Versäumnisklausel** *f* VERSICH errors and omissions clause; **Irrtumswahrscheinlichkeit** *f* MATH level of significance

IRU *abbr* (*internationaler Fernfahrerverband*) TRANSP IRU (*International Road Transport Union*)

IS *abbr* (*integrierter Schaltkreis*) COMP IC (*integrated circuit*)

ISA *abbr* (*Internationales Zuckerübereinkommen*) VW ISA (*International Sugar Agreement*)

ISBN *abbr* (*internationale Standardbuchnummer*) MEDIEN ISBN (*International Standard Book Number*)

ISCO *abbr* (*internationale Standardklassifikation der Berufe*) VW ISCO (*international standard classification of occupations*)

ISD *abbr* (*Internationaler Sozialdienst*) SOZIAL ISS (*International Social Service*)

ISDN *abbr* (*integriertes Dienstleistungsdatennetz*) COMP, KOMM ISDN (*Integrated Services Digital Network*)

ISO *abbr* (*Internationale Organisation für Normung*) GESCHÄFT ISO (*International Standards Organization*)

Isokosten *pl* VW isocost

Isolationismus *m* POL isolationism

isolationistisch *adj* POL isolationist

isolieren *vt* GESCHÄFT insulate, isolate

isoliert *adj* GESCHÄFT, POL isolated; **~es Marktgleichgewicht** *nt* VW isolated market equilibrium; **~er Staat** *m* POL isolated state; **~e Volkswirtschaft** *f* VW enclave economy

Isolierung *f* GESCHÄFT quarantine

Isolierzelle *f* SOZIAL adjustment center (*AmE*), adjustment centre (*BrE*)

ISO: **ISO-Papierformat** *nt* MEDIEN, V&M ISO paper size

Isoquante *f* VW equal product curve, isoquant

isothermisch: **~er Kühltransport** *m* TRANSP temperature-controlled transport

ISSN *abbr* (*internationale Standardseriennummer*) MEDIEN ISSN (*International Standard Serial Number*)

Ist- *in cpds* GESCHÄFT, IND, PERSON, RECHNUNG, VERWALT, VW actual; **Ist-Ausgaben** *f pl* RECHNUNG actual expenditure; **Ist-Beschäftigung** *f* IND actual output; **Ist-Bestand** *m* BANK actual balance, GESCHÄFT actual inventory (*AmE*), actual stock (*BrE*), RECHNUNG actual balance; **Ist-Betrag** *m* BANK, RECHNUNG actual amount, actual balance; **Ist-Erlöse** *m pl* **über Soll-Erlöse** RECHNUNG favorable variance (*AmE*), favourable variance (*BrE*), favorable difference (*AmE*), favourable difference (*BrE*); **Ist-Investitionen** *f pl* BANK actual investment; **Ist-Kosten** *pl* RECHNUNG actual cost, VERWALT effective cost; **Istkostenrechnung** *f* RECHNUNG actual cost system; **Ist-Leistung** *f* IND actual output; **Ist-Menge** *f* IND real volume; **Ist-Stunden** *f pl* PERSON actual man-hours; **Ist-System** *nt* **der Rechnungslegung** RECHNUNG cash accounting, cash basis of accounting; **Ist-Volumen** *nt* IND real volume; **Ist-Zahlen** *f pl* RECHNUNG actual figures; **Ist-**

Zeit *f* IND actual time

IT *abbr* (*Informationstechnik, Informationstechnologie*) COMP IT (*information technology*)

Iteration *f* COMP iteration

ITF *abbr* (*internationale Transportarbeiter-Föderation*) TRANSP ITF (*International Transport Workers' Federation*)

IUOTO *abbr* (*Internationaler Verband amtlicher Fremdenverkehrsorganisationen*) PERSON IUOTO (*International Union of Official Travel Organizations*)

I. v. *abbr* (*Irrtum vorbehalten*) GESCHÄFT E&OE (*errors and omissions excepted*)

IWF *abbr* (*Internationaler Währungsfonds*) VW IMF (*International Monetary Fund*)

IWÜ *abbr* (*Internationale Weizenübereinkunft*) VW IWA (*International Wheat Agreement*)

IZLO *abbr* (*Internationale Zivilluftfahrtorganisation*) TRANSP ICAO (*International Civil Aviation Organization*)

J

J. *abbr* (*Jahr*) GESCHÄFT yr (*year*)

Jachtmakler, in *m,f* PERSON yacht broker

Jagd: ~ **machen auf Führungspersonal** *phr* MGMNT headhunt

Jahr *nt* (*J.*) GESCHÄFT year (*yr*); ◆ **dieses** ~ (*cf heuer Öst, Sch*) GESCHÄFT this year; **pro** ~ GESCHÄFT per annum (*p.a.*)

Jahr: **Jahrbuch** *nt* MATH abstract, MEDIEN yearbook, V&M annual; **sich über viele Jahre erstreckendes Ausgabenpaket** *nt* FINANZ multi-year spending envelope; **sich über viele Jahre erstreckendes Mittelpaket** *nt* FINANZ multi-year resource envelope; **Jahresabonnement** *nt* GESCHÄFT annual subscription; **Jahresabrechnung** *f* RECHNUNG yearly settlement

Jahresabschluß *m* FINANZ accounts, RECHNUNG annual accounts, balance sheet (*B/S*), financial statement; ~ **und Budgetberichterstattung** *f* FINANZ financial statement and budget report (*FSBR*); ~ **einer Unternehmung** RECHNUNG company accounts; ◆ **den** ~ **feststellen** FINANZ agree the accounts; **dem** ~ **zustimmen** FINANZ agree the accounts

Jahresabschluß: **Jahresabschlußarbeiten** *f pl* RECHNUNG year-end procedures; **Jahresabschlußbericht** *m* FINANZ, VERWALT financial report; **Jahresabschlußdividende** *f* RECHNUNG year-end dividend; **Jahresabschlußprognose** *f* FINANZ estimated financial report; **Jahresabschlußprüfung** *f* RECHNUNG year-end audit; **Jahresabschlußprüfungsplan** *m* RECHNUNG annual audit plan

Jahr: **Jahresarbeitslohn** *m* PERSON annual wage; **Jahresauftrag** *m* GESCHÄFT annual order; **Jahresaufstellung** *f* **diskontierbarer Wechsel** GESCHÄFT annual statement of bankable bills; **Jahresausgleich** *m* **durchführen** GESCHÄFT annualize

Jahresbasis *f* MATH annual basis; ◆ **auf** ~ **umgerechnet** FINANZ, GESCHÄFT annualized; **auf** ~ **umgerechneter Zinssatz** *m* MATH annualized interest rate; **auf** ~ **umrechnen** FINANZ, GESCHÄFT annualize

Jahr: **Jahresbeitrag** *m* GESCHÄFT annual subscription; **Jahresbericht** *m* FINANZ financial report, RECHNUNG annual report, year-end closing, RECHT annual return, VERWALT financial report; **Jahresbilanz** *f* FINANZ annual statement of condition; **Jahresendberichtigung** *f* RECHNUNG year-end adjustment; **Jahresende** *nt* RECHNUNG year-end, year ended; **Jahresertrag** *m* GESCHÄFT annual proceeds, RECHNUNG annual yield; **Jahresgebühr** *f* RECHNUNG annual fee; **Jahresgehalt** *nt* GESCHÄFT, PERSON salary, yearly salary; **Jahresgewinn** *m* FINANZ annual net cash inflow, RECHNUNG annual earnings; **Jahresgewinn** *m* **nach Steuern** RECHNUNG, STEUER profit for the year after tax; **Jahreshauptversammlung** *f* GESCHÄFT, MGMNT annual general meeting (*AGM*); **Jahreshaushaltsbericht** *m* VW comprehensive annual financial report (*CAFR*); **Jahreshöchststand** *m* BÖRSE annual high; **Jahreshonorar** *nt* RECHNUNG annual fee; **Jahreskonferenz** *f* Verkauf V&M annual sales conference; **Jahresleistung** *f* IND annual output; **Jahresmitte** *f* GESCHÄFT midyear; **Jahresprämie** *f* VERSICH annual

premium; **Jahresproduktion** *f* IND annual output; **Jahresrate** *f* FINANZ, GESCHÄFT annual installment (*AmE*), annual instalment (*BrE*), MATH annual rate, RECHNUNG annual installment (*AmE*), annual instalment (*BrE*); **Jahresrendite** *f* RECHNUNG annual return, annual yield; **Jahresrendite** *f* **kurzfristiger unverzinslicher Wertpapiere** BÖRSE bond equivalent yield; **in eine Jahresrente investieren** *phr* VERSICH invest in an annuity; **Jahresrevision** *f* RECHNUNG complete audit; **Jahresschätzungen** *f pl* FINANZ year estimates; **Jahressteuererklärung** *f* RECHNUNG, STEUER annual tax return; **Jahresstunden** *f pl* PERSON annualized hours; **Jahresstundenvertrag** *m* PERSON annual hours contract; **Jahrestag** *m* GESCHÄFT anniversary; **Jahrestiefpunkt** *m* BÖRSE annual low; **Jahrestilgungsbetrag** *m* **einer Abzahlungshypothek** MATH annual mortgage constant; **Jahrestilgungsbetrag** *m* **einer Ratenhypothek** MATH annual mortgage constant; **Jahresüberschadensrückversicherung** *f* VERSICH stop loss insurance; **Jahresüberschuß** *m* RECHNUNG annual net profit; **Jahresumsatz** *m* RECHNUNG annual turnover; **Jahresumsatzbericht** *m* GESCHÄFT annual report; **Jahresurlaub** *m* PERSON *Angestelltenverhältnis* annual leave; **Jahresverdienst** *m* PERSON annual wage; **im Jahresvergleich** *phr* MGMNT, RECHNUNG year-on-year; **Jahresvollversammlung** *f* GESCHÄFT, MGMNT annual general meeting (*AGM*); **Jahreszahlung** *f* GESCHÄFT yearly payment, annual payment; **nicht der Jahreszeit entsprechend** *phr* GESCHÄFT unseasonable

jahreszeitlich: ~**er Wechsel** *m* GESCHÄFT seasonal swing

Jahr: **Jahrgang** *m* MEDIEN *Personen* age group, GESCHÄFT vintage

jährlich 1. *adj* GESCHÄFT year-to-year, yearly, annual; **2.** *adv* GESCHÄFT annually, on a yearly basis, on an annual basis, yearly; ◆ ~ **entlohnen** GESCHÄFT pay by the year; ~ **zahlen** GESCHÄFT pay by the year

jährlich: ~**e Abschreibung** *f* GESCHÄFT, RECHNUNG annual depreciation; ~**er Abschreibungsaufwand** *m* RECHNUNG annual depreciation charge; ~**er Auftrag** *m* GESCHÄFT annual order; ~**e Bestätigung** *f* RECHNUNG annual certificate; ~**er Bewertungsplan** *m* FINANZ annual evaluation plan; ~**er Cashflow** *m* RECHNUNG annual cash flow; ~**er Einnahmeüberschuß** *m* RECHNUNG annual cash flow; ~ **erneuerbare Risikoversicherung** *f* VERSICH annually renewable term insurance; ~**er Freibetrag** *m* STEUER annual exemption; ~**e Gehaltsüberprüfung** *f* PERSON annual salary review; ~**e Gesamtbelastung** *f* FINANZ annual percentage rate (*APR*); ~**e Inertgassystemübersicht** *f* UMWELT annual inert gas system survey (*AIGSS*); ~**e Konjunkturumfrage** *f* vw Economic Trends Annual Survey (*BrE*) (*ETAS*); ~**e Maschinenprüfung** *f* TRANSP annual machinery survey (*AMS*); ~**e Mietkosten** *m pl* STEUER annual rental charges; ~**e Mietpreise** *m pl* STEUER annual rental charges; ~**e Prüfung** *f* **der automatischen Steuerung** TRANSP annual automated controls survey; ~**e Rate** *f* GESCHÄFT annual installment (*AmE*), annual instalment (*BrE*); ~**e Revision** *f* **der Gehälter** PERSON *Angestelltenverhältnis* annual salary

review; ~e **Rückzahlung** *f* GESCHÄFT annual repayment;
~er **Schuldendienst** *m* BANK annual debt service; ~e
Steuererklärung *f* RECHNUNG, STEUER annual tax
return; ~e **Tilgungsrate** *f* VERSICH annual amortization;
~er **Umsatzüberschuß** *m* RECHNUNG annual net cash
inflow; ~er **Verkaufsbericht** *m* GESCHÄFT annual sales
report; ~e **Zahlung** *f* GESCHÄFT annual payment; ~e
Zuweisung *f* RECHNUNG annual appropriation

Jährling *m* VW yearling (*BrE*)

Jahrzehnt *nt* GESCHÄFT decade

Jamaika-Abkommen *nt* VW *IWF* Jamaica Agreement

Janson-Klausel *f* VERSICH Janson Clause

Japanisierung *f* VW japanization

Jargon *m* GESCHÄFT jargon

jederzeit *adv* GESCHÄFT at all times; ~ **abrufbares
Kapital** *nt* BANK callable capital; ~ **fristlos kündbares
Mietverhältnis** *nt* GRUND, RECHT tenancy at will;
~ **fristlos kündbares Pachtverhältnis** *nt* GRUND,
RECHT tenancy at will; ~ **verfügbares Geld** *nt*
GESCHÄFT ready money

Jet-lag *nt* TRANSP jetlag

jeweilig: ~e **Umstände** *m pl* PERSON relativities

J-förmige: ~ **Häufigkeitskurve** *f* MATH J-shaped frequency curve

Jingle *m* V&M jingle

JIT *abbr* (*just-in-time, Just-in-Time-Produktion*) IND, PER-
SON JIT (*just-in-time, just-in-time production*)

J-Kurve *f* MATH, VW J curve

Job *m* COMP job, batch job, PERSON job; ~ **Enlargement**
nt PERSON job enlargement; ~ **Enrichment** *nt* PERSON
job enrichment; ~ **Hopper** *m* PERSON job hopper, job
jumper; ~ **Sharing** *nt* PERSON *Teilzeitarbeit* job sharing;
~ **Sharing Programm** *nt* PERSON *Teilzeitarbeit* job share
scheme

Jobben *nt* PERSON jobbing

Jobber *m* BÖRSE jobber (*dat*) (*BrE*)

Job: **Jobeingabe** *f* COMP job entry; **Jobsteuerung** *f*
COMP job control; **Jobwarteschlange** *f* COMP job queue

Joint- *in cpds* GESCHÄFT joint; **Joint Director** *m* PERSON
joint director; **Joint Venture** *nt* BÖRSE, GESCHÄFT,
MGMNT, RECHNUNG, VW joint venture (*JV*); **Joint-
Venture-Bank** *f* BANK joint-venture bank; **Joint-Venture-Recht** *nt* RECHT *Vertragsrecht* joint venture law

Joker *m* COMP wild card

Jota *nt obs* GESCHÄFT iota

Journal *nt* GESCHÄFT, RECHNUNG daybook (*d.b.*), journal; ♦ **ins ~ eintragen** RECHNUNG journalize

Journal: **Journalbuchung** *f* RECHNUNG journal entry;
Journaleintrag *m* RECHNUNG journal entry

Joystick *m* COMP joystick

Jr. *abbr* (*Junior*) GESCHÄFT, RECHT jnr. (*junior*), jr (*junior*)

Jubiläumsausgabe *f* MEDIEN anniversary publication

Jubiläumsband *m* MEDIEN anniversary publication

Jubiläumsschrift *m* MEDIEN anniversary publication

Jugendausbildungsprogramm *nt* PERSON *Arbeit* youth
training (*BrE*) (*YT*), youth training scheme (*BrE*) (*obs*)
(*YTS*)

Jumbo *m infrml* TRANSP jumbo (*infrml*); **Jumbo-Jet** *m
infrml* TRANSP jumbo jet (*infrml*); **Jumbopackung** *f*
V&M jumbo pack

jung: ~e **Aktie** *f* BÖRSE new share; ~e **Demokratien** *f pl*
GESCHÄFT new democracies; ~es **Geschäftsfeld** *nt*
GESCHÄFT fledgling commercial field; ~es
Unternehmen *nt* VW development stage enterprise;
~er **Wirtschaftsbereich** *m* GESCHÄFT fledgling commercial field; ~er **Wirtschaftszweig** *m* IND infant
industry

Jungarbeiter, in *m,f* PERSON young worker

Jungfern- *in cpds* TRANSP inaugural, maiden;
Jungfernfahrt *f* TRANSP inaugural cruise, maiden
voyage, inaugural sailing; **Jungfernflug** *m* TRANSP
inaugural flight, maiden flight

Junggeselle *m* RECHT single man

Junggesellin *f* RECHT single woman

jüngst *adj* V&M *Entwicklung* latest; ~e **Erweiterung** *f*
GESCHÄFT *d. Produktpalette*, V&M latest addition; ~e
Schätzung *f* GESCHÄFT latest estimate (*L/E*); ~e
Statistiken *f pl* MATH latest statistics

Jungunternehmer, in *m,f* GESCHÄFT young entrepreneur

Junikaufoption *f* BÖRSE June call

Junior *m* (*Jr.*) GESCHÄFT, RECHT junior (*jnr., jr.*);
~ **Manager** *m* PERSON junior manager;
Juniorpartner, in *m,f* GESCHÄFT, RECHT junior partner;
Juniorposition *f* PERSON junior position

Juniverkaufsoption *f* BÖRSE June put

Juridifikation *f* PERSON juridification

Juridifizierung *f* PERSON juridification

Jurisprudenz *f* RECHT jurisprudence

juristisch *adj* RECHT legal; ~e **Fakultät** *f* SOZIAL
Universität law school; ~e **Person** *f* PATENT, RECHT
legal person, juridical person, *Rechtspersönlichkeit* legal
entity, VERWALT corporate body; ~e **Tätigkeiten** *f pl*
RECHT legal services

Jury *f* GESCHÄFT jury, panel of judges; ~ **der
Führungsmeinung** MATH jury of executive opinion

justierbar *adj* GESCHÄFT adjustable

justifiabel *adj* GESCHÄFT actionable

just-in-time *phr* (*JIT*) IND, PERSON just-in-time (*JIT*),
just-in-time production (*JIT*)

Just-in-Time-Produktion *f* (*JIT*) IND, PERSON just-in-
time (*JIT*), just-in-time production (*JIT*)

Justiz *f* RECHT justice

Justizminister *m* RECHT Attorney General (*AmE*) (*Atty
Gen*)

Juwelier, in *m,f* GESCHÄFT jeweler (*AmE*), jeweller (*BrE*)

K

Kabel *nt* IND, KOMM, MEDIEN cable; **Kabelfernsehen** *nt* MEDIEN cable television; **Kabelkurs** *m* VW cable rate; **Kabelprogramm** *nt* MEDIEN *Fernsehen* cable program (*AmE*), cable programme (*BrE*)

Kabeltelegramm: Ihr ~ *phr* KOMM your cable (*y/c*)

Kabine *f* KOMM *Telefon* booth, TRANSP cabin; **Kabinengebühren** *f pl* TRANSP cabin charge; **Kabinenzuteilung** *f* TRANSP cabin allocation

Kabinett *nt* POL cabinet

Kabotage *f* TRANSP cabotage

Kader *m* PERSON *Fachmann* specialist, POL cadre

Käfig *m* TRANSP *Fracht* cage container (*c*); **Käfigbehälter** *m* TRANSP cage container (*c*); **Käfigcontainer** *m* TRANSP cage container (*c*); **Käfiglagerkarte** *f* TRANSP cage inventory record (*CIR*)

Kai *m* IMP/EXP, TRANSP quay, wharf; ♦ **ab ~** (*x-Kai*) TRANSP ex quai (*x-quay*); **am ~ abgeliefert** IMP/EXP, TRANSP delivered at docks (*DD*), delivered docks (*DD*); **~-Kai** IMP/EXP, TRANSP port to port (*P to P*), quay to quay; **von ~ zu Kai** IMP/EXP, TRANSP port to port (*P to P*), quay to quay

Kai: Kaiempfangsschein *m* IMP/EXP, TRANSP dock receipt; **Kaigebühren** *f pl* IMP/EXP, TRANSP pierage, quayage, wharfage; **Kaigeld** *nt* IMP/EXP, TRANSP pierage, quayage, wharfage

Kaldor: ~sche Gesetze *nt pl* VW Kaldor's laws; **Kaldor-Hicks-Kompensationsprinzip** *nt* VW Kaldor-Hicks compensation principle

Kalender *m* GESCHÄFT calendar; **~-Spread** *m* BÖRSE calendar spread; **Kalendertag** *m* GESCHÄFT calendar day; **Kalenderuhr** *f* COMP clock-calendar; **Kalenderwoche** *f* (*KW*) GESCHÄFT calendar week; **~-Zinsspanne** *f* BÖRSE calendar spread

Kaliber *m* PERSON caliber (*AmE*), calibre (*BrE*)

Kalibrierung *f* GESCHÄFT, TRANSP calibration

Kalkulation *f* FINANZ cost estimating, costing, MATH calculation; **Kalkulationsbasis** *f* GESCHÄFT base of calculation; **Kalkulationsgrundlage** *f* GESCHÄFT base of calculation; **Kalkulationspreise** *m pl* RECHNUNG budget prices; **Kalkulationsspanne** *f* VW pricing margin; **Kalkulationstabelle** *f* BÖRSE, COMP, FINANZ, RECHNUNG, VERWALT spreadsheet; **Kalkulationsverfahren** *nt* FINANZ costing technique; **Kalkulationszinsfuß** *m* FINANZ adequate target rate, RECHNUNG internal rate of discount

kalkulatorisch: ~e Abschreibung *f* RECHNUNG physical depreciation; **~e Bewertung** *f* RECHNUNG pricing of input factors; **~er Gewinn** *m* RECHNUNG income budget; **~e Kosten** *pl* FINANZ imputed costs; **~e Wagnisse** *nt pl* FINANZ imputed risks; **~e Zinsen** *m pl* RECHNUNG imputed interest charge

kalorienarm *adj* V&M low-calorie

kältebeständig *adj* GESCHÄFT resistant to cold

Kältetechnik *f* IND refrigeration engineering

Kaltlagerung *f* IND cold storage

Kaltstart *m* COMP cold boot, GESCHÄFT cold start

Kamera *f* MEDIEN, V&M camera

kameralistisch: ~e Buchführung *f* RECHNUNG government accounting

Kamin *m* IND smokestack

Kammer *f* POL chamber, house, RECHT chamber

Kämmerer *m* VERWALT financial officer

Kampagne *f* POL, V&M campaign; ♦ **eine ~ führen** POL wage a campaign

Kampf *m* BÖRSE, GESCHÄFT battle; **~ um Stimmrechte** BÖRSE proxy battle (*AmE*)

kämpfen: ~ um *vt* GESCHÄFT battle for; **kämpfe nicht gegen den Börsenticker** *phr* BÖRSE don't fight the tape

kanadisch: ~e Prime Rate *f* VW Canadian Prime Rate

Kanal *m* COMP, MEDIEN channel, TRANSP canal, V&M channel; **der ~** TRANSP the Channel, the English Channel; **Kanalauswahl** *f* V&M channel selection; **Kanalgebühren** *f pl* TRANSP canal dues, canal fees; **Kanalgeld** *nt* TRANSP Channel money (*BrE*)

kanalisieren *vt* GESCHÄFT *Gelder* channel

Kanaltunnel *m* TRANSP Channel Tunnel

Kandidat, in *m,f* PERSON *Bewerbung* applicant, candidate, POL *Wahl* candidate, nominee; **Kandidatenliste** *f* PERSON shortlist, POL list of candidates, slate (*AmE*), *Präsidentschaftswahl* ticket (*AmE*)

Kandidatur *f* POL *Wahl* candidacy, candidature, nomination

kandidieren *vi* POL stand for election

Kanisteröl *nt* IND case oil (*co*)

Kannbestimmung *f* POL authorization

Kantinenwesen *nt* GESCHÄFT catering

Kanton *m* *Sch* POL canton

Kantonalbank *f* *Sch* BANK cantonal bank

Kanzlei *f* RECHT chambers, office

Kanzler *m* POL chancellor

Kapazität *f* COMP *Kondensator* capacitance, GESCHÄFT capacity, potential, PERSON, VW capacity; **Kapazitätsauslastung** *f* TRANSP load factor, VERSICH, VW capacity charge, capacity utilization rate, capacity utilization; **Kapazitätsausnutzung** *f* VERSICH, VW capacity charge, capacity utilization, capacity utilization rate; **Kapazitätseffekt** *m* VW capacity effect; **Kapazitätsfaktor** *m* MATH, VW load factor; **an der Kapazitätsgrenze** *f* RECHNUNG full to capacity; **Kapazitätslinie** *f* VW transformation curve; **Kapazitätsmangel** *m* GESCHÄFT undercapacity; **Kapazitätsreserve** *f* GESCHÄFT idle capacity, IND, TRANSP, VW spare capacity; **Kapazitätsverhältnis** *nt* VW capacity ratio

Kapital *nt* FINANZ assets, capital, funds, RECHT corpus; **~ aus ausgegebenen Aktien** BÖRSE, FINANZ, RECHNUNG issued share capital; **~ des Kontrahenten** FINANZ counterparty capital; **~, Vermögen, Management, Ertrag, Liquidität** FINANZ, VW capital, assets, management, earnings, liquidity (*BrE*) (*CAMEL*); ♦ **~ auflösen** FINANZ unlock funds; **~ erhöhen** VW reinforce capital; **aus etw ~ schlagen** FINANZ cash in on sth; **in etw ~ stecken** FINANZ pump funds into sth

Kapital: Kapitalabfindung *f* BÖRSE, FINANZ cash

settlement; **Kapitalabfluß** *m* FINANZ, RECHNUNG, VW cash outflow, outflow, capital outflow, exodus of capital; **Kapitaländerung** *f* GESCHÄFT alteration of capital

Kapitalanlage *f* FINANZ stake, capital investment

Kapitalanlagegesellschaft *f* BÖRSE, FINANZ investment company; ~ **mit festgelegten Anteilen** BÖRSE fixed-investment trust (*AmE*), nondiscretionary trust; ~ **mit geschlossenem Anlagefonds** FINANZ closed-end investment company (*CEIC*)

Kapitalanlage: **Kapitalanlagegüter** *nt pl* VW capital assets; **Kapitalanlagekonto** *nt* BANK capital asset account; **Kapitalanlagen** *f pl* FINANZ assets, capital assets; **Kapitalanlagenberatergesetz** *nt* FINANZ Investment Advisers Act; **Kapitalanlagepreismodell** *nt* BÖRSE, FINANZ, VW capital asset pricing model (*CAPM*)

Kapital: **Kapitalanlegergruppe** *f* FINANZ investor group; **Kapitalanlegerkonsortium** *nt* BÖRSE syndicate of investors; **Kapitalansammlung** *f* VW capital accumulation; **Kapitalaufbringung** *f* FINANZ capital raising; **Kapitalaufnahme** *f* FINANZ capital raising, equity borrowing; **Kapitalaufwandverhältnis** *nt* FINANZ capital-outlay ratio; **Kapitalausstattung** *f* **mit geringem Eigenkapitalanteil** RECHNUNG thin capitalization; **Kapitalbedarf** *m* FINANZ financial requirements, capital needs, capital requirement

Kapitalbeschaffung *f* BANK, BÖRSE, FINANZ capital raising, fund-raising, capital procurement; **Kapitalbeschaffungskosten** *pl* BANK, BÖRSE, FINANZ capital procurement cost, cost of funds; **Kapitalbeschaffungstransaktion** *f* BANK, BÖRSE, FINANZ capital-raising operation

Kapitalbeteiligung *f* BÖRSE equity sharing, PERSON *von Arbeitnehmern* capital sharing; ~ **eines Anteilseigners** BÖRSE equity ownership; ~ **eines Kreditgebers** BÖRSE equity kicker; ♦ **eine ~ erwerben in** BÖRSE take an equity stake in; **eine ~ haben** BÖRSE have an equity stake

Kapitalbeteiligung: **Kapitalbeteiligungsfonds** *m* FINANZ equity holding, BÖRSE equity investment fund

Kapital: **Kapitalbetrag** *m* FINANZ principal sum, capital sum; **Kapitalbewegung** *f* FINANZ capital flow; **Kapitalbilanz** *f* VW balance of capital movements; **Kapitalbildung** *f* FINANZ, VW accumulation of capital, capital formation, capital accumulation; **Kapitalbindung** *f* FINANZ capital lockup, RECHNUNG capital commitment; **Kapitalbudget** *nt* VW capital budget; **Kapitaldeckung** *nt* BANK capital cover; **Kapitaleinkommen** *nt* FINANZ, RECHNUNG, STEUER unearned income; **Kapitaleinlage** *f* RECHNUNG capital stock; **Kapitaleinlage** *f* **über Nennwert** RECHNUNG investment above nominal value; **Kapitaleinleger** *m* GESCHÄFT contributor of capital; **Kapitaleinsatz** *m* RECHNUNG capital commitment; **vom Kapitaleinsatz unabhängiger technischer Fortschritt** *m* VW *Produktion* disembodied technical progress; **Kapitalentnahme** *f* BANK withdrawal of capital; **Kapitalertrag** *m* FINANZ, RECHNUNG, VW return on capital (*ROC*); **Kapitalertragsteuer** *f* STEUER capital gains tax (*CGT*), dividend tax; **Kapitalfinanzierungsplanung** *f* FINANZ capital funding planning; **Kapitalflucht** *f* VW capital flight, flight of capital; **Kapitalfluß** *m* FINANZ capital flow, cash flow, flow of funds, RECHNUNG flow, funds flow; **Kapitalflußrechnung** *f* FINANZ cash flow statement, RECHNUNG application of funds statement,

funds statement; **Kapitalfonds** *m* FINANZ capital fund; **Kapitalgesellschaft** *f* GESCHÄFT public limited company (*BrE*) (*plc*, *PLC*), publicly listed company; **Kapitalgesellschaft** *f* **mit unbeschränkter Haftung** GESCHÄFT unlimited company; **Kapitalgewinn** *m* FINANZ, RECHNUNG, STEUER, VW capital gains, capital profit, business corporation, VERWALT business corporation; **Kapitalgewinnsteuer** *f* STEUER capital gains tax (*CGT*); **Kapitalgewinn** *m* **nach Steuern** *m* RECHNUNG, STEUER capital gains after tax; **Kapitalgruppe** *f* BÖRSE family of funds; **Kapitalgut** *nt* FINANZ capital asset; **Kapitalgüter** *nt pl* FINANZ investment goods, GESCHÄFT capital goods; **Kapitalherabsetzung** *f* FINANZ capital write-down, RECHNUNG, VERWALT reduction in capital; **Kapitalherkunft** *f* FINANZ source of capital; **Kapitalhilfe** *f* VW capital aid; **Kapitalintensität** *f* PERSON *Produktivitätsmessung* employee ratios, VW capital-labor ratio (*AmE*), capital-labour ratio (*BrE*)

kapitalintensiv *adj* FINANZ, VW capital-intensive; ~**e Industrie** *f* FINANZ, IND, VW capital-intensive industry

kapitalisierbar *adj* FINANZ realizable

kapitalisieren *vt* FINANZ capitalize, realize

Kapitalisierung *f* FINANZ capitalization; ~ **von Leasingverträgen** RECHNUNG capitalization of leases; **Kapitalisierungseffekt** *m* STEUER, VW *einer Steuer* capitalization effect; **Kapitalisierungsfaktor** *m* FINANZ, VW capitalization rate (*cap rate*); **Kapitalisierungssatz** *m* FINANZ, VW capitalization rate (*cap rate*)

Kapitalismus *m* VW capitalism

Kapitalist, in *m,f* VW capitalist; **Kapitalistenklasse** *f* VW capitalist class

kapitalistisch *adj* VW capitalist, capitalistic

Kapital: **Kapitalkoeffizient** *m* FINANZ, VW capital-output ratio; **Kapitalkonsolidierung** *f* VW capital consolidation; **Kapitalkonto** *nt* BANK, VW capital account (*C/A*); **Kapitalkonto** *nt* **von Eigenheimbesitzern** BANK homeowner's equity account; **Kapitalkosten** *pl* FINANZ, VW capital costs; **Kapitalkraft** *f* BANK financial strength, FINANZ financial standing

kapitalkräftig *adj* GESCHÄFT *Firma* substantial

Kapitalmarkt *m* FINANZ, VW capital market; **Kapitalmarktbeeinflussung** *f* RECHNUNG capital market influence; **Kapitalmarktrendite** *f* BÖRSE capital market yield; **Kapitalmarktzins** *m* BANK capital market interest rate

Kapital: **Kapitalnutzung** *f* VW capital utilization; **Kapitalnutzungskosten** *pl* VW capital user costs; **Kapitalobligationen** *f pl* BÖRSE capital bonds (*BrE*); **Kapitalproduktivität** *f* VW capital productivity; **Kapitalrationierung** *f* FINANZ capital rationing; **Kapitalrendite** *f* FINANZ, RECHNUNG, VW return on capital employed (*ROCE*), return on investment (*ROI*), return on capital (*ROC*); **Kapitalreserve** *f* RECHNUNG capital reserves; **Kapitalrisiko** *nt* FINANZ capital risk; **Kapitalrückflußrechnung** *f* FINANZ payback method; **Kapitalrückführung** *f* VW repatriation of funds; **Kapitalrücklage** *f* FINANZ share premium account, RECHNUNG capital reserves, capital paid in excess of par value, capital surplus, share premium reserve; **Kapitalrückzahlung** *f* FINANZ liquidating dividend; **Kapitalspritze** *f* *infrml* VW injection of new capital

kapitalsteuerpflichtig: ~er Gewinn *m* STEUER chargeable capital gains

Kapital: **Kapitalstock** *m* FINANZ capital fund, capital stock; **Kapitalstrom** *m* VW flow of funds; **Kapitalstruktur** *f* FINANZ, RECHNUNG, VW capital structure, financial structure; **Kapitalstrukturkennziffer** *f* BANK, RECHNUNG gearing ratio (*BrE*), leverage ratio (*AmE*); **Kapitalsumme** *f* FINANZ capital sum; **Kapitaltheorie** *f* VW capital theory; **Kapitaltransfer** *m* BANK funds transfer; **Kapitalübertragung** *f* FINANZ capital transfer; **Kapitalübertragungssteuer** *f* STEUER capital transfer tax (*BrE*) (*CTT*); **Kapitalumschichtung** *f* FINANZ recapitalization; **Kapitalumschlag** *m* RECHNUNG asset turnover, VERWALT equity turnover; **Kapitalumstrukturierung** *f* BÖRSE capital reorganization; **Kapitalveräußerungsverlust** *m* FINANZ, VW capital loss; **Kapitalverkehr** *m* FINANZ capital transaction, capital flow; **Kapitalverkehrsbilanz** *f* VW capital account, balance on capital account, balance of capital movements; **Kapitalverlust** *m* FINANZ, VW capital loss, leakage

kapitalvermehrend: ~er technischer Fortschritt *m* VW capital-augmenting technical progress

Kapital: **Kapitalverminderung** *f* FINANZ capital write-down; **Kapitalvermögen** *nt* STEUER capital assets; **Kapitalverschleiß** *m* VW capital consumption, capital consumption allowance; **Kapitalverzinsung** *f* FINANZ, RECHNUNG, VW rate of return, return on capital employed (*ROCE*), return on capital (*ROC*); **Kapitalwert** *m* BÖRSE principal value, FINANZ actual cash value (*a.c.v.*), net present value (*NPV*), RECHNUNG capital value, net present value (*NPV*), fair value, VERSICH cash value, VW capital value, net present value (*NPV*), capitalized value; **Kapitalwertmethode** *f* VW present value method; **Kapitalwertminderung** *f* FINANZ, VW capital loss; **Kapitalwertzuwachs** *m* FINANZ, VW capital profit; **Kapitalzinsen** *m pl* BANK simple interest; **Kapitalzufluß** *m* RECHNUNG inflow, VW capital inflow; **Kapitalzuführung** *f* VW injection of new capital; **Kapitalzuschuß** *m* FINANZ grant; **Kapitalzustrom** *m* FINANZ cash inflow; **Kapitalzuteilung** *f* FINANZ capital allotment, VW capital rationing; **Kapitalzuwachs** *m* BÖRSE capital growth, VW capital increase, capital gain, capital gains; **Kapitalzuwachs** *m* nach Steuern FINANZ, VW capital gains after tax

Kapitän *m* PERSON, TRANSP captain, master; **Kapitäneigner** *m* PERSON master owner; **Kapitänspatent** *nt* TRANSP *Schiffahrt* master's certificate

Kapitel *nt* RECHT *eines Gesetzes* section

Karat *nt* IND *Gold* carat

kardinal: ~er Nutzen *m* VW cardinal utility

Karenzurlaub *m* PERSON *für Mütter* maternity leave, *für Väter* paternity leave

Kargoversicherung *f* VERSICH cargo insurance

Karriere *f* PERSON career; ◆ jdn für eine schnelle ~ vorsehen PERSON *Mitarbeiter* fast-track sb

Karriere: **Karriereaussichten** *f pl* PERSON career prospects; **Karriereentwicklungsdarlehen** *nt* PERSON Career Development Loan (*CDL*) (*BrE*); **Karriereerwartungen** *f pl* PERSON career expectations; **Karriereleiter** *f* PERSON promotion ladder; **die Kar-**

riereleiter erklimmen *phr* PERSON climb the promotion ladder; **Karriereplanung** *f* PERSON career management, career planning; **Karriereziel** *nt* PERSON *berufliche Entwicklung* career goals

Karte *f* COMP *Hardware* card, FREI, GESCHÄFT ticket, PERSON card index, TRANSP ticket; ◆ seine Karten auf den Tisch legen *infrml* GESCHÄFT show one's hand (*infrml*); seine ~ stechen PERSON punch the time clock

Kartei *f* COMP index file, VERWALT card index, index-card file, card catalog (*AmE*), card catalogue (*BrE*), index file; **Karteikarte** *f* COMP data card

Kartell *nt* PERSON cartel, RECHT combine, VW restrictive practices, cartel; ~ mit gemeinsamer Einkaufs- oder Verkaufsorganisation VW cartel with joint purchasing or marketing organization; ~ höherer Ordnung VW pool; **Kartellamt** *nt* V&M Office of Fair Trading (*OFT*); **Kartellausschuß** *m* FINANZ cartel commission; **Kartellbehörde** *f* V&M Office of Fair Trading (*OFT*); **Kartellgericht** *nt* RECHT Restrictive Practices Court (*BrE*); **Kartellgesetz** *nt* RECHT antimonopoly law, antitrust law, antitrust act; **Kartellgesetzgebung** *f* RECHT antimonopoly laws, antitrust acts, antitrust laws; **Kartellkommission** *f* FINANZ, POL antitrust commission; **Kartellrecht** *nt* RECHT antimonopoly law, antitrust law, cartel law, competition laws

Karte: **Kartenablage** *f* COMP card bin; **Kartenbesitzer, in** *m,f* FREI, TRANSP ticket holder; **Kartendatei** *f* COMP, VERWALT index file; **Karteninhaber, in** *m,f* BANK cardholder; **Karteninhabergebühr** *f* BANK cardholder fee; **Kartenleser** *m* COMP card reader; **Kartenmischer** *m* COMP collator; **Kartenschwarzhändler, in** *m,f* FREI ticket tout; **Kartenverkaufsstelle** *f* FREI, GESCHÄFT, TRANSP booking office, ticket agency, ticket office; **Kartenvorverkaufsstelle** *f* FREI ticket agency

Karton *m* IND *Pappe* cardboard, *Packung* carton

kaschiert: ~e Pappe *f* IND pasteboard

Käseblatt *nt* *infrml* MEDIEN rag (*infrml*)

Kassa *f obs* BÖRSE, FINANZ, VERSICH, VW cash; **Kassageschäft** *nt* BÖRSE spot transaction; **Kassageschäfte** *nt pl* BÖRSE cash dealings; **Kassakredit** *m* FINANZ spot credit; **Kassakurse** *m pl* BÖRSE cash market rates; **Kassakurs** *m* und **Terminkurs** *m* des Pfundes VW pound spot and forward; **Kassamarkt** *m* BÖRSE spot market, cash market; am Kassamarkt verkaufen *phr* BÖRSE sell spot; **Kassamarktwechselkurse** *m pl* BÖRSE cash market rates; **Kassamonat** *m* BÖRSE spot month; **Kassanotierung** *f* BÖRSE spot quotation; **Kassaposition** *f* BÖRSE spot position; **Kassaschaden** *m* VERSICH cash loss; **Kassa- und Termin- Dollarkurs** *m* FINANZ dollar spot and forward; **Kassaware** *f* BÖRSE spot commodity

Kasse *f* BANK cash desk, FINANZ cash, FREI *Sportveranstaltung* ticket office, *Theater* box office, GESCHÄFT *Zahlstelle* cash desk, till, *Bargeld* cash, cash on hand, V&M *Supermarkt* checkout, checkout lane, till, vw cash; ~ gegen Dokumente IMP/EXP cash against documents (*c.a.d., CAD*); ~ vor Lieferung GESCHÄFT cash before delivery (*CBD*); ~ für Schmiergelder FINANZ, POL slush fund; ◆ die ~ BANK the Exchequer (*BrE*) (*Exch.*); ~ machen FINANZ cash up *infrml* (*BrE*), RECHNUNG balance the cash; per ~ verkaufen BÖRSE sell spot

Kasse: **Kassenabstimmung** *f* VW reconciliation of cash; **Kassenabteilung** *f* FINANZ cashiering department

(*BrE*); **Kassenanweisung** *f* BANK bank check (*AmE*), bank cheque (*BrE*), V&M cash order (*co*); **Kassenausgang** *m* RECHNUNG cash disbursement; **Kassenausgangsbuch** *nt* RECHNUNG cash payments journal; **Kassenauszahlung** *f* RECHNUNG cash disbursement; **Kassenbeleg** *m* RECHNUNG cash record, cash voucher, V&M sales record; **Kassenbericht** *m* RECHNUNG cash statement; **Kassenbestand** *m* FINANZ cash in hand, RECHNUNG cash balance; **Kassenbestände** *m pl* RECHNUNG cash holdings; **Kassenbestand** *m* **und Verbindlichkeiten** *f pl* BANK cash and debt position; **Kassenbon** *m* GESCHÄFT sales slip; **Kassenbuch** *nt* BANK book, RECHNUNG, VERWALT cash book, cash journal, petty cash book; **Kassenbuchung** *f* RECHNUNG, VERWALT cash entry; **Kassenbudget** *nt* RECHNUNG cash forecast; **Kassendefizit** *nt* FINANZ cash deficit; **Kassendispositionsmethode** *f* MGMNT cash management technique; **Kasseneingänge** *m pl* RECHNUNG cash receipts; **Kasseneinnahmen** *f pl* RECHNUNG cash receipts; **Kasseneinnahmenbuch** *nt* RECHNUNG cash receipts journal; **Kassenfluß** *m* FINANZ cash flow; **Kassenführer, in** *m,f* PERSON cash manager, cashier; **Kassenhaltung** *f* FINANZ, RECHNUNG cash management; **Kassenhaltungspolitik** *f* vw policy of optimum; **Kassenkonto** *nt* BANK, RECHNUNG cash account; **Kassenleistungen** *f pl* SOZIAL, VERSICH health benefits; **Kassenplan** *m* RECHNUNG cash forecast; **Kassenraum** *m* VERWALT cash office; **Kassensaldo** *m* RECHNUNG cash balance; **Kassenschalter** *m* BANK cash desk; **Kassenscheck** *m* BANK cashier's check (*AmE*), cashier's cheque (*BrE*), counter check (*AmE*), counter cheque (*BrE*); **Kassenschlager** *m* *infrml* GESCHÄFT money-spinner (*infrml*), MEDIEN, V&M *Buch, Film* blockbuster (*infrml*); **Kassenstand** *m* RECHNUNG cash position; **Kassenstelle** *f* FINANZ cashiering department (*BrE*); **Kassenstreifen** *m* BANK till receipt; **Kassenüberschuß** *m* FINANZ cash surplus, over; **Kassenverwaltung** *f* FINANZ, RECHNUNG cash management; **Kassenvorschußsystem** *nt* RECHNUNG imprest system; **Kassenzettel** *m* GESCHÄFT sales slip

Kassette *f* COMP, MEDIEN cassette; **Kassettengerät** *nt* COMP, MEDIEN cassette player; **Kassettenrecorder** *m* COMP, MEDIEN cassette recorder, cassette tape recorder

kassieren *vt* GESCHÄFT collect, encash, *infrml Anerkennung* receive, *infrml verdienen* pull in (*infrml*)

Kassierer, in *m,f* BANK teller, V&M *Kassenführer* cashier

Kassiererkarte *f* BANK bank teller card

Kästchen: das ~ ankreuzen *phr* GESCHÄFT check the box (*AmE*), tick the box (*BrE*)

Kaste *f* POL class, caste

Kasten *m* TRANSP, V&M box, case; **~ für Verbesserungsvorschläge** GESCHÄFT suggestion box; **Kastenanhänger** *m* TRANSP box trailer

Kat *m* (*Katalysator*) UMWELT *in einem Fahrzeug* cat (*catalytic converter*)

Katalog *m* GESCHÄFT catalog (*AmE*), catalogue (*BrE*); **Katalogpreis** *m* GESCHÄFT catalog price (*AmE*), catalogue price (*BrE*), V&M list price

Katalysator *m* GESCHÄFT catalyst, UMWELT (*Kat*) *in einem Fahrzeug* catalytic converter (*cat*)

Kataster *m* GRUND land register (*BrE*), plat book (*AmE*); **Katasteramt** *nt* GRUND *Grundbuchamt* land registry; **Katasterplan** *m* GRUND plat, cadastral survey

Katastrophe *f* VERSICH catastrophe, disaster; **Katastrophendeckung** *f* VERSICH catastrophe cover; **Katastrophenhilfswerk** *nt* **der Vereinten Nationen** VW United Nations Disaster and Relief Organization (*UNDRO*); **Katastrophenklausel** *f* VERSICH disaster clause; **Katastrophenreserve** *f* VERSICH catastrophe reserve; **Katastrophenrisiko** *nt* VERSICH catastrophe hazard, catastrophe risk; **Katastrophenrisikopolice** *f* VERSICH catastrophe policy; **Katastrophenrücklage** *f* VERSICH catastrophe reserve; **Katastrophenschaden** *m* GESCHÄFT catastrophic loss; **Katastrophentheorie** *f* MATH catastrophe theory

Kategorie *f* GESCHÄFT category, PATENT category, class, STEUER class

kategorisch: ~ erklären *phr* GESCHÄFT state categorically

kategorisiert: ~e Aktie *f* BÖRSE classified stock

Kathodenstrahlröhre *f* (*CRT*) COMP *Bildschirme* cathode ray tube (*CRT*)

Katona-Effekt *m* VW Katona effect

Kauf *m* GESCHÄFT purchase; **~ zur Abrechnung** BÖRSE purchase for settlement; **~ zum Börsenschluß** BÖRSE closing purchase (*BrE*); **~ in Fremdwährung** RECHNUNG purchase denominated in foreign currency; **~ auf Hausse** BÖRSE bull buying; **~ auf Kredit** V&M credit sale; **~ auf Lieferung** BÖRSE forward buying; **~ auf Probe** V&M sale on approval; **~ mit Rückgaberecht** V&M sale or return, on sale or return; **~ zur sofortigen Lieferung** BÖRSE, FINANZ cash purchase; **~ unter Eigentumsvorbehalt** V&M conditional sales agreement; **~ unter Inzahlungnahme** GESCHÄFT part exchange; **~ und Verkauf** *m* **von Effekten** BÖRSE portfolio management; **~ von Wirtschaftsgütern** GESCHÄFT purchase of assets; ♦ **einen ~ vornehmen** GESCHÄFT make a purchase

Kauf: **Kaufabrechnung** *f* BÖRSE bought note; **Kaufangebot** *nt* GESCHÄFT bid; **Kaufanreiz** *m* V&M sales appeal, sales incentive

kaufen *vt* GESCHÄFT *erwerben* purchase, buy, *bestechen* bribe

Kaufentscheidung *f* GESCHÄFT purchase decision

Käufer, in *m,f* GESCHÄFT buyer, purchaser, V&M shopper, purchaser; **~ von Kunst** MEDIEN art buyer; **~ von Sendezeit** MEDIEN, V&M airtime buyer; **Käuferkonzentration** *f* V&M buyer concentration; **Käuferkredit** *m* BANK buyer credit; **Käufermarkt** *m* BÖRSE, GRUND, VW buyer's market; **Käuferoption** *f* BÖRSE buyer's option; **Käuferreaktion** *f* V&M buyer response; **Käuferreaktion** *f* **in Routinesituationen** V&M routine response behavior (*AmE*), routine response behaviour (*BrE*); **Käuferschichten** *f pl* V&M buying classes; **Käuferunlust** *f* V&M consumer resistance; **Käuferverhalten** *nt* V&M buyer behavior (*AmE*), buyer behaviour (*BrE*)

Kauf: **Kaufflut** *f* GESCHÄFT buying surge; **Kauffrau** *f* GESCHÄFT businesswoman, merchant (*mcht*), *Ladenverkäuferin* saleswoman; **Kaufgewohnheiten** *f pl* GESCHÄFT buying habits; **Kauf- und-Halte-Strategie** *f* BÖRSE buy-and-hold strategy; **Kaufhaus** *nt* V&M department store; **Kaufinteressent, in** *m,f* V&M prospective buyer; **Kaufkosten** *pl* RECHNUNG purchase cost

Kaufkraft *f* GESCHÄFT spending power, purchasing power, VW buying power, *einer Währung* purchasing power; **~ des Geldes** VW value of money; **~ des Kunden** V&M

consumer buying power; ◆ **an ~ verlieren** VW *Währung* depreciate

Kaufkraft: **Kaufkraftparität** *f* VW purchasing power parity (*PPP*)

käuflich: ~er Erwerb *m* FINANZ purchase acquisition

kauflustig *adj* GESCHÄFT eager to buy

Kauf: **Kaufmann** *m* (*Kfm*) GESCHÄFT businessman, merchant (*mcht*), *Ladenverkäufer* salesman

kaufmännisch *adj* GESCHÄFT commercial; **~e Analyse** *f* FINANZ commercial analysis; **~e Ausbildung** *f* PERSON commercial training; **~er Beruf** *m* GESCHÄFT commercial occupation; **~es Bestätigungsschreiben** *nt* RECHT *Vertragsrecht* confirmation notes, letter of confirmation; **~er Direktor** *m*, **~e Direktorin** *f* MGMNT, PERSON business manager, commercial director; **~er Geschäftsverkehr** *m* RECHT *Vertragsrecht* business dealings; **~er Leiter** *m*, **~e Leiterin** *f* MGMNT, PERSON commercial manager; **~es &-Zeichen** *nt* COMP, MEDIEN ampersand; **~es Unternehmen** *nt* IMP/EXP trading company

Kauf: **Kaufmotiv** *nt* V&M buying motive

kaufmotivierend: ~er Faktor *m* V&M purchasing motivator

Kaufoption *f* BÖRSE call option, GESCHÄFT buyer's option; **~ am Terminkontraktmarkt** BÖRSE long futures position; ◆ **mit ~** BÖRSE at call

Kaufoption: **Kaufoptionsdelta** *nt* BÖRSE call delta; **Kaufoptionssicherungsgeschäft** *nt* BÖRSE call-selling hedge

Kauf: **Kaufpreis** *m* GESCHÄFT price (*pr.*), buying price, purchase price, V&M purchase price; **Kaufprozeß** *m* GESCHÄFT buying process; **Kaufsignal** *nt* V&M buying signal; **Kaufübernahmefazilität** *f* FINANZ purchase underwriting facility (*PUF*); **Kaufunlust** *f* V&M sales resistance; **Kaufverhalten** *nt* V&M buying behavior (*AmE*), buying behaviour (*BrE*); **Kaufverhalten** *nt* **in Routinesituationen** V&M routine response behavior (*AmE*), routine response behaviour (*BrE*); **Kauf- und Verkaufsabkommen** *nt* VW buy-and-sell agreement; **Kauf- und Verkaufsaufträge entgegennehmen** *phr* BÖRSE make a market; **Kauf- und Verkaufsstrategie** *f* BÖRSE buy-and-write strategy; **Kaufverpflichtung** *f* GRUND, RECHT *Enteignungsbeschluß* highway order, V&M obligation to buy; **ohne Kaufverpflichtung** *phr* V&M no obligation to buy; **Kaufvertrag** *m* GRUND bargain and sale, RECHT contract of sale, V&M sales contract; **Kaufwelle** *f* GESCHÄFT buying surge; **Kaufwunsch** *m* V&M desire to purchase; **Kaufzwang** *m* V&M compulsive buying

Kaution *f* FINANZ security, GRUND *Mietvorauszahlung* key money, deposit, PATENT deposit, RECHT bail bond, caution money, bail, VERSICH fidelity guarantee; **~ zur Ausübung einer bestimmten Tätigkeit** VERSICH position schedule bond; ◆ **jdn gegen ~ freilassen** RECHT release sb on bail; **jdn durch ~ aus der Haft freibekommen** RECHT bail sb out, bale sb out; **die ~ stellen für jdn** RECHT bail sb out, bale sb out

Kaution: **Kautionsverpflichtung** *f* RECHT *Treuhänder* fiduciary bond; **Kautionsversicherungspolice** *f* VERSICH fidelity bond

Kautschukmilch *f* IND latex

kB *abbr* (*Kilobyte*) COMP kB (*kilobyte*)

KByte *abbr* (*Kilobyte*) COMP kB (*kilobyte*)

Kehrtwende *f* GESCHÄFT, POL *Methode, Meinung* about-face (*AmE*), about-turn (*BrE*)

Kehrtwendung *f* GESCHÄFT, POL *Methode, Meinung* about-face (*AmE*), about-turn (*BrE*)

Keil *m* TRANSP wedge; **Keilpalette** *f* TRANSP key pallet

Kellerwechsel *m* BÖRSE kite

Kennedy-Runde *f* VW Kennedy Round

Kenner *m* GESCHÄFT authority, expert; **~ eines Unternehmens** GESCHÄFT corporate insider

Kennsatzklausel *f* RECHT, TRANSP *Fracht* label clause (*LC*)

Kenntnis *f* GESCHÄFT acquaintance, knowledge; ◆ **in ~** GESCHÄFT aware; **etw zur ~ bringen** RECHT *Vertragsrecht* give notice of sth; **~ von etw geben** RECHT give notice of sth; **jdn von etw in ~ setzen** GESCHÄFT acquaint sb with sth; **in voller ~ der Sachlage** RECHT in full knowledge of the facts

kenntnisreich *adj* GESCHÄFT knowledgeable, well-informed, POL well-informed

Kennung *f* COMP label, answerback code

Kennwort *nt* GESCHÄFT, V&M watchword

Kennzeichen *nt* BANK hallmark, COMP flag, symbol, GESCHÄFT, PATENT, V&M symbol

kennzeichnen *vt* GESCHÄFT brand, V&M label, VW earmark

kennzeichnend *adj* GESCHÄFT specific; **~er Teil** *m* PATENT characterizing portion

Kennzeichnung *f* FINANZ marking; **Kennzeichnungsklausel** *f* RECHT, TRANSP *Fracht* label clause (*LC*)

Kennziffer *f* GESCHÄFT reference number; **Kennzifferanzeige** *f* V&M blind advertisement; **Kennziffernanalyse** *f* MATH ratio analysis

Keogh-Plan *m* FINANZ Keogh Plan

Kern *m* COMP core, GESCHÄFT *eines Problem* core, gist, IND center (*AmE*), centre (*BrE*), PATENT gist; **Kernbereich** *m* GESCHÄFT flagship site; **Kerndefinition** *f* GESCHÄFT core definition; **Kernfächer** *nt pl* SOZIAL core curriculum; **Kernfinanzierung** *f* FINANZ core funding; **Kernfirma** *f* VW core firm; **Kernforschungszentrum** *nt* IND nuclear science center (*AmE*) (*NSC*), nuclear science centre (*BrE*) (*NSC*); **Kerngeschäft** *nt* FINANZ bottom line, GESCHÄFT grassroots; **Kerninflation** *f* VW core inflation; **Kerninflationsrate** *f* VW core inflation rate; **Kernkraft** *f* IND nuclear energy, nuclear power; **Kernkraftwerk** *nt* (*KKW*) IND nuclear power station; **Kernphysiker, in** *m,f* IND, PERSON nuclear physicist; **Kernprodukt** *nt* V&M core product; **Kernpunkt** *m* GESCHÄFT focal point; **Kernreaktor** *m* IND nuclear reactor (*NR*); **Kernreaktoranlage** *f* IND nuclear plant, nuclear power station; **Kernregion** *f* VW core region; **Kernspeicher** *m* COMP core storage, core memory; **Kernstadt** *f* GRUND, UMWELT, VW inner city; **Kernstunden** *f pl* IND, VERWALT core hours; **Kernumfang** *m* COMP *Speicher* core size; **Kernzeit** *f* IND core hours, PERSON *Gleitzeit* core time, VERWALT core hours

Kerosin *nt* TRANSP aviation turbine fuel, kerosene

Kesselraum *m* GESCHÄFT boiler room (*AmE*)

Kette *f* COMP string, IND chain

ketten *vt* COMP concatenate

Kette: **Kettenabwanderung** *f* GESCHÄFT chain migration; **Kettenbanksystem** *nt* BANK chain banking

(*AmE*); **Kettenladen** *m* V&M chain store; **Kettenproduktion** *f* IND chain production

Keynes: ~sche Allgemeine Theorie *f* VW Keynes' general theory; **~scher Effekt** *m* VW Keynes effect; **~sche Erwartungen** *f pl* VW Keynes expectations; **~sches Gleichgewicht** *nt* VW Keynesian equilibrium

keynesianisch *adj* VW Keynesian; **~e Wirtschaftstheorie** *f* VW Keynesian economics

Keynesianismus *m* VW Keynesianism

Keynes: ~sches Kreuzdiagramm *nt* VW Keynesian cross diagram; **~sche Lehre** *f* VW Keynesian economics; **~sche Politik** *f* VW Keynesian policy; **Keynes-Plan** *m* VW Keynes Plan

Keypad *nt jarg* COMP keypad

Kfm. *abbr* (*Kaufmann*) GESCHÄFT businessman, mcht (*merchant*), *Ladenverkäufer* salesman

Kfz *abbr* (*Kraftfahrzeug*) GESCHÄFT vehicle; **Kfz-Haftpflichtversicherung** *f* TRANSP, VERSICH third-party motor vehicle insurance; **Kfz-Steuer** *f* STEUER, TRANSP motor vehicle tax, road tax (*BrE*); **Kfz-Versicherung** *f* TRANSP, VERSICH automobile insurance (*AmE*), motor insurance (*BrE*)

kg *abbr* (*Kilogramm*) GESCHÄFT kg (*kilogram, kilogramme*)

KG *abbr* (*Kommanditgesellschaft*) BÖRSE limited partnership, private limited partnership, public limited partnership, GRUND resyndication limited partnership (*AmE*), RECHT limited partnership, private limited partnership, public limited partnership

KGV *abbr* (*Kurs-Gewinn-Verhältnis*) FINANZ P/E ratio (*price-earnings ratio*), PER (*price-earnings ratio*), RECHNUNG price-earnings multiple

KI *abbr* (*künstliche Intelligenz*) COMP AI (*artificial intelligence*)

Kiel *m* TRANSP keel

Kies *m infrml* GESCHÄFT bread (*infrml*), dosh (*infrml*) (*BrE*), dough (*infrml*), money, wampum (*infrml*) (*AmE*)

Kilo *nt* (*Kilogramm*) GESCHÄFT kilo (*kilogram, kilogramme*); **Kilobyte** *nt* (*KByte*) COMP kilobyte (*kB*); **Kilogramm** *nt* (*kg, Kilo*) GESCHÄFT kilogram (*kg, kilo*), kilogramme (*kg, kilo*); **Kiloliter** *m* (*kl*) GESCHÄFT kiloliter (*AmE*) (*kl*), kilolitre (*BrE*) (*kl*)

Kilometer *m* (*km*) GESCHÄFT kilometer (*AmE*) (*km*), kilometre (*BrE*) (*km*); **~ pro Stunde** (*km/h*) GESCHÄFT kilometers per hour (*AmE*) (*km/h, kmph*), kilometres per hour (*BrE*) (*km/h, kmph*); **Kilometergeld** *nt* STEUER ≈ mileage allowance, ≈ motor mileage allowance (*BrE*), TRANSP per-kilometer rate (*AmE*), per-kilometre rate (*BrE*); **Kilometersatz** *nt* TRANSP per-kilometer rate (*AmE*), per-kilometre rate (*BrE*)

Kilo: Kilotonne *f* (*kt*) GESCHÄFT kiloton (*kt*), kilotonne (*kt*); **Kilowatt** *nt* (*kW*) GESCHÄFT kilowatt (*kW*); **Kilowattstunde** *f* (*kWh*) GESCHÄFT kilowatt-hour (*kWh*)

Kind *nt* SOZIAL, STEUER, VERSICH child; ♦ **auf Kinder ausgerichtet** SOZIAL child-centered (*AmE*), child-centred (*BrE*)

Kinder- *in cpds* SOZIAL, STEUER, VERSICH child; **Kinderbetreuungseinrichtungen** *f pl* PERSON childcare facilities; **Kinderermäßigung** *f* FREI reduction for children; **Kinderfreibetrag** *m* SOZIAL, STEUER child allowance (*BrE*), children's allowance (*AmE*); **Kindergarten** *m* SOZIAL kindergarten, nursery school, preschool center (*AmE*), preschool centre (*BrE*);

Kindergeld *nt* SOZIAL, STEUER child allowance (*AmE*), child benefit (*BrE*), family allowance (*BrE*); **Kinderlebensversicherung** *f* VERSICH child's insurance; **Kinderlebensversicherung** *f* mit aufgeschobenem Leistungstermin VERSICH child's deferred assurance

kinderorientiert *adj* SOZIAL child-centered (*AmE*), child-centred (*BrE*)

kinderreich: ~e Familie *f* V&M large family

Kinder-: Kinderspiel *nt infrml* GESCHÄFT child's play (*infrml*), walkover (*infrml*); **Kinderunfallversicherung** *f* VERSICH child's accident insurance; **Kinderzulage** *f* SOZIAL, STEUER child allowance (*AmE*), child benefit (*BrE*), family allowance (*BrE*)

kindgemäß *adj* SOZIAL child-centered (*AmE*), child-centred (*BrE*)

Kino *nt* FREI, MEDIEN cinema (*BrE*), movie theater (*AmE*); **Kinofilm** *m* FREI, MEDIEN film, motion picture (*AmE*), movie (*AmE*), picture; **Kinoreklame** *f* V&M film advertising, cinema advertising (*BrE*), motion picture advertising (*AmE*); **Kinowerbung** *f* V&M film advertising, cinema advertising (*BrE*), motion picture advertising (*AmE*)

Kippanhänger *m* TRANSP tilt trailer

Kippschalter *m* COMP toggle, toggle switch

Kippschaltung *f* COMP flip-flop

Kiste *f* IMP/EXP, TRANSP box, case, crate; **Kistenrate** *f* TRANSP box rate; **Kistenverpackung** *f* TRANSP case packaging

Kitsch *m* V&M kitsch, trashy goods (*infrml*) (*AmE*)

kitzlig: in einer ~en Situation *phr* PERSON in the hot seat

KKW *abbr* (*Kernkraftwerk*) IND nuclear power station

kl *abbr* (*Kiloliter*) GESCHÄFT kl (*kiloliter AmE, kilolitre BrE*)

Klafter *m or nt obs* IND fathom (*fm*)

klagbar *adj* RECHT enforceable, actionable; **nicht ~** *adj* RECHT unenforceable, non-actionable; **nicht ~er Vertrag** *m* RECHT unenforceable contract

Klagbarkeit *f* RECHT enforceability, actionability

Klage *f* RECHT *Zivilprozeß* suit, lawsuit, action, complaint; **~ ohne feindliche Absicht** RECHT friendly suit; **~ im ordentlichen Zivilprozeß** RECHT legal action; **~ wegen irreführender Werbung** V&M false advertising claim; ♦ **eine ~ begründen** RECHT substantiate a claim; **~ erheben** RECHT enter a writ, issue a writ against sb; **gegen jdn ~ erheben** RECHT bring an action against sb; **gegen jdn öffentlich ~ erheben** RECHT bring an accusation against sb; **~ im ordentlichen Zivilprozeß erheben** RECHT take legal action

Klage: Klagebegründung *f* RECHT statement of claim; **Klageerwiderung** *f* GESCHÄFT answer; **Klagegrund** *m* RECHT cause of action

klagen *vi* RECHT sue

Klage: Klagenabwehr *f* gegen Versicherte VERSICH defence of suit against insured (*BrE*), defense of suit against insured (*AmE*)

Kläger, in *m,f* RECHT plaintiff

Klage: Klagerücknahme *f* RECHT abandonment of a complaint; **Klageschrift** *f* RECHT bill; **Klageverfahren** *nt* RECHT complaints procedure

Klammer *f* COMP, MEDIEN bracket, parenthesis

Klang *m* COMP, MEDIEN sound; **Klangeffekte** *m pl* MEDIEN sound effects

Klappcontainer *m* TRANSP collapsible container (*coltainer*)

Klappentext *m* MEDIEN blurb

klar *adj* GESCHÄFT clear, coherent; ♦ **etw ~ darstellen** GESCHÄFT make sth clear; **~ umrissen** GESCHÄFT clearcut

klar: **~e Denkweise** *f* GESCHÄFT clear thinking; **~e Linie** *f* MGMNT *eines Unternehmens* direction

klären *vt* GESCHÄFT *Frage* settle

Klarierung *f* IMP/EXP clearance, customs clearance; **~ von Schiffen** IMP/EXP, TRANSP clearance of ship; **Klarierungsagent** *m* IMP/EXP clearing agent

klarmachen *vt* GESCHÄFT spell out, *erklären* make clear, *erläutern* throw light on

Klarsichtpackung *f* V&M blister pack, bubble pack

Klarsichtverpackung *f* V&M blister packaging, bubble packaging

Klärung *f* UMWELT purification

Klasse *f* GESCHÄFT class, PATENT category, class, POL class, STEUER bracket, class; **Klasseneinteilung** *f* MATH class division; **Klassengrenze** *f* MATH class boundary; **Klassenhäufigkeit** *f* MATH class frequency; **Klassenkampf** *m* VW class struggle; **Klassenobjekt** *nt* GESCHÄFT class object; **Klassenspartheorie** *f* VW *Cambridge-Theorie des Wachstums* class savings theory; **Klassenzertifikat** *nt* TRANSP classification certificate; **Klassenzimmerbefragung** *f* V&M hall test

Klassifikation *f* GESCHÄFT, VERWALT classification; **~ nach Objekt** GESCHÄFT classification by object; **Klassifikationsgesellschaft** *f* GESCHÄFT classification society

klassifizieren *vt* GESCHÄFT, VERWALT categorize, classify

klassifiziert: **nicht ~** *adj* FINANZ not rated

Klassifizierung *f* GESCHÄFT categorization, classification, V&M rating, VERWALT categorization, classification; **~ von Emittenten** FINANZ rating; **~ von Schuldtiteln** FINANZ rating

klassisch: **~e Anlage** *f* BANK straight investment; **~es Beispiel** *nt* GESCHÄFT classic example; **~e Dichotomie** *f* VW classical dichotomy; **~es Modell** *nt* VW classical model; **~e Nationalökonomie** *f* VW classical economics; **~e Spartheorie** *f* VW classical savings theory

Klausel *f* PERSON, RECHT, VERSICH clause; **~ über allgemeine Ausschlüsse** VERSICH general exclusions clause; **~ zur Beitragsbefreiung** VERSICH noncontribution clause; **~ für böswillige Beschädigung** VERSICH malicious damage clause; **~ für eingestürzte Gebäude** VERSICH fallen building clause; **~ über die Erklärung der Vertragsaufhebung** VERSICH notice of cancellation clause; **~ zur Gefahrtragung** RECHT clause for the bearing of risk; **~ über höhere Gewalt** RECHT, VERSICH force majeure clause; **~ der Nichtversicherung** VERSICH not to insure clause; **~ über Schadensabwendung und Schadensminderung** VERSICH sue and labor clause (*AmE*) (*S/LC*), sue and labour clause (*BrE*) (*S/LC*); **~ über Schiffsverkauf** VERSICH sale of vessel clause; **~ vorsätzlicher oder böswilliger Taten** VERSICH malicious acts clause; ♦ **ohne Klauseln** GESCHÄFT no strings attached

Klebekarton *m* IND pasteboard

Kleidung *f* GESCHÄFT apparel (*AmE*), clothing (*BrE*); **Kleidungs- und Strickwarenherstellung** *f* IND apparel and wool industry (*AmE*), clothing trade (*BrE*); **Kleidungsstück** *nt* GESCHÄFT garment

Klein- *in cpds* FINANZ, GESCHÄFT, RECHNUNG petty, small

klein *adj* FINANZ, GESCHÄFT, RECHNUNG petty, small; ♦ **in ~en Gruppen kommen** GESCHÄFT trickle in; **in ~en Mengen kaufen** GESCHÄFT buy in small quantities

klein: **~e Ausgaben** *f pl* FINANZ petty expenses, RECHNUNG petty cash, petty expenses; **~er Betrieb** *m* IND workshop; **~er Handkoffer** *m* GESCHÄFT valise; **~e Holding** *f* STEUER personal holding company (*AmE*) (*PHC*); **~e Kasse** *f* RECHNUNG petty cash; **der ~e Mann** *m* GESCHÄFT the man in the street; **~e und mittelständische Unternehmen** *nt pl* (*KMU*) GESCHÄFT small and medium-sized enterprises (*SME*); **~er Spekulant** *m*, **~e Spekulantin** *f* BÖRSE small speculator; **~e Spesen** *f pl* FINANZ petty expenses; **~e technische Panne** *f* GESCHÄFT, POL, VW glitch; **~e Tiger** *m pl infrml* VW little dragons (*infrml*); **~es Unternehmen** *nt* GESCHÄFT small business, small enterprise, small firm, V&M *Werbeagentur* shop

Klein-: **Kleinaktien** *f pl* BÖRSE penny shares (*BrE*), penny stock (*AmE*); **Kleinanleger, in** *m,f* FINANZ small investor; **Kleinanzeige** *f* V&M classified ad (*BrE*), classified advertisement, small, small ad; **Kleinanzeigenwerbung** *f* V&M classified display advertising; **Kleinauflage** *f* IND short run (*SR*); **Kleinbauer** *m* VW smallholder; **Kleinbetrieb** *m* GESCHÄFT small business, small firm, small enterprise, PERSON small employer; **Kleinbuchstabe** *m* COMP, MEDIEN lower-case letter

kleinere: **~ Forderungen** *f pl* RECHT small claims

Klein-: **Kleinfirma** *f* GESCHÄFT small business, small firm, small enterprise

kleingedruckt *adj* RECHT *in einem Vertrag* in small print

Klein-: **Kleingeld** *nt* GESCHÄFT loose change, small change, peanuts (*infrml*); **Kleinindustrie** *f* IND small industry; **Kleininserat** *nt* V&M classified ad (*BrE*), classified advertisement, small, small ad; **Kleinkonjunktur** *f* VW boomlet (*infrml*); **Kleinlochstreifenleser** *m* COMP tag reader; **Kleinobligation** *f* BÖRSE baby bond; **Kleinplakat** *nt* **mit Werbung zum Aufstellen** V&M shelf talker; **Kleinrad** *nt* TRANSP pinion; **Kleinrechner** *m* COMP microcomputer

.kleinste: **~r gemeinsamer Nenner** *m* GESCHÄFT lowest common denominator; **~s Glied** *nt* VW least term; **~ oberste Schranke** *f* VW least upper bound

Klein-: **Kleintastatur** *f* COMP keypad; **Kleinunternehmen** *nt* GESCHÄFT small business, small enterprise, small firm; **Kleinunternehmerkapitalismus** *m* VW lemonade-stand capitalism

Klemme: **aus der ~ helfen** *phr infrml* GESCHÄFT bail out, bale out; **in der ~ sitzen** *phr infrml* GESCHÄFT be in a jam (*infrml*), be in a fix (*infrml*), be in a tight spot (*infrml*)

klicken *vi* COMP *Maustaste* click

Klient, in *m,f* GESCHÄFT client

Klima *nt* SOZIAL, UMWELT, VW climate; **Klimaanlage** *f* GESCHÄFT air conditioning; **mit Klimaanlage ausgestattet** *adj* GESCHÄFT air-conditioned, **mit Klimaanlage austatten** *phr* GESCHÄFT air-condition

klimatisieren *vt* GESCHÄFT air-condition

klimatisiert *adj* GESCHÄFT air-conditioned

Klimatisierung *f* GESCHÄFT air conditioning

klingend: **in ~er Münze zahlen** *phr* GESCHÄFT pay in specie

Klinkenputzer *m infrml* GESCHÄFT, V&M door-to-door salesman

Klinkenputzerin *f infrml* GESCHÄFT, V&M door-to-door saleswoman

Klischee *nt* GESCHÄFT *Redewendung* cliché, MEDIEN *Typographie* block; **ein ~ umgebender Text** *m* MEDIEN runaround; **Klischeeabzug** *m* V&M block pull

Klon *m* COMP, GESCHÄFT clone, IND clone, knock-off (*infrml*)

klonen *vt* COMP clone

Klub *nt* GESCHÄFT club; **Klubgut** *nt* VW club good; **Klubtheorie** *f* VW theory of clubs

klug *adj* GESCHÄFT knowledgeable; **~er Kopf** *m infrml* GESCHÄFT child prodigy, whiz kid (*infrml*)

Klumpenauswahlverfahren *nt* V&M *Marktforschung* cluster sampling, cluster analysis

km *abbr* (*Kilometer*) GESCHÄFT km (*kilometer AmE, kilometre BrE*)

km/h *abbr* (*Kilometer pro Stunde*) GESCHÄFT km/h (*kilometers per hour AmE, kilometres per hour BrE*), kmph (*kilometers per hour AmE, kilometres per hour BrE*)

KMU *abbr* (*kleine und mittelständische Unternehmen*) GESCHÄFT SME (*small and medium-sized enterprises*)

knapp 1. *adj* VW scarce, GESCHÄFT concise; ♦ **~ an Bargeld** FINANZ cash-poor; **über ein ~es Budget verfügen** FINANZ be on a tight budget; **~ bei Kasse sein** GESCHÄFT be skint; **~ werden** GESCHÄFT run short; **2.** *adv* ♦ **nach ~ bemessenem Zeitplan arbeiten** GESCHÄFT work to a very tight schedule

knapp: **~e Deckung** *f* MEDIEN scant coverage

Knappheit *f* VW scarcity, shortage; **Knappheitsindex** *m* VW scarcity index

knausern: **~ und sparen** *phr* GESCHÄFT scrimp and save

Knebelregelung *f* POL *zur Schließung einer Debatte* gag rule

Knebelungsvertrag *m* RECHT *Vertragsrecht* adhesion contract

Knete *f infrml* GESCHÄFT bread (*infrml*), dosh (*infrml*) (*BrE*), dough (*infrml*), money, wampum (*infrml*) (*AmE*)

knifflig: **~es Problem** *nt* GESCHÄFT tricky situation; **in einer ~en Situation** *phr* PERSON in the hot seat

Knopf *m* COMP knob

Knoten *m* COMP *Rechner* node, GESCHÄFT knot

Know-how *nt infrml* GESCHÄFT, PATENT know-how (*infrml*); **Know-how-Vertrag** *m* RECHT *geistiges Eigentum* know-how agreement

Koalition *f* POL *Regierung* alliance, coalition; **Koalitionsbündnis** *nt* POL coalition alliance; **Koalitionsfreiheit** *f* POL freedom of association; **Koalitionspartei** *f* POL *von mehreren Parteien* coalition party; **Koalitionsrecht** *nt* POL right to associate; **Koalitionsregierung** *f* POL coalition government

Koaxialkabel *nt* COMP coaxial cable

Kodebox *f* IMP/EXP code box

Kodex *m* COMP code, GESCHÄFT rule book, RECHT code

Kodier- *in cpds* RECHNUNG coding

kodieren *vt* COMP encode, encrypt

Kodier-: **Kodierhandbuch** *nt* RECHNUNG coding manual; **Kodiersystem** *nt* RECHNUNG coding system

Kodierung *f* BANK encoding, COMP encryption, *Programmiersprache* coding

kodifizieren *vt* PATENT, RECHT codify

kodifiziert: **~es Recht** *nt* GESCHÄFT codified law, PATENT, RECHT statute law

Kodirektor, in *m,f* MGMNT co-director, co-manager

Kodizil *nt* RECHT codicil

koedukativ *adj* SOZIAL *Schule, Schulwesen* coeducational (*co-ed*)

Koeffizient *m* MATH coefficient

Koffer *m* FREI, TRANSP case, suitcase; **Kofferkuli** *m* FREI, TRANSP baggage trolley; **Kofferraum** *m* TRANSP boot (*BrE*), trunk (*AmE*)

kognitiv *adj* GESCHÄFT cognitive; **~e Arbeitsplatzanalyse** *f* VERWALT cognitive ergonomics; **~es Verhalten** *nt* MGMNT, V&M cognitive behavior (*AmE*), cognitive behaviour (*BrE*)

Kohäsion *f* GESCHÄFT cohesion; **Kohäsionsfonds** *m* VW cohesion fund

Kohle *f* GESCHÄFT *infrml Geld* bread (*infrml*), cash, dosh (*infrml*) (*BrE*), dough (*infrml*), wampum (*infrml*) (*AmE*), IND, UMWELT carbon, coal

Kohle: **Kohleindustrie** *f* IND, UMWELT coal industry; **Kohlekai** *m* TRANSP coal berth; **Kohlenantrieb** *m* TRANSP coal propulsion; **Kohlenbergbau** *m* IND, UMWELT *Grube* coal mine, *Industrie* coal industry, coal mining

Kohlendioxyd *nt* IND, TRANSP, UMWELT carbon dioxide; **Kohlendioxydanlage** *f* TRANSP carbon dioxide system; **Kohlendioxydemissionen** *f pl* IND, TRANSP, UMWELT carbon dioxide emissions; **Kohlendioxydsteuer** *f* (*CO$_2$-Steuer*) STEUER carbon dioxide tax (*CO$_2$ tax*)

Kohle: **Kohlengrube** *f* IND, UMWELT coal mine; **Kohlengrubegarantiebedingungen** *f pl* TRANSP colliery guarantee terms; **Kohlenlagerstätte** *f* UMWELT coal deposit; **Kohlenmonoxyd** *nt* IND, TRANSP, UMWELT carbon monoxide; **Kohlensäuresystem** *nt* TRANSP carbon dioxide system; **Kohlenschiff** *nt* TRANSP collier; **Kohlenstoffemissionen** *f pl* IND, UMWELT carbon emissions; **Kohlenwasserstoff** *m* UMWELT hydrocarbon; **Kohlenzeche** *f* IND, UMWELT coal mine; **Kohlepapier** *nt* KOMM carbon paper; **Kohlereserve** *f* UMWELT coal reserves; **Kohletransporter** *m* TRANSP coal carrier; **Kohlevorkommen** *nt* UMWELT coal deposit; **Kohlevorrat** *m* UMWELT coal deposit

Kolchos *m or nt* VW Russian collective farm, kolkhoz

Kolchose *f* VW Russian collective farm, kolkhoz

Kollaboration *f* POL collaboration

kollaborieren *vt* POL collaborate

Kollage *f* V&M collage

kollationieren *vt* GESCHÄFT collate

kollationierend *adj* GESCHÄFT collating

Kollege *m* PERSON colleague, fellow worker, RECHT adjunct

Kollegin *f* PERSON colleague, fellow worker, RECHT adjunct

Kollektiv- *in cpds* GESCHÄFT collective

kollektiv *adj* GESCHÄFT collective; **~er Beschluß** *m* MGMNT collective decision; **~es Beschwerdeverfahren** *nt* PERSON collective grievance procedure (*BrE*); **~e Entlassung** *f* PERSON collective dismissal; **~es Investitionsunternehmen** *nt* FINANZ collective investment undertaking

Kollektiv-: **Kollektivbedürfnissse** *nt pl* SOZIAL, VW social wants; **Kollektivgut** *nt* VW social good, collective good

kollektivieren *vt* VW collectivize

Kollektivierung *f* VW collectivization; **~ der Landwirtschaft** VW collectivization of agriculture

Kollektiv-: **Kollektivinvestitionsvereinbarung** *f* FINANZ collective investment undertaking; **Kollektivschlichtung** *f* PERSON collective conciliation (*BrE*); **Kollektivunfallversicherung** *f* VERSICH collective accident insurance; **Kollektivversicherung** *f* VERSICH collective insurance; **Kollektivvertrag** *m* PERSON collective agreement; **Kollektivzeichen** *nt* PATENT collective mark, composite mark; **Kollektivzeichnung** *f* BANK joint signature

Kollision *f* TRANSP, VERSICH collision; **Kollisionschaden** *m* TRANSP contact damage; **Kollisionsdeckung** *f* VERSICH collision coverage; **Kollisionsklausel** *f* VERSICH collision clause, running-down clause (*RDC*); **Kollisionsklausel** *f* **bei beiderseitigem Verschulden** VERSICH both-to-blame collision clause; **Kollisionsversicherung** *f* VERSICH collision insurance

Kolludieren *nt* RECHT collusion

Kollusion *f* VW collusion

Kolon *nt* COMP, MEDIEN *Doppelpunkt* colon

Kolonie *f* POL colony

Kolonnenführer *m* PERSON *Militär* group leader

Kolumne *f* MEDIEN *Druck* column

Kombi *m* *infrml* (*Kombiwagen*) TRANSP estate car (*BrE*), estate (*BrE*) (*infrml*), station wagon (*AmE*); **Kombianhänger** *m* TRANSP composite trailer; **Kombifahrkarte** *f* TRANSP combined ticket

Kombinat *nt* VW combine

Kombination *f* GESCHÄFT combination; **~ politischer Mittel** MGMNT, POL policy mix; **~ von Sätzen** TRANSP combination of rates; **~ verschiedener Versicherungsdeckungen** VERSICH comprehensive insurance policy, comprehensive insurance; **Kombinationsausgabe** *f* MEDIEN combined issue; **Kombinationsgebühr** *f* TRANSP combination charge; **Kombinationssatz** *m* TRANSP combination rate; **Kombinationstarif** *m* V&M combination rate; **Kombinationsticket** *nt* FREI combined ticket; **Kombinationstransportdokument** *nt* TRANSP combined transport document (*CTD*); **Kombinationstransportunternehmer** *m* TRANSP combined transport operator (*CTO*); **Kombinationsverkaufsförderung** *f* V&M tie-in promotion

kombinieren *vt* GESCHÄFT combine

kombiniert *adj* GESCHÄFT combined, TRANSP multimodal; **~e Absatzförderung** *f* V&M cross merchandising; **~er Abschluß** *m* FINANZ combined financial statement; **~e Akzelerator- und Multiplikatorwirkung** *f* VW accelerator-multiplier interaction; **~e Baisseoptionsposition** *f* BÖRSE straddle; **~e Bilanz** *f* FINANZ combined balance sheet; **~e Geschäftsversicherung** *f* VERSICH combined shop insurance; **~e Gewinn- und Verlustrechnung** *f* RECHNUNG combined statement of income; **~e Glasversicherung** *f* VERSICH comprehensive glass insurance; **~e Haftpflichtversicherung** *f* VERSICH comprehensive liability insurance; **~er Handel** *m* GESCHÄFT combined trade; **~e Krankenversicherung** *f* VERSICH comprehensive health insurance; **~e Optionsposition** *f* BÖRSE delta-neutral straddle; **~e Police** *f* VERSICH comprehensive policy, mixed policy; **~e Privathaftpflichtversicherung** *f* VERSICH comprehensive personal liability insurance; **~er Tarif** *m* VW two-

part tariff; **~er Transport** *m* TRANSP combined transport (*CT*), combined transport operation, intermodal transport, multimodal transport; **~es Transportkonossement** *nt* TRANSP combined transport bill of lading (*CTBL*); **~er Verkehr** *m* TRANSP multimodal transport, intermodal transport; **~er Verkehrsservice** *m* TRANSP multimodal transport service; **~e Versicherung** *f* VERSICH comprehensive insurance, multi-risk insurance, multiple risk insurance; **~es Warenzeichen** *nt* PATENT combined mark

Kombi-: **Kombischiff** *nt* TRANSP combi carrier, combi ship, combination carrier; **Kombiticket** *nt* FREI, TRANSP combined ticket; **Kombitransportschiff** *nt* TRANSP combi carrier, combi ship, combination carrier; **Kombiwagen** *m* (*Kombi*) TRANSP estate car (*BrE*), estate (*BrE*) (*infrml*), station wagon (*AmE*)

Kombüse *f* TRANSP galley

Komitee *nt* GESCHÄFT committee (*comm*), commission (*comm*); **~ für Frachtverkehrsverfahren** TRANSP cargo traffic procedures committee (*CTPC*); **~ der Hafenbenutzer** TRANSP port users' committee; ♦ **für das ~ eintreten** GESCHÄFT stand for the committee; **für das ~ kandidieren** GESCHÄFT stand for the committee; **einem ~ einen Vorschlag unterbreiten** GESCHÄFT put a suggestion before a committee; **einem ~ einen Vorschlag vorlegen** GESCHÄFT put a suggestion before a committee

Komm. *abbr* (*Kommission*) GESCHÄFT comm. (*commission, committee*)

Komma *nt* COMP, MEDIEN, MATH comma, *in Dezimalzahlen* decimal point

Kommanditgesellschaft *f* (*KG*) BÖRSE limited partnership, private limited partnership, public limited partnership, GRUND resyndication limited partnership (*AmE*), RECHT limited partnership, private limited partnership, public limited partnership; **~ auf Aktien** BÖRSE joint-stock company

Kommanditist, in *m,f* BÖRSE, RECHT limited partner

Kommando *nt* COMP command

kommend: **~es Jahr** *nt* STEUER upcoming year

Kommentar *m* GESCHÄFT commentary

Kommentierung *f* POL *eines Votums* wording

kommerzialisieren *vt* GESCHÄFT commercialize

Kommerzialisierung *f* GESCHÄFT commercialization

kommerziell 1. *adj* GESCHÄFT commercial; **2.** *adv* GESCHÄFT commercially; ♦ **~ lebensfähig** GESCHÄFT commercially viable

kommerziell: **~e Datenverarbeitung** *f* COMP, GESCHÄFT, SOZIAL business data processing; **~e Effizienz** *f* UMWELT, VW commercial efficiency; **~ eingesetzter Computer** *m* COMP commercial computer; **~es Fernsehen** *nt* MEDIEN commercial television; **~ genutzter Brunnen** *m* UMWELT commercial well; **~er Handel** *m* VW commercial trade; **~e Nutzung** *f* GRUND commercial occupancy; **~er Radiosender** *m* MEDIEN commercial radio station; **~e Vermietung** *f* GRUND commercial letting (*BrE*); **~es Wagnis** *nt* MGMNT commercial venture

Kommission *f* (*Komm.*) GESCHÄFT *Komitee* commission (*comm.*), committee (*comm.*), *Provision* commission (*comm.*); **~ für Energie und Umwelt** UMWELT Commission on Energy and the Environment (*CENE*); **~ der Europäischen Gemeinschaft** *obs* VW Commission of the European Community (*obs*) (*CEC*); **~ der Vereinten Nationen für des International Handelsrecht**

RECHT United Nations Commission on International Trade Law (*UNCITRAL*); **~ für Zuschüsse im Commonwealth** vw Commonwealth Grants Commission; ◆ **in ~** IMP/EXP, TRANSP on consignment

Kommissionär *m* PERSON commission agent

kommissionieren *vt* GESCHÄFT commission

kommissioniert: ~e Kapitalverfügbarkeit *f* FINANZ expected funds availability (*EFA*)

Kommission: **auf Kommissionsbasis verkaufen** *phr* V&M sell on commission; **Kommissionsgeschäft** *nt* V&M sale on commission; **Kommissionsgüter** *nt pl* VW commission goods; **Kommissionsmakler, in** *m,f* BÖRSE commission broker (*AmE*); **Kommissionsrückvergütung** *f* FINANZ kickback; **Kommissionsverkauf** *m* V&M consignment sale, consignment selling; **Kommissionsware** *f* V&M consignment goods

Kommunal- *in cpds* GESCHÄFT communal, municipal

kommunal *adj* GESCHÄFT communal, municipal; **~er Eigenbetrieb** *m* PERSON direct labor organization (*AmE*) (*DLO*), direct labour organization (*BrE*) (*DLO*), VERWALT public service corporation (*AmE*); **~e Finanzen** *f pl* POL local government finance; **~e Finanzpolitik** *f* POL local government financial policy; **~es Finanzwesen** *nt* POL local government finance; **~e Schuldverschreibung** *f* BANK municipal notes

Kommunal-: Kommunalanleihe *f* FINANZ local authority loan (*BrE*), muni (*AmE*), municipal loan (*AmE*); **Kommunalbehörde** *f* VERWALT local authority (*BrE*), municipal authority; **Kommunalbesitz** *m* GRUND communal ownership, vw common ownership; **Kommunaleigentum** *nt* GRUND communal ownership; **Kommunalobligation** *f* BANK municipal bond, BÖRSE general obligation bond (*AmE*) (*G-O bond*), municipal bond; **Kommunalobligation** *f* **ohne Zertifikat** BÖRSE certificateless municipal bond; **Kommunalregierung** *f* POL, VERWALT local government, municipal government; **Kommunalschuldverschreibung** *f* BÖRSE municipal bond; **Kommunalsteuer** *f* STEUER local tax; **Kommunalverband** *m* VW Community aid; **Kommunalverwaltung** *f* POL, VERWALT local government, municipal government, municipality; **Kommunalwahl** *f* POL local election; **Kommunalwirtschaft** *f* VW communal economy

Kommune *f* POL municipality, vw commune

Kommunikation *f* GESCHÄFT communication; **~ zwischen Abteilungen** KOMM, VERWALT interdepartmental communication; **~ offener Systeme** (*OSI*) COMP open systems interconnection (*OSI*); **Kommunikationsfähigkeiten** *f pl* PERSON communication skills; **Kommunikationshemmnis** *nt* MGMNT, PERSON communication barrier; **Kommunikationskanal** *m* MGMNT, PERSON channel of communication; **Kommunikationslücke** *f* MGMNT, PERSON communication gap; **Kommunikationsmanagement** *nt* MGMNT, PERSON communication management; **Kommunikationsmedien** *nt pl* MEDIEN, V&M communications media; **Kommunikations-Mix** *nt* V&M communication mix; **Kommunikationsstrategie** *f* KOMM communication strategy; **Kommunikationstechnik** *f* KOMM communication technology; **Kommunikationstheorie** *f* KOMM, MGMNT communications theory; **Kommunikationsverbindung** *f* COMP data link, MGMNT, PERSON communication link;

Kommunikationsverwaltung *f* MGMNT, PERSON communication management; **Kommunikationsweg** *m* MGMNT, PERSON channel of communication; **Kommunikationswissenschaft** *f* KOMM, MGMNT communications theory; **Kommunikationsziel** *nt* V&M communication objective

Kommunikator *m* KOMM communicator

Kommuniqué *nt* KOMM, POL communication, communiqué

Kommunismus *m* POL, VW communism

kommunistisch *adj* POL, VW communist

Kompakt- *in cpds* COMP, TRANSP high-density; **Kompaktbaugruppe** *f* COMP package; **Kompaktfracht** *f* TRANSP high-density cargo, high-density freight

komparativ *adj* VW comparative; **~e Analyse** *f* VW comparative statics; **~er Vorteil** *m* VW comparative advantage

kompatibel *adj* COMP *Hardware, Software*, IND, PERSON compatible

Kompatibilität *f* COMP, IND, PERSON compatibility

Kompensation *f* BÖRSE, FINANZ, IMP/EXP, RECHT, STEUER, VERSICH, VW compensation, offset, offsetting; **Kompensationsabkommen** *nt* VW compensation agreement; **Kompensationsgegengeschäft** *nt* RECHT *Aufrechnungsgeschäft* offset agreement, VW counter purchase, switch; **Kompensationshandel** *m* VW counter trade; **Kompensationskriterium** *nt* VW compensation principle; **Kompensationsprodukt** *nt* IMP/EXP *EG* compensating product; **Kompensationsvertrag** *m* RECHT counter-trade contract; **Kompensationszoll** *m* IMP/EXP, STEUER countervailing duties

kompensatorisch *adj* BÖRSE, IMP/EXP, RECHT, STEUER, VERSICH, VW compensatory; **~e Aktienoptionen** *f pl* BÖRSE compensatory stock option (*BrE*); **~er Budgetausgleich** *m* VW compensatory budgeting

Kompensatorisch: ~e Finanzfazilität *f* FINANZ compensatory financial facility (*CFF*)

kompensatorisch: **~e Finanzierung** *f* KOMM, VW compensatory financing; **~e Fiskalpolitik** *f* STEUER compensatory fiscal policy

kompensieren *vt* FINANZ offset, GESCHÄFT compensate, make up for, RECHNUNG offset; ◆ **jdn für etw ~** GESCHÄFT compensate sb for sth

kompensierend *adj* FINANZ, RECHNUNG offsetting

kompensiert *adj* FINANZ, RECHNUNG offset; **~e Nachfragefunktion** *f* VW compensated demand curve

Kompetenz *f* GESCHÄFT authority, PERSON competency, RECHT competence; **Kompetenzstreitigkeit** *f* MGMNT, PERSON demarcation dispute (*BrE*), RECHT jurisdiction dispute

kompilieren *vt* COMP compile

Komplement *nt* COMP complement

komplementär *adj* GESCHÄFT complementary; **~e Güter** *nt pl* V&M, VW complementary goods, complements, joint goods

Komplementär, in *m,f* GESCHÄFT general partner; **Komplementärnachfrage** *f* V&M, VW joint demand, complementary demand; **Komplementärprodukt** *nt* V&M complementary product; **Komplementärtechnologie** *f* IND complementary technology

komplett *adj* GESCHÄFT complete; **~es Finanzierungspaket** *nt* FINANZ financing package; **~e**

Namenschuldverschreibung *f* BÖRSE fully-registered bond (*AmE*)

Komplettierungsprogramm *nt* UMWELT completion program (*AmE*), completion programme (*BrE*)

Komplettreise *f* FREI, TRANSP inclusive tour (*IT*)

komplex *adj* GESCHÄFT complex; **~e Kapitalstruktur** *f* VW complex capital structure; **~e Wirtschaft** *f* VW complex economy

Komplex *m* GRUND complex

Komplikation *f* GESCHÄFT complication

Komplize *m* RECHT accessory

komplizieren *vt* GESCHÄFT complicate

kompliziert: **~es Geschäft** *nt* BANK complex transaction; **~e Transaktion** *f* BANK complex transaction

Komplizin *f* RECHT accessory

Komponente *f* COMP, GESCHÄFT, IND component, component part

Komposit- *in cpds* TRANSP, VERSICH composite; **Kompositversicherung** *f* VERSICH composite insurance; **Kompositversicherungsgesellschaft** *f* VERSICH composite insurance company

komprimieren *vt* COMP *Dateien*, PERSON, TRANSP compress

Komprimierung *f* COMP, PERSON, TRANSP compression

Kompromiß *m* GESCHÄFT compromise, VW *zwischen Arbeitslosigkeit und Inflation* trade-off; ◆ **sich auf einen ~ einigen** GESCHÄFT split the difference; **durch ~ regeln** GESCHÄFT compromise; **einen ~ schließen** GESCHÄFT compromise

Kompromiß: **Kompromißentscheidung** *f* GESCHÄFT compromise decision

kompromißlos *adj* GESCHÄFT uncompromising; **~es Schlichtungsverfahren** *nt* VW final offer arbitration

Kompromiß: **Kompromißlösung** *f* GESCHÄFT compromise decision

Kondemnation *f* GRUND *Beschlagnahme* condemnation

Kondensation *f* IND, UMWELT condensation

Konditionen *f pl* BANK, FINANZ conditions, terms; **Konditionenbindung** *f* FINANZ commitment to fixed terms; **Konditionengefälle** *nt* BÖRSE rate differential

Konferenz *f* GESCHÄFT conference, convention; **~ der Vereinten Nationen für Umwelt und Entwicklung** UMWELT United Nations Conference on Environment and Development (*UNCED*); **Konferenzbericht** *m* MGMNT conference proceedings; **Konferenzliniensystem** *nt* MGMNT conference system; **Konferenzmitglied** *nt* MGMNT conference member; **Konferenzort** *m* MGMNT conference site, conference venue; **Konferenzprotokoll** *nt* MGMNT conference proceedings; **Konferenzschaltung** *f* KOMM *Telefon* audio conference, audio conferencing, conference call, three-way call (*AmE*); **Konferenzteilnehmer, in** *m,f* MGMNT conference delegate, convention participant; **Konferenztisch** *m* MGMNT conference table, round table

Konfidenz- *in cpds* MATH confidence; **Konfidenzintervall** *nt* MATH confidence interval; **Konfidenzkoeffizient** *m* MATH confidence coefficient; **Konfidenzniveau** *nt* MATH confidence level

Konfiguration *f* COMP configuration; **Konfigurationssteuerung** *f* COMP configuration control

konfigurieren *vt* COMP configure

konfiszieren *vt* GESCHÄFT confiscate, RECHT sequester, sequestrate; ◆ **etw von jdm ~** GESCHÄFT confiscate sth from sb

Konfiszierung *f* GESCHÄFT confiscation, RECHT sequestration

Konflikt *m* GESCHÄFT conflict; ◆ **in ~ geraten mit** GESCHÄFT fall foul of

Konfluenzanalyse *f* MATH confluence analysis (*CA*)

Konföderation *f* POL confederation

konföderiert *adj* POL confederate

Konföderierte(r) *mf* [decl. as adj] POL confederate

konföderieren: **sich ~** *v refl* POL confederate

konform: **~ gehen mit** *phr* GESCHÄFT agree with, be on the same wavelength as (*infrml*)

Konfrontation *f* GESCHÄFT confrontation

konfrontieren *vt* GESCHÄFT confront; ◆ **jdn mit etw ~** GESCHÄFT confront sb with sth

konglomerat: **~er Zusammenschluß** *m* POL, VW conglomerate merger

Kongreß *m* MGMNT congress, convention, POL Congress; **Kongreßabgeordnete(r)** *mf* [decl. as adj] POL Congressman (*AmE*), Congresswoman (*AmE*), Member of Congress (*AmE*); **Kongreßbeschluß** *m* POL Act of Congress (*AmE*); **Kongreßteilnehmer, in** *m,f* MGMNT congress participant, convention participant

Kongruenzprinzip *nt* RECHNUNG matching principle (*AmE*)

königlich: **~e Genehmigung** *f* RECHT Royal Assent (*BrE*)

Königlich: **~es Schiff** *nt* TRANSP Her Majesty's Ship, His Majesty's Ship (*BrE*) (*HMS*)

Konjunktur *f* GESCHÄFT economic activity, economy

konjunkturabhängig *adj* BÖRSE, VW cyclical

Konjunktur: **Konjunkturabschwächung** *f* VW economic slowdown; **Konjunkturanalyse** *f* VW activity analysis; **Konjunkturaufschwung** *m* MGMNT business expansion, VW economic upswing, economic boom; **Konjunkturaussichten** *f pl* VW business outlook, economic outlook, economic prospects; **Konjunkturbarometer** *nt* VW business barometer, economic indicator, business indicator; **Konjunkturbericht** *m* VW economic report

konjunkturell: **~e Abkühlung** *f* VW economic slowdown; **~er Abschwung** *m* VW business slowdown; **~e Arbeitslosigkeit** *f* VW cyclical unemployment; **~e Schwankung** *f* BÖRSE cyclical fluctuation

konjunkturempfindlich *adj* BÖRSE, VW cyclical; **~e Branche** *f* VW cyclical industry; **~es Unternehmen** *nt* BÖRSE cyclical company

Konjunktur: **Konjunkturentwicklung** *f* VW economic development, economic trend; **Konjunkturindikator** *m* VW business indicator, economic indicator; **Konjunkturklima** *nt* VW economic climate; **Konjunkturlage** *f* VW economic conditions, economic situation, state of the economy

konjunkturorientiert: **~e Finanzpolitik** *f* VW active fiscal policy

Konjunktur: **Konjunkturphase** *f* VW trade cycle; **Konjunkturpolitik** *f* POL, VW trade cycle policy; **Konjunkturprognose** *f* VW economic forecasting, business forecasting; **Konjunkturrückgang** *m* VW recession, downtrend, slowdown; **Konjunkturschwankungen** *f pl* VW cyclical variations; **Konjunkturtief** *nt* VW trough, bottom; **Konjunkturtrend** *m* VW economic trend;

Konjunkturverlangsamung f VW business slowdown; **Konjunkturverlauf** m VW economic trend; **Konjunkturzyklus** m VW trade cycle, business cycle, economic cycle

konkludent: ~ **geschlossener Vertrag** m RECHT implied contract; **durch ~es Handeln zustanden gekommener Vertrag** m RECHT implied in fact contract; **~es Verhalten** nt RECHT *Vertragsrecht* action implying intention

konkret: **~er Beweis** m RECHT concrete evidence; **~e Sachen** f pl GESCHÄFT ascertained goods

Konkretisierung f GESCHÄFT application

Konkurrent, in m,f GESCHÄFT competitor, rival

Konkurrenz f GESCHÄFT competition; ♦ **mit der ~ Schritt halten** GESCHÄFT keep in step with one's competitors

Konkurrenz: **Konkurrenzanalyse** f V&M competitor analysis; **Konkurrenzbetrieb** m COMP, KOMM contention; **Konkurrenzerzeugnis** nt V&M rival goods

konkurrenzfähig adj GESCHÄFT competitive; **~er Preis** m V&M competitive price

Konkurrenz: **Konkurrenzfähigkeit** f GESCHÄFT competitiveness; **Konkurrenzgeschäft** nt GESCHÄFT competitive business; **Konkurrenzkampf** m GESCHÄFT rat race (*infrml*), VW competitive thrust

konkurrenzlos adj BÖRSE unmatched, GESCHÄFT unrivaled (*AmE*), unrivalled (*BrE*)

Konkurrenz: **Konkurrenzmarke** f V&M rival brand; **Konkurrenzpreis** m V&M competitive price; **Konkurrenzprodukt** nt V&M rival goods; **Konkurrenztaktik** f MGMNT competitive tactics; **Konkurrenztarif** m V&M competitive rate; **Konkurrenzunternehmen** nt GESCHÄFT competitor

konkurrieren vi GESCHÄFT compete, vie with; ♦ ~ **mit** GESCHÄFT compete with

konkurrierend adj GESCHÄFT competitive; **~er Anspruch** m V&M competitive claim; **~e Bedürfnisse** nt pl GESCHÄFT competing requirements; **nicht ~e Gruppe** f PERSON noncompeting group; **~er Handel** m VW competitive trading; **~e Nachfrage** f VW competitive demand

Konkurs m FINANZ, RECHNUNG bankruptcy, *Zahlungsunfähigkeit* insolvency, liquidation; ~ **auf Antrag des Gemeinschuldners** FINANZ voluntary bankruptcy; ~ **auf Antrag eines Gläubigers** RECHT involuntary bankruptcy; ♦ ~ **anmelden** FINANZ file for bankruptcy; **in ~ gehen** FINANZ fail, go bankrupt, go to the wall (*infrml*); ~ **machen** FINANZ fail, go bankrupt, go to the wall (*infrml*)

Konkurs: **Konkursantrag** m FINANZ petition for relief (*AmE*), petition in bankruptcy (*BrE*); **Konkursaufhebung** f RECHT discharge of a bankrupt, discharge in bankruptcy; **Konkursausschuß** m FINANZ bankruptcy committee; **Konkursbeschluß** m FINANZ order for relief; **Konkursbilanz** f BANK statement of affairs, RECHT administration; **Konkurseinleitungsbeschluß** m FINANZ receiving order (*RO*); **Konkurseröffnung** f FINANZ, RECHNUNG, RECHT adjudication in bankruptcy; **Konkurseröffnungsbeschluß** m FINANZ, RECHNUNG adjudication of bankruptcy order, decree in bankruptcy, RECHT adjudication of bankruptcy order, administration order, decree in bankruptcy; **Konkursgericht** nt RECHT bankruptcy court, super-

intendent of bankruptcy; **Konkursgesetz** nt RECHNUNG, RECHT act of bankruptcy, bankruptcy act; **Konkursgläubiger, in** m,f RECHT, VERSICH creditor in bankruptcy; **Konkursgut** nt RECHT bankruptcy estate; **Konkursmasse** f RECHT bankruptcy property, bankruptcy estate; **Konkursordnung** f RECHNUNG, RECHT act of bankruptcy, bankruptcy act; **Konkursrecht** nt RECHNUNG, RECHT act of bankruptcy, bankruptcy act; **Konkursrichter** m RECHT superintendent of bankruptcy; **Konkursverfahren** nt RECHNUNG bankruptcy, RECHT bankruptcy proceedings; **Konkursverfahren über jds Vermögen eröffnen** phr RECHNUNG, RECHT adjudge sb bankrupt, adjudicate sb bankrupt; **Konkursverwalter, in** m,f BANK assignee in bankruptcy, trustee in bankruptcy, RECHT official receiver, receiver; **Konkursverwaltung** f RECHNUNG receivership

Können nt GESCHÄFT ability

Konnossement nt IMP/EXP, TRANSP bill of lading (*b.l.,* *B/L*), shipping bill, bill; ~ **für kombinierten Transport** TRANSP combined transport bill of lading (*CTBL*); ~ **mit Namensangabe** IMP/EXP, TRANSP bill of lading issued to a named party; ~ **ohne Einschränkungen** IMP/EXP, TRANSP clean bill of lading; ~ **ohne Vorbehalt** IMP/EXP, TRANSP clean bill of lading; ~ **des Spediteurs** IMP/EXP, TRANSP forwarder's bill of lading; **Konnossementbetrug** m IMP/EXP, TRANSP bill of lading fraud; **Konnossementsgarantie** f TRANSP letter of indemnity (*L/I*); **Konnossementsteilschein** m TRANSP delivery order (*D/O*)

Konsens m GESCHÄFT, POL consensus

konsequent adj MGMNT *in seinen Methoden* consistent

Konservatismus m POL conservatism

konservativ adj GESCHÄFT, POL conservative; **~e Partei** f POL Conservative Party (*BrE*); **~e Schätzung** f GESCHÄFT conservative estimate

Konserve f IND, V&M preserved food

Konservierung f UMWELT conservation; **Konservierungsmittel** nt pl IND preservatives; **ohne Konservierungsstoffe** phr IND, V&M no preservatives; **ohne Konservierungs- oder Zusatzstoffe** phr IND, V&M no preservatives or additives

Konsignant, in m,f IMP/EXP, TRANSP consignor

Konsignation f IMP/EXP, TRANSP consignment; ♦ **in ~** IMP/EXP, TRANSP on consignment

Konsignation: **Konsignationsverkauf** m TRANSP consignment sale

konsolidieren vt BANK, FINANZ consolidate, fund, RECHNUNG, VW consolidate

konsolidiert adj BANK, FINANZ, RECHNUNG, VW consolidated; ♦ **auf einer ~en Basis** FINANZ, RECHNUNG on a consolidated basis; **auf nicht ~er Basis** FINANZ, RECHNUNG on an unconsolidated basis

konsolidiert: **~er Abschluß** m RECHNUNG consolidated accounts, consolidated financial statement, group accounts; **~e Bilanz** f RECHNUNG consolidated balance sheet; **~er Cashflow** m RECHNUNG consolidated cash flow; **~er Cashflow-Bericht** m RECHNUNG consolidated cash flow statement; **~er Ertragsfonds** m FINANZ consolidated revenue fund; **~er Finanzstatus** m FINANZ consolidated statement of condition (*AmE*); **~es Konzernvermögen** nt FINANZ consolidated assets; **~e Kredite** m pl FINANZ funded debt; **~e Papiere** nt pl FINANZ consolidated annuities (*BrE*), consolidated stock (*AmE*); **~e Rechnungslegung** f RECHNUNG consolidated accounting (*BrE*); **~er Reingewinn** *m* RECHNUNG consolidated net profit; **~er Satz** *m* TRANSP consolidated rate; **nicht ~e Schuld** *f* FINANZ unfunded debt; **~e Staatsanleihen** *f pl* BANK bank annuities, FINANZ consolidated annuities (*BrE*), consolidated stock (*AmE*); **~er Staatsfonds** *m* VW consolidated fund (*BrE*); **~e Zahlen** *f pl* RECHNUNG consolidated figures

Konsolidierung *f* BANK, FINANZ consolidation, RECHNUNG merger accounting (*BrE*), VW consolidation; **Konsolidierungsdarlehen** *nt* FINANZ consolidation loan; **Konsolidierungsgrundsätze** *m pl* RECHNUNG consolidation method

Konsortial *f* GRUND resyndication limited partnership (*AmE*); **Konsortialbank** *f* BANK, FINANZ agency bank (*BrE*), consortium bank; **Konsortialbeamte(r)** *m* [decl. as adj], **Konsortialbeamtin** *f* BANK syndication official; **Konsortialführer** *m* BANK, FINANZ *Person* syndicate leader, leading underwriter, prime underwriter, *Unternehmen* leading bank, lead bank; **Konsortialführerin** *f* BANK, FINANZ *Person* leading underwriter, syndicate leader, prime underwriter; **Konsortialgebühr** *f* BÖRSE management fee; **Konsortialkapazität** *f* VERWALT syndication capacity; **Konsortialkredit** *m* BANK, FINANZ participation loan, syndicated loan; **Konsortialmitglied** *nt* FINANZ underwriter; **Konsortialnutzen** *m* BÖRSE *Wertpapieremissionen* gross spread; **Konsortialprovision** *f* BANK negotiation fee; **Konsortialspanne** *f* BÖRSE underwriting spread; **Konsortialvertrag** *m* BANK agreement among underwriters, BÖRSE syndicate agreement, underwriting agreement, RECHT *Vertragsrecht* cooperation agreement

Konsortium *nt* BANK, BÖRSE, FINANZ, GRUND, RECHT consortium, syndicate, VERSICH pool

konstant *adj* GESCHÄFT constant, uniform; ♦ **bei ~en Preisen** GESCHÄFT at constant prices

konstant: **~er Dollarplan** *m* GESCHÄFT constant dollar plan (*BrE*); **~es Kapital** *nt* VW constant capital; **~e Prämie** *f* VERSICH level premium; **~er Preis** *m* VW constant price; **~er Schuldendienst** *m* STEUER level debt service (*AmE*); **~er Skalenertrag** *m* VW constant returns to scale

Konstante *f* COMP constant, MATH absolute term, constant

konstituieren *vt* PATENT constitute

konstruieren *vt* IND *Prototyp* develop, MATH construct

konstruiert: **~er Einkommenszufluß** *m* STEUER constructive receipt, constructive receipt of income (*AmE*)

Konstrukteur, in *m,f* IND design engineer

Konstruktion *f* GESCHÄFT construction, design, GRUND construction, IND construction, development; **~ und Nutzung** *f* RECHT construction and use (*BrE*); **Konstruktionsabteilung** *f* GESCHÄFT engineering department; **Konstruktionsautomation** *f* COMP design automation (*DA*); **Konstruktionsbüro** *nt* GESCHÄFT design office; **Konstruktionstechnik** *f* IND design engineering; **Konstruktionsunternehmen** *nt* GESCHÄFT engineering firm; **Konstruktionsverfahren** *nt* IND engineering process; **Konstruktionswerk** *nt* IND engineering works

konstruktiv *adj* GESCHÄFT constructive, positive

Konsul *m* POL consul

konsularisch: **~e Erklärung** *f* POL consular declaration (*CD*)

Konsulat *nt* POL consulate; **Konsulatserklärung** *f* POL consular declaration (*CD*); **Konsulatsfaktura** *f* RECHNUNG, VERWALT certified invoice; **Konsulatsgebühren** *f pl* IMP/EXP, VERWALT consular fees

konsultativ-demokratisch *adj* MGMNT consultative-democratic

konsultieren *vt* GESCHÄFT, MGMNT consult

Konsum *m* V&M, VW consumption (*C*); **Konsumausgaben** *f pl* VW consumer expenditure, high-street spending; **Konsumbedarf** *m* V&M consumer needs; **Konsumbereitschaft** *f* VW propensity to consume

Konsument *m* V&M, VW consumer; **Konsumentengeschäft** *nt* BANK consumer lending; **Konsumentenpräferenz** *f* V&M consumer preference; **Konsumentenrente** *f* VW consumer's surplus; **Konsumentensouveränität** *f* VW consumer sovereignty

Konsumerismus *m* V&M, VW consumerism

Konsum: **Konsumexternalitäten** *f pl* VW external effects of consumption; **Konsumforschung** *f* V&M consumer research; **Konsumfunktion** *f* VW consumption function; **Konsumgenossenschaft** *f* GESCHÄFT consumers' cooperative (*co-op*); **Konsumgesellschaft** *f* VW consumer society; **Konsumgewohnheit** *f* V&M consumer habit

Konsumgüter *nt pl* V&M consumer goods, consumer product; **Konsumgüterindustrie** *f* IND consumer goods industry; **Konsumgütermarkt** *m* V&M consumer market

konsumieren *vt* V&M, VW consume

Konsum: **Konsumkreditmarkt** *m* BANK consumer credit market; **Konsumneigung** *f* VW propensity to consume; **Konsumorientierung** *f* V&M consumer orientation; **Konsumverlagerung** *f* V&M shift in consumption

Kontakt *m* GESCHÄFT contact; ♦ **miteinander in ~ bringen** GESCHÄFT *Personen* put in touch

Kontakt: **Kontaktbericht** *m* V&M call report, contact report (*AmE*); **Kontakter** *m* MEDIEN account executive; **Kontaktfrau** *f*, **Kontaktmann** *m* MEDIEN account executive; **Kontaktperson** *f* GESCHÄFT contact; **Kontaktschaden** *m* TRANSP contact damage

kontaminieren *vt* UMWELT contaminate

Konten *nt pl* BANK, FINANZ, RECHNUNG accounts; ♦ **~ abstimmen** RECHNUNG agree accounts

Konten: **Kontenanalyse** *f* BANK account analysis; **Kontenberichtigung** *f* BÖRSE reconciliation account; **Kontenblatt** *nt* RECHNUNG account form; **Kontenbuch** *nt* RECHNUNG book of accounts; **Kontenform** *f* RECHNUNG account form; **Kontenführung** *f* RECHNUNG accountancy (*accy*); **Kontengliederung** *f* RECHNUNG classification of accounts; **Kontengliederung** *f* **der Bilanz** RECHNUNG account format; **Kontengruppe** *f* RECHNUNG, V&M account group; **Kontenkonflikt** *m* V&M account conflict; **Kontenplan** *m* RECHNUNG chart of accounts, accounting plan; **Kontenrahmen** *m* RECHNUNG chart of accounts; **Kontensatz** *m* RECHNUNG set of accounts; **Kontensystem** *nt* RECHNUNG system of accounts

Konterbande *f obs* IMP/EXP contraband

Konterware *f obs* IMP/EXP contraband, contraband articles, prohibited goods, smuggled goods

kontextabhängig *adj* COMP context-sensitive; **~e Hilfe** *f* COMP *Software* context-sensitive help

kontextsensitiv *adj* COMP context-sensitive; **~e Hilfe** *f* COMP *Software* context-sensitive help

Kontinent *m* POL continent

kontinental *adj* POL continental

Kontingent *nt* GESCHÄFT allocation, quota, RECHNUNG allocation

kontingentieren *vt* GESCHÄFT allocate, RECHNUNG allocate to

Kontingentierung *f* GESCHÄFT quota fixing; **Kontingentierungssystem** *nt* GESCHÄFT quota system

Kontingenz- *in cpds* MATH, MGMNT contingency; **Kontingenztabelle** *f* MATH contingency table; **Kontingenztheorie** *f* MGMNT contingency theory

kontinuierlich: **~er Haushalt** *m* FINANZ continuous budget; **~es Leitungssystem** *nt* MGMNT ongoing management system; **~e Verkaufsförderung** *f* V&M continuous promotion

Kontinuität *f* RECHNUNG consistency, V&M, VW continuity; **Kontinuitätsthese** *f* VW continuity thesis

Konto *nt* (*Kto.*) BANK, RECHNUNG, V&M account (*a/c*); **~ für bestimmte Zwecke** RECHNUNG specified-purpose account (*AmE*); **~ laufender Zahlungen** FINANZ budget account;♦ **à ~** BANK account of (*a/o*), on account (*o/a*); **auf ~ von** BANK account of (*a/o*); **kein ~** BANK no-account (*n/a*); **per ~** *jarg* BANK account of (*a/o*); **ein ~ abschließen** BANK, FINANZ, RECHNUNG balance an account; **ein ~ abstimmen** BANK, FINANZ, RECHNUNG balance an account, rule off, reconcile an account; **ein ~ ausgleichen** BANK, FINANZ, RECHNUNG balance an account, settle an account; **einem ~ einen Betrag gutschreiben** BANK credit a sum to an account

Konto: **Kontoabschluß** *m* FINANZ, RECHNUNG balancing of an account; **Kontoabstimmung** *f* **zwischen Bank und Kunde** BANK bank reconciliation, RECHNUNG account reconciliation, account matching; **Kontoausgleich** *m* BANK settlement of account

Kontoauszug *m* BANK bank statement, account statement, abstract; ♦ **einen ~ machen** BANK draw up a statement of account

Kontoauszug: **Kontoauszugsdrucker** *m* BANK self-service machine that prints bank statements when used with a cash card

Konto: **Kontobewegung** *f* RECHNUNG account movement, account transaction; **Kontobezeichnung** *f* BANK account name, RECHNUNG account name, name of an account, title of an account, vw style of account; **Kontobuch** *nt* RECHNUNG book of account, account book; **Kontoform** *f* RECHNUNG account form

Kontoführung *f* BANK, RECHNUNG account management; **Kontoführungsgebühr** *f* BANK maintenance fee; **Kontoführungskosten** *pl* BANK maintenance charge

Konto: **Kontoinhaber, in** *m,f* BANK account holder

Kontokorrent *nt* BANK checking account (*AmE*) (*C/A*), cheque account (*BrE*) (*C/A*), credit account (*C/A*), current account (*BrE*) (*C/A*), open account; **Kontokorrentgeschäft** *nt* BANK open account business; **Kontokorrentguthaben** *nt* BANK checking account balance (*AmE*), current account balance (*BrE*), checking account surplus (*AmE*), current account surplus (*BrE*); **Kontokorrentinhaber, in** *m,f* BANK checking account holder (*AmE*), current account holder (*BrE*); **Kontokorrentkonto** *nt* BANK checking account (*AmE*) (*C/A*), cheque account (*BrE*) (*C/A*), credit account (*C/A*), current account (*BrE*) (*C/A*); **Kontokorrentkredit** *m* BANK checking account loan (*AmE*), current account loan (*BrE*), open credit; **Kontokorrentkunde** *m* BANK

checking account customer (*AmE*), current account customer (*BrE*); **Kontokorrentvorbehalt** *m* BANK checking account reservation (*AmE*), current account reservation (*BrE*)

Konto: **Kontonummer** *f* BANK, RECHNUNG account number; **Kontostand** *m* BANK account balance, actual balance, balance (*bal.*), RECHNUNG account balance, actual balance, daily closing balance; **Kontoüberziehung** *f* BANK overdraft (*O/D*); **Kontoumsatz** *m* BANK activity, RECHNUNG account turnover; **Kontoverwendung** *f* BANK account operation; **Kontoverwendungskosten** *pl* BANK account operation charge

Kontrahent *m* BÖRSE counterparty (*BrE*), RECHT contracting party, vw counterpart

kontrahieren *vt* GESCHÄFT contract

Kontrahierung *f* VW contracting

Kontrakt *m* BÖRSE, TRANSP, VW contract; **Kontrakteinheit** *f* BÖRSE contract size; **Kontraktgröße** *f* BÖRSE contract size, *Terminkontraktmarkt* trading unit

kontraktiv: **~e Geldpolitik** *f* VW tight monetary policy, tight money policy; **~e Offenmarktpolitik** *f* VW contractionary open market policy

Kontrakt: **Kontraktkurve** *f* VW contract curve; **Kontraktqualität** *f* BÖRSE *im Warenterminhandel* contract grade; **Kontraktsystem** *nt* TRANSP contract system

Kontroll- *in cpds* GESCHÄFT control; **Kontrollabzug** *m* MEDIEN *Druck* proof; **Kontrollabzüge freigeben** *phr* MEDIEN *Druck* pass the proofs; **Kontrollangestellte(r)** *mf* [decl. as adj] V&M checkout assistant, checkout clerk (*AmE*); **Kontrollausschuß** *m* MGMNT, PERSON supervisory board, RECHT committee of inspection; **Kontrollbehörde** *f* RECHT regulatory body; **Kontrollbuch** *nt* RECHNUNG controlling account

Kontrolle *f* GESCHÄFT control, supervision, *Umsatz, Kosten, Ausgaben* tracking, IMP/EXP *Zoll* examination, MGMNT, PERSON supervision, VW control; **~ des Arbeitsablaufs** MGMNT operational audit, operations audit; **~ der Bargeldbestände** RECHNUNG cash control; **~ der Fertigung** IND manufacturing control; **~ der Linienbeschränkungen** GESCHÄFT control of line limits; **~ durch das Mutterland** FINANZ, VW home-country control; **~ der Staatsausgaben** VW public expenditure control; ♦ **unter ~ bringen** VW *Inflation, Arbeitslosigkeit* bring under control; **die ~ übernehmen** GESCHÄFT take control

Kontrolleur *m* IND factory inspector, MGMNT supervisor, PERSON supervisor, tally clerk, checker

Kontroll-: **Kontrollfahrkarte** *f* TRANSP control ticket; **Kontrollfrage** *f* V&M control question; **Kontrollgenehmigung** *f* IMP/EXP surveillance licence (*BrE*) (*SL*), surveillance license (*AmE*) (*SL*); **Kontrollgruppe** *f* V&M control group

kontrollierbar: **nicht ~e Ausgaben** *f pl* FINANZ uncontrollable expenditures

kontrollieren *vt* GESCHÄFT *Kosten* control, *Ausgaben* track, IMP/EXP examine, MGMNT, PERSON supervise, VW *Inflation* control

kontrolliert: **~e Atmosphäre** *f* UMWELT controlled atmosphere; **~e Auflage** *f* V&M audited circulation, controlled circulation; **~er Kurs** *m* VW controlled rates; **~e Rohstoffe** *m pl* BÖRSE controlled commodities; **~er**

Transit *m* TRANSP controlled transit; **~e Waren** *f pl* BÖRSE controlled commodities

Kontroll-: **Kontrollinformationen** *f pl* GESCHÄFT control information; **Kontrolliste** *f* GESCHÄFT checklist, tally register, PERSON tally sheet; **Kontrollkosten** *pl* VW monitoring costs; **Kontrollmaßnahme** *f* VW measure of control; **Kontrollpunkt** *m* IMP/EXP, TRANSP border crossing-point, checkpoint; **Kontrollspanne** *f* GESCHÄFT span of control; **Kontrollstreifen** *m* GESCHÄFT tally roll; **Kontrollsumme** *f* COMP *Datenübertragung* check sum; **Kontrollsystem** *nt* GESCHÄFT tracking system, RECHT regulatory system; **Kontrolluhr** *f* IND, PERSON time clock; **Kontrollvermerk** *m* GESCHÄFT check (*AmE*), tick (*BrE*), check mark (*AmE*), tick mark (*BrE*); **Kontrollzeichen** *nt* GESCHÄFT check (*AmE*), tick (*BrE*), check mark (*AmE*), tick mark (*BrE*); **Kontrollziffer** *f* FINANZ check digit

Kontroverse *f* GESCHÄFT controversy

Konus *m* MATH, TRANSP cone

Konvention *f* GESCHÄFT, RECHT convention

Konventionalstrafe *f* RECHT *wegen Zuwiderhandlung* penalty for noncompliance; **~ wegen Vertragsbruch** RECHT penalty for breach of contract

Konventionalstrafklausel *f* RECHT penalty clause

konventionell: **~e Anleihe** *f* FINANZ straight bond

Konvergenz *f* GESCHÄFT convergence; **Konvergenztheorie** *f* VW convergence hypothesis; **Konvergenzthese** *f* POL convergence thesis

konvergieren *vi* GESCHÄFT converge

Konversion *f* BÖRSE, FINANZ, VW conversion; **Konversionsanleihe** *f* FINANZ conversion loan

konvertibel: **konvertible Devisen** *f pl* POL, VW convertible currency, hard currency

Konvertibilität *f* FINANZ, POL, VW convertibility

konvertierbar: **~e Emission** *f* **von Wertpapieren** FINANZ convertible issue; **~e Währung** *f* POL, VW convertible currency, hard currency

Konvertierbarkeit *f* FINANZ, POL, VW convertibility

konvertieren *vt* BÖRSE, COMP, FINANZ, VW convert; ◆ **~ in** [+acc] BÖRSE, COMP, FINANZ, VW convert into

Konvertierung *f* BÖRSE, COMP, FINANZ, VW conversion; **Konvertierungskosten** *pl* RECHNUNG conversion cost; **Konvertierungspapier** *nt* FINANZ conversion issue; **Konvertierungsprämie** *f* BÖRSE conversion premium

Konzentration *f* GESCHÄFT, VW concentration; **Konzentrationsmaß** *nt* VW concentration ratio

konzentrieren *vt* GESCHÄFT concentrate

konzentriert: **~es Banking** *nt* BANK concentration banking

Konzept *nt* GESCHÄFT approach, plan, MGMNT approach, RECHNUNG, V&M concept, VERWALT, VW approach; **~ für ein arbeitendes Unternehmen** RECHNUNG going-concern concept; **~ der Rechnungsabgrenzung** RECHNUNG concept of accrual; **Konzeptwertanalyse** *f* FINANZ value engineering

Konzern *m* GESCHÄFT affiliated group, group of companies, concern, group; ◆ **in einem ~ zusammenfassen** GESCHÄFT affiliate

Konzern: **Konzernabschluß** *m* RECHNUNG consolidated accounts, consolidated financial statement, group accounts; **Konzernbetriebsrat** *m* PERSON combine committee; **Konzernbilanz** *f* FINANZ, RECHNUNG combined financial statement, consolidated balance sheet,

consolidated financial statement; **Konzernbilanzbuchhalter, in** *m,f* RECHNUNG group chief accountant; **Konzernbuchgewinn** *m* FINANZ intercompany profits; **Konzerndiversifizierung** *f* VW conglomerate diversification

konzerneigen: **~e Finanzierungsgesellschaft** *f* VW captive finance company; **~e Versicherungsgesellschaft** *f* VW captive insurance company

Konzern: **Konzerngesellschaft** *f* VW corporate affiliate; **Konzerngewinn** *m* RECHNUNG group profit; **Konzerngoodwill** *m* RECHNUNG goodwill on consolidation

konzernintern *adj* PERSON intergroup, intragroup; **~e Beziehungen** *f pl* PERSON intergroup relations, intragroup relations; **~er Markt** *m* BÖRSE intercompany market

Konzern: **Konzernstruktur** *f* GESCHÄFT group structure; **Konzerntochter** *f* RECHNUNG subsidiary; **Konzernumsatz** *m* FINANZ consolidated sales; **Konzernunternehmen** *nt* GESCHÄFT affiliate, affiliate company; **Konzernverbund** *m* FINANZ affiliated group; **Konzern-Verrechnungskonto** *nt* RECHNUNG intercompany clearing account

Konzertzeichner, in *m,f* BÖRSE stag, free rider

Konzertzeichnung *f* BÖRSE free ride (*infrml*)

Konzession *f* GESCHÄFT concession, franchise, PATENT patent (*pat.*), RECHT concession, licence (*BrE*), license (*AmE*), STEUER concession; **Konzessionen** *f pl* GESCHÄFT concessions

Konzessionär, in *m,f* GESCHÄFT concessionaire, RECHT concessionaire, licensee, STEUER concessionaire

konzessionierbar: **nicht ~** *adj* GESCHÄFT nonconcessional

konzessionieren *vt* GESCHÄFT enfranchise, charter, RECHT license

konzessioniert *adj* GESCHÄFT chartered, franchised, RECHT licensed; **~e Bank** *f* BANK chartered bank; **~er Lebensversicherungsagent** *m* VERSICH chartered life underwriter; **~er Sach- und Schadenversicherungsagent** *m* VERSICH chartered property and casualty underwriter; **~er Wirtschaftsprüfer** *m*, **~e Wirtschaftsprüferin** *f* RECHNUNG certified general accountant, certified public accountant (*AmE*) (*CPA*)

Konzession: **Konzessionsantragsprüfung** *f* RECHT licensing examination; **Konzessionserteiler, in** *m,f* PATENT, RECHT licensor; **Konzessionsexport** *m* IMP/EXP concessional export; **Konzessionsinhaber, in** *m,f* GESCHÄFT concessionaire, franchisee, RECHT licensee; **Konzessionsplanung** *f* FINANZ franchise financing; **Konzessionsrecht** *nt* RECHT licence laws (*BrE*), license laws (*AmE*); **Konzessionssicherheitsleistung** *f* RECHT licence bond (*BrE*), license bond (*AmE*); **Konzessionssteuer** *f* STEUER franchise tax (*AmE*); **Konzessionsurkunde** *f* **einer Bank** BANK bank charter; **Konzessionsvergabenorm** *f* UMWELT licensing standard; **Konzessionsvertrag** *m* RECHT franchise agreement

Konzipierung *f* PATENT drawing up

konzis *adj* GESCHÄFT concise

Kooperation *f* GESCHÄFT, RECHT cooperation; **Kooperationsvertrag** *m* GESCHÄFT, RECHT cooperation agreement

kooperativ *adj* GESCHÄFT, VW cooperative; **~er Föderalismus** *m* POL cooperative federalism

Kooperative *f* MGMNT, PERSON, VW cooperative (*co-op*)

kooperieren *vi* GESCHÄFT cooperate

Koordinatennetz *nt* COMP grid

Koordinator, in *m,f* PERSON coordinator; **~ Arbeitgeber-Arbeitnehmer-Interessen** MGMNT, PERSON director of labour relations (*BrE*), director of labor relations (*AmE*), industrial relations director, industrial relations manager; **~ Export** MGMNT export coordinator

koordinieren *vt* GESCHÄFT coordinate

koordiniert *adj* GESCHÄFT coordinated

Koordinierung *f* GESCHÄFT coordination; **Koordinierungsausschuß** *m* **für multilaterale Exportkontrollen** IMP/EXP coordinating committee for multilateral export controls; **Koordinierungsprovision** *f* BANK arrangement fee

Kopf *m* COMP *Laufwerk* head, KOMM caption, MEDIEN *Druck* head; ♦ **pro ~** GESCHÄFT per capita, per head

Kopf: **Kopfbahnhof** *m* TRANSP railhead, terminus station; **Kopfhörer** *m* MEDIEN earphone; **Kopfjäger, in** *m,f* PERSON headhunter

kopflastig *adj* VERWALT *Organisation* top-heavy

Kopf: **Kopfsteuer** *f* SOZIAL, STEUER capitation, head tax, poll tax (*BrE*) (*obs*), capitation tax; **Kopfzeile** *f* COMP *Textverarbeitung* header

Kopie *f* COMP *Textverarbeitung*, GESCHÄFT copy, KOMM carbon copy (*cc*); **~ des Schreibens als Anlage beigefügt** *phr* KOMM enclosed copy of letter, subjoined copy of letter

kopieren *vt* COMP *Textverarbeitung*, GESCHÄFT copy

Kopierer *m* VERWALT copier

Kopiergerät *nt* VERWALT copier

kopiergeschützt *adj* COMP copy-protected; **~e Diskette** *f* COMP copy-protected disk

Kopierschutz *m* COMP *Disketten* copy protection; ♦ **mit ~ versehen** COMP *Diskette* copy-protected

Koppelvertrag *m* RECHT *Vertragsrecht* barter contract

Kopplung *f* FINANZ tie-in; **Kopplungsgeschäft** *nt* RECHT package deal, V&M tie-in sale, vw interlinked transaction; **Kopplungsverkauf** *m* FREI block booking, V&M block booking, tie-in sale; **Kopplungsvertrag** *m* VW tying arrangement, tying contract

Koprozessor *m* COMP coprocessor

Korb *m* VERWALT basket; **~ für ausgehende Post** VERWALT out-tray; **~ für eingehende Post** VERWALT in-tray; **Korbwährung** *f* VW composite currency; **Korbwährungseinheit** *f* VW composite currency unit

Körper- *in cpds* GESCHÄFT, RECHT, VERSICH body, personal

körperlich *adj* GESCHÄFT physical; **~e Arbeit** *f* PERSON manual work; **~e Durchsuchung** *f* GESCHÄFT physical examination; **~e Inventur** *f* RECHNUNG physical inventory

Körper-: **Körperschaden** *m* RECHT, VERSICH personal injury

Körperschaft *f* VERWALT corporate body; **~ des öffentlichen Rechts** GESCHÄFT public body, public corporation; **Körperschaftssteuer** *f* STEUER company tax, corporate tax, corporation income tax, corporation tax (*BrE*); **Körperschaftssteuerabschlußzahlung** *f* STEUER mainstream tax (*MT*); **Körperschaftssteuerpflicht** *f* STEUER corporation tax liability; **Körperschaftssteuersätze** *m pl* STEUER corporation

tax rates (*BrE*); **Körperschaftssteuer-Vorauszahlung** *f* (*KStVz*) STEUER advance corporation tax (*ACT*) (*BrE*)

Körper-: **Körpersprache** *f* GESCHÄFT, PERSON body language; **Körperverletzung** *f* RECHT, VERSICH personal injury

Korporatismus *m* GESCHÄFT, POL corporatism

korporatistisch *adj* GESCHÄFT corporate; **~er Staat** *m* POL corporate state

korporativ *adj* GESCHÄFT corporate; **~er Staat** *m* POL corporate state

Korpsgeist *m* MGMNT, PERSON esprit de corps

Korr. *abbr* (*Korrespondenz*) KOMM corr. (*correspondence*), communication

korrekt *adj* GESCHÄFT accurate, correct

Korrektheit *f* GESCHÄFT accuracy

Korrektur *f* MEDIEN correction; **Korrekturbogen** *m* MEDIEN proof; **in der Korrekturbogenphase** *phr* MEDIEN at proof stage; **Korrekturlesen** *nt* MEDIEN proofreading; **Korrekturposten** *m* RECHNUNG correcting entry

Korrelation *f* MATH correlation; **Korrelationskoeffizient** *m* MATH correlation coefficient, coefficient of correlation

korrelieren *vt* MATH correlate

Korrespondent, in *m,f* BANK correspondent, MEDIEN correspondent, *in freier Mitarbeit* stringer

Korrespondenz *f* (*Korr.*) KOMM correspondence (*corr.*), communication; **Korrespondenzbank** *f* BANK correspondent bank, respondent bank

korrespondenzfähig: **~es Schriftbild** *nt* COMP near letter quality (*NLQ*)

korrespondieren *vi* GESCHÄFT *entsprechen*, KOMM *in Briefwechseln* correspond

Korridor *m* VW corridor

korrigieren *vt* BANK, MATH adjust, MEDIEN correct

korrigierend: **~e Maßnahme** *f* GESCHÄFT corrective action

korrigiert *adj* MEDIEN corrected; **nicht ~** *adj* MEDIEN uncorrected; **~e Wahrscheinlichkeit** *f* MATH corrected probability

korrodieren *vi* IND, TRANSP corrode

Korrosion *f* IND, TRANSP corrosion

korrosionsbeständig: **~es Material** *nt* IND, TRANSP corrosion-resistant material; **~er Werkstoff** *m* IND, TRANSP corrosion-resistant material

korrosionsfest: **~er Werkstoff** *m* IND, TRANSP corrosion-resistant material

Korrosion: **Korrosionsschäden** *m pl* IND, TRANSP, VERSICH corrosion damage

korrosionssicher: **~er Werkstoff** *m* IND, TRANSP corrosion-resistant material

korrumpieren *vt* GESCHÄFT corrupt

Korruption *f* GESCHÄFT corruption

Kosmetik *f* GESCHÄFT cosmetics

kosten *vt* GESCHÄFT cost

Kosten *pl* GESCHÄFT charge, cost, costs, expenditure, expense, expenses, VW costs; **~ für angewandte Forschung** GESCHÄFT applied research cost; **~ außerhalb der Baustelle** GRUND off-site cost; **~ außerhalb der Hauptzeiten** KOMM, TRANSP off-peak charges; **~ der Betriebsschließung** GESCHÄFT closing-down costs; **~ bis zum Löschen** TRANSP landed cost; **~ für**

die Erweiterung des Versicherungsschutzes VERSICH extension costs; ~ durch Fehlbestand GESCHÄFT stockout cost; ~ und Fracht (*C&F*) IMP/EXP, TRANSP *Lieferklausel* cost and freight (*C&F, CAF, CF*); ~ der Geschäftsstelle BÖRSE agency cost (*BrE*); ~ der Kuppelprodukte RECHNUNG joint product cost; ~ der Kuppelproduktion VW common costs, joint costs; ~ pro Anfrage V&M cost per inquiry; ~ pro gefahrenem Kilometer TRANSP cost per vehicle kilometer (*AmE*), cost per vehicle kilometre (*BrE*); ~ pro Tausend V&M cost per thousand; ~ für Schadensminderung und Schadensabwendung VERSICH *Seeversicherung* sue and labor charges (*AmE*), sue and labour charges (*BrE*); ~ der sozialen Anpassung PERSON social adjustment cost; ~ und Versicherung (*C&I*) IMP/EXP, TRANSP *Lieferklausel* cost and insurance (*C&I*); ~, Versicherung und Fracht IMP/EXP, TRANSP *Lieferklausel* cost, insurance and freight (*CI&F*); ♦ für die ~ aufkommen RECHNUNG meet costs; ~ aufschlüsseln FINANZ, RECHNUNG break down expenses; ~ bestimmten Konten zuordnen RECHNUNG allocate costs to certain accounts; ~ bestimmten Konten zurechnen RECHNUNG allocate costs to certain accounts; ~ auf die geeigneten Konten umlegen RECHNUNG allocate costs to the appropriate accounts; ~ kontrollieren GESCHÄFT control costs; ~ sind per Nachnahme zu erheben GESCHÄFT charge forward (*Ch Fwd*); die ~ steigen auf Milliardenhöhe GESCHÄFT costs are running into billions; ~, die für jdn steuerpflichtig sind STEUER costs taxable to sb; die ~ tragen GESCHÄFT bear the costs, defray the cost, meet costs; die ~ übernehmen GESCHÄFT pay for the expenses; ~ umlegen RECHNUNG assign costs, allocate costs; ~ verrechnen RECHNUNG allocate costs

Kosten: Kostenabbau *m* FINANZ, VW cost reduction; Kostenabweichung *f* FINANZ cost variance; Kostenabweichunganalyse *f* RECHNUNG analysis of cost variances; Kostenanalyse *f* FINANZ, RECHNUNG cost analysis; Kostenart *f* FINANZ type of costs; Kostenartenbeitrag *m* RECHNUNG contribution profit; Kostenartenrechnung *f* FINANZ, RECHNUNG analysis of costs by nature, job cost system; Kostenaufstellung *f* FINANZ cost records; Kostenaufteilung *f* RECHNUNG cost allocation

kostenaufwendig *adj* GESCHÄFT costly

Kosten: Kostenauswertung *f* FINANZ, RECHNUNG cost analysis; Kostenbeitrag *m* GESCHÄFT contribution; Kostenbeleg *m* GESCHÄFT cost records; Kostenbewertung *f* von Lagerbeständen RECHNUNG inventory costing, inventory evaluation; Kostenbewußtsein *nt* GESCHÄFT cost awareness; Kostenblock *m* GESCHÄFT pool of costs; Kostenbuchhaltung *f* RECHNUNG cost accounting

kostendeckend 1. *adj* GESCHÄFT cost-effective; 2. *adv* ♦ ~ arbeiten FINANZ break even

kostendeckend: ~e Menge *f* V&M breakeven quantity; ~e Preisfestsetzung *f* V&M marginal pricing; ~e Preisgestaltung *f* V&M breakeven pricing

Kostendeckungspunkt *m* FINANZ breakeven point; ♦ den ~ erreichen FINANZ break even

Kosten: Kostendegression *f* VW economy of scale; Kostendenken *nt* GESCHÄFT cost consciousness; Kostendruckinflation *f* VW cost-push inflation

kosteneffektiv *adj* GESCHÄFT cost-effective, cost-efficient

Kosten: Kosteneindämmung *f* VW cost containment; Kosteneinschätzung *f* GRUND cost approach

kostenempfindlich *adj* GESCHÄFT cost-sensitive

Kosten: Kostenerfassung *f* BÖRSE cost recording (*BrE*); Kosteneskalationsdeckung *f* VERSICH cost escalation cover (*BrE*); Kostenfaktor *m* RECHNUNG cost factor; Kostenfestsetzung *f* BÖRSE fixing of costs

kostenfrei *adj* GESCHÄFT cost-free, IMP/EXP charges prepaid; ~er Anruf *m* KOMM free call

Kosten: Kostenführer *m* VW cost leader; Kostenfunktionsanalyse *f* RECHNUNG functional analysis of costs; Kostengefüge *nt* FINANZ cost structure; Kostengliederung *f* FINANZ, RECHNUNG breakdown of expenses; eine Kostengliederung aufstellen *phr* FINANZ, RECHNUNG break down expenses

kostengünstig *adj* GESCHÄFT cost-effective, low-cost

kosteninduziert: ~e Inflation *f* VW cost-push inflation

Kosten: Kosteninflation *f* VW cost-push inflation; Kostenisoquante *f* VW isocost; Kostenkontrolle *f* RECHNUNG cost control; Kosten- und Leistungsrechnung *f* RECHNUNG cost accounting

kostenlos *adj* GESCHÄFT at no charge, free, free of charge (*foc*), gratuitous, without charge (*w.c.*); ~er Anruf *m* KOMM Freefone® call, (*BrE*), toll-free call (*AmE*); ~es Anrufen *nt* KOMM free call; ~e ärztliche Versorgung *f* SOZIAL free medical treatment; ~es Darlehen *nt* FINANZ gratuitous loan; ~er Eintritt *m* FREI free admission; ~es Muster *nt* V&M free sample; ~er Versicherungsschutz und Transport *m pl* TRANSP, VERSICH free insurance and carriage; ~e Zeitung *f* MEDIEN free newspaper; ~e Zustellung *f* TRANSP free delivery

Kosten: Kostenmehranfall *m* RECHNUNG underabsorption

kostenminimal: ~er Fluß *m* VW minimal cost flow

Kosten: Kosten-Nutzen-Analyse *f* FINANZ, RECHNUNG, VW cost-benefit analysis; Kostenplan *m* FINANZ expense budget; Kostenplanung *f* nach Verantwortungsbereichen FINANZ responsibility accounting; Kostenprognose *f* VERWALT cost forecast; Kostenprogression *f* VW diseconomy, diseconomy of scale

kostenreagibel *adj* VW cost-sensitive

Kosten: Kostenrechnung *f* FINANZ bill of costs, cost-volume-profit analysis, RECHNUNG cost accounting; Kostenrechnung *f* für Serienfertigung IND process costing; Kostenreduzierung *f* FINANZ, VW cost reduction; Kostensammelblatt *nt* FINANZ job cost sheet; Kostensammelkarte *f* FINANZ job card; Kostenschätzung *f* V&M estimating; Kostensenkung *f* GESCHÄFT cost trimming, cost cutting, cost containment, cost reduction

Kostenstelle *f* RECHNUNG activity element, cost center (*AmE*), cost centre (*BrE*), expense center (*AmE*), expense centre (*BrE*); Kostenstellengliederung *f* RECHNUNG activity classification; Kostenstellengruppen *f pl* RECHNUNG activity coding

Kosten: Kostensteuerung *f* RECHNUNG cost control; Kostenstruktur *f* FINANZ cost structure; Kostenüberschreitung *f* VW cost overrun; Kostenüberwachung *f* RECHNUNG cost control; Kostenumfanggewinnanalyse *f* FINANZ cost-volume-profit analysis; Kostenumlage *f* RECHNUNG allocation of costs, apportionment of costs, cost allocation, cost apportionment; Kostenunterdeckung *f* RECHNUNG underabsorption; **Kostenverhältnis** *nt* FINANZ cost ratio; **Kostenverlauf** *m* FINANZ cost behavior pattern (*AmE*), cost behaviour pattern (*BrE*); **Kostenverrechnung** *f* RECHNUNG cost allocation, allocation of costs; **Kostenverteilung** *f* RECHNUNG cost allocation; **Kostenvoranschlag** *m* GESCHÄFT estimate, RECHNUNG cost forecast, estimated charges; **um Kostenvoranschläge ersuchen** *phr* GESCHÄFT appeal for tenders; **Kostenvorgabe** *f* VW cost objective; **Kostenwirksamkeit** *f* GESCHÄFT cost-effectiveness; **Kosten-Wirksamkeits-Analyse** *f* VW cost-effectiveness analysis; **Kostenziel** *nt* VW cost objective; **Kostenzurechnung** *f* RECHNUNG cost apportionment, VW cost application; **Kostenzuspruch** *m* PATENT awarding of costs

kostspielig *adj* GESCHÄFT costly, expensive, dear, pricey (*infrml*)

Kovarianz *f* MATH covariance

Kraft *f* GESCHÄFT force, IND energy, power; ◆ **in ~** RECHT *Vorschriften, Gesetze* in force; **~ seines Amtes** GESCHÄFT virtute officii; **außer ~ setzen** RECHT *Gesetz* invalidate, *Regel* override; **in ~ setzen** MGMNT *Krisenplan* activate, RECHT *Gesetz* put into force; **in ~ treten** RECHT *Gesetz* come into force, enter into force, take effect

Kraft: **mit Kraftantrieb** *phr* IND mechanized; **Krafterzeugung** *f* IND power generation; **Kraftfahrstraße** *f* TRANSP motorway (*BrE*), expressway (*AmE*), superhighway (*AmE*)

Kraftfahrzeug *nt* (*Kfz*) GESCHÄFT vehicle; **Kraftfahrzeuganschaffungskredit** *m* BANK car loan; **Kraftfahrzeughaftpflichtversicherung** *f* TRANSP, VERSICH third-party motor vehicle insurance; **Kraftfahrzeughersteller** *m* IND, TRANSP car manufacturer; **Kraftfahrzeugindustrie** *f* IND, TRANSP automotive industry, car industry, motor industry; **Kraftfahrzeugprämie** *f* VERSICH motor insurance premium; **Kraftfahrzeugsammelpolice** *f* VERSICH fleet policy; **Kraftfahrzeugsteuer** *f* STEUER, TRANSP motor vehicle tax, road tax (*BrE*); **Kraftfahrzeugvermietung** *f* FREI, TRANSP car hire (*BrE*), car rental (*AmE*), car-hire service (*BrE*), car-rental service (*AmE*); **Kraftfahrzeugversicherung** *f* VERSICH automobile insurance (*AmE*), car insurance, motor insurance (*BrE*), motor vehicle insurance; **Kraftfahrzeugversicherungsvertrag** *m* VERSICH motor vehicle insurance agreement; **Kraftfahrzeugzulassung** *f* TRANSP car registration; **Kraftfahrzeugzuschuß** *m* GESCHÄFT car allowance

Kraft: **Kraftprobe** *f* GESCHÄFT showdown (*infrml*), trial of strength; **Kraftstoff** *m* IND fuel

kraftvoll *adj* GESCHÄFT powerful, vigorous

Kraft: **Kraftwagentransporter** *m* TRANSP car carrier, car transporter; **Kraftwerk** *nt* IND power station, UMWELT generating station; **Kraftwerksleistung** *f* IND power-generating capacity

Kragen *m* VW collar

Kran *m* IND, TRANSP crane

kränkelnd *adj* GESCHÄFT ailing

Kranken- *in cpds* PERSON, SOZIAL, VERSICH sickness; **Krankengeld** *nt* PERSON sick pay, sickness benefit, VERSICH daily compensation; **Krankengeld beziehen** *phr* PERSON draw sickness payments; **Krankengeldregelung** *f* PERSON sick pay scheme

(*BrE*); **Krankengeschichte** *f* SOZIAL health record; **Krankenhausertragsanleihe** *f* FINANZ hospital revenue bond; **Krankenkasse** *f* PERSON, SOZIAL health insurance scheme; **Krankenversicherung** *f* PERSON, SOZIAL, VERSICH health insurance, medical insurance, sickness insurance; **Krankenversicherungsleistungen** *f pl* SOZIAL, VERSICH health benefits; **Krankenversicherungsprämie** *f* PERSON, SOZIAL, VERSICH *private Krankenversicherung* health insurance premium, medical insurance premium, sickness insurance premium; **Krankenversicherungssystem** *nt* PERSON, SOZIAL, VERSICH health insurance scheme

krankgeschrieben: **~ sein** *phr* PERSON be on sick leave

Krankheit *f* PERSON, SOZIAL, VERSICH sickness; **aus Krankheitsgründen abwesend sein** *phr frml* PERSON be absent due to illness, be off sick

kränklich *adj* GESCHÄFT ailing

kreativ *adj* GESCHÄFT creative; **~e Buchführung** *f infrml* RECHNUNG creative accounting; **~es Denken** *nt* MGMNT creative thinking; **~er Föderalismus** *m* POL creative federalism; **~e Strategie** *f* V&M creative strategy; **~e Zerstörung** *f* VW creative destruction

Kreativität *f* GESCHÄFT creativity

Kredit *m* BANK advance, bank accommodation, loan, credit (*Cr*), FINANZ advance, credit (*Cr*), RECHNUNG advance; **~ mit eingeschränktem Rückgriffsrecht** BANK limited-recourse debt; **~ mit fester Laufzeit** BANK fixed-term loan; **~ für einen Spitzenbetrag** FINANZ gap loan; ◆ **auf ~** FINANZ on credit; **etw auf ~ kaufen** V&M buy sth on credit; **~ aufnehmen** BANK borrow funds; **einen ~ aufnehmen** FINANZ contract a loan; **einen ~ aufschieben** RECHNUNG defer a debt; **einen ~ beantragen** BANK, FINANZ apply for a loan; **~ gewähren** BÖRSE lend; **gegen ~** GESCHÄFT on account (*o/a*); **auf ~ verkaufen** V&M sell on credit, sell on trust

Kredit: **Kreditabteilung** *f* BANK, FINANZ credit department, loan department; **Kreditansage** *f* FINANZ credit approval; **Kreditanstalt** *f* FINANZ credit institution; **Kreditantrag** *m* BANK, FINANZ loan application

Kreditaufnahme *f* BANK, FINANZ borrowing; **~ im Ausland** BANK, FINANZ foreign borrowing, borrowing abroad; **~ durch Banken** BANK borrowing by banks; **~ bis zur äußersten Grenze** FINANZ high finance; **~ in Fremdwährung** BANK foreign currency borrowing; **~ am Geldmarkt** FINANZ borrowing in the money market; **Kreditaufnahmebefugnis** *f* FINANZ borrowing power; **Kreditaufnahmegrenze** *f* FINANZ borrowing limit; **Kreditaufnahmevollmacht** *f* FINANZ borrowing authority

Kredit: **Kreditauftrag** *m* V&M credit order; **Kreditausfall** *m* BANK loan default, loan loss; **Kreditausfallrückstellung** *f* BANK loan loss provision; **Kreditauskunft** *f* BANK banker's reference, FINANZ credit information; **Kreditauskunftei** *f* FINANZ credit bureau; **Kreditbank** *f* FINANZ loan bank; **Kreditbearbeitung** *f* FINANZ credit management; **Kreditbearbeitungsgebühr** *f* BANK loan fee

Kreditbedarf *m* BANK, FINANZ borrowing requirement, credit demand, credit requirements; **~ des öffentlichen Dienstes** VW public sector borrowing requirement (*BrE*) (*PSBR*); **~ der öffentlichen Hand** VW public sector borrowing requirement (*BrE*) (*PSBR*); **~ der Regierung** VW central government borrowing requirement

Kredit: **Kreditbedingungen** *f pl* BANK terms of credit, VW credit conditions; **Kreditbeschaffungskosten** *pl* BANK cost of borrowing; **Kreditbeschränkung** *f* BANK, FINANZ, VW credit rationing, credit squeeze; **Kreditbestätigung** *f* BANK facility letter; **Kreditbewilligung** *f* **gegen Sicherheiten** FINANZ security lending; **Kreditbrief** *m* BÖRSE credits; **Kreditbürgschaft** *f* FINANZ loan guarantee; **Kreditbürgschaftsprogramm** *nt* FINANZ loan guarantee scheme; **Kreditbüro** *nt* FINANZ credit bureau; **Kreditdrosselung** *f* BANK, FINANZ, VW credit restriction, credit squeeze; **Krediteinräumung** *f* BANK credit granting; **Krediteinschränkung** *f* BANK, FINANZ, VW credit restriction; **Krediteinzahlungsbeleg** *m* BANK credit account voucher; **Kreditengagement** *nt* FINANZ loan exposure

krediterweitert *adj* BÖRSE credit-enhanced

Kredit: **Kreditexpansion** *f* VW domestic credit expansion (*DCE*); **Kreditfachmann** *m* BÖRSE credit analyst

kreditfähig *adj* BANK creditworthy, sound

Kredit: **Kreditfähigkeit** *f* BANK creditworthiness, FINANZ financial standing, borrowing potential; **Kreditfazilität** *f* BANK, FINANZ borrowing facility, credit facility; **Kreditfazilität zusammenstellen** *phr* BANK, FINANZ arrange a loan

kreditfinanziert *adj* BÖRSE, FINANZ on margin; **~er Effektenkauf** *m* BÖRSE, FINANZ buying on margin

Kredit: **Kreditfinanzierung** *f* BANK, FINANZ loan financing; **Kreditgarantie** *f* BANK credit guarantee; **Kreditgeber, in** *m,f* BANK lender; **Kreditgebühr** *f* GESCHÄFT borrowing fee, RECHNUNG debt charge; **Kreditgeld** *nt* BANK credit money; **Kreditgeschäft** *nt* BANK lending business; **Kreditgeschäft** *nt* **der Banken** BANK bank lending; **Kreditgewährung** *f* BANK granting of credit, lending; **Kredithai** *m* infrml FINANZ loan shark (*infrml*); **Kredithöchstgrenze** *f* BANK credit ceiling, credit limit; **Kreditinanspruchnahme** *f* BANK draw; **Kreditinstitut** *nt* BANK bank (*bk*), FINANZ credit institution, financial institution, lending agency, lending institution, credit agency; **Kreditinstitut** *nt* **für langfristige Kredite** BANK long-term credit bank; **Kreditinstrumentarium** *nt* BÖRSE credit instrument; **Kreditinvestition** *f* FINANZ loan investment

Kreditkarte *f* BANK, FINANZ credit card, SOZIAL affinity card; **Kreditkartenaussteller** *m* FINANZ credit card issuer; **Kreditkartenbestand** *m* BANK credit card portfolio; **Kreditkarteninhaber, in** *m,f* BANK, FINANZ cardholder, credit cardholder; **Kreditkartenkonto** *nt* BANK credit account (*C/A*); **Kreditkartenzahlung** *f* BANK, V&M credit card payment

Kredit: **Kreditkauf** *m* V&M credit sale; **Kreditkäufer, in** *m,f* V&M charge buyer (*BrE*), credit buyer (*AmE*); **Kreditknappheit** *f* BANK, FINANZ, VW credit crunch, credit squeeze; **Kreditkolumne** *f* FINANZ credit column; **Kreditkonditionen** *f pl* BANK credit terms, terms of credit; **Kreditkonto** *nt* BANK checking account (*AmE*) (*C/A*), cheque account (*BrE*) (*C/A*), credit account (*C/A*), current account (*BrE*) (*C/A*); **Kreditkontrolle** *f* BANK credit control; **Kreditkosten** *pl* GESCHÄFT borrowing cost, borrowing fee; **Kreditkunde** *m* V&M charge buyer (*BrE*), credit buyer (*AmE*); **Kreditlinie** *f* BANK credit line, FINANZ line of credit, RECHNUNG credits outstanding, bank facilities; **Kreditlinie** *f* **einer Bank** BANK bank line; **Kreditmakler, in** *m,f* BANK, FINANZ money broker; **Kreditmöglichkeit** *f* BANK, FINANZ borrowing facility, credit facility; **Kreditnachfrage** *f* BANK credit demand, loan demand; **Kreditnehmer, in** *m,f* BANK borrower, FINANZ beneficiary; **Kreditnehmer, in** *m,f* **der Klasse AAA** BÖRSE triple-A-rated borrower

Kreditoren *m pl* RECHNUNG accounts payable, creditors (*BrE*); **Kreditorenabteilung** *nt* FINANZ collection department; **Kreditorenbuch** *nt* RECHNUNG accounts payable ledger, bought ledger (*BrE*); **Kreditorenbuchhalter, in** *m,f* RECHNUNG accounts payable clerk

Kredit: **Kreditplafond** *m* BANK credit ceiling; **Kreditpolitik** *f* BANK lending policy; **Kreditpolitik** *f* **der Banken** BANK bank lending policy; **Kreditportefeuille** *nt* BÖRSE, FINANZ asset portfolio; **Kreditposten** *m* BANK, FINANZ credit; **Kreditpotential** *nt* BANK lending power, FINANZ creditor position; **Kreditprüfer, in** *m,f* BÖRSE credit analyst; **Kreditprüfung** *f* BANK credit analysis; **Kreditrahmen** *m* BANK, FINANZ credit facility; **Kreditreserven** *f pl* FINANZ credit reserves; **Kreditrestriktion** *f* BANK, FINANZ, VW credit crunch, credit squeeze; **Kreditrisiko** *nt* FINANZ credit risk, RECHNUNG risk exposure, V&M credit risk; **Kreditrückzahlung** *f* BANK, FINANZ loan repayment; **Kreditsachbearbeiter, in** *m,f* BANK, FINANZ credit officer, lending officer, loan officer, MGMNT credit controller; **Kreditauskunftei** *f* FINANZ rating agency; **Kreditschöpfungsmultiplikator** *m* VW credit creation multiplier; **Kreditschutzverein** *m* FINANZ credit reference agency; **Kreditseite** *f* FINANZ credit side; **Kreditsicherheiten** *f pl* FINANZ lending securities; **Kreditspalte** *f* FINANZ credit column; **Kredittranche** *f* FINANZ credit tranche; **Kredittranchenfazilität** *f* VW credit tranche facility; **Kreditüberwachung** *f* FINANZ credit surveillance; **Kreditvergabe** *f* BANK lending; **Kreditvergabepolitik** *f* BANK lending policy; **Kreditverknappung** *f* BANK, FINANZ, VW restriction of credit, credit squeeze; **Kreditverrechnung** *f* BANK credit clearing (*BrE*); **Kreditversicherung** *f* FINANZ loan insurance; **Kreditvertrag** *m* FINANZ credit agreement; **Kreditverwaltung** *f* FINANZ credit management; **Kreditvolumen** *nt* BANK loan portfolio, BÖRSE, FINANZ asset portfolio, RECHNUNG outstanding credits; **Kreditwirtschaft** *f* BANK banking industry

kreditwürdig *adj* BANK, FINANZ creditworthy, sound

Kreditwürdigkeit *f* BANK, FINANZ creditworthiness, reliability, financial standing, V&M credit standing; **Kreditwürdigkeitsprüfung** *f* BANK credit analysis, FINANZ credit scoring

Kreditzins *m* BANK lending rate; **~ für erste Adressen** BANK prime rate of interest

Kreditzins: **Kreditzinssatz** *m* BANK bank lending rate, borrowing rate

Kreis *m* GESCHÄFT circle, POL district, municipality; ♦ **der ~ hat sich geschlossen** GESCHÄFT the wheel has come full circle

Kreis: **Kreisdiagramm** *nt* MATH pie chart

Kreiselkompaß *m* TRANSP gyrocompass

Kreis: **Kreiskrankenhaus** *nt* SOZIAL district hospital; **Kreislauf** *m* VW cycle; **Kreistag** *m* POL *Bezirksregierung* district council (*BrE*); **Kreisverkehr** *m* TRANSP roundabout (*BrE*), traffic circle (*AmE*)

Kreuz *nt* MATH, V&M, VW cross; **Kreuzelastizität** *f* **der**

Nachfrage V&M cross elasticity of demand; **Kreuzfaltung** *f* V&M French fold; **Kreuzkurs** *m* VW cross rate; **Kreuzparität** *f* VW cross rate; **Kreuzpreiselastizität** *f* **der Nachfrage** VW cross price elasticity of demand; **Kreuztabellierung** *f* MATH cross tabulation

Kreuzungspunkt *m* VW saddle point

Krieg *m* POL, VERSICH war; **Kriegsanleihe** *f* FINANZ war loan (*BrE*); **Kriegsgefahrrisiko** *nt* VERSICH war risk; **Kriegskasse** *f* *jarg* FINANZ idle balance, war chest (*AmE*); **Kriegsklausel** *f* VERSICH war clause; **Kriegsrisiko** *nt* VERSICH war risk; **Kriegsrisikodeckung** *f* **unter der Bedingung schwimmender Fracht** VERSICH waterborne agreement; **nur gegen Kriegsrisiko versichert** *phr* VERSICH war risk only (*wro*)

Krise *f* GESCHÄFT crisis; **~ im Finanzierungs- und Teilzahlungskreditgeschäft** BANK secondary banking crisis; **~ im Teilzahlungsbankgeschäft** BANK fringe banking crisis; **Krisenmanagement** *nt* MGMNT crisis management; **Krisenmanager** *m* COMP, GESCHÄFT troubleshooter; **Krisenplan** *m* FINANZ, MGMNT contingency plan; **Krisenzentrum** *nt* GESCHÄFT, POL trouble spot

Kriterium *nt* GESCHÄFT criterion, yardstick

Kritik *f* MEDIEN write-up, review

Kritiker, in *m,f* MEDIEN critic; **~ aus der Distanz** GESCHÄFT armchair critic (*infrml*)

Kritikus *m* *infrml, obs* GESCHÄFT armchair critic (*infrml*)

kritisch *adj* GESCHÄFT critical; **~er Bereich** *m* MATH critical region; **~es Bewußtsein** *nt* GESCHÄFT, POL acute awareness; **~er Lagerbestand** *m* RECHNUNG reorder point; **~e Masse** *f* V&M, VW critical mass; **~e Menge** *f* V&M, VW critical mass; **~es Niveau** *nt* GESCHÄFT critical level; **~er Pfad** *m* COMP critical path; **~er Weg** *m* COMP critical path; **~er Wert** *m* MATH critical value; **~er Zeitpunkt** *m* GESCHÄFT juncture

kritisieren *vt* GESCHÄFT criticize, level criticism at

Kronanwalt *m* RECHT Queen's Counsel (*BrE*) (*QC*)

Kronanwältin *f* RECHT Queen's Counsel (*BrE*) (*QC*)

Kronrat *m* RECHT crown council, Privy Council (*BrE*)

kryogen *adj* IND cryogenic

Kryogenik *f* IND cryogenics

Kryotechnik *f* IND cryogenic engineering

KStVz *abbr* (*Körperschaftsteuervorauszahlung*) STEUER ACT (*advance corporation tax*) (*BrE*)

kt *abbr* (*Kilotonne*) GESCHÄFT kt (*kiloton, kilotonne*)

Kto. *abbr* (*Konto*) BANK, RECHNUNG, V&M a/c (*account*)

Kubik- *in cpds* GESCHÄFT cubic (*cu*); **Kubikfuß** *m* GESCHÄFT cubic foot (*cf, cu ft*); **Kubikmeter** *m* (m^3) GESCHÄFT cubic meter (*AmE*) (*cbm, m^3*), cubic metre (*BrE*) (*cbm, m^3*); **Kubiktonnage** *f* TRANSP *Ladefähigkeit eines Schiffes* cubic tonnage (*CT*); **Kubikzentimeter** *m* (*cc, cm^3*) GESCHÄFT cubic centimeter (*AmE*) (*cc, cm^3*), cubic centimetre (*BrE*) (*cc, cm^3*); **Kubikzoll** *m* GESCHÄFT cubic inch (*cu in*)

Kuhhandel *m* *infrml* PERSON, POL *Verhandlung* horse trading (*infrml*)

Kühl- *in cpds* IND cold, refrigerated (*R*), cooled

kühl: ~ aufbewahrt *adj* IND refrigerated (*R*)

Kühl-: Kühlanlage *f* IND cold storage plant; **Kühlcontainer** *m* TRANSP refrigerated container

kühlen *vt* IND refrigerate

Kühl-: Kühlhalle *f* IND cold store; **Kühlhaus** *nt* IND refrigerated warehouse, cold store; **Kühlhausterminal** *nt* TRANSP cold store terminal; **Kühlkastenwagen** *m* TRANSP refrigerated box van; **Kühllastwagen** *m* TRANSP refrigerated lorry (*BrE*), refrigerated truck (*AmE*); **Kühlleistung** *f* IND refrigerated capacity; **Kühlraumlagerung** *f* IND cold storage; **Kühlschiff** *nt* TRANSP reefer, reefer carrier, reefer ship, refrigerated ship, refrigerated vessel

Kühlung *f* IND refrigeration (*R*)

Kulanz *f* GESCHÄFT *von Bedingungen* fairness; **Kulanzentschädigung** *f* FINANZ, VERSICH ex gratia payment; **Kulanzregulierung** *f* FINANZ, VERSICH ex gratia payment; **Kulanzzahlung** *f* FINANZ, VERSICH ex gratia payment

kultivieren *vt* VW *Landwirtschaft* cultivate

Kultivierung *f* VW *Landwirtschaft* cultivation

Kultur *f* GESCHÄFT culture

kulturell *adj* GESCHÄFT cultural; **~es Zentrum** *nt* FREI, MEDIEN cultural center (*AmE*), cultural centre (*BrE*)

Kultur: Kulturschock *m* GESCHÄFT culture shock; **Kulturzentrum** *nt* FREI, MEDIEN cultural center (*AmE*), cultural centre (*BrE*)

kümmern: sich ~ um *phr* GESCHÄFT attend to

kumulativ *adj* BÖRSE, FINANZ, STEUER, VERSICH cumulative (*cum.*); **~es Einkommen** *nt* STEUER cumulative income; **~e Erbschafts- und Schenkungssteuer** *f* STEUER accessions tax; **~e Haftung** *f* VERSICH cumulative liability; **~er Jahressatz** *m* BANK compound annual rate (*BrE*) (*CAR*); **~e Steuer** *f* STEUER cumulative tax; **~e Stimmrechtsabgabe** *f* BÖRSE *bei Hauptversammlungen von Kapitalgesellschaften* cumulative voting; **~e Vorzugsaktien** *f pl* BÖRSE cumulative preference shares (*BrE*), cumulative preferred stock (*AmE*); **~es Wertpapier** *nt* BÖRSE cumulative security

kumulieren *vt* BÖRSE, FINANZ, STEUER, VERSICH accumulate

Kumulierung *f* BÖRSE, FINANZ, STEUER, VERSICH accumulation; **~ von Risiken** VERSICH accumulation of risk; **Kumulierungsbereich** *m* BÖRSE accumulation area

Kumulrisiko *nt* VERSICH accumulation risk

kündbar *adj* GESCHÄFT terminable; **~es Darlehen** *nt* BANK callable loan; **täglich ~er Maklerkredit** *m* BÖRSE broker's loan; **~e Urkunde** *f* BÖRSE renounceable document

Kunde *m* V&M client, customer, account; **~ höchster Bonität** GESCHÄFT blue-chip customer; ◆ **Kunden anreißen** GESCHÄFT tout for customers; **den Kunden kennen** V&M know your customer; **Kunden werben** V&M canvass

Kunde: Kundenabrechnung *f* RECHNUNG customer accounting, customer billing; **Kundenabteilung** *f* V&M customer service; **Kundenakte** *f* FINANZ customer card; **nach Kundenangaben gefertigt** *phr* IND made-to-measure

kundenangepaßt: ~e Tastatur *f* COMP customized keyboard

Kunde: Kundenbasis *f* V&M client base; **Kundenbedürfnisse** *nt pl* V&M customer needs; **Kundenbeeinflussung** *f* V&M suggestion selling; **Kundenberatungsfonds** *m* FINANZ advisory funds (*AmE*); **Kundenbestand** *m* V&M customer base

kundenbestimmt *adj* V&M customer-driven

Kunde: Kundenbesuchszyklus *m* V&M calling cycle;

Kundenbetreuer, in *m,f* V&M account manager; **Kundenbetreuung** *f* V&M customer care, account management; **Kundenbuch** *nt* RECHNUNG accounts receivable ledger, sales ledger (*BrE*); **Kundenbuchhaltung** *f* RECHNUNG accounts receivable accounting

Kundendienst *m* V&M after-sales service, backup service, customer service, post-sales service, sales service; **Kundendienstabteilung** *f* IND maintenance department, V&M customer service department, service department; **Kundendienstleiter, in** *m,f* MGMNT customer relations manager, customer service manager, PERSON after-sales manager, customer relations manager, customer service manager; **Kundendienststunden** *f pl* GESCHÄFT service hours; **Kundendiensttechniker, in** *m,f* PERSON service engineer; **Kundendienstvertreter, in** *m,f* PERSON customer service representative

Kunde: **Kundeneinlage** *f* BANK customer deposit; **auf Kundenfang sein** *phr* GESCHÄFT tout for custom; **Kundenfänger, in** *m,f* GESCHÄFT tout; **Kundenfirma** *f* V&M client firm; **Kundenforschung** *f* V&M customer research; **Kundengruppenmanagement** *nt* V&M account management; **Kundenkarte** *f* COMP service card; **Kundenkartei** *f* V&M customer records; **Kundenkontakter, in** *m,f* V&M field worker; **Kundenkonto** *nt* GESCHÄFT trade account; **Kundenkonto** *nt* **mit Plus- und Minuspositionen** BÖRSE mixed account; **Kundenkreditbank** *f* BANK, FINANZ finance house (*BrE*); **Kundenkreditkarte** *f* BANK, V&M charge card; **Kundenkreditkonto** *nt* BANK credit account (*C/A*), FINANZ budget account; **Kundenleasing** *nt* BANK consumer leasing

kundenorientiert *adj* V&M customer-oriented; **~e Marketingpolitik** *f* V&M client-led marketing policy

Kunde: **Kundenorientierung** *f* V&M customer orientation; **Kundenprofil** *nt* V&M customer profile; **Kundenrabatt** *m* V&M sales discount; **Kundenservice** *m* V&M customer service

kundenspezifisch *adj* V&M customized, custom-made, tailor-made, made-to-order; **~e Dienstleistungen** *f pl* V&M customized service

Kunde: **Kundenstamm** *m* V&M established clientele; **Kundenumfrage** *f* V&M multi-client survey; **Kundenverbindung** *f* V&M customer liaison; **Kundenverlust** *m* V&M loss of custom; **Kundenvertrauen** *nt* V&M *in ein Produkt* customer confidence; **Kundenwerber, in** *m,f* V&M canvasser; **Kundenwerbung** *f* V&M consumer advertising; **etw den Kundenwünschen anpassen** *phr* IND *Produktion* customize sth; **Kundenzeitschrift** *f* V&M external house magazine

kündigen 1. *vt* FINANZ foreclose, *Kredit* call in, GESCHÄFT *Beschäftigungsverhältnis* terminate, *Vertrag* annul, PERSON *stornieren* cancel, RECHT terminate; **2.** *vi* GRUND *Mieter, Pächter* give notice to quit, PERSON *Arbeitnehmer* resign, sign off, *Stellung* hand in one's notice, give in one's notice; ◆ **jdm ~** PERSON *Arbeitgeber* dismiss sb, give sb his notice, *Arbeitnehmer* hand in one's notice to sb

Kündigung *f* FINANZ foreclosure, GESCHÄFT *eines Vertrags* annulment, *eines Beschäftigungsverhältnisses* termination, GRUND notice to quit, PERSON *seitens Arbeitnehmers* resignation, *seitens Arbeitgebers* dismissal, RECHT termination, *Stornierung* cancellation;

~ zum Ausstellungsdatum der Police VERSICH notice of cancellation at anniversary date (*NCAD*); **Kündigungsfrist** *f* PERSON period of notice, notice period; **Kündigungsgrund** *m* PERSON grounds for dismissal; **Kündigungsklausel** *f* BÖRSE call provision; **Kündigungsschreiben** *nt* MGMNT, PERSON pink slip (*AmE*), redundancy letter (*BrE*); **Kündigungsschutz** *m* BÖRSE *Anleiheemissionen* call protection, PERSON, RECHT *Arbeitsrecht* protection against wrongful dismissal; **Kündigungsverfahren** *nt* PERSON dismissal procedure

Kundin *f* V&M client, customer

künftig: **~en Bedarf abschätzen** *phr* GESCHÄFT make an appraisal of future needs

Kunst *f* GESCHÄFT, MEDIEN art; **die ~ des Möglichen** POL the art of the possible; **Kunstakademie** *f* SOZIAL art school; **Kunstdruck** *m* V&M art print; **Kunstdruckpapier** *nt* V&M art matt (*AmE*), art matt paper (*BrE*); **Kunstdünger** *m* UMWELT fertilizer; **Kunstgegenstand** *m* MEDIEN, V&M artwork; **Kunsthandwerkermesse** *f* MEDIEN, V&M artisan fair; **Kunsthochschule** *f* SOZIAL art school

Künstlerarbeit *f* MEDIEN, V&M artwork

künstlerisch: **~e Arbeit** *f* MEDIEN, V&M artwork

künstlich *adj* GESCHÄFT artificial, IND man-made; **~ gehaltener Preis** *m* GESCHÄFT subsidized price, supported price; **~es Hochbieten** *nt* BÖRSE bidding up; **~e Intelligenz** *f* (*KI*) COMP artificial intelligence (*AI*); **~e Marktaktivität** *f* BÖRSE daisy chain; **~e Schranke** *f* VW artificial barrier to entry; **~es Veralten** *nt* V&M artificial obsolescence; **~e Währung** *f* VW artificial currency; **~er Wechselkurs** *m* VW artificial exchange rate

Kunststoff *m* IND, UMWELT synthetic material, man-made substance; **Kunststoffe** *m pl* IND, UMWELT plastics; **Kunststoffmüll** *m* IND, UMWELT plastic waste; **Kunstwährung** *f* RECHNUNG artificial currency

Kupfer *nt* IND copper; **Kupfererz** *nt* IND copper ore; **Kupferklischee** *nt* MEDIEN electrotype

Kupon *m* BÖRSE, V&M coupon (*c., cp.*); ◆ **ohne ~** BÖRSE, GESCHÄFT ex coupon (*ex cp, x-c.*)

Kupon: **Kuponsteuer** *f* STEUER dividend withholding tax

Kuppelprodukte *nt pl* VW joint products

Kuratorium *nt* POL, SOZIAL governing body

Kurier *m* KOMM courier; **Kurierdienst** *m* KOMM courier firm, courier service; **Kurierfirma** *f* KOMM courier firm

Kurs *m* BÖRSE quoted price, rate, price (*pr.*), FINANZ price (*pr.*), MGMNT, PERSON, SOZIAL course, VW *Wertpapiere* price (*pr.*); **~ einschließlich aufgelaufener Zinsen** FINANZ flat; ◆ **den ~ einer Aktie durch Verkäufe drücken** BÖRSE raid the market; **Kurse können sowohl fallen als auch steigen** BÖRSE prices can go down as well as up; **die Kurse sind ins Bodenlose gesunken** VW the bottom has dropped out of the market; **Kurse sind niedriger notiert worden** BÖRSE prices have been marked down; **einen ~ haben von** BÖRSE trade at

Kurs: **Kursabschwächung** *f* BÖRSE decline; **Kursauftrieb** *m* BÖRSE price surge; **Kursbeeinflusser, in** *m,f* BÖRSE manipulator; **Kursblatt** *nt* BÖRSE stock list, daily official list, pink sheets (*AmE*), Stock Exchange Official List (*BrE*); **Kursbuch** *nt* FREI, TRANSP timetable; **Kursdifferenz** *f* BÖRSE tail (*AmE*), VW exchange differences

kursempfindlich: ~e **Informationen** *f pl* BÖRSE, VW price-sensitive information

Kurs: **Kursentwicklung** *f* BÖRSE price move; **Kursfestsetzung** *f* BÖRSE pricing of an issue; **Kursfeststellung** *f* FINANZ marking, price determination; **Kursgefälle** *nt* BÖRSE price differential; **Kurseinbruch** *m* BÖRSE break, market plunge (*AmE*); **Kurseinsturz** *m* BÖRSE market slump

kursgesichert: ~er **Optionsschein** *m* FINANZ covered warrant

Kurs: **Kursgewinn** *m* BÖRSE appreciation, gain; **Kurs-Gewinn-Verhältnis** *nt* (*KGV*) FINANZ price-earnings ratio (*P/E ratio, PER*), RECHNUNG price-earnings multiple

kursieren *vi* KOMM *Informationen, Nachrichten* circulate

Kurs: **Kursindex** *m* BÖRSE share price index; **Kursindexniveau** *nt* BÖRSE price index level; **Kursintervention** *f* VW exchange intervention

kursiv *adj* COMP *Textverarbeitung*, MEDIEN *Typographie* italic

Kursivschrift *f* COMP *Textverarbeitung*, MEDIEN *Typographie* italics

Kurs: **Kurskennzeichen** *nt* FINANZ marking; **Kurslimit** *nt* BÖRSE price ceiling, price limit; **Kursmakler, in** *m,f* BÖRSE broker-dealer; **Kursmanipulation** *f* BÖRSE market rigging; **Kursniveau** *nt* GESCHÄFT price level; **Kursnotierung** *f* BÖRSE quoted price, share quotation, VW foreign exchange table, quoted price; **Kursparität** *f* BANK parity of exchange; **Kursrechnung** *m* BÖRSE bond valuation; **Kursrisikogarantieplan** *m* BANK exchange risk guarantee scheme; **Kursrückgang** *m* BÖRSE decline, VW depreciation; **Kursschwankungen** *f pl* **nutzen** BÖRSE, FINANZ arbitrate; **Kurssicherungsgeschäft** *nt* BÖRSE hedging operation; **Kursspanne** *f* BÖRSE trading range, VW exchange differences; **Kursspielraum** *m* **nach oben** FINANZ upside potential; **Kurstabelle** *f* VW foreign exchange table; **Kursstabilisierung** *f* BÖRSE market stabilization; **Kurssteigerung** *f* BÖRSE appreciation, price advance; **Kurssturz** *nt* BÖRSE, FINANZ plunge; **Kursstützung** *f* FINANZ, VW price support; **Kursstützungsniveau** *nt* FINANZ, VW price support level; **Kurstaxe** *f* BÖRSE estimated price; **Kurstendenz** *f* FINANZ price trend; **Kurstreiber, in** *m,f* BÖRSE market rigger; **Kursuntergrenze** *f* BÖRSE stop-out price (*AmE*); **Kursvariabilität** *f* BÖRSE price volatility; **Kursverfall** *m* VW nosedive; **Kursverlust** *m* BÖRSE price loss; **Kurswagen** *m* TRANSP through coach (*BrE*); **Kurswechsel** *m* GESCHÄFT turnabout; **Kurswert** *m* BÖRSE, FINANZ market value; **unter dem Kurswert** *phr* BÖRSE below-market

kurswertgewichtet: ~er **Index** *m* BÖRSE market-value-weighted index

Kurve *f* MATH curve, graph; ~ **gleicher Produktion** VW equal product curve; **Kurvenschreiber** *m* COMP X-Y plotter; **Kurvenzeichner** *m* COMP plotter

Kurz- *in cpds* GESCHÄFT brief, short, summary, *gedrängt* condensed

kurz 1. *adj* GESCHÄFT brief, short, concise, summary, *gedrängt* condensed; ♦ **von ~em Bestand** GESCHÄFT short-lived; 2. *adv* GESCHÄFT briefly; ♦ ~ **zusammenfassen** GESCHÄFT summarize

kurz: ~er **Börsenauftrieb** *m* BÖRSE flurry of activity; ~e **Frist** *f* GESCHÄFT short notice; ~e **Übersicht** *f* GESCHÄFT summary; ~er **Vermerk** *m* VERWALT memo

(*infrml*), memorandum; ~er **Warnstreik** *m* PERSON hit-and-run strike; **zu** ~e **Kapitaldecke** *f* FINANZ low-geared capital; **auf** ~e **Zeit ausgestelltes Konnossement** *nt* IMP/EXP, TRANSP short form, short form bill of lading

Kurz-: **Kurzarbeit** *f* PERSON *Rezession, Auftragsmangel* short-time working; **Kurzarbeit leisten** *phr* PERSON be on short time; **Kurzbefehl** *m* COMP hot key; **Kurzbericht** *m* GESCHÄFT summary, condensed report, brief, summary report; **Kurzeingabe** *f* COMP keyboard short cut, short key

kürzen *vt* BÖRSE shorten, FINANZ cut, GESCHÄFT truncate, *Ausgaben, Kosten, Provision* prune, whittle down, pare down; ♦ **jds Arbeitslohn** ~ PERSON dock sb's wages

kürzerfristig: ~e **Option** *f* BÖRSE shorter-term option

Kurz-: **Kurzfassung** *f* GESCHÄFT abstract, summary

kurzfristig 1. *adj* GESCHÄFT short-term, short-range, short-dated; 2. *adv* GESCHÄFT in the short run, in the short term; ♦ ~ **lieferbar** GESCHÄFT available at short notice; ~ **verfügbar** GESCHÄFT available at short notice

kurzfristig: ~e **Anlagen** *f pl* VW near cash; ~es **Beteiligungsportefeuille** *nt* BÖRSE short-term investment portfolio; ~es **Darlehen** *nt* BANK call loan, accommodation, accommodation loan; ~e **Einlage** *f* BANK bank demand deposit, bank deposit, BÖRSE short-term deposit; ~ **fälliger Wechsel** *m* FINANZ short bill (*SB*); ~es **Fälligkeitsdatum** *nt* BÖRSE short-range maturity date; ~er **Fälligkeitstermin** *m* BÖRSE short-range maturity date; ~e **Finanzierungsrate** *f* BÖRSE short-date financing rate; ~e **Fluktuation** *f* VW short-term fluctuation; ~er **Frachtbrief** *m* TRANSP short form; ~er **Geldmarkt** *m* BÖRSE short-term money market; ~es **Geldmarktpapier** *nt* erstklassiger Emittenten FINANZ euro commercial paper; ~er **Gewinn** *m* BÖRSE short pull, short-term gain; ~e, **hochliquide Anlagen** *f pl* BÖRSE near cash; ~es **Investitionsgut** *nt* BÖRSE short-term investment asset; ~e **kombinierte Optionsposition** *f* BÖRSE short butterfly, short straddle; ~er **Kredit** *m* BÖRSE, FINANZ short credit, short loan; ~e **Laufzeit** *f* BÖRSE short term; ~er **Leasingvertrag** *m* FINANZ operating lease; ~e **Liquiditätsplanung** *f* RECHNUNG, VW cash budgeting; ~er **Markt** *m* BÖRSE short-term market; ~e **Planung** *f* FINANZ, MGMNT short-range planning, short-term planning; ~e **Schuldtitel** *m* BANK short-term debt; ~e **Schuldverschreibung** *f* BÖRSE short-term bond; ~es **Spekulationsgeschäft** *nt* BÖRSE free ride (*infrml*); ~e **Staatspapiere** *nt pl* BÖRSE shorts; ~es **Sterling-Geldmarktpapier** *nt* BANK, BÖRSE sterling commercial paper (*SCP*); ~er **Terminkontraktzinssatz** *m* BÖRSE short-term interest rate futures contract; ~e **Todesfallversicherung** *f* VERSICH term insurance; ~e **unbesicherte Hypothek** *f* BANK self-amortizing mortgage; ~es, **ungesichertes Darlehen** *nt* FINANZ accommodation; ~e **Verbindlichkeit** *f* BANK current liability, short-term debt, BÖRSE short-term liability, FINANZ floating debt, liquid debt, RECHNUNG short-term liability; ~er **Verlust** *m* BÖRSE short-term loss; ~er **Vertrag** *m* PERSON short-term contract; ~e **Vorauszahlung** *f* RECHNUNG short-term prepayment; ~es **Wertpapier** *nt* BÖRSE short-term security; ~es **Wertpapierportefeuille** *nt* BÖRSE short-term investment portfolio; ~es **Ziel** *nt* GESCHÄFT short-term objective; ~es **Zinssatzrisiko** *nt* BÖRSE short-term interest rate risk

Kurz-: **Kurzfristplanung** *f* FINANZ, MGMNT short-term planning; **Kurzkonnossement** *nt* IMP/EXP, TRANSP short form bill of lading, short form; **Kurzläufer** *m* BANK short-term debt, BÖRSE short

kurzlebig *adj* GESCHÄFT transient, short-lived; **~e Güter** *nt pl* V&M nondurable goods, nondurables; **~e Konsumgüter** *nt pl* V&M perishables, nondurable goods, nondurables, VW soft goods; **~e Verbrauchsgüter** *nt pl* V&M perishables, nondurable goods, nondurables, soft goods; **~er Vermögenswert** *m* RECHNUNG, VW wasting asset; **~es Wirtschaftsgut** *nt* RECHNUNG, VW wasting asset

Kurz-: **Kurznachricht** *f* MEDIEN newsflash; **Kurznachrichten** *f pl* MEDIEN news headlines

kurzschließen *vt* IND short-circuit

Kurz-: **Kurzschluß** *m* IND short-circuit; **Kurzschrift** *f* VERWALT shorthand, stenography; **in Kurzschrift aufnehmen** *phr* VERWALT take down in shorthand

kurzsichtig *adj* GESCHÄFT short-sighted

Kurz-: **Kurzstrecke** *f* TRANSP short haul; **Kurztaste** *f* COMP keyboard short cut, short key

Kürzung *f* BÖRSE shortening, FINANZ cut, GESCHÄFT *von Angaben, Kosten, Provision* cut, pruning, whittling down, paring down, truncation, abatement; **~ des Pensionsplanes** FINANZ curtailment in pension plan

Kurz-: **Kurzzeitfahrzeugpark** *m* TRANSP short-term vehicle park (*STVP*); **Kurzzeitplanung** *f* FINANZ, MGMNT short-range planning

Küste *f* TRANSP, UMWELT coast

Küste: **Küstenfahrt** *f* TRANSP coasting; **Küstenfahrtmakler, in** *m,f* TRANSP coasting broker; **Küstenhandel** *m* TRANSP coasting, coasting trade

küstennah *adj* UMWELT offshore; **~e Installation** *f* IND, UMWELT offshore installation; **~es Ölfeld** *nt* IND, UMWELT offshore oil field

Küste: **Küstenschiff** *nt* TRANSP coaster, home trade ship; **Küstenschiffahrt** *f* TRANSP coasting, coasting trade; **Küstenverkehrszone** *f* TRANSP inshore traffic zone; **Küstenverschmutzung** *f* UMWELT coastal pollution; **Küstenvorland** *nt* RECHT foreshore

Kutter *m* TRANSP *Schiffstyp* cutter

Kuznets-Kurve *f* VW Kuznets curve

kW *abbr* (*Kilowatt*) GESCHÄFT kW (*kilowatt*)

KW *abbr* (*Kalenderwoche*) GESCHÄFT calendar week

kWh *abbr* (*Kilowattstunde*) GESCHÄFT kWh (*kilowatt-hour*)

Kybernetik *f* COMP cybernetics

kybernetisch *adj* COMP cybernetic

L

l *abbr* (*Liter*) GESCHÄFT l (*liter AmE, litre BrE*)

Labor *nt* IND lab (*infrml*) (*laboratory*)

Laboratorium *nt* IND laboratory (*lab*)

Labor: **Laborerfahrung** *f* IND laboratory experience; **Labortechnik** *f* IND laboratory technique

Labour: **~ Party** *f* POL Labour Party (*BrE*); **Labour-Regierung** *f* VERWALT, POL Labour Administration (*BrE*)

ladbar: **~e Schriftart** *f* COMP downloadable font

Lade- *in cpds* GESCHÄFT, TRANSP cargo, load, stowage, loading; **Ladeagent** *m* TRANSP loading agent; **Ladebaum** *m* TRANSP derrick; **Ladebereich** *m* TRANSP stowage area; **Ladebereitschaftsmitteilung** *f* TRANSP notice of readiness; **Ladedeplacement** *nt* TRANSP displacement loaded, displacement tonnage; **Ladeeinheit** *f* TRANSP *Luftfahrt* unit load device (*ULD*); **Ladefähigkeit** *f* TRANSP carrying capacity, deadweight capacity (*dwc*), bulk capacity, cargo tonnage, deadweight tonnage (*dwt*), *eines Schiffes* deadweight (*dw*); **Ladefähigkeit** *f* **nach Anzahl und Länge an Deck** TRANSP carrying capacity in number and length on deck (*CDK*); **Ladefläche** *f* TRANSP bearing surface; **Ladekran** *m* TRANSP cargo derrick; **Lademakler, in** *m,f* PERSON loading broker, TRANSP chartering agent; **das Lademaß überschreitend** *phr* TRANSP out of gage (*AmE*) (*OOG*), out of gauge (*BrE*) (*OOG*)

laden *vt* COMP *Programm* download, load, RECHT issue a summons

Laden 1. *m* V&M shop (*BrE*), store (*AmE*); **~ außerhalb der Stadt** V&M out-of-town store; **im ~ betriebene Verkaufsförderung** *f* V&M in-store promotion; **~ an der Ecke** V&M corner shop (*BrE*), neighborhood store (*AmE*), mom-and-pop store (*AmE*); **~ für zollfreie Waren** FREI, IMP/EXP, STEUER duty-free shop (*BrE*), tax-free shop (*AmE*); **2.** *nt* TRANSP loading (*ldg*)

Laden: **Ladenaufsicht** *f* V&M floorwalker; **Ladendiebstahl** *m* V&M shoplifting, shrinkage

Lade-: **Ladenetz** *nt* TRANSP cargo net

Laden: **Ladenfront** *f* V&M shop front; **Ladeninhaber, in** *m,f* V&M shopkeeper (*BrE*), storekeeper (*AmE*); **Ladenkasse** *f* GESCHÄFT, V&M till; **Ladenpreis** *m* GESCHÄFT, V&M published price; **Ladenschild** *nt* V&M facia; **Ladenschlußzeiten** *f pl* GESCHÄFT shop closing times (*BrE*), store closing times (*AmE*); **Ladentisch** *m* GESCHÄFT counter; **Ladenverkauf** *m* V&M retail sale; **Ladenverkaufsanalyse** *f* V&M retail sales analysis; **Ladenverkehr** *m* V&M shop traffic (*BrE*), store traffic (*AmE*); **Ladenvertrieb** *m* V&M in-store merchandising; **Ladenvorführung** *f* V&M store demonstration

Lade-: **Ladeöl** *nt* TRANSP cargo oil (*co*); **Ladeplattform** *f* TRANSP cargo tray; **Ladepritsche** *f* TRANSP cargo tray; **Ladeprovision** *f* TRANSP address commission; **Laderaum** *m* GESCHÄFT loading space, TRANSP hold; **Laderauminhalt** *m* **für Ballen** TRANSP bale capacity; **Ladeschein** *m* IMP/EXP bill of lading (*b.l., B/L*), shipping note (*S/N*), TRANSP bill of lading (*b.l., B/L*),

consignment note (*C/N, CN*), certificate of shipment, shipping note (*S/N*)

Ladetank *m* TRANSP cargo tank (*CT*); **Ladetankflügel** *m* TRANSP cargo tank wing (*CTW*); **Ladetankzentrum** *nt* TRANSP cargo tank center (*AmE*) (*CTC*), cargo tank centre (*BrE*) (*CTC*)

Ladeverdrängung *f* TRANSP displacement loaded

Ladung *f* IND batch, RECHT summons, writ of summons, service of a writ, TRANSP cargo, lading, load, disembarkation; **~ und Kontrolle** *f* **des Befrachters** TRANSP shipper's load and count (*sl&c*); **~ unter Strafandrohung** RECHT writ of subpoena; **~ und Zählung** *f* **des Befrachters** TRANSP shipper's load and count (*sl&c*); **Ladungsfähigkeit** *f* TRANSP cargo capacity (*CC*); **Ladungskapazität** *f* TRANSP cargo capacity (*CC*); **Ladungskontrolleur** *m* TRANSP, V&M tallyman; **Ladungsmanifest** *nt* TRANSP manifest of cargo, manifest; **Ladungsprüfer, in** *m,f* PERSON checker; **Ladungsversicherung** *f* VERSICH cargo insurance; **Ladungsverzeichnis** *nt* IMP/EXP manifest; **im Ladungsverzeichnis anzeigen** *phr* IMP/EXP manifest; **im Ladungsverzeichnis aufführen** *phr* IMP/EXP manifest; **Ladungszuordnung** *f* TRANSP loading allocation

Laffer-Kurve *f* VW Laffer curve

Lag *m* VW lag

Lag. *abbr* (*Lager*) GESCHÄFT whse (*warehouse*), stock, stockpile, storage, storehouse, IMP/EXP whse (*warehouse*), TRANSP whse (*warehouse*), stockpile, storage, V&M whse (*warehouse*)

Lagan *nt* TRANSP lagan

Lage *f* GESCHÄFT position, situation (*sit.*), status; **~ des Konferenzortes** MGMNT conference site location; **~ des Sitzungsortes** MGMNT conference site location; **~ des Tagungsortes** MGMNT conference site location; **♦ in der ~ sein zu** GESCHÄFT be in a position to; **nach ~ der Dinge** GESCHÄFT, RECHT under the circumstances; **die ~ pessimistisch betrachten** GESCHÄFT take a gloomy view of the situation; **die ~ prüfen** GESCHÄFT size up the situation

Lage: **Lagebericht** *m* FINANZ financial report, GESCHÄFT situation report (*sitrep*), status report, MGMNT status report, VERWALT financial report; **Lageinformation** *f* GESCHÄFT status information

Lager *nt* (*Lag.*) GESCHÄFT stock, stockpile, storage, storehouse, warehouse (*whse*), storeroom, IMP/EXP warehouse (*whse*), storeroom, IND storage, TRANSP stockpile, storage, warehouse (*whse*), VERWALT repository; **♦ nicht auf ~** V&M out of stock (*o.s.*); **ab ~** IMP/EXP, TRANSP ex warehouse (*x-warehouse*); **~ abbauen** VW liquidate inventory; **~ auffüllen** VW restock; **wieder auf ~ nehmen** V&M restock

Lager: **Lagerarbeiter** *m* GESCHÄFT storeman; **Lagerarbeiterin** *f* GESCHÄFT storewoman; **Lageraufseher, in** *m,f* GESCHÄFT, IMP/EXP, TRANSP warehouse supervisor

Lagerbestand *m* TRANSP goods on hand; **~ im Fertigungsbereich** IND manufacturing inventory; **♦ ~ kennzeichen** RECHNUNG mark stock

Lagerbestände *m pl* RECHNUNG inventory stocks; ◆
~ absetzen V&M dispose of stock; **~ nach Alter
aufstellen** RECHNUNG age stocks; **seine ~ aufstocken**
GESCHÄFT replenish stocks
Lagerbeständigkeit *f* V&M shelf life
Lagerbestand: **Lagerbestandsbewertung** *f* GESCHÄFT
stock valuation, RECHNUNG inventory pricing;
Lagerbestandsbuch *nt* RECHNUNG inventory book;
Lagerbestandseinheit *f* GESCHÄFT stockkeeping unit;
Lagerbestandskontrolle *f* GESCHÄFT reserve-stock
control, RECHNUNG inventory control;
Lagerbestandsverzeichnis *nt* IND, RECHNUNG inven-
tory; **Lagerbestandswechsel** *m* V&M stock rotation
Lager: **Lagerbuch** *nt* TRANSP warehouse book (*WB*);
Lagerbuchhaltung *f* RECHNUNG store accounting;
Lagerentnahme *f* RECHNUNG, VERWALT withdrawal
from stocks; **Lagererzeugnis** *nt* V&M stock line;
Lagerfinanzierung *f* RECHNUNG inventory financing;
Lagerfläche *f* GESCHÄFT storage area, V&M shelf space;
Lagergebäude *nt* GESCHÄFT storehouse, warehouse
(*whse*), V&M warehouse (*whse*); **Lagergebühren** *f pl*
GESCHÄFT, TRANSP storage charges; **Lagergeld** *nt*
GESCHÄFT, TRANSP storage charges, IMP/EXP warehouse
charges; **Lagerhalter** *m* GESCHÄFT storeman, store-
keeper, warehouse keeper, warehouse officer;
Lagerhalterin *f* GESCHÄFT storekeeper, warehouse
keeper, warehouse officer;
Lagerhalterhaftpflichtversicherung *f* VERSICH store-
keeper's liability insurance
Lagerhaltung *f* GESCHÄFT storage, IMP/EXP warehousing,
IND storage, warehousing, MGMNT inventory manage-
ment, TRANSP warehousing, VW stockholding;
Lagerhaltungskontrolle *f* GESCHÄFT reserve-stock con-
trol; **Lagerhaltungszyklus** *m* VW inventory cycle
Lager: **Lagerhaus** *nt* GESCHÄFT storehouse, warehouse
(*whse*), IMP/EXP, TRANSP, V&M warehouse (*whse*);
Lagerhauseintrag *m* TRANSP warehouse entry
Lagerist *m* GESCHÄFT stockman (*AmE*), storekeeper,
storeman, warehouseman, IMP/EXP warehouse officer
Lageristin *f* GESCHÄFT stockwoman (*AmE*), storekeeper,
storewoman, IMP/EXP warehouse officer
Lager: **Lagerkapazität** *f* GESCHÄFT storage capacity;
Lagerkontrolle *f* RECHNUNG inventory control, stock
control, VW stock control; **Lagerkontrolleur** *m* PERSON,
RECHNUNG, VW stock controller; **Lagerliste** *f* GESCHÄFT
stock sheet
lagern *vt* GESCHÄFT, IND, TRANSP *Fracht, Waren* store
Lager: **Lagerplanung** *f* RECHNUNG, VW inventory plan-
ning; **Lagerprüfung** *f* RECHNUNG store audit;
Lagerraum *m* TRANSP bay; **Lagerschein** *m* IMP/EXP bill
of store, warehouse receipt (*WR*), IND warehouse
receipt (*WR*), RECHT, TRANSP, V&M warehouse receipt
(*WR*), warehouse warrant (*WW*); **Lagerspesen** *f pl*
GESCHÄFT storage charges, IMP/EXP warehouse charges;
Lagerstätte *f* UMWELT deposit; **Lagerumsatz** *m* IND,
RECHNUNG, VW stock turnover; **Lagerumschlag** *m*
GESCHÄFT, IND stock turnover, RECHNUNG inventory
turnover, stock turnover, turnover, VW stock turnover
Lagerung *f* GESCHÄFT storage, IND, TRANSP storage,
warehousing, UMWELT dumping; **~ von Abfall** UMWELT
waste dumping; **Lagerungsgebühren** *f pl* TRANSP
warehouse charges
Lager: **Lagerverwalter** *m* GESCHÄFT stockman (*AmE*),
storekeeper, storeman, warehouse keeper, warehouse-

man, MGMNT stock controller;
Lagerverwalterhaftpflichtversicherung *f* VERSICH
storekeeper's liability insurance; **Lagerverwalterin** *f*
GESCHÄFT stockwoman (*AmE*), storekeeper, store-
woman, warehouse keeper, warehousewoman, MGMNT
stock controller; **Lagerverwaltung** *f* V&M stock man-
agement; **Lagervorrat** *m* **in der Verkaufsabteilung** V&M
forward stock; **Lagerwirtschaft** *f* RECHNUNG inventory
control, stock control, VW inventory control;
Lagerzugang *m* VERWALT addition to stock
Lag-Reaktion *f* VW lag response
Laie *m* FREI amateur, PERSON layman; **Laienmitglied** *nt*
PERSON lay member
Laisser-faire *nt* VW laisser-faire; **Laisser-faire-
Führungstil** *m* PERSON free-rein leadership; **Laisser-
faire-Liberalismus** *m* VW laisser-faire economy
LAN *abbr* (*lokales Netz*) COMP, KOMM LAN (*local area
network*)
Land *nt* IMP/EXP, POL, TRANSP, VW country; **~ in
Anwartschaft** RECHT land in abeyance; **~ mit
Meistbegünstigungsstatus** VW most favored nation
(*AmE*) (*MFN*), most favoured nation (*BrE*) (*MFN*); ◆
**die von einem ~ aufgenommenen Kredite
abschreiben** BANK write off the debts incurred by a
country; **von ~ eingeschlossen** UMWELT landlocked;
jdn des Landes verweisen POL deport sb, expel sb
Land: **Landarbeiter, in** *m,f* STEUER farm laborer (*AmE*),
farm labourer (*BrE*), VW farmhand; **Landbesitzer, in**
m,f GRUND landowner; **Landbrücke** *f* TRANSP land
bridge; **Landbrückenrate** *f* TRANSP land-bridge rate;
Landebahn *f* TRANSP runway, landing strip;
Landeplatz *m* TRANSP airstrip, landing strip
Länder- *in cpds* BANK, BÖRSE, FINANZ, V&M, VW country;
Länderbericht *m* VW country report; **Ländercode** *m*
BANK country code
Ländereien *f pl* GRUND estates
Länder-: **Länderfonds** *m* BÖRSE country fund;
Ländergruppe *f* V&M cluster of countries;
Länderklassifikation *f* **der Weltbank** VW World Bank
classification of countries; **Länderrisiko** *nt* BÖRSE
country exposure, FINANZ country risk, VERSICH, VW
country exposure
Land: **Landesbank** *f* BANK regional bank; **Landeschein**
m TRANSP landing account (*L/A*); **Landesgericht** *nt*
POL, RECHT state government tribunal; **Landesgrenze** *f*
IMP/EXP, POL national boundary; **Landesplanung** *f*
GESCHÄFT country planning; **Landesregierung** *f* POL
government of a Land or province of a federal state
landesspezifisch *adj* VW country-specific
Land: **Landeswährung** *f* VW national currency;
Landeszentralbankenvorstand *m* VW ≈ Federal
Reserve Board (*AmE*); **Landeszentralbankrat** *m*
BANK ≈ Federal Reserve Board (*AmE*) (*FRB*)
landesweit *adj* GESCHÄFT nationwide
Landeszentralbank *f* BANK, VW ≈ Federal Reserve
Bank (*AmE*) (*FRB*)
Landschaftsschutzamt *nt* UMWELT Countryside Com-
mission (*BrE*)
Landschaftsschutzgebiet *nt* UMWELT environmentally
sensitive zone
Landing: ~ Gear *nt* TRANSP landing gear
ländlich: ~es Entwicklungsgebiet *nt* VW Rural Devel-
opment Area (*BrE*) (*RDA*); **~es Fördergebiet** *nt* VW
Rural Development Area (*BrE*) (*RDA*); **~es Gebiet** *nt*

VW rural area; **~e Gemeinde** *f* VW rural community; **~er Raum** *m* VW rural area; **~ und unerschlossen** *phr* UMWELT greenfield

Land: **Landpacht** *f* GRUND, RECHT tenure in land, land lease, farm tenancy; **Landtransport** *m* TRANSP land carriage; **Landtreuhand** *f* RECHT land trust

landumschlossen *adj* UMWELT landlocked

Landungsbrücke *f* TRANSP landing stage, quay

Landvermesser, in *m,f* GRUND surveyor

Landwirt *m* VW agriculturalist, agriculturist

Landwirtschaft *m* GESCHÄFT agriculture

landwirtschaftlich *adj* BANK, POL, UMWELT, VERSICH, VW agricultural; **~er Beruf** *m* PERSON, VW agricultural job; **~e Betriebseinheit** *f* VW agricultural unit; **~e Darlehensgewährung** *f* BANK agricultural lending; **~es Erzeugnis** *nt* VW agricultural product; **~es Gebäude** *nt* VERSICH, VW agricultural building; **~e Genossenschaft** *f* VW agricultural cooperative, farming cooperative; **~ genutzte Fläche** *f* VW agricultural land; **~e Geräte** *nt pl* VERSICH, VW farm equipment, farm implements; **~er Großbetrieb** *m* VW large-scale farming; **~er Haushalt** *m* VW agricultural household; **~er Mischbetrieb** *m* VW mixed farming; **~er Pächter** *m*, **~e Pächterin** *f* VERSICH, VW agricultural tenant; **~er Pachtvertrag** *m* GRUND farm tenancy; **~e Produkte** *nt* *pl* VW produce; **~e Produktionsgenossenschaft** *f* (*LPG*) VW agricultural production cooperative; **~er Sektor** *m* IND rural sector, VW agricultural sector; **~er Terminkontrakt** *m* BÖRSE agricultural futures contract (*BrE*); **~e Überschüsse** *m pl* VW farm surplus; **~e Versicherung** *f* VERSICH agricultural insurance

Landwirtschaft: **Landwirtschaftsbank** *f* BANK, VW agricultural bank, land bank (*AmE*); **Landwirtschaftsexperte** *m*, **Landwirtschaftsexpertin** *f* VW agriculturalist, agriculturist; **Landwirtschaftsingenieur, in** *m,f* UMWELT agricultural engineer; **Landwirtschaftskredit** *m* BANK agricultural loan; **Landwirtschaftslobby** *f* POL farm lobby, farming lobby; **Landwirtschaftsschau** *f* IND, VW agricultural show

lang *adj* GESCHÄFT long; ♦ **etw auf die ~e Bank schieben** GESCHÄFT put sth off; **mit ~er Laufzeit** VERSICH long-term; **auf ~e Sicht** GESCHÄFT in the long run; **über einen ~en Zeitraum** GESCHÄFT over a period of time; **ein ~es Wochenende machen** GESCHÄFT take a long weekend

lang: **~er Boom** *m* VW long boom; **~er Konjunkturzyklus** *m* VW long wave; **~e Periode** *f* VW long period; **~es Wochenende** *nt* GESCHÄFT long weekend

Länge *f* TRANSP length; **Längenmaß** *nt* GESCHÄFT linear measure

längerfristig: **~er Vermögensgegenstand** *m* BÖRSE longer-term asset

längerfristiger: **~e Option** *f* BÖRSE longer-term option

Langformat *nt* COMP, MEDIEN *Textverarbeitung, Druck* landscape

langfristig *adj* BANK, BÖRSE, FINANZ, GESCHÄFT, RECHNUNG, STEUER, VERSICH, VW long-term, permanent; ♦ **~ gesehen** BANK, GESCHÄFT, VERSICH in the long run, in the long term

langfristig: **~e Anlagen** *f pl* **des Finanzvermögens** FINANZ long-term financial investments; **~e Anleihe** *f* VW long-term bond; **~e Arbeitslosigkeit** *f* VW long-

term unemployment; **~er Betrug** *m* GESCHÄFT long fraud; **~es Darlehen** *nt* BANK fixed loan, long-term loan; **~es Darlehen** *nt* **mit Höchstzinssatz** BÖRSE cap rate loan; **~e Einkommensermittlung** *f* VW lifetime averaging; **~e, festverzinsliche Hypothek** *f* FINANZ permanent financing; **~e Finanzanlage** *f* RECHNUNG long-term financial investment; **~e Finanzierung** *f* FINANZ long-term financing; **~er Geschäftsplan** *m* GESCHÄFT, MGMNT strategic plan; **~er Gewinn** *m* STEUER long-term gain, stock long pull; **~er Haushaltsplan** *m* FINANZ long-term budget; **~er Kredit** *m* BÖRSE, FINANZ funded debt, RECHNUNG long-term credit; **~er Mischverrechnungssatz** *m* FINANZ long-term blended cost rate (*LTB*); **~e Planung** *f* GESCHÄFT long-range planning, long-term planning; **~es Risiko** *nt* VERSICH long tail risk; **~e Schuld** *f* FINANZ long-term debt; **~e Schuldtitel** *m pl* BÖRSE longs; **~e Schuldverschreibung** *f* BÖRSE long bond; **~e Staatspapiere** *nt pl* BÖRSE Treasury stock (*BrE*); **~e Stellage** *f* BÖRSE long straddle; **~er Straddle** *m* BÖRSE long straddle; **~er Trend** *m* GESCHÄFT long-term trend; **~es Unternehmenskonzept** *nt* RECHNUNG going concern-concept; **~e Verbindlichkeit** *f* BÖRSE *Schuld* funded debt, FINANZ funded debt, long-term liability, RECHNUNG long-term liability, RECHT *Schuld* long-term obligation; **~e Verpflichtung** *f* BÖRSE share (*BrE*), stock (*AmE*), FINANZ funded debt, RECHNUNG funded debt, long-term liability, RECHT long-term obligation; **~er Vorzugszins** *m* FINANZ long-term prime rate (*LTPR*); **~e Wirtschaftspolitik** *f* VW economic strategy; **~es Ziel** *nt* GESCHÄFT long-term objective; **~er Zinsschein** *m* BÖRSE long coupon

Langfristplanung *f* GESCHÄFT long-range planning

Langfristrisiko *nt* VERSICH long tail risk

langjährig: **~er Mietvertrag** *m* FINANZ, GRUND long lease; **~er Pachtvertrag** *m* FINANZ, GRUND long lease

Langläufer *m* BÖRSE long bond

langlebig *adj* GESCHÄFT durable, made-to-last; **~e Gebrauchsgüter** *nt pl* V&M *dauerhafte Konsumgüter* consumer durables, durables; **~e Wirtschaftsgüter** *nt pl* GESCHÄFT hard goods

Längs- *in cpds* GESCHÄFT, TRANSP longitudinal, fore and aft

langsam 1. *adj* BÖRSE, GESCHÄFT, TRANSP, VW *wirtschaftliche Erholung* slow; **2.** *adv* BÖRSE, GESCHÄFT, TRANSP slowly; ♦ **~ anziehen** VW edge up; **~ kommen** GESCHÄFT trickle in

langsam: **~er Anstieg** *m* BÖRSE slow rise; **~e Fahrt** *f* TRANSP slow steaming; **~er Rückgang** *m* BÖRSE slow decline; **~er Wandel** *m* POL gradualism

Längs-: **Längsbespannung** *f* TRANSP longitudinal framing; **Längsschnittreihe** *f* MATH longitudinal data; **Längsseitkonnossement** *nt* IMP/EXP *Incoterms* alongside bill of lading

längsseits: **~ Schiff** *phr* TRANSP alongside ship (*A/S*)

Langzeit- *in cpds* GESCHÄFT long-term, long-range, MGMNT, PERSON long-term, VW long-term, long-range; **Langzeitarbeitslose** *pl* PERSON, VW *Arbeitsmarkt* long-term unemployed (*LTU*); **Langzeitmieter** *m* GRUND anchor tenant; **Langzeitpächter** *m* GRUND anchor tenant; **Langzeitplanung** *f* MGMNT long-range planning; **Langzeitprognose** *f* GESCHÄFT long-range forecast; **Langzeitteam** *nt* SOZIAL long-term team; **Langzeittrend** *m* VW long-term trend

Lanham-Gesetz *nt* RECHT *über Warenzeichen* Lanham Act (*AmE*)

Lapanov-Gleichgewicht *nt* VW Lapanov equilibrium

Lappalie *f* GESCHÄFT small change

läppisch: **~es Gerede** *nt* GESCHÄFT small change

Laptop *m* COMP laptop, laptop computer

Lärm- *in cpds* GESCHÄFT, UMWELT noise; **Lärmemission** *f* UMWELT noise emission; **Lärmisolierung** *f* UMWELT noise insulation; **Lärmpegel** *m* UMWELT noise level

Laser *m* BANK, COMP, IND, MEDIEN, VERWALT laser; **Laserbankgeschäft** *nt* BANK laser banking; **Laserdrucker** *m* COMP, MEDIEN *Druck* laser printer; **Laserprinter** *m* COMP, MEDIEN *Druck* laser printer; **Laserscanner** *nt* COMP, MEDIEN *Druck* laser scanner; **Laserstrahl** *m* IND laser beam

Laspeyres-Preisindex *m* VW Laspeyres index

last: **~-in-first-out** *phr* (*LIFO*) PERSON last in first out (*LIFO*)

Last *f* FINANZ burden, TRANSP load, VW burden; ♦ **zu Lasten von** BANK charged to, account of (*a/o*), GESCHÄFT to the disadvantage of, RECHNUNG debited to; **zu Lasten des Charterers** TRANSP charterer's account; **zu Lasten des Empfängers** IMP/EXP, TRANSP carriage forward (*carr fwd*)

Last: **Lastfaktor** *m* TRANSP load factor; **Lastkraftwagen** *m* (*LKW*) TRANSP heavy goods vehicle (*HGV*), lorry (*BrE*), truck (*AmE*); **Lastkraftwagenfahrer, in** *m,f* TRANSP lorry driver (*BrE*), truck driver (*AmE*), trucker (*AmE*); **Lastkraftwagenzug** *m* TRANSP road train; **Lastplan** *m* TRANSP load plan

Lastschrift: *f* BANK debit entry, BÖRSE debits, FINANZ debit, RECHNUNG debit entry, debit; ♦ **eine ~ mit einer Gutschrift verrechnen** RECHNUNG set off a debit against a credit

Lastschrift: **Lastschriftanzeige** *f* GESCHÄFT debit note (*D/N*)

Lastwagen *m* TRANSP lorry (*BrE*), truck (*AmE*); **Lastwagenfahrer, in** *m,f* TRANSP lorry driver (*BrE*), truck driver (*AmE*), trucker (*AmE*); **Lastwagenservice** *m* TRANSP lorry service (*BrE*), truck service (*AmE*), trucking (*AmE*); **Lastwagentransport** *m* TRANSP lorry service (*BrE*), truck service (*AmE*), trucking (*AmE*)

latent: **~e Arbeitslosigkeit** *f* VW concealed unemployment; **~e Nachfrage** *f* V&M latent demand; **~e Steuer** *f* STEUER deferred tax, latent tax

lateral: **~es Denken** *nt* GESCHÄFT, MGMNT lateral thinking

Latex *m* IND latex

Latifundienwirtschaft *f* VW estate economy

Lattenkiste *f* TRANSP crate

Lauf *m* GESCHÄFT *Verlauf* course; **~ der Dinge** GESCHÄFT trend of events; **Laufbahnaussichten** *f pl* PERSON career prospects

laufen *vi* COMP *Programm* run; ♦ **~ lassen** COMP *Programm* run

Laufen: **am ~ halten** *phr* GESCHÄFT keep afloat

laufend 1. *adj* GESCHÄFT ongoing, standing; ♦ **auf dem ~en** GESCHÄFT au fait, up-to-date; **auf dem ~en sein mit** GESCHÄFT be abreast of, be au fait with, be up-to-date on; **auf dem ~en halten** VERWALT *Ablage* keep up to date; **jdn auf dem ~en halten** GESCHÄFT, KOMM keep sb up-to-date, keep sb informed; **2.** *adv* VERWALT constantly, continuously

laufend: **~e Angelegenheit** *f* GESCHÄFT ongoing concern; **~e Arbeit** *f* GESCHÄFT, RECHNUNG, VW work in process (*AmE*) (*WIP*), work in progress (*BrE*) (*WIP*); **~er Arbeitstag** *m* TRANSP running workday, running working day; **~e Ausgaben** *f pl* FINANZ current expenditure, running expense, GESCHÄFT running expense, VW current spending, running expense; **~er Betrag** *m* GESCHÄFT running total; **~e Beurteilung** *f* SOZIAL continuous assessment; **~e Buchprüfung** *f* RECHNUNG continuous audit; **~e Devisenbestände** *m pl* BÖRSE current holdings; **~es Einkommen** *nt* VW current income; **~ emittierter Schatzwechsel** *m* BÖRSE tap bill; **~es Finanzjahr** *nt* STEUER current fiscal year; **~er Finanzplan** *m* STEUER current fiscal plan; **~e Frachtpolice** *f* VERSICH floating cargo policy; **~er Geschäftsbetrieb** *m* VW running operations; **~es Geschäftsjahr** *nt* FINANZ current business year; **~e Instandhaltungskosten** *pl* GRUND maintenance costs; **~e Inventur** *f* FINANZ perpetual inventory, GESCHÄFT continuous inventory, RECHNUNG perpetual inventory, VW continuous stocktaking; **~es Jahr** *nt* GESCHÄFT current year; **~er Kalendertag** *m* TRANSP running day (*rd*); **~e Kapitalbeteiligungen** *f pl* BÖRSE current holdings; **~es Konto** *nt* BANK checking account (*AmE*) (*C/A*), cheque account (*BrE*) (*C/A*), current account (*BrE*); **~e Kontrolle** *f* GESCHÄFT routine check; **~e Kosten** *pl* FINANZ overheads, running expense, GESCHÄFT running cost, running expense, RECHNUNG continuing cost, current cost, overheads, running expense, VW running cost, running expense; **~er Kredit** *m* BANK standing advance; **~e lebenslängliche Kapitalversicherung** *f* VERSICH current assumption whole life insurance; **~e lebenslängliche Todesfallversicherung** *f* VERSICH current assumption whole life insurance; **~e Nachfrage** *f* V&M current demand; **~e Nummer** *f* GESCHÄFT serial number, MATH sequential number; **~e Pflichten** *f pl* GESCHÄFT routine duty; **~e Police** *f* VERSICH open cover (*OC*), open policy; **~e Rendite** *f* BANK current yield; **~e Rente** *f* VERSICH current annuity; **~es Steuerjahr** *nt* STEUER current fiscal year; **~er Steuerplan** *m* STEUER current fiscal plan; **~e Stunde** *f* TRANSP running hour; **~e Summe** *f* GESCHÄFT, RECHNUNG running total; **~e Unkosten** *pl* FINANZ current expenditure; **~e Unterstützung** *f* GESCHÄFT continuing support; **~e Versicherung** *f* VERSICH current insurance, insurance in force; **~e Verstärkung** *f* PERSON *des Personalbestands* continuous reinforcement; **~e Wartung** *f* GESCHÄFT routine maintenance; **~e Zahlungen an Personen** *f pl* VW current grants to persons; **~er Zahlungsplan** *m* FINANZ periodic payment plan

Lauf: **Laufgestell** *nt* TRANSP bogie; **Laufgestellheber** *m* TRANSP bogie lift; **Laufkarte** *f* PERSON job ticket; **Laufwerk** *nt* COMP drive, *Bandkassette* deck

Laufzeit *f* BANK term, BÖRSE life, COMP runtime, FINANZ period of redemption, GESCHÄFT operation time, period, RECHNUNG currency, TRANSP tenor, VW length of time to maturity, running time, maturity band; **~ der Verzinsung** *f* VW number of terms; ♦ **zu einer ~ von dreißig Tagen** FINANZ at thirty days' usance

Laufzeit: **Laufzeiteninkongruenz** *f* BANK maturity mismatch, mismatched maturity; **Laufzeitentransformation** *f* FINANZ maturity transformation; **Laufzeitprämie** *f* VW term premium; **Laufzeitstruktur**

f FINANZ term structure; **Laufzeitwechsel** *m* TRANSP tenor bill

Laufzettel *m* GESCHÄFT *verlorene Gegenstände betreffend* tracer, VERWALT routing slip

Lausanne: **~r Schule** *f* VW Lausanne School

laut *prep* [+dat] GESCHÄFT according to; ◆ **~ Anzeige von** GESCHÄFT as per advice from, as per advice of; **~ Avis von** GESCHÄFT as per advice from, as per advice of; **~ Bericht von** GESCHÄFT as per advice from, as per advice of; **~ Kontoauszug** BANK as per statement; **~ Übereinkunft** GESCHÄFT as per agreement

lauter: **~er Handel** *m* V&M, VW fair trade, fair trading; **~e Werbung** *f* V&M ethical advertising; **~er Wettbewerb** *m* RECHT, VW fair competition

Lautsprecheranlage *f* KOMM public address system (*PA*)

Lautstärke *f* COMP volume

lawinenartig: **~ anwachsen** *phr* GESCHÄFT snowball

Layout *nt* COMP *Textverarbeitung, Datenbank, Graphikanwendungen*, MEDIEN, RECHNUNG, VERWALT layout

Layouter *m* COMP, MEDIEN *Druck*, VERWALT layout man; **Layouterin** *f* COMP, MEDIEN *Druck*, VERWALT layout woman

Layout: **Layout-Plan** *m* VERWALT *Rohskizze, Aufriß* layout chart; **Layout-Steuerzeichen** *nt* COMP *Textverarbeitung, Graphikanwendung* layout character

LBO *abbr* (*leveraged Buyout*) FINANZ leveraged buyout

Learning: **~ by doing** *nt* VW learning-by-doing

Leasing *nt* GESCHÄFT, GRUND *Miete, Pacht* leasing; **~ von Führungskräften** MGMNT executive leasing; **Leasing-Erwerbskosten** *pl* FINANZ lease acquisition cost; **Leasinggesellschaft** *f* GESCHÄFT lease company, leasing company, GRUND leasing company; **Leasingvertrag** *m* FINANZ, GESCHÄFT leasing agreement

Leben *nt* GESCHÄFT, VERSICH life

lebend: **~es Inventar** *nt* GESCHÄFT, VW livestock

Leben: **Lebensart** *f* GESCHÄFT way of life; **Lebensausweis** *m* VERSICH certificate of existence; **Lebensbedingungen** *f pl* SOZIAL living conditions; **Lebensbescheinigung** *f* VERSICH certificate of existence; **Lebensdaten** *pl* PERSON *Lebenslauf, Bewerbung* biographical data; **auf die Lebensdauer eines Dritten** *phr* RECHT pour autre vie; **Lebensersparnisse** *f pl* BANK life savings; **Lebenserwartung** *f* VERSICH life expectancy; **Lebenserwartung** *f eines Produktes* V&M product life expectancy

lebensfähig *adj* FINANZ, GESCHÄFT viable; **nicht ~es Unternehmen** *nt* GESCHÄFT non-viable enterprise, lame duck (*infrml*)

Leben: **Lebensfähigkeit** *f* GESCHÄFT viability; **Lebensgewohnheit** *f* GESCHÄFT way of life

Lebenshaltung *f* GESCHÄFT, SOZIAL, VW cost of living; **Lebenshaltungsindex** *m* GESCHÄFT, SOZIAL, VW cost-of-living index; **Lebenshaltungskosten** *pl* GESCHÄFT, SOZIAL living expenses, VW cost of living; **Lebenshaltungskostenindex** *m* GESCHÄFT, SOZIAL, VW cost-of-living index

Leben: **Lebens- und Krankenversicherung** *f* **gegen berufliche Risiken** VERSICH business exposure life and health insurance (*AmE*)

lebenslang: **~e Anstellung** *f* PERSON job for life, life tenure

lebenslänglich: **~er Nießbrauch** *m* FINANZ life interest;

~er Nießbraucher *m*, **~e Nießbraucherin** *f* GRUND life tenant; **~es Pachtrecht** *nt* GRUND life tenancy; **~e Rente** *m* BÖRSE perpetuity

Leben: **Lebenslauf** *m* PERSON, VERWALT curriculum vitae (*CV*) (*BrE*), résumé (*AmE*)

Lebensmittel *nt pl* GESCHÄFT foodstuffs; **Lebensmitteleinzelhandel** *m* V&M food retailing; **Lebensmitteleinzelhandelsgeschäft** *nt* V&M retail food business; **Lebensmittelgeschäft** *nt* V&M food store, grocery; **Lebensmittelgeschäft** *nt* **außerhalb der Stadt** V&M out-of-town food store; **Lebensmittelgesetz** *nt* RECHT food law; **Lebensmittelkette** *f* VW food chain

lebensmittelverarbeitend: **~e Industrie** *f* IND, UMWELT food-processing industry

Lebensmittel: **Lebesmittelvorrat** *m* VW food supply

Leben: **Lebensnachweis** *m* VERSICH certificate of existence

lebensnotwendig: **~e Güter** *nt pl* V&M necessities

Leben: **Lebensqualität** *f* VW quality of life; **Lebensraum** *m* SOZIAL living space, UMWELT habitat; **Lebensrente** *f* PERSON, VERSICH life annuity; **Lebensrettungseinrichtung** *f* TRANSP life-saving appliance (*LSA*); **Lebensrettungsgerät** *nt* TRANSP life-saving apparatus (*LSA*); **Lebensstandard** *m* VW standard of living; **Lebensstellung** *f* PERSON *Bewerbung* tenured post; **Lebensstil** *m* GESCHÄFT, V&M lifestyle; **Lebensstilkonzept** *nt* V&M lifestyle concept; **Lebensstilsegmentierung** *f* V&M lifestyle segmentation; **Lebensunterhalt** *m* FINANZ bread (*infrml*), GESCHÄFT bread (*infrml*), livelihood, SOZIAL subsistence, VW bread (*infrml*); **seinen Lebensunterhalt verdienen** *phr* GESCHÄFT earn one's keep, PERSON, SOZIAL work for a living, VW earn a living, make a living

Lebensversicherung *f* VERSICH assurance (*BrE*) (*ass.*), life assurance (*BrE*), life insurance; **~ gegen Einmalprämie** VERSICH single-premium life insurance; **~ gegen Zahlung einer Einmalprämie** VERSICH single-premium life insurance; **~ für leitende Angestellte** VERSICH business insurance; **~ ohne Rückkaufswert** VERSICH term policy; **~ auf den Todesfall** VERSICH assurance payable at death (*BrE*), insurance payable at death (*AmE*), whole-life assurance (*BrE*), whole-life insurance (*AmE*); **~ auf den Todes- und Erlebensfall** VERSICH endowment life assurance; **~ der Unterzeichner der Police** GESCHÄFT assurance of subscribers; **~ mit verkürzter Prämienzahlung** VERSICH limited payment life insurance; **Lebensversicherungspolice** *f* VERSICH life assurance policy (*BrE*), life insurance policy; **Lebensversicherungsprämie** *f* VERSICH life insurance premium

Leben: **Lebenszeit** *f* BÖRSE, GESCHÄFT lifetime; **Lebenszeithypothese** *f* VW life-cycle hypothesis (*LCH*)

Lebenszyklus *m* UMWELT, V&M, VW life cycle; **~ einer Familie** V&M family life cycle; **~ eines Produktes** V&M product life cycle; **Lebenszyklusanalyse** *f* V&M life-cycle analysis; **Lebenszyklusbewertung** *f* UMWELT life-cycle assessment (*LCA*); **Lebenszyklushypothese** *f* VW life-cycle hypothesis (*LCH*)

lebhaft 1. *adj* BÖRSE *Handel* brisk, active, FINANZ active, GESCHÄFT *Nachfrage* brisk, V&M active, VW brisk, buoyant; **2.** *adv* FINANZ actively, GESCHÄFT briskly, V&M actively, VW briskly; ◆ **~ gehandelt** BÖRSE active, actively traded, heavily traded *lebhaft*: ~e Dollarnachfrage *f* BANK rush on the dollar; ~ gefragte Aktien *f pl* BÖRSE glamor issue (*AmE*), glamor stock (*AmE*), glamour issue (*BrE*), glamour stock (*BrE*); ~ gehandelte Wertpapiere *nt pl* BÖRSE active securities; ~er Geldmarkt *m* FINANZ active money; ~er Handel *m* BÖRSE broad market, active dealings, active trading, V&M active trading; ~es Treiben *nt* GESCHÄFT hustle and bustle; ~e Umsätze *m pl* BÖRSE active dealings, active trading

LED *abbr* (*Lumineszenzdiode, Leuchtdiode, Lichtemissionsdiode*) COMP LED (*light-emitting diode*)

Lederwaren *f pl* IND leather goods

ledig *adj* RECHT, STEUER single; ~e Frau *f* RECHT single woman; ~er Mann *m* RECHT single man

Leer- *in cpds* GESCHÄFT, TRANSP empty

leer 1. *adj* GESCHÄFT *Gerücht* unfounded, TRANSP empty; **2.** *adv* ♦ ~ fahren TRANSP *Bus, Zug* run empty

leer: ~es Schiff *nt* TRANSP light vessel; ~es Wertpapier *nt* BÖRSE stripped security

Leer-: **Leergewicht** *nt* GESCHÄFT *Eigengewicht* deadweight, *unbeladen* unladen weight, weight when empty, TRANSP unladen weight, tare weight

Leerlauf: im ~ *phr* TRANSP down, idle; **Leerlaufkapazität** *f* IND idle capacity; **Leerlaufzeit** *f* COMP idle time

Leer-: **Leerraum** *m* TRANSP ullage; **Leerrückfahrt** *f* TRANSP *Straße* single back; **einen Leerschritt eingeben** *phr* COMP leave a space; **Leertaste** *f* COMP space bar

Leerverkauf *m* BÖRSE bear sale, going short, short, selling short; ~ eines Haussiers BÖRSE short against the box

Leerverkäufe: ~ der Baissespekulation *m pl* BÖRSE bear raiding; ♦ ~ abschließen BÖRSE sell a bear, sell short; ~ als Baissemanöver tätigen BÖRSE bear the market

Leerverkauf: **Leerverkaufsposition** *f* BÖRSE short position; **Leerverkaufsregel** *f* BÖRSE short-sale rule; **Leerverkaufsverhältnis** *nt* **des amtlichen Kursmaklers** BÖRSE specialist's short-sale ratio

Leer-: **Leerverschiffung** *f* TRANSP idle shipping; **Leerzeichen** *nt* COMP blank, blank character, space; **Leerzeit** *f* VERWALT idle time

legalisiert: ~e Ursprungserklärung *f* IMP/EXP certified declaration of origin

Legalisierung *f* POL authentication

legalistisch *adj* RECHT legalistic

Legalität *f* GESCHÄFT legality

legislativ *adj* RECHT legislative

Legislative *f* RECHT legislature

legitim *adj* GESCHÄFT, RECHT legitimate

lehensfrei *adj* RECHT allodial

Lehr: **Lehranstalt** *f* SOZIAL educational establishment

Lehre *f* PERSON, VW apprenticeship; ~ vom Warenabsatz V&M marketing; ♦ jdn in die ~ geben PERSON *Fachausbildung* apprentice sb; bei jdm in die ~ gehen PERSON be apprenticed to sb

Lehrling *m* PERSON, VW apprentice

Lehr: **Lehrmaschine** *f* SOZIAL *im programmierten Unterricht* teaching machine; **Lehrplan** *m* SOZIAL curriculum; **Lehrstelle** *f* PERSON apprenticeship; **Lehrverhältnis** *nt* PERSON apprenticeship; **Lehrzeit** *f* PERSON apprenticeship

Leibrente *f* VERSICH annuity for life, life annuity; **Leibrentenempfänger, in** *m,f* GRUND life annuitant;

Leibrentenversicherung *f* VERSICH annuity assurance, annuity insurance, insurance annuity

Leicht- *in cpds* GESCHÄFT, IND, TRANSP light

leicht 1. *adj* GESCHÄFT easy, light, slight, TRANSP light; **2.** *adv* GESCHÄFT easily, lightly, slightly; ♦ ~ nachgeben VW *Nachfrage* ease off; ~ verständlich darlegen GESCHÄFT present in an easy format

leicht: ~e Fracht *f* TRANSP light cargo; ~es Geld *nt* VW easy money; ~ liquidierbare Einlagen *f pl* VW near money; ~ verderbliche Güter *nt pl* GESCHÄFT, VW perishable goods; ~ verderbliche Lebensmittel *nt pl* GESCHÄFT perishable foodstuffs; ~ verderbliche Waren *f pl* GESCHÄFT, VW perishable goods, perishables; ~er Verlust *m* GESCHÄFT superficial loss; ~e Wahl *f* MGMNT easy option

Leichter *m* TRANSP *Schiffstyp* lighter carrier

leichtere: ~r Umschlag *m* TRANSP *von Gütern* ease of handling

Leicht-: **Leichtindustrie** *f* IND light industry; **Leichtmatrose** *m* PERSON *Schiffahrt* ordinary seaman; **Leichtmetallcontainer** *m* TRANSP alloy container; **Leichtmetallindustrie** *f* IND light metals industry, aluminium industry (*BrE*), aluminum industry (*AmE*)

leichtverdient: ~es Geld *nt* VW easy money

leiden *vi* GESCHÄFT, PERSON, VW suffer

leidenschaftlich *adj* GESCHÄFT *Debatte* passionate, heated

Leih- *in cpds* BÖRSE, FINANZ loaned

leihen *vt* GESCHÄFT borrow; ♦ ~ von BANK borrow from

Leihen *nt* GESCHÄFT hire

Leih-: **Leihhaus** *nt* FINANZ pawnshop; **Leihkapital** *nt* FINANZ hire of money; **durch Leihkapital finanziertes Leasing** *nt* GRUND leveraged lease; **Leihkurs** *m* einschließlich aufgelaufener Zinsen BÖRSE loaned flat

Leine *f* TRANSP towline

Leinpfad *m* TRANSP towpath

leisten 1. *vt* GESCHÄFT *Hilfe* provide; ♦ sich etw ~ VW afford sth; sich etw ~ können VW be able to afford to buy sth; **2.** *vi* ♦ weniger ~ als möglich PERSON underperform

leistend: zu ~e Schadenssumme *f* VERSICH amount to be paid

Leistung *f* GESCHÄFT service, achievement, performance, IND power, PERSON accomplishment, achievement, RECHNUNG, V&M performance; ~ durch Dritte GESCHÄFT performance by a third party; ~ pro Kopf IND output per head; ~ pro Stunde IND output per hour; ♦ ~ erbringen GESCHÄFT perform

Leistung: **Leistungen** *f pl* GESCHÄFT, VERSICH benefits; **Leistungen** *f pl* der Lebensversicherung zu Lebzeiten VERSICH living benefits of life insurance; **Leistungsabweichung** *f* FINANZ efficiency variance; **Leistungsanreiz** *m* PERSON incentive; **Leistungsanreizmechanismus** *m* VW inducement mechanism; **Leistungsaustauschvertrag** *m* RECHT contract of exchange of goods and services; **Leistungsberechtigte(r)** *mf* [decl. as adj] GRUND beneficiary

Leistungsbeurteilung *f* GESCHÄFT merit rating, MGMNT, PERSON personnel rating, performance appraisal, performance review, performance evaluation, *Gehälterrevision* merit rating; ~ und -bewertung *f* von Führungskräften PERSON, RECHNUNG management audit; **Leistungsbeurteilungsgespräch** *nt* PERSON performance appraisal interview (*PAI*)

Leistung: **Leistungsbewertung** *f* FINANZ performance rating, GESCHÄFT merit rating, MGMNT, PERSON performance appraisal, performance evaluation, performance review, personnel rating, *Gehälterrevision* merit rating

leistungsbezogen: **~e Bezahlung** *f* PERSON incentive pay, incentive wage, performance-related pay (*PRP*), profit-related pay (*PRP*), wage incentive; **~e Gehaltssteigerung** *f* PERSON *Arbeitsentgelt* merit increase, merit raise (*AmE*); **~er Indikator** *m* GESCHÄFT performance-related indicator

Leistungsbilanz *f* RECHNUNG current account (*BrE*), VW balance on current account, current account (*BrE*); **Leistungsbilanzüberschußpolitik** *f* VW beggar-my-neighbor policy (*AmE*), beggar-my-neighbour policy (*BrE*)

Leistung: **Leistungsbonus** *m* FINANZ performance bonus; **Leistungsbudget** *nt* FINANZ performance budget; **Leistungsdauer** *f* VERSICH indemnity period; **Leistungseinschätzung** *f* MGMNT, PERSON performance appraisal; **Leistungseinstufung** *f* FINANZ performance rating; **Leistungsempfänger, in** *m,f* VERSICH beneficiary

leistungsfähig *adj* GESCHÄFT efficient

leistungsfähigere: **~ Version** *f* COMP advanced version

Leistung: **Leistungsfähigkeit** *f* GESCHÄFT ability, efficiency, VW efficiency; **Leistungsfähigkeit** *f* **der Arbeiter** IND production standard; **Leistungsfähigkeitsprinzip** *nt* STEUER, VW ability-to-pay principle; **Leistungsgarantie** *f* GESCHÄFT contract bond, performance bond, V&M performance guarantee; **Leistungsgesellschaft** *f* PERSON meritocracy; **Leistungsgradschätzen** *nt* IND, PERSON performance rating; **Leistungsgruppen bilden** *phr* SOZIAL *Schüler* group by ability; **Leistungshaftung** *f* VERSICH completed operations insurance

leistungshemmend: **~er Effekt** *m* VW disincentive effect; **~er Einfluß** *m* VW disincentive

Leistung: **Leistungshemmnis** *nt* VW disincentive; **Leistungsindikator** *m* PERSON *Betriebswirtschaft* performance indicator; **Leistungskarte** *f* PERSON report card; **Leistungskennzahl** *f* VW measure of performance; **Leistungskontrolle** *f* MGMNT, PERSON performance monitoring; **Leistungskraft** *f* VW efficiency

Leistungslohn *m* PERSON performance-related pay (*PRP*), profit-related pay (*PRP*), incentive wage, incentive pay, wage incentive, *Arbeitsentgelt nach Leistung* payment by results (*PBR*), merit pay, VW efficiency wage; **Leistungslohnprogramm** *nt* MGMNT, PERSON incentive wage plan; **Leistungslohnsystem** *nt* MGMNT, PERSON incentive pay scheme

leistungslos: **~e Bodenwertsteigerung** *f* GRUND unearned increment of land

Leistung: **Leistungsmarketing** *nt* V&M performance marketing; **Leistungsmaßstab** *m* MGMNT, PERSON *Betriebswirtschaft* performance standard; **Leistungsmessung** *f* MGMNT, PERSON *Betriebswirtschaft* performance measurement; **Leistungsminderung** *f* RECHT impairment of performance; **Leistungsmotiv** *nt* MGMNT, PERSON achievement motive; **Leistungsnachweis** *m* PERSON

Schul- oder Universitätsabschluß evidence of achievement; **Leistungsniveau** *nt* SOZIAL ability level

leistungsorientiert: **~e Person** *f* SOZIAL over-achiever

Leistung: **Leistungspaket** *nt* MGMNT, PERSON *Arbeitsentgelt* remuneration package; **Leistungspalette** *f* VW range of services; **Leistungspflichtige(r)** *mf* [decl. as adj] VW contributor; **Leistungspflicht** *f* **der versicherten Klausel** VERSICH duty of assured clause; **Leistungsprämie** *f* FINANZ performance bonus, IND production bonus, PERSON acceleration premium; **Leistungsprovision** *f* V&M incentive commission; **Leistungsprüfung** *f* IND performance testing

leistungsschwach *adj* COMP low-tech; **~er Mitarbeiter** *m*, **~e Mitarbeiterin** *f* PERSON low achiever; **~e Person** *f* PERSON low achiever

Leistungsstandard *m* RECHNUNG performance standard

leistungsstark *adj* GESCHÄFT powerful

Leistung: **Leistungsstörung** *f* RECHT *Verträge* impairment of performance; **Leistungssystem** *nt* PERSON incentive scheme; **Leistungstarif** *m* TRANSP incentive rate; **Leistungsüberblick** *m* GESCHÄFT performance review; **Leistungsüberprüfung** *f* RECHNUNG performance review; **Leistungsüberwachung** *f* GESCHÄFT, IND, MGMNT, PERSON *Betriebswirtschaft* performance monitoring (*PM*); **Leistungsvermögen** *nt* GESCHÄFT potential, capability, SOZIAL ability level; **Leistungsvertrag** *m* GESCHÄFT performance contract; **Leistungsverweigerung** *f* RECHT refusal to fulfil an obligation (*BrE*), refusal to fulfill an obligation (*AmE*); **Leistungsverweigerungsrecht** *nt* RECHT *Vertragsrecht* duress, right to withdraw from performance; **Leistungszahlung** *f* PERSON incentive pay; **Leistungsziel** *nt* MGMNT performance target; **Leistungszulage** *f* PERSON incentive bonus, VW proficiency pay; **Leistungszulage** *f* **im Vergleich zur Zielsetzung** PERSON performance against objectives

Leit- *in cpds* COMP, GESCHÄFT, MEDIEN, VW key, leader, major, central; **Leitartikel** *m* GESCHÄFT editorial, MEDIEN editorial column, leader (*BrE*), leading article (*BrE*), editorial; **Leitartikelschreiber, in** *m,f* MEDIEN leader writer (*BrE*)

leiten *vt* GESCHÄFT be in charge of, lead, manage, MGMNT manage, *Organisation* direct, RECHT *Untersuchung* head, TRANSP route

leitend *adj* GESCHÄFT executive, senior (*Snr*), MGMNT managerial, PERSON, VERWALT managing; **~e(r) Angestellte(r)** *mf* [decl. as adj] GESCHÄFT executive (*exec.*), MEDIEN business manager, MGMNT, PERSON executive (*exec.*), general manager, senior executive, senior officer (*SO*), VERWALT company executive; **~e(r) Büroangestellte(r)** *mf* [decl. as adj] MGMNT chief clerk, head clerk, senior clerk; **~er Direktor** *m*, **~e Direktorin** *f* MGMNT managing director, PERSON general manager, chief executive, managing director; **~er Firmenmitarbeiter** *m*, **~e Firmenmitarbeiterin** *f* MGMNT corporate executive; **Fluglotse** *m* PERSON, TRANSP chief traffic controller; **~er Inspektor** *m*, **~e Inspektorin** *f* MGMNT general manager, PERSON chief inspector (*CI*); **~er Konzernmitarbeiter** *m*, **~e Konzernmitarbeiterin** *f* MGMNT corporate executive; **~er Mitarbeiter** *m* **der Geschäftsführung**, **~e Mitarbeiterin** *f* **der Geschäftsführung** MGMNT, PERSON senior manager; **~er Mitarbeiter** *m* **der Unternehmensleitung**, **~e Mitarbeiterin** *f* **der Unternehmensleitung** MGMNT, PERSON senior manager; **~er Unternehmensmitarbeiter** *m*, **~e Unternehmensmitarbeiterin** *f* MGMNT corporate executive; **~er Verhandlungspartner** *m*, **~e Verhandlungspartnerin** *f* GESCHÄFT point

Leiter 1. *m* FINANZ comptroller, controller, MGMNT manager (*MGR*), PERSON *einer Abteilung* manager (*MGR*), director (*dir.*); **~ der Ablauforganisation** PERSON *Unternehmensverwaltung, Organisation, Hierarchie* operational manager; **~ Abteilung Design** MGMNT chief designer; **~ der Abteilung Industrielle Beziehungen** PERSON director of labor relations (*AmE*), director of labour relations (*BrE*); **~ der Abteilung Marketing** MGMNT marketing director, marketing manager; **~ in der Bankenaufsichtsbehörde** BANK inspector-general of banks; **~ des Bereichs Rechnung und Finanzen** FINANZ, MGMNT, RECHNUNG, VERWALT comptroller, controller; **~ der Beschaffungsabteilung** GESCHÄFT, MGMNT procurement manager; **~ bestimmter Behörden** VERWALT commissioner; **~ im eigenen Betrieb** MGMNT owner-manager; **~ der Einwanderungsbehörde** PERSON chief immigration officer (*CIO*); **~ der Entwicklungsabteilung** MGMNT development director, development manager; **~ Exportmarketing** IMP/EXP, PERSON export marketing manager; **~ der Finanzabteilung** MGMNT, RECHNUNG, VERWALT financial director, PERSON corporate treasurer; **~ Finanzen** PERSON chief financial officer (*CFO*); **~ der Forschungsabteilung** MGMNT research director; **~ Marketing Export** MGMNT export marketing manager; **~ des Nachrichtendienstes** PERSON chief information officer (*CIO*); **~ der obersten Finanzbehörde** STEUER Commissioner of Inland Revenue (*BrE*); **~ Öffentlichkeitsarbeit** PERSON director of public relations (*DPR*); **~ der Personalabteilung** PERSON head of personnel, personnel director; **~ der Personalbeschaffung** PERSON *Arbeitsmarkt, freie Stellen* recruitment manager; **~ der Prüfungsgruppe** RECHNUNG audit head; **~ des Rechnungswesens** FINANZ, MGMNT, RECHNUNG, VERWALT comptroller, controller; **~ der Rechtsabteilung** PERSON general counsel (*AmE*), head of legal department (*BrE*); **~ der Schadenabteilung** PERSON *Ersatzansprüche* claims manager; **~ der technischen Abteilung** PERSON engineering manager; **~ eines Verhandlungsteams** GESCHÄFT point; **~ der Verkaufsförderungsabteilung** PERSON merchandising director; **~ Vertrieb und Entwicklung** PERSON commercial and development manager; **~ der Verwaltung einer Firma** VERWALT company secretary (*BrE*); **~ der volkswirtschaftlichen Abteilung** GESCHÄFT chief economist; **~ des Wareneingangs** MGMNT traffic manager; **2.** *f* GESCHÄFT *Karriere*, IND, TRANSP ladder; ♦ **die ~ erklimmen** PERSON *Karriere* scale the ladder

Leiterin *f* FINANZ comptroller, controller, MGMNT manager (*MGR*), manageress, PERSON *einer Abteilung* manager (*MGR*), manageress, director (*dir.*)

Leiterplatte *f* COMP *Hardware* board

Leit-: **Leitkurs** *m* VW central rate; **Leitsatz** *m* GESCHÄFT governing principle, principle

Leitung *f* GESCHÄFT, PERSON leadership, management, VERWALT administration; **~ einer Gesellschaft** *f* MGMNT corporate management; **~ eines Zivilprozesses** RECHT conduct of law suit; ♦ **die ~ einer Firma übernehmen** GESCHÄFT take adminis-

trative control of a company; **die ~ übernehmen** GESCHÄFT take over

Leitung: **Leitungsaktivierung** *f* KOMM line activation; **Leitungsanpassung** *f* KOMM *Netzwerk* line termination equipment; **Leitungsaufbau** *m* MGMNT management structure; **Leitungsausschuß** *m* PERSON executive committee; **Leitungsbefugnis** *f* MGMNT management competence; **Leitungseffektivität** *f* MGMNT managerial effectiveness; **Leitungsgebaren** *nt* MGMNT management practice; **Leitungsgremium** *nt* PERSON executive committee; **Leitungsinstrument** *nt* MGMNT management aid; **Leitungskollektiv** *nt* MGMNT management team; **Leitungskompetenz** *f* MGMNT executive competence, management competence; **Leitungskontrolle** *f* MGMNT managerial control; **Leitungsmethode** *f* MGMNT management method, management practice, management technique; **Leitungsorganisation** *f* MGMNT chain of command; **Leitungspotential** *nt* MGMNT management potential; **Leitungsprovision** *f* V&M incentive commission; **Leitungsprozeß** *m* MGMNT management operation; **Leitungsschema** *nt* MGMNT management chart; **Leitungsschwäche** *f* MGMNT bad management; **Leitungsstil** *m* MGMNT managerial style; **Leitungsstruktur** *f* MGMNT, PERSON line of command, managerial structure; **Leitungssystem** *nt* MGMNT management system; **Leitungsumbildung** *f* MGMNT management reshuffle; **Leitungsverantwortung** *f* MGMNT accountability in management; **Leitungsvereinbarung** *f* MGMNT management agreement; **Leitungsverhältnis** *nt* MGMNT management ratio

Leit-: **Leitwährung** *f* VW key currency, major currency; **Leitweg** *m* GESCHÄFT routing; **Leitweglenkung** *f* COMP routing; **Leitzins** *m* BANK, FINANZ base lending rate, VW key rate, base lending rate; **Leitzinssatz** *m* FINANZ prime lending rate, VW key rate

lenken *vt* FINANZ regulate, GRUND, RECHT steer, VW regulate

Lenksystem *nt* TRANSP steering system

Lenkung *f* GRUND, RECHT steering; **Lenkungsausschuß** *m* BANK, FINANZ steering committee; **Lenkungs- und Überwachungsverfahren** *nt* VERWALT administrative control procedure

Leontief: **Leontief-Matrix** *f* VW Leontief matrix; **Leontief-Paradoxon** *nt* VW Leontief paradox

Leporellofaltung *f* KOMM, V&M accordion folding

Leporellofalzung *f* V&M concertina fold

leptokurtisch: **~e Verteilungskurve** *f* MATH *Statistik* leptokurtic frequency distribution

Leptokurtosis *f* MATH *Statistik* leptokurtosis

Lernen *nt* SOZIAL learning, study; **~ in kleinen Einheiten** SOZIAL part method

Lerner: **Lerner-Effekt** *m* VW Lerner effect; **Lerner-Index** *m* VW Lerner index; **~scher Monopolgrad** *m* VW Lerner index

Lernkurve *f* PERSON, SOZIAL, VW learning curve

Lesekopf *m* COMP head, read head

lesen *vt* COMP read, *Textverarbeitung* view, MEDIEN, V&M read

Lesen *nt* COMP, MEDIEN, V&M read

Leser, in *m,f* COMP, MEDIEN, V&M reader; **Leserbeteiligung** *f* V&M reader involvement; **Leserdienstkarte** *f* V&M reader service card; **Leserprofil** *nt* V&M readership profile

Leserschaft *f* GESCHÄFT audience, MEDIEN *einer Zeitung*

readership; **~ pro Ausgabe** V&M issue readership; **~ pro durchschnittliche Auflage** V&M average issue readership

Leser: **Leserstudie** f V&M readership survey

Lesestift m COMP *für Strichcodes* optical wand

letzte adj GESCHÄFT final, last; ♦ **in ~r Instanz** GESCHÄFT as a last resort; **in den ~n Jahren** GESCHÄFT in recent years; **das ~ Jahr über ungefähr** GESCHÄFT over the last year or so; **zum ~n Kurs** BÖRSE at market; **des ~n Monats** obs GESCHÄFT ultimo (*ult.*); **auf ~r Position** GESCHÄFT in last position; **während des ~n Jahres ungefähr** GESCHÄFT over the last year or so; **während des ~n Jahrzehnts** GESCHÄFT over the last decade

letzte: **~ Abfertigung** f FREI, TRANSP final check-in; **~r Abrechnungskurs** m GESCHÄFT making-up price (*M/U*); **~r Ausweg** m GESCHÄFT last resort; **~r Bekanntmachungstag** m FINANZ last notice day; **~ Ernte** f VW old crop (*OC*); **~r Frachtführer** m TRANSP last carrier; **~s Gebot** nt GESCHÄFT closing bid; **~r Handelstag** m BÖRSE final trading day, last day of trading, last trading day; **~ Information** f GESCHÄFT update; **~r Korrekturabzug** m MEDIEN final proof; **~r Kündigungstag** m PERSON last notice day; **~r Kurs** m GESCHÄFT making-up price (*M/U*); **~ Rate** f FINANZ final instalment; **~ Ratenzahlung** f FINANZ terminal payment; **~s Schlichtungsangebot** nt PERSON last offer arbitration (*BrE*); **~r Spediteur** m TRANSP last carrier; **~ Stunden** f pl **des Einreichungstermins** BÖRSE last day hours; **~r Teil** m jarg MEDIEN back end (*jarg*); **~r Termin** m GESCHÄFT deadline, latest date; **~r Transportunternehmer** m TRANSP *Transportnehmer, über dessen Route der letzte Teil einer Fracht geht* last carrier; **~r Verkauf** m BÖRSE last sale; **~r Versicherungstag** m VERSICH last safe day (*lsd*); **~ Warnung** f PERSON final warning; **~r Wille** m **und Testament** nt RECHT last will and testament

letztinstanzlich: **~e Kapitalgeber** m pl BANK lender of last resort

letztwillig: **~e Zuwendung** f **von Grundbesitz** GRUND, RECHT devise

Leuchtdiode f (*LED*) COMP light-emitting diode (*LED*)

Leumund m GESCHÄFT reputation

Leverage f BÖRSE, FINANZ gearing (*BrE*), leverage (*AmE*)

leveraged: **~ Buyout** m (*LBO*) FINANZ leveraged buyout

Leverage: **Leverage-Kennziffer** f FINANZ debt ratio, financial leverage ratio

Lewis-Fei-Ranis-Modell nt VW *Begriff der Entwicklungspolitik* Lewis-Fei-Ranis model

Lexikon nt COMP dictionary

liberal adj GESCHÄFT liberal; **~e Handelspolitik** f VW liberal trade policy; **~er Kollektivismus** m POL liberal collectivism

liberalisieren vt GESCHÄFT, RECHT *Handel*, VW liberalize

Liberalisierung f GESCHÄFT, RECHT, VW liberalization; **~ des Handels** GESCHÄFT, RECHT, VW liberalization of trade, trade liberalization

Libertarianismus m VW libertarian economics

Liberty-Schiff nt TRANSP liberty ship

LIBID abbr (*Londoner Interbanknachfragesatz*) BANK, BÖRSE LIBID (*London Interbank Bid Rate*)

LIBOR abbr (*Londoner Interbankangebotssatz*) BANK, BÖRSE LIBOR (*London Interbank Offered Rate*)

Licht nt GESCHÄFT light; ♦ **ans ~ bringen** GESCHÄFT

bring to light; **~ werfen auf** GESCHÄFT shed light on, throw light on

Licht: **Lichtemissionsdiode** f (*LED*) COMP light-emitting diode (*LED*); **Lichtgriffel** m COMP *Eingabegerät* light pen; **Lichtleitfaserkabel** f IND fiberoptic cable (*AmE*), fibreoptic cable (*BrE*); **Lichtleittechnik** f COMP fiberoptics (*AmE*), fibreoptics (*BrE*); **Lichtnetz** nt COMP mains (*BrE*), supply network (*AmE*); **Lichtpause** f GESCHÄFT, VERWALT blueprint; **Lichtstift** m COMP light pen; **Lichtwellenleiter** m KOMM fiberoptics (*AmE*), fibreoptics (*BrE*); **Lichtwellenleitertechnik** f COMP fibreoptics (*AmE*), fibreoptics (*BrE*)

Liebhaberwert m VERSICH affection value

Liefer- in cpds GESCHÄFT delivery, supply; **Lieferangebot** nt GESCHÄFT bid, tender

Lieferant m GESCHÄFT, PERSON contractor, VW provider, supplier; **~ von Delikatessen** GESCHÄFT purveyor of fine foods; **Lieferantenauswahl** f V&M selection of suppliers; **Lieferantenbuch** nt RECHNUNG accounts payable ledger, bought ledger (*infrml*) (*BrE*); **Lieferanteneingang** m GESCHÄFT trade entrance, tradesman's entrance; **Lieferantengläubiger, in** m,f GESCHÄFT trade creditor; **Lieferantenkredit** m IMP/EXP supplier credit; **Lieferantenkreditgeber, in** m,f GESCHÄFT trade creditor; **Lieferantenrisiko** nt VW producer's risk

Liefer-: **Lieferanweisungen** f pl TRANSP forwarding instructions; **Lieferanzeige** f IMP/EXP, TRANSP delivery notice; **Lieferauftrag** m TRANSP delivery order (*D/O*)

lieferbar adj BÖRSE deliverable, GESCHÄFT available, V&M *absetzbar* merchantable; ♦ **nicht ~** GESCHÄFT not available; **in ~em Zustand** RECHT in a deliverable state

lieferbar: **~e Schatzwechsel** m pl BÖRSE deliverable bills; **~es Wertpapier** nt BÖRSE deliverable security

Lieferbarkeit f GESCHÄFT availability

Liefer-: **Lieferbedingungen des Vertrages** f pl IMP/EXP delivery terms of sale; **Lieferbestätigung** f IMP/EXP, TRANSP delivery receipt

Lieferer m VW provider, supplier

Liefer-: **Liefererfüllung** f IMP/EXP, TRANSP delivery performance

lieferfertig: **~e Baumwolle** f BÖRSE, IND spot cotton

Liefer-: **Lieferfrist** f BÖRSE delivery time; **Lieferkredit** m IMP/EXP supplier credit; **Liefermonat** m BÖRSE delivery month

liefern vt BÖRSE *Währung* make delivery of, GESCHÄFT *Information* supply, *Waren, Dienstleistungen* deliver, IMP/EXP consign, TRANSP *Güter* consign, deliver; **nicht ~** vt BÖRSE *Wertpapiere* fail to deliver

Liefer-: **Liefernachweis** m TRANSP proof of delivery (*POD*)

liefernd: **zu ~es Paket** nt GESCHÄFT parcel awaiting delivery

Liefer-: **Lieferort** m TRANSP place of delivery (*POD*); **Lieferpreis** m V&M delivered price, VW supply price; **Lieferschein** m FINANZ, IMP/EXP delivery note, RECHNUNG goods received note, TRANSP delivery note; **Liefersystem** nt BÖRSE delivery system; **Liefertag** m BÖRSE delivery day; **Liefertermin** m BÖRSE delivery date (*d.d.*), FINANZ date of delivery; **Lieferunfähigkeit** f GESCHÄFT failure to deliver

Lieferung f GESCHÄFT, TRANSP delivery; **~ frei Haus** TRANSP delivered domicile; **~ gegen Nachnahme** RECHNUNG, TRANSP cash on delivery; **~ gegen**

Zahlung BÖRSE delivery versus payment; **~ am gleichen Tage** KOMM, TRANSP same-day delivery; **~ nur gegen Barzahlung** RECHNUNG, TRANSP on a cash received basis; **~ und Rücklieferung** *f* TRANSP delivery and redelivery; **~ am vierten Werktag** FINANZ, GESCHÄFT regular way delivery; **~ zwei Tage nach Geschäftsabschluß** BÖRSE *bei einem Devisenkassageschäft* spot delivery; ◆ **eine ~ von etw abnehmen** GESCHÄFT accept delivery of sth, take delivery of sth; **vor der ~ gezogener Wechsel** FINANZ, RECHNUNG advance bill

Lieferung: **Lieferungen** *f pl* GESCHÄFT, VW supplies; **Lieferungsumschlag** *m* GESCHÄFT, TRANSP delivery turnround

Liefer-: **Lieferverzug** *m* GESCHÄFT delayed delivery, RECHT *Handelsvertrag* default in delivery; **Lieferzeit** *f* GESCHÄFT, TRANSP delivery time; **Lieferzeitraum** *m* BÖRSE delivery period

Liege- *in cpds* TRANSP berth; **Liegegeld** *nt* TRANSP demurrage

liegen: **~ bei** *phr* BÖRSE *Kurs* trade at, GESCHÄFT *Angebot, Preis, Gebot* stand at

Liegenschaft *f* GRUND immovable estate; **Liegenschaftsamt** *nt* VERWALT land office (*AmE*); **Liegenschaften** *f pl* RECHT corporeal hereditaments; **Liegenschaftsvertrag** *m* RECHT real agreement

Liegeplatz *m* TRANSP *für stillgelegte Schiffe* lay-up berth; ◆ **am ~ oder nicht** TRANSP whether in berth or not

Liegeplatz: **Liegeplatzkostenerstattung** *f* VERSICH lay-up return

Liege-: **Liegetag** *m* TRANSP lay day; **Liegetage** *m pl* **vor der Rückreise** TRANSP reversible lay days; **Liegewagen** *m* FREI, TRANSP couchette

Liegezeit *f* TRANSP laytime, turnaround (*AmE*), turnround (*BrE*); **~ im Hafen** *f* TRANSP port turnaround time (*AmE*), port turnround time (*BrE*), ship turnaround time (*AmE*), ship turnround time (*BrE*); **~ vor der Rückreise** *f* TRANSP reversible lay time

Liesmich- *in cpds* COMP Readme; **Liesmichdatei** *f* COMP Readme file; **Liesmichdokument** *nt* COMP Readme document

Lifestyle: **~ Merchandising** *nt jarg* V&M *auf einen gewissen Lebensstil abziehende Produktwerbung* lifestyle merchandising (*BrE*)

LIFO *abbr* (*last-in-first-out*) PERSON LIFO (*last in first out*); **LIFO-Dollarwert** *m* STEUER dollar value LIFO; **LIFO-Methode** *f* PERSON, RECHNUNG *Bewertung des Lagerbestands*, STEUER, VW *Bewertung des Vorratsvermögens* last in first out (*LIFO*)

Limit *nt* BÖRSE limit; **Limitauftrag** *m* BÖRSE limit order

limitiert: **~er Jahresbericht** *m* RECHNUNG limited annual statements; **~e Order** *f* BÖRSE limit order; **~er Scheck** *m* RECHNUNG limited check (*AmE*), limited cheque (*BrE*); **~e Stufenflexibilität** *f* **fester Wechselkurse** VW adjustable peg

Lindahl: **Lindahl-Gleichgewicht** *nt* VW Lindahl Equilibrium; **Lindahl-Preis** *m* VW Lindahl price

lindern *vt* GESCHÄFT *Probleme* alleviate

Lineal *nt* GESCHÄFT ruler

linear: **~e Abhängigkeit** *f* MATH linear dependence; **~e Abschreibung** *f* RECHNUNG straight-line depreciation; **~e Beziehung** *f* PERSON linear relationship; **~e Erhöhung** *f* MGMNT linear increase; **~e Optimierung** *f* MATH linear programming; **~e Planungsrechnung** *f* MATH linear programming; **~e Programmierung** *f* COMP, MATH, VW linear programming; **~e Regression** *f* MATH linear regression; **~e Verantwortlichkeit** *f* GESCHÄFT linear responsibility; **~e Verantwortung** *f* MATH linear responsibility

Linearprogramm *m* MATH linear program (*AmE*), linear programme (*BrE*)

Lingua franca *f* GESCHÄFT lingua franca

Linie *f* PERSON line; **Linienassistent, in** *m,f* PERSON line assistant; **Liniendienst** *m* FREI, TRANSP scheduled service; **Liniendirektor, in** *m,f* MGMNT line executive; **Linienflug** *m* FREI, TRANSP scheduled flight; **Linienflugzeug** *nt* TRANSP airliner; **Linienfrachter** *m* TRANSP cargo liner; **Linienfrachtschiff** *nt* TRANSP cargo liner; **Linienfunktion** *f* GESCHÄFT line function; **Linienkontrolle** *f* MGMNT line control; **Linienleitung** *f* MGMNT *Produktionsprozeß* line management; **Linienmanagement** *nt* MGMNT line management; **Linienmanager, in** *m,f* MGMNT, PERSON line manager; **Linienorganisation** *f* MGMNT, PERSON line organization; **Linienschiffahrtskonferenz** *f* TRANSP liner conference; **Linienstelle** *f* PERSON line position; **Linienvollmacht** *f* PERSON *Hierarchie* line authority; **Linienvorgesetzte(r)** *mf* [decl. as adj] IND, MGMNT, PERSON line manager

liniert: **~es Papier** *nt* GESCHÄFT lined paper, ruled paper

linke *adj* GESCHÄFT left-hand; ◆ **zum linken Flügel des politischen Spektrums gehörend** POL left-wing; **am linken Rand ausrichten** COMP, MEDIEN *Text in Textverarbeitung* left justify

Linke *f* POL left

linke: **~r Flügel** *m* POL left; **~ Seite** *f* POL left; **~ Spalte** *f* GESCHÄFT left-hand column; **~ Umschalttaste** *f* COMP left shift key

links *adj* GESCHÄFT on the left, POL on the left, *predicative adjective* left-wing; ◆ **~ ausgerichtet** COMP, MEDIEN left-justified

linksbündig *adj* COMP *Textverarbeitung* flush left, left-justified; ◆ **~ ausrichten** COMP, MEDIEN left justify

linksgerichtet *adj* POL left-wing; **~e politische Gesinnung** *f* POL leftism

linksorientiert *adj* POL left-wing; **~e Haltung** *f* POL leftism

Linksruck *m* POL swing to the left

Lippenbekenntnis: **für etw ein ~ ablegen** *phr* GESCHÄFT pay lip service to sth

liquid *adj* BANK, FINANZ liquid, solvent, GESCHÄFT afloat, RECHNUNG liquid, solvent; **~er Aktivposten** *m* BÖRSE, RECHNUNG available asset; **~e Mittel** *nt pl* FINANZ available funds, liquid funds; **~e Mittel** *nt pl* **des Privatsektors** VW private sector liquidity (*PSL*); **~e Mittel** *nt pl* **und Staatspapiere** *nt pl* FINANZ liquid assets and government securities (*LGS*)

Liquidation *f* FINANZ liquidation, GESCHÄFT liquidation, winding-up, MGMNT winding-up, RECHNUNG liquidation, RECHT liquidation, winding-up, VW dissolution; **Liquidationskassenmitglied** *nt* BÖRSE clearing member (*BrE*); **Liquidationspreis** *m* BÖRSE, FINANZ exit price; **Liquidationstermin** *m* BÖRSE account day, settlement day; **Liquidationsvereinbarung** *f* RECHT *Gesellschaftsrecht* winding-up arrangements; **Liquidationsvertrag** *m* RECHT *Innominatsvertrag bei Personengesellschaften* partnership liquidation contract; **Liquidationswert** *m* FINANZ net asset value (*NAV*), break-up value,

RECHNUNG break-up value, liquidating value, net asset value (*NAV*), winding-up value

Liquidator *m* RECHNUNG liquidator

Liquidierbankenprinzip: **nach dem ~** *phr* RECHNUNG in decreasing liquidity order

liquidieren *vt* GESCHÄFT liquidate, wind up

Liquidität *f* BANK solvency, BÖRSE liquidity, FINANZ assets, earnings, liquidity, management, solvency, RECHNUNG solvency; **~ dritten Grades** FINANZ, RECHNUNG current ratio; **~ ersten Grades** FINANZ cash ratio, quick assets ratio, RECHNUNG acid test, acid test ratio, available cash, liquid ratio, liquidity adequacy, quick assets ratio, VW cash deposits ratio; **~ zweiten Grades** FINANZ current ratio, RECHNUNG quick ratio; **Liquiditätsabschöpfung** *f* VW absorption of liquidity; **Liquiditätsenge** *f* FINANZ cash shortage; **Liquiditätsengpaß** *m* FINANZ liquidity squeeze; **Liquiditätsfalle** *f* VW depression pole, liquidity trap; **Liquiditätsgrad** *m* FINANZ cash ratio, liquidity ratio, solvency ratio, RECHNUNG liquidity ratio, solvency ratio; **Liquiditätshunger** *m* FINANZ liquidity famine; **Liquiditätskennzahl** *f* FINANZ solvency ratio, RECHNUNG current ratio, solvency ratio; **Liquiditätskennziffer** *f* BANK bank cash ratio, FINANZ liquid assets ratio; **Liquiditätsklemme** *f* FINANZ liquidity squeeze; **Liquiditätskrise** *f* BANK liquidity crisis; **Liquiditätsmarge** *f* FINANZ solvency margin; **Liquiditätsplan** *m* RECHNUNG cash forecast; **Liquiditätspräferenz** *f* VW liquidity preference; **Liquiditätsprobleme** *nt pl* RECHNUNG liquidity problems; **Liquiditätsprognose** *f* FINANZ cash forecast; **Liquiditätsquote** *f* FINANZ liquidity ratio; **Liquiditätsreserve** *f* BANK, RECHNUNG cash reserve; **Liquiditätsschwierigkeiten** *f pl* RECHNUNG liquidity problems; **Liquiditätsstatus** *m* BANK cash and debt position; **Liquiditätssteuerung** *f* FINANZ financial engineering, MGMNT asset management, RECHNUNG cash management; **Liquiditätsstreuung** *f* BÖRSE liquidity diversification

Liste *f* COMP register, listing, GESCHÄFT schedule (*AmE*); **~ der Mitwirkenden** MEDIEN credit title; **~ der umsatzstärksten Aktien** BÖRSE most active list; ◆ **eine ~ von etw erstellen** GESCHÄFT keep a tally of; **aus der ~ streichen** GESCHÄFT strike off the list

Liste: **Listenpreis** *m* V&M list price

Liter *m* (*l*) GESCHÄFT liter (*AmE*) (*l*), litre (*BrE*) (*l*)

Lithographie *f* V&M lithography

Live- *in cpds* MEDIEN live; **Live-Programm** *nt* MEDIEN live program (*AmE*), live programme (*BrE*); **Live-Sendung** *f* MEDIEN live broadcast

Livree *f* V&M livery

Lizenz *f* BANK, IMP/EXP licence (*BrE*), license (*AmE*), PATENT patent (*pat.*), RECHT licence (*BrE*), license (*AmE*), permit; ◆ **unter ~** PATENT, RECHT under licence (*BrE*), under license (*AmE*); **unter ~ herstellen** IND manufacture under licence (*BrE*), manufacture under license (*AmE*)

Lizenz: **Lizenzabkommen** *nt* PATENT, RECHT licensing agreement; **Lizenzaustausch** *m* COMP, GESCHÄFT, RECHT cross-licensing; **Lizenzbau** *m* VW licensed construction

lizenzberechtigt: **~e Herstellung** *f* IND manufacturing under licence (*BrE*), manufacturing under license (*AmE*)

Lizenz: **Lizenzerteilung** *f* GESCHÄFT, PATENT licensing

lizenzfähig *adj* IMP/EXP licensable

Lizenz: **Lizenzgeber, in** *m,f* GESCHÄFT, PATENT licensor; **Lizenzgebühr** *f* GESCHÄFT licence fee (*BrE*), license fee (*AmE*), royalty

lizenzieren *vt* RECHT license

lizenziert *adj* RECHT *geistiges Eigentum* licensed; **~e Herstellung** *f* IND manufacturing under licence (*BrE*), manufacturing under license (*AmE*)

Lizenz: **Lizenzinhaber, in** *m,f* GESCHÄFT licence holder (*BrE*), license holder (*AmE*), RECHT *geistiges Eigentum* licensee; **Lizenz- und Kooperationsvertrag** *m* RECHT *Verträge* licence and cooperation agreement (*BrE*), license and cooperation agreement (*AmE*); **Lizenzprüfung** *f* GESCHÄFT licensing examination; **Lizenztrust** *m* UMWELT royalty trust; **Lizenzvergabe** *f* RECHT *Verträge* granting of licence (*BrE*), granting of license (*AmE*); **Lizenzvertrag** *m* RECHT franchise agreement; **Lizenzvoraussetzung** *f* IMP/EXP licensing requirements; **Lizenzvorschriften** *f pl* IMP/EXP licensing requirements

LKW *abbr* (*Lastkraftwagen*) TRANSP HGV (*heavy goods vehicle*), lorry (*BrE*), truck (*AmE*); ◆ **per ~ transportieren** TRANSP truck

LKW: **LKW-Anhänger** *m* TRANSP drawbar trailer; **LKW-Annahmebereich** *m* TRANSP lorry reception area (*BrE*), truck reception area (*AmE*); **LKW-Fahrer, in** *m,f* TRANSP lorry driver (*BrE*), truck driver (*AmE*), trucker (*AmE*); **LKW-Ladungsversicherung** *f* VERSICH motor truck cargo insurance (*AmE*)

LL.B. *abbr* PERSON LLB (*Bachelor of Laws*)

Lloyd's *m* VERSICH Lloyd's (*BrE*), Lloyd's of London (*BrE*)

LMBI *abbr* (*leveraged Management Buy-In*) MGMNT LMBI (*leveraged management buy-in*)

LM-Kurve *f* VW LM curve

LNG: **LNG-Tanker** *m* TRANSP LNG carrier; **LNG-Transporter** *m* TRANSP LNG carrier

Lobby *f* POL lobbying, lobby, lobby group

Lobbyist, in *m,f* RECHT *Interessenvertreter* lobbyist

lobbyistisch: **~e Einflußnahme** *f* POL lobbying

Loch *nt* COMP, GESCHÄFT hole

lochen *vt* COMP punch, IND punch a hole in

Locher *m* COMP *Lochkarten* key punch, GESCHÄFT punch

Loch: **Lochkarte** *f* COMP, GESCHÄFT punch card; **Lochkartencode** *m* COMP, GESCHÄFT punch code; **Lochkartenliste** *f* COMP, GESCHÄFT punch list; **Lochkartenlocher** *m* COMP card punch, key punch, GESCHÄFT card punch; **Lochstreifen** *m* COMP, GESCHÄFT paper tape; ticker tape; **Lochstreifenlocher** *m* COMP, GESCHÄFT tape punch; **Lochstreifenspule** *f* COMP spool

Lock- *in cpds* V&M, VW lure, temptation; **Lockartikel** *m* V&M leader, loss leader, VW lure

locker: **~es Bündnis** *nt* POL confederation

lockern *vt* GESCHÄFT, MGMNT relax, VW *wirtschaftspolitische Bestimmungen* ease

Lockerung *f* GESCHÄFT, MGMNT relaxation, VW *wirtschaftspolitischer Bestimmungen* easing

Lock-: **Lockvogel** *m* BÖRSE lowballer, V&M, VW price leader; **Lockvogelverkaufsaktion** *f* V&M bait and switch selling (*AmE*); **Lockvogelwerbung** *f* V&M bait and switch advertising (*AmE*), bait advertising (*AmE*)

Loco-Preis *m* TRANSP loco

Logbuch *nt* TRANSP log, log book, official log, *Schiffahrt* ship's log, VERWALT log book

Logik *f* GESCHÄFT logic

logisch: ~e **Schlußfolgerung** *f* RECHT right combination

Logistik *f* GESCHÄFT, IND, MATH, TRANSP logistics; **Logistikindustrie** *f* IND, TRANSP logistics industry

logistisch *adj* GESCHÄFT, IND, MATH, TRANSP logistical; **~er Prozeß** *m* MATH logistic process; **~es Verfahren** *nt* IND logistic process; **~er Zyklus** *m* VW logistic cycle

Logo *nt* GESCHÄFT, V&M, VERWALT logo (*logotype*)

Lohn *m* GESCHÄFT, PERSON wage, wages (*BrE*), *Wochenlohn* pay, hire, VW wages; **~ mit Nebenleistungen** VW package pay; **Lohnabschluß** *m* PERSON wage settlement; **Lohnabtretung** *f* GESCHÄFT, PERSON wage assignment; **Lohnangleichung** *f* GESCHÄFT, PERSON wage adjustment; **Lohnanpassung** *f* GESCHÄFT, PERSON wage adjustment; **Lohnanteil** *m* **am Sozialprodukt** VW labor's share of national income (*AmE*), labour's share of national income (*BrE*); **Lohnanteil** *m* **am Volkseinkommen** VW labor's share of national income (*AmE*), labour's share of national income (*BrE*); **Lohnausfall** *m* PERSON loss of pay; **Lohnausschuß** *m* *obs* PERSON pay board, Wages Council (*BrE*)

lohnbezogen: **~er Pensionsplan** *m* **des Staates** VW State Earnings-Related Pension Scheme (*BrE*) (*SERPS*); **~e Sozialversicherungssteuer** *f* STEUER employment tax

Lohn: **Lohndiffusion** *f* VW wage diffusion; **Lohndrift** *f* PERSON, VW wage drift, wage gap, *Arbeit*, VW earnings drift; **Lohndruckinflation** *f* VW wage push inflation

Löhne *m pl* PERSON, VW wages; **~ und Gehälter** *nt pl* PERSON, VW salaries and wages; **~, Gehälter** *nt pl* **und Nebenleistungen** *f pl* PERSON, VW *Arbeitsentgelt, Sonderleistung* salaries, wages and fringe benefits

Lohn: **Lohneinbehaltung** *f* PERSON retention of wages, wage withholding; **Lohneinzelkosten** *pl* PERSON, RECHNUNG, VW direct labor (*AmE*), direct labour (*BrE*); **Lohnempfänger** *m* PERSON wage worker (*AmE*)

löhnen *vt infrml* FINANZ cough up (*infrml*)

lohnend *adj* GESCHÄFT worthwhile, PERSON *Tätigkeit* rewarding; **nicht ~** *adj* GESCHÄFT unrewarding

Lohn: **Lohnerhöhung** *f* PERSON rise in wages, *Arbeitsentgelt* wage increase; **Lohnexplosion** *f* PERSON, VW wage explosion; **Lohnflexibilität** *f* PERSON, VW wage flexibility; **Lohnfondstheorie** *f* VW wages fund theory; **Lohnforderung** *f* PERSON wage claim; **Lohnfortzahlungsgesetz** *nt* RECHT wages act; **Lohngefälle** *nt* PERSON differentials (*BrE*), pay differentials (*BrE*), wage differentials, VW wage differentials; **Lohngefüge** *f* PERSON wage structure; **Lohn- und Gehaltsaufwendungen** *f pl* **im Privatsektor** VERWALT, VW industrial payroll; **auf der Lohn- oder Gehaltsliste stehend** *phr* PERSON on the payroll; **Lohn- und Gehaltspolitik** *f* PERSON, VW *eines Unternehmens* pay policy; **Lohn- und Gehaltsrevision** *f* PERSON pay review, *Arbeitsentgelt* wage and salary survey; **Lohn- und Gehaltsstopp** *m* PERSON, VW *Inflationsbekämpfung* pay freeze, pay pause, wage freeze; **Lohn- und Gehaltswesen** *nt* PERSON *Lohnbuchhaltung* wage and salary administration

lohngekoppelt: **~e Staatspension** *f* VW State Earnings-Related Pension Scheme (*BrE*) (*SERPS*)

Lohn: **Lohngemeinkosten** *pl* PERSON, RECHNUNG indir-

ect labor costs (*AmE*), indirect labour costs (*BrE*); **Lohngleichgewicht** *nt* VW equilibrium wage rate; **Lohngleichheitsgesetz** *nt* PERSON *britisches Arbeitsrecht* Equal Pay Act (*BrE*); **Lohngleichheitsrichtlinie** *f* PERSON *1975 von EG-Kommission erlassen* Equal Pay Directive; **Lohngruppe** *f* PERSON grade; **Lohnindexbindung** *f* PERSON *Arbeitsentgelt* wage indexation; **Lohnindexierung** *f* PERSON threshold agreement; **Lohninflation** *f* VW wage inflation; **Lohnkosten** *pl* RECHNUNG manpower costs, STEUER, VW cost of labor (*AmE*), cost of labour (*BrE*), labor costs (*AmE*), labour costs (*BrE*); **Lohnliste** *f* PERSON *Arbeitsentgelt, Betriebswirtschaft* pay bill (*AmE*), payroll, RECHNUNG payroll; **Lohn-Miet-Verhältnis** *nt* VW wage-rental ratio; **Lohnnachzahlung** *f* PERSON back pay, back payment; **Lohnnebenkosten** *pl* RECHNUNG, VERWALT add-on costs; **Lohnnebenleistung** *f* GESCHÄFT, PERSON fringe benefit; **Lohnniveau** *nt* PERSON *Arbeitsentgelt*, VW wage level; **Lohn- oder Gehaltsliste** *f* PERSON *Arbeitsentgelt* payroll; **Lohnpause** *f* PERSON *Arbeitsentgelt* pay freeze, pay pause, wage freeze; **Lohnpolitik** *f* PERSON, VW wages policy, wage policy; **Lohn-Preis-Indexierung** *f* VW wage-price-indexation; **Lohn-Preis-Inflationsspirale** *f* VW wage-price inflation spiral; **Lohn- und Preisleitlinien** *f pl* PERSON *amerikanische Lohnpolitik* wage-and-price guidelines; **Lohn-Preis-Spirale** *f* VW wage-price spiral; **Lohnquote** *f* VW labor's share of national income (*AmE*), labour's share of national income (*BrE*); **Lohnrunde** *f* PERSON pay round, VW wage round; **Lohnscheck** *m* BANK pay check (*AmE*), pay cheque (*BrE*)

lohnschwach: **~er Betrieb** *m* IND, PERSON unfair shop

Lohn: **Lohnskala** *f* PERSON *Arbeitsentgelt* wage scale; **Lohnspanne** *f* PERSON wage spread; **Lohnstabilisierung** *f* PERSON, VW *Inflationsbekämpfung* wage stabilization; **Lohnsteuer** *f* STEUER employment tax; **Lohn-Steuer-Spirale** *f* STEUER, VW wage-tax spiral; **Lohnstillstand** *m* PERSON pay freeze, pay pause, wage freeze; **Lohnstopp** *m* PERSON *Auftragslage, Inflationsbekämpfung* wage freeze, pay freeze, pay pause; **Lohnstreifen** *m* PERSON *Arbeitsentgelt* pay slip, *Lohnempfänger* itemized pay statement; **Lohnstückkosten** *pl* PERSON, RECHNUNG, VW unit labor costs (*AmE*), unit labour costs (*BrE*); **Lohnstufe** *f* PERSON *Arbeitsentgelt* wage bracket; **Lohnsubvention** *f* VW wage subsidy; **Lohnsystem** *nt* PERSON wage system; **Lohntheorie** *f* VW wage theory; **Lohntüte** *f* PERSON pay packet (*BrE*); **Lohnvereinbarung** *f* PERSON *Arbeitnehmer- oder Arbeitgeberverhandlungen* wage agreement; **Lohnvergütung** *f* **für den Anmarschweg zum Arbeitsplatz** PERSON portal-to-portal pay; **Lohnverhandlung** *f* MGMNT, PERSON, VW collective bargaining; **Lohnverhandlungen** *f pl* MGMNT pay talks, wage negotiations, wage talks, PERSON *Arbeitgeber- oder Arbeitnehmerverhandlungen* wage negotiations, *Arbeitsentgelt* pay talks, *Tarifverhandlungen* wage talks; **Lohnzusatzleistung** *f* PERSON fringe benefit; **Lohnzuschlag** *m* PERSON premium pay

Lokal- *in cpds* GESCHÄFT, MEDIEN, PATENT, V&M regional, local

lokal *adj* COMP, FINANZ, IMP/EXP, KOMM local; **~e Ausfuhrkontrolle** *f* IMP/EXP local export control; **~e Depotverwahrung** *f* FINANZ local custody; **~e Einfuhrkontrolle** *f* IMP/EXP local import control (*LIC*);

~er **Exportausschuß** *m* IMP/EXP Local Export Council (*BrE*) (*LEC*); ~e **Exportkontrolle** *f* IMP/EXP local export control (*LEC*); ~e **Importkontrolle** *f* IMP/EXP local import control (*LIC*); ~es **Netz** *nt* (*LAN*) COMP, KOMM local area network (*LAN*); ~e **Variable** *f* COMP local variable

Lokalisationsparameter *m* MATH central tendency

lokalisieren *vt* COMP *Software* localize, GESCHÄFT trace

Lokalisierer *m* TRANSP locator

Lokal-: **Lokalpatent** *nt* PATENT regional patent; **Lokalpresse** *f* MEDIEN local press; **Lokalreporter, in** *m,f* MEDIEN stringer; **Lokalzeitung** *f* MEDIEN local newspaper

loko *adj* IMP/EXP loco

Lokogeschäft *nt* GESCHÄFT spot business

Lombard- *in cpds* BANK, FINANZ, GESCHÄFT lombard; **Lombarddarlehen** *nt* BANK collateral loan

lombardfähig *adj* BANK acceptable, FINANZ eligible as collateral

Lombard-: **Lombardfenster** *nt* BANK, FINANZ discount window, discount window lending

lombardieren *vt* BANK collateralize

Lombard-: **Lombardkredit** *m* BANK collateral loan, BÖRSE advance on securities, securities loan, GESCHÄFT advance against security; **Lombardsatz** *m* BANK Lombard rate

Lomé-Abkommen *nt* VW Lomé Convention

London: ~er **Börsenvorstand** *m* BÖRSE London Stock Exchange Board; ~er **City** *f* FINANZ the City; ~er **Gold-Fixing** *nt* BANK London gold fixing; ~er **Hafenbehörde** *f* TRANSP Port of London Authority (*PLA*); ~er **Interbankangebotssatz** *m* (*LIBOR*) BANK, BÖRSE London Interbank Offered Rate (*LIBOR*); ~er **Interbanknachfragesatz** *m* (*LIBID*) BANK, BÖRSE London Interbank Bid Rate (*LIBID*); ~er **Internationale Finanzterminbörse** *f* BÖRSE London International Financial Futures Exchange; ~er **Metallbörse** *f* BÖRSE London Metal Exchange (*LME*); ~er **Optionenhandelsbehörde** *f* BÖRSE London Trader Options Exchange; ~er **Termin- und Optionsbörse** *f* BÖRSE London Futures and Options Exchange (*London FOX*); ~er **Wertpapierbörse** *f* BÖRSE London Stock Exchange (*LSE*)

Long- *in cpds* BÖRSE long; **Long-Hedge** *m* BÖRSE long hedge; **sich in einer Long-Position mit Terminkontrakten befinden** *phr* BÖRSE be long in futures

Lorenzkurve *f* VW Lorenz curve

Los *nt* IND batch

Lösch- *in cpds* TRANSP discharging, landing, unloading

löschbar: ~er **programmierbarer Nur-Lese-Speicher** *m* COMP erasable programmable read-only memory (*EPROM*)

Lösch-: **Löschbescheinigung** *f* TRANSP landing certificate

löschen *vt* COMP delete, erase, clear, blank, GESCHÄFT extinguish, PATENT *Warenzeichen im Register* cancel, RECHT *Rechtsverbindlichkeit* discharge, extinguish, TRANSP discharge, land, unload

Lösch-: **Löschgebühr** *f* TRANSP drop-off charge; **Löschgenehmigung** *f* TRANSP landing permit; **Löschkai** *m* TRANSP discharging berth, discharging wharf

Löschplatz *m* TRANSP place of discharge, port of delivery; ~ **zur Abfertigung flüssigen Massenguts** TRANSP bulk liquid berth; ~ **zur Abfertigung von Naß- und Trocken-Bulkladung** TRANSP bulk dry and wet cargo berth; ~ **zur Abfertigung von Trocken-Bulkladung** TRANSP bulk dry cargo berth

Lösch-: **Löschrisiko** *nt* GESCHÄFT, TRANSP, VERSICH unloading risk; **Löschtaste** *f* COMP delete key (*DEL*)

Löschung *f* COMP clearing, deletion, erasure, PATENT *eines Warenzeichens im Register* cancellation, RECHT *Schuld* discharge, extinction, TRANSP discharge, landing, unloading; ~ **der Registrierung** STEUER cancellation of registration; ◆ **Löschung, Speicherung, Lieferung** IMP/EXP landing, storage, delivery (*LSD*)

Löschung: **Löschungskosten** *pl* IMP/EXP landed cost, TRANSP, VERWALT landing charges

Lösch-: **Löschwasserschaden** *m* VERSICH water damage; **Löschzeichen** *nt* COMP delete character (*DEL*)

lose *adj* GESCHÄFT unpacked; ~ **Waren** *f pl* TRANSP bulk, bulk goods

Loseblatt- *in cpds* MEDIEN, VERWALT loose-leaf; **Loseblattausgabe** *f* MEDIEN loose-leaf edition; **als Loseblattsammlung herausgeben** *phr* MEDIEN publish in loose-leaf form

lösen *vt* GESCHÄFT *Vertrag* terminate, *Problem* solve, *Konflikt* resolve

Los: **Losgröße** *f* IND batch size

Lösung *f* GESCHÄFT *eines Vertrags* termination, *eines Problems* solution, MGMNT *eines Problems* solution, *eines Konflikts* resolution; **Lösungsansatz** *m* GESCHÄFT, MGMNT, VERWALT, VW approach

losweise: ~ **Prüfung** *f* VW lot-by-lot inspection

loswerden *vt* GESCHÄFT get rid of, shake off

Lotse *m* PERSON *Schiffahrt* pilot; **Lotsenboot** *nt* TRANSP pilot boat; **Lotsengeld** *nt* TRANSP pilotage

Lotterie *f* GESCHÄFT lottery

Louvre-Abkommen *nt* VW Louvre Accord

Löwenanteil *m* GESCHÄFT the lion's share

Loyalität *f* GESCHÄFT, V&M loyalty; **Loyalitätsfaktor** *m* V&M loyalty factor

LPG *abbr* (*landwirtschaftliche Produktionsgenossenschaft*) VW agricultural production cooperative

LPT *abbr* (*line printer*) COMP LPT (*line printer*)

LQ *abbr* (*Briefqualität*) COMP *Drucker* LQ (*letter quality*); **LQ-Font** *m jarg* COMP letter-quality font

Lucas: ~**sche Angebotsfunktion** *f* VW Lucas supply function

Lücke *f* BÖRSE break, FINANZ, GESCHÄFT gap; ~ **in der Berichterstattung** MEDIEN gap in coverage; ◆ **die ~ schließen** FINANZ bridge the gap

Lücke: **Lückenfinanzierung** *f* FINANZ gap financing

lückenlos: ~ **Prüfung** *f* RECHNUNG block testing, complete audit

Lücke: **Lückenuntersuchung** *f* GESCHÄFT gap study

Luft *f* IND, TRANSP, UMWELT air; ◆ **aus der ~ gegriffen** *infrml* GESCHÄFT unsubstantiated; **jdn an die ~ setzen** *infrml* PERSON dismiss sb, give sb his cards (*infrml*) (*BrE*), give sb the sack (*infrml*)

Luft- *in cpds* GESCHÄFT air, aero-, aerial, aviation; **Luftbildvermessung** *f* TRANSP aerial survey; **Luftchartervertrag** *m* TRANSP aircraft charter agreement

luftdicht *adj* IND airtight

Lüfter *m* IND fan

Luftfahrt *f* TRANSP aviation; **Luftfahrtindustrie** *f* TRANSP aircraft industry; **Luftfahrtkaskoversicherung** *f* VERSICH aircraft hull insurance; **Luftfahrtschau** *f* TRANSP airshow; **Luftfahrtversicherung** *f* VERSICH aviation insurance

Luft-: **Luftfahrzeug** *nt* TRANSP aircraft

Luftfracht *f* TRANSP air freight, air cargo; **Luftfrachtbrief** *m* IMP/EXP, TRANSP air bill of lading, air waybill (*AWB*); **Luftfrachtbrief** *m* **des Spediteurs** IMP/EXP, TRANSP forwarder air waybill (*FAB*); **Luftfracht-Container** *m* TRANSP air-freight container (*ac*); **Luftfrachtführer** *m* TRANSP air carrier, carrier; **Luftfrachtkosten** *pl* TRANSP air-freight charges; **Luftfrachtpapiere** *nt pl* IMP/EXP, TRANSP shipper's letter of instruction for issuing air waybills; **Luftfrachtsammelladung** *f* TRANSP air-freight consolidation; **Luftfrachttarif** *m* TRANSP air-freight charges

Luft-: **Luftkissenboot** *nt* TRANSP hovercraft; **Luftkissenfahrzeug** *nt* TRANSP hovercraft, **Luftkorridor** *m* TRANSP air corridor

Luftpost *f* KOMM air mail; ♦ **per ~** KOMM by air mail

Luftpost: **Luftpostbrief** *m* KOMM aerogramme, air letter, air-mail letter; **Luftpostleichtbrief** *m* KOMM aerogramme, air letter; **Luftpostpapier** *nt* KOMM air-mail paper

Luft-: **Luftqualitätsstandard** *m* UMWELT ambient standard (*AmE*); **Luft- und Raumfahrtindustrie** *f* IND aerospace industry; **Luftroute** *f* TRANSP airway

lufttechnisch: **~e Industrie** *f* IND ventilation industry

Lufttransport *m* TRANSP air transport, airlift;

Lufttransportgesellschaft *f* TRANSP air carrier, carrier; **Lufttransportversicherung** *f* VERSICH air transport insurance

Luftverkehr *m* TRANSP air traffic, air transport; **Luftverkehrscontainer** *m* TRANSP air mode container; **Luftverkehrsgesellschaft** *f* TRANSP air carrier; **Luftverkehrslinie** *f* TRANSP airway; **Luftverkehrsregelung** *f* TRANSP air-traffic control (*ATC*); **Luftverkehrsstraße** *f* TRANSP airway; **Luftverkehrszentrale** *f* TRANSP air-traffic control (*ATC*)

Luft-: **Luftverschmutzung** *f* UMWELT air pollution; **Luftverunreinigung** *f* UMWELT air pollution; **auf dem Luftweg** *phr* KOMM, TRANSP *Beförderungsart* by air; **Luftwerbung** *f* V&M aerial advertising

Luke: **pro ~ pro Tag** *phr* TRANSP per hatch per day; **Lukendeckel** *m* TRANSP hatch cover

lukrativ *adj* GESCHÄFT lucrative

Lumineszenzdiode *m* (*LED*) COMP light-emitting diode (*LED*)

Lundberg-Lag *m* VW Lundberg lag

lustlos *adj* BÖRSE lifeless, GESCHÄFT listless; **~er Markt** *m* BÖRSE flat market, GESCHÄFT stale market

Luxemburg-Effekt *m* VW Luxemburg effect

Luxibor *m* VW Luxibor (*Luxembourg Interbank Offered Rate*)

Luxus *m* V&M *Waren* luxury; **Luxusartikel** *m pl* GESCHÄFT, V&M, VW fancy goods; **Luxusgüter** *nt pl* GESCHÄFT, V&M, VW luxury goods; **Luxuskabine** *f* TRANSP deluxe cabin; **Luxussteuer** *f* STEUER luxury tax

M

m *abbr* (*Meter*) GESCHÄFT m (*meter AmE, metre BrE*)

Machart *f* IND style, *Kleidung* cut

Machbarkeit *f* GESCHÄFT feasibility

machen *vt* GESCHÄFT, PATENT *Erfindung* make

Macht *f* GESCHÄFT power, VW control, leverage; ◆ **an der ~** POL in power; **~ ausüben über** GESCHÄFT, POL exercise power over

Macht: **Machtkampf** *m* POL power struggle; **Machtmißbrauch** *m* GESCHÄFT abuse of power; **Machtpolitik** *f* POL power politics, abuse of power; **Machtteilung** *f* GESCHÄFT division of powers

Macker *m infrml* GESCHÄFT punter (*infrml*)

Macmillan-Lücke *f* FINANZ Macmillan Gap

Mädchen: **~ für alles** *phr infrml* dogsbody (*infrml*)

Mag. *abbr* (*Magazin*) GESCHÄFT, IMP/EXP, TRANSP, V&M whse (*warehouse*)

Magazin *nt* (*Mag.*) GESCHÄFT, IMP/EXP, TRANSP, V&M warehouse (*whse*); **Magazinhalter, in** *m,f* GESCHÄFT, IMP/EXP warehouse keeper; **Magazinverwalter, in** *m,f* GESCHÄFT warehouse officer, warehouse keeper; **Magazinverwaltung** *f* GESCHÄFT, IMP/EXP warehousing

mager: **~es Jahr** *nt* VW lean year

magisch: **~es Viereck** *nt* VW magic quadrilateral

Magister *m*: **~ der Betriebswirtschaft** MGMNT, PERSON Master of Business Administration (*MBA*), Master of Commerce (*MCom*); **~ der Naturwissenschaften** GESCHÄFT Master of Science (*MSc*); **~ der Wirtschaftswissenschaften** PERSON Master of Economics (*MEcon*)

Magistrat *m* GESCHÄFT council, POL municipality

Magistratur *f obs* POL local government

Magnat *m* GESCHÄFT tycoon

Magnet *m* GESCHÄFT magnet

Magnetband *nt* COMP, IND magnetic tape; **Magnetbandaufnahme** *f* MEDIEN tape recording; **Magnetbandaufzeichner** *m* COMP, MEDIEN magnetic tape recorder; **Magnetbandaufzeichnung** *f* MEDIEN tape recording; **Magnetbandspule** *f* COMP spool

Magnet: **Magnetblasenspeicher** *m* COMP bubble memory; **Magnetfilm** *m* V&M magnetic film

magnetisch: **~er Speicher** *m* COMP, IND magnetic storage

Magnet: **Magnetkarte** *f* COMP, IND magnetic card; **Magnetkern** *m* COMP magnetic core; **Magnetplatte** *f* COMP magnetic disk; **Magnetspeicher** *m* COMP, IND magnetic storage; **Magnettonband** *nt* COMP, MEDIEN magnetic tape

Mahnbescheid *m* RECHT *Schuldenbegleichung* reminder

mahnen *vt* FINANZ remind, GESCHÄFT dun, RECHNUNG, RECHT remind

mahnend: **~es Wort** *nt* GESCHÄFT word of warning

Mahnung *f* FINANZ, RECHNUNG reminder

Mahnzettel *m* FINANZ, RECHNUNG prompt note

Mail-Box *f* COMP mailbox

Mailing *nt* V&M mailing

Mailmerge *nt* COMP mailmerge

Mailorder *f* GESCHÄFT, KOMM mail order

makellos *adj* GESCHÄFT *Produkt, Ware* in perfect condition, *Ruf* undamaged

Makler, in *m,f* FINANZ broker; **~ auf eigene Rechnung** BÖRSE pit trader; **~ für Festverzinsliche** BÖRSE bond broker; **~ m pl für festverzinsliche Papiere** BÖRSE bond crowd; **~ m pl für festverzinsliche Schuldverschreibungen** BÖRSE active bond crowd (*AmE*); **vom ~ vermittelte Einlage** *f* BÖRSE brokered deposit; **Maklerabrechnung** *f* GESCHÄFT broker's statement; **Maklerdarlehen** *nt* BANK day loan; **Maklergebühr** *f* BÖRSE brokerage allowance (*AmE*), broker's commission, commission rate, FINANZ commission (*comm*), VERWALT procuration fee; **Maklergeschäft** *nt* GESCHÄFT brokerage; **Maklerkonto** *nt* BÖRSE brokerage account; **Maklerkreditrate** *f* BÖRSE broker call-loan rate (*AmE*); **Maklerprovision** *f* BÖRSE broker's commission, brokerage commission, overriding commission, V&M finder's fee; **Maklerstand** *m* BÖRSE pit; **Maklerstand** *m* **mit geringem Umsatzvolumen** BÖRSE inactive post

Makro *nt* (*Makrobefehl*) COMP macro; **Makrobefehl** *m* (*Makro*) COMP macro; **Makromarketing** *nt* V&M macromarketing; **Makroökonomik** *f* VW macroeconomics

makroökonomisch *adj* VW macroeconomic; **~e Bedarfsliste** *f* VW macroeconomic demand schedule

Makro: **Makrostruktur** *f* GESCHÄFT macroenvironment; **Makroverarbeitung** *f* COMP macrocomputing

Makulatur *f* GESCHÄFT spoilage

malafide *phr* RECHT *unredlich* mala fide

Maloney-Gesetz *nt* RECHT Maloney Act

Malthus: **~sches Bevölkerungsgesetz** *nt* VW Malthusian law of population

Mammutgesellschaft *f* GESCHÄFT, VW mammoth company

Management *nt* FINANZ management, GESCHÄFT, PERSON, VERWALT management; **~ nach dem Ausnahmeprinzip** MGMNT management by exception; **~ nach dem Krisenprinzip** MGMNT crisis management, management by crisis; **~ auf mittlerer Führungsebene** PERSON *Hierarchie* middle management; **~ durch Pflege persönlicher Kontakte** MGMNT management by walking around (*MBWA*); **~ der physischen Verteilung** TRANSP physical distribution management (*PDM*); **~ nach Zielvorgaben** MGMNT, VERWALT management by objectives (*MBO*); **Managementaktivität** *f* MGMNT management operation; **Managementausbildung** *f* MGMNT management training; **Management-Buy-In** *nt* FINANZ, MGMNT management buy-in (*MBO*); **Management-Buy-Out** *nt* FINANZ, MGMNT managment buy-out (*MBO*); **Managementfunktion** *f* MGMNT managerial function; **Managementgrafik** *f* MATH management chart; **Managementhandbuch** MGMNT management guide; **Managementinformation** *f* COMP, MGMNT management information; **Management-Informationssystem** *nt* (*MIS*) COMP, MGMNT management information system (*MIS*); **Management-Organisation** *f* PERSON management organization; **Managementpotential** *nt*

GESCHÄFT management potential; **Managementschulung** f PERSON management training; **Managementservice** m FINANZ, MGMNT management service; **Managementsystem** nt MGMNT management system; **Managementsystem** nt **für Geschäftspolitik und Ausgaben** FINANZ policy and expenditure management system; **Managementtechnik** f MGMNT management technique; **Management-Unterstützung** f PERSON management support; **Managementvertrag** m MGMNT management contract; **Managementzyklus** m MGMNT management cycle

managen vt MGMNT manage

Manager m MGMNT, PERSON manager (*MGR*); **~ und Arbeiter** pl PERSON managers and workers; **~ in Ausbildung** MGMNT, PERSON trainee manager; **~ auf der untersten Leitungsebene** MGMNT, PERSON first-line manager; **~ eines Verantwortungszentrums** RECHNUNG responsibility center manager (*AmE*), responsibility centre manager (*BrE*); **Managerhaftpflichtversicherung** f VERSICH directors' and officers' liability insurance

Managerin f MGMNT, PERSON manager (*MGR*), manageress

Manager: **Managerkrankheit** f PERSON executive stress

Manchester: **Manchester-Liberalismus** m VW Manchester school (*BrE*); **Manchester-Schule** f VW Manchester school (*BrE*)

Mandat nt POL elected office, RECHT mandate

Mangel m GESCHÄFT lack, RECHT *Verträge* defect, VW scarcity, shortage; **~ an Erfahrung** PERSON lack of experience; **~ an Personal** PERSON staff-shortage, short-handedness; **~ an Sorgfalt** RECHT *Verträge* lack of care; ♦ **~ haben an** [+dat] GESCHÄFT be lacking in

Mängeleinrede f RECHT *Vertragsrecht* defence based on warranty for a defect (*BrE*), defense based on warranty for a defect (*AmE*)

Mangel: **Mangelfolgeschaden** m RECHT *Vertragsrecht* consequential harm caused by a defect

Mängelfreiheit f RECHT *Verkaufsrecht* faultlessness

Mängelgewähr: **ohne ~** phr GESCHÄFT, RECHT as is

mangelhaft adj RECHT *Vertragsrecht* defective; **~e Erfüllung** f RECHT *Verträge* defective performance; **~e Leistung** f GESCHÄFT defective service

mangeln vt: **~ an** [+dat] GESCHÄFT lack

mangelnd: **~e Geschäftsfähigkeit** f RECHT *Verträge* lack of capacity

Mängelrüge f RECHT *Vertragsrecht* notice of defect

mangels prep GESCHÄFT in the absence of; ♦ **~ Beweises des Gegenteils** RECHT in the absence of evidence to the contrary, for lack of evidence to the contrary; **~ genauer Informationen** GESCHÄFT in the absence of detailed information

Mangel: **Mangelwirtschaft** f VW shortage economy

Manifest nt IMP/EXP, TRANSP manifest

manifestieren vt IMP/EXP, TRANSP manifest

manifestiert: **nicht ~e Fracht** f TRANSP unmanifested cargo

Manipulation f GESCHÄFT, MGMNT manipulation; **~ des Wortlauts** POL word engineering

Manipulator m GESCHÄFT, IND manipulator

manipulieren vt BÖRSE *Kurs* rig, FINANZ *Zahlen* massage, GESCHÄFT manipulate

manipuliert: **~er Handel** m VW managed trade; **~e**

Kosten pl FINANZ managed costs; **~e Währung** f VW managed currency

Manko nt infrml GESCHÄFT shortage

Mann: **der ~** m **auf der Straße** GESCHÄFT the man in the street; **Mann-Maschinen System** nt VERWALT man-machine system

Mannschaft f MGMNT, PERSON, TRANSP crew, team; **Mannschaftsführer, in** m,f MGMNT, PERSON team leader; **Mannschaftsliste** f TRANSP crew manifest

Mann: **Mannstunde** f MGMNT man-hour

manuell 1. adj GESCHÄFT, PERSON manual; 2. adv GESCHÄFT manually

manuell: **~e Fertigkeit** f PERSON *eines Facharbeiters* manual skill; **~er Papiereinzug** m COMP *Drucker* manual feed; **~e Papierzuführung** f COMP *Drucker* manual feed; **~es System** nt TRANSP manual system (*MS*)

Manuskript nt GESCHÄFT *Zeitung* copy; **Manuskriptaufbereitung** f MEDIEN mark-up

Map f COMP computer map, map

Marge m RECHNUNG margin, VW spread; ♦ **~ ankündigen** BÖRSE post margin; **Margen halten** GESCHÄFT, VW hold margins

marginal 1. adj GESCHÄFT marginal; 2. adv GESCHÄFT marginally

marginal: **~er Beschäftigungszuschuß** m VW marginal employment subsidy; **~er Cashflow** m FINANZ incremental cash flow; **~e Importquote** f IMP/EXP marginal propensity to import (*MPM*); **~e Investitionsquote** f VW marginal propensity to invest; **~er Kapitalkoeffizient** m FINANZ incremental capital-output ratio (*ICOR*); **~e Kapitalkosten** pl VW incremental cost of capital; **~e Konsumquote** f VW marginal propensity to consume (*MPC*); **~e Kosten** pl VW marginal cost; **~e Preisfestsetzung** f RECHNUNG marginal pricing; **~e Signifikanz** f VW marginal significance; **~e Sparquote** f VW marginal propensity to save (*MPS*)

Marginalanalyse f FINANZ marginal analysis, GESCHÄFT incremental analysis, RECHNUNG marginal analysis, VW marginalism

marginalisieren vt VW marginalize

Marginalismus m VW marginalism

Marginalist m VW marginalist

Marginalprinzip nt: **~ der Allokation** VW marginal principle of allocation (*MPA*)

Marine- in cpds PERSON, TRANSP marine; **Marineküstenfunkstelle** f TRANSP coastal naval radio station

Marke f COMP flag, PATENT mark, V&M *eines Produktes* brand; ♦ **~ entwickeln** V&M brand

Marke: **Markenakzeptanz** f V&M brand acceptance; **Markenanteil** m V&M brand share; **Markenartikel** m pl GESCHÄFT, V&M branded goods, genuine article, proprietary goods; **Markenartikelwerbung** f V&M brand promotion; **Markenbestand** m V&M brand portfolio; **Markenbetreuer, in** m,f MGMNT brand manager, product manager, PERSON product manager; **Markenbetreuung** f MGMNT, V&M product management; **Markenbewußtsein** nt GESCHÄFT brand awareness, V&M brand awareness, brand recognition; **Markenbild** nt V&M *Werbestil* brand image; **Markendifferenzierung** f V&M brand differentiation;

Markenentwicklung *f* V&M brand development; **Markenerweiterung** *f* V&M brand extension

markenfrei: ~**es Product** *f pl* GESCHÄFT no-name product; ~**e Waren** *f pl* GESCHÄFT unbranded goods

Marke: **Markenführer** *m* GESCHÄFT top of the line, V&M brand leader; **Markengemeinschaft** *f* V&M brand association; **Markenidentifizierung** *f* V&M brand identification

markenlos *adj* PATENT generic; ~**e Produkte** *nt pl* V&M generic products

Marke: **Markenmarketing** *nt* V&M brand marketing; **Markenname** *m* GESCHÄFT proprietary brand, trade name, V&M brand name, name brand; **Markenpersönlichkeit** *f* V&M brand personality; **Markenpflege** *f* MGMNT, V&M brand management; **Markenportefeuille** *nt* BÖRSE, FINANZ brand portfolio; **Markenportfolio** *nt* BÖRSE, FINANZ brand portfolio; **Markenpositionierung** *f* V&M brand positioning; **Markenpräferenz** *f* V&M brand preference; **Markenprofil** *m* V&M brand properties; **Markenstrategie** *f* FINANZ, V&M *Produktstrategie* brand strategy; **Markentreue** *f* V&M brand loyalty; **Markenwaren** *f pl* GESCHÄFT proprietary goods; **Markenwerbung** *f* V&M brand advertising; **Markenwiedererkennung** *f* V&M brand recognition; **Markenzeichen** *nt* PATENT trademark

Marketing *nt* V&M marketing; ~ **in Marktlücken** V&M niche marketing; ~ **auf mehreren Ebenen** V&M multi-level marketing (*MLM*); ~ **von Unternehmen zu Unternehmen** V&M business-to-business marketing; **Marketingbudget** *nt* V&M marketing budget; **Marketing-Dienstleistungen** *f pl* V&M marketing services; **Marketing-Dienstleistungsmanager, in** *m,f* V&M marketing services manager; **Marketingdirektor, in** *m,f* MGMNT marketing director, marketing manager, PERSON marketing director; **Marketing-Kommunikation** *f* V&M marketing communications; **Marketing-Kommunikationskanal** *m* V&M marketing communications channel; **Marketing-Kommunikationsmanager, in** *m,f* V&M marketing communications manager; **Marketing-Kommunikationsmix** *m* V&M marketing communications mix; **Marketingkonzept** *nt* V&M marketing concept; **Marketingkostenabweichung** *f* V&M marketing cost variance; **Marketingmix** *nt* V&M marketing mix; **Marketingprofil** *nt* V&M marketing profile; **Marketingvereinigung** *f* **für Studentendarlehen** FINANZ student loan marketing association (*Sallie Mae, SLMA*) (*AmE*)

markieren *vt* GESCHÄFT brand

Markierung: **keine** ~ *f* TRANSP no mark (*n/m*); **ohne** ~ *f* TRANSP no mark (*n/m*)

Markov-Kettnmodell *nt* MATH Markov chain model

Markt *m* V&M market, marketplace, vw market; ~ **für britische Staatsanleihepapiere** BÖRSE UK gilts market; ~ **für CDs** BANK certificate of deposit market; **am** ~ **eingeführtes Einlagenzertifikat** BÖRSE seasoned CD; ~ **für Ersatzbeschaffung** GESCHÄFT replacement market; ~ **der Europäischen Gemeinschaft** VW European Community Market; ~ **mit Geld und Brief** BÖRSE two-sided market; ~ **für kurzfristige Wertpapiere** FINANZ discount market; ~ **für minderwertige Gebrauchtwagen** VW *Akerlofs Beispiel zur Illustrierung asymmetrischer Informationen* lemons market; ~ **für mittel- und langfristige Darlehen** FINANZ loan market;

~ **eines monopolistischen Anbietes** V&M captive market; ~ **für namenlose Produkte** V&M generic market; ~ **für Neuemissionen** BÖRSE primary market; ~ **für preiswerte Angebote** V&M low end of the market; ~ **für Qualitätsprodukte** V&M top end of the market; **einen** ~ **schaffen** BÖRSE provide the base for sth; ~ **mit starken Schwankungen** VW jumpy market; ~ **für Sterling Commercial Paper** BÖRSE Sterling Commercial Paper market (*SCP market*); ~ **für Sterling-Geldmarktpapier** BÖRSE Sterling Commercial Paper market (*SCP market*); ~ **für Termingeschäfte** BÖRSE forward market; ~ **für Terminkontrakte auf Börsenindizes** BÖRSE stock index futures market; ~ **umsatzschwacher Papiere** BÖRSE cabinet security (*AmE*); ~ **in US-Schatzpapieren** FINANZ US Treasury market; ~ **ohne Zutritts- und Austrittsschranken** VW contestable market; ◆ **auf dem** ~ GRUND on the market; **einen** ~ **beherrschen** FINANZ control a market; **auf den** ~ **bringen** BÖRSE *Emission* bring out, GESCHÄFT commercialize; **in einen** ~ **eindringen** GESCHÄFT break into a market, V&M, VW penetrate a market; **in jds** ~ **eindringen** GESCHÄFT make inroads into sb's market; **einen** ~ **erobern** V&M penetrate market; **einen** ~ **erproben** V&M prove a market, VW probe a market; **den** ~ **erschließen für** [+acc] BÖRSE tap the market for; **den** ~ **fest im Griff haben** V&M, VW have a stranglehold on the market; **auf dem** ~ **Fuß fassen** GESCHÄFT, V&M get a toehold in the market; **der** ~ **hat einen Tiefstand erreicht** VW the bottom has dropped out of the market; **für den höher entwickelten** ~ V&M *Produkt, Werbung* up-market; **auf den** ~ **kommen** VW enter the market, V&M come onto the market; **vom** ~ **nehmen** GESCHÄFT, V&M take off the market; **vom** ~ **verdrängen** VW shunt to the sideline; **den** ~ **dem Wettbewerb öffnen** V&M open the market up to competition; **einen** ~ **schaffen** BÖRSE provide a market, V&M create a market; **einen** ~ **suchen** BÖRSE seek a market; **am** ~ **vorbei produzieren** GESCHÄFT, V&M fail to fill the needs of the market; **auf einen** ~ **vorstoßen** GESCHÄFT break into a market

Markt: **Marktabschöpfung** *f* V&M market skimming; **Marktaggregation** *f* VW market aggregation; **Marktanalyse** *f* BÖRSE, V&M market analysis; **Marktanalyst** *m* BÖRSE, PERSON, V&M *Volkswirtschaft* market analyst; **Marktangebotspalette** *f* BÖRSE breadth of the market; **Marktanpassung** *f* VW market adjustment; **Marktanteil** *m* GESCHÄFT market share, V&M market share, share of market, slice of the market; **Marktanteile** *m pl* **gegen Gewinnmargen eintauschen** VW trade off market share against profit margins; **Marktaufnahmefähigkeit** *f* BÖRSE market receptiveness; **Marktaustrittsschranke** *f* VW barrier to exit, exit barrier; **Marktaustrittsschranken** *f pl* IMP/EXP barrier to exit; **Marktbasis** *f* V&M market base; **Marktbefrager, in** *m,f* V&M fieldworker

marktbeherrschend: ~**es Unternehmen** *nt* VW market-dominant firm

Markt: **Marktbeherrschung** *f* V&M market domination; **Marktbereich** *m* V&M market area; **Marktbericht** *m* V&M market report

marktbestimmt *adj* GESCHÄFT, V&M market-driven

Markt: **Marktbewegungsauftrag** *m* GESCHÄFT commercial movement order (*CVMO*); **Marktbewertung** *f* V&M market evaluation; **Marktbreite** *f* BÖRSE breadth of the market; **Marktclearing** *nt* VW market clearing;

Marktdiskriminierungskoeffizient *m* VW market discrimination coefficient; **Marktdurchdringung** *f* V&M market penetration, sales penetration; **Marktdynamik** *f* V&M market dynamics; **Markteinschätzung** *f* V&M market appraisal; **Markteinstieg** *m* V&M market entry; **Markteintrittsbarriere** *f* IMP/EXP entry barrier

marktempfindlich *adj* V&M market-sensitive

Markt: **Marktempfindlichkeit** *f* V&M market sensitivity; **Marktentwicklung** *f* V&M market development; **Markterkennung** *f* V&M market recognition; **Markterkundung** *f* V&M market exploration, market test, market testing; **Markterwartung** *f* V&M market anticipation; **Markterweiterung** *f* V&M market expansion

marktfähig *adj* V&M marketable, salable (*AmE*), saleable (*BrE*); **nicht ~** *adj* V&M unmarketable, unsalable (*AmE*), unsaleable (*BrE*); ◆ **~ machen** GESCHÄFT, V&M commercialize

Markt: **Marktfinanzierung** *f* VW raising finance from the public; **Marktform** *f* VW market form; **Marktforscher, in** *m,f* field investigator, market researcher; **Marktforschung** *f* V&M market research, marketing research; **Marktforschung** *f* **vor Ort** V&M field survey; **Marktführer** *m* BÖRSE market outperformer, GESCHÄFT market leader, V&M market leader, leader (*AmE*); **Marktführung** *f* V&M market leadership

marktgängig: **~e Ware** *f* V&M merchantable quality

Markt: **Marktgängigkeit** *f* PERSON fungibility

marktgerecht: **~e Verzinsung** *f* FINANZ fair return

Markt: **Marktgespür** *nt* GESCHÄFT, V&M feel of the market; **Marktgewicht** *m* V&M market weight; **Marktgleichgewicht** *nt* VW market equilibrium; **Marktineffizienz** *f* BÖRSE inefficiency in the market; **Marktinformationen** *f pl* V&M marketing intelligence; **Marktinformationsdienst** *m* **für Gläubiger** FINANZ Dun's Market Identifier (*AmE*); **Marktkapitalisierung** *f* BÖRSE market capitalization; **Marktklima** *nt* BÖRSE market tone; **Marktkonzentration** *f* VW market concentration; **Marktkräfte** *f pl* V&M, VW market forces; **Marktkurs** *m* V&M market rating; **Marktlage** *f* GESCHÄFT market situation

Marktlücke *f* V&M market gap, market niche, niche, niche market; ◆ **eine ~ füllen** GESCHÄFT, V&M fill a gap; **eine ~ schließen** GESCHÄFT fill a gap in the market

Marktlücke: **Marktlückenstudie** *f* V&M gap study, niche study

Markt: **Marktmacher** *m* BÖRSE market maker; **Marktmacht** *f* VW market power; **Marktmachtmißbrauch** *m* VW abuse of market power; **Marktmängel** *m pl* VW market failure; **Marktmechanismus** *m* VW market mechanism; **Marktmeinung** *f* BÖRSE market view; **Markt- und Meinungsforschung** *f* V&M statistical sampling; **Marktmiete** *f* VW market rent; **Marktnachfrage** *f* VW market demand; **Marktöffnung** *f* V&M market opening

marktorientiert *adj* V&M, VW market-oriented; **~e Preisfestsetzung** *f* FINANZ market pricing

Markt: **Marktpenetration** *f* V&M *Durchdringen eines Marktes* market penetration; **Marktplatz** *m* GESCHÄFT, V&M marketplace; **Marktposition** *f* BÖRSE market position; **Marktpotential** *nt* V&M market potential; **Marktpräsenz** *f* V&M market presence

Marktpreis *m* FINANZ going rate, GESCHÄFT price (*pr.*), RECHNUNG actual price, arm's-length price, V&M arm's-length price, market price, price (*pr.*), VERWALT going rate, VW actual price, market price, current price; ◆ **zu Marktpreisen** FINANZ at the market price, GESCHÄFT at the going rate

Marktpreis: **Marktpreismechanismus** *m* VW price mechanism

Markt: **Marktprofil** *nt* V&M market profile; **Marktprognose** *f* GESCHÄFT, V&M market forecast

marktreagibel *adj* BÖRSE market-sensitive, sensitive

Markt: **Marktreifgestaltung** *f* V&M *Produktplannung* product planning; **Marktrisikoprämie** *f* BÖRSE market risk premium; **Marktrückgang** *m* BÖRSE market slump; **Marktsättigung** *f* GESCHÄFT, V&M market saturation; **Marktschaffung** *f* V&M market creation, glut on the market; **Marktschwäche** *f* BÖRSE weak market; **Marktschwemme** *f* GESCHÄFT glut on the market

Marktsegment *nt* V&M market segment; **Marktsegmentgewinn** *m* RECHNUNG segment profit; **Marktsegmentierung** *f* V&M market segmentation; **Marktsegmentierung** *f* **nach Nutzwert** V&M benefit segmentation

Markt: **Marktsektor** *m* V&M market sector; **Marktsinn** *m* GESCHÄFT, V&M feel of the market; **Marktsozialismus** *m* VW market socialism; **Marktstärke** *f* GESCHÄFT, V&M market strength; **Marktsteuerung** *f* MGMNT market management; **Marktstruktur** *f* GESCHÄFT, V&M, VW market structure; **Marktstudie** *f* V&M market study; **Marktteilnehmer, in** *m,f* BÖRSE market participant, trading member; **Markttendenz** *f* V&M market trend; **Markttest** *m* V&M acceptance test, market test, market testing; **Markttransparenz** *f* GESCHÄFT, V&M market transparency; **Markttrend** *m* GESCHÄFT, V&M, VW market trend; **Marktüberblick** *m* FINANZ market review

marktüblich: **~e Rendite** *f* FINANZ, RECHNUNG fair return

Markt: **Marktumfang** *m* BÖRSE breadth of the market; **Marktumfeld** *nt* V&M market environment

Markt: **Marktunterstützung** *f* V&M market support; **Marktuntersuchung** *f* GESCHÄFT market study, V&M *Marktanalyse* market survey, survey research; **Marktverbindung** *f* V&M market connection; **Marktvergleich** *m* GRUND market comparison approach; **Marktverhalten** *nt* V&M market behavior (*AmE*), market behaviour (*BrE*); **Marktverlust** *m* GESCHÄFT, V&M loss of market; **Marktversagen** *nt* VW market failure; **Marktverzerrung** *f* VW market distortion; **Marktvorgang** *m* BÖRSE market operation

Marktwert *m* BÖRSE market value, FINANZ current value, market value, GESCHÄFT actual cash value, RECHNUNG cash value, market value, V&M market value, *Verkaufswert* marketable value, VW current value

marktwertgewichtet: **~er Index** *m* BÖRSE market-value-weighted index

Marktwert: **Marktwertklausel** *f* VERSICH market value clause

Markt: **Marktwiderstand** *m* V&M market resistance; **Marktwirtschaft** *f* VW market economy, market system

marktwirtschaftlich: **~e Ordnung** *f* VW market economy

Markt: **Marktzahlungsbilanz** *f* VW market balance of payments; **Marktzermürbung** *f* V&M market attrition; **Marktzersplitterung** *f* V&M, VW market fragmentation; **Marktziel** *nt* V&M market aim; **Marktzielsetzung** *f* V&M market objective; **Marktzins** *m* VW market rate of interest; **Marktzugangsbeschränkung** *f* IMP/EXP entry barrier; **Marktzulassung** *f* V&M *für pharmazeutische Produkte* marketing authorization; **Marktzutrittsoption** *f* IMP/EXP *für Exporteure auf fremden Märkten* market entry option; **Marktzutrittsschranke** *f* IMP/EXP, VW barrier to entry, entry barrier

Marschroute *f* MGMNT line, policy

Marshall-Lerner-Bedingung *f* VW Marshall-Lerner condition

Marshall-Plan *m* VW Marshall Plan

Martingal *nt* MATH martingale

Marx: ~**sche Ökonomie** *f* VW Marxian economics

Marxismus *m* POL Marxism

Maschine *f* GESCHÄFT, IND machine; ~ **für rationelle Energieanwendung** UMWELT energy-efficient machine; ♦ **mit der** ~ **schreiben** GESCHÄFT, VERWALT type, typewrite

maschinell 1. *adj* COMP machine-based, IND mechanized; **2.** *adv* COMP by machine, IND by machine, mechanically; ♦ ~ **bearbeiten** IND machine; ~ **hergestellt** IND *Produktion* machine-made

maschinell: ~**e Anlagen** *f pl* VW machinery; ~**e Beschickung** *f* IND *Produktion* machine loading; ~**e Buchhaltung** *f* RECHNUNG machine accounting; ~**e Datei** *f* COMP computerized file; ~**e Daten** *pl* V&M mechanical data

Maschine: **Maschinen** *f pl* IND, VW machinery (*mchy*); **Maschinenabzug** *m* V&M machine proof; **Maschinenadresse** *f* COMP machine address; **Maschinenanlage** *f* VW machinery; **Maschinenarbeiter, in** *m,f* IND operator; **Maschinenbau** *m* IND mechanical engineering; **Maschinenbauer, in** *m,f* TRANSP engine builder; **Maschinenbauingenieur, in** *m,f* TRANSP engine designer; **Maschinenbefehl** *m* COMP computer instruction; **Maschinenbruchversicherung** *f* VERSICH engineering assurances; **Maschinencode** *m* IND machine code; **Maschinendynamik** *f* VERWALT machine dynamics; **Maschinenfabrik** *f* IND engineering works

maschinengeschrieben *adj* GESCHÄFT, VERWALT typed, typewritten

maschinengestützt: ~**e Übersetzung** *f* COMP machine-aided translation (*MAT*), machine-assisted translation (*MAT*)

Maschine: **Maschinenlauf** *m* COMP, TRANSP machine run

maschinenlesbar *adj* COMP machine-readable; ~**er Code** *m* COMP machine-readable code

Maschine: **Maschinenpark** *m* VW machinery; **Maschinenprüfung** *f* TRANSP machinery survey (*MS*); **Maschinenraum** *m* COMP *eines Rechenzentrums* computer room, TRANSP engine room; **Maschinenschadenmitversicherungsklausel** *f* VERSICH machinery damage co-ins clause

maschinenschreiben *vi* GESCHÄFT, VERWALT type, typewrite

Maschine: **Maschinenschreiben** *nt* GESCHÄFT, VERWALT typewriting; **Maschinensicherheit** *f* IND machine safety; **Maschinensprache** *f* COMP computer language; **Maschinenstürmer** *m* PERSON Luddite; **Maschinenübersetzung** *f* (*MÜ*) COMP machine translation (*MT*); **Maschinenverleih** *m* IND plant hire; **Maschinenwerkstatt** *f* IND job shop; **Maschinenzeit** *f* COMP computer time, IND machine hours

Maske *f* COMP *Textverarbeitung* form

Maslow: **Maslowsche Bedürfnispyramide** *f* MGMNT *Motivationstheorie* Maslow's hierarchy of needs

Maß *nt* GESCHÄFT measure, MATH measurement, PATENT extent, V&M measure; ~ **des wirtschaftlichen Wohlstands** VW measure of economic welfare (*MEW*); ~ **der Zentraltendenz** MATH central tendency; ♦ **nach** ~ **gefertigt** GESCHÄFT tailor-made, IND made-to-measure

Maß: **Maßband** *nt* GESCHÄFT, VERWALT tape measure, measuring tape

Masse *f* GESCHÄFT bulk, IND substance, PERSON lump, the Lump (*BrE*), V&M mass, VW aggregate, bulk; ♦ **der** ~ **zugänglich machen** GESCHÄFT vulgarize

Maß: **Maße** *nt pl* **und Gewichte** GESCHÄFT weights and measures; **Maßeinheit** *f* GESCHÄFT unit of measure, MATH measurement, TRANSP measure; **Maßeinteilung** *f* GESCHÄFT, TRANSP calibration

Masse: **Massenabsatz** *m* V&M mass marketing; **Massenanreiz** *m* V&M mass appeal; **Massenansturm** *m* GESCHÄFT stampede; **Massenarbeitslosigkeit** *f* VW mass unemployment; **Massenartikel** *m* VW staple commodity; **Massenbeförderung** *f* TRANSP forwarding in bulk; **Massenbewegung** *f* GESCHÄFT stampede, POL mass movement; **Massendrucksachen** *f pl* GESCHÄFT bulk mail; **Massen-Ein/Ausgabe** *f* COMP *Daten* bulk input/output; **Massenentlassung** *f* PERSON mass redundancy, collective dismissal; **Massenerzeugnis** *nt* V&M staple product; **Massenfabrikation** *f* GESCHÄFT, IND, VW wholesale manufacture; **Massenfertigung** *f* IND mass production; **Massenfrachtgut** *nt* TRANSP bulk cargo; **Massengeschäft** *nt* GESCHÄFT bulk business

Massengut *nt* GESCHÄFT bulk commodity; ♦ **mit** ~ **beladen** TRANSP laden in bulk

Massengut: **Massengutcontainer** *m* TRANSP bulk freight container; **Massengutfrachter** *m* TRANSP bulk carrier, intermediate bulk container (*IBC*); **Massengutladung** *f* TRANSP bulk shipment; **Massengutumschlagplatz** *m* TRANSP bulk transhipment center (*AmE*), bulk transhipment centre (*BrE*); **Massengutumschlagzentrum** *nt* TRANSP bulk transhipment center (*AmE*), bulk transhipment centre (*BrE*); **Massengutversand** *m* TRANSP bulk shipment

Masse: **Massenkommunikation** *f* COMP *Datenübertragung* mass communication, MEDIEN mass mailing; **Massenluftpost** *f* KOMM bulk air mail (*BAM*); **Massenmarkt** *m* V&M mass market; **Massenmedien** *nt pl* MEDIEN mass media; **Massenproduktion** *f* IND mass production; **Massenrisiko** *nt* VERSICH mass risk; **Massenschnelltransit** *m* TRANSP mass rapid transit (*MRT*); **Massenspeicher** *m* COMP mass memory, mass storage device, GESCHÄFT, TRANSP bulk storage, mass storage; **Massentransitbahn** *f* TRANSP mass transit railway (*BrE*) (*MTR*), mass transit railroad (*AmE*) (*MTR*); **Massentransitsystem** *nt* TRANSP mass transit system (*AmE*); **Massentransport** *f* TRANSP forwarding in bulk; **Massen-und Intensivtierhaltung** *f* UMWELT factory farming; **Massenverladung** *f* IMP/EXP, TRANSP volume shipping; **Massenwerbung** *f* MEDIEN, V&M mass advertising; **Massenzucht** *f* UMWELT factory farming

maßgearbeitet *adj* IND made-to-measure

maßgebend: ~**e Warengattung** *f* PATENT leading line

maßgeblich *adj* GESCHÄFT prevailing, RECHT

authoritative; **~er Anteil** *m* FINANZ qualifying holding; **~e Einnahmen** *f pl* FINANZ relevant earnings; **~er Wertpapierbestand** *m* FINANZ qualifying holding

maßgeschneidert *adj* COMP *Anwendung* customized, GESCHÄFT tailor-made, tailored, IND made-to-measure, V&M tailored; **~er Dienstvertrag** *m* RECHT tailor-made service contract

Maßhalteappell *m* BANK moral suasion

mäßig: **~ verschuldetes Land** *nt* **mit mittlerem Einkommen** FINANZ moderately indebted middle-income country (*MIMIC*); **~ verschuldetes Land** *nt* **mit niedrigem Einkommen** FINANZ moderately indebted low-income country (*MILIC*)

maßlos *adj* GESCHÄFT *Forderung* excessive, inordinate

Maßnahme *f* BÖRSE move, GESCHÄFT, V&M measure; **~ der staatlichen Wirtschaftslenkung** VW regulation; ♦ **Maßnahmen ergreifen** GESCHÄFT take measures, take action, MGMNT take action, RECHT take measures; **Maßnahmen ergreifen gegen** GESCHÄFT counteract, take action against, take measures against; **Maßnahmen treffen gegen** GESCHÄFT provide against, take action against, take measures against

Maßnahme: **Maßnahmenpaket** *nt* FINANZ set of measures; **Maßnahmenpaket** *nt* **zum Umweltschutz** UMWELT, VW environmental action program (*AmE*), environmental action programme (*BrE*); **Maßnahmenplan** *m* GESCHÄFT, PERSON action plan; **Maßnahmenschlüssel** *m* COMP *Textverarbeitung* action code

maßregeln *vt* RECHT discipline

maßschneidern *vt* COMP *Anwendung* customize

Maßstab *m* GESCHÄFT scale, *Erfolg* yardstick; **~ für Entschädigung** VERSICH measure of indemnity; ♦ **einen ~ setzen** MGMNT *für Erfolg* set the standard

maßstäblich: **~ vergrößern** *phr* GESCHÄFT scale up; **~ verkleinern** *phr* GESCHÄFT scale down

Master- *in cpds* GESCHÄFT master; **Masterband** *nt* COMP master copy

Material *nt* GESCHÄFT material (*MAT*); **~ am Verkaufspunkt** V&M point-of-sale material, POS material; **Materialabrechnung** *f* RECHNUNG materials accounting; **Materialbilanz** *f* VW material balance; **Materialfestigkeit** *f* IND strength of materials; **Materialflußsystem** *nt* VW materials flow system

Material: **Materialtransferbescheinigung** *f* GESCHÄFT materials transfer note; **Materialtransport** *m* GESCHÄFT materials handling; **Materialwirtschaft** *f* TRANSP, VW materials management

Materie *f* GESCHÄFT subject area, IND substance

materiell 1. *adj* GESCHÄFT corporeal, material, physical, RECHNUNG tangible; **2.** *adv* GESCHÄFT corporeally, materially, physically

materiell: **~es Anlagevermögen** *nt* FINANZ tangible fixed assets; **~es Gut** *nt* VW material good; **~es Handelshemmnis** *nt* POL, VW material barrier; **~e Lebenslage** *f* POL, VW economic wellbeing; **~e Rechte** *nt pl* GESCHÄFT substantial rights; **~ rechtliches Gesetz** *nt* RECHT substantive law; **~es Vermögen** *nt* VW tangible assets; **~er Vermögenswert** *m* RECHNUNG tangible capital property; **~e Wirtschaftsgüter** *nt pl* VW physical assets

materiellrechtlich *adv* RECHT on its merits

mathematisch: **~er Erwartungswert** *m* VERSICH actuar-ial expectation; **~e Ökonomie** *f* VW mathematical economics; **~e Programmierung** *f* MATH mathematical programming; **~e Statistik** *f* MATH inferential statistics; **~es Stichprobenverfahren** *nt* MATH statistical sampling; **~e Wahrscheinlichkeit** *f* MATH, VW mathematical probability

Matrix *f* BÖRSE, COMP, GESCHÄFT, MATH, MGMNT matrix; **Matrixdrucker** *m* COMP dot-matrix printer, matrix printer; **Matrixhandel** *m* BÖRSE matrix trading; **Matrixmanagement** *nt* MATH, MGMNT matrix management, matrix organization; **Matrixorganisation** *f* MATH, MGMNT matrix management, matrix organization; **Matrixstruktur** *f* GESCHÄFT, MGMNT grid structure

Matrize *f* GESCHÄFT copy platform, RECHT boilerplate (*jarg*), VERWALT *Schablone* stencil; **Matrizenanalyse** *f* VW matrix analysis

matt: **~ setzen** *vt* GESCHÄFT *Gegner* stymie

Matura *f* Öst, Sch GESCHÄFT, SOZIAL ≈ Advanced level (*BrE*) (*A level*), ≈ High School Diploma (*AmE*)

Maturitätsprüfung *f* Sch GESCHÄFT, SOZIAL ≈ Advanced level (*BrE*) (*A level*), ≈ High School Diploma (*AmE*)

Maus *f* COMP mouse

Mäuse *f pl infrml* GESCHÄFT bread (*infrml*), dosh (*infrml*) (*BrE*), dough (*infrml*), money, wampum (*infrml*) (*AmE*)

Mäuseklavier *nt jarg* COMP DIP switch

mausgesteuert *adj* COMP mouse-driven

Maus: **Maustaste** *f* COMP mouse key; **Maustreiber** *m* COMP mouse driver; **Mausunterlage** *f* COMP mouse mat

Maut *f* TRANSP toll; **Mautbrücke** *f* TRANSP tollbridge

mautfrei *adj* TRANSP toll-free

Maut: **Mautstation** *f* TRANSP tollbooth; **Mautstraße** *f* TRANSP toll road (*BrE*), turnpike (*AmE*)

max. *abbr* (*maximal, maximum*) GESCHÄFT, MATH max. (*maximal, maximum*)

Maximal- *pref* GESCHÄFT, MATH maximal (*max.*), maximum (*max.*)

maximal *adj* (*max.*) GESCHÄFT, MATH maximal (*max.*), maximum (*max.*); **~e Aufmerksamkeit** *f* V&M maximum awareness; **~es Bewußtsein** *nt* V&M maximum awareness; **~e Deckung** *f* BÖRSE maximum coverage; **~er Ertrag** *m* BÖRSE maximum return; **~e Nutzungsdauer** *f* VW machine maximum time; **~e Preisfluktuation** *f* BÖRSE maximum price fluctuation; **~er Tiefgang** *m* TRANSP maximum draft (*AmE*), maximum draught (*BrE*); **~ zulässige Kursfluktuation** *f* BÖRSE daily trading limit

Maximal-: **Maximalbelastung** *f* TRANSP maximum load; **Maximaleffizienz** *f* VW maximum efficiency; **Maximalertrag** *m* VW maximum output; **Maximalzinssatz** *m* FINANZ cap

maximieren *vt* FINANZ, GESCHÄFT, RECHNUNG maximize

Maximierung *f* FINANZ, GESCHÄFT, RECHNUNG maximization; **~ der Nutzenfunktion des Managements** MGMNT managerial utility function maximization

Maximin-Regel *f* VW maximin

maximum *adj* (*max.*) GESCHÄFT, MATH maximal (*max.*), maximum (*max.*)

Maximum *nt* GESCHÄFT, MATH maximum

Maximum-Likelihood-Schätzfunktion *f* MATH maximum likelihood estimator (*MLE*)

MB *abbr* (*Megabyte*) COMP *Speicherplatz* Mb (*megabyte*)

MBI *abbr* (*Management-Buy-In*) FINANZ, MGMNT MBI (*management buy-in*)

MBO *abbr* (*Management-Buy-Out*) FINANZ, MGMNT MBO (*management buyout*)

MByte *abbr* (*Megabyte*) COMP *Speicherplatz* Mb (*megabyte*)

m³ *abbr* (*Kubikmeter*) GESCHÄFT m³ (*cubic meter AmE, cubic metre BrE*), cbm (*cubic meter AmE, cubic metre BrE*)

M3 *abbr* (*Geldvolumen 3*) VW M3 (*money 3*)

Mechanik *f* GESCHÄFT, IND mechanism

mechanisch *adj* IND mechanized; ♦ **auf ~en Betrieb umstellen** GESCHÄFT, IND, TRANSP mechanize

mechanisch: **~e Abfertigungsausrüstung** *f* TRANSP mechanical handling equipment (*MHE*); **~es Buchbinden** *nt* V&M mechanical bookbinding; **~er Farbton** *m* V&M mechanical tint; **~e Förderausrüstung** *f* TRANSP mechanical handling equipment (*MHE*); **~er Teil** *m* IND mechanism; **~es Verkaufsgespräch** *nt* V&M mechanical sales talk; **~e Werkstatt** *f* IND job shop

mechanisieren *vt* GESCHÄFT, IND, TRANSP mechanize

mechanisiert *adj* GESCHÄFT, IND, TRANSP mechanized

Mechanisierung *f* GESCHÄFT, IND, TRANSP *Frachtbeförderung* mechanization

Mechanismus *m* GESCHÄFT, IND mechanism; **~ zur Durchführung von** PATENT apparatus for carrying out

Media- *in cpds* GESCHÄFT, MEDIEN, V&M media

Median *m* MATH median

Media-: **Mediaoption** *f* V&M media option; **Mediaplan** *m* V&M media plan; **Mediaplaner, in** *m,f* V&M media planner; **Mediaplanung** *f* MEDIEN, V&M account planning, media planning

Medien *nt pl* GESCHÄFT, MEDIEN, V&M media; ♦ **in den ~ Bericht erstatten** MEDIEN give media coverage

Medien: **Medienanalyse** *f* V&M media analysis; **Medienauswahl** *f* MEDIEN, V&M media selection; **Medienberater, in** *m,f* V&M media analyst; **Medienbesitzer** *m pl* V&M media owners; **Medienbudget** *nt* MEDIEN media budget; **Medienereignis** *nt* MEDIEN media event; **Medienforschung** *f* V&M media research; **Medienkommission** *f* V&M media commission; **Medienmakler, in** *m,f* V&M media broker; **Medienmischung** *f* V&M media mix; **Medienmix** *f* V&M media mix; **Medienprogramm** *nt* MEDIEN media schedule; **Medienstrategie** *f* V&M media strategy

medienunabhängig *adj* V&M media-independent

Medien: **Medienwerbung** *f* V&M media buying

Medium *nt* GESCHÄFT *Kommunikation*, MEDIEN, V&M medium

medizinisch *adj* GESCHÄFT, SOZIAL medical; **~e Gründe** *m pl* PERSON, SOZIAL medical grounds; **~e Hilfe** *f* GESCHÄFT, SOZIAL medical assistance; **~e Kosten** *pl* GESCHÄFT, SOZIAL medical costs; **~e Technik** *f* IND medical engineering

Meer *nt* TRANSP sea; **Meeresstraße** *f* TRANSP strait

Mega- *pref* COMP, GESCHÄFT, IND mega-; **Megabit** *nt* COMP *Chips* megabit; **Megabyte** *nt* (*MByte*) COMP *Speicherplatz* megabyte (*Mb*); **Megaelektronenvolt** *nt* (*MeV*) GESCHÄFT, IND mega electron volt (*MeV*); **Megaunternehmen** *nt* GESCHÄFT megacorp; **Megawatt** *nt* (*MW*) GESCHÄFT, IND megawatt (*MW*)

Mehr- *in cpds* GESCHÄFT multi-, additional

mehr: **~ als** *phr* GESCHÄFT in excess of sth

Mehrbenutzer- *in cpds* COMP multi-user;

Mehrbenutzerdokument *nt* COMP multi-user document; **Mehrbenutzersystem** *nt* COMP multi-user system

Mehr-: **Mehrbereichsöl** *nt* IND multipurpose oil; **Mehrbetrag** *m* FINANZ, GESCHÄFT, VERSICH, VW surplus, excess (*BrE*)

mehrdeutig *adj* GESCHÄFT ambiguous; **~e Funktion** *f* VW many-valued function

mehrdimensional: **~e Analyse** *f* MATH multivariate analysis; **~e Gradeinteilung** *f* V&M multi-dimensional scaling

Meherlösverwendung *f* FINANZ excess revenue allotment

Mehrfach- *in cpds* GESCHÄFT multiple

mehrfach: **~ segmentierte Verfahren** *nt pl* V&M multi-segmented operation

Mehrfach-: **Mehrfachanbietersystem** *nt* COMP multiple supplier system; **Mehrfachauswahlfrage** *f* V&M multiple choice question; **Mehrfachbestimmtheitsmaß** *nt* MATH coefficient of multiple determination; **Mehrfach-Crew-Levels** *m pl* TRANSP multi-crew levels; **Mehrfachertrag** *m* FINANZ compound yield; **Mehrfachkäufer** *m* V&M multiple buyer; **Mehrfachkorrelation** *f* MATH multiple correlation; **Mehrfachkorrelationskoeffizient** *m* MATH coefficient of multiple correlation; **Mehrfachleserschaft** *f* V&M multiple readership; **Mehrfach-Quote** *f* TRANSP multi-quote; **Mehrfachregression** *f* MATH multiple regression; **Mehrfachregressionsanalyse** *f* FINANZ, MATH, VW multiple regression analysis (*MRA*); **Mehrfachsteuereinheit** *f* COMP cluster controller; **Mehrfachstopp** *m* TRANSP multi-stop; **Mehrfachvertrag** *m* mit einer **Finanzschätzungskreditlinie** FINANZ multiple-contract finance-projected line of credit; **Mehrfachzugriff** *m* COMP, GESCHÄFT multiaccess

Mehr-: **Mehrfamilienhaus** *nt* SOZIAL multi-family dwelling; **Mehrgepäck** *nt* FREI, TRANSP baggage excess, excess baggage

mehrgeschossig *adj* GRUND multistorey (*BrE*), multistory (*AmE*)

Mehrgewichtsgebühr *f* FREI, TRANSP excess baggage charge

mehrgipflig: **~e Häufigkeitskurve** *f* MATH multimodal frequency curve; **~e Verteilung** *f* MATH multimodal distribution

Mehrgleichungsmodell *nt* VW large-scale model

mehrgleisig: **~e Unternehmensführung** *f* MGMNT multiple management

Mehrheit *f* BÖRSE, GESCHÄFT, PERSON, POL, RECHT majority; **Mehrheitsaktienbestand** *m* BÖRSE majority shareholding; **Mehrheitsanteil** *m* GESCHÄFT majority stake; **Mehrheitsbeteiligung** *f* BÖRSE controlling interest, majority shareholding, majority interest, GESCHÄFT majority interest, PERSON controlling interest; **Mehrheitsregierung** *f* POL majority rule; **Mehrheitsvotum** *nt* der Geschworenen RECHT majority verdict; **Mehrheitswahl** *f* GESCHÄFT majority vote

Mehr-: **Mehrjahresausgabenplanung** *f* FINANZ multi-year spending envelope; **Mehrjahresressourcenplanung** *f* FINANZ multi-year resource envelope

mehrjährig *adj* FINANZ, GESCHÄFT multi-year; **~e Umschuldungsvereinbarung** *f* FINANZ multi-year rescheduling agreement (*MYRA*), multi-year restructuring agreement (*MYRA*)

Mehr-: **Mehrkosten** *pl* VW cost overrun;

Mehrkostenversicherung *f* VERSICH additional expense insurance; **Mehrliniensystem** *nt* MGMNT functional management

mehrmalig: ~**er Erwerb** *m* **der gleichen Aktie bei steigendem Kurs** BÖRSE pyramiding

Mehr-: **Mehrmarkenstrategie** *f* V&M multibrand strategy; **Mehrphasensteuer** *f* STEUER multistage tax; **Mehrprogrammbetrieb** *m* COMP multiprogramming; **Mehrprogramming** *nt* COMP multiprogramming; **Mehrprozessorsystem** *nt* COMP multiprocessor

mehrschichtig: ~**es Marketing** *nt* V&M multilevel marketing (*MLM*)

Mehr-: **Mehrspartenversicherung** *f* VERSICH composite insurance; **Mehrstückpackung** *f* GESCHÄFT, V&M banded pack; **Mehrstückpreis** *m* V&M multiple unit pricing

mehrstufig: ~**e Betriebsführung** *f* MGMNT multiple management; ~**es Stichprobensystem** *nt* MATH multistage sampling

Mehrthemenbefragung *f* V&M omnibus survey

Mehrwährungs- *in cpds* BANK multicurrency; **Mehrwährungsanleihe** *f* BANK multicurrency loan; **Mehrwährungsdarlehen** *nt* BANK multicurrency loan

Mehrwegbehälter *m* UMWELT *Flaschen* returnable container

Mehrwegflasche *f* UMWELT, V&M returnable bottle

Mehrwegpackungen *f pl* V&M reusable packs

Mehrwert *m* FINANZ added value, surplus value, GESCHÄFT increased value (*iv*), STEUER added value, V&M added value; **Mehrwertaufstellung** *f* RECHNUNG value-added statements; **Mehrwertbericht** *m* RECHNUNG value-added statements; **Mehrwertdienst** *m* GESCHÄFT, KOMM, VERWALT, V&M, VW added value service; **Mehrwertdienste** *m pl* VW value-added services; **Mehrwertdienstleister** *m* COMP value-added reseller (*VAR*); **Mehrwerterklärung** *f* RECHNUNG value-added statements; **Mehrwertnetz** *nt* COMP value-added network (*VAN*); **Mehrwertrate** *f* BANK rate of surplus value

Mehrwertsteuer *f* (*MwSt.*) GESCHÄFT, STEUER value-added tax (*BrE*) (*VAT*); **von der ~ befreite Betriebsstoffe** *m pl* STEUER zero-rated supplies; **von der ~ befreite Ware** *f* STEUER zero-rated goods; ◆ **von der ~ befreit** STEUER zero-rated, exempt from VAT (*BrE*)

Mehrwertsteuer: **Mehrwertsteuerbefreiung** *f* STEUER exemption from VAT (*BrE*), zero rating, zero rate, zero-rate taxation

mehrwertsteuerfrei *adj* STEUER zero-rated, exempt from VAT (*BrE*)

Mehrwertsteuer: **Mehrwertsteuervoranmeldung** *f* STEUER preliminary VAT return (*BrE*)

Mehrwert: **Mehrwerttheorie** *f* VW surplus approach

Mehr-: **Mehrzuteilungsoption** *f* BÖRSE greenshoe

Mehrzweck- *in cpds* GESCHÄFT multipurpose (*MP*), general-purpose; **Mehrzweckschiff** *nt* TRANSP multipurpose vessel

Meilen *f pl*: ~ **je Gallone** GESCHÄFT miles per gallon (*mpg*); ~ **pro Stunde** GESCHÄFT miles per hour (*mph*); **Meilenstein** *m* GESCHÄFT landmark; **Meilenstein-Diagramm** *nt* MATH milestone chart

Meineid *m* RECHT perjury

meinerseits *adv* GESCHÄFT for my part

M1 *abbr* (*Geldvolumen M1*) VW M1 (*money 1*)

Meinung *f* GESCHÄFT view, opinion, thinking, point of view; ~ **der Geschäftsführung** MGMNT administrative point of view (*APV*); ◆ **anderer ~ sein** GESCHÄFT be of a different opinion, take a different view; **eine ~ äußern** POL deliver an opinion; **seine ~ äußern** GESCHÄFT air one's opinions; **bei seiner ~ bleiben** GESCHÄFT sit tight; **eine andere ~ vertreten** GESCHÄFT be of a different opinion, take a different view

Meinung: **Meinungsaustausch** *m* GESCHÄFT communication, exchange of ideas; **Meinungsbildner** *m* V&M opinion leader; **Meinungsführer** *f* V&M opinion leader; **Meinungsumfrage** *f* RECHNUNG opinion shopping, V&M opinion survey, opinion poll, Gallup poll; **Meinungsumfrage** *f* **nach Beliebtheit bestimmter Personen** GESCHÄFT, MEDIEN popularity poll; **Meinungsverschiedenheit** *f* GESCHÄFT disagreement; **Meinungsverzichtserklärung** *f* RECHNUNG disclaimer of opinion

Meist- *in cpds* GESCHÄFT most; **Meistbegünstigungsklausel** *f* RECHT, VW most favored nation clause (*AmE*), most favoured nation clause (*BrE*); **Meistbietende(r)** *mf* [decl. as adj] BÖRSE, GESCHÄFT best bidder, highest bidder

Meister *m* GESCHÄFT *am Bau*, *Polier* foreman, ganger (*BrE*), PERSON foreman, VW master tradesman

melden 1. *vt* GESCHÄFT report; **2. sich ~** *v refl* GESCHÄFT volunteer; ◆ **sich bei jdm ~** GESCHÄFT report to sb; **es meldet sich niemand** KOMM *Telefon* there's no answer

Melder *m* GESCHÄFT, KOMM messenger

Meldeschwelle *f* STEUER registration threshold

Meldung *f* COMP message, KOMM message feedback, *eine Nachricht übermitteln* message

melken *vt* infrml GESCHÄFT milk (*infrml*)

Memo *nt* (*Memorandum*) GESCHÄFT, POL aide-mémoire, RECHT, VERWALT memo (*memorandum*)

Memorandum *nt* (*Memo*) GESCHÄFT, POL aide-mémoire, RECHT, VERWALT memorandum (*memo*)

Menge *f* GESCHÄFT abundance, bulk, quantity (*qnty*, *qty*), quantum, amount (*amt*), VW aggregate; ~ **zur Erreichung der Gewinnschwelle** VERWALT, VW breakeven quantity; ~ **zur Erreichung des Kostendeckungspunktes** VERWALT, VW breakeven quantity; ◆ **in Mengen von** GESCHÄFT in sets of

Menge: **Mengenanalyse** *f* MGMNT quantitative analysis; **Mengenanpassung** *f* VW price taking; **Mengenbeschränkung** *f* VW quantitative restrictions (*QR*); **Mengenbeschränkungen** *f pl* BANK quantitative controls; **Mengeneffekt** *m* VW quantity effect; **Mengeneinkauf** *m* GESCHÄFT bulk buying; **Mengeneinkäufer, in** *m,f* GESCHÄFT, VW bulk purchaser; **Mengenfertigung** *f* IND mass production; **Mengengeschäft** *nt* GESCHÄFT bulk business; **Mengenindex** *m* GESCHÄFT volume index; **Mengenleistung** *f* IND throughput rate, thruput rate (*AmE*)

mengenmäßig *adj* GESCHÄFT quantitative

Menge: **Mengenpreis** *m* GESCHÄFT, VW bulk price; **Mengenrabatt** *m* GESCHÄFT bulk discount, volume discount, quantity discount, RECHNUNG quantity discount, TRANSP volume rebate, V&M quantity discount; **Mengensteuer** *f* IMP/EXP, STEUER specific tax; **Mengenversand** *m* IMP/EXP TRANSP volume shipping

Menschenrechte *nt pl* RECHT human rights

menschlich: ~**er Verbrauch** *m* UMWELT *von Wasser* human consumption

Menü *nt* COMP, FREI, GESCHÄFT menu

menügesteuert *adj* COMP menu-driven

Menü: **Menükosten** *pl* **der Inflation** VW menu costs of inflation; **Menüleiste** *f* COMP menu bar

mep *abbr* (*mittlerer Arbeitsdruck*) IND mep (*mean effective pressure*)

MEP *abbr* IND (*mittlerer Arbeitsdruck*) mep (*mean effective pressure*), POL (*Mitglied des Europaparlaments*) Euro MP (*European Member of Parliament*), MEP (*Member of the European Parliament*)

Merchantbank *f* BANK merchant bank (*BrE*)

mergen *vt jarg* COMP merge

Meridian *m* GESCHÄFT meridian

meritorisch: ~**e Bedürfnisse** *nt pl* VW merit wants; ~**es Gut** *nt* VW merit good; ~**es Ungut** *nt* VW merit bad

merkantil *adj* GESCHÄFT, VW mercantile

Merkantilismus *m* GESCHÄFT, VW mercantilism

Merkblatt *nt* GESCHÄFT code of practice, instruction leaflet

Merkmal *nt* COMP feature, GESCHÄFT attribute, PATENT feature; **Merkmalsklasse** *f* GESCHÄFT category

mesokurtisch: ~**e Verteilungskurve** *f* MATH mesokurtic

Mesoökonomik *f* VW mesoeconomy

Meß- *in cpds* GESCHÄFT measuring, measurement

Messe *f* GESCHÄFT exhibition, fair, trade fair

messen *vt* GESCHÄFT, MATH, VW measure; ♦ **jds Leistung** ~ PERSON measure sb's performance

Messen *nt* GESCHÄFT, MATH, PERSON, VW measurement

Messe: **Messespedition** *f* IMP/EXP exhibition forwarding

Meß-: **Meßgerät** *nt* COMP test equipment, GESCHÄFT gauge, TRANSP measure; **Meßinstrument** *nt* TRANSP measure

Messung *f* GESCHÄFT, MATH, VW measure, measurement, measuring; ~ **der ökonomischen Wohlfahrt** VW measure of economic welfare (*MEW*)

Meß-: **Meßwert** *m* MATH measurement

Metall *nt* BÖRSE, GESCHÄFT, IND, PERSON, UMWELT, VW metal; **Metallarbeiter** *m* PERSON metalworker; **Metalldose** *f* TRANSP, UMWELT metal can; **Metallerz** *nt* UMWELT metalliferous ore; **Metallgeld** *nt* GESCHÄFT coins, VW hard cash; **Metallhandel** *m* VW metal trading; **Metallhütte** *f* IND smelting works; **Metallindustrie** *f* IND metal industry

metallisch: ~**er Rohstoff** *m* BÖRSE hard commodity

Metall: **Metallmarkt** *m* BÖRSE metal market

Metallurg, in *m,f* PERSON metallurgist

Metall: **Metallverpackung** *f* IND, UMWELT metal packaging

Meta-Marketing *nt* V&M metamarketing

metazentrisch: ~**e Höhe** *f* GESCHÄFT metacentric height

Meter *m* (*m*) GESCHÄFT meter (*AmE*) (*m*), metre (*BrE*) (*m*); ~ **pro Sekunde** GESCHÄFT meters per second (*AmE*) (*m/s*), metres per second (*BrE*) (*m/s*)

Methetik *f* MATH methetics

Methode *f* GESCHÄFT approach, method, system, MGMNT approach, method, policy, VERWALT approach, V&M method, VW approach; ~ **der doppelten Buchführung** RECHNUNG double-entry method; ~ **des gleichgewichtigen Wachstums** GESCHÄFT steady growth method; ~ **der gleitenden Mittelwerte** MATH moving average

method; ~ **der kleinsten Quadrate** MATH least squares method, generalized least squares (*GLS*), VW *Regressionsmodelle* generalized least squares (*GLS*); ~ **des kritischen Pfades** MATH critical path analysis (*CPA*); ~ **der relevanten Kosten** MGMNT relevant cost approach; ~ **des stetigen Wachstums** GESCHÄFT steady growth method; ~ **des Technologietransfers** VW transfer of technology method; ~ **des verketteten Index** VW chain index method; ~ **der Wettbewerbsparität** V&M competitive parity method; ~ **der Zufallsauswahl** V&M random observation method; **Methodenlehre** *f* MGMNT methodology; **Methodentechnik** *f* GESCHÄFT methods engineering; **Methodenuntersuchung** *f* GESCHÄFT methods study; **Methoden und Verfahrensregeln** *f pl* GESCHÄFT systems and procedures; **Methodenvielfalt** *f* MGMNT policy mix

Methodik *f* MGMNT methodology

Methods-Times-Measurement *nt* (*MTM*) MGMNT methods-time measurement (*MTM*)

metrisch: ~**e Messung** *f* GESCHÄFT metrication; ~**es System** *nt* GESCHÄFT metric system; ~**e Tonne** *f* GESCHÄFT metric ton (*mton*)

MEZ *abbr* (*mitteleuropäische Zeit*) GESCHÄFT CET (*Central European Time*)

Mezzanin: **Mezzanin-Ebene** *f* FINANZ mezzanine level; **Mezzanin-Finanzierung** *f* FINANZ mezzanine funding

M-Form *f* VW M-form

mg *abbr* (*Milligramm*) GESCHÄFT mg (*milligram, milligramme*)

MHV *abbr* (*multilaterale Handelsgespräche*) VW MTN (*multilateral trade negotiations*)

Microsoft®: ~**-Plattenbetriebssystem** *nt* (*MS-DOS*) COMP Microsoft® disk operating system (*MS-DOS*)

Midwest: ~ **Börse** *f* BÖRSE Midwest Stock Exchange (*AmE*)

Miet- *in cpds* GESCHÄFT rent, rental; **Mietanlagen** *f pl* VW rental equipment; **Mietbeihilfe** *f* SOZIAL rent allowance, rent rebate; **Mietberechtigung** *f* GRUND *gemeinsames Mietobjekt* cotenancy; **Mietdauer** *f* GRUND rental term

Miete *f* GRUND *Pacht* lease, rent, rental, IMP/EXP *Flugzeug, Schiff* charter, rental (*AmE*), auto hire (*BrE*), SOZIAL rent charge, rent, rental, TRANSP auto hire (*BrE*), charter, rental (*AmE*), VW rent; ~ **auf neunundneunzig Jahre** BANK, GRUND ninety-nine-year lease; ~ **pro Kalendermonat** GRUND rent per calendar month (*rent pcm*)

Miet-: **Mieteigentum** *nt* **in Bruchteilen** GRUND, RECHT tenancy in common; **Mieteinnahme** *f* GRUND *Pachteinnahme* rent receipt, rental; **Mieteinzieher, in** *m,f* GRUND rent collector

mieten *vt* GESCHÄFT *Gerät* hire (*BrE*), rent, lease, GRUND lease, rent, IMP/EXP *Fahrzeug*, TRANSP *Flugzeug, Schiff* charter

Mieten *nt* GESCHÄFT hire

Mieter, in *m,f* GESCHÄFT, GRUND tenant, IMP/EXP, TRANSP *Schiff, Flugzeug* charterer; ~ **eines Ankerplatzes** GRUND anchor tenant; **Mieterrecht** *nt* RECHT tenant right (*BrE*); **Mieterreparaturen** *f pl* SOZIAL tenant's repairs; **Mieterschutz besitzen** *phr* GRUND, PERSON have security of tenure

Miet-: **Mietfinanzierung** *f* BANK lease financing

mietfrei *adj* GRUND, PERSON, SOZIAL rent-free; ~**e Zeit** *f* GRUND rent-free period

Miet-: Mietkauf m RECHT hire purchase (*BrE*) (*HP*); **auf Mietkaufbasis kaufen** *phr* FINANZ buy on hire purchase (*BrE*), buy on the installment plan (*AmE*); **Mietkaufvertrag** m RECHT hire-purchase agreement; **Mietkündigung** f GRUND termination of lease; **Mietleitung** f COMP leased line; **Mietnachlaß** m SOZIAL rent rebate; **Mietpreis** m GRUND rental rate; **Mietpreisstopp** m GRUND rent freeze; **Mietquittung** f GRUND rent receipt; **Mietrecht einräumen** *phr* GRUND grant a tenancy

mietrechtlich: ~ **gebundene Werkswohnung** f SOZIAL, VW tied cottage

Miet-: Mietsachschaden m VERSICH damage to rented property; **Mietsaufkommen-Umsatz-Verhältnis** nt RECHNUNG rental-turnover ratio; **Mietschutz** m GRUND security of tenure; **Mietstufe** f GRUND rental level; **Mietverhältnis** nt GRUND, RECHT tenancy

Mietvertrag m BANK lease, lease agreement, GESCHÄFT rental agreement, RECHT lease, lease agreement; ~ **über gewerblich genutzte Räume** GESCHÄFT commercial lease; ~ **mit gleichbleibendem Zinssatz** FINANZ straight lease; ~ **mit konstantem Zins** FINANZ straight lease; ~ **mit stufenweiser Mieterhöhung** FINANZ step-up lease

Miet-: Mietvorauszahlung f GRUND key money; **Mietwagen** m FREI hire car (*BrE*), hired car (*BrE*), rental car (*AmE*), rented car (*AmE*); **Mietwagenfirma** f FREI, TRANSP car-hire operator (*BrE*), car-rental operator (*AmE*); **Mietzuschuß** m PERSON housing allowance, accomodation allowance, SOZIAL housing allowance, rent allowance, rent rebate

migrationsbedingt: ~**e Arbeitslosigkeit** f VW migration-fed unemployment

Mikro- *pref* GESCHÄFT micro-; **Mikrochip** m COMP microchip, microprocessor; **Mikrodiskette** f COMP microdisk; **Mikroelektronik** f IND *Produktion* micro-electronics

mikroelektronisch *adj* IND *Produktion* microelectronic

Mikro-: Mikrofiche m VERWALT microfiche; **Mikrofilm** m VERWALT microfilm; **Mikrofilmlesegerät** nt VERWALT microfilm reader

Mikrofon nt KOMM microphone

Mikro-: Mikromarketing nt V&M micromarketing; **Mikroökonomie** f VW microeconomics; **Mikroökonomik** f VW microeconomics

mikroökonomisch *adj* VW microeconomic

Mikro-: Mikroproduktionsfunktion f VW microproduction function; **Mikroprogramm** nt COMP microprogram; **Mikroprozessor** m COMP microchip, microprocessor; **Mikrorechner** m COMP microcomputer; **Mikrosekunde** f GESCHÄFT microsecond

milcherzeugend: ~**er Betrieb** m VW dairy farm

mildern vt GESCHÄFT soft-pedal (*infrml*), *Probleme* alleviate

mildernd: ~**e Umstände** m pl RECHT extenuating circumstances, *die sich z.B. reduzierend auf das Strafmaß auswirken* mitigating circumstances

militärisch: ~**-industrieller Komplex** m POL military-industrial complex; ~**er Keynesianismus** m POL, VW military Keynesianism

Mill. *abbr* (*Million*) STEUER million

Milli- *pref* GESCHÄFT, MATH milli-; **Milligramm** nt (*mg*) GESCHÄFT milligram (*mg*), milligramme (*mg*); **Milliliter** m (*ml*) GESCHÄFT milliliter (*AmE*) (*ml*), millilitre (*BrE*)

(*ml*); **Millimeter** m (*mm*) GESCHÄFT millimeter (*AmE*) (*mm*), millimetre (*BrE*) (*mm*); **Millimeterpapier** nt VERWALT graph paper, plotting paper; **Millimeter pro Sekunde** *phr* (*mm/s*) GESCHÄFT millimeters per second (*AmE*) (*mm/s*), millimetres per second (*BrE*) (*mm/s*)

Million f (*Mill.*, *Mio.*) BANK, GESCHÄFT, MATH million; **Millionen-Pfund-Geschäft** nt FINANZ multimillion pound deal

Millionär m GESCHÄFT millionaire

Millionärin f GESCHÄFT millionairess

Milli-: Millisekunde f GESCHÄFT millisecond

Min. *abbr* (*Minimum*) GESCHÄFT, MATH min. (*minimum*)

Minderbetrag m STEUER deficiency

mindergeliefert *adj* TRANSP short-shipped

Minderheit f BÖRSE, GESCHÄFT, RECHNUNG minority; **Minderheitsanteil** m GESCHÄFT minority interest; **Minderheitsbeteiligung** f BÖRSE minority interest, minority investment, minority shareholding, minority stake, GESCHÄFT minority holding, RECHNUNG minority interest, minority participation; **Minderheitsbeteiligung** f **am Gewinn** RECHNUNG minority interests in profit

Minderjährige(r) mf [decl. as adj] RECHT juvenile, minor

Minderlieferung f TRANSP short shipment, VERSICH short delivery (*SD*)

mindern vt GESCHÄFT lessen, RECHT reduce, *Kaufpreis* abate, reduce

Minderung f RECHT *des Kaufpreises* abatement, reduction; ~ **des Kaufpreises wegen Mängeln** RECHT *Vertragsrecht* reduction of price due to defects

minderwertig *adj* GESCHÄFT third-rate, *Arbeit, Waren, Qualität, Kenntnisse* substandard, IND substandard, V&M *von geringer Qualität* low-grade; ~**e Waren** f pl GESCHÄFT third-rate goods, trashy goods (*infrml*) (*AmE*), inferior goods

Mindest- *in cpds* GESCHÄFT minimum; **Mindestangebotslohnsatz** m VW minimum supply price of labor (*AmE*), minimum supply price of labour (*BrE*); **Mindestangebotspreis** m **für Arbeit** VW minimum supply price of labor (*AmE*), minimum supply price of labour (*BrE*); **Mindestanschlußzeit** f TRANSP minimum connecting time (*MCT*); **Mindestbestand** m IND safety stock; **Mindestdarlehen** nt FINANZ floor loan; **Mindesteinkommen** nt FINANZ guaranteed income; **Mindesteinschuß** m BÖRSE minimum margin; **Mindesteinschußzahlung** f BÖRSE margin requirement; **Mindestertrag** m BÖRSE floor return; **Mindestforderung** f GESCHÄFT, POL fallback position; **Mindestfracht** f IMP/EXP, TRANSP minimum freight, minimum bill of lading charge; **Mindestfrachtrate** f TRANSP required freight rate (*RFR*); **Mindestgebühr** f TRANSP minimum charge; **Mindestgehalt** nt GESCHÄFT minimum pay; **Mindestgewinnspanne** f FINANZ, RECHNUNG bottom-line profit margin; **Mindestgrundstücksgebiet** nt GRUND minimum lot area (*AmE*); **Mindestguthaben** nt BANK minimum balance; **Mindesthaltbarkeitsdatum** nt V&M *Lebensmittel* sell-by date; **Mindestkontoführung** f BÖRSE minimum maintenance; **Mindestkosten** pl RECHNUNG least cost; **Mindestkursschwankung** f BÖRSE price tick, tick; **Mindestkursschwankung aufwärts** f BÖRSE plus tick; **Mindestlagerbestand** m IND safety stock; **Mindestlohn** m PERSON minimum wage, reservation wage, SOZIAL living wage; **Mindestlohnsatz** m PERSON union rate; **Mindestmenge** f FINANZ full lot, RECHNUNG round lot; **Mindestnote** m PERSON minimum grade; **Mindestnotierungsgröße** f BÖRSE minimum quote size (BrE) (MQS); **Mindestpachtzahlung** f GRUND *Kapitalleasing* minimum lease payments; **Mindestpensionsverpflichtung** f FINANZ minimum pension liability; **Mindestpreis** m BÖRSE, FINANZ floor, GESCHÄFT knockdown price, *Versteigerung* upset price, VW floor price; **Mindestpreisänderung** f BÖRSE minimum price change; **Mindestpreisrecht** nt BÖRSE, FINANZ floor; **Mindestpreissystem** nt GESCHÄFT trigger pricing; **Mindestqualitätsstandard** m V&M minimum quality standard; **Mindestrendite** f BÖRSE floor return, VW minimum yield

Mindestreserve f BANK reserve requirement

mindestreserveähnlich: ~e **Einlage** f BANK special deposit (BrE), minimum reserve deposit

Mindestreserve: **Mindestreserveanforderung** f BANK reserve requirement; **Mindestreserven** f pl BANK required reserves

mindestreservepflichtig: ~e **Einlage** f FINANZ eligible liability

Mindestreserve: **Mindestreservesatz** m BANK required reserve ratio, reserve ratio, FINANZ reserve-assets ratio; **Mindestreservesoll** nt VW minimum reserve requirement (MRR)

Mindest-: **Mindestsaldo** m **eines Nachschußkontos** BÖRSE maintenance margin; **Mindestsatz** m **an Barmitteln** VW till money; **Mindesttransfer** m GESCHÄFT minimum transfer (MT); **Mindestüberweisung** f GESCHÄFT minimum transfer (MT); **Mindestverbindungszeit** f TRANSP minimum connecting time (MCT); **Mindestverkaufspreis** m V&M reservation price; **Mindestverzinsung** f VW cutoff point; **Mindestzins** m BANK minimum lending rate (BrE) (MLR); **Mindestzinssatz** m BANK minimum lending rate (MLR), base lending rate, BÖRSE floor rate, FINANZ, VW minimum lending rate (MLR); **Mindestzoll** f IMP/EXP peril point

Mineral- in cpds IND, STEUER, UMWELT mineral; **Mineralindustrie** f UMWELT mineral industry; **Mineralölprodukt** nt IND mineral oil product; **Mineralölraffinerie** f IND crude oil refinery; **Mineralölsteuer** f STEUER oil tax

Mini- pref GESCHÄFT mini-; **Miniboom** m infrml VW boomlet (infrml); **Minicomputer** m COMP minicomputer

Minimal- in cpds GESCHÄFT, MATH minimal, minimum

minimal adj GESCHÄFT, MATH minimal, minimum; ~e **Notierungsgröße** f BÖRSE minimum quote size (BrE) (MQS); ~e **Preisfluktuation** f BÖRSE minimum price fluctuation; ~e **Produktivitätsskala** f VW minimum efficiency scale (MES)

Minimal-: **Minimalfracht** f IMP/EXP, TRANSP minimum freight, minimum bill of lading charge; **Minimalkonnossement** nt IMP/EXP, TRANSP minimum bill of lading (min B/L); **Minimallistenüberschrift** f GESCHÄFT minimum list heading (BrE) (MLH); **Minimalstaat** m POL minimal state; **Minimalzustand** m GESCHÄFT, POL minimum state

Minimax- in cpds VW minimax; **Minimaxprinzip** nt MGMNT minimax principle; **Minimax-Regel** f VW maximin rule, minimax rule; **Minimax-Strategie** f VW minimax strategy

minimieren vt FINANZ, GESCHÄFT, RECHNUNG *Risiken* minimize

Minimierung f FINANZ, GESCHÄFT, RECHNUNG *von Risiken* minimization

Minimum nt (Min.) GESCHÄFT, MATH minimum (min.); **Minimumtemperatur** f GESCHÄFT minimum temperature (MT)

Mini-: **Miniseite** f V&M *Seitenreproduktion* minipage; **Miniserie** f MEDIEN miniseries

Minister, in m,f POL minister; ~ **ohne Geschäftsbereich** POL, VERWALT minister without portfolio; ~ **ohne Portefeuille** POL minister without portfolio

Ministerial- in cpds POL, VERWALT ministerial; **Ministerialabteilung** f **für Zölle und Verbrauchssteuern** STEUER Commissioner of Customs and Excise (BrE); **Ministerialerlaß** m POL, RECHT ministerial order

ministeriell: ~es **Bankkonto** nt RECHNUNG departmental bank account; ~es **Programm** nt VERWALT departmental program (AmE), departmental programme (BrE)

Ministerium nt POL, VERWALT administration (admin), department, government department, ministry; ~ **für Entwicklungshilfe** POL, VERWALT, VW Ministry of Overseas Development; ~ **der Finanzen** FINANZ, POL, VW Finance Ministry; ~ **für Landwirtschaft, Fischerei und Nahrungsmittel** POL Ministry of Agriculture, Fisheries and Food; ~ **für Touristik** POL, VERWALT Ministry of Tourism

Minister: **Ministerrat** m **der Europäische Union** POL, VERWALT, VW Council of Ministers

Minus nt MATH *Symbol* minus; **Minuswachstum** nt VW minus growth; **Minuszeichen** nt MATH minus sign

MIS abbr (Management-Informationssystem) COMP, MGMNT MIS (management information system)

Misch- in cpds FINANZ, RECHNUNG, V&M, VERSICH, VW mixed; **Mischbündelung** f V&M mixed bundling

Mischen nt COMP merge

Misch-: **Mischgut** nt VW impure public good, mixed good; **Mischkonzern** m VW conglomerate merger; **Mischkosten** pl RECHNUNG mixed cost; **Mischkredit** m FINANZ mixed credit; **Mischpackung** f V&M composite package; **Mischprämie** f VERSICH combined premium; **Mischrente** f VERSICH hybrid annuity

Mischung f BÖRSE commingling, MEDIEN *aufnehmen auf Tonband oder Schallplatte*, V&M mix; ~ **zwischen Fremd- und Eigenkapitalfinanzierung** FINANZ mezzanine finance; ~ **von Preis- und Rabattpolitik** V&M pricing mix; ~ **verschiedener Kommunikationskanäle** V&M communication mix

Misch-: **Mischwirtschaft** f VW mixed economy; **Mischzins** m BANK blended rate

Mißachtung f RECHT contempt, disregard; ~ **von Bedingungen** GESCHÄFT, RECHT nonobservance of conditions; ~ **des Gerichts** RECHT contempt of court; **unter ~ des Gerichts** phr RECHT in contempt of court

Mißbilligungsantrag m POL motion of censure

Mißbrauch m GESCHÄFT, PATENT abuse, UMWELT misuse, V&M *des Verkäufers* abusive practice, VW abuse; ~ **von Dienstleistungen** GESCHÄFT service abuse; ◆ **einem ~ abhelfen** GESCHÄFT remedy an abuse

mißbrauchen vt GESCHÄFT abuse

mißbräuchlich: ~e **Ausnutzung** f GESCHÄFT, PATENT, VW abuse, ~e **Verhaltensweise** f POL, VW abusive practice

Mißerfolg *m* MGMNT failure; **Mißerfolgsanalyse** *f* MGMNT failure analysis

Mißernte *f* VW crop failure

Missetat *f* RECHT wrongdoing

Missetäter, in *m,f* RECHT tort feasor

mißglückt *adj* GESCHÄFT failed

Mission *f* POL cause

Missionarsarbeit *f* PERSON missionary work

Mißmanagement *nt* MGMNT mismanagement

Mißtrauensantrag *m* POL motion of no confidence

mißverständlich *adj* GESCHÄFT ambiguous

Mißverständnis *nt* GESCHÄFT misapprehension, misunderstanding; ♦ **~ ausschließen** GESCHÄFT preclude misunderstanding

mißverstehen *vt* GESCHÄFT misunderstand

Mißwirtschaft *f* MGMNT mismanagement

mißwirtschaften *vi* MGMNT mismanage

mit *prep* BÖRSE cum

Mitabgabe *f*: **~ von Angeboten** VW competitive tendering

Mitarbeit *f* GESCHÄFT collaboration

mitarbeiten *vt* GESCHÄFT collaborate

Mitarbeiter, in *m,f* GESCHÄFT, PERSON employee, colleague; **~ auf Probe** PERSON probationary employee

Mitarbeiter *m pl* GESCHÄFT, PERSON staff, colleagues, manpower; **~ ohne Anspruch auf Überstundenvergütung** PERSON exempt employees (*AmE*); **~ in Stabs- und Linienfunktion** PERSON *Betriebswirtschaft* staff and line; **Mitarbeiteranalyse** *f* VW manpower analysis; **Mitarbeiterbeteiligung** *f* PERSON employee stock ownership plan (*ESOP*), employee participation scheme, employee shareholding scheme; **Mitarbeiterbeurteilung** *f* MGMNT, PERSON staff appraisal; **Mitarbeiterförderung** *f* MGMNT, PERSON staff development; **Mitarbeiteroptionsplan** *m* BÖRSE all-employee option scheme (*BrE*); **Mitarbeiterprofil** *nt* PERSON employee profile; **Mitarbeiterschulung** *f* MGMNT, PERSON staff training; **Mitarbeiterunterstützung** *f* PERSON manpower aid

Mitbediener *m* IND joint operator

Mitbesitz *m* GRUND co-ownership

mitbestimmt: **~e Wirtschaft** *f* GESCHÄFT economic democracy, POL, VW industrial democracy

Mitbestimmung *f* BÖRSE, PERSON, VW codetermination

Mitdirektor, in *m,f* MGMNT joint director, PERSON joint manager, co-director, co-manager

Miteigentum *nt* BANK, GRUND, RECHT joint ownership co-ownership, joint estate, part ownership

Miteigentümer, in *m,f* BANK, GRUND, RECHT co-owner, joint owner, part owner

Miterbe *m* RECHT co-heir, joint heir

Miterbin *f* RECHT co-heir, joint heir

mitfinanzieren *vt* FINANZ cofinance

Mitgift *f* GRUND dowry

Mitglied *nt* GESCHÄFT affiliate, affiliate member, PERSON *einer Gewerkschaft* member; **~ des Aufsichtsrates** PERSON member of the supervisory board; **~ eines Ausschusses** VERWALT commissioner; **~ des Board** PERSON, MGMNT board member, member of the board; **~ einer Direkt-Clearingstelle** BANK direct clearing member; **~ des Europaparlaments** (*MEP*) POL European Member of Parliament (*Euro MP*), Member of

the European Parliament (*MEP*); **~ des Fahrpersonals** TRANSP crew member, member of the crew; **~ der Führungsebene** VERWALT company executive; **~ kraft Amtes** PERSON ex officio member; **~ einer Liquidationskasse** BANK, BÖRSE, FINANZ clearing member; **~ der Öffentlichkeit** GESCHÄFT member of the public; **~ des Verwaltungsrats** MGMNT member of the board of management; **Mitgliederabwerbung** *f* *zwischen Gewerkschaften* PERSON poaching; **Mitgliederleerverkaufsverhältnis** *nt* BÖRSE member short sale ratio; **Mitgliedsbeitrag** *m* GESCHÄFT membership fee, *für Verein oder Verband* subscription, PERSON affiliation fee

Mitgliedschaft *f* GESCHÄFT membership

Mitglied: **Mitgliedskarte** *f* GESCHÄFT membership card; **Mitgliedsstaat** *m* POL member state (*MS*); **Mitgliedsstaaten** *m pl* **der EU** POL, VW EU member states; **Mitgliedsstaaten** *m pl* **der Europäischen Union** POL, VW European Union member states

mithalten: **~ können mit** *phr* V&M match

mithelfen *vi* GESCHÄFT assist

Mitherausgeber, in *m,f* MEDIEN associate editor

Mithilfe *f* GESCHÄFT assistance

mithören *vt* GESCHÄFT, *heimlich* listen to, listen in on, KOMM tap into, *Telefongespräch* listen to, tap

Mithören *nt* GESCHÄFT tapping

Mitinhaber, in *m,f* GESCHÄFT co-owner

Mitkandidat, in *m,f* POL running mate (*AmE*)

Mitläufer, in *m,f* POL fellow traveler (*AmE*), fellow traveller (*BrE*); **Mitläufereffekt** *m* VW bandwagon effect

mitnehmen *vt* BÖRSE *Gewinn* take

Mitprüfer, in *m,f* RECHNUNG joint auditor

Mitschnitt *m* MEDIEN *Rundfunksendung* air check tape

mitschreiben *vt* GESCHÄFT transcribe

Mitschreibung *f* GESCHÄFT transcription

mitschuldig *adj* GESCHÄFT, RECHNUNG partly responsible, RECHT in pari delicto, implicated, partly responsible, accessory, vw partly responsible

Mittäter, in *m,f* RECHT accessory

Mitte *f* GESCHÄFT, IND center (*AmE*), centre (*BrE*)

mitteilen *vt* GESCHÄFT *angeben* communicate, signify, KOMM advise, PATENT communicate, notify, POL communicate; ♦ **jdm etw ~** GESCHÄFT communicate sth to sb, notify sb of sth, KOMM advise sb of sth; **wir müssen Ihnen leider ~, daß** GESCHÄFT, KOMM we regret to inform you that

Mitteiler *m* KOMM communicator

Mitteilung *f* GESCHÄFT communication, message, KOMM advice, PATENT communication, notification, POL communication; **~ über Aktienzuteilung** BÖRSE allotment letter (*BrE*); **~ bezüglich vorausbezahlter Fahrscheine** TRANSP prepaid ticket advice (*PTA*); **~ über Laufzeit und/oder Belastung** GESCHÄFT, KOMM advice of duration and/or charge (*ADC*); **Mitteilungsblatt** *nt* GESCHÄFT, MEDIEN newsletter

Mittel *nt* FINANZ resources, GESCHÄFT agent, means, IND agent, MEDIEN tool, PERSON resources, VW means, resources; **Mittel** *nt pl* **aus laufender Geschäftstätigkeit** RECHNUNG funds from operations; **Mittel** *nt pl* **und Wege** *m pl* VW ways and means; ♦ **~ bereitstellen** FINANZ, MGMNT, RECHNUNG appropriate funds; **~ bewilligen** FINANZ, MGMNT, RECHNUNG allocate resources, appropriate funds; **~ vereinen** VW pool resources; **über die ~ verfügen, etw zu tun** GESCHÄFT have the means to do sth; **~ zusammenfassen** VW pool resources; **~ zuweisen** FINANZ, MGMNT, RECHNUNG allocate resources, appropriate funds

Mittelamerikanisch: **~e Warenbörse** *f* BÖRSE Mid-America Commodity Exchange

mittelbar: **~er Schaden** *m* VERSICH consequential damage

Mittel: **Mittelbeschaffung** *f* FINANZ fund raising; **Mittelbewilligung** *f* FINANZ, RECHNUNG resource allocation; **Mittelbewilligung** *f* **aus dem Nachtragshaushalt** POL, RECHNUNG parliamentary appropriation; **Mittelbindung** *f* FINANZ, MGMNT, RECHNUNG, VW appropriation of funds; **Mittelbindung** *f* **für den Verteidigungshaushalt** POL government defence appropriations (*BrE*), government defense appropriations (*AmE*); **Mittelbindung** *f* **für Verteidigungszwecke** POL government defence appropriations (*BrE*), government defense appropriations (*AmE*)

mitteleuropäisch: **~e Zeit** *f* (*MEZ*) GESCHÄFT Central European Time (*CET*)

Mittel: **Mittelfrequenzsprechfunk** *m* TRANSP medium-frequency radiotelephony

mittelfristig 1. *adj* BÖRSE medium-dated, FINANZ, GESCHÄFT medium-term; **2.** *adv* GESCHÄFT in the medium term

mittelfristig: **~es Darlehen** *nt* BANK medium-term loan (*MTL*); **~e Euronote** *f* BÖRSE medium-term Euronote; **~e Finanzstrategie** *f* VW medium-term financial strategy (*MTFS*); **~es Handelspapier** *nt* BÖRSE medium-term instrument; **~er Kredit** *m* BANK intermediate-term credit, medium-term loan (*MTL*), FINANZ term loan; **~er Mietvertrag** *m* PERSON *Rechtswesen* contract hire; **~e Obligation** *f* BÖRSE medium-term bond; **~e Schuldtitel** *m pl* BANK, BÖRSE, FINANZ medium-term notes (*MTN*), mediums; **~e Schuldverschreibung** *f* BÖRSE medium-term bond

Mittel: **Mittelherkunft** *f* FINANZ, RECHNUNG source of funds; **Mittelherkunft und -verwendung** *f* FINANZ, RECHNUNG source and application of funds, source and disposition of funds; **Mittelklasse** *f* COMP midrange; **Mittelkurs** *m* BÖRSE mid price, RECHNUNG average rate, VW mean price

mittellos *adj* VW poor

Mittelmanagement *nt* PERSON middle management

mittelmäßig *adj* GESCHÄFT medium, mediocre

Mittelmeer: **Mittelmeerbecken** *nt* GESCHÄFT Mediterranean basin; **Mittelmeerblock** *m* GESCHÄFT Mediterranean bloc

Mittel: **Mittelpunkt** *m* GESCHÄFT center (*AmE*), centre (*BrE*), focus; **Mittelrückfluß** *m* **ins Banksystem** BANK reintermediation; **Mittelsmann** *m* GESCHÄFT intermediary, go-between; **Mittelsorte** *f* VW middling quality

mittelständisch: **~er Betrieb** *m* GESCHÄFT medium-sized enterprise

Mittel: **Mittelstück** *nt* GESCHÄFT, IND center (*AmE*), centre (*BrE*); **Mittelunternehmen** *nt* VW middle market business; **Mittelverfügbarkeit** *f* FINANZ resource availability; **Mittelverteilung** *f* FINANZ, MGMNT, RECHNUNG, VW appropriation of funds, fund appropriation, resource allocation; **Mittelverwendung** *f* RECHNUNG *Kapitalflußrechnung* application of funds; **Mittelwert**

m GESCHÄFT average (*av.*), MATH average (*av.*), mean, mean value, RECHNUNG average (*av.*); **den Mittelwert nehmen** *phr* MATH take an average; **Mittelzuteilung** *f* FINANZ, MGMNT, RECHNUNG, VW appropriation of funds, fund appropriation, resource allocation; **Mittelzuweisung** *f* FINANZ, MGMNT, RECHNUNG apportionment of funds, appropriation of funds, resource allocation, VW appropriation, appropriation of funds

mitternächtlich: **~er Schlußtermin** *m* GESCHÄFT midnight deadline

Mittler *m* GESCHÄFT intermediary

mittlere *adj* GESCHÄFT average, mean, middle; **~r Abschlußkurs** *m* BÖRSE middle strike price; **~ Abweichung** *f* MATH average deviation, mean deviation; **~r Arbeitsdruck** *m* (*MEP*) IND mean effective pressure (*mep*); **~r Ausfallabstand** *m* IND mean time between failures (*MTBF*); **~(r) Beamte(r)** *m* [decl. as adj], **~ Beamtin** *f* PERSON petty official; **~r Betrieb** *m* VW medium account; **~s Einkommen** *nt* VW median income; **~ Einkommenssteuergruppe** *f* VW middle income bracket; **~ Einkommenssteuerklasse** *f* VW middle income bracket; **~ Einkommensstufe** *f* VW middle income bracket; **~r Emissionskurs** *m* BÖRSE middle issue price; **~ Frist** *f* GESCHÄFT intermediate term; **~s Frühlingshochwasser** *nt* TRANSP mean high water at spring (*MHWS*); **~ Führungsebene** *f* MGMNT, PERSON middle management; **~ Führungskraft** *f* MGMNT, PERSON middle manager; **~s Grundstück** *nt* GRUND *abgegrenzt* inside lot; **~s Karriereplateau** *nt* PERSON *Berufslaufbahn* midcareer plateau; **~ Lebensdauer** *f* VERSICH average duration of life; **~ Lebenserwartung** *f* VERSICH average duration of life; **~ Liegezeit** *f* TRANSP average layover, average laytime; **~ Marktposition** *f* V&M middle range of the market; **~ Nutzungsdauer** *f* GESCHÄFT *eines Produktes* average life; **~r Optionsbasispreis** *m* BÖRSE middle strike price; **~ quadratische Abweichung** *f* MATH *Statistik* standard deviation; **~ Qualität** *f* GESCHÄFT good fair average (*gfa*); **~r Quartilabstand** *m* VW quartile deviation

Mittlere: **~ Reife** *f* SOZIAL first public exam in secondary school, ≈ General Certificate of Education (*obs*) (*GCE*), ≈ General Certificate of Secondary Education (*GCSE*)

mittlere: **~s Revisionsdatum** *nt* V&M mean audit date; **~ Zeit** *f* GESCHÄFT mean time (*MT*); **~ Zugriffszeit** *f* COMP average access time

Mitverschulden *nt* RECHT contributory negligence

Mitversicherer *m* VERSICH coinsurer

mitversichern *vt* VERSICH coinsure, insure jointly

mitversichert *adj* VERSICH coinsured; **~e Explosionsklausel** *f* VERSICH inherent explosion clause

Mitversicherte(r) *mf* [decl. as adj] VERSICH additional insured, coinsured

Mitversicherung *f* VERSICH coinsurance, joint insurance

mitwirkend *adj* RECHT contributory; **~es Verschulden** *nt* RECHT contributory negligence

Mitwirkung *f* FINANZ contribution

mitzunehmen: **nicht ~** *phr* GESCHÄFT not to be taken away

Mix *m* GESCHÄFT mix

ml *abbr* (*Milliliter*) GESCHÄFT ml (*milliliter AmE, millilitre BrE*)

mm *abbr* (*Millimeter*) GESCHÄFT mm (*millimeter AmE, millimetre BrE*)

mm/s *abbr* (*Millimeter pro Sekunde*) GESCHÄFT mm/s (*millimeters per second AmE, millimetres per second BrE*)

Möbel *nt pl* GESCHÄFT furniture; **Möbellager** *nt* GESCHÄFT furniture depot, furniture warehouse; **Möbelwagen** *m* TRANSP removal van

mobil *adj* GESCHÄFT mobile, KOMM portable; **~er Arbeiter** *m*, **~e Arbeiterin** *f* PERSON mobile worker; **~e Streikposten** *m pl* PERSON flying pickets; **~es Telefon** *nt* KOMM cellular phone, mobile phone, mobile telephone, mobile, portable phone, portable telephone

Mobiliar *nt* RECHT set of chattels

Mobiliarvermögen *nt* GRUND, RECHT chattels personal, personal estate

Mobilienvermietung *f* IND plant hire

mobilisieren *vt* VW mobilize

Mobilität *f* PERSON, SOZIAL, V&M mobility; **Mobilitätsfalle** *f* VW mobility trap; **Mobilitätsklausel** *f* PERSON mobility clause (*BrE*); **Mobilitätsstatus** *m* VW mobility status

Mobiltelefon *nt* KOMM mobile phone, mobile telephone, mobile, portable phone, portable telephone, cellphone, cellular phone

mobizentrisch: **~er Manager** *m*, **~e Managerin** *f* MGMNT mobicentric manager

Modalitäten *f pl* BANK terms; **~ des Auslandsabsatzes** IMP/EXP terms of export sale

Mode *f* GESCHÄFT, V&M fashion; ♦ **in ~** GESCHÄFT, V&M in fashion, trendy (*infrml*) (*BrE*); **in ~ bringen** GESCHÄFT, V&M bring into fashion; **die ~ festlegen** GESCHÄFT, V&M set the fashion

Mode: **Modeartikel** *m pl* GESCHÄFT fancy goods, V&M fashion goods, fancy goods, VW fancy goods; **Modedesigner, in** *m,f* GESCHÄFT stylist, fashion designer; **Modegeschäft** *nt* GESCHÄFT fashion house; **Modejournal** *nt* GESCHÄFT fashion magazine

Model *nt* GESCHÄFT *Person*, MEDIEN, V&M fashion model

Modell *nt* GESCHÄFT pattern, *Muster* model, IND template, MATH model, PATENT design; **Modellbildung** *f* MATH modeling (*AmE*), modelling (*BrE*); **Modellhaus** *nt* GRUND show house; **Modellprofil** *nt* GESCHÄFT model profile; **Modellwohnung** *f* GRUND show apartment (*AmE*), show flat (*BrE*)

Modem *nt* (*Modulator-Demodulator*) COMP, MATH modem (*modulator-demodulator*); **Modemverbindung** *f* COMP modem link

moderat *adj* VW modest

Moderator *m* MEDIEN *Live-Sendung* presenter, *Nachrichtensendung* anchor, anchorman

Moderatorin *f* MEDIEN *Live-Sendung* presenter, *Nachrichtensendung* anchor, anchorwoman

modern GESCHÄFT, IND, VW advanced, modern, up-to-date; **~e Fabrik** *f* IND advanced factory; **~er Industriestaat** *m* VW advanced industrial state; **~e Technik** *f* IND advanced engineering; **~e Technologie** *f* IND advanced technology; **~e Volkswirtschaft** *f* VW modern economy; **~e Volkswirtschaftslehre** *f* VW modern economics; **~e Wirtschaft** *f* VW modern economy; **~e Wirtschaftswissenschaft** *f* VW new economics

modernisieren *vt* GESCHÄFT modernize, update, MGMNT streamline

modernste: **mit ~r Technologie** *phr* IND, VW technologically advanced

Modernisierung *f* GESCHÄFT modernization, updating, IND, MGMNT streamlining

Mode: **Modeschöpfer** *m* GESCHÄFT couturier, fashion designer; **Modeschöpferin** *f* GESCHÄFT couturière, fashion designer; **Modewort** *nt* GESCHÄFT buzzword (*infrml*)

modifizieren *vt* GESCHÄFT *Kontext*, MATH, RECHNUNG, V&M, VW modify

modifiziert: **~e Abgrenzungsposten** *m pl* RECHNUNG modified accrual; **~er Mittelwert** *m* MATH modified mean; **~e Volkskostenrechnung** *f* VW modified absorption costing; **~er Wiederkauf** *m* V&M modified rebuy

Modifizierung *f* GESCHÄFT, MATH, RECHNUNG, V&M, VW modification

Modularität *f* GESCHÄFT modularity

Modularproduktion *f* IND modular production

Modulation *f* KOMM modulation

Modulator-Demodulator *m* (*Modem*) COMP modulator-demodulator (*modem*)

Modulstruktur *f* VW modular structure

Modus *m* COMP, MATH *Statistik* mode

möglich *adj* GESCHÄFT potential, possible; **~e Verbindlichkeit** *f* GESCHÄFT potential commitment; **~e Verpflichtung** *f* GESCHÄFT potential commitment

Möglichkeit *f* GESCHÄFT opportunity, possibility, *Potential* potential, *Alternative* alternative, POL *Gelegenheit*, VW opportunity; **~ zum Abreagieren** MGMNT abreaction channels; ♦ **Möglichkeiten eröffnen** GESCHÄFT afford possibilities

Mole *f* TRANSP mole

Moment: **im ~** *phr* GESCHÄFT at the present time

Momentum *nt* VW momentum

Monat *m* GESCHÄFT month (*m, MTH*); **einen ~ im voraus** *phr* GESCHÄFT a month in advance; **Monate** *m pl* **nach Datum** GESCHÄFT months after date; **Monate** *m pl* **nach heute** GESCHÄFT months after date; **Monate** *m pl* **nach Sicht** BANK months after sight (*m/s*)

monatlich **1.** *adj* GESCHÄFT monthly; **2.** *adv* GESCHÄFT monthly

monatlich: **~e Ausgaben** *f pl* GESCHÄFT monthly expenses; **~e Ersparnisse** *f pl* PERSON monthly savings; **~er Investitionsplan** *m* BÖRSE monthly investment plan; **~e Ratenzahlung** *f* FINANZ monthly installment (*AmE*), monthly instalment (*BrE*); **~e Teilzahlung** *f* BANK installment (*AmE*), instalment (*BrE*); **~e Verkäufe** *m pl* V&M monthly sales; **~ sich verlängerndes Mietverhältnis** *nt* RECHT month-to-month tenancy; **~ sich verlängerndes Pachtverhältnis** *nt* RECHT month-to-month tenancy; **~e Vermietung** *f* GRUND month-to-month tenancy; **~e Voranmeldung** *f* STEUER monthly prepayment notice; **~e Zinsberechnung** *f* BANK monthly compounding of interest

Monat: **Monatsabschluß** *m* BANK, RECHNUNG end-of-month account; **Monatsaufstellung** *f* FINANZ monthly statement; **Monatsauszug** *m* BANK monthly statement; **Monatsbericht** *m* FINANZ monthly statement, RECHNUNG monthly return; **Monatsende** *nt* RECHNUNG end of month; **Monatserste(r)** *m* [decl. as adj] GESCHÄFT first day of the month; **Monatsertrag** *m* RECHNUNG monthly return; **Monatsfahrkarte** *f* TRANSP commutation ticket (*AmE*), season ticket (*BrE*); **Monatsfrist** *f* GESCHÄFT one month's notice; **Monatsmiete** *f* GRUND monthly rent; **Monatsrate** *f* FINANZ monthly installment (*AmE*), monthly instalment (*BrE*); **in Monatsraten** *phr* RECHNUNG in monthly installments (*AmE*), in monthly instalments (*BrE*); **Monatsultimo** *m* GESCHÄFT end of month

monetär *adj* FINANZ, GESCHÄFT, VW monetary; **~e Entwicklung** *f* VW monetary course; **~er Ertrag** *m* VW pecuniary returns; **~er externer Effekt** *m* VW pecuniary spillover; **~e Größe** *f* FINANZ money measurement

Monetarismus *m* FINANZ, GESCHÄFT, VW gradualist monetarism, monetarism

Monetarist, in *m,f* FINANZ, GESCHÄFT, VW monetarist

monetaristisch: **~er Zahlungsbilanzansatz** *m* FINANZ, GESCHÄFT, VW monetarist approach to the balance of payments, monetary approach to the balance of payments; **~e Zahlungsbilanzauffassung** *f* FINANZ, GESCHÄFT, VW monetarist approach to the balance of payments, monetary approach to the balance of payments

Monetisierung *f* VW monetarization

Monitor *m* COMP, GESCHÄFT monitor

Monitum *nt* GESCHÄFT query

Monnet-Gesetz *nt* VW Monnet's law

Monogramm *nt* GESCHÄFT monogram

Monokultursystem *nt* VW one-crop economy

Monopol *nt* IND, VW monopoly; **Monopol- und Fusionskommission** *f* VW Monopolies and Mergers Commission (*BrE*) (*MMC*); **Monopolgewinn** *m* VW monopoly rent, monopoly profit

Monopolist, in *m,f* VW monopolist

monopolistisch: **~e Konkurrenz** *f* VW monopolistic competition

Monopol: **Monopolkapitalismus** *m* VW monopoly capitalism; **Monopolkommission** *f* FINANZ, POL antitrust commission; **Monopolmacht** *f* VW monopoly power; **Monopolpreis** *m* VW monopoly price; **Monopolstellung** *f* IND monopoly

Monopson *nt* VW monopsony

Monowirtschaft *f* VW mono-economics

Montag: **ab ~** *phr* GESCHÄFT starting from Monday

Montage *f* GESCHÄFT assembling, assembly, IND assembly; **Montageband** *nt* IND, PERSON *Produktion* assembly line; **Montagefirma** *f* IND assembler; **Montageplan** *m* GESCHÄFT, IND assembly program (*AmE*), assembly programme (*BrE*); **Montageprogramm** *nt* GESCHÄFT, IND assembly program (*AmE*), assembly programme (*BrE*); **Montageversicherung** *f* VERSICH erection insurance; **Montagewerk** *nt* IND, PERSON *Massenproduktion* assembly plant

Montanindustrie *f* IND mining industry

Montanunion *f* VW European Coal and Steel Community (*ECSC*)

Monte-Carlo-Methode *f* MATH Monte Carlo method

Monteur *m* PERSON assembler, *Arbeit* mechanic, *Elektro-* electrician, *Installateur* fitter

Moody: **~'s Anlagenbewertung** *f* FINANZ Moody's investment grade (*AmE*); **~'s Anlegerdienst** *m* FINANZ Moody's investor service (*AmE*); **~'s**

Kapitalanlegerservice *m* FINANZ Moody's investor service (*AmE*)

moralisch: **~ vertretbar** *adj* MGMNT ethical

Moralökonomiefaktor *m* POL Whitehouse factor (*jarg*)

Moralwächterfaktor *m* POL Whitehouse factor (*jarg*)

Moratorium *nt* FINANZ moratorium, GESCHÄFT moratorium, standstill agreement

Morgan: **~ Stanley Internationaler Welt-Kapital-Index** *m* BÖRSE Morgan Stanley Capital International World Index

morgen *adv* GESCHÄFT tomorrow; ♦ **~ in einer Woche** GESCHÄFT tomorrow week

Morgenschicht *f* PERSON *Schichtarbeit* day shift

morphologisch: **~e Analyse** *f* FINANZ, MATH morphological analysis

Motiv *nt* GESCHÄFT cause, reason, POL cause

Motivation *f* GESCHÄFT, MGMNT, PERSON, V&M motivation; **Motivationsanalyse** *f* PERSON motivational analysis; **Motivationstheorie** *f* PERSON field theory of motivation; **Motivationstheorie** *f* **der Anwartschaft** PERSON, VERSICH expectancy theory of motivation

Motivator, in *m,f* GESCHÄFT, MGMNT, PERSON motivator

Motivforschung *f* V&M motivational research

motivieren *vt* GESCHÄFT, MGMNT, PERSON, V&M motivate

motivierend *adj* GESCHÄFT, MGMNT, PERSON, V&M motivational

Motivierung *f* GESCHÄFT, MGMNT, PERSON, V&M motivation

Motivirrtum *m* RECHT error in motivation

Motor *m* TRANSP engine, motor; **Motorenbenzin** *nt* TRANSP motor spirit; **Motorhandelsschiff** *nt* TRANSP motor merchant vessel (*M/V*); **Motorhubraum** *m* (*cc*) GESCHÄFT cubic capacity (*cc*)

motorisch *adj* IND automotive

Motor: **Motorraum** *m* TRANSP engine room; **Motorschiff** *nt* TRANSP motor ship (*M, MS*), motor vessel (*M, MV*); **Motortanker** *m* TRANSP motor tanker; **Motortransportbeamte(r)** *m* [decl. as adj], **Motortransportbeamtin** *f* PERSON motor transport officer

MS-DOS® *abbr* (*Microsoft-Plattenbetriebssystem*) COMP MS-DOS® (*Microsoft disk operating system*)

Mt. *abbr* GESCHÄFT MTH (*month*)

MTM *abbr* (*Methods-Times-Measurement*) MGMNT MTM (*methods-time measurement*)

MÜ *abbr* (*Maschinenübersetzung*) COMP MT (*machine translation*)

Mühe: **sich viel ~ geben** *phr* GESCHÄFT go to a lot of trouble; **der ~ wert** *phr* GESCHÄFT worthwhile

Mühle: **ab ~** *phr* (*x-Mühle*) TRANSP ex mill (*x-mill*)

Mühlen: **die ~ der Regierung** *f pl* POL the wheels of government

mühsam: **sich ~ durchschlagen** *phr* GESCHÄFT scrape along (*infrml*); **~es Geschäft** *nt* GESCHÄFT sweated trade

mühselig: **~e Arbeit** *f* PERSON *Arbeitszufriedenheit* slog

Müll *m* GESCHÄFT, UMWELT waste, refuse, rubbish (*BrE*), garbage (*AmE*); ♦ **~ rein, Müll raus** *jarg* (*GIGO*) COMP garbage in, garbage out (*jarg*) (*GIGO*)

Müll: **Müllabfuhr** *f* GESCHÄFT, UMWELT refuse collection; **Müllabladeplatz** *m* GESCHÄFT, UMWELT dumping ground; **Müllbehandlung** *f* GESCHÄFT, UMWELT waste treatment; **Müllbeseitigung** *f* GESCHÄFT, UMWELT refuse disposal; **Müllentsorgung** *f* GESCHÄFT, UMWELT waste disposal; **Müllverbrennung** *f* IND, UMWELT incineration

Multi- *pref* GESCHÄFT multi-; **Multifaserabkommen** *nt* VW multi-fiber arrangement (*AmE*) (*MFA*), multi-fibre arrangement (*BrE*) (*MFA*)

multifunktional *adj* GESCHÄFT all-purpose; **~er Bankautomat** *m* BANK, FINANZ automated teller machine (*ATM*), automatic telling machine (*ATM*)

Multi-: **Multikatoreffekt** *m* VW multiplier effect; **Multikollinearität** *f* MATH, VW multicollinearity

multilateral: **~es Abkommen** *nt* VW multilateral agreement; **~e Auszahlung** *f* VW multilateral disbursement; **~e Behörde** *f* VW multilateral agency; **~e Entwicklungsbank** *f* FINANZ multilateral development bank; **~e Geberorganisation** *f* VW multilateral donor; **~e Genehmigung** *f* TRANSP multilateral permit; **~es Handelsabkommen** *nt* VW multilateral trade agreement; **~e Handelsgespräche** *nt pl* (*MHV*) VW multilateral trade negotiations (*MTN*); **~e Handelsorganisation** *f* VW multilateral trade organization; **~e Hilfe** *f* VW multilateral aid; **~e Investitionsgarantieagentur** *f* FINANZ, VW multilateral investment guarantee agency (*MIGA*); **~e Vereinbarung** *f* VW multilateral agreement; **~e Vereinigung** *f* **für Investitionsgarantien** FINANZ, VW multilateral investment guarantee association (*MIGA*)

Multilateralismus *m* VW multilateralism

multilingual *adj* GESCHÄFT, PERSON multilingual

Multi-: **Multimediaschulung** *f* PERSON multimedia training; **Multimomentaufnahme** *f* MGMNT activity sampling; **Multimomentverfahren** *nt* IND, MATH activity sampling, V&M, VERWALT activity sampling

multinational *adj* BANK, GESCHÄFT, IMP/EXP, TRANSP multinational, transnational; **~e Bank** *f* BANK multinational bank; **~e Besatzung** *f* TRANSP multinational crew; **~er Exportkredit** *m* IMP/EXP multinational export credit; **~e Gesellschaft** *f* GESCHÄFT multinational enterprise (*MNE*); **~er Handelsverkehr** *m* IMP/EXP multinational trading; **~es Unternehmen** *nt* GESCHÄFT transnational corporation, multinational enterprise (*MNE*), multinational company, multinational corporation (*MNC*)

multipel: **multiple Korrelation** *f* MATH *Statistik* multiple correlation; **multiple Regression** *f* MATH multiple regression; **multipler Wechselkurs** *m* VW multiple exchange rate; **multiple Wechselkurse** *m pl* VW multi-currency rate

Multiple-Choice-Frage *f* V&M multiple choice question

Multiplikator *m* VW multiplier; **Multiplikator-Akzelerator-Modell** *nt* VW multiplier accelerator model; **Multiplikatorprinzip** *nt* VW multiplier principle; **Multiplikatorwirkung** *f* **eines ausgeglichenen öffentlichen Haushalts** VW balanced budget multiplier

multiplizieren *vt* MATH multiply

Multi-: **Multitasking** *nt* COMP multitasking; **Multivariatenanalyse** *f* MATH multivariate analysis

Mündel *nt* RECHT ward

Mundell-Fleming-Modell *nt* VW Mundell-Fleming model

mündelsicher: **~e Kapitalanlage** *f* BÖRSE, VW legal investment; **~es Wertpapier** *nt* BANK gilt, BÖRSE gilt-edged stock, legal investment, gilt, FINANZ gilt, VW legal investment

mündlich *adj* GESCHÄFT *Vereinbarung, Angebot, Verspre-* *chen* verbal; **~e Abmachung** *f* GESCHÄFT unwritten agreement; **~e Absprache** *f* GESCHÄFT verbal agreement; **~es Angebot** *nt* GESCHÄFT verbal offer; **~e Mitteilung** *f* GESCHÄFT, MGMNT, PERSON verbal communication, POL oral note; **~e Nachricht** *f* POL oral note; **~e Vereinbarung** *f* GESCHÄFT unwritten agreement, verbal agreement, RECHT oral contract; **~e Verhandlung** *f* PATENT oral proceedings; **~e Warnung** *f* MGMNT, PERSON verbal warning

Mund-zu-Mund: **~ Werbung** *f* V&M word-of-mouth advertising, word-of-mouth marketing

Mundraub *m obs* GESCHÄFT grazing (*jarg*)

Münz- *in cpds* VW coinage; **Münzamt** *nt* VW mint; **Münzanstalt** *f* VW mint

Münze *f* GESCHÄFT coin, token, VW mint, money; **~ der Vereinigten Staaten** BANK United States Mint (*USM*); **Münzen** *f pl* VW coinage

Münz-: **Münzgeld** *nt* VW hard money; **Münzgewinn** *m* FINANZ seigniorage; **Münzparität** *f* FINANZ mint par of exchange, VW mint par; **Münzprägung** *f* VW coinage; **Münzsystem** *nt* VW coinage system; **Münztelefon** *nt* KOMM pay phone (*BrE*), pay station (*AmE*)

Murphys: **~ Gesetz** *nt* GESCHÄFT Murphy's Law

Mußvorschrift *f* VERSICH mandatory provision

Muß-Wissen-Basis *f jarg* MGMNT need-to-know basis

Muster *nt* COMP pattern, GESCHÄFT pattern, sample, template, PATENT design, V&M pattern; **~ der Wirtschaftsaktivität** VW pattern of economic activity; **Musterabschluß** *m* VW pattern settlement; **Musterangebot** *nt* GESCHÄFT sampling offer; **Musterbeispiel** *nt* GESCHÄFT textbook case; **Musterbetrieb** *m* GESCHÄFT textbook operation; **Musterformular** *nt* VERWALT forms design sheet

mustergemäß *adj* GESCHÄFT up-to-sample

mustergetreu *adj* GESCHÄFT up-to-sample

Muster: **Musterkarte** *f* GESCHÄFT pattern, sample, V&M sample card; **Musterkoffer** *m* V&M sample case; **Musterkollektion** *f* GESCHÄFT swatch; **Musterlizenz** *f* IMP/EXP sample licence (*BrE*), sample license (*AmE*); **Musterrechnung** *f* GESCHÄFT specimen invoice; **Mustersatzung** *f* VW model articles of association; **Mustersendung** *f* KOMM sample mailing

Muth-Mills-Modell *nt* VW Muth-Mills model

mutmaßlich *adj* GESCHÄFT probable

Mutter- *in cpds* GESCHÄFT mother, parent; **Muttergesellschaft** *f* GESCHÄFT, RECHNUNG parent company, RECHT holding company; **Mutterkarte** *f* COMP motherboard, mothercard; **Mutterland** *nt* FINANZ, GESCHÄFT home country; **Mutterplatte** *f* COMP motherboard

Mutterschaft- *in cpds* PERSON maternity; **Mutterschaftsgeld** *nt* PERSON maternity pay, maternity benefit, maternity allowance; **Mutterschaftsurlaub** *m* PERSON maternity leave

Mutter-: **Mutterschiff** *nt* TRANSP feeder ship, mother ship; **Mutterschutz** *m* VERSICH *Arbeit* maternity protection

mutwillig: **~e Sachbeschädigung** *f* RECHT malicious mischief

MW *abbr* (*Megawatt*) GESCHÄFT MW (*megawatt*)

MwSt. *abbr* (*Mehrwertsteuer*) GESCHÄFT, STEUER VAT (*value-added tax BrE*); **MwSt.-Befreiung** *f* STEUER exemption from VAT (*BrE*); **MwSt.-eingetragener**

Wertpapierhändler *m*, **Wertpapierhändlerin** *f* STEUER VAT registered trader (*BrE*); **MwSt.-Erklärung** *f* STEUER VAT return (*BrE*); **MwSt.-Kennummer** *f* STEUER VAT registration number (*BrE*); **MwSt.-Zahlung** *f* STEUER VAT payment (*BrE*)

MwSt.-eingetragene

m. W. v. *abbr* (*mit Wirkung von*) GESCHÄFT wef (*with effect from*)

M2 *abbr* (*Geldvolumen 2*) vw M2 (*money 2*)

N

N *abbr* (*Name*) GESCHÄFT name

nach 1. *adj* GESCHÄFT according to; **2.** *prep* GESCHÄFT post

Nachnahme *f* FINANZ, GESCHÄFT, IMP/EXP cash on delivery (*COD*)

Nachahmung *f* IND counterfeit; **~ eines Produkts anhand des Originals** GESCHÄFT reverse engineering

nachaktivieren *vt* VW post-capitalize

Nachbar- *in cpds* GESCHÄFT adjoining, neighbouring (*BrE*), neighboring (*AmE*); **Nachbarland** *nt* GESCHÄFT neighboring country (*AmE*), neighbouring country (*BrE*)

Nachbarschaft *f* GESCHÄFT neighborhood (*AmE*), neighbourhood (*BrE*); **Nachbarschaftseffekt** *m* VW neighborhood effect (*AmE*), neighbourhood effect (*BrE*); **Nachbarschaftsladen** *m* V&M corner shop (*BrE*), neighborhood store (*AmE*), mom-and-pop store (*AmE*)

Nachbar-: **Nachbarstaat** *m* GESCHÄFT neighboring country (*AmE*), neighbouring country (*BrE*)

Nachbearbeitung *f* IND finishing

Nachberatung *f* MGMNT debriefing

Nachbesprechung *f* MGMNT debriefing

nachbestellen *vt* GESCHÄFT reorder

Nachbestellung *f* GESCHÄFT repeat order; **Nachbestellungsformular** *nt* GESCHÄFT reorder form; **Nachbestellungsvordruck** *m* GESCHÄFT reorder form

Nachbildung *f* VW reproduction

Nachbörse *f* BÖRSE, VW after-hours market, kerb market, street dealings

nachbörslich: **~er Handel** *m* BÖRSE after-hours dealing, after-hours trading; **~e Kurse** *m pl* BÖRSE after-hours prices

Nachbuchung *f* RECHNUNG supplementary entry

nachdatieren *vt* KOMM postdate

nachdatiert *adj* KOMM postdated (*PD*)

Nachdruck: **mit ~ äußern** *phr* GESCHÄFT hammer home; **etw ~ verleihen** *phr* GESCHÄFT *Bemerkung* lend weight to

nachdrücklich *adj* GESCHÄFT vigorous

Nacherwerbsklausel *f* BANK after-acquired clause

Nachfaßbrief *m* GESCHÄFT, KOMM *Werbung* follow-up letter

nachfassen *vi* GESCHÄFT, KOMM follow up

nachfassend: **~e Untersuchung** *f* MATH follow-up

Nachfolgekonto *nt* FINANZ succeeding account

nachfolgen *vi* [+dat] GESCHÄFT succeed, trace

nachfolgend *adj* GESCHÄFT subsequent, succeeding; **~es Ereignis** *nt* RECHNUNG subsequent event

Nachfolger, in *m,f* GESCHÄFT follower, replacement (*BrE*), successor

nachforschen *vi* [+dat] GESCHÄFT investigate

Nachforschung *f* GESCHÄFT search; ◆ **Nachforschungen über etw anstellen** GESCHÄFT make investigations into

Nachforschung: **Nachforschungsbericht** *m* PATENT search report

Nachfrage *f* V&M *nach einem Produkt* call, VW demand; **~ nach Arbeitskräften** VW demand for labor (*AmE*), demand for labour (*BrE*), labor demand (*AmE*), labour demand (*BrE*); ◆ **die ~ abwürgen** V&M kill demand; **~ schaffen** VW create demand

Nachfrage: **Nachfrage- und Angebotselastizität** *f* VW elasticity of demand and supply; **Nachfrageausweitung** *f* V&M expansion of demand; **Nachfragebewertung** *f* VW demand assessment; **Nachfrageelastizität** *f* VW elasticity of demand

nachfragegesteuert: **~es Wachstum** *nt* GESCHÄFT demand-led growth

nachfrageinduziert: **~e Inflation** *f* GESCHÄFT, VW demand-pull inflation

Nachfrage: **Nachfrageinflation** *f* GESCHÄFT, VW demand-pull inflation, bottleneck inflation; **Nachfragekurve** *f* VW demand curve; **Nachfragemonopol** *nt* VW monopsony; **Nachfragemuster** *nt* VW demand pattern; **Nachfrageoligopol** *nt* VW demand oligopoly; **Nachfrageprognose** *f* V&M demand forecast; **Nachfragerückgang** *m* VW contractionary pressure; **Nachfrageschrumpfung** *f* V&M contraction of demand; **Nachfragesteuerung** *f* VW demand management; **Nachfragetabelle** *f* VW demand schedule; **Nachfrageüberschuß** *m* VW excess demand; **Nachfrageverschiebung** *f* V&M shift in demand

Nachfrist *f* RECHNUNG days of grace, grace period, RECHT *Verträge* additional respite

nachgeben *vi* BANK *Zinsen* sag, BÖRSE *Kurse* slide, sag, GESCHÄFT give in, *Nachfrage* sag, *Material* give, MGMNT *Auseinandersetzung* back down, V&M *Preise, Verkäufe* sag, VW *Aktienpreise* slacken

Nachgeben *nt* BANK, BÖRSE *der Kurse* slide, *der Zinsen* sagging, GESCHÄFT slippage, V&M sagging, VW *der Aktienpreise* slackening

nachgebend *adj* BANK *Zinsen*, BÖRSE, V&M *Nachfrage* sagging

Nachgebühr *f* KOMM additional charge, postage due; **Nachgebührstempel** *m* KOMM postage-due stamp

nachgelagert *adj* GESCHÄFT, VERWALT downstream; **~e Märkte** *m pl* GESCHÄFT downstream markets

nachgemacht *adj* BANK *Geld* counterfeit, IND man-made

nachgeordnet *adj* BÖRSE derivative, subordinate; **~e Optionsscheinemission** *f* BÖRSE subordinated warrant issue; **~e Schuldverschreibungsemission** *f* BÖRSE subordinated bond issue; **~e Wandelschuldverschreibungsemission** *f* BÖRSE subordinated convertible bond issue

nachgeschaltet: **~e Gesellschaft** *f* GESCHÄFT second tier company

nachhaken *vi* GESCHÄFT come back to, make further enquiries

nachhaltig *adj* GESCHÄFT, UMWELT, VW sustainable; **~e Entwicklung** *f* VW sustainable development; **~es Wachstum** *nt* VW sustainable growth; **~e**

Wachstumsrate *f* VW sustainable economic growth rate; **~e Wirkung** *f* GESCHÄFT, MEDIEN lasting effect

Nachhaltigkeit *f* UMWELT, VW sustainability

Nachhilfeunterricht *m* SOZIAL private tuition

nachhinein: im ~ *phr* VW ex post

Nachhol- *in cpds* GESCHÄFT, MEDIEN, VW backlog, catch-up; **Nachholbedarf** *m* GESCHÄFT backlog demand, VW backlog of demand, catch-up demand, pent-up demand; **Nachholenergie** *f* GESCHÄFT pent-up energy

nachindustriell: ~e Gesellschaft *f* VW post-industrial society

Nachkauf *m* GESCHÄFT repeat purchase

nach-Keynesianisch *adj* VW post-Keynesian

Nachkomme *m* RECHT *Erbe* scion, descendant, issue

nachkommen *vi* [+dat] GESCHÄFT *Entscheidung* act on, *Verpflichtungen* fulfill (*AmE*), fulfil (*BrE*), meet, *Zahlungen* keep up with, RECHT obey

nachkommunistisch *adj* GESCHÄFT post-Communist

Nachkriegs- *in cpds* VW postwar; **Nachkriegsaufschwung** *m* VW postwar boom; **Nachkriegsboom** *m* VW postwar boom; **Nachkriegszeit** *f* VW postwar period

nachladen 1. *vt* COMP reload; **2.** *vi* COMP reload

Nachlaß *m* FINANZ rebate, GESCHÄFT reduction, RECHNUNG trade discount, RECHT abatement, *Erbschaft* deceased estate; **kein ~** V&M no discount (*ND*); **~ außerhalb der Saison** V&M seasonal discount; **~ für frühzeitige Begleichung** FINANZ early-settlement rebate; **~ für frühzeitige Erfüllung einer Forderung** FINANZ early-settlement rebate; **~ nach Zahlung aller Verbindlichkeiten** RECHT residuary estate

nachlassen 1. *vt* GESCHÄFT *Kontrolle* relax, *Preise* reduce, MGMT *Kontrolle* relax; **2.** *vi* BÖRSE run low, GESCHÄFT wane, *Arbeiter, Geschäft, Nachfrage* slack off, slacken off, VW *Wirtschaftsaufschwung* slacken

Nachlassen *nt* GESCHÄFT slack, abatement, VW slackening

nachlassend *adj* VW flagging

nachlaßfähig *adj* TRANSP rebateable

Nachlaß: **Nachlaßgericht** *nt* RECHT probate court

nachlässig *adj* GESCHÄFT careless, slapdash; ♦ **~ sein** PERSON be slack; **~ arbeiten** GESCHÄFT skimp

Nachlaß: **Nachlaßregelung** *f* RECHT *Testament* estate planning; **Nachlaßsteuerfreibetrag** *m* STEUER unified credit; **Nachlaßvermögen** *nt* **vor Abzug der Erbschaftssteuer** STEUER gross estate; **Nachlaßverwalter** *m* GRUND *gerichtlich eingesetzter Treuhänder* estate administrator, estate executor, RECHT estate executor, estate manager, executor (*exec., exor, exr.*), estate administrator, administrator; **Nachlaßverwalterin** *f* RECHT executrix (*exec., exor, exr.*); **Nachlaßverwaltung** *f* GRUND estate administration

Nachmärkte *m pl* GESCHÄFT downstream markets

nachmittags *adv* GESCHÄFT post meridiem (*p.m.*)

Nachporto *nt* KOMM postage due

nachprüfbar *adj* GESCHÄFT, RECHNUNG verifiable

Nachprüfung *f* GESCHÄFT re-examination

nachrangig: ~e Aufgabe *f* COMP *Multitasking* background task; **~es Darlehen** *nt* FINANZ subordinated loan; **~es Eigentumsrecht** *nt* BANK subordinated interest; **~e Emission** *f* BÖRSE junior issue; **~er Gläubiger** *m* BANK junior creditor; **~e Hypothek** *f*

BANK second mortgage, submortgage, FINANZ second mortgage, GRUND junior mortgage (*AmE*); **~es Marktsegment** *nt* FINANZ junior market; **~es Pfandrecht** *nt* RECHT junior lien; **~e Refinanzierung** *f* FINANZ junior refunding; **~e Schuld** *f* FINANZ junior debt; **~er Schuldtitel** *m* FINANZ, GESCHÄFT, IND subordinate debt; **~e Schuldverschreibung** *f* BÖRSE subordinated bond, subordinated debenture; **~e Verarbeitung** *f* COMP *Multitasking* background processing; **~e Verbindlichkeiten** *f pl* FINANZ, GESCHÄFT, IND subordinate debt, RECHNUNG subordinated liabilities; **~es Vermögen** *nt* RECHNUNG subordinated assets; **~es Wertpapier** *nt* BÖRSE junior security (*AmE*); **~er Zins** *m* FINANZ subordinated interest

Nachricht *f* GESCHÄFT communication, KOMM bulletin, MEDIEN piece of news, POL communication

Nachrichten *f pl* GESCHÄFT, MEDIEN news; **jdm die ~ beibringen** *phr* KOMM break the news to sb; **jdm die ~ mitteilen** *phr* KOMM break the news to sb; **~ für die Titelseite** MEDIEN front-page news; **~ aus der Wirtschaft** MEDIEN, VW economic news; **Nachrichtenagentur** *f* GESCHÄFT, KOMM, MEDIEN *Presse* news agency (*BrE*), wire service (*AmE*); **Nachrichtenausschuß** *m* GESCHÄFT committee on information; **Nachrichtenbehandlung** *f* COMP, KOMM message handling; **Nachrichtenbild** *nt* MEDIEN news picture; **Nachrichtenblatt** *nt* V&M bulletin; **Nachrichtenbrett** *nt* KOMM Bulletin board service (*BBS*); **Nachrichtenende** *nt* COMP end of message (*EOM*); **Nachrichtenkonferenz** *f* MEDIEN news conference; **Nachrichtenmagazin** *nt* MEDIEN news magazine; **Nachrichtenquelle** *f* V&M message source; **Nachrichtenredakteur, in** *m,f* MEDIEN news editor; **Nachrichtenredaktion** *f* MEDIEN newsroom; **Nachrichtensatellit** *m* KOMM telecommunications satellite; **Nachrichtensperre** *f* MEDIEN news blackout; **Nachrichtensprecher, in** *m,f* MEDIEN newscaster; **Nachrichtentafel** *f* KOMM bulletin board (*BB*), notice board (*BrE*); **Nachrichtentechnik** *f* KOMM communications; **Nachrichtenübersicht** *f* MEDIEN news round up; **Nachrichtenverarbeitung** *f* VERWALT message processing; **Nachrichtenwesen** *nt* KOMM communications

Nachsatz *m* GESCHÄFT postscript

nachschauen *vt* COMP, GESCHÄFT, VERWALT *Informationen* look up

Nachschießen *nt* BÖRSE, FINANZ remargining

nachschlagen *vt* COMP, GESCHÄFT, VERWALT *Informationen* look up

Nachschlagetabelle *f* COMP lookup table

Nachschrift *f* KOMM postscript (*ps., PS*)

Nachschuß- *in cpds* BÖRSE additional, supplementary; **Nachschußforderung** *f* BÖRSE remargining, further call, additional cover, *Effektenhandel* margin call, GESCHÄFT, RECHNUNG, VERSICH additional payment

nachschüssig: ~e Rente *f* VERSICH annuity immediate

Nachschuß-: **Nachschußzahlung** *f* BÖRSE variation margin

Nachsendeanweisungen *f pl* TRANSP forwarding instructions

Nachsichtakkreditiv *nt* FINANZ term credit

Nachsichtwechsel *m* BANK time bill (*BrE*), time draft (*AmE*), FINANZ term bill

nächste: nächster Monat *m* BÖRSE nearest month; **nächsten Monats** *phr* (*n. M.*) KOMM proximo (*prox.*);

am nächsten Tag *phr* TRANSP next-day; **in nächster Zukunft** *phr* GESCHÄFT in the foreseeable future

nachstellen *vt* GESCHÄFT subordinate

Nachsteuer *f* FINANZ supplementary tax, RECHNUNG, STEUER after-tax basis; **Nachsteuerrendite** *f* RECHNUNG, STEUER after-tax yield

nachsuchen *vt*: ~ **um** GESCHÄFT apply for, request

Nacht- *in cpds* GESCHÄFT night; **Nachtarbeit** *f* PERSON night work; **Nachtarbeitszuschlag** *m* VW night differential; **Nachtausgabe** *f* einer Nachrichtensendung MEDIEN late edition; **Nachtbörse** *f* BÖRSE evening trade

Nachteil *m* GESCHÄFT disadvantage, V&M, VW disutility; **zum ~ von** *phr* GESCHÄFT to the detriment of

nachteilig 1. *adj* GESCHÄFT adverse, disadvantageous, prejudicial, VW adverse; **2.** *adv* GESCHÄFT adversely, VW adversely, disadvantageously; ◆ **sich ~ auswirken** GESCHÄFT be prejudicial to; **~ beeinflußt** GESCHÄFT adversely affected

nachteilig: **~e Geschäftsbedingungen** *f pl* VW adverse trading conditions; **~e Handelsbedingungen** *f pl* VW adverse trading conditions

Nachtrag *m* GESCHÄFT *Vertrag* addendum, IMP/EXP *Schiffahrt* post-entry, KOMM *Briefende* postscript (*ps.*, *PS*); **~ bei Ausscheiden aus der Firma** VERSICH ordinary payroll exclusion endorsement; **~ zur Erweiterung des Versicherungsschutzes** VERSICH extended coverage endorsement; **~ zur Pauschaldeckung gegen Kriminalität** VERSICH comprehensive crime endorsement

Nachträge *m pl* FINANZ Supplementary Estimates (*BrE*), POL supplementaries

nachträglich *adj* GESCHÄFT subsequent, PATENT supplementary; **~e Diskriminierung** *f* VW post-entry discrimination; **~es Image** *nt* V&M afterimage; **~e Unmöglichkeit** *f* der Leistung RECHT *Vertragsrecht* subsequent impossibility of performance; **~e Vergütung** *f* PERSON deferred compensation; **~er Vergütungsplan** *m* PERSON deferred compensation plan

Nachtrag: **Nachtragsetat** *m* FINANZ, POL supplementaries, Supplementary Estimates (*BrE*); **Nachtragshaushalt** *m* FINANZ supplemental budget; **Nachtragszeitraum** *m* STEUER supplementary period

Nacht-: **Nachtreise** *f* FREI overnight travel; **Nachtsafe** *m* BANK night safe; **Nachtschalter** *m* BANK night depository; **Nachtschicht** *f* PERSON night shift, graveyard shift (*infrml*); **eine Nachtschicht mit Personal ausstatten** *phr* PERSON man a night shift; **Nachttresor** *m* BANK night depository, night safe; **Nachtverbindung** *f* TRANSP night trunk; **Nachtwächterstaat** *m* VW night watchman state

Nachverkauf *m* V&M after sales

Nachvermächtnisnehmer *m* RECHT residuary legatee

Nachverrechnung *f* VERSICH adjustment; **Nachverrechnungsprämie** *f* VERSICH adjustment premium

Nachverzollung *f* IMP/EXP, TRANSP post-entry

nachwachsend: **~er Rohstoff** *m* UMWELT, VW renewable resource; **nicht ~er Rohstoff** *m* UMWELT, VW nonrenewable resource

Nachwahl *f* POL by-election

nachweisbar *adj* GESCHÄFT verifiable, *Fehler, Defekt* demonstrable, RECHNUNG verifiable; **~er Berufsverlauf** *m* PERSON *Bewerbung* track record

nachweisen *vt* BANK account for

nachweislich: **~er Erfolg** *m* GESCHÄFT good track record

Nachwirkung *f* GESCHÄFT aftereffect

Nachwuchsförderung *f* MGMNT *Führungskräfte* executive training

Nachzahlung *f* PERSON *Lohn, Gehälter* back pay, back payment

Nachzügler *m* BÖRSE, V&M *in der Mode* laggard (*jarg*)

Nachzugs- *in cpds* BÖRSE, GESCHÄFT deferred (*def.*); **Nachzugsterminkontrakte** *m pl* BÖRSE deferred futures; **Nachzugsterminwaren** *f pl* BÖRSE deferred futures

Nacktoption *f* BÖRSE naked option

Nadelzeit *f* MEDIEN needle time

nagelneu *adj* infrml GESCHÄFT brand-new

nah: **~e Zukunft** *f* GESCHÄFT forseeable future, near future

Nahelegen *nt*: **~ der Kündigung** PERSON dehiring

Nahrungsmittel *nt pl* GESCHÄFT foodstuffs; **Nahrungsmittelhilfe** *f* VW food aid; **Nahrungsmittelindustrie** *f* IND, UMWELT food-processing industry; **Nahrungsmittelüberschuß** *m* VW food surplus; **Nahrungsmittelverarbeitung** *f* IND food processing; **Nahrungsmittelversorgung** *f* VW food supply

Nahverkehr *m* TRANSP short haul; **Nahverkehrsfluggesellschaft** *f* TRANSP commuter airline; **Nahverkehrsflugzeug** *nt* TRANSP commuter aircraft

nah: **~ verwandter Beruf** *m* PERSON closely connected profession

Name *m* (*N*) GESCHÄFT name; **~ und Anschrift** *f* KOMM name and address; **auf den Namen ausgestelltes Konnossement** *nt* IMP/EXP, TRANSP bill of lading issued to a named party, straight bill of lading; ◆ **im Namen von** GESCHÄFT on behalf of; **mit Namen bekannt sein** GESCHÄFT be known by name; **nur dem Namen nach** GESCHÄFT nominally

namenlos *adj* GESCHÄFT anonymous, anonymously

Name: **Namensaktie** *f* BÖRSE personal share, registered share, RECHNUNG registered share; **Namenskonnossement** *nt* IMP/EXP, TRANSP non-negotiable bill of lading, straight bill of lading; **ohne Namensnennung** *phr* GESCHÄFT anonymously; **Namensschild** *nt* GESCHÄFT *an der Person* name badge, *an der Tür* nameplate

namentlich: **~ bekannt sein** *phr* GESCHÄFT be known by name

namhaft *adj* GESCHÄFT renowned, *Geldbetrag* substantial

Nash-Verhandlungen *f pl* VW *Spieltheorie* Nash bargaining

nässegeschützt *adj* GESCHÄFT damp-proof

naß: **nasse Ware** *f* infrml GESCHÄFT wet stock

Naßtextilabfall *m* TRANSP, UMWELT wet textile waste

Nation *f* POL nation

national: **~e Behörde** *f* VERWALT national agency; **~er Durchschnitt** *m* VW national average; **~e Fluggesellschaft** *f* FREI, TRANSP domestic airline, national airline; **~es Gesetz** *nt* RECHT national law; **~e Gesetzgebung** *f* RECHT national legislation; **~es Interesse** *nt* POL national interest; **~es Naturschutzgebiet** *nt* UMWELT national nature reserve; **~e Quote** *f* VW national quota; **~e Schallnorm** *f* UMWELT national noise standard; **~er**

Standardladeschein *m* IMP/EXP, TRANSP national standard shipping note (*NSSN*); **~er standardmäßiger Ladeschein** *m* IMP/EXP, TRANSP national standard shipping note (*NSSN*); **~er standardmäßiger Warenbegleitschein** *m* IMP/EXP, TRANSP national standard shipping note (*NSSN*); **~e Standardversandanzeige** *f* IMP/EXP, TRANSP national standard shipping note (*NSSN*); **~e Vereinigung** *f* **der Schiffsbauer und -reparateure** TRANSP Shipbuilders' and Repairers' National Association (*BrE*)

National: **Nationalbank** *f* BANK national bank (*AmE*)

Nationalismus *m* POL nationalism

National: **Nationalökonomie** *f* POL political economy, vw economics, public economics, political economy

NATO *abbr* (*Nordatlantikpakt*) POL NATO (*North Atlantic Treaty Organization*)

Natur- *in cpds* GESCHÄFT, UMWELT, VW natural

Natural- *in cpds* GESCHÄFT in kind; **Naturalgeld** *nt* BÖRSE commodity standard; **Naturalleistung** *f* GESCHÄFT allowance in kind, payment in kind; **Naturallohn** *m* GESCHÄFT allowance in kind; **Naturalobligation** *f* RECHT *nicht einklagbare Verpflichtung* imperfect obligation; **Naturalpächter** *m* VW sharecropper (*AmE*); **Naturaltausch** *m* VW barter; **Naturalwirtschaft** *f* VW barter economy

Natur-: **Naturkost** *f* SOZIAL health foods

natürlich: **~er Arbeitskräfteabgang** *m* PERSON *Kürzung des Personalbestands* natural wastage; **~e Arbeitslosigkeit** *f* VW natural rate of unemployment; **~es Bevölkerungswachstum** *nt* VW natural population increase; **~e Grenzlinien** *f pl* GRUND metes and bounds; **~e Hilfsquellen** *f pl* UMWELT, VW natural resources; **~es Monopol** *nt* VW natural monopoly; **~e Pause** *f* V&M natural break; **~e Person** *f* PATENT natural person; **~er Preis** *m* VW natural price; **~e Rechte** *nt pl* RECHT natural rights; **~e Ressourcen** *f pl* UMWELT, VW natural resources; **~er Schwund** *m* VW natural wastage; **~er Verschleiß** *m* VW natural wastage, natural wear and tear; **~e Wachstumsrate** *f* VW natural rate of growth; **~e Zahl** *f* COMP natural number; **~er Zins** *m* VW natural rate of interest

naturrechtlich: **~e Ansprüche** *m pl* RECHT natural rights

Natur-: **Naturressourcen** *f pl* UMWELT, VW natural resources; **Naturschätze** *m pl* UMWELT, VW natural resources; **Naturschutz** *m* UMWELT conservation; **Naturschützer, in** *m,f* UMWELT conservationist; **Naturverschwendung** *f* UMWELT natural wastage

Navigation *f* TRANSP navigation

NB *abbr* (*nota bene*) GESCHÄFT NB (*nota bene*), please note

Neben- *in cpds* BÖRSE, GESCHÄFT, PERSON subsidiary, sub-ancillary; **Nebenabrede** *f* GESCHÄFT, IND, PERSON subcontract, RECHT sub agreement, subcontract, supplementary agreement; **Nebenabsprache** *f* VW side deal; **Nebenanschluß** *m* KOMM telephone extension (*X*); **Nebenausgaben** *f pl* GESCHÄFT accessories, accessory charges; **Nebenbedeutung** *f* V&M secondary meaning; **Nebenbedingung** *f* VW constraint; **Nebenbeschäftigung** *f* PERSON sideline job, second job; **Nebeneingang** *m* GESCHÄFT tradesman's entrance; **Nebeneinkünfte** *pl* **der Tätigkeit** PERSON perks of the job; **Nebenentwicklung** *f* IND spin-off; **Nebenerwerb** *m* PERSON secondary employment; **Nebenforderung** *f* RECHNUNG secondary claim; **Nebengebäude** *nt* GRUND outhouse; **Nebengebühren** *f pl* GESCHÄFT accessory charges, accessories; **Nebengleis** *nt* TRANSP *Eisenbahn* bay, side track (*AmE*), siding

nebenamtlich: **~er Geschäftsführer** *m*, **~e Geschäftsführerin** *f* MGMNT non-executive director, outside director

nebenher *adv* GESCHÄFT on the side

Neben-: **Nebenindustrie** *f* IND non-basic industry; **Nebenkasse** *f* RECHNUNG petty cash; **ohne Nebenklauseln** *phr* GESCHÄFT no strings attached; **Nebenkontenbuch** *nt* RECHNUNG subsidiary ledger; **Nebenkontensystem** *nt* RECHNUNG subsidiary accounting system; **Nebenkonto** *nt* RECHNUNG subsidiary account; **Nebenkosten** *pl* FINANZ incidental charge, incidental expenses, PERSON incidental expenses, GRUND carrying charge, RECHNUNG extra charges; **Nebenleistung** *f* PERSON perk (*infrml*), perquisite (*frml*), VERWALT fringe benefit; **Nebenleistungen** *f pl* GESCHÄFT ancillary services; **Nebenlinie** *f* TRANSP *Eisenbahn* branch line, V&M by-line; **Nebenlizenz** *f* GESCHÄFT, PATENT sublicence (*BrE*), sublicense (*AmE*); **Nebenmarkt** *m* BÖRSE fringe market, V&M sideline market; **Nebenprodukt** *nt* GESCHÄFT, IND, V&M *Abfallprodukt* by-product, spin-off, vw by-product, secondary product; **ein Nebenprodukt erzeugen** *phr* VW spin off; **Nebenrisiko** *nt* VERSICH allied peril; **Nebensache** *f* GESCHÄFT peripheral matter

nebensächlich *adj* GESCHÄFT accessory, peripheral, secondary

Neben-: **Nebensaison** *f* GESCHÄFT low season, off-season; **Nebensaisonpreis** *m* FREI low-season fare; **Nebenschaden** *m* TRANSP sympathetic damage; **Nebenstelle** *f* GESCHÄFT suboffice, KOMM telephone extension (*X*); **Nebentarif** *m* TRANSP sideline point; **Nebentätigkeit** *f* PERSON *nicht angemeldet*, VW moonlighting (*infrml*); **Nebenverdienst** *m* GESCHÄFT, PERSON, STEUER additional earnings; **Nebenvereinbarung** *f* VERWALT covenant; **Nebenvertrag** *m* GESCHÄFT, IND, PERSON, RECHT subcontract; **Nebenwahl** *f* POL by-election; **Nebenwirkungen** *f pl* GESCHÄFT side effects, vw spillover

Negativ- *in cpds* GESCHÄFT negative

negativ *adj* FINANZ, GESCHÄFT, RECHNUNG, STEUER, VW adverse, negative; ♦ **eine ~e Werbekampagne führen** V&M go negative (*jarg*); **einen ~en Wahlkampf führen** POL go negative (*jarg*)

negativ: **~es Abzielen** *nt jarg* POL *Wahlkampf*, V&M *Werbung* negative targeting (*jarg*), **~er Angebotsschock** *m* VW adverse supply shock; **~es Betriebskapital** *nt* RECHNUNG negative working capital; **~er Cashflow** *m* FINANZ, RECHNUNG negative cash flow; **~es Eigenkapital** *nt* VW negative net worth; **~e Einkommensteuer** *f* STEUER negative income tax (*NIT*), reverse income tax; **~e Elastizität** *f* VW negative elasticity; **~e Ersparnis** *f* VW dissaving; **~er externer Effekt** *m* VW bad; **~er Firmenwert** *m* GESCHÄFT, RECHNUNG bad will; **~er geldwerter Ausgleichsbetrag** *m* FINANZ negative monetary compensatory amount; **~es Gut** *nt* VW bad; **~e Hebelwirkung** *f* RECHNUNG reverse gearing (*BrE*), reverse leverage (*AmE*); **~e Korrelation** *f* MATH negative correlation; **~er Nettowert** *m* VW deficit net worth; **~er Nutzen** *m* V&M, VW disutility; **~e Opportunitätskosten** *pl* GESCHÄFT avoidable costs; **~e Preisentwicklung** *f* VW adverse price movement; **~e Rückkopplung** *f* COMP negative feedback; **~e Rücklagen** *f pl* RECHNUNG negative reserve; **~er Schrägstrich** *m* COMP *Schriftzeichen* backslash; **~e Steueraufwendungen** *f pl* STEUER negative tax expenditure; **~er Vorteil** *m* GESCHÄFT minus advantage; **~er Währungsausgleichsbetrag** *m* FINANZ negative monetary compensatory amount; **~e Zielbildung** *f* POL, V&M negative targeting; **~es Zinsgefälle** *nt* BÖRSE negative interest rate gap; **~e Zinsstrukturkurve** *f* VW negative yield curve

Negativ-: **Negativamortisierung** *f* FINANZ negative amortization; **Negativdatei** *f* BANK negative file; **Negativerklärung** *f* BANK negative pledge; **Negativklausel** *f* BANK negative pledge clause; **Negativklischee** *nt* V&M reverse plate; **Negativsummenspiel** *nt* VW negative sum game; **Negativzins** *m* BANK interest penalty; **Negativzins** *m* **bei vorzeitiger Verfügung über Kündigungsgelder** BÖRSE, FINANZ early-withdrawal penalty

Negoziierbarkeit *f* GESCHÄFT, VW tradeability

negoziierend: **~e Bank** *f* BANK *Akkreditiv* negotiating bank

Negoziierung *f* GESCHÄFT negotiation

Negoziierungskredit *m* VW negotiation credit

Nehmerbank *f* BANK borrowing bank

neigen *vi*: **~ zu** PERSON lean towards; **dazu ~, etw zu tun** *phr* GESCHÄFT tend to do sth

Neigung *f* GESCHÄFT propensity, tendency, preference, TRANSP slope, VW propensity

Nenn- *in cpds* GESCHÄFT nominal

nennen *vt* GESCHÄFT *Konto* state

nennenswert *adj* GESCHÄFT appreciable

Nenner *m* GESCHÄFT denominator

Nenn-: **Nennmaß** *nt* GESCHÄFT basic size; **Nennpferdestärke** *f* GESCHÄFT nominal horsepower (*NHP*); **Nennrisiko** *nt* BÖRSE face risk

Nennwert *m* BÖRSE principal value, RECHNUNG nominal value, par value, VW denomination (*denom.*); ◆ **über dem ~** BÖRSE, GESCHÄFT above par; **über dem ~ notiert werden** BÖRSE stand at a premium, stand at a discount; **zum ~** BÖRSE at face value, at par, FINANZ, GESCHÄFT at par; **1 % des Nennwerts** BÖRSE, FINANZ point

Nennwert: **Nennwertaktie** *f* BÖRSE par value share

nennwertlos *adj* BÖRSE no-par value; **~e Aktie** *f* BÖRSE no-par stock, no-par-value share, VW nonpar share

Neo- *pref* GESCHÄFT neo-, new; **Neo-Keynesianer, in** *m,f* VW neo-Keynesian, new Keynesian; **Neoklassik** *f* VW neoclassical theory

neoklassisch: **~e Theorie** *f* VW neoclassical theory

Neo-: **Neo-Korporatismus** *m* VW neocorporatism; **Neo-Malthusianer, in** *m,f* VW neo-Malthusian; **Neo-Marxist, in** *m,f* VW neo-Marxist; **Neo-Merkantilismus** *m* VW neomercantilism

Neonschild *nt* GESCHÄFT neon sign

Neo-: **Neoprotektionismus** *m* VW new protectionism; **Neo-Ricardianer, in** *m,f* VW neo-Ricardian

neo-ricardianisch: **~e Theorie** *f* VW neo-Ricardian theory

NEP *abbr* (*Neue Ökonomische Politik*) VW NEP (*New Economic Policy*)

Nepper *m infrml* V&M shark (*infrml*), rip-off merchant (*infrml*)

Nervenzentrum *nt* MGMNT nerve center (*AmE*), nerve centre (*BrE*)

netto *adv* GESCHÄFT net; ◆ **~ erbringen** FINANZ net; **~ verdienen** FINANZ net

netto: **~ realisierte Kapitalgewinne** *m pl* BÖRSE net realized capital gains

Netto- *in cpds* GESCHÄFT net; **Nettoabsatz** *m* RECHNUNG net sales; **Nettoakquisitionen** *f pl* VW net acquisitions; **Nettoallphasenumsatzsteuer** *f* STEUER all-stage net turnover tax; **Nettoanteil** *m* BÖRSE net worth, VW net equity; **Nettoauftragseingang** *m* RECHNUNG net sales; **Nettoauslandsinvestition** *f* RECHNUNG net foreign investment; **Nettoauslandsvermögen** *nt* BANK net foreign assets; **Nettoausleihung** *f* BANK net lending; **Nettoausleihungen** *f pl* **des Staates** VW net lending by the public sector; **Nettoauszahlung** *f* VW net disbursement; **Nettobargeld** *nt* FINANZ net liquid funds; **Nettobargeldbedarf** *m* FINANZ net cash requirement (*NCR*); **Nettobedingungen** *f pl* IMP/EXP, TRANSP net terms (*Nt*); **Nettobeitrag** *m* RECHNUNG net contribution; **Nettobestandhaltekosten** *pl* FINANZ negative carry; **Nettobetrag** *m* VW net amount

Nettobetrieb- *in cpds* RECHNUNG net trading; **Nettobetriebseinkommen** *nt* RECHNUNG net operating income; **Nettobetriebsgewinn** *m* RECHNUNG net operating profit, net trading surplus; **Nettobetriebskapital** *nt* RECHNUNG, VW working capital; **Nettobetriebsverlust** *m* RECHNUNG net operating loss

Netto-: **Nettobuchwert** *m* FINANZ net book value; **Netto-Cashflow** *m* RECHNUNG net cash flow, net cash inflow; **Netto-Delta-Position** *f* BÖRSE position net delta; **Nettodividende** *f* BÖRSE, RECHNUNG net dividend; **Nettoeigenkapital** *nt* RECHNUNG net equity; **Nettoeinkommen** *nt* FINANZ clear profit, PERSON net pay, RECHNUNG below-the-line revenue, clear income; **Nettoeinkünfte** *pl* **von Auslandsimmobilien** GRUND net property income from abroad; **Nettoeinnahmen** *f pl* RECHNUNG net receipts; **Nettoeinnahmen-Pool** *m* TRANSP net receipts pool; **Nettoertrag** *m* RECHNUNG below-the-line revenue; **Nettoertrag** *m* **aus Wertpapieren** VW net security gain; **Nettoerwerb** *m* **finanzieller Vermögenswerte** FINANZ net acquisition of financial assets (*NAFA*); **Nettofonds** *m* BANK net liquid funds; **Nettogeldbedarf** *m* FINANZ net cash requirement (*NCR*); **Nettogewicht** *nt* GESCHÄFT net weight

Nettogewinn *m* FINANZ net profit, RECHNUNG net gain, net income; **~ für das laufende Jahr** RECHNUNG net profit for the current year; **~ je Stammaktie** RECHNUNG net income per share of common stock

Netto-: **Nettogewinner, in** *m,f* VW net gainer

Nettogewinn: **Nettogewinnspanne** *f* FINANZ, RECHNUNG, VW net margin

Netto-: **Nettoinlandsinvestition** *f* RECHNUNG net domestic investment; **Nettoinventarwert** *m* FINANZ, RECHNUNG net asset value (*NAV*)

Nettoinvestition *f* BANK, VW net investment; **Nettoinvestitionsaufwand** *m* VW net capital expenditure, net capital spending; **Nettoinvestitionsausgaben** *f pl* VW net capital expenditure; **Nettoinvestitionsposition** *f* BANK net investment position

Nettokapital *nt* BÖRSE, FINANZ, RECHNUNG, VW net capital; **Nettokapitalaufwand** *m* VW net capital expenditure; **Nettokapitalbedarf** *m* BÖRSE net capital require-ment; **Nettokapitalgewinn** *m* FINANZ, VW net asset value; **Nettokapitalverlust** *m* RECHNUNG net capital loss; **Nettokapitalwert** *m* FINANZ, VW net capital gain

Netto-: **Nettokosten** *pl* RECHNUNG net cost

Nettokredit *m* BÖRSE net credit; **Nettokreditposition** *f* BÖRSE position net credit; **Nettokreditvergabe** *f* **der öffentlichen Hand** VW net lending by the public sector

Netto-: **Nettoliquidität** *f* BANK net liquid funds; **Nettolohn** *m* GESCHÄFT, PERSON take-home pay; **Nettomietfläche** *f* GRUND net leasable area; **Nettomietvertrag** *m* RECHT net lease (*AmE*); **Nettomittelzuweisung** *f* BANK available balance; **Nettonachlaßvermögen** *nt* STEUER net estate; **Nettopachtfläche** *f* GRUND net leasable area; **Nettopachtvertrag** *m* RECHT net lease (*AmE*); **Nettoprämie** *f* BÖRSE net premium; **Nettopreis** *m* V&M net price; **Nettoproduktgewinn** *m* VW direct product profitability (*DPP*); **Nettoproduktionswert** *m* VW net output; **Nettoprovisionseinkommen** *nt* RECHNUNG net commission income; **Nettorealisationswert** *m* RECHNUNG net realizable value; **Nettorealkapital** *nt* **pro Aktie** BÖRSE net tangible assets per share; **Nettoregistertonnage** *f* GESCHÄFT net registered tonnage; **Nettoregistertonne** *f* GESCHÄFT net register ton (*NRT*); **Nettoregistertonnengehalt** *m* GESCHÄFT net register tonnage; **Nettorendite** *f* RECHNUNG net rate of return, net yield; **Nettorendite** *f* **nach Steuern** RECHNUNG, STEUER net rate of return after tax; **Nettoreserveanpassungsbetrag** *m* RECHNUNG net reserve adjustment amount; **Nettosollsaldo** *m* BÖRSE net debit; **Nettosollsaldo** *m* **der Kunden** BÖRSE customers' net debit balance; **Nettosozialprodukt** *nt* VW net national product; **Nettosozialprodukt** *nt* **zu Faktorkosten** VW net national income; **Nettosteuergewinn** *m* RECHNUNG taxable net gain; **Nettostimmenverrechnung** *f* FINANZ net voting, vote netting; **Nettotauschgeschäfts-bedingungen** *f pl* IMP/EXP net barter terms of trade; **Nettotilgungsvolumen** *nt* BANK total net redemptions; **Nettotonnage** *f* GESCHÄFT net tonnage; **Netto-transaktion** *f* BÖRSE net transaction; **Nettoumlaufvermögen** *nt* FINANZ net current assets, RECHNUNG net current assets, net quick assets, net working capital, VW net working capital; **Nettoumsatzrendite** *f* RECHNUNG net profit margin; **Nettoverdienst** *m* PERSON *Arbeitsentgelt* real pay, RECHNUNG net earnings; **Nettoverlust** *m* FINANZ clear loss, RECHNUNG net loss; **Nettovermögen** *nt* FINANZ actual net worth, net equity, RECHNUNG actual net worth, net assets, net recorded assets; **Netto-vermögensaufstellung** *f* RECHNUNG statement of net assets; **Nettovermögensertrag** *m* RECHNUNG return on net assets; **Nettowert** *m* BÖRSE net worth, RECHNUNG net value, net worth; **Nettowohlfahrtsverlust** *m* VW deadweight loss

Nettozins *m* VW pure interest rate; **Nettozinseinkommen** *nt* BANK net interest income; **Nettozinsertrag** *m* FINANZ net interest yield; **Nettozinssatz** *m* BANK face interest rate, net rate; **Nettozinsspanne** *f* RECHNUNG net interest margin

Netz *nt* COMP network, *Strom* mains (*BrE*), supply network (*AmE*); **~ von Verkaufsstellen** V&M network of sales outlets; **Netzadapter** *m* COMP current adaptor (*AmE*), mains adaptor (*BrE*); **Netzanalyse** *f* COMP

network analysis; **Netzanwender** *m* COMP, VW networker; **Netzarchitektur** *f* COMP network architecture; **Netzausfall** *m* COMP power failure; **Netzbrooke** *f* TRANSP cargo net; **Netzsoftware** *f* COMP networking software; **Netzstrom** *m* IND power; **Netzübergang** *m* COMP *Vernetzung* gateway; **Netzübergangsrechner** *m* COMP *Vernetzung* gateway

Netzwerk *nt* COMP network; **an ein ~ angeschlossener Heimarbeiter** *m*, **an ein ~ angeschlossene Heimarbeiterin** *f* COMP, VW networker; **Netz-werkanalyse** *f* MGMNT network analysis; **Netzwerk-betrieb** *m* COMP networking; **Netzwerksoftware** *f* COMP networking software; **Netzwerkvolkswirtschaft** *f* VW networking economy; **Netzwerkvorrechner** *m* COMP front-end computer

neu *adj* BANK hot (*infrml*), GESCHÄFT new (*N*); ♦ **~ für alt** VERSICH new for old; **~e Aufträge sichern** GESCHÄFT secure new orders; **~ booten** *jarg* COMP reboot; **in ~er Eigentümerschaft** GESCHÄFT under new ownership; **~ eingeben** COMP retype; **~es Geld bevorzugt** BÖRSE new money preferred; **~ gestalten** GESCHÄFT reform; **~ gewinnen** UMWELT *Boden, Land* reclaim; **einen ~en Höchstwert festsetzen** VW set a new high; **ein ~es Image schaffen für** V&M re-image; **~ kalkulieren** FINANZ *Schuld* recast; **~ laden** COMP reload; **unter ~er Leitung** VW under new ownership; **eine ~e Leitung haben** MGMNT be under new management; **ein ~es Modell auf den Markt bringen** V&M launch a new model; **~ schreiben** COMP *Software* rewrite; **~ urladen** COMP reboot

Neu- *in cpds* GESCHÄFT new

neu: **~e Cambridge-Wirtschaftstheorie** *f* VW new Cambridge economics (*BrE*); **~e Charter** *f* TRANSP new charter; **~es Deck** *nt* TRANSP new deck (*ND*); **~e Ernte** *f* VW new crop (*N/C*); **~er Föderalismus** *m* POL new federalism

Neu: **~es Gemeinschaftsinstrument** *nt* VW *EG* New Community Instrument (*NCI*)

neu: **~es Geschäft** *nt* GESCHÄFT new business; **~er Inhaber** *m* MGMNT under new management; **~e internationale Arbeitsteilung** *f* VW new international division of labor (*AmE*) (*NIDL*), new international division of labour (*BrE*) (*NIDL*); **~e keynesianische Makroökonomen** *m pl* VW Eclectic Keynesians; **~e klassische Wirtschaftstheorie** *f* VW new classical economics; **~er Kontobericht** *m* BÖRSE new account report

Neu: **~e Linke** *f* POL, VW New Left

neu: **~es Marketing** *nt* V&M remarketing; **~e Mikroökonomik** *f* VW new microeconomics

Neu: **~e Ökonomische Politik** *f* (*NEP*) VW New Economic Policy (*NEP*)

neu: **~er Realismus** *m* PERSON new realism (*BrE*)

Neu: **~e Rechte** *f* POL, VW New Right

neu: **~e Technologien** *f pl* GESCHÄFT, IND new technol-ogies; **~e technologische Errungenschaften** *f pl* IND new technologies; **~e Weltordnung** *f* POL new world order; **~e Weltwirtschaftsordnung** *f* VW New Interna-tional Economic Order (*NIEO*)

Neu: **~er Wirtschaftsmechanismus** *m* VW New Eco-nomic Mechanism

neuabfassen *vt* VERWALT rewrite

Neu-: **Neuaktie** *f* BÖRSE new share

neuanzeigen *vt* COMP *Bildschirm* refresh

neuauferlegen *vt* GESCHÄFT reimpose

Neu-: **Neuauflage** *f* MEDIEN new edition, reprint

neuaufzwingen *vt* GESCHÄFT reimpose

neuaushandeln *vt* GESCHÄFT renegotiate

Neu-: **Neubaugebiet** *nt* GRUND housing development

neubedenken *vt* GESCHÄFT reconsider

Neu-: **Neubelebung** *f* GESCHÄFT, VW revitalization

neuberechnen *vt* MATH recalculate

Neu-: **Neubesiedlung** *f* GESCHÄFT resettlement

neubetonen *vt* GESCHÄFT re-emphasize

neubewerten *vt* RECHNUNG, VW revalue

Neubewertung *f* FINANZ revaluation; **auf ~ beruhender Gewinn** *m* RECHNUNG appreciated surplus; **~ des Vermögens** RECHNUNG revaluation of assets; **~ von Vermögenswerten** FINANZ revaluation of assets; **Neubewertungsreserve** *f* RECHNUNG revaluation reserves

Neu-: **Neuemission** *f* BÖRSE new issue

Neuentwicklung *f* IND, PATENT, V&M innovation

Neuerer *m* IND, PATENT, V&M innovator

neueröffnet *adj* MGMNT under new management

Neuerung *f* IND, PATENT, V&M innovation

Neuerungen: **~ einführen** *phr* IND, PATENT, V&M innovate

neueste: **~r Entwicklungsstand** *m* GESCHÄFT state of the art; **~ Information** *f* GESCHÄFT update; **die ~ Mode** *f* GESCHÄFT the latest fashion; **jdn über etw auf den ~n Stand bringen** *phr* GESCHÄFT bring sb up to date on sth; **~ Technik** *f* IND advanced engineering; **~ Technologie** *f* IND advanced technology

neufassen *vt* GESCHÄFT rewrite

Neu-: **Neufestsetzung** *f* **der Währungsparitäten** VW currency realignment; **Neufestsetzung** *f* **der Wechselkurse** VW parity realignment; **Neugestaltung** *f* FINANZ reorganization

neugewählt *adj* GESCHÄFT newly elected

Neugier *f* V&M curiosity; **~ erregende Kampagne** *f* V&M teaser campaign

Neu-: **Neugründung** *f* GESCHÄFT re-establishment, VW *eines Unternehmens* start-up

Neuheit *f* PATENT novelty; **Neuheitswert** *m* V&M novelty value

Neuigkeit *f* MEDIEN piece of news

Neu-: **Neuland betreten** *phr* GESCHÄFT break new ground; **Neuland erschließen** *phr* GESCHÄFT break new ground; **Neuordnung** *f* MGMNT restructuring; **Neupositionierung** *f* V&M repositioning; **Neuregelung** *f* GESCHÄFT revision; **Neustart** *m* COMP *System, Hardware* restart

neustarten *vt* COMP *System, Hardware* restart

neutral *adj* GESCHÄFT neutral, POL non-aligned; ♦ **~ bis Baisse** BÖRSE neutral to bearish; **~ bis fallend** BÖRSE neutral to bearish; **~ bleiben** GESCHÄFT sit on the fence; **in ~em Umschlag versenden** KOMM send under plain cover; **sich ~ verhalten** GESCHÄFT sit on the fence; **in ~er Verpackung versenden** KOMM send under plain cover

neutral: **~e Aufwendungen** *f pl* RECHNUNG exceptional expenses; **~es Ergebnis** *nt* VW nonoperating result; **~ gedeckte Baisseposition** *f* BÖRSE neutral covered short; **~ gedeckte Hausseposition** *f* BÖRSE neutral covered long; **~es Gleichgewicht** *nt* VW metastable equilibrium; **~er Haushaltsplan** *m* POL neutral budget;

~er technischer Fortschritt *m* VW neutral technical progress

Neutralismus *m* GESCHÄFT neutralism

Neutralität *f* POL neutrality

Neu-: **Neuverfilmung** *f* FREI, MEDIEN *Film* remake

neuverhandelt: **~e Hypothek** *f* GRUND renegotiated rate mortgage

Neu-: **Neuverhandlung** *f* GESCHÄFT renegotiation

neuveröffentlichen *vt* MEDIEN republish

Neu-: **Neuverpackung** *f* TRANSP rebagging

neuverteilen *vt* RECHNUNG reallocate

Neu-: **Neuverteilung** *f* FINANZ reallocation; **Neuzuordnung** *f* COMP reassignment; **Neuzuteilung** *f* FINANZ reallocation; **Neuzuweisung** *f* COMP reallocation

New: **~ Deal** *m* POL New Deal (*AmE*)

Niche *f* PERSON, V&M niche

Nicht- *in cpds* GESCHÄFT non-; **Nichtabzugsfähigkeit** *f* **der Arbeitgeberbeiträge** PERSON nondeductibility of employer contributions; **Nichtanerkennung** *f* STEUER disallowance; **Nichtanfechtbarkeitsklausel** *f* VERSICH noncontestability clause

nichtansässig: **~e Gesellschaft** *f* RECHT nonresident company

Nicht-: **Nichtausführung** *f* RECHT nonexecution

nichtausgeschüttet: **~e Dividende** *f* FINANZ passed dividend

Nichtbank- *in cpds* BANK, FINANZ, VW nonbank; **Nichtbank-Bankgeschäfte** *nt pl* BANK nonbank banking; **Nichtbankeneinlage** *f* FINANZ nonbank deposit; **Nichtbankensektor** *m* FINANZ nonbank sector; **Nichtbankunternehmen** *nt* VW nonfinancial corporation

Nicht-: **Nichtbeeinträchtigungsklausel** *f* GRUND, RECHT nondisturbance clause; **Nichtbefolgung** *f* STEUER failure to comply; **Nichtbesteuerung** *f* STEUER tax umbrella; **Nicht-Bestreiten** *nt* RECHT nolo contendere

nichtbetrieblich: **~e Einnahmen** *f pl* RECHNUNG nonoperating revenue; **~e Kosten** *pl* RECHNUNG nonoperating expense

Nicht-: **Nichtbezahlung** *f* GESCHÄFT nonpayment; **Nichteinhaltung** *f* **einer Anordnung** RECHT noncompliance with an order; **Nichteinlösen** *nt* BANK dishonor (*AmE*), dishonour (*BrE*); **Nichteinmischung** *f* VW nonintervention; **Nichteinmischungspolitik** *f* GESCHÄFT, VW hands-off policy; **Nichterbringung** *f* **der Gegenleistung** GESCHÄFT *Nichtzahlung* failure of consideration

nichtbudgetiert: **~ insgesamt** *adj* FINANZ total nonbudget

Nichterfüllung *f* RECHT nonexecution, nonfulfillment (*AmE*), nonfulfilment (*BrE*), nonperformance; **~ einer Position** BÖRSE fail position; **~ eines Vertrags** RECHT nonfulfillment of contract (*AmE*), nonfulfilment of contract (*BrE*)

Nicht-: **Nichterscheinen** *nt* FREI no-show, GESCHÄFT absence, RECHT *vor Gericht* absence, failure to appear, nonappearance

nichterschienen: **~er Zeuge** *m*, **~e Zeugin** *f* RECHT defaulting witness

Nichterschienene(r) *mf* [decl. as adj] GESCHÄFT, PERSON absentee

nichterwerbswirtschaftlich: ~ ausgerichtetes Unternehmen *nt* VW nonprofit enterprise (*NPE*)

Nicht-: **Nicht-EU-Bürger, in** *m,f* GESCHÄFT non-EU national; **Nichtexperte** *m*, **Nichtexpertin** *f* FREI amateur

nichtfungible: ~ **Waren** *f pl* RECHNUNG nonfungible goods

Nicht-: **Nichthonorieren** *nt* BANK *Wechsel, Scheck* dishonor (*AmE*), dishonour (*BrE*)

Nichtigkeit *f* GESCHÄFT voidance; **Nichtigkeitsklage** *f* RECHT action for cancellation, nullity suit

Nicht-: **Nichtinanspruchnahme** *f* GESCHÄFT failure to take advantage

nichtkommerziell: ~e **Fracht** *f* TRANSP noncommercial cargo

nichtkompensierbar: ~e **Wertminderung** *f* GRUND incurable depreciation

nichtkonsolidiert *adj* RECHNUNG nonconsolidated

nichtkumulativ: ~e **Steuer** *f* STEUER noncumulative tax; ~e **Vorzugsaktie** *f* BÖRSE noncumulative preferred stock (*AmE*)

Nicht-: **Nichtkündbarkeitsklausel** *f* VW noncall provision

nichtlandwirtschaftlich: ~e **Nutzung** *f* GRUND nonagricultural use

Nicht-: **Nichtlebensversicherung** *f* VERSICH nonlife insurance

nichtleitend *adj* PERSON non-executive

nichtlinear: ~e **Beziehung** *f* MATH curvilinear relationship; ~e **Korrelation** *f* MATH curvilinear correlation; ~es **Programmieren** *nt* COMP, MATH nonlinear programming; ~e **Programmierung** *f* COMP, MATH nonlinear programming

nichtmateriell: ~er **Lohn** *m* PERSON nonpecuniary returns

Nicht-: **Nichtmarkt-Sektor** *m* VW nonmarket sector; **Nichtmitglied** *nt* PERSON outsider, VERWALT nonmember; **Nichtmitgliedschaft** *f* PERSON nonmembership

nichtmonetär: ~e **Investition** *f* PERSON nonmonetary investment; ~e **Nachfrageinflation** *f* VW bottleneck inflation

Nicht-: **Nichtnullsummenspiel** *nt* VW non-zero-sum game

nichtobligatorisch: ~e **Ausgaben** *f pl* VW noncompulsory expenditure

nichtöffentlich *adj* GESCHÄFT *Versammlung* closed, RECHT *Beweisaufnahme* in camera

nichtoffiziell: **in** ~er **Eigenschaft** *phr* GESCHÄFT in an unofficial capacity

Nicht-: **Nicht-Öl-Ausgleich** *m* UMWELT, VW nonoil balance; **Nicht-Ölländer** *nt pl* UMWELT, VW nonoil countries

nichtorganisiert *adj* PERSON nonunion; ~e **Arbeiter** *m pl* PERSON nonunion labor (*AmE*), nonunion labour (*BrE*); ~e **Arbeitskräfte** *f pl* PERSON nonunion labor (*AmE*), nonunion labour (*BrE*)

nichtprogrammierbar: ~e **Datenstation** *f* COMP dumb terminal

Nicht-: **Nichtraucherraum** *m* FREI nonsmoking lounge; **Nichtraucherzone** *f* UMWELT no-smoking area; **Nichtregierungsorganisation** *f* (*NRO*) GESCHÄFT nongovernmental organization (*NGO*); **Nichtrohstoffe** *m pl* VW nonbasic commodity

nicht-routinemäßig: ~e **Entscheidung** *f* GESCHÄFT non-routine decision

Nichts *nt* GESCHÄFT *Null* nought

nichts: ~ **Gegenteiliges vorgesehen** *phr* GESCHÄFT not otherwise provided; ~ **Neues bringen** *phr* GESCHÄFT state the obvious

nichtstaatlich: ~e **Organisation** *f* VERWALT nongovernmental organization

Nicht-: **Nicht-Sterling-Gebiet** *nt* VW nonsterling area (*NSA*)

nichttarifär: ~es **Handelshemmnis** *nt* GESCHÄFT, IMP/EXP nontariff barrier (*NTB*), VW nontariff trade barrier, nontariff barrier (*NTB*)

Nicht-: **Nichtverfallbarkeit** *f* RECHT, VW nonforfeiture; **Nichtverfügbarkeit** *f* GESCHÄFT unavailability

nichtvertretbar: ~e **Waren** *f pl* RECHNUNG nonfungible goods

Nicht-: **Nichtvorhandensein** *nt* GESCHÄFT absence; **Nichtzahlung** *f* RECHT failure to pay; **Nichtzahlung** *f* **bei Fälligkeit** GESCHÄFT delinquency; **Nichtzielgleichgewicht** *nt* VW nongoal equilibrium

Nieder- *in cpds* GESCHÄFT low; **Niederbordwagen** *m* TRANSP gondola flat; **Niedergang** *m* GESCHÄFT *in Preise* fall, VW decline; **Niederlage** *f* GESCHÄFT defeat

Niederländisch: **Niederländisch-Britische Handelskammer** *f* GESCHÄFT Netherlands-British Chamber of Commerce (*NBCC*)

niederlassen: **sich** ~ *v refl* GESCHÄFT *Arbeitsstelle, Wohnung, Land* settle, set up, establish oneself, SOZIAL take up; ♦ **sich an einem Ort** ~ VERWALT take up residence in a place

Niederlassung *f* GESCHÄFT branch, V&M field organization; **Niederlassungsfreiheit** *f* GESCHÄFT, POL, VW freedom of establishment; **Niederlassungsrecht** *nt* RECHT right of establishment

niederlegen *vt* RECHT lay down

Niedersächsisch: ~e **Börse** *f* **zu Hannover** BÖRSE Hannover Stock Exchange

Nieder-: **Niederschrift** *f* VERWALT minutes, record

Niederstwert *m* RECHNUNG lower of cost or market

niedertechnologisch *adj* IND *Produktion* low-tech

Niedrig- *in cpds* GESCHÄFT low

niedrig 1. *adj* RECHT low, VW reduced, *Kurse* low; ♦ **zu einem** ~en **Preis kaufen und einem hohen Preis verkaufen** BÖRSE buy low and sell high; 2. *adv* FINANZ, GESCHÄFT, STEUER low; ♦ **zu** ~ **ausweisen** GESCHÄFT underreport; **zu** ~ **besteuern** STEUER undertax; **zu** ~ **bewerten** GESCHÄFT undervalue

niedrig: **zu** ~es **Ausweisen** *nt* GESCHÄFT underreporting; **zu** ~ **bemessenes Kapital** *nt* FINANZ low-geared capital; ~ **bezahlter Arbeitsplatz** *f* VW low-paying job; ~e **Einkommen** *nt pl* STEUER small earnings (*BrE*); **zu** ~e **Kapazität** *f* IND undercapacity; ~e **Ladeplattform** *f* TRANSP beavertail; ~er **Lebensstandard** *m* SOZIAL low standard of living; ~e **Miete** *f* STEUER low rent; ~er **Preis** *m* BÖRSE low price, lower price; ~er **Rauminhalt** *m* TRANSP low cube; **zu** ~e **Veranlagung** *f* STEUER underassessment; ~ **verzinslich** *adj* BÖRSE low-yielding; ~er **Viehwagen** *m* TRANSP cattle float

niedrigere: **auf eine** ~ **Ebene verlagern** *phr* GESCHÄFT, MGMNT downscale; ~ **Einkommensteuergruppe** *f* STEUER, VW lower income bracket; ~ **Einkommensteuerklasse** *f* STEUER, VW lower income bracket; **~ Einkommensstufe** *f* STEUER, VW lower income bracket; **einen niedrigeren Rang einnehmen als** *phr* GESCHÄFT rank below

Niedrig-: **Niedriglohn** *m* PERSON low pay; **Niedriglohnarbeiter, in** *m,f* GESCHÄFT low-wage worker; **Niedriglohnland** *nt* VW country with a low-wage economy

Niedrigpreis *m* GESCHÄFT low price, IMP/EXP thrift price (*AmE*); **Niedrigpreisfestsetzung** *f* V&M pricing down; **Niedrigpreisstrategie** *f* GESCHÄFT penetration pricing; **Niedrigpreiswaren** *f pl* GESCHÄFT bargain goods

niedrigste: **~ Gewinnspanne** *f* FINANZ bottom-line profit margin; **~ Leitungsebene** *f* MGMNT, PERSON first-line management; **~r Bieter** *m* BÖRSE lowest bidder; **~r Kurs** *m* GESCHÄFT rock-bottom price; **~r Preis** *m* BÖRSE lowest price, VW price floor; **~r Stand** *m* FINANZ, VW bottom

Niedrigstkurs *m* BÖRSE *Schatzwechselauktion* stop-out price (*AmE*)

niedrigverzinslich: **~es Darlehen** *nt* BANK low-interest loan; **~es Sparkonto** *nt* BANK *Postsparkasse* ordinary account

Niedrig-: **Niedrigzinspolitik** *f* VW easy money policy, policy of low interest rates

Nießbrauch *m* RECHT *Nutzungsrecht* usufruct; **~ auf Lebenszeit** RECHT life interest; **~ auf Zeit** RECHT limited interest

Nießbrauchberechtigte(r) *mf* [decl. as adj]: **~ auf Lebenszeit** RECHT person entitled under a life interest; **~ auf Zeit** RECHT person entitled under a limited interest

Nießbraucher, in *m,f* RECHT usufructuary; **~ auf Lebenszeit** GRUND life tenant

Nikkei: **Nikkei-Durchschnitt** *m* BÖRSE, FINANZ, VW Nikkei average; **Nikkei-Index** *m* BÖRSE, FINANZ, VW Nikkei index

Nische *f* V&M niche; **Nischenbank** *f* BANK niche bank; **Nischenhandel** *m* GESCHÄFT niche trading

Niveau *nt* GESCHÄFT *der Zinssätze* level; **Niveaugrenzerträge** *m pl* VW returns to scale

Nivellierung *f* VW evening out, leveling out (*AmE*), levelling out (*BrE*)

NLQ-Druckmodus *m* COMP near letter quality (*NLQ*)

n.M. *abbr* (*nächsten Monats*) KOMM prox. (*proximo*)

Nobelpreis *m*: **~ für Wirtschaftswissenschaften** VW Nobel Prize for Economics

noch: **~ nicht abgelaufen** *adj* GESCHÄFT unexpired; **~ nicht abgeschlossene Arbeit** *f* GESCHÄFT, RECHNUNG, VW work in process (*AmE*) (*WIP*), work in progress (*BrE*) (*WIP*); **~ nicht beglichene Aufwendungen** *f pl* RECHNUNG incurred expenses; **~ nicht entschieden** *adj* GESCHÄFT pending; **~ nicht erledigter Auftrag** *m* V&M back order; **~ nie dagewesen** *adj* GESCHÄFT unprecedented; **~ nicht plazierte Wertpapiere** *nt pl* BÖRSE floating securities; **~ nicht verbuchte Einzahlung** *f* **bei einer Bank** BANK deposit in transit; **~ nicht verdiente Prämie** *f* FINANZ, RECHT unearned premium; **~ verfügbare Werbezeit** *f* V&M availability; **~ zu vollziehen** *phr* RECHT executory

Nochgeschäftsoption *f* BÖRSE put of more option

nochmals: **~ erwägen** *phr* GESCHÄFT reconsider

Nomenklatur *f* IMP/EXP nomenclature; **~ des Brüsseler**

Zollrates (*NRZZ*) IMP/EXP Customs Cooperation Council Nomenclature (*CCCN*)

Nominal- *in cpds* GESCHÄFT nominal

nominal *adj* GESCHÄFT nominal; **~es BIP** *nt* (*Bruttoinlandsprodukt*) VW money GDP; **~es Bruttosozialprodukt** *nt* VW nominal GDP; **~es Hauptbuch** *nt* RECHNUNG nominal ledger; **~er Preis** *m* RECHNUNG nominal price

Nominal-: **Nominalgehalt** *nt* GESCHÄFT nominal pay; **Nominalkapital** *nt* RECHNUNG nominal capital; **Nominalkosten** *pl* FINANZ nominal cost; **Nominalkreditzins** *m* FINANZ nominal loan rate; **Nominallohn** *m* PERSON nominal wage; **Nominalsteuersatz** *m* STEUER nominal tax rate; **Nominalvermögen** *nt* RECHNUNG nominal assets; **Nominalverzinsung** *f* BÖRSE, FINANZ nominal yield; **Nominalverzinsung** *f* **von Schuldverschreibungen** BÖRSE bond nominal yield; **Nominalwachstum** *nt* VW nominal growth; **Nominalzinssatz** *m* BANK face interest rate

nominell *adj* FINANZ notional, GESCHÄFT nominal; **~er Maßstab** *m* GESCHÄFT nominal scale; **~e Pferdestärke** *f* GESCHÄFT nominal horsepower (*NHP*); **~er Schaden** *m* RECHT nominal damages

nominieren *vt* GESCHÄFT nominate

No-name: **~~-Produkt** *nt* V&M no-name product

Non-Stop-Flug *m* TRANSP nonstop flight

nonverbal: **~e Kommunikation** *f* GESCHÄFT, MGMNT nonverbal communication

Nordamerikanisch: **~e Freihandelszone** *f* VW North American Free Trade Area (*NAFTA*)

Nordatlantik *m* GESCHÄFT, POL, TRANSP North Atlantic; **Nordatlantikpakt** *m* (*NATO*) POL North Atlantic Treaty Organization (*NATO*); **Nordatlantiktarife** *m pl* TRANSP North Atlantic rates; **Nordatlantikvereinigung** *f* **für Westfracht** TRANSP North Atlantic rates, North Atlantic Westbound Freight Association (*NAWFA*)

Nordisch: **~e Investitionsbank** *f* BANK Nordic Investment Bank (*NIB*)

nordisch: **~e Länder** *nt pl* GESCHÄFT Nordic countries

Nord-Ostsee-Kanal *m* TRANSP Kiel canal

Nordsee *f* GESCHÄFT, TRANSP North Sea; **Nordseegas** *nt* UMWELT, IND North Sea gas

Norm *f* COMP standard (*Std*), GESCHÄFT norm, MGMNT rule; ◆ **über der ~** GESCHÄFT above the norm; **einer ~ entsprechen** GESCHÄFT conform to a standard; **unter der ~ liegend** GESCHÄFT, IND substandard

Normal- *in cpds* GESCHÄFT normal, standard, average

normal *adj* GESCHÄFT normal, standard, average; **~e Arbeitszeiten** *f pl* PERSON regular hours; **~es Einfachticket** *nt* FREI ordinary single; **~e Fahrkarte** *f* FREI ordinary ticket; **~er Flugschein** *m* FREI ordinary ticket; **~e und fristgerechte Lieferung** *f* GESCHÄFT *von Wertpapieren* regular way delivery; **~es Geschäftsjahr** *nt* GESCHÄFT natural business year; **~es Hin- und Rückflugticket** *nt* FREI ordinary return; **~e Kapazität** *f* VW normal sustainable capacity; **~e Liegezeit** *f* TRANSP normal laytime; **~e Marktgröße** *f* BÖRSE normal market size (*BrE*) (*NMS*); **~e und notwendige Geschäftsausgaben** *f pl* STEUER ordinary and necessary business expenses; **~e Pensionierung** *f* PERSON normal retirement; **~es Pensionsalter** *nt* PERSON normal retirement age; **~er Preis** *m* VW normal price;

~e **Springflut** f TRANSP ordinary spring tide (*ost*); ~e **Zeiten** f pl GESCHÄFT regular hours

Normal-: **Normalarbeitszeit** f PERSON standard time; **Normaleinkommen** nt VW standard earnings; **Normalfracht** f TRANSP ordinary cargo; **Normalgewinn** m VW normal profit

normalgroß adj COMP of standard size

Normal-: **Normalgut** nt VW normal good

Normalität f GESCHÄFT normalcy (*AmE*), normality (*BrE*)

Normal-: **Normalkapazität** f VW normal capacity; **Normalkosten** pl FINANZ standard costs; **Normalkostenrechnung** f FINANZ standard costing; **Normalleistung** f GESCHÄFT, PERSON standard performance; **Normalsatz** m STEUER standard rate; **zum Normalsatz** phr STEUER standard-rated; **Normaltarif** m GESCHÄFT normal rate; **Normalverbraucher, in** m,f V&M average consumer; **Normalverteilung** f MATH normal distribution; **Normalzeit** f GESCHÄFT standard time

Normativ nt MGMNT normative

normativ: ~e **Prognose** f GESCHÄFT normative forecasting; ~e **Wirtschaftswissenschaft** f VW normative economics

normen vt GESCHÄFT, RECHT, V&M standardize

Norm: **Normen und Praktiken** f pl GESCHÄFT standards and practices

normgerecht adj RECHT according to the norm

Normkosten pl VERWALT ideal standard cost

Norris-La Guardia-Gesetz nt PERSON Norris-La Guardia Act (*AmE*)

Not f GESCHÄFT, PERSON emergency, SOZIAL hardship, poverty

Nota f obs GESCHÄFT bill (*BrE*), check (*AmE*)

nota bene phr (*NB*) GESCHÄFT nota bene (*NB*), please note

Notar, in m,f RECHT notary public, commissioner for oaths

notariell 1. adj RECHT notarial; **2.** adv RECHT by a notary; ♦ ~ **beglaubigen** RECHT acknowledge, notarize; ~ **beglaubigt** RECHT attested by a notary, notarized, recorded by a notary; ~ **beurkunden** RECHT acknowledge, notarize; ~ **beurkundet** RECHT attested by a notary, notarized, recorded by a notary

notariell: ~e **Beglaubigung** f RECHT acknowledgement by a notary, notarial authentication; ~e **Beurkundung** f RECHT acknowledgement by a notary, notarial authentication

Not: **Notausgang** f PERSON, UMWELT emergency exit, fire exit; **Notdienst** m SOZIAL emergency service, TRANSP skeleton service

Notebook nt COMP notebook

Noten- in cpds BANK, VW note; **Notenausgabe** f BANK note issue

Notenbank f BANK bank of circulation; **Notenbankpolitik** f VW central bank policy; **Notenbankpräsident** m VW central bank governor, Governor of the Bank of England (*BrE*), President of the Federal Reserve Board (*AmE*)

Not: **Notfall** m GESCHÄFT emergency; **Notfracht** f TRANSP distress freight; **Notgeld** nt FINANZ token money; **Notgroschen** m GESCHÄFT, VW nest egg; **einen Not-**

groschen zurücklegen phr GESCHÄFT save for a rainy day; **Nothafen** m TRANSP port of necessity

notierbar adj BÖRSE quotable

notieren vt BÖRSE quote, GESCHÄFT take down, quote; ♦ **etw ~** GESCHÄFT keep a note of sth

Notierung f BÖRSE quotation, *Devisen* rate, FINANZ marking; ~ **einschließlich aufgelaufener Stückzinsen** BÖRSE flat quotation; ~ **ohne Umsätze** BÖRSE nominal quotation; ~ **im Telefonverkehr** BÖRSE street price

Notifikation f PATENT notification

Notifizierungshändler, in m,f BÖRSE reporting dealer

nötig: **die ~en finanziellen Mittel** nt pl FINANZ the necessary funds

Nötigung f RECHT duress, *Zwang* constraint

Notizblock m COMP, GESCHÄFT pad

Notizen f pl MEDIEN mark-up

Not: **Notlandung** f FREI forced landing; **Notleiden** nt BANK *Wechsel* dishonor (*AmE*), dishonour (*BrE*)

notleidend adj BANK *Wechsel* dishonored (*AmE*), dishonoured (*BrE*), ailing, IND ailing, VW depressed, ailing; ~e **Anleihe** f BÖRSE defaulted bond; ~e **Bank** f BANK ailing bank; ~es **Darlehen** nt BANK nonperforming credit; ~es **Gebiet** nt VW depressed area; ~er **Kredit** m BANK bad and doubtful debt (*B&D*), bad loan, nonperforming credit; ~e **Region** f VW depressed region; ~e **Volkswirtschaft** f VW ailing economy; ~e **Währung** f BÖRSE forced currency; ~er **Wechsel** m BANK dishonored bill of exchange (*AmE*), dishonoured bill of exchange (*BrE*)

Not: **Notlösung** f GESCHÄFT makeshift solution; **Notstandsplan** m FINANZ contingency plan; **mit Notstromversorgung durch Batterien** adj COMP battery-backed; **Notstromversorgung** f **mit Batterien** COMP battery backup; **Notverkauf** m GESCHÄFT bail-out; **Notverkäufe** m pl BÖRSE forced liquidation

notwendig adj GESCHÄFT necessary; ♦ **die als ~ erachteten Schritte einleiten** RECHT take such steps as are considered necessary; ~ **erscheinen** GESCHÄFT deem necessary

notwendig: ~e **Arbeit** f VW *marxistische Theorie* indispensable labor (*AmE*), indispensable labour (*BrE*); ~er **Lebensunterhalt** m GESCHÄFT bread and butter (*infrml*); ~e **Ursache** f RECHT causa sine qua non

Novation f RECHT novation

Novellierung f RECHT amendment; **Novellierungsantrag** m POL, RECHT application for amendment

Nr. abbr (*Nummer*) GESCHÄFT, MATH no. (*number*)

NRO abbr (*Nichtregierungsorganisation*) GESCHÄFT NGO (*nongovernmental organization*)

NRZZ abbr (*Zolltarifschema des Rates für die Zusammenarbeit auf dem Gebiete des Zollwesens*) IMP/EXP CCCN (*Customs Cooperation Council Nomenclature*)

nuancieren vt GESCHÄFT nuance

Nuklearindustrie f UMWELT nuclear industry

null adj GESCHÄFT zero, nil; ♦ ~ **Fehler** RECHNUNG zero defects; ~ **und nichtig** RECHT null and void; ~ **und nichtig machen** RECHT render null and void

Null f GESCHÄFT zero, nil; ♦ **auf ~ setzen** COMP zero

Null: **Nullage** f COMP zero state; **Nullbasis-Budget** nt RECHNUNG zero-base budget; **Nullbasis-Budgetierung** f FINANZ, RECHNUNG zero-base budgeting (*ZBB*); **Nullbevölkerungswachstum** nt VW zero population growth (*ZPG*); **Nullgewinn** m FINANZ zero profit;

Nullhypothese _f_ MATH null hypothesis; **Nullkuponanleihe** _f_ BÖRSE zero-coupon bond; **Nullkuponwertpapier** _nt_ BÖRSE zero-coupon security; **Nullmängel** _m pl_ FINANZ zero defects; **Nullmenge** _f_ MATH empty set; **Nullösung** _f_ POL zero option; **Nullsatz** _m_ STEUER zero rating; **Nullserie** _f_ IND, MGMNT pilot production; **Nullsumme** _f_ VW zero sum; **Nullsummenspiel** _nt_ GESCHÄFT, MGMNT, POL, VW zero-sum game; **zum Nulltarif** _phr_ GESCHÄFT, V&M free of charge _(foc)_; **Nullwachstum** _nt_ VW zero growth; **Nullzustand** _m_ COMP zero state

numerieren _vt_ GESCHÄFT number

numerisch _adj_ COMP numeric; **~e Ablage** _f_ GESCHÄFT numerical filing; **~e Flexibilität** _f_ PERSON numerical flexibility; **~e Kontrolle** _f_ FINANZ numerical control; **~e Steuerung** _f_ MATH numerical control; **~es Zeichen** _nt_ MATH numeric character

Nummer _f_ MATH number; **~ des Frachtbriefkontrolletiketts** TRANSP consignment note control label number; ♦ **auf ~ Sicher gehen** GESCHÄFT be on the safe side, play safe

Nummer: **Nummern** _f pl_ MATH numbers _(nos.)_; **Nummernkonto** _nt_ BANK _ohne Namen_ numbered account; **Nummernschild** _nt_ TRANSP license plate _(AmE)_, number plate _(BrE)_

Nuplex _m_ IND nuplex

Nutz- _in cpds_ GESCHÄFT practical; **Nutzanwendung** _f_ GESCHÄFT practical application

nutzbar: **~e Vorräte** _m pl_ UMWELT _Energieressourcen_ extractable reserves

nutzbringend _adj_ GESCHÄFT beneficial, _gewinnbringend_ profitable

Nutz-: **Nutzeneinheit** _f_ VW util

nutzen 1. _vt_ GESCHÄFT utilize, exploit, IND, UMWELT utilize, VW capitalize on; ♦ **zu wenig ~** GESCHÄFT _Ressourcen_ underutilize; **2.** _vi_ GESCHÄFT benefit

Nutzen _m_ FREI benefit, GESCHÄFT advancement, advantage, avails, benefit, value, STEUER emolument, VW utility; ♦ **jdm von ~ sein** GESCHÄFT be useful to sb; **den ~ von etw haben** GESCHÄFT have the use of sth

Nutzen: **Nutzenansatz** _m_ **der Besteuerung** STEUER benefit approach to taxation; **Nutzenentgang** _m_ FINANZ loss of use; **Nutzenfunktion** _f_ VW utility function; **Nutzenmaximierung** _f_ VW utility maximization; **Nutzenmöglichkeitskurve** _f_ VW utility possibility frontier; **Nutzenniveau** _nt_ VW satisfaction level; **Nutzensprinzip** _nt_ STEUER, VW benefit principle

Nutzer _m_ GESCHÄFT user; **Nutzerstrategie** _f_ GESCHÄFT user strategy

Nutz-: **Nutzfahrzeug** _nt_ TRANSP commercial vehicle; **Nutzfläche** _f_ GRUND useable floor space; **Nutzholz** _nt_ IND lumber, timber; **Nutzlast** _f_ TRANSP maximum permitted load

nützlich _adj_ GESCHÄFT advantageous, useful; ♦ **jdm ~ sein** GESCHÄFT be useful to sb

Nützlichkeit _f_ VW utility; **Nützlichkeitslehre** _f_ VW utilitarianism

nutzlos _adj_ GESCHÄFT useless, valueless

Nutznießer, in _m,f_ GRUND, VERSICH beneficiary

Nutz-: **Nutznießung** _f_ **zur gesamten Hand** FINANZ undivided interest; **Nutzpflanze** _f_ GESCHÄFT, UMWELT economically-used plant; **Nutzschwelle** _f_ BÖRSE, FINANZ breakeven point, GESCHÄFT break weight, breakeven point, GRUND, RECHNUNG, VW breakeven point; **Nutzschwellenanalyse** _f_ FINANZ, VW breakeven analysis; **Nutztier** _nt_ GESCHÄFT, UMWELT economically-used animal

Nutzung _f_ GESCHÄFT utilization, GRUND residential occupancy, PATENT use, UMWELT utilization; **~ von Geschäftskontakten** GESCHÄFT networking; **Nutzungsausfall** _m_ VW loss of use; **Nutzungsbedingungen** _f pl_ GESCHÄFT conditions of use; **Nutzungsberechtigung** _f_ GRUND certificate of use

Nutzungsdauer _f_ GESCHÄFT resource time, _Maschine_ useful life, RECHNUNG useful life, STEUER depreciable life, VW depreciable life, service life, useful life; **~ eines Wirtschaftsgutes** RECHNUNG asset life

Nutzung: **Nutzungsrecht** _nt_ RECHT beneficial interest

O

o.a.: **die ~ Adresse** *f* (*die oben angegebene Adresse*) KOMM the above address

OAS *abbr* (*Organisation amerikanischer Staaten*) POL, VW OAS (*Organization of American States*)

Oase *f* FINANZ, GESCHÄFT, STEUER haven

ÖBB *abbr* (*Österreichische Bundesbahn*) TRANSP Austrian Federal Railways, ≈ BR (*British Rail*)

obdachlos *adj* SOZIAL homeless

Obdachlose(r) *mf* [decl. as adj] SOZIAL homeless person

oben *adv* GESCHÄFT above, TRANSP aloft; ♦ **nach ~ keine Begrenzung** BÖRSE unlimited on upside; **von ~ nach unten** MGMNT *Leitungsystem* top down

oben: **die ~ angegebene Adresse** *f* (*die o.a. Adresse*) KOMM the above address

obenerwähnt *adj* KOMM above, above-mentioned, afore-mentioned

obengenannt *adj* KOMM above, above-mentioned, afore-mentioned

Ober- *in cpds* GESCHÄFT outer, upper; **Oberaufsicht** *f* GESCHÄFT superintendence

obere: **~r Bereich** *m* **der Skala** V&M top end of the range; **~r Break-Even-Punkt** *m* BÖRSE upside breakeven point; **am ~n Ende** *phr* GESCHÄFT at the top end; **~s Ende** *nt* **des Bereiches** BÖRSE high end of the range; **~r Goldpunkt** *m* FINANZ, IMP/EXP, VW gold exporting point, gold export point; **~r Leistungsbereich** *m* COMP *Geräte, Computer* high-end; **~ Leitungsebene** *f* MGMNT, PERSON senior management; **~s Management** *nt* MGMNT, PERSON senior management; **~r Marktbereich** *m* V&M top end of the market; **~s Marktsegment** *nt* GESCHÄFT up-market segment; **~s Quartil** *nt* MATH upper quartile

Ober-: **Oberfahrdienstleiter, in** *m,f* PERSON, TRANSP chief traffic controller

oberflächlich: **~r Leiter** *m*, **~e Leiterin** *f* MGMNT one-minute manager; **~er Manager** *m*, **~e Managerin** *f* MGMNT one-minute manager

Obergrenze *f* BÖRSE limit, upper limit, FINANZ *für die Änderung von Zinssätzen* cap; ♦ **die ~ durchstoßen** FINANZ break the ceiling

Ober-: **die Oberhand haben** *phr* GESCHÄFT have the upper hand; **Oberhaus** *nt* POL upper house

oberirdisch *adj* IND, TRANSP, UMWELT above-ground

oberlastig *adj* TRANSP *Schiff* top-heavy

oberste: **~ Betriebsführung** *f* MGMNT top management; **~ Führungskraft** *f* PERSON top executive, *Betriebswirtschaft* chief operating officer (*COO*)

Oberste: **~r Gerichtshof** *m* RECHT Supreme Court

oberste: **~ Leitungsebene** *f* MGMNT top management; **~(r) Standesbeamte(r)** *m* [decl. as adj], **~ Standesbeamtin** *f* VERWALT Registrar General (*BrE*); **~(r) Verwaltungsbeamte(r)** *m* [decl. as adj], **~ Verwaltungsbeamtin** *f* MGMNT *Gemeinde* chief executive; **~ Verwaltungsspitze** *f* PERSON chief executive

Obfrau *f* GESCHÄFT, POL representative

Obhut *f* GESCHÄFT care; **Obhutsschaden** *m* VERSICH damage to goods in custody

obig *adj* KOMM above

Objekt *nt* GRUND property

objektiv *adj* GESCHÄFT objective; **~e Unmöglichkeit** *f* **der Leistung** RECHT *Vertragsrecht* physical impossibility of performance; **~er Wert** *m* VW objective value

Objekt: **Objektschutz** *m* GRUND, IND protection of property, site protection

obliegend *adj* POL incumbent

Obligation *f* BÖRSE, FINANZ bond, debenture; **~ mit aufgeschobener Zinszahlung** BÖRSE deferred interest bond; **~ mit geringem Umsatzvolumen** BÖRSE inactive bond; ♦ **Obligationen verwalten** BÖRSE hold bonds

Obligationär, in *m,f* BÖRSE, FINANZ bondholder, debenture holder, loan holder

Obligation: **Obligationengutschein** *m* BÖRSE bond anticipation note (*BAN*); **Obligationsanleihe** *f* BANK bond loan, BÖRSE debenture loan; **Obligationseigentümer, in** *m,f* BANK bond owner; **Obligationsnummer** *f* BANK bond number; **Obligationsschuld** *f* BÖRSE bonded debt; **Obligationstilgungsfonds** *m* BÖRSE bond sinking fund

obligatorisch *adj* GESCHÄFT compulsory, obligatory, binding, RECHT *Richtlinien* mandatory; **nicht ~** *adj* RECHT *Richtlinien* nonmandatory; **~er Anspruch** *m* RECHT claim based upon a contract; **~e Arbeitsunfallversicherung** *f* VERSICH workers' compensation and employers' liability insuring agreement; **~e Ausgaben** *f pl* VW compulsory expenditure; **~e Einschußsumme** *f* BÖRSE compulsory margin (*BrE*); **~e Einschußmarge** *f* BÖRSE compulsory margin (*BrE*); **~er Notierungszeitraum** *m* BÖRSE mandatory quote period; **~es Recht** *nt* RECHT right in personam; **~es Schiedsgerichtsverfahren** *nt* RECHT compulsory arbitration proceedings; **~er Zusammenschluß** *m* **von Versicherern** VERSICH Fair Access To Insurance Requirements Plan (*AmE*) (*FAIR plan*)

Obligo *nt* BANK, FINANZ exposure, liability; ♦ **ohne ~** BANK, FINANZ without recourse

Obligo: **Obligobuch** *nt* BANK, FINANZ acceptance ledger

Obmann *m* GESCHÄFT, POL representative

Obrigkeit *f obs* GESCHÄFT the authorities

obsiegend: **~e Partei** *f* RECHT prevailing party

Obsoleszenz *f* GESCHÄFT obsolescence

OCR *abbr* (*optische Zeichenerkennung*) COMP OCR (*optical character recognition*)

Ödland *nt* GRUND *nicht angebautes Land* wasteland

OECD *abbr* (*Organisation für wirtschaftliche Zusammenarbeit und Entwicklung*) VW OECD (*Organization for Economic Cooperation and Development*)

OEEC *abbr* (*Organisation für europäische wirtschaftliche Zusammenarbeit*) VW OEEC (*Organization for European Economic Cooperation*)

OEM *abbr* (*Originalgerätehersteller*) COMP OEM (*original equipment manufacturer*)

OEZ *abbr* (*Osteuropäische Zeit*) GESCHÄFT EET (*Eastern European Time*)

offen *adj* COMP open-ended, open, GESCHÄFT open, *rechtlich zulässig* above board, *Aussprache* plain-spoken, frank, V&M over-the-counter (*OTC*); **~es Angebot** *nt* MGMNT open bid; **~e Ausschreibung** *f* GESCHÄFT open tendering; **~e Bevölkerung** *f* VW open population; **~er Buchkredit** *m* RECHNUNG advance account; **~e Charter** *f* TRANSP open charter; **~er Container** *m* TRANSP open container; **~es Dock** *nt* TRANSP open dock; **~e Frachtpolice** *f* VERSICH floating cargo policy; **~er Goldinvestmentfonds** *m* BÖRSE gold mutual fund; **~er Hafen** *m* TRANSP open port; **~e Handelsgesellschaft** *f* GESCHÄFT partnership; **~e Hypothek** *f* BANK, FINANZ open mortgage, open-end mortgage, open-ended mortgage; **~er Investmentfonds** *m* FINANZ open-end fund, open-ended fund, mutual fund (*AmE*); **~er Investmentfonds** *m* **für maximale Kapitalgewinne** BÖRSE maximum capital gains mutual fund; **~e Investmentgesellschaft** *f* FINANZ open-end investment company (*OEIC*), open-ended investment company; **~er Kredit** *m* GESCHÄFT open credit; **~e Lagerung** *f* TRANSP open storage; **~er Maklervertrag** *m* GRUND open listing; **~er Markt** *m* VW open market; **~e Nettoverbindlichkeit** *f* BANK exposed net liability position; **~es Netz** *nt* COMP open network; **~e Police** *f* SOZIAL, VERSICH floater (*AmE*), floating policy; **~e Position** *f* BÖRSE open position, FINANZ exposure; **~e Preisliste** *f* GESCHÄFT open list; **~e Rechnung** *f* GESCHÄFT invoice outstanding; **~e Stelle** *f* PERSON job vacancy; **~e Stellen** *f pl* PERSON *Arbeit* situations vacant (*BrE*) (*sits. vac.*); **~es Ticket** *nt* FREI open ticket; **~es Verteilen** *nt* V&M over-the-counter trading; **~e Verteilung** *f* TRANSP open distribution; **~er Vertrag** *m* RECHT *auf unbestimmte Dauer* open-end contract, open-ended contract; **~e Verwaltungsgesellschaft** *f* FINANZ open-end management company; **~e Volkswirtschaft** *f* VW interdependent economy, open economy; **~er Wagen** *m* TRANSP gondola; **~er Wettbewerb** *m* VW open competition; **~er Zuruf** *m* BÖRSE open outcry

offenbart: **~e Präferenz** *f* VW revealed preference

offengelegt: **nicht ~er Betrag** *m* FINANZ undisclosed sum; **~e Rücklagen** *f pl* RECHNUNG disclosed reserves

Offenheit *f* GESCHÄFT openness, *Aussprache* frankness

Offenlegung *f* BÖRSE, FINANZ disclosure, RECHT discovery; **~ einer Erfindung** PATENT disclosure of an invention

Offenmarkt *m* VW open market; **Offenmarktausschuß** *m* VW Open Market Committee (*AmE*) (*OMC*); **Offenmarktgeschäfte** *nt pl* VW open-market operations; **Offenmarkthandel** *m* VW open-market trading; **Offenmarktsatz** *m* BANK open-market rate

offensichtlich *adj* GESCHÄFT obvious; **nicht ~** *adj* GESCHÄFT nonobvious; **~e Krise** *f* POL manifest crisis

offensiv *adj* GESCHÄFT aggressive

Offensive: **in die ~ gehen** *phr* GESCHÄFT take the offensive

öffentlich 1. *adj* GESCHÄFT public; ♦ **in ~em Eigentum sein** POL, VW be under public ownership; **durch ~e Mittel finanziert** VW financed out of public funds; **2.** *adv* GESCHÄFT publicly; ♦ **zum Ausdruck bringen** GESCHÄFT *Meinung* express publicly; **~ finanziert** VW financed out of public funds; **~ gefördert** GESCHÄFT publicly funded; **~ versteigern** GESCHÄFT sell by auction

öffentlich: **~e Angebotseinholung** *f* GESCHÄFT public invitation to bid, RECHT invitation to make an offer; **~e Angelegenheiten** *f pl* POL public affairs; **~e Anleihen** *f pl* VW government securities; **~er Auftrag** *m* FINANZ public loan, GESCHÄFT public contract, RECHT government contract; **~es Auftragswesen** *nt* VW public procurement; **~e Ausgaben** *f pl* VW public spending, public expenditure, general government expenditure (*BrE*) (*GGE*); **~e Ausschreibung** *f* GESCHÄFT advertised bidding, public invitation to bid, RECHT invitation to make an offer; **~e Bauarbeiten** *f pl* GRUND, IND public works; **~e Bedürfnisse** *f pl* VW public wants; **~ Beihilfe** *f* SOZIAL flat grant; **~e Bekanntmachung** *f* RECHT posting; **~er Dienst** *m* POL civil service (*CS*); **~es Eigentum** *nt* GRUND, RECHT res communis, VW common ownership; **~e Einnahme** *f* VW government revenue; **~e Einrichtung** *f* SOZIAL *zur Verbesserung der Lebensqualität* public amenity; **~e Erklärung** *f* GESCHÄFT official statement; **~e Erschließung** *f* VW public development; **~e Finanzen** *f pl* VW public finances; **~es Finanzwesen** *nt* FINANZ public finance; **~ gebundenes Unternehmen** *nt* VW regulated firm; **~es Gesundheitswesen** *nt* SOZIAL public health; **~es Gut** *nt* VW public good, social good, collective good; **~e Hand** *f* FINANZ, POL public authority; **~er Haushalt** *m* VW government budget; **~er Markt** *m* GESCHÄFT public market; **~e Meinung** *f* GESCHÄFT public opinion; **~e Mittel** *nt pl* FINANZ public resources, public funds; **~es Recht** *nt* RECHT public law; **~-rechtliche Anstalt** *f* RECHT statutory body; **~er Rechtsträger** *m* RECHT public body; **~e Rundfunk- und Fernsehanstalten** *f pl* MEDIEN Public Broadcasting Services (*AmE*) (*PBS*); **~e Schuld** *f* VW public debt; **~er Schuldendienst** *m* FINANZ public debt service; **~e Schule** *f* SOZIAL public school (*AmE*), state school (*BrE*); **~er Sektor** *m* VW public sector; **~es Siegel** *nt* RECHT common seal; **~er Verbrauch** *m* VW public consumption; **~es Vergabewesen** *nt* VW government procurement, public procurement; **~er Verkehr** *m* TRANSP public transport (*BrE*), public transportation (*AmE*); **~es Verkehrsmittel** *nt* TRANSP public service vehicle (*PSV*), people-mover (*infrml*); **~e Verkehrsmittel** *nt pl* TRANSP public transport (*BrE*), public transportation (*AmE*); **~es Verkehrssystem** *nt* TRANSP public transport system (*BrE*), public transportation system (*AmE*); **~es Verkehrswesen** *nt* TRANSP public transport (*BrE*), public transportation (*AmE*); **~e Verschuldung** *f* VW debt obligation, national debt; **~es Versorgungsunternehmen** *nt* VW public utility, public utility company; **~e Versteigerung** *f* GESCHÄFT public auction; **~e Warnung** *f* GESCHÄFT public warning; **~e Wertpapierausschüttung** *f* BÖRSE public distribution of securities; **~es Wirtschaftsunternehmen** *nt* GESCHÄFT, VW public enterprise; **~e Wohlfahrt** *f* SOZIAL public welfare, social welfare; **~es Zeichnungsangebot** *nt* BÖRSE public offering; **~er Zugang** *m* POL, RECHT, VERWALT *zu Informationen* public access; **zur ~en Zeichnung aufgelegte Emission** *f* BÖRSE public offering

Öffentliche *pl infrml* VW governments (*infrml*)

Öffentlichkeit *f* GESCHÄFT public; ♦ **an die ~ bringen** POL air

Öffentlichkeit: **Öffentlichkeitsarbeit** *f* PERSON, V&M public relations (*PR*)

Offerte *f* GESCHÄFT bid, tender

offiziell 1. *adj* GESCHÄFT official; ◆ **in ~er Funktion handeln** MGMNT act in one's official capacity; **2.** *adv* GESCHÄFT officially; ◆ **etw ~ erklären** GESCHÄFT put sth on record

offiziell: **~er Aufbewahrungsort** *m* MEDIEN official depository; **~er Bericht** *m* KOMM bulletin; **~er Besuch** *m* GESCHÄFT official visit; **~er Einreichungstermin** *m* FINANZ formal submission date; **~es Essen** *nt* GESCHÄFT formal dinner; **~e Mitteilung** *f* KOMM formal communication; **~es Schiffstagebuch** *nt* TRANSP official log; **~e Verkaufsankündigung** *f* FINANZ official notice of sale; **~er Wechselkurs** *m* VW official exchange rate; **~e Wirtschaft** *f* POL first economy, vw blue economy (*BrE*), first economy, formal economy, recorded economy

Offizier *m* PERSON officer; **~ vom Dienst** PERSON *Militär* duty officer (*DO*)

off-line 1. *adj* COMP off-line; **2.** *adv* COMP off-line

Off-line- *in cpds* COMP off-line

öffnen 1. *vt* COMP *Datei, Fenster* open; **2. sich ~** *v refl* GESCHÄFT *Möglichkeiten* open up

Öffnungszeiten *f pl* GESCHÄFT, VERWALT opening hours

Offsetdruck *m* MEDIEN offset

Offshore- *in cpds* BANK, FINANZ *Investitionen*, UMWELT *Bohrplattform* offshore; **Offshore-Bankgeschäfte** *nt pl* BANK offshore banking; **Offshore-Bankplatz** *m* BANK offshore place; **Offshore-Dollars** *m pl* BANK offshore dollars; **Offshore-Fonds** *m* FINANZ, STEUER offshore funds; **Offshore-Installation** *f* TRANSP offshore installation; **Offshore-Investition** *f* FINANZ offshore investment; **Offshore-Ölfeld** *nt* IND, UMWELT offshore oilfield; **Offshore-Technologie** *f* IND offshore technology; **Offshore-Zentrum** *nt* BANK offshore center (*AmE*), offshore centre (*BrE*)

ohne *prep* BÖRSE ex (*exclusive of*); ◆ **~ Porto und Verpackung** GESCHÄFT exclusive of post and packing

Öko- *pref* UMWELT eco-, green; **Ökoetikettierung** *f* UMWELT ecolabeling (*AmE*), ecolabelling (*BrE*); **Ökokennzeichnung** *f* UMWELT ecolabelling (*BrE*), ecolabeling (*AmE*)

Ökologie *f* UMWELT ecology

ökologisch *adj* UMWELT ecological; **~e Etikettierung** *f* UMWELT green labeling scheme (*AmE*), green labelling scheme (*BrE*); **~e Frage** *f* UMWELT green issue; **~er Indikator** *m* UMWELT ecological indicator; **~es Merkmal** *nt* UMWELT *von Produkten, die zum Verkauf stehen* ecological character; **~e Partei** *f* UMWELT Green Party; **~ sensibler Bereich** *m* UMWELT environmentally sensitive zone

Ökonom, in *m,f* VW economist

Ökonometrie *f* VW econometrics

Ökonometriker, in *m,f* VW econometrician

ökonometrisch *adj* VW econometric

Ökonomie *f* VW economics; **~ der Kriminalität** SOZIAL, VW economics of crime

ökonomisch 1. *adj* BANK, FINANZ, GESCHÄFT, VERWALT, VW *wirtschaftlich* economic, *sparsam* economical; **2.** *adv* BANK, FINANZ, GESCHÄFT, VERWALT, VW economically

ökonomisch: **~e Aktivität** *f* VW economic activity; **~e Analyse** *f* **des Rechts** RECHT, VW economics of law; **~e Effizienz** *f* VW economic efficiency; **~e Herstellungsgröße** *f* IND economic manufacturing quantity; **~e Methode** *f* VW economic method; **~e Methodologie** *f* VW economic methodology; **~es**

Modell *nt* VW economic model; **~e Programmierung** *f* VW economic programming; **~e Rente** *f* VW rent; **~e Ressourcen** *f pl* VW economic resources; **~er Sachverstand** *m* VW economic intelligence; **~e Stufentheorie** *f* VW theory of economic stages; **~e Theorie** *f* **der Clubs** VW economic theory of clubs

Ökonomismus *m* VW economism

Öko-: **Ökosteuer** *f* STEUER, UMWELT green tax; **Ökosystem** *nt* UMWELT ecosystem

ökotoxikologisch *adj* UMWELT ecotoxicological

Öl *nt* IND, UMWELT oil; ◆ **nach ~ bohren** IND prospect for oil

Öl: **Ölanalytiker, in** *m,f* IND oil analyst; **Ölbohrkonzession** *f* RECHT, UMWELT oil exploration licence (*BrE*), oil exploration license (*AmE*); **Ölbohrlizenz** *f* RECHT, UMWELT oil exploration licence (*BrE*), oil exploration license (*AmE*)

öldicht *adj* IND, TRANSP oiltight

Öl: **Öldollar** *m* IMP/EXP petrodollar; **Öl/Erzschiff** *nt* TRANSP ore/oil ship

ölexportierend: **~es Land** *nt* IND, UMWELT, VW oil-exporting country

Öl: **Ölfeld** *nt* IND, UMWELT *Bohrfeld* oilfield; **Ölfleck** *m* UMWELT oil slick; **Ölförderland** *nt* VW oil-producing country; **Öl- und Gasgesellschaft** *f* RECHT, UMWELT oil and gas limited partnership; **Öl- und Gas-Leasing** *nt* RECHT, UMWELT oil and gas lease; **Ölgeld** *nt* IMP/EXP petrodollar; **Ölgesellschaft** *f* IND petroleum company, oil company; **Ölhafen** *m* IND, TRANSP oil terminal

Oligopol *nt* VW oligopoly

Oligopolist *m* VW oligopolist

oligopolistisch *adj* VW oligopolistic

Oligopson *nt* VW oligopsony

Öl: **Ölknappheit** *f* IND oil shortage; **Ölkrise** *f* VW oil shock; **Öllache** *f* UMWELT oil slick; **Ölleitung** *f* IND oil pipeline; **Ölpipeline** *f* IND oil pipeline; **Ölpreisanstieg** *m* VW oil price increase; **Ölproduzent** *m* VW oil-producing country; **Ölraffinerie** *f* IND, UMWELT oil refinery; **Ölschwemme** *f* UMWELT oil glut; **Ölstandsanzeiger** *m* IND oil gage (*AmE*), oil gauge (*BrE*); **Öltanker** *m* TRANSP oil tanker, oil carrier; **Ölteppich** *m* UMWELT oil slick, oil spill; **Öltransporter** *m* TRANSP oil carrier; **Ölumschlagstelle** *f* IND, TRANSP oil terminal; **Öluntersuchungschemiker, in** *m,f* IND oil analyst; **Ölverschmutzung** *f* UMWELT oil pollution; **Ölverschüttung** *f* UMWELT oil spill; **Ölverseuchung** *f* UMWELT oil pollution

Ombudsfrau *f* BANK Banking Ombudsman (*BrE*), GESCHÄFT, POL ombudsman

Ombudsmann *m* BANK Banking Ombudsman (*BrE*), GESCHÄFT, POL ombudsman

on-line 1. *adj* COMP on-line; **2.** *adv* COMP on-line

On-line- *in cpds* COMP on-line; **On-line-Datenbank** *f* COMP on-line database; **On-line-Datendienst** *m* COMP on-line data service; **On-line-Hilfe** *f* COMP on-line help; **On-line-Tarif** *m* TRANSP on-line rate

OPEC *abbr* (*Organisation erdölexportierender Länder*) POL, UMWELT, VW OPEC (*Organization of Petroleum-Exporting Countries*)

Open-Systems-Interconnection *f* (*OSI*) COMP open systems interconnection (*OSI*)

Operand *m* COMP, MATH operand

Operating-Leasing *nt* RECHT operating leasing

Operation *f* GESCHÄFT operation; **Operations-Research** *nt* (*OR*) MGMNT, V&M operational research (*OR*), operations research (*OR*); **Operationssystem** *nt* **des Managements** MGMNT management operating system

operativ: ~**er Mehrjahresplan** *m* FINANZ multi-year operational plan (*MYOP*); ~**es Personal** *nt* PERSON operational staff; ~**er Rahmenplan** *m* RECHNUNG operating budget

Operator, in *m,f* COMP computer operator, operator

Opfer *nt* SOZIAL casualty; **Opfertheorie** *f* VW sacrifice theory

Opportunismus *m* POL opportunism

Opportunist, in *m,f* POL opportunist

opportunistisch *adj* POL opportunist

Opportunität *f* FINANZ, RECHNUNG, VW opportunity; **Opportunitätskosten** *pl* FINANZ, RECHNUNG, VW opportunity costs, alternative costs; **Opportunitätskostenmatrix** *f* VW matrix of opportunity costs

Opposition *f* GESCHÄFT, POL opposition; **Oppositionspartei** *f* POL opposition

optieren *vi* MGMNT opt; ◆ ~ **für** MGMNT opt for

optimal *adj* GESCHÄFT optimal, optimum; ~**e Arbeitsanstrengung** *f* VW optimal work effort; ~**e Bestellmenge** *f* IND, VW economic order quantity (*EOQ*); ~**e Besteuerung** *f* STEUER optimal taxation; ~**es Depotmanagement** *nt* FINANZ portfolio selection; ~**es Fassungsvermögen** *nt* IND optimum capacity; ~**e Fertigungsmenge** *f* IND, MGMNT, VW economic manufacturing quantity; ~**e Kontrolle** *f* VW optimal control; ~**e Kursstützung** *f* VW optimal peg; ~**es Leistungsvermögen** *nt* IND optimum capacity; ~**e Losgröße** *f* IND, MGMNT, VW economic batch quantity, economic batch size; ~**e Ressourcenallokation** *f* VW optimum allocation of resources; ~**e Stadt** *f* VW optimum city; ~**e Verschmutzungsrate** *f* UMWELT, VW optimal rate of pollution; ~**er Währungsraum** *m* VW optimum currency area; ~**er Zoll** *m* VW optimal tariff

Optimalbetrieb *m* VW optimum firm

Optimalität *f* VW optimality

Optimalkapazität *f* VW optimum capacity

optimieren *vt* GESCHÄFT optimize

Optimierung *f* GESCHÄFT optimization; **Optimierungsproblem** *nt* MATH optimization problem

Optimismus *m* GESCHÄFT optimism

Optimist, in *m,f* GESCHÄFT optimist

optimistisch *adj* GESCHÄFT upbeat, optimistic

Option *f* BÖRSE option, privilege (*AmE*), FINANZ, GESCHÄFT option, call; ~ **auf Kassakontrakte** BÖRSE *Wertpapiersektor* option on actuals; ~ **ohne Substanzwert** BÖRSE extrinsic value; ~ **auf Terminkontrakte** BÖRSE option on futures; ~ **auf Verlängerung** *f* GRUND renewal option; ◆ ~ **ausüben oder aufgeben** BÖRSE fill-or-kill (*AmE*) (*FOK*); **eine** ~ **festsetzen** BÖRSE declare an option; **eine** ~ **gegen eine andere Option verkaufen** BÖRSE write an option against another option; **eine** ~ **übernehmen** BÖRSE take up an option

Option: **Optionensatz** *m* BÖRSE set of options; **Optionsanleihe** *f* BANK warrant bond, BÖRSE bond cum warrant, FINANZ warrant issue; **Optionsgeber** *m* **für eine Verkaufs- und Kaufoption** BÖRSE taker for a put and call; **Optionsgebühr** *f* FINANZ option fee;

Optionsgeschäft *nt* **mit Termindevisen** BÖRSE option forward; **Optionshandel** *m* BÖRSE, VW option-trading; **Optionsinhaber, in** *m,f* BÖRSE option holder; **Optionsmarkt** *m* BÖRSE options market (*OM*); **Optionsnachfrage** *f* BÖRSE option demand; **Optionspreismodell** *nt* BÖRSE option price model (*OPM*); **Optionsschein** *m* BÖRSE, FINANZ, POL equity warrant, warrant; **mit Optionsschein** *phr* BÖRSE cum warrant; **Optionsscheindiskontierung** *f* FINANZ warrant discounting; **Optionsswap** *m* FINANZ swoption; **Options- und Terminkontrakte täglich bewerten** *phr* BÖRSE mark to the market; **Optionsverkäufer, in** *m,f* BÖRSE option writer

optisch: ~**er Leser** *m* COMP optical scanner; ~**e Platte** *f* COMP videodisk, optical disk; ~**e Zeichenerkennung** *f* (*OCR*) COMP optical character recognition (*OCR*)

OR *abbr* (*Operations-Research*) MGMNT, V&M OR (*operational research, operations research*)

orange: ~ **Waren** *f pl* V&M orange goods

ordentlich: ~**es Einkommen** *nt* STEUER ordinary gain, ordinary income; ~**es Gericht** *nt* RECHT court of law; ~**er Gewinn** *m* **vor Steuern** RECHNUNG ordinary profit before taxation; ~**e Sitzung** *f* MGMNT regular meeting

Order *f* V&M commission, order; ◆ **an die** ~ **von** V&M to the order of

Order: **Orderfrachtbrief** *m* IMP/EXP order bill of lading; **Orderkonnossement** *nt* BANK bill to order, IMP/EXP, TRANSP order bill of lading, negotiable bill of lading; **Orderlagerschein** *m* RECHT warehouse warrant (*WW*); **Orderpapier** *nt* BANK order paper

ordinal: ~**e Größe** *f* MATH magnitude; ~**er Nutzen** *m* VW ordinal utility; ~**e Nutzenmessung** *f* VW measurement of ordinal utility

ordinalistisch: ~**e Revolution** *f* VW ordinalist revolution

Ordinalskala *f* MATH ordinal scale

ordnen *vt* FINANZ regulate, GESCHÄFT, VERWALT put in order, VW *Industrie, Markt* regulate

Ordnung *f* GESCHÄFT arrangement; ◆ **etw in** ~ **bringen** GESCHÄFT put sth in order

Ordnung: **Ordnungsdaten** *pl* COMP control data; **Ordnungsdateneingabe** *f* COMP control data entry

ordnungsgemäß 1. *adj* GESCHÄFT regular, orderly; **2.** *adv* GESCHÄFT in due form, regularly; ◆ ~ **darstellen** RECHNUNG present fairly; **sich** ~ **niederlassen** VERWALT take up legal residence; ~ **vorgehen** GESCHÄFT go through the proper channels

ordnungsgemäß: ~**e Zahlung** *f* FINANZ clean payment

Ordnung: **Ordnungsziffer** *f* MATH sequence number

Org. *abbr* (*Organisation*) GESCHÄFT org. (*organization*)

Organ *nt* GESCHÄFT body

Organigramm *nt* MGMNT organigram, organizational chart, organization chart

Organisation *f* (*Org.*) GESCHÄFT organization (*org.*); ~ **der Afrikanischen Einheit** POL Organization of African Unity (*OAU*); ~ **amerikanischer Staaten** POL, VW Organization of American States (*OAS*); ~ **erdölexportierender Länder** (*OPEC*) POL, UMWELT, VW Organization of Petroleum-Exporting Countries (*OPEC*); ~ **für europäische wirtschaftliche Zusammenarbeit** (*OEEC*) VW Organization for European Economic Cooperation (*OEEC*); ~ **für Exportförderung** IMP/EXP export facilitation organization; ~ **mit großer Leitungsspanne** MGMNT flat organization; ~ **für Handelskooperation** VW

Organization for Trade Cooperation (*OTC*); **~ und Methoden** *f pl* (*O&M*) MGMNT organization and methods (*O&M*); **~ ohne Erwerbscharakter** VW non-profit-making organization; **~ der Vereinten Nationen für industrielle Entwicklung** (*UNIDO*) VW United Nations Industrial Development Organization (*UNIDO*); **~ für wirtschaftliche Zusammenarbeit und Entwicklung** (*OECD*) VW Organization for Economic Cooperation and Development (*OECD*); **~ zentralamerikanischer Staaten** POL Organization of Central American States (*OCAS*)

organisationell: ~e Praktikabilität *f* GESCHÄFT organizational convenience

Organisation: **Organisationsausschuß** *m* BANK, FINANZ steering committee; **Organisationseinheit** *f* VERWALT organizational unit; **Organisationsentwicklung** *f* MGMNT organization development, organizational development; **Organisationsform** *f* GESCHÄFT organizational shape; **Organisationskosten** *pl* FINANZ, RECHNUNG organization cost, organization expense; **Organisationskultur** *f* MGMNT organization culture; **Organisationslehre** *f* MGMNT organization theory; **Organisationspathologie** *f* PERSON *Betriebswirtschaft* organizational pathology; **Organisationsplan** *m* MGMNT organization chart, organizational chart, organigram; **Organisationsplanung** *f* MGMNT organization planning; **Organisationspolitik** *f* POL organizational politics; **Organisationspsychologie** *f* MGMNT organizational psychology; **Organisationsstruktur** *f* MGMNT organization structure; **Organisationstalent** *nt* PERSON organizational skills; **Organisationstheorie** *f* MGMNT, VW organization theory; **Organisationstheorien** *f pl* VW organizational economics; **Organisationsumfang** *m* GESCHÄFT organizational size; **Organisationsverhalten** *nt* MGMNT, V&M organizational behavior (*AmE*), organizational behaviour (*BrE*)

Organisator, in *m,f* GESCHÄFT organizer

organisatorisch: ~e Straffung *f* IND, MGMNT streamlining; **~e Veränderung** *f* MGMNT organizational change

organisch *adj* MGMNT, VW *Struktur* organic

organischbiologisch *adj* UMWELT organic; **~e Landwirtschaft** *f* UMWELT organic farming; **~e Lebensmittel** *nt pl* UMWELT organic foodstuffs

organisch: **~es Material** *nt* UMWELT organic material; **~es Wachstum** *nt* VW organic growth; **~e Zusammensetzung** *f* **des Kapitals** VW organic composition of capital

organisieren *vt* GESCHÄFT organize

organisiert: ~e Arbeitskampfmaßnahme *f* PERSON official action (*BrE*); **~e Arbeitskräfte** *f pl* PERSON organized labor (*AmE*), organized labour (*BrE*); **~er Markt** *m* VW organized market; **~er Streik** *m* PERSON *Gewerkschaftsbewegung* official strike; **~es Verbrechen** *nt* RECHT organized crime

Orientierung *f* POL orientation; **Orientierungspreis** *m* V&M target price

original *adj* GESCHÄFT original

Original *nt* GESCHÄFT *eines Schriftstücks* original, top copy, MEDIEN generation, master; ♦ **ein ~ und drei Kopien** VERWALT one top and three copies

original: **~e Adresse** *f* KOMM original address

Original-: **Originalangebot** *nt* GESCHÄFT original bid; **Originalbeleg** *m* VERSICH original slip; **Originaldokument** *nt* RECHT, VERWALT original docu-

ment; **Originaleinschuß** *m* BÖRSE deposit margin; **Originalfaktura** *f* GESCHÄFT original invoice; **Originalgerätehersteller** *m* (*OEM*) COMP original equipment manufacturer (*OEM*); **Originalkopie** *f* GESCHÄFT master copy; **Originalkostenvoranschlag** *m* GESCHÄFT original bid; **Originalofferte** *f* GESCHÄFT original bid; **Originalplan** *m* GESCHÄFT original plan; **Originalrechnung** *f* GESCHÄFT original invoice; **Originalschein** *m* VERSICH original slip; **Originalurkunde** *f* RECHT, VERWALT original document

Ort *m* GESCHÄFT locality, place; **~ der Abnahme** TRANSP place of acceptance (*POA*); **~ des Verkaufs** V&M point-of-sale (*POS*); ♦ **am** IMP/EXP loco; **vor ~** GESCHÄFT local, locally; **an ~ und Stelle** GESCHÄFT on the spot

örtlich 1. *adj* GESCHÄFT local, regional; 2. *adv* GESCHÄFT locally

örtlich: ~er Arbeitsmarkt *m* PERSON, VW local labor market (*AmE*), local labour market (*BrE*); **~e Behörde** *f* VERWALT local authority (*BrE*); **~e Behörden** *f pl* POL local government; **~e Gebietskörperschaft** *f* POL local government, VERWALT municipality; **~e Industrie** *f* IND local industry; **~e Lage** *f* GESCHÄFT site; **~es öffentliches Gut** *nt* VW local public good; **~es Unternehmen** *nt* GESCHÄFT local firm; **~e Verwaltung** *f* POL local government

Örtlichkeit *f* GESCHÄFT place

ortsansässig: ~e Arbeitskräfte *f pl* PERSON, VW local labor (*AmE*), local labour (*BrE*); **~e Firma** *f* GESCHÄFT local firm; **~es Gewerbe** *nt* PERSON *manuelle Arbeit, Facharbeiter* local trades and craftspeople

ortsanwesend: ~e Bevölkerung *f* VW de facto population

ortsfest: ~er Kran *m* IND fixed crane

Ort: **Ortsgebühr** *f* TRANSP local charge; **Ortsgespräch** *nt* KOMM local call; **Ortstarif** *m* KOMM local call rate, PERSON local agreement, district agreement (*BrE*)

ortsüblich: ~e Miete *f* GRUND local rent, fair market rent

Ort: **Ortsverein** *m* PERSON local union; **Ortsvorschrift** *f* RECHT bylaw; **Ortszeit** *f* GESCHÄFT local time, MEDIEN *Übertragung* station time (*AmE*); **Ortszulage** *f* PERSON *Sonderleistung* residential amount

Öse *f* IND *Maschinenbau* eye

OSI *abbr* (*Kommunikation offener Systeme, Open-Systems-Interconnection*) COMP OSI (*open systems interconnection*)

Ost- *in cpds* GESCHÄFT, POL east, eastern; **Ostblock** *m* POL Eastern Bloc

Österreichisch: ~e Bundesbahn *f* (*ÖBB*) TRANSP Austrian Federal Railways, ≈ British Rail (*BR*)

Osteuropa *nt* POL Eastern Europe; **Osteuropabank** *f* VW European Bank for Reconstruction and Development (*EBRD*)

Osteuropäisch: ~e Zeit *f* (*OEZ*) GESCHÄFT Eastern European Time (*EET*)

Ost-: **Ostküste** *f* **der Vereinigten Staaten** GESCHÄFT United States East Coast (*USEC*); **Ostküstenzeit** *f* GESCHÄFT Eastern Standard Time (*AmE*) (*EST*)

östlich *adj* GESCHÄFT eastern; **~e Standardzeit** *f* GESCHÄFT Eastern Standard Time (*AmE*) (*EST*)

Ost-: **Ostsee** *f* TRANSP Baltic Sea

Ottokraftstoff *m* TRANSP motor spirit

Otto-Normalverbraucher *phr infrml* V&M the average punter (*infrml*)

O&M *abbr* (*Organisation und Methoden*) MGMNT O&M (*organization and methods*)

Outplacement *nt* PERSON *Entlassung* outplacement

Output *m* COMP, RECHNUNG output; **Output-Varianz** *f* MATH output variance

outputorientiert: **~es Budget** *nt* POL planning programming budget

Outright-Terminkauf *m* VW outright forward purchase

Outsourcing *nt* MGMNT outsourcing

Overheadprojektor *m* VERWALT overhead projector

Overkill *m* infrml V&M *Kahlschlag* overkill (*infrml*)

Ozean- *in cpds* TRANSP ocean; **Ozeanlinienschiff** *nt* TRANSP ocean liner

Ozon *nt* IND, UMWELT ozone; **Ozonabbau** *m* UMWELT ozone depletion; **Ozonschicht** *f* UMWELT ozone layer

P

p.a. *abbr* (*per annum*) GESCHÄFT p.a. (*per annum*)

p.A. *abbr* (*per Adresse*) GESCHÄFT, IMP/EXP, KOMM c/o (*care of*)

Paarvergleich *m* GESCHÄFT paired comparison

Paasche-Index *m* VW Paasche index

Pacht *f* GRUND lease, tenancy, leasehold; **~ auf Lebenszeit** GRUND life tenancy; **~ auf neunundneunzig Jahre** BANK ninety-nine-year lease; **~ mit Vorkaufsrecht** GRUND lease with option to purchase; **Pachtabtretung** *f* GRUND, RECHT assignment of lease; **Pachtbesitz** *m* GRUND leasehold; **Pachteinnahme** *f* GRUND rental

pachten *vt* GRUND lease

Pächter, in *m,f* GRUND leaseholder, tenant; **Pächterrecht** *nt* RECHT tenant right (*BrE*)

Pacht: **Pachtfischerei** *f* VW share fishing; **Pachtgrundstück** *nt* GRUND leasehold, leasehold property; **Pachtgrundstückswert** *m* GRUND leasehold value; **Pachtgutversicherung** *f* VERSICH leasehold insurance; **Pachtkündigung** *f* GRUND termination; **Pacht- und Leihvertrag** *m* GRUND leaselend; **Pacht- und Mietkündigung** *f* GRUND notice to quit; **Pachtverhältnis** *nt* GRUND, RECHT tenancy; **Pachtvertrag** *m* RECHT lease

Pack- *in cpds* IMP/EXP, IND, TRANSP packing, packaging

Päckchen *nt* KOMM, TRANSP package (*pkg., pkge*), packet (*pkt.*), parcel, *Post* small parcel

packen *vt* COMP *Daten* KOMM, TRANSP pack

Packen 1. *m infrml* GESCHÄFT *Geldscheine* wad, MEDIEN *Zeitungen* stack, bundle; **2.** *nt* IND, TRANSP *Container* stuffing; **~ und Auspacken** GESCHÄFT, IND, TRANSP *Container* stuffing and stripping

Packer *m* IND *Person, Maschine* packer

Pack-: **Packing Kredit** *m* BANK anticipatory packing credit; **Packleinwand** *f* TRANSP tow cloth; **Packliste** *f* IMP/EXP, TRANSP packaging list, packing list; **Packmaschine** *f* IND packer; **Packmaterial** *nt* IND packaging; **Packstück** *nt* V&M package

Packung *f* KOMM, TRANSP pack, package (*pkg., pkge*), V&M banded pack

pacta: **~ sunt servanda** *phr* RECHT *Vertragsrecht* pacta sunt servanda

Pädagogik *f* PERSON, SOZIAL education

p.Adr. *abbr* (*per Adresse*) GESCHÄFT, IMP/EXP, KOMM c/o (*care of*)

pagatorisch: **~e Kosten** *pl* RECHNUNG, VERWALT actual cost; **~e Rechnung** *f* RECHNUNG cash basis of accounting

paginieren *vt* COMP, MEDIEN *Dokument* paginate

Paginierung *f* V&M folio, COMP, MEDIEN *Dokument* pagination

Paket *nt* BÖRSE lot, block, block of shares, holding, FINANZ lot, block, block of shares, holding, package, KOMM, TRANSP package (*pkg., pkge*), packet (*pkt.*), parcel; **Paketgeschäft** *nt* BÖRSE bundled deal; **Pakethandel** *m* BÖRSE block trading

Paketierhof *m* TRANSP bundling yard

Paket: **Paketmarkt** *m* TRANSP parcels market; **Paketpost** *f* KOMM parcel post; **etw per Paketpost versenden** *phr* KOMM send sth by parcel post; **Paketpostversicherung** *f* KOMM, VERSICH parcel post insurance; **Paketsendung** *f* KOMM parcel post; **Paketwagen** *m* TRANSP parcels van

Pakt *m* GESCHÄFT pact, POL alliance; **~ zur engeren wirtschaftlichen Zusammenarbeit** VW Closer Economic Relations Pact

Palette *f* IND, TRANSP pallet, stillage; ♦ **auf Paletten packen** IND, TRANSP palletize

Palette: **Palettengabel** *f* IND, TRANSP pallet fork; **Palettennetz** *nt* IND, TRANSP pallet net; **Palettenspur** *f* IND, TRANSP pallet net

palettieren *vt* IND, TRANSP palletize

palettiert: **~es Verstauen** *nt* IND, TRANSP palletized stowage

Palettierung *f* IND, TRANSP palletization

palettisierbar *adj* IND, TRANSP palletizable

palettisieren *vt* IND, TRANSP palletize

Palettisieren *nt* IND, TRANSP palletization

Palmöl *nt* IND palm oil

Panamax: **~ Schiff** *nt* TRANSP Panamax vessel

Panel *nt* GESCHÄFT, POL, V&M panel; **Paneldaten** *pl* V&M panel data; **Panelerhebung** *f* V&M panel testing

paneuropäisch *adj* POL pan-European; **~es Unternehmen** *nt* GESCHÄFT pan-European company

Panik *f* BÖRSE, FINANZ, MEDIEN panic; **Panikmache** *f* *infrml* BÖRSE, FINANZ, MEDIEN scaremongering; **Panikmacherei** *f* BÖRSE, FINANZ, MEDIEN scare tactics

Panne *f* TRANSP breakdown; **~ haben** *phr* TRANSP break down

Panoramaseite *f* MEDIEN *Druck* center spread (*AmE*), centerfold (*AmE*), centre spread (*BrE*), centrefold (*BrE*)

panschen *vt* GESCHÄFT adulterate, water down

Panzerschrank *m* BANK safe

Paperback *nt* MEDIEN paperback

Papier *nt* GESCHÄFT paper; **~ der Zentralregierung** FINANZ, POL central government item; **Papieraktenvernichter** *m* VERWALT shredder; **Papiereinzug** *m* COMP paper feed; **Papierfabrik** *f* UMWELT paper mill; **Papierführung** *f* COMP paper track; **Papiergeld** *nt* BANK, FINANZ paper money, soft money; **Papiergeld** *nt* **ohne Deckung** FINANZ fiat money; **Papiergold** *nt* BANK paper gold; **Papierindustrie** *f* UMWELT paper industry; **Papierkorbpost** *f* KOMM junk mail; **Papierlocher** *m* VERWALT paper punch; **Papierrand** *m* MEDIEN *einer Seite* margin; **Papierstau** *m* COMP *Drucker* jam; **Papierstreifen** *m* BÖRSE ticker tape; **Papiertransportdrucker** *m* COMP friction-feed printer; **Papierverlauf** *m* MEDIEN *Druck* run of paper (*ROP*); **Papiervorschub** *m* COMP paper throw; **Papierwährung** *f* VW paper currency; **Papierwarenhändler, in** *m,f* VERWALT stationer

Pappe *f* IND fiberboard (*AmE*), fibreboard (*BrE*), V&M cardboard

Paradefall *m* GESCHÄFT textbook case

Paradox *nt* GESCHÄFT paradox; **~ der Sparsamkeit** VW paradox of thrift

Paragraph *m* RECHT paragraph, section

Parallel- *in cpds* BANK, FINANZ, GESCHÄFT parallel

parallel *adj* BÖRSE matched, FINANZ, GESCHÄFT, IND parallel; ♦ **~ zu** GESCHÄFT in parallel with

parallel: **~e Geschäfte** *nt pl* GESCHÄFT parallel trading; **~e Produktionsstätten** *f pl* IND *Produktion* parallel plants

Parallel-: **Parallelanleihe** *f* BANK, FINANZ parallel loan; **Paralleldarlehen** *nt* BANK, FINANZ parallel loan

Parallele *f* GESCHÄFT parallel

Parallel-: **Parallelimport** *m* IMP/EXP parallel import

Parallelismus *m* RECHT *Veträge* parallelism

Parallel-: **Parallelkredit** *m* BANK, FINANZ parallel loan, back-to-back loan; **Parallelschnittstelle** *f* COMP parallel interface; **Parallelüberweisungen** *f pl* BANK back-to-back transfers; **Parallelverarbeitung** *f* COMP parallel processing; **Parallelwährung** *f* GESCHÄFT parallel standard, VW parallel currency; **Parallelwährungsstrategie** *f* VW parallel currency strategy; **Parallelzugriff** *m* COMP parallel access

Parameter *m* COMP, MATH parameter; ♦ **~ festsetzen** MATH set parameters

parameterfrei: **~e Statistik** *f* MATH nonparametric statistics

parametergesteuert: **~e Software** *f* COMP parameter-driven software

Parameter: **Parameterschätzung** *f* MATH estimation of parameters

parametrisch: **~es Programmieren** *nt* COMP parametric programming; **~e Programmierung** *f* MATH parametric programming; **~e Statistik** *f* MATH parametric statistics

parasitär: **~e Stadt** *f* VW parasitic city

Parenthese *f* COMP, MEDIEN parenthesis

Pareto: **Pareto-Analyse** *f* VW Pareto analysis; **Pareto-Effizienz** *f* VW Pareto efficiency; **Pareto-Gesetz** *nt* VW Pareto's Law; **Pareto-Optimalität** *f* VW Pareto optimality

pareto-optimal: **~e Volkswirtschaft** *f* VW first best economy

Pareto: **Pareto-Optimum** *nt* VW Pareto optimum; **Pareto-Verbesserung** *f* VW Pareto improvement

pari: **über ~** *phr* BÖRSE, FINANZ above par; **unter ~** *phr* BÖRSE, FINANZ below par; **zu ~** *phr* BÖRSE, FINANZ at face value, at par

Parikurs *m* BÖRSE, FINANZ par

Paris: **~er Club** *m* VW Paris Club; **~er Finanzterminbörse** *f* BÖRSE Paris Financial Futures Exchange; **~er Handelsoptionsbörse** *f* BÖRSE Paris Trader Options Exchange; **~er Interbankenangebotssatz** *m* BANK Paris Interbank Offered Rate (*PIBOR*); **~er Wertpapierbörse** *f* BÖRSE Paris Stock Exchange

Parität *f* COMP, MATH, RECHT, VERSICH, VW parity

paritätisch: **~ besetzter Betriebsausschuß** *m* IND Joint Industrial Council (*BrE*) (*JIC*); **~e Mitbestimmungsrechte** *nt pl* BÖRSE codetermination rights

Parität: **Paritätsbit** *nt* COMP parity bit; **Paritätsklausel** *f* VERSICH parity clause; **Paritätskontrolle** *f* COMP parity check; **Paritätskurs** *m* VW parity price; **Paritätspreisbildung** *f* VW parity pricing; **Paritätssystem** *nt* VW par value system

Pariwert *m* BÖRSE, FINANZ par

Park- *in cpds* TRANSP parking

Parken *nt* TRANSP car parking

Parkett *nt* BÖRSE trading floor, dealing floor, floor, FINANZ floor, FREI *Theater* stalls (*BrE*), parquet (*AmE*); **Parketthändler** *m* BÖRSE floor trader, floor broker

Park-: **Parkhaus** *nt* GRUND, TRANSP multi storey car park

Parkinson: **~sches Gesetz** *nt* PERSON *Betriebswirtschaft* Parkinson's law

Park-: **Parkmöglichkeit** *f* TRANSP parking facilities; **Parkplatz** *m* TRANSP car park (*BrE*), parking lot (*AmE*); **Park-und-Ride** *nt* (*P&R*) TRANSP park and ride

Parlament *nt* POL Parliament; **~ des Commonwealth** POL Parliament of the Commonwealth

parlamentarisch *adj* POL parliamentary; **~e Geschäftsordnung** *f* POL parliamentary procedure; **~e Haushaltsmittelbereitstellung** *f* FINANZ, POL parliamentary appropriation; **~e Stimme** *f* POL parliamentary vote; **~e Untersuchungskommission** *f* RECHT tribunal of enquiry

Parlament: **Parlamentsmitglied** *nt* POL Member of Congress (*AmE*), Member of Parliament (*BrE*) (*MP*)

Parole *f* GESCHÄFT, V&M watchword

Partei *f* POL *Parlament*, RECHT *eines Vertrages* party; ♦ **~ ergreifen für** GESCHÄFT take sides with

parteiabtrünnig *adj* POL off the reservation (*jarg*) (*AmE*), without the whip (*jarg*) (*BrE*)

Partei: **Parteiautonomie** *f* RECHT *Vertragsrecht* party autonomy

Parteidisziplin: **der ~ unterworfen** *phr* POL on the reservation (*jarg*) (*AmE*), under the whip (*jarg*) (*BrE*); **nicht mehr der ~ unterworfen** *phr* POL off the reservation (*jarg*) (*AmE*), without the whip (*jarg*) (*BrE*)

Partei: **Parteienlandschaft** *f* POL party political scene; **Parteienverkehr** *m* Öst GESCHÄFT office hours, opening hours, VERWALT opening hours; **Parteiideologe** *m*, **Parteiideologin** *f* POL policy maker, guru (*infrml*)

Parteilichkeit *f* GESCHÄFT bias, partiality

Partei: **Parteilinie** *f* POL party line

parteipolitisch *adj* POL party-political; **~er Beitrag** *m* POL political levy; **~e Spende** *f* POL political donation

parteitreu *adj* POL on the reservation (*jarg*) (*AmE*), under the whip (*BrE*)

parteiuntreu *adj* POL off the reservation (*jarg*) (*AmE*), without the whip (*jarg*) (*BrE*)

Partei: **Parteiverhalten** *nt* RECHT behavior of the parties (*AmE*), behaviour of the parties (*BrE*); **Parteiwille** *m* RECHT *Vertragsrecht* party's intention

partes: **~ per millionem** *phr* (*ppm*) GESCHÄFT parts per million (*ppm*)

Partie *f* IND batch

partiell: **~e Arbeitslosigkeit** *f* PERSON *Arbeitsmarkt, Statistik* partial unemployment; **~es Gleichgewicht** *nt* VW partial equilibrium; **~e Gleichgewichtsanalyse** *f* VW partial equilibrium analysis; **~e Regression** *f* VW partial regression; **~e Zuteilung** *f* POL suballotment

Partition *f* COMP *Festplatte* partition

Partizipationshierarchie *f* POL ladder of participation

partizipativ: **~e Finanzplanung** *f* FINANZ, MGMNT participative budgeting; **~er Führungsstil** *m* MGMNT participative leadership; **~es Management** *nt* MGMNT participative management; **partizipativ-demokratisch** *adj* MGMNT participative-democratic; **~e**

Unternehmensführung *f* MGMNT bottom-up management

Partner, in *m,f* GESCHÄFT associate, joint proprietor, partner; ◆ **einen Partner aufnehmen** GESCHÄFT take a partner

Partner: **Partnerlebens- und Krankenversicherung** *f* VERSICH business life and health insurance; **Partnerlebens- und Unfallversicherung** *f* VERSICH partnership life and health insurance; **Partnerrente** *f* VERSICH joint and survivor annuity (*AmE*)

Partnerschaft *f* GESCHÄFT partnership

Partyverkauf *m* V&M party selling

Parzelle *f* GRUND parcel, plot

parzellieren *vt* GRUND divide into small plots

Paß *m* FREI, TRANSP, VERWALT passport

Passage *f* MEDIEN *Buch* passage

Passagier *m* FREI, TRANSP passenger; ◆ **ohne Passagiere fahren** TRANSP *Bus, Zug* run empty

Passagier: **Passagieranalyse** *f* FREI passenger analysis; **Passagierbericht** *m* TRANSP passenger return; **Passagierbetreuung** *f* FREI passenger care; **Passagierdampfer** *m* TRANSP passenger liner; **Passagierdurchsatz** *m* TRANSP passenger throughput, passenger thruput (*AmE*); **Passagierflugzeug** *nt* TRANSP passenger aircraft; **Passagiergebühr** *f* FREI, TRANSP passenger toll; **Passagiergebühren** *f pl* FREI, TRANSP passenger dues

passagierklassifiziert: **~er Verkehr** *m* TRANSP passenger-rated traffic

Passagier: **Passagierkontrolle** *f* FREI passenger control; **Passagierkupon** *m* FREI passenger coupon; **Passagierküstenschiff** *nt* TRANSP home trade passenger ship; **Passagierlift** *m* TRANSP passenger lift; **Passagierlinienschiff** *nt* TRANSP passenger liner; **Passagierliste** *f* TRANSP passenger list; **Passagier-Lounge** *f* TRANSP passenger lounge; **Passagiermakler, in** *m,f* PERSON *Agent für Dampfschiffgesellschaft* runner; **Passagiermarkt** *m* TRANSP passenger market; **Passagiermeilen pro Fahrzeugstunde** *phr* TRANSP passenger miles per vehicle hour; **Passagierschiff** *nt* TRANSP passenger ship; **Passagiersicherheitszertifikat** *nt* TRANSP passenger safety certificate; **Passagierstrategie** *f* TRANSP passenger strategy; **Passagierterminal** *m* TRANSP passenger terminal; **Passagiertonnage** *f* TRANSP passenger tonnage

Passant, in *m,f* GESCHÄFT, V&M *an einem Plakat* passer-by

passé *adj infrml* GESCHÄFT out of date

passend *adj* BÖRSE fit, GESCHÄFT suitable; ◆ **~ für** GESCHÄFT suitable for; applicable to

Passierschein *m* GESCHÄFT entry permit, pass, TRANSP sea letter, VERWALT pass

Paßinhaber, in *m,f* FREI, TRANSP, VERWALT passport-holder

passiv *adj* GESCHÄFT passive, RECHNUNG adverse; **~er Anleger** *m* FINANZ passive investor; **~e Handelsbilanz** *f* IMP/EXP, POL, VW adverse trade balance, trade deficit, unfavorable balance of trade (*AmE*), unfavourable balance of trade (*BrE*); **~er Investor** *m* FINANZ passive investor; **~e Rechnungsabgrenzungsposten** *m pl* RECHNUNG accrued expenses, accrued liability; **~e Tätigkeit** *f* STEUER passive activity; **~er Transithandel** *m* VW passive transit trade

Passivgeschäft *nt* BANK deposit-taking business

Passivsaldo *m* FINANZ debit balance

Paß: **Paßkontrolle** *f* FREI, TRANSP, VERWALT passport check

Pastor *m* PERSON minister

Paßwort *nt* COMP password

Pat. *abbr* (*Patent*) PATENT, RECHT pat. (*patent*)

Patent *nt* (*Pat.*) PATENT, RECHT patent (*pat.*); ◆ **ein ~ anmelden** PATENT take out a patent; **ein ~ erwirken** PATENT take out a patent; **~ angemeldet** PATENT patent pending

Patent: **Patentanfechtung** *f* PATENT *Warenzeichen* opposition; **Patentanmeldung** *f* PATENT patent application; **Patentanmeldung läuft** *phr* PATENT patent pending (*pat. pend.*); **Patentausnützung** *f* PATENT licence (*BrE*), license (*AmE*); **Patentauswertung** *f* IND, PATENT working; **Patentbeschreibung** *f* PATENT patent specification; **Patentdauer** *f* PATENT term of patent, patent life; **Patenteinspruch** *m* PATENT opposition; **Patenterneuerungsgebühr** *f* PATENT patent renewal fee; **Patenterteilung** *f* PATENT, RECHT granting of a patent

patentfähig *adj* PATENT, RECHT patentable; **~e Erfindung** *f* PATENT patentable invention

Patent: **Patentfähigkeit** *f* PATENT, RECHT patentability; **Patentgebühr** *f* PATENT patent royalty, royalty; **Patenthandel** *m* PATENT patent trading

patentierbar *adj* PATENT, RECHT patentable; **~e Erfindung** *f* PATENT patentable invention

Patentierbarkeit *f* PATENT patentability

patentieren *vt* PATENT patent; ◆ **etw ~ lassen** PATENT *Erfindung* take out a patent on sth

patentiert *adj* PATENT patented; **nicht ~** *adj* PATENT unpatented

Patent: **Patentinformationsnetz** *nt* PATENT, RECHT Patent Information Network (*BrE*); **Patentinhaber, in** *m,f* PATENT patent proprietor, patentee; **Patentkooperationsvertrag** *m* PATENT, RECHT Patent Cooperation Treaty (*PCT*); **Patentlösung** *f* GESCHÄFT quick fix; **Patentrecht** *nt* PATENT, RECHT patent law, patent right, right to a patent; **Patentrechte** *nt pl* PATENT, RECHT patent rights; **Patentrolle** *f* PATENT register; **Patentschrift** *f* PATENT patent specification, specification; **Patentschutz** *m* PATENT, RECHT patent protection; **Patentübertragung** *f* PATENT assignment; **Patenturkunde** *f* PATENT patent certificate; **Patentverlängerungsgebühr** *f* PATENT renewal fee; **Patentverletzung** *f* PATENT, RECHT patent infringement; **jdn wegen Patentverletzung verklagen** *phr* PATENT sue sb for infringement of patent; **Patentverwertung** *f* PATENT exploitation; **Patentverzicht** *m* PATENT, RECHT surrender of a patent

Paternalismus *m* MGMNT paternalism

Patrimonialindustrie *f* IND patrimonial industry

Patronatserklärung *f* BÖRSE, FINANZ, GESCHÄFT letter of comfort, comfort letter

Patt: **ein ~ erreichen** *phr* GESCHÄFT reach a stalemate

Pauschal- *in cpds* GESCHÄFT flat-rate, lump sum, package

pauschal *adj* GESCHÄFT across-the-board, flat-rate, all-in, all-inclusive; **~e Absatzprovision** *f* GESCHÄFT override; **~e Aussage** *f* GESCHÄFT blanket statement; **~e Einbehaltung** *f* STEUER flat-rate withholding; **~e**

Erhöhung *f* MGMNT across-the-board increase; **~e Finanzzuweisung** *f* POL block grant; **~e Kürzung** *f* VW meat-axe reduction; **~e Veränderungen** *f pl* MGMNT across-the-board changes; **~er Werkvertrag** *m* bis zur schlüsselfertigen Übergabe RECHT turnkey contract; **~er Zuschuß** *m* VERWALT block grant

Pauschal-: **Pauschalabonnement** *nt* FINANZ flat-rate subscription; **Pauschalabschreibung** *f* FINANZ composite depreciation; **Pauschalangebot** *nt* FREI package deal, VW package offer; **Pauschalarztkostenversicherung** *f* VERSICH blanket medical expense insurance; **Pauschalbetrag** *m* BANK, FINANZ, STEUER, VERSICH lump sum (*ls*); **Pauschalbeträge** *m pl* STEUER Round Sum Allowances (*BrE*); **Pauschalbewilligung** *f* VERWALT block grant; **Pauschalcharter** *f* TRANSP lump sum charter; **Pauschaldeckung** *f* V&M blanket coverage

Pauschale *f* BANK, FINANZ, STEUER, VERSICH lump sum (*ls*)

Pauschal-: **Pauschalfracht** *f* TRANSP lump sum freight; **Pauschalgebühr** *f* BANK, PATENT flat fee, flat-rate fee; **Pauschalgebühren** *f pl* VERWALT flat charges; **Pauschalhaftpflichtversicherung** *f* VERSICH umbrella liability insurance; **Pauschalkautionsversicherung** *f* VERSICH blanket fidelity bond; **Pauschalkosten** *pl* VERWALT flat charges; **Pauschalkrankheitskostenversicherung** *f* VERSICH blanket medical expense insurance; **Pauschalpolice** *f* VERSICH blanket contract, unvalued policy, blanket policy; **Pauschalprämie** *f* VERSICH fixed premium; **Pauschalpreis** *m* GESCHÄFT all-inclusive price, flat-rate price, lump sum price; **Pauschalrate** *f* TRANSP consolidated rate; **Pauschalreise** *f* FREI package tour (*BrE*), inclusive tour (*IT*), package holiday (*BrE*); **Pauschalrente** *f* VERSICH fixed annuity; **Pauschalrückversicherung** *f* VERSICH flat line re-insurance; **Pauschalsachversicherung** *f* VERSICH block policy; **Pauschalsatz** *m* GESCHÄFT blanket rate, composite rate; **Pauschalsteuer** *f* STEUER flat-rate tax, lump sum tax; **Pauschalsteuersatz** *m* STEUER composite rate tax; **Pauschaltarif** *m* GESCHÄFT blanket rate, PERSON, STEUER flat scale, VERWALT inclusive rate; **Pauschalurlaub** *m* FREI package holiday; **Pauschalversicherung** *f* VERSICH blanket insurance, floater (*AmE*); **Pauschalversicherungsvertrag** *m* VERSICH blanket policy, blanket bond; **Pauschalzahlung** *f* PERSON flat rate of pay

Pause *f* FREI *Theater* interval, GESCHÄFT break, pause, IND *Kopie* tracing, KOMM break, MEDIEN *Kopie* tracing, PERSON *Mittagspause* break; ♦ **~ machen** GESCHÄFT take a break

Pause: **Pausenzeichen** *nt* MEDIEN, V&M signature tune

Pay-TV *nt* MEDIEN pay TV

pazifisch: **~e Randgebiete** *nt pl* GESCHÄFT Pacific Rim

p.c. *abbr* (*percentum, Prozent, prozentig*) GESCHÄFT P/C (*percent, per cent*), pc (*percent, per cent*)

PC *abbr* (*Personalcomputer*) COMP PC (*personal computer*); **PC-gestützt** *adj* COMP computer-aided, computer-assisted, computer-based, PC-based; **PC-Kompatibilität** *f* COMP PC-compatibility; **PC-unterstützt** *adj* COMP PC-based

Pearson-Bericht *m* VW Pearson Report

Peer-Gruppe *f* V&M peer group

Pegel *m* IND *Geräusch, Lärm* level

Peilfunkeinrichtung *f* TRANSP direction finder (*DF*)

pekuniär: **~e externe Ersparnisse** *f pl* VW pecuniary external economy; **~e Skalenerträge** *m pl* VW pecuniary economy of scale

Pen-Computer *m* COMP *Palmtop* pen-based computer

pendeln *vi* GESCHÄFT, TRANSP *zur Arbeit* commute

Pendeln *nt* GESCHÄFT, TRANSP *zur Arbeit* commuting

Pendelschiedsverfahren *nt* PERSON flip-flop arbitration, pendulum arbitration

Pendelverkehr *m* TRANSP commutation (*AmE*), shuttle service, commuter traffic

Pendelverkehrdienstleistung *f* TRANSP commuter service

Pendelwanderung *f* VW *der Bevölkerung* circular migration

Pendler, in *m,f* GESCHÄFT, TRANSP commuter

Penetration *f* V&M penetration; **Penetrationspreispolitik** *f* V&M penetration pricing; **Penetrationsrate** *f* V&M penetration rate

Pension *f* FINANZ *Ruhegehalt* pension, retirement pension, retirement pay, retiring allowance, superannuation, *im öffentlichen Dienst* state pension, *Ruhestand* retirement, FREI *Unterkunftskosten* board, *Gästehaus* guest-house, boarding house, PERSON, SOZIAL, VERSICH *Ruhegehalt* pension, retirement pension, retirement pay, retiring allowance, superannuation, *im öffentlichen Dienst* state pension, *Ruhestand* retirement; ♦ **in ~ gehen** SOZIAL *Ruhestand* go into retirement

Pensionär, in *m,f* PERSON, SOZIAL old-age pensioner (*BrE*) (*OAP*), retired person, retiree (*AmE*)

pensionieren *vt* FINANZ, PERSON, SOZIAL, VERSICH pension off; ♦ **sich ~ lassen** PERSON *Ruhestand* retire on a pension

pensioniert *adj* FINANZ, PERSON, SOZIAL, VERSICH *Ruhestand* retired, superannuated

Pensionierung *f* FINANZ, PERSON, SOZIAL, VERSICH retirement; **Pensionierungsalter** *nt* PERSON retirement age; **Pensionierungsentlastung** *f* STEUER retirement relief (*BrE*)

Pension: **Pensionsalter** *nt* PERSON, SOZIAL pensionable age

pensionsberechtigt *adj* FINANZ, PERSON, SOZIAL, VERSICH pensionable, PERSON eligible for retirement

pensionsfähig *adj* FINANZ, PERSON, SOZIAL, VERSICH pensionable; **~es Alter** *nt* PERSON, SOZIAL retiring age

Pension: **Pensionsfonds** *m* FINANZ, RECHNUNG, VERSICH retirement fund, superfund (*AmE*), pension fund, superannuation fund; **Pensionsfreibetrag** *m* STEUER retirement relief (*BrE*); **Pensionsgast** *m* FREI *Unterkunft* paying guest (*PG*); **Pensionsgeschäft** *nt* BÖRSE, FINANZ sale and purchase agreement; **Pensionskasse** *f* FINANZ, RECHNUNG, VERSICH pension fund, retirement fund, superfund (*AmE*); **Pensionskassensystem** *nt* mit Rechtsanspruch FINANZ defined benefit pension plan; **Pensionskonto** *nt* VERSICH superannuation account

Pensionsplan *m* FINANZ, PERSON retirement scheme; **~ mit definierten Beiträgen** FINANZ defined contribution pension plan; **~ ohne Beitragsleistungen der Arbeitnehmer** PERSON noncontributory pension fund, noncontributory pension scheme; **Pensionsplanfinanzierung** *f* FINANZ pension plan funding; **Pensionsplanüberbrückung** *f* FINANZ early-retirement benefit

Pension: **Pensionssatz** *m* BANK, FINANZ repurchase rate; **Pensionssicherungsgesetz** *nt* PERSON employee retirement income security act; **Pensionssystem** *nt* PERSON retirement plan; **Pensionsverbindlichkeit** *f* RECHNUNG pension liability; **Pensionszahlung** *f* STEUER pension payment

Pensum *nt* MGMNT quota; ◆ **sein ~ bewältigen** PERSON *Arbeit* do one's stint

Penthouse *nt* GRUND penthouse

per *prep* KOMM via; ◆ **~ Adresse** (*p.A.*, *p.Adr.*) GESCHÄFT, IMP/EXP, KOMM care of (*c/o*); **~ annum** (*p.a.*) GESCHÄFT per annum (*p.a.*); **~ procura** (*pp.*, *ppa.*) GESCHÄFT, per procurationem (*frml*) (*pp, per pro*)

percentum *adv* (*v.H.*) MATH percent, per cent (*P/C, pc*)

Perestroika *f* POL, VW perestroika

Perforator *m* COMP tape punch

Periode *f* GESCHÄFT period; **~ mit geringen Fehlzeiten** PERSON *Produktionsfähigkeit* bull week; **Periodenabgrenzung** *f* RECHNUNG accrual concept, accrual principle; **Periodeneinkommen** *nt* RECHNUNG accounting income

periodenfremd: **~e Aufwendungen** *f pl* **und Erträge** *m pl* RECHNUNG, VW below-the-line items

periodengerecht: **~e Abgrenzung** *f* RECHNUNG accrual accounting; **~e Aufwands- und Ertragsrechnung** *f* RECHNUNG accrual basis of accounting; **~e Buchung** *f* **von Finanzzusagen** RECHNUNG commitment accounting; **~e Einkommensteuerverbuchung** *f* RECHNUNG, STEUER interperiod income tax allocation; **~er Zinssatz** *m* BANK, RECHNUNG accrual interest rate

Periode: **Periodengewinn** *m* RECHNUNG accounting income

periodisch *adj* GESCHÄFT periodic, periodical; **~e Bestandsaufnahme** *f* RECHNUNG periodic inventory method; **~e festgesetzte Obergrenze** *f* FINANZ period cap; **~e Prüfung** *f* VW repeating audit

periodisiert: **~es Zolldeklarationssystem** *nt* IMP/EXP period entry scheme

peripher *adj* COMP, IND, VW peripheral; **~e Geräte** *nt pl* COMP, IND peripherals, peripheral equipment; **~er Kapitalismus** *m* VW peripheral capitalism; **~es Unternehmen** *nt* VW peripheral firm

Peripherie *f* COMP peripherals, peripheral equipment, GRUND *der Stadt* suburbs, IND peripherals, peripheral equipment; **Peripheriecomputer** *m* COMP peripheral computer; **Peripheriegerät** *nt* COMP, IND peripheral device

permanent: **~e Einkommenshypothese** *f* VW permanent income hypothesis; **~e Inventur** *f* FINANZ, RECHNUNG perpetual inventory; **~e Prüfung** *f* RECHNUNG continuing audit

Permutation *f* MATH permutation

Perso *m* *infrml* VERWALT identity card (*ID card*)

Person *f* GESCHÄFT person; **~ mit ständigem Wohnsitz** RECHT permanent resident

Persona: **~ grata** *f* RECHT persona grata; **~ non grata** *f* RECHT persona non grata

Personal *nt* GESCHÄFT, IND workforce, MGMNT, PERSON personnel, staff, workforce; **~ in Lebensstellung** PERSON tenured staff; ◆ **das ~ abbauen** PERSON *Rationalisierung* trim the workforce; **~ abwerben** MGMNT headhunt; **mit ~ besetzen** PERSON man, staff;

mit ~ besetzt PERSON staffed; **~ freisetzen** PERSON lay off staff; **zu wenig ~ haben** PERSON be short-staffed

Personal: **Personalabbau** *m* PERSON reduction in force (*RIF*), demanning, staff cut-back, shake-out; **Personalabteilung** *f* PERSON personnel department; **Personalakte** *f* VERWALT personal dossier, personal file; **Personalangaben** *f pl* VERWALT personal particulars; **Personalanlagenrechnung** *f* PERSON human asset accounting; **Personalaufwand** *m* PERSON, RECHNUNG staff cost; **Personalauswahlverfahren** *nt* PERSON assessment center (*AmE*), assessment centre (*BrE*); **Personalausweis** *m* POL, VERWALT identity card (*ID card*), *staatlich* national identity card; **Personalbedarfsprognose** *f* PERSON manpower forecast, manpower forecasting; **Personalbelegung** *f* PERSON staffing level; **Personalberater, in** *m,f* PERSON executive search consultant, recruitment consultant; **Personalberatung** *f* PERSON employee counseling (*AmE*), employee counselling (*BrE*); **Personalberatungsunternehmen** *nt* PERSON executive search firm; **Personalbeschaffung** *f* GESCHÄFT staffing, MGMNT staffing, staff resourcing, PERSON staffing, staff resourcing, recruitment

Personalbestand *m* GESCHÄFT, IND workforce, MGMNT, PERSON labor force (*AmE*), labour force (*BrE*), manning level, manpower, staffing level, workforce; ◆ **den ~ erhöhen** PERSON staff-up; **den ~ verringern** PERSON downsize the workforce

Personal: **Personalbeurteilung** *f* MGMNT, PERSON staff appraisal, staff audit; **Personalbogen** *m* VERWALT personal data sheet; **Personalchef, in** *m,f* MGMNT head of personnel (department), PERSON personnel manager, staff manager, personnel director; **Personalcomputer** *m* (*PC*) COMP personal computer (*PC*); **Personaldirektor, in** *m,f* MGMNT, PERSON industrial relations director, personnel director; **Personaleinsatz** *m* PERSON personnel placement, VW manpower assignment; **Personalentwicklung** *f* PERSON human resource development (*HRD*); **Personalfreisetzung** *f* PERSON lay-off; **Personalführung** *f* PERSON staffing; **Personalgemeinkosten** *pl* PERSON personnel overheads; **Personalgeschichte** *f* PERSON case history; **Personalinspektion** *f* PERSON staff inspection

personalintensiv *adj* PERSON people-intensive, personnel-intensive

Personalisierung *f* V&M personalization

Personal: **Personalkosten** *pl* PERSON employment expenses, payroll costs, personnel expenses; **Personalkürzung** *f* MGMNT, PERSON *Rationalisierung* downsizing; **Personalleiter, in** *m,f* MGMNT, PERSON personnel manager, head of personnel, personnel director, staff manager; **Personalleitung** *f* MGMNT, PERSON personnel management, staff management; **Personallücken schließen** *phr* PERSON fill manpower gaps; **Personalmanagement** *nt* PERSON human resource management (*HRM*); **Personalmangel** *m* PERSON shortage of manpower; **unter Personalmangel leiden** *phr* PERSON be short-handed, be short-staffed; **Personalmobilität** *f* PERSON staff mobility; **Personalnebenkosten** *pl* RECHNUNG, VERWALT add-on costs; **Personalorganisation** *f* MGMNT, PERSON job design, staff organization; **Personalplanung** *f* PERSON human resource planning (*HRP*), manpower planning; **Personalpolitik** *f* GESCHÄFT, MGMNT staffing policy, PERSON personnel policy, staffing policy;

Personalprognosen *f pl* PERSON staff forecasting; **Personalrat** *m* MGMNT, PERSON, VERWALT staff council; **Personalschulung** *f* MGMNT, PERSON staff training; **Personalspezifikation** *f* PERSON personnel specification; **Personalstamm** *m* PERSON cadre; **Personalstatut** *nt* RECHT law applicable to the person; **Personalstrategie** *f* PERSON staff strategy; **Personaltransfer** *m* PERSON staff transfer; **Personalvermittlungsbüro** *nt* PERSON agency (*agcy*), employment agency; **Personalvertreter, in** *m,f* PERSON staff representative; **Personalvertretung** *f* PERSON staff association, staff representation; **Personalverwaltung** *f* PERSON personnel administration, human resource administration, personnel management, staff management; **Personalwachstum** *nt* PERSON personnel growth; **Personalwechsel** *m* PERSON staff turnover; **Personalwechselrate** *f* PERSON turnover ratio; **Personalwirtschaft** *f* PERSON manpower management personnel management, staff management; **Personalzusatzkosten** *pl* RECHNUNG, VERWALT add-on costs

Person: **Personenbeförderung** *f* TRANSP passenger transport

personell: ~e **Übersetzung** *f* PERSON featherbedding

personenbezogen: ~e **Kapitalgesellschaft** *f* GESCHÄFT private company

Person: **Personenfähre** *f* TRANSP passenger ferry; **Personengarantieversicherung** *f* VERSICH name bond; **Personengesellschaft** *f* GESCHÄFT joint partnership, partnership, limited company (*BrE*) (*Ltd*); **Personenkraftwagen** *m* (*PKW*) TRANSP passenger car, passenger vehicle; **Personenleistung** *f* IND output per head; **Personenschaden** *m* VERSICH personal injury, physical injury; **Personentarif** *m* TRANSP passenger fare, passenger tariff; **Personenvereinigung** *f* GESCHÄFT association; **Personenverkehr** *m* TRANSP passenger service; **Personenwagen** *m* TRANSP carriage; **Personenzug** *m* TRANSP passenger train, accommodation train (*AmE*)

persönlich 1. *adj* GESCHÄFT personal, private, RECHT *schuldrechtlich, für oder gegen eine Person* in personam; **2.** *adv* GESCHÄFT in person, personally; ♦ **sich ~ bemühen** GESCHÄFT apply in person; **sich ~ bewerben** GESCHÄFT apply in person; **~ haftbar** RECHT personally liable, personally responsible

persönlich: ~ **adressierter Brief** *m* V&M personalized letter; ~e **Bürgschaft** *f* BANK personal guarantee; ~er **Einfluß** *m* GESCHÄFT personal influence; ~es **Einkommen** *nt* VW personal income; ~e **Einkommensverteilung** *f* VW personal income distribution; ~e **Gegenstände** *m pl* GESCHÄFT personal effects; ~es **Gepäck** *nt* IMP/EXP personal baggage; ~es **Gespräch** *nt* V&M personal interview; ~e **Habe** *f* GRUND chattels personal; ~ **haftender Gesellschafter** *m*, ~ **haftende Gesellschafterin** *f* BÖRSE, GESCHÄFT general partner; **ein ~es Interesse an etw haben** *phr* GESCHÄFT have a vested interest in sth; ~es **Kapital** *nt* FINANZ personal money; ~er **Mitarbeiter** *m*, ~e **Mitarbeiterin** *f* MGMNT, PERSON personal assistant (*PA*); ~es **Nettoeinkommen** *nt* VW personal disposable income (*PDI*); ~es **Rentenkonto** *nt* BANK, STEUER individual retirement account (*IRA*); ~es **Sachanlagenvermögen** *nt* GRUND tangible personal property; ~es **verfügbares Einkommen** *nt* **nach Steuern** VW personal disposable income (*PDI*); ~er

Verkauf *m* V&M face-to-face selling; ~er **Wohlstand** *m* VW personal wealth

Persönlichkeit *f* MGMNT personality

Perspektive *f* GESCHÄFT perspective

perspektivlos: ~es **Produkt** *nt* V&M dog

PERT *abbr* (*Methode zur Berechnung und Kontrolle des Arbeitsablaufs*) MGMNT PERT (*program evaluation and review technique AmE, programme evaluation and review technique BrE*)

Pertinenzbaum *m* MGMNT pertinence tree

pervers: ~er **Preis** *m* VW perverse price

Perzentil *nt* MATH percentile

Pessimismus *m* BÖRSE, VW gloom, pessimism

pessimistisch *adj* BÖRSE, VW pessimistic

Pestizid *nt* UMWELT pesticide

Peterprinzip *nt* PERSON Peter principle

Petition *f* RECHT petition

Petrochemie *f* IND, UMWELT petrochemicals industry

Petrodollar *m* BANK, IMP/EXP, VW petrodollar

Petrowährung *f* BANK, IMP/EXP, VW petrocurrency

Petty-Gesetz *nt* VW Petty's law

Pfad *m* COMP path

Pfand *nt* FINANZ collateral, pawn, security, V&M *Flasche* deposit

pfändbar *adj* RECHT distrainable, *Lohn* attachable

Pfandbrief *m* BÖRSE, FINANZ, RECHNUNG mortgage bond; **Pfandbriefinhaber** *m* BÖRSE mortgage bond creditor; **Pfandbriefschuld** *f* BÖRSE mortgage bond debt; **Pfandbrieftilgungsprämie** *f* RECHNUNG mortgage bond redemption premium

pfänden *vt* RECHT impound, levy, attach

Pfand: **Pfandflasche** *f* UMWELT, V&M deposit bottle, returnable bottle; **Pfandhaus** *nt* FINANZ pawnshop; **Pfandleihanstalt** *f* FINANZ pawnshop; **Pfandleiher** *m* FINANZ pawnbroker; **Pfandleihgeschäft** *nt* FINANZ pawnbroking

Pfandrecht *nt* FINANZ, RECHT lien, right of lien, right of distraint; ~ **einer Bank** BANK bank lien; ~ **an beweglichen Sachen** BANK chattel mortgage; ~ **der Bundessteuerbehörde** STEUER federal tax lien (*AmE*); ~ **des Frachtführers** TRANSP carrier's lien; ~ **am Gesamtvermögen** BANK general mortgage; ~ **der Steuerbehörde** STEUER tax lien

Pfand: **Pfandsache** *f* FINANZ pawn; **Pfandschein** *m* FINANZ pawn ticket

Pfändung *f* FINANZ pawnage, RECHT distraint of property, VERSICH attachment; **Pfändungsschuldner** *m* RECHT distrainee, garnishee

Pfand: **Pfandverkauf** *m* RECHT distress sale

Pfarrer *m* PERSON minister

Pfd. *abbr* (*Pfund*) GESCHÄFT lb (*pound*)

Pfeil *m* COMP, GESCHÄFT arrow; ~ **ab** COMP *Cursortasten* down arrow; ~ **zurück** COMP *Cursortasten* back arrow

Pfeiler *m* POL *einer Strategie, Wahlkampagne* plank

Pfeil: **Pfeiltaste** *f* COMP *Tastatur* arrow key

Pfennigfuchser *m* *infrml* RECHNUNG beancounter (*infrml*)

Pferdestärke *f* (*PS*) IND, TRANSP horsepower (*HP*)

Pflege *f* SOZIAL care

pflegen *vt* GESCHÄFT *Markt* service, *Beziehungen* foster

Pflege: **Pflegesatz** *m* SOZIAL hospital daily rate, nursing home daily rate

Pflicht *f* RECHT duty, obligation; **Pflichtaktien** *f pl* BÖRSE qualifying shares; **Pflichtaktien** *f pl* **der Mitglieder des Verwaltungsrates** BÖRSE qualification shares; **Pflichtbeitrag** *m* **des Arbeitnehmers** PERSON employee contribution; **Pflichten** *f pl* **im Rahmen des Arbeitsvertrags** PERSON duties under the employment contract; **Pflichtteil** *m* RECHT *Nachlaß* legitimate portion; **Pflichtverletzung** *f* RECHT breach of duty, breach of trust; **Pflichtvernachlässigung** *f* RECHT dereliction of duty; **Pflichtversicherung** *f* VERSICH compulsory insurance; **Pflichtwerbetext** *m* V&M mandatory copy

Pfund *nt* (*Pfd.*) GESCHÄFT pound (*lb*), VW pound; **~ pro Quadratzoll** IND pounds per square inch (*PSI*); **~ Sterling** BÖRSE *Devisenhandelssprache* cable; **Pfund-Sterling-Auslandsanleihe** *f* BÖRSE bulldog issue (*BrE*), FINANZ bulldog bond (*BrE*)

Pharmaindustrie *f* IND pharmaceutical industry

Pharmaprodukte *nt pl* IND pharmaceuticals

Pharmatitel *m pl* BÖRSE pharmaceuticals

Pharmazeutika *nt pl* IND pharmaceuticals

pharmazeutisch *adj* IND pharmaceutical; **~e Industrie** *f* IND pharmaceutical industry

Phase *f* GESCHÄFT phase, stage

phasenweise *adv* GESCHÄFT in stages

Philadelphia: **~ Wertpapierbörse** *f* BÖRSE Philadelphia Stock Exchange (*AmE*) (*PHLX*)

Phillips-Kurve *f* POL, VW Phillips curve, *Korrelation Arbeitslosenquote-Nominallöhne* political business cycle

Physikalisch-Technisch: **~e Bundesanstalt** *f* MATH ≈ American Institute of Weights and Measures (*AIWM*)

Physiokrat *m* VW physiocrat

physisch: **~es Grenzprodukt** *nt* VW marginal physical product (*MPP*); **~er Sicherungsgegenstand** *m* BANK physical collateral; **~er Wirkungsgrad** *m* VW technical efficiency

PIBOR *abbr* (*Pariser Interbankenangebotssatz*) BANK PIBOR (*Paris Interbank Offered Rate*)

piepsen *vi* COMP beep

Pier *m* TRANSP jetty, pier, wharf; ◆ **ab ~** (*x-Pier*) TRANSP ex quay (*x-quay*)

Pigou: **Pigou-Effekt** *m* VW Pigou effect; **Pigou-Steuer** *f* VW Pigouvian tax; **Pigou-Subvention** *f* VW Pigouvian subsidy

Piktogramm *nt* COMP icon, MATH pictogram

Pilot, in *m,f* PERSON, TRANSP *Luftfahrt* pilot; **Pilotanlage** *f* IND pilot plant; **Pilotfilm** *m* MEDIEN pilot; **Pilotproduktion** *f* MGMNT pilot production; **Pilotprogramm** *nt* GESCHÄFT pilot scheme; **Pilotprojekt** *nt* MGMNT pilot project; **Pilotsendung** *f* MEDIEN pilot

Pint *nt* (*pt*) GESCHÄFT pint (*pt*)

Pionier *m* GESCHÄFT pioneer; **Pionierprodukt** *nt* IND, V&M pioneer product

Pipeline *f* IND, TRANSP *Öl, Gas* pipeline

Piratensender *m* MEDIEN pirate radio

PKW *abbr* (*Personenkraftwagen*) TRANSP passenger car, passenger vehicle; **PKW-Fähre** *f* TRANSP passenger vehicle ferry

plädieren *vi* RECHT plead; ◆ **~ für** GESCHÄFT advocate; **für jdn ~** GESCHÄFT plead for sb

Plädieren *nt* RECHT pleading

Plädoyer *nt* RECHT summing up

Plafondierung *f* BANK capping

Plagiat *nt* COMP, IND, V&M piracy; ◆ **~ begehen** IND pirate

Plakat *nt* MEDIEN *Zeitung* broadsheet, V&M *Werbung* bill, placard, poster; **Plakatankleben verboten** *phr* V&M no bill posting; **Plakatanschlagfläche** *f* V&M stand; **Plakatgröße** *f* V&M poster size; **Plakatierung** *f* V&M billsticking; **Plakatwand** *f* V&M billboard, hoarding; **Plakatwerbung** *f* V&M outdoor advertising, poster advertising, poster display

Plan *m* FINANZ estimates, GESCHÄFT blueprint, plan, program (*AmE*), programme (*BrE*), schedule, RECHNUNG budget layout; **~ für eine Kampagne** V&M campaign plan; **~ zur Konjunkturbelebung** VW recovery plan; **sich über mehrere Jahre erstreckender operativer ~** FINANZ multi-year operational plan (*MYOP*); **~ der sozialen Dividende** VW social dividend scheme; **~ der Staatsausgaben** VW public spending plans; ◆ **nach ~** GESCHÄFT according to schedule; **die Pläne fielen ins Wasser** *infrml* GESCHÄFT the plans came unstuck (*infrml*); **der ~ hat weder Hand noch Fuß** *infrml* GESCHÄFT the plan makes no sense, the plan has no substance; **der ~ ist nicht hieb- und stichfest** *infrml* GESCHÄFT the plan does not hold water (*infrml*); **der ~ ist nicht stichhaltig** GESCHÄFT the plan is not sound; **im ~ liegen** GESCHÄFT be on schedule; **einen ~ realisieren** GESCHÄFT put a plan into action; **auf den ~ treten** MEDIEN, POL appear on the scene; **einen ~ umsetzen** GESCHÄFT put a plan into action

Plan: **Planabweichung** *f* FINANZ budget variance; **Planbogen** *m* MEDIEN broadsheet; **Planeinstellung** *f* STEUER discontinuance of plan

planen *vt* GESCHÄFT plan, *vorschlagen* envisage, propose, *Zeitablauf* schedule

Plan: **Planerfüllungsindikator** *m* GESCHÄFT performance indicator; **Planergebnis** *nt* RECHNUNG budgeted profit; **Planerlös** *m* RECHNUNG budgeted income

plangemäß *adj* GESCHÄFT according to plan, as scheduled

Plan: **Plan-Ist-Vergleich** *m* MGMNT performance against objectives; **Plankontrolle** *f* FINANZ, RECHNUNG budgetary control (*BC*), budgeting control; **Plankosten** *pl* GESCHÄFT budgeted cost, standard cost, predicted costs; **Plankostenrechnung** *f;* GESCHÄFT standard cost accounting, FINANZ standard cost system, RECHNUNG standard cost accounting, standard costing, budget accounting, standard cost system, VERWALT budget accounting

planmäßig *adj* GESCHÄFT systematic, on schedule, according to schedule, TRANSP scheduled; **~e Abfahrt** *f* TRANSP scheduled departure; **~e Ankunft** *f* TRANSP scheduled arrival; **~e Kontrolle** *f* TRANSP routine control

Plan: **Planrevision** *f* FINANZ, RECHNUNG, VW budget review, budgetary adjustment; **Planspiel** *nt* MGMNT management game

Plantage *f* VW plantation

Planung *f* GESCHÄFT planning, projecting, projection, scheduling; **~ der Instandhaltungsarbeiten** VERWALT maintenance planning; **~ der Leitungsnachfolge** MGMNT management succession planning; **~ der Organisation** MGMNT organization planning; **~, Programmierung** *f* **und Budgetierung** *f* (*PPB*) FINANZ, MGMNT, RECHNUNG, VW planning, programming and budgeting (*PPB*); **Planungsabteilung** *f* MGMNT, VERWALT planning department; **Planungsausschuß** *m* GESCHÄFT planning committee; **Planungsbehörde** *f* UMWELT, VERWALT planning authority; **Planungsbüro** *nt* MGMNT, VERWALT planning department; **Planungshorizont** *m* VW planning horizon; **Planungskommission** *f* VW planning commission; **Planungsperiode** *f* FINANZ, RECHNUNG, VW budget period; **Planungs-, Programmierungs- und Budgetierungssystem** *nt* MGMNT planning, programming and budgeting system (*PPBS*); **Planungsstab** *m* V&M plans board; **Planungssume** *m* VW planning total; **Planungsübersicht** *f* POL strategic overview; **Planungszeitraum** *m* VW planning horizon

Plan: **Planverkauf** *m* V&M planned selling; **Planwirtschaft** *f* POL, VW command economy, dirigism, managed economy, planned economy

planwirtschaftlich: **~es System** *nt* POL, VW planned economy

Platine *f* COMP board

Platte *f* COMP disk; **Plattenbetriebssystem** *nt* (*DOS*) COMP disk operating system (*DOS*); **Platteneinheit** *f* COMP disk unit; **Plattenfirma** *f* MEDIEN label, record label; **Plattenlaufwerk** *nt* COMP disk drive; **Plattenstapel** *m* COMP disk pack

Plattform *f* COMP *Betriebssysteme*, IND, TRANSP platform; **Plattformkran** *m* IND platform crane; **Plattformwaage** *f* TRANSP weighbridge; **Plattformwagen** *m* TRANSP platform vehicle

platykurtisch: **~e Verteilungskurve** *f* MATH *Statistik* platykurtic frequency distribution

Platykurtosis *f* MATH *Statistik* platykurtosis

Platz *m* FREI *Flugzeug, Zug* seat, GESCHÄFT slot, *Standort* place, site; **~ am Gang** FREI aisle seat, whiskey seat (*infrml*) (*AmE*); **~ für Wohnwagen** TRANSP trailer park; ◆ **am richtigen ~** GESCHÄFT well-positioned

Platz: **Platzbelegung** *f* V&M *für Werbung* booking

platzen *vi* BANK *Scheck* bounce (*infrml*)

Platz: **Platzgiroverkehr** *m* BANK town clearing; **Platzhandel** *m* VW local trade; **Platzmiete** *f* MEDIEN, V&M *Messen, Ausstellungen* pitch rent; **Platzreservierungssystem** *nt* FREI seat reservation system; **Platzspesen** *pl* TRANSP local charge; **Platzvorschrift** *f* V&M appointed space; **Platzwechsel** *m* BANK town bill

Playback *nt* MEDIEN, V&M playback

plazieren *vt* BÖRSE place, position

plaziert: **nicht ~e Aktien** *f pl* BÖRSE excess shares

Plazierung *f* BÖRSE *im Wertpapiergeschäft* placement, placing, V&M *Anzeige* insertion, positioning; **Plazierungskennziffer** *f* FINANZ placement ratio; **Plazierungskurs** *m* BÖRSE placing price; **Plazierungsprovision** *f* BÖRSE selling concession; **Plazierungsreserve** *f* BÖRSE greenshoe

pleite *adj infrml* BANK, FINANZ, GESCHÄFT bankrupt, *Person* broke (*infrml*), *Unternehmen* bust (*infrml*); ◆ **~ gehen** *infrml* GESCHÄFT go bankrupt, go bust (*infrml*), go to the wall (*infrml*); **~ machen** *infrml* GESCHÄFT go bankrupt, go bust (*infrml*), go to the wall (*infrml*); **~ sein** *infrml* GESCHÄFT be skint (*infrml*)

Pleite *f infrml* GESCHÄFT bankruptcy, *Mißerfolg* flop (*infrml*); ◆ **~ gehen** *infrml* GESCHÄFT go bankrupt, go bust (*infrml*), go to the wall (*infrml*)

Plenarsaal *m* POL plenary chamber

Plenarsitzung *f* POL full session, plenary session

Plombe *f* IMP/EXP, IND seal

Plombierung *f* IMP/EXP, IND sealing

Plotter *m* COMP plotter

plötzlich: **sich ~ ändern** *phr* FINANZ *Finanzplanung*, GESCHÄFT *Richtung, Meinung, Verhalten* veer; **~ fallen** *phr* GESCHÄFT *Preise, Kurse* tumble, plunge; **~er Wandel** *m* GESCHÄFT switchover

Plowden-Ausschuß *m* VW Plowden Committee

Pluralismus *m* PERSON, POL pluralism

plus *prep* GESCHÄFT, MATH plus

Plus *nt* GESCHÄFT plus; **Pluskorrektur** *f* GESCHÄFT *Preise* upward revision; **Pluszeichen** *nt* MATH plus sign

PLZ *abbr* (*Postleitzahl*) KOMM postcode (*BrE*), zip code (*AmE*)

Podium *nt* MEDIEN, POL platform, stage, *Erhöhung* podium, rostrum

Point-of-Sale *m* V&M *Einzelhandel* point-of-sale (*POS*)

Poisson-Verteilung *f* MATH Poisson distribution

Polarisation *f* FINANZ, KOMM polarization

Polarisierung *f* FINANZ, KOMM polarization

Police *f* VERSICH policy; **~ mit beschränktem Risiko** VERSICH limited policy; **~ mit eingeschränktem Gefahrenrisiko** VERSICH limited policy; **~ mit Gewinnbeteiligung** VERSICH participating profit policy; **~ ohne Wertangabe** VERSICH unvalued policy; **~ zum Schutze gegen Urkundenfälschung** VERSICH commercial forgery policy; **~ mit vereinbarter Wertangabe** VERSICH valued policy; **~ mit versicherbarem Interesse** VERSICH interest policy; **Policenablauf** *m* VERSICH lapse; **Policendarlehen** *nt* VERSICH policy loan

Poliklinik *f* SOZIAL outpatients' clinic

Politik *f* MGMNT policy, POL policy, political affairs, politics; **~ des Abwartens** VW wait-and-see policy; **~ in Aktion** POL practical politics; **~ des billigen Geldes** BANK, VW cheap money policy; **~ der Chancengleichheit** PERSON Equal Opportunity Policy (*BrE*); **~ der Dienstleistungsgebühren** VERWALT fee for service policy; **~ gegenseitiger Unterstützung** POL mutual support policy, *abwertend* backscratching (*infrml*) (*BrE*), log-rolling (*AmE*); **~ des großen Knüppels** *infrml* POL policy of the big stick (*infrml*); **~ der kleinen Schritte** POL gradualism; **~ des leichten Geldes** *infrml* VW easy money policy; **~ der offenen Tür** MGMNT, POL open-door policy; **~ des teuren Geldes** VW tight monetary policy, tight money policy; **Politikentscheidung** *f* MGMNT, POL policy decision

Politiker, in *m,f* POL politician

Politik: **Politikgestaltung** *f* MGMNT policy making; **Politikmachen** *nt* MGMNT policy making; **Politikmacher, in** *m,f* POL policy maker

politisch *adj* POL political; ◆ **~e Macht besitzen** POL hold office

politisch: **~e Angelegenheiten** *f pl* POL political affairs; **~es Bewußtsein** *nt* POL political thinking; **~e Beziehungen** *f pl* POL political affairs; **~es Denken** *nt* POL political thinking; **~e Einheit** *f* POL political unity; **~e Einrichtung** *f* POL political institution; **~er Fonds** *m* PERSON political fund; **~e Gruppe** *f* POL political group; **~e Gruppierung** *f* POL political group; **~e Harmonisierung** *f* POL, VW policy harmonization; **~er Hebel** *m* POL leverage; **~e Institution** *f* POL political institution; **~e Kernfrage** *f* POL political issue; **~e**

Klasse *f* POL class; **~es Klima** *nt* POL political climate; **~e Lage** *f* POL political situation; **~e Ökonomie** *f* POL, VW political economy; **~e Partei** *f* POL political party; **~e Praxis** *f* POL political practice; **~es Problem** *nt* GESCHÄFT, POL political issue; **~er Rahmenbericht** *m* POL policy framework paper (*PFP*); **~es Risiko** *nt* POL political risk; **~e Situation** *f* POL political situation; **~e Stabilität** *f* POL political stability; **~er Streik** *m* PERSON political strike; **~es System** *nt* POL political system; **~es Tauwetter** *nt* POL political thaw; **~er Umschwung** *m* POL political change; **~e Union** *f* POL political union; **~e Vereinigung** *f* POL political union; **~e Willenserklärung** *f* POL policy statement; **~e Zusammenarbeit** *f* POL political cooperation

politisieren *vt* POL politicize

Polizei *f* RECHT police force, police; **Polizeigewalt** *f* RECHT police power

polizeilich: **~es Kennzeichen** *nt* TRANSP license plate (*AmE*), number plate (*BrE*); **~er Nachrichtendienst** *m* RECHT police intelligence

Polizei: **Polizeistunde** *f* FREI closing time

Polizist *m* POL policeman

Polizistin *f* POL policewoman

Polling *nt* COMP polling

polnisch: **~e Schreibweise** *f* MATH Polish notation

polypolistisch: **~e Konkurrenz** *f* VW atomistic competition

Polyzentrismus *m* POL polycentrism

pönal: **~e Geldbuße** *f* RECHT punitive damages

pönalisierend: **~er Schadensersatz** *m* RECHT punitive damages

Pool *m* VERSICH pool

Pooling-System *nt* TRANSP pooling system

popularisieren *vt* GESCHÄFT popularize

Popularist *m* POL popularist

Popularität *f* POL popularity rating

Port *m* COMP port

portabel *adj* COMP portable

Portabilität *f* COMP portability

Portefeuille *nt* BANK portfolio, BÖRSE asset portfolio, FINANZ asset portfolio, portfolio, MGMNT, POL, VW portfolio; **Portefeuille-Abschnitt** *m* FINANZ portfolio section; **Portefeuille-Aufteilung** *f* FINANZ portfolio split; **Portefeuille-Einkommen** *nt* BÖRSE portfolio income; **Portefeuille-Strukturierung** *f* BÖRSE asset allocation; **Portefeuille-Umschichtung** *f* FINANZ portfolio turnover; **Portefeuille-Verwaltung** *f* FINANZ, MGMNT portfolio management

Portfolio *nt* BÖRSE, FINANZ, MGMNT, V&M, VERSICH portfolio; **Portfolio-Abteilung** *f* BÖRSE portfolio section; **Portfolio-Abtretung** *f* VERSICH cession of portfolio; **Portfolio-Analyse** *f* V&M portfolio analysis; **Portfolio-Investition** *f* FINANZ portfolio investment; **Portfolio-Management** *nt* BÖRSE, FINANZ portfolio management; **Portfolio-Managementtheorie** *f* BÖRSE, FINANZ portfolio management theory; **Portfolio-Manager, in** *m,f* BÖRSE, FINANZ portfolio manager; **Portfolio-Rückversicherung** *f* VERSICH portfolio reinsurance; **Portfolio-Selektion** *f* FINANZ portfolio selection; **Portfolio-Theorie** *f* BÖRSE, FINANZ portfolio theory; **Portfolio-Übertragung** *f* VERSICH portfolio transfer

portierbar *adj* COMP portable

Porto *nt* KOMM postage; **~ und Verpackung** *f* KOMM postage and packing (*p&p*); ♦ **~ bezahlt** KOMM postpaid (*p.p.*), postage paid

portofrei *adj* KOMM postpaid (*p.p.*), postage paid

Porto: **Portokasse** *f* RECHNUNG petty cash; **Portonachnahme** *f* IMP/EXP, TRANSP carriage forward (*carr fwd, CF*); **Portospesen** *pl* KOMM postage

Porträt *nt* V&M portrait

Position *f* BÖRSE, FINANZ, PERSON, V&M position; **~ mit direktem Kundenkontakt** VERWALT front-of-house job; **~ auf Führungsebene** PERSON executive grade; **~ ohne Aufstiegschancen** PERSON blind-alley job (*AmE*), dead-end job (*BrE*); **~ in einer Sackgasse** PERSON blind-alley job (*AmE*), dead-end job (*BrE*); ♦ **eine ~ abwickeln** BÖRSE liquidate a position; **für eine ~ in Betracht gezogen werden** PERSON *Bewerbung* be considered for a post; **eine ~ eröffnen** BÖRSE position; **eine ~ glattstellen** BÖRSE close out a position; **seine ~ halten** GESCHÄFT stand one's ground; **eine ~ liquidieren** BÖRSE liquidate a position; **eine ~ schließen** BÖRSE close out a position

positionieren *vt* GESCHÄFT position

Positionierer *m* COMP *Grafikprogramm* locator

Positionierung *f* BÖRSE, FINANZ, V&M positioning; **Positionierungstheorie** *f* V&M positioning theory

Position: **Positionsbereinigung** *f* BÖRSE position squaring; **Positionsführung** *f* BÖRSE position-keeping; **Positionsgeber** *m* TRANSP locator; **Positionskonto** *nt* BÖRSE position account; **Positionslimit** *nt* BÖRSE position limit; **Positionsmedien** *nt pl* V&M position media; **Positionsmeldung** *f* POL position paper

positiv 1. *adj* GESCHÄFT positive; **2.** *adv* GESCHÄFT positively

positiv: **~e Antwort** *f* GESCHÄFT positive response; **~e Bestätigung** *f* RECHNUNG positive confirmation; **~er Cashflow** *m* FINANZ, RECHNUNG, STEUER positive cash flow; **~e Diskriminierung** *f* PERSON, POL, VERWALT, VW affirmative action (*AmE*), positive discrimination (*BrE*); **~es Echo** *nt* VW positive feedback; **~e ganze Zahl** *f* MATH positive integer; **~er geldwerter Ausgleichsbetrag** *m* FINANZ positive monetary compensatory amount; **~e Korrelation** *f* MATH positive correlation; **~e Neutralität** *f* POL positive neutrality; **~e Reaktion** *f* VW positive feedback; **~e Rückmeldung** *f* VW positive feedback; **~e Wirtschaftswissenschaften** *f pl* VW positive economics; **~e Zinsertragskurve** *f* VW positive yield curve

Positivsummenspiel *nt* VW positive sum game

Possibilismus *m* POL possibilism

Post *f* KOMM mail (*AmE*), post (*BrE*), *Amt* post office (*PO*); **~ mit unleserlicher Adresse** KOMM mail that is unreadable, nixie mail (*AmE*); ♦ **per ~ versenden** KOMM send by post

Post: **Postadresse** *f* KOMM mailing address; **Postamt** *nt* KOMM post office (*PO*); **Postamtsvorseher, in** *m,f* KOMM Postmaster General (*PMG*); **Postangestellte(r)** *mf* [decl. as adj] KOMM, VERWALT mail clerk (*AmE*), postal worker (*BrE*); **Postanschrift** *f* KOMM mailing address (*AmE*), postal address (*BrE*); **Postanweisung** *f* BANK, FINANZ, GESCHÄFT postal money order (*AmE*), postal note (*Aus*), postal order (*BrE*) (*PO*); **Postarbeiter, in** *m,f* KOMM, VERWALT mail clerk (*AmE*), postal worker (*BrE*); **Postauftrag** *m* KOMM, V&M mail order (*MO*); **Postausgangskorb** *m* VERWALT out-tray; **Postauto** *nt* KOMM mailcar (*AmE*), mail truck (*AmE*), mail van (*BrE*); **Postbank** *f* BANK Girobank (*BrE*); **Postbearbeitung** *f* KOMM, VERWALT mail processing; **Postbegleitschein** *m* KOMM, TRANSP *bei Paketeilsendungen* dispatch note; **Postbote** *m* KOMM mail carrier (*AmE*), mailman (*AmE*), postman (*BrE*)

Pöstchenjäger, in *m,f* PERSON pork chop (*AmE*) (*infrml*)

Pöstchenjägerei *f* PERSON rat race

Post: **Postdienst** *m* KOMM postal service; **Posteingangskorb** *m* VERWALT in-tray; **Posteinlieferung** *f* KOMM mailing, posting; **Posteinlieferungsschein** *m* KOMM certificate of posting

Posten *m* IND batch, PERSON *Stelle* job, post; RECHNUNG, VERWALT entry, item; ~ *m pl* **im Haushaltsplan** FINANZ items in the estimates; ♦ **einen ~ einbuchen** RECHNUNG post an entry; **einen ~ im Hauptbuch verbuchen** RECHNUNG enter an item in the ledger

Post: **Postfach** *nt* KOMM post office box (*PO box*)

postfrei *adj* KOMM postage paid, postpaid (*p.p.*)

Post: **Postgebühr** *f* KOMM postage rate; **Postgebührenstempel** *m* KOMM postage-paid impression (*PPI*); **Postgirokonto** *nt* BANK postal checking account (*AmE*); **Postkarte** *f* KOMM mailing card

post-Keynesianisch *adj* VW post-Keynesian

postkommunistisch *adj* POL, VW post-Communist

postlagernd *adj* KOMM poste restante; ~**er Brief** *m* KOMM poste restante letter

Post: **Postlaufkredit** *m* VW mail credit; **Postlaufzeit** *f* GESCHÄFT turnaround time (*AmE*), turnround time (*BrE*); **Postleitzahl** *f* (*PLZ*) KOMM postcode (*BrE*), zip code (*AmE*); **Postleitzone** *f* KOMM postal zone; **Postliste** *f* KOMM mailing list

PostScript®-Drucker *m* COMP PostScript® printer

Postscriptum *nt* (*P.S.*) KOMM *Briefende* postscript (*ps.*, *PS*)

Post: **Postsendung** *f* **dritter Klasse** KOMM third-class matter (*AmE*); **Postsparkasse** *f* BANK, FINANZ ≈ National Savings Bank (*BrE*) (*NSB*), ≈ post office savings bank (*BrE*); **Postsparkonto** *nt* BÖRSE ≈ National Savings Investment Account (*BrE*); **Postsparzinsen** *m pl* BANK ≈ National Savings Income (*BrE*); **Poststempel** *m* KOMM date stamp, postmark; **Postüberweisung** *f* BANK, KOMM mail transfer (*MT*), RECHNUNG postal remittance

postulieren *vt* GESCHÄFT postulate, premise

Post: **Postverkehr** *m* KOMM postal service; **Postversand** *m* KOMM, V&M mailing, direct mail; **auf dem Postweg** *phr* KOMM by mail (*AmE*), by post (*BrE*)

postwendend *adv* KOMM by return of post

Post: **Postwerbeexemplar** *nt* KOMM, V&M mailing shot, mailshot; **Postwertzeichen** *nt frml* KOMM postage stamp (*frml*); **Postwurfsendung** *f* KOMM, V&M bulk mail, direct mail; **Postzustelladresse** *f* KOMM mailing address, postal address; **Postzustellbereich** *m* KOMM postal zone

Potential *nt* GESCHÄFT potential; ♦ **über ~ verfügen** GESCHÄFT have potential

potentiell 1. *adj* GESCHÄFT potential; **2.** *adv* GESCHÄFT potentially

potentiell: ~**er Anleger** *m*, ~**e Anlegerin** *f* BÖRSE potential investor; ~**er Ausstoß** *m* **einer Volkswirtschaft** VW potential output; ~ **befreite**

Übertragungen *f pl* STEUER potentially exempt transfers (*BrE*) (*PETs*); ~**es Einkommen** *nt* VW potential income; ~**er Gewinn** *m* BÖRSE potential profit; ~**er Käufer** *m*, ~**e Käuferin** *f* V&M potential buyer; ~**er Kunde** *m*, ~**e Kundin** *f* V&M prospective customer; ~**er Nutzer** *m*, ~**e Nutzerin** *f* V&M potential user; ~**es Übernahmeobjekt** *nt* BÖRSE sleeping beauty (*infrml*); ~**er Verbraucher** *m*, ~**e Verbraucherin** *f* V&M prospective customer; ~**er Verkaufsschlager** *m* PERSON sleeper (*infrml*)

pp. *abbr* (*per procura*) GESCHÄFT pp (*per procurationem*), per pro (*per procurationem*)

ppa. *abbr* (*per procura*) GESCHÄFT pp (*per procurationem*), per pro (*per procurationem*)

PPB *abbr* (*Planung, Programmierung und Budgetierung*) FINANZ, MGMNT, RECHNUNG, VW PPB (*planning, programming and budgeting*); ~**-System** *nt* (*Planungs-, Programmierungs- und Budgetierungssystem*) FINANZ, MGMNT, RECHNUNG, VW PPBS (*planning, programming and budgeting system*)

ppm *abbr* (*partes per millionem*) GESCHÄFT ppm (*parts per million*)

Pr. *abbr* (*Preis*) GESCHÄFT pr. (*price*)

PR *abbr* (*Public Relations*) PERSON, V&M PR (*public relations*)

Präambel *f* MGMNT *Rede*, RECHT *Gesetz* preamble

Präferenz- *in cpds* GESCHÄFT preference (*pref.*), preferential; **Präferenzaxiome** *nt pl* VW axioms of preference; **Präferenzgut** *nt* GESCHÄFT preference item; **Präferenzsatz** *m* GESCHÄFT preferential rate

Prägedruck *m* V&M embossing

prägen *vt* VW coin, mint

pragmatisch *adj* GESCHÄFT, POL pragmatic

Pragmatismus *m* POL gradualism

präkodiert *adj* V&M precoded

Praktikant, in *m,f* PERSON trainee, threshold worker (*AmE*); **Praktikantenfluktuation** *f* PERSON trainee turnover

Praktikum *nt* PERSON traineeship

praktisch 1. *adj* GESCHÄFT practical; ♦ ~**e und finanzielle Hilfe erhalten** GESCHÄFT be given practical and financial help; **2.** *adv* GESCHÄFT practically; ♦ **etw ~ erproben** GESCHÄFT put sth to the test; ~ **verwerten** PATENT exploit, work

praktisch: ~**es Angehen** *nt* **von Problemen** POL hands-on session; ~**e Ausbildung** *f* PERSON hands-on training; ~**e Erfahrung** *f* PERSON hands-on experience; ~**e Inangriffnahme** *f* **eines Vorhabens** POL hands-on session; ~**er Nutzen** *m* PERSON practical use; ~**e Politik** *f* POL practical politics; ~ **realisierbare Höchstkapazität** *f* VW maximum practical capacity; ~ **realisierbare Kapazität** *f* VW practical capacity

praktizieren *vi* RECHT practice (*AmE*), practise (*BrE*)

praktizierend *adj* RECHT practicing (*AmE*), practising (*BrE*)

Prämie *f* BÖRSE, FINANZ bounty, premium, MGMNT, PERSON *Gehalt* award, bonus, additional pay, V&M *für das Teilnehmen an einer Meinungsumfrage* incentive fee, VERSICH premium; ~ **oberhalb des Anleihewertes** BÖRSE premium over bond value; ~ **oberhalb des Umwandlungswertes** BÖRSE premium over conversion value; ~ **für organisch-biologische Produkte** VW organic premium; ~ **auf Risikobasis** VERSICH risk-based premium; **Prämienabrechnung** *f* FINANZ premium statement; **Prämienanleihe** *f* BANK, BÖRSE, FINANZ premium bond, prize bond; **Prämienbefreiung** *f* VERSICH exemption from payment of premium; **Prämienberechnungsgrundlage** *f* VERSICH basis of premium calculation; **Prämienberichtigung** *f* VERSICH premium adjustment; **Prämiendepot** *nt* VERSICH deposit premium; **Prämieneinnahme** *f* VERSICH collection of premiums, premium income; **Prämienerhöhung** *f* VERSICH premium increase; **Prämienfälligkeit** *f* FINANZ premium maturity

prämienfrei: ~e Versicherung *f* VERSICH fully paid-up policy

Prämie: **Prämienfreijahre** *nt pl* VERSICH premium holiday; **Prämiengeber** *m* BÖRSE giver of option money; **Prämienhändler, in** *m,f* BÖRSE prize broker; **Prämieninkasso** *nt* VERSICH collection of premiums; **Prämienlohn** *m* BÖRSE premium bonus, PERSON *Arbeit* wage bonus, premium bonus; **Prämienlohnsystem** *nt* PERSON *Arbeit* premium bonus scheme, bonus scheme; **Prämiennotierung** *f* BÖRSE premium quotations; **Prämienplan** *m* **nach Halsey** PERSON Halsey Premium Plan (*AmE*); **Prämienreduzierung** *f* VERSICH reduction of premiums; **Prämienreserve** *f* FINANZ premium reserve; **Prämienrückzahlung** *f* VERSICH canceling return (*AmE*), cancelling return (*BrE*); **Prämiensatz** *m* BÖRSE, VERSICH premium rate; **Prämiensparbrief** *m* FINANZ Premium Savings Bond (*BrE*); **Prämiensparkonto** *nt* BANK bonus savings account; **Prämiensparquote** *f* BANK bonus savings rate; **Prämienstorno** *nt* VERSICH cancellation of premium; **Prämienstundung** *f* VERSICH premium deferral; **Prämienverzug** *m* FINANZ, VERSICH premium default; **Prämienvorauszahlung** *f* VERSICH advance premium; **Prämienzinssatz** *m* BANK bonus rate of interest

Präs. *abbr* (*Präsident*) MGMNT, PERSON, POL Pres. (*President*)

Präsensindikator *m* VW coincident indicator

präsent *adj* GESCHÄFT present, ready

Präsent *nt* MEDIEN, V&M present

Präsentation *f* V&M presentation

Präsident, in *m,f* PERSON president, POL President (*Pres.*); **~ des Konzernvorstands** PERSON president of the group executive board (*AmE*); **~ des Schatzamtes** FINANZ President of the Treasury Board (*AmE*)

Präsidentschaft *f* MGMNT, PERSON chairmanship, POL presidency; **Präsidentschaftswahl-Konjunkturzyklustheorie** *f* VW presidential election cycle theory

Präsidialsitzung *f* MGMNT board meeting

Präsidium *nt* PERSON presidium

Praxeologie *f* VW praxeology

Praxis *f* RECHT practice; **~ der Gewerkschaftszugehörigkeitspflicht** PERSON union-only practice (*BrE*); **~ des Rechnungswesens** RECHNUNG accounting practise; ◆ **in der ~** GESCHÄFT in practice

praxisfremd *adj* SOZIAL academic

Präzedenzfall *m* RECHT precedent

Präzedenzrecht *nt* RECHT case law

Präzision- *in cpds* IND, TRANSP, VW precision; **Präzisionsmaß** *nt* VW modulus of precision; **Präzisionstechnik** *f* IND precision engineering

PR: **PR-Berater, in** *m,f* PERSON, V&M public relations consultant, public relations executive, public relations officer (*PRO*); **PR-Beratung** *f* PERSON, V&M public relations consultancy

Prebisch-Singer-These *f* VW Prebisch-Singer thesis

Preis *m* (*Pr.*) GESCHÄFT charge, price (*pr.*); **~ auf Anfrage** GESCHÄFT price on application; **~ pro Einheit** V&M unit price; **~ für ein Einzelexemplar** V&M cover price; **~ ab Kai** IMP/EXP, TRANSP ex-wharf price; **~ über dem Kurswert** BÖRSE above-market price; **~ ab Werk** IND ex factory price, ex works price; ◆ **ohne ~** GESCHÄFT zero-priced; **zum ~** FINANZ at-the-money; **unter ~ anbieten** V&M underprice; **unter ~ angeboten** V&M underpriced; **die Preise frisieren** *infrml* BÖRSE fake the marks (*infrml*); **die Preise gaben nach** GESCHÄFT *Volumen* prices receded; **die Preise sind herabgesetzt worden** BÖRSE prices have been marked down; **Preise hochschleusen** V&M push up prices; **sich durch zu hohe Preise vom Markt ausschließen** V&M price oneself out of the market; **Preise reduzieren** V&M cut prices; **zu Preisen, die sich von x bis y bewegen** GESCHÄFT at prices ranging from x to y; **zu Preisen, die zwischen x und y schwanken** GESCHÄFT at prices ranging from x to y; **unter ~ verkaufen** V&M undercut

Preis: **Preisabänderung** *f* GESCHÄFT price variance; **Preisabnehmer, in** *m,f* VW price taker; **Preisabrufverfahren** *nt* V&M price look-up procedure; **Preisabsatzfunktion** *f* VW price-demand function; **Preisabsprache** *f* GESCHÄFT common pricing, V&M price-fixing; **Preisabweichung** *f* GESCHÄFT price variance; **Preisänderung** *f* BÖRSE price change; **Preisanfrage** *f* GESCHÄFT price enquiry; **Preisangabe** *f* GESCHÄFT displayed price; **ohne Preisangabe** *phr* GESCHÄFT unpriced; **Preisangeber** *m* GESCHÄFT price marker; **Preisangebot** *nt* BÖRSE price bid; **Preisanreiz** *m* V&M price incentive; **Preisansätze** *m pl* RECHNUNG budget prices; **Preisanstieg** *m* FINANZ, V&M price increase, price advance, price escalation; **Preisaufschlag** *m* GESCHÄFT price supplement, extra charge, V&M mark-up; **Preisaufschwung** *m* BÖRSE rallying; **Preisausschlußprinzip** *nt* VW exclusion principle; **Preisauszeichnungsgesetze** *nt pl* RECHT *Etikettierung* labeling laws (*AmE*), labelling laws (*BrE*); **Preisbereich** *m* V&M, VW price range; **Preisbericht** *m* FINANZ price current (*P/C, pc.*); **Preisberichtigung** *f* V&M pricing review; **Preisbestimmung** *f* V&M price determination

Preisbildung *f* V&M, VW price formation; **~ auf Durchschnittskostenbasis** VERWALT, VW average cost pricing; **~ bei Spitzenbelastung** VW peak-load pricing; **Preisbildungsfaktor** *m* V&M price determinant; **Preisbildungspolitik** *f* V&M pricing policy; **Preisbildungstaktiken** *f pl* V&M pricing tactics; **Preisbildungsvereinbarung** *f* V&M, VW pricing arrangement

Preisbindung *f* FINANZ, RECHT, V&M price maintenance, price-fixing; **~ der zweiten Hand** FINANZ, RECHT, V&M price maintenance, resale price maintenance (*RPM*), retail price maintenance (*RPM*); **Preisbindungsregelung** *f* V&M price maintenance scheme (*AmE*)

Preis: **Preisderegulation** *f* GESCHÄFT price deregulation; **Preisdifferenzierung** *f* PERSON, V&M, VW differential pricing, differential price, price differential; **Preisdiskriminierung** *f* V&M price discrimination; **Preisdiskriminierung** *f* **zweiten Grades** V&M second-degree price discrimination, VW nonlinear pricing;

Preisdruck *m* V&M, VW price pressures, pricing pressure; **Preisdrückung** *f* V&M, VW price cutting; **Preise** *m pl* **für unverarbeitete oder halbverarbeitete Rohstoffe** BÖRSE primary commodity prices; **Preiseffekt** *m* VW price effect; **Preiseinbruch** *m* V&M break in the market; **Preis- und Einkommenspolitik** *f* VW prices and incomes policy; **Preiselastizität** *f* **der Nachfrage** VW price elasticity of demand; **Preisempfehlung** *f* V&M recommended retail price (*RRP*)

preisempfindlich *adj* V&M, VW price-sensitive

Preis: **Preisempfindlichkeit** *f* V&M price sensitivity; **Preisentwicklung** *f* BÖRSE price move; **Preiserhöhung** *f* FINANZ, V&M price increase, mark-up; **Preisermäßigung** *f* V&M allowance; **Preisetikett** *nt* FINANZ, V&M price label, price ticket; **Preisfestlegung** *f* FINANZ, V&M pricing

Preisfestsetzung *f* FINANZ, RECHT, V&M price determination, price-fixing; **~ für Lockartikel** V&M loss leader pricing; **~ für Terminkontrakte** BÖRSE forward pricing; **~ nach Zonen** V&M zone pricing; **Preisfestsetzungspolitik** *f* V&M pricing policy

Preis: **Preisfeststellung** *f* FINANZ, V&M price determination; **Preisfixierer** *m* VW price maker; **Preisflexibilität** *f* VW price flexibility; **Preisführer** *m* V&M, VW price leader; **Preisführerschaft** *f* V&M, VW price leadership

Preisgabe *f* RECHT disclosure, relinquishment, VERSICH abandonment; **~ von Informationen** PERSON disclosure of information; **~ des Schiffs** VERSICH abandonment

Preis: **Preisgarantie** *f* V&M price guarantee; **Preisgefälle** *nt* PERSON, V&M differential price, price differential; **Preisgestaltung** *f* **in Frachtbasissystem** TRANSP basing-point pricing; **Preisgleitklausel** *f* RECHT *Vertragsrecht* escalation clause, sliding-price clause, VERSICH escalation clause, V&M price variation clause

preisgünstig *adj* GESCHÄFT low-priced; **~es Angebot** *nt* GESCHÄFT lowest tender

Preis: **Preisherabsetzung** *f* V&M mark-down, VW rollback; **Preisheraufsetzung** *f* V&M mark-up; **Preishinweis** *m* V&M price cue; **Preisindex** *m* FINANZ, RECHNUNG, VW price index; **Preisindex** *m* **für die Lebenshaltung** SOZIAL, VW cost-of-living index; **Preisindexniveau** *nt* BÖRSE price index level; **Preisinflation** *f* VW price inflation; **Preiskalkulation** *f* IND quantity surveying; **Preiskalkulator** *m* FINANZ pricer, GRUND, IND quantity surveyor; **Preiskartell** *nt* VW price discrimination cartel; **Preiskommission** *f* VW Price Commission (*BrE*); **Preiskonsumkurve** *f* VW price-consumption curve (*PCC*); **Preiskontrolle** *f* VW price control; **der Preiskontrolle unterworfen** *phr* IND, VW subject to price controls

Preiskrieg *m* TRANSP fare war, rate war, V&M, VW price war; ♦ **einen ~ führen** GESCHÄFT, V&M wage a price war

Preis: **Preislage** *f* GESCHÄFT price range; **Preis-Leistungs-Verhältnis** *nt* GESCHÄFT value for money, price-performance ratio

preislich: **~e Wettbewerbsfähigkeit** *f* V&M price competitiveness

Preis: **Preislimit** *nt* GESCHÄFT reserve price; **Preisliste** *f* FINANZ price current (*P/C, pc.*), GESCHÄFT tariff, V&M price schedule; **Preis- und Lohnabkommen** *nt* PERSON prices and incomes agreement; **Preismarke** *f* V&M *Preisschild* price tag; **Preisminderung** *f* RECHT *des Kaufpreises* diminuation; **Preismodell** *nt* **für Kapitalvermögen** BÖRSE, FINANZ, VW capital asset

pricing model (*CAPM*); **Preisnachfrageelastizität** *f* V&M price-demand elasticity; **Preisnachlaß** *m* BÖRSE concession, FINANZ discount (*dis, disc.*), rebate; **Preisniveau** *nt* V&M, VW price level; **Preispolitik** *f* V&M, VW pricing policy; **Preispolitik** *f* **für Lockangebote** V&M leader pricing; **Preisprüfung** *f* RECHNUNG, V&M price auditing; **einen Preispunkt bestimmen** *phr* VW set a price-point; **einen Preispunkt festlegen** *phr* VW set a price-point; **Preis-Qualitäts-Verhältnis** *nt* V&M price-quality ratio; **Preisrate** *f* VW price rate; **Preisreduzierung** *f* FINANZ, V&M, VW price cut; **Preisregelung** *f* V&M, VW valorization; **Preisregulierung** *f* V&M, VW price regulation

Preisrichter, in *m,f* GESCHÄFT adjudicator; ♦ **~ sein bei** GESCHÄFT adjudicate at

Preis: **Preisrückgang** *m* V&M, VW falling prices; **Preisscanner** *m* V&M *computergesteuerte optische Lesehilfe* price scanner; **Preisschere** *f* BÖRSE price gap; **Preisschild** *nt* V&M price label, price sticker, price ticket; **Preisschutz** *m* BÖRSE price protection; **Preissenkung** *f* FINANZ, V&M price cutting, price mark-down, price cut, VW price cut; **Preisskala** *f* V&M price range; **Preisspanne** *f* V&M price margin, price range, price spread; **Preisspektrum** *nt* V&M price range; **Preisstabilisierung** *f* V&M, VW price stabilization; **Preisstabilität** *f* V&M, VW price stability; **Preisstaffelung** *f* VW price staggering; **Preisstarrheit** *f* VW price rigidity; **Preissteigerung** *f* FINANZ, V&M, VW price increase, boost; **Preissteigerungsrücklage** *f* RECHNUNG allowance for inflation; **Preisstopp** *m* V&M, VW price freeze; **Preisstrategie** *f* V&M pricing strategy; **Preisstrategie** *f* **mit antizipierter Inflationskomponente** VW anticipatory pricing; **Preisstruktur** *f* FINANZ, V&M, VW price structure; **Preisstützung** *f* FINANZ price support; **Preissystem** *nt* VW price system; **Preistendenz** *f* FINANZ price trend, VW market trend; **Preistreiber** *m* VW price booster; **Preistreiberei** *f* VW price boosting; **Preis-Twist** *m* POL, VW price twist; **Preisüberwacher, in** *m,f* VW price supervisor; **Preisüberwachung** *f* VW price supervision; **Preisunterbietung** *f* BÖRSE dumping, V&M price cutting, underselling, VW price cutting; **Preisunterschied** *m* PERSON, V&M differential price, price differential

preisunterschreitend *adj* V&M undercutting

Preis: **Preisvereinbarung** *f* FINANZ, RECHT, V&M price-fixing; **Preisverhalten** *nt* BÖRSE price behavior (*AmE*), price behaviour (*BrE*); **Preisverschlechterung** *f* VW price deterioration; **Preisverzeichnis** *nt* FINANZ price current (*P/C, pc.*), VW tariff; **Preiswahrnehmung** *f* VW price perception

preiswert *adj* GESCHÄFT cheap; **~es Darlehen** *nt* BANK low-cost loan

Premiere *f* FREI, MEDIEN premiere, first night, first performance; **Premierenpublikum** *nt* FREI first-night audience, jury

Premierminister, in *m,f* POL prime minister (*PM*)

Presse *f* MEDIEN, POL, V&M press; ♦ **der ~ zuspielen** MEDIEN, POL leak to the press

Presse: **Presseagentur** *f* MEDIEN press agency; **Presseamt** *nt* MEDIEN, POL press office; **Presseausweis** *m* MEDIEN press card; **Pressebericht** *m* MEDIEN press report, write-up; **Presseberichterstattung** *f* MEDIEN press coverage; **Presseerklärung** *f* MEDIEN statement for the press, statement; **Pressefotograf, in** *m,f* MEDIEN press photographer; **Pressefragestunde** *f* POL question time; **Pressekampagne** *f* MEDIEN press campaign; **Pressekonferenz** *f* MEDIEN press conference; **Pressekopie** *f* MEDIEN press copy; **Pressemappe** *f* MEDIEN, V&M press kit, press pack; **Pressemeldung** *f* MEDIEN news item; **Pressemitteilung** *f* MEDIEN press statement; **Pressenotiz** *f* MEDIEN news item; **Pressereferent, in** *m,f* MEDIEN, PERSON information officer (*IO*), press officer; **Pressesprecher** *m* MEDIEN, POL press officer, spokesman, spokesperson; **Pressesprecherin** *f* MEDIEN, POL press officer, spokeswoman, spokesperson; **Pressestelle** *f* MEDIEN press office

pressetauglich: für ~ erklären *phr* MEDIEN pass for press

Presse: **Presseverlautbarung** *f* KOMM, MEDIEN press release; **Pressevorstellung** *f* MEDIEN *Produkt, Buch* press launch, *Theater, Film* preview; **Pressezentrale** *f* MEDIEN newspaper syndicate

Prestige *nt* GESCHÄFT prestige

Pretest *m* V&M acceptance test, pre-test

Primabank *f* BANK prime bank

Primapapier *nt* BÖRSE prime paper

Primär- *in cpds* COMP, GESCHÄFT source, primary

primär 1. *adj* GESCHÄFT primary; **2.** *adv* GESCHÄFT primarily

primär: **~er Arbeitsmarkt** *m* VW primary labor market (*AmE*), primary labour market (*BrE*); **~er Boykott** *m* PERSON primary boycott; **~es Defizit** *nt* VW primary deficit; **~es Eigenkapital** *nt* VW primary capital; **~e Leistungspflicht** *f* RECHT *Vertragsrecht* obligation of performance; **~e Preisdifferenzierung** *f* VW first-degree price discrimination; **~er Sektor** *m* VW primary sector; **~es statistisches Großstadtgebiet** *nt* MATH primary metropolitan statistical area (*AmE*) (*PMSA*); **~er Warenverkehr** *m* BÖRSE, VW primary movements

Primär-: **Primärarbeitsmarkt** *m* VW primary labor market (*AmE*), primary labour market (*BrE*); **Primäraufwand** *m* FINANZ primary input; **Primärcode** *m* COMP source code; **Primärdaten** *pl* V&M primary data; **Primärgeld** *nt* VW primary money; **Primärgeschäft** *nt* GESCHÄFT primary activities; **Primärgüter** *nt pl* GESCHÄFT *Rohstoffe* primary goods; **Primärhändler** *m* VW primary dealer; **Primärliquidität** *f* BANK primary liquidity; **Primärmarkt** *m* BÖRSE issue market, primary market; **Primärmarktbereich** *m* BÖRSE primary market area; **Primärmarkthändler** *m* BÖRSE primary market dealer; **Primärprogramm** *nt* VW master production schedule; **Primärrate** *f* VW primary ratio; **Primärressource** *f* UMWELT primary resource; **Primärziel** *nt* FINANZ primary objective, VW prime goal

Prime-Rate *f* BANK prime rate of interest

primitiv: ~e Wirtschaft *f* VW primitive economy

Prinzip *nt* GESCHÄFT principle; **~ der Folgerichtigkeit** RECHNUNG consistency principle; **~ der garantierten Rückgewinnung des Investitionseinsatzes** FINANZ guaranteed recovery of investment principle (*GRIP*); **~ des minimalen Streuungsverhältnisses** VW least variance ratio; **~ der Periodenabgrenzung** RECHNUNG accrual accounting, principle of accrual; **~ der rechtlichen Selbständigkeit** GESCHÄFT, STEUER, V&M arm's-length principle; ♦ **aus ~** GESCHÄFT on principle

prinzipiell *adv* GESCHÄFT on principle

Priorität *f* GESCHÄFT priority; ♦ **nach ~** GESCHÄFT in order of priority; **zur ~ machen** GESCHÄFT prioritize; **etw ~ verleihen** GESCHÄFT give priority to sth

Priorität: **Prioritätsaktie** *f* FINANZ priority share; **Prioritätsdatum** *nt* RECHT priority date; **Prioritätverlust** *m* PATENT loss of priority

Pritschenwagen *m* TRANSP flat bed

privat 1. *adj* GESCHÄFT private; **2.** *adv* GESCHÄFT privately; ♦ **sich ~ versichern** VERSICH go private (*infrml*)

privat: **~es Abkommen** *nt* RECHT private arrangement; **~er Anleger** *m* BÖRSE private investor; **~e Anstalt** *f* GRUND private institution; **~er Beitrag** *m* VW private contribution; **~e Einrichtung** *f* GRUND private institution, SOZIAL *auf freiwilliger Basis* voluntary agency; **~e Gesundheitsvorsorgeeinrichtung** *f* VERSICH health maintenance organization (*AmE*) (*HMO*); **~e Grenzkosten** *pl* VW marginal private cost; **~er Grenzschaden** *m* VW marginal private damage (*MPD*); **~es Institut** *nt* GESCHÄFT *Agentur* private agency, GRUND private institution; **~e Institution** *f* GRUND private institution; **~e Investition** *f* FINANZ private investment; **~er Kapitalanleger** *m* BANK private investment client; **~es Konto** *nt* RECHNUNG private account; **~e Kosten** *pl* VW private cost; **~e Krankenhausbehandlung** *f* SOZIAL private hospital treatment; **~e Krankenkasse** *f* PERSON, SOZIAL, VERSICH private health fund; **~e Krankenversicherung** *f* PERSON, SOZIAL, VERSICH commercial sickness insurance policy (*AmE*), private health insurance (*BrE*); **~e Krankenversicherung** *f* **für die ärztliche Versorgung** PERSON, SOZIAL, VERSICH Blue Shield (*AmE*); **~e Krankenversicherungsorganisation** *f* VERSICH health maintenance organization (*AmE*) (*HMO*); **~er Krankenversicherungsplan** *m* PERSON, SOZIAL, VERSICH private health scheme (*BrE*); **~e Krankenversicherung** *f* **für stationäre Behandlung** PERSON, SOZIAL, VERSICH Blue Cross (*AmE*); **~es Krankenversicherungssystem** *nt* PERSON, SOZIAL, VERSICH Blue Cross (*AmE*), Blue Shield (*AmE*), private health scheme (*BrE*); **~e Marktwirtschaft** *f* VW private enterprise; **~e Mittel** *pl* FINANZ private means; **~ nutzbares Fahrzeug** *nt* STEUER, TRANSP car available for private use; **~e Organisation** *f* SOZIAL voluntary agency; **~es Register** *nt* RECHNUNG private ledger; **~e Rentenversicherung** *f* FINANZ, SOZIAL personal pension scheme (*BrE*); **~e Rentenversicherung** *f* **mit einer Einmalprämie** FINANZ, SOZIAL single-premium deferred annuity; **~er Sektor** *m* VW private sector; **~e stationäre Behandlung** *f* SOZIAL private hospital treatment; **~e Stellenvermittlung** *f* PERSON *Agentur* employment agency, *Arbeitssuche* job hunting, body-shopping (*infrml*); **~es Unternehmen** *nt* VW private sector company; **~e Vereinbarung** *f* RECHT private arrangement; **~er Verkauf** *m* **eines Aktienpakets** BÖRSE cross; **~e Vermittlungsanlage** *f* KOMM *Telefon* private branch exchange (*PBX*); **~er Vertrag** *m* GESCHÄFT private contract; **~es Zollgutlager** *nt* IMP/EXP bonded warehouse

Privat- *in cpds* GESCHÄFT private; **Privatabkommen** *nt* GESCHÄFT private contract; **Privatanleger** *m* FINANZ private investor; **Privatanschlußgleis** *nt* TRANSP private siding (*BrE*), industry track

privatärztlich: ~er Krankenversicherungstarif *m* PERSON, SOZIAL, VERSICH Blue Shield (*AmE*)

Privat-: **Privatausgaben** *f pl* VW private cost; **Privatbank** *f* BANK personal bank, private bank; **Privatbesitz** *m* GRUND private ownership; **Privatbetrieb** *m* VW private enterprise; **Privatbüro** *nt* VERWALT private office; **Privateigentum** *nt* GRUND private ownership; **Privateinlage** *f* FINANZ private-asset contribution; **Privatfunk** *m* MEDIEN commercial radio, radio; **Privatgepäck** *nt* IMP/EXP personal baggage; **Privatgespräch** *nt* KOMM *Telefonat* private call; **Privathaushalt** *m* GESCHÄFT private household; **Privatinvestitionen** *f pl* VW private sector investment

privatisieren *vt* VW privatize

Privatisierung *f* VW privatization, denationalization; **Privatisierungserlös** *m* VW privatization proceeds; **Privatisierungsprogramm** *nt* VW privatization program (*AmE*), privatization programme (*BrE*)

Privat-: **Privatkrankenversicherung** *f* VERSICH commercial health insurance (*AmE*), private health insurance (*BrE*); **Privatkundeneinlage** *f* BANK retail deposit, retail personal deposit; **Privatkundengeschäft** *nt* **der Banken** BANK consumer banking; **auf das Privatkundengeschäft spezialisierte Bank** *f* BANK retail bank; **Privatmann** *m* GESCHÄFT private individual; **Privatpatient, in** *m,f* SOZIAL private patient; **Privatperson** *f* GESCHÄFT private individual; **Privatplazierung** *f* BANK, FINANZ private placement, private placing; **Privatrecht** *nt* RECHT *Zivilrecht* private law

privatrechtlich: ~**e Bedingungen** *f pl* RECHT private terms (*pt*); ~**es Unternehmen** *nt* RECHT private company

privatschriftlich: **durch** ~**en Vertrag** *phr* RECHT by private contract

Privat-: **Privatschule** *f* GESCHÄFT, SOZIAL private school, public school (*BrE*), independent school (*BrE*); **Privatsekretär, in** *m,f* PERSON, MGMNT, VERWALT confidential secretary, personal secretary (*P/Sec, PS*), private secretary, personal assistant (*PA*); **Privatstraße** *f* TRANSP accommodation road; **Privatunternehmen** *nt* GESCHÄFT private company, private enterprise, privately-owned company, VERWALT *Geschäft, Firma* enterprise; **Privatunternehmer** *m* VW entrepreneur; **Privatunterricht** *m* SOZIAL private tuition; **Privatversicherung** *f* VERSICH commercial insurance; **Privatwirtschaft** *f* GESCHÄFT business community, VW private sector enterprise, private enterprise, private enterprise system, private sector

privatwirtschaftlich: ~**e Gehaltserhöhung** *f* PERSON private sector awards; ~**es System** *nt* VW private enterprise system; ~**es Unternehmen** *nt* GESCHÄFT private sector enterprise

Privileg *nt* GESCHÄFT privilege; ~ **der verzögerten Zahlung** *f* FINANZ skip-payment privilege

privilegiert: ~**e Bank** *f* BANK chartered bank; ~**e Klasse** *f* GESCHÄFT ruling class

pro forma *adj* GESCHÄFT, IMP/EXP, VERWALT pro forma

proaktiv *adj* MGMNT proactive; ~**e Strategie** *f* MGMNT proactive strategy

proamerikanisch *adj* POL pro-American

Proband, in *m,f* PERSON interviewee

Probe *f* COMP sample, test, GESCHÄFT trial, tryout, *Muster* pattern; ♦ **auf** ~ GESCHÄFT on approval (*on appro.*); **etw auf** ~ **kaufen** GESCHÄFT buy sth on approval; **etw auf die** ~ **stellen** GESCHÄFT put sth to the test

Probe: **Probeabo** *nt infrml* (*Probeabonnement*) MEDIEN TS (*trial subscription*); **Probeabonnement** *nt* (*Probeabo*) MEDIEN, V&M trial subscription (*TS*); **Probeabonnent, in** *m,f* MEDIEN, V&M trial subscriber; **Probeabstimmung** *f* V&M straw poll, straw vote; **Probeabzug** *m* MEDIEN proof, pull, proof sheet, repro pull; **Probealarm** *f* PERSON fire drill; **Probeandruck** *m* MEDIEN proof, proof sheet; **Probeangebot** *nt* GESCHÄFT, V&M trial offer; **Probeaufnahme** *f* MEDIEN *Film* screen test, test shot; **Probeauftrag** *m* GESCHÄFT, V&M trial order; **Probebefragung** *f* GESCHÄFT pilot study; **Probebestellung** *f* GESCHÄFT, V&M trial order; **Probebetrieb** *m* MGMNT pilot production; **Probebilanz** *f* RECHNUNG aged trial balance, trial balance, pro forma balance sheet; **Probebilanz** *f* **nach Bilanzstichtag** RECHNUNG post closing trial balance; **Probebild** *nt* MEDIEN proof, proof sheet; **Probebohrung** *f* IND, UMWELT test drilling; **Probebuchprüfung** *f* RECHNUNG sample audit; **Probedaten** *pl* COMP sample data; **Probeerhebung** *f* GESCHÄFT pilot study; **Probeexemplar** *nt* MEDIEN author's specimen copy; **Probefahrt** *f* GESCHÄFT trial run, TRANSP test drive; **Probeflug** *m* TRANSP test flight; **Probekarte** *f* GESCHÄFT sample card; **Probekauf** *m* V&M trial purchase; **Probelauf** *m* GESCHÄFT test run, trial run, pilot run, dry run; **Probenverteilung** *f* an Haushalte V&M house-to-house sampling; **Proberevision** *f* RECHNUNG sample audit; **Probetest** *m* V&M pre-test, pre-testing; **Probeuntersuchung** *f* GESCHÄFT pilot study

probeweise *adv* GESCHÄFT on a trial basis

Probe: **Probezeit** *f* GESCHÄFT trial period, PERSON *Arbeitsvertrag* probationary period, probation period, trial period; **in der Probezugsphase** *phr* MEDIEN at proof stage

probieren *vt* GESCHÄFT try, test, try out

Problem *nt* GESCHÄFT problem, concern; ~ **der Weltverschuldung** VW world debt problem; ♦ **sich mit gelösten Problemen beschäftigen** GESCHÄFT reinvent the wheel; **vor einem** ~ **stehen** MGMNT face a problem

Problem: **Problemanalyse** *f* MATH, MGMNT problem analysis

problematisch *adj* GESCHÄFT problematic

Problem: **Problembereich** *m* GESCHÄFT problem area; **Problembestimmung** *f* COMP problem determination; **Problembeurteilung** *f* MGMNT problem assessment; **Problembewertung** *f* MGMNT problem assessment; **Problemeinschätzung** *f* MGMNT problem assessment; **Problemgebiet** *nt* GESCHÄFT problem area; **Problemgruppe** *f* IND problem batch; **Problemindex** *m* VW discomfort index; **Problemkredit** *m* FINANZ problem loan; **Problemkunde** *m* V&M problem customer

problemlos *adj* GESCHÄFT trouble-free

Problem: **Problemlösung** *f* GESCHÄFT problem solving; **Problemverflechtung** *f* PERSON concatenation of problems; **Problemverkettung** *f* PERSON concatention of problems

prod. *abbr* (*produziert*) GESCHÄFT mfd (*manufactured*)

Produkt *nt* IND, V&M, VW product; ~ **des gehobenen Marktes** V&M up-market product; ~ **mit hoher Wertschöpfung** V&M high added-value product; ~ **des unteren Marktsegments** V&M down-market product; ~ **für den weniger anspruchsvollen Markt** V&M down-market product; ~ **zweiter Generation** V&M second-generation product; ◆ **ein ~ positionieren** GESCHÄFT, V&M position a product; **dieses ~ wird zu billig gehandelt** V&M this product is underpriced

Produkt: **Produktabteilung** *f* GESCHÄFT goods department; **Produktakzeptanz** *f* V&M product acceptance; **Produktanalyse** *f* V&M product analysis; **Produktanpassung** *f* V&M product adaptation; **die Produktbasis verbreitern** *phr* V&M broaden the product base; **Produktbekanntheit** *f* V&M product awareness; **Produktbestand** *m* FINANZ product portfolio; **Produktbewertung** *f* V&M product evaluation

produktbezogen: ~**e Betriebsorganisation** *f* MGMNT product organization

Produkt: **Produktdifferenzierung** *f* V&M product differentiation; **Produktdynamik** *f* V&M product dynamics; **Produkteigenschaft** *f* V&M product attribute; **Produkteinführung** *f* V&M product introduction, product initiation, product launch; **Produktenbörse** *f* BÖRSE mercantile exchange, commodity exchange; **Produktenmakler, in** *m,f* V&M merchandise broker; **Produktentanker** *m* TRANSP product tanker, products carrier; **Produktentransporter** *m* TRANSP products carrier; **Produktentwicklung** *f* V&M product development; **Produktentwicklungszyklus** *m* V&M product development cycle; **Produktfamilie** *f* V&M *von Produkten* family; **Produktfeld** *nt* V&M product field; **Produktforschung** *f* V&M product research; **Produktforschung** *f* **und Entwicklung** IND product research and development; **Produktgeneration** *f* V&M product generation; **Produktgestaltung** *f* V&M product design; **Produktgruppe** *f* V&M product category, product group; **Produkthaftbarkeit** *f* V&M product liability; **Produkthaftpflichtversicherung** *f* **der Hersteller und Bauunternehmer** VERSICH manufacturers' and contractors' liability insurance; **Produkthaftung** *f* VERSICH product liability; **Produkthinweis** *m* V&M product cue; **Produktimage** *nt* V&M product image; **Produktingenieur, in** *m,f* IND, PERSON product engineer; **Produktinvestitionen** *f pl* V&M product portfolio

Produktion *f* IND production, manufacturing capacity, output, shopfloor; ~ **nach dem Baukastensystem** IND modular production; ~ **im Dauerbetrieb** IND continuous process production; ~ **im Dauerverfahren** IND continuous process production; ~ **am Fließband** IND line production; ◆ **die ~ ausweiten** IND expand output; **die ~ erhöhen** IND increase production; **etw in ~ geben** IND put sth into production; **die ~ steigern** IND increase production; **die ~ umschalten** IND switch production

Produktion: **Produktionsabfall** *m* IND, VW production slump; **Produktionsablauf** *m* IND production run; **Produktionsabteilung** *f* IND production department; **Produktionsanlage** *f* IND manufacturing plant, production plant; **Produktionsarbeiter, in** *m,f* IND, PERSON production worker; **Produktionsassistent, in** *m,f* IND, PERSON line assistant; **Produktionsasymmetrie** *f* VW production asymmetry; **Produktionsaufwand** *m* IND production costs; **Produktionsausfall** *m* IND loss of production; **Produktionsausfallversicherung** *f* VERSICH manufacturer's output insurance; **Produktionsausweitung** *f* V&M line expansion; **Produktionsautorität** *f* MGMNT line authority; **Produktionsbasis** *f* IND manufacturing base;

Produktionsbudget *nt* FINANZ operational budget, output budgeting; **Produktionsdirektor, in** *m,f* IND, MGMNT, PERSON production director; **Produktionseinrichtung** *f* IND production facility; **Produktionseinschränkung** *f* IND production cutback; **Produktionseinstellung** *f* IND, V&M phase-out; **Produktionsfaktor** *m* IND, VW factor of production

produktionsfaktorerhöhend: ~**er technischer Fortschritt** *m* IND, VW factor-augmenting technical progress

Produktion: **Produktionsfunktion** *f* VW production function; **Produktionsfunktion** *f* **der konstanten Substitutionselastizität** (*CES-Produktionsfunktion*) VW constant elasticity of substitution production function (*CES production function*); **Produktionsgang** *m* IND production process; **Produktionsgenossenschaft** *f* IND, VW cooperative (*co-op*); **Produktionsgüter** *nt pl* IND industrial goods, VW producer goods; **Produktionsinstandhaltung** *f* VERWALT productive maintenance; **Produktionskapazität** *f* IND manufacturing capacity, production capacity; **Produktionskartell** *nt* VW quota agreement; **Produktionskette** *f* IND chain of production, production chain; **Produktionskomplex** *m* IND production complex; **Produktionskosten** *pl* IND, VW factor costs, production costs, costs of production, cost of goods manufactured, manufacturing cost; **Produktionskürzung** *f* IND production cutback; **Produktionsleistung** *f* IND production rate; **Produktionsleiter, in** *m,f* IND line manager, production director, production manager, MEDIEN production manager, MGMNT, PERSON line manager, production director, production manager; **Produktionsleitung** *f* IND, MGMNT, PERSON line management; **Produktionsmenge** *f* IND, VW output; **Produktionsmethode** *f* IND production method; **Produktionsmöglichkeitenkurve** *f* VW production possibility frontier (*PPF*); **Produktionsökologie** *f* UMWELT production ecology; **Produktionsorganisation** *f* MGMNT, PERSON line organization

produktionsorientiert: ~**e Organisation** *f* GESCHÄFT production-oriented organization

Produktion: **Produktionsplan** *m* IND, MGMNT production schedule; **Produktionsplanbeteiligung** *f* IND share of production plan; **Produktionsplanung** *f* IND, MGMNT production planning, production scheduling, RECHNUNG output budgeting; **Produktionsplanung und -steuerung** *f* IND, MGMNT production planning and control; **Produktionspotential** *nt* VW productive potential; **Produktionsprämie** *f* PERSON *Leistungszulage* output bonus; **Produktionsprogramm** *nt* IND, MGMNT production schedule, V&M product mix; **Produktionsprogrammierung** *f* IND, MGMNT production scheduling; **Produktionsrückgang** *m* IND declining production; **Produktionssektor** *m* VW manufacturing sector; **Produktionsstand** *m* IND production volume; **Produktionsstandard** *m* IND production standard; **Produktionsstatistik** *f* VW census of production; **Produktionssteuerung** *f* IND, MGMNT production management; **Produktionstätigkeit** *f* IND manufacturing activity; **Produktionstechnik** *f* IND production engineering; **Produktionstempo** *nt* IND production rate; **Produktionsumfang** *m* IND production volume; **Produktionsumstellung** *f* IND production changeover; **Produktionsverfahren** *nt* IND production method, production process; **Produktionsverlagerung** *f* IND, MGMNT *Zulieferung von Teilen* outsourcing;

Produktionsverlauf *m* IND production run; **Produktionsvolumen** *nt* IND output volume, production volume; **Produktionsweise** *f* IND production method; **Produktionswerkzeug** *nt* IND production implement; **Produktionsziel** *nt* IND production target; **Produktionsziffern** *f pl* IND production figures; **Produktionszubehör** *nt* IND production equipment; **Produktionszweig** *m* IND, VW manufacturing sector; **Produktionszyklus** *m* IND work cycle

produktiv *adj* IND, PERSON, VERWALT productive; **nicht ~e Arbeitskräfte** *f pl* PERSON unproductive labor (*AmE*), unproductive labour (*BrE*); **~ eingesetztes Kapital** *nt* VW productive capital; **~er Lohn** *m* FINANZ, IND direct labor cost (*AmE*), direct labour cost (*BrE*); **~e Wartung** *f* VERWALT productive maintenance

Produktivität *f* IND productivity, technical efficiency, PERSON productivity; **Produktivitätsabkommen** *nt* IND productivity agreement (*BrE*), PERSON efficiency agreement (*BrE*); **Produktivitätsanreiz** *m* PERSON productivity incentive; **Produktivitätsfeldzug** *m* IND productivity drive; **Produktivitätskampagne** *f* V&M productivity campaign; **Produktivitätsmessung** *f* IND productivity measurement

produktivitätsorientiert: ~er Reallohn *m* VW efficiency real wage; **~e Tarifvereinbarung** *f* PERSON productivity bargaining

Produktivität: **Produktivitätsschock** *m* VW productivity shock; **Produktivitätsspitze** *f* VW productivity peak; **Produktivitätsvereinbarung** *f* IND, RECHT productivity agreement (*BrE*); **Produktivitätsverhandlung** *f* PERSON productivity bargaining; **Produktivitätsvertrag** *m* PERSON productivity agreement; **Produktivitätszuwachs** *m* IND productivity gains; **am Produktivitätszuwachs orientierte Tarifvereinbarung** *f* PERSON productivity bargaining

Produkt: **Produktkenntnis** *f* V&M product knowledge; **Produktklassifikation** *f* IND, V&M product classification; **Produktkompatibilität** *f* V&M product compatibility; **Produktkonzept** *nt* V&M product conception; **Produktkosten** *pl* IND, V&M product cost; **Produktkostenberechnung** *f* RECHNUNG product costing; **Produktleistung** *f* V&M product performance; **Produktleiter, in** *m,f* MGMNT, PERSON product manager; **Produktmanagement** *nt* MGMNT, PERSON product management; **Produktmanager, in** *m,f* MGMNT, PERSON, V&M product manager, brand manager; **Produktmarketing** *nt* V&M product marketing; **Produktmix** *nt* V&M product mix; **Produktmomentformel** *f* MATH product moment formula; **Produktnorm** *f* RECHT product standard; **Produktpalette** *f* V&M array of products, product range, range of products; **Produktpflege** *f* MGMNT, V&M product management; **Produktplanung** *f* IND, MGMNT production planning; **Produktportfolio** *nt* BÖRSE product portfolio; **Produktpositionierung** *f* V&M product positioning; **Produktpräsentation** *f* V&M sales presentation; **Produktprofil** *nt* V&M product profile; **Produktqualitätsdifferenzierung** *f* V&M product quality differentiation; **Produktrentabilität** *f* FINANZ, RECHNUNG, V&M product profitability; **Produktschaffung** *f* V&M product creation; **Produktstandard** *m* V&M product standard; **Produktstrategie** *f* V&M product strategy; **Produkttest** *m* IND, V&M product testing; **Produktüberwachung** *f* MGMNT, V&M product manage-

ment; **Produktverbesserung** *f* V&M product improvement; **Produktverläßlichkeit** *f* V&M product reliability; **Produktvorteil** *m* V&M product benefit, product-plus; **Produktwerbung** *f* V&M product advertising; **Produktwirrwarr** *nt* V&M product clutter; **Produktzyklus** *m* V&M product cycle

Produzent, in *m,f* IND manufacturer (*mfr*), maker; **Produzentengenossenschaft** *f* VW producer cooperative; **Produzentenrente** *f* VW producer's surplus; **Produzentenrisiko** *nt* VW producer's risk

produzieren *vt* IND manufacture, produce, roll out, output

produziert *adj* (*prod.*) IND manufactured (*mfd*), produced

Prof. *abbr* (*Professor*) PERSON Prof. (*Professor*)

Professional *m* GESCHÄFT professional (*pro*)

Professionalisierung *f* GESCHÄFT professionalization

Professionalismus *m* GESCHÄFT professionalism

professionell *adj* GESCHÄFT professional

Professor, in *m,f* (*Prof*) PERSON Professor (*Prof.*)

Profi *m* *infrml* GESCHÄFT pro (*infrml*) (*professional*)

Profil *nt* GESCHÄFT profile

profiliert: wenig ~ *phr* V&M low-profile

Profil: **Profilrisiko** *nt* FINANZ profile risk

Profit *m* GESCHÄFT profit; ♦ **bei einem ~ von** GESCHÄFT at a profit of

Profit-Center *nt* FINANZ, RECHNUNG, VW profit center (*AmE*), profit centre (*BrE*); **Profit-Center-Abrechnung** *f* FINANZ, RECHNUNG profit center accounting (*AmE*), profit centre accounting (*BrE*); **Profit-Center-Rechnungswesen** *nt* FINANZ, RECHNUNG profit center accounting (*AmE*), profit centre accounting (*BrE*)

profitieren 1. *vt* GESCHÄFT benefit; **2.** *vi* GESCHÄFT profit, benefit

Profit: **Profitmacher, in** *m,f* GESCHÄFT profiteer; **Profitmotiv** *nt* FINANZ, VW profit motive; **Profitoptimierung** *f* FINANZ, VW profit optimization; **Profitpolice** *f* VERSICH profits policy

Proformarechnung *f* IMP/EXP, V&M, RECHNUNG, VERWALT pro forma invoice

Prognose *f* GESCHÄFT prognosis, projection, prediction, forecast, forecasting; **Prognoserechnung** *f* RECHNUNG forecasting

prognostizieren *vt* GESCHÄFT predict

prognostiziert *adj* GESCHÄFT predicted

Prognostizierung *f* GESCHÄFT forecasting

Programm *nt* COMP program, GESCHÄFT *Zeitplan* plan, schedule, MEDIEN *Sendung* program (*AmE*), programme (*BrE*), MGMNT *Sitzung* agenda, plan, program (*AmE*), programme (*BrE*), timetable; **~ zur Belebung der Konjunktur** GESCHÄFT recovery program (*AmE*), recovery programme (*BrE*); **~ für öffentliche Arbeiten** GESCHÄFT, SOZIAL public works program (*AmE*), public works programme (*BrE*); **~ der öffentlichen Hand** POL, VW cost-shared program (*AmE*), cost-shared programme (*BrE*); **~ der öffentlichen Hand mit Kostenbeteiligung** POL, VW shared-cost program (*AmE*), shared-cost programme (*BrE*); **~ ohne Verschuldung** FINANZ unleveraged program (*AmE*), unleveraged programme (*BrE*)

Programm: **Programmablauf** *m* COMP program flow; **Programmanpassungskredit** *m* FINANZ program adjustment loan (*AmE*) (*PAL*), programme adjustment loan (*BrE*) (*PAL*)

programmatisch *adj* COMP programmatic

Programm: **Programmauswertungsplan** *m* GESCHÄFT program evaluation plan (*AmE*), programme evaluation plan (*BrE*); **Programmbewertungsplan** *m* GESCHÄFT program evaluation plan (*AmE*), programme evaluation plan (*BrE*); **Programmbibliothek** *f* COMP library, program library; **Programmbudget** *nt* POL planning programming budget; **Programmdatei** *f* COMP program file; **Programmevaluationsplan** *m* GESCHÄFT program evaluation plan (*AmE*), programme evaluation plan (*BrE*)

Programmfehler *m* COMP bug, program bug; ♦ **~ bereinigen in** [+dat] COMP debug; **~ beseitigen in** [+dat] COMP debug; **~ suchen in** [+dat] COMP debug

programmgesteuert: **~e Betriebsführung** *f* MGMNT programmed management

Programm: **Programmhandel** *m* BÖRSE, COMP, VW program trading (*AmE*), programme trading (*BrE*), program trade (*AmE*), programme trade (*BrE*), program deal (*AmE*), programme deal (*BrE*); **Programmhilfe** *f* VW program aid (*AmE*), programme aid (*BrE*)

programmierbar: **~e Funktion** *f* COMP programmable function

programmieren *vt* COMP program, GESCHÄFT, MGMNT program (*AmE*), programme (*BrE*)

Programmieren *nt* COMP computer programming, programming

Programmierer, in *m,f* COMP computer programmer, programmer

Programmiersprache *f* COMP language, programming language

programmiert: **~es Management** *nt* MGMNT programmed management; **~er Unterricht** *m* SOZIAL programmed learning; **~e Unterweisung** *f* COMP programmed instruction

Programmierung *f* COMP programming, computer programming, GESCHÄFT programming

Programm: **Programmpaket** *nt* COMP, FINANZ, MGMNT program package, packaged software; **Programmroutine** *f* COMP routine; **Programmschalter** *m* COMP switch; **Programmstoppbefehl** *m* COMP breakpoint instruction; **Programmstruktur** *f* GESCHÄFT program structure (*AmE*), programme structure (*BrE*); **Programmtest** *m* COMP program testing; **Programmverzahnung** *f* COMP multiprogramming; **Programmvoraussage** *f* GESCHÄFT program forecast (*AmE*), programme forecast (*BrE*); **Programmvorschau** *f* GESCHÄFT program forecast (*AmE*), programme forecast (*BrE*), MEDIEN *Film, Fernsehen* preview, trailer

Progressionswirkung *f* FINANZ, STEUER, VW fiscal drag

progressiv 1. *adj* GESCHÄFT progressive, accelerated; **2.** *adv* GESCHÄFT progressively

Prohibitionsrecht *nt* PATENT prohibition right

Projekt *nt* GESCHÄFT plan, project; **Projektabschätzung** *f* MGMNT project appraisal; **Projektanalyse** *f* FINANZ, MGMNT project analysis; **Projektauswertung** *f* FINANZ, MGMNT project analysis; **Projektbeförderung** *f* TRANSP project forwarding; **Projektbewertung** *f* FINANZ, MGMNT project assessment; **Projektbewilligung** *f* GESCHÄFT project approval; **Projektbindung** *f* VW project link, project-typing; **Projekteinschätzung** *f* FINANZ, MGMNT project assessment; **Projektentwurf** *m*

GESCHÄFT draft project; **Projektfortschrittsplanung** *f* MGMNT program evaluation and review technique (*AmE*) (*PERT*), programme evaluation and review technique (*BrE*) (*PERT*)

projektgebunden: **~es Darlehen** *nt* FINANZ nonrecourse loan; **nicht ~e Hilfe** *f* VW nonproject aid

Projekt: **Projektgenehmigung** *f* GESCHÄFT project approval; **Projekthilfe** *f* VW project aid, program aid (*AmE*), programme aid (*BrE*); **Projektingenieur, in** *m,f* IND, MGMNT, PERSON project engineer

Projektion *f* GESCHÄFT projection; **~ des ungünstigsten Falles** GESCHÄFT worst-case projection

projektiv: **~er Test** *m* V&M projective test

Projekt: **Projektleiter, in** *m,f* MGMNT, PERSON project leader, project manager; **Projektleitung** *f* MGMNT, PERSON project management; **Projektmanagement** *nt* MGMNT, PERSON project management; **Projektmanager, in** *m,f* MGMNT, PERSON project manager; **Projektplanung** *f* MGMNT, PERSON project planning; **Projektstudie** *f* GESCHÄFT feasibility survey, feasibility study, blueprint; **Projektträger** *m* VW project sponsor; **Projektvorbereitungsfazilität** *f* FINANZ project preparation facility (*PPF*)

Pro-Kopf- *in cpds* VW per capita; **Pro-Kopf-BIP** *nt* VW per capita GDP; **Pro-Kopf-Einkommen** *nt* VW income per head, per capita income, income per capita; **Pro-Kopf-Verbrauch** *m* VW consumption per capita

proletarisch *adj* POL, VW proletarian

Prolongation *f* BÖRSE contango; **Prolongationsgebühr** *f* BÖRSE, FINANZ contango rate (*BrE*); **Prolongationsklausel** *f* VERSICH continuation clause (*CC*)

prolongieren *vt* GESCHÄFT prolong, renew, extend

prominent *adj* GESCHÄFT prominent

Prominentenwerbung *f* V&M personality promotion

prompt *adj* GESCHÄFT speedy, prompt, quick; **~e Zahlung** *f* FINANZ prompt payment

Prompt *nt jarg* COMP prompt

Propädeutik *f* SOZIAL *Universität* introductory course

Propaganda *f* POL, V&M propaganda; **Propagandafeldzug** *m* POL, V&M propaganda campaign

Proportional- *in cpds* GESCHÄFT proportional

proportional *adj* GESCHÄFT proportional; **~e Steuer** *f* STEUER standard-rate tax

Proportional-: **Proportionaleinkommensteuer** *f* STEUER proportional income tax; **Proportionalsatz** *m* STEUER flat rate; **Proportionalschrift** *f* COMP, MEDIEN proportionally-spaced printing; **Proportionaltarif** *m* FINANZ proportional rate

Prorata-Klausel *f* VERSICH average clause

Prorata-temporis-Basis *f* RECHNUNG percentage-of-completion basis

Prorationsverrechnung *f* TRANSP proration

Prospekt *m* FREI, MEDIEN, V&M booklet, brochure, pamphlet; **Prospektersatzerklärung** *f* BÖRSE statement in lieu of prospectus

prospektiv: **~e Bewertung** *f* VERSICH prospective rating

protegieren *vt* POL, RECHT *nationale Interessen* protect

Protektion *f* VW protection

Protektionismus *m* VW protectionism

protektionistisch: **~e Politik** *f* VW protectionist policy

Protest *m* GESCHÄFT protest

protestieren 1. *vt* GESCHÄFT *Wechsel, Scheck* protest; **2.** *vi* GESCHÄFT protest, make a protest

protestiert: nicht ~ *adj* BANK, FINANZ *Wechsel, Scheck* unprotested

Protest: Protestkosten *pl* RECHT protest charges; **Proteststimme** *f* POL protest vote; **Proteststreik** *m* PERSON protest strike

Protokoll *nt* COMP protocol, POL protocol, RECHT *bei Gericht* transcript, *bei Polizei* statement, VERWALT log, *einer Sitzung* minutes; **Protokollbuch** *nt* VERWALT minute book

protokollieren *vt* GESCHÄFT give record of, VERWALT record, log, *Sitzung* take the minutes of

Prototyp *m* IND, V&M prototype; **Prototypproduktion** *f* IND pilot production

provinziell: ~es staatliches Unternehmen *nt* VERWALT provincial Crown corporation (*BrE*)

Provinzpresse *f* MEDIEN provincial press

Provision *f* BANK, BÖRSE, FINANZ, V&M commission (*comm*); **~ der Führungsbank** BANK arrangement fee; **~ des Kommissionärs** FINANZ factorage; **~ aus einer Konsortialbeteiligung** FINANZ underwriting commission; **~ der Konsortialführung** BANK management fee; **~ für den Spediteur** TRANSP forwarding agent's commission (*fac*); **~ eines Wertpapierhändlers** BÖRSE turn; **Provisionsbelastung** *f* **bei Ersterwerb** FINANZ front-end loading; **Provisionskonto** *nt* BANK commission account; **Provisionsrechnung** *f* BANK commission account; **Provisionssatz** *m* BANK commission rate; **Provisionsschneiderei** *f* *infrml* BÖRSE churning; **Provisionssystem** *nt* PERSON commission system; **Provisionstabelle** *f* BÖRSE scale of commission

provisorisch 1. *adj* GESCHÄFT temporary; **2.** *adv* GESCHÄFT temporarily

Provisorium *nt* GESCHÄFT temporary measure

Prozedur *f* COMP *Programm* procedure

Prozent *nt* (*p.c.*) GESCHÄFT per cent (*P/C, pc*), percent, percentage; **Prozentanalyse** *f* MATH percentage analysis

prozentig *adj* (*v.H.*) GESCHÄFT per cent, percent (*P/C, pc*)

Prozentsatz *m* MATH percentage; **auf Jahresbasis umgerechneter ~** FINANZ annual percentage rate (*APR*), annualized percentage rate (*APR*); **~ der Wertminderung** FINANZ percentage of depreciation; **~ des Wertverlusts** FINANZ percentage of depreciation

prozentual *adj* MATH percentagewise; **~e Änderung** *f* FINANZ percentage change

Prozent: Prozentverteilung *f* MATH percentage distribution

Prozeß *m* COMP, IND process, RECHT *Verfahren* trial, *Rechtsstreit* litigation, *Fall* case, court case; **~ gleitender Durchschnittswerte** MATH moving-average process; **~ mit Streitgenossen** RECHT joint action; **Prozeßanalyse** *f* VW activity analysis; **Prozeßanwalt** *m*, **Prozeßanwältin** *f* RECHT barrister-at-law (*BrE*), trial attorney (*AmE*), trial lawyer (*AmE*), *Rechtsanwalt* counsel; **Prozeßcomputer** *m* COMP, IND process computer; **Prozeßführung** *f* IND process control; **Prozeßkostenhilfe** *f* RECHT, SOZIAL legal aid

prozessieren *vi* RECHT litigate, proceed, sue, go to court; ♦ **gegen jdn ~** RECHT take sb to court

Prozeß: Prozeßindustrie *f* IND process industry; **Prozeßkosten** *pl* RECHT costs; **Prozeßkostenhilfe** *f* RECHT, SOZIAL legal aid; **Prozeßkostenrechnung** *f*

RECHT bill of costs; **Prozeßleitsystem** *nt* IND process control; **Prozeßleitung** *f* IND process control; **Prozeßlenkung** *f* IND process control; **Prozeßniveau** *nt* RECHNUNG, VERWALT, VW activity level

Prozessor *m* COMP processor

Prozeß: Prozeßpartei *f* RECHT litigant; **Prozeßrechner** *m* COMP, IND process computer; **Prozeßsteuersystem** *nt* IND process control; **Prozeßsteuerung** *f* IND process control

PR: ~-Sachbearbeiter, in *m,f* PERSON, V&M public relations consultant, public relations executive, public relations officer (*PRO*)

Prüf- *in cpds* COMP, IND, MATH, RECHNUNG test, testing, checking, auditing; **Prüfanlage** *f* IND testing plant; **Prüfbarkeit** *f* RECHNUNG auditability; **Prüfbericht** *m* FINANZ audit report, PATENT search report; **Prüfbit** *nt* COMP check bit; **Prüfeinrichtung** *f* IND test equipment

prüfen *vt* GESCHÄFT examine, survey, analyse (*BrE*), analyze (*AmE*), inspect, PATENT search, PERSON examine, RECHNUNG audit; ♦ **~ und für richtig befinden** GESCHÄFT approve

prüfend: zu ~e Akte *f* RECHNUNG audit file

Prüfer, in *m,f* FINANZ comptroller, controller, GESCHÄFT, PATENT, PERSON examiner, RECHNUNG auditor, comptroller, controller, audit agent

prüffähig *adj* RECHNUNG auditable

Prüf-: Prüfgerät *nt* COMP, IND test equipment; **Prüfgröße** *f* MATH, VW test statistic; **Prüfhypothese** *f* MATH alternate hypothesis; **Prüfkette** *f* RECHNUNG audit trail

Prüfling *m* GESCHÄFT test examinee

Prüf-: Prüfliste *f* COMP audit trail; **Prüfmaschine** *f* IND testing equipment; **Prüfmaß** *nt* VW test statistic; **Prüfpanel** *nt* GESCHÄFT control panel; **Prüfspur** *f* RECHNUNG audit trail; **Prüfstand** *m* IND test bench, testbed, testing plant; **Prüftätigkeit** *f* RECHNUNG audit activity (*BrE*)

Prüfung *f* COMP check, test, GESCHÄFT analysis, verification, survey, test, inspection, examination, IND testing, testing procedure, PATENT, PERSON examination, RECHNUNG audit, examination, verification, V&M test; **~ des Antrags** VERSICH examination of proposal; **~ der Betriebsabläufe** MGMNT *zur Verbesserung der Produktion* operational audit, operations audit; **~ an Ort und Stelle** GESCHÄFT spot check; **~ von Personal** PERSON, RECHNUNG manpower audit; **~ des Quellenabzugs** STEUER PAYE audit (*BrE*); **~ des Vorschlags** VERSICH examination of proposal; ♦ **bei ~** GESCHÄFT on examination

Prüfung: Prüfungsablauf *m* RECHNUNG audit work schedule; **Prüfungsauftrag** *m* RECHNUNG audit engagement; **Prüfungsausschuß** *m* PERSON review body, screening board, RECHNUNG audit committee; **Prüfungs- und Beratungsdienst** *m* PATENT *des britischen Patentamtes* Search and Advisory Service (*BrE*); **Prüfungsbericht** *m* RECHNUNG audit report, auditor's certificate, auditor's opinion, auditor's report, auditor's statement; **Prüfungsbeweis** *m* RECHNUNG audit evidence; **Prüfungsergebnis** *nt* SOZIAL exam result; **Prüfungsgebühr** *f* GESCHÄFT survey fee; **Prüfungsgremium** *nt* **für Spitzengehälter** MGMNT, PERSON top salaries review body (*BrE*); **Prüfungsgrundsatz** *m* RECHNUNG audit standard, auditing principle, auditing standard; **Prüfungsgruppe** *f* RECHNUNG audit group, audit team;

Prüfungskette *f* RECHNUNG audit trail; **Prüfungskosten** *pl* RECHNUNG audit costs; **Prüfungskurzbericht** *m* RECHNUNG audit brief; **Prüfungspersonal** *nt* RECHNUNG audit staff (*BrE*); **Prüfungspfad** *m* RECHNUNG audit trail; **Prüfungsphase** *f* GESCHÄFT verification phase; **Prüfungsplan** *m* RECHNUNG audit plan; **Prüfungsprogramm** *nt* RECHNUNG audit program (*AmE*), audit programme (*BrE*), audit schedule; **Prüfungsrichtlinie** *f* RECHNUNG auditing principle, auditing standard; **Prüfungsrisiko** *nt* RECHNUNG audit risk; **Prüfungs-Software** *f* RECHNUNG audit software; **Prüfungsteam** *nt* RECHNUNG audit team; **Prüfungstechnik** *f* RECHNUNG audit technique, auditing technique; **Prüfungsumfang** *m* RECHNUNG audit coverage, audit scope; **Prüfungsunabhängigkeit** *f* RECHNUNG audit independence; **Prüfungsunterlagen** *f pl* RECHNUNG audit working papers; **Prüfungsverfahren** *nt* RECHNUNG auditing procedure; **Prüfungsvermerk** *m* RECHNUNG audit certificate; **Prüfungsvorschriften** *f pl* RECHNUNG audit guide; **Prüfungswesen** *nt* RECHNUNG auditing; **Prüfungszeitplan** *m* RECHNUNG audit work schedule

Prüf-: **Prüfverfahren** *nt* IND testing procedure, PERSON *Bewerbung* screening process; **Prüfzeichen** *nt* COMP check character, VERWALT approval mark; **Prüfziffer** *f* COMP check digit

PS *abbr* (*Pferdestärke*) IND, TRANSP HP (*horsepower*)

P.S. *abbr* (*Postscriptum*) KOMM *Briefende* PS (*postscript*), ps. (*postscript*)

Pseudo- *pref* GESCHÄFT pseudo-

Pseudonym *nt* COMP, GESCHÄFT alias

Pseudo-: **Pseudoproduktionsaufgabe** *f* VW pseudo-production function; **Pseudoproduktionsfunktion** *f* VW pseudo-production function; **Pseudoprodukttest** *m* V&M pseudo-product testing

Psychographie *f* V&M psychographics

Psychologie *f* GESCHÄFT psychology

psychologisch: **~er Blickfang** *m* V&M psychological hook; **~er Preis** *m* V&M psychological price; **~e Preisfestsetzung** *f* V&M psychological pricing; **~er Test** *m* PERSON *Bewerbung* psychological test

Psychometrie *f* PERSON *Bewerbung*, V&M psychometrics

psychometrisch: **~er Test** *m* PERSON, V&M psychometric testing

pt *abbr* (*Pint*) GESCHÄFT pt (*pint*)

Public: **~ Relations** *pl* (*PR*) PERSON, V&M public relations (*PR*); **Public-Choice-Theorie** *f* VW public choice theory; **Public-Domain-Software** *f* COMP public domain software

Publikation *f* MEDIEN publication

Publikum *nt* GESCHÄFT public; **sich in eine Publikumsgesellschaft umwandeln** *phr* FINANZ go public;

Publikumsrenner *m* V&M big seller

publikumswirksam *adj* MEDIEN *Titel* punchy, V&M with a strong appeal

publizieren *vt* MEDIEN, PATENT publish

publiziert *adj* MEDIEN, PATENT published

Publizität *f* BÖRSE, FINANZ disclosure, MEDIEN, V&M publicity; **Publizitätserfordernis** *f* BÖRSE, FINANZ disclosure requirement

Puffer *m* COMP *Daten* stack, buffer, buffer storage, buffer store, TRANSP *Eisenbahn* buffer; **Pufferbereich** *m* COMP buffer area; **Pufferbestand** *m* TRANSP buffer stock; **Pufferspeicher** *m* COMP cache buffer, buffer storage, buffer store, buffer; **Pufferstaat** *m* POL buffer state; **Puffervorrat** *m* VW buffer stock; **Pufferzeit** *f* VW float time; **Pufferzone** *f* GRUND buffer zone

Pull-down-Menü *nt* COMP pull-down menu

Puls *m* KOMM *Telefon* pulse

Pump: **etw auf ~ kaufen** *phr infrml* GESCHÄFT buy sth on tick (*infrml*)

P&I *abbr* (*Reederhaftpflicht*) TRANSP P&I (*protection and indemnity*)

P&R *abbr* (*Park-und-Ride*) TRANSP park and ride

Punkt *m* BÖRSE point, COMP dot, GESCHÄFT point, MEDIEN *Typographie* full stop (*BrE*), period (*AmE*), VERWALT item; ◆ **einen ~ erörtern** GESCHÄFT discuss an item; **der ~ ist noch offen** GESCHÄFT the point is still undecided; **der ~ ist noch unentschieden** GESCHÄFT the point is still undecided; **einen toten ~ erreichen** GESCHÄFT reach a deadlock, reach an impasse

Punkt: **Punktbefehl** *m* COMP dot command; **Punktbewertung** *f* MGMNT, PERSON, VERSICH points rating; **Punktbewertungsmethode** *f* MGMNT, PERSON, VERSICH points-rating method; **Punktelastizität** *f* VW point elasticity; **Punkte pro Zoll** *phr* (*dpi*) COMP *Drucker, Bildschirm* dots per inch (*dpi*)

pünktlich 1. *adj* GESCHÄFT exact, precise, TRANSP punctual; **2.** *adv* TRANSP on time; ◆ **~ verkehren** TRANSP run on time

pünktlich: **~e Rechnungsbezahlung** *f* FINANZ prompt payment of invoices

Pünktlichkeit *f* TRANSP punctuality; **Pünktlichkeitsanalyse** *f* TRANSP punctuality analysis; **Pünktlichkeitsleistung** *f* TRANSP punctuality performance

Punkt: **Punktpreis** *m* BÖRSE point price; **Punktschätzung** *f* MATH point estimate

pyramidenförmig *adj* GESCHÄFT pyramidal

Pyramidenhierarchie *f* PERSON pyramid hierarchy

Pyromanie *f* VERSICH incendiarism

Pyrometer *nt* GESCHÄFT pyrometer

pyrotechnisch: **~e Substanz** *f* IND pyrotechnic substance

Q

q *abbr* (*Quadrat*) GESCHÄFT sq (*square*)

QM *abbr* (*Qualitätsmanagement*) IND quality management

Quadrat *nt* (*q*) GESCHÄFT square (*sq*); **Quadratfuß** *m* GESCHÄFT square foot; **pro Quadratfuß** *phr* GESCHÄFT, GRUND per square foot (*psf*); **Quadratfußzahl** *f* GRUND *eines Gebäudes* square footage; **Quadratkilometer** *m* GESCHÄFT square kilometer (*AmE*), square kilometre (*BrE*); **Quadratmeile** *f* GESCHÄFT square mile; **Quadratmeter** *m* GESCHÄFT square meter (*AmE*), square metre (*BrE*)

Qualifikation *f* GESCHÄFT, PERSON, SOZIAL qualification; ♦ **die ~ für etw haben** GESCHÄFT, PERSON be qualified to do sth

Qualifikation: **Qualifikationsstruktur** *f* VW qualification pattern

qualifizieren: sich ~ *v refl* GESCHÄFT, POL, SOZIAL qualify

qualifiziert *adj* GESCHÄFT advanced, qualified POL, SOZIAL qualified; **~e Ausbildung** *f* SOZIAL advanced training; **~e Mehrheit** *f* POL qualified majority; **~e Mehrheitsabstimmung** *f* POL qualified majority vote; **~er Mehrheitsbeschluß** *m* POL qualified majority vote; **~e Meinung** *f* GESCHÄFT qualified opinion; ♦ **für etw ~ sein** PERSON, POL be eligible for sth

Qualifizierung *f* GESCHÄFT, SOZIAL qualification

Qualität *f* GESCHÄFT, IND, MGMNT, V&M, VW quality; **~ der Arbeitskräfte** VW quality of labor force (*AmE*), quality of labour force (*BrE*); **~ des Arbeitslebens** PERSON quality of working life (*QWL*); **~ der Gewinne** FINANZ quality of earnings

qualitativ 1. *adj* GESCHÄFT, V&M qualitative; **2.** *adv* GESCHÄFT qualitatively

qualitativ: **~e Analyse** *f* V&M qualitative analysis; **~e Forschung** *f* V&M qualitative research; **~e Methode** *f* V&M qualitative methodology

Qualität: **Qualitätsanforderung** *f* IND quality requirement; **Qualitätsarbeit** *f* GESCHÄFT high-quality workmanship; **Qualitätsbenzin** *nt* UMWELT four-star petrol (*BrE*), premium grade gasoline (*AmE*); **Qualitätsgruppe** *f* IND, MGMNT, PERSON quality circle; **Qualitätsgüter** *nt pl* GESCHÄFT quality goods; **Qualitätskontrolle** *f* BANK qualitative control, GESCHÄFT quality control (*QC*), IND process control, quality control (*QC*), V&M quality control (*QC*); **Qualitätskontrolltechnik** *f* MGMNT quality engineering; **Qualitätsleitung** *f* IND quality management; **Qualitätsmanagement** *nt* (*QM*) IND quality management; **Qualitätsmangel** *m* RECHT defect; **Qualitätsmarkt** *m* V&M quality market; **Qualitätsnorm** *f* GESCHÄFT quality standard; **Qualitätsnormen** *f pl* IND, MGMNT quality standard; **Qualitätsprodukt** *nt* V&M high-quality product; **Qualitätssicherung** *f* GESCHÄFT, IND, MGMNT, V&M quality assurance, quality protection; **Qualitätssiegel** *nt* GESCHÄFT seal of quality; **Qualitätsstandard** *m* GESCHÄFT, IND, MGMNT quality standard; **Qualitätsüberwachung** *f* GESCHÄFT, IND quality control (*QC*), MGMNT quality management, V&M quality control (*QC*); **Qualitätsurteil** *nt* GESCHÄFT, IND, MGMNT, V&M quality assessment; **Qualitätsvorschrift** *f* IND quality specification; **Qualitätswaren** *f pl* GESCHÄFT quality goods; **Qualitätszeitschrift** *f* V&M class magazine; **Qualitätszeugnis** *nt* IMP/EXP, TRANSP certificate of quality; **Qualitätszirkel** *m* IND, MGMNT, PERSON quality circle

Quant. *abbr* (*Quantität*) GESCHÄFT, MATH qnty (*quantity*), qty (*quantity*)

Quantifikation *f* MATH, VERWALT quantification

quantifizieren *vt* MATH, VERWALT quantify

Quantität *f* (*Quant.*) GESCHÄFT, MATH quantity (*qnty, qty*)

quantitativ *adj* GESCHÄFT, IND, MATH, MGMNT, V&M, VW quantitative; **~e Analyse** *f* IND, MATH, MGMNT, V&M quantitative analysis; **~e Bestimmung** *f* IND quantitative analysis; **~e Forschung** *f* V&M quantitative research; **~e Methode** *f* V&M quantitative methodology; **~e und qualitative Beschränkungen** *f pl* **der Bankkredite** VW corset (*infrml*); **~e Zielvorgabe** *f* VW quantitative target

Quantität: **Quantitätstheorie** *f* VW quantity theory of money

Quantum *nt* GESCHÄFT quantum

Quarantäne *f* GESCHÄFT, IMP/EXP quarantine; **Quarantänearzt** *m*, **Quarantäneärztin** *f* PERSON health officer; **Quarantänegebühren** *f pl* IMP/EXP quarantine dues; **Quarantänestation** *f* IMP/EXP isolation ward

Quart *f* GESCHÄFT quart (*qt*)

Quartal *nt* GESCHÄFT *des Jahres* quarter (*qtr*); **Quartalsabschluß** *m* RECHNUNG quarter-end accounts

quartalsmäßig *adj* GESCHÄFT quarterly

quartalsweise *adv* GESCHÄFT quarterly

Quarterdeck *nt* TRANSP quarterdeck

Quasi- *pref* GESCHÄFT quasi-

quasi: quasi-autonome nichtstaatliche Organisation *f* VERWALT quasi-autonomous nongovernmental organization (*BrE*) (*quango*)

Quasi-: **Quasigeld** *nt* GESCHÄFT quasi-money; **Quasikontrakt** *m* RECHT quasi-contract; **Quasirente** *f* VW quasi-rent; **Quasiunabhängigkeit** *f* GESCHÄFT quasi-independence

Quellcode *m* COMP source code, GESCHÄFT source language

Quelle *f* COMP, FINANZ, GESCHÄFT source; **Quellenabzugsverfahren** *nt* PERSON *Lohnbuchhaltung*, RECHNUNG, STEUER pay-as-you-earn (*BrE*) (*PAYE*); **Quellenadresse** *f* COMP source address; **Quellenangabe** *f* MEDIEN reference

quellenbesteuert *adj* FINANZ, GESCHÄFT, RECHNUNG, STEUER taxed at source; **~e Erträge** *m pl* RECHNUNG income received under deduction of tax

Quelle: **Quellenbesteuerung** *f* PERSON *von Einkommen aus unselbständiger Tätigkeit* pay-as-you-go (*AmE*); **Quellencode** *m* COMP source code; **Quellendatei** *f* COMP source file; **Quellenprogramm** *nt* COMP source program; **Quellensprache** *f* COMP source language; **Quellensteuer** *f* STEUER withholding tax

Quellsprache _f_ COMP, GESCHÄFT source language

Quer- _in cpds_ GESCHÄFT cross-, transverse; **Querantrieb** _m_ TRANSP transverse propulsion unit; **Querdenker, in** _m,f_ MEDIEN, POL lateral thinker; **Querformat** _nt_ COMP _Textverarbeitung, Drucker_ landscape, landscape format, MEDIEN _Druck_, V&M landscape; **Querrechnen** _nt_ MATH cross-footing; **Querschnitt** _m_ GESCHÄFT cross section, profile; **Querschnittsdaten** _pl_ VW cross-section data; **Quersubvention** _f_ FINANZ, GESCHÄFT cross-subsidy; **Quersubventionieren** _nt_ FINANZ, GESCHÄFT cross-subsidization; **Querträger** _m_ TRANSP cross member, transverse member; **Querverbindung** _f_ MEDIEN, POL connection, link; **Querverbund** _m_ GESCHÄFT interconnection; **Querverweis** _m_ COMP cross-reference; **Querverweisliste** _f_ COMP cross-reference listing

quittieren _vt_ GESCHÄFT _Brief_ acknowledge, _Rechnung_ receipt

Quittung _f_ GESCHÄFT acknowledgement (_ack_), receipt for payment, receipt (_rcpt, recpt_), RECHT _schriftliche Freistellung von einer Verbindlichkeit_ acquittance; ♦ **ohne ~** GESCHÄFT _Rechnung_ unreceipted

Quittung: **Quittungen** _f pl_ BÖRSE receipts; **Quittungsbeleg** _m_ GESCHÄFT supporting receipt

Quorum _nt_ GESCHÄFT quorum

Quote _f_ IMP/EXP, POL quota; ♦ **über die ~ hinausgehend** VW above quota; **Quoten festlegen** IMP/EXP fix quotas

quotenabhängig _adj_ GESCHÄFT subject to quota

Quote: **Quotenaktie** _f_ BÖRSE no-par stock, no par value share; **Quotenauswahl** _f_ V&M quota sample; **Quotenauswahlverfahren** _nt_ GESCHÄFT, V&M quota sampling; **Quotenstichprobe** _f_ V&M quota sample; **Quotensystem** _nt_ GESCHÄFT, IMP/EXP quota system

Quotient _m_ MATH quotient

QWERTY-Tastatur _f_ COMP _englischsprachiges Tastatur-Layout_ qwerty keyboard

QWERTZ-Tastatur _f_ COMP _deutschsprachiges Tastatur-Layout_ qwertz keyboard

R

Rabatt *m* BÖRSE, FINANZ, GESCHÄFT rebate, discount (*dis, disc.*), reduction; **~ für Wiederverkäufer** GESCHÄFT trade allowance; ◆ **mit ~** V&M at a discount (*AAD*)

Rabatt: **Rabattmarke** *f* KOMM trading stamp; **Rabattpreis** *m* FINANZ discount price

Rad *nt* IND, TRANSP wheel

Radar *nt* TRANSP radar; **Radaralarm** *m* BÖRSE radar alert

Radcliffe-Bericht *m* VW Radcliffe Report (*BrE*)

Rad: **Radfahrer, in** *m,f* FREI, TRANSP cyclist

radikal *adj* GESCHÄFT, POL radical

Radikalökonomie *f* VW radical economics

Radio *nt* KOMM radio

radioaktiv: **~er Niederschlag** *m* UMWELT radioactive fallout

Radio: **Radioansage** *f* MEDIEN radio announcement; **Radioapparat** *m* MEDIEN radio set; **Radiogramm** *nt* KOMM radiogram; **Radiohörer, in** *m,f* MEDIEN listener; **Radioprogramm** *nt* MEDIEN radio program (*AmE*), radio programme (*BrE*); **Radiosender** *m* MEDIEN radio station; **Radiowerbung** *f* MEDIEN, V&M radio advertising

Rad: **Radweg** *m* FREI, TRANSP cycle path

Raffination *f* IND refining

Raffinatmetall *nt* UMWELT refined metal

Raffinerie *f* IND refinery; **Raffineriebetrieb** *m* IND refiner

raffinieren *vt* IND refine

Raffinieren *nt* IND refining

raffiniert *adj* IND refined

Rahmen *m* COMP rack, *Datenübertragung* frame, GESCHÄFT, FINANZ framework; **~ des operativen Plans** MGMNT operational plan framework; ◆ **im ~ von** GESCHÄFT within the framework of

Rahmen: **Rahmenabkommen** *nt* GESCHÄFT basic agreement; **Rahmenbedingungen** *f pl* UMWELT environment; **Rahmeneinzelgenehmigung** *f* IMP/EXP open individual licence (*BrE*), open individual license (*AmE*); **Rahmeneinzellizenz** *f* IMP/EXP open individual licence (*BrE*), open individual license (*AmE*); **Rahmengeneraleinfuhrlizenz** *f* IMP/EXP open general import licence (*BrE*) (*OGIL*), open general import license (*AmE*); **Rahmenplan** *m* MGMNT, VW master plan; **Rahmenprojekt** *nt* GESCHÄFT umbrella project; **Rahmenvertrag** *m* GESCHÄFT skeleton contract

RAM *abbr* (*Direktzugriffsspeicher*) COMP RAM (*random access memory*)

Rambouillet-Gipfel *m* VW Rambouillet summit

RAM: **RAM-Disk** *f* COMP RAM disk

Rampe *f* TRANSP ramp; **Rampenpalette** *f* TRANSP ramp stillage

Ramschverkauf *m* V&M jumble sale (*BrE*), rummage sale (*AmE*)

Ramsey: **Ramsey-Ersparnismodell** *nt* VW Ramsey savings model; **Ramsey-Preise** *m pl* VW Ramsey prices; **Ramsey-Sparregel** *f* VW Ramsey saving rule

Rand *m* MEDIEN *einer Seite*, PATENT, V&M margin; ◆ **am ~e des Bankrotts** GESCHÄFT on the verge of bank-

ruptcy; **am ~e des Konkurses** GESCHÄFT on the verge of bankruptcy

Rand: **Randauslösung** *f* VERWALT margin stop; **Randbedingung** *f* MATH boundary condition; **Randbemerkung** *f* VERWALT marginal note; **Randgebiet** *nt* GESCHÄFT outlying district; **Randgebiete** *nt pl* V&M marginal areas; **Randgruppe** *f* V&M *Randbereiche einer Werbekampagne* periphery; **Randgruppen** *f pl* POL marginal groups; **Randmarkt** *m* BÖRSE fringe market

Randomisierung *f* MATH randomization

Rand: **Randproblem** *nt* GESCHÄFT side issue; **Randverteilung** *f* MATH boundary distribution

randvoll *adj* IND at full capacity

Rang *m* FREI circle, GESCHÄFT ranking, PERSON *Hierarchie* echelon; **im ~ vorgehendes Darlehen** *nt* BANK senior loan; ◆ **im ~ nachgehen** BÖRSE rank after

rangälteste: **~r Exportsachbearbeiter** *m*, **~ Exportsachbearbeiterin** *f* PERSON senior export clerk; **~r Importsachbearbeiter** *m*, **~ Importsachbearbeiterin** *f* PERSON senior import clerk

Rang: **Rangfolge** *f* GESCHÄFT ranking, priority

ranghohe: **~r Mitarbeiter** *m* **der Geschäftsführung**, **~ Mitarbeiterin** *f* **der Geschäftsführung** MGMNT, PERSON senior manager; **~r Mitarbeiter** *m* **der Unternehmensleitung**, **~ Mitarbeiterin** *f* **der Unternehmensleitung** MGMNT, PERSON senior manager

ranghöchste: **~r Exportsachbearbeiter** *m*, **~ Exportsachbearbeiterin** *f* MGMNT senior export clerk; **~r Importsachbearbeiter** *m*, **~ Importsachbearbeiterin** *f* MGMNT senior import clerk; **~r Stellvertreter** *m* **des Vorstandsvorsitzenden**, **~ Stellvertreterin** *f* **des Vorstandsvorsitzenden** MGMNT senior vice-president; **~r stellvertretender Generaldirektor** *m*, **~ stellvertretende Generaldirektorin** *f* MGMNT senior vice-president; **~r Vizepräsident** *m*, **~ Vizepräsidentin** *f* MGMNT senior vice-president

Rangierbahnhof *m* TRANSP marshalling yard

rangieren *vi* TRANSP shunt, marshal, VW rank

Rang: **Rangkorrelation** *f* MATH rank correlation

rangmäßig: **~e Bewertung** *f* **von Gütern** VW ranking of commodities

Rang: **Rangordnung** *f* GESCHÄFT ranking, MATH rank order, PERSON *Karriereleiter, Prioritäten* ranking; **Rangordnung** *f* **nach Perzentilen** MATH percentile ranking; **Rangskala** *f* MATH ordinal scale; **Rangverlust** *m* PATENT loss of priority

ranhalten: **sich ~** *v refl infrml* GESCHÄFT buck up (*infrml*)

rapid 1. *adj* GESCHÄFT, VW rapid; ◆ **~en Aufschwung nehmen** VW boom; **2.** *adv* GESCHÄFT, VW rapidly; ◆ **~ steigen** VW *Aktien* boom

Rapprochement *nt* POL rapprochement

rasant *adj* GESCHÄFT rapid, meteoric; **~er Aufstieg** *m* MGMNT, PERSON lightning rise, meteoric rise; **~er technischer Fortschritt** *m* VW rapid technological progress

rasch 1. *adj* GESCHÄFT fast; **2.** *adv* ◆ **~ anwachsen**

experience rapid growth; **~ aufsteigend** GESCHÄFT soaring

rasch: **~er Aufstieg** *m* GESCHÄFT fast track; **~er Ausgabenanstieg** *m* GESCHÄFT spending surge; **~er Kursanstieg** *m* BÖRSE bulge; **~es Tempo** *nt* GESCHÄFT fast pace

Rasse- *in cpds* PERSON, POL, RECHT race; **Rassendiskriminierung** *f* PERSON race discrimination, racial discrimination; **Rassendiskriminierungsverbotsgesetz** *nt* PERSON, RECHT Race Relations Act (*BrE*) (*RRA*); **Rassenschranke** *f* PERSON, POL racial barrier, race barrier

Rast- *in cpds* FREI, TRANSP rest

Raster *m* COMP raster, screen; **Rasterbild** *nt* MEDIEN autotype; **Rasterdrucker** *m* COMP dot printer, MEDIEN screen printing mashine; **Rasterfeld** *nt* COMP grid

Rast-: **Rasthaus** *nt* FREI, TRANSP motorway service station (*BrE*), motorway services (*BrE*); **Raststätte** *f* FREI, TRANSP motorway service station (*BrE*), motorway services (*BrE*)

Rasur *f* GESCHÄFT erasure

Rat *m* GESCHÄFT advice, IND council, MGMNT word of advice, POL, VERWALT council, VW council, *EU* European Council; **~ der europäischen Wirtschaftsverbände** IND Council of European Industrial Federations (*CEIF*); **~ für Europäische wirtschaftliche Zusammenarbeit** VW Council for European Economic Cooperation (*CEEC*); **~ für Finanzberichterstattung** RECHNUNG Financial Reporting Council (*BrE*); **~ für gegenseitige Wirtschaftshilfe** *obs* (*RGW*) VW Council for Mutual Economic Aid (*obs*) (*COMECON*); **~ für Verbraucherberatung** VW Consumers' Consultative Council; ♦ **durch ~ Beihilfe leisten** RECHT counsel; **um ~ fragen** GESCHÄFT seek advice

Rate *f* COMP rate, GESCHÄFT rate, instalment (*BrE*), installment (*AmE*); ♦ **auf Raten** FINANZ on hire purchase (*BrE*), on the installment plan (*AmE*); **in Raten** BANK in installments (*AmE*), in instalments (*BrE*); **eine ~ zahlen** FINANZ pay an installment (*AmE*), pay an instalment (*BrE*)

Rate: **Ratenbetrag** *m* STEUER amount paid by installments (*AmE*), amount paid by instalments (*BrE*); **in Raten gezahlter Betrag** *m* STEUER amount paid by installments (*AmE*), amount paid by instalments (*BrE*); **Ratenkauf** *m* V&M hire-purchase (*BrE*) (*HP*); **Ratenkaufvertrag** *m* FINANZ installment plan agreement (*AmE*), hire-purchase agreement (*BrE*); **Ratenkredit** *m* BANK consumer installment loan (*AmE*), consumer instalment loan (*BrE*), FINANZ installment credit (*AmE*), instalment credit (*BrE*); **Ratenprämienvertrag** *m* VERSICH deferred account; **Ratenvertrag** *m* RECHT installment contract (*AmE*), instalment contract (*BrE*); **Ratenzahlung** *f* BANK installment payment (*AmE*), instalment payment (*BrE*), FINANZ part payment; **Ratenzahlungsplan** *m* BANK installment repayment plan (*AmE*), instalment repayment schedule (*BrE*); **Ratenzahlungsvertrag** *m* STEUER deferred account

Rathaus *nt* GESCHÄFT, POL, VERWALT town hall

ratifizieren *vt* GESCHÄFT *Abkommen* ratify, *Vertrag* approve

Ratifizierung *f* BANK approval, GESCHÄFT ratification

Rating-Agentur *f* BÖRSE rating agency

rational *adj* GESCHÄFT rational; **~e Entscheidung** *f* GESCHÄFT rational decision; **~e Erwartungen** *f pl* VW rational expectations (*RE*); **~er Führungsstil** *m* MGMNT rational management

rationalisieren *vt* FINANZ, GESCHÄFT, IND, MGMNT, VW rationalize, streamline

Rationalisierung *f* FINANZ, IND, MGMNT, VW streamlining, rationalization; **~ von Arbeitsprozessen** IND industrial engineering; **~ des Fuhrparks** TRANSP fleet rationalization; **~ einer Marke** V&M brand rationalization; **Rationalisierungsanleihe** *f* eines Staatsunternehmens FINANZ public enterprise rationalization loan (*PERL*), public enterprise reform loan (*PERL*), public enterprise rehabilitation loan (*PERL*); **Rationalisierungsfachmann** *m* MGMNT efficiency engineer; **Rationalisierungsprogramm** *nt* VW rationalization program (*AmE*), rationalization programme (*BrE*); **Rationalisierungsstudie** *f* IND, MGMNT, VW time and motion study

Rationalität *f* GESCHÄFT rationality

rationalökonomisch *adj* VW rational-economic

rationell *adj* GESCHÄFT efficient; **~es Management** *nt* MGMNT rational management; **~e Nutzung von Ressourcen** UMWELT economical use of resources; **~e Stückzahl** *f* IND economic batch quantity, MGMNT economic batch size, VW economic batch quantity

Rationierung *f* VW rationing

Ratschlag *m* GESCHÄFT piece of advice, MGMNT piece of advice, word of advice

Rätsel *nt* GESCHÄFT puzzle, riddle; **Rätselraten** *nt* GESCHÄFT guessing; **Rätselreklame** *f* V&M *Neugier erregend* teaser ad

Raub- *in cpds* COMP, GESCHÄFT, MEDIEN, UMWELT, VW pirate, stolen; **Raubbau** *m* UMWELT overexploitation; **Raubdruck** *m* GESCHÄFT *Buch* piracy

raubgierig: **~e Geschäftsfrau** *f*, **~er Geschäftsmann** *m* GESCHÄFT predator

Raub-: **Raubkopie** *f* COMP, GESCHÄFT pirate copy, MEDIEN bootleg version, pirate version, pirate copy, RECHT pirate copy, VW bootleg version, pirate version, pirate copy; **Raubkopieren** *nt* COMP software piracy, MEDIEN VW piracy, bootlegging; **Raubpressung** *f* GESCHÄFT *Aufnahme* piracy

Rauch *m* GESCHÄFT fumes

Rauchen: *nt* GESCHÄFT smoking; ♦ **~ ist nicht erlaubt** GESCHÄFT smoking is not permitted; **~ ist nicht gestattet** GESCHÄFT smoking is not permitted; **~ verboten** GESCHÄFT smoking prohibited

Raum *m* GESCHÄFT area, room, VW area; **~ für Verbesserungen** GESCHÄFT scope for improvement; **Raumausstatter, in** *m,f* GRUND interior decorator

räumen: **~ lassen** *vt* GESCHÄFT, SOZIAL evict

Raum: **Raumfähre** *f* TRANSP space shuttle; **den Rauminhalt messen von** *phr* TRANSP cube out

räumlich: **~er Ausgleich** *m* VW spatial equalization; **~es Duopol** *nt* VW spatial duopoly; **~es Monopol** *nt* VW local monopoly, spatial monopoly; **~er Nutzen** *m* eines Gutes VW place utility; **~es Oligopol** *nt* VW spatial oligopoly

Räumlichkeiten *f pl* GRUND premises

Raum: **Raummaß** *nt* TRANSP measure of capacity; **Raummeter** *m* GESCHÄFT cubic meter (*AmE*) (*cbm*), cubic metre (*BrE*) (*cbm*); **Raumordnungspolitik** *f* VW regional planning policy; **Raumtonne** *f* GESCHÄFT, TRANSP measurement ton, measurement tonne

Räumung *f* GRUND, RECHT, SOZIAL eviction, V&M clearance; ◆ **zur ~ zwingen** GRUND, RECHT, SOZIAL evict

Räumung: **Räumungsbefehl** *m* GRUND, RECHT eviction order; **Räumungsklage** *f* GRUND, RECHT action for eviction; **Räumungsverfahren** *nt* GRUND, RECHT eviction proceedings, dispossess proceedings; **Räumungsverkauf** *m* V&M clearance sale, vw liquidation sale

Rauschgifthandel *m* GESCHÄFT, IMP/EXP drug trafficking

rausschmeißen *vt infrml* PERSON sack (*BrE*) (*infrml*); ◆ **jdn ~** *infrml* PERSON give sb the sack (*BrE*) (*infrml*); **rausgeschmissen werden** *infrml* PERSON get the sack (*BrE*) (*infrml*)

Rausschmiß *m infrml* PERSON sack (*BrE*) (*infrml*)

Rauswurf *m infrml* PERSON firing

Rawlsch: **~es Differenzprinzip** *nt* vw Rawlsian difference principle; **~e Gerechtigkeit** *f* vw Rawlsian justice

rd. *abbr* (*rund*) GESCHÄFT about, approx. (*approximately*), ca. (*circa*)

Readme- *in cpds* COMP Readme; **Readme-Datei** *f* COMP Readme file; **Readme-Dokument** *nt* COMP Readme document

Reaganomics *pl* vw Reaganomics

reagibel *adj* vw responsive

reagierend: **nicht ~** *adj* GESCHÄFT *Markt* unresponsive

Reaktion *f* GESCHÄFT, PERSON, POL reaction, vw response; **~ auf Werbung** V&M advertising response; **Reaktionselastizität** *f* V&M response elasticity; **Reaktionsfunktion** *f* V&M response function, vw *Begriff der Preistheorie* reaction function; **Reaktionstraining** *nt* MGMNT, PERSON sensitivity training; **Reaktionszeit** *f* VERWALT reaction time

reaktivieren *vt* COMP reactivate, GESCHÄFT recommission

reaktiviert *adj* COMP reactivated, GESCHÄFT recommissioned (*recmd*)

Reaktor *m* IND nuclear reactor (*NR*)

Real- *in cpds* GESCHÄFT real

real 1. *adj* PERSON, RECHNUNG, VW actual; **2.** *adv* vw in real terms

real: **~e Adresse** *f* COMP real address; **~es Austauschverhältnis** *nt* vw terms of trade; **~er Geldwert** *m* vw real money; **~er Größenvorteil** *m* vw real economy of scale; **~e Nettorendite** *f* **nach Steuern** RECHNUNG, STEUER after-tax real rate of return; **~es Nettosozialprodukt** *nt* vw real net national product; **~er Skaleneffekt** *m* vw real economy of scale; **~er Speicher** *m* COMP real storage; **~es verfügbares Einkommen** *nt* vw direct real income (*DRY*); **~es Wachstum** *nt* vw real growth; **~er Wechselkurs** *m* BÖRSE real exchange rate

Real-: **Realeinkommen** *nt* PERSON real earnings, RECHNUNG real income

realisierbar *adj* BÖRSE realizable, FINANZ viable, realizable, GESCHÄFT *Plan*, MATH viable, RECHNUNG realizable; **~er Nettowert** *m* RECHNUNG, V&M net realizable value; **~er Verkaufserlös** *m* FINANZ net realizable value (*NRV*); **~er Verkaufswert** *m* FINANZ net realizable value (*NRV*)

Realisierbarkeit *f* GESCHÄFT viability, feasibility, MATH viability

realisieren *vt* BÖRSE *Gewinn* realize, GESCHÄFT *Maßnahmen* put into effect, RECHNUNG realize

realisiert: **~e Gewinne** *m pl* FINANZ, RECHNUNG realized gains; **nicht ~e Gewinne** *m pl* FINANZ, RECHNUNG, STEUER unrealized gains, unrealized profit; **~e Kursgewinne** *m pl* BÖRSE capital gains; **nicht ~er Kursverlust** *m* BÖRSE paper loss; **~e Mindestrendite** *f* BÖRSE realized minimum return; **~er Minimalertrag** *m* BÖRSE realized minimum return; **nicht ~er Verlust** *m* RECHNUNG unrealized loss; **~e Verluste** *m pl* FINANZ realized losses

Realisierung *f* BÖRSE *Sicherheiten* liquidation, GESCHÄFT, MGMNT implementation, accomplishment, achievement; **~ einer Strategie** GESCHÄFT, MGMNT strategy implementation; **Realisierungszeit** *f* V&M lead time

Realismus *m* GESCHÄFT, POL, RECHT realism

realistisch *adj* GESCHÄFT realistic

Realität *f* GESCHÄFT actuality

Real-: **Realkasseneffekt** *m* vw wealth effect; **Realkosten** *pl* RECHNUNG real cost; **Reallohn** *m* PERSON, RECHNUNG, vw actual wage, real wage; **Reallohnhypothese** *f* vw real-wage hypothesis; **Realpolitik** *f* POL practical politics, power politics; **Realpreis** *m* vw real price; **Realwachstum** *nt* vw real growth; **Realwachstum** *nt* **des Bruttoinlandsprodukts** vw real GDP growth

realwirtschaftlich: **~e Inflation** *f* vw asset price inflation

Real-: **Realzeit** *f* COMP, RECHNUNG, vw real time

Rechen- *in cpds* COMP computational, computing, calculating; **Rechenfehler** *m* COMP computational error; **Rechengeschwindigkeit** *f* COMP computing speed; **Rechenkünstler, in** *m,f* COMP number cruncher (*infrml*); **Rechenleistung** *f* COMP computing power; **Rechenmaschine** *f* COMP calculating machine, GESCHÄFT calculating machine, calculator

Rechenschaft *f* GESCHÄFT, MGMNT, RECHNUNG, VERWALT account; ◆ **jdn zur ~ ziehen** GESCHÄFT call sb to account, bring sb to book

Rechenschaft: **Rechenschaftsbericht** *m* VERWALT report; **Rechenschaftslegung** *f* RECHNUNG reporting

Rechenschaftspflicht *f* GESCHÄFT, MGMNT, RECHNUNG, VERWALT accountability; **~ der Leitung** MGMNT accountability in management; **~ eines Unternehmens** GESCHÄFT corporate accountability

rechenschaftspflichtig *adj* RECHNUNG, VERWALT accountable; **~e(r) Angestellte(r)** *mf* [decl. as adj] PERSON, RECHNUNG accountable officer (*AmE*), responsible officer

Rechen-: **Rechenschieber** *m* GESCHÄFT slide rule; **Rechenwerk** *nt* COMP calculator; **Rechenzentrum** *nt* COMP computing center (*AmE*), computing centre (*BrE*)

Recherche *f* GESCHÄFT search

recherchieren *vt* GESCHÄFT investigate, search

rechnen 1. *vt* MATH calculate; **2.** *vi* MATH calculate; ◆ **~ mit etw** GESCHÄFT depend on sth, plan on sth, rely on sth; **das rechnet sich nicht** GESCHÄFT it does not pay

Rechn. *abbr* (*Rechnung*) GESCHÄFT inv. (*invoice*)

Rechnen *nt* COMP computing, GESCHÄFT calculating, RECHNUNG reckoning

Rechner *m* COMP computer, GESCHÄFT calculator; **~ der zweiten Generation** COMP second-generation computer

rechnerabhängig *adj* COMP on-line; **~es System** *nt* COMP on-line system

Rechner: **Rechnerbetrieb** *m* COMP computer operation; **Rechnercode** *m* VERWALT computer code; **Rechnerdatei** *f* COMP computer file

rechnerfern *adj* COMP remote; **~es Drucken** *nt* COMP remote printing

rechnergesteuert *adj* COMP computer-controlled, computer-driven, computer-operated

rechnergestützt *adj* COMP computer-based, computer-aided, computer-assisted, PC-based; **~e Ausbildung** *f* COMP computer-based training (*CBT*); **~es Börsenhandelssystem** *nt* BÖRSE computer-assisted trading system (*CATS*); **~es Lernen** *nt* PERSON *Ausbildung* computer-based training

rechnerisch *adj* FINANZ notional; **~er Gewinn** *m* RECHNUNG accounting profit; **~e Rendite** *f* RECHNUNG accounting return, approximate rate of return; ◆ **~ ermitteln** GESCHÄFT evaluate

Rechner: **Rechnerlauf** *m* COMP computer run; **Rechnerphobie** *f* COMP computer phobia; **Rechnerprotokoll** *nt* COMP computer log; **Rechnerraum** *m* COMP computing room; **Rechnersteuerung** *f* COMP computer control

rechnerunabhängig 1. *adj* COMP off-line; **2.** *adv* COMP off-line

rechnerunterstützt *adj* COMP computer-aided, computer-assisted, computer-based, PC-based

Rechner: **Rechnerverbindung** *f* COMP computer line; **Rechnerverbund** *m* COMP computer network

Rechnung *f* COMP calculation, GESCHÄFT (*Rechn.*) invoice (*inv.*), account, bill (*BrE*), check (*AmE*); **~ in einer dritten Währung** RECHNUNG invoice in a third currency; **~ in der Währung des Auslandskäufers** RECHNUNG invoice in the currency of the overseas buyer; **~ in der Währung des Auslandsverkäufers** RECHNUNG invoice in the currency of the overseas seller; ◆ **auf ~** V&M on account; **auf ~ von** BANK, GESCHÄFT account of (*a/o*); **für ~ von** BANK, GESCHÄFT account of (*a/o*); **seine eigene ~ aufstellen** GESCHÄFT set up on one's own account; **die ~ bezahlen** GESCHÄFT pick up the tab (*infrml*); **in die ~ einbeziehen** GESCHÄFT take into account; **in ~ stellen** GESCHÄFT charge, invoice; **die ~ zahlen** GESCHÄFT pay the bill

Rechnung: **Rechnungsabteilung** *f* GESCHÄFT billing department (*AmE*), invoicing department (*BrE*); **Rechnungsaufschub** *m* V&M deferred billing; **Rechnungsausstellung** *f* GESCHÄFT billing; **Rechnungsauszug** *m* BANK abstract of accounts, RECHNUNG statement of account; **Rechnungsbetrag** *m* FINANZ invoice amount, invoicing amount, GESCHÄFT amount of a bill, invoice value (*iv*), amount charged; **Rechnungsbuch** *nt* RECHNUNG invoice book (*IB*); **Rechnungsdatum** *nt* GESCHÄFT, RECHNUNG billing date (*AmE*), date of invoice; **Rechnungseinheit** *f* RECHNUNG unit of account; **Rechnungsführer, in** *m,f* RECHNUNG book-keeper; **Rechnungshof** *m* RECHNUNG EU Court of Auditors, ≈ Committee of Public Accounts (*BrE*)

Rechnungsjahr *nt* FINANZ fiscal year (*FY*), RECHNUNG *öffentlicher Haushalt* accounting period, accounting year, fiscal year (*FY*), STEUER fiscal year (*FY*); **im ~ anfallende Einkünfte** FINANZ current revenues

Rechnung: **Rechnungsleger** *m* RECHNUNG accountable officer (*AmE*)

Rechnungslegung *f* GESCHÄFT billing, PERSON accounting, RECHNUNG accounting, accounting report, VERWALT accounting, financial accounting; **Rechnungslegungsmethode** *f* RECHNUNG accounting method; **Rechnungslegungsmethoden** *f pl* RECHNUNG accounting procedure; **Rechnungslegungsmodell** *nt* FINANZ, RECHNUNG accounting model; **Rechnungslegungswährung** *f* FINANZ reporting currency; **Rechnungslegungszyklus** *m* GESCHÄFT billing cycle

Rechnung: **Rechnungsperiode** *f* STEUER fiscal period; **Rechnungsplan** *m* RECHNUNG accounting plan; **Rechnungspreis** *m* BÖRSE invoice price; **Rechnungspreise** *m pl* RECHNUNG invoice cost and charges; **Rechnungsprüfer, in** *m,f* RECHNUNG accountant, auditor, comptroller, controller; **Rechnungsprüfung** *f* FINANZ audit, RECHNUNG audit, accounting control; **Rechnungsprüfungsausschuß** *m* POL Standing Committee on Public Accounts; **Rechnungsrabatt** *m* V&M invoice discount; **Rechnungssaldo** *m* RECHNUNG balance of invoice; **Rechnungsschreibung** *f* GESCHÄFT billing (*AmE*), invoicing (*BrE*); **Rechnungsstelle** *f* RECHNUNG accounting office; **Rechnungsteller** *m* GESCHÄFT biller; **Rechnungswert** *m* GESCHÄFT invoice value (*iv*); **Rechnungswesen** *nt* PERSON accounting, RECHNUNG accountancy (*acc., accy*), accounting, VERWALT accounting

Recht *nt* RECHT *etwas zu tun* right, *Rechtsordnung* law; **~ auf Arbeit** RECHT *ohne Gewerkschaftszwang* right to work; **~ auf Auskunft** POL *Presse* right to know; **~, sich zu distanzieren** PERSON right to dissociate; **~ auf Entschädigung** RECHT right of redress; **~ der Flagge** RECHT law of the flag; **~ am geistigen Eigentum** RECHT rights; **~ auf ein Geschmacksmuster** RECHT design right; **~e gewährt durch** PATENT rights afforded by; **~ zur gewerkschaftlichen Organisation** PERSON right to organize; **~ der Handelsvertretung** RECHT agency law; **~ der Holzentnahme von fremdem Grund** RECHT *des Pächters für die Dauer des Pachtverhältnisses* estover; **~ auf Inbesitznahme** RECHT *durch Betreten des Grundstücks* right of entry; **~ auf Nießbrauch** RECHT right to usufruct; **~ zum Schutz vor Risiko** RECHT *Vertragsrecht* right of protection from risks; **~ der Stellvertretung** RECHT *Verträge* law of agency; **~ auf Umwandlung einer Zeitrente in eine Barabfindung** VERSICH commutation right; **~ zur Wiederaufnahme** RECHT right of resumption; **~ auf Wiedergutmachung** RECHT right of redress; ◆ **~ in Anspruch nehmen** GESCHÄFT, RECHT take legal advice; **in die Rechte eines anderen eingreifen** RECHT impringe on sb's right; **auf die Rechte eines anderen übregreifen** RECHT impringe on sb's right; **Rechte und Rechtsstreit** RECHT *geistiges Eigentum* rights and actions; **für ~ erkennen** RECHT find; **jdm das ~ erteilen, etw zu tun** GESCHÄFT give sb the right to do sth; **alle Rechte vorbehalten** RECHT all rights reserved; **von einem ~ Gebrauch machen** RECHT exercise a right; **~ und öffentliche Ordnung wiederherstellen** RECHT restore law and order; **~ des Ortes, an dem sich die Sache befindet** RECHT *Vertragsrecht* lex rei sitae; **im ~ sein** GESCHÄFT be in the right; **~ übertragen**

GESCHÄFT, RECHT alienate; **von Rechts wegen** RECHT by law, de jure

recht: ~ **und billig** *phr* GESCHÄFT equitable

rechte: ~ **Spalte** *f* GESCHÄFT right-hand column; ~ **Umschalttaste** *f* COMP right shift key

rechtfertigen 1. *vt* GESCHÄFT *Meinung, Handlung* justify, vindicate; **2. sich** ~ *v refl* GESCHÄFT explain

Rechtfertigung *f* GESCHÄFT justification, explanation, vindication

rechtlich 1. *adj* RECHT *juristisch* legal, *zulässig* lawful; ♦ **eine ~e Vereinbarung unterschreiben** RECHT sign a legal agreement; **2.** *adv* RECHT *zulässig* lawfully, legally; ♦ ~ **durchsetzbar** RECHT legally enforceable; ~ **verpflichtet** RECHT legally bound; ~ **verpflichtet sein, etw zu tun** RECHT be under a legal obligation to do sth; ~ **vertretbar** RECHT justifiable

rechtlich: ~**e Durchsetzbarkeit** *f* **eines Tarifvertrags** PERSON legal enforceability of collective agreement (*BrE*); ~**e Einwendungen** *f pl* RECHT demurrer; ~**e Leistungen** *f pl* RECHT legal services; ~**er Rahmen** *m* RECHT legal harmonization; ~**e Rahmenbedingungen** *f pl* RECHT legal framework; ~**e Rahmenrichtlinien** *f pl* RECHT legal framework; ~**e Verpflichtung** *f* RECHT legal obligation

rechtmäßig: ~**er Besitzer** *m*, ~**e Besitzerin** *f* RECHT rightful owner, true owner; ~**e Bezeichnung** *f* RECHT legal name; ~**er Eigentümer** *m*, ~**e Eigentümerin** *f* RECHT rightful owner, true owner; ~**er Inhaber** *m*, ~**e Inhaberin** *f* RECHT holder in due course; ~**e Mittel** *nt pl* RECHT lawful means; ~**er Name** *m* RECHT legal name

Rechtmäßigkeit *f* GESCHÄFT legality, *Anspruch* legitimacy, RECHT legitimacy

rechts: ~ **ausgerichtet** *adj* COMP right-justified, flush right

Recht: **Rechtsabteilung** *f* RECHT *einer Firma* legal department, legal section; **Rechtsangleichung** *f* RECHT assimilation; **Rechtsanspruch** *m* RECHT legal claim, title; **Rechtsanwalt** *m*, **Rechtsanwältin** *f*, RECHT attorney (*AmE*), attorney-at-law (*AmE*), solicitor (*BrE*), *außergerichtlich und bei Gerichten unterer Instanzen* barrister (*BrE*); **Rechtsauffassung** *f* RECHT legal opinion; **Rechtsbeamte(r)** *m* [decl. as adj], **Rechtsbeamtin** *f* RECHT legal officer; **Rechtsbehelf** *m* RECHT appeal, *bei Vertragsbruch* legal redress, *Vertragsrecht* remedy, *wegen Vertragsverletzung* legal remedy; **Rechtsbeistand** *m* GESCHÄFT advocate, RECHT counsel; **Rechtsbelehrung** *f* RECHT charge; **Rechtsberater, in** *m,f* RECHT legal advisor, legal practitioner; **Rechtsberatung** *f* RECHT legal advice; **Rechtsbeugung** *f* RECHT miscarriage of justice

rechtsbündig *adj* COMP *Textverarbeitung* flush right, right-justified

Recht: **Rechtsschreibhilfe** *f* COMP spellcheck, *Textverarbeitung* spellchecker; **Rechtschreibprüfung** *f* COMP spellcheck, *Textverarbeitung* spellchecker; **Rechtsdokument** *nt* RECHT legal document

rechtserheblich: ~**e Umstände** *m pl* RECHT, VERSICH material circumstances

rechtsfähig: ~**e Gesellschaft** *f* GESCHÄFT joint-stock company; **nicht ~es Unternehmen** *nt* RECHT unincorporated company

Recht: **Rechtsfall** *m* RECHT court case, legal case; **Rechtsformalität** *f* RECHT legal formality;

Rechtsfrage *f* GESCHÄFT legal issue, RECHT point of law

rechtsgerichtet *adj* POL right-wing; ~**e politische Gesinnung** *f* POL rightism

Recht: **Rechtsgeschäft** *nt* RECHT *Verträge* legal transaction; **Rechts- und Geschäftsunfähigkeit** *f* VW legal incapacity; **Rechtsgrundsatz** *m* RECHT legal principle

rechtsgültig: ~**er Anspruch** *m* RECHT *Vertragsrecht* good title; ~**e Versicherung** *f* VERSICH insurance in force

Recht: **Rechtsgutachten** *nt* RECHT legal opinion; **Rechtshilfeberatungsstelle** *f* VERWALT Citizens Advice Bureau (*BrE*) (*CAB*); **mit Rechtshilfevernehmung beauftragter Beamter** *m*, **mit Rechtshilfevernehmung beauftragte Beamtin** *f* RECHT trial examiner; **Rechtsirrtum** *m* RECHT error of law, mistake of law; **Rechtskraft** *f* RECHT legal force

rechtskräftig *adj* GESCHÄFT absolute, final, POL statutory; ~ **entschiedene Sache** *f* RECHT res judicata; ~**e Vollmacht** *f* POL statutory authority

rechtskundig *adj* GESCHÄFT versed in the law, RECHT paralegal, versed in the law

Recht: **Rechtsmangel** *m* GRUND cloud on title (*AmE*), RECHT *Vertragsrecht* bad title, defective title

rechtsmängelfrei: ~**er Grundbesitz** *m* GRUND marketable title, merchantable title; **nicht ~es Liegenschaftsrecht** *nt* GRUND nonmerchantable title, unmarketable title

Recht: **Rechtsmängelgewähr** *f* GESCHÄFT warranty of title; **mit Rechtsmängeln behafteter Rechtstitel** *m* RECHT defective title

Rechtsmittel *nt* GESCHÄFT remedy, RECHT appeal, right of appeal; ♦ **ohne ~** RECHT with no right of appeal; ~ **einlegen** RECHT appeal, STEUER lodge an appeal; ~ **gegen ein Urteil einlegen** RECHT appeal against a judgment

Rechtsmittel: **Rechtsmittelbelehrung** *f* RECHT cautioning as to rights; **Rechtsmittelinstanz** *f* RECHT appeal court, appeals court, court of appeal; **Rechtsmittelverfahren** *nt* RECHT appeals procedure

Recht: **Rechtsnachfolgeklausel** *f* RECHT subrogation clause; **Rechtsnachfolger** *m pl* BANK transferees, PATENT successors in title, RECHNUNG assignees, RECHT *Testament* heirs and assigns; **ohne Rechtsnachteil** *phr* VERSICH without prejudice (*wp*)

rechtsorientiert *adj* POL right-wing; ~**e Haltung** *f* POL rightism

Recht: **Rechtspersönlichkeit** *f* PATENT legal entity; **Rechtspflicht** *f* RECHT *Verträge* consideration; **unter eine Rechtspflicht fallen** *phr* VERWALT come under sb's jurisdiction; **Rechtsruck** *m* POL swing to the right; **Rechtsschutz** *m* RECHNUNG legal protection, protection from litigation; **Rechtsschutzversicherung** *f* VERSICH legal expense insurance; **Rechtsstaatlichkeit** *f* RECHT rule of law; **Rechtsstellung** *f* RECHT legal status; **einen Rechtsstreit** *m* **im Richterzimmer verhandeln** *phr* RECHT hear a case in chambers; **Rechtssystem** *nt* RECHT legal system; **Rechtstitelschutzversicherung** *f* VERSICH title protection insurance; **Rechtsträger** *m* PATENT legal entity; **Rechtsstreit** *m* RECHT litigation; **Rechtsübertragung** *f* VERSICH assignment

rechtsunerheblich *adj* RECHT immaterial

rechtsunwirksam: ~**e Klausel** *f* RECHT inoperative

clause; ~e **Police** *f* VERSICH void policy; ~e **Zahlung** *f* FINANZ, RECHT nugatory payment

rechtsverantwortlich *adj* RECHT responsible in law

rechtsverbindlich *adj* GESCHÄFT hard and fast, RECHT legally binding

Recht: **Rechtsverdreher** *m infrml* POL, RECHT shyster (*infrml*), legal eagle (*infrml*); **Rechtsverhältnis** *nt* RECHT *Verträge* agency (*agcy*); **Rechtsverletzung** *f* RECHT breach, *Beeinträchtigung, Eingriff, Übergriff* encroachment, *Delikt, unerlaubte Handlung* legal wrong; **Rechtsvermutung** *f* PATENT legal presumption; **Rechtsverordnung** *f* RECHT legal enactment, statutory instrument; **Rechtsverwirkung** *f* RECHT *Hindernis, Hemmung, Exklusion* estoppel; **Rechtsvorgänger, in** *m,f* PATENT assignor, legal predecessor, predecessor in title, RECHT assignor; **Rechtsvorschrift** *f* RECHT legal requirement; **Rechtswahlvereinbarung** *f* RECHT *bei Vertragsschluß* choice-of-law clause

rechtswidrig *adj* RECHT unlawful; ~es **Betreten** *nt* RECHT unlawful trespass

rechtswirksam *adj* RECHT legally effective; ♦ **nicht mehr** ~ **sein** RECHT *Vertrag* cease to have effect; ~ **werden** RECHT come into effect, become effective

Recht: **Rechtswirksamkeit** *f* PATENT validity; **Rechtswissenschaft** *f* RECHT jurisprudence

rechtzeitig *adj* GESCHÄFT timely

recycelfähig *adj* UMWELT recyclable; **nicht** ~ *adj* UMWELT nonrecyclable

recyceln *vt* UMWELT recycle

Recycling *nt* UMWELT *von Abfallprodukten* recycling; **Recyclingpapier** *nt* GESCHÄFT, UMWELT recycled paper

Redakteur, in *m,f* MEDIEN editor

Redaktion *f* MEDIEN editing

redaktionell: ~ **aufgemachte Anzeige** *f* MEDIEN, V&M editorial advertisement; ~ **aufgemachte Werbung** *f* MEDIEN, V&M editorial publicity; ~er **Text** *m* MEDIEN, V&M editorial matter

Redaktion: **Redaktionschef, in** *m,f* MEDIEN chief editor; **Redaktionsschluß** *m* MEDIEN *Druck, Zeitung* copy deadline, time of going to press, press date; **Redaktionsteam** *nt* MEDIEN editorial staff; **Redaktionswerbung** *f* MEDIEN, V&M editorial advertising

Rede *f* KOMM address, POL *Wahlkampf* speech; **Redenverfasser** *m* POL speech writer

redigieren *vt* MEDIEN edit

rediskontfähig *adj* BANK, FINANZ, RECHNUNG rediscountable, eligible for discount; ~e **Wechsel** *m pl* BANK eligible bills

Rediskont *m* BANK, FINANZ, RECHNUNG rediscount; **Rediskontfazilität** *f* BANK, FINANZ discount window; **Rediskontfazilität** *f* einer **Zentralbank** BANK discount window lending; **Rediskontierer, in** *m,f* BANK, FINANZ, RECHNUNG rediscounter

Rediskontierung *f* BANK, FINANZ, RECHNUNG rediscounting

Rediskont: **Rediskontsatz** *m* RECHNUNG rediscount rate

redlich: ~es **Geschäftsgebaren** *nt* RECHT clean hands

Redlichkeit *f* VERSICH good faith

Redundanz *f* COMP redundancy; **Redundanzprüfung** *f* COMP redundancy check

reduzieren *vt* BÖRSE shorten, GESCHÄFT *Aktivitäten* wind

down, *Ausgaben* reduce, V&M mark down, VW *Preise, Investitionen* reduce

reduziert *adj* BÖRSE shortened, GESCHÄFT wound down, reduced, V&M marked down, VW reduced; ♦ **zu** ~en **Preisen kaufen** GESCHÄFT buy at a reduced price

reduziert: ~e **Form** *f* VW reduced form equation; ~es **Gewicht** *nt* TRANSP reduced weight (*RW*); ~e **Kosten** *pl* RECHNUNG sunk costs; ~e **Vorlaufzeit** *f* IND reduced lead time

Reduzierung *f* BÖRSE shortening, GESCHÄFT reduction, pruning, winding down, V&M marking down, VW reduction

Reeder, in *m,f* IMP/EXP, TRANSP shipowner, shipping officer; ♦ ~ **trägt Kosten von Laden und Löschen** TRANSP gross terms

Reederei *f* GESCHÄFT shipping business, TRANSP shipping office; **Reedereivertreter, in** *m,f* TRANSP ship's agent

Reeder: **Reederhaftpflicht** *f* (*P & I*) TRANSP protection and indemnity (*P&I*)

reell: ~es **Gewicht** *nt* GESCHÄFT full weight; ~e **Zahl** *f* COMP real number

Reexport *m* IMP/EXP re-exportation

Reexporteur, in *m,f* IMP/EXP re-exporter

Referat *nt* POL portfolio

Referendum *nt* GESCHÄFT referendum

Referent, in *m,f* GESCHÄFT aide, MEDIEN, POL aide, *Vortragender* speaker, VERWALT desk planner; ~ **für Arbeitgeber-Arbeitnehmer-Beziehungen** MGMNT, PERSON *Betriebsklima* industrial relations manager; ~ **für Öffentlichkeitsarbeiten** MGMNT information officer

Referenz *f* PERSON *Bewerbung, Zeugnis* reference, *Person* reference, referee; ♦ **jds Referenzen nachprüfen** PERSON take up sb's references

Referenz: **Referenzbank** *f* BANK reference bank; **Referenzmaterial** *nt* VERWALT reference material; **Referenzniveau** *nt* FINANZ reference level; **Referenzwährung** *f* VW reference currency; **Referenzzyklus** *m* VW reference cycle

refinanzieren *vt* FINANZ fund

Refinanzierung *f* FINANZ refinancing, funding; **Refinanzierungsinstitut** *nt* der **letzten Instanz** BANK lender of last resort; **Refinanzierungskosten** *pl* FINANZ cost of funds; **Refinanzierungskredit** *m* BANK refinance credit; **Refinanzierungsplafond** *m* BANK, FINANZ refinancing line; **Refinanzierungsquelle** *f* FINANZ funding source; **Refinanzierungsstelle** *f* einer **Zentralbank** FINANZ discount window; **Refinanzierungszins** *m* einer **Bank** VW interbank rate

Reflation *f* VW reflation

Reform *f* GESCHÄFT, POL, SOZIAL reform; **Reformhaus** *nt* V&M health-food shop

reformieren *vt* GESCHÄFT, POL, SOZIAL reform

Reform: **Reformkost** *f* SOZIAL health foods; **Reformpaket** *nt* POL reform package; **Reformprogramm** *nt* VW reform program (*AmE*), reform programme (*BrE*)

Refundierungsanleihe *f* FINANZ refunding loan

Reg. *abbr* (*Regierung*) GESCHÄFT govt (*government*), MGMNT admin (*infrml*) (*administration*), POL admin (*infrml*) (*administration*), govt (*government*), VERWALT admin (*infrml*) (*administration*)

Regal *nt* GESCHÄFT, V&M shelf; **Regalauslage** *f* V&M shelf display; **Regalauszeichnung** *f* V&M shelf labeling (*AmE*), shelf labelling (*BrE*), shelf price; **Regalfläche** *f* V&M shelf space; **Regalfüller** *m* V&M shelf filler

rege 1. *adj* BÖRSE, GESCHÄFT, VW brisk; **2.** *adv* BÖRSE, GESCHÄFT, VW briskly

rege: ~ **Investitionstätigkeit** *f* VW high capital spending

Regel *f* GESCHÄFT rule; ◆ **Regeln festlegen** VERWALT lay down the rules; **jdm die Regeln vor Augen halten** GESCHÄFT throw the rule book at sb

regelbar *adj* GESCHÄFT adjustable, controllable; ◆ ~ **abschreiben** RECHNUNG depreciate

regelmäßig: ~**e Ausgaben** *f pl* FINANZ regular expenditure; ~**e Einnahmen** *f pl* FINANZ regular income; ~**e Inspektion** *f* TRANSP continuous survey (*CS*); ~**er Nachtragshaushalt** *m* FINANZ regular Supplementary Estimates; ~**e Prüfung** *nt* TRANSP periodical survey; ~**e Schiffsbesichtigung** *f* TRANSP *durch das Aufsichtsamt* continuous survey (*CS*); ~**e Zahlung** *f* GESCHÄFT regular payment; ◆ **in** ~**en Abständen** GESCHÄFT periodic; ~ **erstellter Bericht** *m* GESCHÄFT regular statement; **in** ~**er Folge** GESCHÄFT sequential; ~ **wiederkehrend** GESCHÄFT periodic

regeln *vt* BÖRSE, FINANZ regulate, GESCHÄFT arrange, RECHT govern, VW regulate

Regeln *f pl* GESCHÄFT rules; ~ **über anständiges Geschäftsgebaren** BÖRSE rules of fair practice; ~ **versus Entscheidungsfreiheit** *f* VW rules versus discretion

regelnd *adj* RECHT regulatory

Regel: **Regelsteuersatz** *m* STEUER basic-rate tax, standard rate (*BrE*)

Regelung *f* COMP automatic control; GESCHÄFT, VW regulation; ~ **des Anspruchs** VERSICH adjustment

regelwidrig *adj* GESCHÄFT abnormal

Regen- *in cpds* UMWELT, VERSICH rain; **Regenbogenpresse** *f* MEDIEN gutter press, tabloid press

regenerieren *vt* GESCHÄFT, VW revive

Regenerierung *f* GESCHÄFT, VW revival

Regen-: **Regenversicherung** *f* VERSICH rain insurance; **Regenwald** *m* UMWELT *tropisch* rainforest

Regierung *f* (*Reg.*) GESCHÄFT government (*govt*), MGMNT administration (*admin*), POL administration (*admin*), Cabinet, government (*govt*), VERWALT administration (*admin*); ◆ **an der** ~ **sein** POL be in office

Regierung: **Regierungsanleihe** *f* BANK tap stock, FINANZ government loan; **Regierungsaufsichtsbehörde** *f* **für Buchführungsgrundsätze** RECHNUNG Governmental Accounting Standards Board (*GASB*); **Regierungsbericht** *m* GESCHÄFT government report; **Regierungsbeziehungen** *f pl* POL government relations; **Regierungseingriff** *m* POL, VERWALT, VW government intervention

regierungsintern *adj* POL, VERWALT intragovernmental

Regierung: **Regierungskommission** *f* **für soziale Entwicklung** POL Cabinet Committee on Social Development (*BrE*), Social Development Committee; **die Regierungsmaschinerie** *f* POL the wheels of government; **Regierungsprogramm** *nt* **mit anteiliger Kostenübernahme** VW cost-shared program (*AmE*), cost-shared programme (*BrE*), shared-cost program (*AmE*), shared-cost programme (*BrE*); **Regierungssitz** *m* POL seat; **Regierungssystem** *nt* POL regime; **Regierungsumbildung** *f* POL Cabinet reshuffle; **Regierungszeit** *f* GESCHÄFT reign

Region *f* GESCHÄFT, VW area, region

Regional- *in cpds* GESCHÄFT regional

regional *adj* GESCHÄFT regional; ~**e Arbeitsplatzprämie** *f* PERSON regional employment premium (*REP*); ~**e Behörde** *f* VERWALT local authority; ~**e Demographie** *f* V&M *Marktforschung* geodemography; ~**e Entwicklung** *f* VW regional development; ~**e Entwicklungsplanung** *f* GESCHÄFT, VERWALT planning policy; ~**er Markt** *m* V&M regional market; ~**e Marktuntersuchung** *f* V&M area sample; ~**er Multiplikator** *m* VW regional multiplier; ~**e Quote** *f* VW regional quota; ~**e Steuerwirkung** *f* RECHNUNG regional tax effect; ~**e Tarifverhandlungen** *f pl* PERSON *Gewerkschaftsbewegung* regional wage bargaining; ~**er Trend** *m* V&M regional trend; ~**e Vertretung** *f* V&M regional representation; ~**es Zentrum** *nt* GESCHÄFT regional center (*AmE*), regional centre (*BrE*); ~**er Zusammenschluß** *m* VW regional grouping

Regional-: **Regionalabkommen** *nt* VW regional agreement; **Regionalbank** *f* BANK regional bank; **Regionalbörse** *f* BÖRSE regional stock exchange; **Regionalentwicklung** *f* VW regional development; **Regionalökonomik** *f* VW regional economics; **Regionalorganisation** *f* MGMNT *eines Unternehmens* regional organization; **Regionalpatent** *nt* PATENT regional patent; **Regionalplanungsgesetz** *nt* RECHT Town and Country Planning Act (*BrE*); **Regionalpolitik** *f* VW regional policy; **Regionalpresse** *f* V&M regional press; **Regionalschaden** *m* VERSICH country damage

Register *nt* COMP *Speicher* register, GESCHÄFT, MEDIEN table of contents, PATENT, VERWALT register; **Registerauszug** *m* PATENT extract from the register; **Registerführer, in** *m,f* VERWALT registrar of companies; **Registerführer, in** *m,f* **im Grundbuchamt** GRUND, RECHT registrar of deeds; **Registergericht** *nt* RECHT court of record (*AmE*); **Registerlöschung** *f* STEUER cancellation of registration; **Registertonnage** *f* GESCHÄFT register tonnage; **Registertonne** *f* GESCHÄFT registered ton

Registratur *f* VERWALT registrar's office, registry

registrieren *vt* COMP register, GESCHÄFT record, register, GRUND *Grundbuch* list, PERSON *Rezeption, Wareneingang* sign in, VERWALT register

Registrierkasse *f* V&M cash register

registriert *adj* GESCHÄFT on record, registered; ~**e Adresse** *f* GESCHÄFT registered address; ~**es Angebot von Wertpapieren im Sekundärmarkt** BÖRSE registered secondary offering; **nicht** ~**e Arbeitskräfte** *f pl* PERSON unregistered labour (*BrE*), unregistered labor (*AmE*); ~**e(r) Bevollmächtigte(r)** *mf* [decl. as adj] BÖRSE registered representative; ~**es Sicherungsrecht** *nt* VW perfected security interest; ~**er Stellenbewerber** *m*, ~**e Stellenbewerbin** *f* GESCHÄFT *for work* registered applicant; ~**er Vertreter** *m*, ~**e Vertreterin** *f* BÖRSE registered representative

Registrierung *f* GESCHÄFT, PATENT registration, VERWALT recording, registration; **Registrierungsausschuß** *m* **der Versicherungsmakler** VERSICH Insurance Brokers' Registration Council (*BrE*) (*IBRC*); **Registrierungsgebühr** *f* GESCHÄFT recording fee, registration fee; **Registrierungsort** *m* VERWALT registry

Regler *m* COMP controller, STEUER regulator

Regreß *m* GESCHÄFT *Wechsel* recourse; ◆ **mit** ~ VERSICH with recourse; **ohne ~** FINANZ, VERSICH without recourse

Regreß: **Regreßanspruch** m FINANZ right of recourse, VERSICH claim of recourse; **Regreßbefugnis** f RECHT power of recourse

Regression f MATH, VW regression; **Regressionsanalyse** f MATH, VW regression analysis; **Regressionskurve** f MATH regression curve

regressiv: **~es Angebot** nt VW regressive supply; **~e Arbeitskräfteangebotskurve** f VW backward-bending labor supply curve (AmE), backward-bending labour supply curve (BrE); **~e Erwartungen** f pl MATH regressive expectations; **~e Steuer** f STEUER regressive tax

Regressivität f FINANZ regressivity

regreßlos adj FINANZ nonrecourse; **~e Exportfinanzierung** f FINANZ nonrecourse export financing

Regreß: **ohne Regreßmöglichkeit** phr BANK without recourse; **Regreßverzichtsvereinbarung** f VERSICH knock-for-knock

regulär adj BANK, FREI, GESCHÄFT, MGMNT across-the-counter, standard, regular; **~es Bankgeschäft** nt BANK standard banking; **~er Dienst** m FREI regular service; **~e Sitzung** f MGMNT regular meeting

regulieren vt BANK standardize, FINANZ regulate, GESCHÄFT adjust, control, RECHT lenken, VW Industrie, Markt regulate

reguliert adj BANK standardized, GESCHÄFT adjusted, controlled, standardized, FINANZ, POL administered, RECHT regulated, VERSICH adjusted, VERWALT Preis administered, VW administered, regulated; **~er Investmentfonds** m FINANZ regulated investment company; **~er Markt** m FINANZ regulated market; **~er Schaden** m VERSICH adjusted claim, settled claim; **~es Unternehmen** nt VW regulated firm

Regulierung f VERSICH eines Schadens adjustment, VW regulation; **~ nach Wahl** VERSICH optional modes of settlement; **Regulierungsbehörde** f VW regulatory agency; **Regulierungskosten** pl VERSICH adjustment costs

Rehabilitation f GESCHÄFT rehabilitation, eines Rufs restoration, whitewashing (infrml), vindication

rehabilitieren vt GESCHÄFT Wiederherstellung eines Rufes restore, whitewash (infrml), vindicate, Ruf, Firma rehabilitate, restore

Reibach: **einen ~ machen** phr infrml FINANZ make a killing

Reibung f GESCHÄFT friction

Reibungskiel m TRANSP rubbing keel

reibungslos 1. adj GESCHÄFT smooth; **2.** adv GESCHÄFT smoothly, without a hitch

reibungslos: **~er Ablauf** m GESCHÄFT smooth running

reich adj GESCHÄFT well-off; VW affluent, prosperous, wealthy; ◆ **~ an Bargeld** adj FINANZ cash-rich; **~ an Öl** VW oil-rich

reich: **~e Erzader** f IND bonanza; **~es Ölvorkommen** nt UMWELT rich oil strike; **~ werden** phr GESCHÄFT prosper, become wealthy, become affluent, thrive

Reichen: **die ~** pl GESCHÄFT the wealthy

reichhaltig: **~es Produktionsprogramm** nt V&M wide range of products; **mit ~em Sortiment** phr GESCHÄFT well-stocked

reichlich 1. adj GESCHÄFT abundant, ample; **2.** adv GESCHÄFT amply

Reichtum m VW affluence, prosperity, wealth

Reichweite f V&M reach; **~ und Häufigkeit** f V&M reach and frequency; **~ des Marktes** V&M market reach; **~ der Werbung** V&M advertising reach; ◆ **in ~** GESCHÄFT within reach; **außer ~ sein** GESCHÄFT be out of range

reif adj FINANZ, GESCHÄFT mature; **~e Volkswirtschaft** f VW mature economy

Reifeprüfung f obs GESCHÄFT, SOZIAL school leaving examination qualifying for higher education ≈ Advanced level (BrE) (A level), ≈ High School Diploma (AmE)

Reihe f BÖRSE series, FINANZ set, GESCHÄFT row, MATH array, TRANSP row; **~ von Maßnahmen** FINANZ set of measures; **~ von Optionen** BÖRSE series of options; ◆ **außer der ~** GESCHÄFT out of order; **der ~ nach** GESCHÄFT in turn, sequentially, seriatim, successively; **in ~ und Glied warten** GESCHÄFT queue (BrE), queue up (BrE), wait in line (AmE)

Reihe: **Reihenfolge** f GESCHÄFT order, sequence, succession; **Reihenhaus** nt GRUND row house (AmE), terraced house (BrE); **Reihenkorrelation** f MATH serial correlation

Rein- in cpds GESCHÄFT net, pure

rein adj GESCHÄFT, UMWELT clean; ◆ **auf ~ geschäftlicher Basis** GESCHÄFT arm's-length

rein: **~er Anschaffungspreis** m RECHNUNG strict cost price; **~er Ballasttank** m TRANSP clean ballast tank; **~e Bündelung** f VW pure bundling; **~er Ergebnisbericht** m TRANSP clean report of findings; **~er Herstellungspreis** m RECHNUNG strict cost price; **~e Holdinggesellschaft** f BANK pure holding company; **~e Inflation** f VW pure inflation; **~er Kapitalismus** m VW pure capitalism; **~es Konnossement** nt IMP/EXP, TRANSP clean bill of lading; **~e Kreditwirtschaft** f VW pure credit economy; **~e Marktwirtschaft** f VW pure market economy; **~e Monopol** nt VW absolute monopoly, perfect monopoly, pure monopoly; **~e Spekulation** f BÖRSE pure play; **~es Verpackungsgewicht** nt GESCHÄFT net tare weight; **ein ~es Versprechen** nt RECHT ex nudo pacto non oritur actio; **~ wirtschaftliche Miete** f VW pure economic rent

Re-Indossament nt BANK re-endorsement

Rein-: **Reinerlös** m FINANZ net profit; **Reinertrag** m FINANZ clear profit, GRUND net proceeds (np), RECHNUNG net yield, VW pure profit; **Reinfall** m BÖRSE flier, GESCHÄFT Film, Theaterstück flop (infrml), plunge, write-off; **Reingewicht** nt GESCHÄFT weight allowed free; **Reingewinn** m FINANZ, RECHNUNG, VW net income, net margin, net profit, pure profit; **Reingewinn** m **plus Abschreibungen** f pl FINANZ cash earnings; **Reingewinn** m **vor Steuern** RECHNUNG net operating profit; **Reinhaltung** f IND, POL, UMWELT Luft, Wasser pollution control

reinigen vt IND refine, UMWELT clean, purify

Reinigung f UMWELT purification; **Reinigungsaufbereitung** f UMWELT cleanup operation

Rein-: **Reinnachlaß** m RECHT residuary estate, Rest residuum; **eine Reinschrift anfertigen** phr GESCHÄFT, MEDIEN, V&M write a fair copy; **Reinvermögen** nt BÖRSE shareholders' equity (AmE), FINANZ, RECHNUNG, VW actual net worth, net assets, net worth; **Reinvermögenbetrag** m RECHNUNG net asset amount

reinvestieren 1. vt BÖRSE, FINANZ reinvest, Gewinne plow back (*AmE*), plough back (*BrE*); **2.** *vi* BÖRSE, FINANZ reinvest, plow back profits into a business (*AmE*), plough back profits into a business (*BrE*)

reinvestiert: **~e Gelder** *nt pl* RECHNUNG ploughback (*BrE*), plowback (*AmE*), ploughed-back profits (*BrE*); **~er Gewinn** *m* RECHNUNG ploughback (*BrE*), plowback (*AmE*), reinvestment

Reinvestition *f* BÖRSE reinvestment; **Reinvestitionsrate** *f* BÖRSE reinvestment rate

reinwaschen *vt* GESCHÄFT, MEDIEN, POL whitewash (*infrml*)

Reise *f* FREI, GESCHÄFT tour, TRANSP voyage (*voy*); **Reiseagentur** *f* FREI travel agency; **Reiseanalyse** *f* TRANSP trip analysis; **Reisebeleg** *m* TRANSP travel voucher; **Reisebericht** *m* TRANSP voyage report; **Reisebeschränkungen** *f pl* TRANSP travel restrictions; **Reisebüro** *nt* FREI travel agency, travel bureau, PERSON travel agent; **Reisebüroangestellte(r)** *mf* [decl. as adj] FREI travel agent; **Reisebürokauffrau** *f*, **Reisebürokaufmann** *m* FREI travel agent; **Reisecharter** *f* TRANSP voyage charter; **Reisechartervertrag** *m* TRANSP voyage charter party (*voyage C/P*); **Reisedokument** *nt* FREI travel document; **Reisefestlegung** *f* TRANSP voyage fixture; **Reisegepäck** *nt* FREI, TRANSP baggage

Reisekosten *pl* GESCHÄFT, PERSON, RECHNUNG, STEUER, TRANSP voyage expenses, travel expenses; **Reisekostenbericht** *m* TRANSP voyage account report; **Reisekostenerstattung** *f* GESCHÄFT reimbursement of travel expenses; **Reisekostenvorschuß** *m* GESCHÄFT, VW travel advance, trip advance; **Reisekostenzuschuß** *m* GESCHÄFT travel allowance, traveling allowance (*AmE*), travelling allowance (*BrE*)

Reisende(r) *mf* [decl. as adj] FREI traveler (*AmE*), traveller (*BrE*), PERSON, V&M drummer (*AmE*), sales representative (*rep, sales rep*)

Reise: **Reiseorganisation** *f* FREI tour organization; **Reisepapier** *m* FREI travel document; **Reisepaß** *m* VERWALT passport; **Reiseplaner** *m* TRANSP journey planner; **Reiseplanung** *f* TRANSP journey planning; **Reisepolice** *f* VERSICH voyage policy; **Reisepreis** *m* für **Hin- und Rückfahrt** FREI return fare (*BrE*), round-trip fare (*AmE*); **Reiseschätzung** *f* TRANSP voyage estimate; **Reisescheck** *m* BANK traveler's check (*AmE*), traveller's cheque (*BrE*); **Reisespesen** *f pl* GESCHÄFT travel allowance, traveling allowance (*AmE*), travelling allowance (*BrE*); **Reisetasche** *f* GESCHÄFT valise; **Reiseunterbrechung** *f* FREI, TRANSP break in journey, stopover; **Reiseunternehmen** *nt* FREI tour operator; **Reiseveranstalter, in** *m,f* FREI tour organizer; **Reiseverkehr** *m* VW travel services; **Reisezyklus** *m* V&M journey cycle

Reißbrett *nt* MGMNT drawing board

reißen: **an sich ~** *phr* GESCHÄFT grab

reißend: **~er Absatz** *m* V&M rapid sales

reißfest *adj* TRANSP *freight, cargo* tear-proof

Reißkraft *f* TRANSP breaking load

Reißwolf *m* COMP, VERWALT paper shredder, shredder

Reiz *m* V&M attraction; **Reizüberflutung** *f* **durch Werbung** V&M advertising overkill

Reklamation *f* GESCHÄFT complaint; **Reklamationsverfahren** *nt* GESCHÄFT complaints procedure

Reklame *f* V&M advertisement, promotion (*promo*);

~ durch Geschenke V&M gift promotion; ◆ **~ machen** V&M advertise; **~ machen für** V&M promote

Reklame: **Reklamefläche** *f* V&M hoarding, *Werbefläche* advertising space; **Reklamemätzchen** *nt pl infrml* V&M stunt advertising; **Reklamepodest** *nt* V&M advertising tower; **Reklamerummel** *m* VW pizazz; **Reklametext** *m* V&M advertising copy

Rekonfiguration *f* COMP, GESCHÄFT reconfiguration

rekonfigurieren *vt* COMP, GESCHÄFT reconfigure

rekonstruieren *vt* COMP *Dateien* rebuild, GESCHÄFT reconstruct

Rekonstruktion *f* GESCHÄFT reconstruction

Rekord- *in cpds* GESCHÄFT, PERSON, V&M, VW record; **Rekordabsatz** *m* V&M record sales; **Rekordbrecher** *m* PERSON *Arbeit, Sport, Wettbewerb* record breaker; **Rekordergebnis** *nt* GESCHÄFT record result; **Rekordhöhe** *f* GESCHÄFT, VW all-time high, record high; **Rekordjahr** *nt* GESCHÄFT bumper year

rekrutieren *vt* GESCHÄFT contract, PERSON *Personal* draw from, recruit

Rekrutierung *f* PERSON recruiting; **~ aus dem einheimischen Arbeitsmarkt** VW internal labor market contracting (*AmE*), internal labour market contracting (*BrE*), internal labor market recruitment (*AmE*), internal labour market recruitment (*BrE*)

Rektakonnossement *nt* IMP/EXP, TRANSP straight bill of lading

rekursiv: **~es System** *nt* VW recursive system

relational: **~e Datenbank** *f* COMP relational database (*RDB*)

relativ 1. *adj* GESCHÄFT relative; **2.** *adv* GESCHÄFT in relative terms

relativ: **~e Adresse** *f* COMP relocatable address; **~e Einkommenshypothese** *f* VW relative income hypothesis; **~er Fehler** *m* COMP relative error; **~e Konzentration** *f* MATH relative concentration; **~er Marktanteil** *m* V&M relative market share; **~er Mehrwert** *m* VW relative surplus value; **~er Preis** *m* VW relative price; **~es Risiko** *nt* VW odds ratio; **~e Veränderung** *f* **des Ertragswertes einer Wohnung** GRUND filtering down

relativierbar *adj* COMP *Speicherbereich* relocatable

Relativismus *m* POL *Marxismus* relativism

Relativpreisniveau *nt* VW relative price level

relevant: **~e Kosten** *pl* RECHNUNG alternative costs; **~er Nettoverdienst** *m* STEUER net relevant earnings

religiös: **~e Diskriminierung** *f* PERSON religious discrimination; **~e Überwachung** *f* PERSON religious discrimination

Rembourskredit *m* FINANZ, IMP/EXP acceptance credit

Remedium *nt* GESCHÄFT remedy, tolerance

Rendite *f* BÖRSE, FINANZ return, yield, nominal yield, GESCHÄFT return, RECHNUNG accounting rate of return, rate of return, STEUER rate of return; **~ auf durchschnittliche Laufzeit** BÖRSE yield to average life; **~ des eingesetzten Kapitals** BÖRSE yield to maturity (*YTM*); **~ auf die Endfälligkeit** BANK, BÖRSE yield to maturity (*YTM*); **~ des investierten Kapitals** FINANZ, RECHNUNG, VW return on capital employed (*ROCE*); **~ einer Kapitalanlage** FINANZ, RECHNUNG, VW return on investment (*ROI*); **~ einer kündbaren Anleihe** GESCHÄFT yield to call; **~ einer langfristigen Anleihe** BÖRSE maturity yield;

~ **nach Steuern** RECHNUNG, STEUER after-tax yield; ~ **vor Steuern** STEUER pre-tax rate of return; **Renditegefälle** *nt* VW yield gap; **Renditeniveau** *nt* STEUER level of return; **Renditeobjekt** *nt* FINANZ income property; **Renditetabellen** *f pl* FINANZ basic books

Rennen: aus dem ~ sein *phr* GESCHÄFT be out of the running

Renner *m infrml* GESCHÄFT fast-moving article, V&M fast-moving article, best seller

Renommee *nt* GESCHÄFT prestige, reputation

renommiert *adj* GESCHÄFT prestigious, renowned

renovieren *vt* GRUND refurbish, renovate

Renovierung *f* GESCHÄFT, GRUND *Altbausanierung* refurbishment, renovation

rentabel *adj* FINANZ viable, GESCHÄFT cost-efficient, commercially viable, *Betrieb* viable, RECHNUNG profitable; **rentable Anlage** *f* FINANZ smart money

Rentabilität *f* BÖRSE return, FINANZ profitability, viability, GESCHÄFT return, RECHNUNG profitability, VW economic viability; ~ **des eingesetzten Kapitals** FINANZ, RECHNUNG, VW rate of return on capital employed (*RORCE*); ~ **des investierten Kapitals** FINANZ, RECHNUNG, VW return on invested capital (*ROIC*); ~ **des Kapitaleinsatzes** FINANZ, RECHNUNG, VW return on capital employed (*ROCE*); **Rentabilitätsanalyse** *f* FINANZ, RECHNUNG profitability analysis; **Rentabilitätskennzahl** *f* FINANZ profitability ratio; **Rentabilitätsprüfung** *f* RECHNUNG efficiency audit; **Rentabilitätsschwelle** *f* MGMNT breakeven point; **Rentabilitätsstudie** *f* GESCHÄFT viability study; **Rentabilitätsziel** *nt* FINANZ adequate target rate

Rent-a-Container *phr* TRANSP Rent-a-Container

Rente *f* FINANZ pension, GESCHÄFT annuity, PERSON pension, SOZIAL old-age insurance benefit (*AmE*), old-age pension, retirement benefit (*BrE*), retirement pension, *im öffentlichen Dienst* state pension, pension, VERSICH annuity, VW *Theorie der Preisbildung, Kapitaltheorie* economic rent; ~ **mit bestimmter Laufzeit** VERSICH annuity certain; ~ **auf Lebenszeit** VERSICH annuity for life; ~ **auf den Überlebensfall** VERSICH annuity in reversion, reversionary annuity; ♦ **in** ~ **gehen** SOZIAL go into retirement; **in eine** ~ **investieren** VERSICH invest in an annuity

Rente: **Rentenalter** *nt* PERSON pensionable age, retirement age; **Rentenansparprogramm** *nt* FINANZ retirement savings program (*AmE*), retirement savings programme (*BrE*); **Rentenanwartschaft** *f* PERSON legal right to future pension payments; **Rentenbeitrag** *m* RECHNUNG pension charges, pension costs; **Rentenberechtigung** *f* FINANZ qualifying annuity; **Rentenbestand** *m* BÖRSE bond holdings; **Rentenempfänger, in** *m,f* FINANZ pension-holder; **Rentenfaktor** *m* VERSICH annuity factor; **Rentenfonds** *m* BÖRSE bond fund, FINANZ *Arbeit* retirement fund, GESCHÄFT annuity fund; **Rentengeschäft** *nt* VERSICH annuity business; **Rentenhandel** *m* BÖRSE bond dealings, bond trading; **Rentenindex** *m* BÖRSE bond index; **Rentennachweis** *m* FINANZ qualifying annuity; **Rentenpapier** *nt* FINANZ government annuity; **Rentenpolice** *f* VERSICH annuity policy; **Rentenrückstände** *m pl* VERSICH annuity payable in arrears; **Rentensparplan** *m* FINANZ retirement savings program (*AmE*), retirement savings

programme (*BrE*); **Rententeilbetrag** *m* VERSICH annuity installment (*AmE*), annuity instalment (*BrE*); **Rententeilzahlung** *f* VERSICH annuity installment (*AmE*), annuity instalment (*BrE*); **Rentenumsätze** *m pl* BÖRSE bond turnover; **Rentenversicherung** *f* VERSICH annuity assurance, annuity insurance; **Rentenversicherung** *f* **mit festgelegter Laufzeit** FINANZ term-certain annuity; **Rentenversicherungspolice** *f* FINANZ, STEUER retirement annuity policy, VERSICH annuity policy; **Rentenversicherungsschein** *m* VERSICH annuity policy; **Rentenversicherungssystem** *nt* VERSICH annuity plan; **auf Rentenwerte spezialisierter Wertpapierhändler** *m*, **auf Rentenwerte spezialisierte Wertpapierhändlerin** *f* BÖRSE bond broker; **Rentenzahlung** *f* FINANZ STEUER payment of annuity, VERSICH annuity installment (*AmE*), annuity instalment (*BrE*); **Rentenzahlungen** *f pl* FINANZ retirement payments

Rentier *m* GESCHÄFT person of independent means, GRUND *Kapitalrentner* rentier

Rentner, in *m,f* PERSON, SOZIAL old-age pensioner (*BrE*) (*OAP*), retired person, retiree (*AmE*)

Renvoi *nt* RECHT *Verträge* renvoi

Reorganisation *f* MGMNT reorganization, VW reconstruction

reorganisieren *vt* MGMNT reorganize, restructure, VW reconstruct

Reparatur *f* GESCHÄFT repair; **Reparaturmaterial** *nt* GESCHÄFT repair kit; **Reparaturmechaniker, in** *m,f* GESCHÄFT mechanic; **Reparaturwagen** *m* TRANSP breakdown van (*BrE*), recovery vehicle; **Reparaturwerkstatt** *f* GESCHÄFT repair shop

reparierbar: nicht ~ *adj* GESCHÄFT beyond repair

repartieren *vt* BÖRSE scale down

repatriieren *vt* VW *Gewinn* repatriate

Report *m* BÖRSE contango, COMP, GESCHÄFT report, VW *Devisenmarkt* discount forex

Reporter, in *m,f* MEDIEN reporter; ~ **vor Ort** MEDIEN on-the-spot reporter

Report: **Reportgenerierung** *f* COMP report generation; **Reportgeschäft** *nt* BÖRSE carry-over business, contango business (*BrE*); **Reportgeschäfte** *nt pl* BÖRSE jobbing in contangos (*BrE*); **Reportnehmer** *m* BÖRSE giver; **es gibt keine Reportnehmer bei diesen Wertpapieren** *phr* BÖRSE there are no givers on these securities; **Reportsatz** *m* BÖRSE carry-over rate, contango rate (*BrE*); **Reportterminal** *m* COMP report terminal

Repräsentant, in *m,f* GESCHÄFT, PATENT representative (*rep.*); **Repräsentantenhaus** *nt* POL House of Representatives (*AmE*)

Repräsentation *f* GESCHÄFT representation; **Repräsentationswerbung** *f* V&M prestige advertising

repräsentativ *adj* GESCHÄFT prestigious, representative; ~**e Stichprobe** *f* MATH adequate sample, representative sample; ~**es Unternehmen** *nt* VW representative firm; ~**e Verbrauchergruppe** *f* V&M consumer panel

Repressalie *f* GESCHÄFT retaliatory measure

repressiv *adj* STEUER repressive; ~**e Steuer** *f* STEUER repressive tax

reprivatisieren *vt* VW denationalize, reprivatize

reprivatisiert *adj* VW denationalized, reprivatized

Reprivatisierung *f* VW denationalization, reprivatization

Reproduktion *f* VW reproduction; **Reproduktionsrate** *f* VW reproduction rate; **Reproduktionswert** *m* RECHNUNG asset value

reproduzieren *vt* GESCHÄFT reproduce

reprofähig *adj* MEDIEN *Vorlage, DTP* camera-ready; **~e Vorlage** *f* MEDIEN *Druck* camera-ready copy (*CRC*)

Reprographie *f* GESCHÄFT reprography

reproreif *adj* MEDIEN camera-ready; **~e Vorlage** *f* MEDIEN *Druck* camera-ready copy (*CRC*)

Republikaner *m pl* POL Republican Party (*AmE*), Grand Old Party (*infrml*) (*AmE*) (*GOP*)

Reserve *f* FINANZ reserve; **~ der Arbeitskräfte** PERSON reserve army of labor (*AmE*), reserve army of labour (*BrE*); ◆ **etw in ~ halten** GESCHÄFT keep sth in reserve

Reserve: **Reserveeinlagen** *f pl* VW reserve deposits (*RD*); **Reserveentnahme** *f* GESCHÄFT withdrawal from stocks; **Reserveguthaben** *nt* BANK, FINANZ reserve assets; **Reservekapazität** *f* IND, TRANSP, VW spare capacity; **Reservekraftwerk** *nt* IND standby power plant; **Reserven** *f pl* GESCHÄFT bottom-up, RECHNUNG reserves; **Reservesystem** *nt* COMP fallback; **Reservewährung** *f* FINANZ, GESCHÄFT reserve currency

reservieren *vt* COMP dedicate, assign, FREI, GESCHÄFT book, make a reservation, reserve, VW earmark; ◆ **~ lassen** GESCHÄFT *Hotel* book up

Reservieren *nt* VW earmarking

reserviert *adj* COMP assigned, dedicated, FREI, GESCHÄFT reserved, booked, *Person* cautious, aloof, VW earmarked; **~er Liegeplatz** *m* TRANSP *Schiffahrt* accommodation berth; **~er Verkehr** *m* TRANSP booked traffic

Reservierung *f* FREI, GESCHÄFT advance booking, booking, reservation; **~ der Fracht** TRANSP reservation of cargo; **~ per Kreditkarte** FREI credit card booking; ◆ **eine ~ vornehmen** FREI make a reservation

Reservierung: **Reservierungsbüro** *nt* FREI, TRANSP booking office, advance booking office; **Reservierungsformular** *nt* FREI reservation form; **Reservierungspreis** *m* V&M reserve; **Reservierungsschalter** *m* GESCHÄFT reservation counter; **Reservierungssystem** *nt* FREI reservation system

Reset-Taste *f* COMP reset button

Reskription *f* *Sch* BÖRSE rescription

Resolution *f* RECHT resolution; ◆ **eine ~ verabschieden** RECHT pass a resolution

resp *abbr* (*respektive*) GESCHÄFT respectively

Respektfrist *f* RECHNUNG grace period

respektieren *vt* GESCHÄFT respect

respektive *adv* (*resp*) GESCHÄFT respectively

Ressort *nt* POL portfolio, government department, VERWALT government department, VW organizational unit

ressortmäßig: **~e Abrechnungsanzeige** *f* FINANZ, MGMNT interdepartmental settlement advice

ressortspezifisch: **~er Plan** *m* GESCHÄFT, MGMNT departmental plan

Ressourcen *f pl* FINANZ, PERSON, VW resources; **Ressourcenaggregation** *f* GESCHÄFT resource aggregation; **Ressourcenallokation** *f* VW allocation of resources; **Ressourcenbewertung** *f* MGMNT resource appraisal; **Ressourcenbewirtschaftung** *f* UMWELT resource management; **Ressourcenmanagement** *nt* GESCHÄFT, MGMNT resource management;

Ressourcenprofil *nt* GESCHÄFT resource profile; **Ressourcentheorie** *f* VW resource economics; **Ressourcenverwaltung** *f* GESCHÄFT, MGMNT resource management

Rest *m* IND residue, MATH remainder, UMWELT residue, V&M *Überbleibsel* oddment; **der ~ der Welt** VW rest of the world (*ROW*); ◆ **ohne ~ teilend** MATH aliquot

Rest: **Restanleihe** *f* BÖRSE salvage bond

Restaurant *nt* GESCHÄFT restaurant; **Restaurantbesitzer, in** *m,f* PERSON restaurateur, restaurant proprietor

restaurieren *vt* UMWELT rehabilitate

Restaurierung *f* UMWELT rehabilitation

Rest: **Restbuchwert** *m* FINANZ book value; **Reste** *m pl* GESCHÄFT remnants; **Resteffekt** *m* GESCHÄFT holdover effect; **Resteladen** *m* V&M outlet store; **Restfamilie** *f* SOZIAL *nach Ehezerwürfnis* residual family; **Restfehler** *m* VW residual error; **Restkapitallaufzeit** *f* BÖRSE stub equity; **Restkaufhypothek** *f* GRUND purchase money mortgage; **Restlaufzeit** *f* BÖRSE term to maturity

restlich *adj* GESCHÄFT remaining; ◆ **~es Geld abrechnen** GESCHÄFT make up the odd money

restlich: **~es Wechselgeld** *nt* GESCHÄFT odd change

restlos: **~ bezahlen** *vt* FINANZ pay in full

Rest: **Restpartie** *f* GESCHÄFT odd lot; **Restposten** *m* GESCHÄFT job lot, remaining stock; **Restposten** *m pl* **der Zahlungsbilanz** VW balance of unclassifiable transactions, *Außenwirtschaft* accommodating items, errors and omissions

Restriktion *f* VW constraint

restriktiv *adj* GESCHÄFT restricted, VW tight; ◆ **~e Wirtschaftspolitik betreiben** VW deflate

restriktiv: **~e Finanzpolitik** *f* STEUER, VW tight fiscal policy; **~e Geldpolitik** *f* VW monetary stringency, money restraint, restrictive monetary policy

Restrukturierung *f* VW *eines Unternehmens* restructuring

Restschuld *f* BANK, FINANZ remaining debt, outstanding debt, unpaid balance; **~ zugunsten des Gläubigers** BANK balance due to creditor; **~ des Schuldners** BANK balance due to debtor; **Restschuldlebensversicherung** *f* VERSICH creditor rights life assurance, creditor rights life insurance; **Restschuldversicherung** *f* VERSICH private mortgage insurance

Rest: **Restwert** *m* FINANZ residual value, terminal value, RECHNUNG written-down value, amortized value, VW salvage value, scrap value

Resultat *nt* GESCHÄFT outcome, result; ◆ **als ~** GESCHÄFT as a result

Resümee *nt* GESCHÄFT summary, RECHT summing up

resümieren 1. *vt* GESCHÄFT summarize; **2.** *vi* GESCHÄFT sum up

Retentionsdatum *nt* GESCHÄFT retention date

Retorsionszwangsräumung *f* GRUND retaliatory eviction

Retour- *in cpds* GESCHÄFT, POL, TRANSP return; **Retouren** *f pl* GESCHÄFT returned goods, V&M sales returns; **Retourfracht** *f* TRANSP cargo homeward

Retter *m*: **~ in der Not** *infrml* FINANZ white knight (*infrml*)

Rettung- *in cpds* BANK, TRANSP rescue; **Rettungsaktion** *f* BANK lifeboat operation (*infrml*)

retuschieren *vt* V&M retouch, *Werbung* mask

Reue *f*: **~ nach dem Kauf** V&M post-purchase remorse

Revalorisierung *f* VW revalorization

Reverse: ~ **Print** *m* COMP reverse printing

reversibel *adj* GESCHÄFT reversible

reversionär: ~**er Faktor** *m* MATH reversionary factor

revidieren *vt* MGMNT overhaul

revidiert *adj* GESCHÄFT amended

Revierfahrt *f* TRANSP estuarial service

Revision *f* FINANZ audit, GESCHÄFT revision, IMP/EXP *Zoll* examination, MGMNT overhaul, RECHNUNG audit, accounting control, auditing, RECHT appeal; **Revisionsabteilung** *f* RECHNUNG auditing department; **Revisionsbericht** *m* RECHNUNG audit report, auditor's certificate, auditor's report, auditor's statement; **Revisionsgericht** *nt* RECHT appeal court, appellate court; **Revisionshandbuch** *nt* RECHNUNG auditing manual; **Revisionsklausel** *f* PERSON *Tarifverhandlungen* reopener clause; **Revisionskunde** *m*, **Revisionskundin** *f* RECHNUNG audit client; **Revisionsverfahren** *nt* RECHNUNG auditing procedure; **Revisionszulassungsbeschluß** *m* RECHT *des Revisionsgericht mit Anordnung der Aktenvorlage* writ of error

Revisor, in *m,f* RECHNUNG *Rechnungsprüfung*, VERWALT comptroller, controller

revolvierend *adj* FINANZ, VW revolving; ~**er Beschaffungsfonds** *m* VW supply revolving fund; ~**er Fonds** *m* FINANZ revolving fund; ~**er Fonds** *m* **für Erdölausgleichszahlung** FINANZ Petroleum Compensation Revolving Fund; ~**er Fonds** *m* **der Rüstungsproduktion** FINANZ defence production revolving fund (*BrE*), defense production revolving fund (*AmE*); ~**er Kredit** *m* BANK evergreen credit; ~**e Kreditlinie** *f* FINANZ revolving line of credit; ~**es Schuldenpapier** *nt* **mit Ratenzahlung** FINANZ certificate of amortized revolving debt (*BrE*) (*CARD*); ~**e Teilzahlungsvereinbarung** *f* BANK revolving charge account

Revolvingkredit *m* FINANZ credit revolving

Rezensent, in *m,f* MEDIEN reviewer

rezensieren *vt* MEDIEN review

Rezension *f* MEDIEN review

Rezept *nt* MGMNT *zur Lösung eines Problems* recipe, SOZIAL *ärztlich* prescription

Rezeption *f* FREI, GESCHÄFT reception, reception area, VERWALT front desk

Rezeptionist, in *m,f* FINANZ, GESCHÄFT receptionist, VERWALT desk clerk

rezeptpflichtig: **nicht** ~ *adj* SOZIAL *Arznei*, V&M over-the-counter (*OTC*)

Rezession *f* BÖRSE slump, GESCHÄFT recession, VW hard landing (*infrml*), recession, slump; ◆ **auf eine** ~ **zusteuern** VW enter recession

Rezession: **Rezessionsloch** *nt* VW recessionary gap; **Rezessionslücke** *f* VW recessionary gap; **Rezessionsphase** *f* VW recessionary phase

rezessionssicher: ~**e Branche** *f* VW recession-proof industry

rezessiv *adj* VW recessionary; ~**e Phase** *f* VW recessionary phase

reziprok *adj* GESCHÄFT reciprocal; ~**es Verhältnis** *nt* MATH reciprocal ratio; ~**er Verzug** *m* BANK, FINANZ cross default; ~**er Wert** *m* MATH reciprocal

R-Gespräch *nt* KOMM collect call (*AmE*), reverse charge call (*BrE*); ◆ ~ **anmelden** KOMM call collect (*AmE*),

reverse the charges (*BrE*); **ein** ~ **annehmen** KOMM accept a collect call (*AmE*), accept a reverse-charge call (*BrE*)

RGW *abbr* (*Rat für gegenseitige Wirtschaftshilfe*) VW COMECON (*obs*) (*Council for Mutual Economic Aid*)

Rheinisch-Westfälisch: ~**e Börse** *f* BÖRSE Düsseldorf Stock Exchange

richten 1. *vt* GESCHÄFT *Kritik, Produkt, Programm* aim, RECHT *Richtlinie* address; ◆ ~ **an** [+acc] RECHT address; ~ **Sie Ihre Beschwerden an** [+acc] GESCHÄFT address your complaints to; **2. sich** ~ *v refl* GESCHÄFT conform; ◆ **sich nach etw** ~ GESCHÄFT *Rat* act on sth

Richter, in *m,f* GESCHÄFT awarder, RECHT judge

richterlich: ~**e Haftprüfung** *f* RECHT habeas corpus; ~ **Zahlungsaufforderung** *f* **mit Konkursdrohung** RECHT bankruptcy notice

Richter: **Richterrecht** *nt* PATENT, RECHT case law; **Richterstuhl** *m* RECHT the Bench; **Richterzimmer** *nt* RECHT chamber

richtig 1. *adj* GESCHÄFT accurate, correct, right; ◆ **auf der** ~**en Fährte sein** GESCHÄFT be on the right track; **die** ~**en Qualifikationen für die Arbeitsstelle haben** PERSON have the right qualifications for the job; **auf der** ~**en Spur** GESCHÄFT on track; **im** ~**en Verhältnis** GESCHÄFT proportionate; **2.** *adv* GESCHÄFT accurately, correctly; ◆ ~ **beraten sein** GESCHÄFT be well advised to

Richtigbefund *m* GESCHÄFT verification, approval; ◆ **nach** ~ GESCHÄFT if found correct, if verified

Richtigkeit *f* GESCHÄFT accuracy, correctness; ◆ **auf** ~ **prüfen** GESCHÄFT, RECHNUNG verify

richtigstellen *vt* GESCHÄFT adjust, *Situation* rectify

Richtigstellung *f* GESCHÄFT adjustment, *einer Situation* rectification

Richtkosten *pl* GESCHÄFT standard cost

Richtlinie *f* FINANZ directive, MGMNT normative, PATENT rule, POL direction, directive, VW regulation, directive; ~ **Z** VW regulation Z (*AmE*); ◆ **Richtlinien aufstellen** MGMNT set the standard

Richtlinie: **Richtlinienentwurf** *m* RECHT *Europäische Union* draft directive

Richtnutzungsdauer *f* GRUND guideline lives

Richtpreis *m* GESCHÄFT, V&M guide price, target price, VW target price; ~ **für den Einzelhandel** V&M recommended retail price (*RRP*)

Richtung *f* TRANSP direction; ◆ **die** ~ **geben** GESCHÄFT set a trend

Richtung: **Richtungskoeffizient** *m* GESCHÄFT, MATH slope

richtungsweisend *adj* GESCHÄFT trendsetting; ◆ ~ **sein** GESCHÄFT set a trend

richtungsweisend: ~**e Stellungnahme** *f* POL position paper

Riesen- *in cpds* GESCHÄFT giant, jumbo, mammoth

riesengroß *adj* GESCHÄFT giant, mammoth, mega, V&M giant

Riesen-: **Riesengröße** *f* V&M mammoth size; **Riesenpackung** *f* V&M jumbo pack; **Riesenreduzierung** *f* V&M mammoth reduction

riesig: ~**e Sensationsschlagzeile** *f* MEDIEN screamer (*infrml*)

Rigger *m* TRANSP rigger

Ring *m* BÖRSE pit; **Ringbolzen** *m* TRANSP eye bolt

ringen *vt*: ~ **um** GESCHÄFT *Existenz* battle for

Risiko *nt* FINANZ exposure, GESCHÄFT hazard, MATH, VERSICH risk, VERWALT exposure, VW venture; ~ **des Frachtführers** TRANSP carrier's risk; **jedes** ~ VERSICH all peril, all risks (*A/R*); ~ **des Kursrückgangs** BÖRSE downside risk; ~ **unehrlichen Verhaltens** VERSICH moral hazard; ~ **des zufälligen Untergangs der Sache** RECHT *Vertragsrecht* risk of accidental destruction; ♦ **auf** ~ BÖRSE at risk; **das** ~ **abdecken** BÖRSE cover the risk; **kein** ~ **bis zur Bestätigung** VERSICH no risk until confirmed (*nr*); **das** ~ **eingehen** GESCHÄFT run the risk of; **ein** ~ **eingehen** GESCHÄFT take a risk; **kein** ~ **eingehen** GESCHÄFT play safe; **auf** ~ **des Empfängers** GESCHÄFT at receiver's risk; ~ **geht mit Eigentum über** RECHT *Vertragsprinzip* risk passes with property; **auf** ~ **des Käufers** BÖRSE at buyer's risk; **kein** ~ **nach Löschung** VERSICH no risk after discharge (*nrad*); **Risiken mischen** VERSICH spread risks; ~ **nach oben** BÖRSE upside risk; **Risiken streuen** VERSICH spread risks; **Risiken verteilen** VERSICH spread risks; **das** ~ **tragen** BÖRSE bear the risk

Risiko: **Risikoabdeckung** *f* VW risk cover; **Risikoabwälzung** *f* VERSICH passing of risk; **Risikoanalyse** *f* FINANZ, VERSICH risk analysis

risikoangepaßt: ~**er Diskontsatz** *m* FINANZ risk-adjusted discount rate

Risiko: **Risikoarbitrage** *f* BÖRSE *Übernahme* risk arbitrage

risikoarm: ~**e Wertpapiere** *nt pl* BÖRSE defensive securities, low-risk securities

Risiko: **Risikoausgleich** *m* VERSICH balancing of portfolio; **Risikoausschluß** *m* RECHT *Verträge* exclusion of risk, TRANSP *Versicherung* exceptions clause, VERSICH exception

risikobehaftet *adj* BANK risky; ~**es Geschäftsunternehmen** *nt* MGMNT business venture; ~**er Vermögenswert** *m* BANK risky asset; ~**er Vertrag** *m* BANK hazardous contract

Risiko: **Risikobeschreibung** *f* VERSICH description of risk; **Risikobeurteilung** *f* MGMNT risk assessment; **Risikobewertung** *f* FINANZ, MGMNT, VERSICH risk assessment

risikobezogen: ~**e Prämie** *f* VERSICH risk-based premium

Risiko: **Risikobündelung** *f* FINANZ repackaging of risks; **Risikoeinschätzung** *f* MGMNT risk assessment; **Risikoeinstufung** *f* VERSICH classification of risks

risikofreudig *adj* GESCHÄFT risky

Risiko: **Risikogewichtung** *f* FINANZ risk weighting; **Risikograd** *m* BÖRSE degree of exposure; **Risikohäufung** *f* VERSICH accumulation of risk; **Risikokapital** *nt* BANK, FINANZ, GESCHÄFT, VW risk capital, venture capital; **Risikokapitalgeber** *m* BANK, FINANZ, GESCHÄFT, VW venture capitalist; **Risikokarte** *f* VERSICH aggregate liability index; **Risikoklassifikation** *f* BANK basic rating; **Risikokontrolle** *f* MGMNT risk monitoring; **Risikokredit** *m* BANK bad and doubtful debt (*B&D*), FINANZ problem loan; **Risikolebensversicherung** *f* VERSICH term insurance; **Risikolebensversicherung** *f* **mit Umtauschrecht** VERSICH convertible term life insurance, term life insurance

risikolos *adj* BÖRSE risk-free; ~**er Geschäftsabschluß** *m* BÖRSE risk-free transaction; ~**es Insidergeschäft** *nt* BÖRSE front running; ~**er Schuldtitel** *m* BÖRSE risk-free

debt instrument; ~**e Schuldurkunde** *f* BÖRSE risk-free debt instrument; ~**e Transaktion** *f* BÖRSE risk-free transaction

Risiko: **Risikomanagement** *nt* BÖRSE, FINANZ, MGMNT risk management; **Risikomanager** *m* VERSICH risk manager

risikomeidend *adj* FINANZ risk-avoiding; ~**es Kapital** *nt* FINANZ risk-avoiding capital

risikominimierend *adj* BÖRSE risk-minimizing

risikoorientiert *adj* GESCHÄFT risk-oriented; ~**es Bankmanagement** *nt* BANK risk-based banking standards

Risiko: **Risikopaket** *nt* FINANZ risk package; **Risikopoolung** *f* VERSICH risk pooling; **Risikoposition** *f* BÖRSE risk position; **Risikoprofil** *nt* VERSICH risk profile

risikoreich *adj* BÖRSE high-risk, GESCHÄFT aggressive; ~**es Unternehmen** *nt* VERSICH venture; ~**e Unternehmung** *f* GESCHÄFT high-risk venture

risikoscheu *adj* GESCHÄFT risk-averse

Risiko: **Risikostreuung** *f* BÖRSE, MGMNT risk management; **Risikoteilung** *f* VERSICH risk sharing

risikotragend: ~**es Kapital** *nt* BANK, FINANZ, VW risk capital, risk-bearing capital

Risiko: **Risikotragung** *f* BANK, FINANZ assumption of the risk; **Risikoübernahme** *f* BANK, FINANZ assumption of the risk, VERSICH underwriting; **Risikoüberwachung** *f* MGMNT risk monitoring; **Risikoumstrukturierung** *f* FINANZ repackaging of risks; **Risikounternehmer** *m* BANK, FINANZ, GESCHÄFT, VW venture capitalist; **Risikoversicherung** *f* VERSICH hazard insurance; **Risikoverteilung** *f* RECHT *in einem Geschäft*, VERSICH risk distribution, risk pooling; **Risikovertrag** *m* VERSICH aleatory contract

riskant *adj* GESCHÄFT, VW risky, touch-and-go; ~**e Sache** *f* GESCHÄFT wildcat venture; ~**er Vertrag** *m* VERSICH hazardous contract

Ristornogebühr *f* GESCHÄFT cancellation fee

Ritzel *nt* TRANSP pinion

Roadshow *f* FINANZ, GESCHÄFT, V&M road show

Robertson: ~**sche Verzögerung** *f* VW Robertsonian lag

Roboter *m* IND robot; ♦ ~ **einsetzen** IND robotize

roboterhaft *adj* IND robot-like; ~**e Verkäufer** *m pl* V&M robot salespeople

Roboter: **Robotertechnik** *f* IND robotics

Robotik *f* IND robotics

robust *adj* GESCHÄFT robust

roh *adj* COMP *Daten, Material* raw

Roh- *in cpds* GESCHÄFT raw; **Rohbilanz** *f* RECHNUNG trial balance; **Rohblatt** *nt* MEDIEN base sheet; **Rohdaten** *pl* COMP, MATH raw data; **Rohgewinn** *m* RECHNUNG gross profit margin; **Rohmaterial** *nt* IND raw material, unmanufactured material

Rohöl *nt* UMWELT, IND crude oil; **Rohölreinigung** *f* IND crude oil washing (*COW*); **Rohöltanker** *m* TRANSP crude oil carrier; **Rohöltransporter** *m* TRANSP crude oil carrier

Roh-: **Rohpetroleum** *nt* UMWELT crude petroleum

Rohr- *in cpds* IND, KOMM, TRANSP pipe; **Rohrlegerschiff** *nt* TRANSP pipe-laying ship; **Rohrleitung** *f* IND *für Gas und Erdöl*, KOMM, TRANSP pipeline

Rohstoff *m* IND raw material, VW basic commodity, commodity, primary commodity; ♦ ~**e gegen Fertig-**

erzeugnisse handeln GESCHÄFT trade raw materials for manufactured goods

Rohstoff: **Rohstoffabkommen** *nt* VW commodity agreement; **Rohstoffhandel** *m* VW commodity trade; **Rohstoffkartell** *nt* VW commodity cartel; **Rohstoffmarkt** *m* VW commodity market; **Rohstoffmünzgeld** *nt* VW hard commodity; **Rohstoffpreis** *m* BÖRSE, VW commodity price; **Rohstoffpreisindex** *m* BÖRSE commodities price index

Roll- *in cpds* COMP, FINANZ, IND, TRANSP scrolling, rolling, moving; **Rollbahn** *f* TRANSP runway; **Rollbalken** *m* COMP *Bildschirmdarstellung* scroll bar; **Rollbehälter** *m* TRANSP roll-on container; **Rollcontainer** *m* TRANSP roll-on container

Rolle *f* GESCHÄFT role; **~ der Regierung** POL government role; ♦ **eine ~ spielen bei** [+dat] GESCHÄFT play a part in, be a factor in

rollen *vt* COMP *Bildschirm* scroll

Rolle: **Rollenbesetzung** *f* MGMNT role set

rollend: **~er Fußsteig** *m* GESCHÄFT travelator; **~e Optionsposition** *f* BÖRSE rolling options position; **~er Plan** *m* GESCHÄFT rolling plan

Rolle: **Rollenspiel** *nt* MGMNT role-playing

Roll-: **Rollfuhrunternehmen** *nt* TRANSP haulage contractor, hauler (*AmE*), haulier (*BrE*); **Rollgeld** *nt* TRANSP cartage, drayage (*AmE*), haulage, trucking charges (*AmE*); **Roll-on-Lift-off** *phr* (*Ro-Lo*) TRANSP roll-on-lift-off (*ro-lo*); **Roll-on-Roll-off** *phr* (*Ro-Ro*) TRANSP roll-on-roll-off (*ro-ro*)

Rollover- *in cpds* BANK rollover; **Rollover-Kredit** *m* BANK rollover loan; **Rollover-Kredit** *m* **auf CD-Basis** BANK certificate of deposit rollover; **Rollover-Quote** *f* BANK rollover ratio

Roll-: **Rollpfeil** *m* COMP scroll arrow; **Rollprogramm** *nt* FINANZ, MGMNT rolling program (*AmE*), rolling programme (*BrE*); **Rollsteig** *m* TRANSP moving pavement (*BrE*), travelator (*BrE*), travolator (*AmE*); **Rollswap** *m* FINANZ roller swap; **Rolltreppe** *f* GESCHÄFT escalator, moving stairway (*BrE*)

ROM *abbr* (*Festspeicher*) COMP ROM (*read-only memory*)

Römisch: **~e Verträge** *m pl* POL, VW Treaty of Rome

Rooker Wise: **~ Nachtrag** *m* FINANZ Rooker Wise Amendment; **~ Novelle** *f* FINANZ Rooker Wise Amendment

Ro-Ro-Schiff *nt* IMP/EXP roll-on/roll-off ship

rosa: **~ Wirtschaft** *f* VW pink economy (*jarg*)

rosig *adj* GESCHÄFT *Aussichten* rosy

Rost: **Rostbildung** *f* IND corrosion; **Rostgürtel** *m* IND rustbelt (*AmE*); **Rostschleuder** *f infml* TRANSP rust bucket (*infml*)

Rot- *in cpds* GESCHÄFT red

rot: **~e Klausel** *f* BANK *Vorschußakkreditiv* red clause; **~e Waren** *f pl* V&M red goods; **in den ~en Zahlen** *phr* BANK, GESCHÄFT, RECHNUNG in the red, below the line; **~e Zahlen schreiben** *phr* BANK, GESCHÄFT operate in the red

Rotation- *in cpds* BANK, GESCHÄFT, V&M rotation; **Rotationsdruck** *m* V&M web-offset; **Rotationsklausel** *f* BANK rotation clause; **Rotationstiefdruck** *m* V&M rotogravure; **im Rotationsverfahren** *phr* GESCHÄFT in rotation

Rot-: **Rotbuch** *nt* FINANZ Red Book (*infrml*) (*AmE*)

Roten: **in den ~** *phr infrml* BANK, GESCHÄFT in the red

Rot-: **Rot-Grün-System** *nt* IMP/EXP *Zollabfertigung* red and green system

Round Table *m* MGMNT round table

Route *f* TRANSP route; **Routenabweichungsklausel** *f* VERSICH deviation clause (*D/C*); **Routenbescheinigung** *f* TRANSP routing certificate; **Routenzertifikat** *nt* TRANSP routing certificate

Routine *f* COMP, GESCHÄFT routine

routinemäßig *adj* GESCHÄFT as a matter of routine, routine

Rubrik *f* MEDIEN *Druck* heading

Rück- *in cpds* GESCHÄFT back, reverse, KOMM reply; **Rückanschlag** *m* IND backstop; **Rückantwort** *f* GESCHÄFT, KOMM business reply card (*BRC*), business reply mail (*BRM*); **Rückantwortmedium** *nt* V&M *Postversand* reply vehicle; **Rückantwortträger** *m* V&M *Postversand* reply device; **Rückbehaltungsrecht** *nt* RECHT possessory lien, right of retention, VW possessory lien; **Rückbelastung** *f* BANK charge back, BÖRSE, RECHNUNG billback; **Rückbuchung** *f* GESCHÄFT reversing (*REV*), RECHNUNG reversal (*AmE*), reverse entry, writing back, cancellation

rückdatieren *vt* GESCHÄFT *Dokument, Scheck* antedate, backdate, predate

rückdatiert *adj* GESCHÄFT backdated, predated

Rück-: **Rückdatierung** *f* GESCHÄFT backdating, predating; **Rückdeckungsversicherung** *f* VERSICH business insurance, employer's pension, liability insurance

Rücken *m* MEDIEN backstrip, *eines Buchs* spine

Rück-: **Rückentwicklung** *f* VW retrogression **Rückerwerbsrecht** *nt* *eines Schuldners* FINANZ right of redemption

Rückerstattung *f* BANK, FINANZ, GESCHÄFT, PATENT repayment, refund, RECHT *des Kaufpreises* restitution, VW, STEUER refund, remission; **~ im Garantiefall** GESCHÄFT return of guarantee; **~ eines zuviel gezahlten Betrages** GESCHÄFT return of amount overpaid; **Rückerstattungsbeschluß** *m* RECHT *Vertragsrecht* restitution order; **Rückerstattungspflichtige(r)** *mf* [decl. as adj] RECHT restitutor; **Rückerstattungsvergleich** *m* RECHT *Vertragsrecht* restitution compromise

Rück-: **Rückfahrkarte** *f* FREI return ticket (*BrE*), round-trip ticket (*AmE*); **Rückfahrt** *f* GESCHÄFT return, TRANSP homeward voyage; **Rückfalltat** *f* RECHT second offence (*BrE*), second offense (*AmE*); **Rückflug** *m* FREI return flight; **Rückflugschein** *m* FREI return ticket (*BrE*); **Rückfluß** *m* FINANZ amortization; **Rückfluß** *m* **auf das investierte Kapital** VW return on capital employed; **Rückforderung** *f* FINANZ clawback; **Rückforderung** *f* **gewährter Steuervergünstigungen** STEUER clawback; **Rückfracht** *f* IMP/EXP inward cargo, TRANSP back freight, return cargo (*r/c*), return freight; **Rückfrachtabteilung** *f* IMP/EXP inward freight department; **Rückfrage** *f* GESCHÄFT query; **Rückführung** *f* VW *Gewinn* repatriation; **Rückführung** *f* **ausländischen Kapitals** VW repatriation of overseas funds; **Rückgabe** *f* GESCHÄFT return; **Rückgaberecht** *nt* GESCHÄFT right of return; **Rückgabewert** *m* RECHNUNG surrender value; **Rückgang** *m* GESCHÄFT dip, *Preise* fall, VW retrogression, shrinkage, *Arbeit* decline, *Ausgaben* drop; **Rückgang** *m* **der Währungsreserven** BÖRSE fall in foreign exchange reserves; **Rückgänge** *m pl*, **Kündigungen** *f pl* **und Vorauszahlungen** *f pl* FINANZ droppages, cancellations and prepayments (*DCP*)

rückgängig 1. *adj* GESCHÄFT *Preise, Kurse* declining; **2.** *adv* ◆ **~ machen** RECHT annul, cancel, *vertragliche Vereinbarung* rescind, VW reverse course

rückgängig: **~ zu machende Abschreibung** *f* RECHNUNG recapturable depreciation

Rückgängigmachung *f* RECHT annulment, cancellation, *Vertrag* rescission; **~ überhöhter Abschreibungen** STEUER depreciation recapture

rückgestellt *adj* RECHNUNG accrued

rückgewinnbar: **~es Material** *nt* UMWELT recoverable material, recyclable material

rückgewinnen *vt* UMWELT recover, recycle

Rück-: **Rückgewinnung** *f* COMP recovery, UMWELT recovery, recycling; **Rückgewinnung** *f* **der Basis** STEUER recovery of basis; **Rückgewinnung** *f* **der Gemeinkosten** RECHNUNG overheads recovery; **Rückgrat** *nt* GESCHÄFT backbone; **Rückgrat** *nt* **der Wirtschaft** VW backbone of the economy

Rückgriff *m* GESCHÄFT, VERSICH recourse, backup; ◆ **mit ~** GESCHÄFT, VERSICH with recourse; **ohne ~** GESCHÄFT, VERSICH without recourse

Rückgriff: **Rückgrifflinie** *f* BANK backup line

Rück-: **Rückkanal** *m* COMP reverse channel

Rückkauf *m* FINANZ buy-back; **Rückkaufgeschäft** *nt* GESCHÄFT buy-back agreement; **Rückkaufpreis** *m* **von Anteilen** BANK *Investmentfonds* bid rate; **Rückkaufsklausel** *f* RECHT buy-back clause; **Rückkaufsprämie** *f* RECHNUNG redemption premium; **Rückkaufvereinbarung** *f* BÖRSE, FINANZ, GESCHÄFT repossession (*repo*), repurchase agreement (*RP*), RECHT *Vertrag*, VW buy-back agreement; **Rückkaufwert** *m* FINANZ *einer Versicherungspolice* cash-in value, RECHNUNG surrender value; **Rückkaufwert** *m* **einer Police** VERSICH cash surrender value

Rück-: **Rückkehr** *f* GESCHÄFT return; **Rückkopplung** *f* COMP feedback; **Rückladung** *f* TRANSP back load, cargo homeward, return load

Rücklage *f* FINANZ reserve, handbag, purse; **~ für ungewisse künftige Ereignisse** RECHNUNG contingency provision; **Rücklagen** *f pl* RECHNUNG, VERSICH earned surplus, reserves, retained income, retained profits, balance sheet reserves; **Rücklagenbildung** *f* RECHNUNG creation of reserves; **Rücklagenmanagement** *nt* MGMNT contingency management; **Rücklagentilgung** *f* FINANZ sinking-fund method; **Rücklagenzuweisung** *f* **für Gehaltserhöhungen** PERSON salary adjustment reserve allotment (*SARA*); **Rücklagevermögen** *nt* BANK, FINANZ reserve assets

rückläufig *adj* BÖRSE depressed, shrinking, GESCHÄFT downward, VW declining; **nicht ~** *adj* BÖRSE undepressed; **~er Aktienmarkt** *m* BÖRSE shrinking market, soft market, down-market, VW soft market; **~e Konjunktur** *f* VW declining economic activity; **~er Kurs** *m* FINANZ decreasing rate; **~er Markt** *m* BÖRSE declining market, V&M down-market; **~e Tendenz** *f* VW declining trend; **~e Verkaufsergebnisse** *nt pl* V&M sales slump

Rück-: **Rücklaufplanung** *f* V&M response projection; **Rücklaufquote** *f* V&M response rate; **Rücklaufrate** *f* **von Werbekupons** V&M advertising conversion rate

rückliefern *vt* GESCHÄFT *bei Unzustellbarkeit* redeliver, return

Rück-: **Rücklieferung** *f* GESCHÄFT, TRANSP redelivery, return delivery; **Rücknahme** *f* **einer Klage** RECHT abandonment of a complaint; **Rücknahmekurs** *m* BANK repurchase rate; **Rücknahmewert** *m* BÖRSE bid value; **Rückplanung** *f* MGMNT backward scheduling; **Rückprämie** *f* BÖRSE put, put option, put premium, VERSICH canceling return (*AmE*), cancelling return (*BrE*); **Rückreise** *f* FREI return leg, GESCHÄFT return; **Rückruf** *m* BÖRSE recall

rückrufen *vi* GESCHÄFT call in

Rück-: **einen Rückschlag erleiden** *phr* GESCHÄFT suffer a setback; **Rückschritt** *m* COMP backspace, GESCHÄFT step back; **Rückschrittzeichen** *nt* COMP backspace character; **Rückseite** *f* GESCHÄFT, MEDIEN back section, *Blatt, Münze* verso (*vo.*); **Rückseitendruck** *m* MEDIEN backing up; **Rücksendungen** *f pl* V&M sales returns; **Rücksetzen** *nt* COMP reset; **Rücksetztaste** *f* COMP reset button

Rücksichtnahme *f* VERSICH consideration

rücksichtslos: **~er Wettbewerb** *m* GESCHÄFT predatory competition

Rück-: **Rücksprache** *f* PERSON *mit Kollegen* consultation

Rückstand *m* GESCHÄFT, IND residue, slippage, work backlog, UMWELT residue; ◆ **im ~** GESCHÄFT in arrears; **im ~ sein** GESCHÄFT be in arrears, lag behind; **in ~ geraten** GESCHÄFT fall behind schedule

Rück-: **Rückstände** *m pl* BÖRSE, FINANZ arrearages, arrears, GESCHÄFT arrears

rückständig *adj* FINANZ, GESCHÄFT, VERWALT overdue, in arrears; ◆ **~ sein** GESCHÄFT be in arrears

rückständig: **~e Dividende** *f* BÖRSE dividend in arrears, overdue dividend, FINANZ passed dividend; **~e Miete** *f* PERSON back rent; **~e Rente** *f* VERSICH annuity payable in arrears; **~e Zahlung** *f* FINANZ overdue payment, RECHNUNG payment in arrears; **~e Zahlungen** *f pl* FINANZ arrearages; **~e Zinsen** *m pl* RECHNUNG back interest

rückstellen *vi* RECHNUNG accrue

Rückstellung *f* BANK, FINANZ, GESCHÄFT, RECHNUNG, STEUER provision; **~ für Abschreibungen** RECHNUNG provision for depreciation; **~ für Darlehensverlust** BANK provision for loan loss; **~ für Devisenschwankungen** GESCHÄFT allowance for exchange fluctuations; **~ für Nebenkosten** FINANZ incidentals allowance; **~ für notleidende Kredite** BANK, FINANZ bad loan provision; **~ für Risikokredite** BANK, FINANZ bad loan provision; **~ für satzungsgemäße Kostenüberschreitung** RECHNUNG reserve for statutory overruns; **~ für zweifelhafte Forderungen** BANK, FINANZ bad debt provision, RECHNUNG doubtful-debt provision, bad debt provision, VW reserve for doubtful accounts; **Rückstellungen** *f pl* RECHNUNG balance sheet reserves; **Rückstellungen** *f pl* **für Dividendenzahlungen** RECHNUNG accrued dividend, funding; **Rückstellungskonto** *nt* RECHNUNG appropriation account

Rück-: **Rückstufung** *f* PERSON *niedrigere Gehaltsstufe* downgrading, grading back, *niedrigere Position* demotion; **Rückstufung** *f* **von Arbeitsplätzen** PERSON dilution of labor (*AmE*), dilution of labour (*BrE*); **Rücktaste** *f* COMP backspace; **Rücktausch** *m* VW retranslation; **Rücktrag** *m* RECHNUNG carry-back

rücktragen *vt* FINANZ, RECHNUNG carry back

Rücktritt *m* PERSON resignation, VERWALT resignation, retirement; **~ zum Ausstellungsdatum der Police**

VERSICH notice of cancellation at anniversary date (*NCAD*); **Rücktrittsgesuch** *nt* PERSON letter of resignation, resignation; **sein Rücktrittsgesuch einreichen** *phr* PERSON hand in one's resignation; **Rücktrittsklausel** *f* RECHT *Vertrag* opt-out clause, cancellation clause, canceling clause (*AmE*), contracting out clause, escape clause, cancelling clause (*BrE*), VERSICH cancellation provision clause, VERWALT escape clause; **Rücktrittsrecht** *nt* RECHT right of rescission; **Rücktrittsschreiben** *nt* PERSON letter of resignation

Rück-: **Rückübereignung** *f* GRUND reconveyance; **Rückumschlag** *m* KOMM self-addressed envelope; **Rückumtausch** *m* VW retranslation; **Rückvergütung** *f* FINANZ rebate, GESCHÄFT refund, reimbursement, PATENT refund; **Rückversetzung** *f* **älterer Menschen in untere Führungsebenen** PERSON decruitment; **Rückversicherungsbestand** *m* VERSICH portfolio reinsurance; **Rückversicherungsgesellschaft** *f* VERSICH reinsurance company

rückverzweigen *vi* COMP *Daten, Programm* re-enter

Rück-: **Rück- und Vorprämiengeschäft** *nt* BÖRSE *im Wertpapierhandel* put and call

rückwandeln *vt* COMP reconvert

Rück-: **Rückwandlung** *f* COMP reconversion; **Rückwaren** *f pl* GESCHÄFT returned goods, returns, V&M sales returns

rückwärtig: **~er Buchdeckel** *m* MEDIEN back cover; **~e Konstruktion** *f* GESCHÄFT reverse engineering

Rückwärts- *in cpds* GESCHÄFT reverse, backwards, TRANSP *Schiffahrt* astern; **Rückwärtsentwicklung** *f* GESCHÄFT reverse engineering; **Rückwärtsintegration** *f* IND, MGMNT, VW backward integration; **Rückwärtsplanung** *f* MGMNT backward scheduling; **Rückwärtsterminierung** *f* MGMNT backward scheduling

rückwirkend 1. *adj* GESCHÄFT retroactive, retrospective; **2.** *adv* GESCHÄFT retroactively, retrospectively; ◆ **~ in Kraft treten lassen** RECHT backdate

rückwirkend: **~e Anpassung** *f* VW retroactive adjustment; **~e Einstufung** *f* POL *als Verschlußsache* retroactive classification; **~e Entlohnung** *f* PERSON backdated pay; **~es Gesetz** *nt* RECHT ex post facto law, law with retroactive effect, retroactive law; **~er Nachlaß** *m* TRANSP retrospective rebate

Rück-: **Rückwirkung** *f* GESCHÄFT repercussion, RECHT retroactivity, retrospectivity, STEUER reachback

rückzahlbar *adj* BANK, BÖRSE, FINANZ redeemable, reimbursable, repayable, amortizable, GESCHÄFT redeemable, reimbursable, repayable; **nicht ~** *adj* BÖRSE irredeemable; **~e Aktie** *f* BÖRSE redeemable share; **~e Staatssubvention** *f* FINANZ, RECHNUNG revolving fund; **~e Vorzugsaktie** *f* BÖRSE redeemable preference share

rückzahlen *vt* BANK, BÖRSE, FINANZ, GESCHÄFT repay, redeem, refund, reimburse

Rückzahlung *f* BANK repayment, FINANZ amortization, repayment, GESCHÄFT refund, reimbursement, repayment, STEUER remission; **~ innerhalb von fünf Jahren** BANK, GESCHÄFT repayment over five years; ◆ **Rückzahlungen verteilen** FINANZ spread repayments

Rückzahlung: **Rückzahlungsagio** *nt* RECHNUNG redemption premium; **Rückzahlungsanspruch** *m* STEUER repayment claim; **Rückzahlungsanspruch** *m* **aus der Einkommensteuer** STEUER income tax

repayment claim; **Rückzahlungsbetrag** *m* BÖRSE redemption amount, RECHNUNG amount repayable; **Rückzahlung** *f* **einer Schuld** FINANZ repayment of a debt, extinction of a debt; **Rückzahlungsfähigkeit** *f* BANK ability to repay; **Rückzahlungsmaßnahme** *f* FINANZ payback provision; **Rückzahlungsmittel** *nt* VW medium of redemption; **Rückzahlungsrecht** *nt* FINANZ right of redemption; **Rückzahlungsrendite** *f* BANK, BÖRSE, GESCHÄFT redemption yield, yield to maturity (*YTM*); **Rückzahlungstermin** *m* BÖRSE redemption date; **Rückzahlungsverpflichtung** *f* FINANZ sinking-fund requirements; **Rückzahlungszeitraum** *m* FINANZ repayment term

Rückzieher: **einen ~ machen** *phr infrml* GESCHÄFT, MGMNT back-pedal, backtrack, back down, back out

Rück-: **Rückzugsposition** *f* POL fallback position

Ruder: **ans ~ kommen** *phr* GESCHÄFT, POL come to the fore; **Ruderhaus** *nt* TRANSP wheelhouse

Ruf *m* COMP call, GESCHÄFT reputation, standing, KOMM call; ◆ **~ schädigen** GESCHÄFT disparage

Ruf: **Rufbericht** *m* KOMM call report; **Rufnummer** *f* **zum Nulltarif** KOMM, V&M Freefone number (*BrE*), toll-free number (*AmE*); **Rufweiterschaltung** *f* COMP, KOMM call forwarding

Ruhegehalt *nt* FINANZ, SOZIAL pension, retirement pay, retirement pension, retiring allowance, superannuation, *im öffentlichen Dienst* state pension; **Ruhegehaltkonto** *nt* VERSICH superannuation account

ruhen *vi* GESCHÄFT *Gesetz, Regel* be in abeyance, *nicht wirksam sein* be suspended

ruhend: **~e Erbschaft** *f* RECHT estate in abeyance

Ruhe: **sich zur ~ setzen** *phr* GESCHÄFT retire from business

Ruhestand *m* GESCHÄFT, PERSON retirement; ◆ **in den ~ treten** GESCHÄFT, PERSON retire; **in den ~ versetzen** FINANZ, PERSON pension off

Ruhestand: **Ruhestandkonto** *nt* VERSICH superannuation account

ruhig *adj* GESCHÄFT quiet

ruinös: **~e Konkurrenz** *f* VW cutthroat competition

Run *m* BANK run; **~ auf die Banken** BANK run on the banks

rund 1. *adj* GESCHÄFT approximately (*approx.*), round, (*rd.*) circa (*ca.*); ◆ **~ um die Uhr** GESCHÄFT around-the-clock, round-the-clock (*BrE*), twenty-four-hour; **2.** *adv* (*rd.*) GESCHÄFT about

Runde *f* VW round

rund: **~e Klammern** *f pl* COMP, MEDIEN *Typographie* round brackets; **in ~en Zahlen** *phr* FINANZ, GESCHÄFT in round figures

Rundfunk *m* KOMM radio; ◆ **im ~ senden** MEDIEN broadcast; **durch ~ verbreiten** MEDIEN broadcast

Rundfunk: **Rundfunkbehörde** *f* V&M radio authority; **Rundfunkprogramm** *nt* MEDIEN radio program (*AmE*), radio programme (*BrE*); **Rundfunksendung** *f* MEDIEN broadcast, radio broadcast; **Rundfunksprecher, in** *m,f* MEDIEN radio announcer; **Rundfunkwerbung** *f* MEDIEN radio advertising

Rundreise *f* FREI, GESCHÄFT tour; **Rundreise-Chartervertrag** *m* TRANSP round charter party (*round C/P*) **Rundreise-Frachtvertrag** *m* TRANSP round charter party (*round C/P*)

Rundschreiben *nt* KOMM circular

Rund-um-die-Uhr-Handel *m* BÖRSE all-day trading, twenty-four-hour trading (*BrE*)

Rundungsfehler *m* MATH rounding error

runterladen *vt* COMP download, load

Rybczynski-Theorem *nt* VW Rybczynski theorem

S

S. *abbr* (*Seite*) COMP, GESCHÄFT p (*page*)

Sach- *in cpds* GESCHÄFT physical, tangible; **Sachanlagegüter** *nt pl* VW physical assets; **Sachanlagekonto** *nt* RECHNUNG fixed asset account; **Sachanlagen** *f pl* RECHNUNG tangible assets, VW fixed assets; **Sachanlagevermögen** *nt* FINANZ tangible fixed assets, VW physical assets; **Sachaufwand** *m* VERWALT administrative expenses

Sachbearbeiter, in *m,f* PERSON clerk, executive; ~ **für Einfuhrpapiere** PERSON import documentation supervisor; ~ **für Funkwerbung** MEDIEN, V&M *für Werbesendung* time buyer; ~ **im Verkauf** MGMNT, PERSON, V&M sales executive; ~ **eines Werbeetats** MEDIEN account executive

Sach-: **Sachbezug** *m* GESCHÄFT, PERSON allowance in kind, benefit in kind, nonmonetary compensation, nonmonetary reward, payment in kind, STEUER, VERSICH benefit in kind; **Sachbezüge** *m pl* PERSON nonpecuniary returns

sachdienlich *adj* GESCHÄFT pertinent, suitable, RECHT pertinent; ~**es Gesetz** *nt* RECHT *Gewerkschaftsgesetz* relevant act; ~**e Unterlagen** *f pl* RECHT, VERWALT relevant documents, supporting documents

Sach-: **Sachdividende** *f* FINANZ commodity dividend, dividend payable in kind, property dividend

Sache *f* GESCHÄFT business, matter; ♦ **zur ~ kommen** GESCHÄFT talk business; **einer ~ den letzten Schliff geben** GESCHÄFT put the final touch to sth; **einer ~ von Nutzen** GESCHÄFT a benefit to sth; **die ~ spricht für sich selbst** GESCHÄFT res ipsa loquitur; **einer ~ zustimmen** GESCHÄFT put one's seal to sth

Sach-: **Sachentlohnung** *f* GESCHÄFT payment in kind; **Sachfehler** *m* GESCHÄFT factual error; **Sachgebiet** *nt* GESCHÄFT, PERSON area of expertise, subject area; **Sachhilfe** *f* FINANZ, VW *Entwicklungsländer* aid in kind; **Sachinvestition** *f* BANK real investment; **Sachkapital** *nt* VW nonmonetary capital, real capital; **Sachkenntnis** *f* GESCHÄFT expertise

sachkundig *adj* GESCHÄFT expert, informed; ~**e Entscheidung** *f* MGMNT informed decision

Sach-: **Sachlage** *f* GESCHÄFT circumstances; **Sachleistung** *f* GESCHÄFT allowance in kind, benefit in kind, payment in kind, PERSON, STEUER benefit in kind, VERSICH allowance in kind, benefit in kind, payment in kind, VW noncash benefit, noncash contribution, payment in kind; **Sachleistungsobligation** *f* FINANZ payment-in-kind bond (*PIK bond*)

sachlich *adj* GESCHÄFT, RECHT objective, *auf Tatsachen beruhend* factual, *zur Sache gehörig* pertinent

Sach-: **Sachlieferung** *f* GESCHÄFT performance in kind; **Sachmangel** *m* RECHT *Vertragsrecht* defect, redhibitory defect; **Sachmängelhaftung** *f* RECHT liability for material defects, warranty of quality; **Sachregister** *nt* VERWALT subject index; **Sachschaden** *m* GRUND property damage; **Sachverhalt** *m* GESCHÄFT circumstances, RECHT *Tatumstände* res gestae, statement of affairs; **Sachverhalt** *m* **für ein Zwischenurteil** RECHT special case; **Sachvermögen** *nt* VW nonfinancial assets, tangible wealth; **Sachversicherer** *m* VERSICH property insurer; **Sachversicherung** *f* VERSICH business insurance; **Sachverstand** *m* GESCHÄFT expertise, PERSON *Einstufung des intellektuellen Niveaus* analytical training

sachverständig: ~**er Zeuge** *m*, ~**e Zeugin** *f* RECHT expert witness

Sach-: **Sachverständige(r)** *mf* [decl. as adj] GESCHÄFT expert, GRUND appraiser; **Sachverständigenrat** *m* **für Wirtschaftsfragen** VW Council of Economic Advisers (*CEA*); **Sachwalter, in** *m,f* RECHT person supervising debtor's transactions during composition proceedings, creditors' trustee

Sachwert *m* FINANZ intrinsic value, GESCHÄFT physical asset, tangible asset, STEUER asset value, VW intrinsic value; ♦ **in Sachwerten** GESCHÄFT in kind; **in Sachwerten bezahlen** FINANZ pay in kind

Sackleinwand *f* TRANSP tow cloth

Safe *m oder nt* BANK safety deposit box, safe; **Safemiete** *f* BANK safe deposit fee

Saison- *in cpds* GESCHÄFT seasonal; **Saisonabhängigkeit** *f* **der Nachfrage** VW seasonality of demand; **Saisonabschluß** *m* GESCHÄFT tail end of the season

saisonal *adj* GESCHÄFT seasonal; ~ **angeglichener Preis** *m* FINANZ seasonally-adjusted figure; ~**er Faktor** *m* VW seasonal factor

Saison-: **Saisonarbeiter, in** *m,f* PERSON seasonal worker

saisonbedingt *adj* GESCHÄFT seasonal; ~**e Arbeitslosigkeit** *f* PERSON seasonal unemployment; ~**e Konzentration** *f* V&M seasonal concentration

saisonbereinigt *adj* FINANZ, GESCHÄFT, PERSON, VW seasonally adjusted; **nicht** ~**e Beschäftigungsziffer** *f* PERSON, VW seasonally-unadjusted employment figure; ~**er Preis** *m* FINANZ seasonally-adjusted figure; ~**e Zahl** *f* FINANZ seasonally-adjusted figure

Saison-: **Saisonbereinigung** *f* FINANZ, GESCHÄFT, PERSON, VW seasonal adjustment; **Saisonbewegung** *f* VW seasonal fluctuation; **Saisonkredit** *m* BANK seasonal loan; **Saisonsatz** *m* V&M seasonal rate; **Saisonschlußverkauf** *m* V&M end-of-season sale; **Saisonschwankung** *f* VW seasonal fluctuation, seasonal variation

säkular: ~**e Stagnationstheorie** *f* VW theory of secular stagnation; ~**er Trend** *m* VW secular trend

Saldenanerkenntnis *f* RECHNUNG reconciliation statement

Saldenausgleich *m* BANK settlement of balance

Saldenbuch *nt* FINANZ, RECHNUNG balance book

Saldenstandausweis *m* BANK clearing balance statement

saldieren *vt* BANK, FINANZ, RECHNUNG balance, settle; ♦ **etw mit etw** ~ GESCHÄFT balance sth with sth

Saldo *m* BANK account balance, RECHNUNG account balance, balance of account, bottom line; ~ **nicht aufgliederbarer Transaktionen** VW errors and omissions; ~ **zu ihren Gunsten** BANK balance in your favor (*AmE*), balance in your favour (*BrE*); ~ **statistisch nicht aufgliederbarer Transaktionen** VW accommodating items; ♦ **per** ~ GESCHÄFT net, on balance; **einen ~ von etw ausweisen** RECHNUNG show a balance of sth

Saldo: **Saldovortrag** *m* FINANZ, RECHNUNG balance brought down (*b/d.*), balance brought forward (*b/f*), balance carried forward (*b/f*), carry-over

Sammel- *in cpds* GESCHÄFT, TRANSP collective, general, bulk, consolidated; **Sammelauftrag** *m* GESCHÄFT bulk order; **Sammelbediener, in** *m,f* IMP/EXP, TRANSP groupage operator; **Sammelbestellung** *f* GESCHÄFT joint order, collective order, VW multicopy order; **Sammelbuch** *nt* RECHNUNG general journal; **Sammelbuchung** *f* VERWALT compound entry; **Sammelfinanzierung** *f* FINANZ block funding; **Sammelfrachtdienst** *m* TRANSP consolidated cargo service (*CCS*); **Sammelgut-Container-Service** *m* TRANSP consolidated-cargo container service; **Sammelgut-Service** *m* TRANSP consolidated cargo service (*CCS*); **Sammeljournal** *nt* RECHNUNG general journal; **Sammelkonto** *nt* RECHNUNG control account, controlling account

Sammelladung *f* IMP/EXP groupage, TRANSP consolidation, groupage, mixed consignment; **Sammelladungsagent, in** *m,f* TRANSP groupage agent; **Sammelladungsdepot** *nt* TRANSP groupage depot; **Sammelladungsfrachtrate** *f* TRANSP groupage rate; **Sammelladungsimporteur, in** *m,f* PERSON import groupage operator; **Sammelladungskonnossement** *nt* IMP/EXP, TRANSP groupage bill of lading

Sammel-: **Sammellager** *nt* TRANSP consolidation depot; **Sammellieferung** *f* TRANSP multi-delivery; **Sammelmappe** *f* VERWALT loose-leaf binder

sammeln *vt* RECHNUNG compile

Sammeln *nt*: **~ alter Aktien und Wertpapiere** BÖRSE scripophily

Sammel-: **Sammelobjekt** *nt* GESCHÄFT collectible; **Sammelplatz** *m* GESCHÄFT rallying point; **Sammelposition** *f* VERWALT compound item; **Sammelpunkt** *m* GESCHÄFT rallying point; **Sammeltarif** *m* GESCHÄFT blanket rate; **Sammeltransportkonnossement** *nt* **des Spediteurs** GESCHÄFT freight forwarder's combined transport bill of lading; **Sammelverpackung** *f* TRANSP composite packaging; **Sammelversicherungsschein** *m* VERSICH comprehensive policy

Sammlung *f* RECHNUNG compilation; **~** *f* **von Informationen für Elektronikartikel** GESCHÄFT electronic news gathering

Sample *nt* MATH sample

sämtlich *adj* RECHT all; **~e Einzelheiten** *f pl* GESCHÄFT full particulars

Sand: **~ ins Getriebe streuen** *phr* GESCHÄFT, VW throw a spanner in the works

Sandwich: **Sandwich-Leasing** *nt* GRUND *mittlere Lage zwischen zwei anderen Grundstücken* sandwich lease (*infrml*)

sanft: **~e Landung** *f* VW soft landing; **~e Technologie** *f* UMWELT soft technology, VW small-scale technology, soft technology

sanieren *vt* FINANZ restructure, GRUND redevelop, UMWELT rehabilitate, VW redevelop, refloat, *Unternehmen* restructure

Sanierung *f* FINANZ capital reconstruction, financial adjustment, financial restructuring, restructuring, GRUND redevelopment, UMWELT *von Deponien* rehabilitation, VW *eines Unternehmens* recapitalization,

rehabilitation, reorganization, restructuring, redevelopment; **Sanierungsanleihe** *f* **für Notfälle** FINANZ emergency reconstruction loan (*ERL*); **Sanierungsbilanz** *f* VW recapitalization balance sheet; **Sanierungsgewinne** *m pl* VW recapitalization gains

Sankt-Florians-Prinzip *nt* POL, UMWELT NIMBY principle

Sanktion *f* RECHT, VW sanction

sanktionieren *vt* GESCHÄFT sanction

Satellit *m* COMP, KOMM, MEDIEN satellite; **Satellitenfernsehen** *nt* MEDIEN satellite television; **Satellitenkommunikation** *f* KOMM satellite communications; **Satellitenrechner** *m* COMP satellite computer; **Satellitenstadt** *f* GRUND overspill town, satellite town; **Satellitenverbindung** *f* KOMM satellite communication; **Satellitenverkehr** *m* KOMM satellite communications; **Satellitübertragung** *f* MEDIEN satellite broadcasting

Satisfaktion *f* RECHT amends

Sattel- *in cpds* GESCHÄFT, TRANSP, VW saddle; **Sattelauflieger** *m* TRANSP semi-trailer; **Sattelpunkt** *m* VW saddle point

sättigen *vt* V&M, VW *Markt* saturate

Sättigung *f* V&M, VW saturation, VW absorption; **Sättigungsgüter** *nt pl* VW inferior goods; **Sättigungskampagne** *f* V&M saturation campaign; **Sättigungspunkt** *m* V&M saturation point, VW saturation point, absorption point; **den Sättigungspunkt erreichen** *phr* GESCHÄFT reach saturation point

Satz *m* COMP typesetting, FINANZ, VW rate; **ein ~ Wechsel** *m* FINANZ bills in a set, set of bills; ◆ **in Sätzen von** GESCHÄFT in sets of

Satz: **Satzaufbaufehlermeldung** *f* COMP syntax error message; **Satzfehler** *m* MEDIEN literal; **Satzhöhe** *f* COMP *Textdruck* page depth; **Satzkante** *f* MEDIEN *einer Seite* margin; **Satzkorrekutur** *f* MEDIEN mark-up; **Satzrand** *m* MEDIEN *einer Seite* margin; **Satzspiegel** *m* V&M type area; **Satztechnik** *f* GESCHÄFT *Druckereiwesen* typesetting

Satzung *f* BANK bylaw, RECHT articles of association (*BrE*), articles of incorporation (*AmE*) *einer Gesellschaft* memoranda and articles, memoranda and articles of association (*BrE*)

satzungsgemäß *adj* RECHT by statute; **nicht ~** *adj* RECHT *nicht gesetzlich bestimmt* nonstatutory

satzungsmäßig: **~e Gewinnverteilung** *f* RECHNUNG statutory appropriation

Satzvorbereitung *f* MEDIEN mark-up

sauber *adj* GESCHÄFT clean; **~er Ballasttank** *m* IMP/EXP, TRANSP clean ballast tank; **~er Befundbericht** *m* TRANSP clean report of findings; **~es Floaten** *nt* VW clean float; **~e Technologie** *f* UMWELT clean technology; **~e Unterschrift** *f* GESCHÄFT clean signature

sauer: **saurer Niederschlag** *m* UMWELT *Schnee, Hagel, Nebel* acid precipitation; **saurer Regen** *m* UMWELT acid rain

Säuglingssterblichkeit *f* GESCHÄFT, SOZIAL infant mortality

Saugpost *f* VERWALT absorbent paper

Säule- *in cpds* MATH bar; **Säulendiagramm** *nt* MATH bar chart, bar graph; **Säulenschaubild** *nt* MATH bar chart, bar graph

säumig *adj* FINANZ, GESCHÄFT, RECHT defaulting, delinquent, in default; **~e Partei** *f* RECHT *Vertragsrecht* defaulting party, party in default; **~er Zahler** *m* FINANZ dilatory payer, slow payer

Säumnis *f* FINANZ default, delay, delinquency; **Säumnisurteil** *nt* RECHT default judgment

Säureablagerung *f* UMWELT acid deposit

Sauregurkenzeit *f* infrml GESCHÄFT slack season, MEDIEN dead season, silly season (*BrE*)

Say: **~sches Theorem** *nt* VW Say's law

SBB abbr (*Schweizerische Bundesbahn*) TRANSP Swiss Federal Railways, ≈ BR (*British Rail*)

SB-Bankautomat *m* BANK, FINANZ automated teller machine (*ATM*), automatic telling machine (*ATM*), automatic teller

scannen *vt* COMP *elektronisch* scan

Scannen *nt* COMP scanning

Scanner *m* COMP scanner

Schablone *f* COMP, GESCHÄFT, IND template; ◆ **in ~ halten** vw *die Preise* hold in check

Schachtelprivileg *nt* STEUER affiliation privilege, intercorporate privilege (*AmE*)

Schachtelung *f* COMP, TRANSP nesting

Schaden *m* PATENT, RECHT damage, VERSICH claim, damage; **~ ohne Rechtsverletzung** GESCHÄFT damnum sine injuria; **Schäden** *m pl* **durch wiederholte Belastung** PERSON repetitive strain injury (*RSI*); ◆ **zum ~ von** GESCHÄFT to the detriment of; **~ abschätzen** GESCHÄFT appraise damages; **einen ~ decken** FINANZ cover a loss; **~ erleiden** vw suffer damage; **~ nehmen** vw suffer damage; **einen ~ regulieren** VERSICH adjust a claim; **~ taxieren** GESCHÄFT appraise damages; **jdm Schäden bis zu £10.000 zugestehen** VERSICH award sb £10,000 damages

Schaden: **Schadenabteilung** *f* VERSICH claims department; **Schadenabwicklung** *f* VERSICH claim settlement; **Schadenakte** *f* VERSICH claims file; **Schadenbearbeitungskosten** *pl* VERSICH claims expenses; **Schadenbearbeitungsverfahren** *nt* VERSICH claims procedure; **Schadenbetrag** *m* VERSICH amount of damage, amount of loss; **Schadenbeweis** *m* RECHT, VERSICH proof of loss; **Schadendurchschnitt** *m* VERSICH average claim;

Schadenexzedent *m* VERSICH excess of loss; **Schadenexzedentenrückversicherung** *f* VERSICH excess of loss reinsurance; **Schadenexzedentenrückversicherungsvertrag** *m* VERSICH excess of loss reinsurance treaty

Schaden: **Schadenfestsetzung** *f* VERSICH adjustment; **Schadenfeuer** *nt* VERSICH hostile fire; **Schadenfreiheitsrabatt** *m* VERSICH no-claims bonus (*BrE*); **Schadenhaftung** *f* RECHT *Vertragsrecht* liability for damage; **Schadenhöhe** *f* VERSICH amount of loss, extent of damage; **Schadenmeldeformular** *nt* VERSICH claim form; **Schadenminderungskosten** *pl* VERSICH *Seeversicherung* sue and labor charges (*AmE*), sue and labour charges (*BrE*); **Schadennachlaufproblem** *nt* VERSICH long tail risk; **Schadennachweis** *m* RECHT, VERSICH proof of loss; **Schadenquote** *f* VERSICH loss ratio; **Schadenregulierer** *m* GESCHÄFT assessor, VERSICH assessor, claims adjuster

Schadenregulierung *f* VERSICH claim settlement, claims adjustment, claims settlement; **Schadenregulierungsfonds** *m* VERSICH claims settlement fund; **Schadenregulierungsklausel** *f* VERSICH adjustment

clause; **Schadenregulierungskosten** *pl* VERSICH claims expenses, loss adjustment expense

Schaden: **Schadenreserve** *f* VERSICH claims reserve; **Schadenrückstellung** *f* VERSICH claims reserve; **Schadensabschätzung** *f* VERSICH appraisal of damage; **Schadensabwendung** *f* **und Schadensminderung** *f* VERSICH sue and labor (*AmE*), sue and labour (*BrE*); **Schadensachverständige(r)** *mf* [decl. as adj] PERSON loss adjuster; **Schadensaufmachung** *f* VERSICH average adjustment, average statement; **Schadensaufnahme** *f* VERSICH damage report; **Schadensbearbeitung** *f* VERSICH claims procedure, claims handling; **Schadensbeauftrage(r)** *mf* [decl. as adj] PERSON *Versicherungswesen* claims handler, claims inspector; **Schadensbegleichung** *f* VERSICH claims payment; **Schadensbegrenzung** *f* GESCHÄFT damage limitation; **Schadensbericht** *m* VERSICH damage report

Schadensersatz *m* GESCHÄFT compensation in damages, RECHT damages, *Vertragsrecht* compensation for damage, VERSICH reparation for damage; ◆ **~ fordern** RECHT, VERSICH claim compensation; **~ leisten** VERSICH indemnify; **~ verlangen** RECHT claim ~ **zahlen** PATENT compensate sb for sth, VERSICH award damages

Schadensersatz: **Schadensersatzanspruch** *m* RECHT *Vertragsrecht* claim for damages, claim of compensation, damage claim, VERSICH claim for compensation; **Schadensersatzansprüche stellen** *phr* RECHT claim damages; **Schadensersatzerlangung** *f* RECHT *Vertragsrecht* recovery of damage; **Schadensersatzerwirkung** *f* RECHT *Vertragsrecht* recovery of damage; **eine Schadensersatzforderung einreichen** *phr* RECHT file a claim for damages; **Schadensersatzklage** *f* RECHT action for damages, *bei übler Nachrede* action for libel, VERSICH action for damages; **Schadensersatzleistungen** *f pl* GESCHÄFT, KOMM, POL compensatory financing; **Schadensersatzvereinbarung** *f* VW compensation agreement; **Schadensersatzvertrag** *m* RECHT, VERSICH contract of indemnity; **Schadensersatzzahlung** *f* VERSICH reparation for damage

Schaden: **Schadensfall** *m* VERSICH claim

schadensfrei *adj* GESCHÄFT, VERSICH free of damage (*fod*)

Schaden: **Schadensgutachter** *m* GESCHÄFT, VERSICH assessor; **Schadenshöhe** *f* VERSICH amount of loss; **Schadensminderung** *f* RECHT mitigation of damages; **Schadenspauschalierung** *f* RECHT *Vertragsrecht* liquidated damage; **Schadensregulierer** *m* VERSICH adjustment bureau (*AmE*), average adjuster (*AA*); **Schadenssachbearbeiter, in** *m,f* VERSICH claims adjuster; **Schadensschätzung** *f* VERSICH appraisal of damage; **Schadensstifter, in** *m,f* RECHT tort feasor; **Schadenstufe** *f* VERSICH degree of damage; **Schadensumme** *f* VERSICH amount of damage, amount of loss; **Schadensursache** *f* GESCHÄFT cause of loss; **Schadens- und Verlustersatz** *m* VERSICH compensation for loss or damage; **Schadenteilungsabkommen** *nt* VERSICH knock-for-knock; **Schadenumfang** *m* VERSICH extent of damage; **Schadenversicherung** *f* VERSICH casualty insurance, indemnity insurance; **Schadenzahlung** *f* VERSICH claims payment; **Schadenzahlungen** *f pl* GESCHÄFT, KOMM, POL, VERSICH compensatory financing

schädigen *vt* GESCHÄFT, VW *Währungskaufkraft* impair

Schädigung f RECHT, VERSICH damage, detriment, impairment

schädlich adj GESCHÄFT detrimental, harmful, prejudicial; **~e Auswirkung** f RECHT detrimental effect, harmful effect; **~es Gas** nt UMWELT noxious gas; **~e Konsumgüter** nt pl **und Dienstleistungen** f pl vw illth

Schadloshaltung f RECHT, VERSICH indemnification, indemnity; **Schadloshaltungsklausel** f RECHT Vertrag hold-harmless clause; **Schadloshaltungsvereinbarung** f RECHT hold-harmless agreement (AmE)

Schadstoff m UMWELT pollutant; **Schadstoffausstoß** m UMWELT car exhaust emissions; **Schadstoffbekämpfung** f IND, POL, UMWELT pollution control; **Schadstoffkontrolle** f IND, POL, UMWELT pollution control

schaffen vt GESCHÄFT Möglichkeiten create, infrml Erfolg haben pull off (infrml); ◆ **etw ~** GESCHÄFT succeed

Schaffung f GESCHÄFT creation, PERSON making; **~ von Arbeitsplätzen** PERSON job creation

Schäkel m TRANSP shackle

Schall- in cpds KOMM, UMWELT sound; **Schallabgabe** f UMWELT noise emission; **Schalldämmung** f KOMM, UMWELT sound insulation; **Schallschutz** m KOMM, UMWELT sound insulation

Schalt- in cpds COMP switching

Schalten nt COMP switching

Schalter m COMP switch, GESCHÄFT counter, window; **Schalterstunden** f pl BANK banking hours

Schalt-: **Schaltfläche** f COMP Microsoft push button; **Schaltjahr** nt GESCHÄFT leap year; **Schaltkreis** m COMP circuit; **Schalttafel** f COMP switchboard

Schank- in cpds RECHT bar; **Schankerlaubnis** f RECHT publican's licence (BrE); **Schankgesetze** nt pl RECHT licensing laws; **Schankwirtschaft** f RECHT licensed premises (BrE)

scharf: **~ ansteigen** phr GESCHÄFT Preis shoot up, skyrocket, soar; **~ kalkuliert** phr V&M with a low margin; **~ kalkulierter Preis** n V&M keen price; **~e Konkurrenz** f GESCHÄFT tough competition; **~er Wettbewerb** m GESCHÄFT stiff competition, bitter competition, vw stiff competition; **in ~em Wettbewerb** phr vw in close competition

Schatten m GESCHÄFT, POL, VW shadow; **Schattenkabinett** nt POL shadow cabinet (BrE); **Schattenpreis** m BANK accounting price, RECHNUNG shadow price; **Schattenwirtschaft** f vw black economy, cash economy, hidden economy, informal economy, moonlight economy, parallel market economy, second economy, shadow economy, underground economy

Schattierung f COMP shading

Schätz- in cpds MATH, VERSICH estimating, estimation, appraised, estimated

Schatz m GESCHÄFT treasure; **Schatzamt** nt FINANZ, POL treasury, vw Her Majesty's Treasury (BrE), Treasury, Department of the Treasury (AmE), the Exchequer (BrE) (Exch.); **Schatzanweisung** f FINANZ Exchequer bond (BrE), treasury note (AmE)

schätzbar adj GESCHÄFT appreciable, assessable, rateable

Schatzbriefe m pl BÖRSE, FINANZ National Savings

schätzen vt GESCHÄFT appraise, Projekt appreciate, value, estimate, guesstimate (infrml), GRUND appraise, STEUER veranlagen assess; ◆ **jdn hoch ~** GESCHÄFT have a high regard for sb

Schätzer m GESCHÄFT assessor, estimator, valuer, GRUND appraiser, VERSICH assessor

Schätz-: **Schätzfunktion** f MATH estimator; **Schätzgleichung** f MATH estimating equation

Schatz: **Schatzkanzler** m FINANZ, POL, VW Chancellor of the Exchequer (BrE), Secretary of the Treasury (AmE); **Schatzkanzler** m **im Schattenkabinett** m POL shadow chancellor (BrE); **Schatzobligation** f FINANZ Treasury bond (AmE)

Schätz-: **Schätzpreis** m BÖRSE estimated price; **Schätzstichproben** f pl MATH estimation sampling

Schätzung f GESCHÄFT appraisal, estimation, projection, GRUND apportionment, appraisement, valuation, STEUER assessment; **zu hohe ~** FINANZ, RECHNUNG, vw overestimate; ◆ **nach niedrigster ~** GESCHÄFT at the lowest estimate

Schätzungen f pl GESCHÄFT estimates

Schatzwechsel m BANK bill, FINANZ Treasury bill (AmE) (T-bill), bill; **~ mit drei-monatiger Laufzeit** FINANZ Treasury bill (AmE) (T-bill)

Schätz-: **Schätzwert** m MATH ballpark figure (infrml), VERSICH appraised value, estimated value, **Schätzwerte** m pl FINANZ estimates

Schau- in cpds GESCHÄFT display, show; **Schaubild** nt GESCHÄFT chart, graph

Schauermann m PERSON hatchman, stevedore (stvdr), TRANSP stevedore (stvdr)

Schaufenster nt GESCHÄFT window, V&M shop window, shop front; **Schaufensterauslage** f GESCHÄFT window display, V&M display, window display; **Schaufensterbummel** m GESCHÄFT window-shopping; **Schaufensterdekoration** f GESCHÄFT, V&M window-dressing; **Schaufensterplakat** nt GESCHÄFT window bill; **Schaufensterscheibe** f V&M shop window

Schau-: **Schaukasten** m V&M showcase; **Schaupackung** f V&M display pack

Scheck m BANK check (AmE), cheque (BrE); **~ ohne ausreichende Deckung** BANK not sufficient funds check (AmE), not sufficient funds cheque (BrE); **~ ohne Deckung** BANK uncovered check (AmE), uncovered cheque (BrE); **~ zugunsten Dritter** m BANK third-party check (AmE), third-party cheque (BrE); ◆ **einen ~ ausstellen** BANK raise a check (AmE), raise a cheque (BrE), draw a check (AmE), draw a cheque (BrE), write out a check (AmE), write out a cheque (BrE); **einen ~ auf jdn ausstellen** BANK make a check payable to sb (AmE), make a cheque payable to sb (BrE); **einen ~ durchkreuzen** BANK cross a check (AmE), cross a cheque (BrE); **einen ~ einlösen** vt BANK cash a check (AmE), cash a cheque (BrE); **einen ~ nicht einlösen** BANK dishonor a check (AmE), dishonour a cheque (BrE); **einen ~ zur Einlösung vorlegen** BANK present a check for payment (AmE), present a cheque for payment (BrE); **~ in Höhe von** BANK check in the amount of (AmE), cheque to the amount of (BrE); **einen ~ kreuzen** BANK cross a check (AmE), cross a cheque (BrE); **einen ~ zur Verrechnung austellen** BANK cross a check (AmE), cross a cheque (BrE); **einen ~ zur Zahlung vorlegen** BANK present a check for payment (AmE), present a cheque for payment (BrE); **~ zugunsten von jdm** BANK check in favor of sb (AmE), cheque in favour of sb (BrE)

Scheck: **Scheckabschnitt** m BANK check stub (AmE), cheque stub (BrE), check counterfoil (AmE), cheque counterfoil (*BrE*); **Scheckanforderungsformular** *nt* RECHNUNG check requisition (*AmE*), cheque requisition (*BrE*); **Scheckausgabe** *f* BANK, FINANZ check issue (*AmE*), cheque issue (*BrE*); **Scheckausgangsbuch** *nt* BANK, RECHNUNG check register (*AmE*), cheque register (*BrE*)

Scheckausstellung *f* BANK, FINANZ check issue (*AmE*), cheque issue (*BrE*); **Scheckausstellungsgerät** *nt* BANK check-writer machine (*AmE*), cheque-writer machine (*BrE*); **Scheckausstellungsmaschine** *f* BANK check-writer machine (*AmE*), cheque-writer machine (*BrE*)

Scheck: **Scheckbuch** *nt* BANK check book (*AmE*), cheque book (*BrE*); **Scheckeinlösungssystem** *nt* BANK check payment system (*AmE*), cheque payment system (*BrE*); **Scheckfälschung** *f* BANK check forgery (*AmE*), cheque forgery (*BrE*); **Scheckformular** *nt* BANK check form (*AmE*), cheque form (*BrE*), blank check (*AmE*), blank cheque (*BrE*); **Scheckheft** *nt* BANK check book (*AmE*), cheque book (*BrE*); **Scheckkarte** *f* BANK bank card, banker's card, check card (*AmE*), cheque card (*BrE*); **Scheckkodiermaschine** *f* BANK, FINANZ check writer (*AmE*), check writer machine (*AmE*), cheque writer (*BrE*), cheque writer machine (*BrE*); **Scheckkonto** *nt* BANK checking account (*AmE*) (*C/A*), cheque account (*BrE*) (*C/A*), current account (*BrE*); **Scheckkredit** *m* BANK check credit (*AmE*), cheque credit (*BrE*); **Scheckliste** *f* BANK, RECHNUNG check register (*AmE*), cheque register (*BrE*); **Scheckreiterei** *f* BANK check kiting (*AmE*), cheque kiting (*BrE*); **Scheckschreibmaschine** *f* FINANZ check writer machine (*AmE*), cheque writer machine (*BrE*); **Scheckschutzgerät** *nt* BANK check protector (*AmE*), cheque protector (*BrE*); **Scheckschutzmaschine** *f* BANK check protector (*AmE*), cheque protector (*BrE*); **Schecksicherungsgerät** *nt* BANK check protector (*AmE*), cheque protector (*BrE*); **Schecksperre** *f* FINANZ check embargo (*AmE*), stop order, stopping of a cheque (*BrE*); **Scheckverrechnung** *f* BANK check clearing (*AmE*), cheque clearing (*BrE*); **Scheckverrechnungssystem** *nt* BANK check-clearing system (*AmE*), cheque-clearing system (*BrE*); **Scheckvordruck** *m* BANK check form (*AmE*), cheque form (*BrE*); **Scheckzahlung** *f* BANK check payment (*AmE*), cheque payment (*BrE*)

Schedulensteuer *f* STEUER schedular tax (*BrE*)

scheffeln *vt infrml* GESCHÄFT rake in (*infrml*)

Scheidemünze *f* BANK token coin

Schein *m* BANK, FINANZ *Geld* note (*BrE*), bill (*AmE*), KOMM advice, TRANSP ticket

Schein- *in cpds* GESCHÄFT quasi-, illusory, bogus, sham; **Scheinaktienoption** *f* BÖRSE phantom share option

scheinbar: **~ einwandfreier Besitztitel** *m* GRUND color of title (*AmE*), colour of title (*BrE*); **~ einwandfreier Rechtstitel** *m* GRUND color of title (*AmE*), colour of title (*BrE*); **~ unabhängiger Kandidat** *m*, **~ unabhängige Kandidatin** *f* POL captive candidate; ♦ **~ als** GESCHÄFT deemed to be

Schein-: **Scheinfirma** *f* GESCHÄFT bogus firm, *Übungsfirma für Ausbildung* paper company (*infrml*), street name; **Scheingeschäft** *nt* BÖRSE wash sale, FINANZ sham transaction, RECHT *Vertragsrecht* fictitious transaction, fictitious bargain; **Scheingesellschaft** *f* RECHT *Vertragsrecht* dummy corporation, VW ostensible company; **Scheingewinn** *m* FINANZ illusory profit; **Scheinhandel** *m* BÖRSE sham trading;

Scheinkäufer, in *m,f* V&M mystery shopper (*jarg*); **Scheinproblem** *nt* VW pseudo-problem; **Scheinunabhängigkeit** *f* GESCHÄFT quasi-independence; **Scheinvariable** *f* VW dummy variable; **Scheinverkauf** *m* VW simulated sale; **Scheinvollmacht** *f* RECHT apparent authority; **Scheinvorgang** *m* GESCHÄFT dummy activity

scheitern *vi* GESCHÄFT fail, *Plan* fall apart; **~ lassen** *vt* GESCHÄFT *Mission, Versuch* abort

Scheitern *nt* PERSON *von Verhandlungen* breakdown; **~ von Tarifverhandlungen** MGMNT, PERSON failure to agree (*FTA*)

Schema *nt* PATENT form

Schengen-Abkommen *nt* POL Schengen Agreement

Schenkung *f* RECHT, STEUER gift, donation; **~ in Erwartung des Todes** STEUER gift in contemplation of death; **~ zu Lebzeiten** STEUER lifetime gift (*BrE*), transfer of property inter vivos; **~ von Todes wegen** RECHT gift causa mortis, STEUER gift in contemplation of death; **~ unter Lebenden** RECHT gift inter vivos, STEUER lifetime gift (*BrE*), transfer of property inter vivos; **Schenkungsbeistand** *m* STEUER Gift Aid (*BrE*); **Schenkungshilfe** *f* STEUER Gift Aid (*BrE*); **Schenkungssteuer** *f* STEUER gift tax; **Schenkungsurkunde** *f* RECHT gift deed

Scherenheber *m* TRANSP scissor lift

Schicht *f* COMP layer, PERSON shift; **Schichtarbeit** *f* PERSON daywork, shiftwork; **Schichtarbeiter, in** *m,f* PERSON dayworker, shiftworker; **Schichtarbeit machen** *phr* PERSON work in shifts; **Schichtenpappe** *f* IND pasteboard

Schichtung *f* V&M stratification

Schicht: **Schichtwechsel** *m* PERSON shift rotation; **Schichtzuschlag** *m* PERSON shift differential

schicken *vt* GESCHÄFT *Bestellung* send in, IMP/EXP consign, KOMM dispatch, TRANSP dispatch, consign; ♦ **jdn nach etw ~** GESCHÄFT send sb for sth

Schickeria: **die ~** *f infrml* GESCHÄFT smart set

Schickschuld *f* RECHT *Vertragsrecht* obligation to be performed at the debtor's place of business

Schieber, in *m,f infrml* GESCHÄFT jobber (*AmE*), profiteer, racketeer, trafficker, spir (*infrml*)

Schied- *in cpds* GESCHÄFT, PERSON, RECHT arbitral; **Schiedsabkommen** *nt* GESCHÄFT, RECHT arbitration agreement; **Schiedsabrede** *f* GESCHÄFT, RECHT arbitration agreement; **Schiedsausschuß** *m* GESCHÄFT arbitration committee

Schiedsgericht *nt* GESCHÄFT arbitration tribunal, RECHT court of arbitration; **Schiedsgerichtshof** *m* GESCHÄFT arbitration tribunal; **Schiedsgerichtsklausel** *f* GESCHÄFT arbitration clause; **Schiedsgerichtsverfahren** *nt* IND arbitration, arbitration proceedings, PERSON *Rechtsstreit* arbitration

schiedsgerichtlich: **~ entscheiden** *phr* GESCHÄFT, PERSON, RECHT arbitrate

Schied-: **Schiedsklausel** *f* GESCHÄFT arbitration clause; **Schiedsrichter, in** *m,f* GESCHÄFT adjudicator, awarder, RECHT *Schiedsgericht* arbitrator, referee, arbiter; **Schiedsspruch** *m* PERSON arbitral award, RECHT award; **Schiedsstelle** *f* BÖRSE, GESCHÄFT arbitration board; **Schiedsvereinbarung** *f* GESCHÄFT, RECHT arbitration agreement; **Schiedsverfahren** *nt* IND, PERSON *Rechtsstreit* arbitration, arbitration proceedings; **Schiedsvertrag** *m* GESCHÄFT arbitration agreement schief: ~e **Häufigkeitskurve** f MATH skewed frequency curve

Schiefe f MATH *einer Verteilung* skewness

Schiene: **Schienenkopf** m TRANSP railhead; **Schienennetz** nt TRANSP railroad network (*AmE*), railway network (*BrE*), railroad system (*AmE*), railway system (*BrE*); **Schienenverkehr** m TRANSP rail traffic

Schiff nt MEDIEN *Druck* galley, TRANSP ship, vessel; **jedes ~** VERSICH any one vessel (*AOV*); ♦ **ab ~** IMP/EXP, TRANSP ex ship (*x-ship*); **das ~ aufgeben** TRANSP abandon ship

Schiffahrt f IMP/EXP, KOMM, TRANSP shipping; **Schiffahrtsgesetzgebung** f RECHT navigation laws; **Schiffahrtskommission** f **der Vereinigten Staaten** TRANSP United States Maritime Commission (*USMC*); **Schiffahrtskonferenz** f TRANSP conference line; **Schiffahrtslinie** f TRANSP shipping line; **Schiffahrtsministerium** nt TRANSP *Teil des US-Verkehrsministeriums* Maritime Administration (*AmE*) (*MARAD*); **Schiffahrtsplan** m TRANSP sailing schedule; **Schiffahrtsregister** f TRANSP register of shipping, shipping register; **Schiffahrtsroute** f TRANSP shipping lane; **Schiffahrtsweg** m TRANSP shipping lane

Schiff: **Schiffsagentur** f TRANSP shipping agency; **Schiffsankergrund** m TRANSP naval anchorage; **Schiffsankunftsmeldung** f IMP/EXP ship's inward report; **Schiffsaufgabe** f VERSICH abandonment; **Schiffsbau** m IND, TRANSP shipbuilding; **Schiffsbauer** m IND, TRANSP naval architect, shipbuilder; **Schiffsbauindustriegebiet** nt IND Maritime Industrial Development Area (*MIDA*); **Schiffsbauingenieur** m IND, TRANSP naval architect; **Schiffsbaumeister** m IND, TRANSP *Marinerang* naval architect; **Schiffsbelader** m TRANSP stevedore (*stvdr*); **Schiffsbrief** m TRANSP sea letter; **Schiffsdokumente** nt pl RECHT, TRANSP ship's papers; **Schiffseigner** in m,f IMP/EXP, TRANSP shipowner; **Schiffseignerhaftung** f RECHT, TRANSP, VERSICH *Schiffahrt* shipowner's liability (*SOL*); **Schiffseintragung** f TRANSP nautical registration; **Schiffsfrachtvertrag** m TRANSP, V&M contract of affreightment; **Schiffsingenieur, in** m,f PERSON *Schiffahrt* marine engineer; **Schiffskaskoversicherer** m VERSICH hull underwriter; **Schiffskaskoversicherung** f VERSICH hull insurance; **Schiffskonstruktion** f IND, TRANSP ship planning; **Schiffslieferschein** m IMP/EXP, TRANSP ship's delivery order; **Schiffsmakler, in** m,f IMP/EXP, TRANSP charter broker, chartering broker, shipbroker, shipping officer, vessel broker, shipping agent, VERSICH shipbroker; **Schiffsmakler und Spediteur** m IMP/EXP, PERSON, TRANSP shipping and forwarding agent (*S&FA*); **Schiffsmanagement** nt TRANSP ship management; **Schiffspapiere** nt pl RECHT, TRANSP ship's papers; **Schiffspaß** m TRANSP sea letter; **Schiffspfandrecht** nt RECHT maritime lien; **Schiffsplan** m TRANSP ship plan; **Schiffsraum** m TRANSP hold; **Schiffsregister** nt TRANSP Register Book; **Schiffsregisterbrief** m TRANSP certificate of registry; **Schiffsreise** f TRANSP passage; **Schiffsreling** f TRANSP ship's rail; **Schiffssonderprüfung** f **mit Datum** TRANSP *Schiffahrt* ship's special survey; **Schiffsspezifikation** f TRANSP ship specification; **Schiffstagebuch** nt TRANSP ship's log; **Schiffsüberfahrt** f TRANSP vessel crossing; **Schiffsüberführungsgebühr** f IMP/EXP address commission; **Schiffsumbau** m TRANSP ship conversion; **Schiffsveräußerungsklausel** f VERSICH sale of vessel clause; **Schiffsverkehr** m **zwischen fremden Ländern** TRANSP cross trade; **Schiffsverlust** m TRANSP craft loss (*c/l*); **Schiffsverwaltung** f TRANSP ship management; **Schiffszettel** m IMP/EXP, TRANSP shipping note (*S/N*); **Schiffszulassung** f TRANSP nautical registration; **Schiffumlaufzeit** f TRANSP ship turnaround time (*AmE*), ship turnround time (*BrE*); **Schiffverkehrsangebot** nt TRANSP vessel traffic services; **Schiffverkehrsmanagement** nt TRANSP vessel traffic management system

Schild nt GESCHÄFT nameplate, sign, *Etikett* label; ~ **mit gesammelten Daten** TRANSP consolidated data plate

Schilderung f RECHT representation

Schinderei f GESCHÄFT, POL hard graft

Schirmherr m FREI sponsor; **Schirmherrschaft** f FREI sponsorship; **die Schirmherrschaft übernehmen** phr [+gen] FREI sponsor

Schlachthof m GESCHÄFT abattoir, slaughterhouse

schlafend: ~e **Wirtschaft** f VW sleeping economy

Schlaf- in cpds FREI, TRANSP sleep, sleeping; **Schlafgemeinde** f PERSON bedroom community (*AmE*); **Schlafstadt** f PERSON dormitory suburb; **Schlafwagen** m TRANSP sleeper, sleeping car

Schlag: **Schlagbaumtheorem** nt VW turnpike theorem

schlagend: ~er **Beweis** m PATENT conclusive evidence

Schlag: **Schlagschere** f COMP *zum Durchtrennen der Papierperforation* burster; **Schlagzeile** f MEDIEN head, *Zeitung* headline, V&M catch line, VERWALT header; **Schlagzeilenwerbung** f V&M display advertising

Schlange f VW snake; ♦ ~ **stehen** GESCHÄFT queue (*BrE*), queue up (*BrE*), wait in line (*AmE*), stand in line (*AmE*)

schlau: ~er **Bürokrat** m POL mandarin

schlecht 1. adj GESCHÄFT *Qualität* bad, poor; ♦ **die ~e Lage zu spüren bekommen** VW feel the pinch (*infrml*); ~e **Presse haben** GESCHÄFT have a bad press; **2.** adv GESCHÄFT, PERSON, MGMNT badly, poorly; ♦ ~ **entlohnen** GESCHÄFT, PERSON underpay; ~ **verwalten** MGMNT mismanage

schlecht: ~e **Adressen** f pl VW marginal accounts; ~ **ausgeschossene Seite** f MEDIEN badly-imposed page; ~e **Führung** f MGMNT bad management; ~es **Geschäft** nt GESCHÄFT bad bargain, bad buy; ~e **Gesundheit** f GESCHÄFT ill health; ~er **Kauf** m GESCHÄFT bad bargain, bad buy; ~es **Management** nt MGMNT bad management; ~er **Ruf** m GESCHÄFT bad name, bad reputation, bad will; ~er **Service** m V&M poor service; ~e **Verwaltung** f MGMNT mismanagement

schlechter: ~ **bezahlt** adj PERSON lower-paid

Schlechterfüllung f RECHT *Vertragsrecht* defective performance, inferior performance, malperformance, misperformance

schlechtergestellt adj GESCHÄFT worse off

schlechthin adv GESCHÄFT, RECHT per se

Schleich- in cpds V&M, VW camouflaged, masked

schleichend: ~er **Ausgabenanstieg** m VERWALT outlay creep; ~e **Erhöhung** f **durch Heraufstufung** PERSON grade creep; ~e **Gehaltserhöhung** f PERSON grade drift; ~e **Inflation** f VW creeping inflation; ~e **Steuererhöhung** f VW tax-bracket creep; ~e **Übernahme** f BÖRSE creeping tender; ~es **Übernahmeangebot** nt FINANZ creeping tender

Schleich-: **Schleichwerbung** f MEDIEN plug (*infrml*),

V&M camouflaged advertising, plug (*infrml*), VW masked advertising

Schlemmeratlas *m* FREI good food guide

Schlepp- *in cpds* TRANSP drag, tow, towage, towing; **Schleppboot** *nt* TRANSP tug, tugboat; **Schleppeinrichtung** *f* TRANSP towing gear

schleppen *vt* TRANSP drag, tow, tug

Schleppen *nt* TRANSP dredging, towing

schleppend: **~er Absatz** *m* VW poor market

Schlepper *m* GESCHÄFT runner, TRANSP towboat, towing boat, V&M bagman (*infrml*) (*AmE*); **Schlepperführer** *m* TRANSP tugmaster

Schlepp-: **Schleppgebühr** *f* TRANSP towage charges, towage dues; **Schlepprollbock** *m* TRANSP towing dolly; **Schlepptau** *nt* TRANSP towing hawser, towline; **Schlepptrosse** *f* TRANSP towing hawser; **Schleppunternehmer** *m* TRANSP towage contractor; **Schleppzug** *m* TRANSP tow

Schleuderpreis *m* GESCHÄFT knockdown price

Schleuse- *in cpds* GESCHÄFT, TRANSP lock; **Schleusenhafen** *m* GESCHÄFT wet dock; **Schleusenkammer** *f* TRANSP lock chamber; **Schleusenkanal** *m* TRANSP lock canal

schlichten **1.** *vt* FINANZ conciliate, GESCHÄFT *Konflikt* settle, PERSON *Arbeitskonflikt* conciliate; **2.** *vi* PERSON *Arbeitsstreitigkeit* arbitrate, conciliate

Schlichter, in *m,f* PERSON conciliation officer (*BrE*), *bei Arbeitskonflikten* conciliator, RECHT arbiter

Schlichtung *f* GESCHÄFT *eines Streites* adjustment, IND arbitration, PERSON arbitrage, conciliation, VW mediation; **~ von Auseinandersetzungen** PERSON grievance arbitration; **~ von Lohnstreitigkeiten** PERSON wage arbitration; **Schlichtungsamt** *nt* GESCHÄFT arbitration board; **Schlichtungsausschuß** *m* BÖRSE, GESCHÄFT, IND, PERSON arbitration board, board of arbitration, conciliation board; **Schlichtungs- und Schiedskommission** *f* PERSON *australische Gewerkschaftsbewegung* Conciliation and Arbitration Commission; **Schlichtungsstelle** *f* BÖRSE, GESCHÄFT, IND, PERSON arbitration board, board of arbitration, conciliation board; **Schlichtungsvereinbarung** *f* VW reconciliation bill (*AmE*); **Schlichtungsverfahren** *nt* PERSON grievance procedure

schließen *vt* COMP *Datei* close, GESCHÄFT close down, shut down

Schließfach *nt* BANK safe-deposit box, GESCHÄFT left-luggage locker (*BrE*), KOMM post office box (*PO box*); **~ für Gepäckaufbewahrung** GESCHÄFT left-luggage locker (*BrE*)

Schließung *f* GESCHÄFT *Geschäft* closing down, closure, shutdown

Schlitz *m* MEDIEN slot; **Schlitzohr** *nt* jarg GESCHÄFT wheeler-dealer (*infrml*)

Schlot *m* IND smokestack

schludrig *adj* infrml GESCHÄFT slapdash, slipshod (*infrml*); ◆ **~ arbeiten** infrml GESCHÄFT skimp (*infrml*), scamp (*infrml*); **~e Arbeit leisten** GESCHÄFT skimp (*infrml*), scamp (*infrml*)

Schluß *m* GESCHÄFT *der Liste* tail, V&M final; **~ der Debatte** POL *Parlament* gag rule; ◆ **einen ~ ziehen** GESCHÄFT draw a conclusion

Schluß: **Schlußbestand** *m* RECHNUNG closing inventory, ending inventory; **Schlußbilanz** *f* RECHNUNG final

balance; **Schlußdividende** *f* FINANZ final dividend, VERSICH terminal bonus; **Schlußeinheit** *f* BÖRSE unit of trading; **Schlußeintrag** *m* RECHNUNG closing entry

Schlüssel *m* COMP *Ordnungsbegriff* key; **~ zur Arbeitsplatzbewertung** PERSON job-evaluation scale; **~ für gefährliche Chemikalien** TRANSP hazchem code; **Schlüsseldaten** *pl* GESCHÄFT key data

schlüsselfertig *adj* GESCHÄFT *Projekt*, IMP/EXP *Lieferklausel*, VW turnkey

Schlüssel: **Schlüsselfolge** *f* COMP *Datensuche* key sequence; **Schlüsselindustrie** *f* IND, VW basic industry, essential industry, key industry; **Schlüsselphase** *f* GESCHÄFT key stage; **Schlüsselwort** *nt* COMP *Datensuche* keyword; **Schlüsselwortsuche** *f* COMP keyword search

schlußfolgernd: **~es Denken** *nt* MGMNT deductive reasoning

Schlußfolgerung *f* GESCHÄFT, MGMNT conclusion; ◆ **über seine ~ berichten** GESCHÄFT report one's conclusions

Schluß: **Schlußformulierung** *f* **einer Rede** POL wrap-up (*AmE*); **Schlußkurs** *m* BÖRSE, FINANZ close, closing price, closing quotation; **Schlußnote** *f* BÖRSE bought note, purchase and sale statement (*P&S*), contract note; **Schlußnotierung** *f* BÖRSE closing price, closing quotation; **Schlußquote** *f* RECHNUNG liquidation dividend; **Schlußrechnung** *f* RECHNUNG final accounts; **Schlußschein** *m* BÖRSE bought note, purchase and sale statement (*P&S*), contract note; **Schlußtermin** *m* GESCHÄFT closing date; **Schlußverkauf** *m* GESCHÄFT end-of-season sale; **Schlußwert** *m* BÖRSE settlement price; **Schlußwort** *nt* MEDIEN, V&M *Epilog in der Werbung* tagline; **Schlußzeile** *f* V&M baseline

schmieren: **jdn ~** *phr* infrml GESCHÄFT grease sb's palm (*infrml*), oil sb's palm (*infrml*)

Schmiergeld *nt* FINANZ sweetener (*infrml*), GESCHÄFT boodle (*infrml*), bribe, payoff, bribery, POL graft (*infrml*), RECHT *Arbeitgeber-Arbeitnehmerverhältnis* kickback, TRANSP dirty money, VERWALT corporate pay off; ◆ **Schmiergelder annehmen** RECHT graft (*infrml*)

Schmiergeld: **Schmiergelderfonds** *m* FINANZ, POL slush fund

Schmöker *m* MEDIEN page-turner

Schmuck *m* GESCHÄFT jewelry (*AmE*), jewellery (*BrE*)

schmuggeln *vt* IMP/EXP, RECHT smuggle

Schmuggelware *f* IMP/EXP contraband articles, prohibited goods, contraband, RECHT smuggled goods

Schmuggler, in *m,f* IMP/EXP, RECHT smuggler

schmutzig: **~es Floaten** *nt* VW dirty floating; **~es Floating** *nt* VW managed floating system

Schmutztitel *m* MEDIEN bastard face

Schnäppchen *nt* GESCHÄFT bargain, V&M snip; **Schnäppchenjäger** *m* infrml V&M bargain hunter (*infrml*); **Schnäppchensucher** *m* infrml V&M bargain hunter (*infrml*)

Schneeballsystem *nt* V&M pyramid selling

Schneegürtel *m* IND, VW snowbelt (*AmE*)

Schneiderei *f* GESCHÄFT tailoring

schneidern *vt* GESCHÄFT tailor to

Schnell- *in cpds* GESCHÄFT fast, high-speed

schnell **1.** *adj* GESCHÄFT fast, quick, rapid, speedy; ◆ **die ~e Mark machen** infrml GESCHÄFT earn a fast buck (*infrml*); **2.** *adv* GESCHÄFT fast, speedily; ◆ ~ **Karriere machen** PERSON be on the fast track; ~ **vorankommen** GESCHÄFT make headway; **~es Wachstum erfahren** VW experience rapid growth; **so ~ wie möglich** TRANSP fast as can (*fac*); ~ **zunehmend** GESCHÄFT soaring

schnell: ~**er Anstieg** *m* BÖRSE fast rise; **sich sehr ~ entwickelnde Industrie** *f* IND runaway industry; ~**er Prämienverfall** *m* BÖRSE rapid premium decay; ~**er Pufferspeicher** *m* COMP cache storage, cache store; ~**er Rückgang** *m* BÖRSE fast decline; ~**er Umsatz** *m* FINANZ quick returns; ~**en Veränderungen unterworfene Industrie** *f* IND runaway industry; ~**er Verkauf** *m* GESCHÄFT quick sale

Schnell-: **Schnellberatung** *f* **am Telefon** COMP hotline; **Schnelldrucker** *m* COMP high-speed printer

schneller: ~ **werden** *vi* GESCHÄFT gather speed, speed up

Schnell-: **Schnellgang** *m* TRANSP overdrive; **Schnellgericht** *nt* SOZIAL fast food; **Schnellimbiß** *m* V&M fast food restaurant; **Schnellspeicher** *m* COMP high-speed memory; **Schnelltaste** *f* COMP hot key; **Schnell-Transit-System** *nt* TRANSP rapid transit system

schnellumschlagend: ~**e Ware** *f* V&M fast-moving consumer goods (*FMG*)

Schnell-: **Schnellverfahren** *nt* GESCHÄFT expedited procedure, summary proceedings

schnellwachsend *adj* VW fast-growing; ~**e Inflation** *f* VW spiralling inflation

Schnittstelle *f* COMP *EDV-Systeme, Geräte*, GESCHÄFT interface

Schnüffler *m* GESCHÄFT muckraker

schnurlos *adj* KOMM *Telefon* cordless; ~**e digitale Fernsprechverbindungen** *f* *pl* KOMM cordless digital telecommunications; ~**es Telefon** *nt* KOMM cordless telephone, mobile phone, mobile telephone

Schockinflation *f* VW shock inflation

Schöffe *m* RECHT juror

Schöffen *m* *pl* RECHT jury

Schöffengericht *nt* RECHT jury

Schöffin *f* RECHT juror

Schoner *m* TRANSP *Schiffahrt* schooner

schönfärben *vt* GESCHÄFT whitewash (*infrml*)

Schönheitsreparaturen *f* *pl* GRUND home improvement

Schönschrift *f* COMP *Drucker* letter quality (*LQ*), letter-quality font; **Schönschriftdrucker** *m* COMP letter-quality printer, near-letter-quality printer

schöpferisch: ~**es Marketing** *nt* V&M creative marketing

Schornstein *m* IND smokestack; **Schornsteinindustrie** *f* GESCHÄFT, IND smokestack industry

Schott *nt* TRANSP bulkhead

Schraffierung *f* COMP shading

Schräg- *in cpds* GESCHÄFT diagonal, slanting; **Schrägstrich** *m* COMP *Schriftzeichen*, MEDIEN *Typographie* slash; **Schrägverziehung** *f* TRANSP racking

Schranke *f* GESCHÄFT, VW barrier

schrankenlos: ~**es Risiko** *nt* BÖRSE unbounded risk; ~**er Wettbewerb** *m* GESCHÄFT free-for-all

Schrankkoffer *m* TRANSP trunk (*TRK*)

Schraube: **Schraubenantrieb** *m* TRANSP *Schiffahrt* screw propulsion; **Schraubendampfer** *m* TRANSP steamship

Schreib- *in cpds* COMP head, writing, typing RECHNUNG, VERWALT writing, typing; **Schreibarbeit** *f* VERWALT paperwork

schreiben *vt* COMP, GESCHÄFT write

Schreiben *nt* KOMM letter; ~ **mit Diktiergerät** *nt* GESCHÄFT audiotyping

Schreiber, in *m,f* RECHT clerk

Schreib-: **Schreibfehler** *m* COMP, GESCHÄFT, MEDIEN typing error, typographical error (*typo*), RECHNUNG clerical error, VERWALT clerical error, typing error, typographical error (*typo*)

schreibgeschützt *adj* COMP *Datei, Diskette* write-protected

Schreib-: **Schreibkraft** *f* GESCHÄFT, VERWALT typist; **Schreibkraft** *f* **in Ausbildung** VERWALT trainee typist; **Schreiblesekopf** *m* COMP read-write head

Schreibmaschine *f* GESCHÄFT, VERWALT typewriter; ~ **mit Lochstreifensteuerung** VERWALT automatic typewriter; ~ **mit Speicher** VERWALT memory typewriter; **Schreibmaschinenkugelkopf** *m* GESCHÄFT, VERWALT typewriter ball

Schreib-: **Schreibpapier** *nt* GESCHÄFT writing pad; **mit Schreibschutz versehen** *phr* COMP write-protect; **Schreibtisch** *m* COMP desk; **Schreibwaren** *f* *pl* GESCHÄFT stationery; **Schreibwarenhändler, in** *m,f* VERWALT stationer; **Schreibzimmer** *nt* PERSON secretarial pool, typing pool

Schrift *f* COMP *Typographie* font, typefont, GESCHÄFT, KOMM handwriting, writing, MEDIEN *Publikation* paper, publication, *Typographie* font, typefont; **Schriftart** *f* COMP, MEDIEN typeface, typefont, font; **Schriftart** *f* **mit variabler Schriftgröße** COMP, MEDIEN variable-size font; **Schriftbild** *nt* COMP, GESCHÄFT appearance; **Schriftdatei** *f* COMP *Lichtsatz* font file; **Schriftfamilie** *f* COMP, MEDIEN *Drucker* font family; **in Schriftform** *phr* GESCHÄFT, KOMM in writing; **Schriftleitung** *f* MEDIEN editorship

schriftlich 1. *adj* GESCHÄFT, KOMM written, in writing; ◆ **einen ~en Antrag senden** GESCHÄFT send a written request; **eine ~e Aussage beschwören** RECHT swear on affidavit that; **~e Erlaubnis erhalten** KOMM obtain permission in writing; **ein ~es Gesuch senden** GESCHÄFT send a written request; **2.** *adv* GESCHÄFT, KOMM in writing; ◆ ~ **antworten** GESCHÄFT, KOMM write back; ~ **niederlegen** GESCHÄFT set down

schriftlich: ~**e Abschlußvereinbarung** *m* STEUER closing agreement (*AmE*); ~**e Absichtserklärung** *f* MGMNT letter of intent; ~**es Angebot** *nt* GESCHÄFT written offer; ~**e Annahmeerklärung** *f* VERSICH acceptance slip; **bestätigen** *phr* GESCHÄFT acknowledge receipt by letter; ~**er Beweis** *m* RECHT written evidence; ~**e Erklärung** *f* GESCHÄFT, RECHT written declaration; ~**e Vereinbarung** *f* GESCHÄFT, RECHT written agreement; ~**e Vollmacht** *f* RECHT power of attorney (*PA*); ~**e Warnung** *f* PERSON written warning; ~**er Zahlungsbefehl** *m* RECHNUNG written order to pay

Schrift: **Schriftmontage** *f* MEDIEN paste-up; **Schriftsatz** *m* COMP typesetting, MEDIEN lettering, RECHT brief; **Schriftsetzen** *nt* COMP typesetting; **Schriftsetzer, in** *m,f* COMP, MEDIEN, V&M typographer; **Schriftstil** *m* COMP *Textverarbeitung* style; **Schrifttyp** *m* VERWALT lettertype; **Schriftzeichen** *nt* COMP graphic character; **Schriftzug** *m* MEDIEN lettering

Schritt *m* GESCHÄFT step; ◆ **Schritte ergreifen** GESCHÄFT take steps; ~ **halten mit** GESCHÄFT be abreast of, keep abreast of, keep pace with, keep up with; **Schritte**

unternehmen GESCHÄFT, MGMNT take action, take steps

Schritt: **Schrittmacher** *m* GESCHÄFT trendsetter, pacesetter; **Schrittmethode** *f* COMP steps method

schrittweise 1. *adj* GESCHÄFT gradual; 2. *adv* GESCHÄFT gradually, progressively, step by step; ♦ ~ **abbauen** GESCHÄFT phase out; ~ **anheben** GESCHÄFT phase in; ~ **aufheben** GESCHÄFT phase out; ~ **einführen** GESCHÄFT phase in

schrittweise: ~r **Abbau** *m* GESCHÄFT phasing out

schröpfen *vt infrml* GESCHÄFT bleed sb (*infrml*)

Schrott *m* IND scrap; **Schrottlager** *nt* IND scrap yard; **Schrottplatz** *m* IND scrap yard; **Schrottwert** *m* FINANZ residual value, vw salvage value; **etw zum Schrottwert verkaufen** *phr* GESCHÄFT sell sth for scrap

Schrumpf- *in cpds* GESCHÄFT shrink

schrumpfen *vi* vw contract

schrumpfend: ~e **Gewinne** *m pl* GESCHÄFT shrinking profits; ~e **Industrie** *f* IND ailing industry; ~e **inflatorische Lücke** *f* vw narrowing inflation gap; ~er **Markt** *m* GESCHÄFT shrinking market

Schrumpf-: **Schrumpfung** *f* vw downswing; **Schrumpfverpackung** *f* GESCHÄFT shrink-packaging, shrink-wrapping

Schub *m* IND batch; **Schubblock** *m* TRANSP thrust block

Schublade- *in cpds* GESCHÄFT, MEDIEN, MGMNT contingency; **Schubladenplan** *m* GESCHÄFT, MGMNT contingency plan; **Schubladenplanung** *f* GESCHÄFT, MGMNT contingency planning

Schub: **Schubschlepper** *m* TRANSP push-tow barge; **Schubverband** *m* TRANSP tow

Schufterei *f* GESCHÄFT, POL hard graft

Schuh- *in cpds* GESCHÄFT shoe

Schul- *in cpds* GESCHÄFT, PERSON, SOZIAL school; **Schulabgänger** *mf* PERSON school leaver (*BrE*); **Schulabschluß** *m* PERSON school leaving; **Schulausbildung** *f* PERSON schooling; **Schulbildung** *f* SOZIAL education

Schuld *f* GESCHÄFT debt, RECHT blame, fault, liability; ♦ **eine ~ abarbeiten** FINANZ work off a debt; **jdm eine ~ erlassen** RECHT release sb from a debt; ~ **fällig an** RECHNUNG debt due to; **die ~ ist fällig am** RECHNUNG debt due by; ~ **haben** RECHT be at fault; **eine ~ nachweisen** RECHNUNG prove a debt; **eine ~ übertragen** RECHNUNG transfer a debt; **auf eine ~ verzichten** FINANZ forego a debt

Schuld: **Schuldanerkenntnis** *f* BANK, FINANZ, GESCHÄFT acknowledgement of debt, acknowledgement of indebtness, due bill (*AmE*), promissory note (*P/N, PN*); **Schuldanerkenntnisschein** *m* GESCHÄFT confessed judgment note (*AmE*); **Schuldbefreiung** *f* FINANZ discharge of debt; **Schuldbeitritt** *m* RECHT *Vertragsrecht*, vw collateral promise; **Schuldbewußtsein** *nt* GESCHÄFT consciousness of guilt, RECHT mens rea

schulden *vt* GESCHÄFT owe

Schulden *f pl* FINANZ, GESCHÄFT, VW debt; ~ **der öffentlichen Hand** vw public debt; ♦ **ohne ~** GESCHÄFT afloat; ~ **anhäufen** BANK run up a debt; ~ **begleichen** GESCHÄFT even up; **in ~ geraten** BANK run into debt, GESCHÄFT run up a debt, get into debt; ~ **machen** BANK run up a debt, incur debts, GESCHÄFT get into debt, RECHNUNG incur debts; ~ **streichen** FINANZ delete a debt; **jds ~ übernehmen** GESCHÄFT take over sb's debts; ~ **zurückzahlen** vw pay off one's debts

Schulden: **Schuldenberg** *m* vw mountain of debt; **Schuldendienst** *m* RECHNUNG debt service; **Schuldendienstindikatoren** *m pl* RECHNUNG debt service indicators; **Schuldenerlaß** *m* vw debt relief

schuldenfrei 1. *adj* FINANZ clean, clear of debts, debt-free, GESCHÄFT afloat, clean, clear of debts, debt-free, RECHNUNG clean, clear of debts, debt-free; 2. *adv* GESCHÄFT afloat

schuldenfrei: ~es **Eigentum** *nt* GRUND unencumbered property

Schulden: **Schuldenlast** *f* GRUND encumbrance, vw burden of debts, debt burden; **Schuldenmanagement** *nt* vw debt management; **Schuldenmanager, in** *m,f* vw debt manager; **Schuldenrate** *f* BÖRSE liability rate; **Schuldenstreichung** *f* GESCHÄFT deletion of debts; **Schuldenstrukturpolitik** *f* vw debt management; **Schuldenswap** *m* FINANZ debt swap; **Schuldentausch** *m* FINANZ debt swap; **Schuldentilgung** *f* FINANZ amortization, debt redemption, satisfaction of a debt, RECHNUNG debt retirement

Schuld: **Schulderlaß** *m* RECHT release of debt, remission of debt

schuldhaft *adj* RECHT culpable; ~es **Unterlassen** *nt* RECHT nonfeasance

schuldig *adj* RECHT guilty; ♦ **sich ~ bekennen** RECHT *im Sinne der Anklage* plead guilty; **jdn für ~ befinden** RECHT find sb guilty; **jdn für nicht ~ befinden** RECHT find sb not guilty; **jdn für ~ erklären** RECHT find sb guilty; **jdn für nicht ~ erklären** RECHT find sb not guilty; ~ **sein** [+dat] GESCHÄFT owe

Schuldiger, in *m,f* RECHT guilty person

Schuldigerklärung: **über ~ absprechen** *phr* RECHT plea-bargain

Schuld: **Schuldlosigkeit** *f* VERSICH no fault

Schuldner, in *m,f* FINANZ borrower, GESCHÄFT, RECHNUNG debtor, RECHT *Verpflichteter* obligor, VERWALT debtor; ~ **der Klasse AAA** BÖRSE triple-A-rated borrower; ♦ **den ~ in Verzug setzen** RECHT give the debtor a notice of default

Schuldner: **Schuldnerabteilung** *f* VERWALT debtor department; **Schuldnerverzug** *m* RECHT *Vertragsrecht* debtor's delay, default of the debtor

Schuld: **Schuldposten** *m* BÖRSE, FINANZ, GRUND debit, RECHNUNG liability item; **Schuldrecht** *nt* RECHT *Vertragsrecht* law governing contractual obligations

schuldrechtlich *adj* RECHT in personam; ~er **Anspruch** *m* RECHT claim based upon contract or tort; ~e **Klage** *f* *jarg* RECHT actio in personam (*jarg*)

Schuldschein *m* BANK acknowledgement of indebtness, promissory note (*PN, P/N*), FINANZ promissory note (*PN, P/N*), GESCHÄFT I owe you (*IOU*), VERSICH bond; ~ **mit hoher Resttilgung vor Fälligkeit** BANK balloon note; ~ **zugunsten des Konkursverwalters** FINANZ receiver's certificate

Schuld: **einen Schuldspruch fällen** *phr* RECHT find sb guilty; **Schuldtitel** *m* FINANZ paper (*infrml*), RECHT enforceable legal document; **Schuldtitel** *m pl* **mit kurzer Laufzeit** BÖRSE shorts; **Schuldurkunde** *f* GESCHÄFT certificate of indebtedness, debt instrument; **Schuldverhältnis** *nt* RECHT *Vertragsrecht* obligation

Schuldverschreibung *f* BÖRSE, FINANZ bond, debenture, loan stock (*BrE*); ~ **zum Hausbau** GRUND housing bond; ~ **zugunsten einer Bank** BANK bank debenture; **Schuldverschreibungsurkunde** f BÖRSE bond indenture

Schuld: **Schuldwechsel** m pl RECHNUNG notes payable, bills payable; **Schuldzinsen** m pl FINANZ debit interest

Schul-: **Schulentlassungszeugnis** nt SOZIAL school leaving certificate, Certificate of Secondary Education (*CSE*) (*BrE*) (*obs*); **Schulgeld** nt SOZIAL school fees, tuition fees

schulintern: ~**e Beurteilung** f SOZIAL *eines Schülers* internal school assessment

schulisch: ~**e Ausbildung** f PERSON schooling

Schulung f GESCHÄFT training; ~ **von Führungskräften** MGMNT executive training; **Schulungsagentur** f PERSON Training Agency (*BrE*) (*TA*); **Schulungsbehörde** f PERSON Training Agency (*BrE*) (*TA*); **Schulungsleiter, in** m,f MGMNT training manager; **Schulungsprogramm** nt IND, MGMNT training package, PERSON training package, training program (*AmE*), training programme (*BrE*); **Schulungszentrum** nt PERSON training center (*AmE*), training centre (*BrE*)

Schund m GESCHÄFT trashy goods (*infrml*) (*AmE*); **Schundblatt** nt MEDIEN rag (*infrml*)

Schutt m GESCHÄFT rubble; ♦ **in ~ und Asche fallen** GESCHÄFT go to rack and ruin (*infrml*)

Schütt- *in cpds* GESCHÄFT bulk

Schüttgut nt GESCHÄFT bulk goods, bulk material, bulk commodity, TRANSP bulk, bulk goods; ♦ **mit ~ beladen** TRANSP laden in bulk

Schüttgut: **Schüttgutcontainer** m TRANSP bulk container; **Schüttgutcontainerschiff** nt TRANSP bulk container ship

Schütt-: **Schüttladung** f TRANSP bulk cargo; **Schüttwinkel** m TRANSP angle of repose

Schutz m RECHT *geistiges Eigentum*, UMWELT, VW protection; ~ **geistigen Eigentums** PATENT, RECHT intellectual property rights; ~ **vor vorzeitiger Kündigung** BÖRSE call protection; ~ **durch Zölle** IMP/EXP, VW tariff protection; ♦ **unter dem ~ von** GESCHÄFT under the umbrella of

Schutz: **Schutzausrüstung** f GESCHÄFT safety equipment; **Schutzbestimmung** f FINANZ protective covenant; **Schutzdauer** f *eines Patents* PATENT term of patent

schützen 1. vt GESCHÄFT *Geheimnis* safeguard, RECHT *nationale Interessen* protect; ♦ ~ **vor** GESCHÄFT screen, shield, STEUER shelter; **2. sich ~** v refl GESCHÄFT protect oneself

schützend adj GESCHÄFT protecting; **zu ~e Eigenschaft** f PATENT feature desired to be protected; **zu ~es Merkmal** nt PATENT feature desired to be protected

Schutz: **Schutzfrist** f PATENT term of patent; **Schutzhelm** m PERSON hard hat; **Schutzimpfung** f SOZIAL vaccination; **Schutzklausel** f BÖRSE hedge clause, RECHT safeguard; **Schutzmarke** f GESCHÄFT trademark, PATENT mark, trademark; **Schutzmaßnahme** f GESCHÄFT safety precaution; **Schutzschiedsspruch** m PERSON protective award; **Schutzumschlag** m GESCHÄFT, V&M wrapper; **Schutzzeichen** nt PATENT mark; **Schutzzoll** m IMP/EXP protective duties, VW protective duties, protective tariff

schutzzollbedürftig: ~**e Industrie** f IND infant industry

Schutz: **Schutzzollpolitik** f IMP/EXP, VW protectionism;

Schutzzollsystem nt **im Handel** IMP/EXP, VW trade protectionism

schwach adj GESCHÄFT *Nachfrage, Absatz* slack, RECHT *hinfällig* weak, VW poor, slack, weak; ~**es Geschäftsprofil** nt GESCHÄFT low profile; ~**er Markt** m BÖRSE weak market; ~**e Umsätze** f pl VW light selling; ~**e zyklische Erholung** f VW modest cyclical recovery

schwächen vt GESCHÄFT *Einfluß, Macht* undermine, weaken, VW *Währung* weaken

Schwächenanalyse f RECHNUNG weakness investigation

Schwachstelle f GESCHÄFT danger point, potential trouble spot

Schwall m GESCHÄFT spate

schwanken vi GESCHÄFT *Ergebnis* sway, *Preise* fluctuate, yo-yo

schwankend adj BÖRSE erratic, GESCHÄFT unsteady, VW volatile; ~**er Zinssatz** m **für Ausleihungen** FINANZ variable lending rate (*VLR*)

Schwankung f GESCHÄFT *Markt* swing, variability, MATH variability, VW variation, fluctuation, variability, *Wechselkursschwankung* move; **Schwankungsbreite** f BÖRSE range, VW band of fluctuation; **Schwankungsfonds** m VERSICH equalization fund; **Schwankungsrückstellung** f VERSICH equalization fund

Schwarz- *in cpds* GESCHÄFT black

schwarz adj GESCHÄFT black: ~**es Brett** nt PERSON *Mitteilungen* bulletin board, notice board (*BrE*); ~**er Freitag** m BÖRSE Black Friday; ~**es Gold** nt IND, UMWELT black gold; ~**e Liste** f GESCHÄFT, IND, PERSON *Gewerkschaftsbewegung* blacklist; ~**er Montag** m BÖRSE Black Monday; ♦ **auf die ~e Liste setzen** IND, KOMM blacklist, PERSON blacklist, *Gewerkschaftsbewegung* black; **der Schwarze Peter bleibt an mir hängen**; ~ **sehen** GESCHÄFT be pessimistic; **in den ~en Zahlen** FINANZ, RECHNUNG *Gewinn- und Verlustrechnung* above the line

Schwarz-: **Schwarzarbeit** f PERSON moonlighting (*infrml*), unrecorded employment; **Schwarzarbeiter, in** m,f PERSON fly-by-night worker (*infrml*), moonlighter; **Schwarzfahren** nt TRANSP fare-dodging; **Schwarzfahrer, in** m,f TRANSP fare-dodger, free rider; **Schwarzgeld** nt STEUER black money; **Schwarzhandel** m GESCHÄFT black trading, VW black market; **Schwarzhändler, in** m,f GESCHÄFT trafficker, *Veranstaltungskarten* tout (*infrml*); **Schwarzmarkt** m VW black market; **auf dem Schwarzmarkt kaufen** phr VW buy on the black market; **Schwarzpulver** nt IND black powder; **Schwarzweißbildschirm** m COMP monochrome screen

Schwebe: **in der ~** phr GESCHÄFT in abeyance, in suspense

schwebend adj GESCHÄFT in abeyance, in suspense, pending; ~**er Fall** m RECHT lis pendens; ~**e Geschäfte** nt pl GESCHÄFT, VW pending business; ~**e Schuld** f FINANZ floating debt, unfunded debt; ~ **unwirksam** phr RECHT provisionally invalid

Schwebesitz m TRANSP suspension seat

Schwebstoff m IND suspended solid

Schwedisch: ~**e Schule** f VW Swedish School

Schwefel m UMWELT sulfur (*AmE*), sulphur (*BrE*); **Schwefelausstoß** m UMWELT sulfur emission (*AmE*), sulphur emission (*BrE*); **Schwefeldioxid** nt UMWELT sulfur dioxide (*AmE*), sulphur dioxide (*BrE*)

Schweigegeld nt GESCHÄFT hush money

schweigend: die ~e Mehrheit *f* POL the silent majority

Schweinetrog *m* POL pork barrel (*AmE*) (*infrml*)

Schweinezyklus *m* VW hog cycle

Schweißeisenkabel *nt* TRANSP wrought-iron cable

Schweizerisch: ~e Bundesbahn *f* (*SBB*) TRANSP Swiss Federal Railways, ≈ British Rail (*BR*); **~e Nationalbank** *f* VW Swiss National Bank

Schwelle *f* COMP, FINANZ, GESCHÄFT, PERSON, STEUER, UMWELT threshold; **Schwellenland** *nt* IND, VW newly industrialized country (*NIC*); **Schwellenpopulation** *f* VW threshold population; **Schwellenpreis** *m* GESCHÄFT threshold price, IMP/EXP trigger price, PERSON threshold price; **Schwellenpunkt** *m* BÖRSE threshold point; **Schwellentarif** *f* PERSON threshold rate; **Schwellenvereinbarung** *f* PERSON threshold agreement; **Schwellenwert** *m* COMP threshold value, GESCHÄFT threshold level

Schwemme *f* GESCHÄFT, VW glut

Schwenkung *f* GESCHÄFT, POL *Methode, Meinung* about-face (*AmE*), about-turn (*BrE*)

Schwer- *in cpds* GESCHÄFT heavy

schwer 1. *adj* GESCHÄFT difficult, hard; ♦ **~ zu handhaben** GESCHÄFT unmanageable; **jdm das Leben ~ machen** GESCHÄFT make things difficult for sb; **2.** *adv* ♦ **~ arbeiten** PERSON labor (*AmE*), labour (*BrE*), toil

schwer: **~er Diebstahl** *m* RECHT grand larceny; **~er Fehler** *m* COMP *Programme*, GESCHÄFT fatal error; **~es Heizöl** *nt* UMWELT heavy fuel; **~er Justizirrtum** *m* RECHT gross miscarriage of justice; **~e Verfehlung** *f* PERSON gross misconduct

schwerbehindert: ~er Arbeitnehmer *m*, **~e Arbeitnehmerin** *f* PERSON severely-disabled worker

Schwergut *nt* TRANSP deadweight cargo; **Schwergutfahrzeug** *nt* TRANSP heavy goods vehicle (*HGV*); **Schwergutmastkran** *m* TRANSP heavy lift mast crane; **Schwergutschiff** *nt* TRANSP heavy lift ship; **Schwerguttraverse** *f* TRANSP heavy lifting beam; **Schwergutverkehr** *m* TRANSP heavy goods traffic

Schwer-: **Schwerindustrie** *f* IND heavy industry, heavy engineering; **Schwerkraftmodell** *nt* VW gravity model; **Schwerlastzug** *m* TRANSP juggernaut; **Schwermaschine** *f* IND heavy industrial plant; **Schwermetallkonzentration** *f* UMWELT heavy metal concentration; **Schwerpunkt** *m* TRANSP center of gravity (*AmE*), centre of gravity (*BrE*); **Schwerpunkt** *m* **des Vertragsverhältnisses** RECHT emphasis of the contract; **Schwertransportjet** *m* TRANSP heavy jet

schwerwiegend *adj* GESCHÄFT deep-seated

Schwestergesellschaft *f* GESCHÄFT, VW affiliated company, associated company, sister company

Schwesterschiff *nt* TRANSP sister ship

schwierig *adj* GESCHÄFT sticky, vexed, hard, *Lage* difficult, tough

Schwierigkeit *f* GESCHÄFT difficulty, snag (*infrml*); ♦ **Schwierigkeiten loswerden** GESCHÄFT get out of trouble

Schwimm- *in cpds* TRANSP floating; **Schwimmdock** *nt* TRANSP wet dock

schwimmend *adj* GESCHÄFT, IMP/EXP, KOMM, TRANSP afloat

Schwimm-: **Schwimmlage** *f* TRANSP trim

Schwindel *m* GESCHÄFT swindle; **Schwindelfirma** *f* GESCHÄFT bogus company; **Schwindelgeschäft** *nt*

GESCHÄFT swindle; **Schwindelunternehmen** *nt* BÖRSE bubble (*infrml*), GESCHÄFT bogus company, wildcat venture

schwinden *vi* VW shrink

Schwindler *m* RECHT con-man, crook (*infrml*); **Schwindlertrick** *m* GESCHÄFT confidence trick

Schwingungszwischenraum *m* TRANSP swing clearance

schwören 1. *vt* RECHT swear; **2.** *vi* RECHT swear

Schwund *m* TRANSP ullage, VW leakage, shrinkage; **~ der Gewinnspanne** RECHNUNG margin shrinkage

Schwungkraft: ~ gewinnen *phr* GESCHÄFT gain momentum

Scitovsky-Paradoxon *nt* VW Scitovsky reversal test

scrollen *vi* COMP scroll

s.d. *abbr* (*siehe dies*) GESCHÄFT q.v. (*quod vide*)

See- *in cpds* IMP/EXP, TRANSP, VERSICH marine, maritime; **Seeanker** *m* TRANSP sea anchor; **Seeaufsichtsbeamte(r)** *m*, **Seeaufsichtsbeamtin** *f* [decl. as adj] PERSON marine superintendent; **Seebetrug** *m* TRANSP maritime fraud; **Seedienst** *m* TRANSP maritime service; **Seefähigkeit** *f* TRANSP seaworthiness; **Seefracht** *f* TRANSP ocean freight; **Seefrachtbrief** *m* IMP/EXP, TRANSP bill of lading (*b.l., B/L*), ocean bill of lading, on deck bill of lading, sea waybill; **für Seefrachtbrief übernommen** *phr* IMP/EXP received for shipment bill of lading; **Seegefahr** *f* VERSICH maritime peril; **Seegefahranalytiker,in** *m,f* PERSON, VERSICH marine risk analyst; **Seegefahren** *f pl* TRANSP, VERSICH sea risks; **Seehafen** *m* TRANSP deepwater harbor (*AmE*), deepwater harbour (*BrE*), sea port; **Seehafenspediteur** *m* IMP/EXP, TRANSP shipping officer, shipping agent; **Seehandel** *m* GESCHÄFT sea trade, IMP/EXP maritime trade; **Seekanal** *m* TRANSP maritime canal; **Seekonnossement** *nt* IMP/EXP ocean bill of lading, on deck bill of lading, TRANSP ocean bill of lading; **Seemann** *m* PERSON, TRANSP mariner, sailor, seaman; **Seemannsordnung** *f* TRANSP ship's articles; **Seemeile** *f* GESCHÄFT nautical mile; **Seepfandrecht** *nt* TRANSP maritime lien; **Seeprotest** *m* RECHT ship's protest, TRANSP protest; **Seeräuberei** *f* TRANSP marine piracy; **Seerecht** *nt* RECHT maritime law, *Seehandelsrecht* sea law; **Seereise** *f* TRANSP voyage (*voy'*); **Seerisiko** *nt* VERSICH maritime risk; **Seeschaden** *m* TRANSP *Schiffahrt*, VERSICH sea damage (*SD*); **Seeschadens- und Schutzversicherung** *f* VERSICH ocean marine protection and indemnity insurance; **Seeschiffahrt** *f* TRANSP maritime shipping; **Seeschiffahrtsstraße** *f* TRANSP sea route; **Seetransport** *m* TRANSP sea transport; **Seetransportgeschäft** *nt* IMP/EXP, TRANSP shipping trade; **Seetransportkomitee** *nt* (*MTC*) TRANSP Maritime Transport Committee (*MTC*); **Seetüchtigkeit** *f* TRANSP seaworthiness; **Seeunfall** *m* VERSICH accident at sea; **Seeverfrachter** *m* TRANSP sea carrier; **Seeverkehr** *m* TRANSP sea transport; **Seeversand** *m* TRANSP maritime shipping; **Seewurf** *m* TRANSP jetsam

Seeversicherung *f* VERSICH marine insurance, sea insurance; **Seeversicherungsbetrug** *m* VERSICH marine insurance fraud; **Seeversicherungspolice** *f* VERSICH term policy, marine insurance policy (*MIP*); **Seeversicherungsschein** *m* VERSICH marine insurance policy certificate

See-: **Seewechsel** *m* IMP/EXP, TRANSP bottomry bond;

Seeweg m TRANSP sea route; **auf dem Seewege** phr TRANSP seaborne

Segel nt TRANSP sail; **Segelfahrt** f TRANSP sailing; **Segeltuchüberzug** m TRANSP canvas cover (CC); **Segelwindrose** f TRANSP sailing card

Segment nt COMP, MATH, MGMNT, RECHNUNG, V&M Markt segment

segmentieren vt COMP, MATH, MGMNT, RECHNUNG, V&M segment

Segmentierung f COMP, MATH, MGMNT, RECHNUNG, V&M eines Marktes segmentation; **Segmentierungsstrategie** f V&M segmentation strategy

segmentorientiert: ~e **Berichterstattung** f RECHNUNG segmental reporting

Segment: **Segmentspanne** f RECHNUNG segment margin

Sehgewohnheiten f pl MEDIEN viewing habits

Seite f (S.) COMP, GESCHÄFT page (p); ♦ **an der** ~ MATH collateral

Seite: **Seitenabzug** m MEDIEN, V&M page proof; **Seitenbahnsteig** m TRANSP bay; **Seitengebäude** nt GRUND outhouse; **Seitengleis** nt TRANSP railway siding (BrE), sidetrack (AmE); **Seitenlänge** f COMP Drucker, Textverarbeitung page length; **Seitenrad** nt TRANSP side wheel; **Seitenrand** m COMP, MEDIEN margin; **Seitenspeichergerät** nt COMP DTP paging device; **Seitenumbruch** m COMP page break; **Seitenvorschub** m COMP form feed (FF); **Seitenzahl** f COMP page number

seitlich adj GESCHÄFT lateral, MATH collateral

Sek. abbr (Sekunde) GESCHÄFT sec, sec. (second)

Sekretär, in m,f PERSON Büroarbeit, VERWALT secretary (sec.)

Sekretariat nt PERSON, POL secretariat, VERWALT secretary's office, secretariat; ~ **der Finanzbehörde** POL, VW Treasury Board Secretariat; ~ **des Finanzministeriums** POL, VW Treasury Board Secretariat; **Sekretariatskräfte** f pl PERSON secretarial staff

Sektor m COMP Magnetplatte, GESCHÄFT sector; ♦ **in Sektoren aufteilen** COMP Magnetplatte sector

sektoral adj MGMNT, VW sectoral; ~e **Arbeitslosigkeit** f MGMNT, VW sectoral unemployment; ~e **Strategie** f MGMNT sectoral strategy; ~e **Strukturpolitik** f IND Produktion industrial policy; ~er **Wirtschaftsplan** m RECHNUNG sectoral accounting plan

Sekundär- in cpds GESCHÄFT secondary

sekundär adj GESCHÄFT secondary; ~e **Bankdienstleistungen** f pl BANK fringe banking; ~es **Bedürfnis** nt V&M secondary need; ~e **Gesetzgebung** f RECHT secondary legislation

Sekundarabschluß m SOZIAL Certificate of Secondary Education (BrE) (obs) (CSE)

Sekundär-: **Sekundärarbeitsmarkt** m PERSON secondary labor market (AmE), secondary labour market (BrE); **Sekundärdaten** pl V&M secondary data; **Sekundäreinkommen** nt FINANZ secondary income; **Sekundärforschung** f V&M desk research; **Sekundärgeschäft** nt GESCHÄFT secondary activity; **Sekundärleserschaft** f V&M pass-along readership, secondary readership; **Sekundärmarkt** m BÖRSE aftermarket, VW second market; **Sekundärprodukt** nt V&M derivative product; **Sekundärschutz** m IND secondary protection; **Sekundärsektor** m VW secondary sector; **Sekundärsprengstoff** m TRANSP secondary explosive

sekundärstatistisch: ~e **Auswertung** f V&M desk research

Sekunde f (Sek.) GESCHÄFT second (sec, sec.)

sekundengenau: ~e **Abstimmung** f GESCHÄFT split-second timing

Selbst- in cpds GESCHÄFT self-; **Selbstbeherrschung** f GESCHÄFT, POL self-control

selbständig adj COMP stand-alone, GESCHÄFT self-sufficient, unaffiliated, PERSON self-employed, POL self-governing, STEUER self-employed, VW self-sufficient, unaffiliated; ♦ **sich ~ machen** GESCHÄFT start in business

selbständig: ~e **Besteuerung** f STEUER independent taxation (BrE); ~es **Einzelhandelsgeschäft** nt GESCHÄFT independent store (AmE); ~e(r) **Erwerbstätige(r)** mf [decl. as adj] PERSON self-employed worker; ~e **Nation** f POL self-governing nation; ~e **Tätigkeit** f PERSON, STEUER self-employment; ~er **Unternehmer, ~e Unternehmerin** f STEUER independent contractor

Selbständige(r) mf [decl. as adj] PERSON self-employed person

Selbst-: **Selbstanlasser** m PERSON self-starter

Selbstbedienung f V&M self-service, self-selection; **Selbstbedienungsgepäckwagen** m FREI self-help passenger luggage trolley; **Selbstbedienungsgeschäft** nt V&M self-service store; **Selbstbedienungsgroßhändler, in** m,f V&M cash and carry wholesaler

Selbstbehalt m VERSICH deductible (AmE), excess (BrE), excess insurance, retention; ♦ **zum** ~ GESCHÄFT at owner's risk

Selbstbehalt: **Selbstbehaltsgrenze** f VERSICH excess point; **Selbstbehaltsklausel** f VERSICH deductible clause, franchise clause, own-risk clause

Selbst-: **Selbstbehauptungstraining** nt PERSON assertiveness training

Selbstbeschränkung f GESCHÄFT self-restraint; ~ **bei Lohnforderungen** PERSON voluntary policy, Tarifverhandlungen wage restraint, POL, VW wage restraint; **Selbstbeschränkungsabkommen** nt VW orderly market agreement (OMA)

Selbst-: **Selbstbild** nt V&M self-image; **Selbstentlader** m TRANSP, UMWELT tipper; **Selbstentzündung** f IND spontaneous combustion

selbsternannt adj GESCHÄFT self-styled

selbsterzeugend adj GESCHÄFT self-generating

selbstfahrend adj IND automotive

Selbst-: **Selbstfernwahl** f KOMM direct distance dialing (AmE) (DDD), subscriber trunk dialling (BrE) (STD)

selbstfinanzierend adj FINANZ, RECHNUNG self-financing

selbstfinanzierte: ~ **Renten** f pl FINANZ, PERSON internally funded pensions

Selbstfinanzierung f FINANZ, RECHNUNG autofinancing, self-financing, internal financing; **Selbstfinanzierungsquote** f BÖRSE self-financing ratio

selbstgenügsam adj GESCHÄFT self-contained

selbstgenutzt: ~e **Eigentumswohnung** f GRUND condominium (AmE), owner-occupied flat (BrE), owner-occupied apartment (AmE); ~es **Vermögensrecht** nt RECHT beneficial ownership

Selbst-: **Selbsthilfe** f GESCHÄFT, PERSON self-help; **Selbstkontrahieren** nt FINANZ, RECHT Vertragsrecht self-dealing; **Selbstkosten** *pl* RECHNUNG cost, cost of sales, total production cost; **Selbstkostenpreis** *m* RECHNUNG cost price

selbstladend *adj* IND, TRANSP self-loading; **~er Anhänger** *m* TRANSP self-loading trailer

Selbst-: **Selbstmanagement** *nt* MGMNT self-management, PERSON autogestion, self-management; **Selbstmotivation** *f* MGMNT, PERSON self-motivation; **Selbstpflücken** *nt* V&M *landwirtschaftliche Produkte* pick-your-own (*BrE*)

Selbststeuerung *f* COMP automatic control; ♦ **~ eingetragen** TRANSP automatic control certified (*ACC*), **~ zugelassen** TRANSP automatic control certified (*ACC*)

selbsttätig: **~e Kupplung** *f* TRANSP automatic coupling

selbsttragend *adj* GESCHÄFT self-supporting; **~e Schuld** *f* FINANZ self-supporting debt

Selbst-: **Selbstüberwachungsorganisation** *f* BÖRSE self-regulating organization (*SRO*), self-regulatory organization (*SRO*); **Selbstverbrauch** *m* GESCHÄFT private consumption; **Selbstverbrennung** *f* TRANSP spontaneous combustion; **Selbstverpflegung** *f* FREI self-catering; **Selbstversicherung** *f* VERSICH self-insurance; **Selbstversicherungsfonds** *m* VERSICH self-insurance fund

selbstversorgend *adj* GESCHÄFT, VW self-reliant, self-sufficient

Selbst-: **Selbstversorgung** *f* VW self-sufficiency, self-supply

selbstverwaltet: **~er Betrieb** *m* MGMNT *durch die Arbeitnehmer* labor-managed firm (*AmE*), labour-managed firm (*BrE*)

Selbst-: **Selbstverwaltung** *f* GESCHÄFT autonomy, MGMNT self-management, PERSON autogestion, self-management, POL self-government; **Selbstverwaltungskörperschaft** *f* GESCHÄFT self-regulating organization (*SRO*), self-regulatory organization (*SRO*); **Selbstverwirklichung** *f* MGMNT, PERSON self-actualization; **Selbstwahl** *f* KOMM direct dialing (*AmE*), direct dialling (*BrE*); **Selbstwählferndienst** *m* KOMM direct distance dialing (*AmE*) (*DDD*), subscriber trunk dialling (*BrE*) (*STD*); **Selbstwählfernverkehr** *m* KOMM international direct dialing (*AmE*) (*IDD*), international direct dialling (*BrE*) (*IDD*)

selbstzerlegend: **~e Palette** *f* TRANSP self-demounting pallet

selektiv *adj* GESCHÄFT selective; **~e Aufmerksamkeit** *f* V&M selective attention; **~e Beschäftigungssteuer** *f* STEUER Selective Employment Tax; **~e Finanzhilfe** *f* VW Selective Financial Assistance (*BrE*); **~e Positionierung** *f* V&M selective positioning; **~e Regionalhilfe** *f* VW regional selective assistance (*RSA*); **~er Verkauf** *m* V&M selective selling; **~e Wahrnehmung** *f* V&M selective perception

Seltenheitswert *m* VW scarcity value

semantisch: **~er Unterschied** *m* V&M semantic differential

Seminar *nt* MGMNT, PERSON seminar, workshop; **~ mit Übernachtung** MGMNT, PERSON residential course, seminar

sen. *abbr* (*senior*) GESCHÄFT, RECHT Snr (*senior*)

Senat *m* POL senate

Senator *m* POL senator

Sende- *in cpds* GESCHÄFT, KOMM transmitting;

Sendeaufruf *m* COMP polling; **Sendedatum** *nt* V&M air date, **Sendetermin** *m* V&M air date

senden *vt* COMP *Daten, Information* send, GESCHÄFT broadcast, KOMM transmit, MEDIEN *Fernsehprogramm, Rundfunkprogramm* broadcast

Sende-: **Sendeplatz** *m* MEDIEN *Radio* availability; **Sendeprobe** *f* MEDIEN air check

Sender *m* KOMM forwarder (*fwdr*), *Funkgerät* transmitter, TRANSP forwarder (*fwdr*); **Sendermelodie** *f* MEDIEN, V&M signature tune; **Sendernetz** *nt* MEDIEN *Rundfunkübertragung* networking

Sende-: **Sendeschluß** *m* MEDIEN closedown; **Sendeunterbrechung** *f* **für Werbedurchsagen** KOMM, V&M station break (*AmE*); **Sendeunterbrechung** *f* **für Werbung** KOMM, V&M break, station break (*AmE*); **Sendezeit** *f* MEDIEN airtime, slot, station time (*AmE*), V&M advertising time, airtime

Sendung *f* GESCHÄFT broadcasting, KOMM transmission, TRANSP consignment; ♦ **auf ~** MEDIEN, V&M on the air

senior *adj* (*sen.*) GESCHÄFT, RECHT senior (*Snr*)

Seniorität *f* PERSON seniority

senken *vt* GESCHÄFT *Preise, Steuern nachlassen* abate, VW *Preise, Ausgaben* cut, lower, reduce

senkrecht *adj* TRANSP upright

Senkrechtstarter *m* *infrml* MGMNT high flier, whiz kid (*infrml*)

Senkung *f* VW cut

Sensationswerbung *f* V&M advertising gimmick

sensibel *adj* BÖRSE sensitive

sensibilisieren *vt* GESCHÄFT sensitize

Sensitivität *f* GESCHÄFT sensitivity; **Sensitivitätsanalyse** *f* FINANZ, MATH sensitivity analysis; **Sensitivitätstraining** *nt* MGMNT, PERSON sensitivity training

Sensor- *in cpds* COMP touch-, touch-sensitive

sensoraktiviert *adj* COMP touch-activated

Sensor-: **Sensorbildschirm** *m* COMP touch-sensitive screen; **mit Sensoreingabe** *phr* COMP touch-activated; **Sensortaste** *f* COMP touch key

separat *adj* GESCHÄFT self-contained, separate; **~er Kunde** *m* BÖRSE separate customer

sequentiell *adj* COMP, MATH sequential; **~e Externalität** *f* VW sequential externality; **~es Stichprobenverfahren** *nt* MATH sequential sampling

Sequenzanalyse *f* FINANZ sequential analysis

Sequestration *f* RECHT sequestration

sequestrieren *vt* RECHT sequester, sequestrate

Serie *f* GESCHÄFT *von Produkten* family, range, RECHNUNG batch; ♦ **in ~ hergestellt** IND mass-produced, produced in serial form, serialized

seriell 1. *adj* COMP serial; **2.** *adv* COMP serially, in series; ♦ **~ hergestellt** IND mass-produced

seriell: **~es Abtastgerät** *nt* COMP serial reader; **~er Adapter** *m* COMP serial adaptor; **~er Anschluß** *m* COMP serial port; **~er Betrieb** *m* COMP serial operation; **~er Drucker** *m* COMP serial printer; **~er Rechner** *m* COMP serial computer; **~e Verarbeitung** *f* COMP serial processing; **~er Zugriff** *m* COMP sequential access, serial access

seriell-parallel *adj* COMP serial-parallel

Serie: **Serienanfertigung** *f* IND batch production, mass production; **Serienanleihe** *f* FINANZ serial bond; **Serienbau** *m* IND batch production; **Serienfabrikation** *f* GESCHÄFT, IND, VW wholesale manufacture; **Serienmarke** *f* PATENT associated mark

serienmäßig: **~e Herstellung** *f* IND batch production, mass production

Serie: **Seriennummer** *f* GESCHÄFT serial number; **Serienprodukte** *nt pl* VW series-produced goods; **Serienproduktion** *f* IND batch production, mass production, large-scale production

serifenlos *adj* COMP, MEDIEN sansserif; **~er Buchstabe** *m* COMP, MEDIEN sansserif; **~e Schrift** *f* COMP, MEDIEN sansserif

Server *m* COMP server

Service *m* GESCHÄFT service; **~ rund um die Uhr** GESCHÄFT twenty-four-hour service; ♦ **~ nicht eingeschlossen** GESCHÄFT service not included

Service: **Serviceabteilung** *f* IND maintenance department; **Servicehandbuch** *nt* GESCHÄFT service handbook; **Serviceschiff** *nt* TRANSP service boat; **Servicestunden** *f pl* GESCHÄFT service hours; **Serviceunternehmen** *nt* COMP, GESCHÄFT service bureau

seßhaft *adj* GESCHÄFT settled; ♦ **~ werden** GESCHÄFT take up a permanent place of residence

Set *nt* COMP *Daten* set

Setz- *in cpds* MEDIEN setting, typesetting

setzen *vt* GESCHÄFT set, *Unterschrift* affix, append

Setzen *nt* COMP *Druck*, GESCHÄFT *Schrift* typesetting; **~ einer Seite** MEDIEN page setting

Setzer, in *m,f obs* COMP, MEDIEN, V&M typesetter

Setz-: **Setzfehler** *m jarg* COMP, GESCHÄFT typing error, typographical error (*typo*), MEDIEN setting error, typing error, typographical error (*typo*), VERWALT typing error, typographical error (*typo*); **Setzschiff** *nt* MEDIEN *Druck* galley

sexuell: **~e Belästigung** *f* PERSON *am Arbeitsplatz* sexual harassment; **~e Diskriminierung** *f* PERSON, RECHT sex discrimination; **~es Klischeedenken** *nt* PERSON *Diskriminierung, Gleichberechtigung* sex stereotyping

Shapley-Wert *m* VW *Spieltheorie* Shapley value

Shareware *f* COMP shareware

Shuttle *nt* TRANSP shuttle; **Shuttleverkehr** *m* TRANSP shuttle service commuter traffic

SIBOR *abbr* (*Singapur Interbankenangebotssatz*) BANK SIBOR (*Singapore Interbank Offered Rate*)

Sichanschließen *nt* POL accession

sicher *adj* BANK, FINANZ, VW good, safe, secure; **~e Ankunft** *f* TRANSP safe arrival (*s/a*); **~e Anlage** *f* BANK safe investment; **~es Gefühl** *nt* **für Gewinnwirtschaftung** GESCHÄFT acquisitive instinct; **~er Hafen** *m* TRANSP safe port; **~e Kapitalanlage** *f* BANK secure investment; **~er Liegeplatz** *m* TRANSP safe berth; **~e Reserven** *f pl* UMWELT recoverable reserves; **~er Vermögenswert** *m* FINANZ safe asset

Sicherheit *f* COMP security, FINANZ surety, security, GESCHÄFT safety, guaranty, PERSON, VERWALT security, VW collateral, certainty; **~ am Arbeitsplatz** PERSON safety at work; **~ des Arbeitsplatzes** PERSON job security, security of employment; **als ~ zu hinterlegender Barbetrag** FINANZ good-faith deposit; **~ im Straßenverkehr** TRANSP road safety; ♦ **gegen eine ~ ausleihen** BÖRSE lend against security; **als ~ halten** VERSICH hold as a security; **~ leisten für** BANK stand security for

Sicherheit: **Sicherheitsabschirmung** *f* GESCHÄFT protective safety screen; **Sicherheitsagentur** *f* VERWALT Mutual Security Agency (*MSA*); **Sicherheitsausschuß** *m* SOZIAL *privat* Safety Committee (*AmE*), *staatlich* Safety Commission (*AmE*); **Sicherheitsbeauftragte(r)** *mf* [decl. as adj] PERSON *Arbeitsschutzgesetz, EG Direktive 1989* safety officer; **Sicherheitsbestand** *m* GESCHÄFT safety stock; **Sicherheitsbestimmungen** *f pl* GESCHÄFT safety regulations; **Sicherheitsdienst** *m* VERWALT security service; **Sicherheitsempfänger, in** *m,f* GESCHÄFT, RECHT warrantee; **Sicherheitsfonds** *m* FINANZ provident fund; **Sicherheitsgrenze** *f* GESCHÄFT safety margin; **Sicherheitsgurt** *m* TRANSP safety belt; **Sicherheitsingenieur, in** *m,f* GESCHÄFT safety engineer; **Sicherheitsleck** *nt* GESCHÄFT security leak

Sicherheitsleistung *f* FINANZ good-faith deposit, RECHT bail, VERSICH deposit surety, VW collateral security; **~ des Berufungsklägers** RECHT appeal bond; **~ bei Gericht** RECHT judicial bond; **~ bei gerichtlicher Anordnung** RECHT injunction bond; ♦ **jdn gegen ~ aus der Haft entlassen** RECHT release sb on bail

Sicherheit: **Sicherheitsmanagement** *nt* MGMNT, PERSON *Arbeitsschutzgesetz* safety management; **Sicherheitsmaßnahme** *f* GESCHÄFT safety measure, VERWALT security measure; **Sicherheitsnorm** *f* GESCHÄFT, IND safety standard; **eine Sicherheitspanne berücksichtigen** *phr* RECHNUNG allow for a margin of error; **Sicherheitsprüfung** *f* GESCHÄFT safety check; **Sicherheitsrecht** *nt* RECHT *Vertragsrecht* right of protection from risks, security right; **Sicherheitsrisiko** *nt* GESCHÄFT safety hazard, VERSICH security risk; **Sicherheitsrücklage** *f* MGMNT contingency reserve; **Sicherheitsspanne** *f* RECHNUNG margin of error, safety margin; **Sicherheitsstandard** *m* GESCHÄFT, IND safety standard; **Sicherheitsstandort** *m* TRANSP *Öltanker* protective location; **Sicherheitssumme** *f* GESCHÄFT retention money; **Sicherheitechniker, in** *m,f* GESCHÄFT safety engineer

sicherheitstechnisch: **~e Anforderung** *f* IND safety requirement

Sicherheit: **Sicherheitsüberprüfung** *f* GESCHÄFT, POL vetting; **Sicherheitsverwaltung** *f* MGMNT, PERSON safety management; **Sicherheitsvorkehrung** *f* GESCHÄFT safety precaution; **Sicherheitsvorschriften** *f pl* GESCHÄFT safety regulations, safety code; **Sicherheitszertifikat** *nt* IND safety equipment certificate; **Sicherheitszuschlag** *m* FINANZ, PERSON margin of safety; **Sicherheitszuschlag** *m* **für Bunker** TRANSP safety surplus of bunkers

sichern *vt* BÖRSE secure, COMP *Datei* save, *Daten* back up, GESCHÄFT *Vermögenswerte* safeguard, VERSICH indemnify

Sichernde(r) *m* [decl. as adj] BÖRSE hedger

sicherstellen *vt* RECHT ensure, impound, VERSICH indemnify

Sicherung *f* COMP backing up, GESCHÄFT safeguarding, securing; **Sicherungsdatei** *f* COMP backup file; **Sicherungsgegenstand** *m* VW collateral, collateral security; **Sicherungsgeschäft** *nt* BÖRSE safe hedge, VW posthedging transaction; **Sicherungsgeschäft** *nt* **für den Kauf einer Verkaufsoption** BÖRSE put buying hedge; **Sicherungshandel** *m* BÖRSE hedge trading; **Sicherungshypothek** *f* BANK trust mortgage; **Sicherungskoeffizient** *m* BÖRSE hedge ratio; **Sicherungskopie** *f* COMP backup copy, backup, security backup, security copy; **Sicherungsnehmer** *m* FINANZ secured party; **Sicherungsoperation** *f* FINANZ hedging operation; **Sicherungspolster** *nt* TRANSP securing pad; **Sicherungsspeicher** *m* COMP backup memory; **Sicherungsstrategie** *f* BÖRSE hedging strategy; **Sicherungszeitraum** *m* BÖRSE hedge period; **Sicherungsziel** *nt* BÖRSE hedging goal

Sicht *f* FINANZ sight, GESCHÄFT viewpoint; ◆ **bei ~** FINANZ at sight (*a/s*), RECHNUNG on demand (*O/D*); **nach ~** FINANZ after sight (*A/S*)

Sicht: **Sichtanleihe** *f* BANK on demand bond

sichtbar *adj* FINANZ, GESCHÄFT, IMP/EXP visible; **~e Auswirkung** *f* GESCHÄFT visual impact; **~e Ein- und Ausfuhren** *f pl* VW visibles; **~er Export** *m* IMP/EXP, VW visible export; **~e Hand** *f* VW visible hand; **~er Import** *m* IMP/EXP, VW visible import; **~e Posten** *m pl* VW visibles; ◆ **~ sein** GESCHÄFT be in evidence

Sicht: **Sichteinlage** *f* BANK call deposit, sight deposit, bank demand deposit, demand deposit; **Sichteinlagen** *f pl* BANK bank money, call deposit; **Sichteinlagenkonto** *nt* BANK call account

sichten *vt* COMP *Textverarbeitung, Druck* preview

Sicht: **Sichtkurs** *m* FINANZ sight rate, vw demand price; **Sichttratte** *f* BANK at sight draft (*AmE*), sight draft (*S/ D*); **Sichtwechsel** *m* BANK sight draft (*S/D*), sight bill, FINANZ demand draft (*DD*), sight bill, GESCHÄFT demand draft (*DD*), RECHNUNG bill payable at sight

Siebdruck *m* V&M silk screening

Siebener-Gruppe *f* (*G7*) vw Group of Seven

siegeln *vt* GESCHÄFT affix

Siegelwachs *nt* GESCHÄFT sealing wax

siegreich *adj* GESCHÄFT *Kandidat* winning

siehe: **~ dies** *phr* (*s.d.*) GESCHÄFT quod vide (*q.v.*)

Signal *nt* GESCHÄFT signal; **Signalausfall** *m* COMP dropout

Signalisierung *f* KOMM signaling (*AmE*), signalling (*BrE*)

Signal: **Signalleuchte** *f* COMP signal light; **Signallicht** *nt* COMP signal light; **Signalwirkung** *f* POL announcement effect

Signifikanz *f* GESCHÄFT significance; **Signifikanzniveau** *nt* MATH *Statistik* level of significance; **Signifikanztest** *m* MATH significance test

Signum *nt* V&M, VERWALT logotype (*logo*)

Silbentrennung *f* COMP *Textverarbeitung* hyphenation

Silber- *in cpds* FINANZ, IND, UMWELT silver; **Silbererz** *nt* UMWELT, IND silver ore; **Silberring** *m* FINANZ silver ring (*jarg*); **Silberwährung** *f* FINANZ silver standard

Silizium- *in cpds* COMP, IND silicon; **Siliziumchip** *m* COMP, IND silicon chip

Silo *m* TRANSP bin container; **~ unter Zollverschluß** GESCHÄFT bonded elevator; **Silo-Container** *m* TRANSP bin-type container

Simulant, in *m,f* PERSON malingerer

Simulation *f* GESCHÄFT simulation, PERSON malingering; **Simulationsmodell** *nt* VW simulation model, simulation modeling (*AmE*), simulation modelling (*BrE*)

simulieren *vt* COMP, GESCHÄFT, VW simulate

Simultan- *in cpds* COMP, GESCHÄFT, MEDIEN simultaneous

simultan *adj* GESCHÄFT simultaneous

Simultan-: **Simultansendung** *f* MEDIEN simultaneous broadcast (*simulcast*); **Simultanübersetzung** *f* KOMM simultaneous translation; **Simultanverarbeitung** *f*

COMP *eines Problems durch mehere Rechner* multiprocessing

Sinekure *f* PERSON sinecure

Singapur: **~ Interbankenangebotssatz** *m* (*SIBOR*) BANK Singapore Interbank Offered Rate (*SIBOR*); **Singapur-Dollar-Rechnung** *f* FINANZ Singapore dollar invoice

sinken *vi* BANK sag, BÖRSE sag, slip back, GESCHÄFT decrease, diminish, sag, *Zahlen* fall away, vw *Preis* decline, fall, shrink

Sinken *nt* GESCHÄFT *in Preise* fall

sinkend: **~er Anteil** *m* vw declining share; **~e Zinsen** *m pl* vw declining interest rates

Sinn: **~ machen** *phr* GESCHÄFT make sense

sinngemäß **1.** *adj* GESCHÄFT analogical, analogous, corresponding; **2.** *adv* RECHT mutatis mutandis

sinnlos *adj* GESCHÄFT fruitless

sinnvoll *adj* GESCHÄFT fruitful; ◆ **~ sein** GESCHÄFT make sense

Sit-in *nt* PERSON sit-in

Sittengesetz *nt* RECHT moral law

sittenwidrig *adj* GESCHÄFT unconscionable; **~es Rechtsgeschäft** *nt* RECHT transaction contrary to public policy; **~er Vertrag** *m* RECHT unconscionable contract

Situation *f* GESCHÄFT circumstances, situation (*sit.*); ◆ **sich an eine ~ anpassen** GESCHÄFT adjust oneself to a situation

Sitz *m* POL seat, RECHT registered office, domicile, STEUER domicile; **~ einer Gesellschaft** RECHT registered office; **~ einer Vertretung** GESCHÄFT agency (*agcy*); ◆ **mit ~ in** [+dat] GESCHÄFT based in; **seinen ~ haben in** [+dat] GESCHÄFT be based in

sitzend *adj* GESCHÄFT sedentary

Sitz: **Sitzstreik** *m* PERSON *Arbeitskonflikt* sit-down strike, sit-in strike, stay-in strike

Sitzung *f* COMP session, MGMNT conference, meeting, POL session; ◆ **die ~ beenden** GESCHÄFT, POL adjourn, rise; **eine ~ einberufen** VERWALT call a meeting

Sitzung: **Sitzungsbericht** *m* VERWALT conference proceedings; **Sitzungsgeld** *nt* PERSON attendance fees; **Sitzungsort** *m* MGMNT, VERWALT conference site; **Sitzungsperiode** *f* POL session; **Sitzungsprotokoll** *nt* VERWALT conference proceedings; **Sitzungsraum** *m* VERWALT boardroom; **Sitzungsteilnehmer, in** *m,f* MGMNT conference delegate, convention participant

Skala *f* GESCHÄFT scale; **Skalarorganisation** *f* MGMNT scalar organization; **Skalarprinzip** *nt* PERSON *Lohnskala* scalar principle

Skalenerträge *m pl* vw economy of scale, returns to scale

Skandalpresse *f* MEDIEN gutter press

Skantrierungstag *m* BÖRSE name day

Skelett- *in cpds* TRANSP skeleton; **Skelettanhänger** *m* TRANSP skeletal trailer; **Skelettbehälter** *m* TRANSP skeleton case; **Skelettcontainer** *m* TRANSP skeleton case

Skepsis *m* GESCHÄFT scepticism (*BrE*), skepticism (*AmE*)

Skeptiker, in *m,f* GESCHÄFT sceptic (*BrE*), skeptic (*AmE*)

skeptisch *adj* GESCHÄFT sceptical (*BrE*), skeptical (*AmE*)

Skizze *f* GESCHÄFT sketch

Skonto *m or nt* (*Skto.*) BÖRSE discount (*dis, disc.*), FINANZ cash discount, discount (*dis, disc.*), settlement discount, GESCHÄFT cash discount, RECHNUNG trade discount; ◆ **mit ~** V&M at a discount (*AAD*)

Skontrierungstag *m* BÖRSE ticket day (*BrE*)

skrupellos *adj* GESCHÄFT unscrupulous

Skto. *abbr* (*Skonto*) FINANZ, GESCHÄFT dis (*discount*)

Slave-Palette *f* TRANSP slave pallet

Slogan *m* V&M slogan

Slot *m jarg* COMP slot

Slumpflation *f jarg* VW slumpflation

Slutsky- *in cpds* VW Slutsky; **Slutsky-Effekt** *m* VW Slutsky effect; **Slutsky-Gleichung** *f* VW Slutsky equation

Smartcard *f* BANK, COMP smart card

Sneak: ~ **Preview** *f* MEDIEN *Kino* sneak preview

Sockel *m* V&M plinth

sofern *conj* GESCHÄFT provided that; ◆ ~ **nicht anders angegeben** GESCHÄFT, RECHT unless otherwise specified; ~ **nicht anders vereinbart** GESCHÄFT, RECHT unless otherwise agreed; ~ **nicht verursacht durch** VERSICH unless caused by

Sofort- *in cpds* BANK, GESCHÄFT, TRANSP, VW spot, same-day, immediate, emergency

sofort *adv* GESCHÄFT immediately, instantly, on the spot; ~ **auszahlbare Ersparnisse** *f pl* FINANZ liquid savings; ~ **fällige Forderung** *f* FINANZ liquid debt; ~ **verfügbare Ware** *f* TRANSP actuals

Sofort-: **Soforthilfe** *f* VW emergency aid

sofortig *adj* GESCHÄFT instant (*inst.*); ~**er Einzug** *m* GRUND immediate occupancy; ~**e Geldüberweisung** *f* BANK immediate money transfer (*IMT*); ~**er Lieferungsmonat** *m* BÖRSE spot delivery month; ~**er Monetarismus** *m* VW instant monetarism; ~**e Rechnungsbegleichung** *f* FINANZ prompt payment of invoices; ~**e Zahlungsklausel** *f* FINANZ, VERSICH simultaneous payments clause; ◆ **zur** ~**en Kenntnisnahme** GESCHÄFT for immediate attention; **zur** ~**en Veröffentlichung** MEDIEN for immediate release; ~**en Zuschlag erhalten** GESCHÄFT bid off

Sofort-: **Sofortkredit** *m* BANK spot credit; **Sofortlieferung** *f* KOMM, TRANSP same-day delivery; **Sofortrabatt** *m* GESCHÄFT, KOMM immediate rebate

Softcopy *f jarg* COMP soft copy

Softsektorierung *f* COMP soft sectoring

Software *f* COMP software; ~ **im Bündel** COMP bundled software; ~ **für persönliche Finanzplanung** COMP, FINANZ personal financial planning software; **Software-Anwendung** *f* COMP software application; **Software-Entwicklung** *f* COMP software engineering; **Software-Firma** *f* COMP software house, software company; **Software-Freigabe** *f* COMP software release

softwaregesteuert *adj* COMP software-driven

Software: **Software-Haus** *nt* COMP software company, software house; **Software-Ingenieur, in** *m,f* COMP software engineer; **Software-Lizenz** *f* COMP computer software licence (*BrE*), computer software license (*AmE*); **Software-Paket** *nt* COMP software package; **Software-Release** *m* COMP software release; **Software-Schutzeinrichtung** *f* COMP *Stecker am Druckerport* dongle; **Software-Sprache** *f* COMP software language; **Software-Unternehmen** *nt* COMP software company, software house; **Software-Verfall** *m* COMP software rot

sogenannt *adj* GESCHÄFT so-called

Solarenergie *f* UMWELT solar power

Solawechsel *m* BANK, FINANZ promissory note (*P/N, PN*)

Solidarismus *m* VW solidarism

Solidaritätshandlung *f* PERSON *Arbeiterbewegung, Gewerkschaften* solidarity action

solide *adj* BANK sound, GESCHÄFT *Firma* substantial; ◆ **auf** ~**r Basis** GESCHÄFT on solid ground; **auf** ~**r Grundlage** GESCHÄFT on a sound footing

solide: ~**s Großunternehmen** *nt* GESCHÄFT blue chip company; ~**r Preis** *m* GESCHÄFT bona fide price

Soll *nt* GESCHÄFT debit; ◆ **im** ~ GESCHÄFT below the line

Soll: **Sollergebnis** *nt* RECHNUNG budgeted profit; **Sollertrag** *m* RECHNUNG budgeted income; **Soll-Ist-Vergleich** *m* VERWALT, VW actual versus target comparison; **Soll-Kennziffer** *f* RECHNUNG budget standard; **Sollkosten** *pl* FINANZ budgetary costs, GESCHÄFT predicted costs, VERWALT ideal standard cost, VW budgetary costs, predicted costs; **Sollsaldo** *m* FINANZ debit balance; **Sollseite** *f* GESCHÄFT debit, RECHNUNG debit side, left column, debtor; **Sollspalte** *f* FINANZ debit column, RECHNUNG debtor; **Sollvorgabe** *f* GESCHÄFT target; **Sollzins** *m* BANK borrowing rate; **Sollzinsen** *m pl* FINANZ debit interest, RECHNUNG interest charge; **Sollzinssatz** *m* BANK borrowing rate

Solow-Rest *m* VW Solow residual

solvent *adj* GESCHÄFT able to pay, solvent; ~**er Schuldner** *m* BANK solvent debtor

Solvenz *f* BANK, FINANZ, RECHNUNG ability to pay, solvency, VW ability to pay

Sommer- *in cpds* GESCHÄFT summer; **Sommerpause** *f* POL *Parlament* summer recess (*BrE*); **Sommerschlußverkauf** *m* V&M summer sale; **Sommerzeit** *f* GESCHÄFT daylight saving time, summer time

Sonder- *in cpds* GESCHÄFT special, exceptional; **Sonderabgabe** *f* GESCHÄFT surcharge; **Sonderabschreibung** *f* RECHNUNG accumulated depreciation, exceptional write-off; **Sonderabschreibung** *f* **auf das Anlagevermögen** STEUER relief on business assets

Sonderangebot *nt* GESCHÄFT bargain, V&M introductory offer, premium offer, special offer, *für zwei komplementäre Produkte* banded offer; ◆ **zu Sonderangebotsbedingungen** V&M on bargain-basement terms

Sonderangebot: **Sonderangebotspackung** *f* V&M money-off pack

Sonder-: **Sonderarbitragekonto** *nt* BÖRSE special arbitrage account; **Sonderausführung** *f* TRANSP special type; **Sonderausschuß** *m* POL select committee, special committee; **Sonderbeauftragte(r)** *mf* [decl. as adj] STEUER special commissioner (*BrE*); **Sonderbedingung** *f* STEUER special provision (*BrE*), TRANSP exceptional item; **Sonderberichterstatter** *m* MEDIEN assignment man; **Sonderbezirksanleihe** *f* BÖRSE special district bond; **Sonderdividende** *f* BÖRSE extra (*ex.*), extra dividend, special dividend; **Sondereinzelgenehmigung** *f* IMP/EXP, TRANSP specific individual licence (*BrE*) (*SIL*), specific individual license (*AmE*) (*SIL*); **Sondereinzelkosten** *pl* **des Vertriebs** GESCHÄFT direct cost of sales; **Sondererstattung** *f* STEUER blue return; **Sonderfakturierung** *f* RECHNUNG extra billing; **Sonderformular** *nt* BÖRSE preferential form; **Sondergesellschafter, in** *m,f* RECHT special partner; **Sonderjournal** *nt* RECHNUNG special journal; **Sonderkauf** *m* V&M special purchase; **Sonderkonditionen** *f pl* VW special conditions; **Sonderkonditionen** *f pl* **für den Handel** GESCHÄFT special terms for the trade; **Sonderkonto** *nt* RECHNUNG

special account; **Sonderkurs** *m* BÖRSE put through; **Sondermüll** *m* UMWELT hazardous waste; **Sonderposten** *m* FINANZ extraordinary items; **Sonderpreis** *m* FREI, GESCHÄFT, V&M bargain rate, concessionary rate; **Sonderprüfung** *f* TRANSP *Schiffahrt* special survey; **Sonderqualität** *f* GESCHÄFT exceptional quality; **Sonderreserve** *f* RECHNUNG special reserve; **Sonderrücklagen** *f pl* BANK excess reserves, RECHNUNG special-purpose reserve, VERSICH special contingency reserve; **Sondersitzung** *f* GESCHÄFT, MGMNT special meeting; **Sondertarifangebot** *nt* **für Geschäftsreisende** FINANZ *Fluggesellschaften* business package; **Sondervereinbarung** *f* GESCHÄFT special arrangement; **Sondervergütung** *f* FINANZ bonus, PERSON benefit; **Sonderverkauf** *m* V&M bargain sale; **Sonderversicherung** *f* **gegen mehrfache Gefahren** VERSICH special multiperil insurance (*SMP*); **Sondervertretungsvollmacht** *f* GESCHÄFT express agency; **Sondervorzugsaktien** *f pl* BÖRSE prior-preferred stock; **Sonderwahl** *f* POL by-election; **Sonderwechselkurs** *m* **für den Handel** VW special commercial exchange rate; **Sonderwirtschaftszone** *f* VW Special Economic Zone; **Sonderzahlung** *f* BÖRSE, VERWALT bonus payment; **Sonderzelle** *f* SOZIAL adjustment center (*AmE*), adjustment centre (*BrE*); **Sonderziehungsrechte** *nt pl* (*SZR*) BANK special drawing rights (*SDR*); **Sonderzuschlag** *m* VERSICH particular charge; **Sonderzuteilung** *f* GESCHÄFT special-purpose allotment; **Sonderzwischenprüfung** *f* TRANSP special intermediate survey;
Sonn-: **außer an Sonn- und Feiertagen** *phr* GESCHÄFT, TRANSP Sundays and holidays excepted (*S&H/exct, SHEX*); **Sonn- und Feiertage ausgenommen** *phr* GESCHÄFT Sundays and holidays excepted (*S&H/exct, SHEX*); **Sonn- und Feiertage eingeschlossen** *phr* GESCHÄFT, TRANSP Sundays and holidays included (*SHINC*)
Sonne- *in cpds* GESCHÄFT, UMWELT solar; **Sonnenenergie** *f* UMWELT solar power; **Sonnengürtel** *m* IND sunbelt (*AmE*)
sonst: **unter ~ gleichen Umständen** *phr* VW other things being equal
sonstig: ~e **Aktiva** *pl* FINANZ other assets; ~e **Angelegenheiten** *f pl* GESCHÄFT any other competent business (*AOCB*); ~e **Aufwendungen** *f pl* RECHNUNG sundry expenses; ~e **Erträge** *m pl* RECHNUNG other income; ~e **Forderungen** *f pl* RECHNUNG other receivables; **in** ~er **Hinsicht** *phr* GESCHÄFT in other respects; ~e **Kontokorrenteinlagen** *f pl* FINANZ other checkable deposits (*OCD*); ~e **Kosten** *pl* MGMNT, VERWALT add-on costs; ~e **Sichteinlagen** *f pl* (*OCD*) other checkable deposits (*OCD*); ~e **Tätigkeiten** *f pl* VW non-key jobs; ~e **Verbindlichkeiten** *f pl* RECHNUNG other liabilities; ~e **Verpflichtungen** *f pl* RECHNUNG other liabilities
Sonstiges *nt* GESCHÄFT any other business (*AOB*), sundries
Sorge *f* GESCHÄFT diligence
sorgen: ~ **für** *phr* GESCHÄFT cater for
Sorgfalt *f* GESCHÄFT care
sorgfältig 1. *adj* GESCHÄFT prudent; **2.** *adv* GESCHÄFT accurately; ♦ ~ **behandeln** GESCHÄFT handle with care; ~ **prüfen** GESCHÄFT examine carefully
Sorte *f* GESCHÄFT grade, quality, *Marke* brand, make
Sorten *f pl* FINANZ foreign notes and coins;

Sortenankaufskurs *m* BANK buying rate of exchange; **Sortenkurs** *m* VW cash exchange rate
Sortenzettel *m* GESCHÄFT bordereau
Sortier- *in cpds* COMP collating, collator, sort; **Sortiercode** *m* COMP collator code; **Sortierdatei** *f* COMP sort file
sortieren *vt* COMP sort, GESCHÄFT classify, sort, grade
Sortierer *m* COMP sorter
Sortier-: **Sortierfach** *nt* VERWALT pigeonhole; **Sortierfolge** *f* COMP collating sequence; **Sortiergerät** *nt* COMP card sorter, sorter; **Sortiernummer** *f* COMP collator number; **Sortierschlüssel** *m* COMP sort key
Sortierung *f* COMP sort
Sortiment *nt* GESCHÄFT assortment of goods, choice, range of goods, V&M *Lieferprogramm* line; **Sortimentmarke** *f* PATENT associated mark; **Sortimentsbeschränkung** *f* GESCHÄFT, VW variety reduction; **Sortimentseinschränkung** *f* GESCHÄFT, VW variety reduction; **Sortimentsverkleinerung** *f* GESCHÄFT, VW variety reduction
Soundtrack *m jarg* KOMM, MEDIEN soundtrack (*jarg*)
Source-Computer *m* COMP source computer
Sourcing-Experte *m* V&M sourcing expert
Sourcing-Expertin *f* V&M sourcing expert
souverän *adj* POL self-governing; ~er **Staat** *m* POL self-governing nation
Souverän *m* POL sovereign
Sozial- *in cpds* GESCHÄFT social
sozial *adj* GESCHÄFT social; ~e **Abfindung** *f* **im Kündigungsfall** PERSON redundancy severance pay; ~ **aufsteigend** *adj* PERSON upwardly mobile; ~er **Diskontsatz** *m* FINANZ social rate of discount; ~e **Einrichtung** *f* POL social organization; ~e **Grenzkosten** *pl* VW marginal social cost; ~er **Grenzschaden** *m* VW marginal social damage (*MSD*); ~e **Gruppe** *f* GESCHÄFT social grade; ~e **Kategorie** *f* V&M social category; ~e **Klasse** *f* GESCHÄFT social grade; ~e **Kosten** *pl* SOZIAL social cost, VW bad, social cost; ~e **Kosten** *pl* **der Arbeitslosigkeit** PERSON, VW social cost of unemployment; ~es **Marketingkonzept** *nt* V&M societal marketing concept; ~e **Marktwirtschaft** *f* VW social market economy; ~e **Organisation** *f* POL social organization; ~e **Schichtung** *f* SOZIAL social stratification; ~er **Status** *m* SOZIAL social status; ~es **Wohl** *nt* SOZIAL social welfare; ~er **Wohnungsbau** *m* SOZIAL council housing (*BrE*), low-cost housing, publicly assisted housing; ~e **Zinsrate** *f* FINANZ social rate of discount
Sozial-: **Sozialabteilung** *f* PERSON, SOZIAL welfare department; **Sozialarbeiter, in** *m,f* PERSON, SOZIAL social worker; **Sozialausgaben** *f pl* FINANZ social spending; **Sozialcharta** *f* GESCHÄFT Social Charter; **Sozialdemokratie** *m* POL social democracy; **Sozialdiagnose** *f* SOZIAL, V&M social analysis; **Sozialfonds** *m* FINANZ, VW social capital; **Sozialfürsorge** *f* SOZIAL public welfare, social welfare; **Sozialfürsorgeteufelskreis** *m* SOZIAL welfare trap; **Sozialgewicht** *nt* VW social weight
Sozialhilfe *f* SOZIAL social welfare, welfare, *Geld* welfare benefits, income support (*BrE*), supplementary benefit; ♦ ~ **beziehen** PERSON receive income support (*BrE*), be on social security, be on welfare (*AmE*), SOZIAL be on welfare (*AmE*)

Sozialhilfe: **Sozialhilfekultur** *f* SOZIAL dependency culture

Sozial-: **Sozialinvestitionen** *f pl* VW social capital investments

Sozialisation *f* PERSON, SOZIAL socialization

Sozialismus *m* POL, VW socialism

Sozialist *m* POL, VW socialist

sozialistisch *adj* POL, VW socialist; **~e Wirtschaft** *f* POL, VW socialist economy

Sozial-: **Sozialkapital** *nt* FINANZ, VW social capital, social overhead capital; **Sozialkostenrechnung** *f* RECHNUNG social accounting; **Sozialkredit** *m* GESCHÄFT social credit; **Sozialkunde** *f* SOZIAL *Schulfach* social studies; **Soziallasten** *f pl* SOZIAL, VW social cost

Sozialleistungen *f pl* PERSON, SOZIAL employee benefits; **~ mit Gegenleistung** VW workfare

Sozial-: **Sozialliberalismus** *m* VW social liberalism; **Soziallohn** *m* PERSON social wage (*BrE*); **Sozialpolitik** *f* SOZIAL social policy

sozialpolitisch *adj* POL, SOZIAL sociopolitical

Sozial-: **Sozialprodukt** *nt* VW aggregate output, national product, social product

sozialtechnisch: **~es System** *nt* VERWALT socio-technical system

Sozial-: **Sozialvereinbarung** *f* PERSON *Sozialvertrag zwischen Regierung und autonomen Gruppen* Social Contract (*BrE*)

Sozialversicherung *f* PERSON social security, National Insurance (*BrE*) (*NI*), SOZIAL social insurance, social security; **Sozialversicherungsbeitrag** *m* PERSON, SOZIAL social security contributions; **Sozialversicherungsbeiträge** *m pl* STEUER National Insurance Contributions (*BrE*) (*NICs*); **Sozialversicherungsgläubiger, in** *m,f* RECHNUNG social security creditor; **Sozialversicherungsleistung** *f* PERSON Social Security benefit

Sozial-: **Sozialvertrag** *m* PERSON *zwischen Regierung und autonomen Gruppen* social contract

sozialwirtschaftlich: **~es Klima** *nt* VW socioeconomic climate

Sozial-: **Sozialwohnung** *f* SOZIAL council flat (*BrE*), council housing (*BrE*), low-cost housing, subsidized housing

soziokulturell *adj* V&M sociocultural

soziometrisch *adj* MATH, V&M sociometric

sozioökonomisch *adj* SOZIAL, V&M, VW socioeconomic; **~e Gruppen** *f pl* V&M socioeconomic groups; **~er Status** *m* VW socioeconomic status

Space-Shuttle *nt* TRANSP space shuttle

Spalte *f* COMP, GESCHÄFT, MEDIEN column; **in Spalten angeordnetes Grundbuch** RECHNUNG columnar journal; ◆ **~ verschieben** COMP *Tabellenkalkulation* column move

spalten 1. *vt* GESCHÄFT, POL, VERWALT *Partei, Organisation* split up; **2. sich ~** *v refl* GESCHÄFT VERWALT *Organisation* split up

Spalte: **Spaltenlänge** *f* MEDIEN column inches; **Spaltenüberschrift** *f* RECHNUNG column heading; **Spaltenzentimeter** *m pl* MEDIEN, V&M column centimeters (*AmE*), column centimetres (*BrE*)

Spaltung *f* GESCHÄFT *zwischen Parteien* friction

Spanholzplatte *f* GESCHÄFT chipboard

Spanne *f* VERWALT margin; **~ zwischen Gesichtsfeld und Gehörfeld** VERWALT eye-voice span; **~ zwischen Lieferungen** BÖRSE interdelivery spread; **~ zwischen verschiedenen Lieferungen** BÖRSE intercommodity spread

spannend: **~es Buch** *nt* MEDIEN page-turner

Spannung *f* COMP power, GESCHÄFT *zwischen Parteien* friction, IND, UMWELT power, voltage; **Spannungsausfall** *m* COMP power failure; **Spannungsregler** *m* UMWELT voltage regulator; **Spannungsstoß** *m* COMP power surge

Spannweite *f* GESCHÄFT, STEUER, VW band

Spar- *in cpds* GESCHÄFT savings; **Sparbrief** *m* BANK savings bond (*AmE*), savings certificate; **Sparbuch** *nt* BANK bank book, passbook, account book, RECHNUNG account book; **Spareinlage** *f* BANK savings deposit; **Spareinlagen** *f pl* GESCHÄFT savings; **mit Spareinlagen verbunden** *adj* GESCHÄFT savings-linked

sparen 1. *vt* BANK *Geld* put away, GESCHÄFT *Geld* save, save up; **2.** *vi* GESCHÄFT save; ◆ **~ an** [+dat] GESCHÄFT skimp

Sparen *nt* GESCHÄFT saving; **~ im Abbuchungsverfahren** BANK direct deposit; **~ über vermögensbildende Leistungen** FINANZ contractual savings

Spar-: **Sparfunktion** *f* VW savings function; **Spargeld** *nt* BANK savings deposit; **Sparkasse** *f* BANK savings bank, thrift bank (*AmE*); **Sparkonto** *nt* BANK deposit account (*BrE*) (*D/A*), FINANZ thrift account (*AmE*); **Sparkonto** *nt* **mit laufender Verzinsung** BANK current savings account; **Sparkonto** *nt* **mit Tageszinsen** BANK daily interest savings account; **Sparmaßnahme** *f* VERWALT economy measure; **als Sparmaßnahme** *phr* GESCHÄFT as an economy measure; **Sparneigung** *f* VW propensity to save; **Sparpackung** *f* GESCHÄFT, V&M economy-sized packet, economy pack; **Sparprämienanleihe** *f* FINANZ Premium Savings Bond (*BrE*); **Sparpreis** *m* GESCHÄFT, V&M budget price; **Sparprogramm** *nt* **der öffentlichen Hand** VW economic austerity; **Sparquote** *f* VW propensity to save, savings ratio, savings-to-income ratio

sparsam 1. *adj* GESCHÄFT economical; **2.** *adv* GESCHÄFT economically

sparsam: **~e Haushaltsführung** *f* MGMNT good housekeeping; **~es Wirtschaften** *nt* MGMNT good housekeeping

Sparsamkeit *f* VW economy

Spar-: **Spartarif** *m* FREI, TRANSP economy ticket

Sparte *f* V&M division, VW line of business; **Spartenmanager, in** *m,f* PERSON division manager; **Spartenorganisation** *f* GESCHÄFT divisionalization

Spar-: **Sparwesen** *nt* BÖRSE National Savings (*BrE*); **Sparzinsen** *m pl* BANK bank deposit rate, interest on saving deposits

Spät- *in cpds* GESCHÄFT late

spät: **~er Börsenticker** *m* BÖRSE late tape; **~e Mehrheit** *f* V&M *bei der Einführung eines Produktes* late majority

Spät-: **Spätausgabe** *f* MEDIEN *Zeitung* final

später 1. *adj* GESCHÄFT later; ◆ **zu einem ~en Termin** GESCHÄFT at a later date, at a subsequent date; **2.** *adv* GESCHÄFT later; ◆ **~ datieren** KOMM postdate; **was auch immer ~ eintritt** GESCHÄFT whichever is later

später: **~e Versicherungsleistungen** *f pl* **und Zahlungen** *f pl* VERSICH deferred benefits and payments; **~e Zahlung** *f* **der Jahresrente** VERSICH deferred payment annuity

spätestens *adv* GESCHÄFT at the latest

Spät-: **Spätfolge** *f* GESCHÄFT aftereffect; **Spätkapitalismus** *m* VW late capitalism; **Spätnachmittagsendezeit** *f* MEDIEN early fringe; **Spätschaden** *m* VERSICH belated claim

Spearman: **~sche Rangkorrelationsformel** *f* MATH Spearman's rank correlation formula

Spediteur *m* GESCHÄFT warehouse keeper, warehouse officer, IMP/EXP, TRANSP carrier, forwarder (*fwdr*), forwarding agent, freight forwarder, hauler (*AmE*), haulier (*BrE*), transport agent; **~, der einen kombinierten Transport durchführt** TRANSP combined transport operator (*CTO*); **~ im kombinierten Verkehr** TRANSP multimodal transport operator; **Spediteurkonnossement** *nt* IMP/EXP, TRANSP forwarding agent's bill of lading, house bill of lading; **Spediteurluftfrachtbrief** *m* IMP/EXP, TRANSP house air waybill (*HAWB*)

Spedition *f* IMP/EXP, TRANSP carrier haulage, conveyance, truckage; **Speditionsbetrieb** *m* TRANSP road haulage company, road haulage contractor; **Speditionsfirma** *f* TRANSP forwarding agency, shipping agency; **Speditionskosten** *pl* TRANSP carrying charge; **Speditionsunternehmen** *nt* IMP/EXP, TRANSP forwarding company, transport company

Speicher *m* COMP memory, storage, GESCHÄFT, IMP/EXP, TRANSP storehouse, storeroom, warehouse (*whse*), V&M warehouse (*whse*); **Speicherausdruck** *m* COMP memory print-out; **Speicherauszug** *m* COMP dump, memory dump, storage dump; **Speicherauszug** *m* **der Änderungen** COMP change dump; **Speicherbelegung** *f* COMP storage map; **Speicherbereich** *m* COMP area, storage area; **Speicherchip** *m* COMP memory chip; **Speichererweiterung** *f* COMP memory extension; **Speichererweiterungskarte** *f* COMP memory expansion board

speicherfressend *adj* COMP *Programm, Vorgang* memory-hungry (*infrml*)

Speicher: **Speichergebühren** *f pl* IMP/EXP warehouse charges; **Speichergerät** *nt* COMP storage device; **Speicherkapazität** *f* COMP memory capacity, GESCHÄFT storage capacity; **Speicherkarte** *f* COMP memory card; **Speicherkosten** *pl* TRANSP warehouse charges; **Speichermedium** *nt* COMP storage medium; **Speichermodul** *nt* COMP memory bank

speichern *vt* COMP *Daten* store

Speichern *nt* COMP storage; **~ der Bildschirmdarstellung** COMP screen capture

Speicherplatz *m* COMP storage space, memory location; **~ auf Diskette** COMP disk space; **~ auf Platte** COMP disk space; **Speicherplatzbedarf** *m* COMP storage requirements

speicherresident *adj* COMP *Programm* resident, memory-resident

Speicherung *f* COMP storage

Speicher: **Speichervermittlung** *f* COMP, KOMM message switching; **Speicherverwalter, in** *m,f* GESCHÄFT warehouse keeper, warehouse officer; **Speicherzuweisung** *f* COMP storage allocation

Speisewagen *m* FREI restaurant car

Spekulant *m* BANK venture capitalist, BÖRSE position trader, FINANZ venture capitalist, *Aktien* stag, GESCHÄFT, VW venture capitalist; **~ in Terminkontrakten** BÖRSE scalper

Spekulation *f* GESCHÄFT speculation; **~ an der Börse** BÖRSE play; **~ ohne Deckung** BÖRSE overtrading; ♦ **auf ~** GESCHÄFT on speculation (*on spec*)

Spekulation: **Spekulationshandel** *m* BÖRSE speculative trading; **Spekulationshaus** *nt* GRUND spec house; **Spekulationskapital** *nt* BANK venture capital, FINANZ risk-bearing capital, venture capital, GESCHÄFT, VW venture capital; **Spekulationskasse** *f* FINANZ, VW idle balance, idle money; **Spekulationsmotiv** *nt* VW asset motive; **Spekulationspapiere** *nt pl* BÖRSE cats and dogs; **Spekulationssteuer** *f* STEUER tax on speculative profits, windfall tax

spekulationsweise *adv* PERSON *Arbeitsuche* on speculation (*on spec*)

Spekulation: **Spekulationswert** *m* BÖRSE hot issue (*AmE*)

spekulativ *adj* GESCHÄFT aggressive, speculative; ♦ **zu ~en Zwecken den Markt aufkaufen** BÖRSE cornering the market

spekulativ: **~e Geldnachfrage** *f* VW speculative demand for money

spekulieren *vi* BÖRSE take a flier, play, speculate, GESCHÄFT speculate

Spende *f* SOZIAL, STEUER donation, voluntary contribution

spenden *vt* SOZIAL, STEUER contribute, donate, make a donation

Spende: **Spendensammlung** *f* SOZIAL charity fundraising

Spendiereffekt *m* VW treat effect

Sperr- *in cpds* BANK blocked, BÖRSE waiting, GESCHÄFT bulky, TRANSP restricted, measurement

Sperre *f* GESCHÄFT ban, IMP/EXP, VW ban, boycott; **~ einer Aktienemission** BÖRSE stop order

sperren *vt* BANK *Konto* block, COMP *Datei* lock, FINANZ *Guthaben, Konto* freeze, GESCHÄFT inhibit; ♦ **jds Zuschuß ~** GESCHÄFT stop sb's allowance

Sperr-: **Sperrfrist** *f* BÖRSE *US-Wertpapieremissionen* waiting period; **Sperrgebiet** *nt* TRANSP restricted area; **Sperrgut** *nt* GESCHÄFT bulky goods, TRANSP measurement freight, measurement goods, V&M bulky goods

Sperrholz *nt* IND plywood

sperrig *adj* GESCHÄFT bulky; **~e Ladung** *f* GESCHÄFT bulky cargo; **~e Massenprodukte** *nt pl* V&M low-margin high-space goods

Sperr-: **Sperrklinkeneffekt** *m* VW ratchet effect; **Sperrkonto** *nt* BANK blocked account

Spesen *pl* FINANZ bank charges, RECHNUNG expenses, out-of-pocket expenses; ♦ **~ aufgliedern** FINANZ break down expenses; **jdm wenig ~ geben** GESCHÄFT put sb on short allowance; **~ werden übernommen** GESCHÄFT expenses all paid

Spesen: **Spesenkasse** *f* RECHNUNG imprest fund; **Spesenkonto** *nt* PERSON, RECHNUNG expense account; **Spesenpauschale** *f* RECHNUNG expense allowance; **Spesenzettel** *m* GESCHÄFT cost records

Spezial- *in cpds* GESCHÄFT special, specific; **Spezialartikel** *m* GESCHÄFT speciality, specialty (*AmE*), V&M speciality goods, specialty goods (*AmE*); **Spezialausbildung** *f* PERSON specific training; **Spezialausführung** *f* TRANSP special type; **Spezialclearing** *nt* BANK special clearing (*BrE*); **Spezialgebiet** *nt* GESCHÄFT speciality, specialty (*AmE*)

spezialisieren: **sich ~ auf** *v refl* [+acc] GESCHÄFT specialize in

spezialisiert *adj* GESCHÄFT, IND specialized

Spezialisierung *f* GESCHÄFT specialization

Spezialistentum *nt* GESCHÄFT professionalism

Spezialität *f* GESCHÄFT speciality, specialty (*AmE*); **Spezialitäteneinzelhändler, in** *m,f* V&M speciality retailer, specialty retailer (*AmE*)

Spezial-: **Spezialvertreter, in** *m,f* GESCHÄFT subagent

speziell 1. *adj* GESCHÄFT specific; **2.** *adv* GESCHÄFT specially, specifically

speziell: **~es Angebot** *nt* V&M specific offer; **~e Befugnis** *f* POL special warrant; **~ gebaut** *adj* GRUND, TRANSP purpose-built; **~ gebaute Tonnage** *f* TRANSP purpose-built tonnage; **~e nichtbörsenfähige Anleihe** *f* BÖRSE special nonmarketable bond; **~e Steueranleihe** *f* BÖRSE, STEUER special tax bond; **~e Steuern** *f pl* STEUER, VW narrow-based taxes (*AmE*); **~e Verpflichtung** *f* GESCHÄFT specific commitment; **nicht ~ vorgesehen** *phr* GESCHÄFT not specially provided for (*nspf*); **~e Zahlung** *f* GESCHÄFT specific payment

Speziessachen *f pl* GESCHÄFT ascertained goods

Spezifikation *f* MATH specification

spezifisch *adj* GESCHÄFT specific; **~er Egalitarismus** *m* VW specific egalitarianism; **~es Gewicht** *nt* IND specific gravity (*SG*); **~e Investitionsanleihe** *f* FINANZ specific investment loan (*SIL*); **~es Investitionsdarlehen** *nt* FINANZ specific investment loan (*SIL*); **~es Leistungsgewicht** *nt* TRANSP power to weight ratio; **~e Verpflichtung** *f* RECHT specific obligation; **~er Zoll** *m* IMP/EXP specific duty, STEUER fixed duty, specific duty

Spezifität *f*: **~ eines Wirtschaftsgutes** VW asset specificity

spezifiziert *adj* GESCHÄFT, RECHNUNG specified; **~er Tarif** *m* TRANSP specified rate

spiegeln: **sich ~ in** *v refl* [+dat] GESCHÄFT be reflected in

Spiel *nt* GESCHÄFT game, play; ♦ **ins ~ kommen** GESCHÄFT come into play

Spiel: **Spielkasino** *nt* FREI casino; **Spielraum** *m* GESCHÄFT area, scope, MGMNT *der Gedanken* latitude, RECHNUNG margin of error; **Spielregeln** *f pl* GESCHÄFT ground rules; **Spielschulden** *f pl* GESCHÄFT gambling debts; **Spieltheorie** *f* MGMNT, PERSON, VW game theory; **Spielverderber** *m* POL *Präsidentschaftswahlen* spoiler (*AmE*)

Spinnwebtheorem *nt* VW *Modell der Preisbildung* cobweb theorem

Spionage *f* IND, POL espionage

Spiral- *in cpds* TRANSP, V&M spiral, comb; **Spiralbindung** *f* V&M comb binding

Spirale *f* VW spiral; **~ nach unten** GESCHÄFT downward spiral

Spitze *f* COMP *Rechner* front end, GESCHÄFT top of the tree (*infrml*), top, spearhead, VW peak; **an der ~ des Fortschritts** *phr* GESCHÄFT in the vanguard of progress; **Spitzenbeamte(r)** *m* [decl. as adj], **Spitzenbeamtin** *f* VERWALT top-ranking official; **Spitzencomputer** *m* COMP front-end computer, high-end computer; **Spitzeneffizienz** *f* VW top-level efficiency; **Spitzengespräch** *nt* MGMNT top-level talks; **der Spitzenklasse** *phr* GESCHÄFT high-class; **Spitzenkraft** *f* GESCHÄFT, PERSON high achiever, top hand (*AmE*); **Spitzenleistungstechnik** *f* COMP advanced technology;

Spitzenmanagement *nt* MGMNT top management; **Spitzenmann** *m* *infrml* GESCHÄFT, PERSON high achiever, top hand (*AmE*); **Spitzenmarke** *f* GESCHÄFT top of the line, V&M brand leader; **Spitzenpapier** *nt* FINANZ blue chip; **Spitzenposition** *f* V&M *in einem Markt* prime position; **Spitzenpreis** *m* GESCHÄFT top price; **Spitzenprodukt** *nt* GESCHÄFT top-rank product; **Spitzenqualität** *f* GESCHÄFT top quality

Spitzenreiter *m* GESCHÄFT front runner; ♦ **~ sein** GESCHÄFT be top of the league

Spitze: **Spitzenstellung** *f* GESCHÄFT top of the range

Spitzensteuersatz *m* STEUER top rate of tax; ♦ **zum ~** STEUER at the top rate

Spitze: **Spitzentarif** *m* GESCHÄFT peak rate; **Spitzentechnologie** *f* IND high technology industry; **Spitzenunternehmen** *nt* GESCHÄFT high flier; **Spitzenwert** *m* BÖRSE high flier, VW record high; **Spitzenwerte** *m pl* **und Nachzügler** *m pl* BÖRSE leaders and laggards; **Spitzenzeit** *f* TRANSP, UMWELT peak period, V&M *Fernsehzuschauer* peak time

Splitter- *in cpds* MGMNT, PERSON, POL fragmented, splinter, splintered; **Splitterbehörde** *f* MGMNT splintered authority; **Splittergewerkschaft** *f* PERSON splinter union; **Splittergruppe** *f* PERSON *innerhalb einer Organisation* faction, POL splinter group; **Splitterverhandlung** *f* PERSON fragmented bargaining

sponsern *vt* V&M *Werbung* sponsor

Sponsern *nt* V&M *Werbung* sponsorship

Sponsor *m* FINANZ backer, V&M *Werbung* sponsor; **Sponsorenfernsehen** *nt* MEDIEN, V&M sponsored television

Sponsoring *nt* SOZIAL *von Wohltätigkeitsveranstaltungen* charity sponsorship, V&M *Werbung* sponsorship

Sponsor: **Sponsor-Nachfrage** *f* VW sponsor demand

Spontan- *in cpds* GESCHÄFT impulse

spontan *adj* GESCHÄFT, V&M spontaneous, impulse; ♦ **eine ~e Entscheidung treffen** GESCHÄFT make a snap decision

spontan: **~e Erinnerung** *f* V&M spontaneous recall; **~ gekaufte Waren** *f pl* V&M impulse goods; **auf ~e Kaufreaktion abgestellte Werbung** *f* V&M direct action advertising, direct response advertising; **~e Reaktion** *f* V&M unprompted response

Spontaneität *f* POL spontaneity

Spontan-: **Spontankauf** *m* V&M impulse buy, impulse purchase; **Spontanverkauf** *m* V&M impulse sale

SPOOL-Datei *f* COMP spool file

sporadisch *adj* GESCHÄFT sporadic; **~es Verkehrsangebot** *nt* TRANSP sporadic service

Sporen: **sich die ~ verdienen** *phr* GESCHÄFT win one's spurs

Sport *m* FREI sport; **Sport- und Fitneßcenter** *nt* FREI health club; **Sport- und Fitneßstudio** *nt* FREI health club; **Sportveranstaltung** *f* FREI, GESCHÄFT sporting event

Spot-Chartervertrag *m* TRANSP spot charter

Spottpreis *m* GESCHÄFT bargain price, knockdown price

Sprach- *in cpds* COMP speech, voice

sprachaktiviert *adj* COMP voice-activated

Sprache *f* V&M language; ♦ **zur ~ bringen** GESCHÄFT mention

Sprach-: **Spracherkennung** *f* COMP speech recognition,

voice recognition; **Spracherkennungssoftware** *f* COMP speech recognition software

sprachgesteuert *adj* COMP voice-actuated

Sprach-: **Sprachpost** *f* COMP voice mail; **Sprachverarbeitung** *f* COMP speech processing

Spreading *nt* BÖRSE spreading; **Spreading-Vereinbarung** *f* BÖRSE spreading agreement

Spreadsheet *nt* BÖRSE, COMP, FINANZ, RECHNUNG, VERWALT spreadsheet

Sprech- *in cpds* GESCHÄFT, TRANSP, V&M speech, voice; **Sprechblase** *f* GESCHÄFT balloon line

sprechen: ~ **von** *phr* GESCHÄFT *erwähnen* refer to; ~ **zu** *phr* GESCHÄFT *Thema, Problem* address; **zu** ~ *phr* GESCHÄFT available; **nicht zu** ~ *phr* GESCHÄFT unavailable

Sprecher *m* GESCHÄFT speaker, MEDIEN, POL spokesman, spokesperson

Sprecherin *f* GESCHÄFT speaker, MEDIEN, POL spokeswoman, spokesperson

Sprech-: **Sprechfehler** *m* KOMM slip of the tongue, fluff (*infrml*); **Sprechfunk** *m* KOMM radiotelephony (*RT*); **Sprechfunkgerät** *nt* KOMM radiophone (*RP*)

Spreng- *in cpds* IND, TRANSP explosive; **Sprengkörper** *m* TRANSP explosive article; **Sprengpulver** *nt* IND *Bergbau* black powder; **Sprengzünder** *m* IND detonator

spricht: **es** ~ **für sich selbst** *phr* GESCHÄFT, RECHT res ipsa loquitur

Springflut *f* TRANSP spring tide

Sprit *m* IND industrial spirits

Spruchband *nt* V&M banner

spruchberechtigt *adj* RECHT entitled to adjudicate

Spruchgericht *nt* RECHT court entitled to adjudicate

Sprung *m* GESCHÄFT jump; **Sprungadresse** *f* COMP *Programm* branch address

sprunghaft *adj* BÖRSE *Kursbewegungen*, GESCHÄFT erratic; ~ **ansteigen** *phr* GESCHÄFT *Gewinn, Preise* skyrocket, soar; ~**er Aufschwung** *m* VW boom; ~ **erhöhen** *phr* GESCHÄFT escalate

Sprung: **Sprungkosten** *pl* RECHNUNG step cost, step-variable cost

Spulen *nt* COMP spooling

Spur *f* GESCHÄFT shadow, sign, VW shadow; ~ **eines Beweises** GESCHÄFT scrap of evidence

spürbar *adj* GESCHÄFT appreciable

SQC *abbr* (*statistische Qualitätskontrolle*) MATH SQC (*statistical quality control*)

St. *abbr* GESCHÄFT (*Stück*) pc. (*piece*), pcs (*pieces*), (*Stunde*) h (*hour*), hr (*hour*)

Staat *m* POL state; ~ **der Registrierung** TRANSP state of registry; **Staaten** *m pl* **in Afrika, im karibischen Raum und im Pazifischen Ozean** (*AKP-Staaten*) vw African, Caribbean and Pacific states (*ACP states*); **Staatenbund** *m* POL confederation

staatenlos *adj* POL stateless, VERWALT nationless, VW stateless; ~**e Währung** *f* VW stateless currency

staatl. *abbr* (*staatlich*) GESCHÄFT nat. (*national*)

staatlich 1. *adj* (*staatl.*) GESCHÄFT governmental, national (*nat.*); ♦ ~**e Ansprüche erlassen** STEUER grant administrative relief; **unter** ~**er Aufsicht** VERWALT government-controlled; **mit** ~**er Hilfe** POL, VW state-aided; **2.** *adv* GESCHÄFT by the state; ♦ ~ **finanziert** FINANZ government-financed; ~ **gefördert** FINANZ government-supported, government-sponsored; ~ **gelenkt**

POL government-regulated; ~ **unterstützt** FINANZ government-backed

staatlich: ~**e Anleihe** *f* FINANZ sovereign loan; ~**e Bauvorhaben** *nt pl* GESCHÄFT, VW public works; ~**e Bruttoausgaben** *f pl* VW gross national expenditure; ~**es Darlehen** *nt* FINANZ sovereign loan; ~**e Einflußnahme** *f* **auf die Berichterstattung** POL managed news; ~**er Eingriff** *m* POL, VERWALT, VW government intervention; ~**e Einkommensübertragung** *f* VERWALT government transfer payment; ~**e Einlagenversicherung** *f* VERSICH Federal Deposit Insurance Corporation (*FDIC*) (*AmE*); ~**e Entwicklungshilfe** *f* vw official development assistance (*ODA*); ~**e Finanzierung** *f* FINANZ government finance; ~**es Förderprogramm** *nt* FINANZ direct spending program (*AmE*), direct spending programme (*BrE*); ~**e Förderung** *f* SOZIAL government aid; ~**e Förderung** *f* **für Unternehmensneugründungen** FINANZ enterprise allowance (*BrE*); ~**e Forschungsbeihilfe** *f* FINANZ government research grant; ~ **gefilterte Information** *f* POL word engineering; ~ **gelenkte Nachrichten** *f pl* POL managed news; ~**e Gesellschaft** *f* GESCHÄFT publicly owned company; ~**er Gesundheitsdienst** *m* POL, SOZIAL Medicaid (*AmE*), Medicare (*AmE*), National Health Service (*BrE*) (*NHS*); ~**e Hilfe** *f* SOZIAL state help; ~**e Intervention** *f* GESCHÄFT state intervention, PERSON statutory policy (*BrE*), POL, VERWALT, VW government intervention, state intervention; ~**e Investition** *f* FINANZ government investment; ~**er Investor** *m* FINANZ public investor; ~**er Kommunalobligationsfonds** *m* FINANZ single-state municipal bond fund; ~**e Kontrolle** *f* VW state control; ~**e Landwirtschaftsbank** *f* BANK Federal Land Bank (*AmE*); ~**e Lohnkontrolle** *f* VW wage control; ~**e Lotterie** *f* FINANZ national lottery; ~**e Mittel** *nt pl* VERWALT government funds; ~**e Münze** *f* VW ≈ Royal Mint (*BrE*); ~**e Planung** *f* MGMNT central planning; ~**e Preisfestsetzung** *f* VW public pricing; ~**e Prüfung** *f* PERSON, SOZIAL public examination; ~**er Rechnungsprüfer** *m*, ~**e Rechnungsprüferin** *f* FINANZ comptroller, controller; ~**es Rechnungswesen** *nt* RECHNUNG government accounting; ~ **regulierte Preisfestsetzung** *f* VW administered pricing; ~**es Risiko** *nt* FINANZ sovereign risk; ~**e Schule** *f* SOZIAL public school (*AmE*), state school (*BrE*); ~**er Sektor** *m* VW public sector; ~**er Sparbrief** *m* BANK National Savings Certificate (*BrE*); ~**e Subvention** *f* VW state subsidy, government grant; ~ **subventionierte Exportkredite** *m pl* FINANZ officially-supported export credits; ~**e Transferzahlung** *f* VERWALT government transfer payment; ~**es Unternehmen** *nt* FINANZ, GESCHÄFT, VERWALT, VW government enterprise, government-controlled corporation, public enterprise, state enterprise, state-owned enterprise, state-run enterprise; ~**e Zuweisung** *f* VW government grant

Staat: **Staatsangehörige(r)** *mf* [decl. as adj] POL citizen; **Staatsangehörigkeit** *f* POL citizenship, nationality

Staatsanleihe *f* BÖRSE government stock, funded debt, FINANZ public loan, government annuity, government loan, vw government bond; **Staatsanleihenmarkt** *m* BANK federal funds market (*AmE*); **Staatsanleihepapiere** *nt pl* BÖRSE gilt-edged stock

Staatsanwalt *m* RECHT crown prosecutor (*BrE*), district attorney (*AmE*) (*DA*), public prosecutor

Staatsanwältin *f* RECHT crown prosecutor (*BrE*), district attorney (*AmE*) (*DA*), public prosecutor

Staatsanwaltschaft *f* RECHT Crown Prosecution Service (*BrE*), office of the district attorney (*AmE*), public prosecutor's office; **die ~** *f* RECHT the prosecution

Staat: **Staatsauftrag** *m* GESCHÄFT, RECHT government contract, public contract; **Staatsausgaben** *f pl* VW government expenditure, public expenditure, public spending, national expenditure; **Staatsbetrieb** *m* GESCHÄFT, VW government enterprise, public enterprise, publicly owned company, state-owned enterprise

Staatsbürger, in *m,f* POL citizen, VERWALT national; **~ zweiter Klasse** GESCHÄFT second-class citizen

Staatsbürgerschaft *f* POL citizenship

Staat: **Staatsdarlehen** *nt* STEUER Crown loan (*BrE*); **Staatsdefizit** *nt* VW federal deficit (*AmE*); **Staatsdienst** *m* GESCHÄFT civil service (*CS*), VERWALT public service

staatseigen *adj* GESCHÄFT government-owned; **~e Gesellschaft** *f* VERWALT Crown corporation (*BrE*)

Staat: **Staatseigentum** *nt* FINANZ, POL, VW public ownership, state ownership; **Staatseinnahme** *f* POL revenue; **Staatsfeinde** *m pl* RECHT enemies of the state, King's enemies (*BrE*), Queen's enemies (*BrE*); **Staatsfinanzen** *f pl* VW public finances; **Staatsfinanzierung** *f* VW government finance; **Staatsgewalt** *f* GESCHÄFT the authorities, public authority; **Staatsgrenze** *f* GESCHÄFT national border, IMP/EXP, POL national boundary; **Staatshandelsorganisation** *f* GESCHÄFT state trading organization; **Staatshaushalt** *m* VW budget, government budget, state budget; **den Staatshaushalt ausgleichen** *phr* FINANZ balance the budget; **Staatskapitalismus** *m* POL *Marxismus*, VW state capitalism; **Staatskasse** *f* BANK the Exchequer (*BrE*) (*Exch.*), POL public purse, VW public purse, treasury; **Staatslotterie** *f* FINANZ national lottery; **Staatsoberhaupt** *nt* POL head of state; **Staatsobligationen** *f pl* VW government obligations (*BrE*), governments (*infrml*) (*AmE*)

Staatspapier: **~e** *nt pl* BANK, BÖRSE, FINANZ bank annuities, gilt-edged securities, gilts (*BrE*); **Staatspapiermarktmacher** *m pl* BÖRSE gilt-edged market makers (*GEMMS*)

staatspolitisch *adj* GESCHÄFT political, relating to national policy

Staat: **Staatsprüfung** *f* PERSON, SOZIAL degree, state examination; **Staatsquote** *f* VW public spending ratio; **Staatsrente** *f* FINANZ consolidated annuities (*BrE*), consolidated stock (*AmE*); **Staatssäckel** *m infrml* POL state coffers, VW public purse

Staatsschuld *f* VW Gross National Debt (*AmE*), national debt, debt obligation; **Staatsschuldendienst** *m* VW consolidated fund standing services (*BrE*); **Staatsschuldverschreibung** *f* FINANZ government bond (*BrE*), public bond (*AmE*), state bond (*AmE*)

Staat: **Staatssekretär, in** *m,f* PERSON, POL undersecretary of state

staatssozialistisch: **~e Volkswirtschaft** *f* VW Soviet-type economy

Staat: **Staatssteuer** *f* VW tax; **Staatstheorie** *f* VW state theory; **Staatstitel** *m pl* FINANZ gilt-edged securities; **Staatsunternehmen** *nt* VW state-owned enterprise; **Staatsurkunden** *f pl* VERWALT public records

Staatsverschuldung *f* FINANZ public debt, VW debt obligation, *Devisenbilanz* official financing;

Staatsverschuldungskosten *pl* FINANZ public debt charges; **Staatsverschuldungspaket** *nt* FINANZ public debt envelope

Staat: **Staatsvertrag** *m* GESCHÄFT, POL treaty; **Staatszuschuß** *m* FINANZ government grant, government subsidy, grant-in-aid

Stab *m* PERSON staff; ♦ **~ und Linie** PERSON line and staff

Stab: **Stabdiagramm** *nt* GESCHÄFT, MATH bar chart

stabil *adj* GESCHÄFT *Preise* sticky, *Währung* firm, stable, TRANSP, V&M, VW *Währung* firm, stable; **~es Gleichgewicht** *nt* VW stable equilibrium, strong equilibrium; **~ halten** *phr* VW stabilize; **~er Markt** *m* FINANZ, VW stable market; **~e Rate** *f* TRANSP stable rate

Stabilisator *m* TRANSP antiroll suspension, VW stabilizer

stabilisieren **1.** *vt* VW stabilize; **2. sich ~** *v refl* VW stabilize

stabilisierend: **~er Faktor** *m* VW steadying factor; **~er Regelmechanismus** *m* VW built-in flexibility

stabilisiert: **~er Preis** *m* VW stabilized price; **~er Wechselkurs** *m* FINANZ stabilized currency

Stabilisierung *f* VW stabilization

Stabilität *f* GESCHÄFT *von Märkten, Preisen* firmness, stability; **Stabilitätspolitik** *f* VW stabilization policy; **Stabilitätszone** *f* PERSON, SOZIAL *ohne Streß* stability zone

Stablinie: **Stablinienmanagement** *nt* PERSON line and staff management; **Stablinienorganisation** *f* MGMNT line and staff organization, *Hierarchie* staff organization, PERSON staff organization

Stab: **Stabsleiter, in** *m,f* PERSON staff manager

Stack *m* COMP stack

Stackelberg: **~sches Duopolmodell** *nt* VW Stackelberg duopoly model

Stadium *nt* GESCHÄFT phase, stage

Stadt *f* POL city; ♦ **außerhalb der ~** V&M out-of-town

Stadt: **Stadtbezirk** *m* POL borough, municipality borough (*AmE*)

Städtebau *m* GRUND, POL, VERWALT city planning, town planning (*TP*), urban development

städtebaulich: **~e Planung** *f* GRUND, POL, VERWALT city planning, town planning (*TP*), urban development

Stadt: **Stadtentwicklungsgebiet** *nt* POL, VERWALT Urban Programme Area; **Stadterneuerung** *f* POL, VERWALT urban renewal; **Stadtgebiet** *nt* POL, VERWALT urban area; **Stadthaus** *nt* GRUND *Reihenhaus oder Doppelhaus mit gemeinsamer Wand zum Nebenhaus* town house

städtisch: **~e Anleihe** *f* FINANZ local authority loan (*BrE*); **~es Krankenhaus** *nt* SOZIAL district hospital; **~e Schule** *f* SOZIAL public school (*AmE*)

Stadt: **Stadtkern** *m* GRUND, UMWELT, VW inner city; **Stadtmagistrat** *m* POL city council; **Stadtmitte** *f* GESCHÄFT town center (*AmE*), town centre (*BrE*); **Stadtökonomie** *f* VW urban economics; **Stadtparlament** *nt* POL, VERWALT borough council (*BrE*); **Stadtplaner, in** *m,f* GESCHÄFT, GRUND, POL, VERWALT city planner, town planner, urban planner; **Stadtplanung** *f* GRUND, POL, VERWALT city planning, town planning (*TP*), urban development; **Stadtrat** *m* POL, VERWALT *Einrichtung* borough council (*BrE*), common council (*AmE*), town council, councilman (*AmE*), town councillor, city council; **Stadträtin** *f* POL, VERWALT councilwoman (*AmE*), town councillor; **Stadtsanierung** *f* GESCHÄFT, VW urban renewal;

Stadtsanierungsgebiet *nt* GESCHÄFT Urban Programme Area (*BrE*); **Stadtsubvention** *f* GESCHÄFT City Grant (*BrE*); **Stadtteil** *m* POL, VERWALT borough; **Stadtteil** *m* **mit Geschwindigkeitsbegrenzung** TRANSP restricted area; **Stadtverordnete(r)** *mf* [decl. as adj] GESCHÄFT town councillor; **Stadtverwaltung** *f* POL, VERWALT municipal administration, municipal corporation (*BrE*), municipal government (*AmE*), town administration; **Stadtzentrum** *nt* GESCHÄFT city center (*AmE*), city centre (*BrE*), town center (*AmE*), town centre (*BrE*); **außerhalb des Stadtzentrums** *phr* V&M outside the city center (*AmE*), outside the city centre (*BrE*)

Staff: ~ **Captain** *m* PERSON staff captain

Staffel- *in cpds* FINANZ, GRUND, PERSON graduated; **Staffelmiete** *f* GRUND graduated lease

staffeln *vt* GESCHÄFT *Kosten* stagger

Staffel-: **Staffeltarif** *m* PERSON graduated wage

Staffelung *f* GESCHÄFT *Arbeitszeit* stagger; ~ **der Urlaubszeiten** PERSON staggered holidays (*BrE*), staggered vacations (*AmE*), staggering of vacations (*AmE*), staggering of holidays (*BrE*)

Staffel-: **Staffelzahlungen** *f pl* FINANZ graduated payments; **Staffelzinsen** *f pl* FINANZ graduated interest

Stagflation *f* VW stagflation

Stagfock-Derrick *m* TRANSP jumbo derrick

Stagnation *f* VW stagnation

stagnieren *vi* VW stagnate

stagnierend *adj* VW stagnant; **nicht** ~ *adj* BÖRSE undepressed

Stahl *m* IND, TRANSP steel; **Stahlabdeckung** *f* TRANSP steel covers; **Stahlaktien** *f pl* BÖRSE steel securities, steel shares (*BrE*), steels, steelstocks (*AmE*); **Stahlarbeiter** *m* IND steelworker, PERSON steel-collar worker; **Stahlbaufirma** *f* IND fabricator; **Stahldeckel** *m* TRANSP steel covers; **Stahlhütte** *f* IND steelworks; **Stahlindustrie** *f* IND steel industry

stahlintensiv *adj* IND steel-intensive

Stahl: **Stahlkammer** *f* BANK safety vault; **Stahlpreise** *m pl* **mit Frachtbasis Pittsburgh** VW Pittsburgh-plus (*AmE*); **Stahlwerk** *m* IND steelworks; **Stahlwerker** *m* IND steelworker; **Stahlwerte** *m pl* BÖRSE steel securities, steel shares (*BrE*), steels, steelstocks (*AmE*)

Stall *m* FREI stable

Stamm- *in cpds* COMP, FINANZ, GESCHÄFT, PERSON, VW main, master root, nominal, share, head, original, parent, core, common

Stammaktie *f* BÖRSE common share (*AmE*), common stock (*AmE*), equity share (*AmE*), ordinary share (*BrE*); **Stammaktienäquivalent** *nt* BÖRSE common shares equivalent (*BrE*), common stock equivalent (*AmE*)

stammaktiengleich: ~**es Papier** *nt* BÖRSE common shares equivalent (*BrE*), common stock equivalent (*AmE*)

Stammaktie: **Stammaktien** *f pl* **mit großem Anteil an Vorzugsaktien** FINANZ leveraged stock; **Stammaktienindex** *m* BÖRSE All Ordinaries Index

Stamm-: **Stammanteil** *m* BÖRSE, RECHNUNG stockholders' equity, VW common stock (*AmE*); **Stammbaum** *m* GESCHÄFT, MGMNT family tree; **Stammbelegschaft** *f* PERSON core workforce (*BrE*),

Betriebswirtschaft skeleton staff; **Stammdatei** *f* COMP master file, main file

stammen: ~ **aus** *phr* GESCHÄFT originate in, stem from

Stämmen: **nach** ~ *phr* RECHT per stirpes

Stamm-: **Stammhaus** *nt* GESCHÄFT company headquarters, head office (*HO*), original firm, parent company; **Stammkapital** *nt* FINANZ *GmbH* capital stock (*AmE*), nominal capital, share capital, capital fund, RECHNUNG capital; **Stammkapitalbeteiligung** *f* GESCHÄFT, VERWALT equity interest; **Stammpersonal** *m* COMP cadre; **Stammverzeichnis** *nt* COMP root directory

Stand *m* BÖRSE post (*AmE*), stand, GESCHÄFT *Rang* rank, *der Verhandlungen* stage, level, V&M *bei einer Ausstellung* stand; ~ **der Dinge** GESCHÄFT state of affairs; ~ **der Technik** GESCHÄFT state of the art, PATENT prior art; ♦ **einen** ~ **mit Personal besetzen** PERSON man a stand

Standard *m* BÖRSE standard (*Std*), COMP default, GESCHÄFT standard grade; ~ **der Lebenshaltungskosten** GESCHÄFT budget standard; **Standardabweichung** *f* FINANZ, MATH standard deviation; **Standardausfuhrabschöpfung** *f* IMP/EXP standard export levy

Standardausgaben: **Standardausgabenbewertung** *f* FINANZ, VW standard spending assessment (*SSA*); **Standardausgabenobjekt** *nt* POL, VW standard object of expenditure; **Standardausgabenposten** *m* POL, VW standard object of expenditure

Standard: **Standardaustauscheinrichtungen** *f pl* TRANSP standard interchange facilities (*SIT*); **Standardbeleg** *m* TRANSP standard slip; **Standardbrief** *m* V&M standard letter; **Standarddesign** *nt* IND *eines Schiffs* standard design (*SD*); **Standardeinnahmeobjekt** *nt* POL standard object of revenue; **Standardeinstellung** *f* COMP *Betriebssystem* default; **Standardexportabgabe** *f* IMP/EXP standard export levy; **Standardfehler** *m* MATH standard error; **Standardfehler** *m* **des arithmetischen Mittels** MATH standard error of the mean; **Standardfrachthandelsklassifizierung** *f* TRANSP standard freight trade classification (*SFTC*); **Standardgerät** *nt* COMP default device; **Standardherstellungskosten** *pl* FINANZ standard costs

standardisieren *vt* GESCHÄFT, RECHNUNG, RECHT, V&M standardize

standardisiert *adj* GESCHÄFT, RECHNUNG, RECHT, V&M standardized; ~**e Fertigungsmethode** *f* GESCHÄFT standard operating procedure (*s.o.p., SOP*); ~**e Qualität** *f* GESCHÄFT standard grade; ~**er statistischer Bereich** *m* **einer Großstadt** MATH Standard Metropolitan Statistical Area (*SMSA*); ~**e Verkaufspräsentation** *f* V&M standardized sales presentation

Standardisierung *f* GESCHÄFT, RECHNUNG, RECHT, V&M standardization; ~ **der Buchführung** RECHNUNG accounting harmonization (*BrE*); **Standardisierungsabkommen** *nt* GESCHÄFT standardization agreement

Standard: **Standardkonstruktion** *f* IND *eines Schiffs* standard design (*SD*)

Standardkosten *pl* FINANZ cost standard, RECHNUNG standard costs; **Standardkostensystem** *nt* GESCHÄFT standard cost system

Standard: **Standardlaufwerk** *nt* COMP default drive; **Standardleistung** *f* GESCHÄFT, PERSON standard performance; **Standardmaschinencode** *m* COMP standard object code; **Standardobjekt** *nt* POL, VW standard object; **Standardobjektcode** *m* POL, VW standard object code; **Standardoption** *f* COMP default option; **Standard-Portfeuille-Risikoanalyse** *f* FINANZ standard portfolio analysis of risk (*SPAR*); **Standardposten** *m* POL, VW standard object; **Standardpreis** *m* V&M standard price; **Standardration** *f* POL standard allotment; **Standardschätzfehler** *m* MATH standard error of estimate; **Standardschiffszettel** *m* IMP/EXP, TRANSP standard shipping note; **Standardsorte** *f* PERSON basic grade; **Standardsteuersatz** *m* STEUER basic-rate tax; **Standardunternehmen** *nt* GESCHÄFT off-the-shelf company; **Standardunterschriftskarte** *f* BANK standard specimen signature card; **Standardverfahren** *nt* GESCHÄFT standard operating procedure (*s.o.p., SOP*); **Standard- und Verhaltensnormen** *f pl* RECHT standards and practices; **Standardversandanzeige** *f* IMP/EXP, TRANSP standard shipping note; **Standardvertrag** *m* GESCHÄFT standard agreement, RECHT standard contract, standard-form contract; **Standardvertrag** *m* **mit einseitig auferlegten Bedingungen** RECHT *Vertragsrecht* adhesion contract; **Standardverzeichnis** *nt* COMP default directory; **Standardverzeichnis** *nt* **von Werbeagenturen** V&M standard directory of advertisers; **Standardware** *f* BÖRSE standard commodity; **Standardwerbesendung** *f* V&M audiovisual commercial (*av-commercial*); **Standardwert** *m* BÖRSE blue chip, leader, leading stock; **Standardzuweisung** *f* POL standard allotment

Standby- *in cpds* PERSON standby; **Standby-Fazilität** *f* FINANZ standby facility; **Standby-Kredit** *m* BANK, FINANZ standby credit; **Standby-Ticket** *nt* TRANSP standby ticket

Stand: **Standesamt** *nt* VERWALT office for recordation of personal status (*AmE*), office for registration of personal status (*BrE*), register office, registrar's office, registry office; **Standesethik** *f* MGMNT *Geschäftsführung* ethics

standesgemäß *adj* MGMNT ethical

Stand: **Standesordnung** *f* GESCHÄFT code of ethics; **Standesrichtlinien** *f pl* RECHT *Verhalten von Rechtsanwälten* code of professional responsibility, ethics of the profession

standeswidrig: ~**es Verhalten** *nt* GESCHÄFT breach of professional etiquette, RECHT *Arzt, Rechtsanwalt* professional misconduct

Stand: **Standfestigkeit** *f* FINANZ staying power

ständig *adj* GESCHÄFT *dauerhaft* persistent; ~ **abweichender Wechselkurs** *m* VW misaligned rate of exchange; ~**e Adresse** *f* KOMM permanent address; ~**er Ausschuß** *m* POL standing committee; ~**e Beteiligung** *f* RECHNUNG permanent participation; ~**e Forschung** *f* V&M continuous research; ~ **steigend** *phr* GESCHÄFT *Nachfrage* ever-increasing

Ständig: ~**er Vertreter** *m* **Großbritanniens bei der Europäischen Gemeinschaft** POL, VW United Kingdom Permanent Representative to the European Economic Community

ständig: ~ **vorrätige Ware** *f* V&M open stock; ~**er Wohnsitz** *m* RECHT permanent residence; **ohne** ~**en Wohnsitz** *phr* VERWALT nonpatrial (*obs*) (*BrE*)

Stand: **Standleitung** *f* COMP dedicated line, leased line

Standort *m* GESCHÄFT site, location, IND premises; ~ **der**

Anlage GESCHÄFT plant location; ~ **von besonderem wissenschaftlichen Interesse** UMWELT Site of Special Scientific Interest (*BrE*) (*SSSI*); **jeder** ~ VERSICH any one location (*AOLOC*); ~ **von Plakatwand** V&M hoarding site; **Standortanpassung** *f* COMP localization; **Standortbedingungen** *f pl* VW locational conditions; **Standortbescheinigung** *f* IND Industrial Development Certificate; **Standortbestimmung** *f* IND siting; **Standorterklärung** *f* POL position paper; **Standortfestlegung** *f* IND siting

standortgebunden: ~**e Industrie** *f* IND locked-in industry; ~**es Wissen** *nt* IND locked-in knowledge

Standort: **Standortklärung** *f* POL position paper; **Standortklausel** *f* TRANSP location clause; **Standortlizenz** *f* COMP site licence (*BrE*), site license (*AmE*); **Standortplanung** *f* COMP site planning; **Standortprüfung** *nt* GESCHÄFT site audit; **Standorttheorie** *f* VW economics of location, location theory

standortungebunden: ~**e Industrie** *f* IND footloose industry

Standort: **Standortwahl** *f* IND siting, UMWELT site selection

Standpunkt *m* GESCHÄFT viewpoint, point, point of view, position, MGMNT attitude; ~ **der Unternehmensleitung** MGMNT administrative point of view (*APV*); ♦ **einen** ~ **vertreten** GESCHÄFT take up a position, POL deliver an opinion; **seinen** ~ **vertreten** RECHT argue one's case

Stange: **von der** ~ *phr* GESCHÄFT off-the-peg

Stapel *m* IND, MEDIEN batch, TRANSP slipway; **Stapelausrüstung** *f* TRANSP stacking fitting; **Stapeldatei** *f* COMP batch file; **Stapeleinrichtung** *f* TRANSP post stacker, stacker; **Stapelexport** *m* IMP/EXP staple export; **Stapelfernverarbeitung** *f* COMP remote batch processing; **Stapelförderer** *m* TRANSP stacker; **Stapelgitterbehälter** *m* TRANSP box pallet; **Stapellauf** *m* TRANSP launch, launching; **Stapelrechner** *m* COMP batch computer

Stapelung *f* TRANSP stacking; ~ **von Fracht** TRANSP stacking of cargo

Stapel: **Stapelverarbeitung** *f* COMP batch processing, batch job; **Stapelwaren** *f pl* GESCHÄFT staple commodities, staple goods, staples

stark 1. *adj* GESCHÄFT high-strength, *Argument* forceful, *Indikator* strong, *Nachfrage* great, *Rückgang* marked; ♦ **ein** ~**er Anhänger sein von** POL be a strong supporter of; **auf** ~**er Ausgangsbasis verhandeln** GESCHÄFT negotiate from strength; **2.** *adv* GESCHÄFT strongly; ♦ ~ **beeindrucken** GESCHÄFT score a hit; ~ **diversifiziert** GESCHÄFT broadly diversified; **sich** ~ **erholen** BÖRSE *Markt* rally strongly; ~ **fallen** GESCHÄFT *Preise, Kurse* tumble

stark: ~**er Aufschwung** *m* GESCHÄFT boom; ~**e Baissespekulation** *f* BÖRSE strong bearish play; **zu** ~**e Belastung** *f* FINANZ overcommitment; ~**e Dollarnachfrage** *f* GESCHÄFT run on the dollar; ~**e Fremdfinanzierung** *f* FINANZ high leverage (*AmE*); ~**e Haussespekulation** *f* BÖRSE strong bullish play; ~**es Image** *nt* GESCHÄFT high image; ~**e Konkurrenz** *f* V&M strong competition; ~**e Nachfrage** *f* VW heavy demand; ~**er Nutzer** *m* COMP heavy user; ~ **schwankende Aktien** *f pl* BÖRSE yo-yo stock (*infrml*); ~ **spekulierender Investmentfonds** *m* BÖRSE hedge fund; **zu** ~**e Verpflichtung** *f* FINANZ overcommitment; ~ **verschul-**

detes Land *nt* **mit Durchschnittseinkommen** FINANZ heavily indebted middle-income country (*HIC*); **~ verschuldetes Land** *nt* **mit mittlerem Einkommen** FINANZ, VW severely indebted middle-income country (*SIMIC*); **~ verschuldetes Land** *nt* **mit niedrigem Einkommen** FINANZ, VW severely indebted low-income country (*SILIC*); **~es Wachstum** *nt* VW rapid growth; **~es Zeichenpapier** *nt* V&M cartridge paper

Stärke *f* GESCHÄFT force, VW resilience; **~ des Dollars** BÖRSE strength of the dollar

stärken *vt* GESCHÄFT, VW bolster

stärkste: am ~n betroffener Bereich *m* GESCHÄFT ground zero

Starkstrom *m* IND heavy current, high-voltage current, power

Stärkung *f* GESCHÄFT reinforcement, VW strengthening

starr: ~er Preis *m* VW inflexible price, sticky price

Starrheit *f* VW inflexibility, rigidity; **~ des Arbeitsmarktes** VW labor-market rigidities (*AmE*), labour-market rigidities (*BrE*); **~ der Löhne** VW wage rigidity

Start *m* COMP start, TRANSP takeoff; **Startbahn** *f* TRANSP runway; **Startbit** *nt* COMP start bit

starten 1. *vt* COMP *Datei* start, PERSON, V&M launch; **2.** *vi* TRANSP take off

Start: **Startkapital** *nt* FINANZ seed capital, seed money, start-up capital; **Startkosten** *pl* FINANZ, RECHNUNG start-up costs

Statik *f* IND hydrostatics, statics

Station *f* COMP, TRANSP station (*stn*)

stationär: ~es Gleichgewicht *nt* VW stationary equilibrium; **~e Volkswirtschaft** *f* VW stationary economy, stationary state economy; **~er Zustand** *m* VW stationary state

stationiert *adj* GESCHÄFT based, located; ♦ **~ sein in** [+dat] GESCHÄFT be based in

statisch *adj* VW no-growth, static; **~e Abzinsung** *f* RECHNUNG *Barwertmethode einer Rente* static discounting method; **~es Modell** *nt* VW static model; **~es Risiko** *nt* MATH, VERSICH static risk

Statistik *f* MATH statistics, STEUER Statistical Return (*BrE*); **Statistiken** *f pl* MATH statistical returns

Statistiker, in *m,f* MATH statistician

Statistik: **Statistik-Software** *f* COMP, MATH statistical software

statistisch *adj* GESCHÄFT, MATH, VW statistical; **~er Bericht** *m* STEUER Statistical Return (*BrE*); **~es Bundesamt** *m* VW ≈ Census Bureau (*AmE*), ≈ Federal Statistical Office, ≈ Central Statistical Office (*BrE*) (*CSO*); **~ erfassen** *phr* GESCHÄFT, STEUER, V&M collect statistics; **~e Fertigungskontrolle** *f* MATH statistical process control; **~e Grundgesamtheit** *f* MATH statistical population; **~e Inferenz** *f* MATH statistical inference; **~er Jahresbericht** *m* MATH annual abstract of statistics; **~e Kontrolle** *f* MATH statistical control; **~e Menge** *f* V&M population; **~e Population** *f* MATH statistical population; **~e Qualitätskontrolle** *f* (*SQC*) MATH statistical quality control (*SQC*); **~ signifikant** *adj* MATH statistically significant; **~e Signifikanz** *f* MATH statistical significance; **~e Stichprobe** *f* V&M census sample; **~e Streuung** *f* MATH statistical spread; **~e Tabelle** *f* V&M data sheet; **~er Warenkorb** *m* GESCHÄFT commodity basket; **~e Zahlungsbilanz** *f* VW accounting balance of payments

stattfinden *vi* GESCHÄFT take place

stattgeben *vi* GESCHÄFT *Anspruch* allow, sustain, *Wunsch* grant

statthaft *adj* GESCHÄFT allowable

Status *m* COMP, GESCHÄFT state, status; **~ quo** *m* PERSON, RECHT status quo; **Statusgüter** *nt pl* VW positional goods; **Statusmeldung** *f* COMP status message; **Statusprüfung** *f* V&M status inquiry; **Status-quo-Klausel** *f* PERSON status quo clause; **Statussymbol** *nt* GESCHÄFT status symbol; **Statuszeile** *f* COMP status line, status bar

Statut *nt* RECHT statute

statutarisch *adj* RECHT by statute

Statut: **Statuten** *nt pl* RECHT *Satzung einer Kapitalgesellschaft* articles of association (*BrE*), articles of incorporation (*AmE*), charter, *Satzung eines Vereins* rules, constitution, *von öffentlich-rechtlichen Körperschaften* bylaws; **nach den Statuten vorgeschriebener Aktienbesitz** *m* BÖRSE qualifying shares

Stau *m* TRANSP traffic jam; **Stauanordnung** *f* TRANSP stowage order

Staubschutzhaube *f* COMP dust cover

stauen *vt* TRANSP stow

Stauen *nt* TRANSP stowage

Stauer *m* TRANSP stevedore (*stvdr*)

Stau: **Staufaktor** *m* GESCHÄFT stowage factor; **Staugebühr** *f* TRANSP stowage; **Staugeld** *nt* TRANSP stowage; **Staugutkontrolleur** *m* TRANSP tallyman; **Stauplan** *m* TRANSP stowage plan, cargo plan

Stauung *f* GESCHÄFT congestion, TRANSP traffic jam

Stau: **Stauwasser** *nt* TRANSP slack water

Std. *abbr* (*Stunde*) GESCHÄFT h (*hour*), hr (*hour*)

Stechkarte *f* IND, PERSON time card; ♦ **seine ~ in die Stechuhr stecken** IND, PERSON clock in, punch the time clock

Stechuhr *f* IND, PERSON time clock

Stecker *m* COMP plug; ♦ **den ~ herausziehen von** GESCHÄFT unplug

Steckkarte *f* COMP *Hardware* board, card

Steckplatz *m* COMP slot

stehen: ~ bei *phr* GESCHÄFT *Angebot, Gebot, Preis* stand at; **~ für** *phr* GESCHÄFT *Initialen* stand for sth; **über etw ~** *phr* GESCHÄFT precede

stehend *adj* TRANSP upright; **~e Spanne** *f* BÖRSE perpendicular spread

steigen *vi* GESCHÄFT *Preise* go up, hike (*AmE*), increase, rise; ♦ **wieder ~** VW rise again

Steigen *nt* GESCHÄFT *Preise* rise

steigend *adj* GESCHÄFT mounting, VW buoyant, rising; ♦ **in ~er Reihenfolge** GESCHÄFT in ascending order

steigend: **~e Arbeitslosigkeit** *f* VW rising unemployment; **~e Kosten** *pl* VW rising costs; **~e Nachfrage** *f* VW growing demand; **~er Zinssatz** *m* VW rising interest rate

steigern *vt* FINANZ *Einnahmen* boost, GESCHÄFT accelerate, *Bemühungen* strengthen, *Wert* raise, increase, UMWELT *Bewußtsein* raise, V&M *Verkaufszahlen* boost, VW *Nachfrage, Exporte, Exportvolumen* boost, *Inflation* fuel, *Kaufkraft einer Währung* enhance, *Wirtschaft* inflate

Steigerung *f* BÖRSE run-up, GESCHÄFT advance, boom, increase, rise, *Inflationsrate* speed-up; **~ der Aufträge** GESCHÄFT boom in orders

steil 1. *adj* GESCHÄFT, VW steep; **2.** *adv* GESCHÄFT, VW steeply

steiler: ~ **werden** *phr* MATH *Kurve* steepen

Steinkohlen- *in cpds* IND coal; **Steinkohlenbergwerk** *nt* IND colliery; **Steinkohlengrube** *f* IND colliery; **Steinkohlenkraftwerk** *nt* IND coal-fired power station; **Steinkohlenschacht** *m* IND colliery; **Steinkohlenzeche** *f* IND colliery

Steinschlagschaden *m* VERSICH damage by falling stones

Stellage *f* BÖRSE straddle, spread, put and call; **Stellagegeschäft** *nt* **auf der Grundlage von drei Terminkontrakten** BÖRSE butterfly spread

Stellbereich *m* TRANSP standage area

Stelle *f* COMP digit, PERSON position, post; ◆ **an ~ von** GESCHÄFT, RECHT pro; **eine ~ besetzen** PERSON fill a vacancy; **sich um eine ~ bewerben** PERSON *Arbeitsmarkt* apply for a post; **eine ~ höher einstufen** PERSON upgrade a post; **eine ~ suchen** PERSON look for a job; **an die ~ treten von** GESCHÄFT replace sb, RECHT supersede; **seine ~ verlieren** PERSON lose one's job

stellen 1. *vt* PATENT, RECHT *Anspruch, Antrag* submit; ◆ **Anspruch ~** PATENT, RECHT claim; **2. sich ~** *v refl* GESCHÄFT *Kritik, Angriffen* face

Stelle: **Stellenanforderung** *f* PERSON job requirement; **Stellenangebot** *nt* PERSON job offer; **eine Stellenanzeige aufgeben** *phr* V&M advertise a job; **Stellenanzeigen** *f pl* V&M recruitment advertising; **Stellenausschreibung** *f* PERSON *Arbeitsmarkt* job advertisement; **Stellenbeschreibung** *f* PERSON job description; **Stellenbesetzung** *f* PERSON staffing; **Stellenbewerber, in** *m,f* PERSON *Arbeitsmarkt* applicant; **Stellengesuch** *nt* PERSON application, job application; **Stellenplan** *m* VW position chart; **Stellenplanung** *f* MGMNT manpower planning, PERSON staff planning; **Stellensuche** *f* PERSON *Arbeitsmarkt* job hunting, job search; **Stellensuchende(r)** *mf* [decl. as adj] PERSON job hunter; **Stellentausch** *m* PERSON job rotation; **Stellenvermittlung** *f* GESCHÄFT employment agency, PERSON job placement; **Stellenvermittlung** *f* **für Aushilfskräfte** PERSON *Gelegenheitsarbeit* temping agency

Steller-Pol *m* TRANSP actuator pole

Stellung *f* BÖRSE position, rank, standing, status, PERSON job, position, post, situation (*sit.*), VERWALT position, status; ◆ **sich um eine ~ bewerben** PERSON *Arbeitsmarkt* put in a job application; **jdn aus seiner ~ verdrängen** PERSON oust sb from their job

Stellung: **Stellungnahme** *f* GESCHÄFT opinion; **eine Stellungnahme abgeben** *phr* POL *Parlament* deliver an opinion; **Stellungssuchende(r)** *mf* [decl. as adj] PERSON job hunter

stellvertretend *adj* GESCHÄFT acting, deputizing; **~er Abteilungsleiter** *m*, **~e Abteilungsleiterin** *f* PERSON, MGMNT assistant head of section (*BrE*) (*AHS*), deputy head of department, assistant section head (*BrE*); **~er Direktor** *m*, **~e Direktorin** *f* MGMNT, PERSON assistant director, assistant manager, deputy director, deputy manager; **~er Gemeindedirektor** *m*, **~e Gemeindedirektorin** *f* MGMNT deputy chief executive; **~er Generaldirektor** *m*, **~e Generaldirektorin** *f* MGMNT assistant general manager, vice-president, PERSON *Unternehmensleitung* assistant director general (*ADG*), deputy chief executive, deputy managing director; **~er**

geschäftsführender Direktor *m*, **~e geschäftsführende Direktorin** *f* MGMNT deputy managing director; **~er Geschäftsführer** *m* **eines Geldinstitutes**, **~e Geschäftsführerin** *f* **eines Geldinstitutes** BANK assistant cashier (*BrE*), assistant teller (*AmE*); **~er Hauptgeschäftsführer** *m*, **~e Hauptgeschäftsführerin** *f* MGMNT deputy managing director; **~er Leiter** *m*, **~e Leiterin** *f* MGMNT, PERSON assistant manager, deputy director, deputy manager; **~er Minister** *m*, **~e Ministerin** *f* VERWALT deputy minister; **~es Mitglied** *nt* GESCHÄFT alternate member (*AmE*); **~es Mitglied** *nt* **des Verwaltungsrats** MGMNT deputy member of the board of management; **~er Tagungsleiter** *m*, **~e Tagungsleiterin** *f* MGMNT vice-chairman; **~er Versammlungsleiter** *m*, **~e Versammlungsleiterin** *f* MGMNT vice-chairman; **~e(r) Verwaltungsratsvorsitzende(r)** *mf* [decl. as adj] MGMNT deputy chairman of the board of management; **~e(r) Vorsitzende(r)** *mf* [decl. as adj] MGMNT, PERSON deputy chairman, executive vice-president, vice-chairman, vice-president; **~e(r) Vorsitzende(r)** *mf* [decl. as adj] **des Aufsichtsrates** MGMNT deputy chairman of the supervisory board; **~er Vorstand** *m* **der Geschäftsleitung** MGMNT deputy chairman of the board of management; **~e(r) Vorstandsvorsitzende(r)** *mf* [decl. as adj] MGMNT deputy chairman of the managing board, vice-president

Stellvertreter, in *m,f* GESCHÄFT alternate member (*AmE*), deputy, *Stimmausübung* proxy, PERSON stand-in, RECHT *Bevollmächtigter* agent, *Vertragsrecht* private attorney; **~ des Hauptgeschäftsführers** MGMNT *einer Gesellschaft* deputy chief executive; **~ eines Kandidaten** POL surrogate; **~ des Vorstandsvorsitzenden** MGMNT deputy chairman of the managing board, vice-president; **Stellvertreterrecht** *nt* RECHT agency law; **Stellvertreterstimme** *f* POL proxy vote

Stellvertretung *f* GESCHÄFT agency (*agcy*), representation

Stempel *m* GESCHÄFT stamp; **Stempelkarte** *f* IND clock card; **Stempelkissen** *nt* GESCHÄFT stamp pad; **Stempelmaschine** *f* KOMM stamping machine

stempeln 1. *vt* GESCHÄFT stamp, KOMM *Brief* postmark; **2.** *vi* PERSON clock in, SOZIAL *infrml* be on the dole ' (*infrml*)

Stempel: **Stempelsteuergesetz** *nt* RECHT Stamp Act (*BrE*); **Stempeluhr** *f* IND, PERSON time clock; **die Stempeluhr umgehen** *phr* PERSON ride the clock (*AmE*)

Steno *f infrml* VERWALT shorthand; **Stenographie** *f* VERWALT shorthand; **Stenograph, in** *m,f* VERWALT stenographer

stenographieren *vt* VERWALT take down in shorthand

Steno: **Steno- und Schreibmaschinenkenntnisse** *f pl* PERSON, VERWALT shorthand and typing skills; **Stenotypist, in** *m,f* PERSON, VERWALT shorthand typist

Sterbe- *in cpds* GESCHÄFT, VERSICH death, mortality; **Sterbegeld** *nt* VERSICH contribution to funeral expenses; **Sterberisiko** *nt* VERSICH death risk; **Sterbetabelle** *f* VERSICH mortality table; **Sterbeurkunde** *f* GESCHÄFT death certificate

Sterblichkeit- *in cpds* VERSICH mortality; **Sterblichkeitsrate** *f* VERSICH expected mortality; **Sterblichkeitstafel** *f* VERSICH mortality table; **Sterblichkeitsüberhang** *m* VERSICH excess mortality

Sterling *m* BANK, BÖRSE, FINANZ Sterling; **~ Commercial**

Paper BANK, BÖRSE sterling commercial paper (*SCP*); **Sterlingauslandsanleihe** *f* BANK bulldog loan (*BrE*); **Sterling-Bezugsrechtsschein** *m* für Staatsanleihen BÖRSE sterling warrant into gilt-edged stock (*BrE*) (*SWING*); **Sterlinggebiet** *nt* GESCHÄFT Sterling Area; **Sterlingguthaben** *nt* FINANZ sterling balance; **Sterling-Handelspapier** *nt* BANK, BÖRSE sterling commercial paper (*SCP*); **Sterlingsaldo** *m* FINANZ sterling balance

Sternnetz *nt* COMP star network

stetig 1. *adj* GESCHÄFT steady; **2.** *adv* GESCHÄFT steadily

stetig: **~es inflationsfreies Wachstum** *nt* VW sustained non-inflationary growth (*SNIG*); **~es nichtinflationäres Wachstum** *nt* VW sustained non-inflationary growth (*SNIG*); **~ steigender Markt** *m* GESCHÄFT hardening market; **~e Zufallsvariable** *f* MATH continuous variable

stets: **~ erwartungstreue Schätzfunktion** *f* MATH absolutely unbiased estimator

Steuer *f* IMP/EXP levy, STEUER tax, duty, imposition, VW tax; **~ zum einheitlichen Grundtarif** STEUER basic-rate tax; **~ der Lohnnebenleistungen** STEUER fringe benefits tax; **~ der Lohnzusatzleistungen** STEUER fringe benefits tax; **~ mit negativen Leistungsanreizen** STEUER repressive tax; ♦ **jdm eine ~ auferlegen** STEUER impose a tax on sb; **von der ~ freistellen** STEUER exempt sb from tax

Steuer: **Steuerabgrenzung** *f* STEUER deferral of taxes; **Steuerabzug** *m* STEUER tax deduction; **unter Steuerabzug empfangenes Einkommen** *nt* STEUER income received under deduction of tax; **Steueramortisation** *f* STEUER, VW tax capitalization; **Steuerangleichung** *f* STEUER fiscal approximation; **Steueranrechnung** *f* STEUER, VW tax credit; **Steueranreiz** *m* STEUER tax incentive, tax stimuli; **Steueraufkommen** *nt* FINANZ revenue from taxes, STEUER inland revenue (*BrE*), internal revenue (*AmE*), tax receipt, tax take, tax yield; **Steueraufrechnung** *f* STEUER tax offset; **Steueraufwand** *m* STEUER tax expenditure; **Steueraufwendung** *f* STEUER, VW tax expenditure; **Steuerausgleichskonto** *nt* STEUER tax equalization account; **Steuerausgleichsplan** *m* STEUER tax equalization scheme; **Steuerausweichung** *f* GESCHÄFT, STEUER, VW tax avoidance; **Steuerausweichung** *f* bei **Wertpapieren** FINANZ bond washing

steuerbar: **~e Güter** *nt pl* STEUER excisable goods

Steuer: **Steuerbeamte(r)** *m* [decl. as adj], **Steuerbeamtin** *f* GESCHÄFT, STEUER tax collector; **Steuerbefehl** *m* COMP control command

steuerbefreit: **~e Hilfs- und Betriebsstoffe** *m pl* STEUER exempt supplies; **~e Vermögenswerte** *m pl* STEUER exempt assets

Steuer: **Steuerbefreiung** *f* STEUER exemption from tax, tax exemption

steuerbegünstigt *adj* STEUER eligible for tax relief, tax-privileged, tax-sheltered; **~es Anlagekonto** *nt* BANK tax-sheltered account; **~e Investmentgesellschaft** *f* STEUER, VW regulated investment company; **~es Leasing** *nt* FINANZ, STEUER true lease

Steuer: **Steuerbehörde** *f* BANK, FINANZ fiscal authority, STEUER fiscal authority, Inland Revenue (*BrE*) (*IR*), Internal Revenue Authority (*AmE*), tax authority, taxman; **Steuerbehörden** *f pl* BANK, FINANZ, STEUER fiscal authorities; **Steuerbelastung** *f* STEUER tax burden, tax load; **Steuerbelastungswirkung** *f* STEUER

fiscal incidence; **Steuerbeleg** *m* BÖRSE, STEUER tax voucher; **Steuerbemessungsgrundlage** *f* STEUER, VW basis of assessment, tax basis

Steuerberater, in *m,f* GESCHÄFT, PERSON, RECHNUNG accountant, STEUER tax consultant; **Steuerberaterbüro** *nt* STEUER tax consultant's bureau

Steuer: **Steuerbereinigung** *f* GESCHÄFT tax adjustment; **Steuerberichtigung** *f* GESCHÄFT tax adjustment; **Steuerbezirk** *m* STEUER tax district (*BrE*)

Steuerbord *nt* TRANSP *Schiffahrt* starboard; **Steuerbordseite** *f* TRANSP *Schiffahrt* starboard side

Steuer: **Steuerbürgschaft** *f* STEUER tax bond; **Steuereingangsstufe** *f* STEUER tax threshold; **Steuereinnahmen** *f pl* STEUER inland revenue (*BrE*), internal revenue (*AmE*), tax receipt; **Steuerelastizität** *f* STEUER, VW tax elasticity; **Steuererhebungskosten** *pl* STEUER administrative cost, administrative costs; **Steuererklärung** *f* STEUER return, tax declaration, tax return; **seine Steuererklärung einreichen** *phr* STEUER file one's tax return; **Steuererlaß** *m* STEUER abatement of taxes, tax remission

Steuererleichterung *f* STEUER tax concession, tax relief; **~ für Firmenwagen** STEUER tax relief for business cars; **~ an der Quelle** STEUER tax relief at source

Steuerermäßigung *f* STEUER tax reduction; **~ für Eigenheime** STEUER homestead tax exemption (*AmE*); **~ des Restbestandes** STEUER holdover relief; **~ für Verluste** STEUER allowance for loss

Steuer: **Steuererstattungsanspruch** *m* STEUER right to a tax refund; **Steuerexil** *nt* STEUER tax exile

steuerfrei *adj* STEUER exempt from taxation, tax-exempt, tax-free; **~er Betrag** *m* STEUER tax-free allowance; **~es Einkommen** *nt* STEUER nontax income, tax-free income; **~es Rentensparkonto** *nt* BANK, STEUER individual retirement account (*AmE*) (*IRA*); **~es Sparkonto** *nt* BANK Tax Exempt Special Savings Account (*BrE*) (*TESSA*); **~es Sparkonto** *nt* zur **privaten Altersvorsorge** BANK, STEUER individual retirement account (*AmE*) (*IRA*); **~es Wertpapier** *nt* STEUER tax-exempt security

Steuer: **Steuerfreibetrag** *m* STEUER allowance (*BrE*), tax credit (*AmE*), tax relief, tax-free amount

Steuerfreiheit *f* STEUER exemption from taxes, tax exemption, *Diplomaten* immunity from taxes; **~ bis zur Anlagenabschreibung** FINANZ free depreciation; ♦ **~ beanspruchen** STEUER claim exemption from taxes, claim immunity from tax

Steuer: **Steuerfreijahre** *nt pl* STEUER tax holiday; **Steuergläubiger, in** *m,f* RECHNUNG taxation creditor; **aus Steuergründen vorübergehend gegründete Gesellschaft** *f* STEUER collapsible corporation (*AmE*); **Steuer-Grundfreibetrag** *m* STEUER tax threshold; **Steuergutschein** *m* STEUER tax anticipation bill (*AmE*) (*TAB*), tax anticipation note (*AmE*) (*TAN*), tax credit certificate (*BrE*), tax-reserve certificate (*AmE*); **Steuergutschrift** *f* STEUER tax credit (*AmE*); **Steuerharmonisierung** *f* STEUER, VW tax harmonization; **Steuerhinterziehung** *f* STEUER defrauding the Revenue (*BrE*), fiscal evasion, tax evasion; **Steuerimmunität** *f* STEUER, VW tax immunity; **Steuerinflation** *f* VW tax inflation, taxflation (*jarg*); **Steuerinländer, in** *m,f* STEUER resident for tax purposes, resident taxpayer; **Steuerinzidenz** *f* STEUER incidence of taxation, tax incidence, fiscal incidence;

Steuerjahr *nt* FINANZ, RECHNUNG, STEUER assessment year, fiscal year (*FY*), tax year; **Steuerkeil** *m* VW tax wedge; **Steuerkraft** *f* STEUER, VW taxable capacity; **Steuerlast** *f* STEUER tax burden, tax charge, tax load; **Steuerlastankündigung** *f* STEUER announcement of tax burden

steuerlich *adj* RECHNUNG, STEUER fiscal; **~e Abschreibung** *f* RECHNUNG, STEUER tax return depreciation, tax write-off, capital allowance (*BrE*); **~ absetzbare Kosten** *pl* RECHNUNG allowable expenses; **~ nicht absetzbare Position** *f* STEUER disallowable item (*BrE*); **~e Absetzung** *f* STEUER tax deduction (*AmE*); **~ abzugsfähig** *adj* RECHNUNG, STEUER tax-deductible; **~ abzugsfähige Ausgaben** *f pl* STEUER tax-deductible expenditure (*AmE*), tax-deductible expenses (*BrE*); **~er Anreiz** *m* STEUER fiscal inducement, tax incentive, VW tax incentive; **~e Belastungsgrenze** *f* STEUER, VW taxable capacity; **~e Beschränkung** *f* STEUER tax restriction; **~er Druck** *m* STEUER tax pressure; **jdn ~ erfassen** *phr* STEUER bring sb within the tax net; **~ motivierter Absatz** *m* **von Wertpapieren** STEUER tax selling; **~e Planung** *f* STEUER fiscal projection; **~e Position** *f* STEUER fiscal position; **~er Standpunkt** *m* VW fiscal stance; **~er Überschuß** *m* STEUER fiscal surplus; **~ unterbewerten** *phr* STEUER underassess; **~e Vergünstigung** *f* STEUER tax concession; **~e Verlustberücksichtigung** *f* STEUER allowance for loss; **~er Verlustrücktrag** *m* RECHNUNG, STEUER tax loss carryback; **~er Verlustvortrag** *m* STEUER tax loss carryforward; **~e Vermögensbewertung** *f* STEUER assessed valuation (*AmE*); **~e Vorhersage** *f* STEUER fiscal projection; **~ wirksam** *adj* STEUER tax-efficient; **~er Wohnsitz** *m* STEUER residence for tax purposes, tax domicile

Steuer: **Steuerliste** *f* STEUER assessment roll, list of tax assessments, tax roll; **Steuerlücke** *f* STEUER tax loophole; **Steuermannsquittung** *f* IMP/EXP, TRANSP mate's receipt; **Steuermarke** *f* STEUER tax disc (*BrE*), tax disk (*AmE*), revenue stamp, tax stamp; **Steuermobilität** *f* VW fiscal mobility; **Steuermultiplikator** *m* VW fiscal multiplier

Steuern *f pl* STEUER taxes, taxation; **~ auf Einnahmen aus Erdölgewinnung** STEUER petroleum revenue tax (*PRT*); **~ der Einzelstaaten** STEUER state tax (*AmE*); ♦ **nach ~** RECHNUNG, STEUER after tax, after-tax basis; **ohne ~** VW exclusive of tax; **vor ~** STEUER before tax, pre-tax, exclusive of tax; **~ abführen** STEUER pay tax; **~ einziehen** STEUER collect taxes

Steuernachlaß *m* STEUER abatement of taxes, tax abatement, tax relief; **~ des Restbetrages** STEUER holdover relief

Steuer: **Steuerneutralität** *f* STEUER fiscal neutrality; **Steuernummer** *f* STEUER taxpayer's reference number; **Steueroase** *f* STEUER, VW tax haven

steuerorientiert: **~e Einkommenspolitik** *f* STEUER, VW tax-based incomes policy (*TIP*)

Steuer: **Steuerpfandrecht** *nt* STEUER tax lien; **Steuerpfändung** *f* STEUER tax foreclosure

steuerpflichtig *adj* RECHT liable to pay a tax, liable to pay taxes, liable to tax, STEUER assessable, taxable, liable to pay a tax, liable to pay taxes, liable to tax, subject to taxation, *Gemeindesteuer* rateable (*BrE*); **~es Einkommen** *nt* STEUER assessable income, taxable income; **~e Einkünfte** *pl* STEUER assessable income; **~er Gewinn** *m* RECHNUNG taxable profit; **~e Quote** *f*

STEUER taxable quota; **~e Sozialversicherungsleistung** *f* STEUER taxable social security benefit; **nicht ~e Umsätze** *m pl* STEUER nontaxable transactions

Steuer: **Steuerplanung** *f* STEUER tax planning; **Steuerpolitik** *f* POL fiscal policy, STEUER taxation policy; **Steuerposition** *f* STEUER tax position; **Steuerprognose** *f* STEUER fiscal projection; **Steuerprogramm** *nt* COMP control program; **Steuerprojektion** *f* STEUER fiscal projection; **Steuerprozedur** *f* COMP control procedure; **Steuerrate** *f* STEUER tax installment (*AmE*), tax instalment (*BrE*); **Steuerreform** *f* VW tax reform; **Steuerreformgesetz** *nt* STEUER tax reform act; **Steuerrichtlinien** *f pl* STEUER tax guidelines; **Steuerrolle** *f* STEUER assessment roll, list of tax assessments, tax roll; **Steuerrückstände** *m pl* STEUER back tax, tax arrears; **Steuerrückstellung** *f* RECHNUNG, STEUER tax provision; **Steuerrückzahlung** *f* STEUER tax refund; **Steuerruder** *nt* TRANSP rudder; **Steuersatz** *m* STEUER rate of taxation, tax rate; **Steuerschlupfloch** *nt* STEUER tax loophole; **Steuer-Software** *f* COMP, STEUER tax software; **Steuerstrategie** *f* STEUER, VW tax strategy; **Steuerstruktur** *f* STEUER, VW tax structure; **Steuersystem** *nt* VW system of taxation; **Steuertarif** *m* STEUER tax schedule; **Steuertilgung** *f* STEUER, VW tax capitalization; **Steuertransparenz** *f* STEUER tax transparency; **Steuerüberwälzung** *f* STEUER shifting of taxes; **Steuerumgeher** *m* STEUER tax dodger (*infrml*)

Steuerumgehung *f* GESCHÄFT, STEUER, VW avoidance of tax, tax avoidance, tax dodging (*infrml*); **gegen ~ gerichtete Vorschriften** *f pl* STEUER anti-avoidance legislation

Steuerung *f* COMP *Befehl, Taste* control; **~ des Angebots** VW supply control; **~ des Materialflusses** TRANSP materials management; **~ von Vertrieb und Verkauf** V&M merchandising; **Steuerungsanzeige** *f* COMP *Programme* audit window; **Steuerungstaste** *f* (*STRG-Taste*) COMP control key (*CTRL key*); **Steuerungszeichen** *nt* COMP control character

Steuer: **Steuerveranlagung** *f* STEUER tax assessment

Steuervergünstigung *f* STEUER tax concession, tax privilege, tax relief; **~ für Hypothekentilgung an der Quelle** FINANZ Mortgage Income Relief at Source (*MIRAS*)

Steuer: **Steuerverlust** *m* STEUER revenue loss; **Steuervermeidung** *f* GESCHÄFT, STEUER, VW avoidance of tax, tax avoidance; **Steuervermeidungsvorschriften** *f pl* STEUER anti-avoidance legislation; **Steuerverwaltung** *f* VERWALT tax administration; **Steuervorauszahlung** *f* STEUER advance payment of taxes; **Steuervorschlag** *m* STEUER tax proposal; **Steuerwert** *m* STEUER taxable value; **Steuerwirkung** *f* RECHNUNG tax influence, STEUER effect of taxation, fiscal incidence; **Steuerzahler** *m* GESCHÄFT, RECHNUNG, STEUER taxpayer; **Steuerzweck** *m* RECHNUNG tax purpose

steuerwirksam: **~e Investition** *f* STEUER tax-efficient investment

Steward *m* FREI flight attendant

Stewardess *f* FREI flight attendant

Stich- *in cpds* BÖRSE declaration, FINANZ call, cutoff, GESCHÄFT effective, spot, random, key, target, MATH random, POL final, run-off, decisive, V&M random

stichhaltig *adj* GESCHÄFT *Argument* valid

Stichprobe *f* GESCHÄFT spot check, random test, MATH sample, V&M random test; ◆ **eine ~ entnehmen** MATH take a sample

Stichproben *f pl* V&M random sampling; **Stichprobenabweichung** *f* MATH sampling deviation

stichprobenartig: **~e Untersuchung** *f* VW accidental sampling

Stichproben: **Stichprobendurchschnitt** *m* MATH sample mean; **Stichprobenentnahme** *f* MATH sample drawing; **Stichprobenerhebung** *f* V&M poll; **Stichprobenfehler** *m* MATH sampling error; **Stichprobengitter** *nt* MATH sampling grid; **Stichprobenpunkt** *m* V&M sampling point; **Stichprobenrahmen** *m* MATH sampling frame

Stich-: **Stichtag** *m* BÖRSE date of record, declaration day, FINANZ call date, cutoff date, GESCHÄFT deadline, effective date, key date, target date, RECHNUNG cutoff date (*AmE*), reporting date; **Stichtagsinventurmethode** *f* RECHNUNG periodic inventory method; **Stichtagsvermögen** *nt* RECHNUNG current asset; **Stichwahl** *f* POL decisive ballot, final ballot, run-off (*AmE*), run-off election (*AmE*), second ballot

Stift *m* COMP pin, *Graphiktablett* stylus, TRANSP gudgeon

Stiftung *f* RECHT *Dotation* endowment, vw foundation

Stil *m* GESCHÄFT class, MGMNT style; **~ des Hauses** GESCHÄFT house style; ◆ **einem ~ angleichen** GESCHÄFT stylize

stilisieren *vt* GESCHÄFT stylize

stilisiert: **~es Faktum** *nt* vw stylized fact

Stilist, in *m,f* GESCHÄFT stylist

still: **~er Gesellschafter** *m*, **~e Gesellschafterin** *f* FINANZ, GESCHÄFT, RECHT, VW silent partner (*AmE*), sleeping partner (*BrE*); **~e Reserven** *f pl* VERSICH balance sheet reserves; **~e Rücklage** *f* FINANZ, RECHNUNG secret reserve; **~e Rücklagen** *f pl* BANK hidden reserves; **~e Saison** *f* GESCHÄFT slack period; **~er Teilhaber** *m*, **~e Teilhaberin** *f* FINANZ, GESCHÄFT, RECHT, VW silent partner (*AmE*), sleeping partner (*BrE*)

stillegen *vt* FINANZ immobilize, GESCHÄFT, IND close down, shut down, UMWELT decommission; ◆ **stillgelegt werden** IND close down, shut down

Stillegung *f* FINANZ immobilization, GESCHÄFT closing down, closure, shutdown, UMWELT *eines Kernkraftwerkes* decommissioning

stillgelegt *adj* GESCHÄFT closed down, shut down, TRANSP laid-up, UMWELT *Kernkraftwerk* decommissioned; **~es Bankkonto** *nt* BANK dormant account

Stillhalte- *in cpds* GESCHÄFT standby, standstill; **Stillhalteabkommen** *nt* GESCHÄFT standstill agreement; **Stillhaltevereinbarung** *f* GESCHÄFT standby agreement, standstill agreement

Stillschweigen: **etw mit ~ übergehen** *phr* GESCHÄFT pass sth over in silence

stillschweigend *adj* RECHT *Annahme* implicit, implied, tacit; **~e Bedingung** *f* GESCHÄFT implied condition; **~e dienstbarkeitsähnliche Verpflichtung** *f* RECHT implied easement; **~e Mängelhaftung** *f* RECHT implied warranty; **~es Übereinkommen** *nt* RECHT tacit agreement; **nach ~er Vereinbarung** *phr* RECHT by tacit agreement; **~e Verlängerung** *f* GESCHÄFT tacit renewal; **~e Verpflichtung** *f* RECHT implied obligation; **~e Vollmacht** *f* RECHT implied agency

Stillstand *m* VW stagnation, standstill; ◆ **zum ~ kommen** GESCHÄFT come to a standstill

Stillstand: **Stillstandszeit** *f* COMP, GESCHÄFT dead time, downtime, idle time, lost time, PERSON stoppage, VERSICH idle time

stillstehend *adj* GESCHÄFT, TRANSP down, idle

Stimm- *in cpds* BÖRSE, FINANZ, MGMNT, PERSON, POL ballot, vote, voting; **Stimmabgabe** *f* MGMNT, PERSON voting; **Stimmabgabe** *f* **im Auftrag** POL proxy vote; **Stimmabgabe** *f* **per Post** POL postal vote

stimmberechtigt: **~e Aktie** *f* BÖRSE, FINANZ voting share, voting stock; **~es Kapital** *nt* BÖRSE voting capital; **~es Treuhandzertifikat** *nt* BÖRSE voting trust certificate

Stimm-: **Stimmbevollmächtigte(r)** *mf* [decl. as adj] RECHT proxyholder

Stimme *f* PERSON, POL vote; ◆ **seine ~ nicht abgeben** POL *bei einer Wahl* abstain, **sich der ~ enthalten** POL *bei einer Wahl* abstain

stimmen: **~ für** *phr* PERSON, POL vote for; **~ gegen** *phr* PERSON, POL vote against

Stimme: **Stimmenaufgliederung** *f* POL *Wahl* vote structure; **Stimmenhäufung** *f* BÖRSE cumulative voting; **durch Stimmenmehrheit besiegen** *phr* GESCHÄFT outvote

Stimm-: **Stimmenthaltung** *f* GESCHÄFT, POL abstention

Stimme: **Stimmenverrechnungsertrag** *m* FINANZ vote-netting revenue

Stimmrecht *nt* BÖRSE, FINANZ right to vote, voting power, PERSON voting right, POL franchise, suffrage, voting right

stimmrechtslos: **~e Aktie** *f* BÖRSE nonvoting share, nonvoting stock, A-share (*BrE*)

Stimmrecht: **Stimmrechtsübertragung** *f* FINANZ transfer of voting rights; **Stimmrechtsvollmacht** *f* PERSON voting proxy

Stimmung *f* BÖRSE mood, tone; **Stimmungsbarometer** *nt* vw barometer; **Stimmungsbeeinflussung** *f* V&M mood conditioning

stimmungserzeugend: **~e Werbung** *f* V&M mood advertising

Stimm-: **Stimmverrechnung** *f* FINANZ net voting, vote netting; **Stimmzettel** *m* PERSON ballot paper, *geheime Abstimmung* voting paper

stimulieren *vt* GESCHÄFT, PERSON, VW *Vertrauen, Nachfrage* stimulate

stimulierend *adj* PERSON, VW stimulating, stimulative; **~e Maßnahme** *f* VW stimulative measure

Stipendium *nt* VERWALT grant

Stippvisite *f jarg* POL flying visit, *Wahlkampf in USA* whistle-stop (*jarg*)

stochastisch: **~e Modellierung** *f* MGMNT stochastic simulation; **mit ~er Netzplantechnik** *f* MGMNT program evaluation and review technique (*AmE*) (*PERT*), programme evaluation and review technique (*BrE*) (*PERT*); **~er Prozeß** *m* GESCHÄFT stochastic process; **~e Simulation** *f* MGMNT stochastic simulation; **~er Term** *m* MATH stochastic term; **~e Variable** *f* MATH *Statistik* chance variable, random variable

Stockdividende *f* RECHNUNG free issue of new shares (*BrE*), stock dividend (*AmE*)

stocken *vi* vw falter, stagnate

stockend *adj* vw stagnant

Stockholm: **~er Schule** *f* vw Stockholm School, Swedish School

Stockung *f* vw hold-up

Stoff *m* GESCHÄFT subject matter, IND material substance, PATENT subject matter; **Stoffsack** *m* **mit Papierfutter** TRANSP paper-lined textile bag

Stolper-Samuelson-Theorem *nt* VW Stolper Samuelson theorem

Stolperstein *m* GESCHÄFT stumbling block

Stop- *in cpds* BÖRSE, COMP, VW stop; **Stop-and-go-Inflationszyklus** *m* VW stop-go cycle of inflation; **Stop-and-go-Politik** *f* VW stop-go policy (*BrE*); **Stop-Bit** *nt* COMP stop bit; **Stop-Limit-Order** *f* BÖRSE stop limit order; **Stop-Loss** *m* BÖRSE stop loss; **Stop-Loss-Auftrag** *m* BÖRSE selling stop order; **Stop-Loss-Order** *f* BÖRSE stop loss order; **Stop-Order** *f* BÖRSE stop order

Stopp- *in cpds* COMP, TRANSP breakpoint, stop; **Stoppbefehl** *m* COMP breakpoint instruction; **Stoppsignal** *nt* COMP, TRANSP stop signal; **Stopptag** *m* FINANZ record date; **Stoppzeit** *f* COMP stop time

Stör- *in cpds* COMP, MATH disturbance; **Störimpuls** *m* COMP glitch; **Störvariable** *f* MATH disturbance variable

stornieren *vt* GESCHÄFT *Auftrag* cancel, RECHNUNG *Buchung* reverse, RECHT *Vertrag* cancel

Stornierung *f* GESCHÄFT cancellation, reversing (*REV*), RECHNUNG cancellation, reversal (*AmE*), RECHT cancellation; **Stornierungsdatum** *nt* TRANSP *Chartervertrag* canceling date (*AmE*), cancelling date (*BrE*)

Storno *m or nt* RECHNUNG contra entry, reversing entry; **~ vor Vertragsablauf** VERSICH flat cancellation; **Stornoabschlag** *m* VERSICH surrender charge; **Stornoabzug** *m* VERSICH surrender charge; **Stornobuchung** *f* RECHNUNG contra entry, reversing entry, cancellation; **Stornogebühr** *f* VERSICH cancellation fee

Stör-: **Störterm** *m* MATH disturbance variable

Störung *f* COMP interference, GESCHÄFT disturbance, TRANSP breakdown

störungsfrei *adj* GESCHÄFT smooth; **~es Wachstum** *nt* VW undisturbed growth

Störung: **Störungssuche** *f* COMP troubleshooting

stoßen: **~ auf** *vt* [+acc] GESCHÄFT *Problem* encounter

Stoßwirkung *f* GESCHÄFT impact

St. Petersburg Paradox *nt* VW St Petersburg paradox

Str. *abbr* (*Straße*) GESCHÄFT St (*street*), Rd (*road*)

Straddle- *in cpds* BÖRSE straddle; **Straddle-Baisse-Position** *f* BÖRSE long straddle position; **Straddlekombination** *f* BÖRSE straddle combination; **eine Straddle-Position erwerben** *phr* BÖRSE take a straddle position

Straf- *in cpds* RECHT penalty, sentence; **Strafanzeige** *f* RECHT *Strafrecht* complaint

strafbar *adj* RECHT liable to prosecution, punishable; **~es Fahrlässigkeitsdelikt** *nt* RECHT criminal negligence; **~e Handlung** *f* RECHT criminal offence (*BrE*), criminal offense (*AmE*), offence (*BrE*), offense (*AmE*)

Strafe *f* RECHT penalty; ◆ **mit einer ~ belegen** RECHT penalize; **~ über jdn verhängen** RECHT pass sentence on sb

Straf-: **Straferlaß** *m* RECHT remission of a penalty

strafmündig *adj* RECHT accountable

straff: **~e Betriebsführung** *f* MGMNT tight ship (*infrml*); **~e Fiskalpolitik** *f* STEUER, VW tight fiscal policy

straffen *vt* VW *Organisation, Unternehmen* streamline, take up the slack (*infrml*)

Straffung *f* VW streamlining, tightening

Straf-: **Strafherabsetzung** *f* RECHT reduction of sentence

strafrechtlich: **~ verfolgbar** *phr* RECHT prosecutable; **~ verfolgen** *phr* RECHT prosecute

Straf-: **Strafregister** *nt* RECHT police record; **Straftat** *f* RECHT crime, criminal offence (*BrE*), criminal offense (*AmE*); **Straftäter, in** *m,f* RECHT criminal, **Strafumwandlung** *f* RECHT commutation of a sentence

Strafurteil *nt* RECHT sentence, *Geschworenengericht* verdict; ◆ **~ vertagen** RECHT adjourn sentence

Straf-: **Strafzins** *m* BANK interest penalty, negative interest, penalty interest, penalty rate, FINANZ interest penalty

Strahlungschaden *m* VERSICH damage caused by radiation

Strahlungsverseuchung *f* UMWELT radiation pollution

stranden *vi* TRANSP *Schiff* run aground, run ashore

Strandgut *nt* TRANSP jetsam, *Wrackteile* wreckage, VERSICH salvage goods, stranded goods

Strandung *f* TRANSP shipwreck

Strandvogt *m* PERSON, TRANSP receiver of the wreck

Strang *m* MEDIEN ribbon

strapazierfähig: **~ sein** *phr* GESCHÄFT, IND stand up to wear

Strap-Option *f* BÖRSE strap option

Straße *f* (*Str.*) GESCHÄFT street (*St*), road (*Rd*); **an der ~ gelegene Anschlagstelle** V&M *für Plakate* roadside site; **Straßenbau** *m* VW road building; **Straßenbaustelle** *f* TRANSP roadworks; **Straßenbenutzungsgebühr** *f* GESCHÄFT, TRANSP road toll, road-use tax, toll; **Straßenfahrzeug** *nt* **mit Dieselmotor** TRANSP diesel-engined road vehicle (*BrE*) (*DERV*); **Straßenfront** *f* GRUND frontage; **Straßengüterverkehr** *m* TRANSP road haulage, road transport; **Straßenhändler, in** *m,f* GESCHÄFT, V&M hawker, pedlar, huckster (*AmE*) (*infrml*), street trader (*BrE*), street vendor (*AmE*); **Straßennetz** *nt* TRANSP road network

Straßentransport *m* TRANSP road haulage, road transport, motor freight; **Straßentransportunternehmen** *nt* TRANSP road haulage company

Straße: **Straßenverkäufer, in** *m,f* GESCHÄFT hawker, huckster (*AmE*) (*infrml*), pedlar, street trader (*BrE*), street vendor (*AmE*); **Straßenverkehr** *m* TRANSP road traffic; **Straße-Schiene-Transport** *m* TRANSP piggyback traffic (*AmE*), road-rail transport (*BrE*)

Strategie *f* GESCHÄFT strategy, game plan, VW strategy; **~ des Möglichen** POL possibilism; **Strategiebestimmung** *f* VW strategy formulation

strategisch *adj* GESCHÄFT, MGMNT, VW strategic; **~es Bündnis** *nt* MGMNT strategic alliance; **~e Frage** *f* MGMNT strategic issue; **~e Frühaufklärung** *f* MGMNT, UMWELT, VERWALT, VW environmental assessment, environmental scanning; **~e Geschäftseinheit** *f* MGMNT strategic business unit; **~e Innovation** *f* V&M strategic innovation; **~e Interdependenz** *f* MGMNT strategic interdependence; **~er Plan** *m* GESCHÄFT, MGMNT strategic plan; **~e Planung** *f* GESCHÄFT, MGMNT strategic planning; **~e Preispolitik** *f* V&M strategic pricing; **~e Steuerplanung** *f* STEUER strategic tax planning; **~er Unternehmensbereich** *m* MGMNT strategic business unit; **~e Unternehmenseinheit** *f* MGMNT strategic business unit; **~e Unternehmensplanung** *f* MGMNT corporate strategic planning; **~e Verflechtung** *f* MGMNT strategic interdependence

Streben *nt* GESCHÄFT ambition; **~ nach größtmöglicher Gleichheit aller Menschen** POL egalitarianism

Streber, in *m,f infrml* PERSON *Karriere, Laufbahn* eager beaver (*infrml*)

Strecke *f* GESCHÄFT distance, IND drift, roadway, TRANSP *Eisenbahn* line, track; **Streckenabschnitt** *m* TRANSP route section; **Streckenanalyse** *f* TRANSP route analysis; **Streckenanweisung** *f* TRANSP route order; **Streckenfestlegung** *f* TRANSP routing; **Streckenkapazität** *f* TRANSP route capacity; **Streckennetz** *nt* TRANSP railroad network (*AmE*), railway network (*BrE*), railroad system (*AmE*), railway system (*BrE*); **Streckenoption** *f* TRANSP route option; **Streckenorder** *f* TRANSP route order; **Streckenplanung** *f* TRANSP route planning

streichen *vt* BANK cancel, withdraw, GESCHÄFT delete, erase

Streichung *f* BANK cancellation, withdrawal, FINANZ cancellation, RECHT deletion; **~ aus dem Leistungsangebot** BÖRSE delisting

Streifband *nt* VERWALT postal wrapper; **Streifbanddepot** *nt* FINANZ individual safe custody of securities, securities deposited under wrapper

Streifenanzeige *f* V&M band advertising

Streifendurchlauf *m* COMP *Lochstreifen* tape feed

streifenweise: **~ Grundstückserschließung** *f* GESCHÄFT strip development

Streik *m* GESCHÄFT, IND, PERSON industrial action, primary action, strike, walkout (*infrml*), *Arbeitskonflikt* strike action; **~, Aufruhr und innere Unruhen** *f pl*, RECHT strikes, riots and civil commotions (*SR&CC*); ♦ **im ~** GESCHÄFT, IND, PERSON *Arbeitskonflikt* on strike; **zum ~ aufrufen** GESCHÄFT, IND, PERSON *Arbeitskampfmaßnahme, Gewerkschaftsbewegung* bring out on strike, call a strike; **einen ~ auslösen** GESCHÄFT, IND, PERSON trigger off a strike; **einen ~ ausrufen** GESCHÄFT, IND, PERSON call a strike; **einen ~ organisieren** GESCHÄFT, IND, PERSON stage a strike; **in den ~ treten** GESCHÄFT, IND, PERSON go out on strike, take industrial action, walk out

Streik: **Streikabstimmung** *f* GESCHÄFT, IND, PERSON *Arbeitskonflikt* strike ballot; **Streikausruf** *m* GESCHÄFT, IND, PERSON strike call; **Streikausschuß** *m* GESCHÄFT, IND, PERSON strike committee; **Streikbrecher, in** *m,f* GESCHÄFT, IND, PERSON *Arbeitskonflikt* blackleg (*BrE*), scab (*BrE*) (*infrml*), strikebreaker; **Streikbruch** *m* GESCHÄFT, IND, PERSON strikebreaking; **Streikdrohung** *f* GESCHÄFT, IND, PERSON strike threat

streiken *vi* GESCHÄFT, IND, PERSON hit the bricks (*AmE*), *Arbeitskonflikt, Gewerkschaftsbewegung* go on strike, strike, turn out on strike, walk out, take industrial action

Streikende(r) *mf* [decl. as adj] GESCHÄFT, IND, PERSON *Arbeitskonflikt* striker

Streik: **Streikfonds** *m* GESCHÄFT, IND, PERSON strike fund; **Streikkasse** *f* GESCHÄFT, IND, PERSON strike fund; **Streikklausel** *f* GESCHÄFT, IND, PERSON strike clause

Streikposten *m* GESCHÄFT, IND, PERSON *Arbeitskonflikt* picket; ♦ **~ aufstellen** GESCHÄFT, IND, PERSON picket; **~ nicht beachten** GESCHÄFT, IND, PERSON cross a picket line

Streik: **Streikrecht** *nt* GESCHÄFT, IND, PERSON right to strike; **Streikverbot** *nt* GESCHÄFT, IND, PERSON ban on strikes, prohibition of a strike; **Streikverbotsklausel** *f* GESCHÄFT, IND, PERSON no-strike clause; **Streikverzichtabkommen** *nt* GESCHÄFT, IND, PERSON no-strike agreement; **Streikverzichtabkommen** *nt* **mit einer einzigen Gewerkschaft** GESCHÄFT, IND, PERSON single-union no-strike agreement (*BrE*); **Streikzahlungen** *f pl* GESCHÄFT, IND, PERSON strike benefits, *von der Gewerkschaft an die streikenden Mitglieder* strike pay

Streit *m* GESCHÄFT contest, controversy, dispute; **~ der Bullionisten** BANK *britische Wirtschaftspolitik 1797–1825* Bullionist controversy

streiten *vi*: **~ um** GESCHÄFT battle for; **mit jdm über etw ~** *phr* GESCHÄFT be at variance with sb about sth

Streit: **einen Streitfall schiedsgerichtlich beilegen** *phr* RECHT submit a dispute to arbitration; **Streitfrage** *f* RECHT issue; **Streitgegenstand** *m* GESCHÄFT bone of contention, RECHT matter in dispute, subject matter of the action

streitig: **~ sein** *phr* GESCHÄFT be at issue

Streitigkeit *f* PERSON dispute; **~ von Gewerkschaften untereinander** interunion dispute; **Streitigkeiten schlichten** *phr* PERSON settle a dispute

Streit: **Streitpunkt** *m* RECHT issue; **Streitverkünder, in** *m,f* RECHT applicant of interpleader, person serving a third party notice; **Streitverkündigung** *f* RECHT interpleader, third-party notice

streng **1.** *adj* GESCHÄFT *Maßnahme, Programm* severe, strict, stringent; **2.** *adv* GESCHÄFT severely, strictly, stringently; ♦ **etw ~ bewachen** GESCHÄFT keep a close watch on sth; **~ nach Vorschrift** GESCHÄFT by the book

streng: **~e Abgrenzung** *f* **der Berufsgruppen** PERSON *Gewerkschaftsbewegung* demarcation; **~ geheim** *adj* GESCHÄFT top-secret; **~e Kontrolle** *f* RECHT tight control; **~ vertraulich** *adj* GESCHÄFT private and confidential, strictly confidential

Streß *m* GESCHÄFT, PERSON stress; **den Streßfaktor in Betracht ziehen** *phr* PERSON *Arbeitsentgelt, Zeiteinteilung* take account of the stress factor; **Streß-Interview** *nt* PERSON stress interview

Streudiagramm *nt* MATH, MGMNT scatter diagram, scattergram

Streuplaner *m* PERSON media buyer

Streuung *f* BÖRSE distribution, diversification, MATH dispersion, scatter, V&M spread; **Streuungskoeffizient** *m* MATH coefficient of variation

STRG-Taste *f* (*Steuerungstaste*) COMP CTRL key (*control key*)

Strich- *in cpds* COMP, V&M bar, line; **über dem Strich** *phr* FINANZ, RECHNUNG above the line; **unter dem Strich** *phr* V&M below the line; **Strichätzung** *f* MEDIEN, V&M line block

Strichcode *m* COMP bar code; **Strichcodelesegerät** *nt* COMP bar code scanner; **Strichcodeleser** *m* COMP bar code reader, bar code scanner

strichcodiert: **~e Artikelnummer** *f* COMP bar-coded identification number; **~es Erzeugnis** *nt* V&M bar-coded product

Strich-: **Strichcodierung** *f* COMP bar code marking; **Strichgrafik** *f* COMP bar graphics; **Strichliste** *f* PERSON tally sheet; **Strichzeichnung** *f* MEDIEN, V&M line drawing

Stricke: **wenn alle ~ reißen** *phr* GESCHÄFT as a last resort

String *m jarg* COMP string

strittig: ~ **sein** *phr* PERSON be in dispute

Stroh- *in cpds* IND, STEUER straw, shell; **Strohfirma** *f* STEUER shell company; **Strohmann** *m* BÖRSE nominee, MEDIEN frontman, RECHT dummy; **Strohmannname** *m* BÖRSE nominee name; **Strohmanngesellschaft** *f* BÖRSE nominee company; **Strohmannkonto** *nt* BÖRSE nominee account; **Strohpappe** *f* IND strawboard; **Strohzellstoffpappe** *f* IND strawboard

Strom *m* COMP power, TRANSP flow; ~ **aus Wasserkraftwerk** UMWELT hydroelectric power; ♦ **gegen den ~ schwimmen** GESCHÄFT buck the trend (*infrml*), go against the stream

Strom: **Stromausfall** *m* COMP power failure

strömen *vi* IND flow

Strom: **Stromerzeugung** *f* IND electricity generation; **Stromfluß** *m* IND flow; **Stromgröße** *f* VW flow; **Stromlieferung** *f* IND electricity supply, supply of electric current; **Stromschleife** *f* COMP current loop

Strömung: **Strömungsgröße** *f* VW flow; **Strömungskupplung** *f* IND hydraulic coupling (*HC*); **Strömungslinie** *f* MATH flow line

Strom: **Stromverbrauch** *m* IND electricity consumption

Stromversorgung: **Stromversorgungseinheit** *f* TRANSP power pack; **Stromversorgungsindustrie** *f* IND electricity industry; **Stromversorgungsnetz** *nt* COMP mains (*BrE*), supply network (*AmE*)

Strong: **Strong-Berufsinteresse-Fragebogen** *m* PERSON *Bewerbung* Strong Vocational Interest Blank; **Strong-Campbell Berufsinteresse-Formular** *nt* PERSON *Die 1974er Revision des Strong-Berufsinteresse-Fragebogens von 1927* Strong-Campbell Interest Inventory

strudeln *vt* FINANZ churn, twist

Struktur *f* GESCHÄFT structure; ~ **des Votums** POL vote structure; ~ **des Wahlergebnisses** POL vote structure; ~ **des Warenhandels** VW commodity trade structure; **Strukturangleichung** *f* MGMNT structural adjustment

Strukturanpassung *f* MGMNT structural adjustment; **Strukturanpassungsfazilität** *f* FINANZ structural adjustment facility (*SAF*); **Strukturanpassungskredit** *m* VW structural adjustment loan; **Strukturanpassungspolitik** *f* VW structural adjustment policy

Struktur: **Strukturdefizit** *nt* VW structural deficit

strukturell: ~**e Arbeitslosigkeit** *f* PERSON, VW structural unemployment; ~**e Bereinigung** *f* MGMNT structural adjustment; ~**e Inflation** *f* VW structural inflation

Struktur: **Strukturfonds** *m* VW structural funds; **Strukturführungsleistungsmodell** *nt* VW structure conduct performance model (*SCP*)

strukturieren *vt* GESCHÄFT structure

strukturiert *adj* GESCHÄFT structured; ~**es Interview** *nt* V&M guided interview; ~**e Programmierung** *f* COMP structured programming; ~**es Vorstellungsgespräch** *nt* PERSON *Bewerbung* structured interview

Strukturierung *f* GESCHÄFT structuring

Struktur: **Strukturkrise** *f* VERWALT structural crisis; **Strukturmodell** *nt* VW structural model; **Strukturveränderung** *f* MGMNT structural change; **Strukturwandel** *m* MGMNT structural change

Stück *nt* BÖRSE denomination, GESCHÄFT item, piece, unit, IND *Vieh* head; ♦ **je** ~ GESCHÄFT, V&M apiece; **pro** ~ GESCHÄFT, V&M apiece

Stückelung *f* VW denomination (*denom.*); ♦ **die** ~ **angeben von** VW denominate

Stück: **Stückezuteilung** *f* BÖRSE allotment of securities (*BrE*)

Stückgut *nt* TRANSP *Eisenbahn* breakbulk cargo (*AmE*), loose cargo, mixed carload (*AmE*), part-load, less than container load (*BrE*) (*LCL*), less than carload (*AmE*) (*LCL*), lot (*AmE*), *Schiff* general cargo (*g.c.*), mixed cargo; **Stückgut- und Container-Liegeplatz** *m* TRANSP general cargo and container berth; **Stückgutdepot** *nt* TRANSP LCL depot

Stückgutfracht *f* TRANSP break bulk cargo, general cargo (*g.c.*), package freight (*AmE*); ♦ ~ **abladen** TRANSP break bulk; ~ **aufteilen** TRANSP break bulk

Stückgutfracht: **Stückgutfrachtagent, in** *m,f* TRANSP break bulk agent; **Stückgutfrachtmakler, in** *m,f* TRANSP break bulk agent; **Stückgutfrachtumsatzplatz** *m* TRANSP break bulk center (*AmE*), break bulk centre (*BrE*); **Stückgutfrachtumschlagplatz** *m* TRANSP break bulk center (*AmE*), break bulk centre (*BrE*); **Stückgutfrachtzentrum** *nt* TRANSP break bulk center (*AmE*), break bulk centre (*BrE*)

Stückgut: **Stückgutliegeplatz** *m* TRANSP general cargo berth; **Stückgutrate** *f* TRANSP general cargo rate; **Stückgutsendung** *f* TRANSP less than carload (*AmE*) (*LCL*), less than container load (*BrE*) (*LCL*); **Stückguttarif** *m* TRANSP general cargo rate; **Stückguttür** *f* TRANSP LCL door

Stück: **Stückkosten** *pl* RECHNUNG cost per unit, unit cost, VW average costs; **Stückliste** *f* IND bill of goods

Stücklohn *m* PERSON *Akkordarbeit* piece wage; **Stücklohnarbeit** *f* IND jobbing; **zum Stücklohnsatz** *phr* PERSON at piece rate

Stück: **Stückpreis** *m* GESCHÄFT unit price; **Stücksteuer** *f* STEUER per-unit tax

Stückzinsen *m pl* BANK interest accrued, BÖRSE accrued interest, broken period interest, FINANZ running interest, broken period interest, RECHNUNG broken period interest; ♦ **plus** ~ BÖRSE *Vermerk auf einer Effektenabrechnung* and interest

Student, in *m,f* PERSON, SOZIAL student; ~ **im Grundstudium** SOZIAL undergraduate

Studentverteilung *f* MATH *Statistik* Student's t-distribution

Studie *f* GESCHÄFT, PERSON, SOZIAL study; ~ **zur Auslegung der Anlage** GESCHÄFT plant layout study; ~ **über Herkunfts- und Bestimmungsort** V&M origin and destination study; ~ **zur Werksplanung** GESCHÄFT plant layout study; **Studienfahrt** *f* SOZIAL field trip, study day; **Studiengebühr** *f* SOZIAL tuition fee; **Studiengruppe** *f* GESCHÄFT study group; **Studienreise** *f* SOZIAL study trip; **Studientag** *m* SOZIAL study day

studieren 1. *vt* GESCHÄFT examine carefully, study; **2.** *vi* PERSON read for a university degree, study for a university degree

Studio *nt* GESCHÄFT studio

Studium *nt* GESCHÄFT, PERSON study

Stufe *f* GESCHÄFT bracket, phase, stage; ♦ **in Stufen** GESCHÄFT in stages, by stages

Stufe: **Stufen** *f pl* **der Beteiligungshierarchie** POL ladder of participation

stufenweise *adv* GESCHÄFT by stages, gradually, in graduated stages

Stufe: **Stufenwertzahlenverfahren** *nt* VERSICH points-rating method

stumm: ~**er Verkäufer** *m* V&M silent salesperson

Stunde f (*St.*, *Std.*) GESCHÄFT hour (*h*, *hr*); **Stundenkilometer** m pl GESCHÄFT kilometers per hour (*AmE*) (*km/h, kmph*), kilometres per hour (*BrE*) (*km/h, kmph*); **Stundenleistung** f IND output per hour; **Stundenlohn** m PERSON hourly wage, wage per hour; **Stundenlohnempfänger, in** m,f PERSON hourly paid employee, hourly worker; **Stundenvergütung** f PERSON hourly compensation

stundenweise: ~ **bezahlt werden** phr PERSON *Arbeitsmarkt* be paid by the hour; ~ **Bezahlung** f PERSON hourly pay

Stundung f STEUER extension of time for payment; ~ **von Forderungen** FINANZ prolongation of debt; **Stundungsdienst** m GESCHÄFT extension services; **Stundungsfrist** f STEUER period of extension; **Stundungsvertrag** m RECHT letter of respite; **Stundungszinsen** m pl FINANZ interest charged for deferred payment

Sturz m POL overthrow

stürzen 1. vt POL *Regierung* overthrow, tumble; **2.** vi BÖRSE, VW *Markt* slump, *Preise, Kurse* drop, fall, tumble, collapse

Sturzsee f TRANSP green sea

Stütz- in cpds GESCHÄFT support

Stütze f PERSON unemployment benefit (*BrE*), unemployment compensation (*AmE*), dole (*infrml*) (*BrE*), unemployment pay, POL plank

stützen 1. vt GESCHÄFT *Währung* bolster, peg, reinforce, support, underpin, back, MGMNT support, VW *Währung* bolster, peg, prop up, reinforce, support, underpin; **2. sich ~ auf** v refl [+acc] GESCHÄFT *Entscheidung* be based on

Stütz-: **Stützpunkt** m GESCHÄFT base; **Stützsystem** nt VW pegging system

Stützung f GESCHÄFT support, VW backing; **Stützungsfazilität** f GESCHÄFT backup facilities; **Stützungsgeschäft** nt GESCHÄFT support activity; **Stützungsinstrument** nt VW pegging device; **Stützungskäufe** m pl BÖRSE backing, FINANZ support buying, support operations; **Stützungskäufe** m pl **der Notenbanken** VW buying in; **Stützungskredit** m BANK, FINANZ standby credit, supporting credit; **Stützungsmaßnahme** f MGMNT support activity; **Stützungspreis** m GESCHÄFT supported price

Subaktivität f GESCHÄFT, VW subactivity

subjektiv adj GESCHÄFT, V&M subjective; ~**es Recht** nt RECHT legal right; ~**es Risiko** nt VERSICH moral hazard; ~**e Unmöglichkeit** f **der Leistung** RECHT *Vertragsrecht* inability to perform; ~**e Wahrnehmung** f V&M subjective perception

subkompakt adj GESCHÄFT subcompact

Subkontrakt m GESCHÄFT, IND, PERSON, RECHT subcontract

Submission f GESCHÄFT submission, bid, tender; ~ **von Arbeitsplätzen** VW *innerhalb einer Firma* notification of vacancies; **Submissionsangebot** nt GESCHÄFT tender; **Submissionsangebot** nt **im verschlossenen Umschlag** GESCHÄFT sealed-bid tendering; **Submissionsschluß** m BÖRSE bid closing date; **Submissionsverfahren** nt GESCHÄFT competitive bidding procedure; **Submissionsvergabe** f MGMNT award; **Submissionsverkauf** m V&M sale by tender; **auf dem Submissionsweg** phr VERWALT by tender

suboptimieren vi GESCHÄFT, VW suboptimize

Suboptimierung f FINANZ, GESCHÄFT, VW suboptimization

Subroutine f COMP, GESCHÄFT subroutine

subsidiär adj GESCHÄFT secondary, subsidiary

Subsidiarität f GESCHÄFT, VW subsidiarity

Subsistenz f SOZIAL subsistence; **Subsistenzwirtschaft** f VW subsistence farming

subskribieren vt GESCHÄFT *Zeitungen, Bücher* subscribe to

Subskript nt COMP *Tabelle* subscript

Subskription f COMP, FINANZ, GESCHÄFT subscription; **Subskriptionspreis** m GESCHÄFT subscription price

Substanz f VW substance; **Substanzbildung** f VW accumulation of capital; **Substanzerhöhung** f BÖRSE capital growth; **Substanzwert** m FINANZ intrinsic value, RECHNUNG asset value, VW intrinsic value

substantiell: ~**er Vertrag** m PERSON substantive agreement

substituieren vt VW substitute

Substituierung f VW substitution

Substitut, in m,f GESCHÄFT sub-agent, sub-representative

Substitution f VW substitution; ~ **von Bankkrediten durch handelbare Wertpapiere** BANK, BÖRSE, FINANZ securitization; **Substitutionseffekt** m VW substitution effect; **Substitutionselastizität** f VW elasticity of substitution; **Substitutionskoeffizient** m VW substitution coefficient

subtrahieren 1. vt MATH subtract; **2.** vi MATH subtract

Subunternehmer, in m, f PERSON subcontractor; ♦ **an einen Subunternehmer vergeben** RECHT subcontract

Subvention f FINANZ subsidy, government subsidy, grant

subventionieren vt VW subsidize

subventioniert adj VW subsidized; **nicht ~** adj GESCHÄFT unsubsidized; ~**es Darlehen** nt BANK low-cost loan; ~**er Export** m VW subsidized export; ~**er Preis** m GESCHÄFT subsidized price, supported price, VW pegged price; ~**er Wohnungsbau** m SOZIAL subsidized housing

Subventionierung f VW subsidization

Subvention: **Subventionsantrag** m GESCHÄFT application for subsidies; **Subventionsniveau** nt VW level of support

Suche f GESCHÄFT search; ~ **nach Führungskräften** MGMNT executive search; ♦ **auf der ~ nach etw sein** GESCHÄFT be on the lookout for sth, be in search of sth

suchen vt COMP *Datenbank* find, *Datei, Dokument* search, GESCHÄFT search, *Zustimmung* seek

Suchen nt COMP, GESCHÄFT search; **Suchen/Ersetzen** nt COMP *Textverarbeitung* search and replace

Suchschlüssel m COMP search key;

Suchzettel m GESCHÄFT tracer

Südpazifiktarife m pl TRANSP South Pacific rates

Suggestivfrage f V&M leading question

sukzessiv adj GESCHÄFT gradual, successive

Sukzessivlieferungsvertrag m RECHT apportioned contract, contract for delivery by installments (*AmE*), contract for delivery by instalments (*BrE*), multiple delivery contract

Summe f FINANZ total, GESCHÄFT footing (*AmE*), aggregate, total, amount (*amt*), MATH footing (*AmE*), VW aggregate, amount (*amt*), total; ~ **der liquiden Mittel** RECHNUNG cash on hand; ~ **der Passiva** RECHNUNG total liabilities; ~ **der Standardausgaben**

vw total standard spending; ~ **der Verbindlichkeiten** RECHNUNG total liabilities; **Summenanpassung** *f* VERSICH adjustment of sum insured; **Summenanpassungsklausel** *f* VERSICH adjustment clause; **Summendifferenzversicherung** *f* VERSICH difference in limits insurance; **Summenexzedentenrückversicherung** *f* VERSICH excess of line reinsurance

summenproportional: ~**er Beitragsteil** *m* VERSICH basic premium

Summe: **Summenzählwerk** *nt* GESCHÄFT totalizator; **Summenzuwachs** *m* VERSICH extra dividend, reversionary bonus

Summer *m* COMP buzzer

summieren *vt* MATH, RECHNUNG sum up

Super- *pref* GESCHÄFT super-; **Superbenzin** *nt* UMWELT four-star petrol (*BrE*), premium grade gasoline (*AmE*); **Supercomputer** *m* COMP supercomputer; **Superdividende** *f* FINANZ superdividend, surplus dividend; **Superkraftstoff** *m* UMWELT four-star petrol (*BrE*), premium grade gasoline (*AmE*); **Supermacht** *f* POL superpower

Supermarkt *m* V&M supermarket; ~ **einer Ladenkette** V&M chain superstore; ~ **unter einem Dach** V&M one-stop shopping center (*AmE*), one-stop shopping centre (*BrE*)

Super-: **Supermultiplikator** *m* VW super multiplier; **Superneutralität** *f* VW superneutrality; **Superprovision** *f* VERSICH overriding commission; **Superstandort** *m* V&M super site; **Supertanker** *m* TRANSP supertanker; **Super-VGA** *abbr* (*Super-Videografikadapter*) COMP SVGA (*super video graphics adapter*); **Super-Videografikadapter** *f* (*Super-VGA*) COMP super video graphics adapter (*SVGA*); **Super-Videografikanordnung** *f* COMP super video graphics array (*SVGA*)

Supervisor *m* COMP *Steuerroutine* supervisor

supranational *adj* GESCHÄFT, POL, VW supranational

suspendieren *vt* GESCHÄFT *Handel, Autorisation, Genehmigung*, PERSON suspend

Suspension *f* GESCHÄFT, PERSON suspension

Suspenskollator *m* GESCHÄFT suspense collator

Süßwasser *nt* UMWELT fresh water

SV *abbr* (*Sozialversicherung*) PERSON NI (*National Insurance*)

Swap *m* BÖRSE, GESCHÄFT swop; **Swapgeschäft** *nt* BÖRSE, GESCHÄFT swop; **Swaplinie** *f* FINANZ swop line; **Swapmarkt** *m* BÖRSE swop market; **Swapsatz** *m* VW forward margin, swoprate; **Swaptermingeschäft** *nt* BÖRSE forward swop

Swatch *f* GESCHÄFT swatch

Swing *m* BANK swing; **Swing-Grenze** *f* BANK swing credit margin; **Swing-Überschreitung** *f* BANK swing overdraft

Switch- *in cpds* BÖRSE, GESCHÄFT, V&M, VW switch; **Switch-Geschäft** *nt* VW switch; **Switch-Handel** *m* BÖRSE, GESCHÄFT switch trading; **Switch-Verkauf** *m* BÖRSE, V&M switch selling

symbiotisch: ~**es Marketing** *nt* V&M symbiotic marketing

Symbol *nt* COMP icon, symbol, GESCHÄFT, PATENT, V&M symbol; ◆ **nach ~** COMP *Sortierung* by icon

symbolisch *adj* COMP, GESCHÄFT, POL, V&M symbolic; ~**e**

Assoziation *f* V&M symbolic association; ~**e Bezahlung** *f* BANK, GESCHÄFT token payment

Symmetrie *f* BÖRSE, MATH symmetry

symmetrisch *adj* BÖRSE, MATH symmetric; ~**e Häufigkeitskurve** *f* MATH symmetrical frequency curve

Sympathie- *in cpds* PERSON sympathetic, sympathy; **Sympathieaktion** *f* PERSON sympathetic action, sympathy action; **Sympathiemaßnahme** *f* PERSON sympathetic action; **Sympathiestreik** *m* PERSON sympathetic strike, sympathy strike

Sympathisant, in *m,f* POL *Kommunismus* fellow traveler (*AmE*), fellow traveller (*BrE*), sympathizer

Symposium *nt* GESCHÄFT symposium

synchron *adj* COMP synchronous; **nicht ~** *adj* VW out of sync; ~**er Konjunkturindikator** *m* VW coincident indicator; ~**es Marketing** *nt* V&M syncro marketing

Synchronisation *f* GESCHÄFT dubbing, synchronization (*sync*)

synchronisieren *vt* GESCHÄFT synchronize, V&M dub, synchronize

synchronisiert *adj* GESCHÄFT synchronized

Synchronisierung *f* V&M dubbing

Synchronsystem *nt* IND synchronous system (*Sy*)

Syndikalismus *m* PERSON syndicalism

Syndikat *nt* FINANZ, GESCHÄFT consortium, syndicate, VW cartel with joint purchasing or marketing organization; ◆ **das ~ brechen** BÖRSE break the syndicate

Syndikat: **Syndikatsmitglied** *nt* FINANZ member of a syndicate

Syndikus *m* PERSON legal advisor; ~ **einer Unternehmung** *m* PERSON general counsel (*AmE*), head of legal department (*BrE*); **Syndikusanwalt** *m*, **Syndikusanwältin** *f* RECHT company's solicitor (*BrE*), corporate lawyer (*AmE*), legal advisor, staff lawyer

syndiziert: ~**e Anleihe** *f* FINANZ syndicated loan; ~**er Swap** *m* FINANZ syndicated swap

Synergie *f* GESCHÄFT, VW synergism, synergy

Synergismus *m* GESCHÄFT, VW synergism

Synopse *f* GESCHÄFT, MEDIEN, V&M synopsis

Syntax *f* COMP syntax; **Syntaxfehler** *m* COMP syntax error; **Syntaxfehlermeldung** *f* COMP syntax error message

Synthese *f* GESCHÄFT synthesis

synthetisch *adj* COMP synthetic, GESCHÄFT synthetic, composite, IND man-made, synthetic; ~**e Anleihe** *f* BÖRSE synthetic bond; ~**er Anreiz** *m* VW synthetic incentive; ~**er Frühindikator** *m* VW composite leading index

System *nt* COMP, GESCHÄFT system, POL regime, VERWALT system; ~ **der Arbeitsplatzbewertung** PERSON job evaluation scheme; ~ **zur Beurteilung der Risiken im Aktivgeschäft** BANK risk asset system; ~ **flexiber Entgeltgestaltung** PERSON cafeteria benefit plan; ~ **der freien Marktwirtschaft** VW free enterprise system; ~ **zur Informationswiedergewinnung** COMP information retrieval system; ~ **für kombinierten Transport** TRANSP intermodal transport system; ~ **lehensfreien Grundbesitzes** RECHT allodial system; ~ **der mehrstufigen Betriebsführung** PERSON *Management* multiple management plan; ~ **vorgegebener Bewegungszeiten** FINANZ, MGMNT, VW predetermined motion time system (*PMTS*); ~ **auf Wissensbasis** COMP knowledge-based system (*KBS*); **Systemanalyse**

f COMP systems analysis; **Systemanalytiker** *m* COMP program analyst, software engineer, systems analyst, systems engineer; **Systemanforderung** *f* COMP system requirement; **Systemansatz** *m* COMP systems approach

systematisch *adj* GESCHÄFT systematic; **~er Arbeitsplatzwechsel** *m* PERSON job rotation; **~e Auswahl** *f* MATH systematic sampling; **~er Fehler** *m* MATH bias; **~e Kostenbasis** *f* RECHNUNG systematic cost basis; **~es Risiko** *nt* BÖRSE systematic risk

systematisieren *vt* GESCHÄFT systematize

System: **Systemaufforderung** *f* COMP prompt; **Systemblockade** *f* COMP *Datenzugriff* deadlock; **Systemdatei** *f* COMP system file; **Systemdiskette** *f* COMP system disk; **Systementwicklung** *f* COMP system development, systems engineering; **Systementwurf** *m* COMP system design, systems design; **Systeme** *nt pl* **und Verfahren** *nt pl* COMP systems and procedures

systemgeleitet: **~es Unternehmen** *nt* GESCHÄFT, MGMNT system-managed company

System: **Systemmanagement** *nt* MGMNT systems management

systemorientiert: **~e Buchprüfung** *f* RECHNUNG system-based audit, systems-based auditing

System: **Systemplanung** *f* COMP, GESCHÄFT systems planning; **Systemprogrammierer, in** *m,f* COMP systems programmer; **Systemprogrammierung** *f* COMP systems programming; **Systemsoftware** *f* COMP *Betriebssystem* system software; **Systemtheorie** *f* MGMNT systems theory; **Systemumstellung** *f* COMP migration; **Systemurband** *nt* COMP master copy; **Systemversagen** *nt* COMP system failure; **Systemversorger** *m* FINANZ system-provider; **Systemverwalter, in** *m,f* COMP *Netzwerk* system administrator, administrator; **Systemverwaltung** *f* COMP systems management; **Systemzusammenbruch** *m* COMP abnormal system end

Szenario *nt* MGMNT scenario; **~ für den günstigsten Fall** GESCHÄFT, VW best-case scenario; **~ für den ungünstigsten Fall** GESCHÄFT, VW worst-case scenario

SZR *abbr* *(Sonderziehungsrechte)* BANK SDR *(special drawing rights)*

T

t *abbr* (*Tonne*) GESCHÄFT t (*ton, tonne*)

Tabak *m* STEUER, V&M tobacco; **Tabakerzeugnisse** *nt pl* STEUER, V&M tobacco products; **Tabakprodukte** *nt pl* STEUER, V&M tobacco products; **Tabakwaren** *f pl* STEUER, V&M tobacco products

tabellarisch 1. *adj* COMP, MATH, MEDIEN tabular; **2.** *adv* COMP, MATH, MEDIEN in tabular form; ♦ **~ angeordnet** COMP, MATH, MEDIEN in tabulated form; **~ anordnen** COMP, MATH, MEDIEN tabulate; **~ zusammenstellen** GESCHÄFT *Daten* schedule

tabellarisch: **~e Anordnung** *f* COMP, MATH, MEDIEN tabulation; **~er Bericht** *m* VERWALT tabular report; **~e Darstellung** *f* MATH chart; **~er Lebenslauf** *m* VERWALT personal data sheet

tabellarisieren *vt* COMP, MATH, MEDIEN tabulate

Tabelle *f* COMP, MATH, MEDIEN table; **~ von Nominalwerten** BÖRSE table of par values; **Tabellenführer sein** *phr* GESCHÄFT be top of the league; **Tabellenkalkulation** *f* BÖRSE, COMP, FINANZ, RECHNUNG, VERWALT spreadsheet; **Tabellenkalkulationsprogramm** *nt* COMP spreadsheet program

Tabelliermaschine *f* VERWALT tabulating machine

Tabellierung *f* COMP, MATH, MEDIEN tabulation; **Tabellierungsabteilung** *f* VERWALT tabulating department

Tabulator *m* COMP *Textverarbeitung* tab; **Tabulatoreinstellung** *f* COMP tab setting; **Tabulatorstelle** *f* COMP tab stop; **eine Tabulatorstelle weiterspringen** *phr* COMP tab

Tachograph *m* TRANSP tachograph

Tadelsantrag *m* POL motion of censure

Tag *m* GESCHÄFT day; **~ mit verbilligtem Tarif** KOMM, TRANSP off-peak day; ♦ **pro ~** GESCHÄFT per diem, per day; **den ganzen ~ dauernd** GESCHÄFT around-the-clock (*AmE*), round-the-clock (*BrE*); **~ und Nacht geöffnet** GESCHÄFT open all hours; **einen ~ Sonderurlaub nehmen** PERSON take an extra day off; **von ~ zu Tag** GESCHÄFT day by day

Tag: **Tage** *m pl* **nach Akzept** GESCHÄFT days after acceptance (*D/A*); **Tagebau** *m* IND opencast mining (*BrE*), strip mining (*AmE*); **Tagebuch** *nt* RECHNUNG daybook, journal; **Tagegeld** *nt* GESCHÄFT daily allowance, PERSON attendance fees, attendance money, VERSICH per diem allowance; **Tagelöhner, in** *m,f obs* PERSON daily paid worker

tagen *vi* POL *Parlament, Ausschuß* sit

Tages- *in cpds* GESCHÄFT daily, per day; **Tagesakkord** *m* PERSON measured day work (*MDW*); **Tagesauftrag** *m* BÖRSE day order; **Tagesauszug** *m* RECHNUNG daily position statement; **Tagesbericht** *m* **über Kundenbesuche** V&M daily report of calls; **Tagesentschädigung** *f* VERSICH daily allowance

Tagesgeld *nt* BANK, FINANZ call money, daily loan, day loan, overnight money, money at call, federal funds (*AmE*), fed funds (*AmE*); **Tagesgeldausleihung** *f* BANK, FINANZ overnight loan; **Tagesgeldsatz** *m* BANK call money rate, call rate, daily money rate, interbank rate, overnight rate, FINANZ call money rate, call rate, daily money rate, overnight rate, VW interbank rate

Tages-: **Tageskurs** *m* BANK rate of the day, today's rate, BÖRSE actual price, current price, daily quotation, going price, ruling price, FINANZ today's rate; **zu Tageskursen** *phr* BÖRSE at ruling prices; **Tagesnettogewinn** *m* FINANZ net daily surplus; **Tagesnettoverlust** *m* FINANZ net daily loss

Tagesordnung *f* MGMNT, VERWALT agenda; ♦ **eine ~ aufstellen** MGMNT, VERWALT draw up an agenda; **etw auf die ~ setzen** MGMNT, VERWALT put sth on the agenda; **auf der ~ stehen** MGMNT, VERWALT be on the agenda

Tagesordnung: **Tagesordnungspunkte** *m pl* MGMNT, VERWALT items on the agenda

Tages-: **Tagespolitik** *f* POL current affairs; **Tagespreis** *m* BÖRSE ruling price, actual price; **zu Tagespreisen** *phr* BÖRSE at ruling prices; **Tagesschicht** *f* PERSON *Schichtarbeit* day shift; **Tagesspekulation** *f* BÖRSE day trading; **Tagesstempel** *m* KOMM postmark, VERWALT date stamp; **Tagesumsatz** *m* BÖRSE daily volume; **Tageswert** *m* FINANZ, RECHNUNG market value; **Tageszins** *f* BANK daily interest; **Tageszinseinlage** *f* BANK daily interest deposit; **Tageszinskonto** *nt* BANK daily interest account

tageweise: **~ Anstellung** *f* **von Arbeitskräften** PERSON recurrent spot contracting; **~ Verzinsung** *f* BANK continuous compounding, continuous interest

taggenau: **~e Zinsabrechnung** *f* BANK daily balance interest calculation

taggleich *adj* IMP/EXP, TRANSP *Lieferung* same-day; **~e Regulierung** *f* BÖRSE daily settlement

täglich 1. *adj* GESCHÄFT daily, day-to-day; ♦ **seine ~e Arbeit verrichten** GESCHÄFT go about one's daily business; **2.** *adv* GESCHÄFT daily

täglich: **~er Abschlußsaldo** *m* RECHNUNG daily closing balance; **~er Besuchsbericht** *m* V&M daily report of calls; **~es Brot** *nt* GESCHÄFT bread and butter; **~es Geld** *nt* BANK call money, day-to-day money; **~ kündbares Darlehen** *nt* BANK day-to-day loan; **~e Preisobergrenze** *f* BÖRSE daily price limit; **~ verfügbare Einlage** *f* BANK daily interest

Tag: **Tag- und Nachtdienst** *m* GESCHÄFT around-the-clock service (*AmE*), round-the-clock service (*BrE*)

Tagung *f* MGMNT, VERWALT conference, congress, convention, session; **Tagungsbericht** *m* VERWALT conference proceedings, conference report; **Tagungshotel** *nt* VERWALT convention hotel; **Tagungsleiter** *m* MGMNT, PERSON chairman, chairperson; **Tagungsleiterin** *f* MGMNT, PERSON chairwoman, chairperson; **Tagungsort** *m* MGMNT, VERWALT conference site, conference venue; **Tagungsprotokoll** *nt* VERWALT conference proceedings; **Tagungsteilnehmer, in** *m,f* MGMNT conference delegate, convention participant

Tagwechsel *m* FINANZ day bill

Takler *m* TRANSP rigger

Takt *m* COMP clock pulse, clock signal, IND cycle, timed sequence

taktisch: ~**er Plan** *m* GESCHÄFT tactical plan; ~**e Planung** *f* GESCHÄFT tactical planning; ~**e Preispolitik** *f* V&M tactical pricing

Takt: **Taktrate** *f* COMP clock rate

Talfahrt *f* BÖRSE, VW *Konjunktur* downswing

Tallymann *m* TRANSP tally clerk

Talon *m* BÖRSE apron, coupon sheet, renewal coupon, talon

Talsohle *f* VW bottom, economic tailspin, floor, trough

Tandem: **im ~ arbeiten** *phr* MGMNT operate in tandem

Tank *m* TRANSP tank (*ta*); **Tankanlage** *f* TRANSP tank farm; **Tank-Container** *m* TRANSP tank container; **Tankdecke** *f* TRANSP tank top

Tanker *m* TRANSP tanker

Tank: **Tankfahrzeug** *nt* TRANSP tank truck (*AmE*), tanker lorry (*BrE*); **Tanklager** *nt* TRANSP tank farm; **Tanklastwagen** *m* TRANSP tank truck (*AmE*), tanker lorry (*BrE*); **Tankmotorschiff** *nt* TRANSP tanker motor vessel; **Tankschiffbroker** *m* PERSON tanker broker; **Tankstelle** *f* TRANSP service station; **Tanktainer** *m* TRANSP tanktainer (*ta*); **Tankwagen** *m* TRANSP tank truck (*AmE*), tanker lorry (*BrE*)

Tante-Emma-Laden *m* V&M corner shop (*BrE*), neighborhood store (*AmE*), mom-and-pop store (*AmE*)

Tantieme *f* MEDIEN, PATENT author's fee, royalty, MGMNT, PERSON management bonus, percentage of annual profits, profit-sharing bonus, tantième

Tap-Emission *f* BANK, BÖRSE tap issue

Tara *f* IND, TRANSP tare (*t.*), tare weight

tarieren *vt* IND, TRANSP tare

Tarierung *f* IND, TRANSP taring

Tarif *m* GESCHÄFT tariff, rates, rate, scale of charges, IMP/EXP customs, tariff; ~ **für bestimmte Ware** IMP/EXP specific commodity rate; ~ **für konkrete Ware** IMP/EXP specific commodity rate; ~ **für Mustersendung** KOMM sample rate; ~ **unter Kosten** TRANSP rate below cost; **Tarifabschluß** *m* PERSON wage settlement; **Tarifangleichung** *f* PERSON wage adjustment; **Tarifausgaben** *f pl* RECHNUNG tariff expenditure; **Tarifausschlußklausel** *f* PERSON *Gewerkschaftsbewegung* union membership agreement (*UMA*); **Tarifautonomie** *f* VW autonomous wage bargaining, autonomy in collective bargaining, free collective bargaining; **Tarifbeitrag** *m* VERSICH premium rate; **Tariffestsetzung** *f* FINANZ, STEUER fixing of tariffs, rate fixing, rating, tariffication; **Tarifflexibilität** *f* GESCHÄFT rate flexibility; **Tarifformulierung** *f* GESCHÄFT rates formulation; **Tarifgleichgewicht** *nt* vw equilibrium wage rate

tarifieren *vt* GESCHÄFT classify, rate

Tarif: **Tarifkampf** *m* GESCHÄFT tariff war; **Tarifklasse** *f* TRANSP rate class; **Tarifkommission** *f* PERSON Wages Council (*BrE*); **Tarifkonflikt** *m* PERSON industrial dispute

tariflich 1. *adj* PERSON collectively agreed, contractual; **2.** *adv* ◆ **jdn ~ niedriger einstufen** PERSON *Arbeitnehmer* demote sb

tariflich: ~**e Abgabe** *f* STEUER scale charge; ~**e Klausel** *f* PERSON labor clause (*AmE*), labour clause (*BrE*)

Tarif: **Tariflohn** *m* PERSON union rate; **Tariflohneffekt** *m* FINANZ, PERSON union wage effect; **Tariflohnreduktion**

f TRANSP *Luftfrachtklassifizierung* reduced class rate (*R*); **Tarifniveau** *nt* STEUER tariff level; **Tarifpartei** *m pl* PERSON bargaining unit; **Tarifpartner** *m pl* PERSON both sides of industry, parties to a collective agreement, unions and management, bargaining table; **Tarifprämie** *f* VERSICH tabular premium; **Tarifpreisgestaltung** *f* TRANSP fare pricing; **Tarifrunde** *f* PERSON negotiating round, pay round, round of wage negotiations, wage bargaining round; **Tarifsatz** *m* IMP/EXP tariff rate; **Tarifstrategie** *f* TRANSP rates strategy; **Tarifstruktur** *f* TRANSP rates structure; **Tariftrend** *m* TRANSP rate trend; **Tarifüberprüfung** *f* TRANSP rates review; **Tarifvereinbarung** *f* **mit Produktivitätsbezug** VW productivity bargaining

Tarifverhandlung *f* PERSON, VW collective bargaining, collective negotiations, negotiations for collective agreement (*BrE*), union contract negotiations (*AmE*); **Tarifverhandlungen** *f pl* **auf Betriebsbasis** PERSON workplace bargaining, workshop bargaining; **Tarifverhandlungen** *f pl* **für den gesamten Industriezweig** PERSON single-table bargaining (*BrE*); **Tarifverhandlungen** *f pl* **für mehrere Betriebe** PERSON multi-plant bargaining; **Tarifverhandlungen** *f pl* **mit mehreren Gewerkschaften** PERSON multi-union bargaining; **Tarifverhandlungen** *f pl* **auf Verbandsebene** PERSON multi-employer bargaining

Tarifvertrag *m* PERSON *Gewerkschaftsbewegung* collective agreement, collective bargaining agreement, collective labor agreement (*AmE*), collective labour agreement (*BrE*), union agreement (*AmE*), union contract (*AmE*); ~ **mit einer Gewerkschaft** PERSON single-union agreement (*BrE*), single-union deal (*BrE*); ~ **mit offener Laufzeit** PERSON open-ended agreement; **Tarifvertragsverhandlungen** *f pl* **für das Gesamtunternehmen** PERSON company bargaining

Tasche *f* GESCHÄFT case, *Gepäck* bag, *Aktentasche* briefcase, *Kleidung* pocket; **Taschenbuch** *nt* MEDIEN paperback, soft-cover book; **Taschengeld** *nt* GESCHÄFT pocket money, spending money, pin money; **Taschenrechner** *m* COMP hand calculator, pocket calculator

Tastatur *f* COMP keyboard; ~ **für Sehgeschädigte** COMP tactile keyboard

tastaturbetrieben *adj* COMP keyboard-operated

tastaturgesteuert *adj* COMP keyboard-operated

Taste *f* COMP key; ~ **für negativen Schrägstrich** COMP backslash key; **Tastenanschlag** *m* COMP keystroke; **Tastenanschlagsfrequenz** *f* COMP, VERWALT keystroke rate; **Tastendruck** *m* COMP keystroke; **Tastenfeld** *nt* COMP keypad; **Tastenkürzel** *nt* COMP keyboard short cut, short key; **Tastensperre** *f* COMP keylock; **Tastentelefon** *nt* KOMM push-button telephone, *für Tonwahl* touch-tone phone

Tat *f* GESCHÄFT action

tätig *adj* GESCHÄFT active, busy; ◆ ~ **sein** GESCHÄFT act; ~ **sein als** GESCHÄFT trade as, do business as, RECHT *Anwalt* practice as (*AmE*), practise as (*BrE*); ~ **werden** GESCHÄFT act, take action, MGMNT take action

tätig: ~**er Teilhaber** *m*, ~**e Teilhaberin** *f* MGMNT active partner

tätigen *vt* V&M *Abschluß* close, transact, effect

Tätigkeit *f* GESCHÄFT action, activity, PERSON *Arbeit*, *Beruf* occupation; **Tätigkeitsbereich** *m* GESCHÄFT field of action, range of activity, sphere of action;

Tätigkeitsbericht *m* GESCHÄFT activity report, progress report; **Tätigkeitsfunktion** *f* VW employment function; **Tätigkeitsgruppe** *f* PERSON job cluster; **Tätigkeitsprofil** *nt* PERSON job profile

Tätigwerden *nt* GESCHÄFT action

Tatsache *f* GESCHÄFT fact; ◆ **den Tatsachen ins Auge sehen** GESCHÄFT face the facts; **Tatsachen verdrehen** GESCHÄFT gerrymander

Tatsache: **Tatsachenbeweis** *m* RECHT factual evidence; **Tatsachenfeststellung** *f* GESCHÄFT fact-finding

tatsächlich *adj* COMP actual, effective, GESCHÄFT factual, actual; ◆ **den ~en Verhältnissen entsprechend** RECHNUNG true and fair

tatsächlich: **~e Adresse** *f* COMP absolute address, actual address; **~er Arbeitslosenstand** *m* VW actual level of unemployment; **~e Arbeitslosigkeit** *f* VW actual level of unemployment; **~e Ausgaben** *f pl* RECHNUNG actual expense; **~e Barauszahlungen** *f pl* RECHNUNG actual cash disbursement; **~e Bezahlung** *f* VW pocket out; **~es Bruttogewicht** *nt* TRANSP actual gross weight; **~es Defizit** *nt* VW actual deficit; **~e Einnahmen** *f pl* **des laufenden Monats** RECHNUNG this month's actuals; **~es Ergebnis** *nt* GESCHÄFT actual outcome; **~er Gewinn je Aktie** *phr* BÖRSE primary earnings per share; **~e Kassenausgänge** *m pl* RECHNUNG actual cash disbursement; **~e Kosten** *pl* RECHNUNG actual cost, real cost; **~er Kreditausfall** *m* BANK loan default; **~er Luftfrachtführer** *m* TRANSP actual carrier; **~er Lufttransport** *m* TRANSP actual carrier; **~e Reichweite** *f* V&M net reach; **~e Schuld** *f* BANK effective debt; **~er Spediteur** *m* TRANSP actual carrier; **~er Steuersatz** *m* STEUER effective tax rate; **~er Transportunternehmer** *m* TRANSP actual carrier; **~er Verfrachter** *m* TRANSP actual carrier; **~er Verlust** *m* VW actual deficit; **~e Wachstumsrate** *f* VW actual rate of growth; **~e Zahlen** *f pl* VW actual figures; **~e Zuhörerschaft** *f* MEDIEN, V&M net audience

TAURUS *abbr* BÖRSE TAURUS (*BrE*) (*obs*) (*Transfer & Automated Registration of Uncertified Stock*)

Tausch *m* GESCHÄFT barter, exchange (*exch.*), swop, switch, switching, VW exchange (*exch.*); **~ von Vermögenswertung** RECHNUNG, VERWALT asset swap; **Tausch-Effizienz** *f* VW exchange efficiency

tauschen *vt* GESCHÄFT barter, exchange, swop, switch; ◆ **etw gegen etw ~** GESCHÄFT barter sth for sth

Tausch: **Tauschgeschäft** *nt* FINANZ exchange (*exch.*), GESCHÄFT barter transaction, exchange (*exch.*), exchange deal, VW exchange (*exch.*), swop; **Tauschgewinne** *m pl* VW gains from exchange, gains from trade; **Tauschhandel** *m* VW barter trade, barter transaction, counter-trading, barter; **Tauschhandel treiben** *phr* GESCHÄFT, VW barter; **Tauschhandels-abkommen** *nt* VW barter agreement; **Tauschmittel** *m* VW medium of exchange

Täuschung *f* RECHT *Vertragsrecht* fraudulent misrepresentation

Tausch: **Tauschwert** *m* VW exchange value, value in exchange; **Tauschwirtschaft** *f* VW barter economy, exchange economy, nonmonetary economy

Tausend *nt* GESCHÄFT thousand (*k*)

Tauziehen *nt* GESCHÄFT tug-of-war

Taxe *f* BÖRSE appraised value, GESCHÄFT estimate, estimated price, valuation, STEUER tax, VERSICH agreement of insured value, loss to be paid, VW tax

Taxi *nt* TRANSP cab (*AmE*), taxi (*BrE*)

taxieren *vt* GESCHÄFT appraise, assess, estimate, rate, value

taxiert: **~e Police** *f* VERSICH valued policy; **~er Versicherungswert** *m* VERSICH agreed value

Taxi: **Taxigebühr** *f* TRANSP cab charge (*AmE*), taxi charge (*BrE*); **Taxikonzession** *f* TRANSP hack license (*AmE*), licence to operate a taxi (*BrE*); **Taxistand** *m* TRANSP cab stand (*AmE*), taxi rank (*BrE*), taxi stand (*BrE*)

Tax: **Taxkurs** *m* BÖRSE approximate price; **Taxwert** *m* BÖRSE appraised value

TBN *abbr* (*Gesamtbasenzahl*) IND *Chemie* TBN (*total base number*)

Team *nt* MGMNT, PERSON team; ◆ **im ~ arbeiten** PERSON work as part of a team

Team: **Teamarbeit** *f* MGMNT, PERSON teamwork; **Teambesprechung** *f* MGMNT team briefing; **Teambildung** *f* MGMNT, PERSON team building; **Teamleiter, in** *m,f* MGMNT, PERSON team leader

Technik *f* IND technology, engineering; **Technik- und Konstruktionsabteilung** *f* IND engineering and design department

technisch 1. *adj* GESCHÄFT technical; **2.** *adv* GESCHÄFT technically; ◆ **~ ausgereift** IND high-tech; **~ fortgeschritten** IND, VW technologically advanced

technisch: **~e Aktienanalyse** *f* BÖRSE technical analysis; **~er Anlagenbetreuer** *m* COMP, IND site engineer; **~e Anlagen und Maschinen** *f pl* IND plant and machinery; **~er Assistent** *m*, **~e Assistentin** *f* PERSON technical assistant (*TA*); **~e Bearbeitung** *f* IND *eines Projekts* engineering; **~e Bedarfsprämie** *f* VERSICH burning cost, pure burning cost, pure loss cost; **~er Berater** *m*, **~e Beraterin** *f* IND, PERSON engineering consultant; **~e Beratungsfirma** *f* IND consulting engineer; **~er Bereich** *m* PATENT technical field; **~e Betreuung** *f* COMP, IND technical support; **~e Chartanalyse** *f* BÖRSE chartism; **~e Daten** *pl* GESCHÄFT technical data; **~er Direktor** *m*, **~e Direktorin** *f* MGMNT, PERSON technical director, technical manager, vice president engineering (*AmE*); **~e Einzelheit** *f* GESCHÄFT technicality; **~er Fortschritt** *m* IND engineering progress, technological advance, technological progress, PATENT improvement in the art, progress of the arts; **~e Frage** *f* RECHT technical point; **~es Handelshemmnis** *nt* POL technical barrier, VW technical barrier to trade; **~e Handelsschranke** *f* POL technical barrier; **~e Hilfe** *f* COMP, IND technical assistance; **~e Hilfe** *f* **für Exportfirmen** IMP/EXP technical help to exporters (*THE*); **~e Hilfeleistung** *f* COMP, IND technical support

Technisch: **~e Hochschule** *f* (*TH*) SOZIAL college of advanced technology (*BrE*) (*CAT*), technical university

technisch: **~er Leiter** *m*, **~e Leiterin** *f* MGMNT, PERSON technical manager; **~e Lücke** *f* IND technological gap; **~e Neuerung** *f* IND technological innovation; **~er Patentanwalt** *m*, **~e Patentanwältin** *f* PATENT patent agent; **~es Profil** *nt* GESCHÄFT technical profile; **~er Rückstand** *m* IND technological gap; **~e Schwierigkeit** *f* GESCHÄFT technical hitch; **~e Störung** *f* GESCHÄFT technical hitch

Technisch: **~er Überwachungs-Verein** *m* (*TÜV*) TRANSP ≈ Ministry of Transport test (*BrE*) (*MOT*)

technisch: **~e Unterlagen** *f pl* IND technical data; **~e Unterstützung** *f* COMP, IND technical support; **~er Verkäufer** *m* PERSON technical salesman, technical salesperson; **~e Verkäuferin** *f* PERSON technical saleswoman, technical salesperson; **~e Versicherung** *f* VERSICH engineering insurance; **~er Vertreter** *m* PERSON technical salesman, technical salesperson; **~e Vertreterin** *f* PERSON technical saleswoman, technical salesperson; **~e Zusammenarbeit** *f* IND technical cooperation; **~e Zusammenarbeit** *f* **zwischen den Entwicklungsländern** vw *Vereinte Nationen* technical cooperation among developing countries (*TCDC*)

technokratisch *adj* GESCHÄFT technocratic

Technologie *f* IND technics, engineering, technology; **Technologiepark** *m* IND science park; **Technologietransfer** *m* IND, VW technology transfer (*TT*), transfer of technology; **Technologiezentrum** *nt* IND technology park

technologisch 1. *adj* IND technological; **2.** *adv* IND technologically; ◆ **~ hochentwickelt** IND, VW technologically advanced

technologisch: **~er Fortschritt** *m* IND technological advance; **~e Prognose** *f* IND technological forecast, technological forecasting; **~e Rente** *f* IND technological rent; **~e Verbesserung** *f* IND technological innovation; **~er Vorsprung** *m* IND technological edge; **~er Wandel** *m* IND technological change; **~e Zusammenarbeit** *f* GESCHÄFT technology cooperation, IND technological cooperation

Teerpapier *nt* IND, KOMM waterproof paper

Teil 1. *m* GESCHÄFT part, piece, portion, RECHT party; **~ der Gesetzgebung** RECHT piece of legislation; ◆ **als ein ~ von** GESCHÄFT as a proportion of; **2.** *nt* IND component

Teil: **Teilakzept** *nt* GESCHÄFT partial acceptance; **Teilausbuchung** *f* RECHNUNG partial write-off; **Teilausschuß** *m* POL split commission; **Teilbasis** *f* FINANZ partial basis; **Teilbelastung** *f* GRUND, RECHT partial release; **Teileanalyse-Ausbildung** *f* GESCHÄFT part-analysis training

teilen *vt* COMP divide, GESCHÄFT share; ◆ **etw mit jdm ~** GESCHÄFT share sth with sb; **etw mit jdm zu gleichen Teilen ~** GESCHÄFT go halves with sb

Teil: **Teilentschädigung** *f* RECHNUNG partial consideration; **Teilerhebung** *f* V&M sample study, sample survey; **Teilfreigabe** *f* RECHT partial release; **Teilfreistellung** *f* RECHT partial taking

Teilhaber, in *m,f* GESCHÄFT associate, partner, co-partner; ◆ **einen Teilhaber aufnehmen** GESCHÄFT take a partner

Teilhaber: **Teilhaberlebens- und Krankenversicherung** *f* VERSICH business life and health insurance; **Teilhaberschaft** *f* GESCHÄFT partnership

Teil: **Teilhafter, in** *m,f* GESCHÄFT limited partner; **Teilinformationen** *f pl* GESCHÄFT segment information; **Teilkaskoversicherung** *f* VERSICH third party, fire and theft; **Teilladung** *f* TRANSP part-load; **Teillieferung** *f* BÖRSE partial delivery, GESCHÄFT part-shipment, partial consignment; **Teillieferungsvertrag** *m* RECHT installment contract (*AmE*), instalment contract (*BrE*); **Teilliquidation** *f* VW *von Investmentanteilen* partial withdrawal; **Teillöschung** *f* PATENT, RECHT *eines Warenzeichens* part-cancellation; **Teilmarkt** *m* V&M market segment; **Teilmenge** *f* GESCHÄFT subset; **Teilmonopol** *nt* vw shared monopoly

teilnehmen *vi* GESCHÄFT participate; ◆ **~ an** [+dat]

MGMNT *Sitzung* attend; **an etw ~** GESCHÄFT take part in sth

teilnehmend *adj* GESCHÄFT attending, participating; **~es Beförderungsunternehmen** *m* TRANSP participating carrier; **~er Spediteur** *m* TRANSP participating carrier

Teilnehmer, in *m,f* COMP *Netz, Datenbank* subscriber, GESCHÄFT participant, KOMM subscriber; **~ am Handel** BÖRSE trading party; **~ an einem Kartell** vw cartalist; **Teilnehmerfernwahl** *f* KOMM direct distance dialing (*AmE*) (*DDD*), subscriber trunk dialling (*BrE*) (*STD*); **Teilnehmerzahl** *f* GESCHÄFT number of participants, turnout, KOMM number of subscribers

Teil: **Teilprogramm** *nt* COMP subprogram; **Teilräumung** *f* GRUND partial eviction; **Teilrückstellung** *f* RECHNUNG partial provision basis; **Teilschaden** *m* VERSICH partial loss (*PL*); **Teiltarif** *m* TRANSP sectional rate

Teilung *f* GESCHÄFT division, separation, splitting; **~ von Margen** BÖRSE splitting spreads

Teil: **Teilunwirksamkeitsklausel** *f* RECHT *Handelsvertrag* partial invalidity

teilvariabel: **teilvariable Kosten** *pl* FINANZ, RECHNUNG, vw semi-fixed costs, semi-variable costs, semi-variable expense

Teil: **Teilverlust** *m* VERSICH partial loss (*PL*)

teilweise *adj* GESCHÄFT partial; **~ Annahme** *f* GESCHÄFT partial acceptance; **~r Gesamtschaden** *m* VERSICH partial total loss (*PTL*); **~r Totalschaden** *m* VERSICH partial total loss (*PTL*); **~r Totalverlust** *m* VERSICH partial total loss (*PTL*)

Teil: **Teilwert** *m* RECHNUNG going-concern value, partial value, STEUER value of an asset as part of an enterprise

Teilzahlung *f* BANK installment (*AmE*), installment payment (*AmE*), instalment (*BrE*), instalment payment (*BrE*), payment on account, GESCHÄFT part payment; **~ als Anerkennung einer Zahlungsverpflichtung** GESCHÄFT token payment; ◆ **als ~** GESCHÄFT as part payment

Teilzahlung: **Teilzahlungsbank** *f* FINANZ consumer finance company, finance house (*BrE*); **Teilzahlungsgeschäft** *nt* GESCHÄFT tally trade (*BrE*); **Teilzahlungskredit** *m* BANK installment loan (*AmE*), instalment loan (*BrE*), FINANZ installment credit (*AmE*), instalment credit (*BrE*); **Teilzahlungskreditgeschäft** *nt* BANK fringe banking; **Teilzahlungsplan** *m* BANK installment repayment plan (*AmE*), instalment repayment schedule (*BrE*); **Teilzahlungsverkauf** *m* V&M installment sale (*AmE*), instalment sale (*BrE*); **Teilzahlungsvertrag** *m* FINANZ credit sale agreement, hire-purchase agreement (*BrE*); **Teilzahlungszinsen** *m pl* BANK add-on interest

Teilzeit- in *cpds* PERSON part-time; **Teilzeitarbeit** *f* PERSON part-time work, part-time job; **Teilzeitarbeiter, in** *m,f* PERSON part-time worker, part-timer, part-time employee; **Teilzeitarbeitskraft** *f* PERSON part-time worker, part-timer, part-time employee; **Teilzeitbeschäftigung** *f* PERSON part-time employment; **Teilzeitkraft** *f* PERSON part-time worker, part-timer, part-time employee; **Teilzeitstudie** *f* TRANSP half-time survey (*HT*); **Teilzeitübersicht** *f* TRANSP half-time survey (*HT*)

Teil: **Teilziel** *nt* V&M target segment; **Teilzuweisung** *f* POL suballotment

Tel. *abbr* (*Telefon*) GESCHÄFT, KOMM tel. (*telephone*); **Tel.-**

Nr. *abbr* (*Telefonnummer*) GESCHÄFT, KOMM tel. no. (*telephone number*), phone number

Tele- *pref* COMP, KOMM, VW tele-; **Telearbeit** *f* COMP, PERSON telework, telecommuting; **Telearbeiter, in** *m,f* COMP, PERSON teleworker; **Telebanking** *nt* BANK telebanking; **Tele-Einkauf** *m* COMP, V&M electronic shopping

Telefon *nt* (*Tel.*) GESCHÄFT, KOMM phone, telephone (*tel.*); ◆ **am ~** KOMM over the telephone; **per ~** KOMM over the telephone

Telefon: **Telefonanruf** *m* KOMM phone call; **Telefonbuch** *nt* KOMM phone book, telephone book, telephone directory; **Telefongespräch** *nt* KOMM phone call, telephone conversation (*telcon*); **Telefonhandel** *m* BÖRSE interoffice dealings, interoffice trading, telephone dealing; **Telefonhörer** *m* KOMM telephone receiver

Telefonieren *nt* KOMM phoning

telefonisch *adj* KOMM by telephone, over the telephone, telephonic; ◆ **~ Geschäfte tätigen** MGMNT do business over the phone; **eine ~e Nachricht hinterlassen** KOMM leave a telephone message

telefonisch: **~er Auftragsdienst** *m* GESCHÄFT answering service; **~e Befragung** *f* V&M telephone interviewing; **~e Nachricht** *f* KOMM telephone message; **~e Reservierung** *f* FREI telephone booking

Telefonist, in *m,f* KOMM, PERSON switchboard operator, telephone operator

Telefon: **Telefonkarte** *f* KOMM phone card; **Telefon-Marketing** *nt* V&M phone marketing; **Telefonnummer** *f* (*Tel. Nr.*) GESCHÄFT, KOMM phone number, telephone number (*tel. no.*); **Telefonrechnung** *f* KOMM telephone bill; **Telefonverkauf** *m* V&M telephone sales, telephone selling, telesales; **Telefonverkehr** *m* BÖRSE interoffice dealings, interoffice trading, telephone traffic; **Telefonverzeichnis** *nt* KOMM telephone directory; **nicht im Telefonverzeichnis aufgeführt** *phr* KOMM ex-directory (*BrE*), unlisted (*AmE*); **Telefonzelle** *f* KOMM call box, telephone booth, telephone box

Telegraf *m* KOMM telegraph

telegrafisch *adj* KOMM telegraphic; **~e Adresse** *f* KOMM telegraphic address (*TA*); **~e Auszahlung** *f* BANK, FINANZ cable transfer, telegraphic transfer (*TT*); **~e Eilüberweisung** *f* BANK, FINANZ express telegraphic money transfer; **~e Geldanweisung** *f* BANK, FINANZ telegraphic money order (*TMO*); **~e Geldüberweisung** *f* BANK, FINANZ telegraphic money order (*TMO*); **~e Überweisung** *f* BANK, FINANZ cable transfer, telegraphic transfer (*TT*)

Telegramm *nt* KOMM cable, cablegram (*frml*), telegram, telemessage (*TMESS*); **Telegrammadresse** *f* KOMM cable address, telegraphic address (*TA*)

Tele-: **Telekommunikation** *f* KOMM telecommunications; **Telekommunikation und Automatik** *f* (*Telematik*) COMP, KOMM telematics; **Telekonferenz** *f* COMP, KOMM, V&M teleconference; **Telemarketing** *nt* FINANZ, KOMM, V&M telemarketing; **Telemarkt** *m* FINANZ, KOMM, V&M telemarket; **Telematik** *f* (*Telekommunikation und Automatik*) COMP, KOMM telematics; **Teleshopping** *nt* FINANZ teleshopping; **Teletext**® *m* COMP, MEDIEN Teletext®; **Televerkauf** *m* FINANZ, KOMM, V&M telesales; **Televerkaufsperson** *f* FINANZ, KOMM, V&M telesales person

Television *f* (*TV*) MEDIEN television (*TV*)

Telex *nt* KOMM, VERWALT *Maschine* telex (*tx.*), *Nachricht*

teleprinter message (*BrE*), teletype message (*AmE*); **Telexdienst** *m* KOMM Teletex®

Tel quel *phr* GESCHÄFT sale as is, sale with all faults, tel quel; **Tel quel-Kurs** *m* BÖRSE tel quel rate

Tempo *nt* GESCHÄFT velocity, *Trend* pace, VW rate; **~ der Veränderung** GESCHÄFT pace of change; ◆ **das ~ festlegen** GESCHÄFT set the pace

temporär *adj* GESCHÄFT temporary; **~es Gleichgewicht** *nt* VW temporary equilibrium

Tempo: **Tempowechsel** *m* GESCHÄFT change of pace

Tendenz *f* GESCHÄFT tendency, trend

tendenziös *adj* GESCHÄFT biased, tendentious

Tendenz: **Tendenzwende** *f* FINANZ turnabout, turnaround (*AmE*), turnround (*BrE*)

Tender *m* GESCHÄFT tender; **Tenderaufruf** *m* BÖRSE, FINANZ appeal for tenders; **Tender-Gruppe** *f* FINANZ tender panel; **Tenderverfahren** *nt* BÖRSE tender system

tendieren *vi* BÖRSE, FINANZ tend; ◆ **~ zu** GESCHÄFT tend toward; **dazu ~, etw zu tun** GESCHÄFT tend to do sth

Termin *m* GESCHÄFT appointed time, appointment, *Frist* deadline, time limit, RECHT time limit; ◆ **einen ~ einhalten** GESCHÄFT meet a deadline; **auf ~ kaufen** BÖRSE buy for the account, purchase forward; **nach Vereinbarung** GESCHÄFT by appointment only; **auf ~ verkaufen** BÖRSE sell for the account, sell forward, GESCHÄFT sell for future delivery; **zu einem ~ in der Zukunft** GESCHÄFT at some future date

Termin: **Terminabgabe** *f* STEUER, TRANSP port liner terms charge (*PLTC*); **Terminablage** *f* BANK tickler file

Terminal *nt* COMP terminal, TRANSP air terminal, terminal; **Terminaldurchsatz** *m* TRANSP terminal throughput, terminal thruput (*AmE*); **Terminalgebühren** *f pl* TRANSP terminal charges; **Terminalmanager, in** *m, f* TRANSP terminal manager; **Terminalverkehr** *m* TRANSP terminal traffic

Termin: **Terminbearbeiter** *m,* **Terminbearbeiterin** *f* PERSON traffic manager (*TM*); **Terminbörse** *f* **für Rohölkontrakte** BÖRSE International Petroleum Exchange (*IPE*); **Termindruck** *m* GESCHÄFT, MGMNT time pressure; **Termineinlage** *f* BANK fixed deposit (*BrE*), term deposit, time deposit (*AmE*); **Termingebühr** *f* STEUER, TRANSP port liner terms charge (*PLTC*); **Termingeld** *nt* BANK fixed-term deposit; **Termingeld** *nt* **mit variabler Laufzeit** BANK flexible-term deposit

termingerecht *adj* GESCHÄFT on schedule

Termin: **Termingeschäft** *nt* BÖRSE, FINANZ financial futures, forward exchange transaction, forward operation, dealings for the account, dealing in futures; **Termingeschäfte** *nt pl* BÖRSE, FINANZ futures; **Terminhändler** *m* BÖRSE, FINANZ futures trader; **Terminkapitalverzinsung** *f* BÖRSE forward investment return; **Terminkauf** *m* BÖRSE forward buying, forwarding, GESCHÄFT term purchase; **Terminkaufoption** *f* BÖRSE long butterfly call

Terminkontrakt *m* BÖRSE, FINANZ forward contract, futures contract; **~ kurz vor Fälligkeit** BÖRSE nearby contract; **~ auf US-Treasury bonds** BÖRSE bond futures contract (*AmE*); ◆ **Terminkontrakte kaufen** BÖRSE go long

Terminkontrakt: **Terminkontrakte** *m pl* BÖRSE, FINANZ futures; **Terminkontrakte** *m pl* **auf Aktienbasis** BÖRSE equity-related futures; **Terminkontraktgeschäfts-**

abschluß *m* BÖRSE, FINANZ futures transaction; **Terminkontrakthandel** *m* BÖRSE, FINANZ futures trading; **Terminkontraktkaufoptionen** *f pl* BÖRSE, FINANZ long calls; **Terminkontraktkursänderung** *f* BÖRSE futures price change; **Terminkontraktmarkt** *m* BÖRSE, FINANZ futures market; **Terminkontraktpreis** *m* BÖRSE, FINANZ futures price

Termin: **Terminkontrolle** *f* MGMNT progress control; **Terminkurs** *m* BÖRSE forward rate; **Terminlieferung** *f* GESCHÄFT future delivery; **auf Terminlieferung kaufen** *phr* GESCHÄFT buy for future delivery; **Terminmarkt** *m* BÖRSE, FINANZ forward market, futures market

Terminologie *f* GESCHÄFT terminology

Termin: **Terminorder** *f* GESCHÄFT future order; **Terminpapier** *nt* BÖRSE forward security; **Terminplan** *m* IND, MGMNT production schedule; **Terminplananalyse** *f* MGMNT timetable analysis; **Terminplaner** *m* GESCHÄFT organizer; **Terminplanung** *f* IND, MGMNT calendar management, production scheduling; **Terminposition** *f* BÖRSE forward position; **Terminsicherung** *f* BÖRSE forward cover; **Terminsollzinssatz** *m* BÖRSE forward borrowing rate; **Terminswapgeschäft** *nt* FINANZ forward swap; **Terminüberwachung** *f* V&M traffic department; **Terminverfolgung** *f* IND production control; **Terminverkauf** *m* FINANZ forward sale, future sale; **Terminverkaufsoption** *f* BÖRSE long butterfly put; **Terminverlagerung** *f* VW shifting of target dates; **Terminversicherung** *f* VERSICH term policy; **Terminverwaltung** *f* MGMNT calendar management; **Terminware** *f* BÖRSE forward commodity, future commodity, futures

Terotechnologie *f* VW terotechnology

terrestrisch *adj* MEDIEN *Übertragungstechnik* terrestrial

Territorium *nt* POL territory

Terrorismus *m* POL terrorism

tertiär: **~es Bildungswesen** *nt* SOZIAL tertiary education; **~s Produkt** *nt* VW tertiary product; **~er Sektor** *m* VW tertiary sector

Tertiärgeschäft *nt* GESCHÄFT tertiary activities

Test *m* GESCHÄFT test; **~ zur Güte der Anpassung** MATH goodness-of-fit test

Testament *nt* RECHT will; **ohne ~** RECHT intestate

testamentarisch: **~ errichtete Stiftung** *f* RECHT testamentary trust; **~er Grundstückserbe** *m* GRUND, RECHT devisee; **~e Übertragung** *f* **von Grundbesitz** GRUND, RECHT devise

testamentslos *adj* RECHT intestate

Testament: **Testamentsnachtrag** *m* RECHT codicil; **Testamentsvollstrecker** *m* RECHT executor (*exec.*, *exor, exr.*), executrix (*exec., exor, exr.*); **etw zur Testamentsvollstreckung bewerten** *phr* RECHT value sth for probate

Testat *nt* RECHNUNG audit certificate, audit report, auditor's certificate, auditor's opinion, auditor's report, auditor's statement, RECHT attestation

Test: **Testaufgabe** *f* GESCHÄFT test problem; **Testeinführung** *f* V&M pilot launch

testen *vt* GESCHÄFT test, try out

Test: **Testgebiet** *nt* V&M test area; **Testgerät** *nt* COMP, IND test equipment; **Testieren** *nt* RECHT attestation

testiert: **~er Abschluß** *m* RECHNUNG certified financial statement; **~e Einzelbilanz** *f* RECHNUNG individual

company audited accounts; **~e Ursprungserklärung** *f* IMP/EXP certified declaration of origin

Testimonial-Anzeige *f* V&M testimonial advertisement

Test: **Testmarktaktion** *f* V&M sales test; **Testperson** *f* GESCHÄFT testee; **Testprüfung** *f* GESCHÄFT test audit; **Testtransport** *m* TRANSP test transit

teuer *adj* GESCHÄFT costly, dear, expensive, pricey (*infrml*)

Teuerung *f* V&M, VW rise in prices, price rise; **Teuerungszulage** *f* PERSON *Arbeit* cost-of-living allowance, cost-of-living adjustment (*AmE*) (*COLA*), cost of living supplement; **Teuerungszuschlag** *m* PERSON, *Arbeit* cost-of-living allowance, cost-of-living adjustment (*AmE*) (*COLA*)

Teufelskreis *m* VW vicious circle, vicious cycle

Text *m* COMP, MEDIEN, V&M text body matter, copy; **Textabteilung** *f* V&M copy department

textanschließend: **~e Anzeige** *f* V&M next-to-reading matter

Text: **Textanzeige** *f* V&M advertorial, reader; **Textbearbeiter** *m* V&M copy-adaptor; **Textbearbeitung** *f* COMP text editing; **Texteditor** *m* COMP text editor; **nicht Textiert** *adj* RECHNUNG unaudited

Textil- *in cpds* IND textile

Textilien *pl* IND textiles

Textil-: **Textilindustrie** *f* IND textile industry, apparel industry (*AmE*), clothing industry (*BrE*); **Textilwaren** *f pl* IND, V&M dry goods; **Textil- und Wollindustrie** *f* IND textile industry, apparel and wool industry (*AmE*), clothing trade (*BrE*)

Text: **Textmodus** *m* COMP text mode

textsicher *adj* VERWALT letter-perfect, word-perfect

Textverarbeitung *f* COMP word processing, text processing; **Textverarbeitungsabteilung** *f* COMP word processing center (*AmE*), word processing centre (*BrE*); **Textverarbeitungsarbeitsplatz** *m* COMP word processing center (*AmE*), word processing centre (*BrE*); **Textverarbeitungssoftware** *f* COMP word processing software; **Textverarbeitungssystem** *nt* COMP word processing system, word processor (*WP*); **Textverarbeitungszentrum** *nt* COMP word processing center (*AmE*), word processing centre (*BrE*)

T-Formular *nt* IMP/EXP *Zoll* T form

TH *abbr* (*Technische Hochschule*) SOZIAL CAT (*BrE*) (*college of advanced technology*), technical university

Theke *f* V&M trade counter; **~ für Sonderangebote** V&M bargain counter

Thema *nt* GESCHÄFT subject, topic, subject matter

thematisch: **~e Werbung** *f* V&M theme advertising

Themenpark *m* FREI theme park

Theonomie *f* VW theonomy

Theorem *nt* GESCHÄFT theorem; **~ von Bayes** MGMNT, V&M, VW Bayes' theorem; **~ der Überkapazität** VW excess capacity theorem

theoretisch **1.** *adj* GESCHÄFT theoretical, *Frage* academic; **2.** *adv* GESCHÄFT theoretically, in theory

theoretisch: **~e Maximalkapazität** *f* GESCHÄFT theoretical maximum capacity

Theorie *f* GESCHÄFT theory; **~ des allgemeinen Gleichgewichts** VW general equilibrium analysis; **~ der bevorzugten Wohngebiete** FINANZ preferred habitat theory; **~ der Differentialrente** VW differential theory of rent; **~ der Eigentumsrechte** VW theory of property rights; ~ **der komparativen Kosten** VW theory of comparative costs; ~ **der Regulierung** VW Regulation School; ~ **des schwächsten Glieds** GESCHÄFT weakest link theory; ~ **des segmentierten Arbeitsmarkts** VW segmented labor market theory (*AmE*) (*SLM*), segmented labour market theory (*BrE*) (*SLM*); ~ **des Sickereffekts** VW trickle-down theory; ~ **des stillschweigend geschlossenen Vertrags** VW implicit contract theory; ~ **der Überwachung staatlicher Unternehmen** GESCHÄFT regulatory theory; ~ **der Wahlentscheidung** VW social choice theory; ~ **der zentralen Orte** VW central place theory

Thermalcontainer *m* TRANSP thermal container

thermisch: ~**e Energie** *f* IND, UMWELT thermal energy

thesaurieren *vt* FINANZ, RECHNUNG *Gewinn* accumulate, plough back (*BrE*), plow back (*AmE*)

thesauriert: ~**e Gewinne** *m pl* FINANZ, RECHNUNG ploughed-back profits (*BrE*), profit retentions, retained earnings

Thiebout-Hypothese *f* VW Thiebout hypothesis

Thomson-Bericht *m* VW Thomson Report

Ticket *nt* TRANSP ticket; **Ticket-Analyse** *f* TRANSP ticket analysis

Tidebecken *nt* TRANSP tidal dock

tief *adj* GESCHÄFT low

Tief *nt* BÖRSE, VW bottom, trough

Tiefe *f* GESCHÄFT depth; **Tiefenanalyse** *f* MGMNT depth analysis; **Tiefenbefragung** *f* POL *Wahlforschung* depth polling; **Tiefenprüfung** *f* MGMNT depth analysis

Tiefflieger *m infrml* MGMNT low flier

Tiefgang *m* TRANSP draft (*AmE*), draught (*BrE*)

tiefgekühlt *adj* IND deep-frozen, quick-frozen, refrigerated (*R*)

tiefgreifend: ~**e Diskussion** *f* GESCHÄFT in-depth discussion

Tief: **Tiefkontaktinterview** *nt* V&M depth interview; **Tiefkühlfach** *nt* IND deep-freeze; **Tieflader** *m* TRANSP low loader (*lo*); **Tiefpunkt** *m* BÖRSE, VW bottom, low, nadir; **Tiefstand** *m* BÖRSE, VW bottom, low; **einen Tiefstand erreichen** *phr* BÖRSE hit a low, reach a low, trough

Tiefstkurs *m* BÖRSE, VW lowest price, low

Tiefstpreis *m* BÖRSE, VW lowest price, rock-bottom price, bottom price

Tieftemperaturflüssigkeit *f* IND cryogenic liquid

Tiefwasser *nt* TRANSP deepwater; **Tiefwasseranlegeplatz** *m* TRANSP deepwater berth; **Tiefwasserhafen** *m* TRANSP deepwater harbor (*AmE*), deepwater harbour (*BrE*); **Tiefwasserstraße** *f* TRANSP deepwater route

Tierhalterhaftung *f* VERSICH animal keeper's liability

tilgbar *adj* BANK *Schulden, Hypothek* repayable, amortizable, BÖRSE redeemable (*red.*), repayable, FINANZ, RECHNUNG amortizable

tilgen *vt* BANK *Schulden, Hypothek* repay, pay back, amortize, pay off, BÖRSE redeem, FINANZ liquidate, *Schulden* acquit, satisfy, amortize, GESCHÄFT extinguish, RECHNUNG liquidate, *Schulden* acquit, satisfy, amortize

Tilgung *f* BANK repayment, BÖRSE redemption, FINANZ, RECHNUNG repayment, liquidation, *Schuld* satisfaction, amortization, amortizement, debt retirement, redemption, clearance, UMWELT extinction; ~ **einer Anleihe** FINANZ amortization of a loan, redemption of a loan;

~ **vor dem Fälligkeitstermin** FINANZ redemption before due date; ~ **öffentlicher Schulden** VW public sector debt repayment (*BrE*) (*PSDR*); ~ **einer Schuld** FINANZ satisfaction of a debt; ~ **von Verbindlichkeiten** VW payment of debts; ♦ **zur ~ von** BANK, FINANZ in settlement of

Tilgung: **Tilgungsanleihe** *f* BÖRSE redemption bond, FINANZ amortization loan, sinking-fund bond issue, sinking-fund loan; **Tilgungsart** *f* RECHNUNG amortization method; **Tilgungsaufschub** *m* VERWALT extension; **Tilgungsbetrag** *m* BÖRSE redemption amount; **Tilgungsfonds** *m* FINANZ amortization fund, redemption fund, sinking fund

tilgungsfrei: ~**e Zeit** *f* FINANZ grace period, period of grace

Tilgung: **Tilgungsfrist** *f* FINANZ period of redemption; **Tilgungshypothek** *f* BANK direct reduction mortgage, amortized mortgage loan, FINANZ level-payment mortgage (*AmE*), redemption mortgage; **Tilgungsmittel** *nt pl* VW medium of redemption, redemption funds; **Tilgungsmodalitäten** *f pl* FINANZ terms of redemption; **Tilgungsperiode** *f* FINANZ repayment period; **Tilgungsplan** *m* FINANZ amortization schedule, call schedule, redemption table; **Tilgungsrate** *f* FINANZ amortization installment (*AmE*), amortization instalment (*BrE*), redemption installment (*AmE*), redemption instalment (*BrE*), sinking-fund installment (*AmE*), sinking-fund instalment (*BrE*); **Tilgungsrücklage** *f* FINANZ amortization reserve, amortization fund, sinking-fund reserve; **Tilgungstermin** *m* BÖRSE redemption date, FINANZ repayment date; **Tilgungsverpflichtungen** *f pl* FINANZ redemption commitments, sinking-fund requirements; **Tilgungszahlung** *f* BANK level repayment, RECHNUNG amortization expense, VW redemption payment

Timer *m* COMP timer

Timeshare- *in cpds* GRUND timeshare; **Timeshare-Bauunternehmer, in** *m,f* GRUND timeshare developer; **Timeshare-Eigentum** *nt* GRUND timeshare property

Timesharing *nt* GRUND, PERSON time-sharing; **auf Timesharing-Basis** *phr* GRUND on a time-sharing basis; **Timesharing-Betrieb** *m* GRUND time-sharing company

Tintenstrahldrucker *m* COMP ink-jet printer

Tip *m* GESCHÄFT tip-off, tip, hint, pointer

tippen 1. *vt infrml* COMP, VERWALT type, typewrite; **2.** *vi infrml* COMP, VERWALT type, typewrite

Tippfehler *m* COMP, GESCHÄFT, MEDIEN, VERWALT typing error, typographical error (*typo*)

Tippgeschwindigkeit *f* COMP, VERWALT typing speed

TIPS *abbr* BÖRSE, VW TIPS (*Treasury Inflation Protection Securities*)

Tisch *m* GESCHÄFT counter; **Tischcomputer** *m* COMP desktop computer; **Tischgerät** *nt* COMP desktop unit

Titel *m* BÖRSE security, MEDIEN *Zeitschrift* heading, title, RECHT title; **Titelblatt** *nt* MEDIEN title page, front page; **Titelgeschichte** *f* MEDIEN lead story; **Titelschutzversicherung** *f* VERSICH title protection insurance; **Titelseite** *f* MEDIEN title page, face page, front page; **Titelzeile** *f* VERWALT header

titulieren *vt* GESCHÄFT address

T-Konto *nt* RECHNUNG T-account

Tobin-Steuer *f* STEUER, VW Tobin tax

Tobit-Modell *nt* VW Tobit model

Tochter- *in cpds* GESCHÄFT subsidiary; **Tochterfirma** *f*

GESCHÄFT subsidiary firm; **Tochtergesellschaft** *f* GESCHÄFT affiliated company, associated company, subsidiary, subsidiary company (*BrE*), subsidiary corporation (*AmE*); **Tochterinstitut** *nt* BANK banking subsidiary; **Tochterunternehmen** *nt* GESCHÄFT subsidiary firm

Todesfall *m* SOZIAL fatality, VERSICH death; **Todesfallrisiko** *nt* VERSICH death risk; **Todesfallversicherung** *f* VERSICH assurance payable at death (*BrE*), insurance payable at death (*AmE*), straight-life insurance (*AmE*), whole-life assurance (*BrE*), whole-life insurance (*AmE*); **Todesfallversicherungspolice** *f* VERSICH straight-life insurance policy (*AmE*), whole-life assurance policy (*BrE*), whole-life insurance policy (*AmE*)

Todesopfer *nt* SOZIAL *bei Unfall, Krieg* casualty, fatality

Tokio-Runde *f* VW Tokyo Round

Tokioter: ~ **Interbankenangebotssatz** *m* BANK Tokyo Interbank Offered Rate (*TIBOR*)

Toleranz *f* GESCHÄFT, IND allowance, tolerance; **Toleranzgrenzenveto** *nt* POL line item veto (*AmE*); **Toleranzniveau** *nt* FINANZ tolerance level

Ton *m* COMP, KOMM, MEDIEN sound

Tonband *nt* IND, MEDIEN magnetic tape; **Tonbandanlage** *f* MEDIEN tape unit; **Tonbandaufnahme** *f* MEDIEN tape recording

Ton: **Tonbildschau** *f* MEDIEN film strip; **Toneffekte** *m pl* MEDIEN sound effects

Toner *m* COMP toner

Tonnage *f* IND, TRANSP tonnage; **Tonnagenbeleg** *m* IMP/EXP, TRANSP tonnage dues slip; **Tonnagenberechnung** *f* TRANSP tonnage calculation; **Tonnagenmarke** *f* TRANSP tonnage mark

Tonne *f* (*t*) GESCHÄFT *Gewicht* ton (*t*), tonne (*t*), IND *Behälter* drum, barrel, UMWELT *für Müll* rubbish bin (*BrE*), trashcan (*AmE*), garbage can (*AmE*); **Tonnengehalt** *m* TRANSP tonnage measurement

Ton: **Tonsignal** *nt* COMP beep; **ein Tonsignal ausgeben** *phr* COMP beep; **Tonspur** *f* KOMM, MEDIEN soundtrack

Tool *nt jarg* COMP tool

Top-Down-Modell *nt* VW top-down linkage model

Top-Down-Untersuchung *f*: ~ **der Bedingungen einer Investition** FINANZ top-down approach to investing

Toplader-Container *m* TRANSP top-loader container

Top-Management *nt* MGMNT top management; **Top-Management-Lösung** *f* MGMNT top management approach

Tor *nt* FREI gate

Toronto-Gesamtindex *m* BÖRSE Toronto Composite

Tortendiagramm *nt* COMP *Grafikverarbeitung* pie chart

Total- *in cpds* GESCHÄFT total

total *adj* GESCHÄFT complete, total, all-out; **~er Mangel** *m* VW absolute scarcity

Total-: **Totalschaden** *m* VERSICH total loss (*T/L*), *Auto* write-off; **Totalstatistik** *f* GESCHÄFT census

Totalverlust *m* GESCHÄFT dead loss, VERSICH total loss (*T/L*); ♦ **nur bei ~** VERSICH total loss only (*TLO*); **~ eingeschlossen** VERSICH comprised total loss; **nur gegen ~ versichert** VERSICH total loss only (*TLO*)

tot: **~es Inventar** *nt* VERWALT dead stock; **den ~en Punkt überwinden** *phr* GESCHÄFT break the deadlock

Toto *m or nt* FREI pools

Tourismus *m* FREI tourism; **Tourismusgeschäft** *nt* FREI tourist trade

Tourist, in *m,f* FREI tourist; **~ aus Übersee** FREI overseas tourist

Tourist: **Touristenabgabe** *f* STEUER tourist tax; **Touristenattraktion** *f* FREI tourist attraction; **Touristeninformation** *f* FREI tourist information office, tourist information bureau; **Touristenklasse** *f* FREI, TRANSP economy class, tourist class; **Touristensaison** *f* FREI tourist season; **Touristenticket** *nt* FREI, TRANSP economy ticket; **Touristenvisum** *nt* VERWALT tourist visa

Touristikbranche *f* FREI tourist trade

Tourorganisation *f* FREI tour organization

Tourorganisator *m* FREI tour organizer

toxikologisch *adj* UMWELT toxicological

Toxin *nt* UMWELT toxin

toxisch *adj* UMWELT toxic

Toxizität *f* UMWELT toxicity

Trabantenstadt *f* GRUND, SOZIAL, VW overspill town, satellite town, new town

Trackball *m* COMP *Zeigegerät* trackball

Trade-off *m* VW trade-off

Tradition *f* GESCHÄFT tradition

traditionell *adj* GESCHÄFT traditional

Tragbalken *m* IND girder

tragbar *adj* GESCHÄFT *annehmbar* acceptable, reasonable, *Gerät* portable, V&M hand-held; **~es Funkgerät** *nt* KOMM walkie-talkie; **~er PC** *m obs* COMP laptop, laptop computer; **~er Rechner** *m* COMP portable computer; **~es Telefon** *nt* KOMM mobile phone, mobile telephone, portable phone, portable telephone

Tragbarkeit *f* GESCHÄFT *Annehmbarkeit* acceptability, *Gerät* portability

tragen *vt* GESCHÄFT *Kosten* bear, defray, carry, *Last, Belastung* shoulder

Träger *m* IND girder; **Trägerfrequenz** *f* COMP carrier

Tragetasche *f* V&M bag, carrier bag, shopping bag

Tragetüte *f* V&M bag, carrier bag, shopping bag

Tragfähigkeit *f* TRANSP deadweight capacity (*dwc*), deadweight cargo capacity (*dwcc*), deadweight tonnage (*dwt*), carrying capacity, tons deadweight, tonnes deadweight

Tragflügelboot *nt* TRANSP hydrofoil, jetfoil

Trägheit *f* V&M inertia; **Trägheitseffekt** *m* POL inertia effect; **Trägheitsverkauf** *m* V&M inertia selling; **Trägheitsverkäufer** *m* V&M inertia salesman; **Trägheitsverkäuferin** *f* V&M inertia saleswoman

Traktorzuführung *f* COMP *Einzelblatteinzug* tractor feed

Transaktion *f* GESCHÄFT transaction; **~ am offenen Markt** VW open-market operations; **~ zwischen unabhängigen Partnern** GESCHÄFT, STEUER, V&M arm's-length transaction; **Transaktionsanalyse** *f* FINANZ, MGMNT transactional analysis (*TA*); **Transaktionsbilanz** *f* RECHNUNG transaction balance report; **Transaktionskasse** *f* VW transactions balance, transactions holdings; **Transaktionskosten** *pl* VW transactions costs; **Transaktionskostenökonomie** *f* VW transaction cost economics; **Transaktionsmanagement** *nt* FINANZ, MGMNT transaction management; **Transaktionsmanagement-Software** *f* COMP transaction management software; **Trans-**

aktionsrisiko *nt* BÖRSE transaction exposure; **Transaktionsverarbeitung** *f* COMP transaction processing

transeuropäisch *adj* POL transeuropean

Transeuropanetz *nt* KOMM, TRANSP transeuropean network

Transfer *m* COMP, PERSON, TRANSP, VW transfer (*tr.*, *tfr*); **~ an eine andere Gewerkschaft** PERSON transfer of engagement (*BrE*); **Transfereinkommen** *nt* VW nonfactor income, transfer income; **Transfermanifest** *nt* TRANSP transfer manifest; **Transferproblem** *nt* VW transfer problem; **Transferrate** *f* COMP *Daten* transfer rate; **Transferzahlung** *f* VW transfer payment

Transformation *f* MATH, VW transformation; **Transformationskurve** *f* VW transformation curve; **Transformationsproblem** *nt* VW transformation problem

transformieren *vt* GESCHÄFT transform, MATH transformieren

Transit *m* FREI, IMP/EXP, TRANSP transit; **Transitdokument** *nt* IMP/EXP, TRANSP transit document; **Transithandel** *m* IMP/EXP, TRANSP transit trade, VW merchant trading, third-country trade; **Transitkarte** *f* FREI, TRANSP transit card; **Transitklausel** *f* VERSICH transit clause; **Transitkredit** *m* BANK transit credit; **Transitlager** *nt* GESCHÄFT bonded warehouse, IMP/EXP transit shed, transit store; **Transitluftfrachtbrief** *m* IMP/EXP, TRANSP through air waybill (*TAWB*); **Transitmarkt** *m* FINANZ transit market

transitorisch: **~e Einnahmen** *f pl* VW transitory income; **~er Posten** *m pl* RECHNUNG *Aktiva* deferred item, prepaid expenses

Transit: **Transitpapier** *nt* IMP/EXP, TRANSP transit document; **Transitraum** *m* FREI, TRANSP transit lounge; **Transitrechte** *nt* *pl* transit rights; **Transitreisende(r)** *mf* [decl. as adj] FREI, TRANSP transit passenger; **Transitverkehr** *m* TRANSP transit traffic; **Transitvermerk** *m* IMP/EXP transit bond note

transkribieren *vt* COMP transcribe

Transkription *f* COMP transcription

Transmissionsmechanismus *m* VW transmission mechanism

transnational *adj* GESCHÄFT transnational; **~e Gesellschaft** *f* VW transnational corporation (*TNC*)

Transparent *nt* VERWALT *Durchscheinbild* transparency, V&M *Werbung* banner, neon sign

Transponder *m* KOMM transponder

Transport *m* TRANSP haulage, transit, transport, transportation, conveyance, truckage; **~ von Rückfracht** TRANSP back haul; ◆ **auf ~ befindlich** TRANSP in transit; **beim ~ beschädigt** TRANSP damaged in transit

transportabel *adj* TRANSP transportable

Transport: **Transportanweisung** *f* TRANSP transport instruction, transport instruction form; **Transportart** *f* TRANSP transport mode; **Transportband** *nt* IND conveyor belt; **Transportbehälter** *m* TRANSP container, tote bin; **Transportdokument** *nt* TRANSP transport document, transportation document; **Transporteinrichtungen** *f pl* TRANSP transportation equipment

Transporter *m* TRANSP carrier; **~ von Flüssigerdgas** TRANSP liquefied natural gas carrier; **~ von Flüssiggas** TRANSP liquid petroleum gas carrier

transportfähig *adj* TRANSP transportable

Transport: **Transportfahrzeug** *nt* TRANSP transportation

car; **Transportgut** *nt* TRANSP cargo; **Transporthaftung** *f* VERSICH carrier's liability

transportieren *vt* TRANSP transport, forward (*fwd*), convey, carry

Transport: **Transportkonditionen** *f pl* IMP/EXP terms of shipment; **Transportkontingent** *nt* TRANSP transport quota

Transportkosten *pl* TRANSP carriage; ◆ **~ bezahlt** IMP/EXP, TRANSP carriage paid (*carr pd*)

Transport: **Transportmittel** *nt* TRANSP means of conveyance, means of transport, modes of transport; **Transportmitwirkung** *f* TRANSP, VERSICH instrumentalities of transportation; **Transportmöglichkeiten** *f pl* TRANSP transport facilities; **Transport-Notkarte** *f* TRANSP transport emergency card (*trem card*); **Transportpapiere** *nt pl* IMP/EXP, TRANSP dispatch papers, shipping documents, shipping papers; **Transportquote** *f* TRANSP transport quota; **Transportschaden** *m* TRANSP damage in transit; **Transport- und Spediteurkosten** *pl* TRANSP carriage; **Transport- und Spediteurkosten** *pl* **zu Lasten des Empfängers** IMP/EXP, TRANSP carriage forward (*carr fwd, CF*); **Transportsystem** *nt* TRANSP transport system, transportation system; **Transportunternehmen** *nt* IMP/EXP, TRANSP forwarding company, haulage company, haulage contractor; **Transportunternehmer** *m* IND *Europäisches Leistungsnetz* common carrier, TRANSP carrier, hauler (*AmE*), haulier (*BrE*); **Transportvermittlung** *f* TRANSP, VERSICH instrumentalities of transportation; **Transportversicherung** *f* VERSICH maine insurance, transport insurance; **Transportverteilungsanalyse** *f* TRANSP transport distribution analysis (*TDA*); **Transportwesen** *nt* TRANSP transport, transportation; **Transportzeit** *f* TRANSP handling time, movetime, transit time

Trassant *m* BANK drawer, drafter

Trassat *m* BANK acceptor, drawee

Tratte *f* BANK draft (*dft*), FINANZ bill, bill of exchange (*B/E*); ◆ **eine ~ zur Annahme vorlegen** BANK present a draft for acceptance; **eine ~ avisieren** BANK advise a draft

Trawler *m* TRANSP trawler

treffen *vt* GESCHÄFT meet, VW hit

Treffen *nt* GESCHÄFT meeting

Trefferquote *f* V&M hit rate, strike rate

Treffgenauigkeit *f* MATH accuracy

Treffpunkt *m* GESCHÄFT meeting place, meeting point, venue

treibend: **~es Ölfeld** *nt* UMWELT spillage

treiben *vt* GESCHÄFT spur

Treiber *m* COMP driver

Treibhauseffekt *m* UMWELT greenhouse effect

Treibhausgas *nt* UMWELT greenhouse effect gas

Treibstoff *m* TRANSP fuel; **Treibstoff-Bedingungen** *f pl* TRANSP fuel terms (*ft*); **Treibstoffsteuer** *f* STEUER fuel tax; **Treibstoffzuschlag** *m* TRANSP fuel surcharge

Trend *m* GESCHÄFT tendency, trend; **~ im Inland** VW national trend; ◆ **gegen den ~ laufen** GESCHÄFT buck the trend (*infrml*)

Trend: **Trendanalyse** *f* VW trend analysis

trendanführend: **~es Unternehmen** *nt* VW barometric firm leadership

Trend: **Trendführerschaft** *f* VW barometric firm leadership; **Trendrate** *f* VW underlying rate; **Trendsetter** *m* GESCHÄFT trendsetter; **Trendwende** *f* GESCHÄFT trend reversal; **eine Trendwende herbeiführen** *phr* GESCHÄFT reverse a trend

trennen *vt* COMP decollate, deleave, GESCHÄFT separate, segregate

Trennmauer *f* GRUND party wall

Trennung *f* GESCHÄFT separation, segregation, GRUND severance, POL *Rasse, Geschlecht* segregation

Tresor *m* BANK safe deposit vault, safe, strongroom; **im ~ liegende Gelder** *nt pl* BANK vault cash, vault reserve (*AmE*); **Tresorfach** *nt* BANK safety deposit box

Treue *f* GESCHÄFT fidelity; **Treueprämie** *f* PERSON fidelity bonus; **Treuerabatt** *m* V&M fidelity rebate, loyalty discount, loyalty rebate

Treugeber *m* RECHT settlor, transferor, trustor (*AmE*)

Treu: auf ~ und Glauben *phr* RECHT bona fide, good faith

Treuhand *f* BANK, RECHT trust; **Treuhandabkommen** *nt* GESCHÄFT trust agreement; **Treuhandabteilung** *f* **der Bank** BANK bank trust department; **Treuhandbank** *f* BANK trust bank; **Treuhandbankgeschäft** *nt* BANK trust banking

Treuhänder, in *m,f* RECHT trustee, fiduciary; **~ eines offenen Investmentfonds** BANK mutual fund custodian

treuhänderisch *adj* RECHT fiduciary; **~er Verwalter** *m* RECHT bailee; **~ verwaltetes Konto** *nt* FINANZ discretionary account, RECHNUNG managed account; **~ verwaltetes Vermögen** *nt* VW trust fund; **~ verwaltete Wertpapiere** *nt pl* BÖRSE securities held in trust

Treuhand: **Treuhanderklärung** *f* RECHT declaration of trust; **Treuhandfonds** *m* VW trust fund; **Treuhandgeschäft** *nt* BANK fiduciary investment, fiduciary operation, fiduciary banking; **Treuhandhinterlegungsvereinbarung** *f* RECHT escrow agreement; **Treuhandklausel** *f* RECHT escrow clause; **Treuhandkonto** *nt* BANK custodial account, fiduciary account, agency account; **Treuhandkontogebühr** *f* BANK custodian account fee; **Treuhandquittung** *f* RECHNUNG trust receipt; **Treuhandschaft** *f* RECHT trusteeship; **Treuhandstatus** *m* BÖRSE trustee status; **Treuhandurkunde** *f* RECHT trust instrument; **Treuhandvereinbarung** *f* RECHT trust agreement; **Treuhandverhältnis** *nt* **unter lebenden Personen** RECHT inter vivos trust; **Treuhandvermögen** *nt* VW trust; **Treuhandvertrag** *m* RECHT trust agreement, escrow agreement; **Treuhandverwahrung** *f* RECHT escrow; **Treuhandverwalter, in** *m,f* FINANZ escrow agent; **Treuhandverwaltung** *f* RECHT trust; **in Treuhandverwaltung geben** *phr* RECHT place in trust

treuwidrig: ~e Verfügung *f* RECHT breach of trust

Tribunal *nt* RECHT forum, tribunal

triftig: ~er Grund *m* GESCHÄFT valid reason

Trinkgeld *nt* GESCHÄFT tip

Trinkwasser *nt* UMWELT drinking water

Trittbrettfahrer, in *m,f* *infrml* GESCHÄFT free rider (*infrml*), TRANSP free rider (*AmE*) (*infrml*)

Trocken- *in cpds* IND, TRANSP dry

trocken: er ist noch nicht ~ hinter den Ohren *phr infrml* PERSON he's still wet behind the ears (*infrml*)

Trocken-: **Trockenbatterie** *f* IND dry battery; **Trockendock** *nt* TRANSP dry dock, graving dock; **Trockenfracht** *f* TRANSP dry cargo, dry freight; **Trockengewicht** *nt* TRANSP dry weight

Trockenheit *f* UMWELT drought

Trocken-: **Trockenladung** *f* TRANSP dry cargo; **Trockenmaß** *nt* GESCHÄFT dry measure; **Trockenmassengutladung** *f* TRANSP dry bulk cargo

Trödelmarkt *m* GESCHÄFT second-hand market

Troika *f* POL *Regierung* troika (*AmE*)

Trommel *f* IND drum, cylinder; **Trommeldrucker** *m* COMP drum printer; **Trommelplotter** *m* COMP drum plotter

tropisch: ~er Regenwald *m* UMWELT tropical rain forest

trostlos *adj* GESCHÄFT, VW bleak

Troygewicht *nt* GESCHÄFT troy weight

Troy-Unze *f* FINANZ *Gold* troy ounce

trübe *adj* GESCHÄFT, VW bleak; **~e Aussichten** *f pl* GESCHÄFT bleak outlook

Trumpf *m* GESCHÄFT trump; **Trumpfkarte** *f* GESCHÄFT trump card

Trust *m* RECHT trust; ◆ **in einem ~ zusammenfassen** RECHT trustify

T-Test *m* MATH T-test

Tüchtigkeit *f* GESCHÄFT efficiency, industry

Tunnel *m* GESCHÄFT tunnel; **Tunnelgebühr** *f* TRANSP tunnel toll

Turbinendampfer *m* TRANSP turbine steamship

turboelektrisch *adj* IND turbo-electric

Turbokupplung *f* IND hydraulic coupling (*HC*)

Turnaround *m* GESCHÄFT corporate turnaround

Türschild *nt* VERWALT nameplate

TÜV *abbr* (*Technischer Überwachungs-Verein*) TRANSP ≈ MOT (*BrE*) (*Ministry of Transport test*)

TV *abbr* (*Television*) MEDIEN TV (*television*); **TV-Netz** *nt* MEDIEN TV network

Tycoon *m* GESCHÄFT tycoon

Type *f* COMP, MEDIEN type; **Typenhebel** *m* COMP typebar; **Typenrad** *nt* COMP *Drucker* daisy wheel; **Typenraddrucker** *m* COMP daisy-wheel printer

typisch 1. *adj* GESCHÄFT typical; **2.** *adv* GESCHÄFT typically

typisieren *vt* GESCHÄFT standardize, typify

typisiert *adj* GESCHÄFT, RECHT, V&M standardized; **~er Versicherungsschein** *m* VERSICH block policy

Typist, in *m,f* VERWALT typist

Typograph, in *m,f* COMP, V&M typographer

Typologie *f* V&M typology

typologisch: ~e Analyse *f* V&M typological analysis

U

u.A.w.g. *abbr* (*um Antwort wird gebeten*) KOMM RSVP (*répondez s'il vous plaît*)

U-Bahn *f* TRANSP subway (*AmE*), tube (*BrE*), underground (*BrE*)

übel: **üble Nachrede** *f* RECHT defamation, libel; **jdn wegen übler Nachrede verklagen** *phr* RECHT sue sb for libel

Übel *nt* VW bad

üben *vt* GESCHÄFT exercise

Über- *in cpds* GESCHÄFT, VERWALT, VW excess, over-

überaltert *adj* GESCHÄFT, VW obsolete, outdated; **~e Gesellschaft** *f* VW overaged population, overly aged population

Über-: **Überalterung** *f* V&M *eines Produkts durch den sich ändernden Geschmack oder technische Überholtheit* functional obsolescence; **Überaltung** *f* **der Bevölkerung** VW ageing of the population, superannuation of the population; **Überangebot** *nt* GESCHÄFT, VW glut, oversupply; **ein Überangebot an** *phr* GESCHÄFT a glut of; **Überansammlung** *f* VW overaccumulation

überanstrengen *vt* PERSON overwork

überarbeiten 1. *vt* GESCHÄFT revise, MEDIEN revise, rework; **2. sich ~** *v refl* PERSON overwork

überarbeitet *adj* GESCHÄFT, MEDIEN revised; **~e Ausgabe** *f* MEDIEN revised edition; **~e Fassung** *f* MEDIEN revised version

Über-: **Überarbeitung** *f* MEDIEN revision, PERSON overwork, VERWALT revision; **Überbau** *m* RECHT encroachment upon adjoining land, structure extending over a boundary; **Überbeanspruchung** *f* **der Sinne** MGMNT sensory overload; **Überbeschäftigung** *f* VW overemployment

überbesetzen *vt* PERSON *Abteilung, Station* overman, overstaff

überbesetzt *adj* PERSON overmanned, *Unternehmen, Organisation* overstaffed

Über-: **Überbesetzung** *f* PERSON overmanning, *einer Abteilung, eines Unternehmens* overstaffing

überbetrieblich: **~e Zusatzrente** *f* FINANZ supplementary intercompany pension scheme

überbewerten *vt* FINANZ overestimate, overrate, overstate, RECHNUNG overestimate, overvalue, VW overestimate, overvalue, overstate

überbewertet *adj* GESCHÄFT *Wertpapiere* top-heavy, RECHNUNG, VW overrated, overvalued; **~e Währung** *f* VW overvalued currency

Überbewertung *f* FINANZ overstatement, overestimate, overestimation, RECHNUNG overvaluation, overestimate, overestimation, VW *einer Währung* overrating, overstatement, overvaluation, overestimate, overestimation

überbezahlen *vt* GESCHÄFT, PERSON overpay

überbezahlt *adj* GESCHÄFT, PERSON *Arbeitsmarkt* overpaid

Überbezahlung *f* PERSON overpayment

überbieten *vt* V&M *Auktion* outbid, overbid

Überblick *m* GESCHÄFT survey, overview, review; ♦ **einen ~ geben über** GESCHÄFT, MGMNT review

Überbord- *in cpds* TRANSP *Schiffahrt* overside, overboard; **Überbord-Entladung** *f* TRANSP overside discharge; **Überbord-Ladung** *f* TRANSP overside loading

Überbringer, in *m,f* BANK bearer; **Überbringerklausel** *f* BÖRSE bearer clause; **Überbringerscheck** *m* BANK bearer check (*AmE*), bearer cheque (*BrE*); **Überbringerscheckformular** *nt* BANK counter check form (*AmE*), counter cheque form (*BrE*)

überbrücken *vt* GESCHÄFT bridge, tide over

Überbrückung *f* FINANZ bridging; **Überbrückungsfazilität** *f* BANK bridging facility; **Überbrückungsfinanzierung** *f* FINANZ bridge finance; **Überbrückungskredit** *m* BANK adjustment credit, bridge loan (*AmE*), bridging advance, bridging loan (*BrE*), interim loan, bridge-over loan, FINANZ accommodation, accommodation loan, IMP/EXP accommodatory credit, RECHNUNG accommodating credit, VW adjustment credit; **einen Überbrückungskredit aufnehmen** *phr* FINANZ take an accommodation credit; **Überbrückungsmittel** *nt pl* **bereitstellen** FINANZ bridging pension scheme; **Überbrückungspension** *f* FINANZ bridging pension scheme

überbuchen 1. *vt* FREI, TRANSP, VERWALT *Flüge, Hotels* overbook; **2.** *vi* FREI, TRANSP, VERWALT *Flüge, Hotels* overbook

Überbuchen *nt* FREI, TRANSP, VERWALT *Flüge, Hotels* overbooking

überbucht *adj* FREI, TRANSP, VERWALT *Flüge, Hotels* overbooked

Überbuchung *f* FREI, TRANSP, VERWALT *Flüge, Hotels* overbooking

überdenken *vt* GESCHÄFT rethink

Überdruck *m* V&M overprint

überdrucken *vt* V&M overprint

überdurchschnittlich *adj* GESCHÄFT better than average; **~es Wachstum** *nt* VW above-average growth

übereignen *vt* GRUND convey, RECHT assign, transfer; ♦ **etw ~** RECHT transfer ownership of sth

Übereignung *f* RECHT assignment, transfer (*tr.*, *tfr*); **Übereignungsvertrag** *m* RECHT bill of sale

übereinkommen *vi* GESCHÄFT *Zustimmung, Vereinbarung* agree; ♦ **mit jdm ~** GESCHÄFT agree with sb, come to an agreement with sb, come to an arrangement with sb, come to an understanding with sb

Über-: **Übereinkommen** *nt* GESCHÄFT agreement, arrangement, understanding; **Übereinkunft** *f* GESCHÄFT agreement, accord, *Übereinkunft mit Gläubigern* arrangement; **zu einer Übereinkunft kommen** *phr* GESCHÄFT come to an arrangement

übereinstimmen 1. *vi* GESCHÄFT agree, conform, RECHT coincide, *Meinung* concur; **nicht ~** GESCHÄFT disagree, lack consistency; **2. ~ mit** GESCHÄFT, RECHT be in agreement with, coincide with

übereinstimmend *adj* GESCHÄFT, RECHT concurrent, congruent; ♦ **~ mit** GESCHÄFT congruent with, in accordance with, in agreement with, RECHT consistent with

Übereinstimmung *f* GESCHÄFT agreement, conformity, congruence, consensus, consistency, PATENT unity, RECHT accord, compliance, meeting of the minds; **~ mit den Buchhaltungsvorschriften** RECHNUNG conformity to accounting rules; **~ des europäischen Patents** PATENT unity of European patent; ♦ **in ~ mit** RECHT *gemäß gesetzlicher Vorschriften* in accordance with, in agreement with, in compliance with; **in ~ bringen** GESCHÄFT agree, coordinate

Übereinstimmung: **Übereinstimmungsprüfung** *f* GESCHÄFT consistency check

Überfahrt *f* TRANSP passage

überfällig *adj* GESCHÄFT, RECHNUNG overdue; **~er Betrag** *m* RECHNUNG amount overdue; **~er Flug** *m* TRANSP missing flight; **~e Forderung** *f* FINANZ delinquent account, overdue account, RECHNUNG overdue claim

überfinanzieren *vt* FINANZ overfund

Überfinanzierung *f* FINANZ overfunding

überflügeln *vt* VW *Konkurrenz* outcompete

Überfluß *m* GESCHÄFT, VW abundance, affluence; ♦ **im ~ vorhanden sein** GESCHÄFT be in abundance

Überfluß: **Überflußgesellschaft** *f* GESCHÄFT, VW affluent society

überflüssig *adj* GESCHÄFT redundant, expendable

Überfluß: **Überflußwirtschaft** *f* VW economy of abundance

Überfüllungshypothese *f* VW crowding hypothesis

Übergabe *f* GESCHÄFT delivery, handing-over, handover; **Übergabetermin** *m* GRUND completion date; **Übergabevereinbarung** *f* IND equipment handover agreement

Übergang *m* GESCHÄFT passing, transformation, transition; **Übergangsautomatenschein** *m* TRANSP transitional automated ticket (*TAT*); **Übergangsbestimmungen** *f pl* STEUER transitional provisions; **Übergangskonto** *nt* BANK, RECHNUNG suspense account; **Übergangsperiode** *f* GESCHÄFT transition period; **Übergangsrente** *f* FINANZ interim pension; **Übergangsstadium** *nt* VW stage of transition, transitional stage

übergangsweise *adj* GESCHÄFT transitional

Übergang: **Übergangswirtschaft** *f* VW transitional economy; **Übergangszeit** *f* GESCHÄFT, VW period of transition, transition period, transitional period

übergeben 1. *adj* GESCHÄFT delivered, surrendered, handed over; **2.** *vt* BANK transfer, GESCHÄFT deliver, hand over, vest, PERSON transfer

übergeben: **~e Arbeit** *f* PERSON *in Werkvertrag* contract work

Übergeber, in *m,f* BANK bailor, transferor, transferrer

übergehen *vt* COMP skip; ♦ **~ auf** [+acc] RECHT pass into the ownership of, pass to

übergeordnet *adj* GESCHÄFT, RECHT senior (*Snr*); **~e Kommission** *f* FREI overriding commission

Übergepäck *nt* FREI, GESCHÄFT, TRANSP excess baggage

Übergewicht *nt* TRANSP excess weight, over-pivot weight, overweight; **Übergewichtsbereich** *m* TRANSP over-pivot area

Übergewinnsteuer *f* STEUER excess profits tax

übergreifen *vt* RECHT encroach; ♦ **auf jds Rechte ~** RECHT encroach upon sb's rights

übergreifend: **~er Vertrag** *m* RECHT *Vertragsrecht* overlapping contract

Übergreifung *f* GESCHÄFT encroachment

Überhang *m* BÖRSE overhang, FINANZ surplus, GESCHÄFT excess, surplus, GRUND hangout, RECHNUNG, VW surplus; **Überhangmandat** *nt* POL excess mandate

überhitzt: **~e Volkswirtschaft** *f* VW overheated economy

überhitzen: **sich ~** *v refl* VW overheat

Überhitzung *f* VW overheating

überhöhen *vt* GESCHÄFT *Risiko* inflate, V&M overcharge, VW overextend

überhöht *adj* GESCHÄFT *Preis* excessive, too high, VW overcharged, overextended; **~e Gebühren** *f pl* BANK excessive charge; **~e Kosten** *pl* FINANZ, GESCHÄFT, V&M excessive charge; **~e Zinsen** *m pl* BANK, FINANZ excessive interest

überholen *vt* GESCHÄFT outdate, outpace, recondition, TRANSP overhaul

Überholspur *f* TRANSP fast lane

überholt *adj* GESCHÄFT dated, outdated, out of date, outmoded, outpaced, reconditioned

Überholung *f* GESCHÄFT, TRANSP overhaul; **Überholungsgleis** *nt* TRANSP siding (*BrE*), sidetrack (*AmE*)

Überkapazität *f* GESCHÄFT overcapacity, IND, VW excess capacity; **Überkapazitätentheorem** *nt* VW excess capacity theorem

überkapitalisieren *vt* FINANZ, GESCHÄFT overcapitalize

überkapitalisiert *adj* BÖRSE highly geared, FINANZ top-heavy, GESCHÄFT overcapitalized, *Wirtschaft* top-heavy

Überkapitalisierung *f* FINANZ, GESCHÄFT overcapitalization

Überkompensation *f* PERSON *Psychologie* overcompensation

überkompensieren *vt* GESCHÄFT, PERSON overcapitalize

Überkreuzverflechtung *f* BÖRSE interlocking shareholding: **~ des Vorstands** MGMNT interlocking directorate

überladen *vt* TRANSP overload, overweight

Überladen *nt* TRANSP overloading

Überlagerung *f* COMP overlay

Überlandtransport *m* TRANSP overland transport

überlappen *vi* COMP overlap

Überlappung *f* COMP overlap

überlassen *vt* RECHT abandon, give up, leave, relinquish

Überlassung *f* GESCHÄFT, RECHT abandonment, giving up, leaving, relinquishment; **~ von Tagesgeld** BANK, FINANZ overnight loan; **Überlassungsvertrag** *m* GRUND quitclaim deed

überlasten *vt* KOMM congest, PERSON overburden, overstrain

überlastet: **~es Ballungsgebiet** *nt* VW congested urban area

Überlastung *f* KOMM congestion, PERSON overburdening, overstrain, overstress

Überlauf *m* COMP overflow, IND *Produktion* overrun; **Überlaufeffekt** *m* GESCHÄFT spillover effect

überlaufen 1. *vt* IND overrun; **2.** *vi* COMP overflow

überleben 1. *vt* GESCHÄFT survive; **2.** *vi* GESCHÄFT survive

Überleben- *in cpds* RECHT, VERSICH survivorship, survival; **Überlebensfall** *m* RECHT *Grundbesitz* survivorship; **Überlebensprozeß** *m* VW survival process; **Überlebensrente** *f* GRUND survivorship annuity,

VERSICH joint and survivor annuity (*AmE*), annuity in reversion, reversionary annuity; **Überlebensstrategie** *f* GESCHÄFT, VW survival strategy; **Überlebensversicherung** *f* VERSICH survivorship insurance; **Überlebensversicherungsklausel** *f* VERSICH common disaster clause (*AmE*), survivor policy, survivorship clause (*AmE*)

überlegen 1. *adj* GESCHÄFT superior; ◆ **jdm ~ sein** GESCHÄFT have the edge over sb; **2.** *vt* GESCHÄFT consider, think about

Überlegung *f* GESCHÄFT consideration

überlesen *vt* COMP skip

Überliegezeit *f* TRANSP demurrage

übermäßig 1. *adj* GESCHÄFT excessive, exorbitant; **2.** *adv* GESCHÄFT excessively, unduly; ◆ **~ steigern** VW *Geldumlauf* inflate

übermäßig: **~e Abhängigkeit** *f* GESCHÄFT overdependence; **~e Steuerbelastung** *f* STEUER excess burden of a tax

übermitteln *vt* COMP *Dateien an einen fernen Rechner* upload, KOMM transmit, *elektronisch* send

Übermittler *m* KOMM *einer Meldung* transmitter, RECHT conveyor, notifier

Übermittlung *f* KOMM transmission, RECHT conveyance, *Vertragsrecht* notification; **~ von Signalen** KOMM signaling (*AmE*), signalling (*BrE*)

Übernachtung *f* FREI overnight stay; **~ mit Frühstück** FREI bed and breakfast (*b&b*)

Übernahme *f* BANK, BÖRSE acquisition, takeover, FINANZ absorption, buyout, GESCHÄFT acquisition, takeover, *eines Unternehmens* absorption, MGMNT *einer Methode* adoption, RECHNUNG, STEUER acquisition, TRANSP absorption, VW takeover, acquisition; **~ einer Anleihe** BÖRSE bond underwriting; **~ von Arbeiten als Zulieferant** PERSON subcontracting; **~ des Delkredererisikos** VERSICH credit protection insurance (*BrE*); **vor der ~ erzielte Gewinne** RECHNUNG pre-acquisition profits; **~ der Frachtkosten** TRANSP *durch den Verkäufer* freight costs absorption; **~ durch Fremdfinanzierung** GESCHÄFT leveraged buyout; **~ mit hoher Fremdfinanzierung** GESCHÄFT high-leveraged takeover (*AmE*) (*HLT*); **~ einer Hypothek** BANK mortgage assumption; **~ eines Unternehmens** BÖRSE shell operation, RECHNUNG acquisition of assets; **~ nach Vorverhandlung** FINANZ bear hug takeover; **Übernahmeabwehr-Klausel** *f* FINANZ porcupine provisions; **Übernahmeangebot** *nt* BÖRSE, FINANZ, RECHNUNG bid, takeover bid (*TOB*), tender offer; **Übernahmebeleg** *m* VERSICH line slip; **Übernahmebescheinigung** *f* **des Spediteurs** IMP/EXP, TRANSP forwarder's certificate of receipt; **Übernahmekonnossement** *nt* TRANSP receipt for shipment bill of lading; **Übernahmekonsortialvereinbarung** *f* FINANZ purchase group agreement; **Übernahmekonsortium** *nt* FINANZ underwriting syndicate; **Übernahmekursfestsetzung** *f* FINANZ, V&M, VW transfer pricing; **Übernahmepolitik** *f* BÖRSE acquisition policy; **Übernahmepreis** *m* VW target price; **Übernahmepreissetzung** *f* RECHNUNG transfer pricing; **Übernahmeprofil** *nt* BANK acquisition profile; **Übernahmeprovision** *f* BANK underwriting fee, FINANZ underwriting commission; **Übernahmesatz** *m* GESCHÄFT take-up rate; **Übernahmespesen** *f pl* FINANZ underwriting fee; **Übernahmestempel** *m* VER-

SICH line stamp (*BrE*); **Übernahmeverlust** *m* VW loss on takeover; **Übernahmeversuch** *m* BÖRSE bid; **Übernahmevertrag** *m* BÖRSE underwriting agreement

übernational *adj* GESCHÄFT, POL, VW supranational

übernehmen *vt* FINANZ carry, GESCHÄFT take over, accept, absorb, *Verantwortung* take on, *Verpflichtung* assume, *Arbeit* take in (*infrml*), *Aufgabe, Verantwortung* undertake, *Ideen, Methode* borrow, *Kosten* absorb, *Verpflichtungen* shoulder, KOMM *Anruf* accept, VW absorb

übernehmend: **~e Firma** *f infrml* VW absorbing company; **~e Gesellschaft** *f* FINANZ transferee company, GESCHÄFT purchasing company, acquiring company, transferee company, VW absorbing company

übernommen: **~e Arbeit** *f* PERSON contract work; **~e Gesellschaft** *f* FINANZ, GESCHÄFT, RECHNUNG, VW acquired company, acquisition, purchased company

Über-: **Überplazierung** *f* BANK overplacing; **Überproduktion** *f* IND, VW overproduction

überprüfen *vt* GESCHÄFT check, review, screen, MGMNT review, overhaul, PATENT examine, POL vet

überprüft: **nicht ~** *adj* GESCHÄFT unscreened, *Angaben, Zahlen* unchecked; **~es Gepäck** *nt* FREI, TRANSP baggage checked

Überprüfung *f* GESCHÄFT screening, search, MGMNT review, PATENT examination; **~ der Fernsehkonsumenten** V&M television consumer audit; **~ einer Hypothese** MATH hypothesis testing

überquellen *vi* GESCHÄFT spill over

überragend *adj* GESCHÄFT pre-eminent, paramount, *Wichtigkeit* overriding, POL *Wichtigkeit* overriding, paramount

überreden *vt* GESCHÄFT persuade, win over

Überredung *f* GESCHÄFT persuasion; **Überredungskunst** *f* GESCHÄFT power of persuasion

überregional: **~e Herstellermarke** *f* V&M national brand; **~e Kampagne** *f* V&M national campaign; **~e Presse** *f* MEDIEN national press; **~e Tageszeitung** *f* MEDIEN national newspaper

überreichlich *adj* GESCHÄFT ample, super abundant

Überrepräsentation *f* V&M overrepresentation

überrepräsentieren *vt* V&M overrepresent

Überreste *m pl* GESCHÄFT remnants

uberrimae fidei *phr* GESCHÄFT *Vertrag* uberrimae fidei

Überrollungsentlastung *f* STEUER rollover relief

überschätzen *vt* FINANZ, RECHNUNG, VW overestimate, overrate, overvalue

überschätzt *adj* FINANZ, RECHNUNG, VW overestimated, overrated, overvalued

Überschätzung *f* FINANZ, RECHNUNG, VW overestimation, overvaluation, overrating

überschießend: **~er Preis** *m* VW overshooting price

überschneiden: **sich ~** *v refl* GESCHÄFT, PERSON *Daten, Urlaub*, V&M overlap

Überschneidung *f* GESCHÄFT, PERSON *Daten, Urlaub*, V&M overlap

überschneidungsfrei: **~e Adressenliste herstellen** *phr* V&M merge and purge

Überschneidung: **Überschneidungsklausel** *f* VERSICH other insurance clause

überschreiben *vt* PATENT, RECHT transfer

Überschreiben *nt* COMP *Drucker* strikeover

Überschreibung *f* PATENT transfer (*tr.*, *tfr*)

überschreiten *vt* IMP/EXP *Grenze* cross, RECHNUNG overspend, VW overrun

Überschreitung *f* VW overrun; **~ der Haushaltsansätze** RECHNUNG overspend; ♦ **in ~ der satzungsgemäßen Befugnisse** RECHT ultra vires

Überschrift *f* KOMM caption, MEDIEN *Zeitschriftenartikel* title, leading line, RECHNUNG heading, VERWALT header; **~ über volle Seitenbreite** MEDIEN banner headline, streamer

überschuldet *adj* BANK, RECHNUNG, VW heavily in debt, heavily mortgaged

Überschuldung *f* BANK, RECHNUNG, VW excessive debts, heavy mortgaging

Überschuß *m* FINANZ surplus, GESCHÄFT, RECHNUNG, VW surplus, overage; **~ an Arbeitskräften** PERSON surplus labor (*AmE*), surplus labour (*BrE*); **~ des Vermögens über die Schulden** RECHNUNG surplus of assets over liabilities; ♦ **im ~** VW in surplus; **einen ~ aufweisen** RECHNUNG *Gewinn* show a surplus

Überschuß: **Überschußaktien** *f pl* BÖRSE excessive shares; **Überschußbeteiligung** *f* VERSICH capital bonus

überschüssig *adj* GESCHÄFT excess, surplus; **~e landwirtschaftliche Nutzfläche** *f* UMWELT redundant farmland

Überschuß: **Überschußkapazität** *f* IND surplus capacity, VW excess capacity; **Überschußreserve** *f* BANK, FINANZ excess cash; **Überschußreserven** *f pl* BANK excess reserves, VW idle money; **Überschußrückstellung** *f* VERSICH bonus reserve; **Überschußtheorie** *f* VW vent for surplus

überschwappen *vi* GESCHÄFT spill over

Übersee- *in cpds* GESCHÄFT overseas; **Überseefiliale** *f* IMP/EXP overseas branch; **Überseehilfe** *f* VW overseas aid

überseeisch: **~e Einrichtung** *f* GESCHÄFT overseas body; **~e Firma** *f* GESCHÄFT overseas company; **~e Gebiete** *nt pl* POL *der Europäischen Union* overseas countries and territories (*OCTs*); **~es Sterlinggebiet** *nt* VW overseas sterling area (*OSA*)

Übersee-: **Überseekoffer** *m* TRANSP trunk (*TRK*); **Überseekunde** *m* V&M overseas customer; **Überseemakler** *m* PERSON *Arbeit* deep-sea broker; **Überseemarkt** *m* VW overseas market; **Überseetarifbestimmung** *f* IMP/EXP overseas tariff regulation; **Überseetarife** *m pl* **und -bestimmungen** *f pl* IMP/EXP overseas tariff and regulations (*OTAR*)

übersenden *vt* KOMM send, ship, TRANSP consign, convey, forward (*fwd*), ship

Übersendung *f* KOMM, IMP/EXP shipment, TRANSP consignation, conveyance, forwarding, shipment

übersetzen *vt* KOMM translate

Übersetzen *nt* KOMM translating

Übersetzer, in *m,f* KOMM, GESCHÄFT translator

Übersetzung *f* KOMM translation; **~ von Arbeitsplätzen** PERSON featherbedding; **Übersetzungsprogramm** *nt* COMP compiler, *Softwarepaket* translator

Übersicht *f* GESCHÄFT survey, chart, outline, summary, synopsis, MEDIEN synopsis, PATENT abstract, V&M synopsis

Überspekulation *f* BÖRSE overtrading

überspekulieren *vi* BÖRSE overtrade

überspringen *vt* COMP skip, GESCHÄFT *Preise*, PERSON leapfrog

Überspringen *nt* COMP skip, GESCHÄFT *Preise*, PERSON *Stufen auf der Karriereleiter* leapfrogging

überstaatlich *adj* GESCHÄFT, POL, VW supranational

überstehen *vt* GESCHÄFT survive, VW *Rezession* weather

übersteigen *vt* GESCHÄFT, VW exceed

Übersterblichkeit *f* VERSICH excess mortality

überstimmen *vt* GESCHÄFT, POL outvote, *Leute* overrule

überstimmt: **~ sein** *phr* GESCHÄFT, POL be outvoted

Überstunden *f pl* PERSON *Arbeitszeit* overtime (*OT*), overtime hours; ♦ **~ machen** PERSON *Arbeitszeit* work overtime

Überstunden: **Überstundenausgleich** *m* PERSON *Arbeit* compensatory time; **Überstundenstopp** *m* PERSON *Rezession, Auftragsmangel* overtime ban; **Überstundenvergütung** *f* PERSON *Arbeitszeit* overtime pay; **Überstundenzuschlag** *m* PERSON overtime premium

überteuert *adj* GESCHÄFT, V&M overpriced

Über-: **Überteuerung** *f* GESCHÄFT, V&M excessive charge, overcharge (*o/c*)

Übertrag *m* FINANZ *Saldo* balance brought down (*b/d*), balance brought forward (*b/f*), balance carried forward (*b/f*), carry-over, GESCHÄFT carried forward, RECHNUNG *Saldo* balance brought down (*b/d*), balance brought forward (*b/f*), balance carried forward (*b/f*), carry-over

übertragbar *adj* BÖRSE transferable, GESCHÄFT negotiable, RECHT *Vertragsrecht* assignable VERSICH negotiable; **nicht ~** *adj* BÖRSE untransferable, GESCHÄFT unnegotiable, RECHT unassignable, VERSICH not negotiable; **~er Abhebungsauftrag** *m* BANK, FINANZ negotiable order of withdrawal (*AmE*) (*NOW*); **~er Abrechnungsbereich** *m* RECHNUNG transferable account area (*TAA*); **nicht ~er Befrachtungsvertrag** *m* TRANSP nondemise charter party; **nicht ~es Konnossement** *nt* IMP/EXP, TRANSP non-negotiable bill of lading, straight bill of lading; **~er Kredit** *m* RECHNUNG assignable credit; **~e Kreditinstrumente** *nt pl* FINANZ transferable loan instruments (*TLI*); **~e Kreditzertifikate** *nt pl* FINANZ transferable loan certificates (*TLC*); **nicht ~er Ladeschein** *m* IMP/EXP, TRANSP direct bill of lading; **nicht ~e Schuldtitel** *m pl* BANK nontransferable debentures; **~es Wertpapier** *nt* BANK negotiable instrument, FINANZ transferable security; **nicht ~es Wertpapier** *nt* BANK non-negotiable instrument, FINANZ nontransferable security; **~e Wertpapiere** *nt pl* BÖRSE transferable securities; **nicht ~es Wissen** *nt* POL, RECHT, VW tacit knowledge; **~e Zahlungsanweisung** *f* BANK, FINANZ negotiable order of withdrawal (*AmE*) (*NOW*)

Übertragbarkeit *f* BÖRSE assignability, transferability

Übertrag: **Übertragbestände** *m pl* GESCHÄFT carry-over stocks; **Übertrageffekt** *m* MEDIEN carry-over effect

übertragen *vt* BANK bring forward, BÖRSE transfer, COMP transmit, FINANZ assign, *balance* bring forward, carry down, carry forward, GESCHÄFT broadcast, transcribe, extend, GRUND transfer, KOMM transmit, MEDIEN *Veranstaltung* broadcast, MGMNT *Verantwortung, Macht* delegate, RECHNUNG assign, bring forward, RECHT *Rechte* confer, *Unterschreiben eines Dokumentes, durch das ein Besitz auf jdm anderen übergeht* assign, *Eigentum* convey, VW *Mittel* transfer; ♦ **zu ~** RECHNUNG to be carried forward; **etw auf jdn ~** GESCHÄFT, RECHT vest sth in sb

übertragend *adj* GESCHÄFT, KOMM transmitting; **~e Gesellschaft** *f* GESCHÄFT transferrer company

Übertragende(r) *mf* [decl. as adj] RECHT transferrer, grantor

Übertragung *f* BÖRSE transfer (*tr.*, *tfr*), COMP transmission, FINANZ assignment, GESCHÄFT broadcasting, transcription, *Verbindlichkeiten, Verantwortung* transfer (*tr.*, *tfr*), GRUND transfer (*tr.*, *tfr*), KOMM transmission, MGMNT *Befugnisse, Verantwortung* delegation, PATENT transfer (*tr.*, *tfr*), RECHNUNG assignment, RECHT assignment, confernment, conferral, grant, VW transfer (*tr.*, *tfr*); **~ von Erschließungsrechten** *f* GRUND transfer of development rights; **~ von Vermögen** *f* RECHNUNG transfer of assets; **Übertragungsadresse** *f* COMP transfer address; **Übertragungsbilanz** *f* RECHNUNG acquisition accounting; **Übertragungsempfänger, in** *m,f* BANK transferee; **Übertragungsformular** *nt* RECHT *Vertragsrecht* transfer form; **Übertragungsgebühren** *f pl* RECHT transfer fees; **Übertragungskosten** *pl* RECHNUNG transmission expenses; **Übertragungsurkunde** *f* RECHT *Vertragsrecht* bill of sale, deed; **Übertragungswirtschaft** *f* VW grants economics

übertreffen *vt* GESCHÄFT surpass, exceed, top, VW *Wirtschaftswachstum, Handelsvolumen, Wirtschaftsleistung* outperform

übertreiben *vt* GESCHÄFT exaggerate, overshoot

übertrieben 1. *adj* GESCHÄFT exaggerated; **2.** *adv* ♦ **~ Hilfe geben** GESCHÄFT spoon-feed

übertrieben: **~e Verkaufspolitik** *f* V&M overselling; **~e Werbung** *f* GESCHÄFT, V&M hype, puff

überurbanisieren *vt* VW overurbanize

überurbanisiert *adj* VW overurbanized

Überurbanisierung *f* VW overurbanization

überversichern *vt* VERSICH overinsure

überversichert *adj* VERSICH overinsured

Überversicherung *f* VERSICH overinsurance

Überversorgung *f* VW overprovision

übervorteilen *vt* GESCHÄFT get the better of

überwachen *vt* COMP, FINANZ monitor, GESCHÄFT monitor, supervise, survey, MGMNT, PERSON monitor, supervise, TRANSP, V&M control, monitor

überwachend *adj* COMP, FINANZ, GESCHÄFT, MGMNT, PERSON supervisory

Überwachung *f* COMP, FINANZ monitoring, GESCHÄFT, MGMNT, PERSON supervision, follow-up, RECHT *elektronische Überwachung* surveillance, VERWALT, V&M control; **Überwachungsausschuß** *m* POL watchdog committee; **Überwachungslizenz** *f* IMP/EXP surveillance licence (*BrE*) (*SL*), surveillance license (*AmE*) (*SL*); **Überwachungsorganisation** *f* GESCHÄFT *Verbraucherverbände* watchdog; **Überwachungsstelle** *f* GESCHÄFT board control; **Überwachungssystem** *nt* GESCHÄFT tracking system

überwälzen *vt* STEUER shift, VW *Kosten* pass along, pass on

Überwälzung *f* STEUER shifting, VW pass-along

überwechseln: **~ zu** *vi* GESCHÄFT switch to

überweisen *vt* BANK, FINANZ, VW *Geld* remit, transfer

Überweisung *f* BANK money transmission, payment transfer, transfer (*tr.*, *tfr*), FINANZ, VW remittance, transfer (*tr.*, *tfr*); **~ zum Inkasso** BANK remittance for

collection; **~ per Luftpost** BANK, VW air mail transfer (*AMT*); ♦ **per ~ zahlen** BANK pay by giro

Überweisung: **Überweisungen** *f pl* **der einbehaltenen Beträge** STEUER PAYE remittances (*BrE*); **Überweisungen** *f pl* **von Geldern** FINANZ funds transfers; **Überweisungsanzeige** *f* FINANZ remittance, remittance advice; **Überweisungsauftrag** *m* BANK, FINANZ bank giro credit (*BrE*), banker's order, transfer order, GESCHÄFT remittance order; **Überweisungsbeleg** *m* BANK transfer of funds voucher; **Überweisungsträger** *m* GESCHÄFT remittance slip

überwiegen *vi* GESCHÄFT outweigh

überwinden *vt* GESCHÄFT overcome

überzahlt: **~er Betrag** *m* GESCHÄFT amount overpaid; **~e Einfuhrbescheinigung** *f* IMP/EXP overpaid entry certificate (*OEC*); **~e Summe** *f* GESCHÄFT amount overpaid

überzeugen *vt* GESCHÄFT convince, persuade

überzeugend *adj* GESCHÄFT *Vertreter* convincing, persuasive, powerful, VW compelling; **nicht ~** *adj* GESCHÄFT unconvincing, unimpressive; **~er Beweis** *m* PATENT conclusive evidence

überzeugt: **~ sein von** *phr* GESCHÄFT be convinced of, be positive about

Überzeugung *f* GESCHÄFT conviction, persuasion

überziehen *vt* BANK *Konto* overdraw, VW overextend; ♦ **Konto ~** BANK run up an overdraft

Überziehung *f* BANK overdraft (*O/D*); **Überziehungskredit** *m* BANK bank overdraft, overdraft facility; **Überziehungskreditsatz** *m* BANK overdraft rate; **Überziehungsmöglichkeit** *f* BANK overdraft facility

überzogen *adj* BANK overdrawn (*O/D*), VW overextended; **~e Werbung** *f* GESCHÄFT, V&M puff

ubi remedium ibi ius *phr* GESCHÄFT ubi remedium ibi jus

üblich *adj* GESCHÄFT widespread, customary, normal, usual, standard; ♦ **unter dem ~en Vorbehalt** RECHT with the usual proviso; **zu den ~en Fristen** GESCHÄFT on usual terms

üblich: **~er Abgang** *m* **an Arbeitskräften** IND natural wastage; **~e Abnutzung** *f* GESCHÄFT fair wear and tear; **~e Investitionspraxis** *f* FINANZ normal investment practice; **~e Miete** *f* GRUND fair market rent, fair rent; **~er Mietwert** *m* GRUND fair rental value; **~e Pacht** *f* GRUND fair market rent; **~er Pachtwert** *m* GRUND fair rental value; **~e Praxis** *f* GESCHÄFT standard practice; **~e Rechnungslegungsverfahren** *nt pl* VW regular accounting practices; **~e Tara** *f* STEUER customary tare; **~er Wettbewerbspreis** *f* FINANZ ordinary competitive price

übrig: **die ~e Welt** *f* VW rest of the world (*ROW*)

Übung: **aus der ~** *phr* GESCHÄFT rusty

U-Form *f* VW U-form

Uhr *f* GESCHÄFT clock, IND clock; **Uhrmachergewerbe** *nt* IND watch trade

U-Hypothese *f* VW U-hypothesis

UKW *abbr* (*Ultrakurzwelle*) GESCHÄFT, KOMM, MEDIEN VHF (*very high frequency*); **UKW-Sprechfunk** *m* KOMM, TRANSP VHF radiotelephony

Ultimatum: **jdm ein ~ stellen** *phr* GESCHÄFT give sb an ultimatum

Ultimoabschluß *m* BANK, RECHNUNG end-of-month account

Ultimoausgleich *m* FINANZ, RECHNUNG end-of-year

adjustment, year-end adjustment; **~ für antizipatori-sche Passiva** FINANZ year-end adjustments for accrued expenses

Ultrakurzwelle *f* (*UKW*) GESCHÄFT, KOMM, MEDIEN very high frequency (*VHF*); **Ultrakurzwellensprechfunk** *m* TRANSP very high frequency radiotelephony

umändern *vt* GESCHÄFT alter

Umänderung *f* GESCHÄFT alteration

Umbau *m* GRUND conversion, VW reconstruction

umbauen *vt* GRUND convert, VW reconstruct

umbenennen *vt* COMP rename

umbesetzen *vt* GESCHÄFT, PERSON, VERWALT reassign, reorganize, shake up

Umbesetzung *f* GESCHÄFT, PERSON, VERWALT reassign-ment, reorganization, shake-up; **~ des Kabinetts** POL reshuffle

umbrechen *vt* GESCHÄFT break down, MEDIEN *Seiten* paginate

Umbruch *m* GESCHÄFT upheaval, MEDIEN making-up into pages

umbuchen *vt* BANK, RECHNUNG transfer

Umbuchung *f* BANK money transmission, payment transfer, transfer (*tr.*, *tfr*), RECHNUNG book transfer, transfer (*tr.*, *tfr*); **Umbuchungsauftrag** *f* TRANSP change request

umerziehen *vt* GESCHÄFT, PERSON re-educate

Umerziehung *f* GESCHÄFT, PERSON re-education

Umfang *m* COMP *Daten, Speicher* volume, GESCHÄFT bulk, gage (*AmE*), gauge (*BrE*), scale, volume PATENT scope, extent, VW size; **~ des Einzelhandelsgeschäfts** VW volume of retail sales (*BrE*); **~ der Entschädigung** VERSICH measure of indemnity; **~ der Mindestkursschwankung** BÖRSE tick size; **~ der Schadloshaltung** VERSICH measure of indemnity

umfangreich *adj* GESCHÄFT, VW large-scale; **~e Werbekampagne** *f* V&M heavy advertising

umfassen *vt* GESCHÄFT comprise, encompass

umfassend *adj* GESCHÄFT, PERSON comprehensive, RECHT *Lizenzen* blanket, VERSICH comprehensive; **~e Diskussion** *f* GESCHÄFT in-depth discussion; **~es Haushaltsabstimmungsgesetz** *nt* FINANZ, STEUER Omnibus Budget Reconciliation Act (*AmE*) (*OBRA*); **~ längerfristige Bankgarantie** *f* BANK comprehensive extended-term banker's guarantee (*CXBG*); **~e Marktinformationen** *f pl* V&M market intelligence; **~e Versicherung** *f* **gegen mehrere Gefahren** VERSICH comprehensive insurance

Umfeld *nt* GESCHÄFT environment; **Umfeldanalyse** *f* MGMNT, UMWELT environmental analysis; **Umfeldüberwachung** *f* IND environmental control; **Umfelduntersuchung** *f* UMWELT environment scan

Umfinanzierung *f* FINANZ financial adjustment

umformen *vt* IND, VERSICH transform

umformulieren *vt* POL, VERWALT redraft

Umformulierung *f* POL, VW redraft

Umformungsindustrien *f pl* IND transformation indus-tries

Umfrage *f* GESCHÄFT survey, V&M enquiry, poll; ◆ **eine ~ durchführen** GESCHÄFT, V&M carry out a survey; **eine ~ veranstalten** GESCHÄFT, V&M hold an opinion poll

Umfrage: **Umfragebetrieb** *m* COMP polling

umfragen *vt* V&M enquire

umgebaut *adj* GRUND converted

Umgebung *f* COMP *Software* environment, GESCHÄFT *der Stadt* environs, surrounding area, neighbourhood (*BrE*), neighborhood (*AmE*); **Umgebungstemperatur** *f* GESCHÄFT ambient temperature

umgehen *vt* STEUER avoid

umgehend *adv* GESCHÄFT, KOMM as soon as possible (*a.s.a.p.*)

Umgehungsstraße *f* TRANSP ring road

umgegeben *adj* GESCHÄFT surrounded

umgekehrt 1. *adj* GESCHÄFT reversed; **2.** *adv* MATH inversely

umgekehrt: **~e Hebelwirkung** *f* RECHNUNG reverse leverage (*AmE*); **~e J-förmige Häufigkeitskurve** *f* VW reverse J-shaped frequency curve; **~e Kausalitätshypothese** *f* VW reverse caution hypothesis; **~er Markt** *m* BÖRSE inverted market; **~er Schrägstrich** *m* COMP backslash; **~e Skala** *f* BÖRSE inverted scale

umgeladen *adj* TRANSP transshipped

umgeschlagen *adj* TRANSP transshipped

umgestalten *vt* GESCHÄFT transform, MGMNT reorganize

Umgestaltung *f* GESCHÄFT transformation, MGMNT reorganization

umgruppieren *vt* GESCHÄFT redeploy, regroup

Umgruppierung *f* GESCHÄFT redeployment, regrouping

Umhüllende *f* MATH envelope curve

Umhüllung *f* IND clothing, *Verpackung* wrapping; **Umhüllungsverfahren** *nt pl* **und -vorschriften** *f pl* GESCHÄFT envelope procedures and rules

umkämpfen *vt* POL *Wahlkreis* contest, V&M *Entscheidung* contest, dispute

umkämpft *adj* POL, V&M contested, disputed

Umkehranzeige *f* COMP *Bildschirm* reverse video

umkehren *vt* MATH invert, VW reverse

umkippen *vi* GESCHÄFT go negative (*jarg*)

Umkippen *nt* TRANSP tipping, UMWELT tipping, *Wasser* extinction

Umkleidekabine *f* GESCHÄFT fitting room

Umlade- *in cpds* IMP/EXP, TRANSP transshipment; **Umladeerklärung** *f* IMP/EXP *Reexport*, TRANSP trans-shipment entry; **Umladefracht** *f* IMP/EXP, TRANSP transshipment freight; **Umladekonnossement** *nt* IMP/EXP, TRANSP transshipment bill of lading; **Umladelieferschein** *m* IMP/EXP, TRANSP transshipment delivery order

umladen *vt* TRANSP reload, transship

Umlade-: **Umladeschein** *m* IMP/EXP transshipment bond; **Umladeurkunde** *f* TRANSP transshipment bond

Umladung *f* TRANSP reloading, transshipment

Umlage *f* FINANZ contribution, levy, RECHNUNG alloca-tion

Umlauf *m* VW circulation; **im ~ befindliche Aktien** *f pl* BÖRSE shares outstanding; ◆ **im ~** GESCHÄFT afloat; **im ~ sein** KOMM *Informationen, Nachrichten* circulate; **in ~ setzen** BANK, FINANZ issue; **aus dem ~ ziehen** GESCHÄFT, FINANZ, VW withdraw from circulation

umlaufend *adj*: **~er Text** *m* MEDIEN runaround

umlauffähig: **~es Wertpapier** *nt* BÖRSE, RECHT negotiable instrument

Umlauf: **Umlauffonds** *m* FINANZ revolving fund; **Umlaufgeschwindigkeit** *f* FINANZ velocity of circulation, VW cash transactions velocity; **Umlaufgeschwindigkeit** *f* **des Geldes** VW velocity of circulation of money; **Umlaufmedium** *nt* FINANZ circulating medium; **Umlaufpreis** *m* BÖRSE afloat price; **Umlaufrendite** *f* BANK current yield, vw running yield; **Umlaufvermögen** *nt* RECHNUNG current assets, floating assets; **Umlaufvermögen** *nt* **und Staatspapiere** *nt* *pl* FINANZ liquid assets and government securities (*LGS*); **Umlaufzeit** *f* GESCHÄFT, TRANSP time of circulation, turnaround time (*AmE*), turnround time (*BrE*)

umlegen *vt* BÖRSE *Aktien* apportion, GESCHÄFT prorate, assess, RECHNUNG apply to, *Geld* allocate to, vw *Mittel, Gelder* allocate

umleiten *vt* TRANSP divert, reconsign, reroute

Umleitung *f* TRANSP route diversion, rerouting

Umorganisation *f* FINANZ, GESCHÄFT reorganization, revamp, shake-up

umorganisieren *vt* FINANZ, GESCHÄFT shake up, reorganize, revamp

umorganisiert *adj* FINANZ, MGMNT reorganized

Umorientierung *f* GESCHÄFT refocusing

umpacken *vt* IMP/EXP repackage

Umpacken *nt* IMP/EXP, V&M repackaging

umprogrammieren *vt* COMP reprogram

umrechnen *vt* FINANZ convert, vw *Währung* translate

Umrechnung *f* FINANZ conversion, vw translation, translating; **~ von Fremdwährungen** vw foreign currency translation; **Umrechnungsdifferenz** *f* GESCHÄFT *Währungen* translation differential, RECHNUNG translation difference, vw translation differential; **Umrechnungsfaktor** *m* MATH conversion factor; **Umrechnungsfaktor** *m* **für Arbeitnehmerbeitrag** VERSICH conversion factor for employee contributions; **Umrechnungsgewinn** *m* FINANZ transferee gains, translation profit, vw translation profit; **Umrechnungskurs** *m* FINANZ, vw conversion price, conversion rate, exchange rate, rate of exchange; **Umrechnungsmethode** *f* **zum geltenden Satz** RECHNUNG closing rate method (*BrE*), current rate method (*AmE*); **Umrechnungsrisiko** *nt* BÖRSE transaction exposure, transaction risk; **Umrechnungssatz** *m* FINANZ conversion rate; **Umrechnungstabelle** *f* GESCHÄFT ready reckoner; **Umrechnungsverlust** *m* FINANZ, vw translation loss

umreißen *vt* GESCHÄFT outline

Umsatz *m* BÖRSE activity, dealings, turnover, volume of trade, GESCHÄFT volume, transaction, turnover, V&M sales, billing, vw volume of trade; **~ in Aktien** BÖRSE equity turnover; **~ im Termingeschäft** GESCHÄFT futures sales; ◆ **~ bringen** V&M pull in sales

Umsatz: **Umsatzanalyse** *f* **im Einzelhandel** V&M retail sales analysis; **Umsatzanalyst** *m* V&M sales analyst; **Umsatzaufwendungen** *f* *pl* RECHNUNG cost of goods sold, cost of sales; **Umsatzertrag** *m* RECHNUNG sales revenue; **Umsatzgeschwindigkeit** *f* BÖRSE rate of turnover, turnover rate; **Umsatzhäufigkeit** *f* GESCHÄFT turnover rate; **Umsatzkosten** *pl* vw cost of goods sold; **Umsatz-Leverage** *nt* RECHNUNG operating leverage (*AmE*)

umsatzlos *adj* BÖRSE flat, inactive; **~er Anstieg** *m* GESCHÄFT dead rise (*DR*); **~es Konto** *nt* BANK inactive account, dead account, dormant account, V&M dormant account

Umsatz: **Umsatzpacht** *f* GRUND *Einzelhandel* percentage lease; **Umsatzplanung** *f* V&M anticipated sales; **Umsatzprovisionsmethode** *f* V&M percentage-of-sales

method; **Umsatzquote** *f* GESCHÄFT turnover rate; **Umsatzrendite** *f* FINANZ return on sales, percentage return on sales, profit margin, profit-turnover ratio, RECHNUNG profit-turnover ratio; **Umsatzrentabilität** *f* FINANZ percentage return on sales, profit margin, profit-turnover ratio, return on sales, RECHNUNG profit-turnover ratio; **Umsatzschätzung** *f* V&M sales estimate

umsatzschwach: **~es Papier** *nt* BÖRSE cabinet security; **~e Wertpapierspezialität** *f* BÖRSE cabinet security

umsatzstark *adj* BÖRSE high-volume

Umsatzsteuer *f* (*USt*) BÖRSE transactions tax, STEUER turnover tax; ◆ **nicht mit ~ veranschlagt** STEUER zero-rated, zero-rate

Umsatz: **Umsatzträger, in** *m,f* vw performer; **Umsatzüberschuß** *m* RECHNUNG funds from operations; **Umsatzvolumen** *nt* RECHNUNG volume (*vol.*); **Umsatzziel** *nt* V&M sales objective

umschalten *vt* COMP *zwischen zwei Zuständen* toggle

Umschalten *nt* COMP *Tastatur* shift

Umschalttaste *f* COMP shift key

umschichten *vt* FINANZ shift, switch, GESCHÄFT regroup, RECHNUNG reallocate

Umschichtung *f* FINANZ shifting, switching, GESCHÄFT regrouping, RECHNUNG reallocation; **~ von Verbindlichkeiten** BÖRSE liability management

Umschlag *m* KOMM envelope, TRANSP transshipment, turnaround (*AmE*), turnround (*BrE*), handling (*hdlg*); **~ mit Sichtfenster** V&M window envelope

umschlagen *vt* TRANSP handle, transship, turn over

Umschlag: **Umschlaghäufigkeit** *f* **des Eigenkapitals** VERWALT equity turnover, **Umschlagkai** *m* TRANSP commercial dock (*CD*); **Umschlagplatz** *m* GESCHÄFT place of transshipment, rail and water terminal, terminal; **Umschlagseite** *f* V&M cover page, inside front; **Umschlagserleichterung** *f* TRANSP ease of handling; **Umschlagsgeschwindigkeit** *f* FINANZ velocity of circulation; **Umschlagshäufigkeit** *f* **des Lagerbestands** FINANZ rate of inventory turnover; **Umschlagzeit** *f* GESCHÄFT, IND turnaround time (*AmE*), turnround time (*BrE*), vw replacement period, turnaround time (*AmE*), turnround time (*BrE*)

umschlossen: **~er Hafen** *m* TRANSP enclosed port; **~er Hofraum** *m* GRUND, RECHT curtilage

umschreibbar: **~es Wertpapier** *nt* FINANZ transferable security

umschreiben *vt* BÖRSE *Namenspapiere* transfer, COMP transcribe, *Software* rewrite, GESCHÄFT adapt, alter, GRUND convey, MEDIEN *Druck* rewrite

Umschreiber *m* KOMM *Datenverarbeitung* transcriber

Umschreibung *f* BÖRSE *Wertpapiere* transfer, GESCHÄFT altering, adaptation, transcription, GRUND conveyance; **~ eines Flugscheins** TRANSP rerouting; **~ eines Frachtbriefs** TRANSP rerouting; **Umschreibungsbeamte(r)** *m* [decl. as adj], **Umschreibungsbeamtin** *f* FINANZ *für Aktien* registrar of transfers

umschulden *vt* FINANZ fund, refinance, reschedule, restructure, roll over

Umschuldung *f* FINANZ debt refinancing, debt refunding, debt rescheduling, debt restructuring, debt swap, financial restructuring

umschulen *vt* GESCHÄFT re-educate, PERSON retrain

Umschulung *f* PERSON occupational retraining, retraining, vocational retraining; **Umschulungslehrgang** *m* PERSON retraining course

umschwenken *vi* GESCHÄFT veer

Umschwung *m* FINANZ, GESCHÄFT turnabout, turnaround (*AmE*), turnround (*BrE*), POL *Meinung* reversal, swing

umsehen: sich ~ *v refl* V&M shop around; ♦ **sich nach dem besten Preis ~** V&M shop around for the best price

Umsetz *m* BÖRSE amount of business

umsetzen *vt* COMP convert, GESCHÄFT execute, sell, turn over, transact, PERSON shift, transfer, V&M turn over

Umsetzung *f* COMP conversion, GESCHÄFT execution, PERSON transfer (*tr., tfr*), transferral; **~ einer bestimmten Politik** POL policy execution

umsichtig *adj* GESCHÄFT cautious, prudent

umsiedeln *vt* GESCHÄFT *Standort, Betrieb*, IND, VW relocate, resettle

Umsiedlung *f* GESCHÄFT, IND, VW relocation, resettlement

Umspannungsindustrien *f pl* IND transformation industries

Umstand *m* RECHT circumstance, fact, factor; ♦ **unter gar keinen Umständen** GESCHÄFT not on any terms; **unter den gegebenen Umständen** GESCHÄFT, RECHT under the circumstances; **unter keinen Umständen** GESCHÄFT, RECHT under no circumstances

Umsteigemöglichkeit *f* TRANSP interchange

umsteigen *vi* TRANSP change, transfer

Umsteigung *f* TRANSP transfer (*tr., tfr*)

umstellen 1. *vt* GESCHÄFT switch; **2. sich ~ auf** *v refl* [+acc] GESCHÄFT switch over

Umstellung *f* GESCHÄFT switchover, switch, switching, RECHT *EU Recht* changeover, conversion, transposal; **~ auf** GESCHÄFT switchover to; **~ auf Container** TRANSP containerization; **~ auf Maschinen** IND *Produktion* mechanization; **Umstellungsfehler** *m* GESCHÄFT transposition error

umsteuerbar: nicht ~e Liegezeit *f* TRANSP nonreversible laytime

umstritten *adj* GESCHÄFT controversial

umstrukturieren *vt* BANK *Darlehen* refloat, FINANZ, GESCHÄFT, MGMNT, VW *Unternehmen* reorganize, reshape, reshuffle, restructure

umstrukturiert *adj* BANK refloated, FINANZ, MGMNT reorganized

Umstrukturierung *f* BANK reflotation, FINANZ, GESCHÄFT, MGMNT, VW reorganization, reshuffle, restructuring, shakedown (*infrml*) (*AmE*), structural transformation; **~ des Unternehmens** GESCHÄFT company reconstruction

Umsturz *m* POL overthrow, subversion

umstürzen *vt* POL overthrow, subvert

Umtausch *m* FINANZ conversion, exchange (*exch.*), GESCHÄFT change, VW conversion, exchange (*exch.*); **~ von Obligationen vor Fälligkeit** BÖRSE advance refunding

umtauschbar: ~e Waren *f pl* GESCHÄFT returnable goods; **~es Wertpapier** *nt* FINANZ convertible security

umtauschen *vt* BANK, BÖRSE, FINANZ *Währung* convert, exchange, GESCHÄFT change, VW *Währung* convert, exchange

Umtausch: **Umtauschparität** *f* BÖRSE conversion parity (*BrE*); **Umtauschrecht** *nt* BÖRSE exchange privilege;

Umtauschverhältnis *nt* BÖRSE conversion ratio; **Umtauschwert** *m* BÖRSE exchange value, FINANZ exchange ratio

Umwälzung *f* GESCHÄFT upheaval

umwandelbar *adj* BÖRSE, FINANZ, GESCHÄFT, KOMM, MGMNT, RECHT commutable, convertible, transformable

Umwandelbarkeit *f* RECHT commutability

umwandeln *vt* BÖRSE, FINANZ, GESCHÄFT change, commute, convert, transform, KOMM *Code* transcode, MGMNT reorganize, RECHT *Strafurteil* change, commute, convert; ♦ **~ in** [+acc] BÖRSE, COMP, FINANZ, GESCHÄFT, VW convert into

Umwandler *m* COMP *Datenverarbeitung* transducer

Umwandlung *f* COMP, GESCHÄFT change, conversion, transformation, MGMNT reorganization, RECHT *eines Strafurteils* change, conversion, VERSICH commutation, transformation; **~ in Fußgängerzone** V&M pedestrianization; **~ von Geld in Wirtschaftsgüter** VW commodification

Umweg *m* GESCHÄFT detour, TRANSP indirect route; **Umwegproduktion** *f* VW indirect production, roundabout production

Umwelt *f* UMWELT environment; **Umweltaktionsprogramm** *nt* UMWELT environmental action program (*AmE*), environmental action programme (*BrE*); **Umweltbedingungen** *f pl* UMWELT environmental conditions; **Umweltbelastung** *f* UMWELT environmental load, acid rain pollution

umweltbewußt *adj* UMWELT environmentally aware, environment-conscious, green

Umwelt: **Umweltdeterminismus** *m* UMWELT environmental determinism; **Umweltförderung** *f* GESCHÄFT, UMWELT environmental development; **Umweltfragen** *f pl* UMWELT environmental issues

umweltfreundlich *adj* UMWELT compatible with the environment, environmentally beneficial, environmentally friendly; **~es Produkt** *nt* UMWELT environmentally friendly product, green product; **~e Technologie** *f* UMWELT clean technology, green technology

Umwelt: **Umweltgüte** *nt pl* UMWELT environmental quality; **Umwelthygiene** *f* UMWELT environmental health; **Umweltkontrolle** *f* IND, POL, UMWELT environmental control, pollution control; **Umweltlobby** *f* POL environmental lobby; **Umweltmanagement** *nt* MGMNT, POL, UMWELT environmental management; **Umweltmanagementsystem** *nt* UMWELT environmental management system; **Umweltminister, in** *m,f* POL, UMWELT Secretary of State for the Environment; **Umweltnorm** *f* UMWELT environmental standard; **Umweltpolitik** *f* POL, UMWELT environmental policy; **Umweltproblem** *nt* UMWELT environmental problem; **Umweltprognose** *f* UMWELT environmental projection; **Umweltprüfung** *f* UMWELT environmental assessment; **Umweltqualität** *f* UMWELT environmental quality; **Umweltqualitätsnorm** *f* UMWELT environmental quality standard; **Umweltsanierung** *f* UMWELT environmental cleanup operation; **Umwelt-Scanner** *m* UMWELT environmental scanner; **Umweltschaden** *m* GESCHÄFT, POL, UMWELT environmental damage

Umweltschutz *m* IND, POL, UMWELT environmental control, environmental protection, pollution control, protection of the environment; **Umweltschutzbehörde** *f* POL, UMWELT Environmental Protection Agency (*AmE*) (*EPA*); **Umweltschutzbehörde** *f* **der Vereinig-**

ten Staaten POL, UMWELT United States Environmental Protection Agency (*AmE*) (*EPA*); **Umwelt-schutzbewegung** *f* UMWELT environmentalism
Umweltschützer, in *m,f* UMWELT environmentalist
Umweltschutz: **Umweltschutzpapier** *nt* UMWELT recycled paper
Umwelt: **Umweltsteuer** *f* POL, STEUER, UMWELT environmental tax, pollution tax; **Umweltstudie** *f* MGMNT, UMWELT environmental study; **Umweltüberwachung** *f* IND, UMWELT pollution monitoring; **Umwelt-untersuchung** *f* MGMNT environmental analysis, UMWELT environment scan; **Umwelt- und Verbraucher-schutzdienst** *m* UMWELT *EWG* Environment and Consumer Protection Service (*ECPS*); **Umweltver-schmutzer** *m* UMWELT polluter; **Umweltver-schmutzungskontrolle** *f* IND, UMWELT pollution control; **Umweltverschmutzungsüberwachung** *f* IND, UMWELT pollution monitoring; **Umweltverträglich-keitsprüfung** *f* GESCHÄFT environmental impact analysis, environmental impact assessment; **Umweltverträglichkeitsstudie** *f* UMWELT *eines Vorhabens* environmental-impact study

umziehen *vi* GRUND, TRANSP move house, relocate, move
Umzug *m* GESCHÄFT, TRANSP move, moving, relocation, removal; **Umzugskostenbeihilfe** *f* PERSON allowance for moving costs (*AmE*), allowance for removal (*BrE*), relocation assistance; **Umzugs- und Zuzugsfreiheit** *f* POL freedom of movement
UN *abbr* (*United Nations*) vw UN (*United Nations*), UNO (*United Nations Organization*)
unabdingbar: ~e **Bestimmung** *f* VERSICH mandatory provision
unabhängig *adj* GESCHÄFT arm's length, self-contained, self-sufficient, unaffiliated, POL independent, vw self-sufficient, unaffiliated, STEUER, V&M arm's length; ♦ ~ **von** GESCHÄFT independent of, irrespective of
unabhängig: ~er **Anspruch** *m* PATENT independent claim; ~er **Buchprüfer** *m*, ~e **Buchprüferin** *f* RECHNUNG independent auditor; ~es **Einzelhandelsgeschäft** *nt* V&M independent retailer; ~e **Gewerkschaft** *f* GESCHÄFT, PERSON independent union, unaffiliated union; ~er **Makler** *m*, ~e **Maklerin** *f* BÖRSE independent broker, two-dollar broker (*AmE*); ~er **Sachverständiger** *m*, ~e **Sachverständige** *f* PERSON independent expert; ~e **Untersuchung** *f* RECHT independent inquiry; ~er **Untersuchungsausschuß** *m* PERSON Independent Review Committee (*BrE*); ~e **Variablen** *f pl* MATH independent variables
Unabhängige(r) *mf* [decl. as adj] POL independent
Unabhängigkeit *f* GESCHÄFT, PERSON, POL independence; **Unabhängigkeitszertifikat** *nt* PERSON certificate of independence
unabsehbar *adj* GESCHÄFT unforeseeable, unpredictable
unabsichtlich *adj* GESCHÄFT inadvertent, unintentional
unanfechtbar *adj* GESCHÄFT unassailable, *Vertrag, Beweis* unimpeachable, *Plan, Argument* watertight, PATENT incontestable, RECHT unappealable
Unanfechtbarkeit *f* GESCHÄFT, PATENT, RECHT incontestability, non-appealability; **Unanfechtbarkeitsklausel** *f* VERSICH incontestable clause
unangebracht *adj* GESCHÄFT inappropriate, unreasonable
unangemeldet: ~er **Besuch** *m* V&M cold call, cold calling

unangemessen *adj* GESCHÄFT inappropriate, unsuitable, *Forderung, Preis* unreasonable, inadequate
unangenehm *adj* GESCHÄFT disagreeable
unangepaßt: ~e **Bilanz** *f* RECHNUNG ungeraed balance sheet
unaufgefordert *adj* GESCHÄFT unsolicited; ~e **Aussage** *f* RECHT unsolicited testimonial; ~e **Bewerbung** *f* PERSON unsolicited application
unausgebildet *adj* PERSON, SOZIAL unskilled, untrained
unausgeglichen: ~e **Arbeitsweise** *f* PERSON unbalanced working; ~er **Handel** *m* vw unbalanced trade
unausgetestet *adj* COMP nondebugged
unausgewogen: ~er **Posten** *m* GESCHÄFT uneven lot
unbeabsichtigt *adj* GESCHÄFT unintended, unintentional
unbeantwortet *adj* GESCHÄFT unacknowledged
unbearbeitet *adj* COMP *Daten* raw, IND unfinished, untreated, unworked
unbebaut: ~es **Gelände** *nt* GRUND open space; ~es **Grundstück** *nt* GRUND undeveloped land (*BrE*), vacant lot (*AmE*); ~es **Land** *nt* GRUND raw land, vacant land
unbedeutend *adj* GESCHÄFT negligible, slight, nominal
unbedingt *adj* COMP, GESCHÄFT unconditional; ~e **Beachtung** *f* **von Treu und Glauben** VERSICH utmost good faith
unbefriedigend *adj* GESCHÄFT unsatisfactory
unbefristet *adj* GESCHÄFT unlimited; ~e **Flugreservierung** *f* TRANSP open-ended flight reservation; ~er **Vertrag** *m* FINANZ evergreen
unbefugt *adj* GESCHÄFT unauthorized, without authorization; ~er **Eingriff** *m* RECHT interference
unbeglaubigt *adj* RECHT unauthenticated, uncertified; ~e **Unterschrift** *f* RECHT unauthenticated signature
unbegleitet: ~es **Gepäck** *nt* FREI, TRANSP unaccompanied baggage
unbeglichen *adj* FINANZ, GESCHÄFT *Rechnung, Schuld* due, outstanding, unpaid, unsettled, RECHNUNG unpaid
unbegrenzt *adj* GESCHÄFT indefinite, unlimited; ♦ **nach oben** ~ BÖRSE unlimited on the upside
unbegrenzt: ~e **Dauer** *f* FINANZ perpetuity; ~e **Geldstrafe** *f* RECHT unlimited fine; ~e **Haftung** *f* GESCHÄFT, RECHT unlimited liability; ~e **Kilometerzahl** *f* TRANSP unlimited mileage; ~e **Steuerbürgschaft** *f* BÖRSE unlimited tax bond (*AmE*)
unbegründet *adj* GESCHÄFT *Anschuldigung* unfounded, groundless, unsubstantiated, RECHT without just cause
unbekannt *adj* GESCHÄFT not known, unknown, ~en **Ursprungs** GESCHÄFT of unknown origin
unbelastet *adj* GRUND unencumbered; ~es **Eigentumsrecht** *nt* RECHT clear title (*AmE*); ~e **Immobilie** *f* GRUND unencumbered estate
unbelegt: ~e **Taste** *f* COMP, KOMM, VERWALT *auf einer Tastatur* dead key
unbeliebt *adj* GESCHÄFT unpopular; ~e **Aktie** *f* FINANZ out-of-favor stock (*AmE*), out-of-favour stock (*BrE*); ~e **Industrie** *f* FINANZ out-of-favor industry (*AmE*), out-of-favour industry (*BrE*)
unbemerkt: ~ **bleiben** *vi* GESCHÄFT go unnoticed
unbenannt *adj* COMP unnamed, untitled
unbenutzt *adj* GESCHÄFT unused
unberechenbar *adj* GESCHÄFT incalculable, unpredictable
unberechtigt *adj* GESCHÄFT, RECHT unauthorized, unjus-

tified; **~e Durchsuchung** *f* **und Beschlagnahme** *f* GESCHÄFT search and seizure

unbereinigt *adj* MATH unadjusted

unberücksichtigt: **~ lassen** *phr* MGMNT disregard, ignore

unbeschädigt *adj* GESCHÄFT *Waren* sound, undamaged

unbeschränkt *adj* BÖRSE clean, GESCHÄFT absolute, unlimited, unrestricted; **~es Akkreditiv** *nt* BANK unlimited letter of credit; **~es Akzept** *nt* FINANZ unqualified acceptance; **~e Haftung** *f* GESCHÄFT, RECHT unlimited liability; **~es Kontingent** *nt* GESCHÄFT unrestricted quota; **~e Vollmacht** *f* **des Geschäftsführers** FINANZ plenary powers

unbesehen: **~ klariert** *phr* IMP/EXP *Zollabfertigung* cleared without examination (*CWE*)

unbesetzt: **für eine ~e Stelle arbeiten** *phr* GESCHÄFT, PERSON work for abeyance; **~e Stellen** *f pl* **an einer Maschine** IND *Produktion* unattended machinery spaces, unmanned machinery spaces

unbesichert: **~es Darlehen** *nt* BANK unsecured advance; **~er Kredit** *m* **mit fester Laufzeit** BANK unsecured fixed-term loan

unbeständig *adj* GESCHÄFT inconsistent, unstable, unsteady

unbestätigt *adj* GESCHÄFT unacknowledged, unconfirmed, unverified, unvouched for

unbestimmt *adj* GESCHÄFT indefinite, indeterminate, undetermined; **~e Liegezeit** *f* TRANSP indefinite laytime

Unbestimmtheit *f* GESCHÄFT, VW uncertainty

unbestreitbar *adj* GESCHÄFT unassailable, *Tatsache* incontestable, unquestionable

unbeweglich: **~es Inventar** *nt* GRUND fixtures; **~es Vermögen** *nt* GRUND immovable property, real property; **~e Vermögensgegenstände** *m pl* RECHT corporeal hereditaments; **~e Wertpapieremission** *f* BÖRSE sticky deal

unbewertet *adj* GESCHÄFT unassessed

unbewiesen *adj* GESCHÄFT unproven, unverified

unbewohnt *adj* GRUND uninhabited, unoccupied, vacant

unbezahlt *adj* FINANZ, GESCHÄFT unpaid, unsettled, owing, RECHNUNG unpaid; ♦ **~e Schecks verbuchen** BANK book unpaid checks (*AmE*), book unpaid cheques (*BrE*)

unbezahlt: **~e Verbindlichkeit** *f* RECHNUNG creditors (*BrE*), payables (*AmE*); **~e Verpflichtung** *f* RECHNUNG undischarged commitment

unbillig *adj* GESCHÄFT inequitable, unjust

unbrauchbar *adj* GESCHÄFT unserviceable (*U/S*); **~e Daten** *f* COMP garbage (*AmE*); **~er Stimmzettel** *m* POL spoiled voting paper, spoilt voting paper, spoiled ballot paper, spoilt ballot paper

UNCTAD *abbr* (*Welthandelskonferenz der Vereinten Nationen*) VW UNCTAD (*United Nations Conference on Trade and Development*); **UNCTAD-Konvention** *f* **über kombinierten Verkehr** VW UNCTAD multimodal transport convention (*UNCTAD MMO*)

undatiert *adj* GESCHÄFT undated

undeutlich *adj* GESCHÄFT indistinct, unclear, *Schrift* illegible; **~ geschriebene Ziffer** *f* GESCHÄFT blind figure

undicht: **~e Stelle** *f* MEDIEN, POL leak

undifferenziert *adj* GESCHÄFT undifferentiated; **~es**

Marketing *nt* V&M undifferentiated marketing; **~e Produkte** *nt pl* V&M undifferentiated products

UNDP *abbr* (*Entwicklungsprogramm der Vereinten Nationen*) VW UNDP (*United Nations Development Programme*)

undurchführbar *adj* GESCHÄFT unfeasible, unpracticable, unworkable

undurchsichtig: **~e Struktur** *f* GESCHÄFT daisy-chain scheme; **~er Unternehmenskomplex** *m* BÖRSE daisy chain

Und-Zeichen *nt* COMP, MEDIEN ampersand

unehrlich *adj* GESCHÄFT dishonest

uneigennützig *adj* PERSON, VW altruistic

Uneigennützigkeit *f* VW altruism

uneinbringlich *adj* FINANZ, GESCHÄFT unrecoverable, RECHNUNG, STEUER uncollectable; **~e Forderung** *f* BANK, FINANZ bad debt, RECHNUNG uncollectable account; **~e und zweifelhafte Forderung** *f* BANK bad and doubtful debt (*B&D*)

uneingelöst: **~er Scheck** *m* BANK dishonored check (*AmE*), dishonoured cheque (*BrE*)

uneingeschränkt *adj* BANK, FINANZ unrestricted, unconditional, unqualified, *Wettbewerb, Rechte* uncurtailed, GESCHÄFT unrestricted, unconditional, unqualified, *Wettbewerb, Rechte* uncurtailed, all-out; **~es Akzept** *nt* BANK clean acceptance, general acceptance, GESCHÄFT unconditional acceptance; **~e Annahme** *f* FINANZ unqualified acceptance; **~e Beihilfe** *f* FINANZ unconditional grant; **~es Eigentumsrecht** *nt* GRUND absolute title; **~e Erklärung** *f* RECHNUNG unqualified opinion; **~er Erlaß** *m* FINANZ unconditional remission; **~er Zugang** *m* GESCHÄFT unrestricted access

uneinheitlich: **~ tendierender Markt** *m* BÖRSE sideways market

Uneinigkeit *f* RECHNUNG variance; **Uneinigkeitsanalyse** *f* RECHNUNG variance analysis

uneins: **mit jdm über etw ~ sein** *phr* GESCHÄFT be at variance with sb about sth, disagree with sb

unelastisch: **~es Angebot** *nt* VW fixed supply, inelastic supply; **~e Nachfrage** *f* VW fixed demand, inelastic demand

Unelastizität *f* VW inelasticity; **~ der Preise** VW price inelasticity

unendlich *adj* UMWELT infinite

unentgeltlich: **~e finanzielle Hilfe** *f* FINANZ grant-in-aid; **~e Übertragung** *f* STEUER gratuitous transfer

unentschieden *adj* GESCHÄFT undecided, RECHT pending

unentschlossen *adj* GESCHÄFT indecisive, undecided

unerfahren *adj* GESCHÄFT inexperienced, unfledged

unerfüllt *adj* GESCHÄFT *Bedingung, Versprechen* unfulfilled

unergiebig *adj* BANK lying idle (*infrml*), BÖRSE unproductive, GESCHÄFT unprofitable

unerkannt *adj* GESCHÄFT unidentified, unrecognized

unerläßlich *adj* GESCHÄFT indispensable; **~e Sache** *f* RECHT causa sine qua non

unerlaubt: **sich ~ entfernen** *phr* GESCHÄFT take French leave, go AWOL; **~e Handlung** *f* RECHT unlawful act, *zivilrechtlich* civil wrong; **~ kopiertes Produkt** *nt* V&M bootleg version, pirated product; **~es Streikpostenstehen** *nt* PERSON unlawful picketing

unerledigt *adj* GESCHÄFT outstanding; **~e Angelegenheit** *f* GESCHÄFT outstanding matter; **~e Arbeit** *f* GESCHÄFT arrears of work; **~e Aufträge** *m pl* GESCHÄFT, IND backlogged orders, unfilled orders, outstanding orders, work backlog

unerprobt *adj* GESCHÄFT untested, untried

unerreichbar *adj* GESCHÄFT *Ziel* inaccessible, unattainable, KOMM unattainable

unerreicht *adj* GESCHÄFT unequaled (*AmE*), unequalled (*BrE*), unrivaled (*AmE*), unrivalled (*BrE*); **~e Rekordleistung** *f* GESCHÄFT all-time record

unerschlossen *adj* GESCHÄFT *Ressourcen, Markt* untapped, GRUND undeveloped, VW unexploited; **~es Grundstück** *nt* VW raw land, undeveloped land

unerschöpflich *adj* GESCHÄFT unfailing, UMWELT *Reserven* inexhaustible; **~e externe Effekte** *m pl* UMWELT undepletable externality

unersetzbar *adj* FINANZ irrecoverable, GESCHÄFT irreplaceable

unersetzlich *adj* FINANZ irrecoverable, GESCHÄFT irreplaceable, *Verlust* irreparable

unerwartet *adj* GESCHÄFT unanticipated, unforeseen, without warning; **~er Gewinn** *m* GESCHÄFT, VW unexpected profit, windfall profit; **~ hoher Verlust** *m* VW shock loss; **~es Nebenergebnis** *nt* GESCHÄFT, POL fallout; **~er Verlust** *m* VW unexpected loss, windfall loss

unerwünscht *adj* GESCHÄFT undesirable, unwanted

unfähig *adj* GESCHÄFT, PERSON, RECHT incapable, incompetent, unable; ♦ **~, etw zu tun** GESCHÄFT unable to do sth, unfit to do sth

Unfähigkeit *f* GESCHÄFT disablement, inability, incapability, incapacity, incompetence

unfair: **~e Maßregelung** *f* PERSON victimization; **~e Praktiken** *f pl* **im Arbeitsleben** PERSON unfair labor practice (*AmE*), unfair labour practice (*BrE*); **~e Preisunterbietung** *f* VW third-degree price discrimination

Unfall *m* GESCHÄFT accident, casualty, PERSON, VERSICH accident; **~ beim Transport** VERSICH accident to conveyance; **Unfallentschädigung** *f* PERSON *Arbeitsunfall* workers' compensation; **Unfallgefahr** *nt* VERSICH accident risk; **Unfallhaftpflicht** *f* **des Arbeitgebers** STEUER employer's liabilities; **Unfallmeldung** *f* PERSON notice; **Unfallrisiko** *nt* VERSICH accident risk; **Unfallverhütung** *f* PERSON accident prevention; **Unfallversicherer** *m* VERSICH accident insurer; **Unfallversicherung** *f* PERSON, VERSICH accident insurance, worker compensation insurance, casualty insurance; **Unfallversicherungsbereich** *m* PERSON, VERSICH *Arbeit* zone of employment

unfertig: **~e Erzeugnisse** *nt pl* GESCHÄFT, RECHNUNG, VW partly finished goods, work in process (*AmE*) (*WIP*), work in progress (*BrE*) (*WIP*)

unformatiert *adj* COMP unformatted

unfreiwillig: **~e Arbeitslosigkeit** *f* VW involuntary unemployment; **~e Liquidation** *f* FINANZ compulsory liquidation, involuntary liquidation

ung. *adv* (*ungefähr*) GESCHÄFT about, approximately (*approx.*), circa (*ca.*)

ungastlich *adj* GESCHÄFT inhospitable

ungeachtet *adv* GESCHÄFT notwithstanding

ungebremst *adj* VW undamped

ungebunden *adj* POL non-aligned, non-committed, VW untied

ungedämpft *adj* VW undamped

ungedeckt *adj* BANK *Kredit* unsecured, FINANZ uncovered; **~e Baisse-Optionsposition** *f* BÖRSE naked short option position; **~e Baisse-Verkaufsoption** *f* BÖRSE naked short puts; **~e Kaufoption** *f* BÖRSE naked call option, uncovered call option; **~e Notenausgabe** *f* BANK fiduciary currency; **~er Notenumlauf** *m* FINANZ fiduciary currency; **~e Option** *f* BÖRSE naked option; **~es Optionsgeschäft** *nt* BÖRSE uncovered option; **~er Saldo** *m* FINANZ uncovered balance; **~er Scheck** *m* BANK bad check (*AmE*), bad cheque (*BrE*), kite (*AmE*), bounced check (*AmE*), bounced cheque (*BrE*), uncovered check (*AmE*), uncovered cheque (*BrE*), dud check (*AmE*), dud cheque (*BrE*), check without sufficient funds (*AmE*), cheque without sufficient funds (*BrE*), check without provision (*AmE*), cheque without provision (*BrE*); **~er Sicherungsverlust** *m* BÖRSE uncovered hedge loss; **~er Verkauf** *m* BÖRSE writing naked; **~er Verkäufer** *m* **einer Option** BÖRSE naked writer; **~e Verkaufsoption** *f* BÖRSE naked put, uncovered put; **~er Vorschuß** *m* BANK uncovered advance; **~e Zeitspanne** *f* FINANZ times uncovered

ungeeignet *adj* GESCHÄFT inappropriate, ineligible, unsuitable, unsuited

ungefähr *adv* (*ung.*) GESCHÄFT about, approximately (*approx.*), circa (*ca.*)

ungeklärt *adj* GESCHÄFT unaccounted for, MGMNT *Frage, Problem* unresolved

ungekürzt *adj* GESCHÄFT, MEDIEN *Text* unabridged; **~e Summe** *f* GESCHÄFT full amount

ungelernt *adj* PERSON, SOZIAL unskilled, untrained; **~er Arbeiter** *m* PERSON laborer (*AmE*), labourer (*BrE*); **~e Arbeitskräfte** *f pl* PERSON, VW manual labor (*AmE*), manual labour (*BrE*), unskilled labor (*AmE*), unskilled labour (*BrE*), unskilled workers; **~e Hilfskräfte** *f pl* PERSON, VW unskilled labor (*AmE*), unskilled labour (*BrE*), unskilled workers

ungelocht *adj* COMP blank

ungelöst *adj* MGMNT *Frage, Problem* unresolved

ungenannt *adj* GESCHÄFT anonymous, undisclosed

Ungenauigkeit *f* GESCHÄFT inaccuracy

ungenießbar *adj* GESCHÄFT unpalatable

ungenügend *adj* BANK, FINANZ insufficient, GESCHÄFT unsatisfactory; ♦ **~ bemannt** PERSON *Industrie, Unternehmen* understaffed

ungenügend: **~e Deckung** *f* FINANZ insufficient funds (*I/F*); **~e Erzeugung** *f* IND underproduction; **~ gedeckter Kredit** *m* BANK overextended credit; **~e Produktion** *f* IND underproduction; **~e Vorräte** *m pl* GESCHÄFT stock shortage

ungenutzt *adj* GESCHÄFT unused, *Ressourcen* untapped, PERSON idle; **~e Kapazität** *f* IND, VW idle capacity, surplus capacity; **~e Tonnage** *f* TRANSP idle tonnage; **~e Zeit** *f* PERSON idle time

ungeordnet: **~e Marktverhältnisse** *nt pl* BÖRSE disorderly market

ungeprüft *adj* GESCHÄFT untested, untried

ungerade *adj* COMP, GESCHÄFT odd

ungerecht *adj* GESCHÄFT unfair, unjust, RECHT inequitable; **~e Behandlung** *f* PERSON victimization

ungerechterweise *adv* GESCHÄFT unduly

ungerechtfertigt *adj* GESCHÄFT unwarranted, *Forderung, Preis* unreasonable, PERSON unfair, RECHT unjustified; **~e Drohung** *f* RECHT unjustified threat; **~e Entlassung**

f PERSON unfair dismissal, wrongful dismissal, RECHT wrongful dismissal

ungeregelt: **~er Freiverkehr** *m* BÖRSE off-board trading, vw third market

ungerippt: **~es Papier** *nt* VERWALT wove paper

ungeschult *adj* PERSON, SOZIAL unschooled, untrained

ungeschützt *adj* GESCHÄFT unscreened, PATENT unprotected, PERSON vulnerable; **~e Datei** *f* COMP scratch file

ungesichert *adj* BÖRSE unhedged, unsecured; **~e Anleihe** *f* BÖRSE debenture bond, plain bond issue, unsecured bond issue; **~es Darlehen** *nt* BANK, FINANZ straight loan; **~e Kaufoption** *f* BÖRSE uncovered call; **~e Long- oder Short-Position** *f* BÖRSE naked position; **~e Restfinanzierung** *f* FINANZ mezzanine finance

ungestempelt: **~e gesicherte Schuldverschreibungen** *f pl* BÖRSE unstamped debentures

ungestört *adj* GESCHÄFT undisturbed; **~er Besitz** *m* GRUND, RECHT quiet enjoyment, quiet possession

ungesund *adj* vw unsound; **~es Risiko** *nt* GESCHÄFT, VERSICH unsound risk

ungeteilt *adj* GESCHÄFT undivided; **~er Besitz** *m* GRUND undivided property

ungewiß *adj* GESCHÄFT contingent, doubtful, uncertain; **ungewisses künftiges Ereignis** *nt* GESCHÄFT contingency

Ungewißheit *f* GESCHÄFT, VW uncertainty; ◆ **in ~ sein** GESCHÄFT be in abeyance, be in suspense

ungewogen *adj* GESCHÄFT *Index* unweighted

ungewöhnlich 1. *adj* GESCHÄFT unusual; **2.** *adv* GESCHÄFT unusually

ungewöhnlich: **~er Artikel** *m* GESCHÄFT unusual item; **~ hoher Spekulationsgewinn** *m* BÖRSE killing (*infrml*)

ungezielt *adj* V&M untargeted; **~e Kundenwerbung** *f* V&M cold canvass, cold canvassing; **~er Versand** *m* V&M cold mailing

ungezwungen *adj* GESCHÄFT informal

ungleich: **~er Tausch** *m* GESCHÄFT unequal exchange

Ungleichgewicht *nt* FINANZ imbalance, vw disequilibrium; **~ der Handelsbilanz** vw disequilibrium in the balance of trade

ungleichgewichtig: **~es Wachstum** *nt* vw unbalanced growth

Ungleichgewicht: **Ungleichgewichtspreis** *m* VW disequilibrium price; **Ungleichgewichtstheorie** *f* vw disequilibrium economics

Ungleichheit *f* vw inequality

ungleichmäßig *adj* BÖRSE erratic, GESCHÄFT uneven

Ungleichung *f* MATH inequality

Unglück *nt* GESCHÄFT, VERSICH accident

ungültig *adj* GESCHÄFT invalid, void; ◆ **für ~ erklären** RECHT *Vertragsklausel* annul, invalidate, rescind, declare null and void; **~ geworden** GESCHÄFT expired; **~ machen** GESCHÄFT invalidate; **~ werden** GESCHÄFT expire

ungültig: **~er Frachtbrief** *m* TRANSP stale bill of lading; **~e Klausel** *f* RECHT inoperative clause; **~e Police** *f* VERSICH void policy; **~er Stimmzettel** *m* POL spoiled voting paper, spoilt voting paper, spoiled ballot paper, spoilt ballot paper

Ungültigkeit *f* GESCHÄFT invalidity, RECHT invalidity, nullity; **Ungültigkeitserklärung** *f* RECHT cancellation, declaration of invalidity, invalidation, rescission

Ungültigmachung *f* GESCHÄFT invalidation

ungünstig *adj* GESCHÄFT *Preis, Bedingungen* adverse, unfavorable (*AmE*), unfavourable (*BrE*), vw adverse; **~e Geschäftsbedingungen** *f pl* vw adverse trading conditions; **~e Handelsbedingungen** *f pl* vw adverse trading conditions; **~er Wechselkurs** *m* FINANZ unfavorable exchange (*AmE*), unfavourable exchange (*BrE*), unfavorable rate of exchange (*AmE*), unfavourable rate of exchange (*BrE*)

UNHCR *abbr* (*Hochkommissariat der Vereinten Nationen für Flüchtlinge*) vw UNHCR (*United Nations High Commission for Refugees*)

unheilbar: **~er Mangel** *m* RECHT *Vertragsrecht* incurable defect, irremediable defect

UNIDO *abbr* (*Organisation der Vereinten Nationen für industrielle Entwicklung*) vw UNIDO (*United Nations Industrial Development Organization*)

unilateral: **~es Abkommen** *nt* vw unilateral agreement

unintelligent: **~e Datenstation** *f* COMP dumb terminal

Union *f* POL union

UNITAR *abbr* (*Institut der Vereinten Nationen für Ausbildung und Forschung*) PERSON UNITAR (*United Nations Institute for Training and Research*)

Unitas: **~ Gesamtaktienindex** *m* BÖRSE Unitas all share index

United: **~ Nations** *f pl* (*UN*) POL United Nations (*UN*), United Nations Organization (*UNO*)

universal *adj* FINANZ all-purpose, universal

Universal- *in cpds* GESCHÄFT universal, all-purpose; **Universalbank** *f* BANK universal bank; **Universal-Container** *m* TRANSP universal container (*U*)

Universalismus *m* GESCHÄFT universalism

Universal-: **Universal-Luftfrachtbrief** *m* IMP/EXP, TRANSP universal air waybill (*UAWB*)

universell: **~e Lebensversicherung** *f* VERSICH composite life insurance; **~e Lebensversicherungspolice** *f* VERSICH composite life policy

Universität *f* SOZIAL university; **Universitätsabschluß** *m* PERSON degree; **Universitätsdiplom** *nt* PERSON, SOZIAL degree

unklar *adj* RECHT ambiguous, uncertain, unclear; **~e Signale** *m pl* GESCHÄFT mixed signals

UN-Kode *m* IMP/EXP code-UN

unkontrollierbar *adj* FINANZ, GESCHÄFT unmanageable, *Inflation, Kosten* uncontrollable, vw uncontrollable

unkontrolliert *adj* FINANZ, GESCHÄFT, VW *Angaben, Zahlen* unchecked, uncontrolled; **~e inflationäre Wirtschaft** *f* vw unchecked inflationary economy

unkörperlich: **~er Rechtsgegenstand** *m* PATENT *Wechsel, Patente* chose in action; **~es Vermögen** *nt* RECHNUNG intangible property

Unkorrektheit *f* GESCHÄFT inaccuracy

unkündbar *adj* BÖRSE irredeemable, FINANZ uncallable, RECHT *Vertrag* nonterminable; **~e Anleihe** *f* vw non-callable bond; **~e Pacht** *f* GRUND hereditary lease

unlauter: **~es Geschäft** *nt* GESCHÄFT unfair trade; **~es Geschäftsgebaren** *nt* GESCHÄFT unfair trading practices; **~er Wettbewerb** *m* GESCHÄFT unfair trading practices

unleserlich *adj* GESCHÄFT illegible; **~er Abzug** *m* MEDIEN, V&M dirty proof; **~e Anschrift** *f* KOMM illegible address

unlimitiert *adj* BÖRSE, GESCHÄFT unlimited; **~e Wertpapiere** *nt pl* BÖRSE unlimited securities

unlösbar *adj* GESCHÄFT insoluble

unmittelbar *adj* GESCHÄFT direct; **~er Besitz** *m* RECHT actual possession, SOZIAL actual possession, direct possession; **~e Familie** *f* BÖRSE immediate family; **~e Gefahr** *f* VERSICH imminent danger, imminent peril; **~e Haftung** *f* RECHT direct liability; **~er Monetarismus** *m* VW instant monetarism; **~e Rechtsbeziehung** *f* RECHT privity; **~e(r) Vorgesetzte(r)** *mf* [decl. as adj] PERSON first-line supervisor; **~es Ziel** *nt* GESCHÄFT immediate aim

unmodern *adj* GESCHÄFT out of fashion

Unmöglichkeit *f* RECHT impossibility; **~ der Leistung** RECHT impossibility of performance; **Unmöglichkeitstheorem** *nt* VW impossibility theorem

unnachgiebig *adj* GESCHÄFT uncompromising; **~es Verhandeln** *nt* GESCHÄFT hard bargaining

unökonomisch *adj* GESCHÄFT uneconomic, uneconomical

unorthodox: ~e Finanzierungsmethode *f* FINANZ creative financing

unparteiisch *adj* GESCHÄFT impartial, unbiased, unprejudiced, POL independent; **~er Gutachter** *m*, **~e Gutachterin** *f* VW nonpartisan expert

unpassend *adj* GESCHÄFT unreasonable, *zeitlich* untimely

unpfändbar *adj* FINANZ nonleviable

Unpfändbarkeit *f* RECHT *nicht der Zwangsvollstreckung unterworfen* judgment proof

unpopulär *adj* GESCHÄFT unpopular

unproduktiv *adj* IND, MGMNT idle, nonproductive, unproductive; **~e Arbeitskräfte** *f pl* PERSON unproductive labor (*AmE*), unproductive labour (*BrE*); **~es Darlehen** *nt* BANK nonproductive loan

unqualifiziert *adj* PERSON unqualified

unquittiert *adj* GESCHÄFT *Rechnung* unreceipted

unrealistisch *adj* GESCHÄFT unrealistic

Unrecht *nt* RECHT wrong; ◆ **zu ~** GESCHÄFT wrongly; **~ haben** GESCHÄFT be in the wrong

unrechtmäßig *adj* RECHT illegal, unlawful, wrongful; **~er Gewinnanteil** *m* RECHT illegal dividend

unreduzierbar *adj* GESCHÄFT irreducible

unreell *adj* GESCHÄFT dubious; **~e Firma** *f* FREI bucket shop; **~e Maklerfirma** *f* FINANZ bucket shop

unregelmäßig: ~ gehandelte Aktien *f pl* BÖRSE inactive stock; **~e Wartung** *f* GESCHÄFT sporadic maintenance; **~ zusammengewachsene Siedlung** *f* GRUND cluster housing

Unregelmäßigkeit *f* GESCHÄFT anomaly, irregularity

unreif *adj* BÖRSE, FINANZ, PERSON immature, unfledged

unrein: ~es Konnossement *nt* IMP/EXP, TRANSP claused bill of lading, dirty bill of lading, foul bill of lading

unrentabel *adj* BANK idle, FINANZ unprofitable, GESCHÄFT unremunerative, unprofitable, uneconomic, uneconomical, VW uneconomic, unprofitable

unrichtig *adj* GESCHÄFT false, incorrect, wrong; **~e Altersangabe** *f* VERSICH misstatement of age

Unruhe: Unruheherd *m* GESCHÄFT, POL trouble spot; **Unruhen** *f pl* POL commotion, disorders, riots, unrest

unsachgemäß: ~er Machtgebrauch *m* POL abuse of power

unsauber: ~e Geschäftsmethoden *f pl* RECHT shady practices (*infrml*)

unschätzbar *adj* GESCHÄFT invaluable

unselbständig: ~e Beschäftigung *f* PERSON dependent employment, dependent personal services

unseriös *adj* GESCHÄFT dubious, untrustworthy, PERSON untrustworthy

unsicher *adj* IND unsafe, VW insecure, instable, uncertain

Unsicherheit *f* GESCHÄFT uncertainty, IND danger, VW insecurity, instability, uncertainty

unsichtbar: ~e Arbeitslosigkeit *f* VW hidden unemployment; **~e Ein- und Ausfuhren** *f pl* FINANZ, VW invisible balance, invisibles; **~e Exporte** *m pl* IMP/EXP, VW invisible exports; **~e Hand** *f* VW invisible hand; **~er Handel** *m* FINANZ invisibles, VW invisible trade, invisibles; **~e Importe** *m pl* IMP/EXP, VW invisible imports; **~e Lieferungen** *f pl* GESCHÄFT invisible supply

unsortiert *adj* GESCHÄFT ungraded, unsorted (*u/s*)

unstet *adj* GESCHÄFT, VW unsteady

unstetig *adj* GESCHÄFT, VW volatile

Unstimmigkeit *f* GESCHÄFT friction

unstrukturiert *adj* GESCHÄFT unstructured; **~es Interview** *nt* PERSON *Bewerbung* unstructured interview

unsubventioniert *adj* GESCHÄFT unsubsidized

untauglich *adj* PERSON incompetent, unfit, unsuitable

unteilbar: ~e Exporte *m pl* IMP/EXP indivisible exports; **~e Last** *f* TRANSP indivisible load

Unteilbarkeit *f* VW indivisibility

unten *adv* GESCHÄFT below; ◆ **nach ~** COMP down; **~ erwähnt** GESCHÄFT mentioned below, undermentioned (*u/m*); **nach ~ korrigieren** GESCHÄFT revise downward; **nach ~ revidieren** GESCHÄFT revise downward

Unter- *in cpds* GESCHÄFT sub-, under-

unter: ~ anderem *phr* GESCHÄFT inter alia

Unter-: Unterabteilung *f* MGMNT subdivision; **Unteragent, in** *m,f* GESCHÄFT subagent; **Unterakkreditiv** *nt* BANK back-to-back credit

Unterauftrag *m* GESCHÄFT, IND, PERSON, RECHT subcontract, order unit; ◆ **Unteraufträge vergeben** GESCHÄFT, IND, PERSON, RECHT subcontract

Unterauftrag: Unterauftragnehmer, in *m,f* GESCHÄFT, IND, PERSON, RECHT subcontractor

unterbeschäftigt *adj* PERSON underemployed

Unter-: Unterbeschäftigung *f* PERSON, VW underemployment

unterbesetzt *adj* PERSON undermanned, understaffed, TRANSP undermanned

Unterbesetzung *f* PERSON undermanning, understaffing

unterbevölkert *adj* GESCHÄFT underpopulated

unterbewerten *vt* BÖRSE *Aktie* underprice, FINANZ undervalue, GESCHÄFT underestimate, undervalue, RECHNUNG, VW understate, undervalue

unterbewertet *adj* BÖRSE underpriced, FINANZ undervalued, GESCHÄFT underestimated, undervalued, RECHNUNG, VW understated, undervalued; **~e Währung** *f* FINANZ, VW undervalued currency

Unterbewertung *f* BÖRSE underpricing, FINANZ undervaluation, GESCHÄFT underestimation, undervaluation, RECHNUNG, VW *einer Währung* understatement, undervaluation

unterbezahlen *vt* GESCHÄFT, PERSON underpay

unterbezahlt: ~e Schwerarbeit *f* PERSON sweatshop labor (*AmE*), sweatshop labour (*BrE*)

unterbieten *vt* GESCHÄFT underbid, undercut, under-quote, vw *Konkurrenz* underprice, *Preise* undercut

Unterbieten *nt* GESCHÄFT *Preis* undercutting

unterbinden *vt* GESCHÄFT inhibit

unterbrechen *vt* COMP interrupt, GESCHÄFT disrupt, suspend, *Verhandlungen, Gespräche* break off, MGMNT *Sitzung* adjourn

Unterbrechung *f* COMP *Programme* interruption, GESCHÄFT suspension, MGMNT *einer Sitzung* adjournment, TRANSP breakdown; **~ von Sendungen für Werbung** MEDIEN commercial break

unterbrechungsfrei: ~e Stromversorgung *f* COMP uninterruptible power supply (*UPS*)

unterbreiten *vt* GESCHÄFT, MGMNT submit; ◆ **~ Sie bitte Ihre Angebote** GESCHÄFT please submit your quotations

Unterbreitung *f* GESCHÄFT, VW *Angebote* submission

unterbringen *vt* BÖRSE, FINANZ place, FREI *in Unterkünften aller Art*, GESCHÄFT, SOZIAL *in einer Wohnung* accommodate

Unterbringung *f* BÖRSE, FINANZ placement, placing, FREI, GESCHÄFT, SOZIAL accommodation

unterbrochen: ~e Arbeitsschicht *f* PERSON split shift

Unterdeck *nt* TRANSP lower deck

Unterdepot *nt* RECHNUNG security deposit subdivision

unterdrücken *vt* COMP suppress, GESCHÄFT bottle up, POL oppress, stamp, vw *Inflation* stamp out, suppress

unterdrückt *adj* COMP suppressed, GESCHÄFT bottled-up, POL oppressed, vw suppressed

Unterdrückung *f* COMP suppression, POL oppression, suppression, vw suppression

unterdurchschnittlich 1. *adj* GESCHÄFT below the mark, below-average, *Arbeit, Ware, Qualität, Kenntnisse* substandard, IND substandard, vw *Wachstum* lower than average; **2.** *adv* ◆ **sich ~ entwickeln** vw underperform

untere: ~r Bereich *m* BÖRSE low end of the range; **~r Break-Even-Punkt** *m* BÖRSE downside breakeven point; **~ Führungsebene** *f* VERWALT lower management; **~r Goldpunkt** *m* FINANZ, IMP/EXP, vw gold export point, gold import point; **~r Interventionspunkt** *m* GESCHÄFT selling point, vw *Wechselkurs* floor; **~ Leitungsebene** *f* MGMNT, PERSON first-line management; **~r Marktbereich** *m* V&M low end of the market; **~s Marktsegment** *nt* V&M down-market segment, down market; **~ Preisklasse** *f* GESCHÄFT down-market segment; **~s Quartil** *nt* MATH lower quartile; **~r Speicherbereich** *m* COMP low memory

Untereintrag *m* COMP subentry

unterentwickelt: ~es Land *nt* GESCHÄFT, POL, VW underdeveloped country; **~er Staat** *m* GESCHÄFT, POL, vw underdeveloped country

Unterentwicklung *f* GESCHÄFT, IND, vw underdevelopment

Unterfrachtvertrag: einen ~ abschließen *phr* TRANSP subcharter

Unterführung *f* TRANSP *für Fußgänger* subway

Untergebene *pl* [decl. as adj] PERSON down-the-line personnel, down-the-line staff, subordinates

untergehen *vi* GESCHÄFT *Unternehmen* fail, go under

untergeordnet *adj* GESCHÄFT inferior, subordinate, MGMNT junior, PERSON menial, subsidiary; **~e Führungsebene** *f* MGMNT junior management; **~e Tätigkeit** *f* PERSON menial job

untergliedern *vt* GESCHÄFT, MGMNT subdivide

untergliedert *adj* GESCHÄFT broken down, subdivided, MGMNT subdivided

Untergliederung *f* GESCHÄFT breakdown, MGMNT subdivision

untergraben *vt* GESCHÄFT erode, *Einfluß, Macht* undermine

Untergraben *nt* GESCHÄFT erosion

Untergrundbahn *f* TRANSP subway (*AmE*), tube (*BrE*), underground (*BrE*)

Untergrundwirtschaft *f* vw black economy, cash economy, hidden economy, underground economy

Untergruppe *f* GESCHÄFT subgroup

Unterhalt *m* RECHT maintenance (*BrE*), support (*AmE*)

unterhalten *vt* RECHT maintain, support, VERWALT *Geschäftsstelle* maintain; ◆ **ein Konto ~ bei** BANK bank with

unterhaltend: sich selbst ~ *phr* GESCHÄFT self-supporting

Unterhalt: Unterhaltsbeihilfe *f* SOZIAL cost-of-living allowance; **Unterhaltszuschuß** *m* PERSON, SOZIAL subsistence allowance (*BrE*) (*sub*)

Unterhaltung *f* FREI entertainment; **Unterhaltungsindustrie** *f* FREI, MEDIEN show business

Unter-: Unterhändler, in *m,f* MGMNT negotiator; **Unterkapazität** *f* GESCHÄFT undercapacity

unterkapitalisiert *adj* BÖRSE low-geared, FINANZ underfunded, GESCHÄFT, IND undercapitalized

Unter-: Unterkapitel *nt* MEDIEN, STEUER subchapter; **Unterklasse** *f* vw underclass; **Unterkonto** *nt* RECHNUNG auxiliary account, detail account, subaccount, subsidiary account

Unterkunft *f* FREI, PERSON, SOZIAL accommodation; **Unterkunftsvergütung** *f* PERSON accommodation allowance

Unterlagen *f pl* GESCHÄFT records, supporting documents; **~ über die berufliche Laufbahn** VERWALT career record; **~ über den beruflichen Werdegang** VERWALT career record

Unterlagspapier *nt* IND, KOMM waterproof paper

unterlassen *vt* RECHT omit to do

Unterlassen *nt* RECHT neglect, omission; **~ einer Mitteilung** VERSICH nondisclosure

Unterlassung *f* RECHT failure to act, omission

Unterlieferant *m* PERSON subcontractor

unterliegen *vt* RECHT be subject to

Unterlizenz *f* GESCHÄFT, PATENT sublicence (*BrE*), sublicense (*AmE*)

untermauern *vt* GESCHÄFT reinforce

Unter-: Untermiete *f* GESCHÄFT sublease; **Untermieter, in** *m,f* GRUND subtenant, underlessee

unternehmen *vt* vw undertake

Unternehmen *nt* GESCHÄFT business, concern, firm, organization (*org.*), *Aktion* undertaking, operation, *Projekt* enterprise, establishment, VERWALT *Geschäft, Firma* enterprise; **~ in Arbeitnehmerhand** MGMNT employee-owned firm; **~ zur Aufspürung von Führungskräften** PERSON executive search firm; **im Besitz der Arbeitnehmer befindliches ~** MGMNT employee-owned firm; **~ einer besonderen Kategorie** BANK special bracket firm; **~ ohne eigene Rechtspersönlichkeit** RECHT unincorporated company; **~ für gemeinschaftliche Investition in**

übertragbaren Wertpapieren FINANZ undertakings for collective investment in transferable securities; **~ auf der grünen Wiese** PERSON greenfield site company (*BrE*); **~ mit hohen Liquiditätsreserven** VW cash cow; **~ der öffentlichen Hand** VW publicly listed company; **~ des öffentlichen Interesses** VW public interest company; **~ in Privatbesitz** VW privately-owned company; ♦ **~ gründen** GESCHÄFT establish a company; **ein ~ wieder hochbringen** VW nurse a business

Unternehmen: **Unternehmensangelegenheiten** *f pl* GESCHÄFT corporate affairs; **Unternehmensaufkäufer** *m* FINANZ corporate raider; **Unternehmensberater, in** *m,f* COMP, MGMNT management consultant; **Unternehmensberatung** *f* MGMNT management consulting; **Unternehmensberatungsfirma** *f* MGMNT management consultancy; **Unternehmensbereich** *m* VW division, functional area, group; **Unternehmensbesichtigung** *f* V&M facility visit; **Unternehmensbesteuerung** *f* STEUER corporate taxation; **Unternehmensbeteiligungsgruppe** *f* GESCHÄFT group of affiliated companies; **Unternehmenserfolg** *m* FINANZ, GESCHÄFT profit performance; **Unternehmensersparnisse** *f pl* FINANZ corporate savings; **Unternehmensertrag** *m* RECHNUNG corporate earning; **Unternehmensfinanzierung** *f* FINANZ corporate financing, business finance; **Unternehmensfinanzierungsausschuß** *m* FINANZ corporate financing committee; **Unternehmensform** *f* VERWALT business form; **Unternehmensforschung** *f* MGMNT, V&M operational research (*OR*), operations research (*OR*); **Unternehmensführung** *f* MGMNT business management, management, VERWALT business management, administration; **Unternehmensgeist** *f* GESCHÄFT spirit of enterprise; **Unternehmensgewinn** *m* RECHNUNG corporate profit; **Unternehmensgrafik** *f* FINANZ business graphics; **Unternehmensgründung** *f* BÖRSE company promotion, GESCHÄFT company formation; **Unternehmensgruppe** *f* GESCHÄFT group of companies, RECHNUNG group, V&M venture team; **Unternehmensimage** *nt* GESCHÄFT, V&M corporate image; **Unternehmensinvestition** *f* FINANZ corporate investment; **Unternehmenskonsum** *m* VW firm consumption; **Unternehmenskonzentration** *f* IND industrial concentration: **Unternehmensleitung** *f* MGMNT corporate management, management, operations management, venture management, VERWALT administration; **Unternehmensliquidität** *f* FINANZ company liquidity; **Unternehmensmodell** *nt* FINANZ, RECHNUNG corporate model; **Unternehmensneuorganisation** *f* GESCHÄFT company reorganization; **Unternehmensphilosophie** *f* GESCHÄFT company philosophy, company policy, corporate identity, corporate philosophy; **Unternehmensplan** *m* GESCHÄFT, VW corporate plan; **Unternehmensplanung** *f* GESCHÄFT corporate planning, MGMNT business planning; **Unternehmenspolitik** *f* GESCHÄFT, VW business policy, corporate policy; **Unternehmensportefeuille** *nt* BÖRSE, FINANZ business portfolio; **Unternehmensprofil** *nt* GESCHÄFT company profile; **Unternehmensrentabilität** *f* RECHNUNG overall rate of return; **Unternehmensrisikoausschluß** *m* VERSICH business risk exclusion; **Unternehmensspitze** *f* MGMNT, PERSON senior management, top management; **Unternehmensstatistik** *f* VW census of business (*AmE*); **Unternehmensstrategie** *f* GESCHÄFT, MGMNT, VW business strategy, company strategy, corporate strategy;

Unternehmensverwaltung *f* MGMNT administration, business management, VW business management; **Unternehmenswachstum** *nt* GESCHÄFT corporate growth; **Unternehmenswert** *m* RECHNUNG going-concern value; **Unternehmensziel** *nt* GESCHÄFT, V&M company objective, corporate goal, corporate objective, business objective; **Unternehmenszusammenschluß** *m* BÖRSE, FINANZ merger, VW business combination; **Unternehmenszweck** *m* GESCHÄFT corporate mission, company purpose

Unternehmer *m* GESCHÄFT operator, businessman, MGMNT entrepreneur, PERSON, RECHT contractor, GESCHÄFT, VW entrepreneur; **~ im Güterkraftverkehr** TRANSP hauler (*AmE*), haulier (*BrE*), trucking contractor (*AmE*); **~ des kombinierten Transports** TRANSP freight forwarder's combined transport (*FCT*); **Unternehmerfreiheit** *f* VW free enterprise; **Unternehmergeist** *m* MGMNT entrepreneurial spirit; **Unternehmergewinn** *m* RECHNUNG corporate earning; **Unternehmerhaftpflicht** *f* STEUER employer's liabilities

Unternehmerin *f* GESCHÄFT operator, businesswoman, MGMNT entrepreneur, PERSON, RECHT contractor, GESCHÄFT, VW entrepreneur

unternehmerisch *adj* VW entrepreneurial; **~es Risiko** *nt* GESCHÄFT entrepreneurial risk

Unternehmer: **Unternehmerreingewinn** *m* VW pure profit; **Unternehmerrisiko** *nt* BÖRSE, GESCHÄFT businessman's risk, entrepreneurial risk; **Unternehmerverband** *m* GESCHÄFT, VW trade association; **Unternehmerwagnis** *nt* GESCHÄFT entrepreneurial risk

Unternehmung *f* GESCHÄFT operation, *Projekt* enterprise, VERWALT establishment, VW *Geschäft, Firma* enterprise, venture; **Unternehmungsgeist** *m* GESCHÄFT *Initiative* enterprise

unteroptimieren *n* GESCHÄFT, VW suboptimize

Unteroptimierung *f* FINANZ, GESCHÄFT, VW suboptimization

unterordnen *vt* GESCHÄFT, POL, VW subordinate

Unterordnung *f* GESCHÄFT, POL, VW subordination; **Unterordnungsvereinbarung** *f* VERWALT subordination agreement

Unter-: **Unterpacht** *f* GESCHÄFT sublease; **Unterpächter, in** *m,f* GRUND underlessee; **Unterparagraph** *m* VERWALT subparagraph

unterprivilegiert *adj* GESCHÄFT, SOZIAL underprivileged

unterproduzieren *vt* IND underproduce

Unterprogramm *nt* COMP subprogram, subroutine, GESCHÄFT subroutine

unterproportional *adv* MATH under-proportionately

unterqualifiziert *adj* GESCHÄFT, PERSON underqualified

unterrepräsentieren *vt* GESCHÄFT underrepresent

Unterricht *m* GESCHÄFT class, lesson

unterrichten *vt* GESCHÄFT brief, notify, inform

unterrichtet: **~ sein über** *phr* GESCHÄFT be informed about

Unterricht: **Unterrichtsplan** *m* SOZIAL curriculum; **Unterrichtsstunde** *f* SOZIAL lesson

unterschätzen *vt* GESCHÄFT underestimate, underrate, undervalue

Unterschätzung *f* GESCHÄFT underestimation, undervaluation

unterscheiden 1. *vt* GESCHÄFT differentiate; ♦

~ zwischen [+dat] GESCHÄFT differentiate between, make a distinction between; **2. sich ~ von** *v refl* GESCHÄFT differ from

unterscheidend: ~ nach Groß- und Kleinbuchstaben *phr* COMP case-sensitive

Unterscheidung *f* GESCHÄFT differentiation, distinction, PATENT distinctiveness; ◆ **~ machen zwischen** GESCHÄFT draw a distinction between

unterscheidungsfähig *adj* PATENT distinctive

Unterscheidung: **Unterscheidungsvermögenstest** *m* V&M discrimination test

Unterschicht *f* vw underclass

unterschiedlich *adj* GESCHÄFT different, differing, varying; ◆ **in ~em Maße** GESCHÄFT with varying degrees

unterschiedlich: **~es Pensionierungsalter** *nt* PERSON multiple retirement ages; **~e Steuerinzidenz** *f* STEUER differential tax incidence

unterschlagen *vt* FINANZ misappropriate, GESCHÄFT *Gelder*, RECHT embezzle

Unterschlagung *f* FINANZ misappropriation, GESCHÄFT, RECHT embezzlement; **~ von Geldern** RECHNUNG, RECHT misappropriation of money, defalcation

unterschreiben *vt* GESCHÄFT *Vertrag* sign, undersign; ◆ **auf der punktierten Linie ~** VERWALT sign on the dotted line

unterschreiten *vt* GESCHÄFT undercut, vw undershoot

Unterschreitung *f* GESCHÄFT undercutting, vw undershooting

unterschrieben *adj* GESCHÄFT, KOMM signed (*sgd*); **nicht ~** *adj* GESCHÄFT, KOMM unsigned; ◆ **~ und mit Siegel versehen** RECHT signed and sealed

Unterschrift *f* COMP, GESCHÄFT, KOMM, RECHT, VERWALT signature; ◆ **ohne ~** COMP, GESCHÄFT, KOMM, RECHT, VERWALT unsigned

unterschriftsberechtigt: ~ sein *phr* BANK have signing authority

Unterschrift: **Unterschriftskarte** *f* BANK specimen signature card

unterschwellig: ~e Werbung *f* V&M subliminal advertising

unterste: ~r Bereich *m* V&M bottom end of the range; **~ Ebene** *f* PERSON *der Organisation* bottom; **~ Führungsschicht** *f* MGMNT, PERSON first-line managers; **~ Gewinnmarge** *f* FINANZ bottom-line profit margin

unterstehen: jdm ~ *phr* GESCHÄFT report to sb

unterstellen *vt* GESCHÄFT assume, presume, subordinate, vw put under the control of; ◆ **jdm direkt unterstellt sein** GESCHÄFT *Organisation, Unternehmenshierarchie* be directly responsible to sb

unterstellt: ~es Einkommen *nt* RECHNUNG imputed income; **~e Transaktion** *f* vw imputation; **~e Vertragsbestimmungen** *f pl* RECHT terms of a contract

Unterstellung *f* GESCHÄFT presumption

unterstreichen *vt* COMP *Text*, MEDIEN underline, underscore

Unterstreichung *f* COMP underline, underscore

unterstützen *vt* COMP support, GESCHÄFT back up, *fördern* promote, aid, support, encourage, subsidize, sponsor, *Projekt* back, MGMNT support, SOZIAL benefit, vw back up, aid

Unterstützung *f* COMP support, GESCHÄFT aid, boost, backing, backup, encouragement, promotion, subsidi-

zation, sponsorship, MGMNT support, SOZIAL benefit, vw *finanziell* backing, support; ◆ **mit ~ von** GESCHÄFT through the agency of

Unterstützung: **Unterstützungsabkommen** *nt* GESCHÄFT standby agreement; **Unterstützungsaktivitäten** *f pl* GESCHÄFT support activities; **Unterstützungsempfänger,in** *m,f* GESCHÄFT pauper; **Unterstützungsfonds** *m* **für die Belegschaft** PERSON staff provident fund, staff welfare fund; **Unterstützungskasse** *f* FINANZ provident fund; **Unterstützungsleistung** *f* GESCHÄFT, SOZIAL support service; **Unterstützungsmaßnahme** *f* MGMNT support activity; **Unterstützungszeitraum** *m* SOZIAL, VERSICH duration of benefits

untersuchen *vt* GESCHÄFT examine, inspect, investigate, study, survey, MGMNT, RECHT, V&M enquire, investigate

Untersuchung *f* GESCHÄFT study, survey, examination, IMP/EXP examination, MGMNT, PERSON study, RECHT, V&M *Ermittlung, Nachforschung* analysis, enquiry, investigation; **~ der betrieblichen Aufwendungen** RECHNUNG company expenditure survey (*AmE*); **~ der Staatsausgaben** vw public expenditure survey; **~ der Werbewirksamkeit** V&M impact study; **Untersuchungsauftrag** *m* GESCHÄFT fact-finding mission; **Untersuchungsausschuß** *m* POL *Parlament* committee of inquiry, select committee, RECHT commission of inquiry, investigating committee; **Untersuchungsbeauftragte(r) einer Gewerkschaft** *mf* [decl. as adj] PERSON union safety officer; **Untersuchungsgebühr** *f* FINANZ survey fee; **Untersuchungsgruppe** *f* GESCHÄFT *Marktforschung*, V&M focus group; **Untersuchungshaft** *f* RECHT custody; **sich in Untersuchungshaft befinden** *phr* RECHT be on remand; **in Untersuchungshaft behalten** *phr* RECHT remand in custody; **Untersuchungslabor** *nt* IND research laboratory

Untertage-: Untertagearbeit *f* IND underground working, underground mining

unterteilen *vt* GESCHÄFT, MGMNT subdivide

unterteilt *adj* GESCHÄFT, MGMNT subdivided; **~er Bildschirm** *m* COMP split screen

Unter-: **Unterteilung** *f* MGMNT subdivision; **Untertitel** *f* MEDIEN subtitle, V&M subhead, *Film* subtitle; **Unterveranlagung** *f* STEUER underassessment; **Untervergabe** *f* GESCHÄFT *Auftrag*, vw subcontracting

untervergeben *vt* GESCHÄFT *Auftrag* subcontract

Unter-: **Untervermietung** *f* GESCHÄFT sublease; **Unterverpachtung** *f* GESCHÄFT sublease; **Unterverpfändung** *f* BANK submortgage; **Untervertrag** *m* GESCHÄFT, IND, PERSON, RECHT subcontract; **Untervertreter,in** *m,f* GESCHÄFT subagent; **Unterverzeichnis** *nt* COMP subdirectory

unterwegs *adv* BANK in transit, GESCHÄFT en route; ◆ **~ nach** TRANSP bound for; **~ sein** TRANSP be on the road

Unterwerfung *f* POL, vw submission; **Unterwerfungsentscheidung** *f* RECHT consent decree

unterworfen: ~ sein *phr* GESCHÄFT be subjected to

unterzeichnen *vt* GESCHÄFT sign, undersign

Unterzeichner,in *m,f* POL, RECHT signatory; ◆ **~ von etw sein** POL, RECHT be a signatory to sth

Unterzeichnung *f* GESCHÄFT signature; **~ des Grundstücksvertrages** GRUND, RECHT real estate closing (*AmE*); ◆ **zur ~** GESCHÄFT, VERWALT for signature

Unterzug *m* TRANSP girder

untilgbar *adj* BÖRSE irredeemable

unübertroffen *adj* GESCHÄFT unrivaled (*AmE*), unrivalled (*BrE*)

unumgänglich *adj* GESCHÄFT unavoidable

ununterbrochen: ~e Forschung *f* V&M continuous research

unverändert *adj* BÖRSE unaltered, GESCHÄFT unaltered, unchanged

unverarbeitet *adj* COMP, GESCHÄFT unprocessed

unveräußerlich *adj* RECHT *unverkäuflich* inalienable

unverbindlich *adj* GESCHÄFT *Angebot* not binding, subject to confirmation, without engagement, without obligation; ~e Preisempfehlung *f* V&M recommended retail price (*RRP*); ~er Vertrag *m* GESCHÄFT nudum pactum

unverbürgt *adj* GESCHÄFT unvouched for, unwarranted, unauthenticated

unverdient *adj* GESCHÄFT, RECHNUNG, STEUER unearned; ~er Wertzuwachs *m* FINANZ, GRUND unearned increment

unveredelt *adj* GESCHÄFT unimproved

Unvereinbarkeit *f* FINANZ, RECHT variance

unvergleichlich *adj* GESCHÄFT unique, unparalleled

unverhältnismäßig *adj* ~ hoch *adj* GESCHÄFT excessive

unverheiratet *adj* RECHT, STEUER single

unverhohlen: ~e Diskriminierung *f* PERSON direct discrimination (*BrE*)

unverkäuflich *adj* GESCHÄFT unsalable (*AmE*); V&M not for sale; ~e Ware *f* V&M dead stock

unverkauft *adj* GESCHÄFT unsold, *Bestände* undisposed of; ~e Ware *f* V&M dead stock, unsold goods

unverlangt: ~e Güter *pl* und Dienstleistungen *f pl* V&M unsolicited goods and services

unvermeidbar: ~es Risiko *nt* BÖRSE inherent risk; ~es Wertpapierrisiko *nt* BÖRSE systematic risk

unvermeidlich *adj* GESCHÄFT inevitable, unavoidable

unvermindert *adj* VW undamped

unveröffentlicht *adj* GESCHÄFT, MEDIEN unpublished

unverpackt *adj* GESCHÄFT unpacked, IND *Produktion* in bulk, loose; ~e Ware *f* GESCHÄFT bulk goods

unversehrt *adj* GESCHÄFT undamaged, sound, intact

unversicherbar *adj* VERSICH uninsurable; ~es Risiko *nt* VERSICH prohibited risk; ~er Titel *m* VERSICH uninsurable title

unversichert *adj* VERSICH unassured, uninsured; ~e Risiken *nt pl* VERSICH excepted risks

unverteilbar: ~e Rücklage *f* RECHNUNG undistributable reserves

unverteilt: ~er Gewinn *m* RECHNUNG undistributed income, undistributed profit, undivided profit; ~e Zuteilung *f* GESCHÄFT undistributed allotment

Unverträglichkeit *f* COMP, GESCHÄFT incompatibility

unverzinslich 1. *adj* BANK noninterest-earning; **2.** *adv* ◆ ~ leihen BANK borrow interest-free

unverzinslich: ~e Einlage *f* BANK non-interest-bearing deposit, non-interest-earning deposit; ~e Werte *m pl* BÖRSE non-interest-bearing securities

unverzollt *adj* IMP/EXP, STEUER duty unpaid, in bond (*IB*)

unverzüglich 1. *adj* GESCHÄFT immediate, prompt; ◆ zur ~en Lieferung GESCHÄFT for immediate delivery; **2.** *adv* GESCHÄFT immediately, at once, promptly, without delay

unvollkommen: ~er Markt *m* VW imperfect market; ~e Verbindlichkeit *f* RECHT imperfect obligation

unvollständig 1. *adj* GESCHÄFT incomplete, RECHT *Dokument, Vertrag* inchoate, TRANSP *Lieferung* shortlanded; **2.** *adv* GESCHÄFT incompletely; ◆ ~ geliefert TRANSP short-shipped

unvollständig: ~e Lieferung *f* GESCHÄFT short delivery (*SD*); ~es Warenset *nt* V&M broken lot (*AmE*); ~er Wettbewerb *m* VW imperfect competition

unvollzogen *adj* RECHT executory

unvoreingenommen *adj* GESCHÄFT unbiased, unprejudiced, without prejudice

unvorhergesehen *adj* GESCHÄFT unanticipated, unforeseen; ~e Ausgaben *f pl* RECHNUNG unforeseeable expenditure; ~e Umstände *m pl* GESCHÄFT unforeseen circumstances

unvorhersehbar *adj* GESCHÄFT unforeseeable, *Schwierigkeiten* unpredictable

unvorteilhaft *adj* GESCHÄFT unfavorable (*AmE*), unfavourable (*BrE*)

unwesentlich *adj* GESCHÄFT immaterial, insignificant, irrelevant; ~er Wert *m* BÖRSE extrinsic value

unwiderlegbar *adj* RECHT irrebuttable, irrefutable

unwiderruflich *adj* BANK irrevocable, GESCHÄFT *Entscheidung* irreversible, RECHT irrevocable; ~es Akkreditiv *nt* BANK irrevocable letter of credit (*ILOC*); ~er Kredit *m* BANK irrevocable credit; ~e Kreditgrenze *f* BANK irrevocable credit line; ~er Kreditrahmen *m* BANK irrevocable credit line; ~e Prozeßvollmacht *f* RECHT warrant of attorney; ~es Treuhandverhältnis *nt* RECHT irrevocable trust

unwirklich *adj* GESCHÄFT artificial

unwirtlich *adj* GESCHÄFT inhospitable

unwirtschaftlich *adj* GESCHÄFT inefficient, uneconomic, uneconomical, VW inefficient, restrictive, uneconomic; ~e Arbeitspraktiken *f pl* PERSON, VW restrictive practices

Unwirtschaftlichkeit *f* GESCHÄFT, VW inefficiency

Unwissenheit *f* RECHT ignorance; ◆ sich auf ~ berufen RECHT plead ignorance

Unze *f* GESCHÄFT ounce (*oz*)

unzeitgemäß *adj* GESCHÄFT untimely

Unzufriedenheit *f* PERSON discontent; ~ am Arbeitsplatz PERSON discontent in the workplace

unzulänglich *adj* GESCHÄFT inadequate, insufficient, substandard, IND substandard

unzulässig 1. *adj* GESCHÄFT unsuitable, RECHT illegal, inadmissable; **2.** *adv* ◆ ~ gebrauchen GESCHÄFT abuse; ~ verwenden RECHT *Gelder* misapply

unzulässig: ~e Beeinflussung *f* GESCHÄFT undue influence; ~er Nachdruck *m* GESCHÄFT *Buch*, RECHT piracy; ~e Operation *f* COMP illegal operation; ~es Zeichen *nt* COMP illegal character

unzureichend *adj* GESCHÄFT insufficient, unsatisfactory

unzustellbar *adj* KOMM undeliverable; ~er Brief *m* KOMM dead letter; ~e Post *f* VW nixie mail (*AmE*), mail that is unreadable; ~er Scheck *m* BANK undeliverable check (*AmE*), undeliverable cheque (*BrE*)

unzuverlässig *adj* GESCHÄFT, PERSON unreliable

unzweckmäßig *adj* GESCHÄFT inexpedient, unsuitable

unzweifelhaft *adj* GESCHÄFT unquestionable

updaten *vt jarg* COMP actualize, update; ◆ **etw ~** *jarg* FINANZ, GESCHÄFT bring sth up to date

üppig *adj* GESCHÄFT abundant

Urabstimmung *f* PERSON strike ballot, strike vote

urbanisieren *vt* GESCHÄFT, VW urbanize

urbanisiert *adj* GESCHÄFT, VW urbanized

Urbanisierung *f* GESCHÄFT, VW urbanization

Urbanistik *f* VW urban economics

Urbarmachung *f* VW cultivation

Urbelege *m pl* RECHNUNG accounting papers

Urheberrecht *nt* COMP, RECHT copyright

urheberrechtlich *adj* RECHT copyright; **~ geschützt** *adj* GESCHÄFT proprietary, RECHT copyright reserved, protected by copyright; **~ geschütztes Werk** *nt* RECHT copyright material; **~ geschützte Werke** *nt pl* RECHT copyrighted works

Urheberrecht: **Urheberrechtsgesetz** *nt* GESCHÄFT Copyright Act; **Urheberrechtsschutz** *m* VW protection by copyright

Urk. *abbr* (*Urkunde*) PATENT, RECHT cert. (*certificate*)

Urkunde *f* (*Urk.*) FINANZ certificate (*cert.*), instrument, PATENT, RECHT, VERWALT certificate (*cert.*), instrument, legal document, *Grundstück, beurkundeter Vertrag* deed; **~ mit beschränkten Rechten** RECHT *Grundbesitz* deed restriction; **~ über besitzloses Pfandrecht** BANK letter of hypothecation; **~ in doppelter Ausfertigung** GESCHÄFT certificate in duplicate, charta partita; **~ über Sicherungsverträge** VW chattel paper; **Urkundenbetrug** *m* RECHT documentary fraud

Urkundenfälschung *f* RECHT adulteration of documents, falsification of documents; ◆ **~ begehen** RECHT alter a document, falsify a document; **jdn wegen ~ belangen** RECHT prosecute sb for forgery

urkundlich: **~e Unterlagen** *f pl* VERWALT dossier

Urladediskette *f* COMP boot disk

urladen *vt* COMP *Computer* bootstrap, boot up

Urlaub *m* FREI, PERSON holiday (*BrE*), vacation (*AmE*), leave, holiday leave (*BrE*), leave period; ◆ **auf ~** FREI on holiday (*BrE*), on vacation (*AmE*); **im ~** FREI on holiday (*BrE*), on vacation (*AmE*); **in ~** PERSON on leave; **in ~ gehen** FREI, GESCHÄFT, PERSON go on holiday (*BrE*), take a holiday (*BrE*), take a vacation (*AmE*), take leave

Urlauber, in *m,f* FREI holiday-maker (*BrE*), vacationer (*AmE*), vacationist (*AmE*)

Urlaub: **Urlaubsanspruch** *m* PERSON holiday entitlement; **Urlaubsaufteilung** *f* PERSON staggered holidays (*BrE*), staggered vacations (*AmE*), staggering of vacations (*AmE*), staggering of holidays (*BrE*); **Urlaubs- und Freizeitversicherung** *f* VERSICH holiday and leisure insurance; **Urlaubsgeld** *nt* PERSON *Arbeit* holiday allowance (*BrE*), holiday bonus (*BrE*), holiday pay (*BrE*), vacation allowance (*AmE*), vacation bonus (*AmE*), vacation pay (*AmE*); **Urlaubszeit** *f*

FREI holiday period, leave period, vacation period (*AmE*)

Urlehre *f* UMWELT primary standard, primary resource

Urmaß *nt* UMWELT primary resource, primary standard, standard measure

Ursache *f* GESCHÄFT, POL cause; ◆ **~, ohne die es nicht geht** RECHT causa sine qua non

Ursprung *m* COMP parent, source, FINANZ, GESCHÄFT source; ◆ **seinen ~ haben** GESCHÄFT originate

ursprünglich: **~er Auftrag** *m* V&M original order; **~e Laufzeit** *f* BÖRSE original maturity

Ursprung: **Ursprungsauszeichnung** *f* V&M informative labeling (*AmE*), informative labelling (*BrE*); **Ursprungsbeleg** *m* COMP master document; **Ursprungsbescheinigung** *f* IMP/EXP certificate of origin (*clo, co*); **Ursprungsbezeichnung** *f* IMP/EXP designation of origin, PATENT indication of source; **Ursprungsdatei** *f* COMP source file; **Ursprungsdaten** *nt pl* COMP source data; **Ursprungsdiskette** *f* COMP source disk; **Ursprungserklärung** *f* IMP/EXP declaration of origin; **Ursprungs- und Frachtzeugnis** *nt* IMP/EXP certificate of origin and consignment (*C/OC*); **Ursprungshinweis** *m* PATENT certification mark; **Ursprungsland** *nt* GESCHÄFT, IMP/EXP country of origin (*COO*); **im Ursprungsland beschädigt** *phr* IMP/EXP country-damaged; **Ursprungsprogramm** *nt* COMP source program; **Ursprungssprache** *f* COMP source language; **Ursprungsvermerk** *m* PATENT indication of source; **Ursprungszertifikat** *nt* IMP/EXP certificate of origin (*clo, co*); **Ursprungszeugnis** *nt* FINANZ, IMP/EXP certificate of origin (*clo, co*), IND certificate of manufacture

Urteil *nt* GRUND, RECHT judgment; ◆ **ein ~ anfechten** RECHT appeal against a judgment; **~ erlassen** RECHT pass judgment; **jds ~ entgegen** RECHT against sb's judgment

urteilen *vi* GESCHÄFT adjudicate

urteilsbefugt *adj* RECHT entitled to adjudicate; **~e Tribunale** *nt pl* RECHT tribunals entitled to adjudicate

Urteil: **Urteilsstaat** *m* RECHT state where the judgment was rendered; **eine Urteilsverkündung vorbehalten** *phr* RECHT reserve judgment; **Urteilsvermögen** *nt* GESCHÄFT, RECHT judgment

Uruguay-Runde *f* VW Uruguay Round

Usance *f* TRANSP usance; **Usancekredit** *m* BANK usance credit

User *m* COMP user

Usowechsel *m* BANK bill at usance, usance bill

USt *abbr* (*Umsatzsteuer*) BÖRSE transactions tax, STEUER turnover tax; **USt-Voranmeldung** *f* STEUER preliminary VAT return (*BrE*)

Utilitarismus *m* VW utilitarianism

UWG *abbr* (*Gesetz gegen Wettbewerbsbeschränkungen*) RECHT, VW Fair Trading Act

V

Vakuum *nt* IND vacuum; ◆ **das ~ füllen** GESCHÄFT fill the vacuum

Vakuum: **Vakuumverpackung** *f* IND vacuum packaging

Valdez-Prinzipien *nt pl* UMWELT Valdez principles

validieren *vt* COMP validate

Valoren *f pl* BÖRSE securities, GESCHÄFT valuables; **Valorenverlust** *m* VERSICH loss of specie; **Valorenversicherung** *f* VERSICH insurance of valuables

Valorisation *f* FINANZ, VW valorization

valorisieren *vt* FINANZ, VW valorize

Valorisierung *f* FINANZ, VW valorization

Valuta *f* BANK *Währung* currency, *Wertstellung* value, *Datum* value date, vw medium of exchange; **Valutawechsel** *m* BANK bill (*BrE*), currency draft

Valutenarbitrage *f* BÖRSE currency arbitrage

Valutierungsgewinn *m* BANK float

variabel 1. *adj* GESCHÄFT adjustable, subject to change, variable; **2.** *adv* ◆ **~ verzinslich** FINANZ adjustable, floating-rate, variable-rate, VERSICH adjustable

variabel: **variable Ausgaben** *f pl* FINANZ, RECHNUNG, TRANSP, VW variable expenses, variable costs; **variable Durchschnittskosten** *pl* VW average variable costs; **variabler Einschuß** *m* BÖRSE variation margin; **variable Gebühr** *f* GESCHÄFT variable charge (*VC*); **variable Gemeinkosten** *pl* FINANZ variable overhead cost; **variables Hypothekendarlehen** *nt* BANK adjustable mortgage loan (*AML*); **variables Kapital** *nt* FINANZ variable capital; **variable Kosten** *pl* FINANZ, RECHNUNG, VW variable costs, variable expenses; **variabler Kurs** *m* FINANZ variable rate; **variables Produktionssystem** *nt* IND floating production system; **variables Programm** *nt* FINANZ rolling program (*AmE*), rolling programme (*BrE*); **~ verzinsliche Aktie** *f* BÖRSE drop-lock stock; **~ verzinsliche Anleihe** *f* BÖRSE floating-rate note (*FRN*); **~ verzinsliche Hypothek** *f* BANK, GRUND variable-rate mortgage, adjustable rate mortgage (*ARM*), flexible-payment mortgage (*FPM*); **~ verzinslicher Schuldschein** *m* BANK variable-rate demand note; **variabler Zins** *m* BANK, FINANZ, VW variable rate; **variable Zinsen** *f pl* BANK, FINANZ, VW variable rates of interest; **variabler Zinssatz** *m* **für Ausleihungen** FINANZ variable lending rate (*VLR*)

Variabilität *f* GESCHÄFT, MATH, VW variability

Variable *f* COMP, GESCHÄFT, MATH variable; **Variablenauswahl** *f* MATH variables sampling

Variante *f* GESCHÄFT version

Varianz *f* MATH variance; **~ der Stichprobe** MATH sampling variance; **Varianzanalyse** *f* (*ANOVA*) MATH analysis of variance (*ANOVA*)

Variation *f* GESCHÄFT variation; **~ der Finanzierungsquoten** VW trading on the equity; **Variationskoeffizient** *m* MATH *Statistik* coefficient of variation

variieren 1. *vt* GESCHÄFT vary; **2.** *vi* GESCHÄFT vary

Variometer *nt* IND variometer

Vaterdatei *f* COMP *Datensicherung* father file

Vaterschaftsurlaub *m* PERSON paternity leave

VDR *abbr* (*Verband Deutscher Reeder*) TRANSP ≈ AASO (*Association of American Shipowners*)

VdZ *abbr* (*Verwaltung der Zollunion*) IMP/EXP ACU (*administration of the customs union*)

Veblen-Gut *nt* VW Veblen good

vegetativ: **~e Steuerung** *f* VW vegetative control

Vektor *m* MATH vector; **Vektorautoregression** *f* MATH vector autoregression (*VAR*)

Ventilator *m* IND fan

ventilieren *vt* IND ventilate

verabredet *adj* GESCHÄFT agreed; **~es Oligopol** *nt* VW collusive oligopoly

Verabredung *f* GESCHÄFT appointment; ◆ **eine ~ einhalten** GESCHÄFT keep an appointment; **eine ~ mit jdm treffen** GESCHÄFT make an appointment with sb

verabschieden *vt* GESCHÄFT *Resolution* adopt, PERSON *entlassen* dismiss, POL adopt, RECHT *Resolution* adopt, *Gesetz* pass, VERWALT adopt, VW *Budget* adopt

verabschiedet *adj* GESCHÄFT *Resolution* adopted, PERSON dismissed, RECHT *Resolution* adopted, *Gesetz* passed, VW *Budget* adopted

Verabschiedung *f* GESCHÄFT *einer Resolution* adoption, PERSON *Entlassung* dismissal, RECHT *einer Resolution* adoption, *eines Gesetzes* passing, VW *eines Budgets* adoption; **~ des Jahresabschlusses** *f* RECHNUNG approval of the accounts; ◆ **vor ~ des Haushalts** VW pre-Budget

verallgemeinert: **~es Tarif- und Präferenzsystem** *nt* IMP/EXP generalized system of tariffs and preferences (*GSTP*)

veralten *vi* GESCHÄFT become obsolete

Veralterung *f* GESCHÄFT obsolescence; **Veralterungsklausel** *f* VERSICH obsolescence clause

veraltet *adj* GESCHÄFT obsolete, outdated, outmoded; **~es Produkt** *nt* V&M obsolescent product; **~er Wirtschaftszweig** *m* VW old-line industry

veränderlich: **~er Zinssatz** *m* **für Hypotheken** BANK floating interest rate

verändern 1. *vt* GESCHÄFT alter, change, modify; **2. sich ~** *v refl* GESCHÄFT change; ◆ **sich beruflich ~** GESCHÄFT change one's job

verändert *adj* GESCHÄFT altered (*alt.*)

Veränderung *f* GESCHÄFT alteration, change, variance, variation; **~ des Preisniveaus** GESCHÄFT price level change

verankern *vt* RECHT *in Gesetz* enshrine, embody, lay down

veranlagen *vt* STEUER assess

veranlagt *adj* STEUER assessed; **nicht ~** *adj* STEUER unassessed

Veranlagung *f* STEUER assessment; **~ eines Fehlbetrages** STEUER assessment of deficiency; **Veranlagungsjahr** *nt* RECHNUNG, STEUER year of assessment; **Veranlagungsliste** *f* STEUER assessment roll;

Veranlagungszeitraum *m* (*Vz*) FINANZ, RECHNUNG, STEUER assessment year, income year, tax year

veranlassen *vt* GESCHÄFT bring about, cause, prompt

Veranlassung *f* GESCHÄFT cause, occasion

veranschlagen *vt* RECHNUNG estimate

veranschlagt *adj* RECHNUNG budgeted, estimated; **~e Ausgaben** *f pl* RECHNUNG budgeted cost; **~er Handelsertrag** *m* FINANZ estimated trading account

Veranschlagung *f* RECHNUNG estimation

veranstalten *vt* GESCHÄFT organize, MGMNT *Konferenz, Tagung* stage, hold

Veranstaltung *f* FREI event; **Veranstaltungsort** *m* MGMNT, VERWALT conference venue; **Veranstaltungszentrum** *nt* FREI entertainment complex

verantworten: zu ~ *phr* GESCHÄFT chargeable

verantwortlich *adj* GESCHÄFT accountable, answerable, responsible; ♦ **~ für** GESCHÄFT answerable for, responsible for; **~ gegenüber** GESCHÄFT answerable to; **jdn für etw ~ machen** GESCHÄFT hold sb responsible for sth

Verantwortlichkeit *f* GESCHÄFT responsibility, accountability

Verantwortung *f* GESCHÄFT responsibility; **~ für das Budget** POL budgetary powers; ♦ **die ~ für etw übernehmen** GESCHÄFT assume responsibility for sth, take responsibility for sth; **keine ~ für etw übernehmen** GESCHÄFT assume no responsibility for sth, take no responsibility for sth

Verantwortung: **Verantwortungsbereich** *m* GESCHÄFT area of responsibility; **Verantwortungsbereich** *m* **der Linie** MGMNT linear responsibility; **Verantwortungsgefühl** *nt* GESCHÄFT sense of responsibility; **Verantwortungsrechnung** *f* FINANZ, RECHNUNG responsibility accounting

verantwortungsvoll *adj* GESCHÄFT responsible; **~e Stellung** *f* PERSON *Hierarchie* position of authority

Verantwortung: **Verantwortungszentrum** *nt* FINANZ, MGMNT responsibility center (*AmE*), responsibility centre (*BrE*)

verarbeitbar *adj* COMP processable; **nicht ~** *adj* COMP unprocessable

verarbeiten *vt* COMP *Daten*, IND *Produktion* process

verarbeitend: ~e Industrie *f* IND manufacturing industry, processing industry

Verarbeitung *f* COMP processing, IND manufacturing, process; **~ im Hintergrundmodus** COMP *Multitasking* background processing; **Verarbeitungsansatz** *m* V&M incipient processing; **Verarbeitungsbetrieb** *m* IND processing plant; **Verarbeitungskosten** *pl* RECHNUNG conversion cost; **Verarbeitungsrechner** *m* COMP host; **Verarbeitungsstufe** *f* IND processing stage

verarmt *adj* FINANZ impoverished, poverty-stricken

Verarmungswachstum *nt* VW immiserizing growth

verauktionieren *vt* *infrml* GESCHÄFT sell by auction

verausgaben *vt* FINANZ disburse, expend, GESCHÄFT spend

verausgabt *adj* FINANZ disbursed; **nicht ~es Guthaben** *nt* RECHNUNG unspent cash balance; **nicht ~er Saldo** *m* RECHNUNG unspent cash balance

Verausgabung *f* FINANZ disbursement

Veräußerer *m* GESCHÄFT seller, GRUND vendor, RECHT assignee, transferor, grantor

veräußerlich *adj* GESCHÄFT salable (*AmE*), saleable (*BrE*), GRUND, RECHT alienable

veräußern *vt* FINANZ divest, GESCHÄFT sell, alienate, GRUND alienate, RECHT alienate, transfer, divest

veräußernd: ~e Gesellschaft *f* GESCHÄFT vendor company

Veräußerung *f* GESCHÄFT disposal, realization, sale, GRUND alienation, RECHT alienation, transfer (*tr.*, *tfr*); **~ einer Tochtergesellschaft** FINANZ, RECHT divestiture; **~ von Vermögen** RECHNUNG realization of assets; **Veräußerungsbefugnis** *f* RECHT power of sale; **Veräußerungsbeschränkung** *f* RECHT restraint of alienation; **Veräußerungserlös** *m* VW proceeds on disposal

Veräußerungsgewinn *m* RECHNUNG gain on disposal, STEUER capital gain, gain on disposal; ♦ **~ erzielen** STEUER make a capital gain

Veräußerung: **Veräußerungskurs** *m* **des Termingeschäftes** BÖRSE futures liquidation rate; **Veräußerungswert** *m* FINANZ residual value, RECHNUNG liquidating value, VW salvage value

verbal: ~e Fügung *f* POL word engineering

Verband *m* GESCHÄFT association, league; **~ Deutscher Reeder** (*VDR*) TRANSP association of German shipowners, ≈ AASO (*Association of American Shipowners*); **~ Europäischer Spediteure** TRANSP European Shippers' Council (*ESC*); **~ Südostasiatischer Nationen** POL, VW Association of South-East Asian Nations (*ASEAN*); **~ der Terminmakler und -händler** BÖRSE Association of Futures Brokers and Dealers (*AFBD*); **Verbandsbank** *f* BANK credit union; **Verbandskasten** *m* SOZIAL first-aid kit; **Verbandsmarke** *f* PATENT collective mark, PERSON certification mark; **Verbandszeichen** *nt* PATENT collective mark; **Verbandszeitung** *f* MEDIEN trade journal

verbergen *vt* GESCHÄFT conceal, hide

verbessern *vt* COMP upgrade, enhance, GESCHÄFT correct, enhance, improve, revise

verbessert *adj* COMP enhanced, upgraded, GESCHÄFT enhanced, improved, revised, MEDIEN revised; **nicht ~** *adj* GESCHÄFT *Situation* unimproved; **~er Grafikadapter** *m* (*EGA-Karte*) COMP enhanced graphics adapter (*EGA*); **~e Grafikanordnung** *f* COMP enhanced graphics array (*EGA*)

Verbesserung *f* BANK advance, COMP enhancement, GESCHÄFT enhancement, improvement, GRUND *Melioration* betterment, PATENT correction, RECHNUNG advance; **~ der Fertigkeiten** PERSON upskilling; **~ der Handelsbilanz** VW improvement in balance of trade; **~ der Kenntnisse** PERSON upskilling; **Verbesserungsauflage** *f* PERSON improvement notice (*BrE*)

verbesserungsfähig *adj* GESCHÄFT upgradable

Verbesserung: **Verbesserungsinvestition** *f* VW capital deepening; **Verbesserungspatent** *nt* PATENT improvement patent

verbieten *vt* COMP prohibit, GESCHÄFT disallow, RECHT ban, forbid, outlaw, prohibit

verbilligen *vt* GESCHÄFT cheapen, *Preis* reduce

verbilligt *adj* GESCHÄFT lower-priced, reduced; **~e Fahrkarte** *f* FREI, TRANSP excursion ticket

verbinden 1. *vt* COMP, GESCHÄFT link, connect, IND *Maschinen* bind; ♦ **~ mit** COMP, KOMM connect with; **2. sich ~ mit** *v refl* GESCHÄFT associate with, unite with

verbindlich *adj* GESCHÄFT authentic, firm, obligatory, RECHNUNG authentic, RECHT authoritative, *Entscheidung* binding; **~es Angebot** *nt* GESCHÄFT binding offer, firm offer, binding tender; ~e **Kursnotierung** *f* VW firm quotation; ~e **Offerte** *f* GESCHÄFT binding offer, firm offer; ~e **schiedsrichterliche Entscheidung** *f* RECHT binding arbitration; ~e **Vereinbarung** *f* RECHT binding agreement

Verbindlichkeit *f* RECHNUNG liability, RECHT commitment, liability, obligation; ◆ **ohne ~** GESCHÄFT without prejudice; **eine ~ hypothekarisch sichern** BANK secure a debt by mortgage

Verbindlichkeiten *f pl* RECHNUNG accounts payable, payables (*AmE*); **~ beim Jahresabschluß** RECHNUNG payables at year-end (*AmE*); **~ aus Lieferungen und Leistungen** RECHNUNG trade accounts payable (*AmE*); ◆ **~ übernehmen** RECHNUNG take over liabilities

Verbindlichkeit: **Verbindlichkeitskosten** *pl* BÖRSE liability cost

Verbindung *f* COMP, GESCHÄFT connection, link, KOMM circuit, liaison, PERSON joinder; ◆ **in ~ mit** GESCHÄFT in conjunction with; **in ~ mit jdm bleiben** KOMM keep in touch with sb; **eine ~ herstellen** GESCHÄFT forge a link; **sich in ~ setzen** GESCHÄFT liaise

Verbindungen *f pl* GESCHÄFT relations, KOMM communications; ◆ **~ mit jdm abbrechen** GESCHÄFT sever links with sb; **~ aufbauen mit** GESCHÄFT build links with

Verbindung: **Verbindungslinie** *f* V&M linkline; **Verbindungsmöglichkeiten** *f pl* KOMM communications; **Verbindungszeit** *f* COMP connection time

verborgen *adj* GESCHÄFT concealed; ~er **Mangel** *m* RECHT hidden defect; ~er **Schaden** *m* VERSICH hidden damage

Verbot *nt* GESCHÄFT ban, *Untersagung* prohibition; ◆ **ein ~ verhängen über** RECHT place a ban on

verboten: ~e **Ware** *f* IMP/EXP prohibited goods

Verbot: **Verbotsrecht** *nt* PATENT prohibition right

Verbrauch *m* VW consumption (*C*); **Verbrauch- und Aufwandsteuern** *f pl* STEUER excise duties, excise taxes

verbrauchen *vt* UMWELT expend, *Naturschätze* use, V&M consume

Verbraucher, in *m,f* V&M, VW consumer; **am ~ orientierte Marketingpolitik** *f* V&M consumer-led marketing policy; **Verbraucherantwort** *f* V&M consumer response; **Verbraucherausgaben** *f pl* VW consumer spending; **Verbraucherbefragung** *f* V&M consumer survey; **Verbraucherberatungsdienst** *m* V&M consumer advisory service; **Verbrauchererwartung** *f* V&M consumer expectation; **Verbraucherfrage** *f* V&M consumer issue; **Verbrauchergewohnheit** *f* V&M consumer habit; **Verbrauchergroßmarkt** *m* V&M hypermarket; **Verbraucherkredit** *m* BANK consumer loan; **Verbraucherkreditgesetz** *nt* RECHT Consumer Credit Protection Act (*AmE*), VERWALT Consumer Credit Act (*BrE*); **Verbrauchermacht** *f* VW consumer sovereignty; **Verbrauchermagazin** *nt* MEDIEN, V&M consumer magazine; **Verbrauchermarke** *f* V&M consumer brand; **Verbrauchermarketing** *nt* V&M consumer marketing; **Verbrauchernachfrage** *f* V&M consumer demand; **Verbrauchernutzen** *m* V&M consumer benefit; **Verbraucherorganisation** *f* V&M consumer organization

verbraucherorientiert: ~es **Produkt** *nt* V&M consumer-oriented product

Verbraucher: **Verbraucherpanel** *nt* V&M consumers' panel; **Verbraucherpolitik** *f* V&M consumer policy;

Verbraucherpreis *m* V&M consumer price; **Verbraucherpreisindex** *m* VW consumer price index (*CPI*); **Verbraucherprodukt** *nt* V&M consumer product; **Verbraucherprofil** *nt* V&M consumer profile; **Verbraucherreaktion** *f* V&M consumer reaction; **Verbraucherrecht** *nt* RECHT consumer law; **Verbraucherschutz** *m* RECHT, V&M consumer protection, consumerism; **Verbraucherschutzbewegung** *f* VW consumerism; **Verbraucherschützer** *m* RECHT, V&M consumerist; **Verbraucherschutzgesetz** *nt* RECHT, V&M law on the protection of consumers; **Verbraucherschutzgesetzgebung** *f* RECHT, V&M consumer protection legislation; **Verbrauchertest** *m* V&M consumer test; **Verbrauchertrend** *m* V&M consumer trend; **Verbrauchertreue** *f* V&M consumer loyalty

Verbrauchertum *nt* V&M consumerism

Verbraucher: **Verbraucherüberwachungsorganisation** *f* V&M consumer watchdog; **Verbraucherumfrage** *f* V&M consumer survey; **Verbraucherunternehmen** *nt* V&M consumer company; **Verbraucherverband** *m* V&M consumer organization, Consumers' Association (*CA*); **Verbraucherverhalten** *nt* V&M consumer behavior (*AmE*), consumer behaviour (*BrE*), consumer patterns; **Verbraucherwahl** *f* V&M consumer choice; **Verbraucherwerbung** *f* V&M consumer advertising; **Verbraucherwunsch** *m* V&M consumer want; **Verbraucherzufriedenheit** *f* GESCHÄFT consumer satisfaction

Verbrauch: **Verbrauchsartikel** *m* V&M article of consumption; **Verbrauchsausgaben** *f pl* VW consumer expenditure; **Verbrauchsausgaben-Erhebung** *f* VW consumer expenditure survey (*AmE*)

verbrauchsbedingt: ~e **Wertminderung** *f* RECHNUNG physical depreciation, physical deterioration

Verbrauch: **Verbrauchsgegenstand** *m* V&M article of consumption; **Verbrauchsgewohnheiten** *f pl* VW consumption pattern; **Verbrauchsgut** *nt* V&M consumer product; **Verbrauchsgüter** *nt pl* V&M consumer goods, consumer products, consumption goods; **Verbrauchssteuer** *f* IMP/EXP, STEUER commodity tax, excise, purchase tax, excise duty; **Verbrauchssteuergarantie** *f* IMP/EXP, STEUER excise bond; **Verbrauchssteuerharmonisierung** *f* IMP/EXP harmonization of excise duties

verbrauchsteuerpflichtig: ~e **Güter** *nt pl* STEUER excisable goods

verbraucht: **nicht ~** *adj* FINANZ *Mittel* unspent; **nicht ~es Guthaben** *nt* FINANZ unexpended balance; **nicht ~er Saldo** *m* FINANZ unexpended balance

verbrecherisch *adj* RECHT criminal, felonious

verbreiten *vt* KOMM *Informationen* spread, circulate, disseminate, MEDIEN *Zeitung* circulate, distribute

Verbreitung *f* KOMM *von Informationen* circulation, dissemination, MEDIEN *einer Zeitung* distribution, V&M circulation; **~ von Innovationen** V&M diffusion of innovations

Verbrennung *f* IND, UMWELT *von Müll* incineration; **Verbrennungsanlage** *f* IND, UMWELT combustion plant, incineration plant

verbrieft: ~es **Grundkapital** *nt* RECHNUNG *in der Bilanz* balance sheet value of shares; ~e **Leistungen** *f pl* VERSICH vested benefits; ~e **Versicherungsleistungen** *f pl* VERSICH vested benefits

verbuchen *vt* RECHNUNG enter, post, enter on the books, recognize; ◆ **zu ~** RECHNUNG accountable

Verbuchung *f* RECHNUNG entry, posting

Verbund *m* GESCHÄFT association, VW combine; **eine im ~ existierende Gesellschaft** *f* GESCHÄFT federated company

verbunden *adj* BANK affiliated, BÖRSE linked, GESCHÄFT affiliated, associated, IND allied, PERSON affiliated; ◆ **~ mit** COMP coupled with, GESCHÄFT affiliated to, associated with

verbunden: **~e Gesellschaft** *f* VW associate company; **~e Gewerbezweige** *m pl* IND allied trades; **~e Industriezweige** *m pl* IND allied industries; **~e Lebensversicherung** *f* VERSICH joint life assurance (*BrE*), joint life insurance (*AmE*); **~e Nachfrage** *f* VW joint demand, complementary demand; **~es Unternehmen** *nt* BÖRSE constituent company, GESCHÄFT affiliate, associated company, related company, VW affiliate company

verbünden: sich ~ mit *v refl* POL ally oneself with

Verbündete(r) *mf* [decl. as adj] POL ally

Verbund: **Verbundnetz** *nt* COMP mixed network, interconnection, IND National Grid (*BrE*); **Verbundverpackung** *f* TRANSP composite packaging; **Verbundvorteile** *m pl* VW economies of scope; **Verbundwerbeschau** *f* V&M tie-in display; **Verbundwerbung** *f* V&M association advertising, combined advertising, tie-in advertising

Verdacht: auf ~ *phr* GESCHÄFT on speculation (*on spec*)

verdanken *vi* +*dat* GESCHÄFT owe

verdecken *vt* GESCHÄFT conceal

verdeckt *adj* GESCHÄFT concealed, hidden; **~e Arbeitslosigkeit** *f* VW concealed unemployment, camouflaged unemployment; **~e Inflation** *f* VW camouflaged inflation, hidden inflation; **~e Steuer** *f* STEUER hidden tax; **~e Treuhand** *f* RECHT blind trust (*AmE*)

Verderb *m* GESCHÄFT *Waren* spoilage

verderben *vt* GESCHÄFT *Waren* deteriorate, perish, spoil

verderblich *adj* GESCHÄFT *Waren* perishable

verdeutlichen *vt* GESCHÄFT spell out

verdichten *vt* COMP collate

verdienen *vt* GESCHÄFT bring in, gain, PERSON earn

Verdienst *m* PERSON earnings, income; **Verdienstspanne** *f* V&M margin; **Verdienstspanne** *f* **der Bank** BANK banker's turn; **Verdienstspanne** *f* **des Jobbers** BÖRSE jobber's turn; **Verdienstvorhersage** *f* PERSON earnings forecast

verdient: ~er Betrag *m* VERSICH amount to be paid; **~e Prämie** *f* VERSICH earned premium

Verdoorn-Gesetz *nt* RECHT Verdoorn's law

verdoppeln 1. *vt* MATH double; **2. sich ~** *v refl* MATH double

Verdoppelung *f* GESCHÄFT duplication

verdrängen *vt* GESCHÄFT drive out, oust, *ersetzen* replace, supersede; ◆ **jdn aus seiner Stellung ~** PERSON oust sb from their job

Verdrängungstonnage *f* TRANSP displacement tonnage

Verdrängungswettbewerb *m* GESCHÄFT predatory competition, VW crowding out, destructive competition, predatory pricing policy, cutthroat competition

verdreifachen *vt* GESCHÄFT triple

Verdunkelung *f* RECHT collusion

veredeln *vt* IND finish, *Erdöl* refine

Veredelung *f* IND finishing, *Erdöl* refinement; **Veredelungserzeugnis** *nt* IND processed product

Verein *m* GESCHÄFT association, society; **~ für Kapitalanlageinteressenten** BÖRSE investment club

vereinbar *adj* GESCHÄFT compatible, RECHT *Aussagen* consistent; ◆ **~ mit** GESCHÄFT compatible with, RECHT consistent with

vereinbaren *vt* BANK arrange, GESCHÄFT arrange, *Preis, Verkaufsbedingungen* agree, agree upon, agree on, *vertraglich* stipulate

vereinbarend: zu ~er Satz *m* TRANSP rate to be agreed (*RTBA*)

Vereinbarkeit *f* GESCHÄFT compatibility

vereinbart *adj* GESCHÄFT, RECHT, VERSICH agreed; ◆ **wie ~** GESCHÄFT as agreed **zu einem ~en Preis** GESCHÄFT at an agreed price; **zum ~en Preis** GESCHÄFT at an agreed price

vereinbart: **~e Barwertklausel** *f* VERSICH agreed valuation clause; **~e Bewertungsklausel** *f* VERSICH agreed valuation clause; **~e Gebühr** *f* TRANSP agreed rate; **~e Koordination** *f* VW negotiated coordination; **~er Preis** *m* GESCHÄFT agreed price, TRANSP agreed rate; **~e Summe** *f* GESCHÄFT agreed sum; **~er Tarif** *m* TRANSP agreed rate; **~er Wert** *m* VERSICH agreed value; **~er Zahlungsbeginn** *m* VERSICH attachment date; **~e Zeit** *f* RECHT *Vertragsrecht* agreed period

Vereinbarung *f* GESCHÄFT *Abmachung* agreement, arrangement, accord, *Abschluß* bargain, *Voraussetzung* stipulation, RECHT executory agreed; **~ für ausgewählte Händler** BÖRSE selected dealer agreement; **~ einer Bankgarantie** BANK standby agreement; **~ von Bietern** GESCHÄFT knockout agreeement; **~ zur Sicherheit am Arbeitsplatz** PERSON job security agreement; **~ ohne zusätzliche einschränkende Bedingungen** GESCHÄFT agreement with no strings attached; ◆ **nach ~** GESCHÄFT by arrangement; **eine ~ mit jdm haben** V&M have an understanding with sb; **eine ~ treffen** GESCHÄFT enter into an agreement, make an arrangement

Vereinbarung: **Vereinbarungsentwurf** *m* RECHT draft agreement

vereinbarungsgemäß *adj* GESCHÄFT as per agreement

vereinfachen *vt* GESCHÄFT simplify

vereinfacht *adj* GESCHÄFT simplified; **~es Abfertigungsverfahren** *nt* IMP/EXP *Zoll* simplified clearance procedure (*SCP*); **~e betriebliche Altersversorgung** *f* PERSON simplified employee pension plan

Vereinfachung *f* GESCHÄFT simplification, IND, VW streamlining; **~ des Arbeitsplatzes** PERSON job simplification; **~ der Lohnstruktur** PERSON banding

vereinheitlichen *vt* GESCHÄFT standardize, unify

vereinheitlicht *adj* GESCHÄFT standardized, unified; **~e Formblätter** *nt pl* VERWALT aligned forms; **~e Herstellung** *f* IND standardized production

Vereinheitlichung *f* GESCHÄFT standardization, unification

vereinigen: sich ~ mit *v refl* GESCHÄFT unite with

vereinigt *adj* GESCHÄFT united, unified

Vereinigung *f* GESCHÄFT assembling, association, grouping, unification, POL union; **~ internationaler Schiffseigner** TRANSP International Shipowners' Association (*INSA*); **Vereinigungsfreiheit** *f* POL freedom of association

Vereint: **~e Nationen** *f pl* (*VN*) POL United Nations (*UN*), United Nations Organization (*UNO*)

vereinzelt *adj* GESCHÄFT sporadic

vereiteln *vt* RECHT defeat, frustrate, obstruct

Vereitelung *f* RECHT frustration; **~ des Vertragszwecks** RECHT frustration of purpose

Verelendung *f* VW immiseration; **Verelendungswachstum** *nt* VW immiserizing growth

vererbbar *adj* RECHT inheritable; **~e Vermögensgegenstände** *m pl* RECHT incorporeal hereditaments

Verfahren *nt* COMP *Programm* procedure, GESCHÄFT process, procedure, IND process, technique, MGMNT method, RECHT *Rechtsstreit* suit, proceedings, action, VERWALT procedure; **~ zur Bearbeitung von Frachtansprüchen** TRANSP cargo claims procedure; **~ gegen Unbekannt** RECHT action against persons unknown; **~ zur Regelung arbeitsrechtlicher Streitigkeiten** PERSON dispute procedure; **~ wegen Amtsanmaßung** RECHT *öffentliche Klage* quo warranto; ♦ **ein ~ gegen jdn anstrengen** RECHT bring a lawsuit against sb; **ein ~ für ungültig erklären** RECHT extinguish an action

verfahren: **~e Situation** *f* PERSON *Verhandlungen* deadlock, standoff, POL standoff

Verfahren: **Verfahrensanalyse** *f* GESCHÄFT process analysis; **Verfahrensantrag** *m* RECHT petition; **Verfahrenscode** *m* BÖRSE code of procedure; **Verfahrenskosten** *pl* RECHT costs of proceedings; **Verfahrensordnung** *f* RECHT rules of court, rules of practice, rules of procedure

verfahrensrechtlich *adj* GESCHÄFT procedural; **~e Frage** *f* MGMNT procedural issue; **~es Problem** *nt* MGMNT procedural issue; **~e Verzögerung** *f* MGMNT procedural delay

Verfahren: **Verfahrensregeln** *f pl* GESCHÄFT procedures, RECHT procedural rules, rules of procedure; **Verfahrensregeln** *f pl* **bei Entlassung** PERSON redundancy procedure; **Verfahrensregeln** *f pl* **zur Vermeidung von Arbeitskonflikten** PERSON dispute procedure; **Verfahrenstechnik** *f* IND process engineering; **Verfahrensvereinbarung** *f* PERSON procedure agreement, procedural agreement; **Verfahrensweise** *f* MGMNT course of action, policy, PERSON procedure

Verfall *m* BANK *Zeit* expiry, maturity, expiration, GRUND disrepair, dilapidation, decay, RECHT forfeit, forfeiture, lapse

verfallbar *adj* RECHT forfeitable; **nicht ~** *adj* RECHT, VW nonforfeitable

verfallen **1.** *adj* BANK due, expired, mature, FINANZ mature, GRUND dilapidated, RECHT lapsed, forfeited; **2.** *vi* BANK become due, expire, mature, FINANZ mature, GRUND become dilapidated, decay, RECHT lapse, VW *Preise* collapse

verfallen: **~es Konnossement** *nt* IMP/EXP stale bill of lading; **~e Mittel** *nt pl* RECHNUNG lapsed funds; **~e Sicherheit** *f* VERSICH forfeited security

verfallend *adj* IND ailing; **~e Industrie** *f* IND ailing industry, declining industry

Verfall: **Verfallgeschwindigkeit** *f* **des Zeitwertes** BÖRSE time value rate of decay; **Verfallsdatum** *nt* BANK *Wechsel* due date, GESCHÄFT expiration date (*AmE*), expiry date (*BrE*), PERSON date of expiry; **Verfallsdatum** *nt* **des Termingeschäftes** BÖRSE futures expiration date (*AmE*); **Verfallserklärung** *f* RECHT forfeiture; **Verfallsgeschwindigkeit** *f* BÖRSE rate of decay; **Verfallsklausel** *f* RECHT canceling clause (*AmE*), cancelling clause (*BrE*), forfeiture clause; **Verfallsmonat** *m* BÖRSE expiration month; **Verfallsrhythmus** *m* BÖRSE expiration cycle; **Verfallstag** *m* BÖRSE, GESCHÄFT date of maturity (*DOM*), PERSON date of expiry; **Verfallzeit** *f* BÖRSE cutoff time

verfälschen *vt* GESCHÄFT adulterate, RECHT *Original* falsify

Verfälschung *f* GESCHÄFT forgery

verfassen *vt* RECHT *Gesetz* draw up

Verfassen *nt* GESCHÄFT drafting; **~ eines Szenarios** MGMNT scenario-writing

Verfassung *f* POL, RECHT constitution

verfassungsgemäß *adj* POL, RECHT constitutional

verfassungsmäßig *adj* POL, RECHT constitutional; **~e Gründung** *f* POL constitutional foundation; **~er Streik** *m* PERSON constitutional strike

verfassungswidrig *adj* POL, RECHT unconstitutional; **~er Streik** *m* PERSON unconstitutional strike

verfechten *vt* GESCHÄFT advocate, support

Verfechter, in *m,f* GESCHÄFT advocate, champion, supporter

Verfehlung *f* PERSON misconduct

verfeinern *vt* IND refine

verfeinert *adj* IND refined

Verfeinerung *f* IND refinement

Verfilmung *f* MEDIEN filming, *eines Werkes* cinematographic adaptation; **Verfilmungsrechte** *nt pl* RECHT film rights

verflechten *vt* GESCHÄFT integrate, interlace, interlink

Verflechtung *f* GESCHÄFT integration, interlacing, interlocking, linkage, interdependence; **~ mit nachgelagerten Wirtschaftszweigen** VW forward linkage; **~ mit vorgelagerten Wirtschaftszweigen** VW backward linkage; **~ des Vorstands** MGMNT interlocking directorate

verfolgen *vt* GESCHÄFT *Plan* pursue, *Ausgaben* track, MGMNT, PERSON *Kurs* follow, RECHT prosecute, SOZIAL *Kurs* follow, TRANSP trace

Verfolgung *f* GESCHÄFT pursuit, RECHT prosecution; ♦ **in ~ dieses Ziels** GESCHÄFT in furtherance of this goal

Verfolgungsrecht *nt* RECHT *an unterwegs befindlichen Waren* right of stoppage in transitu

Verfrachter, in *m,f* TRANSP carrier; **~ von Sammelladungen** TRANSP consolidator

Verfremdungseffekt *m* V&M alienation effect

verfrüht *adj* GESCHÄFT premature

verfügbar *adj* GESCHÄFT available; **nicht ~** *adj* GESCHÄFT not available, unavailable; **~e Arbeitskräfte** *f pl* VW labor supply (*AmE*), labour supply (*BrE*); **~e Barliquidität** *f* FINANZ, RECHNUNG cash in hand, cash on hand; **~e Barmittel** *nt pl* FINANZ, RECHNUNG cash in hand, cash on hand, cash holdings; **~er Cashflow** *m* RECHNUNG available cash flow; **~es Einkommen** *nt* FINANZ, STEUER available income, disposable income, vw final income, personal disposable income (*PDI*); **~e Mittel** *nt pl* FINANZ, RECHNUNG available cash, available funds; **~e Mittel** *nt pl* **des Haushaltssektors** FINANZ personal sector liquid assets; **~er Saldo** *m* BANK, RECHNUNG available balance; **~er Speicherplatz** *m*

COMP available disk space; **~er Vermögenswert** *m* BÖRSE, RECHNUNG available asset; **~e Ware** *f* GESCHÄFT stock in hand; **~e Zeit** *f* COMP available time, GESCHÄFT time frame, MGMNT time budget

Verfügbarkeit *f* GESCHÄFT availability; **Verfügbarkeitsthese** *f* VW availability thesis

verfügend *adj* POL, RECHT executive

Verfügung *f* GESCHÄFT disposal, PATENT rule, RECHT decree, order, writ; **Verfügungsentwurf** *m* RECHT draft order; **Verfügungsgeschäft** *nt* RECHT *Vertragsrecht* disposition; **Verfügungsgewalt** *f* RECHT power of disposal, power of disposition; **Verfügungsmöglichkeit** *f* über **Bereitstellungskredit** FINANZ standby facility; **Verfügungsrahmen** *m* BANK, PERSON, VW cash limit; **Verfügungsrecht** *nt* RECHT jus disponendi, right of disposal, right to dispose of

verführend: **~e Kommunikation** *f* V&M persuasive communication

Vergabe *f* GESCHÄFT allocation, award; **~ im Submissionswege** BÖRSE allocation by tender (*BrE*); **~ von Zulieferungsverträgen** GESCHÄFT subcontracting

vergangen: **~es Jahr** *nt* GESCHÄFT past year

Vergangenheit: **in der ~ liegender Leistungsanspruch** *m* FINANZ past service benefit (*AmE*)

vergeben *vt* GESCHÄFT *Arbeit* allocate, award, *Auftrag* place, PERSON contract out, VW *Arbeit an Subunternehmer* farm out

Vergehen *nt* RECHT misdemeanour (*BrE*), misdemeanor (*AmE*), offence (*BrE*), offense (*AmE*)

vergehen: **sich ~ gegen** *v refl* RECHT infringe, offend against

Vergeltung *f* GESCHÄFT retaliation, RECHT retaliation, retribution, *Völkerrecht* retortion; ◆ **als ~ für** RECHT in retaliation for

Vergeltung: **Vergeltungsmaßnahme** *f* GESCHÄFT reprisal, retaliatory measure

Vergemeinschaftlichung *f* GRUND communication

vergesellschaften *vt* GRUND, POL, VW communize, nationalize

Vergesellschaftung *f* GRUND, VW, POL communization, nationalization

vergeuden *vt* GESCHÄFT *Zeit, Geld* squander, waste

vergeudet: **~er Frachtraum** *m* TRANSP waste cube

Vergeudung *f* GESCHÄFT *Zeit, Geld* squandering, wastage

vergewissern: **sich ~ über** *v refl* [+acc] GESCHÄFT *Preis* ascertain

Vergleich *m* GESCHÄFT comparison, arrangement, RECHT comparison, composition, compromise agreement, accord; **~ innerhalb eines Mediums** MEDIEN, V&M intramedia comparison; **~ schließen** RECHT arrange; **~ über Totalschaden** VERSICH arranged total loss; **~ zwischen verschiedenen Medien** MEDIEN, V&M intermedia comparison; ◆ **einen ~ schließen** GESCHÄFT come to an arrangement, compromise, effect a compromise

vergleichbar *adj* GESCHÄFT comparable; **~er Unternehmensertrag** *m* STEUER corporate equivalent yield; **~e Unternehmensrendite** *f* STEUER corporate equivalent yield; **~er Wert** *m* VW comparable worth (*CW*)

Vergleichbarkeit *f* GESCHÄFT comparability; **~ der Bezahlung** PERSON pay comparability

vergleichen **1.** *vt* GESCHÄFT compare, MEDIEN *Schriftstücke* collate; ◆ **~ mit** GESCHÄFT compare to; **2. sich ~** *v refl* RECHT arrange, compound; ◆ **sich ~ mit** BANK settle

vergleichend *adj* GESCHÄFT comparative; **~e Analyse** *f* VW comparative statics; **~e Aufstellungen** *f pl* FINANZ comparative statements; **~e Werbung** *f* V&M comparative advertising

Vergleich: **Vergleichsausschuß** *m* PERSON board of conciliation (*BrE*); **Vergleichsbasis** *f* RECHNUNG comparable basis; **Vergleichsbeschluß** *m* VW order for relief; **Vergleichsbilanz** *f* RECHT statement of affairs; **Vergleichsgrundstücke** *nt pl* GRUND comparables (*AmE*); **Vergleichsjahr** *nt* FINANZ, VW base year; **Vergleichs- und Konkursrecht** *nt* RECHT insolvency legislation; **Vergleichsmarke** *f* VW benchmark; **Vergleichsstatistik** *f* MATH benchmark statistics; **Vergleichstest** *m* GESCHÄFT comparison test; **Vergleichsverfahren** *nt* PERSON conciliation procedure, conciliation proceedings, RECHT arrangement proceedings, composition proceedings

vergleichsweise *adj* GESCHÄFT comparatively

Vergnügung *f* FREI amusement, entertainment; **Vergnügungscenter** *nt* FREI entertainment complex; **Vergnügungseinkauf** *m* V&M pleasure shopping; **Vergnügungsindustrie** *f* FREI, MEDIEN show business; **Vergnügungsreise** *f* GESCHÄFT junket (*infrml*), TRANSP junket (*infrml*), pleasure trip; **Vergnügungssteuer** *f* STEUER entertainment tax

vergr. *abbr* (*vergriffen*) GESCHÄFT sold out, MEDIEN op (*out of print*)

vergriffen *adj* (*vergr.*) GESCHÄFT sold out, MEDIEN out of print (*op*)

vergrößern *vt* GESCHÄFT enlarge, augment, increase, add to

vergrößert: **~e Kopie** *f* KOMM enlarged copy

Vergrößerung *f* GESCHÄFT addition, augmentation, increase, TRANSP jumboization

Vergünstigung *f* MGMNT, PERSON concession, perk (*infrml*), perquisite (*frml*), privilege; **~ für leitende Angestellte** MGMNT, PERSON executive perquisite (*frml*) (*executive perk*)

vergüten *vt* BANK allow

Vergütung *f* GESCHÄFT remuneration, STEUER emolument; **~ für leitende Angestellte** MGMNT executive compensation, executive remuneration; **~ für schnelles Entladen** KOMM, TRANSP dispatch money; **Vergütungsplan** *m* **der Anleger** BÖRSE investors' compensation scheme (*BrE*)

verhaften *vt* RECHT arrest, take into custody

Verhaftung *f* RECHT arrest

Verhalten *nt* PERSON behavior (*AmE*), behaviour (*BrE*), conduct; **Verhaltensänderung** *f* PERSON *Psychologie* behavior modification (*AmE*), behaviour modification (*BrE*); **Verhaltensforschung** *f* MGMNT, V&M behavioral research (*AmE*), behavioural research (*BrE*); **Verhaltensgitter** *nt* MGMNT managerial grid; **Verhaltenskodex** *m* GESCHÄFT code of conduct, code of ethics, code of practice; **Verhaltenslinie** *f* VW behavior line (*AmE*), behaviour line (*BrE*); **Verhaltensregeln** *f pl* GESCHÄFT code of practice; **Verhaltensskala** *f* V&M attitude scale; **Verhaltensstudie** *f* V&M attitude survey;

Verhaltenswissenschaft *f* MGMNT, V&M behavioral science (*AmE*), behavioural science (*BrE*)

Verhältnis *nt* GESCHÄFT relationship, MATH proportion, RECHNUNG ratio; **~ Aufwand zu Umsatzerlös** VW expense ratio; **~ von Auslandsverschuldung zu Exporten** VW ratio of external debt to exports; **~ zwischen direkten und indirekten Steuern** STEUER, VW direct-indirect taxes ratio; **~ Dividende zu Aktienkurs** FINANZ dividend-price ratio; **~ Einschuß-Kapital** BÖRSE gearing (*BrE*), leverage (*AmE*); **~ zwischen Ersparnissen und Einkommen** FINANZ savings-to-income ratio; **~ von Fremd- zu Eigenkapital** FINANZ gearing (*BrE*), leverage (*AmE*); **~ zwischen Fremd- und Eigenkapital** FINANZ gearing ratio (*BrE*), leverage ratio (*AmE*); **~ Gebäudefläche-Grundstücksfläche** GRUND floor-area ratio; **~ des geringen Wertes zu hohem Gewicht** TRANSP low value to high weight ratio; **~ von Gewinn zu Dividenden** RECHNUNG dividend cover; **~ von hohem Wert zu geringem Gewicht** TRANSP high value to low weight ratio; **~ von Kapital zu Arbeitskosten** VW capital-labor ratio (*AmE*), capital-labour ratio (*BrE*); **~ Lagervorräte zu Forderungen** VW ratio of merchandise to receivables; **~ der leitenden Angestellten zur Belegschaft** MGMNT, PERSON *Unternehmensstruktur* management ratio; **~ von Obligationen und Vorzugsaktien zu Stammaktie** BÖRSE gearing (*BrE*), leverage (*AmE*); **~ Preis-Qualität** GESCHÄFT quality-price ratio; **~ von Reingewinn zum Eigenkapital** RECHNUNG net income to net worth ratio; **~ von Technologie und Markt** GESCHÄFT technology and market interface; **~ Vorräte zur Gesamtproduktion** GESCHÄFT stock output ratio; **~ Wert zu Gewicht** TRANSP value to weight ratio; ♦ **im ~ zu** GESCHÄFT relative to, MATH in proportion to; **über seine Verhältnisse leben** GESCHÄFT live beyond one's means

verhältnismäßig 1. *adj* GESCHÄFT pro rata, proportionate, proportional, relative; **2.** *adv* GESCHÄFT pro rata, proportionately, proportionally, relatively

verhältnismäßig: **~e Konsolidierung** *f* RECHNUNG proportional consolidation

Verhältnismäßigkeit *f* GESCHÄFT proportionality

Verhältnis: **Verhältniswahl** *f* POL proportional representation

verhandelbar *adj* GESCHÄFT negotiable, RECHT prosecutable

verhandeln 1. *vt* GESCHÄFT negotiate, RECHT *Fall* hear; **2.** *vi* GESCHÄFT negotiate; ♦ **~ mit** GESCHÄFT deal with; **mit jdm ~** GESCHÄFT bargain with sb

Verhandlung *f* GESCHÄFT negotiation, negotiations, bargaining, RECHT proceedings; **~ zwischen unabhängigen Partnern** GESCHÄFT arm's-length bargaining; **Verhandlungsebene** *f* PERSON bargaining level; **Verhandlungsform** *f* PERSON bargaining form; **Verhandlungsmacht** *f* GESCHÄFT bargaining power; **Verhandlungsmaschinerie** *f* PERSON negotiating machinery; **Verhandlungsniederschrift** *f* GESCHÄFT protocol; **Verhandlungspaket** *nt* PERSON package deal

Verhandlungspartner, in *m,f* GESCHÄFT negotiating partner, party to a negotiation, PERSON *Gewerkschaften* bargaining agent, bargaining partner

Verhandlung: **Verhandlungsposition** *f* GESCHÄFT bargaining position, negotiation position; **Verhandlungsprozedur** *f* PERSON negotiating procedure; **Verhandlungsrahmen** *m* PERSON scope of bargaining; **Verhandlungsspielraum** *m* PERSON bargaining range, bargaining scope, negotiating range, room to negotiate; **Verhandlungsstärke** *f* GESCHÄFT bargaining power; **Verhandlungsstrategie** *f* GESCHÄFT negotiation strategy; **Verhandlungsstruktur** *f* PERSON bargaining structure; **Verhandlungstheorie** *f* **des Lohns** PERSON bargaining theory of wages; **Verhandlungstisch** *m* GESCHÄFT round table, bargaining table, conference table, negotiating table

verhängen *vt* RECHT impose

Verhängung *f* RECHT imposition; **~ einer Geldbuße** RECHT imposition of a fine

verheimlichen *vt* GESCHÄFT conceal

verheimlicht *adj* GESCHÄFT concealed

verheiratet *adj* RECHT, STEUER married

Verheiratetenabzug *m* STEUER marriage deduction

verhindern *vt* GESCHÄFT prevent, provide against, RECHT *Annahme eines Gesetzentwurfes* block

Verhinderung *f* GESCHÄFT prevention; **~ der Entstehung von Schadensersatzansprüchen** VERSICH claims prevention; **~ von Seebetrug** TRANSP maritime fraud prevention

verhüten *vt* GESCHÄFT prevent

Verhütung *f* GESCHÄFT prevention

verifizieren *vt* GESCHÄFT verify

Verifizierung *f* GESCHÄFT verification

verjähren *vi* RECHT become prescribed (*AmE*), become statute-barred, fall under the statute of limitations

verjährt *adj* RECHT barred by the lapse of time, statute-barred, time-barred; **~es Konnossement** *nt* IMP/EXP stale bill of lading

Verjährung *f* RECHT *Vertragsrecht* limitation, limitation of actions, limitation of time, negative prescription, statute of limitations; **Verjährungsfrist** *f* RECHT term of limitation

Verkauf *m* GESCHÄFT sale, selling, vending, V&M sale, sales department, selling, vending; **~ von Anlagen** FINANZ negative investment; **~ mit anschließender Rückmiete** GESCHÄFT sale and leaseback; **~ aufgrund von Erinnerungswerbung** V&M repeat sales; **~ durch Auktion** V&M auction sale; **~ zum Ausgleich** BÖRSE evening up, selling for the settlement; **~ auf Baisse** BÖRSE bear sale; **für den ~ bestimmte Anbaufrucht** *f* UMWELT cash crop; **~ des Betriebs an Teile der Belegschaft** PERSON employee buyout; **~ durch Dritte** V&M third-party sale; **~ vor Fertigstellung** GRUND presale; **~ von Kaufoptionen** BÖRSE call writing; **~ zur Lieferung** BÖRSE sale for delivery; **~ von Produkten zum gleichen Preis** V&M price lining; **~ auf Ratenzahlung** GESCHÄFT installment sale (*AmE*), instalment sale (*BrE*); **~ zu Schleuderpreisen** V&M dumping; **~ von Spezialartikeln** V&M speciality selling; **~ mit Umtauschrecht** V&M sale or exchange; **~ unter Druck** V&M pressure selling; **~ unter Eigentumvorbehalt** BANK Romalpa sale; **~ unter Einstandspreis** V&M loss-pricing; **~ unter dem Ladentisch** *infrml* V&M under-the-counter sale (*infrml*); **~ durch Versteigerung** V&M sale by auction; **~ von Waren** V&M sale of goods; ♦ **einen ~ tätigen** BÖRSE make a sale

verkaufen 1. *vt* FINANZ realize, GESCHÄFT sell, sell off, sell up; ♦ **zu ~** V&M for sale; **gegen etw ~** BÖRSE write against sth; **zu viel ~** V&M oversell; **2. sich ~** *v refl* GESCHÄFT *Produkte* sell

Verkäufer *m* PERSON, V&M salesman, salesperson, vendor, *Laden* shop assistant (*BrE*), sales clerk (*AmE*); **~ einer Rückprämie** BÖRSE giver for a put; **~ einer ungedeckten Kaufoption** BÖRSE uncovered call writer; **~ einer ungedeckten Option** BÖRSE uncovered writer; **~ einer Verkaufsoption** BÖRSE put writer; **Verkäuferfinanzierung** *f* FINANZ vendor finance

Verkäuferin *f* PERSON, V&M saleswoman, salesperson, vendor, *Laden* shop assistant (*BrE*), sales clerk (*AmE*)

Verkäufer: **Verkäufermarkt** *m* BÖRSE, GRUND, VW seller's market; **Verkäuferoption** *f* BÖRSE seller's option (*S. O.*)

verkäuflich *adj* FINANZ realizable, GESCHÄFT marketable, vendible, V&M saleable

Verkauf: **Verkaufsabteilung** *f* V&M sales department; **Verkaufsagent** *m* PERSON, V&M sales agent; **Verkaufsaktion** *f* V&M sales campaign; **Verkaufsanalyse** *f* V&M sales analysis; **Verkaufsangebot** *nt* V&M announcement of sale; **Verkaufsankündigung** *f* V&M announcement of sale; **Verkaufsanstrengungen** *f pl* V&M sales effort, sales push; **Verkaufsargument** *nt* V&M selling point, sales pitch; **Verkaufsausrüstung** *f* V&M sales kit; **Verkaufsaussichten** *f pl* V&M sales prospects; **Verkaufsautomat** *m* GESCHÄFT slot machine, vending machine; **Verkaufsbedingungen** *f pl* V&M conditions of sale, terms of sale; **Verkaufsbereich** *m* V&M sales area; **Verkaufs- und Berichterstattungsvereinbarung** *f* V&M sell and report agreement; **Verkaufsbestand** *m* V&M sales portfolio; **Verkaufsbuch** *nt* V&M sold ledger; **Verkaufsbüro** *nt* V&M sales office; **Verkaufschef, in** *m,f* MGMNT, PERSON, V&M sales manager, sales director; **Verkaufsdirektor, in** *m,f* MGMNT, PERSON, V&M sales executive, sales manager; **Verkaufserfolg** *m* V&M sales record, track record; **Verkaufserlös** *m* V&M proceeds of sales, sales receipt, sales returns; **Verkaufsertrag** *m* RECHNUNG, V&M return on sales; **Verkaufsetat** *m* V&M sales budget; **Verkaufsfiliale** *f* V&M branch store; **Verkaufsfläche** *f* V&M selling space, shop floor; **Verkaufsförderer, in** *m,f* PERSON, V&M development director

verkaufsfördernd *adj* V&M promotional; **~es Programm** *nt* V&M promotional platform

Verkaufsförderung *f* V&M promotion (*promo*), sales promotion; **~ im Laden** V&M store promotion; **~ durch Nachlässe** V&M below-the-line promotion; **~ durch Symbolfigur** V&M character merchandising; **~ am Verkaufsort** V&M point-of-sale promotion; **Verkaufsförderungsbonus** *m* V&M promotional allowance; **Verkaufsförderungsbudget** *nt* V&M promotional budget; **Verkaufsförderungskosten** *pl* FINANZ, V&M promotion cost; **Verkaufsförderungsmix** *nt* V&M promotion mix; **Verkaufsförderungspolitik** *f* V&M promotional policy

Verkauf: **Verkaufsforschung** *f* V&M sales research; **Verkaufsgebiet** *nt* V&M sales area, trading area; **Verkaufsgespräch** *nt* V&M sales talk, pitch; **Verkaufsgewandtheit** *f* V&M salesmanship; **Verkaufsgüter** *nt pl* V&M sales goods; **Verkaufshandbuch** *nt* V&M sales manual; **Verkaufshilfe** *f* V&M sales aid; **Verkaufshöhepunkt** *m* BÖRSE selling climax; **Verkaufsinstrumente** *nt pl* V&M sales tools; **Verkaufsinterview** *nt* V&M sales interview; **Verkaufsjournal** *nt* V&M sold daybook, sold ledger; **Verkaufskampagne** *f* V&M sales campaign; **Verkaufskladde** *f* V&M sold daybook; **Verkaufskommissionär** *m* PERSON commission merchant, commission salesman; **Verkaufskontenbuch** *nt*

RECHNUNG sales ledger; **Verkaufskontingent** *nt* V&M sales quota; **Verkaufskonto** *nt* BANK trading account; **Verkaufskontrolle** *f* V&M sales control; **Verkaufskosten** *pl* FINANZ cost of sales, cost ratio, RECHNUNG selling expenses; **Verkaufskurs** *m* BÖRSE sellers' rate; **Verkaufskurs** *m* **der Bank** BANK bank selling rate; **Verkaufsleiter, in** *m,f* MGMNT, PERSON, V&M sales executive, sales director; **Verkaufs- und Lieferbedingungen** *f pl* GESCHÄFT terms and conditions; **Verkaufs- und Lieferbedingungen** *f pl* **einer Emission** BÖRSE terms and conditions of an issue; **Verkaufsmanagement** *nt* V&M sales management; **Verkaufsmerkmal** *nt* V&M sales feature; **Verkaufsmodell** *nt* V&M mock-up; **Verkaufsniederlassung** *f* V&M sales agency; **Verkaufsoffensive** *f* V&M sales offensive; **Verkaufsoptionsdelta** *nt* BÖRSE put delta; **Verkaufsordner** *m* V&M sales folder; **Verkaufsorganisation** *f* V&M sales organization; **Verkaufsorientierung** *f* V&M sales orientation; **Verkaufsort** *m* V&M point-of-sale (*POS*); **Verkaufspersonal** *nt* V&M sales force, sales personnel; **Verkaufsplanung** *f* V&M sales planning; **Verkaufspolitik** *f* V&M sales approach, sales policy, selling policy; **Verkaufsportefeuille** *nt* V&M sales portfolio; **Verkaufsposition** *f* **am Optionsmarkt** BÖRSE short option position; **Verkaufsposition** *f* **am Terminkontraktmarkt** BÖRSE short futures position; **Verkaufspotential** *nt* V&M sales potential; **Verkaufsprämie** *f* V&M push money (*AmE*), sale commission; **Verkaufspreis** *m* V&M selling price; **Verkaufsproduktion** *f* VW cash crop; **Verkaufsprogramm** *nt* V&M sales platform; **Verkaufsprospekt** *m* V&M sales literature; **Verkaufsprovision** *f* BÖRSE selling concession, FINANZ selling commission, V&M sale commission, selling commission; **Verkaufsprovision** *f* **als Anreiz** V&M incentive commission; **Verkaufspsychologie** *f* V&M psychology of selling; **Verkaufspunkt** *m* V&M point-of-sale (*POS*); **Verkaufsrechnung** *f* GESCHÄFT invoice, sales invoice; **Verkaufsreichweite** *f* V&M sales coverage; **Verkaufsschalter** *m* V&M trade counter; **Verkaufsschlager** *m* MEDIEN *Buch, Schallplatte* best seller, V&M hot-selling line, top-selling article; **Verkaufsschulung** *f* V&M sales training; **Verkaufssicherungsgeschäft** *nt* BÖRSE short hedge; **Verkaufsstelle** *f* V&M point of purchase, point-of-sale (*POS*), sales outlet, outlet; **Verkaufsstellenleiter, in** *m,f* V&M sales office manager; **Verkaufssyndikat** *nt* BÖRSE distributing syndicate; **Verkaufstalent** *nt* V&M salesmanship; **Verkaufstätigkeit** *f* V&M sales activity; **Verkaufstechnik** *f* V&M sales technique; **Verkaufstheke** *f* V&M trade counter; **Verkaufstisch** *m* V&M trade counter; **Verkaufsstrategie** *f* V&M sales strategy; **Verkaufsumfrage** *f* V&M sales enquiry; **Verkaufsurkunde** *f* RECHT bill of sale; **Verkaufsvertreter, in** *m,f* PERSON, V&M sales representative (*rep, sales rep*); **Verkaufsvolumen** *nt* V&M sales volume; **Verkaufsvoraussage** *f* V&M sales forecast; **Verkaufsvorschlag** *m* V&M selling proposition; **Verkaufsvorsprung** *m* V&M sales lead; **Verkaufswert** *m* FINANZ current value, V&M sale value; **Verkaufswettbewerb** *m* V&M sales contest; **Verkaufswiderstand** *m* V&M sales resistance; **Verkaufswirksamkeitstest** *m* V&M sales effectiveness test; **Verkaufsziel** *nt* V&M sales goal, sales objective, sales target; **Verkaufszone** *f* V&M trading area; **Verkaufszusage** *f* V&M promise to sell

verkauft: **~e Auflage** *f* V&M net paid circulation; **~e**

Kaufoption *f* BÖRSE written call; **~e Option** *f* BÖRSE written option; **~e Verkaufsoption** *f* BÖRSE written put

Verkehr *m* BÖRSE dealing, trading, KOMM communications, TRANSP traffic, transport, transportation, VW *Banknoten* circulation; **Verkehrsamt** *nt* FREI tourist office, Tourist Board (*BrE*); **Verkehrsanalyse** *f* TRANSP traffic analysis; **Verkehrsanbindung** *f* TRANSP transport link

verkehrsarm: **~er Tag** *m* KOMM, TRANSP off-peak day

Verkehr: **Verkehrsaufkommen** *nt* TRANSP volume of traffic; **Verkehrsdichte** *f* TRANSP traffic density; **Verkehrseinrichtung** *f* TRANSP transport facilitation; **Verkehrseinrichtungen** *f pl* TRANSP transport facilities; **Verkehrsfluß** *m* TRANSP traffic flow; **Verkehrsgemisch** *nt* TRANSP traffic mixture; **Verkehrsgesetz** *nt* RECHT, TRANSP Transport Act (*BrE*); **Verkehrsgrenze** *f* TRANSP plying limit

verkehrsgünstig *adj* GESCHÄFT accessible, with easy access to public transport

Verkehr: **Verkehrshinweis** *m* TRANSP traffic forecast; **Verkehrskontrolle** *f* TRANSP traffic control; **Verkehrskontrollturm** *m* TRANSP traffic control tower; **Verkehrslenkungsprogramm** *nt* TRANSP traffic separation scheme; **Verkehrsminister, in** *m,f* TRANSP Secretary of State for Transport (*BrE*); **Verkehrsmittelwerbung** *f* TRANSP, V&M transport advertising, transportation advertising; **Verkehrsnetz** *nt* TRANSP communications; **Verkehrspapier** *nt* VW chattel paper; **Verkehrsplanung** *f* TRANSP traffic planning; **Verkehrspotential** *nt* TRANSP traffic potential; **Verkehrsrechte** *nt pl* TRANSP traffic rights; **Verkehrsschiff** *nt* TRANSP service boat; **Verkehrssondermitteilung** *f* TRANSP special traffic notice (*STN*); **Verkehrsstau** *m* TRANSP traffic jam, traffic congestion; **Verkehrstote** *m pl* TRANSP road fatalities; **Verkehrstrend** *m* TRANSP traffic trend

verkehrsüblich: **~e Sorgfalt** *f* RECHT due diligence, ordinary care, ordinary diligence

Verkehr: **Verkehrsverbindung** *f* TRANSP communications, transport link, connection; **Verkehrsverein** *m* FREI tourist office, Tourist Board (*BrE*); **Verkehrswert** *m* FINANZ market value; **Verkehrswertschätzung** *f* FINANZ estimate of current market value; **Verkehrswesen** *nt* TRANSP transport system; **Verkehrszählung** *f* TRANSP traffic count; **Verkehrszeichen** *nt* TRANSP traffic sign

verketten *vt* COMP chain, concatenate

Verkettung *f* COMP chaining, concatenation

verklagen *vt* RECHT sue; ◆ **jdn ~** RECHT bring an action against sb, sue sb

verklappen *vt* UMWELT dump

Verklappung *f* UMWELT dumping; **Verklappungsstandards** *m pl* UMWELT dumping standards

verklausulieren *vt* RECHT guard by clauses, hedge in by clauses

verklausuliert: **~er Frachtbrief** *m* IMP/EXP claused bill of lading

verkleben *vt* VERWALT tape

verkleiden *vt* IND cover

Verkleidung *f* IND cover

verkleinern *vt* GESCHÄFT scale down, reduce in size, MGMNT, PERSON *Personalbestand* downsize, slim down

Verkleinerung *f* GESCHÄFT reduction in size, scaling-down, MGMNT, PERSON *Personalbestand* downsizing

Verknüpfungsmodell *nt* VW linkage model (*BrE*)

verkörpern *vt* PATENT, RECHT embody

Verkörperung *f* PATENT, RECHT embodiment

verkraften *vt* GESCHÄFT *Schlag* absorb

verkürzen *vt* BÖRSE shorten, GESCHÄFT abridge, curtail, reduce, shorten

Verkürzung *f* GESCHÄFT abridgement, curtailment, reduction, shortening

verl. *abbr* (*verlängert*) GESCHÄFT lengthened

Verlade- *in cpds* IMP/EXP, KOMM, TRANSP lading, load, loading, shipment, stevedoring; **Verladeabteilung** *f* TRANSP stevedoring department; **Verladeanweisung** *f* GESCHÄFT, TRANSP broker's order (*BrE*); **Verladebescheinigung** *f* IMP/EXP, TRANSP mate's receipt; **Verladedatum** *nt* TRANSP loading date, date of shipment, day of shipment; **Verladehafen** *m* TRANSP port of loading, lading port; **Verladekai** *m* TRANSP loading dock

verladen: **nicht ~e Fracht** *f* TRANSP shut-out cargo

Verladen *nt* IMP/EXP, KOMM, TRANSP loading, shipment, shipping

Verlader *m* IMP/EXP, KOMM, TRANSP loading agent, forwarder (*fwdr*), shipper

Verlade-: **Verladestation** *f* TRANSP terminal

Verladung *f* IMP/EXP, KOMM, TRANSP loading (*ldg*), shipment, shipping; **~ in Container** TRANSP containerization; **~ und Lieferung** TRANSP loading and delivery (*ldg & dly*); **Verladungsspediteur** *m* IMP/EXP loading agent

Verlag *m* MEDIEN publisher, publishing house

Verlagerung *f* GESCHÄFT *eines Unternehmens* displacement, relocation, shifting

Verlag: **Verlagssystem** *nt* VW domestic system; **Verlagswesen** *nt* MEDIEN book trade, publishing trade

verlangen *vt* GESCHÄFT call for, charge, claim, request, require; ◆ **etw von jdm ~** GESCHÄFT require sth of sb

Verlangen *nt* GESCHÄFT request, V&M desire; **~ von Miete** GRUND rent seeking; ◆ **auf ~** GESCHÄFT on demand (*O/D*); **auf ~ rückzahlbar** BANK, FINANZ repayable on demand

verlängern *vt* BANK extend, BÖRSE lengthen, GESCHÄFT extend, renew

verlängert *adj* (*verl.*) GESCHÄFT extended, lengthened, prolonged; **~er Aufschub** *m* RECHNUNG extended deferment; **~er Eigentumsvorbehalt** *m* RECHT extended reservation of title; **~e Garantiezeit** *f* V&M extended guarantee

Verlängerung *f* GESCHÄFT extension, renewal; **Verlängerungsbestätigung** *f* VERSICH confirmation of renewal; **Verlängerungsgebühr** *f* BANK extension fee; **Verlängerungsklausel** *f* BANK renewal clause, FINANZ evergreen clause, VERSICH continuation clause (*CC*); **Verlängerungskosten** *pl* VERSICH extension costs; **Verlängerungsstück** *nt* BANK allonge

verlangsamen 1. *vt* BÖRSE roll down, VW *Wachstum* decelerate, slow down, slow; **2. sich ~** *v refl* VW *Wachstum* decelerate, slow down, slow

Verlangsamung *f* VW deceleration, slowdown

verlangt: **nicht ~e Dividende** *f* RECHNUNG unrequired dividend

verlassen 1. *vt* COMP *Programm, Betriebszustand* abort, GESCHÄFT abandon, leave, GRUND *Wohnung* vacate; **2.**

sich ~ auf *v refl* [+acc] GESCHÄFT *Person* depend on, rely on

Verlassen *nt* GESCHÄFT leaving, abandonment, TRANSP *des Flugzeuges* deplaning

verläßlich *adj* GESCHÄFT reliable

Verlauf: im ~ von *phr* GESCHÄFT in the course of

Verlaufsanalyse *f* FINANZ sequential analysis

verlegen *vt* GESCHÄFT *Unternehmen* relocate, MEDIEN publish; ♦ **~ nach** MGMNT *Sitzungsort* adjourn to

Verleger, in *m,f* MEDIEN publisher

Verlegung *f* GESCHÄFT relocation

verleihen *vt* BANK lend, GESCHÄFT hire out, RECHT *Titel, Rechte* bestow, confer, vest

Verleihung *f* BANK lending, GESCHÄFT hiring out, RECHT *Titel, Rechte* bestowal, conferment, conferral

Verleitung *f* RECHT inducement; **~ zum Vertragsbruch** RECHT interference with contract

verletzen *vt* PATENT infringe, violate, RECHT *Gesetze, Vorschriften* violate, injure, interfere with, infringe

Verletzer *m* PATENT, RECHT infringer, violator

verletzlich *adj* GESCHÄFT vulnerable

Verletzte(r) *mf* [decl. as adj] RECHT aggrieved party, injured party, wronged party

Verletzung *f* PATENT infringement, violation, PERSON *Körper* injury, RECHT infringement, violation; **von allen anderen Einwirkungen unabhängige ~** VERSICH *Krankenversicherung* injury independent of all other means; **~ der Berufspflicht** RECHT *Arzt, Rechtsanwalt* malpractice; **~ der Geheimhaltung** GESCHÄFT breach of confidence, breach of secrecy; **~ einer Gewährleistungspflicht** RECHT breach of warranty; **~ der Sicherheitsvorschriften** RECHT safety violation; **~ der Treuepflicht** RECHT breach of trust; **~ einer wesentlichen Vertragsbestimmung** RECHT breach of condition (*BrE*); ♦ **in ~ von** GESCHÄFT in violation of

verleumden *vt* RECHT *mündlich* slander, *schriftlich* libel; ♦ **jdn ~** RECHT defame sb's credit, defame sb's reputation

verleumderisch *adj* RECHT defamatory, *schriftlich* libellous (*BrE*), libelous (*AmE*), *mündlich* slanderous

Verleumdung *f* GESCHÄFT backbiting, RECHT defamation, *mündlich* slander, *schriftlich* libel; **Verleumdungsgesetz** *nt* RECHT libel law; **Verleumdungsklage** *f* RECHT action for libel; **Verleumdungsverfahren** *nt* RECHT libel proceedings, slander action

verlieren *vt* GESCHÄFT forfeit, RECHT *Schutz* lose

verlockend *adj* GESCHÄFT enticing

verloren: eine ~e Schlacht kämpfen *phr* GESCHÄFT fight a losing battle; **~e Zeit aufholen** *phr* GESCHÄFT make up for lost time

Verlust *m* BANK loss, GESCHÄFT wastage, IMP/EXP forfeiting, PATENT damage, RECHNUNG charge off, RECHT loss, VW leakage; **als ~ abgebuchte Forderung** RECHNUNG bad debt loss; **~ bei abschreibungsfähigen Vermögenswerten** RECHNUNG loss on depreciable property; **~ des Anspruchs** RECHT loss of claim; **~ aus Kapitalvermögen** STEUER passive loss; **~ aus langfristigem Geschäft** STEUER long-term loss; **~ auf dem Transport** TRANSP loss in transit; **~ durch uneinbringbare Forderungen** VW bad debt loss; ♦ **einen ~ abdecken** FINANZ cover a loss; **einen ~ ausweisen** RECHNUNG report a loss, show a loss; **einen ~ erleiden**

RECHNUNG sustain a loss, RECHT suffer loss; **Verluste hinnehmen** VW lose out; **einen ~ erwirtschaften** VW run a deficit; **einen ~ in Kauf nehmen** BÖRSE take a loss; **~ machen** VW run a deficit; **einen ~ melden** RECHNUNG report a loss; **einen ~ tragen** FINANZ carry a loss, stand a loss; **~ bei Verschleißanlagen** RECHNUNG loss on depreciable property

Verlust: **Verlustabschluß** *m* FINANZ debit balance; **Verlustabzug** *m* STEUER loss deduction; **Verlustanerkennung** *f* RECHNUNG recognition of loss; **Verlustausgleich** *m* FINANZ cross-subsidization, STEUER loss compensation; **Verlustbelastung** *f* GESCHÄFT burden of losses; **Verlusterklärung** *f* VERSICH notice of abandonment; **Verlustfunktion** *f* MATH loss function; **Verlustgeschäft** *nt* VW losing bargain, money-losing deal; **Verlustpreissystem** *nt* V&M losspricing; **Verlustquote** *f* BANK loss ratio; **Verlustrisiko** *nt* aus Währungsumrechnungen FINANZ, VW translation risk; **Verlustrücklage** *f* FINANZ loss contingency; **Verlustrückstellung** *f* MGMNT contingency reserve, RECHNUNG loss provision; **Verlustrücktrag** *m* RECHNUNG carry-back, carry-back of loss, carry-over loss, loss carry-back; **Verlustrücktrags-Verlustvortragssystem** *nt* STEUER carry-back carry-forward system; **Verlustträger** *m* V&M lossmaker; **Verlustvortrag** *m* RECHNUNG carry-over loss, historical loss, loss carry-forward, losses carried forward, STEUER allowance for loss; **Verlustwahrscheinlichkeit** *f* VW loss probability

vermachen *vt* GRUND devise, RECHT bequeath, devise, dispose by will

Vermächtnis *nt* RECHT bequest, legacy, testamentary gift; ♦ **jdm ein ~ aussetzen** RECHT leave a legacy to sb, make a bequest to sb

Vermächtnis: **Vermächtnisnehmer, in** *m,f* GRUND devisee, RECHT beneficiary, devisee, legatee

vermehren *vt* GESCHÄFT augment

Vermehrung *f* GESCHÄFT augmentation

vermeidbar: ~e Kosten *pl* GESCHÄFT avoidable costs; **~es Risiko** *nt* FINANZ avoidable risk, unsystematic risk

vermeiden *vt* GESCHÄFT avoid, prevent, STEUER avoid

Vermeidung *f* GESCHÄFT avoidance, prevention

Vermerk *m* GESCHÄFT entry, note, RECHT *Urkunde, Wechsel* endorsement, indorsement

vermerken *vt* RECHT endorse, indorse; ♦ **etw ~** VERWALT enter, make a note of sth, note

vermessen *vt* GRUND survey

Vermesser, in *m,f* GRUND surveyor

Vermessung *f* GESCHÄFT, GRUND survey; **Vermessungsgebühr** *f* GRUND survey fee; **Vermessungspunkt** *m* GRUND monument (*AmE*)

vermietbar: ~e Fläche *f* GRUND rentable area

vermieten *vt* GRUND let (*BrE*), rent out (*AmE*); ♦ **zu ~** GRUND *Werbung in Schildern und Anzeigen* for rent (*AmE*), to let (*BrE*)

Vermietung *f* GRUND let, letting; **~ ganzer Betriebsanlagen** IND plant hire; **~ von Monat zu Monat** GRUND month-to-month tenancy; **~ auf Monatsbasis** GRUND month-to-month tenancy

Vermischung *f* GESCHÄFT mixture; **~ von Fremdgeld mit eigenen Mitteln** RECHT commingling of funds

vermitteln *vi* PERSON mediate; ♦ **~ zwischen** [+dat] PERSON mediate between

Vermittler, in *m,f* PERSON intermediary, mediator, conciliation officer (*BrE*); ~ **von Hypothekenkrediten** FINANZ mortgage broker (*AmE*)

Vermittlung *f* GESCHÄFT procurement, *Telefon* switchboard, KOMM *Telefon* exchange, PERSON *zwischen zwei Parteien bei Streitigkeiten* mediation, *Arbeit* placement, POL, VERWALT, VW government intervention; ◆ **durch ~ von** GESCHÄFT through the agency of

Vermittlung: **Vermittlungsausschuß** *m* PERSON mediation committee, conference board; **Vermittlungsbüro** *nt* FINANZ middle office; **Vermittlungsprovision** *f* GESCHÄFT finder's fee; **Vermittlungsstelle** *f* GESCHÄFT agency (*agcy*), PERSON mediation board, mediation committee

Vermögen *nt* FINANZ assets, capital, GESCHÄFT power, RECHNUNG assets, capital, VW money; ~ **mit begrenzter Nutzungsdauer** RECHNUNG, VW wasting asset; ◆ ~ **für einen Scheck zurückbehalten** BANK hold funds for a check (*AmE*), hold funds for a cheque (*BrE*)

Vermögen: **Vermögensabgabe** *f* VW capital levy, levy on property; **Vermögensaufstellung** *f* FINANZ financial statement, RECHNUNG schedule of assets (*AmE*), RECHT statement of affairs; **Vermögensaufstellung** *f* **des Konkursschuldners** BANK statement of affairs; **die Vermögensaufstellung vorbereiten** *phr* FINANZ prepare a schedule of assets, prepare the statement of net assets; **Vermögensaufzehrung** *f* FINANZ negative saving; **Vermögensauskunft** *f* V&M status inquiry; **Vermögensbesteuerung** *f* STEUER assessed valuation (*AmE*); **Vermögensbewertung** *f* RECHNUNG asset valuation, STEUER assessment; **Vermögensbilanz** *f* RECHNUNG asset and liability statement; **Vermögensbildung** *f* FINANZ, VW capital accumulation, capital formation; **Vermögenseinbuße** *f* FINANZ actual loss, VERSICH economic loss; **Vermögenseinziehung** *f* RECHT seizure of property; **Vermögensertrag** *m* BÖRSE asset return; **Vermögenserträge** *m pl* BÖRSE asset return, FINANZ investment income; **Vermögensgegenstand** *m* VW property; **Vermögensgegenstände** *m pl* RECHNUNG assets; **Vermögensgruppe** *f* RECHNUNG group of assets

vermögensgesichert: ~**e Anlage** *f* BANK, FINANZ asset-based investment

vermögensrechtlich *adj* FINANZ pecuniary

Vermögen: **Vermögensschaden** *m* FINANZ damage to property, financial damage, pecuniary damage, financial loss, VERSICH economic loss; **Vermögensschadenversicherer** *m* VERSICH property insurer; **Vermögensseite** *f* RECHNUNG asset side; **Vermögenssteuer** *f* FINANZ, STEUER, VW capital income tax, property tax, wealth tax; **Vermögensumstrukturierung** *f* VW restructuring of assets; **Vermögensverwalter, in** *m,f* BANK, BÖRSE, FINANZ trustee, asset manager, fund manager, RECHT custodian of property; **Vermögensverwalter, in** *m,f* **mit Geschäftsführungsbefugnis** RECHT receiver and manager

Vermögensverwaltung *f* BANK, BÖRSE, FINANZ asset management, fund management, investment management, portfolio management, property management; **Vermögensverwaltungsgebühr** *f* BANK agency fee, management fee; **Vermögensverwaltungskonto** *nt* FINANZ asset management account (*AMA*); **Vermögensverwaltungsservice** *m* BANK portfolio management service; **Vermögensverwaltungstheorie** *f* BÖRSE portfolio management theory; **Vermögensverwaltungsvertrag** *m* **zur Umgehung der Erbschaftssteuer** STEUER bypass trust

Vermögenswert *m* FINANZ, RECHNUNG asset value, assets; ~ **mit geringem Umsatzvolumen** BÖRSE inactive asset; ◆ **Vermögenswerte flüssigmachen** BÖRSE realize assets

Vermögenswert: **durch Vermögenswerte gesicherte Anlage** *f* FINANZ asset-backed investment

Vermögen: **Vermögenszugang** *m* RECHNUNG asset addition; **Vermögenszuwachs** *m* VW capital appreciation; **Vermögenszuwachssteuer** *f* FINANZ, RECHNUNG, STEUER, VW capital income tax

vermuten *vt* GESCHÄFT, MEDIEN presume

vermutet: ~**e Steuer** *f* STEUER presumptive tax

vermutlich *adj* GESCHÄFT, RECHT alleged

Vermutung *f* GESCHÄFT, RECHT presumption, assumption; ◆ **auf die ~ hin** GESCHÄFT on speculation (*on spec*)

vernetzen *vt* COMP network

vernetzt: ~**es Arbeiten** *nt* COMP networking

Vernichtung *f* UMWELT destruction, VW *von Arbeitsplätzen* abolition; **Vernichtungswettbewerb** *m* VW cutthroat competition

vernünftig 1. *adj* GESCHÄFT rational, reasonable, sensible; **2.** *adv* GESCHÄFT rationally, reasonably, sensibly

vernünftig: ~**er Mensch** *m* GESCHÄFT reasonable person; ~**er Preis** *m* GESCHÄFT reasonable price

vernünftigerweise *adv* GESCHÄFT reasonably

veröffentlichen *vt* MEDIEN issue, publish, PATENT publish

veröffentlicht *adj* MEDIEN, PATENT published; ~**er Abschluß** *m* RECHNUNG published accounts; ~**er Fahrpreis** *m* TRANSP published fare; ~**e Gebühr** *f* TRANSP published charge; ~**e Information** *f* GESCHÄFT published information; ~**er Tarif** *m* TRANSP published rate

Veröffentlichung *f* MEDIEN publication

verordnet: ~**es Programm** *nt* MEDIEN mandated program (*AmE*), mandated programme (*BrE*)

Verordnung *f* GESCHÄFT regulation, RECHT ordinance, edict

verpachten *vt* GRUND lease, let on lease, rent

Verpachtung *f* GRUND renting

verpacken *vt* GESCHÄFT pack, wrap

Verpacken *nt* GESCHÄFT packing, packaging; ~ **von Massengut in Einheiten** TRANSP bulk unitization

Verpacker *m* IND *Person, Maschine* packer

verpackt: ~**e Ware** *f* V&M packaged goods

Verpackung *f* GESCHÄFT wrapper, packing, wrapping, IND packaging, V&M wrapper, wrapping; **auf der ~ aufgedruckter Preisnachlaß** *m* V&M on-pack price reduction; ~ **aus Holzfaserplatte** IND fiberboard case (*AmE*), fibreboard case (*BrE*); ~ **für kombinierten Transport** TRANSP intermodal packaging; ◆ **auf der ~** V&M on-pack

Verpackung: **Verpackungsanweisung** *f* IND, TRANSP packing instruction; **Verpackungscode** *m* V&M package code; **Verpackungsdesign** *nt* V&M package design; **Verpackungsgesetze** *nt pl* GESCHÄFT, RECHT packaging laws; **Verpackungsgewicht** *nt* GESCHÄFT tare weight; **Verpackungskosten** *pl* IND, V&M packaging cost; **Verpackungsmaterial** *nt* IND, V&M packaging material; **Verpackungszertifikat** *nt* TRANSP packaging certificate

verpassen *vt* GESCHÄFT miss

verpfänden *vt* FINANZ pawn, pledge, GRUND hypothecate, mortgage

Verpfänder, in *m,f* FINANZ pawner, pledger

verpfändet *adj* FINANZ in pawn, in pledge, pawned, pledged, hypothecated, mortgaged; **nicht ~** *adj* GRUND unmortgaged

Verpfändung *f* FINANZ pawning, pledging, GRUND hypothecation, mortgaging; **Verpfändungsbescheinigung** *f* BANK hypothecation certificate, letter of hypothecation; **Verpfändungserklärung** *f* BANK letter of hypothecation

verpflegen *vt* GESCHÄFT cater for

Verpflegung *f* FREI *Unterkunft* board, PERSON, V&M catering; **Verpflegungsstelle** *f* V&M commissary (*AmE*)

verpflichten 1. *vt* GESCHÄFT oblige, obligate (*AmE*), sign up, RECHT bind, engage; ♦ **jdn ~, etw zu tun** GESCHÄFT oblige sb to do sth; **2. sich ~** *v refl* GESCHÄFT sign up; ♦ **sich zu etw ~** GESCHÄFT commit oneself to; **sich ~, etw zu tun** GESCHÄFT undertake to do sth

verpflichtend *adj* GESCHÄFT obligatory

verpflichtet *adj* GESCHÄFT, RECHT committed, obligated, obliged; ♦ **~ gegenüber** GESCHÄFT answerable to; **~ sein, etw zu tun** GESCHÄFT be committed to do sth; **~ sein zu** GESCHÄFT be obliged to

Verpflichtete(r) *mf* [decl. as adj] RECHT debtor, obligor, VERSICH liable party

Verpflichtung *f* GESCHÄFT liability, obligation, RECHT commitment, engagement, undertaking; ♦ **ohne ~** V&M without obligation; **ohne jegliche ~ unsererseits** GESCHÄFT, RECHT without any liability on our part

Verpflichtung: **Verpflichtungsdokument** *nt* RECHT commitment document; **Verpflichtungsermächtigung** *f* FINANZ budgetary appropriation, commitment authority, POL budgetary appropriation, RECHNUNG appropriation; **Verpflichtungskontrolle** *f* RECHT *Staatsrecht* commitment control; **Verpflichtungsprotokoll** *nt* RECHT commitment record

verpulvern *vt* *infrml* GESCHÄFT *Geld* blow (*infrml*)

verrechnen *vt* BANK clear, FINANZ offset, set against, set off, *Verluste* absorb, carry back, RECHNUNG apply to, offset, set against, set off, *Verluste* absorb, carry back

verrechnend *adj* FINANZ, RECHNUNG offsetting

verrechnet *adj* BANK cleared (*cld*), FINANZ absorbed, offset, RECHNUNG allocated; **~e Gemeinkosten** *pl* FINANZ absorbed overheads, RECHNUNG applied overheads; **~e Kosten** *pl* RECHNUNG applied cost

Verrechnung *f* BANK clearing, FINANZ, RECHNUNG absorption, offset, offsetting, set-off, carry-back; **~ gleicher Kaufs- und Verkaufsaufträge** BÖRSE accepted pairing; **~ von Verlusten** RECHNUNG carry-back of loss; ♦ **zur ~** BANK account payee; **nur zur ~** BANK account payee only, for deposit only, not negotiable, unnegotiable

Verrechnung: **Verrechnungsabkommen** *nt* BANK agreement of clearing, clearing agreement; **Verrechnungsbericht** *m* BANK clearing report

verrechnungsfähig: **~e Positionen** *f pl* BANK, RECHNUNG clearing items

Verrechnung: **Verrechnungsgesellschaft** *f* BANK clearing corporation (*AmE*); **Verrechnungskonto** *nt* BANK settlement account, RECHNUNG allocation account,

clearing account, offset account; **Verrechnungspreis** *m* BANK accounting price, GESCHÄFT transfer price; **Verrechnungsscheck** *m* BANK account-only check (*AmE*), account-only cheque (*BrE*), collection-only check (*AmE*), collection-only cheque (*BrE*), crossed check (*AmE*), crossed cheque (*BrE*), non-negotiable cheque, voucher; **Verrechnungstag** *m* BANK clearing day

verrichten *vt* GESCHÄFT perform

Verrichtung *f* GESCHÄFT performance

verringern *vt* FINANZ cut, GESCHÄFT diminish, *Bestand* scale down, work down, *Ausgaben* reduce, MGMNT, PERSON *Personalbestand* downsize, VW reduce, run down

verringert *adj* MGMNT, PERSON *Personalbestand* downsized, VW reduced

Verringerung *f* FINANZ cut, GESCHÄFT reduction, reduction in size, scaling-down, MGMNT, PERSON *Personalbestand* downsizing, scaling-down, VW reduction; **~ des Kapitals** BÖRSE reduction in capital

Vers. *abbr* (*Versicherung*) RECHNUNG, VERSICH ins. (*insurance*)

Versagen *nt* COMP failure, fault, GESCHÄFT fault, IND breakdown; **~ der Regulierungskommissionen** VW regulatory capture

Versal *m* COMP, MEDIEN upper case

Versammlung *f* GESCHÄFT convention, gathering, MGMNT meeting, POL assembly, convention; **Versammlungsleiter** *m* MGMNT, PERSON chairman, chairperson; **Versammlungsleiterin** *f* MGMNT, PERSON chairwoman, chairperson

Versand *m* IMP/EXP, KOMM, TRANSP consignment, consignation, dispatch, dispatching, shipment, shipping; **~ an einen bestimmten Empfänger** IMP/EXP direct transportation; ♦ **bei ~** IMP/EXP, KOMM, TRANSP on shipment

Versand: **Versandabteilung** *f* KOMM, TRANSP despatch department, dispatch department, forwarding department, traffic department; **Versandanschrift** *f* TRANSP shipping address; **Versandanweisungen** *f pl* TRANSP shipping instructions; **Versandanzeige** *f* IMP/EXP consignment note (*C/N, CN*), delivery note, shipping note (*S/N*), KOMM advice note, TRANSP consignment note (*C/N, CN*), delivery note, shipping note (*S/N*); **Versandbahnhof** *m* TRANSP forwarding station; **Versandbedingungen** *f pl* IMP/EXP terms of shipment

versandbereit *adj* TRANSP ready for shipment

Versand: **Versandbereitstellungskredit** *m* BANK packaging credit, packing credit; **Versandbestellung** *f* KOMM, V&M mail order, order by post (*BrE*), order by mail (*AmE*)

versandfrei *adj* IMP/EXP, KOMM, TRANSP free dispatch (*fd*)

Versand: **Versandfreigabe** *f* TRANSP release for shipment; **Versandgebühr** *f* KOMM dispatching charge; **Versandhafen** *m* TRANSP shipping port; **Versandhandel** *m* KOMM, V&M mail order; **Versandhauskatalog** *m* V&M mail-order catalog (*AmE*), mail-order catalogue (*BrE*); **Versandlager** *nt* TRANSP dispatch bay; **Versandlagerraum** *m* TRANSP dispatch bay; **Versandland** *nt* TRANSP country of dispatch; **Versandliste** *f* IMP/EXP packaging list, packing list; **Versandpapiere** *nt pl* IMP/EXP, TRANSP dispatch papers, shipping documents, shipping papers; **Versandprospekt** *m* **ohne Umschlag** V&M self-mailer; **Versandrechnung** *f* IMP/EXP, KOMM shipping invoice;

Versandschein *m* IMP/EXP transit bond note, KOMM, TRANSP dispatch note; **Versandstelle** *m* TRANSP forwarding department; **Versandtag** *m* TRANSP day of shipment, date of shipment; **Versandunternehmen** *nt* V&M mail-order business; **Versandverkauf** *m* V&M mail-order selling; **Versandvorschriften** *f pl* TRANSP shipping instructions

versäumen *vt* RECHT *unterlassen* fail, omit, *vernachlässigen* neglect

Versäumnis *nt* RECHT default, failure, omission

Versäumnisklausel *f* VERSICH neglect clause

Versch. *abbr* (*Verschiedenes*) GESCHÄFT misc. (*miscellaneous*), RECHNUNG sundries

verschachteln *vt* COMP *Programmcode* nest

verschachtelt *adj* COMP *Programmcode* nested

Verschachtelung *f* COMP *Programmcode* nesting

verschärfen *vt* GESCHÄFT intensify, tighten, tighten up, *Bestimmungen* stiffen

Verschärfung *f* GESCHÄFT intensification, tightening-up

verschenken *vt* V&M give away

verschicken *vt* GESCHÄFT send out, IMP/EXP, KOMM, TRANSP send, *Fracht* ship

verschieben *vt* GESCHÄFT move, postpone, shift

Verschiebung *f* COMP *Adressen im Speicher* relocation, GESCHÄFT postponement; **~ der Angebotskurve** VW shift in supply curve; **~ der Nachfragekurve** VW shift in demand curve

verschieden *adj* GESCHÄFT diverse; **~e Ausgaben** *f pl* RECHNUNG sundry expenses; **~e Konten** *nt pl* RECHNUNG sundry accounts; **~e Kosten** *pl* RECHNUNG miscellaneous expenses; **~e Medien** *nt pl* V&M mixed media; **~e Möglichkeiten** *f pl* GESCHÄFT range of options

Verschiedenes *nt* (*Versch.*) GESCHÄFT miscellaneous (*misc.*), RECHNUNG sundries

Verschiedenheit *f* GESCHÄFT diversity, PATENT distinctiveness

verschifft *adj* IMP/EXP, KOMM shipped, TRANSP afloat, shipped

Verschiffung *f* IMP/EXP, KOMM, TRANSP shipment, shipping; **Verschiffungsbescheinigung** *f* IMP/EXP, TRANSP certificate of shipment; **Verschiffungsdokumente** *nt pl* IMP/EXP, TRANSP shipping documents, shipping papers; **Verschiffungshafen** *m* TRANSP port of shipment; **Verschiffungskonnossement** *nt* IMP/EXP, TRANSP shipped bill; **Verschiffungsorder** *f* GESCHÄFT broker's order (*BrE*)

verschlechtern: sich ~ *v refl* GESCHÄFT deteriorate, worsen, VW retrogress

Verschlechterung *f* GESCHÄFT deterioration, worsening, depreciation, VW *Münzen* debasement

verschleiern *vt* GESCHÄFT conceal, cover up, disguise

verschleiert *adj* GESCHÄFT concealed; **~e Pläne** *m pl* GESCHÄFT hidden agenda; **~e Vermögenswerte** *m pl* RECHNUNG concealed assets

Verschleierung *f* GESCHÄFT concealment, RECHNUNG window-dressing; **~ der Verluste** BÖRSE concealment of losses

Verschleiß *m* GESCHÄFT *technisch* loss in value from normal use, wear and tear, VW erosion

verschleißen *vt* VW erode

Verschleiß: Verschleißrate *f* GESCHÄFT attrition rate; **Verschleißteile** *nt pl* COMP expendables, IND spare part

verschlossen: etw ~ halten *phr* GESCHÄFT keep sth under wraps (*infrml*)

Verschluß *m* TRANSP locking

verschlüsseln *vt* COMP encode, encrypt

verschlüsselt: ~e Dateneingabe *f* COMP coded data entry

Verschlüsselung *f* BANK encoding, COMP *Daten, Text* encryption

Verschluß: Verschlußsache *f* POL *Dokumente* classified information

verschmelzen 1. *vt* FINANZ merge, amalgamate, consolidate, fuse; **2.** *vi* FINANZ merge, amalgamate

Verschmelzung *f* FINANZ amalgamation, combination, consolidation, fusion, merger, VERWALT amalgamation

Verschmutzer *m* UMWELT polluter

verschmutzt *adj* UMWELT polluted; **~e Luft** *f* UMWELT polluted air

Verschmutzung *f* UMWELT contamination, pollution; **~ auf niedrigem Niveau** UMWELT background pollution; **Verschmutzungsgebühr** *f* UMWELT pollution charge

verschollen: ~es Schiff *nt* TRANSP missing vessel

Verschollene(r) *mf* [decl. as adj] RECHT missing person

verschönern *vt* GESCHÄFT, GRUND decorate, refurbish

Verschönerung *f* GESCHÄFT, GRUND decoration, refurbishment

verschreiben: sich ~ *v refl* VERWALT mistype

verschrotten *vt* IND scrap

Verschrottung *f* IND scrapping

Verschrottungs-: ~ und Bauvorschriften *f pl* TRANSP scrap and build regulations

verschulden 1. *vt* BANK become indebted, run into debt, RECHT be responsible for; **2. sich ~** *v refl* BANK, GESCHÄFT, RECHNUNG incur debts

Verschulden *nt* COMP, GESCHÄFT fault, RECHT blame; **Verschuldenspotential** *nt* GESCHÄFT borrowing potential

verschuldet *adj* VW indebted; ♦ **~ sein** FINANZ be indebted

verschuldet: ~es Unternehmen *nt* RECHNUNG leveraged company

Verschuldung *f* FINANZ indebtedness, level of debt; **~ des Bundes** VW indebtedness of the federal government; **~ der öffentlichen Hand** VW public debt; **~ pro Kopf der Bevölkerung** VW per capita debt; **Verschuldungsgrad** *m* BANK leverage ratio (*AmE*), FINANZ debit ratio, debt ratio, debt equity ratio, gearing (*BrE*), leverage (*AmE*), RECHNUNG leverage ratio (*AmE*), debt equity ratio, VERWALT debt equity ratio; **Verschuldungsgrenze** *f* GESCHÄFT borrowing allocation, borrowing ceiling; **Verschuldungskoeffizient** *m* FINANZ debt equity ratio

verschweigen *vt* RECHT conceal, fail to disclose

Verschweigen *nt* RECHT *von Information* concealment, VERSICH nondisclosure

verschwenden *vt* GESCHÄFT squander, waste

Verschwender, in *m,f* GESCHÄFT spendthrift

verschwenderisch: ~e Ausgaben *f pl* FINANZ, GESCHÄFT wasteful expenditure

Verschwendung *f* GESCHÄFT prodigality, squandering; **~ von Geld** FINANZ, GESCHÄFT wasteful spending

verschwören: sich ~ *v refl* GESCHÄFT, RECHT conspire, plot

Verschwörung *f* GESCHÄFT, RECHT conspiracy, plot

versehen: **~ mit** *vt* GESCHÄFT affix, append

versenden *vt* GESCHÄFT send out, KOMM, TRANSP consign, convey, dispatch

Versender, in *m,f* IMP/EXP, KOMM consignor, sender, TRANSP consignor, sender, shipper

Versendung *f* IMP/EXP consignment, shipping, GESCHÄFT dispatch, KOMM dispatch, shipping, TRANSP shipping, conveyance, dispatch, dispatching

versetzen *vt* GESCHÄFT, PERSON redeploy, relocate, transfer, VERWALT redeploy, transfer

versetzt *adj* PERSON, VERWALT posted, relocated, transferred; ◆ **~ angeordnet** GESCHÄFT staggered

Versetzung *f* GESCHÄFT, PERSON, VERWALT *von Arbeitnehmern* posting, redeployment, relocation, transfer (*tr.*, *tfr*); **Versetzungsprämie** *f* PERSON redeployment premium

verseuchen *vt* UMWELT contaminate

verseucht *adj* UMWELT contaminated

versicherbar *adj* VERSICH insurable; **~es Interesse** *nt* VERSICH insurable interest; **~es Risiko** *nt* VERSICH insurable risk; **~er Titel** *m* VERSICH insurable title

Versicherbarkeit *f* VERSICH insurability

Versicherer *m* FINANZ carrier, VERSICH insurance company, insurer, underwriter (*U/W*); **~ auf Gegenseitigkeit** VERSICH mutual insurer

versichern *vt* VERSICH assert, assure (*BrE*), insure, underwrite; ◆ **sich ~ lassen** VERSICH take out an insurance policy

versichert *adj* VERSICH insured; **nicht ~** *adj* VERSICH unassured (*BrE*), uninsured; ◆ **Seien Sie ~, daß** GESCHÄFT rest assured that

versichert: **~e Gefahr** *f* VERSICH insured peril; **~es Kapital** *nt* VERSICH capital assured; **~es Konto** *nt* VERSICH insured account; **die ~e Person** *f* VERSICH the insured

Versicherte: **der ~** *m* [decl. as adj], **die ~** *f* [decl. as adj] VERSICH the insured

Versicherung *f* (*Vers.*) GESCHÄFT assertion, RECHNUNG insurance (*ince*, *ins.*), VERSICH assurance (*BrE*) (*ass.*), insurance (*ince*, *ins.*), cover; **~ auf Aktien** VERSICH proprietary insurance; **~ für Ausrüstungsvertreiber** VERSICH equipment dealer insurance; **~ für Ausrüstungsvertriebsgesellschaften** VERSICH equipment dealer insurance; **~ der Eigentumsrechte** VERSICH title insurance; **~ zu erhöhter Prämie** VERSICH rated policy; **~ von Fertigerzeugnissen und abgeschlossenen Dienstleistungen** VERSICH products and completed operations insurance; **~ für die Finanzierung eines Warenlagers** VERSICH floor plan insurance; **~ mit garantiertem Einkommen** VERSICH guaranteed income contract (*GIC*); **~ gegen alle Gefahren** VERSICH all-risk insurance; **~ gegen Erpressung** VERSICH extortion insurance; **~ gegen mehrere Gefahren** VERSICH multiple peril insurance; **~ gegen Rechtsmängel bei Grundstückserwerb** VERSICH title insurance; **~ auf Gegenseitigkeit** VERSICH mutual insurance; **~ gegen Überschwemmungsschäden** VERSICH flood insurance; **~ gegen Vandalismus und böswilligen Schaden** VERSICH vandalism and malicious mischief insurance; **~ gegen Vandalismus und vorsätzliche Beschädigung** VERSICH vandalism and malicious mischief insurance; **~ gegen Vermögensabwertung** VERSICH property depreciation insurance; **~ gegen**

Wirtschaftskriminalität VERSICH business crime insurance; **~ mit gestaffelten Prämienzahlungen** GESCHÄFT graded premium policy; **~ mit Gewinnbeteiligung** VERSICH with-profits endowment assurance; **~ für Haftung bei Brandschäden** VERSICH fire legal liability insurance (*AmE*); **~ für Hauseigentümer** VERSICH homeowner's policy; **~ zur Kompensation von Einkommensverlusten** VERSICH loss of income insurance; **~ nach Taxe** VERSICH valued policy; **~ auf den Todes- und Erlebensfall** VERSICH endowment assurance, endowment insurance, endowment life assurance, endowment life insurance; **~ auf den Todesfall** VERSICH life insurance policy; **~ mit Überschußbeteiligung** VERSICH participating insurance; **~ der Unterzeichner der Police** GESCHÄFT assurance of subscribers; **~ für Werterhöhungen und Qualitätsverbesserungen** VERSICH improvements and betterments insurance; **~ wichtiger Urkunden** VERSICH valuable papers insurance; ◆ **eine ~ abschließen** VERSICH take out an insurance policy; **durch ~ gedeckt sein** VERSICH be covered by insurance

Versicherung: **Versicherungsangebot** *nt* **zur Deckung in Fremdwährung** VERSICH tender to contract cover; **Versicherungsanspruch** *m* VERSICH insurance claim; **Versicherungsanzeige** *f* VERSICH advice card; **Versichrungsaufsicht** *f* VERSICH Superintendent of Insurance; **Versicherungsausweis** *m* VERSICH insurance certificate; **Versicherungsbedingungen** *f pl* VERSICH terms and conditions; **Versicherungsbeginn** *m* VERSICH *einer Police* commencement; **Versicherungsbegleichung** *f* VERSICH insurance settlement; **Versicherungsbeitrag** *m* VERSICH insurance premium; **Versicherungsbestand** *m* VERSICH business in force, insurance portfolio; **Versicherungsbestätigung** *f* VERSICH certificate of insurance (*c/i*); **Versicherungsbetrag** *m* VERSICH sum assured; **Versicherungsbonus** *m* VERSICH capital bonus; **Versicherungsbranche** *f* VERSICH class of insurance; **Versicherungsdokument** *nt* VERSICH insurance policy certificate; **Versicherungsende** *nt* VERSICH lapse; **Versicherungsfactoring** *nt* VERSICH insurance factoring

versicherungsfähig *adj* VERSICH held covered, insurable; **nicht ~** *adj* VERSICH uninsurable; **nicht ~er Titel** *m* VERSICH uninsurable title

Versicherung: **Versicherungsfähigkeit** *f* VERSICH insurability; **Versicherungsgeber, in** *m,f* VERSICH underwriter (*U/W*); **Versicherungsgesellschaft** *f* VERSICH insurance company; **Versicherungsgesellschaft** *f* **mit gesetzlicher Rücklage** VERSICH legal reserve life insurance company; **Versicherungsgewerbe** *nt* VERSICH insurance industry; **Versicherungsgruppe** *f* GESCHÄFT syndicate; **Versicherungskonto** *nt* VERSICH underwriting account (*U/a*); **Versicherungskosten** *pl* VERSICH insurance charge, insurance cost; **Versicherungslasten** *f pl* VERSICH insurance charge; **Versicherungsleistung** *f* VERSICH benefit, insurance benefit, insurance settlement; **Versicherungsmaklergeschäft** *nt* VERSICH insurance broking; **Versicherungsmarkt** *m* VERSICH insurance market; **Versicherungsmathematik** *f* VW actuarial theory

versicherungsmathematisch *adj* VERSICH actuarial; **~es Defizit** *nt* VERSICH actuarial deficit; **~e Leistungspflicht** *f* VERSICH actuarial liability; **~er Schaden** *m* VERSICH actuarial loss

Versicherungspolice f VERSICH insurance policy; ~ **mit Gewinnbeteiligung** VERSICH participating profit policy; ~ **ohne Wertangabe der Fracht** VERSICH open cargo insurance policy (*OP*); ~ **mit periodischer Wertangabe** FINANZ reporting policy; ~ **zum Schutz gegen Geschäftsrisiken** VERSICH commercial form; ~ **zum Schutz von Geschäftsgrundstücken** VERSICH commercial property policy

Versicherung: **Versicherungsprämie** f VERSICH insurance premium; **Versicherungsschein** m VERSICH insurance policy

Versicherungsschutz m VERSICH insurance cover (*BrE*), insurance coverage (*AmE*); ~ **gegen Insolvenz der Projektteilnehmer** VERSICH project participants insolvency cover; ~ **gegen Strandung** VERSICH cover against stranding; ~ **gewerblich genutzter Kraftfahrzeuge** VERSICH business automobile policy (*AmE*); ~ **bei Zusammenstößen** VERSICH collision coverage; ♦ **ohne** ~ VERSICH bare

Versicherung: **Versicherungssparte** f VERSICH class of insurance; **Versicherungssumme** f GESCHÄFT sum insured, VERSICH face amount, face of policy, sum assured; **Versicherungssystem** nt VERSICH insurance scheme

versicherungstechnisch adj VERSICH actuarial; ~**es Defizit** nt VERSICH actuarial deficit; ~**e Leistungspflicht** f VERSICH actuarial liability; ~**er Schaden** m VERSICH actuarial loss

Versicherung: **Versicherungsunternehmen** nt VERSICH insurance company; **Versicherungsunternehmen** nt **mit gesetzlicher Reserve** VERSICH legal reserve life insurance company; **Versicherungsurkunde** f VERSICH insurance certificate; **Versicherungsverein** m **auf Gegenseitigkeit** (*VVaG*) FINANZ benefit society, friendly society (*BrE*), VERSICH mutual benefit society, mutual insurance company, mutual insurance society (*BrE*); **Versicherungsvermittlungsgeschäft** nt VERSICH insurance broking; **Versicherungsvertrag** m VERSICH insurance contract; **Versicherungsverträge abschließen** phr VERSICH write business; **Versicherungsvertrag** m **gegen Vermögensschaden und Unglücksfall** VERSICH property and casualty policy insuring agreement; **Versicherungswirtschaft** f VERSICH insurance industry; **Versicherungszertifikat** nt VERSICH certificate of insurance (*c/i*), insurance certificate; **Versicherungszweig** m VERSICH class of insurance, line of business

versiegeln vt GESCHÄFT, KOMM, RECHT seal

versiegelt adj GESCHÄFT, KOMM, RECHT sealed, under seal; ♦ **in** ~**em Umschlag** GESCHÄFT in a sealed envelope

versiegelt: ~**es Angebot** nt GESCHÄFT sealed tender

Version f COMP, GESCHÄFT version

versöhnen vt FINANZ conciliate, reconcile

versorgen: ~ **mit** vt GESCHÄFT *Informationen* furnish, provide, supply

versorgend: **sich selbst** ~ adj GESCHÄFT self-supporting

Versorgung f COMP supply, FREI *mit Speisen und Getränken* catering, provision; ~ **und Nachschub** m COMP logistics; **Versorgungsbereich** m IND utilities sector; **Versorgungsbetrieb** m IND utility; **Versorgungsunternehmen** nt VERWALT public service corporation (*AmE*), public utility; **Versorgungswert** m FINANZ utility revenue bond

verspätet adj GESCHÄFT delayed, late; ~**e Annahme** f RECHT *Liefervertrag* late acceptance; ~**e Zahlung** f FINANZ late payment

Verspätung f GESCHÄFT delay, lateness, PERSON lateness

versprechen vt GESCHÄFT promise, undertake

Versprechen nt GESCHÄFT promise, undertaking; **Versprechensurkunde** f STEUER deed of covenant (*BrE*)

Versprecher m infrml KOMM slip of the tongue, fluff (*infrml*)

verstaatlichen vt GESCHÄFT nationalize

verstaatlicht: ~**er Industriezweig** m IND, VW nationalized industry; ~**er Sektor** m IND nationalized sector

Verstaatlichung f VW nationalization

verstädtern vt VW urbanize

Verstädterung f VW urbanization

verständigen 1. vt GESCHÄFT notify, inform; **2. sich** ~ v refl RECHT come to an agreement, come to an understanding

Verständigung f GESCHÄFT information (*inf., info*), RECHT agreement, understanding

verständlich adj GESCHÄFT coherent

Verständlichkeit f GESCHÄFT coherence

verstärken vt GESCHÄFT strengthen, *Wirkung* reinforce

Verstärker m TRANSP booster

verstärkt: ~**e Sensibilisierung** f GESCHÄFT, POL acute awareness

Verstärkung f GESCHÄFT reinforcement, strengthening; ~ **des Markenprofils** V&M brand reinforcement

verstecken vt COMP *Datei*, RECHT conceal, hide

versteckt: ~**er Arbeitskräfteüberschuß** m VERWALT concealed surplus of labor (*AmE*), concealed surplus of labour (*BrE*); ~**e Arbeitslosigkeit** f PERSON *Arbeitsmarkt, Statistik* disguised unemployment, VW concealed unemployment; ~**e Datei** f COMP hidden file; ~**e Inflation** f VW hidden inflation; ~**er Mangel** m RECHT latent defect, *Vertragsrecht* hidden defect; ~**er Preisanstieg** m V&M hidden price increase; ~**er Schaden** m VERSICH hidden damage; ~**es Vermögen** nt RECHNUNG hidden assets; ~**er Vermögenswert** m RECHNUNG hidden asset; ~**er Wert** m V&M hidden value

verstehen 1. vt GESCHÄFT understand; **2.** vi GESCHÄFT understand

versteigern vt GESCHÄFT, V&M, VW auction off

Versteigerung f V&M, VW auction, public sale (*P/S*)

verstellbar adj GESCHÄFT, TRANSP adjustable

Verstellung f GESCHÄFT simulation

verstetigen vt VW *Schwankungen, Fluktuationen* smooth out

Verstetigung f VW increasing steadiness

versteuern vt GESCHÄFT, RECHNUNG, STEUER, VW pay tax

versteuernd: **zu** ~**es Einkommen** nt GESCHÄFT, RECHNUNG, STEUER, VW taxable income

versteuert adj GESCHÄFT, RECHNUNG, STEUER, VW net of taxes, tax paid; ~**es Einkommen** nt FINANZ, STEUER final income

Versteuerung f GESCHÄFT, RECHNUNG, STEUER, VW payment of tax

Verstopfung f TRANSP congestion, traffic jam

Verstoß m PATENT, RECHT breach, infringement, offence (*BrE*), offense (*AmE*), violation; ~ **gegen die Standesregeln** GESCHÄFT unprofessional conduct

verstoßen 1. *vt* RECHT violate; **2.** *vi* ◆ ~ **gegen** RECHT break, infringe, offend, violate

verstrichen: ~e **Zeit** *f* COMP elapsed time

Versuch *m* GESCHÄFT experiment, trial, attempt

versuchen *vt* GESCHÄFT attempt, test, try

Versuch: **Versuchsabteilung** *f* V&M research department; **Versuchsanlage** *f* IND *Produktion* pilot plant; **Versuchsbohrung** *f* **nach Erdöl** UMWELT wildcat drilling; **Versuchslauf** *m* GESCHÄFT pilot run; **Versuchspostversand** *m* V&M test mailing; **Versuchsproduktion** *f* GESCHÄFT pilot production; **Versuchsstadt** *f* GESCHÄFT test town; **Versuchsstand** *m* GESCHÄFT, IND testbed; **Versuchswerbung** *f* V&M advertising test; **Versuch-und-Irrtum-Methode** *f* VW trial and error method

versus *prep* (*vs.*) GESCHÄFT versus (*v, vs*)

vertagen 1. *vt* GESCHÄFT postpone, MGMNT *Sitzung*, RECHT *mündliche Verhandlung* adjourn; **2. sich** ~ *v refl* GESCHÄFT *Parlament* rise

Vertagung *f* GESCHÄFT postponement, MGMNT, RECHT adjournment; **Vertagungsdebatte** *f* POL adjournment debate (*BrE*)

verteidigen *vt* GESCHÄFT *Meinung, Handlung* defend, vindicate, RECHT vindicate

Verteidiger, in *m,f* RECHT counsel for the defence (*BrE*), defending counsel (*BrE*), attorney for the defense (*AmE*), defense attorney (*AmE*), defense lawyer (*AmE*)

Verteidigung *f* GESCHÄFT vindication, POL defence (*BrE*), defense (*AmE*), RECHT defence (*BrE*), defense (*AmE*), vindication; ~ **gegen Übernahme** BÖRSE Pac-Man defense (*AmE*); ◆ **die** ~ **führen** RECHT lead for the defence (*BrE*), lead for the defense (*AmE*)

Verteidigung: **Verteidigungsberater, in** *m,f* POL defence advisor (*BrE*) (*DA*), defense advisor (*AmE*) (*DA*); **Verteidigungsgüterindustrie** *f* VW defence industry (*BrE*), defense industry (*AmE*); **Verteidigungsministerium** *nt* POL, VERWALT Ministry of Defence (*BrE*) (*MOD*); **Verteidigungszeuge** *m*, **Verteidigungszeugin** *f* RECHT witness for the defence (*BrE*), witness for the defense (*AmE*)

verteilen *vt* BÖRSE, FINANZ *Aktien* apportion, distribute, GESCHÄFT *Arbeit, Geld* share out, PATENT apportion, RECHNUNG allot, apportion, *Kosten* spread, TRANSP distribute, VW spread, *Mittel, Gelder* allocate

Verteiler *m* IMP/EXP, TRANSP distributor; **Verteilerzentrum** *nt* TRANSP distribution center (*AmE*), distribution centre (*BrE*)

Verteilnetz *nt* COMP distribution network

verteilt *adj* COMP distributed, GESCHÄFT allocated; **nicht** ~ *adj* GESCHÄFT undisposed of; ~e **Datenbank** *f* COMP distributed database (*DDB*); ~e **Datenverarbeitung** *f* COMP distributed computing, distributed data processing (*DDP*); **nicht** ~er **Gewinn** *m* GESCHÄFT unappropriated surplus; ~es **System** *nt* COMP distributed system

Verteilung *f* BÖRSE, FINANZ apportionment, distribution, PATENT apportionment, RECHNUNG allotment, apportionment, TRANSP distribution, allotment, VW distribution; ~ **durch den Handel** V&M physical distribution; ~ **der Kosten** RECHNUNG apportionment of costs; ~ **der Rückvergütung** VERSICH allotment of bonus; ~ **der Verantwortungsbereiche** FINANZ allocation of responsibilities; ~ **des Volkseinkommens** VW distribution of national income; ~ **der**

Werbeausgaben V&M assignment of advertising expenditure; ~ **des Wohlstands** VW wealth distribution; **Verteilungseffekt** *m* VW spread effect

verteilungsfrei: ~e **Statistik** *f* MATH nonparametric statistics

Verteilung: **Verteilungsgewicht** *nt* VW distributional weight; **Verteilungskette** *f* IND chain of distribution; **Verteilungsmanagement** *nt* **durch den Handel** TRANSP physical distribution management (*PDM*)

verteuern *vt* RECHNUNG pay tax

vertiefen *vt* GESCHÄFT *Beziehung* deepen, *Kluft* widen

vertieft *adj* GESCHÄFT widened

Vertiefung *f* GESCHÄFT widening

Vertikal- *in cpds* GESCHÄFT vertical

vertikal *adj* GESCHÄFT vertical (*vert*); ~e **Analyse** *f* RECHNUNG vertical analysis; ~er **Aufbau** *m* GESCHÄFT, MGMNT vertical organization; ~e **Bilanz** *f* RECHNUNG vertical balance sheet; ~e **Diskriminierung** *f* VW vertical discrimination; ~e **Expansion** *f* GESCHÄFT vertical expansion; ~er **Finanzausgleich** *m* STEUER general revenue sharing (*AmE*), VW revenue sharing (*AmE*); ~e **Fusion** *f* GESCHÄFT, VW vertical amalgamation, vertical merger; ~e **Gründung** *f* GESCHÄFT vertical formation; ~e **Integration** *f* GESCHÄFT, VW vertical integration, IND, MGMNT, VW backward vertical integration; ~e **Kommunikation** *f* GESCHÄFT vertical communication; ~e **Mobilität** *f* PERSON, VW vertical mobility; ~e **Planung** *f* GESCHÄFT, MGMNT vertical planning; ~e **Preisbindung** *f* FINANZ, RECHT resale price maintenance (*RPM*), VERWALT administered price, VW resale price maintenance (*RPM*); ~e **Spezialisierung** *f* GESCHÄFT vertical specialization; ~er **Spread** *m* BÖRSE perpendicular spread; ~er **Unternehmenszusammenschluß** *m* GESCHÄFT, VW vertical business combination; ~e **Vorwärtsintegration** *f* VW forward vertical integration; ~er **Zusammenschluß** *m* GESCHÄFT, VW vertical amalgamation

vertikalisiert: ~er **Frachtraum** *m* TRANSP verticalized cargo space

Vertikal-: **Vertikalkonzern** *m* VW vertical combination; **Vertikalzugriff** *m* TRANSP vertical access

Vertrag *m* GESCHÄFT agreement, contract, pact, treaty, POL treaty, accord, RECHT agreement, *schriftliche Vereinbarung* contract, covenant, deed; **das auf den** ~ **anzuwendende Recht** RECHT proper law of the contract; ~ **über den Austausch von Lieferungen und Leistungen** RECHT contract of exchange of goods and services; ~ **zur Bereitstellung von Versorgungsdiensten** GESCHÄFT public service contract; ~ **mit Erstversicherer** VERSICH leading underwriter agreement; ~ **über die Europäische Union** (*VEU*) GESCHÄFT European Union Treaty; ~ **zwischen Fluglinien** TRANSP interline agreement; ~ **über Frachttermingeschäfte** BÖRSE, FINANZ freight futures contract; ~ **mit Generalunternehmen** RECHT prime contract; ~ **über Haftpflichtversicherung** VERSICH liability insuring agreement; ~ **mit Schutzwirkung für Dritte** RECHT contract with protective effect; ~ **auf unbestimmte Dauer** RECHT open-end contract; ~ **auf Unternehmensebene** PERSON company level agreement; ~ **zugunsten Dritter** RECHT contract for the benefit of a third party; ~ **über die Zusammenarbeit im Patentwesen** RECHT Patent Cooperation Treaty (*PCT*); ◆ **einen** ~ **aufheben** RECHT cancel a contract, rescind a contract; **etw in einen ~ einfügen** RECHT *Klausel, Bestimmung, Bedingung* build sth into a contract; **im ~ miteingeschlossene Rechte und Pflichten** RECHT implied terms of a contract; **einen ~ schließen mit** GESCHÄFT enter into a contract with; **einem ~ zustimmen** RECHT agree to a contract

vertraglich 1. *adj* RECHT contractual; ◆ **die ~en Bestimmungen ändern** RECHT vary the terms of a contract; **2.** *adv* RECHT by contract; ◆ **~ ausschließen** RECHT *Renten* contract out; **~ festlegen** GESCHÄFT stipulate

vertraglich: **~e Einbehaltung** *f* GESCHÄFT contract holdback; **~er Fälligkeitsmonat** *m* BÖRSE contract delivery month (*BrE*); **~er Geltungsbereich** *m* PERSON scope of agreement; **~er Kreditzins** *m* BÖRSE contractual loan rate; **~er Liefermonat** *m* BÖRSE contract delivery month (*BrE*); **~er Liefertermin** *m* BÖRSE contract delivery date (*BrE*); **~ vereinbarte Hypothek** *f* BANK conventional mortgage; **~ vereinbarte Miete** *f* GRUND contract rent; **~ vereinbarter Preis** *m* STEUER contract price (*AmE*); **~ Verpflichtete(r)** *mf* [decl. as adj] RECHT covenantor; **~ verpflichtete Partei** *f* RECHT party liable under contract; **~e Verpflichtungserklärung** *f* RECHT contractual formal obligation; **~e Wartung** *f* GESCHÄFT contract maintenance; **~es Wettbewerbsverbot** *nt* RECHT covenant not to compete; **~e Zahlung** *f* FINANZ contractual payment

verträglich *adj* GESCHÄFT compatible

Verträglichkeit *f* COMP compatibility, GESCHÄFT chemistry, compatibility

Vertrag: **Vertragsanfechtung** *f* VERSICH avoidance; **Vertragsangebot** *nt* RECHT offer of a contract, tender to contract (*TTC*); **Vertragsarbeit** *f* PERSON work by contract; **Vertragsaufhebung** *f* RECHT annulment of contract, resolution of contract; **Vertragsbearbeiter, in** *m,f* PERSON contracts officer; **Vertragsbedingungen** *f pl* RECHT conditions of contract, terms of contract, conditions; **Vertragsbeendigung** *f* RECHT termination; **Vertragsbeginn** *m* RECHT commencement of contract; **Vertragsbereitschaft** *f* RECHT readiness to contract; **Vertragsbestimmung** *f* RECHT contractual, provision, stipulation; **Vertragsbestimmungen** *f pl* GESCHÄFT, RECHT articles of agreement; **Vertragsbeziehung** *f* RECHT contractual relationship; **Vertragsbruch** *m* PERSON, RECHT breach of agreement, breach of contract, *Völkerrecht* violation of a treaty; **Vertragsbruch** *m* **ohne Folgeschaden** RECHT injuria sine damno

vertragsbrüchig *adj* RECHT in breach of contract

Vertrag: **Vertragsdauer** *f* RECHT contract period, duration of contract; **Vertragseingriff** *m* RECHT interference with contract; **Vertragseinhaltung** *f* RECHT adherence to contract, compliance with contract, observance of contract; **Vertragsentwurf** *m* RECHT draft agreement, draft contract; **Vertragserfüllung** *f* RECHT discharge of a contract, fulfillment of contract, performance of contract, VERWALT execution of contract; **Vertragserfüllungsgarantie** *f* RECHT guarantee for fulfillment of contract (*AmE*), guarantee for fulfilment of contract (*BrE*); **Vertragsergänzung** *f* RECHT supplement; **Vertragsfinanzierung** *f* FINANZ single finance; **Vertragsfrachtführer** *m* TRANSP contract carrier; **Vertragsfreiheit** *f* RECHT contractual freedom, freedom of contract

vertragsgebunden: **~er Plan** *m* BÖRSE contractual plan

Vertrag: **Vertragsgegenstand** *m* RECHT subject matter of contract

vertragsgemäß *adj* GESCHÄFT as per agreement; **nicht ~** *adj* GESCHÄFT, VW nonconforming; **~e Erfüllung** *f* RECHT specific performance

Vertrag: **Vertragsgrundlage** *f* RECHT basis of agreement, basis of contract; **Vertragshafen** *m* TRANSP treaty port; **Vertragshändler, in** *m,f* GESCHÄFT franchised dealer (*BrE*), RECHT authorized dealer; **Vertragsinhalt** *m* RECHT contents of contract; **Vertrags-Joint Venture** *nt* GESCHÄFT contract joint venture; **Vertragsklage** *f* RECHT action based on contract; **Vertragsklausel** *f* RECHT contract clause, stipulation; **Vertragslizenz** *f* IMP/EXP contract licence (*BrE*), contract license (*AmE*)

vertragsmäßig: **nicht ~e Ware** *f* VW nonconforming goods

Vertrag: **Vertragspartei** *f* PERSON party to an agreement, RECHT contract party, contracting party, contractor, party to a contract; **Vertragspartner, in** *m,f* RECHT contract party; **Vertragspflicht** *f* RECHT contractual obligation, obligation under a contract; **Vertragspreis** *m* STEUER contract price (*AmE*), VW target price; **Vertragspunkte** *m pl* GESCHÄFT, RECHT articles of agreement; **Vertragsrahmen** *m* PERSON scope of agreement; **Vertragsrecht** *nt* RECHT law of contract; **Vertragsrückversicherung** *f* VERSICH treaty reinsurance; **Vertragsschließende(r)** *mf* [decl. as adj] GESCHÄFT contractor; **Vertragsstaat** *m* PATENT contracting state; **Vertragsstrafe** *f* RECHT contractual penalty, penalty, liquidated damage

vertragstreu: **~e Partei** *f* FINANZ nondefaulting party, RECHT nondefaulting party, observant party

Vertrag: **Vertragsvereinbarung** *f* RECHT contract agreement; **Vertragsverhältnis** *nt* GESCHÄFT contractual relationship; **Vertragsverhandlungen** *f pl* PERSON, RECHT contract bargaining, contract negotiations; **Vertragsverletzung** *f* PERSON breach of contract, RECHT breach of contract, violation of contract; **Vertragsverpflichtung** *f* GESCHÄFT contractual liability, RECHT contractual duty, contractual obligation; **Vertragsvollmacht** *f* IMP/EXP contract licence (*BrE*), contract license (*AmE*); **Vertragsvorbereitung** *f* V&M pre-approach; **Vertragswert** *m* BÖRSE value of the contract

vertragswidrig *adj* RECHT contrary to the contract

Vertrag: **Vertragswille** *m* **der Parteien** RECHT intention of the contracting parties

vertrauen *vt* GESCHÄFT, RECHT rely on, trust

Vertrauen *nt* GESCHÄFT confidence, reliance; **~ in den Markt** V&M market confidence; ◆ **~ brechen** VW break confidence

Vertrauen: **Vertrauensbruch** *m* GESCHÄFT breach of confidence, breach of trust; **Vertrauensintervall** *nt* MATH *Statistik* confidence interval; **Vertrauenskoeffizient** *m* MATH confidence coefficient; **Vertrauensmißbrauch** *m* GESCHÄFT abuse of confidence, abuse of trust; **Vertrauensniveau** *nt* MATH *Statistik* confidence level; **Vertrauensschadenversicherung** *f* VERSICH commercial guaranty insurance, fidelity insurance, *Angestelltendeckung* commercial blanket bond; **Vertrauensverletzung** *f* GESCHÄFT breach of confidence, breach of trust

vertrauenswürdig *adj* GESCHÄFT trustworthy, reliable

Vertrauen: **Vertrauenswürdigkeit** *f* GESCHÄFT trustworthiness, reliability

vertraulich *adj* GESCHÄFT confidential, private, private and confidential, RECHT confidential; **~er Bericht** *m* VERWALT confidential report; **~e Information** *f* RECHT confidential information

Vertraulichkeit *f* RECHT confidentiality

vertraut *adj* GESCHÄFT au fait, familiar; ♦ **~ sein mit** GESCHÄFT be acquainted with, be au fait with, be familiar with; **jdn mit der Lage ~ machen** GESCHÄFT acquaint sb with the situation; **jdn mit etw ~ machen** GESCHÄFT acquaint sb with sth, acquaint sb of sth; **sich mit etw ~ machen** GESCHÄFT acquaint oneself with sth

vertraut: **~es Markenzeichen** *nt* PATENT, V&M wellknown mark; **~es Warenzeichen** *nt* PATENT, V&M well-known mark

Vertrautheit *f* V&M familiarity

Vertrautsein *nt* GESCHÄFT acquaintance

vertreiben *vt* GESCHÄFT, V&M distribute, market, sell

vertretbar *adj* GESCHÄFT fungible, justifiable; **~e Sachen** *f pl* vw fungibles

vertreten *vt* GESCHÄFT advocate, represent, POL *einen Wahlbezirk* hold; ♦ **zu wenig ~** GESCHÄFT *unterrepräsentieren* underrepresent

Vertreter, in *m,f* GESCHÄFT agent (*agt*), door-to-door salesman, representative (*rep.*), alternate member (*AmE*), alternate, PATENT assignee, representative (*rep.*), PERSON drummer (*infrml*) (*AmE*), sales representative (*rep, sales rep*), salesperson, salesman, *Abgesandter* delegate, RECHT *Vertragsrecht* agent (*agt*), V&M agent (*agt*), representative (*rep.*), sales representative (*rep, sales rep*), salesperson, salesman, door-to-door salesman, vw substitute; **~ einer außerparlamentarischen Interessengruppe** POL lobby group; **~ für das Frachtgeschäft** GESCHÄFT freight sales representative (*BrE*); **~ in geschäftlichen Angelegenheiten** GESCHÄFT business agent (*AmE*); **~ der Herstellerfirma** V&M manufacturer's agent; **~ des Metallismus** V&M metallist; **Vertreterbesuch** V&M *Kundenbesuch* sales call; **Vertreterbezirk** *m* V&M agent's territory; **Vertreterfahrtenbuch** *nt* TRANSP, V&M agent's vehicle record (*AVR*); **Vertretergebühr** *f* GESCHÄFT, IMP/EXP agency fee; **Vertreterprovision** *f* GESCHÄFT, IMP/EXP, V&M agency fee, agent's commission; **Vertretertagung** *f* V&M sales meeting

Vertretung *f* BÖRSE agency (*agcy*), GESCHÄFT agency (*agcy*), commercial agency, representation, PERSON, RECHNUNG, RECHT, V&M, VERWALT agency (*agcy*); ♦ **eine ~ gründen** GESCHÄFT create an agency

Vertretung: **Vertretungsbeziehung** *f* PERSON, RECHNUNG agency relationship; **Vertretungserfahrung** *f* V&M agency experience; **Vertretungstheorie** *f* BÖRSE, MGMNT, POL, VERWALT, VW agency theory; **Vertretungsverhältnis** *nt* PERSON, RECHNUNG agency (*agcy*); **Vertretungsvertrag** *m* RECHT agency agreement

Vertrieb *m* GESCHÄFT, TRANSP, V&M distribution; **~ durch ausgewählte Händler** V&M selective distribution; **~ nach dem Schneeballsystem** vw multi-level distributorship, pyramid selling; **Vertriebsabteilung** *f* MEDIEN circulation department; V&M marketing department; **Vertriebsbüro** *nt* TRANSP distribution office (*DO*), dock operations (*DO*); **Vertriebsdepot** *nt* TRANSP distribution depot; **Vertriebsdirektor, in** *m,f* MGMNT, PERSON, V&M sales director, sales executive;

Vertriebsfirma *f* IMP/EXP, TRANSP distributor; **Vertriebshändler** *m* IMP/EXP, TRANSP distributor; **Vertriebsingenieur, in** *m,f* PERSON sales engineer; **Vertriebskosten** *pl* GESCHÄFT, IND, TRANSP distribution costs, V&M marketing costs, sales costs; **Vertriebskostenanalyse** *f* V&M distribution cost analysis; **Vertriebsleistung** *f* TRANSP distributive ability; **Vertriebsleiter, in** *m,f* MGMNT, PERSON distribution manager, sales executive, TRANSP distribution manager, V&M sales executive; **Vertriebsleitung** *f* MGMNT physical distribution management (*PDM*), sales management; **Vertriebsnetz** *nt* GESCHÄFT distribution network; **Vertriebsorganisation** *f* IMP/EXP, TRANSP distributor; **Vertriebsplanung** *f* GESCHÄFT distribution planning, V&M market planning; **Vertriebspolitik** *f* GESCHÄFT distribution policy, TRANSP distribution policy, V&M sales policy; **Vertriebsprovision** *f* V&M distribution allowance; **Vertriebs- und Umsatzplan** *m* V&M marketing and sales plan; **Vertriebsunternehmen** *nt* IMP/EXP, TRANSP distributor; **Vertriebs- und Verkaufstätigkeit** *f* V&M merchandising service; **Vertriebszentrum** *nt* TRANSP distribution center (*AmE*), distribution centre (*BrE*)

vertuschen *vt* GESCHÄFT cover up

verunglimpfend: **~e Werbung** *f* V&M disparaging copy

Verunglimpfung *f* RECHT disparagement

verunreinigen *vt* UMWELT contaminate

Verunreinigung *f* IND, UMWELT pollution; **~ auf niedrigem Niveau** UMWELT background pollution

veruntreuen *vt* FINANZ misappropriate, peculate, RECHT *öffentliche Gelder* defalcate, embezzle

Veruntreuung *f* FINANZ misappropriation, RECHT peculation, *öffentliche Gelder* defalcation, embezzlement

verursachen *vt* GESCHÄFT spark off, *Kosten* incur, *Kostenanstieg* cause, trigger

Verursacherprinzip *nt* UMWELT polluter pays principle

verurteilen *vt* RECHT adjudge, condemn, *strafrechtlich* convict, sentence

Verurteilung *f* RECHT condemnation, *strafrechtlich* conviction, sentencing

vervielfachen *vt* GESCHÄFT duplicate, MATH multiply

Vervielfältigung *f* GESCHÄFT duplication, MATH multiplication, MEDIEN generation, vw reproduction

Vervollkommnung *f* GESCHÄFT improvement, perfection; **~ der Technologie** GESCHÄFT advance of technology; **Vervollkommnungspatent** *nt* PATENT improvement patent

vervollständigen *vt* GESCHÄFT complete, supplement

vervollständigt *adj* GESCHÄFT completed, supplemented

Verw. *abbr* (*Verwaltung*) GESCHÄFT, MGMNT, VERWALT admin (*infrml*) (*administration*), management

verwahren *vt* GESCHÄFT enshrine, RECHT hold in custody, keep in custody, keep in safe custody, *gerichtlich* impound

Verwahrer, in *m,f* BANK, RECHT bailee, custodian, depositary, safekeeper (*AmE*)

verwahrlost *adj* GESCHÄFT neglected; ♦ **in ~em Zustand** GESCHÄFT in a state of neglect

Verwahrung *f* BANK bailment, custody, deposit, safekeeping, *gerichtlich* impoundment, RECHT deposit, custody, safekeeping, bailment, *gerichtlich* impoundment

Verwahrzeitraum *m* BÖRSE holding period

verwalten *vt* GESCHÄFT, MGMNT, POL, RECHT administer, manage

verwaltend *adj* GESCHÄFT, MGMNT, POL managing, VERWALT administrative

Verwalter *m* GESCHÄFT, MGMNT, PERSON, POL administrator, manager

Verwalterin *f* GESCHÄFT, MGMNT, PERSON, POL administrator, manageress

verwaltet: ~**e Kosten** *pl* RECHNUNG managed costs; ~**es Vermögen** *nt* GESCHÄFT agency fund

Verwaltung GESCHÄFT administration (*admin*), management; ~ **der Finanzen** VERWALT financial administration; ~ **für internationale Zusammenarbeit** GESCHÄFT International Cooperation Administration (*ICA*); ~ **von Kapitalanlagen** FINANZ investment management; ~ **eines offenen Investmentfonds** BÖRSE, FINANZ unit trust management (*BrE*); ~ **wichtiger Akten** MGMNT vital records management; ~ **der Zollunion** (*VdZ*) IMP/EXP administration of the customs union (*ACU*); **Verwaltungsanteil** *m* RECHNUNG administrative activity element; **Verwaltungsausgaben** *f pl* VERWALT administrative expenses; **Verwaltungsausschuß** *m* GESCHÄFT administrative committee, prudential committee (*AmE*), MGMNT management committee; **Verwaltungsbeamte(r)** *m* [decl. as adj], **Verwaltungsbeamtin** *f* PERSON administration officer (*AO*); **Verwaltungsbehörde** *f* GESCHÄFT administrative authority, POL administration VERWALT administrative agency; **Verwaltungsbuchführung** *f* RECHNUNG government accounting; **Verwaltungsdienst** *m* GESCHÄFT civil service, public service; **Verwaltungsfachmann** *m* PERSON administrator; **Verwaltungsgebühr** *f* BANK management fee, VERSICH administrative charge, administrative fee; **Verwaltungsgemeinkosten** *pl* FINANZ administration expenses, administrative overheads, RECHNUNG administrative activity element, administrative overheads, general expenses, STEUER administrative cost, administrative costs; **Verwaltungsgesellschaft** *f* VW management company; **Verwaltungsgremium** *nt* PERSON administrative board; **Verwaltungskonto** *nt* VERSICH underwriting account (*U/a*); **Verwaltungskosten** *pl* FINANZ administration expenses, GESCHÄFT administrative cost, administrative costs, VERWALT administration costs, administrative burden; **Verwaltungslehre** *f* VERWALT administrative theory; **Verwaltungsleiter, in** *m,f* MGMNT, PERSON administrator

verwaltungsmäßig *adj* GESCHÄFT, MGMNT, VERWALT administrative; ~**e Verfügungskosten** *pl* VERWALT administrative costs of regulation, compliance costs

Verwaltung: **Verwaltungspersonal** *nt* PERSON administrative staff; **Verwaltungsproduktionsverhältnis** *nt* FINANZ, IND, VERWALT administration-production ratio; **Verwaltungsrat** *m* MGMNT board of directors, governing body, executive board; **Verwaltungsratsposten** *m* PERSON *Betriebswirtschaft* directorate, directorship; **Verwaltungsratssitzung** *f* MGMNT board meeting; **Verwaltungsratsvorsitzende(r)** *mf* [decl. as adj] MGMNT, PERSON chairman of the administrative board, chairman of the board of directors, chairman of the board of management, chairperson of the board; **Verwaltungsrecht** *nt* RECHT, VERWALT administrative law; **Verwaltungssitz** *m* MGMNT head office (*HO*); **Verwaltungssystem** *nt* MGMNT management system; **Verwaltungstätigkeit** *f* VERWALT administrative work

verwaltungstechnisch *adj* GESCHÄFT, MGMNT, VERWALT administrative; ~**es Kontrollverfahren** *nt* VERWALT administrative control procedure

Verwaltung: **Verwaltungstheorie** *f* MGMNT administrative theory; **Verwaltungsurkunde** *f* GRUND *Vermögensverwaltung* guardian deed; **Verwaltungsvertrag** *m* FINANZ investment contract, VW business management agreement; **Verwaltungsvorschriften** *f pl* RECHT administrative provisions, administrative regulations; **Verwaltungszentrum** *nt* VERWALT administrative center (*AmE*), administrative centre (*BrE*)

verwandeln *vt* GESCHÄFT change, convert; ♦ ~ **in** [+acc] GESCHÄFT convert into; ~ **zu** GESCHÄFT convert into

Verwandlung *f* GESCHÄFT change, conversion

verwandt *adj* IND allied, PATENT associated, RECHT related, SOZIAL cognate; ~**e Berufe** *m pl* IND allied trades; ~**e Fächer** *nt pl* SOZIAL cognate disciplines; ~**e Fachrichtungen** *f pl* SOZIAL cognate disciplines; ~**e Handwerke** *nt pl* IND allied trades; ~**e Industriebereiche** *m pl* IND allied industries; ~**es Warenzeichen** *nt* PATENT associated mark

verwässern *vt* BÖRSE dilute, GESCHÄFT *Idee, Politik, Aussage* water down

verwässert: ~**e Aktien** *f pl* BÖRSE watered shares; ~**es Kapital** *nt* FINANZ watered capital

Verwässerung *f* BÖRSE, FINANZ dilution; ~ **des Aktienkapitals** BÖRSE dilution of equity

verweigern *vt* GESCHÄFT deny, refuse, reject

verweigert *adj* GESCHÄFT denied, refused, rejected

Verweigerung *f* GESCHÄFT denial, refusal, rejection; ~ **des Bestätigungsvermerks** GESCHÄFT denial of opinion

Verweil- *in cpds* TRANSP turnaround; **Verweildauer** *f* TRANSP turnaround time (*AmE*), turnround time (*BrE*); **Verweilzeit** *f* TRANSP turnaround time (*AmE*), turnround time (*BrE*)

Verweis *m* GESCHÄFT reference (*ref.*), PERSON reprimand

verweisen *vt* GESCHÄFT refer to; ♦ ~ **auf** [+acc] GESCHÄFT refer to; **jdn auf etw** ~ GESCHÄFT refer sb to sb

Verweistabelle *f* COMP lookup table

Verweisung *f* GESCHÄFT reference (*ref.*), referral

verwendbar *adj* GESCHÄFT applicable, usable; ♦ ~ **bis** GESCHÄFT sell by; ~ **für** GESCHÄFT applicable to

Verwendbarkeit *f* GESCHÄFT appropriateness

verwenden *vt* GESCHÄFT apply, employ, make use of, use, utilize

Verwendung *f* GESCHÄFT, PATENT application, utilization; ~ **von Geldern** RECHNUNG use of funds; ~ **von Mitteln** RECHNUNG use of funds; ~ **im öffentlichen Interesse** PATENT public use; ~ **des Reingewinns** RECHNUNG, VERWALT appropriation of income; **Verwendungsfähigkeit** *f* GESCHÄFT adaptability

verwerten *vt* FINANZ liquidate, GESCHÄFT, IND, PATENT, UMWELT exploit, utilize

verwertet *adj* FINANZ, GESCHÄFT, IND, PATENT exploited, liquidated, utilized; ~**e Kapazität** *f* IND utilized capacity

Verwertung *f* FINANZ, GESCHÄFT, IND, PATENT exploitation, liquidation, working

verwestlicht: ~ **werden** *phr* GESCHÄFT become westernized

verwirken *vt* RECHT, VERSICH forfeit

verwirklichen 1. *vt* GESCHÄFT realize, *Ziel* materialize; **2. sich ~** *v refl* GESCHÄFT come to fruition

Verwirklichung *f* GESCHÄFT implementation; **~ einer Strategie** GESCHÄFT, MGMNT strategy implementation

verwirkt: ~e Sicherheit *f* VERSICH forfeited security

Verwirkung *f* RECHT forfeiture; **~ des Versicherungsanspruchs** VERSICH forfeiture

Verwüstung *f* UMWELT desertification

verzahnen *vt* GESCHÄFT interlink

verzahnt: ~e Verarbeitung *f* COMP concurrent processing

Verzehr *m* GESCHÄFT consumption; ♦ **nicht zum ~ geeignet** GESCHÄFT unfit for consumption

Verzeichnis *nt* COMP directory, *Datenbank* index, GESCHÄFT catalog (*AmE*), catalogue (*BrE*), schedule (*AmE*), PATENT, VERWALT register; **~ der zum Börsenhandel zugelassenen Wertpapiere** BÖRSE stock list; **~ fauler Kunden** *infrml* GESCHÄFT black book; **~ mündelsicherer Wertpapieranlagen** BÖRSE approved list of investments; **~ der zollpflichtigen Ladung** IMP/EXP, STEUER dutiable cargo list

verzerren *vt* VW distort

verzerrt *adj* MATH biased; **~e Auswahl** *f* MATH selection bias

Verzerrung *f* GESCHÄFT distort, MATH bias, VW distortion

Verzicht *m* GESCHÄFT relinquishment, PATENT waiving, RECHT *auf ein Recht* abandonment, disclaimer, waiving, relinquishment, renunciation, STEUER waiving, VERSICH sacrifice

verzichten: ~ auf *vt* [+acc] GESCHÄFT forego, *Macht, Freiheit* renounce, *Recht, Forderung, Anspruch* abandon, IMP/EXP *Zollgüter* abandon, PATENT waive, abandon, RECHT abandon, relinquish, waive, STEUER waive, VERSICH sacrifice

Verzicht: Verzichtklausel *f* VERSICH abandonment clause; **Verzichtserklärung** *f* VERSICH disclaimer; **Verzichtserklärungsklausel** *f* VERSICH waiver clause

verzinsen 1. *vt* BANK pay interest on; **2. sich ~** *v refl* BANK bear interest, yield interest

verzinslich: ~e Einlage *f* BANK interest-bearing deposit; **~es Einlagenkonto** *nt* FINANZ money market deposit account (*AmE*) (*MMDA*); **~er Ertrag** *m* BÖRSE interest-bearing yield; **~er Handelsbestand** *m* BÖRSE interest-bearing trading portfolio; **~es Instrument** *nt* BÖRSE interest-bearing instrument; **~es Kontokorrentkonto** *nt* BANK, FINANZ negotiable order of withdrawal account (*AmE*), NOW account (*AmE*); **~e mindestreservepflichtige Einlagen** *f pl* BANK interest-bearing eligible liabilities (*BrE*) (*IBELS*); **~e Rendite** *f* BÖRSE interest-bearing yield; **~e Schuldverschreibung** *f* BÖRSE active bond, interest-bearing bond; **~es Steuerzertifikat** *nt* STEUER certificate of tax deposit (*CTD*); **~e Verbindlichkeiten** *f pl* BANK, RECHNUNG interest-bearing liabilities; **nicht ~e Wertpapiere** *nt pl* BÖRSE non-interest-bearing securities

verzinst: ~es Sparkonto *nt* BANK, FINANZ negotiable order of withdrawal account (*AmE*), NOW account (*AmE*)

Verzinsung *f* BANK payment of interest, BÖRSE, GESCHÄFT return; **~ der Aktiva** BÖRSE asset return; **Verzinsungsverbot** *nt* BANK ban of interest payments

verzögern *vt* GESCHÄFT delay

verzögert: ~e Auslieferung *f* GESCHÄFT delayed delivery;

~e Reaktion *f* GESCHÄFT lag response; **~es Risiko** *nt* BANK lag risk; **~e Variable** *f* MATH lagged variable

Verzögerung *f* COMP delay, GESCHÄFT delay, lag, VW time lag, lag; **Verzögerungstaktik** *f* GESCHÄFT delaying tactics

verzollen *vt* IMP/EXP, TRANSP, VW clear through customs

Verzollung *f* IMP/EXP, TRANSP clearance, customs clearance, VW clearing; **Verzollungsgruppe** *f* IMP/EXP clearance group (*CG*); **Verzollungswert** *m* IMP/EXP *Ware* current domestic value (*CDV*)

Verzug *m* GESCHÄFT, RECHT *bei vertraglicher Leistung* default, delay; **in ~ befindliche Partei** *f* RECHT *Vertragsrecht* party in default; **Verzugsfall** *m* FINANZ event of default; **Verzugsschaden** *m* RECHT *Vertragsrecht* damage caused by default; **Verzugstage** *m pl* GESCHÄFT days after date (*dd, d.d.*); **Verzugszinsen** *m pl* BANK default interest, interest on arrears, interest on overdue accounts

verzweigen *vt* COMP branch

Verzweigung *f* COMP *eines Programms* branch

Veterinär- *in cpds* IMP/EXP veterinary; **Veterinäraufsicht** *f* IMP/EXP veterinary control; **Veterinärkontrolle** *f* IMP/EXP veterinary control; **Veterinärzeugnis** *nt* IMP/EXP veterinary certificate

Veto *nt* GESCHÄFT, POL veto

Vetternwirtschaft *f* GESCHÄFT, PERSON nepotism

VEU *abbr* (*Vertrag über die Europäische Union*) GESCHÄFT European Union Treaty

VGA *abbr* (*Videografikadapter*) COMP VGA (*video graphics adapter*); **VGA-Karte** *f* COMP VGA card

VGR *abbr* (*Volkswirtschaftliche Gesamtrechnung*) RECHNUNG System of National Accounts (*SNA*)

v.H. *abbr* (*vom Hundert*) GESCHÄFT pc (*per cent*), P/C (*per cent*)

via *prep* KOMM via

Video *nt* KOMM, MEDIEN video; **Videoaufnahme** *f* KOMM, MEDIEN video cassette recording, videotape recording (*VTR*); **Videoband** *nt* KOMM, MEDIEN videotape; **auf Videoband aufzeichnen** *phr* KOMM, MEDIEN video tape; **Videobildschirm** *m* COMP, KOMM, V&M video display; **Videoeinkauf** *m* V&M video shopping; **Videografikadapter** *m* (*VGA*) COMP video graphics adapter (*VGA*); **Video-Grafikanordnung** *f* COMP video graphics adapter (*VGA*); **Videokamera** *f* KOMM, MEDIEN video camera; **Videokarte** *f* COMP video card; **Videokassette** *f* KOMM, MEDIEN video cassette; **Videokonferenz** *f* COMP, KOMM, V&M video conference, video conferencing; **Videokopierdiebstahl** *m* MEDIEN, RECHT video piracy; **Videomonitor** *m* COMP, KOMM, MEDIEN video monitor; **Videoplatte** *f* COMP video disk; **Videorekorder** *m* KOMM, MEDIEN video cassette recorder (*VCR*), videotape recorder (*VTR*); **Videotext** *m* COMP, KOMM Videotex®, Teletext®, teletex

Vieh *nt* GESCHÄFT cattle; **Viehcontainer** *m* TRANSP cattle container; **Viehhof** *m* GESCHÄFT stockyard; **Viehtransporter** *m* TRANSP cattle lorry (*BrE*), cattle truck (*AmE*); **Viehtransportwagen** *m* TRANSP cattle lorry (*BrE*), cattle truck (*AmE*); **Viehzüchter** *m* GESCHÄFT stockbreeder, stockman (*AmE*)

Viel- *in cpds* GESCHÄFT multiple

Vielfache(s) *nt* [decl. as adj] MATH multiple

Viel-: Vielschutzversicherung *f* VERSICH multiple protection insurance; **Vielseher** *m* V&M *Fernsehen* heavy viewer; **Vielseitigkeit** *f* COMP, GESCHÄFT, V&M versatility

vielstaatlich: ~e Gerichtsbarkeit *f* RECHT multi-jurisdiction

vielversprechend 1. *adj* GESCHÄFT up-and-coming, promising; **2.** *adv* ♦ ~ **beginnen** GESCHÄFT *Plan, Projekt* get off to a flying start

Vielzweck- *in cpds* COMP, GESCHÄFT multipurpose (*MP*)

Vierfach- *in cpds* MATH quadruple

vierfach *adj* GESCHÄFT in quadruplicate; ♦ **in ~er Ausfertigung** GESCHÄFT in quadruplicate

Vierfach-: **Vierfachstapler** *m* TRANSP quadruple stacker

Vierfarbendruck *m* V&M four-color set (*AmE*), four-colour set (*BrE*)

Viermächteabkommen *nt* GESCHÄFT, POL quadripartite agreement

Vierte: ~ **Richtlinie** *f* **zum Gesellschaftsrecht** RECHT *EU* Fourth Company Law Directive

vierte: ~s **Quartal** *nt* GESCHÄFT fourth quarter (*4Q*)

Vierteilen *nt* PERSON quartering

Viertel *nt* GESCHÄFT *des Jahres* quarter (*qtr*); ♦ **um ein ~ gestiegener Kurs** BÖRSE quarter up price

Viertel: **Vierteljahresrate** *f* RECHNUNG quarterly installment (*AmE*), quarterly instalment (*BrE*); **Vierteljahresschrift** *f* GESCHÄFT, MEDIEN quarterly

vierteljährlich 1. *adj* GESCHÄFT quarterly; **2.** *adv* GESCHÄFT quarterly; ♦ ~ **entlohnen** GESCHÄFT pay by the quarter; ~ **zahlen** GESCHÄFT pay by the quarter

vierteln *vt* GESCHÄFT quarter

Viertel: **Viertelseitenanzeige** *f* V&M quarter page advertisement

24-Stunden-Service *m* KOMM, TRANSP same-day service

vierzehn: ~ **Tage** *m pl* GESCHÄFT fortnight

vierzehntägig *adj* GESCHÄFT biweekly, fortnightly

Vierzigtagehausrecht *nt* GESCHÄFT, TRANSP quarantine

Vignette *f* TRANSP, V&M vignette

VIP *abbr* (*sehr wichtige Person, bedeutende Persönlichkeit, hohes Tier*) GESCHÄFT VIP (*very important person*); **VIP-Lounge** *f* TRANSP executive lounge

virenbefallen *adj* COMP infected by a virus

virenfrei *adj* COMP virus-free

virtuell *adj* COMP virtual; ~e **Festplatte** *f* COMP RAM disk

Virus *m or nt* COMP virus

Visby: ~ **Regeln** *f pl* TRANSP Visby Rules

Vision *f* GESCHÄFT, MGMNT vision

Visitation *f* GESCHÄFT visitation

Visitenkarte *f* GESCHÄFT business card, visiting card

Viskosität *f* GESCHÄFT viscosity

Visum *nt* VERWALT visa; ~ **zur einmaligen Einreise** VERWALT single entry visa; ~ **zur mehrmaligen Einreise** VERWALT multi-entry visa

Vitrine *f* V&M showcase

Vizepräsident, in *m,f* (*VP*) MGMNT, PERSON, POL vice president (*VP, veep*)

VN *abbr* (*Vereinte Nationen*) VW UN (*United Nations*), UNO (*United Nations Organization*)

Vol. *abbr* (*Volumen*) BÖRSE, GESCHÄFT turnover, vol. (*volume*), RECHNUNG, VW vol. (*volume*)

Volk *nt* POL nation, people

Völkerrecht *nt* RECHT international law

völkerrechtlich: ~es **Abkommen** *nt* GESCHÄFT, POL treaty

Volk: **Volksbewegung** *f* GESCHÄFT grass-roots movement; **Volkeinkommen** *nt* VW aggregate income, national income; **Volksentscheid** *m* GESCHÄFT referendum; **Volksgesundheit** *f* GESCHÄFT public health; **Volkskapitalismus** *m* POL, VW popular capitalism; **Volkspension** *f* PERSON demogrant; **Volksschulabschluß** *m obs* SOZIAL Certificate of Secondary Education (*BrE*) (*obs*) (*CSE*)

Volksvermögen *nt* VW national wealth; **Volksvermögensrechnung** *f* VW national balance sheet

Volkswirt, in *m,f* PERSON Bachelor of Economics (*BEcon*), VW economist

Volkswirtschaft *f* POL political economy, VW national economy, *Wirtschaft eines Landes* economy

volkswirtschaftlich 1. *adj* BANK, FINANZ, GESCHÄFT, POL, VERWALT economic, VW aggregate, economic; **2.** *adv* BANK, FINANZ, GESCHÄFT, POL, VERWALT, VW economically

volkswirtschaftlich: ~e **Gesamtrechnung** *f* RECHNUNG macroeconomic accounting, national accounting, V&M national account, VW macroeconomic accounting, national accounting

Volkswirtschaftlich: ~e **Gesamtrechnung** *f* (*VGR*) RECHNUNG System of National Accounts (*SNA*)

volkswirtschaftlich: ~e **Institution** *f* VW economic institution; ~e **Kosten** *pl* VW bad, external cost; ~e **Kosten** *pl* **des Monopols** VW social cost of monopoly; ~e **Opportunitätskosten** *pl* **von Devisen** BÖRSE social opportunity cost of foreign exchange; ~e **Theorie** *f* VW economic theory

Volkswirtschaft: **Volkswirtschaftslehre** *f* VW public economics, economics

Volk: **Volkszählung** *f* GESCHÄFT, MATH population census, census of population

Voll- *in cpds* GESCHÄFT full

voll 1. *adj* GESCHÄFT full, complete; ♦ **zum ~en Ausgleich** RECHNUNG in full settlement, full to capacity; ~e **Bereitstellung von Mitteln beschließen** POL vote full supply; ~e **Beteiligung zugesagt** GESCHÄFT full interest admitted (*fia*); **in ~em Gange sein** POL be in full swing; **bei ~er Kapazität** GESCHÄFT at full capacity; **mit ~er Kraft arbeiten** IND go full steam; **bei ~er Leistungsfähigkeit** GESCHÄFT at full capacity; **ein ~es Programm haben** GESCHÄFT work to a very tight schedule; **2.** *adv* GESCHÄFT fully, completely; ♦ **nicht ~ ausgeben** GESCHÄFT *vorhandene Mittel*, VW underspend; ~ **ausgelastet** RECHNUNG full to capacity; ~ **bezahlt** GESCHÄFT fully paid (*f.p.*); ~ **finanzieren** FINANZ mortgage out; ~ **finanziert** VERWALT fully funded; **etw ~ nutzen** GESCHÄFT make full use of sth; **nicht ~ tragen** RECHNUNG underabsorb; **nicht ~ übernehmen** RECHNUNG underabsorb; **sich ~ verausgaben** GESCHÄFT *bei der Arbeit* work flat out (*infrml*)

voll: ~er **Börsenschluß** *m* BÖRSE full lot, *Obligationen mit einem Nennwert von $ 1000* round lot (*AmE*); ~e **Deckung** *f* GESCHÄFT, VERSICH, VERWALT full coverage; ~ **eingezahlte Aktie** *f* BÖRSE fully-paid share; ~ **eingezahltes Kapital** *nt* FINANZ paid-up capital; ~er **Eintrittspreis** *m* GESCHÄFT adult price, full entrance fee; ~er **Fahrpreis** *m* TRANSP adult fare; ~es **Gewicht** *nt* GESCHÄFT full weight; ~e **Haftung** *f* GESCHÄFT full liability; ~er **Havarieeinschluß** *m* VERSICH general average in full; ~e **hundert Aktien** *f pl* BÖRSE full lot,

Obligationen mit einem Nennwert von $ 1000 round lot (*AmE*); **~e Reichweite** *f* **und Last** TRANSP full reach and burden; **~er Satz** *m* PERSON full rate; **~e Sicherheitsrücklage** *f* **für große Havarie** VERSICH general average in full; **~er Steuerfreibetrag** *m* STEUER full exemption; **~er Terminkalender** *m* MGMNT busy schedule; **~er Versicherungsschutz** *m* VERSICH full coverage; **nicht ~e Wiedereinholung** *f* **von Gemeinkosten** RECHNUNG underrecovery of overhead costs; **~er Wortlaut** *m* GESCHÄFT *Text* text in full

Voll-: **Vollabschreibung** *f* **im esten Jahr** FINANZ free depreciation; **Volladdierwerk** *nt* COMP *Hardware* full adder

Vollast: zur ~ *phr* IND at full capacity

Voll-: **Vollauslastung** *f* IND full capacity; **Vollbeschäftigung** *f* VW full employment; **Vollbeschäftigungsbudget** *nt* VW *Finanzwirtschaft* full-employment budget; **Vollbringung** *f* GESCHÄFT achievement

vollenden *vt* GESCHÄFT accomplish, achieve, complete

vollendet *adj* GESCHÄFT accomplished, completed, achieved; **~e Tatsache** *f* GESCHÄFT fait accompli

Vollendung *f* GESCHÄFT accomplishment, achievement, completion

Voll-: **Vollhafter** *m* GESCHÄFT general partner

völlig: **~e Verarmung** *f* VW absolute poverty; **~e Verknappung** *f* VW absolute scarcity; **~er Wechsel** *m* GESCHÄFT switchover

Voll-: **Volljährigkeit** *f* RECHT majority

vollkaskoversichert *adj* VERSICH comprehensively covered; ◆ **~ sein** TRANSP, VERSICH have complete vehicle insurance, have fully comprehensive cover

Voll-: **Vollkaskoversicherungspolice** *f* VERSICH fully comprehensive insurance policy, fully comprehensive cover, fully comprehensive insurance

vollkommen *adj* GESCHÄFT perfect, accomplished; **~er Markt** *m* VW perfect market; **~es Monopol** *nt* VW absolute monopoly; **~e Preisdiskriminierung** *f* VW perfect price discrimination

Vollkosten *pl* FINANZ, RECHNUNG full cost; **Vollkostenbasis** *f* RECHNUNG absorbed basis, full cost basis; **Vollkostenkalkulation** *f* RECHNUNG full costing, VW full-cost pricing, mark-up pricing; **Vollkostenmethode** *f* FINANZ, RECHNUNG full-cost method; **Vollkostenprinzip** *nt* RECHNUNG full costing; **Vollkostenrechnung** *f* FINANZ absorption, absorption costing, full costing; **Vollkostenvertrag** *m* GESCHÄFT cost-plus contract

Vollmacht *f* BÖRSE *Stimmrecht* proxy, *Wechselrecht* authority, procuration, GESCHÄFT mandate, POL warrant, RECHT mandate, power of attorney (*PA*); **~ zum Verkauf von Aktien** BÖRSE stock power; ◆ **~ erteilen** GESCHÄFT authorize; **jdm eine ~ erteilen** RECHT confer authority on sb, give sb a power of attorney, grant sb a power of attorney, vest sb with authority; **jdm stellvertretende ~ erteilen** GESCHÄFT give vicarious authority to sb; **seine ~ überschreiten** RECHT act ultra vires, exceed one's authority

Vollmacht: **Vollmachterteilung** *f* RECHT authorization; **Vollmachtsanweisung** *f* RECHT proxy statement; **Vollmachtsstatut** *nt* RECHT *Vertragsrecht* lex auctoritatis

vollmachtsüberschreitend 1. *adj* RECHT ultra vires; **2.** *adv* RECHT ultra vires

Vollmacht: **Vollmachtsübertragung** *f* GESCHÄFT delegation of authority; **Vollmachtsurkunde** *f* RECHT letter of attorney, procuratory letter, *administrativ* power of attorney (*PA*)

Voll-: **Vollmitglied** *nt* GESCHÄFT full member; **Vollpension** *f* FREI full board; **Vollschutz** *m* PATENT full protection

vollständig 1. *adj* GESCHÄFT complete, entire, in full; **2.** *adv* GESCHÄFT completely; ◆ **~ abgeschrieben sein** GESCHÄFT be a write-off (*infrml*); **~ ausgeschüttet** BÖRSE fully distributed; **~ und ausschließlich** RECHT wholly and exclusively; **~ bewertet** BÖRSE fully valued; **~ zahlbar bei Zuteilung** FINANZ payment in full on allotment

vollständig: **~ freier Gabelstapler** *m* TRANSP full free fork-lift truck; **~e Freistellung** *f* STEUER full exemption; **nicht ~ gezeichnet** *adj* FINANZ undersubscribed; **~e Konkurrenz** *f* VW perfect competition, pure competition; **~er Name** *m* GESCHÄFT full name; **~e Notierung** *f* BÖRSE full quotation; **~e Offenlegung** *f* RECHT full disclosure; **~es Preisangebot** *nt* BÖRSE full quotation; **~er Text** *m* GESCHÄFT text in full; **~er Wettbewerb** *m* VW perfect competition, pure competition

Voll-: **Vollständigkeit** *f* RECHNUNG completeness

vollstreckbar *adj* RECHT enforceable

Voll-: **Vollstreckbarkeit** *f* RECHT enforceability; **Vollstreckbarkeit** *f* **eines Tarifvertrags** PERSON legal enforceability of collective agreement (*BrE*)

vollstrecken *vt* RECHT execute, *Urteil* enforce

Vollstreckung *f* RECHT enforcement, execution; **~ eines Urteils in einem anderen Staat** RECHT extension of a judgment for enforcement; **Vollstreckungsanweisung** *f* GESCHÄFT enforcement order; **Vollstreckungsbeamte(r)** *m* [decl. as adj], **Vollstreckungsbeamtin** *f* RECHT bailiff; **Vollstreckungsgläubiger** *m* GRUND, RECHT judgment creditor; **Vollstreckungspfandrecht** *nt* RECHT involuntary lien; **Vollstreckungsschuldner** *m* RECHT judgment debtor (*AmE*); **Vollstreckungsverfahren** *nt* GESCHÄFT enforcement procedure, RECHT enforcement proceedings, execution proceedings, executory proceedings

Voll-: **Volltext** *m* GESCHÄFT text in full

vollwertig: **~er Ersatz** *m* VW perfect substitute

Voll-: **Vollwertkost** *f* SOZIAL health foods

vollzählig: **~ machen** *phr* GESCHÄFT bring up to strength

Vollzeit- *in cpds* PERSON full-time; **Vollzeitarbeitskraft** *f* PERSON full-time employee, full-timer; **Vollzeitbeschäftigung** *f* PERSON full-time employment; **Vollzeitkraft** *f* PERSON full-time employee, full-timer

vollziehen *vt* RECHT accomplish, carry out, enforce, execute

vollziehend *adj* POL, RECHT executive

Vollziehung *f* RECHT accomplishment, enforcement, execution

Voll-: **Vollzugsbeamte(r)** *m* [decl. as adj], **Vollzugsbeamtin** *f* RECHT law enforcement official

Volontär, in *m,f* PERSON unpaid trainee, volunteer

Volontariat *nt* PERSON period of training, *Stelle* traineeship

Volontär: **Volontärstelle** *f* PERSON placement

Volumen *nt* (*Vol.*) BÖRSE, GESCHÄFT turnover, volume (*vol.*), RECHNUNG, VW volume (*vol.*); **Volumenfrachtvertrag** *m* TRANSP volume contract of affreightment (*Volcoa*); **Volumengebühr** *f* TRANSP volume charge

volumenreich *adj* BÖRSE high-volume

Volumen: **Volumenverhältnis** *nt* VW volume ratio

vor *prep* GESCHÄFT ante, before, prior to

Vorabkosten *pl* VW front-end costs

Vorabwerbung *f* MEDIEN advance publicity

vorangehen *vi* GESCHÄFT take the lead, precede, MGMNT *mit gutem Beispiel* take the lead

vorangehend *adj* GESCHÄFT preceding

Vorankündigung *f* GESCHÄFT advance notice; **~ einer Emission** BÖRSE red-herring prospectus; **~ eines Emissionsprospektes** BÖRSE red herring

Voranmeldung *f* GESCHÄFT advance notice, PATENT previous application; ◆ **nur nach Voranmeldung** GESCHÄFT by appointment only

Voranschlag *m* FINANZ preliminary budget, GESCHÄFT *Kosten* cost estimate, estimate

vorantreiben *vt* GESCHÄFT expedite, spur, PERSON *Arbeit, Prozeß* drive, expedite, speed up

Vorantreiben *nt* GESCHÄFT speed-up

Vorarbeit *f* GESCHÄFT preparatory work; **Vorarbeiten** *f pl* GESCHÄFT groundwork

Vorarbeiter, in *m,f* GESCHÄFT ganger (*BrE*), MGMNT supervisor, PERSON *Fertigungsbetrieb, Bearbeitungsbetrieb* charge hand, foreman, head foreman, overseer, supervisor; **~ der Produktion** MGMNT line supervisor

Voraus- *in cpds* GESCHÄFT advance, forward, preliminary

voraus *adv* GESCHÄFT ahead; ◆ **im ~** GESCHÄFT anticipated, in advance, up front; **im ~ aufgezeichnet** FREI, MEDIEN prerecorded; **im ~ aufgezeichnete Sendung** MEDIEN pick-up (*jarg*), prerecorded broadcast; **im ~ bestellen** GESCHÄFT book in advance; **im ~ bezahlt** GESCHÄFT, KOMM paid in advance, postpaid (*p.p.*); **im ~ gewählte Kampagne** V&M preselected campaign; **etw im ~ planen** GESCHÄFT plan ahead for sth; **im ~ vereinbart** GESCHÄFT pre-arranged; **im ~ zahlbar** GESCHÄFT payable in advance

Voraus-: **Vorausanzeige** *f* RECHT advance notice; **Vorausbenachrichtigung** *f* RECHT advance notice

vorausberechnen *vt* FINANZ precompute, GESCHÄFT predict

vorausberechnet *adj* GESCHÄFT predicted

vorausbestellen *vt* GESCHÄFT book in advance

vorausbestimmen *vt* GESCHÄFT predetermine

vorausbezahlt *adj* FINANZ, GESCHÄFT, TRANSP, V&M prepaid (*ppd*); **~e Auslagen** *f pl* TRANSP advanced charge, advanced disbursement; **~e Fracht** *f* IMP/EXP, TRANSP freight prepaid (*frt ppd*); **~e Gebühr** *f* TRANSP advanced charge, advanced disbursement, prepaid charge; **~e Kosten** *pl* TRANSP prepaid charges, V&M prepaid costs; **~e Zinsen** *m pl* FINANZ prepaid interest

vorausdenkend *adj* GESCHÄFT forward-thinking

Voraus-: **Vorausbestellung** *f* GESCHÄFT advance order; **Vorausdisposition** *f* TRANSP, VERWALT advance arrangement; **Vorausfaktura** *f* GESCHÄFT, IMP/EXP pro forma invoice

vorausgehen *vt* GESCHÄFT precede, predate

vorausgeplant *adj* GESCHÄFT preplanned

Voraus-: **Vorauskasse** *f* GESCHÄFT prepayment, advance payment, money up front

vorausplanen *vt* GESCHÄFT preplan

Voraus-: **Vorausplanung** *f* FINANZ, GESCHÄFT forward planning, TRANSP preplanning; **Vorausplazierung** *f* BÖRSE advance selling; **Vorausprämie** *f* VERSICH advance premium; **Vorausrechnung** *f* FINANZ advance bill, advance invoice, RECHNUNG advance bill; **Vorausregistrierung** *f* BÖRSE shelf registration (*AmE*)

voraussagbar *adj* GESCHÄFT foreseeable, predictable

Voraus-: **Voraussage** *f* GESCHÄFT forecast, prediction; **Vorausschätzung** *f* GESCHÄFT preliminary estimate; **Vorausschau** *f* GESCHÄFT prediction

vorausschauend *adj* GESCHÄFT forward-looking

voraussehen *vt* GESCHÄFT anticipate

voraussetzen *vt* GESCHÄFT assume, presume, suppose; ◆ **vorausgesetzt, daß** GESCHÄFT provided that

Voraussetzung *f* GESCHÄFT assumption, supposition, premise, prerequisite, presumption; **~ für Stichwahl** POL *Präsidentschaftswahlen* run-off (*AmE*), run-off election (*AmE*); ◆ **unter der ~, daß** GESCHÄFT on condition that, on the premise that, on the understanding that

voraussichtlich *adj* GESCHÄFT presumable, probable, prospective; **~e Abfahrtszeit** *f* TRANSP estimated time of departure (*ETD*); **~~er Ablauf** *m* RECHNUNG estimated lapse; **~ Ablegezeit** *f* TRANSP estimated time of sailing (*ETS*); **~ Ankunftstermin** *m* TRANSP estimated time of arrival (*ETA*); **~e Ankunftszeit** *f* TRANSP estimated time of arrival (*ETA*); **~es Datum** *nt* GESCHÄFT expected date; **~er Jahresbericht** *m* FINANZ estimated financial report; **~er Kunde** *m*, **~e Kundin** *f* GESCHÄFT prospective customer; **~e Sterblichkeit** *f* VERSICH expected mortality; **~e Veranlagung** *f* VERSICH prospective rating; **~e Verkäufe** *m pl* V&M anticipated sales; **~er Verwahrzeitraum** *m* V&M anticipated holding period

Vorauswahl *f* GESCHÄFT, PERSON shortlist; ◆ **eine ~ treffen** GESCHÄFT, PERSON shortlist

vorauszahlen *vt* BANK, FINANZ, RECHNUNG, STEUER prepay .

Vorauszahlung *f* BANK, FINANZ, GESCHÄFT advance, advance payment, money up front, RECHNUNG payment in advance, prepayment, STEUER prepayment; ◆ **eine ~ leisten** BANK make an advance payment

Vorauszahlung: **Vorauszahlungen** *f pl* **und Stundungen** *f pl* **im Auslandszahlungsverkehr** BÖRSE leads and lags; **Vorauszahlungsprämie** *f* VERSICH deposit premium

Vorbedingung *f* GESCHÄFT precondition, prerequisite

Vorbehalt *m* GESCHÄFT reservation, RECHNUNG qualification, SOZIAL qualification period, TRANSP exceptions clause, VERSICH exception; ◆ **ohne ~** GESCHÄFT outright, RECHNUNG without qualification

vorbehalten: sich ~ *v refl* GESCHÄFT reserve

vorbehaltlich *prep* GESCHÄFT subject to, RECHT provided that, subject to, with the proviso that, VERSICH *Veränderung, Zustimmung* subject to; ◆ **~ anderslautender Bestimmungen** GESCHÄFT except as otherwise herein provided (*eohp*); **~ Bruchschaden** VERSICH subject to breakage; **~ großer Havarie** VERSICH unless general

vorbehaltlos *adj* BÖRSE clean

Vorbehalt: **Vorbehaltsklausel** *f* GESCHÄFT exceptions clause, reservation, RECHT conditional clause, exceptions clause, proviso clause, saving clause

vorbehaltslos *adj* RECHNUNG without qualification; **~e Bestätigung** *f* RECHNUNG positive confirmation

***Vorbehalt*: Vorbehaltspreis** *m* GESCHÄFT *Auktion* reserve price

vorbehandeln *vt* UMWELT pre-treat

Vorbehandlung *f* UMWELT pre-treatment

Vorbemerkung *f* PATENT preamble, RECHT preliminary statement; **Vorbemerkungen** *f pl* MEDIEN preliminary pages

Vorbenutzung *f* PATENT prior use; **Vorbenutzungsfall** *m* PATENT prior use

vorbereiten *vt* GESCHÄFT, MGMNT prepare, V&M make ready

vorbereitend: **~e Arbeiten** *f pl* GESCHÄFT preparatory work, IND make-ready work; **~e Maßnahme** *f* GESCHÄFT preliminary

Vorbereitung *f* GESCHÄFT, MGMNT preparation; **~ zur Fertigung** IND industrial engineering; ◆ **in ~ sein** KOMM be in the pipeline, MEDIEN in preparation

***Vorbereitung*: Vorbereitungssitzung** *f* MGMNT warm-up session

Vorbestellung *f* FREI advance booking, booking, reservation, GESCHÄFT *Waren* advance order, MEDIEN subscription

vorbeugen *vt* GESCHÄFT, MGMNT, RECHT prevent

Vorbeugung *f* GESCHÄFT prevention

vorbeugend *adj* GESCHÄFT, MGMNT preventive; **~e Instanthaltung** *f* MGMNT preventive maintenance; **~e Maßnahme** *f* GESCHÄFT, RECHT preventive measure; **~e Prüfung** *f* GESCHÄFT preventive inspection; **~e Wartung** *f* MGMNT preventive maintenance

Vorbildung *f* PERSON background, SOZIAL educational background

Vorbörse *f* BÖRSE before-hours dealings

vorbörslich *adj* BÖRSE before official hours

vorbringen *vt* GESCHÄFT set forth, *Problem* air, RECHT *Anspruch, Antrag* submit

vordatieren *vt* GESCHÄFT foredate, *Dokument, Scheck* postdate

vordatiert *adj* GESCHÄFT postdated (*PD*); **~e Ausgabe** *f* V&M *einer Zeitung* predate

vordere: **~r Klappentext** *m* MEDIEN inside front cover

Vordergrund *m* COMP *Programme* foreground; **Vordergrundprogramm** *nt* COMP *Multiprogrammverarbeitung* foreground program

Vordermann: **auf ~ bringen** *phr jarg* GESCHÄFT revamp (*infrml*), lick into shape (*infrml*)

Vorderseite *f* MEDIEN front page, recto (*ro.*)

vorderste: **~ Front** *f* V&M leading edge

vordringlich: **~er Auftrag** *m* GESCHÄFT rush job

Vordruck *m* GESCHÄFT printed form, blank form, PATENT form

vorehelich: **~er Vertrag** *m* RECHT prenuptial agreement, prenuptial contract

Voreigentümer, in *m,f* PATENT predecessor in title

voreilig *adj* GESCHÄFT premature; **~es Handeln** *nt* BÖRSE gun jumping

voreingenommen *adj* GESCHÄFT biased, prejudiced

Voreingenommenheit *f* GESCHÄFT bias, prejudice

voreingestellt *adj* COMP preset

Vorentwurf *m* FINANZ preliminary draft, RECHT rough draft, V&M rough

vorerwähnt *adj obs* GESCHÄFT, KOMM above

Vorfahrt *f* TRANSP right of way

vorfakturieren *vt* V&M prebill

Vorfakturierung *f* V&M prebill, prebilling

Vorfälligkeit *f* BANK prepayment; **Vorfälligkeitsentschädigung** *f* BANK prepayment penalty; **Vorfälligkeitsklausel** *f* BANK acceleration clause

Vorfeld *nt* GESCHÄFT run-up, TRANSP *am Flughafen* apron; ◆ **im ~** IND at the forefront; **im ~ von** GESCHÄFT in the run-up to

Vorfilm *m* FREI trailer

vorführen *vt* GESCHÄFT *Unterhaltung* perform, produce, V&M demonstrate, present

Vorführraum *m* MEDIEN viewing room

Vorführung *f* GESCHÄFT performance, production, V&M demonstration, presentation

Vorgabe *f* MGMNT performance target; **Vorgabekosten** *pl* FINANZ, RECHNUNG budgetary costs, budgeted cost, vw budgetary costs, ideal standard cost, target cost; **Vorgabezeit** *f* GESCHÄFT standard time, PERSON *Arbeitsvorbereitung, Produktionsplanung* allowed time

Vorgang *m* GESCHÄFT operation, transaction, *Akten* case, case file, file, record, IND process; **Vorgangsakte** *f* GESCHÄFT case file

vorgeben *vt* GESCHÄFT simulate, predetermine

vorgedruckt: **~es Formular** *nt* GESCHÄFT printed form; **~e Steuererklärung** *f* STEUER printed return

vorgefertigt *adj* GRUND prefabricated

vorgegeben *adj* BÖRSE, GESCHÄFT, MGMNT predetermined

vorgehen *vt* GESCHÄFT transact

Vorgehen *nt* GESCHÄFT action, approach, procedure, MGMNT, VERWALT, VW approach; **Vorgehensweise** *f* GESCHÄFT approach, modus operandi (*MO*), MGMNT, VERWALT, VW approach

vorgelagert 1. *adj* GESCHÄFT upstream; **2.** *adv* GESCHÄFT upstream

vorgelegt: **~e Gebühr** *f* TRANSP advanced charge

vorgeordnet *adj* VW upstream

Vorgeschichte *f* PERSON *Bewerber, Unternehmen* previous history, V&M case history

vorgeschlagen *adj* GESCHÄFT proposed

vorgeschrieben: **~e Barreserve** *f* BANK fractional cash reserve; **~e Mindestreserve** *f* BANK fractional reserve; **~er Preis** *m* GESCHÄFT prescribed price

vorgesehen: **~er Beginn** *m* GESCHÄFT scheduled start; **~e Frist** *f* GESCHÄFT prescribed time; **~e Tagesordnung** *f* GESCHÄFT business to be transacted; **~e Zeit** *f* GESCHÄFT prescribed time

vorgesetzt *adj* GESCHÄFT senior (*Snr*)

Vorgesetzte(r) *mf* [decl. as adj] GESCHÄFT senior, PERSON chief, superior

vorgetäuscht *adj* GESCHÄFT artificial, fictitious

vorhaben *vt* GESCHÄFT, MGMNT aim, plan, propose

Vorhaben *nt* GESCHÄFT, MGMNT aim, plan, proposition

vorhanden *adj* GESCHÄFT available; **nicht ~** *adj* GESCHÄFT not available, unavailable

vorher: **~ aufgezeichnet** *phr* FREI, MEDIEN prerecorded; **~ ermitteln** *phr* BÖRSE, GESCHÄFT, MGMNT predetermine; **~ ermittelt** *adj* BÖRSE, GESCHÄFT, MGMNT predetermined

vorhergehend *adj* GESCHÄFT preceding; **~es Jahr** *nt*

GESCHÄFT previous year; ~er **Zeitraum** *m* RECHNUNG prior period

vorhergesagt *adj* GESCHÄFT predicted

vorhergesehen *adj* GESCHÄFT predicted

vorherig *adj* GESCHÄFT previous, prior; ~er **Eigentümer** *m*, ~e **Eigentümerin** *f* PATENT predecessor in title; ~e **Zusage** *f* GESCHÄFT prior consent

vorherrschen *vi* GESCHÄFT prevail

Vorhersage *f* GESCHÄFT forecast, prediction, projection, prognostication, MATH forecast, RECHNUNG, V&M forecasting

vorhersagen *vt* GESCHÄFT forecast, predict, project, prognosticate, MATH, RECHNUNG, V&M forecast

vorhersehbar *adj* GESCHÄFT predictable; ~e **Laufzeit** *f* RECHNUNG predictable life; ~es **Risiko** *nt* BÖRSE foreseeable risk

vorhersehen *vt* GESCHÄFT forecast, foresee, predict

Vorjahr *nt* GESCHÄFT preceding year, previous year; ♦ **als im ~ zugeflossen behandeltes Einkommen** STEUER constructive receipt of income (*AmE*)

Vorjahr: **Vorjahresanpassung** *f* RECHNUNG prior year adjustment

Vorkalkulation *f* RECHNUNG preliminary calculation, preliminary costing

Vorkalkulator *m* RECHNUNG cost estimator

vorkalkulieren *vt* BÖRSE, GESCHÄFT, MGMNT, RECHNUNG estimate

vorkalkuliert *adj* BÖRSE, GESCHÄFT, MGMNT, RECHNUNG estimated; ~er **Preis** *m* BÖRSE estimated price

Vorkalkulierung *f* GESCHÄFT, RECHNUNG

Vorkämpfer, in *m,f* GESCHÄFT pioneer, champion, IND pioneer

Vorkasse *f* GESCHÄFT advance payment, RECHNUNG cash in advance

Vorkaufsrecht *nt* BÖRSE right of preemption, GESCHÄFT option, RECHT, VW pre-emptive right (*AmE*), right of first refusal

Vorkennzeichen *nt* PATENT precharacterizing portion

vorkennzeichnend: ~er **Teil** *m* PATENT precharacterizing portion

Vorkommen *nt* UMWELT deposit

vorladen *vt* RECHT cite, issue a summons, summon

Vorladung *f* RECHT citation, summons

Vorlage *f* GESCHÄFT *Wechsel* production, presentation, submission, POL bill; **~ von Abschlüssen** FINANZ, VERWALT financial reporting; **~ von Empfehlungsschreiben** V&M credentials presentation; **~ für den Nachtragshaushalt** POL, VW supply bill; ♦ **bei ~** FINANZ at sight (*a/s*), on presentation, RECHNUNG on demand (*O/D*), RECHT on presentation; **gegen ~** FINANZ at sight (*a/s*), on presentation, RECHNUNG on demand (*O/D*), RECHT on presentation; **gegen ~ der Dokumente** GESCHÄFT against documents

Vorlauf *m* TRANSP *Fracht* on-carriage

vorläufig **1.** *adj* GESCHÄFT, PATENT, RECHT, VERSICH ad interim, for the time being, interim, provisional, temporary; **2.** *adv* GESCHÄFT ad interim, provisionally; ♦ **~ unwirksam** RECHT in abeyance

vorläufig: ~e **Annahme** *f* GESCHÄFT provisional acceptance; ~e **Auftragserteilung** *f* BÖRSE, GESCHÄFT letter of intent; ~er **Börseneinführungsprospekt** *m* BÖRSE red-herring prospectus; ~e **Deckungszusage** *f* VERSICH binder (*AmE*), cover note (*BrE*) (*C/N, CN*), memor-

andum of insurance; ~e **Differenz** *f* RECHNUNG temporary difference; ~e **Einstellung** *f* VERWALT points of suspension; ~er **Emissionsprospekt** *m* BÖRSE preliminary prospectus; ~e **Klausel** *f* RECHT draft clause; ~er **Plan** *m* GESCHÄFT tentative plan; ~e **Police** *f* VERSICH provisional policy; ~e **Rechnung** *f* GESCHÄFT, IMP/EXP pro forma invoice, provisional invoice; ~e **Schätzung** *f* GESCHÄFT tentative estimate; ~er **Schutz** *m* PATENT provisional protection; ~er **Status** *m* RECHT temporary status; ~e **Tagesordnung** *f* GESCHÄFT tentative agenda; ~e **Unterstützung** *f* PERSON interim relief; ~e **Untersuchung** *f* RECHT preliminary investigation; **~ unwirksam** *phr* RECHT in abeyance; ~e **Versicherungspolice** *f* VERSICH binder (*AmE*), cover note (*BrE*) (*C/N, CN*), memorandum of insurance; ~es **Zertifikat** *nt* BÖRSE scrip; ~e **Zollangabe** *f* IMP/EXP bill of sight

Vorlauf: **Vorlaufkosten** *pl* RECHNUNG preproduction cost; **Vorlaufzeit** *f* IND lead time, V&M gap between product conception and introduction

vorlegen *vt* BÖRSE tender, GESCHÄFT *Bericht* render, table (*BrE*), present, PATENT submit, POL lay, *Gesetz, Entwurf* introduce, table (*BrE*), RECHT *Beweis* present, produce, adduce, submit, *Gesetz, Entwurf* introduce

Vorlegung *f* BÖRSE tender, GESCHÄFT *Wechsel* presentation, PATENT submission, POL introduction, RECHT presentation, production, submission; **bei ~** *phr* FINANZ at sight (*a/s*)

vorliegend: ~e **Aufträge** *m pl* GESCHÄFT orders on hand; ~e **Sache** *phr* GESCHÄFT matter at hand

vormerken *vt* GESCHÄFT pencil in

Vormerkliste *f* GESCHÄFT waiting list

Vormerkmal *nt* PATENT precharacterizing portion

vormittags *adv* GESCHÄFT ante meridiem (*am*), in the morning

Vormundschaft *f* SOZIAL guardianship; ♦ **unter ~ stellen** SOZIAL place under guardianship

vorn: **von ~ beginnen** *phr* GESCHÄFT build up from scratch

Vor-: **~ und Nachteile** *m pl* GESCHÄFT advantages and disadvantages, pros and cons; **die ~ und Nachteile abwägen** *phr* GESCHÄFT weigh the pros and cons

vornehm *adj* GESCHÄFT prestigious

vornherein: **von ~** *phr* GESCHÄFT a priori

Vorort *m* GESCHÄFT suburb

Vorprämie *f* BÖRSE, GESCHÄFT call, call option, premium for the call

Vorpremiere *f* MEDIEN *Kino* sneak preview

Vorprodukt *nt* GESCHÄFT primary product, IND intermediate good, intermediate product

Vorprüfung *f* GESCHÄFT, PATENT preliminary examination

Vorrang *m* GESCHÄFT preference (*pref.*), priority, PATENT priority; ♦ **~ haben vor** GESCHÄFT take priority over

Vorrang: **Vorrangbriefpost** *f* KOMM first-class mail

vorrangig *adj* GESCHÄFT overriding, prior, priority; ~e **Hypothek** *f* BANK, FINANZ, GRUND prior mortgage, senior mortgage; ~er **Schuldtitel** *m* BANK senior debt; ~e **Umschuldung** *f* BÖRSE senior refunding; ~e **Verbindlichkeit** *f* BANK senior debt; ~es **Wertpapier** *nt* BÖRSE, FINANZ senior security

Vorrat *m* COMP *Befehle* repertoire, GESCHÄFT stock, stockpile, TRANSP stockpile

vorrätig *adj* GESCHÄFT, V&M, VW in stock (*i.s.*); ◆ **nicht ~** V&M out of stock (*o.s.*); **solange ~** V&M while stocks last

Vorrat: **Vorratsaktien** *f pl* BÖRSE company's own shares, shares held in treasury, treasury stock; **Vorratsbewertung** *f* GESCHÄFT stock valuation, RECHNUNG inventory valuation; **Vorratsbewirtschaftung** *f* RECHNUNG inventory control; **Vorratshaltung** *f* GESCHÄFT stockpiling; **Vorratskammer** *f* IMP/EXP, TRANSP storeroom; **Vorratslager** *nt* GESCHÄFT stock in hand, VW buffer stock; **Vorratsraum** *m* IMP/EXP, TRANSP storeroom; **Vorratsvermögen** *nt* GESCHÄFT inventories, stock in hand; **Vorratswirtschaft** *f* GESCHÄFT stockpiling, VW inventory management

vorraussagbar *adj* GESCHÄFT foreseeable

vorraussichtlich: **~e Technologie** *f* GESCHÄFT, IND technological forecasting

Vorrechner *m* COMP front-end computer

Vorrecht *nt* BÖRSE preferential right, privilege (*AmE*), PATENT priority, RECHT prerogative; **~ der Geschäftsleitung** PERSON management prerogative; **~ der Unternehmensleitung** PERSON managerial prerogative, right to manage; ◆ **ohne ~** GESCHÄFT without privilege (*x pri*); **mit Vorrechten ausgestattetes Wertpapier** BÖRSE, FINANZ senior security

Vorrede *f* GESCHÄFT preamble

Vorredner, in *m,f* GESCHÄFT last speaker, preceding speaker, previous speaker

Vorreiter, in *m,f* GESCHÄFT, IND pioneer

Vorrichtung *f* GESCHÄFT appliance, IND apparatus

vorrollen 1. *vt* COMP *Text auf Bildschirm* scroll down; **2.** *vi* COMP *auf Bildschirm* scroll down

Vorruhestand *m* GESCHÄFT, PERSON early retirement; **Vorruhestandsregelung** *f* PERSON *Arbeit* early-retirement scheme; **Vorruhestandsrente** *f* FINANZ early-retirement annuity, early-retirement benefit, preretirement pension

vorsätzlich: **~ falsche Behauptung** *f* **einer Tatsache** RECHT, VERSICH fraudulent misrepresentation; **~e Herbeiführung** *f* **des Schadenfalles** RECHT, VERSICH act of wilfully bringing about an insured loss

Vorschau *f* FREI forecast, projection, GESCHÄFT prognostication, MEDIEN trailer

vorschießen *vt* GESCHÄFT advance

Vorschlag *m* GESCHÄFT proposal, suggestion; ◆ **der ~ gilt noch immer** GESCHÄFT the proposal still stands; **einen ~ machen** GESCHÄFT make a suggestion; **als ~ unterbreiten** MGMNT propose, submit a proposal; **Vorschläge einbringen** MGMNT put forward proposals

vorschlagen *vt* GESCHÄFT propose, suggest, MGMNT *Projekt* put forward, *Treffen, Sitzung* propose

Vorschlag: **Vorschlagswesen** *nt* MGMNT suggestion scheme

vorschreiben *vt* MGMNT enjoin, RECHT *Erfordernisse* prescribe, provide

Vorschrift *f* GRUND prescription, MGMNT, PATENT rule, RECHT provision, VW regulation; **Vorschriften** *f pl* GESCHÄFT set rules, RECHT rules and regulations

vorschriftsmäßig: **nicht ~e Benutzung** *f* GRUND, RECHT nonconforming use; **~er Preis** *m* GESCHÄFT prescribed price

Vorschub *m* RECHT aid; ◆ **~ leisten** RECHT *Verbrechen* aid and abet

Vorschulerziehungszentrum *nt* SOZIAL preschool center (*AmE*), preschool centre (*BrE*)

Vorschuß *m* BANK advance, FINANZ *aus öffentlichen Mitteln* imprest, GESCHÄFT advance, PERSON, RECHNUNG advance, RECHT retainer, TRANSP advance; ◆ **auf ~** GESCHÄFT on a retainer; **als ~ geben** GESCHÄFT advance; **einen ~ zahlen** BANK make an advance

Vorschuß: **Vorschußakkreditiv** *nt* TRANSP red clause credit

vorschüssig: **~e Rente** *f* VERSICH annuity due, annuity payable in advance

Vorschuß: **Vorschußkasse** *f* RECHNUNG imprest fund; **Vorschußkonto** *nt* RECHNUNG imprest account; **Vorschußsumme** *f* GESCHÄFT sum advanced; **Vorschußwechsel** *m* BANK collateral bill; **Vorschußzahlung** *f* GESCHÄFT advance; **Vorschußzinsen** *m pl* BÖRSE, FINANZ early-withdrawal penalty

vorscrollen 1. *vt* COMP *Text auf Bildschirm* scroll down; **2.** *vi* COMP *auf Bildschirm* scroll down

vorsehen *vt* FINANZ ring-fence, VW earmark, ring-fence

Vorserie *f* GESCHÄFT, IND pilot production

vorsichtig *adj* GESCHÄFT cautious, conservative, prudent; **~e Ausgabenwirtschaft** *f* V&M defensive spending (*BrE*); **~e Haushaltsplanung** *f* V&M defensive budgeting (*BrE*); **~e Schätzung** *f* GESCHÄFT tentative estimate, conservative estimate, safe estimate

Vorsichtsmaßnahme: **als ~** *phr* GESCHÄFT as a precautionary measure

Vorsichtsprinzip *nt* RECHNUNG principle of caution, principle of conservatism; **~ in der Buchhaltung** RECHNUNG conservative accounting

Vorsitz *m* GESCHÄFT chairmanship, MGMNT chairmanship, presidency, POL presidency; ◆ **den ~ führen** MGMNT be in the chair, *Sitzung* chair a meeting; **den ~ haben** GESCHÄFT preside

vorsitzen *vi* [+dat] GESCHÄFT *Sitzung, Versammlung, Kommission* preside over

Vorsitzende(r) *mf* [decl. as adj] MGMNT, PERSON chairman, chairperson, chairwoman, *von Gewerkschaft* leader, president, POL *von Partei* leader; **Vorsitzender** *m* **und Generaldirektor** *m*, **Vorsitzende** *f* **und Generaldirektorin** *f* MGMNT chairman and general manager; **Vorsitzender** *m* **und geschäftsführender Direktor** *m*, **Vorsitzende** *f* **und geschäftsführende Direktorin** *f* MGMNT, PERSON chairperson and chief executive (*AmE*), chairperson and managing director (*BrE*); **Vorsitzender** *m* **und Hauptgeschäftsführer** *m*, **Vorsitzende** *f* **und Hauptgeschäftsführerin** *f* MGMNT chairman and general manager; **~ des Vorstandsgremiums** PERSON managing director (*BrE*) (*MD*)

Vorsorge *f* GESCHÄFT provision; ◆ **~ treffen für** GESCHÄFT make provision for

Vorsorge: **Vorsorgemaßnahmen** *f pl* **zur Instandhaltung** VERWALT preventive maintenance; **Vorsorgemaßnahmen** *f pl* **zur Werkserhaltung** GESCHÄFT preventive maintenance; **Vorsorgemotiv** *nt* GESCHÄFT precautionary motive; **Vorsorgemotiv** *nt* **der Geldnachfrage** VW precautionary demand for money; **Vorsorgesparen** *nt* VW precautionary saving

vorsorglich *adj* RECHT cautionary

Vorspann *m* MEDIEN *Film, Fernsehen* trailer, *Druck* header, lead

Vorspiegelung *f* RECHT pretence; ~ **falscher Tatsachen** RECHT, VERSICH fraudulent misrepresentation

Vorsprung *m* GESCHÄFT edge; **einen ~ haben** *phr* GESCHÄFT have a head start

vorspulen *vt* COMP *Band* advance

Vorstadt *f* GESCHÄFT suburb

Vorstand *m* GESCHÄFT, MGMNT *einer Gesellschaft* board of directors, board of management, executive board, RECHNUNG, VERWALT board of directors; ~ **der Geschäftsleitung** MGMNT chairman of the board of directors, chairman of the board of management; ♦ **den ~ absetzen** MGMNT unseat the board; ~ **der Londoner Wertpapierbörse** London Stock Exchange Board; **in den ~ wählen** GESCHÄFT elect to the board

Vorstand: **Vorstandsbüro** *nt* VERWALT executive office; **auf Vorstandsebene** *phr* VERWALT at boardroom level; **Vorstandsgremium** *nt* PERSON management board; **Vorstandskontrolle** *f* MGMNT board control; **Vorstandsmitglied** *nt* MGMNT PERSON director, member of the board; **Vorstandspension** *f* FINANZ, PERSON top-hat pension (*infrml*), top-hat scheme (*infrml*); **Vorstandssekretär, in** *m,f* PERSON executive secretary; **Vorstandssitzung** *f* GESCHÄFT, MGMNT board meeting; **Vorstandsvorsitzende(r)** *mf* [decl. as adj] MGMNT *eines Unternehmens*, PERSON chairperson and chief executive (*AmE*), chairperson and managing director (*BrE*), *Geschäftsleitung* president, chairperson of the executive committee, chief executive; **Vorstandszimmer** *nt* MGMNT boardroom

vorstellen: **sich ~** *v refl* GESCHÄFT, MGMNT envision

Vorstellung *f* GESCHÄFT, MGMNT vision, *des Unternehmens* presentation

Vorsteuer *f* STEUER input tax, prior tax, turnover tax

Vorstrafe *f* RECHT previous conviction, past conviction; ♦ **keine Vorstrafen** RECHT clean record

Vorstudie *f* GESCHÄFT pilot study, feasibility study

vortäuschen *vt* GESCHÄFT simulate, RECHT make a pretence of

Vortäuschung *f* GESCHÄFT simulation, RECHT pretence

Vorteil *m* GESCHÄFT advantage, avails, benefit, edge, MGMNT benefit; ~ **durch Preisdifferenz** VW differential advantage

vorteilhaft *adj* GESCHÄFT advantageous, beneficial

Vorteilhaftigkeit *f* V&M favorability (*AmE*), favourability (*BrE*)

Vorteil: **Vorteilsprinzip** *nt* STEUER, VW benefit principle

Vortrag *m* FINANZ balance brought down (*b/d.*), balance brought forward (*b/f*), balance carried forward (*b/f*), GESCHÄFT carried forward, RECHNUNG amount brought forward; ~ **über die Hintergründe** MEDIEN background paper; ♦ **einen ~ halten** SOZIAL deliver a lecture; **es gibt keinen ~ wegen Korruption** RECHT there is no suggestion of corruption

vortragen *vt* BANK bring forward, FINANZ *Saldo* bring forward, carry forward, RECHNUNG bring forward

vorübergehend *adj* GESCHÄFT transient, temporary; **nur ~ Ansässige(r)** *mf* [decl. as adj] VERWALT temporary resident; **~e Arbeitslosigkeit** *f* PERSON temporary unemployment; **~e Aufenthaltsgenehmigung** *f* RECHT temporary residence; **~e Einfuhr** *f* IMP/EXP temporary importation; ♦ **~e Bereitstellung von Mitteln beschließen** POL vote interim supply

voruntersuchen *vt* PATENT make a preliminary examination of

Voruntersuchung *f* PATENT preliminary examination

Vorurteil *nt* GESCHÄFT bias, prejudice; ~ **des Interviewers** V&M interviewer bias

Vorverkauf *m* FREI, GESCHÄFT, TRANSP advance booking, V&M advance sale; ♦ **im ~ besorgen** GESCHÄFT book in advance

Vorverkauf: **Vorverkaufsauftrag** *m* BÖRSE presale order; **Vorverkaufsvertrag** *m* GRUND binder

vorverkauft: **~e Schuldverschreibung** *f* BÖRSE bond sold prior to issue

vorverlegen *vt* GESCHÄFT bring forward, put forward, *Fälligkeitstermin* accelerate

Vorverlegung *f* GESCHÄFT bringing forward; ~ **der Fälligkeit** BANK acceleration of maturity

vorverpacken *vt* V&M prepackage

vorverpackt *adj* V&M prepackaged

Vorverpackung *f* V&M prepackaging

Vorvertrag *m* GESCHÄFT letter of understanding, RECHT *Vertragsrecht* preliminary agreement, tentative agreement

vorvertraglich: **~e Anzeigepflicht** *f* VERSICH material representation

Vorwahl *f* KOMM area code, dialing code (*AmE*), dialling code (*BrE*); **Vorwahlnummer** *f* KOMM area code, dialing code (*AmE*), dialling code (*BrE*); **Vorwahlstimme** *f* **für Kandidaten einer anderen Partei** POL crossover vote

Vorwarnung: **ohne ~** *phr* GESCHÄFT without previous warning

Vorwärtsintegration *f* VW forward integration

vorweggenommen: **~e Antwort** *f* GESCHÄFT anticipatory response; **~er Bedarf** *m* VW anticipated demand; **~e Reaktion** *f* VW anticipatory response; **~er Vertrag** *m* RECHT anticipatory contract

Vorwegnahme *f* GESCHÄFT anticipation

vorwegnehmen *vt* GESCHÄFT anticipate

Vorzeichnungsdarlehen *nt* FINANZ *Versicherungsgewerbe* fronting loan

vorzeitig 1. *adj* GESCHÄFT anticipated, untimely, premature; ♦ **zum ~en Ruhestand bewegen** PERSON force into early retirement; **2.** *adv* GESCHÄFT prematurely, KOMM ahead of schedule; ♦ **~ fällig stellen** BANK *Wechsel* accelerate; **sich ~ pensionieren lassen** GESCHÄFT, PERSON take early retirement

vorzeitig: **~e Ausübung** *f* **eines Rechtes** BÖRSE early exercise; **~e Gewinne** *m pl* STEUER abortive benefits; **nicht ~ kündbare Anleihe** *f* BÖRSE noncallable bond; **~e Rente** *f* FINANZ bridging pension scheme, early-retirement benefit, preretirement pension; **~er Rückkauf** *m* BANK anticipated redemption; **~e Rückzahlung** *f* BANK advance repayment, GESCHÄFT advance repayment, anticipated repayment; **~e Tilgung** *f* FINANZ anticipated redemption, redemption before due date, RECHNUNG accelerated amortization; **~es Tilgungsprivileg** *nt* FINANZ prepayment privilege; **~e Zahlung** *f* GESCHÄFT payment before due date

Vorzug *m* GESCHÄFT preference (*pref.*), priority

Vorzugsaktie *f* BÖRSE, FINANZ preference share (*BrE*), preferred stock (*AmE*); ~ **mit Gewinnbeteiligung** BÖRSE, FINANZ participating preference share (*BrE*), participating preferred stock (*AmE*); ~ **ohne kumulativen Dividendenanspruch** BÖRSE, FINANZ noncumulative preferred stock (*AmE*); **~ ohne Nachbezugsrecht** BÖRSE, FINANZ noncumulative preference share (*BrE*), noncumulative preferred stock (*AmE*)

Vorzug: **Vorzugsangebot** *nt* V&M premium, VW preference offer; **Vorzugsbehandlung** *f* GESCHÄFT preferential treatment; **Vorzugsdividende** *f* RECHNUNG preference dividend (*BrE*), preferred dividend (*AmE*); **Vorzugseinheit** *f* GRUND prime unit; **Vorzugskonditionen** *f pl* GESCHÄFT concessions, preferential terms; **Vorzugslage** *f* GRUND prime site; **Vorzugspatent** *nt* PATENT prior patent; **Vorzugspreis** *m* GESCHÄFT bargain price, VW preferential price; **Vorzugsrecht** *nt* PATENT, RECHT priority right; **Vorzugszinsen** *m pl* BANK preferential interest rates; **Vorzugszinssatz** *m* BANK preferential interest rate; **Vorzugszuteilung** *f* BÖRSE priority allocation

Votum *nt* MGMNT, POL vote

VP *abbr* (*Vizepräsident*) MGMNT, PERSON, POL VP (*vice president*), veep (*AmE*) (*infrml*)

vs. *abbr* (*versus*) GESCHÄFT v (*versus*), vs (*versus*)

Vulgär-Keynesianismus *m* VW bastard Keynesianism

VVaG *abbr* (*Versicherungsverein auf Gegenseitigkeit*) FINANZ benefit society, friendly society (*BrE*), VERSICH mutual benefit society, mutual insurance company, mutual insurance society (*BrE*)

Vz. *abbr* (*Veranlagungszeitraum*) FINANZ, RECHNUNG, STEUER assessment year, income year

W

W *abbr* (*Woche*) GESCHÄFT wk. (*week*)

Wa. *abbr* (*Waren*) PATENT gds (*goods*), TRANSP frt (*freight*), VW gds (*goods*)

WAB *abbr* (*Währungsausgleichsbetrag*) VW MCA (*Monetary Compensatory Amount*)

Wachmann *m* PERSON watchman

wachsen *vi* BANK *Konto* swell, GESCHÄFT *Fonds*, VW grow

Wachstum *nt* BANK, GESCHÄFT, VW growth; **Wachstumsaktie** *f* BÖRSE growth stock; **Wachstumsanalyse** *f* MGMNT incremental analysis; **Wachstumsbranche** *f* VW growth industry; **Wachstumsfonds** *m* **für aufstrebende Märkte** FINANZ Emerging Markets Growth Fund (*EMGF*); **Wachstumsfonds** *m* **für Schwellenländer** FINANZ Emerging Markets Growth Fund (*EMGF*); **Wachstumsgleichgewicht** *nt* VW balanced growth, steady-state growth; **Wachstumsindex** *m* VW growth index; **Wachstumsindustrie** *f* IND growth industry; **Wachstumsmotor** *m* VW engine of growth; **Wachstumspfad** *m* GESCHÄFT growth path; **Wachstumspol** *m* VW growth pole; **Wachstumspotential** *nt* GESCHÄFT growth potential

Wachstumsrate *f* BÖRSE, COMP, VW growth rate; **~ der Volkswirtschaft** VW economic growth rate

wachstumsstark: **~es Produkt** *nt* **mit großem Marktanteil** V&M star product

Wachstum: **Wachstumsstrategie** *f* GESCHÄFT, VW growth strategy; **Wachstumstheorie** *f* **des Unternehmens** VW growth theory of the firm

wackelig *adj infrml* GESCHÄFT shaky (*infrml*); **~er Parlamentssitz** *m* POL marginal constituency (*BrE*)

wagemutig *adj* GESCHÄFT enterprising

wagen 1. *vt* GESCHÄFT risk, take the risk of, venture; **2. sich ~ auf** *v refl* [+acc] GESCHÄFT *Projekt* venture on

Wagen- *in cpds* TRANSP wagon; **Wagenbestand** *m* TRANSP fleet, pool of vehicles; **Wagendecke** *f* TRANSP tilt; **Wagenladungstarif** *m* TRANSP wagonload rate; **Wagenrücklauf** *m* COMP *Drucker* carriage return (*CR*); **Wagenstandsgeld** *nt* TRANSP track storage charge

Waggon *m* TRANSP freight car (*AmE*), goods wagon (*BrE*); **Waggonfrachtrate** *f* TRANSP carload rate; **Waggonwaage** *f* TRANSP track scales

Wagner: **~sches Gesetz** *nt* VW Wagner's law

Wagnis *nt* VW risk, venture; **Wagnisausgleich** *m* VERSICH balancing of portfolio; **Wagniskapital** *nt* BANK, FINANZ, GESCHÄFT, VW risk capital, venture capital; **Wagniskapitalgesellschaft** *f* BANK, FINANZ, GESCHÄFT, VW venture capital company; **Wagniskapitalismus** *m* BANK, FINANZ, GESCHÄFT, VW venture capitalism; **Wagniskapitalkommanditgesellschaft** *f* BANK, FINANZ, GESCHÄFT, VW venture capital limited partnership

Wahl *f* COMP selection, GESCHÄFT *Auswahl* choice, *Möglichkeit* alternative, PERSON *das Wählen* vote, *geheim* ballot, POL vote, voting; **~ des Arbeitsplatzes** VW movement of labor (*AmE*), movement of labour (*BrE*); **~ des Verbrauchers** V&M consumer choice; **durch ~ zu vergebendes Amt** *nt* POL elected office;

~ des Vorsitzenden GESCHÄFT election for chairman; ◆ **zur ~ gehen** POL turn out to vote

Wahl: **Wahlbeteiligung** *f* POL voter turnout; **Wahlgang** *m* PERSON, POL ballot

wählen 1. *vt* GESCHÄFT choose, *Vorgehensweise* elect, MGMNT opt, PERSON vote, POL vote, vote for, *Partei, Kandidat* elect; **2.** *vi* GESCHÄFT take one's pick (*infrml*), POL *Stimmen* vote, *Wahlen abhalten* hold elections

Wähler, in *m,f* POL voter

Wahl: **Wahlergebnis** *nt* POL vote, election results

Wähler: **Wählerliste** *f* GESCHÄFT, POL electoral register

Wählerschaft *f* GESCHÄFT, POL electorate

Wähler: **Wählerverzeichnis** *nt* GESCHÄFT, POL electoral roll

wahlfrei: **~e Plazierung** *f* VERSICH facultative placing

Wahl: **Wahlfreiheit** *f* POL freedom of choice; **Wahlkabine** *f* POL polling booth, voting booth; **Wahlkampagne** *f* GESCHÄFT, POL election campaign; **Wahlkreisschiebungen** *f pl infrml* POL gerrymander; **Wahllokal** *nt* POL polling station; **Wahlmöglichkeit** *f* GESCHÄFT option; **Wahlnebenstellanlage** *f* KOMM *Telefon* private automatic branch exchange (*BrE*) (*PABX*); **Wahlparadoxon** *nt* VW paradox of voting; **Wahlrecht** *nt* POL right to vote, suffrage; **Wahlschuld** *f* RECHT *Vertragsrecht* alternative obligation; **Wahltag** *m* POL polling day

Wählton *m* KOMM dial tone (*AmE*), dialling tone (*BrE*)

Wahl: **Wahlurne** *f* PERSON ballot box; **Wahlverfahren** *nt* PERSON, POL voting procedures; **Wahlzettel** *m* PERSON ballot paper

wahr: **~e Sonnenzeit** *f* **am Schiff** TRANSP apparent time at ship (*ATS*)

wahrgenommen: **~er Nutzen** *m* GESCHÄFT perceived benefit

wahrnehmen *vt* GESCHÄFT *Gelegenheit* utilize, perceive, *Frist, Termin* observe

Wahrnehmung *f* GESCHÄFT perception; **Wahrnehmungsmöglichkeiten** *f pl* V&M *Rundfunkwerbung* opportunities to hear (*OTH*), *Fernsehwerbung* opportunities to see (*OTS*)

wahrscheinlich *adj* GESCHÄFT likely, probable, MATH probable; **~e Abweichung** *f* MATH *Statistik* probable error (*p.e.*); **~es Ergebnis** *nt* GESCHÄFT likely outcome; **~er Fehler** *m* MATH probable error (*p.e.*)

Wahrscheinlichkeit *f* GESCHÄFT likelihood, MATH chance, probability; **Wahrscheinlichkeitsrechnung** *f* MATH calculus of probabilities, calculation of probabilities, VW calculation of probabilities; **Wahrscheinlichkeitsstichprobe** *f* MATH probability sample; **Wahrscheinlichkeitstheorie** *f* MATH, MGMNT probability theory

Währung *f* BANK, FINANZ currency, VW currency, exchange (*exch.*), coinage; **Währungsabkommen** *nt* VW exchange rate agreement (*ERA*); **Währungsabwertung** *f* VW currency depreciation **auf Währungsanlagen spezialisierter Investmentfonds** *m* FINANZ managed currency fund; **Währungsanleihe** *f* VW currency bond; **Währungsaufwertung** *f* VW

currency appreciation, currency revaluation; **Währungsausgabe** *f* BANK currency issue
Währungsausgleich *m* BANK currency adjustment, FINANZ monetary compensation, VW exchange equalization; **Währungsausgleichsbetrag** *m* IMP/EXP, FINANZ monetary compensatory amount, (*WAB*) VW Monetary Compensatory Amount (*MCA*); **Währungsausgleichsfaktor** *m* TRANSP *Zuschlag für Fracht* currency adjustment factor (*CAF*); **Währungsausgleichsfonds** *m* VW *Außenwirtschaft* exchange equalization account (*EEA*)
Währung: **Währungsbehörden** *f pl* BANK monetary authorities; **Währungsbeistand** *m* VW monetary support; **Währungsblock** *m* VW block, monetary bloc; **Währungs- und Bunkerausgleichsfaktor** *m* TRANSP currency and bunker adjustment factor (*CABAF*); **Währungscode** *m* BANK currency code; **Währungsdarlehen** *nt* BANK currency borrowing; **Währungseinheit** *f* FINANZ monetary unit, VW currency unit; **Währungseinlagen** *f pl* FINANZ currency deposits; **Währungsfragen** *f pl* VW monetary policy; **Währungsgarantieplan** *m* BANK exchange risk guarantee scheme
währungsgebunden *adj* FINANZ currency-linked
Währung: **Währungsgewinne** *m pl* FINANZ transferee gains; **Währungsklausel** *f* RECHT foreign currency clause; **Währungskonto** *nt* BANK currency account, foreign exchange account, FINANZ currency account; **Währungskorb** *m* FINANZ currency cocktail, basket of currencies, VW basket of currencies, currency basket; **Währungsleerposition** *f* BANK short position in a currency; **Währungsmischung** *f* BANK currency mix; **Währungsparität** *nt* BÖRSE par value of currency; **Währungsspekulation** *f* FINANZ foreign exchange speculation; **Währungspolitik** *f* VW monetary policy; **Währungsreform** *f* VW currency reform; **Währungsreserven** *f pl* VW currency reserves, foreign exchange reserves, monetary reserves, reserve balances; **Währungsrisiko** *nt* FINANZ translation risk, VW currency risk, foreign exchange risk, translation risk; **Währungsschlange** *f* VW currency snake; **Währungsstandard** *m* VW monetary standard; **Währungsswap** *m* **auf der Pari-Forward-Basis** FINANZ cross-currency swap; **Währungssymbol** *nt* COMP currency symbol; **Währungsunion** *f* VW monetary union; **Währungszone** *f* GESCHÄFT currency zone
Wald *m* GESCHÄFT forest; **Wald-Feld-Bau** *m* UMWELT agroforestry; **Wald- und Forstwirtschaft** *f* GESCHÄFT forestry; **Waldgebiet** *nt* GESCHÄFT, UMWELT woodlands; **Waldland** *nt* GESCHÄFT, UMWELT woodlands
Walkie-talkie *nt* KOMM walkie-talkie
Walras: **~sches Gesetz** *nt* VW Walras's law; **~sche Stabilität** *f* VW Walrasian stability
Walze *f* TRANSP drum, cylinder
WAN *abbr* (*großflächiges Netz, Weitverkehrsnetz*) COMP, KOMM WAN (*wide-area network*)
Wandel- *in cpds* BANK, FINANZ convertible; **Wandelanleihe** *f* FINANZ convertible bond, convertible issue, conversion loan
wandelbar *adj* BANK convertible; **~es Wertpapier** *nt* **mit Nullkupon** BÖRSE zero-coupon convertible security
Wandelbarkeit *f* FINANZ convertibility, GESCHÄFT commutability
wandeln *vt* BANK, FINANZ convert, RECHT cancel, rescind

Wandel-: **Wandelobligation** *f* FINANZ convertible bond; **Wandelschuldverschreibung** *f* FINANZ convertible bond
Wander- *in cpds* GESCHÄFT traveling (*AmE*), travelling (*BrE*), itinerant; **Wanderarbeiter, in** *m,f* PERSON itinerant worker, VW migrant worker; **Wanderausstellung** *f* V&M traveling exhibition (*AmE*), traveling fair (*AmE*), travelling exhibition (*BrE*), travelling fair (*BrE*); **Wanderkino** *nt* FREI roadshow
Wanderung *f* POL, VW migration
Wandler *m* COMP *Prozeßrechner* transducer
Wandlung *f* RECHT *Vertragsrecht* rescission of contract for work and labor (*AmE*), rescission of contract for work and labour (*BrE*), rescission of sale; **Wandlungsaufgeld** *nt* BÖRSE conversion premium
wandlungsfähig *adj* BÖRSE, FINANZ convertible, GESCHÄFT adaptable; **~es nachrangiges Darlehen** *nt* FINANZ convertible subordinated loan; **~er Schuldtitel** *m* BÖRSE convertible loan stock
Wandlung: **Wandlungskurs** *m* FINANZ, VW conversion price; **Wandlungsparität** *f* BÖRSE conversion parity (*BrE*); **Wandlungsverhältnis** *nt* BÖRSE conversion ratio
Ware *f* GESCHÄFT, VW article, commodity, product; **~ zur Ansicht** GESCHÄFT goods on approval; **~ zum Wiederverkauf** RECHNUNG goods held for re-sale; **die ~ wurde noch nicht zugestellt** GESCHÄFT the goods remain undelivered
Waren *f pl* (*Wa.*) PATENT goods (*BrE*) (*gds*), TRANSP freight (*frt*), V&M *Handelsgut* commodities, merchandise, VW goods (*BrE*) (*gds*); **~ und Dienstleistungen** *f pl* VW goods and services; **~ mit Lagerschein** GESCHÄFT goods covered by warrant; **~, die den Marktbestimmungen unterliegen** BÖRSE regulated commodities; **~ des nichttäglichen Bedarfs** GESCHÄFT shopping goods; **~ ohne Markenzeichen** GESCHÄFT unbranded goods; **~ des täglichen Bedarfs** V&M convenience goods; **~ unter Zollverschluß** IMP/EXP, VW bonded goods (*B/G, b/g*); ◆ **seine ~ absetzen** GESCHÄFT sell one's wares; **~ zur Einlagerung eintragen** GESCHÄFT enter goods for warehousing; **~ auf Kredit liefern** GESCHÄFT supply goods on trust; **~ durch Schutzzölle schützen** GESCHÄFT protect goods; **~ zu Spekulationszwecken aufkaufen** V&M corner the market
Waren: **Warenanalyse** *f* BÖRSE commodity analysis (*BrE*); **Warenannahme** *f* GESCHÄFT receiving department, GESCHÄFT, TRANSP receipt of goods (*ROG*); **Warenannahmeschein** *m* RECHNUNG, TRANSP goods received note; **Warenannahmestelle** *f* GESCHÄFT delivery point, reception area; **Warenausfuhr** *f* IMP/EXP, VW visible export, export (*exp.*); **Warenausgang** *m* GESCHÄFT outgoing goods; **Warenausgangsbuch** *nt* V&M sales journal; **Warenausgangskonto** *nt* V&M sales account; **Warenauslage** *f* KOMM display; **Warenaustauschverhältnis** *nt* VW commodity terms of trade; **Warenbegleitschein** *m* TRANSP consignment note (*C/N, CN*); **Warenbeschreibung** *f* V&M trade description; **Warenbestand** *m* GESCHÄFT inventories, stock in hand; **Warenbestandseinheit** *f* GESCHÄFT stockkeeping unit; **Warenbevorschussung** *f* BANK advance against goods, GESCHÄFT advance against goods, advance on commodities; **Warenbörse** *f* BÖRSE commodity exchange; **Wareneinfuhr** *f* IMP/EXP, VW visible import; **Wareneingang** *m* GESCHÄFT incoming goods, stock receipt; **Wareneingangsbuch** *nt* V&M purchase book; **Wareneinheit** *f* **mit Steuerpräferenz**

STEUER tax preference item; **Warenempfang** *m* GESCHÄFT, TRANSP receipt of goods (*ROG*); **Warenempfänger, in** *m,f* RECHT *Vertragsrecht* consignee of goods; **Warenempfangsabteilung** *f* GESCHÄFT receiving department; **Warenempfangsschein** *m* IMP/EXP, TRANSP delivery receipt; **Warenerwerb** *m* STEUER acquisition of goods; **Warenexportauftrag** *m* IMP/EXP export of goods order; **Warenfetischismus** *m* VW commodity fetishism; **Warenfluß** *m* GESCHÄFT commodity flow; **Warenforderungen** *f pl* RECHNUNG trade accounts receivable; **Warengeldsystem** *nt* BÖRSE commodity standard; **Warengeschäfte** *nt pl* VW commodity trade; **Warengläubiger, in** *m,f* GESCHÄFT trade creditor; **Warengruppe** *f* PATENT category; **Warenhandel** *m* VW commodity trade; **Warenhandelsbilanz** *f* VW visible trade balance; **Warenhaus** *nt* GESCHÄFT one-stop shopping center (*AmE*), one-stop shopping centre (*BrE*); **Warenhausausverkauf** *m* V&M department store; **Warenhausdiebstahl** *m* V&M shoplifting, shrinkage; **Warenhauskette** *f* V&M department store chain; **Warenkaufvertrag** *m* RECHT *über bewegliche Sachen* contract for the sale of goods; **Warenkontrolle** *f* V&M merchandise control; **Warenkorb** *m* GESCHÄFT *statistische Bezeichnung* shopping basket, VW basket of commodities, basket of products, market basket; **Warenkredit** *m* BANK commodity credit, trade credit; **Warenkreditversicherung** *f* VERSICH commercial credit insurance (*AmE*); **Warenlager** *nt* GESCHÄFT, IMP/EXP, TRANSP goods depot, warehouse (*whse*), depot (*dpt*), V&M warehouse (*whse*); **Warenlieferung** *f* GESCHÄFT delivery of goods; **Warenliste** *f* GESCHÄFT tally register; **Warenlombard** *m* BANK, GESCHÄFT advance on goods; **Warenmarke** *f* PATENT mark; **Warenmischung** *f* TRANSP commodity mix; **Warennorm** *f* RECHT product standard; **Warenpapier** *nt* BÖRSE commodity paper; **Warenpapiere** *nt pl* IMP/EXP, TRANSP shipping documents; **Warenpreisindex** *m* BÖRSE commodity index (*BrE*); **Warenproben** *f pl* VW merchandise samples; **Warenreservenwährung** *f* VW commodity reserve currency; **Warenrisiko** *nt* RECHT, TRANSP, VERSICH risk in the goods; **Warenrücksendungen und Gutschriften** *f pl* V&M purchase returns and allowances; **Warensortiment** *nt* GESCHÄFT assortment of goods, V&M array of products; **Warensteuer** *f* IMP/EXP commodity tax, excise; **Warenterminbörse** *f* BÖRSE commodity futures exchange; **Warentermingeschäft** *nt* BÖRSE commodities futures (*BrE*); **Warenterminkontrakt** *m* BÖRSE commodities futures (*BrE*); **Warenumsatz** *m* V&M sales turnover; **Warenumschlag** *m* GESCHÄFT stock turn; **Warenverkaufsbuch** *nt* V&M sales book; **Warenverkehr** *m* VW merchandise movements; **Warenverkehrsbescheinigung** *f* IMP/EXP movement certificate; **Warenverzeichnis** *nt* IND bill of goods, PATENT specification of goods; **Warenverzeichnissätze** *m pl* IMP/EXP commodity classification rates (*CCR*); **Warenvorräte** *m pl* GESCHÄFT inventories; **Warenwechsel** *m* BANK commercial bill, trade bill, GESCHÄFT trade acceptance; **Warenzeichen** *nt* GESCHÄFT, PATENT, RECHNUNG, RECHT *Gütezeichen* trademark, mark; **Warenzeichenvertreter, in** *m,f* RECHT trademark agent; **Warenzugänge** *m pl* GESCHÄFT incoming goods

warm: **wie ~e Semmeln weggehen** *phr infrml* GESCHÄFT sell like hot cakes (*infrml*)

Wärme *f* IND thermal power

Wärmekraftwerk *nt* IND thermal power station

Warmluftventilator *m* IND thermostatic fan

Warmstart *m* COMP warm restart

Warn- *in cpds* GESCHÄFT warning; **Warnanlage** *f* GESCHÄFT warning device; **Warnanzeige** *f* GESCHÄFT warning indicator

warnen: **jdn vor etw ~** *phr* GESCHÄFT put sb on guard against sth, warn sb against sth

Warn-: **Warnfenster** *nt* COMP *Programme* alert box; **Warngerät** *nt* GESCHÄFT warning device, warning indicator; **Warngrenze** *f* IMP/EXP *Zoll* peril point, warning limit; **Warnschild** *nt* GESCHÄFT warning sign; **Warnstreik** *m* PERSON token stoppage, token strike; **Warnton** *m* COMP beep

Warnung *f* GESCHÄFT word of warning, PERSON warning

Warschau: **~er Abkommen** *nt* TRANSP Warsaw Convention

Warte- *in cpds* GESCHÄFT waiting; **Wartehalle** *f* **eines Flughafens** TRANSP departure lounge; **Warteliste** *f* FREI, GESCHÄFT, TRANSP waiting list

Warteraum *m* TRANSP waiting room, departure lounge, transit lounge; **~ im Flughafengebäude** TRANSP departure lounge; **~ für Reisende der Business-Class** TRANSP executive lounge

Warteschlange *f* COMP queue, GESCHÄFT line (*AmE*), queue (*BrE*), TRANSP holding pattern, VW line-up; **Warteschlangenmodell** *nt* VW queueing system; **Warteschlangentheorie** *f* GESCHÄFT waiting line theory, MATH, VW queueing theory

Warte-: **Warteschleifenkanzler** *m* POL *der Opposition* shadow chancellor (*BrE*); **Wartezeit** *f* GESCHÄFT waiting time

Wartung *f* COMP, IND maintenance, servicing, GESCHÄFT service, TRANSP maintenance, servicing; **~, Reparatur und Überholung** *phr* TRANSP maintenance, repair and overhaul (*MRO*); ◆ **~ nicht inbegriffen** GESCHÄFT service not included

Wartung: **Wartungsabteilung** *f* IND maintenance department; **Wartungsaufschub** *m* GRUND deferred maintenance; **Wartungsfirma** *f* GESCHÄFT service company; **Wartungsjob** *m*, PERSON *COP* service job; **Wartungsmannschaft** *f* PERSON maintenance crew; **Wartungsplan** *m* GESCHÄFT maintenance schedule; **Wartungsvertrag** *m* COMP, GESCHÄFT service contract; **Wartungsvertrag** *m* **für Wohnungsgebäude** VERSICH residential service contract

Wäsche *f* FINANZ, GESCHÄFT *Geld* laundering

waschen *vt* FINANZ, GESCHÄFT *Geld* launder

Waschräume *m pl* GESCHÄFT rest rooms (*AmE*)

Waschzettel *m* MEDIEN, V&M *eines Buches* blurb

Wasser: **Wasseraufbereitung** *f* UMWELT water treatment

wasserdicht *adj* UMWELT, IND watertight, waterproof; **~es Papier** *nt* IND, KOMM waterproof paper

Wasserkraft *f* UMWELT white coal; **Wasserkraftstrom** *m* UMWELT hydroelectric power; **Wasserkraftwerk** *nt* IND *Produktion* hydroelectric power station

Wasser: **Wasserleitung** *f* IND, TRANSP, UMWELT water pipe; **Wasserreinigung** *f* IND, TRANSP, UMWELT water purification; **Wasserschaden** *m* GESCHÄFT, VERSICH water damage; **Wasserstoff** *m* (*H*) IND, UMWELT hydrogen (*H*); **Wasserstraße** *f* TRANSP waterway; **Wassertransport** *m* TRANSP water transportation;

Wasserversorgung *f* IND, UMWELT water system, water supply; **Wasserwerk** *nt* IND waterworks

Wasserzeichen *nt* VW watermark; ◆ **mit ~ versehen** VW watermarked

WBS *abbr* (*Warenbegleitschein*) TRANSP CN, C/N (*consignment note*)

WDW *abbr* (*Wirtschaftsverband Deutscher Werbeagenturen*) V&M ≈ AAAA (*American Association of Advertising Agencies*)

Weberei *f* IND weaving mill

Weberhandwerk *nt* IND weaving trade

Webstuhl *m* IND weaving loom

Wechsel *m* BANK draft (*dft*), FINANZ promise to pay, bill, bill of exchange (*B/E*), note, paper (*infrml*); **~ zum Einzug** BANK bill for collection; **~ in der Grundstücksnutzung** GRUND land-use succession; **~ im Management** MGMNT change of management; **~ ohne Dokumentensicherung** FINANZ, VW clean bill; **~ mit Rückkaufsvereinbarung** RECHNUNG notes under repurchase agreement; **~ eines Satzes** FINANZ bills in a set; **mit Weiterverkaufsvereinbarung gekaufte ~** *m pl* RECHNUNG bills purchased under resale agreement; ◆ **einen ~ akzeptieren** RECHT accept a bill; **einen ~ mit Akzept versehen** RECHT accept a bill; **einen ~ zur Annahme vorlegen** BANK present a bill for acceptance; **einen ~ zur Diskontierung vorlegen** BANK present a bill for discount; **einen ~ honorieren** FINANZ honor a bill (*AmE*), honour a bill (*BrE*)

Wechsel: **Wechselbank** *f* BANK acceptance house; **Wechselbestand** *m* BANK bill holding; **Wechselbürge** *m*, **Wechselbürgin** *f* FINANZ collateral acceptor, guarantor of a bill; **Wechseldeckung** *f* BANK bill cover; **Wechseldiskont** *m* BANK bank discount; **Wechseldiskontierung** *f* RECHNUNG discounting of bills (*BrE*), discounting of notes (*AmE*); **Wechseldiskontsatz** *m* FINANZ bill rate; **Wechseleinzug** *m* RECHNUNG collection of a bill; **Wechselforderungen** *f pl* RECHNUNG notes receivable (*AmE*), bills receivable (*BrE*); **Wechselfrist** *f* BANK term draft, FINANZ usance bill; **zu einer Wechselfrist von dreißig Tagen** *phr* FINANZ at thirty days' usance; **Wechselgebühr** *f* BANK exchange charge; **Wechselgeld** *nt* BANK float, GESCHÄFT change; **Wechselgeldautomat** *nt* GESCHÄFT change dispenser; **Wechselgeschäft** *nt* VW agiotage; **Wechselinkasso** *nt* RECHNUNG collection of a bill; **Wechseljournal** *nt* RECHNUNG bill book; **Wechselkonto** *nt* BANK acceptance account

Wechselkurs *m* FINANZ, VW exchange rate, foreign exchange rate, rate of exchange; **~ für Touristen** VW tourist exchange rate; **Wechselkursanpassung** *f* VW exchange rate adjustment; **Wechselkursbewegungen** *f pl* VW exchange rate movements; **Wechselkursfreigabe** *f* FINANZ floating; **Wechselkursgewinne** *m pl* VW gain; **Wechselkursmechanismus** *m* VW Exchange Rate Mechanism (*ERM*); **Wechselkursparität** *f* BANK exchange rate parity, parity of exchange; **Wechselkursparität herstellen** *phr* BÖRSE bring parity; **Wechselkurssystem** *nt* VW exchange rate system; **Wechselkursvereinbarung** *f* VW exchange rate agreement (*ERA*); **Wechselkursverlust** *m* VW loss on exchange; **Wechselkurszielzone** *f* VW exchange rate target zone

wechseln 1. *vt* GESCHÄFT, VW change; ◆ **~ zu** GESCHÄFT switch over to; **2.** *vi* GESCHÄFT vary

Wechsel: **Wechselobligo** *nt* BANK acceptance liability; **Wechselportefeuille** *nt* BANK bill portfolio, bill holding; **Wechselportfolio** *nt* BANK bill portfolio; **Wechselrate** *f* FINANZ bill rate; **Wechselreiterei** *f* BÖRSE drawing and redrawing of bills, kite-flying, kiting; **Wechselrembours** *m* FINANZ, IMP/EXP acceptance credit; **Wechselschicht** *f* PERSON rotating shift, *Fertigungsbetrieb* alternating shift

wechselseitig 1. *adj* GESCHÄFT mutual, reciprocal; **2.** *adv* GESCHÄFT mutually, reciprocally

wechselseitig: **~er Anschluß** *m* GESCHÄFT interconnection; **~e Bürgschaft** *f* BANK cross guarantee; **~er Kredit** *m* FINANZ back tax; **~e Kurssicherung** *f* BÖRSE cross hedging; **~e Lieferbeziehungen** *f pl* V&M reciprocal buying

Wechsel: **Wechselstrom** *m* (*WS*) GESCHÄFT alternating current (*ac*); **Wechselstube** *f* BANK, FREI bureau de change, foreign exchange office; **Wechselverbindlichkeiten** *f pl* RECHNUNG bills payables, notes payable (*AmE*); **Wechselverfallbuch** *nt* RECHNUNG bill book; **Wechselverhältnis-Kennzahl** *f* BÖRSE correlation ratio (*BrE*); **Wechselwähler** *m* POL *trotz Parteizugehörigkeit* swing voter, switcher

Weg *m* TRANSP road (*Rd*); **~ des geringsten Widerstands** GESCHÄFT path of least resistance; ◆ **auf den ~ bringen** GESCHÄFT get off the ground (*infrml*); **auf dem ~ sein nach** GESCHÄFT be heading for; **den ~ bahnen für** GESCHÄFT pave the way for; **den ~ bereiten für** GESCHÄFT pioneer; **aus dem ~ räumen** GESCHÄFT smooth out

Wegbereiter, in *m,f* GESCHÄFT, IND pioneer

wegen *prep* [+gen] GESCHÄFT on account of

Wegerecht *nt* RECHT right of way

Wegfall *m* GESCHÄFT discontinuance; **~ der Geschäftsgrundlage** RECHT *Vertrag* frustation of contract

Weggang: **~ vermerken** *phr* VERWALT book out

weggeben *vt* V&M give away

weglassen *vt* GESCHÄFT omit, MEDIEN edit out

weglegen *vt* GESCHÄFT file away

wegnehmen *vt* GESCHÄFT take away

wegschnappen *vt* GESCHÄFT snap up

Wegweiser *m* TRANSP signpost

Wegwerfgesellschaft: **die ~** *f* GESCHÄFT the throwaway society, the waste society

Weg-Ziel-Theorie *f* MGMNT path-goal theory

wehrlos *adj* VW vulnerable

weichmachen *vt* *infrml* GESCHÄFT soften up

weich: **~es Angebot** *nt* GESCHÄFT soft offer; **~e Kosten** *pl* GESCHÄFT soft cost; **~e Landung** *f* VW soft landing; **~e Technologie** *f* IND intermediate technology, UMWELT soft technology, VW small-scale technology, soft technology; **~e Tour** *f* V&M soft sell; **~e Währung** *f* GESCHÄFT, VW soft currency

Weichensteller *m* GESCHÄFT switcher

Weichware *f* BÖRSE soft commodity

Weihnachtsgeld *nt* GESCHÄFT, PERSON Christmas bonus

Wein- *in cpds* IND, V&M, VW wine; **Weinabfüllung** *f* IND wine-bottling; **Weinanbau** *m* VW wine growing; **Weinanbaugebiet** *nt* VW wine-growing district, wine-producing area; **Weinbauer, in** *m,f* VW wine grower; **Weinbaugebiet** *nt* VW wine-growing district, wine-producing area; **Weinberg** *m* GESCHÄFT vineyard;

Weinernte *f* GESCHÄFT vintage, VW wine harvest; **Weinertrag** *m* GESCHÄFT vintage; **Weingut** *nt* GESCHÄFT winery; **Weinhandel** *m* GESCHÄFT wine trade; **Weinhändler, in** *m,f* GESCHÄFT vintner, wine merchant; **Weinindustrie** *f* IND wine industry; **Weinkarte** *f* FREI wine list; **Weinkellerei** *f* GESCHÄFT winery; **Weinkellner** *m* FREI, PERSON wine waiter; **Weinlager** *nt* IMP/EXP *Lagerkontrolle* wine warehouse; **Weinlese** *f* VW wine harvest; **Wein- und Spirituosengeschäft** *nt* V&M liquor store (*AmE*), off-licence (*BrE*), package store (*AmE*)

weiß: **~er Markt** *m* VW white market; **~es Rauschen** *nt* MATH white noise; **~e Revolution** *f* VW white revolution; **~e Ware** *f pl* GESCHÄFT, V&M white goods

Weißblech *nt* IND tin plate

Weißbuch *nt* POL white paper (*BrE*); **~ der Staatsausgaben** VW Public Expenditure White Paper (*BrE*) (*PEWP*)

Weiß-nicht-Stimme *f* POL bullet vote, don't-know vote

Weisung *f* POL, RECHT direction, directive, instruction, order

weisungsgebunden *adj* PERSON, VERWALT accountable; **~e(r) Angestellte(r)** *mf* [decl. as adj] PERSON accountable officer (*AmE*)

Weisung: **Weisungsgewalt** *f* GESCHÄFT authority; **Weisungskette** *f* MGMNT chain of command

weit: **~ aufgefächert** *phr* GESCHÄFT broadly diversified; **etw ~ interpretieren** *phr* GESCHÄFT give a loose interpretation of sth; **~es Oligopol** *nt* VW loose oligopoly

weitblickend *adj* GESCHÄFT far-seeing, far-sighted

Weiter- *in cpds* GESCHÄFT onward, further, re-

weiter: **~e Informationen** *f pl* GESCHÄFT further information; **für ~e Anweisungen** *phr* GESCHÄFT for further instructions (*FFI*); **ohne ~e Bedingungen** *phr* GESCHÄFT *Vereinbarung* no strings attached; **bei ~er Betrachtung** *phr* GESCHÄFT upon further consideration; **bei ~er Überlegung** *phr* GESCHÄFT upon further consideration; **~ zu verfolgende Angelegenheiten** *f pl* GESCHÄFT matters to be followed up

Weiter-: **Weiterbearbeitung** *f* PATENT processing; **Weiterbeförderung** *f* TRANSP reforwarding

Weiterbildung *f* PERSON, SOZIAL continual professional education, further education; **~ von Führungskräften** GESCHÄFT, MGMNT, PERSON executive training, management training, management development; **~ der Mitarbeiter** MGMNT staff development, staff training, PERSON staff training; **~ für Mitarbeiter** IND training within industry (*TWI*); **~ des Personals** MGMNT staff development, staff training, PERSON staff training; **Weiterbildungsprogramm** *nt* IND, MGMNT, PERSON training package

Weiter-: **Weiterflug** *m* TRANSP onward flight

weiterführend: **~e Schule** *f* SOZIAL college of further education (*BrE*) (*CFE*)

Weiter-: **Weitergabe** *f* VW passing-on

weitergeben *vt* VW *Kosten an den Verbraucher* pass on

Weiter-: **Weiterleihen** *nt* FINANZ on-lending

weiterleiten *vt* GESCHÄFT pass on, transmit, KOMM *Sendung, Dokument* forward (*fwd*), RECHT *Fall* refer to

Weiter-: **Weiterleitung** *f* GESCHÄFT transmission

weiteruntersuchen *vt* MGMNT *Gedanken* follow up

weiterverarbeiten *vt* IND, VW reprocess, manufacture

weiterverarbeitend: **~e Industrie** *f* IND manufacturing industry, processing industry

Weiter-: **Weiterverkauf** *m* BÖRSE, GESCHÄFT resale; **Weiterverpfändung** *f* BÖRSE rehypothecation; **Weiterversicherung** *f* VERSICH continued insurance, reinstatement

weitgehend *adv* GESCHÄFT largely

weitreichend *adj* GESCHÄFT far-reaching, wide-ranging, *Planung, Voraussagen* long-range, POL wide-ranging

weitsichtig *adj* GESCHÄFT far-seeing, far-sighted

weitverbreitet *adj* GESCHÄFT widespread

Weitverkehrsnetz *nt* (*WAN*) COMP, KOMM, MGMNT wide-area network (*WAN*)

Weizenmodell *nt* VW corn model

Well- *in cpds* IND, TRANSP corrugated; **Wellbehälter** *m* TRANSP corrugated container; **Wellblechcontainer** *m* TRANSP corrugated container

Wellenenergie *f* IND, UMWELT wave power

Wellenlänge: **die gleiche ~ haben wie** *phr infrml* GESCHÄFT be on the same wavelength as (*infrml*)

Well-: **Wellpappe** *f* V&M corrugated board

Welt *f* GESCHÄFT world; ♦ **in der ganzen Welt** GESCHÄFT all over the world

Welt: **Weltanschauung** *f* PERSON *Persönlichkeit, Neigungen* Weltanschauung; **Weltbank** *f* BANK International Bank for Reconstruction and Development (*IBRD*), World Bank; **Weltenergiekonferenz** *f* POL, UMWELT World Power Conference; **Weltexporte** *m pl* IMP/EXP world exports; **Weltfinanzzentrum** *nt* VW global financial center (*AmE*), global financial centre (*BrE*); **Weltgesundheitsorganisation** *f* (*WHO*) SOZIAL, VW World Health Organization (*WHO*); **Weltgewerkschaftsbund** *m* PERSON World Federation of Trade Unions (*WFTU*)

Welthandel *m* GESCHÄFT international trade, VW world trade; **Welthandels- und Entwicklungskonferenz** *f* **der Vereinten Nationen** (*UNCTAD*) VW United Nations Conference on Trade and Development (*UNCTAD*); **Welthandelsroute** *f* TRANSP world trade route; **Welthandelszentrum** *nt* V&M, VW world trade center (*AmE*) (*WTC*), world trade centre (*BrE*) (*WTC*)

Welt: **Welthungerhilfeprogramm** *nt* (*WFP*) SOZIAL, VW World Food Programme (*WFP*); **Weltklasse** *f* GESCHÄFT world class; **Weltmarkt** *m* VW world market, global market; **Weltorganisation** *f* **für geistiges Eigentum** PATENT, RECHT World Intellectual Property Organization (*WIPO*); **Weltorganisation** *f* **für Meteorologie** UMWELT World Meteorological Organization (*WMO*); **Weltpreis** *m* VW world price; **Weltrang** *m* GESCHÄFT world class; **Weltstrategie** *f* GESCHÄFT global strategy; **Weltsystemperspektive** *f* VW world systems perspective; **Welttextilabkommen** *nt* VW multi-fiber arrangement (*AmE*) (*MFA*), multi-fibre arrangement (*BrE*) (*MFA*)

weltumspannend **1.** *adj* GESCHÄFT global, worldwide; **2.** *adv* GESCHÄFT globally

weltumspannend: **~es Finanzzentrum** *nt* VW global financial center (*AmE*), global financial centre (*BrE*)

Welt: **Weltverband** *m* VW world confederation; **Weltverband** *m* **zum Schutz wildlebender Tiere** (*WWF*) UMWELT World Wide Fund for Nature (*WWF*); **Weltverbrauch** *m* UMWELT, VW world consumption; **Weltwährungsreserven** *f pl* VW international liquidity; **Weltwährungsreservever-**

mögen *nt* FINANZ world monetary reserve assets; **Weltwährungssystem** *nt* FINANZ world monetary system, VW international monetary system

weltweit *adv* GESCHÄFT all over the world, globally, on an international scale, worldwide; ♦ ~ **reichend** GESCHÄFT on a worldwide scale

weltweit: ~ **führendes Unternehmen** *nt* GESCHÄFT, IND, V&M world leader; ~**e Inflation** *f* VW world inflation; ~**e Luftfrachtgüter-Klassifizierung** *f* TRANSP Worldwide Air Cargo Commodity Classification (*WACCC*); ~**es Marketing** *nt* V&M global marketing

Weltweit: ~**e Organisation** *f* **der VN-Verbände** VERWALT World Federation of United Nations Associations (*WFUNA*)

weltweit: ~**es Schuldenproblem** *nt* VW world debt problem

Weltweit: **Weltweit-Service** *m* TRANSP *Schiffahrt* round-the-world service (*Rws*)

weltweit: ~**er Tankerfrachttarif** *m* TRANSP Worldscale; ~**er Universitätsdienst** *m* SOZIAL World University Service (*WUS*); ~**er Wohlstand** *m* SOZIAL, VW world welfare

Weltwirtschaft *f* VW world economy; **Weltwirtschaftsgipfel** *m* POL, VW world economic summit; **Weltwirtschaftsgruppierungen** *f pl* VW world economic groupings; **Weltwirtschaftskrise** *f* VW Great Depression

Wende *f* GESCHÄFT, POL turnabout, turnaround (*AmE*), turnround (*BrE*); **Wendebecken** *nt* TRANSP turning basin; **Wendekreis** *m* TRANSP turning circle

wenden 1. *vt* FINANZ turn around, turn round; **2. sich** ~ **an** *v refl* [+acc] GESCHÄFT *Öffentlichkeit* appeal to, *Person* refer to; ♦ **sich an etw** ~ GESCHÄFT be aimed at sth; **sich an jdn** ~ GESCHÄFT be aimed at sb

Wende: **Wendepunkt** *m* GESCHÄFT turning point; **Wendezeit** *f* TRANSP port turnaround time (*AmE*), port turnround time (*BrE*), *Liegezeit im Hafen* turnaround (*AmE*), turnround (*BrE*)

Wendung: **eine** ~ **nehmen** *phr* GESCHÄFT *zum Guten oder Schlechten* take a turn

wenig: **zu** ~ **ausgeben** *phr* FINANZ, POL, VW underspend

weniger *adv* GESCHÄFT less

Wenigseher *m pl* V&M light viewers

Wenn-dann-Spiele *nt pl* GESCHÄFT what-if games

Werbe- *in cpds* PERSON, V&M public relations (*PR*), publicity, advertising, promotional; **Werbeabonnement** *nt* GESCHÄFT complimentary subscription; **Werbeabteilung** *f* V&M advertising department, art department, creative department, publicity department; **Werbeagent, in** *m,f* V&M advertising agent; **Werbeagentur** *f* V&M advertising agency, public relations agency, PR agency; **Werbeaktion** *f* V&M promotional exercise; **Werbeantwortdienst** *m* V&M business reply service; **Werbeaufwand** *m* V&M advertising expenditure, advertising expense; **Werbeausgaben** *f pl* V&M publicity expenses; **Werbebarometer** *nt* V&M advertising thermometer; **Werbebeilage** *f* V&M advertising supplement, stuffer; **Werbebereich** *m* V&M advertising zone; **Werbebestimmungen** *f pl* V&M advertising regulations; **Werbeblatt** *nt* V&M leaflet; **Werbebranche** *f* V&M advertising trade; **Werbebroschüre** *f* GESCHÄFT booklet; **Werbebudget** *nt* V&M advertising budget; **Werbebudgetprüfung** *f* V&M advertising budget review; **Werbecode** *m* V&M advertising

code; **Werbedesigner, in** *m,f* V&M art designer, commercial designer; **Werbeeinnahmen** *f pl* V&M advertising revenue; **Werbeeinnahmen** *f pl* **durch die Medien** V&M advertising revenue by media; **Werbeetat** *m* V&M advertising budget; **Werbeetatüberprüfung** *f* V&M advertising budget review; **Werbeerfolg** *m* V&M advertising effectiveness; **Werbefachmann** *m* PERSON advertising man (*adman*), publicity man; **Werbefeldzug** *m* V&M advertising campaign; **Werbefernsehen** *nt* MEDIEN commercial television; **Werbefläche** *f* V&M advertising space; **Werbeflugblatt** *nt* V&M sales leaflet; **Werbeforschung** *f* V&M advertising research; **Werbefritze** *m* *infrml* PERSON adman (*infrml*), V&M huckster (*AmE*) (*infrml*); **Werbegag** *m* V&M advertising gimmick, publicity stunt; **Werbegeschenk** *nt* V&M business gift, free gift, incentive pack; **Werbegespräch** *nt* V&M advertising talk; **Werbegrafik** *f* V&M graphic design; **Werbegrafiker, in** *m,f* V&M graphic designer, commercial artist; **Werbegroßanlage** *f* V&M spectacular; **Werbeindustrie** *f* V&M advertising industry; **Werbekampagne** *f* V&M advertising campaign; **Werbekanal** *m pl* V&M advertising channel; **Werbekodex** *m* V&M code of advertising practice (*CAP*); **Werbekonzept** *nt* V&M advertising concept; **Werbekosten** *pl* V&M advertising expenditure, advertising expense; **Werbekosten** *pl* **pro verkauftem Produkt** V&M advertising cost per product sale; **Werbekriterien** *nt pl* V&M advertising criteria; **Werbeleiter, in** *m,f* PERSON, V&M advertising manager, publicity manager; **Werbematerial** *nt* V&M *Prospektmaterial* publicity material, sales literature; **Werbemelodie** *f* V&M advertising jingle; **Werbemittel** *nt pl* MEDIEN, V&M advertising medium; **Werbemix** *nt* V&M promotional mix

werben *vt* GESCHÄFT, V&M *Kunden* win; ♦ ~ **für** V&M *Produkt* advertise, promote

werbend *adj* GESCHÄFT promotional

Werbe-: **Werbenummer** *f* GESCHÄFT, MEDIEN *Zeitschrift* complimentary copy; **Werbeplakat** *nt* GESCHÄFT advertising poster, poster, V&M poster, *Schaufenster* show card; **Werbepolitik** *f* GESCHÄFT, V&M promotional policy, advertising policy; **Werbepreis** *m* GESCHÄFT knockdown price; **Werbeprogrammziele** *nt pl* V&M advertising program objectives (*AmE*), advertising programme objectives (*BrE*); **Werbeprospekt** *m* V&M hand-out; **Werbereise** *f* V&M advertising tour; **Werbeschreiben** *nt* V&M sales letter; **Werbeschrift** *f* FREI, GESCHÄFT brochure; **Werbeschwelle** *f* V&M advertising threshold

Werbesendung *f* MEDIEN, V&M commercial, commercial break; ~ **im Fernsehen** MEDIEN, V&M television commercial; ~ **im Radio** MEDIEN, V&M radio commercial

Werbe-: **Werbeslogan** *m* V&M advertising slogan

Werbespot *m* MEDIEN *Rundfunk, Fernsehen*, V&M ad (*infrml*), commercial, advertisement, spot; ~ **für die gesamte Zuhörerschaft** V&M total audience package; ~ **für die gesamte Zuschauerschaft** V&M total audience package

Werbe-: **Werbespruchband** *nt* **an einem Flugzeug** V&M aeroplane banner (*BrE*), airplane banner (*AmE*); **Werbestatistiken** *f pl* V&M advertising statistics; **Werbestrategie** *f* V&M advertising strategy; **Werbetaktiken** *f pl* V&M advertising tactics; **Werbetechnik** *f* V&M advertising technique; **Werbetest** *m* V&M sales test; **Werbetext** *m* V&M

advertising copy, advertising text; **Werbetexter, in** *m,f*
GESCHÄFT copy writer; **Werbetextstrategie** *f* V&M copy
strategy; **Werbethema** *nt* V&M advertising theme;
Werbetour *f* V&M advertising tour

Werbeträger *m* MEDIEN, V&M advertising medium,
advertising vehicle; **Werbeträgeranalyse** *f* MEDIEN,
vw media analysis

Werbe-: **Werbetrick** *m* V&M gimmick; **Werbeumsatz** *m*
V&M advertising turnover; **Werbeunterbrechung** *f*
MEDIEN commercial break; **Werbevieh** *nt* V&M admass,
admass society; **Werbewaffe** *f* V&M advertising weapon;
Werbewert *m* V&M advertising value;
Werbewertprüfung *f* V&M pre-test, pre-testing;
Werbewesen *nt* PERSON publicity, V&M advertising,
publicity; **Werbewirksamkeit** *f* V&M advertising effec-
tiveness; **Werbezeit** *f* V&M advertising time;
Werbezeitschriften *f pl* MEDIEN *kostenlos* give-away
magazines, free magazines; **Werbezuschuß** *m* V&M *des
Händlers* advertising allocation budget

werblich: ~**e Unterstützung** *f* V&M advertising support

Werbung *f* GESCHÄFT ad (*infrml*), V&M advertisement,
advertising, billing, publicity, *Anzeige, Inserat* advert
(*infrml*); ~ **einer Fluggesellschaft** V&M airline advertising; ~ **mit Gutschein für zweites Erzeugnis** V&M cross
couponing; ~ **für Industrieerzeugnisse** V&M industrial
advertising; ~ **mit Lockartikeln** V&M bait advertising
(*AmE*); ~ **für Markenartikel** V&M brand promotion;
~ **der öffentlichen Hand** V&M public service advertising; ~ **für Spezialartikel** V&M speciality advertising;
~ **für Spezialerzeugnisse** V&M speciality advertising;
~ **von Unternehmen zu Unternehmen** V&M business-
to-business advertising; ~ **nach dem Verkauf** V&M post-
purchase advertising; ~ **am Verkaufsort** V&M point-of-
sale advertising, POS advertising; ~ **am Verkaufspunkt**
V&M point-of-sale promotion, POS promotion, point-
of-sale advertising, POS advertising; ~ **an einem
Verkehrsknotenpunkt** V&M head-on position; ◆ **ohne
~** GESCHÄFT *Produkt* unadvertised; ◆ **machen für** V&M
advertise for; ~ **treiben** V&M advertise

Werbung: **Werbungsdeckung** *f* V&M advertising coverage; **Werbungsmittler, in** *m,f* V&M space broker

Werdegang *m obs* PERSON *Eignungsprüfung, Bewerbung*
background

Werft-Rollbock *m* TRANSP yard dolly

Werk *nt* IND factory, industrial plant, works; ◆ **ab ~**
GESCHÄFT ex factory, IMP/EXP ex factory, ex mill (*x-
mill*), ex works (*EXW*), TRANSP ex factory, ex mill (*x-
mill*), free at point of dispatch, ex works (*EXW*)

Werk: **Werksanlage** *f* **im Grünen** IND greenfield site
factory; **Werksbesichtigung** *f* V&M facility visit;
Werkserhaltung *f* GESCHÄFT plant maintenance;
Werksgelände *nt* GESCHÄFT factory site;
Werksinspektor, in *m,f* IND factory inspector;
Werksleiter, in *m,f* IND, MGMNT, PERSON plant manager,
works manager; **Werksleitung** *f* IND, MGMNT plant
management; **Werk/Speicher** *phr* IMP/EXP house/depot;
Werkspionage *f* IND industrial espionage;
Werksplanung *f* IND plant layout study;
Werksprüfer, in *m,f* IND factory inspector;
Werkssiedlung *f* vw company town

Werkstatt *f* GESCHÄFT shop floor, *Ausbildung* workshop,
IND *für Einzelaufträge* workshop; ◆ **in der ~** IND,
PERSON on the shop floor

Werkstatt: **Werkstattfertigung** *f* IND intermittent pro-

duction, job shop production; **Werkstattkreis** *m* IND,
MGMNT, PERSON *Industrial Engineering* quality circle;
Werkstattwagen *m* TRANSP *Bergung* breakdown van
(*BrE*), recovery vehicle, tow truck (*AmE*), *Wartung*
maintenance vehicle

Werkstechniker, in *m,f* IND site engineer

Werkstoff *m* IND material (*MAT*); **Werkstoffestigkeit** *f*
IND strength of materials

Werk: **Werkstück** *nt* IND component; **Werkswohnung** *f*
GRUND factory-owned apartment, factory-owned flat
(*BrE*), job-related accommodation, PERSON job-related
accommodation; **Werkszeitung** *f* MEDIEN house journal, in-house magazine; **an Werktagen** *phr* GESCHÄFT
on weekdays; **Werkvertrag** *m* GESCHÄFT, RECHT service
contract, works contract

Werkzeug *nt* COMP, GESCHÄFT, IND tool; ◆ **mit Werkzeugen ausstatten** IND tool up; **die Werkzeuge
niederlegen** PERSON down tools

Werkzeug: **Werkzeugleiste** *f* COMP tool bar; **Werkzeugmacher** *m* IND toolmaker; **Werkzeugmacherei** *f*
IND toolroom; **Werkzeugmaschine** *f* IND machine tool

Werner-Bericht *m* vw Werner Report

wert *adj* GESCHÄFT useful, valuable; ◆ ~ **sein** BÖRSE be
worth

Wert *m* GESCHÄFT worth, value; ~ **al Pari** RECHNUNG par
value; **über den Daumen gepeilter ~** *infrml* GESCHÄFT
ballpark figure; ~ **pro Einheit** GESCHÄFT unit value;
~ **eines Punktes** BÖRSE value of one point; ~ **als
Seepolice** VERSICH value as marine policy (*VMP*);
~ **wie in Ursprungspolice** VERSICH value as in original
policy (*VOP*); ~ **einer Währung** vw currency value;
~ **eines Wirtschaftsgutes** FINANZ asset value; ◆ **an
~ gewinnen** BÖRSE gain value; **den ~ mindern** vw
lower the value; **im ~ sinken** BÖRSE go down in value;
im ~ steigen RECHNUNG appreciate; **sich unter
~ verkaufen** GESCHÄFT undersell oneself; **an
~ verlieren** RECHNUNG, vw *Vermögenswerte, Aktiva*
depreciate; **im ~ verringern** BÖRSE write down

Wertanalyse *f* FINANZ value analysis (*VA*), RECHNUNG
value engineering, V&M value analysis (*VA*); ~ **im
Entstehungsstadium** FINANZ value engineering

Wertangabe *f* IMP/EXP, TRANSP declaration of value; ~ **für
Transport** TRANSP declared value for carriage; ~ **für
Zoll** IMP/EXP declared value for customs; ◆ **ohne ~** IMP/
EXP no value declared (*NVD*)

Wert: **Wertanpassung** *f* RECHNUNG valuation adjustment; **Wertaufbewahrungsmittel** *nt* vw store of value

Wertberichtigung *f* RECHNUNG provision, reserve, valuation adjustment, valuation allowance, allowance; ~ **auf
Beteiligungen** RECHNUNG allowable business investment loss; ~ **auf uneinbringliche Forderungen** BANK,
FINANZ bad debt provision, RECHNUNG allowance for
bad debts, provision for bad debts, bad debt provision;
~ **auf Vorratsvermögen** RECHNUNG inventory valuation adjustment; **Wertberichtigungen** *f pl* **auf
Beteiligungen** FINANZ *im Jahresabschluß* investment
reserve system; **Wertberichtigungen** *f pl* **auf das
Sachanlagevermögen** RECHNUNG accumulated depreciation; **Wertberichtigungsbuchung** *f* RECHNUNG
reserve entry; **Wertberichtigungskonto** *nt* RECHNUNG
absorption account, contra account, offset account,
valuation account

Wert: **Wertbescheinigung** *f* IMP/EXP certificate of value
(*BrE*) (*C/V*); **Wertbestimmung** *f* **des Lagerbestands**

RECHNUNG valuation of inventory, valuation of stocks; **Wertbezeichnung** *f* VW denomination (*denom.*); **Wertbrief** *m* KOMM insured letter; **Wertdifferenzversicherung** *f* VERSICH difference in value insurance; **Werteinbuße** *f* GRUND depreciation; **Werterhöhung** *f* GESCHÄFT increase in value; **Werterhöhungen** *f pl* **während der Pachtzeit** FINANZ, GRUND leasehold improvements; **Wertfortschreibung** *f* STEUER adjustment of assessed value; **Wertfracht** *f* TRANSP ad valorem freight

wertfrei *adj* GESCHÄFT without charge (*w.c.*)

Wert: **Wertgegenstände** *m pl* GESCHÄFT valuables; **Wertgesetz** *nt* VW law of value; **Wertkette** *f* FINANZ value chain; **Wertkonnossement** *nt* TRANSP ad valorem bill of lading; **Wertkonzept** *nt* FINANZ value concept

wertlos *adj* GESCHÄFT valueless, worthless; **~er Anstieg** *m* GESCHÄFT dead rise (*DR*)

wertmindernd: **~es Unternehmen** *nt* VW value subtractor

Wert: **Wertminderung** *f* GRUND, RECHNUNG, VW depreciation, impairment of value; **Wertpaket** *nt* KOMM insured parcel, registered parcel

Wertpapier *nt* (*WP*) BANK, BÖRSE, FINANZ, GESCHÄFT, RECHNUNG share (*BrE*), stock (*AmE*), security, bond, commercial paper (*CP*); **~ mit Dividendengarantie** BÖRSE guaranteed security; **~ mit kurzer Restlaufzeit** BÖRSE maturing security; **~ mit laufender Zinszahlung** FINANZ pass-through security; **~ mit schwachen Umsätzen** BÖRSE cabinet security (*AmE*), low-volume security; **Wertpapierabteilung** *f* BÖRSE securities department; **Wertpapieranalyse** *f* BÖRSE, FINANZ securities analysis, investment analysis; **Wertpapieranalytiker, in** *m,f* BÖRSE chartist, security analyst, technical analyst; **Wertpapierangebot** *nt* **im Sekundärmarkt** BÖRSE secondary distribution; **Wertpapierbestand** *m* BANK holding of securities, investment portfolio, portfolio, securities holdings, securities portfolio, BÖRSE investment portfolio, securities holdings, securities portfolio, FINANZ portfolio, investment portfolio, VW portfolio; **Wertpapierbörse** *f* BÖRSE, FINANZ, VW stock exchange (*stk exch*); **Wertpapierbörse** *f* **~ in Toronto** BÖRSE Toronto Stock Exchange

Wertpapiere *nt pl* BANK investments, BÖRSE investments, securities, FINANZ, VW investments; **~ des Anlagevermögens** FINANZ long-term financial investments; **durch ~ gesicherte Industrieobligation** *f* BÖRSE collateral trust bond; **~ mit kurzer Laufzeit** BÖRSE securities of short maturity date; **~ der öffentlichen Hand** VW government securities; **~ im Portefeuille** BÖRSE securities in portfolio; ♦ **~ gesucht** BÖRSE securities wanted; **~ halten** BÖRSE carry; **~ kaufen** BÖRSE go long

Wertpapier: **Wertpapier-Eigen- und Großhandel** *m* BÖRSE jobbing; **Wertpapieremission** *f* BÖRSE security flotation, security issue; **Wertpapier- und Emissionsgeschäft** *nt* BANK investment banking; **Wertpapiergeschäft** *nt* BÖRSE securities business; **Wertpapierhandel** *m* BÖRSE securities trade; **Wertpapierhändler, in** *m,f* BÖRSE market maker, securities dealer, investment dealer, jobber (*obs*) (*BrE*), FINANZ investment dealer; **Wertpapierhaus** *nt* BÖRSE securities house; **Wertpapierkauf** *m* **gegen Kredit** BÖRSE margin trading; **Wertpapierkonto** *nt* BÖRSE securities account; **Wertpapierkredit** *m* BÖRSE advance

on securities; **Wertpapierkreditaufnahme** *f* BANK securities borrowing; **Wertpapierkreditfähigkeit** *f* BÖRSE borrowing power of securities; **Wertpapierkurs** *m* BÖRSE security price; **Wertpapierkursgefüge** *nt* BÖRSE security price structure; **Wertpapierlombardierung** *f* BANK securities borrowing, FINANZ security borrowing; **Wertpapiermarkt** *m* BÖRSE, FINANZ securities market; **Wertpapiermarktlinie** *f* BÖRSE security market line

wertpapiermäßig: **~e Unterlegung** *f* **von Verbindlichkeiten** BANK, BÖRSE, FINANZ securitization

Wertpapier: **Wertpapiermillionär, in** *m,f* GESCHÄFT millionaire on paper; **Wertpapierpaket** *nt* BÖRSE block; **Wertpapierpensionsgeschäft** *nt* FINANZ repossession (*repo*), *vom Geldgeber initiiert* reverse repurchase agreement, GESCHÄFT repossession (*repo*), repurchase agreement; **Wertpapierportefeuille** *nt* BANK, BÖRSE investment portfolio, securities portfolio, FINANZ investment portfolio

Wertpapierposition *f* BÖRSE position; ♦ **eine ~ erwerben** BÖRSE take a position; **eine ~ halten** BÖRSE hold a position; **eine ~ verwerten** BÖRSE liquidate a position

Wertpapier: **Wertpapiersteuer** *f* STEUER securities tax; **Wertpapiertermingeschäft** *nt* BÖRSE forward transaction in securities; **Wertpapierverwaltung** *f* FINANZ securities administration (*AmE*), portfolio management, MGMNT portfolio management

Wert: **Wertparadoxon** *nt* VW paradox of value; **Wertsachen** *f pl* GESCHÄFT items of value, valuables; **Wertschätzung** *f* GRUND *Bewertung* appraisal, appraisement; **Wertschöpfung** *f* FINANZ, STEUER, VERWALT added value, VW added value, value added; **Wertsendung** *f* KOMM insured letter, registered letter, RECHT *Vertragsrecht* consignment with value declared; **Wertsenkung** *f* BÖRSE fall in value; **Wertsicherungsklausel** *f* VERSICH escalation clause; **Wertsteigerung** *f* FINANZ increase in value, GRUND appreciation, betterment, RECHNUNG, STEUER appreciation; **Wertstellungsgewinn** *m* BANK float; **Wertsteuer** *f* FINANZ ad valorem tax, IMP/EXP, STEUER ad valorem duty (*ad val.*), ad valorem tax, VW ad valorem tax; **Wertsteuersatz** *m* IMP/EXP ad valorem tariff, STEUER ad valorem rate, ad valorem tariff; **Werturteil** *nt* GESCHÄFT value judgment; **Wert- und Ursprungszertifikat** *nt* IMP/EXP certificate of value and origin (*BrE*) (*CVO*); **Wert- und Ursprungszeugnis** *nt* IMP/EXP certificate of value and origin (*BrE*) (*CVO*); **Wertverlust** *m* GRUND, RECHNUNG, VW depreciation; **Wertvorschlag** *m* FINANZ, RECHNUNG decrease in value, value proposal; **Wertzoll** *m* IMP/EXP, STEUER ad valorem customs duty, ad valorem duty (*ad val.*), customs duty ad valorem, VW ad valorem tariff; **Wertzolltarif** *m* IMP/EXP, STEUER ad valorem tariff; **Wertzuschlag** *m* TRANSP valuation charge, value surcharge; **Wertzuschreibung** *f* RECHNUNG appreciation in value

Wertzuwachs *m* BÖRSE, FINANZ capital growth, capital gain, capital gains, increase in value, growth in value, GESCHÄFT increment, gain, RECHNUNG, STEUER appreciation; **~ eines Effektenbestandes** RECHNUNG holding gains; **Wertzuwachssteuer** *f* FINANZ, RECHNUNG, STEUER capital gains tax

Wesensmerkmal *nt* PATENT characterizing portion, essential feature

wesentlich *adj* GESCHÄFT substantial, RECHT material; ♦

im ~en GESCHÄFT substantially, essentially; **sich über die ~en Vertragsbestandteile einigen** RECHT agree upon the essential terms of contract

wesentlich: ~e **Änderung** *f* **des Vertragsinhaltes** RECHT material alteration; ~e **Aussichten** *f pl* V&M key prospects; ~er **Bestandteil** *m* GESCHÄFT component part, integral part; ~e **Beteiligung** *f* BÖRSE control stock; STEUER, VW material interest, substantial investment; ~e **Eigenschaft** *f* PATENT essential feature; **im ~en erbrachte Leistung** *f* RECHT doctrine of substantial performance; ~es **Handelshemmnis** *nt* POL material barrier, vw material balance; ~es **Merkmal** *nt* PATENT essential feature; ~er **Programmpunkt** *m* **einer Agenda** POL plank; **die ~en Punkte** *m pl* GESCHÄFT the essentials; ~e **Umstände** *m pl* VERSICH material circumstances; ~e **Vertragsbedingung** *f* RECHT *Vertragsrecht* condition, stipulation going to the root of the contract

Wesentliche: **das** ~ *nt* GESCHÄFT the essentials, gist

Wesentlichkeit *f* GESCHÄFT importance, RECHNUNG materiality level, materiality

Westen: **nach** ~ **fahrend** *phr* TRANSP westbound; **nach** ~ **laufend** *phr* TRANSP westbound

Westeuropa *nt* GESCHÄFT Western Europe

Westeuropäisch: ~e **Union** *f* (*WEU*) POL, VERWALT Western European Union (*WEU*)

westlich *adj* vw western-style; ♦ ~ **ausgerichtet werden** GESCHÄFT become westernized; ~en **Typs** VW *Wirtschaftssystem* western-style

westlich: ~e **Industriestaaten** *m pl* VW Western industrialized nations

Wettbewerb *m* GESCHÄFT competition, contest, PERSON *freie Marktwirtschaft*, V&M competition, vw competition, competitive process; **auf** ~ **beruhende Taktik** MGMNT competitive tactics; ~ **unter Bietern** GESCHÄFT knockout competition; ♦ **mit jdm im** ~ **stehen** GESCHÄFT compete against sb

Wettbewerber, in *m,f* GESCHÄFT, V&M, VW competitor

wettbewerbintensiv: ~er **Markt** *m* VW competitive market

wettbewerblich *adj* GESCHÄFT, STEUER, V&M arm's length

Wettbewerb: **Wettbewerbsanreiz** *m* V&M, VW competitive stimulus

wettbewerbsbeschränkend *adj* FINANZ, V&M, VW anticompetitive; ~e **Praktiken** *f pl* V&M, VW anticompetitive practices, restrictive practices; ~es **Verhalten** *nt* RECHT, VW *Vertragsrecht* restraint on trade, restrictive practices, restrictive trade practices; ~e **Verhaltensweisen** *f pl* GESCHÄFT, VW restrictive practices

Wettbewerb: **Wettbewerbsbeschränkung** *f* VW restraint on trade; **Wettbewerbsbeschränkungen** *f pl* VW restrictive practices

wettbewerbsentzerrend: ~e **Subvention** *f* POL corrective subsidy

wettbewerbsfähig *adj* VW competitive; **nicht** ~es **Angebot** *nt* BÖRSE noncompetitive bid; ~er **Preis** *m* V&M, VW competitive price

Wettbewerb: **Wettbewerbsfähigkeit** *f* GESCHÄFT, V&M, VW competitiveness

wettbewerbsfeindlich *adj* VW detrimental to effective competition

Wettbewerb: **Wettbewerbsfreiheit** *f* VW freedom of

competition, free competition; **Wettbewerbsgesetze** *nt pl* POL, RECHT competition laws

wettbewerbsintensiv *adj* GESCHÄFT highly competitive, intensely competitive

Wettbewerb: **Wettbewerbslage** *f* VW competitive position; **Wettbewerbsmarkt** *m* VW competitive market, free and open market; **Wettbewerbsnorm** *f* GESCHÄFT norm for competition; **Wettbewerbsparität** *f* V&M competitive parity; **Wettbewerbspolitik** *f* POL competition policy; **Wettbewerbsposition** *f* GESCHÄFT, VW competitive position; **Wettbewerbspreis** *m* RECHNUNG, V&M arm's-length price, vw competitive price; **Wettbewerbspreisbildung** *f* GESCHÄFT competitive pricing; **Wettbewerbsprozeß** *m* VW competitive process; **Wettbewerbsrecht** *nt* RECHT cartel law; **Wettbewerbsregeln** *f pl* GESCHÄFT, RECHT, VW rules of competition, trade practice rules; **Wettbewerbsreiz** *m* V&M, VW competitive stimulus

wettbewerbsschädlich *adj* FINANZ, VW anticompetitive

Wettbewerb: **Wettbewerbsstrategie** *f* GESCHÄFT, V&M, VW competitive strategy; **Wettbewerbstaktik** *f* VW competitive tactics; **Wettbewerbsverzerrung** *f* VW distortion of competition; **Wettbewerbsvorsprung** *m* VW competitive advantage, competitive edge; **Wettbewerbsvorstoß** *m* VW competitive thrust; **Wettbewerbsvorteil** *m* VW competitive advantage; **einen Wettbewerbsvorteil gegenüber jdm haben** *phr* VW have a competitive advantage over sb, have a competitive edge over sb

wettbewerbswidrig: ~es **Verhalten** *nt* VW anticompetitive practices

wetteifern: ~ **mit** *phr* GESCHÄFT vie with

wetten 1. *vt* FREI bet, wager; **2.** *vi* FREI bet, wager

Wetten *nt* FREI betting

Wetter *nt* GESCHÄFT weather; **Wetterbericht** *m* GESCHÄFT weather report; **Wetterdeck** *nt* TRANSP weather deck; **nach Wetterlage mögliche Arbeitstage, Freitag und Feiertage ausgeschlossen** *phr* TRANSP weather working days, Friday and holidays excluded (*wwdFHEx*); **nach Wetterlage mögliche Arbeitstage, Sonn- und Feiertage ausgeschlossen** *phr* TRANSP weather working days, Sundays and holidays excluded (*wwdSHEx*); **nach Wetterlage möglicher Arbeitstag** *m* TRANSP weather working day (*wwd*)

wettmachen *vt* GESCHÄFT recoup

Wettstreit *m* GESCHÄFT contest

WEU *abbr* (*Westeuropäische Union*) POL, VERWALT WEU (*Western European Union*)

WFP *abbr* (*Welthungerhilfeprogramm*) VW WFP (*World Food Programme*)

WGA *abbr* (*Wirtschaftsvereinigung Groß- und Außenhandel*) IMP/EXP ≈ BEHA (*British Export Houses' Association*)

Wharton-Modell *nt* VW Wharton model

WHO *abbr* (*Weltgesundheitsorganisation*) SOZIAL, VW WHO (*World Health Organization*)

wichtig *adj* GESCHÄFT important, significant; ~e **aktuelle Nachrichten** *f pl* MEDIEN front-page news; ~es **Amt** *nt* PERSON high office, important office; ~er **Devisenmarkt** *m* FINANZ major foreign exchange market; **sehr** ~e **Fracht** *f* TRANSP very important cargo (*VIC*); **sehr** ~es **Objekt** *nt* TRANSP very important object (*VIO*); ~e **Person** *f* (*VIP*) GESCHÄFT very important person (*VIP*); **~e Währung** *f* VW major currency

Wicklung *f* TRANSP *Fasern* convolute winding

Widerklage *f* RECHT counterclaim, cross-complaint (*AmE*), cross-suit

widerlegbar *adj* RECHT confutable, rebuttable

widerrechtlich: **~e Aneignung** *f* RECHT misappropriation; **~es Betreten** *nt* **von Privateigentum** RECHT trespass on private property; **~ verwenden** *phr* FINANZ misappropriate; **~e Verwendung** *f* FINANZ misappropriation; **~e Verwendung** *f* **von Geldern** GESCHÄFT misappropriation of funds

Widerruf *m* FINANZ revocation, PATENT rescission, revocation, RECHT *Vertragsaufhebung* cancellation

widerrufbar: **~e Abschreibung** *f* RECHNUNG recapturable depreciation; **~es Treuhandverhältnis** *nt* FINANZ revocable trust; **~er Trust** *m* FINANZ revocable trust

widerrufen *vt* FINANZ revoke, PATENT *Lizenz* rescind, revoke, RECHT *Vertrag* cancel

widerruflich *adj* GESCHÄFT revocable

Widerruflichkeit *f* RECHT revocability; **~ von Erklärungen** RECHT *Vertragsrecht* revocability of declarations

Widerrufstag *m* TRANSP *Chartervertrag* canceling date (*AmE*), cancelling date (*BrE*)

widersetzen: **~ sich** *v refl* [+dat] GESCHÄFT oppose

widerspiegeln 1. *vt* GESCHÄFT reflect; **2. sich ~ in** *v refl* [+dat] GESCHÄFT be reflected in

widersprechen *vi* [+dat] GESCHÄFT *Antrag* counter, conflict, RECHT contradict, deny the truth of, *Einspruch erheben* protest against, oppose

Widerspruch *m* PATENT objection, protest, RECHT contradiction, *Einspruch* opposition; ♦ **ohne ~** FINANZ unprotested; **in ~ stehen** GESCHÄFT conflict; **zu jdm wegen etw im ~ stehen** GESCHÄFT be at variance with sb about sth

widersprüchlich: **~e Aussagen** *f pl* RECHT conflicting evidence; **~es Beweismaterial** *nt* RECHT conflicting evidence

Widerstand *m* GESCHÄFT resistance, opposition

widerstandsfähig *adj* GESCHÄFT robust

Widerstandslinie *f* BÖRSE resistance level

widerstreitend: **~e Ansprüche** *m pl* RECHT *Vertragsrecht* contending claims, interfering claims; **~e Interessen** *f pl* GESCHÄFT clashing interests, conflicting interests

widmen: **sich etw ~** *phr* GESCHÄFT *Problem, Aufgabe* address oneself to

widrig *adj* GESCHÄFT adverse

wie: **~ bereits erwähnt** *phr* KOMM as mentioned above; **~ berichtet** *phr* KOMM *in einem Dokument, in den Medien* as reported; **~ besichtigt** *phr* GESCHÄFT, RECHT as is

Wieder- *in cpds* GESCHÄFT re-

wiederankurbeln *vt* VW *Wirtschaft* stimulate

Wieder-: **Wiederanlagevorrecht** *nt* BÖRSE reinvestment privilege; **Wiederanlauf** *m* COMP rerun, reset, VW restart

wiederanlaufen: **~ lassen** *vt* COMP *Uhr, Daten* reset, VW restart

Wieder-: **Wiederanlaufprogramm** *nt* COMP restart program

wiederanlegen *vt* BÖRSE reinvest

Wieder-: **Wiederannäherung** *f* POL rapprochement;

Wiederanstieg *m* **der Preise** GESCHÄFT resurgence in prices; **Wiederaufbau** *m* VW rebuilding, reconstruction

wiederaufbauen *vt* COMP rebuild

Wieder-: **Wiederaufbauplan** *m* VW recovery plan; **Wiederaufbauprogramm** *nt* GESCHÄFT recovery program (*AmE*), recovery programme (*BrE*)

wiederaufblühen *vi* GESCHÄFT, VW revive

Wieder-: **Wiederaufblühen** *nt* GESCHÄFT, VW revival; **Wiederauffinden** *nt* **von Informationen** COMP information retrieval; **Wiederaufforstung** *f* UMWELT reafforestation; **Wiederaufführung** *f* FREI revival

wiederaufgebaut *adj* GESCHÄFT, IND, VW rebuilt (*RBT*)

wiederauflegen *vt* GESCHÄFT *Produkt, Programm* relaunch

Wieder-: **Wiederaufnahme** *f* COMP resumption, FREI revival, GESCHÄFT re-admission, POL *Beziehungen* re-establishment, resumption, RECHT revival, *Verfahren* reopening, resumption, SOZIAL *Patienten* re-admission

wiederaufnehmen *vt* COMP resume, FREI revive, GESCHÄFT re-admit, POL *Beziehungen* re-establish, resume, *als Mitglied* re-admit, RECHT revive, *Verfahren* reopen, resume, SOZIAL *Patienten* re-admit

Wiederausfuhr *f* IMP/EXP re-exportation; **Wiederausfuhrgüter** *nt pl* IMP/EXP goods for re-export; **Wiederausfuhrhändler, in** *m,f* IMP/EXP re-exporter

Wiederausgleich *m*: **~ von Verlusten** RECHNUNG recovery of losses

wiederbeleben *vt* GESCHÄFT, VW revive, restart

Wiederbelebung *f* GESCHÄFT, VW restart, revival

Wiederbeschaffung *f* GESCHÄFT replacement; **Wiederbeschaffungsklausel** *f* VERSICH replacement clause; **Wiederbeschaffungskosten** *pl* RECHNUNG, VW replacement costs; **Wiederbeschaffungskostenrechnung** *f* RECHNUNG replacement cost accounting, replacement costing; **Wiederbeschaffungsplanung** *f* FINANZ replacement planning; **Wiederbeschaffungspreis** *m* V&M replacement price; **Wiederbeschaffungswert** *m* RECHNUNG replacement value, VERSICH cost of replacement

wiedereinbringen *vt* GESCHÄFT recover

Wieder-: **Wiedereinbringen** *nt* **von Verlusten** RECHNUNG making-up for losses

wiedereinführen *vt* GESCHÄFT, V&M *Programm, Produkt* relaunch

Wieder-: **Wiedereinführung** *f* GESCHÄFT, V&M relaunch

wiedereingliedern *vt* RECHT rehabilitate, VW resettle

Wiedereingliederung *f* GESCHÄFT, POL resettlement, RECHT rehabilitation, reintegration; **Wiedereingliederungsfonds** *m* **des Europarats** BANK Council of Europe Resettlement Fund (*CERF*)

Wieder-: **Wiedereinrichtung** *f* GESCHÄFT refocusing

Wiedereinsetzung *f* GESCHÄFT reinstatement, re-establishment; **~ in den vorigen Stand** GESCHÄFT, RECHT restitutio in integrum

wiedereinstellen *vt* GESCHÄFT, PERSON *ehemaligen Mitarbeiter* re-employ, reinstate, re-engage, take back

Wieder-: **Wiedereinstellung** *f* GESCHÄFT, PERSON reinstatement, re-employment, *eines entlassenen Arbeitnehmers* re-engagement

wiedererkennen *vt* GESCHÄFT recognize

Wieder-: **Wiedererkennungseffekt** *m* GESCHÄFT halo effect; **Wiedererkennungstest** *m* V&M recognition test

wiedererlangen *vt* VW recover, retrieve

wiedergeben *vt* GESCHÄFT *Bericht* give back, reproduce

wiedergewählt: nicht ~es Kongreßmitglied *nt* POL lame duck (*AmE*) (*infrml*)

wiedergewinnen *vt* COMP *Daten, Datei* retrieve, GESCHÄFT recover

wiedergutmachen *vt* RECHT make amends, make good, redress

Wiedergutmachung *f* RECHT amends, compensation, indemnification, redress; ◆ **~ verlangen** RECHT seek redress

wiederhereinholen *vt* GESCHÄFT *Vermögenswerte* recover

wiederhergestellt *adj* GESCHÄFT, IND rebuilt (*RBT*)

wiederherstellbar: nicht ~ *adj* COMP unrecoverable

wiederherstellen *vt* COMP *Datei* recover, restore, GESCHÄFT restore, *Balance* redress, RECHT reinstate, replace

Wiederherstellung *f* COMP *von Datei* recovery, restoration, GESCHÄFT re-establishment, restitutio in integrum, RECHT reinstatement, replacement, *ursprünglicher Zustand* restitutio in integrum, UMWELT rehabilitation; **Wiederherstellungskosten** *pl* RECHNUNG replacement costs, reproduction costs

wiederholen *vt* GESCHÄFT reiterate, repeat, rerun, MEDIEN repeat

Wiederholung *f* GESCHÄFT reiteration, repetition, rerun, MEDIEN repeat; **Wiederholungsbefragung** *f* MEDIEN, V&M *Medienforschung* tracking study; **Wiederholungsbudget** *nt* VW rollover budget; **Wiederholungsdarlehen** *nt* BANK repeater loan; **Wiederholungsgeschäft** *nt* GESCHÄFT repeat business; **Wiederholungskäufe** *m pl* V&M repeat buying; **Wiederholungslauf** *m* COMP rerun; **Wiederholungsprüfung** *f* GESCHÄFT re-examination; **Wiederholungsrabatt** *m* V&M rebate granted for repeat advertising; **Wiederholungsrate** *f* V&M *Anzahl der Käufer, die nach einmaligem Kauf zurückkehren* repeat rate

Wieder-: Wiederinbesitznahme *f* BÖRSE, GESCHÄFT, GRUND, RECHT repossession (*repo*); **Wiederinkraftsetzung** *f* RECHT *Gesetz* re-enactment, revival; **Wiederinstandsetzung** *f* GESCHÄFT repair; **Wiederkauf** *m* RECHT buy-back construction; **Wiederkehr** *f* GESCHÄFT return

wiederkehrend: ~e Arbeitsunfähigkeit *f* PERSON *Krankheit* recurrent disability; **~e Aufwendungen** *f pl* GESCHÄFT period cost

wiedervereinigt *adj* GESCHÄFT unified

Wieder-: Wiedervereinigung *f* GESCHÄFT reunification

Wiederverkauf *m* BÖRSE, GESCHÄFT resale

wiederverkaufen *vt* BÖRSE, GESCHÄFT resell

Wiederverkäufer, in *m,f* BÖRSE, GESCHÄFT reseller, *Einzelhändler* retailer; **~ mit Mehrwertdienstleistungen** COMP value-added reseller (*VAR*); **Wiederverkäufermarkt** *m* V&M reseller market; **Wiederverkäuferrabatt** *f* BÖRSE reallowance

Wiederverkauf: Wiederverkaufspreis *m* V&M resale price; **Wiederverkaufspreisbindung** *f* FINANZ, RECHT, V&M retail price maintenance (*RPM*); **Wiederverkaufsrecht** *nt* V&M right of resale; **Wiederverkaufswert** *m* V&M resale value

Wieder-: Wiederverpackung *f* IMP/EXP, V&M repacking

wiederverwendbar: ~e Packungen *f pl* V&M reusable packs

wiederverwenden *vt* GESCHÄFT, UMWELT, V&M recycle, reuse

Wieder-: Wiederverwendung *f* GESCHÄFT, UMWELT recycling, reuse

wiederverwertbar *adj* GESCHÄFT, UMWELT recyclable, reusable; **nicht ~** *adj* GESCHÄFT, UMWELT nonrecyclable

wiederverwerten *vt* GESCHÄFT, UMWELT recycle, reuse

Wieder-: Wiederverwertung *f* GESCHÄFT, UMWELT recycling, reuse; **Wiederwahl** *f* GESCHÄFT re-election

wie: ~ folgt *phr* GESCHÄFT as follows

Wiegeschein *m* GESCHÄFT weight note

Wien: ~er Börsenkammer *f* BÖRSE Viennese Stock Exchange; **~er Schule** *f* VW Austrian School of Economics

wie: ~ oben *phr* KOMM as above; **~ oben erwähnt** *phr* KOMM as mentioned above

wild: ~er Anschlag *m* V&M fly posting; **~e Flucht** *f* GESCHÄFT stampede; **~er Streik** *m* PERSON *Arbeitskampf* illegal strike, unauthorized strike, wildcat strike

Willen: Willenseinigung *f* GESCHÄFT consensus ad idem, consensus agreement, RECHT meeting of the minds; **Willenserklärung** *f* RECHT declaration of intent, mutual consent

Williams-Gesetz *nt* RECHT Williams act

willkommen: ~ heißen *phr* GESCHÄFT welcome

willkürlich *adj* GESCHÄFT arbitrary; **~e Aufteilung** *f* **der Wahlbezirke** *infrml* POL gerrymander (*infrml*); **~er Ausschluß** *m* **von Bankkunden** FINANZ redlining

Winchesterplatte *f obs* COMP *Festplatte* Winchester disk (*obs*)

Windenergie *f* UMWELT wind power

Windenkopf *m* TRANSP gypsy

windunterstützt: ~er Schiffsantrieb *m* TRANSP wind-assisted ship propulsion

Wink *m* GESCHÄFT tip-off

Winkel *m* MATH angle

Winterschlußverkauf *m* V&M January sales, winter sales

Winzer, in *m,f* GESCHÄFT, VW wine grower, vintner

wirbeln *vi* FINANZ churn, twist

wirken *vi* GESCHÄFT act

wirklich: ~ bezahlte Steuern *f pl* RECHNUNG taxes actually paid; **~er Eigentümer** *m*, **~e Eigentümerin** *f* RECHT rightful owner, true owner

Wirklichkeit *f* GESCHÄFT actuality

wirklichkeitsnah *adj* GESCHÄFT realistic

Wirklichkeitssinn *m* GESCHÄFT sense of realism

wirksam *adj* GESCHÄFT effective; **~es Begrenzen** *nt* **von Risiken** FINANZ risk management; ◆ **~ werden** GESCHÄFT take effect, RECHT become effective, come into force, *in Kraft treten* come into operation; **~ werden ab** [+dat] GESCHÄFT take effect from

Wirksamkeit *f* GESCHÄFT effect, effectiveness, efficiency; ◆ **die ~ fördern** GESCHÄFT promote efficiency

Wirkung *f* GESCHÄFT effect, impression; **~ auf die Buchführung** RECHNUNG accounting effect; ◆ **mit ~ von** (*m. W. v.*) GESCHÄFT with effect from (*wef*)

Wirkung: Wirkungsbereich *m* STEUER impacted area; **Wirkungserstreckung** *f* RECHT *Vertragsrecht* efficient range; **Wirkungsgebiet** *nt* STEUER impacted area; **Wirkungshierarchie** *f* V&M hierarchy of effects; **Wirkungskreis** *m* GESCHÄFT sphere of activity, scope of application; **Wirkungsmultiplikator** *m* VW impact multiplier; **Wirkungsverhältnis** *nt* UMWELT efficiency ratio; **Wirkungsverzögerung** *f* STEUER, VW time lag **Wirtschaft** *f* VW economy

wirtschaftlich 1. *adj* BANK, FINANZ economic, efficient, GESCHÄFT economic, efficient, commercial, VERWALT, VW economic, efficient; **2.** *adv* VW economically; ◆ ~ **angemessen darstellen** RECHNUNG *Rechnungsprüfung* present fairly; ~ **gestalten** GESCHÄFT rationalize; ~ **unabhängig** GESCHÄFT self-supporting

wirtschaftlich: ~**e Abschreibung** *f* GRUND functional depreciation; ~**er Anreiz** *m* VW economic incentive; ~**er Aufschwung** *m* GESCHÄFT takeoff, VW boom; ~**er Auftrag** *m* VW economic mission; ~**e Ausdehnung** *f* GESCHÄFT, VW economic expansion; ~**er Eigentümer** *m*, ~**e Eigentümerin** *f* RECHT beneficial owner; ~**e Entwicklung** *f* GESCHÄFT commercial development, POL economic devolution, VW economic development; ~**e Erschütterungen** *f pl* GESCHÄFT economic upheavals; ~**er Fortschritt** *m* GESCHÄFT economic advancement, VW economic progress; ~**es Gut** *nt* VW economic good; ~**e Hauptsektoren** *f pl* VW main economic sectors; ~**e Integration** *f* POL, VW economic integration; ~**e Inzidenz** *f* STEUER economic incidence; ~**es Klima** *nt* VW economic climate, economic weather; ~**e Konzentration** *f* IND industrial concentration; ~**e Kriterien** *nt pl* VW economic criteria; ~**e Lebensdauer** *f* FINANZ, GESCHÄFT, V&M economic life; ~**e Losgröße** *f* IND economic batch quantity, economic order quantity (*EOQ*), economic manufacturing quantity, MGMNT economic batch size; ~**er Nutzen** *m* VW economic benefit; ~**e Nutzungsdauer** *f* FINANZ, GESCHÄFT economic life, RECHNUNG useful economic life, V&M economic life, VW useful economic life; ~**es Paradigma** *nt* VW economic paradigm; ~**er Preis** *m* V&M economic price; ~**es Prüfungswesen** *nt* RECHNUNG auditing; ~**e Rahmenbedingungen** *f pl* VW business conditions; ~**er Ressourceneinsatz** *m* UMWELT economical use of recources; ~**es Risiko** *nt* VERSICH commercial risk; ~ **rückständiges Gebiet** *nt* VW economically backward area; ~**e Stellung** *f* VW economic position; ~**es Umfeld** *nt* VW business conditions; ~**e Unmöglichkeit** *f* GESCHÄFT commercial impracticability; ~**es Veralten** *nt* VW economic obsolescence; ~**e Vereinfachung** *f* IND rationalization; ~**er Wert** *m* VW want-satisfying ability, economic value; ~**es Wohl** *nt* RECHNUNG economic value, SOZIAL economic welfare

Wirtschaftlich: ~**e Zusammenarbeit** *f* **zwischen den Entwicklungsländern** (*ECDC*) VW economic cooperation among developing countries (*ECDC*)

wirtschaftlich: ~**e Zuteilung** *f* VW efficient allocation

Wirtschaftlichkeit *f* FINANZ profitability, GESCHÄFT economic efficiency, cost-effectiveness, IND rationalization, UMWELT, VW economy, efficiency, economic efficiency; **Wirtschaftlichkeitsprüfung** *f* RECHNUNG efficiency audit; **Wirtschaftlichkeitsrechnung** *f* BÖRSE investment appraisal, FINANZ capital budgeting, capital expenditure evaluation, investment appraisal, VW economy calculation, evaluation of economic efficiency, capital budget

Wirtschaft: **Wirtschaftsaktivität** *f* VW economic activity; **Wirtschaftsanalyse** *f* VW economic analysis; **Wirtschaftsaufschwung** *m* GESCHÄFT, VW economic expansion; **Wirtschaftsaussichten** *f pl* VW economic prospects; **Wirtschaftsberater, in** *m,f* BANK, FINANZ, POL, VERWALT, VW economic adviser; **Wirtschafts-**

bericht *m* VW economic report; **Wirtschaftsbetrieb** *m* IND industrial plant; **Wirtschaftsdaten** *pl* VW economic data; **Wirtschaftsdemokratie** *f* GESCHÄFT, PERSON, VW economic democracy; **Wirtschaftsdiplom** *nt* GESCHÄFT Diploma of Economics (*DipEcon*); **Wirtschaftsdynamik** *f* IND industrial dynamics; **Wirtschaftsentwicklungsgebiet** *nt* VW enterprise zone (*EZ*); **Wirtschaftsfinanzierung** *f* FINANZ industrial finance; **Wirtschaftsforschung** *f* GESCHÄFT commercial research, V&M, VW economic research; **Wirtschaftsgebiet** *nt* VW economic area; **Wirtschaftsgeographie** *f* VW economic geography; **Wirtschaftsgesetzgebung** *f* VW economic laws; **Wirtschaftsgipfel** *m* POL, VW *der G7* economic summit; **Wirtschaftsgut** *nt* FINANZ capital asset, VW commodity, economic good; **Wirtschaftsgut** *nt* **mit begrenzter Nutzungsdauer** RECHNUNG wasting asset, VW limited-life asset, wasting asset; **Wirtschaftsgüter** *nt pl* RECHNUNG assets; **Wirtschaftshochschule** *f* SOZIAL graduate school of business; **Wirtschaftsinformatik** *f* COMP, GESCHÄFT, SOZIAL business data processing; **Wirtschaftsjahr** *nt* FINANZ fiscal year (*FY*), RECHNUNG business year, financial year, fiscal year (*FY*), STEUER accounting year, fiscal year (*FY*); **Wirtschaftsjournalismus** *m* FINANZ financial journalism; **Wirtschaftskapitän** *m* *infrml* GESCHÄFT, PERSON *Industrie, Wirtschaft* captain of industry (*infrml*); **Wirtschaftsklima** *nt* GESCHÄFT economic climate; **Wirtschaftskreise** *m pl* GESCHÄFT business circles; **Wirtschaftskreislauf** *m* VW circular flow, cycle; **Wirtschaftskriminalität** *f* VW economic crime; **Wirtschaftskrise** *f* VW depression; **Wirtschaftslage** *f* FINANZ economic conditions, economic situation, GESCHÄFT business situation, POL economic situation, VW economic conditions, economic situation; **Wirtschaftsministerium** *nt* POL Department of Commerce (*AmE*), Department of Trade and Industry (*BrE*) (*DTI*); **Wirtschaftsmission** *f* MGMNT economic mission; **Wirtschaftsmodell** *nt* VW economic model; **Wirtschaftsnachrichten** *f pl* MEDIEN, VW economic news; **Wirtschaftsplanung** *f* GESCHÄFT, MGMNT, POL, UMWELT, VW economic planning; **Wirtschaftsplanungsabteilung** *f* VW economic planning unit; **Wirtschaftspolitik** *f* POL, VW economic policy; **Wirtschaftspolitik** *f* **des gütlichen Zuredens** BANK moral suasion

wirtschaftspolitisch: ~**e Lage** *f* FINANZ, POL, VW economic situation; ~**e Seelenmassage** *f* *infrml* POL jawboning (*AmE*)

Wirtschaft: **Wirtschaftspresse** *f* V&M business press; **Wirtschaftsprognose** *f* POL, VW economic forecasting; **Wirtschaftsprognose** *f* **für das VK** POL, VW UK economic forecasting

Wirtschaftsprüfer, in *m,f* GESCHÄFT, PERSON, RECHNUNG accountant

Wirtschaftsprüfung *f* FINANZ, RECHNUNG audit; **Wirtschaftsprüfungsfirma** *f* RECHNUNG accounting firm, accounting practice

Wirtschaft: **Wirtschaftspsychologie** *f* VW economics and psychology; **Wirtschaftsrecht** *nt* RECHT economic law, business law; **Wirtschaftsreform** *f* POL, VW economic reform; **Wirtschaftssanktionen** *f pl* POL economic sanctions, trade sanctions, VW trade sanctions; **Wirtschaftssektor** *m* GESCHÄFT business sector; **Wirtschafts- und Sozialausschuß** *m* VW Economic & Social Commission; **Wirtschafts- und Sozialrat** *m*

(*WSR*) vw Economic and Social Council (*ECOSOC*); **Wirtschaftsspionage** *f* IND industrial espionage; **Wirtschaftsstrategie** *f* GESCHÄFT commercial strategy; **Wirtschaftssystem** *nt* POL, VW economic system; **Wirtschaftsteil** *m* GESCHÄFT business pages, MEDIEN *einer Zeitung* economic section; **Wirtschaftsunion** *f* FINANZ, POL, VW economic union; **Wirtschaftsunternehmen** *nt* GESCHÄFT business enterprise, VERWALT *Geschäft, Firma* enterprise; **Wirtschaftsverband** *m* GESCHÄFT trade association; **Wirtschaftsverband von Deutscher Werbeagenturen** V&M ≈ American Association of Advertising Agencies (*AAAA*); **Wirtschaftsverbrechen** *nt* RECHT white-collar crime, vw economic crime; **Wirtschaftsvereinigung** *f* **Groß- und Außenhandel** (*WGA*) IMP/EXP ≈ British Export Houses' Association (*BEHA*); **Wirtschaftsverkehr** *m* GESCHÄFT commerce; **Wirtschaftsvorschau** *f* GESCHÄFT, VW business outlook; **Wirtschaftswachstum** *nt* VW economic growth; **Wirtschafts- und Währungsunion** *f* GESCHÄFT, VW Economic and Monetary Union (*EMU*); **Wirtschaftswissenschaft** *f* VW economics; **Wirtschaftswissenschaft** *f* **als Rhetorik** VW economics as rhetoric; **Wirtschaftswissenschaftler, in** *m,f* vw economist

wirtschaftswissenschaftlich: **~e Fakultät** *f* SOZIAL graduate school of business

Wirtschaft: **Wirtschaftszeitschrift** *f* vw business journal; **Wirtschaftszeitung** *f* VW business paper; **Wirtschaftszentrum** *nt* V&M business center (*AmE*), business centre (*BrE*); **Wirtschaftszweig** *m* IND industry, vw industry, trade

Wirtshaus: **im ~ getätigtes Geschäft** *nt* V&M wet sell

wissenbasiert: **~es System** *nt* *jarg* COMP knowledge-based system (*KBS*)

Wissensbasis: *f* SOZIAL knowledge base

Wissenschaft *f* GESCHÄFT science; **~ der Unternehmensführung** MGMNT management science

Wissenschaftler, in *m,f* PERSON *akademische Ausbildung* scientist

wissenschaftlich *adj* GESCHÄFT *naturwissenschaftlich* scientific, SOZIAL *Nachwuchs* academic; **~e Arbeitsorganisation** *f* MGMNT scientific management; **~e Betriebsführung** *f* MGMNT scientific management; **~es Management** *nt* MGMNT scientific management; **~er Meinungsaustausch** *m* GESCHÄFT symposium; **~es Programmieren** *nt* COMP, MATH scientific programming; **~es Zentrum** *nt* **für Kerntechnik** IND nuclear science center (*AmE*) (*NSC*), nuclear science centre (*BrE*) (*NSC*)

Witwenfreibetrag *m* STEUER widow's bereavement allowance

Witwenpflichtteil *m* RECHT dower

Woche *f* (*W*) GESCHÄFT week (*wk.*); ◆ **eine ~ für das Problem ansetzen** MGMNT allot a week to the problem; **eine ~ für das Problem vorsehen** MGMNT allot a week to the problem; **etw um eine ~ verschieben** GESCHÄFT postpone sth for a week; **eine ~ im voraus** GESCHÄFT a week in advance

Wochenausweis *m* BANK weekly return

Wochenend- *in cpds* GESCHÄFT, TRANSP weekend; **Wochenendfrachttarif** *m* TRANSP weekend freight tariff; **Wochenendheimfahrtenvergütung** *f* GESCHÄFT weekend travel home allowance; **Wochenendrückfahrt** *f* TRANSP weekend return

Woche: **Wochenlohn** *m* PERSON *Arbeitsentgelt* weekly wage; **Wochenmiete** *f* GRUND weekly rent

wöchentlich: **~e Bezahlung** *f* PERSON weekly pay; **~e Lohntüte** *f* *obs* PERSON weekly wage packet, weekly pay packet

Wohl *nt* PERSON, SOZIAL welfare

wohlbegründet *adj* GESCHÄFT, RECHT well-grounded

wohlbekannt: **~es Markenzeichen** *nt* PATENT, V&M well-known trademark; **~es Warenzeichen** *nt* PATENT, V&M well-known trademark

Wohlfahrt *f* PERSON, SOZIAL welfare; **Wohlfahrtsbehörde** *f* PERSON, SOZIAL welfare agency; **Wohlfahrtsdienste** *m pl* PERSON, SOZIAL welfare services; **Wohlfahrtsempfänger, in** *m,f* PERSON, SOZIAL *Sozialwesen* person receiving benefit (*BrE*), social security recipient, welfare recipient (*AmE*), SOZIAL social security recipient; **Wohlfahrtsfalle** *f* SOZIAL welfare trap; **Wohlfahrtsgesetzgebung** *f* PERSON, POL, SOZIAL welfare legislation; **Wohlfahrtsökonomik** *f* vw welfare economics; **Wohlfahrtsoptimum** *nt* vw bliss point; **Wohlfahrtsstaat** *m* POL, SOZIAL welfare state, VW nanny state (*infrml*), welfare state

wohlfahrtsstaatlich *adj* POL, SOZIAL welfarist

Wohlfahrt: **Wohlfahrtstheorie** *f* vw welfare economics; **Wohlfahrtsunterstützung** *f* PERSON, SOZIAL *Sozialwesen* welfare payments

wohlhabend *adj* GESCHÄFT, VW prosperous, affluent, wealthy, well-off, well-to-do

Wohlhabende: **die Wohlhabenden** *pl* GESCHÄFT the wealthy

wohlmeinend *adj* GESCHÄFT, SOZIAL well-meaning

Wohlstand *m* VW prosperity, wealth, affluence; **~ der Nationen** vw Wealth of Nations; **Wohlstandsgesellschaft** *f* GESCHÄFT, VW affluent society; **Wohlstandsindikator** *m* VW prosperity indicator

wohltätig: **~e Organisation** *f* SOZIAL, STEUER charity; **~e Stiftung** *f* SOZIAL, STEUER charitable foundation, charitable trust, charity

Wohltätigkeit *f* SOZIAL, STEUER charity; **Wohltätigkeitsfonds** *m* SOZIAL, STEUER charity fund; **Wohltätigkeitsveranstaltung** *f* SOZIAL benefit, charity event; **Wohltätigkeitsverein** *m* GESCHÄFT, SOZIAL benefit club, benefit society

wohlwollend: **~-autoritär** *adj* MGMNT benevolent-authoritative; **~er Kapitalismus** *m* POL benevolent capitalism

Wohn- *in cpds* GRUND residential, building; **Wohnbevölkerung** *f* vw resident population; **Wohnblock** *m* GRUND apartment building (*AmE*), block of flats (*BrE*); **Wohneigentum** *nt* GRUND home ownership

wohnen: **~ und arbeiten** *phr* RECHT reside and work

Wohn-: **Wohngebäude** *nt* GESCHÄFT, SOZIAL residential accommodation; **Wohngebiet** *nt* GRUND residential area; **Wohngeld** *nt* PERSON, SOZIAL housing allowance, rent subsidy, residence allowance

wohnhaft *adj* PERSON, RECHT domiciled, ordinarily resident

Wohn-: **Wohnhaus** *nt* GRUND dwelling, residential building; **Wohnhauskomplex** *m* GRUND housing complex; **Wohnkomplex** *m* GRUND housing complex; **Wohnnutzung** *f* GRUND residential occupancy; **Wohnraum** *m* GESCHÄFT, PERSON, SOZIAL *in einem Haus*

living space, residential accommodation, STEUER living accommodation; **Wohnsiedlung** *f* GRUND housing estate; **Wohnsitz** *m* RECHT, STEUER domicile; **Wohnsitzstaat** *m* STEUER country of residence

Wohnung *f* GRUND apartment (*AmE*), flat (*BrE*), PERSON, SOZIAL accommodation, STEUER living accommodation; **Wohnungsamt** *nt* SOZIAL accommodation bureau (*AmE*), housing department (*BrE*), housing office

Wohnungsbau *m* GESCHÄFT housing, GRUND housebuilding, housing construction, residential construction; **Wohnungsbaubeihilfe** *f* SOZIAL *subventionierter Wohnungsbau* housing subsidy; **Wohnungsbaudarlehen** *nt* BANK home equity loan, home loan, housing loan; **Wohnungsbauhypothek** *f* BANK house mortgage, housing mortgage loan; **Wohnungsbauverordnung** *f* GRUND housing code

Wohnung: **Wohnungseigentum** *nt* GRUND home ownership; **Wohnungsinstandsetzungsdarlehen** *nt* BANK home improvement loan; **Wohnungsmakler, in** *m,f* SOZIAL estate agent, house agent; **Wohnungsmarkt** *m* GRUND housing market; **Wohnungsnot** *f* GRUND housing shortage; **Wohnungsvermittlung** *f* SOZIAL accommodation agency (*BrE*), accommodation bureau (*AmE*), housing department (*BrE*); **Wohnungswirtschaft** *f* IND housing industry

Wohn-: **Wohnverhältnisse** *nt pl* SOZIAL living conditions; **Wohnvorort** *m* PERSON *Sozialwesen, Stadtplanung* bedroom community (*AmE*), dormitory suburb, residential suburb; **Wohnzuschuß** *m* PERSON accomodation allowance; **Wohnzwecke** *m pl* GRUND residential occupancy

Wölbung *f* MATH kurtosis

Woll- *in cpds* GESCHÄFT wool; **Wollhandel** *m* GESCHÄFT wool trade; **Wollhändler, in** *m,f* GESCHÄFT wool merchant; **Wollindustrie** *f* IND wool industry

Workaholic *m* PERSON workaholic

Work-in *nt* PERSON work-in

Workstation *f jarg* COMP, GESCHÄFT work station

Wort *nt* GESCHÄFT term, word; ♦ **für jdn ein ~ einlegen** GESCHÄFT put in a word for sb; **bei etw ein ~ mitreden** GESCHÄFT have a say in sth

Wort: **Wort- und Bildzeichen** *nt* PATENT word and device mark

Wörter: *nt pl* **~ pro Minute** (*WpM*) VERWALT words per minute (*wpm*)

Wörterzählung *f* COMP, MEDIEN word count

wortgetreu: **~er Bericht** *m* GESCHÄFT verbatim account

Wort: **Wortlänge** *f* COMP word length; **Wortlaut** *m* GESCHÄFT, RECHT *Vertrag* wording; **Wortlaut** *m* **einer Abstimmung** GESCHÄFT wording of a vote

WP *abbr* (*Wertpapier*) BANK, FINANZ, GESCHÄFT CP (*commercial paper*)

WpM *abbr* (*Wörter pro Minute*) VERWALT wpm (*words per minute*)

Wrack *nt* TRANSP wreck

WS *abbr* (*Wechselstrom*) GESCHÄFT ac (*alternating current*)

WSR *abbr* (*Wirtschafts- und Sozialrat*) VW ECOSOC (*Economic and Social Council*)

Wucher *m* BANK, FINANZ usurious money-lending, usury

Wucherer *m* FINANZ usurer

wucherisch *adj* BANK, FINANZ usurious

Wucher: **Wuchermiete** *f* RECHT extortionate rent, rackrent; **Wucherzinsen** *m pl* BANK, FINANZ excessive interest, usurious interest

Wuchsaktie *f* BÖRSE growth stock

Wühltisch *m* V&M bargain counter

Wunder: **sein blaues ~ erleben** *phr* GESCHÄFT get more than one bargains for

Wunderkind *nt* GESCHÄFT child prodigy, whiz kid (*infrml*), wunderkind

Wunsch *m* GESCHÄFT ambition, request, V&M desire; ♦ **auf allgemeinen ~** GESCHÄFT by popular request

würdigen: **zu ~ verstehen** *phr* GESCHÄFT appreciate

Wurzel *f* COMP *Baumstruktur* root; **Wurzelsegment** *nt* COMP *Datenbank* root segment; **Wurzelverzeichnis** *nt* COMP root directory

WWF *abbr* (*Weltverband zum Schutz wildlebender Tiere*) UMWELT WWF (*World Wide Fund for Nature*)

WYSIWYG *abbr* (*wirklichkeitsgetreue Darstellung auf dem Bildschirm*) COMP *Textverarbeitung* WYSIWYG (*what you see is what you get*)

X

X-Effizienz *f* VW X efficiency

xerographisch *adj* VERWALT xerographic

Xerokopie® *f* VERWALT Xerox®

xerokopieren® *vt* VERWALT Xerox®

x-Fabrik *phr* (*ab Fabrik*) GESCHÄFT, IMP/EXP, TRANSP ex factory, ex works (*EXW*), x-mill (*ex mill*)

X-Form *f* VW X-form

x-Hafendamm *phr* (*ab Hafendamm*) TRANSP x-wharf (*ex wharf*)

x-Kai *phr* (*ab Kai*) TRANSP x-quay (*ex quay*)

x-Mühle *phr* (*ab Mühle*) TRANSP x-mill (*ex mill*)

x-Pier *phr* (*ab Pier*) TRANSP x-quay (*ex quay*)

x%: unter der ~-Grenze *phr* GESCHÄFT below the x% mark; **zwischen ~ und y% liegen** *phr* GESCHÄFT range from x% to y%

x-Schiff *abbr* (*ex Schiff*) IMP/EXP, TRANSP x-ship (*ex ship*)

XY-Plotter *m* VERWALT X-Y plotter

x-Zinssatz *m* FINANZ x-interest

Y

Yard *nt* GESCHÄFT *Maß* yard (*yd*)

Yumpie *m* GESCHÄFT yumpie (*young upwardly mobile professional*) (*infrml*) (*AmE*)

Yuppie *m* GESCHÄFT yuppie (*young upwardly mobile professional*) (*infrml*) (*BrE*)

Z

Z. *abbr* (*Zahlung*) GESCHÄFT PYT (*payment*)

Zähflüssigkeit *f* GESCHÄFT viscosity

Zahl *f* KOMM cipher, MATH figure, number; **~ der abgegebenen Stimmen** GESCHÄFT *Abstimmung, Wahl* total votes cast; **~ der Abonnenten** GESCHÄFT number of subscribers; **~ der Eingetragenen** GESCHÄFT enrollment (*AmE*), enrolment (*BrE*); **~ der Zeichen pro Zoll** COMP character pitch

zahlbar *adj* GESCHÄFT due, due and payable, payable, vw payable; ◆ **~ am** FINANZ *Datum* payable on; **~ bei Auftragserteilung** GESCHÄFT cash with order (*cwo*); **~ bei Bestellung** GESCHÄFT cash with order (*cwo*); **~ drei Monate ab dato** GESCHÄFT payable three months after date; **~ bei Sicht** FINANZ payable at sight, GESCHÄFT payable at sight, payable on demand

zahlbar: **~es Eilgeld** *nt* IMP/EXP dispatch payable

Zählblatt *nt* TRANSP tally sheet

zahlen 1. *vt* GESCHÄFT clear; **2.** *vi* GESCHÄFT make a payment of, pay, stump up (*infrml*) (*BrE*), PATENT *Gebühr* pay, vw pony up (*infrml*); ◆ **wir ~ Spitzenlöhne** PERSON *Stellenangebote, Werbungssprache* top wages paid

zählen 1. *vt* MATH count; **2.** *vi* MATH count

Zahlen *f pl* MATH numbers (*nos.*); ◆ **in nicht bereinigten ~** GESCHÄFT in unadjusted figures; **an diesen ~ läßt sich der wirtschaftliche Fortschritt messen** GESCHÄFT these figures are a yardstick of the economy's progress; **Ihre ~ stimmen mit unseren überein** RECHNUNG your figures are in agreement with ours; **in unbereinigten ~** GESCHÄFT in unadjusted figures

zahlend: **zu ~er Betrag** *m* VERSICH amount to be paid; **~er Gast** *m* FREI, GESCHÄFT paying guest (*PG*); **~es Mitglied** *nt* PERSON paid-up member (*BrE*); **~e Nutzlast** *f* TRANSP actual payload; **zu ~er Schuldschein** *m* FINANZ note receivable

Zahlen: **Zahlenfressen** *nt infrml* COMP number crunching (*infrml*); **Zahlenfresser** *m infrml* COMP number cruncher (*infrml*); **Zahlenverarbeitung** *f* FINANZ, RECHNUNG, VW number processing, number crunching (*infrml*)

Zählerpreis *m* GESCHÄFT meter rate, meterage (*AmE*)

Zahl: **Zahlkarte** *f* BANK payment card; **Zahlmeister, in** *m,f* PERSON *Schiffahrt, Luftfahrt* purser; **Zahlstelle** *f* STEUER paying agent; **Zahlstellenbank** *f* BANK *Scheck* paying bank; **Zahltag** *m* PERSON *Arbeitsentgelt* payday

Zahlung *f* FINANZ *Schuld* satisfaction, GESCHÄFT clearance, payment (*PYT*), settlement; **~ anstelle einer Kündigungsfrist** PERSON pay in lieu of notice; **eine ~ aufschieben** RECHNUNG defer payment; **~ durch Empfänger** FINANZ, GESCHÄFT, IMP/EXP cash on delivery (*COD*); **~ in Etappen** FINANZ stage payment; **~ gegen offene Rechnung** FINANZ clean payment; **~ laut Vertrag** *f* RECHNUNG contract payment; **~ im Namen Dritter** *f* RECHNUNG payment on behalf of others; **~ netto Kasse** RECHT *Vertragsrecht* clean payment; **~ in Raten** RECHNUNG payment by installment (*AmE*), payment by instalment (*BrE*); **~ unter Protest** RECHT payment under protest; **~ bei Verschiffung** TRANSP cash on shipment (*COS*); **~ der Versicherungssumme** VERSICH indemnity payment; **nicht zur ~ vorgelegter Scheck** *m* BANK unpresented check (*AmE*), unpresented cheque (*BrE*); ◆ **gegen ~** GESCHÄFT against payment; **~ zum Begleichen einer Schuld anbieten** RECHT tender money in discharge of debt; **eine ~ einziehen** FINANZ collect a payment; **gegen ~ erhalten** FINANZ receive versus payment; **in ~ geben** BÖRSE, GESCHÄFT trade in; **ohne ~ keine Leistung** VERSICH pay as paid policy; **in ~ nehmen** GESCHÄFT take in (*infrml*); **eine ~ zurückverfolgen** BANK trace a payment

Zahlungen *f pl* GESCHÄFT payments; ◆ **~ einstellen** FINANZ, GESCHÄFT suspend payments; **mit den ~ der Hypothek auf dem laufenden bleiben** FINANZ keep up payment on one's mortgage

Zahlung: **Zahlungsanweisung** *f* FINANZ order to pay; **Zahlungsaufforderung** *f* BÖRSE call, FINANZ request for payment, GESCHÄFT demand note, request for payment, vw request to pay; **Zahlungsaufschub** *m* FINANZ moratorium; **Zahlungsauftrag** *m* BANK, FINANZ banker's order, payment order (*p.o.*), RECHNUNG order to pay, payment order (*p.o.*); **Zahlungsbedingungen** *f pl* BANK terms of payment; **Zahlungsbefehl** *m* RECHT order for payment of a debt; **Zahlungsbelastung** *f* STEUER burden of payment; **Zahlungsbestätigung** *f* RECHT *Vertragsrecht* confirmation of payment

Zahlungsbilanz *f* VW balance of payments (*BOP*), external account; **~ ex post** VW accounting balance of payments; **Zahlungsbilanzauffassung** *f* FINANZ, GESCHÄFT, VW monetarist approach to the balance of payments, monetary approach to the balance of payments; **Zahlungsbilanzdefizit** *nt* VW balance of payments deficit (*BOP deficit*); **Zahlungsbilanzgleichgewicht** *nt* VW balance of payments equilibrium; **Zahlungsbilanzüberschuß** *m* IMP/EXP external surplus, VW balance of payments surplus (*BOP surplus*); **Zahlungsbilanzverschlechterung** *f* FINANZ worsening in the balance of payments

Zahlung: **Zahlungseinstellung** *f* BANK, GESCHÄFT cessation of payment, suspension of payments; **Zahlungsempfänger, in** *m,f* GESCHÄFT creditor beneficiary, RECHNUNG payee; **Zahlungserinnerung** *f* FINANZ prompt note; **Zahlungserleichterungen** *f pl* BANK easy terms of payments; **Zahlungsermächtigung** *f* FINANZ, POL budgetary appropriation, RECHNUNG appropriation

zahlungsfähig *adj* GESCHÄFT able to pay, solvent; ◆ **wieder ~ erklären** GESCHÄFT whitewash (*infrml*)

zahlungsfähig: **~er Schuldner** *m* BANK solvent debtor

Zahlung: **Zahlungsfähigkeit** *f* FINANZ, GESCHÄFT ability to pay, solvency, liquidity; **Zahlungsfähigkeitsprinzip** *nt* STEUER, VW ability-to-pay principle; **Zahlungsfloat** *f* vw float time; **Zahlungsfrist** *f* VW period of payment; **Zahlungsfristverlängerung** *f* RECHT extension of time for payment; **Zahlungsgarant** *m* im Außenhandelsverkehr VW confirming house; **Zahlungsgarantie** *f* RECHNUNG payment guarantee, RECHT payment bond, payment guaranty

zahlungshalber *adj* RECHT on account of payment

Zahlung: **Zahlungskarte** *f* BANK charge card; **Zahlungsklausel** *f* RECHT payment clause; **Zahlungslast** *f* STEUER burden of payment; **Zahlungsmethode** *f* V&M payment method, payment type; **Zahlungsmittel** *nt* BANK means of payment; **Zahlungsmodalitäten** *f pl* BANK terms of payment; **Zahlungsmodus** *m* FINANZ method of payment; **Zahlungsort** *m* RECHT *Vertragsrecht* place of payment; **Zahlungsplan** *m* RECHNUNG cash income and outgoings plan; **Zahlungspotential** *nt* BANK, FINANZ, RECHNUNG, VW ability to pay; **Zahlungsrückstände** *m pl* RECHNUNG backlog of payments, payments in arrears; **Zahlungssäumnis** *f* RECHT failure to pay; **Zahlungssystem** *nt* VW payment system

zahlungsunfähig *adj* BANK, FINANZ, GESCHÄFT bankrupt, RECHNUNG insolvent, unable to pay; ♦ **jdn für ~ erklären** FINANZ, GESCHÄFT, RECHNUNG, RECHT adjudge sb bankrupt, adjudicate sb bankrupt; **~ sein** GESCHÄFT be bankrupt

zahlungsunfähig: **~er Schuldner** *m* BANK bad debtor, defaulting debtor; **~er Spekulant** *m* BÖRSE lame duck (*infrml*)

Zahlungsunfähigkeit *f* RECHNUNG insolvency, RECHT inability to pay, insolvency; **Zahlungsunfähigkeitsklausel** *f* VERSICH insolvency clause

Zahlung: **Zahlungsverkehr** *m* FINANZ funds transfers, monetary transactions, money transactions, payment transactions; **Zahlungsverlängerung** *f* BANK extended payment; **Zahlungsverpflichtung** *f* BANK, FINANZ obligation to pay; **Zahlungsversprechen** *nt* GESCHÄFT I owe you (*IOU*); **Zahlungsversprechen** *nt* **mit auflösender Bedingung** BANK conditional bond; **Zahlungsverzug** *m* FINANZ default in payment, failure to pay on due date; **die Zahlungsvollmacht festlegen** *phr* VERWALT set forth the spending authority; **Zahlungsweise** *f* FINANZ method of payment; **Zahlungsziel** *nt* GESCHÄFT credit period, period of payment, term of payment; **Zahlungszusicherung** *f* GESCHÄFT promise to pay

Zahnarztkostenversicherung *f* VERSICH dental insurance

Zange *f* TRANSP tongs

Zankapfel *m* GESCHÄFT bone of contention

z.B. *abbr* (*zum Beispiel*) GESCHÄFT e.g. (*exempli gratia, for example*)

Z-Diagramm *nt* MATH Z chart

ZE *abbr* (*Zentraleinheit*) COMP CPU (*central processing unit*)

Zeche *f* GESCHÄFT bill (*BrE*), check (*AmE*), IND colliery, mine; ♦ **die ~ bezahlen** GESCHÄFT pick up the tab (*infrml*)

Zeche: **Zechenbetriebstag** *m* IND colliery working day; **Zechengesellschaft** *f* IND mining company

Zedent, in *m,f* PATENT assignor, RECHT assignor, transferor, transferrer, cedent, STEUER transferor, transferrer, VERSICH cedent, *Unternehmen* ceding company, original insurer

zedieren *vt* RECHT cede, VERSICH assign, cede, transfer

zedierend: **~e Gesellschaft** *f* VERSICH ceding company

Zehnergruppe *f* (*G10*) VW Group of Ten (*G10*)

zehnfach *adv* MATH ten times

Zehnfache: **um das ~ ansteigen** *phr* GESCHÄFT increase tenfold

Zeichen *nt* COMP character, token, GESCHÄFT signal, MATH *Symbol* sign, MEDIEN character; ♦ **unser ~** GESCHÄFT our reference (*our ref.*)

Zeichen: **Zeichenanordnung** *f* COMP character array; **Zeichenbetrieb** *m* COMP byte mode; **Zeichendichte** *f* COMP character density, *Datenträger* packing density; **Zeichendrucker** *m* COMP serial printer; **Zeichenfolge** *f* COMP string; **Zeichenkette** *f* COMP character string; **Zeichenmaßstab** *m* GESCHÄFT plotting scale; **Zeichenstift** *m* COMP plotting pen; **Zeichentisch** *m* COMP plotting board, GESCHÄFT plotting table; **Zeichentrick** *m* V&M animatic; **Zeichenumschaltung** *f* COMP case shift; **Zeichenvorrat** *m* COMP character set

zeichnen *vt* BÖRSE *Aktien* draw, subscribe, GESCHÄFT design, sign, VERSICH underwrite

Zeichner, in *m,f* BÖRSE allottee, subscriber, GESCHÄFT draftsman, VERSICH underwriter (*U/W*)

zeichnerisch: **~e Darstellung** *f* V&M pictorial presentation

Zeichnung *f* GESCHÄFT design, drawing, signature, signing, RECHNUNG subscription, VERSICH underwriting; **~ von Wertpapieren** BÖRSE application; **Zeichnungsangebot** *nt* BÖRSE subscription offer, tender; **ein Zeichnungsangebot machen** *phr* FINANZ invite subscriptions for; **Zeichnungsberechtigte(r)** *mf* [decl. as adj] BANK signing officer; **Zeichnungsberechtigung** *f* VERWALT authority to sign, power to sign; **Zeichnungsbetrag** *m* BÖRSE amount of the subscription, application money, FINANZ subscription money; **Zeichnungserklärung** *f* KOMM letter of application; **Zeichnungsgebühr** *f* BANK application fee, subscription charges; **Zeichnungskurs** *m* BÖRSE offering price; **Zeichnungsprivileg** *nt* BÖRSE subscription privilege; **Zeichnungsrate** *f* FINANZ take-up rate; **Zeichnungsrecht** *nt* BÖRSE application right, subscription right; **Zeichnungstermin** *m* FINANZ subscription day; **Zeichnungsvollmacht** *f* VW signing authority; **Zeichnungsvorrecht** *nt* BÖRSE subscription privilege; **Zeichnungszettel** *m* FINANZ signing slip

zeigen *vt* GESCHÄFT *demonstrieren* show

Zeiger *m* COMP *Speicheradressen* pointer

Zeigestock *m* GESCHÄFT pointer

Zeile *f* V&M line; **Zeilenabstand** *m* MEDIEN *Textverarbeitung* line space; **Zeilendrucker** *m* COMP line printer; **Zeilendurchschuß** *m* MEDIEN *Textverarbeitung* line space; **Zeileneditor** *m* COMP *Programme* line editor; **Zeilenendzeichen** *nt* COMP end-of-line character; **Zeilenpreis** *m* MEDIEN line rate; **Zeilenschaltung** *f* (*ZS*) COMP *Tastatur* carriage return (*CR*); **Zeilenschiff** *nt* MEDIEN *Druck* galley; **Zeilenumbruch** *m* COMP *Textverarbeitung* word wrap, wraparound; **Zeilenvorschub** *m* COMP line feed (*lf*); **Zeilenzahl** *f* MEDIEN lineage; **Zeilenzentimeter** *m* V&M single column centimetre (*BrE*), single column centimeter (*AmE*)

Zeit *f* GESCHÄFT time; ♦ **in der ~ von** GESCHÄFT over the period of; **vor der ~** GESCHÄFT with time to spare; **zu allen Zeiten** GESCHÄFT at all times; **mit der ~ gehen** GESCHÄFT be abreast of the times; **seit langer ~** GESCHÄFT long-standing; **zu dieser ~** GESCHÄFT im letzten Jahr GESCHÄFT this time last year; **um diese ~ nächste Woche** GESCHÄFT *nächste Woche gleiche Zeit* this time next week

zeitabhängig: **~e Kosten** *pl* RECHNUNG period expense

Zeitalter *nt*: ~ **der elektronischen Rechner** COMP computer age

zeitanteilig: ~**er Ferienwohnungs-Kaufvertrag** *m* GRUND, RECHT timeshare sale contract

Zeit: **Zeitarbeit machen** *phr* GESCHÄFT, PERSON temp; **Zeitarbeitskraft** *f* GESCHÄFT, PERSON temp, temporary worker; **Zeitarbitrage** *f* GESCHÄFT time arbitrage; **Zeitaufwand** *m* GESCHÄFT billing for the time spent

zeitaufwendig *adj* GESCHÄFT, MGMNT time-consuming

Zeit: **Zeitberechnung** *f* COMP timing; **Zeit- und Bewegungsstudie** *f* GESCHÄFT time and motion study; **Zeitcharter** *f* TRANSP time charter (*T/C*); **Zeitchartervertrag** *m* TRANSP time charter party (*time C/P*)

Zeitdauer *f* GESCHÄFT period; ~ **der Betriebsstockung** IND, VW downtime; ~ **der Versicherungsleistungen** VERSICH duration of benefits; ◆ **über eine** ~ GESCHÄFT over a period of time; **über eine lange** ~ GESCHÄFT over the long term

Zeit: **Zeitdruck** *m* GESCHÄFT, MGMNT time pressure; **Zeitfahrkarte** *f* TRANSP commutation ticket (*AmE*), season ticket (*BrE*); **Zeitfracht** *f* TRANSP time freight; **Zeitgeber** *m* COMP timer

zeitgemäß *adj* GESCHÄFT timely, up-to-date

zeitgleich: ~**e externe Effekte** *m pl* VW contemporaneous externality; ~**e Externalitäten** *f pl* VW contemporaneous externality

Zeit: **Zeithorizont** *m* MGMNT time horizon; **Zeitkarte** *f* TRANSP commutation ticket (*AmE*), season ticket (*BrE*); **Zeitkarteninhaber, in** *m,f* TRANSP commutation ticket holder (*AmE*), season ticket holder (*BrE*); **Zeitkomponente** *f* GESCHÄFT time component

zeitlich 1. *adj* GESCHÄFT temporal, *Reihenfolge* chronological; ◆ **im** ~**en Rahmen** GESCHÄFT within the allotted time frame; **2.** *adv* GESCHÄFT temporally, timewise, *Reihenfolge* chronologically; ◆ ~ **begrenzt** GESCHÄFT for a limited period of time; ~ **geplant** TRANSP scheduled; ~ **auf dem laufenden bleiben** GESCHÄFT be abreast of the times; ~ **übereinstimmen** GESCHÄFT synchronize

zeitlich: ~**e Abgrenzungen** *f pl* RECHNUNG timing differences; ~**e Abstimmung** *f* COMP timing; ~ **befristeter Vertrag** *m* PERSON fixed-term contract, fixed-term deal, fixed-term agreement; ~ **begrenzter Pachtbesitz** *m* FINANZ, GRUND tenancy for years; ~ **beschränkte Aufenthaltsgenehmigung** *f* VERWALT temporary residence permit; ~ **beschränktes Aufenthaltsvisum** *nt* VERWALT temporary residence visa; ~ **festgelegtes Backup** *nt jarg* COMP timed backup; ~ **festgelegte Sicherung** *f* COMP timed backup; ~**er Rahmen** *m* FINANZ timescale, GESCHÄFT time frame, timescale MGMNT timescale, VW timescale; ~**er Rückstand** *m* **bei Innovationseinführung** GESCHÄFT lead-time delay; ~**e Übereinstimmung** *f* GESCHÄFT synchronization (*sync*); ~**e Verzögerung** *f* STEUER time lag

Zeit: **Zeitlimit** *nt* GESCHÄFT time limit; **Zeitlohn** *m* VW time rate; **Zeitlohnarbeit** *f* PERSON daywork, time work; **Zeitmaßstab** *m* FINANZ, GESCHÄFT, MGMNT, VW timescale; **Zeit- und Methodenstudie** *f* GESCHÄFT time and methods study; **Zeitnahme** *f* GESCHÄFT timing, MGMNT *mit Stoppuhr* stopwatch studies; **Zeitnische** *f* GESCHÄFT slot; **Zeitplan** *m* FINANZ timescale, GESCHÄFT timescale, schedule, MGMNT time budget, timescale, timetable, VW

timescale; **im Zeitplan liegen** *phr* GESCHÄFT be on schedule; **Zeitplaner** *m* GESCHÄFT organizer; **Zeitplanung** *f* MGMNT time management; **Zeitplanungsgestaltung** *f* MGMNT timetable planning

Zeitpunkt *m* GESCHÄFT *Termin* time; ◆ **zu einem frühen** ~ GESCHÄFT at an early stage; **zum** ~ **des Korrekturlesens** MEDIEN at proof stage

Zeit: **Zeitraffer** *m* V&M stop motion; **Zeitrahmen** *m* GESCHÄFT time frame

zeitraubend *adj* GESCHÄFT time-consuming

Zeitraum *m* GESCHÄFT time span, RECHT time limit, TRANSP time band, VW period; ~ **bis zur Fälligkeit** BÖRSE days to maturity; ~ **bis zur Lieferung** BÖRSE days to delivery; ~ **vor Rückzahlung der Hälfte einer Anleihe** BÖRSE half-life; ◆ **für den** ~ RECHNUNG for the period

Zeit: **Zeitreihe** *f* MATH, VW time series; **Zeitreihenanalyse** *f* VW time series analysis; **Zeit- und Reisepolice** *f* VERSICH mixed policy; **Zeitrente** *f* VERSICH annuity certain, term annuity; **Zeitrisiko** *nt* VERSICH time risk; **Zeitschrift** *f* MEDIEN journal, magazine, periodical; **Zeitsegment** *nt* V&M time segment

Zeitspanne *f* GESCHÄFT period of time, time span, VW time span; ~ **vom Bau bis zur vollständigen Vermietung** GRUND rent-up period; ~ **zwischen Produktionkonzeption und -einführung** V&M gap between product conception and introduction

zeitsparend *adj* COMP, GESCHÄFT time-saving

Zeit: **Zeitsperre** *f* COMP timeout; **Zeitstudie** *f* GESCHÄFT work time study, PERSON work time study, IND study, work time study, MATH time study, PERSON work time study; **Zeitteilung** *f* GRUND, VW timeshare; **Zeitüberschreibung** *f* COMP timeout

Zeitung *f* GESCHÄFT newspaper; **Zeitungsanzeige** *f* V&M newspaper advertising; **Zeitungsausschnitt** *m* MEDIEN press cutting, press clipping (*BrE*); **Zeitungsausschnittsdienst** *m* V&M clipping service (*AmE*), cutting service (*BrE*); **Zeitungsredakteur, in** *m,f* MEDIEN copy editor, copy reader (*AmE*); **Zeitungssyndikat** *nt* MEDIEN newspaper syndicate (*AmE*); **Zeitungsverleger** *m* MEDIEN newspaper publisher; **Zeitungswerbung** *f* V&M *Anzeige* newspaper advertising, *Werbung in der Presse* press advertisement

Zeit: **unter der Zeitverschiebung leiden** *phr* TRANSP be jetlagged; **Zeitversicherungspolice** *f* VERSICH time policy; **Zeitvertrag** *m* TRANSP time agreement; **Zeitverwendungsumfrage** *f* VW time budget survey

zeitverzögert: ~**e Wirkung** *f* **einer bestimmten Politik** POL policy lag

zeitweilig 1. *adj* GESCHÄFT temporary; **2.** *adv* GESCHÄFT temporarily; ◆ ~ **aufheben** GESCHÄFT *Handel, Autorisation, Genehmigung* suspend; ~ **außer Kraft sein** GESCHÄFT *Gesetz, Regel* be in abeyance; ~ **aussetzen** RECHT suspend

zeitweilig: ~**e Aufhebung** *f* GESCHÄFT suspension; ~**e Aussetzung** *f* RECHT suspension; ~**e Gewinnrealisierung** *f* RECHNUNG percentage-of-completion method; ~**er Schutz** *m* PATENT provisional protection

Zeitwert *m* BÖRSE *der Restlaufzeit einer Option* time value, FINANZ current value, actual cash value (*a.c.v.*), RECHNUNG market value, fair value, VW current value; **Zeitwertberichtigung** *f* RECHNUNG fair value adjustments; **Zeitwertklausel** *f* VERSICH market value clause; **Zeitwertmethode** *f* FINANZ present value method

Zeit: **Zeitzone** *f* GESCHÄFT time zone; **Zeitzwang** *m* PERSON time constraint

Zellaufbau *m* IND cell organization

Zelle *f* COMP *Speicher, Tabellenkalkulation,* TRANSP cell; **Zellencontainerschiff** *nt* TRANSP cellular container ship; **Zellenführer** *m* TRANSP cell guide; **Zellenschiff** *nt* TRANSP cellular vessel

zellular *adj* GESCHÄFT, KOMM cellular; **~es Funkgerät** *nt* KOMM cellular radio; **~es Telefon** *nt* KOMM cellphone, cellular phone

zensieren *vt* GESCHÄFT censor, MEDIEN exercise censorship over, censor

Zensieren *nt* GESCHÄFT, MEDIEN censorship

Zensierung *f* GESCHÄFT, MEDIEN censorship

Zensur *f* GESCHÄFT, MEDIEN censorship

Zensus *m* GESCHÄFT census

Zentiliter *m* (*cl*) GESCHÄFT centiliter (*AmE*) (*cl*), centilitre (*BrE*) (*cl*)

Zentimeter *m* (*cm*) GESCHÄFT centimeter (*AmE*) (*cm*), centimetre (*BrE*) (*cm*)

Zentner *m* (*Ztr.*) GESCHÄFT hundredweight (*AmE*) (*cwt*)

Zentral- *in cpds* GESCHÄFT central, centralized

zentral: **~er Aspekt** *m* **einer Politik** POL plank; **~er Dachfonds** *m* FINANZ umbrella fund; **~er Einkauf** *m* V&M central buying; **~es Frachtbuchungsbüro** *nt* TRANSP central freight booking office; **~es Frachtbüro** *nt* TRANSP central freight bureau (*CFB*); **~er Geschäftsbezirk** *m* GESCHÄFT, VW central business district (*CBD*); **~es Gewerbegebiet** *nt* GESCHÄFT, VW central business district (*CBD*); **~e Notenbank** *f* VW central bank; **~e Planung** *f* MGMNT central planning; **~es Reservierungsbüro** *nt* FREI central reservation office; **~es Reservierungssystem** *nt* FREI central reservation system; **~e Schiedskommission** *f* MGMNT, PERSON Central Arbitration Committee (*BrE*) (*CAC*); **~e Schlichtungsstelle** *f* MGMNT, PERSON Central Arbitration Committee (*BrE*) (*CAC*); **~e statistische Erfassung** *f* **im Großstadtbereich** VERWALT Consolidated Metropolitan Statistical Area (*AmE*) (*CMSA*); **~e Zweigstelle** *f* BANK hub branch

Zentralamerikanisch: **~er Gemeinsamer Markt** *m* VW Central American Common Market (*CACM*)

Zentral-: **Zentralamt** *nt* **für Statistik** VW ≈ Central Bureau of Statistics (*AmE*)

Zentralbank *f* BANK, VW central bank, Federal Reserve Board (*AmE*) (*FRB*)

zentralbankfähig: **~e Aktiva** *pl* FINANZ eligible assets; **~e Wechsel** *m pl* BANK eligible bills, eligible papers

Zentralbank: **Zentralbankfazilität** *f* BANK Central Bank Facility (*BrE*) (*CBF*); **Zentralbankgeld** *nt* BANK fed funds (*AmE*), federal funds (*AmE*); **Zentralbankgeldmenge** *f* VW monetary base; **Zentralbankgeschäft** *nt* BANK central bank transactions; **Zentralbankgeschäfte** *nt pl* VW central bank transactions; **Zentralbankguthaben** *nt* **der Geschäftsbanken** BANK, VW bankers' deposits (*BrE*); **Zentralbankoperationen** *f pl* VW central bank transactions; **Zentralbanksystem** *nt* BANK, FINANZ, VW Federal Reserve System (*AmE*) (*the Fed*); **Zentralbankvorstand** *m* VW Federal Reserve Board (*FRB*) (*AmE*)

Zentrale *f* GESCHÄFT switchboard, company headquarters, MGMNT head office (*HO*), headquarters (*HQ*)

Zentraleinheit *f* (*ZE*) COMP processor, *Hardware* central processing unit (*CPU*)

zentralfinanziert: **~es Programm** *nt* RECHNUNG centrally financed program (*AmE*), centrally financed programme (*BrE*)

Zentral-: **Zentralinstitut** *nt* GESCHÄFT centralized institution

Zentralisation *f* GESCHÄFT centralization

zentralisieren *vt* GESCHÄFT centralize

zentralisiert *adj* GESCHÄFT centralized

Zentralisierung *f* GESCHÄFT centralization

Zentral-: **Zentrallagerstelle** *f* GESCHÄFT primary point (*AmE*); **Zentralregierung** *f* GESCHÄFT, POL central government; **Zentralregister** *nt* BÖRSE Central Register; **Zentralverwaltung** *f* VERWALT administrative center (*AmE*), administrative centre (*BrE*); **Zentralverwaltungswirtschaft** *f* VW centrally planned economy (*CPE*)

Zentrum *nt* GESCHÄFT focus, IND center (*AmE*), centre (*BrE*); **~ für Wirtschafts- und Gesellschaftsdaten** SOZIAL Centre for Economic and Social Information (*CESI*); **Zentrum-Peripherie-System** *nt* VW center periphery system (*AmE*), centre periphery system (*BrE*)

zerbrechen *vt* GESCHÄFT break up

zerbrechlich *adj* TRANSP fragile

zerlegen *vt* BANK *Kosten* unbundle, IND break down, disassemble, V&M knock down

Zerlegung *f* BANK *Kosten* unbundling, IND disassembly

Zero-Bond *m* BÖRSE zero-coupon bond

Zero-Realzins *m* FINANZ zero real interest

zerrüttet: **~e Finanzen** *f pl* VW shattered finance

Zerschlagung *f* GESCHÄFT, VERWALT break-up

Zersplitterung *f* VW fragmentation; **~ durch die Medien** V&M media fragmentation

zerstören *vt* GESCHÄFT destroy

Zerstörung *f* GESCHÄFT demolition, destruction, dissolution, UMWELT *des Regenwaldes* destruction

zerstörungsfrei: **~e Prüfung** *f* IND nondestructive testing

zerstreuen *vt* GESCHÄFT break up

Zertifikat *nt* BÖRSE, GESCHÄFT certificate (*cert.*); **~ bezüglich der Passagierzahl** TRANSP passenger number certificate

Zession *f* GESCHÄFT cession, RECHT assignment, transfer (*tr., tfr*), cession, VERSICH cession

Zessionar *m* BANK assignee, transferee, PATENT assignee, RECHT, VERSICH assignee, transferee

Zettel *m* V&M leaflet

Zeug: **das ~ haben für** *phr* GESCHÄFT have the makings of

Zeuge *m* GESCHÄFT, RECHT witness; **~ der Anklage** *m* RECHT witness for the prosecution; **~ der Staatsanwaltschaft** RECHT witness for the prosecution; **~ der Verteidigung** RECHT *Entlastungszeuge* witness for the defence (*BrE*), witness for the defense (*AmE*); ♦ **~ von etw sein** RECHT witness sth; **als ~ aussagen** RECHT give evidence as a witness; **jdn als Zeugen anrufen** RECHT call sb as a witness

Zeuge: **Zeugenaussage** *f* RECHT attestation, evidence, statement of witness, testimony

Zeugin *f* GESCHÄFT, RECHT witness; **~ der Anklage**

RECHT witness for the prosecution; **~ der Staatsanwaltschaft** RECHT witness for the prosecution; **~ der Verteidigung** RECHT *Entlastungszeuge* witness for the defence (*BrE*), witness for the defense (*AmE*)

Zeugnis *nt* PERSON *schriftliche Empfehlung von einem Arbeitgeber* reference; ♦ **~ ablegen für** RECHT give evidence on behalf of

z. Hd. *abbr* (*zu Händen*) GESCHÄFT, IMP/EXP, KOMM attn (*attention*)

z. Hd. v. *abbr* (*zu Händen von*) GESCHÄFT, IMP/EXP, KOMM c/o (*care of*)

zick-zack *phr* VW stop and go

Zickzackfaltung *f* V&M accordion folding

Zickzackpolitik *f* VW stop-go policy (*BrE*)

ziehen *vt* BÖRSE draw, COMP *Maus, Fenster* drag

Ziel *nt* COMP destination, target, GESCHÄFT aim, object, target, objective, MGMNT goal, V&M mission, target; ♦ **zum ~ bestimmen** GESCHÄFT target; **das ~ nicht erreichen** GESCHÄFT underperform; **das ~ verfehlen** GESCHÄFT fall short of target; **mit dem ~, etw zu tun** GESCHÄFT with a view to doing sth

Ziel: **Zielbereich** *m* VW target zone; **Zielbestimmung** *f* GESCHÄFT targeting; **Zielbildung** *f* MGMNT goal setting; **Zielcomputer** *m* COMP target computer; **Zielfeld** *nt* COMP target field; **Zielfirma** *f* GESCHÄFT target company; **Zielformulierung** *f* GESCHÄFT, MGMNT policy formulation, statement of objectives; **Zielfunktion** *f* MATH objective function; **die Zielfunktion optimieren** *phr* GESCHÄFT optimize the objective function

zielen: **~ auf** [+acc] *vt* GESCHÄFT aim

zielgerichtet: **~es Marketing** *nt* V&M *am Bestimmungsort orientiert* destination marketing

zielgesteuert: **~e Unternehmensführung** *f* MGMNT, VERWALT management by objectives (*MBO*)

Zielgleichgewicht *nt* VW goal equilibrium

Zielgruppe *f* GESCHÄFT focus group, V&M audience, target, focus group; ♦ **als ~ haben** GESCHÄFT target

Zielgruppe: **Zielgruppenauswahl** *f* V&M market target selection; **Zielgruppenindex** *m* V&M target group index; **Zielgruppenuntersuchung** *f* GESCHÄFT, V&M focus group survey

Ziel: **Zielhafen** *m* GESCHÄFT terminal; **Zielhierarchie** *f* GESCHÄFT hierarchy of objectives; **Zielhörerschaft** *f* MEDIEN, V&M target audience; **Zielindifferenz** *f* VW neutrality of goals; **Zielindikatoren** *m pl* GESCHÄFT objective indicators; **Zielkäufer, in** *m,f* GESCHÄFT, V&M target buyer; **Zielkongruenz** *f* MGMNT *Übereinstimmung von Ziel und Handlung* goal congruence; **Zielkorridor** *m* VW *des Geldmengenwachstums* target range; **Zielkundenkreis** *m* GESCHÄFT target audience; **Ziellaufwerk** *nt* COMP destination drive; **Zielleserschaft** *f* GESCHÄFT, MEDIEN, V&M *Zielpublikum* target audience

ziellos 1. *adj* GESCHÄFT aimless; 2. *adv* GESCHÄFT at random, randomly

Zielmarkt *m* GESCHÄFT, V&M target market

zielorientiert: **~e Budgetierung** *f* RECHNUNG performance budgeting; **~e Budgetplanung** *f* RECHNUNG performance budgeting; **~es Marketing** *nt* V&M target marketing; **~es Verkaufen** *nt* V&M objective selling

Ziel: **Zielort** *m* GESCHÄFT place of destination; **Zielpreis** *m* GESCHÄFT target price; **Zielpreisbildung** *f* GESCHÄFT target pricing; **Zielpreisfestsetzung** *f* GESCHÄFT target

pricing; **Zielprogrammierung** *f* MGMNT goal programming; **Zielsetzung** *f* GESCHÄFT, MGMNT goal setting, objective setting, V&M target setting; **Zielsprache** *f* COMP, GESCHÄFT *Übersetzung* target language; **Zielstellung** *f* GESCHÄFT target setting; **Zielsuche** *f* FINANZ, GESCHÄFT, MGMNT goal-seeking; **Zielsystem** *nt* VW goal system; **Zieltermin** *m* GESCHÄFT target date; **Zielvariable** *f* POL goal variable, VW target variable; **Zielvorgaben** *f pl* GESCHÄFT defined goals and objectives; **Zielwechsel** *m* BANK time bill (*BrE*), time draft (*AmE*); **Zielzone** *f* VW target zone; **Zielzuschauerschaft** *f* MEDIEN, V&M target audience

Ziffer *f* KOMM cipher, MATH figure; **Zifferntastatur** *f* COMP numeric keypad

Zimmervermittlung *f* SOZIAL accommodation agency

Zinn *nt* IND tin; **Zinnaktien** *f pl* BÖRSE tin shares; **Zinnerz** *nt* UMWELT, IND tin ore; **Zinnpreis** *m* BÖRSE tin price

Zins *m* BANK, BÖRSE, FINANZ, RECHNUNG, VW interest (*int.*); **~ für erste Adressen** BANK, VW base rate; **Zinsangabe** *f* BÖRSE indication of interest; **Zinsanpassung** *f* BANK interest rate adjustment; **Zinsanpassungsdatum** *nt* BANK interest roll-over date; **Zinsaufwand** *m* RECHNUNG interest paid; **Zinsausgleichssteuer** *f* STEUER Interest Equalization Tax (*IET*); **Zinsbegrenzung** *f* **nach oben** FINANZ cap

zinsbegünstigt: **~e Anlage** *f* FINANZ, VW *von den USA gewährter zinsloser Kredit an ein Entwicklungsland* soft loan

Zins: **Zinsbelastung** *f* FINANZ interest charge; **Zinsberechnung** *f* **für tägliche Guthaben** BANK daily balance interest calculation; **Zinsbewegung** *f* BANK interest rate movement; **Zinsbogen** *m* FINANZ interest coupon

zinsbringend *adj* BANK, FINANZ, RECHNUNG interest-bearing

Zins: **Zinseinkommen** *nt* BANK, FINANZ interest income, RECHNUNG earned interest; **Zinseinkünfte** *pl* BANK, FINANZ interest income; **Zinselastizität** *f* **der Ersparnisse** VW interest elasticity of savings

zinsempfindlich: **~e Ausgaben** *f pl* FINANZ interest-sensitive expenditure; **~e Police** *f* VERSICH interest-sensitive policy

Zinsen *m pl* BANK, BÖRSE, FINANZ, RECHNUNG, VW interest (*int.*); **~ bezogen auf die effektive Anzahl von Kalendertagen** BANK exact interest; ♦ **~ abwerfen** FINANZ bear interest, yield interest; **~ auflaufen lassen** BANK accrue interest; **~ berechnen** BANK charge interest; **auf ~ borgen** BANK borrow at interest; **~ bringen** FINANZ bear interest, yield interest; **~ tragen in Höhe von** RECHNUNG bear an interest of

Zins: **Zinserhöhungsklausel** *f* FINANZ, PERSON escalator clause, escalation clause; **Zinsertrag** *m* BANK interest received, RECHNUNG income from interest, interest earned, interest received; **Zinserträge** *m pl* BANK, RECHNUNG interest received; **Zinsertragsvergleich** *m* BÖRSE yield comparison; **Zinseszins** *m* BANK, FINANZ, RECHT, VW compound interest; **Zinsformel** *f* BANK interest formula

zinsfrei *adj* BANK, FINANZ interest-free, RECHT allodial; ♦ **~ borgen** BANK borrow interest-free

Zinsfuß *m* BANK, BÖRSE, FINANZ, RECHNUNG, VW interest rate, rate of interest; **interner ~** BANK, BÖRSE, FINANZ, RECHNUNG, VW capitalization rate

zinsgebunden *adj* BANK interest-linked; **~er Kredit** *m* BANK fixed-rate loan

Zins: **Zinsgefälle** *nt* BANK interest rate differential, BÖRSE rate differential; **Zinsgrundtendenz** *f* VW general interest tendency

zinsgünstig: **~er Kredit** *m* FINANZ, VW *von den USA gewährter zinsloser Kredit an ein Entwicklungsland* soft loan

Zins: **Zinsinstrument** *nt* BÖRSE interest rate instrument; **Zinskartell** *nt* BANK interest rate cartel; **Zinsklausel** *f* RECHT *Vertragsrecht* interest clause; **Zinskontrakt** *m* BÖRSE interest rate contract; **Zinskontraktrisiko** *nt* BÖRSE interest rate exposure, **Zinskupon** *m* FINANZ interest coupon; **Zinslast** *f* RECHNUNG interest burden

zinslos: **~ borgen** *phr* BANK borrow interest-free; **~er Überziehungskredit** *m* BANK swing loan

Zins: **Zinsnachlaß** *m* VW interest relief; **Zinsobergrenze** *f* BÖRSE ceiling rate, VW rate ceiling, capitalization rate, cap rate

zinsreagibel: **zinsreagible Ausgaben** *f pl* FINANZ interest-sensitive expenditure

Zins: **Zinsrisiko** *nt* BANK interest rate risk, BÖRSE interest rate exposure, FINANZ interest risk; **Zinsrückstand** *m* RECHNUNG back interest; **Zinsrückstände** *m pl* BANK arrears of interest, interest arrearage

Zinssatz *m* BANK, FINANZ, GESCHÄFT, VW interest rate, rate of interest; **~ für Ausleihungen** BANK lending rate; **~ für Bankkredite** BANK bank loan rate; **~ nach Gebührenabzug** FINANZ interest rate net of all charges; **~ für kurzfristige Kredite** VW short-term interest rate; ◆ **einen ~ festschreiben** BÖRSE lock in a rate; **den ~ neu festsetzen** BANK, FINANZ roll over; **einen ~ nach oben begrenzen** BANK cap an interest rate

Zinssatz: **Zinssätze** *m pl* **auf Spareinlagen** BANK bank deposit rate; **Zinssatz-x** *m* FINANZ x-interest

Zins: **Zinsschein** *m* BÖRSE bond coupon, FINANZ interest coupon, coupon (*c., cp.*); **Zinsspanne** *f* BANK interest margin, interest spread, interest rate range, BÖRSE interest rate range, FINANZ interest margin, interest rate range, GESCHÄFT, RECHNUNG, VW interest rate range; **Zinsstruktur** *f* VW interest rate structure, term structure of interest rates; **Zinsswap** *m* BÖRSE, FINANZ interest rate swap; **Zinsterminkontrakt** *m* BÖRSE interest rate contract, interest rate futures contract, interest-rate future, forward rate agreement (*FRA*), future rate agreement (*FRA*), short-term interest rate futures contract; **Zinsterminkontraktpreise** *m pl* BÖRSE interest rate futures prices; **Zins- und Tilgungszahlungen auf Hypothekenkredite** *f pl* FINANZ mortgage servicing

zinstragend *adj* BANK, FINANZ, RECHNUNG interest-bearing

Zinsuntergrenze *f* BÖRSE floor rate

zinsvariabel: **zinsvariable Anleihe** *f* BANK floater, floating-rate note (*FRN*); **zinsvariables Darlehen** *nt* BANK floating-rate loan; **zinsvariable Einlage** *f* BÖRSE floating-rate deposit; **zinsvariable Investition** *f* BÖRSE floating-rate investment; **zinsvariabler Schuldtitel** *m* BÖRSE floater (*AmE*), floating-rate note (*FRN*), FINANZ rolling-rate note

Zins: **Zinsvorteil** *m* BÖRSE interest rate advantage; **Zinszahlung** *f* BANK interest payment; **Zinszahlungsverbot** *nt* BANK ban on interest payments; **Zinszuschlag** *m* BANK, RECHNUNG additional interest; **Zinszuschuß** *m* FINANZ interest rate subsidy

zirka *adv* (*ca.*) GESCHÄFT about, approximately (*approx.*), circa (*ca.*)

Zirkakurs *m* BÖRSE approximate price

zirkulierend *adj* GESCHÄFT afloat

Zirkumflex *m* COMP *Schriftzeichen* circumflex

Zitat *nt* GESCHÄFT, MEDIEN *von Buch* quotation

zitieren *vt* GESCHÄFT *von Buch* cite, quote

zivil: **~er Markt** *m* GESCHÄFT commercial market

Zivilluftfahrt *f* VW civil aviation

Zivilprozeß *m* RECHT civil action, legal suit; ◆ **einen ~ anstrengen** RECHT file a lawsuit

Zivilrecht *nt* RECHT *bürgerliches Recht* civil law

zivilrechtlich: **~er Anspruch** *m* RECHT *Vertragsrecht* civil claim; **~e Haftung** *f* RECHT *auf der Grundlage von Zivilrecht* civil liability; **~er Status** *m* RECHT civil status

Zivilverwaltung *f* GESCHÄFT civil service (*CS*)

zögern *vi* VW falter, hesitate

zögernd: **~e Inflation** *f* VW hesiflation

Zoll *m* FREI customs, GESCHÄFT customs, inch (*in*), *Gebühr* duty, IMP/EXP customs duty, STEUER duty, tariff; **durch den ~ abzufertigende Exportgüter** *nt pl* IMP/EXP customs pre-entry exports; **durch den ~ abzufertigende Importgüter** *nt pl* IMP/EXP customs pre-entry imports

Zollabfertigung *f* IMP/EXP clearance, customs clearance, customs declaration (*CD*); **~ von Warenladungen** IMP/EXP clearance of cargo goods, customs cargo clearance; ◆ **mit oder ohne ~** IMP/EXP whether cleared customs or not (*wccon*)

Zollabfertigung: **Zollabfertigungsbeamte(r)** *m* [decl. as adj], **Zollabfertigungsbeamtin** *f* PERSON customs clearance agent; **Zollabfertigungscode** *m* IMP/EXP customs transaction code; **Zollabfertigungshafen** *m* IMP/EXP port of entry; **Zollabfertigungsstatus** *m* IMP/EXP customs clearance status (*CCS*)

Zoll: **Zollabgabe** *f* IMP/EXP customs duty; **Zolladressat** *m* IMP/EXP customs consignee; **Zollagent** *m* IMP/EXP customs broker, PERSON clearance agent; **Zollagentur** *f* IMP/EXP customs agency; **Zollager** *nt* GESCHÄFT bond store, IMP/EXP bonded warehouse; **Zollagergut** *nt* IMP/EXP bonded goods (*B/G, b/g*); **Zollamt** *nt* IMP/EXP customs collector, STEUER revenue office, VW Bureau of Customs

zollamtlich: **~er Abwicklungscode** *m* IMP/EXP customs transaction code; **~e Bewertung** *f* IMP/EXP customs valuation; **~e Freigabe einer Fracht/Ladung** *f* IMP/EXP customs cargo clearance; **~e Überwachung** *f* IMP/EXP customs control

Zoll: **Zollangaben** *f pl* IMP/EXP customs entry; **Zollausschlußgebiet** *nt* IMP/EXP free zone; **Zollaussetzung** *f* IMP/EXP, STEUER duty suspension; **Zollbeamte(r)** *m* [decl. as adj], **Zollbeamtin** *f* IMP/EXP customs officer, PERSON customs officer, HM Customs Officer (*BrE*), STEUER revenue officer; **Zollbeamte(r)** *m* [decl. as adj] **im Zollgutlager**, **Zollbeamtin** *f* **im Zollgutlager** TRANSP warehouse officer, warehouse keeper; **Zollbegleitschein** *m* IMP/EXP bond note; **Zollbegleitscheinheft** *nt* IMP/EXP carnet, *für den internationalen Güterkraftverkehr* Transport International Routier carnet (*TIR carnet*); **Zollbehörde** *f* STEUER customs; **Zollbestimmungen** *f pl* IMP/EXP customs regulations; **Zollbewertung** *f* IMP/EXP customs valuation; **Zollbürgschaft** *f* FINANZ customs declaration, customs guaranty; **Zolldeklaration** *f* BANK, IMP/EXP customs report, bill of entry (*B/E*), customs entry, entry; **Zolldeklarierung** *f* IMP/EXP customs declaration (*CD*); **Zolldepositenkonto** *nt* IMP/EXP duty deposit account (*DDA*); **Zolldurchfuhrschein** *m* IMP/EXP transshipment bond; **Zolldurchgangsschuppen** *m* IMP/EXP transit shed; **Zolldurchlauf** *m* IMP/EXP customs clearance

Zölle *m pl* STEUER customs duties; **~ und Abgaben** *f pl* IMP/EXP, STEUER, VW customs and excise duties; ◆ **~ hinterziehen** STEUER evade customs duty

Zoll: **Zolleinfuhrerklärung** *f* BANK, IMP/EXP bill of entry (*B/E*); **Zolleinfuhrschein** *m* IMP/EXP jerque note; **Zolleingangsdeklaration** *f* IMP/EXP inward manifest; **Zolleingangsschein** *m* BANK, IMP/EXP bill of entry (*B/E*); **Zolleinnehmer, in** *m,f* PERSON, STEUER collector (*BrE*); **Zolleinschlußgebiet** *nt* IMP/EXP, RECHT bonded area; **Zollerhebung** *f* STEUER collection of customs duties; **Zollerklärung** *f* BANK bill of entry (*B/E*), customs entry, IMP/EXP bill of entry (*B/E*), customs entry, customs declaration (*CD*); **Zollerlaubnisschein** *m* IMP/EXP bill of sight; **Zollfaktura** *f* IMP/EXP customs invoice; **Zollformalitäten** *f pl* IMP/EXP customs formalities

zollfrei *adj* IMP/EXP, STEUER duty-free (*BrE*), tax-free (*AmE*), tariff-free, uncustomed; **~e Einfuhrmenge** *f* IMP/EXP import allowance; **~er Hafen** *m* IMP/EXP free port; **~e Waren** *f pl* IMP/EXP, STEUER duty-free goods (*BrE*)

Zoll: **Zollfreibetrag** *m* IMP/EXP, STEUER duty-free allowance (*BrE*); **Zollfreiladen** *m* IMP/EXP, STEUER duty-free shop (*BrE*), tax-free shop (*AmE*); **Zollfreischreibung** *f* IMP/EXP, RECHT agreed customs exemption

zollfremd: **~es Handelshemmnis** *nt* GESCHÄFT, IMP/EXP, VW nontariff barrier (*NTB*)

Zoll: **Zollgebühr** *f* IMP/EXP customs duty, tariff; **Zollgericht** *nt* RECHT *Zollrecht* customs court (*AmE*); **Zollgesetz** *nt* IMP/EXP Customs and Excise Act (*AmE*), customs law, Tariff Act (*BrE*), tariff law, RECHT customs code (*CC*); **Zollgesetzgebung** *f* RECHT tariff legislation; **Zollgutlager** *nt* GESCHÄFT, IMP/EXP warehouse (*whse*), TRANSP warehouse (*whse*), bonded warehouse, V&M warehouse (*whse*); **Zollhafen** *m* GESCHÄFT, TRANSP point of entry; **Zollinhaltserklärung** *f* IMP/EXP customs declaration (*CD*); **Zollkontingent** *nt* GESCHÄFT, IMP/EXP, VW tariff quota; **Zollkontrolle** *f* IMP/EXP customs check, customs control; **etw durch die Zollkontrolle schmuggeln** *phr* IMP/EXP, RECHT smuggle sth through customs; **Zollkrieg** *m* GESCHÄFT tariff war; **Zollmakler, in** *m,f* PERSON customs-house broker; **Zollmauer** *f* IMP/EXP tariff wall

Zöllner, in *m,f* IMP/EXP, PERSON customs officer

Zoll: **Zollordnung** *f* IMP/EXP customs regulations; **Zollpapiere** *nt pl* **für vorübergehende Ausfuhr** IMP/EXP sample licence (*BrE*), sample license (*AmE*); **Zollpassierschein** *m* STEUER bill of sufferance; **Zollpassierscheinheft** *nt* IMP/EXP carnet

zollpflichtig *adj* IMP/EXP, STEUER dutiable; **nicht ~** *adj* IMP/EXP, STEUER duty-free (*BrE*), tax-free (*AmE*); **~e Fracht** *f* IMP/EXP, STEUER dutiable cargo; **~e Güter** *f pl* IMP/EXP bonded goods (*B/G, b/g*); **~e Ladung** *f* IMP/EXP dutiable cargo

Zoll: **Zollprüfer, in** *m,f* IMP/EXP examiner; **Zollrechnung** *f* IMP/EXP customs invoice; **Zollrückschein** *m* GESCHÄFT, IMP/EXP drawback; **Zollrückvergütung** *f* GESCHÄFT, IMP/EXP drawback; **Zollsatz** *m* IMP/EXP tariff rate;

Zollschranke *f* GESCHÄFT customs barrier, tariff wall, IMP/EXP entry barrier, tariff barrier, tariff wall, VW tariff barrier; **Zollschutz** *m* IMP/EXP, VW tariff protection; **Zollspeicher** *m* GESCHÄFT bonded warehouse; **Zolltarif** *m* GESCHÄFT tariff schedule, IMP/EXP customs tariff, VW tariff; **Zolltarifsatz** *m* IMP/EXP tariff; **Zolltransaktionscode** *m* IMP/EXP customs transaction code; **Zollunion** *f* VW customs union

zollunwichtig: **~e Waren** *f pl* IMP/EXP commissary goods

Zoll: **Zollvereinbarungen** *f pl* GESCHÄFT customs arrangements; **Zollverfahren** *nt* IMP/EXP customs procedure; **Zollverkehr** *m* IMP/EXP customs procedure; **unter Zollverschluß** *phr* GESCHÄFT bonded, in bond, IMP/EXP bonded; **Zollvorschriften** *f pl* IMP/EXP customs regulations

Zollwert *m* IMP/EXP customs value; **~ pro Bruttokilogramm** IMP/EXP customs value per gross kilogram (*CVGK*); **~ pro Bruttopfund** IMP/EXP customs value per gross pound (*CVGP*); ◆ **ohne ~** IMP/EXP no customs value (*n.c.v.*)

Zollwert: **Zollwertfestsetzung** *f* IMP/EXP customs valuation

Zoll: **Zollzaun** *m* IMP/EXP customs fence; **Zollzugeständnis** *nt* VW concessional aid; **Zollzulassungsnummer** *f* IMP/EXP customs registered number (*CRN*)

zonal: **~e Distribution** *f* V&M phased distribution, zonal distribution

Zone *f* COMP, GESCHÄFT zone; **~ A** FINANZ Zone A; **~ B** FINANZ Zone B; **Zone-A-Kreditinstitut** *nt* FINANZ Zone A credit institution; **Zone-B-Kreditinstitut** *nt* FINANZ Zone B credit institution

zoomen *vt* COMP, MEDIEN zoom in

Zoomen *nt* COMP, MEDIEN zooming

Zoomobjektiv *nt* COMP, MEDIEN zoom

Z-Punkt *m* MATH Z score

ZS *abbr* (*Zeilenschaltung*) COMP *Tastatur* CR (*carriage return*)

Ztr. *abbr* (*Zentner*) GESCHÄFT cwt (*hundredweight*)

Zubehör *nt* GESCHÄFT trimmings, V&M accessories; ◆ **ohne ~** GESCHÄFT with no trimmings

zubereitet: **~e Lebensmittel** *nt pl* IND processed foods

Zubereitung *f* IND *Lebensmittel* processing, production

zubilligen *vt* GESCHÄFT allow

Zucker- *in cpds* IND sugar; **Zuckerbrot und Peitsche** *phr* MGMNT carrot and stick

zuerkennen 1. *vt* RECHT award to; **2.** *vi* RECHT adjudicate

Zuerkennung *f* RECHT adjudication, award; **~ von Kosten** PATENT awarding of costs

Zufahrt: **ohne ~** *phr* GRUND landlocked

Zufall *m* GESCHÄFT accident, coincidence; ◆ **vom ~ abhängig** VERSICH aleatoric

zufällig *adj* GESCHÄFT accidental, incidental; **nicht ~e Stichprobe** *f* VW nonrandom sample; **~er Verlust** *m* VERSICH fortuitous loss

Zufall: **Zufallsabweichung** *f* MATH, VW random variation; **Zufallsauswahl** *f* MATH random selection

zufallsabhängig *adj* VERSICH aleatory

zufallsbedingt: **~es Stichprobenverfahren** *nt* VW accidental sampling

Zufall: **Zufallsbeobachtungsmethode** *f* MATH, MGMNT random observation method; **Zufallseinfluß** *m* VW random factor; **Zufallsfaktor** *m* VW random factor;

Zufallsfehler *m* MATH, VERWALT random error; **Zufallsgewinn** *m* GESCHÄFT, VW windfall gain; **Zufallsprüfung** *f* MATH random check; **Zufallsstichprobe** *f* MATH, V&M random sample; **Zufallsstichprobenauswahl** *f* MATH random selection; **Zufallsstichprobenverfahren** *nt* MATH random sampling; **Zufallsvariable** *f* MATH chance variable, random variable; **Zufallsverlust** *m* VERSICH fortuitous loss; **Zufallswahl** *f* FINANZ contingencies vote; **Zufallszahl** *f* COMP, MATH random number; **Zufallszahlengenerator** *m* MATH random number generator

Zufluchtsland *nt* POL asylum

Zufluchtsort *m* FINANZ, GESCHÄFT, STEUER haven

zufolge *prep* GESCHÄFT, RECHT according to

zufrieden *adj* GESCHÄFT satisfied

Zufriedenheit *f* GESCHÄFT contentment, satisfaction; **~ mit der beruflichen Tätigkeit** MGMNT job satisfaction

zufriedenstellen *vt* GESCHÄFT please, satisfy

zufriedenstellend *adj* GESCHÄFT satisfactory

Zufriedenstellung *f* GESCHÄFT satisfaction

zuführen *vt* COMP feed, FINANZ *Mittel* allocate to

Zuführung *f* COMP feed, RECHNUNG allocation; **~ an die Rücklage** RECHNUNG appropriation to a reserve; **~ zu den Rücklagen** RECHNUNG allocation to reserves; **Zuführungen zu den Rückstellungen** RECHNUNG allocations to provisions; **Zuführungsgeschwindigkeit** *f* COMP feed rate

Zug- *in cpds* IND, TRANSP train, traction, V&M feature, attraction

Zugabe *f* V&M bonus pack, free gift; **~ gegen eingesandten Kupon** V&M mail-in premium

Zugang *m* GESCHÄFT access, RECHNUNG addition, SOZIAL intake, VERWALT addition; **~ von flüssigen Mitteln** FINANZ cash inflow; ♦ **~ zu Informationen haben** GESCHÄFT have access to information; **~ zum Kapitalkonto** RECHNUNG, VW addition to capital account; **sich ~ verschaffen zu** GESCHÄFT gain entry to

Zugänge *m pl* RECHNUNG accruals, additions

zugänglich *adj* GESCHÄFT accessible; ♦ **allgemein ~** GESCHÄFT free-for-all (*infrml*)

Zugänglichkeit *f* COMP, GESCHÄFT accessibility

Zugang: **Zugangsbeschränkung** *f* IMP/EXP, VW barrier to entry, restriction to entry, entry restriction; **Zugangsjahr** *nt* RECHNUNG year of acquisition; **Zugangsschutzsystem** *nt* COMP firewall; **Zugangsstraße** *f* TRANSP accommodation road

Zug-: **Zugartikel** *m* V&M leader (*AmE*); **Zugbruttogewicht** *nt* TRANSP gross train weight (*GTW*)

zugeben *vt* GESCHÄFT admit, *Fehler* acknowledge

zugeflossen: **~e Einkünfte** *pl* RECHNUNG income received

zugegen: **~ sein** *phr* GESCHÄFT be present; **nicht ~** *phr* GESCHÄFT, PERSON absent

zugehörig *adj* RECHT appurtenant; **~e Explosionsversicherungsklausel** *f* VERSICH inherent explosion clause

Zugehörigkeit *f* GESCHÄFT affiliation, membership

Zügel: **die ~ der Geldpolitik straffen** *phr* VW tighten the monetary reins; **die ~ locker lassen** *phr* MGMNT have a loose rein, slacken the reins; **die ~ lockern** *phr* VW have a loose rein, slacken the reins

zugelassen *adj* COMP approved, FINANZ licensed; **nicht**

~er Broker *m* BÖRSE unlicensed broker; **~er Devisenhändler** *m*, **~e Devisenhändlerin** *f* BÖRSE authorized dealer, licensed foreign exchange dealer; **nicht ~e Firma** *f* BÖRSE unlisted company; **~e Räumlichkeiten** *f pl* IMP/EXP approved premises; **~er Wirtschaftsprüfer** *m* RECHNUNG certified accountant (*BrE*), certified general accountant, certified public accountant (*AmE*) (*CPA*), chartered accountant (*BrE*)

zügellos *adj* GESCHÄFT *Wettbewerb* uncurbed

Zügelung *f* GESCHÄFT, POL containment

zugerechnet: **~es Einkommen** *nt* VW imputed income; **~e Zinsen** *m pl* STEUER imputed interest

zugesagt *adj* FINANZ *Gelder* committed, VERSICH approved

zugeschnitten *adj* GESCHÄFT, V&M *auf die Bedürfnisse des Verbrauchers* tailor-made, tailored; **~es Holz** *nt* IND lumber

zugesichert *adj* VERSICH warranted (*Wld*)

zugestanden *adj* GESCHÄFT admitted, granted

Zugeständnis *nt* GESCHÄFT acknowledgement (*ack*), admission, GRUND concession, PERSON giveback; ♦ **Zugeständnisse machen** GESCHÄFT make allowances for

zugeteilt: **nicht ~** *adj* BÖRSE unallotted, COMP unallocated; **~e Leistungen** *f pl* FINANZ allocated benefits

zugewiesen: **nicht ~** *adj* COMP unallocated

Zugewinn *m* BANK, RECHT after-acquired property

Zug-: **Zugfährendeck** *nt* TRANSP train ferry deck

zügig *adj* GESCHÄFT speedy

Zug-: **Zugkraft** *f* V&M *Reklamewirkung* attention value; **Zugmaschine** *f* TRANSP tractive machine; **Zugnummer** *f* TRANSP train number; **Zugpassagier** *m* TRANSP rail traveler (*AmE*), rail traveller (*BrE*)

zugreifen: **~ auf** *vt* [+acc] COMP *Datensatz, Information, Maschine* access

Zugreisende(r) *mf* [decl. as adj] TRANSP rail traveler (*AmE*), rail traveller (*BrE*)

Zugriff *m* COMP, VW access; **Zugriffsberechtigung** *f* COMP *Programme, Dateien* access right; **Zugriffsfähigkeit** *f* COMP, GESCHÄFT accessibility; **Zugriffskontrolle** *f* COMP access control; **Zugriffsmöglichkeit** *f* COMP, GESCHÄFT accessibility; **Zugriffsunterschiede** *m pl* COMP, VW access differential; **Zugriffszeit** *f* COMP *Zeitdauer zwischen Datenanforderung und Datenanzeige* access time

zugrundeliegend: **~e Nettovermögen** *nt pl* FINANZ underlying net assets; **~e Termingeschäfte** *nt pl* BÖRSE underlying futures; **~er Terminkontrakt** *m* BÖRSE underlying futures contract; **~e Terminkontrakte** *m pl* BÖRSE underlying futures; **~er Trend** *m* GESCHÄFT, VW underlying trend; **~e Vermögen** *nt pl* FINANZ underlying assets; **~e Währung** *f* GESCHÄFT basic currency; **~es Wertpapier** *nt* BÖRSE underlying security

Zug-um-Zug: **Zug-um-Zug-Abwicklung** *f* RECHT *Vertragsrecht* performance upon counter-performance; **Zug-um-Zug-Erfüllung** *phr* RECHT *Vertragsrecht* contemporaneous performance; **Zug-um-Zug-Order** *f* BÖRSE alternative order; **Zug-um-Zug-Zahlung** *f* GESCHÄFT pay as paid

zugunsten: **~ von** *phr* GESCHÄFT in favor of (*AmE*), in favour of (*BrE*); **~ von jdm entscheiden** *phr* GESCHÄFT give a ruling in favor of sb (*AmE*), give a ruling in favour of (*BrE*)

Zug-: **Zugwagen** *m* TRANSP railroad car (*AmE*), railway coach (*BrE*)

Zuhörer *m pl* FREI, KOMM, MEDIEN audience

zukleben *vt* GESCHÄFT, KOMM tape

Zukunft *f* GESCHÄFT future

zukünftig 1. *adj* GESCHÄFT future, V&M *Kunden* prospective; ◆ **zu einem ~en Termin** GESCHÄFT at some future date; **2.** *adv* GESCHÄFT in future

zukünftig: **~e Ansprüche** *m pl* GESCHÄFT future interest (*BrE*); **~e Gewinne** *m pl* STEUER future gains; **~e Steuergutschrift** *f* RECHNUNG future tax credits

Zukunftstrends *m pl* GESCHÄFT future trends

Zuladungsfaktor *m* TRANSP load factor

Zulage *f* PERSON *Gefahrenzulage* allowance, bonus, premium; **~ bei Eheschließung** STEUER marriage penalty (*AmE*)

zulassen *vt* GESCHÄFT admit of, accredit, approve, enfranchise, PERSON *Organisation* allow, RECHT endorse, indorse

zulässig *adj* GESCHÄFT admissible, allowable, PATENT admissible, RECHT permissible, permitted, *Beweis, Zeuge, Berufung* admissible; **~er Abschreibungssatz** *m* RECHNUNG depreciation allowance; **~e Abweichung** *f* GESCHÄFT allowance; **~er Anspruch** *m* PATENT admissible claim; **~e Arbeitsbelastung** *f* IND safe working load; **~e Beanspruchung** *f* IND safe working load; **~e Fangquote** *f* UMWELT *Fischfang* total allowable catches (*TACs*); **~er Fehler** *m* GESCHÄFT permissible error; **~e Forderung** *f* PATENT admissible claim, VERSICH allowable claim; **~es Gepäck** *m* TRANSP free baggage allowance; **~es Gewicht** *nt* TRANSP free allowance of luggage; **~e Menge** *f* IMP/EXP quantity permitted; **~es Schwankungslimit** *nt* BÖRSE daily trading limit

Zulässigkeit *f* RECHT admissibility

Zulassung *f* GESCHÄFT admission, admittance, approval, PATENT *eines Patents* licence (*BrE*), license (*AmE*), RECHT *als Anwalt* admission; **~ zur Börsennotierung** BÖRSE admission to quotation; **~ für Personenbeförderung** TRANSP passenger certificate (*BrE*) (*PC*); **~ von Wertpapieren** BÖRSE, FINANZ admission of securities; **Zulassungsfrist** *f* SOZIAL *Universität* qualification period; **Zulassungsgebühr** *m* GESCHÄFT admission fee; **Zulassungsprüfung** *f* GESCHÄFT entrance examination; **Zulassungsschein** *m* **für Personenbeförderung** TRANSP passenger certificate (*BrE*) (*PC*); **Zulassungsvorschriften** *f pl* BÖRSE listing requirements

zuletzt: **~ eingestellt, zuerst entlassen** *phr* (*LIFO*) PERSON, RECHNUNG, STEUER, VW last in first out (*LIFO*)

Zulieferauftrag *m* GESCHÄFT, IND, PERSON, RECHT subcontract

Zulieferindustrie *f* GESCHÄFT supply industry

Zulieferungsvertrag *m* GESCHÄFT, IND, PERSON, RECHT subcontract

zumachen *vt* GESCHÄFT close down, shut down

Zumutbarkeit *f* GESCHÄFT appropriateness

Zunahme *f* GESCHÄFT augmentation, increase, rise

Zünder *m* GESCHÄFT igniter

zunehmen *vi* GESCHÄFT augment, intensify, *Inflation, Wachstum* accelerate, increase, VW accelerate

zunehmend 1. *adj* GESCHÄFT *Inflation, Wachstum* increasing, accelerating; **2.** *adv* GESCHÄFT increasingly

zunehmend: **~e Inflation** *f* VW accelerating inflation; **~e ökologische Orientierung** *f* UMWELT *der Bevölkerung* greening (*jarg*); **~e Skalenerträge** *m pl* VW increasing returns to scale; **~er Wettbewerb** *m* VW mounting competition

Zunft *f* PERSON guild

Zungenspesen *pl* GESCHÄFT conduct money

zunutze: **sich ~ machen** *phr* GESCHÄFT take advantage of

zuordnen *vt* [+dat] COMP *Speicherplatz, Gerät* allocate to, GESCHÄFT group along with

Zuordnung *f* COMP *Speicherplatz, Gerät* allocation

zupackend *adj* GESCHÄFT enterprising

zurechenbar: **~ zu** *phr* GESCHÄFT attributable to; **~es Einkommen** *nt* VW imputed income; **~e Kenntnis** *f* RECHT constructive notice (*AmE*); **~e Kosten** *pl* VW separable costs

zurechnen *vt* [+dat] GESCHÄFT *Ausgaben* charge to, RECHNUNG assign *Einkommen* apply to, *Gelder* allocate to; ◆ **Kosten ~** RECHNUNG assign costs

Zurechnung *f* RECHNUNG allocation, assignment

Zürich: **~er Wertpapierbörse** *f* BÖRSE Zürich Stock Exchange

Zurrung *f* TRANSP lashing

zurück: **~ an Absender** *phr* KOMM return to sender; **~ an Aussteller** *phr* GESCHÄFT refer to drawer (*RD*)

Zurückbehaltung *f* GRUND retainage, VERSICH retention; **Zurückbehaltungsrecht** *nt* RECHT *Vertragsrecht* right of retention, VW *Vertragsrecht* lien; **Zurückbehaltungsrecht** *m* **einer Bank** BANK bank lien

zurückbleiben *vi* GESCHÄFT fall behind, lag, lag behind

zurückbringen *vt* GESCHÄFT return

zurückbuchen *vt* GESCHÄFT write back

Zurückbuchung *f* RECHNUNG writing back

zurückdatieren *vt* GESCHÄFT *Dokument, Scheck* antedate, predate

zurückerhalten *vt* VW recover

zurückfahren *vi* GESCHÄFT *Produktion* wind down

zurückführen *vt* UMWELT recycle, VW *Verschuldung* reduce; ◆ **etw ~ auf etw** GESCHÄFT attribute sth to sth

zurückgeben *vt* GESCHÄFT return

zurückgegeben: **~es Buch** *nt* MEDIEN returned book

zurückgehalten *adj* GESCHÄFT bottled-up; **~er Lohn** *m* PERSON holdback pay

zurückgehen *vi* BÖRSE run back, slip, VW retrogress, decline

zurückgehend: **~e Gewinne** *m pl* GESCHÄFT shrinking profits

zurückgestaut: **~e Inflation** *f* VW suppressed inflation

zurückgestellt: **~es Einkommen** *nt* FINANZ deferred credit, deferred income, deferred revenue; **~e Erträge** *m pl* FINANZ deferred revenue; **~er Rabatt** *m* IMP/EXP, TRANSP deferred rebate

zurückgreifen: **~ auf** *phr* [+acc] GESCHÄFT fall back on

zurückhalten 1. *vt* GESCHÄFT restrain, withhold; **2. sich ~** *v refl* GESCHÄFT keep a low profile

zurückhaltend *adj* GESCHÄFT cautious, low-key, aloof

Zurückhaltung *f* GESCHÄFT, POL containment, restraint, TRANSP detention, V&M low profile; **~ bei Ausgaben** VW underspending

zurückkaufen *vt* BÖRSE buy back, VW *Schuld* repurchase

zurückkehren *vi* GESCHÄFT return

zurückkommen *vi* GESCHÄFT return

zurückkonvertieren *vt* COMP reconvert

zurücklegen *vt* BANK *Geld* put away

Zurücknahme *f* PATENT revocation

zurücknehmbar *adj* GESCHÄFT revocable

zurücknehmen *vt* GESCHÄFT take back, PATENT *Lizenz* revoke, VW *Schulden* repurchase

zurückrollen 1. *vt* COMP *Text auf Bildschirm* scroll up; **2.** *vi* COMP *auf Bildschirm* scroll up

zurückrufen 1. *vt* GESCHÄFT, KOMM, V&M call back; **2.** *vi* BÖRSE recall, KOMM *Telefon* return sb's call

Zurückschieben *nt* TRANSP pushback

zurückschlagen *vi* GESCHÄFT fight back

zurückschreiben *vi* GESCHÄFT, KOMM write back

zurückscrollen 1. *vt* COMP *Text auf Bildschirm* scroll up; **2.** *vi* COMP *auf Bildschirm* scroll up

zurücksenden *vt* V&M *Waren an den Verkäufer* return

zurücksetzen *vt* COMP *Band, Lochstreifen* backspace, *Uhr, Zähler, Daten* reset

zurückspulen *vt* COMP *Band*, MEDIEN *Kassette, Band* rewind

zurückstecken *vi* GESCHÄFT soft-pedal (*infrml*)

zurückstellen *vt* GESCHÄFT shelve, put on the back burner (*infrml*), postpone, table (*AmE*)

Zurückstellung *f* GESCHÄFT postponement

Zurückstoßen *nt* TRANSP pushback

zurücktragen *vt* FINANZ, RECHNUNG carry back

zurücktreten *vi* GESCHÄFT back out, step back, resign *Vertrag, Vereinbarung* back out of, PERSON, POL stand down; ◆ **~ von** GESCHÄFT *Vertrag, Vereinbarung* back out of, withdraw from, RECHT withdraw from

zurückübertragen *vt* FINANZ reassign

zurückverfolgen *vt* GESCHÄFT trace back

Zurückverfolgung *f* GESCHÄFT retracement

zurückverkaufen *vt* BÖRSE sell back

zurückverweisen: ~ an *vt* [+acc] GESCHÄFT, PERSON refer back to

zurückweichen *vi* GESCHÄFT back off

zurückweisen *vt* GESCHÄFT reject, repudiate, turn away, PATENT reject, turn away, RECHT *Anspruch* dismiss, reject, repudiate

Zurückweisung *f* GESCHÄFT, PATENT rejection, RECHT dismissal, repudiation, *Vertragsrecht* rejection

zurückzahlen *vt* BANK *Schulden, Hypothek* amortize, pay back, pay off, repay, FINANZ pay back, repay, wipe off, GESCHÄFT refund, repay, RECHNUNG *Schulden, Hypothek* amortize, pay back, pay off, repay

zurückziehen 1. *vt* FINANZ revoke, GESCHÄFT *Angebot* withdraw; **2. sich ~** *v refl* GESCHÄFT withdraw, *von Versprechen* backtrack, back off

Zurückziehung *f* FINANZ, GESCHÄFT, VW withdrawal

Zusage *f* FINANZ, GESCHÄFT commitment

zusagen *vt* GESCHÄFT promise

Zusammenarbeit *f* GESCHÄFT collaboration, cooperation, GRUND cooperative (*co-op*), KOMM liaison, POL collaboration; **~ mit Drittländern** VW third-country cooperation; ◆ **in ~ mit** GESCHÄFT in association with

zusammenarbeiten *vi* GESCHÄFT cooperate, liaise, work together, pull together, collaborate, PERSON work together, POL collaborate; ◆ **~ mit** GESCHÄFT, MGMNT work in partnership with, PERSON work alongside

Zusammenarbeit: Zusammenarbeitsfähigkeit *f* COMP interoperability

zusammenbrechen *vi* BANK fail, COMP break down, GESCHÄFT *System*, VW *Markt* collapse

zusammenfallen: ~ mit *vt* GESCHÄFT coincide with

zusammenfassen 1. *vt* GESCHÄFT sum up, totalize, VW consolidate, unite; **2.** *vi* GESCHÄFT sum up

zusammenfassend: ~e Darstellung *f* GESCHÄFT executive summary, summary statement

Zusammenfassend: ~e Meldungen *f pl* (*MwSt.*) STEUER aggregate sales listings (*ASL*) (*BrE*)

Zusammenfassung *f* FINANZ conspectus, GESCHÄFT conspectus, summary, synopsis, MEDIEN synopsis, RECHT *Exzerpt*, V&M synopsis, VW abstract; **~ der Hintergründe** FINANZ background paper; **~ von Massengut in Einheiten** TRANSP bulk unitization; **~ der Vorsitzenden** MGMNT chairman's brief; **~ des Vorsitzenden** MGMNT *bei einer Veranstaltung* chairman's brief

zusammenfügen *vt* VERWALT *Dateien* merge

zusammengebrochen *adj* COMP *Systemabsturz* down, GESCHÄFT collapsed

zusammengefaßt *adj* GESCHÄFT consolidated, summarized, V&M condensed; **~er Börsenticker** *m* BÖRSE consolidated tape; **~e Darstellung** *f* GESCHÄFT résumé, summary

Zusammengefaßt: ~e Europäische Einheit *f* FINANZ European Composite Unit (*EURCO*)

zusammengeklebt: ~e Pappe *f* IND pasteboard

zusammengesetzt *adj* GESCHÄFT composite; **~er Ertrag** *m* FINANZ compound yield; **~e Hypothese** *f* MATH composite hypothesis; **~er Index** *m* VW composite index; **~er Index** *m* der Frühindikatoren BÖRSE BÖRSE composite leading index; **~e Journalbuchung** *f* RECHNUNG compound journal entry; **~e Nachfrage** *f* VW composite demand; **~e Rendite** *f* BANK composite yield; **~e Spanne** *f* BANK composite spread; **~es Warenzeichen** *nt* PATENT composite mark

zusammengestellt *adj* GESCHÄFT structured; **~e Lieferung** *f* TRANSP consolidated delivery

Zusammenhalt *m* GESCHÄFT cohesion, coherence

Zusammenhang *m* GESCHÄFT coherence, cohesion, context; ◆ **etw in ~ mit etw bringen** GESCHÄFT associate sth with sth

zusammenhängend *adj* GESCHÄFT coherent; **nicht miteinander ~e Ereignisse** *nt pl* GESCHÄFT disjoint events

zusammenklappen *vt* GESCHÄFT, TRANSP collapse

Zusammenkunft *f* GESCHÄFT assembly, meeting

Zusammenlaufen *nt* BÖRSE convergence

zusammenlegbar: ~er Container *m* TRANSP collapsible container (*coltainer*)

zusammenlegen *vt* GESCHÄFT, TRANSP collapse, VERWALT *Dateien* merge, vw amalgamate

Zusammenlegung *f* BÖRSE commingling

zusammenpassend *adj* V&M matching

zusammenrechnen *vt* GESCHÄFT tally up, MATH add up

Zusammenrechnung *f* MATH addition

zusammenschließen 1. *vt* GESCHÄFT unite; **2. sich ~** *v refl* BÖRSE merge, GESCHÄFT *Unternehmen* join together, amalgamate, combine with, unite, VW amalgamate

Zusammenschluß *m* GESCHÄFT assembling, combination, PERSON amalgamation; **~ von Investoren zur Beeinflussung des Effekte** BÖRSE pool

zusammenschmelzen *vt* IND smelt

zusammensetzen: **sich ~ aus** *v refl* GESCHÄFT be composed of

Zusammensetzung *f* IND make-up; **~ des Personals** TRANSP crew manning

zusammenstellen *vt* GESCHÄFT compile, structure, RECHNUNG compile

Zusammenstellung *f* GESCHÄFT compilation, structure, structuring, RECHNUNG compilation; **~ katalytischer Maßnahmen** VW catalytic policy mix; **~ einer oder mehrerer Arbeitsgruppen** COMP team building; **Zusammenstellungsfracht** *f* TRANSP assembly cargo

Zusammenstoß *m* TRANSP *Verkehrsunfall* crash

zusammenstoßen *vi* TRANSP *Auto* crash

Zusammenstreichen *nt* GESCHÄFT pruning

Zusammenströmen *nt* GESCHÄFT confluence

zusammentragen *vt* GESCHÄFT collect

Zusammentreffen *nt*: **~ von Umständen** GESCHÄFT conjunction of circumstances

zusammenwirken *vi* GESCHÄFT combine

Zusammenwirken *nt* GESCHÄFT, VW synergy

zusammenzählen *vt* GESCHÄFT tot up (*BrE*), totalize, tally up, MATH *Zahlen* add, add up, sum up, RECHNUNG sum up

Zusatz *m* COMP add-on, GESCHÄFT adjunct, additive, annex (*AmE*), annexe (*BrE*), MGMNT add-on, PATENT, POL amendment, RECHNUNG add-on; ♦ **~ zu** GESCHÄFT in addition to

Zusatz: **Zusatzabkommen** *nt* GESCHÄFT supplemental agreement; **Zusatzaktien** *f pl* BÖRSE excessive shares; **Zusatzannuität** *f* FINANZ wraparound annuity; **Zusatzausrüstung** *f* COMP, MGMNT add-on equipment; **Zusatzbedingungen** *f pl* VERSICH additional conditions; **Zusatzbesteuerung** *f* STEUER windfall profits tax; **Zusatzdarlehen** *nt* FINANZ front-end loan; **Zusatzdividende** *f* BÖRSE extra dividend

Zusätze *m pl* RECHT *Vertrag* additional terms; ♦ **ohne jegliche ~** GESCHÄFT free of all additives

Zusatz: **Zusatzeigenschaft** *f* PATENT additional feature; **Zusatzfinanzierung** *f* FINANZ front-end finance, front-end financing; **Zusatzfrist** *f* PATENT extension of time limits; **Zusatzgebühr** *f* RECHNUNG additional charge; **Zusatzgerät** *nt* COMP attachment; **Zusatzgeräte** *nt pl* COMP, MGMNT add-on equipment; **Zusatzhypothek** *f* BANK wraparound mortgage; **Zusatzkarte** *f* COMP *Hardware* add-on board, add-on card; **Zusatzklausel** *f* RECHT additional clause; **Zusatzkosten** *pl* IND on costs, MGMNT add-on costs, RECHNUNG stand-alone cost; **Zusatzleistung** *f* V&M accessorial service

zusätzlich *adj* FINANZ collateral, GESCHÄFT additional, ancillary, supplementary, accessory, IMP/EXP, PATENT, STEUER, TRANSP supplementary; ♦ **~e Arbeit annehmen** PERSON *Auftragslage, Existenzminimum* take in extra work; **~e Fabrikarbeiter einstellen** PERSON *Auftragslage* take on hands; **~es Personal einstellen** PERSON *Beschäftigungslage* take on additional staff

zusätzlich: **~e Abtretung** *f* VERSICH collateral assignment; **~e Angelegenheit** *f* PATENT additional matter; **~e Arbeitskräfte** *f pl* PERSON additional labor (*AmE*), additional labour (*BrE*); **~e Darlehensvergütung** *f* FINANZ kicker (*infrml*) (*AmE*); **~e Dienstleistung** *f* V&M accessorial service; **~e Dienstleistungen** *f pl* GESCHÄFT ancillary services; **~er Dienstleistungstarif** *m* TRANSP supplementary service tariff (*SST*); **~e Eigenschaft** *f*

PATENT additional feature; **~e Einbehaltung** *f* STEUER backup withholding (*AmE*); **~ eingezahltes Kapital** *nt* RECHNUNG additional paid-in capital, paid-in surplus (*AmE*); **~er Einschuß** *m* BÖRSE additional margin; **~e Finanzierungsfazilität** *f* FINANZ Supplementary Financing Facility; **~e Finanzierungsvorkehrungen** *f pl* VW additional financial facilities; **~e Gelder** *nt pl* FINANZ, GESCHÄFT fresh money; **~er Grundfreibetrag** *m* STEUER additional personal allowance; **~e Kapitalkosten** *pl* FINANZ incremental cost of capital; **~e Kredite** *m pl* FINANZ, GESCHÄFT fresh money; **~e Kreditfazilitäten** *f pl* VW additional financial facilities; **~es Merkmal** *nt* PATENT additional feature; **~e Mittel** *nt pl* GESCHÄFT fresh money; **~e Schicht** *f* PERSON *Schichtarbeit* relief shift, swing shift; **~e Sicherheit** *f* VERSICH additional security; **~er Spezialeinlagenplan** *m* FINANZ supplementary special deposits scheme; **~e Steuereinbehaltung** *f* STEUER backup withholding (*AmE*); **~er Versicherungsschutz** *m* VERSICH extended cover, extended coverage; **~e Warengarantie** *f* IMP/EXP supplementary stocks guarantee; **~e Zession** *f* VERSICH collateral assignment; **~e Zinsen** *m pl* BANK, RECHNUNG additional interest; **~e Zollordnung** *f* IMP/EXP Customs Additional Code (*CAC*)

Zusätzliches *nt* POL supplementaries

Zusatz: **Zusatzmarkt** *m* BÖRSE fringe market; **Zusatzmaterial** *nt* PATENT additional matter; **Zusatzmerkmal** *nt* PATENT additional feature; **Zusatzpatent** *nt* PATENT improvement patent; **Zusatzporto** *nt* GESCHÄFT extra postage, TRANSP extra freight; **Zusatzrente** *f* FINANZ supplementary pension scheme; **Zusatzschutzurkunde** *f* GESCHÄFT, PATENT supplementary protection certificate (*SPC*); **Zusatzspeicher** *m* COMP add-on memory; **Zusatzsteuer** *f* FINANZ supplementary tax; **Zusatztechnologie** *f* GESCHÄFT supplemental technology; **Zusatzvereinbarung** *f* GESCHÄFT supplemental agreement; **Zusatzversicherung** *f* VERSICH additional insurance, collateral insurance; **Zusatzvertrag** *m* GESCHÄFT supplemental agreement; **Zusatzwerbung** *f* V&M accessory advertising

Zuschauer *m pl* FREI, KOMM, MEDIEN audience; **Zuschauerzahl** *f* FREI, MEDIEN number of spectators, number of viewers

Zuschlag *m* BANK add-on, FREI excess fare, GESCHÄFT surcharge, *Vertrag, Ausschreibung* acceptance, MGMNT *Auftrag* award, PERSON allowance, RECHNUNG additional charge, extra charge, TRANSP excess fare; VERSICH addition; **~ für verspätete Steuerzahlung** STEUER penalty for late tax payment; **~ wegen Hafenüberfüllung** STEUER, TRANSP congestion surcharge; **~ für Zahlungsverzug** STEUER default surcharge (*BrE*); ♦ **den ~ erteilen** GESCHÄFT accept a bid, accept a tender

Zuschlag: **Zuschlagskalkulation** *f* IND job order costing, PERSON job costing, RECHNUNG job cost system; **Zuschlagsklausel** *f* **für höhere Produktivität** RECHT acceleration clause premium; **Zuschlagswert** *m* TRANSP surcharge value

zuschneiden: **~ auf** *vt* [+acc] GESCHÄFT tailor to

Zuschnitt *m* GESCHÄFT tailoring

zuschreibbar *adj* MEDIEN, POL attributable; **nicht ~** *adj* MEDIEN, POL not for attribution (*AmE*), on lobby terms (*BrE*)

zuschreiben *vt* GESCHÄFT ascribe, attribute, RECHNUNG

apply to, write up; ◆ **jdm etw ~** GESCHÄFT attach sth to sb, attribute sth to sb

Zuschreibung *f* RECHNUNG *Bilanz* appreciation in value, revaluation, write-up

Zuschuß *m* FINANZ categorical grant, grant-in-aid, subsidy, RECHT, VERWALT, VW *finanzieller Art* grant; **~ an Entwicklungsländer** VW categorical grant, grant-in-aid; **~ zum Lebensunterhalt** GESCHÄFT, POL sustaining grant

Zuschüsse *m pl* PERSON allowances (*BrE*)

Zusendung *f* TRANSP consignment

zusichern *vt* GESCHÄFT assure, guarantee, promise, warrant

Zusichernde(r) *mf* [decl. as adj] GESCHÄFT, RECHT *der Gewährleistende* warranter

Zusicherung *f* GRUND covenant, RECHT warranty, *Zusage* undertaking; **~ der Mindestqualität** GESCHÄFT warranty of merchantability

Zuspätkommen *nt* PERSON lateness

zuspielen *vt* [+dat] GESCHÄFT, MEDIEN, POL *Information* leak

zusprechen **1.** *vt* [+dat] RECHT adjudge to, award to; **2.** *vi* RECHT adjudicate

Zust. *abbr* (*Zustellung*) KOMM D (*delivery*)

zustande: ~ bringen *phr* GESCHÄFT bring about

Zustand *m* COMP state, status, GESCHÄFT status, VW shape; **~ nationaler Einheit** GESCHÄFT nationhood; **~ totaler Erschöpfung** PERSON burnout; **~ der Volkswirtschaft** VW state of the economy; **~ der Weltwirtschaft** VW shape of the world economy

Zustandekommen *nt*: **~ eines Vertrages** RECHT formation of a contract

zuständig *adj* PERSON in charge, responsible, RECHT competent; ◆ **~ für** GESCHÄFT in charge of; **~ sein für** GESCHÄFT be in charge of

zuständig: **~e Partei** *f* RECHT *Vertrag* competent party

Zuständigkeit *f* GESCHÄFT competence, PERSON competency, RECHT competence, jurisdiction; **~ für den Etat** POL budgetary powers; **~ des Gerichts** RECHT competency of the court; **Zuständigkeitsverteilung** *f* MGMNT allocation of responsibilities

Zustand: **Zustandsbericht** *m* GESCHÄFT, MGMNT status report; **Zustandsüberwachung** *f* TRANSP condition monitoring (*CM*)

Zustellabteilung *f* V&M traffic department

Zustelladresse *f* GESCHÄFT forwarding address

zustellbar: **nicht ~e Post** *f* KOMM nixie mail (*AmE*)

Zustelldienst *m* TRANSP delivery service

zustellen *vt* RECHT *Mandat* serve

Zustellgebühr *f* TRANSP delivery charge

Zustellung *f* KOMM *Post, Brief* delivery (*D*)

zustimmen *vi* [+dat] GESCHÄFT *Entscheidung, Dokument, Plan* approve, *Projekt, Plan* agree to, consent, POL *Gesetzentwurf* accede

Zustimmung *f* GESCHÄFT accession, approval (*appro*), assent, consent, sanction, acceptance, POL accession, assent, V&M adoption; **Zustimmungsprozeß** *m* V&M adoption process

Zustrom *m* GESCHÄFT confluence, RECHNUNG *von Geldern, von Kapital* inflow

zuteilen *vt* BÖRSE scale down, *Aktien* apportion, FINANZ *Geld* allot, allocate, KOMM allocate, RECHNUNG apportion, VW allocate

Zuteilung *f* FINANZ allotment, distribution, RECHNUNG allocation, apportionment, assignment; **~ von Gratisaktien anstelle einer Bardividende** FINANZ scrip dividend; **Zuteilungsanzeige** *f* BÖRSE allotment letter; **Zuteilungsbenachrichtigung** *f* KOMM letter of allotment; **Zuteilungsbetrag** *m* FINANZ allotment money; **Zuteilungsempfänger, in** *m,f* BÖRSE allottee; **Zuteilungskurs** *m* FINANZ allotment price; **Zuteilungsschein** *m* KOMM letter of allotment

Zutrauen *nt* GESCHÄFT reliance

zutreffend *adj* GESCHÄFT accurate, applicable; ◆ **nicht ~** GESCHÄFT not applicable (*N/A*)

Zutritt *m* BÖRSE entry, GESCHÄFT access, admission, admittance; ◆ **jdm ~ erteilen zu** GESCHÄFT give sb access to; **kein ~** GESCHÄFT no admittance; **~ verboten** GESCHÄFT no admittance; **jdm den ~ versagen** GESCHÄFT bar sb

zuverlässig *adj* GESCHÄFT reliable; **~e Nachrichten** *f pl* MEDIEN reliable news; **~e Quelle** *f* GESCHÄFT reliable source

Zuverlässigkeit *f* GESCHÄFT reliability; **Zuverlässigkeitsprüfung** *f* GESCHÄFT reliability test

zuviel: **~ berechneter Betrag** *m* V&M overcharge (*o/c*); **~ produzieren** *phr* IND overproduce

Zuwachs *m* FINANZ accession, GESCHÄFT accrual, addition, growth, increase, increment; **Zuwachsmindestreservesatz** *m* VW marginal reserve requirements; **Zuwachsrate** *f* BÖRSE growth rate, VW rate of increase

zuwege: **~ bringen** *phr* GESCHÄFT bring about

zuweisen *vt* COMP assign, *Speicherplatz, Gerät* allocate to, FINANZ *Geld* allocate, allot, KOMM allocate, RECHNUNG assign, *Mittel* allot, appropriate for, VW *Mittel für ein Projekt* appropriate, allocate; ◆ **Kosten ~** RECHNUNG allocate costs

Zuweisung *f* COMP allocation, FINANZ allotment, GESCHÄFT, KOMM allocation, RECHNUNG allocation, allotment, assignment, TRANSP allotment, VW *von Mitteln* appropriation; **~ an die Rücklage** RECHNUNG appropriation to a reserve

zuwenden: **sich etw ~** *v refl* GESCHÄFT *Problem, Thema, Sache* address oneself to sth

Zuwendungsempfänger, in *m,f* RECHT creditor beneficiary

zuwiderlaufend *adj* GESCHÄFT alien

zuzurechnend *adj* [+dat] GESCHÄFT attributable to

zuzuschreiben *adj* [+dat] GESCHÄFT attributable to

Zwang *m* RECHT constraint, VW compulsion, constraint, duress

zwanglos *adj* GESCHÄFT informal; **~e Zusammenkunft** *f* VERWALT informal meeting

Zwang: **Zwangsabzug** *m* GESCHÄFT compulsory deduction; **Zwangsarbeit** *f* STEUER forced labor (*AmE*), forced labour (*BrE*); **Zwangsausschreibung** *f* POL compulsory competitive tendering (*BrE*); **Zwangsenteignung** *f* GRUND compulsory margin; **Zwangsenteignungsgesetz** *nt* RECHT Compulsory Purchase Act (*BrE*); **Zwangsentlassung** *f* PERSON compulsory redundancy (*BrE*); **Zwangsersparnisse** *f pl* FINANZ forced savings; **Zwangshaftpflichtversicherung** *f* VERSICH compulsory third party insurance; **Zwangshypothek** *f* RECHT judgment lien (*AmE*); **Zwangsinvestition** *f* FINANZ involuntary investment; **Zwangskauf** *m* GESCHÄFT compulsory purchase; **Zwangsliquidation** *f* FINANZ compulsory liquidation, involuntary liquidation; **Zwangsliquidierung** *f* FINANZ compulsory liquidation, involuntary liquidation; **Zwangslizenz** *f* PATENT compulsory licence (*BrE*), compulsory license (*AmE*); **Zwangspensionierung** *f* PERSON compulsory retirement (*BrE*), mandatory retirement (*AmE*), VERWALT compulsory retirement; **Zwangsräumung** *f* GRUND actual eviction, RECHT ejectment, *Grundbesitz* eviction; **Zwangsschlichtung** *f* PERSON compulsory arbitration (*BrE*); **Zwangssparen** *nt* FINANZ compulsory saving (*BrE*), vw forced saving; **Zwangsvergleich** *m* RECHT legal settlement; **Zwangsverkauf** *m* RECHT forced sale, *Enteignung* compulsory surrender; **Zwangsversicherung** *f* VERSICH compulsory insurance; **Zwangsversteigerung** *f* RECHT forced sale, foreclosure sale (*AmE*), sale by court order, sale under an execution; **Zwangsversteigerung** *f* **zur Deckung von Steuerschulden** STEUER tax sale; **Zwangsverwalter, in** *m,f* RECHT official receiver, receiver, sequestrator; **Zwangsverwaltung** *f* FINANZ receivership, RECHT sequestration; **der Zwangsverwaltung unterstellen** *phr* RECHT *Konkursverwaltung* place under sequestration, put into receivership; **die Zwangsverwaltung veranlassen** *phr* RECHT go into receivership; **Zwangsverwertung** *f* **von Vorräten** RECHT forced sale of stock; **Zwangsvollstreckung** *f* FINANZ foreclosure, RECHT judicial foreclosure; **Zwangsvorladung** *f* RECHT *förmliche Ladung* subpoena; **Zwangswährung** *f* FINANZ, vw forced currency

zwangsweise: **~ Liquidation** *f* GESCHÄFT compulsory liquidation

Zweck *m* GESCHÄFT aim, purpose, MGMNT goal, objective; **~ der Erfindung** PATENT nature of the invention; ♦ **zu diesem ~** GESCHÄFT ad hoc; **einem ~ dienen** GESCHÄFT serve a purpose

Zweck: **Zweckbau** *m* GRUND purpose-built block; **Zweckbindung** *f* FINANZ, vw ringfencing, earmarking; **Zweckbindung** *f* **von Gewinnen oder Rücklagen** RECHNUNG appropriation; **Zweckbindung vornehmen** *phr* FINANZ, vw ring-fence

zweckdienlich *adj* GESCHÄFT expedient

Zweckdienlichkeit *f* FINANZ instrumentality, GESCHÄFT expediency

zweckentfremdet: **~e Mittel** *nt pl* vw misused funds

Zweckentfremdung *f* FINANZ misappropriation

Zweckfahrzeug *nt* TRANSP purpose-built vehicle

zweckgebunden *adj* FREI earmarked, vw appropriated; **~es Darlehen** *nt* BÖRSE purpose loan; **nicht ~e, einbehaltene Erträge** *m pl* FINANZ unappropriated retained earnings; **~e Finanzzuweisung** *f* POL categorical grant; **nicht ~er Gewinn** *m* FINANZ unappropriated profit; **nicht ~e Haushaltsmittel** *nt pl* FINANZ, RECHNUNG general fund; **~ Mittel** *nt pl* FINANZ earmarked funds; **~e, offene Rücklagen** *f pl* FINANZ surplus reserves; **~er Scheck** *m* BANK earmarked check (*AmE*), earmarked cheque (*BrE*); **~er Wohnungsbau** *m* GRUND purpose-built block; **~er Zuschuß** *m* POL categorical grant, grant-in-aid; **~e Zuweisung** *f* GESCHÄFT special purpose allotment

Zweckholz *nt* IND lumber

zwecklos *adj* GESCHÄFT aimless

zweckmäßig *adj* GESCHÄFT advisable, suitable, useful, rational; ♦ **etw ~er gestalten** GESCHÄFT rationalize

zweckmäßigste: **~ Instrumente** *f pl* GESCHÄFT best practical means (*bpm*)

Zweckmäßigkeitsgrund: **aus Zweckmäßigkeitsgründen** *phr* GESCHÄFT on grounds of expediency

zwecks: **~ Anweisung zum Hafen zurückkehren** *phr* TRANSP *Schiffahrt* return to port for orders

zweckwidrig *adj* GESCHÄFT unsuitable

zweiachsig: **~es Fahrzeug** *nt* TRANSP two-axle vehicle

Zweibettzimmer *nt* FREI twin room, twin-bedded room

Zweifach: **um das ~e ansteigen** *phr* GESCHÄFT increase twofold

zweifach: **~e Methode** *f* **der kleinsten Quadrate** vw two-stage least squares method; **~e Verantwortung** *f* PERSON dual responsibility

zweifarbig *adj* V&M two-color (*AmE*), two-colour (*BrE*)

Zweifel *m* GESCHÄFT doubt

zweifelhaft *adj* GESCHÄFT shady (*infrml*); **~e Forderung** *f* BANK, FINANZ, RECHNUNG bad debt, doubtful debt; **aus ~en Forderungen herrührender Verlust** *m* BANK, FINANZ bad debt loss; **~e Schuldner** *m pl* RECHNUNG doubtful debtors

zweifelnd: **~e Haltung** *f* GESCHÄFT scepticism (*BrE*), skepticism (*AmE*)

Zweig- *in cpds* BANK, GESCHÄFT, VERWALT branch, affiliated; **Zweigbetrieb** *m* GESCHÄFT branch operation; **Zweigbüro** *nt* GESCHÄFT suboffice; **Zweigfirma** *f* GESCHÄFT affiliated firm; **Zweiggeschäft** *nt* V&M branch store

zweigipflig: **~e Verteilung** *f* MATH *Statistik* bimodal distribution

Zweig-: **Zweigniederlassung** *f* BANK agency (*agcy*), agency bank (*BrE*), agent bank, GESCHÄFT affiliated firm; **Zweigpostamt** *nt* KOMM sub-post office; **Zweigstelle** *f* BANK branch, GESCHÄFT branch, suboffice, VERWALT branch office (*BO*), vw sub-branch; **Zweigstellennetz** *nt* BANK branch network; **Zweigwerk** *nt* GESCHÄFT branch operation

zwei: **alle ~ Jahre** *phr* GESCHÄFT biennial

zweijährig *adj* GESCHÄFT biennial

zweijährlich *adj* GESCHÄFT biennial

Zweiklassenschiff *nt* TRANSP two-class vessel

zwei: **in ~ Lager gespaltenes Gremium** *nt* POL split commission

zweimal: **~ anklicken** *phr* COMP *Maus* double-click; **~ jährlich** *phr* GESCHÄFT biannual; **~ im Monat** *phr* GESCHÄFT bimonthly; **~ wöchentlich** *phr* GESCHÄFT biweekly

zweimetallisch *adj* IND, UMWELT bimetallic; **~er Standard** *m* IND bimetallic standard

zwei: **alle ~ Monate** *phr* GESCHÄFT bimonthly

Zweirichtungsdrucker *m* COMP bidirectional printer

zweischichtig: **~es System** *nt* GESCHÄFT two-tier system

zwei: **~ Seiten** *f pl* V&M double front

zweiseitig *adj* COMP two-sided, POL bilateral; **~es Handelsabkommen** *nt* vw bilateral trade agreement; **~er Handelsvertrag** *m* vw bilateral trade treaty; **~es Monopol** *nt* vw bilateral monopoly; **~e Referenz** *f* PERSON bilateral reference; **~er Test** *m* MATH two-tailed test; **~e Varianzanalyse** *f* MATH two-way analysis of variance; **~es Verrechnungsabkommen** *nt* vw bilateral clearing agreement; **~er Vertrag** *m* RECHT dual contract

zweispurig: ~es Deck *nt* TRANSP two-lane deck

zweistellig *adj* VW *Inflationsrate* double digit; ~e Inflationsrate *f* FINANZ, VW double digit inflation, double figure inflation, two-digit inflation

Zwei-Steuersatz-System *nt* STEUER two-rate system

Zweistufensystem *nt* GESCHÄFT two-tier system

zweistufig: ~e Stichprobe *f* MATH double sample; ~e Tarifverhandlungen *f pl* PERSON *Tarifvertrag* two-tier bargaining

Zweitakkreditiv *nt* BANK back-to-back credit

Zweitbeschäftigung *f* PERSON secondary employment

Zweitbesetzung *f* IND joint operator

zweitbeste *adj* VW second best

zweite: ~r Arbeitsmarkt *m* VW dual labor market (*AmE*), dual labour market (*BrE*); ~ Generation *f* MEDIEN second generation; ~s Halbjahr *nt* GESCHÄFT second half of the year; ~ Hälfte *f* GESCHÄFT *Monatshälfte* last half (*lh*); ~ Hälfte *f* des Jahres GESCHÄFT second half of the year; aus ~r Hand *phr* GESCHÄFT preowned, second-hand; ~ Hypothek *f* BANK, FINANZ second mortgage; ~ Lesung *f* RECHT *eines Gesetzes, einer Richtlinie etc.* second reading; ~ Lombardierung *f* BÖRSE rehypothecation; ~r Maschinist *m*, ~ Maschinistin *f* IND joint operator; ~ Obligation *f* FINANZ second debenture; ~s Quartal *nt* GESCHÄFT second quarter (*2Q*); ~ Vervielfältigung *f* MEDIEN second generation

Zweite: ~ Welt *f* VW Second World; ~r Weltkrieg *m* POL World War II, Second World War

Zweiteilung *f* GESCHÄFT two-way split

Zweithypothekengeschäft *nt* FINANZ second mortgage lending

zweitgrößte *adj* GESCHÄFT second largest

zweitklassig *adj* GESCHÄFT second-class, second-rate; ~es Geldmarktpapier *nt* FINANZ second-class paper

zweitrangig *adj* BÖRSE, GESCHÄFT, PERSON secondary

Zweitwohnsitz *m* RECHT second domicile, second residence

Zweitwohnung *f* GRUND second home

Zweiwegeverkehr *m* TRANSP two-way scheme

zwei: ~ Wochen *f pl* GESCHÄFT fortnight

zweizeilig *adj* COMP *Textverarbeitung* double-spaced

zwingen *vt* GESCHÄFT force, oblige

zwingend *adj* GESCHÄFT *Maßnahme* stringent, compulsory, stringently, VW compelling; ~er Beweis *m* RECHT conclusive evidence, VERWALT conclusive proof

Zwischen- in *cpds* GESCHÄFT ad interim (*frml*), transitional, intermediate; **Zwischenablage** *f* COMP *Windows, Speicher* clipboard; **Zwischenaudit** *nt* VERWALT interim audit; **Zwischenbankeinlagen** *f pl* BANK, FINANZ interbank deposits; **Zwischenbericht** *m* RECHNUNG interim report

zwischenbetrieblich: ~er Vergleich *m* MGMNT inter-firm comparison

Zwischen-: **Zwischenbilanz** *f* VERWALT interim balance; **Zwischen-Depot-Transfer** *m* TRANSP interdepot transfer; **Zwischendividende** *f* BÖRSE interim dividend; **Zwischeneintrag** *m* RECHNUNG suspense entry; **Zwischenerzeugnis** *nt* VW intermediate good, intermediate product; **Zwischenfinanzierung** *f* BANK intermediate financing, FINANZ intermediate financing, bridge finance; **Zwischenhandel** *m* GESCHÄFT intermediate trade, VW transit trade; **Zwischenkonto** *nt* RECHNUNG suspense account; **Zwischenkredit** *m* BANK bridge-over loan, interim loan, intermediate loan, FINANZ intermediate credit; **Zwischenlandung** *f* FREI, TRANSP stopover; **Zwischenmedium** *nt* V&M transient medium

zwischenmenschlich: ~e Beziehungen *f pl* GESCHÄFT, PERSON human relations

Zwischen-: **Zwischenprodukt** *nt* GESCHÄFT industrial product; **Zwischenspediteur** *m* GESCHÄFT subagent; **Zwischenspiel** *nt* GESCHÄFT interplay

zwischenstaatlich *adj* GESCHÄFT government-to-government, interstate (*AmE*), POL intergovernmental; ~e Beziehungen *f pl* POL government relations; ~er Handel *m* GESCHÄFT interstate commerce (*AmE*); ~es Komitee *nt* für europäische Auswanderung (*ICEM*) SOZIAL Intergovernmental Committee for European Migration (*ICEM*); ~e Organisation *f* POL intergovernmental organization; ~e Vorbereitungsgruppe *f* POL intergovernmental preparatory group (*IPG*)

Zwischen-: **Zwischenstadium** *nt* FINANZ intermediate stage; **Zwischenstation** *f* FREI, TRANSP stopover; **Zwischenstufe** *f* BÖRSE mezzanine bracket; **Zwischensumme** *f* MATH subtotal; **Zwischenübersicht** *f* VERSICH intermediate survey (*INT*); **Zwischenurteil** *nt* RECHT *vorläufiges Urteil, bevor das endgültige Urteil gefällt wird* interlocutory decree; **Zwischenvertrag** *m* GESCHÄFT interim agreement; **Zwischenzeit** *f* GESCHÄFT, POL interim; **in der Zwischenzeit** *phr* GESCHÄFT ad interim

zwischenzeitlich *adj* GESCHÄFT ad interim

Zwischen-: **Zwischenzielvariable** *f* VW target variable

zyklisch *adj* BÖRSE cyclical; ~e Adreßfolge *f* COMP *Speicher* wraparound; ~er Handel *m* VW cyclical trade; ~e Nachfrage *f* VW cyclical demand; ~e Schwankungen *f pl* VW cyclical variations; ~e Werte *m pl* BÖRSE cyclical shares

Zykloidenpropeller *m* TRANSP cycloidal propeller

Zyklus *m* VW cycle

Zylinder *m* COMP *Laufwerk* cylinder, IND drum, cylinder

Anhang Deutsch–Englisch/
German–English appendix

Inhalt/Contents

Geschäftsbriefe und -dokumente/
Business correspondence and documents

Stellenbewerbung/Job application

Bewerbung für die Stelle einer Technischen Übersetzerin

Sehr geehrte Frau Finkbeiner,

ich möchte mich für die Stelle einer Technischen Übersetzerin bewerben, die Sie in der Frankfurter Allgemeinen Zeitung vom 27. März ausgeschrieben haben.

Ich habe an der Universität München Anglistik und Germanistik studiert und an der Universität Heidelberg ein Aufbaustudium in Technischer Übersetzung abgeschlossen. Nach meinem Studium war ich als Technische Übersetzerin bei der Firma Manz Maschinenbau GmbH tätig, wo ich unter anderem für das Übersetzen von technischen Dokumenten, Gebrauchsanweisungen und Werbematerial zuständig war.

Seit ich aus familiären Gründen nach Ulm umgezogen bin, arbeite ich freiberuflich als Technische Übersetzerin. Unter meinen Kunden befanden sich im letzten Jahr die Deutsche Bundespost und die Ulmer Stadtverwaltung.

Im Laufe meines Studiums und meiner beruflichen Tätigkeiten konnte ich mir gute Kenntnisse im Gebrauch von verschiedenen Softwarepaketen sowie französische und spanische Sprachkenntnisse aneignen. Weitere Einzelheiten können Sie meinem Lebenslauf und den beigefügten Zeugniskopien entnehmen.

Ich würde gerne wieder eine feste Stellung annehmen und bin sehr daran interessiert, für ein großes, internationales Unternehmen wie das Ihre zu arbeiten. Ich würde mich sehr freuen, wenn Sie meine Bewerbung in die engere Wahl ziehen und mir Gelegenheit zu einem persönlichen Gespräch geben würden.

Mit freundlichen Grüßen

Susanne Schneider

Anlagen:
Lebenslauf mit Lichtbild
4 Zeugniskopien

Lebenslauf/Curriculum vitae

Name:	Susanne Schneider
Adresse:	Hauptstraße 25
	89013 Ulm
	Tel: 0731/531468

Geburtsdatum:	8. April 1966
Geburtsort:	Friedrichshafen

Eltern:	Herbert Schneider, Kaufmann
	Gerda Schneider, geb. Krüger
Familienstand:	ledig

Schulbildung und Studium

1973–1977	Grundschule in Friedrichshafen
1977–1986	Friedrich-Schiller-Gymnasium, Friedrichshafen Leistungskurse: Deutsch und Englisch Abitur Mai 1986 (Note 2,1)
1986–1991	Universität München Studium der Anglistik und Germanistik Magisterprüfung Juli 1991 (Note 1,9)
1991–1993	Universität Heidelberg Aufbaustudiengang Technische Übersetzung Diplomprüfung März 1993 (Note 2,2)

Berufserfahrung

Oktober 1993– März 1995	Technische Übersetzerin Manz Maschinenbau GmbH, Mainz
seit April 1995	freiberufliche Übersetzungstätigigkeit (unter anderem für Deutsche Bundespost, Stadtverwaltung Ulm, Fischler Formenherstellung KG)

Kenntnisse und Fähigkeiten

Französisch:	fließend in Wort und Schrift
Spanisch:	Grundkenntnisse
EDV-Kenntnisse:	Textverarbeitung (Word for Windows) und Tabellenkalkulation (Excel)
Führerschein Klasse 3	

Persönliche Interessen

Klassische Musik, Skifahren, Kochen

Arbeitsvertrag/Contract of employment

Sehr geehrter Herr Heute,

in Anlehnung an die bereits geführten Gespräche bestätigen wir Ihnen nachfolgenden Arbeitsvertrag, der zwischen Ihnen und der Manz Maschinenbau GmbH – im folgenden Manz genannt – geschlossen wird.

1. **Vertragsbeginn und Aufgabenbereich**
    1.1. Sie werden von Manz mit Wirkung vom 4. Oktober 1996 als Servicefachkraft im Innendienst in der Niederlassung Mainz eingestellt.

    1.2. Sie erklären sich bereit, auch andere Ihrer Vorbildung und Qualifikation entsprechende oder gleichwertige Aufgaben zu übernehmen.

2. **Arbeitszeit und Vergütung**
    2.1. Ihre regelmäßige wöchentliche Arbeitszeit beträgt 38 Stunden. Die Einzelheiten ergeben sich aus den jeweils gültigen Arbeitszeitregelungen.

    2.2. Ihre Vergütung setzt sich wie folgt zusammen:

Grundlohn (38 Std./Woche), Lohngruppe 7	: DM 3.240,–
Erschwerniszulage 5%	: DM 162,–
Freiwillige Zulage	: DM 200,–
Monatlicher Gesamtlohn brutto	: DM 3.602,–

    Die Höhe der Leistungszulage bestimmt sich nach Ihrer jeweiligen Leistungsbeurteilung. Die freiwillige Zulage kann bei allgemeinen und individuellen Lohnänderungen bzw. Eingruppierungen angerechnet werden.

3. **Vertragsdauer**
    Die Probezeit beträgt sechs Monate. Der Vertrag wird auf unbestimmte Dauer abgeschlossen. Es gelten die gesetzlichen Kündigungsfristen. Manz behält sich vor, Sie nach erfolgter Kündigung unter Fortzahlung der Vergütung lt. Ziffer 2.2. von der Arbeit freizustellen.

    Das Arbeitsverhältnis endet ohne Kündigung mit Ablauf des Monats, in dem Sie das 65. Lebensjahr vollenden oder vorher mit dem Ende des Kalendermonats, in dem Sie Erwerbs- oder Berufsunfähigkeitsrente oder vorgezogenes Altersruhegeld beziehen (variable Altersgrenze).

4. **Urlaub**
    Ihr Urlaubsanspruch ist in der Betriebsvereinbarung über Urlaubsgeld/Jahresurlaub und Arbeitsjubiläum geregelt. Hieraus ergibt sich zur Zeit ein Anspruch auf 30 Arbeitstage pro Kalenderjahr.

5. **Dienstreisen und Nutzung von Firmenfahrzeugen**
    Bei Dienstreisen haben Sie Anspruch auf Ersatz der Auslagen gemäß den Bestimmungen der Reisekostenrichtlinien in ihrer jeweils gültigen Fassung. Wird Ihnen ein Firmenfahrzeug zur Verfügung gestellt, richtet sich dessen Nutzung nach der jeweils gültigen Firmenwagenordnung.

6. **Nebentätigkeit**
Während der Dauer dieses Vertrages stellen Sie Ihre berufliche Tätigkeit ganz in den Dienst von Manz. Nebenbeschäftigungen, für die üblicherweise ein Entgelt bezahlt wird, bedürfen der vorherigen schriftlichen Zustimmung von Manz.

7. **Geheimhaltung**
Sie sind verpflichtet, geschäftliche Angelegenheiten und Unterlagen vertraulicher Natur geheimzuhalten und ausschließlich für betriebliche Zwecke zu verwerten. Diese Verpflichtung besteht auch nach Ende des Vertragsverhältnisses fort.

8. **Rückgabe von Firmeneigentum**
Die in Ihrem Besitz befindlichen Gegenstände und Unterlagen bleiben Eigentum von Manz und sind jederzeit auf Verlangen herauszugeben. Im Falle der Beendigung des Vertragsverhältnisses sind diese unaufgefordert zurückzugeben. Die Geltendmachung eines Zurückhaltungsrechtes wird hiermit ausgeschlossen.

9. **Sonstige Bestimmungen**
Die gegenseitigen Rechte und Pflichten ergeben sich aus diesem Vertrag. Im übrigen wird das Arbeitsverhältnis durch die gesetzlichen Bestimmungen, die betrieblichen Vereinbarungen und Regelungen in ihrer jeweils gültigen Fassung und die Arbeitsanweisungen bestimmt.

10. **Ausschlußfristen**
Ansprüche aus dem Arbeitsverhältnis verfallen, wenn sie nicht innerhalb einer Ausschlußfrist von drei Monaten nach Fälligkeit, spätestens jedoch drei Monate nach Beendigung des Vertragsverhältnisses schriftlich geltend gemacht wurden.

11. **Schlußbestimmungen**
Jede Kündigung, Änderung oder Aufhebung dieses Vertrages bedarf der Schriftform. Sollten einzelne Vereinbarungen dieses Vertrages unwirksam sein, so wird dadurch die Wirksamkeit der übrigen Vereinbarungen nicht berührt.

Mainz, den 1. Oktober 1996

Manz Maschinenbau GmbH   Einverstanden:

                                          ....
i.V. R. Ritter   i.V. D. Dreher   Datum/Unterschrift Mitarbeiter

Mahnung/Reminder

**Fällige Forderungen DM 4.591,20
lt. Kontoauszug vom 20.05.1996**

Sehr geehrte Damen und Herren,

unsere schriftlichen und telefonischen Anmahnungen konnten Sie bisher nicht dazu bewegen, die längst fälligen Forderungen auszugleichen.

Wir fordern Sie letztmals dazu auf, Ihren Zahlungsverpflichtungen nachzukommen und den fälligen Saldo in Höhe von DM 4.591,20 laut beiliegendem Kontoauszug bis

spätestens 27.05.1996

mit Verrechnungsscheck auszugleichen.

Sollten bis zu diesem Termin keine Zahlungsmittel von Ihnen vorliegen, werden wir die Angelegenheit unverzüglich an unsere Rechtsabteilung weiterleiten. Ebenso wären wir in diesem Fall gezwungen, Sie ab diesem Zeitpunkt nur noch gegen Vorauskasse zu beliefern. Wir hoffen, daß dieser Schritt nicht notwendig sein wird.

Falls es einen Grund für die Nichtbezahlung der Rechnungen gibt, steht Ihnen Herr Hägele (Tel. 040/823556) zur Verfügung.

Hochachtungsvoll,

Haug und Söhne KG
Hamburg

Jahresbilanz/Balance sheet

Konzernbilanz zum 31. Dezember 1996

AKTIVA	31.12.96	31.12.95
	TDM	**TDM**
A. ANLAGEVERMÖGEN		
I. Immaterielle Vermögensgegenstände		
1. Gewerbliche Schutzrechte und ähnliche Rechte und Werte sowie Lizenzen an solchen Rechten und Werten	2.298	1.878
2. Geleistete Auszahlungen	21	42
	2.319	**1.920**
II. Sachanlagen		
1. Grundstücke, grundstücksgleiche Rechte und Bauten einschließlich der Bauten auf fremden Grundstücken	135.258	123.802
2. Technische Anlagen und Maschinen	26.343	22.466
3. Andere Anlagen, Betriebs- und Geschäftsausstattung	39.621	39.012
4. Geleistete Anzahlungen und Anlagen im Bau	8.331	14.276
	209.553	**199.556**
III. Finanzanlagen		
1. Anteile an verbundenen Unternehmen	23.723	20.145
2. Ausleihungen an verbundene Unternehmen	2.265	2.895
3. Beteiligungen an assoziierten Unternehmen	2.598	2.007
4. Beteiligungen	571	713
5. Ausleihungen an Unternehmen, mit denen ein Beteiligungsverhältnis besteht	1.100	1.070
6. Wertpapiere des Anlagevermögens	1.065	1.067
7. Sonstige Ausleihungen	2.351	2.471
	33.673	**30.368**
	245.545	**231.844**
B. UMLAUFVERMÖGEN		
I. Vorräte		
1. Roh-, Hilfs- und Betriebsstoffe	15.688	16.934
2. Unfertige Erzeugnisse, unfertige Leistungen	24.984	17.522
3. Fertige Erzeugnisse und Waren	869.525	796.154
4. Geleistete Anzahlungen	1.213	4.511
	911.410	**835.121**
II. Forderungen und sonstige Vermögensgegenstände		
1. Forderungen aus Lieferungen und Leistungen	374.641	401.669
2. Forderungen gegen verbundene Unternehmen	1.744	2.417
3. Forderungen gegen Unternehmen, mit denen ein Beteiligungsverhältnis besteht	156	271

	31.12.96	31.12.95
4. Sonstige Vermögensgegenstände	24.551	47.799
	401.092	**452.156**
III. Wertpapiere: Sonstige Wertpapiere	76	31
IV. Schecks, Kassenbestand, Postbankguthaben, Guthaben bei Kreditinstituten	25.643	19.112
	1.338.221	**1.306.420**
C. RECHNUNGSABGRENZUNGSPOSTEN	8.192	5.003
	1.591.958	**1.543.267**

PASSIVA	31.12.96	31.12.95
	TDM	**TDM**
A. EIGENKAPITAL		
I. Gezeichnetes Kapital	50.400	50.400
II. Kapitalrücklage	125.700	125.700
III. Gewinnrücklagen		
1. Rücklage für Anteile eines herrschenden Unternehmens	19.140	18.710
2. Andere Gewinnrücklagen	67.882	66.013
	87.022	**84.723**
IV. Konzernbilanzgewinn	6.773	6.586
V. Anteile anderer Gesellschafter	7.312	7.440
	277.207	**274.849**
B. SONDERPOSTEN MIT RÜCKLAGEANTEIL	2.377	1.265
C. RÜCKSTELLUNGEN		
1. Rückstellungen für Pensionen	123.337	137.377
2. Steuerrückstellungen	560	1.390
3. Sonstige Rückstellungen	117.020	119.475
	240.917	**258.242**
D. VERBINDLICHKEITEN		
1. Verbindlichkeiten gegenüber Kreditinstituten	526.184	462.945
2. Erhaltene Anzahlungen auf Bestellungen	44.119	42.632
3. Verbindlichkeiten aus Lieferungen und Leistungen	321.765	310.770
4. Verbindlichkeiten aus der Annahme gezogener Wechsel und der Ausstellung eigener Wechsel	0	259
5. Verbindlichkeiten gegenüber verbundenen Unternehmen	1.488	1.112
6. Verbindlichkeiten gegenüber Unternehmen, mit denen ein Beteiligungsverhältnis besteht	8	6
7. Sonstige Verbindlichkeiten	174.744	179.311
	1.068.308	**997.035**
E. RECHNUNGSABGRENZUNGSPOSTEN	3.149	11.876
	1.591.958	**1.543.267**

Berufsbezeichnungen in der Wirtschaft/
Job titles used in commerce

in Deutschland *in Germany*	in Großbritannien und in den Vereinigten Staaten *in the UK and US*
Abteilungsleiter,in *m,f*	department head, departmental manager, division head, section head
Agenturvertreter,in *m,f*	agency representative
Aktieninhaber,in *m,f*	shareholder *BrE*, stockholder *AmE*
Aktionär,in *m,f*	shareholder *BrE*, stockholder *AmE*
Anlagenverwalter,in *m,f*	asset manager
Anteilseigner,in *m,f*	shareholder *BrE*, stockholder *AmE*
Assistent,in *m,f* im Rechnungswesen	assistant controller
Atelierleiter,in *m,f*	art manager
Aufseher,in *m,f*	supervisor
Aufsichtsbeamte(r) *m* [decl. as adj], Aufsichtsbeamtin *f*	*public sector* supervisor
Aufsichtsratsvorsitzende(r) *mf* [decl. as adj]	chairman of the board, chairman of the supervisory board
Aufsichtsratmitglied *nt*	top executive
Ausbildende(r) *mf* [decl. as adj]	training officer
Ausbildungsleiter,in *m,f*	training officer
Außendienstleiter,in *m,f*	field sales manager
Baustellenleiter,in *m,f*	site foreman
Berater,in *m,f*	consultant
Bereichsleiter,in *m,f*	area manager, division head, division manager, divisional director
beschränkt haftender Gesellschafter *m*, beschränkt haftende Gesellschafterin *f*	limited partner
Betriebsführer,in *m,f*	plant manager
Betriebsleiter,in *m,f*	chief operating officer, manager, operational manager, plant manager, production manager, works manager
Bürochef,in *m,f*	chief clerk, head clerk, office manager, senior clerk
Büroleiter,in *m,f*	chief clerk, head clerk, office manager, senior clerk
Chef,in *m,f* Management	chief operating officer
Chef,in *m,f* des Rechnungswesens	controller, comptroller
Chefkonstrukteur,in *m,f*	chief designer
Chefsekretär,in *m,f*	personal assistant
Direktor,in *m,f*	director, manager
Direktor,in *m,f* Export	export director
Direktor,in *m,f* ohne Geschäftsbereich	non-executive director, outside director
Direktor,in *m,f* der Produktionsabteilung	production director, production manager
Direktor,in *m,f* der technischen Abteilung	technical director
Direktor,in *m,f* der Werbeabteilung	advertising director
Disponent *m*	procurement manager
ehrenamtlicher Präsident *m*, ehrenamtliche Präsidentin *f*	honorary president *BrE*
Ehrenpräsident,in *m,f*	honorary president *BrE*
Ehrenvorsitzende(r) *mf* [decl. as adj]	honorary chairman

in Deutschland *in Germany*	in Großbritannien und in den Vereinigten Staaten *in the UK and US*
Ehrenvorsitzende(r) *mf* [decl. as adj] des Verwaltungsrats	honorary chairman of the board of directors
Eigentümer-Unternehmer,in *m,f*	owner-manager
Einkäufer,in *m,f*	procurement manager
Einkaufschef,in *m,f*	chief buyer, purchasing executive
Einkaufsleiter,in *m,f*	head buyer, purchasing manager
Ermittlungsbeamte(r) *m* [decl. as adj], Ermittlungsbeamtin *f*	investigation officer
erster Vizepräsident *m*, erste Vizepräsidentin *f*	first vice-president
Exportdirektor,in *m,f*	export director
Exportleiter,in *m,f*	export manager
Exportsachbearbeiter,in *m,f*	export coordinator
Fabrikationsleiter,in *m,f*	production manager
Fabrikleiter,in *m,f*	plant manager
Fahrdienstleiter,in *m,f*	traffic superintendent
Fertigungsleiter,in *m,f*	production manager
Finanzdirektor,in *m,f*	treasurer *AmE*
Finanzleiter,in *m,f*	financial manager
Finanzvorstand *m*	vice-president finance *AmE*, financial director, financial executive
Forschungsdirektor,in *m,f*	research director
Fuhrparkleiter,in *m,f*	fleet manager, motor transport officer
Führungskraft *f* mit Linienfunktion	line executive
Gebietsleiter,in *m,f*	area manager, regional manager, territory manager
gehobene Führungskraft *f*	senior executive
Gemeindedirektor,in *m,f*	chief executive

Generaldirektor,in *m,f*	chief executive, director general, general executive
	    manager, president, *insurance* general manager,
	    managing director *BrE*

geschäftsführender Direktor *m*, geschäftsführende Direktorin *f*	executive director
geschäftsführender Gesellschafter *m*, geschäftsführende Gesellschafterin *f*	managing partner
geschäftsführender Vizepräsident *m*, geschäftsführende Vizepräsidentin *f*	executive vice-president
Geschäftsführer,in *m,f*	director, *shop* manager
Gesellschafter,in *m,f*	partner
Gesprächsleiter,in *m,f*	chair
Großkunden-Betreuer,in *m,f*	national accounts manager
Gruppenleiter,in *m,f*	team leader
Handlungsbevollmächtigte(r) *mf* [decl. as adj]	registered manager
Hauptbuchhalter,in *m,f*	chief accountant
Haupteinkäufer,in *mf*	chief buyer, head buyer
Hauptgeschäftsführer,in *m,f*	general manager, managing director *BrE*, chief operating officer
Herstellungsleiter,in *m,f*	production manager
höhere(r) Beamte(r) *m* [decl. as adj], höhere Beamtin *f*	*public sector* senior officer
höhere(r) Staatsbeamte(r) *m* [decl. as adj], höhere Staatsbeamtin *f*	senior civil servant
Importdirektor,in *m,f*	import director
Importleiter,in *m,f*	import manager
Inspektor,in *m,f*	inspector
Kassenführer,in *m,f*	cash manager
Kontrolleur,in *m,f*	supervisor
Importverkaufsleiter,in *m,f*	import sales executive
Innendienst-Verkaufsleiter,in *m,f*	indoor sales manager

in Deutschland *in Germany*	in Großbritannien und in den Vereinigten Staaten *in the UK and US*
kaufmännischer Direktor *m*, kaufmännische Direktorin *f*	commercial director
kaufmännischer Leiter *m*, kaufmännische Leiterin *f*	commercial manager
Kodirektor,in *m,f*	co-director, co-manager
Kolonnenführer,in *m,f*	group leader
Kommanditist,in *m,f*	limited partner
Komplementär,in *m,f*	*in limited partnership* general partner
Kontakter,in *m,f*	*PR, advertising, finance* account executive
Koordinator,in *m,f* Arbeitgeber-Arbeitnehmer-Interessen	director of labour relations *BrE*, director of labor relations *AmE*, industrial relations director, industrial relations manager
Koordinator,in *m,f* Export	export coordinator
Kreditsachbearbeiter,in *m,f*	credit controller
Kundendienstleiter,in *m,f*	customer relations manager, customer service manager
Kundenbetreuer,in *m,f*	account manager
Kundendienstleiter,in *m,f*	after-sales manager, consumer relations manager
Lagerkontrolleur,in *m,f*	stock controller
Lagerverwalter,in *m,f*	stock controller
leitende(r) Angestellte(r) *mf* [decl. as adj]	executive, executive manager, executive officer, senior executive, *commercial* general manager *BrE*
leitende(r) Büroangestellte(r) *mf* [decl. as adj]	chief clerk, head clerk, senior clerk
leitender Direktor *m*, leitende Direktorin *f*	chief executive, managing director *BrE*
leitender Inspektor *m*, leitende Inspektorin *f*	general manager *BrE*, chief inspector
leitender Mitarbeiter *m* der Geschäftsführung, leitende Mitarbeiterin *f* der Geschäftsführung	senior manager
leitender Vorarbeiter *m*, leitende Vorarbeiterin *f*	head foreman
Leiter,in *m,f*	director, manager
Leiter,in *m,f* der Ablauforganisation	operational manager
Leiter,in *m,f* Abteilung Design	chief designer
Leiter,in *m,f* der Abteilung Marketing	marketing director
Leiter,in *m,f* der Beschaffungsabteilung	procurement manager
Leiter,in *m,f* im eigenen Betrieb	owner-manager
Leiter,in *m,f* der Entwicklungsabteilung	development director, development manager
Leiter,in *m,f* Export	export manager
Leiter,in *m,f* der Forschungsabteilung	research director
Leiter,in *m,f* Marketing Export	export marketing manager
Leiter,in *m,f* für Öffentlichkeitsarbeit	director of public relations
Leiter,in *m,f* der Personalabteilung	personnel director, head of personnel
Leiter,in *m,f* der Rechtsabteilung	head of legal department *BrE*, general counsel *AmE*
Leiter,in *m,f* der Schadenabteilung	claims manager
Leiter,in *m,f* der technischen Abteilung	engineering manager
Leiter,in *m,f* der Verkaufsförderungsabteilung	merchandising director
Leiter,in *m,f* Vertrieb und Entwicklung	commercial and development manager
Leiter,in *m,f* des Wareneingangs	traffic manager
Linienmanager,in *m,f*	line executive, line manager
Manager,in *m,f*	manager
Manager,in *m,f* in Ausbildung	trainee manager
Markenbetreuer,in *m,f*	brand manager, product manager
Marketingdirektor,in *m,f*	marketing director
Marketing-Sachbearbeiter,in *m,f*	marketing officer
Meister,in *m,f*	foreman
Mitdirektor,in *m,f*	co-director, co-manager, joint director, joint manager
Miteigentümer,in *m,f*	co-owner
Mitglied *nt* des Aufsichtsrats	member of the supervisory board
Mitglied *nt* des Verwaltungsrats	member of the board of management
mittlere Führungskraft *f*	middle manager

in Deutschland *in Germany*	in Großbritannien und in den Vereinigten Staaten *in the UK and US*
Nachlaßverwalter,in *m,f*	*estate, inheritance* administrator
nachrückende Führungskraft *f*	junior manager
nebenamtlicher Geschäftsführer *m*, nebenamtliche	
Geschäftsführerin *f*	non-executive director, outside director
oberste Führungskraft *f*	top executive
oberste(r) Verwaltungsbeamte(r) *m* [decl. as adj],	
oberste Verwaltungsbeamtin *f*	chief executive
Personalbeschaffung *f*	recruitment consultant
Personalchef,in *m,f*	personnel director, head of personnel, staff manager
Personaldirektor,in *m,f*	personnel director
Personalleiter,in *m,f*	personnel director, head of personnel, staff manager
Personalreferent,in *m,f*	personnel officer
persönlich haftender Gesellschafter *m*, persönlich	
haftende Gesellschafterin *f*	*in limited partnership* general partner
PR-Berater,in *m,f*	public relations executive, public relations officer
PR-Direktor,in *m,f*	director of public relations
PR-Sachbearbeiter,in *m,f*	public relations executive, public relations officer
Präsident,in *m,f*	president
Pressereferent,in *m,f*	press officer
Pressesprecher,in *m,f*	press officer
Privatsekretär,in *m,f*	confidential secretary, personal secretary, private secretary
Produktionsarbeiter,in *m,f*	production worker
Produktionsdirektor,in *m,f*	production director
Produktionsleiter,in *m,f*	line manager, production director, production manager, product manager
Produktmanager,in *m,f*	product manager
Projektleiter,in *m,f*	project leader, project manager
Projektmanager,in *m,f*	project manager
Prokurist,in *m,f*	registered manager
ranghöchster Exportsachbearbeiter *m*, ranghöchste	
Exportsachbearbeiterin *f*	senior export clerk
ranghöchster Importsachbearbeiter *m*, ranghöchste	
Importsachbearbeiterin *f*	senior import clerk
ranghöchster stellvertretender Generaldirektor *m*,	
ranghöchste stellvertretende Generaldirektorin *f*	senior vice-president *AmE*
ranghöchster Stellvertreter *m* des Vorstands-	
vorsitzenden, ranghöchste Stellvertreterin *f* des	
Vorstandsvorsitzenden	senior vice-president *AmE*
ranghöchster Vizepräsident *m*, ranghöchste	
Vizepräsidentin *f*	senior vice-president *AmE*
Referent,in *m,f* für Öffentlichkeitsarbeit	*public sector* information officer
Sachbearbeiter,in *m,f*	executive
Sachbearbeiter,in *m,f* für Einfuhrpapiere	import documentation supervisor
Sachbearbeiter,in *m,f* im Importverkauf	industrial relations director
Sachbearbeiter,in *m,f* im Verkauf	sales executive
Sachbearbeiter,in *m,f* eines Werbeetats	*PR, advertising* account executive
Schadensbeauftragte(r) *mf* [decl. as adj]	claims inspector
Spartenmanager,in *m,f*	division head, division manager
Staatssekretär,in *m,f*	undersecretary of state
stellvertretender Abteilungsleiter *m*, stellvertretende	assistant head of section *BrE*, assistant section head
Abteilungsleiterin *f*	*BrE*, deputy head of department, assistant manager
stellvertretender Direktor *m*, stellvertretende	assistant director, assistant manager, deputy director,
Direktorin *f*	deputy manager
stellvertretender Gemeindedirektor *m*, stellvertretende	
Gemeindedirektorin *f*	*public sector* deputy chief executive

in Deutschland *in Germany*	in Großbritannien und in den Vereinigten Staaten *in the UK and US*
stellvertretender Generaldirektor *m*, stellvertretende Generaldirektorin *f*	deputy chief executive, deputy managing director, assistant director general, assistant general manager
stellvertretender Geschäftsführer *m*, stellvertretende Geschäftsführerin *f*	*shop* assistant manager
stellvertretender Hauptgeschäftsführer *m*, stellvertretende Hauptgeschäftsführerin *f*	deputy chief executive, deputy managing director
stellvertretender Leiter *m*, stellvertretende Leiterin *f*	deputy director, deputy manager
stellvertretendes Mitglied *nt* des Verwaltungsrats	deputy member of the board of management
stellvertretender Tagungsleiter *m*, stellvertretende Tagungsleiterin *f*	vice-chairman
stellvertretender Versammlungsleiter *m*, stellvertretende Versammlungsleiterin *f*	vice-chairman
stellvertretende(r) Verwaltungsratsvorsitzende(r) *mf* [decl. as adj]	deputy chairman of the board of management
stellvertretende(r) Vorsitzende(r) *mf* [decl. as adj]	deputy chairman, vice-chairman
stellvertretende(r) Vorsitzende(r) *mf* [decl. as adj] des Aufsichtsrats	deputy chairman of the supervisory board
stellvertretender Vorstand *m* der Geschäftsleitung	deputy chairman of the board of management
Syndikus *m*	general counsel *AmE*
Systemverwalter,in *m,f*	*software* administrator
Tagungsleiter,in *m,f*	chairman, chairperson
Teamleiter,in *m,f*	team leader
technischer Direktor *m*, technische Direktorin *f*	technical director
technischer Leiter *m*, technische Leiterin *f*	technical manager
Teilhaber,in *m,f*	partner
Terminüberwacher,in *m,f*	traffic manager
unmittelbare(r) Vorgesetzte(r) *mf* [decl. as adj]	first-line supervisor
Verkaufschef,in *m,f*	sales director, sales manager
Verkaufsdirektor,in *m,f*	sales manager
Verkaufsleiter,in *m,f*	sales director, sales manager
Vermögensverwalter,in *m,f*	asset manager
Versammlungsleiter *m*	chairman, chairperson
Versammlungsleiterin *f*	chairwoman, chairperson
Versandleiter,in *m,f*	traffic manager, transport controller
Versandleitung *f*	traffic executive
Vertragsbearbeiter,in *m,f*	contracts officer
Vertragsleiter,in *m,f*	contracts manager, distribution manager
Vertriebschef,in *m,f*	sales manager
Vertriebsdirektor,in *m,f*	sales director, sales manager
Vertriebsleiter,in *m,f*	sales manager
Verwalter,in *m,f*	administrator
Verwaltungsangestellte(r) *mf* [decl. as adj]	*commerce* administration officer
Verwaltungsbeamte(r) *m* [decl. as adj], Verwaltungsbeamtin *f*	*public sector* administration officer
Verwaltungsfachmann *m*, Verwaltungsfachfrau *f*	administrator
Verwaltungsleiter,in *m,f*	administrator
Verwaltungsratsvorsitzende(r) *mf* [decl. as adj]	chairman of the administrative board, chairman of the board of directors, chairman of the board of management
Vizepräsident,in *m,f*	vice-president (veep *AmE*)
Vorarbeiter,in *m,f*	foreman, supervisor, overseer, *construction industry* charge hand
Vorarbeiter,in *m,f* der Produktion	line supervisor
Vorsitzende(r) *mf* [decl. as adj]	chair, chairman, chairwoman, chairperson, president
Vorsitzender und Generaldirektor *m*, Vorsitzende und Generaldirektorin *f*	chairman and general manager

in Deutschland *in Germany*	in Großbritannien und in den Vereinigten Staaten *in the UK and US*
Vorsitzender und geschäftsführender Direktor *m*, Vorsitzende und geschäftsführende Direktorin *f*	chairman and managing director *BrE*
Vorsitzender und Hauptgeschäftsführer *m*, Vorsitzende und Hauptgeschäftsführerin *f*	chairman and general manager
Vorstand *m* der Geschäftsleitung	chairman of the board of directors, chairman of the board of management
Vorstandsmitglied *nt*	director

Vorstandsvorsitzende(r) *mf* [decl. as adj]	chairman and managing director *BrE*, chairman and
	    chief executive *AmE*, chairman of the executive
	    committee

Werbeleiter,in *m,f*	advertising manager, publicity manager
Werksleiter,in *m,f*	plant manager, works manager

Börsenplätze/Stock exchanges

Deutscher Name *German name*	Land, Stadt *Country, city*	Englischer Name *English name*
	Deutschland *Germany*	
Baden-Württembergische Wertpapierbörse zu Stuttgart	Stuttgart	Stuttgart Securities Exchange
Bayerische Börse	München	Bavarian Stock Exchange
Berliner Wertpapierbörse	Berlin	Berlin Securities Exchange
Deutsche Börse	Frankfurt	German Stock Exchange
Deutsche Terminbörse (DTB)	Frankfurt	German Futures Exchange
Hamburger Kaffeebörse	Hamburg	Hamburg Coffee Exchange
Hanseatische Wertpapierbörse	Hamburg	Hanseatic Securities Exchange
Niedersächsische Börse zu Hannover	Hannover	Hanover Stock Exchange
Rheinisch-Westfälische Börse	Düsseldorf	Düsseldorf Stock Exchange
	Österreich *Austria*	
Wiener Börsenkammer	Wien	Viennese Stock Exchange
	Schweiz *Switzerland*	
Genfer Börse	Genf	Geneva Stock Exchange
Schweizer Börse für Optionen und Finanztermine	Zürich	Swiss Options and Financial Futures Exchange
Züricher Börse	Zürich	Zürich Stock Exchange
	Frankreich *France*	
Pariser Börse	Paris	Paris Stock Exchange
Pariser Finanzterminbörse	Paris	Paris Financial Futures Exchange
Pariser Handelsoptionsbörse	Paris	Paris Trader Options Exchange

Finanz- und Wirtschaftsindizes/
Financial and economic indexes

Deutscher Name	Englischer Name
German name	*English name*

Allgemeiner Anwendungsbereich

Aktienindex *m*	share index, stock index
Aktienpreisindex *m*	share price index, stock price index
allgemeiner leitender Index *m*	composite leading index
Anspannungsindex *m*	employment index
Arbeitslosenzahl *f*	unemployment rate
Arbeitslosenziffer *f*	unemployment rate
Baukostenindex *m*	construction cost index
Börsenindex *m*	market index, stock market index
Börsenkursindex *m*	stock exchange price index
Börsenpreisindex *m*	stock market price index
bereinigter Index *m*	adjusted index
Beschäftigungsindex *m*	employment index
Besoldungsgruppe *f*	salary grade
Bruttosozialprodukt *nt*	gross national product
Bruttovolkseinkommen *nt*	gross national income
Diffusionsindex *m*	diffusion index
Einzelhandelspreisindex *m*	retail price index
Elendsindex *m*	discomfort index, misery index
Erzeugerpreisindex *m*	producer price index
Gehaltsklasse *f*	salary grade
Gehaltsstufe *f*	salary grade
Gesamtführungsindex *m*	composite index
gewichteter Börsenindex *m*	price-weighted index
gewichteter Index *m*	weighted index
gewogener Index *m*	weighted index
Großhandelspreisindex *m*	wholesale price index
Handelsbilanz *f*	balance of trade
Herfindahl-Hirschman-Index *m*	Herfindahl-Hirschman index
impliziter Preisindex *m*	implied price index
Index *m* der Frühindikatoren	index of leading indicators
Index *m* der Spätindikatoren	index of lagging indicators
Indexbindung *f*	index linking, index linkage
Indexkoppelung *f*	index linking, index linkage
Indexverbindung *f*	index linking, index linkage
Indexzahl *f*	index number
Inflationsrate *f*	rate of inflation
Kurspreisindex *m*	share price index, stock price index
Laspeyres-Preisindex *m*	Laspeyre's index
Lebenshaltungsindex *m*	cost-of-living index
Lebenshaltungskostenindex *m*	cost-of-living index
Lerner-Index *m*	Lerner index
Mengenindex *m*	volume index

Deutscher Name *German name*	Englischer Name *English name*
Nettosozialprodukt *nt*	net national product
Paasche-Index *m*	Paasche index
Preisindex *m*	price index
Preisindex *m* für die Lebenshaltung	cost-of-living index
Preisindexniveau *m*	price index level
Problemindex *m*	discomfort index, misery index
Pro-Kopf-Einkommen *nt*	income per capita
Rentenindex *m*	bond index
Staatsausgaben *f pl*	national expenditure
Verbraucherpreisindex *m*	consumer price index
Wachstumsindex *m*	growth index
zusammengesetzter Index *m*	composite index
zusammengesetzter Index *m* der Frühindikatoren	composite leading index
Asien	
Wertpapierbörsenindex *m* von Thailand	SET index
Australien	
Stammaktienindex	All Ordinaries Index
Deutschland	
Deutscher Aktienindex *m* (DAX)	German shares index
FAZ Index *m*	index of the Frankfurter Allgemeine Zeitung
Europa	
Eurodollar-Index *m*	Eurodollar Index
Finnland	
Unitas Gesamtaktienindex *m*	Unitas All Share Index
Großbritannien	
Financial Times Index *m*	Financial Times Index (FT Index)
Index *m* der industriellen Produktion	Index of Industrial Production
Hong Kong	
Hang Seng Index *m*	Hang Seng Index
International	
Divisia-Geldindex *m*	Divisia money Index
Morgan Stanley internationaler Welt-Kapital-Index *m*	Morgan Stanley Capital International World Index
Italien	
Comit-Index *m*	Comit index
Neuseeland	
Barclays Index *m*	Barclays Index
Niederlande	
CBS-Tendenzindex *m*	CBS Tendency Index
Vereinigte Staaten	
Dow-Jones Index *m*	Dow-Jones index
New Yorker Börsengesamtindex *m*	New York Stock Exchange Composite Index

Länder/Countries

Land *Country*	Haupstadt *Capital*	Einwohner *Inhabitant*	Offizielle Sprache(n) *Official language(s)*	Währung *Currency*
Afghanistan *nt*	Kabul *nt*	Afghane *m*, Afghanin *f*	Paschtu, Dari	Afghani *m*
Afghanistan	*Kabul*	*Afghan*	*Pushtu, Dari*	*afghani*
Ägypten *nt*	Kairo *nt*	Ägypter,in *m,f*	Arabisch	ägyptisches Pfund *nt*
Egypt	*Cairo*	*Egyptian*	*Arabic*	*Egyptian pound*
Albanien *nt*	Tirana *nt*	Albaner,in *m,f*	Albanisch/Toskisch	Lek *m*
Albania	*Tirana*	*Albanian*	*Albanian*	*lek*
Algerien *nt*	Algier *nt*	Algerier,in *m,f*	Arabisch, Französisch	Algerischer Dinar *m*
Algeria	*Algiers*	*Algerian*	*Arabic, French*	*dinar*
Andorra *nt*	Andorra la Vella *nt*	Andorraner,in *m,f*	Katalanisch, Französisch, Spanisch	Französischer Franc *m*, Spanische Peseta *f*
Andorra	*Andorra la Vella*	*Andorran*	*Catalan, French, Spanish*	*French franc, peseta*
Angola *nt*	Luanda *nt*	Angolaner,in *m,f*	Portugiesisch	Neuer Kwanza *m*
Angola	*Luanda*	*Angolan*	*Portuguese*	*New kwanza*
Antigua und Barbuda *pl*	St. Johns *nt*	Antiguaner,in *m,f*, Barbudianer,in *m,f*	Englisch	Ostkaribischer Dollar *m*
Antigua and Barbuda	*St. John's*	*Antiguan, Barbudian*	*English*	*East Caribbean dollar*
Äquatorial-Guinea/Malabo *nt* Äquatorialguinea *nt*		aus Äquatorial-Guinea	Spanisch	CFA-Franc *m*
Equatorial Guinea	*Malabo*	*Equatorial Guinean*	*Spanish*	*C.F.A. franc*
Argentinien *nt*	Buenos Aires *nt*	Argentinier,in *m,f*	Spanisch	Peso *m*
Argentina	*Buenos Aires*	*Argentinian/Argentine*	*Spanish*	*peso*
Armenien *nt*	Jerewan *nt*	Armenier,in *m,f*	Armenisch	Dram *m*
Armenia	*Yerevan*	*Armenian*	*Armenian*	*dram*
Aserbaidshan/ Aserbeidshan *nt*	Baku *nt*	Aserbaidschaner,in *m,fl* Aserbeidschaner,in *m,f*	Aseri, Russisch, Türkisch	Manat *m*
Azerbaijan	*Baku*	*Azeri/Azerbaijani*	*Azeri, Russian, Turkish*	*manat*
Äthiopien *nt*	Addis Abeba *nt*	Äthiopier,in *m,f*	Amharisch	Birr *m*
Ethiopia	*Addis Ababa*	*Ethiopian*	*Amharic*	*birr*
Australien *nt*	Canberra *nt*	Australier,in *m,f*	Englisch	Australischer Dollar *m*
Australia	*Canberra*	*Australian*	*English*	*Australian dollar*
die Bahamas *pl*	Nassau *nt*	Bahamer,in *m,fl* Bahamaner,in *m,f*	Englisch	Bahama-Dollar *m*
Bahamas	*Nassau*	*Bahamian*	*English*	*Bahamian dollar*
Bahrain *nt*	Manama *nt*	Bahrainer,in *m,f*	Arabisch	Bahrain-Dinar *m*
Bahrain/Bahrein	*Manama*	*Bahraini*	*Arabic*	*dinar*
Bangladesch *nt*	Dacca *nt*	Bangladeshi *mf*	Bengali	Taka *m*
Bangladesh	*Dhaka*	*Bangladeshi*	*Bengali*	*taka*
Barbados *nt*	Bridgetown *nt*	Barbadier,in *m,f*	Englisch	Barbados-Dollar *m*
Barbados	*Bridgetown*	*Barbadian*	*English*	*Barbados dollar*
Belgien *nt*	Brüssel *nt*	Belgier,in *m,f*	Französisch, Flämisch, Deutsch	Belgischer Franc *m*
Belgium	*Brussels*	*Belgian*	*French, Flemish, German*	*Belgian franc*
Belize *nt*	Belmopan *nt*	Belizer,in *m,f*	Englisch, Spanisch, Kreolisch	Belize-Dollar *m*
Belize	*Belmopan*	*Belizean*	*English, Spanish, Creole*	*Belize dollar*

Land *Country*	Haupstadt *Capital*	Einwohner *Inhabitant*	Offizielle Sprache(n) *Official language(s)*	Währung *Currency*
Benin *nt*	Porto Novo *nt*	Beniner,in *m,f*	Französisch	CFA-Franc *m*
Benin	*Porto Novo*	*Beninese*	*French*	*C.F.A. franc*
die Bermudas/ Bermudainseln *pl*	Hamilton *nt*	von den Bermudas	Englisch	US-Dollar *m*
Bermuda	*Hamilton*	*Bermudan/Bermudian*	*English*	*US dollar*
Bhutan *nt*	Thimphu *nt*	Bhutaner,in *m,f*	Dzonga	Ngultrum *m*, indische Rupie *f*
Bhutan	*Thamphu*	*Bhutanese/Bhutani*	*Dzongka*	*ngultrum, Indian rupee*
Bolivien *nt*	La Paz *nt*	Bolivianer,in *m,f*	Spanisch, indianische Sprachen	Boliviano *m*
Bolivia	*La Paz*	*Bolivian*	*Spanish, Indian languages*	*Bolivianio*
Bosnien-Herzegovina *nt*	Sarajevo *nt*	Bosnier,in *m,f*	Serbokroatisch	Dinar *m*
Bosnia-Herzegovina	*Sarajevo*	*Bosnian*	*Serbo-Croat*	*dinar*
Botswana *nt*	Gaborone *nt*	Botswaner,in *m,f*	Englisch, Setswana	Pula *m*
Botswana	*Gaborone*	*Botswanan*	*English, Setswana*	*pula*
Brasilien *nt*	Brasilia *nt*	Brazilianer,in *m,f*	Portugiesisch	Cruzeiro Real *m*
Brazil	*Brasilia*	*Brazilian*	*Portuguese*	*cruzeiro real*
Brunei *nt*	Bandar Seri Begawan *nt*	Bruneier,in *m,f*	Malaiisch, Englisch	Brunei-Dollar *m*
Brunei	*Bandar Seri Begawan*	*Brunei/Bruneian*	*Malay, English*	*Brunei dollar*
Bulgarien *nt*	Sofia *nt*	Bulgare *m*, Bulgarin *f*	Bulgarisch	Lew *m*
Bulgaria	*Sofia*	*Bulgarian*	*Bulgarian*	*lev*
Burkina Faso *nt*	Ouagadougou *nt*	Burkiner,in *m,f*	Französisch, Mossi	CFA-Franc *m*
Burkina Faso	*Ouagadougou*	*Burkinabe*	*French, Mossi*	*C.F.A. franc*
Burundi *nt*	Bujumbura *nt*	Burundier,in *m,f*	Ki-Rundi, Französisch	Burundi-Franc *m*
Burundi	*Bujumbura*	*Burundian*	*Kirundi, French*	*Burundi franc*
Chile *nt*	Santiago *nt*	Chilene *m*, Chilenin *f*	Spanisch	Chilenischer Peso *m*
Chile	*Santiago*	*Chilean*	*Spanish*	*peso*
China *nt*	Peking *nt*	Chinese *m*, Chinesin *f*	Mandarin, chinesische Sprachen	Renminbi Yuan *m*
China	*Beijing/Peking*	*Chinese*	*Mandarin, Chinese languages*	*Renminbi yuan*
Costa Rica *nt*	San José *nt*	Costaricaner,in *m,f*	Spanisch	Costa-Rica-Colón *m*
Costa Rica	*San José*	*Costa Rican*	*Spanish*	*colón*
Dänemark *nt*	Kopenhagen *nt*	Däne *m*, Dänin *f*	Dänisch	Dänische Krone *f*
Denmark	*Copenhagen*	*Dane*	*Danish*	*Danish krone*
Deutschland *nt*	Berlin *nt*	Deutsche(r) *mf* [decl. as adj]	Deutsch	Deutsche Mark *f*
Germany	*Berlin*	*German*	*German*	*German Mark*
Djibouti/ Dschibuti *nt*	Djibouti/ Dschibuti *nt*	aus Djibouti	Arabisch, Französisch	Franc *m* de Djibouti
Djibouti	*Djibouti*	*Djibuti/Djibutian*	*Arabic, French*	*Djibouti franc*
Dominica *nt*	Roseau *nt*	aus Dominica	Englisch	Ostkaribischer Dollar *m*
Dominica	*Roseau*	*Dominican*	*English*	*East Caribbean dollar*
die Dominikanische Republik *f*	Santo Domingo *nt*	Dominikaner,in *m,f*	Spanisch	Dominikanischer Peso *m*
Dominican Republic	*Santo Domingo*	*Dominican*	*Spanish*	*Dominican peso*

Land _Country_	Haupstadt _Capital_	Einwohner _Inhabitant_	Offizielle Sprache(n) _Official language(s)_	Währung _Currency_
Ecuador/ Ekuador _nt_	Quito _nt_	Ecuadorianer,in _m,f/_ Ekuadorianer,in _m,f_	Spanisch	Sucre _m_
Ecuador	_Quito_	_Ecuadorian/ Ecuadoran_	_Spanish_	_sucre_
die Elfenbeinküste/ Côte-d'Ivoire _f_	Yamoussoukro _nt_	von der Elfenbeinküste	Französisch	CFA-Franc _m_
Ivory Coast	_Yamoussoukro_	_Ivorian_	_French_	_C.F.A. franc_
El Salvador _nt_	San Salvador _nt_	Salvadorianer,in _m,f_	Spanisch	El-Salvador-Colón _m_
El Salvador	_San Salvador_	_Salvadoran/Salvadorean_	_Spanish_	_colón_
England _nt_	London _nt_	Engländer,in _m,f_	Englisch	Pfund Sterling _nt_
England	_London_	_Englishman, English-woman_	_English_	_Sterling pound_
Eritrea _nt_	Asmara _nt_	Eritreer,in _m,f_	Arabisch, Englisch	Birr _m_
Eritrea	_Asmara_	_Eritrean_	_Arabic, Englisch_	_Ethiopian birr_
Estland _nt_	Tallinn _nt_	Este _m_, Estin _f_	Estnisch	Estnische Krone _f_
Estonia	_Tallinn_	_Estonian_	_Estonian_	_kroon_
die Fidschiinseln _pl_	Suva _nt_	Fidschianer,in _m,f_	Englisch	Fidschi-Dollar _m_
Fiji	_Suva_	_Fijian_	_English_	_Fiji dollar_
Finnland _nt_	Helsinki _nt_	Finne _m_, Finnin _f_	Finnisch, Schwedisch	Finnmark _f_
Finland	_Helsinki_	_Finn_	_Finnish, Swedish_	_markka_
Frankreich _nt_	Paris _nt_	Franzose _m_, Französin _f_	Französisch	Französischer Franc _m_
France	_Paris_	_Frenchman, Frenchwoman_	_French_	_French franc_
Gabun _nt_	Libreville _nt_	Gabuner,in _m,f_	Französisch	CFA-Franc _m_
Gabon	_Libreville_	_Gabonese_	_French_	_C.F.A. franc_
Gambia _nt_	Banjul _nt_	Gambier,in _m,f_	Englisch	Dalasi _m_
Gambia	_Banjul_	_Gambian_	_English_	_dalasi_
Georgien _nt_	Tiflis _nt_	Georgier,in _m,f_	Georgisch	Kupon _m_
Georgia	_Tbilisi_	_Georgian_	_Georgian_	_Kupon_
Ghana _nt_	Accra _nt_	Ghanaer,in _m,f_	Englisch	Cedi _m_
Ghana	_Accra_	_Ghanaian_	_English_	_cedi_
Grenada _nt_	St. George's _nt_	von Grenada	Englisch	Ostkaribischer Dollar _m_
Grenada	_St. George's_	_Grenadian_	_English_	_East Caribbean dollar_
Griechenland _nt_	Athen _nt_	Grieche _m_, Griechin _f_	Griechisch	Drachme _f_
Greece	_Athens_	_Greek_	_Greek_	_drachma_
Guatemala _nt_	Guatemala-Stadt _nt_	Guatemalteke _m_, Guatemaltekin _f_	Spanisch	Quetzal _m_
Guatemala	_Guatemala City_	_Guatemalan_	_Spanish_	_quetzal_
Guinea _nt_	Conakry _nt_	Guineer,in _m,f_	Französisch	Guinea-Franc _m_
Guinea	_Conakry_	_Guinean_	_French_	_Guinean franc_
Guinea-Bissau _nt_	Bissau _nt_	aus Guinea-Bissau	Spanisch	Guinea-Bissau Peso _m_
Guinea-Bissau	_Bissau_	_from Guinea-Bissau_	_Spanish_	_Guinea-Bissau peso_
Guyana _nt_	Georgetown _nt_	Guyaner,in _m,f_	Englisch	Guyana-Dollar _m_
Guyana	_Georgetown_	_Guyanese/Guyanan_	_English_	_Guyana dollar_
Haiti _nt_	Port-au-Prince _nt_	Haitianer,in _m,f_	Französisch	Gourde _m_
Haiti	_Port-au-Prince_	_Haitian_	_French_	_gourde_
Honduras _nt_	Tegucigalpa _nt_	Honduraner,in _m,f_	Spanisch	Lempira _m_
Honduras	_Tegucigalpa_	_Honduran_	_Spanish_	_lempira_

| Land | Haupstadt | Einwohner | Offizielle Sprache(n) | Währung |
Country	Capital	Inhabitant	Official language(s)	Currency
Hong Kong *nt*	Victoria *nt*	aus Hong Kong	Englisch	Hong-Kong-Dollar *m*
Hong Kong	*Victoria*	*from Hong Kong*	*English*	*Hong Kong dollar*
Indien *nt*	Neu-Delhi *nt*	Inder,in *m,f*	Hindi, Englisch	Indische Rupie *f*
India	*New Delhi*	*Indian*	*Hindi, English*	*Indian rupee*
Indonesien *nt*	Jakarta *nt*	Indonesier,in *m,f*	Bahasa Indonesisch	Rupiah *f*
Indonesia	*Jakarta*	*Indonesian*	*Bahasa Indonesia*	*Indonesian rupiah*
der Iran *m*	Teheran *nt*	Iraner,in *m,f*	Iranisch	Rial *m*
Iran	*Tehran/Teheran*	*Iranian*	*Iranian*	*rial*
der Irak *m*	Bagdad *nt*	Iraker,in *m,f*	Arabisch	Irak-Dinar *m*
Iraq/Irak	*Baghdad*	*Iraqi/Iraki*	*Arabic*	*Iraqi dinar/Iraki dinar*
Irland *nt*	Dublin *nt*	Ire *m*, Irin *f l* Irländer,in *m,f*	Gälisch, Englisch	Irisches Pfund *nt*
Ireland	*Dublin*	*Irishman, Irishwoman*	*Irish Gaelic, English*	*Irish pound/punt*
Island *nt*	Reykjavik *nt*	Isländer,in *m,f*	Isländisch	Isländische Krone *f*
Iceland	*Reykjavik*	*Icelander*	*Icelandic*	*Icelandic krona*
Israel *nt*	Jerusalem *nt*	Israeli *mf*	Hebräisch, Arabisch	Neuer Israel Schekel *m*
Israel	*Jerusalem*	*Israeli*	*Hebrew, Arabic*	*New shekel*
Italien *nt*	Rom *nt*	Italiener,in *m,f*	Italienisch	Italienische Lira *f*
Italy	*Rome*	*Italian*	*Italian*	*lira*
Jamaika *nt*	Kingston *nt*	Jamaikaner,in *m,f*	Englisch	Jamaika-Dollar *m*
Jamaica	*Kingston*	*Jamaican*	*English*	*Jamaica dollar*
Japan *nt*	Tokio *nt*	Japaner,in *m,f*	Japanisch	Yen *m*
Japan	*Tokyo*	*Japanese*	*Japanese*	*yen*
der Jemen *m*	Sana *nt*	Jemenit,in *m,f*	Arabisch	Jemen-Rial *m*
Yemen	*San'a*	*Yemeni*	*Arabic*	*Yemeni dinar*
Jordanien *nt*	Amman *nt*	Jordaner,in *m,f*	Arabisch	Jordan-Dinar *m*
Jordan	*Amman*	*Jordanian*	*Arabic*	*Jordan dinar*
Kambodscha *nt*	Phnom Penh *nt*	Kambodschaner,in *m,f*	Khmer	Riel *m*
Cambodia	*Phnom Penh*	*Cambodian*	*Khmer*	*riel*
Kamerun *nt*	Yaoundé *nt*	Kameruner,in *m,f*	Französisch, Englisch	CFA-Franc *m*
Cameroon	*Yaoundé*	*Cameroonian*	*French, English*	*C.F.A. franc*
Kanada *nt*	Ottawa *nt*	Kanadier,in *m,f*	Englisch, Französisch	Kanadischer Dollar *m*
Canada	*Ottawa*	*Canadian*	*English, French*	*Canadian dollar*
die Kapverden/ Kapverdische Inseln *pl*	Praia *nt*	Kapverdier, in *m,f*	Portugiesisch	Kap-Verde-Escudo *m*
Cape Verde Islands	*Praia*	*Cape Verdean*	*Portuguese*	*Cape Verde escudo*
Kasachstan *nt*	Almaty *nt*	Kasache *m*, Kasachin *f*	Kasachisch	Tenge *m*
Kazakhstan	*Alma-Ata*	*Kazakh/Kazak*	*Kazakh*	*Tenge*
Katar *nt*	Dauha *nt*	aus Katar	Arabisch	Katar-Riyal *m*
Qatar	*Doha*	*Qatari*	*Arabic*	*Qatar riyal*
Kenia *nt*	Nairobi *nt*	Kenianer,in *m,f*	Swahili, Englisch	Kenia-Schilling *m*
Kenya	*Nairobi*	*Kenyan*	*Swahili, English*	*shilling*
Kirgistan *nt*	Bischkek *nt*	Kirgise *m*, Kirgisin *f*	Kirgisisch *nt*	Kirgistan Som *m*
Kyrgyzstan	*Bishkek*	*Kyrgyz*	*Kyrgyz*	*som*
Kiribati	Bairiki *nt*	aus Kiribati	Englisch, Gilbertesisch	Australischer Dollar *m*
Kiribati	*Bairiki*	*from Kiribati*	*English, Gilbertese*	*Australian dollar*

Land	Haupstadt	Einwohner	Offizielle Sprache(n)	Währung
Country	*Capital*	*Inhabitant*	*Official language(s)*	*Currency*
Kolumbien *nt*	Bogota *nt*	Kolumbianer,in *m,f*	Spanisch *nt*	Kolumbianischer Peso *m*
Colombia	*Bogotá*	*Colombian*	*Spanish*	*peso*
die Komoren *pl*	Moroni *nt*	Komorer,in *m,f*	Französisch, Arabisch	Komoren-Franc *m*
Comoros	*Moroni*	*Comorian/Comoran*	*French, Arabic*	*Comorian franc*
Kongo *m*	Brazzaville *nt*	Kongolese *m*, Kongolesin *f*	Französisch	CFA-Franc *m*
Congo	*Brazzaville*	*Congolese*	*French*	*C.F.A. franc*
Kroatien *nt*	Zagreb *nt*	Kroate *m*, Kroatin *f*	Serbokroatisch	Kuna *m*
Croatia	*Zagreb*	*Croat/Croatian*	*Serbo-Croat*	*kuna*
Kuba *nt*	Havanna *nt*	Kubaner,in *m,f*	Spanisch	Kubanischer Peso *m*
Cuba	*Havana*	*Cuban*	*Spanish*	*Cuban peso*
Kuwait *nt*	Kuwait-Stadt *nt*	Kuwaiter,in *m,f*	Arabisch	Kuwait-Dinar *m*
Kuwait	*Kuwait City*	*Kuwaiti*	*Arabic*	*Kuwaiti dinar*
Laos *nt*	Vientiane *nt*	Laote *m*, Laotin *f*	Lao	Kip *m*
Laos	*Vientiane*	*Laotian*	*Lao*	*kip*
Lesotho *nt*	Maseru *nt*	Lesother,in *m,f*	Sotho, Englisch	Loti *m*
Lesotho	*Maseru*	*Mosotho/Basotho*	*Sotho, English*	*loti*
Lettland *nt*	Riga *nt*	Lette *m*, Lettin *f*	Lettisch	Lat *m*
Latvia	*Riga*	*Latvian*	*Latvian*	*lats*
Libanon *nt*	Beirut *nt*	Libanese *m*, Libanesin *f*	Arabisch	Libanesisches Pfund *nt*
Lebanon	*Beirut*	*Lebanese*	*Arabic*	*Lebanese pound*
Liberien *nt*	Monrovia *nt*	Liberianer,in *m,f/* Liberier,in *m,f*	Englisch	Liberianischer Dollar *m*
Liberia	*Monrovia*	*Liberian*	*English*	*Liberian dollar*
Libyen *nt*	Tripolis *nt*	Libyer,in *m,f*	Arabisch	Libyscher Dinar *m*
Libya	*Tripoli*	*Libyan*	*Arabic*	*Libyan dinar*
Liechtenstein *nt*	Vaduz *nt*	Liechtensteiner,in *m,f*	Deutsch	Schweizer Franken *m*
Liechtenstein	*Vaduz*	*Liechtensteiner*	*German*	*Swiss franc*
Litauen *nt*	Vilnius/Wilna *nt*	Litauer,in *m,f*	Litauisch	Litas *m*
Lithuania	*Vilnius*	*Lithuanian*	*Lithuanian*	*litas*
Luxemburg *nt*	Luxemburg *nt*	Luxemburger,in *m,f*	Französisch, Deutsch	Luxemburgischer Franc *m*
Luxembourg	*Luxembourg*	*Luxemburger*	*French, German*	*Luxembourg franc*
Madagaskar *nt*	Antananarivo *nt*	Madegasse *m*, Madegassin *f*	Malagassy, Französisch	Madagaskar-Franc *m*
Madagascar	*Antananarivo*	*Madagascan*	*Malagasy, French*	*Malagasy franc*
Makedonien/ Mazedonien *nt*	Skopje *nt*	Makedonier,in *m,f/* Mazedonier,in *m,f*	Makedonisch/ Mazedonisch	Makedonischer Dinar *m*
Macedonia	*Skopje*	*Macedonian*	*Macedonian*	*dinar*
Malawi *nt*	Lilongwe *nt*	Malawier,in *m,f*	Englisch	Malawi-Kwacha *m*
Malawi	*Lilongwe*	*Malawian*	*English*	*kwacha*
Malaysia *nt*	Kuala Lumpur *nt*	Malaysier,in *m,f*	Malaiisch	Ringgit *m*
Malaysia	*Kuala Lumpur*	*Malaysian/Malay*	*Malay*	*Malaysian ringgit*
die Malediven *pl*	Malé *nt*	Maledive *m*, Maledevin *f*	Divehi	Rufiyaa *f*
Maldives	*Malé*	*Maldivian*	*Divehi*	*Maldivian rupee*
Mali *nt*	Bamako *nt*	Malier,in *m,f*	Französisch	CFA-Franc *m*
Mali	*Bamako*	*Malian*	*French*	*C.F.A. franc*
Malta *nt*	Valletta *nt*	Malteser,in *m,f*	Maltesisch, Englisch	Maltesische Lira *nt*
Malta	*Valletta*	*Maltese*	*Maltese, English*	*Maltese lira*

Land *Country*	Haupstadt *Capital*	Einwohner *Inhabitant*	Offizielle Sprache(n) *Official language(s)*	Währung *Currency*
Marokko *nt*	Rabat *nt*	Marokkaner,in *m,f*	Arabisch, Französisch	Dirham *m*
Morocco	*Rabat*	*Moroccan*	*Arabic, French*	*dirham*
die Marshall- Inseln *pl*	Dalap-Uliga- Darrit *nt*	von den Marshall- Inseln	Kajin-Majol	US-Dollar *m*
Marshall Islands	*Dalap-Uliga- Darrit*	*from the Marshall Islands*	*Marshallese/Kahjin- Majol*	*US dollar*
Mauretanien *nt*	Nouakchott *nt*	Mauretanier,in *m,f*	Arabisch, Französisch	Ouguiya *nt*
Mauritania	*Nouakchott*	*Mauritanian*	*Arabic, French*	*ouguiya*
Mauritius *nt*	Port Louis *nt*	Mauritier,in *m,f*	Englisch, Französisch	Mauritius-Rupie *f*
Mauritius	*Port Louis*	*Mauritian*	*English, French*	*Mauritian rupee*
Mexiko *nt*	Mexiko-Stadt *nt*	Mexikaner,in *m,f*	Spanisch	Neuer Mexika- nischer Peso *m*
Mexico	*Mexico City*	*Mexican*	*Spanish*	*Mexican new peso*
Mikronesien *nt*	Kolonia	aus Mikronesien	Englisch	US-Dollar *m*
Micronesia	*Kolonia*	*from Micronesia*	*English*	*US dollar*
Moldawien *nt*	Kischinew *nt*	Moldawier,in *m,f*	Rumänisch	Lei *m*
Moldova	*Kishinyev*	*Moldovan*	*Romanian/Rumanian*	*Moldovan leu*
Monaco *nt*	Monaco-Ville *nt*	Monegasse *m*, Monegassin *f*	Französisch	Französischer Franc *m*
Monaco	*Monaco*	*Monegasque*	*French*	*French franc*
die Mongolei *f*	Ulan Bator *nt*	Mongole *m*, Mongolin *f*	Mongolisch	Tugrik *m*
Mongolia	*Ulaanbaatar/ Ulan Bator*	*Mongolian*	*Khalkha, Mongol*	*tugrik*
Montenegro *nt*	Podgorica *nt*	Montenegriner,in *m,f*	Serbokroatisch	Dinar *m*
Montenegro	*Podgorica*	*Montenegrin*	*Serbo-Croat*	*dinar*
Mozambique/ Mosambik *nt*	Maputo *nt*	aus Mozambique	Portugiesisch	Metical *m*
Mozambique	*Maputo*	*Mozambican*	*Portuguese*	*metical*
Myanmar/ Burma *nt*	Yangon/Rangun *nt*	Birmane *m*, Birmanin *f*/ Burmese *m*, Burmesin *f*	Birmanisch/Burmesisch	Kyat *m*
Myanmar/Burma	*Yangon/Rangoon*	*Burmese*	*Burmese*	*kyat*
Namibia *nt*	Windhuk *nt*	Namibier,in *m,f*	Englisch, Afrikaans	Namibischer Dollar *m*
Namibia	*Windhoek*	*Namibian*	*English, Afrikaans*	*Namibian dollar*
Nauru *nt*	Yaren *nt*	Nauruer,in *m,f*	Englisch, Nauruisch	Australischer Dollar *m*
Nauru	*Yaren District*	*from Nauru*	*English, Naurian*	*Australian dollar*
Nepal *nt*	Katmandu *nt*	Nepalese *m*, Nepalesin *f*	Nepalesisch, Nepali	Nepalesische Rupie *f*
Nepal	*Kathmandu*	*Nepalese, Nepali*	*Nepali*	*Nepali rupee*
Neuseeland *nt*	Wellington *nt*	Neuseeländer,in *m,f*	Englisch, Maori	Neuseeland-Dollar *m*
New Zealand	*Wellington*	*New Zealander*	*English, Maori*	*New Zealand dollar*
Nicaragua *nt*	Managua *nt*	Nicaraguaner,in *m,f*	Spanisch	Córdoba *m*
Nicaragua	*Managua*	*Nicaraguan*	*Spanish*	*cordoba*
die Niederlande *pl*/Holland *nt*	Amsterdam	Niederländer,in *m,f*/ Holländer,in *m,f*	Niederländisch	Gulden *m*
the Netherlands/ Holland	*Amsterdam*	*Dutchman, Dutch- woman/Netherlander*	*Dutch*	*guilder*
Niger *nt*	Niamey *nt*	Nigrer,in *m,f*	Französisch	CFA-Franc *m*
Niger	*Niamey*	*from Niger*	*French*	*C.F.A. franc*
Nigeria *nt*	Abuja *nt*	Nigerianer,in *m,f*	Englisch	Naira *m*
Nigeria	*Abuja*	*Nigerian*	*English*	*naira*
Nordirland *nt*	Belfast *nt*	Irländer,in *m,f*/ Ire *m*, Irin *f*	Gälisch, Englisch	Pfund Sterling *nt*
Northern Ireland	*Belfast*	*Irishman, Irishwoman*	*Irish Gaelic, English*	*Sterling pound*

| Land | Haupstadt | Einwohner | Offizielle Sprache(n) | Währung |
Country	*Capital*	*Inhabitant*	*Official language(s)*	*Currency*
Nordkorea *nt*	Pjöngyang *nt*	Nordkoreaner,in *m,f*	Koreanisch	Won *m*
North Korea	*Pyongyang*	*North Korean*	*Korean*	*won*
Norwegen *nt*	Oslo *nt*	Norweger,in *m,f*	Norwegisch	Norwegische Krone *f*
Norway	*Oslo*	*Norse (pl only)*	*Norwegian*	*Norwegian krone*
Oman *nt*	Maskat *nt*	Omaner,in *m,f*	Arabisch	Rial Omani *m*
Oman	*Muscat*	*Omani*	*Arabic*	*Omani rial*
Österreich *nt*	Wien *nt*	Österreicher,in *m,f*	Deutsch	Österreichischer Schilling *m*
Austria	*Vienna*	*Austrian*	*German*	*schilling*
Pakistan *nt*	Islamabad *nt*	Pakistani *mfl* Pakistaner,in *m,f*	Urdu, Englisch	Pakistanische Rupie *f*
Pakistan	*Islamabad*	*Pakistani*	*Urdu, English*	*Pakistan rupee*
Panama *nt*	Panama-Stadt *nt*	Panamaer,in *m,fl* Panamese *m*, Panamesin *f*	Spanisch	Balboa *m*
Panama	*Panama City*	*Panamanian*	*Spanish*	*balboa*
Papua-Neuguinea *nt*	Port Moresby *nt*	Papua *mf*	Englisch	Kina *m*
Papua New Guinea	*Port Moresby*	*from Papua New Guinea/Papuan*	*English*	*kina*
Paraguay *nt*	Asunción *nt*	Paraguayer,in *m,f*	Spanisch	Guarani *m*
Paraguay	*Asunción*	*Paraguayan*	*Spanish*	*guarani*
Peru *nt*	Lima *nt*	Peruaner,in *m,f*	Spanisch, Ketschua	Nuevo Sol *m*
Peru	*Lima*	*Peruvian*	*Spanish, Quechua*	*nuevo sol*
die Philippinen *pl*	Manila *nt*	Filipino *mfl* Philippine *m*, Philippinin *f*	Filipino, Englisch	Philippinischer Peso *m*
Philippines	*Manila*	*Philippine/Filipino*	*Filipino, English*	*Philippine peso*
Polen *nt*	Warschau *nt*	Pole *m*, Polin *f*	Polnisch	Zloty *m*
Poland	*Warsaw*	*Pole*	*Polish*	*zloty*
Portugal *nt*	Lissabon *nt*	Portugiese *m*, Portugiesin *f*	Portugiesisch	Escudo *m*
Portugal	*Lisbon*	*Portuguese*	*Portuguese*	*escudo*
Puerto Rico *nt*	San Juan *nt*	Puertoricaner,in *m,f*	Spanisch, Englisch	US-Dollar *m*
Puerto Rico	*San Juan*	*Puerto Rican*	*Spanish, English*	*US dollar*
Ruanda/Rwanda *nt*	Kigali *nt*	Ruander,in *m,fl* Rwander,in *m,f*	Französisch, Kinyarwanda	Rwanda-Franc *m*
Rwanda	*Kigali*	*Rwandan, Rwandese*	*French, Kinyarwanda*	*Rwanda franc*
Rumänien *nt*	Bukarest *nt*	Rumäne *m*, Rumänin *f*	Rumänisch	Lei *m*
Romania/Rumania	*Bucharest*	*Romanian/Rumanian*	*Romanian/Rumanian*	*Romanian leu*
Rußland *nt*	Moskau *nt*	Russe *m*, Russin *f*	Russisch	Rubel *m*
Russia	*Moscow*	*Russian*	*Russian*	*rouble*
Saint Kitts und Nevis *pl*	Basseterre *nt*	von Saint Kitts und Nevis	Englisch	Ostkaribischer Dollar *m*
Saint Kitts and Nevis	*Basseterre*	*from Saint Kitts and Nevis*	*English*	*East Caribbean dollar*
Saint Lucia *nt*	Castries *nt*	von Saint Lucia	Englisch	Ostkaribischer Dollar *m*
Saint Lucia	*Castries*	*Saint Lucian*	*English*	*East Caribbean dollar*

Land	Haupstadt	Einwohner	Offizielle Sprache(n)	Währung
Country	*Capital*	*Inhabitant*	*Official language(s)*	*Currency*
Saint Vincent *nt* und die Grenadinen *pl*	Kingstown *nt*	von Saint Vincent und den Grenadinen	Englisch	Ostkaribischer Dollar *m*
Saint Vincent and the Grenadines	*Kingstown*	*Vincentian*	*English*	*East Caribbean dollar*
die Salomonen *pl*	Honiara *nt*	von den Salomonen	Englisch	Salomonen-Dollar *m*
Solomon Islands	*Honiara*	*from the Solomon Islands*	*English*	*Solomon Islands dollar*
Sambia *nt*	Lusaka *nt*	Sambesi *mf*	Englisch *nt*	Kwacha *m*
Zambia	*Lusaka*	*Zambian*	*English*	*kwacha*
San Marino *nt*	San Marino *nt*	Sanmarinese *m*, Sanmarinesin *f*	Italienisch *nt*	Italienische Lira *f*
San Marino	*San Marino*	*San Marinese*	*Italian*	*Italian lira*
São Tomé und Principe *nt*	São Tomé *nt*	von São Tomé	Portugiesisch	Dobra *m*
São Tomé and Principe	*São Tomé*	*from São Tomé*	*Portuguese*	*dobra*
Saudi-Arabien *nt*	Riad *nt*	Saudi *mfl* Saudiaraber,in *m,f*	Arabisch	Saudi-Riyal *m*
Saudi Arabia	*Riyadh*	*Saudi/Saudi Arabian*	*Arabic*	*riyal*
Schottland *nt*	Edinburg *nt*	Schotte *m*, Schottin *f*	Englisch	Pfund Sterling *nt*
Scotland	*Edinburgh*	*Scot/Scotsman, Scotswoman*	*English*	*Sterling pound*
Schweden *nt*	Stockholm *nt*	Schwede *m*, Schwedin *f*	Schwedisch	Schwedische Krone *f*
Sweden	*Stockholm*	*Swede*	*Swedish*	*Swedish krona*
die Schweiz *f*	Bern *nt*	Schweizer,in *m,f*	Französisch, Deutsch, Italienisch	Schweizer Franken *m*
Switzerland	*Bern*	*Swiss*	*French, German, Italian*	*Swiss franc*
Senegal *nt*	Dakar *nt*	Senegalese *m*, Senegalesin *f*	Französisch	CFA-Franc *m*
Senegal	*Dakar*	*Senegalese*	*French*	*C.F.A. franc*
Serbien *nt*	Belgrad *nt*	Serbe *m*, Serbin *f*	Serbokroatisch	Dinar *m*
Serbia	*Belgrade*	*Serb*	*Serbo-Croat*	*dinar*
die Seychellen *pl*	Victoria *nt*	von den Seychellen	Englisch, Französisch, Kreolisch	Seychellen-Rupie *f*
Seychelles	*Victoria*	*Seychellois/Seselwa*	*English, French, Creole*	*Seychelles rupee*
Sierra Leone *f*	Freetown *nt*	Sierraleoner,in *m,f*	Englisch	Leone *m*
Sierra Leone	*Freetown*	*Sierra Leonean*	*English*	*leone*
Singapur *nt*	Singapur *nt*	Singapurer,in *m,f*	Englisch, Malaiisch, chinesische Sprachen, Tamil	Singapur-Dollar *m*
Singapore	*Singapore*	*Singaporean*	*English, Malay, Chinese languages, Tamil*	*Singapore dollar*
die Slowakei *f*	Bratislava/ Preßburg *nt*	Slowake *m*, Slowakin *f*	Slowakisch	Slowakische Krone *f*
Slovakia	*Bratislava*	*Slovak*	*Slovak*	*Slovak koruna*
Slowenien *nt*	Ljubljana/ Laibach *nt*	Slowenier,in *m,fl* Slowene *m*, Slowenin *f*	Slowenisch	Tolar *m*
Slovenia	*Ljubljana*	*Slovenian/Slovene*	*Slovene*	*tolar*
Somalia *nt*	Mogadishu *nt*	Somali *mfl* Somalier,in *m,f*	Somali, Arabisch	Somalia-Shilling *m*
Somalia	*Mogadishu*	*Somali*	*Somali, Arabic*	*Somali shilling*
Spanien *nt*	Madrid *nt*	Spanier,in *m,f*	Spanisch	Peseta *f*
Spain	*Madrid*	*Spaniard*	*Spanish*	*peseta*

Land / *Country*	Haupstadt / *Capital*	Einwohner / *Inhabitant*	Offizielle Sprache(n) / *Official language(s)*	Währung / *Currency*
Sri Lanka *nt*	Colombo *nt*	Srilanker,in *m,f*	Singhalesisch, Tamil, Englisch	Sri-Lanka-Rupie *f*
Sri Lanka	*Colombo*	*Sri Lankan*	*Singhalese, Tamil, English*	*Sri Lanka rupee*
Südafrika *nt*	Pretoria *nt*	Südafrikaner,in *m,f*	Afrikaans, Englisch	Rand *m*
South Africa	*Pretoria*	*South African*	*Afrikaans, English*	*rand*
Sudan *nt*	Khartum *nt*	Sudaner,in *m,fl* Sudanese *m,* Sudanesin *f*	Arabisch	Sudanesisches Pfund *nt*
Sudan	*Khartoum*	*Sudanese*	*Arabic*	*Sudanese pound*
Südkorea *nt*	Seoul *nt*	Südkoreaner,in *m,f*	Koreanisch	Won *m*
South Korea	*Seoul*	*South Korean*	*Korean*	*won*
Surinam *nt*	Paramaribo *nt*	Surinamer,in *m,f*	Niederländisch, Englisch	Surinam-Gulden *m*
Surinam	*Paramaribo*	*Surinamese*	*Dutch, English*	*Surinam guilder*
Swasiland *nt*	Mbabane *nt*	Swasi *mf*	Swazi, Englisch	Lilangeni *m*
Swaziland	*Mbabane*	*Swazi*	*Si-Suati, English*	*lilangeni*
Syrien *nt*	Damaskus *nt*	Syrier,in *m,fl* Syrer,in *m,f*	Arabisch	Syrisches Pfund *nt*
Syria	*Damascus*	*Syrian*	*Arabic*	*Syrian pound*
Tadschikistan *nt*	Duschanbe *nt*	Tadschike *m,* Tadschikin *f*	Tadschikisch	Rubel *m*
Tajikistan	*Dushanbe*	*Tajik*	*Tajik*	*rouble*
Taiwan *nt*	Taipeh *nt*	Taiwaner,in *m,f*	Mandarin, chinesische Sprachen	Taiwan-Dollar *m*
Taiwan	*Taipei*	*Taiwanese*	*Mandarin, Chinese languages*	*Taiwan dollar*
Tansania *nt*	Dodoma *nt*	Tansanier,in *m,f*	Swahili, Englisch	Tanzania-Schilling *m*
Tanzania	*Dodoma*	*Tanzanian*	*Swahili, English*	*Tanzanian shilling*
Thailand *nt*	Bangkok *nt*	Thailänder,in *m,fl* Thai *mf*	Thai	Baht *m*
Thailand	*Bangkok*	*Thai*	*Thai*	*baht*
Togo *nt*	Lomé *nt*	Togoer,in *m,f*	Französisch	CFA-Franc *m*
Togo	*Lomé*	*Togolese*	*French*	*C.F.A. franc*
Tonga *nt*	Nuku'alofa *nt*	Tongaer,in *m,f*	Englisch, Tonga	La'anga *m*
Tonga	*Nuku'alofa*	*Tongan*	*English, Tongan*	*pa'anga*
Trinidad und Tobago *nt*	Port of Spain *nt*	von Trinidad und Tobago	Englisch	Trinidad-und-Tobago-Dollar *m*
Trinidad and Tobago	*Port of Spain*	*Trinidadian, Tobagoan/Tobagodian*	*English*	*Trinidad and Tobago dollar*
der Tschad *m*	N'Djamena *nt*	Tschader,in *m,f*	Arabisch, Französisch	CFA-Franc *m*
Chad	*N'Djamena*	*Chadian*	*Arabic, French*	*C.F.A. franc*
die Tschechische Republik *f*	Prag *nt*	Tscheche *m*, Tschechin *f*	Tschechisch	Tschechische Krone *f*
Czech Republic	*Prague*	*Czech*	*Czech*	*Czech koruna*
Tunesien *nt*	Tunis *nt*	Tunesier,in *m,f*	Arabisch	Tunesischer Dinar *m*
Tunisia	*Tunis*	*Tunisian*	*Arabic*	*dinar*
die Türkei *f*	Ankara *nt*	Türke *m*, Türkin *f*	Türkisch	Türkische Lira *f*
Turkey	*Ankara*	*Turk*	*Turkish*	*Turkish lira*
Turkmenistan *nt*	Aschchabad *nt*	Turkmene *m,* Turkmenin *f*	Turkmenisch	Manat *m*
Turkmenistan	*Ashkhabad*	*Turkmen*	*Turkmen*	*Turkmenian manat*
Tuvalu *nt/* Ellice-Inseln *pl*	Funafuti *nt*	Tuvaluer,in *m,f*	Englisch	Australischer Dollar *m*
Tuvalu	*Funafuti*	*from Tuvalu*	*English*	*Australian dollar*

Land *Country*	Haupstadt *Capital*	Einwohner *Inhabitant*	Offizielle Sprache(n) *Official language(s)*	Währung *Currency*
Uganda *nt*	Kampala *nt*	Ugander,in *m,f*	Swahili, Englisch	Uganda-Shilling *m*
Uganda	*Kampala*	*Ugandan*	*Swahili, English*	*Uganda shilling*
die Ukraine *f*	Kiew *nt*	Ukrainer,in *m,f*	Ukrainisch	Karbowanez *m*
Ukraine	*Kiev*	*Ukrainian*	*Ukrainian*	*karbovanet*
Ungarn *nt*	Budapest *nt*	Ungar,in *m,f*	Ungarisch	Forint *m*
Hungary	*Budapest*	*Hungarian*	*Hungarian*	*forint*
Uruguay *nt*	Montevideo *nt*	Uruguayer,in *m,f*	Spanisch	Peso Uruguayo *m*
Uruguay	*Montevideo*	*Uruguayan*	*Spanish*	*peso*
Usbekistan *nt*	Taschkent *nt*	Usbeke *m*, Usbekin *f*	Usbekisch	Usbekistan-Sum *m*
Uzbekistan	*Tashkent*	*Uzbek*	*Uzbek*	*som*
Vanuatu *nt/* Neue Hebriden *pl*	Vila *nt*	aus Vanuatu	Englisch, Französisch, Bislama	Vatu *m*
Vanuatu	*Port Vila*	*from Vanuatu*	*English, French, Bislama*	*vatu*
Venezuela *nt*	Caracas *nt*	Venezolaner,in *m,f*	Spanisch	Bolivar *m*
Venezuela	*Caracas*	*Venezuelan*	*Spanish*	*bolivar*
die Vereinigten Arabischen Emirate *nt pl*	Abu Dhabi *nt*	aus den Vereinigten Arabischen Emiraten	Arabisch	Dirham *m*
United Arab *Emirates*	*Abu Dhabi*	*from the United Arab* *Emirates*	*Arabic*	*dirham*
Vereinigtes Königreich/ Großbritannien *nt*	London *nt*	Brite *m*, Britin *f*	Englisch	Pfund Sterling *nt*
United Kingdom/ *Great Britain*	*London*	*Briton*	*English*	*Sterling pound*
die Vereinigte Staaten *m pl* von Amerika	Washington, D.C. *nt*	Amerikaner,in *m,f*	Englisch	US-Dollar *m*
United States of *America*	*Washington, D.C.*	*American*	*English*	*dollar*
Vietnam *nt*	Hanoi *nt*	Vietnamese *m*, Vietnamesin *f*	Vietnamesisch	Dong *m*
Vietnam	*Hanoi*	*Vietnamese*	*Vietnamese*	*dong*
Wales *nt*	Cardiff *nt*	Waliser,in *m,f*	Englisch, Walisisch	Pfund Sterling *nt*
Wales	*Cardiff*	*Welshman, Welshwoman*	*English, Welsh*	*Sterling pound*
Weißrußland *nt*	Minsk *nt*	Weißrusse *m*, Weißrussin *f*	Weißrussisch	Weißrussischer Rubel *m*
Belarus	*Minsk*	*Belarussian*	*Belarussian*	*Belarussian rouble*
Westsamoa *nt*	Apia *nt*	aus Westsamoa	Englisch, Samoanisch	Tala *m*
Western Samoa	*Apia*	*from Western Samoa*	*English, Samoan*	*tala*
Zaire/Zaïre *nt*	Kinshasa *nt*	Zairer,in *m,f*	Französisch	Neuer Zaïre *m*
Zaïre	*Kinshasha*	*Zaïrese/Zairean*	*French*	*New zaïre*
die Zentralafrika- nische Republik *f*	Bangui *nt*	aus der Zentralafrikanischen Republik	Französisch, Sango	CFA-Franc *m*
Central African *Republic*	*Bangui*	*from the Central African* *Republic*	*French, Sango*	*C.F.A. franc*
Zimbabwe/ Simbabwe *nt*	Harare *nt*	Zimbabwer,in *m,f/* Simbabwer,in *m,f*	Englisch	Zimbabwe-Dollar *m*
Zimbabwe	*Harare*	*Zimbabwean*	*English*	*Zimbabwe dollar*
Zypern *nt*	Nikosia *nt*	Zypriot,in *m,f*	Griechisch, Türkisch	Zypern-Pfund *nt*
Cyprus	*Nicosia*	*Cypriot*	*Greek, Turkish*	*Cyprus pound*

Alle Sprachen in dieser Tabelle sind neutrum/All languages listed in this table are neuter

Kardinal- und Ordinalzahlen/ Cardinal and ordinal numbers

Kardinalzahlen *Cardinal*	Deutsch *German*	Englisch *English*	Ordinalzahlen *Ordinal*	Deutsch *German*	Englisch *English*
1	eins	one	1.	erste	first
2	zwei	two	2.	zweite	second
3	drei	three	3.	dritte	third
4	vier	four	4.	vierte	fourth
5	fünf	five	5.	fünfte	fifth
6	sechs	six	6.	sechste	sixth
7	sieben	seven	7.	siebte	seventh
8	acht	eight	8.	achte	eighth
9	neun	nine	9.	neunte	ninth
10	zehn	ten	10.	zehnte	tenth
11	elf	eleven	11.	elfte	eleventh
12	zwölf	twelve	12.	zwölfte	twelfth
13	dreizehn	thirteen	13.	dreizehnte	thirteenth
14	vierzehn	fourteen	14.	vierzehnte	fourteenth
15	fünfzehn	fifteen	15.	fünfzehnte	fifteenth
16	sechzehn	sixteen	16.	sechzehnte	sixteenth
17	siebzehn	seventeen	17.	siebzehnte	seventeenth
18	achtzehn	eighteen	18.	achtzehnte	eighteenth
19	neunzehn	nineteen	19.	neunzehnte	nineteenth
20	zwanzig	twenty	20.	zwanzigste	twentieth
21	einundzwanzig	twenty-one	21.	einundzwanzigste	twenty-first
22	zweiundzwanzig	twenty-two	22.	zweiundzwanzigste	twenty-second
23	dreiundzwanzig	twenty-three	23.	dreiundzwanzigste	twenty-third
24	vierundzwanzig	twenty-four	24.	vierundzwanzigste	twenty-fourth
25	fünfundzwanzig	twenty-five	25.	fünfundzwanzigste	twenty-fifth
30	dreißig	thirty	30.	dreißigste	thirtieth
40	vierzig	forty	40.	vierzigste	fortieth
50	fünfzig	fifty	50.	fünfzigste	fiftieth
60	sechzig	sixty	60.	sechzigste	sixtieth
70	siebzig	seventy	70.	siebzigste	seventieth
80	achtzig	eighty	80.	achtzigste	eightieth
90	neunzig	ninety	90.	neunzigste	ninetieth
100	(ein)hundert	hundred	100.	(ein)hundertste	one hundredth
101	(ein)hundert- (und)eins	one hundred and one	101.	(ein)hundert- (und)erste	one hundred and first
156	(ein)hundertsechs- undfünfzig	one hundred and fifty-six	156.	(ein)hundertsechs- undfünfzigste	one hundred and fifty- sixth
200	zweihundert	two hundred	200.	zweihundertste	two hundredth
300	dreihundert	three hundred	300.	dreihundertste	three hundredth
400	vierhundert	four hundred	400.	vierhundertste	four hundredth
1 000	(ein)tausend	one thousand	1 000.	(ein)tausendste	one thousandth

Kardinalzahlen _Cardinal_	Deutsch _German_	Englisch _English_	Ordinalzahlen _Ordinal_	Deutsch _German_	Englisch _English_
1 001	(ein)tausend-(und)eins	one thousand and one	1 001.	(ein)tausend-(und)erste	one thousand and first
1 247	eintausend-zweihundert-(und)sieben-undvierzig	one thousand, two hundred and forty-seven	1 247.	(ein)tausend-zweihundert-(und)sieben-undvierzigste	one thousand, two hundred and forty-seventh
2 000	zweitausend	two thousand	2 000.	zweitausendste	two thousandth
3 000	dreitausend	three thousand	3 000.	dreitausendste	three thousandth
10 000	zehntausend	ten thousand	10 000.	zehntausendste	ten thousandth
20 000	zwanzigtausend	twenty thousand	20 000.	zwanzigtausendste	twenty thousandth
100 000	(ein)hunderttausend	one hundred thousand	100 000.	(ein)hundert-tausendste	one hundred thousandth
200 000	zweihunderttausend	two hundred thousand	200 000.	zweihundert-tausendste	two hundred thousandth
1 000 000	eine Million	one million	1 000 000.	(ein)millionste	one millionth
10 000 000	zehn Millionen	ten million(s)			
100 000 000	(ein)hundert Millionen	one hundred million(s)			
1 000 000 000	eine Milliarde	one thousand million(s) (_BrE_) (one billion _AmE_)			
1 000 000 000 000	eine Billion	one billion (_BrE_) (one trillion _AmE_)			

ENGLISH–GERMAN DICTIONARY

WÖRTERBUCH ENGLISCH–DEUTSCH

A

AA *abbr* INS (*average adjuster*) *marine insurance* Dispacheur *m*, Havariekommissar *m*, Schadensregulierer *m*, TRANSP (*Automobile Association*) britischer Kraftfahrerverband, ≈ ADAC (*Allgemeiner Deutscher Automobil-Club*)

AAA *abbr* TRANSP (*American Automobile Association*) amerikanischer Kraftfahrerverband, ≈ ADAC (*Allgemeiner Deutscher Automobil-Club*)

AAAA *abbr* (*American Association of Advertising Agencies*) S&M amerikanischer Verband der Werbeagenturen, ≈ WDW (*Wirtschaftsverband Deutscher Werbeagenturen*)

AAA: ~ **bond** *abbr* (*triple-A bond*) STOCK höchstklassifizierte Schuldverschreibung, Bond *m* bester Bonitätseinstufung

AACCA *abbr* (*Associate of the Association of Certified and Corporate Accountants*) ACC, GEN COMM Mitglied des Verbands der Wirtschaftsprüfer

AAD *abbr* (*at a discount*) S&M mit Rabatt, mit Skonto

AAIA *abbr* (*Associate of the Association of International Accountants*) ACC, GEN COMM Mitglied der Vereinigung der internationalen Wirtschaftsprüfer

AAR *abbr* (*against all risks*) INS gegen alle Gefahren

ABAA *abbr* (*Associate of the British Association of Accountants and Auditors*) ACC, GEN COMM Mitglied des britischen Verbands der Wirtschaftsprüfer und Rechnungsprüfer

abandon *vt* GEN COMM *plan, project* aufgeben, fallenlassen, *right, claim* verzichten auf [+acc], *person, place* verlassen, IMP/EXP *goods in customs* verzichten auf [+acc], INS abandonnieren, LAW *right* aufgeben, überlassen, verzichten auf [+acc], PATENTS fallenlassen, verzichten auf [+acc], STOCK *option* abandonnieren, aufgeben; ♦ ~ **any claim** LAW jeglichen Anspruch fallenlassen; ~ **ship** TRANSP das Schiff aufgeben

abandonee *n* INS, LAW Person, zu deren Gunsten etwas aufgegeben wird, *marine insurance* Empfänger abandonnierter Gegenstände

abandoner *n* INS, LAW *marine insurance* Abandonist *m*

abandonment *n* GEN COMM Verlassen *nt*, HRM Aufgabe *f*, INS *marine* Abandon *m*, Abandonnement *nt*, Preisgabe *f* des Schiffs, Schiffsaufgabe *f*, LAW *of right* Abandon *m*, Preisgabe *f*, Überlassung *f*, Verzicht *m*, PATENTS *of patent right* Aufgabe *f*; ~ **clause** *n* INS Abandonerklärung *f*, Verzichtklausel *f*; ~ **of a complaint** *n* LAW Rücknahme *f* einer Klage, Klagerücknahme *f*; ~ **of a position** *n* HRM Aufgabe *f* einer Stellung

A-base *n* Can ACC Rückstellungen für laufende Projekte

abate *vt* ENVIR abstellen, *noise* bekämpfen, GEN COMM *tax, price* senken, ermäßigen, *nuisance* beheben, LAW *sentence* erlassen, herabsetzen, mindern, *writ, action* einstellen

abated: ~ **contribution** *n* BrE ECON, POL *to the EU* ermäßigter Beitrag *m*

abatement *n* GEN COMM Nachlassen *nt*, Kürzung *f*, *of nuisance* Behebung *f*, *of tax* Ermäßigung *f*, LAW *of contract* Minderung *f*, *of price* Rabatt *m*, Herabsetzung

f, Nachlaß *m*; ~ **of taxes** *n* TAX Steuererlaß *m*, Steuernachlaß *m*

abattoir *n* GEN COMM Schlachthof *m*

abbreviate *vt* GEN COMM, INS abkürzen

abbreviation *n* GEN COMM, INS Abkürzung *f*

ABC *abbr* (*Australian Broadcasting Corporation, American Broadcasting Company*) MEDIA australische bzw. amerikanische Rundfunk- und Fernsehanstalt, ≈ ARD (*Arbeitsgemeinschaft der öffentlich-rechtlichen Rundfunkanstalten der Bundesrepublik Deutschland*)

ABCC *abbr* (*Association of British Chambers of Commerce*) IND Vereinigung der britischen Industrie- und Handelskammern, ≈ DIHT (*Deutscher Industrie- und Handelstag*)

ABC: ~ **method** *n* ADMIN *inventory management* ABC-Verfahren *nt*

abeyance: **be in** ~ *phr* GEN COMM *law, rule* ruhen, in der Schwebe sein, schweben, schwebend sein, in Ungewißheit sein, zeitweilig außer Kraft sein, LAW *property* vorläufig unwirksam sein

abide by *vt* GEN COMM *rule, decision* befolgen, festhalten an [+dat], sich abfinden mit, einhalten

ability *n* GEN COMM Befähigung *f*, Fähigkeit *f*, Geschick *nt*, Können *nt*, Leistungsfähigkeit *f*, HRM Befähigung *f*, Geschick *nt*; ~ **grouping** *n* WEL Eingruppierung *f* nach Leistung, Fähigkeitsgruppe *f*; ~ **level** *n* WEL *of worker, student* Begabungsstufe *f*, Fähigkeitsniveau *nt*, Intelligenzstufe *f*, Leistungsniveau *nt*, Leistungsvermögen *nt*; ~ **to pay** *n* ACC, BANK, ECON, FIN Solvenz *f*, Zahlungsfähigkeit *f*, Zahlungspotential *nt*, HRM, LAW, TAX Zahlungsfähigkeit *f*; ~**-to-pay principle** *n* ECON, TAX *principle of taxation* Zahlungsfähigkeitsprinzip *nt*, Leistungsfähigkeitsprinzip *nt*; ~ **to repay** *n* BANK Rückzahlungsfähigkeit *f*; ~ **to work** *n* ECON, HRM Arbeitsfähigkeit *f*, Erwerbsfähigkeit *f*

able *adj* GEN COMM fähig; ♦ **be ~ to afford to buy sth** ECON sich etw leisten können; **be ~ to meet the demands** GEN COMM den Anforderungen entsprechen; ~ **to pay** GEN COMM solvent, zahlungsfähig; ~ **to work** ECON, HRM arbeitsfähig, erwerbsfähig

abnormal *adj* GEN COMM abnorm, anormal, außergewöhnlich, regelwidrig; ~ **discount** *n* GEN COMM außergewöhnlicher Preisnachlaß *m*; ~ **indivisible load** *n* TRANSP anormale unteilbare Last *f*; ~ **risk** *n* INS anormales Risiko *nt*, erhöhtes Risiko *nt*; ~ **system end** *n* COMP Absturz *m*, Systemzusammenbruch *m*

aboard *adv* IMP/EXP, TRANSP an Bord

abolish *vt* ACC aufheben, ADMIN abschaffen, aufheben, beseitigen, ECON, GEN COMM abbauen, abschaffen, aufheben, beseitigen, LAW abschaffen; ♦ ~ **gradually** GEN COMM abbauen

abolishment *n* ACC, ADMIN Abschaffung *f*, ECON Abschaffung *f*, Aufhebung *f*, GEN COMM, LAW Abschaffung *f*

abolition *n* ACC *of trade control* Abschaffung *f*, Aufhebung *f*, Beseitigung *f*, ADMIN Aufhebung *f*, Beseitigung *f*, ECON Beseitigung *f*, *of job* Vernichtung *f*, *of trade control* Aufhebung *f*, Abschaffung *f*, GEN

COMM *of trade control*, LAW Abschaffung *f*, Beseitigung *f*; **~ of tariffs** *n* ECON Abschaffung *f* von Zöllen, Aufhebung *f* von Zöllen; **~ of trade barriers** *n* ECON Beseitigung *f* von Handelsschranken

abort 1. *n* COMP Abbruch *m*; **2.** *vt* COMP abbrechen, *program, operation* verlassen, GEN COMM *mission, trial, launch* abbrechen, scheitern lassen; **3.** *vi* COMP aussteigen (*infrml*)

abortive: **~ benefits** *n pl* TAX vorzeitige Gewinne *m pl*

about *adv* GEN COMM etwa, ungefähr (*ung.*), zirka (*ca.*), rund (*rd.*)

about: **~-face** *AmE*, **~-turn** *n BrE* GEN COMM, POL Kehrtwendung *f*, Kehrtwende *f*, Schwenkung *f*

above 1. *adj* COMMS, GEN COMM obengenannt, obig, obenerwähnt, vorerwähnt (*obs*); ♦ **the ~ address** *n* COMMS die oben angegebene Adresse *f* (*die o.a. Adresse*) **2.** *adv* COMMS, GEN COMM darüber hinaus, hinaus, oben; **3.** *prep* GEN COMM oberhalb; ♦ **~ average** ECON, GEN COMM über dem Durchschnitt, überdurchschnittlich; **~ board** GEN COMM *action, deal* ehrlich, *person* offen; **~ the line** ACC, FIN *profit and loss accounts* in den schwarzen Zahlen, über dem Strich, im Haben; **~ the norm** GEN COMM *work, produce, quality, knowledge* über der Norm; **~ par** FIN, STOCK über dem Nennwert, über pari; **~ quota** ECON über die Quote hinausgehend

above: **~-average growth** ECON überdurchschnittliches Wachstum *nt*; **~-ground** *adj* ENVIR, IND, TRANSP oberirdisch; **~-market price** *n* STOCK *options on currency futures* Preis *m* über dem Kurswert; **~-mentioned** *adj* COMMS obenerwähnt, obengenannt

ABP *abbr* (*Associated British Ports*) TRANSP Vereinigung britischer Häfen

abreaction: **~ channels** *n pl* COMMS, HRM Abreaktionskanäle *m pl*, MGMNT Möglichkeit *f* zum Abreagieren

abreast: **be ~ of** *phr* GEN COMM *latest developments* auf dem laufenden sein mit, Schritt halten mit; **be ~ of the times** *phr* GEN COMM mit der Zeit gehen, zeitlich auf dem laufenden bleiben

abridge *vt* COMMS *contents* abkürzen, GEN COMM verkürzen

abridgement *n* COMMS *of contents* Abkürzung *f*, GEN COMM Beeinträchtigung *f*, Verkürzung *f*

abroad *adv* GEN COMM im Ausland; ♦ **from ~** GEN COMM ausländisch

abrogate *vt* ADMIN, LAW *contract* aufheben

abrogation *n* ADMIN, LAW *of Community Law* Außerkraftsetzung *f*, Aufhebung *f*

ABS *abbr* (*American Bureau of Shipping*) TRANSP amerikanische Klassifikationsgesellschaft für die Schiffahrt

abscond *vi* LAW *debtor* sich entziehen

absence *n* FIN Fehlen *nt*, GEN COMM *lack* Nichtvorhandensein *nt*, *being elsewhere* Abwesenheit *f*, Fehlen *nt*, Fernbleiben *nt*, Nichterscheinen *nt*, HRM Abwesenheit *f*, LAW *nonappearance* Nichterscheinen *nt*, *non-presence* Abwesenheit *f*; ♦ **in sb's ~** GEN COMM in jds Abwesenheit; **in the ~ of** GEN COMM mangels, *news* bei Fehlen von; **in the ~ of detailed information** GEN COMM mangels genauer Informationen; **in the ~ of evidence to the contrary** LAW mangels Beweises des Gegenteils, in Ermangelung eines Gegenbeweises

absence: **~ of consideration** *n* FIN, GEN COMM Fehlen *nt* der Gegenleistung; **~ of formal requirements** *n* LAW *contracts* Formfreiheit *f*; **~ of next of kin** *n* LAW erbenloser Nachlaß *m*; **~ of a quorum** *n* MGMNT Beschlußunfähigkeit *f*; **~ time** *n* HRM Abwesenheitszeit *f*; **~ without leave** *n* HRM eigenmächtige Abwesenheit *f*

absent *adj* GEN COMM, HRM abwesend, fern, nicht zugegen; ♦ **be ~ due to illness** HRM aus Krankheitsgründen abwesend sein (*infrml*); **go ~ without leave** GEN COMM sich unerlaubt entfernen

absentee *n* GEN COMM, HRM Abwesende(r) *mf* [decl. as adj], Nichterschienene(r) *mf* [decl. as adj]

absenteeism *n* HRM Absentismus *m*

absentee: **~ rate** *n* GEN COMM, HRM Abwesenheitsrate *f*

absolute *adj* COMMS, COMP, ECON absolut, GEN COMM absolut, rechtskräftig, *verdict, decree* endgültig, *power, authority* unbeschränkt, LAW *contract* bedingungslos, *court order, decree* endgültig, MATH, TAX absolut; ♦ **in ~ terms** ECON absolut, in absoluten Größen

absolute: **~ address** *n* COMMS absolute Adresse *f*, COMP absolute Adresse *f*, echte Adresse *f*, tatsächliche Adresse *f*; **~ addressing** *n* COMMS, COMP absolute Adressierung *f*; **~ class frequency** *n* MATH *statistics* absolute Klassenhäufigkeit *f*; **~ concentration** *n* ECON absolute Konzentration *f*; **~ deviation** *n* MATH *statistics* absolute Abweichung *f*; **~ error** *n* MATH *statistics* absoluter Fehler *m*; **~ frequency** *n* MATH *statistics* absolute Häufigkeit *f*; **~ gift** *n* LAW bedingungslose Schenkung *f*; **~ income hypothesis** *n* ECON absolute Einkommenshypothese *f*; **~ limit** *n* GEN COMM absolutes Limit *nt*, *within prescribed time limits* äußerste Frist *f*

absolutely: **~ unbiased estimator** *n* MATH *statistics* stets erwartungstreue Schätzfunktion *f*

absolute: **~ measure** *n* MATH dimensionslose Maßzahl *f*; **~ monopoly** *n* ECON echtes Angebotsmonopol *nt*, reines Monopol *nt*, vollkommenes Monopol *nt*; **~ poor** *n pl* ECON absolut Arme *pl*; **~ poverty** *n* ECON absolute Armut *f*, absolute Mittellosigkeit *f*, völlige Verarmung *f*; **~ scarcity** *n* ECON absoluter Mangel *m*, völlige Verknappung *f*, totaler Mangel *m*; **~ surplus value** *n* ECON absoluter Mehrwert *m*; **~ tax incidence** *n* TAX absolute Steuerinzidenz *f*, absolute Steuerwirkung *f*, absoluter Steuereffekt *m*; **~ term** *n* MATH Konstante *f*; **~ title** *n* PROP uneingeschränktes Eigentumsrecht *nt*

absorb *vt* ACC absorbieren, verrechnen, ECON *purchasing power* abschöpfen, GEN COMM absorbieren, *cost* abfangen, auffangen, übernehmen, verkraften, *business, company* aufnehmen, übernehmen, *import* in sich aufnehmen, *staff, management* eingliedern, *stock, merchandise* aufnehmen; ♦ **~ overhead** ACC Gemeinkosten verrechnen; **~ a used car surplus** GEN COMM einen Gebrauchtwagenüberschuß abschöpfen

absorbed *adj* FIN *cost accounting* verrechnet; **~ basis** *n* ACC Vollkostenbasis *f*; **~ overheads** *n pl* FIN verrechnete Gemeinkosten *pl*; ♦ **be ~** POL *ethnic minority* assimiliert werden

absorbent: **~ paper** *n* ADMIN Saugpost *f*

absorbing: **~ capacity** *n* STOCK *of security market* Aufnahmefähigkeit *f*; **~ company** *n* ECON übernehmende Firma *f* (*infrml*), übernehmende Gesellschaft *f*

absorption *n* ACC Verrechnung *f*, ECON Abschöpfung *f*, Absorption *f*, inländische Gesamtnachfrage *f*, Aufnahme *f*, Sättigung *f*, FIN *of a company* Auflösung *f*, Übernahme *f*, Verrechnung *f*, Vollkostenrechnung *f* GEN COMM *of costs, profits, business* Absorption *f*, Aufnahme *f*, Übernahme *f*, *of resources* Bindung *f*, TRANSP Übernahme *f*; **~ account** *n* ACC Wertberichtigungskonto *nt*; **~ approach** *n* ECON Absorptionstheorie *f*;

~ capacity *n* ECON, GEN COMM *of market* Aufnahmefähigkeit *f*; **~ costing** *n* FIN *cost accounting* Vollkostenrechnung *f*; **~ of liquidity** *n* ECON Liquiditätsabschöpfung *f*; **~ point** *n* ECON Sättigungspunkt *m*

absorptive: **~ capacity** *n* ECON, GEN COMM *of market* Aufnahmefähigkeit *f*, Absorptionskapazität *f*

abstain *vi* GEN COMM sich enthalten, POL *from voting* sich der Stimme enthalten, seine Stimme nicht abgeben

abstention *n* GEN COMM, POL Enthaltung *f*, Stimmenthaltung *f*

abstinence *n* ECON Abstinenz *f*; **~ theory of interest** *n* ECON Abstinenztheorie *f* des Zinses

abstract *n* ECON *summary* Abstrakt *nt*, Kurzfassung *f*, Zusammenfassung *f*, GEN COMM *of document* Auszug *m*, Kurzfassung *f*, LAW *extract* Auszug *m*, Zusammenfassung *f*, MATH *statistics* Jahrbuch *nt*, PATENTS Auszug *m*, Übersicht *f*; **~ of accounts** *n* BANK Kontoauszug *m*, Rechnungsauszug *m*; **~ labor** *AmE*, **~ labour** *BrE n* HRM abstrakte Arbeitskräfte *f pl*

ABT *abbr* (*American Board of Trade*) GEN COMM amerikanische Handelskammer, ≈ DIHT (*Deutscher Industrie- und Handelstag*)

abundance *n* ECON Überfluß *m*, GEN COMM Ergiebigkeit *f*, Fülle *f*, Menge *f*, Überfluß *m*; ♦ **be in ~** GEN COMM im Überfluß vorhanden sein

abundant *adj* GEN COMM reichlich, üppig

abuse 1. *n* ECON, GEN COMM, PATENTS Mißbrauch *m*, mißbräuchliche Ausnutzung *f*; **2.** *vt* GEN COMM *privilege, power, trust* unzulässig gebrauchen, mißbrauchen

abuse: **~ of administrative authority** *n* GEN COMM Amtsmißbrauch *m*; **~ of confidence** *n* GEN COMM Vertrauensmißbrauch *m*; **~ of market power** *n* ECON Marktmachtmißbrauch *m*; **~ of power** *n* GEN COMM Machtmißbrauch *m*, POL unsachgemäßer Machtgebrauch *m*; **~ of trust** *n* GEN COMM Vertrauensmißbrauch *m*

abusive: **~ practice** *n* ECON, POL mißbräuchliche Verhaltensweise *f*, S&M *of seller* Mißbrauch *m*

ac *abbr* GEN COMM (*alternating current*) WS (*Wechselstrom*), TRANSP (*air-freight container*) Luftfracht-Container *m*

a/c *abbr* (*account*) ACC Kto. (*Konto*), BANK Bankkonto *nt*, Kto. (*Konto*), S&M Kto. (*Konto*)

AC *abbr* ECON (*advanced country*) hochentwickeltes Land *nt*, HRM (*assistant controller*) Hilfsrevisor *m*

ACA *abbr* (*Accredited Chartered Accountant*) ACC amtlich zugelassener Wirtschaftsprüfer *m*, amtlich zugelassene Wirtschaftsprüferin *f*

academic *adj* GEN COMM hypothetisch, WEL akademisch, praxisfremd, theoretisch, wissenschaftlich; **~ question** *n* GEN COMM hypothetische Frage *f*; **~ research** *n* GEN COMM, WEL *in science* Hochschulforschung *f*

ACAS *abbr BrE* (*Advisory, Conciliation and Arbitration Service*) HRM Beratungs-, Schlichtungs- und Schiedsgerichtsstelle für Arbeitsstreitigkeiten

ACB *abbr* (*adjusted cost base*) ACC angepaßte Bewertungsgrundlagen *f pl* für die Kostenrechnung

acc. *abbr* (*accountancy*) ACC, ADMIN, HRM Buchführung *f*, Buchhaltung *f*, Rechnungswesen *nt*

ACC *abbr* IND (*American Chamber of Commerce*) amerikanische Handelskammer, TRANSP (*acceptable container condition*) *shipping* annehmbarer Container-Zustand *m*,

(*automatic control certified*) Selbststeuerung eingetragen, Selbststeuerung zugelassen

ACCA *abbr* (*Associate of the Chartered Association of Certified Accountants*) ACC Mitglied des Verbands öffentlich zugelassener Wirtschaftsprüfer

accede *vi* POL zustimmen; ♦ **~ to** POL beitreten; **~ to an office** POL ein Amt antreten; **~ to a treaty** POL sich einem Abkommen anschließen

accelerate 1. *vt* BANK *maturity* vorverlegen, vorzeitig fällig stellen, GEN COMM beschleunigen, forcieren, steigern; **2.** *vi* ECON, GEN COMM *growth, inflation, work rate* sich beschleunigen, zunehmen

accelerated *adj* GEN COMM beschleunigt, *training course* progressiv; **~ amortization** *n* ACC beschleunigte Amortisation *f*, vorzeitige Tilgung *f*; **~ company tax depreciation** *n* TAX *in Germany* betriebliche vorzeitige Abschreibung *f*; **~ conversion** *n* BANK *of debenture* beschleunigte Umwandlung *f*; **~ depreciation** *n* ACC, FIN beschleunigte Abschreibung *f*; **~ growth** *n* ECON beschleunigtes Wachstum *nt*, forciertes Wirtschaftswachstum *nt*; **~ motion** *n* S&M beschleunigte Bewegung *f*; **~ redemption** *n* GEN COMM beschleunigter Rückkauf *m*; **~ surface post** *n* COMMS Eilzustellung *f* auf dem Landweg

accelerating: **~ inflation** *n* ECON zunehmende Inflation *f*

acceleration *n* ECON Akzeleration *f*, *in rate* Beschleunigung *f*, GEN COMM *in rate* Beschleunigung *f*; **~ clause** *n* BANK *mortgages* Vorfälligkeitsklausel *f*; **~ clause premium** *n* LAW Zuschlagsklausel *f* für höhere Produktivität; **~ coefficient** *n* ECON Akzelerationskoeffizient *m*; **~ of maturity** *n* BANK Vorverlegung *f* der Fälligkeit; **~ premium** *n* HRM Leistungsprämie *f*; **~ principle** *n* ECON *investment hypothesis* Akzelerationsprinzip *nt*

accelerator *n* ECON Akzelerator *m*; **~ card** *n* COMP Beschleunigerkarte *f*; **~-multiplier interaction** *n* ECON kombinierte Akzelerator- und Multiplikatorwirkung *f*

accept *vt* BANK *bill, credit card* akzeptieren, annehmen, COMMS *call* akzeptieren, annehmen, entgegennehmen, übernehmen, GEN COMM abnehmen, akzeptieren, anerkennen, entgegennehmen, übernehmen; ♦ **~ a bid** GEN COMM den Zuschlag erteilen; **~ a bill** LAW einen Wechsel akzeptieren, einen Wechsel mit Akzept versehen; **~ a collect call** *AmE*, **~ a reverse-charge call** *BrE* COMMS ein R-Gespräch annehmen; **~ a tender** GEN COMM den Zuschlag erteilen; **~ delivery** GEN COMM eine Lieferung abnehmen; **~ liability** GEN COMM Haftung anerkennen, Haftung übernehmen; **~ liability for sth** GEN COMM Haftung für etw anerkennen, INS für etw haften, LAW für etw haften, Haftung für etw anerkennen, Haftung für etw übernehmen; **~ on presentation** GEN COMM *bill* akzeptieren bei Vorlage

acceptability *n* ECON *of money* Annehmbarkeit *f*, Brauchbarkeit *f*, GEN COMM Annehmbarkeit *f*, Brauchbarkeit *f*, Tragbarkeit *f*

acceptable *adj* BANK beleihbar, lombardfähig, ECON annehmbar, GEN COMM akzeptabel, annehmbar, tragbar, TRANSP annehmbar; **~ container condition** *n* (*ACC*) TRANSP *shipping* annehmbarer Container-Zustand *m*; **~ price** *n* GEN COMM annehmbarer Preis *m*; **~ quality** *n* GEN COMM annehmbare Qualität *f*; **~ quality level system** *n* (*AQL system*) IND DIN 40080 AQL-System *nt*

acceptance *n* BANK *completed bill* Annahme *f*, Akzept *nt*, akzeptierter Wechsel *m*, FIN Akzept *nt*, Akzeptierung *f*, GEN COMM *of bid, tender* Zuschlag *m*, *of contract, goods* Annahme *f*, *assent* Billigung *f*, Einwilligung *f*, Zustimmung *f*, *of invitation* Annahme *f*, *goods* Abnahme *f*, IND Annahme *f*, INS Abnahme *f*, Annahme *f*, LAW *of contract, goods* Annahme *f*, MEDIA *approval of product* Annahme *f*, *of manuscript* Abnahme *f*, POL Akzeptanz *f*, S&M *of brand* Abnahme *f*, Akzeptanz *f*, TRANSP Abnahme *f*; **~ account** *n* BANK Akzeptkonto *nt*, Wechselkonto *nt*; **~ against documents** *n* BANK, GEN COMM Akzept *nt* gegen Dokumente; **~ as performance** *n* LAW *contracts* Erfüllungsannahme *f*; **~ bank** *n* BANK Akzeptbank *f*; **~ bill** *n* BANK Dokumententratte *f*, zum Akzept vorgelegter Wechsel *m*; **~ by intervention** *n* GEN COMM Interventionsakzept *nt*, Interventionsannahme *f*; **~ certificate** *n* TRANSP Abnahmebescheinigung *f*, Abnahmezeugnis *nt*; **~ charge** *n* FIN Akzeptgebühr *f*; **~ commission** *n* BANK Akzeptprovision *f*; **~ commitments** *n pl* FIN Akzeptverbindlichkeiten *f pl*; **~ credit** *n* BANK Akzeptkredit *m*, FIN, IMP/EXP Akzept-Akkreditiv *nt*, Wechselrembours *m*, Rembourskredit *m*; **~ duty** *n* BANK Annahmepflicht *f*; **~ facility** *n* BANK Akzeptkredit *m*, Akzeptfazilität *f*; **~ fee** *n* BANK Akzeptgebühr *f*; **~ for honor** *AmE*, **~ for honour** *BrE* *n* GEN COMM Ehrenakzept *nt*, Ehrenannahme *f*; **~ house** *n* BANK Diskontbank *f*, Akzepthaus *nt*, Wechselbank *f*; **~ ledger** *n* BANK, FIN Akzeptebuch *nt*, Beleggrundbuch *nt*, Obligobuch *nt*; **~ liabilities** *n pl* FIN Akzeptverbindlichkeiten *f pl*; **~ liability** *n* BANK Akzeptlinie *f*, Wechselobligo *nt*; **~ line** *n* *AmE* BANK Akzeptlinie *f*, Akzeptkreditrahmen *m*; **~ of lump sum settlement** *n* FIN Annahme *f* einer Abfindung, Annahme *f* einer Pauschalentschädigung; **~ market** *n* BANK Akzeptmarkt *m*; **~ price** *n* BANK Akzeptpreis *m*; **~ of proposal** *n* INS Antragsannahme *f*; **~ region** *n* IND Annahmebereich *m*; **~ register** *n* BANK *of bank* chronologisches Akzeptverzeichnis *nt*; **~ slip** *n* INS Annahmeschein *m*, schriftliche Annahmeerklärung *f*

acceptances: **~ outstanding** *n pl* ACC eigene Akzepte *nt pl*, FIN Akzeptumlauf *m*

acceptance: **~ supra protest** *n* GEN COMM Ehrenakzept *nt*, Ehrenannahme *f*; **~ test** *n* S&M Markttest *m*, Pretest *m*; **~ trial** *n* IND Abnahmeprüfung *f*, S&M Abnahmetest *m*, TRANSP Abnahmeprüfung *f*

accepted *adj* BANK, COMP akzeptiert, GEN COMM akzeptiert, anerkannt, angenommen, mit Akzept versehen; **~ draft** *n* BANK akzeptierter Wechsel *m*; **~ lot** *n* GEN COMM *of goods* angenommene Lieferung *f*; **~ pairing** *n* S&M *market research* vereinbarte Abrechnung von Kauf- und Verkaufsaufträgen, STOCK Verrechnung *f* gleicher Kaufs- und Verkaufsaufträge

accepting *adj* BANK *banker*, FIN akzeptgebend, akzeptierend; **~ bank** *n* BANK, FIN akzeptgebende Bank *f*, akzeptierende Bank *f*; **~ banker** *n* BANK, FIN Akzeptbank *f*, akzeptierende Bank *f*; **~ house** *n* BANK, FIN Akzeptbank *nt*, akzeptierende Bank *f*, Akzepthaus *nt*

acceptor *n* BANK *of bill* Akzeptant *m*, Bezogene(r) *mf* [decl. as adj], Trassat *m*, LAW *of contract* Akzeptant *m*; **~'s bill** *n* FIN Akzeptantenwechsel *m*

access 1. *n* COMP, ECON Zugriff *m*, GEN COMM Zutritt *m*, Zugang *m*; ♦ **give sb ~ to** GEN COMM jdm Zutritt erteilen zu; **2.** *vt* COMP *database, information, machine* zugreifen auf [+acc]

access: **~ control** *n* COMP *auditing* Zugriffskontrolle *f*; **~ differential** *n* COMP, ECON Zugriffsunterschiede *m pl*

accessibility *n* COMP, GEN COMM *of information* Zugriffsfähigkeit *f*, Zugriffsmöglichkeit *f*, *of public places for the disabled* Zugänglichkeit *f*, Erreichbarkeit *f*

accessible *adj* GEN COMM *location* erreichbar, verkehrsgünstig, zugänglich

accession *n* FIN Zuwachs *m*, GEN COMM Akzession *f*, Zustimmung *f*, POL *agreement* Zustimmung *f*, *to office* Antritt *m*, *to treaty* Beitreten *nt*, Beitritt *m*, Sichanschließen *nt*; **accessions tax** *n* TAX kumulative Erbschafts- und Schenkungssteuer *f*; **~ to the EU** *n* ECON EU-Beitritt *m*

accessorial: **~ service** *n* S&M zusätzliche Dienstleistung *f*, Zusatzleistung *f*

accessories *n pl* GEN COMM Nebenausgaben *f pl*, Nebengebühren *f pl*, S&M Zubehör *nt*

accessory 1. *adj* GEN COMM *additional* hinzukommend, zusätzlich, *subordinate* nebensächlich, LAW akzessorisch, mitschuldig; **2.** *n* LAW Komplize *m*, Komplizin *f*, Helfershelfer, in *m,f*, Mittäter, in *m,f*

accessory: **~ advertising** *n* S&M begleitende Werbeaktion *f*, Zusatzwerbung *f*; **~ charges** *n pl* GEN COMM Nebenausgaben *f pl*, Nebengebühren *n pl*; **~ undertaking** *n* LAW akzessorische Verpflichtung *f*

access: **~ right** *n* COMP Zugriffsberechtigung *f*; **~ time** *n* COMP *between request and data shown* Zugriffszeit *f*

accident *n* GEN COMM *air, rail* Unglück *nt*, *on road, at home, work* Unfall *m*, *chance* Zufall *m*, HRM Unfall *m*, INS Unfall *m*, Unglück *nt*

accidental *adj* GEN COMM zufällig, **~ sampling** *n* ECON stichprobenartige Untersuchung *f*, zufallsbedingtes Stichprobenverfahren *nt*

accident: **~ at sea** *n* INS Havarie *f*, Seeunfall *m*, TRANSP Havarie *f*; **~ insurance** *n* HRM, INS Unfallversicherung *f*; **~ insurer** *n* INS Unfallversicherer *m*; **~ prevention** *n* HRM Unfallverhütung *f*; **~ risk** *n* INS Unfallgefahr *f*; Unfallrisiko *nt*; **~ to conveyance** *n* INS Unfall beim Transport *m*

accommodate *vt* BANK *with loan* gewähren [+dat], GEN COMM *do a favour for* eine Gefälligkeit erweisen, *oblige* entgegenkommen, *provide lodging for* unterbringen [+acc], LEIS *provide lodging for* unterbringen, TRANSP *contain* aufnehmen, WEL *provide lodging for* beherbergen, unterbringen

accommodating: **~ credit** *n* ACC Überbrückungskredit *m*; **~ items** *n pl* ECON Restposten *m pl* der Zahlungsbilanz, Saldo *m* statistisch nicht aufgliederbarer Transaktionen; **~ transactions** *n pl* ECON Ausgleichstransaktionen *f pl*

accommodation *n* BANK Gefälligkeit *f*, FIN Gefälligkeit *f*, kurzfristiges, ungesichertes Darlehen *nt*, Überbrückungskredit *m*, GEN COMM *adaptation, compromise* Anpassung *f*, *financial* geldliche Hilfe *f*, kurzfristiges Darlehen *nt*, *obliging attitude* Entgegenkommen *nt*, Gefälligkeit *f*, *lodging* Unterbringung *f*, PROP Behausung *f*, HRM, LEIS *lodging* Unterkunft *f*, WEL *lodging* Behausung *f*, Unterbringung *f*, Unterkunft *f*, Wohnung *f*; **~ acceptance** *n* GEN COMM Gefälligkeitsakzept *nt*; **~ address** *n* *BrE* COMMS Deckadresse *f*; **~ agency** *n* WEL *for flats, houses* Wohnungsvermittlung *f*, *for rooms* Zimmervermittlung *f*; **~ allowance** *n* HRM Unterkunftsvergütung *f*, Wohnzuschuß *m*, Mietzuschuß *m*; **~ berth** *n* TRANSP *shipping* reservierter Liegeplatz *m*;

~ **bill** *n* FIN, GEN COMM Finanzwechsel *m*, Gefälligkeitswechsel *m*; ~ **bureau** *n* AmE (*cf housing department BrE*) WEL Abteilung *f* Wohnraumlenkung, Wohnungsamt *nt*, Wohnungsvermittlung *f*; ~ **draft** *n* FIN Gefälligkeitswechsel *m*, GEN COMM Gefälligkeitstratte *f*; ~ **endorsement** *n* FIN, GEN COMM Gefälligkeitsindossament *nt*; ~ **loan** *n* FIN Überbrückungskredit *m*, kurzfristiges, ungesichertes Darlehen *nt*, Gefälligkeitsdarlehen *nt*; ~ **note** *n* BANK Gefälligkeitswechsel *m*; ~ **paper** *n* GEN COMM Gefälligkeitspapier *nt*; ~ **party** *n* FIN Gefälligkeitsadresse *f*, Gefälligkeitsbeteiligte(r) *mf* [decl. as adj]; ~ **payment** *n* BANK Gefälligkeitszahlung *f*; ~ **road** *n* TRANSP Anliegerweg *m*, Privatstraße *f*, Zugangstraße *f*; ~ **train** *n* AmE TRANSP Bummelzug *m*, Personenzug *m*

accommodative: ~ **policy** *n* ECON, POL *central bank* akkommodierende Geldpolitik *f*, akkommodierende Politik *f*, anpassende Geldpolitik *f*, anpassende Politik *f*

accommodatory: ~ **credit** *n* IMP/EXP Überbrückungskredit *m*

accompanied *adj* GEN COMM begleitet; ~ **baggage** *n* LEIS, TRANSP begleitetes Gepäck *nt*

accompany *vt* GEN COMM *escort* begleiten, geleiten [+acc], einhergehen mit

accompanying *adj* GEN COMM begleitend; ~ **document** *n* ADMIN, COMMS, TRANSP Begleitschein *m*, Begleitpapier *nt*, Begleitdokument *nt*; ~ **letter** *n* ADMIN, COMMS Begleitbrief *m*, Begleitschreiben *nt*

accomplish *vt* GEN COMM ausführen, vollenden, vollziehen

accomplished *adj* GEN COMM vollendet, vollkommen

accomplishment *n* GEN COMM *of task* Ausführung *f*, Vollendung *f*, *of objectives* Realisierung *f*, HRM *feat* Leistung *f*, LAW Vollziehung *f*

accord *n* GEN COMM Absprache *f*, Vereinbarung *f*, LAW *treaty* Vertrag *m*, Übereinkunft *f*, Vergleich *m*, Übereinstimmung *f*

accordance: **in** ~ **with** *phr* GEN COMM *standard, regulation* übereinstimmen mit, gemäß, im Einklang mit, LAW in Übereinstimmung mit, gemäß; **in** ~ **with your instructions** *phr* GEN COMM gemäß Ihren Anweisungen

accordingly *adv* GEN COMM demgemäß, entsprechend, folglich

according: ~ **to** *phr* GEN COMM, LAW gemäß, laut, nach, zufolge; ~ **to the norm** *phr* IND, LAW normgerecht; ~ **to plan** *phr* GEN COMM plangemäß; ~ **to schedule** *phr* GEN COMM nach Plan, planmäßig, TRANSP *journey* fahrplanmäßig

accordion: ~ **folding** *n* COMMS, S&M *advertising* Zickzackfaltung *f*, Leporellofaltung *f*

account *n* (*a/c*) ACC *book-keeping* Konto *nt* (*Kto.*), BANK Bankkonto *nt*, Konto *nt* (*Kto.*), GEN COMM *bill* Rechnung *f* *invoice* Faktura *f* (*obs*), *customer* Kunde *m*, *report* Bericht *m*, Darstellung *f*, S&M Etat *m*, Konto *nt* (*Kto.*), STOCK Abrechnungszeitraum *m*; ♦ ~ **of** (*a/o*) BANK à Konto, zu Lasten von, auf Konto von, per Konto (*jarg*), für Rechnung von, auf Rechnung von; **on** ~ (*o/a*) BANK à Konto, GEN COMM gegen Kredit, S&M auf Rechnung; **on** ~ **of** GEN COMM wegen; **on** ~ **of payment** LAW zahlungshalber; **on no** ~ GEN COMM auf keinen Fall; ~ **payee** BANK *on cheque* zur Verrechnung; ~ **payee only** BANK *on cheque* nur zur Verrechnung

account for *vt* GEN COMM berücksichtigen, *expenses* nachweisen, abrechnen, *inflation* bereinigen

accountability *n* ACC, ADMIN, GEN COMM, MGMNT Rechenschaftspflicht *f*, Verantwortlichkeit *f*; ~ **in management** *n* MGMNT Leitungsverantwortung *f*, Rechenschaftspflicht *f* der Leitung

accountable *adj* ACC *transaction* buchungspflichtig, rechenschaftspflichtig, zu verbuchen, ADMIN, HRM weisungsgebunden, rechenschaftspflichtig, GEN COMM verantwortlich, haftbar, LAW strafmündig; ~ **advance** *n* ACC, HRM buchungspflichtiger Vorschuß *m*, buchungspflichtige Vorauszahlung *f*; ~ **officer** *n* AmE HRM weisungsgebundene(r) Angestellte(r) *mf* [decl. as adj], rechenschaftspflichtige(r) Angestellte(r) *mf* [decl. as adj], Rechnungsleger *m*; ~ **receipt** *n* ACC buchungspflichtiger Beleg *m*, Buchungsbeleg *m*

account: ~ **analysis** *n* BANK Kontenanalyse *f*

accountancy *n* (*accy*) ACC *business* Rechnungswesen *nt*, Kontenführung *f*, Buchführung *f*, Buchhaltung *f*; ~ **profession** *n* ACC Beruf *m* des Buchhalters, Steuerberaters, Wirtschaftsprüfers oder Buchprüfers; ~ **services** *n pl* ACC Leistungen des Buchhalters, Steuerberaters, Wirtschaftsprüfers oder Buchprüfers

accountant *n* ACC, GEN COMM, HRM *general* Buchhalter, in *m,f*, *for tax* Steuerberater, in *m,f*, *external advisor* Wirtschaftsprüfer, in *m,f*, Rechnungsprüfer, in *m,f*

Accountant: ~ **General** *n* (*AG*) ACC Bilanzbuchhalter, in *m,f*, ADMIN, HRM Generalbevollmächtigte(r) *mf* [decl. as adj], Handlungsbevollmächtigte(r) *mf* [decl. as adj]

accountant: ~**'s professional liability insurance** *n* ACC, INS Haftpflichtversicherung *f* des Buchhalters

account: ~ **balance** *n* ACC, BANK Kontostand *m*, Saldo *m*; ~ **book** *n* ACC, BANK Sparbuch *nt*, Kontobuch *nt*; ~ **conflict** *n* S&M Kontenkonflikt *m*; ~ **day** *n* GEN COMM Abrechnungstag *m*, STOCK Liquidationstermin *m*

accounted: ~ **for** *phr* GEN COMM angerechnet, *document, financial statement* ausgewiesen

account: ~ **executive** *n* MEDIA *advertising* Kontakter *m*, Kontaktmann *m*, Kontaktfrau *f*, Sachbearbeiter, in *m,f* eines Werbeetats; ~ **form** *n* ACC Kontoform *f*, Bilanzformblatt *nt*, *balance sheet* Kontenform *f*, Kontenblatt *nt*; ~ **format** *n* ACC Kontengliederung *f* der Bilanz, Bilanzgliederung *f*, Aufgliederung *f* der Bilanz; ~ **group** *n* ACC, S&M Kontengruppe *f*; ~ **holder** *n* BANK Kontoinhaber, in *m,f*; ~ **in balance** *n* ACC ausgeglichenes Konto *nt*

accounting *n* ACC, ADMIN, HRM Buchführung *f*, Buchhaltung *f*, Rechnungslegung *f*, Rechnungswesen *nt*; ~ **analysis** *n* ACC Auswertung *f* der Rechnungslegung; ~ **balance of payments** *n* ECON statistische Zahlungsbilanz *f*, Zahlungsbilanz *f* ex post; ~ **by functions** *n* ACC, ADMIN Abteilungserfolgsrechnung *f*, *direct costing* Grenzplankostenrechnung *f*; ~ **change** *n* ACC Änderung *f* in der Buchführung, Buchhaltungsumstellung *f*; ~ **clerk** *n* ACC, ADMIN, HRM Buchhalter, in *m,f*; ~ **control** *n* ACC *auditing* Rechnungsprüfung *f*, Revision *f*; ~ **conventions** *n pl* ACC, ADMIN Buchhaltungs- und Bilanzierungsrichtlinien *f pl*; ~ **costs** *n pl* ACC Alternativkosten *pl*; ~ **cycle** *n* ACC Buchhaltungskreislauf *m*; ~ **data** *n pl* ACC Buchungsdaten *pl*, Buchungszahlen *f pl*, *published accounting data produced by companies* Abschlußzahlen *f pl*; ~ **department** *n* ACC Buchhaltungsabteilung *f*, Buchhaltung *f*; ~ **directives law** *n* ACC, LAW Bilanzrichtliniengesetz *nt*; ~ **doctrines** *n pl* ACC, ADMIN Buchführungsrichtlinien *f pl*, Bilanzauffassungen *f pl*; ~ **effect** *n* ACC *of* *application of rules or change in rules* Wirkung *f* auf die Buchführung; **~ entry** *n* ACC Buchung *f*; **~ equation** *n* ACC Bilanzgleichung *f*; **~ error** *n* ACC Buchungsfehler *m*; **~ exchange on the assets side** *n* ACC Aktivtausch *m*; **~ fees** *n pl* ACC Buchhaltungsgebühren *f pl*; **~ firm** *n* ACC Wirtschaftsprüfungsfirma *f*; **~ for inflation** *n* ACC, ECON Inflationsbereinigung *f*; **~ fraud** *n* ACC Bilanzdelikt *nt*; **~ harmonization** *n* ACC Standardisierung *f* der Buchführung; **~ identity** *n* ACC Bilanzgleichung *f*, *accounting principles* Bilanzidentität *f*; **~ income** *n* ACC *net profit* Periodengewinn oder -verlust *m*, *revenue* Periodeneinkommen *nt*, Periodengewinn *m*; **~ information** *n* ACC Buchungsdaten *pl*; **~ law** *n* ACC, LAW *in Germany* Bilanzrichtliniengesetz *nt*; **~ method** *n* ACC Buchhaltungsmethode *f*, Rechnungslegungsmethode *f*; **~ model** *n* ACC, FIN Rechnungslegungsmodell *nt*, Buchführungsmodell *nt*; **~ office** *n* ACC Buchhaltung *f*, Buchhaltungsabteilung *f*, Rechnungsstelle *f*; **~ officer** *n* (*AO*) ACC, ADMIN, HRM Buchhalter, in *m,f*; **~ package** *n* COMP Abrechnungspaket *nt*; **~ papers** *n pl* ACC Urbelege *m pl*; **~ period** *n* ACC Rechnungsjahr *nt*, FIN Bilanzierungsperiode *f*, STOCK Abrechnungsperiode *f*, Börsenhandelsperiode *f*; **~ plan** *n* ACC Bilanzgliederung *f*, Kontenplan *m*, Rechnungsplan *m*; **~ policy** *n* ACC Bilanzierungs- und Bewertungsverfahren *nt*; **~ practice** *n* ACC Praxis *f* des Rechnungswesens, Buchprüfertätigkeit *f*, *office* Buchhaltungsbüro *nt*, Buchhaltungspraxis *f*; **~ price** *n* BANK Schattenpreis *m*, Verrechnungspreis *m*; **~ principles** *n pl* ACC Bilanzierungsgrundsätze *m pl*, Buchführungsgrundsätze *m pl*

Accounting: **~ Principles Board** *n AmE* (*APB*) ACC Ausschuß für Wirtschaftsprüferrichtlinien

accounting: **~ procedure** *n* ACC Buchungsverfahren *nt pl*, Rechnungslegungsmethoden *f pl*; **~ profit** *n* ACC Buchgewinn *m*, rechnerischer Gewinn *m*; **~ rate of return** *n* ACC Rendite *f*; **~ ratio** *n* ACC Bilanzkennzahl *f*, ADMIN finanzwirtschaftliche Kennzahl *f*; **~ records** *n pl* ACC Buchführungsunterlagen *f pl*, Geschäftsbücher *nt pl*; **~ report** *n* ACC Abschlußrechnung *f*, Rechnungslegung *f*; **~ and reporting law** *n* ACC, LAW *in Germany* Bilanzrichtliniengesetz *nt*; **~ return** *n* ACC rechnerische Rendite *f*; **~ rules** *n pl* ACC Bilanzierungsgrundsätze *m pl*, Buchführungsgrundsätze *m pl*; **~ software** *n* ACC, COMP Buchhaltungssoftware *f*

Accounting: **~ Standards Board** *n BrE* ACC Ausschuß für Wirtschaftsprüferrichtlinien

accounting: **~ standard setting** *n* ACC Festlegung *f* der Rechnungslegungsgrundsätze; **~ system** *n* ACC Buchführungssystem *nt*; **~ treatment** *n* ACC buchtechnische Behandlung *f*; **~ value** *n* ACC Buchwert *m*; **~ year** *n* ACC Abrechnungsperiode *f*, Geschäftsjahr *nt*, Haushaltsjahr *nt*, Rechnungsjahr *nt*, FIN Bilanzjahr *nt*, TAX Geschäftsjahr *nt*, Haushaltsjahr *nt*, Wirtschaftsjahr *nt*; **~ year ended** *n* ACC abgeschlossenes Bilanzjahr *nt*, abgeschlossenes Geschäftsjahr *nt*, abgeschlossenes Haushaltsjahr *nt*, abgeschlossenes Rechnungsjahr *nt*, TAX abgeschlossenes Geschäftsjahr *nt*, abgeschlossenes Haushaltsjahr *nt*, abgeschlossenes Wirtschaftsjahr *nt*

account: **~ management** *n* ACC, BANK Kontoführung *f*, S&M Kundenbetreuung *f*, Kundengruppenmanagement *nt*; **~ manager** *n* (*AM*) S&M Account-Manager, in *m,f*, *advertising* Kundenbetreuer, in *m,f*; **~ matching** *n* ACC Abstimmung *f* von Konten, Kontoabstimmung *f*; **~ movement** *n* ACC Kontobewegung *f*; **~ name** *n* ACC,

BANK Kontobezeichnung *f*; **~ number** *n* ACC, BANK Kontonummer *f*; **--only check** *AmE*, **--only cheque** *BrE* *n* BANK Verrechnungsscheck *m*; **~ operation** *n* BANK Kontoverwendung *f*; **~ operation charge** *n* BANK Kontoverwendungskosten *pl*; **~ planning** *n* MEDIA, S&M *advertising* Mediaplanung *f*; **~ reconciliation** *n* ACC Abstimmung *f* von Konten, Kontoabstimmung *f*; **~ rendered** *n* ACC, ADMIN erteilte Rechnung *f*, ausgestellte Rechnung *f*

accounts *n pl* ACC, BANK Konten *nt pl*, FIN *company accounts* Jahresabschluß *m*, Konten *nt pl*, Geschäftsbücher *nt pl*; **~ appraisal** *n* ACC *auditing* Abschlußbewertung *f*; **~ certification** *n* ACC *auditing* Bestätigungsvermerk *m*; **~ department** *n* ACC, ADMIN Buchhaltung *f*, Buchhaltungsabteilung *f*; **~ payable** *n pl* ACC Kreditoren *m pl*, Verbindlichkeiten *f pl*; **~ payable clerk** *n* ACC Kreditorenbuchhalter, in *m,f*; **~ payable ledger** *n* ACC Kreditorenbuch *nt*, Lieferantenbuch *nt*; **~ receivable** *n pl* (*A/R*) ACC Außenstände *m pl*, Forderungen *f pl*, Debitoren *m pl*; **~ receivable account** *n* ACC Debitorenkonto *nt*; **~ receivable accounting** *n* ACC Kundenbuchhaltung *f*, Debitorenbuchhaltung *f*; **~ receivable collection period** *n* ACC, FIN Debitorenumschlag *m*; **~ receivable financing** *n* ACC, FIN Factoring *n*, Finanzierung *f* durch Forderungsabtretung; **~ receivable ledger** *n* ACC Debitorenbuch *nt*, Kundenbuch *nt*; **~ receivable statement** *n* ACC Debitorenkontoauszug *m*, Debitorenaufstellung *f*; **~ receivable turnover** *n* ACC Debitorenumschlag *m*

account: **~ stated** *n* ACC anerkannter Kontokorrentauszug *m*, anerkannter Rechnungsabschluß *m*; **~ statement** *n* BANK *issued by bank* Kontoauszug *m*; **~ transaction** *n* ACC Geschäft *nt* mit aufgeschobener Erfüllung, Kontobewegung *f*, STOCK Geschäft *nt* mit aufgeschobener Erfüllung; **~ turnover** *n* ACC Kontoumsatz *m*

accredit *vt* GEN COMM bestätigen, zulassen, *authorize* akkreditieren, *guarantee* ausstellen, S&M, WEL akkreditieren

accreditation *n* WEL *qualification* Akkreditierung *f*

accredited *adj* S&M akkreditiert, anerkannt, bevollmächtigt; **~ advertising agency** *n* S&M anerkannte Werbeagentur *f*

Accredited: **~ Chartered Accountant** *n* (*ACA*) ACC amtlich zugelassener Wirtschaftsprüfer *m*, amtlich zugelassene Wirtschaftsprüferin *f*

accrual *n* ACC aufgelaufene Zinsen *m pl*, BANK, ECON Ansammlung *f*, GEN COMM Zuwachs *m*, LAW Anwachsung *f*; **~ accounting** *n* ACC Prinzip *nt* der Periodenabgrenzung, periodengerechte Abgrenzung *f*; **~ basis of accounting** *n* ACC Fälligkeitsbasis *f*, periodengerechte Aufwands- und Ertragsrechnung *f*; **~ concept** *n* ACC Grundsatz *m* der Periodenabgrenzung, Periodenabgrenzung *f*; **~ of interest** *n* ACC, BANK Auflaufen *nt* von Zinsen; **~ interest rate** *n* ACC, BANK periodengerechter Zinssatz *m*; **~ principle** *n* ACC Grundsatz *m* der Periodenabgrenzung, Periodenabgrenzung *f*

accruals *n pl* ACC *assets* antizipative Aktiva *pl*, *receipts* Zugänge *m pl*, Einnahmen *f pl*, aktive Rechnungsabgrenzung *f*

accrue *vi* ACC auflaufen, rückstellen, abgrenzen, entstehen, BANK auflaufen, FIN anhäufen, auflaufen, entstehen, GEN COMM auflaufen, entstehen, STOCK auflaufen; ◆ ~ **interest** BANK Zinsen auflaufen lassen

accrued *adj* ACC antizipativ, rückgestellt, *interest* aufgelaufen, entstanden, BANK antizipativ, aufgelaufen, FIN, STOCK aufgelaufen; ~ **asset** *n* ACC antizipativer Aktivposten *m*; ~ **charges** *n pl* BANK antizipative Passiva *pl*; ~ **compound interest** *n* BANK aufgelaufene Zinseszinsen *m pl*; ~ **dividend** *n* ACC, BANK aufgelaufene Dividende *f*, STOCK *distributed* aufgelaufene Dividende *f*, *not yet distributed* aufgelaufene, aber noch nicht ausgeschüttete Dividende *f*; ~ **expense** *n* ACC antizipative Passiva *nt pl*; ~ **expenses** *n pl* ACC antizipative Passiva *nt pl*, passive Rechnungsabgrenzungsposten *m pl*, GEN COMM aufgelaufene Kosten *pl*; ~ **income** *n* ACC antizipative Aktiva *nt pl*, aktive Rechnungsabgrenzungsposten *m pl*; ~ **interest** *n* (*AI*) FIN aufgelaufene Zinsen *m pl*, STOCK Stückzinsen *m pl*; ~ **interest payable** *n* ACC aufgelaufene Zinsverbindlichkeiten *f pl*; ~ **interest receivable** *n* ACC aufgelaufene Zinsforderungen *f pl*; ~ **liability** *n* ACC entstandene Verbindlichkeit *f*, passive Rechnungsabgrenzungsposten *m pl*; ~ **revenue** *n* ACC antizipative Aktiva *nt pl*, aktive Rechnungsabgrenzungsposten *m pl*

accruing *adj* FIN *expense, revenue* auflaufend, *interest* entstehend

accumulate 1. *vt* ECON akkumulieren, FIN anhäufen, kumulieren, GEN COMM akkumulieren, anhäufen, *profit* thesaurieren, INS, STOCK, TAX kumulieren; **2.** *vi* ACC, BANK, FIN auflaufen, GEN COMM auflaufen, sich anhäufen, *profit* thesaurieren, STOCK auflaufen

accumulated *adj* ACC akkumuliert, aufgelaufen, FIN *dividends, depreciation* aufgelaufen, STOCK aufgelaufen; ~ **deficit** *n* ACC aufgelaufener Verlust *m*; ~ **depletion** *n* ACC eingetretene Substanzverringerung *f*; ~ **depreciation** *n* ACC *special write-down* akkumulierte Abschreibung *f*, *systematic depreciation* Sonderabschreibung *f*, Wertberichtigungen *f pl* auf das Sachanlagevermögen; ~ **interest** *n* ACC aufgelaufene Zinsen *m pl*; ~ **profits** *n pl* ACC *on balance sheet* aufgelaufener Betriebsgewinn *m*, Gewinnvortrag *m*, Bilanzgewinn *m*, einbehaltener Gewinn *m*; ~ **surplus** *n* ACC aufgelaufener Gewinn *m*, Gewinnvortrag *m*

accumulation *n* ECON Akkumulation *f*, FIN Aufzinsung *f*, Kumulierung *f*, GEN COMM *of capital, wealth, interest* Akkumulation *f*, Ansammlung *f*, Bildung *f*, INS Häufung *f*, Kumulierung *f*, MATH Aufzinsung *f*, STOCK, TAX Kumulierung *f*; ~ **area** *n* STOCK Kumulierungsbereich *m*; ~ **of capital** *n* ECON, FIN Kapitalbildung *f*, Substanzbildung *f*; ~ **factor** *n* MATH Aufzinsungsfaktor *m*; ~ **risk** *n* INS Kumulrisiko *nt*; ~ **of risk** *n* INS Kumulierung *f* von Risiken, Risikohäufung *f*

accumulator *n* COMP Akkumulator *m*

accuracy *n* ACC, ADMIN *of figures* Genauigkeit *f*, *of balance sheet figures* Bilanzwahrheit *f*, GEN COMM *of figures, data, judgment* Richtigkeit *f*, *of report, document, aim* Genauigkeit *f*, Korrektheit *f*, MATH *of figures* Treffgenauigkeit *f*

accurate *adj* GEN COMM *description, figures, estimate* exakt, genau, *judgment* richtig, zutreffend, *report, aim* einwandfrei, korrekt

accurately *adv* GEN COMM genau, richtig, sorgfältig

accusation *n* LAW Anklage *f*

accuse *vt* LAW anklagen

accy *abbr* (*accountancy*) ACC, ADMIN, HRM Buchführung *f*, Buchhaltung *f*, Rechnungswesen *nt*, Kontenführung *f*

ACD *abbr* (*automated cash dispenser, automatic cash dispenser*) GAA (*Geldausgabeautomat*), Geldautomat *m*, Bancomat *m* (*Sch*)

ACE *abbr* (*Amex Commodities Exchange*) FIN, STOCK Amex Warenbörse *f*

ACH *abbr* (*Automated Clearing House*) FIN automatisierte Abrechnungsstelle *f*, automatisches Clearinghaus *nt*, computergestützte Clearingstelle *f*, automatisiertes Clearinghaus im Gironetz des Massenzahlungsverkehrs

achievable *adj* GEN COMM erreichbar

achieve *vt* GEN COMM *growth, level, objective* erreichen, erzielen, vollenden

achieved *adj* GEN COMM vollendet

achievement *n* GEN COMM *feat* Errungenschaft *f*, Großtat *f*, Leistung *f*, *of aim, objective* Vollbringung *f*, Vollendung *f*, Realisierung *f*, Ausführung *f*, HRM Leistung *f*; ~ **motive** *n* HRM Leistungsmotiv *nt*; ~ **quotient** *n* GEN COMM Erfolgsquotient *m*; ~ **test** *n* GEN COMM Erfolgstest *m*

acid: ~ **deposit** *n* ENVIR Säureablagerung *f*; ~ **precipitation** *n* ENVIR saurer Niederschlag *m*; ~ **rain** *n* ENVIR saurer Regen *m*; ~ **rain pollution** *n* ENVIR Umweltbelastung *f* durch sauren Regen; ~ **test** *n* ACC Liquidität *f* ersten Grades; ~ **test ratio** *n* ACC Liquidität *f* ersten Grades

ACIS *abbr* BrE (*Associate of the Chartered Institute of Secretaries*) ADMIN Mitglied des Verbands staatlich zugelassener Sekretärinnen und Sekretäre

ack *abbr* (*acknowledgement*) COMMS, GEN COMM *of signature, initials on document* Bestätigung *f*, Empfangsbestätigung *f*, *receipt* Quittung *f*

acknowledge *vt* COMMS, COMP *message, order* bestätigen, GEN COMM anerkennen, *mistake* eingestehen, zugeben, *letter* quittieren, *with initials* abzeichnen, *debt, authority, right* bestätigen, LAW notariell beurkunden, *debt, authority, right* bestätigen, notariell beglaubigen; ◆ ~ **receipt by letter** COMMS brieflich bestätigen, schriftlich bestätigen, den Empfang durch Brief bestätigen; ~ **receipt of sth** COMMS, GEN COMM *mail, goods* den Empfang von etw bestätigen

acknowledged *adj* GEN COMM anerkannt, bestätigt, *initials* abgezeichnet

acknowledgement *n* (*ack*) BANK Anerkenntnis *nt*, COMMS *of signature, initials on document* Bestätigung *f*, Empfangsbestätigung *f*, Gegenzeichnung *f*, Abzeichnung *f*, FIN Anerkenntnis *nt*, GEN COMM *of request for goods* Anerkenntnis *f*, Bestätigung *f*, *of payment* Empfangsbestätigung *f*, Anerkennung *f*, *of mistake* Zugeständnis *nt*, Eingeständnis *nt*, *proof of payment* Quittung *f*, LAW Anerkenntnis *nt*, Beurkundung *f*; ~ **by a notary** *n* LAW notarielle Beglaubigung *f*, notarielle Beurkundung *f*; ~ **of debt** *n* BANK, FIN, GEN COMM Schuldanerkenntnis *nt*, LAW Anerkenntnis *nt*; ~ **of indebtness** *n* BANK Schuldanerkenntnis *f*, Schuldschein *m*, FIN, GEN COMM Schuldanerkenntnis *f*; ~ **of order** *n* COMMS, GEN COMM *sent by seller to customer* Auftragsbestätigung *f*; ~ **of receipt** *n* COMMS Empfangsbestätigung *f*, GEN COMM Annahmebestätigung *f*, Empfangsbestätigung *f*

ACM *abbr* (*Andean Common Market*) ECON Andenmarkt *m*, gemeinsamer Markt *m* der Anden

ACMA *abbr* BrE (*Associate of the Chartered Institute of*

Management Accountants) ACC Mitglied des Instituts der betrieblichen Rechnungsprüfer

ACOP *abbr* (*approved code of practice*) GEN COMM anerkannter Praxiscode *m*, anerkannter Verhaltenskodex *m*

A: ~ **countries** *n pl* IMP/EXP A-Länder *nt pl*

acoustic: ~ **memory** *n* COMP akustischer Speicher *m*; ~ **storage** *n* COMP akustischer Speicher *m*; ~ **store** *n* COMP akustischer Speicher *m*

ACP: ~ **states** *n pl* (*African, Caribbean and Pacific states*) ECON AKP-Staaten *m pl* (*Staaten in Afrika, im karibischen Raum und im Pazifischen Ozean*)

acquaint: ~ **sb of sth** *phr* COMMS jdn über etw informieren, jdn von etw informieren, GEN COMM jdn von etw in Kenntnis setzen, jdn mit etw vertraut machen; ~ **sb with sth** *phr* COMMS jdn über etw informieren, jdn von etw informieren, GEN COMM jdn von etw in Kenntnis setzen, jdn mit etw vertraut machen; ~ **oneself with sth** *phr* GEN COMM sich in etw einarbeiten, sich mit etw vertraut machen; ~ **sb with the situation** *phr* GEN COMM jdn mit der Lage vertraut machen

acquaintance *n* GEN COMM *friend* Bekannte(r) *mf* [decl. as adj], *circle of friends* Bekanntenkreis *m*, *with person* Bekanntschaft *f*, *with subject* Kenntnis *f*, Vertrautsein *nt*

acquainted: **be** ~ **with** *phr* GEN COMM *fact, situation* vertraut sein mit, *person* bekannt sein mit

acquire *vt* ACC anschaffen, sich aneignen, aufkaufen, erwerben, erlangen, FIN *reputation* erwerben, GEN COMM anschaffen, sich aneignen, aufkaufen, erwerben, erlangen, PROP, STOCK *option* erwerben; ♦ ~ **an interest in sth** GEN COMM Anteil an etw erwerben, eine Beteiligung an etw erwerben, sich an etw beteiligen

acquired *adj* GEN COMM erlangt, erworben; ~ **company** *n* GEN COMM *takeover* übernommene Gesellschaft *f*; ~ **rights** *n pl* GEN COMM *vested rights* Besitzstand *m*; ~ **share** *n* STOCK erworbene Aktie *f*; ~ **surplus** *n* FIN Gewinnvortrag beim Erwerb eines Unternehmens

acquiring: ~ **authority** *n* PROP *compulsory purchase* erwerbende Behörde *f*; ~ **company** *n* GEN COMM erwerbende Gesellschaft *f*, übernehmende Gesellschaft *f*

acquisition *n* ACC *a subsidiary acquired by takeover* übernommene Gesellschaft *f*, Akquisition *f*, Anschaffung *f*, Aufkauf *m*, Übernahme *f*, BANK Übernahme *f*, ECON *a subsidiary acquired by takeover* Akquisition *f*, *of company* Aufkauf *m*, übernommene Gesellschaft *f*, *of goods* Erwerb *m*, Übernahme *f*, FIN *a subsidiary acquired by takeover* Erwerb *m*, Aufkauf *m*, übernommene Gesellschaft *f*, Akquisition *f*, GEN COMM Ankauf *m*, *of company* Übernahme *f*, *company* Anschaffung *f*, *of goods* Erwerb, INS Akquisition *f*, LAW Anschaffung *f*, *relating to spouses* Erwerb *m*, S&M Akquisition *f*, STOCK *a subsidiary acquired by takeover* Aufkauf *m*, *of company* Übernahme *f*, *of goods* Erwerb *m*, TAX *of goods* Erwerb *m*, *of company* Übernahme *f*; ~ **accounting** *n* ACC Übertragungsbilanz *f*, *method of consolidation* Anschaffungswertprinzip *nt*; ~ **agent** *n* INS Abschlußvermittler, in *m,f*; ~ **of assets** *n* ACC Übernahme *f* eines Unternehmens, FIN Eigentumsbildung *f*; ~ **commission** *n* INS Abschlußprovision *f*; ~ **costs** *n pl* ACC, GEN COMM, INS, S&M Akquisitionskosten *pl*, Anschaffungskosten *pl*; ~ **of goods** *n* TAX Warenerwerb *m*; ~ **of ownership by occupancy** *n* LAW

Aneignung *f*, Ersitzung *f*; ~ **of participations** *n* FIN Beteiligungserwerb *m*; ~ **policy** *n* STOCK Übernahmepolitik *f*; ~ **profile** *n* BANK Übernahmeprofil *nt*; ~ **of shareholdings** *n* STOCK Beteiligungskäufe *m pl*; ~ **of stock** *n* STOCK Beteiligungserwerb *m*; ~ **value** *n* ACC, GEN COMM, LAW Anschaffungswert *m*

acquisitive *adj* GEN COMM *person, society* erwerbsorientiert, erwerbssüchtig, gewinnsüchtig; ~ **instinct** *n* GEN COMM sicheres Gefühl *nt* für Gewinnerwirtschaftung

acquisitiveness *n* GEN COMM Gewinnsucht *f*

acquit *vt* ACC tilgen, FIN *debt, duty* abtragen, tilgen, LAW *accused* freisprechen

acquittal *n* LAW *for debt* Befreiung *f* von Verbindlichkeiten, *of accused* Freispruch *m*

acquittance *n* LAW *proof of payment* Quittung *f*

across: ~-**the-board** *adj* GEN COMM allgemein, generell, pauschal; ~-**the-board changes** *n pl* MGMNT allgemeine Veränderungen *f pl*, pauschale Veränderungen *f pl*; ~-**the-board cut** *n* HRM *in prices, wages, taxes*, MGMNT Globalkürzung *f*; ~-**the-board export promotion** *n* ECON generelle Exportförderung *f*; ~-**the-board increase** *n* HRM *in prices, wages, taxes* allgemeine Erhöhung *f*, MGMNT allgemeine Erhöhung *f*, generelle Erhöhung *f*, pauschale Erhöhung *f*; ~-**the-board investigation** *n* ACC *auditing* generelle Prüfung *f*; ~-**the-counter** *adj* BANK, GEN COMM, LEIS, MGMNT *sales* regulär

ACSS *abbr* (*Automated Clearing Settlement System*) BANK automatisches Clearingssystem *nt*, automatisches Verrechnungssystem *nt*

ACT *abbr* BrE (*advance corporation tax*) TAX KStVz (*Körperschaftssteuer-Vorauszahlung*)

act 1. *n* GEN COMM *deed* Akt *m*, Handlung *f*, LAW *statute* Gesetz *nt*, *action of a person* Handlung *f*, POL Akte *f*, Beschluß *m*; **2.** *vi* GEN COMM agieren, funktionieren, handeln, tätig sein, tätig werden, wirken; ♦ ~ **in good faith** LAW in gutem Glauben handeln; ~ **in one's official capacity** MGMNT in offizieller Funktion handeln; ~ **in the interest of an absent person** LAW *contracts* im Interesse einer abwesenden Person handeln; ~ **on sb's behalf** LAW *on behalf of particular person* im Namen von jdm handeln, im Auftrag von jdm handeln, *on behalf of unspecified person* im Auftrag Dritter handeln, in fremdem Namen handeln; ~ **on sth** GEN COMM *advice, suggestion* sich nach etw richten, *decision* etw nachkommen; ~ **ultra vires** LAW seine Vollmacht überschreiten; ~ **under pressure** GEN COMM unter Druck handeln

act: ~ **of acknowledgement** *n* LAW Beurkundung *f*; ~ **of bankruptcy** *n* ACC, LAW Konkursordnung *f*, Konkursgesetz *nt*, Konkursrecht *nt*; ~ **of cession** *n* GEN COMM, LAW Abtretungsakt *m*, Abtretungshandlung *m*

Act: ~ **of Congress** *n* AmE POL Kongreßbeschluß *m*

act: ~ **of honor** *AmE*, ~ **of honour** *BrE* *n* LAW Ehrenannahme *f* eines Wechsels

acting *adj* GEN COMM amtierend, geschäftsführend, stellvertretend, MGMNT amtierend; ~ **allowance** *n* GEN COMM Handlungsbefugnis *f*, Handlungserlaubnis *f*; ~ **director** *n* MGMNT amtierender Direktor *m*, amtierende Direktorin *f*, geschäftsführender Direktor *m* (*GD*), geschäftsführende Direktorin *f* (*GD*); ~ **partner** *n* MGMNT aktiver Gesellschafter *m*, aktive Gesellschafterin *f*, geschäftsführender Partner *m*, geschäftsführende Partnerin *f*, tätiger Teilhaber *m*, tätige Teilhaberin *f*

actio in personam *n* LAW *jarg* schuldrechtliche Klage *f* (*jarg*)

actio in rem *n* LAW *jarg* dingliche Klage *f* (*jarg*)

action *n* ADMIN, COMP Aktion *f*, ECON Aktion *f*, Handlung *f*, GEN COMM Aktion *f*, Handlung *f*, Tat *f*, Tätigkeit *f*, Tätigwerden *nt*, Vorgehen *nt*, LAW Klage *f*, Verfahren *nt*; ◆ **out of ~** GEN COMM außer Betrieb

actionability *n* LAW Klagbarkeit *f*

actionable *adj* GEN COMM *remark, offence, allegation* belangbar, einklagbar, justifiabel, LAW klagbar

action: **~ against persons unknown** *n* LAW Verfahren *nt* gegen Unbekannt; **~ based on contract** *n* LAW Vertragsklage *f*; **~ based on liability** *n* LAW *contracts* Haftungsklage *f*; **~ code** *n* COMP Aktionscode *m*, Maßnahmenschlüssel *m*; **~ for cancellation** *n* LAW *contract* Aufhebungsklage *f*, Aufhebungsverfahren *nt*, Nichtigkeitsklage *f*; **~ for damages** *n* INS, LAW Schadensersatzklage *f*; **~ for eviction** *n* LAW, PROP Räumungsklage *f*; **~ for libel** *n* LAW Verleumdungsklage *f*, Beleidigungsklage *f*, Schadensersatzklage *f*; **~ for rescission** *n* LAW Anfechtungsklage *f*, Aufhebungsklage *f*; **~ for specific performance** *n* LAW *contracts* Erfüllungsklage *f*; **~ implying intention** *n* LAW *contracts* konkludentes Verhalten *nt*; **~ message** *n* COMP Aktionsnachricht *f*; **~-oriented** *adj* GEN COMM handlungsorientiert; **~ parameter** *n* ADMIN Aktionsparameter *m*; **~ plan** *n* GEN COMM, HRM Maßnahmenplan *m*; **~ program** *AmE*, **~ programme** *BrE* *n* ECON, GEN COMM Aktionsprogramm *nt*, Handlungsprogramm *nt*; **~ research** *n* MGMNT Aktionsforschung *f*, anwendungsbezogene Forschung *f*; **~ scope** *n* ECON, MGMNT Handlungsspielraum *m*

activate *vt* ACC, COMP, GEN COMM aktivieren, IND *button, switch* aktivieren, betätigen, drücken, *mechanism* in Betrieb setzen, MGMNT *contingency plan, procedure* in Kraft setzen, aktivieren

active *adj* ACC *debt* ausstehend, COMP *computer, peripheral* aktiv, arbeitend, FIN *capital, assets* aktiv, lebhaft, GEN COMM *person* arbeitend, aktiv, tätig, HRM *person*, IMP/EXP, INS, LAW aktiv, MGMNT aktiv, geschäftsführend, S&M *market* lebhaft, STOCK *market* gängig, lebhaft, *securities* lebhaft gehandelt, TAX aktiv; ◆ **in ~ employment** HRM aktiv tätig

active: **~ balance of payments** *n* ECON, FIN aktive Zahlungsbilanz *f*; **~ bond** *n* STOCK verzinsliche Schuldverschreibung *f*; **~ bond crowd** *n* *AmE* STOCK Makler *m pl* für festverzinsliche Schuldverschreibungen; **~ business** *n* GEN COMM aktives Unternehmen *nt*; **~ capital** *n* FIN arbeitendes Kapital *nt*; **~ circulation of bank notes** *n* ECON Banknotenumlauf *m*; **~ computer** *n* COMP arbeitende Rechneranlage *f*; **~ dealings** *n pl* STOCK lebhafte Umsätze *m pl*, lebhafter Handel *m*; **~ file** *n* COMP aktive Datei *f*; **~ fiscal policy** *n* ECON aktive Fiskalpolitik *f*, konjunkturorientierte Finanzpolitik *f*; **~ life table** *n* INS Aktivitätsordnung *f*

actively *adv* FIN, S&M, STOCK lebhaft; **~ traded** *adj* STOCK lebhaft gehandelt

active: **~ management** *n* GEN COMM aktives Management *nt*; **~ money** *n* FIN lebhafter Geldmarkt *m*; **~ partner** *n* MGMNT aktiver Gesellschafter *m*, aktive Gesellschafterin *f*, geschäftsführender Partner *m*, geschäftsführende Partnerin *f*, tätiger Teilhaber *m*, tätige Teilhaberin *f*; **~ population** *n* HRM *workers* aktive Bevölkerung *f*; **~ program** *n* COMP aktuelles Programm *nt*; **~ reinsurance** *n* INS aktive Rückversicherung *f*; **~ securities** *n pl* STOCK lebhaft gehandelte Wertpapiere *nt pl*; **~ share** *n* STOCK gängige Aktie *f*; **~ trade balance** *n* ECON, IMP/EXP aktive Handelsbilanz *f*; **~ trading** *n* S&M lebhafter Handel *m*, STOCK lebhafte Umsätze *m pl*, lebhafter Handel *m*; **~ window** *n* COMP aktives Fenster *nt*

activist *n* ECON, POL Aktivist, in *m,f*

activity *n* BANK *account* Kontoumsatz *m*, ECON Beschäftigung *f*, FIN Aktivität *f*, HRM Beschäftigung *f*, GEN COMM Aktivität *f*, Tätigkeit *f*, *duties* Aufgabengebiet *nt*, STOCK Umsatz *m*; **~ accounting** *n* ACC Abteilungserfolgsrechnung *f*, *direct costing* Grenzplankostenrechnung *f*; **~ analysis** *n* ECON Konjunkturanalyse *f*, Prozeßanalyse *f*, GEN COMM Aktivitätsanalyse *f*; **~-based costing** *n* *BrE* ACC auslastungsorientierte Kostenrechnung *f*, beschäftigungsorientierte Kostenrechnung *f*; **~ chart** *n* MGMNT Arbeitsplanungsbogen *m*; **~ classification** *n* ACC Kostenstellengliederung *f*; **~ coding** *n* ACC Kostenstellengruppen *f pl*; **~ element** *n* ACC Kostenstelle *f*; **~ level** *n* ACC, ADMIN, ECON Beschäftigungsgrad *m*, Prozeßniveau *nt*; **~ rate** *n* ECON Erwerbsquote *f*; **~ ratio** *n* FIN Aktivitätskennzahl *f*, betriebswirtschaftliche Kennziffer *f*; **~ report** *n* GEN COMM Tätigkeitsbericht *m*; **~ sampling** *n* ADMIN *statistics*, IND, MATH Multimomentverfahren *nt*, MGMNT Multimomentaufnahme *f*, S&M *industrial engineering* Multimomentverfahren *nt*; **~ total** *n* GEN COMM Gesamtaktivitäten *f pl*

Act: **~ of Parliament** *n* *BrE* LAW Gesetz *nt*

act: **~ of recording** *n* FIN Aufzinsung *f*

ACTU *abbr* (*Australian Council of Trade Unions*) HRM australischer Gewerkschaftsbund, ≈ DGB (*Deutscher Gewerkschaftsbund*)

actual *adj* FIN aktiv, aktuell, GEN COMM effektiv, real, tatsächlich, echt, gegenwärtig, Ist-; **~ address** *n* COMP echte Adresse *f*, tatsächliche Adresse *f*; **~ amount** *n* ACC, BANK *outlay, expenditure* Ist-Betrag *m*, FIN ausmachender Betrag *m*; **~ assets** *n pl* FIN Aktivvermögen *nt*; **~ balance** *n* ACC, BANK *outlay, expenditure* Ist-Betrag *m*, Ist-Betrag *m*, Kontostand *m*; **~ carrier** *n* TRANSP tatsächlicher Spediteur *m*, tatsächlicher Transportunternehmer *m*, *air transport* tatsächlicher Luftfrachtführer *m*, tatsächlicher Lufttransport *m*, *water transport* tatsächlicher Verfrachter *m*; **~ cash disbursement** *n* ACC effektiver Zahlungsausgang *m*, tatsächliche Barauszahlungen *f pl*, tatsächliche Kassenausgänge *m pl*; **~ cash value** *n* (*a.c.v.*) FIN Barwert *m*, Kapitalwert *m*, Zeitwert *m*, GEN COMM Marktwert *m*; **~ cost** *n* ACC, ADMIN Ist-Kosten *pl*, pagatorische Kosten *pl*, tatsächliche Kosten *pl*; **~ cost system** *n* ACC *accounting principle* Istkostenrechnung *f*; **~ deficit** *n* ECON tatsächlicher Verlust *m*, tatsächliches Defizit *nt*; **~ earnings** *n pl* ACC, HRM Effektivlohn *m*, Effektivverdienst *m*; **~ eviction** *n* PROP Zwangsräumung *f*; **~ expenditure** *n* ACC Ist-Ausgaben *f pl*; **~ expense** *n* ACC tatsächliche Ausgaben *f pl*; **~ figures** *n pl* ACC Ist-Zahlen *f pl*, ECON tatsächliche Zahlen *f pl*; **~ gross weight** *n* TRANSP tatsächliches Bruttogewicht *nt*; **~ instruction** *n* COMP echter Befehl *m*; **~ inventory** *n* *AmE* (*cf actual stock BrE*) GEN COMM Ist-Bestand *m*; **~ investment** *n* BANK Ist-Investitionen *f pl*

actuality *n* GEN COMM Realität *f*, Wirklichkeit *f*

actualize *vt* COMP aktualisieren, updaten *(jarg)*, FIN, GEN COMM aktualisieren

actual: ~ **key** *n* COMP Adreßschlüssel *m*; ~ **level of unemployment** *n* ECON tatsächliche Arbeitslosigkeit *f*, tatsächlicher Arbeitslosenstand *m*, aktuelle Arbeitslosigkeit *f*; ~ **loss** *n* FIN Vermögenseinbuße *f*; ~ **man-hours** *n pl* HRM Ist-Stunden *f pl*; ~ **net worth** *n* ACC, FIN Nettovermögen *nt*, Reinvermögen *nt*, haftendes Eigenkapital *nt*; ~ **outcome** *n* GEN COMM tatsächliches Ergebnis *nt*; ~ **output** *n* IND Ist-Beschäftigung *f*, Ist-Leistung *f*; ~ **payload** *n* TRANSP *net weight* zahlende Nutzlast *f*; ~ **possession** *n* LAW, WEL unmittelbarer Besitz *m*; ~ **price** *n* ACC Marktpreis *m*, ECON Marktpreis *m*, STOCK Tageskurs *m*, Tagespreis *m*; ~ **quotation** *n* STOCK effektiver Wertpapierkurs *m*; ~ **rate of growth** *n* ECON tatsächliche Wachstumsrate *f*

actuals *n pl* STOCK *futures* Basisinstrument *nt*, Basiswert *m*, TRANSP *freight market* sofort verfügbare Ware *f*

actual: ~ **stock** *n BrE (cf actual inventory AmE)* GEN COMM Ist-Bestand *m*; ~ **time** *n* IND Ist-Zeit *f*; ~ **versus target comparison** *n* ADMIN, ECON Soll-Ist-Vergleich *m*; ~ **wage** *n* ACC, ECON, HRM Effektivlohn *m*, Reallohn *m*

actuarial *adj* INS versicherungsmathematisch, versicherungstechnisch; ~ **deficit** *n* INS versicherungsmathematisches Defizit *nt*, versicherungstechnisches Defizit *nt*; ~ **expectation** *n* INS mathematischer Erwartungswert *m*; ~ **liability** *n* INS versicherungsmathematische Leistungspflicht *f*, versicherungstechnische Leistungspflicht *f*; ~ **loss** *n* INS versicherungsmathematischer Schaden *m*, versicherungstechnischer Schaden *m*; ~ **theory** *n* ECON Versicherungsmathematik *f*

actuate *vt* IND *machine, system, device* in Gang setzen

actuator: ~ **pole** *n* TRANSP *engineering* Steller-Pol *m*

actus reus *n* LAW actus reus *m (frml)*

ACU *abbr (administration of the customs union)* IMP/EXP VdZ *(Verwaltung der Zollunion)*

acute: ~ **awareness** *n* GEN COMM, POL *of particular factor* geschärftes Bewußtsein *nt*, kritisches Bewußtsein *nt*, verstärkte Sensibilisierung *f*

a.c.v. *abbr (actual cash value)* FIN Kapitalwert *m*, Zeitwert *m*

ad *n infrml (advert, advertisement)* GEN COMM Werbung *f*, MEDIA, S&M *in print* Annonce *f*, Anzeige *f*, Inserat *nt*, *on television, radio* Werbespot *m*

a/d *abbr (after date)* GEN COMM ab Ausstellungsdatum, ab dato, ab heute, dato nach heute, nach Ausstellungsdatum

AD *abbr (above deck)* TRANSP *shipping* auf Deck befindlich

adapt **1.** *vt* GEN COMM anpassen, *text* bearbeiten, umschreiben; **2.** *vi* GEN COMM sich anpassen; ♦ ~ **to** GEN COMM sich anpassen an [+acc]

adaptability *n* GEN COMM Anpassungsfähigkeit *f*, *of product, machine, system* Verwendungsfähigkeit *f*, HRM Anpassungsfähigkeit *f*

adaptable *adj* GEN COMM anpassungsfähig, wandlungsfähig

adaptation *n* GEN COMM Adaption *f*, Angleichung *f*, Anpassung *f*, Umschreibung *f*

adapted: ~ **technology** *n* ADMIN, ECON angepaßte Technik *f*

adapting *n* GEN COMM *text* Bearbeitung *f*

adaptive *adj* COMP, ECON, GEN COMM adaptiv; ~ **control** *n* COMP *system* adaptive Regelung *f*; ~ **expectations** *n pl* ECON adaptive Erwartungen *f pl*; ~ **filtering** *n* GEN COMM *business administration* adaptives Filtern *nt*

adaptor *n* COMP Adapter *m*

ADAS *abbr BrE (Agricultural Development and Advisory Service)* ECON landwirtschaftlicher Entwicklungs- und Beratungsdienst

AD-AS *abbr (aggregate demand-aggregate supply)* ECON Gesamtnachfrage-Gesamtangebot

ADB *abbr (African Development Bank)* BANK, FIN AEB *(Afrikanische Entwicklungsbank)*

ADC *abbr* COMMS *(advice of duration and/or charge)* Anzeige *f* der Dauer und/oder Belastung, Mitteilung *f* über Laufzeit und/oder Belastung, COMP *(analog-to-digital converter) hardware* Analog-Digital-Wandler *m*, GEN COMM *(advice of duration and/or charge)* Anzeige *f* der Dauer und/oder Belastung, Mitteilung *f* über Laufzeit und/oder Belastung

add *vt* GEN COMM anfügen, beifügen, MATH *points* hinzufügen, *column, figures* addieren, aufsummieren, hinzurechnen, zusammenzählen, *figures* hinzuzählen, MEDIA einfügen, hinzufügen

add in *vt* GEN COMM *details, figures, statement* einfügen, einsetzen, hinzufügen

add to *vt* GEN COMM *increase* vergrößern

add up **1.** *vt* ACC, MATH *bill, column of figures* aufsummieren, zusammenrechnen, *sum total* zusammenzählen, *figures, results* addieren; **2.** *vi* ACC, MATH *figures, results* aufgehen, stimmen

add up to *vi* GEN COMM betragen, sich belaufen auf [+acc]

add-carry *n* COMP Additionsübertrag *m*

added: ~ **value** *n* ADMIN, ECON Wertschöpfung *f*, FIN Mehrwert *m*, Wertschöpfung *f*, S&M *special offer* Mehrwert *m*, TAX Wertschöpfung *f*, Mehrwert *m*; ~ **value service** ADMIN, COMMS, ECON, GEN COMM, S&M Mehrwertdienst *m*

addendum *n* GEN COMM Nachtrag *m*

adding *n* MATH Addieren *nt*; ~ **counter** *n* COMP Addierwerk *nt*; ~ **machine** *n* COMP, FIN Addiermaschine *f*, Additionsmaschine *f*

add: ~ **instruction** *n* COMP Addierbefehl *m*

addition *n* ACC *new asset* Anlagenzugang *m*, *to fixed assets* Zugang *m*, ADMIN Zugang *m*, COMP Addition *f*, GEN COMM Addition *f*, Beigabe *f*, Ergänzung *f*, Hinzufügung *f*, Vergrößerung *f*, Zuwachs *m*, INS Zuschlag *m*, MATH Addition *f*, Zusammenrechnung *f*, Hinzufügung *f*, MEDIA *text amendment* Einfügung *f*, Hinzufügung *f*; ♦ **in** ~ **to** GEN COMM zusätzlich zu; **no** ~, **no correction** GEN COMM ohne Ergänzung, ohne Korrektur

additional *adj* GEN COMM zusätzlich; ~ **charge** *n* ACC Zusatzgebühr *f*, Zuschlag *m*, COMMS Nachgebühr *f*; ~ **clause** *n* LAW Zusatzklausel *f*; ~ **conditions** *n pl* INS Zusatzbedingungen *f pl*; ~ **cover** *n* STOCK Nachschußforderung *f*; ~ **earnings** *n pl* GEN COMM, HRM, TAX Nebenverdienst *m*; ~ **expense insurance** *n* INS Mehrkostenversicherung *f*; ~ **extended coverage** *n* INS erweiterter Versicherungsschutz *m*, Gebäudenachversicherung *f* gegen zusätzliche Risiken; ~ **feature** *n* PATENTS zusätzliche Eigenschaft *f*, zusätzliches Merkmal *nt*, Zusatzeigenschaft *f*, Zusatzmerkmal *nt*; ~ **financial facilities** *n pl* ECON *balance of payments* zusätzliche Kreditfazilitäten *f pl*, zusätzliche Finanzierungsvorkehrungen *f pl*; **~ insurance** *n* INS Zusatzversicherung *f*; **~ insured** *n* INS Mitversicherte(r) *mf* [decl. as adj]; **~ interest** *n* ACC, BANK Zinszuschlag *m*, zusätzliche Zinsen *m pl*; **~ labor** *AmE*, **~ labour** *BrE* *n* HRM zusätzliche Arbeitskräfte *f pl*; **~ margin** *n* STOCK zusätzlicher Einschuß *m*; **~ matter** *n* PATENTS zusätzliche Angelegenheit *f*, Zusatzmaterial *nt*; **~ paid-in capital** *n* ACC zusätzlich eingezahltes Kapital *nt*; **~ pay** *n* HRM Prämie *f*; **~ payment** *n* ACC, GEN COMM, INS Nachschußforderung *f*; **~ personal allowance** *n* TAX zusätzlicher Grundfreibetrag *m*; **~ premium** *n* (*AP*) INS Beitragszuschlag *m*, Prämienzuschlag *m*, Zuschlagsprämie *f*; **~ respite** *n* LAW *trade contracts* Nachfrist *f*; **~ security** *n* INS zusätzliche Sicherheit *f*; **~ terms** *n pl* LAW *contracts* Zusätze *m pl*; **~ voluntary contribution** *n* (*AVC*) INS, TAX freiwillige Zuzahlung *f*, freiwillige Zusatzleistung *f*; **~ worker hypothesis** *n* HRM Hypothese *f* zusätzlicher Arbeitnehmer

addition: **~ of fixed asset units** *n* ACC Anlagenzugang *m*

additions *n pl* ACC Zugänge *m pl*

addition: **~ slip** *n* GEN COMM Additionsstreifen *m*; **~ table** *n* COMP Additionstabelle *f*; **~ theorem** *n* MATH Additionstheorem *nt*; **~ theorems of probability** *n pl* MATH *statistics* Additionssätze *m pl* der Wahrscheinlichkeit; **~ to age** *n* INS Alterszuschlag *m*; **~ to capital account** *n* ACC, ECON Zugang *m* zum Kapitalkonto; **~ to plant and equipment** *n* ACC Anlagenzugang *m*; **~ to stock** *n* ADMIN Auffüllung *f* der Lagervorräte, Lagerzugang *m*

additive *n* GEN COMM Zusatz *m*; **~ marginal costs** *n pl* ADMIN, ECON additive Grenzkosten *pl*; **~ property** *n* MATH *statistics* Additivität *f*; **~ random walk process** *n* MATH *statistics* additiver Zufallsprozeß *m*

add: **~ lister** *n* GEN COMM Addiermaschine *f*; **~ listing machine** *n* GEN COMM Additionsmaschine *f*

add-on *n* ACC Zusatz *m*, BANK Zuschlag *m*, COMP Zusatz *m*, GEN COMM Ergänzung *f*, MGMNT Zusatz *m*, STOCK Ergänzung *f*; **~ basis** *n* GEN COMM Ergänzungsgrundlage *f*; **~ board** *n* COMP Zusatzkarte *f*; **~ card** *n* COMP Zusatzkarte *f*; **~ CDs** *n pl* BrE (*add-on domestic certificates of deposit*) STOCK Ergänzungsinlandseinlagenzertifikate *nt pl*; **~ costs** *n pl* ACC, ADMIN Lohnnebenkosten *pl*, Personalnebenkosten *pl*, Personalzusatzkosten *pl*, MGMNT sonstige Kosten *pl*, Zusatzkosten *pl*; **~ domestic certificates of deposit** *n pl* BrE (*add-on CDs*) STOCK Ergänzungsinlandseinlagenzertifikate *nt pl*; **~ equipment** *n* COMP, MGMNT Zusatzausrüstung *f*, Zusatzgeräte *nt pl*; **~ interest** *n* BANK Teilzahlungszinsen *m pl*; **~ memory** *n* COMP Zusatzspeicher *m*; **~ sales** *n pl* BrE S&M *market research* Anschlußaufträge *m pl*; **~ yield** *n* STOCK Ergänzungsrendite *f*; **~ yield equivalent** *n* STOCK *Treasury bills* Ergänzungsverzinsungswert *m*

address 1. *n* COMMS *of person, company, building, computer* Adresse *f*, Anschrift *f*, *talk, speech* Ansprache *f*, Rede *f*, COMP *location of data in computer memory* Adresse *f*, GEN COMM Adresse *f*, Anschrift *f*, Aufschrift *f*, S&M Adresse *f*; **2.** *vt* COMMS *parcel, envelope*, COMP adressieren, GEN COMM *person* anreden, ansprechen, titulieren, *comment, remark* adressieren, *problem* angehen, LAW *directive, complaint* richten an [+acc]; ◆ **~ as above** GEN COMM Anschrift wie oben; **~ oneself to sth** GEN COMM *issue, problem* etw aufgreifen, sich etw zuwenden, *problem, matter in hand, task* sich etw

widmen; **~ your complaints to** GEN COMM richten Sie Ihre Beschwerden an

addressable *adj* GEN COMM adressierbar

address: **~ book** *n* COMMS Adreßbuch *nt*; **~ bus** *n* COMP Adreßbus *m*; **~ capacity** *n* COMP Adressenkapazität *f*; **~ card** *n* COMP Adressierkarte *f*; **~ commission** *n* IMP/EXP *shipping* Schiffsüberführungsgebühr *f*, TRANSP *shipping* Ladeprovision *f*; **~ constant** *n* COMP Adreßkonstante *f*

addressee *n* COMMS Adressat, in *m,f*, Empfänger, in *m,f*; ◆ **to ~ only** COMMS eigenhändig

addresser *n* COMMS Aussteller, in *m,f*

address: **~ field** *n* COMMS Anschriftfeld *nt*, COMP Adreßfeld *nt*, Adressenfeld *nt*; **~ file** *n* COMP Adreßdatei *f*, Adressendatei *f*; **~ generation** *n* COMP Adressenerzeugung *f*; **~ index** *n* COMP Adreßindex *m*; **~ information** *n* GEN COMM Adressenangaben *f pl*

addressing *n* COMP Adressierung *f*, Adressiermethode *f*, Adressierverfahren *nt*; **~ machine** *n* GEN COMM Adressiermaschine *f*; **~ mode** *n* COMP Adressierungsart *f*; **~ system** *n* COMP Adressiersystem *f*

address: **~ label** *n* COMMS Adreßaufkleber *m*, Adreßetikett *nt*, Anhängadresse *f*; **~ line** *n* S&M Adressenzeile *f*; **~ marker** *n* COMP Adreßmarke *f*; **~ modification** *n* COMP Adressenänderung *f*, Adreßmodifikation *f*

Addressograph® *n* GEN COMM Adressiermaschine *f*

address: **~ register** *n* COMP Adreßregister *nt*; **~ selection** *n* COMP Adressenauswahl *f*; **~ space** *n* COMP Adreßraum *m*; **~ space administration** *n* COMP Adreßraumverwaltung *f*

add: **~ statement** *n* COMP Additionsanweisung *f*

adduce *vt* LAW *evidence* anführen, vorlegen

adequacy *n* GEN COMM *of report, explanation, description* Angemessenheit *f*

adequate *adj* ACC angemessen, ECON hinreichend, FIN ausreichend, GEN COMM *explanation, funds, report, supply, technique* adäquat, angemessen, auskömmlich, ausreichend, HRM angemessen, INS ausreichend, LAW adäquat, ausreichend; **~ care** *n* LAW ausreichende Sorgfalt *f*; **~ causal nexus** *n* LAW adäquater Kausalzusammenhang *m*; **~ funding** *n* GEN COMM angemessene Finanzierung *f*

adequately: **~ funded** *adj* ACC fristenkongruent finanziert, fristgerecht finanziert, FIN ausreichend finanziert; **~ insured** *adj* INS ausreichend versichert

adequate: **~ sample** *n* MATH *statistics* repräsentative Stichprobe *f*; **~ target rate** *n* FIN *profit* Kalkulationszinsfuß *m*, interner Zinsfuß *m*, Rentabilitätsziel *nt*, *rate of interest* angestrebte Kapitalverzinsung *f*

ADG *abbr* (*assistant director general*) HRM stellvertretender Generaldirektor *m*, stellvertretende Generaldirektorin *f*

adhere: **~ to** *phr* GEN COMM *contract* einhalten, *principle* befolgen, festhalten an [+dat]

adherence *n* GEN COMM, LAW Befolgung *f*, Einhaltung; **~ to contract** *n* LAW Vertragseinhaltung *f*

adhesion: **~ contract** *n* LAW *type of contract* Knebelungsvertrag *m*, Standardvertrag *m* mit einseitig auferlegten Bedingungen

adhesive: **~ envelope** *n* ADMIN gummierter Briefumschlag *m*; **~ label** *n* ADMIN gummiertes Etikett *nt*, GEN COMM Aufkleber *m*, Aufklebezettel *m*

ad hoc *phr* GEN COMM ad hoc, aus dem Augenblick heraus, fallweise, zu diesem Zweck; ~ **committee** *n* GEN COMM ad hoc Ausschuß *m*

ad idem *phr* GEN COMM ad idem

ad interim *phr* GEN COMM ad interim, einstweilig, vorläufig, in der Zwischenzeit, zwischenzeitlich

adjoining *adj* GEN COMM *room, building* angrenzend, benachbart, aneinandergrenzend

adjoint *adj* MATH adjungiert; ~ **of a matrix** *n* MATH adjungierte Matrix *f*

adjourn 1. *vt* LAW *case* vertagen, MGMNT *meeting* unterbrechen, vertagen; ◆ ~ **sentence** LAW Strafurteil vertagen; **2.** *vi* GEN COMM, POL *parliament* die Sitzung beenden; ~ **to** MGMNT *somewhere else* sich begeben

ajourned: the meeting stands ~ *phr* GEN COMM die Sitzung ist vertagt

adjournment *n* LAW Vertagung *f*, MGMNT *of decision* Aufschub *m*, Aufschiebung *f*, *of meeting* Unterbrechung *f*, Vertagung *f*; ~ **debate** *n* BrE POL Vertagungsdebatte *f*

adjudge: ~ **sb to be sth** *phr* LAW jdn für etw erklären; ~ **heavy damages** LAW hohen Schadensersatz zusprechen; ~ **sb bankrupt** *phr* ACC, LAW jdn für zahlungsunfähig erklären, jdn gerichtlich für Bankrott erklären, jdn offiziell für Bankrott erklären, Konkursverfahren über jds Vermögen eröffnen; ~ **sth to sb** *phr* LAW jdm etw zusprechen

adjudicate 1. *vt* GEN COMM entscheiden; ◆ ~ **sb bankrupt** ACC, LAW jdn für zahlungsunfähig erklären, jdn gerichtlich für Bankrott erklären, jdn offiziell für Bankrott erklären, Konkursverfahren über jds Vermögen eröffnen; **2.** *vi* GEN COMM entscheiden, urteilen, LAW zuerkennen, zusprechen; ◆ ~ **at** GEN COMM *claim, contest* Preisrichter sein bei

adjudication: ~ **in bankruptcy** *n* ACC, FIN, LAW Eröffnung *f* des Konkursverfahrens, Konkurseröffnung *f*; ~ **of bankruptcy order** *n* ACC, FIN, LAW Konkurseröffnungsbeschluß *m*

adjudicator *n* GEN COMM Gutachter, in *m,f*, Preisrichter, in *m,f*, Schiedsrichter, in *m,f*

adjugate: ~ **of a matrix** *n* MATH adjungierte Matrix *f*

adjunct *n* GEN COMM *person* Beigeordnete(r) *mf* [decl. as adj], Kollege *m*, Kollegin *f*, Mitarbeiter, in *m,f*, *thing* Beigabe *f*, Zusatz *m*, LAW *person* Kollege *m*, Kollegin *f*; ~ **professor** *n* AmE HRM außerordentlicher Professor *m*

adjust 1. *vt* ACC bereinigen, BANK bereinigen, *correct* berichtigen, korrigieren, ECON *price, schedule, timetable* berichtigen, bereinigen, GEN COMM regulieren, einstellen auf, richtigstellen, berichtigen, INS *average* ändern, einstellen, angleichen, anpassen, MATH *figures* korrigieren, berichtigen; ◆ ~ **a claim** INS eine Forderung regulieren, einen Anspruch regulieren, einen Schaden regulieren; ~ **downwards** ECON *prices* nach unten angleichen, nach unten anpassen, MATH nach unten angleichen; ~ **oneself to a situation** GEN COMM sich an eine Situation anpassen; ~ **to** ECON, GEN COMM, INS angleichen an [+acc], anpassen an [+acc], MATH angleichen an [+acc]; ~ **upwards** ECON *prices* nach oben angleichen, nach oben anpassen, MATH hochregeln; **2.** *vi* ACC abgrenzen, ECON *wages, prices* sich einpendeln

adjustable *adj* FIN *mortgage rate* variabel verzinslich, GEN COMM regelbar, *hours, rate* variabel, *appliance, position, speed* einstellbar, justierbar, verstellbar INS

policy variabel verzinslich, TRANSP verstellbar; ~ **mortgage loan** *n* (*AML*) BANK variables Hypothekendarlehen *nt*; ~ **peg** *n* ECON *exchange rates* limitierte Stufenflexibilität *f* fester Wechselkurse; ~ **rate mortgage** *n* (*ARM*) BANK, PROP variabel verzinsliche Hypothek *f*

adjusted *adj* ACC angepaßt, bereinigt, berichtigt, BANK, ECON, FIN reguliert, GEN COMM bereinigt, berichtigt, reguliert, INS reguliert, MATH berichtigt, STOCK angepaßt; ◆ ~ **for inflation** ECON inflationsbereinigt

adjusted: ~ **balance sheet** *n* ACC berichtigte Bilanz *f*; ~ **capital ratio** *n* BANK bereinigtes Kapitalverhältnis *nt*; ~ **claim** *n* INS regulierter Schaden *m*; ~ **cost base** *n* AmE (*ACB*) ACC angepaßte Bewertungsgrundlagen *f pl* für die Aufwandsrechnung; ~ **cost basis** *n* ACC angepaßte Bewertungsgrundlagen *f pl* für die Aufwandsrechnung; ~ **exercise price** *n* BrE STOCK angepaßter Basispreis *m*; ~ **index** *n* ACC bereinigter Index *m*; ~ **selling price** *n* ACC angepaßter Verkaufspreis *m*, S&M berichtigter Verkaufspreis *m*; ~ **trial balance** *n* ACC berichtigte Rohbilanz *f*, berichtigte Saldenbilanz *f*, Berichtigungsbuchung *f*, berichtigte Probebilanz *f*

adjusting: ~ **assessment** *n* LAW, TAX Berichtigungsfeststellung *f*; ~ **entry** *n* ACC Berichtigungsbuchung *f*, GEN COMM Berichtigungseintrag *m*

adjustment *n* ACC *of statistics, error* Berichtigung *f*, *accrual accounting* Abgrenzung *f*, BANK Berichtigung *f*, ECON *wages* Gehaltsangleichung *f*, Lohnangleichung *f*, *of prices, rates, charges, wages* Anpassung *f*, GEN COMM *to situation* Angleichung *f*, Anpassung *f*, Assimilation *f*, *regulation* Ausgleich *m*, Einstellung *f*, Berichtigung *f*, INS Anpassung *f*, Aufteilung *f* von Schäden auf mehrere Versicherer, Beilegung *f*, Bereinigung *f*, Berichtigung *f*, *payment* Entschädigungsleistung *f*, Nachverrechnung *f*, Regelung *f* des Anspruchs, Regulierung *f*, *error* Richtigstellung *f*, *fixing* Schadenfestsetzung *f*, Schlichtung *f*, LAW, PATENTS Berichtigung *f*; ~ **account** *n* ACC *accrual accounting* Berichtigungskonto *nt*; ~ **of assessed value** *n* TAX Wertfortschreibung *f*, Fortschreibung *f*; ~ **of average** *n* INS Havarieregulierung *f*; ~ **bond** *n* AmE STOCK Gewinnschuldverschreibung *f*; ~ **bureau** *n* AmE INS Schadensregulierer *m*; ~ **center** AmE, ~ **centre** BrE *n* WEL Einzelzelle *f*, Isolierzelle *f*, Sonderzelle *f*, *for young offenders* Besserungsanstalt *f* (*obs*), Erziehungsheim *nt*; ~ **clause** *n* INS Schadenregulierungsklausel *f*, Summenanpassungsklausel *f*; ~ **costs** *n pl* INS Regulierungskosten *pl*; ~ **credit** *n* BANK, ECON Überbrückungskredit *m*; ~ **gap** *n* ECON Anpassungslücke *f*; ~ **measure** *n* GEN COMM Anpassungsmaßnahme *f*; ~ **premium** *n* INS Beitragsnachverrechnung *f*, Nachverrechnungsprämie *f*; ~ **speed** *n* ECON Anpassungsgeschwindigkeit *f*; ~ **of sum insured** *n* INS Anpassung *f* der Versicherungssumme, Summenanpassung *f*; ~ **of tariff rates** *n* IMP/EXP Angleichung *f* von Zollsätzen; ~ **trigger** *n* GEN COMM auslösender Impuls *m*

Adk *abbr* (*awning deck*) TRANSP *shipping* Sonnendeck *nt*

adman *n* *infrml* (*advertising man*) HRM Anzeigenbearbeiter *m*, Werbefachmann *m*, Werbefritze *m* (*infrml*)

admass *n* S&M Werbevieh *nt*; ~ **society** *n* S&M Werbevieh *nt*

admin *abbr* (*infrml*) (*administration*) ADMIN Reg. (*Regie-*

rung), Verw. (*Verwaltung*), GEN COMM, MGMNT Verw. (*Verwaltung*), POL Reg. (*Regierung*)

administer *vt* GEN COMM, LAW, MGMNT, POL *programme* verwalten

administered *adj* ADMIN, ECON, POL *price* administriert, reguliert; ~ **inflation** *n* ECON administrierte Inflation *f*; ~ **price** *n* ADMIN vertikale Preisbindung *f*; ~ **pricing** *n* ECON administrierte Preisfestsetzung *f*, staatlich regulierte Preisfestsetzung *f*

administration *n* (*admin*) ADMIN Unternehmensführung *f*, Unternehmensleitung *f*, Verwaltung *f* (*Verw.*), *managing* Leitung *f*, Bewirtschaftung *f*, ECON Durchführung *f*, *government department* Ministerium *nt*, GEN COMM, MGMNT Verwaltung *f* (*Verw.*), *of business* Unternehmensverwaltung *f*, POL *authorities* Verwaltung *f* (*Verw.*), Verwaltungsbehörde *f*, *department* Ministerium *nt*, *government* Regierung *f* (*Reg.*), Administration *f*, *term in office* Amtsperiode *f*, *executive* Exekutive *f*; ~ **costs** *n pl* ADMIN Verwaltungskosten *pl*; ~ **of the customs union** *n* (*ACU*) IMP/EXP Verwaltung *f* der Zollunion (*VdZ*); ~ **expenses** *n pl* FIN Verwaltungsgemeinkosten *pl*, Verwaltungskosten *pl*; ~ **lag** *n* ECON Durchführungsverzögerung *f*; ~ **officer** *n* (*AO*) HRM Verwaltungsbeamte(r) *m* [decl. as adj], Verwaltungsbeamtin *f*; ~ **order** *n* ADMIN *of estate* Anordnung *f* der Vermögensverwaltung, LAW *of estate* Anordnung *f* der Nachlaßverwaltung, Konkursbeschluß *m*, Konkurseröffnungsbeschluß *m*; ~-**production ratio** *n* ADMIN, FIN, IND Verwaltungsproduktionsverhältnis *nt*

administrative *adj* ADMIN, GEN COMM administrativ, verwaltungsmäßig, verwaltungstechnisch, verwaltend, Verwaltungs-; ~ **activity element** *n* ACC Verwaltungsanteil *m*, Verwaltungsgemeinkosten *pl*; ~ **agency** *n* ADMIN Verwaltungsbehörde *f*, Behörde *f*; ~ **audit** *n* ACC Innenrevision *f*, interne Revision *f*; ~ **authority** *n* GEN COMM Verwaltungsbehörde *f*; ~ **barriers to trade** *n pl* IMP/EXP *international trade* administrative Handelshemmnisse *nt pl*; ~ **board** *n* HRM Verwaltungsgremium *nt*; ~ **burden** *n* ADMIN Verwaltungskosten *pl*; ~ **center** *AmE*, ~ **centre** *BrE n* ADMIN Verwaltungszentrum *nt*, Zentralverwaltung *f*, Hauptverwaltung *f*; ~ **charge** *n* INS Verwaltungsgebühr *f*; ~ **committee** *n* GEN COMM Verwaltungsausschuß *m*; ~ **control procedure** *n* ADMIN Lenkungs- und Überwachungsverfahren *nt*, verwaltungstechnisches Kontrollverfahren *nt*; ~ **cost** *n* GEN COMM Verwaltungskosten *pl*, TAX *of collecting tax* Steuererhebungskosten *pl*, Verwaltungsgemeinkosten *pl*; ~ **costs** *n pl* GEN COMM Verwaltungskosten *pl*, TAX *of collecting tax* Steuererhebungskosten *pl*, Verwaltungsgemeinkosten *pl*; ~ **costs of regulation** *n* ADMIN Durchführungskosten *pl* von Verwaltungsvorschriften, verwaltungsmäßige Verfügungskosten *pl*; ~ **decision** *n* LAW Bescheid *m*; ~ **expenses** *n pl* ADMIN Verwaltungsausgaben *f pl*, allgemeine Verwaltungskosten *pl*, Sachaufwand *m*; ~ **fee** *n* INS Verwaltungsgebühr *f*; ~ **fine** *n* INS, LAW Bußgeld *nt*; ~ **handling** *n* GEN COMM administrative Abwicklung *f*; ~ **law** *n* ADMIN, LAW Verwaltungsrecht *nt*; ~ **office** *n* ADMIN Dienststelle *f*; ~ **and organizational controls** *n pl BrE* ACC *auditing* administrative und organisatorische Kontrollen *f pl*; ~ **overheads** *n pl* ACC, FIN Verwaltungsgemeinkosten *pl*; ~ **point of view** *n* (*APV*) MGMNT Ansicht *f* der Geschäftsführung, Meinung *f* der Geschäftsführung, Standpunkt *m* der Unternehmensleitung; ~ **protectionism** *n* IMP/EXP *international trade* administrativer Protektionismus *m*; ~ **provisions** *n pl* LAW Verwaltungsvorschriften *f pl*; ~ **regulations** *n pl* LAW Verwaltungsvorschriften *f pl*; ~ **staff** *n pl* HRM Verwaltungspersonal *nt*; ~ **theory** *n* ADMIN Verwaltungslehre *f*, MGMNT Verwaltungstheorie *f*; ~ **work** *n* ADMIN Verwaltungstätigkeit *f*

administrator *n* COMP *network* Systemverwalter, in *m,f*, GEN COMM, HRM Verwalter, in *m,f*, Verwaltungsfachmann *m*, Verwaltungsleiter, in *m,f*, LAW *of an estate* Nachlaßverwalter, in *m,f*, MGMNT Verwalter, in *m,f*, Verwaltungsleiter, in *m,f*, POL Verwalter, in *m,f*

admissibility *n* LAW Zulässigkeit *f*

admissible *adj* GEN COMM *idea, plan, document* erlaubt, zulässig, LAW *evidence, witness, appeal*, PATENTS zulässig; ~ **claim** *n* PATENTS zulässige Forderung *f*, zulässiger Anspruch *m*

admission *n* GEN COMM *to place* Eintritt *m*, Zulassung *f*, Zutritt *m*, *to profession, society* Aufnahme *f*, Eintritt *m*, Zulassung *f*, *cost of going into a place* Eintritt *m*, Eintrittsgeld *nt*, *confession* Eingeständnis *nt*, Zugeständnis *nt*, Geständnis *nt*, LAW *to profession* Zulassung *f*, *confession of guilt* Geständnis *nt*; ♦ ~ **free** GEN COMM, LEIS Eintritt frei, freier Eintritt; **by one's own** ~ GEN COMM nach eigenem Eingeständnis

admission: ~ **fee** *n* GEN COMM *to place* Eintritt *m*, Eintrittsgebühr *f*, Eintrittsgeld *nt*, Eintrittspreis *m to organization, society* Aufnahmegebühr *f*, Eintrittsgebühr *f*, Zulassungsgebühr *f*; ~ **of securities** *n* FIN, STOCK Zulassung *f* von Wertpapieren; ~ **to listing** *n* STOCK Börseneinführung *f*, Börsenzulassung *f*; ~ **to quotation** *n* STOCK Zulassung *f* zur Börsennotierung

admit *vt* GEN COMM *let in* hereinlassen, hineinlassen, *acknowledge* zugeben, einräumen, *a claim* anerkennen, HRM *new partner to business* aufnehmen; ♦ ~ **sb to the bar** *AmE* LAW jdn als Anwalt zulassen; ~ **of** GEN COMM *allow* zulassen

admittance *n* GEN COMM Eintritt *m*, Zutritt *m*, Zulassung *f*; ♦ **no** ~ GEN COMM Eintritt verboten, kein Zutritt, Zutritt verboten

admitted *adj* GEN COMM zugestanden

adopt *vt* ADMIN *annual accounts* feststellen, *procedure* beschließen, ECON *budget* verabschieden, GEN COMM, LAW, POL *annual accounts* feststellen, *procedure* beschließen, *resolution* verabschieden; ♦ ~ **a joint stance** GEN COMM gemeinsame Haltung einnehmen

adopted *adj* ECON *budget*, GEN COMM, LAW *resolution* verabschiedet

adoption *n* ADMIN *annual accounts* Feststellung *f*, ECON *of single currency* Annahme *f*, *of budget* Verabschiedung *f*, GEN COMM, LAW *annual accounts* Feststellung *f*, *of resolution* Verabschiedung *f*, MGMNT *of method* Anwendung *f*, Übernahme *f*, POL *annual accounts* Feststellung *f*, *of resolution* Verabschiedung *f*, S&M Zustimmung *f*; ~ **process** *n* S&M *of product by customer* Zustimmungsprozeß *m*

ADP *abbr* (*automatic data processing*) COMP ADV (*automatisierte Datenverarbeitung*)

ADR *abbr* ACC, LAW (*asset depreciation range*) betriebsgewöhnliche Nutzungsdauer *f*

adrate *n* S&M Anzeigenpreis *m*

adult *n* GEN COMM, HRM Erwachsene(r) *mf* [decl. as adj]

adulterate *vt* GEN COMM verfälschen, *wine* panschen

adulteration: ~ **of documents** *n* LAW Urkundenfälschung *f* *adult*: ~ **fare** *n* TRANSP voller Fahrpreis *m*; ~ **population** *n* GEN COMM erwachsene Bevölkerung *f*; ~ **price** *n* GEN COMM *at exhibition, play, film* Eintrittspreis *m* für Erwachsene, voller Eintrittspreis *m*

ad val. *abbr* (*ad valorem duty*) IMP/EXP, TAX Wertsteuer *f*, Wertzoll *m*

ad valorem: ~ **bill of lading** *n* IMP/EXP ad valorem Frachtbrief *m* (*frml*), ad valorem Ladebrief *m* (*frml*), TRANSP Wertkonnossement *nt*; ~ **customs duty** *n* IMP/ EXP, TAX Wertzoll *m*, ad valorem Zoll *m* (*frml*); ~ **duty** *n* (*ad val.*) IMP/EXP, TAX Wertsteuer *f*, Wertzoll *m*; ~ **freight** *n* TRANSP Wertfracht *f*; ~ **rate** *n* TAX Wertsteuersatz *m*; ~ **tariff** *n* ECON Wertzoll *m*, IMP/EXP, TAX Wertsteuersatz *m*, Wertzolltarif *m*; ~ **tax** *n* ECON, FIN, IMP/EXP, TAX Wertsteuer *f*

advance 1. *n* ACC, BANK Darlehen *nt*, Kredit *m*, *down payment* Anzahlung *f*, *on wages* Bevorschussung *f*, Vorschuß *m*, GEN COMM *forward movement*, Fortschritt *m*, Verbesserung *f*, *payment* Anzahlung *f*, Vorschuß *m*, Vorschußzahlung *f*, Bevorschussung *f*, *in prices, rent* Steigerung *f*, Anstieg *m*, Erhöhung *f*, *loan* Darlehen *nt*, *prepayment* Vorauszahlung *f*, *credit* Kredit *m*, HRM Vorschuß *m*, S&M Erhöhung *f*, STOCK Anstieg *m*, Befestigung *f*, TRANSP Vorschuß *m*; ♦ **in** ~ GEN COMM im voraus; **2.** *vt* ADMIN *person* befördern, COMP *tape* vorspulen, GEN COMM *price, rate* erhöhen, heraufsetzen, hinaufsetzen, *wages* vorschießen, als Vorschuß geben; ♦ ~ **a claim** LAW einen Anspruch geltend machen; **3.** *vi* GEN COMM *prices* anziehen, *person, society, civilization* Fortschritte machen, *work* fortschreiten, STOCK *prices* anziehen, *stocks* befestigen

advance: ~ **account** *n* ACC offener Buchkredit *m*; ~ **against a document credit** *n* BANK, IMP/EXP Akkreditivbevorschussung *f*; ~ **against goods** *n* BANK, GEN COMM Warenlombard *m*, Warenbevorschussung *f*; ~ **against security** *n* GEN COMM Lombardkredit *m*; ~ **arrangement** *n* ADMIN, TRANSP *shipping* Vorausdisposition *f*; ~ **bill** *n* ACC, FIN vor der Lieferung *f* gezogener Wechsel, Vorausrechnung *f*; ~ **billing** *n* ACC Ausstellen *nt* einer Vorausrechnung; ~ **booking** *n* GEN COMM, LEIS, TRANSP *of seat in aircraft, train, of table in restaurant, of hotel room* Reservierung *f*, Vorbestellung *f*, *of seat in theatre, sports stadium* Reservierung *f*, Vorbestellung *f*, Vorverkauf *m*; ~ **booking office** *n* LEIS, TRANSP Reservierungsbüro *nt*; ~ **corporation tax** *n* BrE (*ACT*) TAX Körperschaftssteuer-Vorauszahlung *f* (*KStVz*)

advanced *adj* COMP *software, system* erweitert, fortgeschritten, höher, ECON hochentwickelt, fortgeschritten, modern, GEN COMM angehoben, erhöht, *book, film* fortschrittlich, modern, *courses* qualifiziert, WEL höher; ~ **charge** *n* TRANSP vorausbezahlte Auslagen *f pl*, vorausbezahlte Gebühr *f*, vorgelegte Gebühr *f*; ~ **country** *n* (*AC*) ECON hochentwickeltes Land *nt*; ~ **disbursement** *n* TRANSP vorausbezahlte Auslagen *f pl*, vorausbezahlte Gebühr *f*; ~ **economy** *n* ECON, GEN COMM hochentwickelte Volkswirtschaft *f*, Industrienation *f*; ~ **education** *n* WEL höhere Bildung *f*; ~ **engineering** *n* IND fortschrittliche Technik *f*, moderne Technik *f*, neueste Technik *f*; ~ **factory** *n* IND Fabrik *f* auf dem neuesten Stand, fortschrittlicher Betrieb *m*, moderne Fabrik *f*; ~ **industrial state** *n* ECON moderner Industriestaat *m*; ~ **language** *n* COMP höhere Programmiersprache *f*

Advanced: ~ **level** *n* BrE (*A level, cf High School Diploma AmE*) GEN COMM, WEL Abschluß der Sekundarstufe, ≈ Abitur *nt*, ≈ Hochschulreife *f*, ≈ Matura *f* (*Öst, Sch*), ≈ Maturitätsprüfung *f* (*Sch*), ≈ Reifeprüfung *f* (*obs*)

advanced: ~ **organic economy** *n* ECON *agriculture* fortgeschrittene biologische Agrarwirtschaft *f*; ~ **technology** *n* COMP Spitzenleistungstechnik *f*, Hochleistungstechnik *f*, IND hochentwickelte Technologie *f*, moderne Technologie *f*, neueste Technologie *f*; ~ **training** *n* HRM fortgeschrittene Ausbildung *f*, WEL qualifizierte Ausbildung *f*; ~ **version** *n* COMP höhere Version *f*, leistungsfähigere Version *f*

advance: ~ **freight** *n* (*AF*) TRANSP Frachtvorauszahlung *f*, Frachtvorschuß *m*; ~ **of freight** *n* TRANSP Frachtvorauszahlung *f*; ~ **guaranty** *n* BrE GEN COMM, STOCK Anzahlungsgarantie *f*; ~ **holder** *n* BANK Darlehensnehmer, in *m,f*; ~ **invoice** *n* FIN Vorausrechnung *f*

advancement *n* ADMIN Förderung *f*, GEN COMM *new methods* Entwicklung *f*, *promotion* Beförderung *f*, Förderung *f*, Nutzen *m*, HRM *personal progress* Aufstieg *m*, *promotion* Beförderung *f*, *vocational* Aufstieg *m*, Fortbildung *f*

advance: ~ **notice** *n* GEN COMM Vorankündigung *f*, Voranmeldung *f*, LAW Vorausanzeige *f*, Vorausbenachrichtigung *f*; ~ **on collateral** *n* GEN COMM Beleihungskredit *m*; ~ **on commodities** *n* GEN COMM Warenbevorschussung *f*; ~ **on goods** *n* BANK, GEN COMM Warenlombard *m*; ~ **on salary** *n* HRM Gehaltsvorschuß *m*; ~ **on securities** *n* STOCK Lombardkredit *m*, Effektenlombard *m*, Wertpapierkredit *m*; ~ **order** *n* GEN COMM Vorausbestellung *f*, Vorbestellung *f*; ~ **payment** *n* GEN COMM Vorauszahlung *f*, Vorkasse *f*; ~ **payment bond** *n* STOCK Anzahlungsgarantie *f*; ~ **payment guarantee** *n* IMP/EXP Anzahlungsgarantie *f*; ~ **payment of taxes** *n* TAX Steuervorauszahlung *f*; ~ **premium** *n* INS Prämienvorauszahlung *f*, Vorausprämie *f*; ~ **publicity** *n* MEDIA Vorabwerbung *f*; ~ **refunding** *n* STOCK *government securities, municipal bonds* Umtausch *m* von Obligationen vor Fälligkeit; ~ **repayment** *n* BANK, GEN COMM vorzeitige Rückzahlung *f*; ~ **sale** *n* S&M Vorverkauf *m*; ~ **security** *n* STOCK Anzahlungsgarantie *f*; ~ **selling** *n* STOCK *security* Vorausplazierung *f*; ~ **of technology** *n* GEN COMM Vervollkommnung *f* der Technologie

advancing *adj* GEN COMM, STOCK *prices* anziehend

advantage *n* GEN COMM Nutzen *m*, Gewinn *m*, Vorteil *m*; ~ **of incumbency** *n* GEN COMM Amtsbonus *m*

advantageous *adj* GEN COMM nützlich, günstig, *lucrative* vorteilhaft, gewinnbringend

advantages: ~ **and disadvantages** *n pl* GEN COMM Für *nt* und Wider *nt*, Vor- und Nachteile *m pl*

adverse *adj* ACC passiv, negativ, ECON nachteilig, negativ, ungünstig, FIN negativ, GEN COMM *reaction, factor, conditions* entgegenwirkend, nachteilig, ungünstig, widrig, TAX negativ

adversely *adv* GEN COMM, ECON nachteilig; ~ **affected** *adj* GEN COMM nachteilig beeinflußt

adverse: ~ **movement** *n* STOCK *in the price of bonds* defizitäre Bewegung *f*; ~ **price movement** *n* ECON negative Preisentwicklung *f*; ~ **selection** *n* INS Antiselektion *f*, Gegenauslese *f*; ~ **supply shock** *n* ECON negativer Angebotsschock *m*; ~ **trade balance** *n* ECON, IMP/EXP, POL passive Handelsbilanz *f*; ~ **trading**

conditions n pl ECON nachteilige Geschäftsbedingungen f pl, nachteilige Handelsbedingungen f pl, ungünstige Geschäftsbedingungen f pl, ungünstige Handelsbedingungen f pl

advert n infrml (advertisement) MEDIA, S&M in print Annonce f, Inserat nt, Anzeige f, on television, radio Werbespot m

advertise 1. vt MEDIA, S&M Werbung f treiben, in print inserieren, house, car per Annonce zum Verkauf anbieten, annoncieren, product, service, political party werben für, Werbung machen für, Reklame machen für; ♦ ~ **a job** MEDIA, S&M in the press eine Stellenanzeige aufgeben; **2.** vi MEDIA, S&M Werbung machen, Reklame machen, werben; ♦ ~ **for** MEDIA, S&M werben für, Werbung machen für, Reklame machen für, in print inserieren für; ~ **for bids** GEN COMM, S&M, STOCK ausschreiben

advertised: ~ **bidding** n GEN COMM Ausschreibung f, öffentliche Ausschreibung f

advertisement n (ad, advert) MEDIA, S&M in print Annonce f, Inserat nt, Anzeige f, on television, radio Werbespot m

advertiser n S&M Inserent, in m,f

advertising n MEDIA, S&M business Werbewesen nt, Werbung f, Reklame f, advertisements Werbung f, Reklame f; ~ **agency** n S&M Werbeagentur f; ~ **agent** n S&M Werbeagent, in m,f; ~ **allocation budget** n S&M Werbezuschuß m; ~ **appeal** n S&M ansprechende Werbung f

Advertising: ~ **Association** n BrE S&M britischer Werbeverband, ≈ Bund Deutscher Werbeberater und Werbeleiter (BDW)

advertising: ~ **budget** n S&M Werbeetat m, Werbebudget nt; ~ **budget review** n S&M Werbeetatüberprüfung f, Werbebudgetprüfung f; ~ **campaign** n S&M Werbefeldzug m, Werbekampagne f; ~ **channel** n S&M Werbekanal m pl; ~ **code** n S&M Werbecode m; ~ **concept** n S&M Werbekonzept nt; ~ **conversion rate** n S&M Rücklaufrate f von Werbekupons; ~ **copy** n S&M Reklametext m, Werbetext m; ~ **copywriter** n HRM Anzeigenbearbeiter, in m,f; ~ **cost per contact sale** n S&M Werbekosten f pro verkauftem Produkt; ~ **coverage** n S&M Werbungsdeckung f; ~ **criteria** n pl S&M Werbekriterien nt pl; ~ **department** n S&M Anzeigenabteilung f, of a magazine Werbeabteilung f; ~ **director** n HRM, S&M Direktor, in m,f der Werbeabteilung; ~ **effectiveness** n S&M Werbeerfolg m, Werbewirksamkeit f; ~ **expenditure** n S&M Werbeaufwand m, Werbekosten pl, Ausgaben f pl für Werbung; ~ **expense** n S&M Werbeaufwand m, Werbekosten pl, Ausgaben f pl für Werbung; ~ **gimmick** n S&M Werbegag m, Sensationswerbung f; ~ **industry** n S&M Werbeindustrie f; ~ **jingle** n S&M Werbemelodie f; ~ **journal** n GEN COMM Anzeigenblatt nt; ~ **man** n (adman) HRM Anzeigenbearbeiter m, Werbefachmann m; ~ **manager** n HRM, S&M Werbeleiter, in m,f; ~ **medium** n MEDIA, S&M Werbemittel nt pl, Werbeträger m; ~ **overkill** n S&M Reizüberflutung f durch Werbung; ~ **policy** n GEN COMM, S&M Werbepolitik f; ~ **poster** n GEN COMM Werbeplakat nt; ~ **price** n S&M Einführungspreis m; ~ **program objectives** AmE, ~ **programme objectives** BrE n pl S&M Anzeigenwerbezweck m, Werbeprogrammziele nt pl; ~ **rates** n pl S&M Anzeigentarife m pl; ~ **reach** n S&M Reichweite f der Werbung; ~ **regulations** n pl S&M

Werbebestimmungen f pl; ~ **research** n S&M Werbeforschung f; ~ **response** n S&M Reaktion f auf Werbung; ~ **revenue** n S&M Werbeeinnahmen f pl; ~ **revenue by media** n S&M Werbeeinnahmen f pl durch die Medien; ~ **schedule** n S&M Einschaltplan m; ~ **slogan** n S&M Werbeslogan m; ~ **space** n S&M Reklamefläche f, Werbefläche f, in magazine Anzeigenraum m; ~ **space buyer** n S&M Inserent, in m,f

Advertising: ~ **Standards Authority** n BrE (ASA) S&M Behörde für Werbeethik, ≈ Deutscher Werbeausschuß (DWA)

advertising: ~ **statistics** n pl S&M Werbestatistiken f pl; ~ **strategy** n S&M Werbestrategie f; ~ **supplement** n S&M Werbebeilage f; ~ **support** n S&M werbliche Unterstützung f; ~ **tactics** n pl S&M Werbetaktiken f pl; ~ **talk** n S&M Werbegespräch nt; ~ **technique** n S&M Werbetechnik f; ~ **test** n S&M Versuchswerbung f; ~ **text** n S&M Werbetext m; ~ **theme** n S&M Werbethema nt; ~ **thermometer** n S&M Werbebarometer nt; ~ **threshold** n S&M Werbeschwelle f; ~ **time** n S&M Werbezeit f, Sendezeit f; ~ **tour** n S&M Werbereise f, Werbetour f; ~ **tower** n S&M Reklamepodest nt; ~ **trade** n S&M Werbebranche f; ~ **turnover** n S&M Werbeumsatz m; ~ **value** n S&M Werbewert m; ~ **vehicle** n MEDIA, S&M Werbeträger m; ~ **weapon** n S&M Werbewaffe f; ~ **zone** n S&M Werbebereich m

advertorial n S&M Textanzeige f

advice n COMMS notification Anzeige f, Mitteilung f, note Bescheinigung f, Schein m, GEN COMM Beratung f, Rat m, notification Anzeige f, Benachrichtigung f, note Avis m or nt, INS stock Anzeige f; ♦ **as per ~ from** GEN COMM laut Anzeige von, laut Avis von, laut Bericht von; **as per ~ of** GEN COMM laut Anzeige von, laut Avis von, laut Bericht von; **no ~** (N/A) GEN COMM kein Avis, ohne Avis, ~ **enclosed** COMMS Benachrichtigung beigefügt

advice: ~ **card** n INS marine Anzeige f über abgeschlossene Versicherung, Versicherungsanzeige f; ~ **of collection** n BANK Inkassoanzeige f, Inkassobenachrichtigung f; ~ **of deal** n STOCK Ausführungsanzeige f; ~ **of delivery** n COMMS Empfangsbescheinigung f, Empfangsschein m; ~ **of duration and/or charge** n (ADC) COMMS, GEN COMM Anzeige f der Dauer und/oder Belastung, Mitteilung f über Laufzeit und/oder Belastung; ~ **note** n COMMS Benachrichtigungsnotiz f, delivery Versandanzeige f

advisable adj GEN COMM angebracht, zweckmäßig, empfehlenswert

advise vt COMMS mitteilen, GEN COMM inform benachrichtigen, avisieren, give advice to beraten, recommend empfehlen, MGMNT give advice to beraten; ♦ ~ **a draft** BANK eine Tratte avisieren; ~ **on** GEN COMM avisieren; ~ **sb of sth** COMMS jdm etw mitteilen, jdn von etw benachrichtigen

advised: ~ **bill** n BANK avisierter Wechsel m

advising: ~ **bank** n BANK avisierende Bank f

advisor n GEN COMM, HRM Berater, in m,f

advisory adj GEN COMM beratend; ♦ **in an ~ capacity** GEN COMM als Berater, beratend

advisory: ~ **activity** n GEN COMM Beratungstätigkeit f; ~ **board** n ADMIN of company Beirat m, HRM beratendes Gremium nt; ~ **body** n GEN COMM beratendes Gremium nt, Beratungsstelle f; ~ **capacity** n GEN COMM beratende Aufgabe f, beratende Funktion f; ~ **committee** n GEN

COMM beratendes Gremium *nt*, Beratungsausschuß *m*, Gutachterkommission *f*, POL *European Commission* Gutachterkommission *f*, beratendes Gremium *nt*, Beratungsausschuß *m*, Beirat *m*, beratender Ausschuß *m*

Advisory: ~, Conciliation and Arbitration Service *n* BrE (*ACAS*) HRM Beratungs-, Schlichtungs- und Schiedsgerichtsstelle für Arbeitsstreitigkeiten

advisory: **~ contract** *n* GEN COMM Beratervertrag *m*; **~ function** *n* HRM beratende Aufgabe *f*, beratende Funktion *f*; **~ funds** *n pl* AmE FIN Beratungsfonds *m*, Kundenberatungsfonds *m*; **~ group** *n* GEN COMM Beratergruppe *f*; **~ service** *n* FIN, GEN COMM Beratungsdienst *m*, Beratungsstelle *f*, Gutachtertätigkeit *f*; **~ voice** *n* GEN COMM Gutachterstimme *f*; **~ work** *n* HRM Beratungsarbeit *f*

advocacy: ~ advertising *n* S&M defensive Werbung *f*, Interessenwerbung *f*

advocate 1. *n* GEN COMM Rechtsbeistand *m*, Anwalt *m*, Fürsprecher, in *m,f*, Verfechter, in *m,f*; **2.** *vt* GEN COMM *a plan or proposal* befürworten, eintreten für, plädieren für, verfechten, vertreten

AEA *abbr* (*American Economic Association*) ECON amerikanischer Wirtschaftsverband, ≈ BWR (*Bundeswirtschaftsrat*)

aerial: ~ advertising *n* S&M Luftwerbung *f*; **~ survey** *n* TRANSP *aviation* Luftbildvermessung *f*

aerodrome *n* BrE (*cf airdrome AmE*) TRANSP *aviation* Flugplatz *m*, Flughafen *m*

aerogramme *n* COMMS *letter* Aerogramm *nt*, Luftpostbrief *m*, Luftpostleichtbrief *m*

aeroplane *n* BrE (*cf airplane AmE*) TRANSP Flugzeug *nt*; **~ banner** *n* BrE (*cf airplane banner AmE*) S&M *advertising* von Flugzeug gezogenes Werbespruchband *nt*, Werbespruchband *nt* an einem Flugzeug

aerosol *n* ENVIR *spray can* Aerosol *nt*

aerospace: ~ industry *n* IND Luft- und Raumfahrtindustrie *f*

AF *abbr* (*advance freight*) TRANSP Frachtvorauszahlung *f*, Frachtvorschuß *m*

AFBD *abbr* (*Association of Futures Brokers and Dealers*) STOCK Verband der Terminmakler und -händler

AFC *abbr* (*airflex clutch*) TRANSP Airflex-Kupplung *f*

AfDB *abbr* (*African Development Bank*) BANK, FIN AEB (*Afrikanische Entwicklungsbank*)

AFDC *abbr* AmE (*Aid to Families with Dependent Children*) WEL Unterstützung bedürftiger Familien mit unterhaltsberechtigten Kindern

affair *n* GEN COMM *incident, event* Angelegenheit *f*

affect *vt* ECON *have effect on* einwirken auf [+acc], GEN COMM *detrimentally* beeinträchtigen, angreifen, *influence decisions* beeinflussen, *be of concern* angehen, LAW *findings* berühren, beeinflussen

affection: ~ value *n* INS Affektionswert *m* (*obs*), Liebhaberwert *m*

affective: ~ behavior *AmE*, **~ behaviour** *BrE* *n* GEN COMM affektives Verhalten *nt*

affiliate 1. *n* GEN COMM *organization* verbundenes Unternehmen *nt*, Beteiligungsgesellschaft *f*, Konzernunternehmen *nt*, *person* Mitglied *nt*; **2.** *vt* GEN COMM angliedern, in einem Konzern zusammenfassen; ♦ **~ oneself** GEN COMM sich anschließen

affiliate: **~ company** *n* GEN COMM verbundenes Unternehmen *nt*, Beteiligungsgesellschaft *f*,

Konzernunternehmen *nt*, *associated* Schwestergesellschaft *f*, *subsidiary* Tochtergesellschaft *f*

affiliated *adj* BANK, GEN COMM, HRM angegliedert, angeschlossen, eingegliedert, verbunden; ♦ **~ to** GEN COMM angegliedert an [+acc], angeschlossen an [+acc], verbunden mit

affiliated: **~ bank** *n* BANK angeschlossene Bank *f*; **~ company** *n* GEN COMM *associated* Schwestergesellschaft *f*, *subsidiary* Tochtergesellschaft *f*; **~ firm** *n* GEN COMM Zweigfirma *f*, Zweigniederlassung *f*; **~ group** *n* FIN Konzernverbund *m*, GEN COMM Konzern *m*; **~ person** *n* GEN COMM *in society* eingegliederte Person *f*; **~ trade union** *n* HRM angeschlossene Gewerkschaft *f*

affiliate: **~ member** *n* GEN COMM Mitglied *nt*

affiliation *n* GEN COMM Angliederung *f*, geschäftliche Verbindung *f*, *membership* Zugehörigkeit *f*; **~ fee** *n* HRM Mitgliedsbeitrag *m*; **~ privilege** *n* TAX Schachtelprivileg *nt*

affinity: ~ card *n* WEL Kreditkarte *f*

affirmation *n* BrE LAW *warranted qualities, contract law* Bekräftigung *f*, bindendes Versprechen *nt*

affirmative *adj* GEN COMM bejahend; **~ action** *n* AmE ADMIN, ECON, HRM (*cf positive discrimination BrE*) in recruiting aktive Förderungsmaßnahmen *f pl*, positive Diskriminierung *f*, (*cf equal opportunity BrE*) Chancengleichheit

affix *vt* COMMS *label* aufkleben, *attachment* anbringen, *seal* beidrücken, GEN COMM ankleben, *label* anheften, aufkleben, befestigen an [+dat], setzen, versehen mit, *signature, seal, stamp* aufdrücken, siegeln, S&M aufkleben

afflicted *adj* GEN COMM behaftet

affluence *n* ECON Reichtum *m*, Überfluß *m*, Wohlstand *m*

affluent *adj* ECON *person* reich, wohlhabend; **~ society** *n* ECON, GEN COMM Überflußgesellschaft *f*, Wohlstandsgesellschaft *f*

AFFM *abbr* (*Australian Financial Futures Market*) STOCK australische Finanzterminbörse

afford: ~ sth *vt* ECON sich etw leisten; ♦ **~ possibilities** GEN COMM *provide* Möglichkeiten eröffnen

affordable *adj* GEN COMM bezahlbar, erschwinglich; **~ price** *n* S&M erschwinglicher Preis *m*

affreight *vt* TRANSP *vehicle* befrachten

AFL-CIO *abbr* (*American Federation of Labor-Congress of Industrial Organizations*) HRM Dachverband der amerikanischen Gewerkschaften, ≈ DGB (*Deutscher Gewerkschaftsbund*)

afloat *adj* COMMS schwimmend, verschifft, GEN COMM in circulation im Umlauf, zirkulierend, *free of debt* schuldenfrei, ohne Schulden, *on ship* schwimmend, verschifft, *solvent* liquid, liquide, schuldenfrei, IMP/EXP, TRANSP schwimmend, verschifft; **~ price** *n* STOCK Umlaufpreis *m*

aforementioned *adj* COMMS obenerwähnt, obengenannt

A4 *n* COMMS, GEN COMM *paper size* DIN A4 *nt*

AFRASEC *abbr* (*Afro-Asian Organization for Economic Cooperation*) ECON, POL AFRASEC (*Afro-asiatische Organisation für wirtschaftliche Zusammenarbeit*)

African: ~, Caribbean and Pacific states *n pl* (*ACP states*) ECON *party to the Lomé Convention* Staaten *m pl* in Afrika, im karibischen Raum und im Pazifischen Ozean (*AKP-Staaten*); **~ Development Bank** *n* (*AfDB,*

ADB) BANK, FIN Afrikanische Entwicklungsbank *f* (*AEB*)

Afro-Asian: **~ Organization for Economic Cooperation** *n* (*AFRASEC*) ECON, POL Afro-asiatische Organisation *f* für wirtschaftliche Zusammenarbeit (*AFRASEC*)

AFT *abbr* (*automatic funds transfer*) ACC, BANK, FIN automatischer Zahlungsverkehr *m*, automatisierter Überweisungsverkehr *m*

AFTA *abbr* (*Asian Free Trade Area*) ECON, POL Asiatische Freihandelszone *f*, Malaysia, Singapur, Indonesien, Philippinen, Thailand und Burma

after: **~-acquired clause** *n* BANK *in mortgage agreement* Nacherwerbsklausel *f*; **~-acquired property** *n* BANK, LAW *in bankruptcy* Zugewinn *m*; **~ date** *phr* (*a/d*) GEN COMM ab Ausstellungsdatum, ab dato, ab heute, dato nach heute, nach Ausstellungsdatum

aftereffect *n* GEN COMM Folgeerscheinung *f*, Nachwirkung *f*, Spätfolge *f*

after: **~-hours dealing** *n* STOCK nachbörslicher Handel *m*; **~-hours market** *n* STOCK Nachbörse *f*; **~-hours prices** *n pl* STOCK nachbörsliche Kurse *m pl*; **~-hours rally** *n* STOCK Erholung *f* im nachbörslichen Verkehr; **~-hours trading** *n* STOCK Handel *m* an der Nachbörse, nachbörslicher Handel *m*

afterimage *n* S&M *advertising* nachträgliches Image *nt*

after: **~-market** *n* S&M Anschlußmarkt *m*, STOCK Sekundärmarkt *m*

aftermath: **in the ~ of** *phr* GEN COMM *war, disaster* im Anschluß an

after: **~ sales** *n pl* S&M *auction* Nachverkauf *m*; **~-sales manager** *n* HRM Kundendienstleiter, in *m,f*; **~-sales service** *n* S&M Kundendienst *m*; **~ sight** *phr* (*A/S*) FIN nach Sicht; **~ tax** *phr* ACC, TAX nach Steuern *f pl*; **~-tax basis** *n* ACC, TAX nach Steuern *f pl*, nach Abzug von Steuern *f pl*, nach Berücksichtigung *f* der Steuern, Nachsteuer *f*; **~-tax bond yield** *n* ACC, TAX Anleiherendite *f* nach Steuern; **~-tax dividend** *n* ACC, TAX Dividende *f* nach Steuern; **~-tax income** *n* ACC, TAX Ertrag *m* nach Steuern, Gewinn *m* nach Steuern; **~-tax profit** *n* ACC, TAX Gewinn *m* nach Steuern; **~-tax real rate of return** *n* ACC, TAX reale Nettorendite *f* nach Steuern; **~-tax yield** *n* ACC, TAX Nachsteuerrendite *f*, Rendite *f* nach Steuern

AG *abbr* ACC (*Accountant General*) Bilanzbuchhalter, in *m,f*, ADMIN, HRM (*agent general*) Generalbevollmächtigte(r) *mf* [decl. as adj], Generalvertreter, in *m,f*, Handlungsbevollmächtigte(r) *mf* [decl. as adj], POL (*agent general*) Vertreter bestimmter Commonwealth-Länder in London

against *prep* GEN COMM gegen, gegenüber; ♦ **~ all risks** (*AAR*) INS gegen alle Gefahren; **~ documents** GEN COMM gegen Dokumente, gegen Vorlage der Dokumente; **~ payment** GEN COMM gegen Bezahlung, gegen Zahlung; **~ sb's judgment** LAW entgegen jds Urteil; **~ text** S&M *advertising* Gegendarstellung *f*

agcy *abbr* (*agency*) ACC, ADMIN, GEN COMM Agentur *f*, Geschäftsstelle *f*, Vertretung *f*, MEDIA, S&M Agentur *f*, STOCK Geschäftsstelle *f*, Vertretung *f*, TRANSP Agentur *f*

age 1. *n* GEN COMM Alter *nt*; 2. *vt* ACC *accounts* nach ihrer Fälligkeit aufschlüsseln; ♦ **~ stocks** ACC Lagerbestände nach Alter aufstellen; 3. *vi* GEN COMM altern

age: **~ at entry** *n* INS Abschlußalter *nt*, Beitrittsalter *nt*, Eintrittsalter *nt*; **~ at expiry** *n* INS Abgangsalter *nt*, Endalter *nt*; **~ at withdrawal** *n* INS Austrittsalter *nt*;

~ bracket *n* MEDIA, S&M *market research* Altersgruppe *f*; **~ distribution** *n* ECON, HRM, POL Altersaufbau *m*, Altersgliederung *f*, Altersstruktur *f*, Altersverteilung *f*

aged: **~ trial balance** *n* ACC nach Fälligkeit aufgeschlüsselte Saldenbilanz *f*, Probebilanz *f*

age: **~-earnings profile** *n* HRM Alter/Einkommensprofil *nt*, Alter/Einkommensübersicht *f*; **~ group** *n* MEDIA *market research, statistics* Altersgruppe *f*, Altersklasse *f*, Jahrgang *m*, S&M, *market research* Altersgruppe *f*

ageing: **~ of the population** *n* ECON Überalterung *f* der Bevölkerung; **~ population** *n* ECON alternde Bevölkerung *f*; **~ of receivables** *n* ACC Aufschlüsselung *f* der Forderungen nach Fälligkeit

age: **~ inventories** *n pl* ACC Inventar *nt* nach Alter aufstellen

ageism *n* ECON Altersdiskriminierung *f*, Diskriminierung *f* aufgrund des Alters

age: **~ limit** *n* GEN COMM Altersgrenze *f*

agency *n* (*agcy*) ACC Agentur *f*, Vertretung *f*, ADMIN Agentur *f*, Geschäftsstelle *f*, Vertretung *f*, BANK Zweigniederlassung *f*, ECON Behörde *f*, Dienststelle *f*, GEN COMM Sitz *m* einer Vertretung, Agentur *f*, Geschäftsstelle *f*, *employment* Vermittlungsstelle *f*, *representation* Stellvertretung *f*, Vertretung *f*, *means* Bevollmächtigung *f*, HRM Vertretung *f*, Vertretungsverhältnis *nt*, *employment* Personalvermittlungsbüro *nt*, LAW *contracts, transaction* Agentur *f*, Amt *nt*, Behörde *f*, Dienststelle *f*, Vertretung *f*, MEDIA, S&M Agentur *f*, Vertretung *f*, STOCK Geschäftsstelle *f*, Vertretung *f*, TRANSP Agentur *f*; **~ account** *n* BANK Treuhandkonto *nt*; **~ agreement** *n* LAW Vertretungsvertrag *m*, S&M Agenturvertrag *m*; **~ bank** *n* BANK Konsortialbank *f*, Zweigniederlassung *f*, FIN Konsortialbank *f*; **~ billing** *n* MEDIA Agenturwerbung *f*; **~ broker** *n* STOCK Effektenbroker, in *m,f*; **~ business** *n* GEN COMM Agenturgeschäft *nt*; **~ by ratification** *n* LAW Genehmigung *f* eines Vertreters, Genehmigung *f* einer Vertretung; **~ commission** *n* BANK Bonifikation *f*, GEN COMM Agenturvergütung *f*, Provision *f*

Agency: **~ Compliance Board** *n* TRANSP *aviation, IATA* Gremium *nt* zur Feststellung der Übereinstimmung mit Agenturvorschriften

agency: **~ cost** *n BrE* STOCK Kosten *pl* der Geschäftsstelle; **~ experience** *n* S&M *advertising* Vertretungserfahrung *f*; **~ fee** *n* BANK Abwicklungsgebühr *f*, Vermögensverwaltungsgebühr *f*, GEN COMM Agenturkosten *pl*, Vertretergebühr *f*, Vertreterprovision *f*, IMP/EXP Vertretergebühr *f*, Vertreterprovision *f*, S&M Vertreterprovision *f*; **~ fund** *n* GEN COMM verwaltetes Vermögen *nt*, LAW Amtsfonds *m*, MEDIA Agenturfonds *m*; **~ law** *n* LAW Recht *nt* der Handelsvertretung, Stellvertreterrecht *nt*; **~ relationship** *n* ACC, HRM Vertretungsverhältnis *nt*, Vertretungsbeziehung *f*; **~ representative** *n* S&M *advertising* Agenturvertreter, in *m,f*; **~ selling** *n AmE* BANK, STOCK Effektenemission *f* auf fremde Rechnung; **~ shop** *n* ADMIN, HRM Unternehmen, das auch von nicht organisierten Arbeitnehmern Gewerkschaftsbeiträge einzieht; **~ superintendent** *n AmE* INS Bezirksdirektor, in *m,f*; **~ theory** *n* ADMIN, ECON, MGMNT, POL, STOCK Vertretungstheorie *f*; **through the ~ of** *phr* GEN COMM durch Vermittlung von, mit Unterstützung von; **~ trade** *n* GEN COMM Agenturhandel *m*; **~ with full service** *n* MEDIA, S&M *advertising* Agentur *f* mit komplettem Serviceangebot, Agentur *f* mit umfassen-

dem Service; ~ **worker** *n* INS Außendienstarbeiter, in
m,f

agenda *n* ADMIN Tagesordnung *f*, MGMNT Agenda *f*,
Programm *nt*, Tagesordnung *f*; ◆ **be on the ~** ADMIN,
MGMNT auf der Agenda stehen, auf der Tagesordnung
stehen

agent *n* (*agt*) GEN COMM *person* Handelsvertreter, in *m,f*,
Vertreter, in *m,f*, Beauftragte(r) *mf* [decl. as adj],
Bevollmächtigte(r) *mf* [decl. as adj], *thing* Mittel *nt*,
IND *person* Händler, in *m,f*, *means* Mittel *nt*, *liquid*
Agens *nt*, LAW *contracts* Handelsvertreter und Eigen-
händler *m*, Handelsvertreterin und Eigenhändlerin *f*,
authorized person Stellvertreter, in *m,f*, *contracts*
Vertreter, in *m,f*, S&M Vertreter, in *m,f*; ~ **bank** *n* BANK
Zweigniederlassung *f*; ~**'s commission** *n* GEN COMM,
IMP/EXP, S&M Vertreterprovision *f*; ~ **general** *n* (*AG*)
ADMIN, HRM Generalbevollmächtigte(r) *mf* [decl. as
adj], Generalvertreter, in *m,f*, Handlungsbevollmäch-
tigte(r) *mf* [decl. as adj], POL Vertreter bestimmter
Commonwealth-Länder in London; ~**'s territory** *n* S&M
advertising Vertreterbezirk *m*; ~**'s vehicle record** *n*
(*AVR*) S&M, TRANSP Vertreterfahrtenbuch *nt*

age: ~ **pyramid** *n* ECON Alterspyramide *f*, Bevölkerungs-
pyramide *f*; ~ **ranking of fixed assets** *n* FIN
Altersaufbau *m* des Anlagevermögens; ~**-specific** *adj*
ADMIN *death rate* altersspezifisch

agglomeration *n* ECON Ballungsraum *m*, Ballungszentrum *nt*, Agglomeration *f*; ~ **economy** *n* ECON
Agglomerationsvorteil *m*

aggregate 1. *adj* ECON *amount, demand* gesamt, gesamtwirtschaftlich, volkswirtschaftlich; **2.** *n* ECON Aggregat
nt, Masse *f*, Menge *f*, Summe *f*, GEN COMM Summe *f*,
MATH *statistics* Aggregat *nt*; ◆ **in the ~** GEN COMM
insgesamt; **3.** *vt* MATH sich belaufen auf [+acc]

aggregate: ~ **balance** *n* ACC Gesamtsaldo *m*; ~ **book
value** *n* ACC Gesamtbuchwert *m*; ~ **concentration** *n*
ECON gesamtwirtschaftliche Konzentration *f*; ~ **data** *n*
pl ACC Daten *pl*, ECON aggregierte Zahlen *f pl*,
aggregiertes Zahlenmaterial *nt*; ~ **demand-aggregate
supply** *n* (*AD-AS*) ECON Gesamtnachfrage-Gesamtangebot; ~ **demand curve** *n* ECON
Gesamtnachfragekurve *f*; ~ **depreciation** *n* ECON
Gesamtabschreibung *f*, *capital stock* gesamtwirtschaftliche Wertminderung *f*; ~ **exercise price** *n* STOCK
Gesamtbasispreis *m*; ~ **income** *n* ECON Volkseinkom-
men *nt*; ~ **liability index** *n* INS Risikokarte *f*; ~ **output** *n*
ECON Sozialprodukt *nt*; ~ **production** *n* ECON
Gesamtproduktion *f*, gesamtwirtschaftliche Produktion
f; ~ **risk** *n* GEN COMM Gesamtrisiko *nt*; ~ **sales listings**
n pl BrE (*ASL*) TAX *VAT* Zusammenfassende Mel-
dungen *f pl* (*MwSt.*); ~ **statement** *n* ACC
Gesamtabrechnung *f*; ~ **supply curve** *n* ECON
Gesamtangebotskurve *f*; ~ **table** *n* INS Aggregattafel *f*;
~ **value** *n* TAX *of individual's estate at time of death*
Gesamtwert *m*; ~ **value added** *n* ECON gesamtwirtschaftliche Wertschöpfung *f*; ~ **wealth formation** *n*
ECON gesamtwirtschaftliche Vermögensbildung *f*

aggregation *n* ECON, FIN, MATH *statistics* Aggregation *f*;
~ **problem** *n* ECON *economic accounting* Aggregationsproblem *nt*

aggressive *adj* GEN COMM initiativ, offensiv, risikoreich,
spekulativ, S&M *campaign* aggressiv; ~ **advertising** *n*
S&M aggressive Werbung *f*; ~ **investment** *n* FIN hoch-
spekulative Anlage *f*; ~ **marketing** *n* S&M aggressives

Marketing *nt*; ~ **pricing** *n* S&M *marketing* aggressive
Preispolitik *f*

aggrieved: ~ **party** *n* LAW geschädigte Partei *f*, Geschä-
digte(r) *mf* [decl. as adj], Verletzte(r) *mf* [decl. as adj]

agio *n* ECON, FIN, STOCK *foreign bills of exchange* Agio *nt*,
Aufgeld *nt*; ~ **account** *n* ECON Aufgeldkonto *nt*

agiotage *n* ECON Börsenspiel *nt*, Devisenhandel *m*,
Wechselgeschäft *nt*, FIN, STOCK *foreign bills of exchange*
Agiotage *f*

agio: ~ **theory of interest** *n* ECON Abstinenztheorie *f*

AGM *abbr* (*annual general meeting*) GEN COMM HV
(*Hauptversammlung*)

agree 1. *vt* ACC abstimmen, FIN zustimmen, GEN COMM
books in Übereinstimmung bringen, abstimmen, *report,
proposal* sich einigen auf [+acc], sich einigen über
[+acc]; ◆ ~ **accounts** ACC Konten abstimmen; ~ **the
accounts** FIN den Jahresabschluß feststellen, dem
Jahresabschluß zustimmen; **2.** *vi* GEN COMM *reach
agreement* sich absprechen, Absprache treffen, *tally*
übereinstimmen, *figures, statements* übereinkommen,
people einverstanden sein, *reach mutual understanding*
sich vereinbaren, *share opinion* sich einigen; ◆ ~ **to do
sth** GEN COMM sich bereit erklären, etw zu tun; sich
einverstanden erklären, etw zu tun

agree on *vt* GEN COMM *price, terms of sale* sich einigen
auf [+acc], sich einigen über [+acc], vereinbaren; ◆
~ **the essential terms of contract** LAW sich über die
wesentlichen Vertragsbestandteile einigen

agree to *vt* GEN COMM *discount* annehmen, *project, plan*
zustimmen, *terms* einverstanden sein mit, sich einverstanden erklären mit, *come to terms about*
einwilligen in [+acc]; ◆ ~ **a contract** LAW einem Vertrag
zustimmen

agree upon *vt* GEN COMM *price, terms of sale* sich einigen
auf [+acc], sich einigen über [+acc], vereinbaren

agree with *vt* GEN COMM einverstanden sein mit, konform
gehen mit; ◆ ~ **sb** GEN COMM mit jdm übereinkommen;
~ **sb on sth** GEN COMM jdm in etw zustimmen, jdm in
etw beipflichten

agreed *adj* GEN COMM *time, place, total* vereinbart,
beschlossen, abgemacht, verabredet, INS, LAW vereinbart; ◆ **at an ~ price** GEN COMM *contract* zu einem
vereinbarten Preis, zum vereinbarten Preis; **be ~** GEN
COMM *people* einverstanden sein, gleicher Meinung sein

agreed: ~ **customs exemption** *n* IMP/EXP, LAW
Zollfreischreibung *f*; ~ **period** *n* LAW *contract* vereinbarte Zeit *f*; ~ **price** *n* GEN COMM abgemachter Preis *m*,
vereinbarter Preis *m*; ~ **rate** *n* TRANSP *fee* vereinbarte
Gebühr *f*, *freight rate* vereinbarter Preis *m*, vereinbarter
Tarif *m*; ~ **sum** *n* GEN COMM abgemachte Summe *f*,
vereinbarte Summe *f*; ~ **takeover** *n* ECON frei vereinbarte Übernahme *f*; ~ **valuation clause** *n* INS
vereinbarte Barwertklausel *f*, vereinbarte Bewertungsklausel *f*; ~ **value** *n* INS Festwert *m*, taxierter
Versicherungswert *m*, vereinbarter Wert *m*; ~ **value
insurance** *n* INS Festwertversicherung *f*

agreement *n* GEN COMM *between people* Übereinkommen
nt, Vereinbarung *f*, Einigung *f*, Übereinkunft *f*, Einigkeit *f*, Beipflichten *nt*, *between figures* Übereinstimmung
f, *treaty, contract* Vertrag *m*, Abkommen *nt*, LAW
Vertrag *m*, Verständigung *f*; ◆ **as per ~** GEN COMM
laut Übereinkunft, vereinbarungsgemäß, vertragsgemäß; **come to an ~** LAW sich verständigen; **come to
an ~ with sb** GEN COMM mit jdm übereinkommen; **in**

~ **with** GEN COMM übereinstimmend mit, in Übereinstimmung mit

agreement: ~ **among underwriters** n BANK Emissionsvertrag m, Konsortialvertrag m; ~ **of clearing** n BANK Clearingabkommen nt, Verrechnungsabkommen nt; ~ **for exclusiveness** n LAW sales Alleinvertriebsvertrag m; ~ **of insured value** n INS Taxe f; ~ **on export** n IMP/EXP, LAW Exportvertrag m; ~ **of service** n LAW Dienstvertrag m, Dienstleistungsvertrag m; ~ **with no strings attached** n GEN COMM Vereinbarung f ohne zusätzliche einschränkende Bedingungen

agricultural adj ECON, ENVIR, GEN COMM agrarisch, agrarwirtschaftlich, landwirtschaftlich, Agrar-; ~ **bank** n BANK, ECON Agrarbank f, Landwirtschaftsbank f; ~ **building** n ECON, INS landwirtschaftliches Gebäude nt; ~ **commodities market** n ECON Agrarmarkt m; ~ **commodity** n ECON agrarischer Rohstoff m; ~ **cooperative** n ECON Agrargenossenschaft f, landwirtschaftliche Genossenschaft f; ~ **credit** n GEN COMM Agrarkredit m

Agricultural: ~ **Development and Advisory Service** n BrE (ADAS) ECON landwirtschaftlicher Entwicklungs- und Beratungsdienst

agricultural: ~ **engineer** n ENVIR Landwirtschaftsingenieur, in m,f; ~ **export subsidy** n ECON Agrarexportbeihilfe f; ~ **futures contract** n BrE STOCK CME landwirtschaftlicher Terminkontrakt m

Agricultural: ~ **Holdings Act** n BrE LAW Gesetz über Agrarholdings

agricultural: ~ **household** n ECON, INS landwirtschaftlicher Haushalt m; ~ **insurance** n INS landwirtschaftliche Versicherung f

agriculturalist n ECON Landwirt m, Landwirtschaftsexperte m, Landwirtschaftsexpertin f

agricultural: ~ **job** n ECON, HRM landwirtschaftlicher Beruf m; ~ **land** n ECON landwirtschaftlich genutzte Fläche f; ~ **lending** n BANK landwirtschaftliche Darlehensgewährung f; ~ **levy** n ECON Agrarabschöpfung f; ~ **loan** n BANK Landwirtschaftskredit m, Agrardarlehen nt

Agricultural: ~ **Marketing Board** n BrE ECON Behörde für Agrarmarketing, ≈ Centrale Marketing-Gesellschaft f der deutschen Agrarwirtschaft mbH (CMA)

agricultural: ~ **policy** n ECON Agrarpolitik f; ~ **price support** n ECON Agrarpreisstützung f; ~ **product** n ECON Agrarerzeugnis nt, Agrarprodukt nt, landwirtschaftliches Erzeugnis nt; ~ **production** n ECON Agrarproduktion f; ~ **production cooperative** n ECON landwirtschaftliche Produktionsgenossenschaft f (LPG); ~ **sector** n ECON Agrarsektor m, landwirtschaftlicher Sektor m; ~ **sector adjustment loan** n BrE (ASAL) FIN Anpassungsdarlehen nt für den Agrarsektor; ~ **show** n ECON, IND, S&M Agrarmesse f, Landwirtschaftsschau f; ~ **subsidy** n ECON Agrarsubventionen f pl, Agrarzuschüsse f pl; ~ **tenant** n ECON, INS landwirtschaftlicher Pächter m, landwirtschaftliche Pächterin f

agricultural: ~ **unit** n ECON landwirtschaftliche Betriebseinheit f; ~ **wages board** n BrE HRM Behörde f zur Festsetzung von Landarbeiterlöhnen

agriculture n GEN COMM Landwirtschaft f

Agriculture: ~ **Miscellaneous Provisions Act** n BrE LAW Landwirtschaftsgesetz (verschiedene Bestimmungen)

agriculturist n ECON Landwirt m, Landwirtschaftsexperte m, Landwirtschaftsexpertin f

agrochemical n ENVIR Agrochemikalie f

agroforestry n ENVIR Wald-Feld-Bau m, Forstwirtschaft f

agroindustry n IND Agroindustrie f

agronomist n ENVIR Agronom, in m,f

agronomy n ENVIR Agronomie f

aground adv TRANSP shipping auf Grund, aufgelaufen, auf Grund gelaufen

agt abbr (agent) GEN COMM Handelsvertreter, in m,f, Vertreter, in m,f, Bevollmächtigte(r) mf [decl. as adj], S&M Vertreter, in m,f

AHC Banks: n pl BrE BANK dem Accepting Houses Committee angeschlossene Akzeptbanken

ahead adv GEN COMM voraus; ♦ ~ **of schedule** COMMS vorzeitig, FIN vor Fälligkeit, früher als geplant

AHS abbr (assistant head of section) HRM stellvertretender Abteilungsleiter m, stellvertretende Abteilungsleiterin f

AI abbr COMP (artificial intelligence) KI (künstliche Intelligenz), FIN (accrued interest) aufgelaufene Zinsen m pl

AIA abbr (Associate of the Institute of Actuaries) INS Mitglied des Instituts der Versicherungsmathematiker

AIB abbr (American Institute of Bankers) BANK amerikanisches Institut der Bankfachleute

AIBD abbr (Association of International Bond Dealers) STOCK Verband der internationalen Rentenhändler

AIBOR abbr BrE (Amsterdam Interbank Offered Rate) BANK Amsterdamer Interbankenangebotssatz m

AICPA abbr (American Institute of Certified Public Accountants) ACC amerikanisches Institut der öffentlich zugelassenen Wirtschaftsprüfer

AICS abbr (Associate Institute of Chartered Shipbrokers) HRM Mitglied des Instituts der konzessionierten Schiffsmakler

aid 1. n BANK development Entwicklungshilfe f, Beihilfe f, COMP, ECON, FIN Hilfe f, GEN COMM Beistand m, Unterstützung f, LAW Vorschub m, Beihilfe f; **2.** vt ECON developing country Beihilfe leisten, unterstützen, Entwicklungshilfe leisten, development, understanding fördern, person unterstützen, FIN developing country Beihilfe leisten, Entwicklungshilfe leisten, development, company Beihilfe leisten, GEN COMM company, person unterstützen; ♦ ~ **and abet** LAW Beihilfe leisten, crime Vorschub leisten

AID abbr AmE (Agency for International Development) ECON Behörde für internationale Entwicklung

AIDA abbr (attention, interest, desire, action) GEN COMM Aufmerksamkeit, Interesse, Wunsch, Aktion

aid: ~ **development loan** n BrE BANK Entwicklungshilfekredit m; ~ **donor** n ECON, FIN for development Entwicklungshilfeorganisation f, Geberland nt

aide n GEN COMM Referent, in m,f, Berater, in m,f

aided: ~ **recall** n S&M market research gestützte Erinnerung f; ~ **recall test** n S&M market research Erinnerungstest m mit Gedächtnisstütze, Gedächtnistest m

aide-mémoire n GEN COMM Gedächtnisstütze f, POL Aide-mémoire nt, Memorandum nt (Memo)

aid: ~-**financed project** n ECON, FIN development Entwicklungshilfeprojekt nt; ~ **in kind** n ECON, FIN for development Sachhilfe f; ~ **loan** n BANK for development

Entwicklungshilfekredit *m*; ~ **money** *n* ECON, FIN *for development* Hilfsgelder *nt pl*; ~ **program** *AmE*, ~ **programme** *BrE* *n* ECON, FIN *for development* Hilfsprogramm *nt*; ~ **scheme** *n* ECON, FIN *for development* Hilfsprojekt *nt*, Hilfsprogramm *nt*

Aid: ~ **to Families with Dependent Children** *n AmE* (*AFDC*) WEL Unterstützung bedürftiger Familien mit unterhaltsberechtigten Kindern

AIFTA *abbr* ECON (*Anglo-Irish Free Trade Area Agreement*) anglo-irisches Freihandelsabkommen, HRM (*Associate Institute of the Freight Trades Association*) Assoziiertes Institut der Frachthandelsvereinigung

AIGSS *abbr* (*annual inert gas system survey*) ENVIR jährliche Inertgassystemübersicht *f*

ailing *adj* BANK, ECON notleidend, GEN COMM kränkelnd, kränklich, IND verfallend, notleidend; ~ **bank** *n* BANK notleidende Bank *f*; ~ **economy** *n* ECON notleidende Volkswirtschaft *f*; ~ **industry** *n* IND Industrie *f* im Niedergang, Industrierückgang *m*, verfallende Industrie *f*, schrumpfende Industrie *f*

aim 1. *n* GEN COMM Bestreben *nt*, Vorhaben *nt*, Ziel *nt*, Zweck *m*; **2.** *vt* GEN COMM *criticism, product, programme* zielen auf [+acc], ausrichten [+acc], richten, *intend* vorhaben, S&M *intend to achieve* anstreben; ◆ ~ **sth at sb** GEN COMM etw gegen jdn richten

aimed: **be** ~ **at sb** *phr* GEN COMM auf jdn abgezielt sein, sich an jdn wenden; **be** ~ **at sth** *phr* GEN COMM auf etw abgezielt sein, sich an etw wenden

aimless *adj* GEN COMM ziellos, zwecklos

AIMS *abbr* (*American Institute of Merchant Shipping*) TRANSP amerikanisches Institut der Handelsschiffahrt

AInstM *abbr* (*Associate of the Institute of Marketing*) HRM Mitglied des Instituts für Marketing

air 1. *n* ENVIR, IND, TRANSP Luft *f*; ◆ **by** ~ COMMS, TRANSP *mode of transport, goods, mail* auf dem Luftweg, per Flugzeug; **on the** ~ MEDIA, S&M auf Sendung; **2.** *vt* GEN COMM *concern* vorbringen, *idea, proposal* bekanntgeben, POL an die Öffentlichkeit bringen; ◆ ~ **one's opinions** GEN COMM seine Meinung äußern; ~ **one's views** GEN COMM seine Ansichten äußern, seine Ansichten kundtun

air: ~ **bill of lading** *n* IMP/EXP, TRANSP Luftfrachtbrief *m*

airborne: ~ **time** *n* TRANSP Flugzeit *f*

airbrush: ~ **technique** *n* S&M *advertising* Airbrushtechnik *f*

air: ~ **bus** *n* TRANSP Airbus *m*; ~ **cargo** *n* TRANSP Luftfracht *f*; ~ **carrier** *n* TRANSP Luftfrachtführer *m*, Lufttransportgesellschaft *f*, Luftverkehrsgesellschaft *f*; ~ **check** *n* MEDIA *broadcast* Sendeprobe *f*; ~ **check tape** *n* MEDIA *broadcast* Mitschnitt *m*; ~-**condition** *vt* GEN COMM klimatisieren, mit Klimaanlage austatten; ~-**conditioned** *adj* GEN COMM klimatisiert, mit Klimaanlage ausgestattet; ~ **conditioning** *n* GEN COMM Klimaanlage *f*, Klimatisierung *f*; ~ **corridor** *n* TRANSP Flugkorridor *m*, Luftkorridor *m*

aircraft *n* TRANSP Flugzeug *nt*, Luftfahrzeug *nt*; ~ **charter agreement** *n* TRANSP Luftchartervertrag *m*; ~ **hull insurance** *n* INS Flugzeugversicherung *f*, Luftfahrtkaskoversicherung *f*; ~ **industry** *n* TRANSP Luftfahrtindustrie *f*, Flugzeugindustrie *f*; ~ **kilometers** *AmE*, ~ **kilometres** *BrE* *n pl* TRANSP Flugkilometer *m pl*, Flugzeugkilometer *m pl*; ~ **manifest** *n* TRANSP Frachtmanifest *nt* des Luftfahrzeugs; ~ **operator** *n* TRANSP Flugzeugbetreiber *m*;

~ **passenger insurance** *n* INS Fluggastversicherung *f*, Flugzeuginsassenversicherung *f*; ~ **turnaround time** *AmE*, ~ **turnround time** *BrE* *n* TRANSP Flugzeug-Umschlagzeit *f*

aircrew *n* HRM, LEIS Flugzeugbesatzung *f*

air: ~ **date** *n* S&M *for broadcast* Sendedatum *nt*, Sendetermin *m*

airdrome *n AmE* (*cf aerodrome BrE*) TRANSP *aviation* Flugplatz *m*, Flughafen *m*

air: ~ **fare** *n* LEIS, TRANSP Flugpreis *m*

airfield *n* TRANSP Flugplatz *m*

airflex: ~ **clutch** *n* (*AFC*) TRANSP Airflex-Kupplung *f*

air: ~ **freight** *n* TRANSP *mode of shipment* Luftfracht *f*; ~-**freight charges** *n pl* TRANSP Luftfrachttarif *m*, Luftfrachtkosten *pl*; ~-**freight consolidation** *n* TRANSP Luftfrachtsammelladung *f*; ~-**freight container** *n* (*ac*) TRANSP Luftfracht-Container *m*; ~ **hostess** *n* LEIS, TRANSP Flugbegleiterin *f*; ~ **letter** *n* COMMS Aerogramm *nt*, Luftpostbrief *m*, Luftpostleichtbrief *m*

airlift *n* TRANSP Lufttransport *m*

airline *n* TRANSP Fluggesellschaft *f*, Fluglinie *f*; ~ **advertising** *n* S&M Werbung *f* einer Fluggesellschaft

airliner *n* TRANSP Linienflugzeug *nt*

air: ~ **mail** *n* COMMS Luftpost *f*; **by** ~ **mail** *phr* COMMS per Luftpost; ~-**mail letter** *n* COMMS Luftpostbrief *m*; ~-**mail paper** *n* COMMS Luftpostpapier *nt*; ~-**mail transfer** *n* (*AMT*) BANK, ECON Überweisung *f* per Luftpost; ~ **mode container** *n* TRANSP Luftverkehrscontainer *m*; ~ **passenger** *n* LEIS, TRANSP Fluggast *m*, Flugreisende(r) *mf* [decl. as adj]

airplane *n AmE* (*cf aeroplane BrE*) TRANSP Flugzeug *nt*; ~ **banner** *n AmE* (*cf aeroplane banner BrE*) S&M *advertising* von Flugzeug gezogenes Werbespruchband *nt*, Werbespruchband *nt* an einem Flugzeug

air: ~ **pocket stock** *n* STOCK Aktien, die von einer plötzlichen Kursschwäche betroffen sind; ~ **pollution** *n* ENVIR Luftverschmutzung *f*, Luftverunreinigung *f*

airport *n* TRANSP Flughafen *m*, Flugplatz *m*; ~ **advertising** *n* S&M Flughafenwerbung *f*

Airport: ~ **Associations Coordinating Council** *n* TRANSP koordinierender Rat der Flughafenverbände

airport: ~ **hotel** *n* LEIS Flughafenhotel *nt*; ~ **tax** *n* TAX Flughafengebühr *f*

airshow *n* TRANSP Flugschau *f*, Luftfahrtschau *f*

air: ~ **steward** *n* LEIS, TRANSP Flugbegleiter *m*; ~ **stewardess** *n* LEIS, TRANSP Flugbegleiterin *f*

airstrip *n* TRANSP Landeplatz *m*

air: ~ **terminal** *n* TRANSP Flughafenabfertigungsgebäude *nt*, Terminal *nt*

airtight *adj* IND *container, seal* hermetisch abgeschlossen, luftdicht

airtime *n* MEDIA, S&M *for broadcast* Sendezeit *f*, *for television advertising* Fernsehwerbezeit *f*; ~ **buyer** *n* MEDIA, S&M *radio, TV* Käufer, in *m,f* von Sendezeit

air: ~ **traffic** *n* TRANSP Flugverkehr *m*, Luftverkehr *m*; ~-**traffic control** *n* (*ATC*) TRANSP *activity* Flugsicherung *f* (*FS*), Luftverkehrsregelung *f*, *building* Flugsicherungszentrale *f*, Luftverkehrszentrale *f*; ~-**traffic controller** *n* TRANSP Fluglotse *m*; ~-**traffic control system** *n* TRANSP Flugsicherungssystem *nt*; ~ **transport** *n* TRANSP Lufttransport *m*, Luftverkehr *m*, Beförderung *f* auf dem Luftweg

Air: ~ **Transport Association of America** *n* (*ATA*)

TRANSP amerikanische Lufttransportvereinigung, ≈ Deutscher Luftfahrverband (*DLV*)

air: ~ **transport insurance** *n* INS Lufttransportversicherung *f*; ~ **travel** *n* LEIS, TRANSP Flugreise *f*; ~ **traveler** *AmE*, ~ **traveller** *BrE* *n* LEIS, TRANSP Fluggast *m*, Flugreisende(r) *mf* [decl. as adj]

airway *n* TRANSP Flugkorridor *m*, Luftroute *f*, Fluglinie *f*, Flugroute *f*, Flugstraße *f*, Flugstrecke *f*, Luftverkehrslinie *f*, Luftverkehrsstraße *f*

air: ~ **waybill** *n* (*AWB*) IMP/EXP, TRANSP Luftfrachtbrief *m*

airworthiness: ~ **certification** *n* TRANSP Flugtüchtigkeitszeugnis *nt*, Flugtauglichkeitsbescheinigung *f*

airworthy *adj* TRANSP flugtauglich

aisle *n* GEN COMM *in cinema, shop, train, aircraft* Durchgang *m*, Gang *m*; ~ **seat** *n* LEIS Platz am Gang *m*

AIWM *abbr* (*American Institute of Weights and Measures*) MATH amerikanisches Institut für Maße und Gewichte, ≈ Physikalisch-Technische Bundesanstalt *f*

aka *abbr* (*also known as*) COMMS, GEN COMM auch bekannt als, auch bekannt unter, al (*alias*)

alarm *n* GEN COMM *warning* Alarm *m*; ~ **equipment** *n* COMP Alarmeinrichtung *f*; ~ **signal** *n* GEN COMM Alarmsignal *nt*, Alarmzeichen *nt*

aleatoric *adj* INS aleatorisch, vom Zufall abhängig

aleatory *adj* INS aleatorisch, zufallsabhängig, LAW, S&M aleatorisch; ~ **advertising** *n* S&M aleatorische Werbung *f*; ~ **contract** *n* INS aleatorischer Vertrag *m*, Risikovertrag *m*, LAW aleatorischer Vertrag *m*

alert *n* GEN COMM Alarmbereitschaft *f*, Alarmzustand *m*; ♦ **give the** ~ GEN COMM Alarm schlagen

alert: ~ **box** *n* COMP Hinweisfenster *nt*, Warnfenster *nt*

A: ~ **level** *n* *BrE* (*Advanced level, cf High School Diploma AmE*) WEL Abschluß der Sekundarreife, ≈ Abitur *nt*, ≈ Hochschulreife *f*, ≈ Matura *f* (*Öst, Sch*), ≈ Maturitätsprüfung *f* (*Sch*), ≈ Reifeprüfung *f* (*obs*)

algorithm *n* COMP, MATH Algorithmus *m*

algorithmic *adj* COMP, MATH algorithmisch

algorithmization *n* COMP, MATH Algorithmisierung *f*

alias *n* COMP Pseudonym *nt*, GEN COMM angenommener Name *m*, Pseudonym *nt*

alien 1. *adj* GEN COMM fremd, zuwiderlaufend; ♦ ~ **from** GEN COMM andersartig als; **2.** *n* LAW Ausländer, in *m,f*

alienable *adj* LAW, PROP *transferable* veräußerlich

alienate *vt* FIN *capital* abziehen, GEN COMM abwerben, entfremden, *property* rechtsgeschäftlich übertragen, veräußern, LAW veräußern, abziehen, abwerben, *property* rechtsgeschäftlich übertragen, PROP veräußern

alienation *n* ADMIN *work* Arbeitsentfremdung *f*, ECON Eigentumsübertragung *f*, Entfremdung *f*, FIN *capital* Abzug *m*, HRM Entfremdung *f*, LAW Veräußerung *f*, PROP Veräußerung *f*, S&M Abwerbung *f*; ~ **effect** *n* S&M *in film, picture* Abwerbungswirkung *f*, Verfremdungseffekt *m*

alien: ~ **corporation** *n* LAW ausländische Gesellschaft *f*; ~ **registration card** *n* ADMIN Ausländeranmeldeschein *m*

align *vt* COMP auf gleiche Höhe bringen, ausrichten, ECON angleichen, anpassen, GEN COMM ausrichten, gruppieren, angleichen, anpassen; ♦ ~ **with** ECON angleichen an [+acc], LAW anpassen an [+acc]

aligned: ~ **forms** *n pl* ADMIN angeglichene Formulare *f*

pl, aufeinander abgestimmte Formulare *nt pl*, vereinheitlichte Formblätter *nt pl*

alignment *n* GEN COMM Ausrichtung *f*, Gruppierung *f*, Angleichung *f*, Anpassung *f*; ~ **of tariff rates** *n* IMP/EXP Angleichung *f* von Zollsätzen

aliquot *adj* MATH aliquot, ohne Rest teilend; ~ **parts** *n pl* MATH aliquote Teile *f pl*

all *adj* GEN COMM alle, LAW *contracts* sämtlich; ♦ **at** ~ **times** GEN COMM jederzeit, zu allen Zeiten

all-day: ~ **trading** *n* STOCK Rund-um-die-Uhr-Handel *m*, ganztägiger Handel *m*

allegation *n* GEN COMM, LAW Behauptung *f*

alleged *adj* GEN COMM, LAW angeblich, vermutlich

all-employee: ~ **option scheme** *n* *BrE* STOCK Mitarbeiteroptionsplan *m*

alleviate *vt* GEN COMM *problems* lindern, mildern

alliance *n* GEN COMM *union* Bund *m*, POL Bündnis *nt*, *compact* Pakt *m*, Allianz *f*, *union, coalition* Bund *m*, Koalition *f*

allied *adj* IND verbunden, verwandt; ~ **industries** *n pl* IND verbundene Gewerbe *nt pl*, verwandte Industriebereiche *m pl*, verbundene Industriezweige *m pl*; ~ **peril** *n* INS Nebenrisiko *nt*; ~ **trades** *n pl* IND verwandte Berufe *m pl*, verwandte Handwerke *nt pl*, verbundene Gewerbezweige *m pl*

alligator: ~ **spread** *n* STOCK *investment banking, securities, options* sehr große Kursspanne *f*

all-in *adj* GEN COMM *price* alles eingeschlossen, alles inbegriffen, gesamt, global, pauschal, LAW einschließlich aller Rechte

all-inclusive *adj* GEN COMM *rate* alles eingeschlossen, alles inbegriffen, gesamt, global, pauschal; ~ **price** *n* GEN COMM Pauschalpreis *m*

all-lines: ~ **insurance** *n* INS *policy* Allbranchenversicherung *f*

all-loss: ~ **insurance** *adj* INS *policy* Gesamtversicherung *f*, Globalversicherung *f*

allocate *vt* COMMS *shares* zuteilen, zuweisen, ECON *funds, resources* umlegen, aufteilen, zuteilen, zuweisen, verteilen, FIN *money, duties* bereitstellen, zuweisen, zuteilen, GEN COMM *work* aufteilen, kontingentieren, vergeben, LAW *classify* aufschlüsseln; ~ **to** *vt* ACC *money, duties* kontingentieren, umlegen, zurechnen, *to reserves* einstellen in [+acc], COMP *storage space, machine* zuführen, zuordnen, zuweisen; ♦ ~ **costs** ACC Kosten umlegen, Kosten verrechnen, Kosten zuweisen; ~ **costs to certain accounts** ACC Kosten bestimmten Konten zuordnen, Kosten bestimmten Konten zurechnen; ~ **costs to the appropriate accounts** ACC Kosten auf die geeigneten Konten umlegen; ~ **resources** ACC, FIN, MGMNT Mittel bewilligen, Mittel zuweisen

allocated *adj* ACC verrechnet, GEN COMM verteilt; ~ **benefits** *n pl* FIN *personal* zugeteilte Leistungen *f pl*; ~ **material** *n* GEN COMM auftragsgebundenes Material *nt*

allocation *n* ACC Zuweisung *f*, *of funds to reserve* Zuführung *f*, *amount allocated* Kontingent *nt*, Umlage *f*, Zuteilung *f*, Zurechnung *f*, ADMIN Allokation *f*, COMMS *shares* Zuweisung *f*, COMP Zuweisung *f*, Zuordnung *f*, ECON Allokation *f*, FIN *of money to person* Bereitstellung *f*, GEN COMM Kontingent *nt*, *of contract* Auftragsvergabe *f*, *of duties* Aufgabenverteilung *f*, *of resources* Zuweisung *f*, *of funds, resources* Bestimmung *f*, Aufschlüsselung *f*, Bereitstellung *f*, Aufteilung *f*,

Vergabe *f*, HRM, MGMNT *of duties* Aufgabenverteilung *f*; ~ **account** *n* ACC Verrechnungskonto *nt*; ~ **by tender** *n* BrE STOCK Vergabe *f* im Submissionswege; ~ **of costs** *n* ACC Aufteilung *f* der Kosten, Kostenverrechnung *f*, Kostenumlage *f*; ~ **of earnings** *n* HRM Erfolgszurechnung *f*; ~ **of overheads** *n* ACC Gemeinkostenverrechnung *f*, ADMIN Gemeinkostenumlage *f*; ~ **of resources** *n* ECON Allokation *f* von Ressourcen, Ressourcenallokation *f*; ~ **of responsibilities** *n* FIN Verteilung *f* der Verantwortungsbereiche, GEN COMM, HRM Aufgabenzuweisung *f*, Aufgabenverteilung *f*, MGMNT Aufgabenverteilung *f*, Zuständigkeitsverteilung *f*; ~ **of social costs** *n* ADMIN, ECON Allokation *f* externer Kosten, Internalisierung *f* von Sozialkosten

allocations: ~ **to provisions** *n pl* ACC Zuführungen *f pl* zu den Rückstellungen

allocation: ~ **to the lowest tenderer** *n* S&M Berücksichtigung *f* des billigsten Angebots; ~ **to a provision** *n* GEN COMM Bestätigung *f* einer Bestimmung; ~ **to reserves** *n* ACC Zuführung *f* zu den Rücklagen, Einstellung *f* in die Rücklagen; ~ **of work** *n* HRM Arbeitsverteilung *f*

allocative: ~ **efficiency** *n* ECON Allokationseffizienz *f*; ~ **mechanism** *n* ADMIN, ECON Allokationsmechanismus *m*

allodial *adj* LAW lehensfrei, zinsfrei; ~ **system** *n* LAW System *nt* lehensfreien Grundbesitzes

allonge *n* BANK *on bill of exchange* Allonge *f*, Ansatzstück *nt*, Verlängerungsstück *nt*

All: ~ **Ordinaries Index** *n* STOCK Stammaktienindex *m*

allot *vt* ACC *allocate* zuweisen, *distribute* verteilen, FIN *money* zuteilen, zuweisen; ♦ ~ **a week to the problem** MGMNT eine Woche für das Problem vorsehen, eine Woche für das Problem ansetzen; ~ **shares** STOCK *to employee, applicant* Aktien zuteilen

allotment *n* ACC *allocation* Zuweisung *f*, *distribution* Verteilung *f*, FIN *of money* Zuteilung *f*, Zuweisung *f*, TRANSP *shipping* Verteilung *f*, Zuweisung *f*; ~ **of bonus** *n* INS Bonuszuteilung *f*, Verteilung *f* der Rückvergütung; ~ **letter** *n* BrE STOCK Mitteilung *f* über Aktienzuteilung, Zuteilungsanzeige *f*; ~ **money** *n* FIN Zuteilungsbetrag *m*; ~ **price** *n* FIN Zuteilungskurs *m*; ~ **of securities** *n* STOCK Stückezuteilung *f*

allottee *n* STOCK Bezugsberechtigte(r) *mf* [decl. as adj], Zeichner, in *m,f*, Zuteilungsempfänger, in *m,f*

all-out *adj* GEN COMM uneingeschränkt, total, *effort* gesamt; ~ **strike** *n* HRM Globalstreik *m*

allow *vt* BANK vergüten, erlauben, GEN COMM *action, change* erlauben, genehmigen, gestatten, *claim* anerkennen, stattgeben, bewilligen, zubilligen, einräumen, *grant money, resources* gewähren, HRM zulassen, INS *claim* anerkennen, gewähren, LAW, PATENTS erlauben

allow for *vt* GEN COMM berücksichtigen; ♦ ~ **a margin of error** ACC Fehlergrenze einkalkulieren, eine Sicherheitsspanne berücksichtigen

allowable *adj* GEN COMM erlaubt, statthaft, zulässig, TAX absetzbar, abzugsfähig; ~ **business investment loss** *n* ACC Wertberichtigung *f* auf Beteiligungen; ~ **catch** *n* ECON *fishery* erlaubte Fangquote *f*; ~ **claim** *n* INS zulässige Forderung *f*; ~ **expenses** *n pl* ACC steuerlich absetzbare Kosten *pl*

allowance *n* ACC Rückstellung *f*, Wertberichtigung *f*, GEN COMM Anrechnung *f*, *tolerance* Toleranz *f*, zulässige Abweichung *f*, HRM Zuschlag *m*, Zulage *f*, IND Toleranz *f*, S&M *for damaged or lost goods* Abzug *m*, *discount* Preisermäßigung *f*, TAX Steuerfreibetrag *m*, Freibetrag *m*; ~ **for bad debts** *n* ACC Wertberichtigung *f* auf uneinbringliche Forderungen; ~ **for depreciation** *n* ACC Abschreibung *f*, Absetzung *f* für Abnutzung (*AfA*), Abschreibungsbetrag *m*; ~ **for exchange fluctuations** *n* GEN COMM Rückstellung *f* für Wechselkursschwankungen; ~ **for inflation** *n* ACC Preissteigerungsrücklage *f*; ~ **for loss** *n* TAX Verlustvortrag *m*, Berücksichtigung *f* der Verluste, steuerliche Verlustberücksichtigung *f*; ~ **for moving costs** *n* AmE (*cf allowance for removal BrE*) HRM Umzugskostenbeihilfe *f*; ~ **for removal** BrE *n* (*cf allowance for moving costs AmE*) HRM Umzugskostenbeihilfe *f*; ~ **in kind** *n* GEN COMM Naturalleistung *f*, Naturallohn *m*, Sachbezug *m*, Sachleistung *f*, HRM Sachbezug *m*, INS Sachleistung *f*

allowances *n pl* BrE HRM Zuschüsse *m pl*

allowed *adj* GEN COMM bewilligt; ~ **time** *n* HRM *for job* Vorgabezeit *f*

alloy: ~ **container** *n* TRANSP *shipping* Leichtmetallcontainer *m*

all-purpose *adj* FIN *financial statement* universal, GEN COMM multifunktional

all-risk: ~ **cover** *n* INS Allgefahrendeckung *f*; ~ **insurance** *n* INS Gesamtversicherung *f*, Globalversicherung *f*, Versicherung *f* gegen alle Gefahren

all-round: ~ **price** *n* GEN COMM Gesamtpreis *m*

all-savers: ~ **certificate** *n* AmE BANK steuerbegünstigtes, nicht übertragbares Sparzertifikat von US-Depositenbanken

all-sector: ~ **average** *n* ECON *growth* Durchschnitt *m* aller Sektoren

All: ~ **Share Index** *n* BrE (*Financial Times Actuaries All Shares Index*) STOCK Aktienindex der Financial Times, ≈ FAZ Index (*Aktienindex der Frankfurter Allgemeinen Zeitung*)

all-stage: ~ **gross turnover tax** *n* TAX Bruttoallphasenumsatzsteuer *f*; ~ **net turnover tax** *n* TAX Nettoallphasenumsatzsteuer *f*

all-time: ~ **high** *n* ECON Rekordhöhe *f*, GEN COMM historischer Rekord *m*, Höchstkurs *m*, Rekordhöhe *f*, absoluter Höchststand *m*, STOCK absoluter Höchststand *m*, Höchstkurs *m*; ~ **record** *n* GEN COMM unerreichte Rekordleistung *f*, historischer Rekord *m*

ally 1. *n* POL Verbündete(r) *mf* [decl. as adj]; **2.** *vt* ~ **oneself with** POL sich verbünden mit

aloft *adv* TRANSP *shipping* oben

alongside *adv* (*A/S*) TRANSP daneben; ~ **bill of lading** *n* IMP/EXP Längsseitkonnossement *nt*; ~ **ship** (*A/S*) TRANSP längsseits Schiff

aloof *adj* GEN COMM reserviert, zurückhaltend

alpha *n* STOCK Alpha *nt*

Alpha/Beta: ~ **testing** *n* S&M Alpha-Beta-Testverfahren *nt*

alphabetical *adj* GEN COMM alphabetisch; ♦ **in ~ order** GEN COMM in alphabetischer Reihenfolge

alphanumeric *adj* (*A/N*) COMP, GEN COMM alphanumerisch; ~ **data** *n pl* COMP alphanumerische Daten *pl*; ~ **keyboard** *n* COMP alphanumerische Tastatur *f*

alphanumerics *n pl* COMP alphanumerische Daten *pl*

alpha: ~ **stage** *n* FIN Alpha-Stadium *nt*; ~ **stock** *n* STOCK Alpha-Wert *m*, Alpha-Aktie *f*; ~ **test** *n* COMP Alphatest *m*

Alpine: ~ **countries** *n pl* GEN COMM Alpenländer *nt pl*

also: ~ **known as** *phr* (*aka*) COMMS, GEN COMM alias (*al*), auch bekannt als, auch bekannt unter

alt. *abbr* (*altered*) GEN COMM geändert, verändert

alter *vt* GEN COMM ändern, umändern, umschreiben, verändern; ♦ ~ **a document** LAW Urkundenfälschung begehen

alteration *n* GEN COMM Änderung *f*, Veränderung *f*, Umänderung *f*; ~ **of capital** *n* GEN COMM Änderung *f* des Grundkapitals, Kapitaländerung *f*

alterations: ~ **and improvements** *n pl* ACC *annual accounts* Änderungen und Verbesserungen *f pl*

altered *adj* (*alt.*) GEN COMM geändert, verändert

altering *n* GEN COMM *of document* Umschreibung *f*, Änderung *f*

alternate 1. *adj* GEN COMM *by turns* abwechselnd, *successive* alternierend, aufeinanderfolgend; **2.** *n* GEN COMM Vertreter, in *m,f*; **3.** *vi* GEN COMM alternieren, sich abwechseln

alternate: ~ **hypothesis** *n* MATH Prüfhypothese *f*

Alternate: ~ **key** *n* (*Alt key*) COMP Alt-Taste *f*

alternate: ~ **member** *n AmE* GEN COMM *stand-in* Ersatzfrau *f*, Ersatzmann *m*, stellvertretendes Mitglied *nt*, Stellvertreter, in *m,f*, Vertreter, in *m,f*; ~ **press** *n* MEDIA alternative Presse *f*

alternating: ~ **current** *n* (*ac*) GEN COMM Wechselstrom (*WS*) *m*; ~ **shift** *n* HRM Wechselschicht *f*

alternative 1. *adj* GEN COMM *possibility, activity, answer*, MGMNT *strategy, solution* alternativ; **2.** *n* GEN COMM *option from several* Alternative *f pl*, Wahl *f*, Möglichkeit *f*, *option from two* Alternative *f*, Entweder-Oder *nt*; ♦ **there is no ~** (*TINA*) GEN COMM es gibt keine Alternative

alternative: ~ **costs** *n pl* ACC relevante Kosten *pl*, ECON, FIN Alternativkosten *pl*, Opportunitätskosten *pl*, Grenzkosten *pl*; ~ **economic strategy** *n* ECON alternative Wirtschaftsstrategie *f*; ~ **energy** *n* ENVIR alternative Energie *f*; ~ **hypothesis** *n* MATH *statistical testing* Alternativhypothese *f*; ~ **mortgage instrument** *n* BANK alternative Form einer Hypothek, die nicht als Standardanleihe mit festem Zinssatz und festen Tilgungsraten aufgenommen wird; ~ **obligation** *n* LAW Wahlschuld *f*; ~ **order** *n* STOCK Zug-um-Zug-Order *f*; ~ **proposal** *n* MGMNT Alternativvorschlag *m*; ~ **reorganization** *n* FIN Alternativsanierung *f*; ~ **route** *n* COMP Alternativweg *m*; ~ **solution** *n* GEN COMM Alternativlösung *f*; ~ **substitution** *n* ADMIN, GEN COMM alternative Substitution *f*; ~ **technology** *n* ENVIR, IND *production* alternative Technologie *f*; ~ **use** *n* PROP alternative Nutzung *f*

Alt: ~ **key** *n* (*Alternate key*) COMP Alt-Taste *f*

altruism *n* ECON Altruismus *m*, Uneigennützigkeit *f*

altruistic *adj* ECON altruistisch, uneigennützig

Alu. *abbr* (*aluminium BrE, aluminum AmE*) ENVIR, IND Alu (*Aluminium*)

aluminium *n BrE* (*Alu.*) ENVIR, IND Aluminium *nt* (*Alu*); ~ **covers** *n pl BrE* TRANSP *shipping* Aluminiumabdeckungen *f pl*; ~ **industry** *n BrE* GEN COMM Aluminiumindustrie *f*, IND Leichtmetallindustrie *f*

aluminum *AmE see aluminium BrE*

always: ~ **accessible on arrival** *phr* TRANSP *shipping* bei

Ankunft immer zugänglich; ~ **reachable on arrival** *phr* TRANSP *shipping* bei Ankunft immer zugänglich

am *abbr* (*ante meridiem*) GEN COMM vormittags

AM *abbr* (*account manager*) S&M Account-Manager *m*

AMA *abbr* (*asset management account*) FIN Anlagenverwaltungskonto *nt*, Vermögensverwaltungskonto *nt*

amalgamate 1. *vt* ECON, GEN COMM *companies, activities, shares* fusionieren, zusammenlegen, FIN verschmelzen; **2.** *vi* ECON, GEN COMM fusionieren, sich zusammenschließen, FIN verschmelzen, STOCK fusionieren

amalgamated: ~ **bank** *n* BANK fusionierte Bank *f*

amalgamating: ~ **corporation** *n* BANK fusionierende Gesellschaft *f*

amalgamation *n* ADMIN, FIN Fusion *f*, Verschmelzung *f*, HRM Zusammenschluß *m*, STOCK Fusion *f*

amass *vt* GEN COMM *money, property, goods* anhäufen, ansammeln

amateur *n* LEIS *sport* Amateur *m*, Laie *m*, Nichtexperte *m*, Nichtexpertin *f*

ambassador *n* POL Abgesandte(r) *mf* [decl. as adj], Botschafter, in *m,f*, Gesandte(r) *mf* [decl. as adj]

ambient: ~ **standard** *n* ENVIR *air pollution* Grenzwert *m*, Luftqualitätsstandard *m*; ~ **temperature** *n* GEN COMM Umgebungstemperatur *f*

ambiguous *adj* GEN COMM mehrdeutig, mißverständlich, LAW unklar

ambition *n* GEN COMM Ambition *f*, Begierde *f*, Ehrgeiz *m*, Streben *nt*, Wunsch *m*

ambitious *adj* GEN COMM *person, plan* ehrgeizig

amend *vt* COMP *text* abändern, GEN COMM *conditions* abändern, *text* abändern, berichtigen, LAW abändern

amended *adj* GEN COMM abgeändert, revidiert, berichtigt; ~ **tax return** *n* TAX amendierte Steuererklärung *f*, geänderte Steuererklärung *f*

amending: ~ **statute** *n* LAW Änderungsgesetz *nt*

amendment *n* LAW Änderung *f*, Novellierung *f*, PATENTS *addition* Zusatz *m*, Ergänzung *f*, *change* Änderung *f*, Abänderung *f*, POL *to law, constitution* Änderung *f*, Abänderung *f*, Berechtigung *f*, *addition* Zusatz *m*

amends *n* LAW Wiedergutmachung *f*, Satisfaktion *f*

American: ~ **Association of Advertising Agencies** *n* (*AAAA*) S&M amerikanischer Verband der Werbeagenturen, ≈ Wirtschaftsverband *m* Deutscher Werbeagenturen (*WDW*); ~ **Automobile Association** *n* (*AAA*) TRANSP amerikanische Kraftfahrervereinigung, ≈ Allgemeiner Deutscher Automobil-Club *m* (*ADAC*); ~ **Board of Trade** *n* (*ABT*) GEN COMM amerikanische Handelskammer, ≈ Deutscher Industrie- und Handelstag *m* (*DIHT*); ~ **Broadcasting Company** *n* (*ABC*) MEDIA amerikanische Rundfunk- und Fernsehanstalt, ≈ Arbeitsgemeinschaft *f* der öffentlich-rechtlichen Rundfunkanstalten der Bundesrepublik Deutschland (*ARD*); ~ **Bureau of Shipping** *n* (*ABS*) TRANSP amerikanische Klassifikationsgesellschaft, amerikanische Schiffahrtsbehörde; ~ **Chamber of Commerce** *n* (*ACC*) IND amerikanische Handelskammer, ≈ Industrie- und Handelskammer *f* (*IHK*); ~ **clause** *n* INS *marine* Amerika-Klausel *f*, amerikanische Klausel *f*; ~ **dry quart** *n* GEN COMM amerikanische Viertelgallone *f*; ~ **Economic Association** *n* (*AEA*) ECON amerikanischer Wirtschaftsverband, ≈ Bundeswirtschaftsrat (*BWR*); ~ **Federation of Labor-Congress of Industrial**

Organizations *n* (*AFL-CIO*) HRM Dachverband der amerikanischen Gewerkschaften, ≈ Deutscher Gewerkschaftsbund (*DGB*); ~ **Institute of Accountants** *n* ACC amerikanisches Buchprüferinstitut; ~ **Institute of Bankers** *n* (*AIB*) BANK amerikanisches Institut der Bankfachleute; ~ **Institute of Certified Public Accountants** *n* (*AICPA*) ACC amerikanisches Institut der öffentlich zugelassenen Wirtschaftsprüfer; ~ **Institute of Merchant Shipping** *n* (*AIMS*) TRANSP amerikanisches Institut der Handelsschiffahrt; ~ **Institute of Weights and Measures** *n* (*AIWM*) MATH amerikanisches Institut für Maße und Gewichte, ≈ Physikalisch-Technische Bundesanstalt *f*; ~ **liquid quart** *n* GEN COMM amerikanische flüssige Viertelgallone *f*; ~ **Management Association** *n* MGMNT amerikanischer Managementverband; ~ **Marketing Association** *n* S&M amerikanischer Marketingverband; ~ **Merchant Marine Institute** *n* (*AMMI*) TRANSP amerikanisches Handelsmarine-Institut; ~ **National Standards Institute** *n* (*ANSI*) LAW amerikanischer staatlicher Normenverband, ≈ Deutsches Institut *nt* für Normung (*DIN*); ~ **Newspaper Publishers' Association** *n* (*ANPA*) MEDIA amerikanischer Verband der Zeitungsverleger; ~ **option** *n* STOCK amerikanische Option *f*; ~ **parity** *n* ECON amerikanische Parität *f*; ~ **short ton** *n* GEN COMM amerikanische Tonne *f*; ~ **Society for Testing and Materials** *n* (*ASTM*) GEN COMM amerikanische Gesellschaft für Versuche und Materialen, ≈ Deutscher Normenausschuß *m* (*DNA*); ~ **Standard Code for Information Interchange** *n* (*ASCII*) COMP ASCII-Code *m* (*ASCII*); ~ **Standards Authority** *n* GEN COMM amerikanische Normenbehörde, ≈ Deutsches Institut *nt* für Normung (*DIN*); ~ **Statistical Association** *n* (*ASA*) MATH amerikanische statistische Vereinigung, ≈ Deutsche Statistische Gesellschaft *f* (*DStG*); ~ **Stock Exchange** *n* FIN, STOCK (*AMEX, ASE*) zweitgrößte amerikanische Wertpapierbörse mit Sitz in New York, ≈ Deutsche Börse *f*; ~ **terms** *n pl* ECON amerikanische Parität *f*, *grain trade* amerikanische Bedingungen *f pl*; **in ~ terms** *phr* ECON *currency exchange* zu amerikanischen Bedingungen

AMEX *abbr* (*American Stock Exchange*) STOCK zweitgrößte amerikanische Wertpapierbörse mit Sitz in New York

Amex: ~ **Commodities Exchange** *n* (*ACE*) FIN, STOCK Amex Warenbörse *f*

amicable *adj* GEN COMM einvernehmlich, *manner, performance* gütlich, *person* freundschaftlich; ~ **settlement** *n* GEN COMM gütliche Beilegung *f*, LAW außergerichtlicher Vergleich *m*, gütliche Beilegung *f*; ~ **settlement of dispute** *n* GEN COMM Akkord *m*

amicably *adv* GEN COMM, LAW gütlich, einvernehmlich

amidships *adv* TRANSP mittschiffs

AMIEx *abbr* (*Associate Member of the Institute of Export*) HRM assoziiertes Mitglied des Instituts für Export

AML *abbr* (*adjustable mortgage loan*) BANK variables Hypothekendarlehen *nt*

AMMI *abbr* (*American Merchant Marine Institute*) TRANSP amerikanisches Handelsmarine-Institut

among. ~ **those present** *phr* GEN COMM unter den Anwesenden

Amoroso-Robinson: ~ **relation** *n* ECON Amoroso-Robinson-Relation *f*

amortizable *adj* ACC abschreibbar, abschreibungsfähig, tilgbar, BANK, FIN tilgbar, amortisierbar, rückzahlbar

amortization *n* ACC Abschreibung *f*, Amortisation *f*, Amortisierung *f*, Tilgung *f*, BANK Amortisierung *f*, FIN Rückfluß *m*, Rückzahlung *f*, Schuldentilgung *f*, Tilgung *f*; ~ **adjustment** *n* ACC Amortisationsanpassung *f*; ~ **expense** *n* ACC Tilgungszahlung *f*; ~ **fund** *n* FIN Amortisationsfonds *m*, Tilgungsfonds *m*, Tilgungsrücklage *f*; ~ **installment** *AmE*, ~ **instalment** *BrE* *n* FIN Tilgungsrate *f*; ~ **loan** *n* FIN Amortisationsanleihe *f*, Tilgungsanleihe *f*; ~ **of a loan** *n* FIN Tilgung *f* einer Anleihe, GEN COMM Darlehensrückzahlung *f*; ~ **method** *n* ACC Tilgungsart *f*; ~ **reserve** *n* FIN Tilgungsrücklage *f*; ~ **schedule** *n* ACC Amortisationsplan *m*, FIN Tilgungsplan *m*

amortize *vt* ACC *asset* abschreiben, amortisieren, *debt, mortgage* abtragen, tilgen, zurückzahlen, BANK *asset* abschreiben, amortisieren, *debt, mortgage* abtragen, tilgen, zurückzahlen

amortized: ~ **mortgage loan** *n* BANK Tilgungshypothek *f*, Annuitätenhypothek *f*, Amortisationshypothek *f*; ~ **value** *n* ACC amortisierter Wert *m*, Restwert *m*

amortizement *n* ACC Abschreibung *f*, Amortisation *f*, Tilgung *f*

amount *n* (*amt*) GEN COMM *of money* Betrag *m*, Summe *f*, *of goods* Menge *f*, *of people* Anzahl *f*; ♦ **the ~ standing to your account** BANK Ihr Kontostand

amount to *vi* GEN COMM betragen, sich belaufen auf [+acc]

amount: ~ **brought forward** *n* ACC Vortrag *m*; ~ **of business** *n* GEN COMM Geschäftsumfang *m*, Geschäftsvolumen *nt*, STOCK Umsatz *m*, gehandeltes Volumen *nt*, Handelsumfang *m*; ~ **charged** *n* GEN COMM *quantity* berechnete Menge *f*, *value* berechnete Summe *f*, Rechnungbetrag *m*; ~ **of damage** *n* INS Schadenbetrag *m*, Schadenshöhe *f*, Schadensumme *f*; ~ **due** *n* FIN fälliger Betrag *m*, geschuldeter Betrag *m*; ~ **invested** *n* ACC angelegter Betrag *m*; ~ **of loss** *n* INS Schadenbetrag *m*, Schadenshöhe *f*, Schadensumme *f*; ~ **outstanding** *n* ACC, GEN COMM ausstehender Betrag *m*; ~ **overdue** *n* ACC überfälliger Betrag *m*; ~ **overpaid** *n* GEN COMM überzahlte Summe *f*, überzahlter Betrag *m*; ~ **paid** *n* GEN COMM gezahlter Betrag *m*; ~ **paid by installments** *AmE*, ~ **paid by instalments** *BrE* *n* GEN COMM, TAX Ratenbetrag *m*, in Raten gezahlter Betrag *m*; ~ **paid out** *n* ACC ausgezahlter Betrag *m*, Auszahlung *f*; ~ **payable on settlement** *n* ACC bei Erfüllung *f* zahlbarer Betrag; ~ **repayable** *n* ACC Rückzahlungsbetrag *m*; ~ **of the subscription** *n* STOCK Zeichnungsbetrag *m*; ~ **to be invested** *n* BANK Investitionssumme *f*; ~ **to be paid** *n* INS *marine* verdienter Betrag *m*, zu leistende Schadensumme *f*, zu zahlender Betrag *m*; ~ **of work** *n* MGMNT Arbeitspensum *nt*

ampersand *n* COMP, MEDIA Et-Zeichen *nt*, Und-Zeichen *nt*, kaufmännisches &-Zeichen *nt*

ample *adj* GEN COMM reichlich, überreichlich

amply *adv* GEN COMM reichlich

AMS *abbr* (*annual machinery survey*) TRANSP *shipping* jährliche Maschinenprüfung *f*

Amsterdam: ~ **Interbank Offered Rate** *n BrE* (*AIBOR*) BANK Amsterdamer Interbankenangebotssatz *m*

amt *abbr* (*amount*) ECON, FIN, GEN COMM *of money* Betrag *m*, Summe *f*, *of goods* Menge *f*

AMT *abbr* (*air mail transfer*) BANK, ECON Überweisung *f* per Luftpost

amusement *n* LEIS Vergnügung *f*

A/N *abbr* (*alphanumeric*) COMP, GEN COMM alphanumerisch

analog 1. *adj* COMP analog; **2.** *n* GEN COMM Gegenstück *nt*, Analogon *nt*, entsprechendes Stück *nt*

analog: ~ **channel** *n* COMP Analogkanal *m*; ~ **computer** *n* COMP Analogrechner *m*

analogical *adj* GEN COMM analog, sinngemäß

analog: ~ **monitor** *n* COMP *hardware* Analogbildschirm *m*

analogous *adj* GEN COMM analog, ähnlich, sinngemäß, entsprechend, parallel

analog: ~ **representation** *n* GEN COMM Analog-Repräsentation *f*, analoge Darstellung *f*; ~**-to-digital converter** *n* (*ADC*) COMP *hardware* Analog-Digital-Wandler *m*

analyse *vt* BrE ACC, COMP, ECON, FIN analysieren, GEN COMM analysieren, *sales, costs, results* prüfen, HRM analysieren, MGMNT analysieren, auswerten, S&M, TRANSP analysieren

analyser *n* BrE COMP Analyseprogramm *nt*

analysis *n* ACC, COMP, ECON, FIN Analyse *f*, GEN COMM *account, report* Analyse *f*, Prüfung *f*, HRM Analyse *f*, MGMNT Auswertung *f*, Untersuchung *f*, Analyse *f*, TRANSP Analyse *f*; ~ **book** *n* ACC Analysenbuch *nt*; ~ **of costs by nature** *n* ACC *annual accounts*, FIN Kostenartenrechnung *f*; ~ **of cost variances** *n* ACC Kostenabweichnungsanalyse *f*; Abweichungsanalyse *f*; ~ **of time series** *n* GEN COMM, MATH Zeitreihenanalyse *f*; ~ **of variance** *n* (*ANOVA*) MATH Varianzanalyse *f* (*ANOVA*)

analyst *n* MGMNT, STOCK Analytiker, in *m,f*, Wertpapieranalytiker, in *m,f*

analytic *adj* GEN COMM analytisch; ~ **accounting** *n* ACC analytisches Rechnungswesen *nt*

analytical *adj* GEN COMM analytisch; ~ **audit** *n* ACC analytische Prüfung *f*; ~ **auditing** *n* ACC analytische Prüfung *f*; ~ **review** *n* ACC analytischer Bericht *m*; ~ **training** *n* HRM Sachverstand *m*

analytic: ~ **job evaluation** *n* IND analytische Arbeitsbewertung *f*; ~ **process** *n* MGMNT Analyseverfahren *nt*

analyze *AmE see* analyse *BrE*

analyzer *AmE see* analyser *BrE*

anarchism *n* GEN COMM Anarchielehre *f*, POL Anarchielehre *f*, Anarchismus *m*

anarcho: ~**-communism** *n jarg* POL Anarcho-Kommunismus *m* (*jarg*); ~**-syndicalism** *n jarg* POL Anarcho-Syndikalismus *m* (*jarg*)

anarchy: ~ **of production** *n* POL Anarchie *f* der Produktion

anchor *n* MEDIA *broadcaster* Moderator, in *m,f*

anchorman *n* MEDIA *broadcaster* Moderator *m*

anchor: ~ **tenant** *n* PROP Langzeitmieter, in *m,f*, Langzeitpächter, in *m,f*, Mieter, in *m,f* eines Ankerplatzes, S&M Absatzmagnet *m*

anchorwoman *n* MEDIA *broadcaster* Moderatorin *f*

ancillary *adj* GEN COMM ergänzend, zusätzlich, Neben-, Zusatz-; ~ **operation** *n* MGMNT Hilfsoperation *f*; ~ **operations** *n pl* GEN COMM ergänzende Tätigkeiten *f pl*; ~ **service** *n* GEN COMM Hilfsdienst *m*; ~ **services** *n pl* GEN COMM zusätzliche Dienstleistungen *f pl*, Nebenleistungen *f pl*

ANCOM *abbr* (*Andean Common Market*) ECON Andenmarkt *m*, gemeinsamer Markt *m* der Anden

Andean: ~ **Common Market** *n* (*ANCOM*) ECON Andenmarkt *m*, gemeinsamer Markt *m* der Anden; ~ **Pact** *n* ECON Andenpakt *m*

anecdotal *adj* WEL anekdotisch

ANF *abbr* (*arrival notification form*) TRANSP *shipping* Ankunftsanzeige *f*

angel *n infrml* GEN COMM *investor in a film* Geldgeber, in *m,f*, *investor in the theatre* Geldgeber, in *m,f*, Theater-Sponsor, in *m,f*

angle *n* MATH Winkel *m*; ~ **of repose** *n* TRANSP *of stockpiled material* Schüttwinkel *m*

Anglo- *pref* GEN COMM anglo-; ~**French** *adj* GEN COMM anglo-französisch; ~**Irish Free Trade Area Agreement** *n* (*AIFTA*) ECON anglo-irisches Freihandelsabkommen *n*

animal: ~ **keeper's liability** *n* INS Tierhalterhaftung *f*

animatic *n* S&M *advertising* Zeichentrick *m*

annex 1. *n* AmE *see* annexe *BrE*; **2.** *vt* GEN COMM *territory, land, country* annektieren

annexe *n* BrE GEN COMM *document* Anhang *m*, Zusatz *m*, *building* Anbau *m*, LAW Anhang *m*, Anlage *f*

anniversary *n* GEN COMM Gedenkfeier *f*, Jahrestag *m*; ~ **publication** *n* MEDIA Jubiläumsausgabe *f*, Jubiläumsband *m*, Jubiläumsschrift *f*

announce *vt* GEN COMM *over intercom* durchsagen, *cut in base rates* auflegen, *profit, figures* bekanntmachen, ankündigen, bekanntgeben; ♦ ~ **the details** GEN COMM die Einzelheiten bekanntgeben

announcement *n* GEN COMM Bekanntgabe *f*, Bekanntmachung *f*; ~ **advertising** *n* S&M Einführungswerbung *f*; ~ **effect** *n* POL Ankündigungseffekt *m*, Signalwirkung *f*; ~ **of an engagement** *n* GEN COMM Bekanntgabe *f* einer Vereinbarung, Bekanntgabe *f* eines Abkommens; ~ **letter** *n* GEN COMM Ankündigungsschreiben *nt*; ~ **of sale** *n* S&M Verkaufsangebot *nt*, Verkaufsankündigung *f*; ~ **of tax burden** *n* TAX Steuerlastankündigung *f*

annual 1. *adj* GEN COMM jährlich; **2.** *n* ECON, GEN COMM, S&M Jahrbuch *nt*

annual: ~ **abstract of statistics** *n* MATH statistischer Jahresbericht *m*; ~ **accounts** *n pl* ACC Bilanz *f*, Jahresabschluß *m*; ~ **amortization** *n* INS jährliche Tilgungsrate *f*; ~ **appropriation** *n* ACC jährliche Zuweisung *f*; ~ **audit plan** *n* ACC Jahresabschlußprüfungsplan *m*; ~ **automated controls survey** *n* TRANSP *of ship* jährliche Prüfung *f* der automatischen Steuerung; ~ **basis** *n* ECON, GEN COMM, MATH *statistics* Jahresbasis *f*; ~ **cash flow** *n* ACC, ADMIN jährlicher Cashflow *m*, jährlicher Einnahmeüberschuß *m*; ~ **certificate** *n* ACC *audit* jährliche Bestätigung *f*; ~ **debt service** *n* BANK jährlicher Schuldendienst *m*; ~ **depreciation** *n* ACC, GEN COMM jährliche Abschreibung *f*; ~ **depreciation charge** *n* ACC jährlicher Abschreibungsaufwand *m*; ~ **earnings** *n pl* ACC, ADMIN Jahresgewinn *m*; ~ **evaluation plan** *n* FIN jährlicher Bewertungsplan *m*; ~ **exemption** *n* TAX jährlicher Freibetrag *m*; ~ **fee** *n* ACC Jahresgebühr *f*, Jahreshonorar *nt*; ~ **general meeting** *n* (*AGM*) GEN COMM Hauptversammlung *f* (*HV*), Jahreshauptversammlung *f*, Jahresvollversammlung *f*; ~ **high** *n* STOCK Jahreshöchststand *m*; ~ **hours contract** *n* HRM Jahresstundenvertrag *m*; ~ **inert gas system survey** *n* (*AIGSS*) ENVIR jährliche Inertgassystemübersicht *f*; ~ **installment** *AmE*, ~ **instalment** *BrE n* ACC Jahresrate *f*, FIN Annuität *f*, Jahresrate *f*, GEN COMM jährliche Rate *f*, Jahresrate *f* annualize *vt* FIN, GEN COMM annualisieren, auf Jahresbasis umrechnen, TAX Jahresausgleich *m* durchfüren

annualized *adj* FIN, GEN COMM annualisiert, auf Jahresbasis umgerechnet; ~ **hours** *n pl* HRM Jahresstunden *f pl*; ~ **hours system** *n* HRM Arbeitsstundensystem *nt* auf Jahresbasis; ~ **interest rate** *n* MATH auf Jahresbasis umgerechneter Zinssatz *m*; ~ **percentage rate** *n* (*APR*) FIN *of interest* effektiver Jahreszins *m*, auf Jahresbasis umgerechneter Prozentsatz *m*

annual: ~ **leave** *n* HRM Jahresurlaub *m*; ~ **low** *n* STOCK Jahrestiefpunkt *m*

annually *adv* GEN COMM jährlich; ~ **renewable term insurance** *n* INS jährlich erneuerbare Risikoversicherung *f*

annual: ~ **machinery survey** *n* (*AMS*) TRANSP *shipping* jährliche Maschinenprüfung *f*; ~ **meeting** *n* GEN COMM, MGMNT Hauptversammlung *f* (*HV*); ~ **mortgage constant** *n* MATH Jahrestilgungsbetrag *m* einer Ratenhypothek, Jahrestilgungsrate *f* einer Abzahlungshypothek; ~ **net cash inflow** *n* ACC Netto-Cashflow *m*, jährlicher Umsatzüberschuß *m* ACC Jahresüberschuß *m*; ~ **order** *n* GEN COMM jährlicher Auftrag *m*, Jahresauftrag *m*; ~ **output** *n* IND Jahresleistung *f*, Jahresproduktion *f*; ~ **payment** *n* GEN COMM Jahreszahlung *f*, jährliche Zahlung *f*; ~ **percentage rate** *n* (*APR*) FIN *of interest* effektiver Jahreszins *m*, auf Jahresbasis umgerechneter Prozentsatz *m*; ~ **premium** *n* INS Jahresprämie *f*; ~ **proceeds** *n pl* ADMIN, GEN COMM Jahresertrag *m*; ~ **rate** *n* FIN, MATH Jahresrate *f*; ~ **rental charges** *n pl* TAX jährliche Mietkosten *pl*, jährliche Mietpreise *m pl*; ~ **repayment** *n* GEN COMM jährliche Rückzahlung *f*; ~ **report** *n* ACC Geschäftsbericht *m*, Jahresbericht *m*; ~ **return** *n* ACC Jahresrendite *f*, LAW *legal document* Jahresbericht *m*; ~ **salary review** *n* HRM jährliche Revision *f* der Gehälter, jährliche Gehaltsüberprüfung *f*; ~ **sales conference** *n* S&M Jahreskonferenz *f* Verkauf; ~ **sales report** *n* GEN COMM *showing turnover* jährlicher Verkaufsbericht *m*, Jahresumsatzbericht *m*; ~ **statement of bankable bills** *n* BANK Jahresaufstellung *f* diskontierbarer Wechsel; ~ **statement of condition** *n* ACC, FIN Jahresbilanz *f*; ~ **subscription** *n* GEN COMM Jahresabonnement *nt*, Jahresbeitrag *m*; ~ **tax return** *n* ACC, TAX Jahressteuererklärung *f*, jährliche Steuererklärung *f*; ~ **turnover** *n* ACC Jahresumsatz *m*; ~ **wage** *n* HRM Jahresverdienst *m*, Jahresarbeitslohn *m*, garantierter Jahreslohn *m*; ~ **yield** *n* ACC Jahresertrag *m*, Jahresrendite *f*

annuity *n* FIN Annuität *f*, GEN COMM, INS Rente *f*; ~ **assurance** *n* INS Leibrentenversicherung *f*, Rentenversicherung *f*; ~ **business** *n* INS Rentengeschäft *nt*; ~ **certain** *n* INS Rente *f* mit bestimmter Laufzeit, Zeitrente *f*; ~ **due** *n* INS vorschüssige Rente *f*; ~ **factor** *n* INS Rentenfaktor *m*; ~ **for life** *n* INS Leibrente *f*, Rente *f* auf Lebenszeit; ~ **fund** *n* GEN COMM Rentenfonds *m*; ~ **immediate** *n* INS nachschüssige Rente *f*; ~ **in reversion** *n* INS Rente *f* auf den Überlebensfall, Anwartschaftsrente *f*, Überlebensrente *f*; ~ **installment** *AmE*, ~ **instalment** *BrE* *n* INS Rententeilbetrag *m*, Rententeilzahlung *f*, Rentenzahlung *f*; ~ **insurance** *n* INS Leibrentenversicherung *f*, Rentenversicherung *f*; ~ **payable in advance** *n* INS vorschüssige Rente *f*; ~ **payable in arrears** *n* INS rückständige Rente *f*, Rentenrückstände *m pl*; ~ **plan** *n* INS Rentenversicherungssystem *nt*; ~ **policy** *n* INS Rentenversicherungspolice *f*, Rentenversicherungsschein *m*, Rentenpolice *f*

annul *vt* GEN COMM *contract* annullieren, kündigen, *decision* annullieren, aufheben, LAW annullieren, aufheben, für ungültig erklären, rückgängig machen

annulling *adj* BANK, GEN COMM annullierend, LAW *clause* aufhebend

annulment *n* GEN COMM *of contract* Annullierung *f*, Kündigung *f*, *of decision* Annullierung *f*, Aufhebung *f*, LAW Rückgängigmachung *f*, *invalidation* Annullierung *f*, Aufhebung *f*; ~ **of contract** *n* LAW Vertragsaufhebung *f*

anomaly *n* GEN COMM *in system* Abweichung *f*, Anomalie *f*, Unregelmäßigkeit *f*; ~ **switch** *n* STOCK Umschichtung des Portefeuilles bei starken Kursschwankungen

anomie *n* HRM Anomie *f*

anonymity *n* GEN COMM Anonymität *f*

anonymous *adj* GEN COMM anonym, namenlos, ungenannt

anonymously *adv* GEN COMM ohne Namensnennung, anonym, namenlos

anonymous: ~ **product testing** *n* S&M anonymer Produkttest *m*

ANOVA *abbr* (*analysis of variance*) MATH ANOVA (*Varianzanalyse*)

ANPA *abbr* (*American Newspaper Publishers' Association*) MEDIA amerikanischer Verband der Zeitungsverleger

ANSI *abbr* (*American National Standards Institute*) LAW amerikanischer staatlicher Normenverband, ≈ DIN (*Deutsches Institut für Normung*)

answer 1. *n* COMP, GEN COMM Antwort *f*, LAW Antwort *f*, Erwiderung *f*, Klageerwiderung *f*; ◆ **get an ~** GEN COMM Antwort erhalten; **in ~ to your letter** COMMS in Beantwortung Ihres Schreibens (*frml*); **there's no ~** COMMS *telephone* es meldet sich niemand; 2. *vt* GEN COMM *invitation, advertisement* antworten auf, erwidern auf, *letter, question* beantworten, antworten auf; ◆ **~ sb** GEN COMM jdm antworten; ~ **to sb** GEN COMM jdm antworten; 3. *vi* GEN COMM antworten, erwidern

answer for *vt* GEN COMM *individual* garantieren für, *safety of product* haften für

answerable *adj* GEN COMM haftbar, verantwortlich, LAW haftbar; ◆ ~ **for** GEN COMM verantwortlich für; ~ **to** GEN COMM verpflichtet gegenüber, verantwortlich gegenüber

answerback: ~ **code** *n* ADMIN, COMMS, COMP Kennung *f*, Antwortcode *m*

answering: ~ **machine** *n* COMMS, COMP, GEN COMM Anrufbeantworter *m*; ~ **service** *n* GEN COMM Fernsprechauftragsdienst *m*, telefonischer Auftragsdienst *m*

answer: ~ **mode** *n* COMP Antwortmodus *m*

answerphone *n* COMMS, COMP, GEN COMM Anrufbeantworter *m*

answer: ~ **print** *n* S&M Antwortvordruck *m*, Antwortkarte *f*

antagonistic: ~ **conditions of production** *n pl* POL antagonistische Produktionsbedingungen *f pl*; ~ **growth** *n* ECON antagonistisches Wachstum *nt*

ante *prep* GEN COMM vor

antedate *vt* GEN COMM *document, cheque* rückdatieren, zurückdatieren

antedating *n* GEN COMM Rückdatierung *f*

ante: ~ **meridiem** *phr* (*am*) GEN COMM vormittags

anthropometry *n* ADMIN Anthropometrie *f*

anti-avoidance: ~ **legislation** *n* TAX gegen Steuerumgehung gerichtete Vorschriften *f pl*, Steuervermeidungsvorschriften *f pl*

anticipate *vt* GEN COMM *problem, delay, development* erwarten, antizipieren, voraussehen, vorwegnehmen, STOCK eskomptieren

anticipated *adj* GEN COMM voraussichtlich, erwartet, *repayment* im voraus, vor Fälligkeit, vorzeitig; ~ **cost** *n* ACC Antizipationsaufwand *m*; ~ **demand** *n* ECON Bedarfsvorwegnahme *f*, vorweggenommener Bedarf *m*; ~ **holding period** *n* STOCK voraussichtlicher Verwahrzeitraum *m*, erwartete Besitzdauer *f*; ~ **profit** *n* ACC erwarteter Gewinn *m*; ~ **redemption** *n* BANK vorzeitiger Rückkauf *m*, FIN, STOCK *bond* Ablösung *f*, vorzeitige Tilgung *f*; ~ **repayment** *n* GEN COMM vorzeitige Rückzahlung *f*; ~ **sales** *n pl* S&M voraussichtliche Verkäufe *m pl*, geplante Umsätze *m pl*, Umsatzplanung *f*

anticipation *n* ECON *expectation* Erwartung *f*, GEN COMM *expectation* Erwartung *f*, *action in advance* Vorwegnahme *f*, IMP/EXP Antizipation *f*, LAW, MATH Erwartung *f*; ~ **equivalence** *n* IMP/EXP Antizipationsäquivalenz *f*

anticipatory: ~ **breach of contract** *n* LAW antizipierter Vertragsbruch *m*; ~ **contract** *n* LAW vorweggenommener Vertrag *m*; ~ **hedge** *n* STOCK antizipatives Sicherungsgeschäft *nt*; ~ **packing credit** *n* BANK Packing Kredit *m*, Akkreditivbevorschussung *f*; ~ **pricing** *n* ECON Preisstrategie *f* mit antizipierter Inflationskomponente; ~ **response** *n* ECON vorweggenommene Reaktion *f*, GEN COMM vorweggenommene Antwort *f*

anticompetitive *adj* ECON, FIN, S&M wettbewerbsbeschränkend, wettbewerbsschädlich; ~ **practices** *n pl* ECON, S&M wettbewerbsbeschränkende Praktiken, wettbewerbswidriges Verhalten *nt*

anticyclic: ~ **advertising** *n* S&M antizyklische Werbung *f*

anticyclical *adj* ECON antizyklisch; ~ **policy** *n* ECON antizyklische Fiskalpolitik *f*, antizyklische Politik *f*

antidumping *n* POL Antidumping *nt*; ~ **agreement** *n* POL Antidumpingabkommen *nt*, Antidumpingvereinbarung *f*; ~ **legislation** *n* POL Antidumpinggesetzgebung *f*

antifouling: ~ **system** *n* TRANSP *marine engineering* Antifouling-System *nt*

antiglare *adj* COMP blendfrei

anti-inflationary *adj* ECON anti-inflationär

anti-inflation: ~ **stance** *n* ECON anti-inflationäre Haltung *f*

antimonopoly: ~ **law** *n* LAW Kartellgesetz *nt*, Kartellrecht *nt*; ~ **laws** *n pl* LAW Kartellgesetzgebung *f*

antitheft: ~ **device** *n* GEN COMM, TRANSP Diebstahlsicherung *f*

antitrust: ~ **acts** *n pl* LAW Antitrustrecht *nt*, Kartellgesetze *nt pl*, Kartellgesetzgebung *f*, Kartellrecht *nt*; ~ **commission** *n* FIN, POL Kartellkommission *f*, Monopolkommission *f*; ~ **law** *n* LAW Antitrustrecht *nt*, Kartellgesetz *nt*, Kartellrecht *nt*; ~ **laws** *n pl* LAW Antitrustrecht *nt*, Kartellgesetzgebung *f*

anti-union: ~ **legislation** *n* HRM antigewerkschaftliche Gesetzgebung *f*

antivirus: ~ **software** *n* COMP Antiviren-Software *f*

ANZTAC *abbr* (*Australia and New Zealand Trade Advisory Committee*) ECON Beratender Ausschuß für den Handel mit Australien und Neuseeland

ANZUS *abbr* (*Australia, New Zealand and United States*) ECON ANZUS-Pakt *m*

a/o *abbr* (*account of*) BANK, GEN COMM à Konto, zu Lasten von, auf Konto von, per Konto (*jarg*), für Rechnung von, auf Rechnung von

AO *abbr* (*accounting officer*) ACC, ADMIN, HRM Buchhalter, in *m,f*

AOB *abbr* (*any other business*) GEN COMM Sonstiges *nt*

AOCB *abbr* (*any other competent business*) GEN COMM sonstige Angelegenheiten *f pl*, Sonstiges *nt*

AOLOC *abbr* (*any one location*) INS *marine* jeder Standort *m*

AON: ~ **clause** *n* (*all or nothing clause*) STOCK *tender* Alles-oder-Nichts-Klausel *f*

A1 *adj* GEN COMM, TRANSP erstklassig

AOS *abbr* (*any one steamer*) INS *marine* jeder Frachter *m*

AOV *abbr* (*any one vessel*) INS *marine* jedes Schiff *nt*

AP *abbr* INS (*additional premium*) Beitragszuschlag *m*, Prämienzuschlag *m*, Zuschlagsprämie *f*

APACS *abbr* BrE (*Association for Payment Clearing Services*) ECON Scheckverrechnungsstelle der größten britischen Banken

apart: ~ **from** *prep* GEN COMM abgesehen von, außer, ausgenommen

apartment *n* AmE (*cf flat BrE*) PROP Wohnung *f*; ~ **building** *n* AmE (*cf block of flats BrE*) PROP Appartementhaus *nt*, Wohnblock *m*

APB *abbr* AmE (*Accounting Principles Board*) ACC Ausschuß für Wirtschaftsprüferrichtlinien

APC *abbr* (*average propensity to consume*) ECON *accounting* durchschnittliche Konsumquote *f*

APEC *abbr* (*Asia Pacific Economic Cooperation*) ECON APEC-Staaten *m pl*

aphorism *n* GEN COMM Aphorismus *m*, Gedankensplitter *m*

apiece *adv* GEN COMM, S&M je Stück, pro Stück

apologize *vi* GEN COMM sich entschuldigen; ♦ ~ **for** GEN COMM sich entschuldigen für; ~ **to** GEN COMM sich entschuldigen bei; ~ **to sb for sth** GEN COMM sich gegenüber jdm für etw entschuldigen

apology *n* GEN COMM Entschuldigung *f*

apparatchik *n infrml* POL Apparatschik *m* (*infrml*)

apparatus *n* GEN COMM Instrument *nt*, IND Aggregat *nt*, Apparat *m*, Einrichtung *f*, Instrument *nt*, Vorrichtung *f*; ♦ ~ **for carrying out** PATENTS Apparat *m* zur Durchführung von, Einrichtung *f* zur Durchführung von, Mechanismus *m* zur Durchführung von

apparel *n* AmE (*cf clothing BrE*) GEN COMM Gewand *nt*, Kleidung *f*; ~ **industry** *n* AmE (*cf clothing industry BrE*) IND Bekleidungsindustrie *f*, Textilindustrie *f*; ~ **and wool industry** *n* AmE (*cf clothing trade BrE*) IND Kleidungs- und Strickwarenherstellung *f*, Textil- und Wollindustrie *f*, Bekleidungsbranche *f*

apparent: ~ **authority** *n* LAW Scheinvollmacht *f*, *contracts* Anscheinsvollmacht *f*; ~ **defect** *n* LAW *contracts* erkennbarer Mangel *m*; ~ **good order of the goods** *n* TRANSP augenscheinlich guter Zustand *m* der Waren, einwandfreier äußerer Zustand *m* der Waren

appeal 1. *n* GEN COMM *attraction* Anreiz *m*, Anklang *m*, *call* Appell *m*, Aufruf *m*, Ersuchen *nt*, LAW Rechtsbehelf *m*, Rechtsmittel *nt*, Beschwerde *f*, Revision *f*, Berufung *f,* Anfechtung *f,* PATENTS Berufung *f,* Beschwerde *f,* Einspruch *m,* S&M *of product* Anziehungskraft *f;* **2.** *vi* LAW Rechtsmittel einlegen

appeal against *vt* LAW *judgment, ruling* Berufung *f* einlegen, anfechten; ♦ **~ a decision** LAW Beschwerde führen, eine Entscheidung anfechten; **~ a judgment** LAW Rechtsmittel gegen ein Urteil einlegen, ein Urteil anfechten

appeal for *vt* GEN COMM ersuchen um; ♦ **~ funds** FIN, GEN COMM um Gelder ersuchen, um Geldmittel dringend ersuchen, um Mittel werben; **~ tenders** GEN COMM um Angebote ersuchen, um Kostenvoranschläge ersuchen

appeal to *vt* GEN COMM *attract* Anklang finden bei, gefallen [+dat], *ask for support* Aufruf richten an [+acc], sich wenden an [+acc]

appeal: **~ bond** *n* LAW Sicherheitsleistung *f* des Berufungsklägers; **~ court** *n* LAW Berufungsgericht *nt,* Rechtsmittelinstanz *f,* Revisionsgericht *nt;* **~ for funds** *n* FIN Spendenappell *m,* Spendenaufruf *m;* **~ for tenders** *n* FIN, STOCK Aufforderung *f* zur Angebotsabgabe, Tenderaufruf *m;* **~ proceedings** *n pl* LAW Berufungsverfahren *nt;* **~ product** *n* GEN COMM, S&M Anreizprodukt *nt*

appeals: **~ procedure** *n* LAW Rechtsmittelverfahren *nt*

appear *vi* GEN COMM, MEDIA erscheinen; ♦ **~ in court** LAW vor Gericht erscheinen; **~ on the scene** MEDIA, POL auf den Plan treten

appearance *n* COMP, GEN COMM Aussehen *nt,* Darstellungsart *f,* Erscheinungsbild *nt,* Schriftbild *nt*

appellate: **~ court** *n* LAW Berufungsgericht *nt,* Revisionsgericht *nt*

append *vt* COMMS beifügen, COMP *file, data* anhängen, GEN COMM beifügen, *signature* setzen, versehen mit

appendix *n* GEN COMM Anhang *m,* Anlage *f*

appliance *n* GEN COMM *action* Anwendung *f, device* Gerät *nt,* Vorrichtung *f*

applicable *adj* GEN COMM geeignet, verwendbar, zutreffend; **not ~** *adj* (*N/A*) GEN COMM nicht zutreffend; ♦ **~ to** GEN COMM anwendbar auf, passend für, verwendbar für

applicant *n* FIN Aktienzeichner, in *m,f,* GEN COMM *for licence* Anmelder, in *m,f, for grant* Antragsteller, in *m,f,* HRM *for job* Stellenbewerber, in *m,f,* Bewerber, in *m,f,* Kandidat, in *m,f,* LAW Antragsteller, in *m,f,* ersuchende Stelle *f,* PATENTS *for patents* Anmelder, in *m,f,* Antragsteller, in *m,f,* STOCK *for shares* Aktienzeichner, in *m,f;* **~ entrepreneur** *n* GEN COMM Antragsteller, in *m,f* für Unternehmensgründung; **~ for shares** *n* FIN Aktienzeichner, in *m,f,* Anteilszeichner, in *m,f,* STOCK Aktienzeichner, in *m,f;* **~ of interpleader** *n* LAW Streitverkünder, in *m,f*

application *n* COMP Anwendung *f,* GEN COMM *for job, licence* Bewerbung *f, of technique, law* Anwendung *f,* Verwendung *f, for grant* Ersuchen *nt,* Antrag *m, of idea* Konkretisierung *f,* HRM *for job* Stellengesuch *nt,* Bewerbung *f,* Bewerbungsschreiben *nt,* PATENTS *of idea, technique* Verwendung *f, for registration* Anmeldung *f,* STOCK *for shares* Zeichnung *f* von Wertpapieren; ♦ **~ turned down on the grounds of unsuitability** HRM Absage *f* mangels Eignung

application: **~ of accounting rules** *n* ACC Anwendung *f* der Buchhaltungsvorschriften; **~ control** *n* ACC *auditing* Anwendungskontrolle *f;* **~ design** *n* IND Anwendungs-

entwurf *m;* **~ fee** *n* BANK Zeichnungsgebühr *f;* **~ for admission** *n* GEN COMM, STOCK *to the stock exchange* Aufnahmeantrag *m;* **~ for amendment** *n* LAW, POL Änderungsantrag *m,* Antrag *m* auf Abänderung, Novellierungsantrag *m;* **~ for export licence** *BrE,* **~ for export license** *AmE n* IMP/EXP Antrag *m* auf Ausfuhrgenehmigung; **~ for listing** *n* STOCK Antrag *m* auf Börsenzulassung; **~ form** *n* ADMIN Bewerbungsformular *nt,* GEN COMM Anmeldeformular *nt,* IMP/EXP Antragsformular *nt;* **~ for quotation** *n* STOCK Antrag *m* auf Börsennotierung; **~ for shares** *n* STOCK Aktienzeichnung *f;* **~ for subsidies** *n* GEN COMM Subventionsantrag *m,* Antrag *m* auf Zuschüsse; **~ for the supply of funding** *n* POL Antrag *m* auf Bereitstellung von Mitteln; **~ of funds** *n* ACC Mittelverwendung *f;* **~ of funds statement** *n* ACC Ausweis *m* über die Verwendung des Kapitals, Kapitalflußrechnung *f;* **~ money** *n* STOCK Zeichnungsbetrag *m;* **~ procedure** *n* GEN COMM Anmeldeverfahren *nt;* **~ of the quota system** *n* GEN COMM Anwendung *f* der Quotenregelung; **~ right** *n* STOCK Zeichnungsrecht *nt*

applications: **~ engineering** *n* IND Anwendungstechnik *f;* **~ package** *n* COMP Anwendungspaket *nt;* **~ program** *n* COMP *software* Anwendungsprogramm *nt;* **~ programmer** *n* COMP *software* Anwendungsprogrammierer, in *m,f;* **~ software** *n* COMP Anwendungssoftware *f;* **~ terminal** *n* COMP Anwendungsterminal *nt*

applied *adj* GEN COMM *research* angewandt; **~ cost** *n* ACC verrechnete Kosten *pl;* **~ economic research** *n* ECON angewandte Wirtschaftsforschung *f;* **~ overheads** *n pl* ACC verrechnete Gemeinkosten *pl;* **~ research** *n* MGMNT angewandte Forschung *f,* anwendungsbezogene Forschung *f;* **~ research cost** *n* GEN COMM Kosten *pl* für angewandte Forschung

apply 1. *vt* GEN COMM anwenden, gebrauchen, verwenden, LAW *law* anwenden; **2.** *vi* GEN COMM *rule* anwendbar sein, Anwendung finden; ♦ **~ at the office** GEN COMM im Büro vorstellig werden; **~ in person** GEN COMM sich persönlich bemühen, sich persönlich bewerben

apply for *vt* GEN COMM nachsuchen um, *passport, licence* beantragen; HRM *job, employment* sich bewerben um, PATENTS anmelden; ♦ **~ a loan** BANK, FIN ein Darlehen beantragen, einen Kredit beantragen; **~ a post** HRM *employment* sich um eine Stelle bewerben; **~ shares** STOCK Aktien zeichnen

apply to *vt* ACC *a period* zuschreiben, *attribute* umlegen, verrechnen, zurechnen; ♦ **apply expenses to a period** ACC Ausgaben auf einen bestimmten Zeitraum abgrenzen, Aufwendungen einer Periode zuschreiben; **apply income to a period** ACC Erträge einer Periode abgrenzen

appoint *vt* GEN COMM *person* einstellen, ernennen, *date, place* festlegen, HRM *person* einstellen, *committee* berufen, bestimmen, LAW *annual auditor, liquidator* bestellen; ♦ **~ as attorney-in-fact** ACC, LAW bevollmächtigen

appointed *adj* GEN COMM *agent, chairman* ernannt, LAW *annual auditor, liquidator* bestellt; ♦ **at the ~ time** GEN COMM zum festgesetzten Zeitpunkt

appointed: **~ day** *n* GEN COMM festgesetzter Termin *m;* **~ representative** *n* LAW bestellter Vertreter *m,* bestellte Vertreterin *f;* **~ space** *n* S&M *advertising* Platzvorschrift *f*; ~ **stockist** *n* S&M bestellter Fachhändler *m*, bestellte Fachhändlerin *f*; ~ **time** *n* GEN COMM Termin *m*

appointee *n* GEN COMM *executive* Ernannte(r) *mf* [decl. as adj]

appointment *n* GEN COMM *of person* Ernennung *f*, Bestellung *f*, *with doctor, lawyer* Termin *m*, *to meet* Verabredung *f*, HRM *to a job* Berufung *f*, LAW Bestellung *f*; ♦ **by ~ only** GEN COMM nur nach Absprache, Termin nach Vereinbarung, nur nach Voranmeldung; ~ **vacant** HRM freie Stelle *f*

apportion *vt* ACC *costs* aufteilen, verteilen, zuteilen, FIN aufteilen, verteilen, GEN COMM aufschlüsseln, aufteilen, PATENTS aufteilen, verteilen, PROP *land, property* aufteilen, STOCK *shares* umlegen, verteilen, zuteilen; ♦ ~ **the average** INS *marine* Havarie aufteilen

apportioned: ~ **contract** *n* LAW Sukzessivlieferungsvertrag *m*; ~ **material** *n* GEN COMM auftragsgebundenes Material *nt*

apportionment *n* ACC Aufteilung *f*, Verteilung *f*, Zuteilung *f*, FIN *public finance* Aufteilung *f*, Verteilung *f*, GEN COMM Aufschlüsselung *f*, Aufteilung *f*, PATENTS Aufteilung *f*, Verteilung *f*, PROP Aufteilung *f*; ~ **of costs** *n* ACC Kostenumlage *f*, Verteilung *f* der Kosten; ~ **of funds** *n* ACC, FIN, MGMNT Mittelzuweisung *f*

appraisal *n* ADMIN *business* Unternehmensbewertung *f*, GEN COMM *evaluation* Schätzung *f*, Beurteilung *f*, Begutachtung *f*, Gutachten *nt*, Auswertung *f*, HRM Bewertung *f*, MGMNT *of project* Beurteilung *f*, Bewertung *f*, Einschätzung *f*, PROP Schätzung *f*, Wertschätzung *f*; ~ **of damage** *n* INS Schadensabschätzung *f*, Schadensschätzung *f*; ~ **increment** *n* ACC Bewertungszuschreibung *f*, GEN COMM Bewertungsverbesserung *f*; ~ **interview** *n* HRM Beurteilungsgespräch *nt*; ~ **report** *n* GEN COMM Gutachten *nt*; ~ **right** *n* AmE STOCK Recht auf Barabfindung der Aktionäre, die einer Fusion nicht zugestimmt haben; ~ **rights** *n pl* AmE STOCK Bewertungsrechte *nt pl*

appraise *vt* GEN COMM schätzen, beurteilen, begutachten, auswerten, taxieren, HRM bewerten, MGMNT *project* beurteilen, bewerten, einschätzen, PROP schätzen; ♦ ~ **damages** GEN COMM Schaden abschätzen, Schaden taxieren

appraised: ~ **value** *n* INS Schätzwert *m*, PROP geschätzter Wert *m*, STOCK Taxe *f*, Taxwert *m*

appraisement *n* PROP Schätzung *f*, Wertschätzung *f*

appraiser *n* PROP Schätzer *m*, amtlicher Schätzer *m*, Sachverständige(r) *mf* [decl. as adj]

appreciable *adj* GEN COMM *noticeable* deutlich, nennenswert, spürbar, *assessable* abschätzbar, schätzbar, *considerable* beträchtlich, *perceptible* bewertbar

appreciate 1. *vt* ECON *increase the value of* aufwerten, GEN COMM *understand the significance of* schätzen, zu würdigen verstehen; **2.** *vi* ACC, PROP im Wert steigen

appreciated: ~ **surplus** *n* ACC auf Neubewertung beruhender Gewinn *m*, höher bewerteter Überschuß *m*

appreciation *n* ACC *of property*, PROP Wertsteigerung *f*, Wertzuwachs *m*, STOCK *of share* Kursgewinn *m*, Kurssteigerung *f*, TAX Wertsteigerung *f*, Wertzuwachs *m*, ECON *of currency* Aufwertung *f*; ~ **in value** *n* ACC Wertzuschreibung *f*, Zuschreibung *f*

apprentice 1. *n* ECON Auszubildende(r) *mf* [decl. as adj] (*Azubi*), Lehrling *m*, HRM Lehrling *m*, Auszubildende(r) *mf* [decl. as adj] (*Azubi*), Eleve *m*, Elevin *f* (*obs*); **2.** *vt* HRM *person* in die Lehre geben

apprenticed: **be ~ to sb** *phr* HRM bei jdm in die Lehre gehen

apprenticeship *n* HRM Berufsausbildung *f*, Lehre *f*, Lehrverhältnis *nt*, Lehrzeit *f*, *place* Lehrstelle *f*, Berufsausbildungsplatz *m*

appro *n* (*approval*) GEN COMM Billigung *f*, Zustimmung *f*; ♦ **on ~** (*on approval*) GEN COMM *goods* auf Probe, zur Ansicht *f*

approach 1. *n* ADMIN, ECON, GEN COMM, MGMNT Ansatz *m*, Forschungsansatz *m*, Lösungsansatz *m*, Konzept *nt*, Denkansatz *m*, Betrachtungsweise *f*, Methode *f*, Vorgehen *nt*, Vorgehensweise *f*; **2.** *vt* GEN COMM *deal with* behandeln

appropriate *vt* ACC bereitstellen, ECON *allocate* bewilligen, zuweisen, *take possession of* beschlagnahmen, Besitz ergreifen von, FIN *make available* bereitstellen, LAW *property* sich aneignen, Besitz ergreifen von; ♦ ~ **funds** ACC, FIN, MGMNT Mittel bereitstellen, Mittel bewilligen, Mittel zuweisen; ~ **for** ACC genehmigen, zuweisen

appropriated *adj* ECON bewilligt, genehmigt, *for a purpose* zweckgebunden

appropriate: ~ **nature of prices** *n* GEN COMM Angemessenheit *f* von Preisen

appropriateness *n* GEN COMM Verwendbarkeit *f*, Zumutbarkeit *f*

appropriate: ~ **technology** *n* ENVIR geeignete Technologie *f*, einschlägige Technologie *f*

appropriation *n* ACC *of funds* Bestimmung *f*, *of funds to reserve* Zweckbindung *f*, Bereitstellung *f*, Ausgabenbewilligung *f*, *for commitment* Verpflichtungsermächtigung *f*, *for payment* Zahlungsermächtigung *f*, ECON *of funds* Mittelzuweisung *f*, Zuweisung *f*, Bestimmung *f*, Geldzuweisung *f*, FIN *of funds* Bereitstellung *f*; ~ **account** *n* ACC Bereitstellungskonto *nt*, Durchgangskonto *nt* zur Aufnahme des Gewinnvortrags, Gewinnverteilungskonto *nt*, Rückstellungskonto *nt*; ~ **act** *n* FIN Ausgabebudget *nt*, Haushaltsgesetz *nt*; ~ **of advertising** *n* S&M genehmigter Werbeetat *m*; ~ **bill** *n* ACC Bewilligung *f* von Geldern, ECON Ausgabebudget *nt*, FIN Ausgabebudget *nt*, Haushaltsgesetz *nt*, POL Bewilligungsgesetz *nt*, Gesetz *nt* zur Bewilligung von Geldern; ~ **of earnings** *n* ACC, ADMIN Gewinnverwendung *f*, buchmäßige Gewinnverteilung *f*; ~ **of funds** *n* ACC, ECON, FIN, MGMNT Mittelbindung *f*, Mittelverteilung *f*, Mittelzuteilung *f*, Mittelzuweisung *f*; ~ **of income** *n* ACC, ADMIN Gewinnverwendung *f*, Verwendung *f* des Reingewinns

appropriations: ~ **bill** *n* AmE ACC Bewilligungsvorlage *f*; ~ **committee** *n* FIN Bewilligungsausschuß *m*

appropriation: ~ **to a reserve** *n* ACC Bedienung *f* der Rücklage, Einstellung *f* in die Rücklage, Zuführung *f* an die Rücklage, Zuweisung *f* an die Rücklage

approval *n* (*appro*) BANK *of loan* Genehmigung *f*, FIN Akzeptanz *f*, Annahme *f*, Gutbefund *m*, GEN COMM *of contract, request* Ratifizierung *f*, *of decision, document, plan* Bestätigung *f*, Zustimmung *f*, Billigung *f*, Genehmigung *f*, *machine, process* Zulassung *f*, Genehmigung *f*, Zustimmung *f*, *acceptance* Akzeptanz *f*, Billigung *f*, LAW Billigung *f*; ♦ **for ~** GEN COMM zur Genehmigung; **have the ~** GEN COMM die Genehmigung haben von; **on ~** (*on appro*) GEN COMM *goods* auf Probe, zur Ansicht

approval: ~ **of the accounts** *n* ACC Verabschiedung *f* des Jahresabschlusses; ~ **mark** *n* TRANSP *road vehicles*

Genehmigungszeichen *nt*, Prüfzeichen *nt*; ~ **process** *n* BANK Genehmigungsprozess *m*

approve *vt* BANK *loan* genehmigen, GEN COMM *accounts* prüfen und für richtig befinden, *contract, request* ratifizieren, *decision, document, plan* bestätigen, zustimmen, billigen, genehmigen, *dealer* zulassen

approved *adj* COMP *device, software* genehmigt, zugelassen, GEN COMM *decision, document, plan* bestätigt, zugestimmt, gebilligt, genehmigt, INS *marine* genehmigt, zugesagt; ♦ ~ **of** GEN COMM akzeptiert

approved: ~ **bill of exchange** *n* STOCK erstklassiger Wechsel *m*; ~ **code of practice** *n* (*ACOP*) GEN COMM anerkannter Praxiscode *m*, anerkannter Verhaltenskodex *m*; ~ **delivery facility** *n* STOCK anerkannte Lieferstelle *f*; ~ **list of investments** *n* STOCK Verzeichnis *nt* mündelsicherer Wertpapieranlagen; ~ **place** *n* ADMIN genehmigter Ort *m*; ~ **premises** *n pl* IMP/EXP zugelassene Räumlichkeiten *f pl*; ~ **price** *n* GEN COMM, POL *by agency* genehmigter Preis *m*; ~ **profit-sharing scheme** *n BrE* HRM genehmigter Gewinnbeteiligungsplan *m*; ~ **status** *n BrE* TAX *by the Inland Revenue* anerkannte Finanzlage *f*; ~ **voucher** *n* ACC anerkannter Beleg *m*

approving *adj* GEN COMM bejahend, genehmigend, Genehmigungs-

approx. *abbr* (*approximately*) GEN COMM annähernd, ca. (*zirka*), etwa, rd. (*rund*), ung. (*ungefähr*)

approximate *vt* GEN COMM, MATH annähern

approximately *adv* (*approx.*) GEN COMM, MATH annähernd, etwa, ungefähr (*ung.*), rund (*rd.*), zirka (*ca.*)

approximate: ~ **price** *n* STOCK Annäherungskurs *m*, Taxkurs *m*, Zirkakurs *m*; ~ **rate of return** *n* ACC rechnerische Rendite *f*

approximation *n* GEN COMM, MATH annähernd richtiges Ergebnis *nt*, annähernde Gleichheit *f*, Annäherung *f*, grober Ansatz *m*, *procedure* Annäherungsverfahren *nt*, LAW *of laws within the EU* Angleichung *f*, POL *of policies within the EU* Annäherung *f*, Harmonisierung *f*, *procedure* Annäherungsverfahren *nt*, grober Ansatz *m*

appurtenant *adj* LAW zugehörig; ~ **structures** *n pl* INS *insurance coverage for* dazugehörige Gebäudeteile *m pl*

APR *abbr* (*annualized percentage rate*) FIN effektiver Jahreszins *m*, auf Jahresbasis umgerechneter Prozentsatz *m*

a priori *adj* GEN COMM a priori (*frml*), grundsätzlich, von vornherein; ~ **statement** *n* GEN COMM Apriori-Erklärung *f*

apron *n* STOCK Talon *m*, Abschnitt *m*, Allonge *f*, TRANSP *at airport* Vorfeld *nt*

APS *abbr* (*average propensity to save*) ECON *accounting* durchschnittliche Sparneigung *f*

APT *abbr* (*arbitrage pricing theory*) STOCK Arbitragepreis-Theorie *f*

aptitude *n* HRM *of individual* Befähigung *f*, Eignung *f*; ~ **test** *n* HRM, S&M Eignungsprüfung *f*, Eignungstest *m*

APV *abbr* (*administrative point of view*) MGMNT Ansicht *f* der Geschäftsführung, Meinung *f* der Geschäftsführung, Standpunkt *m* der Unternehmensleitung

AQL system *abbr* (*acceptable quality level system*) IND *DIN 40080* AQL-System *nt*

AR *abbr* (*average revenue*) ACC, FIN Durchschnittserlös *m*, Durchschnittsertrag *m*

A/R *abbr* ACC (*accounts receivable*) Debitoren *m pl*,

Forderungen *f pl*, INS (*all risks*) alle Gefahren *f pl*, jedes Risiko *nt*

Arab: ~ **Common Market** *n* ECON gemeinsamer Arabischer Markt *m*

Arabic: ~ **numerals** *n pl* MATH arabische Zahlen *f pl*

arbiter *n* LAW *arbitration* Schiedsrichter, in *m,f*, Schlichter, in *m,f*

arbitrage *n* BANK Arbitrage *f* HRM Schlichtung *f*; ~ **bonds** *n pl AmE* STOCK Arbitrageschuldverschreibungen *f pl*; ~ **calculation** *n* FIN Arbitragerechnung *f*; ~ **clause** *n* IMP/EXP Arbitrageklausel *f*; ~ **dealer** *n* STOCK Arbitragehändler, in *m,f*; ~ **dealing** *n* STOCK Arbitragegeschäft *n*, Arbitragehandel *m*, Arbitrage-Transaktion *f*; ~ **house** *n* STOCK Arbitragefirma *f*; ~ **in securities** *n BrE* STOCK Effektenarbitrage *f*; ~ **margin** *n BrE* STOCK Arbitragespanne *f*, internationales Zinsgefälle *nt*; ~ **operation** *n* STOCK Arbitragegeschäft *nt*, Arbitrage-Transaktion *f*; ~ **pricing theory** *n* (*APT*) STOCK Arbitragepreis-Theorie *f*

arbitrager *n* FIN, HRM Arbitrageur *m*, STOCK Arbitragehändler, in *m,f*, Arbitrageur *m*

arbitrage: ~ **stocks** *n pl* STOCK Arbitragewerte *m pl*; ~ **support points** *n pl* FIN Arbitrage-Interventionspunkte *m pl*; ~ **trader** *n* STOCK Arbitragehändler, in *m,f*; ~ **trading** *n* STOCK Arbitragegeschäft *nt*, Arbitragehandel *m*; ~ **transaction** *n* STOCK Arbitragegeschäft *nt*, Arbitrage-Transaktion *f*

arbitrageur *n* FIN, HRM Arbitrageur *m*, STOCK Arbitragehändler, in *m,f*, Arbitrageur *m*

arbitraging *n* GEN COMM Arbitragegeschäft *nt*, Arbitragehandel *m*

arbitral: ~ **award** *n* HRM Schiedsspruch *m*

arbitrary *adj* GEN COMM *decision* eigenmächtig, willkürlich

arbitrate 1. *vt* FIN *using fluctuations in market rates* arbitrieren, Kursschwankungen *f pl* nutzen, GEN COMM, HRM, LAW *dispute* schiedsgerichtlich entscheiden, schlichten, STOCK *using fluctuations in market rates* arbitrieren, Kursschwankungen *f pl* nutzen; **2.** *vi* FIN Arbitragegeschäfte machen, GEN COMM, LAW *in dispute* schlichten, STOCK Arbitragegeschäfte machen

arbitration *n* HRM, IND Schiedsverfahren *nt*, Schiedsgerichtsverfahren *nt*, Schlichtung *f*, Arbitration *f*, LAW Arbitrage *f*, Schlichtung *f*; ~ **agreement** *n* GEN COMM, LAW Schiedsabkommen *nt*, Schiedsabrede *f*, Schiedsvereinbarung *f*, Schiedsvertrag *m*; ~ **board** *n* GEN COMM Einigungsamt *nt*, Schiedsstelle *f*, Schlichtungsamt *nt*, Schlichtungsausschuß *m*, Schlichtungsstelle *f*, HRM, IND Schlichtungsausschuß *m*, Schlichtungsstelle *f*, STOCK Schlichtungsausschuß *m*, Schlichtungsstelle *f*, Schiedsstelle *f*; ~ **clause** *n* GEN COMM Arbitrageklausel *f*, Schiedsgerichtklausel *f*, Schiedsklausel *f*; ~ **committee** *n* GEN COMM Schiedsausschuß *m*; ~ **of exchange** *n* FIN Arbitragerechnung *f*, Devisenarbitrage *f*; ~ **proceedings** *n pl* HRM Schiedsverfahren *nt*, IND Schiedsverfahren *nt*, Schiedsgerichtsverfahren *nt*; ~ **tribunal** *n* GEN COMM Schiedsgericht *nt*, Schiedsgerichtshof *m*

arbitrator *n* LAW Schiedsrichter, in *m,f*

arc *n* MATH Bogen *m*; ~ **elasticity** *n* MATH Bogenelastizität *f*

architect *n* PROP Architekt, in *m,f*; ~**'s liability** *n* INS Architektenhaftung *f*

architecture *n* COMP, PROP Architektur *f*

archival: ~ **storage** n COMP Archivierung f

archive 1. n ADMIN Archivbestände m pl, COMP Archiv nt; **2.** vt ADMIN, COMP archivieren

archive: ~ **copy** n COMP Archivkopie f; ~ **file** n COMP Archivdatei f; ~ **storage** n ADMIN Archiv nt

archivist n ADMIN Archivar, in m,f

area n COMP Speicherbereich m, Bereich m, ECON surface size Fläche f, region Region f, Raum m, Gebiet nt, GEN COMM in town Gebiet nt, of knowledge Bereich m, Gebiet nt, scope, extent Spielraum m, space Raum m, region Region f

area: ~ **of application** n GEN COMM Anwendungsbereich m; ~ **code** n COMMS telephone Vorwahl f, Vorwahlnummer f; ~ **of expertise** n GEN COMM, HRM of professional Fachgebiet nt, Sachgebiet nt; ~ **of industrial concentration** n ECON industrielles Ballungsgebiet nt; ~ **manager** n MGMNT Bereichsleiter, in m,f, Gebietsleiter, in m,f; ~ **office** n ADMIN Bezirksbüro nt, BANK Filiale f; ~ **of operations** n HRM Arbeitsbereich m; ~ **rehabilitation** n GEN COMM Altbausanierung f; ~ **of responsibility** n GEN COMM Aufgabenbereich m, Geschäftsbereich m, Verantwortungsbereich m; ~ **salesman** n GEN COMM, HRM Gebietsverkäufer m; ~ **saleswoman** n GEN COMM, HRM Gebietsverkäuferin f; ~ **sample** n S&M Flächenstichprobe f, regionale Marktuntersuchung f

argue: ~ **one's case** phr LAW seinen Standpunkt vertreten

arise vi GEN COMM auftauchen; ◆ **should the occasion ~** GEN COMM gegebenenfalls

arithmetic: ~ **mean** n MATH arithmetisches Mittel nt; ~ **progression sequence** n MATH arithmetische Folge f

ARM abbr (adjustable rate mortgage) ECON, PROP variabel verzinsliche Hypothek f

armchair: ~ **critic** n infrml GEN COMM Kritiker, in m,f aus der Distanz, Kritikus m (infrml, obs)

arm: ~**'s-length** adj GEN COMM, S&M, TAX wettbewerblich, auf Basis von Marktpreis, auf rein geschäftlicher Basis, unabhängig; ~**'s-length bargaining** n GEN COMM Verhandlung f zwischen unabhängigen Partnern; ~**'s-length competition** n GEN COMM, S&M, TAX freier Wettbewerb m; ~**'s-length price** n ACC, S&M Wettbewerbspreis m, Marktpreis m; ~**'s-length principle** n GEN COMM, S&M, TAX Prinzip nt der rechtlichen Selbständigkeit, Grundsatz m der Unabhängigkeit, LAW Drittvergleichsgrundsatz m, S&M, TAX Prinzip nt der rechtlichen Selbständigkeit, Grundsatz m der Unabhängigkeit; ~**'s-length transaction** n GEN COMM, S&M, TAX Abschluß m auf Basis von Marktpreisen, Transaktion f zwischen unabhängigen Partnern

arrange vt BANK loan aushandeln, vereinbaren, GEN COMM anordnen, einrichten, festsetzen, date ausmachen, details regeln, vereinbaren, meeting ansetzen, LAW Vergleich m schließen, sich vergleichen; ◆ **~ a loan** BANK, FIN ein Darlehen aushandeln, Kreditfazilität zusammenstellen, Bankkredit m aufnehmen; ~ **for sth to be done** GEN COMM etw erledigen

arranged: **be ~ for** phr GEN COMM anberaumt sein für; ~ **total loss** n INS marine Vergleich m über Totalschaden

arrangement n GEN COMM organization Gliederung f, agreement Übereinkommen nt, Übereinkunft f, Vereinbarung f, in dispute gütliche Einigung f, Vergleich m, ordering Anordnung f, Ordnung f; ◆ **by ~** GEN COMM nach Vereinbarung; **come to an ~** GEN COMM with one's creditors einen Vergleich schließen, zu einer Übereinkunft kommen, zu einer Einigung gelangen mit; **come to an ~ with sb** GEN COMM sich mit jdm arrangieren, mit jdm übereinkommen

arrangement: ~ **fee** n BANK Koordinierungsprovision f, Provision f der Führungsbank; ~ **proceedings** n pl LAW Vergleichsverfahren nt

arrangements: **make ~** phr GEN COMM Vereinbarungen treffen, abmachen

arranger n FIN Arrangeur m

array n COMP of figures, data Bereich m, GEN COMM Datenreihe f, MATH Anordnung f, Reihe f; ~ **processor** n COMP computer capable of performing an array function in one step Feldrechner m; ~ **of products** n S&M Produktpalette f, Warensortiment nt

arrearages n pl FIN Rückstände m pl, rückständige Zahlungen f pl, STOCK Rückstände m pl

arrears n pl FIN, GEN COMM, STOCK Rückstände m pl; ◆ **be in ~** ADMIN, FIN, GEN COMM im Rückstand sein, rückständig sein; **in ~** ADMIN, FIN, GEN COMM im Rückstand, rückständig

arrears: ~ **of interest** n BANK Zinsrückstände m pl; ~ **of work** n pl GEN COMM unerledigte Arbeit f

arrest 1. n INS marine Aufbringen nt, LAW cargo Beschlagnahme f, Verhaftung f; **2.** vt LAW verhaften

arrival n GEN COMM, TRANSP action Ankunft f, person Ankommende(r) mf [decl. as adj], letter Eingang m; ~ **date** n TRANSP of consignment Ankunftsdatum nt, Ankunftstag m; ~ **notification form** n (ANF) TRANSP shipping Ankunftsanzeige f

arrive vi COMMS, GEN COMM letter eingehen, person ankommen

arrived: ~ **notification form** n TRANSP Eingangsbenachrichtigung f

arrow n COMP, GEN COMM Pfeil m; ~ **key** n COMP for moving the cursor Pfeiltaste f

arson n INS, LAW Brandlegung f, Brandstiftung f

art n GEN COMM, MEDIA Kunst f; ~ **buyer** n MEDIA Käufer, in m,f von Kunst; ~ **department** n S&M advertising Werbeabteilung f; ~ **designer** n S&M advertising Werbedesigner, in m,f

article n ECON Ware f, GEN COMM Ware f, small object Ware f, Gegenstand m, Artikel m, LAW part of law Artikel m; ~ **of consumption** n GEN COMM Gebrauchsgegenstand m, Verbrauchsgegenstand m, S&M Verbrauchsartikel m; ~ **for personal use** n GEN COMM customs Artikel m des persönlichen Bedarfs, Gegenstand m des persönlichen Bedarfs

articled: ~ **clerk** n BrE LAW Anwaltsreferendar, in m,f

articles: ~ **of agreement** n pl GEN COMM, LAW Vertragsbestimmungen f pl, Vertragspunkte m pl, TRANSP of shipping, crew Heuerbedingungen f pl, Heuervertrag m; ~ **of association** BrE, ~ **of incorporation** AmE n pl LAW corporation Gründungsurkunde f, Gesellschaftsvertrag m, Satzung f, Statuten nt pl

artificial adj GEN COMM künstlich, falsch, unwirklich, vorgetäuscht; ~ **barrier to entry** n ECON market künstliche Schranke f; ~ **currency** n ECON künstliche Währung f, Kunstwährung f; ~ **exchange rate** n ECON künstlicher Wechselkurs m; ~ **intelligence** n (AI) COMP künstliche Intelligenz f (KI); ~ **obsolescence** n S&M künstliches Veralten nt

artisan: ~ **fair** n MEDIA, S&M Kunsthandwerkermesse f

art: ~ **manager** n S&M *advertising* Atelierleiter, in *m,f*; ~ **matt** *AmE*, ~ **matt paper** *BrE* n S&M *advertising* Kunstdruckpapier *nt*; **the ~ of the possible** n POL die Kunst *f* des Möglichen; ~ **print** n S&M *advertising* Kunstdruck *m*; ~ **school** n WEL Kunstakademie *f*, Kunsthochschule *f*

Arts: ~ **Council** n *BrE* LEIS, MEDIA britischer Kulturausschuß

arts: ~ **sponsorship** n LEIS, MEDIA, S&M Förderung *f* der Kunst

artwork n MEDIA, S&M *production of works of art* Künstlerarbeit *f*, künstlerische Arbeit *f*, *object* Kunstgegenstand *m*, *illustrations* Bildmaterial *nt*

a/s *abbr* (*at sight*) FIN bei Sicht, bei Vorlage, gegen Vorlage, bei Vorlegung

A/S *abbr* FIN (*after sight*) nach Sicht, TRANSP (*alongside ship*) längsseits Schiff

ASA *abbr* MATH (*American Statistical Association*) amerikanische statistische Vereinigung, ≈ DStG (*Deutsche Statistische Gesellschaft*), S&M (*Advertising Standards Authority*) Behörde für Werbeethik, ≈ DWA (*Deutscher Werbeausschuß*)

as: ~ **above** *phr* COMMS wie oben; ~ **advertised on TV** *phr* S&M wie in der TV-Werbung gezeigt; ~ **agreed** *phr* GEN COMM wie vereinbart

ASAL *abbr* (*agricultural sector adjustment loan*) FIN Anpassungsdarlehen *nt* für den Agrarsektor

a.s.a.p. *abbr* (*as soon as possible*) COMMS, GEN COMM baldmöglichst, so bald wie möglich, umgehend

ASC *abbr* (*Australian Securities Commission*) STOCK australische Börsenaufsichtsbehörde

ascendancy n HRM *advancement* Aufstieg *m*

ascending: **in ~ order** *phr* GEN COMM in steigender Reihenfolge

ascertain *vt* ADMIN *final statements* feststellen, ECON erheben, ermitteln, GEN COMM *price* ermitteln, feststellen, sich vergewissern über [+acc], MATH erheben, ermitteln

ascertained: ~ **fact** n GEN COMM festgestellte Tatsache *f*; ~ **goods** n pl GEN COMM konkrete Sachen *f pl*, Speziessachen *f pl*

ascertainment n GEN COMM Ermittlung *f*, Feststellung *f*

ASCII *abbr* (*American Standard Code for Information Interchange*) COMP ASCII (*ASCII-Code*); ◆ **in ~** COMP im ASCII-Code, in ASCII

ASCII: ~ **file** n COMP ASCII-Datei *f*

as: ~ **a consequence of** *phr* GEN COMM infolge

ascribe *vt* GEN COMM beimessen, zuschreiben; ◆ ~ **sth to sb** GEN COMM jdm etw beimessen

ASE *abbr* (*American Stock Exchange*) FIN, STOCK zweitgrößte amerikanische Wertpapierbörse mit Sitz in New York (AMEX)

ASEAN *abbr* (*Association of South-East Asian Nations*) ECON Verband *m* Südostasiatischer Nationen

as: ~ **amended** LAW in der Fassung von; ~ **an economy measure** *phr* GEN COMM als Sparmaßnahme; ~ **follows** *phr* GEN COMM wie folgt; ~ **a function of** *phr* GEN COMM als Funktion von

A-share n *BrE* STOCK Aktie *f* drittbester Klassifizierung, stimmrechtslose Aktie *f*

Asian: ~ **Free Trade Area** n (*AFTA*) ECON, POL Asiatische Freihandelszone *f*, Malaysia, Singapur, Indonesien, Philippinen, Thailand und Burma

Asia: ~ **Pacific Economic Cooperation** n (*APEC*) ECON APEC-Staaten *m pl*

Asiatic: ~ **mode of production** n ECON asiatische Produktionsweise *f*

a similibus ad similia *phr* GEN COMM a similibus ad similia

as: ~ **is** *phr* GEN COMM, LAW wie die Ware liegt und steht, ohne Mängelgewähr, wie besichtigt

ask *vt* GEN COMM *person* fragen, *question* Frage *f* stellen; ◆ ~ **for an expert opinion** GEN COMM ein Gutachten einholen; ~ **for sth** COMMS, COMP etw anfordern, GEN COMM um etw bitten, etw anfordern; ~ **sb for sth** GEN COMM jdn um etw angehen, jdn um etw bitten

asked n PROP Angebotspreis *m*, STOCK Brief *m*; ~ **price** n ACC Ausgabepreis *m*, STOCK Angebotskurs *m*, Briefkurs *m*; ~ **and bid** n STOCK *selling and buying price* Brief *m* und Geld *nt*

ASL *abbr* *BrE* (*aggregate sales listings*) TAX *VAT* Zusammenfassende Meldungen *f pl* (*MwSt.*)

as: ~ **a last resort** *phr* GEN COMM in letzter Instanz, wenn alle Stricke reißen (*infrml*); ~ **the law stands at present** *phr* LAW beim gegenwärtigen Rechtsstand; ~ **mentioned above** *phr* COMMS wie bereits erwähnt, wie oben erwähnt; ~ **part payment** *phr* GEN COMM als Teilzahlung

aspect n GEN COMM *of question, topic* Aspekt *m*, Gesichtspunkt *m*, *appearance* Aussehen *nt*, Erscheinung *f*; ~ **ratio** n COMP Bildkantenverhältnis *nt*, Bildschirmformat *nt*

aspiration: ~ **level** n ECON, S&M Anspruchsniveau *nt*

aspire: ~ **to** *vt* S&M anstreben

as: ~ **a precautionary measure** *phr* GEN COMM als Vorsichtsmaßnahme; ~ **reported** *phr* COMMS, MEDIA *in document, media* Berichten zufolge, wie berichtet

ass. *abbr* *BrE* (*assurance*) INS Lebensversicherung *f*, Versicherung *f*

assay: ~ **sth** *phr* GEN COMM *purity of metals* den Feingehalt von etw feststellen, den Feingehalt von etw prüfen, den Gehalt von etw bestimmen

as: ~ **scheduled** *phr* GEN COMM nach Plan, plangemäß

assembler n COMP Assembler *m*, Assemblierprogramm *nt*, HRM Monteur *m*, IND Montagefirma *f*

assembling n GEN COMM Montage *f*, *of firms* Vereinigung *f*, Zusammenschluß *m*

assembly n GEN COMM Montage *f*, *of people* Zusammenkunft *f*, IND Baugruppe *f*, Bausatz *m*, Montage *f*, POL Versammlung *f*; ~ **cargo** n TRANSP Zusammenstellungsfracht *f*; ~ **line** n HRM, IND *production* Band *nt*, Fließband *nt*, Montageband *nt*; ~ **line work** n HRM, IND Fließbandarbeit *f*; ~ **line worker** n HRM, IND Fließbandarbeiter, in *m,f*; ~ **plant** n HRM, IND Montagewerk *nt*; ~ **program** n COMP Assembler *m*, Assemblierprogramm *nt*, GEN COMM *AmE see assembly programme BrE*; ~ **programme** n *BrE* GEN COMM Montageplan *m*, Montageprogramm *nt*

assent n GEN COMM *acquiescence* Beipflichten *nt*, Einwilligung *f*, Hinnehmen *nt*, Zustimmung *f*, *to proposal* Billigung *f*, POL *of parliament* Zustimmung *f*, *signature* Einverstandensein *nt*, *to motion* Billigung *f*

assert *vt* GEN COMM behaupten, versichern; ◆ ~ **a claim** LAW *contract law* einen Anspruch geltend machen

assertion n GEN COMM Behauptung *f*, Versicherung *f*

assertiveness n HRM Durchsetzungsvermögen *nt*, Selbstbehauptung *f*; **~ training** *n* HRM Selbstbehauptungstraining *nt*

assertory: **~ oath** *n* LAW assertorischer Eid *m*, eidliche Versicherung *f*

assess *vt* GEN COMM begutachten, einschätzen, taxieren, *proposal, offer* bewerten, *fine, tax* bemessen, beurteilen, *for tax* veranlagen, *income, price, value* festsetzen, umlegen, *value, capacity* beurteilen, TAX schätzen, veranlagen

assessable *adj* GEN COMM schätzbar, TAX steuerpflichtig; **~ income** *n* TAX steuerpflichtige Einkünfte *pl*, steuerpflichtiges Einkommen *nt*

assessed *adj* TAX veranlagt; **~ valuation** *n* AmE TAX *property* steuerliche Vermögensbewertung *f*, Vermögensbesteuerung *f*

assessment *n* GEN COMM Begutachtung *f*, Bemessung *f*, Beurteilung *f*, Einschätzung *f*, *of proposal, offer* Bewertung *f*, TAX Schätzung *f*, Veranlagung *f*, Vermögensbewertung *f*; **~ of compensation** LAW Feststellung *f* der Höhe des Schadensersatzes; **~ center** *AmE*, **~ centre** *BrE n* HRM Assessment Center *nt*, Personalauswahlverfahren *nt*; **~ of deficiency** *n* TAX Festsetzung *f* eines Fehlbetrages, Veranlagung *f* eines Fehlbetrages; **~ ratio** *n* PROP Bemessungsverhältnis *nt*; **~ roll** *n* TAX *property* Steuerliste *f*, Steuerrolle *f*, Veranlagungsliste *f*; **~ year** *n* ACC, FIN, TAX Steuerjahr *nt*, Veranlagungszeitraum *m* (*Vz*)

assessor *n* GEN COMM, INS Schätzer *m*, Schadenregulierer *m*, Schadensgutachter, in *m,f*

asset *n* ACC Aktivposten *m*, Aktivum *nt*; **~ account** *n* ACC Aktivkonto *nt*, Bestandskonto *nt*; **~ addition** *n pl* ACC Vermögenszugang *m*; **~ allocation** *n* STOCK Portefeuille-Strukturierung *f*; **~-backed investment** *n* FIN durch Vermögenswerte gesicherte Anlage *f*; **~-based investment** *n* BANK, FIN vermögensgesicherte Anlage *f*; **~ coverage** *n* ACC, FIN akzessorische Besicherung *f*; **~ depreciation range** *n* (*ADR*) ACC, LAW *property* betriebsgewöhnliche Nutzungsdauer *f*; **~ diversification** *n* FIN Anlagenstreuung *f*; **~ exposure** *n* BANK Ausleihungen *f pl*; **~ item** *n* ACC Aktivposten *m*; **~ and liability management** *n* BANK, FIN Aktiv-Passiv-Management *nt*, Aktiv- und Passivsteuerung *f*; **~ and liability statement** *n* ACC Bilanz *f*, Finanzstatus *m*, Vermögensbilanz *f*; **~ life** *n* ACC Nutzungsdauer *f* eines Wirtschaftsgutes; **~ management** *n* ACC Anlagenverwaltung *f*, Anlagenwirtschaft *f*, BANK Vermögensverwaltung *f*, FIN Aktiv-Management *nt*, Anlagenverwaltung *f*, Anlagenwirtschaft *f*, Vermögensverwaltung *f*, MGMNT Liquiditätssteuerung *f*, Anlagenverwaltung *f*, Anlagenwirtschaft *f*; STOCK Vermögensverwaltung *f*; **~ management account** *n* (*AMA*) FIN Anlagenverwaltungskonto *nt*, Vermögensverwaltungskonto *nt*; **~ management company** *n* ADMIN, FIN Anlagenverwaltungsgesellschaft *f*; **~ manager** *n* BANK, FIN Vermögensverwalter, in *m,f*, STOCK Anlageverwalter, in *m,f*, Vermögensverwalter, in *m,f*; **~ motive** *n* ECON *monetary economics* Spekulationsmotiv *nt*; **~ portfolio** *n* FIN, STOCK Bestand *m* an Anlagewerten, Kreditportefeuille *nt*, Kreditvolumen *nt*, Portefeuille *nt*; **~ price inflation** *n* ECON realwirtschaftliche Inflation *f*; **~ return** *n* STOCK Vermögensertrag *m*, Vermögensrendite *f*, Anlagenverzinsung *f*

assets *n pl* ACC Aktiva *nt pl*, Vermögen *nt*, Vermögensgegenstände *m pl*, Vermögenswert *m*, Wirtschaftsgüter

nt pl, FIN Anlagen *f pl*, Ausleihungen *f pl*, Kapitalanlagen *f pl*, Vermögen *nt*, *capital* Kapital *nt*, *liquidity* Liquidität *f*, *profit* Gewinn *m*, Vermögenswert *m*

asset: **~ sale** *n* ACC, ADMIN Anlagenverkauf *m*

assets: **~ eligible for the money market** *n pl* BANK, FIN geldmarktfähige Aktiva *nt pl*; **~ held abroad** *n pl* GEN COMM ausländisches Vermögen *nt*, Auslandsaktiva *nt pl*, Auslandsvermögen *nt*

asset: **~ side** *n* ACC *of balance sheet* Aktivseite *f*, Vermögensseite *f*

assets: **~ and liabilities management** *n* BANK, FIN Aktiv-Passiv-Management *nt*, Aktiv- und Passivsteuerung *f*

asset: **~ specificity** *n* ECON Spezifität *f* eines Wirtschaftsgutes; **~ stripping** *n* *infrml* ACC, ECON Ausschlachten *nt* von Unternehmen (*infrml*), FIN Anlagenausschlachtung *f*

assets: **~ under construction** *n pl* ACC *annual accounts* im Bau befindliche Anlagen *f pl*

asset: **~ swap** *n* ACC, ADMIN Aktivtausch *m*, Tausch *m* von Vermögenswerten, BANK Asset Swap *m*; **~ turnover** *n* ACC, FIN *financial analysis ratio* Kapitalumschlag *m*; **~ valuation** *n* ACC Anlagenbewertung *f*, Vermögensbewertung *f*; **~ value** *n* ACC Vermögenswert *m*, FIN Vermögenswert *m*, Wert *m* eines Wirtschaftsgutes, TAX *total value of assets* Reproduktionswert *m*, Sachwert *m*, Substanzwert *m*

assign *vt* ACC *cede* abtreten, *transfer* übertragen, *allocate* zurechnen, zuteilen, zuweisen, COMP reservieren, zuweisen, FIN übertragen, HRM *new post* einweisen, INS abtreten, zedieren, LAW übereignen, abtreten; **~ costs** *vt* ACC Kosten aufteilen, Kosten umlegen, Kosten zurechnen

assignability *n* LAW Abtretbarkeit *f*, STOCK Übertragbarkeit *f*

assignable *adj* LAW *contracts* übertragbar, abtretbar, begebbar; **~ credit** *n* ACC übertragbarer Kredit *m*

assigned *adj* COMP belegt, reserviert; **~ material** *n* GEN COMM auftragsgebundenes Material *nt*

assignee *n* ACC Beauftragte(r) *mf* [decl. as adj], Forderungsübernehmer, in *m,f*, Rechtsnachfolger *m pl*, BANK, INS Zessionar *m*, LAW Abtretungsempfänger, in *m,f*, Veräußerer *m*, Zessionar *m*, PATENTS Forderungsübernehmer, in *m,f*, Zessionar *m*, Vertreter, in *m,f*, Beauftragte(r) *mf* [decl. as adj]; **~ in bankruptcy** *n* BANK Konkursverwalter, in *m,f*

assignment *n* ACC *receivables* Abtretung *f*, Übertragung *f*, Zurechnung *f*, Zuteilung *f*, Zuweisung *f*, COMP Belegung *f*, FIN Übertragung *f*, INS Abtretung *f*, Rechtsübertragung *f*, LAW Abtretung *f*, Übereignung *f*, Übertragung *f*, Zession *f*, PATENTS Abtretung *f*, Patentübertragung *f*, Zession *f*; **~ of activities** *n* GEN COMM Aufgabenverteilung *f*, HRM Aufgabenverteilung *f*, Arbeitsverteilung *f*, MGMNT Aufgabenverteilung *f*; **~ of advertising expenditure** *n* S&M Verteilung *f* der Werbeausgaben; **~ of claims** *n* ACC Forderungsabtretung *f*; **~ day** *n* STOCK Abtretungstermin *m*; **~ of debts** *n* ACC Forderungsabtretung *f*; **~ document** *n* LAW *contracts* Abtretungserklärung *f*; **~ of income** *n* TAX Einkommensverschiebung *f*; **~ of lease** *n* LAW Pachtabtretung *f*; **~ man** *n* MEDIA Sonderberichterstatter *m*

assignor *n* GEN COMM, INS Abtretende(r) *mf* [decl. as

adj], LAW, PATENTS Rechtsvorgänger, in *m,f,* Zedent, in *m,f*

assimilate *vt* ACC angleichen, anpassen, LAW *Community law* angleichen, STOCK aufnehmen

assimilation *n* ACC Angleichung *f,* Anpassung *f,* Assimilation *f,* GEN COMM Assimilation *f,* LAW *by EC member states of laws enacted at Community level* Angleichung *f,* Rechtsangleichung *f,* STOCK Aufnahme *f*

assist *vi* GEN COMM mithelfen

assistance *n* ECON Hilfe *f,* GEN COMM Beistand *m,* Mithilfe *f*

assistant *n* (*asst*) GEN COMM, HRM Assistent, in *m,f,* Gehilfe *m,* Gehilfin *f,* Hilfskraft *f;* ~ **cashier** *n* BrE (*cf assistant teller AmE*) BANK Hilfskassierer, in *m,f,* stellvertretender Geschäftsführer *m,* stellvertretende Geschäftsführerin *f;* ~ **controller** *n* (*AC*) HRM Hilfsrevisor *m,* MGMNT Assistent, in *m,f* im Rechnungswesen; ~ **director** *n* HRM, MGMNT stellvertretender Direktor *m,* stellvertretende Direktorin *f;* ~ **director general** *n* (*ADG*) HRM stellvertretender Generaldirektor *m,* stellvertretende Generaldirektorin *f;* ~ **general manager** *n* MGMNT stellvertretender Generaldirektor *m,* stellvertretende Generaldirektorin *f;* ~ **head of section** *n* BrE (*AHS*) HRM, MGMNT stellvertretender Abteilungsleiter *m,* stellvertretende Abteilungsleiterin *f;* ~ **manager** *n* HRM, MGMNT stellvertretender Direktor *m,* stellvertretende Direktorin *f,* stellvertretender Abteilungsleiter *m,* stellvertretende Abteilungsleiterin *f,* stellvertretender Leiter *m,* stellvertretende Leiterin *f;* ~ **teller** *n* AmE (*cf assistant cashier BrE*) BANK Hilfskassierer, in *m,f,* stellvertretender Geschäftsführer *m,* stellvertretende Geschäftsführerin *f;* ~ **to manager** *n* MGMNT Betriebsassistent, in *m,f*

assisted: ~ **area** *n* ECON Fördergebiet *nt*

associate **1.** *n* GEN COMM Gesellschafter, in *m,f,* Partner, in *m,f,* Teilhaber, in *m,f;* **2.** *vt* ♦ ~ **sth with sth** GEN COMM etw in Zusammenhang mit etw bringen; **3.** *vi* ♦ ~ **with** GEN COMM sich verbinden mit

Associate: ~ **of the Association of Certified and Corporate Accountants** *n* (*AACCA*) ACC Mitglied des Verbands der Wirtschaftsprüfer; ~ **of the Association of International Accountants** *n* (*AAIA*) ACC Mitglied der Vereinigung der internationalen Wirtschaftsprüfer; ~ **of the British Association of Accountants and Auditors** *n* (*ABAA*) ACC Mitglied des britischen Verbands der Wirtschaftsprüfer und Rechnungsprüfer; ~ **of the Chartered Association of Certified Accountants** *n* (*ACCA*) ACC Mitglied des Verbands öffentlich zugelassener Wirtschaftsprüfer; ~ **of the Chartered Institute of Management Accountants** *n* BrE (*ACMA*) ACC Mitglied des Instituts der betrieblichen Rechnungsprüfer; ~ **of the Chartered Institute of Secretaries** *n* BrE (*ACIS*) ADMIN Mitglied des Verbands staatlich geprüfter Sekretärinnen und Sekretäre

associate: ~ **company** *n* ECON verbundene Gesellschaft *f*

associated *adj* GEN COMM verbunden, PATENTS verwandt; ♦ ~ **with** GEN COMM verbunden mit

Associated: ~ **British Ports** *n* (*ABP*) TRANSP Vereinigung britischer Häfen

associated: ~ **company** *n* ECON, GEN COMM angegliederte Gesellschaft *f,* Beteiligungsgesellschaft *f,* Schwestergesellschaft *f,* Tochtergesellschaft *f,* assoziiertes Unternehmen *nt,* verbundenes Unternehmen *nt;* ~ **company abroad** *n* FIN, GEN COMM Auslandsbeteili-

gung *f;* ~ **country** *n* ECON *international, EU* assoziiertes Land *nt;* ~ **employer** *n* HRM assoziierter Arbeitgeber *m,* assoziierte Arbeitgeberin *f;* ~ **enterprise** *n* GEN COMM assoziiertes Unternehmen *nt;* ~ **mark** *n* PATENTS assoziiertes Warenzeichen *nt,* Serienmarke *f,* Sortimentmarke *f,* verwandtes Warenzeichen *nt*

associate: ~ **editor** *n* MEDIA Mitherausgeber, in *m,f*

Associate: ~ **of the Institute of Marketing** *n* (*AInstM*) HRM Mitglied des Instituts für Marketing; ~ **Member of the Institute of Export** *n* (*AMIEx*) HRM Assoziiertes Mitglied des Instituts für Export

association *n* GEN COMM Gesellschaft *f,* Handelsgesellschaft *f,* Personenvereinigung *f,* Vereinigung *f, professional group, pressure group* Interessenverband *m, cooperative* Genossenschaft *f, non-profit-making* Verband *m,* Verein *m,* Bund *m,* Verbund *m,* IMP/EXP Handelsgesellschaft *f;* ♦ **in** ~ **with** GEN COMM gemeinsam mit, in Zusammenarbeit *f* mit

association: ~ **advertising** *n* S&M Verbundwerbung *f*

Association: ~ **of British Chambers of Commerce** *n* (*ABCC*) IND Vereinigung der britischen Industrie- und Handelskammern, ≈ Deutscher Industrie- und Handelstag *m* (*DIHT*); ~ **for Payment Clearing Services** *n* BrE (*APACS*) ECON Scheckverrechnungsstelle der größten britischen Banken; ~ **of Futures Brokers and Dealers** *n* (*AFBD*) STOCK Verband *m* der Terminmakler und -händler; ~ **of International Bond Dealers** *n* (*AIBD*) STOCK Verband *m* der internationalen Rentenhändler; ~ **of Scientific, Technical and Managerial Staff** *n* BrE (*ASTMS*) HRM Gewerkschaft für wissenschaftliches, technisches und leitendes Personal; ~ **of South-East Asian Nations** *n* (*ASEAN*) ECON, POL Verband *m* Südostasiatischer Nationen

as: ~ **soon as possible** *phr* (*a.s.a.p.*) COMMS, GEN COMM baldmöglichst, so bald wie möglich, umgehend

assort *vt* S&M assortieren

assortment *n* GEN COMM Auswahl *f;* ~ **of goods** *n* GEN COMM Sortiment *nt,* Warensortiment *nt*

asst *abbr* (*assistant*) GEN COMM Gehilfe *m,* Gehilfin *f,* HRM Assistent, in *m,f,* Hilfskraft *nt*

assume *vt* GEN COMM *take on* übernehmen, annehmen, unterstellen, *suppose* annehmen, *presuppose* voraussetzen; ♦ ~ **responsibility for sth** GEN COMM die Verantwortung für etw übernehmen; ~ **no responsibility for sth** GEN COMM keine Verantwortung für etw übernehmen

assumed *adj* GEN COMM angenommen

assumption *n* GEN COMM *taking on* Übernahme *f,* Annahme *f,* Vermutung *f, supposition* Voraussetzung *f;* ~ **of liability** *n* INS, LAW *contracts* Haftungsübernahme *f;* ~ **of mortgage** *n* BANK Hypothekenübernahme *f;* ~ **of the risk** *n* BANK, FIN Risikoübername *f,* Risikotragung *f,* LAW *contracts* Gefahrübernahme *f*

assurance *n* BrE (*ass.*) INS Lebensversicherung *f,* Versicherung *f;* ~ **payable at death** *n* BrE (*cf whole-life insurance AmE*) INS Lebensversicherung *f* auf den Todesfall, Todesfallversicherung *f;* ~ **of subscribers** *n* GEN COMM Eigentumsübertragung *f* der Unterzeichner der Urkunde, Eigentumsübertragungsurkunde *f* der Unterzeichner, *insurance policy* Lebensversicherung *f* der Unterzeichner der Police, Versicherung *f* der Unterzeichner der Police

assure *vt* GEN COMM zusichern, INS versichern

ASTM *abbr* (*American Society for Testing and Materials*)

GEN COMM amerikanische Gesellschaft für Materialprüfung, ≈ Deutscher Normenausschuß *m* (*DNA*)

ASTMS *abbr BrE* (*Association of Scientific, Technical and Managerial Staff*) HRM Gewerkschaft für wissenschaftliches, technisches und leitendes Personal

asylum *n* LAW, POL *refuge* Asyl *nt*, *country*, Asylstaat *m*, Asyl *nt*, Zufluchtsland *nt*; ~ **application** *n* LAW, POL Asylantrag *m*; ~ **seeker** *n* LAW, POL Asylbewerber, in *m,f*

asymmetric: ~ **information** *n* INS asymmetrische Auskunft *f*, asymmetrische Information *f*

asymmetry *n* GEN COMM Asymmetrie *f*

asynchronous *adj* COMP asynchron; ~ **communication** *n* COMP asynchrone Kommunikation *f*

ATA *abbr* (*Air Transport Association of America*) TRANSP amerikanische Lufttransportvereinigung, ≈ DLV (*Deutscher Luftfahrverband*)

ATC *abbr* (*air-traffic control*) TRANSP *activity* FS (*Flugsicherung*), Luftverkehrsregelung *f*, *building* Flugsicherungszentrale *f*, Luftverkehrszentrale *f*

ATM *abbr* (*automated teller machine, automatic telling machine*) BANK, FIN automatischer Bankschalter *m*, multifunktionaler Bankautomat *m*, SB-Bankautomat *m*

atmosphere *n* ENVIR, GEN COMM Atmosphäre *f*

atomistic: ~ **competition** *n* ECON atomistische Konkurrenz *f*, polypolistische Konkurrenz *f*

at: ~ **once** *phr* GEN COMM unverzüglich; ~ **or better** *phr* STOCK zum angegebenen Kurs oder besser

ATS *abbr* BANK (*automatic transfer service*) automatischer Überweisungsverkehr *m*, automatischer Verrechnungsdienst *m*

attach *vt* COMP *file, data* anhängen, hinzufügen, LAW pfänden; ♦ ~ **importance to sth** GEN COMM etw Bedeutung beimessen; ~ **sth to sb** GEN COMM *remark* jdm etw zuschreiben

attachable *adj* LAW pfändbar

attachment *n* COMP *hardware* Anlage *f*, Zusatzgerät *nt*, GEN COMM Ansatzstück *nt*, INS Beschlagnahme *f*, Pfändung *f*, LAW dinglicher Arrest *m*; ~ **date** *n* INS *marine* Fristenbeginn *m*, vereinbarter Zahlungsbeginn *m*; ~ **procedure** *n* LAW Arrestverfahren *nt*

attack 1. *n* GEN COMM, IND Angriff *m*; **2.** *vt* GEN COMM, IND angreifen

attained: ~ **age** *n* INS erreichtes Alter *nt*

attempt 1. *n* GEN COMM Versuch *m*; **2.** *vt* GEN COMM versuchen

attend *vt* MGMNT *meeting* teilnehmen an [+dat]

attend to *vt* GEN COMM *customer* bedienen, abfertigen, *problem* sich kümmern um

attendance: ~ **bonus** *n* HRM Anwesenheitsprämie *f*; ~ **fees** *n pl* HRM Sitzungsgeld *nt*, Tagegeld *nt*; ~ **figures** *n pl* GEN COMM Besucherzahlen *f pl*; ~ **money** *n* HRM Tagegeld *nt*

attended *adj* GEN COMM *at event* besucht

attending *adj* GEN COMM teilnehmend

attention *n* GEN COMM Aufmerksamkeit *f*, Beachtung *f*, S&M Aufmerksamkeit *f*; ♦ **for the ~ of** (*FAO*) COMMS, GEN COMM, IMP/EXP zu Händen (*z. Hd.*), zu Händen von (*z. Hd. v.*)

attention: ~ **factor** *n* S&M *advertising* Aufmerksamkeitsfaktor *m*; ~ **getter** *n* S&M *advertising* Blickfang *m*; ~, **interest, desire, action** *n* (*AIDA*) GEN COMM

Aufmerksamkeit *f*, Interesse *f*, Wunsch *m*, Aktion *f*; ~ **value** *n* S&M *advertising* Zugkraft *f*

attest *vt* LAW bezeugen

attest to *vt* LAW bekunden, beurkunden, bezeugen, beglaubigen

attestation *n* LAW Bestätigung *f*, Testieren *nt*, Testat *nt* Zeugenaussage *f*

attested: ~ **by a notary** *phr* LAW notariell beglaubigt, notariell beurkundet

attitude *n* GEN COMM Haltung *f*, MGMNT Einstellung *f*, Haltung *f*, Standpunkt *m*, S&M *about products, ideas* Einstellung *f*; ~ **scale** *n* S&M *market research* Verhaltensskala *f*; ~ **survey** *n* S&M *market research* Verhaltensstudie *f*

attn *abbr* (*attention*) COMMS, GEN COMM *on letter* z. Hd. (*zu Händen*)

attorney *n AmE* (*cf barrister BrE*) LAW Anwalt *m*, Anwältin *f*, Rechtsanwalt *m*, Rechtsanwältin *f*; ~**-at-law** *n AmE* (*cf barrister BrE*) LAW Rechtsanwalt *m*, Rechtsanwältin *f*; ~ **for the defense** *n AmE* (*cf counsel for the defence BrE*) LAW Verteidiger, in *m,f*

Attorney: ~ **General** *n* (*Atty Gen*) LAW *BrE* Generalstaatsanwalt *m*, Generalstaatsanwältin *f*, *AmE* Justizminister *m*

attorney: ~**-in-fact** *n* LAW Bevollmächtigte(r) *mf* [decl. as adj], Beauftragte(r) *mf* [decl. as adj]

attornment *n AmE* LAW Fortsetzung *f* des Pachtvertrags

attract *vt* GEN COMM *orders* hereinholen; ♦ ~ **new business** ECON Aufträge beschaffen, Aufträge hereinholen; ~ **sb's attention** GEN COMM jds Aufmerksamkeit auf sich lenken, jds Aufmerksamkeit auf sich ziehen, jds Aufmerksamkeit erregen, jds Aufmerksamkeit erwecken

attractive *adj* GEN COMM *for investors*, STOCK attraktiv, günstig; ~ **offer** *n* GEN COMM attraktives Angebot *nt*, günstiges Angebot *nt*; ~ **terms** *n pl* GEN COMM attraktive Ausstattung *f*, attraktive Bedingungen *f pl*

attributable: *adj* MEDIA, POL *comment* zuschreibbar; ♦ **be ~ to sb** GEN COMM zu jdm zurechenbar sein, jdm zuzurechnend sein, jdm zuzuschreiben sein

attribute 1. *n* COMP *programming language* Attribut *nt*, GEN COMM Eigenschaft *f*, Merkmal *nt*, IND Attribut *nt*; **2.** *vt* ♦ ~ **sth to sb** GEN COMM *importance, intelligence* jdm etw beimessen, *remark* jdm etw zuschreiben; ~ **sth to sth** GEN COMM *success, failure* etw auf etw zurückführen

attribute: ~ **sampling** *n* ACC *auditing* Eigenschaftskontrolle *f* durch Stichproben, MATH *statistics*, MEDIA *market research* Attributkontrolle *f*

attribution: **not for ~** *phr AmE* (*cf on lobby terms BrE*) MEDIA, POL nicht zuschreibbar

attrition *n* HRM *natural wastage* Arbeitskräfteabgang *m*; ~ **rate** *n* GEN COMM Abnutzungsgrad *m*, Verschleißrate *f*

Atty Gen *abbr* (*Attorney General*) LAW *BrE* Generalstaatsanwalt *m*, Generalstaatsanwältin *f*, *AmE* Justizminister *m*

atypical: ~ **worker** *n* HRM Arbeitnehmer, der nicht in einem dauerhaften, festen, ganztägigen, ununterbrochenen Beschäftigungsverhältnis mit nur einem Arbeitgeber steht

auction 1. *n* ECON, GEN COMM, S&M Auktion *f*, Versteigerung *f*; **2.** *vt* ECON, GEN COMM, S&M versteigern

auction off *vt* ECON, GEN COMM, S&M versteigern

auction: ~ **market** n ECON Auktionsmarkt m; ~ **room** n GEN COMM Auktionslokal nt; ~ **sale** n S&M Verkauf m durch Auktion

audience n COMMS Zuhörer m pl, GEN COMM for the press Leserschaft f, MEDIA, LEIS for television Zuschauer m pl, Zuhörer m pl, S&M advertising Zielgruppe f

audio: ~ **conference** n COMMS Fernsprechkonferenz f, Konferenzschaltung f, GEN COMM Fernsprechkonferenz f; ~ **conferencing** n COMMS Fernsprechkonferenz f, Konferenzschaltung f, GEN COMM Fernsprechkonferenz f

audiotyping n GEN COMM Schreiben nt mit Diktiergerät

audiovisual adj COMMS, GEN COMM, MEDIA, S&M audiovisuell; ~ **aids** n pl COMMS audio-visuelle Hilfen f pl, COMP audio-visuelle Hilfsmittel nt pl, MEDIA audio-visuelle Unterstützung f; ~ **commercial** n (av-commercial) S&M Standardwerbesendung f; ~ **display** n S&M audio-visuelle Anzeige f; ~ **equipment** n S&M audio-visuelle Ausrüstung f

audit 1. n ACC, FIN Abschlußprüfung f, Buchprüfung f, Prüfung f, Rechnungsprüfung f, Revision f, Wirtschaftsprüfung f, by government audit agency Haushaltskontrolle f, quality audit Audit nt; **2.** vt ACC, FIN accounts prüfen, Bücher prüfen, Bücher revidieren

audita altera parte: ~ **procedure** n GEN COMM Anhörung f der Gegenpartei, Anhörung f der Gegenseite

auditability n ACC Prüfbarkeit f

auditable adj ACC prüffähig

audit: ~ **activity** n BrE ACC Prüftätigkeit f; ~ **agent** n ACC Prüfer, in m,f; ~ **brief** n ACC Prüfungskurzbericht m

Audit: ~ **Bureau of Circulation** n S&M advertising Auflagenüberwachungsstelle m

audit: ~ **certificate** n ACC Bestätigungsvermerk m, Prüfungsvermerk m, Testat nt; ~ **client** n ACC auditing Revisionskunde m, Revisionskundin f; ~ **committee** n ACC Prüfungsausschuß m; ~ **costs** n pl ACC Prüfungskosten pl; ~ **coverage** n ACC Prüfungsumfang m

audited: ~ **accounts** n pl ACC geprüfter Abschluß m; ~ **circulation** n S&M kontrollierte Auflage f

auditee n ACC company geprüftes Unternehmen nt

audit: ~ **engagement** n ACC Prüfungsauftrag m; ~ **evidence** n ACC Prüfungsbeweis m; ~ **file** n ACC zu prüfende Akte f; ~ **group** n ACC Prüfungsgruppe f; ~ **guide** n ACC Prüfungsvorschriften f pl; ~ **head** n ACC Leiter, in m,f der Prüfungsgruppe; ~ **independence** n ACC Prüfungsunabhängigkeit f

auditing n ACC Buchprüfung f, Prüfungswesen nt, Revision f, wirtschaftliches Prüfungswesen nt; ~ **department** n ACC Revisionsabteilung f, within company Buchprüfungsabteilung f; ~ **manual** n ACC Revisionshandbuch nt; ~ **principle** n ACC Prüfungsgrundsatz m, Prüfungsrichtlinie f; ~ **procedure** n ACC Prüfungsverfahren nt, Revisionsverfahren nt; ~ **standard** n ACC Prüfungsgrundsatz m, Prüfungsrichtlinie f; ~ **technique** n ACC Prüfungstechnik f

auditor n ACC Bilanzprüfer, in m,f, Buchprüfer, in m,f, Prüfer, in m,f, Rechnungsprüfer, in m,f, quality audit Auditor m; ~**'s certificate** n ACC Bestätigungsvermerk m, Prüfungsbericht m, Revisionsbericht m, Testat nt; ~**'s operational standard** n ACC Abschlußprüferrichtlinie f; ~**'s opinion** n ACC Bestätigungsvermerk m, Prüfungsbericht m, Testat nt; ~**'s report** n ACC Bestätigungsvermerk m, Prüfungsbericht m, Revisionsbericht m, Testat nt; ~**'s statement** n ACC

Bestätigungsvermerk m, Prüfungsbericht m, Revisionsbericht m, Testat nt

audit: ~ **plan** n ACC Prüfungsplan m; ~ **program** AmE, ~ **programme** BrE n ACC Prüfungsprogramm nt; ~ **report** n ACC Bestätigungsvermerk m, Prüfungsbericht m, Revisionsbericht m, Testat nt, FIN Prüfbericht m; ~ **risk** n ACC Prüfungsrisiko nt; ~ **schedule** n ACC Prüfungsprogramm nt; ~ **scope** n ACC Prüfungsumfang m; ~ **software** n ACC, COMP Prüfungs-Software f; ~ **staff** n BrE ACC Prüfungspersonal nt; ~ **standard** n ACC Prüfungsgrundsatz m; ~ **team** n ACC Prüfungsgruppe f, Prüfungsteam nt; ~ **technique** n ACC Prüfungstechnik f; ~ **trail** n ACC Prüfkette f, Prüfspur f, Prüfungskette f, Prüfungspfad m, COMP Prüfliste f; ~ **window** n COMP Steuerungsanzeige f; ~ **working papers** n pl ACC Prüfungsunterlagen f pl; ~ **work schedule** n ACC Prüfungsablauf m, Prüfungszeitplan m

au fait adj GEN COMM vertraut, auf dem laufenden; ♦ **be ~ with** GEN COMM vertraut sein mit, auf dem laufenden sein mit

augment 1. vt GEN COMM income vergrößern, vermehren; **2.** vi GEN COMM zunehmen

augmentation n GEN COMM Vergrößerung f, Vermehrung f, Zunahme f

AUSTRA abbr (Australian Committee on Trade Procedures and Facilitation) ECON australischer Ausschuß für Handelsverfahren und Handelsförderung

Australia: ~ **and New Zealand Trade Advisory Committee** n (ANZTAC) ECON Beratender Ausschuß für den Handel mit Australien und Neuseeland

Australian: ~ **Broadcasting Corporation** n (ABC) MEDIA australische Rundfunk- und Fernsehanstalt, ≈ Arbeitsgemeinschaft f der öffentlich-rechtlichen Rundfunkanstalten der Bundesrepublik Deutschland (ARD); ~ **Committee on Trade Procedures and Facilitation** n (AUSTRA) ECON australischer Ausschuß für Handelsverfahren und Handelsförderung; ~ **Council of Trade Unions** n (ACTU) HRM australischer Gewerkschaftsbund, ≈ Deutscher Gewerkschaftsbund m (DGB)

Australia: ~, **New Zealand and United States** n pl (ANZUS) ECON ANZUS-Pakt m

Australian: ~ **Financial Futures Market** n (AFFM) STOCK australische Finanzterminbörse; ~ **Securities Commission** n (ASC) STOCK australische Börsenaufsichtsbehörde; ~ **Stock Exchange** n STOCK australische Wertpapierbörse

Austrian: ~ **School of Economics** n ECON Wiener Schule f

autarchic adj ECON, GEN COMM autark

autarky n ECON, GEN COMM Autarkie f

authentic adj ACC, GEN COMM, LAW text verbindlich

authenticate vt ACC, GEN COMM beurkunden, LAW beglaubigen claim glaubhaft machen, STOCK beglaubigen

authenticated: ~ **document** n LAW beglaubigte Urkunde f

authentication n ACC, GEN COMM Beurkundung f, LAW Beglaubigung f, of claims Glaubhaftmachung f, POL of documents Legalisierung f, STOCK Bestätigung f durch eine amtliche Stelle, Beglaubigung f, Echtheitsbescheinigung f

authoritarian: ~ **management** n HRM, MGMNT

autoritäres Management *nt*; ~ **society** *n* ECON autoritäre Gesellschaft *f*, autoritäres System *nt*

authoritative *adj* LAW maßgeblich, *text* verbindlich

authorities: the ~ *n pl* GEN COMM die Obrigkeit *f* (*obs*), die Staatsgewalt *f*

authority *n* GEN COMM Amtsgewalt *f*, Befugnis *f*, Weisungsgewalt *f*, Kompetenz *f*, *person, expert* Autorität *f*, HRM *of managers* Autorität *f*, PATENTS *national* Amt *nt*, Behörde *f*, STOCK Vollmacht *f*; ~ **structure** *n* ADMIN, GEN COMM Autoritätsstruktur *f*; ~ **to buy** *n* GEN COMM *on behalf of a third party* Ankaufsermächtigung *f*; ~ **to purchase** *n* FIN Authority to Purchase *f*, GEN COMM Ankaufsermächtigung *f*, Einkaufsvollmacht *f*, IMP/EXP Authority to Purchase *f*; ~ **to sign** *n* GEN COMM *on behalf of a third party* Zeichnungsberechtigung *f*

authorization *n* BANK Autorisation *f*, Befugnis *f*, Erlaubnis *f*, Ermächtigung *f*, Genehmigung *f*, GEN COMM Autorisation *f*, Bevollmächtigung *f*, Erlaubnis *f*, Ermächtigung *f*, Genehmigung *f*, LAW Bevollmächtigung *f*, *delegation of power* Vollmachterteilung *f*, PATENTS Erlaubnis *f*, Genehmigung *f*, POL Kannbestimmung *f*; ~ **center** *AmE*, ~ **centre** *BrE* *n* BANK Authorisierungszentrale *f*, Genehmigungsstelle *f*; ~ **code** *n* BANK Genehmigungs-Code *m*; ~ **for expenditure** *n* ACC Ausgabenbewilligung *f*; ~ **number** *n* BANK Genehmigungsnummer *f*

authorize *vt* GEN COMM *person* autorisieren, bevollmächtigen, ermächtigen, Vollmacht erteilen, *action* bewilligen, erlauben, genehmigen, LAW beauftragen

authorized *adj* GEN COMM bewilligt, *person* befugt, bevollmächtigt, erlaubt; ~ **agent** *n* GEN COMM bevollmächtigter Vertreter *m*, bevollmächtigte Vertreterin *f*, Bevollmächtigte(r) *mf* [decl. as adj]; ~ **bank** *n* BANK Devisenbank *f*; ~ **capital** *n* ECON genehmigtes Kapital *nt*, autorisiertes Aktienkapital *nt*, autorisiertes Grundkapital *nt*, FIN Grundkapital *nt*, *unissued capital* bedingtes Kapital *nt*; ~ **capital stock** *n* FIN Grundkapital *nt*; ~ **credit** *n* BANK genehmigter Kredit *m*; ~ **dealer** *n* LAW Vertragshändler, in *m,f*, STOCK zugelassener Devisenhändler *m*, zugelassene Devisenhändlerin *f*; ~ **expenditure** *n* ACC bewilligte Ausgaben *f pl*; ~ **representative** *n* GEN COMM, HRM bevollmächtigter Vertreter *m*, bevollmächtigte Vertreterin *f*; ~ **share capital** *n* ACC, FIN genehmigtes Kapital *nt*, autorisiertes Aktienkapital *nt*; ~ **shares** *n pl* STOCK genehmigte Aktien *f pl*; ~ **stock** *n* STOCK genehmigtes Aktienkapital *nt*

author: ~'**s fee** *n* MEDIA, PATENTS Tantieme *f*; ~'**s specimen copy** *n* GEN COMM Belegexemplar *nt*, MEDIA Probeexemplar *nt*

auto- *pref* GEN COMM Auto-

autobank: ~ **card** *n* BANK Geldautomatenkarte *f*

autoboot *n* COMP automatisches Booten *nt*, automatisches Urladen *nt*

autocorrelation *n* ECON *econometrics* Autokorrelation *f*

autoduplication *n* COMP automatische Duplikation *f*

autoeconomy *n* ECON Automobilwirtschaft *f*

autofeed *n* COMP automatischer Einzug *m*

autofinancing *n* FIN Eigenfinanzierung *f*, Selbstfinanzierung *f*

autogestion *n* HRM Arbeiterselbstverwaltung *f*, Selbstmanagement *nt*, Selbstverwaltung *f*

auto: ~ **hire** *n* BrE (*cf rental AmE*) IMP/EXP, TRANSP Autovermietung *f*, Miete *f*

autoloading *n* COMP automatisches Laden *nt*

auto-login *n* COMP automatische Anmeldung *f*

auto-logon *n* COMP automatische Anmeldung *f*

automate *vt* COMP automatisieren, IND automatisch fertigen, automatisieren

automated: ~ **cash dispenser** *n* (*ACD*) BANK Geldausgabeautomat *m* (*GAA*), Geldautomat *m*, Bancomat *m* (*Sch*)

Automated: ~ **Clearing House** *n* (*ACH*) FIN automatisierte Abrechnungsstelle *f*, automatisches Clearinghaus *nt*, computergestützte Clearingstelle *f*, automatisiertes Clearinghaus im Gironetz des Massenzahlungsverkehrs; ~ **Clearing Settlement System** *n* (*ACSS*) BANK automatisches Verrechnungssystem *nt*, automatisches Clearingssystem *nt*

automated: ~ **teller card** *n* BANK Geldautomatenkarte *f*; ~ **teller machine** *n* (*ATM*) BANK, FIN automatischer Bankschalter *m*, multifunktionaler Bankautomat *m*, SB-Bankautomat *m*; ~ **teller machine statement** *n* BANK, FIN Bankautomaten-Kontoauszug *m*

automatic *adj* GEN COMM, IND automatisch; ~ **adjustment point** *n* HRM *of salaries* automatische Gehaltsregulierung *f*

automatically *adv* GEN COMM, IND automatisch

automatic: ~ **billing machine** *n* GEN COMM Fakturiermaschine *f*; ~ **cash dispenser** *n* (*ACD*) BANK Geldausgabeautomat *m* (*GAA*), Geldautomat *m*, Bancomat *m* (*Sch*); ~ **check-off** *n* AmE ECON, HRM *labour economics* Einzug von Gewerkschaftsbeiträgen durch Arbeitgeber; ~ **control** *n* COMP Regelung *f*, Selbststeuerung *f*; ~ **control certified** *phr* (*ACC*) TRANSP Selbststeuerung eingetragen, Selbststeuerung zugelassen; ~ **coupling** *n* TRANSP *road transport* selbsttätige Kupplung *f*; ~ **data processing** *n* (*ADP*) COMP automatisierte Datenverarbeitung *f* (*ADV*); ~ **debit transfer system** *n* FIN Bankabrufverfahren *nt*, Einzugsverfahren *nt*; ~ **fare collection** *n* TRANSP automatischer Fahrpreiseinzug *m*; ~ **fiscal stabilizer** *n* ECON automatischer fiskalpolitischer Konjunkturstabilisator *m*; ~ **funds transfer** *n* (*AFT*) ACC, BANK, FIN automatischer Zahlungsverkehr *m*, automatisierter Überweisungsverkehr *m*, elektronischer Zahlungsverkehr *m*; ~ **maritime radio telex service** *n* TRANSP *shipping, terrestrial service* automatischer Seefunk-Telex-Dienst *m*; ~ **merchandising** *n* S&M *vending machine sales* Automatenverkauf *m*; ~ **redialing** *AmE*, ~ **redialling** *BrE* *n* COMMS automatische Wahlwiederholung *f*; ~ **reinvestment** *n* STOCK automatische Wiederanlage *f*; ~ **reset** *n* COMP automatisches Rücksetzen *nt*; ~ **stabilizer** *n* ECON, POL *fiscal policy* automatischer Stabilisator *m*; ~ **teller** *n* BANK, FIN automatischer Bankschalter *m*, Bankautomat *m*, SB-Bankautomat *m*, Geldautomat *m*; ~ **telling machine** *n* (*ATM*) BANK, FIN automatischer Bankschalter *m*, multifunktionaler Bankautomat *m*, SB-Bankautomat *m*; ~ **transfer** *n* BANK automatische Überweisung *f*, elektronische Überweisung *f*; ~ **transfer service** *n* BrE (*ATS*) BANK automatischer Überweisungsverkehr *m*, automatischer Verrechnungsdienst *m*, elektronische Überweisung *f*, elektronischer Zahlungsverkehr *m* für Überweisungen (*EZÜ*); ~ **typewriter** *n* ADMIN Schreibmaschine *f* mit Lochstreifensteuerung; ~ **updating** *n* COMP automatische Aktualisierung *f*; ~ **vending machine** *n* GEN COMM Automat *m*; ~ **withdrawal** *n* STOCK automatische Abhebung *f*

automation n COMP Automation f, Automatisierung f

automobile n GEN COMM, IND, TRANSP Automobil nt

Automobile: ~ **Association** n BrE (AA) TRANSP britische Kraftfahrervereinigung, ≈ Allgemeiner Deutscher Automobil-Club m (ADAC)

automobile: ~ **insurance** n AmE (cf motor insurance BrE) INS Autoversicherung f, Kraftfahrzeugversicherung f, Kfz-Versicherung f

automotive adj IND motorisch, selbstfahrend; ~ **industry** n IND Autoindustrie f, Kraftfahrzeugindustrie f, TRANSP Kraftfahrzeugindustrie f; ~ **stock** n STOCK Automobilwerte m pl

autonomous adj GEN COMM autonom; ~ **consumption** n ECON autonomer Konsum m; ~ **expenditure** n ECON autonome Ausgaben f pl; ~ **investment** n ECON autonome Investition f; ~ **wage bargaining** n ECON, HRM, MGMNT Tarifautonomie f; ~ **work groups** n pl BrE HRM autonome Arbeitsgruppen f pl

autonomy n GEN COMM Autonomie f, Selbstverwaltung f; ~ **in collective bargaining** n ECON, HRM, MGMNT Tarifautonomie f

autopark n COMP of head, hard disk drive automatisches Parken nt

autorestart n COMP automatischer Neustart m

autosave n COMP automatisches Sichern nt

autostart n COMP automatischer Start m

autotype n MEDIA Rasterbild nt

aux. abbr (auxiliary) COMP memory, program, GEN COMM Hilfs-, IND engine Zusatz-

auxiliary adj (aux.) COMP memory, program, GEN COMM Hilfs-, IND engine Zusatz-; ~ **account** n ACC Unterkonto nt; ~ **memory** n COMP Hilfsspeicher m; ~ **storage** n COMP hardware Hilfsspeicher m

av. abbr (average) ACC, GEN COMM, MATH Durchschnitt m, Mittelwert m

availability n ECON of monetary reserves Disponibilität f, GEN COMM Lieferbarkeit f, Verfügbarkeit f, MEDIA radio Sendeplatz m, S&M of time on radio, TV noch verfügbare Werbezeit f; ~ **of jobs** n ECON Arbeitsplatzangebot nt; ~ **thesis** n ECON Verfügbarkeitsthese f

available adj GEN COMM obtainable erhältlich, lieferbar, able to be contacted erreichbar, ready for use verfügbar, vorhanden; **not** ~ GEN COMM person nicht zu erreichen, nicht erreichbar, product nicht lieferbar; ~ **on a current basis** GEN COMM aktuell verfügbar; ~ **for discounting** ACC diskontfähig; ♦ ~ **at short notice** GEN COMM kurzfristig lieferbar, kurzfristig verfügbar; **make** ~ GEN COMM money bereitstellen

available: ~ **asset** n ACC, STOCK liquider Aktivposten m, verfügbarer Vermögenswert m; ~ **balance** n ACC, BANK Nettomittelzuweisung f, verfügbarer Saldo m; ~ **cash** n ACC, FIN Barliquidität f, Liquidität f ersten Grades, verfügbare Mittel nt pl; ~ **cash flow** n ACC verfügbarer Cashflow m; ~ **disk space** n COMP verfügbarer Speicherplatz m; ~ **funds** n pl ACC, FIN flüssige Mittel nt pl, liquide Mittel nt pl, verfügbare Mittel nt pl; ~ **income** n FIN, TAX verfügbares Einkommen nt; ~ **time** n COMP verfügbare Zeit f

avails n pl GEN COMM Ertrag m, Nutzen m, Vorteil m

AVC abbr (additional voluntary contribution) INS, TAX freiwillige Zusatzleistung f, freiwillige Zuzahlung f

av: ~~**commercial** n (audiovisual commercial) S&M Standardwerbesendung f

avdp. abbr (avoirdupois) GEN COMM weight Avoirdupois nt, Handelsgewicht nt

average 1. adj GEN COMM durchschnittlich, normal; **2.** n (av.) ACC, GEN COMM Durchschnitt m, Mittelwert m, INS maritime Havarie f, MATH Durchschnitt m, Mittelwert m, STOCK Durchschnittskurs m, Aktienindex m; ♦ **at an** ~ GEN COMM durchschnittlich, im Durchschnitt; **with** ~ (W.A.) INS maritime einschließlich Havarie; **3.** vt ACC, MATH calculate the average of den Durchschnitt ermitteln von

average out 1. vt FIN costs, profit ausgleichen, austarieren, den Durchschnitt ermitteln von, output durchschnittlich befragen; **2.** vi FIN costs, profit sich ausgleichen

average: ~ **access time** n COMP mittlere Zugriffszeit f; ~ **adjuster** n (AA) INS maritime Dispacheur m, Havariekommissar m, Schadensregulierer m; ~ **adjustment** n INS Dispache f, Schadensaufmachung f; ~ **agent** n INS maritime Havarieagent m, Havariekommissar m; ~ **amount** n GEN COMM Durchschnittsbetrag m; ~ **balance** n BANK calculating interest charges durchschnittliches Guthaben nt; ~ **bond** n STOCK Havariebond m, Havarieverpflichtungsschein m; ~ **charges** n pl INS Havariegeld nt; ~ **claim** n INS Durchschnittsschaden m, Schadendurchschnitt m; ~ **clause** n INS Freizeichnungsklausel f, Havarieklausel f, Prorata-Klausel f; ~ **collection period** n ACC Durchschnittsdauer f der Außenstände; ~ **compensation** n ACC Durchschnittsentgelt nt; ~ **consumer** n S&M Normalverbraucher, in m,f; ~ **contribution** n INS Havarieeinschuß m; ~ **cost of claims** n INS Durchschnittskosten pl eines Schadens, durchschnittliche Schadenkosten pl; ~ **cost pricing** n ADMIN, ECON Preisbildung f auf Durchschnittskostenbasis; ~ **costs** n pl ACC, ADMIN Durchschnittskosten pl, durchschnittliche Kosten pl, ECON Durchschnittskosten pl, Stückkosten pl; ~ **deposit** n FIN durchschnittliche Einzahlung f; ~ **deviation** n MATH mittlere Abweichung f; ~ **duration of life** n INS mittlere Lebensdauer f, mittlere Lebenserwartung f; ~ **earning** n HRM Durchschnittsverdienst m; ~ **expenses** n pl INS Havariespesen pl; ~ **fixed cost** n ACC durchschnittliche Fixkosten pl; ~ **hourly earnings** n pl HRM Durchschnitts-Stundenverdienst m, durchschnittlicher Stundenlohn m; ~ **income** n HRM Durchschnittseinkommen nt; ~ **interest rate** n BANK Durchschnittsverzinsung f, durchschnittlicher Zinssatz m; ~ **issue readership** n S&M Leserschaft f pro durchschnittlicher Auflage; ~ **layover** n TRANSP mittlere Liegezeit f; ~ **laytime** n TRANSP shipping durchschnittliche Liegezeit f, mittlere Liegezeit f; ~ **LIBOR** n BANK durchschnittlicher LIBOR-Satz m, Durchschnitts-LIBOR m; ~ **life** n GEN COMM of machine, product betriebsgewöhnliche Nutzungsdauer f, mittlere Nutzungsdauer f; ~ **market price** n FIN, GEN COMM, STOCK Durchschnittskurs m, Durchschnittsmarktpreis m; ~ **mark-up** n GEN COMM durchschnittlicher Preisaufschlag f; ~ **maturity** n STOCK of security durchschnittliche Laufzeit f; ~ **pay** n ACC Durchschnittseinkommen nt, Durchschnittsentgelt nt, HRM Durchschnittsentgelt nt; ~ **premium** n INS Durchschnittsprämie f; ~ **premium system** n INS Durchschnittsprämiensystem nt; ~ **propensity to consume** n (APC) ECON accounting durchschnittliche Konsumquote f; ~ **propensity to save** n (APS) ECON accounting durchschnittliche Sparneigung f; **the**

~ punter *n infrml* S&M Otto-Normalverbraucher *m* (*infrml*)

averager *n* STOCK Person, die Aktien zu verschiedenen Kursen und Zeitpunkten kauft, um den Durchschnittspreis zu optimieren

average: **~ rate** *n* ACC, STOCK Durchschnittskurs *m*, Durchschnittssatz *m*; **~ reader** *n* MEDIA, S&M Durchschnittsleser, in *m,f*; **~ revenue** *n* (*AR*) ACC, FIN Durchschnittserlös *m*, Durchschnittsertrag *m*; **~ size of loss** *n* INS durchschnittliche Schadenshöhe *f*, Durchschnittsschaden *m*; **~ sold circulation** *n* MEDIA durchschnittlicher Absatz *m*; **~ statement** *n* INS Dispache *f*, Schadensaufmachung *f*; **~ stater** *n* INS Dispacheur *m*; **~ tax rate** *n* TAX durchschnittlicher Steuersatz *m*, Durchschnittssteuersatz *m*; **~ total cost** *n* ACC durchschnittliche Gesamtkosten *pl*; **~ unit cost** *n* ACC durchschnittliche Stückkosten *pl*; **~ utilization** *n* IND durchschnittliche Auslastung *f*; **~ variable costs** *n pl* ECON variable Durchschnittskosten *pl*; **~ wage** *n* HRM Durchschnittslohn *m*; **~ working week** *BrE*, **~ workweek** *AmE n* HRM durchschnittliche Arbeitswoche *f*; **~ yield** *n* ACC, FIN Durchschnittsertrag *m*, Durchschnittsrendite *f*

averaging *n* FIN Durchschnittsmethode *f*, GEN COMM, STOCK, TAX *income* Durchschnittsbildung *f*; **~ formula** *n* BANK Durchschnittsmethode *f*

aviation *n* TRANSP Flugwesen *nt*, Luftfahrt *f*; **~ fuel** *n* TRANSP Flugbenzin *nt*, Flugkraftstoff *m*; **~ insurance** *n* INS Luftfahrtversicherung *f*; **~ risk** *n* INS Flugrisiko *nt*; **~ spirit** *n* TRANSP Flugbenzin *nt*, Flugkraftstoff *m*; **~ trip life insurance** *n* INS Flugreiselebensversicherung *f*; **~ turbine fuel** *n* TRANSP Flugturbinenkraftstoff *m*, Kerosin *nt*

avoid *vt* GEN COMM vermeiden, LAW anfechten, annullieren, aufheben, PATENTS anfechten, TAX umgehen, vermeiden

avoidable: **~ costs** *n pl* GEN COMM Differenzkosten *pl*, negative Opportunitätskosten *pl*, vermeidbare Kosten *pl*; **~ risk** *n* FIN vermeidbares Risiko *nt*

avoidance *n* GEN COMM Vermeidung *f*, INS *marine* Anfechtung *f*, Vertragsanfechtung *f*, LAW Anfechtung *f*, Annullierung *f*, Aufhebung *f*; **~ clause** *n* LAW Anfechtungsklausel *f*; **~ of tax** *n* TAX Steuerumgehung *f*, Steuervermeidung *f*

avoirdupois *n* (*avdp.*) GEN COMM *weight* Avoirdupois *nt*, Handelsgewicht *nt*

AVR *abbr* (*agent's vehicle record*) S&M, TRANSP Vertreterfahrtenbuch *nt*

avulsion *n* PROP Grundstücksübertragungsmethode *f*

award 1. *n* GEN COMM Erteilung *f*, Vergabe *f*, HRM Prämie *f*, LAW außergerichtliche Entscheidung *f*, Schiedsspruch *m*, MGMNT *bonus* Zuschlag *m*, *of contract* Auftragserteilung *f*, Submissionsvergabe *f*, Zuschlag *m*; **2.** *vt* GEN COMM *contract* erteilen, geben, vergeben, *pay rise* gewähren; **~ to sb** LAW *costs, damages* jdm bemessen, jdm zuerkennen, jdm zusprechen; ♦ **~ damages** INS Schadensersatz zahlen; **~ sb £10,000 damages** INS jdm Schäden bis zu £10.000 zugestehen

awarded *adj* GEN COMM erteilt

awarder *n* GEN COMM Richter, in *m,f*, Schiedsrichter, in *m,f*

awarding: **~ of costs** *n* PATENTS Kostenzuspruch *m*, Zuerkennung *f* von Kosten

aware *adj* GEN COMM in Kenntnis

awareness: **~ level** *n* S&M Bekanntheitsebene *f*

awash: **~ with cash** *phr infrml* GEN COMM mit Bargeld überschwemmt, im Geld schwimmen (*infrml*)

away: **~ from the market** *phr* STOCK außerhalb der Börse

AWB *abbr* (*air waybill*) IMP/EXP, TRANSP Luftfrachtbrief *m*

axial: **~ composition** *n* GEN COMM, S&M *advertising* axiale Komposition *f*

axioms: **~ of preference** *n pl* ECON Präferenzaxiome *nt pl*

axis *n* MATH, TRANSP Achse *f*

axle: **~ weight** *n* TRANSP Achsgewicht *nt*

azimuth *n* MATH Abweichung *f*

B

B *abbr* (*bale*) IND, TRANSP *bundle* Ballen *m*, *unit of mass* Bale *nt*

BAA *abbr* (*British Airports Authority*) TRANSP britische Flughafenbehörde, ≈ Bundesanstalt *f* für Flugsicherung (*BFS*)

baby: ~ **bond** *n* STOCK Baby Bond *nt*, Kleinobligation *f*; ~ **boom** *n* ECON Babyboom *m*; ~ **boomers** *n pl* S&M *target audience* geburtenstarke Jahrgänge *m pl*

BACC *abbr* (*British-American Chamber of Commerce*) ECON, GEN COMM britisch-amerikanische Handelskammer

Bachelor *n* HRM niedrigster akademischer Grad in GB und USA, Bakkalaureus *m*; ~ **of Business Administration** *n* HRM Betriebswirt, in *m,f*; ~ **of Commerce** *n* (*BCom*) HRM Handelswirt *m*; ~ **of Economics** *n* (*BEcon*) HRM Volkswirt, in *m,f*; ~ **of Industrial Design** *n* (*BID*) HRM Bakkalaureus *m* für Industriedesign, Bakkalaureus *m* für industrielles Design; ~ **of Laws** *n* (*LLB*) HRM, LAW, WEL Bakkalaureus *m* der Rechtswissenschaft, Bakkalaureus *m* des Rechts; ~ **of Science** *n* (*BSc*) HRM Bakkalaureus *m* der Naturwissenschaften; ~ **of Science in Business Administration** *n* (*BSBA*) HRM Betriebswirt, in *m,f*

back *vt* ECON *support* unterstützen, *currency* decken, GEN COMM *support* stützen, unterstützen, *approve* befürworten, LAW *endorse* indossieren

back down *vi* GEN COMM einen Rückzieher machen (*infrml*), *in argument* nachgeben

back off *vi* GEN COMM zurückweichen, sich zurückziehen

back out *vi* GEN COMM zurücktreten, *of contract, deal* aussteigen (*infrml*), einen Rückzieher machen (*infrml*); ◆ ~ **of** GEN COMM *contract, deal* aussteigen aus (*infrml*), zurücktreten von

back up *vt* COMP *file, data* sichern, ECON, GEN COMM unterstützen, beistehen, befürworten

back: ~ **arrow** *n* COMP *key* Backspace-Taste *f*, Pfeil zurück *m*

backbencher *n BrE* POL Hinterbänkler *m*

backbench: ~ **MP** *n BrE* POL Hinterbänkler *m*

backbiting *n* GEN COMM Verleumdung *f*

backbone *n* GEN COMM Rückgrat *nt*; ~ **of the economy** *n* ECON Rückgrat *nt* der Wirtschaft

back: ~-**channel** *n AmE* POL geheimer Kanal *m*; ~ **cover** *n* GEN COMM hinterer Buchdeckel *m*, rückwärtiger Buchdeckel *m*; ~ **data information** *n* S&M Back-Data-Informationen *f pl*

backdate *vt* GEN COMM rückdatieren, LAW rückwirkend in Kraft treten lassen

backdated *adj* GEN COMM rückdatiert; ~ **pay** *n* HRM rückwirkende Entlohnung *f*

backdating *n* GEN COMM Rückdatierung *f*

backdoor: ~ **financing** *n* ECON, POL *public finance* Finanzierung *f* durch die Hintertür; ~ **lending** *n* ECON Kredite der Bank von England an die Diskontbanken zu Marktpreis; ~ **operation** *n* ECON Stützung des britischen Geldmarkts durch die Bank von England; ~ **selling** *n* S&M Verkauf unter Umgehung der festgelegten Absatzwege

backdrop *n* ECON, GEN COMM, POL Hintergrund *m*

backed: ~ **bill of exchange** *n* STOCK avalierter Wechsel *m*; ~ **by** *phr* FIN *big name retailer* finanziell unterstützt durch

back: ~ **end** *n jarg* MEDIA letzter Teil *m* (*jarg*)

backer *n* FIN Geldgeber,in *m,f*, Sponsor *m*, Hintermann *m*, GEN COMM Befürworter, in *m,f*, *of foreign bill of exchange* Geldgeber,in *m,f*, Indossant *m*

back: ~ **freight** *n* TRANSP Rückfracht *f*

background *n* COMP *of screen*, ECON, GEN COMM *to situation* Hintergrund *m*, HRM *professional, academic, personal* Werdegang *m* (*obs*), Vorbildung *f*, *experience* Erfahrung *f*, POL *to situation* Hintergrund *m*; ~ **art** *n* PATENTS Hintergrundkenntnisse *f pl*; ~ **color** *AmE*, ~ **colour** *BrE n* COMP Hintergrundfarbe *f*; ~ **field** *n* COMP *of screen* Hintergrundfeld *nt*; ~ **information** *n* GEN COMM Hintergrundinformation *f*; ~ **paper** *n* FIN Hintergrundpapier *nt*, Zusammenfassung *f* der Hintergründe, MEDIA Vortrag *m* über die Hintergründe; ~ **picture** *n* COMP *of screen* Bildhintergrund *m*; ~ **pollution** *n* ENVIR Verschmutzung *f* auf niedrigem Niveau, Verunreinigung *f* auf niedrigem Niveau; ~ **printing** *n* COMP *of low priority* Drucken *nt* im Hintergrundmodus; ~ **processing** *n* COMP *of low priority* nachrangige Verarbeitung *f*, Verarbeitung *f* im Hintergrundmodus, HRM *of employee's job history* Verarbeitung der Informationen über den Werdegang; ~ **story** *n* MEDIA *in newspaper* Hintergrundbericht *m*; ~ **task** *n* COMP *of low priority* nachrangige Aufgabe *f*

back: ~ **haul** *n* TRANSP *shipping* Transport *m* von Rückfracht

backing *n* ECON Unterstützung *f*, *of a currency* Stützung *f*, Deckung *f*, GEN COMM *support* Unterstützung *f*, *approval* Befürwortung *f*, LAW *endorsement* Indossament *nt*, STOCK Stützungskäufe *m pl*; ~ **syndicate** *n* FIN Auffangkonsortium *nt*; ~ **up** *n* MEDIA *print* Rückseitendruck *m*, COMP *of file, data* Sicherung *f*

back: ~ **interest** *n* ACC rückständige Zinsen *m pl*, Zinsrückstand *m*; ~ **issue** *n* MEDIA *of newspaper, magazine* alte Ausgabe *f*, alte Nummer *f*; ~ **load** *n* TRANSP Rückladung *f*

backlog *n* GEN COMM Arbeitsrückstand *m*, Auftragsrückstand *m*; ~ **demand** *n* GEN COMM Nachholbedarf *m*; ~ **of demand** *n* ECON Nachholbedarf *m*; ~ **of final orders** *n* GEN COMM Bestand *m* an festen Aufträgen

backlogged: ~ **orders** *n pl* GEN COMM Auftragsbestand *m*, unerledigte Aufträge *m pl*

backlog: ~ **order books** *n* GEN COMM Auftragsbestand *m*; ~ **of orders** *n* GEN COMM Auftragsbestand *m*, Auftragsrückstand *m*; ~ **of payments** *n* ACC Zahlungsrückstände *m pl*; ~ **of work** *n* GEN COMM Arbeitsrückstand *m*

back: ~ **margin** *n* MEDIA hinterer Rand *m*; ~ **number** *n* MEDIA *of newspaper, magazine* alte Ausgabe *f*, alte Nummer *f*; ~ **order** *n* S&M noch nicht erledigter Auftrag *m*; ~ **pay** *n* HRM Lohnnachzahlung *f*, Nachzahlung *f*; ~ **payment** *n* HRM Lohnnachzahlung *f*, Nachzahlung *f*

back-pedal *vi* GEN COMM, MGMNT einen Rückzieher machen (*infrml*)

back: ~ **rent** *n* HRM rückständige Miete *f*

backscratching *n* *BrE infrml* (*cf* *log-rolling AmE*) POL Politik *f* gegenseitiger Unterstützung, Bildung *f* von Seilschaften (*infrml*)

back: ~ **section** *n* GEN COMM, MEDIA *of magazines* Rückseite *f*

backslash *n* COMP Backslash *m* (*jarg*), inverser Schrägstrich *m*, negativer Schrägstrich *m*, umgekehrter Schrägstrich *m*; ~ **key** *n* COMP Backslash-Taste *f* (*jarg*), Taste *f* für negativen Schrägstrich

backspace 1. *n* COMP Rückschritt *m*, Backspace-Taste *f*, Rücktaste *f*; **2.** *vi* COMP zurücksetzen

backspace: ~ **character** *n* COMP Rückschrittzeichen *nt*

backspread *n* STOCK *options* Arbitrage *f* bei unternormalen Kursdifferenzen, Arbitrage *f* bei unternormalen Preisdifferenzen

backstop *n* IND Anschlag *m*, Begrenzungsanschlag *m*, Gegenhalter *m*, hinterer Anschlag *m*, Rückanschlag *m*

backstrip *n* MEDIA *of book* Buchrücken *m*, Rücken *m*, *print* Buchdruck *m*

back: ~ **tax** *n* TAX Steuerrückstände *m pl*; **~-to-back credit** *n* BANK Gegenakkreditiv *nt*, Gegenkredit *m*, Unterakkreditiv *nt*, Zweitakkreditiv *nt*; **~-to-back loan** *n* FIN wechselseitiger Kredit *m*, Parallelkredit *m*; **~-to-back transaction** *n* BANK Gegengeschäft *nt*; **~-to-back transfers** *n pl* BANK Parallelüberweisungen *f pl*

backtrack *vi* GEN COMM, MGMNT *from plan, promise* sich zurückziehen, einen Rückzieher machen (*infrml*)

backup *n* COMP Sicherungskopie *f*, Backup *nt*, GEN COMM Rückgriff *m*, *support* Unterstützung *f*, INS Rückgriff *m*; ~ **copy** *n* COMP *of file, data* Sicherungskopie *f*; ~ **credit line** *n* *AmE* BANK *for commercial paper issues* Auffang-Kreditlinie *f*; ~ **facilities** *n pl* GEN COMM *installations* Deckungslinie *f*, Stützungsfazilität *f*; ~ **facility** *n* COMP Backup-Einrichtung *f*; ~ **file** *n* COMP *electronic copy* Sicherungsdatei *f*; ~ **line** *n* BANK Auffanglinie *f*, Deckungslinie *f*, Rückgrifflinie *f*, FIN Deckungsfazilität *f*, Deckungslinie *f*; ~ **memory** *n* COMP Sicherungsspeicher *m*; ~ **service** *n* GEN COMM Hilfsdienst *m*, S&M Kundendienst *m*; ~ **support** *n* STOCK Anschlußaufträge *m pl*; ~ **utility program** *n* COMP Backup-Dienstprogramm *nt*; ~ **withholding** *n* *AmE* TAX zusätzliche Einbehaltung *f*, zusätzliche Steuereinbehaltung *f*; ~ **withholding tax** *n* *AmE* TAX Anschlußquellensteuer *f*

backwardation *n* STOCK Deport *m*; ~ **business** *n* STOCK Deportgeschäft *nt*; ~ **rate** *n* FIN Deportsatz *m*

backward: **~-bending labor supply curve** *AmE*, **~-bending labour supply curve** *BrE* *n* ECON anomale Kurve *f* des Arbeitskräfteangebots, regressive Arbeitskräfteangebotskurve *f*; **~-bending supply curve** *n* ECON anomale Angebotskurve *f*; ~ **integration** *n* ECON, IND, MGMNT Rückwärtsintegration *f*; ~ **linkage** *n* ECON beschaffungsseitige Verflechtung *f*, Verflechtung *f* mit vorgelagerten Wirtschaftszweigen; ~ **scheduling** *n* MGMNT Rückwärtsplanung *f*, Rückwärtsterminierung *f*, Rückplanung *f*; ~ **vertical integration** *n* ECON, IND, MGMNT vertikale Integration *f*

backwash: ~ **effect** *n* ECON Aushöhlungseffekt *m*

backyard: **not in my ~** *phr* (*NIMBY*) ENVIR, POL nicht bei uns

BACS *abbr* BANK (*Banks Automated Clearing Services*) automatischer Banken-Abrechnungsdienst *m*, automatisiertes Banken-Clearing-System *nt*, automatisches Banken-Verrechnungssystem *nt*, *BrE* (*Banks Automated*

Clearing System) Gesellschaft für elektronischen Zahlungsverkehr

bad 1. *adj* GEN COMM *quality* schlecht; **2.** *n* ECON Übel *nt*, negatives Gut *nt*, negativer externer Effekt *m*, volkswirtschaftliche Kosten *pl*, soziale Kosten *pl*

bad: ~ **bargain** *n* GEN COMM schlechter Kauf *m*, schlechtes Geschäft *nt*; ~ **break** *n* *infrml* GEN COMM Fauxpas *m*; ~ **buy** *n* GEN COMM schlechter Kauf *m*, schlechtes Geschäft *nt*; ~ **check** *AmE*, ~ **cheque** *BrE n* BANK ungedeckter Scheck *m*; ~ **debt** *n* ACC zweifelhafte Forderung *f*, BANK, FIN uneinbringliche Forderung *f*, zweifelhafte Forderung *f*; ~ **debt loss** *n* ACC als Verlust abgebuchte Forderung *f*, BANK aus zweifelhaften Forderungen herrührender Verlust *m*, ECON Verlust *m* durch uneinbringliche Forderungen, FIN aus zweifelhaften Forderungen herrührender Verlust *m*; ~ **debtor** *n* BANK zahlungsunfähiger Schuldner *m*, zahlungsfähige Schuldnerin *f*; ~ **debt provision** *n* ACC, BANK, FIN Rückstellung *f* für zweifelhafte Forderungen, Rückstellung *f* für Risikokredite, Wertberichtigung *f* auf uneinbringliche Forderungen; ~ **debt recovery** *n* ACC Eingang *m* von bereits als Verlust abgebuchten Forderungen; ~ **and doubtful debt** *n* (*B&D*) BANK notleidender Kredit *m*, Risikokredit *m*, uneinbringliche und zweifelhafte Forderung *f*; ~ **investment** *n* BANK, FIN Fehlinvestition *f*; ~ **loan** *n* BANK notleidender Kredit *m*; ~ **loan provision** *n* BANK, FIN Rückstellung *f* für notleidende Kredite, Rückstellung *f* für Risikokredite

badly: **~-imposed page** *n* MEDIA *print* schlecht ausgeschossene Seite *f*; ~ **in debt** *phr* BANK hoch verschuldet

bad: ~ **management** *n* MGMNT Leitungsschwäche *f*, schlechte Führung *f*, schlechtes Management *nt*; ~ **name** *n* GEN COMM schlechter Ruf *m*; ~ **paper** *n* *infrml* BANK fauler Wechsel *m* (*infrml*); ~ **reputation** *n* GEN COMM schlechter Ruf *m*; ~ **sector** *n* COMP Fehlersektor *m*, fehlerhafter Sektor *m*; ~ **title** *n* LAW *contracts* Rechtsmangel *m*; ~ **will** *n* ACC *consolidated accounts* negativer Firmenwert *m*, GEN COMM negativer Firmenwert *m*, schlechter Ruf *m*; ~ **work** *n* GEN COMM Ausschuß *m*, fehlerhafte Arbeit *f*

BAEC *abbr* (*British Agricultural Export Council*) IMP/EXP britischer Rat für Agrarexporte

bag *n* LEIS, TRANSP Tasche *f*, S&M *packaging* Tragetasche *f*, Trägetüte *f*

baggage *n* LEIS, TRANSP Gepäck *nt*, Reisegepäck *nt*; ~ **allowance** *n* IMP/EXP, LEIS, TRANSP Freigepäck *nt*; ~ **check** *n* LEIS, TRANSP Gepäckschein *m*, Gepäckkontrolle *f*; ~ **checked** *n* LEIS, TRANSP aufgegebenes Gepäck *nt*, TRANSP überprüftes Gepäck *nt*; ~ **excess** *n* LEIS, TRANSP Mehrgepäck *nt*; ~ **handling** *n* LEIS, TRANSP Gepäckabfertigung *f*, Gepäckbeförderung *f*; ~ **reclaim area** *n* LEIS, TRANSP Gepäckausgabe *f*; ~ **tag** *n* LEIS, TRANSP Gepäckanhänger *m*, Gepäckaufkleber *m*; ~ **trolley** *n* LEIS, TRANSP Kofferkuli *m*; ~ **vehicle** *n* LEIS, TRANSP Gepäckwagen *m*

bagging *n* TRANSP *of cargo* Einsacken *nt*

bagman *n* *AmE infrml* FIN *person accepting a bribe* Bestochene(r) *mf* [*decl. as adj*], POL Kassierer oder Verteiler von Schutz- oder Schmiergeldern, S&M Schlepper *m* (*infrml*)

bail *n* LAW Auslösung *f*, Kaution *f*, Bürgschaft *f*, Sicherheitsleistung *f*

bail out 1. *vt* LAW die Kaution stellen für, gegen Kaution freibekommen; **2.** *vi infrml* GEN COMM *escape from an awkward situation* aussteigen (*infrml*); ◆ **bail sb out** GEN COMM *infrml* jdm aus der Klemme helfen, LAW die Kaution für jdn stellen, jdn durch Kaution aus der Haft freibekommen

bail: **~ bond** *n* LAW Haftkaution *f*, Kaution *f*, Bürgschaftsurkunde *f*

bailee *n* LAW treuhänderischer Verwalter *m*, treuhänderische Verwalterin *f*, Verwahrer, in *m,f*

bailiff *n* LAW *law officer* Gerichtsdiener *m*, Gerichtsvollzieher *m*, Vollstreckungsbeamte(r) *m* [decl. as adj], Vollstreckungsbeamtin *f*, PROP *estate, land supervisor* Gutsverwalter, in *m,f*

bailing: **~ out** *n* STOCK Abstoßen *nt*, Aussteigen *nt* (*infrml*)

bailment *n* BANK Verwahrung *f*, GEN COMM Hinterlegung *f*, Hinterlegungsvertrag *m*, LAW *of deposit* Hinterlegungsvertrag *m*, Verwahrung *f*, *release on bail* Haftentlassung *f* gegen Sicherheitsleistung

bailor *n* BANK, GEN COMM *in safekeeping* Einleger, in *m,f*, Hinterleger, in *m,f*, Übergeber, in *m,f*

bail-out *n* GEN COMM Notverkauf *m*

bait: **~ advertising** *n* AmE S&M Lockvogelwerbung *f*, Werbung *f* mit Lockartikeln; **~ and switch advertising** *n* AmE S&M *consumer deception* Lockvogelwerbung *f*; **~ and switch selling** *n* AmE S&M Lockvogelverkaufsaktion *f*

bal. *abbr* (*balance*) ACC Saldo *m*, BANK Kontostand *m*, Saldo *m*, FIN Saldo *m*

balance 1. *n* (*bal.*) ACC, BANK, FIN *of account* Kontostand *m*, GEN COMM *equilibrium* Ausgleich *m*; **2.** *vt* ACC, BANK, FIN *add up* abschließen, saldieren, *equalize* ausgleichen, *pay off* begleichen; ◆ **~ an account** *n* ACC, BANK, FIN ein Konto abschließen, ein Konto abstimmen, ein Konto ausgleichen; **~ the books** ACC die Bücher abschließen, die Bilanz ziehen; **~ the budget** FIN den Haushalt ausgleichen, den Staatshaushalt ausgleichen; **~ the cash** *infrml* ACC Kasse machen (*infrml*); **~ sth against sth** ACC etw gegen etw aufrechnen, GEN COMM etw mit etw ausgleichen

balance out *vt* ACC, BANK, FIN, GEN COMM ausgleichen; **2.** *vi* ACC, BANK, FIN, GEN COMM sich ausgleichen

balance: **~ of account** *n* ACC Saldo *m*; **~ book** *n* ACC, FIN Saldenbuch *nt*; **~ brought down** *n* (*b/d*) ACC, FIN Saldovortrag *m*, Vortrag *m*, Übertrag *m*; **~ brought forward** *n* (*b/f*) ACC, FIN Saldovortrag *m*, Übertrag *nt*, Vortrag *m*; **~ of capital movements** *n* ECON Kapitalverkehrsbilanz *f*, Kapitalbilanz *f*; **~ carried forward** *n* (*b/f*) ACC, FIN Saldovortrag *m*, Übertrag *nt*, Vortrag *m*

balanced *adj* ACC ausgeglichen; **~ budget** *n* ECON, FIN ausgeglichener Haushalt *m*, ausgeglichenes Budget *nt*; **~ budget multiplier** *n* ECON Multiplikatorwirkung eines ausgeglichenen öffentlichen Haushalts; **~ growth** *n* ECON Gleichgewichtswachstum *nt*, gleichgewichtiges Wachstum *nt*, Wachstumsgleichgewicht *nt*; **~ portfolio** *n* STOCK ausgewogener Wertpapierbestand *m*

balance: **~ due to creditor** *n* BANK Restschuld *f* zugunsten des Gläubigers; **~ due to debtor** *n* BANK Restschuld *f* zugunsten des Schuldners; **~ for official financing** *n* (*BOF*) ECON *balance of payments* Devisenbilanz *f*; **~ in bank** *n* BANK Bankguthaben *nt*, Habensaldo *m*; **~ in current account** *n* ECON Leistungsbilanz *f*; **~ of invisible trade** *n* ECON

Dienstleistungsbilanz *f*; **~ of invoice** *n* ACC Rechnungssaldo *m*; **~ in your favor** *AmE*, **~ in your favour** *BrE n* BANK Saldo *m* zu ihren Gunsten; **~ item** *n* ACC Bilanzposten *m*; **~ on capital account** *n* ECON Kapitalverkehrsbilanz *f*; **~ on current account** *n* ECON Leistungsbilanz *f*; **~ on services** *n* ECON Dienstleistungsbilanz *f*; **~ of payments** *n* (*BOP*) ECON Zahlungsbilanz *f*; **~ of payments deficit** *n* ECON Defizit *nt* der Zahlungsbilanz, Zahlungsbilanzdefizit *nt*; **~ of payments equilibrium** *n* ECON Zahlungsbilanzgleichgewicht *nt*; **~ of payments surplus** *n* ECON Zahlungsbilanzüberschuß *m*; **~ of power** *n* GEN COMM Gleichgewicht *nt* der Kräfte

balances: **~ abroad** *n pl* BANK Auslandsguthaben *nt pl*

balance: **~ sheet** *n* (*B/S*) ACC Bilanz *f*, Jahresabschluß *m*, Abschlußblatt *nt*; **off the ~ sheet** ACC, ECON, FIN bilanzunwirksam; **~ sheet auditor** *n* ACC Bilanzprüfer, in *m,f*; **~ sheet format** *n* ACC Bilanzformblatt *nt*; **~ sheet for settlement purposes** *n* ACC Auseinandersetzungsbilanz *f*; **~ sheet item** *n* ACC Bilanzposten *m*; **~ sheet ratio** *n* ACC Bilanzkennzahl *f*; **~ sheet reserves** *n pl* ACC, INS Rücklagen *f pl*, Rückstellungen *f pl*, stille Reserven *f pl*; **~ sheet supplement** *n* ACC Bilanzanlage *f*; **~ sheet value of shares** *n* ACC *accounting value of shareholders' equity* verbrieftes Grundkapital *nt*; **~ of trade** *n* ECON, GEN COMM Handelsbilanz *f*; **~ of unclassifiable transactions** *n* ECON Restposten *m pl* der Zahlungsbilanz

balancing 1. *adj* GEN COMM ausgleichend; **2.** *n* ACC, FIN Ausbuchung *f*, Abgleich *m*, Bilanzierung *f*, GEN COMM Bilanzziehung *f*

balancing: **~ of an account** *n* ACC, FIN Kontoabschluß *m*, Bilanzierung *f*; **~ against** *n* ACC Aufrechnung *f*; **~ item** *n* ECON Ausgleichsposten *m*; **~ of portfolio** *n* INS Gefahrenausgleich *m*, Risikoausgleich *m*, Wagnisausgleich *m*

bale *n* (*B*) IND *bundle* Ballen *m*, Ballenware *f*, *unit of mass* Bale *nt*, TRANSP *bundle* Ballen *m*, *unit of mass* Bale *nt*; **~ capacity** *n* TRANSP *shipping* Laderauminhalt *m* für Ballen; **~ cubic meters** *AmE*, **~ cubic metres** *BrE n pl* (*BC*) IND Ballenkubikmeter *m pl*

bale out *see bail out*

baling *n* TRANSP *shipping* Verpacken von Waren in Ballen

ballast *n* IND *shipping* Ballast *m*

balloon *n* BANK hoher Restbetrag *f* einer Anleihe; **~ advertising** *n* S&M Fesselballonwerbung *f*; **~ interest** *n* STOCK hoher Zins *m*; **~ line** *n* GEN COMM *advertising* Sprechblase *f*; **~ loan** *n* BANK Darlehen mit Abschlußzahlung, die die Darlehenshöhe übersteigt; **~ note** *n* BANK Schuldschein *m* mit hoher Resttilgung vor Fälligkeit; **~ payment** *n* BANK hohe Abschlußzahlung *f*, überdurchschnittlich hohe Tilgungszahlung bei Fälligkeit der Abschlußzahlung; **~ repayment** *n* BANK überdurchschnittlich hohe Tilgungszahlung *f* bei Fälligkeit der Abschlußzahlung

ballot *n* HRM, POL *method of voting* Wahl *f*, Wahlgang *m*; **~ box** *n* HRM Wahlurne *f*; **~ paper** *n* HRM Stimmzettel *m*, Wahlzettel *m*

ballpark: **~ figure** *n infrml* GEN COMM über den Daumen gepeilter Wert *m* (*infrml*)

Baltic: **The ~** *n BrE* (*Baltic Mercantile & Shipping Exchange*) STOCK Londoner Frachten- und Warenbörse; **~ Exchange** *n BrE* (*Baltic Mercantile & Shipping*

Exchange) STOCK Londoner Frachten- und Warenbörse; ~ **Freight Index** *n* (*BFI*) IMP/EXP *shipping* Londoner Frachtenindex; ~ **Futures Exchange** *n* STOCK Baltische Terminbörse *f*; ~ **International Freight Futures Exchange** *n BrE* (*BIFFEX*) STOCK internationale Frachtterminbörse in London; ~ **Mercantile & Shipping Exchange** *n BrE* (*The Baltic, Baltic Exchange*) STOCK Londoner Frachten- und Warenbörse; ~ **Sea** *n* GEN COMM Ostsee *f*

BAM *abbr* (*bulk air mail*) COMMS Massenluftpost *f*

bamboo: ~ **curtain** *n* POL Bambusvorhang *m*

ban 1. *n* ECON Sperre *f*, GEN COMM Sperre *f*, Verbot *nt*, IMP/EXP Sperre *f*, *on exports* Ausfuhrverbot *nt*, LAW Verbot *nt*; ~ **on strikes** *n* GEN COMM, HRM, IND Streikverbot *nt*; **2.** *vt* LAW verbieten

BAN *abbr* (*bond anticipation note*) STOCK Obligationengutschein *m*

band *n* ECON *currency rates*, TAX *VAT* Bandbreite *f*, Spannweite *f*; ~ **advertising** *n* S&M Streifenanzeige *f*

b&b *abbr* (*bed and breakfast*) LEIS Übernachtung *f* mit Frühstück

B&D *abbr* (*bad and doubtful debt*) BANK notleidender Kredit *m*, Risikokredit *m*, uneinbringliche und zweifelhafte Forderung *f*

banded: ~ **offer** *n* S&M *for two products* gebündeltes Angebot *nt*, Sonderangebot *nt*; ~ **pack** *n* COMMS Packung *f*, GEN COMM, S&M *for same product* Mehrstückpackung *f*, *for two different products* Packung *f*

band: ~ **of fluctuation** *n* ECON *currency rate* Schwankungsbreite *f*

banding *n* HRM Vereinfachung *f* der Lohnstruktur

band: ~ **saw** *n* IND Bandsäge *f*

bandwagon: ~ **effect** *n* ECON Mitläufereffekt *m*

bandwidth *n* COMP Bandbreite *f*, HRM *flexitime* Bandbreite *f* der Arbeitszeit, MEDIA *radio* Bandbreite *f*

bank 1. *n* (*bk*) BANK Bank *f*, Bankinstitut *nt*, Geldinstitut *nt*, Kreditinstitut *nt*; **2.** *vt* BANK *money* einzahlen, zur Bank bringen; **3.** *vi* ♦ ~ **with** BANK ein Konto unterhalten bei

bankable *adj* BANK bankfähig, diskontfähig, ~ **asset** *n* BANK bankfähiger Vermögenswert *m*; ~ **bill** *n* BANK bankfähiger Wechsel *m*, diskontierbarer Wechsel *m*; ~ **paper** *n* BANK diskontfähiger Wechsel *m*

bank: ~ **acceptance** *n* BANK Bankakzept *nt*, Bankwechsel *m*; ~ **accommodation** *n* BANK Bankdarlehen *nt*, Bankkonto *nt*, Kredit *m*; ~ **account** *n* BANK Bankkonto *nt*; ~ **address** *n* BANK Bankadresse *f*; ~ **advance** *n* BANK Bankdarlehen *nt*, Bankkredit *m*; ~ **advice** *n* BANK Bankavis *nt*, Bankanzeige *f*; ~ **annuities** *n pl* BANK konsolidierte Staatsanleihen *f pl*, Staatspapiere *nt pl*, FIN, STOCK Staatspapiere *nt pl*; ~ **assets** *n pl* ACC bankfähige Vermögenswerte *m pl*, BANK Bankvermögen *nt*; ~ **audit** *n* BANK Bankrevision *f*, Bankkontrolle *f*; ~ **balance** *n* ACC Guthabensaldo *m*, BANK Bankguthaben *nt*, Banksaldo *nt*, Guthabensaldo *m*, FIN Guthabensaldo *m*; ~ **bill** *n* BANK *AmE* (*cf banknote BrE*) *note* Banknote *f*, Geldschein *m*, *of exchange* Bankakzept *nt*, Bankscheck *m*, Bankwechsel *m*, *draft* Banktratte *f*; ~ **bond** *n* BANK Bankanleihe *f*, Bankobligation *f*; ~ **book** *n* BANK *customer* Bankbuch *nt*, Sparbuch *nt*, FIN Bankbuch *nt*; ~ **branch** *n* BANK Bankfiliale *f*; ~ **capital** *n* BANK Bankkapital *nt*; ~ **card** *n* BANK Bankkarte *f*, Scheckkarte *f*; ~ **cash ratio** *n* BANK Liquiditätskennziffer *f*; ~ **certificate** *n* BANK

Bankzertifikat *nt*; ~ **charges** *n pl* BANK Bankgebühren *f pl*, Bankkosten *pl*, FIN Spesen *pl*; ~ **charter** *n* BANK Konzessionsurkunde *f* einer Bank

Bank: ~ **Charter Act** *n BrE* BANK Gesetz zur Regelung der Notenausgabe der Bank von England

bank: ~ **check** *AmE*, ~ **cheque** *BrE* *n* BANK Bankscheck *m*, Kassenanweisung *f*; ~ **of circulation** *n* BANK Notenbank *f*; ~ **clearing** *n* BANK Banken-Clearing *nt*, Bankenabrechnung *f*; ~ **clerk** *n* BANK Bankangestellte(r) *mf* [decl. as adj]; ~ **code** *n* BANK routing Bankleitzahl *f* (*BLZ*); ~ **commission** *n* BANK Bankprovision *f*; ~ **crash** *n* BANK Bankenkrach *m*, Bankzusammenbruch *m*; ~ **credit** *n* BANK Bankkredit *m*; ~ **credit transfer** *n* BANK Banküberweisung *f*; ~ **debenture** *n* BANK Schuldverschreibung *f* zugunsten einer Bank; ~ **debts** *n pl* BANK Bankverbindlichkeiten *f pl*; ~ **demand deposit** *n* BANK kurzfristige Einlage *f*, Sichteinlage *f*; ~ **deposit** *n* BANK Bankeinlage *f*, kurzfristige Einlage *f*; ~ **deposit insurance** *n* BANK *Banking Act of 1935* Depotversicherung *f*, Einlagenversicherung *f*, INS Bankeinlagenversicherung *f*; ~ **deposit monies** *n pl* BANK Bankeinlagen *f pl*; ~ **deposit rate** *n* BANK Einlagenzins *m*, Sparzinsen *m pl*, Zinssätze *m pl* auf Spareinlagen; ~ **discount** *n* BANK Bankdiskont *m*, Wechseldiskont *m*; ~ **discount rate** *n* BANK Bankdiskont *m*, Bankdiskontsatz *m*, Wechseldiskont *m*; ~ **draft** *n* (*B/Dft*) BANK Bankakzept *nt*, Bankscheck *m*, Banktratte *m*, Bankwechsel *m*; ~ **efficiency** *n* BANK Bankeffizienz *f*; ~**endorsed** *adj* BANK bankenindossiert, bankgiriert

Bank: ~ **of England** *n* (*B of E, BE*) BANK, ECON englische Zentralbank, ≈ Deutsche Bundesbank *f* (*BBk*)

banker *n* BANK Bankangestellte(r) *mf* [decl. as adj], Bankkauffrau *f*, Bankkaufmann *m*, Banker, in *m,f* (*infrml*), Bankier *m*; ~**'s acceptance** *n* BANK Bankakzept *nt*; ~**'s bill** *n* BANK Bankwechsel *m*; ~**'s card** *n* BANK Scheckkarte *f*; ~**'s check** *AmE*, ~**'s cheque** *BrE* *n* BANK Bankscheck *m*; ~**'s deposit rate** *n* BANK, FIN Zinssatz für Einlagen mit 7-tägiger Kündigung

bankers': ~ **deposits** *n pl BrE* BANK, ECON Zentralbankguthaben *nt* der Geschäftsbanken

banker: ~**'s draft** *n* BANK, FIN Bankakzept *nt*, Banktratte *f*, Bankwechsel *m*; ~**'s order** *n* BANK Bankanweisung *f*, Überweisungauftrag *m*, Zahlungsauftrag *m*, *standing order* Dauerauftrag *m*, FIN *standing order* Überweisungauftrag *m*, Zahlungsauftrag *m*; ~**'s reference** *n* BANK Bankauskunft *f*, Bankreferenz *f*, Kreditauskunft *f*; ~**'s turn** *n* BANK Verdienstspanne *f* der Bank

bank: ~ **examination** *n AmE* BANK Bankrevision *f*; ~ **examiner** *n AmE* BANK Bankrevisor, in *m,f*; ~ **facilities** *n pl* ACC Bankfazilitäten *f pl*, Kreditlinie *f*; ~**financed** *adj* BANK bankenfinanziert; ~ **financing** *n* BANK Bankfinanzierung *f*; ~ **float** *n* BANK Bankfloat *m*, Bankvalutierungsgewinn *m*

Bank: ~ **for International Settlements** *n* (*BIS*) BANK, ECON Bank *f* für Internationalen Zahlungsausgleich (*BIZ*)

bank: ~ **giro** *n BrE* BANK Banküberweisung *f*, Bankgiro *nt*, bargeldlose Zahlung *f*; ~ **giro credit** *n BrE* BANK Überweisungauftrag *m*; ~ **giro credit system** *n BrE* BANK automatisiertes Banküberweisungssystem *nt*, bargeldloser Zahlungsverkehr *m*; ~ **group** *n AmE* (*cf banking group BrE*) BANK Bankengruppe *f*, Bankenkette *f*, Bankenkonsortium *nt*, Bankkonzern *m*;

~ **guarantee** *n* BANK Bankbürgschaft *f*, Bankgarantie *f*, Einlagengarantie *f*; ~ **holding company** *n* BANK, GEN COMM Bank-Holdinggesellschaft *f*, Bankholding *nt*

Bank: ~ **Holding Company Act** *n* AmE BANK *of 1956* Gesetz *nt* über Bank-Holdinggesellschaften

bank: ~ **holiday** *n* BrE (*cf legal holiday AmE, cf statutory holiday AmE*) GEN COMM, HRM, LAW Bankfeiertag *m*, allgemeiner Feiertag *m*, gesetzlicher Feiertag *m*

banking *n* BANK Bankgeschäft *nt*, Bankwesen *nt*, Bankgewerbe *nt*; ~ **arrangements** *n pl* BANK Bankabsprachen *f pl*; ~ **audit** *n* BANK Bankrevision *f*; ~ **auditor** *n* BANK Bankrevisor, in *m,f*; ~ **business** *n* BANK Bankbetrieb *m*, Bankgeschäft *nt*; ~ **center** AmE, ~ **centre** BrE *n* BANK Bankplatz *m*; ~ **charges** *n pl* BANK Bankgebühren *f pl*; ~ **circles** *n pl* BANK Bankkreise *m pl*; ~ **community** *n* BANK Bankkreise *m pl*; ~ **day** *n* ACC Banktag *m*; ~ **establishment** *n* BANK Bank *f*, Bankhaus *nt*, Bankinstitut *nt*; ~ **group** *n* BrE (*cf bank group AmE*) BANK Bankengruppe *f*, Bankenkette *f*, Bankenkonsortium *nt*, Bankkonzern *m*; ~ **hours** *n pl* BANK Banköffnungszeiten *f pl*, Schalterstunden *f pl*; ~ **house** *n* BANK Bank *f*, Bankhaus *nt*, Bankinstitut *nt*; ~ **industry** *n* BANK Bankgewerbe *nt*, Kreditwirtschaft *f*; ~ **interest** *n* BANK Bankbeteiligung *f*; ~ **network** *n* BANK Banknetz *nt*

Banking: ~ **Ombudsman** *n* BrE BANK Ombudsfrau *f*, Ombudsmann *m*

banking: ~ **operation** *n* BANK Bankgeschäft *nt*; ~ **operations** *n pl* BANK Bankbetrieb *m*

Banking: ~ **School** *n* BrE BANK Gruppe *f* von Bankern

banking: ~ **sector** *n* BANK Bankensektor *m*; ~ **services** *n pl* BANK Bankdienstleistungen *f pl*; ~ **subsidiary** *n* BANK Banktochter *f*, Tochterinstitut *nt*

Banking: ~ **Supervision Division** *n* BrE BANK Bankenaufsicht der Bank von England

banking: ~ **system** *n* BANK, FIN Bankenapparat *m*, Bankensystem *nt*; ~ **transaction** *n* BANK Bankgeschäft *nt*, Banktransaktion *f*; ~ **transfer system** *n* BANK bargeldloser Zahlungsverkehr *m*, Giroverkehr *m*

bank: ~ **interest** *n* BANK Bankzinsen *m pl*; ~ **of issue** *n* BANK Emissionsbank *f*; ~ **lending** *n* BANK Ausleihungen *f pl*, Kreditgeschäft *nt* der Banken, Bankkredite *m pl*; ~ **lending policy** *n* BANK Kreditpolitik *f* der Banken; ~ **lending rate** *n* BANK Kreditzinssatz *m*; ~ **lien** *n* BANK Pfandrecht *nt* einer Bank, Zurückbehaltungsrecht *m* einer Bank; ~ **line** *n* BANK Kreditlinie *f* einer Bank; ~ **liquidity** *n* BANK Bankenliquidität *f*; ~ **loan** *n* BANK Bankdarlehen *nt*, Bankkredit *m*; ~ **loan rate** *n* BANK Zinssatz *m* für Bankkredite; ~ **manager** *n* FIN Bankdirektor, in *m,f*; ~ **messenger** *n* BANK Bankbote *m*, Bankbotin *f*; ~ **money** *n* BANK Buchgeld *nt*, Giralgeld *nt*, Sichteinlagen *f pl*

banknote *n* BrE (*cf bank bill AmE*) BANK Banknote *f*, Geldschein *m*; ~ **trading** *n* BANK Banknotenhandel *m*

bank: ~ **officer** *n* BANK Bankangestellte(r) *mf* [decl. as adj], Bankbeamte(r) *m* [decl. as adj], Bankbeamtin *f*; ~ **overdraft** *n* BANK Überziehungskredit *m*; ~ **paper** *n* BANK Bankpapier *nt*, Bankwechsel *m*; ~ **post bill** *n* (*BPB*) BANK Solawechsel der Bank von England; ~ **rate** *n* BANK Diskontsatz *m*, FIN Diskontsatz *m* der Notenbank; ~ **reconciliation** *n* BANK Kontoabstimmung *f* zwischen Bank und Kunde; ~ **remittance** *n* BANK Banküberweisung *f*; ~ **requirements** *n pl* BANK Bankvorschriften *f pl*; ~ **reserve** *n* BANK Bankreserve

f, Bankrücklage *f*; ~ **return** *n* BrE BANK *Bank of England* Bankausweis *m*

bankroll *n* AmE BANK Banknotenbündel *nt*

bank: ~ **routing number** *n* BANK Bankleitzahl *f* (*BLZ*); ~ **run** *n* BANK Botengang *m*; ~ **runner** *n* BANK Bankbote *m*, Bankbotin *f*

bankrupt *adj* ACC, BANK, FIN, GEN COMM bankrott, zahlungsunfähig, insolvent, pleite (*infrml*); ◆ **be** ~ GEN COMM bankrott sein, zahlungsunfähig sein; **go** ~ FIN in Konkurs gehen, Konkurs machen, GEN COMM bankrott gehen, bankrott machen, pleite gehen (*infrml*), pleite machen (*infrml*)

bankruptcy *n* ACC Konkurs *m*, Konkursverfahren *nt*, BANK, ECON Pleite *f* (*infrml*), FIN Konkurs *m*, GEN COMM, STOCK Pleite *f* (*infrml*); ~ **act** *n* ACC, LAW Konkursgesetz *nt*, Konkursordnung *f*, Konkursrecht *nt*; ~ **committee** *n* FIN Konkursausschuß *m*; ~ **court** *n* LAW Konkursgericht *nt*; ~ **estate** *n* LAW Konkursmasse *f*; ~ **notice** *n* LAW richterliche Zahlungsaufforderung *f* mit Konkursdrohung; ~ **proceedings** *n pl* LAW Konkursverfahren *nt*; ~ **property** *n* LAW Konkursmasse *f*

Banks: ~ **Automated Clearing Services** *n* (*BACS*) BANK automatisierter Banken-Abrechnungsdienst *m*, elektronisches Banken-Clearing-System *nt*, automatisches Banken-Verrechnungssystem *nt*

bank: ~ **securities** *n pl* BANK Bankwertpapiere *nt pl*; ~ **selling rate** *n* BANK, FIN, STOCK Abgabesatz *m* der Bank, Verkaufskurs *m* der Bank, Bankbriefkurs *m*; ~ **service charge** *n* BANK Bankgebühr *f*, Bearbeitungsgebühr *f*; ~ **settlement system** *n* BANK Bankabrechnungsverkehr *m*; ~ **settlement voucher** *n* BANK Bankabrechnungsbeleg *m*; ~ **shares** *n pl* BANK Bankaktien *f pl*, Bankwerte *m pl*; ~ **statement** *n* BANK *of bank's financer* Bankauszug *m*, *of customer account* Kontoauszug *m*; ~ **switching** *n* COMP Bankauswahlverfahren *nt*; ~ **teller** *n* BANK Bankkassierer, in *m,f*; ~ **teller card** *n* BANK Kassiererkarte *f*; ~-**to-bank lending** *n* BANK Interbank-Kreditgeschäft *nt*; ~ **transaction** *n* BANK Bankgeschäft *nt*; ~ **transfer** *n* BANK Banküberweisung *f*; ~ **trust department** *n* BANK Treuhandabteilung *f* der Bank; ~ **turnovers** *n pl* FIN Bankumsätze *m pl*

banner *n* S&M *in procession* Spruchband *nt*, Transparent *nt*; ◆ **in** ~ **headlines** MEDIA in Balkenüberschriften

banner: ~ **headline** *n* MEDIA Balkenüberschrift *f*, Schlagzeilen *f pl*; ~ **year** *n* GEN COMM erfolgreiches Jahr *nt*

ban: ~ **on export** *n* IMP/EXP Ausfuhrsperre *f*, Ausfuhrstopp *m*; ~ **on imports** *n* IMP/EXP Einfuhrsperre *f*, Einfuhrstopp *m*, Einfuhrverbot *nt*; ~ **on interest payments** *n* BANK *in deposits of nonresidents* Verzinsungsverbot *nt*, Zinszahlungsverbot *nt*; ~ **on strikes** *n* HRM Streikverbot *nt*

bar 1. *n* BANK Ausschluß *m*, LAW Anwaltschaft *f*, Anwaltsberuf *m*; 2. *vt* ◆ ~ **sb** GEN COMM jdn ausschließen, jdm den Zutritt versagen, LAW jdn ausschließen

BARB *abbr* (*Broadcasters Audience Research Board*) MEDIA Ausschuß für Rundfunk-Höreranalysen

bar: ~ **chart** *n* GEN COMM, MATH *statistics* Balkendiagramm *nt*, Säulendiagramm *nt*, Säulenschaubild *nt*, Stabdiagramm *nt*

Barclays: ~ **Index** *n* STOCK Barclays Index *m*

bar: ~ **code** *n* COMP Strichcode *m*; ~~-**coded identifica-**

tion number *n* COMP strichcodierte Artikelnummer *f*; **~-coded product** *n* S&M strichcodiertes Erzeugnis *nt*; **~ code marking** *n* COMP Strichcodierung *f*; **~ code reader** *n* COMP Strichcodeleser *m*; **~ code scanner** *n* COMP Strichcodelesegerät *nt*, Strichcodeleser *m*

bare *adj* INS ohne Versicherungsschutz; **~-bones version** *n* COMP Basismodell *nt*; **~ contract** *n* LAW einfacher Vertrag *m*; **~ necessities** *n pl* ECON Grundbedürfnisse *nt pl*

bargain 1. *n* FIN Abschluß *m*, Börsengeschäft *nt*, Geschäft *nt*, GEN COMM *deal* Geschäft *nt*, Handel *m*, *agreement* Vereinbarung *f*, *transaction* Abschluß *m*, *article bought cheaply* guter Kauf *m*, Schnäppchen *nt* (*infrml*), *cheap article* billige Ware *f*, *special offer* Sonderangebot *nt*, S&M günstiger Kauf *m*, STOCK Abschluß *m*; **2.** *vi* GEN COMM *negotiate* handeln; ♦ **~ about** GEN COMM, S&M handeln um, *haggle* feilschen um; **~ down** GEN COMM *price* herunterhandeln auf [+acc]; **~ over sth** GEN COMM *haggle* um etw feilschen, um etw handeln; **~ with sb** GEN COMM mit jdm verhandeln

bargain: **~ basement** *n* S&M *store* Abteilung *f* für Sonderangebote; **on ~-basement terms** *phr* S&M zu Sonderangebotsbedingungen; **~ counter** *n* S&M Theke *f* für Sonderangebote, Wühltisch *m*; **~ goods** *n pl* GEN COMM Niedrigpreiswaren *f pl*; **~ hunter** *n infrml* S&M Schnäppchenjäger *m* (*infrml*), Schnäppchensucher *m* (*infrml*)

bargaining *n* GEN COMM Handeln *nt*, Verhandlung *f*; **~ agent** *n* HRM *unions* Verhandlungspartner, in *m,f* bei Tarifverhandlungen; **~ form** *n* HRM Verhandlungsform *f*; **~ level** *n* HRM Verhandlungsebene *f*; **~ partner** *n* HRM *unions* Verhandlungspartner, in *m,f*; **~ position** *n* GEN COMM Verhandlungsposition *f*; **~ power** *n* GEN COMM Verhandlungsmacht *f*, Verhandlungsstärke *f*; **~ range** *n* HRM Verhandlungsspielraum *m*; **~ scope** *n* HRM Verhandlungsspielraum *m*; **~ structure** *n* HRM Verhandlungsstruktur *f*; **~ table** *n* GEN COMM Verhandlungstisch *m*, HRM *unions* Tarifpartner *m pl*; **~ theory of wages** *n* ECON Verhandlungstheorie *f* des Lohns, Bargaining-Theorie *f* des Lohns; **~ unit** *n* HRM gewerkschaftliche Verhandlungsgruppe *f*, Tarifpartei *f*

bargain: **~ offer** *n* GEN COMM, S&M günstiges Angebot *nt*; **~ price** *n* GEN COMM Ausverkaufspreis *m*, Gelegenheitspreis *m*, Spottpreis *m*, Vorzugspreis *m*; **~ rate** *n* GEN COMM, LEIS, S&M Sonderpreis *m*; **~ and sale** *n* PROP Abtretungsvertrag *m*, Eigentumsübertragung *f*, Kaufvertrag *m*; **~ sale** *n* S&M Sonderverkauf *m*, Ausverkauf *m*

bar: **~ graph** *n* GEN COMM, MATH *statistics* Balkendiagramm *nt*, Säulendiagramm *nt*, Stabdiagramm *nt*

barometer *n* ECON *measuring trends* Stimmungsbarometer *nt*, Barometer *nt*; **~ stock** *n* STOCK Barometer-Aktie *f*

barometric: **~ firm leadership** *n* ECON trendanführendes Unternehmen *nt*, Trendführerschaft *f*

barred: **~ by the lapse of time** *phr* LAW verjährt

barrel *n* ENVIR Barrel *nt*, IND Tonne *f*, TRANSP Barrel *nt*, Faß *nt*

barrels: **~ per day** *n pl* (*b/d*) ECON, IND *oil industry* Barrel *nt pl* pro Tag

barrier *n* ECON Hindernis *nt*, Hürde *f*, Schranke *f*, GEN COMM Barriere *f*, Beschränkung *f*, Schranke *f*; **~ to entry** *n* ECON, IMP/EXP Marktzutrittsschranke *f*,

Zugangsbeschränkung *f*; **~ to exit** *n* ECON, IMP/EXP Marktaustrittsschranke *f* Marktaustrittsschranken *f pl*; **~ to trade** *n* ECON Handelshemmnis *nt*, Handelsrestriktion *f*, Handelsschranke *f*, Handelshindernis *nt*

barrister *n* BrE (*cf attorney AmE*) LAW Anwalt *m*, Anwältin *f*, Rechtsanwalt *m*, Rechtsanwältin *f*; **~-at-law** *n* BrE LAW Prozeßanwalt *m*

Barron's: **~ Group Stock Averages** *n pl* AmE STOCK Barron Aktiengruppendurchschnittswerte *m pl*

barter 1. *n* ECON, GEN COMM Naturaltausch *m*, Tauschhandel *m*, Bartergeschäft *nt*, Tausch *m*; **2.** *vt* ECON, GEN COMM tauschen; ♦ **~ sth for sth** GEN COMM etw gegen etw tauschen, etw gegen etw eintauschen; **3.** *vi* ECON, GEN COMM tauschen, Tauschhandel treiben

barter: **~ agreement** *n* ECON *international trade* Tauschhandelsabkommen *nt*; **~ contract** *n* LAW Koppelvertrag *m*; **~ economy** *n* ECON Bartergeschäft *nt*, Naturalwirtschaft *f*, Tauschwirtschaft *f*; **~ trade** *n* ECON Tauschhandel *m*; **~ transaction** *n* ECON Bartergeschäft *nt*, Tauschgeschäft *nt*, *international trade* Tauschhandel *m*

baryta: **~ paper** *n* ADMIN Barytpapier *nt*

base 1. *n* COMP *hardware* Basis *f*, GEN COMM Basis *f*, Stützpunkt *m*; **2.** *vt* ♦ **~ on** GEN COMM basieren auf [+dat], gründen auf [+acc]

base: **~ address** *n* COMP Basisadresse *f*

baseband *n* COMP Basisband *nt*

base: **~ budget** *n* ACC Basisbudget *nt*, Grundetat *m*; **~ of calculation** *n* GEN COMM Kalkulationsbasis *f*, Kalkulationsgrundlage *f*; **~ capital** *n* ECON Grundkapital *nt*; **~ configuration** *n* COMP Grundausstattung *f*, Grundkonfiguration *f*; **~ currency** *n* ECON Bezugswährung *f*

based *adj* GEN COMM ansässig, stationiert; ♦ **be ~ in** GEN COMM *company* seinen Sitz haben in [+dat], ansässig sein in [+dat], stationiert sein in [+dat], *person, work in* arbeiten in [+dat]; **be ~ on** GEN COMM *decision, opinion* basieren auf [+dat], beruhen auf [+dat], sich stützen auf [+acc]

base: **~ date** *n* STOCK *for comparison of share prices, returns* Basisdatum *nt*, Bezugstermin *m*; **~ lending rate** *n* BANK, ECON, FIN Leitzins *m*, Eckzins *m*, Mindestzinssatz *m*, Basiszins *m*

baseline *n* COMP, MATH *of diagram* Bezugslinie *f*, Grundlinie *f*, S&M *advertisement* Baseline *f*, Schlußzeile *f*

base: **~ load** *n* IND *energy* Grundlast *f*; **~ load power station** *n* IND Grundlastkraftwerk *nt*; **~ pay** *n* AmE ECON, HRM Grundlohn *m*, Ecklohn *m*, Grundgehalt *nt*; **~ pay rate** *n* ECON, HRM Ecklohn *m*, Ecklohntarif *m*; **~ price** *n* GEN COMM, TAX Ausgangspreis *m*, Grundpreis *m*; **~ product** *n* IND Hauptprodukt *nt*, Grundprodukt *nt*, wichtigstes Erzeugnis *nt*; **~ rate** *n* BANK, ECON, FIN Leitzins *m*, Zins *m* für erste Adressen, GEN COMM, IND Grundtarif *m*; **~ rent** *n* PROP Grundmiete *f*; **~ salary** *n* AmE HRM Grundgehalt *nt*; **~ sheet** *n* MEDIA Rohblatt *nt*; **~ weight** *n* MATH Basisgewicht *nt*; **~ year** *n* ECON, FIN Basisjahr *nt*, Vergleichsjahr *nt*; **~ year analysis** *n* ECON Basisjahranalyse *f*

BASIC *abbr* (*beginner's all-purpose symbolic instruction code*) COMP BASIC (*Beginner's All-Purpose Symbolic Instruction Code*)

basic: **~ agreement** *n* GEN COMM Rahmenabkommen *nt*;

~ **amount** *n* GEN COMM Grundbetrag *m*; ~ **arithmetical operations** *n pl* MATH Grundrechnungsarten *f pl*, Grundrechenarten *f pl*; ~ **balance** *n* ECON *balance of payments* Grundbilanz *f*; ~ **books** *n pl* FIN Renditetabellen *f pl*; ~ **commodity** *n* ECON Grundstoff *m*, Rohstoff *m*; ~ **concept** *n* GEN COMM *term* Grundbegriff *m*; ~ **currency** *n* GEN COMM zugrundeliegende Währung *f*; ~ **definition** *n* GEN COMM Grunddefinition *f*; ~ **earnings per share** *n pl* FIN Betriebsgewinn *m* pro Aktie; ~ **foodstuffs** *n pl* GEN COMM Grundnahrungsmittel *nt pl*; ~ **goods sector** *n* GEN COMM Grundstoffsektor *m*; ~ **grade** *n* HRM Standardsorte *f*; ~ **income** *n* FIN Grundeinkommen *nt*, Grundverdienst *m*; ~ **industry** *n* ECON, IND *primary industry* Grundindustrie *f*, Grundstoffindustrie *f*, Schlüsselindustrie *f*; ~ **input/output operating system** *n* (*BIOS*) COMP *software* Basiseingabe/Ausgabesystem *nt*; ~ **limits of liability** *n pl* INS Grundhaftungsgrenzen *f pl*, grundlegende Haftungsgrenzen *f pl*; ~ **material** *n* ECON Grundstoff *m*; ~ **media** *n pl* MEDIA Basismedien *nt pl*; ~ **message** *n* S&M *advertising* Grundaussage *f*; ~ **needs** *n pl* ECON Grundbedürfnisse *nt pl*; ~ **pay** *n* BrE ECON, HRM Ecklohn *m*, Grundlohn *m*, Grundgehalt *nt*; ~ **piece rate** *n* IND Akkordrichtsatz *m*; ~ **premium** *n* INS Grundprämie *f*, summenproportionaler Beitragsteil *m*; ~ **price** *n* GEN COMM Basispreis *m*, Grundpreis *m*, STOCK Erwerbskurs *m*; ~ **rate** *n* HRM Grundlohn *m*, Ecklohntarif *m*, S&M Anzeigengrundpreis *m*, TAX Eingangssatz *m*; ~-**rate tax** *n* TAX Steuer *f* zum einheitlichen Grundtarif, Grundtarifsteuer *f*; ~ **rating** *n* BANK Risikoklassifikation *f*; ~ **relief** *n* TAX Grundfreibetrag *m*; ~ **research** *n* GEN COMM, S&M Basisforschung *f*, Grundlagenforschung *f*; ~ **research cost** *n* S&M Basisforschungskosten *pl*

basics *n pl* ECON Grundbedürfnisse *nt pl*, GEN COMM Grundlagen *f pl*, Grundinformationen *f pl*, Grundsachverhalt *m*

basic: ~ **salary** *n* ECON, HRM Grundgehalt *nt*; ~ **size** *n* GEN COMM Bezugsmaß *nt*, genormte Größe *f*, Nennmaß *nt*, IND Bezugsmaß *nt*; ~ **standard of reporting** *n* ACC Berichterstattungsgrundsatz *m*; ~ **technique** *n* GEN COMM Grundtechnik *f*; ~ **time limit** *n* GEN COMM Ecktermin *m*; ~ **trend** *n* GEN COMM Grundtendenz *f*; ~ **unit** *n* GEN COMM Grundeinheit *f*; ~ **wage** *n* ECON, HRM Grundlohn *m*, Ecklohn *m*; ~ **weight scales** *n pl* GEN COMM Basisgewichtstabellen *f pl*

basing: ~-**point pricing** *n* TRANSP Preisgestaltung *f* im Frachtbasissystem

basis *n* STOCK *of currency futures* Basis *f*, TAX Basis *f*, Grundlage *f*; ♦ **on the** ~ **of** GEN COMM auf der Basis von, HRM aufgrund von

basis: ~ **of agreement** *n* LAW Vertragsgrundlage *f*; ~ **of assessment** *n* ECON, TAX Steuerbemessungsgrundlage *f*; ~ **of calculation** *n* FIN Berechnungsgrundlage *f*; ~ **of contract** *n* LAW Vertragsgrundlage *f*; ~ **for assessment** *n* GEN COMM, TAX Bemessungsgrundlage *f*; ~ **for discussion** *n* GEN COMM Diskussionsbasis *f*, Diskussionsgrundlage *f*; ~ **point** *n* FIN, STOCK Basispunkt *m*, 1/100 *nt* eines Prozentpunkts vom Nennwert; ~ **point value ratio** *n* STOCK *interest rate futures* Basispunkt-Wertverhältnis *nt*; ~ **of premium calculation** *n* INS Prämienberechnungsgrundlage *f*; ~ **price** *n* FIN Grundpreis *m*; ~ **risk** *n* FIN Basisrisiko *nt*; ~ **swap** *n* FIN Basisswap *m*

basket *n* ADMIN Korb *m*; ~ **of commodities** *n* ECON Warenkorb *m*; ~ **of currencies** *n* ECON, FIN Währungskorb *m*, internationaler Währungskorb *m*, STOCK internationaler Währungskorb *m*; ~ **of products** *n* ECON Warenkorb *m*

Basle: ~ **Concordat on Banking Supervision** *n* BANK Baseler Konkordat *nt*

bastard: ~ **face** *n* MEDIA *printing* Schmutztitel *m*; ~ **Keynesianism** *n* ECON Vulgär-Keynesianismus *m*

batch *n* ACC *of invoices* Serie *f*, COMP *group of items* Batch *m*, IND abgeteilte Menge *f*, Charge *f*, Ladung *f*, Los *nt*, Partie *f*, Posten *m*, Stapel *m*, Schub *m*, MEDIA *letters* Bündel *nt*, Stapel *m*; ~ **computer** *n* COMP *group of items* Stapelrechner *m*; ~ **control** *n* COMP Gruppenabstimmung *f*; ~ **file** *n* COMP Stapeldatei *f*; ~ **job** *n* COMP Job *m*, Stapelverarbeitung *f*; ~ **processing** *n* COMP Stapelverarbeitung *f*; ~ **production** *n* IND Serienanfertigung *f*, Serienbau *m*, Serienproduktion *f*, serienmäßige Herstellung *f*; ~ **size** *n* IND Losgröße *f*, Chargengröße *f*

bathtub: ~ **theorem** *n* ECON Badewannentheorem *nt*

battered: ~ **letter** *n* MEDIA *print*, S&M beschädigter Buchstabe *m*

battery *n* COMP Batterie *f*, IND *of automobile* Akkumulator *m*, Batterie *f*; ~-**backed** *adj* COMP mit Notstromversorgung durch Batterien; ~ **backup** *n* COMP Batterienotstromversorgung *f*, Notstromversorgung *f* mit Batterien

battle 1. *n* GEN COMM, STOCK Kampf *m*; **2.** *vi* ♦ ~ **for** GEN COMM streiten um, *existence* kämpfen um, ringen um

baud *n* COMP Baud *nt*; ~ **rate** *n* COMP Baud-Rate *f*

bay *n* TRANSP *on rail platform* Seitenbahnsteig *m*, *on rail siding* Nebengleis *nt*, *recess* Lagerraum *m*

Bayesian: ~ **approach to decision-making** *n* ECON, MGMNT, S&M Bayes-Regel *f* der Entscheidungsfindung; ~ **decision theory** *n* ECON, MGMNT, S&M Bayesianische Entscheidungstheorie *f*; ~ **method** *n* ECON, MGMNT, S&M Bayes-Regel *f*

Bayes': ~ **theorem** *n* ECON, MGMNT, S&M Theorem *nt* von Bayes

BB *abbr* COMMS (*bulletin board*) Anschlagbrett *nt*, Anzeigenbrett *nt*, Nachrichtentafel *f*, POL *AmE* (*Bureau of the Budget*) Haushaltsabteilung *f* des Schatzamtes der Vereinigten Staaten

BBA *abbr* (*British Bankers' Association*) BANK britischer Bankenverband

BBC *abbr* (*British Broadcasting Corporation*) MEDIA BBC (*British Broadcasting Corporation*), ≈ ARD (*Arbeitsgemeinschaft der öffentlich-rechtlichen Rundfunkanstalten der Bundesrepublik Deutschland*)

BBS *abbr* (*Bulletin Board Service*) COMMS BBS (*Bulletin Board Service*), Nachrichtenbrett *nt*

BC *abbr* ACC (*budgetary control*) Budgetkontrolle *f*, Haushaltskontrolle *f*, Etatkontrolle *f*, Finanzkontrolle *f*, Plankontrolle *f*, ADMIN (*British Council*) staatliche geförderte Einrichtung zur Verbreitung der britischen Kultur, ≈ Goethe-Institut *nt*, FIN (*budgetary control*) Budgetkontrolle *f*, Haushaltskontrolle *f*, Etatkontrolle *f*, Finanzkontrolle *f*, Plankontrolle *f*, GEN COMM (*bale cubic meters AmE*, *bale cubic metres BrE*) Ballenkubikmeter *m pl*

BCC *abbr* (*British Chamber of Commerce*) GEN COMM britische Handelskammer, ≈ DIHT (*Deutscher Industrie- und Handelstag*)

BCom *abbr* (*Bachelor of Commerce*) HRM Handelswirt *m*

b/d *abbr* ACC (*balance brought down*) Saldovortrag *m*, Vortrag *m*, ECON (*barrels per day*) *oil industry* Barrel pro Tag, FIN (*balance brought down*) Saldovortrag *m*, Vortrag *m*, Übertrag *m*

B/D *abbr* (*bank draft*) BANK Bankscheck *m*, Banktratte *m*, Bankwechsel *m*

B/Dft *abbr* (*bank draft*) BANK Bankscheck *m*, Banktratte *m*, Bankwechsel *m*

bdi *abbr* (*both dates inclusive*) GEN COMM beide Daten eingeschlossen

BE *abbr* (*Bank of England*) BANK, ECON englische Zentralbank, ≈ BBk (*Deutsche Bundesbank*)

B/E *abbr* BANK, FIN (*bill of exchange*) Tratte *f*, Wechsel *m*, IMP/EXP (*bill of entry*) Deklarationsschein *m*, Einfuhrdeklaration *f*, Einfuhrerklärung *f*, Zolldeklaration *f*, Zolleinfuhrerklärung *f*, Zolleingangsschein *m*, Zollerklärung *f*

BEA *abbr* (*Bureau of Economic Analysis*) ECON Amt für Wirtschaftsanalyse

beancounter *n infrml* ACC Erbsenzähler *m* (*infrml*), Pfennigfuchser *m* (*infrml*)

bear 1. *n* FIN, STOCK Baissespekulant *m*, Baissier *m*, Contremineur *m*; **2.** *vt* GEN COMM *costs* bestreiten, tragen; ♦ **~ a date** GEN COMM das Datum tragen, datiert sein; **~ in mind** GEN COMM berücksichtigen; **~ interest** BANK sich verzinsen, FIN Zinsen abwerfen, Zinsen bringen; **~ an interest of** ACC Zinsen tragen in Höhe von; **~ the market** STOCK Leerverkäufe als Baissemanöver tätigen; **~ the risk** STOCK das Risiko tragen; **3.** *vi* STOCK auf Baisse spekulieren

bear: **~ account** *n* STOCK Baisseposition *f*; **~ call spread** *n* STOCK *options* Baissespread *m* mit Kaufoptionen; **~ covering** *n* STOCK Deckungskauf *m* des Baissiers

bearer *n* BANK *of negotiable instrument* Inhaber, in *m,f*; Überbringer, in *m,f*; **~ bond** *n* FIN Inhaberobligation *f*, Inhaberschuldverschreibung *f*; **~ check** *AmE*, **~ cheque** *BrE* *n* BANK Inhaberscheck *m*, Überbringerscheck *m*; **~ clause** *n* STOCK Inhaberklausel *f*, Überbringerklausel *f*; **~ debenture** *n* STOCK Inhaberobligation *f*, Inhaberschuldverschreibung *f*; **~ form** *n* STOCK Inhaberformular *nt*; **~ marketable bond** *n* STOCK börsengängige Industrieobligation *f*, börsengängige Industrieschuldverschreibung *f*; **~ share** *n* STOCK Inhaberaktie *f*; **~ stock** *n* STOCK Inhaberaktie *f*; **~ warrant** *n* STOCK Inhaberoptionsschein *m*

bear: **~ hug takeover** *n* FIN Übernahme *f* nach Vorverhandlung

bearing: **~ surface** *n* TRANSP *shipping* Ladefläche *f*

bearish: **~ downward movement** *n* STOCK Baissebewegung *f*

bearishness *n* STOCK Baissestimmung *f*, Baisseströmung *f*, Baissetendenz *f*

bearish: **~ signal formation** *n* STOCK *in point and figure analysis* Baissesignal *nt*; **~ tone** *n* STOCK *of market* Baissestimmung *f*, Baisseströmung *f*, Baissetendenz *f*

bear: **~ market** *n* STOCK Baissemarkt *m*; **~ operation** *n* STOCK Baissespekulation *f*; **~ position** *n* STOCK Baisseengagement *nt*; **~ put spread** *n* STOCK *options* Baisseverkaufsspanne *f*; **~ raiding** *n* STOCK Leerverkäufe *m pl* der Baissespekulation; **~ sale** *n* STOCK Leerverkauf *m*, Verkauf *m* auf Baisse; **~ speculation** *n* STOCK Baissespekulation *f*; **~ transaction** *n* STOCK Baissegeschäft *nt*, Baissespekulation *f*

beat down *vt* GEN COMM *price* herunterhandeln auf [+acc]

Beaufort: **~ scale** *n* ENVIR Beaufort Skala *f*

beavertail *n* TRANSP niedrige Ladeplattform *f*

become *vi* GEN COMM werden; ♦ **~ affluent** GEN COMM reich werden; **~ dilapidated** PROP verfallen; **~ due** BANK fällig werden, verfallen; **~ effective** LAW rechtswirksam werden, wirksam werden; **~ indebted** BANK verschulden; **~ known** GEN COMM bekanntwerden; **~ obsolete** GEN COMM veralten; **~ prescribed** *AmE* LAW verjähren; **~ statute-barred** LAW verjähren; **~ wealthy** GEN COMM reich werden; **~ westernized** GEN COMM verwestlicht werden, westlich ausgerichtet werden

BEcon *abbr* (*Bachelor of Economics*) HRM Volkswirt, in *m,f*

bed: **~ and breakfast** *n* (*b&b*) LEIS Übernachtung *f* mit Frühstück

bedroom: **~ community** *n AmE* HRM Wohnvorort *m*, Schlafgemeinde *f*

Beeb: **the ~** *n BrE infrml* (*British Broadcasting Corporation*) MEDIA BBC (*British Broadcasting Corporation*)

beep 1. *n* COMP *audible warning noise* Tonsignal *nt*, Warnton *m*; **2.** *vi* COMP ein Tonsignal ausgeben, piepsen

before *prep* GEN COMM vor; **~ official hours** STOCK vorbörslich; **~ tax** TAX vor Abzug der Steuern, vor Steuern

before: **~-hours dealings** *n pl* STOCK Vorbörse *f*; **~-tax cash flow** *n* ACC, FIN, TAX Cashflow *m* vor Steuern

beggar: **~-my-neighbor policy** *AmE*, **~-my-neighbour policy** *BrE* *n* ECON Leistungsbilanzüberschußpolitik *f*, Beggar-my-neighbour-Politik *f*, GEN COMM Export *m* von Arbeitslosigkeit

begin 1. *vt* GEN COMM anfangen, antreten, beginnen; **2.** *vi* GEN COMM anfangen, beginnen

beginner: **~'s all-purpose symbolic instruction code** *n* (*BASIC*) COMP BASIC

beginning *n* GEN COMM Beginn *m*; **~ of file** COMP Dateianfang *m*; **~ inventory** *n* ACC Anfangsbestand *m*; **~ of the legal capacity** *n* LAW Beginn der Rechtsfähigkeit *m*

BEHA *abbr* (*British Export Houses' Association*) IMP/EXP Vereinigung britischer Exportunternehmen, ≈ WGA (*Wirtschaftsvereinigung Groß- und Außenhandel*)

behalf: **on ~ of** *phr* GEN COMM im Namen von

behavior *AmE see* behaviour *BrE*

behavioral *AmE see* behavioural *BrE*

behaviour *n BrE* HRM Verhalten *nt*

behavioural: **~ research** *n BrE* MGMNT, S&M Verhaltensforschung *f*; **~ science** *n BrE* MGMNT, S&M Verhaltenswissenschaft *f*

behaviour: **~ line** *n BrE* ECON *microeconomics* Verhaltenslinie *f*; **~ modification** *n BrE* HRM Verhaltensänderung *f*; **~ of the parties** *n BrE* LAW Parteiverhalten *nt*

belated: **~ claim** *n* INS Spätschaden *m*

Belfast: **~ Stock Exchange** *n* STOCK Belfaster Börse *f*

Belgium-Luxembourg: **~ Economic Union** *n* (*BLEU*) ECON belgisch-luxemburgische Wirtschaftsunion *f*

belief *n* S&M *advertising* Ansicht *f*

belittle *vt* GEN COMM herabsetzen

belittling *n* GEN COMM Herabsetzung *f*

bell: **~-shaped curve** n MATH *statistics* Glockenkurve f

bellwether n STOCK führender Wert m

below: **~-average** adj GEN COMM unter dem Durchschnitt, unterdurchschnittlich; **~ the gangway** phr POL *House of Commons* unter der Querpassage, wo die prominenteren Mitglieder des Hauses sitzen; **~ the line** phr ACC, GEN COMM im Soll, in den roten Zahlen, unter dem Strich; **~-the-line-promotion** n S&M Verkaufsförderung f durch Nachlässe; **~ the mark** phr GEN COMM unterdurchschnittlich; **~-market** adj STOCK *price* unter dem Börsenkurs, unter dem Kurswert; **~ par** phr STOCK unter pari; **~-the-line items** n pl ACC, ECON periodenfremde Aufwendungen f pl und Erträge m pl; **~-the-line revenue** n ACC Nettoeinkommen nt, Nettoertrag m; **~ the x% mark** phr GEN COMM unter der x%-Grenze

belt: **loosen one's ~** phr FIN Geld großzügiger ausgeben

Bench: **the ~** n LAW Richterstuhl m

benchmark n COMP *test of performance* Benchmark f, Bezugsmarke f, Bezugspunkt m, Fixpunkt m, ECON Bezugspunkt m, Vergleichsmarke f, GEN COMM Bezugsmarke f, Fixpunkt m; **~ figure** n GEN COMM Ausgangszahl f; **~ method** n FIN Eckwertmethode f; **~ reserve** n AmE BANK Benchmarkreserve f; **~ statistics** n pl MATH Vergleichsstatistik f; **~ test** n COMP Benchmarktest m

beneficial adj GEN COMM gewinnbringend, nutzbringend, vorteilhaft; **~ interest** n LAW Nutzungsrecht nt; **~ owner** n LAW wirtschaftlicher Eigentümer m, wirtschaftliche Eigentümerin f; **~ ownership** n LAW selbstgenutztes Vermögensrecht nt

beneficiary n FIN Begünstigte(r) mf [decl. as adj], Kreditnehmer, in m,f, INS Anspruchsberechtigte(r) mf [decl. as adj], Begünstigte(r) mf [decl. as adj], Berechtigte(r) mf [decl. as adj], Bezugsberechtigte(r) mf [decl. as adj], Nutznießer, in m,f, Leistungsempfänger, in m,f, LAW Anspruchsberechtigte(r) mf [decl. as adj], Begünstigte(r) mf [decl. as adj], Berechtigte(r) mf [decl. as adj], *under a will* Vermächtnisnehmer, in m,f, PROP Bedachte(r) mf [decl. as adj], Begünstigte(r) mf [decl. as adj], Berechtigte(r) mf [decl. as adj], Empfangsberechtigte(r) mf [decl. as adj], Leistungsberechtigte(r) mf [decl. as adj], Nutznießer, in m,f; **~ clause** n INS Begünstigungsklausel f

benefit 1. n GEN COMM *gain* Gewinn m, Nutzen m, *advantage* Vorteil m, *financial assistance* Beihilfe f, HRM *allowance* Beihilfe f, *privilege* Sondervergütung f, INS Versicherungsleistung f, LEIS Gewinn m, Nutzen m, MGMNT *advantage* Vorteil m, WEL *event* Wohltätigkeitsveranstaltung f, *social security aid* Unterstützung f; ♦ **be a ~ to sth** GEN COMM einer Sache von Nutzen sein; **2.** vt GEN COMM jdn fördern, jdm guttun, jdm nutzen, profitieren, LAW jdn begünstigen, WEL unterstützen; **3.** vi GEN COMM begünstigen, profitieren

benefit: **~ approach to taxation** n TAX Nutzenansatz m der Besteuerung; **~-based pension plan** n INS gehaltsgebundenes Rentensystem nt; **~ club** n WEL Wohltätigkeitsverein m; **~ in kind** n GEN COMM, HRM, INS, TAX *from employment* Sachbezug m, Sachleistung f; **~ of insurance clause** n INS marine Begünstigungsklausel f, Bezugsberechtigungsklausel f; **~ principle** n ECON, TAX *public finance* Äquivalenzprinzip nt, Nutzenprinzip nt, Vorteilsprinzip nt; **~-received principle** n ECON, TAX Äquivalenzprinzip nt

benefits n pl GEN COMM Leistungen f pl, HRM Aufwandsentschädigung f, INS Leistungen f pl

benefit: **~ segmentation** n S&M *advertising* Marktsegmentierung f nach Nutzwert; **~ society** n FIN AmE (*cf friendly society* BrE) Bausparkasse f, Versicherungsverein m auf Gegenseitigkeit (*VVaG*), GEN COMM Wohltätigkeitsverein m; **~ tax** n TAX Gebühr f

Benelux n ECON Benelux-Wirtschaftsunion f

benevolent: **~-authoritative** adj MGMNT *leadership style* wohlwollend-autoritär; **~ dictator** n ECON wohlmeinender Diktator m

bequeath vt LAW *legacy* vermachen

bequest n LAW Vermächtnis nt

Bergson: **~ social welfare function** n ECON, WEL Bergsons gesellschaftliche Wohlfahrtsfunktion

Berne: **~ Union** n INS Berner Union f

berth: **no ~ list** n (*NBL*) TRANSP *shipping* keine Liegeplatzliste f

Bertrand: **~ duopoly model** n ECON Bertrandsches Duopol-Modell nt

BESO abbr (*British Executive Service Overseas*) ADMIN britischer Führungskräftedienst in Übersee

best adj GEN COMM beste; ♦ **at ~** STOCK *price, selling order* zum Höchstpreis, bestens, *buying order* billigst

best: **~ alternative** n GEN COMM beste Alternative f; **~ bid** n GEN COMM bestes Angebot nt, bestes Gebot nt, Höchstgebot nt; **~ bidder** n GEN COMM Höchstbietende(r) mf [decl. as adj], Meistbietende(r) mf [decl. as adj], STOCK Meistbietende(r) mf [decl. as adj]; **~-case scenario** n ECON, GEN COMM Szenario nt für den günstigsten Fall, günstigste Situation f; **~ choice** n GEN COMM beste Wahl f; **~ efforts** n pl STOCK *of underwriter* bloße Übernahme f des Vertriebs einer Neuemission; **~ option** n GEN COMM beste Möglichkeit f

bestow vt LAW verleihen

bestowal n LAW Verleihung f

best: **~ possible** adj GEN COMM bestmöglich; **~ practical means** n pl (*bpm*) GEN COMM beste angewandte Mittel nt pl, zweckmäßigste Instrumente nt pl; **~ price** n GEN COMM Bestpreis m; **~ profferer** n GEN COMM bester Anbieter m; **~ seller** n MEDIA *book* Bestseller m, Verkaufsschlager m, S&M Bestseller m, Renner m (*infrml*)

Best: **~'s Rating** n AmE INS Einstufung der Kreditwürdigkeit für Versicherungen

best: **~ time available** n S&M bestmögliche Zeit f

bet 1. vt LEIS wetten; **2.** vi LEIS wetten

beta n AmE STOCK Beta nt; **~ coefficient** n AmE STOCK Beta-Koeffizient m; **~ error** n MATH *statistics* Beta-Fehler m, Fehler m zweiter Ordnung; **~ factor** n BrE STOCK Beta-Koeffizient m; **~ site** n COMP Beta-Standort m; **~ stock** n STOCK Beta-Aktie f; **~ test** n COMP *software* Betatest m; **~ version** n COMP *software* Beta Version f

betterment n PROP *improvement* Verbesserung f, *increase in value* Wertsteigerung f

better: **~-off** adj GEN COMM bessergestellt; **~ offer** n GEN COMM günstigeres Angebot nt; **~ than average** phr GEN COMM überdurchschnittlich, besser als der Durchschnitt; **~ than expected** phr GEN COMM besser als erwartet; **~ than predicted** phr GEN COMM besser als vorhergesagt

betting *n* LEIS Wetten *nt*

beyond: ~ **repair** *phr* GEN COMM irreparabel, nicht reparierbar, nicht mehr auszubessern

b/f *abbr* (*balance brought forward, balance carried forward*) ACC, FIN Saldovortrag *m*, Übertrag *nt*, Vortrag *m*

BFI *abbr* BrE (*Baltic Freight Index*) IMP/EXP *shipping* Londoner Frachtenindex

B5: ~ **letter** *n* COMMS, GEN COMM *paper size* DIN B5 Format *nt*

b/g *abbr* (*bonded goods*) IMP/EXP Güter *nt pl* unter Zollverschluß, Waren *f pl* unter Zollverschluß, zollpflichtige Güter *f pl*, Zollagergut *nt*

B/G *abbr* (*bonded goods*) IMP/EXP Güter *nt pl* unter Zollverschluß, Waren *f pl* unter Zollverschluß, zollpflichtige Güter *f pl*, Zollagergut *nt*

BH *abbr* (*bill of health*) WEL Gesundheitszeugnis *nt*

BHC *abbr* (*British High Commission*) ADMIN britisches Hochkommissariat

bhp *abbr* (*brake horsepower*) TRANSP effektive Pferdestärke *f*, Effektivleistung *f*

BHRA *abbr* (*British Hotels and Restaurants Association*) LEIS Vereinigung britischer Hotels und Restaurants

biannual *adj* GEN COMM *twice a year* zweimal jährlich, halbjährlich

bias *n* GEN COMM Befangenheit *f*, Parteilichkeit *f*, Voreingenommenheit *f*, *prejudice* Vorurteil *nt*, MATH *statistics* systematischer Fehler *m*, Verzerrung *f*

biased *adj* GEN COMM tendenziös, voreingenommen, MATH verzerrt

BIC *abbr* (*British Importers' Confederation*) IMP/EXP britischer Importeurverband

bicycle *n* GEN COMM, INS, TRANSP Fahrrad *nt*

bid 1. *n* ACC, FIN Übernahmeangebot *nt*, GEN COMM Gebot *nt*, Kaufangebot *nt*, Lieferangebot *nt*, Offerte *f*, *tender* Angebot *nt*, STOCK *offer* Übernahmeangebot *nt*, Übernahmeversuch *m*, *price* Geldkurs *m*; ♦ ~ **is received** GEN COMM Angebot liegt vor, Angebot geht ein; **2.** *vi* GEN COMM *for project, contract* Angebot machen, sich bewerben, *at auction* bieten, MGMNT *for project, contract* sich bewerben; ♦ ~ **for** GEN COMM *contract* anbieten; ~ **on** *AmE* GEN COMM *contract* anbieten

bid away *vt* HRM *poach employee* abwerben

bid off *vi* GEN COMM sofortigen Zuschlag erhalten

BID *abbr* (*Bachelor of Industrial Design*) HRM Bakkalaureus *m* für Industriedesign, Bakkalaureus *m* für industrielles Design

bid: ~ **and asked quotations** *n pl* STOCK Geld- und Briefkurse *m pl*; ~ **closing** *n* STOCK Einreichungsschluß *m*; ~ **closing date** *n* STOCK Einreichungsschluß *m*, Submissionsschluß *m*

bidder *n* FIN *in a tender offer* Bewerber, in *m,f*, Bietende(r) *mf* [decl. as adj], GEN COMM Bietende(r) *mf* [decl. as adj], Bewerber, in *m,f*, Bieter, in *m,f*, Ausschreibungsbeteiligte(r) *mf* [decl. as adj], Anbieter, in *m,f*

bidding *n* GEN COMM *submission of bid* Abgabe *f* von Angeboten, Abgabe *f* von Geboten; ~ **association** *n* S&M Anbietergemeinschaft *f*; ~ **period** *n* GEN COMM Ausschreibungsfrist *f*; ~ **procedure** *n* GEN COMM Ausschreibungsverfahren *nt*; ~ **requirements** *n pl* GEN COMM Ausschreibungsbedingungen *f pl*; ~ **technique**

n ECON Abgabe *f* von Angeboten; ~ **up** *n* STOCK künstliches Hochbieten *nt*

bidirectional: ~ **printer** *n* COMP bidirektionaler Drucker *m*, Zweirichtungsdrucker *m*

bid: ~ **offer spread** *n* STOCK Spanne *f* zwischen Ausgabe- und Rücknahmekurs; ~ **opening** *n* GEN COMM Angebotseröffnung *f*; ~ **price** *n* ECON Angebotspreis *m*, STOCK Geldkurs *m*; ~ **rate** *n* BANK Angebotskurs *m*, Geldkurs *m*, Rückkaufpreis *m* von Anteilen; ~ **rent** *n* PROP gebotene Miete *f*

BIDS *abbr* (*British Institute of Dealers in Securities*) STOCK britisches Wertpapierhändlerinstitut

bid: ~ **value** *n* STOCK Rücknahmewert *m*

biennial *adj* GEN COMM *every two years* alle zwei Jahre, zweijährlich, zweijährig

BIF *abbr* (*British Industries Fair*) IND britische Industriemesse

BIFFEX *abbr* BrE (*Baltic International Freight Futures Exchange*) STOCK internationale Frachtterminbörse

Big: ~ **Bang** *n* STOCK *on London Stock Exchange* Deregulierung des britischen Wertpapiermarktes am 27. Oktober 1986

big: ~ **bank** *n* BANK Großbank *f*

Big: ~ **Board** *n* *infrml* STOCK New Yorker Börse *f*

big: ~ **business** *n* GEN COMM Großbetrieb *m*, Großindustrie *f*; ~ **cheese** *n* *infrml* BrE hohes Tier *nt* (*infrml*); ~ **company** *n* GEN COMM Großunternehmen *nt*; ~ **customer** *n* GEN COMM Großkunde *m*, Großkundin *f*; ~ **figure** *n* STOCK *foreign exchange* erste Stellen des Devisenkurses

Big: ~ **Four** *n pl* BrE BANK die großen vier Clearing-Banken: Barclays, Lloyds, Midland, National Westminister

big: ~ **income earner** *n* FIN, HRM Bezieher, in *m,f* eines hohen Einkommens, Großverdiener, in *m,f*; ~ **industrial user** *n* GEN COMM, IND Großabnehmer, in *m,f*; ~ **investor** *n* FIN Großanleger, in *m,f*; ~**-name** *adj* GEN COMM bekannt; ~ **name** *n* GEN COMM großer Name *m*; ~ **seller** *n* S&M Publikumsrenner *m*

bigwig *n* *infrml* POL Bonze *m* (*infrml*)

bilateral *adj* ECON bilateral, POL bilateral, zweiseitig; ~ **aid** *n* ECON bilaterale Entwicklungshilfe *f*; ~ **clearing agreement** *n* ECON *international trade between countries* zweiseitiges Verrechnungsabkommen *nt*; ~ **contract** *n* LAW gegenseitiger Vertrag *m*; ~ **disbursement** *n* ECON *development assistance* bilaterale Auszahlung *f*; ~ **donors** *n pl* ECON *of development assistance* bilaterale Geberinstitutionen *f pl*

bilateralism *n* ECON *international trade*, POL Bilateralismus *m*

bilateral: ~ **loan** *n* BANK *development* bilaterale Anleihe *f*; ~ **mistake** *n* GEN COMM bilateraler Fehler *m*; ~ **monopoly** *n* ECON bilaterales Monopol *nt*, zweiseitiges Monopol *nt*; ~ **reference** *n* HRM zweiseitige Referenz *f*; ~ **road agreement** *n* TRANSP bilaterales Verkehrsabkommen *nt*

bilaterals *n pl* ECON jährliche Verhandlungen zwischen dem Finanzminister und den anderen Ministern über Staatsausgaben, Chefgespräche *nt pl*

bilateral: ~ **trade agreement** *n* ECON bilaterales Handelsabkommen *nt*, zweiseitiges Handelsabkommen *nt*; ~ **trade treaty** *n* ECON bilateraler Handelsvertrag *m*, zweiseitiger Handelsvertrag *m*

bill *n* BANK, FIN *payable, receivable draft* Wechsel *m*,

Valutawechsel *m*, Tratte *f*, *Treasury* Schatzwechsel *m*, *AmE* (*cf note BrE*) *serving as money* Banknote *f*, Schein *m*, GEN COMM *BrE* (*cf check AmE*) *invoice* Rechnung *f*, Zeche *f*, Nota *f* (*obs*), Faktura *f* (*obs*), LAW *legislation* Gesetzesvorlage *f*, *writ* Klageschrift *f*, POL Vorlage *f*, S&M *advertising poster* Plakat *nt*, TRANSP Frachtbrief *m*, Konnossement *nt*; ♦ **no ~ posting** S&M *advertising* Plakatankleben verboten

bill: **~ at double usance** *n* GEN COMM Doppelusowechsel *m*, doppelter Usowechsel *m*; **~ at usance** *n* BANK Usowechsel *m*

billback *n* ACC, STOCK Rückbelastung *f*

billboard *n* S&M Plakatwand *f*; **~ advertising** *n* S&M Anschlagwerbung *f*

bill: **~ book** *n* ACC Wechseljournal *nt*, Wechselverfallbuch *nt*; **~ of charges** *n* ACC Gebührenrechnung *f*; **~ of costs** *n* FIN Gebührenrechnung *f*, Kostenrechnung *f*, LAW Prozeßkostenrechnung *f*; **~ cover** *n* BANK Wechseldeckung *f*; **~ discounted** *n* BANK Diskontwechsel *m*; **~ drawn by a bank on a debtor** *n* FIN Debitorenziehung *f*; **~ of entry** *n* (*B/E*) BANK, IMP/EXP *customs* Deklarationsschein *m*, Einfuhrdeklaration *f*, Einfuhrerklärung *f*, Zolldeklaration *f*, Zolleinfuhrerklärung *f*, Zolleingangsschein *m*, Zollerklärung *f*

biller *n* GEN COMM *machine* Fakturiermaschine *f*, *person* Rechnungsteller *m*

bill: **~ of exchange** *n* (*B/E*) FIN *payable, receivable* Tratte *f*, Wechsel *m*; **~ for collection** *n* BANK Einzugswechsel *m*, Inkassowechsel *m*, Wechsel *m* zum Einzug; **~ for discount** *n* BANK Diskontwechsel *m*; **~ of freight** *n* TRANSP Frachtbrief *m*; **~ of goods** *n* IND Stückliste *f*, Warenverzeichnis *nt*; **~ of health** *n* (*BH*) WEL Gesundheitszeugnis *nt*; **~ holding** *n* BANK Wechselbestand *m*, Wechselportefeuille *nt*

billing *n* GEN COMM Fakturierung *f*, Rechnungslegung *f*, Rechnungsausstellung *f*, Rechnungsschreibung *f*, Abrechnung *f*, S&M *billposting* Werbung *f*, *advertising agency* Gesamtetat *m*, Umsatz *m*; ♦ **get top ~** LEIS die Hauptattraktion sein

billing: **~ of customers** *n* ACC Ausstellen *nt* und Zusenden *nt* von Rechnungen; **~ cycle** *n* GEN COMM Rechnungslegungszyklus *m*, Fakturierzyklus *m*; **~ date** *n* ACC Rechnungsdatum *nt*, GEN COMM Fakturendatum *nt* (*obs*), Rechnungsdatum *nt*; **~ department** *n* AmE (*cf invoicing department BrE*) GEN COMM Fakturierabteilung *f*, Rechnungsabteilung *f*; **~ for the time spent** *n* GEN COMM *invoice* Zeitaufwand *m*

bill: **~ of lading** *n* (*b.l.*, *B/L*) IMP/EXP, TRANSP *freight* Frachtbrief *m* (*FB*), Konnossement *nt*, Ladeschein *m*, *maritime* Seefrachtbrief *m*; **~ of lading fraud** *n* IMP/EXP, TRANSP Konnossementbetrug *m*; **~ of lading ton** *n* IMP/EXP, TRANSP Frachtbrieftonne *f*; **~ of lading tonne** *n* IMP/EXP, TRANSP Frachtbrieftonne *f*; **~ to order** *n* BANK Orderkonnossement *nt*; **~ payable** *n* ACC fälliger Wechsel *m*, Schuldwechsel *m*, Wechselverbindlichkeiten *f pl*; **~ payable at sight** *n* ACC Sichtwechsel *m*; **~ portfolio** *n* BANK Wechselportefeuille *nt*, Wechselportfolio *nt*; **~ rate** *n* FIN Wechseldiskontsatz *m*, Wechselrate *f*; **~ receivable** *n* ACC Besitzwechsel *m*; **~ of sale** *n* LAW *contracts, trade law* Übereignungsvertrag *m*, Verkaufsurkunde *f*, Übertragungsurkunde *f*; **~ of sight** *n* IMP/EXP *customs* vorläufige Zollangabe *f*, Zollerlaubnisschein *m*; **~ of sufferance** *n* TAX Zollpassierschein *m*

bills: **~ in a set** *n pl* FIN ein Satz *m* Wechsel, Wechsel *m pl* eines Satzes; **~ payable** *n pl* ACC Schuldwechsel *m pl*, Akzeptobligo *nt*; **~ purchased under resale agreement** *n pl* ACC *balance sheet* mit Weiterverkaufsvereinbarung gekaufte Wechsel *m pl*; **~ receivable** *n pl* BrE (*cf notes receivable AmE*) ACC Besitzwechsel *m pl*, Wechselforderungen *f pl*

billsticking *n* S&M *posters* Plakatierung *f*, Anschlagwerbung *f*

BIM *abbr* (*British Institute of Management*) MGMNT britisches Institut für Unternehmensführung

bimetallic *adj* ENVIR, IND bimetallisch, zweimetallisch; **~ standard** *n* IND zweimetallischer Standard *m*

bimetallism *n* ECON *currency* Bimetallismus *m*

bimodal: **~ distribution** *n* MATH *statistics* bimodale Verteilung *f*, zweigipflige Verteilung *f*; **~ frequency curve** *n* MATH bimodale Verteilungskurve *f*

bimonthly *adj* GEN COMM *every two months* alle zwei Monate, *twice a month* zweimal im Monat

binary *adj* COMP, MATH binär; **~ addition** *n* COMP Binäraddition *f*; **~-coded decimal** *n* COMP binär codierte Dezimalziffer *f*; **~ coding** *n* COMP Binärkodierung *f*; **~ digit** *n* COMP, MATH Binärziffer *f*, Bit *nt*; **~ file** *n* COMP Binärdatei *f*; **~ number** *n* COMP Binärzahl *f*, MATH Binärzahl *f*, Dualzahl *f*; **~ operator** *n* COMP Binäroperator *m*; **~ search** *n* COMP Binärsuche *f*, dichotomisches Suchen *nt*; **~-to-decimal conversion** *n* COMP Binär-Dezimal-Umwandlung *f*

bin: **~ container** *n* TRANSP Bunker *m*, Silo *m*

bind *vt* IND *machinery* binden, verbinden, LAW verpflichten

binder *n* COMP Binder *m*, INS begrenzte Frist *f*, vorläufige Versicherungspolice *f*, vorläufige Deckungszusage *f*, PROP Vorverkaufsvertrag *m*

binding *adj* LAW *contracts* bindend, *decision* verbindlich; ♦ **not ~** GEN COMM freibleibend, ohne Gewähr, unverbindlich

binding: **~ agreement** *n* LAW verbindliche Vereinbarung *f*; **~ arbitration** *n* LAW verbindliche schiedsrichterliche Entscheidung *f*; **~ bid** *n* GEN COMM bindendes Angebot *nt*; **~ effect** *n* LAW bindende Wirkung *f*; **~ offer** *n* GEN COMM bindendes Angebot *nt*, Festangebot *nt*, festes Angebot *nt*, verbindliche Offerte *f*, verbindliches Angebot *nt*; **~ promise** *n* GEN COMM bindende Zusage *f*; **~ tender** *n* GEN COMM bindendes Angebot *nt*, verbindliches Angebot *nt*

binomial *adj* ECON binomisch; **~ charge** *n* ECON binomische Belastung *f*

bin: **~-type container** *n* TRANSP *shipping* Silo-Container *m*

bio- *pref* ENVIR, IND Bio-, biologisch

biochip *n* COMP Biochip *m*

biocontrol *n* ENVIR Biokontrolle *m*

biodegradability *n* ENVIR biologische Abbaubarkeit *f*

biodegradable *adj* ENVIR biologisch abbaubar

biodiversity: **~ treaty** *n* LAW, ENVIR Artenschutzabkommen *nt*

bioeconomics *n* ECON Bioökonomie *f*

bioengineering *n* IND Biotechnik *f*

biographical: **~ data** *n pl* HRM biographische Daten *pl*, Lebensdaten *pl*

biological *adj* ENVIR, IND biologisch, Bio-

BIOS *abbr* (*basic input/output operating system*) COMP *software* Basiseingabe/Ausgabesystem *nt*

biotechnology *n* IND Biotechnologie *f*

biotope *n* ENVIR Biotop *nt*

bipolar *adj* COMP bipolar; **~ transistor** *n* COMP *hardware* bipolarer Transistor *m*

Birmingham: **~ Stock Exchange** *n* STOCK Börse in Birmingham

birth: **~ certificate** *n* GEN COMM Geburtsurkunde *f*

BIS *abbr* (*Bank for International Settlements*) BANK, ECON BIZ (*Bank für Internationalen Zahlungsausgleich*)

BISRA *abbr* (*British Iron & Steel Research Association*) IND britische Forschungsgesellschaft für Eisen und Stahl

bit *n* COMP Bit *nt*, Bitabbildung *f*, MATH Bit *nt*; **~ configuration** *n* COMP Bitkonfiguration *f*; **~ density** *n* COMP Bitdichte *f*; **~ location** *n* COMP Bitposition *f*; **~-mapped character** *n* COMP Bitabbildungszeichen *nt*; **~-mapped graphics** *n pl* COMP Bitabbildung *f*; **~ rate** *n* COMP Bitrate *f*

bits: **~ per inch** *n pl* (*bpi*) COMP Bits *nt pl* pro Zoll (*BPI*); **~ per second** *n pl* (*bps*) COMP Bits *nt pl* pro Sekunde (*BPS*)

bit: **~ string** *n* COMP Bitfolge *f*

bitter: **~ competition** *n* GEN COMM erbitterter Wettbewerb *m*, scharfer Wettbewerb *m*

biweekly *adj* GEN COMM *every two weeks* vierzehntägig, *twice a week* zweimal wöchentlich

bk *abbr* BANK Bk. (*Bank*)

b.l. *abbr* (*bill of lading*) IMP/EXP, TRANSP *freight* FB (*Frachtbrief*), Konnossement *nt*, Ladeschein *m*, maritime Seefrachtbrief *m*

B/L *abbr* (*bill of lading*) IMP/EXP, TRANSP *freight* FB (*Frachtbrief*), Konnossement *nt*, Ladeschein *m*, maritime Seefrachtbrief *m*

black *vt* BrE HRM *blacklist* auf die schwarze Liste setzen, *boycott* boykottieren

blackboard: **~ trading** *n* STOCK Handel *m* an der Tafel

black: **~ book** *n* ECON *takeover bids* Abwehrplan gegen feindliche Übernahmeversuche, GEN COMM Verzeichnis *nt* fauler Kunden (*infrml*); **~ box** *n* COMP Black-Box *f*; **~ economy** *n* ECON Schattenwirtschaft *f*, Untergrundwirtschaft *f*

Black: **~ Friday** *n* STOCK schwarzer Freitag *m*

black: **~ gold** *n* ENVIR, IND *oil* schwarzes Gold *nt*

blacklegs *n pl* BrE *infrml* GEN COMM, HRM, IND Streikbrecher, in *m,f*, gewalttätige Streikbrecher *m pl*

blacklist 1. *n* GEN COMM, HRM, IND schwarze Liste *f*; **2.** *vt* GEN COMM, HRM, IND auf die schwarze Liste setzen

blackmail 1. *n* GEN COMM Erpressung *f*; **2.** *vt* GEN COMM erpressen

black: **~ market** *n* ECON Schwarzhandel *m*, Schwarzmarkt *m*

Black: **~ Monday** *n* STOCK schwarzer Montag *m*

black: **~ money** *n* TAX Schwarzgeld *nt*

blackout *n* COMP *complete loss of electrical supply* Blackout *m* (*jarg*), Gesamtausfall *m* der Stromversorgung

black: **~ powder** *n* IND *mining* Schwarzpulver *nt*, Sprengpulver *nt*

Black-Scholes: **~ option pricing model** *n* STOCK Black-Scholes Optionspreismodell *nt*

black: **~ trading** *n* GEN COMM Schwarzhandel *m*

blame *n* LAW Schuld *f*, Verschulden *nt*

blank 1. *adj* COMP blank, *punch card* ungelocht; **2.** *n* COMP Leerzeichen *nt*; **3.** *vt* COMP löschen

blank: **~ character** *n* COMP Leerzeichen *nt*; **~ check** AmE, **~ cheque** BrE *n* BANK Blankoscheck *m*, Scheckformular *nt*; **~ endorsement** *n* STOCK Blankoindossament *nt*

blanket *adj* LAW *licence* umfassend; **~ agreement** *n* GEN COMM, HRM Generalvertrag *m*; **~ ban** *n* GEN COMM allgemeines Verbot *nt*; **~ bond** *n* INS Pauschalversicherungsvertrag *m*, STOCK durch Gesamthypothek besicherte Schuldverschreibung *f*; **~ contract** *n* INS Generalpolice *f*, Globalpolice *f*, Pauschalpolice *f*, LAW Generalvertrag *m*; **~ coverage** *n* S&M Pauschaldeckung *f*; **~ fidelity bond** *n* INS Pauschalkautionsversicherung *f*; **~ insurance** *n* INS Pauschalversicherung *f*; **~ medical expense insurance** *n* INS Pauschalarztkostenversicherung *f*, Pauschalkrankheitskostenversicherung *f*; **~ mortgage** *n* BANK Gesamthypothek *f*; **~ order** *n* GEN COMM Abrufauftrag *m*, Blankoauftrag *m*; **~ policy** *n* INS Pauschalpolice *f*, Pauschalversicherungsvertrag *m*; **~ rate** *n* GEN COMM Pauschalsatz *m*, Pauschaltarif *m*, Gruppentarif *m*, Sammeltarif *m*; **~ recommendation** *n* STOCK allgemeine Empfehlung *f*; **~ statement** *n* GEN COMM allgemeine Aussage *f*, pauschale Aussage *f*; **~ statute** *n* GEN COMM allgemeine Gesetzesvorschrift *f*, allgemeine Vorschrift *f*

blank: **~ form** *n* GEN COMM Blankett *nt*, Blankoformular *nt*, Formblatt *nt*, Vordruck *m*; **~ order** *n* GEN COMM Blankoauftrag *m*; **~ receipt** *n* GEN COMM Blankobeleg *m*, Blankoquittung *f*; **~ signature** *n* BANK Blankounterschrift *f*

bleak *adj* ECON, GEN COMM trostlos, trübe; **~ outlook** *n* GEN COMM *for the economy* trübe Aussichten *f pl*

bleed *vt* *infrml* GEN COMM *person* auspressen (*infrml*), ausquetschen (*infrml*), schröpfen (*infrml*)

blended: **~ rate** *n* BANK *of interest* Durchschnittssatz *m*, Mischzins *m*

blending *n* IND ausgewogene Mischung *f*

BLEU *abbr* (*Belgium-Luxembourg Economic Union*) ECON belgisch-luxemburgische Wirtschaftsunion *f*

blighted: **~ area** *n* PROP *of city* heruntergekommenes Wohnviertel *nt*

blight: **~ notice** *n* PROP Ankündigung *f* eines Zwangserwerbs

blind *adj* S&M blind; **~ advertisement** *n* S&M Chiffreanzeige *f*, Kennzifferanzeige *f*; **~-alley job** *n* AmE (*cf dead-end job BrE*) HRM Beruf *m* ohne Aufstiegsmöglichkeiten, Position *f* ohne Aufstiegschancen, Position *f* in einer Sackgasse; **~ faith** *n* GEN COMM *in the integrity of a party* blinder Glaube *m*, blindes Vertrauen *nt*; **~ figure** *n* GEN COMM undeutlich geschriebene Ziffer *f*; **~ person's allowance** *n* BrE TAX Blindenfreibetrag *m*; **~ product test** *n* S&M Anzeigenerinnerungstest *m*; **~ test** *n* S&M Blindtest *m*, anonymer Test *m*; **~ trust** *n* AmE LAW verdeckte Treuhand *f*

blink *vi* COMP *cursor* blinken; **~ meter** *n* S&M Gerät zum Messen der Wimpernschlagfrequenz

bliss: **~ point** *n* ECON *social welfare* Wohlfahrtsoptimum *nt*

blister: **~ pack** *n* S&M Klarsichtpackung *f*,

Blisterpackung *f*; ~ **packaging** *n* S&M *of goods* Klarsichtverpackung *f*

BLL *abbr* (*Bachelor of Laws*) HRM Bakkalaureus *m* der Rechtswissenschaft, Bakkalaureus *m* des Rechts

bloc *n* POL *union of countries or political parties* Block *m*

block 1. *n* COMP *section* Block *m*, ECON *currency* Währungsblock *m*, FIN *of shares* Paket *nt*, MEDIA Klischee *nt*, STOCK Wertpapierpaket *nt*, Aktienpaket *nt*, Paket *nt*; **2.** *vt* BANK *account* sperren, *freeze credit balance* einfrieren, COMP blocken, ECON *currency* blokkieren, GEN COMM *competition* hemmen, LAW blockieren, *vote, bill* verhindern

blockade *n* HRM Blockade *f*

block: ~ **booking** *n* LEIS, S&M Kopplungsverkauf *m*, Gesamtauftrag *m*, Gruppenbuchung *f*

blockbuster *n* *infrml* MEDIA, S&M Kassenschlager *m* (*infrml*)

blockbusting *n* *AmE infrml* PROP diskriminierendes und gesetzwidriges Verfahren, bei dem eine Partei gezwungen wird, ein Haus an einen Angehörigen einer ethnischen Minderheit zu verkaufen, damit die Nachbarn veranlaßt werden, ihre Häuser aus Furcht vor ethnischer Überfremdung zu sehr niedrigen Preisen zu veräußern, Blockbusting *nt*

block: ~ **coefficient** *n* TRANSP *shipping* Blockkoeffizient *m*; ~ **diagram** *n* COMP Blockdiagramm *nt*

blocked *adj* BANK *funds* eingefroren, ECON *currency* blockiert, GEN COMM *vote, bill* blockiert, verhindert; ~ **account** *n* BANK gesperrtes Konto *nt*, Sperrkonto *nt*

block: ~ **of flats** *n* BrE (*cf apartment building AmE*) PROP Appartementhaus *nt*, Wohnblock *m*; ~ **funding** *n* ACC *public sector* Blockfinanzierung *f*, FIN *public sector* Sammelfinanzierung *f*, TAX *public sector* Gruppenfinanzierung *f*; ~ **grant** *n* ADMIN Pauschalbewilligung *f*, pauschaler Zuschuß *m*, POL pauschale Finanzzuweisung *f*; ~ **mode** *n* COMP Blockmodus *m*; ~ **move** *n* COMP *data or word processing* Blockverschiebung *f*; ~ **policy** *n* INS Generalpolice *f*, Pauschalsachversicherung *f*, typisierter Versicherungsschein *m*; ~ **pull** *n* S&M Klischeeabzug *m*; ~ **sampling** *n* ACC Blockstichprobe *f*; ~ **of shares** *n* FIN, STOCK Paket *nt*; ~ **testing** *n* ACC *auditing* lückenlose Prüfung *f*; ~ **time** *n* TRANSP *aviation* Blockzeit *f*; ~ **trading** *n* STOCK Blockhandel *m*, Pakethandel *m*; ~ **transfer** *n* COMP Blocktransfer *m*; ~ **voting** *n* HRM Blockabstimmung *f*

blow *vt* *infrml* GEN COMM *all one's money* verpulvern (*infrml*); ♦ ~ **the whistle on sb** *infrml* LAW jdn auffliegen lassen (*infrml*)

blown: ~-**up balance sheet** *n* ACC aufgeblähte Bilanz *f*

blowout *n* *AmE* S&M Abverkauf *m* zu Schleuderpreisen

bluebook *n* BrE ACC, ECON, POL Blaubuch *nt*

blue: ~ **chip** *n* ECON, FIN erstklassiges Wertpapier *nt*, goldgerändertes Papier *nt* (*infrml*), Spitzenpapier *nt*, STOCK Standardwert *m*; ~-**chip company** *n* GEN COMM solides Großunternehmen *nt*; ~-**chip customer** *n* GEN COMM erstklassiger Kunde *m*, erste Adresse *f*, Kunde *m* höchster Bonität; ~-**chip industrials** *n pl* STOCK führende Industriewerte *m pl*; ~-**chip stock** *n* STOCK erstklassige Aktie *f*, goldgerändete Aktie *f* (*infrml*); ~-**collar worker** *n* ECON Arbeiter, in *m,f*, gewerbliche Arbeitnehmerin *f*, gewerblicher Arbeitnehmer *m*

Blue: ~ **Cross** *n* *AmE* (*cf private health scheme BrE*) HRM, INS, WEL *hospital plan* privates Krankenversiche-

rungssystem *nt*, private Krankenversicherung *f* für stationäre Behandlung

blue: ~ **economy** *n* BrE ECON offizielle Wirtschaft *f*

Blue: ~ **laws** *n pl* *AmE* LAW *Sunday trading* Gesetze gegen die Aufhebung der Sonntagsruhe

blueprint *n* ADMIN *printing* Lichtpause *f*, GEN COMM Plan *m*, Lichtpause *f*, Projektstudie *f*

blue: ~ **return** *n* TAX Sondererstattung *f*

Blue: ~ **Shield** *n* *AmE* (*cf private health scheme BrE*) HRM, INS, WEL *medical-surgical plan* privates Krankenversicherungssystem *nt*, private Krankenversicherung *f* für die ärztliche Versorgung, privatärztlicher Krankenversicherungstarif *m*

blurb *n* MEDIA *print* Klappentext *m*, Waschzettel *m*, S&M *publicity* Waschzettel *m*

BMLA *abbr* (*British Maritime Law Association*) LAW britischer Verband für Schiffahrtsrecht

BMRB *abbr* (*British Market Research Bureau*) S&M britische Marktforschungsagentur

BNC/ICC *abbr* (*British National Committee of the International Chambers of Commerce*) GEN COMM britisches nationales Komitee der internationalen Handelskammern

BO *abbr* (*branch office*) ADMIN Zweigstelle *f*

board *n* COMP *hardware* Leiterplatte *f*, Platine *f*, Steckkarte *f*, GEN COMM Behörde *f*, LEIS *accommodation* Pension *f*, Verpflegung *f*, POL Beirat *m*; ~ **of arbitration** *n* GEN COMM, HRM, IND Schlichtungsausschuß *m*, Schlichtungsstelle *f*, STOCK Schlichtungsausschuß *m*, Schlichtungsstelle *f*; ~ **broker** *n* STOCK Börsenmakler, in *m,f*; ~ **of conciliation** *n* BrE HRM Vergleichsausschuß *m*; ~ **control** *n* GEN COMM Überwachungsstelle *f*; ~ **of directors** *n* ACC, ADMIN, GEN COMM Firmenvorstand *m*, Vorstand *m*, MGMNT Aufsichtsrat *m*, Direktorium *nt*, Verwaltungsrat *m*, Vorstand *m*; ~ **of equalization** *n* TAX Ausgleichsbehörde *f*, Ausgleichsstelle *f*

Board: ~ **of Governors of the Federal Reserve System** *n* *AmE* ECON Direktorium *nt* des Zentralbankensystems

boarding: ~ **card** *n* TRANSP *at airport* Bordkarte *f*; ~ **gate** *n* TRANSP *at airport* Flugsteig *m*; ~ **house** *n* LEIS Gästehaus *nt*, Pension *f*; ~ **pass** *n* TRANSP *at airport* Bordkarte *f*

board: ~ **of investment** *n* GEN COMM Investitionsausschuß *m*; ~ **of management** *n* GEN COMM, MGMNT Direktorium *nt*, Vorstand *m*; ~ **meeting** *n* GEN COMM Vorstandssitzung *f*, MGMNT Aufsichtsratssitzung *f*, Präsidialsitzung *f*, Verwaltungsratssitzung *f*, Vorstandssitzung *f*; ~ **member** *n* HRM Mitglied *nt* des Board; ~ **of realtors** *n* *AmE* PROP Leitungsgremium der US-Immobilienmakler

boardroom *n* ADMIN Sitzungsraum *m*, MGMNT Führungsetage *f*, Vorstandszimmer *nt*, STOCK Börsensaal *m*; ♦ **at** ~ **level** ADMIN auf Vorstandsebene

board: ~ **of trade** *n* *AmE* ECON, GEN COMM, LAW Handelskammer *f* (*HK*)

Board: ~ **of Trade** *n* BrE (*BOT*) ECON Handelsministerium *nt*

body *n* GEN COMM *group* Gruppe *f*, *organization* Gremium *nt*, Organ *nt*; ~ **copy** *n* S&M Fließtext *m*; ~ **of creditors** *n* ACC Gesamtheit *f* der Gläubiger, Gläubigergemeinschaft *f*; ~ **language** *n* GEN COMM, HRM Körpersprache *f*; ~ **matter** *n* S&M Text *m*; ~ **shopping** *n* *infrml* HRM private Stellenvermittlung *f*

BOF *abbr* ECON (*Balance for Official Financing*) *accounting* Devisenbilanz *f*; COMP (*beginning of file*) Dateianfang *m*

B of E *abbr* (*Bank of England*) BANK, ECON englische Zentralbank, ≈ BBk (*Deutsche Bundesbank*)

bogie *n* TRANSP Drehgestell *nt*, Laufgestell *nt*; **~ lift** *n* TRANSP Laufgestellheber *m*

bogus: **~ company** *n* GEN COMM Schwindelfirma *f*; **~ firm** *n* GEN COMM Scheinfirma *f*

boilerplate *n* LAW *draft contract* Matrize *f*

boiler: **~ room** *n* AmE GEN COMM Kesselraum *m*, INS illegale Organisation für den Vertrieb zweifelhafter Wertpapiere

bold *adj* COMP *font* fett; **~ face** *n* COMP, MEDIA *printing*, S&M fette Schrift *f*, fetter Satz *m*, fettgedruckte Schrift *f*

boldface: **~ character** *n* COMP, MEDIA, S&M fettgedrucktes Zeichen *nt*

bold: **~ printing** *n* COMP, MEDIA Fettdruck *m*; **~ type** *n* COMP, MEDIA, S&M *printing* fette Schrift *f*, fetter Buchstabe *m*

bolster *vt* ECON, GEN COMM stützen, stärken

bomb: **~ scare** *n* POL Bombendrohung *f*

bona fide *adj* LAW, GEN COMM gutgläubig, auf Treu und Glauben; **~ clause** *n* GEN COMM *of letter of credit* bona fide Klausel *f*; **~ holder** *n* STOCK gutgläubige Inhaberin *f*, gutgläubiger Inhaber *m*; **~ offer** *n* GEN COMM gutgläubiges Angebot *nt*; **~ price** *n* GEN COMM angemessener Preis *m*, solider Preis *m*; **~ purchaser** *n* GEN COMM gutgläubiger Erwerber *m*

bonanza *n* GEN COMM Goldgrube *f* (*infrml*), Hochkonjunktur *f*, IND *mining* reiche Erzader *f*

bona vacantia *n* LAW *property* erbenloser Nachlaß *m*, herrenloses Gut *nt*

bond *n* ACC, BANK Wertpapier *nt*, ECON Anleihe *f*, FIN Anleihe *f*, Obligation *f*, Schuldverschreibung *f*, Wertpapier *nt*, INS Schuldschein *m*, STOCK Schuldverschreibung *f*, Wertpapier *nt*; ♦ **in ~** *adv* GEN COMM unter Zollverschluß; (*IB*) IMP/EXP unverzollt

bond: **~ anticipation note** *n* (*BAN*) STOCK Obligationengutschein *m*; **~ broker** *n* STOCK Makler, in *m,f* für Festverzinsliche, auf Rentenwerte spezialisierter Wertpapierhändler *m*, auf Rentenwerte spezialisierte Wertpapierhändlerin *f*, Fondsmakler, in *m,f*; **~ capital** *n* STOCK Anleihekapital *nt*; **~ certificate** *n* STOCK Anleiheschein *m*, Bond-Zertifikat *nt*; **~ conversion** *n* STOCK Anleihekonversion *f*; **~ costs** *n pl* STOCK Anleihekosten *pl*; **~ coupon** *n* STOCK Anleihekupon *m*, Zinsschein *m*; **~ creditor** *n* STOCK Anleihegläubiger, in *m,f*; **~ crowd** *n* STOCK Makler *m pl* für festverzinsliche Papiere; **~ cum warrant** *n* STOCK Anleihe *f* mit Optionsschein, Optionsanleihe *f*; **~ dealings** *n pl* STOCK Rentenhandel *m*; **~ debt** *n* STOCK Anleiheschuld *f*; **~ denomination** *n* STOCK Anleihestückelung *f*

bonded *adj* GEN COMM, IMP/EXP unter Zollverschluß; **~ area** *n* IMP/EXP, LAW Zolleinschlußgebiet *nt*; **~ cargo** *n* IMP/EXP, TRANSP Fracht *f* unter Zollverschluß; **~ debt** *n* STOCK Anleiheschuld *f*, Anleiheverbindlichkeit *f*, Obligationsschuld *f*; **~ elevator** *n* GEN COMM Silo *m* unter Zollverschluß; **~ goods** *n pl* (*B/G, b/g*) ECON, IMP/EXP Güter *nt pl* unter Zollverschluß, Waren *f pl* unter Zollverschluß, zollpflichtige Güter *nt pl*, Zollagergut *nt*; **~ indebtedness** *n* STOCK Anleiheverbindlichkeiten *f pl*; **~ warehouse** *n* GEN COMM Transitlager *nt*, Zollspeicher

m, IMP/EXP Freilager *nt*, privates Zollgutlager *nt*, Zollager *nt*, TRANSP Zollgutlager *nt*

bond: **~ equivalent yield** *n* STOCK Jahresrendite *f* kurzfristiger unverzinslicher Wertpapiere; **~ ex warrants** *n* STOCK Anleihe *f* ohne Optionsscheine; **~ features** *n pl* STOCK Anleiheausstattung *f*; **~ financing** *n* STOCK Anleihefinanzierung *f*; **~ flotation** *n* STOCK Anleiheemission *f*; **~ fund** *n* STOCK Rentenfonds *m*; **~ futures contract** *n* AmE STOCK Terminkontrakt *m* auf US-Treasury bonds; **~ holdings** *n pl* STOCK Rentenbestand *m*; **~ indenture** *n* STOCK Anleihevertrag *m*, Schuldverschreibungsurkunde *f*; **~ index** *n* STOCK Rentenindex *m*

bonding: **~ cost** *n* STOCK Anleihekosten *pl*

bond: **~ issue** *n* STOCK Anleiheemission *f*; **~ issue operation** *n* STOCK Anleihegeschäft *nt*; **~ issuing price** *n* STOCK Ausgabekurs *m*; **~ loan** *n* BANK Obligationsanleihe *f*; **~ market rally** *n* STOCK Erholung *f* am Rentenmarkt; **~ nominal yield** *n* STOCK Nominalverzinsung *f* von Schuldverschreibungen; **~ note** *n* IMP/EXP Zollbegleitschein *m*; **~ number** *n* BANK Obligationsnummer *f*; **~ owner** *n* BANK Obligationseigentümer, in *m,f*; **~ portfolio** *n* BANK Anleiheportefeuille *nt*; **~ power** *n* STOCK Anleiheberechtigung *f*; **~ premium** *n* STOCK Anleiheemissionsagio *nt*; **~ principal** *n* STOCK Anleihekapital *nt*; **~ proceeds** *n pl* STOCK Anleiheerlös *m*; **~ rating** *n* STOCK Anleihebewertung *f*, bonitätsmäßige Einstufung *f* einer Anleihe, bonitätsmäßige Klassifizierung *f* einer Anleihe; **~ rating agency** *n* STOCK Anleihebewertungs-Vertretung *f*; **~ redemption premium** *n* ACC Anleihetilgungsprämie *f*; **~ sales** *n pl* STOCK Absatz *m* festverzinslicher Wertpapiere; **~ sinking fund** *n* STOCK Anleihetilgungsfonds *m*, Obligationstilgungsfonds *m*; **~ sold prior to issue** *n* STOCK vorverkaufte Schuldverschreibung *f*

bonds: **~ outstanding** *n pl* STOCK Anleiheumlauf *m*; **~ payable** *n pl* STOCK Anleiheverbindlichkeiten *f pl*

bond: **~ store** *n* GEN COMM Zollager *nt*; **~ terms** *n pl* STOCK Anleiheausstattung *f*, Anleihemodalitäten *f pl*; **~ trading** *n* STOCK Rentenhandel *m*; **~ turnover** *n* STOCK Rentenumsätze *m pl*; **~ underwriting** *n* STOCK Übernahme *f* einer Anleihe; **~ valuation** *n* STOCK Anleihebewertung *f*, Kursrechnung *m*; **~ volume** *n* FIN Anleihevolumen *nt*; **~ with warrants attached** *n* STOCK Anleihe *f* mit beigehefteten Optionsscheinen; **~ washing** *n* FIN, TAX Steuerausweichung *f* bei Wertpapieren; **~ yield** *n* STOCK Anleiherendite *f*

bone: **~ of contention** *n* GEN COMM Streitgegenstand *m*, Zankapfel *m*

bonus *n* FIN Bonus *m*, Extradividende *f*, Sondervergütung *f*, GEN COMM Bonifikation *f*, HRM Prämie *f*, Zulage *f*; **~ in cash** *n* INS Bardividende *f*; **~ increment** *n* IND Akkordzuschlag *m*; **~ issue** *n* BrE FIN, STOCK Ausgabe *m* von Gratisaktien, Gratisaktie *f*; **~ pack** *n* S&M Zugabe *f*; **~ payment** *n* ADMIN, STOCK Sonderzahlung *f*; **~ rate of interest** *n* BANK Prämienzinssatz *m*; **~ reserve** *n* GEN COMM Dividendenrücklage *f*, INS Überschußrückstellung *f*; **~ savings account** *n* BANK Prämiensparkonto *nt*; **~ savings rate** *n* BANK Prämiensparquote *f*; **~ scheme** *n* HRM Prämienlohnsystem *nt*; **~ share** *n* FIN Aufstockungsaktie *f*

boodle *n infrml* GEN COMM Bestechungsgeld *nt*, Schmiergeld *nt* (*infrml*)

book 1. *n* ACC Buch *nt*, BANK Geschäftsbuch *nt*, Kassenbuch *nt*, MEDIA Buch *nt*, STOCK *of bond dealer* Buch *nt*, Gesamtumsatz *m*; ◆ **by the ~** GEN COMM streng nach Vorschrift; **2.** *vt* GEN COMM *ticket, place* bestellen, buchen, reservieren, LEIS reservieren; ◆ **~ early** GEN COMM frühzeitig buchen, frühzeitig reservieren; **~ in advance** GEN COMM im voraus bestellen, im Vorverkauf besorgen, vorausbestellen; **~ sb out** ADMIN auschecken (*infrml*), Weggang vermerken, MGMNT ihn auswärts in Arbeit geben; **~ unpaid checks** *AmE*, **~ unpaid cheques** *BrE* BANK unbezahlte Schecks verbuchen; **3.** *vi* GEN COMM bestellen, buchen

book in *vi* LEIS *at airport* Buchung aufgeben, sich anmelden, sich einchecken, *at hotel* sich anmelden, sich eintragen, sich einchecken

book up *vt* LEIS *hotel* reservieren lassen

book: **~ of account** *n* ACC Kontobuch *nt*; **~ of accounts** *n* ACC Kontenbuch *nt*; **~ cost** *n* ACC Buchwert *m*; **~ debt** *n* ACC Buchforderung *f*; **~ depreciation** *n* ACC Buchwertabschreibung *f*, bilanzielle Abschreibung *f*

booked *adj* GEN COMM, LEIS reserviert; **~ traffic** *n* TRANSP reservierter Verkehr *m*; **~ up** *adj* GEN COMM, LEIS, TRANSP *full* ausgebucht, ausverkauft

book: **~ entry** *n* ACC Bucheintrag *m*; **~ entry securities** *n pl* STOCK buchmäßig verwaltete Wertpapiere *nt pl*; **~ of final entry** *n* ACC, FIN *general ledger* Hauptbuch *nt*; **~ of first entry** *n* ACC, FIN *original entry* Grundbuch *nt*

bookie *n infrml* LEIS *sport* Buchmacher *m*

booking *n* GEN COMM Buchung *f*, Eintragung *f*, Engagement *nt*, Reservierung *f*, LEIS Reservierung *f*, Vorbestellung *f*, S&M *of advertising space* Platzbelegung *f*; **~ fee** *n* GEN COMM Buchungsgebühr *f*; **~ of new orders** *n* GEN COMM Auftragseingang *m*; **~ note** *n* TRANSP Buchungsanzeige *f*; **~ office** *n* LEIS Kartenverkaufsstelle *f*, Reservierungsbüro *nt*, TRANSP Reservierungsbüro *nt*, *rail* Fahrkartenausgabe *f*, Fahrkartenschalter *m*, Kartenverkaufsstelle *f*; **~ orders** *n pl* GEN COMM Bestelltätigkeit *f*; **~ system** *n* LEIS Buchungssystem *nt*, S&M Auftragssystem *nt*

book: **~ inventory** *n* ACC Buchinventur *f*, *perpetual inventory* permanente Inventur *f*, STOCK *of bond dealer* Gesamtumsatz *m*; **~-keeper** *n* ACC Buchhalter, in *m,f*, Rechnungsführer, in *m,f*, ADMIN, HRM Buchhalter, in *m,f*; **~-keeping** *n* ACC, ADMIN, HRM Buchführung *f*, Buchhaltung *f*

booklet *n* GEN COMM Werbebroschüre *f*, MEDIA, S&M Prospekt *m*

book: **~ loss** *n* ACC buchmäßiger Verlust *m*, Buchverlust *m*

bookmaker *n* LEIS *sport* Buchmacher *m*

book: **~ of original entry** *n* ACC Grundbuch *nt*; **~ of prime entry** *n* ACC, FIN Grundbuch *nt*; **~ profit** *n* ACC Buchgewinn *m*, buchmäßiger Gewinn *m*, Gewinn *m*; **~ receivables** *n pl* ACC Buchforderung *f*; **~ reviewer** *n* MEDIA *print* Bücherrezensent, in *m,f*, Buchkritiker, in *m,f*; **~ royalty** *n* MEDIA *print* Buchhonorar *nt*

books *n pl* ACC Bücher *nt pl*; ◆ **in the ~** ACC in den Büchern

book: **~ of secondary entry** *n* ACC, FIN Hauptbuch *nt*; **~ token** *n* S&M Büchergutschein *m*; **~ trade** *n* MEDIA Buchhandel *m*, Verlagswesen *nt*; **~ transfer** *n* ACC Umbuchung *f*; **~ value** *n* FIN Buchwert *m*, Restbuch-

wert *m*; **~ value before adjustment** *n* ACC Bruttobuchwert *m*; **~ value of investment** *n* ACC Beteiligungswert *m*

Boolean *adj* COMP aussagenlogisch, boolesch; **~ algebra** *n* MATH *prog* Algebra *f* der Logik, boolesche Algebra *f*; **~ logic** *n* MATH Algebra *f* der Logik; **~ variable** *n* COMP *progamming* boolesche Variable *f*

boom 1. *n* ECON Boom *m*, Hausse *f*, Hochkonjunktur *f*, wirtschaftlicher Aufschwung *m*, *prices* sprunghafter Aufschwung *m*, GEN COMM Boom *m*, Aufschwung *m*, Steigerung *f*, starker Aufschwung *m*, STOCK Hausse *f*; **2.** *vi* ECON rapiden Aufschwung nehmen, rapid steigen

boom: **~ in orders** *n* GEN COMM Auftragsboom *m*, Steigerung *f* der Aufträge

boomlet *n* (*infrml*) ECON Kleinkonjunktur *f*, Miniboom *m* (*infrml*)

boost 1. *n* ECON Auftrieb *m*, Preissteigerung *f*, GEN COMM *upward trend* Auftrieb *m*, Erhöhung *f*, Förderung *f*, *support* Unterstützung *f*; **2.** *vt* ECON *demand, exports* ankurbeln, steigern, FIN *earnings*, S&M *sales* steigern

booster *n* TRANSP *dangerous classified cargo movement* Verstärker *m*; **~ training** *n* HRM auffrischende Ausbildung *f*

boot *n BrE* (*cf trunk AmE*) TRANSP *of vehicle* Kofferraum *m*

boot off *vt infrml* GEN COMM ausbooten (*infrml*), ausschließen

boot out *vt infrml* GEN COMM ausbooten (*infrml*), ausschließen

boot up 1. *vt* COMP booten, urladen; **2.** *vi* COMP booten, urladen

boot: **~ disk** *n* COMP Bootdiskette *f* (*jarg*), Urladediskette *f*

booth *n* COMMS Kabine *f*

bootleg: **~ version** *n* ECON, MEDIA Raubkopie *f*, S&M Raubkopie *f*, unerlaubt kopiertes Produkt *nt*

bootlegging *n* ECON, MEDIA Raubkopieren *nt*

bootstrap *vt* COMP booten (*jarg*), urladen

boot-up *n* COMP Booten *nt* (*jarg*)

BOP *abbr* (*balance of payments*) ECON Zahlungsbilanz *f*; **~ deficit** *n* ECON Defizit *nt* der Zahlungsbilanz, Zahlungsbilanzdefizit *nt*; **~ surplus** *n* ECON Zahlungsbilanzüberschuß *m*

border: **~ control** *n* ECON, IMP/EXP Grenzkontrolle *f*; **~ crossing-point** *n* TRANSP Grenzübergang *m*, Kontrollpunkt *m*

bordereau *n* GEN COMM Inhaltsvermerk *m*, Sortenzettel *m*

bordering: **~ state** *n* LAW Anliegerstaat *m*

borderline: **~ case** *n* GEN COMM Grenzfall *m*

border: **~ trade** *n* IMP/EXP Grenzhandel *m*; **~ traffic** *n* GEN COMM Grenzverkehr *m*

born: **~ leader** *n* GEN COMM, HRM, MGMNT geborene Führerin *f*, geborener Führer *m*, geborene Leiterin *f*, geborener Leiter *m*

borough *n* ADMIN Stadtteil *m*, POL *district* Bezirk *m*, Stadtbezirk *m*, *in London* Stadtteil *m*, *town* selbstverwaltete Stadt, Gemeinde *f*; **~ council** *n BrE* (*cf common council AmE*) ADMIN, POL Stadtrat *m*, Gemeinderat *m*, Stadtparlament *nt*

borrow 1. *vt* BANK *money* aufnehmen, GEN COMM *idea, method* übernehmen, STOCK *money* aufnehmen; ◆ **~ at call** BANK auf Abruf borgen, Darlehen auf Abruf aufnehmen; **~ at interest** BANK auf Zinsen borgen; **~ funds** BANK Fremdmittel aufnehmen, Geld aufnehmen, Geldmittel leihen, Kredit aufnehmen; **~ interest-free** BANK unverzinslich leihen, zinsfrei borgen, zinslos borgen; **~ money** BANK Geld aufnehmen, Geld leihen; **~ money from sb** GEN COMM Geld von jdm borgen, Geld von jdm leihen; **2.** *vi* BANK Kredit aufnehmen, Darlehen aufnehmen **~ from a bank** BANK Bankkredit aufnehmen; **~ in the Euromarket** GEN COMM Eurokredit aufnehmen, im Euromarkt Kredit aufnehmen

borrowed: **~ capital** *n* BANK aufgenommenes Kapital *nt*, Fremdkapital *nt*, Fremdmittel *nt pl*, FIN Fremdmittel *nt pl*; **~ funds** *n pl* BANK Fremdmittel *nt pl*, FIN aufgenommene Mittel *nt pl*, Fremdmittel *nt pl*; **~ reserves** *n pl* BANK ausgeliehene Mittel *nt pl*, ECON geliehene Währungsreserven *f pl*; **~ stock** *n* STOCK geliehene Aktien *f pl*

borrower *n* BANK Darlehensempfänger, in *m,f*, Darlehensnehmer, in *m,f*, Kreditnehmer, in *m,f*, mortgage Hypothekenschuldner, in *m,f*, FIN Schuldner, in *m,f*; **~'s own funding** *n* FIN Eigenleistung *f*

borrowing *n* BANK Aufnahme *f* von Geldern, Darlehensaufnahme *f*, Fremdfinanzierung *f*, Kreditaufnahme *f*, FIN Kreditaufnahme *f*; **~ abroad** *n* BANK, FIN Kreditaufnahme *f* im Ausland, GEN COMM äußere Verschuldung *f*, externe Verschuldung *f*; **~ allocation** *n* GEN COMM Verschuldungsgrenze *f*; **~ authority** *n* FIN Kreditaufnahmevollmacht *f*; **~ bank** *n* BANK aufnehmende Bank *f*, Nehmerbank *f*; **~ by banks** *n* BANK Kreditaufnahme *f* durch Banken; **~ ceiling** *n* GEN COMM Verschuldungsgrenze *f*; **~ cost** *n* GEN COMM Kreditkosten *pl*; **~ external funds** *n* GEN COMM Aufnahme *f* von Fremdmitteln; **~ facility** *n* BANK, FIN Kreditfazilität *f*, Kreditmöglichkeit *f*; **~ fee** *n* GEN COMM Kreditgebühr *f*, Kreditkosten *pl*; **~ in the money market** *n* FIN Kreditaufnahme *f* am Geldmarkt, STOCK Inanspruchnahme *f* des Geldmarktes, Mittelaufnahme *f* am Geldmarkt; **~ limit** *n* FIN Kreditaufnahmegrenze *f*; **~ potential** *n* FIN Kreditfähigkeit *f*, Verschuldenspotential *nt*; **~ power** *n* FIN Kreditaufnahmebefugnis *f*; **~ power of securities** *n* STOCK Wertpapierkreditfähigkeit *f*; **~ rate** *n* BANK Darlehenszinssatz *m*, Kreditzinssatz *m*, Sollzins *m*, Sollzinssatz *m*; **~ ratio** *n* ACC Fremdfinanzierungsquote *f*; **~ requirement** *n* BANK Finanzierungsbedarf *m*, Fremdmittelbedarf *m*, Kreditbedarf *m*, FIN Kreditbedarf *m*

borrowings *n pl* BANK aufgenommene Kredite *m pl*, Direktkredite *m pl*, Fremdkapital *nt*

boss *n infrml* GEN COMM Chef, in *m,f*, Boß *m* (*infrml*); ♦ **be one's own ~** *infrml* HRM sein eigener Herr sein

Boston: **~ Stock Exchange** *n* AmE STOCK Bostoner Börse *f*

BOT *abbr* BrE (*Board of Trade*) ECON Handelsministerium *nt*

BOTB *abbr* (*British Overseas Trade Board*) GEN COMM britische Behörde für Überseehandel

both: **~ dates inclusive** *phr* (*bdi*) GEN COMM beide Daten eingeschlossen; **~ sides of industry** *n pl* HRM Tarifpartner *m pl*; **~-to-blame collision clause** *n* INS *maritime insurance* Kollisionsklausel *f* bei beiderseitigem Verschulden

bottled: **~-up** *adj* GEN COMM *price increase* unterdrückt, zurückgehalten

bottleneck *n* ECON, GEN COMM Flaschenhals *m*, *in supply* Engpaß *m*; **~ inflation** *n* ECON Nachfrageinflation *f*, nichtmonetäre Nachfrageinflation *f*

bottle up *vt* GEN COMM unterdrücken

bottom *n* ECON Konjunkturtief *nt*, Talsohle *f*, Tief *nt*, Tiefstand *m*, niedrigster Stand *m*, FIN niedrigster Stand *m*, GEN COMM Tiefpunkt *m*, Tiefstand *m*, HRM *of organization* unterste Ebene *f*, STOCK Tiefpunkt *m*, Tiefstand *m*; ♦ **the ~ has dropped out of the market** ECON die Kurse sind ins Bodenlose gesunken, der Markt hat einen Tiefstand erreicht

bottom: **~ end of the range** *n* S&M *marketing* unterster Bereich *m*; **~ fisher** *n* STOCK *type of investor* Anleger, der mit Tiefstand-Aktien spekuliert; **~ line** *n* ACC Endgewinn *m*, Endverlust *m*, Saldo *m*, FIN Endgewinn *m*, *overall result* Endergebnis *nt*, Endverlust *m*, *main activity* Kerngeschäft *nt*, Grundgeschäft *nt*, Hauptsparte *f*; **~-line profit margin** *n* ACC Mindestgewinnspanne *f*, FIN Mindestgewinnspanne *f*, niedrigste Gewinnspanne *f*, unterste Gewinnmarge *f*; **~ price** *n* ECON, GEN COMM äußerster Preis *m*, Tiefstpreis *m*

bottomry *n* TRANSP Bodmerei *f*; **~ bond** *n* IMP/EXP, INS, TRANSP *shipping* Bodmereibrief *m*, Seewechsel *m*

bottom: **~-up** *n* GEN COMM finanzielle Reserven *f pl*, Reserven *f pl*; **~-up approach** *n* FIN *to investing* Aggregationsmethode *f*; **~-up linkage model** *n* ECON interregionales Aggregationsmodell *nt*; **~-up management** *n* MGMNT partizipative Unternehmensführung *f*; **~-up method** *n* MATH Aggregationsmethode *f*

bought: **~ book** *n* ACC Einkaufsjournal *nt*; **~ day book** *n* ACC Einkaufstagesjournal *nt*; **~ journal** *n* ACC Einkaufsjournal *nt*; **~ ledger** *n* BrE ACC Einkaufbuch *nt*, Kreditorenbuch *nt*, Lieferantenbuch *nt*; **~ note** *n* STOCK Effektenkaufabrechnung *f*, *of broker* Kaufabrechnung *f*, Schlußnote *f*, Schlußschein *m*

Boulewareism *n* AmE HRM ultimatives Angebot der Arbeitgeberseite bei Tarifverhandlungen

bounce *vi infrml* BANK *cheque* platzen

bounce: **~-back** *n* GEN COMM Bieten *nt* eines neuen Anreizes zum Kauf, Bieten *nt* eines neuen Kaufanreizes

bounced: **~ check** AmE, **~ cheque** BrE *n* BANK, GEN COMM geplatzter Scheck *m*, ungedeckter Scheck *m*

boundary *n* GEN COMM Begrenzung *f*, PROP Grenze *f*; **~ condition** *n* MATH Randbedingung *f*; **~ distribution** *n* MATH Randverteilung *f*

bounded: **~ rationality** *n* ECON eingeschränkte Rationalität *f*

bound: **~ for** *phr* TRANSP bestimmt für, unterwegs nach

bounty *n* FIN *shares to employee* Prämie *f*, STOCK *shares to employee* Bonus *m*, Prämie *f*

bourse *n* ECON, FIN, STOCK *continental Europe* Effektenbörse *f*

boutique *n* S&M Boutique *f*

box *n* S&M, TRANSP Kasten *m*, Kiste *f*

boxcar *n* AmE (*cf goods truck BrE*) TRANSP *rail* Güterwagen *m*

box: **~ container** *n* TRANSP *shipping* Box-Container *m*; **~ number** *n* COMMS, HRM *advertisement* Chiffrennummer *f*; **~ office** *n* LEIS *theatre* Kasse *f*; **~-office takings** *n pl* LEIS *theatre* Einnahmen *f pl*; **~ pallet** *n* TRANSP Boxpalette *f*, Stapelgitterbehälter *m*; **~ rate** *n* TRANSP Kistenrate *f*; **~ trailer** *n* TRANSP Kastenanhänger *m*

boycott 1. *n* ECON Ächtung *f*, Boykott *m*, Sperre *f*, HRM Boykott *m*, IMP/EXP Sperre *f*, LAW Boykott *m*, Ächtung *f*; **2.** *vt* ECON, HRM, LAW boykottieren

BPA *abbr* (*British Ports Association*) TRANSP Vereinigung britischer Häfen

b.p.b. *abbr* (*bank post bill*) BANK Solawechsel der Bank von England, Bankpostwechsel *m*

BPF *abbr* (*British Plastics Federation*) IND britischer Kunstoffverband

bpi *abbr* (*bits per inch*) COMP BPI (*Bits pro Zoll*)

bpm *abbr* (*best practical means*) GEN COMM beste angewandte Mittel *nt pl*, zweckmäßigste Instrumente *nt pl*

bps *abbr* (*bits per second*) COMP BPS (*Bits pro Sekunde*)

BR *abbr obs* (*British Rail*) TRANSP staatliche britische Eisenbahngesellschaft vor Privatisierung, ≈ DB (*Deutsche Bundesbahn*) (*obs*), ≈ ÖBB (*Österreichische Bundesbahn*), ≈ SBB (*Schweizerische Bundesbahn*)

bracket *n* COMP *parenthesis* Klammer *f*, GEN COMM Stufe *f*, Intervall *nt*, MEDIA *parenthesis* Klammer *f*, TAX Klasse *f*

Brady: **~ Commission** *n* AmE STOCK Brady Ausschuß *m*

brainchild *n infrml* GEN COMM Geistesprodukt *nt*, Erfindung *f*

brain: **~ drain** *n infrml* HRM Abwanderung *f* von Wissenschaftlern

brainstorming *n* MGMNT *creativity method* Brainstorming *nt*, Ideenfindung *f*, Ideensitzung *f*

brainwave *n infrml* GEN COMM Gedankenblitz *m* (*infrml*)

brake: **~ horsepower** *n* (*bhp*) TRANSP effektive Pferdestärke *f*, Effektivleistung *f*

branch 1. *n* ADMIN Branche *f*, BANK *of bank* Filiale *f*, Zweigstelle *f*, COMP Verzweigung *f*, GEN COMM Filiale *f*, Geschäftsstelle *f*, Niederlassung *f*, Zweigstelle *f*; **2.** *vt* COMP verzweigen

branch: **~ address** *n* COMP Sprungadresse *f*; **~ bank** *n* BANK Filialbank *f*; **~ banking** *n* BANK Filialbankwesen *nt*; **~ banking system** *n* BANK Filialbanksystem *nt*; **~ of a business** *n* GEN COMM Geschäftszweig *m*; **~ economy** *n* ECON Volkswirtschaft, die wesentlich von außen bestimmt wird, weil viele Betriebe Tochtergesellschaften ausländischer Unternehmen sind; **~ of industry** *n* IND Industriezweig *m*; **~ line** *n* TRANSP *rail* Anschlußbahn *f*, Anschlußlinie *f*, Nebenlinie *f*; **~ manager** *n* BANK Filialleiter, in *m,f*; **~ network** *n* BANK Filialnetz *nt*, Geschäftsstellennetz *nt*, Zweigstellennetz *nt*; **~ number** *n* BANK Filialnummer *f*; **~ office** *n* (*BO*) ADMIN Zweigstelle *f*, GEN COMM Filiale *f*, Agentur *f*; **~ office manager** *n* GEN COMM, HRM Direktor, in *m,f* einer Niederlassung, Filialleiter, in *m,f*, Filialvorsteher, in *m,f*, MGMNT Direktor, in *m,f* einer Niederlassung, Filialleiter, in *m,f*, Filialvorsteher, in *m,f*; **~ operation** *n* GEN COMM Filialbetrieb *m*, Filiale *f*, Zweigbetrieb *m*, *manufacturing* Zweigwerk *nt*; **~ store** *n* S&M Zweiggeschäft *nt*, Verkaufsfiliale *f*

brand 1. *n* ECON Handelsmarke *f*, GEN COMM Fabrikat *nt*, Sorte *f*, S&M *of product, service* Marke *f*; **2.** *vt* GEN COMM kennzeichnen, markieren, brandmarken, S&M Marke entwickeln

brand: **~ acceptance** *n* S&M Markenakzeptanz *f*; **~ advertising** *n* S&M Markenwerbung *f*; **~ association** *n* S&M Markengemeinschaft *f*; **~ awareness** *n* GEN COMM, S&M Markenbewußtsein *nt*; **~ development** *n*

S&M Markenentwicklung *f*; **~ differentiation** *n* S&M Markendifferenzierung *f*

branded: **~ goods** *n pl* GEN COMM, S&M Markenartikel *m pl*

brand: **~ extension** *n* S&M Markenerweiterung *f*; **~ identification** *n* S&M Markenidentifizierung *f*; **~ image** *n* S&M Markenbild *nt*; **~ leader** *n* S&M Markenführer *m*, Spitzenmarke *f*; **~ loyalty** *n* S&M Markentreue *f*; **~ management** *n* MGMNT, S&M Markenpflege *f*; **~ manager** *n* MGMNT, S&M Markenbetreuer, in *m,f*, Produktmanager, in *m,f*; **~ marketing** *n* S&M Markenmarketing *nt*; **~ name** *n* S&M Markenname *m*, Gütezeichen *nt*, Handelsbezeichnung *f*; **~-new** *adj* GEN COMM fabrikneu, nagelneu (*infrml*), ganz neu; **~ personality** *n* S&M Markenpersönlichkeit *f*; **~ portfolio** *n* FIN Markenportefeuille *nt*, Markenportfolio *nt*, S&M Markenbestand *m*, STOCK Markenportefeuille *nt*, Markenportfolio *nt*; **~ positioning** *n* S&M Markenpositionierung *f*; **~ preference** *n* S&M Markenpräferenz *f*; **~ promotion** *n* S&M Markenartikelwerbung *f*, Werbung *f* für Markenartikel; **~ properties** *n pl* S&M Markenprofil *m*, Eigenschaften *f pl* einer Marke; **~ rationalization** *n* S&M Rationalisierung *f* einer Marke; **~ recognition** *n* S&M Markenwiedererkennung *f*, Markenbewußtsein *nt*; **~ reinforcement** *n* S&M Verstärkung *f* des Markenprofils; **~ share** *n* S&M Markenanteil *m*; **~ strategy** *n* FIN, S&M Markenstrategie *f*

brass *n pl infrml* HRM hohe Tiere *nt pl* (*infrml*)

BRB *abbr obs* (*British Railways Board*) TRANSP staatliche britische Eisenbahnverwaltung vor Privatisierung

BRC *abbr* (*business reply card*) COMMS, GEN COMM Rückantwort *f*

BRE *abbr* (*business reply envelope*) COMMS, GEN COMM Freiumschlag *m*

breach 1. *n* LAW Rechtsverletzung *f*, Verstoß *m*, PATENTS Verstoß *m*; ♦ **in ~ of contract** LAW vertragsbrüchig; **2.** *vt* GEN COMM *market* Fuß fassen in

breach: **~ of agreement** *n* HRM, LAW Vertragsbruch *m*; **~ of condition** *n* BrE LAW Verletzung *f* einer wesentlichen Vertragsbestimmung; **~ of confidence** *n* GEN COMM Verletzung *f* der Geheimhaltung, Vertrauensbruch *m*, Vertrauensverletzung *f*; **~ of contract** *n* HRM, LAW Vertragsbruch *m*, Vertragsverletzung *f*; **~ of duty** *n* LAW Pflichtverletzung *f*; **~ of professional etiquette** *n* GEN COMM standeswidriges Verhalten *nt*; **~ of secrecy** *n* GEN COMM Bruch *m* der Geheimhaltung, Verletzung *f* der Geheimhaltung, **~ of trust** *n* GEN COMM Vertrauensbruch *m*, Vertrauensverletzung *f*, LAW Pflichtverletzung *f*, Verletzung *f* der Treuepflicht, treuwidrige Verfügung *f*; **~ of warranty** *n* LAW Garantieverletzung *f*, Verletzung einer Gewährleistungspflicht *f*

bread *n infrml* GEN COMM *money* Brötchen *nt* (*infrml*), Geld *nt*, Kies *m* (*infrml*), Knete *f* (*infrml*), Kohle *f* (*infrml*), Lebensunterhalt *m*, Mäuse *f pl* (*infrml*); **~ and butter** *n infrml* GEN COMM tägliches Brot *nt*, notwendiger Lebensunterhalt *m*; **~-and-butter issue** *n infrml* BrE POL Grundanliegen *nt*; **~-and-butter letter** *n infrml* GEN COMM Dankesbrief *m* für erwiesene Gastfreundschaft, Dankschreiben *nt*; **~-and-butter line** *n infrml* GEN COMM Grundgeschäft *nt*; **~-and-butter technique** *n infrml* GEN COMM Grundtechnik *f*

breadth: ~ **of the market** *n* STOCK Marktumfang *m*, Marktbreite *f*, Marktangebotspalette *f*

breadwinner *n* ECON Ernährer, in *m,f*

break 1. *n* COMMS *for news bulletin* Bruch *m*, Pause *f*, *for commercials* Sendeunterbrechung *f*, GEN COMM *infrml stroke of good luck* Chance *f*, glückliche Gelegenheit *f*, Pause *f*, HRM *in work* Pause *f*, POL *from party* Abfall *m*, S&M *in broadcast for commercials* Sendeunterbrechung *f*, STOCK *in accounts of brokerage firm* Lücke *f*, Kurseinbruch *m*; **2.** *vt* ECON *monopoly*, GEN COMM *contract, promise*, HRM *strike* brechen, LAW *contract, law* brechen, verstoßen gegen, STOCK *syndicate* brechen; ◆ ~ **bulk** TRANSP Bulkfracht teilen, Stückgutfracht aufteilen, Bulkfracht aufteilen, *shipping* Bulkfracht entladen, Stückgutfracht abladen, Bulkfracht abladen, Bulkfracht ausladen; ~ **the ceiling** FIN die Obergrenze durchstoßen; ~ **confidence** ECON Vertrauen brechen; ~ **the deadlock** GEN COMM den toten Punkt überwinden; ~ **new ground** GEN COMM Neuland betreten, Neuland erschließen; ~ **the news to sb** COMMS jdm die Nachricht mitteilen, *bad news* jdm die Nachricht beibringen; ~ **ranks** HRM aus dem Glied treten; **3.** *vi* COMMS, MEDIA *news* bekanntwerden, POL *from party* abfallen; ◆ ~ **even** ADMIN, ECON die Gewinnschwelle erreichen, FIN den Kostendeckungspunkt erreichen, kostendeckend arbeiten

break down 1. *vt* ACC, FIN, GEN COMM *costs, figures* aufschlüsseln, aufgliedern, umbrechen, IND *machinery* zerlegen; ◆ ~ **expenses** ACC, FIN eine Kostengliederung aufstellen, Kosten aufschlüsseln, Spesen aufgliedern; **2.** *vi* COMP *crash* zusammenbrechen, GEN COMM *plans, negotiations* scheitern, IND *machinery* ausfallen, versagen, TRANSP Panne haben

break into *vt* GEN COMM *funds, stocks* angreifen; ◆ ~ **a market** GEN COMM in einen Markt eindringen, auf einen Markt vorstoßen

break off *vt* GEN COMM *negotiations, talks* abbrechen, unterbrechen

break up 1. *vt* GEN COMM zerbrechen, *disband* auflösen, zerstreuen; **2.** *vi* GEN COMM *disband* sich auflösen; ◆ **the meeting broke up** *phr* GEN COMM die Sitzung wurde abgebrochen

breakage *n* GEN COMM Bruch *m*; ~ **clause** *n* INS Bruchklausel *f*; ~ **of glass risk** *n* INS Glasbruchrisiko *nt*

breakaway: ~ **union** *n* HRM abtrünnige Gewerkschaft *f*

break: ~ **bulk agent** *n* TRANSP Bulkfrachtmakler, in *m,f*, Stückgutfrachtagent, in *m,f*, Stückgutfrachtmakler, in *m,f*; ~ **bulk cargo** *n* TRANSP *shipping* Stückgutfracht *f*, Stückgut *nt*; ~ **bulk center** *AmE*, ~ **bulk centre** *BrE n* TRANSP *shipping* Bulkfrachtumsatzplatz *m*, Bulkfrachtumschlagplatz *m*, Stückgutfrachtumsatzplatz *m*, Stückgutfrachtumschlagplatz *m*, Stückgutfrachtzentrum *nt*

breakdown *n* ACC Aufgliederung *f*, COMP *of system* Absturz *m*, Ausfall *m*, GEN COMM *analysis* Aufgliederung *f*, Aufstellung *f*, Untergliederung *f*, HRM *analysis* Aufschlüsselung *f*, *failure* Scheitern *nt*, IND Versagen *nt*, MGMNT *analysis* Aufschlüsselung *f*, TRANSP *failure* Ausfall *m*, *interruption* Unterbrechung *f*, Betriebsunterbrechung *f*, *rail* Panne *f*, Störung *f*; ~ **of expenses** *n* ACC, FIN Kostengliederung *f*; ~ **van** *n* BrE (*cf tow truck AmE*) TRANSP Abschleppwagen *m*, Bergungsfahrzeug *nt*, Reparaturwagen *m*, Werkstattwagen *m*

breakeven: ~**analysis** *n* ECON, FIN Break-Even-Analyse

f, Deckungsbeitragsrechnung *f*, Deckungspunktanalyse *f*, Nutzschwellenanalyse *f*, *profits* Gewinnschwellenanalyse *f*; ~ **level of income** *n* ECON Basiseinkommen *nt* des Haushalts; ~ **point** *n* ACC, ECON Break-Even-Punkt *m*, Ertragsschwelle *f*, Nutzschwelle *f*, *profits* Gewinnschwelle *f*, FIN, *costs* Break-Even-Punkt *m*, *profits* Deckungspunkt *m*, Gewinnschwelle *f*, Nutzschwelle *f*, Kostendeckungspunkt *m*, GEN COMM Ertragsschwelle *f*, Nutzschwelle *f*, *of profits* Gewinnschwelle *f*, MGMNT Rentabilitätsschwelle *f*, PROP, STOCK Break-Even-Punkt *m*, Nutzschwelle *f*, *of profits* Gewinnschwelle *f*; ~ **pricing** *n* S&M kostendeckende Preisgestaltung *f*; ~ **quantity** *n* ADMIN, ECON Menge *f* zur Erreichung der Gewinnschwelle, Menge *f* zur Erreichung des Kostendeckungspunktes, Break-Even-Stückzahl *f*, IND Akkord *m*, S&M kostendeckende Menge *f*; ~ **weight** *n* TRANSP Deckungsgewicht *nt*

breaking: ~ **away** *n* POL *from party* Abfall *m*; ~ **down** *n* GEN COMM *analysis* Aufschlüsselung *f*; ~ **load** *n* TRANSP Bruchbelastung *f*, Bruchlast *f*, Reißkraft *f*

break: ~ **in journey** *n* LEIS, TRANSP Reiseunterbrechung *f*; ~ **in the market** *n* S&M Preiseinbruch *m*; ~~**out** *n* GEN COMM, STOCK *of total* Aufgliederung *f*

breakpoint *n* COMP bedingter Programmstopp *m*; ~ **instruction** *n* COMP bedingter Programmstopp *m*, Programmstoppbefehl *m*, Stoppbefehl *m*; ~ **sale** *n* FIN Breakpunkt-Verkauf *m*

breakthrough *n* ADMIN, ECON Durchbruch *m*

break: ~~**up** *n* ADMIN, GEN COMM Auflösung *f*, Zerschlagung *f*, Aufteilung *f*; ~~**up value** *n* ACC Abbruchwert *m*, Liquidationswert *m*, FIN Liquidationswert *m*; ~ **weight** *n* GEN COMM Nutzschwelle *f*

Bretton: ~ **Woods Agreement** *n* ECON Bretton Woods-Abkommen *nt*; ~ **Woods Conference** *n* ECON Bretton Woods-Konferenz *f*

bribe 1. *n* FIN Bestechungsgeld *nt*, GEN COMM Bestechung *f*, Bestechungsgeld *nt*, Bestechungsgelder *nt pl*, Bestechungsgeschenk *nt*, Schmiergeld *nt* (*infrml*); **2.** *vt* GEN COMM bestechen, kaufen

bribe: ~ **money** *n* GEN COMM Bestechungsgeld *nt*

bribery *n* GEN COMM Bestechung *f*

bridge 1. *n* TRANSP *of ship* Brücke *f*; **2.** *vt* ◆ ~ **the gap** ECON, GEN COMM die Lücke schließen, *in time* überbrücken

bridge: ~ **finance** *n* FIN Zwischenfinanzierung *f*, Überbrückungsfinanzierung *f*; ~ **loan** *n* AmE (*cf bridging loan BrE*) BANK Überbrückungskredit *m*, Zwischenkredit *m*; ~~**over loan** *n* BANK Überbrückungskredit *m*, Zwischenkredit *m*

bridgeware *n* COMP Bridgeware *f* (*jarg*), Bridge-Programm *nt*

bridging *n* FIN Überbrückung *f*; ~ **advance** *n* BANK Überbrückungskredit *m*, Zwischenkredit *m*; ~ **facility** *n* BANK Überbrückungsfazilität *f*; ~ **loan** *n* BrE (*cf bridge loan AmE*) BANK Überbrückungskredit *m*, Zwischenkredit *m*; ~ **pension scheme** *n* FIN Überbrückungspension *f*, vorzeitige Rente *f*; ~ **software** *n* COMP Bridgeware *f* (*jarg*), Bridge-Programm *nt*

brief 1. *adj* GEN COMM *summary* kurz; **2.** *n* GEN COMM Auftrag *m*, Instruktionen *f pl*, Kurzbericht *m*, LAW Schriftsatz *m*; **3.** *vt* COMMS informieren, GEN COMM anweisen, informieren, instruieren, unterrichten, LAW mit der Vertretung eines Falles betrauen, instruieren

briefcase *n* GEN COMM Aktentasche *f*, Tasche *f*

briefing *n* GEN COMM Anweisungen *f pl*, MGMNT Einweisung *f*; ~ **session** *n* GEN COMM Einsatzbesprechung *f*

briefly *adv* GEN COMM kurz

brightness *n* COMP Helligkeit *f*

bring *vt* LAW *action* erheben; ◆ ~ **an accusation against sb** LAW gegen jdn öffentlich Klage erheben; ~ **an action against sb** LAW gegen jdn ein Verfahren anstrengen, gegen jdn Klage erheben, jdn verklagen; ~ **a lawsuit against sb** LAW gegen jdn ein Verfahren anstrengen, gegen jdn Klage erheben, jdn verklagen; ~ **into fashion** GEN COMM, S&M in Mode bringen; ~ **into play** GEN COMM aufbieten, einsetzen; ~ **parity** STOCK *currency futures* Wechselkursparität herstellen; ~ **pressure to bear on sb** GEN COMM auf jdn Druck ausüben; ~ **sb to book** GEN COMM jdn zur Rechenschaft ziehen; ~ **sb up to date about sth** GEN COMM jdn über etw auf den neuesten Stand bringen; ~ **sth up to date** GEN COMM etw aktualisieren, etw updaten (*jarg*); ~ **sb within the tax net** TAX jdn steuerlich erfassen; ~ **to an end** GEN COMM zu Ende bringen; ~ **to bear against** GEN COMM, LAW *new law* anwenden gegen; ~ **to light** GEN COMM ans Licht bringen, enthüllen; ~ **under control** ECON *inflation, unemployment* unter Kontrolle bringen; ~ **up to strength** GEN COMM vollzählig machen

bring about *vt* GEN COMM zustande bringen, zuwege bringen, bewirken, *arrange* veranlassen

bring down *vt* GEN COMM *prices, inflation* ermäßigen, herabsetzen

bring forward *vt* ACC, BANK, FIN *balance* übertragen, vortragen, GEN COMM *date, meeting* vorverlegen; ◆ ~ **a claim** LAW einen Anspruch geltend machen

bring in *vt* GEN COMM *revenue, sales* einbringen, hereinbringen, verdienen, LAW *legislation* einbringen, einführen

bring out *vt* STOCK *new issue* auf den Markt bringen; ◆ ~ **on strike** GEN COMM, HRM, IND *workers* zum Streik aufrufen

brisk *adj* ECON, GEN COMM *demand*, STOCK *trading* lebhaft, rege

briskly *adv* ECON. GEN COMM, STOCK lebhaft, rege

British: ~ **Agricultural Export Council** *n* (*BAEC*) IMP/EXP britischer Rat für Agrarexporte; ~ **Airports Authority** *n* (*BAA*) TRANSP britische Flughafenbehörde, ≈ Bundesanstalt *f* für Flugsicherung (*BFS*); ~**-American Chamber of Commerce** *n* (*BACC*) ECON, GEN COMM britisch-amerikanische Handelskammer; ~ **Bankers' Association** *n* (*BBA*) BANK britischer Bankenverband; ~ **Broadcasting Corporation** *n* (*BBC, the Beeb*) MEDIA British Broadcasting Corporation *f* (*BBC*), ≈ Arbeitsgemeinschaft der öffentlich-rechtlichen Rundfunkanstalten der Bundesrepublik Deutschland (*ARD*); ~ **Chamber of Commerce** *n* (*BCC*) GEN COMM britische Handelskammer, ≈ Deutscher Industrie- und Handelstag *m* (*DIHT*); ~ **Code of Advertising Practice** *n* S&M britischer Kodex für Werbepraktiken; ~ **Code of Promotion Practice** *n* S&M britischer Kodex für Praktiken der Verkaufsförderung; ~ **Council** *n* (*BC*) ADMIN staatliche geförderte Einrichtung zur Verbreitung der britischen Kultur, ≈ Goethe-Institut *nt*; ~ **Executive Service Overseas** *n* (*BESO*) ADMIN britischer Führungskräftedienst in Übersee; ~ **Export Houses' Association** *n* (*BEHA*) IMP/EXP Vereinigung britischer Exportunternehmen, ≈ Wirtschaftsvereinigung

f Groß- und Außenhandel (*WGA*); ~ **High Commission** *n* (*BHC*) ADMIN britisches Hochkommissariat; ~ **Hotels and Restaurants Association** *n* (*BHRA*) LEIS Vereinigung britischer Hotels und Restaurants; ~ **Importers' Confederation** *n* (*BIC*) IMP/EXP britischer Importeurverband; ~ **Industries Fair** *n* (*BIF*) IND britische Industriemesse; ~ **Institute of Dealers in Securities** *n* (*BIDS*) STOCK britisches Wertpapierhändlerinstitut; ~ **Institute of Management** *n* (*BIM*) MGMNT britisches Institut für Unternehmensführung; ~ **Iron & Steel Research Association** *n* (*BISRA*) IND britische Forschungsgesellschaft für Eisen und Stahl; ~ **Maritime Law Association** *n* (*BMLA*) LAW britischer Verband für Schiffahrtsrecht; ~ **Market Research Bureau** *n* (*BMRB*) S&M britische Marktforschungsagentur; ~ **National Committee of the International Chambers of Commerce** *n* (*BNC/ICC*) GEN COMM britisches nationales Komitee der internationalen Handelskammern; ~ **Overseas Trade Board** *n* (*BOTB*) GEN COMM britische Behörde für Überseehandel; ~ **Plastics Federation** *n* (*BPF*) IND britischer Kunststoffverband; ~ **Ports Association** *n* (*BPA*) TRANSP Vereinigung britischer Häfen; ~ **quart** *n* GEN COMM britische Viertelgallone *f*; ~ **Rail** *n obs* (*BR*) TRANSP staatliche britische Eisenbahngesellschaft vor Privatisierung, ≈ Deutsche Bundesbahn *f* (*obs*) (*DB*), ≈ Österreichische Bundesbahn *f* (*ÖBB*), ≈ Schweizerische Bundesbahn *f* (*SBB*); ~ **Railways Board** *n obs* (*BRB*) TRANSP staatliche britische Eisenbahnverwaltung vor Privatisierung; ~ **Savings Bonds** *n pl* STOCK Sparbonds; ~ **Shippers' Council** *n* (*BSC*) TRANSP britischer Spediteurverband; ~ **Shipping Federation** *n* (*BSF*) TRANSP britischer Schiffahrtsverband; ~ **Standard** *n* (*BS*) IND, LAW britische Norm, ≈ Deutsche Industrienorm *f* (*DIN*); ~ **Standard Code of Practice** *n* (*BSCP*) LAW britische Standesrichtlinien; ~ **Standards Institution** *n* (*BSI*) ADMIN, IND, LAW britischer staatlicher Normenverband, ≈ Deutsches Institut *nt* für Normung (*DIN*); ~ **Standard Specification** *n* (*BSS*) IND, LAW *m*, britische Normvorschrift; ~ **Standard Time** *n* GEN COMM britische Normalzeit *f*; ~ **Summer Time** *n* GEN COMM britische Sommerzeit *f*; ~ **Technology Group** *n* IND britischer Technologiekonzern; ~ **Telecom** *n* (*BT*) COMMS britische Telefongesellschaft; ~ **Tourist Authority** *n* (*BTA*) LEIS britische Fremdenverkehrszentrale; ~ **Travel Association** *n* (*BTA*) LEIS britischer Reiseverkehrsverband; ~ **Venture Capital Association** *n* FIN britischer Wagniskapital-Beteiligungsverband; ~ **Waterways Board** *n* (*BWB*) TRANSP britische Wasserstraßenverwaltung

BRM *abbr* (*business reply mail*) COMMS, GEN COMM Rückantwort *f*, Freiumschlag *m*

broadband *n* COMP Breitband *nt*, HRM Gehaltsstruktur *f* mit wenigen Stufen

broad: ~ **banding** *n* BrE HRM Anwendung einer Gehaltsstruktur mit wenigen Stufen; ~**-based** *adj* TAX auf breiter Bemessungsgrundlage, breit fundiert, allgemein; ~**-brush** *adj* POL grob umrissen

broadcast 1. *n* MEDIA *radio* Rundfunksendung *f*, *TV* Fernsehsendung *f*; **2.** *vt* GEN COMM *make known* durchgeben, senden, durchsagen, MEDIA *radio* durch Rundfunk verbreiten, im Rundfunk senden, senden, übertragen, *TV* im Fernsehen senden, übertragen

Broadcasters: ~ **Audience Research Board** *n* (*BARB*) MEDIA Ausschuß für Rundfunk-Höreranalysen

broadcasting n GEN COMM, MEDIA Übertragung f, Sendung f

broadly adv GEN COMM breit; ◆ ~ **diversified** GEN COMM range of products stark diversifiziert, weit aufgefächert

broad: ~ **market** n STOCK aufnahmefähiger Markt m, lebhafter Handel m; ~ **masses** n pl POL breite Masse f; ~ **money** n BANK Geldmenge f M3, Geldmenge f in ihrer weitesten Abgrenzung

broadsheet n MEDIA newspaper Flugblatt nt, großformatige Zeitung f (obs), leaflet großformatiges Flugblatt nt, Großprospekt m, Planbogen m, poster Plakat nt; ~ **newspaper** n MEDIA Flugblatt nt, großformatige Zeitung f (obs)

broad: ~ **tape** n AmE STOCK insurance, real estate, securities aktiver Börsenticker m

brochure n GEN COMM, LEIS, S&M Broschüre f, Prospekt m, Werbeschrift f

broke adj infrml GEN COMM bankrott, pleite (infrml); ◆ **go** ~ infrml GEN COMM bankrott machen, pleite machen (infrml)

broken: ~ **down** adj GEN COMM aufgeschlüsselt, untergliedert; ~ **lot** n AmE S&M unvollständiges Warenset nt; ~ **period interest** n ACC, FIN, STOCK Stückzinsen m pl

broker n FIN Börsenhändler, in m,f, Makler, in m,f, Broker m

brokerage n GEN COMM Maklergeschäft nt, STOCK Courtage f; ~ **account** n STOCK Brokerkonto nt, Courtagekonto nt, Maklerkonto nt; ~ **allowance** n AmE STOCK Maklergebühr f; ~ **commission** n STOCK Maklerprovision f; ~ **statement** n STOCK Courtagerechnung f

broker: ~ **call-loan rate** n AmE STOCK Maklerkreditrate f; ~~**dealer** n STOCK Broker m, Händler, in m,f, Kursmakler, in m,f

brokered: ~ **deposit** n STOCK vom Makler vermittelte Einlage f

broker: ~ **fund** n BrE STOCK Brokerfonds m; ~'s **commission** n STOCK Courtage f, Maklergebühr f, Maklerprovision f; ~'s **loan** n STOCK täglich kündbarer Maklerkredit m; ~'s **order** n GEN COMM, TRANSP Verladeanweisung f, Verschiffungsorder f, STOCK Brokerauftrag m; ~'s **statement** n GEN COMM Maklerabrechnung f, STOCK Courtagerechnung f

Brookings: ~ **Institution** n AmE ECON Brookings-Institut nt

brown: ~ **goods** n pl S&M braune Ware f

browse vt COMP document, database blättern, durchsuchen

browsing n COMP Durchsuchen nt

Brundtland: ~ **Report** n ECON Bericht m der Brundtland-Kommission, Brundtland-Bericht m

brush up vt GEN COMM language, skill aufbessern, auffrischen

BS abbr (British Standard) IND, LAW ≈ DIN (Deutsche Industrienorm)

B/S abbr (balance sheet) ACC Bilanz f, Jahresabschluß m

BSBA abbr (Bachelor of Science in Business Administration) HRM Betriebswirt, in m,f

BSc abbr (Bachelor of Science) HRM Bakkalaureus m der Naturwissenschaften

BSC abbr (British Shippers' Council) TRANSP britischer Spediteurverband

BSCP abbr (British Standard Code of Practice) LAW britische Standesrichtlinien

BSF abbr (British Shipping Federation) TRANSP britischer Schiffahrtsverband

BSI abbr (British Standards Institution) ADMIN, IND, LAW britischer staatlicher Normenverband, ≈ DIN (Deutsches Institut für Normung)

BSS abbr (British Standard Specification) IND, LAW britische Normvorschrift

BT abbr (British Telecom) COMMS britische Telefongesellschaft

BTA abbr LEIS (British Travel Association) britischer Reiseverkehrsverband, (British Tourist Authority) britische Fremdenverkehrszentrale

bubble n infrml STOCK Schwindelunternehmen nt; ~ **memory** n COMP Magnetblasenspeicher m; ~ **pack** n S&M Klarsichtpackung f; ~ **packaging** n S&M Klarsichtverpackung f; ~ **policy** n ECON, ENVIR Blasenpolitik f, Glockenpolitik f; ~ **sort** n COMP Bubblesort nt

buck 1. n infrml GEN COMM Dollar m; ◆ **the** ~ **stops here** GEN COMM der Schwarze Peter bleibt bei mir hängen; 2. vt ◆ ~ **the trend** infrml GEN COMM gegen den Strom schwimmen, gegen den Trend laufen

buck up vi infrml GEN COMM aufleben, sich ranhalten (infrml)

bucket: ~ **shop** n FIN unreelle Maklerfirma f, LEIS unreelle Firma f, STOCK mit betrügerischen Mitteln arbeitende Maklerfirma f

bucks n pl infrml GEN COMM Kohle f (infrml)

Buddhist: ~ **economics** n ECON buddhistische Wirtschaftsform f

budget 1. n ACC, ECON, FIN, POL Budget nt, Etat m, Finanzplan m, Haushaltsplan m, of government Staatshaushalt m; 2. vi ACC, ECON, FIN, POL Etat aufstellen, einplanen, etatisieren

budget for vt ACC, FIN etatisieren, im Haushalt veranschlagen, im Haushalt vorsehen

budget: ~ **account** n FIN Konto nt laufender Zahlungen, Kundenkreditkonto nt; ~ **accounting** n ACC, ADMIN Plankostenrechnung f; ~ **allotment** n FIN Haushaltszuweisung f; ~ **analysis** n ACC, FIN Haushaltsanalyse f; ~ **appropriation** n FIN Ausgabenbewilligung f, Etatansatz m, POL governmental accounting Bewilligung f von Haushaltsmitteln

budgetary adj ACC, ECON, FIN haushaltsmäßig; ~ **account** n ACC, ECON, FIN Haushaltskonto nt, Haushaltsrechnung f; ~ **adjustment** n ACC, ECON, FIN Budgetberichtigung f, Haushaltsanpassung f, Planrevision f; ~ **appropriation** n FIN, POL of government Ausgabenbewilligung f, bewilligte Haushaltsmittel nt pl, Haushaltsbewilligung f, for commitment Verpflichtungsermächtigung f, for payment Zahlungsermächtigung f; ~ **constraint** n ACC Etateinschränkung f; ~ **control** n (BC) ACC, FIN Budgetkontrolle f, Haushaltskontrolle f, Etatkontrolle f, Finanzkontrolle f, Plankontrolle f; ~ **costs** n pl ACC Vorgabekosten pl, ECON, FIN Budgetkosten pl, Sollkosten pl, Vorgabekosten pl; ~ **cut** n ACC, ECON, FIN Haushaltskürzung f; ~ **deficit** n ECON, FIN Haushaltsdefizit nt, GEN COMM, POL Deckungslücke f, Haushaltsdefizit nt; ~ **expenditure** n FIN, POL of government Haushaltsausgaben f pl; ~ **period** n FIN, POL of government Haushaltsjahr nt, Finanzperiode f,

Haushaltsperiode *f*; ~ **planning** *n* FIN, POL *of government* Haushaltsplanung *f*, Finanzplanung *f*; ~ **policy** *n* POL Haushaltspolitik *f*; ~ **position** *n* ACC Haushaltsposition *f*; ~ **powers** *n pl* POL Haushaltsbefugnisse *f pl*, Verantwortung *f* für das Budget, Zuständigkeit *f* für den Etat; ~ **revenue** *n* FIN Haushaltseinnahmen *f pl*, POL im Etat veranschlagte Einnahmen *f pl*; ~ **spending** *n* FIN, POL *of government* Haushaltsausgaben *f pl*, im Etat veranschlagte Ausgaben *f pl*; ~ **statement** *n* POL *of government* Haushaltsübersicht *f*, Haushaltsabschluß *m*; ~ **submission** *n* ACC, ECON, FIN Haushaltsvorlage *f*; ~ **surplus** *n* ECON, FIN, GEN COMM, POL Haushaltsüberschuß *m*

budget: ~ **authority** *n AmE* FIN Ausgabeermächtigung *f*, POL *agency* Haushaltsbehörde *f*

Budget: ~ **Box** *n BrE* ECON, POL Koffer, in dem der Schatzkanzler den Haushaltsentwurf von 11, Downing Street zu den Houses of Parliament trägt

budget: ~ **ceiling** *n* ACC Haushaltsplafond *m*, ECON Ausgabengrenze *f*; ~ **constraint** *n* ACC, ECON, FIN Budgetrestriktion *f*; ~ **control** *n* ACC, FIN Budgetkontrolle *f*, Etatkontrolle *f*, Finanzkontrolle *f*, Haushaltskontrolle *f*, Plankontrolle *f*; ~ **cut** *n* ACC, ECON, FIN Haushaltskürzung *f*; ~ **cuts** *n pl* FIN Budgeteinsparungen *f pl*; ~ **cutting** *n* ACC, ECON, FIN, GEN COMM, POL Haushaltskürzung *f*; ~ **deficit** *n* GEN COMM Haushaltsdefizit *nt*

budgeted *adj* ACC veranschlagt, im Haushalt vorgesehen; ~ **cost** *n* ACC budgetierte Kosten *pl*, veranschlagte Ausgaben *f pl*, Vorgabekosten *pl*, FIN Vorgabekosten *pl* GEN COMM Plankosten *pl*; ~ **income** *n* ACC Sollertrag *m*, Planerlös *m*; ~ **profit** *n* ACC Planergebnis *nt*, Sollergebnis *nt*

budget: ~ **equation** *n* ECON *for the household* Bilanzgleichung *f*; ~ **expenditure** *n* ECON Haushaltsausgabe *f*; ~ **incidence** *n* ECON Budgetinzidenz *f*

budgeting *n* ACC, ADMIN, ECON, FIN Aufstellung *f* eines Haushaltsplanes, Budgetierung *f*, Etatisierung *f*, Finanzplanung *f*, Haushaltsplanung *f*

budget: ~ **layout** *n* ACC Plan *m*; ~ **level** *n* ACC Haushaltshöhe *f*; ~ **line** *n* ECON Bilanzgerade *f*; ~ **mortgage** *n AmE* BANK Hypothek bei der monatlich sowohl Zins- und Kapitalrückzahlungen als auch Steuer- und Versicherungsabgaben fällig werden; ~ **paper** *n* POL *of government* Haushaltsvorlage *f*; ~ **payment** *n* ECON *development aid* Entwicklungshilfe *f*; ~ **period** *n* ACC, ECON, FIN Haushaltsjahr *nt*, Budgetperiode *f*, Haushaltsperiode *f*, Planungsperiode *f*, POL Haushaltsperiode *f*; ~ **preparation** *n* ACC, ECON, FIN, MGMNT Budgetausarbeitung *f*, Budgeterstellung *f*, Haushaltsaufstellung *f*; ~ **price** *n* GEN COMM, S&M *specially reduced* Sparpreis *m*; ~ **prices** *n pl* ACC *used in establishing budget* Preisansätze *m pl*, Kalkulationspreise *m pl*; ~ **proposal** *n* ACC, ECON, FIN Haushaltsvorlage *f*

Budget: ~ **purdah** *n BrE* ECON, POL Hauptzeitraum der Aufstellung des Haushaltsplans

budget: ~ **reduction** *n* ACC, FIN Etatkürzung *f*; ~ **resolution** *n AmE* POL Haushaltsbeschluß *m*, Haushaltsverabschiedung *f*; ~ **review** *n* ACC, ECON, FIN Budgetrevision *f*, Berichtigung *f* der Planungsrechnung, Planrevision *f*

Budget: ~ **speech** *n BrE* ECON, POL Haushaltsrede *f* des Schatzkanzlers, Haushaltsrede *f* des Finanzministers

budget: ~ **standard** *n* ACC Soll-Kennziffer *f*, FIN Budgetstandard *m*, Haushaltsstandard *m*, GEN COMM Budgetstandard *m*, Haushaltsstandard *m*, Standard *m* der Lebenshaltungskosten; ~ **surplus** *n* ECON, FIN, GEN COMM, POL Haushaltsüberschuß *m*; ~ **system** *n* ACC, ADMIN Budgetierungssystem *nt*, betriebliches Planungswesen *nt*, Budgetwesen *nt*; ~ **variance** *n* ACC Etatabweichung *f*, FIN Planabweichung *f*; ~ **year** *n* ACC, FIN, POL Haushaltsjahr *nt*

buffer *n* COMP *circuit* Pufferspeicher *m*, *temporary data storage area* Puffer *m*, TRANSP Puffer *m*; ~ **area** *n* COMP Pufferbereich *m*; ~ **state** *n* POL Pufferstaat *m*; ~ **stock** *n* ECON Ausgleichslager *nt*, Puffervorrat *m*, Vorratslager *nt*, TRANSP Ausgleichsvorrat *m*, Pufferbestand *m*; ~ **storage** *n* COMP Puffer *m*, Pufferspeicher *m*; ~ **store** *n* COMP Puffer *m*, Pufferspeicher *m*, ECON Ausgleichslager *nt*; ~ **zone** *n* PROP Pufferzone *f*

bug *n* COMP Programmfehler *m*

build *vt* IND, PROP bauen; ◆ ~ **links with** GEN COMM Verbindungen aufbauen mit; ~ **sth into a contract** LAW *clause, stipulation, provison* etw in einen Vertrag einfügen

build in *vt* GEN COMM *time* einbauen

build up *vt* GEN COMM *firm* aufbauen, herstellen, errichten, *reserves* aufstocken, PROP *land* bebauen; ◆ ~ **from scratch** GEN COMM von vorn beginnen

building *n* GEN COMM Gebäude *nt*, IND Bau *m*, Bebauung *f*, PROP Bau *m*, Bebauung *f*, Gebäude *nt*; ~ **block concept** *n* IND Baukastenprinzip *nt*; ~ **code** *n* LAW, PROP Bauordnung *f*, Bauvorschriften *f pl*; ~ **expert** *n* IND, PROP Bausachverständige(r) *mf* [decl. as adj]; ~ **industry** *n* IND, PROP Bauindustrie *f*, Bauwesen *nt*; ~ **line** *n* LAW Bebauungsgrenze *f*, PROP Baulinie *f*; ~ **loan agreement** *n* BANK Baudarlehensvertrag *m*; ~ **and loan association** *n AmE* (*cf building society BrE*) BANK, FIN Bausparkasse *f*; ~ **lot** *n* PROP Baugrundstück *nt*; ~ **materials** *n pl* IND, PROP Baubedarf *m*, Baumaterial *nt*, Baustoff *m*; ~ **mortgage** *n* FIN Bauhypothek *f*; ~ **permit** *n AmE* PROP Baugenehmigung *f*; ~ **plan** *n* GEN COMM Bebauungsplan *m*; ~ **regulations** *n pl* LAW, PROP Bauvorschriften *f pl*; ~ **repair** *n* PROP Gebäudereparatur *f*; ~ **site** *n* IND, PROP Bau *m*, Bauplatz *m*, Baustelle *f*

Building: ~ **Societies Act** *n BrE* BANK Gesetz über die Liberalisierung der britischen Bausparkassen; ~ **Societies Association** *n BrE* BANK Verband der britischen Bausparkassen; ~ **Societies Commission** *n BrE* FIN Bausparkassenausschuß

building: ~ **society** *n BrE* (*cf building and loan association AmE, savings and loan association AmE*) BANK, FIN Bausparkasse *f*

build: ~-**up** *n* GEN COMM Ansammlung *f*

built: ~-**in** *adj* COMP, ECON eingebaut; ~-**in check** *n* COMP automatische Geräteprüfung *f*, Geräteselbstprüfung *f*; ~-**in flexibility** *n* ECON automatischer Konjunkturstabilisator *m*, stabilisierender Regelmechanismus *m*; ~-**in inflator** *n* ECON automatischer Inflationsverstärker *m*; ~-**in obsolescence** *n* ECON, S&M geplanter Verschleiß *m*, geplantes Veralten *nt*; ~-**in stabilizer** *n* ECON automatischer Konjunkturstabilisator *m*, automatischer Regelmechanismus *m*, automatischer Stabilisator *m*; ~-**in test** *n* COMP automatische Geräteprüfung *f*, Geräteselbstprüfung *f*; ~-**up area** *n* PROP bebaute Fläche *f*, bebautes Gebiet *nt*, geschlossene

Ortschaft *f*; **~-up vehicle** *n* TRANSP Fahrzeug *nt* mit Aufbauten

bulge *n* STOCK rascher Kursanstieg *m*

bulk *n* ECON Größe *f*, Großteil *m*, Masse *f*, GEN COMM *volume* Umfang *m*, Masse *f*, *majority* Menge *f*, Hauptteil *m*, größter Teil *m*, TRANSP *items to be carried* lose Waren *f pl*, Schüttgut *nt*; ◆ **in ~** IND unverpackt

bulk: **~ air mail** *n* (*BAM*) COMMS Massenluftpost *f*; **~ billing** *n* WEL Direktabrechnung *f*; **~ business** *n* GEN COMM größter Teil *m* des Geschäftes, Massengeschäft *nt*, Mengengeschäft *nt*; **~ buyer** *n* GEN COMM Großabnehmer *m*; **~ buying** *n* GEN COMM Mengeneinkauf *m*; **~ capacity** *n* TRANSP Ladefähigkeit *f*; **~ cargo** *n* TRANSP Massenfrachtgut *nt*, Schüttladung *f*; **~ cargo trade** *n* TRANSP Bulkhandel *m*; **~ carrier** *n* TRANSP Massengutfrachter *m*; **~ commodity** *n* GEN COMM Schüttgut *nt*, Massengut *nt*; **~ container** *n* TRANSP Behälter *m* für staubförmige Güter, Schüttgutcontainer *m*; **~ container ship** *n* TRANSP Schüttgutcontainerschiff *nt*; **~ discount** *n* GEN COMM Mengenrabatt *m*; **~ dry cargo berth** *n* TRANSP *shipping* Löschplatz *m* zur Abfertigung von Trocken-Bulkladung; **~ dry and wet cargo berth** *n* TRANSP *shipping* Löschplatz *m* zur Abfertigung von Naß- und Trocken-Bulkladung; **~ freight container** *n* TRANSP *shipping* Massengutcontainer *m*; **~ goods** *n pl* GEN COMM Schüttgut *nt*, unverpackte Ware *f*, TRANSP *items to be carried* lose Waren *f pl*, Schüttgut *nt*

bulkhead *n* TRANSP *in aircraft, ship* Schott *nt*

bulk: **~ input/output** *n* COMP Massen-Ein/Ausgabe *f*; **~ licence** *BrE*, **~ license** *AmE* IMP/EXP Bulklizenz *f*; **~ liquid berth** *n* TRANSP *shipping* Löschplatz *m* zur Abfertigung flüssigen Massenguts; **~ liquid container** *n* TRANSP *shipping* Container *m* für flüssiges Massengut; **~ mail** *n* COMMS Postwurfsendung *f*, GEN COMM Massendrucksachen *f pl*; **~ material** *n* GEN COMM Schüttgut *nt*; **~ order** *n* GEN COMM Großauftrag *m*, Sammelauftrag *m*; **~ package** *n* GEN COMM Großpackung *f*; **~ price** *n* ECON, GEN COMM Mengenpreis *m*; **~ purchase** *n* GEN COMM Großeinkauf *m*; **~ purchaser** *n* ECON, GEN COMM Großeinkäufer, in *m,f*, Mengeneinkäufer, in *m,f*, Großabnehmer *m*; **~ shipment** *n* TRANSP Massengutladung *f*, Massengutversand *m*; **~ storage** *n* GEN COMM Großlager *nt*, Massenspeicher *m*, TRANSP Massenspeicher *m*; **~ transhipment center** *AmE*, **~ transhipment centre** *BrE* *n* TRANSP Massengutumschlagplatz *m*, Massengutumschlagzentrum *nt*; **~ unitization** *n* TRANSP *shipping* Verpacken *nt* von Massengut in Einheiten, Zusammenfassung *f* von Massengut in Einheiten

bulky *adj* GEN COMM sperrig; **~ cargo** *n* GEN COMM sperrige Ladung *f*; **~ goods** *n pl* GEN COMM, S&M Sperrgut *nt*

bull *n* FIN Haussespekulant *m*, Haussier *m*, STOCK Haussier *m*; ◆ **go a ~** STOCK auf Hausse spekulieren

bull: **~ account** *n* STOCK Hausseengagement *nt*, Hausseposition *f*; **~-and-bear bond** *n* *BrE* STOCK Aktienindexanleihe *f*; **~ buying** *n* STOCK Haussekauf *m*, Kauf *m* auf Hausse; **~ call spread** *n* STOCK *options* Haussekündigungsspread *m*

bulldog: **~ bond** *n* *BrE* FIN Pfund-Sterling-Auslandsanleihe *f*; **~ edition** *n* *AmE* MEDIA *print* Frühausgabe *f* einer Zeitung; **~ issue** *n* *BrE* STOCK Pfund-Sterling-

Auslandsanleihe *f*; **~ loan** *n* *BrE* BANK Sterlingauslandsanleihe *f*

bullet *n* BANK Anleihe *f* ohne laufende Tilgung, endfällige Anleihe *f*, COMP Bullet *m* (*jarg*)

bulletin *n* COMMS Nachricht *f*, offizieller Bericht *m*, S&M Nachrichtenblatt *nt*; **~ board** *n* (*BB*) COMMS Anschlagbrett *nt*, Anzeigenbrett *nt*, Nachrichtentafel *f*, HRM schwarzes Brett *nt*

bulletin: **~ board service** *n* (*BBS*) COMMS Bulletin Board Service *m* (*jarg*) (*BBS*), Nachrichtenbrett *nt*

bullet: **~ loan** *n* BANK Anleihe *f* mit Endfälligkeit; **~ repayment** *n* BANK Anleihentilgung in einer Gesamtsumme; **~ vote** *n* POL Weiß-nicht-Stimme *f*

bullion *n* BANK Edelmetallbarren *m*

bullionist: **~ controversy** *n* BANK Streit *m* der Bullionisten

bullion: **~ market** *n* STOCK Goldbarrenmarkt *m*; **~ stock** *n* GEN COMM Edelmetallbestand *m*

bullish: **~ movement** *n* ECON, FIN, STOCK Hausse *f*

Bullock: **~ report** *n* *BrE* HRM Bullock Report *m*

bull: **~ position** *n* STOCK Hausseengagement *nt*, Hausseposition *f*; **~ put spread** *n* STOCK *options* Hausseverkaufsspread *m*; **~ speculation** *n* STOCK Haussespekulation *f*; **~ transaction** *n* STOCK Haussegeschäft *nt*; **~ week** *n* HRM Periode *f* mit geringen Fehlzeiten

bumper: **~ year** *n* GEN COMM Rekordjahr *nt*

bunches *n pl* *BrE* *infrml* GEN COMM Ausverkaufswaren *f pl*

bunch: **~ graph** *n* MATH Büschelkarte *f*

bunching *n* TAX Bündelung *f*

bunch: **~ map** *n* MATH Büschelkarte *f*

bundle 1. *n* MEDIA Packen *m*, TRANSP Bündel *nt*; 2. *vt* COMP, S&M bündeln

bundled: **~ with** *phr* COMP im Bündel mit; **~ deal** *n* STOCK Paketgeschäft *nt*; **~ software** *n* COMP Software *f* im Bündel

bundling *n* COMP, S&M Bundling *nt*, Bündeln *nt*; **~ yard** *n* TRANSP Paketierhof *m*

buoyant *adj* ECON *rising* steigend, *stock market* belebt, lebhaft, aktiv; **~ forces** *n pl* ECON Auftriebskräfte *f pl*; **~ tax** *n* TAX sich erhöhende Steuer *f*, anwachsende Steuer *f*

burden 1. *n* ADMIN Gemeinkosten *pl*, ECON Auflage *f*, Belastung *f*, Gemeinkosten *pl*, Last *f*, FIN Last *f*, GEN COMM Belastung *f*, LAW Belastung *f*, Auflage *f*, TAX Belastung *f*; 2. *vt* LAW belasten

burden: **~ of debts** *n* ECON Schuldenlast *f*; **~ of losses** *n* GEN COMM Verlustbelastung *f*; **~ of payment** *n* TAX Zahlungsbelastung *f*, Zahlungslast *f*; **~ of proof** *n* LAW Beweislast *f*

bureau *n* ADMIN *office* Büro *nt*, Amtszimmer *nt*, *government department* Amt *nt*, Behörde *f*, Dienststelle *f*

Bureau: **~ of the Budget** *n* (*BB*) POL Haushaltsabteilung des Schatzamtes der Vereinigten Staaten

bureaucracy *n* ADMIN, HRM Bürokratie *f*, Bürokratismus *m*

bureaucrat *n* ADMIN, HRM Bürokrat *m*

bureaucratic *adj* ADMIN, HRM bürokratisch

bureaucratization *n* ADMIN, HRM Bürokratisierung *f*

Bureau: **~ of Customs** *n* ECON Zollamt *nt*

bureau: **~ de change** *n* BANK, LEIS Wechselstube *f*

Bureau: ~ **of Economic Analysis** *n* (*BEA*) ECON Amt für Wirtschaftsanalyse; ~ **of Labour Statistics** *n* BrE HRM Amt für Arbeitsstatistik

burglar: ~ **alarm** *n* GEN COMM Alarmanlage *f*

burglary *n* LAW Einbruchdiebstahl *m*, Einbruch *m*

burning: ~ **cost** *n* INS Bedarfsprämie *f*, technische Bedarfsprämie *f*

burnout *n* HRM Zustand *m* totaler Erschöpfung

burst: ~ **advertising** *n* S&M erfolglose Werbung *f*; ~ **campaign** *n* S&M geplatzte Kampagne *f*

burster *n* COMP *for paper* Schlagschere *f*

burst: ~ **mode** *n* COMP Blockbetrieb *m*, Burstmodus *m*

bus *n* COMP *hardware* Bus *m*

business *n* GEN COMM *affairs to be attended to* Angelegenheit *f*, *commerce* Geschäfte *nt pl*, *enterprise, company* Geschäft *nt*, Unternehmen *nt*, *firm* Betrieb *m*, Firma *f*, *links, relations* Geschäftsverbindungen *f pl*; ♦ **on ~** GEN COMM geschäftlich; **do ~** GEN COMM Geschäfte tätigen; **do ~ as** GEN COMM *name* tätig sein als; **do ~ over the phone** MGMNT telefonisch Geschäfte tätigen; **go out of ~** GEN COMM die Geschäftstätigkeit einstellen; ~ **to ~** GEN COMM von Geschäft zu Geschäft, von Unternehmen zu Unternehmen; ~ **is at a low ebb** GEN COMM das Geschäft hat einen Tiefststand erreicht; ~ **is slack** GEN COMM das Geschäft ist ruhig; ~ **transferred to** GEN COMM Geschäftsübertragung auf; **what line of ~ are you in?** GEN COMM in welcher Branche sind Sie tätig?

business: ~ **account** *n* BANK Geschäftskonto *nt*; ~ **acquaintance** *n* GEN COMM, MGMNT Geschäftsbekanntschaft *f*, Geschäftsfreund, in *m,f*; ~ **activity** *n* GEN COMM Geschäftstätigkeit *f*; ~ **acumen** *n* MGMNT Geschäftsverstand *m*; ~ **address** *n* GEN COMM Geschäftsadresse *f*; ~ **administration** *n* ADMIN Betriebswirtschaft *f*, Betriebswirtschaftslehre *f*; ~ **administrator** *n* ADMIN Betriebswirt *m*; ~ **affairs** *n pl* GEN COMM geschäftliche Angelegenheiten *f pl*; ~ **agent** *n* AmE GEN COMM Gewerkschaftsvertreter, in *m,f*, Vertreter, in *m,f* in geschäftlichen Angelegenheiten, IND *trade union official* Gewerkschaftsvertreter, in *m,f*; ~ **assets** *n pl* ACC, FIN, GEN COMM Betriebsvermögen *nt*, Geschäftsvermögen *nt*; ~ **automobile policy** *n* AmE INS Versicherungsschutz *m* gewerblich genutzter Kraftfahrzeuge; ~ **bank** *n* BANK Geschäftsbank *f*; ~ **barometer** *n* ECON Konjunkturbarometer *m*; ~ **to be transacted** *n* GEN COMM *at meeting* vorgesehene Tagesordnung *f*; ~ **call** *n* GEN COMM Dienstgespräch *nt*; ~ **canvasser** *n* GEN COMM Geschäftsreisende(r) *mf* [decl. as adj], Geschäftsvertreter, in *m,f*; ~ **capital spending** *n* ACC, ECON Anlageinvestitionen *f pl*; ~ **card** *n* GEN COMM Geschäftskarte *f*, Visitenkarte *f*, MGMNT Geschäftskarte *f*; ~ **center** *AmE*, ~ **centre** *BrE* *n* GEN COMM *district* Geschäftsviertel *nt*, Geschäftszentrum *nt*, S&M *in airport* Geschäftszentrum *nt*, Handelszentrum *nt*, Wirtschaftszentrum *nt*; ~ **charges** *n pl* GEN COMM Betriebsausgaben *f pl*; ~ **circles** *n pl* GEN COMM Geschäftskreise *m pl*, Wirtschaftskreise *m pl*; ~ **class** *n* LEIS, TRANSP Businessklasse *f*; ~ **closure insurance** *n* INS Betriebsstillstandsversicherung *f*, Betriebsunterbrechungsversicherung *f*; ~ **college** *n* HRM Handelsakademie *f*; ~ **combination** *n* ACC Firmenzusammenschluß *m*, Geschäftszusammenschluß *m*, ECON Unternehmenszusammenschluß *m*; ~ **community** *n* GEN COMM Privatwirtschaft *f*,

Geschäftswelt *f*; ~ **computer** *n* COMP betrieblicher Rechner *m*, Geschäftscomputer *m*; ~ **computing** *n* COMP betriebliches Rechnerwesen *nt*; ~ **concern** *n* GEN COMM Geschäftsbetrieb *m*, Handelsunternehmen *nt*; ~ **conditions** *n pl* ECON wirtschaftliche Rahmenbedingungen *f pl*, wirtschaftliches Umfeld *nt*, GEN COMM Geschäftsbedingungen *f pl*; ~ **connection** *n* GEN COMM Geschäftsverbindung *f*, befreundete Firma *f*; ~ **connections** *n pl* GEN COMM Geschäftsverkehr *m*; ~ **convention** *n* GEN COMM Geschäftskonvention *f*; ~ **corporation** *n* ADMIN, ECON Kapitalgesellschaft *f*; ~ **corporation law** *n* AmE LAW Gesetz *nt* über Kapitalgesellschaften; ~ **creation** *n* GEN COMM Geschäftsgründung *f*; ~ **crime insurance** *n* INS Versicherung *f* gegen Wirtschaftskriminalität; ~ **cycle** *n* ECON Konjunkturzyklus *m*; ~ **data processing** *n* COMP, GEN COMM, WEL Wirtschaftsinformatik *f*, kommerzielle Datenverarbeitung *f*; ~ **dealings** *n pl* GEN COMM Geschäftsverbindungen *f pl*, LAW *transactions* kaufmännischer Geschäftsverkehr *m*; ~ **decision** *n* GEN COMM Geschäftsentscheidung *f*; ~ **development** *n* GEN COMM, MGMNT Geschäftsentwicklung *f*, geschäftliche Entwicklung *f*; ~ **diversification** *n* MGMNT Geschäftsdiversifizierung *f*; ~ **economist** *n* GEN COMM Betriebswirt *m*; ~ **enterprise** *n* GEN COMM Gewerbebetrieb *m*, gewerbliches Unternehmen *nt*, Handelsunternehmen *nt*, Wirtschaftsunternehmen *nt*, Firma *f* (*Fa.*); ~ **equipment and furnishing** *n* GEN COMM Betriebs- und Geschäftsaustattung *f*; ~ **ethics** *n pl* GEN COMM Geschäftsethik *f*; ~ **etiquette** *n* GEN COMM Geschäftsetikette *f*; ~ **expansion** *n* ECON Konjunkturaufschwung *m*, MGMNT Geschäftserweiterung *f*, Geschäftsausdehnung *f*; ~ **expenses** *n pl* GEN COMM Betriebsausgaben *f pl*; ~ **experience** *n* GEN COMM Geschäftserfahrung *f*; ~ **exposure life and health insurance** *n* AmE INS Lebens- und Krankenversicherung *f* gegen berufliche Risiken; ~ **exposures liability** *n* LAW *commercial* Haftung *f* für Geschäftsrisiken; ~ **failure** *n* GEN COMM Insolvenz *f*, geschäftlicher Zusammenbruch *m*; ~ **finance** *n* FIN Finanzwirtschaft *f*, Unternehmensfinanzierung *f*; ~ **forecasting** *n* ECON Konjunkturprognose *f*; ~ **form** *n* ADMIN *organization* Unternehmensform *m*, *paper* Formblatt *nt*, Geschäftsformular *nt*; ~ **generalist** *n* GEN COMM Allround-Geschäftsfrau *f*, Allround-Geschäftsmann *m*; ~ **gift** *n* S&M Werbegeschenk *nt*; ~ **goods** *n pl* GEN COMM Geschäftswaren *f pl*; ~ **graphics** *n pl* COMP Geschäftsgrafik *f*, FIN Unternehmensgrafik *f*, MEDIA Geschäftsgrafik *f*; ~ **indicator** *n* ECON Konjunkturbarometer *nt*, Konjunkturindikator *m*; ~ **in force** *n* INS Versicherungsbestand *m*; ~ **insurance** *n* INS Lebensversicherung *f* für leitende Angestellte, Rückdeckungsversicherung *f*, Sachversicherung *f*; ~ **interest** *n* GEN COMM Geschäftsinteresse *nt*; ~ **interruption** *n* GEN COMM Betriebsunterbrechung *f*, Geschäftsunterbrechung *f*; ~ **interruption insurance** *n* INS Betriebsunterbrechungsversicherung *f*; ~ **interruption policy** *n* INS Betriebsunterbrechungspolice *f*; ~ **journal** *n* ECON Wirtschaftszeitschrift *f*; ~ **law** *n* LAW Wirtschaftsrecht *nt*; ~ **lending to outside parties** *n* FIN Aktivkredit *m*; ~ **letter** *n* GEN COMM Geschäftsbrief *m*; ~ **liability** *n* LAW geschäftliche Haftung *f*; ~ **liability insurance** *n* INS Betriebshaftpflichtversicherung *f*, Geschäftshaftpflichtversicherung *f*; ~ **library** *n* GEN COMM Geschäftsbibliothek *f*; ~ **life and health insurance** *n* INS Partnerlebens- und Krankenversicherung *f*, Teilhaberlebens- und Krankenversicherung *f*; ~ **loan** *n* BANK gewerblicher Kredit *m*; ~ **loss** *n* ACC Geschäftsverlust *m*; ~ **lunch** *n* GEN COMM Geschäftsessen *nt*; ~ **machine** *n* GEN COMM Büromaschine *f*; ~ **magnate** *n* FIN Großindustrielle(r) *mf* [decl. as adj]

businessman *n* GEN COMM Geschäftsmann *m*, Kaufmann *m*, Unternehmer *m*

business: ~ **management** *n* ADMIN Betriebsleitung *f*, Geschäftsleitung *f*, ECON, MGMNT Betriebsführung *f*, Geschäftsführung *f*, Unternehmensführung *f*, *of estates, assets, money* Unternehmensverwaltung *f*; ~ **management agreement** *n* ECON, MGMNT Verwaltungsvertrag *m*; ~ **manager** *n* ADMIN, HRM, MGMNT Angestellte(r) *mf* [decl. as adj] in leitender Position, Hauptabteilungsleiter, in *m,f*, Geschäftsführer, in *m,f*, kaufmännischer Direktor *m*, kaufmännische Direktorin *f*, leitende(r) Angestellte(r) *mf* [decl. as adj]

businessman: ~'s **risk** *n* GEN COMM, STOCK Unternehmerrisiko *nt*

business: ~ **meeting** *n* GEN COMM geschäftliches Treffen *nt*; ~ **objective** *n* S&M Unternehmensziel *nt*; ~ **office** *n* ADMIN, LAW Geschäftslokal *nt*; ~ **operations** *n pl* GEN COMM Geschäftsbetrieb *m*, Geschäftstätigkeit *f*; ~ **opportunity** *n* GEN COMM Geschäftschance *f*, geschäftliche Möglichkeit *f*; ~ **organization** *n* GEN COMM Betriebsstruktur *f*, Firmenorganisation *f*; ~**-oriented** *adj* GEN COMM geschäftlich ausgerichtet, geschäftsorientiert; ~ **outlook** *n* ECON Geschäftsaussichten *f pl*, Konjunkturaussichten *f pl* GEN COMM Geschäftslage *f*, Geschäftsprognose *f*, Wirtschaftsvorschau *f*; ~ **owner's policy** *n* INS Geschäftseigentümerpolice *f*, Geschäftsinhaberpolice *f*; ~ **package** *n* COMP Geschäftspaket *nt*, FIN Sondertarifangebot *nt* für Geschäftsreisende, GEN COMM Geschäftspaket *nt*; ~ **pages** *n pl* GEN COMM *of newspaper* Wirtschaftsteil *m*; ~ **paper** *n* BANK Handelswechsel *m*, MEDIA, S&M *newspaper* Wirtschaftszeitung *f*; ~ **people** *n pl* GEN COMM Geschäftsleute *pl*; ~ **plan** *n* MGMNT Geschäftsplan *m*; ~ **plan consulting** *n* GEN COMM Beratung *f* zur Realisierung von Geschäftsvorhaben; ~ **plan guide** *n* GEN COMM Anleitung *f* für Geschäftsvorhaben; ~ **planning** *n* MGMNT Betriebsplanung *f*, Unternehmensplanung *f*; ~ **policy** *n* ADMIN, ECON Geschäftspolitik *f*, Unternehmenspolitik *f*, Grundsätze *m pl* der Unternehmenspolitik, Geschäftsmethoden *f pl*; ~ **portfolio** *n* ECON Geschäftsfelder-Portfolio *nt*, FIN, STOCK Unternehmensportefeuille *nt*; ~ **practice** *n* GEN COMM Geschäftspraxis *f*; ~ **premises** *n pl* GEN COMM Geschäftsgebäude *nt*, Geschäftslokal *nt*, Geschäftsräume *m pl*, gewerbliche Räume *m pl*; ~ **press** *n* MEDIA, S&M Wirtschaftspresse *f*; ~ **property and liability insurance package** *n* INS Geschäftsgrundstücks- und Haftpflichtversicherungspaket *nt*; ~ **proposition** *n* ECON Geschäftsvorschlag *m*, GEN COMM Geschäftsvorschlag *m*, geschäftlicher Vorschlag *m*; ~ **quarter** *n* GEN COMM *of town, city* Geschäftsviertel *nt*; ~ **recovery** *n* GEN COMM Geschäftserholung *f*; ~ **regulations** *n pl* GEN COMM Handelsvorschriften *f pl*, Betriebsvorschriften *f pl*; ~ **relations** *n pl* ECON Geschäftsbeziehungen *f pl*, Geschäftsverbindungen *f pl*, GEN COMM Geschäftsbeziehungen *f pl*, MGMNT Geschäftsbeziehungen *f pl*, geschäftliche Beziehungen *f pl*; ~ **reply card** *n* (*BRC*) COMMS, GEN COMM Rückantwort *f*; ~ **reply envelope** *n* (*BRE*) ADMIN, COMMS Freiumschlag *m*; ~ **reply mail** *n* (*BRM*) ADMIN,

COMMS Freiumschlag *m*, Rückantwort *f*; ~ **reply service** *n* S&M Werbeantwortdienst *m*; ~ **risk exclusion** *n* INS Unternehmensrisikoausschluß *m*; ~ **routine** *n* GEN COMM Geschäftsroutine *f*; ~ **school** *n* GEN COMM, WEL Handelsschule *f*; ~ **secret** *n* HRM Geschäftsgeheimnis *nt*, Dienstgeheimnis *nt*; ~ **sector** *n* GEN COMM Wirtschaftssektor *m*; ~ **segment reporting** *n* ACC, ADMIN Geschäftsfeld-Berichterstattung *f*, Berichterstattung *f* über einzelne Geschäftsbereiche; ~ **sense** *n* GEN COMM Geschäftssinn *m*; ~ **service** *n* ADMIN, GEN COMM Dienstleistung *f*; ~ **situation** *n* GEN COMM Wirtschaftslage *f*; ~ **slowdown** *n* ECON Konjunkturverlangsamung *f*, konjunktureller Abschwung *m*; ~ **strategy** *n* ECON, GEN COMM, MGMNT Geschäftsstrategie *f*, Unternehmensstrategie *f*; ~ **stream** *n* ECON Geschäftsfluß *m*, GEN COMM Geschäftsrichtung *f*; ~ **studies** *n pl* ECON Betriebswirtschaft *f*, Betriebswirtschaftslehre *f*; ~ **system** *n* ECON, GEN COMM Geschäftssystem *nt*; ~**-to-business advertising** *n* S&M Werbung *f* von Unternehmen zu Unternehmen; ~**-to-business marketing** *n* S&M Marketing *nt* von Unternehmen zu Unternehmen; ~ **tout** *n* GEN COMM Geschäftswerber, in *m,f*; ~ **travel** *n* TRANSP Geschäftsreise *f*; ~ **travel market** *n* TRANSP Geschäftsreisenmarkt *m*; ~ **trend** *n* GEN COMM Geschäftstrend *m*; ~ **trip** *n* GEN COMM, TRANSP Dienstreise *f*, Geschäftsreise *f*; ~ **unit** *n* GEN COMM Geschäftseinheit *f*; ~ **venture** *n* MGMNT risikobehaftetes Geschäftsunternehmen *nt*; ~ **volume** *n* GEN COMM Geschäftsumfang *m*, Geschäftsvolumen *nt*

businesswoman *n* GEN COMM Geschäftsfrau *f*, Kauffrau *f*, Unternehmerin *f*

business: ~ **world** *n* GEN COMM Geschäftswelt *f*; ~ **year** *n* ACC Wirtschaftsjahr *nt*, GEN COMM Geschäftsjahr *nt*

bus: ~ **mailing** *n* COMP Busmailing *nt* (*jarg*); ~ **shuttle** *n* TRANSP Buspendelverkehr *m*

bust *adj infrml* GEN COMM bankrott, pleite (*infrml*); **go ~** *infrml* ACC bankrott machen, BANK bankrott machen, pleite gehen (*infrml*), Pleite machen (*infrml*), ECON pleite gehen (*infrml*), Pleite machen (*infrml*), FIN bankrott machen, GEN COMM pleite gehen (*infrml*), Pleite machen (*infrml*), LAW bankrott machen, STOCK pleite gehen (*infrml*), Pleite machen (*infrml*)

busy *adj AmE* COMMS (*cf engaged BrE*) *telephone line, signal, tone* besetzt, COMP *machine* belegt, in Betrieb GEN COMM *person* belebt, beschäftigt, tätig; ♦ **be ~ doing sth** GEN COMM mit etw beschäftigt sein

busy: ~ **schedule** *n* MGMNT voller Terminkalender *m*; ~ **signal** *n AmE* (*cf engaged tone BrE*) COMMS *telephone* Besetztzeichen *nt*

butane *n* IND Butan *nt*; ~ **gas** *n* IND Butangas *nt*

butterfly: ~ **effect** *n* STOCK Strategie beim Handel mit Optionen; ~ **spread** *n* STOCK Butterfly-Spread *m*

butter: ~ **mountain** *n* ECON *agricultural* Butterberg *m*

buy 1. *vt* ECON anschaffen, beziehen, einkaufen, erwerben GEN COMM kaufen, abnehmen; ♦ ~ **airtime** S&M Fernsehwerbezeit kaufen; ~ **for the account** STOCK auf Termin kaufen; ~ **sth on approval** GEN COMM etw auf Probe kaufen; ~ **on the bad news** STOCK aufgrund von schlechten Nachrichten kaufen; ~ **on the black market** auf dem Schwarzmarkt kaufen ECON; ~ **on close** STOCK zum Börsenschluß kaufen; ~ **sth on credit** S&M etw auf Kredit kaufen; ~ **on a falling market** STOCK auf einem Baissemarkt kaufen; ~ **for future delivery** GEN COMM auf Terminlieferung kaufen; ~ **on hire purchase** *BrE* (*cf buy on the installment plan AmE*) FIN, S&M auf Abzahlungsbasis kaufen, auf Mietkaufbasis kaufen, auf Abzahlung kaufen; ~ **on the installment plan** *AmE* (*cf buy on hire purchase BrE*) FIN, S&M auf Abzahlungsbasis kaufen, auf Mietkaufbasis kaufen, auf Abzahlung kaufen; ~ **in large quantities** GEN COMM in großen Mengen kaufen; ~ **low and sell high** STOCK günstig ein- und teuer verkaufen, zu einem niedrigen Preis kaufen und einem hohen Preis verkaufen; ~ **at market** STOCK an der Börse kaufen; ~ **at a reduced price** GEN COMM zu reduzierten Preisen kaufen; ~ **shares on the open market** STOCK Aktien auf dem offenen Markt kaufen; ~ **in small quantities** GEN COMM in kleinen Mengen kaufen; ~ **sth on spec** *infrml* GEN COMM etw auf gut Glück kaufen (*infrml*); ~ **sth on tick** *infrml* GEN COMM etw auf Pump kaufen (*infrml*); ~ **at the top of the market** S&M zu Höchstpreisen kaufen; **2.** *vi* ECON, GEN COMM kaufen

buy back *vt* GEN COMM, STOCK zurückkaufen

buy in *vt* GEN COMM Deckungskäufe vornehmen, sich eindecken mit, einkaufen, *at auction* selbst ersteigern, STOCK Deckungskäufe vornehmen; ◆ ~ **sth in** GEN COMM *stock up with* sich mit etw eindecken

buy off *vt* GEN COMM *company* abfinden, aufkaufen

buy out *vt* GEN COMM *company* aufkaufen, *partner, shareholder* auszahlen

buy up *vt* GEN COMM *company* aufkaufen

buy: ~**-and-hold strategy** *n* STOCK Kauf-und-Halte-Strategie *f*; ~**-and-sell agreement** *n* ECON *business interests of deceased or disabled proprietor* Kauf- und Verkaufsabkommen *nt*; ~**-and-write strategy** *n* STOCK Kauf- und Verkaufsstrategie *f*; ~**-back** *n* FIN Rückkauf *m*; ~**-back agreement** *n* ECON *international trade* Rückkaufvereinbarung *f*, GEN COMM *transaction* Rückkaufgeschäft *nt*, LAW *contract* Rückkaufvereinbarung *f*; ~**-back clause** *n* LAW Rückkäufsklausel *f*; ~**-back construction** *n* LAW Wiederkauf *m*

buyer *n* GEN COMM Aufkäufer, in *m,f*, Einkäufer, in *m,f* Erwerber, in *m,f*, Käufer, in *m,f*; ~ **behavior** *AmE*, ~ **behaviour** *BrE* *n* S&M Käuferverhalten *nt*; ~ **concentration** *n* S&M Käuferkonzentration *f*; ~ **credit** *n* BANK Beschaffungskredit *m*, Käuferkredit

m; ~ **response** *n* S&M Käuferreaktion *f*; ~**'s market** *n* ECON, PROP, STOCK Käufermarkt *m*; ~**'s option** *n* GEN COMM Kaufoption *f*, STOCK Käuferoption *f*; ~**'s rate** *n* STOCK Ankaufssatz *m*, Geldkurs *m*, Geld *nt*

buying *n* ADMIN Beschaffungswesen *nt*, Einkauf *m*; ~ **behavior** *AmE*, ~ **behaviour** *BrE* *n* S&M Kaufverhalten *nt*; ~ **classes** *n pl* S&M Käuferschichten *f pl*; ~ **commission** *n* S&M Einkaufsprovision *f*; ~ **habits** *n pl* GEN COMM, S&M Kaufgewohnheiten *f pl*; ~ **in** *n* ECON Stützungskäufe *m pl* der Notenbanken, LAW *contracts* Deckungskauf *m*; ~**-in price** *n* ECON *EC* Einkaufspreis *m*; ~ **motive** *n* S&M Kaufmotiv *nt*; ~ **on margin** *n* FIN kreditfinanzierter Effektenkauf *m*, STOCK Effektenkauf *m* mit Einschuß, kreditfinanzierter Effektenkauf *m*; ~ **pattern** *n* S&M Kaufverhalten *nt*; ~ **power** *n* ECON, GEN COMM Kaufkraft *f*; ~ **price** *n* GEN COMM Kaufpreis *m*; ~ **process** *n* GEN COMM Kaufprozeß *m*; ~ **rate** *n* FIN Ankaufkurs *m*, Geldkurs *m*; ~ **rate of exchange** *n* BANK Ankaufskurs *m*, Ankaufssatz *m*, Geldkurs *m*, Sortenankaufskurs *m*; ~ **signal** *n* S&M Kaufsignal *nt*; ~ **surge** *n* GEN COMM Kaufflut *f*, Kaufwelle *f*; ~ **syndicate** *n* S&M Einkaufssyndikat *nt*; ~ **up** *n* GEN COMM Aufkauf *m*

buyout *n* FIN Aufkauf *m*, Buy-out *m*, Übernahme *f*, STOCK Aufkauf *m*, Buy-out *m*

buzzer *n* COMP Summer *m*

buzzword *n* *infrml* GEN COMM Modewort *nt*

BWB *abbr* (*British Waterways Board*) TRANSP britische Wasserstraßenverwaltung

by-election *n* POL Nachwahl *f*, Nebenwahl *f*, Sonderwahl *f*

bylaw *n* BANK Geschäftsordnung *f*, Satzung *f*, LAW Ortsvorschrift *f*; ~ **laws** *n pl* LAW Statuten *nt pl*

by-line *n* MEDIA, S&M Nebenlinie *f*

bypass: ~ **trust** *n* TAX Vermögensverwaltungsvertrag *m* zur Umgehung der Erbschaftssteuer

by-product *n* ECON *of principal commodity*, GEN COMM, IND, S&M Nebenprodukt *nt*

bystander *n* LAW Außenstehende(r) *mf* [decl. as adj]

byte *n* COMP Byte *nt*; ~ **mode** *n* COMP Zeichenbetrieb *m*

C

c *abbr* (*cage container*) TRANSP Käfig *m*, Käfigbehälter *m*, Käfigcontainer *m*

c. *abbr* (*coupon*) GEN COMM Bon *m*, Gutschein *m*, S&M Kupon *m*, STOCK Kupon *m*, Zinsschein *m*

C *abbr* (*consumption*) ECON Konsum *m*, Verbrauch *m*

ca. *abbr* (*circa*) GEN COMM ca. (*zirka*), ung. (*ungefähr*), rd. (*rund*)

CA *abbr* GEN COMM (*Consumers' Association*) Verbraucherverband *m*, MATH (*confluence analysis*) Konfluenzanalyse *f*, S&M (*Consumers' Association*) Verbraucherverband *m*

C/A *abbr* ACC (*check account AmE, checking account AmE, cheque account BrE, current account*) Girokonto *nt*, Kontokorrentkonto *nt*, (*current account*) Kreditkonto *nt*, BANK (*check account AmE, checking account AmE, cheque account BrE*) Girokonto *nt*, Kontokorrent *nt*, Kontokorrentkonto *nt*, (*capital account*) Kapitalkonto *nt*, (*credit account*) Kundenkreditkonto *nt*, ECON (*capital account*) *balance of payments* Kapitalkonto *nt*, Kapitalverkehrsbilanz *f*

CAA *abbr BrE* (*Civil Aviation Authority*) TRANSP Behörde für Zivilluftfahrt

CAAS *abbr* (*computer-aided advertising system*) S&M computergestützte Werbung *f*

cab *n AmE* (*cf taxi BrE*) TRANSP Taxi *nt*

CAB *abbr* ADMIN *BrE* (*Citizens Advice Bureau*) Rechtshilfeberatungsstelle *f*, TRANSP *AmE* (*Civil Aeronautics Board*) oberste amerikanische Behörde der Zivilluftfahrt

CABAF *abbr* (*currency and bunker adjustment factor*) TRANSP *shipping* Währungs- und Bunkerausgleichsfaktor *m*

cabin *n* TRANSP *on ship or aircraft* Kabine *f*; ~ **allocation** *n* TRANSP *shipping* Kabinenzuteilung *f*; ~ **charge** *n* TRANSP *shipping* Kabinengebühren *f pl*

cabinet *n* POL Kabinett *nt*

Cabinet *n* POL Regierung *f* (*Reg.*); ~ **Committee on Social Development** *n BrE* POL Regierungskommission *f* für soziale Entwicklung

cabinet: ~ **crowd** *n* STOCK *low volume securities* Markt *m* umsatzschwacher Papiere, Händler *m pl* umsatzschwacher Wertpapierspezialitäten

Cabinet: ~ **reshuffle** *n* POL Regierungsumbildung *f*

cabinet: ~ **security** *n AmE* STOCK *low volume securities* umsatzschwaches Papier *nt*, umsatzschwache Wertpapierspezialität *f*

cabin: ~ **staff** *n* TRANSP *on ship* Bordpersonal *nt*

cable *n* COMMS *wiring* Kabel *nt*, *message* Telegramm *nt*, ECON, IND, MEDIA, S&M Kabel *nt*, STOCK *AmE jarg* Pfund-Kurs in Dollar *nt*; ~ **address** *n* COMMS Telegrammadresse *f*

cablegram *n frml* COMMS Telegramm *nt*

cable: ~ **program** *AmE*, ~ **programme** *BrE n* MEDIA Kabelprogramm *nt*; ~ **rate** *n* ECON *international trade* Kabelkurs *m*; ~ **television** *n* MEDIA Kabelfernsehen *nt*; ~ **transfer** *n* BANK, FIN telegrafische Auszahlung *f*, telegrafische Überweisung *f*

cabotage *n* TRANSP Kabotage *f*

cab: ~ **stand** *n AmE* (*cf taxi rank BrE*) TRANSP Taxistand *m*

CAC *abbr* HRM (*Central Arbitration Committee*) zentrale Schlichtungsstelle *f*, zentrale Schiedskommission *f*, IMP/EXP (*Customs Additional Code*) zusätzliche Zollordnung *f*, MGMNT (*Central Arbitration Committee*) zentrale Schiedskommission *f*, zentrale Schlichtungsstelle *f*, WEL (*Consumers' Advisory Council*) Rat für Verbraucherberatung

cache *n* COMP Cache *m*; ~ **buffer** *n* COMP Pufferspeicher *m*; ~ **memory** *n* COMP Cache-Speicher *m*; ~ **storage** *n* COMP Cache-Speicher *m*, schneller Pufferspeicher *m*; ~ **store** *n* COMP Cache-Speicher *m*, schneller Pufferspeicher *m*

CACM *abbr* (*Central American Common Market*) ECON Zentralamerikanischer Gemeinsamer Markt *m*

c.a.d. *abbr* (*cash against documents*) IMP/EXP Barzahlung *f* gegen Dokumente, Kasse *f* gegen Dokumente

CAD *abbr* COMP (*computer-aided design, computer-assisted design*) *development* CAD (*computerunterstützte Entwicklung, computerunterstützte Konstruktion, computerunterstützter Entwurf, computerunterstütztes Konstruieren*), IMP/EXP (*cash against documents*) Barzahlung *f* gegen Dokumente, Kasse *f* gegen Dokumente, IND (*computer-aided design, computer-assisted design*) CAD (*computerunterstützte Entwicklung, computerunterstützte Konstruktion, computerunterstützter Entwurf, computerunterstütztes Konstruieren*)

cadastral: ~ **survey** *n* PROP *of property* Katasterplan *m*

cadastre *n* TAX Grundstückswertregister *nt*

CAD/CAM *abbr* (*computer-aided design and manufacturing, computer-assisted design and manufacturing*) COMP, IND CAD/CAM (*computerunterstützte Entwicklung und Fertigung*)

CADD *abbr* (*computer-aided design and drafting, computer-assisted design and drafting*) COMP, IND CADD (*computerunterstütztes Konstruieren und technisches Zeichnen*)

cadre *n* HRM Personalstamm *m*, Stammpersonal *nt*, POL Kader *m*

CAE *abbr* (*computer-aided engineering, computer-assisted engineering*) COMP, IND CAE (*computerunterstütztes Ingenieurwesen*)

CAF *abbr* IMP/EXP, TRANSP (*cost and freight*) C&F (*Kosten und Fracht*), (*currency adjustment factor*) *surcharge on freight* Währungsausgleichsfaktor *m*

cafeteria: ~ **benefit plan** *n AmE* HRM A-la-carte-Vergütungssystem *nt*, System *nt* flexiber Entgeltgestaltung

CAFR *abbr* (*comprehensive annual financial report*) ADMIN, ECON Gesamtjahresabschluß *m*, Jahreshaushaltsbericht *m*

cage *n AmE* STOCK Abwicklungsstelle *f*; ~ **container** *n* (*c*) TRANSP *shipping* Käfig *m*, Käfigbehälter *m*, Käfigcontainer *m*; ~ **inventory record** *n* (*CIR*) TRANSP Käfiglagerkarte *f*

CAI *abbr* (*computer-aided instruction, computer-assisted* *instruction*) COMP CAI (*computerunterstützter Unterricht*)

Cairn: ~'s **Group** *n* ECON *agricultural* Cairns-Gruppe *f*

CAL *abbr* (*computer-aided learning, computer-assisted learning*) COMP CAL (*computerunterstütztes Lernen*)

calculable *adj* MATH berechenbar

calculate 1. *vt* GEN COMM ansetzen, berechnen, ausrechnen, durchrechnen, MATH berechnen, errechnen, rechnen; **2.** *vi* MATH rechnen

calculating *n* GEN COMM, MATH Rechnen *nt*; ~ **machine** *n* COMP, GEN COMM Rechenmaschine *f*

calculation *n* GEN COMM Rechnung *f*, Berechnung *f*, Berechnen *nt*, Kalkulation *f*; ~ **of probabilities** *n* ECON, MATH Wahrscheinlichkeitsrechnung *f*

calculator *n* COMP Rechenwerk *nt*, GEN COMM Rechenmaschine *f*, Rechner *m*

calculus: ~ **of probabilities** *n* MATH *theory* Wahrscheinlichkeitsrechnung *f*

calendar *n* GEN COMM Kalender *m*; ~ **day** *n* GEN COMM Kalendertag *m*; ~ **management** *n* MGMNT Terminverwaltung *f*, Terminplanung *f*; ~ **spread** *n* STOCK Kalender-Spread *m*, Kalender-Zinsspanne *f*; ~ **week** *n* GEN COMM Kalenderwoche *f* (*KW*)

caliber *AmE see* calibre *BrE*

calibration *n* GEN COMM, TRANSP Maßeinteilung *f*, Kalibrierung *f*, Eichung *f*

calibre *n BrE* HRM *of staff* Format *nt*, Kaliber *m*

call 1. *n* COMMS Anruf *m*, Ruf *m*, COMP Aufruf *m*, FIN *capital* Abruf *m*, Einforderung *f*, Option *f*, GEN COMM Gespräch *nt*, *call option* Vorprämie *f*, S&M Nachfrage *f*, STOCK Kaufoption *f*, Vorprämie *f*, *request to pay* Zahlungsaufforderung *f*; ♦ **at** ~ STOCK mit Kaufoption; **2.** *vt* COMMS anrufen, COMP aufrufen; ♦ ~ **a meeting** ADMIN eine Sitzung einberufen; ~ **a strike** HRM, IND einen Streik ausrufen, zum Streik aufrufen; ~ **collect** *AmE* (*cf reverse the charges BrE*) COMMS R-Gespräch anmelden; ~ **into play** GEN COMM aufbieten, einsetzen; ~ **sb as a witness** LAW jdn als Zeugen anrufen; ~ **sb to account** GEN COMM jdn zur Rechenschaft ziehen; ~ **sb to the bar** *BrE* LAW jdn als Anwalt zulassen; ~ **sb toll-free** *AmE* COMMS jdn gebührenfrei anrufen

call back 1. *vt* COMMS zurückrufen; **2.** *vi* COMMS zurückrufen

call in *vt* ECON *remove banknotes from circulation*, FIN aufrufen, *credit* kündigen, GEN COMM rückrufen

call on *vt* GEN COMM aufsuchen

call out *vt* GEN COMM ausrufen

call up *vt* COMMS anrufen, FIN aufrufen

CALL *abbr* (*computer-aided language learning, computer-assisted language learning*) COMP CALL (*computerunterstütztes Lernen von Sprachen*)

callable: ~ **capital** *n* BANK jederzeit abrufbares Kapital *nt*; ~ **loan** *n* BANK kündbares Darlehen *nt*

call: ~ **account** *n* BANK Sichteinlagenkonto *nt*; ~ **analysis** *n* S&M Auswertung *f* von Anrufen, Auswertung *f* von Vertreterbesuchen; ~ **box** *n* COMMS Telefonzelle *f*; ~ **charge** *n* COMMS Gesprächsgebühr *f*; ~ **date** *n* FIN *IMF & international banking* Stichtag *m*; ~ **delta** *n* STOCK Kaufoptionsdelta *nt*; ~ **deposit** *n* BANK Sichteinlage *f*, Sichteinlagen *f pl*

called: ~-**in** *adj* STOCK eingezogen; ~-**in share** *n* STOCK eingezogene Aktie *f*; ~-**up share capital** *n* ACC, FIN

eingefordertes Kapital *nt*, STOCK zur Einzahlung aufgerufenes Aktienkapital *nt*

call: ~ **exercise price** *n* STOCK Basispreis *m* einer Kaufoption; ~ **for redemption of securities** *n* ACC Aufforderung *f* zur Einlösung von Wertpapieren; ~ **for tender** *n* ADMIN Aufforderung *f* zur Angebotsabgabe; ~ **forwarding** *n* COMMS *telephone company service*, COMP Rufweiterschaltung *f*; ~ **frequency** *n* S&M *of calls paid to customer* Häufigkeit *f* von Vertreterbesuchen, *of phone calls received* Anrufhäufigkeit *f*

calling *n* GEN COMM Aufforderung *f*, Einberufung *f*; ~ **cycle** *n* S&M Kundenbesuchszyklus *m*; ~ **forward notice** *n* TRANSP Abrufen *nt* einer Versandnotiz; ~ **program** *n* COMP Abrufprogramm *nt*

call: ~-**in of a loan** *n* FIN Anleihekündigung *f*; ~ **loan** *n* BANK kurzfristiges Darlehen *nt*; ~ **money** *n* BANK tägliches Geld *nt*, Tagesgeld *nt*; ~ **money rate** *n* BANK, FIN Tagesgeldsatz *m*; ~ **option** *n* GEN COMM Vorprämie *f*, STOCK Kaufoption *f*, Vorprämie *f*; ~ **protection** *n* STOCK Schutz *m* vor vorzeitiger Kündigung, Kündigungsschutz *m*; ~ **provision** *n* STOCK Kündigungsklausel *f*; ~ **rate** *n* BANK *of interest*, FIN Tagesgeldsatz *m*; ~ **report** *n* COMMS Rufbericht *m*, S&M Kontaktbericht *m*; ~ **schedule** *n* FIN Tilgungsplan *m*; ~-**selling hedge** *n* STOCK Kaufoptionssicherungsgeschäft *nt*; ~ **sign** *n* TRANSP *shipping* Funkrufzeichen *nt*; ~'s **strike** *n* STOCK Basispreis *m* einer Kaufoption; ~ **writing** *n* STOCK Verkauf *m* von Kaufoptionen

CAM *abbr* (*computer-aided manufacturing, computer-assisted manufacturing*) COMP, IND CAM (*computerunterstützte Fertigung*)

Cambridge: ~ **controversies** *n pl* ECON Cambridge-Kontroversen *f pl*; ~ **Economic Policy Group** *n* ECON Cambridge-Ökonomen *m pl*; ~ **school** *n* ECON Cambridge Schule *f*

CAMEL *abbr BrE* (*capital, assets, management, earnings, liquidity*) ECON, FIN Kapital, Vermögen, Management, Ertrag, Liquidität

camera *n* MEDIA, S&M Kamera *f*; ♦ **in** ~ LAW nicht-öffentlich, *meeting* unter Ausschluß der Öffentlichkeit

camera: ~-**ready** *adj* MEDIA reprofähig, reproreif; ~-**ready copy** *n* (*CRC*) MEDIA reprofähige Vorlage *f*, reproreife Vorlage *f*

camouflaged: ~ **advertising** *n* S&M Schleichwerbung *f*; ~ **inflation** *n* ECON verdeckte Inflation *f*; ~ **unemployment** *n* ECON verdeckte Arbeitslosigkeit *f*

campaign *n* GEN COMM Initiative *f*, POL, S&M Kampagne *f*; ~ **plan** *n* S&M Plan *m* für eine Kampagne, Aktionsplan *m*

can *n* S&M Dose *f*, Blechdose *f*

Canadian: ~ **Prime Rate** *n* ECON kanadische Prime Rate *f*

canal *n* TRANSP Kanal *m*; ~ **dues** *n pl* TRANSP *shipping* Kanalgebühren *f pl*; ~ **fees** *n pl* TRANSP *shipping* Kanalgebühren *f pl*

cancel *vt* BANK annullieren, streichen, COMP abbrechen, GEN COMM *order* annullieren, stornieren, HRM kündigen, LAW aufheben, auflösen, stornieren, wandeln, widerrufen, rückgängig machen, PATENTS löschen; ♦ ~ **a contract** LAW einen Vertrag aufheben; ~ **an entry** ADMIN, GEN COMM, LAW Eintragung löschen

cancel out 1. *vt* ACC, MATH aufheben, ausgleichen; **2.** *vi* ACC, MATH sich aufheben, sich ausgleichen

canceled *AmE see* cancelled *BrE*

canceling *AmE see cancelling BrE*

cancellation *n* ACC Stornierung *f*, Stornobuchung *f*, Rückbuchung *f* BANK Annullierung *f*, Streichung *f*, FIN *of debt* Streichung *f*, GEN COMM Annullierung *f*, *of order* Stornierung *f*, *of appointment* Absage *f*, LAW Widerruf *m*, Rückgängigmachung *f*, Ungültigkeitserklärung *f*, Aufhebung *f*, Auflösung *f*, Kündigung *f*, Stornierung *f*, PATENTS *of entry* Löschung *f*; ~ **clause** *n* LAW *of contract* Rücktrittsklausel *f*; ~ **fee** *n* INS Stornogebühr *f*, Ritornogebühr *f*; ~ **of premium** *n* INS Prämienstorno *nt*; ~ **provision clause** *n* INS Rücktrittsklausel *f*; ~ **of registration** *n* TAX *VAT* Löschung *f* der Registrierung

cancelled: ~ **cheque** *n BrE* BANK annullierter Scheck *m*

cancelling: ~ **clause** *n BrE* LAW Rücktrittsklausel *f*, Verfallsklausel *f*; ~ **date** *n BrE* TRANSP *charter contract* Stornierungsdatum *nt*, Widerrufstag *m*; ~ **return** *n BrE* INS Prämienrückzahlung *f*, Rückprämie *f*

C&D *abbr* (*collected and delivered*) GEN COMM eingezogen und ausgeliefert

C&E *abbr* (*Customs & Excise*) IMP/EXP britische Zoll- und Steuerbehörde

C&F *abbr* (*cost and freight*) IMP/EXP, TRANSP *Incoterms* C&F (*Kosten und Fracht*)

C&I *abbr* (*cost and insurance*) IMP/EXP, TRANSP *Incoterms* C&I (*Kosten und Versicherung*)

candidacy *n* POL Kandidatur *f*

candidate *n* HRM, POL Kandidat, in *m,f*

candidature *n* POL Kandidatur *f*

C&U: ~ **regulations** *n pl* (*construction and use regulations*) IND *road transport* Bau- und Anwendungsbestimmungen *f pl*, Bau- und Verwendungsbestimmungen *f pl*

canned: ~ **presentation** *n* S&M auf Band aufgenommene Präsentation *f*; ~ **program** *n* COMP Fertigprogramm *nt*

canons: ~ **of taxation** *n pl* TAX Besteuerungsgrundsätze *m pl*

canton *n* POL *in Switzerland* Kanton *m*

cantonal: ~ **bank** *n* BANK *in Switzerland* Kantonalbank *f*

canvas: ~ **cover** *n* (*CC*) TRANSP Segeltuchüberzug *m*

canvass *vi* S&M Kunden werben

canvasser *n* GEN COMM Akquisiteur *m*, S&M Kundenwerber, in *m,f*

canvassing: ~ **costs** *n pl* ACC, GEN COMM, INS, S&M Akquisitionskosten *pl*

cap 1. *abbr* (*capital letter*) COMP, MEDIA Großbuchstabe *m*; **2.** *n* ECON Grenze *f*, Begrenzung *f*, FIN Zinsbegrenzung *f* nach oben, *on interest rate* Obergrenze *f*, Höchstzinssatz *m* bei Cap-Floatern, Cap *m*, Maximalzinssatz *m*, GEN COMM Obergrenze *f*; **3.** *vt* ◆ ~ **an interest rate** BANK einen Zinssatz nach oben begrenzen

CAP *abbr* ECON, POL (*Common Agricultural Policy*) GAP (*gemeinsame Agrarpolitik*), S&M (*code of advertising practice*) Werbekodex *m*

capability *n* GEN COMM Fähigkeit *f*, Leistungsvermögen *nt*

capable *adj* GEN COMM fähig; ◆ ~ **of** GEN COMM fähig zu; ~ **of development** GEN COMM entwicklungsfähig

capacitance *n* COMP *hardware* Kapazität *f*

capacity *n* ECON *production* Kapazität *f*, GEN COMM, HRM *personal, professional* Befähigung *f*, Kapazität *f*; ◆ **at full** ~ GEN COMM bei voller Kapazität, bei voller Leistungsfähigkeit, IND bis auf den letzten Rest gefüllt, das ganze Fassungsvermögen gefüllt, randvoll, zur Vollast

capacity: ~ **charge** *n* ECON, INS Kapazitätsauslastung *f*, Kapazitätsausnutzung *f*; ~ **effect** *n* ECON Kapazitätseffekt *m*; ~ **ratio** *n* ECON Kapazitätsverhältnis *nt*; ~ **to work** *n* GEN COMM Arbeitsfähigkeit *f*; ~ **utilization** *n* ECON Kapazitätsauslastung *f*, Kapazitätsausnutzung *f*, IND *data processing* Bestückung *f*, INS Kapazitätsauslastung *f*, Kapazitätsausnutzung *f*; ~ **utilization rate** *n* ECON Kapazitätsauslastung *f*, Kapazitätsausnutzung *f*, IND *data processing* Bestückungsausbau *m*, INS Kapazitätsauslastung *f*, Kapazitätsausnutzung *f*

CAP: ~ **charges** *n pl* ECON Belastungen *f pl* im Rahmen der gemeinsamen Agrarpolitik

capex *abbr* (*capital expenditure*) ACC, FIN aktivierungspflichtiger Aufwand *m*, Anlagekosten *pl*, Investitionsaufwand *m*

CAP: ~ **goods** *n pl* ECON unter die gemeinsame Marktordnung fallende Agrargüter *nt pl*

cap: ~ **issue** *n* (*capitalization issue*) STOCK Ausgabe *f* von Gratisaktien

capital *n* ACC Aktienkapital *nt*, Grundkapital *nt*, Stammkapital *nt* Vermögen *nt*, FIN Kapital *nt*, Vermögen *nt*, Gewinn *m*; ~ **account** *n* (*C/A*) BANK Kapitalkonto *nt*, ECON *balance of payments* Kapitalkonto *nt*, Kapitalverkehrsbilanz *f*, FIN Kapitalkonto *nt*; ~ **accumulation** *n* ECON, FIN Kapitalansammlung *f*, Kapitalbildung *f*, Vermögensbildung *f*; ~ **adequacy** *n* BANK erforderliche Kapitaldecke *f*, angemessene Kapitalausstattung *f*, FIN *of investment firms and credit institutions* ausreichende Kapitalausstattung *f*; ~ **aid** *n* ECON *development aid* Kapitalhilfe *f*; ~ **allotment** *n* FIN *governmental* Kapitalzuteilung *f*; ~ **allowance** *n BrE* ACC Abschreibung *f*, Abschreibungsbetrag *m*, steuerliche Abschreibung *f*, TAX steuerliche Abschreibung *f*; ~ **and reserves** *n pl* ACC Eigenmittel *nt pl*, Eigenkapital *nt*; ~ **appreciation** *n* ECON Vermögenszuwachs *m*; ~ **asset** *n* FIN *investment* Anlagegut *nt*, Kapitalgut *nt*, Wirtschaftsgut *nt*; ~ **asset account** *n* BANK Kapitalanlagekonto *nt*; ~ **asset pricing model** *n* (*CAPM*) ECON, FIN, STOCK Kapitalanlagepreismodell *nt*, Preismodell *nt* für Kapitalvermögen; ~ **assets** *n pl* ECON Kapitalanlagegüter *nt pl*, GEN COMM Anlagegüter *nt pl*, FIN Kapitalanlagen *f pl*, TAX Anlagegüter *nt pl*, Anlagekapital *nt*, Anlagevermögen *nt*, fixe Anlagen *f pl*, Kapitalvermögen *nt*; ~, **assets, management, earnings, liquidity** *phr BrE* (*CAMEL*) ECON, FIN Kapital, Vermögen, Management, Ertrag, Liquidität; ~ **assured** *n* INS versichertes Kapital *nt*; ~–**augmenting technical progress** *n* ECON kapitalvermehrender technischer Fortschritt *m*; ~ **bonds** *n pl BrE* STOCK Kapitalobligationen *f pl*; ~ **bonus** *n* INS Überschußbeteiligung *f*, Versicherungsbonus *m*; ~ **budget** *n* ACC Investitionshaushalt *m*, Investitionsplan *m*, ADMIN Investitionsplan *m*, ECON Finanzbudget *nt*, Kapitalbudget *nt*, *for investment* Investitionsplanung *f*, Wirtschaftlichkeitsrechnung *f*, Investitionsrechnung *f*; ~ **budgeting** *n* ACC Budgetierung *f* der Investitionen, Investitionsrechnung *f*, ECON Investitionsrechnung *f*, FIN Wirtschaftlichkeitsrechnung *f*; ~ **commitment** *n* ACC finanzielles Engagement *nt*, Investitionsvolumen *nt*, Kapitalbindung *f*, Kapitaleinsatz *m*, FIN Investitionsvolumen *nt*; ~ **consolidation** *n* ECON Kapitalkonsolidierung *f*; ~ **consumption** *n* ECON Abschreibung *f*, Abschreibungen *f pl*, Kapitalverschleiß *m*; ~ **consumption allowance** *n*

ECON Abschreibung *f*, Kapitalverschleiß *m*; ~ **costs** *n pl* ECON Finanzierungskosten *pl*, Investitionskosten *pl*, Kapitalkosten *pl*; ~ **cover** *n* BANK Kapitaldeckung *nt*; ~ **deepening** *n* ECON Verbesserungsinvestition *f*; ~ **employed** *n* ACC, FIN Anlagekapital *nt*, eingesetztes Kapital *nt*, investiertes Kapital *nt*; ~ **expenditure** *n* (*capex*) ACC, FIN aktivierungspflichtiger Aufwand *m*, Anlagekosten *pl*, Investitionsaufwand *m*; ~ **expenditure appraisal** *n* ECON Investitionsrechnung *f*; ~ **expenditure budget** *n* ACC Investitionsbudget *nt*, Investitionsplan *m*; ~ **expenditure evaluation** *n* FIN Wirtschaftlichkeitsrechnung *f*; ~ **expenditure vote** *n* POL *governmental* Abstimmung *f* über Investitionen, Investitionsausgaben *f pl*; ~ **flight** *n* ECON Kapitalflucht *f*; ~ **flow** *n* FIN Kapitalfluß *m*, Kapitalbewegung *f*, Kapitalverkehr *m*; ~ **formation** *n* ECON, FIN Kapitalbildung *f*, Vermögensbildung *f*; ~ **fund** *n* FIN Gesamtkapitalausstattung *f* einer Unternehmung, Kapitalfonds *m*, Kapitalstock *m*, Stammkapital *nt*, Grundkapital *nt*; ~ **funding planning** *n* FIN Kapitalfinanzierungsplanung *f*; ~ **gain** *n* TAX Kapitalzuwachs *m*, Wertzuwachs *m*, Veräußerungsgewinn *m*; ~ **gains** *n pl* ACC Gewinn *m* aus der Veräußerung von Kapitalanlagegütern, Kapitalgewinn *m*, ECON, FIN Kapitalzuwachs *m*, Wertzuwachs *m*, Kapitalgewinn *m*, STOCK realisierte Kursgewinne *m pl*, TAX Kapitalgewinn *m*; ~ **gains after tax** *n pl* ACC, TAX Kapitalzuwachs *m* nach Steuern, Kapitalgewinn *m* nach Steuern; ~ **gains distribution** *n* STOCK Ausschüttung *f* realisierter Kursgewinne, Ausschüttung *f* von Kapitalgewinnen, Gewinnausschüttung; ~ **gains tax** *n* (*CGT*) TAX Kapitalertragsteuer *f*, Wertzuwachssteuer *f*, Kapitalgewinnsteuer *f*; ~ **goods** *n pl* GEN COMM Anlagegüter *nt pl*, Investitionsgüter *nt pl*, Kapitalgüter *nt pl*; ~ **growth** *n* STOCK Kapitalzuwachs *m*, Substanzerhöhung *f*, Wertzuwachs *m*; ~ **income tax** *n* ECON, FIN, TAX Vermögensteuer *f*, Vermögenszuwachssteuer *f*; ~ **increase** *n* ECON Erhöhung *f* des Kapitals, Kapitalzuwachs *m*; ~ **inflow** *n* ECON Kapitalzufluß *m*; ~ **intensive** *adj* ECON anlagenintensiv, kapitalintensiv, FIN kapitalintensiv; ~ **intensive industry** *n* ECON, FIN, IND kapitalintensive Industrie *f*

Capital: ~ **International World Index** *n* STOCK Internationaler Welt-Kapital-Index *m*

capital: ~ **investment** *n* ECON Anlageninvestition *f*, Investition *f*, FIN Kapitalanlage *f*; ~ **investment appraisal** *n* FIN Investitionsrechnung *f*; ~ **investment strategy** *n* FIN Investitionsstrategie *f*

capitalism *n* ECON Kapitalismus *m*

capitalist 1. *adj* ECON kapitalistisch; **2.** *n* ECON Kapitalist, in *m,f*

capitalistic *adj* ECON kapitalistisch

capitalization *n* ACC Aktivierung *f*, Kapitalisierung *f*, COMP *in capital letters* Großschreibung *f*, ECON Kapitalisierung *f*, Ausgabe *f* von Wertpapieren, Kapitalausstattung *f*, FIN Kapitalausstattung *f*, Kapitalisierung *f*, Aktivierung *f*, GEN COMM, MEDIA Großschreibung *f*, STOCK Börsenkapitalisierung *f*; ~ **effect** *n* ECON, TAX Kapitalisierungseffekt *m*; ~ **issue** *n* (*cap issue*) STOCK Ausgabe *f* von Gratisaktien, Emission *f* von Gratisaktien; ~ **of leases** *n* ACC Kapitalisierung *f* von Leasingverträgen; ~ **rate** *n* (*cap rate*) ECON *interest rate* FIN Interner Zinsfuß *m*, Kapitalisierungsfaktor *m*, Kapitalisierungssatz *m*;

~ **ratio** *n* FIN Anteil *m* der Wertpapiergattungen am Gesamtnominalkapital, GEN COMM Anlageintensität *f*

capitalize *vt* GEN COMM kapitalisieren, aktivieren, MEDIA *typography* großschreiben

capitalize on *vt* GEN COMM aktivieren, nutzen

capitalized: ~ **value** *n* ECON Kapitalwert *m*

capital: ~**-labor ratio** *AmE*, ~**-labour ratio** *BrE* *n* ECON Kapitalintensität *f*, Verhältnis *nt* von Kapital zu Arbeitskosten; ~ **lease** *n* FIN, GEN COMM aktivierungspflichtiger Leasingvertrag *m*, Finanzierungs-Leasing *nt*; ~ **lease agreement** *n* GEN COMM Finanzierungs-Leasingvertrag *m*; ~ **letter** *n* (*cap*) COMP, MEDIA Großbuchstabe *m*; ~ **letters** *n pl* (*caps*) COMP, MEDIA Großbuchstaben *m pl*; ~ **levy** *n* ECON Vermögensabgabe *f*; ~ **lockup** *n* FIN Kapitalbindung *f*; ~ **loss** *n* ECON, FIN Kapitalveräußerungsverlust *m*, Kapitalwertminderung *f*, Kapitalverlust *m*; ~ **market** *n* ECON, FIN Kapitalmarkt *m*; ~ **market influence** *n* ACC *on theory and practice* Kapitalmarktbeeinflussung *f*; ~ **market interest rate** *n* BANK Kapitalmarktzins *m*; ~ **market yield** *n* STOCK Kapitalmarktrendite *f*; ~ **needs** *n pl* FIN Kapitalbedarf *m*; ~ **outflow** *n* ACC, ECON, FIN Kapitalabfluß *m*; ~ **outlay** *n* ECON Investitionsaufwand *m*, Investitionsausgaben *f pl*; ~**-outlay ratio** *n* ECON Anteil *m* investiver Ausgaben, Investitionsquote *f*, FIN Kapitalaufwandverhältnis *nt*; ~**-output ratio** *n* ECON, FIN Kapitalkoeffizient *m*; ~ **paid in excess of par value** *n* ACC Agio *nt*, Kapitalrücklage *f*; ~ **procurement** *n* BANK, FIN, STOCK Kapitalbeschaffung *f*; ~ **procurement cost** *n* BANK, FIN, STOCK Kapitalbeschaffungskosten *pl*; ~ **productivity** *n* ECON Kapitalproduktivität *f*; ~ **profit** *n* ACC, ECON Kapitalgewinn *m*, FIN, GEN COMM Gewinn *m* aus Kapitalvermögen, Kapitalgewinn *m*, Kapitalwertzuwachs *m*, TAX Kapitalgewinn *m*; ~ **program** *AmE*, ~ **programme** *BrE* *n* FIN Investitionsprogramm *nt*; ~ **project** *n* ACC, FIN Investitionsprojekt *nt*, Investitionsvorhaben *nt*; ~ **project evaluation** *n* ECON Bewertung *f* eines Investitionsprojekts, FIN Investitionsrechnung *f*, Investitionsprojektsbewertung *f*; ~ **raising** *n* BANK Kapitalbeschaffung *f*, FIN Kapitalaufbringung *f*, Kapitalaufnahme *f*, Kapitalbeschaffung *f*, STOCK Kapitalbeschaffung *f*; ~**-raising operation** *n* BANK, FIN, STOCK Kapitalbeschaffungstransaktion *f*; ~ **ratio** *n* BANK Eigenkapitalquote *f*; ~ **rationing** *n* ECON Kapitalzuteilung *f*, FIN Begrenzung *f* der Kapitalbeschaffungsmöglichkeiten, Kapitalrationierung *f*; ~ **reconstruction** *n* FIN Sanierung *f*; ~ **reorganization** *n* STOCK Kapitalumstrukturierung *f*; ~ **requirement** *n* FIN Kapitalbedarf *m*; ~ **requirements** *n pl* FIN Finanzierungsbedarf *m*; ~ **reserves** *n pl* ACC *not available for distribution* Gewinnrücklagen *f pl*, gesetzliche Rücklagen *f pl*, Kapitalrücklage *f*, Kapitalreserve *f*; ~ **resources** *n pl* ECON Kapitalausstattung *f*, Eigenmittel *nt pl*; ~ **risk** *n* FIN Kapitalrisiko *nt*; ~ **sharing** *n* HRM Kapitalbeteiligung *f*; ~ **spending** *n* ECON Investitionsausgaben *f pl*; ~ **stock** *n* *AmE* (*cf share capital BrE*) ACC Kapitaleinlage *f*, ECON Kapitalstock *m*, FIN Geschäftskapital *nt*, Stammkapital *nt*, Grundkapital *nt*; ~ **stock issued** *n* STOCK ausgegebenes Kapital *nt*; ~ **strategy** *n* FIN Investitionsstrategie *f*; ~ **structure** *n* ACC, ECON, FIN Kapitalstruktur *f*; ~ **sum** *n* FIN Kapitalbetrag *m*, Kapitalsumme *f*; ~ **surplus** *n* ACC Agiorücklage *f*, Kapitalrücklage *f*, STOCK Aktienemissionsagio *nt*;

~ **theory** n ECON Kapitaltheorie f; **~-to-asset ratio** n ACC Eigenkapitalquote f; ~ **transaction** n FIN Kapitalverkehr m; ~ **transfer** n FIN Kapitalübertragung f; ~ **transfer tax** n BrE (CTT) TAX Erbschafts- und Schenkungssteuer f, Kapitalübertragungssteuer f; ~ **user costs** n pl ECON Kapitalnutzungskosten pl; ~ **utilization** n ECON Kapitalnutzung f; ~ **value** n ACC, ECON, FIN Kapitalwert m; ~ **widening** n ECON Erweiterungsinvestition f; ~ **write-down** n FIN Kapitalherabsetzung f, Kapitalverminderung f

capitation n TAX, WEL Kopfsteuer f; ~ **tax** n TAX, WEL Kopfsteuer f

CAP: ~ **levy** n ECON Abschöpfung f im Rahmen der gemeinsamen Agrarpolitik

CAPM abbr (capital asset pricing model) ECON, FIN, STOCK Kapitalanlagepreismodell nt, Preismodell nt für Kapitalvermögen

capping n BANK of interest rate Festlegung f einer Obergrenze, Plafondierung f

cap: ~ **rate** n (capitalization rate) ECON interest rate FIN Höchstzins m, Zinsobergrenze f, Kapitalisierungsfaktor m, Kapitalisierungssatz m; ~ **rate loan** n STOCK Anleihe f mit Zinshöchstsatz, langfristiges Darlehen nt mit Höchstzinssatz

caps n pl (capital letters) COMP, MEDIA Großbuchstaben m pl

captain n HRM, TRANSP of ship, aircraft Kapitän m; ~ **of industry** n GEN COMM Wirtschaftskapitän m (infrml), Industriekapitän m (infrml), HRM Großindustrielle(r) mf [decl. as adj], Industrieführer m

caption n COMMS of document Einleitungsformel f, Kopf m, Überschrift f, MEDIA heading Bildertext m, above picture Bildüberschrift f, under picture Bildunterschrift f, S&M above picture Bildüberschrift f, under picture Bildunterschrift f

captive: ~ **candidate** n POL scheinbar unabhängige Kandidatin f, scheinbar unabhängiger Kandidat m; ~ **finance company** n ECON konzerneigene Finanzierungsgesellschaft f; ~ **insurance company** n INS konzerneigene Versicherungsgesellschaft f; ~ **market** n S&M Eigenbedarfsmarkt m, Markt m eines monopolistischen Anbieters

CAQ abbr (computer-aided quality assurance) COMP, IND computerunterstützte Qualitätssicherung f

CAR abbr BrE (compound annual rate) BANK of interest kumulativer Jahressatz m

car: ~ **allowance** n GEN COMM Kraftfahrzeugzuschuß m, Fahrzeugpauschale f; ~ **available for private use** n TAX, TRANSP privat nutzbares Fahrzeug nt; ~ **carrier** n IND, TRANSP ship Autotransportschiff nt, road vehicle Autotransporter m, Kraftwagentransporter m

carat n IND of gold, of diamond Karat nt

carbon n ENVIR, IND Kohle f; ~ **copy** n (cc) COMMS Durchschlag m, Kopie f, GEN COMM Durchschrift f; ~ **dioxide** n ENVIR, IND, TRANSP Kohlendioxyd nt; ~ **dioxide emissions** n pl ENVIR, IND, TRANSP Kohlendioxydemissionen f pl; ~ **dioxide system** n TRANSP shipbuilding, engineering Kohlensäuresystem nt, Kohlendioxydanlage f; ~ **dioxide tax** n (CO_2 tax) TAX Kohlendioxydsteuer f (CO_2-Steuer); ~ **emissions** n pl ENVIR, IND, TRANSP Kohlenstoffemissionen f pl; ~ **monoxide** n ENVIR, IND, TRANSP Kohlenmonoxyd nt;

~ **paper** n COMMS Durchschlagpapier nt, Kohlepapier nt

carboy n IND, TRANSP Glasballon m

card n COMP hardware Karte f, Steckkarte f, HRM Karte f, Visitenkarte f, Geschäftskarte f

CARD abbr BrE (certificate of amortized revolving debt) FIN, GEN COMM revolvierendes Schuldenpapier nt mit Ratenzahlung

card: ~ **bin** n COMP Kartenablage f

cardboard n IND, S&M Karton m, Pappe f

card: ~ **catalog** AmE, ~ **catalogue** BrE n ADMIN Kartei f

cardholder n BANK, FIN Karteninhaber, in m,f, of credit card Kreditkarteninhaber, in m,f; ~ **fee** n BANK, FIN Karteninhabergebühr f

cardinal: ~ **utility** n ECON kardinaler Nutzen m

card: ~ **index** n ADMIN Kartei f; ~ **punch** n COMP, GEN COMM Lochkartenlocher m; ~ **reader** n COMP Kartenleser m; ~ **sorter** n COMP Sortiergerät nt

cards n pl infrml GEN COMM Entlassungspapiere f pl; ◆ **get one's** ~ BrE infrml GEN COMM gekündigt werden; **give sb his cards** BrE infrml GEN COMM jdn an die Luft setzen (infrml), jdn entlassen

care n GEN COMM supervision Aufsicht f, Betreuung f, Sorgfalt f, Obhut f, WEL Pflege f; ◆ ~ **of** (c/o) COMMS, GEN COMM, IMP/EXP bei, per Adresse (p. A., p. Adr.), zu Händen von (z. Hd. v.)

care: ~ **and control** n WEL Aufmerksamkeit f und Kontrolle f

career n HRM Karriere f, berufliche Laufbahn f, Beruf m; ~ **advancement** n HRM beruflicher Aufstieg m, berufliches Fortkommen nt, berufliches Weiterkommen nt; ~ **adviser** n HRM Berufsberater, in m,f; ~ **counseling** AmE, ~ **counselling** BrE n HRM Berufsberatung f; ~ **development** n HRM Aufstieg m, berufliche Entwicklung f

Career: ~ **Development Loan** n BrE (CDL) HRM Karriereentwicklungsdarlehen nt

career: ~ **development prospects** n pl HRM Aufstiegschancen f pl; ~ **expectations** n pl HRM Karriereerwartungen f pl; ~ **goals** n pl HRM Karriereziel nt; ~ **guidance** n HRM Berufsberatung f; ~ **management** n HRM Karriereplanung f; ~-**oriented training** n HRM berufsbezogene Aus- und Weiterbildung f; ~ **path** n HRM beruflicher Werdegang m; ~ **planning** n HRM Karriereplanung f; ~ **prospects** n pl HRM Laufbahnaussichten f pl, Karriereaussichten f pl; ~ **record** n ADMIN Unterlagen f pl über den beruflichen Werdegang, Unterlagen f pl über die berufliche Laufbahn

careless adj GEN COMM nachlässig

caret n MEDIA, S&M symbol Einschaltzeichen nt

car: ~ **exhaust emissions** n pl ENVIR Abgas nt, Auspuffemissionen f pl, Schadstoffausstoß m; ~ **ferry** n TRANSP Autofähre f

cargo n TRANSP Beförderungsgut nt, Ladung f, Frachtgut nt, Transportgut nt, Fracht f; ~ **accounting device** n TRANSP Frachtabrechnungsvorrichtung f; ~ **agent** n TRANSP Frachtagent, in m,f; ~ **assembly** n TRANSP Frachtzusammenstellung f; ~ **boat** n TRANSP Frachter m; ~ **capacity** n (CC) TRANSP Frachtkapazität f, Ladungsfähigkeit f, Ladungskapazität f; ~ **center** AmE, ~ **centre** BrE n TRANSP Frachtumschlagplatz m; ~ **claim** n TRANSP Frachtanspruch m; ~ **claims**

procedure n TRANSP Verfahren nt zur Bearbeitung von Frachtansprüchen; **~ clearance** n IMP/EXP Frachtabfertigung f; **~ configuration** n TRANSP Frachtkonfiguration f, Frachtzusammenstellung f; **~ declaration** n TRANSP Frachterklärung f; **~ delivery terms** n pl TRANSP Frachtlieferbedingungen f pl; **~ derrick** n TRANSP Frachtderrick m, Ladekran m; **~ disassembly** n TRANSP Frachtzerlegung f; **~ dues** n pl TRANSP Frachtgebühren f pl; **~ handling charge** n (CHC) TRANSP Frachtladekosten pl, Frachtumschlagkosten pl, Güterverladungskosten pl; **~ handling equipment** n TRANSP Frachtumschlagausrüstung f, Güterverladungsanlagen f pl; **~ homeward** n TRANSP Rückladung f, Retourfracht f; **~ in isolation** n TRANSP abgesonderte Fracht f; **~ insurance** n INS Gütertransportversicherung f, Kargoversicherung f, Ladungsversicherung f; **~ liner** n TRANSP Linienfrachter m, Linienfrachtschiff nt; **~ manifest** n TRANSP Frachtmanifest nt; **~ marking symbol** n TRANSP Frachtmarkierungssymbol nt; **~ mix** n TRANSP Frachtmischung f; **~ net** n TRANSP cargo handling equipment Ladenetz nt, Netzbrooke f; **~ oil** n (co) TRANSP Frachtöl nt, Ladeöl nt; **~ outward** n TRANSP abgehende Fracht f; **~ plan** n TRANSP Frachtplan m, Stauplan m; **~ plane** n TRANSP Frachtflugzeug nt; **~ ship safety equipment certificate** n TRANSP Ausrüstungssicherheitszeugnis nt für Frachtschiffe; **~ shut-out** n TRANSP Frachtausschluß m; **~ stowage** n TRANSP Frachtladeraum m; **~ superintendent** n HRM Frachtaufseher, in m,f; **~ surveyor** n HRM Frachtsachverständige(r) mf [decl. as adj]; **~ tag** n TRANSP Frachtanhänger m; **~ tank** n (CT) TRANSP Ladetank m; **~ tank center** AmE, **~ tank centre** BrE n (CTC) TRANSP Ladetankzentrum nt; **~ tank wing** n (CTW) TRANSP Ladetankflügel m; **~ tonnage** n TRANSP Frachtraum m, Ladefähigkeit f; **~ tonne kilometers used** AmE, **~ tonne kilometres used** BrE n pl TRANSP Frachttonnenkilometerzahl f; **~ traffic procedures committee** n (CTPC) TRANSP Komitee nt für Frachtverkehrsverfahren; **~ transfer** n TRANSP Frachttransfer m; **~ transit** n TRANSP Frachttransit m; **~ tray** n TRANSP cargo handling equipment Ladeplattform f, Ladepritsche f; **~ vessel** n TRANSP Frachter m

car: **~ hire** n BrE (cf car rental AmE) LEIS, TRANSP Autovermietung f, Kraftfahrzeugvermietung f; **~-hire operator** n BrE (cf car-rental operator AmE) LEIS, TRANSP Mietwagenfirma f; **~-hire service** n BrE (cf car-rental service AmE) LEIS, TRANSP Autovermietung f, Kraftfahrzeugvermietung f; **~ industry** n IND, TRANSP Automobilindustrie f, Kraftfahrzeugindustrie f; **~ insurance** n INS Kraftfahrzeugversicherung f

carload: **~ rate** n TRANSP Waggonfrachtrate f

car: **~ loan** n BANK Kraftfahrzeuganschaffungskredit m; **~ manufacturer** n IND, TRANSP Autohersteller m, Kraftfahrzeughersteller m

carnet n IMP/EXP customs Carnet nt, Zollbegleitscheinheft nt, Zollpassierscheinheft nt; **~ system** n IMP/EXP EC Carnetsystem nt

car: **~ pallet** n TRANSP shipping Autopalette f; **~ park** n BrE (cf parking lot AmE) TRANSP Parkmöglichkeit f, Parkplatz m; **~ parking** n TRANSP Parken nt; **~ phone** n COMMS Autotelefon nt; **~ pool** n TRANSP Fuhrpark m; **~ registration** n TRANSP Kraftfahrzeugzulassung f; **~ rental** n AmE (cf car hire BrE) LEIS, TRANSP

Autovermietung f, Kraftfahrzeugvermietung f; **~-rental operator** n AmE (cf car-hire operator BrE) LEIS, TRANSP Mietwagenfirma f; **~-rental service** n AmE (cf car-hire service BrE) LEIS, TRANSP Autovermietung f, Kraftfahrzeugvermietung f

carr fwd abbr (carriage forward) IMP/EXP, TRANSP Frachtkosten pl per Nachnahme, Transport- und Spediteurkosten pl zu Lasten des Empfängers, Portonachnahme f

carriage n TRANSP act Beförderung f, charge Beförderung f, Transport- und Spediteurkosten pl, Frachtgeld nt, of persons and goods Transportkosten pl, BrE rail coach Personenwagen m; **♦ ~ and insurance paid** (CIP) IMP/EXP, INS, TRANSP Incoterms frachtfrei versichert, named place of destination Fracht und Versicherung bezahlt; **~ free** IMP/EXP frachtfrei (frfr.), frei Haus, TRANSP frachtfrei (frfr.); **~ paid** (carr pd) IMP/EXP named place of destination, TRANSP Fracht bezahlt, frachtfrei (frfr.)

carriage: **~ charge** n TRANSP shipping Frachtgeld nt; **~ expenses** n pl TRANSP shipping Beförderungskosten pl, Frachtkosten pl; **~ forward** n (carr fwd, CF) IMP/EXP, TRANSP Frachtkosten pl per Nachnahme, Transport- und Spediteurkosten pl zu Lasten des Empfängers, Portonachnahme f

Carriage: **~ of Goods by Road Act** n BrE LAW 1965 Gesetz nt zum Güterkraftverkehr; **~ of Goods by Sea Act** n BrE (COGSA) LAW 1924, 1971 Gesetz nt zur Seefrachtbeförderung

carriage: **~ inward** n GEN COMM, TRANSP Eingangsfracht f; **~ return** n (CR) COMP Wagenrücklauf m, Zeilenschaltung f (ZS)

carriageway n BrE TRANSP Fahrbahn f

carried: **~ forward** phr ACC zu übertragen, GEN COMM bookkeeping Übertrag m, Vortrag m

carrier n COMP Trägerfrequenz f, FIN Versicherer m, IMP/EXP Beförderer m, Spediteur m, TRANSP Beförderungsunternehmer m, Transportunternehmer m, Frachtführer m, Verfrachter, in m,f, Transporter m, Beförderungsunternehmen nt, Spediteur m, by air Fluglinie f, Lufttransportgesellschaft f, Luftfrachtführer m, Fluggesellschaft f; **~ bag** n S&M Tragetüte f, Tragetasche f; **~ haulage** n IMP/EXP Spedition f, TRANSP Frachtunternehmen nt, Spedition f; **~'s haulage** n (CH) TRANSP Transportkosten pl; **~'s liability** n INS Frachtführer-Haftpflicht f, Transporthaftung f; **~'s lien** n TRANSP Pfandrecht nt des Frachtführers; **~'s risk** n TRANSP Risiko nt des Frachtführers

carrot: **~ and stick** phr infrml MGMNT in negotiations Zuckerbrot nt und Peitsche f (infrml)

carr pd abbr (carriage paid) IMP/EXP, TRANSP Fracht bezahlt, frfr. (frachtfrei), Transportkosten trägt

carry 1. vt FIN übernehmen, GEN COMM tragen, transport befördern, transportieren, S&M keep in stock führen, STOCK Wertpapiere halten, TRANSP goods befördern, transportieren; **♦ ~ a loss** FIN einen Verlust tragen; **~ on piggyback** TRANSP combined transport huckepack befördern

carry back vt ACC, FIN losses rücktragen, verrechnen, zurücktragen

carry down vt ACC, FIN balance übertragen

carry forward vt ACC, FIN balance übertragen, vortragen

carry out vt GEN COMM abwickeln, ausführen, durchführen, LAW vollziehen, PATENTS complete zum

Abschluß bringen, *invention* ausführen, durchführen; ◆ **~ a survey** GEN COMM, S&M eine Umfrage durchführen; **~ trials on new equipment** GEN COMM die neue Ausrüstung erproben

carry: **~-back** *n* ACC Rücktrag *m*, *of loss* Verrechnung *f*, Verlustrücktrag *m*, FIN Verrechnung *f*; **~-back carry-forward system** *n* TAX Verlustrücktrags-Verlustvortragssystem *nt*; **~-back of loss** *n* ACC Verlustrücktrag *m*, Verrechnung *f* von Verlusten

carrying: **~ as assets** *n* ACC, FIN Aktivierung *f*; **~ capacity** *n* TRANSP *population* Tragfähigkeit *f*, *of shipping* Ladefähigkeit *f*; **~ capacity in number and length on deck** *n* TRANSP *shipping* (*CDK*) Ladefähigkeit *f* nach Anzahl und Länge an Deck; **~ charge** *n* PROP Nebenkosten *pl*, TRANSP *of commodities* Speditionskosten *pl*, Transportkosten *pl*; **~ out** *n* GEN COMM, PATENTS *invention* Ausführung *f*, Durchführung *f*; **~ value** *n* ACC Bilanzwert *m*, Buchwert *m*

carry: **~-over** *n* ACC, FIN Saldovortrag *m*, Übertrag *nt*; **~-over business** *n* STOCK Reportgeschäft *nt*; **~-over effect** *n* MEDIA Übertrageffekt *m*; **~-over loss** *n* ACC Verlustrücktrag *m*, Verlustvortrag *m*; **~-over rate** *n* STOCK Reportsatz *m*; **~-over stocks** *n pl* GEN COMM Übertragbestände *m pl*

cartage *n* TRANSP Rollgeld *nt*

cartalist *n* ECON Teilnehmer, in *m,f* an einem Kartell

car: **~ tax** *n* TAX Autosteuer *f*

cartel *n* ECON, HRM Kartell *nt*; **~ commission** *n* FIN Kartellausschuß *m*; **~ with joint purchasing or marketing organization** *n* ECON Kartell *nt* mit gemeinsamer Einkaufs- oder Verkaufsorganisation, Syndikat *nt*; **~ law** *n* LAW Kartellrecht *nt*, Wettbewerbsrecht *nt*

carton *n* IND Karton *m*

car: **~ transporter** *n* TRANSP *road vehicle* Autotransporter *m*, Kraftwagentransporter *m*

cartridge: **~ paper** *n* S&M starkes Zeichenpapier *nt*

carving: **~ note** *n* BrE TRANSP *shipping* Beschriftungs-Bescheinigung *f*; **~-up** *n* S&M Aufteilung *f*

car: **~ worker** *n* IND, TRANSP Automobilarbeiter, in *m,f*

case *n* GEN COMM Tasche *f*, *file* Vorgang *m*, IMP/EXP Kiste *f*, LAW Fall *m*, Prozeß *m*, LEIS *for spectacles* Etui *nt*, *for documents* Koffer *m*, S&M Kasten *m*, TRANSP Kiste *f*, Koffer *m*, Kasten *m*; ◆ **in this ~** GEN COMM in diesem Fall

CASE *abbr* (*computer-aided software engineering, computer-assisted software engineering*) COMP CASE (*computerunterstützte Software-Erstellung*)

casebound *adj* MEDIA *book* eingebunden, gebunden, in fester Decke gebunden, mit festem Einband

case: **~ file** *n* GEN COMM Fallordner *m*, Vorgang *m*, Vorgangsakte *f*; **~ history** *n* GEN COMM Fallbeispiel *nt*, HRM Personalgeschichte *f*, S&M *advertising* Fallgeschichte *f*, WEL *of person* Vorgeschichte *f*; **~ law** *n* LAW Fallrecht *nt*, Präzedenzrecht *nt*, Richterrecht *nt*, PATENTS Richterrecht *nt*; **~ method** *n* GEN COMM Fallmethode *f*; **~ notes** *n pl* GEN COMM Fallnotizen *f pl*; **~ oil** *n* (*co*) IND Faßöl *nt*, Kanisteröl *nt*; **~ packaging** *n* TRANSP Kistenverpackung *f*; **~ papers** *n pl* GEN COMM Akte *f*, Fallunterlagen *f pl*; **~ of relief** *n* LAW Entlassungsgründe *m pl*, *transactions* Entlastungsgründe *m pl*; **~-sensitive** *adj* COMP unterscheidend nach Groß- und Kleinbuchstaben; **~ shift** *n* COMP Buchstaben-Ziffern Umschaltung *f*, Zeichenumschaltung *f*; **~ study** *n* GEN COMM, MGMNT, S&M Fallstudie *f*; **~ study method** *n* MGMNT *formulation of policy* Fallmethode *f*, Fallstudienmethode *f*

cash 1. *adj* GEN COMM bar; **2.** *adv* GEN COMM bar; **3.** *n* GEN COMM Bargeld *nt*, Barmittel *nt pl*, Geldmittel *nt pl*, Kasse *f*, Kohle *f* (*infrml*), Kassa *f* (*obs*); ◆ **for ~** (*flc*) GEN COMM in bar, gegen Barzahlung; **in ~** GEN COMM bar, in bar; **on a ~ basis** GEN COMM gegen Barzahlung, auf Basis von Barzahlung; **on a ~ received basis** ACC *supplies only for cash*, TRANSP Lieferung nur gegen Barzahlung; **~ with order** (*cwo*) GEN COMM zahlbar bei Auftragserteilung, zahlbar bei Bestellung; **4.** *vt* BANK, FIN einlösen; ◆ **~ a check** *AmE*, **~ a cheque** *BrE* BANK einen Scheck einlösen

cash in 1. *vt* STOCK *bonds* aus einem Geschäft aussteigen, gegen bar verkaufen; **2.** *vi* ◆ **~ on sth** FIN aus etw Kapital schlagen

cash up *vi* FIN Kasse machen, GEN COMM abrechnen

cashable *adj* BANK einlösbar; **~ check** *AmE*, **~ cheque** *BrE* *n* BANK Barscheck *m*

cash: **~ account** *n* ACC, BANK Kassenkonto *nt*; **~ accounting** *n* ACC Einnahmen-Ausgaben-Rechnung *f*, Ist-System *nt* der Rechnungslegung; **~ acknowledgement** *n* FIN Bargeldanweisung *f*; **~ against documents** *n* (*CAD*) IMP/EXP Barzahlung *f* gegen Dokumente, Kasse *f* gegen Dokumente; **~ assets** *n pl* FIN Barvermögen *nt*; **~ balance** *n* ACC Barguthaben *nt*, Geldbestand *m*, *takings* Kassenbestand *m*, Kassensaldo *m*, BANK Bankguthaben *nt*; **~ basis of accounting** *n* ACC Buchführung *f* auf Einnahmen- und Ausgabenbasis, Einnahmen-Ausgaben-Rechnung *f*, Ist-System *nt* der Rechnungslegung, pagatorische Rechnung *f*; **~ before delivery** *n* (*CBD*) GEN COMM Barzahlung *f* vor Lieferung, Kasse *f* vor Lieferung, IMP/EXP Barzahlung *f* vor Lieferung; **~ benefit** *n* ADMIN Geldleistung *f*, INS Bardividende *f*, Geldleistung *f*; **~ bonus** *n* INS Bardividende *f*; **~ book** *n* ACC, ADMIN Kassenbuch *nt*; **~ budget** *n* ACC Einnahmen-Ausgaben-Planung *f*; **~ budgeting** *n* ACC, ECON Einnahmen-Ausgaben-Planung *f*, kurzfristige Liquiditätsplanung *f*; **~ buyer** *n* S&M Barkäufer, in *m,f*; **~ card** *n* BANK Bargeldkarte *f*, Geldautomatenkarte *f*; **~ and carry wholesaler** *n* S&M Selbstbedienungsgroßhändler, in *m,f*; **~ certificate** *n* FIN Bargeldzertifikat *nt*; **~ collection** *n* FIN Bargeldeinzug *m*; **~ contribution** *n* ACC Bareinlage *f*; **~ control** *n* ACC Kontrolle *f* der Bargeldbestände; **~ conversion cycle** *n* FIN Bargeldzyklus *m*; **~ cow** *n* ECON Unternehmen *nt* mit hohen Liquiditätsreserven; **~ cow products** *n pl* GEN COMM Cash-Cow-Produkte *nt pl*, ertragsstarke Produkte *nt pl*; **~ credit** *n* (*C/C*) GEN COMM Barkredit *m*; **~ crop** *n* ECON Agrarprodukt *nt* für den Export, Cash-Crop *nt*, Verkaufsproduktion *f*, ENVIR für den Verkauf bestimmte Anbaufrucht *f*; **~ deal** *n* ACC Bargeschäft *nt*; **~ dealings** *n pl* STOCK Kassageschäfte *nt pl*; **~ and debt position** *n* BANK Kassenbestand *m* und Verbindlichkeiten *f pl*, Liquiditätsstatus *m*; **~ deduction** *n* GEN COMM Barabzug *m*; **~ deficit** *n* FIN Kassendefizit *nt*; **~ deposit** *n* ACC Bareinlage *f*, Barsicherheit *f*, S&M Anzahlung *f*; **~ deposit acknowledgement** *n* FIN Bestätigung *f* der Barhinterlegung; **~ deposits ratio** *n* BANK Barreservesatz *m*, ECON Liquidität *f* ersten Grades; **~ desk** *n* BANK Kasse *f*, Kassenschalter *m*, GEN COMM Kasse *f*; **~ disbursement** *n* ACC

Kassenausgang *m*, Kassenauszahlung *f*; ~ **discount** *n*
FIN, GEN COMM Barzahlungsrabatt *m*, Skonto *m or nt*,
S&M Barzahlungsrabatt *m*; ~ **dispenser** *n* BANK Geld-
ausgabeautomat *m* (*GAA*), Geldautomat *m*, Bancomat
m (*Sch*); **~-dispensing machine** *n* BANK Geldausgabe-
automat *m* (*GAA*), Geldautomat *m*, Bancomat *m* (*Sch*);
~ **distribution** *n* FIN Barausschüttung *f*; ~ **dividend** *n*
FIN ausgeschüttete Dividende *f*, Barausschüttung *f*,
Bardividende *f*; ~ **drain** *n* FIN Abgang *m* von flüssigen
Mitteln; ~ **drawdown** *n* ACC, BANK Barabhebung *f*,
Barentnahme *f*; ~ **earnings** *n pl* FIN Bareinnahmen *f pl*,
Barverdienst *m*, Reingewinn *m* plus Abschreibungen *f*
pl; ~ **economy** *n* ECON Schattenwirtschaft *f*, Untergrundwirtschaft *f*; ~ **entry** *n* ACC, ADMIN
Kassenbuchung *f*; ~ **equivalence** *n* S&M Barwert *m*;
~ **equivalents** *n pl* FIN Bargegenwerte *m pl*;
~ **exchange rate** *n* ECON Sortenkurs *m*; ~ **flow** *n* ACC
Barmittelstrom *m*, FIN Barmittelstrom *m*, Kapitalfluß
m, Kassenfluß *m*, Cashflow *m*, Gewinn *m* und
Abschreibungen *f pl*; ~ **flow forecast** *n* ACC Cashflow-Prognose *f*; ~ **flow problem** *n* ACC, FIN
Barmittelproblem *nt*, Cashflow-Problem *nt*; ~ **flow**
statement *n* FIN Cashflow-Bericht *m*,
Kapitalflußrechnung *f*; ~ **forecast** *n* ACC
Kassenbudget *nt*, Kassenplan *m*, Liquiditätsplan *m*,
FIN Liquiditätsprognose *f*; ~ **generation** *n* FIN Beschaf-
fung *f* von Barmitteln; ~ **holdings** *n pl* ACC
Bargeldbestände *m pl*, Kassenbestände *m pl*, verfügbare
Barmittel *nt pl*
cashier *n* HRM Kassenführer, in *m,f*, S&M Kassierer, in
m,f
cashiering: ~ **department** *n* BrE FIN Kassenabteilung *f*,
Kassenstelle *f*
cashier: ~'**s check** *AmE*, ~'**s cheque** *BrE n* BANK
Bankscheck *m*, Barscheck *m*, Kassenscheck *m*; ~'**s**
error allowance *n* GEN COMM Fehlertoleranz *f* des
Kassierers
cash: ~ **in advance** *n* ACC Vorkasse *f*; ~ **in bank** *n* BANK
Bankguthaben *nt*; ~ **income and outgoings plan** *n* ACC
Zahlungsplan *m*; ~ **inflow** *n* FIN Barmittelzufluß *m*,
Kapitalzustrom *m*, Zugang *m* von flüssigen Mitteln;
~ **in hand** *n* ACC Barguthaben *nt*, verfügbare Barmittel
nt pl, FIN Kassenbestand *m*, verfügbare Barmittel *nt pl*,
GEN COMM Bargeld *nt*; ~ **in transit** *n* ACC government
accounting durchlaufende Zahlungsmittel *nt pl*; **~-in**
value *n* FIN Rückkaufwert *m*; ~ **journal** *n* ACC, ADMIN
Kassenbuch *nt*
cashless: ~ **pay** *n* HRM bargeldlose Lohn- und Gehaltszahlung *f*; ~ **payment** *n* BANK bargeldlose Zahlung *f*;
~ **payment system** *n* BANK bargeldloser Zahlungsverkehr *m*; ~ **society** *n* ECON bargeldlose Gesellschaft *f*
cash: ~ **limit** *n* BANK, ECON, HRM Ausgabenbegrenzung *f*,
Ausgabenbeschränkung *f*, Barmittelbegrenzung *f*, Ver-
fügungsrahmen *m*; ~ **loss** *n* INS Barschaden *m*,
Kassaschaden *m*; ~ **management** *n* ACC
Finanzmanagement *nt*, Gelddisposition *f*,
Kassenhaltung *f*, Liquiditätssteuerung *f*,
Kassenverwaltung *f*, FIN Abstimmung *f* laufender
Einnahmen und Ausgaben, Kassenhaltung *f*,
Kassenverwaltung *f*; ~ **management account** *n*
(*CMA*) FIN Gelddispositionskonto *nt*, Investitions-
Girokonto-Kombination *f*; ~ **management system** *n*
BANK Finanz-Disposystem *nt*; ~ **management**
technique *n* MGMNT Gelddispositionsmethode *f*,
Kassendispositionsmethode *f*; ~ **manager** *n* HRM

Kassenführer, in *m,f*; ~ **market** *n* STOCK Kassamarkt
m; ~ **market rates** *n pl* STOCK Kassakurse *m pl*,
Kassamarktwechselkurse *m pl*; ~ **messenger**
insurance *n* INS Botenberaubungsversicherung *f*;
~ **needs** *n pl* FIN Bargeldbedarf *m*; ~ **office** *n* ADMIN
Kassenraum *m*; ~ **on the barrel head** *n AmE infrml* (*cf*
cash on the nail BrE) GEN COMM Bargeld *nt* auf die
Klaue (*infrml*); ~ **on delivery** *n* (*COD*) ACC Lieferung *f*
gegen Nachnahme, FIN, GEN COMM, IMP/EXP Zahlung *f*
durch Empfänger, Barzahlung *f* bei Lieferung (*c.o.d.*),
TRANSP *trade law* Lieferung *f* gegen Nachnahme; ~ **on**
hand *n* ACC Barbestand *m*, Summe *f* der liquiden
Mittel, verfügbare Barliquidität *f*, FIN verfügbare
Barliquidität *f*, GEN COMM Barbestand *m*, Kasse *f*;
~ **on the nail** *n BrE infrml* (*cf cash on the barrel head*
AmE) GEN COMM Bargeld *nt* auf die Klaue (*infrml*);
~ **on shipment** *n* (*COS*) TRANSP Zahlung *f* bei Verschiffung; ~ **operation** *n* FIN Bartransaktion *f*; ~ **order**
n (*co*) S&M Bestellung *f* mit vereinbarter Barzahlung,
Kassenanweisung *f*; ~ **outflow** *n* ACC, ECON, FIN
Kapitalabfluß *m*; ~ **payment** *n* BANK Auszahlung *f* in
bar, Barzahlung *f*, FIN Barauszahlung *f*; ~ **payments**
journal *n* ACC Kassenausgangsbuch *nt*; ~ **payout** *n* FIN
Bardividende *f*; **~-poor** *adj* FIN knapp an Bargeld;
~ **position** *n* ACC Barposition *f*, Bestand *m* an liquiden
Mitteln, Kassenstand *m*, FIN Barliquidität *f*; ~ **price** *n*
GEN COMM Barpreis *m*; ~ **purchase** *n* FIN Bareinkauf
m, Kauf *m* zur sofortigen Lieferung, STOCK Bareinkauf
m, Kauf *m* zur sofortigen Lieferung; ~ **ratio** *n* FIN
Barliquidität *f*, Deckungsgrad *m*, Liquidität *f* ersten
Grades, Liquiditätsgrad *m*; ~ **receipts** *n pl* ACC
Bareinnahmen *f pl*, Kasseneingänge *m pl*,
Kasseneinnahmen *f pl*; ~ **receipts journal** *n* ACC
Kasseneinnahmenbuch *nt*; ~ **record** *n* ACC
Kassenbeleg *m*; ~ **refunding date** *n* STOCK *interest rate*
futures Barerstattungsdatum *nt*; ~ **register** *n* S&M
Registrierkasse *f*; ~ **register slip** *n* GEN COMM Bon *m*;
~ **requirement** *n pl* ACC Baranforderung *f*, Bedarf *m* an
liquiden Mitteln, Geldbedarf *m*; ~ **reserve** *n* ACC, BANK
Barreserve *f*, Barmittelrücklage *f*, Liquiditätsreserve *f*;
~ **resources** *n pl* FIN Ausstattung *f* mit Barmitteln,
flüssige Mittel *nt pl*; **~-rich** *adj* FIN reich an Bargeld;
~ **risk** *n* STOCK Barmittelrisiko *nt*; **~-settled** *adj* GEN
COMM *delivery procedure* bar abgerechnet; ~ **settlement**
n FIN Barabfindung *f*, Geldabfindung *f*,
Kapitalabfindung *f*, STOCK Barabfindung *f*,
Barregulierung *f*, Geldabfindung *f*, Kapitalabfindung
f; ~ **shortage** *n* FIN Bargeldknappheit *f*, Liquiditätsenge *f*; ~ **squeeze** *n* FIN Bargeldknappheit *f*;
~ **statement** *n* ACC Kassenbericht *m*; **~-strapped** *adj*
FIN finanziell schwach, in finanziellen Schwierigkeiten;
~ **surplus** *n* ACC Bargeldüberschuß *m*, FIN
Kassenüberschuß *m*; ~ **surrender value** *n* INS
Barablösungswert *m*, Barwert *m* einer Lebensversiche-
rung, Rückkaufwert *m* einer Police; ~ **transaction** *n*
ACC Bargeschäft *nt*, Barverkauf *m*, FIN Bartransaktion
f, GEN COMM Barverkauf *m*; ~ **transactions velocity** *n*
ECON Umlaufgeschwindigkeit *f*; ~ **transfer** *n* BANK, FIN
Barüberweisung *f*; ~ **value** *n* ACC Barwert *m*,
Marktwert *m*, INS Kapitalwert *m*; ~ **value life**
insurance *n AmE* INS Barablösungswert *m*, Barwert
m einer Lebensversicherung; ~ **voucher** *n* ACC
Kassenbeleg *m*; ~ **withdrawal** *n* ACC, BANK
Barabhebung *f*, Barentnahme *f*
casino *n* LEIS Spielkasino *nt*

cask *n* (*ck*) TRANSP Faß *nt*

cassette *n* COMP, MEDIA Kassette *f*; **~ player** *n* COMP, MEDIA Kassettengerät *nt*; **~ recorder** *n* COMP, MEDIA Kassettenrecorder *m*; **~ tape recorder** *n* COMP, MEDIA Kassettenrecorder *m*

cast up *vt* ACC, MATH addieren, aufaddieren

caste *n* POL Kaste *f*

casual: **~ labor** *AmE see casual labour BrE*; **~ laborer** *AmE see casual labourer BrE*; **~ labour** *BrE n* HRM Gelegenheitsarbeit *f*; **~ labourer** *n BrE* HRM Aushilfskraft *f*, Gelegenheitsarbeiter, in *m,f*

casualty *n* GEN COMM *sth damaged* Unfall *m*, WEL *injured person* Opfer *nt*, *dead person* Todesopfer *nt*; **~ insurance** *n* INS Bezeichnung aller Versicherungssparten außer der Lebensversicherung, Schadensversicherung *f*, Unfallversicherung *f*

casual: **~ work** *n* HRM Gelegenheitsarbeit *f*; **~ worker** *n* HRM Aushilfskraft *f*, Gelegenheitsarbeiter, in *m,f*

cat *n* (*catalytic converter*) ENVIR Kat *m* (*Katalysator*)

CAT *abbr* COMP (*computer-aided testing, computer-assisted testing*) computerunterstütztes Prüfen *nt*, computerunterstütztes Testen *nt*, (*computer-aided teaching, computer-assisted teaching*) computerunterstützter Unterricht *m*, (*computer-aided translation, computer-assisted translation*) computerunterstützte Übersetzung *f*, WEL (*college of advanced technology*) TH (*Technische Hochschule*)

catalog *AmE see catalogue BrE*

catalogue *n BrE* GEN COMM Katalog *m*, Verzeichnis *nt*; **~ buying** *n BrE* S&M Einkauf *m* im Versandhandel, Einkauf *m* im Versandhaus, Fernkauf *m*; **~ price** *n BrE* GEN COMM Katalogpreis *m*

catalyst *n* GEN COMM Katalysator *m*

catalytic: **~ converter** *n* (*cat*) ENVIR Katalysator *m* (*Kat*); **~ policy mix** *n* ECON Zusammenstellung *f* katalytischer Maßnahmen

catastrophe *n* INS Katastrophe *f*; **~ cover** *n* INS Extremschadensdeckung *f*, Katastrophendeckung *f*; **~ hazard** *n* INS Katastrophenrisiko *nt*; **~ policy** *n* INS Katastrophenrisikopolice *f*; **~ reserve** *n* INS Katastrophenrücklage *f*, Katastrophenreserve *f*; **~ risk** *n* INS Katastrophenrisiko *nt*; **~ theory** *n* MATH Katastrophentheorie *f*

catastrophic: **~ loss** *n* GEN COMM Katastrophenschaden *m*

catch up *vi* ECON, GEN COMM aufholen

catching: **~-up process** *n* ECON Aufholprozeß *m*

catch: **~ line** *n* S&M *advertising* Schlagzeile *f*

catchment: **~ area** *n* S&M Einzugsbereich *m*

catch: **~-up demand** *n* ECON Nachholbedarf *m*; **~-up effect** *n* HRM Ausgleichseffekt *m*; **~-up increase** *n* HRM ausgleichende Lohnerhöhung *f*

catchy *adj* MEDIA, S&M einprägsam

categorical: **~ grant** *n* ECON Zuschuß *m* an Entwicklungsländer, FIN Zuschuß *m*, zweckgebundene Finanzzuweisung *f*, zweckgebundener Zuschuß *m*

categorically: **~ needy** *adj* WEL ausgesprochen bedürftig

categories: **~ of construction types** *n pl* INS Bauartenkategorien *f pl*, Bauartenklassen *f pl*

categorization *n* ADMIN Klassifizierung *f*, GEN COMM Einreihung *f*, Einstufung *f*

categorize *vt* ADMIN klassifizieren, GEN COMM einreihen, einstufen, klassifizieren

category *n* GEN COMM Kategorie *f*, Merkmalsklasse *f*, PATENTS Kategorie *f*, Klasse *f*, *of goods* Warengruppe *f*

cater for *vt* GEN COMM *needs, requirements* abgezielt sein auf, sorgen für, verpflegen

catering *n* GEN COMM Gaststättenwesen *nt*, Kantinenwesen *nt*, HRM Verpflegung *f*, LEIS Bewirtung *f*, Gastronomie *f*, Versorgung *f*, S&M Verpflegung *f*; **~ trade** *n* LEIS Gastronomie *f*, Hotel- und Gaststättengewerbe *nt*

cathode: **~ ray tube** *n* (*CRT*) COMP Kathodenstrahlröhre *f* (*CRT*)

CATS *abbr* (*computer-assisted trading system*) STOCK rechnergestütztes Börsenhandelssystem *nt*

cats: **~ and dogs** *n pl* STOCK Spekulationspapiere *nt pl*

cattle *n* GEN COMM Vieh *nt*; **~ container** *n* TRANSP Viehcontainer *m*; **~ float** *n* TRANSP niedriger Viehwagen *m*; **~ lorry** *n BrE* (*cf cattle truck AmE*) TRANSP Viehtransporter *m*, Viehtransportwagen *m*; **~ truck** *n* AmE (*cf cattle lorry BrE*) TRANSP Viehtransporter *m*, Viehtransportwagen *m*

causa sine qua non *n* LAW notwendige Ursache *f*, unerläßliche Sache *f*, Ursache *f*, ohne die es nicht geht

cause 1. *n* GEN COMM *reason* Ursache *f*, Veranlassung *f*, Motiv *nt*, POL Ursache *f*, *purpose, common cause* Mission *f*, Motiv *nt*; **2.** *vt* GEN COMM veranlassen, verursachen

cause: **~ of action** *n* LAW *for claim* Klagegrund *m*; **~ of cancellation** *n* INS Abgangsursache *f*, Annullierungsgrund *m*; **~ of liability** *n* INS Haftungsgrund *m*, Haftungsklage *f*, LAW *contract* Haftungsgrund *m*; **~ of loss** *n* GEN COMM Schadensursache *f*

cautionary *adj* LAW vorsorglich

cautioning: **~ as to rights** *n* LAW Rechtsmittelbelehrung *f*

caution: **~ money** *n* LAW Kaution *f*

cautious *adj* GEN COMM vorsichtig, reserviert, umsichtig, *reticent* zurückhaltend

caveat *n* GEN COMM, LAW Vorbehalt *m*, PATENTS Einspruch *m*; **~ subscriptor** *phr* LAW Gewährleistungshaftung *f* des Abnehmers; **~ venditor** LAW Gewährleistungshaftung *f* des Verkäufers

CB *abbr* *BrE* (*container base*) TRANSP *shipping* Containerboden *m*

CBD *abbr* ECON (*central business district*) zentraler Geschäftsbezirk *m*, zentrales Gewerbegebiet *nt*, FIN (*cash before delivery*) Barzahlung *f* vor Lieferung, Kasse *f* vor Lieferung, GEN COMM (*cash before delivery*) Barzahlung *f* vor Lieferung, Kasse *f* vor Lieferung, (*central business district*) zentraler Geschäftsbezirk *m*, zentrales Gewerbegebiet *nt*, IMP/EXP (*cash before delivery*) Barzahlung *f* vor Lieferung

CBF *abbr BrE* (*Central Bank Facility*) BANK Zentralbankfazilität *f*

CBI *abbr* (*Confederation of British Industry*) IND Verband der britischen Industrie, ≈ BDI (*Bundesverband der Deutschen Industrie*)

cbm *abbr* (*cubic meter AmE, cubic metre BrE*) GEN COMM cbm (*Kubikmeter*), m³ (*Kubikmeter*)

CBO *abbr* (*Congressional Budget Office*) FIN, POL Haushaltsabteilung des Kongresses der Vereinigten Staaten von Amerika

CBOE *abbr* (*Chicago Board Options Exchange*) STOCK Optionsbörse in Chicago

CBS: ~ **Tendency index** *n* STOCK *in Holland* CBS-Tendenzindex *m*

CBT *abbr* COMP (*computer-based training*) computergestützte Ausbildung *f*, rechnergestützte Ausbildung *f*, STOCK (*Chicago Board of Trade*) Handelskammer von Chicago

cc *abbr* COMMS (*carbon copy*) Durchschlag *m*, Kopie *f*, GEN COMM (*cubic centimeter AmE, cubic centimetre BrE*) cc (*Kubikzentimeter*), cm³ (*Kubikzentimeter*), (*cubic capacity*) cc (*Motorhubraum*)

CC *abbr* ECON (*Chamber of Commerce*), GEN COMM (*Chamber of Commerce*) HK (*Handelskammer*), INS (*continuation clause*) Prolongationsklausel *f*, Verlängerungsklausel *f*, LAW (*customs code*) Zollgesetz *nt*, POL (*civil commotion*) Aufruhr *m*, Bürgerunruhen *f pl*, innere Unruhe *f*, TRANSP (*canvas cover*) Plane *f*, Segeltuchüberzug *m*, (*cargo capacity*) Frachtkapazität *f*, Ladungsfähigkeit *f*, Ladungskapazität *f*, (*container control*) Containerkontrolle *f*

C/C *abbr* FIN (*clean credit*) einfaches Akkreditiv *nt*, GEN COMM (*cash credit*) Barkredit *m*

CCA *abbr* ACC (*current cost accounting*) ACC Bilanzierung *f* auf der Basis des Wiederbeschaffungswertes, Buchführung *f* zum Tageswert

CCC *abbr* ECON (*Commodity Credit Corporation*) *agricultural* US-Preisstützungsbehörde für die Landwirtschaft, IMP/EXP (*Customs Cooperation Council*) Rat *m* für die Zusammenarbeit auf dem Gebiete des Zollwesens, BZR (*Brüsseler Zollrat*)

CCCN *abbr* (*Customs Cooperation Council Nomenclature*) IMP/EXP Nomenklatur *f* des Brüsseler Zollrates, NRZZ (*Zolltarifschema des Rates für die Zusammenarbeit auf dem Gebiete des Zollwesens*)

CCI *abbr* (*Chamber of Commerce and Industry*) ECON IHK (*Industrie- und Handelskammer*)

CCR *abbr* (*commodity classification rates*) IMP/EXP Güterverzeichnissätze *m pl*, Warenverzeichnissätze *m pl*

CCS *abbr* IMP/EXP (*customs clearance status*) Zollabfertigungsstatus *m*, TRANSP (*consolidated cargo service*) Sammelfrachtdienst *m*, Sammelgut-Service *m*

CCT *abbr* (*common customs tariff*) IMP/EXP GZT (*gemeinsamer Zolltarif*)

cd *abbr* (*cum dividend*) STOCK einschließlich Dividende

CD *abbr* ADMIN (*consular declaration*) konsularische Erklärung *f*, Konsulatserklärung *f*, COMP, GEN COMM, MEDIA (*compact disc*) CD (*Compact Disc*), IMP/EXP (*customs declaration*), Zollabfertigung *f*, Zolldeklarierung *f*, Zollerklärung *f*, Zollinhaltserklärung *f*, TRANSP (*commercial dock*) shipping Handelskai *m*, Umschlagkai *m*

CDC *abbr* (*Commonwealth Development Corporation*) ECON Commonwealth-Entwicklungsgesellschaft

CDL *abbr BrE* (*Career Development Loan*) HRM Karriereentwicklungsdarlehen *nt*

CD-ROM *abbr* (*compact disc read-only memory*) COMP, MEDIA *hardware* CD-ROM (*Compact Disc-Festwertspeicher*)

CDV *abbr* (*current domestic value*) IMP/EXP aktueller Inlandswert *m*, Inlandswert *m*, Verzollungswert *m*

CEA *abbr* (*Council of Economic Advisers*) ECON Sachverständigenrat *m* für Wirtschaftsfragen

CEAC *abbr* (*Committee for European Airspace Coordination*) IND Ausschuß *m* für die Koordinierung des europäischen Luftraums

cease 1. *vt* GEN COMM aufhören, einstellen, beenden; ♦ ~ **to have effect** LAW *contract* nicht mehr rechtswirksam sein; **2.** *vi* GEN COMM aufhören, enden

CEC *abbr obs* (*Commission of the European Community*) ECON EG-Kommission *f* (*obs*) (*Kommission der Europäischen Gemeinschaft*)

CED *abbr* (*Committee for Economic Development*) ECON Ausschuß *m* für wirtschaftliche Entwicklung

cede *vt* INS abgeben, abtreten, zedieren, LAW abtreten, zedieren

cedent *n* INS, LAW Zedent, in *m,f*, Abtretende(r) *mf* [decl. as adj]

ceding: ~ **company** *n* INS abgebende Gesellschaft *f*, Zedent *m*, zedierende Gesellschaft *f*

CEEC *abbr* (*Council for European Economic Cooperation*) ECON Rat *m* für Europäische wirtschaftliche Zusammenarbeit

CEIC *abbr* (*closed-end investment company*) FIN Kapitalanlagegesellschaft *f* mit geschlossenem Anlagefonds

CEIF *abbr* (*Council of European Industrial Federations*) IND Rat *m* der europäischen Industrieverbände

ceiling *n* ACC Höchstgrenze *f*, FIN Höchstbetrag *m*; ~ **price** *n* ECON äußerster Kurs *m*, Höchstpreis *m*; ~ **rate** *n* STOCK *interest rate futures* Zinsobergrenze *f*

cell *n* COMP Zelle *f*, TRANSP *container securing* Containerzelle *f*, Zelle *f*; ~ **guide** *n* TRANSP *container securing* Containerstaugerüst *nt*, Zellenführer *m*; ~ **organization** *n* IND Zellaufbau *m*

cellphone *n* COMMS zellulares Telefon *nt*, mobiles Telefon *nt*, Mobiltelefon *nt*, Handy *nt* (*infrml*)

cellular *adj* COMMS, GEN COMM zellular; ~ **container ship** *n* TRANSP Zellencontainerschiff *nt*; ~ **phone** *n* COMMS zellulares Telefon *nt*, mobiles Telefon *nt*, Mobiltelefon *nt*; ~ **radio** *n* COMMS zellulares Funkgerät *nt*; ~ **vessel** *n* TRANSP Zellenschiff *nt*

CEMA *abbr BrE* (*Customs and Excise Management Act*) LAW Gesetz zur Zoll- und Verbrauchssteuerhandhabung

CEN *abbr* (*European Committee for Standardization*) ECON CEN (*Europäisches Komitee für Normung*)

CENE *abbr* (*Commission on Energy and the Environment*) ENVIR Kommission *f* für Energie und Umwelt

CENELEC *abbr* (*European Committee for Electrotechnical Standardization*) ECON Europäisches Komitee *f* für elektrotechnische Normung (*CENELEC*)

censor *vt* GEN COMM, MEDIA zensieren

censorship *n* GEN COMM, MEDIA Zensur *f*, Zensieren *nt*, Zensierung *f*

census *n* GEN COMM Großzählung *f*, Totalstatistik *f*, Zensus *m*

Census: ~ **Bureau** *n AmE* ECON statistisches Bundesamt *nt*

census: ~ **of business** *n AmE* ECON Unternehmensstatistik *f*; ~ **of manufacturers** *n AmE* IND, MATH Erzeugerstatistik *f*; ~ **of population** *n* ECON, MATH Volkszählung *f*, Bevölkerungsstatistik *f*; ~ **of production** *n* ECON Produktionsstatistik *f*; ~ **of retail trade** *n AmE* ECON Einzelhandelsstatistik *f*; ~ **sample** *n* S&M statistische Stichprobe *f*

center *AmE see* centre *BrE*

centerfold *AmE see* centrefold *BrE*

centiliter *AmE see* centilitre *BrE*

centilitre *BrE n* (*cl*) GEN COMM Zentiliter *m* (*cl*)

centimeter *AmE see* centimetre *BrE*

centimetre *BrE n* (*cm*) GEN COMM Zentimeter *m* (*cm*)

Central: ~ **American Common Market** *n* (*CACM*) ECON Zentralamerikanischer Gemeinsamer Markt *m*; ~ **Arbitration Committee** *n BrE* (*CAC*) HRM, MGMNT zentrale Schiedskommission *f*, zentrale Schlichtungsstelle *f*

central: ~ **bank** *n* BANK Zentralbank *f*, ECON zentrale Notenbank *f*

Central: ~ **Bank Facility** *n BrE* (*CBF*) BANK Zentralbankfazilität *f*

central: ~ **bank policy** *n* ECON Notenbankpolitik *f*; ~ **bank transactions** *n pl* BANK Zentralbankgeschäft *nt*, ECON Zentralbankgeschäfte *nt pl*, Zentralbankoperationen *f pl*

Central: ~ **Bureau of Statistics** *n AmE* ECON Zentralamt *nt* für Statistik

central: ~ **business district** *n* (*CBD*) ECON *of city*, GEN COMM zentraler Geschäftsbezirk *m*, zentrales Gewerbegebiet *nt*; ~ **buying** *n* S&M zentraler Einkauf *m*

Central: ~ **European Time** *n* (*CET*) GEN COMM mitteleuropäische Zeit *f* (*MEZ*)

central: ~ **freight booking office** *n* TRANSP *aviation* zentrales Frachtbuchungsbüro *nt*; ~ **freight bureau** *n* (*CFB*) TRANSP zentrales Frachtbüro *nt*; ~ **government** *n* GEN COMM, POL Zentralregierung *f*; ~ **government borrowing requirement** *n* ECON Kreditbedarf *m* der Regierung; ~ **government item** *n* FIN Papier *nt* der Zentralregierung

centralization *n* GEN COMM Zentralisation *f*, Zentralisierung *f*

centralize *vt* GEN COMM zentralisieren

centralized *adj* GEN COMM zentralisiert; ~ **institution** *n* GEN COMM Zentralinstitut *nt*

centrally: ~ **financed program** *AmE*, ~ **financed programme** *BrE n* ACC zentralfinanziertes Programm *nt*; ~ **planned economy** *n* (*CPE*) ECON Zentralverwaltungswirtschaft *f*

central: ~ **place theory** *n* ECON *population* Theorie *f* der zentralen Orte; ~ **planning** *n* MGMNT staatliche Planung *f*, zentrale Planung *f*; ~ **processing unit** *n* (*CPU*) COMP *hardware* Zentraleinheit *f* (*ZE*); ~ **rate** *n* ECON *of currencies in EMS* Leitkurs *m*

Central: ~ **Register** *n BrE* STOCK *of Securities and Investment Board* Zentralregister *nt*

central: ~ **reservation office** *n* LEIS zentrales Reservierungsbüro *nt*; ~ **reservation system** *n* LEIS zentrales Reservierungssystem *nt*

Central: ~ **Risk Service** *n* FIN Evidenzzentrale *f*; ~ **Standard Time** *n AmE* (*CST*) GEN COMM Zentrale Standardzeit *f*; ~ **Statistical Office** *n BrE* (*CSO*) ECON statistisches Zentralbüro, ≈ statistisches Bundesamt *nt*

central: ~ **tendency** *n* MATH Lokalisationsparameter *m*, Maß *nt* der Zentraltendenz

centre *n BrE* GEN COMM Mitte *f*, *point, focus* Mittelpunkt *m*, *part* Mittelstück *nt*, *of town* Zentrum *nt*, IND Kern *m*, Mitte *f*, Mittelstück *nt*

centrefold *n BrE* MEDIA *print* Doppelseite *f*, Panoramaseite *f*

Centre: ~ **for Economic and Social Information** *n* (*CESI*) WEL Zentrum *nt* für Wirtschafts- und Gesellschaftsdaten

centre: ~ **of gravity** *n BrE* TRANSP *of load, vehicle* Schwerpunkt *m*; ~ **periphery system** *n BrE* ECON

Zentrum-Peripherie-System *nt*; ~ **spread** *n BrE* MEDIA *print* Doppelseite *f*, Panoramaseite *f*

Centronics®: ~ **interface** *n* COMP *hardware* Centronics®-Schnittstelle *f*

CEO *abbr AmE* (*chief executive officer*) HRM Chief-Executive-Officer *m*, oberste Verwaltungsspitze *f*

cereal *n* STOCK Getreide *nt*

CERF *abbr* (*Council of Europe Resettlement Fund*) BANK Wiedereingliederungsfonds *m* des Europarats

cert. *abbr* (*certificate*) COMMS Besch. (*Bescheinigung*), Best. (*Bestätigung*), GEN COMM Besch. (*Bescheinigung*), Zertifikat *nt*, LAW, PATENTS Urk. (*Urkunde*) *f*, STOCK Anteilsschein *m*, Zertifikat *nt*

certain: ~ **conditions** *n pl* GEN COMM bestimmte Bedingungen *f pl*; ~ **point** *n* GEN COMM *in a statement* bestimmter Punkt *m*

certainty *n* ECON, GEN COMM *being certain* Bestimmtheit *f*, Gewißheit *f*, Sicherheit *f*, *sth certain* Gewißheit *f*

certificate *n* (*cert.*) ADMIN Urkunde *f*, COMMS Bescheinigung *f* (*Besch.*), Bestätigung *f* (*Best.*), FIN Urkunde *f* (*Urk.*), GEN COMM Bescheinigung *f* (*Besch.*), Zertifikat *nt*, LAW, PATENTS Urkunde *f* (*Urk.*), STOCK Anteilsschein *m*, Zertifikat *nt*; ~ **in duplicate** *n* GEN COMM Urkunde *f* in doppelter Ausfertigung; ~ **of airworthiness** *n* TRANSP Flugtüchtigkeitszeugnis *nt*, Flugtauglichkeitsbescheinigung *f*; ~ **of amortized revolving debt** *n BrE* (*CARD*) FIN revolvierendes Schuldenpapier *nt* mit Ratenzahlung; ~ **of analysis** *n* TRANSP Analysenzertifikat *nt*; ~ **of competency** *n* TRANSP *shipping* Befähigungsnachweis *m*; ~ **of compliance** *n* ADMIN Bescheinigung *f* über Ordungsmäßigkeit, GEN COMM Einwilligungsbescheinigung *f*; ~ **of conditioning** *n* TRANSP Beschaffenheitsbestätigung *f*; ~ **of deposit** *n* FIN Einlagenzertifikat *nt*, GEN COMM Depositenzertifikat *nt* (*CD*); ~ **of deposit market** *n* BANK Markt *m* für CDs, CD-Markt *m*; ~ **of deposit roll-over** *n* BANK Rollover-Kredit *m* auf CD-Basis; ~ **of existence** *n* INS Lebensausweis *m*, Lebensbescheinigung *f*, Lebensnachweis *m*; ~ **of health** *n* WEL Gesundheitszeugnis *nt*; ~ **of incorporation** *n* LAW *company law* amtliche Registrierungsbescheinigung *f*, *corporation law* Gründungsurkunde *f*; ~ **of indebtedness** *n* GEN COMM Schuldurkunde *f*; ~ **of independence** *n* HRM Unabhängigkeitszertifikat *nt*; ~ **of inspection** *n* TRANSP Beschaffenheitszeugnis *nt*; ~ **of insurance** *n* (*c/i*) INS Versicherungsbestätigung *f*, Versicherungszertifikat *nt*

certificateless: ~ **municipal bond** *n* STOCK Kommunalobligation *f* ohne Zertifikat

certificate: ~ **of manufacture** *n* IND Ursprungszeugnis *nt*; ~ **of occupancy** *n* PROP Abnahmebescheinigung *f*; ~ **of origin** *n* FIN (*c/o, co*) Ursprungszeugnis *nt*, IMP/EXP (*c/o, co*) Herkunftsbescheinigung *f*, Ursprungsbescheinigung *f*, Ursprungszertifikat *nt*, Ursprungszeugnis *nt*; ~ **of origin and consignment** *n* (*C/OC*) IMP/EXP Ursprungs- und Frachtzeugnis *nt*; ~ **of ownership** *n* GEN COMM Eigentumsurkunde *f*, PROP Eigentumsbescheinigung *f*, Eigentumsnachweis *m*, Eigentumsurkunde *f*; ~ **of posting** *n* COMMS Posteinlieferungsschein *m*; ~ **of pratique** *n* IMP/EXP *permission to land aircraft or ship* Freigabezeugnis *nt*; ~ **of qualification** *n* LAW Befähigungsnachweis *m*; ~ **of quality** *n* IMP/EXP, TRANSP Qualitätszeugnis *nt*; ~ **of registration** *n* LAW *intellectual property*

Eintragungsbescheinigung *f*; ~ **of registry** *n* TRANSP *shipping* Schiffsregisterbrief *m*

Certificate: ~ **of Secondary Education** *n BrE obs* (*CSE*) WEL Sekundarabschluß *m*, Volksschulabschluß *m* (*obs*)

certificate: ~ **of shipment** *n* IMP/EXP, TRANSP Ladeschein *m*, Verschiffungsbescheinigung *f*; ~ **of survey** *n* TRANSP *shipping* Besichtigungsschein *m*; ~ **of tax deposit** *n* (*CTD*) TAX verzinsliches Steuerzertifikat *nt*; ~ **of title** *n* PROP Eigentumsnachweis *m*; ~ **of use** *n* PROP Nutzungsberechtigung *f*; ~ **of value** *n BrE* (*C*/*V*) IMP/EXP Wertbescheinigung *f*; ~ **of value and origin** *n BrE* (*CVO*) IMP/EXP Wert- und Ursprungszertifikat *nt*, Wert- und Ursprungszeugnis *nt*; ~ **of weight** *n* TRANSP Gewichtsbescheinigung *f*, Gewichtsnota *f*

certification *n* GEN COMM Bestätigung *f*, LAW *for product* Beglaubigung *f*, Bescheinigung *f*; ~ **mark** *n* GEN COMM Gütemarke *f*, Gütezeichen *nt*, HRM *labour relations* Anerkennung *f* einer Gewerkschaft, Verbandsmarke *f*, LAW Gütemarke *f*, Gütezeichen *nt*, PATENTS Gütezeichen *nt*, Ursprungshinweis *m*

Certification: ~ **Officer** *n BrE* (*CO*) ADMIN, HRM Bevollmächtigungsbeamte(r) *m* [decl. as adj], Bevollmächtigungsbeamtin *f*

certified *adj* ADMIN, LAW amtlich beglaubigt; ~ **accountant** *n BrE* ACC zugelassener Wirtschaftsprüfer *m*, zugelassene Wirtschaftsprüferin *f*; ~ **accounts** *n pl* ACC beglaubigte Buchhaltung *f*; ~ **check** *AmE*, ~ **cheque** *BrE n* BANK bestätigter Scheck *m*, von einer Bank garantierter Scheck *m*, gedeckter Scheck *m*, ECON bankbestätigter Scheck *m*; ~ **copy** *n* ADMIN amtlich beglaubigte Kopie *f*, LAW beglaubigte Abschrift *f*, beglaubigte Kopie *f*; ~ **declaration of origin** *n* IMP/EXP legalisierte Ursprungserklärung *f*, testierte Ursprungserklärung *f*; ~ **employee benefit specialist** *n AmE* HRM amtlich zugelassener Sondervergütungsexperte *m*, amtlich zugelassene Sondervergütungsexpertin *f*; ~ **financial planner** *n* FIN amtlich zugelassener Finanzierungsplaner *m*, amtlich zugelassene Finanzierungsplanerin *f*; ~ **financial statement** *n* ACC Abschluß *m* mit Bestätigungsvermerk, testierter Abschluß *m*; ~ **general accountant** *n* ACC konzessionierter Wirtschaftsprüfer *m*, konzessionierte Wirtschaftsprüferin *f*, zugelassener Wirtschaftsprüfer *m*, zugelassene Wirtschaftsprüferin *f*; ~ **invoice** *n* ACC, ADMIN Konsulatsfaktura *f*; ~ **mail** *n AmE* (*cf registered post BrE*) COMMS Einschreiben *nt*; ~ **public accountant** *n AmE* (*CPA*) ACC konzessionierter Wirtschaftsprüfer *m*, konzessionierte Wirtschaftsprüferin *f*, zugelassener Wirtschaftsprüfer *m*, zugelassene Wirtschaftsprüferin *f*; ~ **true copy** *n* LAW beglaubigte Abschrift *f*, beglaubigte Kopie *f*

certify *vt* LAW beglaubigen

certifying: ~ **officer** *n* ADMIN beglaubigende(r) Beamte(r) *m* [decl. as adj], beglaubigende Beamtin *f*

CESI *abbr* (*Centre for Economic and Social Information*) WEL Zentrum *nt* für Wirtschafts- und Gesellschaftsdaten

CES: ~ **production function** *n* (*constant elasticity of substitution production function*) ECON CES-Produktionsfunktion *f* (*Produktionsfunktion der konstanten Substitutionselastizität*)

cessation *n* GEN COMM Einstellung *f*; ~ **of interest** *n BrE* BANK Einstellung *f* von Zinszahlungen; ~ **of payment** *n* BANK, GEN COMM Zahlungseinstellung *f*; ~ **of payment of premiums** *n* INS Einstellung *f* der Prämienzahlung

cession *n* GEN COMM, INS, LAW Abtretung *f*, Zession *f*; ~ **of portfolio** *n* INS Portfolio-Abtretung *f*

cestui que trust *n* LAW Begünstigte(r) *mf* [decl. as adj]

CET *abbr* ECON (*common external tariff*) gemeinsamer Außenzoll *m*, GEN COMM (*Central European Time*) MEZ (*mitteleuropäische Zeit*)

CETA *abbr AmE* (*Comprehensive Employment and Training Act*) HRM amerikanisches Gesetz zur Ausbildung von Jugendlichen

ceteris paribus *phr* GEN COMM unter sonst gleichen Umständen, ceteris paribus, ceteris paribus-Klausel *f*

cf *abbr* (*cubic foot*) GEN COMM Kubikfuß *m*

CF *abbr* IMP/EXP, TRANSP (*carriage forward*) Frachtkosten *pl* per Nachnahme, Transport- und Spediteurkosten *pl* zu Lasten des Empfängers, Portonachnahme *f*, (*cost and freight*) C&F (*Kosten und Fracht*)

CFB *abbr* (*central freight bureau*) TRANSP zentrales Frachtbüro *nt*

CFC *abbr* (*chlorofluorocarbon*) ENVIR FCKW (*Fluorchlorkohlenwasserstoff*)

CFE *abbr BrE* (*college of further education*) GEN COMM Handelsschule *f*, WEL Berufsfachschule *f*, Berufsschule *f*, *commercial* Handelsschule *f*, *for domestic sciences* Haushaltungsschule *f*, *technical* höhere Handelsschule *f*, weiterführende Schule *f*

CFF *abbr* (*compensatory financial facility*) FIN Sonderfazilität des Internationalen Währungsfonds, Kompensatorische Finanzfazilität *f*

CFO *abbr* (*chief financial officer*) HRM Finanzleiter, in *m,f*, Finanzdirektor, in *m,f*, Leiter, in *m,f* Finanzen

CFS *abbr AmE* (*container freight station*) TRANSP *shipping* Containerfrachtstation *f*, Containerpackstation *f*

CFTC *abbr AmE* (*Commodity Futures Trading Commission*) STOCK US-Aufsichtsbehörde für den Warenterminhandel

CG *abbr* IMP/EXP (*clearance group*) Verzollungsgruppe *f*

CGA *abbr* (*color graphics adapter AmE,colour graphics adapter BrE*) COMP CGA-Karte *f*, Farbgrafikadapter *m*, (*color graphics array AmE,colour graphics array BrE*) Farbgrafikanordnung *f*

CGCB *abbr* (*Committee of Governors of Central Banks*) BANK, POL Gouverneursausschuß *m* der Zentralbanken

CGI *BrE abbr* (*City and Guilds Institute*) ECON Londoner Prüfungsinstitut für technische und Handwerksbetriebe

CGT *abbr* (*capital gains tax*) TAX Kapitalertragsteuer *f*, Kapitalgewinnsteuer *f*

CH *abbr* (*carrier's haulage*) TRANSP Transportkosten *pl*

chain 1. *n* IND Kette *f*; **2.** *vt* COMP verketten, TRANSP *cargo handling* anketten

chain: ~ **banking** *n AmE* BANK Filialbankwesen *nt*, Kettenbanksystem *nt*; ~ **of command** *n* MGMNT Dienstweg *m*, Leitungsorganisation *f*, Weisungskette *f*; ~ **of distribution** *n* IND Verteilungskette *f*, Distributionskette *f*; ~ **index method** *n* ECON *accounting* Methode *f* des verketteten Index

chaining *n* COMP Verkettung *f*

chain: ~ **migration** *n* GEN COMM Kettenabwanderung *f*; ~ **production** *n* IND Kettenproduktion *f*; ~ **of production** *n* IND Produktionskette *f*; ~ **store** *n* S&M Kettenladen *m*, Filialkette *f*, Filiale *f*; ~ **superstore** *n* S&M Supermarkt *m* einer Ladenkette

chair 1. *n* GEN COMM Gesprächsleiter, in *m,f*; ◆ **be in the**

~ MGMNT *for meetings* den Vorsitz führen; **2.** *vt* ♦ **~ a meeting** MGMNT den Vorsitz führen

chairman *n* HRM, MGMNT Tagungsleiter, in *m,f*, Versammlungsleiter, in *m,f*, Vorsitzende(r) *mf* [decl. as adj]; **~'s brief** *n* MGMNT Zusammenfassung *f* der Vorsitzenden, Zusammenfassung *f* des Vorsitzenden; **~ of the administrative board** *n* HRM, MGMNT Verwaltungsratsvorsitzende(r) *mf* [decl. as adj]; **~ of the board** *n* MGMNT Aufsichtsratsvorsitzende(r) *mf* [decl. as adj], HRM Verwaltungsratsvorsitzende(r) *mf* [decl. as adj]; **~ of the board of directors** *n* MGMNT Verwaltungsratsvorsitzende(r) *mf* [decl. as adj], Vorstand *m* der Geschäftsleitung; **~ of the board of management** *n* MGMNT Verwaltungsratsvorsitzende(r) *mf* [decl. as adj], Vorstand *m* der Geschäftsleitung; **~ and chief executive** *n* AmE (*cf chairman and managing director BrE*) HRM, MGMNT Vorsitzender und geschäftsführender Direktor *m*, Vorsitzende und geschäftsführende Direktorin *f*, Vorstandsvorsitzende(r) *mf* [decl. as adj]; **~ of the executive committee** *n* HRM, MGMNT Vorstandsvorsitzende(r) *mf* [decl. as adj]; **~ and general manager** *n* MGMNT Vorsitzender und Generaldirektor *m*, Vorsitzende und Generaldirektorin *f*, Vorsitzender und Hauptgeschäftsführer *m*, Vorsitzende und Hauptgeschäftsführerin *f*; **~ and managing director** *n* BrE (*cf chairman and chief executive AmE*) HRM, MGMNT Vorsitzender und geschäftsführender Direktor *m*, Vorsitzende und geschäftsführende Direktorin *f*, Vorstandsvorsitzende(r) *mf* [decl. as adj]; **~ of the supervisory board** *n* MGMNT Aufsichtsratsvorsitzende(r) *mf* [decl. as adj]; **~ of works council** *n* GEN COMM, HRM Betriebsratsvorsitzende(r) *mf* [decl. as adj]

chairmanship *n* HRM Präsidentschaft *f*, MGMNT Präsidentschaft *f*, Vorsitz *m*

chairperson *n* HRM, MGMNT Tagungsleiter, in *m,f*, Versammlungsleiter, in *m,f*, Vorsitzende(r) *mf* [decl. as adj]

chairwoman *n* HRM, MGMNT Tagungsleiterin *f*, Versammlungsleiterin *f*, Vorsitzende *f* [decl. as adj]

challenge 1. *n* GEN COMM Herausforderung *f*, LAW Anfechtung *f*; **2.** *vt* GEN COMM herausfordern, LAW anfechten

chamber *n* LAW Kammer *f*, Richterzimmer *nt*, POL Kammer *f*

Chamber: ~ of Commerce *n* (*CC*) ECON, GEN COMM, LAW Handelskammer *f* (*HK*); **~ of Commerce and Industry** *n* (*CCI*) ECON Industrie- und Handelskammer *f* (*IHK*)

chambers *n pl* LAW Kanzlei *f*

Chamber: ~ of Trade *n* ECON, GEN COMM, LAW Handelskammer *f* (*HK*)

champion *n* GEN COMM Verfechter, in *m,f*, Vorkämpfer, in *m,f*

chance *n* GEN COMM Chance *f*, MATH Möglichkeit *f*, Wahrscheinlichkeit *f*

chancellor *n* POL Kanzler *m*

Chancellor: ~ of the Exchequer *n* BrE ECON, FIN, POL Finanzminister *m*, Schatzkanzler *m*

chance: ~ variable *n* MATH *statistics* stochastische Variable *f*, Zufallsvariable *f*

change 1. *n* COMP Umwandlung *f*, ECON *in supply or demand* Änderung *f*, GEN COMM *conversion* Verwandlung *f*, *alteration* Änderung *f*, *transformation* Umwandlung *f*, Veränderung *f*, *amendement* Abände-

rung *f*, *swap* Umtausch *m*, *in coins* Wechselgeld *nt*, LAW *of sentence* Umwandlung *f*; **2.** *vt* ECON *supply or demand* ändern, *money* wechseln, einwechseln, GEN COMM *convert* verwandeln, *alter* ändern, verändern, *transform* umwandeln, verändern, *amend* abändern, *swap* umtauschen, *money* wechseln, einwechseln, LAW *sentence* umwandeln; ♦ **~ one's job** GEN COMM sich beruflich verändern; **~ hands** S&M *money, goods, business* den Besitzer wechseln; **3.** *vi* GEN COMM *alter* sich verändern, TRANSP *buses, trains* umsteigen

change: **~ of address** *n* COMMS Änderung *f* der Anschrift, Adressenänderung *f*; **~ of beneficiary provision** *n* INS *life insurance* Änderung *f* der Begünstigungsklausel; **~ dispenser** *n* GEN COMM Wechselgeldautomat *nt*; **~ dump** *n* COMP Speicherauszug *m* der Änderungen; **~ file** *n* COMP Änderungsdatei *f*, Bewegungsdatei *f*; **~ of management** *n* MGMNT Wechsel *m* im Management; **~over** *n* LAW Umstellung *f*; **~ of pace** *n* GEN COMM Tempowechsel *m*; **~ request** *n* TRANSP *aviation* Änderungsanfrage *f*, Änderungsantrag *m*, Änderungsbitte *f*, Änderungsgesuch *nt*, Umbuchungsauftrag *f*

channel 1. *n* COMP, MEDIA, S&M Kanal *m*; **2.** *vt* GEN COMM kanalisieren

Channel: the ~ *n* TRANSP der Kanal

channel: **~ of communication** *n* HRM, MGMNT Kommunikationskanal *m*, Kommunikationsweg *m*; **~ of distribution** *n* S&M Absatzkanal *m*, Absatzweg *m*; **~ for orders** *n* S&M Auftragsweg *m*

Channel: **~ money** *n* BrE TRANSP *shipping* Kanalgeld *nt*

channel: **~ of sales** *n* S&M Absatzkanal *m*; **~ selection** *n* S&M Kanalauswahl *f*

Channel: **~ Tunnel** *n* TRANSP Kanaltunnel *m*

chaos: ~ research *n* IND Chaosforschung *f*

CHAPS *abbr* AmE (*Clearing House Automated Payments System*) BANK Automatisiertes Real Time-Settlementsystem der Banken, Automatisiertes Zahlungssystem *nt* der Clearinghouses

chapter *n* GEN COMM *of organization* Abschnitt *m*

character *n* COMP, MEDIA Zeichen *nt*, S&M *of area, shop, product* Charakter *m*; **~ array** *n* COMP Zeichenanordnung *f*; **~-at-a-time printer** *n* COMP Einzelzeichendrucker *m*; **~ density** *n* COMP Zeichendichte *f*; **~ firmness** *n* HRM charakterliche Zuverlässigkeit *f*

characteristic *adj* GEN COMM bezeichnend

characterizing: ~ portion *n* PATENTS charakteristisches Merkmal *nt*, kennzeichnender Teil *m*, Wesensmerkmal *nt*

character: **~ merchandising** *n* S&M *advertising* Verkaufsförderung *f* durch Symbolfigur; **~ pitch** *n* COMP Zahl *f* der Zeichen pro Zoll; **~ set** *n* COMP Zeichenvorrat *m*; **~ string** *n* COMP Character-String *m* (*jarg*), Zeichenkette *f*

charge 1. *n* ACC Belastung *f*, ECON Abgabe *f*, Belastung *f*, *fee* Gebühr *f*, FIN Gebühr *f*, GEN COMM Abgabe *f*, Anrechnung *f*, Kosten *pl*, Preis *m*, LAW Anklage *f*, Belastung *f*, Rechtsbelehrung *f*; ♦ **at no ~** GEN COMM kostenlos, gebührenfrei; **in ~** HRM zuständig; **be in ~ of** GEN COMM zuständig sein für, leiten; **2.** *vt* ACC, BANK belasten, GEN COMM anrechnen, *fee* verlangen, *amount* in Rechnung stellen, berechnen, LAW belasten, anklagen, S&M berechnen; ♦ **~ as an expense** ACC als Aufwand verrechnen; **~ as present operating cost** ACC als Aufwand verrechnen; ~ **forward** (*Ch Fwd*) GEN COMM Kosten sind per Nachnahme zu erheben; ~ **interest** BANK Zinsen berechnen; ~ **to capital** ACC aktivieren

charge against *vt* ACC belasten; ◆ ~ **the operations of an accounting period** ACC als Aufwand verrechnen

charge off *vt* ACC abbuchen, ausbuchen

charge to *vt* GEN COMM *expenses* zurechnen

charge with *vt* GEN COMM beauftragen

chargeable *adj* GEN COMM anrechenbar, zu berechnen, zu verantworten, LAW, TAX abgabenpflichtig; ~ **assets** *n pl* TAX *capital gains tax* anrechenbare Vermögenswerte *m pl*; ~ **capital gains** *n pl* TAX kapitalsteuerpflichtiger Gewinn *m*; ~ **goods** *n pl* TAX abgabenpflichtige Waren *f pl*

charge: ~ **account** *n* BANK Abzahlungskonto *nt*; ~ **back** *n* BANK Ausgleichsbuchung *f*, Rückbelastung *f*; ~ **buyer** *n BrE* (*cf credit buyer AmE*) S&M Kreditkäufer, in *m,f*, Kreditkunde *m*; ~ **card** *n* BANK, S&M Zahlungskarte *f*, Kundenkreditkarte *f*

charged *adj* ACC, BANK belastet; ◆ ~ **against** GEN COMM belastet; ~ **off** ACC ausgebucht; **be ~ on top of** TAX am höchsten belastet sein mit; ~ **to** BANK *account, person* zu Lasten von

charge: ~ **hand** *n* HRM Vorarbeiter, in *m,f*; ~ **off** *n* ACC Abbuchung *f*, Ausbuchung *f*, Verlust *m*

charges *n pl* ACC Aufwendungen *f pl*, BANK, ECON, FIN Gebühren *f pl*; ◆ ~ **prepaid** IMP/EXP gebührenfrei, kostenfrei; ~ **on banking transactions** *n pl* BANK Bankgebühren *f pl*, Gebühren *f pl* für Bankgeschäfte

charitable *adj* GEN COMM, TAX, WEL wohltätige Stiftung *f*; ~ **trust** *n* TAX, WEL wohltätige Stiftung *f*

charity *n* TAX, WEL *beneficence* Wohltätigkeit *f*, *organization* wohltätige Organisation *f*, wohltätige Stiftung *f*; ~ **event** *n* WEL Wohltätigkeitsveranstaltung *f*; ~ **fund** *n* TAX Wohltätigkeitsfonds *m*; ~ **fundraising** *n* WEL Spendensammlung *f*; ~ **sponsorship** *n* WEL Sponsoring *nt*

chart *n* COMP *diagram, graph* Diagramm *nt*, GEN COMM *table* Übersicht *f*, *diagram, graph* Diagramm *nt*, *showing progress* Schaubild *nt*, MATH Diagramm *nt*, Grafik *f*, tabellarische Darstellung *f*; ~ **of accounts** *n* ACC Kontenplan *m*, Kontenrahmen *m*

charta partita *n* GEN COMM Urkunde *f* in doppelter Ausfertigung

charter 1. *n* IMP/EXP Miete *f*, LAW *company law* Gesellschaftssatzung *f*, Gründungsurkunde *f*, Statuten *nt pl*, TRANSP Charter *f*, Miete *f*; **2.** *vt* GEN COMM konzessionieren, IMP/EXP, TRANSP *vehicle* befrachten, chartern, mieten

charter: ~ **broker** *n* IMP/EXP, TRANSP *shipping* Befrachtungsmakler, in *m,f*, Schiffsmakler, in *m,f*; ~ **contract** *n* TRANSP Chartervertrag *m*

chartered *adj* GEN COMM konzessioniert; ~ **accountant** *n BrE* ACC zugelassener Wirtschaftsprüfer *m*, zugelassene Wirtschaftsprüferin *f*; ~ **bank** *n* BANK konzessionierte Bank *f*, privilegierte Bank *f*; ~ **company** *n* GEN COMM privilegierte Handelsgesellschaft, Schutzbriefgesellschaft; ~ **financial consultant** *n* FIN geprüfter Finanzberater *m*, geprüfte Finanzberaterin *f*; ~ **flight** *n* TRANSP Charterflug *m*

Chartered: ~ **Institute of Transport** *n BrE* TRANSP konzessioniertes Transportinstitut

chartered: ~ **life underwriter** *n* INS konzessionierter

Lebensversicherungsagent *m*; ~ **plane** *n* LEIS Charterflugzeug *nt*, Chartermaschine *f*, gechartertes Flugzeug *m*; ~ **property and casualty underwriter** *n* INS konzessionierter Sach- und Schadenversicherungsagent *m*

charterer *n* IMP/EXP, TRANSP Befrachter *m*, Charterer *m*, Mieter, in *m,f*; ◆ ~ **pays dues** (*cpd*) IMP/EXP, TRANSP *shipping* Befrachter zahlt Abgaben; ~'**s account** TRANSP zu Lasten des Charterers

charter: ~ **flight** *n* TRANSP Charterflug *m*

chartering *n* IMP/EXP, TRANSP Chartern *nt*; ~ **agent** *n* TRANSP Charteragent *m*, Lademakler, in *m,f*; ~ **broker** *n* IMP/EXP, TRANSP *shipping* Befrachtungsmakler, in *m,f*, Schiffsmakler, in *m,f*

charter: ~ **party** *n* (*C/P*) TRANSP *shipping* Charterpartie *f*, Chartervertrag *m*; ~ **party bill of lading** *n* TRANSP *shipping* Chartervertrag-Konnossement *nt*; ~ **party fraud** *n* TRANSP Chartervertragsbetrug *m*; ~ **party freight** *n* TRANSP Chartervertragsfracht *f*; ~ **plane** *n* TRANSP Charterflugzeug *nt*, Chartermaschine *f*, gechartertes Flugzeug *nt*

chartism *n* STOCK technische Chartanalyse *f*

chartist *n* STOCK Wertpapieranalytiker, in *m,f*

chart: ~ **point** *n* MATH Interventionspunkt *m*

chattel: ~ **mortgage** *n* BANK Pfandrecht *nt* an beweglichen Sachen; ~ **paper** *n* ECON Urkunde *f* über Sicherungsverträge, Verkehrspapier *nt*

chattels *n pl* LAW bewegliche Güter *nt pl*; ~ **personal** *n pl* LAW Mobiliarvermögen *nt*, PROP bewegliches Vermögen *nt*, Mobiliarvermögen *nt*, persönliche Habe *f*

CHC *abbr* (*cargo handling charge*) TRANSP Frachtladekosten *pl*, Frachtumschlagkosten *pl*, Güterverladungskosten *pl*

cheap *adj* GEN COMM billig, preiswert

cheapen *vt* GEN COMM verbilligen

cheap: ~ **fare** *n* TRANSP Fahrkarte *f* zum verbilligten Tarif; ~ **imitation** *n* IND billige Imitation *f*; ~ **money** *n* BANK billiges Geld *nt*; ~ **money policy** *n* BANK, ECON Politik *f* des billigen Geldes

cheat *vt* GEN COMM beschwindeln, betrügen

check 1. *n* BANK *AmE see cheque BrE*, GEN COMM *examination* Prüfung *f*, *AmE* (*cf bill BrE*) *invoice* Rechnung *f*, Überprüfung *f*, Zeche *f*, Nota *f* (*obs*), Faktura *f* (*obs*), *AmE* (*cf tick BrE*) *mark* Haken *m*, Häkchen *nt*, Kontrollzeichen *nt*, Kontrollvermerk *m*; **2.** *vt* GEN COMM überprüfen, *examine* nachprüfen, checken *restrain* unter Kontrolle halten, *AmE* (*cf tick BrE*) *mark* abhaken, TRANSP *ticket* kontrollieren; ◆ ~ **the box** *AmE* (*cf tick the box BrE*) GEN COMM das Kästchen ankreuzen; ~ **thoroughly** GEN COMM *examine* gründlich überprüfen, durchchecken

check in 1. *vt* LEIS *luggage* abfertigen lassen; **2.** *vi* LEIS *at airport, hotel* sich anmelden, sich einchecken

check off *vt AmE* (*cf tick off BrE*) GEN COMM *on list* abhaken

check out *vi* LEIS *of hotel* sich abmelden, *leave hotel* abreisen

check: ~ **bit** *n* COMP Prüfbit *nt*

checkbook *AmE see chequebook BrE*

check: ~ **box** *n AmE* (*cf tick box BrE*) COMP, GEN COMM Auswahlfeld *nt*; ~ **character** *n* COMP Prüfzeichen *nt*; ~ **digit** *n* COMP Prüfziffer *f*, FIN Kontrollziffer *f*

checker *n* HRM Kontrolleur *m*, Ladungsprüfer, in *m,f*,

S&M *AmE* (*cf supervisor BrE*) Aufsichtsbeamte(r) *m* [decl. as adj], Aufsichtsbeamtin *f*

checking: **~ account** *n AmE* BANK (*C/A, cf cheque account BrE, cf current account BrE, cf credit account*) Girokonto *nt*, Kontokorrentkonto *nt*, Kontokorrent *nt*, laufendes Konto *nt*, Scheckkonto *nt*; **~ account balance** *n AmE* BANK Kontokorrentguthaben *nt*; **~ account customer** *n AmE* BANK Kontokorrentkunde *m*; **~ account holder** *n AmE* BANK Kontokorrentinhaber, in *m,f*; **~ account loan** *n AmE* BANK Kontokorrentkredit *m*; **~ account reservation** *n AmE* BANK Kontokorrentvorbehalt *m*; **~ account surplus** *n AmE* BANK Kontokorrentguthaben *nt*

check list *n* GEN COMM Aufnahmebogen *m*, Checkliste *f*, Kontrolliste *f*

check: **~ mark** *n AmE* (*cf tick mark BrE*) GEN COMM Haken *m*, Häkchen *nt*, Kontrollzeichen *nt*, Kontrollvermerk *m*; **~-off** *n AmE* HRM Einziehung der Gewerkschaftsbeiträge durch Arbeitgeber

checkout *n* LEIS *hotel* Abmeldung *f*, S&M *in store* Ausgangskasse *f*, Kasse *f*; **~ assistant** *n* S&M Kontrollangestellte(r) *mf* [decl. as adj]; **~ clerk** *n AmE* S&M Kontrollangestellte(r) *mf* [decl. as adj]; **~ lane** *n* S&M Kasse *f*, Ausgangskasse *f*

checkpoint *n* COMP bedingter Programmstopp *m*, TRANSP *on the border, customs* Grenzübergang *m*, Kontrollpunkt *m*

check: **~ price** *n* STOCK Ankaufssatz *m*

checkroom *n AmE* (*cf left-luggage office BrE*) TRANSP Gepäckaufbewahrung *f*, Gepäckaufbewahrungsstelle *f*, Garderobe *f*

checksum *n* COMP *data transfer* Kontrollsumme *f*

Chemical: **~ Industries Association** *n* IND Verband der chemischen Industrie

chemical: **~ industry** *n* IND Chemieindustrie *f*, chemische Industrie *f*; **~ input** *n* ENVIR *agriculture* chemischer Eintrag *m*

chemicals *n pl* ENVIR, IND Chemie *f*, Chemikalien *f pl*, TRANSP Chemikalien *f pl*

chemical: **~ tanker** *n* TRANSP Chemikalientanker *m*; **~ works** *n pl* IND Chemiewerke *nt pl*

chemistry *n* ENVIR Chemie *f*, GEN COMM *between people* Chemie *f* (*infrml*), Verträglichkeit *f*, IND Chemie *f*

cheque *n BrE* BANK Scheck *m*; **~ account** *n BrE* BANK (*C/A, cf checking account AmE, cf credit account, cf current account BrE*) Girokonto *nt*, Kontokorrent *nt*, Kontokorrentkonto *nt*, laufendes Konto *nt*, Scheckkonto *nt*

chequebook *n BrE* BANK Scheckbuch *nt*, Scheckheft *nt*

cheque: **~ card** *n BrE* BANK *guarantee* Scheckkarte *f*; **~ clearing** *n BrE* BANK Scheckverrechnung *f*; **~ clearing system** *n BrE* BANK Scheckverrechnungssystem *nt*; **~ counterfoil** *n BrE* BANK Scheckabschnitt *m*; **~ credit** *n BrE* BANK Scheckkredit *m*; **~ embargo** *n BrE* BANK, FIN Schecksperre *f*; **~ forgery** *n BrE* BANK Scheckfälschung *f*; **~ form** *n BrE* BANK Scheckformular *nt*, Scheckvordruck *m*; **~ in favour of sb** *n BrE* BANK Scheck *m* zugunsten von jdm; **~ issue** *n BrE* BANK, FIN Scheckausgabe *f*, Scheckausstellung *f*; **~ kiting** *n BrE* BANK Ausstellung *f* eines noch nicht gedeckten Schecks, Scheckreiterei *f*; **~ payment** *n BrE* BANK Scheckzahlung *f*; **~ payment system** *n BrE* BANK Scheckeinlösungssystem *nt*; **~ protector** *n BrE* BANK *device* Scheckschutzgerät *nt*, Scheckschutzmaschine *f*;

~ register *n BrE* ACC, BANK Scheckausgangsbuch *nt*, Scheckliste *f*; **~ requisition** *n BrE* ACC, BANK Scheckanforderungsformular *nt*; **~ signer** *n BrE* ADMIN automatische Ausfertigung *f* der Scheckunterschrift; **~ stub** *n BrE* BANK Scheckabschnitt *m*; **~ to the amount of** *n BrE* BANK Scheck *m* in Höhe von; **~ without provision** *n BrE* BANK ungedeckter Scheck *m*; **~ without sufficient funds** *n BrE* BANK ungedeckter Scheck *m*; **~ writer** *n BrE* BANK *device* Scheckkodiermaschine *f*, Scheckausstellungsgerät *nt*, Scheckausstellungsmaschine *f*, Scheckschreibmaschine *f*; **~ writer machine** *n BrE* BANK Scheckkodiermaschine *f*, Scheckausstellungsgerät *nt*, Scheckausstellungsmaschine *f*, Scheckschreibmaschine *f*

Ch Fwd *abbr* (*charge forward*) GEN COMM Kosten sind per Nachnahme zu erheben

Chicago: **~ Board Options Exchange** *n* (*CBOE*) STOCK Optionsbörse in Chicago; **~ Board of Trade** *n* (*CBT*) STOCK Handelskammer von Chicago; **~ Mercantile Exchange** *n* (*CME*) STOCK Produktenbörse in Chicago; **~ School** *n* ECON Chicagoer Schule *f*; **~ Stock Exchange** *n* STOCK Wertpapierbörse in Chicago

chief *n* HRM Vorgesetzte(r) *mf* [decl. as adj]; **~ accountant** *n* ACC erster Buchhalter *m*, erste Buchhalterin *f*, Hauptbuchhalter, in *m,f*, Bilanzbuchhalter, in *m,f*; **~ accounting officer** *n* ACC, FIN Hauptbuchhalter, in *m,f*; **~ assets** *n pl* STOCK Hauptvermögenswerte *m pl*; **~ buyer** *n* MGMNT Einkaufschef, in *m,f* S&M *customer*, Hauptkunde *m*, Hauptkundin *f*, *of company* Haupteinkäufer, in *m,f*; **~ clerk** *n* MGMNT Bürochef, in *m,f*, Büroleiter, in *m,f*, leitende(r) Büroangestellte(r) *mf* [decl. as adj]; **~ designer** *n* MGMNT Chefkonstrukteur, in *m,f*, Leiter, in *m,f* Abteilung Design; **~ economist** *n* GEN COMM Leiter, in *m,f* der volkswirtschaftlichen Abteilung; **~ editor** *n* MEDIA Redaktionschef, in *m,f*, Chefredakteur, in *m,f*; **~ engineer** *n* HRM *on ship* erster Maschinist *m*, erste Maschinistin *f*; **~ executive** *n* HRM oberste Verwaltungsspitze *f*, Vorstandsvorsitzende(r) *mf* [decl. as adj], MGMNT Generaldirektor, in *m,f*, leitender Direktor *m*, leitende Direktorin *f*, *of local authority* oberste(r) Verwaltungsbeamte(r) *m* [decl. as adj], oberste Verwaltungsbeamtin *f*, Gemeindedirektor, in *m,f*, *of business* Vorstandsvorsitzende(r) *mf* [decl. as adj], Generalbevollmächtigte(r) *mf* [decl. as adj], Hauptgeschäftsführer, in *m,f*; **~ executive officer** *n AmE* (*CEO*) HRM Chief-Executive-Officer *m*, Hauptgeschäftsführer, in *m,f*; **~ financial officer** *n* (*CFO*) HRM Finanzleiter, in *m,f*, Leiter, in *m,f* Finanzen, Finanzchef, in *m,f*, Finanzleiter, in *m,f*; **~ immigration officer** *n* (*CIO*) HRM Leiter, in *m,f* der Einwanderungsbehörde; **~ information officer** *n* (*CIO*) HRM Leiter, in *m,f* des Nachrichtendienstes; **~ inspector** *n* (*CI*) HRM leitender Inspektor *m*, leitende Inspektorin *f*; **~ negotiator** *n* GEN COMM Chefunterhändler, in *m,f*; **~ officer** *n* HRM *on ship* erster Offizier *m*; **~ operating officer** *n* (*COO*) HRM oberste Führungskraft *f*, MGMNT Chef, in *m,f*, Hauptgeschäftsführer, in *m,f*; **~ place of business** *n* GEN COMM, HRM Hauptgeschäftssitz *m*; **~ of staff** *n* HRM Generalstabschef *m*; **~ steward** *n* HRM *on ship* Chefsteward *m*; **~ stewardess** *n* HRM *on ship* Chefstewardess *f*; **~ sub** *n BrE infrml* (*chief subeditor*) MEDIA Chefredakteur, in *m,f*; **~ subeditor** *n BrE* (*chief sub*)

MEDIA *print* Chefredakteur, in *m,f*; ~ **traffic controller** *n* HRM *of air traffic* leitender Fluglotse *m*, *of rail traffic* Oberfahrdienstleiter, in *m,f*; ~ **value** *n* (*CV*) GEN COMM Höchstwert *m*, Höchstpreis *m*, Hauptpreis *m*, Hauptwert *m*

child *n* ECON, INS, TAX, WEL Kind *nt*; ~'**s accident insurance** *n* INS Kinderunfallversicherung *f*; ~ **allowance** *n* TAX, WEL *BrE* (*cf children's allowance AmE*) *yearly tax rebate* Kinderfreibetrag *m*, *AmE* (*cf child benefit BrE*) *monthly payments* Kindergeld *nt*, Kinderzulage *f*; ~ **benefit** *n BrE* (*cf child allowance AmE*) TAX, WEL *monthly payments* Kindergeld *nt*, Kinderzulage *f*

childcare: ~ **facilities** *n* *pl* HRM Kinderbetreuungseinrichtungen *f pl*

child: ~~**centered** *AmE*, ~~**centred** *BrE adj* WEL auf Kinder ausgerichtet, kinderorientiert, *environment* kindgemäß, *politics* familienpolitisch; ~'**s deferred assurance** *n* INS Kinderlebensversicherung *f* mit aufgeschobenem Leistungstermin; ~'**s insurance** *n* INS Kinderlebensversicherung *f*; ~'**s play** *n infrml* GEN COMM Kinderspiel *nt* (*infrml*); ~'**s prodigy** *n* GEN COMM Genie *nt*, kluger Kopf *m* (*infrml*), Wunderkind *nt*

children: ~'**s allowance** *n AmE* (*cf child benefit BrE*) TAX, WEL *yearly tax rebate* Kinderfreibetrag *m*

Chinese: ~ **money** *n BrE jarg* STOCK eine Zahlung, die in Wertpapieren anstelle von Bargeld gemacht wird; ~ **walls** *n pl* BANK, FIN, STOCK *insider trading* Informationsbarriere *f*, innere Abschottung *f*, Auskunftsperre *f*

chip *n* COMP Chip *m*; ~~**based card** *n* COMP Chipkarte *f*

chipboard *n* GEN COMM Graupappe *f*, Hartfaserplatte *f*, Holzspanplatte *f*, Spanholzplatte *f*

chip: ~ **card** *n* COMP Chipkarte *f*

CHIPS *abbr AmE* (*Clearing House Interbank Payments System*) BANK internes elektronisches Abrechnungssystem der New Yorker Banken

chi: ~ **square** *n* MATH *statistics* Chi-Quadrat *nt*; ~~**squared distribution** *n* MATH *statistics* Chi-Quadrat-Verteilung *f*; ~~**square test** *n* MATH *statistics* Chi-Quadrat-Test *m*

chlorofluorocarbon *n* (*CFC*) ENVIR Fluorchlorkohlenwasserstoff *m* (*FCKW*)

choice *n* GEN COMM *choosing, thing chosen* Wahl *f*, *assortment* Auswahl *f*, Sortiment *nt*; ~~**of-law clause** *n* LAW Rechtswahlvereinbarung *f*; ~ **variable** *n* ECON *decision theory* Entscheidungsvariable *f*

choose *vt* GEN COMM wählen

chose *n* LAW Gegenstand *nt* des beweglichen Vermögens; ~ **in action** *n* LAW Forderungsrecht *nt*, PATENTS unkörperlicher Rechtsgegenstand *m*

Christmas: ~ **bonus** *n* GEN COMM, HRM Weihnachtsgeld *nt*

chronological *adj* GEN COMM zeitlich

chronologically *adv* GEN COMM zeitlich

chunk: ~ **of stock** *n infrml* STOCK Aktienpaket *nt*

churn *vi* FIN strudeln, wirbeln

churning *n* STOCK *infrml* Provisionsschneiderei *f* (*infrml*), FIN Gaunerei *f*, Provisionsschneiderei *f*

c/i *abbr* (*certificate of insurance*) INS Versicherungsbestätigung *f*, Versicherungszertifikat *nt*

CI *abbr* (*chief inspector*) HRM leitender Inspektor *m*, leitende Inspektorin *f*

CI&F *abbr* (*cost, insurance and freight*) IMP/EXP, TRANSP Kosten, Versicherung und Fracht

CIFAS *abbr BrE* (*Credit Industry Fraud Avoidance System*) FIN Betrugskontrollsystem innerhalb der Kreditindustrie

CIF: ~ **contract** *n* IMP/EXP cif-Vertrag *m*; ~ **landed** *n* IMP/EXP cif einschließlich Löschen

CIM *abbr* (*computer-integrated manufacture, computer-integrated manufacturing*) COMP, IND CIM (*computerintegrierte Fertigung, computerintegrierte Herstellung*)

Cincinnatti: ~ **Stock Exchange** *n* STOCK Cincinnatti Wertpapierbörse

cinema *n BrE* (*cf movie theater AmE*) LEIS, MEDIA Kino *nt*, Filmtheater *nt*; ~ **advertising** *n BrE* S&M Filmwerbung *f*, Kinoreklame *f*, Kinowerbung *f*

cinematographic: ~ **adaptation** *n* MEDIA *of a work* Verfilmung *f*

CIO *abbr* HRM (*Congress of Industrial Organizations*) Industriegewerkschaftsverband, ≈ DGB (*Deutscher Gewerkschaftsbund*), (*chief immigration officer*) Leiter, in *m,f* der Einwanderungsbehörde, (*chief information officer*) Leiter, in *m,f* des Nachrichtendienstes

CIP *abbr* (*carriage and insurance paid*) IMP/EXP Fracht und Versicherung bezahlt, *Incoterms* frachtfrei versichert

cipher *n* COMMS *code* Ziffer *f*, Code *m*, Chiffre *f*, *number* Zahl *f*

CIR *abbr* (*cage inventory record*) TRANSP Käfiglagerkarte *f*

circa *adv* (*ca.*) GEN COMM ungefähr (*ung.*), zirka (*ca.*), rund (*rd.*)

circle *n* GEN COMM *political, business* Kreis *m*, LEIS *in theatre* Rang *m*; ~ **of acquaintances** *n* GEN COMM Bekanntenkreis *m*

circuit *n* COMMS Verbindung *f*, COMP Schaltkreis *m*, LAW Gerichtsbezirk *m*; ~ **board assembly** *n* COMP Bestückungsbetrieb *m*

circular *n* COMMS Rundschreiben *nt*; ~ **flow** *n* ECON Wirtschaftskreislauf *m*; ~ **migration** *n* ECON *of population* Pendelwanderung *f*

circulate 1. *vt* COMMS *information*, MEDIA *newspaper, magazine* verbreiten; **2.** *vi* COMMS *information, news* im Umlauf sein, kursieren

circulating: ~ **capital** *n* ECON Betriebskapital *nt*; ~ **medium** *n* FIN Umlaufmedium *nt*

circulation *n* COMMS Verbreitung *f*, ECON Umlauf *m*, Verkehr *m*, MEDIA *of newspaper, magazine* Auflage *f*, Auflagenhöhe *f*, S&M Verbreitung *f*; ~ **breakdown** *n* GEN COMM, MEDIA *of newspaper, magazine* Auflageneinbruch *m*; ~ **department** *n* MEDIA *of newspaper, magazine* Vertriebsabteilung *f*; ~ **manager** *n* MEDIA *of newspaper, magazine*, MGMNT Vertriebsleiter, in *m,f*

circumflex *n* COMP *accent* Zirkumflex *m*

circumstance *n* LAW Umstand *m*

circumstances *n pl* GEN COMM Sachlage *f*, Sachverhalt *m*, Situation *f*; ◆ **under the** ~ GEN COMM, LAW nach Lage der Dinge, unter den gegebenen Umständen; **under no** ~ GEN COMM, LAW unter keinen Umständen

circumstantial: ~ **evidence** *n* LAW Indizienbeweis *m*

CIS *abbr* (*Commonwealth of Independent States*) POL GUS (*Gemeinschaft Unabhängiger Staaten*)

citation *n* LAW Vorladung *f*, PATENTS Entgegenhaltung *f*

cite *vt* GEN COMM zitieren, LAW vorladen, PATENTS entgegenhalten

citizen *n* POL Bürger, in *m,f*, Staatsangehörige(r) *mf* [decl. as adj], Staatsbürger, in *m,f*; **~ bonds** *n pl* STOCK Bürgeranleihen *f pl*

Citizens: **~ Advice Bureau** *n BrE* (*CAB*) ADMIN Rechtshilfeberatungsstelle *f*

Citizen: **~'s Charter** *n BrE* POL Bürgercharta *f*

citizenship *n* POL Staatsangehörigkeit *f*, Staatsbürgerschaft *f*

city *n* POL Stadt *f*; ◆ **outside the ~ center** *AmE*, **outside the ~ centre** *BrE* S&M außerhalb des Stadtzentrums

City: the ~ *n* FIN Londoner City *f*

city: **~ center** *AmE*, **~ centre** *BrE n* GEN COMM Innenstadt *f*, Stadtzentrum *nt*; **~ council** *n* POL Stadtmagistrat *m*, Stadtrat *m*

City: **~ Grant** *n BrE* GEN COMM *government aid* Stadtsubvention *f*; **~ and Guilds Institute** *n* (*CGI*) ECON britische Prüfungsinstitution für technische und Handwerksbetriebe

city: **~ planner** *n* ADMIN, GEN COMM, POL, PROP Stadtplaner, in *m,f*; **~ planning** *n* ADMIN, POL, PROP Städtebau *m*, städtebauliche Planung *f*, Stadtplanung *f*

civil: **~ action** *n* LAW Zivilprozeß *m*

Civil: **~ Aeronautics Board** *n AmE* (*CAB*) TRANSP oberste Zivilluftfahrtbehörde

civil: **~ aviation** *n* ECON Zivilluftfahrt *f*

Civil: **~ Aviation Authority** *n BrE* (*CAA*) TRANSP Zivilluftfahrtbehörde

civil: **~ claim** *n* LAW *contract* zivilrechtlicher Anspruch *m*; **~ commotion** *n* (*CC*) INS, POL Aufruhr *m*, Bürgerunruhen *f pl*, innere Unruhe *f*

civilian: **~ employment** *n* HRM bürgerlicher Beruf *m*

civil: **~ law** *n* LAW Zivilrecht *nt*; **~ liability** *n* LAW zivilrechtliche Haftung *f*; **~ penalty** *n AmE* INS, LAW Bußgeld *nt*; **~ rights** *n pl* LAW *incorporated in the constitution of a country* Bürgerrechte *nt pl*; **~ servant** *n* HRM Beamte(r) *m* [decl. as adj], Beamtin *f*; **~ servant on limited appointment** *n* HRM Beamte(r) *m* [decl. as adj] auf Zeit, Beamtin *f* auf Zeit; **~ service** *n* (*CS*) GEN COMM öffentlicher Dienst *m*, Staatsdienst *m*, Zivilverwaltung *f*

Civil: **~ Service Commission** *n BrE* (*CSC*) ADMIN Berufsbeamtenausschuß *m*

civil: **~ status** *n* LAW zivilrechtlicher Status *m*; **~ war** *n* POL Bürgerkrieg *m*; **~ wrong** *n* LAW unerlaubte Handlung *f*

ck *abbr* (*cask*) TRANSP Faß *nt*

cl *abbr* (*centiliter AmE, centilitre BrE*) GEN COMM cl (*Zentiliter*)

c/l *abbr* (*craft loss*) TRANSP *shipping* Schiffsverlust *m*

CL *abbr* (*Corporation of Lloyd's*) INS *marine* Lloyd's Versicherung *f*

claim 1. *n* GEN COMM Beanspruchung *f*, Behauptung *f*, INS Anspruch *m*, Forderung *f*, Schaden *m*, Schadensfall *m*, LAW, PATENTS Beanspruchung *f*, TAX, WEL Anspruch *m*; **2.** *vt* GEN COMM beanspruchen, behaupten, fordern, verlangen, LAW, PATENTS beanspruchen, Anspruch stellen, WEL beantragen; ◆ **~ compensation** INS, LAW Schadensersatz fordern; **~ damages** LAW Schadensersatzansprüche stellen; **~ exemption from taxes** TAX Steuerfreiheit beanspruchen; **~ immunity from tax** TAX Steuerfreiheit beanspruchen; **3.** *vi* INS Ansprüche geltend machen, LAW Schadensersatz verlangen; ◆ **~ against sb** INS, LAW einen Anspruch gegen jdn erheben

claimant *n* HRM Antragsteller, in *m,f*, INS Anspruchsberechtigte(r) *mf* [decl. as adj], Anspruchsteller, in *m,f*, Forderungsberechtigte(r) *mf* [decl. as adj], Geschädigte(r) *mf* [decl. as adj], LAW Anspruchsberechtigte(r) *mf* [decl. as adj], Forderungsberechtigte(r) *mf* [decl. as adj]

claim: **~ based upon a contract** *n* LAW obligatorischer Anspruch *m*; **~ based upon contract or tort** *n* LAW schuldrechtlicher Anspruch *m*; **~ of compensation** *n* LAW Entschädigungsanspruch *m*, Schadensersatzanspruch *m*; **~ for adjustment** *n* LAW Ausgleichsanspruch *m*; **~ for compensation** *n* INS Schadensersatzanspruch *m*; **~ for damages** *n* LAW Schadensersatzanspruch *m*; **~ for indemnification** *n* INS Ersatzanspruch *m*; **~ form** *n* INS Schadenmeldeformular *nt*; **~ for refund** *n* TAX Erstattungsanspruch *m*; **~ in rem** *n* LAW *contracts* dinglicher Anspruch *m* (*frml*); **~ paid** *n* INS bezahlter Schaden *m*; **~ of recourse** *n* INS Regreßanspruch *m*

claims: **~ adjuster** *n* INS Dispacheur *m*, Schadenregulierer *m*, Schadenssachbearbeiter, in *m,f*; **~ adjustment** *n* INS *marine damages* Dispache *f*, Schadenregulierung *f*; **~ department** *n* INS Schadenabteilung *f*; **~ of different categories** *n pl* PATENTS Ansprüche *m pl* unterschiedlicher Kategorien, Ansprüche *m pl* unterschiedlicher Klassen, Ansprüche *m pl* verschiedener Klassen

claim: **~ settlement** *n* INS Schadenabwicklung *f*, Schadenregulierung *f*

claims: **~ expenses** *n pl* INS Schadenbearbeitungskosten *pl*, Schadenregulierungskosten *pl*; **~ file** *n* INS Schadenakte *f*; **~ handler** *n* HRM Schadensbeauftrage(r) *mf* [decl. as adj]; **~ handling** *n* INS Schadensbearbeitung *f*; **~ incurring fees** *n pl* PATENTS gebührenpflichtige Ansprüche *m pl*; **~ inspector** *n* HRM Schadensbeauftrage(r) *mf* [decl. as adj]; **~ and liabilities** *n pl BrE* FIN Forderungen und Verbindlichkeiten *f pl*; **~ limit** *n* INS Höchstanspruch *m*, Anspruchsgrenze *f*; **~ manager** *n* HRM Leiter, in *m,f* der Schadenabteilung; **~ payment** *n* INS Schadensbegleichung *f*, Schadenzahlung *f*; **~ prevention** *n* INS Verhinderung *f* der Entstehung von Schadensersatzansprüchen; **~ procedure** *n* INS Behandlung *f* von Ansprüchen, Schadensbearbeitung *f*, Schadenbearbeitungsverfahren *nt*; **~ reserve** *n* INS Schadenrückstellung *f*, Schadenreserve *f*; **~ of the same category** *n pl* PATENTS Ansprüche *m pl* derselben Kategorie, Ansprüche *m pl* derselben Klasse; **~ settlement** *n* INS Schadenregulierung *f*; **~ settlement fund** *n* INS Schadenregulierungsfonds *m*

claim: **~ to delivery** *n* TRANSP Auslieferungsanspruch *m*; **~ to an inheritance** *n* LAW Erbanspruch *m*; **~ to protection against abridgment of legal rights** *n* LAW Abwehranspruch *m*

clapped: **~ out** *adj BrE infrml* GEN COMM ausgedient, ausgeleiert, abgetakelt (*infrml*)

clashing: **~ interests** *n pl* GEN COMM widerstreitende Interessen *f pl*

class *n* GEN COMM *category* Klasse *f*, *for education* Klasse *f*, Unterricht *m*, *quality, style* Stil *m*, PATENTS *International Patent Classification, Nice Classification* Klasse *f*, Kategorie *f*, POL *in society* Gesellschaftsklasse *f*, Gesellschaftsschicht *f*, Klasse *f*, politische Klasse *f*, Bewußtseinsklasse *f*, Einstufung *f*, gesellschaftlicher Rang *m*, Kaste *f*, TAX Kategorie *f*, Klasse *f*; **~ action** *n* LAW Gruppenklage *f*

Class: **~ A shares** *n pl AmE* STOCK Aktien *f pl* der

Kategorie A; ~ **B shares** *n pl AmE* STOCK Aktien *f pl* der Kategorie B

class: ~ **boundary** *n* MATH *statistics* Klassengrenze *f*; ~ **of construction** *n* INS Bauart *f*, Bauklasse *f*; ~ **division** *n* MATH *statistics* Klasseneinteilung *f*; ~ **frequency** *n* MATH *statistics* Klassenhäufigkeit *f*

classical: ~ **dichotomy** *n* ECON klassische Dichotomie *f*; ~ **economics** *n* ECON klassische Nationalökonomie *f*; ~ **model** *n* ECON klassisches Modell *nt*; ~ **savings theory** *n* ECON *econometrics* klassische Spartheorie *f*

classic: ~ **example** *n* GEN COMM klassisches Beispiel *nt*

classification *n* ADMIN Einstufung *f*, Klassification *f*, Klassifizierung *f*, GEN COMM Klassifizierung *f*, *analysis* Aufgliederung *f*, Aufschlüsselung *f*, Einteilung *f*, Klassifikation *f*, *arrangement* Einstufung *f*, HRM Einstufung *f*; ~ **of accounts** *n* ACC Kontengliederung *f*; ~ **by object** *n* GEN COMM Einordnung *f* nach Objekt, Klassifikation *f* nach Objekt; ~ **certificate** *n* TRANSP *shipping* Klassenzertifikat *nt*; ~ **of occupations** *n* INS Berufsgruppenklassifikation *f*; ~ **of risks** *n* INS Gefahrenklassifikation *f*, Risikoeinstufung *f*; ~ **society** *n* GEN COMM Klassifikationsgesellschaft *f*

classified: ~ **ad** *n BrE* (*classified advertisement*) GEN COMM, MEDIA Annonce *f*, S&M *small ad* Inserat *nt*, Kleinanzeige *f*, Kleininserat *nt*; ~ **advertisement** *n* (*classified ad*) GEN COMM, MEDIA, *small ad* S&M Annonce *f*, Kleinanzeige *f*, Kleininserat *nt*, Inserat *nt*; ~ **display advertising** *n* S&M Kleinanzeigenwerbung *f*; ~ **information** *n* POL *document* Verschlußsache *f*; ~ **stock** *n* STOCK kategorisierte Aktie *f*

classify *vt* ADMIN einstufen, klassifizieren, GEN COMM aufgliedern, eingliedern, einordnen, einteilen, einstufen, klassifizieren, sortieren, *analysis* aufschlüsseln, *customs* tarifieren

class: ~ **of insurance** *n* INS Versicherungsbranche *f*, Versicherungssparte *f*, Versicherungszweig *m*; ~ **magazine** *n* S&M Qualitätszeitschrift *f*, anspruchsvolle Zeitschrift *f*; ~ **object** *n* GEN COMM Klassenobjekt *nt*; ~ **of risk** *n* INS Gefahrenklasse *f*; ~ **savings theory** *n* ECON *econometrics* Klassenspartheorie *f*; ~ **struggle** *n* ECON Klassenkampf *m*

clause *n* HRM Klausel *f*, INS Bestimmung *f*, Klausel *f*, LAW Klausel *f*; **all or nothing** ~ *n* (*AON clause*) STOCK *tender* Alles-oder-Nichts-Klausel *f*; ~ **of arbitration** *n* LAW Arbitrageklausel *f*

claused: ~ **bill of lading** *n* IMP/EXP *shipping* mit Klauseln abgesicherter Frachtbrief *m*, unreines Konnossement *nt*, verklausulierter Frachtbrief *m*, einschränkendes Konnossement *nt*, TRANSP *shipping* unreines Konnossement *nt*

clause: ~ **for the bearing of risk** *n* LAW Klausel *f* zur Gefahrtragung

clawback *n* FIN Rückforderung *f*, TAX *of tax relief* Rückforderung *f* gewährter Steuervergünstigungen

Clayton: ~ **Act** *n* ECON *1914 Kartellgesetzgebung* amerikanisches Antitrust-Gesetz

cld *abbr* (*cleared*) BANK abgerechnet, verrechnet, FIN abgerechnet

clean 1. *adj* ACC schuldenfrei, ENVIR *car* rein, FIN schuldenfrei, GEN COMM rein, schuldenfrei, sauber, STOCK vorbehaltlos, unbeschränkt; **2.** *vt* ENVIR reinigen, dekontaminieren

clean: ~ **acceptance** *n* BANK uneingeschränktes Akzept *nt*

Clean: ~ **Air Act Amendments** *n pl AmE* ENVIR *1970* Ergänzungen des Gesetzes über die Reinhaltung der Luft

clean: ~ **ballast tank** *n* TRANSP *shipping* reiner Ballasttank *m*, sauberer Ballasttank *m*; ~ **bill** *n* ECON, FIN Wechsel *m* ohne Dokumentensicherung; ~ **bill of health** *n* GEN COMM Attest *nt* ohne gesundheitliche Einschränkungen; ~ **bill of lading** *n* IMP/EXP echtes Konnossement *nt*, Frachtbrief *m* ohne Vorbehalt, Konnossement *nt* ohne Einschränkungen, reines Konnossement *nt*, Konnossement *nt* ohne Vorbehalt, TRANSP reines Konnossement *nt*, Konnossement *nt* ohne Einschränkungen, Konnossement *nt* ohne Vorbehalt; ~ **credit** *n* (*C/C*) FIN einfaches Akkreditiv *nt*; ~ **float** *n* ECON sauberes Floaten *nt*; ~ **hands** *n pl* GEN COMM ehrliches Geschäftsgebaren *nt*, LAW redliches Geschäftsgebaren *nt*; ~ **payment** *n* FIN nicht dokumentäre Zahlung *f*, ordnungsgemäße Zahlung *f*, Zahlung *f* gegen offene Rechnung, LAW *contracts* Zahlung *f* netto Kasse; ~ **record** *n* LAW keine Vorstrafen *f pl*; ~ **report of findings** *n* TRANSP reiner Ergebnisbericht *m*, sauberer Befundbericht *m*; ~ **signature** *n* GEN COMM saubere Unterschrift *f*; ~ **technology** *n* ENVIR saubere Technologie *f*, umweltfreundliche Technologie *f*

cleanup: ~ **fund** *n* INS *life insurance* Gewinnrückstellung *f*; ~ **operation** *n* ENVIR Reinigungsaufbereitung *f*, Umweltsanierung *f*, *soil remediation* Altlastensanierung *f*

clear 1. *adj* GEN COMM klar; ♦ **make sth** ~ GEN COMM etw klar darstellen; **2.** *vt* BANK *cheque* verrechnen, *funds* abrechnen, COMP löschen, GEN COMM *account, debt* zahlen; ♦ ~ **through customs** IMP/EXP, TRANSP abfertigen, verzollen

clearance *n* FIN Abrechnung *f*, Tilgung *f*, GEN COMM *of account, debt* Zahlung *f*, IMP/EXP *customs* Klarierung *f*, Verzollung *f*, Zollabfertigung *f*, S&M Räumung *f*, TRANSP Verzollung *f*; ~ **agent** *n* HRM Zollagent *m*; ~ **of cargo goods** *n* IMP/EXP Zollabfertigung *f* von Warenladungen; ~ **group** *n* (*CG*) IMP/EXP Verzollungsgruppe *f*; ~ **inwards** *n* IMP/EXP Einklarierung *f*, Einfuhrerklärung *f*, Eingangsdeklarierung *f*; ~ **outwards** *n* IMP/EXP Ausfuhrerklärung *f*, Ausgangsdeklarierung *f*; ~ **sale** *n* S&M Räumungsverkauf *m*; ~ **of ship** *n* IMP/EXP, TRANSP Klarierung *f* von Schiffen

clear: ~~**cut** *adj* GEN COMM deutlich, klar umrissen; ~ **of debts** *adj* ACC, FIN, GEN COMM schuldenfrei

cleared *adj* (*cld*) BANK abgerechnet, verrechnet, FIN abgerechnet; ♦ ~ **without examination** (*CWE*) IMP/EXP unbesehen klariert

cleared: ~ **check** *AmE*, ~ **cheque** *BrE n* BANK abgerechneter Scheck *m*

clear: ~ **income** *n* ACC Nettoeinkommen *nt*

clearing *n* BANK Abrechnungsverfahren *m*, Abrechnungsverkehr *m*, Giroverkehr *m*, Abrechnung *f*, Clearing *nt*, Verrechnung *f*, COMP Löschung *f*, ECON *customs* Verzollung *f*, GEN COMM Behebung *f*; ~ **account** *n* ACC Verrechnungskonto *nt*; ~ **agent** *n* IMP/EXP Abfertigungsagent *m*, Klarierungsagent *m*; ~ **agreement** *n* BANK Verrechnungsabkommen *nt*; ~ **balance statement** *n* BANK Saldenstandausweis *m*; ~ **bank** *n* BANK, FIN Abrechnungsbank *f*, Clearingbank *f*, Girobank *f*; ~ **center** *AmE*, ~ **centre** *BrE n* BANK Clearingstelle *f*, Clearingzentrale *f*; ~ **corporation** *n* *AmE* BANK Verrechnungsgesellschaft *f*, Clearinggesellschaft *f*; **~ day** *n* BANK Verrechnungstag *m*; **~ house** *n* FIN Abrechnungsstelle *f*, Clearinghaus *nt*, TRANSP *aviation* Abrechnungsstelle *f*, Clearingstelle *f*

Clearing: **~ House Automated Payments System** *n BrE* (*CHAPS*) BANK Automatisiertes Real Time-Settlementsystem der Banken, Automatisiertes Zahlungssystem *nt* der Clearinghouses

clearing: **~ house funds** *n pl* BANK, ECON am Interbankenmarkt gehandelte Geschäftsbankenguthaben *nt pl*

Clearing: **~ House Interbank Payments System** *n* (*CHIPS*) BANK internes elektronisches Abrechnungssystem der New Yorker Banken

clearing: **~ items** *n pl* ACC, BANK verrechnungsfähige Positionen *f pl*, GEN COMM Ausverkaufwaren *f pl*; **~ market** *n* ECON Gleichgewichtsmarkt *m*; **~ the market** *n* STOCK Abwicklung *f* aller Kauf- und Verkaufsaufträge; **~ member** *n* BANK, FIN Mitglied *nt* einer Liquidationskasse, STOCK *currency options* Liquidationskassenmitglied *nt*, Mitglied *nt* einer Liquidationskasse; **~ report** *n* BANK Verrechnungsbericht *m*; **~ transactions** *n pl* BANK Clearingverkehr *m*

clear: **~ loss** *n* FIN Nettoverlust *m*; **~ profit** *n* FIN Nettoeinkommen *nt*, Reinertrag *m*; **~ thinking** *n* GEN COMM klare Denkweise *f*; **~ title** *n AmE* LAW unbelastetes Eigentumsrecht *nt*

clerical *adj* HRM *ecclesiastical* geistlich; **~ error** *n* ACC, ADMIN Schreibfehler *m*; **~ personnel** *n* HRM Büropersonal *nt*, Angestellte(n) *pl* [decl. as adj], Büroangestellte(n) *pl* [decl. as adj]; **~ staff** *n* HRM Büropersonal *nt*, Angestellte(n) *pl* [decl. as adj], Büroangestellte(n) *pl* [decl. as adj]; **~ work** *n* HRM Büroarbeit *f*; **~ worker** *n* HRM Angestellte(r) *mf* [decl. as adj], Büroangestellte(r) *mf* [decl. as adj]; **~ work measurement** *n* (*CWM*) HRM Bewertung *f* von Büroarbeiten

clerk *n* HRM Angestellte(r) *mf* [decl. as adj], Büroangestellte(r) *mf* [decl. as adj], Sachbearbeiter, in *m,f*, LAW Schreiber, in *m,f*

cliché *n* GEN COMM Klischee *nt*

click *vt* COMP *mouse button* anklicken, klicken

client *n* GEN COMM Auftraggeber, in *m,f*, Klient, in *m,f*, S&M *of advertising agency* Kunde *m*, Kundin *f*; **~ account** *n* ACC Anderkonto *nt*; **~ agreement letter** *n BrE* FIN Einverständnisschreiben *nt* des Kunden; **~ base** *n* S&M Kundenbasis *f*; **~ firm** *n* S&M Kundenfirma *f*; **~-led marketing policy** *n* S&M kundenorientierte Marketingpolitik *f*

client/server *n* COMP Client/Server *m* (*jarg*)

climate *n* ECON, ENVIR, WEL Klima *nt*

climb *vi* ECON *unemployment* ansteigen; ♦ **~ the promotion ladder** HRM die Karriereleiter erklimmen

clip: **~ art** *n* COMP Bildvorlage *f*, Clipart *nt* (*jarg*)

clipboard *n* COMP Clipboard *nt* (*jarg*), Zwischenablage *f*

clipping *n AmE* (*cf cutting BrE*) MEDIA *from newspaper* Ausschnitt *m*; **~ service** *n AmE* (*cf cutting service BrE*) S&M Zeitungsausschnittsdienst *m*

clock *n* GEN COMM, IND Uhr *f*

clock in *vi* HRM, IND Arbeitszeit registrieren, Arbeitsanfang registrieren, seine Stechkarte in die Stechuhr stecken, anstempeln, stempeln

clock off *vi* HRM, IND abstempeln, Arbeitsende registrieren

clock on *vi* HRM, IND Arbeitszeit registrieren, Arbeitsan-

fang registrieren, seine Stechkarte in die Stechuhr stecken, anstempeln, stempeln

clock out *vi* HRM, IND abstempeln, Arbeitsende registrieren

clock: **~-calendar** *n* COMP *hardware* Kalenderuhr *f*; **~ card** *n* HRM, IND Stechkarte *f*, Stempelkarte *f*; **~ pulse** *n* COMP Takt *m*; **~ rate** *n* COMP Taktrate *f*; **~ signal** *n* COMP Takt *m*

clone 1. *n* COMP, GEN COMM, IND Klon *m*; **2.** *vt* COMP klonen, Hardware billig, ohne Autorisierung nachbauen

close 1. *adj* GEN COMM *cooperation, relationship* eng; ♦ **in ~ competition** ECON in scharfem Wettbewerb; **in ~ touch** GEN COMM in engem Kontakt; **2.** *n* FIN Schlußkurs *m*, STOCK Börsenschluß *m*, amtlicher Börsenschluß *m*, *closing price* Schlußkurs *m*; **3.** *vt* ACC *books* abschließen, FIN *file, session* schließen, *deal* tätigen, *sale* einstellen; ♦ **~ a gap** FIN eine Lücke schließen

close down 1. *vt* GEN COMM *branch, company* schließen, zumachen (*infrml*), IND *permanently* stillegen; **2.** *vi* GEN COMM *branch, company* schließen, zumachen (*infrml*), IND *permanently* stillgelegt werden, MEDIA *radio, television* das Programm beenden

close out *vt* ACC abbuchen, ausbuchen, INS *policy* ausstellen; ♦ **~ a position** STOCK eine Position schließen, eine Position glattstellen

close: **~ company** *n BrE* ECON, GEN COMM Gesellschaft *f* mit geringer Mitgliederzahl; **~ correlation** *n* MATH enge Korrelation *f*

closed *adj* GEN COMM geschlossen, *account* abgeschlossen, *ended* aufgehoben, *not public* nichtöffentlich; ♦ **~ to the public** LAW unter Ausschluß der Öffentlichkeit

closed: **~ account** *n* ACC abgeschlossenes Konto *nt*, ausgeglichenes Konto *nt*, BANK, FIN abgeschlossenes Konto *nt*; **~ box container** *n* TRANSP *shipping* geschlossener Container *m*; **~ circuit** *n* COMP geschlossener Stromkreis *m*; **~ container** *n* TRANSP *shipping* geschlossener Container *m*; **~ corporation** *n AmE* ECON Familiengesellschaft *f*, Gesellschaft *f* mit beschränkter Mitgliederzahl, Gesellschaft *f* mit geringer Mitgliederzahl, GEN COMM Gesellschaft *f* mit geringer Mitgliederzahl; **~ down** *adj* GEN COMM stillgelegt; **~ economy** *n* ECON geschlossene Volkswirtschaft *f*; **~-end fund** *n* FIN geschlossener Investmentfonds *m*, Investmentfonds *m* mit begrenzter Emissionshöhe; **~-end investment company** *n* (*CEIC*) FIN Kapitalanlagegesellschaft *f* mit geschlossenem Anlagefonds; **~-end investment fund** *n* FIN Investmentfonds *m* mit begrenzter Emissionshöhe; **~-end investment trust** *n* FIN Investmentgesellschaft *f* mit begrenzter Emissionshöhe; **~-end management company** *n BrE* FIN geschlossene Investmentgesellschaft *f*; **~-end mortgage** *n* BANK abgeschlossene Hypothek *f*; **~-end mutual fund** *n* STOCK geschlossener Investmentfonds *m*; **~-loop adaptation** *n* COMP adaptive Regelung *f* mit Rückführung; **~-out** *adj* STOCK abgewickelt

close-down *n* MEDIA *of broadcast* Sendeschluß *m*

closed: **~ position** *n* FIN geschlossene Position *f*, STOCK glattgestellte Position *f*; **~ question** *n* GEN COMM Alternativfrage *f*, S&M *market research* Alternativfrage *f*, gebundene Frage *f*; **~ season** *n* MEDIA *print, broadcast* Sauregurkenzeit *f* (*infrml*); **~ shop** *n* ECON, HRM gewerkschaftspflichtiger Betrieb *m*; **~ union** *n*

HRM Gewerkschaft *f* mit Mitgliedersperre; ~ **vehicle deck** *n* TRANSP *shipping* geschlossenes Fahrzeugdeck *nt*
close: ~ **examination** *n* GEN COMM genaue Prüfung *f*
closely: ~ **connected profession** *n* HRM nah verwandter Beruf *m*; **~-held corporation** *n* AmE ECON, GEN COMM Gesellschaft *f* mit beschränkter Mitgliederzahl, Gesellschaft *f* mit geringer Mitgliederzahl, Gesellschaft *f* mit beschränktem Aktionärskreis
Closer: ~ **Economic Relations Pact** *n* ECON *Australia* Pakt zur engeren wirtschaftlichen Zusammenarbeit
closing *n* FIN Auflösung *f*, PROP Auflassung *f*; ~ **address** *n* GEN COMM *of conference*, POL Abschlußrede *f*; ~ **agreement** *n* AmE TAX endgültige Vereinbarung *f*, schriftliche Abschlußvereinbarung *m*; ~ **balance** *n* BANK Endsaldo *m*; ~ **bid** *n* GEN COMM Höchstgebot *nt*, letztes Gebot *nt*; ~ **costs** *n pl* FIN Abschlußkosten *pl*, PROP *real estate* Auflassungskosten *pl*; ~ **date** *n* GEN COMM Abgabefrist *f*, Anmeldeschluß *m*, Schlußtermin *m*, MEDIA Einsendeschluß *m*, PROP Auflassungsdatum *nt*, S&M Einsendeschluß *m*; ~ **down** *n* GEN COMM *of branch, company* Schließung *f*, Stillegung *f*; **~-down costs** *n pl* GEN COMM Kosten *pl* der Betriebsschließung; **~-down sale** *n* GEN COMM Ausverkauf *m* wegen Geschäftsaufgabe; ~ **entry** *n* ACC Abschlußbuchung *f*, Schlußeintrag *m*; ~ **inventory** *n* ACC Endbestand *m*, Schlußbestand *m*; ~ **out** *n* ACC Ausbuchung *f*; ~ **price** *n* FIN Schlußkurs *m*, STOCK Schlußkurs *m*, Schlußnotierung *f*; ~ **purchase** *n* BrE STOCK Abschlußkauf *m*, Kauf *m* zum Börsenschluß; ~ **quotation** *n* FIN Schlußkurs *m*, STOCK Schlußkurs *m*, Schlußnotierung *f*; ~ **range** *n* STOCK Glattstellungsbereich *m*; ~ **rate method** *n* BrE (*cf current rate method AmE*) ACC *currency translation for consolidated accounts* Fremdwährungsumrechnung *f* zu Stichtagskursen, Umrechnungsmethode *f* zum geltenden Satz; ~ **speech** *n* GEN COMM *of conference*, POL Abschlußrede *f*; ~ **statement** *n* PROP Auflassungsurkunde *f*; ~ **time** *n* LEIS *in pub* Polizeistunde *f*
closure *n* GEN COMM Einstellung *f*, *of branch, company* Schließung *f*, Stillegung *f*
cloth: **~-cap pension** *n* BrE HRM Rentenversicherungssystem, vor allem für Arbeiter, dem die gesamten Rentenansprüche bei Pensionierung als Pauschalbetrag ausbezahlt werden können
clothing *n* BrE (*cf apparel AmE*) GEN COMM Kleidung *f*, IND Umhüllung *f*, *uniform, overall* Bekleidung *f*; ~ **industry** *n* BrE (*cf apparel industry AmE*) IND Bekleidungsindustrie *f*; ~ **trade** *n* BrE (*cf apparel and wool industry AmE*) IND Kleidungs- und Strickwarenherstellung *f*, Textil- und Wollindustrie *f*, Bekleidungsbranche *f*
cloud: ~ **on title** *n* AmE PROP Rechtsmangel *m*
CLSB *abbr* BrE (*Committee of London and Scottish Bankers*) BANK Komitee der Londoner und schottischen Bankiers
club *n* GEN COMM Klub *nt*; ~ **class** *n* TRANSP Club-Klasse *f*; ~ **good** *n* ECON Club-Gut *nt*, Klubgut *nt*
Club: ~ **of Rome** *n* ECON *1968 onwards* Club *m* of Rome
cluster *n* COMP *of hard disk*, GEN COMM Cluster *m*; ~ **analysis** *n* S&M *market research* Clusteranalyse *f*, Klumpenauswahlverfahren *nt*; ~ **controller** *n* COMP Clustersteuereinheit *f*, Mehrfachsteuereinheit *f*; ~ **of countries** *n* S&M Ländergruppe *f*; ~ **housing** *n* PROP unregelmäßig zusammengewachsene Siedlung *f*

clustering *n* S&M Clustering *nt*
cluster: ~ **sample** *n* S&M *market research* Clustereinheit *f*; ~ **sampling** *n* MATH *statistics* Clusteranalyse *f*, S&M *market research* Clusteranalyse *f*, Klumpenauswahlverfahren *nt*
cm *abbr* (*centimeter AmE, centimetre BrE*) GEN COMM cm (*Zentimeter*)
cm³ *abbr* (*cubic centimeter AmE, cubic centimetre BrE*) GEN COMM cm³ (*Kubikzentimeter*), cc (*Kubikzentimeter*)
CM *abbr* ECON (*common market* gemeinsamer Markt *m*, TRANSP (*condition monitoring*) *shipping* Zustandsüberwachung *f*
CMA *abbr* (*cash management account*) FIN Gelddispositionskonto *nt*, Investitions-Girokonto-Kombination *f*
CME *abbr* (*Chicago Mercantile Exchange*) STOCK Produktenbörse in Chicago
CMO *abbr* (*collateralized mortgage obligation*) BANK, FIN private Schuldverschreibung mit Erträgen aus hypotharisch gesicherten Forderungen des Wertemittenten
CMSA *abbr* AmE (*Consolidated Metropolitan Statistical Area*) ADMIN zentrale statistische Erfassung *f* im Großstadtbereich
CN *abbr* FIN, GEN COMM (*credit note*) Gutschein *m*, Gutschrift *f*, Gutschriftsanzeige *f*, INS (*cover note*) Deckungsbestätigung *f*, Deckungsgrundlage *f*, Deckungszusage *f*, vorläufige Deckungszusage *f*, vorläufige Versicherungspolice *f*, TRANSP (*consignment note*) FB (*Frachtbrief*), Ladeschein *m*, Versandanzeige *f*, WBS (*Warenbegleitschein*)
C/N *abbr* FIN, GEN COMM (*credit note*) Gutschein *m*, Gutschrift *f*, Gutschriftsanzeige *f*, INS (*cover note*) Deckungsbestätigung *f*, Deckungsgrundlage *f*, Deckungszusage *f*, vorläufige Deckungszusage *f*, vorläufige Versicherungspolice *f*, TRANSP (*consignment note*) FB (*Frachtbrief*), Ladeschein *m*, Versandanzeige *f*, WBS (*Warenbegleitschein*)
CNS *abbr* BrE (*continuous net settlement*) STOCK fortlaufende Nettoabrechnung *f*
co *abbr* FIN (*certificate of origin*) Ursprungszeugnis *nt*, IMP/EXP (*certificate of origin*) Herkunftsbescheinigung *f*, Ursprungsbescheinigung *f*, Ursprungszertifikat *nt*, Ursprungszeugnis *nt*, IND (*case oil*) Faßöl *nt*, Kanisteröl *nt*, S&M (*cash order*) Bestellung *f* mit vereinbarter Barzahlung, Kassenanweisung *f*, TRANSP (*cargo oil*) Frachtöl *nt*, Ladeöl *nt*
c/o *abbr* COMMS (*care of*) p.A. (*per Adresse*), p.Adr. (*per Adresse*), z. Hd. v. (*zu Händen von*), FIN (*certificate of origin*) Ursprungszeugnis *nt*, GEN COMM (*care of*), p.A. (*per Adresse*), p.Adr. (*per Adresse*), z. Hd. v. (*zu Händen von*), IMP/EXP (*care of*), p.A. (*per Adresse*), p.Adr. (*per Adresse*), z. Hd. v. (*zu Händen von*), (*certificate of origin*) Herkunftsbescheinigung *f*, Ursprungsbescheinigung *f*, Ursprungszertifikat *nt*, Ursprungszeugnis *nt*
Co. *abbr* (*company*) ECON, GEN COMM, LAW Fa. (*Firma*), Gesellschaft *f*; ♦ **and ~** GEN COMM und Co.
CO *abbr* BrE (*Certification Officer*) ADMIN, HRM Bevollmächtigungsbeamte(r) *m* [decl. as adj], Bevollmächtigungsbeamtin *f*
coach: ~ **class** *n* TRANSP Busklasse *f*
coal *n* ENVIR, IND Kohle *f*; ~ **berth** *n* TRANSP *shipping* Kohlekai *m*; ~ **carrier** *n* TRANSP *shipping* Kohletransporter *m*; ~ **deposit** *n* ENVIR Kohlenlagerstätte *f*, Kohlevorkommen *nt*, Kohlevorrat

m; ~-**fired power station** *n* IND Steinkohlenkraftwerk *nt*; ~ **industry** *n* ENVIR, IND Kohleindustrie *f*, Kohlenbergbau *m*

coalition *n* POL *government* Koalition *f*; ~ **alliance** *n* POL Koalitionsbündnis *nt*; ~ **government** *n* POL Koalitionsregierung *f*; ~ **party** *n* POL Koalitionspartei *f*

coal: ~ **mine** *n* ENVIR, IND Bergwerk *nt*, Kohlengrube *f*, Kohlenzeche *f*, Kohlenbergbau *m*; ~ **mining** *n* ENVIR, IND Kohlenbergbau *m*; ~ **mining subsidence** *n* IND Bergschäden *m pl*; ~ **propulsion** *n* TRANSP *shipping* Kohlenantrieb *m*; ~ **reserves** *n pl* ENVIR Kohlereserve *f*

coarse: ~ **screen** *n* S&M Grobraster *nt*

Coase *n* ECON Coase *nt*; ~ **theorem** *n* ECON Coase-Theorem *nt*

coast *n* ENVIR, TRANSP Küste *f*

coastal: ~ **naval radio station** *n* TRANSP Marineküstenfunkstelle *f*; ~ **pollution** *n* ENVIR Küstenverschmutzung *f*

coaster *n* TRANSP *vessel* Küstenschiff *nt*

coasting *n* TRANSP *shipping* Küstenfahrt *f*, Küstenhandel *m*, Küstenschiffahrt *f*; ~ **broker** *n* TRANSP *shipping* Küstenfahrtmakler, in *m,f*; ~ **trade** *n* TRANSP *shipping* Küstenhandel *m*, Küstenschiffahrt *f*

coaxial: ~ **cable** *n* COMP *hardware* Koaxialkabel *nt*

Cobb: ~ **Douglas production function** *n* ECON Cobb-Douglas-Funktion *f*, Cobb-Douglas-Produktionsfunktion *f*

COBOL *abbr* (*common business-oriented language*) COMP COBOL (*allgemeine kaufmännisch orientierte Programmiersprache*)

cobweb: ~ **theorem** *n* ECON Cobweb-Theorem *nt*, Spinnwebtheorem *nt*

C/OC *abbr* (*certificate of origin and consignment*) IMP/EXP Ursprungs- und Frachtzeugnis *nt*

COD *abbr* (*cash on delivery*) FIN, GEN COMM, IMP/EXP Barzahlung *f* bei Lieferung (*c.o.d.*), Zahlung *f* durch Empfänger, Nachnahme *f*

code *n* COMP Code *m*, Kode *m*, LAW Kodex *m*; ~ **of advertising practice** *n* (*CAP*) S&M Werbekodex *m*; ~ **of arbitration** *n* STOCK Arbitragecode *m*; ~ **box** *n* IMP/EXP Kodebox *f*

codec *n* (*coder-decoder*) COMP Codec *m* (*Codierer-Decodierer*)

code: ~ **check** *n* COMP Codeprüfung *f*; ~ **of conduct** *n* GEN COMM Verhaltenskodex *m*

coded: ~ **data entry** *n* COMP verschlüsselte Dateneingabe *f*

code: ~ **element** *n* COMP Codeelement *nt*; ~ **of ethics** *n* GEN COMM Ehrenkodex *m*, Standesordnung *f*, Verhaltenskodex *m*; ~ **line** *n* COMP Codierlinie *f*, Codierzeile *f*; ~ **name** *n* COMP Codebezeichnung *f*, Codename *m*; ~ **of practice** *n* GEN COMM Merkblatt *nt*, Verhaltenskodex *m*, Verhaltensregeln *f pl*; ~ **of procedure** *n* STOCK Verfahrenscode *m*; ~ **of professional responsibility** *n* LAW Standesrichtlinien *f pl*

coder: ~-**decoder** *n* (*codec*) COMP Codierer-Decodierer *m* (*Codec*)

code: ~ **set** *n* COMP Codeliste *f*; ~ **sheet** *n* COMP Codeseite *f*; ~ **table** *n* COMP Codetabelle *f*

codetermination *n* ECON, HRM, STOCK Mitbestimmung *f*; ~ **at plant level** *n* HRM, MGMNT betriebliche Mitbestimmung *f*; ~ **rights** *n pl* STOCK paritätische Mitbestimmungsrechte *nt pl*

code-UN *n* IMP/EXP UN-Kode *m*

codicil *n* LAW Kodizil *nt*, Testamentsnachtrag *m*

codified: ~ **law** *n* GEN COMM kodifiziertes Recht *nt*, geschriebenes Recht *nt*

codify *vt* LAW, PATENTS kodifizieren

coding *n* ACC *identification of account* Benennung *f*, COMP *programming language* Codieren *nt*, Codierung *f*; ~ **manual** *n* ACC Kodierhandbuch *nt*; ~ **system** *n* ACC Kodiersystem *nt*

co-director *n* MGMNT Mitdirektor, in *m,f*, Kodirektor, in *m,f*

co-ed *adj* (*coeducational*) WEL gemischt, koedukativ

coeducational *adj* (*co-ed*) WEL gemischt, koedukativ; ~ **high school** *n* WEL gemischte Oberschule *f*, gemischtes Gymnasium *nt*

coefficient *n* MATH Koeffizient *m*; ~ **of correlation** *n* MATH *statistics* Korrelationskoeffizient *m*; ~ **of determination** *n* MATH *statistics* Bestimmtheitsmaß *nt*; ~ **of multiple correlation** *n* MATH *statistics* Mehrfachkorrelationskoeffizient *m*; ~ **of multiple determination** *n* MATH *statistics* Mehrfachbestimmtheitsmaß *nt*; ~ **of variation** *n* ACC Abweichungskoeffizient *m*, MATH *statistics* Streuungskoeffizient *m*, Variationskoeffizient *m*

cofinance *vt* FIN mitfinanzieren

cognate *adj* WEL verwandt; ~ **disciplines** *n pl* WEL verwandte Fächer *nt pl*, verwandte Fachrichtungen *f pl*

cognition *n* MGMNT Erkenntnis *f*, Erkenntnistätigkeit *f*

cognitive *adj* GEN COMM kognitiv; ~ **behavior** *AmE*, ~ **behaviour** *BrE n* MGMNT, S&M kognitives Verhalten *nt*; ~ **consonance** *n* MGMNT Gedankengleichheit *f*; ~ **dissonance** *n* MGMNT Gedankenverschiedenheit *f*; ~ **ergonomics** *n* ADMIN kognitive Arbeitsplatzanalyse *f*

COGSA *abbr BrE* (*Carriage of Goods by Sea Act*) LAW Gesetz *nt* zur Seefrachtbeförderung

coheir *n* LAW Miterbe *m*, Miterbin *f*

coherence *n* GEN COMM Einheitlichkeit *f*, Zusammenhalt *m*, Zusammenhang *m*, Verständlichkeit *f*

coherent *adj* GEN COMM einheitlich, klar, zusammenhängend, verständlich

cohesion *n* GEN COMM Kohäsion *f*, Zusammenhalt *m*, Zusammenhang *m*; ~ **fund** *n* ECON EU Kohäsionsfonds *m*

coin 1. *n* GEN COMM Geldstück *nt*, Münze *f*; **2.** *vt* ECON *money* ausprägen, prägen

coinage *n* ECON Münzprägung *f*, *currency* Währung *f*, *coins* Hartgeld *nt*, Münzen *f pl*; ~ **system** *n* ECON Hartgeldsystem *nt*, Münzsystem *nt*

coincide *vi* GEN COMM gleichlaufen, LAW übereinstimmen; ♦ ~ **with** GEN COMM übereinstimmen mit, sich decken mit, zusammenfallen mit

coincidence *n* GEN COMM Zufall *m*

coincident: ~ **indicator** *n* ECON *econometrics* Präsensindikator *m*, synchroner Konjunkturindikator *m*

coin: ~-**machine insurance** *n* INS Automatenversicherung *f*

coins *n pl* GEN COMM Hartgeld *nt*, Metallgeld *nt*

coinsurance *n* INS Mitversicherung *f*

coinsure *vt* INS mitversichern

coinsured 1. *adj* INS mitversichert; **2.** *n* INS Mitversicherte(r) *mf* [decl. as adj]

coinsurer *n* INS Mitversicherer *m*

COLA *abbr* (*cost-of-living adjustment*) ECON, HRM Teuerungszulage *f*, Teuerungszuschlag *m*

cold: ~ **boot** *n* COMP Kaltstart *m*; ~ **call** *n* S&M *by sales representative* unangemeldeter Besuch *m*; ~ **calling** *n* S&M *by sales representative* unangemeldeter Besuch *m*; ~ **canvass** *n* S&M ungezielte Kundenwerbung *f*; ~ **canvassing** *n* S&M ungezielte Kundenwerbung *f*; ~ **mailing** *n* S&M ungezielter Versand *m*; ~ **start** *n* GEN COMM Kaltstart *m*; ~ **storage** *n* IND Kühlraumlagerung *f*, Kaltlagerung *f*; ~ **storage plant** *n* IND Kühlanlage *f*; ~ **store** *n* IND Kühlhalle *f*, Kühlhaus *nt*; ~ **store terminal** *n* TRANSP *shipping* Kühlhausterminal *nt*; ~ **type** *n* MEDIA *printing* Fotosatz *m*

collaborate *vt* GEN COMM mitarbeiten, zusammenarbeiten, POL kollaborieren, zusammenarbeiten

collaboration *n* GEN COMM Mitarbeit *f*, Zusammenarbeit *f*, POL Kollaboration *f*, Zusammenarbeit *f*

collaborative *adj* GEN COMM, HRM gemeinsam

collage *n* S&M Kollage *f*

collapse 1. *vt* GEN COMM, TRANSP *carton, folding construction* flachfalten, zusammenklappen, zusammenlegen; **2.** *vi* ECON *market* zusammenbrechen, *prices* stürzen, verfallen, GEN COMM *system* zusammenbrechen, STOCK *market* stürzen

collapsed *adj* GEN COMM *company* zusammengebrochen

collapsible: ~ **container** *n* (*coltainer*) TRANSP Klappcontainer *m*, zusammenlegbarer Container *m*; ~ **corporation** *n* AmE TAX aus Steuergründen vorübergehend gegründete Gesellschaft *f*

collar *n* ECON Kragen *m*

collate *vt* COMP verdichten, GEN COMM kollationieren, MEDIA *documents, papers* vergleichen

collateral 1. *adj* FIN zusätzlich, GEN COMM *measures* flankierend, *phenomenon* begleitend, MATH an der Seite, seitlich; **2.** *n* ECON Sicherheit *f*, Sicherungsgegenstand *m*, FIN Pfand *nt*

collateral: ~ **acceptance** *n* FIN *by bank* Avalakzept *nt*; ~ **acceptor** *n* FIN Wechselbürge *m*, Wechselbürgin *f*; ~ **assignment** *n* INS zusätzliche Abtretung *f*, zusätzliche Zession *f*; ~ **bill** *n* BANK Vorschußwechsel *m*; ~ **insurance** *n* INS Zusatzversicherung *f*

collateralize *vt* BANK *securities* lombardieren, FIN besichern

collateralized: ~ **mortgage obligation** *n* (*CMO*) BANK, FIN private Schuldverschreibung mit Erträgen aus hypothekarisch gesicherten Forderungen des Wertemittenten

collateral: ~ **loan** *n* BANK besichertes Darlehen *nt*, *securities* Lombarddarlehen *nt*, Lombardkredit *m*; ~ **loan business** *n* FIN Banklombardgeschäft *nt*; ~ **promise** *n* ECON, LAW *contracts* Schuldbeitritt *m*; ~ **security** *n* ECON Sicherheitsleistung *f*, Sicherungsgegenstand *m*, FIN dingliche Sicherheit *f*, LAW akzessorische Sicherheit *f*; ~ **trust bond** *n* STOCK durch Wertpapiere gesicherte Industrieobligation *f pl*

collating *adj* COMP Sortier-, GEN COMM kollationierend; ~ **sequence** *n* COMP Sortierfolge *f*

collator *n* COMP *punched cards* Kartenmischer *m*; ~ **code** *n* COMP Sortiercode *m*; ~ **number** *n* COMP Sortiernummer *f*

colleague *n* GEN COMM Arbeitskamerad, in *m,f* (*obs*), Arbeitskollege *m*, Arbeitskollegin *f*, Mitarbeiter, in *m,f*, HRM Kollege *m*, Kollegin *f*, Mitarbeiter, in *m,f*

colleagues *n pl* GEN COMM, HRM Mitarbeiter *m pl*

collect *vt* GEN COMM *statistics, data* erfassen, *information* zusammentragen, beschaffen, *receivables, tax* einziehen, eintreiben, *cash* kassieren, STOCK *premium* einlösen, einziehen; ♦ ~ **a debt** FIN eine Forderung einziehen, eine Forderung liquidieren; ~ **a payment** FIN eine Zahlung einziehen; ~ **statistics** GEN COMM, S&M, TAX statistisch erfassen; ~ **sums due** FIN fällige Beträge einziehen; ~ **taxes** TAX Steuern einziehen

collect: ~ **call** *n* AmE (*cf reverse charge call BrE*) COMMS *telephone* R-Gespräch *nt*

collected *adj* GEN COMM eingezogen; ♦ ~ **and delivered** (*C&D*) GEN COMM *object* eingezogen und ausgeliefert

collectible *n* GEN COMM Sammelobjekt *nt*

collecting: ~ **bank** *n* FIN einziehende Bank *f*, Inkassobank *f*; ~ **commission** *n* INS Inkassoprovision *f*

collection *n* ACC Einzug *m*, Inkasso *nt*, BANK Einziehung *f*, Einzug *m*, Inkasso *nt*, FIN Einziehung *f*, Inkasso *nt*, INS Inkasso *nt*, GEN COMM *of statistics, information* Erfassung *f*, Erhebung *f*, Beschaffung *f*, *tax, receivables* Eintreibung *f*, STOCK *of premium* Einlösung *f*, Einziehung *f*, TAX *of public money* Einziehung *f*; ~ **of accounts** *n* ACC Forderungseinziehung *f*; ~ **of a bill** *n* ACC Einziehung *f* eines Rechnungsbetrages, *bill of exchange* Wechseleinzug *m*, Wechselinkasso *nt*; ~ **charge** *n* GEN COMM Einzugsgebühr *f*, Inkassogebühr *f*, TRANSP Inkassogebühr *f*; ~ **of commercial documents** *n* LAW *contracts* Dokumenteninkasso *nt*; ~ **costs** *n pl* GEN COMM Einzugskosten *pl*, Einzugsspesen *pl*, INS Inkassokosten *pl*; ~ **of customs duties** *n* TAX Zollerhebung *f*; ~ **department** *n* FIN Inkassoabteilung *f*, Kreditorenabteilung *f*; ~-**only check** *AmE*, ~-**only cheque** *BrE n* BANK Verrechnungsscheck *m*; ~ **of public money** ECON, GEN COMM Beschaffung *f* öffentlicher Mittel; ~ **period** *n* ACC Forderungsumschlag *m*; ~ **of debt** Forderungsumschlag *m*; ~ **of premiums** *n* INS Beitragseinzug *m*, Prämieneinnahme *f*, Prämieninkasso *nt*; ~ **ratio** *n* ACC Forderungsumschlag *m*; ~ **tariff** *n* IMP/EXP Inkassotarif *m*

collective *adj* GEN COMM gemeinsam, gemeinschaftlich, kollektiv, Kollektiv-, Sammel-; ~ **accident insurance** *n* INS Gruppenunfallversicherung *f*, Kollektivunfallversicherung *f*; ~ **agreement** *n* HRM Kollektivvertrag *m*, Tarifvertrag *m*; ~ **bargaining** *n* ECON, HRM Lohnverhandlung *f*, Tarifverhandlung *f*, MGMNT Lohnverhandlung *f*; ~ **bargaining agreement** *n* HRM Tarifvertrag *m*; ~ **conciliation** *n* BrE HRM Kollektivschlichtung *f*; ~ **decision** *n* MGMNT kollektiver Beschluß *m*; ~ **dismissal** *n* HRM kollektive Entlassung *f*, Massenentlassung *f*; ~ **good** *n* ECON öffentliches Gut *nt*, Kollektivgut *nt*; ~ **grievance procedure** *n* BrE HRM kollektives Beschwerdeverfahren *nt*; ~ **insurance** *n* INS Gruppenversicherung *f*, Kollektivversicherung *f*; ~ **investment undertaking** *n* FIN kollektives Investitionsunternehmen *nt*, Kollektivinvestitionsvereinbarung *f*; ~ **labor agreement** *AmE*, ~ **labour agreement** *BrE n* HRM Tarifvertrag *m*

collectively *adv* GEN COMM als Gesamtheit, gemeinsam, insgesamt; ~ **agreed** *adj* HRM *wages* tariflich

collective: ~ **mark** *n* PATENTS Kollektivzeichen *nt*, Verbandsmarke *f*, Verbandszeichen *nt*; ~ **negotiations** *n pl* ECON, HRM Tarifverhandlung *f*; ~ **order** *n* GEN COMM Sammelbestellung *f*; ~ **ownership** *n* ECON, POL Gemeineigentum *nt*; ~ **securities deposit** *n* FIN Effektensammeldepot *nt*

collectivization *n* ECON Kollektivierung *f*; **~ of agriculture** *n* ECON Kollektivierung *f* der Landwirtschaft

collectivize *vt* ECON kollektivieren

collector *n* BrE HRM, TAX Zolleinnehmer, in *m,f*; **~'s office** *n* IMP/EXP Inkassobüro *nt*

college: **~ of advanced technology** *n* BrE (*CAT*) WEL Technische Hochschule *f* (*TH*), **~ of further education** *n* BrE (*CFE*) GEN COMM Handelsschule *f*, WEL Berufsfachschule *f*, Berufsschule *f*, *commercial* Handelsschule *f*, *for domestic sciences* Haushaltungsschule *f*, *technical* weiterführende Schule *f*, höhere Handelsschule *f*

collier *n* TRANSP *ship* Kohlenschiff *nt*

colliery *n* IND Steinkohlenbergwerk *nt*, Steinkohlengrube *f*, Steinkohlenzeche *f*, Zeche *f*, *shaft* Steinkohlenschacht *m*; **~ guarantee terms** *n pl* TRANSP Kohlengrubegarantiebedingungen *f pl*; **~ working day** *n* IND Zechenbetriebstag *m*

collision *n* INS, TRANSP Kollision *f*; **~ clause** *n* INS *marine* Kollisionsklausel *f*; **~ coverage** *n* INS Kollisionsdeckung *f*, Versicherungsschutz *m* bei Zusammenstößen; **~ insurance** *n* INS Kollisionsversicherung *f*

collusion *n* ECON heimliche Absprache *f*, Kollusion *f*, LAW Kolludieren *nt*, Verdunkelung *f*

collusive: **~ bidding** *n* ECON Anbieterabsprache *f*; **~ oligopoly** *n* ECON heimliches Oligopol *nt*, verabredetes Oligopol *nt*; **~ tendering** *n* ECON Anbieterabsprache *f*

colon *n* COMP, MEDIA Kolon *nt*

colony *n* POL Kolonie *f*

color *AmE see* colour *BrE*

colour *n* BrE COMP, MEDIA Farbe *f*; **~ display** *n* BrE COMP Farbanzeige *f*, Farbbildschirm *m*, Farbdisplay *nt* (*jarg*); **~ graphics adapter** *n* BrE (*CGA*) COMP Farbgrafikadapter *m*; **~ separation** *n* BrE S&M Farbtrennung *f*; **~ supplement** *n* BrE MEDIA *of newspaper* Farbbeilage *f*; **~ of title** *n* BrE PROP glaubwürdiger Eigentumsanspruch *m*, scheinbar einwandfreier Besitztitel *m*, scheinbar einwandfreier Rechtstitel *m*

coltainer *n* (*collapsible container*) TRANSP *shipping* Klappcontainer *m*, zusammenlegbarer Container *m*

column *n* COMP Spalte *f*, MEDIA Kolumne *f*, Spalte *f*

columnar: **~ bookkeeping** *n* ACC amerikanische Buchführung *f*; **~ journal** *n* ACC in Spalten angeordnetes Grundbuch *nt*

column: **~ centimeters** *AmE*, **~ centimetres** *BrE n pl* MEDIA, S&M Spaltenzentimeter *m pl*; **~ heading** *n* ACC Spaltenüberschrift *f*; **~ inches** *n pl* MEDIA Spaltenlänge *f*; **~ move** *n* COMP *spreadsheet command* Spalte verschieben

co-manager *n* MGMNT Mitdirektor, in *m,f*; Kodirektor, in *m,f*

combat *vt* GEN COMM *unemployment, drug trafficking* bekämpfen

comb: **~ binding** *n* S&M Spiralbindung *f*

combi: **~ carrier** *n* (*combination carrier*) TRANSP Kombischiff *nt*, Kombitransportschiff *nt*

combination *n* FIN Verschmelzung *f*, GEN COMM Kombination *f*, Zusammenschluß *m*; **~ carrier** *n* (*combi carrier*) TRANSP Kombischiff *nt*, Kombitransportschiff *nt*; **~ charge** *n* TRANSP Kombinationsgebühr *f*; **~ rate** *n*

S&M Kombinationstarif *m*, TRANSP Kombinationssatz *m*; **~ of rates** *n* TRANSP Kombination *f* von Sätzen

combine 1. *n* ECON Kombinat *nt*, Verbund *m*, LAW Firmenzusammenschluß *m*, Kartell *nt*; **2.** *vt* GEN COMM zusammenfassen, kombinieren; **3.** *vi* GEN COMM sich zusammenschließen, zusammenwirken

combine: **~ committee** *n* HRM Konzernbetriebsrat *m*

combined *adj* GEN COMM kombiniert; **~ advertising** *n* S&M Verbundwerbung *f*; **~ balance sheet** *n* FIN kombinierte Bilanz *f*; **~ financial statement** *n* ACC, FIN kombinierter Abschluß *m*, Konzernbilanz *f*; **~ issue** *n* MEDIA *print* Kombinationsausgabe *f*; **~ mark** *n* PATENTS *word and device* kombiniertes Warenzeichen *nt*; **~ premium** *n* INS Mischprämie *f*; **~ shop insurance** *n* INS kombinierte Geschäftsversicherung *f*; **~ statement of income** *n* ACC kombinierte Gewinn- und Verlustrechnung *f*; **~ ticket** *n* TRANSP Kombifahrkarte *f*, Kombiticket *nt*, Kombinationsticket *nt*; **~ trade** *n* GEN COMM kombinierter Handel *m*; **~ transport** *n* (*CT*) TRANSP kombinierter Transport *m*; **~ transport bill of lading** *n* (*CTBL*) TRANSP kombiniertes Transportkonnossement *nt*, Konnossement *nt* für kombinierten Transport; **~ transport document** *n* (*CTD*) TRANSP Beleg *m* für kombinierten Transport, Kombinationstransportdokument *nt*; **~ transport operation** *n* TRANSP kombinierter Transport *m*; **~ transport operator** *n* (*CTO*) TRANSP Kombinationstransportunternehmer *m*

combi: **~ ship** *n* TRANSP Kombischiff *nt*, Kombitransportschiff *nt*

combustion: **~ plant** *n* ENVIR, IND Verbrennungsanlage *f*

come out *vi* MEDIA *book, magazine* erscheinen

come to *vi* GEN COMM *amount to* betragen, sich belaufen auf [+acc]

COMECON *abbr obs* (*Council for Mutual Economic Aid*) ECON COMECON, RGW (*Rat für gegenseitige Wirtschaftshilfe*)

COMET *abbr* (*Common Market Medium Term Model*) ECON *econometrics* COMET-Modell *nt*

comfortable *adj* GEN COMM *circumstances* auskömmlich

comfort: **~ letter** *n* BANK, GEN COMM, STOCK Patronatserklärung *f*

Comit: **~ Index** *n* STOCK *Milan Stock Exchange* Comit-Index *m*

comm. *abbr* GEN COMM (*commission*) Komm. (*Kommission*), (*committee*) Ausschuß *m*, Komitee *nt*

comma *n* ADMIN Beistrich *m*, COMP, MATH, MEDIA Komma *nt*

command 1. *n* COMP Befehl *m*, Kommando *nt*, GEN COMM, HRM Befehl *m*; **2.** *vt* GEN COMM *order* anordnen; ◆ **~ a certain price** ECON einen bestimmten Preis fordern

command: **~ economy** *n* ECON, POL Befehlswirtschaft *f*, Planwirtschaft *f*; **~ file** *n* COMP Befehlsdatei *f*; **~ key** *n* COMP Befehlstaste *f*; **~ line** *n* COMP Befehlszeile *f*

commence 1. *vt* GEN COMM beginnen; **2.** *vi* GEN COMM beginnen

commencement *n* GEN COMM Beginn *m*, INS *of policy* Inkrafttreten *nt*, Versicherungsbeginn *m*; **~ of contract** *n* LAW Vertragsbeginn *m*; **~ of coverage** *n* INS Beginn *m* der Deckung, Beginn *m* des Versicherungsschutzes

commensurate *adj* ACC angemessen, GEN COMM angemessen, entsprechend, HRM angemessen; **~ charge** *n*

GEN COMM angemessene Gebühr *f*, Gebühr *f* gleicher Höhe, gleich große Gebühr *f*

comment *vt* GEN COMM bemerken

commentary *n* GEN COMM Berichterstattung *f*, Erläuterung *f*, Kommentar *m*

comments: ~ **field** *n* COMP Bemerkungsfeld *nt*

commerce *n* ECON Handel *m*, GEN COMM Handel *m*, Handelsverkehr *m*, Wirtschaftsverkehr *m*

commercial 1. *adj* GEN COMM kaufmännisch, wirtschaftlich, kommerziell, gewerblich; ♦ **no ~ value** (*n.c.v.*) GEN COMM ohne Handelswert; **2.** *n* MEDIA *print, broadcast*, S&M Werbespot *m*

commercial: ~ **account** *n* ACC Geschäftskonto *nt*; ~ **activity** *n* IND gewerbliche Tätigkeit *f*; ~ **acumen** *n* GEN COMM Geschäftssinn *m*, Geschäftstüchtigkeit *f*; ~ **advantage** *n* GEN COMM Handelsvorteil *m*; ~ **agency** *n* GEN COMM Vertretung *f*, Auskunftei *f*; ~ **agency report** *n* LAW *contracts* Handelsauskunft *f*; ~ **agent** *n* GEN COMM Agent *m*, Handelsvertreter, in *m,f*; ~ **agreement** *n* GEN COMM, LAW Handelsabkommen *nt*; ~ **analysis** *n* FIN kaufmännische Analyse *f*; ~ **and development manager** *n* HRM Leiter, in *m,f* Vertrieb und Entwicklung; ~ **artist** *n* S&M *advertising* Werbegrafiker, in *m,f*; ~ **bank** *n* BANK, ECON, FIN Geschäftsbank *f*, Handelsbank *f*; ~ **bill** *n* BANK *retail* Handelswechsel *m*, Warenwechsel *m*, STOCK Handelswechsel *m*; ~ **blanket bond** *n* INS *employee cover* Vertrauensschadenversicherung *f*; ~ **break** *n* MEDIA *radio, TV* Unterbrechung *f* von Sendungen für Werbung, Werbeunterbrechung *f*; ~ **broker** *n* AmE PROP Handelsmakler, in *m,f*; ~ **business** *n* GEN COMM Handelsgeschäft *nt*; ~ **cargo** *n* TRANSP Handelsfracht *f*; ~ **center** AmE, ~ **centre** BrE *n* S&M Handelsmetropole *nt*, Handelszentrum *nt*

Commercial: ~ **Code** *n* LAW Handelsgesetzbuch *nt* (*HGB*)

commercial: ~ **computer** *n* COMP handelsüblicher Computer *m*, kommerziell eingesetzter Computer *m*; ~ **concern** *n* GEN COMM Handelsangelegenheit *f*; ~ **contract** *n* LAW *trade law* Handelsvertrag *m*; ~ **credit insurance** *n* AmE INS Handelskreditversicherung *f*, Warenkreditversicherung *f*; ~ **designer** *n* S&M *advertising* Werbedesigner, in *m,f*; ~ **developer** *n* PROP Bauunternehmer, in *m,f*; ~ **development** *n* GEN COMM wirtschaftliche Entwicklung *f*; ~ **director** *n* HRM, MGMNT kaufmännischer Direktor *m*, kaufmännische Direktorin *f*; ~ **dock** *n* (*CD*) TRANSP *shipping* Handelskai *m*, Umschlagkai *m*; ~ **efficiency** *n* ECON, ENVIR kommerzielle Effizienz *f*; ~ **employee** *n* HRM Handlungsgehilfe *m*, Handlungsgehilfin *f*; ~ **establishment** *n* GEN COMM Handelseinrichtung *f*, LAW *contracts* Handelsniederlassung *f*; ~ **forgery policy** *n* INS Police *f* zum Schutze gegen Urkundenfälschung; ~ **form** *n* INS Versicherungspolice *f* zum Schutz gegen Geschäftsrisiken; ~ **guaranty insurance** *n* INS Vertrauensschadenversicherung *f*; ~ **health insurance** *n* AmE (*cf private health insurance* BrE) INS Privatkrankenversicherung *f*; ~ **hedgers** *n pl* STOCK gewerbliche Hedger *m pl*; ~ **impracticability** *n* GEN COMM wirtschaftliche Unmöglichkeit *f*; ~ **insurance** *n* INS Betriebsversicherung *f*, Handelsrisikoversicherung *f*, Privatversicherung *f*; ~ **interest** *n* ECON Geschäftsinteresse *nt*; ~ **invoice** *n* ACC Faktura *f* (*obs*), Handelsrechnung *f*, GEN COMM, LAW *contracts* Handelsrechnung *f*

commercialism *n* ECON, GEN COMM Handelsgeist *m*

commercialization *n* GEN COMM Kommerzialisierung *f*

commercialize *vt* GEN COMM kommerzialisieren, auf den Markt bringen, marktfähig machen

commercial: ~ **law** *n* GEN COMM Handelsrecht *nt*, Handelsgesetz *nt*; ~ **lease** *n* GEN COMM Mietvertrag *m* über gewerblich genutzte Räume; ~ **lending** *n* BANK gewerbliche Ausleihungen *f pl*; ~ **letting** *n* BrE PROP kommerzielle Vermietung *f*; ~ **loan** *n* BANK gewerblicher Kredit *m*

commercially *adv* GEN COMM geschäftlich, kommerziell; ♦ ~ **viable** GEN COMM kommerziell lebensfähig, rentabel

commercial: ~ **manager** *n* HRM, MGMNT kaufmännischer Leiter *m*, kaufmännische Leiterin *f*; ~ **marine** *n* TRANSP Handelsmarine *f*; ~ **market** *n* GEN COMM ziviler Markt *m*; ~ **occupancy** *n* PROP geschäftliche Nutzung *f*, kommerzielle Nutzung *f*; ~ **occupation** *n* GEN COMM kaufmännischer Beruf *m*; ~ **officer** *n* GEN COMM Geschäftsleiter, in *m,f* für Commerce; ~ **paper** *n* (*CP*) BANK, FIN, GEN COMM, STOCK Handelspapier *nt*, Wertpapier *nt*; ~ **partner** *n* GEN COMM Handelspartner, in *m,f*; ~ **policy** *n* ECON, IMP/EXP Handelspolitik *f*; ~ **port** *n* TRANSP Handelshafen *m*; ~ **property** *n* PROP Geschäftsgebäude *nt*; ~ **property policy** *n* INS Versicherungspolice *f* zum Schutz von Geschäftsgrundstücken; ~ **radio** *n* MEDIA Werbefunk *m*, Privatfunk *m*, kommerzieller Rundfunk *m*; ~ **radio station** *n* MEDIA kommerzieller Radiosender *m*; ~ **registration** *n* GEN COMM, LAW Handelsregister-Eintragung *f*, HR-Eintragung *f*

Commercial: ~ **Relations and Exports** *n pl* BrE (*CRE*) IMP/EXP Handelsbeziehungen *f pl* und Exporte *m pl*

commercial: ~ **representation** *n* GEN COMM Handelsvertretung *f*; ~ **representative** *n* GEN COMM, HRM Handelsvertreter, in *m,f*; ~ **research** *n* GEN COMM Wirtschaftsforschung *f*; ~ **risk** *n* INS wirtschaftliches Risiko *nt*; ~ **risk analysis** *n* FIN, INS Analyse *f* des betriebswirtschaftlichen Risikos; ~ **sickness insurance policy** *n* AmE (*cf private health insurance* BrE) HRM, INS, WEL private Krankenversicherung *f*; ~ **stock** *n* GEN COMM Handelsbestand *m*; ~ **storage** *n* TRANSP geschäftsmäßige Lagerung *f*, gewerbliche Lagerung *f*; ~ **strategy** *n* ECON Handelsstrategie *f*, GEN COMM Handelsstrategie *f*, Wirtschaftsstrategie *f*; ~ **targets** *n pl* GEN COMM Handelsziel *nt*, Handelszielstellung *f*; ~ **television** *n* MEDIA Werbefernsehen *nt*, kommerzielles Fernsehen *nt*; ~ **television channel** *n* MEDIA kommerzieller Fernsehkanal *m*; ~ **trade** *n* ECON kommerzieller Handel *m*; ~ **training** *n* HRM kaufmännische Ausbildung *f*; ~ **traveler** AmE, ~ **traveller** BrE *n* GEN COMM Geschäftsreisende(r) *mf* [decl. as adj], Handelsreisende(r) *mf* [decl. as adj]; ~ **usage** *n* GEN COMM, LAW *contracts* Handelsbrauch *m*; ~ **use** *n* GEN COMM, PROP gewerbliche Nutzung *f*; ~ **value** *n* LAW *contracts* Handelswert *m*; ~ **value movement order** *n* (*CVMO*) GEN COMM Marktwertbewegungsauftrag *m*; ~ **vehicle** *n* TRANSP Nutzfahrzeug *nt*; ~ **venture** *n* MGMNT Handelsspekulation *f*, kommerzielles Wagnis *nt*; ~ **well** *n* ENVIR gewerblich genutzter Brunnen *m*, kommerziell genutzter Brunnen *m*; ~ **world** *n* GEN COMM Geschäftswelt *f*

commingling *n* STOCK *securities, trust banking* Mischung *f*, Zusammenlegung *f*; ~ **of funds** *n* LAW Vermischung *f* von Fremdgeld mit eigenen Mitteln

commissary *n* AmE ADMIN Beauftragte(r) *mf* [decl. as

adj], S&M Verpflegungsstelle *f*; ~ **goods** *n pl* IMP/EXP zollunwichtige Waren *f pl*

commission 1. *n* (*comm.*) ADMIN, BANK *payment* Provision *f*, *body* Ausschuß *m*, ECON *body* Ausschuß *m*, FIN *payment* Provision *f*, Maklergebühr *f*, *body* Ausschuß *m*, GEN COMM *order* Order *f*, *body* Kommission *f* (*Komm.*), Ausschuß *m*, *payment* Provision *f*, MGMNT Ausschuß *m*, Komitee *nt*, Kommission *f* (*Komm.*), POL Ausschuß *m*, Gremium *nt*, S&M *order* Order *f*, Provision *f*, STOCK Provision *f*; **2.** *vt* ECON bestellen, in Auftrag geben, GEN COMM beauftragen, kommissionieren

commission: ~ **account** *n* BANK Provisionskonto *nt*, Provisionsrechnung *f*; ~ **agent** *n* HRM Kommissionär *m*; ~ **broker** *n AmE* STOCK Kommissionsmakler, in *m,f*

commissioner *n* ADMIN Beauftragte(r) *mf* [decl. as adj], Leiter, in *m,f* bestimmter Behörden, Mitglied *nt* eines Ausschusses

Commissioner: ~ **of Customs and Excise** *n BrE* TAX Ministerialabteilung *f* für Zölle und Verbrauchssteuern

commissioner: ~ **for oaths** *n BrE* LAW Notar, in *m,f*; ~ **for the rights of trade union members** *n BrE* (*CROTUM*) HRM Kommissar für die Rechte von Gewerkschaftsmitgliedern

Commissioner: ~ **of Inland Revenue** *n BrE* TAX Leiter *m* der obersten Finanzbehörde

Commission: ~ **of the European Community** *n obs* (*CEC*) ECON Kommission *f* der Europäischen Gemeinschaft (*obs*) (*EG-Kommission*)

commission: ~ **goods** *n pl* ECON Kommissionsgüter *nt pl*

commissioning *n* TRANSP Inbetriebnahme *f*

commission: ~ **of inquiry** *n* HRM Ermittlungsausschuß *m*, LAW Untersuchungsausschuß *m*; ~ **merchant** *n* HRM Verkaufskommissionär *m*

Commission: ~ **on Energy and the Environment** *n* (*CENE*) ENVIR Kommission *f* für Energie und Umwelt

commission: ~ **on guaranty** *n* FIN Avalprovision *f*; ~ **rate** *n* BANK Courtage *f*, Provisionssatz *m*, STOCK Maklergebühr *f*; ~ **salesman** *n* HRM Verkaufskommissionär *m*; ~ **system** *n* HRM Provisionssystem *nt*

Commission: ~ **White Paper** *n* LAW Europäische Gesetzesvorlage *f*

commit: ~ **oneself to sth** *phr* GEN COMM sich an etw binden, sich zu etw verpflichten

commitment *n* FIN, GEN COMM Zusage *f*, LAW Verbindlichkeit *f*, Verpflichtung *f*, LEIS *theatre* Engagement *nt*; ~ **accounting** *n* ACC *government* periodengerechte Buchung *f* von Finanzzusagen; ~ **authority** *n* FIN Verpflichtungermächtigung *f*, Bereitstellungsermächtigung *f*; ~ **control** *n* LAW Verpflichtungskontrolle *f*; ~ **document** *n* LAW Verpflichtungsdokument *nt*; ~ **fee** *n* BANK Bereitstellungsprovision *f*; ~ **interest** *n* FIN Bereitstellungszins *m*; ~ **record** *n* LAW Verpflichtungsprotokoll *nt*; ~ **to fixed terms** *n* FIN Konditionenbindung *f*

committed *adj* FIN zugesagt, GEN COMM, LAW verpflichtet; ♦ **be ~ to do sth** GEN COMM verpflichtet sein, etw zu tun

committed: ~ **costs** *n pl* ACC fixe Kosten *pl*

committee *n* (*comm.*) GEN COMM Ausschuß *m*, Komitee *nt*, Kommission *f* (*Komm.*), POL Ausschuß *m*, Gremium *nt*; ~ **chairman** *n* GEN COMM Ausschußvorsitzende(r) *m* [decl. as adj]; ~ **chairwoman** *n* GEN COMM Ausschußvorsitzende *f*

Committee: ~ **for Economic Development** *n* (*CED*)

ECON Ausschuß *m* für wirtschaftliche Entwicklung; ~ **for European Airspace Coordination** *n* (*CEAC*) IND Ausschuß *m* für die Koordinierung des europäischen Luftraums; ~ **of Governors of Central Banks** *n* (*CGCB*) BANK, POL Gouverneursausschuß *m* der Zentralbanken

committee: ~ **of inquiry** *n* POL Untersuchungsausschuß *m*; ~ **of inspection** *n* LAW Kontrollausschuß *m*, *financial* Gläubigerausschuß *m*

Committee: ~ **of London and Scottish Bankers** *n* (*CLSB*) BANK *clearing banks* Komitee der Londoner und schottischen Bankiers

committee: ~ **meeting** *n* GEN COMM Ausschußsitzung *f*; ~ **member** *n* GEN COMM Ausschußmitglied *nt*

Committee: ~ **on Consumer Policy** *n* LAW Ausschuß *m* für Verbraucherpolitik

committee: ~ **on information** *n* GEN COMM Informationskomitee *nt*, Nachrichtenausschuß *m*

Committee: ~ **of Permanent Representatives of the EC** *n* (*COREPER*) ECON *EU* Ausschuß *m* der Ständigen Vertreter (*AStV*); ~ **of Public Accounts** *n BrE* ACC Ausschuß für öffentliches Rechnungswesen, *parliamentary committee* ≈ Rechnungshof *m*; ~ **of the Regions** *n* LAW Ausschuß *m* der Regionen; ~ **of Shipowners Associations of the European Community** *n* ADMIN Ausschuß *m* für die Schiffseigner der Europäischen Gemeinschaft; ~ **on Standardization Principles** *n* LAW Ausschuß *m* für Standardisierungsfragen

commodification *n* ECON *of money* Umwandlung *f* von Geld in Wirtschaftsgüter

commodities *n pl* S&M Waren *f pl* (*Wa.*); ~ **futures** *n pl BrE* STOCK Warentermingeschäft *nt*, Warenterminkontrakt *m*; ~ **price index** *n* STOCK Rohstoffpreisindex *m*

commodity *n* ECON *article of commerce* Wirtschaftsgut *nt*, Ware *f*, *raw materials* Rohstoff *m*, GEN COMM Ware *f*, Handelsware *f*, Handelsgut *nt*, Gebrauchsartikel *m*; ~ **agreement** *n* ECON Rohstoffabkommen *nt*; ~ **analysis** *n BrE* STOCK Warenanalyse *f*; ~ **approach** *n* S&M *to marketing* güterbezogener Ansatz *m*; ~ **basket** *n* GEN COMM statistischer Warenkorb *m*; ~ **cartel** *n* ECON Rohstoffkartell *nt*; ~ **classification rates** *n pl* (*CCR*) IMP/EXP Güterverzeichnissätze *m pl*, Warenverzeichnissätze *m pl*; ~ **concentration** *n* IMP/EXP Anteil *m* des Warenhandels am Außenhandel; ~ **credit** *n* BANK Warenkredit *m*

Commodity: ~ **Credit Corporation** *n AmE* (*CCC*) ECON *agricultural* US-Preisstützungsbehörde für die Landwirtschaft

commodity: ~ **dividend** *n* FIN Sachdividende *f*; ~ **exchange** *n* STOCK Warenbörse *f*, Produktenbörse *f*

Commodity: ~ **Exchange of New York** *n* (*COMEX*) STOCK New Yorker Warenbörse *f*

commodity: ~ **fetishism** *n* ECON Warenfetischismus *m*; ~ **flow** *n* GEN COMM Warenfluß *m*; ~ **futures exchange** *n* STOCK Warenterminbörse *f*

Commodity: ~ **Futures Trading Commission** *n* (*CFTC*) STOCK US-Aufsichtsbehörde für den Warenterminhandel

commodity: ~ **index** *n BrE* STOCK Warenpreisindex *m*; ~ **market** *n* ECON Gütermarkt *m*, Rohstoffmarkt *m*; ~ **mix** *n* TRANSP Warenmischung *f*; ~ **paper** *n* STOCK Warenpapier *nt*; ~ **price** *n* ECON, STOCK Rohstoffpreis *m*; ~ **rate** *n* TRANSP Einzelfrachttarif *m*; ~ **reserve currency** *n* ECON Warenreservenwährung *f*; ~ **stabili-**

zation schemes *n pl* ECON Abkommen *nt* zur Stabilisierung der Rohstoffpreise; **~ standard** *n* STOCK Naturalgeld *nt*, Warengeldsystem *nt*; **~ tax** *n* IMP/EXP Verbrauchssteuer *f*, Warensteuer *f*, TAX Verbrauchssteuer *f*; **~ terms of trade** *n* ECON Warenaustauschverhältnis *nt*; **~ trade** *n* ECON Rohstoffhandel *m*, Warenhandel *m*, Warengeschäfte *nt pl*; **~ trade structure** *n* ECON Struktur *f* des Warenhandels

common *adj* GEN COMM *policy, decision* gemeinsam; ◆ **by ~ consent** GEN COMM einstimmig

common: **~ access resources** *n pl* ECON Allmenderessourcen *f pl*

Common: **~ Agricultural Policy** *n* (*CAP*) ECON, POL gemeinsame Agrarpolitik *f* (*GAP*); **~ Agricultural Policy levy** *n* ECON Abschöpfung *f* im Rahmen der gemeinsamen Agrarpolitik

commonality *n* HRM, IND *staff* Arbeiterschaft *f*, Belegschaft *f*

common: **~ area** *n* PROP Gemeindeland *nt*; **~ cargo tank** *n* TRANSP gemeinsamer Ladetank *m*; **~ carrier** *n* IND *European energy networks* Transportunternehmer, in *m,f*, TRANSP Frachtführer, in *m,f*; **~ code of practice** *n* GEN COMM allgemeiner Verhaltenskodex *m*; **~ costs** *n pl* ECON Gemeinkosten *pl*, Kosten *pl* der Kuppelproduktion; **~ council** *n AmE* (*cf borough council BrE*) ADMIN, POL Stadtrat *m*; **~ currency** *n* ECON Gemeinschaftswährung *f*; **~ customs tariff** *n* (*CCT*) IMP/EXP Gemeinsamer Zolltarif *m* (*GZT*); **~ denominator** *n* GEN COMM *in decision-making* gemeinsamer Nenner *m*; **~ directive** *n* LAW gemeinsame Richtlinie *f*; **~ disaster clause** *n AmE* INS *life insurance* Hinterbliebenenversicherungsklausel *f*, Überlebensversicherungsklausel *f*; **~ distinguishing factor** *n* HRM *in aggregated union voting* gemeinsamer Nenner *m*; **~ elements** *n pl* PROP *of a condominium* Gemeinschaftsfläche *f*; **~ external tariff** *n* (*CET*) ECON gemeinsamer Außenzoll *m*; **~ language** *n* GEN COMM gemeinsame Sprache *f*; **~ law** *n* HRM, LAW Common Law *nt*, gemeines Recht *nt*; **~ learnings** *n pl* WEL allgemeines Wissen *nt*

Common: **~ Market** *n* (*CM*) ECON gemeinsamer Markt *m*; **~ Market Medium Term Model** *n* (*COMET*) ECON *econometrics* COMET-Modell *nt*

common: **~ business-oriented language** *n* (*COBOL*) COMP allgemeine kaufmännisch orientierte Programmiersprache *f* (*COBOL*); **~ ownership** *n* ECON öffentliches Eigentum *nt*, Kommunalbesitz *m*; **~ policy** *n* GEN COMM, POL gemeinsame Politik *f*; **~ pricing** *n* GEN COMM Preisabsprache *f*; **~ revenue** *n* FIN allgemeine Einnahmen *f pl*; **~ seal** *n* LAW öffentliches Siegel *nt*; **~ sense** *n* GEN COMM gesunder Menschenverstand *m*; **~ service cost distribution system** *n* ACC Hilfskostenumlagesystem *nt*; **~ share** *n AmE* STOCK Stammaktie *f*; **~ shares equivalent** *n BrE* (*cf common stock equivalent AmE*) STOCK Stammaktienäquivalent *nt*, stammaktiengleiches Papier *nt*; **~ stock** *n AmE* (*cf ordinary shares BrE*) ECON Stammanteil *m*, STOCK Stammaktie *f*; **~ stock equivalent** *n AmE* (*cf common shares equivalent BrE*) STOCK Stammaktienäquivalent *nt*, stammaktiengleiches Papier *nt*; **~ stock fund** *n* FIN, STOCK Aktieninvestmentfonds *m*; **~ system** *n* TAX *EU* gemeinsames System *nt*; **~ user facility** *n* GEN COMM allgemeine Nutzereinrichtung *f*

commonwealth *n* ECON Commonwealth *nt*

Commonwealth: **~ Development Corporation** *n* (*CDC*) ECON Commonwealth-Entwicklungsgesellschaft *f*; **~ Grants Commission** *n* ECON *in Australia* Kommission *f* für Zuschüsse im Commonwealth; **~ of Independent States** *n* (*CIS*) POL Gemeinschaft *f* Unabhängiger Staaten (*GUS*); **~ preference** *n* IMP/EXP Commonwealthpräferenz *f*

commotion *n* POL Unruhen *f pl*

communal *adj* GEN COMM kommunal, Kommunal-; **~ economy** *n* ECON Kommunalwirtschaft *f*; **~ ownership** *n* PROP Gemeinschaftsbesitz *m*, Gemeinschaftseigentum *nt*, Kommunalbesitz *m*, Kommunaleigentum *nt*

commune *n* ECON Kommune *f*

communicate *vt* PATENTS, POL mitteilen; **~ sth to sb** *phr* GEN COMM jdm etw mitteilen

communication *n* COMMS Kommuniqué *nt*, Kommunikation *f*, *by letter* Korrespondenz *f* (*Korr.*), GEN COMM *communicating* Kommunikation *f*, *by letter* Korrespondenz *f* (*Korr.*), *exchange of views* Gedankenaustausch *m*, Meinungsaustausch *m*, *piece of news* Nachricht *f*, *message* Mitteilung *f*, PATENTS Benachrichtigung *f*, Mitteilung *f*, POL Kommuniqué *nt*, Mitteilung *f*, Nachricht *f*, Kommunikation *f*; **~ barrier** *n* HRM, MGMNT Kommunikationshemmnis *nt*; **~ gap** *n* HRM, MGMNT Kommunikationslücke *f*; **~ link** *n* HRM, MGMNT Kommunikationsverbindung *f*; **~ management** *n* HRM, MGMNT Kommunikationsmanagement *nt*, Kommunikationsverwaltung *f*; **~ mix** *n* S&M Kommunikations-Mix *nt*, Mischung *f* verschiedener Kommunikationskanäle; **~ objective** *n* S&M Kommunikationsziel *nt*

communications *n pl* COMMS Nachrichtentechnik *f*, Nachrichtenwesen *nt*, Verbindungen *f pl*, Verbindungsmöglichkeiten *f pl*, Verkehr *m*, TRANSP Verbindungen *f pl*, Verkehrsverbindung *f*, Verbindungsmöglichkeiten *f pl*, Verkehrsnetz *nt*

communication: **~ skills** *n pl* HRM Kommunikationsfähigkeiten *f pl*

communications: **~ media** *n pl* MEDIA, S&M Kommunikationsmedien *nt pl*; **~ network** *n* COMP Datenübertragungsnetz *nt*; **~ theory** *n* COMMS, MGMNT Kommunikationstheorie *f*, Kommunikationswissenschaft *f*

communication: **~ strategy** *n* COMMS Kommunikationsstrategie *f*; **~ technology** *n* COMMS Kommunikationstechnik *f*

communicator *n* COMMS Mitteiler *m*, Kommunikator *m*

communiqué *n* COMMS, POL Kommuniqué *nt*

communism *n* ECON, POL Kommunismus *m*

communist *adj* ECON, POL kommunistisch

community *n* GEN COMM Gemeinde *f*, Gemeinschaft *f*, Gemeinwesen *nt*

Community: **~ action** *n* GEN COMM Gemeinschaftsmaßnahme *f*, Gemeinschaftsaktion *f*; **~ aid** *n* ECON Gemeinschaftshilfe *f*, Hilfe *f* der Gemeinschaft, *EU* Kommunalverband *m*

community: **~ association** *n* PROP Gemeindeverband *m*

Community: **~ budget** *n* ECON Gemeinschaftsbudget *nt*, Gemeinschaftshaushalt *m*; **~ Charter of Fundamental Social Rights of Workers** *n* HRM Gemeinschaftssatzung *f* zu grundlegenden Sozialrechten der Arbeiter; **~ goods** *n pl* IMP/EXP EG-Waren *f pl*,

Gemeinschaftswaren *f pl*; ~ **imports** *n pl* IMP/EXP EG-Importe *m pl*, Gemeinschaftseinfuhren *f pl*

community: ~ **of interests** *n* GEN COMM Interessengemeinschaft *f*; ~ **jobs** *n pl* ECON Arbeitsplätze *m pl*; ~ **network** *n* COMMS Gemeinschaft *f*; ~ **program** *AmE*, ~ **programme** *BrE* *n* HRM Gemeinschaftsprogramm *nt*, Arbeitsbeschaffungsmaßnahmen *f pl* (*ABM*); ~ **property** *n* LAW Gemeinschaftsgut *nt*; ~ **spirit** *n* GEN COMM Gemeinschaftsgeist *m*, Gemeinschaftssinn *m*

Community: ~ **transit** *n* (*CT*) IMP/EXP, TRANSP EG-Durchfuhr *f*, EG-Transit *m*; ~ **treatment** *n* IMP/EXP Behandlung *f* gemäß EG-Richtlinien, Gemeinschaftsbehandlung *f*

communization *n* ECON, POL, PROP *bringing into public ownership* Vergemeinschaftlichung *f*, Vergesellschaftung *f*

communize *vt* ECON, POL *bring into public ownership* in Gemeineigentum überführen, vergesellschaften, PROP in Gemeinschaftseigentum überführen

commutability *n* GEN COMM Wandelbarkeit *f*, LAW Umwandelbarkeit *f*

commutable *adj* COMMS, FIN umwandelbar, GEN COMM ablösbar, umwandelbar, LAW umwandelbar, abänderbar, MGMNT, STOCK umwandelbar

commutation *n* INS Umwandlung *f*, TRANSP öffentliche Verkehrsmittel *nt pl*, Pendelverkehr *m*; ~ **right** *n* INS Recht *nt* auf Umwandlung einer Zeitrente in eine Barabfindung; ~ **of a sentence** *n* LAW Strafumwandlung *f*; ~ **ticket** *n* *AmE* (*cf season ticket BrE*) TRANSP Abonnementsfahrkarte *f*, Zeitfahrkarte *f*, Zeitkarte *f*, *monthly* Monatsfahrkarte *f*, *rail* Eisenbahnabonnement *nt*; ~ **ticket holder** *n* *AmE* (*cf season ticket holder BrE*) TRANSP Zeitkarteninhaber, in *m,f*

commute 1. *vt* GEN COMM ablösen, umwandeln, LAW *sentence* umwandeln, *decision* abändern; **2.** *vi* GEN COMM, TRANSP *to work* pendeln

commuter *n* GEN COMM Pendler, in *m,f*, TRANSP Berufsverkehrsteilnehmer, in *m,f*, Pendler, in *m,f*; ~ **aircraft** *n* TRANSP Nahverkehrsflugzeug *nt*; ~ **airline** *n* TRANSP Nahverkehrsfluggesellschaft *f*; ~ **belt** *n* GEN COMM Einzugsgebiet *nt*; ~ **service** *n* TRANSP Pendelverkehrdienstleistung *f*; ~ **tax** *n* *AmE* TAX Gemeindebesteuerung *f* von Pendlern

commuting *n* GEN COMM, TRANSP *to work* Pendeln *nt*

compact: ~ **disc** *n* (*CD*) COMP, GEN COMM, MEDIA Compact Disc *f* (*CD*); ~ **disc read-only memory** *n* (*CD-ROM*) COMP Compact Disc-Festwertspeicher *m* (*CD-ROM*)

Companies: ~ **Act** *n* *BrE* LAW Aktiengesetz *nt*, Gesetze *nt pl* über Aktiengesellschaften; ~ **Code** *n* LAW *in Australia* Gesellschaftsrecht *nt*; ~ **Registration Office** *n* (*CRO*) GEN COMM Gesellschafts-Registeramt *nt*, Gesellschaftsregisterstelle *f*, *in Germany* Handelsregister *nt*, LAW *contracts* Gesellschaftsregister *nt*

company *n* (*Co*) ECON Gesellschaft *f*, GEN COMM Gesellschaft *f*, Firma *f* (*Fa.*), LAW *contracts, trade law* Gesellschaft *f*; ~ **accounts** *n pl* ACC Jahresabschluß *m* einer Unternehmung; ~**'s affairs** *n pl* GEN COMM Firmenangelegenheiten *f pl*, Geschäftslage *f* des Unternehmens; ~ **agreement** *n* HRM Gesellschaftsvertrag *m*; ~ **bargaining** *n* HRM Tarifvertragsverhandlungen *f pl* für das Gesamtunternehmen; ~ **benefits** *n pl* HRM

betriebliche Sozialleistungen *f pl*; ~ **capital** *n* GEN COMM Gesellschaftskapital *nt*; ~ **car** *n* TRANSP Firmenwagen *m*; ~ **credit card** *n* TAX Firmenkreditkarte *f*; ~ **employee** *n* HRM Belegschaftsangehörige(r) *mf* [decl. as adj]; ~ **executive** *n* ADMIN Führungskraft *f*, leitende(r) Angestellte(r) *mf* [decl. as adj], Mitglied *nt* der Führungsebene; ~ **expenditure survey** *n* *AmE* ACC Untersuchung *f* der betrieblichen Aufwendungen; ~ **formation** *n* GEN COMM Unternehmensgründung *f*, Gesellschaftsgründung *f*; ~ **goal** *n* GEN COMM Unternehmensziel *nt*; ~ **headquarters** *n* GEN COMM Zentrale *f*, Stammhaus *nt*; ~ **in liquidation** *n* LAW Abwicklungsfirma *f*; **the ~ is rated triple-A** *phr* STOCK die Firma ist erstklassig bewertet worden; ~ **law** *n* LAW Gesellschaftsrecht *nt*; ~ **lease agreement** *n* LAW Betriebspachtvertrag *m*; ~ **level agreement** *n* HRM Vertrag *m* auf Unternehmensebene; ~ **liquidity** *n* FIN Unternehmensliquidität *f*; ~ **logo** *n* GEN COMM, S&M Firmenlogo *nt*; ~ **meeting** *n* GEN COMM Aktionärsversammlung *f*; ~ **model** *n* GEN COMM Firmenmodell *nt*; ~ **objective** *n* GEN COMM Unternehmensziel *nt*; ~**-owned** *adj* GEN COMM firmeneigen; ~ **pension plan** *n* ADMIN Betriebsrentensystem *f*, betriebliche Altersversorgung *f*; ~ **philosophy** *n* GEN COMM Unternehmensphilosophie *f*; ~ **planning** *n* GEN COMM betriebliche Planung *f*, Unternehmensplanung *f*; ~ **policy** *n* GEN COMM Unternehmensphilosophie *f*; ~ **profile** *n* GEN COMM Unternehmensprofil *nt*; ~ **promotion** *n* ADMIN Unternehmensgründung *f*; ~ **purpose** *n* GEN COMM Unternehmenszweck *m*; ~ **reconstruction** *n* GEN COMM Umstrukturierung *f* des Unternehmens; ~ **reorganization** *n* GEN COMM Unternehmensneuorganisation *f*; ~ **results** *n pl* GEN COMM Geschäftsergebnisse *f pl*; ~ **seal** *n* LAW Firmensiegel *nt*; ~ **secretary** *n* *BrE* ADMIN Leiter, in *m,f* der Verwaltung einer Firma; ~ **service contract** *n* GEN COMM *shipping* Firmenwartungsvertrag *m*; ~**'s health insurance scheme** *n* HRM, INS Betriebskrankenkasse *f*; ~**'s own field organization** *n* IMP/EXP firmeneigener Außendienst *m*; ~**'s own shares** *n pl* STOCK Vorratsaktien *f pl*; ~**-specific card** *n* FIN firmenspezifische Karte *f*; ~**'s representative** *n* MGMNT Firmenvertretung *f*; ~**'s solicitor** *n* *BrE* LAW Firmenanwältin *f*, Firmenanwalt *m*, Syndikusanwältin *f*, Syndikusanwalt *m*; ~ **strategy** *n* ECON, GEN COMM, MGMNT Unternehmensstrategie *f*; ~ **structure** *n* GEN COMM Gesellschaftsstruktur *f*, Aufbau *m* eines Unternehmens; ~ **tax** *n* TAX Körperschaftsteuer *f*; ~ **town** *n* ECON Stadt, die von einem Unternehmen abhängig ist, Werkssiedlung *f*; ~ **union** *n* HRM Betriebsgewerkschaft *f*, gelbe Gewerkschaft *f*; ~ **vehicle** *n* TRANSP Firmenfahrzeug *nt*

comparability *n* GEN COMM Vergleichbarkeit *f*

comparable *adj* GEN COMM vergleichbar; ~ **basis** *n* ACC *of reporting* Vergleichsbasis *f*

comparables *n pl* *AmE* PROP *similar properties* Vergleichsgrundstücke *nt pl*

comparable: ~ **worth** *n* (*CW*) ECON vergleichbarer Wert *m*, HRM gleiche Produktivität *f*

comparative *adj* ECON komparativ, GEN COMM *value* vergleichend; ~ **advantage** *n* ECON komparativer Vorteil *m*; ~ **advertising** *n* S&M vergleichende Werbung *f*; ~ **earnings analysis** *n* FIN Erfolgsvergleichsrechnung *f*; ~ **evaluation sheet** *n* GEN COMM Angebotsanalyse *f*

comparatively *adv* GEN COMM vergleichsweise

comparative: ~ **negligence** *n* LAW anspruchminderndes

Mitverschulden *nt*; ~ **statements** *n pl* FIN vergleichende Aufstellungen *f pl*; ~ **statistics** *n pl* ECON komparative Analyse *f*, vergleichende Analyse *f*

compare *vt* GEN COMM vergleichen; ◆ ~ **like with like** GEN COMM Gleiches mit Gleichem vergleichen; ~ **sth to sth** GEN COMM etw mit etw vergleichen

comparison *n* GEN COMM, LAW Vergleich *m*; ~ **test** *n* GEN COMM Vergleichstest *m*

compartmentalize 1. *vt* GEN COMM *agricultural common market* abschotten, einteilen; **2.** *vi* MGMNT Bereiche bilden

compartmentation *n* ECON, GEN COMM *of agricultural common market* Abschottung *f*

compatibility *n* COMP Austauschbarkeit *f*, Kompatibilität *f*, Verträglichkeit *f*, GEN COMM Verträglichkeit *f*, Vereinbarkeit *f*, HRM Kompatibilität *f*, IND *of products* gegenseitige Verträglichkeit *f*, Kompatibilität *f*

compatible *adj* COMP kompatibel, GEN COMM vereinbar, verträglich, HRM, IND kompatibel; ◆ ~ **with** GEN COMM vereinbar mit; ~ **with the environment** ENVIR umweltfreundlich

compelling *adj* ECON überzeugend, zwingend

compensate *vt* GEN COMM kompensieren, HRM *pay* abfinden, entschädigen, INS entschädigen; ◆ ~ **for** GEN COMM abfinden, abgelten, ausgleichen, PATENTS entschädigen für, Schadensersatz zahlen; ~ **sb for sth** GEN COMM *damages* jdn für etw entschädigen, jdn für etw kompensieren

compensated: ~ **demand curve** *n* ECON kompensierte Nachfragefunktion *f*

compensating *adj* GEN COMM ausgleichend, STOCK ausgleichend, deckend; ~ **balance** *n* BANK Ausgleichsbilanz *f*; ~ **common tariff** *n* ECON gemeinsamer Ausgleichszoll *m*; ~ **errors** *n pl* ACC sich gegenseitig aufhebende Buchungsfehler *m pl*; ~ **income** *n BrE* STOCK Arbeitslohn *m*; ~ **loss** *n BrE* STOCK Ausgleichsverlust *m*; ~ **product** *n* IMP/EXP Kompensationsprodukt *nt*; ~ **tariff** *n* IMP/EXP Ausgleichszoll *m*; ~ **wage differential** *n* HRM zum Ausgleich des Lohngefälles

compensation *n* ECON Ausgleich *m*, Entschädigung *f*, Kompensation *f*, *indemnification* Abstandsgeld *nt*, Entgelt *nt*, GEN COMM Ausgleich *m*, Abgeltung *f*, HRM Arbeitsentgelt *nt*, Abfertigung *f*, IMP/EXP Kompensation *f*, INS Entschädigung *f*, Kompensation *f*, LAW Kompensation *f*, Wiedergutmachung *f*, STOCK, TAX Kompensation *f*; ~ **agreement** *n* ECON *international trade* Entgeltvereinbarung *f*, Kompensationsabkommen *nt*, Schadensersatzvereinbarung *f*; ~ **for damage** *n* LAW *contracts* Schadensersatz *m*; ~ **for loss or damage** *n* INS Entschädigung *f* für Verlust und Schaden, Schadens- und Verlustersatz *m*; ~ **fund** *n BrE* STOCK Ausgleichsfonds *m*, Entschädigungsfonds *m*; ~ **in damages** *n* GEN COMM Schadensersatz *m*; ~ **money** *n* HRM Entschädigungsbetrag *m*; ~ **principle** *n* ECON Kompensationskriterium *nt*; ~ **tax** *n* TAX Ausgleichsabgabe *f*

compensatory *adj* ECON, GEN COMM, IMP/EXP, INS, LAW, STOCK, TAX kompensatorisch; ~ **amount** *n* ECON Entschädigungszahlung *f*, INS Entschädigungssumme *f*; ~ **budgeting** *n* ECON kompensatorischer Budgetausgleich *m*; ~ **concessions** *n pl* IMP/EXP Ausgleichszugeständnisse *nt pl*; ~ **damages** *n pl* LAW adäquater Schadensersatz *m*; ~ **finance** *n* ECON *fiscal policy* antizyklische Finanzpolitik *f*, GEN COMM finanz-

politische Ausgleichsregelung *f*, POL Ausgleichsfinanzierung *f*, finanzpolitische Ausgleichsregelung *f*, *indemnification* finanzielle Entschädigung *f*; ~ **financial facility** *n* (*CFF*) FIN Kompensatorische Finanzfazilität *f*, Sonderfazilität des Internationalen Währungsfonds; ~ **financing** *n* COMM Schadenzahlungen *f pl*, Schadensersatzleistungen *f pl*, *facilities* kompensatorische Finanzierung *f*, *for damage, dismissal* finanzielle Abfindung *f*, ECON *international facilities for balance of payments* kompensatorische Finanzierung *f*, GEN COMM Schadensersatzleistungen *f pl*, Schadenzahlungen *f pl*, *facilities* Ausgleichsfinanzierung *f*, *for damage, dismissal* Abfindung *f*, INS Schadenzahlungen *f pl*, POL Schadenzahlungen *f pl*, Schadensersatzleistungen *f pl*, *for damage, dismissal* finanzielle Abfindung *f*, *facilities* Ausgleichsfinanzierung *f*; ~ **fiscal policy** *n* TAX kompensatorische Fiskalpolitik *f*; ~ **levy** *n* IMP/EXP Ausgleichsabgabe *f*, Ausgleichszahlung *f*, Anteilszoll *m*; ~ **payment** *n* TAX Ausgleichszahlung *f*; ~ **principle of taxation** *n* FIN Äquivalenzprinzip *nt*; ~ **stock option** *n BrE* STOCK kompensatorische Aktienoptionen *f pl*; ~ **tax** *n* TAX Ausgleichsabgabe *f*; ~ **time** *n* HRM Überstundenausgleich *m*

compete *vi* GEN COMM konkurrieren; ◆ ~ **against sb** GEN COMM mit jdm im Wettbewerb stehen; ~ **with** GEN COMM konkurrieren mit

competence *n* GEN COMM *authority* Befugnis *f*, *responsibility* Zuständigkeit *f*, *ability* Fähigkeit *f*, LAW *ability* Kompetenz *f*, *responsibility* Zuständigkeit *f*

competency *n* GEN COMM *authority* Befugnis *f*, *responsibility* Zuständigkeit *f*, *ability* Fähigkeit *f*, LAW *ability* Kompetenz *f*, *responsibility* Zuständigkeit *f*; ~ **of the court** *n* LAW Zuständigkeit *f* des Gerichts

competent *adj* GEN COMM fähig, LAW zuständig; ~ **party** *n* LAW *contract* zuständige Partei *f*

competing: ~ **requirements** *n pl* GEN COMM konkurrierende Bedürfnisse *nt pl*

competition *n* ECON Wettbewerb *m*, GEN COMM Konkurrenz *f*, Wettbewerb *m*, HRM, S&M Wettbewerb *m*

competition: ~ **laws** *n pl* POL, LAW Wettbewerbsgesetze *nt pl*, Kartellrecht *nt*; ~ **policy** *n* POL Wettbewerbspolitik *f*

competitive *adj* ECON wettbewerbsfähig, GEN COMM konkurrierend, konkurrenzfähig; ◆ **have a ~ advantage over sb** ECON einen Wettbewerbsvorteil gegenüber jdm haben

competitive: ~ **advantage** *n* ECON Wettbewerbsvorsprung *m*, Wettbewerbsvorteil *m*; ~ **bid** *n* S&M Gegenangebot *nt*; ~ **bidding procedure** *n* GEN COMM Submissionsverfahren *nt*; ~ **business** *n* GEN COMM Konkurrenzgeschäft *nt*; ~ **claim** *n* S&M konkurrierender Anspruch *m*; ~ **demand** *n* ECON konkurrierende Nachfrage *f*; ~ **devaluation** *n* ECON Abwertung *f* aus Wettbewerbsgründen; ~ **edge** *n* ECON Wettbewerbsvorsprung *m*; ~ **examination** *n* HRM Ausscheidungswettbewerb *m*; ~ **exploitation** *n* ECON, ENVIR, GEN COMM Ausbeutung *f* auf Wettbewerbsbasis; ~ **fringe** *n* ECON kleine einflußlose Firmen in einem von großen Anbietern bestimmten Markt; ~ **market** *n* ECON Wettbewerbsmarkt *m*, wettbewerbsintensiver Markt *m*

competitiveness *n* GEN COMM Konkurrenzfähigkeit *f*, Wettbewerbsfähigkeit *f*

competitive: ~ **parity** *n* S&M Wettbewerbsparität *f*;

~ parity method *n* S&M Methode *f* der Wettbewerbs-parität; **~ position** *n* ECON Wettbewerbslage *f*, Wettbewerbsposition *f*, GEN COMM Wettbewerbsposition *f*; **~ price** *n* ECON freier Marktpreis *m*, Wettbewerbspreis *m*, wettbewerbsfähiger Preis *m*, S&M Konkurrenzpreis *m*, wettbewerbsfähiger Preis *m*, konkurrenzfähiger Preis *m*; **~ pricing** *n* GEN COMM Wettbewerbspreisbildung *f*; **~ process** *n* ECON Wettbewerb *m*, Wettbewerbsprozeß *m*; **~ rate** *n* S&M Konkurrenztarif *m*; **~ stimulus** *n* ECON, S&M Wettbewerbsanreiz *m*, Wettbewerbsreiz *m*; **~ strategy** *n* ECON, GEN COMM, S&M Wettbewerbsstrategie *f*; **~ tactics** *n pl* ECON Wettbewerbstaktik *f*, MGMNT auf Wettbewerb beruhende Taktik *f*, Konkurrenztaktik *f*; **~ tendering** *n* ECON Mitabgabe *f* von Angeboten, S&M Ausschreibung *f*; **~ thrust** *n* ECON Konkurrenzkampf *m*, Wettbewerbsvorstoß *m*; **~ trading** *n* ECON konkurrierender Handel *m*

competitor *n* ECON *country, product* Konkurrent, in *m,f*, Wettbewerber, in *m,f*, *company* Wettbewerber, in *m,f*, GEN COMM *person, country, product* Konkurrent, in *m,f*, Wettbewerber, in *m,f*, *company* Konkurrent, in *m,f*, Wettbewerber, in *m,f*, Konkurrenzunternehmen *nt*, HRM *person* S&M *person, country, product* Wettbewerber, in *m,f*, *company* Konkurrent, in *m,f*, Wettbewerber, in *m,f*; **~ analysis** *n* S&M Analyse *f* konkurrierender Produkte, Konkurrenzanalyse *f*

compilation *n* ACC Sammlung *f*, Zusammenstellung *f*, GEN COMM Zusammenstellung *f*

compile *vt* ACC sammeln, zusammenstellen, COMP kompilieren, GEN COMM zusammenstellen

compiler *n* COMP Compiler *m*, Übersetzungsprogramm *nt*

complain *vi* GEN COMM sich beschweren

complaining: **~ party** *n* LAW *contracts* beschwerdeführende Partei *f*

complaint *n* GEN COMM Beschwerde *f*, Reklamation *f*, LAW *civil action* Klage *f*, *criminal law* Strafanzeige *f*; **~ proceedings** *n pl* LAW Beschwerdeverfahren *nt*

complaints: **~ procedure** *n* GEN COMM Reklamationsverfahren *nt*, LAW Klageverfahren *nt*

complement 1. *n* COMP Komplement *nt*; **2.** *vt* GEN COMM ergänzen

complementary *adj* GEN COMM ergänzend, komplementär; **~ demand** *n* ECON Komplementärnachfrage *f*, verbundene Nachfrage *f*, S&M Komplementärnachfrage *f*; **~ goods** *n pl* ECON, S&M komplementäre Güter *nt pl*; **~ product** *n* S&M Komplementärprodukt *nt*; **~ technology** *n* IND Komplementärtechnologie *f*

complements *n pl* ECON, S&M komplementäre Güter *nt pl*

complete 1. *adj* GEN COMM komplett, vollständig, total, voll; **2.** *vt* FIN abwickeln, GEN COMM vollenden, vervollständigen, ergänzen, *sale, order* abschließen, beenden, PROP *sale* abschließen, LAW *contract* erfüllen, abschließen

complete: **~ audit** *n* ACC Jahresrevision *f*, lückenlose Prüfung *f*

completed *adj* GEN COMM *supplemented* ergänzt, vervollständigt, *finished* vollendet, abgeschlossen, LAW beschlossen, *contract* erfüllt, abgeschlossen; **~ contract method** *n* ACC Grundsatz *m* der Gewinnrealisierung; **~ operations insurance** *n* INS *property* Leistungshaftung *f*

completely *adv* GEN COMM vollständig

completeness *n* ACC *of data* Vollständigkeit *f*

complete: **~ picture** *n* GEN COMM geschlossenes Bild *nt*; **~ refund offer** *n* S&M Angebot *nt* der vollständigen Rückerstattung

completion *n* GEN COMM Abschluß *m*, Beenden *nt*, Beendigung *f*, Fertigstellung *f*, Vollendung *f*; **~ basis** *n* ACC Fertigstellungsbasis *f*; **~ bond** *n* AmE LAW *property* Fertigstellungsgarantie *f*; **~ date** *n* GEN COMM Fertigstellungstermin *m*, PROP *of house purchase* Einzugstermin *m*, Übergabetermin *m*; **~ deadline** *n* LAW *contracts* Erfüllungsfrist *f*; **~ program** *AmE*, **~ programme** *BrE n* ENVIR Ausführungsprogramm *nt*, Fertigstellungsprogramm *nt*, Komplettierungsprogramm *nt*

complex 1. *adj* GEN COMM komplex; **2.** *n* PROP *of buildings* Komplex *m*

complex: **~ capital structure** *n* ECON komplexe Kapitalstruktur *f*; **~ economy** *n* ECON komplexe Wirtschaft *f*; **~ transaction** *n* BANK komplizierte Transaktion *f*, kompliziertes Geschäft *nt*

compliance *n* GEN COMM, LAW Einhaltung *f*, Erfüllung *f*, Übereinstimmung *f*, PATENTS Übereinstimmung *f*; ♦ **in ~ with** LAW in Übereinstimmung mit

compliance: **~ audit** *n* ACC Erfüllungsprüfung *f*; **~ with contract** *n* LAW Vertragseinhaltung *f*; **~ costs** *n pl* ACC Erfüllungskosten *pl*, ADMIN verwaltungsmäßige Verfügungskosten *pl*, ENVIR Erfüllungskosten *pl*; **~ system** *n* TAX Erfüllungsmethode *f*, Erfüllungssystem *nt*; **~ test** *n* GEN COMM Erfüllungstest *m*

complicate *vt* GEN COMM komplizieren

complication *n* GEN COMM Komplikation *f*

complimentary: **~ close** *n* COMMS *of letter* Grußformel *f*; **~ copy** *n* MEDIA *book* Freiexemplar *nt*, *magazine* Werbenummer *f*; **~ subscription** *n* GEN COMM Werbeabonnement *nt*; **~ ticket** *n* LEIS Freikarte *f*

compliment: **~ slip** *n* COMMS Empfehlungszettel *m*, S&M höfliche Begleitnotiz *f*

comply *vi* GEN COMM einwilligen; ♦ **~ with** GEN COMM *conditions* erfüllen, *standards* entsprechen [+dat], LAW *rule* einhalten, *law* befolgen

component *n* COMP Komponente *f*, GEN COMM Komponente *f*, IND Bestandteil *m*, Komponente *f*, Teil *nt*, Werkstück *nt*, Bauteil *nt*; **~ factory** *n* IND Bestückungsbetrieb *m*, Fertigungsbetrieb *m*; **~ part** *n* COMP *electronic* Bauteil *nt*, Komponente *f*, GEN COMM *of system* wesentlicher Bestandteil *m*, Bestandteil *m*, Komponente *f*, IND Bestandteil *m*, Einzelteil *nt*, Komponente *f*

composed: **be ~ of** *phr* GEN COMM sich zusammensetzen aus

composite *adj* GEN COMM gemischt, zusammengesetzt, synthetisch; **~ commodity** *n* ECON Güterbündel *nt*; **~ currency** *n* ECON Korbwährung *f*; **~ currency unit** *n* ECON Korbwährungseinheit *f*; **~ demand** *n* ECON zusammengesetzte Nachfrage *f*; **~ depreciation** *n* FIN Gruppenabschreibung *f*, Pauschalabschreibung *f*; **~ hypothesis** *n* MATH *statistics* zusammengesetzte Hypothese *f*; **~ index** *n* ECON, FIN zusammengesetzter Index *m*; **~ insurance** *n* INS Kompositversicherung *f*, Mehrspartenversicherung *f*; **~ insurance company** *n* INS Kompositversicherungsgesellschaft *f*; **~ leading index** *n* ECON synthetischer Frühindikator *m*, STOCK zusammengesetzter Index *m* der Frühindikatoren; **~ leading indicator** *n* STOCK *statistics*

Gesamtfrühindikator *m*; **~ life insurance** *n* INS allgemeine Lebensversicherung *f*, universelle Lebensversicherung *f*; **~ life policy** *n* INS allgemeine Lebensversicherungspolice *f*, universelle Lebensversicherungspolice *f*; **~ mark** *n* PATENTS Kollektivzeichen *nt*, zusammengesetztes Warenzeichen *nt*; **~ package** *n* S&M Mischpackung *f*; **~ packaging** *n* TRANSP Sammelverpackung *f*, Verbundverpackung *f*; **~ rate** *n* GEN COMM Pauschalsatz *m*; **~ rate tax** *n* TAX allgemeiner Steuersatz *m*, Pauschalsteuersatz *m*; **~ spread** *n* BANK zusammengesetzte Spanne *f*; **~ trailer** *n* TRANSP *road vehicle* Kombianhänger *m*; **~ variation** *n* ACC Abweichung *f* zweiten Grades; **~ yield** *n* BANK zusammengesetzte Rendite *f*

composition *n* LAW Beschaffenheit *f*, Vergleich *m*, *with creditor* Gesamtvergleich *m* mit Gläubigern; **~ proceedings** *n pl* LAW Akkord *m*, Vergleichsverfahren *nt*

compound *vi* LAW *agree* sich vergleichen; **~ annual growth** *n* ECON Gesamtjahreswachstum *nt*; **~ annual rate** *n* BrE *(CAR)* BANK *of interest* kumulativer Jahressatz *m*; **~ duty** *n* IMP/EXP *customs* gemischter Wertzoll *m*; **~ entry** *n* ACC Gesamteintrag *m*, ADMIN Sammelbuchung *f*; **~ growth rate** *n* ECON Gesamtwachstumsrate *f*; **~ interest** *n* BANK, ECON, FIN, LAW *contracts* Zinseszins *m*; **~ interest bond** *n* FIN Anleihe *f* mit Staffelzinsen; **~ item** *n* ADMIN Sammelposition *f*; **~ journal entry** *n* ACC zusammengesetzte Journalbuchung *f*; **~ yield** *n* FIN Mehrfachertrag *m*, zusammengesetzter Ertrag *m*

comprehensive *adj* GEN COMM *report, review* inhaltsreich, *answer* umfassend, HRM, INS umfassend; **~ agreement** *n* HRM Gesamtvertrag *m*; **~ annual financial report** *n* *(CAFR)* ECON Gesamtjahresabschluß *m*, Jahreshaushaltsbericht *m*; **~ bank guarantee** *n* BANK globale Bankgarantie *f*; **~ budget** *n* FIN Gesamthaushalt *m*; **~ crime endorsement** *n* INS Nachtrag *m* zur Pauschaldeckung gegen Kriminalität

Comprehensive: ~ Employment and Training Act *n* *AmE (CETA)* HRM amerikanisches Gesetz zur Ausbildung von Jugendlichen

comprehensive: **~ extended-term banker's guarantee** *n* *(CXBG)* BANK umfassende längerfristige Bankgarantie *f*; **~ general liability insurance** *n* INS Betriebs- und Produkthaftpflichtversicherung *f*; **~ glass insurance** *n* INS kombinierte Glasversicherung *f*; **~ health-care system** *n* WEL Gesundheitsfürsorgegesamtplan *m*; **~ health insurance** *n* INS kombinierte Krankenversicherung *f*; **~ insurance** *n* INS Kombination *f* verschiedener Versicherungsdeckungen, kombinierte Versicherung *f*, umfassende Versicherung *f* gegen mehrere Gefahren; **insurance policy** *n* INS Kombination *f* verschiedener Versicherungsdeckungen; **~ liability insurance** *n* INS kombinierte Haftpflichtversicherung *f*

comprehensively: ~ covered *adj* INS vollkaskoversichert

comprehensive: **~ personal liability insurance** *n* INS kombinierte Privathaftpflichtversicherung *f*; **~ policy** *n* INS gebündelte Versicherung *f*, kombinierte Police *f*, Sammelversicherungsschein *m*; **~ responsibility** *n* GEN COMM Gesamtverantwortung *f*; **~ school** *n* WEL Gesamtschule *f*; **~ school education** *n* WEL Gesamtschulbildung *f*

compress *vt* COMP *file, data*, HRM *salary*, TRANSP komprimieren

compression *n* COMP *of file, data*, HRM *of salary* Komprimierung *f*, TRANSP Druck *m*, Komprimierung *f*

comprise *vt* GEN COMM beinhalten, einschließen, bestehen aus, umfassen

comprised: ~ total loss *n* INS *marine* einschließlich Totalverlust *m*, Totalverlust *m* eingeschlossen

comprised: **be ~ of** *phr* GEN COMM bestehen aus

compromise 1. *n* GEN COMM Kompromiß *m*; **2.** *vt* GEN COMM *project* durch Kompromiß regeln; **3.** *vi* GEN COMM einen Vergleich schließen, einen Kompromiß schließen

compromise: **~ agreement** *n* LAW Vergleich *m*; **~ decision** *n* GEN COMM Kompromißentscheidung *f*, Kompromißlösung *f*

comptroller *see controller*

Comptroller: ~ of the Currency *n* *AmE* BANK staatlicher Währungsprüfer, Währungskommissar; Bankenaufsichtsbehörde; **~ General** *n* *AmE* ACC Hauptcontroller *m*

compulsion *n* ECON Zwang *m*

compulsive: ~ buying *n* S&M Kaufzwang *m*

compulsory *adj* GEN COMM *power* obligatorisch, *regulation* zwingend; **~ arbitration** *n* BrE HRM *labour disputes* Zwangsschlichtung *f*; **~ arbitration proceedings** *n pl* LAW obligatorisches Schiedsgerichtsverfahren *nt*; **~ competitive tendering** *n* BrE POL Zwangsausschreibung *f*; **~ deduction** *n* GEN COMM Zwangsabzug *m*; **~ expenditure** *n* ECON obligatorische Ausgaben *f pl*; **~ insurance** *n* INS Pflichtversicherung *f*, Zwangsversicherung *f*; **~ licence** BrE, **~ license** *AmE* *n* PATENTS Zwangslizenz *f*; **~ liquidation** *n* FIN unfreiwillige Liquidation *f*, Zwangsliquidation *f*, Zwangsliquidierung *f*, GEN COMM zwangsweise Liquidation *f*; **~ margin** *n* BrE STOCK obligatorische Einschußsumme *f*, obligatorische Einschußzahlung *f*; **~ purchase** *n* GEN COMM Zwangskauf *m*, PROP Zwangsenteignung *f*

Compulsory: ~ Purchase Act *n* BrE LAW Zwangsenteignungsgesetz *nt*

compulsory: **~ purchase order** *n* BrE PROP Anordnung *f* zur Zwangsenteignung; **~ redundancy** *n* BrE HRM Zwangsentlassung *f*; **~ retirement** *n* BrE *(cf mandatory retirement AmE)* ADMIN, HRM Zwangspensionierung *f*; **~ saving** *n* BrE FIN Zwangssparen *nt*; **~ surrender** *n* LAW *in Scotland* Zwangsverkauf *m*; **~ third party insurance** *n* INS Zwangshaftpflichtversicherung *f*

computation *n* COMP Berechnung *f*

computational: ~ error *n* COMP Rechenfehler *m*

computation: **~ of time limits** *n* LAW Berechnung *f* der Fristen

compute *vt* COMP berechnen

computer *n* COMP Computer *m*, *calculating machine* Rechner *m*; **~ accounting** *n* ACC Buchführung *f* per Computer, Buchhaltung *f* per Computer; **~ age** *n* COMP Computerzeitalter *nt*, Zeitalter *nt* der elektronischen Rechner; **~-aided** *adj* COMP computergestützt, computerunterstützt, PC-gestützt, rechnergestützt, rechnerunterstützt; **~-aided advertising system** *n* *(CAAS)* S&M computergestützte Werbung *f*; **~-aided design** *n* *(CAD)* COMP, IND *development* computerunterstützte Entwicklung *f* *(CAD)*, computerunterstützte Konstruktion *f* *(CAD)*, computerunterstütztes Entwerfen *nt* *(CAD)*, computerunterstütztes Konstruieren *nt* (*CAD*); **~-aided design and manufacturing** *n* (*CAD/CAM*) COMP, IND computerunterstützte Entwicklung und Fertigung *f* (*CAD/CAM*); **~-aided engineering** *n* (*CAE*) COMP, IND computerunterstütztes Ingenieurwesen *nt* (*CAE*); **~-aided instruction** *n* (*CAI*) COMP computerunterstützter Unterricht *m* (*CAI*); **~-aided language learning** *n* (*CALL*) COMP computerunterstütztes Lernen *nt* von Sprachen (*CALL*); **~-aided learning** *n* (*CAL*) COMP computerunterstütztes Lernen *nt* (*CAL*); **~-aided learning program** *n* COMP computerunterstütztes Ausbildungsprogramm *nt*; **~-aided manufacturing** *n* (*CAM*) IND, COMP computerunterstützte Fertigung *f* (*CAM*); **~-aided quality assurance** *n* (*CAQ*) COMP, IND computerunterstützte Qualitätssicherung *f*; **~-aided software engineering** *n* (*CASE*) COMP computerunterstützte Software-Erstellung *f* (*CASE*); **~-aided teaching** *n* (*CAT*) COMP computerunterstützter Unterricht *m*; **~-aided testing** *n* (*CAT*) COMP computerunterstütztes Prüfen *nt*, computerunterstütztes Testen *nt*; **~-aided translation** *n* (*CAT*) COMP computerunterstützte Übersetzung *f*; **~ animation** *n* S&M Computeranimation *f*; **~-assisted** *adj* COMP computergestützt, computerunterstützt, PC-gestützt, rechnergestützt, rechnerunterstützt; **~-assisted design** *n* (*CAD*) COMP, IND *development* computerunterstützte Entwicklung *f* (*CAD*), computerunterstützte Konstruktion *f* (*CAD*), computerunterstütztes Entwerfen *nt* (*CAD*), computerunterstütztes Konstruieren *nt* (*CAD*); **~-assisted design and manufacturing** *n* (*CAD/CAM*) COMP, IND computerunterstützte Entwicklung und Fertigung *f* (*CAD/CAM*); **~-assisted design and drafting** *n* (*CADD*) COMP, IND computerunterstütztes Konstruieren und technisches Zeichnen *nt* (*CADD*); **~-assisted engineering** *n* (*CAE*) COMP, IND computerunterstütztes Ingenieurwesen *nt* (*CAE*); **~-assisted instruction** *n* (*CAI*) COMP computerunterstützter Unterricht *m* (*CAI*); **~-assisted language learning** *n* (*CALL*) COMP computerunterstütztes Lernen *nt* von Sprachen (*CALL*); **~-assisted learning** *n* (*CAL*) COMP computerunterstütztes Lernen *nt* (*CAL*); **~-assisted learning program** *n* COMP computerunterstütztes Ausbildungsprogramm *nt*; **~-assisted manufacturing** *n* (*CAM*) IND, COMP computerunterstützte Fertigung *f* (*CAM*); **~-assisted software engineering** *n* (*CASE*) COMP computerunterstützte Software-Erstellung *f* (*CASE*); **~-assisted teaching** *n* (*CAT*) COMP computerunterstützter Unterricht *m*; **~-assisted testing** *n* (*CAT*) COMP computerunterstütztes Prüfen *nt*, computerunterstütztes Testen *nt*; **~-assisted trading system** *n* (*CATS*) STOCK rechnergestütztes Börsenhandelssystem *nt*; **~-assisted translation** *n* (*CAT*) COMP computerunterstützte Übersetzung *f*; **~ bank** *n* BANK Computerbank *f*; **~-based** *adj* COMP computergestützt, computerunterstützt, PC-gestützt, rechnergestützt, rechnerunterstützt; **~-based training** *n* (*CBT*) COMP computergestützte Ausbildung *f*, rechnergestützte Ausbildung *f*, HRM rechnergestütztes Lernen *nt*; **~ center** *AmE*, **~ centre** *BrE* *n* COMP Computercenter *nt*; **~ circles** *n pl* COMP Computerkreise *m pl*; **~ code** *n* ADMIN Rechnercode *m*, COMP Computercode *m*; **~ communication** *n* COMP Computerkommunikation *f*; **~ company** *n* COMP Computerhersteller *m*; **~ conferencing** *n* COMP Computerkonferenz *f*; **~ consultant** *n* COMP EDV-Berater, in *m,f*; **~ control**

n COMP *of stocks* Computersteuerung *f*, Rechnersteuerung *f*; **~-controlled** *adj* COMP computergesteuert, rechnergesteuert; **~ crime insurance** *n* INS Computerkriminalitäts-Versicherung *f*, Computermißbrauch-Versicherung *f*; **~ department** *n* COMP EDV-Abteilung *f*; **~ design** *n* COMP *of hardware* Computerdesign *nt*; **~-driven** *adj* COMP computergesteuert, rechnergesteuert; **~ engineer** *n* COMP Computertechniker, in *m,f*; **~ engineering** *n* COMP Computertechnik *f*; **~ environment** *n* COMP Computerumgebung *f*; **~ expert** *n* COMP Computerexperte *m*, Computerexpertin *f*; **~ file** *n* COMP Datei *f*, Rechnerdatei *f*; **~ fraud** *n* LAW Computerbetrug *m*; **~ graphics** *n pl* COMP Computergrafik *f*; **~ hacker** *n* COMP Hacker, in *m,f* (*infrml*); **~ instruction** *n* COMP Befehl *m* in Maschinensprache, Maschinenbefehl *m*; **~-integrated** *adj* COMP computerintegriert; **~-integrated manufacturing** *n* (*CIM*) COMP, IND computerintegrierte Fertigung *f* (*CIM*), computerintegrierte Herstellung *f* (*CIM*)

computerization *n* COMP Computerisierung *f*

computerize *vt* COMP computerisieren

computerized *adj* COMP computerisiert; **~ accounting system** *n* ACC computergestütztes Buchungssystem *nt*; **~ banking** *n* BANK computerisiertes Bankwesen *nt*; **~ file** *n* COMP maschinelle Datei *f*; **~ management** *n* COMP computergestützte Verwaltung *f*

computer: **~ language** *n* COMP Maschinensprache *f*; **~ law** *n* COMP Computergesetz *nt*; **~-leasing business** *n* COMP Computerleasinggeschäft *nt*; **~-leasing firm** *n* COMP Computerleasingfirma *f*; **~ line** *n* COMP Computerverbindung *f*, Rechnerverbindung *f*; **~ literacy** *n* COMP Computerfachkenntnis *f*; **~-literate** *adj* COMP mit guten EDV-Kenntnissen; **~ log** *n* COMP Computerprotokoll *nt*, Rechnerprotokoll *nt*; **~ map** *n* COMP Bildschirmformat *nt*, Map *f*; **~ memory** *n* COMP Computerspeicher *m*; **~ network** *n* COMP Computernetzwerk *nt*, Rechnerverbund *m*; **~-operated** *adj* COMP computergesteuert, rechnergesteuert; **~ operation** *n* COMP Rechnerbetrieb *m*; **~ operator** *n* COMP Computerbediener, in *m,f*, Operator, in *m,f*; **~ output** *n* COMP Ausgabe *f* (*Ausg.*); **~ package** *n* COMP Computerpaket *nt*; **~ paper** *n* COMP Computerpapier *nt*; **~ phobia** *n* COMP Angst *f* vor Computern, Rechnerphobie *f*; **~ print-out** *n* COMP Computerausdruck *m*; **~ program** *n* COMP Computerprogramm *nt*; **~ programmer** *n* COMP Programmierer, in *m,f*; **~ programming** *n* COMP Programmieren *nt*, Programmierung *f*, MATH Programmierung *f*; **~ return** *n* TAX Computersteuererklärung *f*; **~ room** *n* COMP Computerraum *m*, Maschinenraum *m*; **~ run** *n* COMP Computerlauf *m*, Rechnerlauf *m*; **~ science** *n* COMP Informatik *f*; **~ scientist** *n* COMP Computerwissenschaftler, in *m,f*, Informatiker, in *m,f*; **~ screen** *n* COMP Bildschirm *m*; **~ security** *n* COMP Datensicherheit *f*; **~ services** *n pl* COMP Computerservice *m*; **~ services bureau** *n* COMP Computerservice *m*; **~ simulation** *n* COMP Computersimulation *f*; **~ software** *n* COMP Computersoftware *f*; **~ software licence** *BrE*, **~ software license** *AmE* *n* COMP Software-Lizenz *f*; **~ storage** *n* COMP Archivierung *f*; **~ strategy** *n* COMP EDV-Strategie *f*; **~ system** *n* COMP Computersystem *nt*, EDV-System *nt*; **~ technology** *n* COMP Computertechnik *f*; **~ time** *n* COMP Maschinenzeit *f*; **~ vendor** *n* COMP EDV-

Händler, in *m,f*; **~ virus** *n* COMP Computervirus *nt*; **~ whiz-kid** *n* *infrml* COMP Computerwunderkind *nt* (*infrml*); **~ wizard** *n* COMP Computergenie *nt*

computing *n* COMP *subject* Computerwissenschaft *f*, *calculation* Berechnen *nt*, Rechnen *nt*; **~ center** *AmE*, **~ centre** *BrE n* COMP Rechenzentrum *nt*; **~ power** *n* COMP Rechenleistung *f*; **~ room** *n* COMP Rechnerraum *m*; **~ show** *n* COMP Computermesse *f*; **~ speed** *n* COMP Rechengeschwindigkeit *f*

con: **~ artist** *n* *infrml* GEN COMM Betrüger, in *m,f*, Hochstapler, in *m,f*, LAW Hochstapler, in *m,f*

concatenate *vt* COMP *programming* ketten, verketten

concatenation *n* COMP *programming* Verkettung *f*; **~ of problems** *n* HRM Problemverflechtung *f*, Problemverkettung *f*

conceal *vt* COMP verstecken, GEN COMM verbergen, verdecken, verheimlichen, verschleiern, LAW *information* verschweigen, verstecken

concealed *adj* GEN COMM verborgen, verdeckt, verheimlicht, verschleiert; **~ assets** *n pl* ACC verschleierte Vermögenswerte *m pl*; **~ surplus of labor** *AmE*, **~ surplus of labour** *BrE n* ADMIN versteckter Arbeitskräfteüberschuß *m*; **~ unemployment** *n* ECON latente Arbeitslosigkeit *f*, verdeckte Arbeitslosigkeit *f*, versteckte Arbeitslosigkeit *f*

concealment *n* LAW *of information* Verschweigen *nt*; STOCK *of losses* Verschleierung *f*

concentrate *vt* GEN COMM konzentrieren

concentration *n* ECON Konzentration *f*, GEN COMM *attention* Konzentration *f*, *gathering* Ansammlung *f*; **~ banking** *n* BANK konzentriertes Banking *nt*; **~ of industry** *n* IND industrielle Zusammenballung *f*; **~ ratio** *n* ECON Konzentrationsmaß *nt*

concept *n* ACC Konzept *nt*, GEN COMM Begriff *m*, S&M Konzept *nt*; **~ of accrual** *n* ACC Konzept *nt* der Rechnungsabgrenzung; **~ of modular assembly** *n* IND Baukastenprinzip *nt*; **~ test** *n* S&M Akzeptanztest *m* einer Produktidee

conceptual: **~ framework** *n* ACC *basis of accounting standards* Buchungsplan *m*, Buchungsrichtlinien *f pl*; **~ model** *n* ADMIN Denkmodell *nt*

concern 1. *n* GEN COMM *worry* Problem *nt*, *business organization* Konzern *m*, Betrieb *m*, Unternehmen *nt*; 2. *vt* GEN COMM angehen, betreffen

concerning *adv* GEN COMM betrifft, betreffs, in bezug auf

concerted: **~ effort** *n* GEN COMM gemeinsame Bemühung *f*

concertina: **~ fold** *n* S&M Leporellofalzung *f*

concession *n* GEN COMM *distribution right* Konzession *f*, HRM *privilege* Vergünstigung *f*, LAW *of grant, licence* Konzession *f*, MGMNT Vergünstigung *f*, PROP Zugeständnis *nt*, S&M Gewerbeerlaubnis *f*, STOCK Bonifikation *f*, Preisnachlaß *m*, TAX behördliche Zulassung *f*, Konzession *f*

concessionaire *n* GEN COMM Konzessionär, in *m,f*, Konzessionsinhaber, in *m,f*, LAW, TAX Konzessionär, in *m,f*

concessional *adj* GEN COMM zu günstigen Bedingungen; **~ aid** *n* ECON *development assistance* Zollzugeständnis *nt*; **~ export** *n* IMP/EXP Konzessionsexport *m*; **~ terms** *n pl* GEN COMM günstige Konditionen *f pl*

concessionary: **~ rate** *n* GEN COMM, LEIS, S&M Sonderpreis *m*

concessions *n pl* GEN COMM Konzessionen *f pl*, *special treatment* Vorzugskonditionen *f pl*

conciliate *vt* FIN aussöhnen, schlichten, versöhnen, HRM *labour dispute* schlichten

conciliation *n* FIN Aussöhnung *f*, Schlichtung *f*, Versöhnung *f*, HRM, LAW *of labour dispute* Schlichtung *f*

Conciliation: **~ and Arbitration Commission** *n* HRM *in Australia* Schlichtungs- und Schiedskommission *f*

conciliation: **~ board** *n* GEN COMM, HRM, IND, STOCK Schlichtungsausschuß *m*, Schlichtungsstelle *f*; **~ officer** *n* *BrE* HRM Schlichter, in *m,f*, Vermittler, in *m,f*; **~ procedure** *n* HRM Vergleichsverfahren *nt*; **~ proceedings** *n pl* HRM Vergleichsverfahren *nt*

conciliator *n* HRM *in labour dispute* Schlichter, in *m,f*

concise *adj* GEN COMM knapp, konzis, kurz

conclude 1. *vt* GEN COMM *meeting* beenden, schließen, *deal, treaty* abschließen; 2. *vi* GEN COMM *meeting* enden, schließen

conclusion *n* ADMIN, GEN COMM, LAW *of agreement, contract* Abschluß *m*

conclusive *adj* GEN COMM endgültig; **~ evidence** *n* LAW zwingender Beweis *m*, PATENTS überzeugender Beweis *m*, schlagender Beweis *m*; **~ proof** *n* ADMIN zwingender Beweis *m*

concrete: **~ evidence** *n* LAW konkreter Beweis *m*

concur *vi* LAW *agree* übereinstimmen

concurrent *adj* LAW übereinstimmend; **~ processing** *n* COMP verzahnte Verarbeitung *f*

condemn *vt* LAW verurteilen

condemnation *n* LAW Verurteilung *f*, PROP Abbruchanordnung *f*, Kondemnation *f*, *compulsory purchase* Enteignungsrecht *nt* des Staates

condensation *n* ENVIR, IND Kondensation *f*

condensed *adj* GEN COMM kurz, S&M zusammengefaßt; **~ report** *n* GEN COMM Kurzbericht *m*

condition *n* COMP, GEN COMM Bedingung *f*, LAW Auflage *f*, *of contract* Bedingung *f*, wesentliche Vertragsbedingung *f*; ◆ **on ~ that** GEN COMM mit der Auflage, daß, unter der Voraussetzung, daß, unter der Bedingung, daß

conditional *adj* LAW bedingt; **~ acceptance** *n* LAW *contracts* bedingte Annahme *f*; **~ bond** *n* BANK *international banking* Zahlungsversprechen *nt* mit auflösender Bedingung; **~ branch** *n* COMP bedingte Verzweigung *f*; **~ clause** *n* LAW Vorbehaltsklausel *f*; **~ contract** *n* LAW an Bedingungen geknüpfter Vertrag *m*, bedingter Vertrag *m*; **~ employment contract** *n* HRM bedingter Arbeitsvertrag *m*; **~ endorsement** *n* FIN beschränktes Giro *nt*; **~ liabilities and burdens** *n pl* TAX *on property* aufschiebende bedingte Lasten *f pl*; **~ market order** *n* *BrE* STOCK *futures* eingeschränkter Bestensauftrag *m*; **~ offer** *n* LAW *international contract law* bedingtes Angebot *nt*; **~ protection** *n* PATENTS bedingter Schutz *m*; **~ sale** *n* LAW *contracts*, S&M Eigentumsvorbehalt *m*; **~ sales agreement** *n* S&M Kauf *m* unter Eigentumsvorbehalt

condition: **~ monitoring** *n* (*CM*) TRANSP *shipping* Zustandsüberwachung *f*; **~ precedent** *n* *AmE* LAW aufschiebende Bedingung *f*, aufschiebende Voraussetzung *f*

conditions *n pl* GEN COMM Vertragsbedingungen *f pl*, LAW *of contract* Bedingungen *f pl*, Vertragsbedingungen *f pl*; **~ of carriage** *n pl* TRANSP

Beförderungsbedingungen *f pl*; ~ **of contract** *n pl* LAW Vertragsbedingungen *f pl*; ~ **of employment** *n pl* HRM Arbeitsbedingungen *f pl*; ~ **of sale** *n pl* S&M Verkaufsbedingungen *f pl*; ~ **of tender** *n pl* GEN COMM Ausschreibungsbedingungen *f pl*; ~ **of transport** *n* TRANSP Beförderungsbedingungen *f pl*

condition: ~ **subsequent** *n AmE* LAW auflösende Bedingung *f*

conditions: ~ **of use** *n pl* GEN COMM Nutzungsbedingungen *f pl*

condominium *n AmE* (*condo*) PROP Eigentumswohnung *f*

Condorcet: ~ **criterion** *n* POL Condorcet-Kriterium *nt*

conducive: ~ **to** *adj* GEN COMM *growth* dienlich

conduct 1. *n* HRM Führung *f*, Verhalten *nt*, LAW *of lawsuit* Leitung *f*; **2.** *vt* GEN COMM *share sale* durchführen, *business* betreiben

conduct: ~ **money** *n* GEN COMM Zungenspesen *pl*

cone *n* MATH, TRANSP Konus *m*

confectioners: ~, **tobacconists and newsagents** *n pl BrE* (*CTN*) S&M Süßwarenhändler, Tabakhändler und Zeitungsverkäufer *pl*

confederate 1. *adj* POL konföderiert; **2.** *n* POL Konföderierte(r) *m* [decl. as adj]; **3.** *vi* POL sich konföderieren

confederation *n* POL Bund *m*, Konföderation *f*, lockeres Bündnis *nt*, Staatenbund *m*, Eidgenossenschaft *f* (*Sch*)

Confederation: ~ **of British Industry** *n* (*CBI*) IND Verband der britischen Industrie, ≈ Bundesverband der Deutschen Industrie *m* (*BDI*)

confer 1. *vt* LAW *right* übertragen, erteilen, verleihen; ♦ ~ **authority on sb** LAW jdm eine Vollmacht erteilen; ~ **the right on sb to do sth** GEN COMM jdn ermächtigen, etw zu tun; **2.** *vi* GEN COMM, MGMNT sich beraten

conference *n* GEN COMM, MGMNT Konferenz *f*, Tagung *f*, Sitzung *f*; ~ **board** *n* HRM Vermittlungsausschuß *m*; ~ **call** *n* COMMS, GEN COMM Konferenzschaltung *f*; ~ **delegate** *n* MGMNT Tagungsteilnehmer, in *m,f*, Konferenzteilnehmer, in *m,f*, Delegierte(r) *mf* [decl. as adj], Konferenzteilnehmer, in *m,f*, Sitzungsteilnehmer, in *m,f*; ~ **line** *n* TRANSP *shipping* Schiffahrtskonferenz *f*; ~ **member** *n* MGMNT Konferenzmitglied *nt*; ~ **proceedings** *n pl* ADMIN Tagungsbericht *m*, Tagungsprotokoll *nt*, Sitzungsprotokoll *nt*, Sitzungsbericht *m*, Konferenzbericht *m*, Konferenzprotokoll *nt*; ~ **report** *n* ADMIN Tagungsbericht *m*; ~ **site** *n* ADMIN, MGMNT Konferenzort *m*, Sitzungsort *m*, Tagungsort *m*; ~ **site location** *n* GEN COMM, MGMNT Lage *f* des Konferenzortes, Lage *f* des Sitzungsortes, Lage *f* des Tagungsortes; ~ **system** *n* MGMNT Konferenzliniensystem *nt*; ~ **table** *n* GEN COMM Verhandlungstisch *m*, MGMNT Konferenztisch *m*; ~ **venue** *n* ADMIN, MGMNT Konferenzort *m*, Tagungsort *m*, Veranstaltungsort *m*

conferment *n* LAW *of right* Übertragung *f*, Verleihung *f*

conferral *n* GEN COMM Erteilung *f*, LAW *of right* Übertragung *f*, Verleihung *f*

conferred *adj* LAW erteilt

confessed: ~ **judgment note** *n AmE* GEN COMM Schuldanerkenntnisschein *m*

confession *n* LAW *criminal law* Geständnis *nt*

confidence *n* GEN COMM Vertrauen *nt*; ~ **coefficient** *n* MATH Konfidenzkoeffizient *m*, Vertrauenskoeffizient *m*; ~ **game** *n* GEN COMM Betrugsspiel *nt*; ~ **interval** *n* MATH *statistics* Konfidenzintervall *nt*, Vertrauensintervall *nt*; ~ **level** *n* MATH *statistics* Konfidenzniveau *nt*, Vertrauensniveau *nt*; ~ **man** *n* GEN COMM gewerbsmäßiger Schwindler *m*; ~ **trick** *n* GEN COMM Schwindlertrick *m*; ~ **trickster** *n* GEN COMM gewerbsmäßiger Schwindler *m*, gewerbsmäßige Schwindlerin *f*, Betrüger, in *m,f*, Hochstapler, in *m,f*, LAW Hochstapler, in *m,f*

confidential *adj* GEN COMM, LAW vertraulich; ~ **information** *n* LAW vertrauliche Information *f*

confidentiality *n* LAW Vertraulichkeit *f*; ~ **agreement** *n* LAW *intellectual property* Geheimhaltungsvertrag *m*

confidential: ~ **report** *n* ADMIN vertraulicher Bericht *m*; ~ **secretary** *n* ADMIN, HRM, MGMNT Privatsekretär, in *m,f*

configuration *n* COMP Konfiguration *f*; ~ **control** *n* COMP Konfigurationssteuerung *f*

configure *vt* COMP *software, hardware* konfigurieren

confirm *vt* GEN COMM *appointment* bestätigen

confirmation *n* ACC Bestätigung *f*, GEN COMM *of plans* Bestätigung *f*, Billigung *f*, LAW *decision* Bekräftigung *f*, Bestätigung *f*; ~ **notes** *n pl* LAW *contracts* kaufmännisches Bestätigungsschreiben *nt*; ~ **notice** *n* GEN COMM Bestätigungsmitteilung *f*; ~ **of order** *n* COMMS, GEN COMM Auftragsbestätigung *f*; ~ **of payment** *n* LAW *contracts* Zahlungsbestätigung *f*; ~ **of renewal** *n* INS Bestätigung *f* der Erneuerung, Bestätigung *f* der Verlängerung, Erneuerungsbestätigung *f*, Verlängerungsbestätigung *f*

confirmed *adj* GEN COMM bestätigt; ~ **copy** *n* LAW *of legal document* bestätigte Kopie *f*, gleichlautende Abschrift *f*; ~ **credit** *n* BANK bestätigter Kredit *m*; ~ **irrevocable credit** *n* BANK bestätigter unwiderruflicher Kredit *m*; ~ **irrevocable letter of credit** *n* BANK bestätigtes unwiderrufliches Akkreditiv *nt*

confirming: ~ **bank** *n* BANK *international trade* Zahlungsgarantiebank für Auslandsaufträge; ~ **house** *n BrE* ECON *international trade* Exportvertreter, in *m,f*, Zahlungsgarant *m* im Außenhandelsverkehr

confiscate *vt* GEN COMM konfiszieren, IMP/EXP beschlagnahmen; ♦ ~ **sth from sb** GEN COMM etw von jdm beschlagnahmen, etw von jdm konfiszieren

confiscation *n* GEN COMM Konfiszierung *f*, IMP/EXP Beschlagnahme *f*, Beschlagnahmung *f*

conflagration: ~ **area** *n* INS Großbrandbereich *m*

conflict 1. *n* GEN COMM Konflikt *m*; **2.** *vi* GEN COMM in Widerspruch stehen, widersprechen

conflicting: ~ **evidence** *n* LAW widersprüchliche Aussagen *f pl*, widersprüchliches Beweismaterial *nt*; ~ **interests** *n pl* GEN COMM widerstreitende Interessen *f pl*

conflict: ~ **of interest** *n* GEN COMM Interessenkonflikt *m*

confluence *n* GEN COMM *interest* Zusammenströmen *nt*, Zustrom *m*; ~ **analysis** *n* (*CA*) MATH *statistics* Konfluenzanalyse *f*

conform *vi* GEN COMM *to rules* sich richten, *agree, comply with* entsprechen, übereinstimmen; ♦ ~ **to a standard** GEN COMM einer Norm entsprechen

conformity *n* GEN COMM Übereinstimmung *f*; ♦ **in ~ with** GEN COMM, LAW gemäß

conformity: ~ **to accounting rules** *n* ACC Übereinstimmung *f* mit den Buchhaltungsvorschriften

confront *vt* GEN COMM konfrontieren; ♦ ~ **sb with sth** GEN COMM jdn mit etw konfrontieren

confrontation *n* GEN COMM Konfrontation *f*

confutable *adj* LAW widerlegbar

congest *vt* COMMS überlasten

congested: ~ **urban area** *n* ECON überlastetes Ballungsgebiet *nt*

congestion *n* COMMS *telephone lines* Überlastung *f*, ENVIR Verstopfung *f*, GEN COMM *market* Andrang *m*, Stauung *f*, Ansammlung *f*, TRANSP Verstopfung *f*; ~ **surcharge** *n* TAX, TRANSP *shipping* Zuschlag *m* wegen Hafenüberfüllung

conglomerate: ~ **diversification** *n* ECON Konzerndiversifizierung *f*; ~ **merger** *n* ECON konglomerater Zusammenschluß *m*, Mischkonzern *m*

congress *n* MGMNT Kongreß *m*, Tagung *f*

Congress *n* *AmE* ECON konglomerater Zusammenschluß *m*, POL Kongreß *m*; ~ **of Industrial Organizations** *n* *AmE* (*CIO*) HRM *unions* Industriegewerkschaftsverband *m*, ≈ Deutscher Gewerkschaftsverband *m* (*DGB*)

Congressional: ~ **Budget and Impoundment Control Act** *n* *AmE* POL amerikanisches Gesetz zur Kontrolle des Haushaltsdefizits; ~ **Budget Office** *n* *AmE* (*CBO*) FIN, POL Haushaltsabteilung des Kongresses der Vereinigten Staaten von Amerika

congressional: ~ **party** *n* *AmE* POL Fraktion *f*

Congressman *n* *AmE* POL Kongreßabgeordnete(r) *m* [decl. as adj]

congress: ~ **participant** *n* MGMNT Kongreßteilnehmer, in *m,f*

Congresswoman *n* *AmE* POL Kongreßabgeordnete *f* [decl. as adj]

congruence *n* GEN COMM Deckungsgleichheit *f*, Übereinstimmung *f*

congruent *adj* LAW übereinstimmend; ♦ ~ **with** GEN COMM übereinstimmend mit, deckungsgleich mit

conjunction: **in** ~ **with** *phr* GEN COMM in Verbindung mit; ~ **of circumstances** *n* GEN COMM Zusammentreffen *nt* von Umständen

con: ~ **man** *n* *infrml* GEN COMM Betrüger *m*, Hochstapler *m*, LAW Hochstapler *m*, Schwindler *m*

connect *vt* COMMS, COMP verbinden, anschließen; ♦ ~ **with** COMMS, COMP verbinden mit, anschließen an [+acc]

connecting: ~ **carrier** *n* TRANSP Anschlußspediteur *m*; ~ **flight** *n* TRANSP Anschlußflug *m*

connection *n* COMP, GEN COMM Verbindung *f*, MEDIA, POL Querverbindung *f*, TRANSP Anschluß *m*, Verkehrsverbindung *f*; ~ **time** *n* COMP Verbindungszeit *f*

consciousness: ~ **of guilt** *n* GEN COMM Schuldbewußtsein *nt*

consecutive *adj* GEN COMM aufeinanderfolgend; ~ **days** *n pl* GEN COMM aufeinanderfolgende Tage *m pl*

consecutively *adv* MEDIA, PATENTS fortlaufend

consensus *n* GEN COMM Konsens *m*, Übereinstimmung *f*, POL Konsens *m*

consensus ad idem *phr* GEN COMM *mutual assent* Willenseinigung *f*

consensus: ~ **agreement** *n* GEN COMM Willenseinigung *f*

consent 1. *n* GEN COMM Zustimmung *f*, LAW Einverständnis *nt*; **2.** *vi* GEN COMM zustimmen, einwilligen

consent: ~ **decree** *n* LAW Unterwerfungsentscheidung *f*

consequence *n* GEN COMM Auswirkung *f*, Folge *f*

consequential: ~ **damage** *n* INS Folgeschaden *m*, mittel-

barer Schaden *m*; ~ **effect of a court action** *n* LAW Folgewirkung *f* eines Gerichtverfahrens; ~ **harm caused by a defect** *n* LAW *contracts* Mangelfolgeschaden *m*; ~ **loss** *n* INS Folgeschaden *m*; ~ **loss policy** *n* INS Folgeschaden-Police *f*

conservation *n* ENVIR Erhaltung *f*, Konservierung *f*, Naturschutz *m*; ~ **camp** *n* ENVIR Erhaltungscamp *nt*

conservationist *n* ENVIR Naturschützer, in *m,f*

conservatism *n* GEN COMM Grundsatz *m* der Vorsicht, POL Konservatismus *m*; ~ **principle** *n* ACC Grundsatz *m* der Vorsicht

conservative *adj* GEN COMM *spending, estimate* vorsichtig, konservativ, POL konservativ; ~ **accounting** *n* ACC Vorsichtsprinzip *nt* in der Buchhaltung; ~ **estimate** *n* GEN COMM vorsichtige Schätzung *f*, konservative Schätzung *f*

Conservative: ~ **Party** *n* *BrE* POL konservative Partei *f*

consider *vt* GEN COMM überlegen; ♦ ~ **sb for a post** HRM jdn für eine Position in Betracht ziehen

considerable *adj* GEN COMM bedeutend, erheblich, *amount* beträchtlich

consideration *n* ADMIN Gegenleistung *f*, GEN COMM Berücksichtigung *f*, Überlegung *f*, INS Berücksichtigung *f*, Rücksichtnahme *f*, LAW *contracts* Rechtspflicht *f*, *contract* Gegenleistung *f*, STOCK Gegenleistung *f*; ♦ **in** ~ **of** GEN COMM in Anbetracht [+gen]

consign *vt* IMP/EXP liefern, schicken, versenden, TRANSP *goods* übersenden, liefern, schicken, versenden

consignation *n* TRANSP Übersendung *f*, Versand *m*, Zusendung *f*

consignee *n* IMP/EXP, TRANSP Empfänger, in *mf*; ~ **of goods** *n* LAW *contracts* Warenempfänger, in *m,f*

consignment *n* IMP/EXP Konsignation *f*, Versendung *f*, TRANSP Sendung *f*, Versand *m*, Konsignation *f*; ♦ **on** ~ IMP/EXP, TRANSP in Kommission, in Konsignation

consignment: ~ **goods** *n pl* S&M Kommissionsware *f*; ~ **insurance** *n* INS Frachtversicherung *f*; ~ **note** *n* (*CN*) TRANSP Frachtbrief *m*, Ladeschein *m*, Versandanzeige *f*, Warenbegleitschein *m*; ~ **note control label number** *n* TRANSP Nummer *f* des Frachtbriefkontrolletiketts; ~ **sale** *n* S&M Kommissionsverkauf *m*, TRANSP Konsignationsverkauf *m*; ~ **selling** *n* S&M Kommissionsverkauf *m*; ~ **with value declared** *n* LAW *contracts* Wertsendung *f*

consignor *n* COMMS Absender, in *m,f*, IMP/EXP, TRANSP Absender, in *m,f*, Konsignant, in *m,f*, Versender, in *m,f*

consistency *n* ACC *of procedures* Kontinuität *f*, GEN COMM Übereinstimmung *f*; ~ **check** *n* GEN COMM Übereinstimmungsprüfung *f*; ~ **principle** *n* ACC Prinzip *nt* der Folgerichtigkeit

consistent *adj* GEN COMM beständig, LAW *claims, statements* vereinbar, MGMNT *in methods* konsequent; ♦ ~ **with** LAW übereinstimmend mit, vereinbar mit

consolidate 1. *vt* ACC, BANK konsolidieren, ECON konsolidieren, zusammenfassen; **2.** *vi* FIN konsolidieren, verschmelzen

consolidated *adj* ACC, BANK, FIN konsolidiert, GEN COMM zusammengefaßt, konsolidiert, Sammel-; ♦ **on a** ~ **basis** ACC, FIN auf einer konsolidierten Basis

consolidated: ~ **accounting** *n* *BrE* ACC *including foreign currency* konsolidierte Rechnungslegung *f*; ~ **accounts** *n pl* ACC konsolidierter Abschluß *m*, Konzernabschluß *m*; ~ **annuities** *n pl* *BrE* FIN konsolidierte Papiere *nt pl*, konsolidierte Staatsanleihen *f pl*, Staatsrente *f*;

~ **assets** *n pl* FIN konsolidiertes Konzernvermögen *nt*; ~ **audited accounts** *n pl* ACC geprüfter Konzernabschluß *m*; ~ **balance sheet** *n* ACC Gemeinschaftsbilanz *f*, Gesamtbilanz *f*, konsolidierte Bilanz *f*, Konzernbilanz *f*, FIN Konzernbilanz *f*; ~~**cargo container service** *n* TRANSP Sammelgut-Container-Service *m*; ~ **cargo service** *n* (*CCS*) TRANSP Sammelfrachtdienst *m*, Sammelgut-Service *m*; ~ **cash budget** *n* FIN bereinigtes Kassenbudget *nt*; ~ **cash flow** *n* ACC konsolidierter Cashflow *m*; ~ **cash flow statement** *n* ACC konsolidierter Cashflow-Bericht *m*; ~ **data plate** *n* TRANSP Schild *nt* mit gesammelten Daten; ~ **delivery** *n* TRANSP gemeinsame Auslieferung *f*, zusammengestellte Lieferung *f*; ~ **figures** *n pl* ACC konsolidierte Zahlen *f pl*; ~ **financial statement** *n* ACC konsolidierter Abschluß *m*, Konzernabschluß *m*, Konzernbilanz *f*, FIN Konzernbilanz *f*; ~ **fund** *n BrE* ECON konsolidierter Staatsfonds *m*; ~ **fund standing services** *n pl BrE* ECON Staatsschuldendienst *m*

Consolidated: ~ **Metropolitan Statistical Area** *n AmE* (*CMSA*) ADMIN zentrale statistische Erfassung *f* im Großstadtbereich

consolidated: ~ **net profit** *n* ACC konsolidierter Reingewinn *m*; ~ **rate** *n* TRANSP konsolidierter Satz *m*, Pauschalrate *f*; ~ **revenue fund** *n* FIN konsolidierter Ertragsfonds *m*; ~ **sales** *n pl* FIN Konzernumsatz *m*; ~ **statement of condition** *n AmE* FIN konsolidierter Finanzstatus *m*; ~ **stock** *n AmE* FIN konsolidierte Papiere *nt pl*, konsolidierte Staatsanleihen *f pl*, Staatsrente *f*; ~ **tape** *n* STOCK zusammengefaßter Börsenticker *m*; ~ **tax return** *n* TAX *affiliated group* gemeinsame Steuererklärung *f*

consolidation *n* ACC *of accounts* Erstellung *f* eines konsolidierten Abschlusses, BANK, ECON *of holdings, business* Konsolidierung *f*, FIN Verschmelzung *f*, *of holdings, business* Konsolidierung *f*, TRANSP Sammelladung *f*; ~ **depot** *n* TRANSP Sammellager *nt*; ~ **loan** *n* FIN Konsolidierungsdarlehen *nt*; ~ **method** *n* ACC *annual accounts* Konsolidierungsgrundsätze *m pl*

consolidator *n* TRANSP Verfrachter, in *m,f* von Sammelladungen

consols *n pl BrE* FIN, GEN COMM fundierte Staatsanleihe *f*

consortium *n* BANK Konsortium *nt*, FIN Konsortium *nt*, Syndikat *nt*, GEN COMM Interessengemeinschaft *f*, Syndikat *nt*, HRM *ad hoc* Arbeitsgemeinschaft *f*, LAW Konsortium *nt*, *contracts* eheliche Gemeinschaft *f*, PROP, STOCK Konsortium *nt*; ~ **bank** *n* BANK, FIN Konsortialbank *f*; ~ **of banks** *n* BANK Bankenkonsortium *nt*

conspectus *n* FIN, GEN COMM *as regards content, tabular, comparative* Zusammenfassung *f*

conspicuous: ~ **consumption** *n* ECON auffälliger Konsum *m*, Geltungskonsum *m*

conspiracy *n* GEN COMM, LAW Verschwörung *f*

conspire *vi* GEN COMM, LAW sich verschwören

constant 1. *adj* GEN COMM konstant; ◆ **at ~ prices** GEN COMM bei konstanten Preisen; **2.** *n* COMP, MATH Konstante *f*

constant: ~ **capital** *n* ECON konstantes Kapital *nt*; ~ **cost** *n* ADMIN fixe Kosten *pl*; ~ **dollar plan** *n BrE* GEN COMM konstanter Dollarplan *m*; ~ **dollars** *n pl AmE* ECON Basisdollar *m pl*, Dollar *m pl* im Bezugsjahr; ~ **elasticity of substitution production function** *n* (*CES production function*) ECON Produktionsfunktion *f* der konstanten Substitutionselastizität (*CES-Produktionsfunktion*); ~ **issue** *n* STOCK Daueremission *f*

constantly *adv* ADMIN laufend

constant: ~ **payment loan** *n BrE* BANK Darlehen *nt* mit konstanten Raten, Darlehen *nt* mit konstanten Ratenzahlungen; ~ **payment mortgage** *n* FIN Abzahlungshypothek *f*; ~ **price** *n* ECON konstanter Preis *m*; ~ **returns to scale** *n pl* ECON konstanter Skalenertrag *m*; ~ **risk** *n* INS gleichbleibendes Risiko *nt*

constituent: ~ **company** *n* STOCK verbundenes Unternehmen *nt*

constitute *vt* PATENTS *infringement* darstellen, konstituieren

constituted *adj* GEN COMM gegründet (*gegr.*), LAW *a trust* ernannt

constitution *n* LAW Verfassung *f*, Statuten *nt pl*, POL Verfassung *f*

constitutional *adj* LAW, POL verfassungsgemäß, verfassungsmäßig; ~ **foundation** *n* POL verfassungsmäßige Gründung *f*; ~ **strike** *n* HRM verfassungsmäßiger Streik *m*

constrain *vt* GEN COMM beschränken

constrained: ~ **market pricing** *n* ECON gehemmte Marktpreisbildung *f*

constraining: ~ **factor** *n* ECON *restricting production or sale* Engpaßfaktor *m*

constraint *n* ECON Nebenbedingung *f*, Restriktion *f*, Zwang *m*, LAW Nötigung *f*, Zwang *m*

construct *vt* GEN COMM errichten, IND bauen, MATH konstruieren, PROP bauen

construction *n* IND, PROP Auslegung *f*, Bau *m*, Konstruktion *f*; ◆ **under ~** IND im Bau, im Bauzustand

construction: ~ **cost index** *n BrE* STOCK Baukostenindex *m*; ~ **firm** *n* PROP Bauunternehmer, in *m,f*; ~ **industry** *n* IND, PROP Baugewerbe *nt*, Bauindustrie *f*, Bauwesen *nt*; ~ **loan** *n* BANK Baudarlehen *nt*; ~ **project** *n* PROP Bauvorhaben *nt*; ~ **rate** *n* IND Baurate *f*; ~ **site** *n* IND, PROP Bau *m*, Bauplatz *m*, Baustelle *f*; ~ **slump** *n* ECON Baurezession *f*; ~ **subsidies** *n pl* IND *shipping* Bausubventionen *f pl*; ~ **and use** *n BrE* LAW Konstruktion *f* und Nutzung *f*; ~ **and use regulations** *n pl* (*C&U regulations*) IND Bau- und Anwendungsbestimmungen *f pl*, Bau- und Verwendungsbestimmungen *f pl*; ~ **worker** *n* IND Bauarbeiter, in *m,f*

constructive *adj* GEN COMM konstruktiv; ~ **dismissal** *n* HRM Kündigung durch Arbeitnehmer auf Drängen des Arbeitgebers; ~ **eviction** *n* PROP Beeinträchtigung *f* des Besitzes durch den Verpächter; ~ **notice** *n AmE* LAW zurechenbare Kenntnis *f*; ~ **receipt** *n* TAX fingierte Empfangsbestätigung *f*, konstruierter Einkommenszufluß *m*; ~ **receipt of income** *n AmE* TAX als im Vorjahr zugeflossen behandeltes Einkommen *nt*, konstruierter Einkommenszufluß *m*; ~ **total loss** *n* (*CTL*) INS *marine* angenommener Totalverlust *m*; ~ **total loss only** *n* (*CTLO*) INS *marine* angenommener Totalverlust *m*

consul *n* POL Konsul *m*

Consul-General *n* GEN COMM, POL Generalkonsul *m*

consular: ~ **declaration** *n* (*CD*) POL konsularische Erklärung *f*, Konsulatserklärung *f*; ~ **fees** *n pl* ADMIN, IMP/EXP Konsulatsgebühren *f pl*

consulate *n* POL Konsulat *nt*

consult 1. *vt* GEN COMM befragen, konsultieren, MGMNT konsultieren; **2.** *vi* GEN COMM, MGMNT sich beraten

consultancy *n* GEN COMM Beratungsfirma *f*; **~ agreement** *n* GEN COMM Beratervertrag *m*; **~ service** *n* ECON Beratungsdienst *m*; **~ work** *n* GEN COMM Beratungstätigkeit *f*

consultant *n* GEN COMM, HRM Berater, in *m,f*, MGMNT Berater, in *m,f*, Gutachter, in *m,f*; **~ engineer** *n* IND beratende Ingenieurin *f*, beratender Ingenieur *m*

consultation *n* GEN COMM Beratung *f*, *hearing* Anhörung *f*, HRM Rücksprache *f*; ♦ **in ~ with** GEN COMM in Beratung mit

consultative *adj* GEN COMM beratend; **~ body** *n* GEN COMM *committees and boards* beratendes Gremium *nt*; **~ committee** *n* ADMIN beratender Ausschuß *m*

Consultative: ~ Committee *n* ADMIN Beratungsausschuß *m*

consultative: **~-democratic** *adj* MGMNT *leadership style* konsultativ-demokratisch

consulting *n* GEN COMM Beratung *f*; **~ activity** *n* GEN COMM Beratungstätigkeit *f*; **~ agency** *n* ADMIN Beratungsstelle *f*; **~ contract** *n* GEN COMM Beratervertrag *m*; **~ engineer** *n* GEN COMM Beratungsingenieur, in *m,f*, technische Beratungsfirma *f*; **~ firm** *n* GEN COMM Beratungsfirma *f*, Beratungsunternehmen *nt*; **~ service** *n* GEN COMM Beratungsservice *m*

consume *vt* ECON konsumieren, verbrauchen, S&M konsumieren

consumer *n* ECON, S&M Konsument *m*, Verbraucher, in *m,f*; **~ acceptance** *n* S&M Akzeptanz *f*; **~ advertising** *n* S&M Kundenwerbung *f*, Verbraucherwerbung *f*; **~ advisory service** *n* S&M Verbraucherberatungsdienst *m*; **~ banking** *n* BANK Privatkundengeschäft *nt* der Banken; **~ behavior** *AmE*, **~ behaviour** *BrE* *n* S&M Verbraucherverhalten *nt*; **~ benefit** *n* S&M Verbrauchernutzen *m*; **~ brand** *n* S&M Verbrauchermarke *f*; **~ buying power** *n* S&M Kaufkraft *f* des Kunden; **~ choice** *n* S&M Verbraucherwahl *f*, Wahl *f* des Verbrauchers; **~ company** *n* S&M Verbraucherunternehmen *nt*

Consumer: ~ Credit Act *n* *BrE* ADMIN, LAW Verbraucherkreditgesetz *nt*

consumer: **~ credit market** *n* BANK Konsumkreditmarkt *m*

Consumer: ~ Credit Protection Act *n* *AmE* ADMIN, LAW Verbraucherkreditgesetz *nt*

consumer: **~ demand** *n* S&M *market research* Verbrauchernachfrage *f*; **~ durables** *n pl* ECON dauerhafte Konsumgüter *nt pl*, Gebrauchsgüter *nt pl*, S&M *type of goods* langlebige Gebrauchsgüter *nt pl*; **~ equilibrium** *n* ECON Ausgleich *m* der Grenznutzen; **~ expectation** *n* S&M Verbrauchererwartung *f*; **~ expenditure** *n* ECON Konsumausgaben *f pl*, Verbrauchsausgaben *f pl*; **~ expenditure survey** *n* *AmE* ECON *accounting* Verbrauchsausgaben-Erhebung *f*; **~ finance company** *n* FIN Teilzahlungsbank *f*; **~ goods** *n pl* S&M Konsumgüter *nt pl*, Verbrauchsgüter *nt pl*; **~ goods industry** *n* IND Konsumgüterindustrie *f*; **~ habit** *n* S&M Verbrauchergewohnheit *f*, Konsumgewohnheit *f*; **~ hardgoods** *n pl* GEN COMM Gebrauchsgüter *nt pl*; **~ installment loan** *AmE*, **~ instalment loan** *BrE* *n* BANK Ratenkredit *m*, Kundenkredit *m*

consumerism *n* ECON Konsumerismus *m*, Verbraucher-

schutzbewegung *f*, LAW *protection of the interests of consumers* Verbraucherschutz *m*, S&M Konsumerismus *m*, Verbrauchertum *nt*, *protection of the interests of the consumer* Verbraucherschutz *m*

consumer: **~ issue** *n* S&M Verbraucherfrage *f*

consumerist *n* LAW, S&M Verbraucherschützer *m*

consumer: **~ law** *n* LAW Verbraucherrecht *nt*; **~ leasing** *n* BANK Kundenleasing *nt*; **~-led marketing policy** *n* S&M *marketing* am Verbraucher orientierte Marketingpolitik *f*; **~ lending** *n* BANK Konsumentengeschäft *nt*; **~ loan** *n* BANK Verbraucherkredit *m*; **~ loan institute** *n* FIN Finanzierungsgesellschaft *f* für Kleinkredite; **~ loyalty** *n* S&M Verbrauchertreue *f*; **~ magazine** *n* MEDIA, S&M Verbrauchermagazin *nt*; **~ market** *n* S&M Konsumgütermarkt *m*; **~ marketing** *n* S&M *marketing* Verbrauchermarketing *nt*; **~ needs** *n pl* S&M Konsumbedarf *m*; **~ organization** *n* S&M Verbraucherorganisation *f*, Verbraucherverband *m*; **~ orientation** *n* S&M Konsumorientierung *f*; **~-oriented** *adj* S&M benutzerorientiert; **~-oriented product** *n* S&M verbraucherorientiertes Produkt *nt*; **~ panel** *n* S&M *market research* repräsentative Verbrauchergruppe *f*; **~ patterns** *n pl* S&M Verbraucherverhalten *nt*; **~ policy** *n* S&M Verbraucherpolitik *f*; **~ preference** *n* S&M Konsumentenpräferenz *f*; **~ price** *n* S&M Verbraucherpreis *m*; **~ price index** *n* (*CPI*) ECON Verbraucherpreisindex *m*, Index *m* der Verbraucherpreise; **~ product** *n* S&M Verbrauchsgut *nt*; **~ products** *n pl* S&M Konsumgüter *nt pl*, Verbrauchsgüter *nt pl*; **~ profile** *n* S&M Verbraucherprofil *nt*; **~ protection** *n* LAW, S&M Verbraucherschutz *m*; **~ protection legislation** *n* LAW, S&M Verbraucherschutzgesetzgebung *f*; **~ protection legislation of sale** *n* LAW Gesetz *nt* zum Schutz des Verbrauchers beim Kauf; **~ reaction** *n* S&M Verbraucherreaktion *f*; **~ relations manager** *n* MGMNT Kundendienstleiter, in *m,f*; **~ requirement** *n* S&M Anforderung *f* des Verbrauchers; **~ research** *n* S&M Konsumforschung *f*; **~ resistance** *n* S&M Käuferunlust *f*; **~ response** *n* S&M Verbraucherantwort *f*

Consumers': **~ Advisory Council** *n* *AmE* (*CAC*) WEL Rat für Verbraucherberatung; **~ Association** *n* (*CA*) S&M Verbraucherverband *m*

consumer: **~ satisfaction** *n* GEN COMM Verbraucherzufriedenheit *f*

Consumers': **~ Consultative Council** *n* ECON Rat *m* für Verbraucherberatung

consumers': **~ cooperative** *n* (*co-op*) GEN COMM Konsumgenossenschaft *f*

consumer: **~ society** *n* ECON Konsumgesellschaft *f*; **~ sovereignty** *n* ECON Konsumentensouveränität *f*, Verbrauchermacht *f*

consumers': **~ panel** *n* S&M Verbraucherpanel *nt*

consumer: **~ spending** *n* ECON Verbraucherausgaben *f pl*; **~'s surplus** *n* ECON Konsumentenrente *f*; **~ survey** *n* S&M Verbraucherbefragung *f*, Verbraucherumfrage *f*; **~ test** *n* S&M Verbrauchertest *m*; **~ trend** *n* S&M Verbrauchertrend *m*; **~ want** *n* S&M Verbraucherwunsch *m*; **~ watchdog** *n* S&M Verbraucherüberwachungsorganisation *f*

consumption *n* (*C*) ECON Konsum *m*, Verbrauch *m*, GEN COMM Verzehr *m*; **~ function** *n* ECON Konsumfunktion *f*; **~ goods** *n pl* ECON, ENVIR, S&M Verbrauchsgüter *nt* *pl*; **~ pattern** *n* ECON Verbrauchsgewohnheiten *f pl*; **~ per capita** *n* ECON Pro-Kopf-Verbrauch *m*

cont. *abbr* (*continued*) GEN COMM ff. (*fortgesetzt*), fortg. (*fortgesetzt*)

contact *n* GEN COMM *communication* Kontakt *m*, *person* Kontaktperson *f*; **~ damage** *n* TRANSP *shipping* Kollisionschaden *m*, Kontaktschaden *m*; **~ report** *n* AmE S&M Kontaktbericht *m*

contain *vt* GEN COMM *demand, inflation* eindämmen, eingrenzen

container *n* TRANSP Behälter *m*, Container *m*, Transportbehälter *m*; **~ base** *n* (*CB*) TRANSP *shipping* Containerboden *m*; **~ berth** *n* TRANSP *shipping* Containerplatz *m*; **~ bill** *n* IMP/EXP *shipping* Containerkonnossement *nt*, Frachtbrief *m* für Transportbehälter, TRANSP *shipping* Containerkonnossement *nt*; **~ bill of lading** *n* TRANSP Containerfrachtbrief *m*; **~ block** *n* TRANSP *shipping* Containerblock *m*; **~ car** *n* AmE TRANSP *rail* Behälterwagen *m*, Behälterwaggon *m*, Containerwagen *m*, Containerwaggon *m*; **~ control** *n* (*CC*) TRANSP Containerkontrolle *f*; **~ crane** *n* TRANSP Containerkran *m*; **~ depot** *n* TRANSP *shipping* Containerdepot *nt*; **~ dock** *n* TRANSP Containerkai *m*; **~ dues** *n pl* TRANSP *shipping* Containergebühren *f pl*; **~ frame** *n* TRANSP *shipping* Containerrahmen *m*; **~ freight station** *n* (*CFS*) TRANSP *shipping* Containerfrachtstation *f*, Containerpackstation *f*; **~ head** *n* TRANSP *shipping* Containerkopf *m*; **~ import cargo manifest** *n* TRANSP *shipping* Containerimportfracht-Manifest *nt*

containerization *n* TRANSP Umstellung *f* auf Container, Verladung *f* in Container

containerize *vt* TRANSP containerisieren, in Container laden, in Container verpacken

containerized *adj* TRANSP auf Container umgestellt, in Container verladen; **~ shipping** *n* TRANSP Containerspedition *f*, Containerverladung *f*, Containerversand *m*, Containerverschiffung *f*

container: **~ leasing** *n* TRANSP Containerleasing *nt*; **~ line** *n* TRANSP Containerreihe *f*; **~ load** *n* TRANSP Containerladung *f*; **~ market** *n* TRANSP Containermarkt *m*; **~ on flat car** *n* AmE (*cf container on flat wagon BrE*) TRANSP Container *m* auf Plattformwagen, Flachwagencontainer *m*; **~ on flat wagon** *n* BrE (*cf container on flat car AmE*) TRANSP Container *m* auf Plattformwagen, Flachwagencontainer *m*, K-Wagencontainer *m*; **~ operation** *n* TRANSP Containerspedition *f*; **~ operator** *n* TRANSP Containerspediteur *m*, Containerunternehmer *m*; **~ packing certificate** *n* TRANSP Containerverpackungs-Zertifikat *nt*; **~ park** *n* TRANSP Containerpark *m*; **~ partload** *n* TRANSP Containerstückgut *nt*; **~ pool** *n* TRANSP Containerpool *m*; **~ port** *n* TRANSP Containerhafen *m*; **~ service** *n* TRANSP Containerdienst *m*; **~ service tariff** *n* (*CST*) TRANSP Containerdienst-Tarif *m*; **~ ship** *n* TRANSP Containerschiff *nt*; **~ space allocation** *n* TRANSP Containerplatzzuteilung *f*; **~ stack** *n* TRANSP Containerstapel *m*; **~ stuffing** *n* TRANSP Containerfüllung *f*; **~ terminal** *n* TRANSP *shipping* Containerterminal *nt*; **~ traffic** *n* TRANSP Containerverkehr *m*; **~ transport** *n* TRANSP Behältertransport *m*, Containertransport *m*; **~ unstuffing** *n* TRANSP Containerentladung *f*; **~ use** *n* TRANSP Containerverwendung *f*; **~ user analysis** *n* TRANSP Containeranwenderanalyse *f*; **~ utilization** *n* TRANSP Containernutzung *f*; **~ wagon** *n* BrE (*cf*

container car *AmE*) TRANSP *rail* Behälterwagen *m*, Behälterwaggon *m*, Containerwagen *m*, Containerwaggon *m*; **~ yard** *n* (*CY*) TRANSP Containerdepot *nt*

containment *n* ECON *demand, credit* Eindämmung *f*, GEN COMM, POL Begrenzung *f*, Beherrschung *f*, Eingrenzung *f*, Zügelung *f*, Zurückhaltung *f*

contaminate *vt* ENVIR kontaminieren, verseuchen, verunreinigen

contaminated *adj* ENVIR verseucht; **~ site** *n* ENVIR Altlasten *f pl*

contamination *n* ENVIR Verschmutzung *f*

contango *n* STOCK Contango *m*, Prolongation *f*, Report *m*; **~ business** *n* BrE STOCK Reportgeschäft *nt*; **~ rate** *n* FIN Prolongationsgebühr *f*, STOCK Prolongationsgebühr *f*, Reportsatz *m*

contd *abbr* (*continued*) GEN COMM ff. (*fortgesetzt*), fortg. (*fortgesetzt*)

contemplate *vt* LAW beabsichtigen

contemporaneous: **~ externality** *n* ECON zeitgleiche externe Effekte *m pl*, zeitgleiche Externalitäten *f pl*; **~ performance** *n* LAW *contracts* Zug-um-Zug-Erfüllung

contempt: **~ of court** *n* LAW Mißachtung *f* des Gerichts; ◆ **in ~ of court** LAW unter Mißachtung des Gerichts

contending: **~ claims** *n pl* LAW widerstreitende Ansprüche *m pl*

content *n* PATENTS *of the abstract* Inhalt *m*

contention *n* COMMS, COMP Konkurrenzbetrieb *m*, GEN COMM Behauptung *f*

contentment *n* GEN COMM Zufriedenheit *f*

contents *n pl* COMP *of file, document* Inhalt *m*, GEN COMM *of package* Einwaage *f*, Inhalt *m*, Inhaltsausgabe *f*; **~ of contract** *n pl* LAW Vertragsinhalt *m*

contest 1. *n* GEN COMM Wettbewerb *m*, Wettstreit *m*, Streit *m*; **2.** *vt* LAW *will* anfechten, POL, S&M umkämpfen

contestable *adj* GEN COMM bestreitbar, INS, LAW anfechtbar; **~ clause** *n* INS anfechtbare Klausel *f*; **~ market** *n* ECON bestreitbarer Markt *m*, Markt *m* ohne Zutritts- und Austrittsschranken

contestation *n* GEN COMM Bestreiten *nt*, LAW Anfechtung *f*

contested *adj* POL, S&M *market* umkämpft; **~ claim** *n* FIN bestrittener Anspruch *m*

context *n* GEN COMM Zusammenhang *m*; **~-sensitive** *adj* COMP kontextabhängig, kontextsensitiv; **~-sensitive help** *n* COMP *software* kontextabhängige Hilfe *f*, kontextsensitive Hilfe *f*

contiguous *adj* COMP benachbart

continent *n* POL Kontinent *m*

Continent: **the ~** *n* BrE GEN COMM *mainland Europe* das europäische Festland *nt*

continental *adj* POL kontinental; **~ trade** *n* ECON, S&M *international trade* Europahandel *m*

continent: **~ of Europe** *n* GEN COMM europäischer Kontinent *m*

contingencies: **~ vote** *n* FIN Zufallswahl *f*

contingency *n* GEN COMM Eventualverbindlichkeit *f*, ungewisses künftiges Ereignis *nt*; **~ arrangements** *n pl* GEN COMM Alternativvereinbarungen *f pl*; **~ budget** *n* FIN Eventualhaushalt *m*; **~ claims contracting** *n* HRM befristete Einstellung *f*; **~ fund** *n* FIN *personal budgets* außerordentlicher Rücklagenfonds *m*, Delkredere-

Fonds *m*; **~ management** *n* MGMNT Rücklagenmanagement *nt*; **~ payments** *n pl* ACC *budgeting* Beträge *m pl* im Falle eines unvorhergesehenen Ereignisses; **~ plan** *n* FIN Krisenplan *m*, Notstandsplan *m*, GEN COMM Alternativplan *m*, Schubladenplan *m*, MGMNT Ausweichplan *m*, Krisenplan *m*, Schubladenplan *m* (*infrml*); **~ planning** *n* GEN COMM Alternativplanung *f*, Schubladenplanung *f*, MGMNT flexible Planung *f*, Schubladenplanung *f*; **~ provision** *n* ACC Rücklage *f* für ungewisse künftige Ereignisse; **~ reserve** *n* MGMNT Sicherheitsrücklage *f*, Verlustrückstellung *f*; **~ table** *n* MATH *statistics* Kontingenztabelle *f*; **~ theory** *n* MGMNT Kontingenztheorie *f*

contingent *adj* GEN COMM *liability* ungewiß; **~ asset** *n* ACC bedingtes Fremdkapital *nt*, Eventualforderung *f*; **~ business interruption insurance** *n* INS bedingte Betriebsstillstandsversicherung *f*, bedingte Betriebsunterbrechungsversicherung *f*; **~ claim** *n* ACC Eventualforderung *f*; **~ consideration** *n* GEN COMM Eventualvergütung *f*; **~ duty** *n* IMP/EXP Ausgleichszoll *m*; **~ fee** *n* GEN COMM Erfolgshonorar *nt*; **~ liabilities** *n pl* LAW bedingte Verbindlichkeiten *f pl*; **~ liability** *n* ACC, FIN Eventualverbindlichkeit *f*, LAW Eventualverpflichtung *f*, Eventualverbindlichkeit *f*; **~ market** *n* INS bedingter Markt *m*, eventueller Markt *m*; **~ order** *n* STOCK gekoppelter Wertpapierauftrag *m*; **~ right** *n* LAW *contracts* Anwartschaftsrecht *nt*

continual: **~ professional education** *n* HRM, WEL Weiterbildung *f*

continuation: **~ clause** *n* (*CC*) INS Prolongationsklausel *f*, Verlängerungsklausel *f*

continue *vt* GEN COMM *programme* fortführen, fortsetzen

continued *adj* (*cont.*, *contd*) GEN COMM fortgesetzt (*ff.*, *fortg.*); **~ insurance** *n* INS Weiterversicherung *f*; **~ success** *n* GEN COMM *of person, company, product* anhaltender Erfolg *m*

continuing *adj* GEN COMM *investment* anhaltend; ◆ **~ appropriation authorities** FIN Behörden *f pl* für nicht verbrauchte Haushaltsteile

continuing: **~ audit** *n* ACC Dauerprüfung *f*, permanente Prüfung *f*; **~ commitment** *n* GEN COMM fortlaufende Verpflichtung *f*; **~ cost** *n* ACC laufende Kosten *pl*; **~ support** *n* GEN COMM laufende Unterstützung *f*

continuity *n* ECON, S&M Kontinuität *f*; **~ of employment** *n* HRM Beschäftigungskontinuität *f*; **~ thesis** *n* ECON Kontinuitätsthese *f*

continuous *adj* GEN COMM durchgehend, fortlaufend; **~ assessment** *n* WEL laufende Beurteilung *f*; **~ audit** *n* ACC laufende Buchprüfung *f*; **~ budget** *n* FIN kontinuierlicher Haushalt *m*; **~ compounding** *n* BANK tageweise Verzinsung *f*; **~ flow production** *n* IND Fließarbeit *f*, Fließfabrikation *f*, Fließfertigung *f*; **~ form feed** *n* COMP Endloseinzug *m*; **~ forms** *n pl* GEN COMM Endlosformulare *nt pl*; **~ funding** *n* FIN Dauerfinanzierung *f*; **~ interest** *n* BANK tageweise Verzinsung *f*; **~ inventory** *n* GEN COMM laufende Inventur *f*

continuously *adv* ADMIN laufend

continuous: **~ net settlement** *n* BrE (*CNS*) STOCK fortlaufende Nettoabrechnung *f*; **~ process** *n* ECON, IND dynamischer Prozeß *m*, Fließprozeß *m*; **~ process production** *n* IND Produktion *f* im Dauerbetrieb, Produktion *f* im Dauerverfahren; **~ promotion** *n* S&M

advertising kontinuierliche Verkaufsförderung *f*; **~ reinforcement** *n* HRM laufende Verstärkung *f*; **~ research** *n* S&M ständige Forschung *f*, ununterbrochene Forschung *f*; **~ stationery** *n* COMP Endlospapier *nt*; **~ stocktaking** *n* ECON laufende Inventur *f*; **~ survey** *n* (*CS*) S&M Dauermarktanalyse *f*, TRANSP *shipping* Dauerprüfung *f*, regelmäßige Inspektion *f*, regelmäßige Schiffsbesichtigung *f*; **~ variable** *n* MATH *statistics* stetige Zufallsvariable *f*

contra *n* ACC Gegenposten *m*; **~ account** *n* ACC Gegenkonto *nt*, Gegenrechnung *f*, Wertberichtigungskonto *nt*

contraband *n* IMP/EXP Konterbande *f* (*obs*), Konterware *f* (*obs*), Schmuggelware *f*; **~ articles** *n pl* IMP/EXP Konterware *f* (*obs*), Schmuggelware *f*, unter Ein- oder Ausfuhrverbot stehende Waren *f pl*

contra: **~ broker** *n* STOCK Gegenbroker *m*

contract 1. *n* GEN COMM Vertrag *m*, Kontrakt *m*, *order* Auftrag *m*; ◆ **by ~** LAW vertraglich; **2.** *vt* GEN COMM *agree, enter into* kontrahieren, *debts* ansammeln, *workers* rekrutieren; ◆ **~ a loan** FIN eine Anleihe aufnehmen, ein Darlehen aufnehmen, einen Kredit aufnehmen; **3.** *vi* GEN COMM *diminish* abnehmen, schrumpfen

contract away *vt* HRM, LAW abwerben

contract in *vi* FIN, INS *to pension scheme* beitreten, LAW sich anschließen

contract out 1. *vt* HRM *work* außer Haus machen lassen, vergeben, LAW freizeichnen, vertraglich ausschließen; **2.** *vi* FIN, INS *of pension scheme* nicht beitreten, LAW sich nicht anschließen, austreten; ◆ **~ of an agreement** einen Vertrag kündigen

contract: **~ of affreightment** *n* S&M, TRANSP Schiffsfrachtvertrag *m*; **~ agreement** *n* LAW Vertragsvereinbarung *f*; **~ of assignment** *n* LAW *contracts* Abtretungsvertrag *m*; **~ award process** *n* GEN COMM Auftragsvergabe *f*; **~ bargaining** *n* HRM, LAW Vertragsverhandlungen *f pl*; **~ bond** *n* GEN COMM Erfüllungsgarantie *f*, Leistungsgarantie *f*; **~ of carriage** *n* LAW *contracts* Beförderungsvertrag *m*; **~ carrier** *n* TRANSP Vertragsfrachtführer *m*; **~ clause** *n* LAW Vertragsklausel *f*; **~ curve** *n* ECON Kontraktkurve *f*; **~ delivery date** *n* BrE STOCK *currency futures* vertraglicher Liefertermin *m*; **~ delivery month** *n* BrE STOCK *currency futures* vertraglicher Fälligkeitsmonat *m*, vertraglicher Liefermonat *m*

contracted: **~-in rates** *n pl* BrE TAX *National Insurance contributions* Beitrittsgebühren *f pl*, Gebühren *f pl* bei Eintritt; **~-out rates** *n pl* BrE TAX *National Insurance contributions* Austrittsgebühren *f pl*, Gebühren *f pl* bei Austritt

contract: **~ of employment** *n* GEN COMM, HRM Arbeitsvertrag *m*; **~ of exchange of goods and services** *n* LAW *contracts* Leistungsaustauschvertrag *m*, Vertrag *m* über den Austausch von Lieferungen und Leistungen; **~ for delivery by installments** *AmE*, **~ for delivery by instalments** *BrE* *n* LAW Sukzessivlieferungsvertrag *m*; **~ for the sale of goods** *n* LAW Warenkaufvertrag *m*; **~ for services** *n* LAW Dienstleistungsvertrag *m*; **~ grade** *n* STOCK *Eurodollar futures* Kontraktqualität *f*; **~ hire** *n* HRM mittelfristiger Mietvertrag *m*; **~ holdback** *n* GEN COMM vertragliche Einbehaltung *f*; **~ of indemnity** *n* INS *property and liability insurance* Entschädigungsvertrag *m*, Schadensersatzvertrag *m*, LAW Schadensersatzvertrag *m*

contracting n ECON Kontrahierung f; ~ **away** n S&M Abwerbung f; ~ **out** n HRM Aus der staatlichen/firmeneigenen Rentenversicherung austreten und sich anderweitig versichern, Arbeiten vergeben, LAW Freizeichnung f; ~ **out clause** n LAW Rücktrittsklausel f, Freizeichnungsklausel f; ~ **party** n LAW Vertragspartei f; ~ **state** n PATENTS Vertragsstaat m

contraction n ECON Abschwung m

contractionary: ~ **national income gap** n (cf deflationary gap) ECON econometrics deflatorische Lücke f; ~ **open market policy** n ECON kontraktive Offenmarktpolitik f; ~ **pressure** n ECON Deflationsdruck m, Nachfragerückgang m

contraction: ~ **of demand** n S&M Nachfrageschrumpfung f; ~ **of money supply** n ECON Geldverknappung f

contract: ~ **joint venture** n GEN COMM Vertrags-Joint Venture nt; ~ **labor** AmE, ~ **labour** BrE n HRM Arbeitskräfte f pl auf Zeit; ~ **licence** BrE, ~ **license** AmE n IMP/EXP Vertragslizenz f, Vertragsvollmacht f; ~ **maintenance** n GEN COMM vertragliche Wartung f; ~ **negotiations** n pl HRM, LAW Vertragsverhandlungen f pl; ~ **note** n FIN Effektenabrechnung f, STOCK Ausführungsanzeige f, Schlußnote f, Schlußschein n

contractor n GEN COMM Lieferant m, Vertragsschließende(r) mf [decl. as adj], HRM Auftragnehmer m, Lieferant m, Unternehmer, in m,f, LAW party to a contract Vertragspartei f, work Unternehmer, in m,f; ~'**s all risks insurance** n INS Bauleistungsversicherung f

contract: ~ **party** n LAW Vertragspartei f, Vertragspartner, in m,f; ~ **payment** n ACC Zahlung f laut Vertrag; ~ **period** n LAW Vertragsdauer f; ~ **price** n AmE TAX instalment sale Vertragspreis m, vertraglich vereinbarter Preis m; ~ **with protective effect** n LAW Vertrag m mit Schutzwirkung für Dritte; ~ **rent** n PROP vertraglich vereinbarte Miete f; ~ **requiring specific form** n LAW contracts formbedürftiger Vertrag m; ~ **of sale** n LAW Kaufvertrag m; ~ **of service** n BrE HRM Dienstvertrag m; ~ **size** n STOCK currency futures Kontrakteinheit f, Kontraktgröße f

contracts: ~ **manager** n HRM Contracts Manager m; ~ **officer** n HRM Vertragsbearbeiter, in m,f

contract: ~ **specifications** n pl LAW Ausschreibungsbedingungen f pl; ~ **system** n TRANSP shipping Kontraktsystem nt

contractual adj HRM wages tariflich, LAW vertraglich; ~ **duty** n LAW Vertragsverpflichtung f; ~ **formal obligation** n LAW vertragliche Verpflichtungserklärung f; ~ **freedom** n LAW Vertragsfreiheit f; ~ **liability** n GEN COMM Vertragsverpflichtung f; ~ **loan rate** n STOCK Eurodollar futures vertraglicher Kreditzins m; ~ **obligation** n LAW Vertragspflicht f, Vertragsverpflichtung f; ~ **payment** n FIN vertragliche Zahlung f; ~ **penalty** n LAW Vertragsstrafe f; ~ **plan** n STOCK vertragsgebundener Plan m; ~ **relationship** n GEN COMM Vertragsverhältnis nt, LAW Vertragsbeziehung f; ~ **savings** n pl FIN Betriebssparen nt, Sparen nt über vermögensbildende Leistungen; ~ **use** n LAW bestimmungsgemäßer Gebrauch m

contract: ~ **value** n STOCK futures Auftragswert m; ~ **work** n HRM übergebene Arbeit f, übernommene Arbeit f

contracyclical: ~ **policy** n ECON antizyklische Politik f

contra: ~ **deal** n S&M Gegenangebot nt

contradict vt LAW widersprechen

contradiction n LAW Widerspruch m

contra: ~ **entry** n ACC Gegenbuchung f, Storno m or nt, Stornobuchung f

contra preferentem phr GEN COMM gegen den eigentlich Begünstigten

contrary: ~ **to the contract** phr LAW vertragswidrig

contribute 1. vt ECON einbringen, GEN COMM beisteuern, beitragen, TAX, WEL spenden; **2.** vi GEN COMM beisteuern, beitragen, TAX, WEL spenden

contribution n ECON Beitrag m, FIN Mitwirkung f, Umlage f, GEN COMM personal Kostenbeitrag m, personal or financial Beitrag m, TAX Beitrag m; ~ **analysis** n FIN Beitragsanalyse f, Deckungsbeitragsanalyse f; ~ **costing** n ACC Deckungsbeitragsrechnung f; ~ **margin** n ACC Bruttogewinn m, Deckungsbeitrag m; ~ **profit** n ACC cost accounting Kostenartenbeitrag m; ~ **standard** n ECON Beitragsstandard m

contribution: ~ **to funeral expenses** n INS Sterbegeld nt

contributor n ECON Betragsleitende(r) mf [decl. as adj], Leistungspflichtige(r) mf [decl. as adj]; ~ **of capital** n GEN COMM Kapitaleinleger m

contributory adj LAW beitragend, mitwirkend; ~ **negligence** n LAW Mitverschulden nt, mitwirkendes Verschulden nt; ~ **pension fund** n HRM Gruppenversicherung f; ~ **pension plan** n FIN beitragspflichtige Pensionskasse f, beitragspflichtiger Pensionsplan m, beitragspflichtiges Pensionssystem nt; ~ **pension scheme** n FIN beitragspflichtige Pensionskasse f, beitragspflichtiger Pensionsplan m, beitragspflichtiges Pensionssystem nt, HRM Gruppenversicherung f; ~ **sickness fund** n GEN COMM, HRM Gruppenkrankenversicherung f; ~ **value** n INS Beitragswert m

control 1. n ADMIN Überwachung f, COMP Steuerung f, ECON Macht f, supervision Kontrolle f, Aufsicht f, economic planning Bewirtschaftung f, GEN COMM Kontrolle f, Beherrschung f, POL Beherrschung f, S&M direct marketing Überwachung f; **2.** vt ECON inflation kontrollieren, GEN COMM beherrschen, kontrollieren, regulieren, TRANSP, S&M überwachen; ♦ ~ **costs** GEN COMM Kosten kontrollieren; ~ **a market** FIN einen Markt beherrschen; ~ **the purse strings** ECON die Ausgaben kontrollieren; ~ **spending** ECON die Ausgaben kontrollieren

control: ~ **account** n ACC Sammelkonto nt; ~ **character** n COMP Steuerungszeichen nt; ~ **command** n COMP Steuerbefehl m; ~ **data** n pl COMP Ordnungsdaten pl; ~ **data entry** n COMP Ordnungsdateneingabe f; ~ **group** n S&M Kontrollgruppe f; ~ **information** n GEN COMM Kontrollinformationen f pl; ~ **key** n (CTRL key) COMP Steuerungstaste f (CTRL-Taste, STRG-Taste)

controllable adj GEN COMM regelbar; ~ **cost** n ACC beeinflußbare Kosten pl

controlled adj FIN, GEN COMM reguliert; ~ **atmosphere** n ENVIR kontrollierte Atmosphäre f; ~ **circulation** n S&M kontrollierte Auflage f; ~ **commodities** n pl STOCK kontrollierte Rohstoffe m pl, kontrollierte Waren f pl; ~ **company** n ECON, STOCK abhängige Gesellschaft f, beherrschte Gesellschaft f; ~ **economy** n ECON gelenkte Wirtschaft f; ~ **market** n ECON gelenkter Markt m; ~ **rates** n pl ECON rates of currency exchange kontrollierter Kurs m; ~ **transit** n TRANSP kontrollierter Transit m

controller n ACC, ADMIN Controller m, Chef, in m,f des

Rechnungswesens, Leiter, in *m,f* des Rechnungswesens, Leiter, in *m,f* des Bereichs Rechnung und Finanzen, Aufseher, in *m,f*, Prüfer, in *m,f*, Rechnungsprüfer, in *m,f*, Revisor, in *m,f*, staatlicher Rechnungsprüfer *m*, staatliche Rechnungsprüferin *f*, COMP Regler *m*, FIN, MGMNT Controller *m*, Chef, in *m,f* des Rechnungswesens, Leiter, in *m,f* des Rechnungswesens, Leiter, in *m,f* des Bereichs Rechnung und Finanzen, Aufseher, in *m,f*, Prüfer, in *m,f*, Rechnungsprüfer, in *m,f*, Revisor, in *m,f*, staatlicher Rechnungsprüfer *m*, staatliche Rechnungsprüferin *f*

control: ~ **of line limits** *n* GEN COMM Kontrolle *f* der Linienbeschränkungen

controlling: ~ **account** *n* ACC Gegenrechnung *f*, Hauptbuchsammelkonto *nt*, Kontrollbuch *nt*, Sammelkonto *nt*; ~ **company** *n* ECON, STOCK beherrschende Gesellschaft *f*; ~ **interest** *n* HRM, STOCK Mehrheitsbeteiligung *f*

control: ~ **panel** *n* GEN COMM Prüfpanel *nt*; ~ **procedure** *n* COMP Steuerprozedur *f*; ~ **program** *n* COMP Steuerprogramm *nt*; ~ **question** *n* S&M Kontrollfrage *f*; ~ **stock** *n* STOCK ausschlaggebender Aktienanteil *m*, wesentliche Beteiligung *f*

Control: ~ **of Substances Hazardous To Health Regulations** *n* (*COSHH*) HRM britische Gesetzgebung über gesundheitsschädliche Stoffe

control: ~ **ticket** *n* TRANSP Kontrollfahrkarte *f*

controversial *adj* GEN COMM umstritten

controversy *n* GEN COMM Kontroverse *f*, Streit *m*

convene *vt* MGMNT *meeting* einberufen

convenience: ~ **flag** *n* TRANSP *shipping* billige Flagge *f*, billige Handelsflagge *f*; ~ **foods** *n pl* S&M Halbfertig- und Fertiggerichte *nt pl*; ~ **goods** *n pl* GEN COMM, S&M Güter *nt pl* des täglichen Bedarfs, Waren *f pl* des täglichen Bedarfs; ~ **sampling** *n* S&M Ermessensauswahl *f*; ~ **shop** *n* BrE (*cf convenience store AmE*) S&M Bedarfsartikelgeschäft *nt*; ~ **store** *n* AmE (*cf convenience shop BrE*) S&M Bedarfsartikelgeschäft *nt*

convenient: ~ **speed** *n* TRANSP *shipping* geeignete Geschwindigkeit *f*

convenor *n* GEN COMM, HRM Einberufer, in *m,f*

convention *n* GEN COMM Konvention *f*, Grundsatz *m*, Versammlung *f*, *conference* Konferenz *f*, LAW Konvention *f*, MGMNT Konferenz *f*, Tagung *f*, Kongreß *m*, POL Versammlung *f*

conventional *adj* GEN COMM herkömmlich; ~ **cargo** *n* TRANSP herkömmliche Fracht *f*; ~ **mortgage** *n* BANK vertraglich vereinbarte Hypothek *f*

convention: ~ **hotel** *n* ADMIN Tagungshotel *nt*; ~ **participant** *n* MGMNT Tagungsteilnehmer, in *m,f*, Delegierte(r) *mf* [decl. as adj], Konferenzteilnehmer, in *m,f*, Kongreßteilnehmer, in *m,f*, Sitzungsteilnehmer, in *m,f*

converge *vi* GEN COMM *ideas, activities* konvergieren

convergence *n* GEN COMM Konvergenz *f*, STOCK Zusammenlaufen *nt*; ~ **hypothesis** *n* ECON Konvergenztheorie *f*; ~ **thesis** *n* POL Konvergenzthese *f*

conversational: ~ **entry** *n* COMP Dialogeingabe *f*

conversationally *adv* COMP in Dialogbetrieb

conversational: ~ **mode** *n* COMP Dialogmodus *m*; **in** ~ **mode** *phr* COMP in Dialog; ~ **system** *n* COMP Dialogsystem *nt*

conversely *adv* GEN COMM gegenteilig

conversion *n* COMP Konvertierung *f*, Umsetzung *f*, Umwandlung *f*, ECON Konversion *f*, Konvertierung *f*, Umtausch *m*, FIN Konvertierung *f*, Umrechnung *f*, Umtausch *m*, Konversion *f*, GEN COMM Umwandlung *f*, LAW *of sentence* Umstellung *f*, Umwandlung *f*, PROP *of buildings* Umbau *m*, STOCK Konversion *f*, Konvertierung *f*; ~ **cost** *n* ACC Konvertierungskosten *pl*, Verarbeitungskosten *pl*; ~ **factor** *n* MATH Umrechnungsfaktor *m*; ~ **factor for employee contributions** *n* INS *defined benefit pension plan* Umrechnungsfaktor *m* für Arbeitnehmerbeitrag; ~ **issue** *n* FIN Konvertierungspapier *nt*; ~ **loan** *n* FIN Konversionsanleihe *f*, Wandelanleihe *f*; ~ **parity** *n* BrE STOCK Umtauschparität *f*, Wandlungsparität *f*; ~ **premium** *n* STOCK Konvertierungsprämie *f*, Wandlungsaufgeld *nt*; ~ **price** *n* ECON, FIN Umrechnungskurs *m*, Wandlungskurs *m*; ~ **rate** *n* ECON Umrechnungskurs *m*, FIN Umrechnungskurs *m*, Umrechnungssatz *m*; ~ **ratio** *n* STOCK Umtauschverhältnis *nt*, Wandlungsverhältnis *nt*

convert *vt* BANK *money* umtauschen, wandeln, COMP konvertieren, umsetzen, ECON *currency* konvertieren, umtauschen, FIN konvertieren, umrechnen, umtauschen, umwandeln, wandeln, GEN COMM verwandeln, umwandeln, LAW *sentence* umwandeln, PROP umbauen, STOCK konvertieren, umtauschen, umwandeln; ◆ ~ **into** GEN COMM konvertieren in [+acc], umwandeln in [+acc], verwandeln in [+acc], verwandeln zu

converted *adj* PROP umgebaut

convertibility *n* ECON, POL Konvertibilität *f*, Konvertierbarkeit *f*, FIN Konvertibilität *f*, Konvertierbarkeit *f*, Wandelbarkeit *f*

convertible *adj* BANK wandelbar, COMMS umwandelbar, FIN umwandelbar, wandlungsfähig, GEN COMM, LAW umwandelbar, MGMNT umwandelbar, STOCK umwandelbar, wandlungsfähig; ~ **bond** *n* FIN Wandelobligation *f*, Wandelschuldverschreibung *f*, Wandelanleihe *f*; ~ **currency** *n* ECON, POL konvertible Devisen *f pl*, konvertierbare Währung *f*; ~ **issue** *n* FIN konvertierbare Emission *f* von Wertpapieren, Wandelanleihe *f*; ~ **loan stock** *n* STOCK wandlungsfähiger Schuldtitel *m*; ~ **security** *n* FIN handelbares Wertpapier *nt*, umtauschbares Wertpapier *nt*; ~ **subordinated loan** *n* FIN wandlungsfähiges nachrangiges Darlehen *nt*; ~ **term life insurance** *n* INS Risikolebensversicherung *f* mit Umtauschrecht

convey *vt* GEN COMM befördern, IMP/EXP versenden, LAW übertragen, PROP übertragen, übereignen, umschreiben, TRANSP *goods* transportieren, befördern, versenden, übersenden

conveyance *n* IMP/EXP Spedition *f*, LAW Grundstücksübertragung *f*, Übermittlung *f*, PROP Grundstücksübertragung *f*, Umschreibung *f*, TRANSP Spedition *f*, Versendung *f*, Transport *m*, Übersendung *f*; ~ **by agreement** *n* LAW Auflassung *f*; ~ **of goods** *n* TRANSP Gütertransport *m*

conveyor *n* LAW Übermittler *m*; ~ **belt** *n* IND Förderband *nt*, Transportband *nt*

convict *vt* LAW verurteilen

conviction *n* GEN COMM Überzeugung *f*, LAW Verurteilung *f*

convince *vt* GEN COMM überzeugen

convinced: **be** ~ **of** *phr* GEN COMM überzeugt sein von; **be** ~ **that** *phr* GEN COMM fest daran glauben, daß

convincing *adj* GEN COMM überzeugend, glaubhaft

convolute: ~ **winding** n TRANSP *fibre drum* Wicklung f
COO abbr GEN COMM, IMP/EXP (*country of origin*) Herkunftsland nt, Ursprungsland nt, HRM (*chief operating officer*) oberste Führungskraft f
cooling: ~~**off period** n GEN COMM *before signing a contract* Bedenkzeit f, Denkpause f, HRM, INS, STOCK Abkühlungszeit f
co-op n ECON (*cooperative*) Kooperative f, GEN COMM (*consumers' cooperative*) Konsumgenossenschaft f, (*cooperative, cooperative society*) Genossenschaft f, HRM (*cooperative*) Kooperative f, IND (*cooperative*) Produktionsgenossenschaft f, MGMNT (*cooperative*) Kooperative f, PROP (*cooperative*) *apartment block* Genossenschaftswohnung f, *commission arrangement* Zusammenarbeit f
cooperage n TRANSP Faßfabrik f
cooperate vi GEN COMM kooperieren, zusammenarbeiten
cooperation n GEN COMM Kooperation f, Zusammenarbeit f, LAW Kooperation f; ~ **agreement** n GEN COMM *between nations* Kooperationsvertrag m, LAW *contract law* Konsortialvertrag m, Kooperationsvertrag m
cooperative 1. adj ECON kooperativ, *trade, society, agreement* auf Genossenschaftsbasis, GEN COMM *compliant* kooperativ, *helpful* hilfsbereit, HRM, IND, MGMNT *trade, society, agreement* auf Genossenschaftsbasis; **2.** n (*co-op*) ECON Kooperative f, GEN COMM Genossenschaft f, HRM Kooperative f, IND Produktionsgenossenschaft f, MGMNT Kooperative f, PROP *apartment block* Genossenschaftswohnung f, *commission arrangement* Zusammenarbeit f
cooperative: ~ **advertising** n S&M *retailing arrangement* Gemeinschaftswerbung f; ~ **education** n WEL *non-confessional* Gemeinschaftsschulsystem nt; ~ **farming** n ECON genossenschaftlicher Ein- und Verkauf m in der Landwirtschaft; ~ **federalism** n POL kooperativer Föderalismus m; ~ **marketing** n S&M genossenschaftliches Absatzwesen nt; ~ **society** n (*co-op*) GEN COMM Genossenschaft f
Cooperative: ~ **Wholesale Society** n BrE (*CWS*) GEN COMM Konsumgroßhandelsgesellschaft
coordinate vt GEN COMM aneinander angleichen, aufeinander abstimmen, gleichordnen, gleichschalten, in Übereinstimmung bringen, koordinieren
coordinated adj GEN COMM *systems* aufeinander abgestimmt, koordiniert
coordinating: ~ **committee for multilateral export controls** n IMP/EXP Koordinierungsausschuß m für multilaterale Exportkontrollen
coordination n GEN COMM Abstimmung f, Koordinierung f, MGMNT Abstimmung f
coordinator n HRM Koordinator, in m,f
co-owner n BANK Miteigentümer, in m,f, GEN COMM Mitinhaber, in m,f, LAW, PROP Miteigentümer, in m,f
co-ownership n BANK, LAW, PROP Mitbesitz m, Miteigentum nt
co-partner n GEN COMM Teilhaber, in m,f
copier n ADMIN Kopierer m, Kopiergerät nt
copper n IND Kupfer nt; ~ **ore** n IND Kupfererz nt
coprocessor n COMP *hardware* Coprozessor m, Koprozessor m
copy 1. n COMP Kopie f, GEN COMM *reproduction* Abschrift f, Ausgabe f einer Zeitung, Kopie f, Exemplar nt, Manuskript nt, Artikelinhalt m, Ausfertigung f,

Abdruck m, S&M Text m; **2.** vt COMP, GEN COMM *photocopy* kopieren
copy: ~ **adaptor** n GEN COMM Textbearbeiter, in mf; ~ **appeal** n S&M *advertising* Attraktivität f der Anzeigenaussage; ~ **date** n GEN COMM Datum nt der Abschrift, S&M Anzeigenschluß m; ~ **deadline** n GEN COMM Anzeigenschluß m, MEDIA Redaktionsschluß m; ~ **department** n GEN COMM Textabteilung f; ~ **editor** n MEDIA Zeitungsredakteur, in m,f; ~ **from the original** n GEN COMM Abschrift f vom Original; ~ **number** n MEDIA Ausgabe f (*Ausg.*); ~ **platform** n GEN COMM Matrize f; ~~**protected** adj COMP kopiergeschützt, mit Kopierschutz versehen; ~~**protected disk** n COMP Diskette mit Kopierschutz f, kopiergeschützte Diskette f; ~ **protection** n COMP *software* Kopierschutz m; ~ **reader** n MEDIA *print* Zeitungsredakteur, in m,f
copyright 1. adj LAW urheberrechtlich; **2.** n COMP *data, software*, LAW Copyright nt, Urheberrecht nt; ♦ ~ **reserved** LAW urheberrechtlich geschützt
Copyright: ~ **Act** n GEN COMM Urheberrechtsgesetz nt
copyrighted: ~ **works** n pl LAW urheberrechtlich geschützte Werke nt pl
copyright: ~ **material** n LAW *intellectual property* urheberrechtlich geschütztes Werk nt
copy: ~ **strategy** n S&M *advertising* Werbetextstrategie f; ~ **test** n S&M Anzeigenuntersuchung f
copytesting n S&M Copytesten nt
copy: ~ **writer** n GEN COMM Werbetexter, in m,f; ~ **writing** n S&M Abfassung eines Reklametextes f
cordless adj COMMS *mechanism, peripherne* schnurlos; ~ **digital telecommunications** n pl COMMS schnurlose digitale Fernsprechverbindungen f pl; ~ **telephone** n COMMS schnurloses Telephon nt
core n COMP *hardware*, GEN COMM Kern m; ~ **business** n ECON, GEN COMM Hauptgeschäftsbereich m; ~ **curriculum** n WEL Kernfächer nt pl; ~ **definition** n GEN COMM Kerndefinition f; ~ **economy** n ECON führende Volkswirtschaft f; ~ **firm** n ECON Kernfirma f; ~ **funding** n FIN Kernfinanzierung f; ~ **hours** n ADMIN Kernstunden f pl, Kernzeit f, IND Hauptarbeitsstunden f pl, Kernstunden f pl, Kernzeit f; ~ **inflation** n ECON Kerninflation f; ~ **inflation rate** n ECON Kerninflationsrate f; ~ **memory** n COMP Kernspeicher m
COREPER abbr (*Committee of Permanent Representatives of the EC*) ECON EU AStV (*Ausschuß der Ständigen Vertreter*)
core: ~ **product** n S&M Kernprodukt nt; ~ **region** n ECON Kernregion f; ~ **size** n COMP Kernumfang m; ~ **storage** n COMP Kernspeicher m; ~ **time** n HRM Kernzeit f; ~ **workforce** n HRM Stammbelegschaft f
corner 1. n GEN COMM Eckpunkt m einer Matrix; **2.** vt FIN aufkaufen; ♦ ~ **the market** S&M Waren zu Spekulationszwecken aufkaufen, STOCK zu spekulativen Zwecken den Markt aufkaufen
cornerer n FIN Aufkäufer m
corner: ~ **shop** n BrE (*cf neighborhood store AmE, mom-and-pop store AmE*) S&M Nachbarschaftsladen m, Laden m an der Ecke, Geschäft nt mit Artikeln des täglichen Bedarfs, Tante-Emma-Laden m; ~ **solution** n ECON Ecklösung f
cornerstone n GEN COMM Grundstein m
corn: ~ **exchange** n BrE (*cf grain exchange AmE*) STOCK Getreidebörse f; ~ **model** n ECON Weizenmodell nt

corp. *abbr* (*corporation*) GEN COMM Fa. (*Firma*)

corporate *adj* GEN COMM gesellschaftlich, korporatistisch, korporativ, Firmen-; ~ **accountability** *n* GEN COMM Rechenschaftspflicht *f* eines Unternehmens; ~ **account deposit** *n* BANK Firmenkundeneinlage *f*; ~ **advertising** *n* S&M Firmenwerbung *f*; ~ **affairs** *n pl* GEN COMM Unternehmensangelegenheiten *f pl*; ~ **affiliate** *n* ECON Konzerngesellschaft *f*; ~ **assets** *n pl* ADMIN, FIN Gesellschaftsvermögen *nt*; ~ **banking** *n* BANK Firmenkundengeschäft *nt*; ~ **body** *n* ADMIN juristische Person *f*, Körperschaft *f*; ~ **campaign** *n* S&M Firmenkampagne *f*; ~ **client** *n* BANK Firmenkunde *m*, Firmenkundin *f*; ~ **credit** *n* BANK Firmenkundenkredit *m*; ~ **credit card** *n* FIN Firmenkreditkarte *f*; ~ **credit manager** *n* BANK Firmenkundenkreditmanager, in *m,f*; ~ **customer** *n* BANK Firmenkunde *m*, Firmenkundin *f*; ~ **database** *n* COMP Betriebsdatenbank *f*; ~ **data center** *AmE*, ~ **data centre** *BrE* *n* COMP Betriebsdatenzentrum *nt*, Datenzentrum *nt* eines Unternehmens; ~ **earning** *n* ACC Unternehmensertrag *m*, Unternehmergewinn *m*; ~ **earning power** *n* ECON Ertragsfähigkeit *f* eines Unternehmens, Ertragskraft *f* eines Unternehmens; ~ **equivalent yield** *n* TAX vergleichbare Unternehmensrendite *f*, vergleichbarer Unternehmensertrag *m*; ~ **executive** *n* MGMNT leitender Firmenmitarbeiter *m*, leitende Firmenmitarbeiterin *f*, leitender Konzernmitarbeiter *m*, leitende Konzernmitarbeiterin *f*, leitender Unternehmensmitarbeiter *m*, leitende Unternehmensmitarbeiterin *f*; ~ **finance** *n* FIN betriebliches Rechnungswesen *nt*; ~ **financing** *n* FIN Unternehmensfinanzierung *f*; ~ **financing committee** *n* FIN Unternehmensfinanzierungsausschuß *m*; ~ **funds** *n pl* ADMIN Gesellschaftsmittel *nt pl*; ~ **goal** *n* GEN COMM Unternehmensziel *nt*; ~ **governance** *n* ADMIN gesellschaftliche Verwaltung *f*; ~ **growth** *n* GEN COMM Unternehmenswachstum *nt*; ~ **identity** *n* S&M Corporate Identity *nt* (*CI*), Unternehmensphilosophie *f*; ~ **image** *n* GEN COMM, S&M Firmenimage *nt*, Unternehmensimage *nt*; ~ **insider** *n* GEN COMM Kenner *m* eines Unternehmens; ~ **investment** *n* FIN Investitionen *f pl* der Unternehmen, Unternehmensinvestition *f*; ~ **issue** *n* FIN Emission *f* einer Aktiengesellschaft; ~ **law** *n* LAW Gesellschaftsrecht *nt*; ~ **lawyer** *n* *AmE* LAW *who is employed by a company* Syndikusanwalt *m*, Syndikusanwältin *f*, *who represents a company* Firmenanwalt *m*, Firmenanwältin *f*; ~ **lending** *n* BANK Firmenkredite *m pl*; ~ **lending market** *n* BANK Firmenkreditmarkt *m*; ~ **management** *n* MGMNT Firmenleitung *f*, Leitung *f* einer Gesellschaft, Unternehmensleitung *f*; ~ **mission** *n* GEN COMM Unternehmenszweck *m*, MGMNT Geschäftsauftrag *m*; ~ **model** *n* ACC, FIN Unternehmensmodell *nt*; ~ **morality** *n* GEN COMM Geschäftsmoral *f*; ~ **name** *n* GEN COMM Firmenname *m*; ~ **network** *n* COMP betriebliches Netz *nt*; ~ **objective** *n* GEN COMM Unternehmensziel *nt*; ~ **pay off** *n* ADMIN Schmiergeld *nt*; ~ **philosophy** *n* GEN COMM Unternehmensphilosophie *f*; ~ **plagiarism** *n* GEN COMM Diebstahl des geistigen Eigentums einer Unternehmung; ~ **plan** *n* ECON, GEN COMM Unternehmensplan *m*; ~ **planning** *n* GEN COMM Geschäftsplanung *f*, Unternehmensplanung *f*; ~ **policy** *n* ECON, GEN COMM Unternehmenspolitik *f*; ~ **profit** *n* ACC Unternehmensgewinn *m*; ~ **purchasing** *n* S&M Firmeneinkauf *m*; ~ **raider** *n* FIN Unternehmensaufkäufer *m*; ~ **savings** *n pl* FIN Unternehmensersparnisse

f pl; ~ **seal** *n* BANK Gesellschaftssiegel *nt*; ~ **spending** *n* TAX betriebliche Ausgaben *f pl*; ~ **sponsorship** *n* S&M *advertising, promotion* Firmenförderung *f*; ~ **state** *n* POL korporatistischer Staat *m*, korporativer Staat *m*; ~ **strategic planning** *n* MGMNT strategische Unternehmensplanung *f*; ~ **strategy** *n* GEN COMM, MGMNT Unternehmensstrategie *f*; ~ **structure** *n* GEN COMM Firmenstruktur *f*, HRM Betriebsstruktur *f*; ~ **tax** *n* TAX Körperschaftssteuer *f*; ~ **taxation** *n* TAX Unternehmensbesteuerung *f*; ~ **treasurer** *n* HRM Leiter, in *m,f* der Finanzabteilung; ~ **turnaround** *n* GEN COMM Geschäftsumschwung *m* eines Unternehmens, Turnaround *m*; ~ **veil** *n* GEN COMM Haftungsbeschränkung *f*

corporation *n* (*corp.*) GEN COMM Firma *f* (*Fa.*), STOCK (*cf public limited company*) Aktiengesellschaft *f* (*AG*); ~ **income tax** *n* TAX Körperschaftssteuer *f*

Corporation: ~ **of Lloyd's** *n* (*CL*) INS *marine* Lloyd's Versicherung *f*

corporation: ~ **tax** *n* *BrE* TAX Körperschaftssteuer *f*; ~ **tax liability** *n* TAX Körperschaftssteuerpflicht *f*; ~ **tax rates** *n pl* *BrE* TAX Körperschaftssteuersätze *m pl*

corporatism *n* GEN COMM, POL Korporatismus *m*

corporeal *adj* GEN COMM materiell; ~ **hereditaments** *n pl* LAW Liegenschaften *f pl*, unbewegliche Vermögensgegenstände *m pl*

corporeally *adv* GEN COMM materiell

corpus *n* LAW *assets* Kapital *nt*, *civil law* Gegenstand *m* des Verfahrens, Gesetzessammlung *f*

corr. *abbr* (*correspondence*) GEN COMM Korr. (*Korrespondenz*)

correct 1. *adj* GEN COMM korrekt, richtig; 2. *vt* GEN COMM *errors* bereinigen, abändern, verbessern, berichtigen, MEDIA korrigieren; ♦ ~ **a distorted pattern in** GEN COMM entzerren

corrected *adj* GEN COMM berechtigt, bereinigt, MEDIA korrigiert; ~ **invoice** *n* FIN berichtigte Rechnung *f*; ~ **probability** *n* FIN berichtigte Wahrscheinlichkeit *f*, MATH bereinigte Wahrscheinlichkeit *f*, berichtigte Wahrscheinlichkeit *f*, korrigierte Wahrscheinlichkeit *f*

correcting: ~ **entry** *n* ACC Berichtigungsbuchung *f*, Berichtigungseintragung *f*, Korrekturposten *m*, ADMIN Berichtigungsbuchung *f*

correction *n* BANK, ACC Berichtigung *f*, GEN COMM Bereinigung *f*, Berichtigung *f*, Entzerrung *f*, LAW Berichtigung *f*, MEDIA Korrektur *f*, PATENTS Berichtigung *f*, *improvement* Verbesserung *f*; ~ **maintenance** *n* GEN COMM, IND Instandsetzung *f*

corrective: ~ **action** *n* GEN COMM korrigierende Maßnahme *f*; ~ **subsidy** *n* ECON Ausgleichszuschuß *m*, POL Ausgleichszuschuß *m*, *anti-discrimination subsidy* wettbewerbsentzerrende Subvention *f*; ~ **tax** *n* POL Ausgleichssteuer *f*

correctly *adv* GEN COMM richtig

correctness *n* GEN COMM Richtigkeit *f*

correlate *vt* MATH korrelieren

correlation *n* MATH *statistics* Korrelation *f*; ~ **coefficient** *n* MATH *statistics* Korrelationskoeffizient *m*; ~ **ratio** *n* STOCK *interest rate futures* Wechselverhältnis-Kennzahl *f*

correspond *vi* COMMS *exchange letters* korrespondieren, GEN COMM *be similar* gleichkommen; ♦ ~ **to** GEN COMM *be equivalent* entsprechen [+dat]

correspondence *n* (*corr.*) COMMS Briefwechsel *m*, GEN COMM *letters* Korrespondenz *f* (*Korr.*); ~ **college** *n* WEL

Fernakademie *f*; ~ **course** *n* WEL Fernstudium *nt*;
~ **school** *n* WEL Fernakademie *f*, Fernuniversität *f*

correspondent *n* BANK, MEDIA Korrespondent, in *m,f*;
~ **bank** *n* BANK Korrespondenzbank *f*

corresponding *adj* GEN COMM sinngemäß, *equivalent*
entsprechend

corridor *n* ECON Korridor *m*; ~ **traffic** *n* S&M Durchgangsverkehr *m*

corroboration *n* LAW Bekräftigung *f*

corrode *vt* IND, TRANSP einfressen, korrodieren

corrosion *n* IND Einfressen *nt*, Korrosion *f*, Rostbildung
f, TRANSP Korrosion *f*; ~ **damage** *n* IND, INS, TRANSP
Korrosionsschäden *m pl*; ~**-resistant material** *n* IND,
TRANSP korrosionsbeständiger Werkstoff *m*, korrosions-
beständiges Material *nt*, korrosionsfester Werkstoff *m*,
korrosionssicherer Werkstoff *m*

corrugated: ~ **board** *n* S&M Wellpappe *f*; ~ **container** *n*
TRANSP Wellbehälter *m*, Wellblechcontainer *m*

corrupt *vt* GEN COMM korrumpieren

corruption *n* GEN COMM Korruption *f*

corset *n infrml* ECON quantitative und qualitative
Beschränkungen *f pl* der Bankkredite

COS *abbr* (*cash on shipment*) TRANSP Zahlung *f* bei
Verschiffung

COSHH *abbr BrE* (*Control of Substances Hazardous To
Health Regulations*) HRM britische Gesetzgebung über
gesundheitsschädliche Stoffe

cosmetics *n pl* GEN COMM Kosmetik *f*

cost 1. *n* ACC Selbstkosten *pl*, ECON Anschaffungskosten
pl, Aufwand *m*, Buchwert *m*, GEN COMM Kosten *pl*; **2.** *vt*
GEN COMM kosten

cost out *vt* ADMIN die Kosten ermitteln von

cost: ~ **accounting** *n* ACC Betriebskalkulation *f*,
Kostenbuchhaltung *f*, Kostenrechnung *f*, Kosten- und
Leistungsrechnung *f*; ~ **allocation** *n* ACC
Kostenaufteilung *f*, Kostenumlage *f*,
Kostenverrechnung *f*, Kostenverteilung *f*; ~ **analysis** *n*
ACC, FIN Kostenanalyse *f*, Kostenauswertung *f*;
~ **application** *n* ECON Kostenzurechnung *f*;
~ **apportionment** *n* ACC Kostenumlage *f*,
Kostenzurechnung *f*; ~ **approach** *n* PROP
Kosteneinschätzung *f*; ~ **awareness** *n* GEN COMM
Kostenbewußtsein *nt*; ~ **behavior pattern** *AmE*,
~ **behaviour pattern** *BrE n* FIN Kostenverlauf *m*;
~**-benefit analysis** *n* ACC, ECON, FIN Kosten-Nutzen-
Analyse *f*; ~ **of borrowing** *n* BANK
Kreditbeschaffungskosten *pl*; ~ **of carry** *n* STOCK
Bestandshaltekosten *pl*, Carrykosten *pl*; ~ **center**
AmE, ~ **centre** *BrE n* ACC Kostenstelle *f*;
~ **consciousness** *n* GEN COMM Kostendenken *nt*; ~ **of
construction** *n* PROP Bauaufwand *m*, Erstellungskosten
pl; ~ **containment** *n* ECON Kosteneindämmung *f*, GEN
COMM Kostensenkung *f*; ~ **control** *n* ACC
Kostenüberwachung *f*, Kostenkontrolle *f*, Kostensteuerung *f*; ~ **cutting** *n* GEN COMM Kostensenkung *f*; ~ **of
demolition** *n* GEN COMM Abbruchkosten *pl*, Demontagekosten *pl*; ~ **of dismantling** *n* GEN COMM
Abbruchkosten *pl*, Demontagekosten *pl*; ~**-effective**
adj GEN COMM kostendeckend, kostengünstig, kosteneffektiv; ~**-effectiveness** *n* GEN COMM
Kostenwirksamkeit *f*, Wirtschaftlichkeit *f*;
~**-effectiveness analysis** *n* ECON Kosten-Wirksamkeits-Analyse *f*; ~**-efficient** *adj* GEN COMM
kosteneffektiv, rentabel; ~ **escalation cover** *n* INS *UK*

Kosteneskalationsdeckung *f*; ~ **estimate** *n* GEN COMM
Voranschlag *m*; ~ **estimating** *n* FIN Kalkulation *f*;
~ **estimator** *n* ACC Vorkalkulator *m*; ~ **factor** *n* ACC
Kostenfaktor *m*; ~ **forecast** *n* ACC Kostenvoranschlag
m, ADMIN Kostenprognose *f*; ~**-free** *adj* GEN COMM
kostenfrei; ~ **and freight** *phr* (*C&F, CAF, CF*) Incoterms
IMP/EXP *to named port of destination*, TRANSP Kosten
und Fracht *pl* (*C&F*); ~ **of freight** *n* TRANSP *shipping*
Frachtkosten *pl*; ~ **of funds** *n* BANK Kapitalbeschaffungskosten *pl*, FIN Kapitalbeschaffungskosten *pl*,
Refinanzierungskosten *pl*, STOCK Kapitalbeschaffungskosten *pl*; ~ **of goods manufactured** *n* ACC
Herstellungskosten *pl*, Produktionskosten *pl*; ~ **of
goods sold** *n* ACC Umsatzaufwendungen *f pl*, ECON
Umsatzkosten *pl*

costing *n* FIN Kalkulation *f*; ~ **technique** *n* FIN Kalkulationsverfahren *nt*

cost: ~ **and insurance** *n* (*C&I*) IMP/EXP, TRANSP *Incoterms* Kosten und Versicherung *pl* (*C&I*); ~**, insurance
and freight** *phr* (*CI&F*) IMP/EXP, TRANSP *Incoterms*
Kosten, Versicherung und Fracht *pl*; ~ **insurance
freight landed** *phr* TRANSP *cargo delivery* Ausliefe rungs-
kosten, -fracht und -versicherung; ~**, insurance and
freight London terms** *phr* IMP/EXP cif nach Londoner
Bestimmungen; ~ **of issue** *n* ACC *share issue* Emissionskosten *pl*; ~ **of labor** *AmE*, ~ **of labour** *BrE n* ADMIN
Arbeitskosten *pl*, TAX Lohnkosten *pl*; ~ **leader** *n* ECON
Kostenführer *m*; ~ **of living** *n* ECON Lebenshaltungs-
kosten *pl*, Lebenshaltung *f*, GEN COMM, WEL
Lebenshaltung *f*; ~ **of living supplement** *n* WEL
Teuerungszulage *f*; ~ **of a loan** *n* BANK *to lender*
Darlehenskosten *pl*

costly *adj* GEN COMM *action* kostenaufwendig, *materials*
kostspielig, teuer

cost: ~ **method** *n* FIN Bewertungsmethode *f*; ~ **objective**
n ECON Kostenvorgabe *f*, Kostenziel *nt*; ~**-of-living
adjustment** *n* *AmE* (*COLA*) ECON *economic
accounting*, HRM Teuerungszuschlag *m*, Teuerungszulage *f*; ~**-of-living allowance** *n* HRM Teuerungszuschlag
m, Teuerungszulage *f*, WEL Unterhaltsbeihilfe *f*; ~**-of-
living index** *n* ECON Lebenshaltungsindex *m*, Lebenshaltungskostenindex *m*, Preisindex *m* für die
Lebenshaltung, GEN COMM Lebenshaltungsindex *m*,
Lebenshaltungskostenindex *m*, WEL Lebenshaltungsindex *m*, Lebenshaltungskostenindex *m*, Preisindex *m*
für die Lebenshaltung; ~ **overrun** *n* ECON
Kostenüberschreitung *f*, Mehrkosten *pl*; ~ **per inquiry**
n S&M Kosten *pl* pro Anfrage; ~ **per thousand** *n* S&M
Kosten *pl* pro Tausend; ~ **per unit** *n* ACC Stückkosten
pl; ~ **per vehicle kilometer** *AmE*, ~ **per vehicle
kilometre** *BrE n* TRANSP Kosten *pl* pro gefahrenem
Kilometer; ~**-plus contract** *n* GEN COMM
Vollkostenvertrag *m*; ~ **price** *n* ACC Selbstkostenpreis
m; ~**-push inflation** *n* ECON Kostendruckinflation *f*,
kosteninduzierte Inflation *f*, Kosteninflation *f*; ~ **ratio** *n*
FIN Kostenverhältnis *nt*, Verkaufskosten *pl*;
~ **recording** *n pl* STOCK Kostenerfassung *f*; ~ **records**
n pl FIN Kostenaufstellung *f*, GEN COMM Kostenbeleg *m*,
Spesenzettel *m*; ~ **reduction** *n* ECON, FIN Kostenabbau
m, Kostenreduzierung *f*, GEN COMM Kostensenkung *f*;
~ **of replacement** *n* INS Wiederbeschaffungswert *m*;
~**-of-service principle** *n* FIN Äquivalenzprinzip *nt*

costs *n pl* ECON, GEN COMM Kosten *pl*, LAW Gerichtskosten *pl*, Prozeßkosten *pl*; **on** ~ *n pl* IND Gemeinkosten
pl, Zusatzkosten *pl*; ~ **of acquisition or production** *n pl*

ACC Anschaffungs- oder Herstellungskosten *pl* (*AK/HK*); **~ are running into billions** *phr* GEN COMM die Kosten steigen auf Milliardenhöhe; **~ of clearance of debris** *n pl* INS Aufräumungskosten *pl*

cost: **~ of sales** *n* (*cf cost of goods sold*) ACC Selbstkosten *pl*, Umsatzaufwendungen *f pl*, ECON Einstandspreis *m* der verkauften Ware, FIN Verkaufskosten *pl*; **~-sensitive** *adj* ECON kostenreagibel, GEN COMM *customer* kostenempfindlich; **~-shared program** *AmE*, **~-shared programme** *BrE n* ECON Programm *nt* der Öffentlichen Hand, Regierungsprogramm *nt* mit anteiliger Kostenübernahme, POL Programm *nt* der Öffentlichen Hand

costs: **~ of proceedings** *n pl* GEN COMM Verfahrenskosten *pl*; **~ of production** *n pl* IND Produktionskosten *pl*

cost: **~ standard** *n* FIN Standardkosten *pl*

costs: **~ taxable to sb** *n pl* TAX Kosten *pl*, die für jdn steuerpflichtig sind

cost: **~ structure** *n* FIN Kostengefüge *nt*, Kostenstruktur *f*; **~ of transport** *n* TRANSP Beförderungskosten *pl*; **~ of transportation** *n* TRANSP Beförderungskosten *pl*; **~ of treatment** *n* INS Behandlungskosten *pl*; **~ trimming** *n* GEN COMM Kostensenkung *f*; **~ variance** *n* FIN Kostenabweichung *f*; **~ variance analysis** *n* ACC Abweichungsanalyse *f*; **~-volume-profit analysis** *n* FIN Kostenumfanggewinnanalyse *f*, Kostenrechnung *f*

cotenancy *n* PROP Mietberechtigung *f*

cottage: **~ industry** *n* IND Heimindustrie *f*

cotton: **~ exchange** *n* STOCK Baumwollbörse *f*

CO_2: **~ tax** *n* (*carbon dioxide tax*) TAX CO_2-Steuer *f* (*Kohlendioxydsteuer*)

couchette *n* LEIS, TRANSP Liegewagen *m*

cough: **~ up** *vt infrml* FIN aufbringen, herausrücken (*infrml*), löhnen (*infrml*)

council *n* ADMIN, ECON Rat *m*, GEN COMM *local government* Magistrat *m*, IND Rat *m*, POL Beirat *m*, Rat *m*

Council: **~ of Economic Advisers** *n* (*CEA*) ECON Sachverständigenrat *m* für Wirtschaftsfragen; **~ of Europe** *n* POL Europarat *m*; **~ of European Industrial Federations** *n* (*CEIF*) IND Rat der europäischen Industrieverbände; **~ of Europe Resettlement Fund** *n* (*CERF*) BANK Wiedereingliederungsfonds des Europarats *m*

council: **~ flat** *n BrE* WEL Sozialwohnung *f*

Council: **~ for European Economic Cooperation** *n* (*CEEC*) ECON Rat *m* für Europäische wirtschaftliche Zusammenarbeit; **~ for Mutual Economic Aid** *n obs* (*COMECON*) ECON Rat *m* für gegenseitige Wirtschaftshilfe *obs* (*COMECON, RGW*)

council: **~ housing** *n BrE* WEL sozialer Wohnungsbau *m*, Sozialwohnung *f*

councilman *n AmE* ADMIN, POL Stadtrat *m*

Council: **~ of Ministers** *n* ADMIN, ECON, POL Ministerrat *m* der Europäische Union; **~ to the Stock Exchange** *n BrE* STOCK Börsenaufsichtsbehörde *f*, Börsenrat *m*, Börsenzulassungsausschuß *m*

council: **~ tax** *n BrE* (*cf poll tax BrE*) TAX Kommunalabgaben, Gemeindesteuern

councilwoman *n AmE* ADMIN, POL Stadträtin *f*

counsel **1.** *n* LAW *lawyer* Prozeßanwalt *m*, Prozeßanwältin *f*, *legal advice* Rechtsbeistand *m*; **2.** *vt*

LAW *advise* beraten, *criminal law* durch Rat Beihilfe leisten

counsel: **~ for the defence** *n BrE* (*cf attorney for the defense AmE*) LAW Verteidiger, in *m,f*

counseling *AmE see* **counselling** *BrE*

counselling *n BrE* GEN COMM Beratung *f*

counsellor *n BrE* GEN COMM Berater, in *m,f*

counselor *AmE see* **counsellor** *BrE*

count **1.** *vt* GEN COMM anrechnen, MATH zählen; **2.** *vi* GEN COMM zählen

counter **1.** *n* GEN COMM Schalter *m*, *shop, supermarket* Ladentisch *m*, Tisch *m*; **2.** *vt* GEN COMM widersprechen

counteract *vt* GEN COMM Maßnahmen ergreifen gegen

counter: **~-advertising** *n* S&M Abwehrwerbung *f*

counterbalance *vt* ACC aufrechnen, ECON auffangen, GEN COMM aufrechnen

counterbalancing *n* ACC Aufrechnung *f*

counter: **~ check** *AmE*, **~ cheque** *BrE n* BANK Blankobankscheck *m*, Kassenscheck *m*; **~ cheque form** *n BrE* BANK Überbringerscheckformular *nt*

counterclaim *n* LAW Gegenanspruch *m*, Widerklage *f*

countercyclical: **~ fiscal policy** *n* ECON antizyklische Finanzpolitik *f*; **~ policy** *n* ECON antizyklische Politik *f*

counter: **~ deal** *n* BANK Gegengeschäft *nt*

counterfeit **1.** *adj* BANK nachgemacht; **2.** *n* IND *fashion industry* Imitation *f*, Nachahmung *f*, LAW *money* Fälschung *f*

countermeasure *n* GEN COMM Gegenmaßnahme *f*

counteroffer *n* S&M Gegenangebot *nt*

counterpart *n* ECON Kontrahent *m*, GEN COMM Ausfertigung *f*

counterparty *n* STOCK Kontrahent *m*; **~ capital** *n* FIN Kapital *nt* des Kontrahenten

counterperformance *n* LAW *contract law* Gegenleistung *f*

counter: **~ purchase** *n* ECON *international trade* Gegenliefergeschäft *nt*, Kompensationsgegengeschäft *nt*; **~ trade** *n* ECON Kompensationshandel *m*; **~-trade contract** *n* LAW Kompensationsvertrag *m*; **~ trading** *n* ECON Tauschhandel *m*

countervailing: **~ duties** *n pl* IMP/EXP Ausgleichszoll *m*, Kompensationszoll *m*, TAX Kompensationszoll *m*; **~ power** *n* ECON Gegenmacht *f*, gegengewichtige Marktmacht *f*

counting: **~ towards** *adj* GEN COMM anrechenbar auf

country *n* ECON, IMP/EXP, POL, TRANSP Land *nt*; **~ code** *n* BANK Ländercode *m*; **~ damage** *n* INS Regionalschaden *m*; **~-damaged** *adj* IMP/EXP im Ursprungsland beschädigt; **~ of departure** *n* IMP/EXP Ausgangsland *nt*; **~ of destination** *n* IMP/EXP, TRANSP Bestimmungsland *nt*; **~ of dispatch** *n* TRANSP Versandland *nt*; **~ exposure** *n* ECON, INS, STOCK Länderrisiko *nt*; **~ fund** *n* STOCK Länderfonds *m*; **~ with a low-wage economy** *n* ECON Niedriglohnland *nt*; **~ of origin** *n* (*COO*) GEN COMM, IMP/EXP Herkunftsland *nt*, Ursprungsland *nt*; **~ planning** *n* GEN COMM Landesplanung *f*; **~ report** *n* ECON Länderbericht *m*; **~ of residence** *n* TAX Wohnsitzstaat *m*; **~ risk** *n* FIN *provisions* Länderrisiko *nt*

Countryside: **~ Commission** *n BrE* ENVIR Landschaftsschutzamt *nt*

country: **~-specific** *adj* ECON *development aid* landesspezifisch

county *n BrE* (*cf territory*) GEN COMM Grafschaft *f*; **~ court** *n* LAW *civil cases* Amtsgericht *nt*

coupled: ~ **with** *adj* COMP gekoppelt mit, verbunden mit, GEN COMM gekoppelt mit

coupon *n* GEN COMM (*c.*, *cp.*) Bon *m*, Gutschein *m*, *on bond* Anleihezins *m*, S&M (*c.*, *cp.*) *advertising* Kupon *m*, STOCK *money-off* Zinsschein *m*, Kupon *m*; ~ **collection** *n* FIN Einlösung *f* von Zinsscheinen; ~ **sheet** *n* FIN Bogen *m*, STOCK Talon *m*

courier *n* COMMS Kurier *m*; ~ **firm** *n* COMMS Kurierdienst *m*, Kurierfirma *f*; ~ **service** *n* COMMS Kurierdienst *m*

Cournot: ~'**s duopoly model** *n* ECON Cournotsches Dyopol *nt*

course *n* GEN COMM Lauf *m*, HRM, MGMNT, WEL Kurs *m*; ♦ **in the** ~ **of** GEN COMM *negotiations* im Verlauf von

course: ~ **of action** *n* MGMNT Handlungsweise *f*, Verfahrensweise *f*

court *n* LAW Gericht *nt*, Gerichtshof *m*, *courtroom* Gerichtssaal *m*; ♦ **come before** ~ LAW vor Gericht erscheinen; **go to** ~ LAW prozessieren; ~ **is now in session** LAW das Gericht tagt

court: ~ **of appeal** *n* LAW Berufungsgericht *nt*, Rechtsmittelinstanz *f*; ~ **of arbitration** *n* LAW Schiedsgericht *nt*

Court: ~ **of Auditors** *n* ACC Rechnungshof *m*

court: ~ **case** *n* LAW Rechtsfall *m*, Prozeß *m*; ~ **of chancery** *n* LAW Gericht *nt* des Lordkanzlers; ~ **entitled to adjudicate** *n* LAW Spruchgericht *nt*

Court: ~ **of First Instance** *n* LAW *EU* Gericht *nt* erster Instanz; ~ **of Justice** *n* LAW Gerichtshof *m* der Europäischen Union

court: ~ **of law** *n* LAW ordentliches Gericht *nt*; ~ **of petty session** *n* LAW Amtsgericht *nt* in Strafsachen; ~ **procedures** *n pl* LAW Gerichtsverfahren *nt pl*; ~ **proceedings** *n pl* LAW gerichtliches Verfahren *nt*; ~ **of record** *n* *AmE* LAW Registergericht *nt*

courtroom *n* LAW Gerichtssaal *m*

Court: ~ **of Session** *n* LAW *Scotland* Oberstes Gericht für Zivilsachen

couturier *n* GEN COMM Modeschöpfer *m*

couturière *n* GEN COMM Modeschöpferin *f*

covariance *n* MATH *statistics* Kovarianz *f*

covenant *n* ADMIN Nebenvereinbarung *f*, LAW förmliches rechtsverbindliches Versprechen *nt*, Vertrag *m*, PROP Zusicherung *f*; ~ **not to compete** *n* LAW vertragliches Wettbewerbsverbot *nt*

covenantor *n* LAW vertraglich Verpflichtete(r) *mf* [decl. as adj]

cover 1. *n* BANK, FIN Deckung *f*, IND Verkleidung *f*, INS Versicherung *f*, STOCK Deckung *f*; **2.** *vt* BANK, FIN *costs* decken, IND verkleiden, STOCK decken; ♦ ~ **expenses** FIN Ausgaben decken; ~ **a loss** FIN einen Schaden decken, einen Verlust abdecken; ~ **the risk** STOCK das Risiko abdecken

cover up *vt* GEN COMM *truth, information* vertuschen, verschleiern

cover: ~ **against stranding** *n* INS Deckung *f* gegen Strandung, Versicherungsschutz *m* gegen Strandung

coverage *n* ADMIN Erfassung *f*, Geltungsbereich *m*, GEN COMM, MEDIA Deckung *f*

cover: ~ **of assurance** *n* *BrE* INS Deckungskapital *nt*, Deckungsrückstellung *f*

covered: **be** ~ **by insurance** *phr* INS durch Versicherung gedeckt sein; ~ **call** *n* *BrE* STOCK gedeckte Kaufoption *f*; ~ **dry container** *n* TRANSP *shipping* geschlossener Trockencontainer *m*; ~ **gangway** *n* TRANSP *shipping* geschlossene Gangway *f*; ~ **long** *n* STOCK *options* gedeckte Baisseposition *f*; ~ **option** *n* STOCK gedeckte Option *f*; ~ **position** *n* *BrE* STOCK *options* gedeckte Position *f*; ~ **put** *n* STOCK gedeckte Verkaufsoption *f*; ~ **short** *n* STOCK *options* gedeckte Short-Position *f*; ~ **warrant** *n* FIN kursgesicherter Optionsschein *m*; ~ **writer** *n* STOCK gedeckter Optionsverkäufer *m*

covering: ~ **letter** *n* ADMIN, COMMS Begleitschreiben *nt*, Begleitbrief *m*; ~ **purchase** *n* GEN COMM, LAW Deckungskauf *m*, STOCK Deckung *f*

cover: ~ **note** *n* (*CN*) INS Deckungsbestätigung *f*, Deckungsgrundlage *f*, Deckungszusage *f*, vorläufige Deckungszusage *f*, vorläufige Versicherungspolice *f*; ~ **page** *n* S&M Umschlagseite *f*; ~ **price** *n* S&M Preis *m* für ein Einzelexemplar; ~ **ratio** *n* FIN Deckungsgrad *m*, Deckungsquote *f*, INS Deckungssatz *m*

COW *abbr* (*crude oil washing*) IND Rohölreinigung *f*

cowboy: ~ **economy** *n* *AmE infrml* ECON Cowboy-Wirtschaft *f*

Cowles: ~ **Commission** *n* *AmE* GEN COMM Cowles-Kommission *f*

cp. *abbr* (*coupon*) GEN COMM Bon *m*, Gutschein *m*, S&M Kupon *m*, STOCK Kupon *m*, Zinsschein *m*

C/P *abbr* TRANSP (*charter party*) *shipping* Charterpartie *f*, Chartervertrag *m*, (*custom of port*) Hafenusance *f*

CP *abbr* BANK, FIN, GEN COMM (*commercial paper*) Handelspapier *nt*, WP (*Wertpapier*), HRM (*community program AmE, community programme BrE*) Gemeinschaftsprogramm *nt*, STOCK (*commercial paper*) Handelspapier *nt*, WP (*Wertpapier*)

CPA *abbr* ACC (*certified public accountant AmE*) konzessionierter Wirtschaftsprüfer *m*, konzessionierte Wirtschaftsprüferin *f*, zugelassener Wirtschaftsprüfer *m*, zugelassene Wirtschaftsprüferin *f*, MATH (*critical path analysis*) Methode *f* des kritischen Pfades

C/P: ~ **bill of lading** *n* TRANSP *shipping* Chartervertrag-Konnossement *nt*

cpd *abbr* (*charterer pays dues*) IMP/EXP, TRANSP *shipping* Befrachter zahlt Abgaben

CPE *abbr* (*centrally planned economy*) ECON Zentralverwaltungswirtschaft *f*

CPI *abbr* (*consumer price index*) ECON Verbraucherpreisindex *m*, Index *m* der Verbraucherpreise

CPM *abbr* (*critical path method*) MATH CPM-Methode *f*

CPP *abbr* (*current purchasing power*) ECON Gegenwartswert *m* der Kaufkraft

CPS *abbr* ECON (*current population survey*) fortgeschriebene Bevölkerungsstatistik *f*, (*Centre for Policy Studies BrE*) Zentrum *nt* für politische Studien

CPU *abbr* (*central processing unit*) COMP ZE (*Zentraleinheit*)

Cr *abbr* (*creditor*) ADMIN, FIN, GEN COMM Gl. (*Gläubiger*)

CR *abbr* (*carriage return*) COMP Wagenrücklauf *m*, ZS (*Zeilenschaltung*)

craft: ~ **loss** *n* (*c/l*) TRANSP *shipping* Schiffsverlust *m*

craftsman *n* HRM Handwerker, in *m,f*

craft: ~ **union** *n* HRM Fachgewerkschaft *f*

crane *n* IND, TRANSP Kran *m*

crash 1. *n* COMP Absturz *m*, GEN COMM Aufprall *m*, TRANSP Absturz *m*, Aufprall *m*, Zusammenstoß *m*, STOCK Aufprall *m*; **2.** *vi* COMP abstürzen, TRANSP *car* abstürzen, zusammenstoßen; ~ **into** aufprallen auf [+acc]

crate *n* IMP/EXP *air freight* Kiste *f*, TRANSP Lattenkiste *f*, Kiste *f*

crawling: ~ **peg** *n* ECON Gleitparität *f*, STOCK gleitende Wechselkursanpassung *f*

CRC *abbr* (*camera-ready copy*) MEDIA *publishing* reprofähige Vorlage *f*, reproreife Vorlage *f*

CRE *abbr BrE* (*Commercial Relations and Exports*) IMP/EXP Handelsbeziehungen *f pl* und Exporte *m pl*

cream off *vt infrml* GEN COMM *money, demand* absahnen (*infrml*), abschöpfen

cream: ~ **of the crop** *n infrml* HRM Elite *f*

create *vt* COMP erstellen, GEN COMM *opportunities* schaffen, LAW *mortgage* bestellen; ♦ ~ **a market** S&M einen Markt schaffen; ~ **an agency** GEN COMM eine Vertretung gründen; ~ **demand** ECON Nachfrage schaffen; ~ **jobs** ADMIN Arbeitsplätze schaffen

creation *n* GEN COMM Schaffung *f*; ♦ ~ **of reserves** ACC Rücklagenbildung *f*

creative *adj* GEN COMM kreativ; ~ **accounting** *n* ACC aktive Bilanzgestaltung *f*, kreative Buchführung *f* (*infrml*); ~ **department** *n* S&M Werbeabteilung *f*; ~ **destruction** *n* ECON kreative Zerstörung *f*; ~ **federalism** *n* POL kreativer Föderalismus *m*; ~ **financing** *n* FIN unorthodoxe Finanzierungsmethode *f*; ~ **marketing** *n* S&M schöpferisches Marketing *nt*; ~ **strategy** *n* S&M *advertising* kreative Strategie *f*; ~ **thinking** *n* MGMNT kreatives Denken *nt*

creativity *n* GEN COMM Kreativität *f*

credentials: ~ **presentation** *n* S&M Vorlage *f* von Empfehlungsschreiben

credibility *n* S&M Glaubwürdigkeit *f*; ~ **gap** *n* S&M Glaubwürdigkeitslücke *f*

credit 1. *n* (*Cr*) ACC, BANK, FIN Kredit *m*, *sum of money* Kreditposten *m*, *amount possessed* Guthaben *nt*, *allowance* Anrechnung *f*; ♦ **on** ~ FIN auf Kredit; **2.** *vt* ACC, BANK, FIN gutschreiben [+dat]; ♦ ~ **a sum to an account** BANK einem Konto einen Betrag gutschreiben

creditable: ~ **against** *adj* TAX anrechenbar auf; ~ **amount** *n* TAX anrechenbarer Betrag *m*; ~ **assets** *n pl* TAX anrechenbare Vermögenswerte *m pl*

credit: ~ **account** *n* (*C/A, cf cheque account BrE, cf current account BrE, cf checking account AmE*) BANK Girokonto *nt*, Kreditkonto *nt*, Kontokorrent *nt*, Kontokorrentkonto *nt*, Kreditkartenkonto *nt*, Kundenkreditkonto *nt*; ~ **account voucher** *n* BANK Krediteinzahlungsbeleg *m*; ~ **agency** *n* BANK, FIN Kreditinstitut *nt*; ~ **agreement** *n* FIN Kreditvertrag *m*; ~ **analysis** *n* BANK Kreditprüfung *f*, Kreditwürdigkeitsprüfung *f*; ~ **analyst** *n* BANK Bonitätsprüfer, in *m,f*, STOCK Kreditfachmann *m*, Kreditprüfer, in *m,f*; ~ **approval** *n* FIN Kreditansage *f*; ~ **balance** *n* BANK Guthaben *nt*; ~ **bureau** *n* FIN *credit information* Kreditauskunftei *f*, Kreditbüro *nt*; ~ **buyer** *n AmE* (*cf charge buyer BrE*) S&M Kreditkäufer, in *m,f*, Kreditkunde *m*; ~ **by way of bank guaranty** *n* BANK Aval *m*; ~ **card** *n* BANK, FIN Kreditkarte *f*; ~ **card booking** *n* LEIS Reservierung per Kreditkarte *f*; ~ **cardholder** *n* BANK, FIN Kreditkarteninhaber, in *m,f*; ~ **card issuer** *n* FIN Kreditkartenaussteller *m*; ~ **card payment** *n* BANK, S&M Kreditkartenzahlung *f*; ~ **card portfolio** *n* BANK Kreditkartenbestand *m*; ~ **ceiling** *n* BANK Kredithöchstgrenze *f*, Kreditplafond

m; ~ **clearing** *n BrE* BANK Kreditverrechnung *f*; ~ **column** *n* FIN Kreditkolumne *f*, Kreditspalte *f*; ~ **conditions** *n pl* ECON Kreditbedingungen *f pl*; ~ **control** *n* BANK Kreditkontrolle *f*; ~ **controller** *n* MGMNT Kreditsachbearbeiter, in *m,f*; ~ **creation multiplier** *n* ECON Kreditschöpfungsmultiplikator *m*; ~ **crunch** *n* BANK, ECON, FIN Kreditknappheit *f*, Kreditrestriktion *f*; ~ **demand** *n* BANK Kreditnachfrage *f*, Kreditbedarf *m*, FIN Kreditbedarf *m*; ~ **department** *n* BANK, FIN Kreditabteilung *f*

credited: ~ **to** *phr* ACC zur Gutschrift auf, FIN gutgeschrieben auf

credit: ~-**enhanced** *adj* STOCK *securities* krediterweitert; ~ **enhancement** *n* BANK Bonitätsverbesserung *f*; ~ **entry** *n* ACC Gutschrift *f*, Habenbuchung *f*; ~ **facilities** *n pl* ACC Bankfazilitäten *f pl*; ~ **facility** *n* BANK, FIN Kreditfazilität *f*, Kreditmöglichkeit *f*, Kreditrahmen *m*; ~ **granting** *n* BANK Krediteinräumung *f*; ~ **guarantee** *n* BANK Kreditgarantie *f*

Credit: ~ **Industry Fraud Avoidance System** *n BrE* (*CIFAS*) FIN System der Betrugvermeidung innerhalb der Kreditindustrie

credit: ~ **information** *n* FIN Kreditauskunft *f*; ~ **institution** *n* FIN Kreditanstalt *f*, Kreditinstitut *nt*; ~ **instrument** *n* STOCK *interest rate futures* Finanzierungsmittel *nt*, Kreditinstrumentarium *nt*; ~ **limit** *n* BANK Kredithöchstgrenze *f*; ~ **line** *n* BANK Kreditlinie *f*; ~ **management** *n* FIN Kreditbearbeitung *f*, Kreditverwaltung *f*; ~ **memorandum** *n* FIN Einzahlungsbeleg *m*, Gutschrift *f*, Gutschriftsanzeige *f*; ~ **money** *n* BANK Kreditgeld *nt*, FIN Buchgeld *nt*, Giralgeld *nt*; ~ **multiplier** *n* FIN Giralgeldschöpfungsmultiplikator *m*; ~ **note** *n* FIN, GEN COMM (*C/N, CN*) Gutschein *m*, Gutschrift *f*, Gutschriftsanzeige *f*; ~ **officer** *n* BANK, FIN Kreditsachbearbeiter, in *m,f*

creditor *n* (*Cr*) ADMIN, FIN, GEN COMM Gläubiger, in *m,f* (*Gl.*); ~ **beneficiary** *n* GEN COMM Zahlungsempfänger, in *m,f*, INS *life insurance* Begünstigte(r) *mf* [decl. as adj], LAW Zuwendungsempfänger, in *m,f*; ~ **department** *n* ADMIN Gläubigerabteilung *f*

credit: ~ **order** *n* S&M Kreditauftrag *m*

creditor: ~ **in bankruptcy** *n* INS, LAW Konkursgläubiger, in *m,f*; ~ **position** *n* FIN Finanzlage *f* des Gläubigers, Gläubigerstellung *f*, Kreditpotential *nt*; ~ **rights life assurance** *n* INS Restschuldlebensversicherung *f*; ~ **rights life insurance** *n* INS Restschuldlebensversicherung *f*

creditors *n pl BrE* (*cf payables AmE*) ACC Kreditoren *m pl*, unbezahlte Verbindlichkeit *f*

creditor: ~'s **account** *n* FIN aufgenommene Gelder *nt pl*; ~'s **committee** *n* FIN Gläubigerausschuß *m*; ~'s **fault of acception** *n* LAW *contracts* Gläubigerverzug *m*

creditors': ~ **ledger** *n* ACC Gläubigerbuch *nt*; ~ **trustee** *n* LAW Sachwalter, in *m,f*

credit: ~ **period** *n* GEN COMM Zahlungsziel *nt*; ~ **protection** *n* FIN Delkredereschutz *m*; ~ **protection insurance** *n* INS Übernahme *f* des Delkredererisikos; ~ **rationing** *n* BANK, ECON, FIN Drosselung *f* der Kreditgewährung, Kreditbeschränkung *f*; ~ **reference agency** *n* FIN Auskunftei *f*, Kreditschutzverein *m*; ~ **requirements** *n pl* BANK, FIN Kreditbedarf *m*; ~ **reserves** *n pl* FIN Kreditreserven *f pl*; ~ **restriction** *n* BANK, ECON, FIN Kreditdrosselung *f*, Krediteinschränkung *f*, Kreditrestriktion *f*; **~ revolving** *n* FIN Revolvingkredit *m*; **~ risk** *n* FIN, S&M Kreditrisiko *nt*

credits *n pl* STOCK *options on Eurodollar futures* Akkreditive *nt pl*, Kreditbrief *m*

credit: **~ sale** *n* LAW *British contract law* Abzahlungskauf *m* ohne Eigentumsvorbehalt, S&M Kauf *m* auf Kredit, Kreditkauf *m*; **~ sale agreement** *n* FIN Teilzahlungsvertrag *m*; **~ scoring** *n* FIN Kreditwürdigkeitsprüfung *f*; **~ side** *n* ACC Habenseite *f*, FIN Habenseite *f*, Kreditseite *f*; **~ slip** *n* FIN Bon *m*, Einzahlungsbeleg *m*, Einzahlungsschein *m*, Gutschriftzettel *m*

credits: **~ outstanding** *n* ACC Kreditlinie *f*

credit: **~ squeeze** *n* BANK, ECON, FIN Beschränkung *f* der Kreditaufnahme, Kreditbeschränkung *f*, Kreditdrosselung *f*, Kreditknappheit *f*, Kreditrestriktion *f*, Kreditverknappung *f*; **~ standing** *n* BANK Bonität *f*, S&M Kreditwürdigkeit *f*

Credit: **~ Suisse Index** *n* STOCK Schweizer Kreditindex

credit: **~ surveillance** *n* FIN Kreditüberwachung *f*; **~ terms** *n pl* BANK Kreditkonditionen *f pl*; **~ title** *n* MEDIA Liste *f* der Mitwirkenden; **~ tranche** *n* FIN Kredittranche *f*; **~ tranche facility** *n* ECON Kredittranchenfazilität *f*; **~ transfer** *n* BANK Banküberweisung *f*; **~ union** *n* BANK Verbandsbank *f*

creditworthiness *n* BANK Kreditfähigkeit *f*, Kreditwürdigkeit *f*, FIN Bonität *f*, Kreditwürdigkeit *f*

creditworthy *adj* BANK kreditfähig, kreditwürdig, FIN kreditwürdig

creeping: **~ inflation** *n* ECON schleichende Inflation *f*; **~ tender** *n* FIN *takeovers* schleichendes Übernahmeangebot *nt*, STOCK *takeovers* schleichende Übernahme *f*

cremation: **~ expenses insurance** *n* INS Feuerbestattungsversicherung *f*

crew *n* HRM, MGMNT, TRANSP Mannschaft *f*; **~ manifest** *n* TRANSP *shipping* Mannschaftsliste *f*; **~ manning** *n* TRANSP *shipping* Zusammensetzung *f* des Personals; **~ member** *n* TRANSP *shipping* Mitglied *nt* des Fahrpersonals

crime *n* LAW Straftat *f*

criminal 1. *n* LAW Straftäter, in *m,f*,Gauner *m* (*infrml*); **2.** *adj* LAW verbrecherisch; **~ damage** *n* LAW Eigentumsdelikt *nt*; **~ liability** *n* INS, LAW Haftung *f* aus vorsätzlichen Straftaten; **~ negligence** *n* LAW strafbares Fahrlässigkeitsdelikt *nt*; **~ offence** *BrE*, **~ offense** *AmE n* LAW Straftat *f*, strafbare Handlung *f*

crisis *n* GEN COMM Krise *f*; **~ management** *n* MGMNT Krisenmanagement *nt*, Management *nt* nach dem Krisenprinzip

criteria: **~ of a similar nature** *n pl* GEN COMM ähnliche Kriterien *nt pl*

criterion *n* GEN COMM Kriterium *nt*

critic *n* MEDIA Kritiker, in *m,f*

critical *adj* GEN COMM anspruchsvoll, *censorious* kritisch; **~ level** *n* GEN COMM kritisches Niveau *nt*; **~ mass** *n* ECON, S&M kritische Masse *f*, kritische Menge *f*; **~ path** *n* COMP *planning* kritischer Pfad *m*, kritischer Weg *m*; **~ path analysis** *n* (*CPA*) MATH *statistics* Methode *f* des kritischen Pfades; **~ path method** *n* (*CPM*) MATH *statistics* CPM-Methode *f*; **~ path theory** *n* (*cf critical path method*) ECON CPM-Theorie *f*; **~ region** *n* MATH *statistical testing* Ablehnungsbereich *m*, kritischer Bereich *m*; **~ value** *n* MATH *statistics* kritischer Wert *m*

criticize *vt* GEN COMM kritisieren

CRN *abbr* (*customs registered number*) IMP/EXP Zollzulassungsnummer *f*

CRO *abbr* (*Companies Registration Office*) GEN COMM Gesellschafts-Registeramt *nt*, Gesellschaftsregisterstelle *f*, *in Germany* Handelsregister *nt*

crook *n* *infrml* GEN COMM Hochstapler, in *m,f*, LAW Hochstapler, in *m,f*, Schwindler *m*

crop *n* ECON Ernte *f*, Frucht *f*, ENVIR Frucht *f*, GEN COMM, INS Ernte *f*; **~ failure** *n* ECON *agricultural* Mißernte *f*; **~ hail insurance** *n* INS Erntehagelversicherung *f*; **~ rotation** *n* ENVIR Fruchtwechsel *m*, Fruchtfolge *f*

cross 1. *n* ECON, MATH, S&M Kreuz *nt*, STOCK privater Verkauf *m* eines Aktienpakets; **2.** *vt* IMP/EXP *frontier* überschreiten; ♦ **~ a check** *AmE*, **~ a cheque** *BrE* BANK einen Scheck kreuzen, einen Scheck durchkreuzen, einen Scheck zur Verrechnung ausstellen; **~ a picket line** HRM, IND die Streikposten nicht beachten; **~ specially** BANK *cheque* besonders kreuzen

cross: **~-bencher** *n* *BrE* POL *House of Lords* Fraktionslose(r) *mf* [decl. as adj]; **~-border** *adj* GEN COMM grenzüberschreitend; **~-border demerger** *n* ECON grenzüberschreitende Entflechtung *f*; **~-border transaction** *n* FIN grenzüberschreitendes Finanzgeschäft *nt*; **~-border joint venture** *n* MGMNT grenzüberschreitendes Gemeinschaftsunternehmen *nt*, grenzüberschreitendes Joint-Venture *nt*; **~-border merger** *n* ECON grenzüberschreitende Fusion *f*, GEN COMM, STOCK grenzüberschreitende Firmenzusammenschlüsse *m pl*, grenzüberschreitende Fusion *f*; **~-border trade** *n* ECON grenzüberschreitender Handel *m*, internationaler Warenverkehr *m*, IMP/EXP grenzüberschreitender Handel *m*; **~-border trading** *n* ECON, IMP/EXP grenzüberschreitender Handelsverkehr *m*; **~-border transaction** *n* ECON grenzüberschreitende Transaktion *f*, internationales Geschäft *nt*; **~-border transfer** *n* ENVIR, TRANSP *of hazardous waste* grenzüberschreitender Transfer *m*

crosscheck *n* BANK Gegenprüfung *f*

cross: **~-complaint** *n* *AmE* LAW Widerklage *f*; **~ couponing** *n* S&M *sales promotion* Werbung *f* mit Gutschein für zweites Erzeugnis; **~-currency swap** *n* FIN Währungsswap *m* auf der Pari-Forward-Basis; **~ default** *n* BANK, FIN Drittverzug *m*, reziproker Verzug *m*

crossed *adj* BANK nicht gekreuzt; **~ check** *AmE*, **~ cheque** *BrE n* BANK Verrechnungsscheck *m*

cross: **~ elasticity of demand** *n* S&M *marketing* Kreuzelastizität *f* der Nachfrage; **~-footing** *n* MATH *spreadsheet* Querrechnen *nt*; **~ guarantee** *n* BANK wechselseitige Bürgschaft *f*; **~ hedge** *n* STOCK Cross Hedge *m*; **~ hedging** *n* STOCK wechselseitige Kurssicherung *f*; **~ holdings between companies** *n pl* STOCK gegenseitige Kapitalbeteiligung *f* zwischen Unternehmen; **~ liability** *n* INS gegenseitige Haftpflicht *f*, gegenseitige Haftung *f*; **~ licence** *n* LAW *contract law* gegenseitige Lizenz *f*; **~-licensing** *n* COMP *technology transfer* gegenseitiger Austausch *m* von Lizenzen, Lizenzaustausch *m*, GEN COMM, LAW Lizenzaustausch *m*, gegenseitiger Austausch *m* von Lizenzen; **~ member** *n* TRANSP *of container* Querträger *m*; **~ merchandising** *n* S&M kombinierte Absatzförderung *f*

crossover: ~ **vote** n AmE POL presidential elections Vorwahlstimme f für Kandidaten einer anderen Partei
cross: ~ **ownership** n GEN COMM Besitzverflechtung f; ~ **price elasticity of demand** n ECON Kreuzpreiselastizität f der Nachfrage; ~ **rate** n ECON indirekte Parität f, Kreuzparität f; ~**-rate of exchange** n FIN indirekter Wechselkurs m; ~**-reference** n COMP Querverweis m; ~**-reference listing** n COMP Querverweisliste f; ~ **section** n GEN COMM Querschnitt m; ~**-section data** n pl ECON econometrics Querschnittsdaten pl; ~**-subsidization** n FIN Quersubventionieren nt, Verlustausgleich m, GEN COMM Quersubventionieren nt; ~**-subsidy** n FIN, GEN COMM Quersubvention f; ~**-suit** n LAW Widerklage f; ~ **tabulation** n MATH statistical technique Kreuztabellierung f; ~ **trade** n TRANSP shipping Schiffsverkehr m zwischen fremden Ländern
CROTUM abbr BrE (commissioner for the rights of trade union members) HRM Kommissar für die Rechte von Gewerkschaftsmitgliedern
crowd out vt ECON borrowers, investors hinausdrängen, GEN COMM ausschließen
crowding: ~ **hypothesis** n ECON Überfüllungshypothese f; ~ **out** n ECON borrowing, investment Crowding-Out nt, Verdrängungswettbewerb m
Crown: ~ **Agent** n BrE ECON UK government procurement agency britische Beschaffungsbehörde f; ~ **corporation** n BrE ADMIN staatseigene Gesellschaft f
crown: ~ **council** n LAW Kronrat m; ~ **jewels** n pl infrml ECON besonders lukrativer Geschäftsbereich m
Crown: ~ **loan** n BrE TAX Staatsdarlehen nt; ~ **Prosecution Service** n BrE LAW Staatsanwaltschaft f
crown: ~ **prosecutor** n BrE (cf district attorney AmE) LAW Staatsanwältin f, Staatsanwalt m
CRT abbr (cathode ray tube) COMP hardware CRT (Kathodenstrahlröhre)
crude: ~ **oil** n ENVIR, IND Rohöl nt; ~ **oil carrier** n TRANSP Rohöltanker m, Rohöltransporter m; ~ **oil refinery** n IND Mineralölraffinerie f; ~ **oil washing** n (COW) IND Rohölreinigung f; ~ **petroleum** n ENVIR Rohpetroleum nt; ~ **population rate** n ECON allgemeine Bevölkerungswachstumsrate f
cryogenic adj IND kryogen; ~ **engineering** n IND Kryotechnik f; ~ **liquid** n TRANSP engineering Tieftemperaturflüssigkeit f
cryogenics n IND engineering Kryogenik f
CS abbr GEN COMM (civil service) öffentlicher Dienst m, Staatsdienst m, Verwaltungsdienst m, Zivilverwaltung f, TRANSP (continuous survey) shipping Dauerprüfung f, regelmäßige Inspektion f, regelmäßige Schiffsbesichtigung f
CSC abbr BrE (Civil Service Commission) ADMIN Berufsbeamtenausschuß m
CSE abbr BrE obs (Certificate of Secondary Education) WEL Sekundarabschluß m, Volksschulabschluß m (obs)
CSO abbr BrE (Central Statistical Office) ECON statistisches Zentralbüro nt, ≈ statistisches Bundesamt nt
CST abbr GEN COMM (Central Standard Time) Zentrale Standardzeit, TRANSP (container service tariff) Containerdienst-Tarif m
CT abbr GEN COMM (cubic tonnage) Kubiktonnage f, IMP/EXP (Community transit) EG-Durchfuhr f, EG-Transit m, TRANSP (combined transport) kombinierter Transport m, (Community transit) EG-Durchfuhr f, EG-Transit m,

(cargo tank) Ladetank m, (cubic tonnage) Kubiktonnage f
CTBL abbr (combined transport bill of lading) TRANSP kombiniertes Transportkonossement nt, Konnossement nt für kombinierten Transport
CTC abbr (cargo tank center AmE, cargo tank centre BrE) TRANSP Ladetankzentrum nt
CTD abbr TAX (certificate of tax deposit) verzinsliches Steuerzertifikat nt, TRANSP (combined transport document) Beleg m für kombinierten Transport, Kombinationstransportdokument nt
CTL abbr (constructive total loss) INS marine angenommener Totalverlust m
CTLO abbr (constructive total loss only) INS marine angenommener Totalverlust m
CTN abbr (Confectioners, Tobacconists and Newsagents) S&M Süßwaren-, Tabak- und Zeitungshändler
CTO abbr (combined transport operator) TRANSP Kombinationstransportunternehmer m, Spediteur m, der einen kombinierten Transport durchführt
CTPC abbr (cargo traffic procedures committee) TRANSP Komitee nt für Frachtverkehrsverfahren
CTRL: ~ **key** n (control key) COMP keyboard CTRL-Taste f (Steuerungstaste), STRG-Taste f (Steuerungstaste)
CTT abbr BrE (capital transfer tax) TAX Erbschafts- und Schenkungssteuer f, Kapitalübertragungssteuer f
CTW abbr (cargo tank wing) TRANSP shipping Ladetankflügel m
cu abbr (cubic) GEN COMM Kubik; ~ **ft** abbr (cubic foot) GEN COMM Kubikfuß m; ~ **in** abbr (cubic inch) GEN COMM Kubikzoll m
cube out vt TRANSP den Rauminhalt messen von
cube: ~**-cutting** n TRANSP shipping betrügerisches Unterschlagen von Rauminhalt
cubic adj (cu) GEN COMM Kubik-; ~ **capacity** n (cc) GEN COMM Motorhubraum m (cc); ~ **centimeter** AmE, ~ **centimetre** BrE n (cc, cm^3) GEN COMM Kubikzentimeter m (cc, cm^3); ~ **foot** n (cu ft) GEN COMM Kubikfuß m; ~ **inch** n (cu in) GEN COMM Kubikzoll m; ~ **meter** AmE, ~ **metre** BrE n (cbm, m^3) GEN COMM Kubikmeter m (m^3), Raummeter m; ~ **tonnage** n (CT) TRANSP of ship Kubiktonnage f
cue n S&M Hinweis m
cul-de-sac n PROP Sackgasse f
culpable adj LAW schuldhaft
cultivate vt ECON bearbeiten, kultivieren
cultivation n ECON agricultural economics Anbau m, Bearbeitung f, Bebauung f, Bewirtschaftung f, Kultivierung f, Urbarmachung f
cultural adj GEN COMM kulturell; ~ **center** AmE, ~ **centre** BrE n LEIS, MEDIA Kulturzentrum nt, kulturelles Zentrum nt
culture n GEN COMM Kultur f; ~ **shock** n GEN COMM Kulturschock m
cum prep STOCK mit; ♦ ~ **dividend** (cd) STOCK einschließlich Dividende; ~ **and ex** STOCK einschließlich und ausschließlich
cum. abbr (cumulative) FIN, INS, STOCK, TAX kumulativ
cumulative adj (cum.) FIN, INS kumulativ, S&M erfaßt, STOCK, TAX kumulativ; ~ **audience** n S&M erfaßte Gesamthörerzahl f; ~ **income** n TAX income kumulatives Einkommen nt; ~ **liability** n INS kumulative Haftung f; ~ **penetration** n S&M gesteigertes Durch-

dringungsvermögen *nt*; ~ **preference shares** *n pl BrE* (*cf cumulative preferred stock AmE*) STOCK kumulative Vorzugsaktien *f pl*; ~ **preferred stock** *n AmE* (*cf cumulative preference shares BrE*) STOCK kumulative Vorzugsaktien *f pl*; ~ **reach** *n* S&M Gesamtreichweite *f*; ~ **security** *n* STOCK kumulatives Wertpapier *nt*; ~ **tax** *n* TAX kumulative Steuer *f*; ~ **voting** *n* STOCK *stockholders voting system* kumulative Stimmrechtsabgabe *f*, Stimmenhäufung *f*

cum: ~ **warrant** *phr* STOCK mit Bezugsrecht, mit Optionsschein

curb *vt* ECON drosseln, GEN COMM dämpfen

curiosity *n* S&M Neugier *f*

currency *n* ACC Gültigkeit *f*, Laufzeit *f*, BANK gesetzliches Zahlungsmittel *nt*, Valuta *f*, Währung *f*, ECON, FIN gesetzliches Zahlungsmittel *nt*, Währung *f*; ~ **account** *n* BANK Währungskonto *nt*, ECON Devisenkonto *nt*, FIN Devisenkonto *nt*, Währungskonto *nt*; ~ **adjustment** *n* BANK Währungsausgleich *m*; ~ **adjustment factor** *n* (*CAF*) TRANSP *surcharge on freight* Währungsausgleichsfaktor *m*; ~ **appreciation** *n* ECON Währungsaufwertung *f*; ~ **arbitrage** *n* STOCK Devisenarbitrage *f*, Valutenarbitrage *f*; ~ **at a discount** *n* BANK *international banking* auf Devisen entfallenes Aufgeld *nt*; ~ **band** *n* FIN Bandbreite *f*; ~ **basket** *n* BANK Währungskorb *m*; ~ **bond** *n* FIN Währungsanleihe *f*; ~ **borrowing** *n* BANK Währungsdarlehen *nt*; ~ **and bunker adjustment factor** *n* (*CABAF*) TRANSP *shipping* Währungs- und Bunkerausgleichsfaktor *m*; ~ **clause** *n* FIN Effektivklausel *f*; ~ **cocktail** *n* FIN Währungskorb *m*; ~ **code** *n* BANK Währungscode *m*; ~ **contract** *n* STOCK *money market* Devisenvertrag *m*; ~ **of the credit** *n* FIN Akkreditivwährung *f*; ~ **deposits** *n pl* FIN Währungseinlagen *f pl*; ~ **depreciation** *n* ECON Währungsabwertung *f*; ~ **devaluation** *n* ECON Abwertung *f*; ~ **draft** *n* BANK Valutawechsel *m*; ~ **holdings** *n pl* ECON Devisenbestände *m pl*; ~ **in circulation** *n* ECON Bargeldumlauf *m*; ~ **issue** *n* BANK Währungsausgabe *f*; ~-**linked** *adj* FIN währungsgebunden; ~ **market** *n* ECON Devisenbörse *f*, Devisenmarkt *m*, STOCK Devisenmarkt *m*; ~ **mix** *n* BANK Währungsmischung *f*; ~ **realignment** *n* ECON Neufestsetzung *f* der Währungsparitäten; ~ **reform** *n* ECON Währungsreform *f*; ~ **reserves** *n pl* ECON Währungsreserven *f pl*; ~ **restrictions** *n pl* ECON Devisenbeschränkungen *f pl*; ~ **revaluation** *n* ECON Währungsaufwertung *f*; ~ **risk** *n* ECON *macroeconomics* Währungsrisiko *nt*

Currency: ~ **School** *n BrE* ECON Currency-Theorie *f*

currency: ~ **snake** *n* ECON Währungsschlange *f*; ~ **speculation** *n* ECON Devisenspekulation *f*; ~ **stabilization scheme** *n* ECON Abkommen *nt* zur Stabilisierung der Wechselkurse; ~ **standard** *n* STOCK Devisenstandard *m*; ~ **symbol** *n* COMP Währungssymbol *nt*; ~ **unit** *n* ECON Währungseinheit *f*; ~ **value** *n* ECON Wert *m* einer Währung; ~ **zone** *n* GEN COMM Währungszone *f*

current *adj* ECON *exchange rate* aktuell, GEN COMM *exchange rate* aktuell, augenblicklich; ◆ **at ~ prices** STOCK zu gegenwärtigen Börsenkursen, zu gegenwärtigen Preisen

current: ~ **account** *n BrE* ACC *balance of payments* Leistungsbilanz *f*, BANK (*C/A, cf cheque account BrE, cf checking account AmE, cf credit account*) Kreditkonto *nt*, Girokonto *nt*, Kontokorrent *nt*, Kontokorrentkonto

nt, laufendes Konto *nt*, Scheckkonto *nt*, ECON *balance of payments* Leistungsbilanz *f*; ~ **account balance** *n BrE* BANK Kontokorrentguthaben *nt*, GEN COMM aktueller Kontostand *m*; ~ **account customer** *n BrE* BANK Kontokorrentkunde *m*; ~ **account holder** *n BrE* BANK Kontokorrentinhaber, in *m,f*; ~ **account loan** *n BrE* BANK Dispokredit *m*, Dispositionskredit *m*, Kontokorrentkredit *m*; ~ **account reservation** *n BrE* BANK Kontokorrentvorbehalt *m*; ~ **account surplus** *n BrE* (*cf checking account surplus AmE*) BANK Kontokorrentguthaben *nt*; ~ **adaptor** *n AmE* COMP Netzadapter *m*; ~ **affairs** *n pl* GEN COMM aktuelles Zeitgeschehen *nt*, POL aktuelles politisches Geschehen *nt*, Tagespolitik *f*; ~ **annuity** *n* INS laufende Rente *f*; ~ **asset** *n* ACC aktuelles Vermögen *nt*, Stichtagsvermögen *nt*; ~ **assets** *n pl* ACC Umlaufvermögen *nt*; ~ **assumption whole life insurance** *n* INS laufende lebenslängliche Kapitalversicherung *f*, laufende lebenslängliche Todesfallversicherung *f*; ~ **business year** *n* FIN laufendes Geschäftsjahr *nt*; ~ **cost** *n* ACC laufende Kosten *pl*; ~ **cost accounting** *n* (*CCA*) ACC Bilanzierung *f* auf der Basis des Wiederbeschaffungswertes, Buchführung *f* zum Tageswert; ~ **cost basis** *n* ACC aktuelle Bewertungsgrundlagen *f pl* für die Kostenrechnung; ~ **demand** *n* S&M laufende Nachfrage *f*; ~ **dollars** *n pl* ECON heutiger Wert *m* in Dollar, FIN Dollar *m* zum Tageskurs; ~ **domestic value** *n* (*CDV*) IMP/EXP aktueller Inlandswert *m*, Inlandswert *m*, Verzollungswert *m*; ~ **economic trend** *n* ECON gegenwärtiger Wirtschaftstrend *m*; ~ **entry price** *n* FIN aktueller Einstandspreis *m*; ~ **events** *n pl* GEN COMM aktuelle Ereignisse *nt pl*; ~ **expenditure** *n* FIN Betriebskosten *pl*, laufende Ausgaben *f pl*, laufende Unkosten *pl*; ~ **fiscal plan** *n* TAX laufender Finanzplan *m*, laufender Steuerplan *m*; ~ **fiscal year** *n* TAX laufendes Finanzjahr *nt*, laufendes Steuerjahr *nt*; ~ **grants to persons** *n pl* ECON laufende Zahlungen *f pl* an Personen; ~ **holdings** *n pl* STOCK laufende Devisenbestände *m pl*, laufende Kapitalbeteiligungen *f pl*; ~ **income** *n* ECON laufendes Einkommen *nt*; ~ **insurance** *n* INS laufende Versicherung *f*; ~ **liability** *n* BANK kurzfristige Verbindlichkeit *f*; ~ **loop** *n* COMP *transferring of data on older teletypewriters* Stromschleife *f*; ~ **market value** *n* S&M aktueller Marktwert *m*; ~ **operating profit** *n* ACC aktueller Betriebsgewinn *m*; ~ **population survey** *n* (*CPS*) ECON fortgeschriebene Bevölkerungsstatistik *f*; ~ **price** *n* ECON Marktpreis *m*, STOCK Tageskurs *m*; ~ **profitability** *n* FIN aktuelle Ertragslage *f*; ~ **program** *n* COMP aktuelles Programm *nt*; ~ **purchasing power** *n* (*CPP*) ECON Gegenwartswert *m* der Kaufkraft; ~ **rate** *n* GEN COMM aktueller Satz *m*, derzeitiger Satz *m*; ~ **rate method** *n AmE* (*cf closing rate method BrE*) ACC *of currency translation for consolidated accounts* Fremdwährungsumrechnung *f* zu Stichtagskursen, Umrechnungsmethode *f* zum geltenden Satz; ~ **ratio** *n* ACC Liquidität *f* dritten Grades, Liquiditätskennzahl *f*, FIN Liquidität *f* zweiten Grades, Liquidität *f* dritten Grades; ~ **revenues** *n pl* FIN im Rechnungsjahr anfallende Einkünfte *pl*; ~ **risks** *n pl* ECON gegenwärtige Risiken *nt pl*; ~ **savings account** *n* BANK Sparkonto *nt* mit laufender Verzinsung; ~ **spending** *n* ECON laufende Ausgaben *f pl*; ~ **value** *n* ECON Marktwert *m*, Zeitwert *m*, FIN Marktwert *m*, Verkaufswert *m*, Zeitwert *m*; ~ **value accounting** *n* ACC beizulegender Wert *m*;

~ **year** *n* GEN COMM laufendes Jahr *nt*; ~ **yield** *n* BANK laufende Rendite *f*, Umlaufrendite *f*

curriculum *n* WEL Curriculum *nt*, Lehrplan *m*, *education* Unterrichtsplan *m*; ~ **vitae** *n* BrE (*CV, cf résumé AmE*) ADMIN, HRM Lebenslauf *m*

cursor *n* COMP *on screen* Cursor *m*; ~ **control pad** *n* COMP Cursortastenblock *m*

curtail *vt* GEN COMM verkürzen, LAW *rights* beeinträchtigen

curtailment *n* GEN COMM *of programme* Beschränkung *f*, Verkürzung *f*; ~ **in pension plan** *n* FIN Kürzung *f* des Pensionsplanes

curtesy *n* LAW Nießbrauch des Witwers am Grundbesitz der verstorbenen Ehefrau

curtilage *n* LAW, PROP umschlossener Hofraum *m*

curve *n* MATH Kurve *f*, Bogen *m*

curvilinear: ~ **correlation** *n* MATH *statistics* nichtlineare Korrelation *f*; ~ **relationship** *n* MATH *statistics* nichtlineare Beziehung *f*

cushion *vt* GEN COMM *impact* auffangen

cushion: ~ **tire** *AmE*, ~ **tyre** *BrE n* TRANSP *engineering* Ballon-Elastikreifen *m*

custodial: ~ **account** *n* BANK Depotkonto *nt*, Treuhandkonto *nt*

custodian *n* LAW Verwahrer, in *m,f*; ~ **account fee** *n* BANK Treuhandkontogebühr *f*; ~ **fee** *n* BANK Depotgebühr *f*; ~ **of property** *n* LAW Vermögensverwalter, in *m,f*

custodianship: ~ **account** *n* BANK Depotkonto *nt*

custody *n* BANK Verwahrung *f*, LAW Haft *f*, Untersuchungshaft *f*, Verwahrung *f*; STOCK Aufbewahrung *f*; ~ **account** *n* BANK Depotkonto *nt*; ~ **account charge** *n* BANK Depotkontogebühr *f*; ~ **charge** *n* BANK Depotgebühr *f*; ~ **of shares** *n* STOCK Aufbewahrung *f* von Aktien

customary *adj* GEN COMM üblich, gewohnt; ~ **dispatch** *n* TRANSP handelsüblicher Versand *m*; ~ **tare** *n* TAX übliche Tara *f*

custom: ~ **builder** *n* PROP Bauunternehmer, der nach Kundenspezifikationen baut

customer *n* GEN COMM Auftraggeber *m*, S&M Kunde *m*, Kundin *f*; ~ **accounting** *n* ACC Kundenabrechnung *f*; ~ **awareness** *n* S&M Bekanntheitsgrad *m*; ~ **base** *n* S&M Kundenbestand *m*; ~ **billing** *n* ACC Kundenabrechnung *f*; ~ **card** *n* FIN Kundenakte *f*; ~ **care** *n* S&M Kundenbetreuung *f*; ~ **confidence** *n* S&M Kundenvertrauen *nt*; ~ **deposit** *n* BANK Kundeneinlage *f*; ~**-driven** *adj* S&M kundenbestimmt; ~ **liaison** *n* S&M Kundenverbindung *f*; ~ **needs** *n pl* S&M Kundenbedürfnisse *nt pl*; ~**-oriented** *adj* S&M kundenorientiert; ~ **orientation** *n* S&M Kundenorientierung *f*; ~ **profile** *n* S&M Kundenprofil *nt*; ~ **records** *n pl* S&M Kundenkartei *f*; ~ **relations manager** *n* MGMNT Kundendienstleiter, in *m,f*; ~ **research** *n* S&M *market research* Kundenforschung *f*; ~ **service** *n* S&M Kundenabteilung *f*, Kundenservice *m*, S&M Kundendienst *m*; ~ **service department** *n* S&M Kundendienstabteilung *f*; ~ **service manager** *n* MGMNT Kundendienstleiter, in *m,f*; ~ **service representative** *n* HRM Kundendienstvertreter, in *m,f*

customers': ~ **net debit balance** *n* STOCK Nettosollsaldo *m* der Kunden

customize *vt* COMP *hardware, software* an Kundenspezi-

fikationen anpassen, maßschneidern; ♦ ~ **sth** IND etw den Kundenwünschen anpassen

customized *adj* COMP *application* maßgeschneidert, GEN COMM *solution*, S&M kundenspezifisch; ~ **keyboard** *n* COMP kundenangepaßte Tastatur *f*; ~ **service** *n* S&M kundenspezifische Dienstleistungen *f pl*

custom: ~**-made** *adj* S&M kundenspezifisch; ~ **of port** *n* (*C/P*) TRANSP Hafenusance *f*; ~ **and practice** *n* HRM Gepflogenheiten *f pl*

customs *n* GEN COMM Zoll *m*, IMP/EXP Tarif *m*, LEIS Zoll *m*, TAX Einfuhrzölle *m pl*, *agency* Zollbehörde *f*

Customs: ~ **Additional Code** *n* (*CAC*) IMP/EXP zusätzliche Zollordnung *f*

customs: ~ **agency** *n* IMP/EXP Zollagentur *f*

Customs: ~ **& Excise** *n* (*C&E*) IMP/EXP britische Zoll- und Steuerbehörde; ~ **& Excise department** *n* IMP/EXP Amt für Zoll und Verbrauchssteuern

customs: ~ **arrangements** *n pl* GEN COMM Zollvereinbarungen *f pl*; ~ **barrier** *n* GEN COMM Zollschranke *f*; ~ **broker** *n* IMP/EXP *shipping* Zollagent, in *m,f*; ~ **cargo clearance** *n* IMP/EXP Zollabfertigung *f* von Warenladungen, zollamtliche Freigabe *f* einer Fracht/ Ladung; ~ **check** *n* IMP/EXP Zollkontrolle *f*; ~ **clearance** *n* IMP/EXP Klarierung *f*, Verzollung *f*, Zolldurchlauf *m*, Zollabfertigung *f*, TRANSP Verzollung *f*; ~ **clearance agent** *n* HRM Zollabfertigungsbeamte(r) *m* [decl. as adj], Zollabfertigungsbeamtin *f*; ~ **clearance status** *n* (*CCS*) IMP/EXP Zollabfertigungsstatus *m*; ~ **code** *n* (*CC*) LAW Zollgesetz *nt*; ~ **collector** *n* IMP/EXP Zollamt *nt*; ~ **consignee** *n* IMP/EXP Zolladressat *m*; ~ **control** *n* IMP/EXP Zollkontrolle *f*, zollamtliche Überwachung *f*

Customs: ~ **Convention on the International Transit of Goods** *n* (*ITI*) IMP/EXP Zollabkommen *nt* zum internationalen Gütertransport; ~ **Cooperation Council** *n* (*CCC*) IMP/EXP Rat für die Zusammenarbeit auf dem Gebiete des Zollwesens, Brüsseler Zollrat *m* (*BZR*); ~ **Cooperation Council Nomenclature** *n* (*CCCN*) IMP/EXP Zolltarifschema des Rates für die Zusammenarbeit auf dem Gebiete des Zollwesens, Nomenklatur *f* des Brüsseler Zollrates (*NRZZ*)

customs: ~ **court** *n* AmE LAW *customs law* Zollgericht *nt*; ~ **declaration** *n* (*CD*) FIN Zollbürgschaft *f*, IMP/EXP *shipping* Zolldeklarierung *f*, Zollerklärung *f*, Zollinhaltserklärung *f*, Zollabfertigung *f*; ~ **duties** *n pl* TAX Zölle *m pl*; ~ **duty** *n* IMP/EXP Zoll *m*, Zollabgabe *f*, Zollgebühr *f*; ~ **duty ad valorem** *n* IMP/EXP, TAX Wertzoll *m*; ~ **entry** *n* BANK Zolldeklaration *f*, Zollerklärung *f*, IMP/EXP Zollangaben *f pl*, Zolldeklaration *f*, Zollerklärung *f*

Customs: ~ **and Excise Act** *n* AmE IMP/EXP Zollgesetz *nt*

customs: ~ **and excise duties** *n pl* ECON, IMP/EXP, TAX Zölle und Abgaben *f pl*

Customs: ~ **and Excise Management Act** *n* (*CEMA*) LAW Gesetz zur Zoll- und Verbrauchssteuerhandhabung

customs: ~ **fence** *n* IMP/EXP Zollzaun *m*; ~ **formalities** *n pl* IMP/EXP Zollformalitäten *f pl*; ~ **guaranty** *n* FIN Zollbürgschaft *f*; ~**-house broker** *n* HRM Zollmakler, in *m,f*; ~ **invoice** *n* IMP/EXP Zollfaktura *f*, Zollrechnung *f*; ~ **law** *n* IMP/EXP Zollgesetz *nt*; ~ **officer** *n* HRM, IMP/EXP Zöllner, in *m,f*, Zollbeamte(r) *m* [decl. as adj], Zollbeamtin *f*; ~ **pre-entry exports** *n pl* IMP/EXP durch den Zoll abzufertigende Exportgüter *nt pl*; ~ **pre-entry imports** *n pl* IMP/EXP durch den Zoll abzufertigende Importgüter *nt pl*; **~ procedure** *n* IMP/EXP Zollverfahren *nt*, Zollverkehr *m*; **~ registered number** *n* (*CRN*) IMP/EXP Zollzulassungsnummer *f*; **~ regulations** *n pl* IMP/EXP Zollbestimmungen *f pl*, Zollordnung *f*, Zollvorschriften *f pl*; **~ report** *n* BANK, IMP/EXP Zolldeklaration *f*; **~ tariff** *n* IMP/EXP Zolltarif *m*; **~ transaction code** *n* IMP/EXP Zolltransaktionscode *m*, Zollabfertigungscode *m*, zollamtlicher Abwicklungscode *m*; **~ union** *n* ECON Zollunion *f*; **~ valuation** *n* IMP/EXP Zollbewertung *f*, zollamtliche Bewertung *f*, Zollwertfestsetzung *f*; **~ value** *n* IMP/EXP Zollwert *m*; **no ~ value** *n* (*n.c.v.*) IMP/EXP ohne Zollwert; **~ value per gross kilogram** *n* IMP/EXP Zollwert pro Bruttokilogramm *m*; **~ value per gross pound** *n* (*CVGP*) IMP/EXP Zollwert pro Bruttopfund *m*

custom: **~ and trade practices** *n pl* HRM Handelsgepflogenheiten *f pl*, Handelspraktiken *f pl*

cut 1. *n* ECON *in rates* Senkung *f*, FIN Herabsetzung *f*, Kürzung *f*, Verringerung *f*, IND Machart *f*; **2.** *vt* COMP *text block, graphics* ausschneiden, ECON *rates* senken, FIN kürzen, verringern; ◆ **~ and paste** COMP ausschneiden und einfügen; **~ one's losses** FIN die eigenen Verluste reduzieren; **~ prices** S&M Preise reduzieren; **~ spending** ECON Ausgaben kürzen

cut back *vt* FIN einschränken, GEN COMM beschneiden

cut down *vt* HRM, MGMNT *workforce* abbauen

cutback *n* FIN Einschränkung *f*

cutoff: **~ date** *n* ACC, FIN *IMF, international banking* Stichtag *m*; **~ method** *n* ACC Cutoff-Verfahren *nt*; **~ point** *n* ECON *capital budgeting* Ausscheidungsrate *f*, Mindestverzinsung *f*; **~ procedure** *n* ACC Ausscheidungsverfahren *nt*; **~ time** *n* STOCK Verfallzeit *f*

cut: **~ paper** *n* COMP Einzelblatt *nt*

cutter *n* TRANSP *type of ship* Kutter *m*

cutthroat: **~ competition** *n* ECON ruinöse Konkurrenz *f*, Vernichtungswettbewerb *m*, Verdrängungswettbewerb *m*

cutting *n* BANK, FIN *of rates* Herabsetzung *f*, MEDIA *BrE* (*cf clipping AmE*) *from newspaper* Ausschnitt *m*; **~ service** *n BrE* (*cf clipping service AmE*) S&M Zeitungsausschnittsdienst *m*

CV *abbr* ADMIN *BrE* (*curriculum vitae, cf résumé AmE*) Lebenslauf *m*, GEN COMM (*chief value*) Höchstwert *m*, Höchstpreis *m*, Hauptpreis *m*, Hauptwert *m*, HRM *BrE* (*curriculum vitae, cf résumé AmE*) Lebenslauf *m*

C/V *abbr BrE* (*certificate of value*) IMP/EXP Wertbescheinigung *f*

CVGK *abbr* (*customs value per gross kilogram*) IMP/EXP Zollwert *m* pro Bruttokilogramm

CVGP *abbr* (*customs value per gross pound*) IMP/EXP Zollwert *m* pro Bruttopfund

CVMO *abbr* (*commercial value movement order*) GEN COMM Marktwertbewegungsauftrag *m*

CVO *abbr BrE* (*certificate of value and origin*) IMP/EXP Wert- und Ursprungszertifikat *nt*, Wert- und Ursprungszeugnis *nt*

CW *abbr* (*comparable worth*) ECON vergleichbarer Wert *m*, HRM gleiche Produktivität *f*

CWE *abbr* (*cleared without examination*) IMP/EXP unbesehen klariert

CWM *abbr* (*clerical work measurement*) HRM Bewertung *f* von Büroarbeiten

cwo *abbr* (*cash with order*) GEN COMM zahlbar bei Auftragserteilung, zahlbar bei Bestellung

CWS *abbr BrE* (*Cooperative Wholesale Society*) GEN COMM Konsumgroßhandelsgesellschaft *f*

cwt *abbr* (*hundredweight*) GEN COMM Ztr. (*Zentner*)

CXBG *abbr* (*comprehensive extended-term banker's guarantee*) BANK umfassende längerfristige Bankgarantie *f*

CY *abbr* (*container yard*) TRANSP Containerdepot *nt*

cybernetic *adj* COMP kybernetisch

cybernetics *n* COMP Kybernetik *f*

cycle *n* ECON *recurring period* Kreislauf *m*, Wirtschaftskreislauf *m*, Zyklus *m*, IND Takt *m*, INS, TRANSP *bicycle* Fahrrad *nt*; **~ insurance** *n* INS Fahrradversicherung *f*; **~ path** *n* LEIS, TRANSP Radweg *m*; **~ theft insurance** *n* INS Fahrraddiebstahlversicherung *f*

cyclical *adj* ECON, STOCK konjunkturabhängig, konjunkturempfindlich, zyklisch; **~ company** *n* STOCK konjunkturempfindliches Unternehmen *nt*; **~ demand** *n* ECON zyklische Nachfrage *f*; **~ fluctuation** *n* STOCK *in commodity prices* konjunkturelle Schwankung *f*; **~ industry** *n* ECON konjunkturempfindliche Branche *f*; **~ shares** *n pl* STOCK Aktien *f pl* konjunkturreagibler Unternehmen, zyklische Werte *m pl*; **~ stock** *n* ECON Aktien *f pl* konjunkturempfindlicher Unternehmen; **~ trade** *n* ECON zyklischer Handel *m*; **~ unemployment** *n* ECON konjunkturelle Arbeitslosigkeit *f*; **~ variations** *n pl* ECON Konjunkturschwankungen *f pl*, zyklische Schwankungen *f pl*

cyclist *n* LEIS, TRANSP Radfahrer, in *m,f*

cycloidal: **~ propeller** *n* TRANSP *shipping* Zykloidenpropeller *m*

cylinder *n* COMP *hard disk drive* Zylinder *m*, IND Trommel *f*, TRANSP Walze *f*, Zylinder *m*

cymogene *n* IND *dangerous classified cargo* Cymogen *nt*

D

D *abbr* COMMS (*delivery*) Zust. (*Zustellung*), GEN COMM (*delivered*) gel. (*geliefert*)

DA *abbr* COMP (*design automation*) Entwurfsautomatisierung *f*, Konstruktionsautomation *f*, GEN COMM (*documents against acceptance*) DA (*Dokumente gegen Akzept*), D/A (*Dokumente gegen Akzept*), d/a (*Dokumente gegen Akzept*), LAW (*district attorney*) Staatsanwalt *m*, Staatsanwältin *f*, POL (*defence advisor BrE, defense advisor AmE*) Verteidigungsberater, in *m,f*

D/A *abbr* BANK (*deposit account*) Depositenkonto *nt*, Einlagenkonto *nt*, Sparkonto *nt*, COMP (*digital-to-analog*) D/A (*digital-analog*), GEN COMM (*days after acceptance*) Tage *m pl* nach Akzept, (*documents against acceptance*) D/A (*Dokumente gegen Akzept*), DA (*Dokumente gegen Akzept*), d/a (*Dokumente gegen Akzept*)

DAC *abbr* COMP (*digital-to-analog converter*) D/A-Wandler *m* (*Digital-Analog-Wandler*), ECON (*Development Assistance Committee*) Ausschuß *m* für Entwicklungshilfe

DAF *abbr* (*delivered at frontier*) IMP/EXP *Incoterms* geliefert Grenze

DAGAS *abbr* (*Dangerous Goods Advisory Service*) GEN COMM Beratungsdienst für gefährliche Waren

daily 1. *adj* GEN COMM täglich, Tages-; ♦ **go about one's ~ business** GEN COMM seine tägliche Arbeit verrichten; **2.** *adv* GEN COMM täglich

daily: **~ allowance** *n* GEN COMM Tagegeld *nt*, Tagesentschädigung *f*; **~ balance interest calculation** *n* BANK taggenaue Zinsabrechnung *f*, Zinsberechnung *f* für tägliche Guthaben; **~ closing balance** *n* ACC Kontostand *m*, täglicher Abschlußsaldo *m*; **~ compensation** *n* INS Krankengeld *nt*; **~ deposit** *n* BANK täglich verfügbare Einlage *f*; **~ interest** *n* BANK Tageszins *m*; **~ interest account** *n* BANK Tageszinskonto *nt*; **~ interest deposit** *n* BANK Tageszinseinlage *f*; **~ interest savings account** *n* BANK Sparkonto *nt* mit Tageszinsen; **~ loan** *n* BANK, FIN Tagesgeld *nt*; **~ money rate** *n* BANK Tagesgeldsatz *m*; **~ official list** *n* STOCK Kursblatt *nt*; **~ paid worker** *n* HRM Tagelöhner, in *m,f* (*obs*), Hilfsarbeiter, in *m,f*; **~ position statement** *n* ACC Tagesauszug *m*; **~ price limit** *n* STOCK *options* tägliche Preisobergrenze *f*; **~ quotation** *n* STOCK Tageskurs *m*

Daily: **~ Range Factor** *n* (*DRF*) FIN, STOCK Faktor *m* der täglichen Schwankungsbreite

daily: **~ report of calls** *n* S&M täglicher Besuchsbericht *m*, Tagesbericht *m* über Kundenbesuche; **~ settlement** *n* STOCK taggleiche Regulierung *f*; **~ trading limit** *n* STOCK maximal zulässige Kursfluktuation *f*, zulässiges Schwankungslimit *nt*; **~ volume** *n* STOCK Tagesumsatz *m*

dairy: **~ farm** *n* ECON *agricultural* milcherzeugender Betrieb *m*

daisy: **~ chain** *n* STOCK künstliche Marktaktivität *f*, undurchsichtiger Unternehmenskomplex *m*; **--chain scheme** *n* GEN COMM undurchsichtige Struktur *f*;

~ wheel *n* COMP Typenrad *nt*; **--wheel printer** *n* COMP Typenraddrucker *m*

damage *n* INS, LAW Schädigung *f*, Schaden *m*, PATENTS Schaden *m*, Verlust *m*; **~ by falling stones** *n* INS Steinschlagschaden *m*; **~ by pharmaceutical products** *n* INS Arzneimittelschäden *m pl*; **~ caused by default** *n* LAW *contracts* Verzugsschaden *m*; **~ caused by radiation** *n* INS Strahlungsschaden *m*; **~ claim** *n* LAW *contracts* Schadensersatzanspruch *m*

damaged: **~ in transit** *phr* TRANSP beim Transport beschädigt

damage: **~ limitation** *n* GEN COMM Schadensbegrenzung *f*; **~ report** *n* INS *marine* Schadensaufnahme *f*, Schadensbericht *m*

damages *n pl* LAW Schadensersatz *m*, PATENTS *compensation* Abfindung *f*, Entschädigung *f*

damage: **~ to goods in custody** *n* INS Obhutsschaden *m*; **~ to health** *n* INS Gesundheitsschädigung *f*, Gesundheitsschaden *m*; **~ to property** *n* FIN Vermögensschaden *m*; **~ to rented property** *n* INS Mietsachschaden *m*; **~ in transit** *n* TRANSP Transportschaden *m*; **~ whilst loading and unloading** *n* INS Be- und Entladeschaden *m*

damnum sine injuria *phr* GEN COMM Schaden *m* ohne Rechtsverletzung

dampen *vt* ECON *growth* bremsen, dämpfen, GEN COMM *enthusiasm* dämpfen

damp: **--proof** *adj* GEN COMM nässegeschützt, feuchtigkeitsfest

danger *n* HRM Gefahr *f*, IND Unsicherheit *f*; **~ money** *n* HRM Gefahrenzulage *f*

dangerous *adj* GEN COMM gefährlich; **~ cargo** *n* TRANSP Gefahrgut *nt*; **~ cargo compound** *n* TRANSP Gefahrgutzusammensetzung *f*; **~ goods** *n pl* LAW *commercial* Gefahrgüter *nt pl*

Dangerous: **~ Goods Advisory Service** *n* (*DAGAS*) GEN COMM Beratungsdienst für gefährliche Waren

dangerous: **~ goods authority form** *n* TRANSP Genehmigung *f* für Gefahrgütertransport

Dangerous: **~ Goods Board** *n* (*DGB*) GEN COMM *IATA term* Kommission für gefährliches Transportgut

dangerous: **~ goods note** *n* (*DGN*) TRANSP Gefahrgüteranzeige *f*; **~ goods rate** *n* TRANSP Gefahrgutsatz *m*; **~ goods regulations** *n pl* TRANSP Gefahrgutvorschriften *f pl*; **~ waste** *n* ENVIR gefährliche Abfälle *m pl*

danger: **~ point** *n* GEN COMM Schwachstelle *f*, Gefahrenpunkt *m*

DAP *abbr* (*documents against payment*) GEN COMM DZ (*Dokumente gegen Zahlung*)

Dartford: **~ International Freight Terminal** *n* BrE (*DIFT*) TRANSP internationales Frachtterminal in Dartford

dash *n* MEDIA *typography* Gedankenstrich *m*

dashed: **~ line** *n* ADMIN, COMP, MATH gestrichelte Linie *f*

data *n pl* ADMIN, COMP, ECON Daten *pl*; **~ acquisition** *n* COMP Datenerfassung *f*, ECON Datenerfassung *f*, Datenerhebung *f*; **~ bank** *n* COMP Datenbank *f*

database *n* COMP Datenbank *f*; **~ management** *n* COMP

Datenbankverwaltung *f*; **~ management system** *n* (*DBMS*) COMP Datenbankverwaltungssystem *nt* (*DMS*)

data: **~ bit** *n* COMP Datenbit *nt*; **~ broadcasting** *n* COMMS Datenfunk *m*, Datenrundfunk *m*; **~ bus** *n* COMP Datenbus *m*, Datenbusleitung *f*, Datenbusschiene *f*; **~ capture** *n* COMP Datenerfassung *f*; **~ card** *n* COMP Datenkarte *f*, Karteikarte *f*; **~ carrier** *n* COMP Datenträger *m*; **~ collection** *n* COMP Datenerfassung *f*, ECON Datenerhebung *f*; **~ communication** *n* COMP *data transferred between computers* Datenübertragung *f*; **~ communications** *n pl* COMMS Datenübermittlung *f*, Datenkommunikation *f*; **~ communications equipment** *n* (*DCE*) COMP Datenübertragungseinrichtung *f*; **~ compression** *n* COMP *software* Datenkomprimierung *f*; **~ conversion** *n* COMP Datenkonvertierung *f*; **~ editing** *n* COMP Aufbereitung *f* von Daten; **~ entry** *n* COMP Dateneingabe *f*; **~ entry operator** *n* COMP Datenerfasser *m*; **~ entry terminal** *n* COMP Dateneingabestation *f*; **~ field** *n* COMP Datenfeld *nt*; **~ file** *n* COMP Datendatei *f*; **~ flow** *n* COMP Datenfluß *m*; **~ flow chart** *n* MATH Datenflußplan *m*; **~ freight receipt** *n* (*DFR*) TRANSP *shipping* Datenfrachtempfang *m*; **~ gathering** *n* COMP Datenerfassung *nt*; **~ input** *n* COMP Dateneingabe *f*; **~ integrity** *n* COMP Datenintegrität *f*; **~ link** *n* COMP Datenverbindungsabschnitt *m*, Kommunikationsverbindung *f*; **~ management** *n* COMP Datenverwaltung *f*; **~ mining** *n* ECON *econometrics* Datenverbiegung *f*; **~ network** *n* COMP Datennetz *nt*; **~ organization** *n* ECON Aufbereitung *f* von Daten; **~ output** *n* COMP Datenausgabe *f*; **~ packet** *n* COMP Datenpaket *nt*; **~ plate** *n* TRANSP *on container* Datenschild *nt*; **~ post** *n* BrE COMMS Datenpost *f*

Datapost® *n* BrE COMMS britischer Eilpaketdienst

data: **~ post on demand** *phr* BrE COMMS Datenpost *f* auf Abruf, Datenpost *f* auf Verlangen; **~ preparation** *n* ADMIN, COMP Datenaufbereitung *f*; **~ privacy** *n* BrE (*cf data security AmE*) COMP Datensicherheit *f*; **~ processing** *n* (*DP*) ADMIN, COMP Datenverarbeitung *f* (*DV*); **~ processing insurance** *n* INS Datenverarbeitungsversicherung *f*; **~ protection** *n* COMP Datenschutz *m*

Data: **~ Protection Act** *n* BrE LAW *1984* Datenschutzgesetz *nt*

data: **~ rate** *n* COMP Datenübertragungsrate *f*; **~ record** *n* COMP Datensatz *m*; **~ retrieval** *n* COMP Datenwiedergewinnung *f*; **~ security** *n* AmE (*cf data privacy BrE*) COMP Datensicherheit *f*; **~ set** *n* COMP Datensatz *m*; **~ sharing** *n* COMP gemeinsamer *m* Zugriff auf Daten; **~ sheet** *n* S&M statistische Tabelle *f*; **~ storage** *n* COMP Datenspeicher *m*; **~ stream** *n* GEN COMM Datenfluß *m*; **~ structure** *n* COMP Datenstruktur *f*; **~ terminal equipment** *n* (*DTE*) COMP *hardware* Datenendeinrichtung *f*; **~ transfer** *n* COMP Datenübertragung *f*, Datentransfer *m*; **~ transfer rate** *n* COMP Baud *nt*, Datenübertragungsrate *f*; **~ transmission facility** *n* COMP Datenübertragungseinrichtung *f*; **~ type** *n* COMP Datenart *f*; **~ word** *n* COMP Datenwort *nt*

date *n* GEN COMM Datum *nt*; ◆ **at a later ~** GEN COMM zu einem späteren Termin; **by ~** COMP nach Datum; **out of ~** GEN COMM überholt, passé (*infrml*); **~ as postmarked** COMMS Datum *nt* des Poststempels; **to ~** GEN COMM bis dato, bisher, bislang

date: **~ of application** *n* GEN COMM Antragsdatum *nt*

dated 1. *adj* GEN COMM überholt, datiert; **2.** *vt* ◆ **be ~** GEN COMM datiert sein

dated: **~ date** *n* FIN Verzinsungsbeginn bei einer Emission

date: **~ of delivery** *n* FIN Liefertermin *m*; **~ of expiry** *n* HRM Verfallstag *m*, Fälligkeitstermin *m*, Verfallsdatum *nt*; **~ of filing** *n* PATENTS Antragsdatum *nt*; **~ of grant** *n* PATENTS Bewilligungsdatum *nt*, Erteilungsdatum *nt*; **~ of invoice** *n* (*cf billing date*) ACC Rechnungsdatum *nt*, GEN COMM Fakturendatum *nt* (*obs*), Rechnungsdatum *nt*; **~ of issue** *n* GEN COMM Ausstellungstag *m*, INS Ausfertigungsdatum *nt*, Ausgabetag *m*; **~ marking** *n* S&M *prepackaged goods* Datumsangabe *f*; **~ of maturity** *n* (*DOM*) BANK Fälligkeitstermin *m*, Ablauftermin *m*, GEN COMM Fälligkeitsdatum *nt*, STOCK *bill of exchange* Verfallstag *m*; **~ of quotation** *n* GEN COMM Datum *nt* des Angebots; **~ of receipt** *n* GEN COMM Empfangsdatum *nt*, Eingangsdatum *nt*; **~ of record** *n* STOCK *dividends* Stichtag *m*; **~ of registration** *n* PATENTS Eintragungsdatum *nt*; **~ of sailing** *n* TRANSP Abfahrtsdatum *nt*; **~ of shipment** *n* TRANSP Versandtag *m*, Verladedatum *nt*; **~ stamp** *n* ADMIN Bearbeitungsstempel *m*, Tagesstempel *m*, COMMS Poststempel *m*

dating *n* GEN COMM Festsetzung *f* der Laufzeit

dawn: **~ raid** *n jarg* FIN, STOCK aggressives Überraschungsmanöver *nt*

day *n* GEN COMM Tag *m*; ◆ **~ by day** GEN COMM von Tag zu Tag

day: **~ bill** *n* FIN Tagwechsel *m*

daybook *n* (*d.b.*) ACC Journal *nt*, Tagebuch *nt*, GEN COMM Journal *nt*

daylight: **~ saving time** *n* GEN COMM Sommerzeit *f*

day: **~ loan** *n* BANK Tagesgeld *nt*, täglich fälliges Geld *nt*, Maklerdarlehen *nt*; **~ of maturity** *n* ACC Fälligkeitstag *m*; **~ off** *n* HRM arbeitsfreier Tag *m*, dienstfreier Tag *m*; **~ order** *n* STOCK Tagesauftrag *m*; **~ of posting** *n* GEN COMM Aufgabetag *m*; **~ release** *n* WEL tageweise Freistellung zur beruflichen Fortbildung

days: **~ after acceptance** *n pl* (*D/A*) GEN COMM Tage *m pl* nach Akzept; **~ after date** *n pl* (*dd, d.d.*) GEN COMM Verzugstage *m pl*; **~ of grace** *n pl* ACC Nachfrist *f*

day: **~ shift** *n* HRM Morgenschicht *f*, Tagesschicht *f*; **~ of shipment** *n* TRANSP Verladedatum *nt*, Versandtag *m*

days: **~ to delivery** *n pl* STOCK *currency futures* Zeitraum *m* bis zur Lieferung; **~ to maturity** *n pl* STOCK Zeitraum *m* bis zur Fälligkeit

day: **~-to-day** *adj* GEN COMM täglich; **~-to-day loan** *n* BANK täglich kündbares Darlehen *nt*; **~-to-day money** *n* BANK tägliches Geld *nt*; **~ trading** *n* STOCK Tagesspekulation *f*

daywork *n* HRM Zeitlohnarbeit *f*, Schichtarbeit *f*

dayworker *n* HRM Schichtarbeiter, in *m,f*

d.b. *abbr* (*daybook*) GEN COMM Journal *nt*

dB *abbr* (*decibel*) GEN COMM dB (*Dezibel*)

DBMS *abbr* (*database management system*) COMP DMS (*Datenbankverwaltungssystem*)

dc *abbr* (*direct current*) GEN COMM GS (*Gleichstrom*)

DC *abbr* (*developed country*) ECON, IND Industrieland *nt*, Industriestaat *m*

D/C *abbr* (*deviation clause*) INS *marine* Abweichungsklausel *f*, Routenabweichungsklausel *f*

DCA *abbr* (*debt collection agency*) FIN Inkassobüro *nt*

DCE *abbr* COMP (*data communications equipment*)

hardware Datenübertragungseinrichtung *f*, ECON (*domestic credit expansion*) inländischer Zuwachs *m* des Kreditvolumens, Kreditexpansion *f*, FIN inländische Kreditausweitung *f*

DCF *abbr* (*discounted cash flow*) ACC, FIN abgezinster Cash-Flow *m*, diskontierter Bargeldfluß *m*, diskontierter Einnahmeüberschuß *m*

DCO *abbr* (*debt collection order*) FIN Inkassoauftrag *m*

DCom *abbr* (*Doctor of Commerce*) GEN COMM Doktor *m* der Betriebswirtschaft

DComL *abbr* (*Doctor of Commercial Law*) GEN COMM Doktor *m* des Handelsrechts, Doktor *m* des Wirtschaftsrechts

DCP *abbr* (*droppages, cancellations and prepayments*) FIN Rückgänge *m pl*, Kündigungen *f pl* und Vorauszahlungen *f pl*

DCS *abbr* (*departure control system*) TRANSP Abflugkontrollsystem *nt*

dd *abbr* GEN COMM (*days after date*) Verzugstage *m pl*, (*delivered*) gel. (*geliefert*)

d.d. *abbr* GEN COMM (*days after date*) Verzugstage *m pl*, STOCK (*delivery date*) Fälligkeitstermin *m*, Liefertermin *m*

DD *abbr* BANK (*direct debit*) Abbuchung *f* durch Einzugsermächtigung, Einzugsverfahren *nt*, COMP (*double density*) DD (*doppelte Dichte*), FIN (*direct debit*) Abbuchung *f* durch Einzugsermächtigung, Einzugsverfahren *nt*, IMP/EXP, TRANSP (*delivered at docks, delivered docks*) *shipping* am Kai abgeliefert

DDA *abbr* (*duty deposit account*) IMP/EXP Zolldepositenkonto *nt*

DDB *abbr* (*distributed database*) COMP verteilte Datenbank *f*

DDD *abbr* AmE (*direct distance dialing*) COMMS Selbstwählferndienst *m*, Selbstfernwahl *f*, Teilnehmerfernwahl *f*

DDE *abbr* (*direct data entry*) COMP direkte Dateneingabe *f*, (*dynamic data exchange*) dynamischer Datenaustausch *m*

DDP *abbr* COMP (*distributed data processing*) verteilte Datenverarbeitung *f*, IMP/EXP (*delivered duty paid*) geliefert verzollt

DDU *abbr* (*delivered duty unpaid*) IMP/EXP geliefert unverzollt

DE *abbr* BrE obs (*Department of Employment*) ECON, POL Arbeitsministerium *nt*

dead: **~ account** *n* BANK umsatzloses Konto *nt*

deadbeat *n* S&M Kreditkunde, der seine Rechnung nicht bezahlt

dead: **~-end job** *n* BrE (*cf blind-alley job AmE*) HRM Beruf *m* ohne Aufstiegsmöglichkeiten, Position *f* ohne Aufstiegschancen, Position *f* in einer Sackgasse, berufliche Sackgasse *f*

deadfreight *n* (*df*) TRANSP *shipping* Fautfracht *f*, Fehlfracht *f*

dead: **~ key** *n* ADMIN *on keyboard*, COMMS unbelegte Taste *f*, COMP Akzenttaste *f*, unbelegte Taste *f*; **~ letter** *n* COMMS unzustellbarer Brief *m*

Dead: **~ Letter Office** *n* (*DLO*) ADMIN Büro für unzustellbare Sendungen

deadline *n* GEN COMM letzter Termin *m*, Termin *m*, Stichtag *m*, Anmeldeschluß *m*

dead: **~ load** *n* GEN COMM Auftragsüberhang *m*

deadlock *n* COMP Systemblockade *f*, GEN COMM Sackgasse *f*, HRM *negotiations* verfahrene Situation *f*

deadlocked *adj* COMP blockiert

dead: **~ loss** *n* GEN COMM Totalverlust *m*; **~ matter** *n* S&M abgesetztes Manuskript *nt*; **~ rise** *n* (*DR*) GEN COMM *linked with sales* umsatzloser Anstieg *m*, wertloser Anstieg *m*; **~ season** *n* MEDIA Sauregurkenzeit *f* (*infrml*); **~ stock** *n* ADMIN totes Inventar *nt*, S&M unverkäufliche Ware *f*, unverkaufte Ware *f*; **~ time** *n* COMP, GEN COMM Stillstandszeit *f*, HRM, IND Brachzeit *f*

deadweight *n* (*dw*) GEN COMM Leergewicht *nt*, TRANSP *of ship* Deadweight *nt*, Ladefähigkeit *f*; **~ all told** *n* (*dwat*) TRANSP Gesamtdeadweight *nt*, Gesamttragfähigkeit *f*; **~ capacity** *n* (*dwc*) TRANSP Ladefähigkeit *f*, Tragfähigkeit *f*; **~ cargo** *n* GEN COMM Eigengewichtsfracht *f*, TRANSP Gewichtsfracht *f*, Schwergut *nt*; **~ cargo capacity** *n* (*dwcc*) TRANSP Tragfähigkeit *f*; **~ loss** *n* ECON Nettowohlfahrtsverlust *m*; **~ tonnage** *n* (*dwt*) GEN COMM Gesamtzuladungsgewicht *nt*, TRANSP Gesamtzuladungsgewicht *nt*, Ladefähigkeit *f*, Tragfähigkeit *f*

deal *n* GEN COMM Geschäft *nt*, Abschluß *m*, Geschäftsabschluß *m*, Handel *m*

deal with *vt* GEN COMM sich beschäftigen mit, sich befassen mit, *arrangement, crisis* behandeln, *do business with* verhandeln mit

dealer *n* GEN COMM, S&M, STOCK Händler, in *m,f*; **~ audit** *n* S&M Händlerprüfung *f*; **~ brand** *n* S&M Händlermarke *f*; **~ incentive** *n* S&M Händlerwettbewerb *m*; **~ network** *n* STOCK Händlerorganisation *f*, Händlernetz *nt*

dealing *n* S&M *antique, drug* Geschäft *nt*, STOCK Verkehr *m*; **~ floor** *n* STOCK Parkett *nt*, Börsenparkett *nt*; **~ in futures** *n* FIN Termingeschäft *nt*; **~ restrictions** *n pl* ECON Geschäftsbeschränkungen *f pl*

dealings *n pl* MGMNT Geschäfte *nt pl*, Geschäftsbeziehungen *f pl*, STOCK Abschlüsse *m pl*, Umsatz *m*; **~ for the account** *n* STOCK Termingeschäft *nt*; **~ in futures** *n pl* FIN Futuregeschäfte *nt pl*

dear *adj* GEN COMM kostspielig, teuer

death *n* INS Todesfall *m*; **~ benefit** *n* INS Hinterbliebenenrente *f*; **~ certificate** *n* GEN COMM Sterbeurkunde *f*; **~ duty** *n obs BrE* TAX (*cf death tax AmE*) Erbschaftssteuern *f pl*, (*cf inheritance tax AmE*) Erbschaftssteuer *f*; **~ risk** *n* INS Sterberisiko *nt*, Todesfallrisiko *nt*; **~ tax** *n AmE* (*cf death duty BrE*) TAX Erbschaftssteuern *f pl*

debasement *n* ECON *of currency* Entwertung *f*, Verschlechterung *f*

debate 1. *n* GEN COMM Erörterung *f*; **2.** *vt* GEN COMM erörtern

debenture *n* FIN Schuldverschreibung *f*, STOCK Obligation *f*, Schuldverschreibung *f*; **~ bond** *n* STOCK gesicherte oder ungesicherte Anleihe *f* in gleicher Stückelung, ungesicherte Anleihe *f*; **~ loan** *n* STOCK Obligationsanleihe *f*

debit 1. *n* ACC, FIN Belastung *f*, Lastschrift *f*, Schuldposten *m*, Debet *nt* (*obs*), *subtraction* Ausbuchung *f*, Anrechnung *f*, *balance due* Soll *nt*, Sollseite *f*, PROP, STOCK Schuldposten *m*; **2.** *vt* ACC, BANK *account* belasten, abbuchen, GEN COMM abbuchen, ausbuchen

debit: **~ balance** *n* FIN Debetsaldo *m* (*obs*), Passivsaldo *m*, Sollsaldo *m*, Verlustabschluß *m*; **~ column** *n* FIN Debetspalte *f*, Sollspalte *f*

debited *adj* BANK *an account* belastet; **~ to** *adj* ACC *an account* belastet, zu belasten, zu Lasten von

debit: **~ entry** *n* ACC, BANK Lastschrift *f*; **~ interest** *n* FIN Schuldzinsen *m pl*, Sollzinsen *m pl*; **~ memorandum** *n* AmE BANK Belastungsanzeige *f*; **~ note** *n* (*D/N*) GEN COMM Belastungsanzeige *f*, Lastschriftanzeige *f*; **~ ratio** *n* FIN Verschuldungsgrad *m*

debits *n pl* STOCK *options on Eurodollar futures* Lastschrift *f*

debit: **~ side** *n* ACC Sollseite *f*

debottleneck *vt* ECON die Engpässe beseitigen in

debrief *vt* MGMNT eine Abschlußbesprechung durchführen mit

debriefing *n* MGMNT Abschlußbesprechung *f*, Nachberatung *f*, Nachbesprechung *f*

debt *n* ECON, FIN Schulden *f pl*, GEN COMM Schuld *f*, Schulden *f pl*; ◆ **~ due by** ACC die Schuld ist fällig am; **~ due from** ACC fällige Forderung von; **~ due to** ACC Schuld fällig an; **get into ~** GEN COMM Schulden machen, in Schulden geraten; **~ owed by** ACC Forderung an

debt: **~ burden** *n* ECON Schuldenlast *f*; **~ charge** *n* ACC Kreditgebühr *f*; **~ collection agency** *n* (*DCA*) FIN Inkassobüro *nt*; **~ collection order** *n* (*DCO*) FIN Inkassoauftrag *m*; **~ collector** *n* GEN COMM Inkassobeauftragte *f* [decl. as adj], Inkassobeauftragte(r) *n* [decl. as adj]; **~ discount** *n* BANK Damnum *nt*, Disagio *nt*; **~ equity ratio** *n* ACC, ADMIN, FIN Verschuldungsgrad *m*, Verschuldungskoeffizient *m*; **~ equity swap** *n* FIN Debt-Equity-Swap *m*; **~ factoring** *n* FIN Factoring *nt*; **~ financing** *n* ACC, FIN Fremdfinanzierung *f*; **~-free** *adj* ACC, FIN, GEN COMM schuldenfrei; **~ incurred by sb** *n* BANK durch jdn eingegangene Verbindlichkeiten *f pl*; **~ instrument** *n* GEN COMM Schuldurkunde *f*; **~ management** *n* ECON Schuldenmanagement *nt*, *public debt* Schuldenstrukturpolitik *f*; **~ manager** *n* ECON Schuldenmanager, in *m,f*; **~ obligation** *n* ECON *of developing countries* öffentliche Verschuldung *f*, Staatsverschuldung *f*, Staatsschuld *f*

debtor *n* ACC *debit side* Sollseite *f*, *person* Schuldner, in *m,f*, ADMIN, GEN COMM Schuldner, in *m,f*, LAW Verpflichtete(r) *mf* [decl. as adj]; **~'s delay** *n* LAW *contracts* Schuldnerverzug *m*; **~ department** *n* ADMIN Schuldnerabteilung *f*; ◆ **give the ~ a notice of default** LAW den Schuldner in Verzug setzen

debt: **~ ratio** *n* FIN Leverage-Kennziffer *f*, Verschuldungsgrad *m*; **~ redemption** *n* FIN Schuldentilgung *f*; **~ refinancing** *n* FIN Umschuldung *f*; **~ refunding** *n* FIN Umschuldung *f*; **~ relief** *n* ECON Schuldenerlaß *m*; **~ rescheduling** *n* FIN Umschuldung *f*; **~ restructuring** *n* FIN Umschuldung *f*; **~ retirement** *n* ACC Schuldentilgung *f*, Tilgung *f*, FIN Tilgung *f*; **~ service** *n* ACC Annuität *f*, Schuldendienst *m*; **~ service indicators** *n pl* ECON Schuldendienstindikatoren *m pl*; **~ swap** *n* FIN Schuldenswap *m*, Umschuldung *f*, Schuldentausch *m*

debug *vt* COMP austesten, Programmfehler bereinigen in, Programmfehler beseitigen in, Programmfehler suchen in

debugger *n* COMP Debugger *m* (*jarg*), Fehlersuchprogramm *nt*

debugging *n* COMP Fehlerbeseitigung *f*

decade *n* GEN COMM Dekade *f*, Jahrzehnt *nt*

decartelization *n* GEN COMM Dekartellisierung *f*, Dekartellierung *f*

decay 1. *n* PROP Verfall *m*; **2.** *vi* PROP verfallen

deceased: **~ estate** *n* LAW Nachlaß *m*

deceive *vt* S&M irreführen

decelerate *vi* ECON *growth* verlangsamen

deceleration *n* ECON *growth* Verlangsamung *f*

decentralization *n* MGMNT, POL Dezentralisierung *f*

decentralize *vt* MGMNT, POL dezentralisieren

decentralized *adj* MGMNT, POL dezentralisiert; **~ management** *n* MGMNT dezentrale Leitung *f*, dezentralisiertes Management *nt*; **~ market economy** *n* (*DME*) ECON, POL dezentrale Marktwirtschaft *f*; **~ planning** *n* MGMNT dezentrale Planung *f*

deceptive *adj* GEN COMM, LAW, PATENTS, S&M irreführend; **~ advertising** *n* GEN COMM, S&M irreführende Werbung *f*; **~ packaging** *n* S&M irreführende Verpackung *f*

decibel *n* (*dB*) GEN COMM Dezibel *nt* (*dB*)

decide *vt* GEN COMM entscheiden; **~ on** *vt* GEN COMM beschließen

decided *adj* GEN COMM beschlossen, entschieden

decimal *adj* MATH dezimal; **~ to binary conversion** *n* COMP, MATH dezimal-binäre Umwandlung *f*; **~ digit** *n* COMP, MATH Dezimalstelle *f*; **~ notation** *n* MATH Dezimaldarstellung *f*; **~ number** *n* COMP, MATH Dezimalzahl *f*; **~ point** *n* COMP, MATH Dezimalpunkt *m*, Dezimalzeichen *nt*, *Germany* Komma *nt*

decimate *vt* GEN COMM dezimieren

decipher *vt* GEN COMM entziffern

decision *n* GEN COMM Entscheidung *f*, MGMNT Beschluß *m*; ◆ **make a snap ~** GEN COMM eine spontane Entscheidung treffen

decision: **~ analysis** *n* MGMNT Entscheidungsanalyse *f*; **~ maker** *n* MGMNT Entscheidungsträger, in *m,f*; **~ making** *n* MGMNT Entscheiden *nt*, Entscheidungsfindung *f*; **~-making aids** *n pl* GEN COMM Entscheidungshilfen *f pl*; **~-making process** *n* MGMNT Entscheidungsprozeß *m*, Entscheidungsfindungsprozeß *m*; **~-making unit** *n* GEN COMM Entscheidungsträger, in *m,f*, S&M *marketing* entscheidungsfindende Einheit *f*; **~ model** *n* MGMNT Entscheidungsmodell *nt*; **~ package** *n* FIN, MGMNT Entscheidungspaket *nt*; **~ process** *n* MGMNT Entscheidungsprozeß *m*; **~ support system** *n* (*DSS*) MGMNT Entscheidungsfindungssystem *nt*, Entscheidungsunterstützungssystem *nt*; **~ table** *n* COMP Entscheidungstabelle *f*; **~ theory** *n* MGMNT Entscheidungstheorie *f*; **~ tree** *n* HRM, MGMNT Entscheidungsbaum *m*; **~ unit** *n* GEN COMM Entscheidungsträger, in *m,f*

decisive *adj* GEN COMM entschlußfreudig, *measures* entscheidend; **~ ballot** *n* POL Stichwahl *f*; **~ factor** *n* GEN COMM Ausschlag *m*; **~ vote** *n* HRM ausschlaggebende Stimme *f*

deck *n* COMP *for magnetic tapes* Laufwerk *nt*, TRANSP *of ship* Deck *nt*

declaration *n* GEN COMM Erklärung *f*, STOCK Festsetzung *f*; **~ of abandonment** *n* INS Abandonrevers *m*; **~ of accession** *n* POL Beitrittserklärung *f*; **~ of assignment** *n* LAW *contract law* Abtretungserklärung *f*; **~ of avoidance** *n* LAW Aufhebungserklärung *f*; **~ day** *n* STOCK *dividends* Stichtag *m*; **~ of estimated tax** *n* AmE TAX Erklärung *f* über geschätzte Steuereingänge, Erklärung *f* der eingeschätzten Steuereingänge; **~ of**

intent *n* LAW Absichtserklärung *f*, Willenserklärung *f*; **~ of invalidity** *n* LAW Ungültigkeitserklärung *f*; **~ of origin** *n* IMP/EXP Ursprungserklärung *f*; **~ of trust** *n* LAW Treuhanderklärung *f*; **~ of value** *n* IMP/EXP, TRANSP Wertangabe *f*

declare *vt* COMP deklarieren, FIN *dividends* beschließen, IMP/EXP deklarieren, erklären, STOCK festsetzen, TAX deklarieren, erklären; ♦ **~ null and void** LAW für ungültig erklären, annullieren; **~ on oath** LAW eidlich erklären; **~ an option** STOCK eine Option festsetzen; **~ sb not guilty** LAW jdn freisprechen

declared: **~ dividend** *n* FIN ausgewiesene Dividende *f*, beschlossene Dividende *f*; **~ insolvent** *phr* GEN COMM für insolvent erklärt; **~ value for carriage** *n* TRANSP Wertangabe *f* für Transport; **~ value for customs** *n* IMP/EXP erklärter Zollwert *m*, Wertangabe *f* für Zoll

decline 1. *n* ECON Rückgang *m*, *employment* Niedergang *m*, Abnahme *f*, STOCK Kursabschwächung *f*, Kursrückgang *m*; **2.** *vt* GEN COMM, LAW ablehnen; ♦ **~ the offer** LAW *contracts* das Angebot ablehnen; **3.** *vi* ECON abnehmen, sinken, zurückgehen

decline: **~ stage** *n* S&M Degenerationsphase *f*

declining *adj* GEN COMM rückgängig, rückläufig; **~-balance depreciation** *n* FIN Buchwertabschreibung *f*, degressive Abschreibung *f*; **~-balance method** *n* ACC degressive Abschreibung *f*; **~ economic activity** *n* ECON rückläufige Konjunktur *f*; **~ industrial area** *n* ECON Industrieregion *f* im Abwärtstrend; **~ industry** *n* IND Industrie *f* im Niedergang, Industrierückgang *m*, verfallende Industrie *f*; **~ interest rates** *n pl* ECON sinkende Zinsen *n pl*; **~ market** *n* STOCK rückläufiger Markt *m*; **~ production** *n* IND Produktionsrückgang *m*; **~ share** *n* ECON abnehmender Anteil *m*, sinkender Anteil *m*; **~ trend** *n* ECON rückläufige Tendenz *f*

decoder *n* COMP *hardware* Decoder *m* (*jarg*), Decodierwerk *nt*

decollate *vt* COMP trennen

decommission *vt* ENVIR stillegen

decommissioned *adj* ENVIR stillgelegt

decommissioning *n* ENVIR *of nuclear power plant* Stillegung *f*

decommitment *n* ACC Freistellung *f* von Mitteln

decompartmentalization *n* ADMIN Auflösung *f* der Aufteilung in Abteilungen, Abteilungszusammenlegung *f*

DEcon *abbr* (*Doctor of Economics*) GEN COMM Doktor *m* der Wirtschaftswissenschaften

deconcentration *n* ADMIN, BANK Dekartellisierung *f*, Entflechtung *f*

decorate *vt* GEN COMM, PROP verschönern

decoration *n* GEN COMM, PROP Verschönerung *f*; **~ and furnishings** *n pl* GEN COMM, S&M Innenausstattung *f*

decrease *vi* GEN COMM sinken

decrease: **~ in value** *n* ACC, FIN Wertvorschlag *m*; **~ of risk** *n* INS Gefahrverminderung *f*

decreasing: **in ~ liquidity order** *phr* ACC *balance sheet* nach abnehmender Liquidität, nach dem Liquidierbankenprinzip; **~ order** *n* COMM absteigende Folge *f*; **~ rate** *n* FIN rückläufiger Kurs *m*

decree *n* LAW Verfügung *f*, POL Erlaß *m*; **~ in bankruptcy** *n* ACC, LAW Konkurseröffnungsbeschluß *m*

decrement *vt* COMP um eine Einheit vermindern

decruitment *n* HRM Rückversetzung *f* älterer Menschen in untere Führungsebenen

decrypt *vt* COMP entschlüsseln, decodieren

decryption *n* COMMS Decodierung *f*, Entschlüsselung *f*, COMP Entschlüsselung *f*

dedicate *vt* COMP reservieren

dedicated *adj* COMP *hardware* reserviert, *software* dediziert; **~ line** *n* COMP Standleitung *f*

dedomiciling *n* GEN COMM Geschäftssitzverlagerung *f*, Geschäftssitzverlegung *f*

deduct *vt* FIN, INS, MATH, TAX abziehen, in Abzug bringen; ♦ **~ from** FIN, INS, MATH, TAX abziehen von

deductibility: **~ of employer contributions** *n* TAX Abzugsfähigkeit *f* des Arbeitgeberanteils, Abzugsfähigkeit *f* der Arbeitgeberbeiträge

deductible 1. *adj* FIN, TAX abzugsfähig; **2.** *n AmE* (*cf excess BrE*) INS Abzugsfranchise *f*, Selbstbehalt *m*

deductible: **~ clause** *n* INS Selbstbehaltsklausel *f*

deduction *n* GEN COMM, INS Abzug *m*, Anrechnung *f*, TAX abzugsfähiger Betrag *m*, *from income* Absetzung *f*, Abzug *m*; **~ at source** *n* TAX Quellenabzug *m* Abzug *m* an der Quelle; **~ from wages** *n* TAX Lohnabzug *m*, Abzug *m* vom Lohn; **~ new for old** *n* INS Abzüge *m pl* neu für alt

deductive: **~ reasoning** *n* MGMNT schlußfolgerndes Denken *nt*

deed *n* LAW *property* Übertragungsurkunde *f*, Urkunde *f*, förmlicher Vertrag *m*; **~ of assignation** *n* GEN COMM Abtretungsurkunde *f*; **~ of covenant** *n BrE* TAX Schenkungsurkunde *f*, Versprechensurkunde *f*; **~ in lieu of foreclosure** *n* LAW, PROP *property* Grundstücksübereignung *f* anstatt der Vollstreckung; **~ of partnership** *n* LAW Gesellschaftsvertrag *m*; **~ restriction** *n* LAW *property* Urkunde *f* mit beschränkten Rechten

deem: **~ necessary** *vt* GEN COMM notwendig erscheinen

deemed 1. *adj* GEN COMM gehalten für; **2. ~ to be** *vt* GEN COMM scheinen als

deepen *vt* GEN COMM vertiefen

deep: **~-freeze** *n* IND Gefrierschrank *m*, Tiefkühltruhe *f*; **~-frozen** *adj* IND tiefgekühlt; **~-sea broker** *n* HRM Überseemakler *m*; **~-sea shipping lane** *n* TRANSP Hochseeroute *f*

deepwater *n* TRANSP Tiefwasser *nt*; **~ berth** *n* TRANSP *shipping* Tiefwasseranlegeplatz *m*; **~ harbor** *AmE*, **~ harbour** *BrE n* TRANSP *shipping* Seehafen *m*, Tiefwasserhafen *m*; **~ route** *n* TRANSP *shipping* Hochseeroute *f*, Tiefwasserstraße *f*

def. *abbr* (*deferred*) ACC, GEN COMM, HRM, INS aufgeschoben

de facto *adj* LAW de facto; **~ corporation** *n* ECON, LAW faktische Gesellschaft *f*, Arbeitsgemeinschaft *f*; **~ manager** *n* MGMNT De-facto-Manager *m*; **~ population** *n* ECON De-facto-Bevölkerung *f*, ortsanwesende Bevölkerung *f*

defalcate *vt* LAW veruntreuen

defalcation *n* LAW Unterschlagung *f* von Geldern, Veruntreuung *f*

defamation *n* LAW *of character* üble Nachrede *f*, Beleidigung *f*, Ehrverletzung *f*, Verleumdung *f*

defamatory *adj* LAW beleidigend, verleumderisch

defame: **~ sb's credit** *vt* LAW jdn verleumden; **~ sb's reputation** *vt* LAW jdn verleumden

default *n* COMP Standardeinstellung *f*, Standard *m*, FIN

Säumnis *f*, GEN COMM Verzug *m*, LAW Versäumnis *nt*, Verzug *m*, Leistungsstörung *f*; ◆ **in** ~ FIN, GEN COMM, LAW säumig

default: ~ **of the debtor** *n* LAW *contracts* Schuldnerverzug *m*; ~ **device** *n* COMP Standardgerät *nt*; ~ **directory** *n* COMP Standardverzeichnis *nt*; ~ **drive** *n* COMP Standardlaufwerk *nt*

defaulted: ~ **bond** *n* STOCK notleidende Anleihe *f*

default: ~ **in acceptance** *n* LAW Annahmeverzug *m*; ~ **in delivery** *n* LAW *contracts* Lieferverzug *m*

defaulting *adj* FIN, GEN COMM, LAW säumig; ~ **debtor** *n* BANK säumiger Schuldner *m*, in Verzug geratener Schuldner *m*; ~ **party** *n* LAW *contracts* säumige Partei *f*; ~ **witness** *n* LAW nichterschienener Zeuge *m*, nichterschienene Zeugin *f*

default: ~ **interest** *n* BANK Verzugszinsen *m pl*; ~ **judgment** *n* LAW Säumnisurteil *nt*; ~ **option** *n* COMP Standardoption *f*; ~ **in payment** *n* FIN Zahlungsverzug *m*; ~ **surcharge** *n* BrE TAX Zuschlag *m* für Zahlungsverzug

defeasance *n* LAW Nichtigkeitserklärung *f*, STOCK *corporate finance, general* Erlöschen *nt* eines Eigentumsrechtes

defeat 1. *n* GEN COMM Niederlage *f*; **2.** *vt* LAW vereiteln

defect *n* LAW *trade law* Mangel *m*, Qualitätsmangel *m*, Sachmangel *m*

defective *adj* LAW *contracts* fehlerhaft, mangelhaft; ~ **performance** *n* LAW *international contract law* mangelhafte Erfüllung *f*, Schlechterfüllung *f*; ~ **service** *n* GEN COMM *consumer protection* mangelhafte Leistung *f*; ~ **title** *n* LAW mit Rechtsmängeln behafteter Rechtstitel *m*, Rechtsmangel *m*; ~ **units** *n pl* IND Ausschuß *m*

defence *n* BrE GEN COMM Abwehr *f*, LAW Einrede *f*, Verteidigung *f*, POL Verteidigung *f*; ~ **advisor** *n* BrE (*DA*) POL Verteidigungsberater, in *m,f*; ~ **based on warranty for a defect** *n* BrE LAW *contracts* Mängeleinrede *f*; ~ **industry** *n* BrE ECON Rüstungsindustrie *f*; ~ **production revolving fund** *n* BrE FIN revolvierender Fonds *m* der Rüstungsproduktion; ~ **of suit against insured** *n* BrE INS *liability insurance* Klagenabwehr *f* gegen Versicherte

defend *vt* GEN COMM verteidigen

defendant *n* LAW Beklagte(r) *mf* [decl. as adj]

defending: ~ **counsel** *n* BrE (*cf defense attorney AmE*) LAW Verteidiger, in *m,f*

defense *AmE see* **defence** *BrE*; ~ **attorney** *n* AmE (*cf defending counsel BrE, counsel for the defence BrE*) LAW Verteidiger, in *m,f*; ~ **lawyer** *n* AmE (*cf defending counsel BrE, counsel for the defence BrE*) LAW Verteidiger, in *m,f*

defensive: ~ **budgeting** *n* BrE ADMIN, S&M vorsichtige Haushaltsplanung *f*; ~ **conditions** *n pl* GEN COMM Abwehrkonditionen *f pl*; ~ **securities** *n pl* STOCK risikoarme Wertpapiere *nt pl*; ~ **spending** *n* BrE S&M vorsichtige Ausgabenwirtschaft *f*; ~ **strategy** *n* GEN COMM defensive Strategie *f*

defer *vt* GEN COMM *decision* aufschieben, *debt* stunden; ◆ ~ **a debt** ACC einen Kredit verlängern; ~ **payment** ACC eine Zahlung aufschieben

deferment *n* GEN COMM Aufschub *m*

deferral: ~ **of taxes** *n* ACC transitorische Steuerabgrenzung *f*

deferred *adj* (*def.*) ACC *balance sheet* aktivisch abgegrenzt, GEN COMM *shares* aufgeschoben, HRM aufgeschoben, INS abgekürzt, aufgeschoben; ~ **account** *n* INS Ratenprämienvertrag *m*, TAX Ratenzahlungsvertrag *m*; ~ **annuity** *n* INS abgekürzte Lebensversicherung *f*, aufgeschobene Rente *f*; ~ **benefits and payments** *n pl* INS aufgeschobene Versicherungsleistungen und Zahlungen *f pl*, spätere Versicherungsleistungen und Zahlungen *f pl*; ~ **billing** *n* S&M Rechnungsaufschub *m*; ~ **charge** *n* ACC aufgeschobene Ausgaben *f pl*; ~ **compensation** *n* HRM *salary* nachträgliche Vergütung *f*; ~ **compensation plan** *n* HRM nachträglicher Vergütungsplan *m*; ~ **contribution plan** *n* HRM aufgeschobener Gewinnverteilungsplan *m*; ~ **credit** *n* ACC transitorische Passiva *m pl*, zurückgestelltes Einkommen *nt*; ~ **futures** *n pl* STOCK Nachzugsterminkontrakte *m pl*, Nachzugsterminwaren *f pl*; ~ **group annuity** *n* HRM Gruppenversicherung *f*; ~ **income** *n* ACC transitorische Passiva *m pl*, zurückgestelltes Einkommen *nt*; ~ **interest** *n* ACC antizipative Zinsabgrenzung *f*; ~ **interest bond** *n* STOCK Obligation *f* mit aufgeschobener Zinszahlung; ~ **item** *n* ACC transitorischer Posten *m*; ~ **maintenance** *n* PROP *appraisal* Wartungsaufschub *m*; ~ **payment annuity** *n* INS aufgeschobene Zahlung *f* der Jahresrente, spätere Zahlung *f* der Jahresrente; ~ **payments** *n pl* ACC aufgeschobene Zahlungen *f pl*; ~ **profit sharing** *n* HRM aufgeschobene Gewinnbeteiligung *f*; ~ **profit-sharing plan** *n* TAX abgegrenzter Gewinnbeteiligungsplan *m*; ~ **rebate** *n* IMP/EXP, TRANSP *shipping* zurückgestellter Rabatt *m*; ~ **retirement** *n* HRM *work, social welfare* aufgeschobene Pensionierung *f*; ~ **revenue** *n* FIN zurückgestellte Erträge *m pl*, zurückgestelltes Einkommen *nt*; ~ **tax** *n* FIN aufgeschobene Steuer *f*, TAX aufgeschobene Steuer *f*, latente Steuer *f*; ~ **taxation** *n* FIN, TAX aufgeschobene Besteuerung *f*; ~ **tax liabilities** *n pl* FIN, TAX gestundete Steuerverbindlichkeiten *f pl*; ~ **wage increase** *n* HRM *work, industry* aufgeschobene Lohnerhöhung *f*

deficiency *n* GEN COMM Ausfall *m*, Defizit *nt*, Fehlbestand *m*, TAX Fehlbetrag *m*, Minderbetrag *m*; ~ **judgment** *n* LAW Ausfallurteil *nt*; ~ **payment** *n* ECON *agriculture* Agrarpreissubvention *f*, FIN Ausgleichszahlung *f*

deficient *adj* GEN COMM fehlerhaft; ~ **tax installment** *AmE*, ~ **tax instalment** *BrE n* TAX unzureichende Steuerrate *f*

deficit *n* ECON Defizit *nt*, FIN Defizit *nt*, Fehlbetrag *m*; ~ **financing** *n* ECON, FIN Defizit Spending *nt*, Defizitfinanzierung *f*, Finanzierung *f* durch Staatsverschuldung; ~ **net worth** *n* ECON negativer Nettowert *m*; ~ **spending** *n* ECON Defizitfinanzierung *f*, Defizit Spending *nt*; ~ **spending policy** *n* FIN *governmental accounting* Defizitpolitik *f*, Politik *f* des Defizit Spending

defined: ~ **benefit pension plan** *n* FIN *pensions* Pensionskassensystem *nt* mit Rechtsanspruch; ~ **contribution pension plan** *n* FIN *pensions* Pensionsplan *m* mit definierten Beiträgen; ~ **goals and objectives** *n pl* GEN COMM Zielvorgaben *f pl*

definite *adj* GEN COMM bestimmt, eindeutig, konkret

definition *n* GEN COMM, INS Definition *f*; ~ **of items** *n* INS Definition *f* der Einzelposten, Bezeichnung *f* der Posten; ~ **of limits** *n* INS Definition *f* der Deckungssumme, Festlegung *f* der Haftungssumme

deflate *vt* ECON restriktive Wirtschaftspolitik betreiben, deflationieren

deflation *n* ECON Deflation *f*

deflationary *adj* ECON deflationär; **~ gap** *n* (*cf contractionary national income gap*) ECON deflatorische Lücke *f*; **~ pressures** *n pl* ECON deflatorischer Druck *m*

deflator *n* ECON, MATH Deflator *m*

defragmentation *n* COMP *disk* Defragmentierung *f*

defraud *vt* ACC, LAW betrügen, beschwindeln

defrauder *n* ACC, LAW Steuerhinterzieher *m*, Betrüger, in *m,f* (*infrml*)

defrauding: **~ the Revenue** *n BrE* TAX Steuerhinterziehung *f*

defray *vt* GEN COMM begleichen, *costs* tragen; ◆ **~ the expenses** GEN COMM die Kosten übernehmen, für die Spesen aufkommen

defunct: **~ company** *n* ECON erloschene Gesellschaft *f*

defuse *vt* HRM entschärfen

degradation *n* ENVIR Abbau *m*

degree *n* GEN COMM *measure* Grad *m*, HRM, WEL *education* Staatsprüfung *f*, Universitätsabschluß *m*, Hochschulabschluß *m*, Universitätsdiplom *nt*; **~ of damage** *n* INS Grad *m* der Beschädigung, Schadensstufe *f*; **~ of disablement** *n* INS Invaliditätsgrad *m*; **~ of exposure** *n* STOCK *to the market* Umfang *f* offener Positionen, Devisenengagement *nt*, Kreditengagement *nt*, Wertpapierengagement *nt*, Risikograd *m*; **~ of fluctuation** *n* STOCK *in futures price* Grad der Kursschwankungen *m*, Grad der Preisschwankungen *m*, Schwankungsintensität *f*; **~ measure** *n* MATH Gradmaß *nt*; **~ of risk** *n* GEN COMM Gefahrenumfang *m*, Risikograd *m*

degrees: **~ Centigrade** *n pl* GEN COMM Grad Celsius *m pl*; **~ Fahrenheit** *n pl* GEN COMM Grad Fahrenheit *m pl*

degression *n* MATH Degression *f*

degressive: **~ tax** *n* TAX degressive Steuer *f*

dehiring *n AmE* HRM Nahelegen *nt* der Kündigung

de-icing: **~ fluid** *n* TRANSP Enteiser *m*, Enteisungsflüssigkeit *f*

deindustrialization *n* ECON, IND Deindustrialisierung *f*

deintensified: **~ farming** *n* ENVIR deintensivierte Landwirtschaft *f*

de jure *adv* LAW de jure, von Rechts wegen

de jure: **~ population** *n* (*cf de facto population*) ECON De-jure-Bevölkerung *f*

del. *abbr* (*delegation*) GEN COMM Delegation *f*

DEL *abbr* (*delete key*) COMP DEL-Taste *f*, ENTF-Taste *f*, Löschtaste *f*, Löschzeichen *nt*

delay 1. *n* COMP Verzögerung *f*, FIN Säumnis *f*, GEN COMM Verspätung *f*, Verzögerung *f*, Verzug *m*, Aufschub *m*, LAW *in performance from contract* Verzug *m*; **2.** *vt* GEN COMM aufschieben, verzögern

delay: **~ of the creditor** *n* LAW *contracts* Gläubigerverzug *m*

delayed *adj* GEN COMM verspätet; **~ delivery** *n* GEN COMM Lieferverzug *m*, verzögerte Auslieferung *f*

delaying: **~ tactics** *n pl* GEN COMM Verzögerungstaktik *f*

del credere *n* GEN COMM Delkredere *nt*; **~ agent** *n* GEN COMM Delkredere-Agent *m*; **~ guarantee** *n* LAW *contracts* Delkredere-Vereinbarung *f*

deleave *vt* COMP *sheets of paper* trennen

delegate 1. *n* HRM Vertreter, in *mf*, POL Abgeordnete(r) *mf* [decl. as adj] (*Abg.*), Abgesandte(r) *mf* [decl. as adj];

2. *vt* MGMNT *powers, responsibilities* übertragen, delegieren, erteilen

delegated *adj* MGMNT erteilt

delegation *n* (*del.*) GEN COMM *of people* Delegation *f*, MGMNT *of powers, authority* Erteilung *f*, Übertragung *f*; **~ of authority** *n* GEN COMM Vollmachtsübertragung *f*, Delegation *f* von Kompetenzen; **~ of signing authority** *n* GEN COMM Erteilung *f* von Zeichnungsvollmacht

delete *vt* COMP löschen, GEN COMM durchstreichen, streichen; ◆ **~ a debt** FIN Schulden streichen

delete: **~ character** *n* (*DEL*) COMP ENTF-Taste *f*, Löschzeichen *nt*; **~ key** *n* (*DEL*) COMP DEL-Taste *f*, ENTF-Taste *f*, Löschtaste *f*

deletion *n* COMP Löschung *f*, LAW *by-laws provisions* Streichung *f*; **~ of debts** *n* GEN COMM Schuldenstreichung *f*

deliberate 1. *vt* LAW beraten; **2.** *vi* LAW beraten

deliberation *n* LAW Beratung *f*

delict *n* LAW *Scots Law* Delikt *nt*

delimit *vt* COMMS begrenzen

delinquency *n* FIN Säumnis *f*, GEN COMM Nichtzahlung *f* bei Fälligkeit; **~ ratio** *n* ACC Ausfallquote *f*

delinquent *adj* FIN, GEN COMM, LAW säumig; **~ account** *n* FIN überfällige Forderung *f*

delisting *n* STOCK Aufhebung *f* der Börsennotierung, Aufhebung *f* der Börsenzulassung

deliver *vt* GEN COMM *goods, services* übergeben, liefern, TRANSP liefern; ◆ **~ the Budget speech** *BrE* ECON die Haushaltsrede halten; **~ a lecture** WEL einen Vortrag halten; **~ an opinion** POL *parliament* eine Meinung äußern, eine Stellungnahme abgeben, einen Standpunkt vertreten

deliverable *adj* STOCK *T-bills* lieferbar; ◆ **in a ~ state** LAW in lieferbarem Zustand

deliverable: **~ bills** *n pl* STOCK lieferbare Schatzwechsel *m pl*; **~ security** *n* STOCK lieferbares Wertpapier *nt*

delivered *adj* (*dd*) GEN COMM geliefert (*gel.*), übergeben; ◆ **~ at docks** (*DD*) IMP/EXP, TRANSP *shipping* am Kai abgeliefert; **~ at frontier** (*DAF*) IMP/EXP an der Grenze abgeliefert, geliefert Grenze; **~ docks** (*DD*) IMP/EXP, TRANSP am Kai abgeliefert; **~ domicile** TRANSP Lieferung *f* frei Haus; **~ duty paid** (*DDP*) IMP/EXP geliefert verzollt; **~ duty unpaid** (*DDU*) IMP/EXP geliefert unverzollt; **~ ex quay** (*DEQ*) IMP/EXP *Incoterms* geliefert ab Kai; **~ ex ship** (*DES*) IMP/EXP *named port of destination* geliefert ab Schiff; **~ free** COMMS, GEN COMM franko

delivered: **~ price** *n* S&M Lieferpreis *m*, Preis *m* frei Haus

delivering: **~ carrier** *n* TRANSP Auslieferungsspediteur *m*

delivery *n* (*D*) COMMS *of post* Zustellung *f*, GEN COMM Aushändigung *f*, Auslieferung *f*, Lieferung *f*, Übergabe *f*, LAW Übermittlung *f*, TRANSP Auslieferung *f*, Lieferung *f*; **~ charge** *n* TRANSP Zustellgebühr *f*; **~ costs** *n pl* ACC Lieferkosten *pl*, Bezugskosten *pl*; **~ counter** *n* ECON Ausgabeschalter *m*; **~ date** *n* (*d.d.*) *shipping* Empfangsdatum *nt*, STOCK Fälligkeitstermin *m*, Liefertermin *m*; **~ day** *n* GEN COMM Tag *m* der Zustellung, STOCK Liefertag *m*; **~ of goods** *n* GEN COMM Warenlieferung *f*; **~ month** *n* STOCK *futures* Liefermonat *m*; **~ note** *n* FIN Lieferschein *m*, IMP/EXP, TRANSP Lieferschein *m*, Versandanzeige *f*; **~ notice** *n* IMP/EXP, TRANSP Lieferanzeige *f*; **~ order** *n* (*D/O*) TRANSP Auslieferungsauftrag *m*, Konnossementsteilschein *m*, Lieferauftrag *m*; **~ performance** *n* IMP/EXP, TRANSP Liefererfüllung *f*;

~ period *n* GEN COMM Lieferfrist *f*, STOCK Lieferzeitraum *m*; **~ point** *n* GEN COMM Lieferort *m*, Warenannahmestelle *f*; **~ receipt** *n* IMP/EXP, TRANSP Lieferbestätigung *f*, Warenempfangsschein *m*; **~ and redelivery** *n pl* TRANSP Lieferung *f* und Rücklieferung *f*; **~ service** *n* TRANSP Zustelldienst *m*; **~ system** *n* STOCK *futures* Liefersystem *nt*; **~ terms of sale** *n pl* IMP/EXP Lieferbedingungen *f pl*; **~ time** *n* GEN COMM Lieferzeit *f*, STOCK Lieferfrist *f*, TRANSP Lieferzeit *f*; **~ turnround** *n* GEN COMM, TRANSP Lieferungsumschlag *m*; **~ versus payment** *n* STOCK Lieferung *f* gegen Zahlung

Delors: **~ Plan** *n* (*cf Werner Report*) ECON Delors-Plan *m*

Delphi: **~ technique** *n* MGMNT Delphi-Methode *f*

delta *n* FIN, STOCK *options on Eurodollar futures* Delta *nt*; **~ factor** *n* STOCK Delta-Faktor *m*; **~-neutral** *adj* STOCK *options on Eurodollar futures* deltaneutral; **~-neutral straddle** *n* STOCK *options* deltaneutrale Optionsposition *f*, deltaneutraler Straddle *m*, kombinierte Optionsposition *f*; **~-neutral strangle** *n* STOCK *options* deltaneutrale Geldverknappung *f*; **~ stock** *n* STOCK Delta-Aktie *f*

deluxe: **~ cabin** *n* TRANSP *shipping* Luxuskabine *f*

demand 1. *n* GEN COMM Bedarf *f*, Nachfrage *f*, GEN COMM Aufforderung *f*, Bedarf *m*; ◆ **in ~** GEN COMM, HRM gefragt; **on ~** (*O/D*) ACC bei Vorlage, *at sight* bei Sicht, gegen Vorlage, GEN COMM auf Verlangen; **2.** *vt* GEN COMM fordern

demand: **~ analysis** *n* S&M Bedarfsanalyse *f*; **~ assessment** *n* ADMIN, ECON Nachfragebewertung *f*; **~ curve** *n* ECON Nachfragekurve *f*; **~ deposit** *n* BANK Sichteinlage *f*; **~ draft** *n* (*DD*) FIN, GEN COMM Sichttratte *f*, Sichtwechsel *m*; **~ forecast** *n* S&M Nachfrageprognose *f*; **~ for goods** *n* ECON Güternachfrage *f*; **~ for labor** *AmE*, **~ for labour** *BrE* *n* ECON Nachfrage *f* nach Arbeitskräften; **~ for money** *n* ECON Geldnachfrage *f*; **~ for sophisticated products** *n* S&M Nachfrage *f* nach technisch anspruchsvollen Produkten, differenzierte Produktanforderungen *f pl*

demanding *adj* GEN COMM anspruchsvoll

demand: **~-led growth** *n* GEN COMM nachfragegesteuertes Wachstum *nt*; **~ line of credit** *n* FIN Bedarfs-Kreditlinie *f*; **~ management** *n* ECON Nachfragesteuerung *f*; **~ note** *n* GEN COMM *instrument* Zahlungsaufforderung *f*; **~ oligopoly** *n* ECON Nachfrageoligopol; **~ pattern** *n* ECON Nachfragestruktur *f*, Nachfragemuster *nt*; **~ price** *n* ECON Geldkurs *m*, Sichtkurs *m*, STOCK Geldkurs *m*; **~-pull inflation** *n* ECON, GEN COMM Nachfrageinflation *f*, nachfrageinduzierte Inflation *f*; **~ schedule** *n* ECON Nachfragetabelle *f*; **~-shift inflation** *n* ECON Inflation *f* durch Nachfragestrukturveränderungen

demanning *n* HRM Personalabbau *m*

demarcation *n* HRM strenge Abgrenzung *f* der Berufsgruppen; **~ dispute** *n* HRM, MGMNT Kompetenzstreitigkeit *f*

demarketing *n* S&M Antimarketing *nt*

dematerialization *n* ECON, STOCK beleglose Abwicklung *f* von Börsentransaktionen, Dematerialisierung *f*, Elektronisierung *f*

dematerialized *adj* (*cf paperless*) ECON, STOCK *certificates of deposit* beleglos

demerger 1. *n* ECON *of two or more companies* Entflechtung *f*, Entfusionierung *f*, GEN COMM Entfusionierung *f*; **2.** *vt* ECON, GEN COMM entfusionieren

demerit: **~ good** *n* ECON demeritorisches Gut *nt*

de minimis: **~ case** *n* FIN Bagatellfall *m*; **~ rule** *n* LAW *EU* De-minimis-Regel *f*

democracy *n* GEN COMM, POL Demokratie *f*

democratic *adj* GEN COMM, POL demokratisch; **~ centralism** *n* POL demokratischer Zentralismus *m*; **~ management** *n* HRM demokratisches Management *nt*; **~ style of leadership** *n* HRM demokratischer Führungsstil *m*

demogrant *n* HRM Volkspension *f*, Volksrente *f*, Bürgergeld *nt*

demographics *n pl* ECON, MATH Bevölkerungsstatistiken *f pl*

demographic: **~ statistics** *n* ECON, MATH Bevölkerungsstatistik *f*; **~ transition** *n* ECON demographischer Wandel *m*

demography *n* ECON Demographie *f*

demolish *vt* GEN COMM zerstören, PROP abbrechen

demolition *n* GEN COMM Zerstörung *f*, PROP Abbruch *m*, Abriß *m*; **~ cost** *n* GEN COMM Abbruchkosten *pl*

demometrics *n* ECON Demometrie *f*

demonetization *n* ECON Demonetisierung *f*

demonstrable *adj* GEN COMM nachweisbar

demonstrate *vt* GEN COMM *by table, graph* demonstrieren, S&M vorführen

demonstration *n* S&M Vorführung *f*

demoralize *vt* HRM demoralisieren

demote: **~ sb** *vt* HRM *employee* jdn tariflich niedriger einstufen, jdn herunterstufen

demotion *n* HRM Rückstufung *f*

demotivate *vt* HRM demotivieren

demotivation *adj* HRM Demotivation *f*

demountable: **~ system** *n* TRANSP demontierbares System *nt*

demurrage *n* TRANSP Liegegeld *nt*, Überliegezeit *f*

demurrer *n* LAW rechtliche Einwendungen *f pl*

DEn *abbr BrE* (*Department of Energy*) IND, POL Ministerium für Energie

denationalization *n* ECON Privatisierung *f*, Reprivatisierung *f*

denationalize *vt* ECON reprivatisieren

denationalized *adj* ECON reprivatisiert

denial *n* GEN COMM Verweigerung *f*; **~ of opinion** *n* GEN COMM Verweigerung *f* des Bestätigungsvermerks

denied *adj* GEN COMM verweigert

Denison: **~ residual** *n* ECON Denisonscher Rest *m*

Dennison: **~'s law** *n* ECON Dennisonsches Gesetz *nt*

denom. *abbr* (*denomination*) ECON *notes* Bezeichnung *f*, Nennwert *m*, Stückelung *f*, Wertbezeichnung *f*

denominate *vt* ECON denominieren, die Stückelung angeben von

denomination *n* (*denom.*) ECON *coins* Wertbezeichnung *f*, Bezeichnung *f*, Stückelung *f*, Nennwert *m*, STOCK Stücke *nt pl*

denominator *n* GEN COMM Nenner *m*

denounce *vt* LAW auspacken (*infrml*), denunzieren

de novo *adv* LAW de novo

densely: **~ populated** *adj* ECON dicht besiedelt, dichtbevölkert; **~ populated area** *n* ECON dicht besiedeltes Gebiet *nt*, dichtbevölkertes Gebiet *nt*

density *n* PROP Dichte *f*; **~ zoning** *n AmE* LAW *property* Flächennutzungspläne in verdichteten Gebieten

dental: **~ insurance** *n* INS Zahnarztkostenversicherung *f*

deny *vt* GEN COMM verweigern, LAW bestreiten; ◆ **~ the truth of** LAW abstreiten

depart: **~ from sth** *vt* GEN COMM, POL von etw abrücken, von etw abweichen

department *n* (*dept.*) ECON Abteilung *f*, Ministerium *nt*, GEN COMM *in company* Abteilung *f*, MGMNT *administration* Dezernat *nt*, POL Ministerium *nt*

departmental: **~ account** *n* ADMIN dezentralisiertes Rechnungswesen *nt*; **~ assets** *n pl* FIN Abteilungsvermögen *nt*; **~ bank account** *n* ACC *government accounting* Bankkonto *nt* des Ministeriums, ministerielles Bankkonto *nt*; **~ burden** *n* ACC Abteilungsgemeinkosten *pl*; **~ cost estimation** *n* ACC Abteilungskalkulation *f*; **~ costing** *n* ACC Abteilungskostenrechnung *f*, Abteilungsrechnung *f*

Departmental: **~ Entry Processing System** *n BrE* (*DEPS*) IMP/EXP Brancheneinfuhrabfertigungssystem *nt*

departmental: **~ expenditure plan** *n* ADMIN ministerielle Ausgabenplanung *f*, Ausgabenplanung *f* des Ministeriums; **~ expenses** *n pl* ACC Abteilungsgemeinkosten *pl*; **~ head** *n* GEN COMM Abteilungsleiter, in *m,f*; **~ hierarchy** *n* ADMIN Abteilungshierarchie *f*

departmentalization *n* GEN COMM Aufgliederung *f* in Abteilungen

departmental: **~ line object** *n* ADMIN Gegenstand *m* einer Abteilung; **~ management** *n* GEN COMM Abteilungsführung *f*; **~ manager** *n* GEN COMM Abteilungsleiter, in *m,f*; **~ manual** *n* ADMIN Abteilungshandbuch *nt*; **~ object** *n* ADMIN Gegenstand *m* einer Abteilung; **~ organization** *n* ACC Abteilungsorganisation *f*; **~ overheads** *n pl* ACC Abteilungsgemeinkosten *pl*; **~ plan** *n* GEN COMM, MGMNT Abteilungsplan *m*, ressortspezifischer Plan *m*; **~ profit** *n* ACC Abteilungsgewinn *m*, Abteilungsspanne *f*; **~ program** *AmE*, **~ programme** *BrE n* ADMIN ministerielles Programm *nt*; **~ reporting system** *n* ADMIN Berichtssystem *nt* der Ministerien; **~ structure** *n* ADMIN Abteilungsgliederung *f*

departmentation *n* ADMIN Abteilungsgliederung *f*, Abteilungsbildung *f*

Department: **~ of Agriculture** *n AmE* Landwirtschaftsministerium; **~ of Commerce** *n AmE* (*cf Department of Trade and Industry BrE*) POL Handels- und Industrieministerium, Wirtschaftsministerium *nt*; **~ of Education and Science** *n BrE obs* (*DES*) POL Ministerium für Bildung und Wissenschaft; **~ of Employment** *n BrE obs* (*DE*) POL Arbeitsministerium *nt*; **~ of Energy** *n AmE* (*DEn*) POL Ministerium für Energie; **~ of the Environment** *n BrE* (*DOE*) POL Umweltministerium; **~ for Education** *n BrE obs* (*DFE*) POL Ministerium für Bildung; **~ for Education and Employment** *n BrE* (*DfEE*) POL Ministerium für Bildung und Arbeit

department: **~ head** *n* HRM Abteilungsleiter, in *m,f*

Department: **~ of Health** *n BrE* (*DoH*) POL Gesundheitsministerium; **~ of Health, Education and Welfare** *n AmE* (*HEW*) POL Ministerium für Gesundheit, Erziehung und Wohlfahrt; **~ of Health and Human Services** *n AmE* POL Gesundheitsministerium; **~ of Health and Social Security** *n BrE obs* (*DHSS*) POL Gesundheits- und Sozialministerium; **~ of housing and urban development** *n AmE* POL Wohnungs- und Städtebauministerium; **~ of Industry** *n AmE* (*DOI*) POL Industrieministerium; **~ of the Interior** *n AmE* (*cf Home Office BrE*) POL Innenministerium *nt*

department: **~ manager** *n* S&M *in a store* Abteilungsleiter, in *m,f*

Department: **~ of National Savings** *n BrE obs* BANK Postsparkassenbehörde; **~ of Social Security** *n BrE* (*DSS*) POL Sozialministerium

department: **~ store** *n* S&M Kaufhaus *nt*, Warenhaus *nt*; **~ store chain** *n* S&M Warenhauskette *f*; **~ store sale** *n* S&M Warenhausausverkauf *m*

Department: **~ of Trade and Industry** *n* (*DTI*) ECON, GEN COMM, IND Wirtschaftsministerium *nt*, Ministerium für Handel und Industrie; **~ of Transport** *n BrE* (*DTp*) POL Verkehrsministerium; **~ of the Treasury** *n AmE* POL Finanzministerium *nt*, Schatzamt *nt*

departure *n* TRANSP Abfahrt *f*, Abflug *m*, Abgang *m*; **~ control system** *n* (*DCS*) TRANSP Abflugkontrollsystem *nt*; **~ lounge** *n* TRANSP Warteraum *m* im Flughafengebäude, Abflughalle *f*; **~ tax** *n* TAX Ausreisesteuer *f*

depend on *vt* GEN COMM *person* sich verlassen auf [+acc], *event* abhängen von; ◆ **~ sth** GEN COMM mit etw rechnen

dependency: **~ culture** *n* WEL Sozialhilfekultur *f*; **~ ratio** *n* WEL Anteil staatlicher Leistungsempfänger; **~ theory** *n* ECON Dependencia-Theorie *f*

dependent: **~ claim** *n* PATENTS Abhängigkeitsanspruch *m*; **~ coverage** *n* INS abhängige Deckung *f*, abhängiger Versicherungsschutz *m*; **~ economy** *n* ECON abhängige Volkswirtschaft *f*, abhängige Beschäftigung *f*; **~ employment** *n* HRM unselbständige Beschäftigung *f*; **be ~ on** *phr* PATENTS *claim* abhängig sein von; **~ patent** *n* PATENTS abhängiges Patent *nt*; **~ personal services** *n pl* HRM unselbständige Beschäftigung *f*

deplaning *n* TRANSP *leaving aircraft* Verlassen *nt*

depletable: **~ externality** *n* ECON sich erschöpfende Externalität *f*; **~ resource** *n* ECON, ENVIR abbaubarer Rohstoff *m*, endlicher Rohstoff *m*

deplete *vt* ENVIR *raw materials* erschöpfen

deploy *vt* GEN COMM einsetzen

deployment *n* GEN COMM Einsatz *m*

depopulate *vt* GEN COMM entvölkern

depopulation *n* GEN COMM Entvölkerung *f*

deport *vt* POL *alien* abschieben, ausweisen

deportation *n* POL Abschiebung *f*, Ausweisung *f*

deportee *n* POL Abzuschiebende(r) *mf* [decl. as adj]

deposit 1. *n* ACC *paying into a bank* Einzahlung *f*, *downpayment* Anzahlung *f*, BANK Verwahrung *f*, ENVIR Vorkommen *nt*, Lagerstätte *f*, GEN COMM Hinterlegung *f*, Anzahlung *f*, LAW Verwahrung *f*, Hinterlegung *f*, PATENTS Hinterlegung *f*, Depositum *nt*, Kaution *f*, Anzahlung *f*, PROP Kaution *f*, S&M *bottle* Pfand *nt*, STOCK Einschußzahlung *f*; ◆ **for ~ only** BANK nur zur Verrechnung; **2.** *vt* GEN COMM hinterlegen

deposit: **~ account** *n BrE* (*D/A*) BANK Depositenkonto *nt*, Einlagenkonto *nt*, Sparkonto *nt*; **~ administration plan** *n* FIN *pensions* betriebliche Altersversorgung, die ein Unternehmer für seine Mitarbeiter bei einem Versicherungsunternehmen einrichtet; **~ agreement** *n* LAW Hinterlegungsvereinbarung *f*

depositary *n* ADMIN Hinterlegungsstelle *f*, LAW Treuhänder, in *m,f*, Verwahrer, in *m,f*

deposit: **~ balance** *n* BANK Guthabensaldo *nt*; **~ bank** *n*

BANK Depositenbank *f*, Girobank *f*; ~ **banking** *n* BANK Depositengeschäft *nt*; ~ **book** *n* BANK Einlagenbuch *nt*; ~ **bottle** *n* ENVIR, S&M Pfandflasche *f*; ~ **certificate** *n* BANK Einlagenschein *m*, Einlagenzertifikat *nt*, FIN Depotbescheinigung *f*; ~ **currency** *n* BANK, ECON Giralgeld *nt*, Buchgeld *nt*; ~ **facility** *n* ADMIN Hinterlegungsstelle *f*, BANK Einlagenfazilität *f*; ~ **guarantee fund** *n* BANK *Banking Act* Einlagensicherungsfonds *m*; ~ **institution** *n* ADMIN Hinterlegungsstelle *f*; ~ **insurance** *n* INS Depotversicherung *f*; ~ **interest** *n* BANK Einlagenzins *m*; ~ **in transit** *n* BANK noch nicht verbuchte Einzahlung *f* bei einer Bank

deposition *n* LAW *bailment* Hinterlegung *f*, *official statement* beglaubigte schriftliche Zeugenaussage *f*

deposit: ~ **liabilities** *n pl* BANK Einlagenverbindlichkeiten *f pl*; ~ **margin** *n* STOCK Originaleinschuß *m*; ~ **money** *n* BANK, ECON Buchgeld *nt*; ~ **multiplier** *n* ECON *econometrics* Geldschöpfungsmultiplikator *m*

depositor *n* BANK, GEN COMM Einleger, in *m,f*, Einzahler, in *m,f*, Hinterleger, in *m,f*; ~**'s forgery insurance** *n* INS Depositeninhaberversicherung *f* gegen Fälschung, Einzahlerversicherung *f* gegen Fälschung

Depository: ~ **Institutions Deregulation and Monetary Control Act** *n AmE* (*DIDMCA*) POL 1980 Gesetz zur Deregulierung und monetären Überwachung öffentlicher Geldinstitute; ~ **Trust Company** *n AmE* (*DTC*) STOCK Depot-Treuhandgesellschaft *f*

deposit: ~ **passbook** *n* BANK Depositenbuch *nt*; ~ **premium** *n* INS Prämiendepot *nt*, Vorauszahlungsprämie *f*; ~ **rate** *n* BANK Einlagenzins *m*; ~ **receipt** *n* (*DR*) BANK Depotschein *m*, Einzahlungsbeleg *m*

deposits *n pl* BANK Depositen *pl*, Depositengelder *nt pl*, Einlagen *f pl*

deposit: ~ **slip** *n* BANK Depotschein *m*, Einzahlungsschein *m*, GEN COMM Hinterlegungsschein *m*; ~ **surety** *n* INS Sicherheitsleistung *f*; ~**-taking business** *n* BANK Einlagengeschäft *nt*, Passivgeschäft *nt*; ~ **and trust accounts** *n pl* BANK Depositen- und Treuhandkonten *nt pl*

depot *n* (*dept.*) GEN COMM, IMP/EXP, TRANSP Depot *nt*, Warenlager *nt*; ~ **charge** *n* IMP/EXP Depotgebühr *f*

depreciable: ~ **amount** *n* ACC Abschreibungsbetrag *m*; ~ **asset** *n* ACC abnutzbares Vermögen *nt*; ~ **basis** *n* ACC Abschreibungsbasis *f*; ~ **cost** *n* ACC abschreibungsfähige Kosten *pl*; ~ **life** *n* ECON, TAX Abschreibungszeitraum *m*, Nutzungsdauer *f*; ~ **property** *n* ACC abnutzbares Vermögen *nt*; ~ **real estate** *n* PROP abnutzbares unbewegliches Vermögen *nt*

depreciate 1. *vt* ACC, ECON *currency* abwerten, entwerten, *investment, assets* abschreiben; **2.** *vi* ACC, ECON *currency* an Kaufkraft verlieren, *investment, assets* an Wert verlieren

depreciated: ~ **amount** *n* ACC abgeschriebener Betrag *m*

depreciation *n* ACC *special write-down* Wertminderung *f*, Wertverlust *m*, ECON *currency* Entwertung *f*, Kursrückgang *m*, Wertverlust *f*, Wertminderung *f*, GEN COMM Verschlechterung *f*, PROP Abschreibung *f*, Abwertung *f*, Werteinbuße *f*, Wertminderung *f*, Wertverlust *f*; ~ **adjustment** *n* ACC Abschreibungsanpassung *f*; ~ **allowance** *n* ACC zulässiger Abschreibungssatz *m*; ~ **of fixed assets** *n* BANK Abschreibung *f* auf Anlagevermögen; ~ **recapture** *n* TAX Rückgängigmachung *f* überhöhter Abschreibungen; ~ **reserve** *n* ACC Abschreibungsrücklage *f*

depressed *adj* ECON *regions* notleidend, STOCK *commodity prices* rückläufig; ~ **area** *n* ECON notleidendes Gebiet *nt*; ~ **region** *n* ECON notleidende Region *f*

depression *n* ECON Depression *f*, Wirtschaftskrise *f*; ~ **pole** *n* ECON Liquiditätsfalle *f*

deprivation *n* HRM Aberkennung *f*

deprive: ~ **sb of sth** *vt* HRM jdm etw aberkennen

DEPS *abbr BrE* (*Departmental Entry Processing System*) IMP/EXP Brancheneinfuhrabfertigungssystem *nt*

dept. *abbr* GEN COMM (*department*) Abteilung *f*, (*depot*) Depot *nt*, Warenlager *nt*

depth *n* GEN COMM Tiefe *f*, TRANSP *shipping* Geitenhöhe *f*; ◆ **in** ~ GEN COMM ausführlich, gründlich

depth: ~ **analysis** *n* MGMNT Tiefenanalyse *f*, Tiefenprüfung *f*; ~ **interview** *n* S&M *research technique* Tiefkontaktinterview *nt*; ~ **polling** *n* POL Tiefenbefragung *f*

deputizing *adj* GEN COMM stellvertretend

deputy *n* GEN COMM Stellvertreter, in *m,f*, POL Abgeordnete(r) *mf* [decl. as adj] (*Abg.*); ~ **chairman** *n* HRM, MGMNT stellvertretende(r) Vorsitzende(r) *mf* [decl. as adj]; ~ **chairman of the board of management** *n* MGMNT stellvertretende(r) Verwaltungsratsvorsitzende(r) *mf* [decl. as adj], stellvertretender Vorstand *m* der Geschäftsleitung; ~ **chairman of the managing board** *n* MGMNT stellvertretende(r) Vorstandsvorsitzende(r) *mf* [decl. as adj], Stellvertreter, in *m,f* des Vorstandsvorsitzenden; ~ **chairman of the supervisory board** *n* MGMNT stellvertretende(r) Vorsitzende(r) *mf* [decl. as adj] des Aufsichtsrates; ~ **chief executive** *n* MGMNT Stellvertreter, in *m,f* des Hauptgeschäftsführers, stellvertretender Generaldirektor *m*, stellvertretende Generaldirektorin *f*, *public sector* stellvertretender Gemeindedirektor *m*, stellvertretende Gemeindedirektorin *f*; ~ **director** *n* HRM, MGMNT stellvertretender Direktor *m*, stellvertretende Direktorin *f*, stellvertretender Leiter *m*, stellvertretende Leiterin *f*; ~ **head of department** *n* HRM, MGMNT stellvertretender Abteilungsleiter *m*, stellvertretende Abteilungsleiterin *f*; ~ **manager** *n* HRM, MGMNT stellvertretender Direktor *m*, stellvertretende Direktorin *f*, stellvertretender Leiter *m*, stellvertretende Leiterin *f*; ~ **managing director** *n* MGMNT stellvertretender geschäftsführender Direktor *m*, stellvertretende geschäftsführende Direktorin *f*, stellvertretender Hauptgeschäftsführer *m*, stellvertretende Hauptgeschäftsführerin *f*, stellvertretender Generaldirektor *m*, stellvertretende *f*; ~ **member of the board of management** *n* MGMNT stellvertretendes Mitglied *nt* des Verwaltungsrats; ~ **minister** *n* ADMIN stellvertretender Minister *m*, stellvertretende Ministerin *f*

DEQ *abbr* (*delivered ex quay*) IMP/EXP *Incoterms* geliefert ab Kai

derecognition *n BrE* HRM Aberkennung *f*

deregulate *vt* ECON, GEN COMM *international trade* deregulieren

deregulation *n* ECON, GEN COMM *international trade* Deregulierung *f*

dereliction: ~ **of duty** *n* LAW Pflichtvernachlässigung *f*

derivative *adj* STOCK derivativ, nachgeordnet; ~ **instrument** *n* FIN Derivat *nt*, derivatives Instrument *nt*; ~ **product** *n* S&M Derivat *nt*, Sekundärprodukt *nt*

derived: ~ **demand** *n* ECON abgeleitete Nachfrage *f*, derivative Nachfrage *f*

derogation *n* LAW *from a privilege* Beeinträchtigung *f*

derrick *n* TRANSP *shipping* Ladebaum *m*

Derv 1. *abbr* (*diesel-engined road vehicle*) TRANSP Straßenfahrzeug *nt* mit Dieselmotor; **2.** *n* TRANSP *fuel* Dieselkraftstoff *m*, Dieseltreibstoff *m*

DES *abbr* IMP/EXP (*delivered ex ship*) *Incoterms* geliefert ab Schiff, POL (*Department of Education and Science BrE*) (*obs*) Ministerium für Bildung und Wissenschaft

descendant *n* LAW Abkömmling *m*, Nachkomme *m*

descending: ~ **tops** *n pl* STOCK fallende Spitzenwerte *m pl*

describe *vt* GEN COMM beschreiben, darstellen; ♦ ~ **in full detail** GEN COMM ausführlich beschreiben

description *n* GEN COMM Beschreibung *f*, Darstellung *f*, PATENTS Beschreibung *f*; ~ **of operational risk** *n* INS Betriebsrisikobeschreibung *f*; ~ **of risk** *n* INS Risikobeschreibung *f*; ~ **of warranted qualities** *n* LAW *contracts* ausdrückliches Beschreiben *nt* bei zugesicherten Eigenschaften

descriptive *adj* GEN COMM, PATENTS beschreibend; ~ **statistics** *n pl* MATH deskriptive Statistik *f*

deselect *vt* COMP abwählen

desertification *n* ENVIR Verwüstung *f*

design 1. *n* GEN COMM *sketch* Entwurf *m*, Konstruktion *f*, Zeichnung *f*, PATENTS Ausführung *f*, Design *nt*, Modell *nt*, Muster *nt*; **2.** *vt* GEN COMM zeichnen, entwerfen

design: ~ **aids** *n pl* GEN COMM Entwurfshilfen *f pl*

designate *vt* GEN COMM bezeichnen

designated: ~ **investment exchanges** *n pl BrE* STOCK angegebene Investitionsbörsen *f pl*; ~ **office** *n* PATENTS bestimmtes Amt *nt*, designiertes Amt *nt*, genanntes Amt *nt*

designation *n* GEN COMM Bezeichnung *f*; ~ **of origin** *n* IMP/EXP Ursprungsbezeichnung *f*

design: ~ **automation** *n* (*DA*) COMP Entwurfsautomatisierung *f*, Konstruktionsautomation *f*; ~ **engineer** *n* IND Konstrukteur, in *m,f*; ~ **engineering** *n* IND Konstruktionstechnik *f*

designed *adj* GEN COMM entworfen

designer: ~ **product** *n* S&M Designerprodukt *nt*

design: ~ **and layout** *n* S&M *of a store* Design und Layout *nt*; ~ **office** *n* GEN COMM Konstruktionsbüro *nt*; ~ **right** *n* LAW Recht *nt* auf ein Geschmacksmuster

Designs: ~ **Registry** *n BrE* LAW *intellectual property* Geschmacksmusterrolle *f*

desire *n* GEN COMM Begierde *f*, S&M Verlangen *nt*, Wunsch *m*; ~ **to purchase** *n* S&M Kaufwunsch *m*

desk *n* GEN COMM Schreibtisch *m*, STOCK *broker* Desk *nt*, Handelsdesk *nt*

Desk *n AmE* FIN Wertpapierabteilung der New Yorker Federal Reserve Bank

desk: ~ **clerk** *n* ADMIN Rezeptionist, in *m,f*

deskilling *n* HRM Herabstufung *f* von Arbeitsplätzen

desk: ~ **planner** *n* ADMIN Referent, in *m,f*; ~ **research** *n* S&M Sekundärforschung *f*, *market research* sekundärstatistische Auswertung *f*

desktop: ~ **computer** *n* COMP Tischcomputer *m*; ~ **publishing** *n* (*DTP*) COMP, MEDIA Desktop-Publishing *nt* (*DTP*); ~ **unit** *n* COMP Tischgerät *nt*

despatch *see* dispatch

destination *n* COMP Ziel *nt*, GEN COMM Bestimmungsort *m*; ~ **airport** *n* IMP/EXP, TRANSP Bestimmungsflughafen

m; ~ **drive** *n* COMP Ziellaufwerk *nt*; ~ **marketing** *n* S&M zielgerichtetes Marketing *nt*; ~ **port** *n* IMP/EXP, TRANSP Bestimmungshafen *m*

destroy *vt* GEN COMM ausrotten, zerstören

destruction *n* ENVIR *of rainforests* Vernichtung *f*, Zerstörung *f*

destructive: ~ **competition** *n* ECON Verdrängungswettbewerb *m*

detachable *adj* GEN COMM abtrennbar; ~ **front end** *n* TRANSP *trailer* demontierbare Vorderseite *f*

detail 1. *n* GEN COMM Detail *nt*, Einzelheit *f*; **2.** *vt* GEN COMM ausführlich beschreiben

detail: ~ **account** *n* ACC Unterkonto *nt*

detailed *adj* GEN COMM ausführlich; ~ **planning** *n* MGMNT Detailplanung *f*, Feinplanung *f*

details *n pl* GEN COMM Angaben *f pl*, Einzelheiten *f pl*

detail: ~ **strip** *n* ACC Belegstreifen *m*

detain *vt* LAW inhaftieren, TRANSP beschlagnahmen

detention *n* LAW Inhaftierung *f*, TRANSP *of ship, of cargo* Beschlagnahme *f*, Zurückhaltung *f*

deter: ~ **from** *vt* GEN COMM abhalten von

deteriorate 1. *vt* GEN COMM verderben; **2.** *vi* GEN COMM sich verschlechtern

deterioration *n* GEN COMM Verschlechterung *f*

determination *n* LAW *in tribunal* Entscheidung *f*

determine *vt* ECON *price* bestimmen, festlegen, GEN COMM bemessen

deterrent *n* GEN COMM Abschreckungsmittel *nt*

detonator *n* IND Sprengzünder *m*

detour *n* GEN COMM Umweg *m*

detriment *n* INS, LAW Schädigung *f*; ♦ **to the ~ of** GEN COMM zum Nachteil von, zum Schaden von

detrimental *adj* GEN COMM schädlich; ♦ ~ **to effective competition** ECON wettbewerbsfeindlich

detrimental: ~ **effect** *n* LAW schädliche Auswirkung *f*

de-unionization *n* HRM gewerkschaftlichen Einfluß beseitigen

devalorization *n* ECON Abwertung *f*

devaluate *vi* ECON *currency* abwerten

devaluation *n* ECON Abwertung *f*

devalue *vt* ECON abwerten, devaluieren

devanning *n* TRANSP Entladung *f*

develop *vt* COMP *system, software*, IND *prototype, new model* konstruieren, entwickeln, aufschließen, S&M *product*, TRANSP *prototype, new model* entwickeln

developed: ~ **country** *n* (*DC*) ECON, IND Industrieland *nt*, Industriestaat *m*; ~ **economy** *n* ECON entwickelte Volkswirtschaft *f*; ~ **market** *n* S&M entwickelter Markt *m*

developer *n* PROP Erschließungsunternehmen *nt*

developing: ~ **country** *n* ECON Entwicklungsland *nt*

development *n* COMP, ECON Entwicklung *f*, IND *prototype, new model* Entwicklung *f*, Konstruktion *f*, S&M *of product* Entwicklung *f*; ~ **aid** *n* ECON Entwicklungshilfe *f*

developmental: ~ **drilling program** *AmE*, ~ **drilling programme** *BrE n* ECON Bohrversuchsprogramm *nt*, Entwicklungsbohrprogramm *nt*, Erschließungsvorhaben *nt* zur Erdgas- und Erdölförderung

development: ~ **area** *n BrE* ECON Fördergebiet *nt*; ~ **assistance** *n* ECON Entwicklungshilfe *f*

Development: **~ Assistance Committee** *n* (*DAC*) ECON Ausschuß *m* für Entwicklungshilfe

development: **~ bank** *n* BANK Entwicklungsbank *f*; **~ committee** *n* LAW Entwicklungsausschuß *m*; **~ director** *n* HRM Direktor, in *m,f*, Verkaufsförderer, in *m,f*, Leiter, in *m,f* der Entwicklungsabteilung, S&M Verkaufsförderer, in *m,f*; **~ economics** *n* ECON Entwicklungsökonomie *f*; **~ expenditure** *n* FIN Entwicklungskosten *pl*; **~ loan** *n* BANK Entwicklungshilfekredit *m*, Investitionskredit *m*; **~ management** *n* MGMNT Entwicklungsmanagement *nt*; **~ manager** *n* MGMNT Leiter, in *m,f* der Entwicklungsabteilung; **~ planning** *n* ECON Entwicklungsplanung *f*; **~ policy** *n* POL Entwicklungspolitik *f*; **~ potential** *n* GEN COMM Entwicklungspotential *nt*; **~ program** *AmE*, **~ programme** *BrE* *n* FIN Entwicklungsprogramm *nt*, MGMNT Entwicklungsprogramm *nt*, Förderprogramm *nt*; **~ project** *n* ECON Entwicklungsprojekt *nt*; **~ region** *n* ECON Entwicklungsgebiet *nt*; **~ stage enterprise** *n* ECON junges Unternehmen *nt*; **~ strategy** *n* MGMNT Entwicklungsstrategie *f*

deviation *n* LAW *in law* Abweichung *f*; **~ clause** *n* (*D/C*) INS *marine* Abweichungsklausel *f*, Routenabweichungsklausel *f*; **~ fraud** *n* TRANSP *shipping* Deviationsbetrug *m*; **~ policy** *n* MGMNT Abweichungspolitik *f*

device *n* COMP, GEN COMM Gerät *nt*; **~ driver** *n* COMP Gerätetreiber *m*; **~-independent** *adj* COMP geräteunabhängig; **~ mark** *n* PATENTS Bildzeichen *nt*; **~-specific** *adj* COMP gerätespezifisch

devise 1. *n* LAW, PROP letztwillige Zuwendung *f* von Grundbesitz, testamentarische Übertragung *f* von Grundbesitz; **2.** *vt* LAW, PROP vermachen

devisee *n* LAW, PROP testamentarischer Grundstückserbe *m*, Vermächtnisnehmer, in *m,f*

devolution *n* LAW Erbfall *m*

df *abbr* (*deadfreight*) TRANSP Fautfracht *f*, Fehlfracht *f*

DF *abbr* (*direction finder*) TRANSP *shipping* Funkpeilanlage *f*, Funkpeiler *m*, Peilfunkeinrichtung *f*, Funkpeilgerät *nt*

DFE *abbr BrE obs* (*Department for Education*) POL Ministerium für Bildung

DfEE *abbr BrE* (*Department for Education and Employment*) POL Ministerium für Bildung und Arbeit

DFI *abbr* (*direct foreign investment*) ECON, FIN ausländische Direktinvestition *f*, Direktinvestition *f* aus dem Ausland, Direktinvestition *f* im Ausland

DFR *abbr* (*data freight receipt*) TRANSP *shipping* Datenfrachtempfang *m*

dft *abbr* (*draft*) BANK Bankscheck *m*, gezogener Wechsel *m*, Tratte *f*, Wechsel *m*

DFT *abbr* (*direct fund transfer*) BANK elektronischer Überweisungsverkehr *m* der Kreditinstitute

DGB *abbr* (*Dangerous Goods Board*) GEN COMM Kommission für gefährliches Transportgut

DGN *abbr* (*dangerous goods note*) TRANSP Gefahrgüteranzeige *f*

DHSS *abbr BrE obs* (*Department of Health and Social Security*) POL, WEL Gesundheits- und Sozialministerium

DI *abbr AmE* (*Department of Industry*) POL Industrieministerium

diagnosis *n* COMP, GEN COMM Diagnose *f*

diagnostic *adj* COMP, GEN COMM diagnostisch; **~ message** *n* COMP Diagnosemeldung *f*; **~ routine** *n* GEN COMM diagnostische Routine *f*

diagonal: **~ expansion** *n* ECON diagonales Wachstum *nt*

diagram *n* GEN COMM Diagramm *nt*

dialing *AmE see* **dialling** *BrE*

dialling: **~ code** *n BrE* COMMS *telephone* Vorwahl *f*, Vorwahlnummer *f*; **~ tone** *n BrE* (*cf dial tone AmE*) COMMS Wählton *m*

dialog *AmE see* **dialogue** *BrE*

dialogue *n BrE* COMP, GEN COMM Dialog *m*; **~ box** *n BrE* COMP Dialogbox *f*

dial: **~ tone** *n AmE* (*cf dialling tone BrE*) COMMS Wählton *m*

diamond: **~ investment trust** *n* STOCK Diamantinvestmentgesellschaft *f*

dichotomous: **~ question** *n* GEN COMM, S&M Alternativfrage *f*

dictate *vt* ADMIN *shorthand*, GEN COMM diktieren

DIDMCA *abbr AmE* (*Depository Institutions Deregulation and Monetary Control Act*) POL 1980 Gesetz zur Deregulierung und monetären Überwachung öffentlicher Geldinstitute

die *vi* GEN COMM *come to an end* auslaufen; ◆ **~ intestate** BANK, LAW ohne Hinterlassung eines Testaments sterben

diesel *n* TRANSP Diesel *m*; **~-engined road vehicle** *n BrE* (*Derv*) TRANSP Straßenfahrzeug *nt* mit Dieselmotor; **~ fuel** *n* TRANSP Dieselkraftstoff *m*, Dieseltreibstoff *m*; **~ oil** *n* (*DO*) ENVIR, TRANSP Dieselöl *nt*

dies a quo *phr* ACC Anfangstermin *m*

differ *vi* GEN COMM differieren; ◆ **~ from** GEN COMM sich unterscheiden von

difference *n* GEN COMM Differenz *f*; **~ equation** *n* ECON *econometrics* Differenzengleichung *f*; **~ in conditions insurance** *n* INS Bedingungsdifferenzversicherung *f*; **~ in limits insurance** *n* INS Summendifferenzversicherung *f*; **~ in value insurance** *n* INS Wertdifferenzversicherung *f*

different *adj* GEN COMM unterschiedlich; ◆ **be of a ~ opinion** GEN COMM anderer Meinung sein, eine andere Meinung vertreten

differential *n* TRANSP *road transport* Differential *nt*; **~ advantage** *n* ECON Vorteil *m* durch Preisdifferenz; **~ analysis** *n* MGMNT Differenzialanalyse *f*; **~ cost** *n* ECON Differenzkosten *pl*; **~ lock** *n* TRANSP Differentialsperre *f*; **~ price** *n* ECON, S&M Preisdifferenzierung *f*, Preisgefälle *nt*, Preisunterschied *m*; **~ pricing** *n* ECON, S&M Preisdifferenzierung *f*

differentials *n pl BrE* HRM Lohngefälle *nt*

differential: **~ sampling** *n* S&M Anwendung *f* unterschiedlicher Stichprobenverfahren; **~ tax incidence** *n* TAX Differentialinzidenz *f* der Besteuerung, unterschiedliche Steuerinzidenz *f*; **~ theory of rent** *n* ECON Theorie *f* der Differentialrente

differentiate *vt* GEN COMM differenzieren, unterscheiden; ◆ **~ between** GEN COMM unterscheiden zwischen [+dat]

differentiated: **~ goods** *n pl* S&M *marketing* differenzierte Ware *f*; **~ marketing** *n* S&M differenziertes Marketing *nt*; **~ product** *n* S&M differenziertes Produkt *nt*

differentiation *n* GEN COMM Unterscheidung *f*, S&M Differenzierung *f*; **~ strategy** *n BrE* S&M Differenzierungsstrategie *f*

different: ~ **terms** n pl LAW in contract Änderungen f pl

differing adj GEN COMM abweichend, unterschiedlich

difficult adj GEN COMM schwer, schwierig

difficulty n GEN COMM Schwierigkeit f

diffusion n ECON, IND, S&M Diffusion f; ~ **curve** n S&M Diffusionskurve f; ~ **index** n ECON econometrics Diffusionsindex m; ~ **of innovations** n S&M Verbreitung f von Innovationen; ~ **rate** n IND Physics Diffusionsgeschwindigkeit f

DIFT abbr BrE (Dartford International Freight Terminal) TRANSP internationales Frachtterminal in Dartford

digit n COMP Stelle f

digital adj COMMS, COMP digital; ~ **computer** n COMP Digitalrechner m; ~ **data** n pl COMP digitale Daten pl; ~ **data processing** n COMP digitale Datenverarbeitung f; ~ **selective calling** n (DSC) COMMS digitaler Selektivruf m; ~ **sort** n COMP digitale Sortierung f; ~**-to-analog** adj (D/A) COMP digital-analog (D/A); ~**-to-analog converter** n (DAC) COMP Digital-Analog-Wandler m (D/A-Wandler)

digitize vt COMMS, COMP digital darstellen

digits: ~ **deleted** n pl STOCK gelöschte Dezimalstellen f pl auf dem Börsenticker

dilapidated adj PROP verfallen

dilapidation n PROP Baufälligkeit f, Verfall m

dilatory: ~ **payer** n FIN säumiger Zahler m

diligence n GEN COMM Sorge f

Dillon: ~ **Round** n ECON Dillon-Runde f

dilute vt STOCK verwässern

dilution: ~ **of equity** n STOCK Verwässerung f des Aktienkapitals; ~ **of labor** AmE, ~ **of labour** BrE n HRM Einsatz ungelernter Arbeitskräfte anstelle von Facharbeitern, Rückstufung von Arbeitsplätzen f

DIM abbr (Diploma in Industrial Management) GEN COMM Diplom nt für Industriemanagement

diminish 1. vt GEN COMM verringern; **2.** vi GEN COMM sinken

diminishing: ~**-balance method** n ACC degressive Abschreibung f; ~ **marginal rate of substitution** n ECON abnehmende Grenzrate f der Substitution; ~ **returns** n pl ECON abnehmende Erträge m pl, Ertragsrückgang m; ~ **returns to scale** n pl ECON abnehmende Skalenerträge m pl

diminuation n LAW of purchase price Preisminderung f

dimmed adj COMP computer screen abgedunkelt

Dinks abbr infrml (double income no kids) ECON kinderlose Doppelverdiener

diode n COMP hardware Diode f

dip n GEN COMM in profits Rückgang m

DipCOM abbr (Diploma of Commerce) GEN COMM Handelsdiplom nt

DipEcon abbr (Diploma of Economics) GEN COMM Wirtschaftsdiplom nt

dip: ~ **into savings** phr GEN COMM Ersparnisse angreifen

diploma n GEN COMM Diplom nt

Diploma: ~ **of Commerce** n (DipCOM) GEN COMM Handelsdiplom nt

diplomacy n MGMNT Diplomatie f

Diploma: ~ **of Economics** n (DipEcon) GEN COMM Wirtschaftsdiplom nt; ~ **in Industrial Management** n (DIM) GEN COMM Diplom für Industriemanagement; ~ **in Public Administration** n (DipPA) GEN COMM Diplom für

öffentliche Verwaltung; ~ **in Technology** n (DipTech) GEN COMM Diplom für Technologie

diplomatic: ~ **bag** n BrE (cf diplomatic pouch AmE) COMMS, POL Diplomatenpost f; ~ **mission** n POL diplomatische Mission f, diplomatische Vertretung f, diplomatischer Auftrag f; ~ **pouch** n AmE (cf diplomatic bag BrE) COMMS, POL Diplomatenpost f; ~ **service** n POL diplomatischer Dienst m

Diplomatic: ~ **Service Department** n (DSD) POL Abteilung für den diplomatischen Dienst

diplomatic: ~ **service post** n POL diplomatische Dienststelle f

DipPA abbr (Diploma in Public Administration) GEN COMM Diplom für öffentliche Verwaltung

DIP: ~ **switch** n COMP hardware DIP-Schalter m, Mäuseklavier nt (jarg)

DipTech abbr (Diploma in Technology) GEN COMM Diplom für Technologie

dir. abbr HRM (director) Dir. (Direktor), Geschäftsführer, in m,f, Leiter, in m,f, TRANSP (direct) route direkt

direct 1. adj (dir.) GEN COMM direkt, unmittelbar, TRANSP route direkt; ♦ ~ **or held covered** INS marine auf direktem oder indirektem Wege versichert; **2.** vt GEN COMM dirigieren, MGMNT organization leiten

direct: ~ **access** n COMP direkter Zugriff m, Direktzugriff m; ~**-action advertising** n S&M Aktionswerbung f, auf spontane Kaufreaktion abgestellte Werbung f; ~ **advertising** n S&M Direktwerbung f; ~ **arbitrage** n FIN einfache Devisenabfrage f; ~ **bill of lading** n IMP/EXP, TRANSP shipping Direktkonnossement nt, nicht übertragbarer Ladeschein, m nicht begebbarer Namensfrachtbrief m; ~ **booking** n LEIS Direktbuchung f; ~ **call** n COMMS Direktgespräch m, Direktverbindung f; ~ **clearer** n BANK Direktclearingstelle f; ~ **clearing member** n BANK Mitglied nt einer Direkt-Clearingstelle; ~**-connect modem** n COMP hardware Direktanschlußmodem nt; ~ **costing** n ACC, ECON, FIN Direct Costing nt, Deckungsbeitragsrechnung f, Grenzplankostenrechnung f; ~ **costs** n pl ACC, ECON, FIN direkte Kosten pl; ~ **cost of sales** n COMM direkte Umsatzaufwendungen f pl, Sondereinzelkosten f pl des Vertriebs; ~ **data entry** n (DDE) COMP direkte Dateneingabe f, dynamischer Datenaustausch m; ~ **debit** n (DD) BANK, FIN Abbuchung f durch Einzugsermächtigung, Einzugsverfahren nt; ~ **debit authorization** n BANK, FIN Einzugsermächtigung f; ~ **delivery** n TRANSP Direktlieferung f; ~ **deposit** n BANK Direkteinlage, Sparen f im Abbuchungsverfahren nt; ~ **dialing** AmE, ~ **dialling** BrE n COMMS Durchwahl f, Selbstwahl f; ~ **discrimination** n BrE HRM unverhohlene Diskriminierung f; ~ **distance dialing** AmE (DDD, cf subscriber trunk dialling BrE) COMMS Selbstwählferndienst m, Selbstfernwahl f, Teilnehmerfernwahl f

directed: ~ **at** adj GEN COMM ausgerichtet auf [+acc]; ~ **interview** n S&M market research gelenktes Interview nt; ~ **verdict** n LAW binding direction by judges Geschworenengerichtsentscheidung f

direct: ~ **exchange** n ECON direkter Warentausch m; ~ **expenses** n pl ACC direkte Kosten pl, Einzelkosten pl; ~ **export trading** n IMP/EXP direkter Exporthandel m, direktes Exportgeschäft nt, Direktexport m; ~ **financial leasing** n ECON direktes Finanzierungs-Leasing nt; ~ **foreign investment** n (DFI) ECON, FIN ausländische

Direktinvestition *f*, Direktinvestition *f* aus dem Ausland, Direktinvestition *f* im Ausland; ~ **fund transfer** *n* (*DFT*) BANK elektronischer Überweisungsverkehr *m* der Kreditinstitute; ~ **and indirect material** *n* ECON Fertigungsmaterial *nt*; ~ **and indirect taxation** *n* ECON, TAX direkte und indirekte Besteuerung *f*; ~**-indirect taxes ratio** *n* ECON, TAX Verhältnis *nt* zwischen direkten und indirekten Steuern; ~ **insurance** *n* INS Direktversicherung *f*, Erstversicherung *f*; ~ **insurer** *n* INS Direktversicherer *m*, Erstversicherer *m*

direction *n* ECON *of interest rates* Entwicklungsrichtung *f*, LAW Weisung *f*, MGMNT klare Linie *f*, POL Richtlinie *f*, Weisung *f*, TRANSP Richtung *f*; ~ **finder** *n* (*DF*) TRANSP *shipping* Funkpeilanlage *f*, Funkpeiler *m*, Peilfunkeinrichtung *f*, Funkpeilgerät *nt*

directions: ~ **for use** *n pl* GEN COMM Benutzungsanleitung *f*, Gebrauchsanweisung *f*

directive *n* ECON, FIN Richtlinie *f*, LAW Weisung *f*, POL Richtlinie *f*, Weisung *f*; ~ **style of leadership** *n* POL autoritärer Führungsstil *m*

direct: ~ **labor** *AmE*, ~ **labour** *BrE n* ECON, HRM Fertigungslöhne *m pl*, Lohneinzelkosten *pl*; ~ **labour costs** *BrE n pl* ACC direkte Lohnkosten *pl*, FIN, IND Fertigungslohnkosten *pl*; ~ **labour organization** *BrE n* HRM Ausführung von städtischen Dienstleistungen durch Kommunalangestellte und nicht durch privatwirtschaftliche Unternehmen, kommunaler Eigenbetrieb *m*; ~ **liability** *n* LAW unmittelbare Haftung *f*

directly *adv* MATH direkt; ♦ ~ **related to** GEN COMM direkt bezogen auf; **be ~ responsible to sb** GEN COMM *organization hierarchy* jdm direkt unterstellt sein; ~ **transported** IMP/EXP, TRANSP *within EU countries* direkt transportiert

directly: ~ **unproductive profit-seeking activities** *n pl* (*DUP*) ECON direkt unproduktive auf Gewinn gerichtete Aktivitäten *f pl*

direct: ~ **mail** *n* COMMS Postwurfsendung *f*, S&M Direktversand *m*, Postversand *m*, Postwurfsendung *f*; ~ **marketing** *n* S&M Direktmarketing *nt*, individualisierte Absatzpolitik *f*

Direct: ~ **Marketing Association** *n AmE* (*DMA*) S&M Verband für Direktabsatz

direct: ~ **obligation** *n* BANK direkte finanzielle Verpflichtung *f*, direkte Zahlungsverpflichtung *f*

director *n* (*dir.*) HRM Direktor, in *m,f*, Geschäftsführer, in *m,f*, Leiter, in *m,f*, MGMNT Vorstandsmitglied *nt*

directorate *n* HRM Direktorat *nt*, Verwaltungsratsposten *m*

director: ~ **general** *n* HRM Generaldirektor, in *m,f*; ~ **of labor relations** *AmE*, ~ **of labour relations** *BrE n* HRM Leiter, in *m,f* der Abteilung Industrielle Beziehungen, MGMNT Koordinator, in *m,f* Arbeitgeber-Arbeitnehmer-Interessen

Director: ~ **of Public Prosecutions** *n BrE* (*DPP*) LAW Oberstaatsanwalt

director: ~ **of public relations** *n* (*DPR*) HRM *advertising* Leiter, in *m,f* Öffentlichkeitsarbeit; ~**'s report** *n* GEN COMM Bericht *m* des Geschäftsführers; ~**'s shares** *n* STOCK Aktien *f pl* des Boardmitglieds

directors *n pl* MGMNT Führung *f*

directorship *n* HRM Direktorat *nt*, Verwaltungsratsposten *m*

directors': ~ **and officers' liability insurance** *n* INS Haftpflichtversicherung *f* für Geschäftsführung,

Managerhaftpflichtversicherung *f*; ~ **tax** *n* TAX Aufsichtsratssteuer *f*

directory *n* COMP Verzeichnis *nt*, GEN COMM Adreßbuch *nt*; ~ **assistance** *n* COMMS Auskunft *f*; ~ **enquiries** *n pl BrE* COMMS Auskunft *f*; ~ **information** *n AmE* COMMS Auskunft *f*

direct: ~ **outward investment** *n* ECON, FIN Direktinvestitionen *f pl* im Ausland, ausländische Direktinvestition *f*; ~ **participation program** *AmE*, ~ **participation programme** *BrE n* FIN direktes Beteiligungsprogramm *nt*, direktes Kapitalbeteiligungsprogramm *nt*; ~ **payment** *n* BANK *grants* endgültige Zahlung *f*; ~ **placement** *n* BANK Direktplazierung *f*; ~ **port** *n* (*dp*) TRANSP Direkthafen *m*; ~ **possession** *n* WEL unmittelbarer Besitz *m*; ~ **production** *n* ECON direkte Produktion *f*; ~ **product profitability** *n* (*DPP*) ECON Nettoproduktgewinn *m*, S&M direkte Produktrentabilität *f*; ~ **purchase** *n* GEN COMM Beziehungskauf *m*, Direkteinkauf *m*; ~ **real income** *n* (*DRY*) ECON reales verfügbares Einkommen *nt*; ~ **reduction mortgage** *n* BANK Tilgungshypothek *f*; ~ **response** *n* GEN COMM, S&M *telephone selling* Direktantwort *f*; ~ **response advertising** *n* S&M auf spontane Kaufreaktion abgestellte Werbung *f*; ~ **route** *n* TRANSP Direktroute *f*, Direktweg *m*; ~ **sales** *n pl* S&M Direktverkauf *m*; ~ **selling** *n* S&M Direktverkauf *m*, Erzeugerhandel *m*; ~ **spending envelope** *n* FIN direkter Ausgabenumschlag *m*; ~ **spending program** *AmE*, ~ **spending programme** *BrE n* FIN *government* staatliches Förderprogramm *nt*; ~ **tax** *n* TAX direkte Steuer *f*; ~ **trader input** *n* (*DTI*) IMP/EXP direkter Handelsinput *m*, direkte Handelseingabe *f*; ~ **transhipment** *n* TRANSP Direktumladung *f*; ~ **transportation** *n* IMP/EXP Direktversand *m*, Versand *m* an einen bestimmten Empfänger; ~ **workers** *n pl* HRM direkte Arbeiter *m pl*; ~ **yield** *n* BANK, STOCK Direktertrag *m*, Direktrendite *f*

dirigism *n* ECON, POL Dirigismus *m*, Planwirtschaft *f*

dirty: ~ **bill of lading** *n* IMP/EXP, TRANSP *shipping* unreines Konnossement *nt*; ~ **floating** *n* ECON schmutziges Floaten *nt*; ~ **money** *n* TRANSP *shipping* Schmiergeld *nt*; ~ **proof** *n* MEDIA, S&M unleserlicher Abzug *m*

dis *abbr* (*discount*) FIN, GEN COMM Diskont *m*, Preisnachlaß *m*, Rabatt *m*, Skto. (*Skonto*)

disability *n* HRM Behinderung *f*, *of employee* Arbeitsunfähigkeit *f*, INS Erwerbsunfähigkeit *f*; ~ **annuity** *n* INS Erwerbsunfähigkeitsrente *f*, Invalidenrente *f*; ~ **benefit** *n* INS Erwerbsunfähigkeitsrente *f*; ~ **buy-out insurance** *n AmE* INS Invaliditätsübernahmeversicherung *f*; ~ **insurance** *n* INS Invaliditätsversicherung *f*; ~ **insurance income** *n AmE* INS Berufsunfähigkeitsrente *f*, Invalidenrente *f*; ~ **pension** *n* FIN, INS Invaliditätsrente *f*; ~ **percentage table** *n* INS Gliedertaxe *f*, Invaliditätsskala *f*; ~ **replacement insurance** *n AmE* INS Berufsunfähigkeitsrentenversicherung *f*, Invalidenrentenversicherung *f*

disabled *adj* COMP abgeschaltet, ausgeschaltet, HRM behindert; ~ **person** *n* HRM Behinderte(r) *mf* [decl. as adj]; ~ **quota** *n* HRM Behindertenquote *f*

disablement *n* GEN COMM Unfähigkeit *f*; ~ **pension** *n* FIN Arbeitsunfallrente *f*

disadvantage *n* GEN COMM Nachteil *m*; ♦ **to the ~ of** GEN COMM zu Lasten von

disadvantaged *adj* GEN COMM benachteiligt

disadvantageous *adj* GEN COMM nachteilig

disadvantageously *adv* GEN COMM nachteilig

disaffirm *vt* LAW aufheben

disaffirmance *n* LAW Aufhebung *f*

disaffirmation *n* LAW Aufhebung *f*

disaffirmed *adj* LAW aufgehoben

disagio *n* GEN COMM Disagio *nt*

disagree *vi* GEN COMM *with plan* nicht einverstanden sein, *not tally* nicht übereinstimmen; ◆ ~ **with sb** GEN COMM mit jdm über etw uneins sein

disagreeable *adj* GEN COMM unangenehm

disagreement *n* GEN COMM *dispute* Meinungsverschiedenheit *f*

disallow *vt* GEN COMM verbieten, HRM aberkennen

disallowable: ~ **item** *n* BrE TAX *VAT* steuerlich nicht absetzbare Position *f*

disallowance *n* HRM Aberkennung *f*, TAX Nichtanerkennung *f*

disappointing *adj* GEN COMM enttäuschend

disassemble *vt* IND zerlegen

disassembly *n* IND Zerlegung *f*

disaster *n* INS Katastrophe *f*; ~ **clause** *n* INS Katastrophenklausel *f*

disbursable *adj* FIN auszahlbar

disburse *vt* FIN auszahlen, verausgaben, GEN COMM ausgeben

disbursed *adj* FIN verausgabt

disbursement *n* ACC Auszahlung *f*, FIN Verausgabung *f*; ~ **commission** *n* GEN COMM Auszahlungsprovision *f*

disburser *n* FIN Auszahler *m*

disc. *abbr* (*discount*) FIN, GEN COMM Diskont *m*, Preisnachlaß *m*, Rabatt *m*, Skto. (*Skonto*)

discharge 1. *n* GEN COMM Erlöschen *nt*, Erledigung *f*, LAW Löschung *f*, *debt* Befreiung *f* von Verbindlichkeiten, TRANSP Löschung *f*; **2.** *vt* FIN *of debt* befreien, GEN COMM begleichen, ausladen, befreien, HRM entlassen, LAW erlöschen, *legal duty* löschen, *obligations* entlasten von, TRANSP löschen

discharge: ~ **of a bankrupt** *n* LAW Entlastung *f* des Gemeinschuldners, Konkursaufhebung *f*; ~ **of a contract** *n* LAW Vertragserfüllung *f*; ~ **in bankruptcy** *n* LAW Konkursaufhebung *f*; ~ **of debt** *n* FIN Schuldbefreiung *f*; ~ **of lien** *n* LAW Erlöschen *nt* eines Pfandrechts; ~ **port** *n* TRANSP Entladehafen *m*; ~ **of the trustee** *n* LAW Entlastung *f* des Treuhänders

discharged *adj* BANK, FIN, GEN COMM beglichen

discharging *n* GEN COMM Ausladen *nt*; ~ **berth** *n* TRANSP *shipping* Entladekai *m*, Löschkai *m*; ~ **wharf** *n* TRANSP Entladekai *m*, Löschkai *m*

disciplinary *adj* HRM, LAW disziplinarisch, Disziplinar-; ~ **layoff** *n* HRM Disziplinarentlassung *f*; ~ **measures** *n pl* LAW Disziplinarmaßnahmen *f pl*; ~ **procedure** *n* HRM Disziplinarverfahren *nt*; ~ **proceedings** *n pl* LAW Disziplinarverfahren *nt*; ~ **rule** *n* HRM Disziplinarbestimmung *f*, Disziplinarordnung *f*

discipline 1. *n* GEN COMM, HRM Disziplin *f*; **2.** *vt* LAW erziehen, maßregeln

disciplined: ~ **movement** *n* TRANSP disziplinierte Beförderung *f*

disclaim *vt* LAW freizeichnen, aufgeben

disclaimer *n* INS Aufgabe *f* eines Anspruchs, Verzichtserklärung *f*, LAW Aufgabe *f*, *waiver* Verzicht *m*; ~ **clause** *n* INS, LAW Haftungsausschlußklausel *f*; ~ **of opinion** *n* ACC Meinungsverzichtserklärung *f*

disclaiming *n* LAW Aufgeben *nt*

disclose *vt* GEN COMM bekanntgeben, bekanntmachen

disclosed: ~ **reserves** *n pl* ACC offengelegte Rücklagen *f pl*

disclosure *n* ACC Berichterstattung *f*, LAW Preisgabe *f*, FIN, STOCK Offenlegung *f*, Publizität *f*; ~ **of information** *n* HRM Preisgabe *f* von Informationen; ~ **of an invention** *n* PATENTS *part of description* Bekanntgabe *f* einer Erfindung, Offenlegung *f* einer Erfindung; ~ **requirement** *n* ACC Angabepflicht *f*, FIN, STOCK Publizitätserfordernis *f*

discomfort: ~ **index** *n* ECON Elendsindex *m*, Problemindex *m*

discontent *n* HRM Unzufriedenheit *f*; ~ **in the workplace** *n* HRM Unzufriedenheit *f* am Arbeitsplatz

discontinuance *n* GEN COMM Wegfall *m*, Fortfall *m*, LAW *business* Aufgabe *f*; ~ **of plan** *n* TAX Planeinstellung *f*

discontinue *vt* IND einstellen

discontinued *adj* IND eingestellt; ~ **operations** *n pl* IND *factory* eingestellter Betrieb *m*

discontinuous: ~ **variable** *n* MATH *statistics* diskrete Variable *f*

discount 1. *n* BANK Disagio *nt*, Diskont *m*, ECON Diskont *m*, FIN (*dis, disc.*) Diskont *m*, Preisnachlaß *m*, Rabatt *m*, Skonto *m or nt* (*Skto.*), GEN COMM (*dis, disc.*) Rabatt *m*, S&M Diskont, STOCK Abzug *m*, Diskont *m*, Rabatt *m*, Skonto *m or nt* (*Skto.*); ◆ **at a ~** (*AAD*) S&M mit Rabatt, mit Skonto; **at a ~ of** STOCK mit einem Disagio von; **no ~** (*ND*) S&M kein Nachlaß *m*; **2.** *vt* ACC abzinsen, BANK diskontieren, FIN abzinsen, diskontieren, STOCK diskontieren

discountable *adj* BANK *money market papers* diskontfähig, diskontierbar, FIN, STOCK diskontierbar; ~ **bill** *n* FIN diskontfähiger Wechsel *m*

discount: ~ **bill** *n* ACC Diskontwechsel *m*; ~ **business** *n* FIN Diskontgeschäft *nt*; ~ **center** *AmE*, ~ **centre** *BrE n* FIN Diskonthaus *nt*, Diskontzentrale *f*; ~ **charges** *n pl* ACC Diskontspesen *pl*; ~ **dividend reinvestment plan** *n* FIN Diskontdividenden-Reinvestitionsplan *m*

discounted: ~ **bill** *n* BANK Diskontwechsel *m*, diskontierter Wechsel *m*; ~ **cash flow** *n* (*DCF*) ACC, FIN abgezinster Cash-Flow *m*, diskontierter Bargeldfluß *m*, diskontierter Einnahmeüberschuß *m*; ~ **loan** *n* BANK diskontierte Anleihe *f*; ~ **paper** *n* FIN Abzinsungspapier *nt*; ~ **present value** *n* FIN diskontierter Barwert *m*, diskontierter Zeitwert *m*; ~ **share price** *n* STOCK diskontierter Aktienpreis *m*

discounter *n* FIN Diskontgeber, in *m,f*, Diskontierer, in *m,f*, S&M Discounter *m*

discount: ~ **factor** *n* FIN Abzinsungsfaktor *m*; ~ **forex** *n* ECON *international* Report *m*; ~ **house** *n* FIN Diskontbank *f*, Diskonthaus *nt*, S&M Discounter *m*, Diskontladen *m*, Einzelhandelsladen *m* mit Rabattsystem

discounting *n* ACC, FIN Abzinsung *f*, Diskontgeschäft *nt*, Diskontierung *f*; ~ **bank** *n* BANK, FIN Diskontbank *f*; ~ **banker** *n* BANK Diskontbanker *m*, Diskontbankier *m*; ~ **of bills** *n* BrE (*cf discounting of notes AmE*) ACC Wechseldiskontierung *f*; ~ **of notes** *n* AmE (*cf discounting of bills BrE*) ACC Wechseldiskontierung *f*

discount: ~ **instrument** *n* STOCK Diskontinstrument *nt*, Diskontierungsinstrument *nt*; ~ **market** *n* FIN

Diskontmarkt *m*, Markt *m* für kurzfristige Wertpapiere; ~ **market loan** *n* FIN Diskontmarktdarlehen *nt*; ~ **mechanism** *n* FIN Abzinsungsmechanismus *m*; ~ **points** *n pl* BANK Diskontpunkte *m pl*; ~ **price** *n* FIN Rabattpreis *m*; ~ **rate** *n* BANK Diskontsatz *m*; ~ **rate differential** *n* FIN Diskontgefälle *nt*; ~ **shop** *n* BrE (*cf discount store AmE*) S&M Diskontladen *m*, Einzelhandelsladen *m* mit Rabattsystem; ~ **store** *n* AmE (*cf discount shop BrE*) S&M Diskontladen *m*, Einzelhandelsladen *m* mit Rabattsystem; ~ **table** *n* FIN Abzinsungstabelle *f*; ~ **travel** *n* LEIS Billigreisen *f pl*, ermäßigtes Reisen *nt*; ~ **window** *n* BANK, FIN Lombardfenster *nt*, Refinanzierungsstelle *f* einer Zentralbank, Diskontfenster *nt* (*jarg*), Rediskontfazilität *f*; ~ **window lending** *n* BANK Lombardfenster *nt*, Rediskontfazilität *f* einer Zentralbank, FIN Lombardfenster *nt*; ~ **yield** *n* STOCK Diskontertrag *m*

discourage *vt* GEN COMM, HRM entmutigen

discouraged: ~ **worker hypothesis** *n* HRM Hypothese der Entmutigung bei der Arbeitssuche durch verbreitete Arbeitslosigkeit und Einstellungsstopp

discovery *n* LAW *disclosure* Beweisermittlungsverfahren *nt*, Offenlegung *f*; ~ **sampling** *n* MATH Entdeckungsstichprobe *f*

discrepancy *n* GEN COMM Abweichung *f*, Diskrepanz *f*

discretion *n* GEN COMM Ermessen *nt*; ◆ **at the ~ of** GEN COMM nach Ermessen von, nach Gutdünken von

discretionary *adj* ECON, GEN COMM, TAX diskretionär; ~ **account** *n* FIN treuhänderisch verwaltetes Konto *nt*; ~ **authority** *n* BANK Autoritätsbefugnis *f*; ~ **buying power** *n* S&M frei verfügbare Kaufkraft *f*; ~ **cost** *n* ECON diskretionäre Kosten *pl*; ~ **economic policy** *n* ECON diskretionäre Politik *f*; ~ **fiscal policy** *n* ECON diskretionäre Fiskalpolitik *f*; ~ **income** *n* ECON frei verfügbares Einkommen *nt*; ~ **limit** *n* BANK Ermessensgrenze *f*; ~ **order** *n* STOCK Bestens-Auftrag *m*, interessewahrender Auftrag *m*; ~ **spending power** *n* ECON *of government* diskretionäre Ausgabenkompetenz *f*; ~ **trust** *n* LAW Treuhandverhältnis mit uneingeschränkter Ermessensbefugnis

discriminate *vi* ECON, GEN COMM, LAW diskriminieren

discriminate: ~ **against** *vt* ECON, GEN COMM, LAW diskriminieren

discriminating: ~ **monopoly** *n* ECON diskriminierendes Monopol *nt*

discrimination *n* ECON, GEN COMM Diskriminierung *f*, LAW Benachteiligung *f*; ◆ **no ~ factor** GEN COMM kein Diskriminierungsfaktor

discrimination: ~ **in the workplace** *n* HRM Diskriminierung am Arbeitsplatz *f*; ~ **test** *n* S&M Unterscheidungsvermögenstest *m*

discriminatory: ~ **taxation** *n* TAX diskriminierende Besteuerung *f*

discuss *vt* GEN COMM besprechen, diskutieren, erörtern; ◆ ~ **an item** GEN COMM einen Punkt erörtern; ~ **fully** GEN COMM ausdiskutieren

discussion *n* GEN COMM Besprechung *f*, Diskussion *f*, Erörterung *f*; ◆ **under ~** GEN COMM im Gespräch

discussion: ~ **group** *n* S&M Diskussionsgruppe *f*

diseconomy *n* ECON Kostenprogression *f*; **diseconomies of scale** *n* ECON Größennachteile *m pl*, Kostenprogression *f*

disembarkation *n* TRANSP Ausschiffung *f*, Ladung *f*

disembodied: ~ **technical progress** *n* ECON *production* investitionsunabhängiger technischer Fortschritt *m*, vom Kapitaleinsatz unabhängiger technischer Fortschritt *m*

disequilibrium *n* ECON Ungleichgewicht *nt*; ~ **economics** *n* ECON Ungleichgewichtstheorie *f*; ~ **in the balance of trade** *n* ECON Handelsungleichgewicht *nt*, Ungleichgewicht *nt* der Handelsbilanz; ~ **money** *n* ECON Geldungleichgewicht *nt*; ~ **price** *n* ECON Ungleichgewichtspreis *m*

disguise *vt* GEN COMM verschleiern

disguised: ~ **unemployment** *n* HRM *labour market, statistics* versteckte Arbeitslosigkeit *f*

dishonest *adj* GEN COMM unehrlich

dishonor AmE *see* dishonour BrE

dishonored AmE *see* dishonoured BrE

dishonour 1. *n* BrE BANK Akzeptierverweigerung *f*, Annahmeverweigerung *f*, Nichteinlösen *nt*, Nichthonorieren *nt*, Notleiden *nt*; **2.** *vt* BANK nicht einlösen, nicht honorieren; ◆ ~ **a cheque** BrE BANK einen Scheck nicht einlösen

dishonoured *adj* BrE BANK nicht akzeptiert, nicht bezahlt, nicht honoriert, notleidend; ~ **bill of exchange** *n* BrE BANK nicht bezahlter Wechsel *m*, notleidender Wechsel *m*; ~ **cheque** *n* BrE BANK nicht eingelöster Scheck *m*, uneingelöster Scheck *m*

disincentive *n* ECON Leistungshemmnis *nt*, leistungshemmender Einfluß *m*; ~ **effect** *n* ECON Disincentive-Effekt *m*, leistungshemmender Effekt *m*

disinflation *n* ECON Desinflation *f*

disinformation *n* GEN COMM, POL Falschinformation *f* zu Täuschungszwecken, Desinformation *f*

disintegration *n* ECON, GEN COMM Auflösung *f*, Desintegration *f*

disintermediate *vt* BANK, ECON Einlagen abziehen

disintermediation *n* BANK, ECON Bruttoverlust *m* an Einlagegeldern

disinvestment *n* FIN Desinvestition *f*

disjoint: ~ **events** *n pl* GEN COMM nicht miteinander zusammenhängende Ereignisse *nt pl*

disk *n* COMP Diskette *f*, Platte *f*; ~ **drive** *n* COMP *hardware* Floppy-Laufwerk *nt* (*jarg*), Plattenlaufwerk *nt*

diskette *n* COMP Diskette *f*, Floppy *f* (*jarg*); ~ **drive** *n* COMP Diskettenlaufwerk *nt*, Floppy-Laufwerk *nt* (*jarg*); ~ **storage** *n* COMP Diskettenspeicher *m*

disk: ~ **operating system** *n* (*DOS*) COMP Plattenbetriebssystem *nt* (*DOS*); ~ **pack** *n* COMP Plattenstapel *m*; ~ **space** *n* COMP Speicherplatz *m* auf Diskette, Speicherplatz *m* auf Platte; ~ **unit** *n* COMP Platteneinheit *f*

dismantle *vt* ECON abbauen, GEN COMM abbauen, auseinandernehmen

dismantled *adj* GEN COMM, TRANSP demontiert

dismantling *n* ECON *of barriers* Abbau *m*; ◆ ~ **of a law** LAW Aushöhlung *f* eines Gesetzes

dismiss *vt* HRM entlassen, verabschieden, LAW *claim* zurückweisen; ◆ ~ **a notion** LAW einen Antrag ablehnen; ~ **sb** HRM jdn kündigen; ~ **sb without notice** HRM jdn fristlos entlassen

dismissal *n* HRM Entlassung *f*, Kündigung *f*, Verabschiedung *f*, LAW Zurückweisung *f*; ~ **with due notice** *n* HRM fristgerechte Kündigung *f*; ~ **procedure** *n* HRM Kündigungsverfahren *nt*; ~ **with timely notice** *n* HRM fristgerechte Kündigung *f*; ~ **wage** *n* HRM Entlassungsgehalt *nt*; ~ **without notice** *n* HRM fristlose Entlassung *f*

dismissed *adj* HRM gekündigt, verabschiedet; ◆ **be ~** GEN COMM gekündigt werden

disorderly: ~ **market** *n* STOCK ungeordnete Marktverhältnisse *nt pl*

disorders *n pl* POL Unruhen *f pl*

disparage *vt* GEN COMM herabsetzen, Ruf schädigen

disparagement *n* GEN COMM Herabsetzung *f*, LAW Verunglimpfung *f*

disparaging: ~ **copy** *n* S&M herabsetzender Werbetext *m*, verunglimpfende Werbung *f*; ~ **statement** *n* PATENTS herabsetzende Aussage *f*

disparity *n* ECON, GEN COMM Disparität *f*

dispatch 1. *n* COMMS Abfertigung *f*, Versand *m*, Versendung *f*, GEN COMM *execution* Erledigung *f*, Versendung *f*, TRANSP Abfertigung *f*, Versand *m*, Versendung *f*; **2.** *vt* COMMS absenden, befördern, schikken, versenden, COMP abfertigen, GEN COMM *execute* erledigen, versenden, TRANSP absenden, befördern, schicken, versenden

dispatch: ~ **bay** *n* TRANSP Versandlager *nt*, Versandlagerraum *m*, Abfertigungsbucht *f*; ~ **department** *n* COMMS, TRANSP Versandabteilung *f*

dispatcher *n* COMMS, TRANSP Expedient *m*, *aviation* Flugbetriebsregler, in *m,f*

dispatching *n* COMMS Versand *m*, Versendung, TRANSP *aviation* Flugbetriebsregelung *f*; ~ **charge** *n* COMMS Versandgebühr *f*

dispatch: ~ **money** *n* COMMS, TRANSP Beschleunigungsgebühr *f*, Eilgeld *nt*, Vergütung *f* für schnelles Entladen; ~ **note** *n* COMMS, TRANSP Frachtzettel *m*, Postbegleitschein *m*, Versandschein *m*; ~ **papers** *n pl* IMP/EXP, TRANSP Transportpapiere *nt pl*, Versandpapiere *nt pl*; ~ **payable** *n* IMP/EXP, TRANSP zahlbares Eilgeld *nt*

dispensation *n* LAW Dispens *m*

dispersion *n* MATH Streuung *f*

displacement *n* GEN COMM Verlagerung *f*; ~ **loaded** *n* TRANSP *shipping* Ladedeplacement *nt*, Ladeverdrängung *f*; ~ **tonnage** *n* TRANSP Ladedeplacement *nt*, Verdrängungstonnage *f*

display 1. *n* COMMS Auslage *f*, Ausstellung *f*, Warenauslage *f*, COMP Anzeige *f*, Bildschirm *m*, S&M Schaufensterauslage *f*, Display *nt*; **2.** *vt* COMP anzeigen

display: ~ **advertising** *n* S&M Großanzeige *f*, Schlagzeilenwerbung *f*; ~ **article** *n* GEN COMM Ausstellungsstück *nt*; ~ **device** *n* COMP Anzeigeeinheit *f*

displayed: ~ **price** *n* ECON angegebener Preis *m*, ausgehängter Preis *m*, GEN COMM Preisangabe *f*

display: ~ **file** *n* COMP Anzeigedatei *f*, Bilddatei *f*; ~ **material** *n* S&M Displaymaterial *nt*; ~ **monitor** *n* COMP Anzeigebildschirm *m*; ~ **pack** *n* S&M Schaupackung *f*; ~ **setting** *n* COMP Anzeigeeinstellung *f*; ~ **stand** *n* MEDIA *for books, newspapers* Ausstellungsstand *m*; ~ **unit** *n* COMP Anzeigeeinheit *f*

disposable: ~ **income** *n* ECON, TAX verfügbares Einkommen *nt*; ~ **packaging** *n* S&M Einwegverpackung *f*

disposal *n* ENVIR *waste* Entsorgung *f*, GEN COMM Verfügung *f*, Veräußerung *f*; ~ **unit** *n* ENVIR Entsorgungseinrichtung *f*

dispose: ~ **by will** *vi* LAW vermachen; ◆ ~ **of stock** S&M Lagerbestände absetzen

disposition *n* LAW *transactions* Verfügungsgeschäft *nt*

dispossess *vt AmE* PROP Besitz entziehen

dispossess: ~ **proceedings** *n pl* LAW, PROP *property* Räumungsverfahren *nt*

disputable *adj* GEN COMM bestreitbar

dispute 1. *n* GEN COMM *boardroom* Streit *m*, HRM Auseinandersetzung *f*, Streitigkeit *f*; ◆ **be in ~** HRM *with employer* strittig sein; **2.** *vt* LAW *claim* bestreiten, *will* anfechten, S&M umkämpfen

dispute: ~ **procedure** *n* HRM Verfahren *nt* zur Regelung arbeitsrechtlicher Streitigkeiten, Verfahrensregeln *f pl* zur Vermeidung von Arbeitskonflikten; ~ **resolution** *n* HRM Beilegung *f* eines Streitfalls

Disputes: ~ **Committee** *n BrE* HRM Ausschuß *m* zur Beilegung von Streitigkeiten

disregard *vt* MGMNT unberücksichtigt lassen

disrepair *n* PROP Verfall *m*

disrupt *vt* GEN COMM unterbrechen

dissaving *n* ECON Entsparen *nt*, negative Ersparnis *f*

disseminate *vt* COMMS verbreiten

dissemination *n* COMMS *of information* Verbreitung *f*

dissent *n* LAW *contracts* Dissens *m*, abweichende Meinung *f*

dissenting: ~ **opinion** *n* LAW, MGMNT abweichende Meinung *f*; ~ **view** *n* MGMNT abweichende Meinung *f*; ~ **vote** *n* LAW abweichende Meinung *f*, Gegenstimme *f*

dissolution *n* ECON Liquidation *f*, GEN COMM Auflösung *f*, Zerstörung *f*, HRM, LAW, POL *of parliament* Auflösung *f*

dissolve *vt* GEN COMM *partnership*, LAW, POL *parliament* auflösen

distance *n* GEN COMM Strecke *f*, TRANSP Entfernung *f*; ◆ **at an appropriate ~** GEN COMM in angemessener Entfernung

distance: ~ **freight** *n* TRANSP Distanzfracht *f*; ~ **learning** *n* WEL Fernstudium *nt*, Fernunterricht *m*

distant *adj* GEN COMM distanziert

distinction *n* GEN COMM *difference* Unterscheidung *f*, *outstanding quality* erste Qualität *f*

distinctive *adj* PATENTS unterscheidungsfähig

distinctiveness *n* PATENTS Unterscheidung *f*, Verschiedenheit *f*

distinguished *adj* HRM *career* glänzend

distort 1. *n* GEN COMM Verzerrung *f*; **2.** *vt* ECON verzerren

distortion *n* ECON Verzerrung *f*; ~ **of competition** *n* ECON Wettbewerbsverzerrung *f*

distrainable *adj* LAW pfändbar

distrainee *n* LAW Pfändungsschuldner *m*

distraint *n* LAW dinglicher Arrest *m*, *property* Beschlagnahme *f*, Beschlagnahmung *f*; ~ **of property** *n* LAW Beschlagnahme *f* von Eigentum, Pfändung *f*

distressed: ~ **property** *n* PROP gepfändetes Eigentum *nt*

distress: ~ **freight** *n* TRANSP Notfracht *f*; ~ **sale** *n* LAW Pfandverkauf *m*

distributable: ~ **profit** *n* ACC, FIN ausschüttungsfähiger Gewinn *m*

distribute *vt* FIN *dividends* ausschütten, verteilen, MEDIA *newspaper, magazine* verbreiten, S&M vertreiben, STOCK, TRANSP verteilen; ◆ ~ **a dividend** FIN eine Dividende ausschütten

distributed *adj* COMP verteilt; ◆ **when ~** STOCK bei Ausschüttung

distributed: ~ **computing** *n* COMP verteilte Datenverarbeitung *f*; ~ **database** *n* (*DDB*) COMP verteilte Datenbank *f*; ~ **data processing** (*DDP*) *n* COMP verteilte Datenverarbeitung *f*; ~ **profit** *n* ACC, FIN ausgeschütteter Gewinn *m*; ~ **system** *n* COMP verteiltes System *nt*

distributing: ~ **syndicate** *n* STOCK Emissionskonsortium *nt*, Verkaufssyndikat *nt*

distribution *n* ECON Verteilung *f*, FIN Verteilung *f*, Zuteilung *f*, GEN COMM Vertrieb *m*, LAW *estate law* Aufteilung *f*, MEDIA *of newspaper, magazine* Verbreitung *f*, S&M *trade or manufacturer* Distribution *f*, Vertrieb *m*, STOCK *of dividends* Ausschüttung *f*, Streuung *f*, Verteilung *f*, TRANSP *trade or manufacturer* Vertrieb *m*, *of the load* Verteilung *f*

distribution: ~ **allowance** *n* S&M Vertriebsprovision *f*

distributional: ~ **weight** *n* ECON Verteilungsgewicht *nt*

distribution: ~ **area** *n* GEN COMM Absatzgebiet *nt*, STOCK Ausschüttungsbereich *m*; ~ **center** *AmE*, ~ **centre** *BrE* *n* TRANSP Absatzzentrum *nt*, Verteilerzentrum *nt*, Vertriebszentrum *nt*; ~ **channel** *n* GEN COMM Absatzkanal *m*, Absatzweg *m*; ~ **check** *n* S&M Distributionskontrolle *f*; ~ **cost analysis** *n* S&M Vertriebskostenanalyse *f*; ~ **costs** *n pl* FIN *of profit* Ausschüttungskosten *pl*, GEN COMM *company*, IND, TRANSP Vertriebskosten *pl*; ~ **depot** *n* TRANSP Vertriebsdepot *nt*; ~ **manager** *n* HRM, MGMNT, TRANSP Absatzleiter, in *m,f*, Vertriebsleiter, in *m,f*; ~ **of national income** *n* ECON Verteilung *f* des Volkseinkommens; ~ **of net profit** *n* ACC Nettogewinnausschüttung *f*; ~ **network** *n* COMP Verteilnetz *nt*, GEN COMM Vertriebsnetz *nt*; ~ **office** *n* (*DO*) TRANSP Vertriebsbüro *nt*; ~ **planning** *n* GEN COMM Vertriebsplanung *f*, TRANSP Distributionsplanung *f*; ~ **policy** *n* GEN COMM, S&M, TRANSP Absatzpolitik *f*, Vertriebspolitik *f*; ~ **of risk** LAW *in a transaction* Risikoverteilung *f*; ~ **service** *n* TRANSP Distributionsservice *m*; ~ **stock** *n* STOCK Aktien, auf die Erträge ausgeschüttet werden

distributive: ~ **ability** *n* TRANSP Vertriebsleistung *f*; ~ **trades** *n pl* S&M Absatzwirtschaft *f*, Handel *m*

distributor *n* IMP/EXP, TRANSP Agent, in *m,f*, Verteiler *m*, Vertriebsfirma *f*, Vertriebshändler *m*, Vertriebsorganisation *f*, Vertriebsunternehmen *nt*

distributors': ~ **brand** *n* S&M Händlermarke *f*, Gemeinschaftsmarke *f*

district *n* GEN COMM Bezirk *m*, POL Kreis *m*; ~ **agreement** *n* *BrE* HRM Ortstarif *m*; ~ **attorney** *n* *AmE* (*DA*) LAW Staatsanwältin *f*, Staatsanwalt *m*; ~ **council** *n* *BrE* POL Kreistag *m*; ~ **court** *n* *AmE* LAW Amtsgericht *nt*; ~ **hospital** *n* WEL Bezirkskrankenhaus *nt*, Kreiskrankenhaus *nt*, städtisches Krankenhaus *nt*; ~ **manager** *n* HRM Bezirksleiter, in *m,f*, INS Bezirksdirektor, in *m,f*; ~ **officer** *n* (*DO*) HRM Bezirksreferent, in *m,f*; ~ **training officer** *n* (*DTO*) HRM Ausbildender mit besonderer Verantwortung für einen Bezirk

disturbance *n* GEN COMM Störung *f*; ~ **variable** *n* MATH *statistics* Störterm *m*, Störvariable *f*

disutility *n* ECON, S&M Nachteil *m*, negativer Nutzen *m*

div. *abbr* (*dividend*) STOCK Div. (*Dividende*), Gewinnanteil *m*

diverge *vi* GEN COMM *exchange rates* abweichen

divergence *n* GEN COMM Divergenz *f*; ~ **indicator** *n* ECON *international* Abweichungsindikator *m*; ~ **threshold** *n* ECON Abweichungsschwelle *f*, Divergenzschwelle *f*

divergent: ~ **manufacturing** *n* IND divergierende Fertigung *f*; ~ **marketing** *n* S&M divergentes Marketing *nt*; ~ **thinking** *n* MGMNT abweichende Meinung *f*

diverse *adj* GEN COMM verschieden

diversification *n* GEN COMM, HRM, MGMNT Diversifizierung *f*, S&M Diversifikation *f*, STOCK Streuung *f*; ~ **strategy** *n* S&M Diversifikationsstrategie *f*

diversified: ~ **company** *n* ECON breitgefächertes Unternehmen *nt*

diversify *vt* GEN COMM, HRM, MGMNT diversifizieren; ♦ ~ **risk** STOCK das Risiko verteilen

diversity *n* GEN COMM Verschiedenheit *f*

divert *vt* TRANSP umleiten; ~ **custom** *vt* LAW, S&M abwerben

diverting: ~ **custom** *n* LAW, S&M Abwerbung *f*

divest *vt* FIN, LAW abstoßen, veräußern

divestiture *n* FIN, LAW Abstoßen *nt* einer Tochtergesellschaft, Veräußerung *f* einer Tochtergesellschaft

divestment *n* FIN, LAW Besitzentziehung *f*

divide *vt* ACC aufteilen, COMP dividieren, teilen, MATH dividieren, S&M aufteilen; ~ **into small plots** *vt* PROP parzellieren

dividend *n* (*div.*) INS Dividende *f*, STOCK Dividende *f*, Gewinnanteil *m*; ~ **coupon** *n* FIN Dividendenschein *m*; ~ **cover** *n* ACC Verhältnis *nt* von Gewinn zu Dividenden; ~ **exclusion** *n* TAX Dividendenfreibetrag *m*, Dividendensteuerbefreiung *f*; ~ **in arrears** *n* STOCK aufgelaufene Dividende *f*, rückständige Dividende *f*; ~ **income** *n* STOCK Dividendeneinkommen *nt*, Dividendeneinnahme *f*; ~ **payable in kind** *n* FIN Sachdividende *f*; ~ **payout policy** *n* FIN Dividendenpolitik *f*; ~ **payout ratio** *n* ACC Ausschüttungssatz *m*; ~ **per share** *n* *BrE* (*DPS*) FIN Dividende *f* pro Aktie; ~ **policy** *n* FIN Ausschüttungspolitik *f*, STOCK Ausschüttungspolitik *f*, Dividendenpolitik *f*; ~ **price ratio** *n* FIN Verhältnis *nt* Dividende zu Aktienkurs; ~ **requirement** *n* ACC Dividendenbedarf *m*; ~ **reserve fund** *n* ACC Dividendenrücklage *f*; ~ **resolution** *n* FIN Ausschüttungsbeschluß *m*; ~ **rollover plan** *n* STOCK Dividendenrolloverplan *m*

dividends *n pl* ACC, FIN Dividenden *f pl*, Beträge *m pl*; ~ **payable** *n pl* ACC auszuschüttende Dividenden *f pl*

dividend: ~ **stripping** *n* FIN Dividenden-Stripping *nt*; ~ **tax** *n* TAX Dividendensteuer *f*, Kapitalertragsteuer *f*; ~ **voucher** *n* STOCK Dividendenbeleg *m*, Dividendenquittung *f*; ~ **warrant** *n* FIN Dividendenanteilschein *m*, Dividendenberechtigungsschein *m*, Dividendenschein *m*, Dividendenzahlungsanweisung *f*; ~ **withholding tax** *n* TAX auf Dividenden zu zahlende Kapitalertragsteuer *f*, Dividendenquellensteuer *f*, Kuponsteuer *f*; ~ **yield** *n* STOCK Dividendenertrag *m*, Dividendenrendite *f*, Effektivrendite *f*

Divisia: ~ **money index** *n* ECON Divisia-Geldindex *m*

division *n* ACC Aufteilung *f*, ECON Unternehmensbereich *m*, GEN COMM Abteilung *f*, Teilung *f*, S&M Aufteilung *f*, Sparte *f*

divisional: ~ **board of management** *n* HRM, MGMNT Bereichsvorstand *m*; ~ **director** *n* *BrE* HRM Bereichsleiter, in *m,f*

divisionalization *n* GEN COMM Divisionalisierung *f*, Gliederung *f* in Geschäftsbereiche, Spartenorganisation *f*

divisional: ~ **management** n HRM, MGMNT Abteilungs-leitung f, Bereichsleitung f

division: ~ **head** n HRM, MGMNT Abteilungsleiter, in m,f, Bereichsleiter, in m,f, Spartenmanager, in; ~ **of labor** AmE, ~ **of labour** BrE n ECON Arbeitsteilung f; ~ **manager** n HRM, MGMNT Abteilungsleiter, in m,f, Bereichsleiter, in m,f, Spartenmanager, in m,f; ~ **of powers** n GEN COMM Machtteilung f; ~ **of thought** n MGMNT Gedankenaustausch m

DIY abbr (do-it-yourself) LEIS Heimwerken nt

DJIA abbr (Dow Jones Industrial Average) STOCK Dow-Jones-Industrieaktienindex m

DLO abbr ADMIN (Dead Letter Office) Büro für unzu-stellbare Sendungen, HRM (direct labor organization AmE, direct labour organization BrE) Ausführung von städtischen Dienstleistungen durch Kommunalangestellte und nicht durch privatwirtschaftliche Unternehmen, kom-munaler Eigenbetrieb m

DMA abbr AmE (Direct Marketing Association) S&M Verband für Direktabsatz

DME abbr (decentralized market economy) ECON dezen-trale Marktwirtschaft f

D/N abbr (debit note) GEN COMM Belastungsanzeige f, Lastschriftanzeige f

DO abbr ENVIR (diesel oil) Dieselöl nt, Dieselkraftstoff m, Dieseltreibstoff m, HRM (district officer) Bezirksreferent, in m,f, (duty officer) Offizier m vom Dienst, TRANSP (diesel oil) Dieselöl nt, Dieselkraftstoff m, Dieseltreibstoff m, (distribution office) Vertriebsbüro nt, (dock operations) Docktätigkeiten f pl

D/O abbr (delivery order) TRANSP Auslieferungsauftrag m, Konnossementsteilschein m, Lieferauftrag m

DOC abbr AmE (Drive Other Car insurance) INS Fahrerhaftpflichtversicherung f

dock 1. n TRANSP Dock nt; **2.** vt ♦ ~ **sb's wages** HRM pay jds Arbeitslohn kürzen

dock: ~ **charges** n pl TRANSP Dockgebühren f pl; ~ **dues** n pl TRANSP Dockgebühren f pl

docker n BrE (cf longshoreman AmE) HRM, TRANSP Hafenarbeiter m

docking: ~ **survey** n TRANSP Dockprüfung f

dock: ~ **operations** n pl (DO) TRANSP Docktätigkeiten f pl, Vertriebsbüro nt; ~ **receipt** n IMP/EXP, TRANSP Kaiempfangsschein m; ~ **warrant** n (D/W) IMP/EXP shipping, TRANSP Dockempfangsschein m, Docklagerschein m

Doctor n (Dr.) GEN COMM, WEL title Doktor m (Dr.)

doctorate n WEL Doktorgrad m

Doctor: ~ **of Commerce** n (DCom) GEN COMM Doktor m der Betriebswirtschaft; ~ **of Commercial Law** n (DComL) GEN COMM Doktor m des Handelsrechts, Doktor m des Wirtschaftsrechts; ~ **of Economics** n (DEcon) GEN COMM Doktor m der Wirtschaftswissen-schaften; ~ **of Laws** n (LLD) HRM, LAW, WEL Doktor m der Rechte (Dr. jur.); ~ **of Medicine** n (MD) WEL Doktor der Medizin m (Dr. med.); ~ **of Philosophy** n GEN COMM, WEL (DPhil, PhD) Doktorgrad m, Doktor m der Philosophie (Dr. phil.)

doctor: ~'**s degree** n WEL Doktorgrad m

doctrine: ~ **of strict compliance** n BANK Grundsatz m der strikten Bedingungserfüllung; ~ **of substantial performance** n LAW contractual obligations im wesent-lichen erbrachte Leistung f

document n COMP Dokument nt, GEN COMM Beur-kundung f, Dokument nt, LAW Dokument nt, TAX Beleg m

documentary 1. adj GEN COMM dokumentarisch; **2.** n S&M book Dokumentarbericht m, film Dokumentarfilm m, radio, television Dokumentarsendung f

documentary: ~ **credit** n FIN Dokumentenakkreditiv nt; ~ **draft** n ADMIN, GEN COMM, IMP/EXP Dokumententratte f; ~ **evidence** n GEN COMM doku-mentärer Nachweis m; ~ **fraud** n LAW Urkundenbetrug m; ~ **letter of credit** n BANK Dokumentenakkreditiv nt; ~ **remittance** n BANK Dokumentenrimesse f

documentation n COMP, GEN COMM Dokumentation f

document: ~ **code** n COMP Dokumentencode m; ~ **feeder** n COMP Belegvorschub m; ~ **holder** n GEN COMM Dokumenteninhaber, in m,f; ~ **mode** n COMP Dokumentenmodus m; ~ **name** n COMP Dokumentenname m; ~ **rate** n COMP Belegdurchlauf m; ~ **reader** n COMP Belegleser m; ~ **retrieval system** n COMP Dokumentenwiedergewinnungssystem nt

documents: ~ **against acceptance** n pl (DA) GEN COMM Dokumente nt pl gegen Akzept (DA, D/A, d/a); ~ **against payment** n pl (DAP) GEN COMM Dokumente f pl gegen Zahlung (DZ)

document: ~ **signed in blank** n GEN COMM Blankett nt, Blankoformular nt; ~ **of title** n LAW Eigentumsurkunde f

DOE abbr BrE (Department of Environment) POL Umwelt-ministerium

dog n S&M wenig erfolgreiches Produkt nt, perspektiv-loses Produkt nt; ~ **hook** n TRANSP cargo handling equipment Greifhaken m

dogsbody n infrml Handlanger, Mädchen für alles (infrml)

DoH abbr BrE (Department of Health) POL, WEL Gesund-heitsministerium

DOI abbr AmE (Department of Industry) IND, POL Industrieministerium

do: ~-**it-yourself** n (DIY) LEIS Heimwerken nt

dole n BrE infrml ECON, GEN COMM, WEL Arbeitslosenunterstützung f, HRM Arbeits-losenunterstützung f, Stütze f; ♦ **be on the** ~ BrE infrml (cf be on welfare AmE) HRM Arbeitslosenunter-stützung empfangen, WEL Arbeitslosenunterstützung beziehen, stempeln (infrml)

dole: ~ **bludger** n infrml HRM arbeitsscheuer Empfänger m von Arbeitslosenunterstützung

dollar n GEN COMM Dollar m; ~ **area** n ECON Dollarblock m, Dollarraum m; ~ **balance** n ECON Dollarausgleich m; ~ **bid** n STOCK options Dollarkurs m, Dollarsubmis-sionsangebot nt; ~ **bill** n AmE ECON Dollarschein m; ~ **cost averaging** n STOCK Dollardurchschnittskostenmethode f; ~ **drain** n ECON Dollarabfluß m; ~-**for-dollar offset** n STOCK Dollar m; ~ **gap** n ECON Dollarlücke f, Dollarzinsspanne f

dollarization n ECON, FIN, STOCK Dollarisierung f

dollar: ~ **premium** n STOCK options Dollaraufgeld nt, Dollarprämie f; ~ **price** n GEN COMM commodities Dollarpreis m, STOCK Dollarkurs m; ~ **rate** n STOCK Dollarkurs m, Dollarpreis m; ~ **securities** n pl FIN Dollartitel m pl; ~ **shortage** n STOCK Dollarmangel m, Dollarverknappung f; ~ **spot and forward** FIN, STOCK Kassa- und Termin- Dollarkurs m; ~ **standard** n ECON Dollarstandard m; ~ **surplus** n ECON Dollarüberschuß *m*; ~ **transaction** *n* BANK Dollargeschäft *nt*; ~ **value** *n* STOCK Dollarwert *m*; ~ **value LIFO** *n* TAX LIFO-Dollarwert *m*

DOM *abbr* (*date of maturity*) BANK Fälligkeitstermin *m*, Ablauftermin *m*, GEN COMM, STOCK Fälligkeitsdatum *nt*, *bill of exchange* Verfalltag *m*

domain *n* ECON Bereich *m*, Grundbesitz *m*, GEN COMM Bereich *m*, MATH *statistics* Definitionsbereich *m*

Domei *n* HRM Domei *nt*

domestic *adj* ECON einheimisch, inländisch, *trade* Binnen-, *policy* Inland-, TRANSP *network* inländisch, Binnen-, Inland-; ~ **absorption** *n* ECON inländische Absorption *f*; ~ **affairs** *n pl* POL Innenpolitik *f*, innenpolitische Fragen *f pl*; ~ **agreement** *n BrE* HRM Binnenabkommen *nt*; ~ **airline** *n* LEIS Inlandsfluglinie *f*, nationale Fluggesellschaft *f*, TRANSP Inlandsfluglinie *f*; ~ **assets** *n pl* BANK inländische Guthaben *nt pl*, Inlandsguthaben *nt pl*

domestication *n* ECON Domestizierung *f*

domestic: ~ **bank** *n* BANK Inlandsbank *f*; ~ **banking system** *n* BANK inländisches Bankensystem *nt*; ~ **business** *n* GEN COMM Inlandsgeschäft *nt*; ~ **consumption** *n* ENVIR Inlandsverbrauch *m*; ~ **corporation** *n* ECON inländische Kapitalgesellschaft *f*; ~ **court** *n* LAW heimisches Gericht *nt*; ~ **credit expansion** *n* (*DCE*) ECON inländischer Zuwachs *m* des Kreditvolumens, Kreditexpansion *f*, FIN inländische Kreditausweitung *f*; ~ **demand** *n* ECON Binnennachfrage *f*, Inlandsnachfrage *f*; ~ **economy** *n* ECON Binnenwirtschaft *f*; ~ **export financing** *n* IMP/EXP heimische Exportfinanzierung *f*, Inlandsexportfinanzierung *f*; ~ **flight** *n* TRANSP Inlandsflug *m*; ~ **industry** *n* IND *for home market* inländische Industrie *f*, heimischer Wirtschaftszweig *m*, *working from home* Heimarbeit *f*, Heimindustrie *f*; ~ **investment** *n* ECON Inlandsinvestition *f*; ~ **issue** *n* STOCK Inlandsemission *f*; ~ **liabilities** *n pl* BANK Inlandsverbindlichkeiten *f pl*; ~ **market** *n* ECON Binnenmarkt *m*, Inlandsmarkt *m*; ~ **money market** *n* ECON inländischer Geldmarkt *m*; ~ **output** *n* ECON inländische Produktion *f*; ~ **port** *n* TRANSP Inlandshafen *m*; ~ **product** *n* ECON Inlandsprodukt *nt*, GEN COMM inländisches Erzeugnis *nt*; ~ **rate** *n* GEN COMM, STOCK, TRANSP Inlandssatz *m*; ~ **resource cost** *n* (*DRC*) ECON inländische Faktorkosten *pl*; ~ **risks** *n pl* INS Inlandsrisiko *nt*; ~ **sales** *n pl* S&M Inlandsabsatz *m*; ~ **situation** *n* ECON binnenwirtschaftliche Lage *f*; ~ **subsidiary** *n* ECON inländische Tochter *f* (*jarg*), inländische Tochtergesellschaft *f*; ~ **system** *n* ECON Verlagssystem *nt*, Heimarbeit *f*; ~ **trade** *n* ECON Binnenhandel *m*; ~ **waste** *n* ENVIR Hausmüll *m*

domicile *n* GEN COMM Aufenthalt *m*, LAW, TAX *person* Wohnsitz *m*, *firm* Sitz *m*, Gesellschaftssitz *m*

domiciled *adj* LAW wohnhaft

dominance *n* GEN COMM Beherrschung *f*, Dominanz *f*, POL Beherrschung *f*

dominant *adj* GEN COMM dominant, beherrschend; ~ **advertising** *n* S&M dominante Werbung *f*; ~ **position** *n* ECON *abuse of* beherrschende Stellung *f*, herrschende Stellung *f*; ~ **tenement** *n* PROP herrschendes Grundstück *nt*

dominate *vt* GEN COMM *market* beherrschen

donate *vt* TAX, WEL spenden

donation *n* TAX, WEL Spende *f*

dongle *n* COMP Dongle *m* (*jarg*), Software-Schutzeinrichtung *f*

Donoghue: ~'**s Money Fund Average** *n AmE* STOCK Donoghues-Geldfondsdurchschnitt *m*

donor *n* GEN COMM, WEL Geber *m*; ~ **agency** *n* WEL Gebereinrichtung *f*; ~ **aid** *n* ECON *development assistance* Entwicklungshilfe *f*; ~ **country** *n* ECON *of overseas aid* Geberland *nt*; ~ **government** *n* WEL Geberregierung *f*

Donovan: ~ **Commission** *n BrE* HRM, IND Donovan-Kommission *f*

don't: ~-**know vote** *n* POL Weiß-nicht-Stimme *f*

door/depot *adj* TRANSP Haus/Lager

door: ~-**to-door** *adj* TRANSP von Haus zu Haus; ~-**to-door clause** *n* INS von-Haus-zu-Haus-Klausel *f*; ~-**to-door sales** *n pl* S&M Haustürverkauf *m*; ~-**to-door salesman** *n* GEN COMM Klinkenputzer *m* (*infrml*), Vertreter *m*, S&M Haushaltsreisende(r) *m* [decl. as adj], Klinkenputzer *m* (*infrml*), Vertreter *m*; ~-**to-door saleswoman** *n* GEN COMM Klinkenputzerin *f* (*infrml*), Vertreterin *f*, S&M Haushaltsreisende *f* [decl. as adj], Klinkenputzerin *f* (*infrml*), Vertreterin *f*; ~-**to-door selling** *n* S&M Direktverkauf *m* durch Vertreter, ambulanter Verkauf *m*

doors: ~ **open at nine** *phr* GEN COMM *for exhibition, conference* ab neun Uhr geöffnet, Einlaß ab neun Uhr

dormant: ~ **account** *n* BANK stillgelegtes Bankkonto *nt*, umsatzloses Konto *nt*, S&M umsatzloses Konto *nt*

dormitory: ~ **suburb** *n* HRM Wohnvorort *m*, Schlafstadt *f*

DOS *abbr* (*disk operating system*) COMP DOS (*Plattenbetriebsystem*); ~ **prompt** *n* COMP DOS-Prompt *m* (*jarg*), DOS-Eingabeaufforderung *f*

dosh *n BrE infrml* GEN COMM Geld *nt*, Kohle *f* (*infrml*), Knete *f* (*infrml*), Mäuse *f pl* (*infrml*), Kies *m* (*infrml*)

dossier *n* ADMIN urkundliche Unterlagen *f pl*, Dossier *nt*

dot *n* COMP Punkt *m*; ~ **command** *n* COMP Punktbefehl *m*; ~-**matrix printer** *n* COMP *hardware* Matrixdrucker *m*; ~ **printer** *n* COMP Rasterdrucker *m*

dots: ~ **per inch** *n* (*dpi*) COMP Punkte *m pl* pro Zoll (*dpi*)

dotted: ~ **line** *n* ADMIN, COMP, MATH *on graph* gepunktete Linie *f*

double 1. *vt* MATH verdoppeln; **2.** *vi* MATH sich verdoppeln

double: ~ **account** *n* ACC doppeltes Konto *nt*; ~ **acting** *adj* IND *machinery* doppeltwirkend; ~-**barreled quotation** *AmE*, ~-**barrelled quotation** *BrE n* STOCK Angabe *f* von Ankauf- und Verkaufskurs; ~-**click** *n* COMP Doppelklick *m*; ~-**click speed** *n* COMP Doppelklickgeschwindigkeit *f*; ~ **column** *n* MEDIA, S&M Doppelspalte *f*; ~ **counting** *n* FIN Doppelzählung *f*; ~ **damages** *n pl* LAW *award* doppelter Schadensersatz *m*; ~ **decking** *n* TRANSP *of roads* doppelte Fahrbahn *f*; ~-**declining balance** *n* FIN *depreciation* degressive Abschreibung *f*; ~ **density** *n* (*DD*) COMP doppelte Dichte *f* (*DD*); ~-**density disk** *n* COMP Diskette *f* mit doppelter Speicherdichte; ~-**density diskette** *n* COMP Diskette *f* mit doppelter Speicherdichte; ~ **digit** *adj* ECON *inflation* zweistellig; ~ **digit inflation** *n* ECON, FIN zweistellige Inflationsrate *f*; ~-**dipper** *n* HRM Doppelaktivierer *m*; ~-**dipping** *n* HRM Doppelaktivierung; ~ **eagle** *n AmE* GEN COMM Zwanzig-Dollar-Schein; ~ **economic burden** *n* LAW, TAX Doppelbelastung *f*; ~-**entry accounting** *n* ACC doppelte Buchführung *f*; ~-**entry bookkeeping** *n* ACC doppelte Buchführung *f*;

~-entry method n ACC *bookkeeping* Methode f der doppelten Buchführung; **~-entry visa** n ADMIN doppeltes Einreisevisum nt; **~ factorial terms of trade** n pl ECON doppelt faktorales Austauschverhältnis nt; **~ figure inflation** n ECON, FIN zweistellige Inflationsrate f; **~ front** n S&M zwei Seiten f pl; **~ income household** n ECON Doppelverdienerhaushalt m; **~ income no kids** phr infrml (*Dinks*) ECON kinderlose Doppelverdiener; **~ insurance** n INS Doppelversicherung f; **~-page spread** n MEDIA, S&M doppelseitige Anzeige f; **~ precision** n COMP doppelte Genauigkeit f; **~ reduction** n (*DR*) GEN COMM Doppelsenkung f; **~ residency** n LAW, TAX Doppelwohnsitz m, doppelte Ansässigkeit f; **~ room** n LEIS Doppelzimmer nt; **~ sample** n MATH *statistics* zweistufige Stichprobe f; **~-sided** adj COMP doppelseitig; **~-sided disk** n COMP doppelseitige Diskette f; **~-sided diskette** n COMP doppelseitige Diskette f; **~-spaced** adj COMP zweizeilig; **~ spacing** n COMP doppelter Zeilenabstand m; **~ spread advertising** n MEDIA, S&M doppelseitige Anzeige f; **~ staffing** n HRM *industry* Doppelbesetzung f; **~ strike** n COMP doppelter Anschlag m; **~ switching** n ECON doppelte Umschichtung f; **~ tax agreement** n TAX Doppelbesteuerungsabkommen nt; **~ taxation of savings** n TAX doppelte Besteuerung von Spareinlagen f; **~-width passenger gangway** n TRANSP *shipping* Passagiergangway f mit doppelter Breite

doubling n GEN COMM Doppelung f

doubt 1. n GEN COMM Zweifel m, LAW Besorgnis f; **2.** vt GEN COMM bezweifeln

doubt: **~ as to impartiality** n LAW Besorgnis f der Befangenheit

doubtful adj GEN COMM fraglich, ungewiß; **~ debt** n ACC zweifelhafte Forderung f; **~ debtors** n pl ACC zweifelhafte Schuldner m pl; **~-debt provision** n ACC Rückstellung f für zweifelhafte Forderungen

dough n infrml GEN COMM Geld nt, Kohle f (*infrml*), Knete f (*infrml*), Mäuse f pl (*infrml*), Kies m (*infrml*)

dower n LAW Witwenpflichtteil m

Dow: **~ Jones average** n STOCK Dow-Jones-Durchschnitt m; **~ Jones Index** n FIN Dow-Jones-Index m; **~ Jones Industrial Average** n (*DJIA*) STOCK Dow-Jones-Industrieaktienindex m

down 1. adj COMP *direction, position* nach unten, *not in working order* zusammengebrochen, GEN COMM stillstehend, TRANSP im Leerlauf, stillstehend; ◆ **be ~** ECON darnieder liegen, *prices* gefallen sein, *not working* außer Betrieb sein; **2.** vt ◆ **~ tools** HRM *strike, break from work* die Arbeit niederlegen, die Werkzeuge niederlegen

down: **~ arrow** n COMP *keyboard* Pfeil ab m

downgrade vt HRM *job* herunterstufen

downgrading n HRM Rückstufung f, *salary* Herabstufung f

downhill: **go ~** phr GEN COMM *business* den Bach hinuntergehen (*infrml*)

download 1. n COMP Download m; **2.** vt COMP herunterladen, laden, runterladen, downloaden (*jarg*)

downloadable: **~ font** n COMP ladbare Schriftart f

down: **~ market** adj GEN COMM Abwärtstrend m, S&M rückläufiger Markt m, *market position* unteres Marktsegment nt, STOCK rückläufiger Aktienmarkt m; **~-market product** n S&M Produkt nt für den weniger anspruchsvollen Markt, Produkt nt des unteren Marktsegments; **~-market segment** n GEN COMM untere Preisklasse f, S&M unteres Marktsegment nt; **~-market service** n S&M Dienstleistungen f pl eines rückläufigen Marktes

down: **~ payment** n ACC, ADMIN, S&M *advance payment* Anzahlung f

downscale vt MGMNT auf eine niedrigere Ebene verlagern

downside: **~ breakeven point** n STOCK *options* unterer Break-Even-Punkt m, Break-Even-Punkt m nach unten; **~ risk** n STOCK Risiko nt des Kursrückgangs; **~ trend** n FIN Abwärtstrend m

downsize vt HRM, MGMNT abbauen, verkleinern, verringern; ◆ **~ the workforce** HRM den Personalbestand verringern

downsized adj HRM, MGMNT verringert

downsizing n HRM, MGMNT *of workforce* Personalkürzung f, Abbau m, Verkleinerung f, Verringerung f

downstream adv GEN COMM nachgelagert

downstream: **~ float** n GEN COMM Abwärtsbewegung f; **~ markets** n pl GEN COMM Nachmärkte m pl, nachgelagerte Märkte m pl

downswing n ECON Abschwung m, Talfahrt f, Schrumpfung f

down: **~-the-line personnel** n HRM Untergebene pl [decl. as adj]; **~-the-line staff** n HRM Untergebene pl [decl. as adj]

downtime n COMP Ausfallzeit f, Stillstandszeit f, ECON Ausfallzeit f, Zeitdauer f der Betriebsstockung, GEN COMM Stillstandszeit f, HRM Brachzeit f, IND Brachzeit f, Ausfallzeit f, Zeitdauer f der Betriebsstockung

downtrend n ECON Abwärtstrend m, Konjunkturrückgang m

downturn n ECON, GEN COMM Abschwung m; **~ phase** n FIN Baisse f

downward 1. adj GEN COMM *trend* rückläufig; **2.** adv AmE (*cf downwards*) GEN COMM abwärts

downward: **~ communication** n MGMNT Informationsfluß m von oben nach unten; **~ compatibility** n COMP Abwärtskompatibilität f; **~ movement** n GEN COMM Abwärtsbewegung f; **~ pressure** n ECON *on currency, interest rates* Druck m

downward: **~ spiral** n GEN COMM *in wages, prices* Spirale f nach unten; **~ valuation adjustment** n LAW, TAX Bewertungsabschlag m

downzoning n PROP Herabzonung f

dowry n PROP Aussteuer f, Mitgift f

doz. abbr (*dozen*) GEN COMM Dtz. (*Dutzend*), Dtzd. (*Dutzend*)

dozen n (*doz.*) GEN COMM Dutzend nt (*Dtz., Dtzd.*)

dp abbr (*direct port*) TRANSP *shipping* Direkthafen m

DP abbr ADMIN (*data processing*) DV (*Datenverarbeitung*), COMP (*data processing*) DV (*Datenverarbeitung*), GEN COMM, S&M (*dynamic positioning*) dynamische Positionierung f

DPhil abbr (*Doctor of Philosophy*) HRM, WEL Dr. phil. (*Doktor der Philosophie*)

dpi abbr (*dots per inch*) COMP dpi (*Punkte pro Zoll*)

DPP abbr ECON (*direct product profitability*) Nettoproduktgewinn m, LAW (*Director of Public Prosecutions*) Oberstaatsanwalt, S&M (*direct product profitability*) direkte Produktrentabilität f

DPR *abbr* (*director of public relations*) HRM *advertising* Leiter, in *m,f* Öffentlichkeitsarbeit

DPS *abbr BrE* (*dividend per share*) FIN Dividende *f* pro Aktie

Dr. *abbr* (*Doctor*) GEN COMM, WEL *title* Dr. (*Doktor*)

DR *abbr* BANK (*deposit receipt*) Depotschein *m*, Einzahlungsbeleg *m*, GEN COMM (*dead rise*) umsatzloser Anstieg *m*, wertloser Anstieg *m*, (*double reduction*) Doppelsenkung *f*

draft 1. *n* BANK (*dft*) Bankscheck *m*, gezogener Wechsel *m*, Tratte *f*, Wechsel *m*, COMP Entwurf *m*, GEN COMM Ausarbeitung *f*, LAW Entwurf *m*, TRANSP *AmE see* *draught BrE*; ◆ **in ~ form** LAW als Entwurf; **2.** *vt* COMP entwerfen, GEN COMM, HRM abfassen, LAW entwerfen, S&M *advertisement text* abfassen

draft: **~ agreement** *n* LAW Vereinbarungsentwurf *m*, Vertragsentwurf *m*; **~ amendments** *n pl* LAW Änderungsentwurf *m*; **~ budget** *n* ACC Entwurf *m* des Haushaltsplans, Haushaltsentwurf *m*; **~ clause** *n* LAW vorläufige Klausel *f*; **~ contract** *n* LAW Vertragsentwurf *m*; **~ directive** *n* LAW Richtlinienentwurf *m*

drafted *adj* COMP, LAW entworfen

drafter *n* BANK Trassant *m*

draft: **~ for collection** *n* BANK Inkassowechsel *m*; **~ letter** *n* COMMS Briefentwurf *m*; **~ mode** *n* COMP Entwurfsmodus *m*; **~ order** *n* LAW *compulsory purchase* Verfügungsentwurf *m*; **~ printing** *n* COMP Entwurfsdruck *m*; **~ project** *n* GEN COMM Projektentwurf *m*; **~ resolution** *n* LAW Entschließungsentwurf *m*

draftsman *n* GEN COMM Zeichner, in *m,f*

draft: **~ stage** *n* LAW Entwurfsphase *f*

drag *vt* COMP *mouse, window* ziehen, TRANSP schleppen

drain *n* COMP *hardware* Drain *m*, ECON *on or of resources* Abfluß *m*, Abschöpfung *f*, Entzug *m*

DRAM *abbr* (*dynamic random access memory*) COMP *hardware* DRAM (*dynamischer Speicher*)

drama: **~ critic** *n* MEDIA Theaterkritiker, in *m,f*

Dram: **~ Shop Act** *n AmE* LAW *state law for tavernkeepers* Ausschankgesetze

drastic: **~ measures** *n pl* ECON drastische Maßnahmen *f pl*

draught *n BrE* TRANSP *shipping* Tiefgang *m*

draw 1. *n* BANK Kreditinanspruchnahme *f*; **2.** *vt* BANK *money* abheben, entnehmen, ECON, FIN, GEN COMM *money* abheben, STOCK zeichnen, ziehen, LAW *legal document* aufsetzen; ◆ **~ a check** *AmE*, **~ a cheque** *BrE* BANK einen Scheck ausstellen; **~ a conclusion** GEN COMM einen Schluß ziehen; **~ a distinction between** GEN COMM eine Unterscheidung machen zwischen; **~ sickness payments** HRM Krankengeld beziehen

draw from *vt* HRM rekrutieren

draw on *vt* GEN COMM angreifen; ◆ **~ one's savings** FIN auf seine Ersparnisse zurückgreifen

draw up *vt* ACC aufstellen, GEN COMM aufstellen, *plan, will* ausarbeiten, anfertigen, ausstellen, *report* erstellen, INS *marine insurance* aufmachen, LAW aufsetzen, ausfertigen, verfassen; ◆ **~ an agenda** ADMIN, MGMNT eine Tagesordnung aufstellen; **~ a shortlist** HRM eine Auswahlliste aufstellen; **~ a statement of account** BANK einen Kontoauszug machen

drawback *n* GEN COMM, IMP/EXP Zollrückschein *m*, Zollrückvergütung *f*

drawbar: **~ trailer** *n* TRANSP LKW-Anhänger *m*

drawdown *n* BANK Inanspruchnahme *f*

drawee *n* BANK Akzeptant *m*, Bezogene(r) *mf* [decl. as adj], Trassat *m*

drawer *n* BANK Aussteller, in *m,f*, Trassant *m*

drawing *n* GEN COMM Zeichnung *f*; **~ account** *n* BANK Girokonto *nt*; **~ board** *n* MGMNT Reißbrett *nt*; **on the ~ board** *phr* MGMNT im Entwurfsstadium; **~ file** *n* COMP Grafikdatei *f*; **~ officer** *n* BANK Ausstellungsbeamte(r) *m* [decl. as adj], Ausstellungsbeamtin *f*; **~ software** *n* COMP Grafiksoftware *f*; **~ up** *n* ACC Aufstellung *f*, PATENTS *report* Abfassung *f*, Konzipierung *f*; **~-up of a balance sheet** *n* ACC Aufstellung *f* einer Bilanz

drawn: **~ bill** *n* ECON gezogener Wechsel *m*; **~ bond** *n* STOCK ausgeloste Anleihe *f*, ausgeloste Obligation *f*

drayage *n AmE* TRANSP Rollgeld *nt*

DRC *abbr* (*domestic resource cost*) ECON inländische Faktorkosten *pl*

dredging *n* TRANSP *shipping* Schleppen *nt*

dress up *vt* ACC *balance sheet* frisieren (*infrml*)

DRF *abbr* (*Daily Range Factor*) FIN, STOCK Faktor *m* der täglichen Schwankungsbreite

drift *n* IND *mining* Strecke *f*

drilling: **~ platform** *n* ENVIR Bohrinsel *f*, Bohrplattform *f*; **~ program** *AmE*, **~ programme** *BrE* *n* ENVIR Bohrprogramm *nt*

drinking: **~ water** *n* ENVIR Trinkwasser *nt*

drive 1. *n* COMP Laufwerk *nt*, GEN COMM *concerted effort* Antrieb *m*; **2.** *vt* GEN COMM antreiben, vorantreiben; ◆ **~ a hard bargain** GEN COMM hart verhandeln; **driven by** GEN COMM *certain factor* angetrieben von

drive down *vt* ECON *prices* drücken

drive out *vt* GEN COMM verdrängen

Drive: **~ Other Car insurance** *n AmE* (*DOC*) INS Fahrerhaftpflichtversicherung *f*

driver *n* COMP *software, hardware* Treiber *m*, HRM Fahrer, in *m,f*; **~'s cab** *n* TRANSP Fahrerhaus *nt*; **~'s licence** *BrE*, **~'s license** *AmE* *n* TRANSP Führerschein *m*

Driver: **~ and Vehicle Licensing Centre** *n BrE* (*DVLC*) TRANSP britisches Amt für Führerschein- und Kraftfahrzeugzulassungen

drive: **~ time** *n* S&M Dauer *f* eines Werbefeldzugs

driving: **~ force** *n* GEN COMM Antriebskraft *f*; **~ licence** *BrE*, **~ license** *AmE* *n* TRANSP Führerschein *m*

drop 1. *n* GEN COMM *in spending* Rückgang *m*, *rate* Abfall *m*; **2.** *vt* ECON, STOCK *prices* stürzen; **3.** *vi* ECON *rate* abfallen, stürzen, GEN COMM fallen, STOCK *rate* abfallen, stürzen

drop out *vi* GEN COMM aussteigen

drop: **~ in earnings** *n* FIN Ertragsrückgang *m*; **~ in orders** *n* ECON Auftragsrückgang *m*; **~-lock stock** *n* STOCK variabel verzinsliche Aktie *f*; **~-off charge** *n* TRANSP Löschgebühr *f*; **~-out** *n* COMP Signalausfall *m*

droppages: **~, cancellations, and prepayments** *n pl* (*DCP*) FIN Rückgänge *m pl*, Kündigungen *f pl* und Vorauszahlungen *f pl*

drop: **~ shipping** *n AmE* S&M *merchandising* Direktverkauf durch Grossisten *m*

drought *n* ENVIR Dürre *f*, Trockenheit *f*

drug *n* GEN COMM Arzneimittel *nt*, Droge *f*; **~ economy** *n* ECON Drogenwirtschaft *f*; **~ trade** *n* GEN COMM

Arzneimittelhandel *m*; ~ **trafficking** *n* GEN COMM, IMP/ EXP Drogenhandel *m*, Rauschgifthandel *m*

drum *n* COMP Druckwalze *f*, IND Tonne *f*, Trommel *f*, Walze *f*, Zylinder *m*

drummer *n* AmE infrml HRM Reisende(r) *mf* [decl. as adj], Vertreter, in *m,f*, S&M Reisende(r) *mf* [decl. as adj]

drum: ~ **plotter** *n* COMP Trommelplotter *m*; ~ **printer** *n* COMP Trommeldrucker *m*

DRY *abbr* (*direct real income*) ECON reales verfügbares Einkommen *nt*

dry: ~ **battery** *n* IND *shipping* Trockenbatterie *f*; ~ **bulk cargo** *n* TRANSP Trockenmassengutladung *f*; ~ **cargo** *n* TRANSP Trockenfracht *f*, Trockenladung *f*; ~ **dock** *n* TRANSP Trockendock *nt*; ~ **freight** *n* TRANSP Trockenfracht *f*; ~ **goods** *n pl* S&M Textilwaren *f pl*; ~ **measure** *n* GEN COMM Trockenmaß *nt*; ~ **run** *n* GEN COMM Probelauf *m*; ~ **weight** *n* TRANSP Trockengewicht *nt*

DSC *abbr* (*digital selective calling*) COMMS digitaler Selektivruf *m*

DSD *abbr* (*Diplomatic Service Department*) POL Abteilung für den diplomatischen Dienst

DSS *abbr* MGMNT (*decision support system*) Entscheidungsfindungssystem *nt*, Entscheidungsunterstützungssystem *nt*, POL, WEL (*Department of Social Security*) Sozialministerium

DTC *abbr* AmE (*Depository Trust Company*) STOCK Depot-Treuhandgesellschaft *f*

DTE *abbr* (*data terminal equipment*) COMP *hardware* Datenendeinrichtung *f*

DTI *abbr* IND BrE (*Department of Trade and Industry*) Handels- und Industrieministerium, IMP/EXP (*direct trader input*) direkter Handelsinput *m*, direkte Handelseingabe *f*, POL BrE (*Department of Trade and Industry*) Handels- und Industrieministerium

DTO *abbr* (*district training officer*) HRM Ausbildender mit besonderer Verantwortung für einen Bezirk

DTp *abbr* BrE (*Department of Transport*) POL, TRANSP Verkehrsministerium

DTP *abbr* (*desktop publishing*) COMP, MEDIA DTP (*Desktop-Publishing*)

dual: ~ **banking** *n* AmE BANK *chartered banks* duales Bankensystem *nt*; ~ **capacity** *n* STOCK *of stockbrokers as market makers and brokers* Doppelfunktion *f*, gleichzeitige Ausübung *f* von Marketmaker- und Brokerfunktionen; ~ **contract** *n* LAW zweiseitiger Vertrag *m*; ~ **decision hypothesis** *n* ECON Hypothese *f* der dualen Entscheidung; ~ **economy** *n* ECON duale Volkswirtschaft *f*; ~ **exchange rate** *n* ECON dualer Wechselkurs *m*; ~ **federalism** *n* POL dualer Föderalismus *m*, gleichrangiger Föderalismus *m*; ~ **job holder** *n* HRM Doppelverdiener, in *m,f*; ~ **job holding** *n* HRM Doppelverdienen *nt*; ~ **labor market** *AmE*, ~ **labour market** *BrE n* ECON zweiter Arbeitsmarkt *m*, dualer Arbeitsmarkt *m*; ~ **pitch** *n* ADMIN doppelte Typenbreite *f*; ~ **responsibility** *n* HRM zweifache Verantwortung *f*; ~ **sourcing** *n* GEN COMM Doppelakquisition *f*; ~ **status** *n* GEN COMM Doppelstatus *m*

dub *vt* S&M synchronisieren

dubbing *n* S&M Synchronisation *f*, Synchronisierung *f*

dubious *adj* GEN COMM fragwürdig, unreell, unseriös

dud: ~ **check** *AmE*, ~ **cheque** *BrE n* infrml BANK ungedeckter Scheck *m*, fauler Scheck *m* (*infrml*)

due *adj* BANK verfallen, FIN *bill, debt* unbeglichen, GEN COMM *bill, debt* fällig, unbeglichen, zahlbar; ♦ **when** ~ FIN, STOCK bei Fälligkeit; **at** ~ **date** GEN COMM zum Fälligkeitstermin; ~ **and payable** *adj* GEN COMM fällig, zahlbar

due: ~ **bill** *n* AmE BANK, GEN COMM Schuldanerkenntnis *f*, FIN fälliger Wechsel *m*, Schuldanerkenntnis *f*; ~ **capital** *n* FIN fälliges Kapital *nt*; ~ **date** *n* ACC Fälligkeitstag *m*, ADMIN Fälligkeitstermin *m*, BANK Verfallsdatum *nt*, FIN Fälligkeit *f*, GEN COMM Abgabefrist *f*, Fälligkeitsdatum *nt*, LAW *contracts* Fälligkeitszeitpunkt *m*; ~ **date of premium** *n* INS Fälligkeit *f* der Prämie; ~ **date of renewal** *n* INS Fälligkeit *f* der Verlängerung; ~ **diligence** *n* FIN gebührende Sorgfalt *f*, LAW verkehrsübliche Sorgfalt *f*

dumb: ~ **terminal** *n* COMP nichtprogrammierbare Datenstation *f*, unintelligente Datenstation *f*

dummy *n* LAW Strohmann *m*; ~ **activity** *n* GEN COMM Scheinvorgang *m*; ~ **corporation** *n* LAW *trade law* Scheingesellschaft *f*; ~ **variable** *n* ECON *econometrics* Scheinvariable *f*

dump 1. *n* COMP *data transfer* Speicherauszug *m*; 2. *vt* COMP *data* ausgeben, ENVIR *waste* abkippen, *waste at sea* verklappen

dumping *n* ENVIR *of waste* Ablagerung *f*, Lagerung *f*, *waste at sea* Verklappung *f*, GEN COMM Dumping *nt*, S&M Verkauf *m* zu Schleuderpreisen, STOCK Abstoßen *nt*, Dumping *nt*, Preisunterbietung *f*; ~ **ground** *n* ENVIR Deponie *f*, Müllablageplatz *m*, GEN COMM Müllablageplatz *m*; ~ **standards** *n pl* ENVIR Verklappungsstandards *m pl*

dun *vt* GEN COMM mahnen

Dun's: ~ **Market Identifier** *n* FIN Gläubigernummer *f*, Marktinformationsdienst *m* für Gläubiger

duopoly *n* ECON Duopol *nt*

DUP *abbr* (*directly unproductive profit-seeking activities*) ECON direkt unproduktiv auf Gewinn gerichtete Aktivitäten *f pl*

duplex 1. *adj* COMP beidseitig; 2. *n* COMP Duplex *nt*, PROP Doppelhaushälfte *f*

duplex: ~ **computer** *n* COMP Duplexsystem *nt*; ~ **operation** *n* COMP Duplexbetrieb *m*; ~ **printing** *n* COMP beidseitiges Drucken *nt*

duplicate *vt* COMP duplizieren, GEN COMM vervielfachen

duplicated: ~ **record** *n* COMP doppelter Satz *m*

duplication *n* GEN COMM Verdoppelung *f*, Vervielfältigung *f*; ~ **of benefits** *n* INS Doppelzahlung *f* der Versicherungsleistungen

duplicatory *adj* GEN COMM duplikatorisch

Du Pont: ~ **formula** *n* FIN Du-Pont-Formel *f*

durable *adj* GEN COMM dauerhaft, langlebig

durables *n pl* S&M langlebige Gebrauchsgüter *nt pl*

duration *n* FIN durchschnittliche Bindungsdauer *f*, GEN COMM Dauer *f*; ♦ **for the** ~ **of** GEN COMM für die Dauer von

duration: ~ **analysis** *n* FIN Durationsanalyse *f*; ~ **of benefits** *n* INS Dauer *f* der Versicherungsleistungen, Unterstützungszeitraum *m*, Zeitdauer *f* der Versicherungsleistungen, WEL Unterstützungszeitraum *m*; ~ **of contract** *n* LAW *contract law* Vertragsdauer *f*; ~ **of guaranty** *n* GEN COMM Garantiedauer *f*

Durbin-Watson: ~ **statistic** *n* (*DW statistic*) MATH Durbin-Watson-Statistik *f*

duress *n* ECON Zwang *m*, LAW Leistungsverweigerungsrecht *nt*, Nötigung *f*

dust: ~ **cover** *n* COMP Staubschutzhaube *f*

Dutch: ~ **auction** *n* S&M Versteigerung mit laufend erniedrigtem Ausbietungspreis

dutiable *adj* IMP/EXP, TAX abgabenpflichtig, zollpflichtig; ~ **cargo** *n* IMP/EXP, TAX zollpflichtige Fracht *f*, zollpflichtige Ladung *f*; ~ **cargo list** *n* IMP/EXP, TAX Verzeichnis *nt* der zollpflichtigen Ladung; ~ **goods** *n pl* IMP/EXP, TAX abgabenpflichtige Waren *f pl*

duties: ~ **under the employment contract** *n pl* HRM Pflichten *f pl* im Rahmen des Arbeitsvertrags

duty *n* GEN COMM Dienst *m*, Zoll *m*, HRM Aufgabe *f*, LAW Pflicht *f*, TAX indirekte Steuer *f*, Steuer *f*, Zoll *m*; ♦ **on ~** GEN COMM diensttuend, diensthabend

duty: ~ **to assist** *n* LAW, TAX Beistandspflicht *f*; ~ **of assured clause** *n* INS Leistungspflicht *f* der versicherten Klausel; ~ **deposit account** *n* (*DDA*) IMP/EXP Zolldepositenkonto *nt*; ~ **to disclose information** *n* GEN COMM Auskunftspflicht *f*; ~-**free** *adj* IMP/EXP, TAX *goods* nicht zollpflichtig, zollfrei; ~-**free allowance** *n* IMP/EXP, TAX Freigrenze *f*, Zollfreibetrag *m*; ~-**free goods** *n pl* IMP/EXP, TAX zollfreie Waren *f pl*; ~-**free shop** *n* IMP/EXP, TAX Geschäft für zollfreie Waren *nt*, Zollfreiladen *m*, LEIS Duty-Free-Laden *m*, Duty-Free-Shop *m*, Geschäft für zollfreie Waren *nt*, Laden für zollfreie Waren *m*; ~ **officer** *n* (*DO*) HRM Offizier vom Dienst *m*; ~ **rota** *n* GEN COMM Dienstplan *m*; ~ **station** *n* GEN COMM Arbeitsplatz *m*, HRM Dienstort *m*; ~ **suspension** *n* IMP/EXP, TAX Zollaussetzung *f*; ~ **unpaid** *adj* IMP/EXP, TAX unverzollt; ~ **to warn** *n* LAW *imposed on producer* Aufklärungspflicht *f*

DVLC *abbr* BrE (*Driver and Vehicle Licensing Centre*) TRANSP britisches Amt für Führerscheinerteilung und Kraftfahrzeugzulassungen

dw *abbr* (*deadweight*) TRANSP Deadweight *nt*, Ladefähigkeit *f*

D/W *abbr* (*dock warrant*) IMP/EXP, TRANSP Dockempfangsschein *m*, Docklagerschein *m*

dwat *abbr* (*deadweight all told*) TRANSP Gesamtdeadweight *nt*, Gesamttragfähigkeit *f*

dwc *abbr* (*deadweight capacity*) TRANSP Ladefähigkeit *f*, Tragfähigkeit *f*

dwcc *abbr* (*deadweight cargo capacity*) TRANSP Tragfähigkeit *f*

dwelling *n* PROP Wohnhaus *nt*

dwindle *vi* GEN COMM *demand* abnehmen

DW: ~ **statistic** *n* (*Durbin-Watson statistic*) MATH *statistics* Durbin-Watson-Statistik *f*

dwt *abbr* (*deadweight tonnage*) TRANSP Gesamtzuladungsgewicht *nt*, Ladefähigkeit *f*, Tragfähigkeit *f*

dye *vt* IND färben

dyed: ~-**in-the-wool democrat** *n* BrE (*cf yellow-dog democrat AmE*) POL eingefleischter Demokrat *m*

dynamic *adj* GEN COMM *growth, personality* dynamisch

dynamically: ~ **inconsistent policy** *n* POL dynamisch unvereinbare Politik *f*

dynamic: ~ **analysis** *n* ECON dynamische Analyse *f*; ~ **data exchange** *n* (*DDE*) COMP dynamischer Datenaustausch *m*; ~ **evaluation** *n* GEN COMM dynamische Bewertung *f*; ~ **hedging** *n* FIN dynamisches Absichern *nt*, dynamische Absicherung *f*; ~ **management model** *n* MGMNT dynamisches Managementmodell *nt*; ~ **obsolescence** *n* S&M dynamische Veralterung *f*; ~ **positioning** *n* (*DP*) GEN COMM, S&M dynamische Positionierung *f*; ~ **programming** *n* COMP, MATH dynamische Programmierung *f*, dynamisches Programmieren *nt*, GEN COMM dynamische Planung *f*; ~ **random access memory** *n* (*DRAM*) COMP *hardware* dynamischer Speicher *m* (*DRAM*)

dynamism *n* GEN COMM Dynamik *f*

dysfunctional *adj* MGMNT funktionsgestört

E

EA *abbr BrE* (*Employment Act*) HRM Gesetzgebung zur Einschränkung der Macht der britischen Gewerkschaften

EAAA *abbr* (*European Association of Advertising Agencies*) S&M Europäischer Verband *m* der Werbeagenturen

EAEC *abbr* (*European Atomic Energy Community*) IND Europäische Atomgemeinschaft *f* (*EAG, EURATOM*)

eager: ~ **beaver** *n infrml* HRM *person* Streber, in *m,f* (*infrml*); ~ **to buy** *adj* GEN COMM kauflustig

EAGGF *abbr* (*European Agricultural Guidance and Guarantee Fund*) BANK EAGFL (*Europäischer Ausrichtungs- und Garantiefonds für die Landwirtschaft*)

eagle *n AmE* GEN COMM Zehn-Dollar-Schein

EAL *abbr* (*export adjustment loan*) FIN Ausfuhranpassungskredit *m*, Exportangleichungskredit *m*

EAN *abbr* (*European Article Number*) COMP, S&M EAN (*Europäische Artikelnummer*)

E&OE *abbr* (*errors and omissions excepted*) GEN COMM I. v. (*Irrtum vorbehalten*)

earlier: ~ **application** *n* PATENTS frühere Anmeldung *f*; ~ **priority** *n* PATENTS frühere Priorität *f*

early: ~ **adopter** *n* S&M *marketing* Person, die ein Produkt früh annimmt; ~ **edition** *n* MEDIA Frühausgabe *f* einer Zeitung; ~ **exercise** *n* STOCK *options* vorzeitige Ausübung *f* eines Rechtes; ~ **fringe** *n* MEDIA *broadcast* Abendsendezeit *f*, Spätnachmittagssendezeit *f*; ~ **majority** *n jarg* S&M *marketing* frühe Mehrheit *f*; ~ **publication** *n* MEDIA frühe Veröffentlichung *f*, frühzeitige Veröffentlichung *f*; ~ **retirement** *n* GEN COMM, HRM Vorruhestand *m*; ~~**retirement annuity** *n* FIN Vorruhestandsrente *f*; ~~**retirement benefit** *n* FIN Pensionsplanüberbrückung *f*, Vorruhestandsrente *f*, vorzeitige Rente *f*, HRM Frührente *f*; ~~**retirement scheme** *n* HRM Vorruhestandsregelung *f*; ~~**settlement rebate** *n* FIN *consumer credit* Nachlaß *m* für frühzeitige Begleichung, Nachlaß *m* für frühzeitige Erfüllung einer Forderung; ~~**withdrawal penalty** *n* FIN, STOCK Negativzins *m* bei vorzeitiger Verfügung über Kündigungsgelder, Vorschußzinsen *m pl*

earmark *vt* ECON *finance* vorsehen, reservieren, bereitstellen, bestimmen, *funds, resources* kennzeichnen, GEN COMM an einen bestimmten Zweck binden

earmarked *adj* LEIS reserviert, zweckgebunden; ~ **check** *AmE*, ~ **cheque** *BrE n* BANK zweckgebundener Scheck *m*; ~ **funds** *n pl* FIN zweckgebundene Mittel *nt pl*; ~ **gold** *n* ECON im Depot gehaltenes Gold *nt* für Rechnung

earmarking *n* ECON *allocation of public funds* Reservieren *nt*, Zweckbindung *f*, FIN Bereitstellung *f*

earn *vt* ADMIN ertragen, BANK bringen, ECON einbringen, FIN *interest* bringen, *reputation* erwerben, GEN COMM *reputation* erwerben, HRM verdienen; ◆ ~ **a fast buck** *infrml* GEN COMM die schnelle Mark machen (*infrml*); ~ **a living** ECON seinen Lebensunterhalt verdienen; ~ **a salary of £20,000** HRM ein Jahresgehalt in Höhe von £ 20.000 beziehen; ~ **one's keep** GEN COMM seinen Lebensunterhalt verdienen

earned: ~ **income** *n* ADMIN Erwerbseinkommen *nt*; ~ **income allowance** *n* HRM Freibetrag *m* für Einkünfte aus selbständiger Tätigkeit; ~ **income before deductions** *n* HRM, TAX Bruttoarbeitseinkommen *nt*; ~ **interest** *n* ACC Zinseinkommen *nt*; ~ **premium** *n* INS verdiente Prämie *f*; ~ **surplus** *n* ACC, INS Rücklagen *f pl*

earnest: ~ **money** *n* PROP Anzahlung *f*, Draufgabe *f*, Bietungsgarantie *f*

earning: ~ **capacity** *n* GEN COMM Ertragskapazität *f*; ~ **performance** *n* GEN COMM Ertragsleistung *f*; ~ **power** *n* ACC *of a company*, GEN COMM Ertragskraft *f*, HRM Erwerbsfähigkeit *f*; ~ **reserves** *n pl* ACC Gewinnrücklagen *f pl*

earnings *n* ADMIN Ertrag *m*, Gewinn *m*, FIN Einkünfte *pl*, Gewinn *m*, Liquidität *f*, GEN COMM Einkünfte *pl*, HRM Arbeitseinkommen *nt*, Verdienst *m*, TAX Einkommen *nt*; ~ **base** *n* FIN Ertragsbasis *f*; ~ **ceiling** *n* HRM Einkommensmaximum *nt*; ~ **differential** *n* HRM Einkommensgefälle *nt*; ~ **drift** *n* HRM Lohndrift *f*; ~ **forecast** *n* FIN Gewinnprognose *f*, HRM Verdienstvorhersage *f*, GEN COMM Gewinnentwicklung *f*; ~ **performance** *n* ACC, FIN, GEN COMM Gewinnentwicklung *f*; ~ **performance of a stock** *n* FIN Gewinnentwicklung *f* einer Aktie; ~ **per share** *n* (*EPS*) ACC, FIN Gewinn *m* je Aktie; ~ **position** *n* FIN Ertragslage *f*; ~ **ratio** *n* ADMIN, GEN COMM Gewinnkennziffer *f*, STOCK Gewinnkennzahl *f* einer Unternehmung; ~ **report** *n* FIN Gewinn- und Verlustrechnung *f*

earning: ~ **streams** *n pl* FIN Gewinnströme *m pl*

earnings: ~ **yield** *n* FIN Gewinnrendite *f*, STOCK Gewinn *m* je Stammaktie nach Steuern zu Kurs der Stammaktie, Gewinnrendite *f*

earphone *n* MEDIA Kopfhörer *m*

earthing *n BrE* (*cf grounding AmE*) COMP, IND *electricity* Erdung *f*

earthquake: ~ **insurance** *n* INS Erdbebenversicherung *f*

earthworks *n pl* PROP Erdarbeiten *f pl*

ease *vt* ECON *credit controls* erleichtern, *economic policy* lockern

ease off *vi* ECON abflauen, *demand* leicht nachgeben

ease: ~ **of handling** *n* TRANSP leichterer Umschlag *m*, Umschlagserleichterung *f*

easement *n* PROP Grunddienstbarkeit *f*

EASI *abbr* (*European Association for Shipping Informatics*) GEN COMM Europäische Vereinigung *f* für Schiffahrtsinformatik

easily *adv* GEN COMM leicht

easing *n* ECON *of economic policy* Erleichterung *f*, Lokkerung *f*

eastern *adj* GEN COMM östlich

Eastern: ~ **Bloc** *n* POL Ostblock *m*; ~ **Europe** *n* POL Osteuropa *nt*; ~ **European Time** *n* (*EET*) GEN COMM Osteuropäische Zeit *f* (*OEZ*); ~ **Standard Time** *n AmE* (*EST*) GEN COMM Ostküstenzeit *f*, östliche Standardzeit *f*

East: ~ **European Trade Council** *n* GEN COMM East European Trade Council *m*

easy *adj* GEN COMM leicht; ◆ **with ~ access to public transport** GEN COMM verkehrsgünstig

easy: **~ money** *n* ECON leichtes Geld *nt*, leichtverdientes Geld *nt*; **~ money policy** *n* ECON Niedrigzinspolitik *f*, Politik *f* des leichten Geldes; **~ option** *n* MGMNT leichte Wahl *f*; **~ rider** *n* ECON Free-rider-Verhalten *nt*; **~ terms of payments** *n pl* BANK Zahlungserleichterungen *f pl*; **~ to use** *adj* COMP anwenderfreundlich, benutzerfreundlich

EAT *abbr* BrE (*Employment Appeal Tribunal*) HRM Berufungsgericht *nt* für Beschäftigungskonflikte

EBRD *abbr* (*European Bank for Reconstruction and Development*) ECON *development* EBWE (*Europäische Bank für Wiederaufbau und Entwicklung*), Osteuropabank *f*

EC *abbr* (*European Community*) POL EG (*Europäische Gemeinschaft*), (*European Commission*) POL *EU* EuK (*Europäische Kommission*)

ECB *abbr* (*European Central Bank*) ECON EZB (*Europäische Zentralbank*)

ECDC *abbr* (*economic cooperation among developing countries*) ECON ECDC (*Wirtschaftliche Zusammenarbeit zwischen den Entwicklungsländern*)

ECE *abbr* (*Economic Commission for Europe*) ECON *UN* ECE (*Europäische Wirtschaftskommission*)

ECG *abbr* (*European Cooperation Grouping*) LAW EKV (*Europäische Kooperationsvereinigung*)

ECGD *abbr* BrE (*Export Credit Guarantees Department*) IMP/EXP Ausfuhrkreditversicherungsanstalt *f*

echelon *n* HRM Rang *m*

ECJ *abbr* (*European Court of Justice*) LAW EuGH (*obs*) (*Europäischer Gerichtshof*), Gerichtshof *m* der Europäischen Union

Eclectic: **~ Keynesians** *n pl* ECON neue keynesianische Makroökonomen *m pl*

ECNR *abbr* (*European Council for Nuclear Research*) IND Europäischer Kernforschungsrat *m*

eco- *pref* GEN COMM, ENVIR Öko-

ecolabeling *AmE see* ecolabelling *BrE*

ecolabelling *n* *BrE* ENVIR Ökoetikettierung *f*, Ökokennzeichnung *f*

ecological *adj* ENVIR, GEN COMM ökologisch; **~ character** *n* ENVIR *of products for sale* ökologisches Merkmal *nt*; **~ indicator** *n* ENVIR ökologischer Indikator *m*

ecology *n* ENVIR, GEN COMM Ökologie *f*

econometric *adj* ECON ökonometrisch

econometrician *n* ECON Ökonometriker, in *m,f*

econometrics *n* ECON Ökonometrie *f*

economic *adj* ADMIN, BANK, ECON, FIN, GEN COMM ökonomisch, volkswirtschaftlich, wirtschaftlich, POL volkswirtschaftlich; **~ activity** *n* ECON ökonomische Aktivität *f*, Wirtschaftsaktivität *f*, GEN COMM Konjunktur *f*; **~ advancement** *n* GEN COMM wirtschaftlicher Fortschritt *m*; **~ adviser** *n* ADMIN, BANK, ECON, FIN, POL Wirtschaftsberater, in *m,f*; **~ agent** *n* ECON Geschäftsführer, in *m,f*; **~ aid** *n* ECON Entwicklungshilfe *f*

economical *adj* ADMIN, BANK, ECON, FIN ökonomisch, GEN COMM sparsam, ökonomisch

economically *adv* ADMIN, BANK, ECON wirtschaftlich, FIN, GEN COMM *sparingly* sparsam, ökonomisch, volkswirtschaftlich, POL volkswirtschaftlich; **~ backward**

area *n* ECON wirtschaftlich rückständiges Gebiet *nt*; **~-used animal** *n* ENVIR, GEN COMM Nutztier *nt*; **~-used plant** *n* ENVIR, GEN COMM Nutzpflanze *f*

economical: **~ use of resources** *n* ENVIR rationelle Nutzung *f* von Ressourcen, wirtschaftlicher Ressourceneinsatz *m*

economic: **~ analysis** *n* ECON Wirtschaftsanalyse *f*; **~ area** *n* ECON Wirtschaftsgebiet *nt*; **~ austerity** *n* ECON Ausgabenbeschränkung *f*, Sparprogramm *nt* der öffentlichen Hand; **~ base** *n* ECON Exportbasis *f*; **~ batch quantity** *n* ECON, IND, MGMNT rationelle Stückzahl *f*, optimale Losgröße *f*, wirtschaftliche Losgröße *f*; **~ batch size** *n* ECON, IND, MGMNT Losgröße *f*, optimale Losgröße *f*, rationelle Stückzahl *f*, wirtschaftliche Losgröße *f*; **~ benefit** *n* ECON wirtschaftlicher Nutzen *m*; **~ boom** *n* ECON Konjunkturaufschwung *m*; **~ climate** *n* ECON, GEN COMM Konjunkturklima *nt*, wirtschaftliches Klima *nt*, Wirtschaftsklima *nt*

Economic: **~ Commission for Europe** *n* (*ECE*) ECON *UN* Europäische Wirtschaftskommission *f* (*ECE*)

economic: **~ conditions** *n* ECON Konjunkturlage *f*, Wirtschaftslage *f*, FIN Wirtschaftslage *f*; **~ cooperation among developing countries** *n* (*ECDC*) ECON Wirtschaftliche Zusammenarbeit *f* zwischen den Entwicklungsländern; **~ crime** *n* ECON Wirtschaftskriminalität *f*, Wirtschaftsverbrechen *nt*; **~ criteria** *n pl* ECON wirtschaftliche Kriterien *nt pl*; **~ cycle** *n* ECON Konjunkturzyklus *m*; **~ data** *n pl* ECON Wirtschaftsdaten *pl*; **~ democracy** *n* ECON, GEN COMM, HRM *workers' participation* mitbestimmte Wirtschaft *f*, Wirtschaftsdemokratie *f*; **~ development** *n* ECON Konjunkturentwicklung *f*, wirtschaftliche Entwicklung *f*

Economic: **~ Development Committee** *n* (*EDC*) ECON Ausschuß *m* für Wirtschaftsentwicklung

economic: **~ devolution** *n* POL wirtschaftliche Entwicklung *f*; **~ efficiency** *n* ECON, GEN COMM ökonomische Effizienz *f*, Wirtschaftlichkeit *f*; **~ expansion** *n* ECON, GEN COMM Wirtschaftsaufschwung *m*, wirtschaftliche Ausdehnung *f*; **~ forecasting** *n* ECON *econometrics* Konjunkturprognose *f*, Wirtschaftsprognose *f*; **~ freedom** *n* ECON, POL Gewerbefreiheit *f*; **~ geography** *n* ECON Wirtschaftsgeographie *f*; **~ good** *n* ECON Wirtschaftsgut *nt*, wirtschaftliches Gut *nt*; **~ growth** *n* ECON Wirtschaftswachstum *nt*; **~ growth rate** *n* ECON Wachstumsrate *f* der Volkswirtschaft; **~ incentive** *n* ECON wirtschaftlicher Anreiz *m*; **~ incidence** *n* TAX wirtschaftliche Inzidenz *f*; **~ indicator** *n* ECON Konjunkturbarometer *nt*, *econometrics* Konjunkturindikator *m*; **~ institution** *n* ECON volkswirtschaftliche Institution *f*; **~ integration** *n* ECON, POL wirtschaftliche Integration *f*; **~ intelligence** *n* ECON ökonomischer Sachverstand *m*; **~ law** *n* LAW Wirtschaftsrecht *nt*; **~ laws** *n pl* ECON Wirtschaftsgesetzgebung *f*; **~ life** *n* FIN, GEN COMM, S&M wirtschaftliche Lebensdauer *f*, wirtschaftliche Nutzungsdauer *f*; **~ loss** *n* INS Vermögenseinbuße *f*, Vermögensschaden *m*; **~ man** *n* ECON homo oeconomicus *m*; **~ manufacturing quantity** *n* ECON optimale Fertigungsmenge *f*, IND optimale Fertigungsmenge *f*, ökonomische Herstellungsgröße *f*, wirtschaftliche Losgröße *f*, MGMNT optimale Fertigungsmenge *f*; **~ method** *n* ECON ökonomische Methode *f*; **~ methodology** *n* ECON ökonomische Methodologie *f*; **~ mission** *n* ECON wirtschaftlicher Auftrag *m*, MGMNT Wirtschaftsmission *f*; ~ **model** *n* ECON ökonomisches Modell *nt*, Wirtschaftsmodell *nt*

Economic: ~ **and Monetary Union** *n* (*EMU*) ECON Wirtschafts- und Währungsunion *f*

economic: ~ **news** *n* ECON, MEDIA Nachrichten *f pl* aus der Wirtschaft, Wirtschaftsnachrichten *f pl*; ~ **obsolescence** *n* ECON wirtschaftliches Veralten *nt*; ~ **order quantity** *n* (*EOQ*) ECON, IND optimale Bestellmenge *f*, wirtschaftliche Losgröße *f*; ~ **outlook** *n* ECON Konjunkturaussichten *f pl*; ~ **paradigm** *n* ECON wirtschaftliches Paradigma *nt*; ~ **planning** *n* ECON, ENVIR, GEN COMM, MGMNT, POL Wirtschaftsplanung *f*; ~ **planning unit** *n* ECON Wirtschaftsplanungsabteilung *f*; ~ **policy** *n* ECON, POL Wirtschaftspolitik *f*; ~ **position** *n* ECON wirtschaftliche Stellung *f*; ~ **price** *n* S&M wirtschaftlicher Preis *m*; ~ **programming** *n* ECON ökonomische Programmierung *f*; ~ **progress** *n* ECON wirtschaftlicher Fortschritt *m*; ~ **prospects** *n pl* ECON Konjunkturaussichten *f pl*, Wirtschaftsaussichten *f pl*; ~ **recovery loan** *n* (*ERL*) FIN Aufbauanleihe *f*; ~ **reform** *n* ECON, POL Wirtschaftsreform *f*; ~ **rent** *n* ECON Rente *f*; ~ **report** *n* ECON Konjunkturbericht *m*, Wirtschaftsbericht *m*; ~ **research** *n* ECON, S&M Wirtschaftsforschung *f*; ~ **resources** *n pl* ECON ökonomische Ressourcen *f pl*

economics *n* ECON Ökonomie *f*, *of country* Volkswirtschaftslehre *f*, Wirtschaftswissenschaft *f*, Nationalökonomie *f*

economic: ~ **sanctions** *n pl* POL Wirtschaftssanktionen *f pl*

economics: ~ **as rhetoric** *n* ECON *subject* Wirtschaftswissenschaft *f* als Rhetorik; ~ **of crime** *n* ECON Ökonomie *f* der Kriminalität

economic: ~ **section** *n* MEDIA *of newspaper* Wirtschaftsteil *m*

economics: ~ **of education** *n* ECON Bildungsökonomie *f*

economic: ~ **situation** *n* ECON Konjunkturlage *f*, Wirtschaftslage *f*, wirtschaftspolitische Lage *f*

economics: ~ **of law** *n* ECON ökonomische Analyse *f* des Rechts; ~ **of location** *n* ECON Standorttheorie *f*

economic: ~ **slowdown** *n* ECON Konjunkturabschwächung *f*, konjunkturelle Abkühlung *f*

Economic: ~ **and Social Committee** *n* (*ESC*) ECON Wirtschafts- und Sozialausschuß *m*; ~ **and Social Council** *n* (*ECOSOC*) ECON Wirtschafts- und Sozialrat *m* (*WSR*)

economics: ~ **and psychology** *n* ECON Wirtschaftspsychologie *f*

economic: ~ **strategy** *n* ECON langfristige Wirtschaftspolitik *f*; ~ **summit** *n* ECON, POL Wirtschaftsgipfel *m*; ~ **system** *n* ECON, POL Wirtschaftssystem *nt*; ~ **tailspin** *n* ECON Talsohle *f*; ~ **theory** *n* ECON volkswirtschaftliche Theorie *f*; ~ **theory of clubs** *n* ECON ökonomische Theorie *f* der Clubs; ~ **trend** *n* ECON Konjunkturentwicklung *f*, Konjunkturtrend *m*, Konjunkturverlauf *m*, GEN COMM Geschäftstrend *m*

Economic: ~ **Trends Annual Survey** *n* BrE (*ETAS*) ECON *econometrics* jährliche Konjunkturumfrage *f*

economic: ~ **union** *n* ECON, FIN, POL Wirtschaftsunion *f*; ~ **upheavals** *n pl* ECON, GEN COMM, POL wirtschaftliche Erschütterungen *f pl*; ~ **upswing** *n* ECON Konjunkturaufschwung *m*; ~ **value** *n* ACC wirtschaftliches Wohl *nt*, ECON wirtschaftlicher Wert *m*;

~ **viability** *n* ECON Rentabilität *f*, Eigenwirtschaftlichkeit *f*; ~ **weather** *n* ECON wirtschaftliches Klima *nt*; ~ **welfare** *n* WEL wirtschaftliches Wohl *nt*; ~ **wellbeing** *n* ECON, POL materielle Lebenslage *f*

economies *n pl* ADMIN Einsparungen *f pl*; ~ **of scope** *n* ECON Verbundvorteile *m pl*

economism *n* ECON Ökonomismus *m*

economist *n* ECON Ökonom, in *m,f*, Volkswirt, in *m,f*, Wirtschaftswissenschaftler, in *m,f*

economy *n* ADMIN, ECON *of area, country of country* Volkswirtschaft *f*, *thrift of country* Wirtschaftlichkeit *f*, Wirtschaft *f*, Sparsamkeit *f*, GEN COMM Konjunktur *f*; ~ **of abundance** *n* ECON Überflußwirtschaft *f*; ~ **calculation** *n* ECON Wirtschaftlichkeitsrechnung *f*; ~ **class** *n* LEIS, TRANSP Touristenklasse *f*; ~ **measure** *n* ADMIN Sparmaßnahme *f*; ~ **pack** *n* GEN COMM, S&M Sparpackung *f*; ~ **of scale** *n* ECON Degressionsgewinn *m*, Diversifikationsvorteil *m*, Kostendegression *f*, Skalenerträge *m pl*; ~ **of size** *n* ECON Größenvorteil *m*; ~-**sized packet** *n* GEN COMM, S&M Großpackung *f*, Sparpackung *f*; ~ **ticket** *n* LEIS, TRANSP Touristenticket *nt, rate, tariff* Spartarif *m*

ECOSOC *abbr* (*Economic and Social Council*) ECON WSR (*Wirtschafts- und Sozialrat*)

ecosystem *n* ENVIR Ökosystem *nt*

ecotoxicological *adj* ENVIR ökotoxikologisch

ECPD *abbr* (*export cargo packing declaration*) IMP/EXP Exportversandliste *f*

ECPS *abbr* (*Environment and Consumer Protection Service*) ENVIR Umwelt- und Verbraucherschutzdienst *m*

ECSC *abbr* (*European Coal and Steel Community*) ECON EGKS (*Europäische Gemeinschaft für Kohle und Stahl*), Montanunion *f*

ECSI *abbr* (*export cargo shipping instruction*) IMP/EXP Exportversandanweisung *f*

EC: ~ **transit form** *n* TRANSP EG-Transitformular *nt*

ECU *abbr* (*European Currency Unit*) ECON, FIN ECU *f* (*Europäische Währungseinheit*)

ECU: ~ **central rate** *n* FIN ECU-Leitkurs *m*

ed. *abbr* (*edition*) COMP, GEN COMM, MEDIA Ausg. (*Ausgabe*)

ED *abbr obs* (*Employment Department*) POL Arbeitsministerium

EDC *abbr* (*Economic Development Committee*) ECON Ausschuß *m* für Wirtschaftsentwicklung

EDF *abbr* (*European Development Fund*) ECON EEF (*Europäischer Entwicklungsfonds*)

edge *n* GEN COMM Vorsprung *m*, Vorteil *m*; ◆ **have the ~ over sb** GEN COMM jdm überlegen sein

edge up *vi* ECON langsam anziehen

Edge: ~ **Act corporation** *n* AmE ECON Finanzinstitut, über das nur Auslandsoperationen getätigt werden

Edgeworth: ~ **Box** *n* ECON *theory* Edgeworth-Box *f*

EDI *abbr* (*electronic data interchange*) COMMS, COMP EDI (*elektronischer Datenaustausch*)

edict *n* LAW Verordnung *f*

edit *vt* COMP aufbereiten, *data, document* bearbeiten, editieren, MEDIA redigieren; ~ **out** *vt* MEDIA herausnehmen, weglassen

editing *n* MEDIA Redaktion *f*

edition *n* (*ed.*) COMP, GEN COMM, MEDIA Ausgabe *f* (*Ausg.*)

edit: ~ **menu** *n* COMP Edit-Menu *nt*; ~ **mode** *n* COMP Editiermodus *m*

editor *n* COMP *software* Editor *m*, MEDIA Herausgeber, in *m,f*, Redakteur, in *m,f*

editorial *n* GEN COMM, MEDIA Leitartikel *m*; ~ **advertisement** *n* MEDIA, S&M redaktionell aufgemachte Anzeige *f*; ~ **advertising** *n* MEDIA Redaktionswerbung *f*; ~ **column** *n* MEDIA Leitartikel *m*; ~ **matter** *n* S&M redaktioneller Text *m*; ~ **publicity** *n* S&M redaktionell aufgemachte Werbung *f*; ~ **staff** *n* MEDIA Redaktionsteam *nt*

editorship *n* MEDIA Chefredaktion *f*, Schriftleitung *f*

EDP *abbr* (*electronic data processing*) COMP EDV (*elektronische Datenverarbeitung*)

educate *vt* HRM erziehen

educated *adj* HRM ausgebildet, *general knowledge* gebildet

education *n* HRM, WEL Ausbildung *f*, Bildung *f*, Erziehung *f*, *educational theory* Pädagogik *f*, Schulbildung *f*

educational: ~ **advertising** *n* S&M Aufklärungswerbung *f*, belehrende Werbung *f*; ~ **background** *n* WEL Ausbildung *f*, Bildungsweg *m*, Vorbildung *f*; ~ **development** *n* WEL Bildungsentwicklung *f*, Ausbildungsentwicklung *f*; ~ **endowment** *n* INS Ausbildungsbeihilfe *f*, Erziehungsrente *f*; ~ **establishment** *n* WEL Bildungsanstalt *f*, Lehranstalt *f*

Education: ~ **Projects Fund** *n* WEL Fonds für Bildungsprojekte

EEA *abbr* ECON (*exchange equalization account*) Währungsausgleichsfonds *m*, *obs* (*European Economic Area*) EWR (*obs*) (*Europäischer Wirtschaftsraum*)

EEB *abbr* (*European Environmental Bureau*) ENVIR EEB (*Europäisches Umweltbüro*)

EEC *abbr obs* (*European Economic Community*) ECON EWG (*Europäische Wirtschaftsgemeinschaft*) (*obs*)

EEIG *abbr* (*European Economic Interest Grouping*) ECON EWIV (*Europäische Wirtschaftliche Interessenvereinigung*)

EEOC *abbr AmE* (*Equal Employment Opportunity Commission*) HRM amerikanische Kommission für Chancengleichheit auf dem Arbeitsmarkt

EET *abbr* (*Eastern European Time*) GEN COMM OEZ (*Osteuropäische Zeit*)

EF *abbr* (*European Foundation*) GEN COMM Europäische Stiftung *f*

EFA *abbr* (*expected funds availability*) FIN kommissionierte Kapitalverfügbarkeit *f*

EFF *abbr* (*extended fund facility*) FIN erweiterte Fondsfazilität *f*, erweiterte Kreditfazilität *f*

effect 1. *n* GEN COMM Auswirkung *f*, Wirksamkeit *f*, Wirkung *f*; ♦ **come into** ~ LAW rechtswirksam werden; **with** ~ **from** (*wef*) GEN COMM mit Wirkung vom; **2.** *vt* GEN COMM *agreement* erzielen, *sale, purchase* tätigen, *settlement* durchführen; ♦ ~ **a compromise** GEN COMM einen Vergleich schließen

effective *adj* COMP tatsächlich, ECON effektiv, GEN COMM wirksam, effektiv; ~ **control** *n* FIN Effektivkontrolle *f*; ~ **cost** *n* ADMIN Ist-Kosten *pl*; ~ **date** *n* GEN COMM Stichtag *m*, LAW Datum *nt* des Inkrafttretens; ~ **debt** *n* BANK tatsächliche Schuld *f*; ~ **demand** *n* ECON effektive Nachfrage *f*; ~ **exchange rate** *n* ECON effektiver Wechselkurs *m*; ~ **funding rate** *n* STOCK *interest rate futures* Effektivfinanzierungsrate *f*; ~ **horsepower** *n*

(*ehp*) IND effektive Pferdestärke *f*; ~ **interest rate** *n* BANK Effektivzins *m*, effektiver Zins *m*; ~ **loan charges** *n* BANK effektive Kreditgebühr *f*

effectively *adv* GEN COMM effektiv; ~ **closed** *adj* TRANSP *packing term* effektiv geschlossen

effective: ~ **management** *n* MGMNT effektives Management *nt*

effectiveness *n* GEN COMM Wirksamkeit *f*

effective: ~ **rate** *n* ACC *interest* effektiver Zins *m*, BANK Effektivverzinsung *f*, Effektivzins *m*; ~ **rate of assistance** *n* (*ERA*) ECON effektive Hilfsrate *f*; ~ **rate of interest** *n* ECON effektiver Zinssatz *m*; ~ **rate of protection** *n* ECON effektive Protektionsrate *f*; ~ **tax rate** *n* TAX tatsächlicher Steuersatz *m*; ~ **yield** *n* BANK Effektivverzinsung *f*, Effektivzins *m*

effects: **no** ~ *phr* (*NE*) GEN COMM keine Deckung

effect: ~ **of taxation** *n* TAX Steuerwirkung *f*

effectual: ~ **demand** *n* ECON effektive Nachfrage *f*

efficiency *n* ECON *capacity* Leistungsfähigkeit *f*, *effectiveness* Leistungskraft *f*, Wirtschaftlichkeit *f*, GEN COMM *of machine, factory* Leistungsfähigkeit *f*, *of method* Fähigkeit *f*, Effizienz *f*, Wirksamkeit *f*, *of person* Tüchtigkeit *f*; ~ **agreement** *n* BrE HRM Produktivitätsabkommen *nt*; ~ **audit** *n* ACC Rentabilitätsprüfung *f*, Wirtschaftlichkeitsprüfung *f*; ~ **engineer** *n* MGMNT Rationalisierungsfachmann *m*; ~ **of labor** *AmE*, ~ **of labour** *BrE* *n* ECON Arbeitsproduktivität *f*; ~ **ratio** *n* ECON Arbeitsproduktivität *f*, ENVIR Wirkungsverhältnis *nt*; ~ **real wage** *n* ECON produktivitätsorientierter Reallohn *m*; ~ **variance** *n* FIN Leistungsabweichung *f*; ~ **wage** *n* ECON Leistungslohn *m*

efficient *adj* ADMIN, BANK, ECON, FIN *effective* effizient, wirtschaftlich, GEN COMM *person* fähig, effizient, *machine, factory* leistungsfähig, *method, system* rationell, wirtschaftlich; ~ **allocation** *n* ECON effiziente Allokation *f*, wirtschaftliche Zuteilung *f*; ~ **estimator** *n* ECON effiziente Schätzfunktion *f*; ~ **job mobility** *n* ECON effiziente Arbeitsmobilität *f*; ~ **market hypothesis** *n* ECON Hypothese *f* von der Kapitalmarkteffizienz; ~ **portfolio** *n* STOCK effizientes Portefeuille *nt*; ~ **range** *n* LAW *contracts* Wirkungserstreckung *f*

effluent *n* ENVIR Abfluß *m*, Abwasser *nt*, Ausfluß *m*; ~ **fee** *n* ECON Emissionsabgabe *f*

efflux *n* ENVIR Abfluß *m*, Ausfluß *m*

EFL *abbr* (*external financing limit*) FIN Auslandsfinanzierungsgrenze *f*, Fremdfinanzierungsgrenze *f*

EFT *abbr* (*electronic funds transfer*) ADMIN elektronischer Zahlungsverkehr *m*, belegloser Überweisungsverkehr *m*, belegloser Zahlungsverkehr *m*, BANK elektronischer Zahlungsverkehr *m*

EFTA *abbr* (*European Free Trade Association*) ECON EFTA (*Europäische Freihandelszone*)

EFTPOS *abbr* (*electronic funds transfer at point of sale*) BANK, COMP, S&M EFTPOS (*elektronische Geldüberweisung am Verkaufsort*)

EFTS *abbr* (*electronic funds transfer system*) BANK elektronisches Zahlungsverkehrssystem *nt*

e.g. *abbr* (*for example*) GEN COMM z.B. (*zum Beispiel*)

EGA *abbr* COMP (*enhanced graphics adapter*) EGA-Karte *f*, verbesserter Grafikadapter *m*, (*enhanced graphics array*) verbesserte Grafikanordnung *f*

egalitarianism *n* POL Egalitarismus *m*, Gleichmacherei *f* (*infrml*), Streben *nt* nach größtmöglicher Gleichheit aller Menschen

EGM *abbr* (*extraordinary general meeting*) MGMNT außerordentliche Hauptversammlung *f*, außerordentliche Vollversammlung *f*

ehp *abbr* (*effective horsepower*) IND effektive Pferdestärke *f*

EHS *abbr* (*extra high strength*) IND besonders große Stärke *f*

EI *abbr* (*employee involvement*) HRM, IND Arbeitspartizipation *f*

EIB *abbr* (*European Investment Bank*) BANK EIB (*Europäische Investitionsbank*)

EIC *abbr* GEN COMM (*Euro Info Centre*) EIC (*Euro Info Center*), EU-Beratungsstelle *f* für KMU, IND (*electrically insulated coating*) Elektroisolierüberzug *m*, Elektroisolieranstrich *m*, (*equipment installation and checkout*) Geräteeinbau *m* und -abnahme *f*

eigenprices *n pl* ECON Eigenpreise *m pl*

EIS *abbr* BrE (*export intelligence service*) IMP/EXP Ausfuhrnachrichtendienst *m*, Exportnachrichtendienst *m*

EITZ *abbr* (*English Inshore Traffic Zone*) GEN COMM englische Küstenverkehrszone *f*

eject *vt* COMP *card, disk* auswerfen, WEL *tenant* hinauswerfen

ejectment *n* LAW *property* Zwangsräumung *f*

ejusdem generis *phr* GEN COMM ähnlicher Art

elapsed: ~ **time** *n* COMP verstrichene Zeit *f*

elastic: ~ **demand** *n* ECON elastische Nachfrage *f*

elasticity *n* ECON Elastizität *f*; ~ **of anticipation** *n* ECON Erwartungselastizität *f*; ~ **coefficient** *n* ECON Elastizitätskoeffizient *m*; ~ **of demand** *n* ECON Elastizität *f* der Nachfrage, Nachfrageelastizität *f*; ~ **of demand and supply** *n* ECON Nachfrage- und Angebotselastizität *f*; ~ **of expectations** *n* ECON Erwartungselastizität *f*; ~ **of substitution** *n* ECON Substitutionselastizität *f*; ~ **of supply** *n* ECON Angebotselastizität *f*

elastic: ~ **supply** *n* ECON elastisches Angebot *nt*

ELB *abbr* (*export licensing branch*) IMP/EXP Abteilung für Exportlizenzen

ELEC *abbr* (*European League for Economic Cooperation*) ECON Europäische Liga *f* für wirtschaftliche Zusammenarbeit

elect *vt* GEN COMM *course of action*, POL *candidate* wählen; ♦ ~ **to the board** GEN COMM, MGMNT in den Vorstand wählen

elected: ~ **office** *n* POL durch Wahl zu vergebendes Amt *nt*, *parliament* Mandat *nt*

election: ~ **campaign** *n* GEN COMM, POL Wahlkampagne *f*; ~ **for chairman** *n* GEN COMM, POL Wahl *f* des Vorsitzenden; ~ **results** *n pl* POL Wahlergebnis *nt*

electoral: ~ **register** *n* GEN COMM, POL Wählerliste *f*; ~ **roll** *n* GEN COMM, POL Wählerverzeichnis *nt*

electorate *n* GEN COMM, POL Wählerschaft *f*

electric *adj* GEN COMM elektrisch, Elektro-

electrical *adj* GEN COMM elektrisch, Elektro-; ~ **appliance** *n* GEN COMM Elektrogerät *nt*; ~ **engineer** *n* IND Elektroingenieur, in *m,f*; ~ **engineering** *n* IND Elektrobranche *f*, Elektrotechnik *f*; ~ **exemption clause** *n* INS *property insurance* Elektrizitäts-Freistellungsklausel *f*, Elektrizitäts-Freizeichnungsklausel *f*, Elektrizitäts-Haftungsausschlußklausel *f*

electrically: ~ **insulated coating** *n* (*EIC*) IND Elektroisolierüberzug *m*, Elektroisolieranstrich *m*

electrical: ~ **propulsion** *n* TRANSP *engine* Elektroantrieb *m*

electrician *n* HRM Monteur, in *m,f*, Elektriker, in *m,f*

electricity *n* GEN COMM, IND Elektrizität *f*; ~ **consumption** *n* IND Stromverbrauch *m*; ~ **generation** *n* IND Elektrizitätserzeugung *f*, Elektrizitätslieferung *f*, Stromerzeugung *f*; ~ **industry** *n* ECON Elektrizitätswirtschaft *f*, IND Elektrizitätsindustrie *f*, Elektrizitätswirtschaft *f*, Stromversorgungsindustrie *f*; ~ **sector** *n* IND Elektrizitätssektor *m*; ~ **supply** *n* IND Elektrizitätsversorgung *f*, Stromlieferung *f*; ~ **support industry** *n* IND Elektrizitätszulieferungsindustrie *f*

electric: ~ **train** *n* TRANSP elektrischer Zug *m*; ~ **typewriter** *n* ADMIN elektrische Schreibmaschine *f*; ~ **vehicle** *n* TRANSP Elektrofahrzeug *nt*

electrification *n* TRANSP *of railways* Elektrifizierung *f*

electronic *adj* GEN COMM elektronisch; ~ **accounting system** *n* ACC elektronisches Buchhaltungssystem *nt*; ~ **bank** *n* BANK elektronische Bank *f*; ~ **banking** *n* BANK elektronische Abwicklung *f* von Bankgeschäften; ~ **banking service** *n* BANK elektronische Bankleistung *f*, elektronische Bankdienstleistung *f*; ~ **calculator** *n* COMP elektronische Rechenmaschine *f*; ~ **component** *n* COMP *hardware* elektronisches Bauelement *nt*; ~ **data interchange** *n* (*EDI*) COMMS, COMP elektronischer Datenaustausch *m* (*EDI*); ~ **data processing** *n* (*EDP*) COMP elektronische Datenverarbeitung *f* (*EDV*); ~ **document interchange** *n* COMMS elektronischer Dokumentenaustausch *m*; ~ **funds transfer** *n* (*EFT*) ADMIN, BANK elektronischer Zahlungsverkehr *m*, FIN beleglos er Überweisungsverkehr *m*, beleg loser Zahlungsverkehr *m*, elektronischer Zahlungsverkehr *m*; ~ **funds transfer at point of sale** *n* (*EFTPOS*) BANK COMP, S&M elektronische Geldüberweisung am Verkaufsort (*EFTPOS*); ~ **funds transfer system** *n* (*EFTS*) BANK elektronisches Zahlungsverkehrssystem *nt*; ~ **home banking** *n* BANK Homebanking *nt*, elektronische Bankgeschäfte *nt pl* zu Hause; ~ **mail** *n* (*e-mail*) ADMIN elektronische Datenübermittlung *f*, elektronische Post *f* (*E-Mail*), COMP *networks, op sys* elektronische Post *f* (*E-Mail*); ~ **media** *n* S&M elektronische Medien *nt pl*; ~ **news gathering** *n* GEN COMM Sammlung *f* von Informationen für Elektronikartikel; ~ **office** *n* ADMIN, GEN COMM elektronisches Büro *nt*; ~ **payment terminal** *n* (*EPT*) FIN elektronisches Zahlungsterminal *nt*, elektronisches Zahlungsverkehrsterminal *nt*; ~ **point of sale** *n* (*EPOS*) GEN COMM elektronischer POS *m*; ~ **posting board** *n* STOCK elektronische Anschlagstafel *f*; ~ **publishing** *n* COMP elektronisches Publizieren *nt*

electronics *n* IND Elektronik *f*

electronic: ~ **shopping** *n* COMP, S&M Tele-Einkauf *m*

electronics: ~ **industry** *n* IND Elektronikindustrie *f*

electronic: ~ **till** *n* COMP Computerkasse *f*

electrostatic: ~ **printer** *n* COMP *hardware* elektrostatischer Drucker *m*

electrotype *n* MEDIA Kupferklischee *nt*

element *n* GEN COMM *factor* Element *nt*

elementary: ~ **loss** *n* INS Elementarschaden *m*

element: ~ **of risk** *n* GEN COMM Gefahrenelement *nt*

elevation *n* IND Aufriß *m*

elevator: ~ **liability insurance** *n* AmE INS Fahrstuhlhaftpflichtversicherung *f*

eligibility: ~ **requirement** *n pl* GEN COMM

Auswahlanforderungen *f pl*; **~ test** *n* BANK Diskontfähigkeitstest *m*

eligible *adj* GEN COMM anrechnungsfähig; ♦ **~ as collateral** FIN beleihbar, lombardfähig; **be ~ for sth** HRM, POL für etw berechtigt sein, für etw geeignet sein, für etw qualifiziert sein, *for subsidies or grants* für etw anspruchsberechtigt sein, *National Insurance* für etw anrechnungsfähig sein; **~ for discount** ACC, BANK, FIN diskontfähig, rediskontfähig; **~ for retirement** HRM pensionsberechtigt; **~ for tax relief** TAX steuerbegünstigt

eligible: **~ assets** *n pl* FIN zentralbankfähige Aktiva *pl*; **~ bills** *n pl* BANK rediskontfähige Wechsel *m pl*, zentralbankfähige Wechsel *m pl*; **~ insured years** *n pl* HRM anrechnungsfähige Versicherungsjahre *nt pl*; **~ liability** *n* FIN mindestreservepflichtige Einlage *f*; **~ papers** *n pl* BANK zentralbankfähige Wechsel *m pl*; **~ person** *n* HRM Anwartschaftsberechtigte(r) *mf* [decl. as adj]

eliminate *vt* GEN COMM entfernen, ausschalten, *error* beseitigen, *possibility* ausschließen

eliminated *adj* GEN COMM entfernt, ausgeschaltet, beseitigt, *possibility* ausgeschlossen

elimination *n* GEN COMM Ausscheidung *f*, Entfernung *f*, Ausschluß *m*

elite *n* GEN COMM Elite *f*

elsewhere: **not ~ specified** *phr* (*NES*) GEN COMM nicht anderweitig spezifiziert

EMA *abbr* (*European Monetary Agreement*) GEN COMM Europäisches Währungsabkommen *nt* (*EWA*)

e-mail *n* (*electronic mail*) ADMIN elektronische Datenübermittlung *f*; *n* (*electronic mail*) COMP E-Mail *f* (*elektronische Post*)

emancipation *n* LAW Emanzipation *f*

embargo *n* IMP/EXP *imports* Einfuhrsperre *f*, Einfuhrstopp *m*, MEDIA, TRANSP Embargo *nt*; **~ on exports** *n* IMP/EXP Ausfuhrsperre *f*

embark *vi* TRANSP sich einschiffen; ♦ **~ on** GEN COMM *course of action* einschlagen

embarkation *n* TRANSP *shipping* Anbordgehen *nt*, Einbootung *f*, Einschiffung *f*; **~ card** *n* TRANSP Bordkarte *f*; **~ port** *n* GEN COMM Auslaufhafen *m*

embassy *n* POL Botschaft *f*

embed *vt* COMP einbetten

embedded *adj* COMP eingebettet; **~ command** *n* COMP eingebetteter Befehl *m*

embezzle *vt* GEN COMM *funds* unterschlagen, LAW veruntreuen, *funds* unterschlagen

embezzlement *n* GEN COMM Unterschlagung *f*, LAW *of funds* Unterschlagung *f*, Veruntreuung *f*

embezzler *n* GEN COMM Betrüger, in *m,f* (*infrml*)

emblements *n* LAW *agriculture* Ernte *f* auf dem Halm, Feldfrüchte *f pl*

embodied: **~ technical progress** *n* ECON, IND *production* investitionsgebundener technischer Fortschritt *m*

embodiment *n* LAW Verkörperung *f*, PATENTS *of invention* Form *f*, Gestalt *f*

embody *vt* LAW verkörpern, verankern, PATENTS verkörpern

embossing *n* S&M Prägedruck *m*

EMCF *abbr* (*European Monetary Cooperation Fund*) BANK, ECON EFWZ (*Europäischer Fonds für währungspolitische Zusammenarbeit*)

em: **~ dash** *n* MEDIA *typography* Gedankenstrich von der Breite eines Ms

emerge *vi* GEN COMM auftauchen

emergency *n* GEN COMM, HRM Notfall *m*, Not *f*; **~ aid** *n* ECON *development aid* Soforthilfe *f*; **~ exit** *n* ENVIR, HRM Notausgang *m*; **~ powers** *n pl* HRM Ermächtigung *f* zur Anwendung außerordentlicher Maßnahmen; **~ reconstruction loan** *n* (*ERL*) FIN Sanierungsanleihe *f* für Notfälle; **~ service** *n* WEL Bereitschaftsdienst *m*, Notdienst *m*

Emerging: **~ Markets Growth Fund** *n* (*EMGF*) FIN Wachstumsfonds *m* für aufstrebende Märkte, Wachstumsfonds *m* für Schwellenländer

Emerging: **~ Markets Investment Fund** *n* (*EMIF*) FIN Investitionsfonds *m* für aufstrebende Märkte, Investitionsfonds *m* für Schwellenländer

EMF *abbr* (*European Monetary Fund*) ECON EWF (*Europäischer Währungsfonds*)

EMGF *abbr* (*Emerging Markets Growth Fund*) FIN Wachstumsfonds *m* für aufstrebende Märkte, Wachstumsfonds *m* für Schwellenländer

EMI *abbr* (*European Monetary Institute*) ECON, POL Europäisches Währungsinstitut *nt* (*EWI*)

EMIF *abbr* (*Emerging Markets Investment Fund*) FIN Investitionsfonds *m* für aufstrebende Märkte, Investitionsfonds *m* für Schwellenländer

eminent: **~ domain** *n* POL Enteignungsrecht *nt* des Staates

emissary *n* POL Abgesandte(r) *mf* [decl. as adj]

emission *n* ENVIR *of gases* Emission *f*; **~ charges** *n pl* ENVIR *for pollution* Emissionsabgabe *f*; **~ fee** *n* ENVIR *for pollution* Emissionsgebühr *f*; **~ limit** *n* ENVIR Emissionsgrenze *f*; **~ reductions banking** *n* ENVIR *for pollution* Emissionsschutzwall *m*; **~ standard** *n* ENVIR Emissionsstandard *m*

emolument *n* GEN COMM Bezüge *m pl*, Einkünfte *pl*, TAX Gewinn *m*, Nutzen *m*, Vergütung *f*

emotional: **~ appeal** *n* S&M *of an advertisement* emotionale Aufmachung *f*

emphasis *n* GEN COMM Betonung *f*; **~ of the contract** *n* LAW Schwerpunkt *m* des Vertragsverhältnisses

emphasize *vt* GEN COMM betonen, hervorheben

emphatic *adj* GEN COMM emphatisch

empirical *adj* GEN COMM, MATH empirisch

empirics *n* ECON Empirie *f*

employ *vt* GEN COMM *person* anstellen, einstellen, *method* anwenden, verwenden, HRM beschäftigen

employable *adj* HRM arbeitsfähig

employed *adj* HRM beschäftigt

employee *n* GEN COMM, HRM Angestellte(r) *mf* [decl. as adj], Arbeitnehmer, in *m,f*, Beschäftigte(r) *mf* [decl. as adj], Mitarbeiter, in *m,f*, MGMNT Beschäftigte(r) *mf* [decl. as adj]; **~ association** *n* HRM Arbeitnehmerverband *m*; **~ benefits** *n pl* HRM, WEL Sozialleistungen *f pl*; **~ buyout** *n* HRM Verkauf *m* des Betriebs an Teile der Belegschaft; **~ communications** *n pl* HRM Arbeitnehmerkommunikation *f*; **~ contribution** *n* HRM Pflichtbeitrag *m* des Arbeitnehmers; **~ counseling** *AmE*, **~ counselling** *BrE n* HRM Personalberatung *f*; **~ development program** *AmE*, **~ development programme** *BrE n* HRM Fortbildungsprogramm *nt*; **~-elected representation** *n* HRM Arbeitnehmervertretung *f*; **~ involvement** *n* (*EI*) HRM

Arbeitspartizipation *f*; ~ **involvement and participation** *n BrE* HRM Arbeitspartizipation *f*; ~**-owned firm** *n* MGMNT Unternehmen *nt* in Arbeitnehmerhand, im Besitz der Arbeitnehmer befindliches Unternehmen *nt*; ~ **participation scheme** *n* HRM Arbeitnehmerbeteiligung *f*, Mitarbeiterbeteiligung *f*; ~ **profile** *n* HRM Mitarbeiterprofil *nt*; ~ **profit-sharing** *n* HRM Gewinnbeteiligung *f* der Arbeitnehmer; ~ **rate** *n BrE* TAX *National Insurance contributions* Arbeitnehmeranteil *m*, Arbeitnehmerbeitrag *m*; ~ **ratios** *n* HRM Kapitalintensität *f*; ~ **relations** *n pl* HRM, IND, MGMNT innerbetriebliche Beziehungen *f pl*; ~ **retirement income security act** *n* HRM Pensionssicherungsgesetz *nt*

employees *n pl* GEN COMM Belegschaft *f*, HRM, MGMNT Beschäftigte *pl* [decl. as adj]

employees': ~ **committee** *n* HRM Betriebsrat *m*

employee: ~ **contribution** *n* HRM, TAX Arbeitnehmeranteil *m*, Arbeitnehmerbeitrag *m*; ~ **savings premium** *n* HRM Arbeitnehmer-Sparzulage *f*; ~ **shareholding scheme** *n* HRM Arbeitnehmerbeteiligung *f*, Mitarbeiterbeteiligung *f*, Belegschaftsaktien-Beteiligungsplan *m*; ~ **share ownership plan** *n BrE (ESOP)* STOCK Aktienerwerbsplan *m* für Arbeitnehmer, Belegschaftsaktienfonds *m*; ~ **share ownership trust** *n BrE* STOCK Belegschaftsaktienfonds *m*; ~ **stock ownership plan** *n (ESOP)* HRM Mitarbeiterbeteiligung *f*, Aktienerwerbsplan *m* für Arbeitnehmer, Belegschaftsaktienfonds *m*; ~ **turnover** *n* ECON, GEN COMM, HRM Arbeitskräftefluktuation *f*

employer *n* FIN, GEN COMM, HRM, TAX Arbeitgeber *m*, Brötchengeber, in *m,f (infrml)*; ~ **express term** *n* HRM vom Arbeitgeber vorgeschriebene, ausdrückliche Vertragsvereinbarung *f*; ~ **interference** *n* HRM Einsatz *m* unlauterer Arbeitskampfmethoden seitens Arbeitgeber; ~ **rate** *n BrE* TAX *National Insurance* Arbeitgeberanteil *m*, Arbeitgeberbeitrag *m*

employers': ~ **association** *n* GEN COMM, HRM Arbeitgeberverband *m*

employer: ~**'s contribution** *n* FIN, HRM, TAX Arbeitgeberanteil *m*, Arbeitgeberbeitrag *m*; ~**'s legal obligation to fund** *n* HRM *pension* gesetzliche Verpflichtung *f* des Arbeitgebers zur Finanzierung; ~**'s liabilities** *n pl* TAX Arbeitgeberhaftpflicht *f*, Unfallhaftpflicht *f* des Arbeitgebers, Unternehmerhaftpflicht *f*; ~**'s liability coverage** *n* INS Abdeckung *f* von Haftpflichtschäden des Arbeitgebers; ~**'s occupational pension scheme** *n BrE* FIN, HRM *tax* betriebliche Pensionskasse *f*; ~**'s pension** *n* HRM, INS Rückdeckungsversicherung *f*; ~**'s pension commitment** *n* HRM, INS Direktzusage *f*; ~**'s return** *n* TAX Arbeitgeberrückerstattung *f*, Arbeitgeberrückzahlung *f*

employment *n* HRM Arbeitsverhältnis *nt*, Beschäftigung *f*, Dienstverhältnis *nt*; ◆ **on the ~ front** ECON, HRM, POL was den Arbeitsmarkt angeht

Employment: ~ **Act** *n (EA)* HRM Gesetzgebung zur Einschränkung der Macht der britischen Gewerkschaften

employment: ~ **agency** *n* ADMIN, GEN COMM, HRM Arbeitsvermittlung *f*, Personalvermittlungsbüro *nt*, private Stellenvermittlung *f*

Employment: ~ **Appeal Tribunal** *n BrE (EAT)* HRM Berufungsgericht *nt* für Beschäftigungskonflikte

employment: ~ **compensation** *n* HRM, IND, LAW Arbeitslohn *m*; ~ **contract** *n* GEN COMM, HRM Arbeitsvertrag *m*

Employment: ~ **Department** *n obs (ED)* POL Arbeitsministerium

employment: ~ **expenses** *n pl* HRM Personalkosten *pl*; ~ **figures** *n pl* ECON Beschäftigungszahlen *f pl*, GEN COMM Beschäftigtenzahlen *f pl*; ~ **function** *n* ECON Beschäftigungsfunktion *f*, Tätigkeitsfunktion *f*; ~ **income** *n* TAX Arbeitslohn *m*; ~ **index** *n* ECON Anspannungsindex *m*

Employment: ~ **Institute** *n BrE* ECON *policy centre* Londoner Institut für Beschäftigung

employment: ~ **law** *n BrE* HRM, LAW Arbeitsgesetz *nt*; ~ **multiplier** *n* ECON Beschäftigungsmultiplikator *m*; ~ **office** *n* ADMIN, HRM, WEL Arbeitsamt *nt*; ~ **policy** *n* HRM, POL Beschäftigungspolitik *f*

Employment: ~ **Protection Act** *n BrE (EPA)* HRM, LAW Gesetz zum Schutz von Arbeitnehmerrechten

employment: ~ **protection rights** *n pl BrE* HRM Arbeitsschutzrechte *nt pl*; ~ **record** *n* HRM Beschäftigungsnachweis *m*; ~ **relationship** *n* HRM Beschäftigungsverhältnis *nt*, *in EC regulations* Arbeitsverhältnis *nt*; ~ **security** *n* HRM Arbeitsplatzsicherheit *f*; ~ **service** *n AmE (cf Jobcentre BrE)* ADMIN, HRM britisches Arbeitsamt, Arbeitsamt *nt*, Arbeitsvermittlung *f*; ~ **situation** *n* GEN COMM Beschäftigungssituation *f*; ~ **tax** *n* TAX Lohnsteuer *f*, lohnbezogene Sozialversicherungssteuer *f*; ~ **test** *n* HRM *selection* Einstellungstest *m*; ~ **training** *n BrE (ET)* HRM innerbetriebliche Weiterbildung *f*

emporium *n* GEN COMM Handelszentrum *nt*

empower *vt* GEN COMM bevollmächtigen, LAW beauftragen; ◆ ~ **sb to do sth** GEN COMM jdn ermächtigen, etw zu tun

empowered *adj* GEN COMM bevollmächtigt, LAW beauftragt

empty *adj* TRANSP leer; ~ **nesters** *n pl infrml* PROP *housing market* Paar, dessen Kinder einen eigenen Haushalt haben; ~ **set** *n* MATH Nullmenge *f*

EMS *abbr (European Monetary System)* ECON EWS *(Europäisches Währungssystem)*

em: ~ **space** *n* MEDIA *typography* Geviert *nt*

EMU *abbr* ECON *(Economic and Monetary Union)* Wirtschafts- und Währungsunion *f*, *(European Monetary Union)* EWU *(Europäische Währungsunion)*

emulate *vt* COMP *software, protocol*, GEN COMM emulieren

emulation *n* COMP, GEN COMM Emulation *f*; ~ **board** *n* COMP Emulationsplatine *f*; ~ **card** *n* COMP Emulationskarte *f*; ~ **software** *n* COMP Emulationssoftware *f*

emulator *n* COMP Emulator *m*

enable *vt* COMP *software* einschalten, aktivieren, GEN COMM, HRM befähigen

enablement *n* COMP Einschalten *nt*, Aktivierung *f*, GEN COMM Befähigung *f*

enabling: ~ **clause** *n* LAW Ermächtigungsklausel *f*

enact *vt* LAW *legislation* erlassen

enactment *n* LAW *of legislation* Erlaß *m*

encash *vt* ACC, BANK kassieren, STOCK einlösen

encashable *adj* ACC, BANK einkassierbar, STOCK einlösbar

encashment *n* ACC Inkasso *nt*, BANK Einkassierung *f*, Inkasso *nt*, STOCK Einlösung *f*; ~ **schedule** *n* ACC Einlösungstermin *m*, Inkassotermin *m*

encl. *abbr (enclosure)* GEN COMM Anl. *(Anlage)*

enclave: ~ **economy** *n* ECON isolierte Volkswirtschaft *f*

enclose vt COMMS beifügen, beilegen, GEN COMM beifügen, beiheften

enclosed adj COMMS in letter als Anlage, anbei frml, beigeheftet; ♦ **please find** COMMS anbei schicken wir Ihnen; ~ **copy of letter** phr COMMS Kopie des Schreibens als Anlage beigefügt

enclosed: ~ **document** n COMMS mail beigefügtes Dokument nt; ~ **testimonial** n LAW beigefügtes Zeugnis nt

enclosure n (encl.) GEN COMM Anlage f (Anl.)

encode vt COMP verschlüsseln, kodieren

encoding n BANK Verschlüsselung f, Kodierung f

encompass vt GEN COMM umfassen

encounter vt GEN COMM problem stoßen auf [+acc]

encourage vt GEN COMM person ermutigen, trade, industry fördern, unterstützen

encouragement n GEN COMM Ermutigung f, of trade, industry Förderung f, Unterstützung f

encouraging adj GEN COMM ermutigend

encroach vt LAW beeinträchtigen, übergreifen

encroach on vt LAW right beeinträchtigen

encroach upon vt LAW beeinträchtigen; ♦ ~ **sb's rights** LAW auf jds Rechte übergreifen

encroachment n GEN COMM, LAW Beeinträchtigung f, Übergreifung f, Rechtsverletzung f; ♦ ~ **upon adjoining land** LAW Überbau m

encrypt vt COMP kodieren, verschlüsseln

encryption n COMP Kodierung f, Verschlüsselung f

encumber vt LAW belasten

encumbrance n LAW property Belastung f, dingliche Belastung f, Grundstücksbelastung f, PROP Schuldenlast f

end n GEN COMM Ende nt; ♦ **at the ~ of the day** GEN COMM am Ende des Tages; **come to an ~** GEN COMM event ablaufen, zu Ende kommen, zu einem Ende kommen

endanger vt GEN COMM gefährden; ♦ ~ **jobs** HRM Arbeitsplätze gefährden

endangered adj ENVIR gefährdet; ~ **species** n ENVIR gefährdete Art f

en: ~ **dash** n MEDIA typography Gedankenstrich von der Breite eines Ns, Halbgeviertstrich m

end: ~ **consumer** n ECON, S&M Endabnehmer, in m,f, Endverbraucher, in m,f

endeavor AmE, **endeavour** vi BrE GEN COMM sich bemühen

endemic adj GEN COMM endemisch

end: ~ **of file** n (EOF) COMP Dateiende nt; ~ **of financial year** n ACC Ende nt des Finanzjahres

ending: ~ **balance** n ACC, BANK, FIN Abschlußbilanz f; ~ **inventory** n ACC Abschlußinventar nt, Schlußbestand m, Endbestand m

end: ~ **of message** n (EOM) COMP Ende nt der Mitteilung, Nachrichtenende nt; ~ **of month** n ACC, GEN COMM Monatsultimo m, Monatsende nt; ~**-of-file mark** n COMP Dateiendemarke f; ~**-of-line character** n COMP Zeilenendzeichen nt; ~**-of-line goods** n pl S&M Auslaufware f; ~**-of-month account** n ACC, BANK Ultimoabschluß m, Monatsabschluß m; ~**-of-season sale** n GEN COMM Schlußverkauf m, S&M Saisonschlußverkauf m

endogenizing: ~ **the exogenous** n ECON econometrics Endogenisierung f exogener Variablen

endogenous: ~ **variable** n ECON econometrics endogene Variable f

endorse vt BANK, GEN COMM indossieren, LAW vermerken, billigen, zulassen, S&M bestätigen

endorse back vt BANK durch Indossament rückübertragen

endorsee n BANK, LAW, S&M Indossatar m

endorsement n BANK bill, cheque Indossament nt, LAW Indossament nt, Vermerk m, S&M of product Bestätigung f; ~ **stamp** n BANK Indossamentstempel m; ♦ ~ **and delivery** BANK, LAW Indossament und Übergabe

endorser n BANK, LAW, S&M Indossant, in m,f

endorsor see endorser

endowment n LAW gift Stiftung f; ~ **assurance** n INS gemischte Lebensversicherung f, Versicherung f auf den Todes- und Erlebensfall; ~ **effect** n BANK Ausstattungseffekt m; ~ **insurance** n INS gemischte Lebensversicherung f, Versicherung f auf den Todes- und Erlebensfall; ~ **life assurance** n INS gemischte Lebensversicherung f, Lebensversicherung f auf den Todes- und Erlebensfall; ~ **life insurance** n INS gemischte Lebensversicherung f, Versicherung f auf den Todes- und Erlebensfall; ~ **policy** n BrE (cf mortgage life insurance AmE) INS Hypothekentilgungsversicherung f

end: ~ **product** n GEN COMM Endprodukt nt; ~ **result** n FIN, GEN COMM Endergebnis nt; ~ **use** n IMP/EXP Endverbrauch m; ~ **use goods** n pl IMP/EXP Endverbrauchsgüter nt pl; ~**-user** n COMP Benutzer, in m,f, Anwender, in m,f, ECON Endabnehmer, in m,f, Endverbraucher, in m,f, certificate Endanwender m; ~**-user computing** n COMP Benutzer-EDV f; ~ **use trader** n IMP/EXP Endverbrauchshändler, in m,f; ~ **of work** n ADMIN, HRM Arbeitsschluß m

ENEA abbr (European Nuclear Energy Authority) GEN COMM Europäische Atomenergiebehörde f

enemies: ~ **of the state** n pl LAW, POL Staatsfeinde m pl

energy n IND power Energie f (E), Kraft f; ~ **conservation** n ENVIR Energieerhaltung f; ~ **crisis** n ENVIR Energiekrise f; ~ **demand** n ECON Energiebedarf m, Energienachfrage f; ~ **efficiency** n ENVIR, GEN COMM Energieeinsparung f, Energienutzungsgrad m; ~**-efficient machine** n ENVIR Maschine f für rationelle Energieanwendung, energiesparende Maschine f

Energy: ~ **Industries Council** n BrE IND Industrierat für Energie

energy: ~ **management** n ENVIR, MGMNT Energiewirtschaft f; ~ **mutual fund** n ENVIR gemeinsamer Energiefonds m; ~ **policy** n GEN COMM Energiepolitik f; ~ **recovery** n ENVIR recycling Energierückgewinnung f; ~ **reserves** n pl ENVIR Energiereserven f pl, Energieressourcen f pl, Energievorräte m pl; ~ **resources** n pl ENVIR Energieressourcen f pl, Energiequellen f pl; ~ **source** n GEN COMM Energiequelle f; ~ **supply** n GEN COMM Energieversorgung f; ~ **system** n GEN COMM Energiesystem nt; ~ **tax credit** n AmE TAX Energiesteuergutschrift f; ~**-wasting** adj ENVIR energieverschwendend

enforce vt GEN COMM erzwingen, rights durchsetzen, LAW vollstrecken, vollziehen, erzwingen; ♦ ~ **a claim** LAW contract law einen Anspruch durchsetzen

enforceability *n* LAW Klagbarkeit *f*, Vollstreckbarkeit *f*

enforceable *adj* LAW durchsetzbar, einklagbar, klagbar, vollstreckbar; ~ **legal document** *n* LAW Schuldtitel *m*

enforced *adj* LAW erzwungen, durchgesetzt

enforcement *n* LAW Durchsetzung *f*, Vollstreckung *f*, Vollziehung *f*, Geltendmachung *f*; ~ **order** *n* GEN COMM Vollstreckungsanweisung *f*; ~ **procedure** *n* GEN COMM Vollstreckungsverfahren *nt*; ~ **proceedings** *n pl* LAW Vollstreckungsverfahren *nt*

enfranchise *vt* GEN COMM konzessionieren, zulassen

engage *vt* GEN COMM beschäftigen, HRM *staff* einstellen, LAW verpflichten

engaged *adj* COMMS *BrE (cf busy AmE) telephone line* besetzt, GEN COMM *person* beschäftigt; ◆ **be ~ in** MGMNT arbeiten an, sich beschäftigen mit

engaged: ~ **signal** *n BrE (cf busy signal AmE)* COMMS *telephone* Besetztzeichen *nt*; ~ **tone** *n BrE (cf busy signal AmE)* COMMS *telephone* Besetztzeichen *nt*

engagement *n* GEN COMM Engagement *nt*, LAW Verpflichtung *f*; ~ **to sell short** *n* STOCK Baisseengagement *nt*

Engel: ~ **coefficient** *n* ECON Engel-Koeffizient *m*; ~'s **law** *n* ECON Engelsches Gesetz *nt*

engine *n* IND, TRANSP Motor *m*; ~ **builder** *n* IND Maschinenbauer, in *m,f*; ~ **designer** *n* IND *machinery* Maschinenbauingenieur, in *m,f*

engineer *n* HRM, IND Ingenieur, in *m,f*

engineering *n* IND Engineering *nt*, industrielle Planung *f*, Ingenieurwesen *nt*, *technology* Technik *f*, technische Bearbeitung *f*, Technologie *f*; ~ **assurances** *n pl* INS Maschinenbruchversicherung *f*; ~ **consultant** *n* HRM, IND technischer Berater *m*, technische Beraterin *f*; ~ **department** *n* GEN COMM Konstruktionsabteilung *f*; ~ **and design department** *n* IND Technik- und Konstruktionsabteilung *f*; ~ **firm** *n* GEN COMM Konstruktionsunternehmen *nt*

Engineering: ~ **Industries Association** *n AmE* IND amerikanischer Verband der Maschinenindustrie

engineering: ~ **insurance** *n* INS technische Versicherung *f*; ~ **manager** *n* HRM Leiter, in *m,f* der technischen Abteilung; ~ **process** *n* IND Konstruktionsverfahren *nt*; ~ **progress** *n* IND technischer Fortschritt *m*; ~ **works** *n pl* IND Maschinenfabrik *f*, Konstruktionswerk *nt*

engine: ~ **of growth** *n* ECON Wachstumsmotor *m*; ~ **room** *n* TRANSP *ship* Maschinenraum *m*, Motorraum *m*

English: ~ **Channel** *n* TRANSP der Ärmelkanal *m*, der Kanal *m*; ~ **Estates** *n* PROP Grundbesitzbehörde der britischen Regierung; ~ **Heritage** *n BrE* POL englische Denkmalschutzkommission; ~ **Inshore Traffic Zone** *n (EITZ)* TRANSP englische Küstenverkehrszone *f*; ~ **Tourist Board** *n (ETB)* LEIS englischer Fremdenverkehrsverein

enhance *vt* COMP erweitern, verbessern, ECON *purchasing power* erhöhen, steigern, GEN COMM verbessern

enhanced *adj* COMP *quality, features* erweitert, verbessert, GEN COMM verbessert; ~ **graphics adapter** *n (EGA)* COMP verbesserter Grafikadapter *m (EGA-Karte)*; ~ **graphics array** *n (EGA)* COMP verbesserte Grafikanordnung *f*

Enhanced: ~ **Structural Adjustment Facility** *n (ESAF)* FIN erweiterte Strukturanpassungsfazilität *f*

enhancement *n* COMP *of computer system* Erweiterung *f*, Verbesserung *f*, GEN COMM Verbesserung *f*

enjoin *vt* MGMNT vorschreiben

enjoy *vt* GEN COMM *benefits* sich erfreuen, *reputation* genießen

enlarge *vt* GEN COMM vergrößern

enlarged: ~ **copy** *n* GEN COMM vergrößerte Kopie *f*; ~ **edition** *n* GEN COMM erweiterte Ausgabe *f*

enlargement *n* GEN COMM Erweiterung *f*

enquire *vi* COMP abfragen, anfragen, GEN COMM anfragen, LAW, MGMNT untersuchen, S&M erkundigen, umfragen, untersuchen

enquiry *n* COMP Abfrage *f*, Anfrage *f*, GEN COMM Anfrage *f*, S&M Erkundigung *f*, *survey* Umfrage *f*, *study* Untersuchung *f*; ~ **desk** *n* GEN COMM Auskunftsschalter *m*; ~ **file** *n* COMP Abfragedatei *f*; ~ **form** *n* GEN COMM Fragebogen *m*; ~ **office** *n* ADMIN Auskunftei *f*; ~ **program** *n* COMP Abfrageprogramm *nt*; ~ **system** *n* COMP Abfragesystem *nt*; ~ **test** *n* S&M Erkundigungstest *m*; ~ **unit** *n* COMP Abfrageeinheit *f*

enrich *vt* COMMS erweitern, TAX erhöhen

enriched: ~ **program** *AmE*, ~ **programme** *BrE n* GEN COMM erweitertes Programm *nt*

enrichment *n* GEN COMM *of job* Ausweitung *f*, LAW Bereicherung *f*

enrollment *AmE*, **enrolment** *n BrE* GEN COMM *for course* Einschreibung *f*, Eintragung *f*, *number* Zahl *f* der Eingetragenen

en route *adv* GEN COMM unterwegs

enshrine *vt* GEN COMM einschließen, verwahren, LAW verankern

ensure *vt* LAW sicherstellen

enter *vt* ACC verbuchen, COMP *data* eingeben, GEN COMM *etw* vermerken, POL beitreten; ◆ ~ **an appeal** LAW in Berufung gehen; ~ **on the books** ACC buchen, verbuchen; ~ **a debit against** GEN COMM ausbuchen; ~ **goods for warehousing** GEN COMM Waren zur Einlagerung eintragen; ~ **information onto a register** GEN COMM Daten in ein Register eintragen; ~ **an item in the ledger** ACC einen Posten im Hauptbuch verbuchen; ~ **the labor market** *AmE*, ~ **the labour market** *BrE* ECON, HRM auf den Arbeitsmarkt treten, in den Arbeitsmarkt eintreten; ~ **the market** ECON auf den Markt kommen; ~ **a plea** LAW einen Einwand anmelden; ~ **recession** ECON auf eine Rezession zusteuern; ~ **a writ** LAW Klage erheben

enter into *vt* GEN COMM *contract* eingehen; ◆ ~ **an agreement** GEN COMM eine Vereinbarung treffen; ~ **a contract with** GEN COMM einen Vertrag schließen mit; ~ **force** LAW *legislation* in Kraft treten

enter: ~ **key** *n* COMP *keyboard* Enter-Taste *f*

enterprise *n* ADMIN *business firm* Unternehmen *nt*, Unternehmung *f*, Wirtschaftsunternehmen *nt*, Privatunternehmen *nt*, GEN COMM *project* Unternehmen *nt*, Unternehmung *f*, *initiative* Unternehmungsgeist *m*, Initiative *f*; ~ **allowance** *n BrE* FIN staatliche Förderung für Unternehmensneugründungen *f*, Förderbeihilfe *f*, Förderzuschuß *m*, Förderprämie *f*

Enterprise: ~ **Investment Scheme** *n BrE* ECON Existenzgründungs- und Investitionsförderungsprogramm

enterprise: ~ **union** *n* HRM Betriebsgewerkschaft *f*, gelbe Gewerkschaft *f*; ~ **zone** *n (EZ)* ECON Industrieförderdergebiet *nt*, Industriegebiet *nt*, Wirtschaftsentwicklungsgebiet *nt*, ausgewiesene Flächen *f pl* mit besonderem Entwicklungsstatus, Fördergebiet *nt*, Gewerbegebiet *nt*

enterprising *adj* GEN COMM wagemutig, ideenreich, zupackend

entertain *vt* GEN COMM *client* bewirten

entertainment *n* GEN COMM *of client* Bewirtung *f*, LEIS Unterhaltung *f*, Vergnügung *f*; ~ **allowance** *n* ADMIN Aufwandsentschädigung *f*, GEN COMM Bewirtungspauschale *f*; ~ **complex** *n* LEIS Veranstaltungszentrum *nt*, Vergnügungscenter *nt*; ~ **tax** *n* TAX Vergnügungssteuer *f*

entice away *vt* HRM abwerben

enticing *adj* GEN COMM *offer* verlockend

entire *adj* GEN COMM ganz, vollständig

entirety *n* GEN COMM Gesamtheit *f*

entitle *vt* GEN COMM ermächtigen, LAW berechtigen

entitled *adj* LAW *allowed* berechtigt; ◆ ~ **to adjudicate** LAW spruchberechtigt, urteilsbefugt; ~ **to priority** LAW bevorrechtigt

entitlement *n* HRM Anspruch *m*, LAW, WEL Berechtigung *f*; ~ **to the goods** *n* LAW Eigentumsrecht *nt* an den Waren

entrance *n* GEN COMM Eingang *m*, *fee* Eintrittsgeld *nt*, Eintritt *m*, Eintrittsgebühr *f*; ~ **examination** *n* GEN COMM Aufnahmeprüfung *f*, Zulassungsprüfung *f*; ~ **fee** *n* GEN COMM Eintrittsgebühr *f*, Eintrittsgeld *nt*, Eintritt *m*

entrepreneur *n* ECON Unternehmer, in *m,f*, Privatunternehmer *m*, GEN COMM Geschäftsfrau *f*, Geschäftsmann *m* Unternehmer, in *m,f*, MGMNT Unternehmer, in *m,f*

entrepreneurial *adj* ECON unternehmerisch; ~ **risk** *n* GEN COMM unternehmerisches Risiko *nt*, Unternehmerrisiko *nt*, Unternehmerwagnis *nt*; ~ **spirit** *n* MGMNT Unternehmergeist *m*

entrust *vt* GEN COMM anvertrauen; ◆ ~ **sb with the management** ADMIN jdn mit der Geschäftsführung beauftragen; ~ **sb with a specific task** GEN COMM jdn mit einer bestimmten Aufgabe betrauen

entry *n* ACC Posten *m*, Verbuchung *f*, ADMIN Einreise *f*, Eintragung *f*, Posten *m*, BANK Zolldeklaration *f*, ECON Einreise *f*, GEN COMM Vermerk *m*, IMP/EXP Einreise *f*, Zolldeklaration *f*, POL Beitreten *nt*, Beitritt *m*, STOCK *into market* Eintritt *m*, Zutritt *m*; ~ **barrier** *n* ECON Marktzutrittsschranke *f*, Markteintrittsbarriere *f*, Marktzugangsbeschränkung *f*, IMP/EXP *customs* Zollschranke *f*; ~-**level job** *n* HRM Anfangsstellung *f*; ~ **permit** *n* ADMIN Einreisegenehmigung *f*, GEN COMM Eintrittserlaubnis *f*, Passierschein *m*; ~ **price** *n* IMP/EXP Einfuhrpreis *m*, STOCK *futures* Buchungspreis *m*; ~ **processing unit** *n* (*EPU*) IMP/EXP Einfuhrabfertigungsstelle *f*; ~ **restriction** *n* ECON *goods* Zugangsbeschränkung *f*, *persons* Einreisebeschränkung *f*; ~ **stamp** *n* IMP/EXP *on arrival in new country* Einreisestempel *m*; ~ **visa** *n* ADMIN, TRANSP Einreisevisum *nt*

enumerate *vt* GEN COMM aufzählen

enumeration *n* GEN COMM Aufzählung *f*

envelope *n* COMMS Umschlag *m*; ~ **curve** *n* MATH Hüllkurve *f*, Umhüllende *f*; ~ **procedures and rules** *n pl* GEN COMM Umhüllungsverfahren *nt pl* und -vorschriften *f pl*

environment *n* COMP Umgebung *f*, ENVIR Umwelt *f*, GEN COMM Umfeld *nt*, Rahmenbedingungen *f pl*

environmental: ~ **action program** *AmE*, ~ **action programme** *BrE n* ENVIR Maßnahmenpaket *nt* zum Umweltschutz, Umweltaktionsprogramm *nt*; ~ **analysis** *n* ENVIR, MGMNT Umweltuntersuchung *f*, Umfeldanalyse *f*; ~ **assessment** *n* ENVIR strategische Frühaufklärung *f*, Umweltprüfung *f*; ~ **conditions** *n pl* ENVIR Umweltbedingungen *f pl*; ~ **control** *n* ENVIR Umweltschutz *m*, Umweltkontrolle *f*, IND Umweltüberwachung *f*, Umweltkontrolle *f*, POL Umweltschutz *m*; ~ **damage** *n* ENVIR, GEN COMM, POL Umweltschaden *m*; ~ **determinism** *n* ENVIR Umweltdeterminismus *m*; ~ **development** *n* ENVIR, GEN COMM Umweltförderung *f*; ~ **health** *n* ENVIR Umwelthygiene *f*

Environmental: ~ **Health Officer** *n BrE* ENVIR Beauftragte(r) *mf* [decl. as adj] für Umwelthygiene

environmental: ~ **impact analysis** *n* GEN COMM Umweltverträglichkeitsprüfung *f*, Analyse *f* der Umweltwirkungen; ~ **impact assessment** *n* ENVIR Bewertung *f* der Umweltbelastung, Umweltverträglichkeitsprüfung *f*; ~-**impact study** *n* ENVIR Umweltverträglichkeitsstudie *f*

environmentalism *n* ENVIR Umweltschutzbewegung *f*

environmental: ~ **issues** *n pl* ENVIR Umweltfragen *f pl*

environmentalist *n* ENVIR Umweltschützer, in *m,f*

environmental: ~ **load** *n* ENVIR Umweltbelastung *f*; ~ **lobby** *n* POL Interessengruppe *f* für Umweltfragen, Umweltlobby *f*

environmentally: ~ **aware** *adj* ENVIR umweltbewußt; ~ **beneficial** *adj* ENVIR umweltfreundlich; ~-**conscious** *adj* ENVIR umweltbewußt; ~ **friendly** *adj* ENVIR umweltfreundlich; ~-**friendly product** *n* ENVIR umweltfreundliches Produkt *nt*; ~ **sensitive zone** *n* ENVIR ökologisch sensibler Bereich *m*, Landschaftsschutzgebiet *nt*

environmental: ~ **management** *n* ENVIR, MGMNT Umweltmanagement *nt*; ~ **management system** *n* ENVIR, MGMNT Umweltmanagementsystem *nt*; ~ **policy** *n* ENVIR, POL Umweltpolitik *f*; ~ **problem** *n* ENVIR Umweltproblem *nt*; ~ **projection** *n* ENVIR Umweltprognose *f*; ~ **protection** *n* ENVIR, POL Umweltschutz *m*

Environmental: ~ **Protection Act** *n BrE* ENVIR *1990* Umweltschutzgesetz; ~ **Protection Agency** *n AmE* (*EPA*) ENVIR, POL Umweltschutzbehörde *f*

environmental: ~ **quality** *n pl* ENVIR Umweltqualität *f*, Umweltgüte *nt pl*; ~ **quality standard** *n* ENVIR Umweltqualitätsnorm *f*; ~ **scanner** *n* ENVIR Umwelt-Scanner *m*; ~ **scanning** *n* ADMIN, ECON, MGMNT strategische Frühaufklärung *f*; ~ **standard** *n* ENVIR Umweltnorm *f*; ~ **study** *n* ENVIR, MGMNT Umweltstudie *f*; ~ **tax** *n* ENVIR, POL, TAX Umweltsteuer *f*

Environment: ~ **and Consumer Protection Service** *n* (*ECPS*) ENVIR Umwelt- und Verbraucherschutzdienst *m*

environment: ~ **scan** *n* ENVIR Umweltuntersuchung *f*, Umfelduntersuchung *f*

environs *n pl* GEN COMM *of town* Umgebung *f*

envisage *vt* GEN COMM planen

envision *vt* GEN COMM sich vorstellen

EOC *abbr BrE* (*Equal Opportunities Commission*) HRM britische Kommission für Chancengleichheit auf dem Arbeitsmarkt

EOF *abbr* (*end of file*) COMP Dateiende *nt*

eohp *abbr* (*except as otherwise herein provided*) GEN COMM vorbehaltlich anderslautender Bestimmungen

EOM *abbr* COMP (*end of message*) Nachrichtenende *nt*, STOCK (*European Options Market*) Europäischer Optionsmarkt *m*

EOQ *abbr* (*economic order quantity*) ECON optimale Bestellmenge *f*, IND optimale Bestellmenge *f*, wirtschaftliche Losgröße *f*

EP *abbr* IMP/EXP (*export promotion*) Exportförderung *f*, IND (*extreme pressure*) Höchstdruck *m*, POL (*European Parliament*) EP (*Europaparlament*)

EPA *abbr* ENVIR *AmE* (*Environmental Protection Agency*) Umweltschutzbehörde *f*, HRM (*Employment Protection Act*) Gesetz zum Schutz von Arbeitnehmerrechten, IND (*European Productivity Agency*) Europäische Produktivitätsbehörde, LAW (*Employment Protection Act*) Gesetz zum Schutz von Arbeitnehmerrechten, POL *AmE* (*Environmental Protection Agency*) Umweltschutzbehörde *f*

EPC *abbr* (*European Patent Convention*) LAW, PATENTS EPÜ (*Europäisches Patentübereinkommen*)

ephemeralization *n* ECON Ephemeralisierung *f*

EPO *abbr* PATENTS (*European Patent Organization*) EPO (*Europäische Patentorganisation*), (*European Patent Office*) EPA (*Europäisches Patentamt*)

epoch: **~-making** *adj* GEN COMM, IND bahnbrechend

EPOS *abbr* (*electronic point of sale*) COMP, GEN COMM elektronischer POS *m*

EPROM *abbr* (*erasable programmable read-only memory*) COMP *programming language* löschbarer programmierbarer Nur-Lese-Speicher *m*

EPS *abbr* (*earnings per share*) ACC, FIN Gewinn *m* je Aktie

EPT *abbr* (*electronic payment terminal*) FIN elektronisches Zahlungsterminal *nt*

EPU *abbr* ECON (*European Payments Union*), GEN COMM (*European Payments Union*) EZU (*Europäische Zahlungsunion*), IMP/EXP (*entry processing unit*) Einfuhrabfertigungsstelle *f*

equal 1. *adj* MATH gleich; ♦ **all else being ~** GEN COMM ceteris paribus, unter sonst gleichen Umständen; **~ pay for work of equal value** *BrE* HRM gleicher Lohn für gleichwertige Arbeit; **in ~ proportions** GEN COMM zu gleichen Teilen; **of ~ rank** GEN COMM gleichberechtigt, gleichrangig; **on ~ terms** GEN COMM zu den gleichen Bedingungen; **2.** *n* HRM *person* Gleichgestellte(r) *mf* [decl. as adj]; **3.** *vi* MATH gleich sein

Equal: **~ Credit Opportunity Act** *n AmE* LAW *anti-discrimination* Kreditgleichheitsgesetz

equal: **~ employment opportunity** *n* HRM, LAW Chancengleichheit *f* am Arbeitsmarkt

Equal: **~ Employment Opportunity Commission** *n AmE* (*EEOC*) HRM amerikanische Kommission für Chancengleichheit auf dem Arbeitsmarkt

equal: **~ footing** *n* GEN COMM gleiche Basis *f*

equality *n* HRM, LAW, POL Gleichheit *f*; **~ standard** *n* POL Gleichheitsstandard *m*

equalization *n* GEN COMM Ausgleich *m*, Gleichsetzung *f*

Equalization: **~ Board** *n AmE* TAX *property* Steuerausgleichsamt

equalization: **~ fund** *n* INS Ausgleichsfonds *m*, Schwankungsfonds *m*, Schwankungsrückstellung *f*; **~ levy** *n* IMP/EXP *on cross-border EU goods* Ausgleichsabgabe *f*; **~ payment** *n* FIN Ausgleichszahlung *f*; **~ of revenue**

and expenditure *n* FIN Ausgleich *m* von Einnahmen und Ausgabe; **~ store** *n* ECON Ausgleichslager *nt*

equalize *vt* GEN COMM gleichsetzen, ausgleichen

equalizing *adj* GEN COMM gleichsetzend, ausgleichend; **~ wage differential** *n* ECON ausgleichende Lohnzulage *f*

Equal: **~ Opportunities Commission** *n BrE* (*EOC*) HRM britische Kommission für Chancengleichheit auf dem Arbeitsmarkt

equal: **~ opportunity** *n BrE* (*cf affirmative action AmE*) HRM Chancengleichheit *f*; **~ opportunity employer** *n BrE* HRM Arbeitgeber, der Chancengleichheit praktiziert; **~ opportunity policy** *n BrE* HRM Politik *f* der Chancengleichheit

equal: **~ and opposite** *adj* GEN COMM gleich und gegensätzlich; **~ pay** *n* HRM gleicher Lohn *m*

Equal: **~ Pay Act** *n BrE* HRM *1963* Lohngleichheitsgesetz *nt*; **~ Pay Directive** *n* HRM *1975* Lohngleichheitsrichtlinie *f*

equal: **~ product curve** *n* ECON Isoquante *f*, Kurve *f* gleicher Produktion

Equal: **~ Protection of the Laws** *n AmE* LAW *constitutional guarantee* Gleichheit *f* vor dem Gesetz; **~ Rights Amendment** *n AmE* (*ERA*) HRM, LAW Gesetz *nt* zur Gleichberechtigung

equal: **~ value** *n* STOCK *currency futures prices* Gleichwertigkeit *f*; **~ value amendment** *n BrE* HRM *1983* Novelle zur Anerkennung gleichwertiger Arbeitsleistung; **~ voting rights** *n pl* LAW, MGMNT *of partners in company* gleiches Stimmrecht *nt*

Equal: **~ Worth Equal Pay Act** *n* HRM Gesetz über die Gleichheit von Lohn und Leistung

equation *n* MATH Gleichung *f*

equilibrium *n* ECON Gleichgewicht *nt*; **~ basis** *n* STOCK *currency futures* Gleichgewichtsbasis *f*; **~ GNP** *n* ECON güterwirtschaftliches Gleichgewicht *nt*; **~ output** *n* ECON Gleichgewichtsmenge *f*, Gleichgewichtsproduktion *f*; **~ price** *n* ECON Gleichgewichtspreis *m*; **~ wage rate** *n* ECON Lohngleichgewicht *nt*, Tarifgleichgewicht *nt*

equip *vt* COMP ausstatten, GEN COMM ausrüsten, ausstatten, IND bestücken

equipment *n* COMP Ausstattung *f*, GEN COMM Ausrüstung *f*, Ausstattung *f*, IND Bestückung *f*; **~ dealer insurance** *n* INS Versicherung *f* für Ausrüstungsvertreiber, Versicherung *f* für Ausrüstungsvertriebsgesellschaften; **~ failure** *n* GEN COMM Gerätefehler *m*; **~ goods** *n pl* ECON Ausrüstungsgegenstände *m pl*, Investitionsgüter *nt pl*; **~ handover agreement** *n* IND Geräteübergabevertrag *m*, Übergabevereinbarung *f*; **~ installation and checkout** *n* (*EIC*) IND Geräteeinbau *m* und -abnahme *f*; **~ leasing** *n* ECON Investitionsgüter-Leasing *nt*, FIN Ausrüstungsvermietung *f*, IND Geräteleasing *nt*, Geräteverleih *m*, PROP Geräteleasing *nt*; **~ trust bond** *n* FIN durch Maschinen und Ausrüstungsgegenstände gesicherte Schuldverschreibung

equitable *adj* ECON billigkeitsrechtlich, GEN COMM *fair* gerecht, recht und billig, LAW billigkeitsrechtlich; **~ distribution** *n* GEN COMM gerechte Verteilung *f*

equity *n* ACC Aktienkapital *nt*, Eigenkapital *nt*, ECON *fairness* Billigkeit *f*, Eigenkapital *nt*, LAW Billigkeit *f*; ♦ **have an ~ stake** STOCK eine Kapitalbeteiligung haben

equity: **~ accounting** *n* ACC Eigenkapitalmethode *f*; **~ base** *n* ACC Eigenkapitalbasis *f*; **~ borrowing** *n* FIN

Kapitalaufnahme *f*; ~ **capital** *n* FIN Eigenkapital *nt*; ~ **capital base** *n* ACC Eigenkapitalbasis *f*; ~ **and debt capital** *n* LAW Eigen- und Fremdkapital *nt*; ~ **financing** *n* FIN Aktienfinanzierung *f*, Beteiligungsfinanzierung *f*, Eigenfinanzierung *f*; ~ **fund** *n* ACC, STOCK Aktienfonds *m*; ~ **holder** *n* HRM Aktionär, in *m,f*; ~ **holding** *n* FIN Beteiligung *f*, Kapitalbeteiligung *f*, STOCK Aktienbesitz *m*; ~ **interest** *n* ADMIN, GEN COMM Stammkapitalbeteiligung *f*, STOCK Aktienbeteiligung *f*; ~ **investment fund** *n* STOCK Kapitalbeteiligungsfonds *m*; ~ **issue** *n* STOCK Aktienemission *f*, Emission von Stammaktien *f*; ~ **joint venture** *n* GEN COMM Gemeinschaftsunternehmung *f*; ~ **kicker** *n* STOCK Kapitalbeteiligung *f* eines Kreditgebers; ~-**linked mortgage** *n* FIN eigenkapitalgebundene Hypothek *f*, Eigenkapitalhypothek *f*, an das Eigenkapital gebundene Hypothek *f*; ~-**linked policy** *n* STOCK aktiengebundene Politik *f*; ~ **market** *n* STOCK Aktienmarkt *m*; ~ **method of accounting** *n* ACC Bilanzierung *f* langfristiger Beteiligungen; ~ **ownership** *n* STOCK Eigenkapital *nt*, Kapitalbeteiligung *f* eines Anteilseigners; ~ **position** *n* FIN Eigenkapitalausstattung *f*, Eigenkapitaldecke *f*; ~ **of redemption** *n* BANK Ablösungsrecht *nt*, Auslösungsrecht *nt*; ~-**related bonds** *n pl* STOCK aktienähnliche Obligationen *f pl*; ~-**related futures** *n pl* STOCK Terminkontrakte *m pl* auf Aktienbasis, aktienähnliche Termingeschäfte *nt pl*, aktienähnliche Terminkontrakte *m pl*; ~ **return** *n* STOCK Eigenkapitalrentabilität *f* (*EKR*); ~ **share** *n AmE* (*cf ordinary share BrE*) STOCK Stammaktie *f*; ~ **sharing** *n* STOCK Kapitalbeteiligung *f*; ~ **stake** *n* STOCK Aktienbeteiligung *f*; ~ **taxation** *n* TAX Aktienbesteuerung *f*; ~ **trading** *n* STOCK Aktienhandel *m*; ~ **turnover** *n* ADMIN Kapitalumschlag *m*, Umschlaghäufigkeit *f* des Eigenkapitals, STOCK Umsatz *m* in Aktien; ~ **value** *n* BANK Eigenkapitalwert *m*; ~ **warrant** *n* FIN Aktien-Warrant *m*, STOCK Aktienbezugsrechtsschein *m*, Optionsschein *m*

equivalence *n* GEN COMM Äquivalenz *f*

equivalent *adj* GEN COMM äquivalent, gleichwertig; ~ **amount** *n* GEN COMM Gegenwert *m*; ~ **taxable yield** *n* TAX äquivalenter steuerlicher Ertrag *m*

ERA *abbr* ECON (*exchange rate agreement*) Währungsabkommen *nt* Wechselkursvereinbarung *f*, (*effective rate of assistance*) effektive Hilfsrate *f*, HRM, LAW (*Equal Rights Amendment*) Gleichberechtigungsergänzungsgesetz *nt*

eradicate *vt* GEN COMM ausrotten

eradication *n* GEN COMM Ausrottung *f*

erasable: ~ **programmable read-only memory** *n* (*EPROM*) COMP *programming language* löschbarer programmierbarer Nur-Lese-Speicher *m*

erase *vt* COMP löschen, GEN COMM ausradieren, streichen

erasure *n* COMP Löschung *f*, GEN COMM Rasur *f*

ERC *abbr* (*European Registry of Commerce*) GEN COMM EHR (*Europäisches Handelsregister*)

ERDF *abbr* (*European Regional Development Fund*) ECON EFRE (*Europäischer Fonds für regionale Entwicklung*)

erect *vt* GEN COMM *customs barriers* errichten, IND *factories, housing* bauen, *machinery* aufstellen, *scaffolding* aufbauen

erection: ~ **insurance** *n* INS Montageversicherung *f*

ergonomic *adj* COMP, GEN COMM ergonomisch

ergonomically *adv* COMP ergonomisch; ~-**designed** *adj* COMP *work station* ergonomisch konstruiert

ergonomics *n* ADMIN *office* Arbeitsplatzanalyse *f*, Ergonomie *f*, COMP Arbeitswissenschaft *f*, Ergonomie *f*, GEN COMM, HRM Ergonomie *f*

ergonomist *n* GEN COMM Ergonom, in *m,f*

ERL *abbr* FIN (*economic recovery loan*) Aufbauanleihe *f*, (*emergency reconstruction loan*) Sanierungsanleihe *f* für Notfälle

ERM *abbr* (*Exchange Rate Mechanism*) ECON Wechselkursmechanismus *m*

erode *vt* ECON abnutzen, verschleißen, ENVIR erodieren, GEN COMM *power* untergraben, aushöhlen, STOCK aushöhlen

erosion *n* ECON Abnutzung *f*, Verschleiß *m*, ENVIR *of land* Erosion *f*, GEN COMM Untergraben *nt*, Aushöhlung *f*, STOCK *of option's premium or time value* Aushöhlung *f*

ERP *abbr* (*European Recovery Program AmE, European Recovery Programme BrE*) ECON Marshall-Plan, ERP (*Europäisches Wiederaufbauprogramm*)

err *vi* GEN COMM sich irren

errand *n* GEN COMM Botengang *m*, Geschäftsgang *m*

erratic *adj* GEN COMM heftig, sprunghaft, STOCK *performance, work* ungleichmäßig, *price movements* heftig, sprunghaft, schwankend, erratisch

erratum *n* GEN COMM Fehler *m*

erroneous *adj* GEN COMM falsch, irrtümlich

error *n* COMP Fehler *m*, INS, LAW Irrtum *m*, MATH *statistics* Fehler *m*; ~ **control** *n* COMP Fehlerüberwachung *f*; ~-**free** *adj* COMP fehlerfrei; ~ **in motivation** *n* LAW *contracts* Motivirrtum *m*; ~ **of law** *n* LAW Rechtsirrtum *m*; ~ **message** *n* COMP Fehlermeldung *f*; ~ **rate** *n* COMP Fehlerhäufigkeit *f*; ~ **recovery** *n* COMP Fehlerbeseitigung *f*; ~ **report** *n* COMP Fehlerbericht *m*

errors: ~ **and omissions** *n pl* ECON *balance of payments* Saldo *m* nicht aufgliederbarer Transaktionen, Restposten *m pl* der Zahlungsbilanz; ~ **and omissions clause** *n* INS Irrtums- und Versäumnisklausel *f*; ~ **and omissions excepted** *phr* (*E&OE*) GEN COMM Irrtum vorbehalten; ~ **and omissions insurance** *n* ADMIN, INS Haftpflichtversicherung *f*

ES *abbr* (*expert system*) COMP, GEN COMM Expertensystem *nt*

ESA *abbr* (*European Space Agency*) GEN COMM EWO (*Europäische Weltraumorganisation*)

ESAF *abbr* (*Enhanced Structural Adjustment Facility*) FIN IMF erweiterte Strukturanpassungsfazilität *f*

Esc *abbr* (*Escape key*) COMP *keyboard* Abbruchtaste *f*, ESCAPE-Taste *f*

ESC *abbr* ECON (*Economic and Social Committee*) Wirtschafts- und Sozialausschuß *m*, TRANSP (*European Shippers' Council*) Verband *m* Europäischer Spediteure

escalate *vi* GEN COMM *costs* eskalieren, sprunghaft erhöhen, *prices* in die Höhe schnellen

escalation: ~ **clause** *n* ECON, INS Indexklausel *f*, Preisgleitklausel *f*, Wertsicherungsklausel *f*, Zinserhöhungsklausel *f*, LAW *contract law* Preisgleitklausel *f*

escalator *n* GEN COMM *moving staircase* Rolltreppe *f*; ~ **clause** *n* FIN, HRM Zinserhöhungsklausel *f*

escape: ~ **character** *n* COMP Escape-Zeichen *nt*; ~ **clause** *n* ADMIN Rücktrittsklausel *f*, GEN COMM

Befreiungsklausel *f*, LAW *contract* Ausweichklausel *f*, Rücktrittsklausel *f*

Escape: ~ **key** *n* (*Esc*) COMP Abbruchtaste *f*, ESCAPE-Taste *f*

escape: ~ **sequence** *n* COMP Escape-Folge *f*

escheat *n* LAW *property* Heimfall *m*

escort 1. *n* GEN COMM Eskorte *f*, Geleitschutz *m*; **2.** *vt* GEN COMM *visitor* begleiten

escrow *n* LAW Treuhandverwahrung *f*; ~ **account** *n* BANK, FIN Anderkonto *nt*; ~ **agent** *n* FIN Treuhandverwalter, in *m,f*; ~ **agreement** *n* LAW *trusteeship* Treuhandhinterlegungsvereinbarung *f*, Treuhandvertrag *m*; ~ **clause** *n* LAW *shipping* Treuhandklausel *f*

ESF *abbr* (*European Social Fund*) ECON ESF (*Europäischer Sozialfonds*)

ESOP *abbr* (*employee stock ownership plan*) STOCK Aktienerwerbsplan *m* für Arbeitnehmer, Mitarbeiterbeteiligung *f*, Belegschaftsaktienfonds *m*

esp. *abbr* (*especially*) GEN COMM besonders, insb. (*insbesondere*)

especially *adv* (*esp.*) GEN COMM besonders, insbesondere (*insb.*)

espionage *n* IND, POL Spionage *f*

esprit de corps *n* GEN COMM, HRM, MGMNT Gemeinschaftsgeist *m*, Korpsgeist *m*

Esq. *abbr* (*esquire*) GEN COMM Herr *m*

esquire *n* (*Esq.*) GEN COMM Herr *m*

ESRO *abbr* (*European Space Research Organization*) GEN COMM ESRO (*Europäische Organisation für Weltraumforschung*)

essential: ~ **commodities** *n pl* GEN COMM, S&M Güter *nt pl* des täglichen Bedarfs; ~ **feature** *n* PATENTS Wesensmerkmal *nt*, wesentliche Eigenschaft *f*, wesentliches Merkmal *nt*; ~ **foodstuffs** *n pl* GEN COMM Grundnahrungsmittel *nt pl*; ~ **industry** *n* ECON, IND Schlüsselindustrie *f*

essentials: **the** ~ *n pl* GEN COMM das Wesentliche *nt*, die wesentlichen Punkte *m pl*

est. *abbr* (*established*) GEN COMM gegr. (*gegründet*)

EST *abbr AmE* (*Eastern Standard Time*) GEN COMM östliche Standardzeit

establish 1. *vt* GEN COMM anerkennen, *fact, date* festlegen, feststellen, ermitteln; ♦ ~ **a company** GEN COMM Unternehmen gründen; ~ **a direct link** with COMMS eine Direktverbindung herstellen mit; **2.** ~ **oneself** *v refl* GEN COMM sich etablieren, sich niederlassen

established *adj* (*est.*) GEN COMM anerkannt, gegründet (*gegr.*); ~ **brand** *n* S&M bekannte Marke *f*, eingeführte Marke *f*; ~ **clientele** *n* GEN COMM fester Kundenkreis *m*, S&M Kundenstamm *m*; ~ **image** *n* S&M Ansehen *nt*, guter Ruf *m*; ~ **market** *n* S&M etablierter Markt *m*; ~ **product** *n* S&M bekanntes Produkt *nt*, eingeführtes Produkt *nt*; ~ **programmes financing** *BrE*, ~ **programs financing** *AmE n* FIN Finanzierung *f* etablierter Programme

establishment *n* ADMIN Unternehmung *f*, GEN COMM Unternehmen *nt*, Firma *f* (*Fa.*), HRM Betrieb *m*, *new business* Gründung *f*, Geschäftsgründung *f*, Errichtung *f*

Establishment: **the** ~ *n BrE* GEN COMM das Establishment *nt*

estate *n BrE infrml* TRANSP Kombi *m* (*infrml*) (*Kombiwagen*); ~ **in abeyance** *n* LAW ruhende Erbschaft *f*, herrenloses Anwesen *nt*; ~ **administration** *n* PROP Nachlaßverwaltung *f*; ~ **administrator** *n* LAW, PROP *inheritance* Nachlaßverwalter, in *m,f*; ~ **agency** *n BrE* (*cf real-estate office AmE*) PROP Immobilienbüro *nt*; ~ **agent** *n* (*cf realtor AmE*) PROP Grundstücksmakler, in *m,f*, Immobilienmakler, in *m,f*, Wohnungsmakler, in *m,f*; ~ **car** *n BrE* (*cf station wagon AmE*) TRANSP Kombiwagen *m* (*Kombi*); ~ **economy** *n* ECON Latifundienwirtschaft *f*; ~ **executor** *n* LAW, PROP Nachlaßverwalter, in *m,f*; ~ **manager** *n* LAW Nachlaßverwalter, in *m,f*; ~ **planning** *n* LAW *wills* Nachlaßregelung *f*; ~ **in reversion** *n* LAW *property* Heimfallanspruch *m*, Heimfallrecht *nt*; ~ **in severalty** *n* PROP Immobilie als Bruchteilseigentum *f*

estates *n pl* PROP Ländereien *f pl*

estate: ~ **tax** *n AmE* TAX Erbschaftssteuer *f*

estimate 1. *n* ADMIN Haushaltsausgabenansatz *m*, FIN Haushaltsansatz *m*, Haushaltsvoranschlag *m*, GEN COMM Berechnung *f*, Taxe *f*, *of cost* Kostenvoranschlag *m*, Voranschlag *m*; ♦ **at the highest** ~ GEN COMM nach höchster Schätzung; **at the lowest** ~ GEN COMM nach niedrigster Schätzung; **2.** *vt* ACC veranschlagen, GEN COMM taxieren, *cost* berechnen, schätzen, ansetzen, vorkalkulieren, MGMNT, STOCK vorkalkulieren

estimate: ~ **of current market value** *n* FIN Verkehrswertschätzung *f*

estimated *adj* ACC veranschlagt, vorkalkuliert, GEN COMM, MGMNT, STOCK geschätzt, vorkalkuliert; ~ **charges** *n pl* ACC *expenses* Kostenvoranschlag *m*, *fees* Kostenvoranschlag *m*; ~ **financial report** *n* FIN Jahresabschlußprognose *f*, voraussichtlicher Jahresbericht *m*; ~ **lapse** *n* ACC erwarteter Verfall *m*, voraussichtlicher Ablauf *m*; ~ **price** *n* GEN COMM Taxe *f*, Schätzpreis *m*, STOCK Kurstaxe *f*, vorkalkulierter Preis *m*; ~ **realizable value** *n* BANK geschätzter Veräußerungswert *m*; ~ **revenue** *n* ACC geschätztes Einkommen *nt*; ~ **time of arrival** *n* (*ETA*) TRANSP voraussichtliche Ankunftszeit *f*, voraussichtlicher Ankunftstermin *m*; ~ **time of departure** *n* (*ETD*) TRANSP voraussichtliche Abfahrtszeit *f*; ~ **time of sailing** *n* (*ETS*) TRANSP voraussichtliche Abfahrtszeit *f*; ~ **trading account** *n* FIN veranschlagter Handelsertrag *m*; ~ **value** *n* INS geschätzter Wert *m*, Schätzwert *m*; ~ **value of real estate** *n BrE* PROP Grundstückswertschätzung *f*, geschätzter Wert *m* von Grundstücken

estimates *n pl* FIN Ausgabenansätze *m pl*, Etat *m*, Plan *m*, Budget *nt*, GEN COMM Schätzungen *f pl*, Schätzwerte *m pl*

estimating *n* S&M Kostenschätzung *f*; ~ **equation** *n* MATH *statistics* Schätzgleichung *f*

estimation *n* ACC Veranschlagung *f*, Vorkalkulierung *f*, GEN COMM Schätzung *f*, Vorkalkulierung *f*; ♦ **in my** ~ GEN COMM nach meiner Einschätzung; **in one's own** ~ GEN COMM in das Ermessen gestellt, nach eigenem Ermessen

estimation: ~ **of parameters** *n* MATH *statistics* Parameterschätzung *f*; ~ **sampling** *n* MATH *statistics* Schätzstichproben *f pl*

estimator *n* GEN COMM Schätzer *m*, MATH *statistics* Schätzfunktion *f*

estoppel *n* LAW Rechtsverwirkung *f*, Hinderung *f*

estover *n* LAW *property* Recht *nt* der Holzentnahme von fremdem Grund

ET *abbr BrE* (*employment training*) HRM, WEL innerbetriebliche Weiterbildung *f*

ETA *abbr* (*estimated time of arrival*) TRANSP voraussichtliche Ankunftszeit *f*, voraussichtlicher Ankunftstermin *m*

et al. *phr* GEN COMM et al.

ETAS *abbr BrE* (*Economic Trends Annual Survey*) ECON *econometrics* jährliche Konjunkturumfrage *f*

ETB *abbr* (*English Tourist Board*) LEIS englischer Fremdenverkehrsverein

ETC *abbr* (*European Trade Committee*) GEN COMM Europäischer Handelsausschuß *m*

ETD *abbr* (*estimated time of departure*) TRANSP voraussichtliche Abfahrtszeit *f*

ethical *adj* LAW, MGMNT ethisch, moralisch vertretbar, standesgemäß; **~ advertising** *n* S&M lautere Werbung *f*; **~ investment** *n* STOCK ethische Investition *f*; **~ unit trust** *n* FIN Ethikfonds *m*, ethisch motivierter Investmentfonds *m*

ethics *n pl* LAW, MGMNT *business conduct* Ethik *f*, Standesethik *f*; **~ of the profession** *n pl* LAW Standesrichtlinien *f pl*, Berufsethos *nt*

ethnic: **~ monitoring** *n* HRM ethnische Statistik *f*

ETO *abbr* (*European Transport Organization*) TRANSP ETO (*Europäische Transportorganisation*)

ETPO *abbr* (*European Trade Promotion Organization*) GEN COMM Europäische Organisation *f* zur Förderung des Handels

ETS *abbr* (*estimated time of sailing*) TRANSP voraussichtliche Ablegezeit *f*

ETUC *abbr* (*European Trade Union Confederation*) HRM EGB (*Europäischer Gewerkschaftsbund*)

et ux. *phr* LAW und Ehefrau

EU *abbr* (*European Union*) ECON, POL EU (*Europäische Union*)

EUA *abbr* (*European Unit of Account*) ECON, FIN ERE (*Europäische Rechnungseinheit*)

EU: **~ directive** *n* LAW EU-Richtlinie *f*

Euler: **~'s theorem** *n* ECON, MATH Eulersches Theorem *nt*

EU: **~-mark** *n* IND *on goods meeting EU safety standards* EU-Kennzeichnung *f*, EU-Sicherheitskennzeichnung *f*, EU-Markierung *f*; **~ member states** *n pl* ECON, POL Mitgliedsstaaten *m pl* der EU

EURATOM *abbr* (*European Atomic Energy Community*) IND EURATOM (*Europäische Atomgemeinschaft*)

EURCO *abbr* (*European Composite Unit*) FIN Zusammengefaßte Europäische Einheit *f*

Euro- *pref* GEN COMM, POL Euro-

Eurobank *n* BANK Eurobank *f*

Eurobanking *n* BANK Eurobankgeschäfte *nt pl*, Eurobanking *nt*

eurobond *n* BANK Euroanleihe *f*, FIN am Euromarkt begebener Schuldtitel *m*, STOCK Euroanleihe *f*, Eurobond *m*

Eurocapital: **~ market issue** *n* STOCK Eurokapitalmarkt-Emission *f*, Eurokapitalmarktanleihe *f*, Euroanleihe *f*

eurocentric *adj* GEN COMM eurozentrisch

eurocheque *n* BANK, FIN Eurocheque *m* (*EC*), Euroscheck *m*

Euro-clear *n* BANK Euro-Clear *nt*

Euroclear *n* BANK Verrechnungssystem des internationalen Anleihehandels

euro: **~ commercial paper** *n* (*ECP*) FIN kurzfristiges Geldmarktpapier *nt* erstklassiger Emittenten, Euro-Commercial-Paper *nt* (*ECP*)

Euro: **~ Co-op** *abbr* (*European Community of Consumer Cooperatives*) GEN COMM Europäische Gemeinschaft *f* der Konsumgenossenschaften (*EURO COOP*)

eurocurrency *n* BANK, ECON, FIN, STOCK Eurowährung *f*; **~ loan** *n* BANK Euroanleihe *f*, Eurowährungsanleihe *f*, Eurowährungskredit *m*; **~ market** *n* ECON Euromarkt *m*, Fremdwährungsmarkt *m*, Eurogeldmarkt *m*, STOCK Eurogeldmarkt *m*, Eurowährungsmarkt *m*; **~ rates** *n pl* ECON Eurowährungskurse *m pl*

Eurodollar *n* ECON Eurodollar *m*; **~ bond** *n* ECON Eurodollaranleihe *f*; **~ certificates of deposit** *n* BANK Eurodollar-CDs *nt pl*, Eurodollar-Depositenzertifikate *nt pl*; **~ deposit** *n* BANK, ECON Eurodollareinlage *f*; **~ future** *n* STOCK Eurodollar-Termingeschäft *nt*, Eurodollar-Terminkontrakt *m*; **~ index** *n* STOCK Eurodollar-Index *m*; **~ market** *n* ECON Eurodollarmarkt *m*; **~ rate** *n* ECON, STOCK *currency* Eurodollarzins *m*; **~ time deposit** *n* STOCK Eurodollar-Termineinlage *f*; **~ time deposit funds** *n* STOCK Eurodollar-Termineinlagenfonds *m*; **~ time deposit futures contract** *n* STOCK Eurodollar-Termineinlagen-Terminkontrakt *m*

Euroequity *n* ECON Euroequities *pl*

Eurofranc *n* ECON Eurofranc *m*

Euro: **~ Info Centre** *n* (*EIC*) GEN COMM Euro Info Center *nt* (*EIC*), EU-Beratungsstelle *f* für KMU

Euromarket *n* ECON Euromarkt *m*; **~ lending business** *n* FIN Eurokreditgeschäft *nt*

Euromoney *n* BANK Eurogeld *nt*, Eurotagesgeld *nt*

Euro: **~ MP** *n* (*European Member of Parliament*) POL Abgeordnete(r) *mf* [decl. as adj] des Europaparlaments, MEP (*Mitglied des Europaparlaments*)

Euronet *n* COMMS Euronet *nt*

Europallet *n* GEN COMM, TRANSP *for delivery of printed matter* Europalette *f*

Europe *n* GEN COMM Europa *nt*

European *adj* GEN COMM europäisch; **~ affairs** *n pl* GEN COMM, POL Europa betreffende Angelegenheiten *f pl*, europäische Angelegenheiten *f pl*; **~ Agricultural Fund** *n* ECON Europäischer Agrarfonds *m*; **~ Agricultural Guidance and Guarantee Fund** *n* (*EAGGF*) BANK, ECON Europäischer Ausrichtungs- und Garantiefonds *m* für die Landwirtschaft (*EAGFL*); **~ Article Number** *n* (*EAN*) COMP, S&M Europäische Artikelnummer *f* (*EAN*); **~ Association of Advertising Agencies** *n* (*EAAA*) MEDIA, S&M Europäischer Verband *m* der Werbeagenturen; **~ Association for Shipping Informatics** *n* (*EASI*) GEN COMM, TRANSP Europäische Vereinigung *f* für Schiffahrtsinformatik; **~ Atomic Energy Community** *n* (*EAEC, EURATOM*) ECON, POL Europäische Atomgemeinschaft *f* (*EAG, EURATOM*); **~ Bank for Reconstruction and Development** *n* (*EBRD*) ECON Europäische Bank *f* für Wiederaufbau und Entwicklung (*EBWE*), Osteuropabank *f*; **~ Central Bank** *n* (*ECB*) ECON Europäische Zentralbank *f* (*EZB*); **~ Coal and Steel Community** *n* (*ECSC*) ECON Europäische Gemeinschaft *f* für Kohle und Stahl (*EGKS*), Montanunion *f*; **~ Commission** *n* (*EC*) ECON Europäische Kommission *f* (*EuK*); **~ Committee for Electrotechnical**

Standardization n (*CENELEC*) ECON, IND Europäisches Komitee nt für elektrotechnische Normung (*CENELEC*); ~ **Committee for Standardization** n (*CEN*) ECON CEN (*Europäisches Komitee für elektrotechnische Normung*); ~ **Committee of Legal Cooperation** n LAW Europäischer Ausschuß m für Zusammenarbeit in Rechtsfragen; ~ **Community** n (*EC*) POL Europäische Gemeinschaft f (*EG*); ~ **Community of Agricultural Ministers** n ECON Agrarministerrat m; ~ **Community Budget** n ECON EG-Haushalt m; ~ **Community of Consumer Cooperatives** n (*Euro Co-op*) GEN COMM Europäische Gemeinschaft f der Konsumgenossenschaften (*EURO COOP*); ~ **Community Market** n ECON Markt m der Europäischen Gemeinschaft; ~ **Composite Unit** n (*EURCO*) FIN Zusammengefaßte Europäische Einheit f; ~ **Convention on Human Rights** n HRM, POL, WEL Europäische Menschenrechtskonvention f; ~ **Cooperation Grouping** n (*ECG*) LAW Europäische Kooperationsvereinigung f (*EKV*); ~ **Council** n ECON EU Europäischer Rat m, Rat m (*jarg*); ~ **Council for Nuclear Research** n (*ECNR*) IND Europäischer Kernforschungsrat m; ~ **Court of Justice** n (*ECJ*) LAW Europäischer Gerichtshof m (*EuGH*), Gerichtshof m der Europäischen Union; ~ **Currency Unit** n (*ECU*) ECON, FIN Europäische Währungseinheit f (*ECU*); ~ **Development Fund** n (*EDF*) ECON Europäischer Entwicklungsfonds m (*EEF*); ~ **Economic Area** n obs (*EEA*) ECON Europäischer Wirtschaftsraum m (*obs*) (*EWR*); ~ **Economic Community** n obs (*EEC*) ECON Europäische Wirtschaftsgemeinschaft f (*obs*) (*EWG*); ~ **Economic Interest Grouping** n (*EEIG*) ECON Europäische Wirtschaftliche Interessenvereinigung f (*EWIV*); ~ **Energy Charter** n ENVIR, GEN COMM Europäische Energiecharta f; ~ **Environmental Bureau** n (*EEB*) ENVIR Europäisches Umweltbüro nt (*EEB*); ~ **Foundation** n (*EF*) GEN COMM Europäische Stiftung f; ~ **Free Trade Association** n (*EFTA*) ECON Europäische Freihandelszone f (*EFTA*); ~ **Investment Bank** n (*EIB*) BANK Europäische Investitionsbank f (*EIB*); ~ **League for Economic Cooperation** n (*ELEC*) ECON Europäische Liga f für wirtschaftliche Zusammenarbeit; ~ **Member of Parliament** n (*Euro MP*) POL Abgeordnete(r) mf [decl. as adj] des Europaparlaments, Mitglied nt des Europaparlaments (*MEP*); ~ **Mercantile Exchange** n FIN Europäische Handelsbörse f; ~ **Monetary Agreement** n (*EMA*) GEN COMM Europäisches Währungsabkommen nt (*EWA*); ~ **monetary cooperation** n ECON Europäische währungspolitische Zusammenarbeit f; ~ **Monetary Cooperation Fund** n (*EMCF*) BANK, ECON Europäischer Fonds m für währungspolitische Zusammenarbeit (*EFWZ*); ~ **Monetary Fund** n (*EMF*) ECON Europäischer Währungsfonds m (*EWF*); ~ **Monetary Institute** n (*EMI*) ECON, POL Europäisches Währungsinstitut nt (*EWI*); ~ **Monetary System** n (*EMS*) ECON Europäisches Währungssystem nt (*EWS*); ~ **Monetary Union** n (*EMU*) ECON Europäische Währungsunion f (*EWU*); ~ **Nuclear Energy Authority** n (*ENEA*) GEN COMM Europäische Atomenergiebehörde f; ~ **Options Market** n (*EOM*) STOCK Europäischer Optionsmarkt m; ~ **pallet pool** n TRANSP Europäischer Paletten-Pool m; ~ **Parliament** n (*EP*) POL Europäisches Parlament nt, Europaparlament nt; ~ **patent** n PATENTS europäisches Patent nt, Europapatent nt; ~ **patent application** n PATENTS europäische Patentanmeldung f; ~ **Patent Convention** n (*EPC*)

LAW, PATENTS *intellectual property* Europäisches Patentübereinkommen nt (*EPÜ*); ~ **Patent Office** n (*EPO*) PATENTS Europäisches Patentamt nt (*EPA*); ~ **Patent Organization** n (*EPO*) PATENTS Europäische Patentorganisation f (*EPO*); ~ **Payments Union** n (*EPU*) ECON, GEN COMM Europäische Zahlungsunion f (*EZU*); ~ **Recovery Program** AmE, ~ **Recovery Programme** BrE n (*ERP*) ECON Marshall-Plan, Europäisches Wiederaufbauprogramm nt (*ERP*); ~ **Regional Development Fund** n (*ERDF*) ECON Europäischer Fonds m für regionale Entwicklung (*EFRE*); ~ **Registry of Commerce** n (*ERC*) GEN COMM Europäisches Handelsregister nt (*EHR*); ~ **Shippers' Council** n (*ESC*) TRANSP Verband m Europäischer Spediteure; ~ **Single Market** n ECON EU-Binnenmarkt m; ~ **Social Charter** n ECON Europäische Sozialcharta f; ~ **Social Fund** n (*ESF*) ECON Europäischer Sozialfonds m (*ESF*); ~ **Space Agency** n (*ESA*) GEN COMM Europäische Weltraumorganisation f (*EWO*); ~ **Space Research Organization** n (*ESRO*) GEN COMM Europäische Organisation f für Weltraumforschung (*ESRO*); ~ **standard specifications** n GEN COMM europäische Normen f pl (*EN*); ~ **terms** n pl ECON *currency trading* europäisches Austauschverhältnis nt; ~ **Trade Committee** n (*ETC*) GEN COMM Europäischer Handelsausschuß m; ~ **Trade Promotion Organization** n (*ETPO*) GEN COMM Europäische Organisation f zur Förderung des Handels; ~ **Trade Union Confederation** n (*ETUC*) HRM Europäischer Gewerkschaftsbund m (*EGB*); ~ **trading company** n GEN COMM europäische Handelsgesellschaft f; ~ **Transport Organization** n (*ETO*) TRANSP Europäische Transportorganisation f (*ETO*); ~ **Union** n (*EU*) ECON, POL Europäische Union f (*EU*); ~ **Union member states** n ECON, POL Mitgliedsstaaten m pl der Europäischen Union; ~ **Union Treaty** n GEN COMM Vertrag m über die Europäische Union (*VEU*); ~ **Unit of Account** n (*EUA*) ECON, FIN Europäische Rechnungseinheit f (*ERE*); ~ **Year of the Environment** n (*EYE*) ENVIR Europäisches Jahr nt der Umwelt; ~ **zone charge** n (*EZC*) TRANSP *haulage* europäische Zonengebühr f

europhile adj GEN COMM europhil

europhobic adj GEN COMM europhobisch

Euro: **~-rates** n pl BANK Eurokurse m pl

Eurorebel n BrE POL Eurorebell m

Euro: **~-route** n TRANSP Europastraße f

Eurosceptic n BrE POL Euroskeptiker, in m,f

eurosceptical adj BrE POL euroskeptisch

Eurovision n ADMIN Eurovision f

evade vt TAX *taxation* hinterziehen; ♦ ~ **customs duty** TAX Zölle hinterziehen

evaluate vt GEN COMM auswerten, begutachten, bewerten, rechnerisch ermitteln

evaluation n GEN COMM Auswertung f, Bewertung f; ~ **of economic efficiency** n ECON Wirtschaftlichkeitsrechnung f; ~ **questionnaire** n GEN COMM Bewertungsfragebogen m

evasion n GEN COMM Ausweichen nt

evasive adj GEN COMM *action* ausweichend

even 1. adj COMP gerade, *distribution* gleichmäßig; ♦ **on an ~ keel** GEN COMM ausgeglichen; **2.** ~ **out** vi ECON, GEN COMM ausgleichen, *prices* einpendeln; ~ **up** GEN COMM *pay off debt* Schulden begleichen; **3.** ~ **out** vt GEN

COMM *prices* ausgleichen; ~ **up** GEN COMM *sum* aufrunden

evened: **~-out position** *n* BANK, STOCK glattgestellte Position *f*

evening: ~ **class** *n* GEN COMM Abendkurs *m*; ~ **out** *n* ECON Nivellierung *f*; ~ **peak** *n* STOCK Höchststand *m* am Abend; ~ **shift** *n* HRM Abendschicht *f*; ~ **trade** *n* STOCK Nachtbörse *f*; ~ **up** *n* STOCK Verkauf *m* zum Ausgleich

evenly: ~ **spread** *adj* GEN COMM gleichmäßig verteilt

even: **~-numbered** *adj* GEN COMM geradzahlig, MATH *integer* ganzzahlig; ~ **parity** *n* COMP gerade Bitzahl *f*, gerade Parität *f*

event *n* COMP, GEN COMM Ereignis *nt*, LEIS Veranstaltung *f*; ~ **of default** *n* FIN Verzugsfall *m*

events: ~ **subsequent to the closing date** *n pl* ACC Ereignisse *nt pl* nach dem Bilanzstichtag

eventuality *n* GEN COMM Eventualität *f*

evergreen *n* FIN unbefristeter Vertrag *m*; ~ **clause** *n* FIN Verlängerungsklausel *f*; ~ **credit** *n* BANK revolvierender Kredit *m*

ever: **~-increasing** *adj* GEN COMM *demand* ständig steigend

evict *vt* LAW, PROP, WEL *tenants* räumen lassen, zur Räumung zwingen, hinauswerfen (*infrml*)

eviction *n* LAW Räumung *f*, *property* Zwangsräumung *f*, PROP, WEL Räumung *f*; ~ **order** *n* LAW, PROP Räumungsbefehl *m*; ~ **proceedings** *n* LAW, PROP Räumungsverkauf *m*

evidence *n* LAW *lawsuit* Beweis *m*, Zeugenaussage *f*; ◆ ~ **of** GEN COMM Beweis für; **in** ~ GEN COMM deutlich in Erscheinung treten; **be in** ~ GEN COMM sichtbar sein; **give** ~ LAW vor Gericht aussagen; **give** ~ **as a witness** LAW als Zeuge aussagen; **give** ~ **on behalf of** LAW Zeugnis ablegen für; **give** ~ **on oath** LAW unter Eid aussagen; **give** ~ **under oath** LAW unter Eid aussagen

evidence: ~ **accounts** *n* ECON *international countertrade* Evidenzkonto *nt*; ~ **of achievement** *n* HRM Leistungsnachweis *m*; ~ **of formal qualification** *n* GEN COMM Befähigungsnachweis *m*; ~ **of title** *n* LAW *property* Eigentumsnachweis *m*; ~ **of use** *n* PATENTS Gebrauchsnachweis *m*

evident *adj* GEN COMM deutlich, evident

evidentiary *adj* LAW als Beweismittel geltend, beweiserheblich

evolution *n* GEN COMM Entwicklung *f*, Evolution *f*

evolutionary: ~ **theory of the firm** *n* ECON, MGMNT evolutorische Unternehmenstheorie *f*

ex *abbr* GEN COMM (*executed*) ausgeführt, (*examined*) geprüft, (*extra*) Extra *nt*, (*example*) Bsp. (*Beispiel*), (*exclusive of*) ausgenommen, ausschl. (*ausschließlich*), STOCK (*exclusive of*) ohne, (*extra*) Sonderdividende *f*, TRANSP (*exclusive of*) ab, frei

exact **1.** *adj* GEN COMM genau, *figures* exakt, pünktlich, MATH genau, *figures* exakt; **2.** *vt* FIN, GEN COMM *money*, WEL eintreiben, fordern

exacting *adj* GEN COMM *person* anspruchsvoll, *standard* hoch

exact: ~ **interest** *n* BANK Zinsen *m pl* bezogen auf die effektive Anzahl von Kalendertagen, englische Zinsrechnung *f*, Echt/365 (*jarg*)

exactly *adv* GEN COMM genau

exaggerate *vt* GEN COMM übertreiben

ex allotment *adv* FIN ex Bezugsrecht (*exB*)

examination *n* ACC Prüfung *f*, GEN COMM Untersuchung *f*, Prüfung *f*, HRM *of candidate* Prüfung *f*, IMP/EXP *by customs* Kontrolle *f*, Revision *f*, Untersuchung *f*, PATENTS Prüfung *f*, Überprüfung *f*; ◆ **on** ~ GEN COMM bei Prüfung; **under** ~ GEN COMM in Bearbeitung *f*, wird noch geprüft

examination: ~ **of proposal** *n* INS Prüfung *f* des Antrags, Prüfung *f* des Vorschlags

examine *vt* GEN COMM befragen, untersuchen, *application* prüfen, HRM *candidate* prüfen, IMP/EXP kontrollieren, PATENTS überprüfen; ◆ ~ **carefully** GEN COMM eingehend untersuchen, sorgfältig prüfen, studieren

examined *adj* (*ex*) GEN COMM geprüft

examinee *n* HRM Prüfling *m*

examiner *n* GEN COMM, HRM Prüfer, in *m,f*, IMP/EXP *customs* Zollprüfer, in *m,f*, PATENTS Prüfer, in *m,f*

example *n* (*ex.*) GEN COMM Beispiel *nt* (*Bsp.*); ◆ **for** ~ (*e.g.*) GEN COMM zum Beispiel (*z. B.*)

exam: ~ **result** *n* WEL Prüfungsergebnis *nt*

ex ante: ~ **variables** *n pl* ECON ex ante-Variablen *f pl*

exceed *vt* ECON übersteigen, GEN COMM übersteigen, übertreffen; ◆ ~ **one's authority** LAW, MGMNT seine Vollmacht überschreiten

exceeding: **not** ~ *phr* GEN COMM bis zu, höchstens

excellent *adj* GEN COMM, HRM ausgezeichnet, hervorragend

except *prep* GEN COMM außer, ausgenommen; ◆ ~ **as otherwise herein provided** (*eohp*) GEN COMM vorbehaltlich anderslautender Bestimmungen

excepted *adj* GEN COMM ausgenommen; ~ **risks** *n pl* INS unversicherte Risiken *nt pl*

exception *n* GEN COMM *to rule* Ausnahme *f*, INS Risikoausschluß *m*, Vorbehalt *m*; ◆ **with the** ~ **of** GEN COMM ausgenommen, mit Ausnahme von, unter Ausschluß von

exceptional *adj* GEN COMM *case, circumstances* außergewöhnlich; ~ **expenses** *n pl* ACC *balance sheet* außergewöhnliche Ausgaben *f pl*, einmalige Aufwendungen *f pl*, neutrale Aufwendungen *f pl*; ~ **item** *n* TRANSP Sonderbedingung *f*; ~ **quality** *n* GEN COMM Besonderheit *f*, Sonderqualität *f*; ~ **write-off** *n* ACC Sonderabschreibung *f*

exceptions: ~ **clause** *n* GEN COMM, LAW *shipping* Vorbehaltsklausel *f*, TRANSP *shipping* Ausnahmeklausel *f*, Risikoausschluß *m*, Vorbehalt *m*

excess **1.** *adj* GEN COMM überschüssig; **2.** *n* BrE (*cf deductible AmE*) ECON, FIN Mehrbetrag *m*, INS Abzugsfranchise *f*, Exzedent *m*, Mehrbetrag *m*, Selbstbehalt *m*, GEN COMM Überhang *m*; ◆ **in** ~ **of sth** GEN COMM über etw hinaus, mehr als

excess: ~ **baggage** *n* GEN COMM, LEIS, TRANSP Übergepäck *nt*, Mehrgepäck *nt*; ~ **baggage charge** *n* LEIS, TRANSP Gebühr *f* für Mehrgepäck, Gebühr *f* für Übergepäck, Gepäckübergewichtsgebühr *f*, Mehrgewichtsgebühr *f*; ~ **burden of a tax** *n* TAX übermäßige Steuerbelastung *f*; ~ **capacity** *n* ECON freie Kapazität *f*, Überkapazität *f*, Überschußkapazität *f*, IND freie Kapazität *f*, freies Faßvermögen *nt*, Freiraum *m*, Überkapazität *f*, TRANSP freie Kapazität *f*; ~ **capacity theorem** *n* ECON Theorem *nt* der Überkapazität, Überkapazitätentheorem *nt*; ~ **cash** *n* BANK Überschußreserve *f*, FIN Bargeldüberschuß *m*; ~ **demand** *n* ECON Nachfrageüberschuß *m*; ~ **fare** *n* LEIS, TRANSP

Zuschlag *m*; ~ **franchise** *n* INS Abzugsbetrag *m* vom Versicherungswert, Abzugsfranchise *f*; ~ **insurance** *n* INS Franchise *f*, Selbstbehalt *m*

excessive *adj* GEN COMM maßlos, überhöht, übermäßig, unverhältnismäßig hoch; ~ **charge** *n* BANK überhöhte Gebühren *f pl*, FIN, GEN COMM, S&M überhöhte Kosten *pl*, Überteuerung *f*; ~ **debts** *n pl* ACC, BANK, ECON Überschuldung *f*; ~ **interest** *n* BANK, FIN Wucherzinsen *m pl*, überhöhte Zinsen *m pl*

excessively *adv* GEN COMM übermäßig

excess: ~ **liabilities** *n pl* INS Haftung *f* mit Selbstbeteiligung; ~ **of line reinsurance** *n* INS Summenzedentenrückversicherung *f*; ~ **of loss** *n* INS Schadenexzedent *m*; ~ **of loss reinsurance** *n* INS Schadenexzedentenrückversicherung *f*; ~ **of loss reinsurance treaty** *n* INS Schadenexzedentenrückversicherungsvertrag *m*; ~ **mandate** *n* POL Überhangmandat *nt*; ~ **mortality** *n* INS Übersterblichkeit *f*, Sterblichkeitsüberhang *m*; ~ **point** *n* INS Selbstbehaltsgrenze *f*; ~ **profits tax** *n* TAX Übergewinnsteuer *f*; ~ **reserves** *n pl* BANK außerordentliche Reserven *f pl*, Überschußreserven *f pl*, Sonderrücklagen *f pl*; ~ **revenue allotment** *n* FIN Mehrerlösverwendung *f*; ~ **shares** *n pl* STOCK nicht plazierte Aktien *f pl*, Überschußaktien *f pl*, Zusatzaktien *f pl*; ~ **supply** *n* ECON Angebotsüberschuß *m*; ~ **weight** *n* TRANSP Übergewicht *nt*

exch. *abbr* (*exchange*) ECON Umtausch *m*, *foreign currency* Dev. (*Devisen*), Währung *f*, FIN Umtausch *m*

Exch. *abbr BrE* (*the Exchequer*) BANK Fiskus *m*, Staatskasse *f*, POL *GB* Schatzamt *nt*, Finanzministerium *nt*

exchange 1. *n* (*exch.*) COMMS *of information, views* Austausch *m*, Vermittlung *f*, ECON *goods* Tausch *m*, Austausch *m*, Tauschgeschäft *nt*, Umtausch *m*, *foreign currency* Devisen *f pl*, Währung *f*, FIN, GEN COMM Umtausch *m*, Austausch *m*, Tausch *m*, *barter transaction* Tauschgeschäft *nt*, STOCK Börse *f*; ♦ **in** ~ FIN im Tausch *m*; **2.** *vt* BANK umtauschen, COMMS *information, views* austauschen, ECON *currency* umtauschen, wechseln, FIN umtauschen, GEN COMM *letters* austauschen, *places, rooms* tauschen, STOCK umtauschen

exchangeable *adj* COMMS, ECON, GEN COMM austauschbar

exchange: ~ **of acceptances** *n* FIN Akzepttausch *m*; ~ **arbitrage** *n* STOCK Devisenarbitrage *f*; ~ **charge** *n* BANK Wechselgebühr *f*; ~ **contract** *n* LAW Devisenumtauschvertrag *m*; ~ **of contracts** *n* GEN COMM Abschluß des Kaufvertrags bei Immobilienkauf; ~ **control** *n* ECON *government policy* Devisenbewirtschaftung *f*; ~ **control officer** *n* HRM Devisenkontrollreferent, in *m,f*; ~ **cross rate** *n* Kreuzkurs *m*, Cross rate *f*, indirekte Parität *f*; ~ **deal** *n* GEN COMM Tauschgeschäft *nt*; ~ **department** *n* STOCK Devisenabteilung *f*; ~ **differences** *n pl* ECON Kursdifferenz *f*, Kursspanne *f*; ~ **discount** *n* STOCK Devisendiskont *m*; ~ **economy** *n* ECON Tauschwirtschaft *f*; ~ **efficiency** *n* ECON Tausch-Effizienz *f*; ~ **equalization** *n* ECON Währungsausgleich *m*; ~ **equalization account** *n* (*EEA*) ECON Währungsausgleichsfonds *m*; ~ **of ideas** *n* GEN COMM Meinungsaustausch *m*, POL Gedankenaustausch *m*; ~ **of information** *n* GEN COMM Informationsaustausch *m*; ~ **intervention** *n* ECON *international* Devisenmarktintervention *f*, Intervention *f* am Devisenmarkt, Kursintervention *f*; ~ **of know-how** *n* GEN COMM

Erfahrungsaustausch *m*, Austausch *m* von Fachwissen; ~ **margins** *n* FIN *currency rate* Bandbreite *f*; ~ **privilege** *n* STOCK Umtauschrecht *nt*; ~ **rate** *n* ECON, FIN Umrechnungskurs *m*, Wechselkurs *m*; ~ **rate adjustment** *n* ECON Wechselkursanpassung *f*; ~ **rate agreement** *n* (*ERA*) ECON Währungsabkommen *nt*, Wechselkursvereinbarung *f*

Exchange: ~ **Rate Mechanism** *n* (*ERM*) ECON Wechselkursmechanismus *m*

exchange: ~ **rate movements** *n pl* ECON Wechselkursbewegungen *f pl*; ~ **rate parity** *n* BANK Wechselkursparität *f*; ~ **rate system** *n* ECON Wechselkurssystem *nt*; ~ **rate target zone** *n* ECON Wechselkurszielzone *f*; ~ **ratio** *n* FIN Umtauschwert *m*, STOCK Bezugsverhältnis *nt*; ~ **risk guarantee scheme** *n* BANK Kursrisikogarantieplan *m*, Währungsgarantieplan *m*; ~ **of shares** *n BrE* (*cf exchange of stock AmE*) FIN Aktienaustausch *m*

Exchange: ~ **Stabilization Fund** *n* IMP/EXP Ausgleichsfonds *m*

exchange: ~ **of stock** *n AmE* (*cf exchange of shares BrE*) FIN Aktienaustausch *m*; ~ **value** *n* ECON Tauschwert *m*, FIN Börsenwert *m*, STOCK Börsenwert *m*, Umtauschwert *m*

exchequer *n* BANK Geldmittel *nt pl*

Exchequer: **the** ~ *n BrE* (*Exch.*) BANK Fiskus *m*, Staatskasse *f*, POL *GB* Schatzamt *nt*, Finanzministerium *nt*; ~ **bond** *n BrE* (*cf Treasury note AmE*) FIN Schatzanweisung *f*

excisable: ~ **goods** *n pl* IMP/EXP, TAX steuerbare Güter *nt pl*, verbrauchsteuerpflichtige Güter *nt pl*

excise *n* IMP/EXP *tax* Verbrauchsteuer *f*, Warensteuer *f*; ~ **bond** *n* IMP/EXP, TAX *customs* Verbrauchsteuergarantie *f*; ~ **duties** *n pl* TAX Verbrauch- und Aufwandsteuern *f pl*; ~ **duty** *n* IMP/EXP, TAX Verbrauchsteuer *f*; ~ **taxes** *n pl* FIN Akzisen *f pl*, Verbrauch- und Aufwandsteuern *f pl*

excl. *abbr* GEN COMM (*excluding, exclusive*) außer, ausschl. (*ausschließlich*), exkl. (*exklusiv*)

ex claim *adv* LAW ex Anspruch

exclude *vt* GEN COMM ausschließen

excluded: ~ **sector** *n* IND ausgeschlossener Bereich *m*

excluding *prep* (*excl.*) GEN COMM außer, ausschließlich

exclusion *n* GEN COMM Ausschließung *f*, Ausschluß *m*; ♦ **to the** ~ **of** GEN COMM unter Ausschluß von

exclusion: ~ **clause** *n* INS, LAW Haftungsausschlußklausel *f*; ~ **of liability** *n* INS Haftungsausschluß *m*, LAW *contracts* Ausschluß *m* der Gewährleistung, Haftungsausschluß *m*; ~ **principle** *n* ECON Ausschlußprinzip *nt*, Ausschlußprinzip *nt* des Preises, Preisausschlußprinzip *nt*; ~ **of risk** *n* LAW *transactions* Risikoausschluß *m*

exclusive *adj* (*excl.*) GEN COMM *not including* ausschließlich (*ausschl.*), exklusiv (*exkl.*), Exklusiv-, S&M exklusiv (*exkl.*); ♦ ~ **of** (*ex*) GEN COMM ausgenommen, ausschließlich (*ausschl.*); ~ **of loading and unloading** (*xl & ul*) IMP/EXP, TRANSP ausschließlich Laden und Löschen, ausschließlich Be- und Entladung; ~ **of post and packing** COMMS ohne Porto und Verpackung; ~ **of tax** ADMIN, ECON, TAX vor Steuern, ohne Steuern

exclusive: ~ **agency** *n* GEN COMM Alleinvertretung *f*; ~ **agency agreement** *n* LAW *commercial law* Alleinvertretungsvertrag *m*; ~ **agency listing** *n* PROP *real estate* brokers Alleinverkaufsrecht *nt*; ~ **contract** *n* GEN COMM Alleinauftrag *m*; ~ **dealer arrangement** *n* S&M Ausschließlichkeitsvertrag *m*; ~ **dealing right** *n* GEN COMM

Exklusivrecht *nt*; ~ **distribution** *n* POL *restriction on secret files* exklusive Zirkulation *f*; ~ **jurisdiction** *n* LAW alleinige Zuständigkeit *f*, ausschließliche Zuständigkeit *f*; ~ **licence** *BrE*, ~ **license** *AmE n* PATENTS Alleinlizenz *f*, Alleinverkaufsrecht *nt*; ~ **licensing arrangement** *n* PATENTS Ausschließlichkeitsvertrag *m*

exclusively *adv* GEN COMM ausschließlich

exclusive: ~ **marketing** *n* S&M Alleinvertrieb *m*; ~ **monopoly** *n* ECON exklusives Monopol *nt*; ~ **representation** *n* LAW *contracts* Alleinvertretungsrecht *nt*; ~ **right** *n* LAW Exklusivrecht *nt*, Ausschlußrecht *nt*, PATENTS Ausschlußrecht *nt*, Exklusivrecht *nt*, Alleinrecht *nt*; ~ **right-to-sell listing** *n AmE* PROP Alleinverkaufsrecht *nt*; ~ **sales contract** *n* LAW Alleinvertriebsabkommen *nt*; ~ **use** *n* PATENTS ausschließliche Benutzung *f*, ausschließliche Nutzung *f*

exclusivity *n* S&M *of product, boutique* Exklusivität *f*

ex coupon *adv* (*ex cp.*, *x-c.*) GEN COMM, STOCK ex Gratisaktien, ex Kupon, ohne Kupon

ex cp. *abbr* (*ex coupon*) GEN COMM, STOCK ex Gratisaktien, ex Kupon, ohne Kupon

exculpate *vt* BANK entlasten, LAW entlasten, freizeichnen

exculpatory *adj* BANK entlastend, LAW *trustee* entlastend, freizeichnend

excursion: ~ **ticket** *n* LEIS, TRANSP verbilligte Fahrkarte *f*, Ausflugsfahrkarte *f*

excuse *vt* LAW befreien, freistellen

ex-directory *adj BrE* (*cf unlisted AmE*) COMMS *telecommunications* nicht im Telefonverzeichnis aufgeführt

ex div. *abbr* (*ex dividend*) FIN ausschließlich Dividende, ex Dividende, ohne Dividende

ex dividend *adv* (*ex div.*) FIN ausschließlich Dividende, ex Dividende, ohne Dividende

ex docks *adv* TAX frei Dock

exec. *abbr* GEN COMM (*executive*) Führungskraft *f*, leitende(r) Angestellte(r) *mf* [decl. as adj], LAW (*executor, executrix*) *of will* Testamentsvollstrecker, in *m,f*, *administrator of an estate* Nachlaßverwalter, in *m,f*

execute *vt* ADMIN erfüllen, COMP abarbeiten, ausführen, GEN COMM ausführen, durchführen, umsetzen, LAW *carry out* durchführen, vollziehen, *a document* ausfertigen, *a contract* erfüllen, *of a will* vollstrecken, MGMNT *of policy* durchführen, STOCK ausführen; ♦ ~ **orders** STOCK Aufträge ausführen

executed *adj* (*ex*) GEN COMM *fully accomplished or performed* ausgeführt, LAW *contract* erfüllt; ~ **contract** *n* LAW erfüllter Vertrag *m*

execution *n* ADMIN *of contract* Erfüllung *f*, COMP Abarbeiten *nt*, Ausführung *f*, GEN COMM Ausführung *f*, Umsetzung *f*, LAW *of a document* Ausfertigung *f*, *of a contract* Erfüllung *f*, Vollziehung *f*, *of a will* Vollstreckung *f*, MGMNT *of policy* Durchführung *f*, STOCK Ausführung *f*; ~ **proceedings** *n pl* LAW Vollstreckungsverfahren *nt*; ~ **time** *n* COMP Ausführungszeit *f*

executive 1. *adj* GEN COMM *position, director* leitend, LAW, POL *powers* ausführend, verfügend, vollziehend; **2.** *n* (*exec.*) HRM Führungskraft *f*, leitende(r) Angestellte(r) *mf* [decl. as adj], LAW ausführende Gewalt *f*, Exekutive *f*, Sachbearbeiter, in *m,f*, MGMNT Führungskraft *f*, leitende(r) Angestellte(r) *mf* [decl. as adj], POL ausführende Gewalt *f*, Exekutive *f*

executive: ~ **advancement** *n* MGMNT Aufstieg *m* in der Leitungshierarchie; ~ **assistant** *n* ADMIN, HRM Assistent, in *m,f* der Geschäftsleitung,

Geschäftsführungsassistent, in *m,f*; ~ **board** *n* MGMNT Vorstand *m*, UN Verwaltungsrat *m*; ~ **class** *n* LEIS, TRANSP Businessklasse *f*; ~ **committee** *n* HRM Leitungsausschuß *m*, Leitungsgremium *nt*, *of union* Exekutivausschuß *m*, LAW Exekutivausschuß *m*, MGMNT *decision making* Exekutivausschuß *m*, geschäftsführender Vorstand *m*; ~ **compensation** *n* HRM Vergütung *f* für leitende Angestellte, MGMNT Amtsvergütung *f*, Vergütung *f* für leitende Angestellte; ~ **competence** *n* MGMNT Leitungskompetenz *f*; ~ **development** *n* GEN COMM Ausbildung *f* von Führungskräften; ~ **director** *n* ADMIN hauptberuflicher Direktor *m*, hauptberufliche Direktorin *f*, MGMNT Generaldirektor, in *m,f*, geschäftsführender Direktor *m* (*GD*), geschäftsführende Direktorin *f* (*GD*), hauptamtlicher Geschäftsführer *m*, hauptamtliche Geschäftsführerin *f*; ~ **grade** *n* HRM Position *f* auf Führungsebene; ~ **leasing** *n* MGMNT Leasing *nt* von Führungskräften; ~ **lounge** *n* TRANSP *air and ship* Warteraum *m* für Reisende der Business-Class, VIP-Lounge *f*; ~ **manager** *n* HRM Führungskraft *f*, leitende(r) Angestellte(r) *m,f* [decl. as adj]; ~ **manpower strategy** *n* HRM, MGMNT Führungskräftestrategie *f*; ~ **office** *n* HRM Vorstandsbüro *nt*; ~ **perk** *n infrml* (*executive perquisite*) HRM Vergünstigung *f* für leitende Angestellte; ~ **perquisite** *n frml* (*executive perk*) HRM, MGMNT Vergünstigung *f* für leitende Angestellte; ~ **promotion** *n* HRM, MGMNT Beförderung *f* von Führungskräften; ~ **remuneration** *n* HRM Entgelt *nt* für die Unternehmensführung, Vergütung *f* für leitende Angestellte, MGMNT Vergütung *f* für leitende Angestellte; ~ **search** *n* MGMNT Führungskräfte-Marketing *nt*, Suche *f* nach Führungskräften; ~ **search consultant** *n* HRM Personalberater, in *m,f*; ~ **search firm** *n* HRM Personalberatungsunternehmen *nt*, Unternehmen *nt* zur Aufspürung von Führungskräften; ~ **secretary** *n* HRM Vorstandssekretär, in *m,f*; ~ **stress** *n* HRM Managerkrankheit *f*; ~ **suite** *n* HRM Chefsuite *f*; ~ **summary** *n* GEN COMM zusammenfassende Darstellung *f*; ~ **training** *n* HRM, MGMNT Ausbildung *f* von Führungskräften, Nachwuchsförderung *f*, Schulung *f* von Führungskräften, Weiterbildung *f* von Führungskräften; ~ **vice-president** *n* HRM, MGMNT geschäftsführender Vizepräsident *m*, geschäftsführende Vizepräsidentin *f*, stellvertretende(r) Vorsitzende(r) *mf* [decl. as adj]

executor *n* (*exec.*, *exor*, *exr.*) LAW *of will* Testamentsvollstrecker, in *m,f*, *administrator of an estate* Nachlaßverwalter, in *m,f*

executory *adj* LAW noch zu vollziehen, unvollzogen; ~ **agreed** *n* LAW *contracts* Vereinbarung *f*; ~ **proceedings** *n pl* LAW Vollstreckungsverfahren *nt*

executrix *n* (*exec.*, *exor*, *exr.*) LAW *of will* Testamentsvollstreckerin *f*, *administrator of an estate* Nachlaßverwalterin *f*

exempli gratia *adv* (*e.g.*) GEN COMM zum Beispiel (*z.B.*)

ex-employee *n* HRM ehemalige Mitarbeiterin *f*, ehemaliger Mitarbeiter *m*

exempt 1. *adj* GEN COMM, TAX befreit; ♦ ~ **from income tax** TAX einkommenssteuerbefreit; ~ **from taxation** TAX steuerfrei; ~ **from VAT** *BrE* TAX mehrwertsteuerfrei, von der Mehrwertsteuer befreit; **2.** *vt* GEN COMM befreien, freistellen; ♦ ~ **sb from tax** TAX jdn von der Steuer freistellen

exempt: ~ **assets** *n pl* TAX *capital gains tax* steuerbefreite

Vermögenswerte *m pl*; ~ **employees** *n pl AmE* HRM Mitarbeiter *m pl* ohne Anspruch auf Überstundenvergütung

exemption *n* GEN COMM Befreiung *f*; ~ **clause** *n* ADMIN Freistellungsklausel *f*, LAW *contract* Freizeichnungsklausel *f*; ~ **from contributions** *n* WEL Beitragsbefreiung *f*; ~ **from liability clause** *n* INS, LAW Haftungsausschlußklausel *f*; ~ **from payment of premium** *n* INS Beitragsfreistellung *f*, Prämienbefreiung *f*; ~ **from tax** *n* TAX Steuerbefreiung *f*; ~ **from taxes** *n* TAX Steuerfreiheit *f*; ~ **from VAT** *n BrE* TAX MwSt.-Befreiung *f*

exempt: ~ **supplies** *n pl* TAX *VAT* steuerbefreite Hilfs- und Betriebsstoffe *m pl*

exequature *n* LAW *contracts* Exequaturverfahren *nt*, Exequatur *nt*

exercisable *adj* STOCK *options* ausübbar

exercise 1. *n* GEN COMM Anwendung *f*, Ausübung *f*, LAW, STOCK Ausübung *f*; **2.** *vt* GEN COMM anwenden, ausüben, *price restraint* üben, LAW, S&M, STOCK ausüben; ♦ ~ **a right** LAW von einem Recht Gebrauch machen; ~ **censorship over** MEDIA zensieren; ~ **power over** GEN COMM Macht ausüben über

exercise: ~ **deadline** *n* STOCK Ausübungsfrist *f*, Erklärungsfrist *f*; ~ **of occupation** *n* GEN COMM, HRM Berufsausübung *f*; ~ **price** *n* STOCK Basispreis *m*; ~ **procedure** *n* STOCK *options* Ausübungsverfahren *nt*; ~ **of profession** *n* GEN COMM, HRM Berufsausübung *f*; ~ **of rights** *n* STOCK Ausübung *f* von Rechten; ~ **of trade** *n* GEN COMM, HRM Berufsausübung *f*; ~ **of undue authority** *n* GEN COMM Ausübung *f* nicht zustehender Rechte

exert *vt* GEN COMM anwenden

ex factory *adv* GEN COMM, IMP/EXP, TRANSP ab Fabrik (*x-Fabrik*), ab Werk; ~ **clause** *n* GEN COMM Fabrikklausel *f*; ~ **price** *n* IND Preis ab Werk *m*

ex gratia: ~ **payment** *n* FIN freiwillige Zahlung *f*, Kulanzentschädigung *f*, Kulanzregulierung *f*, Kulanzzahlung *f*, HRM Abfindung *f*, INS freiwillige Leistung *f*, Kulanzentschädigung *f*, Kulanzregulierung *f*, Kulanzzahlung *f*

exhaust *vt* ENVIR *natural resources*, GEN COMM *resources, possibilities* erschöpfen

exhaust: ~ **emission** *n* ENVIR Abgasemission *f*; ~ **gas** *n* ENVIR *from vehicles* Abgas *nt*

exhaustive *adj* GEN COMM erschöpfend

exhibit 1. *n* GEN COMM Ausstellungsstück *nt*, LAW *evidence* Beweisstück *nt*, PATENTS, S&M Ausstellungsstück *nt*; **2.** *vt* GEN COMM *goods* ausstellen, PATENTS, S&M *at a fair* ausstellen

exhibition *n* GEN COMM Ausstellung *f*, Messe *f*, PATENTS, S&M Ausstellung *f*; ~ **center** *AmE*, ~ **centre** *BrE n* GEN COMM Ausstellungszentrum *nt*; ~ **forwarding** *n* IMP/EXP Ausstellungsspedition *f*, Messespedition *f*; ~ **risks insurance** *n* INS Ausstellungsversicherung *f*; ~ **room** *n* GEN COMM Ausstellungsraum *m*; ~ **stand** *n* MEDIA Ausstellungsstand *m*

EXIM: ~ **bank** *n* (*export-import bank*) FIN, IMP/EXP Ausfuhr-Einfuhr-Bank *f*

exit 1. *n* GEN COMM Ausgang *m*; **2.** *vt* COMP beenden

exit: ~ **barrier** *n* ECON Marktaustrittsschranke *f*, POL *persons* Ausreisebeschränkung *f*; ~ **interview** *n* ADMIN, HRM Abgangsgespräch *nt*; ~ **price** *n* FIN, STOCK Auf-

lösungspreis *m*, Liquidationspreis *m*; ~ **voice** *n* HRM Absentismus *m*

ex-legal *adj* LAW außerrechtlich

ex nudo pacto non oritur actio *phr* LAW ein reines Versprechen *nt*

exodus: ~ **of capital** *n* FIN Abwanderung *f* von Kapital, Kapitalabfluß *m*

ex officio *adv* HRM von Amts wegen; ~ **member** *n* HRM Mitglied kraft Amtes *nt*

exogenous: ~ **expectations** *n* ECON exogene Erwartungen *f pl*; ~ **variable** *n* ECON exogene Variable *f*

exonerate *vt* GEN COMM befreien

exor *abbr* (*executor, executrix*) LAW *of will* Testamentsvollstrecker, -in *m,f*, *administrator of an estate* Nachlaßverwalter, -in *m,f*

exorbitant *adj* GEN COMM übermäßig, exorbitant

exotic: ~ **currency** *n* ECON exotische Währung *f*

exotics *n pl* STOCK exotische Währungen *f pl*, exotische Papiere *nt pl*

exp. *abbr* (*export*) ECON Ausf. (*Ausfuhr*), Exp. (*Export*), IMP/EXP *process* Ausf. (*Ausfuhr*), Exp. (*Export*), *exported article* Ausfuhrgut *nt*, Exportgut *nt*

expand *vt* ECON *a company* ausweiten, erweitern, expandieren, FIN, GEN COMM erweitern, *activities* ausdehnen, ausweiten; ♦ ~ **output** IND die Produktion ausweiten

expandable *adj* COMP *hardware, software* erweiterbar

expanded *adj* ECON *company* erweitert, expandiert, ausgeweitet, FIN, GEN COMM erweitert; ~ **memory** *n* COMP Erweiterungsspeicher *m*; ~ **type** *n* MEDIA breite Antiquaschrift *f*

expansion *n* ECON *of company* Ausweitung *f*, Erweiterung *f*, Expansion *f*, FIN, GEN COMM *of company* Ausdehnung *f*, Ausweitung *f*, Erweiterung *f*, Expansion *f*

expansionary *adj* ECON *fiscal policy* expansiv

expansion: ~ **board** *n* COMP Erweiterungsplatine *f*; ~ **card** *n* COMP Erweiterungskarte *f*; ~ **of demand** *n* S&M Nachfrageausweitung *f*; ~ **strategy** *n* ECON, GEN COMM Expansionsstrategie *f*

ex parte *adv* GEN COMM einseitig

expatriate: ~ **employee** *n* GEN COMM im Ausland tätige Mitarbeiterin *f*, im Ausland tätiger Mitarbeiter *m*; ~ **executive** *n* GEN COMM im Ausland tätige Führungskraft *f*

expectancy *n* LAW *sales contract* Anwartschaftsrecht *nt*, LAW Erwartungswert *m*; ~ **theory of motivation** *n* HRM, INS Motivationstheorie *f* der Anwartschaft

expectation *n* GEN COMM, ECON, MATH Erwartung *f*; ♦ **in ~ of** GEN COMM in Erwartung von

expected *adj* GEN COMM *result, outcome* erwartet; ~ **actual capacity** *n* ECON erwartete Istkapazität *f*; ~ **date** *n* GEN COMM voraussichtliches Datum *nt*; ~ **funds availability** *n* (*EFA*) FIN kommissionierte Kapitalverfügbarkeit *f*; ~ **mortality** *n* INS Sterblichkeitsrate *f*, voraussichtliche Sterblichkeit *f*; ~ **perils** *n pl* INS erwartete Gefahren *f pl*, erwartete Risiken *nt pl*; ~ **value** *n* MATH Erwartungswert *m*

expect: ~ **sth from sb** *phr* GEN COMM von jdm etw erwarten

expediency *n* GEN COMM *of measures* Zweckdienlichkeit *f*

expedient *adj* GEN COMM zweckdienlich

expedite *vt* GEN COMM beschleunigen, vorantreiben, beschleunigt abfertigen, HRM vorantreiben

expedited: ~ **funds availability** *n* BANK beschleunigte Mittelbereitstellung *f*; ~ **procedure** *n* FIN abgekürztes Verfahren *nt*, GEN COMM abgekürztes Verfahren *nt*, Schnellverfahren *nt*

expel *vt* GEN COMM ausschließen; ~ **sb** *vt* POL jdn des Landes verweisen

expelled *adj* GEN COMM ausgeschlossen, POL *from a country* ausgewiesen; ~ **shareholder** *n* GEN COMM ausgeschlossener Aktionär *m*

expend *vt* ENVIR *resources* verbrauchen, FIN verausgaben, GEN COMM ausgeben, aufwenden

expendable *adj* GEN COMM entbehrlich, *people* überflüssig; ~ **goods** *n pl* GEN COMM Betriebsstoffe *m pl*; ~ **pallet** *n* TRANSP Einwegpalette *f*

expendables *n pl* COMP *paper, peripherals* Verschleißteile *nt pl*

expenditure *n* ADMIN, ECON, FIN, GEN COMM, TAX Aufwand *m*, Aufwendungen *f pl*, Ausgabe *f* (*Ausg.*), Ausgaben *f pl*, Kosten *pl*, Barausgaben *f pl*; ~ **budget** *n* ECON, FIN, GEN COMM Ausgabenetat *m*; ~ **estimates** *n pl* FIN Ausgabenansätze *m pl*; ~ **function** *n* ECON Ausgabenfunktion *f*; ~ **multiplier** *n* ECON Ausgabenmultiplikator *m*; ~ **tax** *n* ECON, TAX Ausgabensteuer *f*

expense *n* ACC, FIN, GEN COMM, TAX Ausgabe *f* (*Ausg.*), Aufwand *m*, Kosten *pl*; ◆ **go to the ~ of** GEN COMM die Ausgabe auf sich nehmen; **go to great ~** GEN COMM sich in große Unkosten stürzen; **at one's own ~** GEN COMM auf eigene Kosten, auf eigene Rechnung

expense: ~ **account** *n* ACC Aufwandskonto *nt*, Spesenkonto *nt*, HRM Spesenkonto *nt*; ~ **allowance** *n* ACC Spesenpauschale *f*, GEN COMM Aufwandsentschädigung *f*; ~ **budget** *n* ACC Etat *m*, FIN Kostenplan *m*; ~ **center** *AmE*, ~ **centre** *BrE* *n* ACC Kostenstelle *f*

expensed *adj* *AmE* ACC ausgebucht, als Aufwand verbucht

expense: ~ **item** *n* ACC Aufwandsposten *m*; ~ **ratio** *n* ECON Verhältnis *nt* Aufwand zu Umsatzerlös

expenses *n pl* ACC Spesen *pl*, Auslagen *f pl*, *statement of income* Aufwendung *f*, Geschäftsausgaben *f pl*, ECON, GEN COMM Auslagen *f pl*, Kosten *pl*; ◆ **all ~ paid** GEN COMM auf Geschäftskosten, Spesen werden übernommen

expensive *adj* GEN COMM kostspielig, teuer

experience 1. *n* GEN COMM *growth* Erfahrung *f*; **2.** *vt* GEN COMM *growth* erfahren, erleben; ◆ ~ **rapid growth** ECON rasch anwachsen, schnelles Wachstum erfahren

experience: ~ **curve** *n* ECON, IND Erfahrungskurve *f*

experienced *adj* GEN COMM, HRM erfahren; ~ **workforce** *n* HRM erfahrene Mitarbeiter *m pl*

experience: ~ **figures** *n* GEN COMM Erfahrungswerte *m pl*; ~ **good** *n* ECON Erfahrung *f*; ~ **loss** *n* FIN, INS Erfahrungsverlust *m*; ~ **rating** *n* INS Erfahrungstarifierung *f*

experiment *n* GEN COMM Experiment *nt*, Versuch *m*

expert 1. *adj* COMP fachmännisch, GEN COMM fachmännisch, sachkundig, HRM erfahren, geschickt; **2.** *n* COMP Experte *m*, Expertin *f*, Fachmann *m*, GEN COMM Autorität *f*, Experte *m*, Expertin *f*, Sachverständige(r) *mf* [decl. as adj], HRM Experte *m*, Expertin *f*, Fachmann *m*

expert: ~ **body** *n* GEN COMM Fachgremium *nt*

expertise *n* GEN COMM Sachkenntnis *f*, Sachverstand *m*, HRM Erfahrung *f*

expert: ~ **knowledge** *n* GEN COMM, HRM Fachwissen *nt*, Fachkenntnisse *f pl*; ~ **network** *n* COMP Expertennetz *nt*; ~ **power** *n* MGMNT Expertengewalt *f*; ~ **system** *n* (*ES*) COMP, GEN COMM Expertensystem *nt*; ~ **valuation** *n* GEN COMM Begutachtung *f*; ~ **witness** *n* LAW sachverständige Zeugin *f*, sachverständiger Zeuge *m*

expiration *n* BANK Verfall *m*, GEN COMM Ende *nt*, Ablauf *m*, STOCK Fälligkeit *f*; ~ **cycle** *n* STOCK Auslaufrhythmus *m*, Verfallsrhythmus *m*; ~ **date** *n* AmE (*cf expiry date BrE*) GEN COMM Verfallsdatum *nt*; ~ **month** *n* STOCK *currency futures* Auslaufmonat *m*, Verfallsmonat *m*; ~ **notice** *n* INS *policy* Fristablaufsbenachrichtigung *f*, Benachrichtigung *f* über einen Fristablauf; ~ **of time** *n* GEN COMM Fristablauf *m*

expire *vi* BANK verfallen, GEN COMM auslaufen, *lapse* ablaufen, ungültig werden; ◆ ~ **in-the-money** STOCK Substanzwert einer Option verfällt; ~ **worthless** STOCK nach Ablauf wertlos sein

expired *adj* BANK verfallen, GEN COMM abgelaufen, ausgelaufen, ungültig geworden; ~ **bill** *n* BANK fälliger Wechsel *m*

expiry *n* BANK Verfall *m*, GEN COMM Ablauf *m*; ~ **date** *n* BrE (*cf expiration date AmE*) GEN COMM Ablauftermin *m*, *of food etc* Verfallsdatum *nt*, HRM Datum *nt* des Erlöschens

explain 1. *vt* GEN COMM erläutern, erklären, rechtfertigen; **2.** *vi* GEN COMM sich rechtfertigen

explanation *n* GEN COMM Erläuterung *f*, Erklärung *f*, Rechtfertigung *f*

explicit *adj* GEN COMM deutlich, explizit; ~ **contract** *n* LAW ausdrücklicher Vertrag *m*; ~ **cost** *n* ECON ausgewiesene Kosten *pl*

explode *vt* COMP auseinanderziehen

exploded: ~ **view** *n* S&M aufgelöste Darstellung *f*, auseinandergezogene Darstellung *f*

exploit *vt* ECON, ENVIR *natural resources* verwerten, ausbeuten, abbauen, FIN, GEN COMM *minerals, land, talent, situation* ausnutzen, verwerten, nutzen, ausbeuten, HRM *workers* ausnutzen, ausbeuten (*jarg*), IND verwerten, PATENTS auswerten, praktisch verwerten, verwerten

exploitation *n* ECON, ENVIR *of vulnerable resource* Abbau *m*, Ausbeutung *f*, *of raw material* Gewinnung *f*, *of rainforests* Abholzung *f*, *of natural resources* Abbau *m*, FIN, GEN COMM, IND Ausbeutung *f*, Ausnutzung *f*, Verwertung *f*, PATENTS Auswertung *f*, Patentverwertung *f*, Verwertung *f*; ~ **in industry** *n* IND industrielle Verwertung *f*, PATENTS industrielle Nutzung *f*

exploited *adj* FIN, GEN COMM verwertet, HRM ausgebeutet, IND, PATENTS verwertet; ~ **resource** *n* ENVIR genutzte Ressource *f*; ~ **workers** *n pl* GEN COMM, HRM ausgebeutete Arbeiter *m pl* (*jarg*)

explosive: ~ **article** *n* TRANSP Sprengkörper *m*; ~ **substance** *n* TRANSP *dangerous classified transported goods* Explosivstoff *m*

exponent *n* MATH Exponent *m*, Hochzahl *f*

exponential *adj* MATH exponentiell, Exponential-; ~ **function** *n* COMP, MATH Exponentialfunktion *f*; ~ **notation** *n* COMP, MATH Exponentialschreibweise *f*; ~ **smoothing** *n* FIN, MATH *forecasting technique* exponentielle Glättung *f*; ~ **trend** *n* ECON Exponentialtrend *m*

export 1. *n* (*exp.*) ECON, IMP/EXP Ausfuhr *f* (*Ausf.*), Warenausfuhr *f*, Export *m* (*Exp.*); **2.** *vt* ECON, IMP/EXP ausführen, exportieren

export: ~ **adjustment loan** *n* (*EAL*) FIN Ausfuhranpassungskredit *m*, Exportangleichungskredit *m*; ~ **agent** *n* HRM Ausfuhragent, in *m,f*

exportation *n* ECON, IMP/EXP Ausfuhr *f*, Ausfuhrhandel *m*, Export *m*

export: ~ **authorization** *n* GEN COMM, IMP/EXP Ausfuhrgenehmigung *f*; ~ **ban** *n* GEN COMM, IMP/EXP Ausfuhrverbot *nt*; ~ **berth** *n* TRANSP *shipping* Exportliegeplatz *m*; ~ **business** *n* IMP/EXP Ausfuhrhandel *m*, Exportwirtschaft *f*, Exportgeschäft *nt*; ~ **cargo packing declaration** *n* (*ECPD*) IMP/EXP Exportversandliste *f*; ~ **cargo shipping instruction** *n* (*ECSI*) IMP/EXP Exportversandanweisung *f*; ~ **catalog** *AmE*, ~ **catalogue** *BrE* *n* S&M Exportkatalog *m*; ~ **clerk** *n* HRM Exportsachbearbeiter, in *m,f*; ~ **club** *n* IMP/EXP Exportklub *m*; ~ **commission agent** *n* IMP/EXP Exportkommissär, in *m,f*; ~ **consignment** *n* IMP/EXP Ausfuhrsendung *f*; ~ **consignment identifying number** *n* IMP/EXP Exportsendungsidentifizierungsnummer *f*, Exportsendungskennnummer *f*, Exportsendungskennzeichen *nt*; ~ **contract** *n* IMP/EXP Ausfuhrvertrag *m*; ~ **control** *n* IMP/EXP Ausfuhrüberwachung *f*, Exportkontrolle *f*; ~ **coordinator** *n* HRM Exportsachbearbeiter, in *m,f*; ~ **credit** *n* IMP/EXP Ausfuhrkredit *m*, Exportkredit *m*

Export: ~ **Credit Guarantees Department** *n BrE* (*ECGD*) IMP/EXP Ausfuhrkreditversicherungsanstalt *f*

export: ~ **credit insurance** *n* IMP/EXP, INS Ausfuhrkreditversicherung *f*, Exportschutzversicherung *f*; ~ **customer** *n* IMP/EXP, S&M Exportkunde *m*, Exportkundin *f*; ~ **data folder** *n* IMP/EXP Exportdatenmappe *f*; ~ **declaration** *n* GEN COMM, IMP/EXP Ausfuhrerklärung *f*; ~ **department** *n* IMP/EXP Exportabteilung *f*; ~ **depot charges** *n pl* IMP/EXP Exportlagergebühren *f pl*; ~ **director** *n* HRM Exportdirektor, in *m,f*; ~ **documentation** *n* IMP/EXP Ausfuhrpapiere *nt pl*, Exportdokumente *nt pl*, Exportunterlagen *f pl*; ~ **documentation procedure** *n* GEN COMM, IMP/EXP Vorschriften *f pl* für Exportunterlagen; ~ **duties and taxes** *n pl* IMP/EXP, TAX Ausgangsabgaben *f pl*; ~ **earnings** *n pl* ECON Exporterlöse *m pl*

exporter *n* HRM, IMP/EXP Exporteur, in *m,f*; ~ **credit** *n* BANK Exportkredit *m*; ~'**s acceptance credit** *n* BANK Export-Rembourskredit *m*, Exportakzeptkredit *m*

export: ~ **facilitation organization** *n* IMP/EXP Organisation *f* für Exportförderung; ~ **factoring** *n* IMP/EXP Exportfactoring *nt*; ~ **fair** *n* IMP/EXP, S&M Exportmesse *f*; ~ **figures** *n pl* IMP/EXP Ausfuhrzahlen *f pl*, Exportziffern *f pl*; ~ **finance** *n* IMP/EXP Exportfinanzierung *f*; ~ **finance house** *n* FIN, IMP/EXP Exportfinanzierungshaus *nt*; ~ **financing** *n* FIN Exportfinanzierung *f*; ~ **of goods order** *n* GEN COMM, IMP/EXP Warenexportauftrag *m*; ~ **house** *n* IMP/EXP Exportfirma *f*, Exportunternehmen *nt*; ~~**import bank** *n AmE* (*EXIM bank*) BANK, FIN, IMP/EXP Ausfuhr-Einfuhr-Bank *f*

exporting *n* IMP/EXP Ausfuhr *f*, Exporttätigkeit *f*; ~ **beneficiary country** *n* IMP/EXP begünstigtes Ausfuhrland *f*

export: ~ **intelligence service** *n BrE* (*EIS*) IMP/EXP Ausfuhrnachrichtendienst *m*, Exportnachrichtendienst *m*; ~~**intensive industry** *n* ECON exportintensive Indu-

strie *f*; ~ **invoice** *n* IMP/EXP Exportrechnung *f*; ~~**led** *adj* ECON *international* exportinduziert; ~~**led economic recovery** *n* ECON exportinduzierter Aufschwung *m*; ~~**led growth** *n* IMP/EXP exportinduziertes Wachstum *nt*; ~ **letter of credit** *n* FIN Exportakkreditiv *nt*; ~ **licence** *n BrE* IMP/EXP Exportlizenz *f*, Ausfuhrbewilligung *f*, Ausfuhrgenehmigung *f*, Exportbewilligung *f*, Exportlizenz *f*; ~ **licence expiry date** *n BrE* IMP/EXP Ablaufdatum *nt* der Exportlizenz, Ablauftag *m* der Ausfuhrgenehmigung, Ablauftermin *m* der Ausfuhrgenehmigung, Exportbewilligungsverfallsdatum *nt*; ~ **licence number** *n BrE* IMP/EXP Ausfuhrgenehmigungskennzeichen *nt*, Exportlizenznummer *f*; ~ **license** *AmE see export licence BrE*; ~ **licensing branch** *n* (*ELB*) IMP/EXP Abteilung für Exportlizenzen; ~ **loan** *n* BANK Exportkredit *m*; ~ **management company** *n AmE* (*cf import/export merchant BrE*) IMP/EXP Außenhandelsunternehmen *nt*; ~ **manager** *n* MGMNT Exportleiter, in *m,f*, Leiter, in *m,f* Export; ~ **market** *n* ECON, IMP/EXP Ausfuhrmarkt *m*, Exportmarkt *m*; ~ **marketing** *n* IMP/EXP, S&M Exportmarketing *nt*, internationales Marketing *nt*; ~ **marketing manager** *n* HRM, IMP/EXP, MGMNT, S&M Leiter, in *m,f* Exportmarketing, Leiter, in *m,f* Marketing Export; ~ **market research** *n* IMP/EXP, S&M Exportmarktforschung *f*; ~ **merchant** *n* HRM, IMP/EXP Exportkauffrau *f*, Exportkaufmann *m*; ~ **office** *n* IMP/EXP Exportbüro *nt*; ~ **order** *n* IMP/EXP, IND Exportauftrag *m*; ~ **order check list** *n* IMP/EXP Checkliste *f* für Exportaufträge; ~~**oriented** *adj* IMP/EXP ausfuhrgerecht, exportgerecht, exportorientiert; ~ **packer** *n* IMP/EXP Exportpacker *m*; ~ **performance** *n* IMP/EXP Exportergebnis *nt*, Exportleistung *f*; ~ **permit** *n* IMP/EXP Ausfuhrbewilligung *f*, Exportgenehmigung *f*; ~ **policy** *n* IMP/EXP Ausfuhrpolitik *f*; ~ **prices** *n pl* ECON, IMP/EXP Exportpreise *m pl*; ~ **prohibition** *n* IMP/EXP Ausfuhrverbot *nt*; ~ **promotion** *n* (*EP*) IMP/EXP Exportförderung *f*; ~ **quota** *n* ECON Ausfuhrkontingent *nt*, Ausfuhrquote *f*, Exportquote *f*; ~ **rebate** *n* TAX Ausfuhrvergütung *f*; ~ **regulations** *n pl* GEN COMM, IMP/EXP Ausfuhrvorschriften *f pl*, Exportbestimmungen *f pl*; ~ **reject** *n* IMP/EXP Exportabfall *m*; ~ **sales** *n pl* IMP/EXP, S&M Exportverkäufe *m pl*; ~ **sales manager** *n* S&M Exportleiter, in *m,f*; ~ **sector** *n* IMP/EXP Exportwirtschaft *f*; ~ **services voucher** *n* IMP/EXP Exportleistungsbeleg *m*; ~ **shed** *n* IMP/EXP Exporthalle *f*; ~ **subsidy** *n* IMP/EXP Ausfuhrbeihilfe *f*, Exportsubvention *f*; ~ **surplus** *n* ECON, IMP/EXP Ausfuhrüberschuß *m*, Exportüberschuß *m*, Exportüberhang *m*; ~ **trade** *n* IMP/EXP Ausfuhrhandel *m*, Exporthandel *m*; ~ **transactions** *n* IMP/EXP Exportgeschäft *nt*; ~ **turnover** *n* IMP/EXP Auslandsumsatz *m*, Exportumsatz *m*

exposed: ~ **net asset position** *n* GEN COMM offene Nettovermögensposition *f*; ~ **net liability position** *n* BANK offene Nettoverbindlichkeit *f*; **in an** ~ **position** *phr* GEN COMM an exponierter Stelle; ~ **sector** *n* GEN COMM exponierter Bereich *m*

exposition *n* STOCK Ausstellung *f*

ex post *adv* ECON ex post, im nachhinein; ~ **facto law** *n* LAW rückwirkende Gesetze *nt pl*; ~ **variables** *n pl* ECON ex post-Variablen *f pl*

exposure *n* ADMIN Obligo *nt*, Risiko *nt*, FIN Obligo *nt*, offene Position *f*, Risiko *nt*, S&M *advertising* Darbietung *f*; ~ **draft** *n* ACC Arbeitspapier *nt*, Diskussionspapier *nt*, POL Arbeitspapier *nt*

express 1. *adj* GEN COMM *unambiguous* ausdrücklich, *delivery* Expreß-; **2.** *vt* GEN COMM *intention* ausdrücken, aussprechen, bekunden, zum Ausdruck bringen; ♦ ~ **publicly** GEN COMM öffentlich zum Ausdruck bringen

express: ~ **agency** *n* GEN COMM Sondervertretungsvollmacht *f*; ~ **authority** *n* LAW ausdrückliche Genehmigung *f*, *for transaction* ausdrückliche Vollmacht *f*; ~ **conditions** *n pl* GEN COMM, LAW ausdrückliche Bedingungen *f pl*; ~ **consignment** *n* GEN COMM, IMP/EXP Expreßgut *nt*; ~ **contract** *n* LAW ausdrücklicher Vertrag *m*; ~ **delivery** *n* COMMS Eilpost *f*, GEN COMM Expreßbeförderung *f*; ~ **freight** *n* BrE (*cf fast freight AmE*) TRANSP Eilfracht *f*

expression *n* COMP *programming language* Ausdruck *m*

express: **mail** *n* BrE (*cf priority mail AmE*) GEN COMM Expreßpost *f*; ~ **mail service** *n* GEN COMM Eilzustellungsdienst *m*; ~ **order** *n* GEN COMM Eilauftrag *m*; ~ **telegraphic money transfer** *n* BANK, FIN telegrafische Eilüberweisung *f*; ~ **term** *n* HRM ausdrückliche Vertragsvereinbarung *f*, GEN COMM *of contract*, LAW ausdrückliche Bedingung *f*; ~ **warranty** *n* GEN COMM ausdrückliche Garantie *f*, LAW ausdrückliche Garantie *f*, *Uniform Contract Act* vertragliche Gewährleistung

expressway *n* AmE (*cf motorway BrE*) TRANSP Autobahn *f*, Autostraße *f*, Kraftfahrstraße *f*

expropriate *vt* ADMIN, LAW enteignen

expropriation *n* ADMIN, LAW Enteignung *f*

expulsion *n* POL Ausweisung *f*

expunge *vt* GEN COMM ausstreichen, durchstreichen, *from record* auslösen

expunged *adj* GEN COMM ausgestrichen, durchgestrichen, *from record* ausgelöst

ex quay *adv* (*x-quay*) TRANSP ab Pier (*x-Pier*), ab Kai (*x-Kai*)

exr. *abbr* (*executor, executrix*) LAW *of will* Testamentsvollstrecker, in *m,f*, *administrator of an state* Nachlaßverwalter, in *m,f*

ex scrip *adv* STOCK ex Gratisaktien

extend *vt* BANK erweitern, prolongieren, verlängern, COMP erweitern, FIN ausdehnen, GEN COMM *deadline* verlängern, *clientele, knowledge* ausdehnen, *carry over* übertragen LAW *rules* erweitern; ♦ ~ **a loan** BANK ein Darlehen herauslegen an [+acc], ein Darlehen gewähren; ~ **the time limit for sth** GEN COMM die Frist für etw verlängern

extended *adj* BANK erweitert, verlängert, COMP erweitert, FIN ausgedehnt, GEN COMM *deadline* verlängert, *clientele, knowledge* ausgedehnt, LAW erweitert; ~ **cover** *n* INS erweiterte Deckung *f*, zusätzlicher Versicherungsschutz *m*; ~ **coverage** *n* INS erweiterte Deckung *f*, zusätzlicher Versicherungsschutz *m*; ~ **coverage endorsement** *n* INS Nachtrag *m* zur Erweiterung des Versicherungsschutzes; ~ **credit** *n* S&M über ein halbes Jahr hinaus gewährter Exportkredit *m*; ~ **deferment** *n* ACC verlängerter Aufschub *m*; ~ **fund facility** *n* (*EFF*) FIN erweiterte Fondsfazilität *f*, erweiterte Kreditfazilität *f*; ~ **guarantee** *n* S&M verlängerte Garantiezeit *f*; ~ **memory** *n* COMP Erweiterungsspeicher *m*; ~ **payment** *n* BANK Zahlungsverlängerung *f*; ~ **program** *AmE*, ~ **programme** *BrE* *n* GEN COMM erweitertes Programm *nt*; ~ **reservation of title** *n* LAW

contracts verlängerter Eigentumsvorbehalt *m*; ~ **terms** *n pl* BANK erweiterte Bedingungen *f pl*; ~ **use test** *n* S&M Dauergebrauchstest *m*

extensible *adj* MGMNT *employment* ausbaufähig

extension *n* ADMIN *of repayments* Tilgungsaufschub *m*, BANK Erweiterung *f*, Verlängerung *f*, COMMS Anschluß *m*, COMP *of filename* Erweiterung *f*, GEN COMM Verlängerung *f*, Ausdehnung *f*, LAW Erweiterung *f*; ~ **costs** *n pl* INS Kosten *pl* für die Erweiterung des Versicherungsschutzes, Verlängerungskosten *pl*; ~ **fee** *n* BANK *installment loan* Verlängerungsgebühr *f*; ~ **for returns** *n* TAX Fristaufschub *m* für Steuererklärungen, Fristverlängerung *f*; ~ **of a judgment for enforcement** *n* LAW Vollstreckung *f* eines Urteils in einem anderen Staat; ~ **of original term** *n* LAW *contracts* Endterminverschiebung *f*, Fristverlängerung *f*; ~ **services** *n pl* FIN Dienste *m pl* der Nebenstelle, GEN COMM Stundungsdienst *m*; ~ **of time** *n* LAW Fristverlängerung *f*; ~ **of time for filing** *n* TAX *tax return* Abgabefristverlängerung *f*, Einreichungsfristverlängerung *f*; ~ **of time for payment** *n* LAW Zahlungsfristverlängerung *f*, Fristverlängerung *f*, TAX Stundung *f*; ~ **of time limits** *n* PATENTS Fristverlängerung *f*, Zusatzfrist *f*

extensive: ~ **farming** *n* ECON *agricultural economics* extensive Bewirtschaftung *f*; ~ **selling** *n* S&M extensiver Verkauf *m*

extent *n* PATENTS *of protection* Maß *nt*, Umfang *m*; ~ **of damage** *n* INS Schadenhöhe *f*, Schadenumfang *m*

extenuating: ~ **circumstances** *n pl* LAW mildernde Umstände *m pl*

external *adj* GEN COMM extern, Außen-, Fremd-; ~ **account** *n* ECON Ausländerkonto *nt*, Auslandskonto *nt*, Zahlungsbilanz *f*; ~ **balance** *n* ECON Außenbilanz *f*; ~ **balance sheet comparison** *n* ACC externer Bilanzvergleich *m*; ~ **bill** *n* BANK Auslandswechsel *m*; ~ **border** *n* GEN COMM Außengrenze *f*; ~ **borrowings** *n pl* ACC, ECON, FIN Auslandsverschuldung *f*, Auslandsschulden *f pl*; ~ **community transit document** *n* IMP/EXP externer gemeinschaftlicher Versandschein *m*; ~ **cost** *n* ACC außerbetriebliche Kosten *pl*, ECON volkswirtschaftliche Kosten *pl*; ~ **debt** *n* ECON, FIN Auslandsverschuldung *f*; ~ **debtor** *n* ACC, ECON, FIN Auslandsschuldner, in *m,f*; ~ **debt ratio** *n* ECON, FIN Auslandsverschuldungsgrad *m*; ~ **debts** *n pl* ACC, ECON, FIN Auslandsschulden *f pl*; ~ **economic aid** *n* ECON Auslandshilfe *f*; ~ **economy** *n* GEN COMM Außenwirtschaft *f*; ~ **economy of scale** *n* ECON externe Nutzen *m pl*, externe Skalenerträge *m pl*; ~ **effects of consumption** *n pl* ECON externe Konsumeffekte *m pl*, Konsumexternalitäten *f pl*, externe Effekte *m pl* des Konsums; ~ **facts** *n pl* GEN COMM äußere Umstände *m pl*; ~ **financing** *n* ACC, FIN Außenfinanzierung *f*, Beteiligungs- und Fremdfinanzierung *f*; ~ **financing limit** *n* (*EFL*) FIN Außenfinanzierungsplafond *m*; ~ **frontier** *n* GEN COMM Außengrenze *f*; ~ **funds** *n pl* ECON, FIN Auslandsgelder *nt pl*; ~ **government policy** *n* ECON Außenwirtschaftspolitik *f* der Regierung; ~ **hard disk** *n* COMP externe Festplatte *f*; ~ **house magazine** *n* MEDIA, S&M Kundenzeitschrift *f*; ~ **improvements** *n pl* PROP *of a property other than buildings* Außenanlagen *f pl*

externality *n* ECON externe Effekte *m pl*, Externalität *f*

externalize *vt* ECON externalisieren

external: ~ **labor market** *AmE*, ~ **labour market** *BrE* *n*

ECON ausländischer Arbeitsmarkt *m*, externer Arbeits-markt *m*; ~ **liabilities** *n pl* ACC, ECON, FIN Auslandsschulden *f pl*; ~ **loan** *n* FIN Auslandsanleihe *f*

externally: ~ **funded pensions** *n pl* BrE FIN extern dotierte Rentenbezüge *m pl*, extern finanzierte Pensionsanteile *m pl* des Arbeitnehmers

external: ~ **market** *n* ECON, GEN COMM Auslandsmarkt *m*; ~ **procedure** *n* TRANSP *transit* externes Verfahren *nt*; ~ **relations** *n pl* GEN COMM Auslandsbeziehungen *f pl*, MGMNT Außenbeziehungen *f pl*, auswärtige Beziehungen *f pl*; ~ **report** *n* GEN COMM externer Bericht *m*; ~ **reporting** *n* ADMIN externes Berichtswesen *nt*; ~ **shock** *n* ECON exogener Schock *m*; ~ **sovereignty** *n* ECON Außensouveränität *f*; ~ **surplus** *n* ECON, IMP/EXP Zahlungsbilanzüberschuß *m*; ~ **tariff** *n* ECON Außenzoll *m*, IMP/EXP *export duty* Außentarif *m*, Außenzoll *m*; ~ **trade** *n* GEN COMM Außenhandel *m*; ~ **trade guarantee** *n* INS Außenhandelsgarantie *f*; ~ **trade indicator** *n* ECON *international trade* Außenhandels-indikator *m*; ~ **trade statistics** *n pl* ECON Außenhandelsstatistik *f*

extinction *n* ENVIR Aussterben *nt*, Umkippen *nt*, GEN COMM Tilgung *f*, LAW Löschung *f*; ~ **of a debt** *n* FIN Rückzahlung *f* einer Schuld

extinguish *vt* GEN COMM löschen, tilgen, LAW *debt* entlasten von, *legal duty* löschen; ♦ ~ **an action** LAW ein Verfahren für ungültig erklären

extort *vt* GEN COMM *money* erpressen

extortionate: ~ **rent** *n* LAW Wuchermiete *f*

extortion *n* FIN Wucher *m*, GEN COMM Erpressung *f*; ~ **insurance** *n* INS Versicherung *f* gegen Erpressung

extra *n* (*ex.*) GEN COMM Extra *nt*, STOCK Sonderdividende *f*; ~ **billing** *n* ACC Sonderfakturierung *f*; ~~**budgetary outlay** *n* GEN COMM außerplanmäßige Ausgaben *f pl*; ~ **charge** *n* ACC Aufpreis *m*, Zuschlag *m*, GEN COMM Aufgeld *nt*, Aufschlag *m*, Preisaufschlag *m*; ~ **charges** *n pl* ACC Nebenkosten *pl*

extract 1. *n* GEN COMM *from document*, LAW Auszug *m*; **2.** *vt* GEN COMM *information* Auszug anfertigen über, herausziehen, gewinnen, IND *minerals, energy resources* fördern

extractable: ~ **reserves** *n pl* ENVIR *energy resources* nutzbare Vorräte *m pl*

extract: ~ **from the land register** *n* PROP Grundbuchauszug *m*; ~ **from the register** *n* PATENTS Auszug *m* aus dem Register, Registerauszug *m*

extraction *n* IND *oil, gas* Förderung *f*, Gewinnung *f*

extractive: ~ **industry** *n* ECON, IND *mining* Grundstoffindustrie *f*

extra: ~ **dividend** *n* INS Bonus *m*, Summenzuwachs *m*, STOCK Bonus *m*, Sonderdividende *f*, Zusatzdividende *f*; ~ **freight** *n* GEN COMM Frachtzuschlag *m*, TRANSP Zusatzporto *nt*; ~ **high strength** *n* (*EHS*) IND Hochfestigkeit *f*

extraordinary: ~ **benefits** *n pl* ACC außerordentliche Zuwendungen *f pl*; ~ **charge** *n* ACC *balance sheets*, FIN außerordentlicher Aufwand *m*; ~ **depreciation** *n* ACC

außerordentliche Abschreibung *f*; ~ **dividend** *n* STOCK außerordentliche Dividende *f*; ~ **expenditure** *n* ACC außerordentliche Aufwendungen *f pl*, außergewöhnliche Aufwendungen *f pl*; ~ **expenses** *n pl* ACC außerordentliche Aufwendungen *f pl*; ~ **gain** *n* ACC außerordentlicher Ertrag *m*; ~ **general meeting** *n* (*EGM*) MGMNT außerordentliche Hauptversammlung *f*, außerordentliche Vollversammlung *f*; ~ **income** *n* ACC außerordentlicher Ertrag *m*; ~ **item** *n* ACC, ADMIN außerordentlicher Posten *m*, FIN außerordentliche Aufwands- oder Ertragsposition *f*, Sonderposten *m*; ~ **loss** *n* ACC außerordentlicher Verlust *m*; ~ **meeting** *n* GEN COMM, MGMNT außerplanmäßige Sitzung *f*, außerplanmäßige Tagung *f*, außerplanmäßiges Treffen *nt*, außerplanmäßige Versammlung *f*

extra: ~ **pay** *n* HRM Gehaltszulage *f*

extrapolation *n* MATH *prediction of values* Extrapolation *f*, Hochrechnung *f*

extrapolative: ~ **expectations** *n* ECON extrapolierende Erwartungen *f pl*

extra: ~ **postage** *n* GEN COMM Zusatzporto *nt*; ~ **tare** *n* GEN COMM Extra-Tara *f*

extraterritorial: ~ **enforcement** *n* LAW exterritoriale Vollstreckung *f*

extreme: ~ **pressure** *n* (*EP*) IND Höchstdruck *m*

extremum *n* ECON Extremwert *m*

extrinsic: ~ **motivation** *n* HRM extrinsische Motivation *f*; ~ **value** *n* STOCK *options* Option *f* ohne Substanzwert, unwesentlicher Wert *m*

ex turpi causa non oritur actio *phr* LAW jede aus illegalen oder unmoralischen Beweggründen vorgenommene Handlung

EXW *abbr* (*ex works*) IMP/EXP, TRANSP *Incoterms* ab Fabrik (*x-Fabrik*), ab Werk

ex warehouse *adv* (*x-warehouse*) IMP/EXP, TRANSP *Incoterms* ab Lager

ex wharf *adv* (*x-wharf*) IMP/EXP, TRANSP *Incoterms* ab Hafendamm (*x-Hafendamm*)

ex works *adv* (*EXW*) IMP/EXP, TRANSP *Incoterms* ab Fabrik (*x-Fabrik*), ab Werk; ~ **export packing** *n* IMP/EXP *cargo delivery*, TRANSP Exportverpackung *f* ab Werk; ~ **price** *n* IND Preis *m* ab Werk

EYE *abbr* (*European Year of the Environment*) ENVIR Europäisches Jahr *nt* der Umwelt

eye: ~~**catching** *adj* S&M *display* auffällig; ~ **contact** *n* S&M *marketing* Blickkontakt *m*

eyewash *n* infrml S&M fauler Zauber *m* (*infrml*), Geschwätz *nt*, Augenwischerei *f* (*infrml*)

eyewitness *n* LAW Augenzeuge *m*

EZ *abbr* (*enterprise zone*) ECON Industriefördergebiet *nt*, Industriegebiet *nt*, Wirtschaftsentwicklungsgebiet *nt*, ausgewiesene Flächen *f pl* mit besonderem Entwicklungsstatus, Fördergebiet *nt*, Gewerbegebiet *nt*

EZC *abbr* (*European zone charge*) TRANSP *haulage* europäische Zonengebühr *f*

F

F *abbr* (*Fahrenheit*) GEN COMM F (*Fahrenheit*)

f.a.a. *abbr* (*free of all average*) GEN COMM, INS, TRANSP frei von Havarie, havariefrei

FAA *abbr AmE* (*Federal Aviation Administration*) TRANSP Bundesluftfahrtbehörde *f*

FAB *abbr* (*forwarder air waybill*) IMP/EXP, TRANSP Luftfrachtbrief *m* des Spediteurs

fabricate *vt* GEN COMM *goods* herstellen

fabricator *n* IND Stahlbaufirma *f*

fac *abbr* TRANSP (*fast as can*) *loading, discharging* so schnell wie möglich, (*forwarding agent's commission*) Provision *f* für Spediteur

facade *n* PROP *of a building* Fassade *f*

face 1. *n* COMP, MEDIA *typography* Schriftart *f*, PROP *of building* Fassade *f*; ◆ **in the ~ of** GEN COMM angesichts; **at ~ value** FIN, STOCK zu pari, zum Nennwert; **2.** *vt* GEN COMM sich stellen; ◆ **~ a problem** MGMNT vor einem Problem stehen; **~ the facts** GEN COMM den Tatsachen ins Auge sehen; **~ up to sb** GEN COMM jdm ins Auge sehen

face: **~ amount** *n* INS Versicherungssumme *f*; **~ interest rate** *n* BANK Nettozinssatz *m*, Nominalzinssatz *m*; **~ page** *n* MEDIA Titelseite *f*; **~ of policy** *n* INS Versicherungssumme *f*; **~ risk** STOCK Nennrisiko *nt*; **~-to-face selling** *n* S&M persönlicher Verkauf *m*

facia *n* S&M Firmenschild *nt*, Ladenschild *nt*

facilitate *vt* GEN COMM, TRANSP einrichten, erleichtern

facilitation *n* GEN COMM Erleichterung *f*, TRANSP *of goods traffic* Erleichterung *f*, Förderung *f*

facilities *n pl* BANK Fazilitäten *f pl*, HRM Einrichtungen *f pl*

facility *n* COMP, GEN COMM Einrichtung *f*; **~ letter** *n* BANK Kreditbestätigung *f*, IMP/EXP Bankbürgschaft *f*; **~ trip** *n* POL Dienstreise *f*; **~ visit** *n* S&M Unternehmensbesichtigung *f*, Werksbesichtigung *f*

facing *n* S&M Aufklebezettel *m*, Facing *nt*

facsimile *n* (*fax*) COMMS, GEN COMM *hardware* Faksimile *nt* (*Fax*), Fernkopie *f* (*dat*), Fernkopierer *m*; **~ signature** *n* GEN COMM Faksimileunterschrift *f*

fact *n* GEN COMM Tatsache *f*, LAW Umstand *m*; **~-finding** *n* GEN COMM Tatsachenfeststellung *f*; **~-finding mission** *n* GEN COMM Untersuchungsauftrag *m*

faction *n* HRM *within an organization* Splittergruppe *f*, POL *within a party* Fraktion *f*

factoblig *abbr* (*facultative/obligatory*) INS *re-insurance* fakultativ/obligatorisch

factor *n* GEN COMM Faktor *m*, LAW Umstand *m*; ◆ **at ~ cost** ECON zu Faktorkosten; **be a ~ in** GEN COMM ein Faktor sein bei, eine Rolle spielen bei

factorage *n* FIN Faktoringgebühr *f*, Faktoringentgelt *nt*, Provision *f* des Kommissionärs

factor: **~ analysis** *n* MATH Faktoranalyse *f*; **~-augmenting technical progress** *n* ECON, IND *production* produktionsfaktorerhöhender technischer Fortschritt *m*; **~ costs** *n pl* ECON, IND *production* Faktorkosten *pl*, Produktionskosten *pl*; **~ endowment** *n* ECON Faktorausstattung *f*

factorial *n* MATH Faktorielle *f*, Fakultät *f*; **~ terms of trade** *n pl* ECON faktorielles Austauschverhältnis *nt*

factor: **~ income** *n* ECON Faktoreinkommen *nt*

factoring *n* ACC *of receivables*, FIN Forderungsverkauf *m*, Factoring *nt*; **~ charge** *n* FIN Factoring-Gebühr *f*, Finanzierungsgebühr *f*; **~ company** *n* FIN Factoring-Unternehmen *nt*, Factoring-Institut *nt*, Faktor *m*; **~ contract** *n* LAW Factoring-Vertrag *m*

factor: **~ market** *n* ECON Faktormarkt *m*; **~ price equalization theorem** *n* ECON Faktorpreisausgleichstheorem *nt*; **~ of production** *n* ECON, IND Produktionsfaktor *m*; **~ productivity** *n* ECON Faktorproduktivität *f*

factory *n* IND Fabrik *f*, Fabrikanlage *f*, Fabrikgebäude *nt*, Fertigungsanlage *f*, Betrieb *m*, Werk *nt*; **~ farming** *n* ECON industriell betriebene Landwirtschaft *f*, ENVIR Massen- und Intensivtierhaltung *f*, *land* Intensivbewirtschaftung *f*, Massenzucht *f*; **~ hand** *n* GEN COMM Fabrikarbeiter, in *m,f*; **~ incentive scheme** *n* HRM Anreizsystem *nt* auf Betriebsebene, betriebliches Anreizsystem *nt*; **~ inspector** *n* IND Fabrikinspektor, in *m,f*, Kontrolleur, in *m,f*, Werksinspektor, in *m,f*, Werksprüfer, in *m,f*; **~ inspectorate** *n* IND, WEL Gewerbepolizei *f*

Factory: **~ Inspectorate** *n BrE* IND, WEL Gewerbeaufsichtsamt *nt*

factory: **~ management** *n* HRM, IND, MGMNT Betriebsleitung *f*; **~ overheads** *n pl* ACC, ECON Fertigungsgemeinkosten *pl*; **~-owned apartment** *n* PROP Betriebswohnung *f*, Werkswohnung *f*; **~-owned flat** *n BrE* PROP Betriebswohnung *f*, Werkswohnung *f*; **~ owner** *n* IND Fabrikbesitzer, in *m,f*; **~ site** *n* GEN COMM Werksgelände *nt*, IND Fabrikgrundstück *nt*; **~ supplies** *n pl* ACC Hilfs- und Betriebsstoffe *m pl*, IND Betriebsstoffe *m pl*

facts: **~ and figures** *n pl* GEN COMM Daten *pl*, Fakten *m pl* und Zahlen *f pl*

factual *adj* GEN COMM tatsächlich, sachlich, LAW sachlich; **~ error** *n* GEN COMM Sachfehler *m*; **~ evidence** *n* LAW Tatsachenbeweis *m*

facultative *adj* GEN COMM fakultativ

facultative/obligatory *adj* (*factoblig*) INS *re-insurance* fakultativ/obligatorisch

facultative: **~ placing** *n* INS *marine* wahlfreie Plazierung *f*

faculty *n* GEN COMM, MATH Fakultät *f*

fad *n* ECON Blase *f*

fahrenheit *n* (*F*) GEN COMM Fahrenheit *nt*

fail 1. *vt* LAW versäumen; **2.** *vi* BANK zusammenbrechen, COMP versagen, GEN COMM *company* in Konkurs gehen, untergehen, Konkurs machen, scheitern; ◆ **~ to comply with an order** LAW einer Anordnung zuwiderhandeln; **~ to deliver** STOCK *securities* nicht liefern; **~ to disclose** LAW verschweigen; **~ to fill the needs of the market** GEN COMM, S&M am Markt vorbei produzieren; **~ to observe the law** LAW nicht nach dem Gesetz handeln, dem Gesetz zuwiderhandeln; **~ to reach an agreement** GEN COMM keine Einigung erzielen; **~ to receive** STOCK nicht erhalten

failed *adj* GEN COMM mißglückt; ~ **takeover bid** *n* FIN gescheiterte Übernahme *f*, gescheitertes Übernahmeangebot *nt*

fail: ~ **position** *n* STOCK Nichterfüllung *f* einer Position

failure *n* BANK Insolvenz *f*, COMP Versagen *nt*, GEN COMM Ausfall *m*, *of firm* Insolvenz *f*, LAW Versäumnis *nt*, MGMNT Mißerfolg *m*; ~ **analysis** *n* MGMNT Mißerfolgsanalyse *f*; ~ **behavior** *AmE*, ~ **behaviour** *BrE n* IND Ausfallverhalten *nt*; ~ **of consideration** *n* GEN COMM Nichterbringung *f* der Gegenleistung; ~ **rate** *n* GEN COMM Ausfallquote *f*; ~ **to accept** *n* GEN COMM Annahmeunterlassung *f*; ~ **to act** *n* LAW Unterlassung *f*; ~ **to agree** *n* (*FTA*) HRM, MGMNT Scheitern *nt* vonTarifverhandlungen; ~ **to appear** *n* LAW *Court* Nichterscheinen *nt*; ~ **to comply** *n* TAX Nichtbefolgung *f*; ~ **to deliver** *n* GEN COMM Lieferunfähigkeit *f*; ~ **to pay** *n* LAW Nichtzahlung *f*, Zahlungssäumnis *f*; ~ **to pay on due date** *n* FIN Zahlungsverzug *m*; ~ **to take advantage** *n* GEN COMM Nichtinanspruchnahme *f*

fair 1. *adj* ACC, GEN COMM, HRM angemessen, LAW gerecht; 2. *n* GEN COMM *trade fair* Ausstellung *f*, Messe *f*

Fair: ~ **Access To Insurance Requirements Plan** *n AmE* (*FAIR plan*) INS obligatorischer Zusammenschluß *m* von Versicherern

fair: ~ **average quality** *n* (*f.a.q.*) GEN COMM, IMP/EXP Durchschnittsqualität *f*, gute Durchschnittsqualität *f*; ~ **business practices** *n pl* GEN COMM angemessene Geschäftspraktiken *f pl*; ~ **competition** *n* ECON, LAW *commercial* lauterer Wettbewerb *m*

Fair: ~ **Credit Reporting Act** *n AmE* LAW Gesetz über nichtdiskriminierende Kreditauskünfte

fair: ~ **day's pay** *n* HRM angemessener Tageslohn *m*; ~ **day's work** *n* HRM angemessene Tagesleistung *f*; ~ **dismissal** *n* HRM Entlassung *f* aus triftigem Grund; ~ **employment** *n* HRM faire Beschäftigung *f*

Fair: ~ **Employment Commission** *n BrE* (*FEC*) HRM *Northern Ireland* Kommission für gerechte Arbeitsbedingungen; ~ **Labor Standards Act** *n AmE* (*FLSA*) LAW Gesetz über Mindestlohnnormen

fair: ~ **market rent** *n* PROP ortsübliche Miete *f*, übliche Miete *f*, übliche Pacht *f*

fairness *n* GEN COMM *of conditions* Kulanz *f*

FAIR: ~ **plan** *n AmE* (*Fair Access To Insurance Requirements Plan*) INS obligatorischer Zusammenschluß *m* von Versicherern

fair: ~ **presentation** *n AmE* (*cf true and fair view BrE*) ACC Buchführung im Sinne der Grundsätze ordnungsgemäßer Buchführung; eine den tatsächlichen Verhältnissen entsprechende Bilanz; ~ **rate of return** *n* ACC, FIN angemessene Verzinsung *f*; ~ **rent** *n* PROP übliche Miete *f*; ~ **rental value** *n* PROP üblicher Mietwert *m*, üblicher Pachtwert *m*; ~ **return** *n* ACC angemessene Verzinsung *f*, marktübliche Rendite *f*, FIN marktübliche Rendite *f*, marktgerechte Verzinsung *f*; ~ **sample** *n* GEN COMM angemessenes Muster *nt*; ~ **share** *n* GEN COMM angemessener Anteil *m*; ~ **trade** *n* S&M *pricing* lauterer Handel *m*

Fair: ~ **Trade Acts** *n pl AmE* S&M Gesetze über die Preisbindung von Markenartikeln

fair: ~ **trading** *n* ECON lauterer Handel *m*

Fair: ~ **Trading Act** *n* ECON, LAW Gesetz *nt* gegen Wettbewerbsbeschränkungen (*UWG*)

fair: ~ **value** *n* ACC *of assets* angemessener Wert *m*, Zeitwert *m*, Kapitalwert *m*; ~ **value adjustments** *n pl* ACC *first consolidation of a subsidiary* Zeitwertberichtigung *f*

Fair: ~ **Wages Resolution** *n BrE* ECON Normallohnresolution

fair: ~ **wear and tear** *n* GEN COMM übliche Abnutzung *f*

fait accompli *n* GEN COMM vollendete Tatsache *f*

faithful *adj* GEN COMM gewissenhaft

fake: ~ **the marks** *phr infrml* STOCK die Preise frisieren (*infrml*)

fall 1. *n* GEN COMM *rate* Abfall *m*, *in price* Niedergang *m*, Sinken *nt*, Rückgang *m*; 2. *vi* GEN COMM *prices* fallen, sinken, stürzen, *rate* abfallen; ♦ ~ **behind schedule** GEN COMM in Rückstand geraten; ~ **foul of** GEN COMM in Konflikt geraten mit; ~ **foul of the law** LAW ein Gesetz verletzen; ~ **short of** GEN COMM *expectations* nicht erfüllen; ~ **short of target** GEN COMM das Ziel verfehlen; ~ **under the statute of limitations** LAW verjähren; ~ **within the scope of** PATENTS in den Bereich fallen von

fall apart *vi* GEN COMM auseinanderbrechen, *plan, negotiations* scheitern

fall away *vi* GEN COMM *numbers* sinken

fall back on *vt* GEN COMM zurückgreifen auf [+acc], Hilfe suchen bei

fall behind *vi* GEN COMM zurückbleiben

fall down *vi* PROP *buildings* einstürzen

fallback *n* COMP Reservesystem *nt*; ~ **option** *n* MGMNT Abschwächungsoption *f*; ~ **position** *n* GEN COMM Mindestforderung *f*, HRM *military* gefestigte Stellung *f* für den taktischen Rückzug, POL Mindestforderung *f*, Rückzugsposition *f*

fallen: ~ **building clause** *n* INS *property* Klausel *f* für eingestürzte Gebäude

fallibility *n* GEN COMM Fehlbarkeit *f*

fallible *adj* GEN COMM fehlbar

fall: ~ **in the bank rate** *n* BANK Diskontsenkung *f*; ~ **in foreign exchange reserves** *n* STOCK Rückgang *m* der Währungsreserven

falling: ~ **prices** *n* ECON fallende Preise *m pl*, Preisrückgang *m*, S&M Preisrückgang *m*, STOCK Baisse *f*; ~ **trend** *n* STOCK fallende Tendenz *f*

fall: ~ **in population** *n* ECON Bevölkerungsrückgang *m*; ~ **in supplies** *n* ECON Angebotsrückgang *m*; ~ **in value** *n* STOCK Wertsenkung *f*

fallout *n* GEN COMM, POL unerwartetes Nebenergebnis *nt*

falsa demonstratio non nocet *phr* GEN COMM eine falsche Beschreibung macht den Gegenstand nicht ungültig

false *adj* GEN COMM falsch, unrichtig ~ **advertising** *n* GEN COMM, S&M irreführende Werbung *f*; ~ **advertising claim** *n* S&M Klage *f* wegen irreführender Werbung; ~ **alarm** *n* GEN COMM Fehlalarm *m*; ~ **economy** *n* ECON falsche Sparsamkeit *f*; ~ **or misleading information** *n* LAW falsche oder irreführende Information *f*; ~ **statement** *n* ADMIN falsche Angaben *f pl*; ~ **witness** *n* LAW *person* falscher Zeuge *m*, falsche Zeugin *f*, *testimony* falsches Zeugnis *nt*

falsely *adv* GEN COMM falsch

falsification *n* ACC Fälschung *f*; ~ **of documents** *n* LAW Urkundenfälschung *f*

falsify *vt* LAW *change the original* verfälschen, fälschen; ◆ **~ a document** LAW Urkundenfälschung begehen

falter *vi* ECON *speech* stocken, *steps* zögern

familiar *adj* GEN COMM vertraut; ◆ **be ~ with** GEN COMM vertraut sein mit, eingearbeitet sein in

familiarity *n* S&M Bekanntheit *f*, Vertrautheit *f*

family *n* GEN COMM *of products* Serie *f*, S&M Produktfamilie *f*; **~ allowance** *n* BrE WEL Familienbeihilfe *f*, Kindergeld *nt*, Kinderzulage *f*; **~ benefits** *n pl* WEL Familienbeihilfen *f pl*; **~ brands** *n pl* S&M Dachmarke *f*; **~ budget** *n* S&M Familienbudget *nt*; **~ business** *n* GEN COMM Familienbetrieb *m*, Familienunternehmen *nt*; **~ circumstances** *n pl* LAW Familienverhältnisse *nt pl*

Family: ~ Expenditure Survey *n* BrE (*FES*) ECON Indexvergleich der Familienlebensunterhaltskosten ≈ Familienbericht *m*

family: ~ fare *n* TRANSP Familienfahrpreis *m*; **~ firm** *n* GEN COMM Familienbetrieb *m*; **~ of funds** *n* STOCK Kapitalgruppe *f*; **~ hour** *n* MEDIA *broadcast* Familienprogramm *nt*; **~ income benefit policy** *n* AmE INS Familienvorsorgeversicherung *f*; **~ life cycle** *n* S&M Lebenszyklus *m* einer Familie; **~ life insurance** *n* INS Familienlebensversicherung *f*; **~ life-style** *n* S&M familiärer Lebensstil *m*; **~-owned business** *n* GEN COMM Familienbetrieb *m*; **~-owned company** *n* ECON Familiengesellschaft *f*; **~ protection policy** *n* INS Familienschutzpolice *f*, Familienschutzversicherung *f*; **~-size pack** *n* GEN COMM, HRM Familienpackung *f*; **~ tree** *n* GEN COMM, MGMNT Stammbaum *m*

famous *adj* GEN COMM berühmt

fan *n* IND Lüfter *m*, Ventilator *m*

fancy: ~ goods *n pl* ECON, GEN COMM, S&M Modeartikel *m pl*, Luxusartikel *m pl*; **~ value** *n* GEN COMM Affektionswert *m*

F&D *abbr* (*freight and demurrage*) IMP/EXP, TRANSP Fracht- und Überliegegeld *nt*

Fannie: ~ Mae *n* AmE *infrml* (*Federal National Mortgage Association*) FIN, PROP Bundesbehörde zur Förderung des Wohneigentums und Verbesserung des Wohnungsniveaus, ≈ Bundeshypothekenanstalt *f*

fanzine *n* MEDIA Fanzeitung *f*

FAO *abbr* COMMS (*for the attention of*) z. Hd. (*zu Händen*), z. Hd. v. (*zu Händen von*), ECON (*Food and Agriculture Organization*) Ernährungs- und Landwirtschaftsorganisation der UN, GEN COMM, IMP/EXP (*for the attention of*) z. Hd. (*zu Händen*), z. Hd. v. (*zu Händen von*)

f.a.q. *abbr* (*fair average quality*) GEN COMM, IMP/EXP Durchschnittsqualität *f*, gute Durchschnittsqualität *f*

fare: ~-dodger *n* TRANSP Schwarzfahrer, in *m,f*; **~-dodging** *n* TRANSP Schwarzfahren *nt*; **~ pricing** *n* TRANSP Tarifpreisgestaltung *f*; **~ war** *n* TRANSP Preiskrieg *m*

farm out *vt* ECON *piece of work* vergeben

Farm: ~ Credit System *n* AmE ECON Agrarkreditsystem *nt*

farm: ~ equipment *n* ECON, INS landwirtschaftliche Geräte *nt pl*

farmer *n* ECON, POL Bauer *m*, Bäuerin *f*

farmers': ~ association *n* GEN COMM Bauernverband *m*

farmhand *n* ECON Landarbeiter, in *m,f*

farm: ~ implements *n pl* ECON, INS landwirtschaftliche Geräte *nt pl*; **~ income** *n* ECON Agrareinkommen *nt*

farming *n* ECON Agrarwirtschaft *f*, Bewirtschaftung *f*; **~ cooperative** *n* ECON landwirtschaftliche Genossenschaft *f*; **~ lobby** *n* POL Landwirtschaftslobby *f*; **~ method** *n* ECON Bewirtschaftungsmethode *f*

farm: ~ laborer AmE, **~ labourer** BrE *n* TAX Landarbeiter, in *m,f*

farmland *n* ECON Ackerland *nt*

farm: ~ loan *n* ECON Agrarkredit *m*; **~ lobby** *n* POL Agrarlobby *f*, Bauerninteressenverband *m*, Bauernlobby *f*, Landwirtschaftslobby *f*; **~ policy** *n* ECON Agrarpolitik *f*; **~ produce** *n* ECON Agrarerzeugnis *nt*, Agrarprodukt *nt*; **~ shop** *n* BrE S&M Geschäft auf einem Bauernhof; **~ structure** *n* ECON Agrarstruktur *f*; **~ subsidy** *n* ECON Agrarsubventionen *f pl*; **~ surplus** *n* ECON Agrarüberschuß *m*, landwirtschaftliche Überschüsse *m pl*; **~ tenancy** *n* PROP Landpacht *f*, landwirtschaftlicher Pachtvertrag *m*

farmstead *n* BrE (*cf homestead AmE*) PROP Gehöft *nt*, Bauernhof *m*

far: ~-reaching *adj* GEN COMM *consequences* weitreichend; **~-seeing** *adj* GEN COMM weitblickend, weitsichtig; **~-sighted** *adj* GEN COMM weitblickend, weitsichtig

FASB *abbr* AmE (*Financial Accounting Standards Board*) ACC Gremium, das die US-Bilanzierungsrichtlinien festlegt

fascism *n* POL Faschismus *m*

fashion *n* GEN COMM, S&M Mode *f*; ◆ **in ~** GEN COMM, S&M hochmodisch, in Mode; **out of ~** GEN COMM altmodisch, unmodern

fashion: ~ designer *n* GEN COMM Modedesigner, in *m,f*, Modeschöpfer, in *m,f*; **~ editor** *n* GEN COMM Herausgeber, in *m,f* von Modezeitschriften; **~ goods** *n pl* S&M Modeartikel *m pl*; **~ house** *n* GEN COMM Modegeschäft *nt*; **~ magazine** *n* GEN COMM Modejournal *nt*; **~ model** *n* GEN COMM, MEDIA, S&M Model *nt*

fast 1. *adj* GEN COMM rasch, schnell; ◆ **be on the ~ track** HRM schnell Karriere machen; **2.** *adv* GEN COMM schnell; ◆ **very ~** GEN COMM rasant; **~ as can** (*fac*) TRANSP *loading, discharging* so schnell wie möglich; **3. ~-track sb** *vt* HRM jdn für eine schnelle Karriere vorsehen

fast: ~ decline *n* STOCK *currency expectations* schneller Rückgang *m*

fasten *vt* GEN COMM befestigen, festschnallen

fastening *n* GEN COMM Befestigung *f*

fast: ~ food *n* WEL Schnellgericht *nt*; **~ food restaurant** *n* S&M Schnellimbiß *m*; **~ freight** *n* AmE (*cf express freight BrE*) TRANSP Eilfracht *f*; **~-growing** *adj* ECON schnellwachsend; **~ lane** *n* TRANSP Überholspur *f*; **~-moving article** *n* GEN COMM, S&M Renner *m* (*infrml*); **~-moving consumer goods** *n pl* (*FMG*) S&M schnellumschlagende Ware *f*; **~ pace** *n* GEN COMM rasches Tempo *nt*; **~ rise** *n* STOCK *currency expectation* schneller Anstieg *m*; **~ track** *n* GEN COMM rascher Aufstieg *m*

FAT *abbr* (*file allocation table*) COMP FAT (*Dateizuordnungstabelle*)

fatal: ~ error *n* GEN COMM schwerer Fehler *m*, gravierender Fehler *m*

fatality *n* WEL Todesfall *m*, Todesopfer *nt*

father: ~ of chapel *n* (*FoC*) HRM *publishing, printing trade* *unions* Betriebsratsvorsitzende(r) *m* [decl. as adj]; **~ file** *n* COMP Vaterdatei *f*

fathom *n (fm)* IND *timber* Klafter *m or nt (obs)*

fault *n* COMP, GEN COMM Fehler *m*, Verschulden *nt*, Versagen *nt*, LAW Schuld *f*; **no ~** *n* INS *damage insurance* Schuldlosigkeit *f*; ♦ **be at ~** LAW Schuld haben

faultless *adj* GEN COMM fehlerfrei

faultlessness *n* LAW *contracts* Fehlerfreiheit *f*, Mängelfreiheit *f*

fault: ~ diagnosis clinic *n* MGMNT Fehlersuchseminar *nt*; **~-tolerant** *n* COMP fehlertolerant; **~-tolerant system** *n* COMP fehlertolerantes System *nt*; **~ tree analysis** *n* GEN COMM Fehlerbaumanalyse *f*

faulty *adj* GEN COMM fehlerhaft; **~ goods** *n pl* S&M fehlerhafte Waren *f pl*; **~ installation** *n* INS fehlerhafte Installation *f*, fehlerhafte Montage *f*

faux-pas *n* GEN COMM Fauxpas *m*, Fehlverhalten *nt*

favor *AmE see favour BrE*

favorability *AmE see favourability BrE*

favorable *AmE see favourable BrE*

favorite *AmE see favourite BrE*

favour 1. *n BrE* GEN COMM Gefallen *m*, Gunst *f*; ♦ **in ~ of** *BrE* GEN COMM *project, suggestion* zugunsten von; **be in ~ of** *BrE* GEN COMM einverstanden sein mit; **2.** *vt BrE* GEN COMM begünstigen, bevorzugen

favourability *n BrE* S&M Vorteilhaftigkeit *f*

favourable *adj BrE* GEN COMM *price, conditions* attraktiv, günstig, STOCK *price, conditions* günstig; **~ balance of trade** *n BrE* ECON, IMP/EXP aktive Handelsbilanz *f*; **~ difference** *n BrE* ACC geplante Kosten *pl* über Ist-Kosten, Isterlöse *m pl* über Soll-Erlöse; **~ economic climate** *n BrE* ECON günstiges Konjunkturklima *nt*, günstiges Wirtschaftsklima *nt*; **~ economic conditions** *n pl BrE* ECON günstige Konjunkturlage *f*, günstige Wirtschaftslage *f*; **~ exchange rate** *n BrE* STOCK günstiger Wechselkurs *m*; **~ rate** *n BrE* ECON günstiger Tarif *m*; **~ trade balance** *n BrE* ECON, IMP/EXP aktive Handelsbilanz *f*; **~ variance** *n BrE* ACC geplante Kosten *pl* über Ist-Kosten, Isterlöse *m pl* über Soll-Erlöse

favourite *n BrE* POL Favorit *m*

fax 1. *n (facsimile)* ADMIN, COMMS, GEN COMM Fax *nt (Faksimile)*, Fernkopierer *m*; **2.** *vt* COMMS, COMP, GEN COMM faxen

fax: ~ machine *n* ADMIN, COMP *hardware* Faxgerät *nt*; **~ transmission** *n* COMMS Faxübermittlung *f*, Faxübertragung *f*

FBIM *abbr (Fellow of the British Institute of Management)* MGMNT Mitglied des britischen Instituts für Unternehmensführung

f/c *abbr (for cash)* GEN COMM bar, in bar, gegen Barzahlung

FCAR *abbr (free of claim for accident reported)* INS *marine* frei von Schadensansprüchen aus dem übermittelten Unfall

FCCA *abbr BrE (Fellow of the Chartered Association of Certified Accountants)* ACC Mitglied des Verbands öffentlich zugelassener Wirtschaftsprüfer

FCGI *abbr (Fellow of the City and Guilds of London Institute)* GEN COMM Mitglied des Londoner Instituts für technische und Handwerksbetriebe

FCIA *abbr BrE (Fellow of the Institute of Insurance Agents)* INS Mitglied des Instituts der Versicherungsvertreter

FCMA *abbr (Fellow of the Chartered Institute of Management Accountants)* ACC Mitglied des Instituts der betrieblichen Rechnungsprüfer

fco. *abbr (franco)* IMP/EXP, TRANSP fr. *(franko, frei)*, fro. *(obs) (franko)*

FCO *abbr* ADMIN *(Foreign and Commonwealth Office BrE)* Amt für Auslands- und Commonwealthangelegenheiten, Außenministerium *nt*, ECON *AmE (Federal Cartel Office)* Bundeskartellamt *nt*, Bundeskartellbehörde *f*

fd *abbr* TRANSP *(free discharge)* freies Löschen *nt*, *(free dispatch)* freier Versand *m*

FD *abbr (free domicile)* IMP/EXP, TRANSP frei Haus, frei ins Haus

FDI *abbr (foreign direct investment)* ECON, FIN ausländische Direktinvestition *f*

FDIC *abbr AmE (Federal Deposit Insurance Corporation)* INS Bundes-Einlagenversicherungsgesellschaft, staatliche Einlagenversicherung *f*

fear: ~ of prejudice *n* LAW Besorgnis *f* der Befangenheit

feasibility *n* GEN COMM Durchführbarkeit *f*, Machbarkeit *f*, Realisierbarkeit *f*; **~ report** *n* COMP Durchführbarkeitsbericht *m*; **~ study** *n* GEN COMM Durchführbarkeitsuntersuchung *f*, Vorstudie *f*, Projektstudie *f*; **~ survey** *n* GEN COMM Projektstudie *f*

feasible *adj* GEN COMM durchführbar

featherbedding *n* HRM personelle Überbesetzung *f*, Überbesetzung *f* von Arbeitsplätzen

feature *n* COMP Merkmal *nt*, MEDIA *in newspaper* Feature *nt*, PATENTS Eigenschaft *f*, Merkmal *nt*; **~ article** *n* MEDIA Dokumentarbericht *m*; **~ desired to be protected** *n* PATENTS zu schützende Eigenschaft *f*, zu schützendes Merkmal *nt*; **~ film** *n* LEIS Hauptfilm *m*

FEC *abbr BrE (Fair Employment Commission)* HRM *Northern Ireland* Kommission für gerechte Arbeitsbedingungen

Fed: the ~ *n AmE (Federal Reserve System)* BANK, ECON, FIN Zentralbanksystem der Vereinigten Staaten, Zentralbanksystem *nt*, die Fed *f (jarg)*

federal *adj* ECON, POL föderal, Bundes-, bundesstaatlich

Federal: ~ Agency Issue *n AmE* FIN Emission *f* der Bundesbehörde; **~ Agency Security** *n AmE* FIN von US-Bundesbehörden emittierter Schuldtitel; **~ Aviation Administration** *n AmE (FAA)* TRANSP Bundesluftfahrtbehörde *f*; **~ Cartel Office** *n AmE (FCO)* ECON Bundeskartellamt *nt*, Bundeskartellbehörde *f*

federal: ~ deficit *n AmE* ECON Staatsdefizit *nt*

Federal: ~ Deposit Insurance Corporation *n AmE (FDIC)* INS Bundes-Einlagenversicherungsgesellschaft, staatliche Einlagenversicherung *f*

federal: ~ election *n* POL Bundeswahl *f*; **~ finance** *n AmE* FIN bundesstaatliches Finanzwesen *nt*; **~ financial program** *AmE*, **~ financial programme** *BrE n* ECON bundesstaatliches Finanzprogramm *nt*, Bundeshaushaltsplanung *f* und -budgetierung *f*, Finanzierungsprogramm *nt* der Bundesregierung

Federal: ~ Flood Insurance *n AmE* INS Bundes-Überschwemmungsversicherung

federal: ~ funds *n AmE* BANK *money market* Tagesgeld *nt*, Zentralbankgeld *nt*; **~ funds market** *n AmE* BANK Staatsanleihenmarkt *m*; **~ funds rate** *n AmE* BANK Tagesgeldsatz zwischen US-Banken; **~ government bond** *n AmE* STOCK Bundesstaatsanleihe *f*

Federal: ~ **Home Loan Bank Board** *n AmE* BANK Bundesaufsichtsbehörde *f* für das Bausparkassenwesen; ~ **Home Loan Bank System** *n AmE* FIN Bausparkassenzentralbanksystem *nt*; ~ **Home Loan Board** *n AmE* FIN Zentralbanksystem der Bausparkassen; ~ **Home Loan Mortgage Corporation** *n AmE* (*Freddie Mac, FHLMC*) PROP eines der drei großen Realkredit-Institute in den USA; ~ **Housing Administration** *n AmE* (*FHA*) PROP Bundesstelle für Wohnungsbau, ≈ Bundeswohnbauverwaltung *f*; ~ **Housing Finance Board** *n AmE* WEL Bundesamt für Wohnungsfinanzierung; ~ **Insurance Contributions Act** *n AmE* (*FICA*) WEL Bundesgesetz über die Sozialversicherungsabgaben; ~ **Intermediate Credit Bank** *n AmE* FIN Bundesbank für Zwischenkredite an die Landwirtschaft

federalism *n* ECON, POL Föderalismus *m*

Federal: ~ **Land Bank** *n AmE* BANK Bundeslandwirtschaftsbank *f*, staatliche Landwirtschaftsbank *f*

federal: ~~**level** *adj* ECON, POL auf Bundesebene

federally: ~ **regulated exchange** *n AmE* STOCK bundesstaatlich regulierte Börse *f*

Federal: ~ **Maritime Board** *n AmE* (*FMB*) IND Bundesseefahrtskomitee; ~ **Maritime Commission** *n AmE* (*FMC*) TRANSP Bundesschiffahrtsbehörde; ~ **National Mortgage Association** *n AmE* (*Fannie Mae, FNMA*) FIN, PROP Bundesbehörde zur Förderung des Wohneigentums und Verbesserung des Wohnungsniveaus, ≈ Bundeshypothekenanstalt *f*; ~ **Open Market Committee** *n AmE* (*FOMC*) ECON Offenmarktausschuß des Federal Reserve System; ~ **Parliament** *n* POL Bundesparlament *nt*; ~ **Power Commission** *n AmE* (*FPC*) IND Bundesenergiekommission; ~ **Reserve Bank** *n AmE* (*FRB*) BANK, ECON *national* amerikanische Zentralbank, ≈ Deutsche Bundesbank *f* (*BBk*), *regional* eine der zwölf regionalen Banken des Federal Reserve System, ≈ Landeszentralbank *f*; ~ **Reserve Board** *n AmE* (*FRB*) BANK, ECON Vorstand des Federal Reserve System, Zentralbankvorstand *m*

federal: ~ **reserve note** *n AmE* BANK Fed-Schuldverschreibung *f* (*jarg*)

Federal: ~ **Reserve System** *n AmE* (*the Fed*) BANK, ECON, FIN Zentralbanksystem der Vereinigten Staaten, Zentralbanksystem *nt*; ~ **Savings and Loan Insurance Corporation** *n AmE* (*FSLIC*) BANK Bundesaufsichtsamt *nt* für Bausparkassen, Bundesversicherungsanstalt *f* für Bauspareinlagen; ~ **Statistical Office** *n* ECON statistisches Bundesamt *m*

federal: ~ **tax lien** *n AmE* TAX Bundessteuerpfandrecht *nt*, Pfandrecht *nt* der Bundessteuerbehörde

Federal: ~ **Trade Commission** *n AmE* (*FTC*) ECON, POL Ausschuß *m* zur Bekämpfung des unlauteren Wettbewerbs, Bundeskartellbehörde *nt*

federal: ~ **tribunal** *n* LAW Bundesgerichtshof *m*

federated: ~ **company** *n* GEN COMM eine im Verbund existierende Gesellschaft *f*

federation *n* POL Föderation *f*

fed: ~ **funds** *n pl AmE* BANK Tagesgeld *nt*, Zentralbankgeld *nt*

fee *n* GEN COMM, PATENTS Gebühr *f*; ~~**based service** *n* BANK Dienstleistung *f* gegen Gebühr

feed 1. *n* COMP Zuführung *f*; **2.** *vt* COMP einführen, zuführen

feedback *n* COMP Rückkopplung *f*, GEN COMM Feedback *nt*

feed: ~ **bin** *n* COMP Einzugsschacht *m*; ~ **hole** *n* COMP *hardware* Führungsloch *nt*; ~ **rate** *n* COMP Zuführungsgeschwindigkeit *f*

feedstocks *n* ECON *agricultural*, IND Einsatzmaterial *nt*

fee: ~~**for-service policy** *n* ADMIN Dienstleistungsgebührenpolitik *f*; ~ **for service policy** *n* ADMIN Politik *f* der Dienstleistungsgebühren; ~ **income** *n* ACC Honorareinkommen *nt*

feel: ~ **of the market** *n* GEN COMM, S&M Marktgespür *nt*, Gespür *nt* für den Markt, Marktsinn *m*; ~ **the pinch** *phr infrml* ECON die schlechte Lage zu spüren bekommen

fee: ~ **simple** *n* PROP Grundstückseigentum *nt*; ~ **simple absolute** *n AmE* PROP Bundeswohnbauverwaltung *f*; ~ **split** *n* ACC Honoraraufteilung *f*

felicific: ~ **calculus** *n* ECON felizifische Berechnung *f*

Fellow: ~ **of the British Association of Accountants and Auditors** *n* ACC Mitglied des britischen Verbands der Wirtschaftsprüfer und Rechnungsprüfer; ~ **of the British Institute of Management** *n* (*FBIM*) MGMNT Mitglied des britischen Instituts für Unternehmensführung; ~ **of the Chartered Association of Certified Accountants** *n BrE* (*FCCA*) ACC Mitglied des Verbands öffentlich zugelassener Wirtschaftsprüfer; ~ **of the Chartered Institute of Management Accountants** *n* (*FCMA*) ACC Mitglied des Instituts der betrieblichen Rechnungsprüfer; ~ **of the City and Guilds of London Institute** *n* (*FCGI*) GEN COMM Mitglied des Londoner Instituts für technische und Handwerksbetriebe; ~ **of the Incorporated Society of Valuers & Auctioneers** *n BrE* (*FSVA*) GEN COMM Mitglied der eingetragenen Gesellschaft der Schätzer und Auktionatoren; ~ **of the Institute of Actuaries** *n* (*FIA*) FIN Mitglied des Instituts der Versicherungsmathematiker; ~ **of the Institute of Bankers** *n* (*FIB*) BANK Mitglied des Instituts der Bankiers; ~ **of the Institute of Chartered Shipbrokers** *n* (*FICS*) HRM Mitglied des Instituts der konzessionierten Schiffsmakler; ~ **of the Institute of Chemistry** *n BrE* (*FIC*) IND Mitglied des Instituts für Chemie; ~ **of the Institute of Commerce** *n* (*FCI*) GEN COMM Mitglied des Instituts für Handel; ~ **of the Institute of Company Accountants** *n* (*FICA*) ACC Mitglied des Instituts der Betriebsbuchhalter; ~ **of the Institute of Export** *n* (*FIEx*) HRM Mitglied des Instituts für Export; ~ **of the Institute of Insurance Agents** *n BrE* (*FCIA*) INS Mitglied des Instituts der Versicherungsvertreter; ~ **of the Institute of Personnel Management** *n* (*FIPM*) HRM Mitglied des Instituts für Personalwirtschaft; ~ **of the Royal Institute of Chartered Surveyors** *n* (*FRICS*) GEN COMM Mitglied des Königlichen Instituts staatlich geprüfter Landvermesser und Baugutachter

fellow: ~ **traveler** *AmE*, ~ **traveller** *BrE n* POL Gesinnungsgenosse *m*, Gesinnungsgenossin *f*, Mitläufer, in *m,f*, Sympathisant, in *m,f*; ~ **worker** *n* HRM Kollege *m*, Kollegin *f*

felonious *adj* LAW verbrecherisch

fend off *vt* GEN COMM *question* abwehren

ferrous *adj* ENVIR eisenhaltig

ferry: ~ **berth** *n* TRANSP *shipping* Fähranleger *m*; ~ **boat** *n* TRANSP Fähre *f*, Fährschiff *nt*; ~ **line manager** *n* HRM Fährbetriebsleiter, in *m,f*; ~ **ramp** *n* TRANSP *shipping* Fährrampe *f*

fertilize *vt* ENVIR düngen

fertilizer *n* ENVIR Düngemittel *nt*, Kunstdünger *m*, Dünger *m*

FES *abbr BrE* (*Family Expenditure Survey*) ECON Indexvergleich der Familienlebensunterhaltskosten ≈ Familienbericht *m*

fetch *vt* GEN COMM *price* erzielen

feudalism *n* POL Feudalismus *m*

FF *abbr* (*form feed*) COMP Belegvorschub *m*, Formularvorschub *m*, Seitenvorschub *m*

FFI *abbr* (*for further instructions*) GEN COMM für weitere Anweisungen

fga *abbr* (*free of general average*) GEN COMM, INS frei von großer Havarie, ohne große Havarie

fh *abbr* (*first half of the month*) GEN COMM erste Monatshälfte *f*

FHA *abbr* BANK, FIN (*Finance Houses Association BrE*) Verband der Londoner Teilzahlungsbanken, PROP (*Federal Housing Administration AmE*) Bundesstelle für Wohnungsbau, ≈ Bundeswohnbauverwaltung *f*

FHBR *abbr BrE* (*Finance House Base Rate*) BANK, FIN Eckzins für Ausleihungen der britischen Teilzahlungsbanken

FHLMC *abbr AmE* (*Federal Home Loan Mortgage Corporation*) PROP eines der drei großen Realkredit-Institute in den USA

fia *abbr* (*full interest admitted*) GEN COMM volle Beteiligung zugesagt

FIA *abbr* (*Fellow of the Institute of Actuaries*) FIN Mitglied des Instituts der Versicherungsmathematiker

fiat: ~ **money** *n* FIN Giralgeld *nt*, Papiergeld *nt* ohne Deckung

FIB *abbr* (*Fellow of the Institute of Bankers*) BANK Mitglied des Instituts der Bankiers

fiberboard *AmE see fibreboard BrE*

fiberglass *AmE see fibreglass BrE*

fiberoptic *AmE see fibreoptic BrE*

fibreboard *n BrE* IND Faserplatte *f*, Holzfaserplatte *f*, Pappe *f*; ~ **case** *n BrE* IND Verpackung *f* aus Holzfaserplatte

fibreglass *n BrE* IND Fiberglas *nt*, *reinforced* Glasseide *f*, *spun* Glasfasern *f pl*; ~ **cover** *n BrE* IND Fiberglasabdeckung *f*, Glaswollabdeckung *f*

fibreoptic: ~ **cable** *n BrE* IND Glasfaserkabel *f*, Lichtleitfaserkabel *f*

fibre: ~ **optics** *n BrE* COMMS *communications technology* Glasfaseroptik *f*, Lichtwellenleiter *m*, COMP Faseroptik *f*, Lichtleittechnik *f*, Lichtwellenleitertechnik *f*, IND Faseroptik *f*

FIBS *abbr* (*financial information and budgeting systems*) FIN finanzielle Informations- und Budgetierungssysteme *nt pl*, finanzielle Informations- und Haushaltsysteme *nt pl*

FIC *abbr BrE* (*Fellow of the Institute of Chemistry*) IND Mitglied des Instituts für Chemie

FICA *abbr* ACC (*Fellow of the Institute of Company Accountants*) Mitglied des Instituts der Betriebsbuchhalter, WEL (*Federal Insurance Contributions Act AmE*) Bundesgesetz über die Sozialversicherungsabgaben

FICS *abbr* (*Fellow of the Institute of Chartered Shipbrokers*) HRM Mitglied des Instituts der konzessionierten Schiffsmakler

fictitious *adj* GEN COMM fiktiv, vorgetäuscht; ~ **bargain** *n* LAW *transactions* Scheingeschäft *nt*; ~ **invoice** *n* GEN COMM fingierte Rechnung *f*; ~ **security price** *n* STOCK Ausweichkurs *m*; ~ **transaction** *n* LAW Scheingeschäft *nt*

FID *abbr* (*International Federation for Documentation*) GEN COMM Internationale Föderation *f* für Dokumentation

fiddle *vt infrml* ACC *a bill* frisieren (*infrml*); ♦ ~ **accounts** *infrml* ACC die Bücher frisieren (*infrml*)

fidelity *n* GEN COMM Treue *f*; ~ **bond** *n* INS Kautionsversicherungspolice *f*; ~ **bonus** *n* HRM Treueprämie *f*; ~ **guarantee** *n* INS Kaution *f*; ~ **insurance** *n* INS Vertrauensschadenversicherung *f*; ~ **rebate** *n* S&M Treuerabatt *m*

fiduciary 1. *adj* LAW treuhänderisch, fiduziarisch; **2.** *n* LAW Treuhänder, -in *m,f*

fiduciary: ~ **account** *n* BANK Treuhandkonto *nt*; ~ **banking** *n* BANK Treuhandgeschäft *nt*, fiduziarisches Bankgeschäft *nt*; ~ **bond** *n* LAW Kautionsverpflichtung *f*; ~ **currency** *n* BANK fiduziärer Notenumlauf *m*, ungedeckte Notenausgabe *f*, FIN ungedeckter Notenumlauf *m*; ~ **investment** *n* BANK Treuhandgeschäft *nt*; ~ **issue** *n* BANK fiduziärer Notenumlauf *m*; ~ **operation** *n* BANK *investment banking* Treuhandgeschäft *nt*

field *n* COMP *word, data processing* Feld *nt*, IND *of research* Gebiet *nt*, Datenfeld *nt*, Gesichtsfeld *nt*, Feld *nt*, S&M Feld *nt*; ~ **of action** *n* GEN COMM Tätigkeitsbereich *m*; ~ **force** *n* S&M Außendienstmitarbeiter *m pl*; ~ **investigator** *n* S&M *market research* Marktforscher, -in *m,f*; ~ **operator** *n* GEN COMM, S&M Außendienstmitarbeiter, -in *m,f*; ~ **organization** *n* ADMIN Außendienstorganisation *f*, S&M *branch* Niederlassung *f*, *sales team* Außendienst *m*; ~ **research** *n* S&M Feldforschung *f*; ~ **sales** *n pl* S&M Außendienstverkauf *m*; ~ **sales force** *n* S&M Außendienstorganisation *f*, Außendienst *m*; ~ **sales manager** *n* HRM Außendienstleiter, -in *m,f*; ~ **selling** *n* S&M Außendienstverkauf *m*; ~ **service** *n* GEN COMM Außendienst *m*; ~ **staff** *n* HRM Außendienstmitarbeiter *m pl*; ~ **survey** *n* S&M Marktforschung *f* vor Ort, Absatzforschung *f*; ~ **testing** *n* S&M Feldversuch *m*; ~ **theory of motivation** *n* HRM Feldtheorie *f* der Motivation, Motivationstheorie *f*; ~ **trip** *n* GEN COMM Geländefahrt *f*, WEL Exkursion *f*; ~ **worker** *n* GEN COMM, S&M Außendienstmitarbeiter, -in *m,f*, Kundenkontakter, -in *m,f*, *market research* Marktbefrager, -in *m,f*

fierce *adj* GEN COMM *competition* heftig

FIEx *abbr* (*Fellow of the Institute of Export*) HRM Mitglied des Instituts für Export

FIFO *abbr* (*first in first out*) ACC Fifo-Methode *f*

fight *vt* GEN COMM bekämpfen; ♦ **don't** ~ **the tape** STOCK *market trends* kämpfe nicht gegen den Börsenticker; ~ **a losing battle** GEN COMM eine verlorene Schlacht kämpfen; ~ **unemployment** GEN COMM die Arbeitslosigkeit bekämpfen

fight back *vi* GEN COMM zurückschlagen

figurative: ~ **device** *n* PATENTS Bildzeichen *nt*

figure *n* MATH Zahl *f*, Ziffer *f*, MEDIA Illustration *f*, PATENTS *of a drawing* Abbildung *f*, Illustration *f*; ♦ **get the** ~ **wrong** GEN COMM falsche Zahlen ermitteln

figurehead *n* GEN COMM Galionsfigur *f*

figure: ~ **number** *n* GEN COMM Betragszahl *f*

FIL *abbr* (*financial intermediary loan*) FIN finanzielle Zwischenanleihe *f*, Intermediärkredit *m*

file 1. *n* ADMIN Akte *f*, Aktenstück *nt*, COMP Datei *f*, GEN COMM Vorgang *m*, PATENTS Akte *f*; ◆ ~ **not found** COMP Datei nicht gefunden; **2.** *vt* ADMIN *document* ablegen, *application* einreichen, PATENTS *application* zu den Akten legen, zu den Akten geben; ◆ ~ **a claim** INS einen Antrag stellen, LAW eine Forderung einreichen, einen Anspruch einreichen; ~ **a claim for damages** LAW eine Schadensersatzforderung einreichen; ~ **a lawsuit** LAW einen Zivilprozeß anstrengen; ~ **one's tax return** TAX seine Steuererklärung einreichen; **3.** *vi* ◆ ~ **for bankruptcy** FIN Konkurs anmelden

file away *vt* ADMIN weglegen, zu den Akten legen

file: ~ **allocation table** *n* (*FAT*) COMP Dateizuordnungstabelle *f* (*FAT*); ~ **compression** *n* COMP Dateikomprimierung *f*; ~ **conversion** *n* COMP Dateikonvertierung *f*; ~ **copy** *n* ADMIN Ablagekopie *f*, Aktenkopie *f*; ~ **directory** *n* COMP Dateiverzeichnis *nt*; ~ **identifier** *n* COMP Dateikennsatz *m*; ~ **management** *n* COMP Dateiverwaltung *f*; ~ **menu** *n* COMP Dateimenü *nt*; ~ **number** *n* GEN COMM Aktenzeichen *nt*; ~ **protection** *n* COMP Dateischutz *m*; ~ **section** *n* COMP Dateiabschnitt *m*; ~ **server** *n* COMP Dateiserver *m*; ~ **sharing** *n* COMP gemeinsame Dateinutzung *f*

filing *n* ADMIN Ablage *f*, Archivierung *f*, GEN COMM *clerical duty* Ablage *f*; ~ **basket** *n* GEN COMM Ablagekorb *m*; ~ **cabinet** *n* ADMIN Aktenschrank *m*; ~ **date** *n* GEN COMM Abgabefrist *f*; ~ **drawer** *n* GEN COMM Ablagefach *nt*; ~ **system** *n* ADMIN Ablagesystem *nt*

fill *vt* HRM *occupy post* innehaben, *take up post* einnehmen, *recruit for post* besetzen; ◆ ~ **a gap** GEN COMM, S&M *in market* eine Marktlücke füllen, eine Marktlücke schließen; ~ **manpower gaps** HRM Personallücken schließen; ~ **-or-kill** *AmE* (*FOK*) STOCK Option ausüben oder aufgeben; ~ **a vacancy** HRM *employer* eine Stelle besetzen; ~ **the vacuum** GEN COMM das Vakuum füllen

fill in 1. *vt* GEN COMM *blanks, form* ausfüllen, *date* eintragen, eintragen in [+acc]; **2.** *vi* ◆ ~ **for sb** HRM für jdn einspringen

fill out *vt* GEN COMM *form* ausfüllen

filler *n* S&M Füllanzeige *f*

fill: ~ **-in** *n* HRM Aushilfe *f*, Aushilfskraft *f*

fills *n pl* MEDIA *print* Füllsel *nt*

film *n* LEIS, MEDIA Film *m*, Kinofilm *m*; ~ **advertising** *n* S&M Filmwerbung *f*, Kinoreklame *f*, Kinowerbung *f*; ~ **festival** *n* MEDIA Filmfestspiele *f pl*; ~ **industry** *n* LEIS Filmbranche *f*, Filmindustrie *f*, MEDIA Filmindustrie *f*

filming *n* MEDIA Verfilmung *f*

film: ~ **-maker** *n* MEDIA Filmemacher *m*; ~ **-making** *n* MEDIA Filmemachen *nt*; ~ **production costs** *n pl* TAX Filmproduktionskosten *pl*; ~ **rights** *n pl* LAW Verfilmungsrechte *nt pl*; ~ **rush** *n* S&M Filmrohfassung *f*; ~ **script** *n* MEDIA Filmdrehbuch *nt*

filmsetter *n* BrE (*cf photosetter AmE*) MEDIA *print* Fotosatzgerät *nt*

filmsetting *n* BrE (*cf photosetting AmE*) MEDIA *print* Fotosatz *m*

film: ~ **strip** *n* MEDIA Tonbildschau *f*; ~ **test** *n* MEDIA Filmprobe *f*

filter *n* COMP Filter *m or nt*

filtering: ~ **down** *n* PROP relative Veränderung *f* des Ertragswertes einer Wohnung

FIMBRA *abbr* BrE (*Financial Intermediaries, Managers and Brokers Association*) FIN Selbstüberwachungsorganisation der Londoner City

final 1. *adj* GEN COMM endgültig, letzte, End-, LAW rechtskräftig; **2.** *n* MEDIA *newspaper* Spätausgabe *f*, S&M *end* Ende *nt*, Schluß *m*

final: ~ **acceptance** *n* GEN COMM *of goods* Endabnahme *f*; ~ **accounts** *n pl* ACC Endabrechnung *f*, Schlußrechnung *f*; ~ **assembly** *n* GEN COMM Endmontage *f*; ~ **balance** *n* ACC Endbestand *m*, Endsaldo *m*, *final balance sheet* Schlußbilanz *f*; ~ **ballot** *n* POL Stichwahl *f*; ~ **check-in** *n* LEIS, TRANSP *for passengers* letzte Abfertigung *f*; ~ **contract settlement price** *n* STOCK *futures* endgültiger Vertragsabrechnungspreis *m*; ~ **date for acceptance** *n* GEN COMM Abgabefrist *f*; ~ **deadline** *n* LAW *contract law* Abgabetermin *m*, Endtermin *m*; ~ **demand** *n* ACC, ECON Endnachfrage *f*; ~ **destination** *n* GEN COMM, IMP/EXP endgültiger Bestimmungsort *m*; ~ **dividend** *n* FIN Schlußdividende *f*, STOCK Abschlußdividende *f*; ~ **examination** *n* WEL Abschlußprüfung *f*; ~ **good** *n* ECON Endprodukt *nt*; ~ **income** *n* ECON verfügbares Einkommen *nt*, FIN, TAX versteuertes Einkommen *nt*; ~ **installment** *AmE*, ~ **instalment** *BrE* *n* FIN Abschlußzahlung *f*, letzte Rate *f*

finalize *vt* GEN COMM abschließen

final: ~ **mortgage payment** *n* FIN Hypothekenabschlußzahlung *f*; ~ **notice** *n* GEN COMM endgültiger Bescheid *m*; ~ **offer arbitration** *n* ECON kompromißloses Schlichtungsverfahren *nt*; ~ **product** *n* GEN COMM Endprodukt *nt*; ~ **proof** *n* MEDIA *printing, photography* Endkorrektur *f*, letzter Korrekturabzug *m*

finals *n pl* WEL Abschlußprüfung *f*

final: ~ **trading day** *n* STOCK letzter Handelstag *m*; ~ **value model** *n* FIN Endwertmodell *nt*; ~ **warning** *n* HRM letzte Warnung *f*

finance 1. *n* FIN Finanzwesen *nt*, Finanzierung *f*; **2.** *vt* FIN finanzieren; ◆ ~ **an export transaction** IMP/EXP ein Exportgeschäft finanzieren; ~ **directly** FIN direkt finanzieren; ~ **the difference** ECON die Differenz finanzieren

Finance: ~ **Act** *n* BrE LAW Haushaltsgesetz *nt*, Steuergesetz *nt*, Finanzgesetz *nt*

finance: ~ **bill** *n* BANK, FIN *bank draft* Finanzwechsel *m*

Finance: ~ **Bill** *n* BrE ECON Finanzvorlage *f*, Haushaltsvorlage *f*

finance: ~ **charge** *n* BANK Finanzierungskosten *pl*; ~ **company paper** *n* FIN Wertpapier eines Factoring-Institutes; ~ **director** *n* MGMNT Finanzdirektor, in *m,f*, Finanzvorstand *m*

financed: ~ **out of public funds** *adj* ECON durch öffentliche Mittel finanziert, öffentlich finanziert

finance: ~ **house** *n* BrE BANK Kundenkreditbank *f*, FIN Finanzierungsgesellschaft *f*, Finanzierungsinstitut *nt*, Kundenkreditbank *f*, Teilzahlungsbank *f*

Finance: ~ **House Base Rate** *n* BrE (*FHBR*) BANK, FIN Eckzins für Ausleihungen der britischen Teilzahlungsbanken; ~ **Houses Association** *n* BrE (*FHA*) BANK, FIN Verband der Londoner Teilzahlungsbanken

finance: ~ **lease** *n* FIN, GEN COMM Finanzierungs-Leasing *nt*

Finance: ~ **Minister** *n* ECON, FIN, POL Finanzminister *m*; ~ **Ministry** *n* ECON, FIN, POL Finanzministerium *nt*, Ministerium *nt* der Finanzen

finance: ~ **sector** *n* FIN Finanzsektor *m*

financial *adj* FIN, TAX finanziell, Finanz-; ◆ **be in**

~ straits FIN sich in finanziellen Schwierigkeiten befinden; **in ~ surplus** ECON finanziell im Plus (*infrml*), im Gewinnbereich, in der Gewinnzone

financial: **~ accounting** *n* ACC Bilanzierung *f*, ADMIN Rechnungslegung *f*, FIN Bilanzierung *f*, Finanzbuchhaltung *f*, Geschäftsbuchhaltung *f*

Financial: **~ Accounting Standards Board** *n AmE* (*FASB*) ACC Gremium, das die US-Bilanzierungsrichtlinien festlegt

financial: **~ adjustment** *n* FIN Umfinanzierung *f*, Sanierung *f*; **~ administration** *n* ADMIN Verwaltung *f* der Finanzen, FIN Finanzverwaltung *f*

Financial: **~ Administration Act** *n* LAW Finanzverwaltungsgesetz *nt*

financial: **~ aid** *n* ECON Finanzhilfe *f*, finanzielle Unterstützung *f*; **~ appraisal** *n* FIN Finanzgutachten *nt*, Finanzbewertung *f*; **~ asset** *n* FIN finanzieller Vermögenswert *m*; **~ assets** *n pl* ECON Finanzanlagen *f pl*; **~ assistance** *n* ECON *from the Government* Finanzhilfe *f*, finanzielle Unterstützung *f*; **~ backer** *n* FIN Geldgeber *m*; **~ backing** *n* FIN finanzielle Unterstützung *f*; **~ balance** *n* ECON finanzielles Gleichgewicht *nt*; **~ budget** *n* ADMIN Finanzbudget *nt*; **~ burden** *n* FIN finanzielle Belastung *f*; **~ capital** *n* FIN Finanzkapital *nt*; **~ center** *AmE*, **~ centre** *BrE n* ECON Finanzzentrum *nt*; **~ circles** *n pl* FIN Finanzkreise *m pl*; **~ claim** *n* ACC finanzieller Anspruch *m*; **~ climate** *n* ECON finanzielle Lage *f*; **~ conglomerate** *n* FIN Finanzkonglomerat *nt*, Finanzierungskonglomerat *nt*; **~ contribution** *n* FIN Beitrag *m*; **~ control** *n* ACC, FIN Finanzkontrolle *f*; **~ controller** *n* ACC *person* Controller *m*, *of an organization* Finanz-Controller *m*; **~ crisis** *n* FIN Finanzkrise *f*; **~ damage** *n* FIN Vermögensschaden *m*; **~ director** *n* HRM Finanzvorstand *m*, MGMNT Finanzdirektor, in *m,f*, Leiter, in *m,f* der Finanzabteilung; **~ disclosure** *n* FIN finanzielle Offenlegung *f*; **~ encumbrance** *n* FIN finanzielle Belastung *f*; **~ engineering** *n* FIN Erstellung *f* eines Finanzierungskonzeptes, Finanzierungstechnik *f*, Liquiditätssteuerung *f*; **~ enterprise** *n* FIN Finanzierungsinstitut *nt*; **~ executive** *n* HRM Finanzvorstand *m*; **~ expenses** *n pl* ADMIN Finanzierungskosten *pl*; **~ field** *n* FIN Finanzbereich *m*, Finanzgebiet *nt*; **~ firm** *n* FIN Finanzfirma *f*; **~ flow** *n* ECON Finanzierungsströme *m pl*; **~ forecasts** *n pl* FIN Finanzprognosen *f pl*; **~ futures** *n* FIN, STOCK Termingeschäft *nt*; **~ futures market** *n* FIN, STOCK Finanzterminmarkt *m*; **~ highlights** *n pl* ACC Finanzhöhepunkte *m pl*; **~ holding company** *n* FIN Finanzholding *f*; **~ incentive** *n* FIN finanzieller Anreiz *m*; **~ information and budgeting systems** *n* (*FIBS*) FIN finanzielle Informations- und Budgetierungssysteme *nt pl*, finanzielle Informations- und Haushaltsysteme *nt pl*; **~ institution** *n* FIN Finanzinstitut *nt*, Geldinstitut *nt*, Kreditinstitut *nt*

Financial: **~ Intermediaries, Managers and Brokers Association** *n BrE* (*FIMBRA*) FIN Selbstüberwachungsorganisation der Londoner City

financial: **~ intermediary loan** *n* (*FIL*) FIN finanzielle Zwischenanleihe *f*, Intermediärkredit *m*; **~ investment** *n* FIN Finanzinvestition *f*, Geld- oder Kapitalanlage *f*; **~ involvement** *n* FIN finanzielle Beteiligung *f*; **~ journalism** *n* FIN Finanzjournalismus *m*, Wirtschaftsjournalismus *m*; **~ leverage ratio** *n* FIN Leverage-Kennziffer *f*; **~ loss** *n* FIN Vermögensschaden *m*, finanzieller Verlust *m*, Ausfall *m*

financially *adv* GEN COMM finanziell; **~ sound** *adj* GEN COMM finanziell gesund

financial: **~ magnate** *n* FIN Finanzmagnat, in *m,f*; **~ management** *n* ACC Finanzmanagement *nt*, Finanzplanung *f*, FIN Finanzplanung *f*, MGMNT Finanzmanagement *nt*, Finanzplanung *f*, Finanzverwaltung *f*, Finanzwesen *nt*, Finanzwirtschaft *f*; **~ management report** *n* FIN Finanzbericht *m*, Finanzplanungsbericht *m*; **~ management system** *n* FIN Finanzmanagement-System *nt*; **~ manager** *n* HRM Finanzvorstand *m*, MGMNT Finanzleiter, in *m,f*; **~ market** *n* FIN Finanzmarkt *m*; **~ means** *n pl* FIN finanzielle Mittel *nt pl*, Finanzierungsmittel *nt pl*, Geldmittel *nt pl*; **~ muscle** *n* ADMIN, S&M Finanzkraft *f*, finanzielle Macht *f*; **~ news** *n pl* FIN Börsenbericht *m*, Börsennachrichten *f pl*; **~ officer** *n* ADMIN *local government* Kämmerer *m*, Außenprüfer, in *m,f*, Betriebsprüfer, in *m,f*, Außenfinanzbeamte(r) *m* [decl. as adj], Außenfinanzbeamtin *f*; **~ participation scheme** *n BrE* HRM Gewinnbeteiligungssystem *nt*; **~ period** *n* ACC Geschäftsjahr *nt*; **~ perspective** *n* ECON Finanzperspektive *f*; **~ planning** *n* ACC, ADMIN, FIN, MGMNT Finanzplanung *f*; **~ policy** *n* FIN Finanzpolitik *f*; **~ position** *n* ACC Finanzlage *f*, Finanzstatus *m*; **~ profit or loss** *n* ACC finanzieller Gewinn oder Verlust *m*; **~ proposal** *n* ECON Finanzvorlage *f*; **~ pyramid** *n* FIN Finanzpyramide *f*; **~ ratio** *n* FIN finanzwirtschaftliche Kennzahl *f*; **~ report** *n* ADMIN, FIN Jahresabschlußbericht *m*, Lagebericht *m*, Bericht *m* über die Vermögenslage, Jahresbericht *m*; **~ reporting** *n* ADMIN, FIN Vorlage *f* von Abschlüssen

Financial: **~ Reporting Council** *n BrE* ACC Rat *m* für Finanzberichterstattung; **~ Reporting Standard** *n* (*FRS*) ACC Grundsätze *m pl* des finanziellen Berichtswesens

financial: **~ requirements** *n pl* FIN Finanzbedarf *m*, Kapitalbedarf *m*; **~ responsibility clause** *n AmE* INS *automobile*, LAW Haftungsklausel *f* für finanzielle Verantwortung; **~ restructuring** *n* FIN Umschuldung *f*, Sanierung *f*; **~ review** *n* FIN finanzieller Überblick *m*, GEN COMM Finanzüberblick *m*; **~ reward** *n* GEN COMM Entgelt *nt*; **~ risk** *n* STOCK finanzielles Risiko *nt*; **~ services** *n pl* FIN Finanzdienstleistungen *f pl*, finanzielle Dienstleistungen *f pl*

Financial: **~ Services Act** *n BrE* (*FSA*) FIN *1986* Finanzdienstleistungsgesetz

financial: **~ signing authority** *n* FIN finanzielle Zeichnungsberechtigung *f*; **~ simulation software** *n* FIN Finanzsimulationssoftware *f*; **~ situation** *n* ACC Finanzlage *f*; **~ sophisticate** *n* HRM finanzwirtschaftlich gebildete Person *f*; **~ stability** *n* FIN finanzielle Stabilität *f*; **~ standard** *n* FIN finanzieller Standard *m*, GEN COMM Finanzierungsstandard *m*; **~ standing** *n* FIN Bonität *f*, Kreditwürdigkeit *f*, finanzielle Lage *f*, Kapitalkraft *f*, Kreditfähigkeit *f*; **~ statement** *n* ACC Abschluß *m*, Finanzausweis *m*, Jahresabschluß *m*, FIN Bericht *m* über die Vermögenslage, Vermögensaufstellung *f*, *liquidity* Finanzstatus *m*; **~ statement and budget report** *n* (*FSBR*) FIN Jahresabschluß- und Budgetberichtstattung *f*; **~ straits** *n pl* ADMIN finanzieller Engpaß *m*; **~ strategy** *n* FIN Finanzierungsstrategie *f*, GEN COMM Finanzstrategie *f*; **~ strength** *n* BANK Finanzkraft *f*, Kapitalkraft *f*; **~ structure** *n* ACC *balance sheet*, ECON, FIN Finanzierungsstruktur *f*, Kapitalstruktur *f*; **~ summary** *n* FIN finanzieller Überblick *m*; ~ **supermarket** *n* FIN Finanz-Supermarkt *m*; ~ **support** *n* ECON finanzielle Unterstützung *f*; ~ **support staff** *n* BANK, FIN finanzielle Beratungsgruppe *f*, Beratungsgruppe *f* Finanzen, Beraterstab *m* Finanzen; ~ **system** *n* FIN Finanzsystem *nt*

Financial: ~ **Times** *n BrE* (*FT*) MEDIA Financial Times *f*; ~ **Times Actuaries All Shares Index** *n BrE* (*All Share Index*) STOCK Aktienindex der Financial Times, ≈ Aktienindex *m* der Frankfurter Allgemeinen Zeitung (*FAZ Index*); ~ **Times Industrial Ordinary Share Index** *n BrE* (*FT Index*) STOCK Industrieaktienindex der Financial Times; ~ **Times Stock Exchange Index** *n* (*FT-SE*) STOCK Aktienindex *m* der Financial Times

financial: ~ **wizard** *n infrml* GEN COMM Finanzgenie *nt* (*infrml*); ~ **year** *n* ACC Bilanzjahr *nt*, Wirtschaftsjahr *nt*, ECON Finanzjahr *nt*, Geschäftsjahr *nt*, Haushaltsjahr *nt*, FIN, TAX Bilanzjahr *nt*; ~ **year then ended** *n BrE* das dann zu Ende gegangene Geschäftsjahr *nt*

financier *n* BANK Finanzexperte *m*, Finanzexpertin *f*, Finanzier *m*, Geldgeber *m*

financing *n* FIN finanzielle Mittel *nt pl*, Finanzierung *f*; ~ **adjustment** *n* FIN Finanzierungsanpassung *f*; ~ **package** *n* FIN Gesamtfinanzierung *f*, Bündel *nt* finanzpolitischer Maßnahmen, komplettes Finanzierungspaket *nt*, Finanzierung *f* aus einer Hand; ~ **plan** *n* FIN Finanzierungsplan *m*; ~ **rate** *n* STOCK *futures pricing* Finanzierungssatz *m*; ~ **through securities** *n* FIN Effektenfinanzierung *f*

find *vt* COMP *database* suchen, LAW für Recht erkennen, entscheiden; ◆ ~ **sb guilty** LAW einen Schuldspruch fällen, jdn für schuldig befinden, jdn für schuldig erklären; ~ **sb not guilty** LAW jdn für nicht schuldig befinden, jdn für nicht schuldig erklären; ~ **the balance** STOCK das Gleichgewicht finden

finder: ~**'s fee** *n* GEN COMM Vermittlungsprovision *f*, S&M Maklerprovision *f*

finding *n* LAW Gerichtsurteil *nt*

findings *n pl* LAW *of fact* festgestellter Sachverhalt *m*, *of investigation, tribunal* Feststellungen *f pl*

fine *n* HRM Geldbuße *f*, LAW *pecuniary penalty* Geldstrafe *f*

fine-tune *vt* ECON feinabstimmen

fine-tuning *n* COMP Feineinstellung *f*, ECON Feinabstimmung *f*, Feinsteuerung *f*

finish *vt* IND veredeln; ◆ ~ **completely** GEN COMM aufbrauchen; ~ **work** GEN COMM die Arbeit beenden, die Arbeit einstellen

finished: ~ **goods** *n pl* GEN COMM Fertigwaren *f pl*; ~ **product** *n* GEN COMM Fertigprodukt *nt*

finishing *n* IND Endbearbeitung *f*, Nachbearbeitung *f*, Veredelung *f*

finite *adj* ENVIR begrenzt

FIPM *abbr* (*Fellow of the Institute of Personnel Management*) HRM Mitglied des Instituts für Personalwirtschaft

firavv *abbr* (*first available vessel*) TRANSP erstes verfügbares Schiff *nt*

fire 1. *n* GEN COMM, INS Feuer *nt*; **2.** *vt infrml* HRM *staff* entlassen, feuern (*infrml*)

fire: ~ **brigade** *n BrE* GEN COMM Feuerwehr *f*; ~ **door** *n* HRM Feuerschutztür *f*; ~ **drill** *n* HRM Feuerwehrübung *f*, Probealarm *m*; ~ **escape** *n* HRM Feuerleiter *f*; ~ **exit** *n* ENVIR, HRM Notausgang *m*

firefighting: ~ **fund** *n* ACC Feuerwehrfonds *m*

fire: ~ **hazard** *n* WEL Brandrisiko *nt*, Feuergefahr *f*; ~ **insurance agreement** *n BrE* INS Feuerversicherungsvertrag *m*; ~ **insuring agreement** *n AmE* INS Feuerversicherungsvertrag *m*; ~ **legal liability insurance** *n AmE* INS Feuerhaftpflichtversicherung *f*, Versicherung *f* für Haftung bei Brandschäden; ~ **prevention** *n* WEL Brandverhütung, Feuerverhütung *f*

fireproof *adj* GEN COMM feuerfest, feuersicher; ~ **construction** *n* INS feuersichere Bauart *f*

fire: ~ **regulations** *n pl* LAW Brandschutzvorschriften *f pl*; ~**-resistant** *adj* GEN COMM feuerfest; ~**-resistant construction** *n* INS feuersichere Bauart *f*; ~ **risk on freight** *n* TRANSP Frachtfeuergefahr *f*; ~ **service** *n* GEN COMM Feuerwehr *f*; ~ **wall** *n* INS, WEL *in building* Brandmauer *f*, Feuerschutzmauer *f*

firewall *n* COMP *network security* Zugangsschutzsystem *nt*, Fire-Wall-Abschottung *f*

firing *n infrml* HRM Rauswurf *m* (*infrml*), Entlassung *f*

firm 1. *adj* ECON *currency* stabil, fest, GEN COMM *order* verbindlich, stabil, S&M, TRANSP stabil; **2.** *n* ECON, GEN COMM Firma *f* (*Fa.*), Unternehmen *nt*; **3.** *vi* STOCK anziehen, sich befestigen, fest tendieren

firm: ~ **belief** *n* GEN COMM feste Überzeugung *f*; ~ **bid** *n* ADMIN Festgebot *nt*; ~ **commitment** *n* STOCK *securities underwriting* feste Übernahmeverpflichtung *f*; ~ **commitment underwriting** *n* STOCK feste Übernahme *f* einer Anleihe durch eine Emissionsbank; ~ **consumption** *n* ECON Unternehmenskonsum *m*; ~ **deal** *n* GEN COMM fester Abschluß *m*

firming *adj* STOCK anziehend

firmly *adv* GEN COMM fest

firmness *n* GEN COMM *market, shares* Stabilität *f*

firm: ~ **offer** *n* GEN COMM Festangebot *nt*, festes Angebot *nt*, verbindliche Offerte *f*, verbindliches Angebot *nt*; ~ **order** *n* S&M Fixauftrag *m*; ~ **price** *n* STOCK feste Notierung *f*, fester Kurs *m*; ~ **quotation** *n* ECON verbindliche Kursnotierung *f*

firmware *n* COMP Firmware *f*

first *adj* GEN COMM erste; ◆ **in the** ~ **instance** GEN COMM an erster Stelle; **every** ~ **day of the month** GEN COMM an jedem Ersten, jeden Ersten

first: ~**-aid kit** *n* WEL Erste-Hilfe-Ausrüstung *f*, Verbandskasten *m*; ~ **available vessel** TRANSP erstes verfügbares Schiff *nt*; ~ **best economy** *n* ECON Modell einer Volkswirtschaft mit Ressourcenallokation nach Pareto-Optimum, pareto-optimale Volkswirtschaft *f*; ~ **bid** *n* GEN COMM Erstgebot *nt*; ~ **carrier** *n* TRANSP erster Spediteur *m*; ~**-class** *adj* STOCK erstklassig, erste Adresse; ~ **class** *n* LEIS, TRANSP erste Klasse *f*; ~**-class mail** *n* COMMS Briefpost *f*, Vorrangbriefpost *f*; ~ **country of destination** *n* IMP/EXP, TRANSP erstes Bestimmungsland *nt*; ~ **day of the month** *n* GEN COMM Monatserste(r) *m* [*decl. as adj*]; ~**-degree price discrimination** *n* ECON primäre Preisdifferenzierung *f*

First: ~ **Development Decade** *n* POL erste Dekade der Entwicklungspolitik

first: ~ **economy** *n* ECON, POL offizielle Wirtschaft *f*; ~**-generation** *adj* IND der ersten Generation; ~ **half of the month** *n* (*fh*) GEN COMM erste Monatshälfte *f*; ~ **half of the year** *n* GEN COMM erste Jahreshälfte *f*; ~ **in first out** *adj* (*FIFO*) ACC Fifo-Methode *f*; ~**-instance fiscal court** *n* TAX Finanzgericht *nt*; ~ **lien** *n* PROP erstrangiges Pfandrecht *nt*; ~**-line management** *n*

HRM, MGMNT niedrigste Leitungsebene *f*, unterste Leitungsebene *f*, unterste Führungsschicht *f*; **~-line manager** *n* HRM, MGMNT Führungskraft *f* auf unterster Leitungsebene, Manager, in *m,f* auf der untersten Leitungsebene, Manager, in *m,f* auf der untersten Leitungsebene; **~-line supervisor** *n* HRM, MGMNT unmittelbare(r) Vorgesetzte(r) *mf* [decl. as adj]; **~ mortgage** *n* BANK erste Hypothek *f*; **~ mortgage loan** *n* BANK Darlehen *nt* für eine erste Hypothek; **~ night** *n* LEIS, MEDIA Premiere *f*; **~-night audience** *n* LEIS Premierenpublikum *nt*; **~ notice day** *n* FIN erster Ankündigungstag *m*, erster Benachrichtigungstag *m*; **~ owner of copyright** *n* LAW *intellectual property* erster Urheberrechtsinhaber *m*, erste Urheberrechtsinhaberin *f*; **~ performance** *n* LEIS, MEDIA Premiere *f*; **~ preference share** *n* STOCK erstrangige Vorzugsaktie *f*; **~ preference stock** *n* STOCK erstrangige Vorzugsaktien *f pl*; **~ quarter** *n* (*1Q*) GEN COMM erstes Quartal *nt*; **~-rate** *adj* GEN COMM erstklassig; **~ reminder** *n* ACC erste Mahnung *f*; **~ vice president** *n* HRM erster Vizepräsident *m*, erste Vizepräsidentin *f*

First: **~ World** *n* ECON Erste Welt *f*, Alte Welt *f*; **~ World War** *n* POL Erster Weltkrieg *m*

fiscal *adj* ECON, TAX fiskalisch, Fiskal-, steuerlich, Steuer-; **~ approximation** *n* TAX Steuerangleichung *f*; **~ austerity** *n* ECON fiskalpolitische Sparmaßnahmen *f pl*; **~ authorities** *n pl* BANK, FIN, TAX Finanzbehörden *f pl*, Steuerbehörden *f pl*, Fiskus *m*; **~ authority** *n* BANK, FIN, TAX Finanzbehörde *f*, Steuerbehörde *f*; **~ barrier** *n* ECON *international trade* fiskalische Schranke *f*; **~ crisis** *n* TAX Haushaltskrise *f*, Finanzkrise *f*; **~ deficit** *n* ACC Haushaltsdefizit *nt*, Finanzdefizit *nt*; **~ dividend** *n* TAX Mittel zur freien Verfügung von Präsident und Kongreß aus dem Zuwachs des Steuervolumens; **~ drag** *n* ECON, FIN, TAX fiskalische Bremse *f*, Progressionswirkung *f*, Bremseffekt *m* der Steuerprogression, Fiscal Drag-Effekt *m*; **~ evasion** *n* TAX Steuerhinterziehung *f*; **~ federalism** *n* TAX Finanzföderalismus *m*; **~ incidence** *n* TAX Steuerinzidenz *f*, Steuerbelastungswirkung *f*, Steuerwirkung *f*; **~ indicator** *n* TAX fiskalischer Indikator *m*; **~ inducement** *n* TAX steuerlicher Anreiz *m*

fiscalist *n* ECON Fiskalist *m*

fiscal: **~ mobility** *n* ECON Steuermobilität *f*; **~ multiplier** *n* ECON Fiskalmultiplikator *m*, Steuermultiplikator *m*; **~ neutrality** *n* TAX Finanzneutralität *f*, Steuerneutralität *f*; **~ period** *n* ACC, TAX Abrechnungsperiode *f*, Buchungszeitraum *m*, Geschäftsperiode *f*, Rechnungsperiode *f*, Geschäftsabschnitt *m*; **~ policy** *n* ECON Fiskalpolitik *f*, POL Steuerpolitik *f*; **~ position** *n* TAX steuerliche Position *f*; **~ projection** *n* TAX fiskalische Planung *f*, fiskalische Vorhersage *f*, steuerliche Planung *f*, steuerliche Vorhersage *f*, Steuerprognose *f*, Steuerprojektion *f*; **~ stance** *n* ECON fiskalischer Standpunkt *m*, steuerlicher Standpunkt *m*; **~ surplus** *n* TAX steuerlicher Überschuß *m*; **~ year** *n* (*FY*) ACC, FIN, TAX Bilanzjahr *nt*, Geschäftsjahr *nt*, Rechnungsjahr *nt*, Steuerjahr *nt*, Wirtschaftsjahr *nt*, *public accounting* Finanzjahr *nt*, Haushaltsjahr *nt*; **~ year ended** *n* TAX abgeschlossenes Geschäftsjahr *nt*, abgeschlossenes Haushaltsjahr *nt*, abgeschlossenes Wirtschaftsjahr *nt*; **~ year then ended** *n* AmE ACC das dann zu Ende gegangene Geschäftsjahr *nt*

Fisher: **~ effect** *n* ECON Fisher-Effekt *m*; **~ theorem** *n* ECON Fisher-Theorem *nt*

fishery *n* ECON Fischereiwirtschaft *f*

fish: **~ farming** *n* ECON Fischzucht *f*

fishing *n* GEN COMM Fischerei *f*; **~ grounds** *n pl* ECON Fanggebiete *nt pl*, Fanggründe *m pl*; **~ industry** *n* IND Fischindustrie *f*, Fischerei *f*; **~ port** *n* IND Fischereihafen *m*

fit **1.** *adj* STOCK passend; ♦ **~ for work** HRM arbeitsfähig; **~ and proper** LAW *person* geeignet; **2.** *vt* GEN COMM einbauen; **3.** *vi* GEN COMM *requirements* entsprechen

fit out *vt* GEN COMM ausstatten, TRANSP ausrüsten

f.i.t. *abbr* (*free of income tax*) TAX einkommensteuerfrei

fit: **~ investment** *n* STOCK geeignete Investition *f*

fitness *n* LEIS, WEL Fitneß *f*

fitter *n* HRM Monteur *m*

fitting: **~ out** *n* TRANSP *shipping* Ausrüstung *f*; **~ room** *n* GEN COMM Umkleidekabine *f*

five: **~-for-one split** *n* BrE STOCK *of shares in capital restructuring* Aktiensplitting *nt* fünf zu eins; **~ hundred dollar rule** *n* STOCK Fünfhundert-Dollar-Regel *f*; **~ percent rule** *n* STOCK Fünf-Prozent-Regel *f*; **~-year formula** *n* BANK Fünfjahresformel *f*; **~-year plan** *n* ACC, ECON Fünfjahresplan *m*

fix **1.** *n* AmE FIN Bestechung *f*; ♦ **be in a ~** *infrml* GEN COMM in der Klemme sitzen (*infrml*); **2.** *vt* GEN COMM festlegen, ansetzen; ♦ **~ quotas** IMP/EXP Quoten festlegen

fixation *n* STOCK Festlegung *f*, Fixierung *f*

fixed *adj* BANK fest, GEN COMM bestimmt, fixiert; **~ allowance** *n* GEN COMM Fixum *nt*; **~ annuity** *n* INS Festrente *f*, Pauschalrente *f*; **~ asset** *n* ACC Anlagegegenstand *m*, Gegenstand *m* des Anlagevermögens; **~ asset account** *n* ACC Sachanlagenkonto *nt*; **~ asset assessment** *n* ACC Bewertung *f* des Anlagevermögens; **~ asset investment** *n* ACC Anlageinvestitionen *f pl*; **~ asset policies** *n pl* ACC das Anlagevermögen betreffende Grundsätze *m pl*; **~ asset policy** *n* ACC Anlagevermögenspolitik *f*; **~ assets** *n pl* ACC Anlagevermögen *nt*, ECON Sachanlagen *f pl*; **~ benefits** *n pl* GEN COMM feste Versorgungsleistungen *f pl*, feste Leistungen *f pl*; **~ capital** *n* ECON Anlagevermögen *nt*, FIN Anlagekapital *nt*; **~ charge** *n* ACC Fixkosten *pl*, Gemeinkosten *pl*, feste Belastung *f*; **~-charge coverage** *n* ACC Fixkostendeckung *f*; **~ costs** *n pl* ACC, ECON fixe Kosten *pl*, Fixkosten *pl*, Gemeinkosten *pl*; **~ demand** *n* ECON unelastische Nachfrage; **~ deposit** *n* (*cf time deposit AmE*) BANK Festgeld *nt*, Termineinlage *f*; **~ disk** *n* COMP *hardware* Festplatte *f* (*HD*); **~ duty** *n* TAX spezifischer Zoll *m*; **~ exchange rate** *n* ECON fester Wechselkurs *m*; **~ expenses** *n pl* ACC Fixkosten *pl*; **~ expiration date** *n* STOCK *options* festgelegter Verfalltag *m*; **~ fee** *n* GEN COMM feste Gebühr *f*; **~ income** *n* STOCK feste Einkünfte *pl*; **~-income investment** *n* STOCK festverzinsliche Kapitalanlage *f*; **~ installment** *AmE*, **~ instalment** *BrE* *n* FIN festgelegte Ratenzahlung *f*, fixe Rate *f*; **~-interest loan** *n* FIN festverzinsliches Darlehen *nt*; **~-interest research** *n* FIN Bond-Analyse *f*; **~-investment trust** *n* AmE (*cf nondiscretionary trust*) STOCK Investmentfonds *m* mit unveränderlichem Portefeuille, Kapitalanlagegesellschaft *f* mit festgelegten Anteilen; **~ loan** *n* BANK langfristiges Darlehen *nt*; **~ maturity** *n* BANK feste Laufzeit *f*; **~ overheads** *n pl* ACC fixe Gemeinkosten *pl*; **~ penalty** *n* TAX *for failing to submit returns* festgelegte Geldbuße *f*, festgesetzte Geldstrafe *f*; **~-period deposit** *n* BANK Festgeld *nt*; **~ plant** *n* IND Betriebsanlage *f*; **~-point number** *n* MATH

Festkommazahl *f*; **~ premium** *n* INS Festprämie *f*, Pauschalprämie *f*; **~ price** *n* ACC, STOCK *put options* Festpreis *m*; **~-price contract** *n* S&M Festpreisauftrag *m*; **~-rate loan** *n* BANK zinsgebundener Kredit *m*, Festzinskredit *m*; **~-rate mortgage** *n* BANK Festsatzhypothek *f*, Festzinshypothek *f*; **~ route** *n* TRANSP feste Fahrtroute *f*; **~ salary** *n* HRM Festgehalt *nt*, Fixum *nt*; **~ supply** *n* ECON unelastisches Angebot *nt*; **~-term agreement** *n* HRM zeitlich befristeter Vertrag *m*; **~-term contract** *n* HRM zeitlich befristeter Vertrag *m*; **~-term deal** *n* HRM zeitlich befristeter Vertrag *m*; **~-term deposit** *n* BANK Termingeld *nt*, Festgeldanlage *f*; **~-term loan** *n* BANK Kredit *m* mit fester Laufzeit; **~ terms** *n pl* ADMIN Festkonditionen *f pl*

fixing: **~ of costs** *n* STOCK Festlegung *f* der Kosten, Kostenfestsetzung *f*; **~ of tariffs** *n* FIN, TAX Tariffestsetzung *f*; **~ of a time limit** *n* LAW *contract law* Fristsetzung *f*; **~-up expense** *n* PROP *preparation of residence for sale* Herrichtungskosten *pl*

fixture: **~ rate** *n* TRANSP *shipping* festgelegter Satz *m*

fixtures *n pl* PROP Grundstücksbestandteile *m pl*, unbewegliches Inventar *nt*; **~ and fittings** *n pl* ACC Anschlüsse *m pl* und unbewegliches Inventar *nt*, GEN COMM Betriebs- und Geschäftseinrichtung *f*, Betriebs- und Geschäftsausstattung *f*

F: **~ key** *n* (*function key*) COMP *keyboard* Funktionstaste *f*

flag 1. *n* COMP Flag *nt* (*jarg*), Kennzeichen *nt*, Fehlerkennzeichen *nt*, Marke *f*, TRANSP *shipping* Flagge *f*; **2.** *vi* ECON, GEN COMM abflauen

flagging *adj* ECON *demand, economy* abflauend, nachlassend

flagship: **~ site** *n* GEN COMM Hauptgeschäftsbereich *m*, Kernbereich *m*; **~ store** *n* S&M Hauptgeschäft *nt*

flare up *vi* GEN COMM *anger, trouble* aufflackern

flash *vi* GEN COMM *signal* blinken

flash: **~ of inspiration** *n* GEN COMM Ideenblitz *m*, Gedankenblitz *m*; **~ item** *n* S&M Artikel *m* im Sonderangebot

flat 1. *adj* GEN COMM *dull* flau, STOCK umsatzlos; **2.** *n* FIN Kurs *m* einschließlich aufgelaufener Zinsen, GEN COMM Großpalette *f*, PROP *BrE* (*cf apartment AmE*) Wohnung *f*

flat: **~ bed** *n* TRANSP Pritschenwagen *m*; **~ cancellation** *n* INS Storno *m or nt* vor Vertragsablauf; **~ car** *n AmE* (*cf flat wagon BrE*) TRANSP *rail* Flachwagen *m*; **~ charges** *n pl* ADMIN Pauschalgebühren *f pl*, Pauschalkosten *pl*; **~ container** *n* TRANSP Flachcontainer *m*; **~ fee** *n* BANK, PATENTS Pauschalgebühr *f*, FIN Einheitstarif *m*, Grundgebühr *f*; **~ grant** *n* WEL Bundeszuschuß *m*, öffentliche Beihilfe *f*; **~ line re-insurance** *n* INS Pauschalrückversicherung *f*; **~ market** STOCK lustloser Markt *m*, relativ stabiler, aber bewegungsloser Markt *m*; **~ organization** *n* MGMNT flache Organisation *f*, Organisation *f* mit großer Leitungsspanne; **~ pay** *n* ADMIN Grundgehalt *nt*; **~ price** *n* STOCK Erwerbskurs *m*; **~ quotation** *n* STOCK Notierung *f* einschließlich aufgelaufener Stückzinsen; **~ rack** *n* TRANSP *container* Flachgestell *nt*; **~-rate** *adj* GEN COMM pauschal, Pauschal-; **~ rate** *n* INS Durchschnittsprämie *f*, S&M Einheitstarif *m*, TAX Proportionalsatz *m*; **~-rate bonus** *n* HRM Einheitsprämie *f*; **~-rate fee** *n* BANK, PATENTS Pauschalgebühr *f*; **~-rate of pay** *n* HRM Pauschalzahlung *f*; **~-rate price** *n* GEN COMM Pauschalpreis *m*; **~-rate subscription** *n* FIN Pauschalabonnement *nt*; **~-rate tax** *n* TAX Pauschalsteuer *f*; **~-rate withholding** *n* TAX pauschale Einbehaltung *f*; **~ scale** *n* HRM, TAX Pauschaltarif *m*

flatten *vi* MATH *curve* abflachen

flattening: **~ of hierarchies** *n* ADMIN, GEN COMM, HRM Abbau der Statusunterschiede zwischen Arbeitern und Angestellten, Abflachen *nt* der Unternehmenshierarchien

flat: **~ wagon** *n BrE* (*cf flat car AmE*) TRANSP *rail* Flachwagen *m*

flaw *n* GEN COMM Fehler *m*

flawed *adj* GEN COMM fehlerhaft

fledgling: **~ commercial field** *n* GEN COMM junges Geschäftsfeld *nt*, junger Wirtschaftsbereich *m*

fleet *n* TRANSP *of company cars* Fahrzeugpark *m*, Fuhrpark *m*, Wagenbestand *m*; **~ manager** *n* HRM Fuhrparkleiter, in *m,f*, *for planes and ships* Flottenleiter, in *m,f*; **~ planning** *n* TRANSP *shipping* Flottenplanung *f*; **~ policy** *n* INS Fuhrparkpolice *f*, Kraftfahrzeugsammelpolice *f*; **~ rationalization** *n* TRANSP Rationalisierung *f* des Fuhrparks; **~ utilization** *n* TRANSP Auslastung *f* des Fuhrparks

flexibility *n* GEN COMM Flexibilität *f*, Anpassungsfähigkeit *f*

flexible *adj* GEN COMM flexibel, anpassungsfähig, beweglich; **~ accelerator** *n* ECON flexibler Akzelerator *m*; **~ budget** *n* ECON flexibles Budget *nt*; **~ exchange rate** *n* ECON flexibler Wechselkurs *m*, frei schwankender Wechselkurs *m*, freier Wechselkurs *m*; **~ firm** *n* ECON flexibles Unternehmen *nt*, GEN COMM bewegliches Unternehmen *nt*; **~-payment mortgage** *n* (*FPM*) BANK, PROP variabel verzinsliche Hypothek *f*; **~ plant** *n* ECON beweglicher Maschinenpark *m*; **~ price** *n* ECON flexibler Preis *m*; **~ schedule** *n* HRM Gleitzeit *f*, flexible Arbeitszeit *f*, flexibles Arbeitszeitprogramm *nt*; **~-term deposit** *n* BANK Termingeld *nt* mit variabler Laufzeit; **~ time** *n* HRM flexible Arbeitszeit *f*, Gleitzeit *f*, gleitende Arbeitszeit *f*; **~ working hours** *n pl* ADMIN Gleitzeit *f*, HRM flexible Arbeitszeit *f*, Gleitzeit *f*, gleitende Arbeitszeit *f*

flexitime *n* HRM flexible Arbeitszeit *f*

flexography *n* S&M Flexodruck *m*

flexprice *n* ECON flexibler Preis *m*

flextime *n* HRM flexible Arbeitszeit *f*, Gleitzeit *f*

flicker 1. *n* COMP *screen* Flimmern *nt*; **2.** *vi* COMP *screen* flackern

flicker: **~-free** *adj* COMP flimmerfrei

flier *n* STOCK Reinfall *m*

flight *n* GEN COMM Flucht *f*, LEIS, TRANSP Flug *m*; **~ attendant** *n* TRANSP Flugbegleiter, in *m,f*, Steward *m*, Stewardess *f*; **~ of capital** *n* ECON Kapitalflucht *f*, FIN Abwanderung *f* von Kapital; **~ coupon** *n* TRANSP Flugschein *m*, Flug-Kupon *m*; **~ information** *n* TRANSP Fluginformation *f*; **~ number** *n* TRANSP Flugnummer *f*; **~ plan** *n* LEIS Flugplan *m*; **~ schedule** *n* LEIS Flugplan *m*; **~ scheduler** *n* TRANSP Flugplaner, in *m,f*; **~ strategy** *n* TRANSP Flugstrategie *f*; **~ time** *n* TRANSP Flugzeit *f*

flipchart *n* GEN COMM Flip-Chart *f*

flip-flop *n* COMP *hardware* Kippschaltung *f*, TRANSP *containers* Flip-Flop *nt*; **~ arbitration** *n* HRM Pendelschiedsverfahren *nt*

float 1. *n* BANK Float *m*, Inkassi *nt pl*,

Wertstellungsgewinn *m*, Valutierungsgewinn *m*, *change* Wechselgeld *nt*; **2.** *vt* FIN auflegen, begeben; ◆ **~ an issue** STOCK eine Anleihe auflegen; **~ a loan** STOCK eine Anleihe auflegen

floater *n* BANK zinsvariable Anleihe *f*, INS Abschreibepolice *f*, Generalpolice *f*, offene Police *f*, Pauschalversicherung *f*, STOCK zinsvariabler Schuldtitel *m*, WEL offene Police *f*

floating *n* FIN *of currency* Floaten *nt*, Floating *nt*, Wechselkursfreigabe *f*; **~ assets** *n pl* ACC Umlaufvermögen *nt*; **~ cargo policy** *n* INS *shipping* laufende Frachtpolice *f*, offene Frachtpolice *f*; **~ debt** *n* FIN schwebende Schuld *f*, kurzfristige Verbindlichkeit *f*; **~ exchange rate** *n* ECON flexibler Wechselkurs *m*, frei schwankender Wechselkurs *m*, freier Wechselkurs *m*, freigegebener Wechselkurs *m*; **~ interest rate** *n* BANK veränderlicher Zinssatz *m* für Hypotheken; **~ marine policy** *n* (*FP*) INS, TRANSP *shipping* Generalpolice *f*; **~-point number** *n* COMP, MATH Gleitkommazahl *f*; **~ policy** *n* INS, WEL Abschreibepolice *f*, Generalpolice *f*, offene Police *f*; **~ production system** *n* IND variables Produktionssystem *nt*; **~ rate** *n* ECON *of exchange* freier Wechselkurs *m*; **~-rate** *adj* FIN variabel verzinslich; **~-rate deposit** *n* STOCK *interest rate futures* zinsvariable Einlage *f*; **~-rate investment** *n* STOCK zinsvariable Investition *f*; **~-rate loan** *n* BANK zinsvariables Darlehen *nt*, Anleihe *f* mit variablem Zinssatz; **~-rate note** *n* (*FRN*) BANK zinsvariable Anleihe *f*, STOCK variabel verzinsliche Anleihe *f*; **~-rate notes** *n* STOCK Emission *f* mit variablem Zinssatz; **~ securities** *n pl* STOCK begebene Wertpapiere *nt pl*, noch nicht plazierte Wertpapiere *nt pl*; **~ time** *n* ECON Pufferzeit *f*, Zahlungsfloat *f*, IMP/EXP Begebungszeit *f*

flood *n* GEN COMM Flut *f*; **~ insurance** *n* INS Hochwasserversicherung *f*, Versicherung *f* gegen Überschwemmungsschäden

floor *n* ECON Talsohle *f*, *exchange rate* unterer Interventionspunkt *m*, FIN, STOCK Mindestpreis *m*, Mindestpreisrecht *nt*, *location of trading* Parkett *nt*; **~-area ratio** *n* PROP Verhältnis *nt* Gebäudefläche-Grundstücksfläche; **~ broker** *n* STOCK *currency exchange trading* Börsenmakler, in *m,f*, Parketthändler *m*

flooring *n* BANK Beleihung *f* von Lagerbeständen, Finanzierung *f* eines Warenlagers

floor: **~ loan** *n* FIN Mindestdarlehen *nt*; **~ official** *n* STOCK Börsenangestellte(r) *mf* [decl. as adj]; **~ plan** *n* PROP *of rooms* Grundriß *m*; **~ plan insurance** *n* INS Versicherung *f* für die Finanzierung eines Warenlagers; **~ planning** *n* BANK Beleihung *f* von Lagerbeständen, Finanzierung *f* eines Warenlagers; **~ price** *n* ECON Mindestpreis *m*; **~ rate** *n* STOCK Mindestzinssatz *m*, Zinsuntergrenze *f*; **~ return** *n* STOCK Mindestertrag *m*, Mindestrendite *f*; **~ space** *n* PROP Grundfläche *f*; **~ trader** *n* STOCK *trading* Parketthändler *m*

floorwalker *n* S&M Empfangschef, in *m,f*, Ladenaufsicht *f*

flop *n* *infrml* GEN COMM Flop *m* (*infrml*), Reinfall *m*, Pleite *f* (*infrml*)

floppy *n* COMP Diskette *f*, Floppy *f* (*jarg*); **~ disk** *n* COMP Diskette *f*, Floppy *f* (*jarg*); **~ disk drive** *n* COMP Diskettenlaufwerk *nt*

flotation *n* STOCK Begebung *f* einer Anleihe, Begebung *f* eines Schuldtitels; **~ cost** *n* STOCK Börseneinführungskosten *pl*, Emissionskosten *pl*

flourish *vi* GEN COMM *business, competition* florieren

flourishing *adj* GEN COMM florierend, flott gehend

flow 1. *n* ACC *of funds* Kapitalfluß *m*, COMP *of data* Fluß *m*, *operations* Ablauf *m*, ECON Stromgröße *f*, Strömungsgröße *f*, Flow-Größe *f* (*jarg*), IND *of electricity* Stromfluß *m*, *of gas* Gasstrom *m*, TRANSP *of goods or traffic* Strom *m*; **2.** *vi* GEN COMM fließen, IND *electricity* fließen, *gas* strömen; ◆ **~ out** ECON *money* abfließen

flowchart *n* COMP Flußdiagramm *nt*, GEN COMM Ablaufdiagramm *nt*, MATH Datenflußplan *m*, MGMNT *algorithm* Arbeitsablaufbogen *m*

flow: **~ concept** *n* STOCK Ablaufkonzept *nt*; **~ control** *n* COMP Flußsteuerung *f*; **~ diagram** *n* MATH Flußdiagramm *nt*

flower: **~ bond** *n* STOCK Staatstitel zur Begleichung von Steuerschulden, Flower Bond *m*

flow: **~ of funds** *n* ACC *balance* Geldstrom *m*, Geldmittelbewegung *f*, ECON Geldstrom *m*, Geldmittelbewegung *f*, Kapitalstrom *m*, FIN Kapitalfluß *m*; **~-of-funds analysis** *n* ECON Geldstromanalyse *f*; **~-of-funds table** *n* FIN *national accounts* Geldstromtabelle *f*; **~ line** *n* IND Ablauflinie *f*, MATH Feldlinie *f*, Strömungslinie *f*, TRANSP *pallets* Flußprinzip *nt*; **~ of orders** *n* GEN COMM Auftragsfluß *m*; **~ process chart** *n* MATH Arbeitsablaufbogen *m*, MGMNT Arbeitsablaufbogen *m*, Arbeitsflußdiagramm *nt*; **~ production** *n* IND Bandfabrikation *f*, Bandproduktion *f*, Fließarbeit *f*, Fließbandarbeit *f*, Fließfabrikation *f*; **~-through credits** *n* BANK, FIN durchlaufende Kredite *m pl*; **~-through share** *n* STOCK Durchlaufaktie *f*

fl.oz. *abbr* (*fluid ounce*) GEN COMM Flüssigunze *f*

FLSA *abbr AmE* (*Fair Labor Standards Act*) LAW Gesetz über Mindestlohnnormen

fluctuate *vi* GEN COMM schwanken

fluctuating: **~ currency** *n* ECON frei schwankender Wechselkurs *m*; **~ exchange rate** *n* ECON frei schwankender Wechselkurs *m*, freier Wechselkurs *m*

fluctuation *n* ECON Schwankung *f*, GEN COMM Fluktuation *f*; **~ band** *n* ECON *ERM* Bandbreite *f*; **~ limit** *n* STOCK Fluktuationsbegrenzung *f*

fluff *n* *infrml* COMMS Sprechfehler *m*, Versprecher *m* (*infrml*)

fluid: **~ ounce** *n* (*fl.oz.*) GEN COMM Flüssigunze *f*

flurry: **~ of activity** *n* STOCK kurzer Börsenauftrieb *m*; **~ of new issue activity** *n* STOCK Emissionsstoß *m*

flush *n* COMP Ausrichtung *f*; **~ left** *adj* COMP *document, printing* linksbündig; **~ right** *adj* COMP *document, printing* rechtsbündig, rechts ausgerichtet

flutter: **have a ~** *phr BrE infrml* LEIS *betting* ein paar Scheinchen riskieren (*infrml*), sein Glück versuchen

flux *n* GEN COMM Fluß *m*

fly: **~-by-night worker** *n* *infrml* HRM Schwarzarbeiter, in *m,f*

flyer *n* COMMS, MEDIA, S&M *advertisement* Flugblatt *nt*

flying: **~ doctor** *n* WEL fliegender Arzt *m*; **~ pickets** *n pl* HRM mobile Streikposten *m pl*; **~ visit** *n* GEN COMM Blitzbesuch *m*, POL Stipvisite *f* (*jarg*)

fly: **~ posting** *n* S&M wilder Anschlag *m*

fm *abbr* (*fathom*) IND *timber* Klafter *m or nt* (*obs*)

FMB *abbr AmE* (*Federal Maritime Board*) IND Bundesseefahrtskomitee

FMC *abbr AmE* (*Federal Maritime Commission*) TRANSP Bundesschiffahrtsbehörde

FMG *abbr* (*fast-moving consumer goods*) S&M schnellumschlagende Ware *f*

FNMA *abbr AmE* (*Federal National Mortgage Association*) FIN, PROP Bundesbehörde zur Förderung des Wohneigentums und Verbesserung des Wohnungsniveaus, ≈ Bundeshypothekenanstalt *f*

fo *abbr* (*for orders*) GEN COMM bei Aufträgen, für Aufträge

FOA *abbr* GEN COMM (*Foreign Operations Administration*) Auslandshilfsamt

fob: ~ **sb off with sth** *phr infrml* S&M jdn mit etw abspeisen (*infrml*); ~ **sth off on sb** *phr infrml* S&M jdm etw andrehen (*infrml*)

foc *abbr* (*free of charge*) GEN COMM gebührenfrei, kostenlos, zum Nulltarif, gratis

FoC *abbr BrE* (*father of chapel*) HRM *publishing, printing trade unions* Betriebsratsvorsitzende(r) *m* [decl. as adj]

focal: ~ **point** *n* GEN COMM *of discussion* Kernpunkt *m*

focus 1. *n* GEN COMM Mittelpunkt *m*, Brennpunkt *m*, Zentrum *nt*; **2.** *vt* GEN COMM einstellen, fokussieren

focus: ~ **group** *n* GEN COMM, S&M *market research* Zielgruppe *f*, Untersuchungsgruppe *f*; ~ **group survey** *n* GEN COMM, S&M *market research* Zielgruppenuntersuchung *f*

fod *abbr* (*free of damage*) GEN COMM, INS frei von Schäden, schadensfrei

FOIA *abbr AmE* (*Freedom of Information Act*) LAW Gesetz *nt* zur Informationspflicht von Behörden

foil *n* MEDIA Folie *f*; ~ **stamping** *n* MEDIA Foliendruck *m*

FOK *abbr AmE* (*fill-or-kill*) STOCK Option ausüben oder aufgeben

folder *n* GEN COMM Faltblatt *nt*

folio *n* S&M Paginierung *f*, *printing* Foliant *m*, Folioblatt *nt*

follow *vt* GEN COMM befolgen, folgen [+dat], folgen auf [+acc], HRM, MGMNT, WEL *course* verfolgen; ◆ ~ **a similar curve** MATH einer ähnlichen Kurve folgen; ~ **a similar pattern** GEN COMM *demand* einem ähnlichen Muster folgen; ~ **suit** GEN COMM dasselbe tun

follow through *vt* GEN COMM *project, scheme* durchziehen (*infrml*), MGMNT bis zum Ende führen, zu Ende verfolgen

follow up *vt* COMMS, GEN COMM nachfassen, MGMNT *plans, suggestions, proposals* weiteruntersuchen

follower *n* GEN COMM Nachfolger, in *m,f*

follow-up *n* GEN COMM Überwachung *f*, Anschluß *m*, MATH nachfassende Untersuchung *f*; ~ **advertising** *n* S&M Anschlußwerbung *f*; ~ **letter** *n* COMMS Erinnerungsschreiben *nt*, Nachfaßbrief *m*, S&M Erinnerungsbrief *m*, Folgebrief *m*; ~ **orders** *n pl* GEN COMM Anschlußaufträge *m pl*; ~ **standard specification** *n* IND Anschlußnorm *f*

FOMC *abbr AmE* (*Federal Open Market Committee*) ECON Offenmarktausschuß des Federal Reserve System

font *n* COMP, MEDIA *typography* Schrift *f*, Schriftart *f*; ~ **family** *n* COMP, MEDIA *typography* Schriftfamilie *f*; ~ **file** *n* COMP *typesetting* Schriftdatei *f*

Food: ~ **and Agriculture Organization** *n* (*FAO*) ECON Ernährungs- und Landwirtschaftsorganisation der UN

food: ~ **aid** *n* ECON *development assistance* Nahrungsmittelhilfe *f*; ~ **chain** *n* ECON

Lebensmittelkette *f*; ~ **law** *n* LAW Lebensmittelgesetz *nt*; ~ **processing** *n* IND Nahrungsmittelverarbeitung *f*; **~-processing industry** *n* ENVIR, IND lebensmittelverarbeitende Industrie *f*, Nahrungsmittelindustrie *f*; ~ **retailing** *n* S&M Lebensmitteleinzelhandel *m*; ~ **store** *n* S&M Lebensmittelgeschäft *nt*

foodstuffs *n pl* GEN COMM Lebensmittel *nt pl*, Nahrungsmittel *nt pl*

food: ~ **supply** *n* ECON Lebensmittelvorrat *m*, Nahrungsmittelversorgung *f*; ~ **surplus** *n* ECON Nahrungsmittelüberschuß *m*

foot *n* (*ft*) GEN COMM Fuß *m*

foot up *vt AmE* MATH *columns of figures* addieren

footage *n* MEDIA Filmlänge *f*, Filmmeter *m*, Gesamtlänge *f*

footer *n* COMP *document* Fußzeile *f*

footing *n AmE* GEN COMM, MATH *adding up of figures* Addieren *nt*, Addition *f*, GEN COMM, MATH *resulting figures* Summe *f*; **on the same ~** *phr* GEN COMM auf gleicher Basis

footloose: ~ **industry** *n* IND standortungebundene Industrie *f*

footnote *n* COMP *document* Fußnote *f*; ~ **disclosure** *n* ACC gesonderter Ausweis *m* als Anmerkung zur Bilanz

Footsie *n BrE* (*FT-SE 100 Share Index*) STOCK Aktienindex der Financial Times

forbid *vt* LAW verbieten; ◆ ~ **an issue** STOCK eine Emission durchsetzen

force 1. *n* GEN COMM Kraft *f*, Stärke *f*; ◆ **come into ~** LAW *regulations, legislation* in Kraft treten, wirksam werden; **in ~** LAW *regulations, legislation* in Kraft; **2.** *vt* GEN COMM durchsetzen, zwingen; ~ **into early retirement** HRM zum vorzeitigen Ruhestand bewegen; ~ **performance** GEN COMM Erfüllung durchsetzen

force down *vt* ECON *interest rates* drücken

forced: ~ **currency** *n* ECON, FIN Zwangswährung *f*, STOCK notleidende Währung *f*; ~ **labor** *AmE*, ~ **labour** *BrE* *n* GEN COMM Zwangsarbeit *f*; ~ **landing** *n* LEIS Notlandung *f*; ~ **liquidation** *n* STOCK Notverkäufe *m pl*; ~ **sale** *n* LAW Zwangsverkauf *m*, Zwangsversteigerung *f*; ~ **sale of stock** *n* LAW Zwangsverwertung *f* von Vorräten; ~ **saving** *n* ECON Zwangssparen *nt*; ~ **savings** *n pl* FIN Zwangsersparnisse *f pl*

forceful *adj* GEN COMM *argument* stark

force: ~ **majeure** *n* INS, LAW höhere Gewalt *f*; ~ **majeure clause** *n* INS, LAW Höhere-Gewalt-Klausel *f*, Klausel *f* über höhere Gewalt

forcible: ~ **entry** *n* LAW *by police* gewaltsames Eindringen *nt*

Fordism *n* ECON Fordismus *m*

fore: **come to the ~** *phr* GEN COMM, POL ans Ruder kommen

forecast 1. *n* GEN COMM Voraussage *f*, Vorhersage *f*, Prognose *f*, LEIS Vorschau *f*, MATH Vorhersage *f*; **2.** *vt* GEN COMM vorhersagen, vorhersehen, MATH, S&M vorhersagen

forecasting *n* ACC Prognoserechnung *f*, Vorhersage *f*, GEN COMM Prognostizierung *f*, Prognose *f*, S&M Vorhersage *f*

foreclose *vt* FIN kündigen; ◆ ~ **a mortgage** ECON, FIN, LAW aus einer Hypothek die Zwangsvollstreckung betreiben

foreclosure *n* FIN Ausschluß *m*, Kündigung *f*,

Zwangsvollstreckung *f*; ~ **sale** *n AmE* LAW Zwangsver-steigerung *f*

foredate *vt* GEN COMM vordatieren

forefront: **at the ~** *phr* IND *of research and development* avantgardistisch, bahnbrechend, im Vorfeld

forego *vt* GEN COMM verzichten auf [+acc]; ◆ ~ **a debt** FIN auf eine Schuld verzichten; ~ **collection of a debt** ACC auf Forderungseinzug verzichten, auf Forderungs-inkasso verzichten

foreground *adj* COMP Vordergrund *m*; ~ **program** *n* COMP Vordergrundprogramm *nt*

foreign *adj* GEN COMM ausländisch, *trade* Außen-, POL auswärtig, Außen-; ~ **account** *n* BANK Auslandskonto *nt*; ~ **affairs** *n pl* POL auswärtige Angelegenheiten *f pl*, *foreign policy* Außenpolitik *f*; ~ **agent** *n* GEN COMM Auslandsvertreter, in *m,f*; ~ **aid** *n* ECON Auslandshilfe *f*; ~ **assets** *n pl* BANK Auslandsguthaben *nt pl*, ECON Auslandswerte *m pl*; ~ **bank** *n* BANK Auslandsbank *f*; ~ **banking** *n* BANK Auslandsbankgeschäfte *nt pl*; ~ **bill** *n* BANK Auslandswechsel *m*; ~ **bond** *n* FIN Auslandsan-leihe *f*; ~ **borrowing** *n* BANK, FIN Kreditaufnahme *f* im Ausland; ~ **branch** *n* BANK Auslandsfiliale *f*, Auslands-niederlassung *f*, GEN COMM, IMP/EXP Auslandsniederlassung *f*; ~ **buying house** *n* IMP/EXP ausländisches Einkaufshaus *nt*; ~ **check issue** *AmE*, ~ **cheque issue** *BrE n* BANK Auslandsscheckausgabe *f*, Ausstellung *f* eines Auslandsschecks, Begebung *f* eines Auslandsschecks

Foreign: ~ **and Commonwealth Office** *n BrE* (*FCO*) ADMIN Amt für Auslands- und Commonwealthangelegen-heiten, Außenministerium *nt*

foreign: ~ **company** *n* GEN COMM ausländisches Unter-nehmen *nt*; ~ **competitor** *n* ECON Auslandskonkurrent *m*; ~**-controlled bank** *n* BANK Bank *f* unter aus-ländischer Kontrolle; ~**-controlled enterprise** *n* GEN COMM in Auslandsbesitz befindliches Unternehmen *nt*; ~ **corporation** *n* LAW ausländische Gesellschaft *f*; ~ **correspondent** *n* MEDIA Auslandskorrespondent, in *m,f*; ~ **country** *n* GEN COMM Ausland *nt*; ~ **currency** *n* BANK, ECON, FIN, LAW Fremdwährung *f*; ~ **currency allowance** *n* FIN Fremdwährungsfreibetrag *m*; ~ **cur-rency borrowing** *n* BANK Fremdwäh-rungskreditaufnahme *f*, Kreditaufnahme *f* in Fremd-währung; ~ **currency clause** *n* LAW Währungsklausel *f*; ~ **currency credit cover account** *n* FIN Akkreditivwährungsdeckungskonto *nt*; ~ **currency loan** *n* ECON Fremdwährungskredit *m*, FIN Fremdwäh-rungsanleihe *f*; ~ **currency loan issue** *n* FIN Fremdwährungsanleihe *f*; ~ **currency outflow** *n* ECON Devisenabfluß *m*; ~ **currency position** *n* ECON *interna-tional trade* Fremdwährungsposition *f*; ~ **currency transaction** *n* ECON, IMP/EXP Devisentransaktion *f*; ~ **currency translation** *n* ECON Umrechnung *f* von Fremdwährungen; ~ **currency translation reserve** *n* ACC *annual accounts* Devisenrücklage *f*; ~ **currency unit** *n* ECON ausländische Währungseinheit *f*; ~ **demand** *n* ECON Auslandsnachfrage *f*; ~ **direct investment** *n* (*FDI*) ECON, FIN ausländische Direktinvestition *f*; ~ **dividends** *n pl* STOCK Auslandsdividenden *f pl*; ~ **employee** *n* ECON, HRM ausländische Arbeitnehmerin *f*, ausländischer Arbeitnehmer *m*

foreigner *n* GEN COMM Ausländer, in *m,f*

foreign: ~ **exchange** *n* (*forex*) GEN COMM Devisen *f pl*; ~ **exchange account** *n* BANK Devisenkonto *nt*, Fremd-währungskonto *nt*, Währungskonto *nt*; ~ **exchange**

advisory service *n* BANK Devisenberatung *f*; ~ **exchange arbitrage** *n* FIN Devisenkursarbitrage *f*, Ausgleichsarbitrage *f*; ~ **exchange broker** *n* FIN Devisenmakler, in *m,f*; ~ **exchange conversion rate** *n* FIN Devisenumrechnungskurs *m*; ~ **exchange dealer** *n* FIN Devisenhändler, in *m,f*; ~ **exchange department** *n* BANK Devisenabteilung *f*; ~ **exchange earner** *n* GEN COMM Devisenbringer, in *m,f*; ~ **exchange hedge** *n* ACC Devisenabsicherung *f*, Devisenschutz *m*; ~ **exchange holdings** *n pl* BANK Devisenbestände *m pl*, Devisenreserven *f pl*; ~ **exchange market** *n* ECON Devisenbörse *f*, Devisenmarkt *m*, STOCK Devisenmarkt *m*; ~ **exchange note** *n* FIN Devisenabrechnung *f*; ~ **exchange office** *n* BANK, LEIS Wechselstube *f*; ~ **exchange rate** *n* ECON Devisenkurs *m*, Wechselkurs *m*; ~ **exchange reserves** *n pl* ECON Währungsreserven *f pl*; ~ **exchange restrictions** *n pl* ECON Devisenbeschränkungen *f pl*; ~ **exchange risk** *n* ECON Währungsrisiko *nt*; ~ **exchange speculation** *n* FIN Währungsspekulation *f*, Devisenspekulation *f*; ~ **exchange table** *n* ECON Kursnotierung *f*, Kurstabelle *f*; ~ **exchange trader** *n* STOCK Devisenhändler, in *m,f*; ~**firm** *n* GEN COMM Auslandsunternehmen *nt*; ~ **gen-eral average** *n* (*fga*) GEN COMM ausländische große Havarie *f*; ~ **investment** *n* ECON Auslandsinvestition *f*; ~ **language** *n* GEN COMM Fremdsprache *f*; ~ **loan** *n* FIN Auslandsanleihe *f*, Auslandskredit *f*; ~ **market** *n* ECON, GEN COMM Auslandsmarkt *m*; ~ **minister** *n* POL Außenminister *m*; ~ **ministry** *n* POL Außenministerium *nt*; ~ **money order** *n* BANK internationale Geldan-weisung *f*; ~ **national** *n* HRM ausländische(r) Staatsangehörige(r) *mf* [decl. as adj]; ~ **notes and coins** *n pl* FIN Sorten *f pl*

Foreign: ~ **Operations Administration** *n AmE* (*FOA*) GEN COMM Auslandshilfsamt

foreign: ~ **operations department** *n* FIN Auslandsab-teilung *f*; ~**-owned** *n* BANK, GEN COMM, TRANSP in ausländischem Besitz; ~**-owned bank** *n* BANK Bank *f* im ausländischen Besitz; ~ **participation** *n* FIN, GEN COMM Auslandsbeteiligung *f*; ~ **policy** *n* ECON, POL Außenpolitik *f*; ~ **product** *n* GEN COMM ausländisches Erzeugnis *nt*, ausländisches Fabrikat *nt*; ~ **relations** *n pl* POL Außenbeziehungen *f pl*; ~ **representative** *n* GEN COMM Auslandsvertreter, in *m,f*; ~ **sales** *n pl* GEN COMM, S&M Auslandsabsatz *m*

Foreign: ~ **Secretary** *n BrE* POL Außenminister, in *m,f*

foreign: ~ **section** *n* STOCK Auslandsabteilung *f*; ~ **ser-vice pay** *n* HRM Auslandszulage *f*; ~**-source income** *n* TAX ausländische Einkünfte *pl*; ~ **subsidiary** *n* GEN COMM, LAW, TAX ausländische Tochtergesellschaft *f*; ~ **trade** *n* ECON Außenhandel *m*, IMP/EXP *carried on by domestic firms* Aktivhandel *m*; ~ **trade contract** *n* LAW Außenhandelsvertrag *m*; ~ **trade firm** *n* ECON Außen-handelsunternehmen *nt*; ~ **trade information agencies** *n pl* IMP/EXP Auskunftstellen *f pl* für den Außenhandel; ~ **trade multiplier** *n* ECON Außenhandelsmultiplikator *m*; ~ **trade organization** *n* (*FTO*) FIN, IMP/EXP Außen-handelsorganisation *f*, Außenhandelsvereinigung *f*; ~ **trade policy** *n* ECON, IMP/EXP, POL Außenhandels-politik *f*; ~ **trade statistics** *n pl* ECON Außenhandelsstatistik *f*; ~ **trade surplus** *n* ECON Außenhandelsüberschuß *m*; ~ **trade zone** *n* ECON Freihandelszone *f*; ~ **venture** *n* GEN COMM Auslands-unternehmung *f*, Auslandsventure *nt*; ~ **worker** *n* ECON, HRM Fremdarbeiter, in *m,f*, Gastarbeiter, in *m,f*, ausländischer Arbeitnehmer *m*, ausländische Arbeitnehmerin *f*

foreman *n* GEN COMM Meister *m*, HRM Meister *m*, Vorarbeiter, in *m,f*

foresee *vt* GEN COMM vorhersehen

foreseeable *adj* GEN COMM *predictable* vorraussagbar; ♦ **in the ~ future** GEN COMM in nächster Zukunft

foreseeable: **~ risk** *n* STOCK vorhersehbares Risiko *nt*

foreshore *n* LAW Küstenvorland *nt*

forest *n* GEN COMM Wald *m*

forestry *n* GEN COMM Wald- und Forstwirtschaft *f*

Forestry: **~ Commission** *n* BrE IND Forstverwaltung

forestry: **~ industry** *n* IND Forstwirtschaft *f*, Forstwirtschaftsindustrie *f*

forex *n* *(foreign exchange)* GEN COMM Devisen *f pl*; **~ trading** *n* BANK *merchant* Devisenhandel *m*

forfaiting *n* ECON *method of international trade finance* Forfaitierung *f*

forfait: **~ system** *n* TAX Forfaitierung-System *nt*

forfeit 1. *n* LAW Verfall *m*; **2.** *vt* GEN COMM verlieren, INS *claim*, LAW *right* verwirken

forfeitable *adj* LAW verfallbar

forfeited *adj* LAW verfallen; **~ security** *n* INS verfallene Sicherheit *f*, verwirkte Sicherheit *f*

forfeiting *n* IMP/EXP Verlust *m*

forfeiture *n* INS Verwirkung *f* des Versicherungsanspruchs, LAW *of right* Verfall *m*, Verfallserklärung *f*, Verwirkung *f*; **~ clause** *n* LAW Verfallklausel *f*

forge *vt* GEN COMM fälschen; ♦ **~ a link** GEN COMM eine Verbindung herstellen

forged: **~ check** *AmE*, **~ cheque** *BrE n* BANK gefälschter Scheck *m*

forgery *n* GEN COMM Fälschung *f*, Verfälschung *f*, LAW Herstellung *f* falschen Beweismaterials

forgivable: **~ loan** *n* FIN erlassbare Anleihe *f*

forgiveness: **~ of debt** *n* *AmE* LAW Schulderlaß *m*

fork out 1. *vt infrml* GEN COMM berappen (*infrml*); **2.** *vi infrml* GEN COMM berappen (*infrml*)

fork: **~-lift truck** *n* TRANSP Gabelstapler *m*

form 1. *n* COMP Maske *f*, LAW Ausgestaltungsform *f*, PATENTS *of the abstract* Form *f*, Gestalt *f*, Schema *nt*, *printed* Formblatt *nt*, Formular *nt*, Vordruck *m*; ♦ **in the ~ of** GEN COMM in Form von; **2.** *vt* GEN COMM *committee, alliance* bilden, *company* gründen; ♦ **~ a partnership** GEN COMM eine Gesellschaft gründen; **~ a quorum** MGMNT beschlußfähig sein

formal *adj* GEN COMM formal, förmlich; **~ agreement** *n* GEN COMM formale Vereinbarung *f*; **~ communication** *n* COMMS offizielle Mitteilung *f*; **~ dinner** *n* GEN COMM offizielles Essen *nt*; **~ economy** *n* ECON offizielle Wirtschaft *f*

formality *n* GEN COMM Formalität *f*

formalization *n* GEN COMM Formalisierung *f*

formalize *vt* GEN COMM formalisieren

formal: **~ management development** *n* MGMNT formelle Weiterentwicklung *f* des Management; **~ notice** *n* GEN COMM förmliche Mitteilung *f*, formelle Mitteilung *f*; **~ notice of default** *n* LAW *contracts* Inverzugsetzung *f*; **~ receipt** *n* GEN COMM formelle Empfangsbestätigung *f*; **~ submission date** *n* FIN offizieller Einreichungstermin *m*; **~ trade links** *n pl* GEN COMM formale Handelsverbindungen *f pl*

format 1. *n* ADMIN, COMP Format *nt*; **2.** *vt* COMP *disk* formatieren

formation: **~ of a contract** *n* LAW Zustandekommen *nt* eines Vertrages

formatting *n* COMP Formatierung *f*

former *adj* GEN COMM ehemalig; **~ buyer** *n* S&M ehemaliger Käufer *m*, ehemalige Käuferin *f*

form: **~ feed** *n* *(FF)* COMP Belegvorschub *m*, Formularvorschub *m*, Seitenvorschub *m*

formless *adj* GEN COMM formlos

formlessness *n* GEN COMM Formlosigkeit *f*

forms: **~ design sheet** *n* ADMIN Musterformular *nt*

formula *n* MATH Formel *f*; **~ funding** *n* FIN Finanzierung *f* nach Plan

formulate *vt* GEN COMM formulieren, LAW *rules, guidelines, conditions* festlegen

formulation *n* MGMNT *of policy* Formulierung *f*

forthcoming *adj* GEN COMM bevorstehend

fortnight *n* GEN COMM zwei Wochen *f pl*, vierzehn Tage *m pl*

fortnightly *adv* GEN COMM vierzehntägig

fortuitous: **~ loss** *n* INS zufälliger Verlust *m*, Zufallsverlust *m*

forum *n* GEN COMM Gerichtshof *m*, Tribunal *nt*, POL Austragungsmodus *m* einer Debatte, Forum *nt*

forward *vt* *(fwd)* COMMS *package, document* weiterleiten, GEN COMM befördern, TRANSP übersenden, *shipping* transportieren; ♦ **please ~** COMMS bitte weiterleiten; **~ freight** TRANSP befrachten

forward: **~ borrowing rate** *n* STOCK *currency futures* Terminsollzinssatz *m*; **~ buying** *n* STOCK Kauf *m* auf Lieferung, Terminkauf *m*; **~ commodity** *n* STOCK Terminware *f*; **~ contract** *n* FIN, STOCK Terminkontrakt *m*; **~ cover** *n* STOCK Terminsicherung *f*; **~ currency deal** *n* ECON, STOCK *international trade* Devisentermingeschäft *nt*

forwarder *n* *(fwdr)* COMMS, IMP/EXP, TRANSP *carrier* Beförderer *m*, Frachtspediteur *m*, Spediteur *m*, *sender* Absender *m*, Sender *m*, Verlader *m*; **~ air waybill** *n* *(FAB)* IMP/EXP, TRANSP Luftfrachtbrief *m* des Spediteurs; **~'s certificate of receipt** *n* *(FCR)* IMP/EXP, TRANSP Übernahmebescheinigung *f* des Spediteurs

forward: **~ exchange** *n* ECON Devisentermingeschäft *nt*, Devisenterminhandel *m*; **~ exchange contract** *n* BANK *currency* Devisenkontrakt *m*; **~ exchange dealing** *n* STOCK Devisenterminhandel *m*, Devisentermingeschäft *nt*; **~ exchange market** *n* STOCK Devisenterminmarkt *m*; **~ exchange rate** *n* ECON, STOCK Devisenterminkurs *m*; **~ exchange trading** *n* STOCK Devisenterminhandel *m*; **~ exchange transaction** *n* FIN, STOCK Termingeschäft *nt*; **~ indicator** *n* ECON Frühindikator *m*

forwarding *n* STOCK Terminkauf *m*, TRANSP Übersendung *f*; **~ address** *n* GEN COMM Zustelladresse *f*; **~ agency** *n* TRANSP Speditionsfirma *f*; **~ agent** *n* IMP/EXP, TRANSP Spediteur *m*; **~ agent's bill of lading** *n* IMP/EXP, TRANSP Spediteurkonnossement *nt*; **~ agent's commission** *n* *(fac)* TRANSP Provision *f* für den Spediteur; **~ agent's receipt** *n* IMP/EXP, TRANSP Übernahmebescheinigung *f* des Spediteurs; **~ in bulk** *n* TRANSP Beförderung *f* in großen Mengen, Massenbeförderung *f*, Massentransport *m*; **~ clerk** *n* HRM *transport* Expedient, in *m,f*; **~ company** *n* IMP/EXP,

TRANSP Speditionsunternehmen *nt*, Transportunternehmen *nt*; ~ **department** *n* TRANSP Versandstelle *f*, Versandabteilung *f*; ~ **instructions** *n pl* TRANSP Lieferanweisungen *f pl*, Nachsendeanweisungen *f pl*; ~ **by rail** *n* TRANSP Bahnversand *m*; ~ **station** *n* TRANSP *rail* Versandbahnhof *m*

forward: ~ **integration** *n* ECON Vorwärtsintegration *f*; ~ **investment return** *n* STOCK *interest rate futures* Terminkapitalverzinsung *f*; ~ **linkage** *n* ECON absatzorientierte Verflechtung *f*, Verflechtung *f* mit nachgelagerten Wirtschaftszweigen; ~**-looking** *adj* GEN COMM *person, project* vorausschauend; ~ **margin** *n* ECON *international trade* Swapsatz *m*; ~ **market** *n* STOCK Markt *m* für Termingeschäfte, Terminmarkt *m*; ~ **operation** *n* STOCK Termingeschäft *nt*; ~ **planning** *n* FIN, GEN COMM Vorausplanung *f*; ~ **position** *n* STOCK Terminposition *f*; ~ **pricing** *n* STOCK Preisfestsetzung *f* für Terminkontrakte; ~ **rate** *n* FIN Devisenterminkurs *m*, STOCK Terminkurs *m*; ~ **rate agreement** *n* (*FRA*) FIN, STOCK Zinsterminkontrakt *m*; ~ **rates** *n pl* STOCK *currency futures* Terminkurse *m pl*; ~ **sale** *n* FIN Terminverkauf *m*; ~ **security** *n* STOCK Terminpapier *nt*; ~ **stock** *n* S&M Lagervorrat *m* in der Verkaufsabteilung; ~ **swap** *n* FIN Terminswapgeschäft *nt*, STOCK Swaptermingeschäft *nt*; ~**-thinking** *adj* GEN COMM vorausdenkend; ~ **transaction in securities** *n* STOCK Wertpapiertermingeschäft *nt*; ~ **vertical integration** *n* ECON vertikale Vorwärtsintegration *f*

fossil: ~ **fuel** *n* ENVIR fossiler Brennstoff *m*

foster *vt* GEN COMM begünstigen, *relationship* pflegen

foul: ~ **bill of health** *n* WEL Gesundheitspaß *m* mit Einschränkungen; ~ **bill of lading** *n* IMP/EXP, TRANSP *shipping* unreines Konnossement *nt*

found *vt* GEN COMM gründen; ♦ **be founded on** GEN COMM beruhen auf [+dat]

foundation *n* ECON *charitable, educational* Stiftung *f*, TRANSP *shipping* Fundierung *f*

found: **if** ~ **correct** *phr* GEN COMM nach Richtigbefund

founder: ~ **member** *n* GEN COMM Gründungsmitglied *nt*

founding: ~ **company** *n* GEN COMM Gründungsgesellschaft *f*

fountain: ~ **pen** *n* GEN COMM Füllfederhalter *m*

four: ~**-color set** *AmE*, ~**-colour set** *BrE n* S&M Vierfarbendruck *m*; ~ **Ps** *n pl* S&M *product, price, promotion, place* Elemente des Marketing-Mix: Produkt, Preis, Kommunikation, Distribution

4Q *abbr* (*fourth quarter*) GEN COMM viertes Quartal *nt*

four: ~**-star petrol** *n BrE* (*cf premium grade gasoline AmE*) ENVIR Qualitätsbenzin *nt*, Superbenzin *nt*, Superkraftstoff *m*

Fourth: ~ **Company Law Directive** *n* LAW Vierte Richtlinie *f* zum Gesellschaftsrecht

fourth: ~ **market** *n* STOCK computergestützter Interbankenmarkt *m* für Wertpapiere; ~ **quarter** *n* (*4Q*) GEN COMM viertes Quartal *nt*

f.p. *abbr* (*fully paid*) GEN COMM voll bezahlt

FP *abbr* (*floating marine policy*) INS Generalpolice *f*

FPA *abbr* (*free of particular average*) INS frei von besonderer Havarie, ohne besondere Havarie

FPC *abbr AmE* (*Federal Power Commission*) IND Bundesenergiekommission

FPM *abbr* (*flexible-payment mortgage*) BANK, PROP variabel verzinsliche Hypothek *f*

FPZ *abbr* (*free port zone*) TRANSP *shipping* Freihafenzone *f*

F/R *abbr* (*freight release*) IMP/EXP *document* Frachtfreigabe-Bescheinigung *f*

FRA *abbr* (*forward rate agreement, future rate agreement*) FIN, STOCK Zinsterminkontrakt *m*

fraction *n* MATH Bruch *m*

fractional: ~ **cash reserve** *n* BANK vorgeschriebene Barreserve *f*; ~ **discretion order** *n* STOCK teilweise interessewahrender Auftrag

fractionalize *vt* MATH fraktionieren

fractional: ~ **lot** *n* STOCK Paket mit weniger als 100 Aktien; ~ **reserve** *n* BANK vorgeschriebene Mindestreserve *f*; ~ **reserve banking** *n* BANK Banksystem, in dem nur ein Teil der Kundeneinlagen als Zentralbankgeld gehalten wird; ~ **share** *n* STOCK Anteilsbruchteil *m*

fragile *adj* TRANSP zerbrechlich

fragmentation *n* COMP *disk* Fragmentierung *f*, ECON *of market* Aufteilung *f*, Fragmentierung *f*, Zersplitterung *f*

fragmented: ~ **bargaining** *n* HRM Splitterverhandlung *f*; ~ **market** *n* GEN COMM aufgeteilter Markt *m*, fragmentierter Markt *m*

frame 1. *n* COMP Frame *m* (*jarg*), Rahmen *m*; **2.** *vt* COMMS begrenzen

frame: ~ **of mind** *n* GEN COMM Gemütsverfassung *f*, Haltung *f*, Einstellung *f*

framework *n* FIN, GEN COMM *institutional* Rahmen *m*

franchise *n* INS Franchise *f*, POL Stimmrecht *nt*, S&M Franchise *nt*, Franchising *nt*, Alleinverkaufsrecht *nt*, Konzession *f*; ~ **agreement** *n* LAW Konzessionsvertrag *m*, Lizenzvertrag *m*; ~ **clause** *n* INS Selbstbehaltsklausel *f*, Franchiseklausel *f*

franchised *adj* GEN COMM konzessioniert; ~ **dealer** *n BrE* GEN COMM Vertragshändler, in *m,f*

franchisee *n* GEN COMM Konzessionsinhaber, in *m,f*, S&M Franchisenehmer, in *m,f*

franchise: ~ **financing** *n* FIN Konzessionsplanung *f*; ~ **gap** *n* ECON Bandbreite *f* zwischen An- und Verkaufskurs; ~ **tax** *n AmE* TAX Konzessionssteuer *f*

franchising *n* S&M Franchising *nt*

franchisor *n* GEN COMM, S&M Franchisegeber, in *m,f*

franco *adv* (*fco.*) IMP/EXP, TRANSP franko (*fr., fro.*), frei (*fr.*)

frank *adj* GEN COMM, POL *discussion* offen

franking: ~ **machine** *n* COMMS Frankiermaschine *f*, GEN COMM Freistempler *m*

fraud *n* ACC, GEN COMM, LAW arglistige Täuschung *f*, Betrug *m*; ~ **squad** *n BrE* GEN COMM Betrugsdezernat *nt*

fraudulence *n* ACC, GEN COMM, LAW Arglist *f*

fraudulent *adj* ACC, GEN COMM, LAW arglistig, betrügerisch; ~ **bankruptcy** *n* ACC, GEN COMM, LAW betrügerischer Bankrott *m*; ~ **entry** *n* ACC, GEN COMM, LAW betrügerische Buchung *f*, betrügerischer Eintrag *m*; ~ **misrepresentation** *n* INS vorsätzlich falsche Behauptung *f* einer Tatsache, Vorspiegelung *f* falscher Tatsachen, LAW Täuschung *f*

FRB *abbr AmE* BANK, ECON (*Federal Reserve Bank*) *national* amerikanische Zentralbank, ≈ Deutsche Bundesbank *f* (*BBk*), *regional* eine der zwölf regionalen Banken des Federal Reserve Systems, ≈ Landeszentralbank *f*, (*Federal Reserve Board*)

Vorstand des Federal Reserve System, Zentralbankvorstand *m*

Freddie: ~ **Mac** *n AmE infrml* (*Federal Home Loan Mortgage Corporation*) PROP eines der drei großen Realkredit-Institute in den USA

free 1. *adj* COMP frei, GEN COMM frei, gratis, kostenlos, IMP/EXP, TRANSP frei; ♦ ~ **access and choice** GEN COMM freier Zugang *m* und freie Wahl *f*; ~ **of address** TRANSP *shipping* ohne Adresse; ~ **of all additives** GEN COMM ohne jegliche Zusätze; ~ **of all average** (*f.a.a.*) GEN COMM, INS, TRANSP frei von Havarie, havariefrei; ~ **of charge** (*foc*) GEN COMM gebührenfrei, kostenlos, zum Nulltarif, gratis; ~ **of claim for accident reported** (*FCAR*) INS *marine* frei von Schadensansprüchen aus dem übermittelten Unfall; ~ **and clear** *AmE* LAW *title to property* frei von Rechten Dritter; ~ **of damage** (*fod*) INS frei von Schäden, schadensfrei; ~ **from defects** GEN COMM fehlerfrei; ~ **of general average** (*fga*) GEN COMM, INS frei von großer Havarie, ohne große Havarie; ~ **of income tax** (*f.i.t.*) TAX einkommensteuerfrei; ~ **of particular average** (*FPA*) INS frei von besonderer Havarie, ohne besondere Havarie; **there's no such thing as a** ~ **lunch** GEN COMM alles Gute hat seinen Preis; **2.** *vt* GEN COMM befreien

free: ~ **admission** *n* LEIS kostenloser Eintritt *m*; ~ **allowance of luggage** *n* IMP/EXP, LEIS, TRANSP Freigepäck *nt*, TRANSP zulässiges Gewicht *nt*; ~ **baggage allowance** *n* IMP/EXP, LEIS Freigepäck *nt*, TRANSP Freigepäck *nt*, zulässiges Gepäck *m*; ~ **baggage limit** *n* IMP/EXP Freigepäckgrenze *f*; ~ **banking** *n* BANK Bankgebührenfreiheit *f*; ~ **call** *n* COMMS kostenfreier Anruf *m*, kostenloses Anrufen *nt*; ~ **choice of employment** *n* LAW freie Wahl *f* des Arbeitsplatzes; ~ **circulation** *n* ENVIR freie Zirkulation *f*; ~ **collective bargaining** *n* ECON Tarifautonomie *f*; ~ **competition** *n* ECON freier Wettbewerb *m*; ~ **delivery** *n* TRANSP freie Lieferung *f*, kostenlose Zustellung *f*; ~ **depreciation** *n* FIN Vollabschreibung *f* im ersten Jahr; ~ **discharge** *n* (*fd*) TRANSP freies Löschen *nt*; ~ **dispatch** *n* (*fd*) COMMS, IMP/EXP, TRANSP freier Versand *m*

freedom *n* LAW Freiheit *f*; ~ **of action** *n* GEN COMM Bewegungsfreiheit *f*, Handlungsfreiheit *f*; ~ **of association** *n* POL Vereinigungsfreiheit *f*, Koalitionsfreiheit *f*; ~ **of choice** *n* GEN COMM, POL Entscheidungsfreiheit *f*, Wahlfreiheit *f*; S&M Entscheidungsfreiheit *f*; ~ **of competition** *n* ECON Wettbewerbsfreiheit *f*; ~ **of contract** *n* LAW Vertragsfreiheit *f*; ~ **of establishment** *n* ECON, GEN COMM, POL *EU* Niederlassungsfreiheit *f*

Freedom: ~ **of Information Act** *n AmE* (*FOIA*) LAW Gesetz *nt* zur Informationspflicht von Behörden

freedom: ~ **of movement** *n* ECON *of workers, employees in EU* Freizügigkeit *f*, GEN COMM Bewegungsfreiheit *f*, POL Umzugs- und Zuzugsfreiheit *f*

freed: ~ **up** *adj* STOCK *securities* freigegeben

free: ~ **enterprise** *n* ECON Unternehmerfreiheit *f*, freies Unternehmertum *nt*; ~ **enterprise economy** *n* ECON freie Marktwirtschaft *f*; ~ **enterprise system** *n* ECON System *nt* der freien Marktwirtschaft

Freefone® *adj BrE* (*cf toll-free AmE*) COMMS gebührenfrei; ~ **call** COMMS gebührenfreier Anruf *m*, kostenloser Anruf *m*, kostenloses Anrufen *nt*; ~ **number** *n BrE* (*cf toll-free number AmE*) COMMS, S&M gebührenfreie Rufnummer *f*, Rufnummer *f* zum Nulltarif

free: ~**-for-all** *adj infrml* GEN COMM allgemein zugänglich; ~**-for-all** *n infrml* GEN COMM allgemeine Rauferei *f* (*infrml*), schrankenloser Wettbewerb *m*; ~ **foreign agency** *n* TRANSP *shipping* freie Auslandsagentur *f*; ~ **format** *n* COMP freies Format *nt*; ~ **gift** *n* S&M Werbegeschenk *nt*, Zugabe *f*; ~ **good** *n* ECON freies Gut *nt*

freehold *n* ADMIN Grundeigentum *nt*, PROP freies Grundeigentum *nt*, Grundeigentum *nt*

freeholder *n* PROP freier Grundeigentümer *m*, freie Grundeigentümerin *f*

freehold: ~ **estate** *n* PROP freies Grundeigentum *nt*; ~ **owner** *n* PROP Grundstückseigentümer, in *m,f*; ~ **property** *n* PROP Grundbesitz *m*, Grundeigentum *nt*

free: ~ **insurance and carriage** INS, TRANSP kostenloser Versicherungsschutz und Transport *m*; ~ **issue of new shares** *n BrE* (*cf stock dividend AmE*) ACC Stockdividende *f*, Gratisaktien *f pl*

freelance *n* HRM Freiberufler, in *m,f*; ~ **contract** *n* HRM Honorarvertrag *m*; ~ **correspondent** *n* MEDIA *broadcast* freiberuflicher Korrespondent *m*, freiberufliche Korrespondentin *f*; ~ **worker** *n* HRM Freiberufler, in *m,f*, Freischaffende(r) *mf* [*decl. as adj*]; ~ **writer** *n* MEDIA freiberuflicher Journalist *m*, freiberufliche Journalistin *f*

freely: ~ **negotiable credit** *n* ECON *international trade* frei begebbares Akkreditiv *nt*

free: ~ **magazines** *n pl* MEDIA Werbezeitschriften *f pl*; ~ **market economy** *n* ECON freie Marktwirtschaft *f*; ~ **medical treatment** *n* WEL kostenlose ärztliche Versorgung *f*; ~ **movement of goods** *n* ECON *EU* freier Warenverkehr *m*; ~ **movement of goods and services** *n* ECON *EU* freier Waren- und Dienstleistungsverkehr *m*; ~ **movement of labor** *AmE*, ~ **movement of labour** *BrE n* ECON, LAW *EU* Freizügigkeit *f* der Arbeitnehmer; ~ **newspaper** *n* MEDIA kostenlose Zeitung *f*; ~ **and open market** *n* ECON Wettbewerbsmarkt *m*; ~ **pass** *n* LEIS *travel, entrance fee* Freikarte *f*; ~ **port** *n* IMP/EXP Freihafen *m*, zollfreier Hafen *m*; ~ **port zone** *n* (*FPZ*) TRANSP Freihafenzone *f*

Freepost® *n BrE* COMMS, GEN COMM ≈ Gebühr bezahlt Empfänger, gebührenfrei

free: ~**-rein leadership** *n* HRM Laisser-faire-Führungsstil *m*; ~ **ride** *n infrml* STOCK Konzertzeichnung *f*, kurzfristiges Spekulationsgeschäft *nt*; ~ **rider** *n infrml* GEN COMM *person who takes advantage*, TRANSP *AmE person who travels without ticket* Trittbrettfahrer, in *m,f*, Schwarzfahrer *m*, STOCK Konzertzeichner *m*; ~ **right of exchange** *n* STOCK freies Umtauschrecht *nt*; ~ **sale agreement** *n* TRANSP *IATA* Freiverkaufsvereinbarung; ~ **sample** *n* S&M kostenloses Muster *nt*

freesheet *n* GEN COMM Anzeigenblatt *nt*

free: ~**-standing** *adj* COMP freistehend; ~ **ticket** *n* LEIS Freikarte *f*; ~ **trade** *n* ECON Freihandel *m*

Free: ~ **Trade Agreement** *n* (*FTA*) ECON *international trade* Freihandelsabkommen *nt*

free: ~**-trade area** *n* ECON, IMP/EXP Freihandelszone *f*; ~**-trade zone** *n* (*FTZ*) ECON, IMP/EXP Freihandelszone *f*

freeze *vt* FIN *account, prices* einfrieren, sperren, TAX einfrieren

freezing *n* FIN *account, prices*, TAX Einfrieren *nt*

free: ~ **zone** *n* ECON Freihafen *m*, Freihafengebiet *nt*, IMP/EXP Freizone *f*, Zollausschlußgebiet *nt*

freight 1. *n* (*frt*) TRANSP *charges for goods* Fracht *f* (*Fr.*),

Frachtkosten *pl*, Frachtgeld *nt*, *goods* Fracht *f* (*Fr.*), Güter *nt pl* (*G.*), Waren *f pl* (*Wa.*); ◆ ~ **all kinds** TRANSP Fracht aller Art; ~ **collect** IMP/EXP, TRANSP Fracht gegen Nachnahme; ~ **forward** (*frt fwd*) IMP/EXP, TRANSP Fracht bezahlt Empfänger, Fracht gegen Nachnahme; ~ **and insurance paid** IMP/EXP, INS, TRANSP *to a named place* Fracht und Versicherung bezahlt; ~ **paid to** TRANSP *a named place* Fracht gezahlt an; ~ **prepaid** (*frt ppd*) IMP/EXP, TRANSP Fracht bezahlt Empfänger, Fracht im voraus bezahlt, frachtfrei (*frfr.*), vorausbezahlte Fracht; **2.** *vt* TRANSP *vehicle* befrachten

freight: ~ **aircraft** *n* TRANSP Frachtflugzeug *nt*; ~ **car** *n* AmE (*cf goods wagon BrE*) TRANSP Güterwagen *m*, Waggon *m*; ~ **container** *n* TRANSP Fracht-Container *m*; ~ **costs absorption** *n* TRANSP Übernahme *f* der Frachtkosten

freighter *n* IMP/EXP *ship* Befrachter *m*, TRANSP *aircraft* Frachtflugzeug *nt*, *ship* Befrachter *m*, Frachter *m*

freight: ~ **forwarder** *n* IMP/EXP Spediteur *m*, TRANSP Frachttransportunternehmen *nt*, Spediteur *m*; ~ **forwarder's combined transport bill of lading** *n* (*FCT*) IMP/EXP, TRANSP Sammeltransportkonossement *nt* des Spediteurs; ~ **futures contract** *n* FIN, STOCK Vertrag *m* über Frachttermingeschäfte, Frachtterminkontrakt *m*; ~ **futures market** *n* STOCK Frachtterminmarkt *m*

freighting *n* IMP/EXP Beförderung *f*, TRANSP Befrachtung *f*

freight: ~ **insurance** *n* INS Frachtversicherung *f*, Gütertransportversicherung *f*; **freight, insurance and shipping charges** *n* (*FIS*) IMP/EXP Fracht-, Versicherungs- und Transportgebühren *f pl*, Fracht-, Versicherungs- und Transportkosten *pl*, Fracht-, Versicherungs- und Versandkosten *pl*; ~ **inward** *n* GEN COMM, TRANSP Eingangsfracht *f*; ~ **manifest** *n* TRANSP Frachtmanifest *nt*; ~ **market** *n* STOCK Frachtbörse *f*, Frachtmarkt *m*; ~ **policy** *n* INS *marine* Frachtpolice *f*, Frachtversicherungspolice *f*; ~ **release** *n* (*F/R*) IMP/EXP *document* Frachtfreigabe-Bescheinigung *f*, *returning of goods* Frachterlaß *m*, Güterfreigabe *f*; ~ **sales representative** *n* BrE GEN COMM Vertreter,in *m,f* für das Frachtgeschäft; ~ **strategy** *n* TRANSP Frachtstrategie *f*; ~ **tariff** *n* TRANSP Frachttarif *m*; ~ **terminal** *n* TRANSP Frachtterminal *nt*; ~ **ton** *n* (*F/T*) TRANSP Gütertonne *f*, Frachttonne; ~ **tonne** *n* (*F/T*) TRANSP Gütertonne *f*, Frachttonne; ~ **traffic** *n* TRANSP Frachtverkehr *m*, Güterverkehr *m*; ~ **train** *n* AmE (*cf goods train BrE*) TRANSP Güterzug *m*; ~ **transport** *n* TRANSP Gütertransport *m*

Freight: ~ **Transport Association** *n* BrE (*FTA*) GEN COMM Frachttransportverband

French: ~ **fold** *n* S&M Kreuzfaltung *f*

frequency *n* COMMS Frequenz *f*, MATH Häufigkeit *f*, MEDIA *radio* Frequenz *f*, S&M *advertising* Häufigkeit *f*; ~ **curve** *n* MATH *statistics* Häufigkeitskurve *f*; ~ **distribution** *n* MATH *statistics* Häufigkeitsverteilung *f*; ~ **modulation** *n* COMMS, MEDIA Frequenzmodulation *f*; ~ **polygon** *n* MATH *statistics* Häufigkeitspolygon *nt*; ~ **table** *n* MATH *statistics* Häufigkeitstabelle *f*

fresh: ~ **money** *n* FIN *world debt*, GEN COMM zusätzliche Mittel *nt pl*, frisches Geld *nt* (*jarg*), zusätzliche Kredite *m pl*; ~ **water** *n* ENVIR Frischwasser *nt*, Süßwasser *nt*; ~ **water allowance** *n* TRANSP *shipping* Binnenschiffahrtsbeihilfe *f*

FRICS *abbr* BrE (*Fellow of the Royal Institute of Chartered Surveyors*) GEN COMM Mitglied des königlichen Instituts staatlich geprüfter Landvermesser und Baugutachter

friction *n* GEN COMM *between parties* Reibung *f*, Spannung *f*, Unstimmigkeit *f*

frictional: ~ **unemployment** *n* (*cf casual unemployment*) ECON friktionelle Arbeitslosigkeit *f*

friction: ~ **feed** *n* COMP Friktionsantrieb *m*, Friktionsführung *f*; ~**-feed printer** *n* COMP *hardware* Friktionsvorschubdrucker *m*, Papiertransportdrucker *m*

Friedman: ~ **theory** *n* ECON Friedman-Theorie *f*

friendly: ~ **agreement** *n* LAW freundschaftliche Vereinbarung *f*; ~ **society** *n* BrE (*cf benefit society*) FIN Bausparkasse *f*, Versicherungsverein *m* auf Gegenseitigkeit (*VVaG*); ~ **suit** *n* LAW Klage *f* ohne feindliche Absicht

Friends: ~ **of the Earth** *n* ENVIR *pressure group* Freunde der Erde

fringe: ~ **banking** *n* BANK sekundäre Bankdienstleistungen *f pl*, Teilzahlungskreditgeschäft *nt*; ~ **banking crisis** *n* BANK Krise *f* im Teilzahlungsbankgeschäft; ~ **benefit** *n* ADMIN Nebenleistung *f*, GEN COMM *salary* Lohnnebenleistung *f*, HRM Lohnnebenleistung *f*, Lohnzusatzleistung *f*; ~ **benefits tax** *n* TAX *on profit-sharing* Gewinnbeteiligungssteuer *f*, Steuer *f* auf Lohnnebenleistungen, Steuer *f* auf Lohnzusatzleistungen; ~ **market** *n* STOCK Nebenmarkt *m*, Zusatzmarkt *m*, Randmarkt *m*; ~ **meeting** *n* GEN COMM Unterredung am Rand des Geschehens

FRN *abbr* (*floating-rate note*) BANK zinsvariable Anleihe *f*, STOCK zinsvariabler Schuldtitel *m*

frontage *n* PROP Frontlänge *f*, Straßenfront *f*

front: ~ **cover** *n* S&M erste Umschlagseite *f*; ~ **desk** *n* ADMIN Rezeption *f*; ~ **end** *n* COMP *hardware, software* Spitze *f*; ~**-end computer** *n* COMP *position* Front-End-Rechner *m*, Vorrechner *m*, Netzwerkvorrechner *m*, Front-End-Prozessor *m*, *performance* Hochleistungscomputer *m*, Spitzencomputer *m*; ~**-end costs** *n pl* ECON *international trade* hohe Anfangskosten *pl*, Anlaufkosten *pl*, Vorabkosten *pl*; ~**-end finance** *n* FIN Zusatzfinanzierung *f*; ~**-end financing** *n* FIN Zusatzfinanzierung *f*; ~**-end load** *n* STOCK hohe Anfangskosten *pl*; ~**-end loading** *n* FIN *investment fund certificate* anfängliche Provisionsbelastung *f*, Provisionsbelastung *f* bei Ersterwerb; ~**-end loan** *n* FIN Zusatzdarlehen *nt*; ~**-end money** *n* FIN hoher Vorschuß *m*; ~**-end payment** *n* HRM Vergütung, die ein Unternehmen einem neuen Mitarbeiter für die durch den Arbeitsplatzwechsel entgangenen Tantiemen zahlt; ~ **foot** *n* AmE PROP ein im Zusammenhang mit Grundstücken verwendetes Flächenmaß: 1 Fuß Breite x 100 Fuß Tiefe (≃ 0,34m x 30,48m); ~**-of-house job** *n* ADMIN Position *f* mit direktem Kundenkontakt

frontier *n* GEN COMM Grenze *f*; ~ **control** *n* ECON, IMP/EXP *of goods* Grenzkontrolle *f*; ~ **customs post** *n* IMP/EXP Grenzzollstelle *f*; ~ **worker** *n* HRM Grenzgänger *m*

fronting *n* INS *marine* Risikoübernahme für Erstversicherung mit Absicht der Rückversicherung; ~ **loan** *n* FIN Vorzeichnungsdarlehen *nt*

frontline: ~ **employees** *n pl* HRM an vorderster Front stehende Mitarbeiter

frontman *n* FIN, GEN COMM, STOCK Strohmann *m*

front: ~ **money** *n* FIN Anfangskapital *nt*; ~ **office** *n* ADMIN, BANK, FIN, GEN COMM Front Office *nt*,

Abteilung *f* mit Kundenkontakt; **~-office clerk** *n* ADMIN, HRM Angestellte(r) *mf* [decl. as adj] im Front Office; **~-office personnel** *n* ADMIN, HRM Büropersonal *nt* im Front Office; **~ page** *n* MEDIA Titelblatt *nt*, Titelseite *f*, Vorderseite *f*; **~-page news** *n* MEDIA *print* Nachrichten *f pl* für die Titelseite, wichtige aktuelle Nachrichten *f pl*; **~ runner** *n* GEN COMM Spitzenreiter *m*; **~ running** *n* STOCK Front-running *nt*, risikoloses Insidergeschäft *nt*

frostbelt *n AmE* IND Frostgürtel *m*

frozen *adj* ECON *assets, credits* eingefroren, gesperrt; **~ account** *n* BANK eingefrorenes Konto *nt*, gesperrtes Konto *nt*; **~ assets** *n pl* FIN eingefrorene Guthaben *nt pl*, eingefrorene Vermögenswerte *m pl*; **~ credits** *n pl* FIN eingefrorene Kredite *m pl*

FRS *abbr* (*Financial Reporting Standard*) ACC Grundsätze *m pl* des finanziellen Berichtswesens

frt *abbr* (*freight*) TRANSP *charges for goods* Fr. (*Fracht*), Frachtkosten *pl*, Frachtgeld *nt*, *goods* Fr. (*Fracht*), G. (*Güter*), Wa. (*Waren*); **~ fwd** *abbr* (*freight forward*) IMP/EXP, TRANSP Fracht bezahlt Empfänger; **~ ppd** *abbr* (*freight prepaid*) IMP/EXP, TRANSP Fracht bezahlt Empfänger, frfr. (*frachtfrei*); **~ ton** *abbr* (*freight ton, freight tonne*) GEN COMM Frachttonne *f*, Gütertonne *f*

fruit: **~ carrier** *n* TRANSP Fruchttransportschiff *nt*; **~ farmer** *n* ECON *agricultural* Fruchtbauer *m*, Fruchtbäuerin *f*; **~ farming** *n* ECON *agricultural* Fruchtanbau *m*

fruition: **come to ~** *phr* GEN COMM sich verwirklichen

fruitless *adj* GEN COMM sinnlos, fruchtlos

fruit: **~ terminal** *n* TRANSP Fruchtumschlagplatz *m*, Fruchtumschlagterminal *nt*

frustrate *vt* LAW vereiteln

frustrated: **~ cargo** *n jarg* TRANSP gescheiterte Fracht *f*

frustration *n* LAW Vereitelung *f*; **~ of contract** *n* LAW Wegfall *m* der Geschäftsgrundlage; **~ of purpose** *n* LAW Vereitelung *f* des Vertragszwecks

FSA *abbr BrE* (*Financial Services Act*) FIN *1986* Finanzdienstleistungsgesetz

FSBR *abbr* (*financial statement and budget report*) FIN Jahresabschluß- und Budgetberichterstattung *f*

FSLIC *abbr AmE* (*Federal Savings and Loan Insurance Corporation*) BANK Bundesaufsichtsamt *nt* für Bausparkassen, Bundesversicherungsanstalt *f* für Bauspareinlagen

F-statistic *n* MATH F-Statistik *f*

FSVA *abbr BrE* (*Fellow of the Incorporated Society of Valuers & Auctioneers*) GEN COMM Mitglied der eingetragenen Gesellschaft der Schätzer und Auktionatoren

ft *abbr* GEN COMM (*foot*) Fuß *m*, TRANSP (*fuel terms*) Treibstoff-Bedingungen *f pl*

FT *abbr BrE* (*Financial Times*) MEDIA Financial Times *f*

F/T *abbr* (*freight ton, freight tonne*) GEN COMM Frachttonne *f*, Gütertonne *f*

FTA *abbr* ECON (*Free Trade Agreement*) *international trade* Freihandelsabkommen *nt*, GEN COMM (*Freight Transport Association*) Frachttransportverband, HRM, MGMNT (*failure to agree*) Scheitern *nt* von Tarifverhandlungen

FTC *abbr AmE* (*Federal Trade Commission*) ECON, POL Ausschuß *m* zur Bekämpfung des unlauteren Wettbewerbs, Bundeskartellbehörde *f*

F-test *n* ECON F-Test *m*

FT: **~ Index** *abbr BrE* (*Financial Times Industrial Ordinary Share Index*) STOCK Aktienindex der Financial Times

FTO *abbr* (*foreign trade organization*) FIN, IMP/EXP Außenhandelsorganisation *f*, Außenhandelsvereinigung *f*

FT-SE *abbr BrE* (*Financial Times Stock Exchange Index*) STOCK Aktienindex *m* der Financial Times; **~ Eurotrack 100 Index** *n BrE* STOCK gewichteter Aktienindex von 100 Aktien in Europa; **~ 100 Share Index** *n BrE* (*Footsie*) STOCK Aktienindex der Financial Times

FTZ *abbr* (*free-trade zone*) ECON, IMP/EXP Freihandelszone *f*

fuel 1. *n* ENVIR Brennstoff *m*, IND Kraftstoff *m*, TAX, TRANSP Brennstoff *m*, Treibstoff *m*; **2.** *vt* ECON *inflation* anheizen, steigern, GEN COMM *inflation* antreiben

fuel: **~ benefits** *n pl BrE* TAX Vergünstigungen bei bestimmten Brennstoffen oder Heizmaterialien; **~ duty rebate** *n BrE* TAX *rural transport* Brennstoff-Steuerrabatt *m*, Heizstoffsteuerrabatt *m*; **~ efficiency** *n* ENVIR Brennstoffersparnis *f*; **~ oil** *n* TRANSP Heizöl *nt*; **~ oil tank farm** *n* TRANSP *shipping* Heizöltankfarm *f*, Heizöltanklager *nt*; **~ scale charges** *n pl* TAX Brennstoffgebührenordnung *f*, Brennstoffgebührentabelle *f*; **~ surcharge** *n* TRANSP *shipping* Treibstoffzuschlag *m*; **~ tax** *n* TAX Brennstoffsteuer *f*, Treibstoffsteuer *f*; **~ terms** *n pl* (*ft*) TRANSP Treibstoff-Bedingungen *f pl*

fulcrum *n* GEN COMM Drehpunkt *m*, Angelpunkt *m*

fulfil *vt BrE* GEN COMM *commitments* erfüllen, *obligations* nachkommen [+dat]; ♦ **~ the expectations** *BrE* GEN COMM den Anforderungen entsprechen, die Erwartungen erfüllen

fulfill *AmE see* fulfil *BrE*

fulfilment *n BrE* S&M *subscriptions* Erfüllung *f*; **~ of contract** *n BrE* LAW *contract law* Vertragserfüllung *f*

full *adj* GEN COMM ganz, umfassend, vollständig, voll; ♦ **~ interest admitted** (*fia*) GEN COMM volle Beteiligung zugesagt; **in ~** GEN COMM vollständig; **in ~ knowledge of the facts** LAW in voller Kenntnis der Sachlage; **in ~ settlement** ACC zum vollen Ausgleich; **be in ~ swing** POL in vollem Gange sein, voll in Gange sein; **~ to capacity** ACC voll ausgelastet, an der Kapazitätsgrenze, zum vollen Ausgleich

full: **~ adder** *n* COMP *hardware* Volladdierwerk *nt*; **~ amount** *n* GEN COMM ungekürzte Summe *f*; **~ board** *n* LEIS Vollpension *f*; **~ capacity** *n* IND Vollauslastung *f*; **~ container load** *n* (*FCL*) TRANSP Vollcontainerladung *f*; **~ cost** *n* ACC, FIN Vollkosten *pl*; **~ cost basis** *n* ACC Vollkostenbasis *f*; **~ costing** *n* ACC Vollkostenkalkulation *f*, Vollkostenprinzip *nt*, FIN Vollkostenrechnung *f*; **~-cost method** *n* ACC, FIN Vollkostenmethode *f*; **~-cost pricing** *n* ECON Vollkostenkalkulation *f*; **~ coupon bond** *n* STOCK Inhaberschuldverschreibung *f* cum Kupon, Inhaberschuldverschreibung *f* mit Kupon; **~ coverage** *n* ADMIN, GEN COMM volle Deckung *f*, INS voller Versicherungsschutz *m*, volle Deckung *f*, MEDIA *of an event* ausführliche Berichterstattung *f*; **~ disclosure** *n* LAW vollständige Offenlegung *f*; **~ duplex** *n* COMP Duplex *nt*; **~ employment** *n* ECON Vollbeschäftigung *f*; **~-employment budget** *n* ECON, POL Vollbeschäftigungsbudget *nt*; **~ entrance fee** *n* GEN COMM *at exhibitions* voller Eintrittspreis *m*; **~ exemption** *n* TAX vollständige Freistellung *f*; **~ free fork-lift truck** *n*

TRANSP *cargo handling* vollständig freier Gabelstapler *m*; ~ **implications** *n pl* GEN COMM gesamte Konsequenzen *f pl*; ~ **liability** *n* GEN COMM volle Haftung *f*; ~ **lot** *n* FIN *money market* Mindestmenge *f*, GEN COMM Gesamtsumme *f*, Gesamtbetrag *m*, STOCK Handelseinheit *f*, volle hundert Aktien *f pl*, voller Börsenschluß *m*; ~ **member** *n* GEN COMM Vollmitglied *nt*; ~ **name** *n* GEN COMM vollständiger Name *m*; ~ **particulars** *n pl* GEN COMM sämtliche Einzelheiten *f pl*; ~ **protection** *n* PATENTS Vollschutz *m*; ~ **quotation** *n* STOCK vollständige Notierung *f*, vollständiges Preisangebot *nt*; ~ **rate** *n* HRM voller Satz *m*; ~~**screen editor** *n* COMP *wordprocessing* Ganzseiteneditor *m*; ~~**screen terminal** *n* COMP *hardware* Datensichtgerät *nt* mit Ganzseitenbildschirm; ~~**service agency** *n* MEDIA, S&M *advertising* Agentur *f* mit umfassendem Service, Agentur *f* mit Allround-Service, Beratung *f* auf allen Gebieten; ~~**service broker** *n* STOCK Broker, der alle üblichen Dienstleistungen anbietet; ~ **session** *n* POL Plenarsitzung *f*; ~ **stop** *n* BrE (*cf period AmE*) MEDIA Punkt *m*; ~~**time** *adj* HRM ganztägig, Vollzeit-; ~~**time employee** *n* HRM Vollzeitarbeitskraft *f*, Vollzeitkraft *f*; ~~**time employment** *n* HRM Ganztagsbeschäftigung *f*, Vollzeitbeschäftigung *f*; ~~**timer** *n* HRM Vollzeitarbeitskraft *f*, Vollzeitkraft *f*; ~ **weight** *n* GEN COMM reelles Gewicht *nt*, volles Gewicht *nt*, Gesamtgewicht *nt*

fully: ~ **comprehensive cover** *n* INS Vollkaskoversicherungspolice *f*; ~ **comprehensive insurance** *n* INS Vollkaskoversicherungspolice *f*; ~ **comprehensive insurance policy** *n* INS Haftpflichtversicherung *f* mit Vollkaskoversicherung; ~ **distributed** *adj* STOCK vollständig ausgeschüttet; ~ **funded** *adj* ADMIN voll finanziert; ~ **paid** *adj* (*f.p.*) GEN COMM voll bezahlt; ~~**paid share** *n* STOCK voll eingezahlte Aktie *f*; ~ **paid-up policy** *n* INS *life policy* beitragsfreie Versicherung *f*, prämienfreie Versicherung *f*; ~~**registered bond** *n* AmE STOCK komplette Namenschuldverschreibung *f*; ~ **valued** *adj* STOCK vollständig bewertet

fumes *n pl* GEN COMM *environment* Rauch *m*

function 1. *n* COMP, GEN COMM Funktion *f*, LEIS Feierlichkeit *f*, MATH Abbildung *f*, Funktion *f*; **2.** *vi* GEN COMM funktionieren

functional *adj* GEN COMM funktional; ~ **analysis** *n* GEN COMM Funktionsanalyse *f*; ~ **analysis of costs** *n* ACC Kostenfunktionsanalyse *f*; ~ **approach** *n* GEN COMM funktionelle Methode *f*; ~ **area** *n* ECON Unternehmensbereich *m*; ~ **authority** *n* HRM funktionale Autorität *f*, funktionales Weisungsrecht *nt*; ~ **costing** *n* ACC funktionelle Kostenbewertung *f*; ~ **currency** *n* ECON gesetzliches Zahlungsmittel *nt*; ~ **depreciation** *n* PROP wirtschaftliche Abschreibung *f*; ~ **financing** *n* FIN funktionelle Finanzierung *f*; ~ **flexibility** *n* HRM Funktionsflexibilität *f*; ~ **income distribution** *n* ECON funktionelle Einkommensverteilung *f*; ~ **layout** *n* GEN COMM funktionelle Struktur *f*; ~ **management** *n* MGMNT Mehrliniensystem *nt*, Funktionsmeistersystem *nt*; ~ **obsolescence** *n* S&M funktionale Obsoleszenz *f*, funktionale Veralterung *f*; ~ **organization** *n* GEN COMM funktionale Organisation *f*, MGMNT funktionsbezogene Organisation *f*; ~ **relations** *n pl* GEN COMM funktionale Beziehungen *f pl*, MGMNT Funktionsbeziehungen *f pl*; ~ **responsibility** *n* GEN COMM funktionale Verantwortung *f*, MGMNT funktionsbezogene Verantwortung *f*

functionary *n* HRM Funktionär, in *m,f*

functioning *n* ADMIN Ablauf *m*

function: ~ **key** *n* (*F key*) COMP *keyboard* Funktionstaste *f*

fund 1. *n* FIN Fonds *m*; **2.** *vt* FIN finanzieren, refinanzieren, konsolidieren, umschulden; ◆ ~ **a loan** BANK eine Anleihe finanzieren, eine Anleihe konsolidieren

fund: ~ **accounting** *n* ACC Buchführung *f* einer gemeinnützigen Organisation

fundamental *adj* GEN COMM fundamental; ~ **analysis** *n* FIN *financial statements, investments* fundamentale Aktienanalyse *f*, Fundamentalanalyse *f*; ~ **equilibrium** *n* ECON fundamentales Gleichgewicht *nt*

fund: ~ **appropriation** *n* ACC *governmental* Bewilligung *f* von Geldern, Mittelverteilung *f*, Mittelzuteilung *f*, ECON, FIN, MGMNT Mittelverteilung *f*, Mittelzuteilung *f*

funded *adj* FIN, STOCK fundiert; ~ **debt** *n* ACC langfristige Verpflichtung *f*, FIN fundierte Schuld *f*, konsolidierte Kredite *m pl*, langfristige Verbindlichkeit *f*, langfristige Verpflichtung *f*, langfristiger Kredit *m*, STOCK Anleiheschuld *f*, fundierte Schuld *f*, langfristige Verbindlichkeit *f*, langfristiger Kredit *m*, Staatsanleihe *f*; ~ **pension plan** *n* AmE (*cf funded retirement plan AmE*) HRM Pensionsplan, der durch ein angesammeltes Treuhandvermögen gedeckt ist; ~ **retirement plan** *n* AmE (*cf funded pension plan AmE*) HRM Pensionsplan, der durch ein angesammeltes Treuhandvermögen gedeckt ist

funding *n* ADMIN Finanzierung *f*, FIN Refinanzierung *f*, Anlage *f* in Staatspapieren, Bildung *f* von Rückstellungen, *project* Finanzierung *f*; ~ **agency** *n* FIN Finanzierungsfiliale *f*; ~ **gap** *n* FIN Finanzierungslücke *f*; ~ **scheme** *n* ADMIN Finanzierungsprogramm *nt*; ~ **source** *n* FIN Finanzierungsquelle *f*, Refinanzierungsquelle *f*

fund: ~~**linked life insurance** *n* INS fondsgebundene Lebensversicherung *f*; ~ **management** *n* BANK *investment banking* Fondsverwaltung *f*, Vermögensverwaltung *f*, FIN, STOCK Vermögensverwaltung *f*; ~ **manager** *n* BANK Vermögensverwalter, in *m,f*, FIN Disponent *m*, *pensions* Vermögensverwalter, in *m,f*, STOCK Vermögensverwalter, in *m,f*; ~~**raising** *n* FIN Geldbeschaffung *f*, Kapitalbeschaffung *f*, Mittelbeschaffung *f*

funds *n pl* BANK Geldmittel *nt pl*, FIN Kapital *nt*; ◆ **no ~** (*NF*) GEN COMM keine Deckung

funds: ~ **abroad** *n pl* BANK Auslandsguthaben *nt pl*; ~ **flow** *n* ACC Geldstrom *m*, Kapitalfluß *m*, Geldmittelbewegung *f*, ECON Geldstrom *m*, Geldmittelbewegung *f*; ~ **from operations** *n pl* ACC Umsatzüberschuß *m*, Mittel *nt pl* aus laufender Geschäftstätigkeit; ~ **statement** *n* ACC Bewegungsbilanz *f*, Kapitalflußrechnung *f*; ~ **transfer** *n* BANK Kapitaltransfer *m*, FIN Überweisung *f* von Geldern, Zahlungsverkehr *m*

fungibility *n* HRM Marktgängigkeit *f*, LAW Fungibilität *f*

fungible *adj* GEN COMM vertretbar, LAW fungibel; ~ **assets** *n* FIN fungible Vermögenswerte *m pl*; ~ **item** *n* LAW *sales contract* Gattungssache *f*

fungibles *n pl* ECON fungible Waren *f pl*, vertretbare Sachen *f pl*, Fungibilien *pl*

furlough *n* AmE HRM Beurlaubung *f*

furnish *vt* GEN COMM bereitstellen, versorgen mit; ◆ ~ **a certificate** ADMIN eine Bescheinigung beibringen

furniture *n* GEN COMM Möbel *nt pl*; ~ **depot** *n* GEN COMM

Möbellager *nt*; ~ **and fittings** *n pl* ACC, GEN COMM Betriebs- und Geschäftsausstattung *f*, Betriebs- und Geschäftseinrichtung *f*; ~ **warehouse** *n* GEN COMM Möbellager *nt*

further: ~ **call** *n* STOCK Nachschußforderung *f*; ~ **education** *n* HRM, WEL Fortbildung *f*, Weiterbildung *f*; ~ **information** *n* GEN COMM weitere Informationen *f pl*; ~ **to** *phr* GEN COMM in bezug auf, im Anschluß an

fuse *vt* ECON fusionieren, FIN fusionieren, verschmelzen, STOCK fusionieren

fusion *n* FIN, STOCK Fusion *f*, Verschmelzung *f*

future 1. *adj* GEN COMM zukünftig; ♦ **at some ~ date** GEN COMM zu einem Termin in der Zukunft, zu einem zukünftigen Termin; **2.** *n* GEN COMM Zukunft *f*; ♦ **at some time in the ~** GEN COMM irgendwann in der Zukunft; **in ~** GEN COMM zukünftig

future: ~ **commodity** *n* STOCK Terminware *f*; ~ **delivery** *n* GEN COMM Terminlieferung *f*; ~ **gains** *n pl* TAX zukünftige Gewinne *m pl*; ~ **interest** *n BrE* GEN COMM *in property, trust* zukünftige Ansprüche *m pl*; ~ **orders** *n pl* GEN COMM Terminorder *f*; ~ **rate agreement** *n (FRA)* FIN, STOCK Zinsterminkontrakt *m*

futures *n pl* FIN, STOCK Termingeschäfte *nt pl*, Terminkontrakte *m pl*, Terminwaren *f pl*

future: ~ **sale** *n* FIN Terminverkauf *m*

futures: ~ **contract** *n* FIN, STOCK Terminkontrakt *m*; ~ **expiration date** *n AmE* STOCK Verfallsdatum *nt* des Termingeschäftes; ~ **liquidation rate** *n* STOCK Veräußerungskurs *m* des Termingeschäftes; ~ **market** *n* STOCK Terminkontraktmarkt *m*, Terminmarkt *m*; ~ **price** *n* STOCK Terminkontraktpreis *m*; ~ **price change** *n* STOCK Terminkontraktkursänderung *f*; ~**-registered broker** *n* STOCK Makler, der für Termingeschäfte registriert ist; ~ **sales** *n pl* GEN COMM Umsatz *m* im Termingeschäft; ~ **trader** *n* FIN, STOCK Terminhändler *m*; ~ **trading** *n* STOCK Terminkontrakthandel *m*; ~ **transaction** *n* FIN, STOCK Terminkontraktgeschäftsabschluß *m*

future: ~ **tax credits** *n pl* ACC zukünftige Steuergutschrift *f*; ~ **trends** *n pl* GEN COMM Zukunftstrends *m pl*

fwd *abbr (forward)* COMMS *package, document* weiterleiten, GEN COMM befördern, TRANSP übersenden, *shipping* transportieren

fwdr *abbr (forwarder)* COMMS, IMP/EXP, TRANSP *carrier* Beförderer *m*, Frachtspediteur *m*, Spediteur *m*, *sender* Absender *m*, Sender *m*, Verlader *m*

FY *abbr (fiscal year)* ACC, FIN, TAX Bilanzjahr *nt*, Geschäftsjahr *nt*, Rechnungsjahr *nt*, Steuerjahr *nt*, Wirtschaftsjahr *nt*, *public accounting* Finanzjahr *nt*, Haushaltsjahr *nt*

G

g *abbr* GEN COMM (*gram, gramme*) g (*Gramm*)

G *abbr* (*gross mass*) GEN COMM Bruttomasse *f*

GA *abbr* GEN COMM (*general authorization*) Generalvollmacht *f*, INS (*general average*) große Havarie *f*, MATH (*general average*) *statistics* Gesamtdurchschnitt *m*

G/A *abbr* (*general average*) INS große Havarie *f*, MATH *statistics* Gesamtdurchschnitt *m*

GAAP *abbr* AmE (*Generally Accepted Accounting Principles*) ACC allgemein anerkannte Grundsätze *m pl* der Rechnungslegung, *in Germany* GoB (*Grundsätze ordnungsgemäßer Buchführung*)

GAAS *abbr* AmE (*Generally Accepted Auditing Standards*) ACC allgemein anerkannte Buchprüfungsnormen *f pl*

GAB *abbr* (*general arrangement to borrow*) ECON, FIN IMF AKV (*Allgemeine Kreditvereinbarungen*)

GAC *abbr* (*general average certificate*) INS Bescheinigung *f* über große Havarie

G/A: **~ con** *abbr* (*general average contribution*) INS Beitrag *m* für große Havarie; **~ dep** *abbr* (*general average deposit*) INS Einschuß *m*

gadget *n* GEN COMM Gerät *nt*, Apparat *m*

GAFTA *abbr* (*Grain and Free Trade Association*) ECON Getreide- und Freihandelsassoziation *f*

gage *AmE see gauge BrE*

gag: **~ order** *n* LAW Beschränkung *f* der Gerichtsberichterstattung; **~ rule** *n* POL Knebelregelung *f*, Schluß *m* der Debatte

gain 1. *n* ECON *on foreign exchange transactions* Wechselkursgewinne *m pl*, STOCK *on position values* Kursgewinn *m*, Wertzuwachs *m*; **2.** *vt* GEN COMM erlangen, verdienen, erhalten; ♦ **~ entry to** GEN COMM sich Zugang verschaffen zu; **~ ground** GEN COMM Boden gewinnen, aufholen; **~ momentum** GEN COMM *trend* Schwungkraft gewinnen; **~ a toehold in the market** *n* S&M auf dem Markt Fuß fassen; **~ value** STOCK an Wert gewinnen; **3.** *vi* STOCK gewinnen

gainful *adj* GEN COMM *business* einträglich, gewinnbringend, *occupation* ertragreich

gain: **~ on disposal** *n* ACC, TAX Veräußerungsgewinn *m*

gains: **~ from exchange** *n pl* ECON Außenhandelsgewinne *m pl*, Tauschgewinne *m pl*; **~ from trade** *n* ECON Außenhandelsgewinne *m pl*, Tauschgewinne *m pl*; **~ and losses** *n pl AmE* (*cf rises and falls BrE*) ECON Gewinne und Verluste *m pl*

gal *abbr* (*gallon*) GEN COMM Gallone *f*

galley *n* MEDIA *print* Schiff *nt*, Setzschiff *nt*, Zeilenschiff *nt*, TRANSP *ship's kitchen* Kombüse *f*

gallon *n* (*gal*) GEN COMM Gallone *f*

galloping: **~ inflation** *n* ECON galoppierende Inflation *f*

Gallup: **~ poll** *n* S&M *market research* Meinungsumfrage *f*, Gallup-Umfrage *f*

gamble: **~ on the stock exchange** *phr* STOCK an der Börse spekulieren

gambling: **~ debts** *n pl* GEN COMM Spielschulden *f pl*

game *n* GEN COMM Spiel *nt*; **~ plan** *n* GEN COMM Strategie *f*; **~ theory** *n* ECON, HRM, MGMNT Spieltheorie *f*

gamma *n* STOCK Gamma *nt*; **~ stock** *n* STOCK Gamma-Aktie *f*

ganger *n BrE* GEN COMM Meister *m*, Vorarbeiter *m*

gang: **~ piecework** *n* HRM Akkordarbeit *f* einer Kolonne

gangway *n* TRANSP *shipping* Gangway *f*

Gantt: **~ chart** *n* COMP Gantt-Karte *f*

GAO *abbr AmE* (*General Accounting Office*) ACC Bundesrechnungshof *m*

gap *n* FIN, GEN COMM Lücke *f*; **~ between product conception and introduction** *n* S&M Vorlaufzeit *f*, Zeitspanne *f* zwischen Produktkonzeption und -einführung; **~ financing** *n* FIN Lückenfinanzierung *f*; **~ in coverage** *n* MEDIA Lücke *f* in der Berichterstattung; **~ loan** *n* FIN Kredit *m* für einen Spitzenbetrag; **~ study** *n* GEN COMM Lückenuntersuchung *f*, S&M Marktlückenstudie *f*

garbage *n* (*cf rubbish BrE*) COMP Datenmüll *m*, unbrauchbare Daten *f*, ENVIR, GEN COMM Abfall *m*, Müll *m*; **~ can** *n AmE* (*cf rubbish bin BrE*) ENVIR Abfalleimer *m*, Tonne *f*; **~ in garbage out** *n jarg* (*GIGO*) COMP Müll rein, Müll raus (*jarg*) (*GIGO*)

garden: **~ apartment** *AmE*, **~ flat** *BrE n* PROP Gartenappartement *nt*, Gartenwohnnung *f*

garment *n* GEN COMM Kleidungsstück *nt*

garnish *vt* LAW Drittschuldnerpfändung vornehmen

garnishee *n* LAW Pfändungsschuldner *m*, Drittschuldner *m*

gas *n* ENVIR, IND Gas *nt*, TRANSP *AmE* (*cf petrol BrE*) *for motor vehicles* Benzin *nt*

GASB *abbr* (*Governmental Accounting Standards Board*) ACC Regierungsaufsichtsbehörde *f* für Buchführungsgrundsätze

gas: **~ company** *n* ENVIR Gasgesellschaft *f*; **~ exploitation** *n* IND Gasauswertung *f*, Gasgewinnung *f*; **~ exploration licence** *BrE*, **~ exploration license** *AmE n* ENVIR Gaserkundungskonzession *f*, Genehmigung *f* zur Gasexploration; **~ industry** *n* ENVIR Gasindustrie *f*, Gaswirtschaft *f*; **~ oil** *n* ENVIR Gasöl *nt*

gasoline *n AmE* (*cf petrol BrE*) ENVIR, TRANSP Benzin *nt*

gas: **~ turbine** *n* TRANSP *shipping* Gasturbine *f*

gasworks *n pl* ENVIR, IND Gasanstalt *f*, Gaswerk *nt*

gate *n* LEIS *entrance* Tor *nt*, Gatter *nt*, *takings* Einnahmen *f pl*, TRANSP *aviation* Flugsteig *m*

gatefold *n* MEDIA, S&M ausschlagbare Anzeigenseite *f*, faltbare Seite *f*, gefaltete Seite *f*

gateway *n* COMP *wide-area networks* Gateway *m* (*jarg*), Netzübergang *m*, Netzübergangsrechner *m*, TRANSP *aviation* Gateway *m*, Haupteinfahrt *f*

gather *vt* GEN COMM *intelligence* gewinnen; ♦ **~ in the stops** STOCK Grenzwerte für eine Neubewertung sammeln; **~ speed** GEN COMM schneller werden, Fahrt aufnehmen

gathering *n* GEN COMM Versammlung *f*

GATT *abbr* (*General Agreement on Tariffs and Trade*) ECON, POL GATT (*Allgemeines Zoll- und Handelsabkommen*)

gauge 1. *n BrE* GEN COMM Eichmaß *nt*, Meßgerät *nt*,

trends Umfang *m*; ◆ **out of ~** *BrE* TRANSP das Lademaß überschreitend; **2.** *vt BrE* GEN COMM abmessen

gavel *n* GEN COMM *auction* Auktionshammer *m*

GAW *abbr* (*guaranteed annual wage*) HRM garantiertes Jahreseinkommen *nt*, jährlicher Mindestlohn *m*

gazump *vt BrE jarg* PROP den Grundstückspreis nachträglich erhöhen

gazumping *n BrE* LAW *property* entgegen mündlicher Zusage ein Haus an einen Höherbietenden verkaufen

Gb *abbr* (*gigabyte*) COMP GB (*Gigabyte*)

g.c. *abbr* (*general cargo*) TRANSP Stückgut *nt*, Stückgutfracht *f*

GCC *abbr* (*German Chamber of Commerce*) GEN COMM Deutsche Handelskammer *f*

GCCUK *abbr* (*German Chamber of Commerce for the UK*) GEN COMM Deutsche Handelskammer *f* für das Vereinigte Königreich

GCE *abbr BrE obs* (*General Certificate of Education*) WEL ≈ Mittlere Reife *f*

GCIC *abbr* (*German Chamber of Industry and Commerce*) GEN COMM Deutsche Industrie- und Handelskammer *f*

GCR *abbr* (*general commodity rate*) STOCK allgemeiner Warenkurs *m*

GCSE *abbr BrE* (*General Certificate of Secondary Education*) WEL ≈ Mittlere Reife *f*

GDP *abbr* (*gross domestic product*) ECON BIP (*Bruttoinlandsprodukt*); **~ per capita** *n* ECON BIP *nt* pro Kopf der Bevölkerung; **~ per head** *n* ECON BIP *nt* pro Kopf der Bevölkerung

gds *abbr BrE* (*goods*) ECON Wa. (*Waren*), PATENTS Art. (*Artikel*), Wa. (*Waren*), TRANSP Fr. (*Fracht*), G. (*Güter*)

GE *abbr* (*general equilibrium*) ECON allgemeines Gleichgewicht *nt*

gearing *n BrE* (*cf leverage AmE*) FIN Hebelwirkung *f*, Leverage *f*, Verschuldungsgrad *m*, Verhältnis *nt* von Fremd- zu Eigenkapital, Fremdkapitalaufnahme *f*, STOCK Fremdkapitalaufnahme *f*, Leverage *f*, Verhältnis *nt* Einschuß-Kapital, Verhältnis *nt* von Obligationen und Vorzugsaktien zu Stammaktie; **~ adjustment** *n BrE* (*cf leverage adjustment AmE*) FIN Anpassung *f* zwischen Fremd- und Eigenkapital; **~ ratio** *n BrE* (*cf leverage ratio AmE*) FIN Verhältnis *nt* zwischen Fremd- und Eigenkapital

gears *n pl* TRANSP Getriebe *nt*

gear: ~ to *phr* GEN COMM anpassen an [+acc]; **~ towards** *phr* GEN COMM ausrichten auf [+acc]

GEM *abbr AmE* (*growing-equity mortgage*) BANK Wachstumshypothek nach Equity-Recht

gen *abbr* (*generator*) GEN COMM Generator *m*

gender: ~ discrimination *n* LAW geschlechtsbezogene Diskriminierung *f*

general *adj* GEN COMM allgemein; **~ acceptance** *n* BANK bedingungslose Annahme *f*, uneingeschränktes Akzept *nt*; **~ accounting** *n* ACC allgemeines Rechnungswesen *nt*

General: ~ Accounting Office *n AmE* (*GAO*) ACC Bundesrechnungshof *m*

general: ~ agent *n* LAW Generalbevollmächtigte(r) *mf* [decl. as adj]

General: ~ Agreement on Tariffs and Trade *n* (*GATT*) ECON, POL Allgemeines Zoll- und Handelsabkommen *nt* (*GATT*)

general: ~ arrangement to borrow *n* (*GAB*) ECON, FIN IMF Allgemeine Kreditvereinbarungen *f pl* (*AKV*);

~ authorization *n* (*GA*) GEN COMM Generalvollmacht *f*; **~ average** *n* (*GA*, *G/A*) INS große Havarie *f*, MATH *statistics* Gesamtdurchschnitt *m*; **~ average adjuster** *n* INS Dispacheur, in *m,f*; **~ average certificate** *n* (*GAC*) INS Bescheinigung *f* über große Havarie; **~ average contribution** *n* (*G/A con*) INS Beitrag *m* für große Havarie; **~ average deposit** *n* (*G/A dep*) INS Einschuß *m*; **~ average in full** *n* INS volle Sicherheitsrücklage *f* für große Havarie, voller Havarieeinschluß *m*; **~ basis of assessment** *n* WEL allgemeine Bemessungsgrundlage *f*; **~ business statistics** *n pl* GEN COMM allgemeine Wirtschaftsdaten *pl*; **~ cargo** *n* (*g.c.*) TRANSP Stückgut *nt*, Stückgutfracht *f*; **~ cargo berth** *n* TRANSP Stückgutliegeplatz *m*; **~ cargo and container berth** *n* TRANSP Stückgut- und Container-Liegeplatz *m*; **~ cargo rate** *n* TRANSP Stückgutrate *f*, Stückguttarif *m*; **~ cargo ship** *n* TRANSP Frachtschiff *nt* für Sammelladung, Frachtschiff *nt* für Stückgut

General: ~ Certificate of Education *n BrE obs* (*GCE*) WEL ≈ Mittlere Reife *f*; **~ Certificate of Secondary Education** *n BrE* (*GCSE*) WEL ≈ Mittlere Reife *f*; **~ Commissioners** *n pl BrE* TAX Berufungsinstanz *f* in Steuersachen, bevollmächtigte Instanz *f* für Steuersachen

general: ~ commodity rate *n* (*GCR*) STOCK allgemeiner Rohstoffkurs *m*, allgemeiner Warenkurs *m*; **~ consumption tax** *n* TAX allgemeine Verbrauchssteuer *f*; **~ contractor** *n* GEN COMM Generalunternehmer, in *m,f*; **~ cost** *n* ACC, ADMIN Gemeinkosten *pl*

General: ~ Council of British Shipping *n* IND ständiges Repräsentativorgan für die britische Seefahrt

general: ~ counsel *n AmE* (*cf head of legal department BrE*) HRM Leiter, in *m,f* der Rechtsabteilung, Syndikus *m* einer Unternehmung; **~ creditor** *n* ACC nicht bevorrechtigter Gläubiger *m*, nicht bevorrechtigte Gläubigerin *f*, nicht bevorrechtigter Konkursgläubiger *m*, nicht bevorrechtigte Konkursgläubigerin *f*

General: ~ Customs Regulations *n pl* IMP/EXP Allgemeine Zollordnung *f* (*AZO*)

general: ~ equilibrium *n* (*GE*) ECON allgemeines Gleichgewicht *nt*; **~ equilibrium analysis** *n* ECON *theoretical model* Theorie *f* des allgemeinen Gleichgewichts; **~ exclusions clause** *n* INS *marine* allgemeine Ausschlußklausel *f*, Klausel *f* über allgemeine Ausschlüsse; **~ executive** *n* MGMNT Generaldirektor, in *m,f*

General: ~ Executive Manager *n* HRM Generaldirektor, in *m,f*

general: ~ expenses *n pl* ACC Gemeinkosten *pl*, Verwaltungsgemeinkosten *pl*; **~ fund** *n* ACC, FIN nicht zweckgebundene Haushaltsmittel *nt pl*; **~ government expenditure** *n BrE* (*GGE*) ECON öffentliche Ausgaben *f pl*, allgemeine Ausgaben *f pl* der öffentlichen Hand; **~ holdover relief** *n BrE* TAX allgemeine Steuerermäßigung *f* bei Restbeständen, allgemeiner Steuernachlaß *m* bei Restbeträgen; **~ holiday** *n* HRM Betriebsferien *pl*, Betriebsurlaub *m*

General: ~ Household Survey *n* (*GHS*) ECON *econometrics* allgemeine Haushaltserhebung *f*

general: ~ indirect cost center *AmE*, **~ indirect cost centre** *BrE n* ACC allgemeine Hilfskostenstelle *f*; **~ interest tendency** *n* ECON allgemeine Zinstendenz *f*, Zinsgrundtendenz *f*

generalist *n* HRM *person* Generalist, in *m,f*

generalized: ~ least squares *n* (*GLS*) ECON

econometrics, MATH *statistics* Methode *f* der kleinsten Quadrate; **~ medium** *n* ECON allgemein akzeptiertes Tausch- und Zahlungsmittel *nt*; **~ system of preferences** *n* (*GSP*) ECON allgemeines Präferenzsystem *nt*; **~ system of tariffs and preferences** *n* (*GSTP*) IMP/EXP allgemeines Zoll- und Präferenzsystem *nt*, verallgemeinertes Tarif- und Präferenzsystem *nt*

general: **~ journal** *n* ACC Sammelbuch *nt*, Sammeljournal *nt*; **~ ledger** *n* ACC, FIN Hauptbuch *nt*; **~ liability insurance** *n* INS allgemeine Haftpflichtversicherung *f*, Betriebshaftpflichtversicherung *f*; **~ lien** *n* PROP allgemeines Zurückbehaltungsrecht *nt*

Generally: **~ Accepted Accounting Principles** *n pl AmE* (*GAAP*) ACC allgemein anerkannte Grundsätze *m pl* der Rechnungslegung, *in Germany* Grundsätze *m pl* ordnungsgemäßer Buchführung (*GoB*); **~ Accepted Auditing Standards** *n pl AmE* (*GAAS*) ACC allgemein anerkannte Buchprüfungsnormen *f pl*

general: **~ management** *n* MGMNT *administration* allgemeine Verwaltung *f*, *managers* Gesamtgeschäftsführung *f*; **~ manager** *n* HRM, MGMNT Generaldirektor, in *m,f*, Hauptgeschäftsführer, in *m,f*, leitende(r) Angestellte(r) *mf* [decl. as adj], leitender Direktor *m*, leitende Direktorin *f*, leitender Inspektor *m*, leitende Inspektorin *f*; **~ market equilibrium** *n* ECON allgemeines Marktgleichgewicht *nt*

General: **~ Medical Council** *n BrE* (*cf State Medical Board of Registration AmE*) GEN COMM Allgemeiner Medizinischer Rat, ≈ Ärztekammer *f*; **~ meeting of shareholders** *n* STOCK Hauptversammlung *f* der Aktionäre

general: **~ merchandise** *n* GEN COMM Gemischtwaren *f pl*; **~ mortgage** *n* BANK Gesamthypothek *f*, Pfandrecht *nt* am Gesamtvermögen; **~ mortgage bond** *n* STOCK Anleihe *f* mit Sicherung durch eine Gesamthypothek; **~ obligation bond** *n AmE* (*G-O bond*) STOCK *municipal bond* Kommunalobligation *f*; **~ operating costs** *n pl* ACC allgemeine Betriebskosten *pl*; **~ partner** *n* GEN COMM Vollhafter *m*, Komplementär, in *m,f*, persönlich haftender Gesellschafter *m*, persönlich haftende Gesellschafterin *f*

General: **~ Policy Committee** *n* (*GPC*) ADMIN *of the GCBS* Ausschuß *m* für allgemeine Richtlinien

general: **~ price level accounting** *n* (*GPLA*) ACC inflationsbereinigte Rechnungslegung *f*; **~ provisions** *n pl* ACC *for bad debts* allgemeine Rückstellungen *f pl*; **~ public** *n* GEN COMM, LAW Allgemeinheit *f*; **~ purpose** *n* (*GP*) GEN COMM allgemeiner Zweck *m*; **~-purpose** *adj* (*GP*) GEN COMM Mehrzweck-; **~-purpose berth** *n* TRANSP *shipping* Allzweckliegeplatz *m*; **~ revenue** *n AmE* TAX *state and local governments* allgemeine Steuermittel *nt pl*; **~ revenue sharing** *n AmE obs* TAX *former US federal program* vertikaler Finanzausgleich *m*; **~ sales tax** *n* TAX allgemeine Umsatzsteuer *f*

General: **~ Secretary** *n* HRM *union* Generalsekretär, in *m,f*

general: **~ service contract** *n BrE* TRANSP *shipping* allgemeiner Dienstvertrag *m*; **~ service department** *n* ACC allgemeine Hilfskostenstelle *f*; **~ service partner** *n* ACC *in firm* allgemeiner Partner *m*, allgemeine Partnerin *f*; **~ statement** *n* ACC, GEN COMM *accounts* Gesamtbilanz *f*, allgemeiner Ausweis *m*; **~ strike** *n* HRM Generalstreik *m*; **~ terms and conditions** *n pl* GEN COMM, LAW allgemeine Geschäftsbedingungen *f pl* (*AGB*); **~ terms and conditions of delivery** *n pl* GEN

COMM allgemeine Lieferbedingungen *f pl*; **~ trader** *n* TRANSP *shipping* allgemeines Handelsschiff *nt*; **~ training** *n* HRM allgemeine Berufsausbildung *f*; **~ transire** *n* IMP/EXP allgemeiner Zollbegleitschein *m*; **~ unemployment** *n* ECON allgemeine Arbeitslosigkeit *f*; **~ union** *n* HRM allgemeine Gewerkschaft *f*; **~ wage level** *n* ECON allgemeines Lohnniveau *nt*

generate *vt* COMP erzeugen, ECON *income* erwirtschaften, GEN COMM *ideas* hervorbringen, *waste, power, profit* erzeugen

generating: **~ station** *n* ENVIR Elektrizitätswerk *nt* (*E-Werk*), Kraftwerk *nt*

generation *n* COMP Generierung *f*, GEN COMM *power, profits* Erzeugung *f*, Generation *f*, *broadcast* Original *nt*, Vervielfältigung *f*; **~ conflict** *n* WEL Generationenkonflikt *m*, Generationskonflikt *m*; **~ gap** *n* WEL Generationenproblem *nt*, Generationsproblem *nt*

generator *n* (*gen*) GEN COMM Generator *m*

generic *adj* GEN COMM gattungsbedingt, PATENTS nicht geschützt, markenlos; **~ brand** *n* S&M Gattungsname *m*; **~ business plan** *n* GEN COMM allgemeiner Geschäftsplan *m*; **~ job grades** *n pl* HRM generische Bezeichnungen *f pl* für Arbeitsplätze; **~ job titles** *n* HRM generische Bezeichnungen *f pl* für Arbeitsplätze; **~ market** *n* S&M Markt *m* für namenlose Produkte; **~ products** *n pl* S&M markenlose Produkte *nt pl*

generous *adj* TAX *allowance* freigebig, großzügig

genetic *adj* GEN COMM genetisch; **~ engineering** *n* GEN COMM Gentechnik *f*

Geneva: **~ Stock Exchange** *n* STOCK Genfer Börse *f*

gentleman: **~'s agreement** *n* LAW Absprache *f* unter Ehrenmännern, Gentleman's-Agreement *nt*

gentrification *n jarg* ECON, ENVIR, WEL Einzug von sozial Höherstehenden in heruntergekommene Wohnviertel, Gentrifizierung *f* (*jarg*)

genuine: **~ article** *n* GEN COMM, S&M Markenartikel *m pl*; **~ occupational qualification** *n BrE* (*GOQ*) HRM echte Berufsqualifikation *f*, echte Berufsqualifizierung *f*

geodemography *n* S&M *market research* regionale Demographie *f*

geographic *adj* GEN COMM geographisch

geographical: **~ area** *n* GEN COMM geographisches Gebiet *nt*; **~ trade structure** *n* ECON geographische Handelsstruktur *f*

geometric: **~ mean** *n* (*GM*) MATH geometrischer Mittelwert *m*, geometrisches Mittel *nt*; **~ progression** *n* MATH geometrische Folge *f*

geopolitical *adj* POL geopolitisch

German: **~ Chamber of Commerce** *n* (*GCC*) GEN COMM Deutsche Handelskammer *f*; **~ Chamber of Commerce for the UK** *n* (*GCCUK*) GEN COMM Deutsche Handelskammer *f* für das Vereinigte Königreich; **~ Chamber of Industry and Commerce** *n* (*GCIC*) GEN COMM Deutsche Industrie- und Handelskammer *f*; **~ economic institutes** *n pl* ECON Deutsche Wirtschaftsforschungsinstitute *nt pl*; **~ economic miracle** *n* ECON deutsches Wirtschaftswunder *nt*; **~ Futures Exchange** *n* STOCK Deutsche Terminbörse *f*; **~ Historical School** *n* WEL Schule deutscher Wirtschaftswissenschaftler des 19. und frühen 20. Jahrhunderts; **~ International Chamber of Commerce** *n* (*GICC*) GEN COMM Internationale Deutsche Handelskammer *f*; **~ Stock Exchange** *n* STOCK Deutsche Börse *f*

Germanischer: ~ **Lloyd** n (GL) TRANSP *shipping* Germanischer Lloyd m (GL)

German: ~ **Red Cross** n WEL Deutsches Rotes Kreuz nt (DRK)

gerrymander 1. n *infrml* POL Wahlkreisschiebungen f pl (*infrml*), willkürliche Aufteilung f der Wahlbezirke; **2.** vt GEN COMM *election, business* Tatsachen verdrehen, POL Wahlbezirke willkürlich aufteilen

Gerschenkron: ~ **effect** n ECON Gerschenkron-Effekt m

gestation: ~ **period** n ECON *of capital* Ausreifungszeit f

get vt GEN COMM anschaffen; ♦ ~ **the better of** GEN COMM übervorteilen; ~ **more than one bargains for** GEN COMM sein blaues Wunder erleben; ~ **rid of** GEN COMM loswerden, ausbooten (*infrml*)

gfa abbr (*good fair average*) GEN COMM gute Durchschnittsqualität f, mittlere Qualität f

G5 abbr (*Group of Five*) ECON G5 (*Gruppe der Fünf, Fünfer-Gruppe*)

GGE abbr BrE (*general government expenditure*) ECON öffentliche Ausgaben f pl, allgemeine Ausgaben f pl der öffentlichen Hand

ghost n AmE *jarg* HRM abwesender Mitarbeiter, der trotzdem als anwesend registriert wird; ~ **writer** n S&M Ghostwriter m

GHS abbr (*General Household Survey*) ECON *econometrics* allgemeine Haushaltserhebung f

giant adj GEN COMM, S&M riesengroß

GIC abbr (*guaranteed income contract*) INS Versicherung f mit garantiertem Einkommen

GICC abbr (*German International Chamber of Commerce*) GEN COMM Internationale Deutsche Handelskammer f

Giffen: ~ **good** n ECON Giffengut nt; ~ **paradox** n ECON Giffen-Paradoxon nt

Gift: ~ **Aid** n BrE TAX Schenkungsbeistand m, Schenkungshilfe f

gift: ~ **causa mortis** n LAW Schenkung f von Todes wegen; ~ **deed** n LAW Schenkungsurkunde f

gifted adj WEL *trainee, learner* begabt

gift: ~ **in contemplation of death** n TAX Schenkung f von Todes wegen, Schenkung f in Erwartung des Todes; ~ **inter vivos** n LAW Schenkung f unter Lebenden; ~ **promotion** n S&M *advertising* Reklame f durch Geschenke; ~ **tax** n TAX Schenkungssteuer f; ~ **token** n GEN COMM Geschenkgutschein m; ~ **voucher** n GEN COMM Geschenkgutschein m

gigabyte n (*Gb*) COMP Gigabyte nt (*GB*)

gigantomania n *jarg* HRM Gigantomanie f (*jarg*)

gigantomaniac adj *jarg* HRM gigantomanisch (*jarg*)

GIGO abbr *jarg* (*garbage-in/garbage-out*) COMP GIGO (*jarg*) (*Müll rein, Müll raus*)

gilt n BrE BANK, FIN, STOCK Staatspapier nt, mündelsicheres Wertpapier nt; ~-**edged market makers** n pl (*GEMMS*) STOCK Staatspapiermarktmacher m pl; ~-**edged securities** n pl BANK, FIN, STOCK Staatspapiere nt pl, Staatstitel m pl; ~-**edged stock** n STOCK mündelsicheres Wertpapier nt, Staatsanleihepapiere nt pl

gimmick n S&M Werbetrick m

Gini: ~ **coefficient** n ECON *econometrics* Gini-Koeffizient m

Ginnie: ~ **Mae** n AmE *infrml* (*Government National Mortgage Association*) FIN, PROP bundesstaatliche Hypothekenkreditanstalt f

girder n IND Tragbalken m, *shipping* Träger m, TRANSP Unterzug m

giro n BANK Giro nt

Girobank n BrE BANK Postbank f

gist n GEN COMM *of conversation* das Wesentliche nt, Hauptinhalt m, PATENTS Kern m

give 1. vt GEN COMM geben; **2.** vi GEN COMM *material* nachgeben

give away vt S&M verschenken, weggeben

give back vt GEN COMM wiedergeben

give in 1. vt GEN COMM *document* einreichen; ♦ ~ **one's notice** HRM kündigen; **2.** vi GEN COMM aufgeben, nachgeben

give up 1. vt LAW überlassen, *claim* verzichten auf [+acc]; ♦ ~ **all claims to sth** INS, STOCK etw abandonnieren; **2.** vi GEN COMM aufgeben, nachgeben

give: ~-**away magazines** n pl MEDIA *print* Werbezeitschriften f pl

giveback n HRM *industrial relations* Zugeständnis nt

given: **at a** ~ **time** phr GEN COMM zu einer angegebenen Zeit, zu einer bestimmten Zeit; ~ **the circumstances** phr GEN COMM unter den gegebenen Umständen; **be** ~ **a clean bill of health** phr WEL als gesund entlassen werden, für völlig gesund erklärt werden; **be** ~ **practical and financial help** phr GEN COMM praktische und finanzielle Hilfe erhalten

giver n STOCK Reportnehmer m; ♦ **there are no givers on these securities** STOCK es gibt keine Reportnehmer bei diesen Wertpapieren

giver: ~ **for a call** n STOCK Erwerber m einer Kaufoption; ~ **for a call of more** n STOCK Erwerber m eines Nochgeschäfts; ~ **for a put** n STOCK Verkäufer m einer Rückprämie; ~ **for a put and call** n STOCK Erwerber m einer Kauf- und Verkaufsoption; ~ **on stock** n STOCK Aktien-Reportnehmer m; ~ **of option money** n STOCK Prämiengeber m

giving: ~ **up** n LAW Aufgeben nt, Überlassung f

GL abbr (*Germanischer Lloyd*) TRANSP *shipping* GL (*Germanischer Lloyd*)

GLAM abbr (*gray, leisured, affluent, married* AmE, *grey, leisured, affluent, married* BrE) ECON *econometrics* sozioökonomische Gruppe im Alter zwischen 45 und 59, die müßig, wohlhabend und verheiratet sind

glamor AmE see *glamour* BrE

glamour: ~ **issue** n BrE STOCK lebhaft gefragte Aktien f pl; ~ **stock** n BrE STOCK lebhaft gefragte Aktien f pl

glare: ~-**free** adj COMP *screen* blendfrei

Glasgow: ~ **Stock Exchange** n STOCK Glasgower Wertpapierbörse f

glass n IND Glas nt; ~ **fiber-reinforced plastic** AmE, ~ **fibre-reinforced plastic** BrE n (*GRP*) IND glasfaserverstärkter Kunststoff m (*GFK*); ~ **insurance** n INS Fensterglasversicherung f, Glasversicherung f; ~-**reinforced cladding** n TRANSP glasverstärkte Plattierung f

Glass: ~ **Steagall Act** n AmE BANK US-Kreditwesengesetz von 1933

glass: ~ **wool** n TRANSP Glaswolle f

gliding: ~ **rate** n STOCK Gleitzoll m; ~ **shift** n HRM Gleitschicht f

glitch n COMP *operating system* Störimpuls m, ECON, GEN COMM kleine technische Panne f, POL *election campaign* elektronische Panne f, kleine technische Panne f

global *adj* GEN COMM *comprehensive* global, *worldwide* weltumspannend; **~ balance** *n* ENVIR globales Gleichgewicht *nt*; **~ bank** *n* BANK globale Bank *f*; **~ custody** *n* FIN Globaldepot *nt*, globale Aufbewahrung *f*; **~ deregulation** *n* ECON globale Deregulierung *f*; **~ financial center** *AmE*, **~ financial centre** *BrE* *n* ECON weltumspannendes Finanzzentrum *nt*, Weltfinanzzentrum *nt*; **~ harmonization** *n* ACC globale Harmonisierung *f*; **~ image** *n* S&M globales Image *nt*

globalization *n* GEN COMM Globalisierung *f*

globalize *vt* GEN COMM globalisieren

globally *adv* GEN COMM *worldwide* weltumspannend, weltweit

Global: **~ Maritime Distress and Safety System** *n* (*GMDSS*) TRANSP *shipping* Globales Seenot- und Sicherheitssystem *nt*

global: **~ market** *n* ECON Weltmarkt *m*; **~ marketing** *n* S&M weltweites Marketing *nt*; **~ memory** *n* COMP globaler Speicher *m*; **~ monetarism** *n* ECON globaler Monetarismus *m*; **~ network** *n* COMP globales Netz *nt*

Global: **~ Positioning System** *n* (*GPS*) TRANSP *shipping* Globales Positionsbestimmungssystem *nt*

global: **~ search** *n* COMP *document, data* globales Suchen *nt*; **~ search and replace** *n* COMP globales Suchen und Ersetzen *nt*; **~ strategy** *n* GEN COMM globale Strategie *f*, Weltstrategie *f*; **~ variable** *n* COMP *prog* globale Variable *f*

gloom *n* ECON, STOCK Pessimismus *m*

gloss *n* MEDIA *photography* Glanz *m*; **~ print** *n* MEDIA *photography* Glanzabzug *m*

glossy *n* *infrml* (*glossy magazine*) MEDIA Hochglanzmagazin *nt*; **~ magazine** *n* (*glossy*) MEDIA Hochglanzmagazin *nt*; **~ paper** *n* COMMS Hochglanzpapier *nt*, GEN COMM, MEDIA Glanzpapier *nt*

GLS *abbr* (*generalized least squares*) ECON, MATH *statistics* Methode *f* der kleinsten Quadrate

glut *n* ECON Schwemme *f*, Überangebot *nt*, GEN COMM Überangebot *nt*, *economy, market* Schwemme *f*; ♦ **a ~ of** GEN COMM ein Überangebot an

glut: **~ of money** *n* GEN COMM Geldschwemme *f*; **~ on the market** *n* GEN COMM, S&M Marktschaffung *f*, Marktschwemme *f*

GM *abbr* ECON, FIN (*gross margin*) Bruttogewinn *m*, Bruttohandelsspanne *f*, Bruttomarge *f*, Bruttospanne *f*, MATH (*geometric mean*) geometrischer Mittelwert *m*, geometrisches Mittel *nt*

GMDSS *abbr* (*Global Maritime Distress and Safety System*) TRANSP *shipping* Globales Seenot- und Sicherheitssystem *nt*

GMT *abbr* (*Greenwich Mean Time*) GEN COMM GMT (*Greenwich Mean Time*)

GNI *abbr* (*gross national income*) ECON Bruttovolkseinkommen *nt*

GNMA *abbr* *AmE* (*Government National Mortgage Association*) FIN, PROP bundesstaatliche Hypothekenkreditanstalt *f*

GNP *abbr* (*gross national product*) ECON BSP (*Bruttosozialprodukt*)

go down *vi* GEN COMM *prices* sinken, fallen; ♦ **~ in value** STOCK im Wert sinken

go out *vi* HRM streiken; ♦ **~ on strike** HRM in den Streik treten

go under *vi* GEN COMM *company* untergehen

go up *vi* GEN COMM *prices* steigen

goal *n* MGMNT Ziel *nt*, Zweck *m*; **~ congruence** *n* MGMNT Zielkongruenz *f*; **~ equilibrium** *n* ECON Zielgleichgewicht *nt*; **~-programming** *n* MGMNT Zielprogrammierung *f*; **~-seeking** *n* FIN, GEN COMM, MGMNT Zielsuche *f*; **~-setting** *n* GEN COMM Zielsetzung *f*, MGMNT Zielbildung *f*, Zielsetzung *f*; **~ system** *n* ECON Zielsystem *nt*; **~ variable** *n* POL Zielvariable *f*

go-and-not-go: **~ gage** *AmE*, **~ gauge** *BrE* *n* IND Attributenkontrolle *f*

go-between *n* GEN COMM Vermittler, in *m,f*

G-O: **~ bond** *n* *AmE* (*general obligation bond*) STOCK Kommunalobligation *f*

go-go: **~ fund** *n* FIN Investmentfonds, der raschen Wertzuwachs anstrebt

going: **at the ~ rate** *phr* GEN COMM zu Marktpreisen; **~ business** *n* ECON erfolgreiches Unternehmen *nt*; **~ concern** *n* GEN COMM arbeitendes Unternehmen *nt*, aktiver Betrieb *m*, erfolgreiches Unternehmen *nt*; **~-concern concept** *n* ACC langfristiges Unternehmenskonzept *nt*; **~-concern value** *n* ACC Teilwert *m*, Unternehmenswert *m*; **~ long** *n* STOCK Erwerb *m* von Options- oder Terminkontrakten, Haussespekulation *f*; **~ price** *n* STOCK Tageskurs *m*, GEN COMM, HRM herrschender Lohnsatz *m*; **~ short** *n* STOCK Baissespekulation *f*, Leerverkauf *m*

gold *n* STOCK Gold *nt*

goldbug *n* ECON Befürworter, in *m,f* des Goldstandards

gold: **~ bullion standard** *n* ECON Goldkernwährung *f*; **~ card** *n* BANK Gold Card *f*; **~ coin** *n* BANK Goldmünze *f*; **~ cover** *n* ECON Golddeckung *f*; **~ credit** *n* STOCK Goldkredit *m*; **~ currency** *n* BANK Goldumlauf *m*, Goldwährung *f*; **~ demonetization** *n* ECON Golddemonetisierung *f*

golden: **~ age path** *n* ECON Golden Age-Wachstumspfad *m*; **~ handcuffs** *n pl* *infrml* HRM, MGMNT Sonderleistungen einer Firma, um Manager länger zu halten, goldene Handschellen *f pl* (*infrml*); **~ handshake** *n* *infrml* HRM hohe Abfindung *f*; **~ hello** *infrml* *n* HRM Einstellungsprämie *f*; **~ parachute** *n* *infrml* FIN großzügige Abfindung *f*; **~ rate** *n* HRM großzügiger Satz *m*; **~ rule** *n* ECON goldene Regel *f*

Golden: **~ Triangle** *n* ECON Goldenes Dreieck *nt*

gold: **~ exchange standard** *n* ECON Golddevisenwährung *f*; **~ exporting point** *n* ECON, FIN, IMP/EXP oberer Goldpunkt *m*, Goldausfuhrpunkt *m*; **~ export point** *n* ECON, FIN, IMP/EXP Goldausfuhrpunkt *m*, oberer Goldpunkt *m*; **~ fixing** *n* BANK Goldfixing *nt*; **~ import** *n* IMP/EXP Goldeinfuhr *f*; **~ import point** *n* ECON, FIN, IMP/EXP Goldeinfuhrpunkt *m*, unterer Goldpunkt *m*; **~ market** *n* ECON Goldmarkt *m*; **~ mining** *n* IND Goldabbau *m*, Goldbergbau *m*, Goldgewinnung *f*; **~-mining company** *n* ENVIR Goldbergwerksgesellschaft *f*; **~ mutual fund** *n* STOCK offener Goldinvestmentfonds *m*; **~ ore** *n* ENVIR, IND Golderz *nt*; **~ point** *n* IMP/EXP Goldpunkt *m*; **~ price** *n* STOCK Goldpreis *m*; **~ producer** *n* IND Goldgewinner *m*, Goldproduzent *m*; **~ reserves** *n* ECON Goldreserven *f pl*; **~ rush** *n* GEN COMM Goldrausch *m*; **~ shortage** *n* ECON Goldknappheit *f*

golds: **~ index** *n* STOCK Geldwert-Index *m*

Goldsmith: **~ banking system** *n* BANK Goldsmith-Banksystem *nt*

gold: **~ standard** *n* ECON Goldstandard *m*

gondola *n* S&M *shop fitting* beiderseitig zugängliches Warenauslageregal *nt*, TRANSP *rail* offener Wagen *m*; **~ flat** *n* TRANSP *type of container* Niederbordwagen *m*

good *adj* BANK *debt*, ECON, FIN sicher, GEN COMM gut; ♦ **in ~ faith** GEN COMM in gutem Glauben; **be in ~ from** LEIS, WEL gut in Form sein; **in ~ repair** GEN COMM in gutem Wartungszustand; **be in ~ shape** LEIS, WEL gut in Stand sein *(jarg)*; **in ~ trim** *infrml* GEN COMM in guter Verfassung, gut in Form *(infrml)*

good: **~ delivery** *n* STOCK einwandfreie Übergabe *f*; **~ fair average** *n* *(gfa)* GEN COMM gute Durchschnittsqualität *f*, mittlere Qualität *f*; **~ faith** *n* INS Redlichkeit *f*, LAW auf Treu und Glauben; **~-faith deposit** *n* FIN als Sicherheit zu hinterlegender Barbetrag *m*, Sicherheitsleistung *f*, STOCK *commodities, securities* gutgläubige Einlage *f*; **~ food guide** *n* LEIS Schlemmeratlas *m*

Goodhart: **~'s law** *n* ECON Goodhart-Gesetz *nt*

good: **~ housekeeping** *n* MGMNT sparsame Haushaltsführung *f*, sparsames Wirtschaften *nt*

Good: **~ Housekeeping Seal** *n* *AmE* S&M *consumer protection* Gütezeichen einer Verbraucherschutzvereinigung

good: **~ money** *n* BANK, ECON *Gresham's law* echtes Geld *nt*

goodness: **~-of-fit test** *n* MATH *statistical procedure* Test *m* zur Güte der Anpassung

good: **~ news** *n pl* GEN COMM gute Nachrichten *f pl*; **~ return** *n* ACC *on an investment* gute Rendite *f*; **~ risk** *n* INS gutes Risiko *nt*

goods *n pl BrE* *(gds)* ECON Waren *f pl* *(Wa.)*, PATENTS Waren *f pl* *(Wa.)*, Artikel *m pl* *(Art.)*, TRANSP Güter *nt pl* *(G.)*, Fracht *f* *(F.)*; ♦ **the ~ remain undelivered** GEN COMM die Ware wurde noch nicht zugestellt

goods: **~ called forward** *n pl* TRANSP abgerufene Ware *f*; **~ covered by warrant** *n pl* GEN COMM Waren *f pl* mit Lagerschein; **~ department** *n* GEN COMM Produktabteilung *f*; **~ depot** *n* GEN COMM, IMP/EXP, TRANSP Warenlager *nt*; **~ of foreign origin** *n pl* GEN COMM ausländische Erzeugnisse *nt pl*; **~ for re-export** *n pl* IMP/EXP Wiederausfuhrgüter *nt pl*; **~ held for re-sale** *n pl* ACC Ware *f* zum Wiederverkauf; **~ on approval** *n pl* GEN COMM Ware *f* zur Ansicht; **~ on hand** *n pl* TRANSP Lagerbestand *m*

good: **~ sound merchantable** *adj BrE* *(gsm)* GEN COMM *quality* gut marktgängig

goods: **~ received note** *n* ACC Lieferschein *m*, Warenannahmeschein *m*, IMP/EXP Güterempfangsbestätigung *f*, TRANSP Eingangsschein *m*, Warenannahmeschein *m*; **~ and services** *n pl* ECON Waren und Dienstleistungen *f pl*; **~ train** *n BrE* *(cf freight train AmE)* TRANSP Güterzug *m*; **~ wagon** *n BrE* *(cf freight car AmE)* TRANSP Güterwagen *m*, Waggon *m*

good: **~-till-canceled order** *AmE*, **~-till-cancelled order** *BrE* *n* STOCK bis zur Annullierung gültiger Auftrag *m*; **~ title** *n* LAW *transactions* rechtsgültiger Anspruch *m*, PROP gültiger Rechtsanspruch *m*, gültiger Rechtstitel *m*; **~ track record** *n* GEN COMM nachweislicher Erfolg *m*; **~ value** *adj* GEN COMM günstig; **~ value for money** *n* GEN COMM gutes Preis-Leistungs-Verhältnis *nt*

goodwill *n* ACC Firmenwert *m*, Geschäftswert *m*, Goodwill *m*, GEN COMM Firmenwert *m*; **~ amortization** *n* ACC Firmenwert-Abschreibung *f*, Goodwill-Abschreibung *f*; **~ on consolidation** *n* ACC Konzerngoodwill *m*

goon: **~ squad** *n AmE infrml* HRM gewalttätige Streikbrecher *m pl*

GOP *abbr AmE infrml* *(Grand Old Party)* POL Republikaner *m pl*

GOQ *abbr BrE* *(genuine occupational qualification)* HRM echte Berufsqualifikation *f*, echte Berufsqualifizierung *f*

gorilla: **~ scale** *n infrml* HRM Hierarchie *f* des Führungspersonals

go-slow *n BrE* *(cf slowdown AmE)* ECON, HRM *workers* Bummelstreik *m*, Arbeit *f* nach Vorschrift

govern *vt* LAW regeln

governing: **~ body** *n* MGMNT Verwaltungsrat *m*, POL, WEL Kuratorium *nt*; **~ principle** *n* GEN COMM Leitsatz *m*

government *n* *(govt)* GEN COMM, POL Regierung *f* *(Reg.)*; **~ accounting** *n* ACC *principles and procedures* kameralistische Buchführung *f*, Verwaltungsbuchführung *f*, staatliches Rechnungswesen *nt*; **~ agency** *n* ADMIN Behörde *f*; **~ aid** *n* WEL Beihilfe *f*, staatliche Förderung *f*

governmental *adj* GEN COMM staatlich *(staatl.)*

Governmental: **~ Accounting Standards Board** *n* *(GASB)* ACC Regierungsaufsichtsbehörde *f* für Buchführungsgrundsätze

government: **~ annuity** *n* FIN Rentenpapier *nt*, Staatsanleihe *f*; **~-backed** *adj* FIN staatlich unterstützt; **~ benefit** *n* WEL Beihilfe *f*; **~ bond** *n* ECON Staatsanleihe *f*, FIN Staatsschuldverschreibung *f*; **~ broker** *n* STOCK Broker, der im Auftrage der Regierung kauft und verkauft; **~ budget** *n* ECON Staatshaushalt *m*, öffentlicher Haushalt *m*; **~ contract** *n* GEN COMM Staatsauftrag *m*, LAW öffentlicher Auftrag *m*, Behördenvertrag *m*, Staatsauftrag *m*; **~-controlled** *adj* ADMIN unter staatlicher Aufsicht; **~-controlled corporation** *n* ADMIN, ECON, FIN, GEN COMM staatliches Unternehmen *nt*; **~ defence appropriations** *BrE*, **~ defense appropriations** *AmE n pl* POL Mittelbindung *f* für Verteidigungszwecke, Verteidigungshaushalt *m*, Mittelbindung *f* für den Verteidigungshaushalt; **~ department** *n* ADMIN, POL Ministerium *nt*, Ressort *nt*; **~ enterprise** *n* ADMIN staatliches Unternehmen *nt*, ECON Staatsbetrieb *m*, staatliches Unternehmen *nt*, FIN staatliches Unternehmen *nt*, GEN COMM Staatsbetrieb *m*, staatliches Unternehmen *nt*; **~ expenditure** *n* ECON, FIN Ausgaben *f pl* der öffentlichen Hand, öffentliche Ausgaben *f pl*, Staatsausgaben *f pl*; **~ finance** *n* FIN staatliche Finanzierung *f*, Staatsfinanzierung *f*; **~-financed** *adj* FIN staatlich finanziert; **~ funds** *n pl* ADMIN staatliche Mittel *nt pl*, WEL öffentliche Mittel *nt pl*; **~ grant** *n* ECON staatliche Zuweisung *f*, FIN Staatszuschuß *m*, staatliche Subvention *f*; **~ intervention** *n* ADMIN, ECON, POL Regierungseingriff *m*, staatliche Intervention *f*, *mediation* Vermittlung *f*, *public order* staatlicher Eingriff *m*; **~ investment** *n* FIN staatliche Investition *f*; **~ loan** *n* FIN Regierungsanleihe *f*, Staatsanleihe *f*

Government: **~ National Mortgage Association** *n AmE* *(Ginnie Mae, GNMA)* FIN, PROP bundesstaatliche Hypothekenkreditanstalt *f*

government: **~ obligations** *n pl BrE* ECON Staatsobligationen *f pl*; **~-owned** *adj* GEN COMM *company* staatseigen; **~ procurement** *n* ECON öffentliches Vergabewesen *nt*, Beschaffungswesen *f*; **~-regulated** *adj* POL staatlich gelenkt, unter Aufsicht der Behörden; **~ relations** *n pl* POL Beziehungen *f pl* zwischen Regierungen, Regierungsbeziehungen *f pl*, *intergovern-*

mental relations zwischenstaatliche Beziehungen *f pl*; **~ report** *n* GEN COMM Regierungsbericht *m*; **~ research grant** *n* FIN staatliche Forschungsbeihilfe *f*; **~ revenue** *n* ECON öffentliche Einnahme *f*, öffentliche Einnahmen *f pl*; **~ role** *n* POL Rolle *f* der Regierung

governments *n pl AmE infrml* ECON Staatsobligationen *f pl*, Öffentliche *pl* (*infrml*)

government: **~ securities** *n pl* ECON öffentliche Anleihen *f pl*, Wertpapiere *nt pl* der öffentlichen Hand; **~-sponsored** *adj* FIN *project* staatlich gefördert; **~ stock** *n* STOCK Staatsanleihe *f*; **~ subsidy** *n* FIN Staatszuschuß *m*, Subvention *f*; **~-supported** *adj* FIN *project* staatlich gefördert; **~-to-government** *adj* GEN COMM zwischenstaatlich; **~ transfer payment** *n* ADMIN staatliche Einkommensübertragung *f*, staatliche Transferzahlung *f*

Governor: **~ of the Bank of England** *n* ECON Gouverneur *m* der Bank von England, Notenbankpräsident *m*; **~ General** *n* POL Generalgouverneur *m*

govt *abbr* (*government*) GEN COMM, POL Reg. (*Regierung*)

GP *abbr* GEN COMM (*general purpose*) allgemeiner Zweck *m*, (*general-purpose*) Mehrzweck-

GPC *abbr* (*General Policy Committee*) ADMIN Ausschuß *m* für allgemeine Richtlinien

GPLA *abbr* (*general price level accounting*) ACC inflationsbereinigte Rechnungslegung *f*

GPS *abbr* (*Global Positioning System*) TRANSP *shipping* Globales Positionsbestimmungssystem *nt*

grab 1. *n* TRANSP *cargo handling equipment* Greifer *m*; **2.** *vt* GEN COMM an sich reißen

grace: **~ days** *n pl* ACC Gnadenfrist *f*, Nachfrist *f*; **~ period** *n* ACC Nachfrist *f*, Respektfrist *f*, FIN tilgungsfreie Zeit *f*

grade 1. *n* GEN COMM Sorte *f*, HRM *of pay scale* Lohngruppe *f*; **2.** *vt* GEN COMM sortieren, *calibrate* einteilen, *classify* einstufen

grade: **~ creep** *n* HRM schleichende Erhöhung *f* durch Heraufstufung

graded: **~ by size** *phr* GEN COMM *produce* nach Größe geordnet; **~ premium policy** *n* GEN COMM *insurance* Versicherung *f* mit gestaffelten Prämienzahlungen

grade: **~ drift** *n* HRM schleichende Gehaltserhöhung *f*

grading: **~ back** *n* HRM Rückstufung *f*

gradual *adj* GEN COMM graduell, sukzessiv, schrittweise

gradualism *n* POL langsamer Wandel *m*, Politik *f* der kleinen Schritte, Pragmatismus *m*

gradualist: **~ monetarism** *n* ECON, FIN, GEN COMM Monetarismus *m*

gradually *adv* GEN COMM allmählich, stufenweise, schrittweise

graduate *n* HRM Akademiker, in *m,f*, Graduierte(r) *mf* [decl. as adj], Hochschulabsolvent, in *m,f*

graduated: **~ interest** *n* FIN Staffelzinsen *f pl*; **~ lease** *n* PROP Staffelmiete *f*; **~ payment mortgage** *n* BANK Hypothek mit gestaffelten, aber steigenden Tilgungsleistungen; **~ payments** *n pl* FIN Staffelzahlungen *f pl*; **~ pension scheme** *n* HRM abgestuftes Sozialrentensystem *nt*; **in ~ stages** *phr* GEN COMM stufenweise; **~ wage** *n* HRM Staffeltarif *m*

graduate: **~ school of business** *n* WEL Wirtschaftshochschule *f*, wirtschaftswissenschaftliche Fakultät *f*

graft 1. *n infrml* POL Bestechungsgeld *nt*, Schmiergeld *nt*; **2.** *vi infrml* LAW Schmiergelder annehmen

Graham: **~ and Dodd method of investing** *n* STOCK Graham-und-Dodd-Investitionsmethode *f*

grain *n* STOCK Getreide *nt*; **~ certificate** *n* TRANSP *shipping* Getreidezertifikat *nt*; **~ crop** *n* ECON Getreideernte *f*; **~ exchange** *n* AmE (*cf corn exchange BrE*) STOCK *silo* Getreidebörse *f*

Grain: **~ and Free Trade Association** *n* (*GAFTA*) ECON Getreide- und Freihandelsassoziation *f*

grain: **~ harvest** *n* ECON Getreideernte *f*; **~ silo** *n* GEN COMM Getreidespeicher *m*; **~ terminal** *n* TRANSP *shipping* Getreideterminal *m*; **~ trade** *n* ECON, IND Getreidehandel *m*

gram *n* (*g*) GEN COMM Gramm *nt* (*g*)

gramme *see* **gram**

Gramm: **~ Rudman Hollings Act** *n* AmE POL Gramm-Rudman-Hollings-Gesetz *nt*

Grammy *n* MEDIA *broadcast award* Grammy *m*

granary *n* TRANSP Getreidesilo *m*, Getreidespeicher *m*

grandfather: **~ clause** *n* AmE POL Besitzstandsklausel *f*

grand: **~ jury** *n* AmE LAW Anklagejury *f*; **~ larceny** *n* AmE LAW schwerer Diebstahl *m*

Grand: **~ Old Party** *n* AmE infrml (*GOP*) POL Republikaner *m pl*

grand: **~ total** *n* GEN COMM Gesamtsumme *f*

grant 1. *n* ADMIN Beihilfe *f*, Zuschuß *m*, *to student* Stipendium *nt*, ECON Zuschuß *m*, FIN Kapitalzuschuß *m*, Subvention *f*, LAW *agreement* Bewilligung *f*, *loan* Erteilung *f*, *property conveyance* Übertragung *f*, *subsidy* Zuschuß *m*, Subvention *f*, PATENTS Bewilligung *f*, Erteilung *f*, Gewährung *f*; ♦ **in ~ form** FIN in Form einer Subvention; **2.** *vt* FIN *credit* bewilligen, erteilen, gewähren, GEN COMM *concessions* gewähren, PATENTS *licence* bewilligen, erteilen, *to request, suggestion, wish* stattgeben; ♦ **~ administrative relief** TAX staatliche Ansprüche erlassen; **~ a delay** LAW *contract* Aufschub gewähren; **~ extended credit** FIN einen erweiterten Kredit gewähren; **~ interim supply** ACC Überbrückungsmittel *nt pl* bereitstellen; **~ a loan** BANK ein Darlehen geben; **~ respite** LAW Aufschub gewähren; **~ sb a power of attorney** LAW jdm eine Vollmacht erteilen; **~ a tenancy** PROP Mietrecht einräumen

granted *adj* FIN bewilligt, erteilt, GEN COMM zugestanden, PATENTS erteilt, bewilligt

grantee *n* LAW *property* Erwerber, in *m,f*

grant: **~-in-aid** *n* ECON Zuschuß *m* an Entwicklungsländer, FIN zweckgebundener Zuschuß *m*, Staatszuschuß *m*, unentgeltliche finanzielle Hilfe *f*, Zuschuß *m*

granting: **~ of credit** *n* BANK Kreditgewährung *f*; **~ of exclusive rights** *n* LAW Einräumung *f* von Exklusivrechten; **~ of licence** *BrE*, **~ of license** *AmE n* LAW Lizenzvergabe *f*; **~ of a patent** *n* LAW, PATENTS Patenterteilung *f*

grantor *n* LAW *property* Veräußerer *m*, Übertragende(r) *mf* [decl. as adj]; **~ trust** *n* LAW vom Errichter der Treuhand beherrschtes Treuhandvermögen

grants: **~ economics** *n* ECON Übertragungswirtschaft *f*; **~ expenditures** *n pl* FIN Ausgaben *f pl* für Kapitalzuschüsse, Ausgaben *f pl* für Subventionen

grapevine *n* GEN COMM Gerüchteküche *f*

graph *n* COMP grafische Darstellung *f*, Graph *m*, GEN COMM Schaubild *nt*, MATH Graph *m*, Kurve *f*

graphic *adj* COMP grafisch

graphical: ~ **editing** n COMP, MEDIA grafisches Editieren nt

graphically: ~ **illustrated** adj GEN COMM grafisch illustriert

graphical: ~ **user interface** n (*GUI*) COMP grafische Benutzerschnittstelle f (*GUI*)

graphic: ~ **character** n COMP Schriftzeichen nt; ~ **data processing** n COMP Grafikdatenverarbeitung f; ~ **design** n S&M advertising Werbegrafik f; ~ **designer** n S&M Werbegrafiker, in m,f

graphics n pl COMP Grafik f; ~ **board** n COMP Grafikbrett nt, Grafiktafel f; ~ **card** n COMP Grafikkarte f; ~ **database** n COMP Grafikdatenbank f; ~ **file** n COMP Grafikdatei f; ~ **display terminal** n COMP grafikfähiger Bildschirm m; ~ **mode** n COMP Grafikmodus m; ~ **printer** n COMP Grafikdrucker m; ~ **software** n COMP Grafiksoftware f

graph: ~ **paper** n ADMIN Millimeterpapier nt

grassroots n pl POL support Basis f, Grassroots pl (jarg); ~ **business** n GEN COMM Kerngeschäft nt; ~ **movement** n GEN COMM Volksbewegung f

grateful adj GEN COMM dankbar

gratify vt GEN COMM desire befriedigen

gratis 1. adj GEN COMM gratis; **2.** adv GEN COMM gratis

gratuitous adj GEN COMM loan kostenlos; ~ **transfer** n TAX unentgeltliche Übertragung f

gratuity n GEN COMM Geldzuweisung f

graveyard: ~ **shift** n infrml HRM Nachtschicht f

graving: ~ **dock** n TRANSP shipping Trockendock nt

gravity: ~ **model** n ECON Schwerkraftmodell nt

gray AmE see grey BrE

grayscale AmE see greyscale BrE

grazing n jarg GEN COMM geringfügiger Ladendiebstahl m, Mundraub m (obs)

grease: ~ **sb's palm** vt infrml GEN COMM jdn bestechen, jdn schmieren (infrml)

great adj GEN COMM groß, stark

Great: ~ **Depression** n ECON Weltwirtschaftskrise f; ~ **Leap Forward** n ECON großer Sprung nach vorn; ~ **Society** n AmE ECON die große Gesellschaft f

green adj ENVIR grün, umweltbewußt

greenback n AmE ECON Dollarschein m

green: ~ **belt** n ENVIR Grüngürtel m; ~ **card** n INS grüne Versicherungskarte f, POL AmE Aufenthaltsgenehmigung f; ~ **currency** n ECON EU agriculture Grüne Währung f

Green: ~ **Discussion Paper** n LAW Informations- und Diskussionspapier nt

green: ~ **energy** n ENVIR grüne Energie f; ~ **product** n ENVIR umweltfreundliches Produkt nt; ~ **technology** n ENVIR umweltfreundliche Technologie f

greenfield adj ENVIR ländlich und unerschlossen; ~ **site company** n BrE HRM Unternehmen nt auf der grünen Wiese; ~ **site factory** n IND Werksanlage f im Grünen

greenhouse: ~ **effect** n ENVIR Treibhauseffekt m; ~ **effect gas** n ENVIR Treibhausgas nt

greening n jarg ENVIR of public opinion zunehmende ökologische Orientierung f

green: ~ **issue** n ENVIR ökologische Frage f; ~ **labeling scheme** AmE, ~ **labelling scheme** BrE n ENVIR of products on sale ökologische Etikettierung f; ~ **light** n GEN COMM authorization grünes Licht nt

greenlining n ENVIR Innenstadtsanierung und Begrünung f

green: ~ **lobby** n ENVIR grüne Lobby f

greenmail n AmE STOCK erpresserischer Kauf m eines Aktienpakets

Green: ~ **Paper** n BrE LAW Informationsbericht m; ~ **Party** n (cf Greens) ENVIR, POL ökologische Partei f, Grüne Partei f

green: ~ **petrol** n ENVIR grünes Benzin nt; ~ **pound** n ECON EU agriculture grünes Pfund nt; ~ **revolution** n ECON agricultural grüne Revolution f

Greens n pl ENVIR, POL Grüne m pl

green: ~ **sea** n TRANSP Sturzsee f; ~ **tax** n ECON Ökosteuer f

greenshoe n STOCK increase of capital stock Mehrzuteilungsoption f, Plazierungsreserve f

Greenwich: ~ **Mean Time** n (*GMT*) GEN COMM Greenwich Mean Time f (*GMT*)

greetings n pl COMMS Grüße m pl

Gresham: ~'s **law** n ECON Greshamsches Gesetz nt

grey: ~ **belt** n BrE jarg ECON grauer Gürtel m; ~-**hair** n infrml GEN COMM erfahrene, ältere Person, alter Hase m (infrml); ~, **leisured, affluent, married** phr BrE (*GLAM*) ECON econometrics sozioökonomische Gruppe im Alter zwischen 45 und 59, die müßig, wohlhabend und verheiratet sind; ~ **market** n BrE ECON, STOCK grauer Markt m; ~ **Monday** n BrE STOCK grauer Montag m

greyscale n BrE COMP Grauskala f

grey: ~ **society** n BrE ECON graue Gesellschaft f

grid n COMP Koordinatennetz nt, Rasterfeld nt; ~ **structure** n FIN Gitterstruktur f, GEN COMM, MGMNT Matrixstruktur f

grievance n HRM Beschwerde f; ~ **arbitration** n HRM Schlichtung f von Auseinandersetzungen; ~ **procedure** n HRM Beschwerdeverfahren nt, Schlichtungsverfahren nt

GRIP abbr (guaranteed recovery of investment principle) FIN Prinzip nt der garantierten Rückgewinnung des Investitionseinsatzes

GRM abbr (gross rent multiplier) PROP Bruttomietemultiplikator m

grocery n S&M Lebensmittelgeschäft nt

gross 1. adj GEN COMM brutto; ♦ ~ **terms** TRANSP shipping Reeder trägt Kosten von Laden und Löschen; **2.** adv GEN COMM brutto; **3.** n MATH 12 dozen Gros nt (obs)

gross: ~ **amount** n ACC Bruttobetrag m, Gesamtbetrag m; ~ **billing** n AmE S&M Bruttofakturierung f; ~ **book value** n ACC Bruttobuchwert m, Buchwert m vor Abschreibungen; ~ **budget** n FIN Bruttoetat m; ~ **cash flow** n FIN Bruttocashflow m, Cashflow m vor Steuern; ~ **circulation** n S&M Bruttoauflagenhöhe f; ~ **debt** n FIN Gesamtschulden f pl; ~ **dividend** n ACC, FIN Bruttodividende f; ~ **dividend yield** n ECON Bruttodividendenertrag m, Bruttodividende f, STOCK Bruttodividendenrendite f; ~ **domestic product** n (*GDP*) ECON Bruttoinlandsprodukt nt (*BIP*); ~ **earnings** n pl HRM Bruttoeinkommen nt, Bruttoverdienst m, Bruttoerlös m

grossed: ~-**up dividend** n FIN erzielte Bruttodividende f

gross: ~ **estate** n TAX Bruttonachlaß m, Bruttovermögen nt, Nachlaßvermögen nt vor Abzug der Erbschaftssteuer; ~ **excess reinsurance policy** n INS

Bruttoexzedentenrückversicherung *f*; ~ **fault** *n* LAW grobes Verschulden *nt*; ~ **fixed capital formation** *n* ACC Bruttoanlageinvestitionen *f pl*, GEN COMM Bruttoanlagenkapitalbildung *f*; ~ **form of charter** *n* TRANSP *maritime* Bruttoform *f* des Chartervertrages; ~ **ignorance** *n* LAW grob fahrlässige Unkenntnis *f*; ~ **income** *n* ACC Bruttoeinkommen *nt*

grossing: ~**-up** *n* ACC Bruttoberechnung *f*, Ermittlung *f* des Bruttobetrages, Errechnung *f* des Bruttobetrags, S&M Bruttoberechnung *f*

gross: ~ **investment** *n* ACC Bruttoinvestitionen *f pl*; ~ **leasable area** *n* AmE PROP Bruttomietfläche *f*; ~ **lease** *n* PROP Bruttomiete *f*, Bruttopacht *f*; ~ **margin** *n* (*GM*) ACC Bruttogewinn *m*, Bruttospanne *f*, ECON, FIN Bruttogewinn *m*, Bruttohandelsspanne *f*, Bruttomarge *f*, Bruttospanne *f*; ~ **mass** *n* (*G*) GEN COMM Bruttomasse *f*; ~ **miscarriage of justice** *n* LAW schwerer Justizirrtum *m*; ~ **misconduct** *n* HRM schwere Verfehlung *f*

Gross: ~ **National Debt** *n* AmE ECON Staatsschuld *f*

gross: ~ **national expenditure** *n* ECON staatliche Bruttoausgaben *f pl*; ~ **national income** *n* (*GNI*) ECON Bruttovolkseinkommen *nt*; ~ **national product** *n* (*GNP*) ECON Bruttosozialprodukt *nt* (*BSP*); ~ **operating revenue** *n* ACC betrieblicher Bruttoertrag *m*; ~ **pay** *n* HRM Bruttolohn *m*; ~ **profit** *n* ACC, ADMIN, ECON, FIN Bruttogewinn *m*; ~ **profit margin** *n* ACC Betriebshandelsspanne *f*, Bruttogewinnspanne *f*, Rohgewinn *m*; ~ **profit method** *n* ACC Vorratsbewertung durch retrograde Kalkulation anhand des Rohgewinns; ~ **profit ratio** *n* ACC Bruttogewinnverhältnis *nt*; ~ **rate** *n* TRANSP Bruttosatz *m*; ~ **reach** *n* S&M Bruttoreichweite *f*; ~ **receipts pool** *n* TRANSP *shipping* Bruttoeinnahmen-Pool *m*; ~ **registered tonnage** *n* GEN COMM, TRANSP *shipping* Bruttoregistertonnage *f*; ~ **register ton**, ~ **register tonne** *n* (*GRT*) GEN COMM, TRANSP Bruttoregistertonne *f*; ~ **rent multiplier** *n* (*GRM*) PROP Bruttomietemultiplikator *m*; ~ **retail price** *n* (*GRP*) S&M Bruttoeinzelhandelspreis *m*; ~ **return** *n* ADMIN Bruttorendite *f*; ~ **sales** *n* ACC Bruttoerlös *m*, Bruttoumsatz *m*; ~ **sales revenue** *n* ACC Bruttoumsatzerlöse *m pl*; ~ **savings** *n pl* FIN Bruttoersparnisse *f pl*; ~ **social product** *n* ECON Bruttosozialprodukt *nt* (*BSP*); ~ **spread** *n* FIN, STOCK Bruttospanne *f*, Konsortialnutzen *m*; ~ **state product** *n* ECON Bruttoinlandsprodukt eines US-Bundesstaates; ~ **tare weight** *n* TRANSP Bruttoverpackungsgewicht *nt*; ~ **ton** *n* GEN COMM *maritime* Bruttotonne *f*; ~ **tonnage** *n* (*GT*) GEN COMM Bruttotonnage *f*; ~ **tonne** *see gross ton*; ~ **trading profit** *n* ACC Bruttowarengewinn *m*; ~ **train weight** *n* (*GTW*) TRANSP *road vehicle* Bruttozuggewicht *nt*, *train* Zugbruttogewicht *nt*; ~ **turnover** *n* ACC Bruttoumsatz *m*; ~ **vehicle weight** *n* (*GVW*) TRANSP *road vehicle* Fahrzeuggesamtgewicht *nt*; ~ **wage** *n* HRM Bruttolohn *m*; ~ **weight** *n* (*gr.wt.*) GEN COMM Bruttogewicht *nt*

ground: get off the ~ *phr infrml* GEN COMM *business, project* in Gang bringen, in Gang kommen, auf den Weg bringen; ~ **control** *n* COMMS, TRANSP Bodenkontrolle *f*; ~ **crew** *n* TRANSP Bodenpersonal *nt*

grounding *n* AmE (*cf earthing BrE*) COMP, IND *electricity* Erdung *f*

ground: ~ **lease** *n* PROP Erbbaurechtsvertrag *m*

groundless *adj* GEN COMM unbegründet

ground: ~ **plan** *n* GEN COMM Grundriß *m*; ~ **rent** *n* ADMIN Bodenrente *f*, PROP Erbbauzins *m*, Grundrente *f*; ~ **rules** *n pl* GEN COMM Grundregeln *f pl*, Spielregeln *f pl*

grounds *n pl* PATENTS *for opposition, revocation* Begründung *f*; ♦ **on** ~ **of expediency** *phr* GEN COMM aus Zweckmäßigkeitsgründen; **on the** ~ **of ill health** HRM *retirement or leave* aus Gesundheitsgründen

grounds: ~ **for dismissal** *n pl* HRM Entlassungsgrund *m*, Kündigungsgrund *m*

ground: ~ **transportation** *n* TRANSP Bodentransport *m*

groundwork *n* GEN COMM Grundlagenarbeit *f*, Vorarbeiten *f pl*

ground: ~ **zero** *n* GEN COMM *point of impact* am stärksten betroffener Bereich *m*

group 1. *n* ACC Gruppe *f*, Unternehmensgruppe *f*, ECON Unternehmensbereich *m*, GEN COMM Konzern *m*; **2.** *vt* GEN COMM gruppieren; ♦ ~ **along with** GEN COMM zuordnen [+dat]; ~ **by ability** WEL Leistungsgruppen bilden

group: ~ **accounts** *n pl* ACC Gruppenabschluß *m*, konsolidierter Abschluß *m*, Konzernabschluß *m*; ~ **of affiliated companies** *n* GEN COMM Unternehmensbeteiligungsgruppe *f*

groupage *n* IMP/EXP, TRANSP Sammelladung *f*; ~ **agent** *n* TRANSP Sammelladungsagent, in *m,f*; ~ **bill of lading** *n* IMP/EXP, TRANSP Gruppenkonnossement *nt*, Gruppierungskonnossement *nt*, Sammelladungskonnossement *nt*; ~ **depot** *n* TRANSP Sammelladungsdepot *nt*; ~ **operator** *n* IMP/EXP, TRANSP Gruppierungsspediteur, in *m,f*, Sammelbediener, in *m,f*; ~ **rate** *n* TRANSP Sammelladungsfrachtrate *f*

group: ~ **annuity contract** *n* ADMIN Betriebsrentensystem *f*; ~ **of assets** *n* ACC Vermögensgruppe *f*; ~ **banking** *n* BANK Gruppenbanking *n*, Holdingbankwesen *nt*; ~ **bonus** *n* HRM Gruppenprämie *f*; ~ **chief accountant** *n* ACC Konzernbilanzbuchhalter, in *m,f*; ~ **of companies** *n* GEN COMM Unternehmensgruppe *f*, Gruppe *f*, Konzern *m*; ~ **of connected clients** *n* FIN Gruppe *f* verbundener Kunden; ~ **contract** *n* GEN COMM Gruppenvertrag *m*; ~ **credit insurance** *n* INS Kollektivlebensversicherung *f* für Darlehensnehmer ungedeckter Kredite; ~ **disability insurance** *n* INS Gruppenerwerbsunfähigkeitsversicherung *f*; ~ **discussion** *n* GEN COMM Gruppengespräch *nt*, S&M Gruppendiskussion *f*; ~ **dynamics** *n pl* HRM Gruppendynamik *f*

Group: ~ **Executive Board** *n* HRM Konzerndirektion *f*; ~ **of Five** *n* (*G5*) ECON Fünfer-Gruppe *f* (*G5*), Gruppe *f* der Fünf (*G5*)

group: ~ **health insurance** *n* INS Gruppenkrankenversicherung *f*; ~ **incentive** *n* HRM Gruppenanreiz *m*; ~ **incentive payment system** *n* ADMIN Gruppenakkordsystem *nt*; ~ **incentive scheme** *n* HRM Anreizsystem *nt* auf Gruppenebene, Gruppenanreizsystem *nt*

grouping *n* GEN COMM *of companies* Gruppierung *f*, Vereinigung *f*, *classification* Eingruppierung *f*, MATH *statistics* Gruppierung *f*

group: ~ **interview** *n* HRM Gruppengespräch *nt*; ~ **leader** *n* HRM Gruppenleiter, in *m,f*, *workers' gang* Kolonnenführer, in *m,f*; ~ **life insurance** *n* INS Gruppenlebensversicherung *f*; ~ **piecework** *n* HRM Gruppenakkord *m*; ~ **profit** *n* ACC Konzerngewinn *m*

Group: ~ **of Seven** *n* (*G7*) ECON *international trade*

Gruppe *f* der sieben führenden Weltwirtschaftsnationen (*G7*), Siebener-Gruppe *f* (*G7*)

group: ~ **structure** *n* GEN COMM Gruppenstruktur *f*, Konzernstruktur *f*

Group: ~ **of Ten** *n* (*G10*) ECON Zehnergruppe *f* (*G10*)

group: ~ **training** *n* HRM Gruppentraining *nt*; ~ **travel** *n* LEIS Gruppenreise *f*; ~ **working** *n* HRM Gruppenarbeit *f*, Gruppenarbeitssystem *nt*

grow *vi* ECON, GEN COMM *funds, business* wachsen

growing *adj* GEN COMM anwachsend; ~ **demand** *n* ECON steigende Nachfrage *f*; **--equity mortgage** *n AmE* (*GEM*) BANK Wachstumshypothek nach Equity-Recht

growth *n* BANK, ECON Wachstum *nt*, GEN COMM Wachstum *nt*, Zuwachs *m*; ~ **accounting** *n* ECON *econometrics* Analyse *f* der Wachstumsdeterminanten; ~ **index** *n* ECON Wachstumsindex *m*; ~ **industry** *n* ECON Wachstumsbranche *f*, IND Wachstumsindustrie *f*; ~ **in value** *n* STOCK Wertzuwachs *m*; ~ **path** *n* GEN COMM Wachstumspfad *m*; ~ **pole** *n* ECON Wachstumspol *m*; ~ **potential** *n* GEN COMM Wachstumspotential *nt*; ~ **rate** *n* COMP, ECON Wachstumsrate *f*, STOCK Wachstumsrate *f*, Zuwachsrate *f*; ~ **stock** *n* STOCK Wachstumsaktie *f*, Wuchsaktie *f*; ~ **strategy** *n* ECON, GEN COMM Wachstumsstrategie *f*; ~ **theory of the firm** *n* ECON Wachstumstheorie *f* des Unternehmens

GRP *abbr* IND (*glass fiber-reinforced plastic AmE, glass fibre-reinforced plastic BrE*) GFK (*glasfaserverstärkter Kunststoff*), S&M (*gross retail price*) Bruttoeinzelhandelspreis *m*

GRT *abbr* (*gross register ton, gross register tonne*) GEN COMM, TRANSP Bruttoregistertonne *f*

gr.wt. *abbr* (*gross weight*) GEN COMM Bruttogewicht *nt*

G7 *abbr* (*Group of Seven*) ECON *international trade* G7 (*Gruppe der sieben führenden Weltwirtschaftsnationen, Siebener-Gruppe*)

gsm *abbr BrE* (*good sound merchantable*) GEN COMM *quality* gut marktgängig

GSP *abbr* (*generalized system of preferences*) ECON allgemeines Präferenzsystem *nt*

G-spool *n* S&M *advertising* G-Prädikat *nt*

GSTP *abbr* (*generalized system of tariffs and preferences*) IMP/EXP allgemeines Zoll- und Präferenzsystem *nt*, verallgemeinertes Tarif- und Präferenzsystem *nt*

GT *abbr* (*gross tonnage*) GEN COMM Bruttotonnage *f*

GTC: ~ **order** *n* (*good-till-cancelled order*) STOCK gültiger Auftrag *m* bis zur Annullierung

G10 *abbr* (*Group of Ten*) ECON G10 (*Zehnergruppe*)

GTW *abbr* (*gross train weight*) TRANSP *rail* Zugbruttogewicht *nt*, *road vehicle* Bruttozuggewicht *nt*

guar *abbr* (*guaranteed*) GEN COMM gar. (*garantiert*), mit Bürgschaft gesichert

guarantee 1. *n* BANK Bürgschaft *f*, Garantie *f*, GEN COMM Garantie *f*, Gewährleistung *f*; ◆ **give a** ~ GEN COMM garantieren; **under** ~ GEN COMM unter Garantie; **2.** *vt* GEN COMM *loan* garantieren, zusichern; **3.** *vi* GEN COMM garantieren für

guarantee: ~ **agreement** *n* BANK Garantieabkommen *nt*

guaranteed *adj* (*guar*) GEN COMM garantiert (*gar.*), mit Bürgschaft gesichert; ◆ ~ **by** BANK per Aval; ~ **not to fade** GEN COMM farbecht

guarantee: ~ **deed** *n* BANK Garantieurkunde *f*

guaranteed: ~ **annual wage** *n* (*GAW*) HRM garantiertes Jahreseinkommen *nt*, jährlicher Mindestlohn *m*; ~ **bill**

of exchange *n* STOCK avalierter Wechsel *m*; ~ **facility** *n* FIN garantierter Kredit *m*; ~ **income** *n* FIN garantiertes Einkommen *nt*, Mindesteinkommen *nt*; ~ **income contract** *n* (*GIC*) INS Versicherung *f* mit garantiertem Einkommen; ~ **insurability** *n* INS *life insurance* garantierte Versicherbarkeit *f*; ~ **investment certificate** *n* FIN garantiertes Investmentzertifikat *nt*; ~ **letter of credit** *n* BANK avaliertes Akkreditiv *nt*; ~ **minimum wage** *n* HRM Garantielohn *m*, garantierter Mindestlohn *m*; ~ **mortgage** *n* BANK Hypothek *f* mit Zins- und Tilgungszahlungsgarantie eines Dritten; ~ **pay** *n* HRM garantierte Mindestzahlung *f*; ~ **price** *n* FIN Garantiepreis *m*; ~ **recovery of investment principle** *n* (*GRIP*) FIN Prinzip *nt* der garantierten Rückgewinnung des Investitionseinsatzes; ~ **security** *n* STOCK Wertpapier *nt* mit Dividendengarantie; ~ **wage** *n* HRM Garantielohn *m*; ~ **week** *n* HRM garantierter Wochenlohn *m*; ~ **weight** *n* TRANSP *stock control* garantiertes Gewicht *nt*

guarantee: ~ **for fulfillment of contract** *AmE*, ~ **for fulfilment of contract** *BrE n* LAW Garantieversprechen *nt*, Vertragserfüllungsgarantie *f*; ~ **letter** *n* STOCK Garantieschreiben *nt*; ~ **liability** *n* ACC Verbindlichkeiten aus Garantien, Bürgschaften und Avalen, Bürgschaftsverpflichtung *f*, Garantieverpflichtung *f*; ~ **of signature** *n* BANK Bestätigung *f* der Echtheit einer Unterschrift; ~ **to purchase** *n* LAW *trade contract* Abnahmeverpflichtung *f*

guarantor *n* BANK, FIN Bürge *m*, Bürgin *f*, GEN COMM Garant *m*; ~ **of a bill** *n* FIN Wechselbürge *m*, Wechselbürgin *f*

guaranty 1. *n* BANK *debt* Bürgschaft *f*, GEN COMM *to undertake obligation* Garantie *f*, Gewährleistung *f*, Sicherheit *f*; ◆ **put sb on** ~ **against sth** GEN COMM jdn vor etw warnen; **2.** *vt* GEN COMM *to undertake obligation* garantieren

guaranty: ~ **bond** *n* STOCK Garantieerklärung *f*; ~ **fund** *n* BANK, INS Deckungskapital *nt*, Garantiefonds *m*; ~ **savings bank** *n* BANK Sparkasse mit zwei verschiedenen Einlagekassen

guard: **be on one's** ~ *phr* GEN COMM auf der Hut sein; ~ **by clauses** *phr* LAW verklausulieren

guard against *vt* GEN COMM *risk* sich absichern gegen

guardian: ~ **deed** *n* PROP Verwaltungsurkunde *f*

guardianship *n* WEL Vormundschaft *f*

guessing *n* GEN COMM Rätselraten *nt*

guesstimate 1. *n infrml* GEN COMM Daumenschätzung *f* (*infrml*), Schätzung *f*; **2.** *vt infrml* GEN COMM schätzen

guest: **--house** *n* LEIS Gästehaus *nt*, Pension *f*

guestworker *n* ECON, HRM Gastarbeiter, in *m,f*, Fremdarbeiter, in *m,f*, ausländischer Arbeitnehmer *m*, ausländische Arbeitnehmerin *f*

GUI *abbr* (*graphical user interface*) COMP GUI (*grafische Benutzerschnittstelle*)

guidance *n* GEN COMM Führung *f*

guide *n* GEN COMM *manual* Handbuch *nt*

guided: ~ **interview** *n* S&M strukturiertes Interview *nt*

guideline: ~ **lives** *n pl* PROP Richtnutzungsdauer *f*, TAX Abschreibungstabellen *f pl*

guide: ~ **price** *n* GEN COMM, S&M Richtpreis *m*

guiding: ~ **principle** *n* GEN COMM Grundprinzip *nt*

guild *n* HRM Gilde *f*, Innung *f*, Zunft *f*

guilty *adj* LAW schuldig; ♦ **be ~ of gross negligence** LAW grob fahrlässig handeln

guilty: **~ person** *n* LAW Schuldige(r) *mf* [decl. as adj]

Gulf: **~ Plus** *n* ECON Frachtbasisabkommen der größten Erdölgesellschaften 1928

gun: **~ jumping** *n* STOCK voreiliges Handeln *nt*

gunslinger *n jarg* FIN aggressiver Käufer *m*

guru *n infrml* POL Parteiideologe *m*, Parteiideologin *f*

gut: **~ feeling** *n infrml* S&M instinktives Gefühl *nt*

gutter *n* MEDIA Bundsteg *m*; **~ press** *n* MEDIA Boulevardpresse *f*, Regenbogenpresse *f*, Skandalpresse *f*

guttersnipe *n* S&M *advertising* Blickfang *m*

GVW *abbr* (*gross vehicle weight*) TRANSP Fahrzeuggesamtgewicht *nt*

H

h *abbr* GEN COMM (*hour*) St. (*Stunde*), Std. (*Stunde*)

H *abbr* (*hydrogen*) ENVIR, IND H (*Wasserstoff*)

ha *abbr* GEN COMM (*hectare*) ha (*Hektar*)

habeas corpus *n* LAW Habeas Corpus, richterliche Haftprüfung *f*

habendum *n* LAW *property* Auflassungsklausel *f*

habitat *n* ENVIR *of wildlife* Lebensraum *m*

hack *vt infrml* COMP *break into systems, computers* unberechtigt in ein Computernetz eindringen, hacken (*infrml*)

hacker *n infrml* COMP Hacker *m* (*infrml*); **~-proof** *adj infrml* COMP *system, computer* geschützt vor unbefugtem Eindringen durch Hacker, hackersicher (*infrml*)

hacking *n infrml* COMP Hacken *nt* (*infrml*)

hack: ~ license *n AmE* (*cf licence to operate a taxi BrE*) TRANSP Taxikonzession *f*

haggle *vi* GEN COMM *bargain* feilschen; ◆ **~ about** GEN COMM feilschen um, handeln um; **~ over** GEN COMM feilschen um, handeln um

Hague: ~ Protocol *n* LAW Haager Protokoll *nt*; **~ Rules** *n pl* TRANSP Haager Regeln *f pl*, *shipping* Haager Vorschriften *f pl*; **The ~ Convention on the Law applicable to Contract for the Sale** *n* LAW Die Haager Konvention über das anwendbare Recht bei internationalen Kaufverträgen

Haig: ~ Simons definition of income *n* ECON Haig-Simons-Einkommensdefinition *f*

half: at ~-price *phr* GEN COMM zum halben Preis; **be on ~-time** *phr* GEN COMM halbtags arbeiten; **~ adder** *n* COMP *hardware* Halbaddierwerk *nt*; **~-board** *n* LEIS Halbpension *f*; **~ a dozen** *n* GEN COMM ein halbes Dutzend *nt*; **~-duplex** *adj* (*HDX*) COMP Halbduplexbetrieb *m*; **~ fare** *n* GEN COMM halber Preis *m*; **~-life** *n* STOCK Zeitraum *m* vor Rückzahlung der Hälfte einer Anleihe; **~-monthly** *adj* GEN COMM halbmonatlich; **~ a strike price interval** *n* STOCK *Eurodollar options* halbe Basispreisabstufung *f*; **~-time survey** *n* (*HT*) TRANSP Halbzeitübersicht *f*, Halbzeitstudie *f*, Teilzeitübersicht *f*, Teilzeitstudie *f*; **go halves with sb** *phr* GEN COMM etw mit jdm zu gleichen Teilen teilen

halftone *n* MEDIA Halbton *m*

half: ~ year *n* GEN COMM halbes Jahr *nt*; **~-yearly** *adj* GEN COMM *dividend* halbjährlich

hallmark *n* BANK Feingehaltsstempel *m*, Gütezeichen *nt*, Kennzeichen *nt*; **~ stamp** *n* BANK Feingehaltsstempel *m*

hall: ~ test *n* S&M *market research* Klassenzimmerbefragung *f*

halo *n* S&M *advertising* Einflußbereich *m*; **~ effect** *n* GEN COMM Wiedererkennungseffekt *m*

Halsey: ~ Premium Plan *n AmE* HRM Prämienplan *m* nach Halsey

hammer: ~ home *vt* GEN COMM *point* mit Nachdruck äußern; **~ the market** *vt* STOCK den Kurs durch Leerverkäufe nach unten drücken

hammer: ~ price *n* GEN COMM Auktionspreis *m*, STOCK realisierter Verkaufspreis der verbleibenden Aktien eines Mitgliedes

hamper *vt* GEN COMM *growth* behindern

hand in *vt* GEN COMM *document* einreichen; ◆ **~ one's notice** HRM kündigen; **~ one's resignation** HRM sein Rücktrittsgesuch einreichen; **~ a petition** ADMIN eine Eingabe machen

hand over *vt* GEN COMM übergeben

handbag *n* FIN Geldbörse *f*, Rücklage *f*

handbill *n* COMMS Handzettel *m*

handbook *n* GEN COMM Handbuch *nt*

hand: ~ calculator *n* COMP Taschenrechner *m*; **~-held** *adj* S&M tragbar, in der Hand zu halten, Hand-

handing: ~-over *n* GEN COMM Aushändigung *f*, Übergabe *f*

handle 1. *n* COMP Griff *m*; **2.** *vt* GEN COMM abwickeln, bearbeiten, sich befassen mit, TRANSP umschlagen; ◆ **~ large sums of money** FIN größere Geldbeträge verwalten; **~ with care** GEN COMM *label on parcels* sorgfältig behandeln

handling *n* (*hdlg*) GEN COMM Abwicklung *f*, Bearbeitung *f*, TRANSP *of goods* Handling *nt*, Umschlag *m*; **~ charge** *n* GEN COMM, S&M Bearbeitungsgebühr *f*; **~ time** *n* GEN COMM Abwicklungszeit *f*, TRANSP Transportzeit *f*

hand: ~ luggage *n* GEN COMM Handgepäck *nt*

handmade *adj* IND *production* handgemacht

hand: ~-out *n* S&M Broschüre *f*, Werbeprospekt *m*

handover *n* GEN COMM Übergabe *f*

hands: in the ~ of *phr* GEN COMM *under the ownership of* in den Händen von; **in the ~ of a third party** *phr* GEN COMM in den Händen Dritter; **be in the ~ of a receiver** *phr* LAW in den Händen eines Konkursverwalters sein; **~-off policy** *n* ECON interventionsfreie Politik *f*, Nichteinmischungspolitik *f*, GEN COMM Nichteinmischungspolitik *f*; **~-on** *adj* ECON interventionistisch, HRM intensiv, praktisch; **~-on experience** *n* HRM praktische Erfahrung *f*; **~-on session** *n* POL praktische Inangriffnahme *f* eines Vorhabens, praktisches Angehen *nt* von Problemen; **~-on training** *n* HRM praktische Ausbildung *f*

hand: ~-woven *adj* IND *production* handgewebt

handwriting *n* COMMS, GEN COMM Handschrift *f*, Schrift *f*

handwritten *adj* COMMS, GEN COMM handgeschrieben, handschriftlich

handyman *n* HRM Handwerker *m*

hang up 1. *vt* COMMS *telephone receiver* auflegen, aufhängen; **2.** *vi* COMMS *finish call* auflegen, aufhängen

hangout *n* PROP Überhang *m*

Hang Seng: ~ Index *n* STOCK Hang-Seng-Index *m*

hansom: ~ cab economy *n* ECON Volkswirtschaft, die jegliche Modernisierung ablehnt

harbor *AmE see* **harbour** *BrE*

harbormaster *AmE see* **harbourmaster** *BrE*

harbour *n BrE* TRANSP Hafen *m*; **~ authority** *n BrE* TRANSP Hafenamt *nt*, Hafenbehörde *f*; **~ dues** *n pl BrE* TAX, TRANSP Hafengebühren *f pl*, Hafengeld *nt*; **~ facilities** *n pl BrE* TRANSP Hafenanlagen *f pl*, Hafeneinrichtungen *f pl*

harbourmaster *n BrE* Hafenmeister *m*

hard *adj* GEN COMM *data, facts* hart, *difficult* schwer, schwierig

hardback 1. *adj* MEDIA *book* gebunden; **2.** *n* MEDIA *book* Buch *nt* mit festem Einband, gebundenes Buch *nt*

hard: ~ **bargaining** *n* GEN COMM unnachgiebiges Verhandeln *nt*; ~ **cash** *n* ECON Hartgeld *nt*, Metallgeld *nt*; ~ **commodity** *n* ECON Rohstoffmünzgeld *nt*, STOCK metallischer Rohstoff *m*; ~ **copy** *n* COMP Ausdruck *m*; ~~**core unemployed** *n* ECON schwer oder nicht vermittelbare Personen, Bodensatz der Arbeitslosen; ~ **cost** *n* FIN *construction, real estate* harte Kosten *pl*

hardcover 1. *adj* MEDIA *book* gebunden; **2.** *n* MEDIA *book* gebundenes Buch *nt*

hard: ~ **currency** *n* ECON, POL harte Währung *f*, konvertible Devisen *f pl*, konvertierbare Währung *f*; ~ **discount** *n* FIN festes Disagio *nt*, Diskont *m*; ~ **disk** *n* COMP *hardware* Festplatte *f*; ~ **disk drive** *n* (*HDD*) COMP Festplattenlaufwerk *nt*; ~ **disk error** GEN COMM, PATENTS Festplattenfehler *m*; ~ **disk management** *n* COMP Festplattenverwaltung *f*; ~ **disk unit** *n* COMP Festplatteneinheit *f*

hardening: ~ **market** *n* GEN COMM stetig steigender Markt *m*

hard: ~ **error** *n* COMP Beschädigung *f* auf der Festplatte; ~ **and fast** *adj* GEN COMM *rules* rechtsverbindlich; ~ **goods** *n pl* GEN COMM langlebige Wirtschaftsgüter *nt pl*; ~ **graft** *n* GEN COMM, POL Schinderei *f*, Schufterei *f*; ~ **hat** *n* HRM Schutzhelm *m*; ~~**headed** *adj* S&M dickköpfig, hartnäckig; ~ **landing** *n infrml* ECON harte Landung *f* (*infrml*), Rezession *f*, GEN COMM harte Landung *f* (*infrml*)

hardliner *n* POL Befürworter, in *m,f* einer unnachgiebigen Politik, Hardliner *m*

hard: ~ **loan** *n* BANK hartes Darlehen *nt*; ~ **money** *n* ECON *coins* Münzgeld *nt*, *currency* harte Währung *f*, Hartgeld *nt*, GEN COMM *non-credit* Bargeld *nt*, POL *financing* harte Währung *f*, von Anfang an finanziell abgesichertes Programm *nt*; ~ **page break** *n* COMP *wordprocessing* fester Seitenumbruch *m*, harter Seitenumbruch *m* (*jarg*); ~ **return** *n* COMP harter Zeilenvorschub *m*; ~ **sell** *n* S&M energische Verkaufstechnik *f*; ~ **selling** *n* S&M energische Verkaufstechnik *f*

hardship *n* ECON Erschwernis *f*, Härte *f*, WEL Erschwernis *f*, Härte *f*, *euphemism* Elend *nt*, Not *f*; ~ **clause** *n* LAW Härteklausel *f*

hardware *n* COMP Hardware *f*; ~ **compatibility** *n* COMP Hardware-Kompatibilität *f*; ~ **configuration** *n* COMP Hardware-Konfiguration *f*; ~ **device** *n* COMP Gerät *nt*; ~ **error** *n* COMP Hardware-Fehler *m*, Hardware-Versagen *nt*; ~ **firm** *n* COMP Hardware-Hersteller *m*; ~ **interrupt** *n* COMP Hardware-Interrupt *m*, Hardware-Unterbrechung *f*; ~ **requirements** *n pl* COMP Hardware-Anforderungen *f pl*; ~ **security** *n* COMP Hardware-Sicherheit *f*; ~ **specialist** *n* COMP Hardware-Spezialist *m*; ~ **upgrade** *n* COMP Hardware-Erweiterung *f*, Hardware-Upgrade *m* (*jarg*)

harmful *adj* GEN COMM schädlich; ~ **effect** *n* LAW schädliche Auswirkung *f*

harmonic: ~ **mean** *n* MATH *statistics* harmonischer Mittelwert *m*, harmonisches Mittel *nt*

harmonization *n* GEN COMM Angleichung *f*, Harmonisierung *f*; ~ **of excise duties** *n* IMP/EXP Verbrauchssteuerharmonisierung *f*; ~ **process** *n* GEN COMM Angleichungsprozeß *m*, Harmonisierungsprozeß *m*

harmonize *vt* ECON, GEN COMM, HRM angleichen, harmonisieren

Harrod: ~ **Domar model** *n* ECON Harrod-Domar-Modell *nt*

harsh: ~ **competition** *n* ECON harter Konkurrenzkampf *m*, harter Wettbewerb *m*

harshly *adv* TAX hart

hatchman *n* HRM *shipping* Schauermann *m*

hat: ~ **money** *n* TRANSP Primage *f*, Primgeld *nt*

haulage *n* TRANSP Beförderung *f*, Transport *m*, *freight charges* Rollgeld *nt*; ~ **company** *n* TRANSP Fuhrunternehmen *nt*, Fuhrunternehmer *m*, Transportunternehmen *nt*; ~ **contractor** *n* TRANSP Fernspediteur *m*, Rollfuhrunternehmen *nt*, Transportunternehmen *nt*

hauler *AmE see* **haulier** *BrE*

haulier *n BrE* IMP/EXP Spediteur *m*, TRANSP Fuhrunternehmer *m*, Spediteur *m*, Transportunternehmer *m*, Rollfuhrunternehmen *nt*, Fuhrunternehmen *nt*

Havana: ~ **Charter** *n* ECON Havanna-Charta *f*

have: ~ **cash in hand** *phr* GEN COMM über Bargeld verfügen; ~ **cash on hand** *phr* FIN über Bargeld verfügen; ~ **a competitive edge over sb** *phr* ECON einen Wettbewerbsvorteil gegenüber jdm haben; ~ **complete vehicle insurance** *phr* INS vollkaskoversichert sein; ~ **excellent references** *phr* HRM über ausgezeichnete Referenzen verfügen, über ausgezeichnete Zeugnisse verfügen; ~ **exclusive agency for** *phr* GEN COMM *a firm, company* die Alleinvertretung haben für; ~ **fully comprehensive cover** *phr* INS vollkaskoversichert sein; ~ **a headcount** *phr* GEN COMM *of people present* abzählen; ~ **a head start** *phr* GEN COMM einen Vorsprung haben; ~ **holdings in a company** *phr* GEN COMM Geschäftsanteile an einem Unternehmen halten; ~ **it out with sb** *phr* GEN COMM sich mit jdm auseinandersetzen; ~ **a loose rein** *phr* ECON, MGMNT die Zügel locker lassen; ~ **money to burn** *phr infrml* GEN COMM Geld wie Heu haben (*infrml*)

haven *n* FIN, GEN COMM, TAX Oase *f*, Zufluchtsort *m*

have: ~ **one's questions ready** *phr* MEDIA Fragen präsent haben; ~ **security of tenure** *phr* HRM, PROP Mieterschutz besitzen; ~ **signing authority** *phr* BANK unterschriftsberechtigt sein; ~ **a stranglehold on the market** *n* S&M den Markt fest im Griff haben; ~ **the sum wrong** *phr* GEN COMM etw falsch addiert haben; ~ **the upper hand** *phr* GEN COMM die Oberhand haben; ~ **a whip-round** *phr BrE infrml* HRM den Hut herumgehen lassen (*infrml*); ~ **a word with sb about sth** *phr* GEN COMM etw mit jdm besprechen

HAWB *abbr* (*house air waybill*) IMP/EXP *aviation*, TRANSP eigener Luftfrachtbrief *m*, Hausluftfrachtbrief *m*, Spediteurluftfrachtbrief *m*

hawker *n* GEN COMM Hausierer *m*, Straßenhändler, in *m,f*, Straßenverkäufer, in *m,f*, S&M Straßenhändler, in *m,f*

hazard *n* GEN COMM Gefahr *f*, Risiko *nt*; ~ **insurance** *n* INS Risikoversicherung *f*

hazardous *adj* GEN COMM gefährlich; ~ **cargo** *n* TRANSP Gefahrgut *nt*; ~ **chemical** *n* (*hazchem*) TRANSP gefährliche Chemikalie *f*; ~ **contract** *n* INS risikobehafteter Vertrag *m*, riskanter Vertrag *m*, LAW aleatorischer

Vertrag *m*; ~ **substance** *n* ENVIR gefährlicher Stoff *m*, gefährliche Substanz *f*; ~ **waste** *n* ENVIR Sondermüll *m*

hazchem *abbr* (*hazardous chemical*) TRANSP gefährliche Chemikalie *f*; ~ **code** *n* TRANSP Schlüssel *m* für gefährliche Chemikalien

h.b. *abbr* (*hours of business*) GEN COMM GeschZ (*Geschäftszeiten*)

HD *abbr* COMP (*high density*) HD (*hohe Speicherdichte*), (*hard disk*) HD (*Festplatte*)

HDD *abbr* COMP (*hard disk drive*) Festplattenlaufwerk *nt*, (*high-density disk*) Diskette *f* mit hoher Speicherdichte

hdlg *abbr* (*handling*) TRANSP Handling *nt*, Umschlag *m*

HDX *abbr* (*half-duplex*) COMP Halbduplexbetrieb *m*

head 1. *n* COMP *of disk drive* Kopf *m*, Lesekopf *m*, GEN COMM *of department* Chef, in *m,f*, IND *livestock* Stück *nt*, MEDIA *of newspaper* Schlagzeile *f*, *of document* Kopf *m*; ♦ **per ~** GEN COMM pro Kopf; **2.** *vt* LAW *inquiry* leiten

head: ~ **accountant** *n* ACC Chefbuchhalter, in *m,f*; ~ **of an agreement** *n* GEN COMM Hauptpunkt *m* eines Vertrages; ~ **of the audit group** *n* ACC Chef, in *m,f* der Prüfungsgruppe; ~ **buyer** *n* GEN COMM Einkaufsleiter, in *m,f*, S&M Haupteinkäufer, in *m,f*; ~ **clerk** *n* LAW Amtmann *m*, Geschäftsleiter, in *m,f* eines Gerichts, MGMNT Bürochef, in *m,f*, Büroleiter, in *m,f*, leitende(r) Büroangestellte(r) *mf* [decl. as adj]; ~ **of department** *n* MGMNT *administration* Abteilungsleiter, in *m,f*, Dezernent, in *m,f*

header *n* ADMIN Überschrift *f*, Schlagzeile *f*, Titelzeile *f*, COMP *typography* Kopfzeile *f*, MEDIA *broadcast* Vorspann *m*

head: ~ **foreman** *n* HRM Vorarbeiter, in *m,f*; ~ **of household** *n* TAX Haushaltsvorstand *m*

headhunt *vt* HRM abwerben, nach Führungskräften suchen, MGMNT Jagd machen auf Führungspersonal, Personal abwerben

headhunted: **be ~** *phr* HRM abgeworben werden

headhunter *n* HRM Abwerber, in *m,f*, Kopfjäger, in *m,f*

headhunting *n* HRM Abwerbung *f*

heading *n* ACC *of balance sheet* Überschrift *f*, MEDIA Rubrik *f*, Titel *m*; ♦ **be ~ for** GEN COMM auf dem Weg sein nach; ~ **into surplus** ECON *balance of payments* Aktivierung *f*

head: ~ **of legal department** *n* BrE (*cf general counsel AmE*) HRM Leiter, in *m,f* der Rechtsabteilung, Syndikus *m* einer Unternehmung

headline *n* MEDIA *newspaper* Schlagzeile *f*; ~ **rate** *n* ECON Preisindex für Einzelhandel und Lebenshaltung

head: ~ **of local tax office** *n* TAX Finanzamtsleiter, in *m,f*; ~ **office** *n* (*HO*) GEN COMM Hauptsitz *m*, Hauptverwaltung *f* (*HV*), Hauptgeschäftssitz *m*, Stammhaus *nt*, HRM Hauptsitz *m*, Hauptverwaltung *f* (*HV*), Hauptgeschäftssitz *m*, Hauptbüro *nt*; ~**-on position** *n* S&M Werbung *f* an einem Verkehrsknotenpunkt; ~ **of personnel (department)** *n* HRM, MGMNT Leiter, in *m,f* der Personalabteilung, Personalleiter, in *m,f*, MGMNT Personalchef, in *m,f*

headquarters *n pl* (*HQ*) BANK, GEN COMM, HRM Hauptbüro *nt*, Hauptsitz *m*, Hauptverwaltung *f* (*HV*), MGMNT Hauptverwaltung *f* (*HV*), Zentrale *f*

head: ~ **of state** *n* POL Staatsoberhaupt *nt*; ~ **tax** *n* TAX, WEL Kopfsteuer *f*

health *n* GEN COMM Gesundheit *f*

Health: ~ **Authority** *n* GEN COMM Gesundheitsbehörde *f*

health: ~ **benefit certificate** *n* ADMIN Gesundheitszertifikat *nt*; ~ **benefits** *n pl* INS, WEL Kassenleistungen *f pl*, Krankenversicherungsleistungen *f pl*; ~ **care industry** *n* IND Gesundheitsindustrie *f*, Gesundheitswesen *nt*; ~ **center** *AmE*, ~ **centre** *BrE n* WEL Ärztezentrum *nt*, Gemeinschaftspraxis *f*, Gesundheitszentrum *nt*; ~ **club** *n* LEIS Fitneß-Club *m*, Sport- und Fitneßcenter *nt*, Sport- und Fitneßstudio *nt*; ~ **economics** *n* ECON Gesundheitsökonomik *f*; ~ **education** *n* GEN COMM Gesundheitserziehung *f*; ~ **farm** *n* WEL Gesundheitsfarm *f*; ~ **foods** *n pl* WEL Biokost *f*, Naturkost *f*, Reformkost *f*, Vollwertkost *f*; ~**-food shop** *n* S&M Bioladen *m*, Reformhaus *nt*; ~ **grounds** *n pl* HRM gesundheitliche Gründe *m pl*; ~ **hazard** *n* WEL Gesundheitsrisiko *nt*; ~ **insurance** *n* HRM, INS, WEL Gesundheitsversicherung *f*, Krankenversicherung *f*; ~ **insurance premium** *n* HRM, INS, WEL Krankenversicherungsprämie *f*; ~ **insurance scheme** *n* HRM, INS, WEL Krankenkasse *f*, Krankenversicherungssystem *nt*; ~ **maintenance organization** *n AmE* (*HMO*) INS private Gesundheitsvorsorgeeinrichtung *f*, private Krankenversicherungsorganisation *f*; ~ **officer** *n* HRM Beamte(r) *m* [decl. as adj] des Gesundheitsamtes, Beamtin *f* des Gesundheitsamtes, Quarantänearzt *m*, Quarantäneärztin *f*, WEL Bedienstete(r) eines Gesundheitsamtes, Amtsarzt *m*, Amtsärztin *f*; ~ **record** *n* WEL Anamnese *f*, Krankengeschichte *f*; ~ **regulations** *n pl* LAW Gesundheitsvorschriften *f pl*; ~ **risk** *n* WEL Gesundheitsgefährdung *f*, Gesundheitsrisiko *nt*; ~ **and safety** *n* HRM Gesundheit und Sicherheit *f*

Health: ~ **and Safety at Work Act** *n* BrE (*HSWA*) LAW 1974 Gesetz zur Sicherheit am Arbeitsplatz; ~ **and Safety Commission** *n* BrE WEL Arbeitsschutzkommission; ~ **and Safety Executive** *n* BrE (*HSE*) WEL Amt für Gesundheit und Sicherheit; ~ **and Safety Inspectorate** *n* BrE WEL Aufsichtsamt für Gesundheit und Sicherheit am Arbeitsplatz

health: ~ **sector** *n* ECON Gesundheitswesen *nt*

healthy *adj* GEN COMM *competition* gesund

hear *vt* LAW anhören, *case* verhandeln; ♦ ~ **a case in chambers** LAW einen Rechtsstreit im Richterzimmer verhandeln

hearing *n* LAW Anhörung *f*

hearsay *n* GEN COMM Gerücht *nt*, LAW Hörensagen *nt*

heated *adj* GEN COMM *debate* leidenschaftlich

heater *n* (*htr*) GEN COMM Heizgerät *nt*

heating: ~ **industry** *n* IND Heizungsindustrie *f*; ~ **surface** *n* (*HS*) GEN COMM Heizoberfläche *f*

heat: ~**-resistant** *adj* GEN COMM hitzebeständig

heavily *adv* GEN COMM, TAX hoch, in hohem Maße; ♦ ~ **in debt** ACC, BANK, ECON überschuldet; ~ **mortgaged** ACC, BANK, ECON hoch belastet, überschuldet; ~ **traded** STOCK lebhaft gehandelt

heavily: ~ **indebted middle-income country** *n* (*HIC*) FIN stark verschuldetes Land *nt* mit Durchschnittseinkommen

heavy *adj* STOCK *market* gedrückt; ~ **advertising** *n* S&M umfangreiche Werbekampagne *f*; ~ **current** *n* IND Starkstrom *m*; ~ **demand** *n* ECON starke Nachfrage *f*; ~ **duties** *n pl* TAX hohe Steuern *f pl*; ~ **engineering** *n* IND Großmaschinenbau *m*, Schwerindustrie *f*; ~ **fuel** *n* ENVIR schweres Heizöl *nt*; ~ **goods traffic** *n* TRANSP Schwergutverkehr *m*; ~ **goods vehicle** *n* (*HGV*)

TRANSP Lastkraftwagen *m* (*LKW*), Schwergutfahrzeug *nt*; **~ industrial plant** *n* IND Großanlage *f*, Schwermaschine *f*; **~ industry** *n* IND Schwerindustrie *f*; **~ jet** *n* TRANSP Großraumflugzeug *nt*, Schwertransportjet *m*; **~ lift ship** *n* TRANSP Schwergutschiff *nt*; **~ metal concentration** *n* ENVIR Schwermetallkonzentration *f*; **~ mortgaging** *n* ACC, BANK, ECON hohe Belastung *f*, Überschuldung *f*; **~ user** *n* COMP extremer Anwender *m*, starker Nutzer *m*; **~ viewer** *n* S&M *marketing* Vielseher *m*

Heckscher-Ohlin: **~ theorem** *n* ECON Heckscher-Ohlin-Theorem *nt*; **~ trade theorem** *n* ECON Heckscher-Ohlin-Theorem *nt*

hectare *n* (*ha*) GEN COMM Hektar *m*

hedge *vt* GEN COMM sichern; ♦ **~ in by clauses** LAW verklausulieren

hedge: **~ against inflation** *n* INS Absicherung *f* gegen Inflation, Inflationssicherung *f*; **~ clause** *n* STOCK Absicherungsklausel *f*, Schutzklausel *f*

hedged: **~ asset** *n* ACC abgesichertes Vermögen *nt*; **~ liability** *n* ACC abgesicherte Verbindlichkeit *f*; **~ tender** *n* STOCK gesicherte Ausschreibung *f*, gesichertes Angebot *nt*

hedge: **~ fund** *n* STOCK stark spekulierender Investmentfonds *m*; **~ management** *n* STOCK Hedge-Verwaltung *f*; **~ manager** *n* STOCK Hedge-Manager *m*; **~ period** *n* STOCK Sicherungszeitraum *m*

hedger *n* STOCK Hedger *m*, Sichernde(r) *m* [decl. as adj]

hedge: **~ ratio** *n* STOCK Sicherungskoeffizient *m*; **~ trading** *n* STOCK Sicherungshandel *m*

hedging: **~ goal** *n* STOCK Sicherungsziel *nt*; **~ operation** *n* FIN Sicherungsoperation *f*, STOCK Kurssicherungsgeschäft *nt*; **~ strategy** *n* STOCK Sicherungsstrategie *f*

hedonic: **~ output** *n* ECON hedonische Produktion *f*; **~ price** *n* ECON hedonischer Preis *m*; **~ wages** *n pl* ECON hedonische Löhne *m pl*

hegemony *n* POL Hegemonie *f*

height *n* (*hgt*) GEN COMM Höhe *f*

heighten *vt* GEN COMM erhöhen

heir *n* LAW Erbe *m*

heiress *n* LAW Erbin *f*

heirs: **~ and assigns** *n* LAW *deeds and wills* Rechtsnachfolger *m pl*

held: **~ covered** *adj* INS *marine* ausreichend versichert, versicherungsfähig

helicopter *n* TRANSP Hubschrauber *m*; **~ money** *n* ECON Hubschraubergeld *nt*

heliport *n* TRANSP Heliport *m*, Hubschrauberflugplatz *m*, Hubschrauberlandeplatz *m*

helistop *n* TRANSP Hubschrauberlandeplatz *m*, Hubschrauberflugplatz *m*

help *n* COMP Hilfe *f*; **~ key** *n* COMP Hilfetaste *f*; **~ mode** *n* COMP Hilfemodus *m*; **~ screen** *n* COMP Hilfebildschirm *m*

hereditary: **~ lease** *n* PROP Erbpacht *f*, unkündbare Pacht *f*

hereof *adv* COMMS hieraus

hereto *adv* COMMS hierzu

hereunder *adv* COMMS hierunter

Herfindahl-Hirschman: **~ index** *n* ECON Herfindahl-Hirschman-Index *m*

Hermes: **~ Model** *n* ECON Hermes-Modell *nt*

hesiflation *n* ECON *macroeconomics* zögernde Inflation *f*

hesitate *vi* ECON zögern

heteroscedasticity *n* MATH *statistics* Heteroskedastizität *f*

heuristic *adj* COMP, GEN COMM, MGMNT *problem-solving* heuristisch

heuristics *n pl* COMP, GEN COMM, MGMNT *problem-solving* Heuristik *f*

HEW *abbr AmE* (*Department of Health, Education and Welfare*) WEL Ministerium für Gesundheit, Soziales und Wohlfahrt

H-form *n* ECON H-Form *f*

hgt *abbr* (*height*) GEN COMM Höhe *f*

HGV *abbr* (*heavy goods vehicle*) TRANSP LKW (*Lastkraftwagen*), Schwergutfahrzeug *nt*

HIC *abbr* (*heavily indebted middle income country*) FIN stark verschuldetes Land *nt* mit Durchschnittseinkommen

Hicks: **~ charts** *n pl* ECON Hicks-Pläne *m pl*

Hicksian: **~ income measure** *n* ECON Hicks-Einkommensbestimmung *f*, Hicks-Einkommensbewertung *f*

hidden *adj* GEN COMM verdeckt; **~ agenda** *n* GEN COMM verschleierte Pläne *m pl*, MGMNT geheime Tagesordnung *f*; **~ asset** *n* ACC versteckter Vermögenswert *m*, verstecktes Vermögen *nt*; **~ damage** *n* INS *maritime* verborgener Schaden *m*, versteckter Schaden *m*; **~ decision** *n* GEN COMM geheime Entscheidung *f*; **~ defect** *n* LAW verborgener Mangel *m*, versteckter Mangel *m*; **~ economy** *n* ECON Schattenwirtschaft *f*, Untergrundwirtschaft *f*; **~ file** *n* COMP versteckte Datei *f*; **~ inflation** *n* ECON verdeckte Inflation *f*, versteckte Inflation *f*; **~ persuaders** *n pl* S&M geheime Verführer *m pl*; **~ price increase** *n* S&M versteckter Preisanstieg *m*; **~ reserves** *n pl* BANK stille Rücklagen *f pl*; **~ tax** *n* TAX verdeckte Steuer *f*; **~ unemployment** *n* ECON unsichtbare Arbeitslosigkeit *f*; **~ value** *n* S&M versteckter Wert *m*

hide *vt* COMP *data* verstecken, GEN COMM verbergen, LAW verstecken

hierarchical: **~ decomposition principle** *n* MGMNT hierarchisches Dekompositionsprinzip *nt*; **~ menu** *n* COMP Baumstruktur *f*, hierarchisches Menü *nt*; **~ task analysis** *n* (*HTA*) MGMNT hierarchische Aufgabenanalyse *f*

hierarchy *n* HRM Hierarchie *f*; **~ of effects** *n* S&M Wirkungshierarchie *f*; **~ of needs** *n* HRM Bedürfnishierarchie *f*; **~ of objectives** *n* GEN COMM Zielhierarchie *f*

high 1. *adj* GEN COMM hoch; ♦ **too ~** GEN COMM *price, estimate* überhöht, zu hoch; **2.** *n* GEN COMM, STOCK Höchstkurs *m*, Höchststand *m*

high: **very ~** *adj* GEN COMM sehr hoch; **~ achiever** *n* GEN COMM, HRM Spitzenkraft *f*, Spitzenmann *m* (*infrml*); **~ added-value product** *n* ECON Produkt *nt* mit hoher Wertschöpfung; **~-caliber** *AmE*, **~-calibre** *BrE adj* HRM *staff, graduates* hochkarätig; **~ capital spending** *n* ECON rege Investitionstätigkeit *f*; **~-class** *adj* GEN COMM der Spitzenklasse, erstklassig

High: **~ Commission** *n BrE* GEN COMM Hoher Ausschuß *m*, Hohe Kommission *f*

high: **~-cost labor** *AmE*, **~-cost labour** *BrE n* HRM Hochlohn-Arbeitskräfte *f pl*

High: **~ Court of Justice** *n* LAW *England and Wales* oberstes erstinstanzliches Zivilgericht

high: **~ credit** *n* FIN Höchstkredit *m*; **~ density** *n* (*HD*) COMP hohe Speicherdichte *f* (*HD*); **~-density cargo** *n* TRANSP Kompaktfracht *f*; **~-density disk** *n* (*HDD*) COMP Diskette *f* mit hoher Speicherdichte; **~-density freight** *n* TRANSP Kompaktfracht *f*; **~ employment surplus** *n* ECON hoher Beschäftigungsüberschuß *m*; **~-end** *adj* COMP *equipment, system* hoher Leistungsbereich *m*, oberer Leistungsbereich *m*; **~-end computer** *n* COMP Hochleistungscomputer *m*, Spitzencomputer *m*; **~ end of the range** *n* STOCK *buying options positions* oberes Ende *nt* des Bereiches

higher: **~ education** *n* GEN COMM höhere Bildung *f*; **~ income bracket** *n* ECON hohe Einkommensgruppe *f*, hohe Einkommensstufe *f*

Higher: **~ National Certificate** *n* BrE (*HNC*) WEL Diplomabschluß *m*, Fachhochschulreife *f*, Fachschulabschluß *m*; **~ National Diploma** *n* BrE (*HND*) WEL Diplomabschluß *m*, Fachhochschulabschluß *m*, höherer Fachschulabschluß *m*

highest: **~ and best use** *n* PROP *appraisal* höchste und beste Nutzung *f*; **~ bid** *n* STOCK Höchstgebot *nt*; **~ bidder** *n* GEN COMM *at auction*, STOCK Meistbietende(r) *mf* [decl. as adj]; **~ price** *n* GEN COMM Höchstkurs *m*, Bestpreis *m*, STOCK Höchstkurs *m*, Höchstpreis *m*; **~ tender** *n* GEN COMM Höchstgebot *nt*

high: **~ executive** *n* HRM hochstehende Führungskraft *f*; **~ finance** *n* FIN Hochfinanz *f*, Kreditaufnahme *f* bis zur äußersten Grenze; **~ flier** *n* GEN COMM *company* Spitzenunternehmen *nt*, HRM *personnel* Hochbegabte(r) *mf* [decl. as adj], Erfolgsmensch *m*, MGMNT *person* Ehrgeizling *m* (*infrml*), Senkrechtstarter *m* (*infrml*), STOCK Spitzenwert *m*; **~-flying stock** *n* STOCK hoch bewertete Aktien *f pl*; **~-frequency radiotelephony** *n* TRANSP *shipping* drahtlose Hochfrequenztelefonie *f*, drahtloses Hochfrequenzfernsprechwesen *nt*, Hochfrequenzsprechfunk *m*; **very ~ frequency** *n* (*VHF*) COMMS, GEN COMM, MEDIA Ultrakurzwelle *f* (*UKW*); **very ~ frequency radiotelephony** *n* TRANSP *shipping* Ultrakurzwellensprechfunk *m*; **~-grade bond** *n* STOCK erstklassige Schuldverschreibung *f*; **~ image** *n* GEN COMM starkes Image *nt*; **~-level decision** *n* GEN COMM Entscheidung *f* auf höchster Ebene; **~-level language** *n* (*HLL*) COMP höhere Programmiersprache *f*; **~ leverage** *n* AmE FIN starke Fremdfinanzierung *f*; **~-leveraged takeover** *n* AmE (*HLT*) GEN COMM Übernahme *f* mit hoher Fremdfinanzierung

highlight *vt* COMP *wordprocessing*, GEN COMM *differences* hervorheben

highlighted *adj* COMP hellerleuchtet, hervorgehoben

highlighting *n* COMP, GEN COMM Hervorhebung *f*

highlights *n pl* GEN COMM Glanzlichter *nt pl*, Highlights *nt pl*

high: **~ loader** *n* TRANSP *vehicle* Hochlader *m*

highly: **~ competitive** *adj* GEN COMM *market* höchst wettbewerbsfähig, *strategy* wettbewerbsintensiv; **~ geared** *adj* STOCK überkapitalisiert; **~ skilled** *adj* HRM hochqualifiziert

high: **~ office** *n* HRM hohes Amt *nt*, wichtiges Amt *nt*; **~-order language** *n* COMP höhere Programmiersprache *f*; **~-pollution area** *n* ENVIR Belastungsgebiet *nt*, hochbelastetes Gebiet *nt*; **~-powered** *adj* GEN COMM *person* hochrangig; **~-powered money** *n* ECON Geldbasis *f*; **~-premium convertible debenture** *n* STOCK Hoch-

prämien-Wandelschuldverschreibung *f*; **~-pressure selling** *n* S&M aggressive Verkaufspolitik *f*; **~ price** *n* STOCK hoher Preis *m*; **~-profile** *adj* S&M hochprofiliert; **~-profile company** *n* S&M hoch angesehenes Unternehmen *nt*; **~-quality product** *n* (*cf upscale product AmE*) GEN COMM hochwertiges Produkt *nt*, S&M Qualitätsprodukt *nt*; **~-quality workmanship** *n* GEN COMM Qualitätsarbeit *f*; **~ rate of investment** *n* ECON hohe Investitionsrate *f*; **~-resolution** *adj* COMP *graphics, scanner, VDU* hochauflösend; **~ return** *n* STOCK *market* hoher Ertrag *m*, hohe Rendite *f*, hohe Verzinsung *f*; **~-rise** *n* PROP, WEL *building* Hochhaus *nt*; **~-risk** *adj* STOCK *market* risikoreich; **~-risk venture** *n* GEN COMM risikoreiche Unternehmung *f*; **~-school diploma** *n* AmE (*cf leaving certificate BrE*) WEL Abschlußzeugnis *nt*

High: **~ School Diploma** *n* AmE (*cf A level BrE, Advanced level BrE*) GEN COMM, WEL Abschluß der Sekundarstufe, ≈ Abitur *nt*, ≈ Hochschulreife *f*, ≈ Matura *f* (*Öst, Sch*), ≈ Maturitätsprüfung *f* (*Sch*), ≈ Reifeprüfung *f* (*obs*)

high: **~-season fare** *n* LEIS Hochsaisonpreis *m*; **~-speed memory** *n* COMP Schnellspeicher *m*; **~-speed printer** *n* COMP Schnelldrucker *m*; **~-speed train** *n* (*HST*) TRANSP Hochgeschwindigkeitszug *m*; **~ standard of living** *n* WEL hoher Lebensstandard *m*; **~ standards** *n pl* GEN COMM hohe Normwerte *m pl*; **~-stream** *adj* IND hochentwickelt; **~ street** *n* BrE S&M Haupteinkaufsstraße *f*, Hauptstraße *f*; **~-street bank** *n* BrE BANK Bankfiliale *f*; **~-street share shop** *n* BrE STOCK Börsenmaklerbüro auf der Hauptstraße; **~-street spending** *n* BrE ECON Ausgaben *f pl*, Konsumausgaben *f pl*; **~-strength** *adj* GEN COMM stark; **~-tech** *adj* COMP, GEN COMM, IND hochtechnologisch, technisch ausgereift; **~ technology** *n* COMP, GEN COMM, IND Hochtechnologie *f*; **~ technology industry** *n* IND Spitzentechnologie *f*; **~-tech stock** *n* STOCK High-Tech-Aktien *f pl*; **~-value clearings** *n pl* BrE BANK Clearing *nt* von hohen Beträgen; **~ value to low weight ratio** *n* TRANSP Verhältnis *nt* von hohem Wert zu geringem Gewicht; **~-voltage current** *n* IND Starkstrom *m*; **~-volume** *adj* STOCK umsatzstark, volumenreich; **~-volume paper clearings** *n pl* BrE BANK Clearingsystem *nt* für den Massenwertpapierverkehr

highway *n* AmE (*cf trunk road BrE*) TRANSP ≈ Bundesstraße *f*, Fernstraße *f*; **~ order** *n* LAW, PROP *compulsory purchase* Kaufverpflichtung *f*

high: **~-yield** GEN COMM ertragreich; **~-yield crops** *n pl* GEN COMM ertragreiche Anbausorten *f pl*; **~-yield financing** *n* FIN Hochzinsfinanzierung *f*

hike 1. *n* GEN COMM *price* Anstieg *m*; **2.** *vt* AmE GEN COMM *price* steigen

hinder *vt* GEN COMM *growth* behindern

hindrance *n* GEN COMM Behinderung *f*

hint *n* ECON, GEN COMM, MGMNT Andeutung *f*, Fingerzeig *m*, Hinweis *m*, Tip *m*, Anflug *m*

hire 1. *n* GEN COMM Mieten *nt*, Leihen *nt*, *wages* Lohn *m*; ♦ **off ~** TRANSP *chartering* ohne Charter, ohne Frachtauftrag; **2.** *vt* GEN COMM mieten, HRM *staff* chartern, einstellen; ♦ **~ and fire** HRM einstellen und entlassen, heuern und feuern (*infrml*)

hire out *vt* GEN COMM verleihen

hire: **~ car** *n* BrE (*cf rental car AmE*) LEIS Mietwagen *m*

hired *adj* HRM *person* eingestellt; ~ **car** *n BrE* (*cf rented car AmE*) LEIS Mietwagen *m*

hire: ~ **of money** *n* FIN Leihkapital *nt*; ~ **purchase** *n BrE* S&M Ratenkauf *m*, LAW Abzahlungskauf *m*, Mietkauf *m*; **on** ~ **purchase** *phr BrE* (*cf on the installment plan AmE*) FIN auf Abzahlungsbasis, auf Raten; ~**-purchase agreement** *n* FIN Ratenkaufvertrag *m*, Teilzahlungsvertrag *m*, LAW Mietkaufvertrag *m*; ~**-purchase contract** *n BrE* FIN Abzahlungsvertrag *m*; ~**-purchase period** *n BrE* FIN Abzahlungszeitraum *m*; ~**-purchase price** *n* GEN COMM Abzahlungspreis *m*; ~**-purchase sale** *n BrE* GEN COMM, S&M Abzahlungsverkauf *m*; ~**-purchase transaction** *n BrE* GEN COMM Abzahlungsgeschäft *nt*; ~ **and reward operator** *n* TRANSP *road haulage* Charter- und Vergütungs-Unternehmer *m*

hiring: ~ **out** *n* GEN COMM Verleihung *f*

histogram *n* MATH Balkendiagramm *nt*, Histogramm *nt*

historical *adj* ACC *accounts, records*, ECON, GEN COMM, PROP, TRANSP historisch; ~ **cost** *n* ACC *costs* Anschaffungskosten *pl* (*AK*), Herstellungskosten (*HK*); ~ **cost concept** *n* ACC Anschaffungswertprinzip *nt*; ~ **loss** *n* ACC angefallener Verlust *m*, Verlustvortrag *m*

historically *adv* ACC, ECON, GEN COMM, PROP, TRANSP historisch

Historical: ~ **School** *n* ECON historische Schule *f*

historical: ~ **trade** *n* TRANSP historischer Handel *m*

historic: ~ **building** *n* PROP historisches Gebäude *nt*; ~ **structure** *n* PROP historisches Gebäude *nt*

hit *vt* ECON treffen, GEN COMM aufprallen auf [+acc]; ◆ ~ **the bid** STOCK einen Geldkurs akzeptieren; ~ **the bricks** *AmE* GEN COMM, HRM, IND streiken; ~ **a low** GEN COMM einen Tiefstand erreichen; ~ **the market** S&M *product* einschlagen

hit: ~**-and-run strike** *n* HRM kurzer Warnstreik *m*; ~ **list** *n infrml* GEN COMM Abschußliste *f* (*infrml*), Hitliste *f* (*infrml*), POL *of tasks, projects* Aktionsliste *f*; ~**-or-miss** *adj infrml* GEN COMM *method* aufs Geratewohl; ~ **rate** *n* S&M Trefferquote *f*

hive off *vt* ECON *shares* abstoßen, ausgründen, GEN COMM *department, section* ausgliedern

hive: ~**-off** *n* GEN COMM *department, section* Ausgliederung *f* von Betriebsteilen

HLL *abbr* (*high-level language*) COMP höhere Programmiersprache *f*

HLT *abbr* (*high-leveraged takeover*) GEN COMM Übernahme *f* mit hoher Fremdfinanzierung

HMC *abbr BrE* (*Her Majesty's Customs*) IMP/EXP britische Zollbehörde

HMC&E *abbr BrE* (*Her Majesty's Customs and Excise*) IMP/EXP, TAX britische Zoll- und Steuerbehörde

HM: ~ **Customs and Excise** *n BrE* (*Her Majesty's Customs and Excise*) IMP/EXP, TAX britische Zoll- und Steuerbehörde; ~ **Customs Officer** *n BrE* HRM Zollbeamte(r) *m* [decl. as adj], Zollbeamtin *f*

HMG *abbr BrE* (*Her Majesty's Government*) POL Regierung Ihrer Majestät

HMO *abbr AmE* (*health maintenance organization*) INS private Gesundheitsvorsorgeeinrichtung *f*, private Krankenversicherungsorganisation *f*

HMS *abbr BrE* (*Her Majesty's Ship*) TRANSP königliches Schiff

HMSO *abbr BrE* (*Her Majesty's Stationery Office*) GEN COMM Staatsverlag, der auch die staatlichen Stellen mit Bürobedarf versorgt

HNC *abbr BrE* (*Higher National Certificate*) WEL Diplomabschluß *m*, Fachhochschulreife *f*, Fachschulabschluß *m*

HND *abbr BrE* (*Higher National Diploma*) WEL Diplomabschluß *m*, Fachhochschulabschluß *m*, höherer Fachschulabschluß *m*

HO *abbr* (*head office*) GEN COMM Hauptbüro *nt*, Hauptsitz *m*, HV (*Hauptverwaltung*), Verwaltungssitz *m*, Zentrale *f*

hoarding *n* S&M Anschlagtafel *f*, Plakatwand *f*, Reklamefläche *f*; ~ **site** *n* S&M Standort *m* von Plakatwand

H of C *abbr BrE* (*House of Commons*) POL britisches Unterhaus, ≈ Bundestag *m*

hog: ~ **cycle** *n* ECON Schweinezyklus *m*

H of L *abbr BrE* (*House of Lords*) POL britisches Oberhaus, ≈ Bundesrat *m*

hold 1. *n* TRANSP *shipping* Laderaum *m*, Schiffsraum *m*; **2.** *vt* GEN COMM *enquiry* durchführen, *referendum* abhalten, MGMNT *conference* veranstalten, abhalten, durchführen, POL *opinion* vertreten, *post* innehaben; ◆ ~ **a position** STOCK eine Wertpapierposition halten; ~ **in-service training** HRM eine innerbetriebliche Schulung abhalten; ~ **as a security** INS als Sicherheit halten; ~ **bonds** STOCK Obligationen verwalten; ~ **elections** POL wählen; ~ **funds for a check** *AmE*, ~ **funds for a cheque** *BrE* BANK Vermögen für einen Scheck zurückbehalten; ~ **in check** ECON *prices* in Schach halten; ~ **in custody** LAW verwahren; ~ **margins** ECON Margen halten, FIN Deckungssummen innehaben, GEN COMM Margen halten; ~ **office** POL im Amt bekleiden, im Amt sein, politische Macht besitzen; ~ **one's ground** GEN COMM sich behaupten; ~ **sb liable for sth** GEN COMM, LAW jdn für etw haftbar machen; ~ **sb responsible for sth** GEN COMM, LAW jdn für etw verantwortlich machen; ~ **the line** COMMS *on telephone* bleiben Sie bitte am Apparat; ~ **an opinion poll** GEN COMM, S&M eine Umfrage veranstalten; ~ **the purse strings** ECON über den Geldbeutel verfügen

holdback *n* PROP einbehaltener Teil *m* der Vertragssumme, Einbehaltung *f*; ~ **pay** *n* HRM zurückgehaltener Lohn *m*

holder: ~ **for value** *n* BANK *of bill of exchange* entgeltlicher Inhaber *m*, entgeltliche Inhaberin *f*; ~ **in due course** *n* LAW rechtmäßiger Inhaber *m*, rechtmäßige Inhaberin *f*; ~ **of an office** *n* HRM Amtsinhaber, in *m,f*; ~ **of record** *n* STOCK eingetragener Wertpapierinhaber *m*, eingetragene Wertpapierinhaberin *f*

hold: ~**-harmless agreement** *n AmE* LAW *contract* Schadloshaltungsvereinbarung *f*; ~**-harmless clause** *n* LAW *contract* Schadloshaltungsklausel *f*

holding *n* LAW Besitzen *nt*, FIN Paket *nt*, STOCK *of shares and stock* Besitz *m*, Paket *nt*; ◆ ~ **the market** *phr* STOCK ständiger Zukauf einer bestimmten Aktie

holding: ~ **company** *n* ACC Dachgesellschaft *f*, Holdinggesellschaft *f*, BANK, FIN, GEN COMM Holdinggesellschaft *f*, LAW Holdinggesellschaft *f*, Muttergesellschaft *f*, STOCK Holdinggesellschaft *f*; ~ **gains** *n pl* ACC Wertzuwachs *m* eines Effektenbestandes; ~ **in a bank** *n* BANK Anteil *m* an einer Bank; ~ **pattern** *n* STOCK Situation, in der nichts passiert, TRANSP *plane* Warteschleife *f*; ~ **period** *n* STOCK

Besitzdauer *f*, Verwahrzeitraum *m*; ~ **of securities** *n* BANK Wertpapierbestand *m*

holdover: ~ **effect** *n* GEN COMM Resteffekt *m*; ~ **relief** *n* TAX Steuerermäßigung *f* des Restbestandes, Steuernachlaß *m* des Restbetrages; ~ **tenant** *n* AmE PROP Mieter, der Auszug verweigert

hold: ~**-up** *n* ECON Stockung *f*

hole *n* COMP, GEN COMM Loch *nt*

holiday *n* BrE (*cf vacation AmE*) HRM, LEIS Ferien *pl*, Urlaub *m*; ◆ **on ~** BrE (*cf on vacation AmE*) LEIS im Urlaub, auf Urlaub; **go on ~** (*cf go on vacation AmE*) GEN COMM, HRM, LEIS Ferien machen, in die Ferien gehen, in Urlaub gehen

holiday: ~ **accommodation** *n* PROP Ferienunterkunft *f*; ~ **allowance** *n* BrE (*cf vacation allowance AmE*) HRM Urlaubsgeld *nt*; ~ **bonus** *n* BrE (*cf vacation bonus AmE*) HRM Urlaubsgeld *nt*; ~ **entitlement** *n* HRM Urlaubsanspruch *m*; ~ **guest** *n* BrE (*cf vacation guest AmE*) LEIS Feriengast *m*; ~ **leave** *n* BrE LEIS Urlaub *m*; ~ **and leisure insurance** *n* INS Ferien- und Freizeitversicherung *f*, Urlaubs- und Freizeitversicherung *f*; ~**-maker** *n* BrE (*cf vacationist AmE*) LEIS Urlauber, in *m,f*; ~ **pay** *n* BrE (*cf vacation pay AmE*) HRM Urlaubsgeld *nt*; ~ **period** *n* LEIS Ferienzeit *f*, Urlaubszeit *f*

home *n* WEL *institution* Heim *nt*; ◆ **at ~ and abroad** GEN COMM im In- und Ausland

home: **one's own ~** *n* PROP Eigenheim *nt*; ~ **affairs** *n pl* POL Inlandsangelegenheiten *f pl*, innere Angelegenheiten *f pl*, *domestic policy* Innenpolitik *f*, innenpolitische Fragen *f pl*; ~ **audit** *n* S&M Hausrevision *f*; ~ **banking** *n* BANK Abwicklung von Bankgeschäften von zu Hause, Home Banking *nt*; ~ **computer** *n* COMP Heimcomputer *m*; ~ **contents insurance** *n* INS Hausratversicherung *f*; ~ **counties** *n pl* GEN COMM, IMP/EXP Grafschaften in Südostengland; ~ **country** *n* FIN, GEN COMM Mutterland *nt*; ~**-country control** *n* ECON, FIN Kontrolle *f* durch das Mutterland; ~ **economics** *n* ECON Hauswirtschaft *f*; ~ **equity loan** *n* BANK Wohnungsbaudarlehen *nt*; ~**-grown** *adj* GEN COMM aus eigenem Anbau, aus Eigenproduktion; ~ **improvement** *n* PROP Eigenheiminvestitionen *f pl*, Hausreparaturen *f pl*, Wohnungsreparaturen *f pl*; ~ **improvement loan** *n* BANK Wohnungsinstandsetzungsdarlehen *nt*

homeless *adj* WEL obdachlos; ~ **person** *n* WEL Obdachlose(r) *mf* [decl. as adj]

home: ~ **loan** *n* BANK Hypothek *f*, Wohnungsbaudarlehen *nt*; ~ **loss payment** *n* PROP finanzielle Unterstützung bei Wohnungsverlust; ~**-made** *adj* GEN COMM aus Eigenproduktion; ~ **market** *n* ECON Binnenmarkt *m*, Inlandsmarkt *m*; ~ **mortgage** *n* BANK Eigenheimhypothek *f*; ~ **mortgage loan** *n* BANK auf dem Eigenheim gesichertes Hypothekendarlehen *nt*

Home: ~ **Office** *n* BrE (*cf Department of the Interior AmE*) POL Innenministerium *nt*

homeowners': ~ **association** *n* PROP Eigentümerverband *m*; ~ **equity account** *n* BANK Kapitalkonto *nt* von Eigenheimbesitzern

home: ~ **ownership** *n* PROP Eigenheimbesitz *m*, Hausbesitz *m*, Wohneigentum *nt*, Wohnungseigentum *nt*

homeowners': ~ **policy** *n* INS Versicherung *f* für Hauseigentümer; ~ **warranty program** *AmE*, ~ **warranty**

programme *BrE* *n* INS Garantieprogramm *nt* für Hauseigentümer

home: ~ **product** *n* GEN COMM Inlandsprodukt *nt*; ~ **production** *n* ECON einheimische Erzeugnisse *nt pl*, Inlandsproduktion *f*; ~ **purchase loan** *n* BANK Eigenheimerwerbsdarlehen *nt*; ~ **sales** *n pl* ADMIN Inlandsumsatz *m*, S&M Inlandsverkäufe *m pl*

homestead *n* AmE (*cf farmstead BrE*) PROP Gehöft *nt*, Bauernhof *m*; ~ **tax exemption** *n* AmE TAX Steuerermäßigung *f* für Eigenheime

home: ~ **study course** *n* WEL Fernstudium *nt*; ~ **trade** *n* ECON Binnenhandel *m*; ~ **trade passenger ship** *n* TRANSP Passagierküstenschiff *nt*; ~ **trade ship** *n* TRANSP Küstenschiff *nt*

homeward: ~ **voyage** *n* TRANSP Heimfahrt *f*, Rückfahrt *f*

homework *n* ECON, HRM Heimarbeit *f*

homeworker *n* HRM Heimarbeiter, in *m,f*

homogeneous *adj* GEN COMM homogen; ~ **good** *n* ECON homogenes Gut *nt*; ~ **market** *n* S&M homogener Markt *m*; ~ **oligopoly** *n* ECON homogenes Oligopol *nt*

homologation *n* IMP/EXP Genehmigung *f*, Homologation *f*

homoscedasticity *n* MATH *statistics* Homoskedastizität *f*

honest *adj* GEN COMM aufrichtig; ~ **broker** *n* POL ehrlicher Makler *m*, ehrlicher Unterhändler *m*

honesty *n* GEN COMM Aufrichtigkeit *f*

honeycomb: ~ **slip** *n* FIN Bienenwabenschein *m*, STOCK *underwriting* Deckungszusage *f* mit vielen Ausschlußklauseln; ~ **slip endorsement** *n* STOCK *underwriting* Indossament in Ergänzung zur Deckungszusage des Brokers

honor *AmE see* **honour** *BrE*

honorarium *n* GEN COMM Honorar *nt*

honorary: **in an ~ capacity** *phr* HRM ehrenamtlich; ~ **chairman** *n* HRM Ehrenvorsitzende(r) *mf* [decl. as adj]; ~ **chairman of the board of directors** *n* MGMNT Ehrenvorsitzende(r) *mf* [decl. as adj] des Verwaltungsrats, Ehrenvorstand *m* der Geschäftsleitung; ~ **membership** *n* HRM Ehrenmitgliedschaft *f*; ~ **president** *n* HRM Ehrenpräsident, in *m,f*, ehrenamtlicher Präsident *m*, ehrenamtliche Präsidentin *f*

honour 1. *n* BrE GEN COMM Auszeichnung *f*; **2.** *vt* BrE BANK *debt, bill* einlösen, honorieren, *cheque* bezahlen, GEN COMM *commitment* erfüllen; ◆ ~ **a bill** *BrE* FIN einen Wechsel honorieren

honours: ~ **graduate** *n* BrE GEN COMM Inhaber, in *m,f* eines akademischen Grades

hook: ~ **up to** *phr infrml* COMP anschließen an [+acc]

horizon: **on the ~** *phr* GEN COMM am Horizont; ~ **analysis** *n* FIN Horizontanalyse *f*

horizontal *adj* GEN COMM horizontal; ~ **amalgamation** *n* ECON, GEN COMM horizontale Fusion *f*, horizontaler Zusammenschluß *m*; ~ **analysis** *n* ACC horizontale Analyse *f*; ~ **balance sheet** *n* ACC horizontale Bilanz *f*; ~ **channel integration** *n* MGMNT horizontale Integration *f*; ~ **combination** *n* ECON, GEN COMM horizontaler Zusammenschluß *m*; ~ **communication** *n* GEN COMM horizontale Kommunikation *f*; ~ **discrimination** *n* ECON horizontale Diskriminierung *f*; ~ **equity** *n* TAX horizontale Steuergerechtigkeit *f*; ~ **expansion** *n* ECON horizontales Wachstum *nt*; ~ **integration** *n* ECON horizontale Integration *f*; ~ **merger** *n* ECON, GEN COMM horizontaler Zusammenschluß *m*; ~ **publication** *n*

MEDIA *print* horizontale Publikation *f*; ~ **specialization** *n* MGMNT horizontale Arbeitsteilung *f*, horizontale Spezialisierung *f*; ~ **union** *n* HRM horizontale Fachgewerkschaft *f*

horsepower *n (HP)* IND, TRANSP Pferdestärke *f (PS)*

horse: ~ **trading** *n* HRM Kuhhandel *m (infrml)*, POL Kuhhandel *m (infrml)*

hospital: ~ **daily rate** *n* WEL Pflegesatz *m*; ~ **revenue bond** *n* FIN Krankenhausertragsanleihe *f*

host *n* COMP Host *m*; ~ **city** *n* GEN COMM Gastgeberstadt *f*; ~ **computer** *n* COMP Host-Computer *m*, Verarbeitungsrechner *m*; ~ **country** *n* ECON, GEN COMM, LEIS Gastland *nt*; ~**-driven** *adj* COMP hauptrechnergesteuert

hostile: ~ **fire** *n* INS Brand *m*, Schadenfeuer *nt*

hot *adj* BANK *bills* neu; ♦ **in the ~ seat** HRM *candidate* in einer kitzligen Situation, in einer knffligen Situation

hot: ~ **bills** *n pl* BANK Schatzwechsel, die in der jeweils zurückliegenden Woche emittiert wurden; ~ **cargo clause** *n* HRM Klausel über Erzeugnisse eines bestreikten Betriebs

hotel *n* LEIS, PROP Hotel *nt*; ~ **accommodation** *n* LEIS Hotelunterbringung *f*, Hotelunterkunft *f*

hotelier *n* LEIS, PROP Hotelier *m*

hotel: ~ **manager** *n* LEIS, PROP Hotelmanager, in *m,f*; ~ **proprietor** *n* LEIS, PROP Hotelbesitzer, in *m,f*; ~ **register** *n* LEIS Hotelregister *nt*, Hotelverzeichnis *nt*

hot: ~ **issue** *n AmE* STOCK Spekulationswert *m*; ~ **key** *n* COMP Taste zum Aufruf von Befehlsfolgen, Hotkey *m (jarg)*, Hotkey-Taste *f (jarg)*, Schnelltaste *f*, Kurzbefehl *m*

hotline *n* COMMS *politics* heißer Draht *m*, COMP Hotline *f*, Schnellberatung *f* am Telefon, POL heißer Draht *m*

hot: ~**-metal setting** *n* MEDIA *printing* Bleisatz *m*; ~ **money** *n* ADMIN, GEN COMM Fluchtgelder *nt pl*, heißes Geld *nt*; ~ **property** *n infrml* S&M *advertising* heiße Ware *f (infrml)*; ~**-selling line** *n* S&M Verkaufsschlager *m*; ~ **shop** *n* S&M hervorragende Agentur *f*; ~ **stock** *n* GEN COMM heiße Ware *f (infrml)*, STOCK neu emittierte Aktien, die stark im Preis steigen; ~ **type** *n* MEDIA *printing* Bleisatz *m*

hour *n (h, hr)* GEN COMM Stunde *f (St., Std.)*

hourly: ~ **compensation** *n* HRM Stundenvergütung *f*; ~ **paid employee** *n* HRM Stundenlohnempfänger, in *m,f*; ~ **pay** *n* HRM stundenweise Bezahlung *f*; ~ **wage** *n* HRM Stundenlohn *m*; ~ **worker** *n* HRM Stundenlohnempfänger, in *m,f*

hours: ~ **of business** *n pl (h.b.)* GEN COMM Geschäftszeiten *f pl*; ~ **of work** *n pl* GEN COMM, HRM Arbeitszeit *f*

house *n* LAW Haus *nt*, POL Kammer *f*, PROP Haus *nt*

House: the ~ *n BrE infrml* STOCK Spitzname für die Londoner Börse

house: ~ **agent** *n* WEL Wohnungsmakler, in *m,f*; ~ **air waybill** *n (HAWB)* IMP/EXP, TRANSP *aviation* eigener Luftfrachtbrief *m*, Hausluftfrachtbrief *m*, Spediteurluftfrachtbrief *m*; ~ **bill of lading** *n* IMP/EXP, TRANSP Spediteurkonnossement *nt*

housebuilding *n* PROP Wohnungsbau *m*

house: ~**-building loan** *n* BANK Baudarlehen *nt*

House: ~ **of Commons** *n BrE (H of C)* POL britisches Unterhaus, ≈ Bundestag *m*

house/depot *phr* IMP/EXP Werk/Speicher, TRANSP Haus/Lager

household *n* GEN COMM Haushalt *m*; ~ **appliance** *n* GEN COMM Haushaltsgerät *nt*; ~ **behavior** *AmE*,

~ **behaviour** *BrE n* ECON Haushaltsverhalten *nt*; ~ **commodities** *n pl* GEN COMM Haushaltswaren *f pl*; ~ **decision-making** *n* ECON Haushaltsentscheidungen *f pl*; ~ **durables** *n pl* S&M dauerhafte Haushaltskonsumgüter *nt pl*; ~ **effects** *n pl* INS Hausrat *m*; ~ **goods** *n pl* GEN COMM Haushaltswaren *f pl*; ~ **name** *n* S&M Haushaltsname *m*

house: ~ **journal** *n* MEDIA Firmenzeitung *f*, Werkszeitung *f*

House: ~ **of Lords** *n BrE (H of L)* POL britisches Oberhaus, ≈ Bundesrat *m*

house: ~ **magazine** *n* S&M Betriebszeitschrift *f*; ~ **mailing** *n* S&M Hausversand *m*; ~ **mortgage** *n* BANK Wohnungsbauhypothek *f*; ~ **prices** *n pl* PROP Hauspreise *m pl*; ~ **purchase** *n* PROP Hauskauf *m*

House: ~ **of Representatives** *n AmE* POL Repräsentantenhaus *nt*, ≈ Bundestag *m*

house: ~ **search** *n* LAW Hausdurchsuchung *f*; ~ **style** *n* GEN COMM Stil *m* des Hauses, MEDIA *print* firmeneigener Stil *m*; ~**-to-house** *phr* IMP/EXP von Haus zu Haus, TRANSP Haus-Haus; ~**-to-house sampling** *n* S&M Probenverteilung *f* an Haushalte; ~**-to-house selling** *n* S&M Haustürverkauf *m*

housewife *n* GEN COMM Hausfrau *f*

housing *n* GEN COMM Wohnungsbau *m*; ~ **allowance** *n* HRM, WEL Mietzuschuß *m*, Wohngeld *nt*; ~ **bond** *n* PROP Schuldverschreibung *f* zum Hausbau; ~ **code** *n* PROP Wohnungsbauverordnung *f*; ~ **complex** *n* PROP Wohnhauskomplex *m*, Wohnkomplex *m*; ~ **construction** *n* PROP Wohnungsbau *m*; ~ **department** *n BrE (cf accommodation bureau AmE)* WEL Wohnungsamt *nt*, Wohnungsvermittlung *f*; ~ **development** *n* PROP *new houses* Neubaugebiet *nt*, *policy* Entwicklung *f* des Wohnwesens; ~ **estate** *n* PROP Wohnsiedlung *f*; ~ **industry** *n* IND Wohnungswirtschaft *f*; ~ **loan** *n* BANK Wohnungsbaudarlehen *nt*; ~ **market** *n* PROP Wohnungsmarkt *m*; ~ **mortgage loan** *n* BANK Wohnungsbauhypothek *f*; ~ **office** *n* WEL Wohnungsamt *nt*; ~ **project** *n AmE* WEL Bauvorhaben *nt*; ~ **scheme** *n BrE* WEL Bauvorhaben *nt*; ~ **shortage** *n* PROP Wohnungsnot *f*; ~ **subsidy** *n* WEL Wohnungsbaubeihilfe *f*

Housing: ~ **and Urban Development Department** *n AmE (HUD Department)* PROP Ministerium für Wohnungs- und Städtebau

hovercraft *n* TRANSP Luftkissenboot *nt*, Luftkissenfahrzeug *nt*

hoverport *n* TRANSP Hafen *m* für Luftkissenboote

HP *abbr* IND *(horsepower)* PS *(Pferdestärke)*, S&M *(hire-purchase BrE)* Mietkauf *m*, Ratenkauf *m*, TRANSP *(horsepower)* PS *(Pferdestärke)*

HQ *abbr (headquarters)* GEN COMM HV *(Hauptverwaltung)*

hr *abbr (hour)* GEN COMM St. *(Stunde)*, Std. *(Stunde)*

HRA *abbr (human resource accounting)* ADMIN, HRM Humankapitalrechnung *f*, Humanvermögensrechnung *f*

HRD *abbr (human resource development)* ADMIN, HRM Personalentwicklung *f*

HRM *abbr (human resources management)* ADMIN, HRM Personalmanagement *nt*

HRP *abbr (human resource planning)* ADMIN, HRM Personalplanung *f*

HS *abbr (heating surface)* GEN COMM Heizoberfläche *f*

HSE *abbr BrE* (*Health and Safety Executive*) WEL Amt für Gesundheit und Sicherheit

HST *abbr* (*high-speed train*) TRANSP Hochgeschwindigkeitszug *m*

HSWA *abbr BrE* (*Health and Safety at Work Act*) LAW *1974* Gesetz zur Sicherheit am Arbeitsplatz

HT *abbr* TRANSP (*half-time survey*) Halbzeitübersicht *f*, Halbzeitstudie *f*, Teilzeitübersicht *f*, Teilzeitstudie *f*

HTA *abbr* (*hierarchical task analysis*) MGMNT hierarchische Aufgabenanalyse *f*

htr *abbr* (*heater*) GEN COMM Heizgerät *nt*

hub: ~ **of activity** *n* GEN COMM Geschäftsmittelpunkt *m*; ~ **branch** *n* BANK zentrale Zweigstelle *f*

huckster *n* AmE *infrml* GEN COMM *street trader* Straßenhändler, in *m,f*, Hausierer, in *m,f*, Straßenverkäufer, in *m,f*, S&M *advertising* Werbefritze *m* (*infrml*)

HUD: ~ **Department** *n* AmE (*Housing and Urban Development Department*) PROP Ministerium für Wohnungs- und Städtebau

huge *adj* GEN COMM *debt* sehr hoch, *order* sehr groß

Hulbert: ~ **rating** *n* FIN Hulbert-Klassifizierung *f*

hull: ~ **insurance** *n* INS *marine* Schiffskaskoversicherung *f*; ~ **underwriter** *n* INS *marine* Schiffskaskoversicherer *m*

human: ~ **asset accounting** *n* HRM Humanvermögensrechnung *f*; ~ **capital** *n* ADMIN Arbeitsvermögen *nt*, ECON Arbeitsvermögen *nt*, Humankapital *nt*; ~ **consumption** *n* ENVIR *of water* menschlicher Verbrauch *m*; ~ **engineering** *n* ADMIN Arbeitsplatzgestaltung *f*, HRM Ergonomie *f*; ~ **factors** *n pl* HRM *industrial psychology* Humanfaktoren *m pl*; ~ **relations** *n pl* GEN COMM, HRM *management theory* Human Relations *pl*, zwischenmenschliche Beziehungen *f pl*; ~ **resource accounting** *n* (*HRA*) ADMIN, HRM Humanvermögensrechnung *f*, Humankapitalrechnung *f*; ~ **resource administration** *n* HRM Personalverwaltung *f*; ~ **resource development** *n* (*HRD*) ADMIN, HRM Personalentwicklung *f*; ~ **resource management** *n* (*HRM*) HRM Personalmanagement *nt*; ~ **resource planning** *n* (*HRP*) HRM Personalplanung *f*; ~ **resources** *n pl* ADMIN, HRM Arbeitskräfte *f pl*, Humankapital *nt*, Humanvermögen *nt*; ~ **resources management** *n* (*HRM*) HRM Personalmanagement *nt*; ~ **rights** *n pl* LAW Menschenrechte *nt pl*; ~-**scale economics** *n* ECON humane Skaleneffekte *m pl*

Humphrey-Hawkins: ~ **Act** *n* AmE POL Humphrey-Hawkins-Gesetz *nt*

hunch *n* S&M inneres Gefühl *nt*

hundredweight *n* AmE (*cwt*) GEN COMM Zentner *m*

hurdle *n* GEN COMM Hürde *f*; ~ **rate** *n* ECON *budgeting*

capital expenditures erwartete Mindestrendite *f*; ~ **rate of return** *n* FIN erforderliche Investitionsrendite *f*, erwartete Mindestrendite *f*

hush: ~ **money** *n infrml* GEN COMM Bestechungsgeld *nt*, Schweigegeld *nt*

hustle *vt* AmE *infrml* GEN COMM *goods* etw ergaunern

hustle: ~ **and bustle** *n* GEN COMM lebhaftes Treiben *nt*

hybrid: ~ **annuity** *n* INS Mischrente *f*; ~ **auction** *n* STOCK gemischte Auktion *f*; ~ **computer** *n* COMP Analog-Digital-Rechner *m*, Hybridcomputer *m*, Hybridrechner *m*; ~ **income tax** *n* TAX hybride Einkommenssteuer *f*

hydraulic *adj* IND hydraulisch; ~ **coupling** *n* (*HC*) IND Hydraulikkupplung *f*, Strömungskupplung *f*, Turbokupplung *f*

hydrocarbon *n* ENVIR Kohlenwasserstoff *m*

hydrocharter *n* TRANSP *shipping* Hydrocharter *f*

hydrodynamic *adj* IND hydrodynamisch

hydroelectric *adj* ENVIR *energy*, IND *power* hydroelektrisch; ~ **power** *n* ENVIR Strom *m* aus Wasserkraftwerk, Wasserkraftstrom *m*; ~ **power station** *n* IND Wasserkraftwerk *nt*

hydrofoil *n* TRANSP Tragflügelboot *nt*

hydrogen *n* (*H*) ENVIR, IND Wasserstoff *m* (*H*)

hydrometer *n* ENVIR Hydrometer *nt*

hydrostatics *n* IND Hydrostatik *f*, Statik *f*

hygroscopic: ~ **substance** *n* ENVIR hygroskopische Substanz *f*

hype *n* GEN COMM, S&M übertriebene Werbung *f*

hyperinflation *n* ECON Hyperinflation *f*

hypermarket *n* S&M Verbrauchergroßmarkt *m*, Großeinkaufszentrum *nt*

hyphenation *n* COMP Silbentrennung *f*

hypothecate *vt* PROP verpfänden

hypothecated *adj* PROP verpfändet

hypothecation *n* PROP *expenditure* Verpfändung *f*; ~ **certificate** *n* BANK Verpfändungsbescheinigung *f*

hypothesis *n* ECON, GEN COMM Hypothese *f*; ~ **testing** *n* MATH *statistics* Hypothesentest *m*, Überprüfung *f* einer Hypothese

hypothetical *adj* GEN COMM hypothetisch; ~ **circumstances** *n pl* GEN COMM hypothetische Umstände *m pl*; ~ **conditions** *n pl* GEN COMM hypothetische Bedingungen *f pl*; ~ **point** *n* GEN COMM hypothetischer Punkt *m*; ~ **question** *n* GEN COMM hypothetische Frage *f*; ~ **situation** *n* GEN COMM hypothetische Lage *f*

hysteresis *n* ECON Hysterese *f*

I

IACS *abbr* (*International Association of Classification Societies*) GEN COMM Internationaler Verband *m* der Klassifizierungsgesellschaften

IAEC *abbr* (*International Association of Environmental Coordinators*) ENVIR Internationale Vereinigung *f* der Umweltkoordinatoren

IAM *abbr BrE* (*Institute of Administrative Management*) MGMNT Institut *nt* für Verwaltungsmanagement

IAPC *abbr* (*International Auditing Practices Committee*) ACC Internationaler Ausschuß *m* für Buchprüfungspraktiken

IAPH *abbr* (*International Association of Ports and Harbours*) IMP/EXP Internationaler Hafenverband *m*

IAPIP *abbr* (*International Association for the Protection of Industrial Property*) LAW Internationaler Verband *m* für gewerbliche Schutzrechte

IASC *abbr* (*International Accounting Standards Committee*) ACC Internationaler Ausschuß *m* für Rechnungslegungsgrundsätze

IATA *abbr* (*International Air Transport Association*) TRANSP IATA (*Internationaler Lufttransportverband*)

IB *abbr* GEN COMM (*invoice book*) Rechnungsbuch *nt*, IMP/EXP (*in bond*) unverzollt

IBC *abbr* (*intermediate bulk container*) TRANSP *shipping* Massengutfrachter *m*

IBEC *abbr* BANK (*International Bank for Economic Cooperation*) Internationale Bank *f* für wirtschaftliche Zusammenarbeit

IBELS *abbr BrE* (*interest-bearing eligible liabilities*) BANK verzinsliche mindestreservepflichtige Einlagen *f pl*

IBF *abbr* (*international banking facility*) BANK internationale Bankfazilität *f*

ibid. *abbr* (*ibidem*) GEN COMM ebd. (*ebenda*)

ibidem *adv* (*ibid.*) GEN COMM ebenda (*ebd.*)

IBOR *abbr* (*interbank offered rate*) BANK Interbankenangebotssatz *m*

IBRC *abbr BrE* (*Insurance Brokers' Registration Council*) INS Registrierungsausschuß *m* der Versicherungsmakler

IBRD *abbr* (*International Bank for Reconstruction and Development*) BANK IBWE (*Internationale Bank für Wiederaufbau und Entwicklung*), Weltbank *f*

IC *abbr* COMP (*integrated circuit*) IS (*integrierter Schaltkreis*), FIN (*investment committee*) Investitionsausschuß *m*, TRANSP (*inland container*) Inlandscontainer *m*

ICA *abbr* ACC (*Institute of Chartered Accountants*) ≈ IdW (*Institut der Wirtschaftsprüfer*), GEN COMM (*International Cooperation Administration*) Verwaltung *f* für internationale Zusammenarbeit, STOCK (*International Commodity Agreement*) internationales Rohstoffabkommen *nt*

ICAEW *abbr* (*Institute of Chartered Accountants in England and Wales*) ACC Institut *nt* der Wirtschaftsprüfer von England und Wales

ICAI *abbr* (*Institute of Chartered Accountants in Ireland*) ACC Institut *nt* der Wirtschaftsprüfer von Irland

ICAO *abbr* (*International Civil Aviation Organization*) TRANSP IZLO (*Internationale Zivilluftfahrtorganisation*)

ICAS *abbr* (*Institute of Chartered Accountants of Scotland*) ACC Institut *nt* der Wirtschaftsprüfer von Schottland

ICC *abbr* ECON (*income-consumption curve*) Einkommenskonsumkurve *f*, (*Interstate Commerce Commission AmE*) US-Bundesverkehrsbehörde, GEN COMM (*International Chamber of Commerce*) Internationale Handelskammer *f*

ICCH *abbr* (*International Commodities Clearing House*) STOCK internationale Clearingstelle *f* für Terminkontrakte London

ICCs *abbr* (*industrial and commercial companies*) ECON gewerblich-industrielle Unternehmen *nt pl*, industrielle und kommerzielle Unternehmen *nt pl*

ICD *abbr* (*inland clearance depot*) IMP/EXP Inlandsabfertigungslager *nt*

iceberg: **~ company** *n jarg* GEN COMM Eisberg-Gesellschaft *f*

ICEM *abbr* (*Intergovernmental Committee for European Migration*) WEL ICEM (*zwischenstaatliches Komitee für europäische Auswanderung*)

ICETT *abbr BrE* (*Industrial Council for Educational & Training Technology*) WEL Industrierat *m* für Fortbildungstechnologie

ICFTU *abbr* (*International Confederation of Free Trade Unions*) HRM, LAW IBFG (*Internationaler Bund Freier Gewerkschaften*)

ICHCA *abbr* (*International Cargo-Handling Coordinating Association*) TRANSP internationaler Verband *m* für die Koordinierung von Frachtangelegenheiten

ICIE *abbr* (*International Centre for Industry and the Environment*) IND internationales Zentrum *nt* für Industrie und Umwelt

ICJ *abbr* (*International Court of Justice*) LAW IGH (*Internationaler Gerichtshof*)

ICMA *abbr BrE* (*Institute of Cost and Management Accountants*) ACC Institut *nt* der Kostenrechner und Wirtschaftsprüfer

icon *n* COMP Icon *nt*, Piktogramm *nt*, Symbol *nt*; ◆ **by ~** COMP nach Symbol

ICOR *abbr* (*incremental capital-output ratio*) FIN marginaler Kapitalkoeffizient *m*

ICRC *abbr* (*International Committee of the Red Cross*) WEL IKRK (*Internationales Komitee vom Roten Kreuz*)

ICS *abbr* TRANSP (*International Chamber of Shipping*) ICS (*Internationale Schiffahrtskammer*), (*Institute of Chartered Shipbrokers*) Institut *nt* für zugelassene Schiffsmakler

ICTB *abbr* (*International Customs Tariffs Bureau*) IMP/EXP Internationales Zolltarifbüro *nt*

ICU *abbr* (*International Clearing Union*) ECON Internationale Clearingunion *f*, Internationale Verrechnungsinstitution *f*

id. *abbr* (*idem*) GEN COMM id. (*idem*)

ID *abbr* COMP (*identification*) ID (*Identifikation*), IMP/EXP,

TAX (*import duty*) Einfuhrzoll *m*, Importabgabe *f*, Importzoll *m*

IDA *abbr* ECON (*International Development Association*) UN IDA (*Internationale Entwicklungsorganisation*), IMP/EXP, TAX (*Import Duty Act*) Importzollgesetz *nt*

IDB *abbr BrE* (*interdealer broker*) BANK Makler, der ausschließlich Geschäfte zwischen Primärhändlern vermittelt

ID: ~ **card** *n* (*identity card*) ADMIN *issued by company* Ausweiskarte *f*, Perso *m* (*infrml*), *issued by state* Personalausweis *m*

IDD *abbr* (*international direct dialing AmE, international direct dialling BrE*) COMMS Selbstwählfernverkehr *m*

ideal *adj* GEN COMM ideal; ~ **capacity** *n* ECON Betriebsoptimum *nt*; ~ **limit** *n* ECON Idealgrenze *f*; ~ **standard cost** *n* ACC, ADMIN Sollkosten *pl*, Normkosten *pl*, Vorgabekosten *pl*

idem *adj* (*id.*) GEN COMM idem (*id.*)

identification *n* (*ID*) COMP Identifikation *f* (*ID*); ~ **number** *n* (*ID-number*) COMP Identifikationsnummer *f* (*ID-Nummer*); ~ **problem** *n* ECON *econometrics* Identifikationsproblem *nt*

identifier *n* COMP Bezeichner *m*, Feldname *m*

identity: ~ **card** *n* (*ID card*) ADMIN *issued by company* Ausweiskarte *f*, Perso *m* (*infrml*), *issued by state* Personalausweis *m*

id est *phr* (*i.e.*) GEN COMM das heißt (*d.h.*)

IDF *abbr* (*interdepartmental flexibility*) HRM bereichsübergreifende Flexibilität *f*, abteilungsübergreifende Flexibilität *f*

idle *adj* ADMIN frei, BANK unrentabel, GEN COMM stillstehend, HRM frei, ungenutzt, IND, MGMNT unproduktiv, TRANSP im Leerlauf, stillstehend; ~ **balance** *n* ECON Spekulationskasse *f*, FIN brachliegende Guthaben *nt pl*, anlagebereite Mittel *nt pl*, *for takeover purposes* Kriegskasse *f* (*jarg*); ~ **capacity** *n* ECON freie Kapazität *f*, ungenutzte Kapazität *f*, GEN COMM Kapazitätsreserve *f*, IND freie Kapazität *f*, Leerlaufkapazität *f*, ungenutzte Kapazität *f*, TRANSP freie Kapazität *f*; ~ **money** *n* ECON brachliegendes Geld *nt*, Spekulationskasse *f*, FIN Überschußreserven *f pl*; ~ **shipping** *n* TRANSP Leerverschiffung *f*; ~ **time** *n* ADMIN Leerzeit *f*, COMP Leerlaufzeit *f*, Stillstandszeit *f*, GEN COMM Stillstandszeit *f*, HRM ungenutzte Zeit *f*, INS Stillstandszeit *f*; ~ **tonnage** *n* TRANSP *shipping* ungenutzte Tonnage *f*

ID: ~ **number** *n* (*identification number*) COMP ID-Nummer *f* (*Identifikationsnummer*)

IDRC *abbr* (*International Development Research Centre*) GEN COMM Internationales Entwicklungsforschungszentrum *nt*

i.e. *abbr* (*id est*) GEN COMM d.h. (*das heißt*)

IEA *abbr* ECON *BrE* (*Institute of Economic Affairs*) Institut für Wirtschaftsangelegenheiten, ENVIR (*International Energy Agency*) IEA (*Internationale Energie-Agentur*)

IET *abbr* (*Interest Equalization Tax*) TAX Zinsausgleichsteuer *f*

I/F *abbr* (*insufficient funds*) FIN ungenügende Deckung *f*

IFAD *abbr* (*International Fund for Agricultural Development*) BANK IFAD (*Internationaler Agrarentwicklungsfonds*)

IFAP *abbr* (*International Federation of Agricultural Producers*) IND internationaler Verband *m* der Produzenten landwirtschaftlicher Erzeugnisse

IFC *abbr* (*International Finance Corporation*) FIN IFC (*Internationale Finanzkorporation*)

IFS *abbr BrE* (*Institute for Fiscal Studies*) TAX Institut für fiskalische Studien

IFTU *abbr* (*International Federation of Trade Unions*) HRM IGB (*Internationaler Gewerkschaftsbund*)

IGLU *abbr* (*index growth linked units*) STOCK indexwachstumsgebundene Fondsanteile *m pl*

ignite *vt* GEN COMM *panic, reaction, dispute* auslösen

igniter *n* GEN COMM Zünder *m*, TRANSP *hazardous cargos* Gefahrgut *nt*

ignorance *n* LAW Unwissenheit *f*

ignorantia juris neminem excusat *phr* LAW Unkenntnis des Gesetzes schützt nicht vor Strafe

ignore *vt* MGMNT unberücksichtigt lassen

ihp *abbr* (*indicated horsepower*) TRANSP indizierte Pferdestärke *f*

IIF *abbr* (*Institute for International Finance*) FIN Internationales Finanzinstitut *nt*, Internationales Finanzwirtschaftsinstitut *nt*

IITA *abbr* (*International Institute for Tropical Agriculture*) ECON Internationales Institut *nt* für tropische Landwirtschaft

I/L *abbr* (*import licence BrE, import license AmE*) IMP/EXP Einfuhrbewilligung *f*, Einfuhrgenehmigung *f*, Importbewilligung *f*, Importgenehmigung *f*, Importlizenz *f*

ILA *abbr* (*international language for aviation*) TRANSP internationale Luftfahrtsprache *f*

illegal *adj* LAW gesetzwidrig, illegal, unrechtmäßig, unzulässig; ~ **alien** *n* LAW illegaler Einwanderer *m*; ~ **character** *n* COMP unzulässiges Zeichen *nt*; ~ **dividend** *n* LAW unrechtmäßiger Gewinnanteil *m*; ~ **immigrant** *n* ADMIN illegaler Einwanderer *m*; ~ **immigration** *n* ADMIN, LAW illegale Einwanderung *f*; ~ **operation** *n* COMP unzulässige Operation *f*; ~ **strike** *n* HRM wilder Streik *m*

illegible *adj* GEN COMM *handwriting* unleserlich, undeutlich; ~ **address** *n* COMMS unleserliche Anschrift *f*

ill: ~ **health** *n* GEN COMM schlechte Gesundheit *f*

illiquid *adj* BANK, FIN fest angelegt, illiquid, nicht flüssig; ~ **assets** *n pl* FIN illiquides Aktivvermögen *nt*

illth *n* ECON schädliche Konsumgüter *nt pl* und Dienstleistungen *f pl*

illusory: ~ **profit** *n* FIN Scheingewinn *m*

illustrate *vt* MEDIA illustrieren

illustration *n* GEN COMM *example* Beispiel *nt*, MEDIA *picture*, PATENTS Illustration *f*

ill: ~ **will** *n* GEN COMM böser Wille *m*

ILO *abbr* HRM (*International Labour Office BrE, International Labor Office AmE*) IAA (*Internationales Arbeitsamt*), IND (*International Labour Organization*) IAO (*Internationale Arbeitsorganisation*)

ILOC *abbr* (*irrevocable letter of credit*) BANK unwiderrufliches Akkreditiv *nt*

ILR *abbr BrE* (*independent local radio*) MEDIA unabhängige lokale Radiosender

image *n* COMP Bild *nt*, S&M Image *nt*; ~ **advertising** *n* S&M Imagewerbung *f*; ~ **audit** *n* S&M Imageprüfung *f*; ~ **file** *n* COMP *computer graphics* Bilddatei *f*; ~ **projection** *n* S&M *marketing* Imageprojektion *f*

imaging *n* S&M Imageanzeige *f*

IMB *abbr* (*International Maritime Bureau*) TRANSP internationales Seefahrtsbüro *nt*

imbalance *n* FIN Ungleichgewicht *nt*, gestörtes Gleichgewicht *nt*

imbalanced: **~ working** *n* HRM unausgeglichene Arbeitsweise *f*

imbalance: **~ of orders** *n* STOCK Auftragsmißverhältnis *nt*; **~ of trade** *n* ECON, IMP/EXP, POL Handelsbilanzungleichgewicht *nt*

IMC *abbr* (*International Maritime Committee*) TRANSP internationales Seerechtskomitee *nt*

IMDG: **~ Code** *abbr* (*International Maritime Dangerous Goods Code*) TRANSP *shipping* internationaler Code *m* für Seegefahrgüter

IMF *abbr* (*International Monetary Fund*) ECON IWF (*Internationaler Währungsfonds*)

IMM *abbr* (*International Monetary Market*) ECON, STOCK internationaler Geldmarkt *m*

immaterial *adj* GEN COMM unwesentlich, LAW rechtsunerheblich, beweisunerheblich

immature *adj* HRM unreif

IMM: **~ CD index** *n* (*International Monetary Market Certificate of Deposit index*) STOCK Internationaler Geldmarkt-Einlagenzertifikat-Index *m*

immediate *adj* GEN COMM augenblicklich, unverzüglich; ♦ **for ~ attention** GEN COMM zur sofortigen Kenntnisnahme; **for ~ delivery** GEN COMM zur unverzüglichen Lieferung; **for ~ release** MEDIA *print* zur sofortigen Veröffentlichung

immediate: **~ access** *n* COMP Direktzugriff *m*; **~ aim** *n* GEN COMM unmittelbares Ziel *nt*; **~ family** *n* STOCK direkte Familie *f*, unmittelbare Familie *f*

immediately *adv* GEN COMM sofort, unverzüglich

immediate: **~ money transfer** *n* (*IMT*) BANK sofortige Geldüberweisung *f*; **~ occupancy** *n* PROP sofortiger Einzug *m*; **~-or-cancel order** *n* STOCK Auftrag *m* zur sofortigen Ausführung; **~ rebate** *n* GEN COMM Sofortrabatt *m*

immigrant *n* ADMIN Einwanderer, in *m,f*; **~ worker** *n* ECON, HRM ausländischer Arbeitnehmer *m*, ausländische Arbeitnehmerin *f*

immigration *n* ECON Einwanderung *f*, Immigration *f*; **~ control** *n* ADMIN Einwanderungskontrolle *f*; **~ officer** *n* (*IO*) GEN COMM Beamte(r) *m* [decl. as adj] der Einwanderungsbehörde, Beamtin *f* der Einwanderungsbehörde, Einwanderungsbeamte(r) *m* [decl. as adj], Einwanderungsbeamtin *f*; **~ official** *n* ADMIN, HRM Einwanderungsbeamte(r) *m* [decl. as adj], Einwanderungsbeamtin *f*; **~ policy** *n* LAW Einwanderungspolitik *f*

imminent: **~ danger** *n* INS drohende Gefahr *f*, akute Gefahr *f*, unmittelbare Gefahr *f*; **~ peril** *n* INS drohende Gefahr *f*, akute Gefahr *f*, unmittelbare Gefahr *f*

immiseration *n* ECON Verelendung *f*

immiserizing: **~ growth** *n* ECON Verelendungswachstum *nt*, Verarmungswachstum *nt*

immobilization *n* FIN Stillegung *f*

immobilize *vt* FIN stilllegen

immovable: **~ estate** *n* PROP Liegenschaft *f*; **~ property** *n* PROP unbewegliches Vermögen *nt*

IMM: **~ T-bill index** *n* (*International Monetary Market Treasury bill index*) STOCK Internationaler Geldmarkt-Schatzwechsel-Index *m*

immune: **~ from** *phr* LAW befreit von

immunity *n* HRM, LAW Immunität *f*; **~ from taxes** *n* TAX Steuerfreiheit *f*

immunization *n* FIN, MGMNT Immunisierungsstrategie *f*

IMO *abbr* (*international money order*) BANK, COMMS, LAW Auslandspostanweisung *f*

imp. *abbr* (*import, importation*) ECON, IMP/EXP Imp. (*Import*), Einf. (*Einfuhr*), Einführung *f*

impact *n* GEN COMM Anstoß *m*, *effect* Auswirkung *f*, Stoßwirkung *f*; ♦ **have an ~ on** GEN COMM sich auswirken auf [+acc]

impacted: **~ area** *n* TAX Wirkungsbereich *m*, Wirkungsgebiet *nt*

impact: **~ effect** *n* ECON Anstoßwirkung *f*; **~ multiplier** *n* ECON Impaktmultiplikator *m*, Wirkungsmultiplikator *m*; **~ printer** *n* COMP Anschlagdrucker *m*; **~ study** *n* S&M Untersuchung *f* der Werbewirksamkeit

impair *vt* ECON, GEN COMM beeinträchtigen, schädigen

impairment *n* INS, LAW Schädigung *f*; **~ of performance** *n* LAW Leistungsminderung *f*, Leistungsstörung *f*; **~ of value** *n* ACC *of security*, ECON, PROP Wertminderung *f*

impartial *adj* GEN COMM unparteiisch

impasse *n* GEN COMM Sackgasse *f*

impede *vt* GEN COMM *growth* behindern

imperfect: **~ competition** *n* ECON unvollständiger Wettbewerb *m*; **~ market** *n* ECON unvollkommener Markt *m*; **~ obligation** *n* LAW Naturalobligation *f*, unvollkommene Verbindlichkeit *f*

impetus *n* GEN COMM Anstoß *m*, Impuls *m*

impinge: **~ on sb's rights** *phr* LAW auf die Rechte eines anderen übergreifen, in die Rechte eines anderen eingreifen

implement *vt* COMP *system* implementieren, GEN COMM *plans* ausführen

implementation *n* COMP Implementierung *f*, ECON Ausführung *f*, Durchführung *f*, GEN COMM Ausführung *f*, Durchführung *f*, Realisierung *f*, LAW Ausführung *f*, Durchführung *f*, MGMNT Realisierung *f*; **~ lag** *n* ECON Durchführungsverzögerung *f*

implementing: **~ ordinance** *n* LAW Durchführungsverordnung *f*, Ausführungsanordnung *f*; **~ regulations** *n pl* LAW Durchführungsbestimmungen *f pl*, Ausführungsbestimmungen *f pl*

implicated *adj* LAW mitschuldig

implications *n pl* GEN COMM Auswirkungen *f pl*

implicit *adj* GEN COMM implizit, LAW *acceptance* stillschweigend; **~ basis of contract** *n* LAW Geschäftsgrundlage *f*; **~ contract theory** *n* ECON Theorie *f* des stillschweigend geschlossenen Vertrags; **~ marginal income** *n* ECON implizites Marginaleinkommen *nt*; **~ price deflator** *n* ECON impliziter Deflator *m*

implied *adj* LAW *acceptance* stillschweigend; **~ agency** *n* LAW stillschweigende Vollmacht *f*; **~ condition** *n* GEN COMM stillschweigende Bedingung *f*; **~ contract** *n* LAW konkludent geschlossener Vertrag *m*; **~ easement** *n* LAW stillschweigende dienstbarkeitsähnliche Verpflichtung *f*; **~ in fact contract** *n* LAW durch konkludentes Handeln zustande gekommener Vertrag *m*; **~ obligation** *n* LAW stillschweigende Verpflichtung *f*; **~ price index** *n* ECON impliziter Preisindex *m*; **~ repo rate** *n infrml* FIN implizite Repo-Rate *f*, geltende Rückkaufrate *f*; **~ terms of a contract** *n pl* LAW im Vertrag miteingeschlossene Rechte und Pflichten *pl*, unterstellte Vertragsbestimmungen *f pl*; **~ warranty** *n*

LAW gesetzliche Gewährleistung *f*, stillschweigende Mängelhaftung *f*

imply *vt* GEN COMM beinhalten, implizieren

import 1. *n* (*imp.*) ECON, IMP/EXP Einfuhr *f* (*Imp.*), Import *m* (*Imp.*); **2.** *vt* COMP *data* importieren, ECON, IMP/EXP, TAX einführen, importieren

import: ~ **admission** *n* IMP/EXP *customs* Einfuhrerlaubnis *f*; ~ **allowance** *n* IMP/EXP zollfreie Einfuhrmenge *f*

importance *n* GEN COMM Bedeutung *f*, Belang *m*, Wesentlichkeit *f*

important *adj* GEN COMM wichtig; **very ~ cargo** *n* (*VIC*) TRANSP sehr wichtige Fracht *f*; **very ~ object** *n* (*VIO*) TRANSP sehr wichtiges Objekt *nt*; ~ **office** *n* HRM hohes Amt *nt*, wichtiges Amt *nt*; **very ~ person** *n* (*VIP*) GEN COMM bedeutende Persönlichkeit *f* (*VIP*), sehr wichtige Person *f* (*VIP*), hohes Tier *nt* (*infrml*) (*VIP*)

importation *n* (*imp.*) ECON, IMP/EXP Einfuhr *f* (*Einf.*), Einführung *f*, Import *m* (*Imp.*)

import: ~ **berth** *n* TRANSP *shipping* Importliegeplatz *m*; ~ **clerk** *n* HRM Importsachbearbeiter, in *m,f*; ~ **depot charges** *n pl* IMP/EXP Importlagergebühren *f pl*; ~ **director** *n* HRM, IMP/EXP, MGMNT Importdirektor, in *m,f*; ~ **documentation supervisor** *n* HRM Sachbearbeiter, in *m,f* für Einfuhrpapiere; ~ **duty** *n* (*ID*) IMP/EXP, TAX Einfuhrzoll *m*, Importabgabe *f*, Importzoll *m*

Import: ~ **Duty Act** *n* (*IDA*) IMP/EXP, TAX Importzollgesetz *nt*

imported *adj* COMP, ECON, IMP/EXP, TAX importiert; ~ **goods** *n pl* ECON Importwaren *f pl*, IMP/EXP Importgüter *nt pl*, Importwaren *f pl*; ~ **inflation** *n* ECON importierte Inflation *f*; ~ **services** *n pl* ECON, TAX importierte Dienstleistungen *f pl*

importer *n* IMP/EXP Importfirma *f*, Importhändler, in *m,f*, Importeur, in *m,f*

import: ~**-export** *n* COMP, IMP/EXP Import-Export *m*

import/export: ~ **merchant** *n* BrE (*cf export management company AmE*) IMP/EXP Außenhandelsunternehmen *nt*

import: ~ **groupage operator** *n* HRM Sammelladungsimporteur, in *m,f*

importing *n* IMP/EXP Importtätigkeit *f*, Einfuhrtätigkeit *f*

import: ~ **letter of credit** *n* FIN, IMP/EXP Importakkreditiv *nt*; ~ **licence** *BrE*, ~ **license** *AmE n* IMP/EXP Einfuhrbewilligung *f*, Einfuhrgenehmigung *f*, Importbewilligung *f*, Importgenehmigung *f*, Importlizenz *f*; ~ **licensing** *n* IMP/EXP Einfuhrgenehmigungsverfahren *nt*, Erteilung *f* von Importlizenzen; ~ **manager** *n* HRM Importleiter, in *m,f*; ~ **penetration ratio** *n* IMP/EXP Importanteil *m*, Importquote *f*; ~ **permit** *n* IMP/EXP Importerlaubnis *f*; ~ **price** *n* ECON Importpreis *m*; ~ **quota** *n* IMP/EXP Einfuhrkontingent *nt*, Importquote *f*; ~ **release note** *n* (*IRN*) IMP/EXP Importfreigabebescheinigung *f*; ~ **sales executive** *n* HRM Importverkaufsleiter, in *m,f*; ~ **shed** *n* IMP/EXP Importhalle *f*, Importschuppen *m*; ~ **substitution** *n* IMP/EXP Importsubstitution *f*; ~ **surplus** *n* ECON, IMP/EXP Importüberschuß *m*; ~ **tariff** *n* IMP/EXP, TAX Einfuhrzoll *m*, Importabgabe *f*, Importzoll *m*; ~ **trade** *n* IMP/EXP Importgeschäft *nt*, Importhandel *m*

impose *vt* GEN COMM *restrictions, penalty*, LAW *limits, restrictions* auferlegen, verhängen; ♦ ~ **a fine on** LAW zu einer Geldstrafe verurteilen; ~ **a tax on sb** TAX jdm eine Steuer auferlegen; ~ **sth on sb** ECON, GEN COMM, POL jdm etw auferlegen

imposition *n* ECON Besteuerung *f*, GEN COMM *burden, request* Auferlegung *f*, LAW Verhängung *f*, TAX Abgabe *f*, Besteuerung *f*, Steuer *f*; ~ **of a fine** *n* LAW Verhängung *f* einer Geldbuße

impossibility *n* LAW Unmöglichkeit *f*; ~ **ab initio** *n* LAW anfängliche Unmöglichkeit *f*; ~ **at the time of making** *n* LAW anfängliche Unmöglichkeit *f*; ~ **of performance** *n* LAW Unmöglichkeit *f* der Leistung; ~ **theorem** *n* ECON Unmöglichkeitstheorem *nt*

impound *vt* LAW beschlagnahmen, pfänden, sicherstellen, verwahren

impound: ~ **account** *n* FIN beschlagnahmtes Konto *nt*, eingefrorenes Konto *nt*

impoundment *n* BANK, LAW Verwahrung *f*

impoverished *adj* FIN verarmt

impression *n* GEN COMM Eindruck *m*, Wirkung *f*

impressionable *adj* GEN COMM beeinflußbar

impressive *adj* GEN COMM beeindruckend

imprest *n* FIN Vorschuß *m*; ~ **account** *n* ACC Vorschußkonto *nt*; ~ **fund** *n* ACC Spesenkasse *f*, kleine Kasse *f*, Vorschußkasse *f*; ~ **system** *n* ACC Kassenvorschußsystem *nt*

imprint *n* MEDIA *of book, newspaper* Impressum *nt*, S&M Abdruck *m*, Aufdruck *m*

imprison *vt* LAW inhaftieren

imprisonment *n* LAW Haft *f*, Inhaftierung *f*, *sentence* Gefängnisstrafe *f*

improve *vt* GEN COMM verbessern; ♦ ~ **profitability** FIN die Ertragskraft verbessern

improved *adj* GEN COMM verbessert; ~ **area** *n* GEN COMM bebaute Fläche *f*; ~ **land** *n* ENVIR, PROP erschlossenes Gelände *nt*, erschlossenes Gebiet *nt*

improvement *n* GEN COMM Verbesserung *f*; ~ **in the art** *n* PATENTS technischer Fortschritt *m*; ~ **in balance of trade** *n* ECON Verbesserung *f* der Handelsbilanz; ~ **notice** *n* BrE HRM *health and safety* Verbesserungsauflage *f*; ~ **patent** *n* PATENTS Verbesserungspatent *nt*, Vervollkommnungspatent *nt*, Zusatzpatent *nt*

improvements: ~ **and betterments insurance** *n* INS Versicherung *f* für Werterhöhungen und Qualitätsverbesserungen

improvise *vi* GEN COMM improvisieren

impulse *adj* GEN COMM, S&M spontan; ~ **buy** *n* S&M Spontankauf *m*; ~ **buyer** *n* GEN COMM, S&M Impulskäufer, in *m,f*; ~ **buying** *n* GEN COMM, S&M Impulskauf *m*; ~ **goods** *n pl* S&M spontan gekaufte Waren *f pl*; ~ **purchase** *n* S&M Spontankauf *m*; ~ **sale** *n* S&M Spontanverkauf *m*

impure: ~ **public good** *n* ECON Mischgut *nt*

imputation *n* ECON fiktive Buchung *f*, unterstellte Transaktion *f*, TAX Anrechnung *f*

imputed: ~ **costs** *n pl* FIN kalkulatorische Kosten *pl*; ~ **income** *n* ACC unterstelltes Einkommen *nt*, fiktives Einkommen *nt*, ECON zugerechnetes Einkommen *nt*, zurechenbares Einkommen *nt*; ~ **interest** *n* TAX *tax law* fiktive Zinsen *m pl*, zugerechnete Zinsen *m pl*; ~ **interest charge** *n* ACC kalkulatorische Zinsen *m pl*; ~ **risks** *n pl* FIN kalkulatorische Wagnisse *nt pl*; ~ **value** *n* ACC fiktiver Wert *m*

IMRO *abbr* BrE (*Investment Management Regulatory*

Organization) STOCK Verband der Anlageberater mit Kontrollfunktion

IMS *abbr* (*Institute of Manpower Studies*) HRM Institut für Personalstudien

IMT *abbr* (*immediate money transfer*) BANK sofortige Geldüberweisung *f*

in *abbr* (*inch*) GEN COMM Inch *m*, Zoll *m*

inability *n* GEN COMM Unfähigkeit *f*; ~ **to pay** *n* LAW Zahlungsunfähigkeit *f*; ~ **to perform** *n* LAW subjektive Unmöglichkeit *f* der Leistung; ~ **to work** *n* HRM Arbeitsunfähigkeit *f*

inaccessible *adj* GEN COMM unerreichbar

inaccuracy *n* GEN COMM Ungenauigkeit *f*, Unkorrektheit *f*

inactive *adj* COMP nicht aktiv, GEN COMM *money* inaktiv, STOCK *market* umsatzlos; ~ **account** *n* BANK umsatzloses Konto *nt*; ~ **asset** *n* STOCK Vermögenswert *m* mit geringem Umsatzvolumen; ~ **bond** *n* STOCK Obligation *f* mit geringem Umsatzvolumen; ~ **post** *n* STOCK Maklerstand *m* mit geringem Umsatzvolumen; ~ **stock** *n* STOCK Aktien *f pl* mit geringem Umsatzvolumen, unregelmäßig gehandelte Aktien *f pl*

inadequate *adj* GEN COMM unangemessen, unzulänglich

inadmissable *adj* LAW unzulässig

inadvertent *adj* GEN COMM unabsichtlich

inalienable *adj* LAW *right* unveräußerlich

in-and-out: ~ **trading** *n* STOCK Handel *m* mit dem Kauf und späteren Verkauf eines Wertpapiers

inappropriate *adj* GEN COMM unangebracht, unangemessen, ungeeignet

inaugural: ~ **cruise** *n* TRANSP Jungfernfahrt *f*; ~ **flight** *n* TRANSP Jungfernflug *m*; ~ **sailing** *n* TRANSP erstmaliges Auslaufen *nt*, Jungfernfahrt *f*; ~ **schedule** *n* TRANSP Antrittszeitplan *m*; ~ **transit** *n* TRANSP Antrittstransit *m*

in-balance *adj* GEN COMM ausgeglichen; ~ **budget** *n* FIN ausgeglichener Haushalt *m*, ausgeglichenes Budget *nt*

in-bond: ~ **manufacturing** *n* IMP/EXP Herstellung *f* unter Zollverschluß

inbound: ~ **investor** *n* ECON inländischer Investor *m*

inc. *abbr* AmE (*incorporated*) GEN COMM amtlich als AG eingetragen

Inc. *abbr* AmE (*Incorporated*) GEN COMM GmbH (*Gesellschaft mit beschränkter Haftung*), Ges.m.b.H. (*Öst*) (*Gesellschaft mit beschränkter Haftung*), AG (*Aktiengesellschaft*)

incalculable *adj* GEN COMM unberechenbar

incapability *n* GEN COMM Unfähigkeit *f*

incapable *adj* GEN COMM, HRM, LAW unfähig

incapacity *n* GEN COMM Unfähigkeit *f*

ince *abbr* (*insurance*) ACC, INS Vers. (*Versicherung*)

incendiarism *n* INS Brandstiftung *f*, Pyromanie *f*

incentive *n* GEN COMM Anreiz *m*, Antrieb *m*, HRM Leistungsanreiz *m*, S&M *sales* Anreiz *m*; ~ **bonus** *n* HRM Leistungszulage *f*; ~ **commission** *n* S&M Leistungsprovision *f*, Verkaufsprovision *f* als Anreiz; ~ **contracting** *n* GEN COMM Abschluß *m* von Leistungsverträgen; ~ **effect** *n* ECON Anreizeffekt *m*; ~ **fee** *n* ADMIN Erfolgshonorar *nt*, S&M Prämie *f*; ~ **pack** *n pl* S&M Werbegeschenk *nt*; ~ **pay** *n* ADMIN Leistungslohn *m*, HRM Leistungszahlung *f*, leistungsbezogene Bezahlung *f*; ~ **pay scheme** *n* HRM Leistungslohnsystem *nt*; ~ **plan** *n* HRM Anreizplan *m*; ~ **rate** *n* TRANSP *freight* Leistungstarif *m*; ~ **scheme** *n* HRM *profit-sharing*

Leistungssystem *nt*, Anreizsystem *nt*; ~ **system** *n* ECON Anreizsystem *nt*; ~ **wage** *n* HRM gewinnbezogene Bezahlung *f*, gewinnbezogenes Arbeitsentgelt *nt*, leistungsbezogene Bezahlung *f*, Leistungslohn *m*; ~ **wage plan** *n* HRM Leistungslohnprogramm *nt*

inch *n* (*in*) GEN COMM Inch *m*, Zoll *m*

inchoate *adj* LAW unvollständig

incidence *n* HRM *rate of occurrence* Häufigkeit *f*; ~ **of taxation** *n* TAX Steuerinzidenz *f*

incidental *adj* GEN COMM zufällig; ~ **charge** *n* FIN Nebenkosten *pl*; ~ **damages** *n pl* LAW Schadensersatz für Kosten, die bei der Vertragserfüllung entstanden sind; ~ **expenses** *n pl* FIN, HRM *for sales staff* Nebenkosten *pl*

incidentals: ~ **allowance** *n pl* FIN Rückstellung *f* für Nebenkosten

incidental: ~ **variation** *n* ACC Abweichung *f* zweiten Grades

incineration *n* ENVIR, IND *of waste* Verbrennung *f*, Müllverbrennung *f*; ~ **plant** *n* ENVIR, IND Verbrennungsanlage *f*

incipient: ~ **processing** *n* S&M Verarbeitungsansatz *m*

incitative: ~ **planning** *n* ECON, POL anreizorientierte Wirtschaftsplanung

incl. *abbr* (*included, including, inclusive*) GEN COMM einschl. (*einschließlich*), inkl. (*inklusive*)

include *vt* GEN COMM einbeziehen, *expenses* einschließen

included *adj* (*incl.*) GEN COMM einschließlich (*einschl.*), inklusive (*inkl.*)

including *prep* (*incl.*) GEN COMM inklusive (*inkl.*)

inclusion *n* GEN COMM Einschluß *m*

inclusive *adj* (*incl.*) GEN COMM einschließlich (*einschl.*), inklusive (*inkl.*); ~ **of** *prep* GEN COMM inklusive (*inkl.*); ~ **rate** *n* ADMIN Pauschaltarif *m*; ~ **terms** *n pl* GEN COMM Inklusivpreise *m pl*; ~ **tour** *n* (*IT*) LEIS Komplettreise *f*, Pauschalreise *f*, TRANSP Komplettreise *f*

income *n* ECON Einkommen *nt*, Einnahmen *f pl*, FIN, GEN COMM Gewinn *m*, Ertrag *m*, Erträge *m pl*, Einkünfte *pl*, HRM Verdienst *m*; ♦ **for ~ tax purposes** TAX für Einkommensteuerzwecke

income: ~ **accounts** *n* ACC Gewinn- und Verlustrechnung *f*; ~ **approach** *n* PROP *appraisal* Einnahmenmethode *f*; ~ **available for fixed charges** *n* ACC Gewinnrücklage *f*; ~ **averaging** *n* FIN, TAX Durchschnittsbesteuerung *f*; ~ **bond** *n* STOCK Gewinnobligation *f*, Gewinnschuldverschreibung *f*, TAX Gewinnschuldverschreibung *f*; ~ **bracket** *n* ADMIN Einkommensgruppe *f*; ~ **budget** *n* ACC kalkulatorischer Gewinn *m*; ~~**consumption curve** *n* (*ICC*) ECON Einkommenskonsumkurve *f*

Income: ~ **and Corporation Taxes Act** *n* BrE TAX Einkommens- und Körperschaftsteuergesetz *nt*

income: ~ **debenture** *n* STOCK Gewinnschuldverschreibung *f*; ~ **differential** *n* ECON Einkommensdifferenz *f*; ~ **distribution** *n* ECON Distribution *f*, FIN Einkommensverteilung *f*; ~ **earned overseas** *n* TAX Auslandseinkünfte *pl*, im Ausland verdientes Einkommen *nt*; ~ **effect** *n* ADMIN, ECON Einkommenseffekt *m*; ~~**elastic** *adj* *jarg* ECON einkommenselastisch; ~~**elasticity of demand** *n* *jarg* ECON Einkommenselastizität *f* der Nachfrage; ~ **and expenditure account** *n* ACC Gewinn- und Verlustrechnung *f*; ~ **and expenses** *n pl* AmE ACC Erträge *m pl* und Aufwendungen *f pl*, Einnahmen und Ausgaben *f pl*; ~ **from discounting** *n* BANK Diskonterträge *m pl*, Erträge *m pl* aus dem

Diskontgeschäft; **~ from interest** *n* ACC Zinsertrag *m*; **~ from investments** *n* ACC Ertrag *m* aus Beteiligungen, Beteiligungserträge *m pl*; **~ from a limited partnership** *n* ACC Gewinnanteile *m pl* aus einer Kommanditgesellschaft; **~ from securities** *n* ACC Erträge *m pl* aus Wertpapieranlagen; **~ from services** *n* ACC Einnahmen *f pl* aus Dienstleistungen; **~ from subsidiaries** *n* FIN Erträge *m pl* aus Beteiligungen an Tochtergesellschaften; **~ from trades and professions** *n* TAX Einkünfte *pl* aus Gewerbebetrieb und selbständiger Arbeit; **~ group** *n* S&M *market research* Einkommensgruppe *f*; **~ in respect of a decedent** *n* AmE TAX Einkommen *nt* unter Berücksichtung eines Verstorbenen, Einkommen *nt* im Hinblick auf einen Verstorbenen; **~ investment company** *n* FIN Einkommensinvestmentgesellschaft *f*; **~ level** *n* ADMIN Einkommensniveau *nt*; **~ per capita** *n* ECON Pro-Kopf-Einkommen *nt*; **~ per head** *n* ECON Pro-Kopf-Einkommen *nt*; **~ property** *n* FIN Renditeobjekt *nt*; **~ received** *n* TAX zugeflossene Einkünfte *pl*; **~ received under deduction of tax** *n* TAX quellenbesteuerte Erträge *m pl*, unter Steuerabzug empfangenes Einkommen *nt*; **~ redistribution** *n* ECON Einkommensumverteilung *f*; **~ replacement** *n* INS Einkommensersatz *m*; **~ splitting** *n* TAX Einkommen-Splitting *nt*; **~-splitting system** *n* TAX Einkommen-Splitting-System *nt*
incomes: **~ policy** *n* ADMIN, ECON, HRM, POL Einkommenspolitik *f*
income: **~ spread** *n* FIN Einkommensspanne *f*; **~ statement** *n* BrE ACC Gewinn- und Verlustrechnung *f*, Erfolgsrechnung *f*, Aufwands- und Ertragsrechnung *f*; **~ and substitution effects** *n pl* ECON Einkommens- und Substitutionseffekt *m*; **~ support** *n* BrE WEL Sozialhilfe *f*; **~ tax** *n* TAX Einkommensteuer *f*; **~ tax gain** *n* TAX Einkommensteuergewinn *m*; **~ tax liability** *n* TAX Einkommensteuerschuld *f*; **~ tax rate band** *n* BrE TAX Einkommensteuersatzspannweite *f*; **~ tax refund** *n* TAX Einkommensteuerrückzahlung *f*, Einkommensteuererstattung *f*; **~ tax repayment claim** *n* TAX Einkommensteuerrückzahlungsanspruch *m*, Rückzahlungsanspruch *m* aus der Einkommensteuer; **~ tax return** *n* ACC Einkommensteuererklärung *f*; **~ tax scale** *n* TAX Einkommensteuergrundtabelle *f*; **~ tax thereon at x %** *n* TAX Einkommensteuer *f* von x %; **~-tested supplement** *n* WEL einkommensabhängige Zulage *f*; **~ velocity of money** *n* ECON Einkommenskreislaufgeschwindigkeit *f* des Geldes; **~ year** *n* LAW, TAX Veranlagungszeitraum *m* (*Vz.*)
incoming: **~ business** *n* GEN COMM Auftragseingang *m*; **~ call** *n* COMMS *phone* ankommender Ruf *m*, Anruf *m*; **~ data** *n pl* COMP Eingangsdaten *pl*; **~ goods** *n pl* GEN COMM Wareneingang *m*, Warenzugänge *m pl*; **~ order** *n* S&M hereinkommender Auftrag *m*
in-company *adj* ECON, HRM, GEN COMM innerbetrieblich
incompatibility *n* COMP, GEN COMM Inkompatibilität *f*, Unverträglichkeit *f*
incompatible *adj* COMP, GEN COMM inkompatibel
incompetence *n* GEN COMM Unfähigkeit *f*
incompetent *adj* GEN COMM unfähig, HRM unfähig, untauglich, LAW unfähig
incomplete *adj* GEN COMM unvollständig
inconsistent *adj* GEN COMM unbeständig
incontestability *n* GEN COMM, LAW, PATENTS Unanfecht-

barkeit *f*; **~ clause** *n* INS *life insurance* Unanfechtbarkeitsklausel *f*
incontestable *adj* GEN COMM unbestreitbar, PATENTS unanfechtbar
inconvertible: **~ money** *n* ECON, POL nicht frei konvertierbare Währung *f*
incorporate *vt* GEN COMM *include* eingliedern, *company* einschließen, *establish* gründen, LAW *company* gründen, MEDIA einbauen
incorporated *adj* AmE (*inc.*) GEN COMM amtlich als AG eingetragen
Incorporated *n* AmE (*Inc.*, *cf limited liability company* BrE, *limited company* BrE) GEN COMM Gesellschaft *f* mit beschränkter Haftung (*GmbH*, *Ges.m.b.H. Öst*), Aktiengesellschaft *f* (*AG*)
incorporation *n* LAW *of a company* Gründung *f*
incorporeal *adj* GEN COMM, LAW immateriell; **~ hereditaments** *n pl* LAW, PROP Grundstücksnebenrechte *nt pl*, immaterielle Vermögensgegenstände *m pl*, vererbbare Vermögensgegenstände *m pl*; **~ property** *n* LAW *property* immaterielle Gegenstände *m pl*, immaterielles Eigentum *nt*
incorrect *adj* GEN COMM falsch, unrichtig
Incoterms *abbr* (*international commercial terms*) ECON Incoterms (*internationale Regeln für die Auslegung von Handelsklauseln*)
increase **1.** *n* GEN COMM Anstieg *m*, Aufstockung *f*, Erhöhung *f*, Steigerung *f*, Vergrößerung *f*, Zunahme *f*, Zuwachs *m*; **2.** *vt* GEN COMM aufstocken, erhöhen, steigen, steigern, vergrößern; ♦ **~ production** IND die Produktion erhöhen, die Produktion steigern; **~ the supply** ECON das Angebot erhöhen; **3.** *vi* ECON ansteigen, GEN COMM zunehmen; ♦ **~ tenfold** GEN COMM um das Zehnfache ansteigen; **~ twofold** GEN COMM um das Zweifache ansteigen
increased: **~ value** *n* (*iv*) GEN COMM erhöhter Wert *m*, Mehrwert *m*
increase: **~ in value** *n* FIN Wertsteigerung *f*, Wertzuwachs *m*, GEN COMM Werterhöhung *f*
increasing **1.** *adj* GEN COMM anwachsend; **2.** *n* GEN COMM Anheben *nt*, Anwachsen *nt*
increasingly *adv* GEN COMM zunehmend
increasing: **~ opportunity costs law** *n* ECON Gesetz *nt* der steigenden Opportunitätskosten; **~ returns to scale** *n pl* ECON zunehmende Skalenerträge *m pl*; **~ steadiness** *n* ECON Verstetigung *f*
increment *n* GEN COMM Wertzuwachs *m*, Zuwachs *m*
incremental *adj* COMP anwachsend, inkremental, GEN COMM *cost*, TAX inkremental; **~ analysis** *n* GEN COMM Grenzwertanalyse *f*, Marginalanalyse *f*, MGMNT Wachstumsanalyse *f*, TAX inkrementale Analyse *f*; **~ capital-output ratio** *n* (*ICOR*) FIN marginaler Kapitalkoeffizient *m*; **~ cash flow** *n* ACC erweiterter Cashflow *m*, FIN marginaler Cashflow *m*; **~ cost** *n* ECON Grenzkosten *pl*; **~ cost of capital** *n* ECON marginale Kapitalkosten *pl*, FIN zusätzliche Kapitalkosten *pl*; **~ oil revenue tax** *n* (*IORT*) TAX inkrementale Ölsteuer *f*; **~ payment** *n* HRM Gehaltszuwachs *m*; **~ scale** *n* HRM Gehaltszuwachstabelle *f*; **~ spending** *n* S&M Grenzausgaben *f pl*; **~ technology** *n* GEN COMM Inkrementaltechnologie *f*
incumbent *adj* HRM innehabend, POL innehabend, obliegend, *minister* amtierend
incur *vt* GEN COMM *costs* verursachen; ♦ **~ debts** ACC,

BANK sich verschulden, Schulden machen; ~ **expenses** ACC Aufwendungen machen

incurable: ~ **defect** n LAW unheilbarer Mangel m; ~ **depreciation** n PROP appraisal nichtkompensierbare Wertminderung f

incurred adj ACC entstanden; ~ **costs** n pl ACC entstandene Ausgaben f pl, entstandene Kosten pl; ~ **expenses** n pl ACC entstandene Aufwendungen f pl, noch nicht beglichene Aufwendungen f pl

indebted adj ECON verschuldet; ◆ be ~ FIN verschuldet sein; be ~ to sb GEN COMM jdm zu Dank verpflichtet sein

indebtedness n FIN Verschuldung f; ~ **to banks** n BANK Bankverbindlichkeiten f pl

indecisive adj GEN COMM unentschlossen

indefinite adj GEN COMM unbegrenzt, unbestimmt; ~ **laytime** n TRANSP shipping unbestimmte Liegezeit f

indemnification n INS Schadloshaltung f, LAW Schadloshaltung f, Wiedergutmachung f

indemnify vt FIN, GEN COMM abfinden, INS entschädigen, Schadensersatz leisten, sichern, sicherstellen; ◆ ~ **shareholders** FIN Aktionäre abfinden

indemnity n INS Entschädigung f, Haftungsfreistellung f, Schadloshaltung f, LAW Abfindung f, Entschädigung f, Schadloshaltung f, against liability Haftungsausschluß m, Haftungsfreistellung f; ~ **against liability** n INS, LAW Haftungsausschluß m, Haftungsfreistellung f; ~ **bond** n ADMIN, LAW Ausfallbürgschaft f, Freistellungsverpflichtung f, Garantieerklärung f; ~ **claim** n LAW Entschädigungsanspruch m; ~ **insurance** n INS Schadenversicherung f; ~ **obligation** n LAW of fulfillment of contract Erfüllungsgarantie f; ~ **payment** n INS Zahlung f der Versicherungssumme; ~ **period** n INS Haftungsdauer f, Leistungsdauer f, LAW Haftungsdauer f

indentation n COMP word processing Einrückung f

indent 1. n COMP word processing Einrückung f; **2.** vt COMP word processing einrücken

indent: ~ **house** n GEN COMM Indenthaus nt

indenture n STOCK Anleihevertrag m

independence n GEN COMM, HRM, POL Unabhängigkeit f

independent 1. adj POL unabhängig, unparteiisch; ◆ ~ **of** GEN COMM unabhängig von; **2.** n INS insurer Außenseiter, in m,f, POL Fraktionslose(r) mf [decl. as adj], Unabhängige(r) mf [decl. as adj]

independent: ~ **auditor** n ACC außerbetrieblicher Revisor m, außerbetriebliche Revisorin f, außerbetrieblicher Wirtschaftsprüfer m, außerbetriebliche Wirtschaftsprüferin f, externer Buchprüfer m, externe Buchprüferin f, unabhängiger Buchprüfer m, unabhängige Buchprüferin f; ~ **broker** n STOCK unabhängiger Makler m, unabhängige Maklerin f; ~ **claim** n PATENTS Hauptanspruch m, unabhängiger Anspruch m; ~ **contractor** n TAX selbständiger Unternehmer m, selbständige Unternehmerin f, unabhängige(r) Sachverständige(r) mf [decl. as adj]; ~ **inquiry** n LAW unabhängige Untersuchung f; ~ **retailer** n S&M unabhängiges Einzelhandelsgeschäft nt

Independent: ~ **Review Committee** n BrE HRM unabhängiger Untersuchungsausschuß m

independent: ~ **school** n (BrE) WEL Privatschule f; ~ **store** n AmE GEN COMM selbständiges Einzelhandelsgeschäft nt; ~ **taxation** n BrE TAX selbständige Besteuerung f

Independent: ~ **Television** n BrE (ITV) MEDIA Netzwerk unabhängiger Fernsehsender; ~ **Television Commission** n BrE (ITC) MEDIA Überwachungsgremium für unabhängige Fernsehsender; ~ **Television Publications** n (ITP) MEDIA unabhängige Fernsehveröffentlichungen

independent: ~ **union** n GEN COMM, HRM unabhängige Gewerkschaft f; ~ **variables** n pl MATH unabhängige Variablen f pl

in-depth adj GEN COMM gründlich; ~ **analysis** n GEN COMM gründliche Analyse f; ~ **business plan** n GEN COMM detaillierter Geschäftsplan m; ~ **discussion** n GEN COMM tiefgreifende Diskussion f, umfassende Diskussion f; ~ **study** n GEN COMM gründliche Untersuchung f

indeterminate adj GEN COMM unbestimmt; ~ **obligation** n LAW Gattungsschuld f

index 1. n COMP Index m, Verzeichnis nt, ECON, STOCK Index m; **2.** vt COMP, MATH indizieren; **3.** vi COMP, ECON, FIN, STOCK, TAX indexieren

indexation n ECON Indexierung f, HRM Indexbindung f; ~ **relief** n TAX for capital gains indexgebundene Entlastung f

index: ~ **basis** n MATH comparative calculation Indexbasis f; ~-**card file** n ADMIN Kartei f; ~ **of coincident indicators** n FIN Index m übereinstimmender Indikatoren

indexed adj COMP, MATH indiziert; ~ **bond** n BANK Indexanleihe f; ~ **life insurance** n INS dynamische Lebensversicherung f, gleitende Lebensversicherung f, indexierte Lebensversicherung f; ~ **loan** n BANK Indexanleihe f; ~ **security investment plan** n STOCK indexierter Wertpapierinvestitionsplan m

index: ~ **file** n ADMIN, COMP Indexdatei f, Kartendatei f, Kartei f; ~ **fund** n STOCK Index-Fonds m; ~ **futures contract** n STOCK Indexterminkontrakt m; ~ **growth linked units** n pl (IGLU) STOCK indexwachstumsgebundene Fondsanteile m pl

indexing n ECON Indexbindung f, STOCK Indexierung f

index: ~ **of lagging indicators** n FIN Index m der Spätindikatoren; ~ **of leading indicators** n FIN Index m führender Indikatoren, Index m der Frühindikatoren, STOCK Trendbarometer der US-Wirtschaft; ~ **lease** n PROP Indexmiete f, Indexpacht f; ~ **linkage** n ECON Indexverbindung f; ~-**linked** adj INS indexiert; ~-**linked gilt** n STOCK indexierte Staatsanleihe f; ~-**linked loan** n FIN indexgebundenes Darlehen nt; ~-**linked stock** n FIN Indexaktie f; ~ **linking** n ECON, HRM Indexbindung f; ~ **of longer leading indicators** n FIN Index m länger führender Indikatoren; ~ **number** n ECON econometrics Indexzahl f, Indexziffer f, MATH Indexzahl f; ~ **option** n STOCK Indexoption f

Index: ~ **and Option Market division** n AmE (IOM division) STOCK Chicago Mercantile Exchange Abteilung des Index- und Optionsmarktes

index: ~ **point** n STOCK Indexpunkt m; ~ **price** n STOCK Indexpreis m; ~ **of shorter leading indicators** n FIN Index m kürzer führender Indikatoren; ~-**tracking fund** n FIN indexorientierter Fonds m

indicate vt GEN COMM angeben, anzeigen

indicated: ~ **yield** n STOCK angegebene Rendite f, angegebene Verzinsung f

indication: ~ **of interest** n STOCK Zinsangabe f; ~ **of source** n PATENTS Ursprungsbezeichnung f, Ursprungsvermerk m

indicative: **be ~ of** *phr* GEN COMM hindeuten auf [+acc]; **~ planning** *n* ECON, MGMNT indikative Planung *f*

indicator *n* COMP Anzeige *f*, ECON *econometrics* Indikator *m*; **~ variable** *n* ECON *econometrics* Indikatorvariable *f*

indifference: **~ curve** *n* ECON Indifferenzkurve *f*

indirect *adj* GEN COMM indirekt; **~ addressing** *n* COMP indirekte Adressierung *f*; **~ authorization** *n* BANK indirekte Vollmacht *f*; **~ costs** *n pl* ACC, ECON, FIN indirekte Kosten *pl*; **~ demand** *n* ECON abgeleitete Nachfrage *f*; **~ discrimination** *n* HRM indirekte Diskriminierung *f*; **~ expenses** *n pl* FIN allgemeine Geschäftskosten *pl*; **~ export trading** *n* IMP/EXP indirekter Exporthandel *m*; **~ labor** *AmE*, **~ labour** *BrE n* HRM Lohngemeinkosten *pl*; **~ labour costs** *n pl BrE* ACC indirekte Lohnkosten *pl*, Lohngemeinkosten *pl*, ECON Fertigungsgemeinkosten *pl*, Gemeinkostenlöhne *m pl*

indirectly *adv* GEN COMM indirekt; ♦ **~ related to** GEN COMM indirekt bezogen auf, indirekt verbunden mit

indirect: **~ production** *n* ECON Umwegproduktion *f*; **~ route** *n* TRANSP Umweg *m*; **~ taxation** *n* TAX indirekte Besteuerung *f*

indiscountable *adj* BANK nicht diskontfähig

indispensable *adj* GEN COMM unerläßlich; **~ labor** *AmE*, **~ labour** *BrE n* ECON *Marxist theory* notwendige Arbeit *f*

indistinct *adj* GEN COMM undeutlich

individual 1. *adj* GEN COMM einzeln, individuell, Einzel-; **2.** *n* GEN COMM *person* Einzelperson *f*

individual: **~ advertising** *n* S&M Alleinwerbung *f*; **~ annuity policy** *n* INS Einzelrentenpolice *f*, Individualrentenpolice *f*, individuelle Rentenpolice *f*; **~ assessment** *n* ADMIN Einzelbewertung *f*; **~ bargaining** *n* HRM Einzeltarifverhandlung *f*; **~ company accounts** *n pl* ACC Einzelbilanz *f*; **~ company audited accounts** *n pl* ACC testierte Einzelbilanz *f*; **~ conciliation** *n* HRM individuelle Schlichtung *f*; **~ consumer** *n* GEN COMM, S&M Einzelverbraucher, in *m,f*; **~ firm** *n* GEN COMM Einzelfirma *f*, Einzelunternehmen *nt*; **~ grievance procedure** *n* HRM individuelles Schlichtungsverfahren *nt*; **~ import licence** *BrE*, **~ import license** *AmE n* IMP/EXP Einzeleinfuhrgenehmigung *f*, Einzelimportlizenz *f*; **~ income** *n* ADMIN Individualeinkommen *nt*; **~ investor** *n* STOCK Einzelanleger, in *m,f*

individualization *n* WEL Individualisierung *f*

individualize *vt* WEL individualisieren

individual: **~ licence** *BrE*, **~ license** *AmE n* IMP/EXP Einzelgenehmigung *f*, Einzellizenz *f*; **~ life insurance** *n* INS Einzellebensversicherung *f*, Individuallebensversicherung *f*

individually *adv* GEN COMM einzeln

individual: **~ order** *n* GEN COMM Einzelauftrag *m*; **~ retirement account** *n AmE* (*IRA*) BANK, TAX persönliches Rentenkonto *nt*, steuerfreies Sparkonto *nt* zur privaten Altersvorsorge, steuerfreies Rentensparkonto *nt*; **~ retirement account rollover** *n* TAX Darlehensverlängerung *f* für steuerfreies Rentensparkonto; **~ safe custody of securities** *n* FIN Streifbanddepot *nt*

indivisibility *n* ECON Unteilbarkeit *f*

indivisible: **~ exports** *n pl* IMP/EXP unteilbare Exporte *m pl*; **~ load** *n* TRANSP unteilbare Last *f*

indoor: **~ sales manager** *n* HRM Innendienstverkaufsleiter, in *m,f*

indorse *see* endorse

indorsee *see* endorsee

indorsement *see* endorsement

indorser *see* endorser

indorsor *see* endorser

induce *vt* ECON, FIN induzieren

induced: **~ draft** *n* FIN induzierter Wechsel *m*; **~ technical progress** *n* ECON induzierter technischer Fortschritt *m*

inducement *n* GEN COMM Anreiz *m*, LAW *to break the law* Verleitung *f*; **~ good** *n* ECON induzierendes Gut *nt*; **~ mechanism** *n* ECON Leistungsanreizmechanismus *m*

induct *vt* HRM einführen

induction *n* GEN COMM Induktion *f*, Einarbeitung *f*, HRM Einführung *f*; **~ course** *n* WEL Einführung *f*, Einführungskurs *m*, Einführungsseminar *nt*

inductive: **~ reasoning** *n* MGMNT induktives Denken *nt*

indulgency: **~ pattern** *n* MGMNT *industrial relations* Duldungsmuster *nt*

industrial *adj* GEN COMM gewerblich, industriell, IND, STOCK *stock market classification* industriell; **~ accident** *n* HRM Arbeitsunfall *m*, Betriebsunfall *m*; **~ action** *n* ECON Arbeitskampf *m*, GEN COMM, HRM, IND Arbeitskampf *m*, Streik *m*; **~ activity** *n* IND gewerbliche Tätigkeit *f*; **~ advertising** *n* S&M Werbung *f* für Industrieerzeugnisse; **~ application** *n* PATENTS gewerbliche Anmeldung *f*; **~ arbitration** *n* HRM gewerbliche Schiedsgerichtsbarkeit *f*; **~ base** *n* IND industrielle Basis *f*; **~ capacity utilization** *n* IND industrielle Kapazitätsnutzung *f*; **~ capitalism** *n* IND Industriekapitalismus *m*, industrieller Kapitalismus *m*; **~ carrier** *n* TRANSP betriebliches Transportunternehmen *nt*; **~ center** *AmE*, **~ centre** *BrE n* IND Industriezentrum *nt*; **~ and commercial companies** *n pl* (*ICCs*) ECON industrielle und kommerzielle Unternehmen *nt pl*, gewerblich-industrielle Unternehmen *nt pl*; **~ concentration** *n* IND Unternehmenskonzentration *f*, wirtschaftliche Konzentration *f*; **~ conflict** *n* HRM Arbeitskonflikt *m*; **~ cooperation** *n* IND gewerbliche Zusammenarbeit *f*, gewerbliche Kooperation *f*; **~ cooperative** *n* IND gewerbliche Genossenschaft *f*

Industrial: **~ Council for Educational & Training Technology** *n BrE* (*ICETT*) WEL Industrierat *m* für Fortbildungstechnologie

industrial: **~ country** *n* ECON, IND Industrieland *nt*; **~ demand** *n* IND industrielle Nachfrage *f*; **~ democracy** *n* ECON mitbestimmte Wirtschaft *f*, POL *government* industrielle Demokratie *f*, mitbestimmte Wirtschaft *f*, *state* demokratischer Industriestaat *m*

Industrial: **~ Development Authority** *n* ECON Behörde für industrielle Entwicklung

industrial: **~ development bond** *n AmE* STOCK Schuldverschreibung zum Zweck der gewerblichen Erschließung

Industrial: **~ Development Certificate** *n* IND Standortbescheinigung *f*

industrial: **~ discharge** *n* ENVIR, IND industrieller Schadstoffausstoß *m*; **~ disease** *n* HRM Berufskrankheit *f*; **~ dispute** *n* HRM Arbeitskonflikt *m*, Arbeitskampf *m*, Tarifkonflikt *m*; **~ dynamics** *n pl* IND Wirtschaftsdynamik *f*; **~ economics** *n pl* ECON gewerbliche Wirtschaft *f*; **~ engineering** *n* IND Betriebstechnik *f*, Fertigungsorganisation *f*, Industrial Engineering *nt*,

Rationalisierung *f* von Arbeitsprozessen, *production planning* Vorbereitung *f* zur Fertigung, *theory* Industriebetriebslehre *f*; **~ equipment** *n* IND Industrieeinrichtungen *f pl*; **~ espionage** *n* GEN COMM Betriebsspionage *f*, IND Industriespionage *f*, Werkspionage *f*, Wirtschaftsspionage *f*; **~ estate** *n* IND Industriegebiet *nt*, Industriegelände *nt*, Industriezone *f*, PROP Gewerbefläche *f*, Gewerbegebiet *nt*, Gewerbepark *m*, Industriegebiet *nt*, Industriepark *m*; **~ fatigue** *n* HRM betriebliche Ermüdung *f*, industrielle Ermüdung *f*; **~ finance** *n* FIN Wirtschaftsfinanzierung *f*; **~ goods** *n pl* ECON Investitionsgüter *nt pl*, IND Industrieprodukte *nt pl*, Investitionsgüter *nt pl*, Produktionsgüter *nt pl*; **~ health** *n* HRM Arbeitshygiene *f*; **~ hygiene** *n* HRM, WEL Arbeitshygiene *f*, Betriebshygiene *f*; **~ incident** *n* HRM, WEL Arbeitszwischenfall *m*; **~ inertia** *n* IND industrielle Flaute *f*; **~ injury** *n* HRM, IND Arbeitsunfall *m*, Berufsunfall *m*; **~ inspection** *n* WEL *inspectorate* Gewerbepolizei *f*

industrialist *n* ECON, IND Industrielle(r) *mf* [decl. as adj]

industrialization *n* ECON, IND Industrialisierung *f*

industrialize *vt* ECON, IND industrialisieren

industrialized *adj* ECON, IND industrialisiert; **~ country** *n* ECON, IND Industrieland *nt*, Industriestaat *m*

industrial: **~ law** *n* BrE HRM, LAW Arbeitsrecht *nt*; **~ marketing** *n* S&M Investitionsgüter-Marketing *nt*; **~ nation** *n* ECON Industrienation *f*; **~ occupancy** *n* PROP betriebliche Nutzung *f*, gewerbliche Nutzung *f*, industrielle Nutzung *f*; **~ organization** *n* (*IO*) ECON Industrieökonomik *f*, IND industrielle Organisation *f*; **~ park** *n* ENVIR, IND Industriepark *m*, Gewerbegebiet *nt*; **~ payroll** *n* ADMIN, ECON Lohn- und Gehaltsaufwendungen *f* im Privatsektor; **~ plant** *n* IND Fabrikanlage *f*, Industrieanlage *f*, Werk *nt*, Wirtschaftsbetrieb *m*; **~ plant engineer** *n* IND Betriebsingenieur, in *m,f*; **~ policy** *n* IND Industriepolitik *f*, sektorale Strukturpolitik *f*; **~ product** *n* GEN COMM Zwischenprodukt *nt*, IND gewerbliches Erzeugnis *nt*, Industrieerzeugnis *nt*; **~ production** *n* ECON Industrieproduktion *f*; **~ property** *n* GEN COMM gewerbliches Eigentum *nt*, PATENTS gewerbliches Eigentum *nt*, gewerbliche Schutzrechte *nt pl*, PROP gewerbliches Eigentum *nt*; **~ property protection** *n* LAW, PATENTS gewerblicher Rechtsschutz *m*; **~ psychology** *n* HRM, IND, MGMNT Arbeitspsychologie *f*, Betriebspsychologie *f*; **~ relations** *n pl* (*IR*) ADMIN, ECON, HRM Arbeitsbeziehungen *f pl*, Arbeitgeber-Arbeitnehmer-Beziehungen *f pl*; **~ relations director** *n* HRM, MGMNT Personaldirektor, in *m,f*, Koordinator, in *m,f* Arbeitgeber-Arbeitnehmer-Interessen; **~ relations manager** *n* HRM, MGMNT Referent, in *m,f* für Arbeitgeber-Arbeitnehmer-Beziehungen, Koordinator, in *m,f* Arbeitgeber-Arbeitnehmer-Interessen

Industrial: **~ Relations Policy Committee** *n* BrE (*IRPC*) HRM Ausschuß für Arbeitgeber-Arbeitnehmer-Beziehungen

industrial: **~ rent** *n* PROP gewerbliche Pacht *f*; **~ research** *n* S&M industrielle Absatzforschung *f*, industrielle Forschung *f*; **~ revolution** *n* ECON industrielle Revolution *f*; **~ safety** *n* ADMIN Arbeitssicherheit *f*, HRM Arbeitsschutz *m*, Betriebssicherheit *f*, IND Betriebssicherheit *f*; **~ safety helmet** *n* IND Industrieschutzhelm *m*; **~ safety regulations** *n pl* IND Arbeitsschutzbestimmungen *f pl*; **~ sector** *n* IND industrieller Bereich *m*, industrieller Sektor *m*; **~ security** *n* FIN *shares* Industriewert *m*, HRM *safety* Betriebssicher-

heit *f*, IND industrielle Sicherheit *f*, Betriebssicherheit *f*; **~ selling** *n* S&M Investitionsgüterverkauf *m*; **~ services** *n pl* IND Industriedienstleistungen *f pl*; **~ share** *n* STOCK Industrieaktie *f*; **~ site** *n* IND Betriebsgelände *nt*, gewerbliches Grundstück *nt*, Industrieareal *nt*, Industriegelände *nt*; **~ society** *n* ECON Industriegesellschaft *f*; **~ source** *n* ENVIR *of pollution* industrieller Ursprung *m*; **~ spirits** *n pl* IND Industriealkohol *m*; **~ strife** *n* HRM Arbeitskonflikt *m*; **~ system** *n* IND industrielles System *nt*; **~ and trade policy adjustment loan** *n* (*ITPAL*) FIN Ausgleichsanleihe *f* für Industrie- und Handelspolitik; **~ training** *n* ADMIN, HRM, IND innerbetriebliche Schulung *f*; **~ tribunal** *n* BrE (*IT, cf labor court AmE*) HRM, LAW Arbeitsgericht *nt*, gewerbliches Schiedsgericht *nt*; **~ union** *n* HRM Industriegewerkschaft *f*; **~ vehicle** *n* TRANSP Industriefahrzeug *nt*; **~ waste** *n* ECON Industriemüll *m*, ENVIR Industrieabfälle *m pl*, Industriemüll *m*, IND gewerbliche Abfälle *m pl*, Industrieabfälle *m pl*, Industriemüll *m*

industry *n* ECON Industrie *f*, Wirtschaftszweig *m*, GEN COMM *efficiency* Tüchtigkeit *f*, IND Industrie *f*, *sector* Branche *f*, Gewerbe *nt*, Wirtschaftszweig *m*; **~ leader** *n* S&M Branchenführer *m*; **~ leadership program** *AmE*, **~ leadership programme** *BrE* *n* MGMNT *public relations* Branchenführerprogramm *nt*; **~ minister** *n* POL Industrieminister, in *m,f*; **~ standard** *n* ECON, IND Industrienorm *f*; **~ track** *n* TRANSP Privatanschlußgleis *nt*; **~-wide agreement** *n* HRM branchenweite Vereinbarung *f*; **~-wide wage agreement** *n* HRM Branchentarifvertrag *m*

inefficiency *n* ECON Ineffizienz *f*, Unwirtschaftlichkeit *f*, GEN COMM Unwirtschaftlichkeit *f*, *person* Ineffizienz *f*; **~ in the market** *n* STOCK Marktineffizienz *f*

inefficient *adj* ECON, GEN COMM ineffizient, unwirtschaftlich

inelastic: **~ demand** *n* ECON unelastische Nachfrage *f*

inelasticity *n* ECON Inelastizität *f*, Unelastizität *f*

inelastic: **~ supply** *n* ECON unelastisches Angebot *nt*

ineligible *adj* GEN COMM ungeeignet; **~ paper** *n* BANK nicht diskontfähiges Papier *nt*

inequality *n* ECON Ungleichheit *f*, MATH Ungleichung *f*

inequitable *adj* GEN COMM unbillig, LAW ungerecht

inertia *n* S&M Trägheit *f*; **~ effect** *n* POL Trägheitseffekt *m*

inertial: **~ inflation** *n* ECON Inertialinflation *f*

inertia: **~ salesman** *n* S&M Trägheitsverkäufer *m*, **~ saleswoman** *n* S&M Trägheitsverkäuferin *f*; **~ selling** *n* S&M Trägheitsverkauf *m*

inevitable *adv* GEN COMM unvermeidlich

inexhaustible *adj* ENVIR *natural resources* unerschöpflich

inexpedient *adj* GEN COMM unzweckmäßig

inexpensive *adj* GEN COMM billig

inexperienced *adj* GEN COMM unerfahren

inf. *abbr* (*information*) GEN COMM Info (*infrml*) (*Information*), Infos (*infrml*) (*Informationen*)

infant: **~ industry** *n* IND junger Wirtschaftszweig *m*, schutzzollbedürftige Industrie *f*; **~ industry argument** *n* ECON, IND Erziehungszoll-Argument *nt*; **~ mortality** *n* GEN COMM, WEL Säuglingssterblichkeit *f*

infected: **~ by a virus** *phr* COMP infiziert, virenbefallen

inferential: **~ statistics** *n* MATH induktive Statistik *f*, Inferenzstatistik *f*, mathematische Statistik *f*

inferior *adj* GEN COMM untergeordnet; **~ goods** *n pl* ECON inferiore Güter *nt pl*, Sättigungsgüter *nt pl*, GEN COMM minderwertige Waren *f pl*; ~ **performance** *n* LAW Schlechterfüllung *f*

inferred: ~ **authority** *n* HRM gefolgerte Autorität *f*

infinite *adj* ENVIR unendlich

inflate *vt* ECON hochtreiben, inflationieren, steigern, aufblähen, übermäßig steigern, GEN COMM *risks* überhöhen

inflation *n* ECON Geldentwertung *f*, Inflation *f*; ◆ ~ **undercuts purchasing power** ECON Inflation untergräbt Kaufkraft

inflation: ~ **accounting** *n* ACC inflationsneutrale Buchführung *f*; ~**-adjusted deficit** *n* ECON inflationsbereinigtes Defizit *nt*; ~**-adjusted income** *n* ECON inflationsbereinigtes Einkommen *nt*

inflationary *adj* ECON inflationär; ~ **expectations** *n pl* ECON Inflationserwartungen *f pl*; ~ **gap** *n* ECON Inflationslücke *f*, inflatorische Lücke *f*; ~ **pressure** *n* ECON Inflationsdruck *m*; ~ **spiral** *n* ECON Inflationsspirale *f*; ~ **trends** *n pl* ECON inflatorische Tendenzen *f pl*

inflation: ~ **endorsement** *n* INS, PROP Inflationsnachtrag *m*, Inflationszusatz *m*; ~ **illusion** *n* ECON Geldillusion *f*

inflationist *n* ECON Inflationist, in *m,f*

inflation: ~ **rate** *n* ECON Inflationsrate *f*; ~ **tax** *n* TAX Inflationssteuer *f*

inflexible: ~ **price** *n* ECON starrer Preis *m*

inflict: ~ **sth on sb** *phr* GEN COMM jdm etw auferlegen

in-flight: ~ **catering** *n* TRANSP Bordverpflegung *f*; ~ **entertainment** *n* TRANSP Bordunterhaltung *f*; ~ **film** *n* TRANSP Bordkino *nt*; ~ **information** *n* TRANSP Bordinformationen *f pl*; ~ **magazine** *n* TRANSP Bordzeitschrift *f*; ~ **meal** *n* TRANSP Bordverpflegung *f*; ~ **music** *n* TRANSP Bordmusik *f*; ~ **service** *n* TRANSP Bordservice *m*

inflow *n* ACC *of funds* Kapitalzufluß *m*, Zustrom *m*; ~ **of orders** *n* GEN COMM Auftragseingang *m*

influence 1. *n* GEN COMM Beeinflussung *f*, Einfluß *m*; **2.** *vt* GEN COMM einwirken auf [+acc], *decision, costs* beeinflussen

influential *adj* GEN COMM einflußreich

info *n* *infrml* (*information*) GEN COMM Info (*infrml*) (*Information*), Infos (*infrml*) (*Informationen*), Benachrichtigung *f*, Verständigung *f*

inform *vt* GEN COMM avisieren, benachrichtigen, informieren, *instruct* unterrichten, *notify* verständigen

informal *adj* GEN COMM *unstructured* formlos, informell, *unofficial* inoffiziell, nicht förmlich, *casual* zwanglos, ungezwungen; ~ **arrangement** *n* GEN COMM informelle Vereinbarung *f*; ~ **economy** *n* ECON Schattenwirtschaft *f*, informelle Wirtschaft *f*; ~ **interview** *n* HRM formlose Befragung *f*

informality *n* HRM Formlosigkeit *f*

informal: ~ **meeting** *n* ADMIN zwanglose Zusammenkunft *f*; ~ **organization** *n* MGMNT formlose Organisation *f*, informelle Organisation *f*

informatics *n* COMP Informatik *f*, Informations- und Dokumentationswissenschaft *f*

information *n* (*inf.*, *info*) GEN COMM Information *f* (*Info*), Informationen (*Infos*), Benachrichtigung *f*, Verständigung *f*; ◆ **have access to** ~ GEN COMM Zugang zu Informationen haben

information: ~ **agreement** *n* GEN COMM Informationsvereinbarung *f*; ~ **bit** *n* COMP Datenbit *nt*, Informationsbit *nt*; ~ **bureau** *n* GEN COMM Auskunft-

stelle *f*; ~ **desk** *n* LEIS Informationsschalter *m*; ~ **flow** *n* COMP, GEN COMM Informationsfluß *m*; ~ **handling** *n* COMP, GEN COMM Informationsbearbeitung *f*, Informationsbehandlung *f*; ~ **highway** *n* COMP Datenautobahn *f* (*jarg*), Infobahn *f* (*jarg*); ~ **network** *n* COMP Datennetz *nt*, Informationsnetz *nt*; ~ **office** *n* GEN COMM Auskunftstelle *f*; ~ **officer** (*IO*) HRM, MEDIA, MGMNT Pressereferent, in *m,f*, *public sector* Referent, in *m,f* für Öffentlichkeitsarbeiten; ~ **processing** *n* COMP Informationsbearbeitung *f*, Informationsverarbeitung *f*; ~ **retrieval** *n* COMP Informationswiedergewinnung *f*; ~ **retrieval system** *n* COMP System *nt* zur Informationswiedergewinnung; ~ **return** *n* TAX Fragebogen *m*; ~ **storage** *n* COMP Informationsspeicherung *f*; ~ **storage capacity** *n* COMP Informationsspeicherkapazität *f*; ~ **superhighway** *n* COMP Datenautobahn *f* (*jarg*), Infobahn *f* (*jarg*); ~ **system** *n* COMP Informationssystem *nt*; ~ **technology** *n* (*IT*) COMP, IND Informationstechnik *f* (*IT*), Informationstechnologie *f* (*IT*), elektronische Datenverarbeitung *f* (*EDV*)

Information: ~ **Technology Export Organization** *n* BrE IMP/EXP Exportorganisation für Informationstechnik

information: ~ **theory** *n* COMP, MATH, MGMNT Informationstheorie *f*; ~ **transfer** *n* COMP Informationsübertragung *f*

informative: ~ **advertising** *n* S&M Informationswerbung *f*; ~ **labeling** *AmE*, ~ **labelling** *BrE* *n* S&M *country of origin* Herkunftsbezeichnung *f*, Ursprungsauszeichnung *f*

informed *adj* GEN COMM *decision, argument* sachkundig, fachkundig, informiert; ◆ **be ~ about** GEN COMM unterrichtet sein über

informed: ~ **decision** *n* MGMNT sachkundige Entscheidung *f*; ~ **public** *n* GEN COMM informierte Öffentlichkeit *f*

informer *n* GEN COMM Denunziant, in *m,f*, Informant, in *m,f*

infrastructural *adj* ECON, TRANSP infrastrukturell

infrastructure *n* ECON, TRANSP Infrastruktur *f*

infringe *vt* LAW vergehen gegen, verstoßen gegen, *rule* verletzen, PATENTS *copyright* verletzen

infringement *n* GEN COMM *of privacy* Eingriff *m*, LAW Verletzung *f*, Verstoß *m*, PATENTS *of copyright* Verletzung *f*

infringer *n* LAW, PATENTS Verletzer *m*

ingenuity *n* GEN COMM Einfallsreichtum *m*

ingot *n* BANK, STOCK Barren *m*

ingress: ~ **and egress** *n* GEN COMM Eingang und Ausgang *m*

inhabitant *n* GEN COMM Einwohner, in *m,f*

inherent: ~ **defect** *n* GEN COMM Beschaffenheitsschaden *m*, LAW *of goods* innerer Mangel *m*; ~ **explosion clause** *n* INS, PROP mitversicherte Explosionklausel *f*, zugehörige Explosionsversicherungsklausel *f*; ~ **risk** *n* STOCK unvermeidbares Risiko *nt*

inherit *vt* LAW erben

inheritable *adj* LAW vererbbar

inheritance *n* FIN Erbschaft *f*, LAW Erbfall *m*, Erbe *nt*; ~ **tax** *n* (*cf death duty BrE*) FIN, TAX Erbschaftssteuer *f*; ~ **tax return** *n* TAX Erbschaftssteuererklärung *f*

inherited: ~ **audience** *n jarg* MEDIA *broadcast* geerbte Zuschauer *m pl*; ~ **burdens** *n pl* ECON Altlasten *f pl*

inhibit *vt* GEN COMM behindern, hemmen, sperren, unterbinden

inhospitable *adj* GEN COMM ungastlich, unwirtlich

in-house *adj* GEN COMM innerbetrieblich, *service, worker* firmeneigen, hauseigen, intern, Innen-; ~ **audit** *n* ADMIN Innenrevision *f*; ~ **magazine** *n* MEDIA Werkszeitung *f*; ~ **software** *n* COMP hauseigene Software *f*; ~ **system** *n* COMP hauseigenes System *nt*; ~ **training** *n* HRM innerbetriebliche Schulung *f*; ~ **valuation** *n* PROP interne Bewertung *f*

initial 1. *adj* GEN COMM anfänglich; **2.** *n* COMMS, MEDIA Initial *nt*, Initiale *f*

initial: ~ **boiling point** *n* IND Anfangstemperatur *f*; ~ **capital** *n* FIN, STOCK Anfangskapital *nt*, Ausgangskapital *nt*, Einlagenkapital *nt*, Gründungskapital *nt*; ~ **deposit** *n* STOCK Einschuß *m*; ~ **dividend** *n* FIN Anfangsdividende *f*; ~ **expenditure** *n* FIN Anfangsausgaben *f pl*; ~ **inventory** *n* ACC Anfangsinventar *f*; ~ **investment** *n* FIN Anfangsauszahlung *f*

initialization *n* COMP *operating system* Initialisierung *f*

initialize *vt* COMP *operating system* initialisieren

initial: ~ **letter** *n* COMMS, MEDIA Initial *nt*, Initiale *f*; ~ **margin level** *n* STOCK Einschußniveau *nt*; ~ **offering price** *n* STOCK Erstausgabepreis *m*; ~ **order** *n* GEN COMM Erstauftrag *m*; ~ **outlay** *n* ACC Anschaffungskosten *pl*; ~ **placing of securities** *n* STOCK Erstplazierung *f*; ~ **public offering** *n AmE* (*IPO*) STOCK erstes öffentliches Zeichnungsangebot *nt*; ~ **quotation** *n* STOCK erster Kurs *m*; ~ **sale** *n* S&M Erstverkauf *m*; ~ **sales of newly issued securities** *n pl* STOCK Erstabsatz *m*; ~ **supply** *n* GEN COMM Erstausstattung *f*; ~ **value** *n* GEN COMM Anfangswert *m*

initiate *vt* COMP *software* auslösen, initiieren

initiative *n* MGMNT Initiative *f*

initiator *n* POL Initiator, in *m,f*

injection *n* ECON Geldzuschuß *m*, Injektion *f*; ~ **of new capital** *n* ECON Kapitalspritze *f* (*infrml*), Kapitalzuführung *f*

injunction: ~ **bond** *n* LAW Sicherheitsleistung *f* bei gerichtlicher Anordnung

injure *vt* LAW verletzen

injured: ~ **party** *n* LAW Geschädigte(r) *mf* [decl. as adj], Verletzte(r) *mf* [decl. as adj]

injuria sine damno *phr* LAW Vertragsbruch *m* ohne Folgeschaden

injury *n* HRM *of an employee* Verletzung *f*; ~ **independent of all other means** *n* INS *health insurance* von allen anderen Einwirkungen unabhängige Verletzung *f*

ink: ~**-jet printer** *n* COMP Ink-Jet-Printer *m* (*jarg*), Tintenstrahldrucker *m*

inland *adj* IMP/EXP, TRANSP inländisch, Binnen-, Inland-; ~ **carrier** *n* IMP/EXP, TRANSP Binnenfrachtführer *m*, Binnentransportfirma *f*, Inlandtransportunternehmen *nt*, Binnenbeförderungsunternehmen *nt*; ~ **clearance depot** *n* (*ICD*) IMP/EXP Inlandsabfertigungslager *nt*; ~ **container** *n* (*IC*) TRANSP Inlandscontainer *m*; ~ **haulage** *n* IMP/EXP, TRANSP Binnentransport *m*, Inlandsfracht *f*, Inlandstransport *m*; ~ **marine insurance** *n* INS Binnentransportversicherung *f*; ~ **postage** *n* COMMS Inlandsporto *nt*; ~ **rail depot** *n* (*IRD*) IMP/EXP, TRANSP Inlandsbahndepot *nt*; ~ **revenue** *n BrE* (*cf internal revenue AmE*) TAX *income from taxes* Steueraufkommen *nt*, Steuereinnahmen *f pl*

Inland: ~ **Revenue** *n BrE* (*IR, cf Internal Revenue*

Authority AmE) TAX Steuerbehörde *f*; ~ **Revenue Office** *n BrE* (*cf Internal Revenue Service AmE*) TAX Finanzamt *nt*

inland: ~ **waterway** *n* TRANSP Binnenschiffahrtsweg *m*; ~ **waterway vessel** *n* TRANSP Binnenschiff *nt*

in-line *adj* GEN COMM ausgeglichen; ~ **budget** *n* FIN ausgeglichener Haushalt *m*, ausgeglichenes Budget *nt*

inmate *n* LAW *of prison* Insasse *m*, Insassin *f*

inner: ~ **city** *n* ECON, ENVIR, PROP Stadtkern *m*, Kernstadt *f*, Innenstadt *f*; ~**-city area** *n* ECON, ENVIR, PROP innerstädtischer Bereich *m*; ~ **harbor** *AmE*, ~ **harbour** *BrE n* TRANSP Binnenhafen *m*, Hafenbecken *nt*

innominate: ~ **contract** *n* LAW Innominatvertrag *m*

innovate *vi* IND, PATENTS, S&M Neuerungen einführen

innovation *n* IND, PATENTS, S&M *production* Innovation *f*, Neuentwicklung *f*, Neuerung *f*; ~ **center** *AmE*, ~ **centre** *BrE n* IND Innovationszentrum *nt*

innovative *adj* IND, PATENTS, S&M innovativ

innovator *n* IND, PATENTS, S&M Innovator, in *m,f*, Neuerer *m*

inoperative: ~ **clause** *n* LAW rechtsunwirksame Klausel *f*, ungültige Klausel *f*

inordinate *adj* GEN COMM maßlos

in-pack: ~ **premium** *n* S&M beigelegter Zugabeartikel *m*

in pari delicto *phr frml* LAW beiderseits schuldig, mitschuldig

in-plant: ~ **training** *n* HRM betriebliche Ausbildung *f*

input 1. *n* COMP *of data, text* Eingabe *f*, GEN COMM Einsatz *m*, Eingabe *f*, Input *m*; **2.** *vt* COMP *data, text* eingeben

input: ~ **cost** *n* ACC Eingabekosten *pl*; ~ **data** *n pl* COMP Eingabedaten *pl*; ~ **device** *n* COMP Eingabegerät *nt*; ~ **factor** *n* FIN Input-Faktor *m*; ~ **form** *n* COMP Eingabemaske *f*; ~ **format** *n* COMP Eingabeformat *nt*; ~ **keyboard** *n* COMP Eingabetastatur *f*; ~ **market** *n* ECON Faktormarkt *m*; ~ **message** *n* COMP Eingabemeldung *f*

input/output *n* (*I/O*) COMP Eingabe-Ausgabe *f* (*E/A*); ~ **analysis** *n* COMP, ECON, FIN, MATH Eingabe-Ausgabe-Analyse *f*, Input-Output-Analyse *f* (*jarg*); ~ **control system** *n* (*IOCS*) COMP Eingabe-Ausgabe-Steuersystem *nt*; ~ **processor** *n* COMP Eingabe-Ausgabe-Prozessor *m*; ~ **table** *n* COMP, ECON, FIN, MATH Eingabe-Ausgabe-Tabelle *f*

inputs *n pl* COMP Eingaben *f pl*, ECON Einsatzgüter *nt pl*

input: ~ **tax** *n* TAX Vorsteuer *f*

in rem *phr* LAW dinglich (*frml*)

ins. *abbr* (*insurance*) ACC, INS Vers. (*Versicherung*)

INSA *abbr* (*International Shipowners' Association*) TRANSP Vereinigung *f* internationaler Schiffseigner

insecure *adj* ECON unsicher

insecurity *n* ECON Unsicherheit *f*

insert *vt* COMP einfügen, MEDIA einbauen

insertion *n* S&M Plazierung *f*

in-service *adj* HRM, IND innerbetrieblich; ~ **training** *n* HRM, IND innerbetriebliche Schulung *f*

inshore: ~ **traffic zone** *n* TRANSP *shipping* Küstenverkehrszone *f*

inside *prep* GEN COMM innerhalb; ~ **back cover** *n* MEDIA *print* hinterer Klappentext *m*; ~ **front** *n* S&M *advertising* Umschlagseite *f*; ~ **front cover** *n* MEDIA *print* vorderer Klappentext *m*; ~ **information** *n* GEN COMM

Informationen *f pl* aus erster Hand, *confidential* Insiderinformation *f*, Interna *pl*, interne Geschäftsinformation *f*; **~ lag** *n* ECON, POL innere Wirkungsverzögerung *f*; **~ lot** *n* PROP mittleres Grundstück *nt*; **~ money** *n* ECON Innengeld *nt*

insider: **~ dealing** *n* FIN, STOCK Insidergeschäfte *nt pl*, Insiderhandel *m*; **~ wage setting** *n* HRM Insiderlohnabschluß *m*

insignificant *adj* GEN COMM unwesentlich

insoluble *adj* GEN COMM *problem* unlösbar

insolvency *n* ACC, BANK, FIN, LAW Überschuldung *f*, Zahlungsunfähigkeit *f*, *bankruptcy* Konkurs *m*, Insolvenz *f*; **~ clause** *n* INS *reinsurance contract* Insolvenzklausel *f*, Zahlungsunfähigkeitsklausel *f*; **~ legislation** *n* LAW Vergleichs- und Konkursrecht *nt*

insolvent *adj* ACC, BANK, FIN, LAW zahlungsunfähig, insolvent

inspect *vt* GEN COMM untersuchen, *check* prüfen

inspection *n* GEN COMM Inspektion *f*, *checking* Prüfung *f*; ◆ **on ~** GEN COMM zur Ansicht

inspection: **~ of files** *n* PATENTS Aktenprüfung *f*; **~ specimen** *n* GEN COMM Ansichtsexemplar *nt*; **~ survey** *n* IND Besichtigung *f*

inspector *n* GEN COMM Inspektor, in *m,f*

inspectorate *n* GEN COMM Aufsichtsbehörde *f*, Inspektion *f*, *office* Aufsichtsamt *nt*

inspector: **~-general of banks** *n* BANK Leiter, in *m,f* in der Bankenaufsichtsbehörde

inst. *abbr* COMMS (*instant*) *of current month* d.M. (*dieses Monats*), GEN COMM (*instant*) immediate sofortig, fristlos, (*installed*) eingebaut, installiert, (*institute*) Institut *nt*

instability *n* ECON Unsicherheit *f*

instable *adj* ECON unsicher

install *vt* COMP installieren, GEN COMM installieren, einbauen, IND aufstellen

installation *n* COMP, GEN COMM Installierung *f*, Installation *f*, IND Aufstellung *f*; **~ diskette** *n* COMP Installationsdiskette *f*

installed *adj* (*inst.*) GEN COMM eingebaut, installiert

installment *n AmE see* instalment *BrE*; ◆ **on the ~ plan** *AmE* (*cf on hire purchase BrE*) FIN auf Abzahlungsbasis, auf Raten

instalment *n BrE* BANK, FIN Rate *f*, Teilzahlung *f*; ◆ **in instalments** *BrE* BANK, FIN in Raten

instalment: **~ bill of exchange** *n BrE* FIN Abzahlungswechsel *m*; **~ commission** *n BrE* INS Folgeprovision *f*; **~ contract** *n BrE* FIN, LAW Abzahlungsvertrag *m*, Ratenvertrag *m*, Teillieferungsvertrag *m*; **~ credit** *n BrE* BANK, FIN Abzahlungskredit *m*, Ratenkredit *m*, Teilzahlungskredit *m*; **~ loan** *n BrE* BANK, FIN Teilzahlungskredit *m*; **~ mortgage** *n BrE* BANK, FIN Abzahlungshypothek *f*; **~ payment** *n BrE* BANK, FIN Ratenzahlung *f*, Teilzahlung *f*; **~ price** *n BrE* BANK, FIN Abzahlungspreis *m*; **~ repayment plan** *n BrE* BANK, FIN Ratenzahlungsplan *m*, Teilzahlungsplan *m*; **~ repayment schedule** *n BrE* BANK, FIN Ratenzahlungsplan *m*, Teilzahlungsplan *m*; **~ sale** *n BrE* S&M Abzahlungsverkauf *m*, Verkauf *m* auf Ratenzahlung, Teilzahlungsverkauf *m*; **~ sale period** *n BrE* S&M Abzahlungszeitraum *m*

instance: **in this ~** *phr* GEN COMM in diesem Fall

instant *adj* (*inst.*) COMMS *of current month* dieses Monats

(*d.M.*), GEN COMM *immediate* sofortig, fristlos; **~ dismissal** *n* HRM fristlose Entlassung *f*

instantly *adv* GEN COMM sofort

instant: **~ monetarism** *n* ECON sofortiger Monetarismus *m*, unmittelbarer Monetarismus *m*

institute *n* (*inst.*) GEN COMM Institut *nt*

Institute: **~ of Administrative Management** *n BrE* (*IAM*) MGMNT Institut für Verwaltungsmanagement; **~ of Bankers** *n* (*IOB*) BANK Institut der Bankiers; **~ of Chartered Accountants** *n BrE* (*ICA*) ACC ≈ Institut *nt* der Wirtschaftsprüfer (*IdW*); **~ of Chartered Accountants in England and Wales** *n* (*ICAEW*) ACC Institut der Wirtschaftsprüfer von England und Wales; **~ of Chartered Accountants in Ireland** *n* (*ICAI*) ACC Institut der Wirtschaftsprüfer von Irland; **~ of Chartered Accountants of Scotland** *n* (*ICAS*) ACC Institut der Wirtschaftsprüfer von Schottland; **~ of Chartered Shipbrokers** *n* (*ICS*) TRANSP Institut der konzessionierten Schiffsmakler

institute: **~ clause** *n* INS *marine* Bedingung der Londoner Seeversicherer

Institute: **~ of Cost and Management Accountants** *n BrE* (*ICMA*) ACC Institut der Kostenrechner und Wirtschaftsprüfer; **~ of Economic Affairs** *n BrE* (*IEA*) ECON Institut für Wirtschaftsangelegenheiten; **~ for Fiscal Studies** *n BrE* (*IFS*) TAX Institut für fiskalische Studien; **~ for International Finance** *n* (*IIF*) FIN internationales Finanzinstitut, internationales Finanzwirtschaftsinstitut; **~ of London Underwriters** *n* INS Institut der Londoner Versicherungsgeber; **~ of Manpower Studies** *n* (*IMS*) HRM Institut für Personalstudien; **~ of Office Management** *n* (*IOM*) MGMNT Institut für Büroorganisation; **~ of Personnel Management** *n BrE* (*IPM*) MGMNT Institut für Personalverwaltung; **~ of Practitioners in Advertising** *n BrE* (*IPA*) S&M Institut für Werbefachleute; **~ of Public Relations** *n BrE* (*IPR*) S&M Institut für Öffentlichkeitsarbeit; **~ of Shipping and Forwarding Agents** *n* (*ISFA*) TRANSP Institut der Versand- und Speditionsagenten

institute: **~ warranty** *n* INS Garantie-Standardsatz *m*, Gewährleistungs-Standardsatz *m*

institution *n* GEN COMM Institution *f*

institutional: **~ advertising** *n* S&M firmeneigene Werbung *f*; **~ economics** *n* ECON Institutionenökonomik *f*; **~ investor** *n* STOCK institutioneller Anleger *m*, institutionelle Anlegerin *f*

institution: **~ incorporated under public law** *n* LAW Anstalt *f* des öffentlichen Rechts

in-store: **~ merchandising** *n* S&M Ladenvertrieb *m*; **~ promotion** *n* S&M im Laden betriebene Verkaufsförderung *f*

instruct *vt* GEN COMM beauftragen, anweisen, LAW *jury* instruieren, belehren

instruction *n* COMP *program* Befehl *m*, GEN COMM Anweisung *f*, Instruktion *f*, HRM *training* Ausbildung *f*, LAW *jury* Instruktion *f*, Belehrung *f*, POL *directive* Weisung *f*; **~ book** *n* GEN COMM Bedienungsanleitung *f*, Betriebsanleitung *f*; **~ leaflet** *n* GEN COMM Merkblatt *nt*; **~ manual** *n* GEN COMM Bedienungshandbuch *nt*, Befehlshandbuch *nt*

instructions: **~ for use** *n pl* GEN COMM Bedienungsanleitung *f*

instrument *n* BANK Handelspapier *nt*, FIN Dokument *nt*, Handelspapier *nt*, GEN COMM Handelspapier *nt*,

Instrument *nt*, IND *implement* Instrument *nt*, STOCK Handelspapier *nt*

instrumental *adj* GEN COMM instrumental, dienlich, förderlich

instrumentalities: **~ of transportation** *n pl* INS, TRANSP Transportmitwirkung *f*, Transportvermittlung *f*

instrumentality *n* FIN Zweckdienlichkeit *f*

instrument: **~ variable** *n* ECON Instrumentenvariable *f*

insufficient *adj* BANK, FIN ungenügend, GEN COMM unzulänglich, unzureichend; **~ funds** *n pl* (*I/F*) FIN ungenügende Deckung *f*

insulate *vt* GEN COMM isolieren; ◆ **~ against** GEN COMM abschirmen, LAW befreien; **~ from** GEN COMM abschotten, LAW befreien

insulating: **~ measures** *n pl* GEN COMM Abwehrmaßnahmen *f pl*

insurability *n* INS Versicherbarkeit *f*, Versicherungsfähigkeit *f*

insurable *adj* INS versicherbar, versicherungsfähig; **~ interest** *n* INS versicherbares Interesse *nt*; **~ risk** *n* INS versicherbares Risiko *nt*; **~ title** *n* INS versicherbarer Titel *m*

insurance *n* (*ince, ins.*) ACC, INS Versicherung *f* (*Vers.*); **~ annuity** *n* INS Leibrentenversicherung *f*; **~ benefit** *n* INS Versicherungsleistung *f*

Insurance: **~ Brokers' Registration Council** *n BrE* (*IBRC*) INS Registrierungsausschuß *m* der Versicherungsmakler

insurance: **~ broking** *n* INS Versicherungsmaklergeschäft *nt*, Versicherungsvermittlungsgeschäft *nt*; **~ certificate** *n* INS Einzelpolice *f*, Versicherungsausweis *m*, Versicherungsurkunde *f*, Versicherungszertifikat *nt*; **~ charge** *n* INS Versicherungskosten *pl*, Versicherungslasten *f pl*; **~ claim** *n* INS Versicherungsanspruch *m*; **~ company** *n* INS Assekurant *m*, Versicherer *m*, Versicherungsgesellschaft *f*, Versicherungsunternehmen *nt*; **~ contract** *n* INS Versicherungsvertrag *m*; **~ cost** *n* INS Versicherungskosten *pl*; **~ cover** *BrE*, **~ coverage** *AmE* *n* INS Deckung *f*, Deckungsumfang *m*, Versicherungsschutz *m*; **~ factoring** *n* INS Versicherungsfactoring *nt*; **~ in force** *n* INS laufende Versicherung *f*, rechtsgültige Versicherung *f*; **~ industry** *n* INS Assekuranz *f*, Versicherungswirtschaft *f*, Versicherungsgewerbe *nt*; **~ market** *n* INS Versicherungsmarkt *m*

Insurance: **~ Ombudsman Bureau** *n BrE* (*IOB*) INS Büro des Versicherungs-Beschwerdekommissars

insurance: **~ payable at death** *n AmE* (*cf whole-life assurance BrE*) INS Lebensversicherung *f* auf den Todesfall, Todesfallversicherung *f*; **~ policy** *n* INS Versicherungsschein *m*, Versicherungspolice *f*; **~ policy certificate** *n* INS Versicherungsdokument *nt*; **~ portfolio** *n* INS Versicherungsbestand *m*; **~ premium** *n* INS Versicherungsbeitrag *m*, Versicherungsprämie *f*; **~ scheme** *n* INS Versicherungssystem *nt*; **~ settlement** *n* INS Versicherungsbegleichung *f*, Versicherungsleistung *f*; **~ of valuables** *n* INS Valorenversicherung *f*

insure *vt* INS versichern; ◆ **~ sb against fire** INS jdn gegen Feuer versichern

insure: **not to ~ clause** *n* INS Klausel *f* der Nichtversicherung

insured *adj* INS versichert; **the ~** *n* INS die versicherte Person *f*, der Versicherte *m* [decl. as adj], die Versicherte *f* [decl. as adj]; **~ account** *n* INS *at a financial institution* versichertes Konto *nt*; **~ letter** *n* COMMS Wertbrief *m*,

Wertsendung *f*; **~ parcel** *n* COMMS Wertpaket *nt*; **~ peril** *n* INS versicherte Gefahr *f*

insure: **~ jointly** *vt* INS mitversichern

insurer *n* INS Versicherer *m*, Assekurant *m*

insurgent 1. *adj* POL aufständisch; **2.** *n* POL Aufständische(r) *mf* [decl. as adj], Aufrührer, in *m,f*

insurrection *n* POL Aufstand *m*

int. *abbr* (*interest*) ACC, BANK, ECON, FIN, STOCK Zins *m*, Zinsen *m pl*

INT *abbr* (*intermediate survey*) INS Zwischenübersicht *f*

intact *adj* GEN COMM *undamaged* unversehrt, intakt, ganz

intake *n* GEN COMM *of new orders* Eingang *m*, WEL *of students* Zugang *m*

intangible *adj* ACC, ECON, FIN, LAW immateriell; **~ assets** *n pl* ACC, FIN immaterielle Aktiva *pl*, immaterielles Vermögen *nt*, immaterielle Vermögenswerte *m pl*; **~ asset worth** *n* ACC, FIN immaterieller Vermögenswert *m*; **~ contribution** *n* GEN COMM immaterieller Beitrag *m*; **~ fixed assets** *n pl* ACC, FIN immaterielles Anlagevermögen *nt*; **~ property** *n* ACC immaterielles Vermögen *nt*, unkörperliches Vermögen *nt*; **~ reward** *n* ECON immaterielle Entlohnung *f*, HRM immaterielle Belohnung *f*; **~ value** *n* ACC immaterieller Wert *m*; **~ wealth** *n* ECON inmaterieller Wohlstand *m*

integral: **~ part** *n* GEN COMM wesentlicher Bestandteil *m*

integrate *vt* GEN COMM eingliedern, integrieren, verflechten

integrated *adj* GEN COMM integriert; ◆ **be ~ into** GEN COMM aufgenommen sein in, integriert sein in

integrated: **~ circuit** *n* (*IC*) COMP integrierter Schaltkreis *m* (*IS*); **~ management system** *n* MGMNT integriertes Führungssystem *nt*, integriertes Managementsystem *nt*; **~ pollution control** *n* (*IPC*) ENVIR integrierte Schadstoffkontrolle *f*, integrierter Umweltschutz *m*; **~ project management** *n* (*IPM*) MGMNT integrierte Projektleitung *f*, integrierte Projektverwaltung *f*, einheitliche Projektleitung *f*, integriertes Projektmanagement *nt*

Integrated: **~ Services Digital Network** *n* (*ISDN*) COMMS, COMP integriertes Dienstleistungsdatennetz *nt* (*ISDN*)

integrated: **~ software** *n* COMP integrierte Software *f*

integration *n* GEN COMM Integration *f*, Verflechtung *f*; **~ with social security** *n* HRM, WEL Integration *f* in die Sozialversicherung

integrative: **~ bargaining** *n* HRM integrative Verhandlungen *f pl*

integrity *n* GEN COMM Integrität *f*

intellectual: **~ property** *n* LAW, PATENTS geistiges Eigentum *nt*; **~ property rights** *n pl* LAW, PATENTS gewerblicher Rechtsschutz *m*, gewerbliche Schutz- und Urheberrechte *nt pl*, Schutz *m* geistigen Eigentums

intelligent: **~ document** *n* COMP intelligentes Dokument *nt*; **~ information retrieval** *n* COMP intelligente Informationswiedergewinnung *f*; **~ terminal** *n* COMP intelligente Datenstation *f*

intensely: **~ competitive** *adj* GEN COMM wettbewerbsintensiv

intensification *n* GEN COMM Intensivierung *f*, Verschärfung *f*

intensify 1. *vt* GEN COMM intensivieren, verschärfen; **2.** *vi* GEN COMM zunehmen

intensive *adj* GEN COMM intensiv; **~ farming** *n* ECON intensive Bewirtschaftung *f*; **~ livestock farming** *n*

ECON intensive Viehwirtschaft *f*; ~ **negotiating** *n* GEN COMM intensives Verhandeln *nt*; ~ **negotiation** *n* STOCK intensive Verhandlung *f*; ~ **production** *n* ECON, IND intensive Produktion *f*, Intensivproduktion *f*; ~ **selling** *n* S&M Intensivverkauf *m*

intent *n* LAW Absicht *f*

intention *n* LAW Absicht *f*; ~ **of the contracting parties** *n* LAW Vertragswille *m* der Parteien; ~ **to deceive** *n* LAW Arglist *f*, arglistige Täuschung *f*; ~ **to undergo commitments** *n* LAW *contracting parties* Bindungswille *m*

intent: ~ **to enrich oneself** *n* LAW Bereicherungsabsicht *f*

inter-account: ~ **dealing** *n* FIN Interkontenhandel *m*

interaction: ~ **matrix** *n* MGMNT Interaktionsmatrix *f*

interactive *adj* COMP, GEN COMM interaktiv; ~ **mode** *n* COMP Dialogmodus *m*; ~ **processing** *n* COMP Dialogverarbeitung *f*; ~ **system** *n* COMP Dialogsystem *nt*

inter alia *adv* GEN COMM unter anderem

interbank: ~ **business** *n* BANK, ECON, FIN Interbankengeschäft *nt*; ~ **deposits** *n pl* BANK, FIN Interbankeneinlagen *f pl*, Zwischenbankeinlagen *f pl*; ~ **exchange rate** *n* BANK, ECON Interbankenwechselkurs *m*; ~ **funds** *n pl* BANK, FIN Interbankmittel *nt pl*; ~ **lending** *n* BANK, FIN Bank-an-Bank-Kredit *m*; ~ **lendings** *n pl* BANK, FIN Bank-an-Bank-Ausleihungen *f pl*; ~ **loan** *n* BANK, FIN Bank-an-Bank-Kredit *m*, Zwischenbankkredit *m*; ~ **market** *n* BANK, ECON Interbankenmarkt *m*; ~ **offered rate** *n* (*IBOR*) BANK, ECON Interbankenangebotssatz *m*; ~ **rate** *n* BANK, ECON Interbankenrate *f*, Refinanzierungszins *m* einer Bank, Tagesgeldsatz *m*; ~ **transactions** *n pl* BANK, ECON, FIN Interbankengeschäft *nt*

interchange 1. *n* GEN COMM *exchange* Austausch *m*, TRANSP *for passengers* Umsteigemöglichkeit *f*; **2.** *vt* GEN COMM austauschen

interchangeable *adj* GEN COMM austauschbar

interchange: ~ **container** *n* TRANSP Austausch-Container *m*; ~ **flight** *n* TRANSP Flug *m* mit Umsteigen; ~ **of know-how** *n* GEN COMM Erfahrungsaustausch *m*; ~ **of letters** *n* COMMS Briefwechsel *m*

InterCity *n* BrE TRANSP *train* Intercity *m*

intercommodity: ~ **spread** *n* STOCK Inter-Lieferungs-Spread *m*, Spanne *f* zwischen verschiedenen Lieferungen

intercompany: ~ **clearing account** *n* ACC Konzern-Verrechnungskonto *nt*; ~ **market** *n* STOCK konzerninterner Markt *m*; ~ **profits** *n pl* FIN Konzernbuchgewinn *m*

interconnection *n* GEN COMM gegenseitige Verbindung *f*, Querverbund *m*, Verbundnetz *nt*, wechselseitiger Anschluß *m*

intercontinental *adj* TRANSP interkontinental

intercorporate: ~ **privilege** *n* AmE TAX Schachtelprivileg *nt*

intercultural: ~ **marketing** *n* S&M interkulturelles Marketing *nt*

interdealer: ~ **broker** *n* BrE (*IDB*) BANK, STOCK Makler, der ausschließlich Geschäfte zwischen Primärhändlern vermittelt

interdelivery: ~ **spread** *n* STOCK *currency futures* Inter-Lieferungs-Spread *m*, Spanne *f* zwischen Lieferungen

interdepartmental *adj* ADMIN *within company, organization* abteilungsübergreifend; ~ **communication** *n* ADMIN, COMMS Kommunikation *f* zwischen Abteilungen; ~ **flexibility** *n* (*IDF*) HRM bereichsübergreifende Flexibilität *f*, abteilungsübergreifende Flexibilität *f*; ~ **settlement** *n* LAW interministerielle Regelung *f*; ~ **settlement advice** *n* FIN, MGMNT ressortmäßige Abrechnungsanzeige *f*

interdependence *n* GEN COMM gegenseitige Abhängigkeit *f*, Interdependenz *f*, Verflechtung *f*

interdependent *adj* GEN COMM gegenseitig abhängig; ~ **economy** *n* ECON interdependente Volkswirtschaft *f*, offene Volkswirtschaft *f*

interdepot: ~ **transfer** *n* TRANSP Zwischen-Depot-Transfer *m*

interest *n* (*int.*) ACC, BANK Zinsen *m pl*, ECON Zins *m*, FIN *holding* Zins *m*, Beteiligung *f*, GEN COMM *on borrowings* Zins *m*, Interesse *nt*, Anteil *m*, Zinsen *m pl*, LAW Interesse *nt*; ♦ **and** ~ STOCK *bond prices* plus Stückzinsen

interest: ~ **accrued** *n* BANK Stückzinsen *m pl*; ~ **arrearage** *n* BANK Zinsrückstände *m pl*; ~ **on arrears** *n* BANK Verzugszinsen *m pl*; ~ **in a bank** *n* BANK Anteil *m* an einer Bank; ~~**bearing** *adj* ACC, BANK, FIN zinsbringend, zinstragend; ~~**bearing bond** *n* STOCK verzinsliche Schuldverschreibung *f*; ~~**bearing deposit** *n* BANK verzinsliche Einlage *f*; ~~**bearing eligible liabilities** *n pl* BrE (*IBELS*) BANK verzinsliche mindestreservepflichtige Einlagen *f pl*; ~~**bearing instrument** *n* STOCK verzinsliches Instrument *nt*; ~~**bearing liabilities** *n pl* ACC, BANK verzinsliche Verbindlichkeiten *f pl*; ~~**bearing trading portfolio** *n* STOCK verzinslicher Handelsbestand *m*; ~~**bearing yield** *n* STOCK *Eurodollar futures* verzinsliche Rendite *f*, verzinslicher Ertrag *m*; ~ **burden** *n* ACC Zinslast *f*; ~ **charge** *n* ACC *on loan* Sollzinsen *m pl*, FIN Zinsbelastung *f*; ~ **charged for deferred payment** *n* FIN Stundungszinsen *m pl*; ~ **clause** *n* LAW Zinsklausel *f*; ~ **coupon** *n* FIN Zinsbogen *m*, Zinskupon *m*, Zinsschein *m*; ~ **earned** *n* ACC *profit and loss account*, BANK Ertragszinsen *m pl*, Habenzinsen *m pl*, Zinsertrag *m*

interested: ~ **party** *n* GEN COMM beteiligte Partei *f*, LAW Beteiligte(r) *mf* [decl. as adj]

interest: ~ **elasticity of savings** *n* ECON Zinselastizität *f* der Ersparnisse

Interest: ~ **Equalization Tax** *n* (*IET*) TAX Zinsausgleichssteuer *f*

interest: ~ **formula** *n* BANK Zinsformel *f*; ~~**free** *adj* BANK, FIN *loan* zinsfrei; ~ **group** *n* GEN COMM Interessengruppe *f*; ~ **income** *n* BANK, FIN Zinseinkommen *nt*, Zinseinkünfte *pl*; ~~**linked** *adj* BANK, FIN zinsgebunden; ~ **margin** *n* BANK, FIN Zinsspanne *f*; ~ **on overdue accounts** *n* BANK Verzugszinsen *m pl*; ~ **paid** *n* ACC *profit and loss account* Zinsaufwand *m*; ~ **payment** *n* BANK Zinszahlung *f*; ~ **penalty** *n* BANK Negativzins *m*, Strafzins *m*; ~ **policy** *n* INS Police *f* mit versicherbarem Interesse; ~ **profit and dividends** *n pl* (*IPD*) ECON Zinsen, Gewinne und Dividenden aus Kapitalanlagen von Inländern; ~ **rate** *n* ACC, BANK, ECON, FIN, STOCK Zinsfuß *m*, Zinssatz *m*; ~ **rate adjustment** *n* BANK Zinsanpassung *f*; ~ **rate advantage** *n* STOCK Zinsvorteil *m*; ~ **rate cartel** *n* BANK Zinskartell *nt*; ~ **rate ceiling** *n* BANK Höchstzins *m*; ~ **rate contract** *n* STOCK *interest rate futures* Zinskontrakt *m*, Zinsterminkontrakt *m*; ~ **rate**

differential n BANK Zinsgefälle nt; **~ rate exposure** n STOCK interest rate futures Zinskontraktrisiko nt, Zinsrisiko nt; **~ rate future** n STOCK Zinsterminkontrakt m pl; **~ rate futures contract** n STOCK Zinsterminkontrakt m; **~ rate futures prices** n pl STOCK Zinsterminkontraktpreise m pl; **~ rate instrument** n STOCK Zinsinstrument nt; **~ rate movement** n BANK Zinsbewegung f; **~ rate net of all charges** n FIN Zinssatz m nach Gebührenabzug; **~ rate range** n ACC, BANK, ECON, FIN, STOCK Zinsspanne f; **~ rate risk** n BANK Zinsrisiko nt; **~ rate structure** n ECON Zinsstruktur f; **~ rate subsidy** n FIN Zinszuschuß m; **~ rate swap** n FIN, STOCK Zinsswap m; **~ received** n ACC, BANK Ertragszinsen m pl, Habenzinsen m pl, Zinsertrag m, Zinserträge m pl; **~ relief** n ECON Zinsnachlaß m; **~ risk** n FIN Zinsrisiko nt; **~ roll-over date** n BANK Zinsanpassungsdatum nt; **~ on saving deposits** n BANK Sparzinsen m pl; **~sensitive expenditure** n FIN zinsempfindliche Ausgaben f pl, zinsreagible Ausgaben f pl; **~-sensitive policy** n INS zinsempfindliche Police f; **~ spread** n BANK Zinsspanne f

interface n COMP Interface nt (jarg), Schnittstelle f, GEN COMM Schnittstelle f

interfere: **~ with** phr LAW contract beeinträchtigen, verletzen

interference n COMP Störung f, GEN COMM Beeinträchtigung f, impairment Interferenz f, LAW unbefugter Eingriff m; **~ with contract** n LAW Verleitung f zum Vertragsbruch, Vertragseingriff m

interfering: **~ claims** n pl LAW widerstreitende Ansprüche m pl

inter-firm: **~ comparison** n MGMNT zwischenbetrieblicher Vergleich m

interfund n ECON Haushalt m

intergenerational: **~ distribution of income** n ECON Einkommensverteilung f zwischen Generationen, intergenerative Einkommensverteilung f; **~ equity** n ECON Generationenvertrag m

intergovernmental adj POL summit zwischenstaatlich

Intergovernmental: **~ Committee for European Migration** n (ICEM) WEL zwischenstaatliches Komitee nt für europäische Auswanderung (ICEM)

intergovernmental: **~ organization** n POL zwischenstaatliche Organisation f; **~ preparatory group** n (IPG) POL zwischenstaatliche Vorbereitungsgruppe f

intergroup adj HRM konzernintern; **~ relations** n pl HRM konzerninterne Beziehungen f pl

interim 1. adj GEN COMM report, job einstweilig, vorläufig; 2. n GEN COMM, POL Interim nt, Zwischenzeit f; ♦ **in the ~** GEN COMM einstweilig

interim: **~ accounts** n pl ACC Interimskonten nt pl; **~ agreement** n GEN COMM Zwischenvertrag m; **~ audit** n ADMIN Zwischenaudit nt; **~ balance** ACC Interimbilanz f, Zwischenbilanz f; **~ dividend** n STOCK Abschlagsdividende f, Interimsdividende f, Zwischendividende f; **~ injunction** n PATENTS einstweilige Verfügung f; **~ loan** n BANK Überbrückungskredit m, Zwischenkredit m; **~ pension** n FIN Übergangsrente f; **~ relief** n HRM vorläufige Unterstützung f; **~ report** n ACC Zwischenbericht m

interindustry: **~ competition** n ECON, IND Inter-Branchen-Konkurrenz f; **~ trade** n ECON, IND innergewerblicher Handel m

interior adj GEN COMM Innen-, domestic Inland-, Binnen-; **~ decorator** n PROP Raumausstatter, in m,f; **~ defect** n LAW of goods innerer Mangel m; **~ robbery policy** n INS Einbruch- und Diebstahlversicherung f

interlace vt GEN COMM verflechten

interlacing n GEN COMM Verflechtung f

interline: **~ agreement** n TRANSP aviation Vertrag m zwischen Fluglinien; **~ carrier** n TRANSP aviation Frachtführer m mit Vertrag zwischen Fluglinien

interlink vt GEN COMM verflechten, verzahnen

interlinked: **~ transaction** n ECON Kopplungsgeschäft nt

interlocking n GEN COMM Verflechtung f; **~ directorate** n MGMNT Überkreuzverflechtung f des Vorstands, Verflechtung f des Vorstands; **~ shareholding** n STOCK Überkreuzverflechtung f des Vorstands

interlocutory: **~ decree** n LAW Zwischenurteil nt

Intermarket: **~ Trading System** n AmE (ITS) STOCK elektronisches Informationssystem der US-Börsen

intermedia: **~ comparison** n MEDIA, S&M intermedialer Vergleich m, Vergleich m zwischen verschiedenen Medien

intermediary n GEN COMM Mittelsmann m, Mittler m, Vermittler, in m,f

intermediate: **~ area** n ECON assisted area Grauzone f; **~ bulk container** n (IBC) TRANSP Massengutfrachter m; **~ container** n TRANSP Zwischencontainer m; **~ credit** n FIN Zwischenkredit m; **~ financing** n BANK, FIN Zwischenfinanzierung f; **~ good** n IND Vorprodukt nt, Zwischenerzeugnis nt; **~ loan** n BANK Zwischenkredit m; **~ product** n IND Vorprodukt nt, Zwischenerzeugnis nt; **~ stage** n FIN Zwischenstadium nt; **~ survey** n (INT) INS Zwischenübersicht f; **~ target** n ECON, POL Etappenziel nt, mittelfristiges Ziel nt; **~ technology** n IND production Technologie, die mit einfachen Werkzeugen und arbeitsintensiven Methoden arbeitet, weiche Technologie f; **~ term** n GEN COMM mittlere Frist f; **~-term credit** n BANK mittelfristiger Kredit m; **~ trade** n GEN COMM Zwischenhandel m

intermediation n FIN Geldanlage f über Banken und Finanzinstitute

intermittent: **~ production** n IND Herstellung f nach Kundenbestellung, Werkstattfertigung f

intermodal: **~ container** n TRANSP Container m für kombinierten Transport; **~ packaging** n TRANSP Verpackung f für kombinierten Transport; **~ transport** n TRANSP intermodaler Verkehr m, kombinierter Verkehr m, kombinierter Transport m; **~ transport law** n LAW, TRANSP Gesetz nt zum kombinierten Verkehr; **~ transport system** n TRANSP intermodales Verkehrssystem nt, System nt für kombinierten Transport

internal adj GEN COMM within country Binnen-, Inland-, within organization innerbetrieblich, intern, Innen-; **~ affairs** n pl POL Innenpolitik f, innenpolitische Fragen f pl; **~ audit** n ACC Innenrevision f, interne Revision f; **~ balance** n ECON binnenwirtschaftliches Gleichgewicht nt; **~ check** n GEN COMM interne Prüfung f; **~ communications** n pl COMMS interne Kommunikation f; **~ consumption** n ECON, ENVIR interner Verbrauch m; **~ control** n ACC interne Kontrolle f; **~ debt** n ECON Inlandsschuld f, interne Schuld f; **~ economy** n ECON Binnenwirtschaft f; **~ economy of scale** n ECON betriebsinterner Größenvorteil m, interne Kostendegression f; **~ expansion** n ECON internes Wachstum nt; **~ fare** n LEIS, TRANSP aviation

Inlandsflugpreis *m*; ~ **feud** *n* MGMNT interner Machtkampf *m*; ~ **financing** *n* FIN Innenfinanzierung *f*, interne Finanzierung *f*, Selbstfinanzierung *f*; ~ **flight** *n* LEIS, TRANSP Inlandsflug *m*; ~ **frontier** *n* GEN COMM interne Grenze *f*; ~ **funding** *n* ACC, FIN eigene Finanzierung *f*; ~ **government policy** *n* ECON, POL Innenpolitik *f* der Regierung; ~ **growth** *n* ECON internes Wachstum *nt*

internalization *n* ECON Internalisierung *f*, STOCK Methode, Aktien zwischen Brokerbüros zu übertragen

internalize *vt* ECON internalisieren

internalizing: ~ **an externality** *n* ECON Internalisierung *f* externer Effekte, Internalisierung *f* sozialer Kosten

internal: ~ **labor market** *AmE*, ~ **labour market** *BrE n* ECON einheimischer Arbeitsmarkt *m*, Inlandsarbeitsmarkt *m*; ~ **labour market contracting** *n BrE* ECON interne Arbeitsmarktbeteiligung *f*, Rekrutierung *f* aus dem einheimischen Arbeitsmarkt; ~ **labour market recruitment** *BrE n* ECON Rekrutierung *f* aus dem einheimischen Arbeitsmarkt; ~ **lines of communication** *n pl* MGMNT innerbetriebliche Kommunikationswege *m pl*

internally: ~ **funded pensions** *n pl* FIN, HRM selbstfinanzierte Renten *f pl*; ~ **generated funds** *n pl* ACC, FIN eigenerwirtschaftete Mittel *nt pl*, intern erwirtschaftete Geldmittel *nt pl*

internal: ~ **market** *n* ECON Binnenmarkt *m*; ~ **power struggle** *n* MGMNT interner Machtkampf *m*; ~ **rate of discount** *n* ACC Kalkulationszinsfuß *m*; ~ **rate of return** *n* (*IRR*) ACC, ECON, FIN interner Zinsfuß *m*; ~ **reporting** *n* MGMNT internes Berichtswesen *nt*; ~ **revenue** *n AmE* (*cf inland revenue BrE*) TAX *income from taxes* Steueraufkommen *nt*, Steuereinnahmen *f pl*

Internal: ~ **Revenue Authority** *n AmE* (*cf Inland Revenue BrE*) TAX Steuerbehörde *f*; ~ **Revenue Service** *n AmE* (*IRS, cf Inland Revenue Office BrE*) TAX Bundessteuerbehörde *f*, Finanzamt *nt*

internal: ~ **school assessment** *n* WEL schulinterne Beurteilung *f*; ~ **search** *n* HRM internes Stellenangebot *nt*; ~ **storage** *n* COMP interner Speicher *m*; ~ **trade** *n* ECON Binnenhandel *m*; ~ **transactions** *n pl* ACC Buchungsvorfälle *m pl*

international *adj* (*intl*) GEN COMM international (*int.*); ◆ **at an ~ level** GEN COMM auf internationaler Ebene; **on an ~ scale** GEN COMM auf internationaler Ebene, weltweit

international, International: **International Accounting Standards Committee** *n* (*IASC*) ACC Internationaler Ausschuß *m* für Rechnungslegungsgrundsätze; **international affairs** *n pl* POL internationale Angelegenheiten *f pl*, *international relations* internationale Beziehungen *f pl*; **international agency** *n* ADMIN internationale Agentur *f*, internationale Behörde *f*, internationale Vertretung *f*; **international agreement** *n* LAW internationales Abkommen *nt*; **International Aid and Loan Bulletin** *n* BANK Internationales Entwicklungshilfe- und Kreditbulletin *nt*; **international airline** *n* LEIS, TRANSP internationale Fluggesellschaft *f*; **international airport** *n* LEIS, TRANSP internationaler Flughafen *m*; **International Air Transport Association** *n* (*IATA*) TRANSP Internationaler Lufttransportverband *m* (*IATA*); **international application** *n* PATENTS internationale Anmeldung *f*; **International Association of Classification Societies** *n* (*IACS*) GEN COMM Internationaler Verband *m* der

Klassifizierungsgesellschaften; **International Association of Environmental Coordinators** *n* (*IAEC*) ENVIR Internationale Vereinigung *f* der Umweltkoordinatoren; **International Association for the Distribution of Food Products** *n* WEL Internationale Vereinigung für die Distribution von Lebensmitteln; **International Association for the Protection of Industrial Property** *n* (*IAPIP*) LAW Internationaler Verband *m* für gewerbliche Schutzrechte; **International Association of Ports and Harbours** *n* (*IAPH*) IMP/EXP Internationaler Hafenverband *m*; **International Auditing Practices Committee** *n* (*IAPC*) ACC Internationaler Ausschuß *m* für Buchprüfungspraktiken; **international auditing standards** *n pl* ACC internationale Grundsätze *m pl* der betriebsinternen Revision, internationale Prüfungsrichtlinien *f pl*; **International Bank for Economic Cooperation** *n* (*IBEC*) BANK, ECON Internationale Bank *f* für wirtschaftliche Zusammenarbeit; **international banking** *n* BANK internationales Bankgeschäft *nt*, internationale Banktätigkeit *f*; **international banking act** BANK, LAW internationale Bankfazilität *f*; **International Banking Act** *n AmE* BANK, LAW *1978* Gesetz, das die Tätigkeit der Auslandsbanken in den Vereinigten Staaten regelt; **international banking facility** *n* (*IBF*) BANK internationale Bankfazilität *f*; **International Bank for Reconstruction and Development** *n* (*IBRD*) BANK Internationale Bank *f* für Wiederaufbau und Entwicklung (*IBWE*), Weltbank *f*; **international business** *n* GEN COMM Auslandsgeschäft *nt*; **international call** *n* COMMS Auslandsgespräch *nt*; **international capital market** *n* STOCK internationaler Kapitalmarkt *m*; **International Cargo-Handling Coordinating Association** *n* (*ICHCA*) TRANSP internationaler Verband *m* für die Koordinierung von Frachtangelegenheiten; **international carriage** *n* TRANSP internationale Beförderung *f*, internationaler Transport *m*; **international cartel** *n* ECON internationales Kartell *nt*; **International Centre for Industry and the Environment** *n* (*ICIE*) ENVIR, IND internationales Zentrum *nt* für Industrie und Umwelt; **International Chamber of Commerce** *n* (*ICC*) GEN COMM Internationale Handelskammer *f*; **International Chamber of Shipping** *n* (*ICS*) TRANSP Internationale Schiffahrtskammer *f* (*ICS*); **International Civil Aviation Organization** *n* (*ICAO*) TRANSP Internationale Zivilluftfahrtorganisation *f* (*IZLO*); **international clearing house** *n* BANK internationale Verrechnungsstelle *f*; **International Clearing Union** *n* (*ICU*) ECON Internationale Clearingunion *f*, Internationale Verrechnungsinstitution *f*; **international commercial terms** *n pl* (*Incoterms*) ECON internationale Regeln *f pl* für die Auslegung von Handelsklauseln (*Incoterms*); **International Committee of the Red Cross** *n* (*ICRC*) WEL Internationales Komitee *nt* vom Roten Kreuz (*IKRK*); **International Commodities Clearing House** *n* (*ICCH*) STOCK Internationale Clearingstelle *f* für Terminkontrakte London; **International Commodity Agreement** *n* (*ICA*) STOCK internationales Rohstoffabkommen *nt*; **international comparison** *n* ECON internationaler Vergleich *m*; **international comparison of the cost of living** *n* ECON internationaler Vergleich *m* der Lebenshaltungskosten; **international competitiveness** *n* ECON internationale Wettbewerbsfähigkeit *f*; **International Confederation of Free Trade Unions** *n* (*ICFTU*) HRM, LAW Internationaler Bund *m* Freier Gewerkschaften (*IBFG*); **international** conference *n* GEN COMM internationale Konferenz *f*; **international conference center** *AmE*, **international conference centre** *BrE n* GEN COMM internationales Kongreßzentrum *nt*, internationales Tagungszentrum *nt*; **international consortium** *n* BANK internationales Konsortium *nt*; **international convention center** *AmE*, **international convention centre** *BrE n* GEN COMM internationales Kongreßzentrum *nt*, internationales Tagungszentrum *nt*; **international convention on carriage of goods by rail** *n* TRANSP internationale Konvention *f* über Schienentransport; **International Cooperation Administration** *n* (*ICA*) GEN COMM Verwaltung *f* für internationale Zusammenarbeit; **International Court of Justice** *n* (*ICJ*) LAW Internationaler Gerichtshof *m* (*IGH*); **international credit** *n* BANK, FIN internationaler Kredit *m*; **international credit club** *n* FIN internationaler Kreditverband *m*; **International Customs Tariffs Bureau** *n* (*ICTB*) IMP/ EXP Internationales Zolltarifbüro *nt*; **international department** *n* FIN, HRM Auslandsabteilung *f*; **International Development Association** *n* (*IDA*) ECON UN Internationale Entwicklungsorganisation *f* (*IDA*); **International Development Research Centre** *n* *BrE* (*IDRC*) GEN COMM internationales Entwicklungsforschungszentrum *nt*; **international direct dialing** *AmE*, **international direct dialling** *BrE n* (*IDD*) COMMS Selbstwählfernverkehr *m*; **international driver's license** *AmE*, **international driving licence** *BrE n* ADMIN, TRANSP internationaler Führerschein *m*; **international driving permit** *n* ADMIN, TRANSP internationaler Führerschein *m*; **international economic cooperation** *n* ECON internationale wirtschaftliche Zusammenarbeit *f*; **International Energy Agency** *n* (*IEA*) ENVIR Internationale Energie-Agentur *f* (*IEA*); **International Federation of Agricultural Producers** *n* (*IFAP*) IND internationaler Verband *m* der Produzenten landwirtschaftlicher Erzeugnisse; **International Federation for Documentation** *n* (*FID*) GEN COMM Internationaler Verband *m* für Dokumentation; **International Federation of Forwarding Agents Associations** *n* TRANSP Internationaler Verband *m* für Speditionsvereinigungen; **International Federation of Freight Forwarders Associations** *n* TRANSP Internationaler Verband *m* der Spediteur-Vereinigungen; **International Federation of Trade Unions** *n* (*IFTU*) HRM Internationaler Gewerkschaftsbund *m*; **International Finance Corporation** *n* (*IFC*) FIN Internationale Finanzkorporation *f* (*IFC*); **international financial management** *n* FIN internationales Finanzmanagement *nt*, internationale Finanzplanung *f*; **international freight forwarder** *n* TRANSP internationaler Spediteur *m*; **International Fund for Agricultural Development** *n* (*IFAD*) BANK Internationaler Agrarentwicklungsfonds *m* (*IFAD*); **international gateway** *n* TRANSP *aviation* internationales Tor *nt*; **international goods regulations** *n pl* TRANSP internationale Warenbestimmungen *f pl*, internationale Warenvorschriften *f pl*; **international hauler** *AmE*, **international haulier** *BrE n* TRANSP internationaler Spediteur *m*; **International Hotel Association** *n* LEIS internationaler Hotelverband *m*; **International Institute for Tropical Agriculture** *n* (*IITA*) ECON Internationales Institut *nt* für tropische Landwirtschaft; **International Institute for Unification of Private Law** *n* LAW Internationales Institut *nt* für die Vereinheitlichung des Privatrechts; **international investment bank** *n* (*IIB*)

BANK internationale Investitionsbank *f* (*IIB*), internationale Investmentbank *f*

internationalism *n* ECON, POL Internationalismus *m*

internationalization *n* ECON, POL Internationalisierung *f*

internationalize *vt* ECON, POL internationalisieren

international, International: **International Labour Office** *n* (*ILO*) HRM Internationales Arbeitsamt *nt* (*IAA*); **International Labour Organization** *n* (*ILO*) IND Internationale Arbeitsorganisation *f* (*IAO*); **international language for aviation** *n* (*ILA*) TRANSP internationale Luftfahrtsprache *f*; **international law** *n* LAW Völkerrecht *nt*; **International League for Creditors** *n* BANK Internationale Gläubigerliga *f*; **international leasing transaction** *n* LAW internationales Leasinggeschäft *nt*; **international liquidity** *n* ECON internationale Liquidität *f*, Weltwährungsreserven *f pl*; **international liquidity ratios** *n pl* BANK internationale Liquiditätskennzahlen *f pl*; **international management** *n* MGMNT internationale Unternehmensführung *f*, internationales Management *nt*; **International Maritime Bureau** *n* (*IMB*) TRANSP internationales Seefahrtsbüro *nt*; **International Maritime Committee** *n* (*IMC*) TRANSP internationales Seerechtskomitee *nt*; **international marketing** *n* S&M internationales Marketing *nt*; **International Monetary Fund** *n* (*IMF*) ECON Internationaler Währungsfonds *m* (*IWF*); **International Monetary Market** *n* (*IMM*) ECON, STOCK internationaler Geldmarkt *m*; **International Monetary Market Certificate of Deposit index** *n* (*IMM CD index*) STOCK Internationaler Geldmarkt-Einlagenzertifikat-Index *m*; **International Monetary Market Three-month Discount index** *n* STOCK Internationaler Geldmarkt-Dreimonats-Diskont-Index *m*; **International Monetary Market Treasury bill index** *n* (*IMM T-bill index*) STOCK Internationaler-Geldmarkt-Schatzwechsel-Index *m*; **international monetary organization** *n* FIN internationale Währungsbehörde *f*; **international monetary system** *n* ECON Weltwährungssystem *nt*; **international money draft** *n* BANK Auslandsgeldanweisung *f*; **international money flow** *n* ECON internationaler Geldstrom *m*, internationaler Kapitalstrom *m*; **international money order** *n* (*IMO*) BANK, COMMS Auslandspostanweisung *f*; **International Oil Pollution Compensation Fund** *n* (*IOPC Fund*) BANK, ENVIR Internationaler Fonds *m* zur Entschädigung für Ölverschmutzung; **international organization** *n* GEN COMM internationale Organisation *f*; **International Organization of Employers** *n* (*IOE*) HRM internationaler Arbeitgeberverband *m*; **International Organization for Legal Metrology** *n* (*OIML*) IND, LAW Internationale Organisation *f* für Eichung; **International Organization of Securities Commissioners** *n* (*IOSCO*) STOCK Internationale Organisation *f* für Wertpapieraufsicht; **international parity** *n* IND internationale Gleichheit *f*; **international payment order** *n* (*IPO*) BANK internationaler Zahlungsauftrag *m*; **international payments** *n pl* BANK, ECON internationaler Zahlungsverkehr *m*; **International Petroleum Exchange** *n* (*IPE*) STOCK Terminbörse *f* für Rohölkontrakte, Internationale Rohölbörse *f*; **international preliminary examining authority** *n* PATENTS internationale Voruntersuchungsbehörde *f*, internationales Prüfamt *nt*; **International Press Institute** *n* (*IPI*) MEDIA Internationales Presseinstitut *nt*; **international registration** *n* PATENTS internationale Eintragung *f*; **international relations** *n* *pl* POL internationale Beziehungen *f pl*; **international reply coupon** *n* (*IRC*) COMMS internationaler Antwortschein *m* für Postsendungen (*IAS*); **international representation** *n* GEN COMM internationale Vertretung *f*; **international reserve** *n* ECON internationale Reserve *f*; **international road haulage permit** *n* ADMIN, TRANSP internationale Güterkraftverkehrsgenehmigung *f*; **International Road Transport Union** *n* (*IRU*) TRANSP internationaler Fernfahrerverband *m* (*IRU*); **international sales contract** *n* LAW Auslandsliefervertrag *m*; **international searching authority** *n* PATENTS internationale Untersuchungsbehörde *f*; **International Securities Regulatory Organization** *n* (*ISRO*) STOCK internationale Wertpapieraufsichtsbehörde *f*; **International Service for National Agricultural Research** *n* (*ISNAR*) ECON internationaler Dienst *m* für nationale Agrarforschung; **International Shipowners' Association** *n* (*INSA*) TRANSP Vereinigung *f* internationaler Schiffseigner; **International Shipping Federation** *n* (*ISF*) TRANSP internationaler Reederverein *m*; **International Shipping Information Service** *n* (*ISIS*) TRANSP internationaler Schiffahrtsinformationsdienst *m*; **International Social Service** *n* (*ISS*) WEL Internationaler Sozialdienst *m* (*ISD*); **international standard** *n* ENVIR, GEN COMM, IND internationale Norm *f*; **International Standard Book Number** *n* (*ISBN*) MEDIA internationale Standardbuchnummer *f* (*ISBN*); **international standard classification of occupations** *n* (*ISCO*) ECON internationale Standardklassifikation *f* der Berufe (*ISCO*); **international standard conditions** *n pl* LAW internationale Standardbedingungen *f pl*; **international-standard hotel** *n* LEIS Hotel *nt* mit internationalem Standard; **International Standard Industrial Classification of all Economic Activities** *n AmE* (*ISIC*) IND Internationale Systematik *f* der Wirtschaftszweige; **International Standard Serial Number** *n* (*ISSN*) MEDIA internationale Standardseriennummer *f* (*ISSN*); **International Standards Organization** *n* (*ISO*) GEN COMM Internationale Organisation *f* für Normung (*ISO*); **International Statistical Institute** *n* (*ISI*) GEN COMM internationales Statistikinstitut *nt*; **International Stock Exchange** *n* (*ISE*) STOCK Internationale Wertpapierbörse *f*; **International Sugar Agreement** *n* (*ISA*) ECON Internationales Zuckerübereinkommen *nt* (*ISA*); **International Sugar Council** *n* (*ISC*) IND Internationaler Zuckerrat *m*; **International Sugar Organization** *n* (*ISO*) IND internationale Zuckerorganisation *f*; **international syndicate** *n* BANK internationales Konsortium *nt*; **International Telecommunications Union** *n* (*ITU*) COMMS internationale Fernmeldeunion *f*, internationaler Fernmeldeverein *m*; **international telegram** *n* COMMS internationales Telegramm *nt*; **International Telegraph and Telephone Consultative Committee** *n* COMMS internationaler Beratungsausschuß *m* für Telegramm und Telefon; **International Tin Council** *n* (*ITC*) IND internationaler Zinnrat *m*; **international trade** *n* GEN COMM Außenhandel *m*, internationales Geschäft *nt*, Welthandel *m*; **international trade center** *AmE*, **international trade centre** *BrE n* GEN COMM internationales Handelszentrum *nt*; **International Trade Commission** *n AmE* (*ITC*) ECON US-Bundesbehörde *f* für den Außenhandel; **international trade law** *n* LAW internationales Handelsgesetz *nt*; **international trade organization** *n* (*ITO*) GEN COMM internationale Außenhandelsorganisation *f*, internationale Handels-

organisation *f*; **international trade policy** *n* ECON internationale Handelspolitik *f*; **international trade theory** *n* ECON Außenhandelstheorie *f*; **international trading certificate** *n* (*ITC*) IMP/EXP internationale Gewerbebescheinigung *f*, internationale Handelsbescheinigung *f*, internationale Handelserlaubnis *f*; **International Transport Workers' Federation** *n* (*ITF*) TRANSP internationale Transportarbeiter-Föderation *f* (*ITF*); **international travel** *n* LEIS, TRANSP internationale Reisetätigkeit *f*; **International Union of Marine Insurance** *n* INS internationale Vereinigung *f* der Seeversicherer; **International Union of Official Travel Organizations** *n* (*IUOTO*) TRANSP Internationaler Verband *m* amtlicher Fremdenverkehrsorganisationen (*IUOTO*); **international wage level** *n* ECON internationales Lohnniveau *nt*; **International Wheat Agreement** *n* (*IWA*) ECON Internationale Weizenübereinkunft *f* (*IWÜ*); **International Wheat Council** *n* ECON Internationaler Weizenrat *m*; **International Wool Secretariat** *n* IND Internationales Wollsekretariat *nt*

internation: **~ equity** *n* ECON internationale Gleichheit *f*

interoffice: **~ dealings** *n pl* STOCK Telefonhandel *m*, Telefonverkehr *m*; **~ trading** *n* STOCK Telefonhandel *m*, Telefonverkehr *m*

interoperability *n* COMP Interoperabilität *f*, Zusammenarbeitsfähigkeit *f*, FIN gegenseitige Benutzbarkeit *f*, IND *of equipment* Interfunktionsfähigkeit *f*

Interparliamentary: **~ Union** *n* (*IPU*) POL interparlamentarische Union *f*

interperiod: **~ income tax allocation** *n* ACC, TAX periodengerechte Einkommensteuerverbuchung *f*

interpersonal: **~ skills** *n pl* HRM interpersonelle Fertigkeiten *f pl*; **~ utility comparison** *n* ECON interpersoneller Nutzenvergleich *m*

interplay *n* GEN COMM Zwischenspiel *nt*

interpleader *n* LAW Streitverkündigung *f*

interpolation *n* MATH Interpolation *f*

inter praesentes *adv* GEN COMM unter den Anwesenden

interpret 1. *vt* COMMS *translate language* dolmetschen, *understand* interpretieren, auslegen, COMP *programming*, GEN COMM *evaluate* auswerten, LAW auslegen; **2.** *vi* COMMS *translate language* dolmetschen

interpretation *n* COMP Auswertung *f*, GEN COMM Interpretation *f*, LAW Auslegung *f*; ♦ **give a loose ~ of sth** GEN COMM etw weit interpretieren

interpretative: **~ regulations** *n pl* LAW Auslegungsrichtlinien *f pl*

interpreter *n* COMMS *of languages* Dolmetscher, in *m,f*, COMP *programming* Interpreter *m*, Interpreterprogramm *nt*

interpreting *n* COMMS *of languages* Dolmetschen *nt*

interpretive: **~ regulations** *n pl* LAW Auslegungsrichtlinien *f pl*

interrelation *n* MATH *statistics* Beziehung *f*

interrogate *vt* GEN COMM ausfragen

interrogatories *n pl* LAW Beweisfragen *f pl*

interrupt *vt* COMP unterbrechen

interruption *n* COMP Unterbrechung *f*; **~ of work** *n* HRM Arbeitsunterbrechung *f*

interstate *adj AmE* GEN COMM zwischenstaatlich; **~ commerce** *n AmE* GEN COMM zwischenstaatlicher Handel *m*

Interstate: **~ Commerce Commission** *n AmE* (*ICC*)

ECON US-Bundesverkehrsbehörde; **~ Land Sales Act** *n* *AmE* PROP zwischenstaatliches Gesetz zum Landverkauf

interunion: **~ dispute** *n* *BrE* HRM Streitigkeit *f* von Gewerkschaften untereinander

interval *n* LEIS *break* Pause *f*, MATH *statistics* Intervall *nt*; **~ estimate** *n* MATH *statistics* Intervallschätzung *f*; **~ scale** *n* MATH *statistics* Intervallskala *f*; **~ service** *n* TRANSP Intervallservice *m*

intervene *vi* ECON, FIN, HRM, POL eingreifen, intervenieren

intervention *n* ECON, FIN, HRM, POL Intervention *f*; **~ currency** *n* ECON, FIN Interventionswährung *f*

interventionist 1. *adj* ECON, POL interventionistisch; **2.** *n* ECON, POL Befürworter, in *m,f* des Intervenierens

intervention: **~ price** *n* ECON, FIN Interventionspreis *m*; **~ rate** *n* ECON, FIN Interventionskurs *m*

interview *n* HRM Einstellungsgespräch *nt*, Interview *nt*

interviewee *n* HRM Befragte(r) *mf* [decl. as adj], Proband, in *m,f*

interviewer: **~ bias** *n* S&M *market research* Vorurteil *nt* des Interviewers

interview: **~ guide** *n* HRM *person* Interview-Führer, in *m,f*, *instructions* Interview-Hilfe *f*

inter vivos: **~ trust** *n* LAW Treuhandverhältnis *nt* unter lebenden Personen

intestate *adj* LAW testamentslos, ohne Testament

in-the-money: **~ call** *n* STOCK Kaufoption, deren Abschlußpreis unter dem Marktpreis des Wertpapiers liegt; **~ option** *n* STOCK Option, deren Abschlußpreis bei einer Kaufoption unter dem Marktpreis, bei einer Verkaufsoption über dem Marktpreis liegt; **~ put** *n* STOCK Verkaufsoption, deren Abschlußpreis über dem Marktpreis des Wertpapiers liegt

intimidate *vt* HRM einschüchtern

intimidation *n* HRM Einschüchterung *f*

intl *abbr* (*international*) GEN COMM int. (*international*)

in-town: **~ store** *n* S&M innerstädtisches Geschäft *nt*

intra-Community: **~ trade** *n* ECON innergemeinschaftlicher Handel *m*

intradepartmental *adj* ADMIN abteilungsintern

intra-EU: **~ trade** *n* ECON Handel *m* innerhalb der EU, Binnenhandel *m*, innergemeinschaftlicher Handel *m*

intragovernmental *adj* ADMIN, POL regierungsintern

intragroup *adj* HRM konzernintern; **~ relations** *n pl* HRM konzerninterne Beziehungen *f pl*

intra-industry: **~ trade** *n* IND brancheninterner Handel *m*

intramedia: **~ comparison** *n* MEDIA, S&M Vergleich *m* innerhalb eines Mediums

intrastate *adj* POL innerstaatlich

intra vires *phr* LAW innerhalb der rechtlichen Befugnisse

in-tray *n* ADMIN Ablage *f* für Eingänge, Korb *m* für eingehende Post, Posteingangskorb *m*

intrinsic: **~ motivation** *n* HRM innere Motivation *f*; **~ value** *n* ECON, FIN innerer Wert *m*, Substanzwert *m*, Sachwert *m*

introduce *vt* GEN COMM einführen, LAW, POL *draft bill* vorlegen, *legislation* einbringen; ◆ **~ a motion** POL einen Antrag stellen

introduction *n* GEN COMM Einleitung *f*, POL Vorlegung *f*, Einführung *f*

introductory: **~ course** *n* WEL Einführungskurs *m*, Einführungsseminar *nt*, Einführungsvorlesung *f*, Propädeutik *f*; **~ offer** *n* S&M *advertising* Sonderangebot

nt; **~ price** *n* S&M Einführungspreis *m*; **~ stage** *n* S&M Einführungsstadium *nt*

intuitive: **~ management** *n* MGMNT intuitive Handlungsweise *f*, intuitives Management *nt*

inv. *abbr* (*invoice*) GEN COMM Rechn. (*Rechnung*), Fakt. (*Faktur*) (*obs*), Faktura *f* (*obs*), Verkaufsrechnung *f*

invalid *adj* GEN COMM ungültig

invalidate *vt* GEN COMM ungültig machen, LAW *judgment* außer Kraft setzen, für ungültig erklären

invalidation *n* GEN COMM Ungültigmachung *f*, LAW Ungültigkeitserklärung *f*

invalidity *n* GEN COMM Ungültigkeit *f*, INS *disability* Invalidität *f*, LAW Ungültigkeit *f*

invaluable *adj* GEN COMM unschätzbar

invent *vt* IND, PATENTS erfinden

invention *n* IND, PATENTS Erfindung *f*

inventive *adj* IND, PATENTS erfinderisch; **~ step** *n* PATENTS Erfindungshöhe *f*

inventor *n* IND, PATENTS Erfinder, in *m,f*

inventories *n pl* GEN COMM Vorratsvermögen *nt*, Warenbestand *m*, Warenvorräte *m pl*

inventory *n* ACC *list of stocks* Inventar *f*, Lagerbestände *m pl*, *stocktaking* Inventur *f*, Bestandsaufnahme *f*, IND *list of goods* Bestandsnachweis *m*, Inventar *f*, Inventarliste *f*, Inventarverzeichnis *nt*, Lagerbestandsverzeichnis *nt*, *stocktaking* Bestandsaufnahme *f*, Inventarliste *f*, Inventur *f*, INS Bestandsverzeichnis *nt*, Inventar *f*, Inventarliste *f*, S&M Bestandsaufnahme *f*, Inventar *nt*, Inventarliste *f*; **~ adjustments** *n pl* ACC Bestandsberichtigungen *f pl*, *finished goods* Abwertung *f* auf Fertigerzeugnisse, *raw materials and supplies* Abwertung *f* auf Roh-, Hilfs- und Betriebsstoffe, Abwertung *f* auf Roh-, Hilfs- und Betriebswaren, *work in progress* Abwertung *f* auf unfertige Erzeugnisse; **~ book** *n* ACC Inventarbuch *nt*, Lagerbestandsbuch *nt*; **~ build-up** *n* ACC Auffüllung *f* von Lagerbeständen; **~ computation** *n* ACC Bestandsberechnung *f*; **~ control** *n* ACC Lagerkontrolle *f*, Lagerwirtschaft *f*, Lagerbestandskontrolle *f*, Bestandskontrolle *f*, Vorratsbewirtschaftung *f*; **~ controller** *n* ACC Bestandskontrolleur, in *m,f*; **~ costing** *n* ACC Kostenbewertung *f* von Lagerbeständen; **~ cycle** *n* ECON Lagerhaltungszyklus *m*; **~ evaluation** *n* ACC Kostenbewertung *f* von Lagerbeständen; **~ file** *n* ADMIN Bestandskartei *f*; **~ financing** *n* ACC Lagerfinanzierung *f*; **~ item** *n* ACC Bestandsposten *m*; **~ management** *n* ECON Vorratswirtschaft *f*, FIN Bestandsverwaltung *f*, Bestandsführung *f*, MGMNT Lagerhaltung *f*, Lagerwirtschaft *f*; **~ planning** *n* ECON Lagerplanung *f*; **~ pricing** *n* ACC Lagerbestandsbewertung *f*; **~ shortage** *n* ECON Bestandsfehlbetrag *m*; **~ shrinkage** *n* ECON Beständeschwund *m*; **~ turnover** *n* ACC Inventarumschlag *m*, Lagerumschlag *m*; **~ valuation** *n* ACC Vorratsbewertung *f*, Bestandsberechnung *f*; **~ valuation adjustment** *n* ACC Berichtigung *f* des Inventarwerts, Wertberichtigung *f* auf Vorratsvermögen

inverse *adj* MATH invers; **~ condemnation** *n* LAW, PROP enteignungsgleicher Eingriff *m*; **~ elasticity rule** *n* ECON inverse Elastizitätsregel *f*

inversely *adv* MATH umgekehrt

invert *vt* MATH invertieren, umkehren

inverted: **~ market** *n* STOCK umgekehrter Markt *m*; **~ scale** *n* STOCK umgekehrte Skala *f*; **~ yield curve** *n* ECON inverse Zinsstrukturkurve *f*

invest 1. *vt* BANK, ECON, FIN *capital*, GEN COMM *time, money*, STOCK *capital* anlegen, investieren; ◆ **~ with** POL *powers* ausstatten mit; **~ money** GEN COMM Geld anlegen, Geld investieren; **2.** *vi* BANK, ECON, FIN, STOCK investieren; **~ in** ECON, FIN investieren in [+acc], anlegen in [+dat]; ◆ **~ in an annuity** INS in eine Jahresrente investieren, in eine Rente investieren; **~ in bonds** STOCK in Anleihen investieren; **~ in property** PROP in Eigentum investieren; **~ in shares** STOCK in Aktien investieren

invested: **~ with power of attorney** *phr* ACC, LAW bevollmächtigt

investee *n* BANK, ECON, FIN, STOCK Investitionsempfänger, in *m,f*

investible *adj* BANK, ECON, FIN, STOCK investierbar

investigate *vt* GEN COMM recherchieren, aufklären, ermitteln, untersuchen, *evaluate* nachforschen, LAW, MGMNT, S&M untersuchen

investigating: **~ committee** *n* LAW Untersuchungsausschuß *m*; **~ officer** *n* HRM Ermittlungsbeamte(r) *m* [decl. as adj], Ermittlungsbeamtin *f*

investigation *n* LAW Untersuchung *f*, Aufklärung *f*

Investigation: **~ Division** *n* BrE TAX *Customs and Excise* Fahndungsabteilung *f*

investigatory: **~ powers** *n pl* LAW *of a court* Ermittlungsbefugnisse *f pl*

investment *n* BANK, ECON, FIN, STOCK Anlage *f*, Investition *f*, Investment *nt*; **~ above nominal value** *n* ACC Kapitaleinlage *f* über Nennwert; **~ account** *n* ACC Anlagenkonto *nt*, BANK Festgeldkonto *nt*; **~ account security** *n* BANK Festgeldkonto-Wertpapier *nt*; **~ activity** *n* ECON Investitionstätigkeit *f*

Investment: **~ Advisers Act** *n* AmE FIN *1940* Kapitalanlageberatergesetz *nt*; **~ Advisory Service** *n* AmE STOCK Anlageberatungsservice *m*

investment: **~ analysis** *n* FIN, STOCK *method* Investitionsrechnung *f*, *of securities* Analyse *f* von Kapitalanlagen, Wertpapieranalyse *f*; **~ appraisal** *n* FIN, STOCK Bewertung *f* einer Kapitalanlage, Investitionsbeurteilung *f*, Wirtschaftlichkeitsrechnung *f*; **~ bank** *n* BANK Investmentbank *f*, Emissionsbank *f*; **~ banker** *n* BANK Investitionsbanker *m*; **~ banking** *n* BANK Wertpapier- und Emissionsgeschäft *nt*; **~ base** *n* BANK Investitionsbasis *f*; **~ budget** *n* ACC, FIN Investitionsbudget *nt*, Investitionsplan *m*; **~ capital** *n* ECON, FIN, STOCK Investitionskapital *nt*; **~ center** AmE, **~ centre** BrE *n* FIN Investitionszentrale *f*, Investmentzentrum *nt*; **~ climate** *n* ECON Investitionsklima *nt*; **~ club** *n* STOCK Verein *m* für Kapitalanlageinteressenten; **~ committee** *n* BrE (*IC*) FIN Investitionsausschuß *m*; **~ company** *n* FIN, STOCK Investitionsgesellschaft *f*, Kapitalanlagegesellschaft *f* Investmentgesellschaft *f*

Investment: **~ Company Act** *n* AmE FIN *1940* ≈ Gesetz *nt* über Kapitalanlagegesellschaften

investment: **~ consultancy** *n* FIN, STOCK Effektenberatungstätigkeit *f*; **~ consultant** *n* FIN, STOCK Anlageberater, in *m,f*; **~ contract** *n* FIN Verwaltungsvertrag *m*; **~ counseling** AmE, **~ counselling** BrE *n* FIN, STOCK Anlageberatung *f*; **~ counsellor** BrE, **~ counselor** AmE *n* FIN, STOCK Anlageberater, in *m,f*; **~ criteria** *n pl* FIN Investitionskriterien *f pl*; **~ curb** *n* FIN Investitionsdrosselung *f*; **~ currency** *n* FIN Anlagedevisen *nt pl*, Anlagewährung

f; **~ dealer** *n* FIN, STOCK Wertpapierhändler, in *m,f*; **~ decision** *n* FIN, STOCK Investitionsentscheidung *f*; **~ deficit** *n* FIN Investitionslücke *f*; **~ department** *n* FIN Effektenabteilung *f*, Effekteninvestmentabteilung *f*; **~ dollar pool system** *n* AmE ECON Dollarsonderfonds für Auslandsinvestitionen; **~ financing** *n* BANK, FIN Anlagefinanzierung *f*, Investitionsfinanzierung *f*; **~ firm** *n* FIN Investmentgesellschaft *f*; **~ fund** *n* BANK, FIN Investitionsfonds *m*; **~ fund for shares** *n* STOCK Aktienfonds *m*, Investmentfonds *m* für Aktien; **~ goal** *n* FIN Anlageziel *nt*; **~ gold coin** *n* FIN Investitionsgoldmünze *f*; **~ goods** *n pl* FIN Investitionsgüter *nt pl*, Kapitalgüter *nt pl*; **~ grade** *n* AmE STOCK Investitionseinstufung *f*; **~ grant** *n* ACC *approval* Investitionsbewilligung *f*; **~ hedger** *n* STOCK Investment-Hedger *m*; **~ history** *n* FIN Investitionsgeschichte *f*; **~ holdings** *n pl* FIN Anteilsbesitz *m*; **~ incentive** *n* BANK Investitionsanreiz *m*; **~ income** *n* FIN Anlageerträge *m pl*, Vermögenserträge *m pl*; **~ interest expense** *n* AmE TAX Beteiligungsausgaben *f pl*; **~ life cycle** *n* STOCK Investitionslebenszyklus *m*; **~ management** *n* BANK Vermögensverwaltung *f*, FIN Anlageverwaltung *f*, Vermögensverwaltung *f*, Abwicklung *f* von Investitionen, Verwaltung *f* von Kapitalanlagen, STOCK Vermögensverwaltung *f*

Investment: **~ Management Regulatory Organization** *n* (*IMRO*) FIN Aufsichtsbehörde *f* für Anlagenberatung, Aufsichtsbehörde *f* für Effektenverwaltung, STOCK Verband der Anlageberater mit eigenen Kontrollfunktionen

investment: **~ mix** *n* FIN Investitionsmix *m*; **~ multiplier** *n* ECON *econometrics* Investitionsmultiplikator *m*; **~ objective** *n* FIN Anlageziel *nt*; **~ opportunity** *n* BANK Investitionsmöglichkeit *f*; **~ policy** *n* ECON, FIN, POL Anlagepolitik *f*, Investitionspolitik *f*; **~ portfolio** *n* BANK, FIN, STOCK Beteiligungsportefeuille *nt*, Effektenportefeuille *nt*, Wertpapierbestand *m*, Wertpapierportefeuille *nt*; **~ program** AmE, **~ programme** BrE *n* FIN Investitionsprogramm *nt*; **~ project** *n* FIN Investitionsprojekt *nt*; **~ property** *n* PROP Investitionsgrundstück *nt*; **~ rate of interest** *n* FIN Anlagezinsfuß *m*; **~ reserve system** *n* FIN Wertberichtigungen *f pl* auf Beteiligungen; **~ restriction** *n* ECON Investitionsbeschränkung *f*; **~ review** *n* FIN Investitionsprüfung *f*; **~ risk** *n* FIN Anlagerisiko *nt*

investments *n pl* BANK, ECON, FIN, STOCK Anlagen *f pl*, Beteiligungen *f pl*, Finanzanlagen *f pl*, Wertpapiere *nt pl*

investment: **~ savings account** *n* BANK Investitionssparkonto *nt*; **~ service** *n* FIN Investitionsservice *m*; **~ services** *n pl* FIN Effektenberatungstätigkeit *f*; **~ software** *n* COMP, FIN Investitionssoftware *f*, Anlageprogramm *nt*; **~ strategy** *n* FIN, STOCK Investitionsstrategie *f*; **~ strategy committee** *n* FIN Investitionsstrategieausschuß *m*; **~ subsidy** *n* ACC Investitionsbeihilfe *f*; **~ trust** *n* BrE FIN Investmentgesellschaft *f*; **~ value of a convertible security** *n* STOCK Investitionswert *m* eines wandlungsfähigen Wertpapiers; **~ yield** *n* BANK Anlagenverzinsung *f*

investor *n* BANK, ECON, FIN, STOCK Anleger, in *m,f*, Investor, in *m,f*; **~ group** *n* BANK, FIN Investorengruppe *f*, Kapitalanlegergruppe *f*; **~ protection** *n* STOCK Anlegerschutz *m*; **~ relations department** *n* STOCK *major public companies* Abteilung *f* für Aktionärspflege

investors': **~ compensation scheme** *n* BrE STOCK Ausgleichsplan *m* der Anleger, Vergütungsplan *m* der Anleger; **~ indemnity account** *n* BANK, FIN Abfindungskonto *nt* für Investoren, Investorenprämienkonto *nt*; ~ **service bureau** *n* FIN Anlegerdienstleistungsbüro *nt*

invisible: ~ **balance** *n* ECON, FIN Bilanz *f* der unsichtbaren Leistungen, Dienstleistungsbilanz *f*, unsichtbare Ein- und Ausfuhren *f pl*; ~ **earnings** *n pl* ECON, FIN Einkünfte *pl* aus unsichtbaren Leistungen; ~ **exports** *n pl* ECON, IMP/EXP *balance of trade* Dienstleistungsexporte *m pl*, unsichtbare Exporte *m pl*; ~ **hand** *n* ECON unsichtbare Hand *f*; ~ **imports** *n pl* ECON, IMP/EXP *balance of trade* Dienstleistungsimporte *m pl*, unsichtbare Importe *m pl*

invisibles *n pl* ECON, FIN unsichtbarer Handel *m*, unsichtbare Ein- und Ausfuhren *f pl*

invisible: ~ **supply** *n* GEN COMM unsichtbare Lieferungen *f pl*; ~ **trade** *n* ECON Dienstleistungsverkehr *m*, unsichtbarer Handel *m*; ~ **trade balance** *n* ECON Dienstleistungsbilanz *f*

invitation *n* GEN COMM Einladung *f*, LAW Aufforderung *f*; ~ **to bid** *n* LAW Ausschreibung *f*; ~ **to make an offer** *n* LAW öffentliche Angebotseinholung *f*, öffentliche Ausschreibung *f*, Aufforderung *f* zur Angebotsabgabe; ~ **to treat** *n* LAW Aufforderung *f* zur Abgabe eines Angebots

invite: ~ **subscriptions** *phr* FIN auflegen; ~ **subscriptions for** *phr* FIN ein Zeichnungsangebot machen; ~ **subscriptions to shares** *phr* STOCK Aktien zur Zeichnung auflegen; ~ **tenders** *phr* GEN COMM ausschreiben, zur Abgabe von Angeboten auffordern, Ausschreibung vornehmen

invoice 1. *n* (*inv.*) GEN COMM Rechnung *f* (*Rechn.*), Faktur *f* (*Fakt.*) (*obs*), Faktura *f* (*obs*), Verkaufsrechnung *f*; **2.** *vt* GEN COMM in Rechnung stellen

invoice: ~ **amount** *n* FIN Rechnungsbetrag *m*; ~ **book** *n* (*IB*) ACC Rechnungsbuch *nt*; ~ **clerk** *n* GEN COMM Fakturist, in *m,f*; ~ **cost and charges** *n pl* ACC Rechnungspreise *m pl*; ~ **discount** *n* S&M Rechnungsrabatt *m*; ~ **in the currency of the overseas buyer** *n* ACC Rechnung *f* in der Währung des Auslandskäufers; ~ **in the currency of the overseas seller** *n* ACC Rechnung *f* in der Währung des Auslandsverkäufers; ~ **in a third currency** *n* ACC *currency not used by buyer or seller* Rechnung *f* in einer dritten Währung; ~ **outstanding** *n* GEN COMM fällige Rechnung *f*, offene Rechnung *f*; ~ **price** *n* STOCK Rechnungspreis *m*

invoices: ~ **not yet received** *n pl* ACC ausstehende Rechnungen *f pl*

invoice: ~ **value** *n* (*iv*) GEN COMM Rechnungsbetrag *m*, Rechnungswert *m*, Fakturawert *m* (*obs*)

invoicing *n* ACC Abrechnung *f*, GEN COMM Fakturierung *f*, Rechnungsschreibung *f*; ~ **amount** *n* FIN Rechnungsbetrag *m*; ~ **department** *n* BrE (*cf billing department AmE*) GEN COMM Fakturierabteilung *f*, Rechnungsabteilung *f*

invoke *vt* LAW *law, penalty* sich berufen auf

involuntary: ~ **bankruptcy** *n* LAW Konkurs *m* auf Antrag eines Gläubigers; ~ **investment** *n* FIN Zwangsinvestition *f*; ~ **lien** *n* LAW Vollstreckungspfandrecht *nt*; ~ **liquidation** *n* FIN unfreiwillige Liquidation *f*, Zwangsliquidation *f*, Zwangsliquidierung *f*; ~ **trust** *n* AmE LAW gesetzliches Treuhandverhältnis *nt*; ~ **unemployment** *n* ECON unfreiwillige Arbeitslosigkeit *f*

involved: ~ **party** *n* LAW Beteiligte(r) *mf* [decl. as adj]

involvement *n* GEN COMM Beteiligung *f*; ~ **of employees**

n HRM, MGMNT Arbeitspartizipation *f*, *in management decisions* betriebliche Mitbestimmung *f*

inward: ~ **bill of lading** *n* IMP/EXP, TRANSP Importkonnossement *nt*; ~ **cargo** *n* IMP/EXP Herfracht *f*, Rückfracht *f*; ~ **charges** *n pl* TRANSP *shipping* Gebühr *f* für heimwärts laufendes Boot; ~ **freight department** *n* IMP/EXP Herfrachtabteilung *f*, Rückfrachtabteilung *f*; ~ **investor** *n* FIN *from overseas* ausländischer Direktinvestor *m*; ~ **manifest** *n* IMP/EXP Zolleingangsdeklaration *f*; ~ **payment** *n* FIN Inlandszahlung *f*; ~ **processing** *n* IMP/EXP aktive Veredelung *f*; ~ **process relief** *n* (*IPR*) IMP/EXP Entlastung *f* der Binnenzollbehandlung

inwards: ~ **mission** *n* S&M Auslandsdelegation *f*

IO *abbr* HRM (*immigration officer*) Einwanderungsbeamte(r) *m* [decl. as adj], Einwanderungsbeamtin *f*, IND (*industrial organization*) industrielle Organisation *f*, MEDIA (*information officer*) Pressereferent, in *m,f*, *public sector* Referent, in *m,f* für Öffentlichkeitsarbeiten

I/O *abbr* (*input/output*) COMP E/A (*Eingabe-Ausgabe*), I/O (*Input-Output*)

IOB *abbr* BANK (*Institute of Bankers*) Institut der Bankiers, INS (*Insurance Ombudsman Bureau*) Büro des Versicherungs-Beschwerdekommissars

IOCS *abbr* (*input/output control system*) COMP Ein-/Ausgabe-System *nt*

IOE *abbr* (*International Organization of Employers*) HRM internationaler Arbeitgeberverband *m*

I/O: ~ **error message** *n* COMP I/O-Fehlermeldung *f*

IOM *abbr* (*Institute of Office Management*) MGMNT Institut für Büroorganisation; ~ **division** *n* AmE (*Index and Option Market division*) STOCK *Chicago Mercantile Exchange* Abteilung des Index- und Optionsmarktes

IOPC: ~ **Fund** *n* (*International Oil Pollution Compensation Fund*) BANK, ENVIR Internationaler Fonds *m* zur Entschädigung für Ölverschmutzung

IORT *abbr* (*incremental oil revenue tax*) TAX inkrementale Ölsteuer *f*

IOSCO *abbr* (*International Organization of Securities Commissioners*) STOCK Internationale Organisation *f* für Wertpapieraufsicht

iota *n* GEN COMM Jota *nt* (*obs*)

IOU *abbr* (*I owe you*) GEN COMM Schuldschein *m*, Zahlungsversprechen *nt*

I owe you *n* (*IOU*) GEN COMM Schuldschein *m*, Zahlungsversprechen *nt*

IPA *abbr* (*Institute of Practitioners in Advertising*) S&M Institut für Werbefachleute

IPC *abbr* (*integrated pollution control*) ENVIR integrierte Schadstoffkontrolle *f*, integrierter Umweltschutz *m*

IPD *abbr* (*interest, profit and dividends*) ECON Zinsen, Gewinne und Dividenden aus Kapitalanlagen von Inländern

IPE *abbr* (*International Petroleum Exchange*) STOCK Terminbörse *f* für Rohölkontrakte

IPG *abbr* (*intergovernmental preparatory group*) POL zwischenstaatliche Vorbereitungsgruppe *f*

IPI *abbr* (*International Press Institute*) MEDIA Internationales Presseinstitut *nt*

IPM *abbr* MGMNT (*integrated project management*) integrierte Projektleitung *f*, integrierte Projektverwaltung *f*, einheitliche Projektleitung *f*, integriertes Projektmanagement *nt*, (*Institute of Personnel Management*) Institut für Personalverwaltung

IPO *abbr* BANK (*international payment order*) internationaler Zahlungsauftrag *m*, STOCK (*initial public offering*) erstes öffentliches Zeichnungsangebot *nt*

IPR *abbr* IMP/EXP (*inward process relief*) Entlastung *f* der Binnenzollbehandlung, S&M (*Institute of Public Relations*) Institut *nt* für Öffentlichkeitsarbeit

ipso facto *adv* GEN COMM ipso facto

IPU *abbr* (*Interparliamentary Union*) POL Interparlamentarische Union *f*

IR *abbr* ADMIN, ECON, HRM (*industrial relations*) Arbeitsbeziehungen *f pl*, Arbeitnehmer-/Arbeitgeberbeziehungen *f pl*, TAX (*Inland Revenue*) Steuerbehörde *f*

IRA *abbr* AmE (*individual retirement account*) BANK, TAX persönliches Rentenkonto *nt*, steuerfreies Sparkonto *nt* zur privaten Altersvorsorge, steuerfreies Rentensparkonto *nt*; **~ rollover** *n* AmE TAX Darlehensverlängerung *f* für steuerfreies Rentensparkonto

IRC *abbr* (*international reply coupon*) COMMS IAS (*internationaler Antwortschein für Postsendungen*)

IRD *abbr* (*inland rail depot*) IMP/EXP, TRANSP Inlandsbahndepot *nt*

IRN *abbr* IMP/EXP (*import release note*) Importfreigabebescheinigung *f*, IND (*iron*) Eisen *nt*

iron *n* (*IRN*) IND Eisen *nt*; **~ law of wages** *n* ECON ehernes Lohngesetz *nt*, eisernes Lohngesetz *nt*, Existenzminimumtheorie *f* des Lohnes; **~ ore** *n* IND Eisenerz *nt*; **~ ore carrier** *n* TRANSP Eisenerzfrachter *m*, Eisenerztransportschiff *nt*

ironworks *n* IND Eisenhütte *f*

IRPC *abbr* BrE (*Industrial Relations Policy Committee*) HRM Ausschuß für Arbeitgeber/Arbeitnehmerbeziehungen

IRR *abbr* (*internal rate of return*) ACC, ECON, FIN interner Zinsfuß *m*

irrebuttable *adj* LAW *presumption* unwiderlegbar

irrecoverable *adj* FIN *loss* unersetzbar, unersetzlich

irredeemable *adj* STOCK nicht rückzahlbar, unkündbar, untilgbar

irreducible *adj* GEN COMM unreduzierbar

irrefutable *adj* LAW unwiderlegbar

irregularity *n* GEN COMM Unregelmäßigkeit *f*; **~ report** *n* IND Bericht *m* über Unregelmäßigkeiten

irrelevant *adj* GEN COMM ohne Belang, belanglos, irrelevant, unwesentlich

irremediable: **~ defect** *n* LAW *goods* unheilbarer Mangel *m*

irreparable *adj* GEN COMM *error, loss, damage* irreparabel, unersetzlich

irreplaceable *adj* GEN COMM unersetzbar, unersetzlich

irrespective: **~ of** *prep* GEN COMM unabhängig von

irreversible *adj* GEN COMM irreversibel, *decision* unwiderruflich

irrevocable *adj* BANK, LAW unwiderruflich; **~ credit** *n* BANK unwiderruflicher Kredit *m*; **~ credit line** *n* BANK unwiderrufliche Kreditgrenze *f*, unwiderruflicher Kreditrahmen *m*; **~ letter of credit** *n* (*ILOC*) BANK unwiderrufliches Akkreditiv *nt*; **~ trust** *n* LAW unwiderrufliches Treuhandverhältnis *nt*

IRS *abbr* AmE (*Internal Revenue Service*) TAX Bundessteuerbehörde *f*, Finanzamt *nt*

IRU *abbr* (*International Road Transport Union*) TRANSP IRU (*internationaler Fernfahrerverband*)

i.s. *abbr* (*in stock*) ECON, GEN COMM, S&M vorrätig

ISA *abbr* (*International Sugar Agreement*) ECON ISA (*Internationales Zuckerübereinkommen*)

ISBN *abbr* (*International Standard Book Number*) MEDIA ISBN (*internationale Standardbuchnummer*)

ISC *abbr* (*International Sugar Council*) IND Internationaler Zuckerrat *m*

ISCO *abbr* (*international standard classification of occupations*) ECON ISCO (*internationale Standardklassifikation der Berufe*)

ISDN *abbr* (*Integrated Services Digital Network*) COMMS, COMP ISDN (*integriertes Dienstleistungsdatennetz*)

ISE *abbr* (*International Stock Exchange*) STOCK Internationale Wertpapierbörse *f*

ISF *abbr* (*International Shipping Federation*) TRANSP internationaler Reederverein *m*

ISFA *abbr* (*Institute of Shipping and Forwarding Agents*) TRANSP Institut der Versand- und Speditionsagenten

ISI *abbr* (*International Statistical Institute*) GEN COMM internationales Statistikinstitut *nt*

ISIC *abbr* AmE (*International Standard Industrial Classification of all Economic Activities*) IND Internationale Systematik *f* der Wirtschaftszweige

ISIS *abbr* (*International Shipping Information Service*) TRANSP internationaler Schiffahrtsinformationsdienst *m*

island: **~ display** *n* S&M *advertising* Inselplazierung *f*; **~ site** *n* S&M *advertising* Inselplazierung *f*

ISNAR *abbr* (*International Service for National Agricultural Research*) ECON internationaler Dienst *m* für nationale Agrarforschung

ISO *abbr* GEN COMM (*International Standards Organization*) ISO (*Internationale Organisation für Normung*), IND (*International Sugar Organization*) internationale Zuckerorganisation *f*

isocost *n* ECON Isokosten *pl*

isolate *vt* GEN COMM, POL isolieren

isolated *adj* GEN COMM, POL isoliert; **~ market equilibrium** *n* ECON isoliertes Marktgleichgewicht *nt*; **~ state** *n* POL isolierter Staat *m*

isolationism *n* POL Isolationismus *m*

isolationist *adj* POL isolationistisch

isolation: **~ ward** *n* IMP/EXP Quarantänestation *f*

ISO: **~ paper size** *n* MEDIA, S&M ISO-Papierformat *nt*

isoquant *n* ECON Isoquante *f*

ISRO *abbr* (*International Securities Regulatory Organization*) STOCK internationale Wertpapieraufsichtsbehörde *f*

ISS *abbr* (*International Social Service*) WEL ISD (*Internationaler Sozialdienst*)

ISSN *abbr* (*International Standard Serial Number*) MEDIA ISSN (*internationale Standardseriennummer*)

issuance: **~ facility** *n* FIN Emissionsfazilität *f*

issue 1. *n* BANK, FIN *bills, money* Ausgabe *f* (*Ausg.*), Emission *f*, *cheque* Ausstellung *f*, Ausfertigung *f*, *loan* Auflegung *f*, GEN COMM *of documents, certificate* Ausstellung *f*, *problem* Gegenstand *m* des Interesses, Gegenstand *m* der Auseinandersetzung, LAW *dispute* Streitfrage *f*, Streitpunkt *m*, *offspring* Nachkomme *m*, Abkömmling *m*, MEDIA *of magazine, newspaper, book* Herausgabe *f*, Ausgabe *f* (*Ausg.*), STOCK *of shares* Ausgabe *f* (*Ausg.*), Emission *f*, Begebungszeit *f*; ♦ **be at ~** GEN COMM streitig sein; **the ~ at stake** GEN COMM das zur Diskussion stehende Problem; **the ~ was**

undersubscribed STOCK die Emission war unterzeichnet; **2.** *vt* BANK, FIN *bills, money* ausgeben, in Umlauf setzen, emittieren, *cheque* ausstellen, ausfertigen, *loan* auflegen, GEN COMM *documents, certificate* ausstellen, MEDIA *magazine, newspaper, book* herausgeben, veröffentlichen, STOCK *shares* ausgeben, emittieren; ♦ **~ a letter of credit** STOCK ein Dokumentenakkreditiv ausstellen; **~ a report** GEN COMM einen Bericht vorlegen; **~ a share at a discount** STOCK eine Aktie unter dem Nennwert emittieren; **~ a summons** LAW laden, vorladen; **~ a writ against sb** LAW eine Klage gegen jdn erheben

issue: **~ card** *n* IND Ausgabekarte *f*, Betriebspaß *m*; **~ costs** *n pl* STOCK Anleihekosten *pl*

issued *adj* BANK, FIN, STOCK ausgegeben, emittiert; ♦ **~ for subscription** FIN aufgelegt; **~ and outstanding** STOCK ausgegeben und ausstehend

issue: **~ date** *n* STOCK Emissionsdatum *nt*

issued: **~ and floating shares** *n pl* STOCK emittierte Aktien *f pl*; **~ share capital** *n* ACC, FIN, STOCK ausgegebenes Aktienkapital *nt*, Kapital *nt* aus ausgegebenen Aktien; **~ shares** *n pl* STOCK ausgegebene Aktien *f pl*

issue: **~ of a loan** *n* FIN Begebung *f* einer Anleihe; **~ market** *n* STOCK Emissionsmarkt *m*, Primärmarkt *m*; **~ premium** *n* STOCK Emissionsagio *nt*; **~ price** *n* FIN Ausgabepreis *m*, Ausgabewert *m*, STOCK Abgabekurs *m*, Emissionskurs *m*

issuer *n* BANK, FIN, STOCK Aussteller, in *m,f*, Emittent *m*

issue: **~ readership** *n* S&M *of publication* Leserschaft *f* pro Ausgabe

issues: **~ with currency options** *n pl* STOCK Emissionen *f pl* mit Devisenoptionen

issue: **~ voucher** *n* GEN COMM Ausgabemarke *f*, Bon *m*, Gutschein *m*

issuing: **~ authority** *n* ADMIN *passport* ausstellende Behörde *f*; **~ bank** *n* BANK Akkreditivbank *f*, akkreditiveröffnende Bank *f*, Emissionsbank *f*; **~ carrier** *n* TRANSP ausstellender Frachtführer *m*; **~ company** *n* STOCK Emittent *m*, emittierende Gesellschaft *f*; **~ date** *n* GEN COMM Ausstellungstag *m*; **~ house** *n* STOCK Emissionshaus *nt*; **~ office** *n* ADMIN ausstellende Dienststelle *f*; **~ price** *n* STOCK Erstausgabepreis *m*

IT *abbr* COMP (*information technology*) IT (*Informationstechnik, Informationstechnologie*), EDV (*elektronische Datenverarbeitung*), HRM, LAW (*industrial tribunal BrE*) Arbeitsgericht *nt*, gewerbliches Schiedsgericht *nt*, LEIS (*inclusive tour*) Komplettreise *f*, Pauschalreise *f*; **~ department** *n* COMP EDV-Abteilung *f*; **~ strategy** *n* COMP EDV-Strategie *f*; **~ system** *n* COMP EDV-System *nt*

italic *adj* COMP, MEDIA *typography* kursiv

italics *n* COMP, MEDIA *typography* Kursivschrift *f*

ITC *abbr* ECON *AmE* (*International Trade Commission*) US-Bundesbehörde für den Außenhandel, IMP/EXP (*international trading certificate*) internationale Gewerbebescheinigung *f*, internationale Handelsbescheinigung *f*, internationale Handelserlaubnis *f*, IND (*International Tin Council*) internationaler Zinnrat, MEDIA (*Independent Television Commission BrE*) Überwachungsgremium für unabhängige Fernsehsender

item *n* ACC *entry* Eintrag *m*, Posten *m*, ADMIN Punkt *m*, Posten *m*, COMP Element *nt*, GEN COMM Stück *nt*, S&M Artikel *m*; **~ analysis** *n* MATH *statistics* Indikatorenanalyse *f*; **~ approved for inclusion** *n* POL zur Aufnahme bewilligte Sache *f*

itemization *n* GEN COMM *invoice* Aufgliederung *f*, Einzelaufzählung *f*

itemize *vt* GEN COMM *invoice* aufgliedern, einzeln aufführen, einzeln nennen

itemized *adj* GEN COMM *invoice* aufgegliedert; **~ deductions** *n pl* TAX einzeln aufgeführte Abzüge *m pl*; **~ pay statement** *n* HRM Lohnstreifen *m*

item: **~ mark-up** *n* S&M Artikelaufschlag *m*; **~ number** *n* S&M Artikelnummer *f*

items: **~ in the estimates** *n pl* FIN Posten *m pl* im Haushaltsplan; **~ on the agenda** *n pl* ADMIN, MGMNT Tagesordnungspunkte *m pl*

item: **~ status** *n* S&M Artikelstatus *m*

items: **~ of value** *n pl* GEN COMM Wertsachen *f pl*

iteration *n* COMP Iteration *f*

ITF *abbr* (*International Transport Workers' Federation*) TRANSP ITF (*internationale Transportarbeiter-Föderation*)

itinerant: **~ selling** *n* S&M ambulanter Handel *m*; **~ worker** *n* HRM Wanderarbeiter, in *m,f*

itinerary *n* TRANSP Fahrstrecke *f*

ITO *abbr* (*international trade organization*) GEN COMM internationale Außenhandelsorganisation *f*, internationale Handelsorganisation *f*

ITPAL *abbr* (*industrial and trade policy adjustment loan*) FIN Ausgleichsanleihe *f* für Industrie- und Handelspolitik

ITS *abbr AmE* (*Intermarket Trading System*) STOCK elektronisches Informationssystem der US-Börsen

ITU *abbr* (*International Telecommunications Union*) COMMS Internationale Fernmeldeunion *f*

ITV *abbr BrE* (*Independent Television*) MEDIA Netzwerk unabhängiger Fernsehsender

IUOTO *abbr* (*International Union of Official Travel Organizations*) HRM IUOTO (*Internationaler Verband amtlicher Fremdenverkehrsorganisationen*)

iv *abbr* GEN COMM (*invoice value*) Rechnungsbetrag *m*, Rechnungswert *m*, Fakturawert *m* (*obs*), (*increased value*) erhöhter Wert *m*, Mehrwert *m*

IWA *abbr* (*International Wheat Agreement*) ECON IWÜ (*Internationale Weizenübereinkunft*)

J

J/A *abbr* (*joint account*) BANK gemeinsames Konto *nt*, Gemeinschaftskonto *nt*

jabbering *n* GEN COMM Gequassel *nt* (*infrml*)

jack up *vt infrml* GEN COMM, S&M *prices* erhöhen

jacket *n* COMP *disk* Hülle *f*

jam *n* COMP *printer* Papierstau *m*; ◆ **be in a ~** *infrml* GEN COMM in der Klemme sitzen (*infrml*)

Jamaica: ~ Agreement *n* ECON Jamaika-Abkommen *nt*

Janson: ~ Clause *n* INS *marine* Janson-Klausel *f*

January: ~ sales *n pl* S&M Winterschlußverkauf *m*

japanization *n* ECON *international trade* Japanisierung *f*

jar *n* S&M Dose *f*

jargon *n* GEN COMM Fachsprache *f*, Jargon *m*

jawboning *n* AmE POL Appell der Regierung an Unternehmen und Gewerkschaften, im gemeinsamen Interesse eine gemäßigte Preis- und Lohnpolitik zu betreiben, wirtschaftspolitische Seelenmassage *f* (*infrml*)

JCCC *abbr BrE* (*Joint Customs Consultative Committee*) IMP/EXP gemeinsamer beratender Zollausschuß

J: ~ curve *n* ECON, MATH *statistics* J-Kurve *f*

JDI *abbr* (*joint declaration of interest*) BANK gemeinsame Bekanntgabe *f* von Interesse

JEC *abbr AmE* (*Joint Economic Committee of Congress*) ECON Wirtschaftsausschuß des US-Kongresses

jeopardize *vt* GEN COMM *endanger* gefährden, *impede* behindern

jerque: ~ note *n* IMP/EXP Zolleinfuhrschein *m*

jetfoil *n* TRANSP *shipping* Tragflügelboot *nt*

jetlag *n* TRANSP Jet-lag *nt*

jetlagged: be ~ *phr* TRANSP unter der Zeitverschiebung leiden

jetsam *n* TRANSP *shipping* Seewurf *m*, Strandgut *nt*

jetty *n* TRANSP Pier *m*

jetway *n* TRANSP *aviation* Fluggastbrücke *f*

jeweler *AmE see* jeweller *BrE*

jewelry *AmE see* jewellery *BrE*

jeweller *n BrE* GEN COMM Juwelier, in *m,f*

jewellery *n BrE* GEN COMM Schmuck *m*

JIC *abbr BrE* (*Joint Industrial Council*) IND gemeinsamer Industrierat, paritätisch besetzter Betriebsausschuß *m*

JICCAR *abbr BrE* (*Joint Industry Committee for Cable Audience Research*) S&M gemeinsamer Industrieausschuß für die Analyse von Kabelanschlußinhabern

JICNARS *abbr BrE* (*Joint Industry Committee for National Readership Survey*) S&M gemeinsamer Industrieausschuß für landesweite Leserschaftsuntersuchungen

JICPAR *abbr BrE* (*Joint Industry Committee for Poster Audience Research*) S&M gemeinsamer Industrieausschuß für die Analyse der Adressaten von Plakatwerbung

JICRAR *abbr BrE* (*Joint Industry Committee for Radio Audience Research*) S&M gemeinsamer Industrieausschuß für die Analyse der Rundfunkhörerschaft

JICTAR *abbr BrE* (*Joint Industrial Committee for Television Advertising Research*) S&M gemeinsamer Industrieausschuß für die Analyse von Fernsehwerbung

jingle *n* MEDIA, S&M *advertising* Erkennungsmelodie *f*, Jingle *m*

JIT *abbr* (*just-in-time, just-in-time production*) HRM, IND JIT (*just-in-time, Just-in-Time-Produktion*)

JLCD *abbr* (*Joint Liaison Committee on Documents*) ADMIN gemeinsamer Verbindungsausschuß für Dokumente

JMC *abbr* (*Joint Maritime Commission*) IND gemeinsame Seefahrtskommission

JMSDC *abbr BrE* (*Joint Merchant Shipping Defence Committee*) IND gemeinsames Komitee zur Verteidigung der Handelsmarine

jnr. *abbr* (*junior*) GEN COMM, LAW Jr. (*Junior*)

job *n* COMP Auftrag *m*, Job *m*, GEN COMM *profession* Beruf *m*, *employment* Arbeitsplatz *m*, *specific project* Aufgabe *f*, HRM Beruf *m*, Posten *m*, *position* Stellung *f*, *employment* Arbeitsplatz *m*, *task* Job *m*, Arbeitsaufgabe *f*, Aufgabe *f*; **~ acceptance schedule** *n* ECON Arbeitsplatzannahmebereitschaft *f*; **~ action** *n jarg* HRM *industrial action* Arbeitskampfmaßnahmen *f pl*; **~ advertisement** *n* HRM Stellenausschreibung *f*; **~ analysis** *n* HRM Arbeitsanalyse *f*, Arbeitsplatzanalyse *f*; **~ application** *n* HRM Bewerbung *f*, Stellengesuch *nt*; **~ appraisal** *n* HRM Arbeitsplatzbewertung *f*; **~ assignment** *n* GEN COMM, HRM, MGMNT Aufgabenverteilung *f*; **~ bank** *n* HRM Arbeitsplatz-Datenbank *f*

jobber *n* GEN COMM Großhändler, in *m,f*, Schieber, in *m,f* (*infrml*), STOCK Jobber *m*, Wertpapierhändler, in *m,f* (*jarg*); **~'s turn** *n* STOCK Verdienstspanne *f* des Jobbers

jobbing *n* GEN COMM Gelegenheitsarbeit *f*, HRM Jobben *nt*, IND *job work* Stücklohnarbeit *f*, Akkordarbeit *f*, *graphic* Akzidenzarbeit *f*, STOCK Großhandel *m*, Wertpapier-Eigen- und Großhandel *m*; **~ in contangos** *n BrE* STOCK Effektenhandel *m* mit Contangos, Reportgeschäfte *nt pl*

job: ~ breakdown *n* HRM Arbeitsunterteilung *f*; **~ candidate** *n* HRM Bewerber, in *m,f*; **~ card** *n* HRM Kostensammelkarte *f*

Jobcentre *n BrE* (*cf employment service AmE*) ADMIN, HRM, WEL Arbeitsamt *nt*, Arbeitsvermittlung *f*

job: ~ challenge *n* HRM Herausforderung *f* durch den Arbeitsplatz, MGMNT berufliche Herausforderung *f*; **~ change** *n* HRM Arbeitsplatzwechsel *m*; **~ characteristics** *n pl* HRM Arbeitsplatzmerkmale *nt pl*; **~ classification** *n* HRM Berufsklassifizierung *f*; **~ club** *n BrE* HRM, WEL Berufsclub des Arbeitsamts für Arbeitslose; **~ cluster** *n* HRM Tätigkeitsgruppe *f*; **~ competence** *n* HRM berufliche Kompetenz *f*; **~ content** *n* HRM Arbeitsinhalt *m*; **~ control** *n* COMP Auftragssteuerung *f*, Jobsteuerung *f*, IND Arbeitsüberwachung *f*; **~ costing** *n* HRM Zuschlagskalkulation *f*; **~ cost sheet** *n* ECON Kostensammelblatt *nt*; **~ cost system** *n* ACC Kostenartenrechnung *f*, Zuschlagskalkulation *f*, FIN Kostenartenrechnung *f*; **~~creating measures** *n pl* HRM Arbeitsbeschaffungsmaßnahmen *f pl* (*ABM*), Arbeitsbeschaffungspraktiken *f pl*; **~ creation** *n* HRM Schaffung *f* von Arbeitsplätzen; **~~creation program** *AmE*, **~~creation programme**

BrE n ECON Arbeitsbeschaffungsprogramm *nt*, Beschäftigungsprogramm *nt*; **~-creation scheme** *n* ECON Arbeitsbeschaffungsprogramm *nt*, Beschäftigungsprogramm *nt*; **~ cycle** *n* IND Arbeitszyklus *m*; **~ database** *n* HRM Arbeitsplatz-Datenbank *f*; **~ description** *n* HRM Arbeitsplatzanalyse *f*, Arbeitsplatzbeschreibung *f*, Stellenbeschreibung *f*; **~ design** *n* HRM, MGMNT Personalorganisation *f*; **~ engineering** *n* HRM Arbeitsplatzgestaltung *f*; **~ enlargement** *n* HRM horizontale Arbeitsfeldvergrößerung *f*, Job Enlargement *nt*, MGMNT Erweiterung *f* des Aufgabengebietes, Erweiterung *f* des Tätigkeitsbereiches, Erweiterung *f* des Tätigkeitsspektrums; **~ enrichment** *n* HRM Arbeitsbereicherung *f*, Job Enrichment *nt*, MGMNT Bereicherung *f* des Aufgabengebietes, Bereicherung *f* des Tätigkeitsbereiches, Bereicherung *f* des Tätigkeitsspektrums; **~ entry** *n* COMP Auftragseingabe *f*, Jobeingabe *f*; **~ evaluation** *n* HRM Arbeitsplatzbewertung *f*; **~-evaluation scale** *n* HRM Schlüssel *m* zur Arbeitsplatzbewertung; **~ evaluation scheme** *n* HRM System *nt* der Arbeitsplatzbewertung; **~ expectations** *n pl* HRM Arbeitsplatzerwartungen *f pl*; **~ flexibility** *n* HRM Arbeitsplatzflexibilität *f*; **~ for life** *n* HRM lebenslange Anstellung *f*; **~ freeze** *n* HRM Einstellungsstopp *m*; **~ handling** *n* COMP Auftragsabwicklung *f*; **~ hopper** *n* HRM Person, die häufig die Arbeitsstelle wechselt, Job Hopper *m*; **~ hopping** *n* HRM häufiger Stellenwechsel *m*; **~ hunter** *n* HRM Stellensuchende(r) *mf* [decl. as adj], Stellungssuchende(r) *mf* [decl. as adj]; **~ hunting** *n* HRM Stellensuche *f*, private Stellenvermittlung *f*; **~ improvement** *n* HRM Arbeitsplatzverbesserung *f*; **~ instruction** *n* HRM Arbeitsanweisung *f*; **~ interest** *n* HRM Berufsinteresse *nt*; **~ jumper** *n* HRM Person, die häufig die Arbeitsstelle wechselt, Job Hopper *m*; **~ legislation** *n* LAW Arbeitsgesetzgebung *f*, Arbeitsrecht *nt*

jobless *adj* ECON, HRM, WEL arbeitslos; **the ~** *n pl* ECON, HRM, WEL die Arbeitslosen *pl*; **~ person** *n* ECON, HRM, WEL Arbeitslose(r) *mf* [decl. as adj]; **~ rate** *n* ECON, HRM Arbeitslosenquote *f*

job: **~ lot** *n* GEN COMM Restposten *m*; **~ market** *n* HRM Arbeitsmarkt *m*; **~ mobility** *n* HRM berufliche Mobilität *f*; **~ offer** *n* HRM Stellenangebot *nt*, Arbeitsplatzangebot *nt*; **~ opportunity** *n* HRM Arbeitsmöglichkeit *f*, Beschäftigungschance *f*, Beschäftigungsmöglichkeit *f*; **~ order** *n* GEN COMM, IND Arbeitsauftrag *m*; **~ order costing** *n* IND Zuschlagskalkulation *f*; **~ order planning** *n* IND Auftragsplanung *f*; **~ performance** *n* HRM Arbeitsleistung *f*; **~ placement** *n* HRM Arbeitsvermittlung *f*, Stellenvermittlung *f*; **~ profile** *n* HRM Tätigkeitsprofil *nt*; **~ prospect** *n* HRM Arbeitsmöglichkeit *f*, Beschäftigungsmöglichkeit *f*; **the ~ queue** *n* COMP Auftragswarteschlange *f*, Jobwarteschlange *f*, ECON, HRM, WEL *unemployed people* die Arbeitslosen *pl*; **~ regulation** *n* HRM Arbeitsregulierung *f*; **~-related accommodation** *n* PROP Betriebswohnung *f*, Werkswohnung *f*; **~-related injury** *n* HRM arbeitsplatzbezogene Verletzung *f*, Betriebsunfall *m*, INS Betriebsunfall *m*; **~ requirement** *n* HRM Stellenanforderung *f*; **~ rotation** *n* HRM Stellentausch *m*, systematischer Arbeitsplatzwechsel *m*; **~ satisfaction** *n* HRM Arbeitszufriedenheit *f*, MGMNT Befriedigung *f* im Beruf, Zufriedenheit *f* mit der beruflichen Tätigkeit

jobs: **~ data** *n pl* GEN COMM Beschäftigtenzahlen *f pl*

job: **~ search** *n* HRM Stellensuche *f*; **~ security** *n* HRM Sicherheit *f* des Arbeitsplatzes, Arbeitsplatzsicherheit *f*; **~ security agreement** *n* HRM Vereinbarung *f* zur Sicherheit am Arbeitsplatz

jobseeker *n* HRM Arbeitssuchende(r) *mf* [decl. as adj]

job: **~ segregation** *n* HRM Arbeitstrennung *f*; **~ share** *n* HRM Arbeitsplatzteilung *f*; **~ share scheme** *n* HRM Job Sharing Programm *nt*; **~ sharing** *n* HRM Arbeitsplatzteilung *f*, Job Sharing *nt*; **~ shift** *n* GEN COMM Arbeitsplatzwechsel *m*; **~ shop** *n* HRM Betrieb *m* mit Kundenauftragsfertigung, IND Maschinenwerkstatt *f*, mechanische Werkstatt *f*; **~ shop production** *n* IND Werkstattfertigung *f*; **~ simplification** *n* HRM Vereinfachung *f* des Arbeitsplatzes; **~ site** *n* GEN COMM Arbeitsplatz *m*; **~ skills** *n pl* HRM berufliche Fähigkeiten *f pl*; **~ spec** *n infrml* HRM Anforderungsprofil *nt*; **~ specialization** *n* HRM berufliche Spezialisierung *f*; **~ specification** *n* HRM Anforderungsprofil *nt*; **~ splitting** *n* HRM Arbeitsplatzteilung *f*; **~ study** *n* HRM Arbeitsanalyse *f*; **~ ticket** *n* HRM Arbeitslaufzettel *nt*, Laufkarte *f*; **~ title** *n* HRM, MGMNT Berufsbezeichnung *f*; **~ vacancy** *n* HRM offene Stelle *f*; **~ value** *n* GEN COMM Arbeitswert *m*

jockey *n* FIN Handlanger *m*

join *vt* HRM *union*, LAW *profession* beitreten; ♦ **~ the dole queue** *BrE* HRM sich in die Schlange der Empfänger von Arbeitslosenunterstützung einreihen; **~ together** GEN COMM *companies* sich zusammenschließen

joinder *n* HRM Verbindung *f*

joining: **~ of the EU** *n* ECON EU-Beitritt *m*

joint *adj* GEN COMM *communiqué* gemeinsam; **~ account** *n (J/A)* BANK gemeinsames Konto *nt*, Gemeinschaftskonto *nt*; **~ account agreement** *n* BANK Gemeinschaftskontovertrag *m*; **~ action** *n* LAW Prozeß *m* mit Streitgenossen; **~ applicant** *n* PATENTS gemeinsamer Anmelder *m*, gemeinsame Anmelderin *f*; **~ assignment** *n* GEN COMM gemeinsame Aufgabe *f*; **~ auditor** *n* ACC Mitprüfer, in *m,f*; **~ auditors** *n pl* ACC *auditing* gemeinsame Prüfer *m pl*; **~ authorization** *n* BANK gemeinsame Befugnis *f*; **~ bank account** *n* BANK gemeinsames Bankkonto *nt*; **~ bond** *n* STOCK gemeinsam emittierte Schuldverschreibung *f*; **~ charge** *n* TRANSP gemeinsame Gebühr *f*; **~ committee** *n* HRM gemeinsamer Ausschuß *m*; **~ consultation** *n* HRM, MGMNT gemeinsame Beratung *f*; **~ consultations** *n pl* GEN COMM Gemeinschaftsberatung *f*; **~ consultative committee** *n* HRM gemeinsamer Beratungsausschuß *m*; **~ costs** *n pl* ECON Kosten *pl* der Kuppelproduktion; **~ custody** *n* BANK gemeinsames Sorgerecht *nt*

Joint: **~ Customs Consultative Committee** *n BrE (JCCC)* IMP/EXP gemeinsamer beratender Zollausschuß *m*

joint: **~ declaration of interest** *n (JDI)* BANK gemeinsame Bekanntgabe *f* von Interesse; **~ demand** *n* ECON Komplementärnachfrage *f*, verbundene Nachfrage *f*; **~ designation** *n* PATENTS gemeinsame Bezeichnung *f*; **~ director** *n* HRM Joint Director *m*, MGMNT Mitdirektor, in *m,f*

Joint: **~ Economic Committee of Congress** *n AmE (JEC)* ECON Wirtschaftsausschuß des US-Kongresses

joint: **~ estate** *n* BANK, LAW, PROP Miteigentum *nt*; **~ fare** *n* TRANSP gemeinsamer Fahrpreis *m*; **~ goods** *n pl* ECON, S&M komplementäre Güter *nt pl*; **~ guarantee** *n* FIN gemeinsame Garantie *f*; **~ heir** *n* LAW Miterbe *m*, Miterbin *f*; **~ heirs** *n pl* LAW Erbengemeinschaft *f*

Joint: ~ **Industrial Committee for Television Advertising Research** *n BrE* (*JICTAR*) S&M gemeinsamer Industrieausschuß für die Analyse von Fernsehwerbung; ~ **Industrial Council** *n BrE* (*JIC*) IND gemeinsamer Industrierat, paritätisch besetzter Betriebsausschuß *m*; ~ **Industry Committee for Cable Audience Research** *n BrE* (*JICCAR*) S&M *TV viewing figures* gemeinsamer Industrieausschuß für die Analyse von Kabelanschlußinhabern; ~ **Industry Committee for National Readership Survey** *n BrE* (*JICNARS*) S&M gemeinsamer Industrieausschuß für landesweite Leserschaftsuntersuchungen; ~ **Industry Committee for Poster Audience Research** *n BrE* (*JICPAR*) S&M gemeinsamer Industrieausschuß für die Analyse der Adressaten von Plakatwerbung; ~ **Industry Committee for Radio Audience Research** *n BrE* (*JICRAR*) S&M gemeinsamer Industrieausschuß für die Analyse der Rundfunkhörerschaft

joint: ~ **insurance** *n* INS Gegenseitigkeitsversicherung *f*, Mitversicherung *f*; ~ **liability** *n* BANK gemeinsame Haftung *f*, gemeinsame Verbindlichkeit *f*, LAW gemeinsame Haftung *f*

Joint: ~ **Liaison Committee on Documents** *n* (*JLCD*) ADMIN gemeinsamer Verbindungsausschuß für Dokumente

joint: ~ **life assurance** *n BrE* (*cf joint life insurance AmE*) INS verbundene Lebensversicherung *f*; ~ **life insurance** *n AmE* (*cf joint life assurance BrE*) INS verbundene Lebensversicherung *f*; ~ **loan** *n* BANK gemeinsame Anleihe *f*

jointly: ~ **liable** *adj* LAW gesamtschuldnerisch haftbar; **be ~ liable** *phr* GEN COMM gemeinsam haften, LAW gemeinsam haftbar sein; ~ **and severally** *adv* LAW *liability* gesamtschuldnerisch

joint: ~ **management** *n* MGMNT gemeinschaftliche Leitung *f*, Gesamtgeschäftsführung *f*; ~ **manager** *n* HRM Mitdirektor, in *m,f*

Joint: ~ **Maritime Commission** *n* (*JMC*) IND gemeinsame Seefahrtskommission; ~ **Merchant Shipping Defence Committee** *n* (*JMSDC*) IND GCBS gemeinsames Komitee zur Verteidigung der Handelsmarine

joint: ~ **negotiation** *n* MGMNT *industrial relations* gemeinsame Verhandlung *f*, Gemeinschaftsverhandlung *f*, gemeinsames Verhandeln *nt*, STOCK gemeinsame Negoziierung *f*, gemeinsame Verhandlung *f*, gemeinsames Verhandeln *nt*; ~ **negotiations** *n* GEN COMM, HRM *industrial relations* gemeinsame Verhandlungen *f pl*, Gemeinschaftsverhandlung *f*; ~ **operator** *n* IND Mitbediener *m*, Zweitbesetzung *f*, zweiter Maschinist *m*, zweite Maschinistin *f*; ~ **order** *n* GEN COMM Sammelbestellung *f*; ~ **owner** *n* BANK, LAW Miteigentümer, in *m,f*, PROP gemeinsamer Eigentümer *m*, gemeinsame Eigentümerin *f*, Miteigentümer, in *m,f*; ~ **ownership** *n* BANK, LAW, PROP Miteigentum *nt*; ~ **partnership** *n* GEN COMM Personengesellschaft *f*; ~ **product cost** *n* ACC Kosten *pl* der Kuppelprodukte; ~ **production committee** *n* HRM gemeinsamer Produktionsausschuß *m*; ~ **products** *n pl* ECON Kuppelprodukte *nt pl*; ~ **promissory note** *n* FIN Gemeinschafts-Solawechsel *m*; ~ **proprietor** *n* GEN COMM Partner, in *m,f*; ~ **rate** *n* TRANSP gemeinsamer Preis *m*; ~ **representation** *n* GEN COMM, HRM, MGMNT Gemeinschaftsvertretung *f*

Joint: ~ **Research Centre** *n* IND *EURATOM* gemeinsames Forschungszentrum

joint: ~ **return** *n* TAX gemeinsame Steuererklärung *f*; ~ **service** *n* TRANSP gemeinsamer Einsatz *m*; ~ **and**

several liability *n* LAW gesamtschuldnerische Haftung *f*; ~ **and several obligation** *n* LAW gesamtverbindliche Verpflichtung *f*; ~ **signature** *n* BANK Kollektivzeichnung *f*; ~ **statement** *n* GEN COMM gemeinsame Erklärung *f*; ~**-stock bank** *n* BANK Aktienbank *f*; ~**-stock company** *n* GEN COMM Aktiengesellschaft *f* (*AG*), rechtsfähige Gesellschaft *f*, STOCK Kommanditgesellschaft *f* auf Aktien; ~ **and survivor annuity** *n AmE* INS Partnerrente *f*, Überlebensrente *f*; ~ **tenancy** *n* LAW Gesamteigentum *nt*; ~ **tenants with right of survivorship** *n pl* STOCK Gesamthauseigentümer *m pl* mit Überlebensfallrecht; ~ **venture** *n* (*JV*) ACC, ECON, GEN COMM Beteiligungsgeschäft *nt*, Gemeinschaftsunternehmen *nt*, Joint Venture *nt*, HRM Arbeitsgemeinschaft *f*, MGMNT, STOCK Joint Venture *nt*, Beteiligungsgeschäft *nt*, Gemeinschaftsunternehmen *nt*; ~**-venture bank** *n* BANK Joint-Venture-Bank *f*; ~**-venture company** *n* MGMNT, STOCK Gemeinschaftsfirma *f*, STOCK Beteiligungsgesellschaft *f*; ~**-venture investment bank** *n* BANK gemeinsame Investitionsbank *f*; ~ **venture law** *n* LAW Joint-Venture-Recht *nt*; ~**-venture merchant bank** *n* BANK gemeinsame Handelsbank *f*; ~ **working party** *n* (*JWP*) HRM gemeinsame Arbeitsgruppe *f*

joker *n AmE* LAW Hintertürchen-Paragraph *m*

jot down *vt* GEN COMM aufschreiben

journal *n* ACC Tagebuch *nt*, *bookkeeping* Journal *nt*, GEN COMM *academic, professional periodical* Journal *nt*, MEDIA *periodical* Zeitschrift *f*; ~ **entry** *n* ACC Journalbuchung *f*, Journaleintrag *m*

journalize *vt* ACC ins Journal eintragen

journal: ~ **voucher** *n* ACC Buchungsbeleg *m*

journey *n* GEN COMM, TRANSP Fahrt *f*; ~ **cycle** *n* S&M Reisezyklus *m*

journeyman *n* HRM Geselle *m*

journey: ~ **planner** *n* TRANSP Reiseplaner *m*; ~ **planning** *n* TRANSP Reiseplanung *f*

joystick *n* COMP Joystick *m*

JP *abbr BrE* (*Justice of the Peace*) HRM Friedensrichter *m*

jr. *abbr* (*junior*) GEN COMM, LAW Jr. (*Junior*)

J-shaped: ~ **frequency curve** *n* MATH *statistics* J-förmige Häufigkeitskurve *f*

judge 1. *n* LAW Richter, in *m,f*; **2.** *vt* GEN COMM beurteilen

judges': ~ **rules** *n pl BrE* LAW Bestimmung zur Vernehmung von Verdächtigen in Untersuchungshaft

judgment *n* GEN COMM *assessing* Beurteilung *f*, *faculty* Urteilsvermögen *nt*, LAW *faculty* Urteilsvermögen, *verdict* Urteil *nt*, *assessing* Beurteilung *f*, PROP Urteil *nt*; ~ **creditor** *n* LAW, PROP Vollstreckungsgläubiger, in *m,f*; ~ **debtor** *n AmE* LAW Vollstreckungsschuldner, in *m,f*; ~ **lien** *n AmE* LAW Zwangshypothek *f*; ~ **proof** *n* LAW Unpfändbarkeit *f*; ~ **sample** *n* S&M *market research* ins Ermessen des Befragers gestellte Repräsentativauswahl

judicial *adj* LAW gerichtlich; ~ **affairs** *n pl* LAW gerichtliche Angelegenheiten *f pl*; ~ **arbitrator** *n* LAW gerichtlicher Schiedsrichter *m*; ~ **bond** *n* LAW Sicherheitsleistung *f* bei Gericht; ~ **foreclosure** *n* LAW gerichtliche Vollstreckung *f* aus einem Grundpfandrecht, Zwangsvollstreckung *f*

judicially *adv* LAW gerichtlich

judicial: ~ **proceedings** *n pl* LAW Gerichtsverfahren *nt pl*

judiciary *n* LAW Gerichtswesen *nt*

juggernaut *n* TRANSP Schwerlastzug *m*

jumble: ~ **sale** *n* BrE S&M Ramschverkauf *m*

jumbo *n* infrml TRANSP Großraum-Jet *m*, Jumbo *m* (*infrml*); ~ **certificate of deposit** *n* STOCK Einlagen-zertifikat mit einer Einlage von mehr als $100.000; ~ **jet** *n* infrml TRANSP Großraum-Jet *m*, Jumbo-Jet *m* (*infrml*); ~ **loan** *n* BANK Großkredit *m*; ~ **pack** *n* S&M Jumbopackung *f*, Riesenpackung *f*

jump *n* GEN COMM *in prices* Sprung *m*

jumpy: ~ **market** *n* ECON Markt *m* mit starken Schwan-kungen

juncture *n* GEN COMM *point in time* kritischer Zeitpunkt *m*

June: ~ **call** *n* STOCK Junikaufoption *f*; ~ **put** *n* STOCK Juniverkaufsoption *f*

junior 1. *n* (*jnr.*, *jr.*) GEN COMM, LAW Junior *m* (*Jr.*); **2.** *adj* MGMNT untergeordnet

junior: ~ **creditor** *n* BANK nachrangiger Gläubiger *m*; ~ **debt** *n* FIN nachrangige Schuld *f*; ~ **issue** *n* STOCK nachrangige Emission *f*; ~ **lien** *n* LAW nachrangiges Pfandrecht *nt*; ~ **management** *n* MGMNT Führungs-nachwuchs *m*, untergeordnete Führungsebene *f*; ~ **manager** *n* HRM Junior Manager *m*; ~ **market** *n* FIN nachrangiges Marktsegment *nt*; ~ **mortgage** *n* AmE PROP nachrangige Hypothek *f*; ~ **partner** *n* GEN COMM, LAW Juniorpartner, in *m,f*; ~ **position** *n* HRM Juniorposition *f*; ~ **refunding** *n* FIN nachrangige Refinanzierung *f*; ~ **security** *n* AmE STOCK nachrangi-ges Wertpapier *nt*

junket *n* infrml GEN COMM, TRANSP Vergnügungsreise *f*

junk: ~ **mail** *n* COMMS Papierkorbpost *f*

juridical: ~ **person** *n* LAW, PATENTS juristische Person *f*; ~ **position** *n* LAW gerichtliche Position *f*

juridification *n* HRM Juridifikation *f*, Juridifizierung *f*

jurisdiction *n* LAW *physical area* Gerichtsbezirk *m*, *range of authority* Zuständigkeit *f*, *responsibility* Gerichts-barkeit *f*; ♦ **come under sb's** ~ ADMIN unter eine Rechtsprechung fallen; **it comes under our** ~ LAW es fällt unter unsere Gerichtsbarkeit

jurisdiction: ~ **dispute** *n* LAW Kompetenzstreitigkeit *f*

jurisprudence *n* LAW Jurisprudenz *f*, *science of law* Rechtswissenschaft *f*

juror *n* LAW Geschworene(r) *mf* [decl. as adj], Schöffe *m*, Schöffin *f*

jury *n* LAW Geschworenengericht *nt*, Schöffengericht *nt*, LEIS *theatre* Premierenpublikum *nt*; **the** ~ *n* LAW die Geschworenen *pl*, die Schöffen *pl*; ~ **of executive opinion** *n* MATH *statistics* Jury *f* der Führungsmeinung; ~ **trial** *n* LAW Geschworenenprozeß *m*

jus disponendi *n* LAW Verfügungsrecht *nt*

just *adj* LAW *appropriate* angemessen, *fair* gerecht; ~ **cause dismissal** *n* HRM Entlassung *f* aus triftigem Grund; ~ **compensation** *n* LAW angemessene Entschä-digung *f*

justice *n* LAW *fairness* Gerechtigkeit *f*, *judicial system* Gerichtsbarkeit *f*, Justiz *f*, *judge* Richter, in *m,f*; ♦ **get** ~ LAW Gerechtigkeit erlangen

Justice: ~ **of the Peace** *n* BrE (*JP*) HRM Friedensrichter *m*

justifiable *adj* GEN COMM berechtigt, vertretbar, LAW berechtigt, rechtlich vertretbar

justification *n* COMP *text* Ausrichtung *f*, GEN COMM *reason* Rechtfertigung *f*

justified *adj* COMP *text* ausgerichtet, GEN COMM *reason* gerechtfertigt; ~ **price** *n* STOCK gerechtfertigter Preis *m*

justify *vt* COMP *text* ausrichten, GEN COMM *reason* rechtfertigen

just: ~**-in-time** *phr* (*JIT*) HRM, IND Just-in-Time-Produk-tion *f* (*JIT*), just-in-time (*JIT*); ~**-in-time production** *n* (*JIT*) HRM, IND Just-in-Time-Produktion *f* (*JIT*), just-in-time (*JIT*); ~**-in-time purchasing** *n* IND fertigungs-synchrone Materialwirtschaft *f*; ~ **noticeable difference** *n* ADMIN gerade feststellbarer Unterschied *m*; ~ **price** *n* ECON gerechter Preis *m*; ~ **wage** *n* ECON gerechter Lohn *m*

juvenile *n* LAW Minderjährige(r) *mf* [decl. as adj]

JV *abbr* (*joint venture*) ACC, ECON, GEN COMM, MGMNT, STOCK Beteiligungsgeschäft *nt*, Gemeinschaftsunter-nehmen *nt*, Joint Venture *nt*

JWP *abbr* (*joint working party*) HRM gemeinsame Arbeits-gruppe *f*

K

k *abbr* (*thousand*) GEN COMM Tausend *nt*

Kaldor-Hicks: ~ **compensation principle** *n* ECON Kaldor-Hicks-Kompensationsprinzip *nt*

Kaldor: ~'s **laws** *n pl* ECON Kaldorsche Gesetze *nt pl*

Katona: ~ **effect** *n* ECON Katona-Effekt *m*

kB *abbr* (*kilobyte*) COMP kB (*Kilobyte*), KByte (*Kilobyte*)

KBS *abbr* (*knowledge-based system*) COMP Expertensystem *nt*, System *nt* auf Wissensbasis, wissensbasiertes System *nt* (*jarg*)

keel *n* TRANSP Kiel *m*

keen: ~ **price** *n* S&M extrem niedriger Preis *m*, scharf kalkulierter Preis *m*

keep 1. *vt* ACC, COMP *records* führen, GEN COMM *maintain* führen, *appointment* einhalten; ◆ ~ **abreast of** GEN COMM *changing conditions and legislation* Schritt halten mit; ~ **afloat** GEN COMM *business* am Laufen halten; ~ **an appointment** GEN COMM eine Verabredung einhalten; ~ **accounts for** ACC Buch führen über; ~ **a close watch on sth** GEN COMM etw streng bewachen; ~ **in custody** LAW verwahren; ~ **in safe custody** LAW verwahren; ~ **in step with one's competitors** GEN COMM mit der Konkurrenz Schritt halten; ~ **in touch with sb** COMMS in Verbindung mit jdm bleiben; ~ **inflation down** ECON die Inflation niedrig halten; ~ **a low profile** GEN COMM sich zurückhalten; ~ **a note of sth** GEN COMM etw notieren; ~ **pace with** GEN COMM Schritt halten mit; ~ **sb informed** COMMS, GEN COMM jdn auf dem laufenden halten; ~ **sb up-to-date** GEN COMM jdn auf dem laufenden halten; ~ **sth in reserve** GEN COMM etw in Reserve halten; ~ **sth under wraps** *infrml* GEN COMM etw verschlossen halten; **a** ~ **tally of** GEN COMM eine Liste von etw erstellen; ~ **track of** GEN COMM *maintain records* Buch führen über; ~ **up to date** ADMIN *filing and* IND *food, goods* sich halten; ◆ ~ **well** IND *food, goods* haltbar sein

keep up 1. *vt* GEN COMM aufrechterhalten; ◆ ~ **payment on one's mortgage** FIN mit den Zahlungen der Hypothek auf dem laufenden bleiben; **2.** *vi* GEN COMM nachkommen; ◆ ~ **with** GEN COMM *payments* nachkommen, *developments* Schritt halten mit

keep: ~-**out price** *n* S&M Abwehrpreis *m*

keg *n* TRANSP Faß *nt*

Kennedy: ~ **Round** *n* ECON Kennedy-Runde *f*

Keogh: ~ **Plan** *n* FIN *pension plan* Keogh-Plan *m*

kerb: ~ **market** *n* FIN, STOCK Freiverkehr *m*, Nachbörse *f*; ~ **weight** *n* TRANSP *of a motor vehicle* Gewicht fahrfertig mit vollem Tank ohne Insassen

kerosene *n* TRANSP Kerosin *nt*

key *n* COMP Schlüssel *m*, *on keyboard* Taste *f*

key in *vt* COMP eingeben

key: ~-**area evaluation** *n* MGMNT Beurteilung *f* nach Schlüsselbereichen

keyboard *n* COMP Tastatur *f*

keyboarder *n* ADMIN, COMP Datentypist, in *m,f*

keyboard: ~-**operated** *adj* COMP tastaturbetrieben, tastaturgesteuert; ~ **short cut** *n* COMP Kurzeingabe *f*, Kurztaste *f*, Tastenkürzel *nt*

key: ~ **currency** *n* ECON Leitwährung *f*; ~ **data** *n pl* GEN COMM Schlüsseldaten *pl*; ~ **date** *n* GEN COMM Stichtag *m*

keyed: ~ **advertisement** *n* S&M Chiffreanzeige *f*

key: ~ **feature** *n* GEN COMM Hauptmerkmal *nt*; ~ **industry** *n* ECON, IND Schlüsselindustrie *f*; ~ **issue** *n* GEN COMM Hauptproblem *nt*

keylock *n* COMP Tastensperre *f*

key: ~ **money** *n* PROP Kaution *f*, Mietvorauszahlung *f*

Keynes: ~ **effect** *n* ECON Keynes-Effekt *m*; ~ **expectations** *n pl* ECON Keynessche Erwartungen *f pl*

Keynes': ~ **general theory** *n* ECON Keynessche Allgemeine Theorie *f*

Keynesian *adj* ECON keynesianisch; ~ **cross diagram** *n* ECON Keynessches Kreuzdiagramm *nt*; ~ **economics** *n* ECON Keynessche Lehre *f*, keynesianische Wirtschaftstheorie *f*; ~ **equilibrium** *n* ECON Keynessches Gleichgewicht *n*

Keynesianism *n* ECON Keynesianismus *m*; **military** ~ *n* ECON militärischer Keynsianismus *m*

Keynesian: ~ **multiplier** *n* ECON *econometrics* Investitionsmultiplikator *m*; ~ **policy** *n* ECON Keynessche Politik *f*

Keynes: ~ **Plan** *n* ECON Keynes-Plan *m*

keypad *n* COMP Keypad *nt* (*jarg*), Kleintastatur *f*, Tastenfeld *nt*

key: ~ **pallet** *n* TRANSP Keilpalette *f*; ~ **person life and health insurance** *n* INS Lebens- und Krankenversicherung für leitende Personen eines Unternehmens; ~ **point** *n* GEN COMM Hauptpunkt *m*; ~ **prospects** *n pl* S&M wesentliche Aussichten *f pl*; ~ **punch** *n* COMP Lochkartenlocher *m*, Locher *m*; ~ **rate** *n* ECON *interest rates* Leitzins *m*, *wage* Leitzinssatz *m*; ~ **sequence** *n* COMP Schlüsselfolge *f*; ~ **stage** *n* GEN COMM *in a process* Schlüsselphase *f*

keystroke *n* COMP Tastenanschlag *m*, Tastendruck *m*; ~ **rate** *n* ADMIN Tastenanschlagsfrequenz *f*

keyword *n* COMP Schlüsselwort *nt*; ~ **search** *n* COMP Schlüsselwortsuche *f*

kg *abbr* (*kilogram, kilogramme*) GEN COMM kg (*Kilogramm*)

kick out *vt jarg* GEN COMM ausbooten (*jarg*)

kickback *n* FIN Kommissionsrückvergütung *f*, LAW *government and private contracts* geheime Provision *f*, *labour relations* Schmiergeld *nt* (*infrml*)

kicker *n AmE infrml* FIN zusätzliche Darlehensvergütung *f*

kidnap: ~ **insurance** *n* INS Entführungsversicherung *f*

Kiel: ~ **canal** *n* TRANSP Nord-Ostsee-Kanal *m*

kill: ~ **demand** *phr* S&M die Nachfrage abwürgen

killing *n infrml* STOCK ungewöhnlich hoher Spekulationsgewinn *m*

kilo *n* (*kilogram, kilogramme*) GEN COMM Kilo *nt* (*Kilogramm*)

kilobyte *n* (*kB*) COMP Kilobyte *nt* (*kB, KByte*)

kilogram *n* (*kg, kilo*) GEN COMM Kilogramm *nt* (*kg, Kilo*)

kilogramme *see* kilogram

kilograms: ~ **per square centimeter** *n pl* (*KC*) GEN COMM Kilogramm *nt pl* pro Quadratzentimeter

kiloliter *AmE*, **kilolitre** *BrE n* (*kl*) GEN COMM Kiloliter *m* (*kl*)

kilometer *AmE*, **kilometre** *BrE n* (*km*) GEN COMM Kilometer *m* (*km*)

kilometres: ~ **per hour** *n pl BrE* (*km/h, kmph*) GEN COMM Kilometer *m* pro Stunde (*km/h*), Stundenkilometer *m pl*

kiloton *n* (*kt*) GEN COMM Kilotonne *f* (*kt*)

kilotonne *see kiloton*

kilowatt *n* (*kW*) GEN COMM Kilowatt *nt* (*kW*); **~-hour** *n* (*kWh*) GEN COMM Kilowattstunde *f* (*kWh*)

kind: **in** ~ *phr* GEN COMM *payment* in natura, in Sachwerten

kindergarten *n* WEL Kindergarten *m*

King: **~'s enemies** *n pl BrE* LAW Staatsfeinde *m pl*

kinked: ~ **demand curve** *n* ECON geknickte Preis-Absatz-Kurve *f*

kite *n* BANK ungedeckter Scheck *m*, FIN Gefälligkeitswechsel *m*, STOCK Kellerwechsel *m*, Gefälligkeitswechsel *m*; **~-flying** *n* STOCK Wechselreiterei *f*

kiting *n* STOCK Wechselreiterei *f*

kitsch *n* S&M Kitsch *m*

kl *abbr* (*kiloliter AmE, kilolitre BrE*) GEN COMM kl (*Kiloliter*)

km *abbr* (*kilometer AmE, kilometre BrE*) GEN COMM km (*Kilometer*)

km/h *abbr* (*kilometers per hour AmE, kilometres per hour BrE*) GEN COMM km/h (*Kilometer pro Stunde*)

kmph *abbr* (*kilometers per hour AmE, kilometres per hour BrE*) GEN COMM km/h (*Kilometer pro Stunde*)

knob *n* COMP Knopf *m*

knock down *vt* GEN COMM *price* herunterhandeln, IND *machinery* zerlegen

knockdown: ~ **price** *n* GEN COMM Schleuderpreis *m*, Spottpreis *m*, Werbepreis *m*, *auction* äußerster Preis *m*, Mindestpreis *m*

knock: **~-for-knock** *n* INS gegenseitige Regreßverzichts-erklärung *f*, Regreßverzichtsvereinbarung *f*, gegenseitiger Regreßverzicht *m*, Schadenteilungsabkommen *nt*

knocking: ~ **copy** *n* S&M herabsetzende Werbung *f*; **~-off time** *n infrml* ADMIN, HRM Arbeitsschluß *m*

knock: **~-off** *n infrml* IND billige Imitation *f*, Klon *m*; **~-on effect** *n* GEN COMM Anstoßwirkung *f*; **~-on financing** *n* FIN Anschubfinanzierung *f*

knockout: ~ **agreement** *n infrml* GEN COMM Vereinbarung *f* von Bietern; ~ **competition** *n* GEN COMM Wettbewerb *m* unter Bietern

knot *n* GEN COMM Knoten *m*

know-how *n infrml* GEN COMM Know-how *nt* (*infrml*), PATENTS Fachkenntnisse *f pl*, Know-how *nt* (*infrml*); ~ **agreement** *n* LAW *intellectual property* Know-how-Vertrag *m*

knowledge *n* GEN COMM *of subject* Bekanntheit *f*, Kenntnis *f*

knowledgeable *adj* GEN COMM gebildet, kenntnisreich, bewandert, klug

knowledge: ~ **base** *n* WEL *social work* Wissensbasis *f*; **~-based system** *n* (*KBS*) COMP Expertensystem *nt*, System *nt* auf Wissensbasis, wissensbasiertes System *nt* (*jarg*)

known: **not** ~ *adj* GEN COMM unbekannt; **be** ~ **by name** *phr* GEN COMM mit Namen bekannt sein, namentlich bekannt sein; ~ **loss** *n* INS bekannter Verlust *m*, erkannter Verlust *m*

kolkhoz *n* ECON russiche landwirtschaftliche Produktionsgenossenschaft, Kolchos *m or nt*, Kolchose *f*

kt *abbr* (*kiloton, kilotonne*) GEN COMM kt (*Kilotonne*)

kudos *n* GEN COMM Ehre *f*

kursmakler *n* ECON amtlicher Kursmakler *m*

kurtosis *n* MATH *statistics* Exzeß *m*, Wölbung *f*

Kuznets: ~ **curve** *n* ECON Kuznets-Kurve *f*

kW *abbr* (*kilowatt*) GEN COMM kW (*Kilowatt*)

kWh *abbr* (*kilowatt-hour*) GEN COMM kWh (*Kilowattstunde*)

L

l *abbr* (*liter AmE, litre BrE*) GEN COMM l (*Liter*)

L/A *abbr* GEN COMM (*letter of authority*) Ermächtigungs-schreiben *nt*, Genehmigungsschreiben *nt*, INS (*Lloyd's Agent*) Lloyd's Agent *m*, Lloyd's Versicherer *m*, TRANSP (*landing account*) *shipping* Landeschein *m*

lab *n infrml* (*laboratory*) IND Labor *nt* (*Laboratorium*)

label 1. *n* COMP Etikett *nt*, Kennung *f*, GEN COMM Schild *nt*, Aufschrift *f*, MEDIA *record company* Plattenfirma *f*, S&M *marketing* Etikett *nt*; **2.** *vt* GEN COMM auszeichnen, S&M auszeichnen, kennzeichnen

label: **~ clause** *n* (*LC*) LAW, TRANSP *cargo* Kennsatz-klausel *f*, Kennzeichnungsklausel *f*

labeled *AmE see* **labelled** *BrE*

labeling *AmE see* **labelling** *BrE*

labelled: **~ file** *n BrE* COMP gekennzeichnete Datei *f*

labelling *n BrE* S&M Auszeichnung *f*, Etikettierung *f*, Kennzeichnung *f*; **~ laws** *n pl BrE* LAW Preisaus-zeichnungsvorschriften *f pl*, Etikettierungsgesetze *nt pl*, Preisauszeichnungsgesetze *nt pl*

labor *AmE see* **labour** *BrE*

laboratory *n* (*lab*) IND Laboratorium *nt* (*Labor*); **~ experience** *n* IND Laborerfahrung *f*; **~ technique** *n* IND Labortechnik *f*

labor: **~ court** *n AmE* (*cf industrial tribunal BrE*) HRM, LAW Arbeitsgericht *nt*, gewerbliches Schiedsgericht *nt*

laborer *AmE see* **labourer** *BrE*

laboring *AmE see* **labouring** *BrE*

Labor: **~ Management Relations Act** *n AmE* HRM, LAW *1947* US-Bundesgesetz zur Regelung der Arbeitgeber-Arbeitnehmer-Beziehungen

labor: **~ union** *n AmE* (*cf trade union BrE*) GEN COMM, HRM, POL Gewerkschaft *f*; **~ unionist** *n AmE* (*cf trade unionist BrE*) GEN COMM, HRM, POL Gewerkschafter, in *m,f*

labour 1. *n BrE* ECON Arbeit *f*, Produktionsfaktor *m* Arbeit HRM Arbeit *f*, Arbeitnehmer *m pl*, *trade unions* Gewerkschaften *f pl*; **2.** *vi BrE* HRM schwer arbeiten

Labour: **~ Administration** *n BrE* ADMIN, POL Labour-Regierung *f*

labour: **~-augmenting technical progress** *n BrE* ECON arbeitsadditiver technischer Fortschritt *m*, arbeitsver-mehrender technischer Fortschritt *m*; **~ clause** *n BrE* HRM tarifliche Klausel *f*, tarifliche Bestimmung *f*, Arbeitsklausel *f*; **~ code** *n BrE* HRM Arbeitskodex *m*; **~ contract** *n BrE* GEN COMM, HRM Arbeitsvertrag *m*; **~ costs** *n pl BrE* ECON Arbeitsaufwand *m*, Arbeits-kosten *pl*, Arbeitslöhne *m pl*, Lohnkosten *pl*; **~ demand** *n BrE* ECON Arbeitsbedarf *m*, Arbeitskräftenachfrage *f*, Nachfrage *f* nach Arbeitskräften; **~ dispute** *n BrE* ECON Arbeitskampf *m*, Arbeitsstreit *m*, arbeitsrecht-liche Streitfrage *f*, HRM, IND Arbeitskampf *m*; **~ disutility theory** *n BrE* ECON Arbeitsertragsrück-gangstheorie *f*, Theorie *f* vom abnehmenden Arbeitsnutzen; **~ economics** *n BrE* ECON Arbeitsöko-nomik *f*, Arbeitsmarkttheorie *f*; **~ efficiency** *n BrE* HRM Arbeitsproduktivität *f*

labourer *n BrE* HRM Hilfsarbeiter, in *m,f*, ungelernter Arbeiter *m*

labour: **~ exchange** *n BrE* ADMIN, HRM Arbeitsamt *nt*; **~ force** *n BrE* ECON Erwerbsbevölkerung *f*, Erwerbs-tätige *pl*, *within a firm* Arbeitskräfte *f pl*, Belegschaft *f*, *of a country* Zahl *f* der Beschäftigten, Beschäftigtenanzahl *f*, HRM Personalbestand *m*, Beleg-schaft *f*, IND Arbeitskraft *f*, Arbeitskräftereserven *f pl*, MGMNT Personalbestand *m*; **~ force participation rate** *n BrE* (*LFPR*) ECON, HRM Erwerbsquote *f*; **~ grading** *n BrE* HRM Arbeitsplatzbewertung *f*

labouring: **~ class** *n BrE* HRM Arbeiterklasse *f*

labour: **~ inspector** *n BrE* WEL Gewerbeaufsichtsperson *f*, Inspizient *m* der Gewerbeaufsicht, Gewerbeaufseher, in *m,f*; **~ inspectorate** *n BrE* WEL Gewerbeaufsichtsamt *nt*; **~-intensive** *adj BrE* ECON *sector*, HRM, IND arbeitsintensiv; **~-intensive industry** *n BrE* HRM arbeitsintensive Industrie *f*; **~ law** *n BrE* HRM, LAW Arbeitsgesetz *nt*, Arbeitsrecht *nt*; **~ legislation** *n BrE* HRM, LAW arbeitsrechtliche Vor-schriften *f pl*; **~-managed firm** *n BrE* MGMNT selbstverwalteter Betrieb *m*, von den Arbeitnehmern geführte Firma *f*, von den Arbeitnehmern geleitete Firma *f*; **~ market** *n BrE* ECON, GEN COMM, HRM Arbeitsmarkt *m*; **~-market levy** *n BrE* ECON Arbeitsmarktabgabe *f*; **~-market policy** *n BrE* ECON, POL Arbeitsmarktpolitik *f*; **~-market rigidities** *n pl BrE* ECON Starrheit *f* des Arbeitsmarktes, Rigidität *f* des Arbeitsmarkts; **~-market situation** *n BrE* GEN COMM Beschäftigungssituation *f*; **~-market theory** *n BrE* ECON Arbeitsmarkttheorie *f*; **~ mobility** *n BrE* ECON, HRM Arbeitsmobilität *f*; **~ movement** *n BrE* HRM Arbeiterbewegung *f*, Gewerkschaftsbewegung *f*; **~-only sub-contracting** *n BrE* HRM Untervermittlung von Arbeitskräften

Labour: **~ Party** *n BrE* POL britische Arbeiterpartei, Labour Party *f*

labour: **~ piracy** *n BrE* HRM Abwerbung *f*; **~ power** *n BrE* HRM Arbeitsvermögen *nt*; **~-process theory** *n BrE* HRM Arbeitsprozeßtheorie *f*; **~ relations** *n pl BrE* ECON, HRM Arbeitsbeziehungen *f pl*, Arbeitgeber-Arbeitneh-mer-Beziehungen *f pl*

Labour: **~ Relations Agency** *n BrE* (*LRA*) HRM *Northern Ireland* Beratungs-, Schlichtungs- und Schiedsgerichts-stelle für Arbeitsstreitigkeiten; **~ Representation Committee** *n BrE* (*LRC*) HRM Arbeitnehmervertretungsausschuß *m*

labour: **~ rules** *n pl BrE* HRM, LAW arbeitsrechtliche Vorschriften *f pl*; **~-saving** *adj BrE* HRM arbeitssparend; **~-saving** *n BrE* HRM Einsparung *f* von Arbeitskräften; **~ shed** *n BrE* ECON, HRM *area from which labour supply is drawn* Arbeitsreserve *f*, Arbeitskräftereservoir *nt*; **~ shortage** *n BrE* HRM Arbeitskräftemangel *m*; **~'s share of national income** *n BrE* ECON Lohnquote *f*, Lohnanteil *m* am Sozialprodukt, Lohnanteil *m* am Volkseinkommen; **~ standard** *n BrE* ECON Arbeits-norm *f*; **~ supply** *n BrE* ECON Arbeitsangebot *nt*, Arbeitskräfteangebot *nt*, verfügbare Arbeitskräfte *f pl*; **~ theory of value** *n BrE* ECON Arbeitswertlehre *f*,

Arbeitswerttheorie *f*; ~ **troubles** *n pl BrE* HRM Arbeiterunruhen *f pl*; ~ **turnover** *n BrE* ECON Arbeitskräftefluktuation *f*, Arbeitsplatzwechsel *m*, GEN COMM, HRM Arbeitskräftefluktuation *f*; ~ **unrest** *n BrE* HRM Arbeiterunruhen *f pl*; ~ **voucher** *n* GEN COMM, IND Arbeitsauftrag *m*; ~ **wastage** *n BrE* HRM Arbeitskräfteabgang *m*

laches *n* LAW Verwirkung von Rechten, die lange nicht in Anspruch genommen worden sind

lack 1. *n* FIN Fehlen *nt*, GEN COMM Mangel *m*, Fehlen *nt*; ◆ **for ~ of evidence to the contrary** LAW mangels Beweises des Gegenteils; **2.** *vt* GEN COMM *confidence, support* mangeln an [+dat], fehlen an [+dat]; ◆ **~ consistency** GEN COMM nicht übereinstimmen

lack: ~ **of capacity** *n* LAW mangelnde Geschäftsfähigkeit *f*; ~ **of care** *n* LAW *transactions* Mangel *m* an Sorgfalt; ~ **of experience** *n* HRM Erfahrungsmangel *m*, Mangel *m* an Erfahrung

lacking: **be ~ in** *phr* GEN COMM Mangel haben an

ladder *n* GEN COMM, IND, TRANSP Leiter *f*; ~ **of participation** *n* POL Partizipationshierarchie *f*, Stufen *f pl* der Beteiligungshierarchie

laden: ~ **in bulk** *phr* TRANSP mit Massengut beladen, mit Schüttgut beladen

Ladies: ~ **and Gentlemen** *phr* GEN COMM Sehr geehrte Damen und Herren, Meine Damen und Herren

lading *n* TRANSP Ladung *f*; ~ **port** *n* TRANSP Verladehafen *m*

Laffer: ~ **curve** *n* ECON Laffer-Kurve *f*

lag 1. *n* ECON Lag *m*, Verzögerung *f*, GEN COMM Verzögerung *f*; **2.** *vi* GEN COMM zurückbleiben; ◆ **~ behind** GEN COMM im Rückstand sein, zurückbleiben

laggard *n jarg* S&M, STOCK Nachzügler *m* (*jarg*)

lagged: ~ **variable** *n* MATH verzögerte Variable *f*

lag: ~ **response** *n* ECON Lag-Reaktion *f*, GEN COMM verzögerte Reaktion *f*; ~ **risk** *n* BANK verzögertes Risiko *nt*

laid: ~-**up** *adj* TRANSP *shipping* stillgelegt

laisser-faire *n* ECON Laisser-faire *nt*; ~ **economy** *n* ECON Laisser-faire-Liberalismus *m*

lame: ~ **duck** *n infrml* GEN COMM *company* nicht lebensfähiges Unternehmen *nt*, POL *AmE* nicht wiedergewähltes Kongreßmitglied *nt*, STOCK zahlungsunfähiger Spekulant *m*

LAN *abbr* (*local area network*) COMMS, COMP LAN (*lokales Netz*)

land 1. *n* ECON Boden *m*, GEN COMM Land *nt*, Grundbesitz *m*; **2.** *vt* TRANSP löschen

land: ~ **acquisition program** *AmE*, ~ **acquisition programme** *BrE n* ECON Bodenbeschaffungsplan *m*; ~ **bank** *n* BANK, ECON Landwirtschaftsbank *f*; ~ **banking** *n* PROP spekulativer Erwerb von Grund und Boden für spätere Nutzung in 5-10 Jahren; ~ **bridge** *n* TRANSP Landbrücke *f*; ~-**bridge rate** *n* TRANSP Landbrückenrate *f*, Landbrückentarif *m*; ~ **carriage** *n* TRANSP Beförderung *f* auf dem Landweg, Landtransport *m*; ~ **certificate** *n* PROP Grundbuchauszug *m*, Grundstücksbescheinigung *f*

Land: ~ **Compensation Act** *n BrE* LAW Grundstücksentschädigungsgesetz *nt*

land: ~ **contract** *n* PROP Grundstücksüberlassungsvertrag *m*, Grundstücksvertrag *m*; ~ **development** *n*

ENVIR, IND, PROP, WEL Erschließung *f* von Bauland; ~ **economy** *n* ECON Immobilienwirtschaft *f*

landed: ~ **cost** *n* IMP/EXP Löschungskosten *pl*, TRANSP Kosten *pl* bis zum Löschen; ~ **property** *n* PROP Grundbesitz *m*; ~ **terms** *n pl* IMP/EXP, TRANSP franko Löschung

landfill: ~ **site** *n* ENVIR Deponiegelände *nt*

land: ~ **improvement** *n* ENVIR, IND, PROP, WEL Grundstückserschließung *f*, *cleaning up* Erschließung *f* von Bauland, Grundstückseinrichtungen *f pl*; ~ **in abeyance** *n* LAW *property* Land *nt* in Anwartschaft, vorübergehend ungenutztes Land

landing *n* TRANSP Löschung *f*; ~ **account** *n* (*L/A*) TRANSP *shipping* Landeschein *m*; ~ **certificate** *n* TRANSP *shipping* Löschbescheinigung *f*; ~ **charges** *n pl* ADMIN, TRANSP Löschungskosten *pl*; ~ **gear** *n* TRANSP *trailer* Landing Gear *nt*; ~ **permit** *n* TRANSP Löschgenehmigung *f*; ~ **stage** *n* TRANSP Landungsbrücke *f*; ~, **storage, delivery** *phr* (*LSD*) IMP/EXP Löschung, Speicherung, Lieferung; ~ **strip** *n* TRANSP *aircraft* Landebahn *f*, Landeplatz *m*

land: ~ **lease** *n* PROP Landpacht *f*

landlocked *adj* ENVIR *country* landumschlossen, von Land eingeschlossen, ohne Meereszugang, PROP ohne Zufahrt; ~ **country** *n* POL Binnenstaat *m*; ~ **state** *n* POL Binnenstaat *m*

landmark *n* GEN COMM Wahrzeichen *nt*, Meilenstein *m*, PROP Grenzzeichen *nt*, Grenzstein *m*; ~ **case** *n* LAW grundlegender Fall *m*

land: ~ **mortgage bank** *n* BANK Hypothekenbank *f*, Bodenkreditanstalt *f*; ~ **office** *n AmE* ADMIN Grundbuchamt *nt*, Liegenschaftsamt *nt*

landowner *n* PROP Landbesitzer, in *m,f*

land: ~ **ownership** *n* ECON Grundbesitz *m*; ~ **reform** *n* ECON *agricultural* Bodenreform *f*; ~ **register** *n* (*cf plat book AmE*) ADMIN, PROP Grundbuch *nt*, Kataster *m*; ~ **registration** *n* PROP Grundbucheintragung *f*; ~ **registry** *n* ADMIN Grundbuchamt *nt*, PROP Katasteramt *nt*; ~ **rent** *n* PROP Grundstücksmiete *f*, Grundstückspacht *f*

landscape 1. *n* COMP Querformat *nt*, *document layout* Langformat *nt*, MEDIA *print*, S&M *advertising* Querformat *nt*; **2.** *vi jarg* ADMIN Bürolandschaft entwerfen

landscape: ~ **format** *n* COMP *document layout* Querformat *nt*

landslide *n* POL Erdrutsch *m*

land: ~ **tax** *n* TAX Grundsteuer *f*; ~, **tenements and hereditaments** *pl* LAW *property* Grundstück *nt*, Lehensbesitz *m* am Grundstück und dingliche Rechte *nt pl*; ~ **transport** *n* TRANSP Beförderung *f* auf dem Landweg; ~ **trust** *n* LAW *property* Landtreuhand *f*; ~ **use** *n* ENVIR *local level* Flächennutzung *f*, Grundstücksbenutzung *f*, *national level* Bodennutzung *f*; ~-**use intensity** *n* ENVIR Bodennutzungsintensität *f*; ~-**use planning** *n* ECON Flächennutzungsplanung *f*; ~-**use regulation** *n* PROP Grundstücksnutzungsvorschrift *f*; ~-**use succession** *n* PROP Grundstücksnutzungswechsel *m*, Wechsel *m* in der Grundstücksnutzung; ~ **value tax** *n* TAX Bodenwertzuwachssteuer *f*

language *n* COMP Programmiersprache *f*, S&M *advertising* Sprache *f*

Lanham: ~ **Act** *n AmE* LAW Lanham-Gesetz *nt*

Lapanov: ~ **equilibrium** *n* ECON Lapanov-Gleichgewicht *nt*

lapping *n* ACC Aufschieben von Kasseneingängen, um die Buchungsunterlagen zu fälschen

lapse 1. *n* ACC, GEN COMM Erlöschen *nt*, INS *policy termination* Policenablauf *m*, Versicherungsende *nt*, LAW Verfall *m*; **2.** *vi* ACC, GEN COMM erlöschen, INS ablaufen, LAW verfallen

lapsed *adj* LAW abgelaufen, verfallen; ~ **funds** *n pl* ACC verfallene Mittel *nt pl*; ~ **option** *n* STOCK abgelaufene Option *f*

lapse: ~ **of time** *n* GEN COMM Fristablauf *m*

laptop *n* COMP Laptop *m*, tragbarer PC *m* (*obs*), Aktentaschencomputer *m* (*obs*); ~ **computer** *n* COMP Laptop *m*, tragbarer PC *m* (*obs*), Aktentaschencomputer *m* (*obs*)

large *adj* GEN COMM groß; ♦ **to a ~ extent** GEN COMM in großem Umfang, in hohem Maße, **in ~ quantities** GEN COMM in großen Mengen, **on a ~ scale** GEN COMM in großem Maße

large: ~ **exposure** *n* FIN Großkredit *m*; ~ **family** *n* S&M kinderreiche Familie *f*

largely *adv* GEN COMM weitgehend

large: ~ **order** *n* GEN COMM Großauftrag *m*; ~ **risk** *n* INS große Gefahr *f*, großes Risiko *nt*; ~~**scale** *adj* ECON, GEN COMM *project* groß angelegt, umfassend, umfangreich; ~~**scale exporter** *n* ECON, IMP/EXP Großexporteur *m*; ~~**scale farming** *n* ECON *agricultural* landwirtschaftlicher Großbetrieb *m*; ~~**scale industry** *n* IND Großindustrie *f*; ~~**scale model** *n* ECON *econometrics* Mehrgleichungsmodell *nt*; ~~**scale production** *n* IND Großserienfertigung *f*, Großproduktion *f*

laser *n* ADMIN, BANK, COMP, IND, MEDIA Laser *m*; ~ **banking** *n* BANK Laserbankgeschäft *nt*; ~ **beam** *n* IND *production* Laserstrahl *m*; ~ **printer** *n* COMP, MEDIA Laserdrucker *m*, Laserprinter *m*; ~ **scanner** *n* COMP, MEDIA *print* Laserscanner *nt*

Laspeyres: ~ **index** *n* ECON *econometrics* Laspeyres-Preisindex *m*

last 1. *adj* GEN COMM letzte; ♦ ~ **in position** GEN COMM auf letzter Position; ~ **in first out** (*LIFO*) HRM last-in-first-out (*LIFO*), LIFO-Methode *f*, zuletzt eingestellt, zuerst entlassen; **over the ~ decade** GEN COMM während des letzten Jahrzehnts; **over the ~ year or so** GEN COMM das letzte Jahr über ungefähr, während des letzten Jahres ungefähr; **2.** *vi* GEN COMM andauern

last: ~ **carrier** *n* TRANSP letzter Frachtführer *m*, letzter Spediteur *m*, letzter Transportunternehmer *m*; ~ **day hours** *n pl* STOCK letzte Stunden *f pl* des Einreichungstermins; ~ **day of trading** *n* STOCK letzter Handelstag *m*; ~ **half** *n* (*lh*) GEN COMM *of the month* zweite Hälfte *f*

lasting: ~ **effect** *n* GEN COMM, MEDIA nachhaltige Wirkung *f*

last: ~~**minute decision** *n* GEN COMM Entscheidung *f* in letzter Minute; ~ **notice day** *n* FIN letzter Bekanntmachungstag *m*, HRM letzter Kündigungstag *m*; ~ **offer arbitration** *n* BrE HRM letztes Schlichtungsangebot *nt*; ~ **resort** *n* GEN COMM letzter Ausweg *m*; ~ **safe day** *n* (*lsd*) INS *marine* letzter Versicherungstag *m*; ~ **sale** *n* STOCK letzter Verkauf *m*; ~ **speaker** *n* GEN COMM Vorredner, in *m,f*; ~ **trading day** *n* STOCK letzter Handelstag *m*; ~ **will and testament** *n* LAW letzter Wille *m* und Testament *nt*

lat. *abbr* (*latitude*) GEN COMM geographische Breite *f*

late *adj* GEN COMM verspätet; ~ **acceptance** *n* LAW *goods, contract of delivery* verspätete Annahme *f*; ~ **capitalism** *n* ECON Spätkapitalismus *m*; ~ **edition** *n* MEDIA *broadcast* Nachtausgabe *f* einer Nachrichtensendung; ~ **majority** *n* S&M späte Mehrheit *f*

lateness *n* GEN COMM Verspätung *f*, HRM Verspätung *f*, Zuspätkommen *nt*

late: ~~**night opening** *n* GEN COMM Dienstleistungsabend *m*

latent: ~ **defect** *n* LAW *property* versteckter Mangel *m*; ~ **demand** *n* S&M latente Nachfrage *f*; ~ **tax** *n* TAX latente Steuer *f*

late: ~ **payment** *n* FIN verspätete Zahlung *f*

later *adj* GEN COMM später

lateral *adj* GEN COMM *movement* seitlich; ~ **integration** *n* ECON horizontale Integration *f*; ~ **suspension file** *n* ADMIN Hängeregistraturmappe *f*; ~ **thinker** *n* MEDIA, POL Querdenker, in *m,f*; ~ **thinking** *n* GEN COMM, MGMNT laterales Denken *nt*

latest *adj* S&M *development* jüngst; ♦ **at the ~** GEN COMM spätestens

latest: ~ **addition** *n* GEN COMM *to product range*, S&M jüngste Erweiterung *f*; ~ **date** *n* GEN COMM letzter Termin *m*; ~ **estimate** *n* (*L/E*) GEN COMM jüngste Schätzung *f*; **the ~ fashion** *n* GEN COMM die neueste Mode *f*; ~ **statistics** *n pl* MATH *statistics* jüngste Statistiken *f pl*

late: ~ **tape** *n* STOCK später Börsenticker *m*

latex *n* IND Kautschukmilch *f*, Latex *m*

latitude *n* (*lat.*) GEN COMM geographische Breite *f*, MGMNT *thinking* Spielraum *m*

launch 1. *n* TRANSP *of ship* Stapellauf *m*; **2.** *vt* FIN *share issue* auflegen, begeben, HRM *career* beginnen, starten, S&M *product* einführen, starten, in Gang setzen, herausbringen; ♦ ~ **a bond coupon** STOCK eine Anleiheemission auflegen; ~ **a bond issue** STOCK eine Anleiheemission auflegen; ~ **a bond offering** FIN eine Anleihe auflegen; ~ **a new model** S&M *marketing* ein neues Modell auf den Markt bringen; ~ **an issue** STOCK eine Emission begeben

launching *n* S&M Einführung *f*, TRANSP *of lifeboats* Aussetzen *nt*, *of ship* Stapellauf *m*; ~ **costs** *n pl* ACC, FIN Anlaufkosten *pl*; ~ **of a loan** *n* FIN Begebung *f* einer Anleihe

launch: ~ **party** *n* MEDIA *for book* Party anläßlich der Veröffentlichung eines Buchs

launder *vt* FIN, GEN COMM *money* waschen

laundering *n* FIN, GEN COMM *money* Wäsche *f*

laundry: ~ **list** *n* AmE *jarg* POL Liste der zu verabschiedenden Gesetzesentwürfe

Lausanne: ~ **School** *n* ECON Lausanner Schule *f*

Lautro *n* BrE (*Life Assurance and Unit Trust Regulatory Organization*) FIN, INS Selbstüberwachungsorganisation der Londoner City

law *n* LAW *legislation* Gesetzgebung *f*, *rule* Gesetz *nt*, *system* Recht *nt*; ♦ **by ~** LAW von Rechts wegen; **in the eyes of the ~** LAW in den Augen des Gesetzes, vor dem Gesetz

law: ~ **of agency** *n* LAW *transactions* Recht *nt* der Stellvertretung; ~ **applicable to the person** *n* LAW Personalstatut *nt*; ~ **of comparative advantage** *n* ECON *international trade* Gesetz *nt* des komparativen Vorteils; ~ **of contract** *n* LAW Vertragsrecht *nt*; ~ **of**

diminishing marginal utility *n* ECON Gesetz *nt* vom abnehmenden Grenznutzen; **~ of diminishing returns** *n* ECON Ertragsgesetz *nt*, Gesetz *nt* der abnehmenden Erträge, Gesetz *nt* vom abnehmenden Ertrag; **~ enforcement official** *n* LAW Vollzugsbeamte(r) *m* [decl. as adj], Vollzugsbeamtin *f*; **~ of equi-marginal returns** *n* ECON Gesetz *nt* vom Ausgleich der Grenznutzen, Grenznutzenausgleichsgesetz *nt*; **~ firm** *n* LAW Anwaltskanzlei *f*; **~ of the flag** *n* LAW *commercial* Recht *nt* der Flagge, Flaggenrecht *nt*

lawful *adj* LAW gesetzmäßig, rechtlich; **~ means** *n pl* LAW rechtmäßige Mittel *nt pl*

law: **~ governing contractual obligations** *n* LAW Recht *nt* der Schuldverhältnisse, Vertragsrecht *nt*, Schuldrecht *nt*; **~ of increasing costs** *n* ECON Gesetz *nt* der steigenden Kosten; **~ of indifference** *n* ECON Gesetz *nt* der Unterschiedslosigkeit der Preise; **~ of large numbers** *n* MATH Gesetz *nt* der großen Zahl; **~ on the protection of consumers** *n* LAW, S&M Verbraucherschutzgesetz *nt*; **~ practice** *n* LAW Anwaltspraxis *f*, Anwaltstätigkeit *f*; **~ of reciprocal demand** *n* ECON Gesetz *nt* der reziproken Nachfrage; **~ of reflux** *n* BANK Gesetz *nt* des Rückflusses; **~ regulating the valuation of property** *n* LAW, PROP, TAX Bewertungsrecht *nt*; **~ relating to nonresidents** *n* LAW Ausländerrecht *nt*; **~ with retroactive effect** *n* LAW rückwirkendes Gesetz *nt*; **~ of satiable wants** *n* ECON erstes Gossensches Gesetz *nt*, Gesetz *nt* der Bedürfnissättigung; **~ school** *n* WEL juristische Fakultät *f*

Law: **~ Society** *n BrE* LAW ≈ Anwaltskammer *f*

lawsuit *n* LAW Klage *f*

law: **~ of supply and demand** *n* ECON Gesetz *nt* von Angebot und Nachfrage; **~ 29** *n jarg* GEN COMM gesunder Menschenverstand *m*; **~ of value** *n* ECON Wertgesetz *nt*; **~ of variable proportions** *n* ECON Ertragsgesetz *nt*, Gesetz *nt* vom abnehmenden Ertragszuwachs

lay **1.** *adj* HRM ehrenamtlich; **2.** *vt* POL vorlegen; ◆ **~ claim to** GEN COMM, LAW, PATENTS Anspruch erheben, beanspruchen; **~ an embargo on** GEN COMM, MEDIA ein Embargo verhängen über [+acc]; **~ the emphasis on** GEN COMM betonen; **~ the ground for sth** GEN COMM die Grundlage für etwas schaffen; **~ a proposal before a committee** GEN COMM einem Ausschuß einen Antrag vorlegen

lay down *vt* LAW *in contract, constitution* niederlegen, verankern, festlegen, *principle, rule, norm* aufstellen; ◆ **~ the rules** ADMIN Regeln festlegen

lay off *vt* HRM *workers* entlassen; ◆ **~ staff** Personal freisetzen

lay out *vt* GEN COMM *spend* ausgeben, *invest* investieren

lay: **~ day** *n* TRANSP *shipping* Liegetag *m*

layer *n* COMP *network, circuitry* Schicht *f*

layman *n* HRM Laie *m*

lay: **~ member** *n* HRM Laienmitglied *nt*; **~-off** *n* HRM Personalfreisetzung *f*; **~ official** *n* HRM *industrial relations* ehrenamtlicher Vertreter *m*, ehrenamtliche Vertreterin *f*; **~-off pay** *n* HRM Abfindung *f*, Entlassungsgeld *nt*, Entlassungszahlung *f*

layout *n* ACC Layout *nt*, *draft* Entwurf *m*, ADMIN, COMP, MEDIA *Druck* Layout *nt*; **~ character** *n* COMP Layout-Steuerzeichen *nt*; **~ chart** *n* ADMIN Layout-Plan *m*; **~ man** *n* ADMIN, COMP, MEDIA Layouter *m*; **~ woman** *n* ADMIN, COMP, MEDIA Layouterin *f*

laytime *n* TRANSP *shipping* Liegezeit *f*

lay: **~-up berth** *n* TRANSP *shipping* Liegeplatz *m*; **~-up return** *n* INS *marine* Liegeplatzkostenerstattung *f*

lb *abbr* (*pound*) GEN COMM Pfd. (*Pfund*)

LC *abbr* GEN COMM (*Library of Congress AmE*) Nationalbibliothek der USA, LAW, TRANSP (*label clause*) *cargo* Kennsatzklausel *f*, Kennzeichnungsklausel *f*

L/C *abbr* (*letter of credit*) BANK Akkreditiv *nt*

LCA *abbr* (*life-cycle assessment*) ENVIR Lebenszyklusbewertung *f*

LCCI *abbr BrE* (*London Chamber of Commerce & Industry*) GEN COMM Londoner Industrie- und Handelskammer

LCE *abbr BrE obs* (*London Commodity Exchange*) STOCK ehemalige Londoner Warenbörse

LCH *abbr* (*life-cycle hypothesis*) ECON Lebenszeithypothese *f*, Lebenszyklushypothese *f*

LCL *abbr* (*less than container load*) TRANSP Stückgut *nt*, Stückgutsendung *f*; **~ depot** *n* TRANSP Stückgutdepot *nt*; **~ door** *n* TRANSP Stückguttür *f*

LDC *abbr* (*less-developed country*) ECON Entwicklungsland *nt*

ldg *abbr* (*loading*) TRANSP Beladen *nt*, Laden *nt*, Verladung *f*; **~ & dly** *abbr* (*loading and delivery*) TRANSP Verladung *f* und Lieferung *f*

LDMA *abbr* (*London Discount Market Association*) BANK Vereinigung der Londoner Diskonthäuser, Finanzmakler und Geldhändler der großen Geschäftsbanken

L/E *abbr* (*latest estimate*) GEN COMM jüngste Schätzung *f*

LEA *abbr* (*Local Enterprise Agency*) WEL Agentur für ortsansässige Unternehmen

lead **1.** *n* MEDIA *main news story* Aufmacher *m*, *opening paragraph of story* Vorspann *m*; **2.** *vt* GEN COMM dirigieren, führen, leiten; ◆ **~ for the defence** *BrE*, **~ for the defense** *AmE n* LAW die Verteidigung führen

lead ~ bank *n* BANK führende Bank *f*, Konsortialführer *m*, FIN Konsortialführer *m*

leader *n* GEN COMM Geschäftsführer, in *m,f*, Anführer *m*, HRM *of trade union* Vorsitzende(r) *mf* [decl. as adj], INS führender Versicherer *m*, Erstversicherer *m*, LAW erster, leitender Anwalt in einem Verfahren, MEDIA *editorial* Leitartikel *m*, POL Vorsitzende(r) *mf* [decl. as adj], S&M *to attract consumers* Lockartikel *m*, Zugartikel *m*, *most successful* Marktführer *m*, STOCK Standardwert *m*; **~ merchandising** *n* S&M Absatzförderung *f* von Lockartikeln; **~ pricing** *n* S&M Preispolitik *f* für Lockangebote

leadership *n* GEN COMM *quality* Leitung *f*, *of a company* Führung *f*, HRM Führung *f*, Leitung *f*, MGMNT Führung

leaders: **~ and laggards** *n pl* STOCK Spitzenwerte und Nachzügler *m pl*

leader: **~ writer** *n BrE* MEDIA Leitartikelschreiber, in *m,f*

lead: **~-free** *adj* ENVIR, TRANSP *petrol* bleifrei; **~-free fuel** *n* ENVIR bleifreier Kraftstoff *m*; **~-free gas** *AmE n* (*cf lead-free petrol BrE*) ENVIR bleifreies Benzin *nt*; **~-free petrol** *BrE n* (*cf lead-free gas AmE*) ENVIR bleifreies Benzin *nt*

leading *adj* GEN COMM, S&M führend; **~ article** *n BrE* MEDIA *editorial* Leitartikel *m*; **~ bank** *n* BANK, FIN Konsortialführer *m*; **~ edge** *n* S&M vorderste Front *f*; **~ indicator** *n* ECON *econometrics* Frühindikator *m*; **~ industries** *n pl* IND führende Industrien *f pl*;

~ industry *n* IND Hauptwirtschaftsbranche *f*; **~ line** *n* MEDIA *headline* Überschrift *f*, PATENTS maßgebende Warengattung *f*, *reference sign* führende Zeile *f*, S&M Führungslinie *f*, *of goods* führende Marke *f*; **~ question** *n* S&M Suggestivfrage *f*; **~ share** *n* STOCK führende Aktie *f*; **~ stock** *n* STOCK Standardwert *m*; **~ underwriter** *n* BANK, FIN *organization* Erstversicherer *m*, *person* Konsortialführer, in *m,f*; **~ underwriter agreement** *n* INS *marine* Abkommen *nt* mit Erstversicherer, Vertrag *m* mit Erstversicherer; **~ underwriters' agreement for marine cargo business** *n* (*LUAMC*) INS *marine* Annahmerichtlinien *f pl* der Erstversicherer für Seefrachtgeschäfte; **~ underwriters' agreement for marine hull business** *n* (*LUAMH*) INS *marine* Annahmerichtlinien *f pl* der Erstversicherer für Schiffskaskogeschäfte

lead: **~ management** *n* FIN Federführung *f*; **~ ore** *n* ENVIR Bleierz *nt*

leads: **~ and lags** *n pl* ECON Leads *pl* und Lags *pl*, vorauseilende und nachhinkende Indikatoren *m pl*, STOCK Vorauszahlungen *f pl* und Stundungen *f pl* im Auslandszahlungsverkehr

lead: **~ slip** *n* INS *marine* Deckungszusage *f* des Erstversicherers; **~ story** *n* MEDIA Titelgeschichte *f*; **~ time** *n* ADMIN, GEN COMM Bearbeitungszeit *f*, IND *plan* Vorlaufzeit *f*, S&M *of new product* Einführungszeit *f*, *plan* Realisierungszeit *f*, *stock* Beschaffungszeit *f*; **~-time delay** *n* GEN COMM zeitlicher Rückstand *m* bei Innovationseinführung

leaf *n* COMMS, MEDIA *paper* Blatt *nt*

leaflet *n* S&M Werbeblatt *nt*, Zettel *m*

league *n* GEN COMM *organization* Verband *m*

leak 1. *n* MEDIA, POL *of information* undichte Stelle *f*; **2.** *vt* MEDIA, POL *information* zuspielen; ♦ **~ to the press** MEDIA, POL der Presse zuspielen; **3.** *vi* MEDIA, POL *information* durchsickern

leak out *vi* MEDIA, POL *information* bekanntwerden, durchsickern

leakage *n* ECON Schwund *m*, Verlust *m*, *of capital* Kapitalverlust *m*, FIN *of capital* Kapitalverlust *m*, MEDIA, POL *of information* Durchsickern *nt*

leaking *n* ENVIR Ausfluß *m*

lean: **~ towards** *vi* HRM neigen zu

lean: **~ year** *n* ECON mageres Jahr *nt*

leapfrog *vi* GEN COMM *prices*, HRM überspringen

leapfrogging *n* HRM *wages* Überspringen *nt*

leap: **~ year** *n* GEN COMM Schaltjahr *nt*

learning: **~-by-doing** *n* ECON Learning by doing *nt*; **~ curve** *n* ECON, HRM, WEL Lernkurve *f*

learn: **~ the ropes** *phr* HRM sich einarbeiten

lease 1. *n* BANK Mietvertrag *m*, LAW *usually commercial* Pachtvertrag *m*, *renting an object* Mietvertrag *m*, PROP Miete *f*, Pacht *f*; **2.** *vt* GEN COMM mieten, PROP *from sb* mieten, pachten, *to sb* verpachten

lease: **~ acquisition cost** *n* FIN Leasing-Erwerbskosten *pl*; **~ agreement** *n* BANK, LAW Mietvertrag *m*; **~ company** *n* GEN COMM Leasinggesellschaft *f*

leased *adj* GEN COMM geleast; **~ line** *n* COMP Mietleitung *f*, Standleitung *f*

lease: **~ financing** *n* BANK Mietfinanzierung *f*, Leasing-Finanzierung *f*

leasehold *n* ACC Pachtbesitz *m*, PROP Pachtgrundstück *nt*

leaseholder *n* GEN COMM Pächter, in *m,f*

leasehold: **~ estate** *n* GEN COMM gemietetes Grundstück *nt*; **~ improvements** *n pl* FIN Werterhöhungen *f pl* während der Pacht, PROP Werterhöhungen *f pl* während der Pachtzeit; **~ insurance** *n* INS Pachtgutversicherung *f*; **~ mortgage** *n* PROP Grundpfandrecht *nt* auf Pachtgrundstück, **~ property** *n* LAW, PROP Pachtgrundstück *nt*; **~ value** *n* PROP Pachtgrundstückswert *m*

leaselend *n* PROP Pacht- und Leihvertrag *m*; **~ with option to purchase** *n* PROP Pacht *f* mit Vorkaufsrecht, Mietvertrag *m* mit Vorkaufsrecht

leasing *n* GEN COMM, PROP Leasing *nt*; **~ agreement** *n* FIN, GEN COMM Leasingvertrag *m*; **~ company** *n* GEN COMM, PROP Leasinggesellschaft *f*

least: **~ cost** *n* ACC Mindestkosten *pl*; **~-favored region** *AmE*, **~-favoured region** *BrE n* ECON am wenigsten bevorzugtes Gebiet *nt*, besonders benachteiligte Region *f*; **~ squares method** *n* MATH *statistics* Methode *f* der kleinsten Quadrate; **~ term** *n* MATH kleinstes Glied *nt*; **~ upper bound** *n* MATH kleinste oberste Schranke *f*; **~ variance ratio** *n* ECON, MATH Prinzip *nt* des minimalen Streuungsverhältnisses

leather: **~ goods** *n pl* IND Lederwaren *f pl*

leave 1. *n* HRM, LEIS Urlaub *m*, Ferien *pl*; ♦ **on ~** HRM in Urlaub; **2.** *vt* GEN COMM austreten aus, verlassen, LAW überlassen; ♦ **~ a legacy to sb** LAW jdm ein Vermächtnis aussetzen; **~ a space** COMP einen Leerschritt eingeben; **~ a telephone message** COMMS eine telefonische Nachricht hinterlassen; **~ the matter open** GEN COMM die Angelegenheit offen lassen

leave: **~ of absence** *n* HRM Beurlaubung *f*; **~ period** *n* HRM Urlaub *m*, Urlaubszeit *f*

leaving *n* GEN COMM Verlassen *nt*, LAW Überlassung *f*; **~ certificate** *n* *BrE* (*cf high-school diploma AmE*) WEL Abschlußzeugnis *nt*; **~ examination** *n* WEL Abschlußprüfung *f*

LEC *abbr BrE* (*Local Export Council*) IMP/EXP örtliche Ausfuhrförderungsgemeinschaft, lokaler Exportausschuß *m*

LED *abbr* (*light-emitting diode*) COMP LED (*Leuchtdiode, Lichtemissionsdiode, Lumineszenzdiode*)

ledger *n* ACC *bookkeeping*, FIN Hauptbuch *nt*; **~ account** *n* ACC, FIN Hauptbuchkonto *nt*; **~ balance** *n* ACC, FIN Hauptbuchkontenstand *m*, Hauptbuchsaldo *m*

ledgerless: **~ accounting** *n* ACC Belegbuchhaltung *f*

left *n* GEN COMM linke Seite *f*, POL Linke *f*, linker Flügel *m*; ♦ **on the ~** GEN COMM, POL links

left: **~ column** *n* ACC Sollseite *f*; **~-hand** *adj* GEN COMM linke; **~-hand column** *n* GEN COMM linke Spalte *f*

leftism *n* POL linksgerichtete politische Gesinnung *f*, linksorientierte Haltung *f*

left-justified *adj* COMP, MEDIA links ausgerichtet, linksbündig

left-justify *vt* COMP, MEDIA am linken Rand ausrichten, linksbündig ausrichten

left: **~-luggage locker** *n* *BrE* GEN COMM Schließfach *nt*, Schließfach *nt* für Gepäckaufbewahrung; **~-luggage office** *n* *BrE* (*cf checkroom AmE*) GEN COMM, TRANSP Gepäckaufbewahrung *f*, Gepäckaufbewahrungsstelle *f*, Garderobe *f*; **~ shift key** *n* COMP linke Umschalttaste *f*; **~-wing** *adj* POL links, linksgerichtet, linksorientiert, zum linken Flügel des politischen Spektrums gehörend

leg *n* MEDIA *print* Abschnitt *m*

legacy *n* LAW Vermächtnis *nt*; **~ duty** *n* *BrE* (*cf legacy tax*

AmE) TAX Erbschaftssteuer *f*; ~ **tax** *n* AmE (*cf legacy duty BrE*) TAX Erbschaftssteuer *f*

legal *adj* LAW *concerning law* rechtlich, juristisch, *lawful* gesetzmäßig; ♦ **be under a ~ obligation to do sth** LAW rechtlich verpflichtet sein, etw zu tun

legal: ~ **action** *n* LAW gerichtliche Schritte *m pl*, Klage *f* im ordentlichen Zivilprozeß; ~ **advice** *n* LAW Rechtsberatung *f*; ~ **advisor** *n* HRM Beistand *m*, Syndikus *m*, LAW Rechtsberater, in *m,f*, Syndikusanwalt *m*, Syndikusanwältin *f*; ~ **aid** *n* LAW, WEL Prozeßkostenhilfe *f*; ~ **case** *n* LAW Rechtsfall *m*; ~ **charges** *n pl* LAW Gerichtskosten *pl*; ~ **claim** *n* LAW Rechtsanspruch *m*; ~ **counsel** *n* LAW Anwalt *m*, Anwältin *f*; ~ **department** *n* LAW Rechtsabteilung *f*; ~ **document** *n* LAW Rechtsdokument *nt*, Urkunde *f*; ~ **eagle** *n* *infrml* LAW, POL Rechtsverdreher *m*; ~ **enactment** *n* LAW Rechtsverordnung *f*; ~ **enforceability of collective agreement** *n* BrE HRM rechtliche Durchsetzbarkeit *f* eines Tarifvertrags; ~ **entity** *n* LAW juristische Person *f*, PATENTS Rechtspersönlichkeit *f*, Rechtsträger *m*

Legal: ~ **Exchange Information Service** *n* (*LEXIS*) LAW juristischer Informationsdienst

legal: ~ **expense insurance** *n* INS *personal* Rechtsschutzversicherung *f*; ~ **fees** *n pl* LAW Anwaltsgebühren *f pl*; ~ **force** *n* LAW Rechtskraft *f*; ~ **formality** *n* LAW Rechtsformalität *f*; ~ **framework** *n* LAW rechtlicher Rahmen *m*, rechtliche Rahmenbedingungen *f pl*, rechtliche Rahmenrichtlinien *f pl*; ~ **harmonization** *n* LAW *EU* Angleichung *f* der Gesetze; ~ **heir** *n* LAW gesetzlicher Erbe *m*; ~ **holiday** *n* AmE (*cf bank holiday BrE*) GEN COMM, HRM, LAW gesetzlicher Feiertag *m*, Bankfeiertag *m*, allgemeiner Feiertag *m*; ~ **immunity** *n* LAW gesetzliche Immunität *f*; ~ **incapacity** *n* ECON Rechts- und Geschäftsunfähigkeit *f*; ~ **investment** *n* ECON, STOCK mündelsichere Kapitalanlage *f*, mündelsicheres Wertpapier *nt*; ~ **issue** *n* GEN COMM Rechtsfrage *f*

legalistic *adj* LAW legalistisch

legality *n* GEN COMM Rechtmäßigkeit *f*, Legalität *f*, Gesetzlichkeit *f*

legalize *vt* LAW beglaubigen, genehmigen

legalized *adj* LAW amtlich beglaubigt, notariell beglaubigt, öffentlich beglaubigt

legal: ~ **liability** *n* LAW gesetzliche Haftpflicht *f*; ~ **list** *n* AmE STOCK von den US-Bundesstaaten veröffentlichtes Verzeichnis von Wertpapieren

legally *adv* LAW rechtlich, gesetzlich; ~ **binding** *adj* LAW rechtsverbindlich; ~ **bound** *adj* LAW rechtlich verpflichtet; ~ **effective** *adj* LAW rechtswirksam; ~ **enforceable** *adj* LAW rechtlich durchsetzbar

legal: ~ **monopoly** *n* ECON gesetzliches Monopol *nt*; ~ **name** *n* LAW *administrative* rechtmäßige Bezeichnung *f*, rechtmäßiger Name *m*, *company* Firmenname *m*, Firmenbezeichnung *f*; ~ **notice** *n* LAW *anouncement* Gerichtsbekanntmachung *f*, *period of notification* gesetzliche Kündigungsfrist *f*; ~ **obligation** *n* LAW rechtliche Verpflichtung *f*; ~ **officer** *n* LAW Rechtsbeamte(r) *m* [decl. as adj], Rechtsbeamtin *f*; ~ **opinion** *n* LAW Rechtsgutachten *nt*, *commercial* Rechtsauffassung *f*; ~ **person** *n* LAW, PATENTS juristische Person; ~ **practitioner** *n* LAW Rechtsberater, in *m,f*; ~ **predecessor** *n* PATENTS Rechtsvorgänger, in *m,f*; ~ **presumption** *n* PATENTS Rechtsvermutung *f*;

~ **principle** *n* LAW Rechtsgrundsatz *m*; ~ **proceedings** *n pl* LAW Gerichtsverfahren *nt pl*; **the ~ profession** *n* LAW Anwaltschaft *f*; ~ **prohibition to capitalize** *n* ACC Aktivierungsverbot *nt*; ~ **protection** *n* ACC Rechtsschutz *m*; ~ **rate of interest** *n* ECON gesetzlicher Zinsfuß *m*; ~ **recognition** *n* LAW gesetzliche Anerkennung *f*; ~ **redress** *n* LAW *breach of contract* Rechtsbehelf *m*; ~ **remedy** *n* LAW *breach of contract* Rechtsbehelf *m*; ~ **requirement** *n* LAW *obligation* gesetzliche Verpflichtung *f*, *regulation* Rechtsvorschrift *f*; ~ **reserve life insurance company** *n* INS Versicherungsgesellschaft *f* mit gesetzlicher Rücklage, Versicherungsunternehmen *nt* mit gesetzlicher Reserve; ~ **reserves** *n* ACC Barreserve *f*, gesetzliche Rücklagen *f pl*, LAW gesetzliche Rücklagen *f pl*; ~ **residence** *n* LAW gesetzlicher Wohnsitz *m*; ~ **revaluation** *n* ACC gesetzliche Aufwertung *f*, gesetzliche Neubewertung *f*; ~ **right** *n* LAW *entitlement* subjektives Recht *nt*; ~ **right to future pension payments** *n* HRM Anwartschaft *f*, Rentenanwartschaft *f*; ~ **section** *n* LAW *of a company* Rechtsabteilung *f*; ~ **services** *n pl* LAW juristische Tätigkeiten *f pl*, rechtliche Leistungen *f pl*; ~ **settlement** *n* LAW Zwangsvergleich *m*; ~ **status** *n* LAW Rechtsstellung *f*; ~ **suit** *n* LAW Zivilprozeß *m*; ~ **system** *n* LAW Rechtssystem *nt*; ~ **tender** *n* FIN, GEN COMM *money* gesetzliches Zahlungsmittel *nt*; ~ **transaction** *n* LAW Rechtsgeschäft *nt*; ~ **transfer** *n* STOCK *of shares* gesetzlich zulässige Übertragung *f*; ~ **wrong** *n* LAW Rechtsverletzung *f*

legatee *n* LAW *property* Vermächtnisnehmer, in *m,f*

legislate *vi* LAW erlassen

legislation *n* LAW Gesetzgebung *f*; ~ **protective of workers and employees** *n* HRM individuelle Arbeitsschutzrechte *nt pl*

legislative *adj* LAW gesetzgebend, legislativ; ~ **power** *n* LAW gesetzgebende Gewalt *f*

legislature *n* LAW *separation of powers* Legislative *f*

legitimacy *n* GEN COMM, LAW Rechtmäßigkeit *f*

legitimate *adj* GEN COMM, LAW legitim, berechtigt; ~ **claim** *n* LAW berechtigter Anspruch *m*; ~ **portion** *n* LAW Pflichtteil *m*

leisure: ~ **center** *AmE*, ~ **centre** *BrE* *n* LEIS Freizeitanlage *f*, Freizeitcenter *nt*, Freizeiteinrichtung *f*, Freizeitpark *m*; ~ **development** *n* WEL Freizeiteinrichtung *f*; ~ **industry** *n* LEIS Freizeitindustrie *f*; ~ **time** *n* LEIS freie Zeit *f*, Freizeit *f*

lemonade: ~~-**stand capitalism** *n* ECON Kleinunternehmerkapitalismus *m*

lemons: ~ **market** *n* ECON Markt *m* für minderwertige Gebrauchtwagen

lend *vt* BANK verleihen, ausleihen, FIN ausleihen, STOCK Kredit gewähren; ♦ ~ **money** FIN Geld leihen; ~ **to** BANK ausleihen an [+acc], ausreichen an [+acc]; ~ **weight to** GEN COMM *argument, assumption* etw Nachdruck verleihen; ~ **against security** BANK, GEN COMM gegen eine Sicherheit ausleihen; ~ **on security** BANK, GEN COMM besicherten Kredit gewähren

lendable: ~ **funds** *n pl* BANK, FIN ausleihungsfähige Mittel *nt pl*

lender *n* BANK Kreditgeber, in *m,f*, Darlehensgeber, in *m,f*, Kapitalgeber, in *m,f*; ~ **of last resort** *n* BANK Lender *m* of last resort, letztinstanzliche Kapitalgeber *m pl*, Refinanzierungsinstitut *nt* der letzten Instanz; ~'s **holder-in-due-course insurance** *n* INS *personal* Versicherung zum Schutz des rechtmäßigen Inhabers von Finanztiteln

lending n BANK Ausleihung f, Darlehensvergabe f, Kreditgewährung f, Kreditvergabe f, Verleihung f; **~ at a premium** FIN Darlehensgewährung f über Pari

lending: **~ agency** n FIN *development aid* Kreditinstitut nt; **~ banker** n BANK Darlehensbank f; **~ business** n BANK Kreditgeschäft nt, FIN Aktivgeschäft nt; **~ ceiling** n GEN COMM Beleihungsgrenze f; **~ institution** n FIN Kreditinstitut nt; **~ limit** n GEN COMM Beleihungsgrenze f; **~ officer** n BANK, FIN Kreditsachbearbeiter, in m,f; **~ policy** n BANK Kreditpolitik f, Kreditvergabepolitik f; **~ power** n BANK Kreditpotential nt; **~ rate** n BANK Kreditzins m, Zinssatz m für Ausleihungen

lendings n FIN Ausleihungen f pl

lending: **~ securities** n pl FIN Kreditsicherheiten f pl

length n TRANSP Länge f; **~ of employment** n HRM Beschäftigungsdauer f

lengthen vt STOCK verlängern

lengthened adj GEN COMM verlängert (*verl.*)

length: **~ of service** n HRM Beschäftigungsdauer f, Dienstalter nt, Dienstzeit f; **~ of time to maturity** n ECON Laufzeit f

Leontief: **~ matrix** n ECON Leontief-Matrix f; **~ paradox** n ECON Leontief-Paradoxon nt

leptokurtic: **~ frequency distribution** n MATH *statistics* hochgipflige Verteilungskurve f, leptokurtische Verteilungskurve f

leptokurtosis n MATH *statistics* Hochgipfligkeit f, Leptokurtosis f

Lerner: **~ effect** n ECON Lerner-Effekt m; **~ index** n ECON Lerner-Index m, Lernerscher Monopolgrad m

less prep GEN COMM *profit and loss account* abzüglich, nach Abzug; **~-developed country** n (*LDC*) ECON Entwicklungsland nt

lessen vt GEN COMM mindern

lesser: **to a ~ extent** phr GEN COMM in geringerem Maße

less: **~-favored** AmE, **~-favoured** BrE adj ECON *area, people* benachteiligt

lesson n GEN COMM Unterricht m, WEL Unterrichtsstunde f

less: **~-than-perfect** adj GEN COMM fehlerhaft

let 1. n PROP Vermietung f; **2.** vt (*cf rent out AmE*) PROP vermieten; ♦ **to ~** BrE (*cf for rent AmE*) PROP zu vermieten; **~ on lease** PROP verpachten; **~ out a contract to sb** GEN COMM an jdn einen Auftrag vergeben

letter n COMMS Brief m, Schreiben nt, COMP, MEDIA Buchstabe m; **~ of advice** n COMMS Ankündigungsschreiben nt, Benachrichtigungsschreiben nt; **~ of allotment** n COMMS *stock exchange* Zuteilungsbenachrichtigung f, Zuteilungsschein m; **~ of apology** n COMMS Entschuldigungsschreiben nt; **~ of application** n COMMS *candidate* Bewerbungsschreiben nt, *investor* Zeichnungserklärung f; **~ of appointment** n HRM Anstellungsschreiben nt; **~ of assignment** n GEN COMM Ernennungsschreiben nt; **~ of attorney** n LAW Vollmachtsurkunde f; **~ of authority** n (*L/A*) GEN COMM Ermächtigungsschreiben nt, Genehmigungsschreiben nt; **~ box** n BrE (*cf mailbox AmE*) ADMIN, COMMS *delivery of post* Briefkasten m; **~ of comfort** n FIN, GEN COMM Patronatserklärung f; **~ of confirmation** n LAW *trade* kaufmännisches Bestätigungsschreiben nt; **~ of**

content n GEN COMM Frachtbrief m; **~ of credit** n (*L/C*) BANK Akkreditiv nt; **~ of enquiry** n COMMS briefliche Anfrage f

letterfoot n COMMS Briefende nt

letterhead n COMMS Briefkopf m

letter: **~ of hypothecation** n BANK Urkunde f über besitzloses Pfandrecht, Verpfändungsbescheinigung f, Verpfändungserklärung f; **~ of indemnity** n (*L/I*) TRANSP Garantieerklärung f, Konnossementsgarantie f

lettering n MEDIA *printing* Aufschrift f, Beschriftung f, Schriftsatz m, Schriftzug m

letter: **~ of intent** n GEN COMM vorläufige Auftragserteilung f, MGMNT schriftliche Absichtserklärung f, STOCK Absichtserklärung f, vorläufige Auftragserteilung f; **~ of introduction** n COMMS Empfehlungsschreiben nt; **~-perfect** adj ADMIN textsicher, sicher in Textbeherrschung

letterpress n S&M *print* Druckerpresse f, *text* Druck m

letter: **~ quality** n (*LQ*) COMP Briefqualität f (*LQ*), Schönschrift f; **~-quality font** n COMP LQ-Font m, Schönschrift f; **~-quality printer** n COMP Schönschriftdrucker m; **~ of recommendation** n HRM Empfehlungsschreiben nt; **~ of renunciation** n STOCK *rights issue* Abtretungsformular nt für Bezugsrechte; **~ of resignation** n HRM Rücktrittsschreiben nt, Rücktrittsgesuch nt; **~ of respite** n LAW *contracts* Stundungsvertrag m; **~ spacing** n MEDIA *print* Buchstabenabstand m; **~ stock** n AmE STOCK Aktien ohne amtliche Zulassung für den Börsenhandel; **~ of subrogation** n BrE COMMS Abtretungserklärung f; **~ of transmittal** n ADMIN Anschreiben nt; **~ tray** n ADMIN Ablagekorb m

lettertype n ADMIN Schrifttyp m

letter: **~ of understanding** n GEN COMM Vorvertrag m

letting n PROP Vermietung f

level 1. n COMP Ebene f, GEN COMM Höhe f, Niveau nt, Stand m, IND *of noise* Pegel m; **2.** vt ♦ **~ criticism at** GEN COMM Kritik äußern an, kritisieren

level off vt ECON abschwächen, GEN COMM abflachen

level out 1. vt GEN COMM ausgleichen; **2.** vi GEN COMM sich ausgleichen

level up vt ECON auf ein höheres Niveau bringen

level: **~ of debt** n FIN Schuldenstand m, Verschuldung f; **~ debt service** n AmE TAX *municipal charter* konstanter Schuldendienst m; **~ of employment** n ECON Beschäftigungsstand m; **~ of expenditure** n ECON Ausgabenniveau nt, Ausgabenhöhe f; **~-headed** adj HRM ausgeglichen

leveling AmE see *levelling* BrE

levelling: **~ out** n BrE ECON Nivellierung f

level: **~ money** n GEN COMM *second-hand car trade* gleicher Geldwert m, gleichbleibendes Geld nt; **~ of orders** n S&M Auftragsbestand m; **~-payment mortgage** n AmE FIN Tilgungshypothek f, Annuitätenhypothek f; **~ premium** n INS gleichbleibende Prämie f, konstante Prämie f; **~ repayment** n BANK Tilgungszahlung f; **~ of return** n TAX Renditeniveau nt; **~ of significance** n MATH *statistics* Irrtumswahrscheinlichkeit f, Signifikanzniveau nt; **~ of support** n ECON *subsidies* Subventionsniveau nt, Höhe f der finanziellen Unterstützung; **~ of training** n HRM Ausbildungsniveau nt, Ausbildungsstand m

leverage n AmE (*cf gearing BrE*) ECON Macht f, politischer Hebel m, FIN Leverage f, Verschuldungsgrad *m*, Hebelwirkung *f*, Verhältnis *nt* von Fremd- zu Eigenkapital, Fremdkapitalaufnahme *f*, *influence* Einfluß *m*, POL Macht *f*, Druck *m*, politischer Hebel *m*, STOCK Fremdkapitalaufnahme *f*, Leverage *f*, Verhältnis *nt* Einschuß-Kapital, Verhältnis *nt* von Obligationen und Vorzugsaktien zu Stammaktie

leverage up *vi* FIN den Fremdkapitalanteil erhöhen

leverage: ~ **adjustment** *n* AmE (*cf gearing adjustment BrE*) FIN Anpassung *f* zwischen Fremd- und Eigenkapital

leveraged: ~ **bid** *n* STOCK fremdfinanziertes Submissionsangebot *nt*; ~ **buyout** *n* FIN fremdfinanziertes Übernahmeangebot *nt*, Leveraged Buy-Out *m* (*LBO*), GEN COMM Übernahme *f* durch Fremdfinanzierung; ~ **company** *n* ACC verschuldetes Unternehmen *nt*; ~ **lease** *n* PROP durch Leihkapital finanziertes Leasing *nt*; ~ **management buy-in** *n* (*LMBI*) FIN, MGMNT fremdfinanziertes Management-Buy-In *nt* (*LMBI*); ~ **management buyout** *n* (*LMBO*) FIN, MGMNT fremdfinanziertes Management-Buy-Out *nt*, fremdfinanzierte Übernahme *f* durch das Management; ~ **stock** *n* FIN Stammaktien *f pl* mit großem Anteil an Vorzugsaktien

leverage: ~ **effect** *n* ECON Hebelwirkung *f*; ~ **fund** *n* ECON Investmentfonds *m*; ~ **lease** *n* FIN Anteilsmiete *f*; ~ **ratio** *n* AmE (*cf gearing ratio BrE*) ACC, BANK Verschuldungsgrad *m*, FIN Verhältnis *nt* zwischen Fremd- und Eigenkapital, Kapitalstrukturkennziffer *f*

levy 1. *n* FIN *action* Erhebung *f*, Umlage *f*, *tax* Abgabe *f*, IMP/EXP *action* Erhebung *f*, *tax* Abgabe *f*, Steuer *f*, LAW Auferlegung *f*, *seizure of tax* Beschlagnahme *f*, Eintreibung *f*; **2.** *vt* GEN COMM *raise, collect* erheben, LAW *seize* pfänden, *impose* auferlegen, TAX eintreiben, erheben

levy: ~ **on property** *n* ECON Vermögensabgabe *f*

Lewis-Fei-Ranis: ~ **model** *n* ECON Lewis-Fei-Ranis-Modell *nt*

lex auctoritatis *n* LAW Vollmachtsstatut *nt*

LEXIS *abbr* (*Legal Exchange Information Service*) LAW juristischer Informationsdienst

lex mercatoria *n* LAW Handelsgesetz *nt*, Handelsrecht *nt*

lex non cogit ad impossibilia *phr* LAW das Gesetz zwingt niemanden, Unmögliches zu tun

lex rei sitae *n* LAW *contracts* Recht *nt* des Ortes, an dem sich die Sache befindet

lex scripta *n* GEN COMM geschriebenes Recht *nt*

lf *abbr* (*line feed*) COMP Zeilenvorschub *m*

LFPR *abbr* ECON, HRM (*labor force participation rate AmE, labour force participation rate BrE*) Erwerbsquote *f*

LGS *abbr* (*liquid assets and government securities*) FIN liquide Mittel und Staatspapiere *nt pl*, Umlaufvermögen und Staatspapiere *nt pl*

lh *abbr* (*last half*) GEN COMM zweite Hälfte *f*

L/I *abbr* (*letter of indemnity*) GEN COMM Garantieerklärung *f*, Konnossementsgarantie *f*

liability *n* ACC Verbindlichkeit *f*, ADMIN, FIN Obligo *nt*, GEN COMM *responsibility* Haftung *f*, Verpflichtung *f*, LAW Haftbarkeit *f*, Haftpflicht *f*, Haftung *f*, Schuld *f*, Verbindlichkeit *f*; ~ **cost** *n* STOCK *interest rate futures* Verbindlichkeitskosten *pl*; ~ **dividend** *n* ACC Dividende *f* in Form von Schuldurkunden; ~ **for breach of warranty** *n* GEN COMM Gewährleistungshaftung *f*; ~ **for damage** *n* LAW Schadenhaftung *f*; ~ **for material defects** *n* LAW Sachmängelhaftung *f*; ~ **insurance** *n*

ADMIN Haftpflichtversicherung *f*, INS Haftpflichtversicherung *f*, Rückdeckungsversicherung *f*; ~ **insuring agreement** *n* INS Haftpflichtversicherungsvertrag *m*, Vertrag *m* über Haftpflichtversicherung; ~ **in tort** *n* GEN COMM Haftung *f* aus unerlaubter Handlung, Deliktshaftung *f* (*frml*); ~ **issuer** *n* STOCK Emittent *m* von Verbindlichkeiten; ~ **item** *n* ACC Schuldposten *m*; ~ **limitation clause** *n* INS, LAW Haftungsbeschränkungsklausel *f*; ~ **management** *n* FIN, STOCK Verschuldungspolitik *f*, *public finance* Debt Management *nt*, Umschichtung *f* von Verbindlichkeiten; ~ **manager** *n* STOCK mit der Passivsteuerung betraute Person; ~ **rate** *n* STOCK *interest rate futures* Schuldenrate *f*; ~ **to be discharged at the domicile of the debtor** *n* LAW Holschuld *f*; ~ **under a guarantee** *n* LAW Garantiehaftung *f*; ~ **under a letter of credit** *n* FIN Akkreditivverpflichtung *f*

liable *adj* GEN COMM haftbar, haftpflichtig, LAW haftbar; ♦ **be ~ for** INS, LAW haften für; ~ **to pay a tax** LAW, TAX steuerpflichtig, abgabenpflichtig; ~ **to pay taxes** LAW, TAX steuerpflichtig, abgabenpflichtig; ~ **to prosecution** LAW strafbar; ~ **to tax** LAW, TAX steuerpflichtig, abgabenpflichtig

liable: ~ **party** *n* INS Verpflichtete(r) *mf* [decl. as adj]

liaise *vi* GEN COMM zusammenarbeiten, sich in Verbindung setzen

liaison *n* GEN COMM *coordination* Verbindung *f*, Zusammenarbeit *f*

LIARS *abbr* (*Lloyd's Instantaneous Accounting Record System*) INS Lloyd's Sofortrechnungsbelegsystem *nt*

libel 1. *n* LAW üble Nachrede *f*, Beleidigung *f*, Verleumdung *f*; **2.** *vt* LAW verleumden

libel: ~ **law** *n* LAW Verleumdungsgesetz *nt*

libellous *adj* BrE LAW beleidigend, verleumderisch

libelous AmE see **libellous** BrE

libel: ~ **proceedings** *n pl* LAW Verleumdungsverfahren *nt*

liberal *adj* ECON freizügig, GEN COMM, POL liberal; ~ **collectivism** *n* POL liberaler Kollektivismus *m*

liberalization *n* ECON, GEN COMM, LAW Liberalisierung *f*; ~ **of trade** *n* ECON, GEN COMM, LAW Handelsliberalisierung *f*, Liberalisierung *f* des Handels

liberalize *vt* ECON, GEN COMM, LAW liberalisieren

liberal: ~ **trade policy** *n* ECON liberale Handelspolitik *f*

libertarian: ~ **economics** *n* ECON Libertarianismus *m*

liberty: **at ~** *phr* AmE HRM *unemployed* arbeitslos; ~ **ship** *n* TRANSP Liberty-Schiff *nt*

LIBID *abbr* (*London Interbank Bid Rate*) BANK, STOCK Zinssatz, zu dem die großen Londoner Banken bereit sind, Geldbankkredite am internationalen Interbankenmarkt aufzunehmen, LIBID (*Londoner Interbanknachfragesatz*)

LIBOR *abbr* (*London Interbank Offered Rate*) BANK, STOCK LIBOR (*Londoner Interbankangebotssatz*)

library *n* COMP Programmbibliothek *f*, GEN COMM *public services* Bibliothek *f*

Library: ~ **of Congress** *n* AmE (*LC*) GEN COMM Nationalbibliothek der USA

library: ~ **rate** *n* AmE (*cf printed paper rate BrE*) COMMS ermäßigtes Porto *nt* für Büchersendungen; ~ **service** *n* GEN COMM *public services* Bibliotheksdienst *m*

LIC *abbr* (*local import control*) IMP/EXP lokale Einfuhrkontrolle *f*, lokale Importkontrolle *f*

licence *n* BrE BANK Lizenz *f*, IMP/EXP Genehmigung *f*, Lizenz *f*, LAW *permit* Lizenz *f*, Konzession *f*, Zulassung *f*, Genehmigung *f*, Erlaubnis *f*, PATENTS Patentausnützung *f*, Zulassung *f*; ◆ **under ~** *BrE* LAW, PATENTS unter Lizenz

licence: **~ bond** *n BrE* LAW *commercial* Konzessionssicherheitsleistung *f*; **~ and cooperation agreement** *n BrE* LAW Lizenz- und Kooperationsvertrag *m*; **~ fee** *n BrE* GEN COMM Lizenzgebühr *f*; **~ holder** *n BrE* GEN COMM Lizenzinhaber, in *m,f*; **~ laws** *n pl BrE* LAW *commercial* Konzessionsrecht *nt*; **~ to operate a taxi** *n BrE* (*cf hack license AmE*) TRANSP Taxikonzession *f*

licensable *adj* IMP/EXP genehmigungspflichtig, lizenzfähig

license 1. *n AmE see licence BrE*; **2.** *vt* GEN COMM erlauben, LAW lizenzieren, konzessionieren, zulassen, genehmigen

licensed *adj* FIN zugelassen, GEN COMM erlaubt, LAW konzessioniert, *intellectual property* geschützt, lizenziert; **~ construction** *n* ECON Lizenzbau *m*; **~ foreign exchange dealer** *n* STOCK zugelassener Devisenhändler *m*, zugelassene Devisenhändlerin *f*; **~ premises** *n pl BrE* LAW Schankwirtschaft *f*

licensee *n* LAW Konzessionär, in *m,f*, *intellectual property* Benutzungsberechtigte(r) *mf* [decl. as adj], Lizenzinhaber, in *m,f*, Konzessionsinhaber, in *m,f*

license: **~ plate** *n AmE* (*cf number plate BrE*) TRANSP Nummernschild *nt*, polizeiliches Kennzeichen *nt*

licensing *n* ECON, PATENTS Lizenzerteilung *f*; **~ agreement** *n* LAW, PATENTS Lizenzabkommen *nt*; **~ examination** *n* GEN COMM *suitability of applicant* Lizenzprüfung *f*, LAW Konzessionsantragsprüfung *f*; **~ laws** *n pl* LAW Schankgesetze *nt pl*; **~ procedure** *n* ECON Genehmigungsverfahren *nt*; **~ requirements** *n pl* IMP/EXP Lizenzvoraussetzung *f*, Lizenzvorschriften *f pl*; **~ standard** *n* ENVIR Konzessionsvergabenorm *f*

licensor *n* GEN COMM Lizenzgeber, in *m,f*, LAW Konzessionserteiler, in *m,f*, PATENTS Konzessionserteiler, in *m,f*, Lizenzgeber, in *m,f*

lick: **~ into shape** *phr* GEN COMM auf Vordermann bringen (*jarg*)

lie: **~ idle** *phr infrml* BANK *money* nicht arbeiten, brachliegen

lien *n* ECON Zurückbehaltungsrecht *nt*, FIN, LAW Pfandrecht *nt*

lieu: **~ days** *n pl* HRM Freizeitausgleich *m*, Freizeitausgleichstage *m pl*

life *n* GEN COMM Lebensdauer *f*, INS Leben *nt*, STOCK *of an option* Laufzeit *f*; **~ annuitant** *n* PROP Leibrentenempfänger, in *m,f*; **~ annuity** *n* HRM Leibrente *f*, Lebensrente *f*; **~ assurance** *n BrE* INS *personal* Lebensversicherung *f*; **~ assurance policy** *n BrE* INS Lebensversicherungspolice *f*

Life: **~ Assurance and Unit Trust Regulatory Organization** *n BrE* (*Lautro*) FIN, INS Selbstüberwachungsorganisation der Londoner City

lifeboat: **~ operation** *n infrml* BANK Rettungsaktion *f*, Sanierung *f*

life: **~ cycle** *n* ECON, ENVIR, S&M *of firm or product* Lebenszyklus *m*; **~~cycle analysis** *n* S&M *marketing* Lebenszyklusanalyse *f*; **~~cycle assessment** *n* (*LCA*) ENVIR Lebenszyklusbewertung *f*; **~~cycle hypothesis** *n* (*LCH*) ECON Lebenszeithypothese *f*, Lebenszyklushypothese *f*; **~ estate** *n* PROP Grundstücksnießbrauch *m*; **~ expectancy** *n* GEN COMM *object* erwartete Nutzungsdauer *f*, INS *person* Lebens-

erwartung *f*; **~ insurance** *n* INS Lebensversicherung *f*; **~ insurance policy** *n* INS Lebensversicherungspolice *f*, Versicherung *f* auf den Todesfall; **~ insurance premium** *n* INS Lebensversicherungsprämie *f*; **~ interest** *n* FIN lebenslänglicher Nießbrauch *m*, LAW dingliches Recht *nt* auf Lebenszeit, Nießbrauch *m* auf Lebenszeit

lifeless *adj* STOCK flau, lustlos

life: **~~saving apparatus** *n* (*LSA*) TRANSP *shipping* Lebensrettungsgerät *nt*; **~~saving appliance** *n* (*LSA*) TRANSP *shipping* Lebensrettungseinrichtung *f*; **~ savings** *n pl* BANK Lebensersparnisse *f pl*

lifestyle *n* GEN COMM, S&M Lebensstil *m*; **~ concept** *n* S&M Lebensstilkonzept *nt*; **~ merchandising** *n BrE* S&M Lifestyle Merchandising *nt* (*jarg*); **~ segmentation** *n* S&M *marketing* Lebensstilsegmentierung *f*

life: **~ tenancy** *n* PROP lebenslängliches Pachtrecht *nt*, Pacht *f* auf Lebenszeit; **~ tenant** *n* PROP lebenslänglicher Nießbraucher *m*, lebenslängliche Nießbraucherin *f*, Nießbraucher, in *m,f* auf Lebenszeit; **~ tenure** *n* HRM lebenslange Anstellung *f*, Anstellung *f* auf Lebenszeit

lifetime *n* GEN COMM, STOCK Lebenszeit *f*; **~ averaging** *n* ECON *taxation of income* langfristige Einkommensermittlung *f*; **~ employment** *n* ECON, HRM Beschäftigung *f* auf Lebenszeit; **~ gift** *n BrE* TAX Schenkung *f* unter Lebenden, Schenkung *f* zu Lebzeiten

LIFO *abbr* (*last in first out*) HRM LIFO (*last-in-first-out*), LIFO-Methode *f*, zuletzt eingestellt, zuerst entlassen

lifted *adj* ECON *price controls*, GEN COMM *restrictions* aufgehoben

lifting *n* GEN COMM *of restrictions, laws*, LAW Aufhebung *f*, TRANSP *car* Hochheben *nt*, Heben *nt*, Hub *m*, Anheben *nt*

light 1. *adj* GEN COMM *interest, trading* gering, *not heavy* leicht, TRANSP leicht; **2.** *n* GEN COMM Licht *m*

light: **~ cargo** *n* TRANSP leichte Fracht *f*; **~~emitting diode** *n* (*LED*) COMP Leuchtdiode *f* (*LED*), Lichtemissionsdiode *f* (*LED*), Lumineszenzdiode *m* (*LED*); **~ engineering** *n* IND Feinmechanik *f*, Feinwerktechnik *f*; **~ industry** *n* IND Leichtindustrie *f*

lightly *adv* GEN COMM leicht

light: **~ metals industry** *n* IND Leichtmetallindustrie *f*

lightning: **~ rise** *n* HRM, MGMNT rasanter Aufstieg *m*; **~ strike** *n* HRM Blitzstreik *m*

light: **~ pen** *n* COMP Lichtgriffel *m*, Lichtstift *m*; **~ selling** *n* ECON schwache Umsätze *f pl*; **~ vessel** *n* TRANSP leeres Schiff *nt*; **~ viewers** *n pl* S&M Wenigseher *m pl*

like: **~~kind property** *n AmE* TAX gleichartige Vermögenswerte *m pl*, gleichartiges Vermögen *nt*

likelihood *n* GEN COMM Wahrscheinlichkeit *f*

likely *adj* GEN COMM wahrscheinlich; **~ outcome** *n* GEN COMM *of negotiations* wahrscheinliches Ergebnis *nt*

LIMEAN *abbr* (*London Interbank Mean Rate*) BANK, STOCK Mittelkurs zwischen LIBID und LIBOR

limit 1. *n* ECON Grenze *f*, STOCK Limit *nt*, Obergrenze *f*; **2.** *vt* GEN COMM begrenzen, beschränken, LAW begrenzen, STOCK *risk* begrenzen, beschränken

limitation *n* GEN COMM Begrenzung *f*, Beschränkung *f*, LAW *of liability* Verjährung *f*; **~ of actions** *n* LAW Verjährung *f*; **~ of liability** *n* INS, LAW Haftungsbeschränkung *f*; **~ on imports** *n* ECON Einfuhrkontingente *nt pl*; **~ on profit distribution** *n*

LAW Ausschüttungssperre *f*; ~ **of time** *n* LAW *sentencing* Verjährung *f*

limited *adj* GEN COMM begrenzt, eingeschränkt; ♦ **for a ~ period of time** GEN COMM zeitlich begrenzt; **in a ~ sphere** GEN COMM in einem begrenzten Bereich; ~ **in time** LAW befristet

limited: ~ **annual statements** *n pl* ACC begrenzter Jahresbericht *m*, limitierter Jahresbericht *m*; ~ **audit** *n* ACC beschränkte Prüfung *f*; ~ **authority** *n* LAW beschränkte Vollmacht *f*; ~ **authorization** *n* IMP/EXP befristete Genehmigung *f*, befristete Zulassung *f*; ~ **check** *AmE*, ~ **cheque** *BrE n* ACC limitierter Scheck *m*; ~ **company** *n BrE* (*Ltd*) GEN COMM Gesellschaft *f* mit beschränkter Haftung (*GmbH, Ges.m.b.H. Öst*), Personengesellschaft *f*; ~ **discretion** *n* STOCK begrenzte Entscheidungsfreiheit *f*, beschränkte Disposition *f*; ~ **distribution** *n* TRANSP begrenzte Verteilung *f*, beschränkte Verteilung *f*; ~ **interest** *n* LAW Nießbrauch *m* auf Zeit; ~ **jurisdiction** *n* LAW begrenzte Zuständigkeit *f*; ~ **liability company** *n BrE* GEN COMM Gesellschaft *f* mit beschränkter Haftung (*GmbH, Ges.m.b.H. Öst*); ~-**life asset** *n* ACC, ECON abnutzbares Wirtschaftsgut *nt*, Wirtschaftsgut *nt* mit begrenzter Nutzungsdauer; ~ **market** *n* ECON begrenzter Markt *m*; ~ **partner** *n* GEN COMM Teilhafter, in *m,f*, LAW Kommanditist, in *m,f*, beschränkt haftender Gesellschafter *m*, beschränkt haftende Gesellschafterin *f*, STOCK Kommanditist, in *m,f*; ~ **partnership** *n* LAW, STOCK *company* Kommanditgesellschaft *f* (*KG*); ~ **payment life insurance** *n* INS *personal* Lebensversicherung *f* mit verkürzter Prämienzahlung; ~ **policy** *n* INS Police *f* mit beschränktem Risiko, Police *f* mit eingeschränktem Gefahrenrisiko; ~-**postponed accounting** *n* IMP/EXP begrenzter Abrechnungsaufschub *m*; ~-**recourse debt** *n* BANK Kredit *m* mit eingeschränktem Rückgriffsrecht; ~-**recourse financing** *n* BANK Finanzierung *f* mit eingeschränktem Rückgriffsrecht; ~ **risk** *n* STOCK begrenztes Risiko *nt*; ~ **tax bond** *n* TAX Kommunalobligation, die durch die Einnahmen aus einer bestimmten Steuer gedeckt ist; ~ **terms** *n pl* INS begrenzte Bedingungen *f pl*, eingeschränkte Bedingungen *f pl*; ~-**trading authorization** *n* STOCK begrenzte Handlungsbevollmächtigung *f*

limiting *adj* GEN COMM beschränkend

limit: ~ **order** *n* STOCK Limitauftrag *m*, limitierte Order *f*; ~ **price** *n* ECON Eintrittssperrenpreis *m*; ~ **up** *phr* STOCK zugestandene minimale und maximale Preisschwankung pro Tag

limousine: ~ **liberal** *n infrml* POL Elfenbeinturmliberale(r) *mf* [decl. as adj] (*infrml*); ~ **liberalism** *n* POL Elfenbeinturmliberalismus *m* (*jarg*)

Lindahl: ~ **Equilibrium** *n* ECON Lindahl-Gleichgewicht *nt*; ~ **price** *n* ECON Lindahl-Preis *m*

line *n* GEN COMM *AmE* (*cf queue BrE*) *of people* Warteschlange *f*, HRM Linie *f*, MGMNT *policy* Marschroute *f*, S&M *advertising* Zeile *f*, *products* Sortiment *nt*, STOCK *of shares* Aktienpaket *nt*, TRANSP *railway* Strecke *f*; ♦ **in ~ with** GEN COMM *inflation, expectations etc* entsprechend; **on ~** COMP, GEN COMM online

line: ~ **activation** *n* COMMS Leitungsaktivierung *f*

lineage *n* MEDIA Zeilenzahl *f*, S&M *origin* Abkunft *f*, Abstammung *f*

linear: ~ **dependence** *n* MATH lineare Abhängigkeit *f*; ~ **increase** *n* MGMNT lineare Erhöhung *f*; ~ **measure** *n* GEN COMM Längenmaß *nt*; ~ **program** *AmE*,

~ **programme** *BrE n* MATH Linearprogramm *m*; ~ **programming** *n* COMP, ECON lineare Programmierung *f*, MATH lineare Optimierung *f*, lineare Planungsrechnung *f*, lineare Programmierung *f*; ~ **regression** *n* MATH *statistics* lineare Regression *f*; ~ **relationship** *n* HRM lineare Beziehung *f*; ~ **responsibility** *n* GEN COMM lineare Verantwortlichkeit *f*, MATH lineare Verantwortung *f*, MGMNT Verantwortungsbereich *m* der Linie

line: ~ **assistant** *n* HRM Linienassistent, in *m,f*, Produktionsassistent, in *m,f*, IND Produktionsassistent, in *m,f*; ~ **of attack** *n* GEN COMM Angriffslinie *f*; ~ **authority** *n* HRM Linienvollmacht *f*, MGMNT Produktionsautorität *f*; ~ **block** *n* MEDIA, S&M Strichätzung *f*; ~ **of business** *n* ECON Sparte *f*, INS Versicherungszweig *m*; ~ **of command** *n* HRM Leitungsstruktur *f*, MGMNT Führungshierarchie *f*, Leitungsstruktur *f*; ~ **control** *n* MGMNT Linienkontrolle *f*; ~ **of credit** *n* FIN Kreditlinie *f*

lined: ~ **paper** *n* GEN COMM liniertes Papier *nt*

line: ~ **drawing** *n* MEDIA *print*, S&M Federzeichnung *f*, Strichzeichnung *f*; ~ **of duty** *n* GEN COMM Aufgabenbereich *m*; ~ **editor** *n* COMP *programming* Editor *m*, Zeileneditor *m*; ~ **executive** *n* MGMNT Führungskraft *f* mit Linienfunktion, Liniendirektor, in *m,f*; ~ **expansion** *n* S&M *product range* Produktionsausweitung *f*; ~ **feed** *n* (*lf*) COMP Zeilenvorschub *m*; ~ **function** *n* GEN COMM Linienfunktion *f*; ~ **item veto** *n* AmE POL Grenzpostenveto *nt*, Toleranzgrenzenveto *nt*; ~ **management** *n* HRM, IND Produktionsleitung *f*, MGMNT Linienleitung *f*, Linienmanagement *nt*, Produktionsleitung *f*; ~ **manager** *n* HRM, IND, MGMNT Linienvorgesetzter *m*, Linienmanager, in *m,f*, Produktionsleiter, in *m,f*, Führungskraft *f* mit Linienfunktion; ~ **object** *n* ADMIN in Abteilungen aufgegliederter Geschäftszweck eines Unternehmens; ~ **of occupation** *n* HRM Berufszweig *m*; ~ **organization** *n* HRM, MGMNT Linienorganisation *f*, Produktionsorganisation *f*; ~ **position** *n* HRM Linienstelle *f*; ~ **printer** *n* COMP Zeilendrucker *m*; ~ **production** *n* IND Produktion *f* am Fließband

liner *n* TRANSP Linienschiff *nt*

line: ~ **rate** *n* MEDIA *print* Zeilenpreis *m*; ~ **relations** *n pl* GEN COMM Branchenverbindungen *f pl*; ~ **relationship** *n* MGMNT Beziehung *f* innerhalb der Linie, Beziehung *f* innerhalb des Fachgebiets; ~ **slip** *n* INS Übernahmebeleg *m*; ~ **space** *n* MEDIA *printing* Durchschuß *m*, Zeilenabstand *m*, Zeilendurchschuß *m*; ~ **and staff** *n* HRM Stab *m* und Linie *f*; ~ **and staff management** *n* HRM Stablinienmanagement *nt*; ~ **and staff organization** *n* MGMNT Stablinienorganisation *f*; ~ **stamp** *n BrE* INS Übernahmestempel *m*; ~ **supervisor** MGMNT Vorarbeiter, in *m,f* der Produktion; ~ **termination equipment** *n* COMMS Leitungsanschluß *m*, Leitungsanpassung *f*, ECON Warteschlange *f*

lingua franca *n* GEN COMM Lingua franca *f*

link 1. *n* COMP, GEN COMM Verbindung *f*, MEDIA, POL Querverbindung *f*; **2.** *vt* COMP *peripherals, connections*, GEN COMM verbinden; ♦ ~ **rates of exchange** STOCK Devisenkurse verbinden

linkage *n* GEN COMM Verflechtung *f*; ~ **model** *n BrE* ECON *econometrics* Verknüpfungsmodell *nt*

linked *adj* STOCK verbunden

linking: ~ **of currencies** *n* ECON Bindung *f* von Währungen; ~ **department** *n* ADMIN Abteilung *f* für Börsenzulassung

linkline *n* S&M Verbindungslinie *f*

lion: **the ~'s share** *n* GEN COMM Hauptanteil *m*, Löwenanteil *m*

liquefied: ~ **natural gas** *n* (*LNG*) ENVIR, IND verflüssigtes Erdgas *nt*, Flüssigerdgas *nt*; ~ **natural gas carrier** *n* TRANSP Transporter *m* von Flüssigerdgas

liquid 1. *adj* ACC liquid, BANK, FIN *funds* flüssig, liquid; **2.** *n* GEN COMM Flüssigkeit *f*

liquid: ~ **assets** *n pl* ACC, FIN flüssige Mittel *nt pl*; ~ **assets and government securities** *n pl* (*LGS*) FIN liquide Mittel *nt pl* und Staatspapiere *nt pl*, Umlaufvermögen und Staatspapiere *nt pl*; ~ **assets ratio** *n* FIN Liquiditätskennziffer *f*

liquidate *vt* ACC abwickeln, tilgen, FIN tilgen, verwerten, GEN COMM liquidieren; ♦ ~ **a position** STOCK eine Position liquidieren, eine Position abwickeln, eine Wertpapierposition verwerten; ~ **inventory** ECON Lager abbauen

liquidated *adj* FIN *debt* getilgt, *options* verwertet; ~ **damage** *n* LAW Schadenspauschalierung *f*, Vertragsstrafe *f*; ~ **damages** *n pl* LAW bezifferter Schadensersatz *m*; ~ **debt** *n* ACC beglichene Schulden *f pl*, getilgte Schulden *f pl*

liquidating: ~ **authority** *n* ACC, LAW Abwickler *m*; ~ **dividend** *n* FIN Kapitalrückzahlung *f*; ~ **value** *n* ACC *of an asset of a company* Liquidationswert *m*, Veräußerungswert *m*

liquidation *n* ACC Auflösung *f*, Konkurs *m*, Liquidation *f*, Tilgung *f*, FIN Konkurs *m*, Liquidation *f*, *of debt* Tilgung *f*, *of option* Verwertung *f*, GEN COMM, LAW Abwicklung *f*, Liquidation *f*, MGMNT Abwicklung *f*, STOCK Ablösung *f*, Realisierung *f*; ~ **dividend** *n* ACC Schlußquote *f*; ~ **period** *n* LAW Abwicklungszeitraum *m*; ~ **procedure** *n* LAW Abwicklungsverfahren *nt*; ~ **sale** *n* ECON Räumungsverkauf *m*

liquidator *n* ACC Abwickler *m*, Liquidator *m*, LAW Abwickler *m*

liquid: ~ **bulk cargo** *n* TRANSP Flüssigmassenfrachtgut *nt*; ~ **cash resources** *n* FIN Barliquidität *f*; ~ **debt** *n* FIN kurzfristige Verbindlichkeit *f*, sofort fällige Forderung *f*; ~ **funds** *n pl* ACC, FIN flüssige Gelder *nt pl*, flüssige Mittel *nt pl*, Barmittel *nt pl*, liquide Mittel *nt pl*

liquidity *n* FIN Zahlungsfähigkeit *f*, Liquidität *f*, STOCK flüssige Mittel *nt pl*, Liquidität *f*; ~ **adequacy** *n* ACC Liquidität *f* ersten Grades; ~ **crisis** *n* BANK Liquiditätskrise *f*; ~ **diversification** *n* STOCK Liquiditätsstreuung *f*; ~ **famine** *n* FIN Liquiditätshunger *m*; ~ **preference** *n* ECON Liquiditätspräferenz *f*; ~ **problems** *n pl* ACC Liquiditätsprobleme *nt pl*, Liquiditätsschwierigkeiten *f pl*; ~ **ratio** *n* ACC Liquiditätsgrad *m*, FIN Liquiditätsquote *f*; ~ **squeeze** *n* FIN Liquiditätsengpaß *m*, Liquiditätsklemme *f*; ~ **trap** *n* ECON Liquiditätsfalle *f*

liquidization *n* STOCK Glattstellung *f*

liquid: ~ **market** *n* STOCK liquider Markt *m*, Börse *f* mit ausreichenden Umsätzen; ~ **measure** *n* GEN COMM Flüssigkeitsmaß *nt*; ~ **petroleum gas** *n* (*LPG*) ENVIR, IND flüssiges Propangas *nt*, Flüssiggas *nt*; ~ **petroleum gas carrier** *n* TRANSP Transporter *m* von Flüssiggas; ~ **ratio** *n* ACC Liquidität *f* ersten Grades; ~ **savings** *n pl* FIN sofort auszahlbare Ersparnisse *f pl*

liquor: ~ **store** *n* AmE (*cf off-licence BrE*) S&M Wein- und Spirituosengeschäft *nt*

lis pendens *n* LAW anhängiger Rechsstreit *m*, anhängiges Verfahren *nt*, schwebender Fall *m*

list 1. *n* GEN COMM Aufstellung *f*; **2.** *vt* COMP aufführen, auflisten, PROP registrieren

listable *adj* STOCK *shares* börsenfähig, kursfähig, TAX steuerpflichtig

list: ~ **of addresses** *n* HRM Adressenliste *f*; ~ **broker** *n* GEN COMM Adressenverlag *m*; ~ **of candidates** *n* POL Kandidatenliste *f*

listed: ~ **bank** *n* BANK börsennotierte Bank *f*; ~ **company** *n* ECON, GEN COMM, STOCK börsennotierte Gesellschaft *f*, börsennotiertes Unternehmen *nt*; ~ **on the stock exchange** *adj* ACC, STOCK an der Börse notiert, börsennotiert; ~ **option** *n* STOCK börsennotierte Option *f*; ~ **securities** *n pl* ECON, STOCK börsennotierte Wertpapiere *nt pl*; ~ **share** *n* STOCK börsennotierte Aktie *f*, börsennotierter Gesellschaftsanteil *m*

listen: ~ **to** *phr* *telephone call* hören, zuhören, GEN COMM hören auf, zuhören; ~ **in on** *phr* COMMS, GEN COMM *telephone call* mithören

listener *n* MEDIA *broadcast* Radiohörer, in *m,f*

listing *n* COMP Auflistung *f*, Liste *f*, LAW *property* Beauftragung *f*, PROP Einschaltung *f* eines Immobilienmaklers, STOCK Börsenzulassung *f*; ~ **agent** *n* AmE PROP Grundstücksmakler, in *m,f*; ~ **broker** *n* AmE PROP Grundstücksmakler, in *m,f*; ~ **committee** *n* STOCK Börsenzulassungsausschuß *m*; ~ **particulars** *n pl* STOCK Angaben *f pl* zur Börsenzulassung; ~ **procedure** *n* STOCK Börsenzulassungsverfahren *nt*; ~ **requirements** *n pl* STOCK Zulassungsvorschriften *f pl*

listless *adj* GEN COMM *market, trading* lustlos

list: ~ **price** *n* S&M *sales, retail* Katalogpreis *m*, Listenpreis *m*, STOCK *shares, securities* Börsenkurs *m*; ~ **of tax assessments** *n* TAX Steuerliste *f*, Steuerrolle *f*

liter *AmE see* litre *BrE*

literal *n* MEDIA *print* Druckfehler *m*, Satzfehler *m*; ~ **error** *n* MEDIA *print* Druckfehler *m*

lithography *n* S&M Lithographie *f*

litigant *n* LAW Prozeßpartei *f*

litigate *vi* LAW prozessieren

litigation *n* LAW Prozeß *m*, Rechtstreit *m*

litre *n* BrE (*l*) GEN COMM Liter *m* (*l*)

litter: ~ **bin** *n* BrE (*cf trashcan AmE*) ENVIR *in public spaces* Abfalleimer *f*

little: ~ **board** *n* *infrml* ECON informeller Begriff für die American Stock Exchange; ~ **dragons** *n pl* *infrml* ECON *Asian countries* kleine Tiger *m pl* (*infrml*), Tigerstaaten *m pl*

live *adj* LEIS *broadcasting* direkt; ~ **broadcast** *n* MEDIA Live-Sendung *f*; ~ **customers** *n pl* S&M echte Kunden *m pl*; ~ **food** *n* IND *health foods* Frischnahrung *f*, Frischkost *f*

livelihood *n* GEN COMM Lebensunterhalt *m*

live: ~ **program** *AmE*, ~ **programme** *BrE* *n* MEDIA *broadcast* Live-Programm *nt*

Liverpool: ~ **Commodity Exchange** *n* STOCK Warenbörse in Liverpool; ~ **Stock Exchange** *n* STOCK Wertpapierbörse in Liverpool

livery *n* S&M Livree *f*

livestock *n* ECON, GEN COMM lebendes Inventar *nt*

living: ~ **accommodation** *n* TAX Wohnraum *m*, Wohnung *f*; ~ **benefits of life insurance** *n* INS Leistungen *f pl* der Lebensversicherung zu Lebzeiten; ~ **conditions** *n pl* WEL Lebensbedingungen *f pl*, Wohnverhältnisse *nt pl*; ~ **expenses** *n pl* GEN COMM, WEL Lebenshaltungskosten *pl*; ~ **space** *n* WEL Lebensraum *m*, Wohnraum *m*; ~ **trust** *n AmE* LAW aktive Treuhand *f*; ~ **wage** *n* ECON Bedürfnislohn *m*, WEL Mindestlohn *m*

LLB *abbr* (*Bachelor of Laws*) HRM, LAW, WEL Bakkalaureus *m* der Rechtswissenschaft, Bakkalaureus *m* des Rechts

LLD *abbr* (*Doctor of Laws*) HRM, LAW, WEL Dr. jur. (*Doktor der Rechte*)

Lloyd's *n BrE* INS Lloyd's *m*; ~ **Agent** *n* (*L/A*) INS *shipping* Lloyd's Agent *m*, Lloyd's Versicherer *m*; ~ **Instantaneous Accounting Record System** *n* (*LIARS*) INS Lloyd's Sofortrechnungsbelegsystem *nt*; ~ **List** *n* TRANSP *shipping* Lloyd's Liste *f*; ~ **Loading List** *n* TRANSP *shipping* Lloyd's Ladeliste *f*; ~ **of London** *n* INS Lloyd's of London *m*; ~ **member** *n* INS *marine* Lloyd's Mitglied, das Risiken mitzeichnet; ~ **Register** *n* (*LR*) INS *marine* Lloyd's Register *nt*; ~ **Register of Shipping** *n* INS Lloyd's Schiffsregister *nt*; ~ **Underwriting Agents' Association** *n* (*LUAA*) INS Verband der Lloyd's-Versicherungsagenten

LMBI *abbr* (*leveraged management buy-in*) FIN, MGMNT LMBI (*fremdfinanziertes Management Buy-In*)

LMBO *abbr* (*leveraged management buyout*) FIN, MGMNT LMBO (*fremdfinanziertes Management Buy-Out*), fremdfinanzierte Übernahme *f* durch das Management

LM: ~ **curve** *n* ECON LM-Kurve *f*

LME *abbr* (*London Metal Exchange*) STOCK Londoner Metallbörse *f*

LNG *abbr* (*liquefied natural gas*) ENVIR, IND verflüssigtes Erdgas *nt*, Flüssigerdgas *nt*; ~ **carrier** *n* TRANSP *shipping* Flüssigerdgastanker *m*, Flüssigmethantanker *m*, LNG-Tanker *m*, LNG-Transporter *m*

lo *abbr* (*low loader*) TRANSP Tieflader *m*

load 1. *n* FIN Aufschlag *m*, GEN COMM Belastung *f*, TRANSP Fracht *f*, Ladung *f*, Last *f*; **2.** *vt* COMP *software* herunterladen, laden, runterladen, downloaden (*jarg*), TRANSP *vehicle* befrachten, auslasten

loader *n* TRANSP Verlader *m*

load: ~ **factor** *n* ECON *manufacturing*, MATH Kapazitätsfaktor *m*, Auslastungsfaktor *m*, TRANSP Auslastung *f*, Lastfaktor *m*, Zuladungsfaktor *m*, Auslastungsfaktor *m*, Kapazitätsauslastung *f*

loading *n* (*ldg*) COMMS Verladen *nt*, HRM Gewichtung *f*, IMP/EXP Verladen *nt*, TRANSP *of a cargo* Verladen *nt*, *of a ship* Laden *nt*, Verladung *f*, Beladen *nt*; ~ **agent** *n* COMMS Verlader *m*, IMP/EXP *shipping* Verlader *m*, Verladungsspediteur *m*, TRANSP *shipping* Verlader *m*, Ladeagent *m*; ~ **allocation** *n* TRANSP Ladungszuordnung *f*; ~ **broker** *n* HRM Lademakler, in *m,f*; ~ **date** *n* TRANSP *shipping* Verladedatum *nt*; ~ **and delivery** *phr* (*ldg & dly*) TRANSP Verladung *f* und Lieferung *f*; ~ **dock** *n* TRANSP Verladekai *m*; ~ **space** *n* GEN COMM Laderaum *m*

load: ~ **port** *n* TRANSP Verladehafen *m*; ~ **sheet** *n* TRANSP Ladedokument *nt*

loan *n* BANK Darlehen *nt*, Kredit *m*, ECON, FIN Anleihe *f*

loan: ~ **account** *n* BANK Darlehenskonto *nt*; ~ **agreement** *n* BANK Darlehensvertrag *m*, STOCK Anleihevertrag *m*; ~ **application** *n* BANK Darlehensantrag *m*, Kreditantrag *m*, FIN Kreditantrag *m*;

~ **authorization** *n* BANK Darlehensbefugnis *f*; ~ **bank** *n* FIN Kreditbank *f*, Darlehenskasse *f*; ~ **capital** *n* ACC, ECON, FIN festverzinsliche Wertpapiere *nt pl*, Fremdkapital *nt*; ~ **charges** *n pl* BANK Darlehenskosten *pl*; ~ **commitment** *n* BANK Darlehenszusage *f*; ~ **company** *n* FIN Darlehensgesellschaft *f*; ~ **crowd** *n* STOCK Maklergruppe, die Aktien borgen oder ausleihen will; ~ **default** *n* BANK Kreditausfall *m*, tatsächlicher Kreditausfall *m*; ~ **demand** *n* BANK Kreditnachfrage *f*; ~ **department** *n* BANK, FIN Kreditabteilung *f*; ~ **discount** *n* BANK Damnum *nt*, Abgeld *nt*, Disagio *nt*

loaned *adj* FIN, STOCK Leih-; ~ **flat** *n* STOCK Leihkurs *m* einschließlich aufgelaufener Zinsen

loan: ~ **exposure** *n* FIN Gesamtausleihungen *f pl*, Kreditengagement *nt*; ~ **fee** *n* BANK Kreditbearbeitungsgebühr *f*; ~ **financing** *n* BANK, FIN Kreditfinanzierung *f*; ~ **with fixed date for repayment** *n* FIN Darlehen *nt* mit festem Rückzahlungstermin; ~ **grant** *n* BANK Darlehensgewährung *f*; ~ **guarantee** *n* FIN Kreditbürgschaft *f*; ~ **guarantee scheme** *n* FIN *for rural development* Kreditbürgschaftsprogramm *m*; ~ **holder** *n* FIN Anleihebesitzer, in *m,f*, Anleihegläubiger, in *m,f*, Obligationär, in *m,f*; ~ **insurance** *n* FIN Kreditversicherung *f*; ~ **investment** *n* FIN Kreditinvestition *f*; ~ **issue** *n* FIN Anleiheemission *f*; ~ **liabilities** *n pl* BANK Darlehensverbindlichkeiten *f pl*; ~ **loss** *n* BANK Kreditausfall *m*; ~ **loss provision** *n* BANK Kreditausfallrückstellung *f*; ~ **market** *n* FIN Geldmarkt *m* für sehr kurzfristige Kredite, Markt *m* für mittel- und langfristige Darlehen; ~ **officer** *n* BANK, FIN Finanzierungsspezialist *m*, Kreditsachbearbeiter, in *m,f*; ~ **portfolio** *n* BANK Anleiheportefeuille *nt*, Darlehensbestand *m*, Kreditvolumen *nt*; ~ **-pricing date** *n* STOCK Datum *nt* für die Festsetzung des Anleihezinssatzes, Festsetzungsdatum *nt* für die Kreditkonditionen; ~ **recipient** *n* BANK Darlehensempfänger, in *m,f*; ~ **repayment** *n* BANK, FIN Darlehenstilgung *f*, Kreditrückzahlung *f*; ~ **repayment schedule** *n* BANK Darlehensrückzahlungsplan *m*; ~ **shark** *n infrml* FIN Kredithai *m* (*infrml*)

loans: ~ **in transit** *n pl* BANK, FIN durchlaufende Kredite *m pl*; ~**, investments and advances** *phr* ACC Darlehen, Investitionen und Vorschußzahlungen

loan: ~ **stock** *n* ACC *securities*, ECON festverzinsliche Wertpapiere *nt pl*, FIN festverzinsliche Wertpapiere *nt pl*, Schuldverschreibung *f*, STOCK Schuldverschreibung *f*, festverzinslicher Schuldtitel *m*

loans: ~ **to related companies** *n pl* ACC *annual accounts* Forderungen *f pl* gegen verbundene Gesellschaften

loan: ~ **-to-value ratio** *n* (*LTV*) FIN Beleihungsquote *f*, Beleihungssatz *m*; ~ **value** *n* INS Beleihungswert *n* einer Lebensversicherung; ~ **write-off** *n* BANK Debitorenausfall *m*; ~ **yield** *n* STOCK Anleiherendite *f*

lobby *n* POL Interessengruppe *f*, Interessenvereinigung *f*, Interessenvertretung *f*, Lobby *f*; ◆ **on ~ terms** *BrE* (*cf not for attribution AmE*) MEDIA, POL nicht zuschreibbar

lobby: ~ **group** *n* POL Interessengruppe *f*, Interessenvereinigung *f*, Interessenvertretung *f*, Lobby *f*, Vertreter *m pl* einer außerparlamentarischen Interessengruppe

lobbying *n* POL Lobby *f*, lobbyistische Einflußnahme *f*

lobbyist *n* LAW Lobbyist, in *m,f*

local 1. *adj* GEN COMM einheimisch, örtlich, vor Ort,

lokal, Lokal-; **2.** *n* STOCK *securities* Börsenmitglied, das nur auf eigene Rechnung handelt

local: ~ **agreement** *n* HRM Ortstarif *m*; ~ **area network** *n* (*LAN*) COMMS, COMP lokales Netz *nt* (*LAN*); ~ **authority** *n* ADMIN regionale Behörde *f*, örtliche Behörde *f*, Kommunalbehörde *f*; ~ **authority loan** *n* BrE FIN *issued by local government* Kommunalanleihe *f*, städtische Anleihe *f*; ~ **call** *n* COMMS Ortsgespräch *nt*; ~ **call rate** *n* COMMS Ortstarif *m*; ~ **charge** *n* TRANSP Ortsgebühr *f*, Platzspesen *pl*; ~ **custody** *n* FIN lokale Depotverwahrung *f*; ~ **election** *n* POL Kommunalwahl *f*

Local: ~ **Enterprise Agency** *n* (*LEA*) WEL Agentur für ortsansässige Unternehmen

local: ~ **export control** *n* IMP/EXP lokale Ausfuhrkontrolle *f*, lokale Exportkontrolle *f*

Local: ~ **Export Council** *n* BrE (*LEC*) IMP/EXP örtliche Ausfuhrförderungsgemeinschaft, lokaler Exportausschuß *m*

local: ~ **firm** *n* GEN COMM ortsansässige Firma *f*, örtliches Unternehmen *nt*; ~ **government** *n* ADMIN örtliche Verwaltung *f*, Gebietskörperschaft *f*, Kommunalverwaltung *f*, Kommunalregierung *f*, POL örtliche Behörden *f pl*, örtliche Gebietskörperschaft *f*, Kommunalregierung *f*, Kommunalverwaltung *f*, Magistratur *f* (*obs*); ~ **government finance** *n* POL kommunale Finanzen *f pl*, kommunales Finanzwesen *nt*; ~ **government financial policy** *n* POL kommunale Haushaltspolitik *f*, kommunale Finanzpolitik *f*; ~ **import control** *n* (*LIC*) IMP/EXP lokale Einfuhrkontrolle *f*, lokale Importkontrolle *f*; ~ **industry** *n* IND örtliche Industrie *f*, ansässige Industrie *f*, hiesige Industrie *f*

locality *n* GEN COMM Ort *m*

localization *n* COMP *software* Standortanpassung *f*

localize *vt* COMP *software* lokalisieren

local: ~ **labor** AmE, ~ **labour** BrE *n* ECON, HRM einheimische Arbeitskräfte *f pl*, ortsansässige Arbeitskräfte *f pl*; ~ **labour market** *n* BrE ECON, HRM örtlicher Arbeitsmarkt *m*, heimischer Arbeitsmarkt *m*

locally *phr* GEN COMM örtlich, vor Ort

local: ~ **monopoly** *n* ECON räumliches Monopol *nt*; ~ **newspaper** *n* MEDIA Lokalzeitung *f*; ~ **press** *n* MEDIA Lokalpresse *f*; ~ **produce** *n* GEN COMM heimisches Erzeugnis *nt*; ~ **public good** *n* ECON örtliches öffentliches Gut *nt*; ~ **rent** *n* ECON ortsübliche Miete *f*; ~ **skills** *n pl* HRM vor Ort verfügbare Fertigkeiten *f pl*; ~ **tax** *n* TAX Gemeindesteuer *f*, Kommunalsteuer *f*; ~ **time** *n* GEN COMM Ortszeit *f*; ~ **trade** *n* ECON Platzhandel *m*; ~ **union** *n* HRM Ortsverein *m*; ~ **variable** *n* COMP lokale Variable *f*; ~ **workers** *n* ECON einheimische Arbeitskräfte *f pl*, ortsansässige Arbeitskräfte *f pl*

located *adj* GEN COMM gelegen, stationiert

location *n* GEN COMM Standort *m*

locational: ~ **conditions** *n* ECON Standortbedingungen *f pl*

location: ~ **clause** *n* TRANSP *shipping* Standortklausel *f*; ~ **theory** *n* ECON Standorttheorie *f*

locator *n* COMP Positionierer *m*, TRANSP Lokalisierer *m*, Positionsgeber *m*

lock *vt* COMP sperren

lock away *vt jarg* STOCK festlegen

lock in *vt* STOCK festlegen, festschreiben; ◆ ~ **a rate** STOCK *interest rate futures* einen Zinssatz festschreiben

lock out *vt* STOCK ausschließen

lock up *vt* FIN *funds* binden

lock: ~ **canal** *n* TRANSP *shipping* Schleusenkanal *m*; ~ **chamber** *n* TRANSP *shipping, canal* Schleusenkammer *f*

locked: **~-in** *adj* GEN COMM, MGMNT festgelegt, STOCK festgelegt, festgeschrieben; **~-in effect** *n* STOCK Festanlage-Effekt *m*; **~-in industry** *n* IND standortgebundene Industrie *f*; **~-in knowledge** *n* ECON gebundenes Fachwissen *nt*, IND standortgebundenes Wissen *nt*; **~-in value** *n* STOCK *of shares allocated to employees* festgeschriebener Wert *m*; **~-out** *adj* HRM ausgesperrt

locking *n* TRANSP *containers* Verschluß *m*

lock: **~-out** *n* GEN COMM, HRM Aussperrung *f*; **~-up option** *n* FIN *corporate takeovers* Anlageoption *f*

loco 1. *adj* IMP/EXP am Ort, loko; **2.** *n* TRANSP Loco-Preis *m*

lodge *vt* HRM einreichen; ◆ ~ **a complaint with sb** GEN COMM Beschwerde bei jdm einlegen; ~ **an appeal** TAX Rechtsmittel einlegen

log 1. *n* ADMIN Protokoll *nt*, TRANSP *shipping, aviation* Logbuch *nt*; **2.** *vt* ADMIN protokollieren

log in *vi* COMP sich anmelden

log off *vi* COMP sich abmelden

log on *vi* COMP sich anmelden

log out *vi* COMP sich abmelden

log: ~ **book** *n* ADMIN *record*, TRANSP Bordbuch *nt*, Logbuch *nt*; ~ **file** *n* COMP Protokolldatei *f*

logic *n* GEN COMM Logik *f*

logical *adj* GEN COMM, IND, MATH, TRANSP logistisch

logistic: ~ **cycle** *n* ECON logistischer Zyklus *m*; ~ **process** *n* IND logistisches Verfahren *nt*, MATH logistischer Prozeß *m*

logistics *n* COMP Versorgung *f* und Nachschub *m*, GEN COMM, IND, MATH, TRANSP Logistik *f*; ~ **industry** *n* IND, TRANSP Logistikindustrie *f*

logo *n* (*logotype*) ADMIN Logo *nt*, Signum *nt*, GEN COMM Firmenzeichen *nt*, Logo *nt*, S&M Firmenschriftzug *m*, Logo *nt*, Signum *nt*

logotype *n* (*logo*) ADMIN Logo *nt*, Signum *nt*, GEN COMM Firmenzeichen *nt*, Logo *nt*, S&M Firmenschriftzug *m*, Logo *nt*, Signum *nt*

log: **~-rolling** *n* AmE (*cf backscratching BrE*) POL Politik *f* gegenseitiger Unterstützung, Bildung *f* von Seilschaften (*infrml*)

Lombard: ~ **rate** *n* BANK Lombardsatz *m*; ~ **Street** *n* BrE FIN Londoner Geldmarkt

Lomé: ~ **Convention** *n* ECON *trade* Lomé-Abkommen *nt*

London: ~ **Chamber of Commerce & Industry** *n* BrE (*LCCI*) GEN COMM Londoner Industrie- und Handelskammer; ~ **Commodity Exchange** *n* BrE *obs* (*LCE*) STOCK ehemalige Londoner Warenbörse; ~ **Discount Market Association** *n* BrE (*LDMA*) BANK Vereinigung der Londoner Diskonthäuser und Geldhändler der großen Geschäftsbanken; ~ **FOX** *n* (*London Futures and Options Exchange*) STOCK Londoner Termin- und Optionsbörse *f*; ~ **Futures and Options Exchange** *n* (*London FOX*) STOCK Londoner Termin- und Optionsbörse *f*; ~ **gold fixing** *n* BANK Londoner Gold-Fixing *nt*; ~ **Interbank Bid Rate** *n* (*LIBID*) BANK, STOCK Zinssatz, zu dem die großen Londoner Banken bereit sind, Geldbankkredite am internationalen Interbankenmarkt aufzunehmen, Londoner Interbanknachfragesatz *m* (*LIBID*); ~ **Interbank Mean Rate** *n* BrE (*LIMEAN*) BANK, STOCK Mittelkurs zwischen LIBOR und LIBID; ~ **Interbank Offered Rate** *n* (*LIBOR*) BANK, STOCK Londoner Interbankangebotssatz *m* (*LIBOR*); ~ **International Financial Futures Exchange** *n* STOCK Londoner Internationale Finanzterminbörse *f*; ~ **International Petroleum Exchange** *n* BrE STOCK Internationale Rohölbörse in London; ~ **Metal Exchange** *n* (*LME*) STOCK Londoner Metallbörse *f*; ~ **Regional Transport** *n* (*LRT*) TRANSP Londoner Regionalverkehr; ~ **School of Economics** *n* BrE (*LSE*) ECON Londoner Wirtschaftshochschule; ~ **Stock Exchange** *n* (*LSE*) STOCK Londoner Wertpapierbörse *f*, ≈ Deutsche Börse *f*; ~ **Stock Exchange Board** *n* STOCK Vorstand *m* der Londoner Wertpapierbörse; ~ **Tourist Board** *n* (*LTB*) LEIS Londoner Touristenbehörde; ~ **Traded Options Market** *n* (*LTOM*) STOCK Londoner börsengehandelter Optionenmarkt; ~ **Trader Options Exchange** *n* STOCK Londoner Optionenhandelsbörse *f*; ~ **weighting** *n* WEL Londoner Ortszuschlag

long 1. *adj* GEN COMM lang; ♦ **be ~ in a currency** ECON *international trade* mit Devisen versorgt sein; **be ~ in futures** STOCK sich in einer Long-Position mit Terminkontrakten befinden; **go ~** STOCK Terminkontrakte kaufen, Wertpapiere kaufen; **in the ~ run** BANK langfristig gesehen, GEN COMM auf lange Sicht, langfristig gesehen, INS langfristig gesehen; **in the ~ term** BANK, GEN COMM, INS langfristig gesehen; **over the ~ term** GEN COMM auf lange Sicht, über eine lange Zeitdauer; **2.** *n jarg* STOCK Person, die weniger verkauft als gekauft hat

long: ~ **bond** *n* STOCK langfristige Schuldverschreibung *f*, Langläufer *m*; ~ **boom** *n* ECON langer Boom *m*; ~ **butterfly call** *n* STOCK *options* Terminkaufoption *f*; ~ **butterfly put** *n* STOCK *options* Terminverkaufsoption *f*; ~ **calls** *n pl* STOCK Terminkontraktkaufoptionen *f pl*; ~ **coupon** *n* STOCK langfristiger Zinsschein *m*; ~-**distance call** *n* COMMS Ferngespräch *nt*; ~-**distance lorry driver** *n* BrE (*cf long-distance truck driver AmE*) TRANSP Fernfahrer, in *m,f*, Fernlastfahrer, in *m,f*; ~-**distance truck driver** *n* AmE (*cf long-distance lorry driver BrE*) TRANSP Fernfahrer, in *m,f*, Fernlastfahrer, in *m,f*

longer: ~-**term asset** *n* STOCK längerfristiger Vermögensgegenstand *m*; ~-**term option** *n* STOCK längerfristigere Option *f*; **no ~ valid** *phr* GEN COMM abgelaufen

longest: ~-**serving employee** *n* GEN COMM Dienstälteste(r) *mf* [decl. as adj]

longevity: ~ **pay** *n* HRM Gehaltserhöhung *f* nach Dauer der Betriebszugehörigkeit

long: ~ **form** *n* ADMIN, IMP/EXP *bill of lading* detailliertes Formular *nt*; ~ **fraud** *n* GEN COMM langfristiger Betrug *m*; ~ **futures position** *n* STOCK *options* Kaufoption *f* am Terminkontraktmarkt; ~ **hedge** *n* STOCK Long-Hedge *m*

longitudinal: ~ **data** *n pl* MATH *statistics* Längsschnittreihe *f*

long: ~-**lasting** *adj* GEN COMM dauerhaft; ~ **lease** *n* FIN, PROP langjähriger Mietvertrag *m*, langjähriger Pachtvertrag *m*; ~ **period** *n* ECON lange Periode *f*; ~ **position** *n* FIN Hausseposition *f*; ~-**range** *adj* ECON, GEN COMM *planning, forecast* weitreichend, Langzeit-; ~-**range forecast** *n* GEN COMM Langzeitprognose *f*; ~-**range planning** *n* GEN COMM langfristige Planung *f*, Langzeitplanung *f*, Langfristplanung *f*; ~ **room** *n* BrE

IMP/EXP Zollbüro, in dem die Dokumente deklarierter Güter kontrolliert werden

longs *n pl* STOCK Langläufer *m pl*, langfristige Schuldtitel *m pl*

longshoreman *n* AmE (*cf docker BrE*) HRM, TRANSP Hafenarbeiter *m*

long: ~-**standing** *adj* GEN COMM seit langer Zeit; ~ **straddle** *n* STOCK *options* langfristige Stellage *f*, langfristiger Straddle *m*; ~ **straddle position** *n* STOCK Straddle-Baisse-Position *f*; ~ **tail risk** *n* INS Langfristrisiko *nt*, langfristiges Risiko *nt*, Schadennachlaufproblem *nt*

long-term *adj* GEN COMM langfristig, mit langer Laufzeit, Langzeit-; ~ **blended cost rate** *n* (*LTB*) FIN langfristiger Mischverrechnungssatz *m*; ~ **bond** *n* ECON langfristige Anleihe *f*; ~ **budget** *n* FIN langfristiger Haushaltsplan *m*; ~ **credit** *n* ACC langfristiger Kredit *m*; ~ **credit bank** *n* BANK Kreditinstitut *nt* für langfristige Kredite; ~ **debt** *n* FIN langfristige Schuld *f*; ~ **financial investment** *n* ACC *annual accounts* langfristige Finanzanlage *f*; ~ **financial investments** *n pl* ACC Wertpapiere *nt pl* des Anlagevermögens, Beteiligungen *f pl*, langfristige Finanzanlagen *f pl*, langfristige Anlagen *f* des Finanzvermögens; ~ **financing** *n* FIN langfristige Finanzierung *f*; ~ **gain** *n* TAX Gewinn *m* aus langfristigem Geschäft, langfristiger Gewinn *m*; ~ **income averaging** *n* TAX langfristige Durchschnittsbesteuerung *f*; ~ **liability** *n* ACC *balance sheets* langfristige Verbindlichkeit *f*, langfristige Verpflichtung *f*, FIN fundierte Schuld *f*, langfristige Verbindlichkeit *f*; ~ **loan** *n* BANK langfristiges Darlehen *nt*; ~ **loss** *n* TAX Verlust *m* aus langfristigem Geschäft; ~ **objective** *n* GEN COMM langfristiges Ziel *nt*; ~ **obligation** *n* LAW *commitment* langfristige Verbindlichkeit *f*, langfristige Verpflichtung *f*; ~ **planning** *n* GEN COMM langfristige Planung *f*, Langfristplanung *f*; ~ **prime rate** *n* (*LTPR*) FIN langfristige Prime Rate *f*, langfristiger Vorzugszins *m*; ~ **team** *n* WEL *social work* Langzeitteam *nt*; ~ **trend** *n* ECON Langzeittrend *m*, GEN COMM langfristiger Trend *m*; ~ **unemployed** *n pl* (*LTU*) ECON, HRM Langzeitarbeitslose *pl* [decl. as adj]; ~ **unemployment** *n* ECON, HRM langfristige Arbeitslosigkeit *f*

long: ~ **ton**, ~ **tonne** *n* GEN COMM Bruttotonne *f*; ~ **wave** *n* ECON langer Konjunkturzyklus *m*; ~ **weekend** *n* GEN COMM langes Wochenende *nt*

look up *vt* ADMIN, COMP, GEN COMM *information* nachschauen, nachschlagen

looker *n* PROP Betrachter, in *m,f*

lookout: **be on the ~ for sth** *phr* GEN COMM auf der Suche nach etw sein; ~ **book** *n* ADMIN, POL Liste von Ausländern, denen die Einreise verweigert wird

looks *n pl* GEN COMM Aussehen *nt*

lookup: ~ **table** *n* COMP Nachschlagetabelle *f*, Verweistabelle *f*

loop *n* AmE *obs* POL engster Beraterkreis des Präsidenten mit Zugang zu Information der höchsten Geheimhaltungsstufe

loophole *n* LAW Gesetzeslücke *f*, Hintertürchen *nt*

loose *adj* IND *not packed* unverpackt; ~ **cargo** *n* TRANSP Bahn Stückgut *nt*; ~ **change** *n* GEN COMM Kleingeld *nt*; ~ **inserts** *n pl* S&M Beilagen *f pl*; ~-**leaf binder** *n* ADMIN Sammelmappe *f*; ~-**leaf edition** *n* MEDIA Loseblattausgabe *f*; ~ **oligopoly** *n* ECON weites Oligopol *nt*

Lorenz: ~ **curve** n ECON Lorenzkurve f

lorry n BrE (cf truck AmE) TRANSP Lastkraftwagen m (LKW), Lastwagen m; ~ **driver** n BrE (cf truck driver AmE, trucker AmE) TRANSP Lastwagenfahrer, in m,f, Lastkraftwagenfahrer, in m,f, LKW-Fahrer, in m,f; **~-mounted crane** n BrE (cf truck-mounted crane AmE) TRANSP Automobilkran m; ~ **reception area** n BrE (cf truck reception area AmE) TRANSP LKW-Annahmebereich m; ~ **service** n BrE (cf truck service AmE) TRANSP Lastwagenservice m, Lastwagentransport m

lose vt LAW protection verlieren; ♦ ~ **ground** GEN COMM in competition an Boden verlieren; ~ **one's job** HRM den Arbeitsplatz verlieren, seine Stelle verlieren

lose out vi ECON Verluste hinnehmen

losing: ~ **bargain** n ECON Verlustgeschäft nt

loss n BANK capital, LAW Verlust m; ~ **adjuster** n HRM insurance Schadensachverständige(r) mf [decl. as adj]; ~ **adjustment expense** n INS Schadenregulierungskosten pl; ~ **carry-back** n ACC taxation Verlustrücktrag m; ~ **carry-forward** n ACC balance sheets, Verlustvortrag m; ~ **of claim** n LAW Verlust m des Anspruchs; ~ **compensation** n TAX Verlustausgleich m; ~ **contingency** n FIN balance sheets Verlustrücklage f; ~ **of custom** n S&M Kundenverlust m; ~ **deduction** n TAX Verlustabzug m; ~ **of earnings** n FIN Ertragsausfall m

losses: ~ **carried forward** n pl ACC Verlustvortrag m

loss: ~ **function** n MATH statistics Verlustfunktion f; ~ **of income** n FIN Einkommensausfall m; ~ **of income insurance** n INS personal Versicherung f zur Kompensation von Einkommensverlusten; ~ **in transit** n TRANSP Verlust m auf dem Transport; ~ **in value of assets** n ACC Anlagenwertverlust m; ~ **in value from normal use** n GEN COMM Verschleiß m; ~ **leader** n S&M marketing Lockartikel m, Lockvogel m; ~ **leader pricing** n S&M sales Lockvogelpreispolitik f, Preisfestsetzung m für Lockartikel

lossmaker n S&M Verlustträger m, Verlustbringer m

loss: ~ **of market** n GEN COMM, S&M Marktverlust m; ~ **on depreciable property** n ACC Verlust m bei abnutzbaren Vermögensgegenständen, Verlust m bei Verschleißanlagen, Verlust m bei abschreibungsfähigen Vermögenswerten; ~ **on exchange** n ECON Wechselkursverlust m; ~ **on takeover** n ECON Übernahmeverlust m; ~ **of pay** n HRM Lohnausfall m; **~-pricing** n S&M marketing Verkauf m unter Einstandspreis, Verlustpreissystem nt; ~ **of priority** n PATENTS Prioritätverlust m, Rangverlust m; ~ **probability** n ECON Verlustwahrscheinlichkeit f; ~ **of production** n IND Produktionsausfall m; ~ **provision** n ACC Verlustrückstellung f; ~ **ratio** n BANK Verlustquote f, INS Schadenquote f; ~ **of specie** n INS Valorenverlust m; ~ **suffered** n LAW eingetretener Verlust m, erlittener Verlust m; ~ **to be paid** n INS Taxe f; ~ **of use** n ECON Nutzungsausfall m, FIN Nutzenentgang m

lost: ~ **tax revenue** n ECON entgangene Steuereinnahmen f pl; ~ **time** n COMP, GEN COMM Stillstandszeit f, IND Brachzeit f; ~ **units** n pl IND Ausschuß m

lot n AmE FIN, STOCK Paket nt, TRANSP Stückgut nt; ~ **and block** n AmE PROP Blockparzellierung f; **~-by-lot inspection** n ECON losweise Prüfung f

Lotharingian: ~ **axis** n ECON Gürtel m der wirtschaftlich starken EU-Städte

lot: ~ **line** n PROP Grundstücksgrenze f, Grundstücksparzellenlinie f

lottery n GEN COMM Lotterie f

Louvre: ~ **Accord** n ECON Louvre-Abkommen nt

low 1. adj ECON niedrig, GEN COMM tief, LAW niedrig; ♦ **with a ~ margin** S&M scharf kalkuliert; **be ~ on** GEN COMM knapp sein an; **2.** adv FIN, GEN COMM, TAX niedrig; **3.** n ECON Tiefstand m, Tiefstkurs m, GEN COMM, STOCK futures price Tiefpunkt m, Tiefstand m

low: ~ **achiever** n HRM leistungsschwacher Mitarbeiter m, leistungsschwache Mitarbeiterin f, leistungsschwache Person f

lowballer n STOCK Lockvogel m

low: **~-calorie** adj S&M kalorienarm; **~-cost** adj GEN COMM kostengünstig, GEN COMM billig; **~-cost housing** n WEL sozialer Wohnungsbau m, Sozialwohnung f; **~-cost loan** n BANK preiswertes Darlehen nt, subventioniertes Darlehen nt; ~ **cube** n TRANSP niedriger Rauminhalt m; **~-density cargo** n TRANSP Fracht f mit geringer Dichte; ~ **end of the market** n S&M marketing Markt m für preiswerte Angebote, unterer Marktbereich m; ~ **end of the range** n STOCK buying options positions unterer Bereich m

lower vt ECON herabsetzen, senken; ♦ ~ **the value** ECON den Wert mindern

lower: **~-case letter** n COMP, MEDIA Kleinbuchstabe m; ~ **of cost or market** n ACC balance sheets Niederstwert m; ~ **deck** n TRANSP of aircraft, ship Unterdeck nt; ~ **income bracket** n ECON, TAX niedrigere Einkommenssteuergruppe f, niedrigere Einkommensteuerklasse f, niedrigere Einkommensstufe f; ~ **management** n ADMIN untere Führungsebene f; **~-paid** adj HRM schlechter bezahlt; ~ **price** n STOCK niedriger Preis m; **~-priced** adj GEN COMM verbilligt; ~ **quartile** n MATH statistics unteres Quartil nt; ~ **than average** phr ECON unterdurchschnittlich

lowering n ECON of inflation rate Herabsetzung f

lowest: ~ **bidder** n STOCK niedrigster Bieter m; ~ **common denominator** n GEN COMM kleinster gemeinsamer Nenner m; ~ **price** n ECON Tiefstpreis m, GEN COMM äußerster Preis m, Tiefstkurs m, Tiefstpreis m pl, STOCK niedrigster Preis m, Tiefstkurs m; ~ **tender** n GEN COMM preisgünstigstes Angebot nt

low: ~ **flier** n MGMNT Tiefflieger m (infrml); **~-geared** adj STOCK unterkapitalisiert, kapitalknapp; **~-geared capital** n FIN zu kurze Kapitaldecke f; **~-grade** adj S&M quality minderwertig; **~-income household** n S&M market research Haushalt m mit geringem Einkommen; **~-interest loan** n BANK niedrigverzinsliches Darlehen nt; **~-key** adj GEN COMM zurückhaltend; **~-margin high-space goods** n pl S&M sperrige Massenprodukte nt pl; ~ **memory** n COMP unterer Speicherbereich m; **the ~-paid** n pl HRM Geringverdiener m pl, Einkommensschwache pl [decl. as adj]; ~ **pay** n HRM Niedriglohn m; **~-paying job** n HRM niedrig bezahlter Arbeitsplatz m; **~-polluting** adj ENVIR technology gering umweltverschmutzend; **~-powered money** n ECON Geld nt mit kleinem Geldschöpfungsmultiplikator; ~ **price** n GEN COMM Niedrigpreis m, STOCK currency futures niedriger Preis m; **~-priced** adj GEN COMM billig, preisgünstig; **~-profile** adj S&M wenig profiliert; ~ **profile** n GEN COMM schwaches Geschäftsprofil nt, S&M Zurückhaltung f; ~ **rent** n TAX niedrige Miete f; **~-risk securities** n pl STOCK risikoarme Wertpapiere nt pl; ~ **season** n

GEN COMM Nebensaison *f*; **~-season fare** *n* LEIS Nebensaisonpreis *m*; **~ standard of living** *n* WEL niedriger Lebensstandard *m*; **~-tech** *adj* COMP leistungsschwach, IND *production* niedertechnologisch, mit weicher Technologie; **~ value to high weight ratio** *n* TRANSP Verhältnis *nt* des geringen Wertes zu hohem Gewicht; **~-volume security** *n* STOCK Wertpapier *nt* mit schwachen Umsätzen; **~-wage worker** *n* GEN COMM Niedriglohnarbeiter, in *m,f*, Hilfsarbeiter, in *m,f*; **~-yielding** *adj* STOCK niedrig verzinslich

loyalty *n* GEN COMM *of customer, employee*, S&M Loyalität *f*; **~ discount** *n* S&M Treuerabatt *m*; **~ factor** *n* S&M Loyalitätsfaktor *m*; **~ rebate** *n* S&M Treuerabatt *m*

LPG *abbr* (*liquid petroleum gas*) ENVIR, IND flüssiges Propangas *nt*, Flüssiggas *nt*; **~ carrier** *n* TRANSP *shipping* Flüssiggastanker *m*, Flüssigpropangastanker *m*

LQ *abbr* (*letter quality*) COMP LQ (*Briefqualität*), Schönschrift *f*

LR *abbr* (*Lloyd's Register*) INS *marine* Lloyd's Register *nt*

LRA *abbr* BrE (*Labour Relations Agency*) HRM *Northern Ireland* Beratungs-, Schlichtungs- und Schiedsgerichtsstelle für Arbeitsstreitigkeiten

LRC *abbr* BrE (*Labour Representation Committee*) HRM Arbeitnehmervertretungsausschuß *m*

LRT *abbr* BrE (*London Regional Transport*) TRANSP Londoner Regionalverkehr

ls *abbr* (*lump sum*) FIN, GEN COMM, HRM Pauschalsumme *f*, Pauschalbetrag *m*, INS Depotzahlung *f*, Einmalzahlung *f*, Pauschalbetrag *m*, Pauschale *f*, TRANSP *freight* Pauschalbetrag *m*, Pauschale *f*

LSA *abbr* TRANSP (*life-saving apparatus*) *shipping* Lebensrettungsgerät *nt*, (*life-saving appliance*) Lebensrettungseinrichtung *nt*

lsd *abbr* (*last safe day*) INS *marine* letzter Versicherungstag *m*

LSD *abbr* (*landing, storage, delivery*) IMP/EXP Löschung, Speicherung, Lieferung

LSE *abbr* ECON (*London School of Economics*) Londoner Wirtschaftshochschule, STOCK (*London Stock Exchange*) Londoner Wertpapierbörse *f*

LTB *abbr* FIN (*long-term blended cost rate*) langfristiger Mischverrechnungssatz *m*, LEIS (*London Tourist Board*) Londoner Touristenbehörde

Ltd *abbr* BrE (*limited company*) GEN COMM GmbH (*Gesellschaft mit beschränkter Haftung*), Ges.m.b.H. (*Öst*) (*Gesellschaft mit beschränkter Haftung*), Personengesellschaft *f*

LTOM *abbr* (*London Traded Options Market*) STOCK Londoner börsengehandelter Optionenmarkt

LTPR *abbr* (*long-term prime rate*) FIN langfristige Prime Rate *f*, langfristiger Vorzugszins *m*

LTU *abbr* (*long-term unemployed*) ECON, HRM Langzeitarbeitslose *pl* [decl. as adj]

LTV *abbr* FIN (*loan-to-value ratio*) Beleihungsquote *f*, Beleihungssatz *m*

LUAA *abbr* (*Lloyd's Underwriting Agents' Association*) INS Verband der Lloyd's-Versicherungsagenten

LUAMC *abbr* (*leading underwriters' agreement for marine cargo business*) INS Annahmerichtlinien *f pl* der Erstversicherer für Seefrachtgeschäfte

LUAMH *abbr* (*leading underwriters' agreement for marine hull business*) INS Annahmerichtlinien *f pl* der Erstversicherer für Schiffskaskogeschäfte

Lucas: **~ supply function** *n* ECON Lucassche Angebotsfunktion *f*

lucky: **~ break** *n* GEN COMM Glücksfall *m*

lucrative *adj* GEN COMM lukrativ

Luddite *n* HRM Maschinenstürmer *m*

luggage *n* BrE LEIS, TRANSP Gepäck *nt*; **~ lockers** *n pl* BrE TRANSP Gepäckaufbewahrungsstelle *f*

lull *n* GEN COMM Flaute *f*

lumber *n* AmE (*cf timber BrE*) IND Bauholz *nt*, Nutzholz *nt*, zugeschnittenes Holz *nt*, Zweckholz *nt*; **~ industry** *n* AmE (*cf timber industry BrE*) Holzindustrie *f*

lump *n* HRM Masse *f*; **the ~** *BrE* HRM *construction industry* Masse *f* der Hilfsarbeiter

lump sum *n* (*ls*) FIN, GEN COMM, HRM Pauschalsumme *f*, Pauschalbetrag *m*, INS Depotzahlung *f*, Einmalzahlung *f*, Pauschalbetrag *m*, Pauschale *f*, TRANSP *freight* Pauschalbetrag *m*, Pauschale *f*; **~ charter** *n* TRANSP *shipping* Pauschalcharter *f*; **~ contract** *n* HRM Auftrag *m* mit Festpreisen; **~ distribution** *n* STOCK Ausschüttung *f* in einer Summe; **~ freight** *n* TRANSP *shipping* Pauschalfracht *f*; **~ price** *n* GEN COMM Pauschalpreis *m*; **~ purchase** *n* FIN Globalkauf *m*; **~ tax** *n* TAX Pauschalsteuer *f*

luncheon: **~ voucher** *n* BrE (*LV*) HRM Essensbon *m*, Essensmarke *f*

Lundberg: **~ lag** *n* ECON Lundberg-Lag *m*

lure *n* ECON Lockartikel *m*

Luxembourg: **~ Interbank Offered Rate** *n* (*Luxibor*) ECON Luxibor *m*

Luxembourg: **~ effect** *n* ECON Luxemburg-Effekt *m*

Luxibor *n* (*Luxembourg Interbank Offered Rate*) ECON Luxibor *m*

luxury *adj* S&M *goods* Luxus *m*; **~ goods** *n pl* ECON, GEN COMM, S&M Luxusgüter *nt pl*; **~ tax** *n* TAX Luxussteuer *f*

LV *abbr* BrE (*luncheon voucher*) HRM Essensbon *m*, Essensmarke *f*

lying: **~ idle** *adj infrml* BANK *money* unergiebig, brachliegend

M

m *abbr* GEN COMM (*meter AmE, metre BrE*) m (*Meter*), (*month*) Monat *m*

m³ *abbr* (*cubic meter AmE, cubic metre BrE*) GEN COMM m³ (*Kubikmeter*), cbm (*Kubikmeter*)

Maastricht: ~ **Summit** *n* GEN COMM Gipfeltreffen *nt* von Maastricht

machine 1. *n* GEN COMM, IND Maschine *f*; **2.** *vt* IND abspanen, maschinell bearbeiten

machine: **by** ~ *adv* COMP, IND maschinell; ~ **accounting** *n* ACC maschinelle Buchhaltung *f*; ~ **address** *n* COMP absolute Adresse *f*, Maschinenadresse *f*; **~-aided translation** *n* (*MAT*) COMP maschinengestützte Übersetzung *f*; **~-assisted translation** *n* (*MAT*) COMP maschinengestützte Übersetzung *f*; **~-based** *adj* COMP maschinell; ~ **code** *n* IND Maschinencode *m*; ~ **downtime** *n* IND Brachzeit *f*; ~ **dynamics** *n pl* ADMIN Maschinendynamik *f*; ~ **hours** *n pl* IND Maschinenzeit *f*; ~ **idle time** *n* IND Brachzeit *f*; ~ **interference time** *n* IND Brachzeit *f*; ~ **loading** *n* IND *production* maschinelle Beschickung *f*; **~-made** *adj* IND maschinell hergestellt; ~ **maximum time** *n* ECON maximale Nutzungsdauer *f*; ~ **operator** *n* HRM, MGMNT Bedienungskraft *f*; ~ **proof** *n* S&M Maschinenabzug *m*; **~-readable** *adj* COMP *bar codes* maschinenlesbar; **~-readable code** *n* COMP maschinenlesbarer Code *m*; ~ **run** *n* COMP, TRANSP Maschinenlauf *m*

machinery *n* (*mchy*) ECON *in factory* Maschinen *f pl*, Apparat *m*, Maschinenpark *m*, maschinelle Anlagen *f pl*, Maschinenanlage *f*, IND Maschinen *f pl*, LAW *of law* Apparat *m*; ~ **damage co-ins clause** *n* INS *hull clause* Maschinenschadenmitversicherungsklausel *f*; ~ **survey** *n* (*MS*) TRANSP *shipping* Maschinenprüfung *f*

machine: ~ **safety** *n* IND Maschinensicherheit *f*; ~ **tool** *n* IND Werkzeugmaschine *f*; ~ **translation** *n* (*MT*) COMP Maschinenübersetzung *f* (*MÜ*)

machining: ~ **procedure** *n* ECON Bearbeitungsverfahren *nt*

Macmillan: ~ **Gap** *n* FIN Macmillan-Lücke *f*

macro *n* COMP *instruction* Makro *nt*, Makrobefehl *m*

macrocomputing *n* COMP Makroverarbeitung *f*

macroeconomic *adj* ECON makroökonomisch; ~ **accounting** *n* ACC, ECON volkswirtschaftliche Gesamtrechnung *f*; ~ **demand schedule** *n* ECON gesamtwirtschaftliche Bedarfsliste *f*, makroökonomische Bedarfsliste *f*; ~ **policy** *n* ECON Wirtschaftspolitik *f*, Gesamtwirtschaftspolitik *f*

macroeconomics *n pl* ECON *econometrics* Makroökonomik *f*

macroenvironment *n* GEN COMM Makrostruktur *f*

macromarketing *n* S&M Makromarketing *nt*

made: ~ **out in** *phr* BANK *dollars* ausgestellt in; **~-to-bearer instrument** *n* ECON Inhaberpapier *nt*; **~-to-last** *adj* GEN COMM langlebig; **~-to-measure** *adj* IND *tailoring* maßgearbeitet, maßgeschneidert, nach Kundenangaben gefertigt, nach Maß gefertigt; **~-to-order** *adj* S&M kundenspezifisch; ~ **up/made down** *n* STOCK Abwicklung von Geschäften eines Insolventen

MAFF *abbr BrE* (*Ministry of Agriculture, Fisheries and Food*) POL Ministerium *nt* für Landwirtschaft, Fischerei und Nahrungsmittel

magazine *n* MEDIA Zeitschrift *f*

magic: ~ **quadrilateral** *n* ECON magisches Viereck *nt*

magistrates: ~ **entitled to adjudicate** *n pl* LAW urteilsbefugte Amtsrichter *m pl*

magnet *n* GEN COMM Magnet *m*

magnetic: ~ **card** *n* COMP, IND Magnetkarte *f*; ~ **core** *n* COMP Magnetkern *m*; ~ **disk** *n* COMP Magnetplatte *f*; ~ **film** *n* S&M Magnetfilm *m*; ~ **storage** *n* COMP, IND *microprocessors* Magnetspeicher *m*, magnetischer Speicher *m*; ~ **tape** *n* COMP Magnetband *nt*, *audio* Magnettonband *nt*, IND Magnetband *nt*, *acoustics* Tonband *nt*, MEDIA Magnettonband *nt*, Tonband *nt*; ~ **tape recorder** *n* COMP, MEDIA Magnetbandaufzeichner *m*

magnitude *n* MATH ordinale Größe *f*

maiden: ~ **flight** *n* TRANSP Jungfernflug *m*; ~ **voyage** *n* TRANSP Jungfernfahrt *f*

mailbox *n* ADMIN, COMMS *AmE* (*cf postbox BrE*) Briefkasten *m*, Briefeinwurf *m*, COMP Mail-Box *f*, *advertising, promotion* elektronische Kommunikation *f*

mailcar *n AmE* (*cf mail van BrE*) COMMS Postauto *nt*

mail: ~ **carrier** *n AmE* (*cf postman BrE*) COMMS Briefträger, in *m,f*, Postbote *m*, Postbotin *f*; ~ **clerk** *n* ADMIN Postangestellte(r) *mf* [decl. as adj]; ~ **credit** *n* ECON Postlaufkredit *m*; ~ **fraud** *n* S&M *advertising* irreführende Werbepost *f*

mailing *n* COMMS Posteinlieferung, Postversand, COMP *dispatch* Aufgabe *f* zur Post, S&M *advertising* Postversand *m*, Mailing *nt*; ~ **address** *n* COMMS Postadresse *f*, Postzustelladresse *f*; ~ **card** *n* COMMS Postkarte *f*; ~ **list** *n* COMMS Adressenliste *f*, Postliste *f*, Verteiler *m*; ~ **shot** *n* COMMS, S&M *advertising* Postwerbeexemplar *nt*

mail: **~-in premium** *n* S&M Zugabe *f* gegen eingesandten Kupon; ~ **interview** *n* ECON, S&M briefliche Befragung *f*

mailman *n AmE* (*cf postman BrE*) COMMS Briefträger *m*, Postbote *m*

mailmerge *n* COMP Mailmerge *nt*

mail: ~ **order** *n* (*MO*) COMMS Mailorder *f*, Versandbestellung *f*, GEN COMM Mailorder *f*, S&M Postauftrag *m*, Versandbestellung *f*, Versandhandel *m*; **~-order business** *n* S&M *firm* Versandhandel *m*, Versandunternehmen *nt*; **~-order catalog** *AmE*, **~-order catalogue** *BrE n* S&M Versandhauskatalog *m*; **~-order selling** *n* S&M Versandverkauf *m*; ~ **processing** *n* ADMIN, COMMS Postbearbeitung *f*

mailshot *n* COMMS, S&M *advertising* Postwerbeexemplar *nt*

mail: ~ **survey** *n* ECON, S&M briefliche Befragung *f*; ~ **that is unreadable** *n BrE* (*cf nixie mail AmE*) COMMS Post *f* mit unleserlicher Adresse; ~ **transfer** *n* (*MT*) BANK *international trade*, ECON briefliche Auszahlung *f*, Postüberweisung *f*; ~ **truck** *n* COMMS Postauto *nt*; ~ **van** *n BrE* (*cf mailcar AmE*) COMMS Postauto *nt*

main: ~ **bidder** *n* ECON Hauptanbieter, in *m,f*; ~ **branch**

n GEN COMM Hauptstelle *f*; ~ **business** *n* GEN COMM Kerngeschäft *nt*, Hauptgeschäft; ~ **cause** *n* LAW Hauptursache *f*; ~ **contractor** *n* ECON Generalunternehmer *m*; ~ **deadline** *n* ECON Haupttermin *m*; ~ **economic sectors** *n pl* ECON wirtschaftliche Hauptsektoren *f pl*

maine: ~ **insurance** *n* INS Transportversicherung *f*

main: ~ **file** *n* COMP Bestandsdatei *f*, Hauptdatei *f*, Stammdatei *f*; ~ **line** *n* TRANSP *AmE* (*cf main road BrE*) Hauptstraße *f*, *rail* Hauptstrecke *f*, Hauptverbindung *f*; **on the ~ line** *adj* TRANSP *railway station* an der Hauptstrecke; ~ **memory** *n* COMP Arbeitsspeicher *m*, Hauptspeicher *m*; ~ **menu** *n* COMP Hauptmenü *nt*; ~ **residence** *n* PROP Hauptwohnsitz *m*; ~ **road** *n* *BrE* (*cf main line AmE*) TRANSP Hauptstraße *f*

mains *n pl* *BrE* (*cf supply network AmE*) COMP Lichtnetz *nt*, Netz *nt*, Stromversorgungsnetz *nt*; ~ **adaptor** *n* *BrE* COMP Netzadapter *m*

main: ~ **screen** *n* COMP Hauptbildschirm *m*

mainstreaming *n* WEL Eingliederung lernbehinderter Kinder in Schulklassen

mainstream: ~ **tax** *n* (*MT*) TAX Körperschaftssteuerabschlußzahlung *f*

main: ~ **street** *n* *AmE* S&M Haupteinkaufsstraße *f*, Hauptstraße *f*

maintain *vt* ADMIN *office* unterhalten, GEN COMM *assert* behaupten, LAW unterhalten

maintenance *n* COMP Wartung *f*, LAW Unterhalt *m*, TRANSP Wartung *f*; ~ **bond** *n* LAW *commercial* Garantieversprechen *nt*; ~ **charge** *n* BANK Kontoführungskosten *pl*; ~ **costs** *n pl* PROP laufende Instandhaltungskosten *pl*; ~ **crew** *n* HRM Wartungsmannschaft *f*; ~ **department** *n* GEN COMM Instandsetzungsabteilung *f*, IND Instandsetzungsabteilung *f*, Wartungsabteilung *f*, *servicing* Kundendienstabteilung *f*, Serviceabteilung *f*; ~ **fee** *n* BANK Kontoführungsgebühr *f*, PROP Instandhaltungskosten *pl*; ~ **margin** *n* STOCK *futures* Mindestsaldo *m* eines Nachschußkontos; ~ **planning** *n* ADMIN Planung *f* der Instandhaltungsarbeiten; ~, **repair and overhaul** *phr* (*MRO*) TRANSP Wartung, Reparatur und Überholung; ~ **and repair work** *n* GEN COMM Ausbesserungen *f pl*; ~ **schedule** *n* GEN COMM Wartungsplan *m*; ~ **vehicle** *n* TRANSP Werkstattwagen *m*

main: ~ **trading partner** *n* ECON Haupthandelspartner, in *m,f*

Majesty: **Her ~'s Customs** *n* *BrE* (*HMC*) IMP/EXP britische Zollbehörde; **Her ~'s Customs and Excise** *n* *BrE* IMP/EXP, TAX (*HM Customs and Excise, HMC&E*) britische Zoll- und Steuerbehörde; **Her ~'s Government** *n* *BrE* (*HMG*) POL Regierung Ihrer Majestät; **On Her ~'s Service** *phr* *BrE* (*OHMS*) ADMIN, POL zu Diensten Ihrer Majestät; *n* *BrE* (*HMS*) TRANSP königliches Schiff; **Her ~'s Stationery Office** *n* *BrE* (*HMSO*) GEN COMM britischer Staatsverlag, der auch die staatlichen Stellen mit Bürobedarf versorgt; **Her ~'s Treasury** *n* *BrE* ECON Schatzamt *nt*, Finanzministerium *nt*

major *adj* GEN COMM führend; ~ **currency** *n* ECON Leitwährung *f*, wichtige Währung *f*; ~ **customer** *n* GEN COMM Großkunde *m*, Großkundin *f*; ~ **foreign exchange market** *n* FIN wichtiger Devisenmarkt *m*

majority *n* GEN COMM, HRM Mehrheit *f*, LAW *age* Volljährigkeit *f*, *greater number* Mehrheit *f*, POL, STOCK Mehrheit *f*; ~ **interest** *n* GEN COMM, STOCK Mehrheits-

beteiligung *f*; ~ **rule** *n* POL Mehrheitsregierung *f*; ~ **shareholding** *n* STOCK Mehrheitsaktienbestand *m*, Mehrheitsbeteiligung *f*; ~ **stake** *n* GEN COMM Mehrheitsbeteiligung *f*, Mehrheitsanteil *m*; ~ **verdict** *n* LAW Mehrheitsvotum *nt* der Geschworenen; ~ **vote** *n* GEN COMM Mehrheitswahl *f*

major: ~ **producer** *n* ECON *of commodity* Hauptproduzent, in *m,f*; ~ **road** *n* TRANSP Hauptstraße *f*; ~ **trading partner** *n* ECON Haupthandelspartner, in *m,f*

make 1. *n* GEN COMM *of machine* Fabrikat *nt*, Sorte *f*, INS, S&M Fabrikat *nt*; 2. *vt* GEN COMM machen, erzielen, PATENTS *invention* machen; ♦ ~ **sb's acquaintance** GEN COMM jds Bekanntschaft machen; ~ **an advance** GEN COMM einen Vorschuß zahlen; ~ **an advance payment** GEN COMM Anzahlung leisten, eine Vorauszahlung leisten; ~ **allowance for** GEN COMM berücksichtigen; ~ **allowances for** GEN COMM *exceptional occurrences* Zugeständnisse machen; ~ **an allowance on** GEN COMM einen finanziellen Zuschuß geben; ~ **amends** LAW wiedergutmachen; ~ **an application for** GEN COMM einen Antrag stellen auf; ~ **an appointment with sb** GEN COMM eine Verabredung mit jdm treffen; ~ **an appraisal of future needs** GEN COMM künftigen Bedarf abschätzen; ~ **an arrangement** GEN COMM eine Vereinbarung treffen; ~ **a bequest to sb** LAW jdm ein Vermächtnis aussetzen; ~ **a bid** GEN COMM bieten; ~ **a capital gain** TAX Veräußerungsgewinn erzielen; ~ **a check payable to sb** *AmE*, ~ **a cheque payable to sb** *BrE* BANK einen Scheck auf jdn ausstellen; ~ **clear** GEN COMM klarmachen; ~ **a comeback** GEN COMM *currency* ein Comeback erleben; ~ **a complete estimate of** GEN COMM auskalkulieren; ~ **a contribution** GEN COMM einen Beitrag leisten; ~ **cuts in spending** ECON Ausgaben kürzen; ~ **a deal** ECON sich arrangieren; ~ **a decision** GEN COMM, MGMNT eine Entscheidung fällen, eine Entscheidung treffen; ~ **delivery of** STOCK *currency* liefern; ~ **a distinction between** GEN COMM unterscheiden zwischen [+dat]; ~ **a donation** TAX, WEL spenden; ~ **a down payment** BANK, ECON Anzahlung leisten; ~ **enquiries** MGMNT, S&M Erkundungen einziehen; ~ **an entry in the accounts** ACC buchen; ~ **an error** GEN COMM einen Fehler machen; ~ **an exception** GEN COMM eine Ausnahme machen; ~ **an exception of** GEN COMM ausnehmen; ~ **a firm offer** LAW ein festes Angebot machen; ~ **the first move** GEN COMM den ersten Schritt tun; ~ **full use of sth** GEN COMM etw auslasten, etw voll nutzen; ~ **further enquiries** GEN COMM nachhaken; ~ **gains** STOCK Gewinne erzielen; ~ **good** LAW wiedergutmachen; ~ **headway** GEN COMM schnell vorankommen; ~ **an impression** GEN COMM einen Eindruck machen; ~ **inroads into sb's market** GEN COMM in jds Markt eindringen; ~ **investigations into** GEN COMM Nachforschungen über etw anstellen; ~ **a killing** *infrml* FIN einen Reibach machen (*infrml*); ~ **a list of** GEN COMM eine Aufstellung anfertigen von; ~ **a living** ECON seinen Lebensunterhalt verdienen; ~ **a loan** BANK ein Darlehen gewähren; ~ **a market** STOCK Geld- und Briefkurse stellen, Kauf- und Verkaufsaufträge entgegennehmen; ~ **a note of sth** GEN COMM etw vermerken; ~ **an objection** GEN COMM einen Einwand erheben; ~ **an offer** GEN COMM Angebot unterbreiten; ~ **sth one's business** GEN COMM sich etw zur Aufgabe machen; ~ **sth one's job** GEN COMM sich etw zur Aufgabe machen; ~ **a payment of** GEN COMM zahlen;

~ **port** TRANSP einen Hafen anlaufen; ~ **a pretence of** LAW vortäuschen; ~ **a profit** ACC Gewinn erzielen, Gewinn machen; ~ **profits** ACC Gewinn machen; ~ **a protest** GEN COMM protestieren; ~ **provision for** GEN COMM Vorsorge treffen für; ~ **public** GEN COMM bekanntmachen; ~ **a purchase** GEN COMM einen Kauf vornehmen; ~ **a request** GEN COMM Bitte vorbringen; ~ **a request to the appropriate authority** GEN COMM einen Antrag bei der zuständigen Behörde stellen; ~ **a reservation** LEIS eine Reservierung vornehmen, reservieren; ~ **a sale** STOCK einen Verkauf tätigen; ~ **a scoop** *infrml* GEN COMM einen Coup landen (*infrml*); ~ **sense** GEN COMM sinnvoll sein, Sinn machen; ~ **a statement** LAW eine Aussage machen; ~ **a suggestion** GEN COMM einen Vorschlag machen; ~ **things difficult for sb** GEN COMM jdm das Leben schwer machen; ~ **a transaction** GEN COMM ein Geschäft durchführen; ~ **a turn** ECON Gewinn machen; ~ **use of** GEN COMM benutzen, verwenden; ~ **a valuation of** GEN COMM bewerten

make out *vt* GEN COMM *invoice, cheque, receipt* ausstellen

make over *vt* INS, LAW abtreten

make up *vt* BANK *account* abschließen, aufstellen, ECON *deficit* ausgleichen, decken, GEN COMM *list* anfertigen, ausgleichen, aufstellen, *lost time* aufholen; ♦ ~ **for** GEN COMM *compensate* kompensieren; ~ **one's accounts** ACC abrechnen; ~ **for lost time** GEN COMM verlorene Zeit aufholen; ~ **the odd money** GEN COMM restliches Geld abrechnen

make: ~**-or-buy decision** *n* GEN COMM Entscheidung *f* über Eigenfertigung oder Kauf

maker *n* GEN COMM Hersteller, in *m,f*, IND Erzeuger, in *m,f*, Fabrikant, in *m,f*, Hersteller, in *m,f*, Produzent, in *m,f*, LAW *of a note* Aussteller, in *m,f*, S&M Hersteller, in *m,f*

make: ~**-ready work** *n* IND vorbereitende Arbeiten *f pl*

makeshift *adj* GEN COMM behelfsmäßig; ~ **solution** *n* GEN COMM Notlösung *f*

make: ~**-up** *n* FIN Abrechnung *f*, IND *garment* Zusammensetzung *f*; ~**-work** *n* AmE ECON Arbeitsbeschaffung *f*

making *n* HRM *of a position* Schaffung *f*, IND *of product* Fabrikation *f*; ♦ ~ **allowance for** GEN COMM unter Berücksichtigung von

makings: have the ~ of *phr* GEN COMM das Zeug haben für

making: ~ **up** *n* BANK Aufstellung *f*, *of accounts* Abschluß *m*; ~**-up of a balance sheet** *n* ACC Aufstellung *f* einer Bilanz; ~ **up for losses** *n* ACC Verluste *m pl* ausgleichen; ~**-up into pages** *n* COMP Seitenumbruch *m*, Umbruch *m*; ~**-up price** *n* (*M/U*) GEN COMM letzter Abrechnungskurs *m*, letzter Kurs *m*

mala fide *adj* LAW bösgläubig, in böser Absicht, malafide

malfunction *n* GEN COMM Funktionsstörung *f*

malicious: ~ **acts clause** *n* INS *hull policy* Klausel *f* vorsätzlicher oder böswilliger Taten; ~ **damage clause** *n* INS *marine, cargo policy* Klausel *f* für böswillige Beschädigung

maliciously *adv* LAW böswillig

malicious: ~ **mischief** *n* LAW mutwillige Sachbeschädigung *f*

malinger *vt* HRM sich drücken

malingerer *n* HRM Simulant, in *m,f*, Scheinkranker *m*

malingering *n* HRM Simulation *f*

mall *n* S&M Einkaufsgalerie *f*

Maloney: ~ **Act** *n* LAW *to amend the Securities Exchange Act of 1934* Maloney-Gesetz *nt*

malperformance *n* LAW *contracts* Schlechterfüllung *f*

malpractice *n* LAW *doctor, lawyer* Verletzung *f* der Berufspflicht

Malthusian: ~ **law of population** *n* ECON Malthussches Bevölkerungsgesetz *nt*

mammoth *adj* GEN COMM riesengroß; ♦ **on a ~ scale** GEN COMM auf breitester Basis

mammoth: ~ **company** *n* ECON, GEN COMM Mammutgesellschaft *f*; ~ **reduction** *n* S&M *sales* Riesenreduzierung *f*; ~ **size** *n* S&M Riesengröße *f*

man *vt* HRM bemannen, mit Personal besetzen; ♦ ~ **a night shift** HRM eine Nachtschicht mit Personal ausstatten; ~ **a stand** HRM einen Stand mit Personal besetzen

manage *vt* GEN COMM *supervise* verwalten, bewerkstelligen, leiten, *manipulate* manipulieren (*infrml*), LAW verwalten, MGMNT leiten, führen, managen, verwalten, POL verwalten; ♦ ~ **sb's affairs** MGMNT jds Geschäfte führen

managed: ~ **account** *n* ACC treuhänderisch verwaltetes Konto *nt*; ~ **costs** *n pl* ACC verwaltete Kosten *pl*, ECON gelenkte Kosten *pl*, FIN manipulierte Kosten *pl*; ~ **currency** *n* ECON manipulierte Währung *f*; ~ **currency fund** *n* FIN auf Währungsanlagen spezialisierte Investmentfonds *m*; ~ **economy** *n* ECON, POL Planwirtschaft *f*; ~ **floating system** *n* ECON schmutziges Floating *nt*, schmutziges Floaten *nt*; ~ **fund** *n* ECON Investmentfonds *m*; ~ **news** *n* POL staatlich gelenkte Nachrichten *f pl*, staatliche Einflußnahme *f* auf die Berichterstattung; ~ **trade** *n* ECON manipulierter Handel *m*

management *n* ADMIN Management *nt*, Verwaltung *f* (*Verw.*), FIN Gewinn *m*, Liquidität *f*, Management *nt*, GEN COMM Unternehmensführung *f*, Leitung *f*, Management *nt*, HRM Leitung *f*, Management *nt*, MGMNT Führung *f*, Unternehmensführung *f*, Unternehmensleitung *f*, Verwaltung *f* (*Verw.*), Bewirtschaftung *f*; ♦ **under new ~** MGMNT Geschäftsübernahme *f*, neuer Inhaber *m*, unter neuer Leitung *f*

management: ~ **accountancy** *n* ACC entscheidungsorientiertes Rechnungswesen *nt*; ~ **accountant** *n* ACC betrieblicher Rechnungsprüfer *m*, betriebliche Rechnungsprüferin *f*; ~ **accounting** *n* ACC entscheidungsorientierte Buchführung *f*, entscheidungsorientiertes Rechnungswesen *nt*, FIN internes Rechnungswesen *nt*; ~ **accounts** *n pl* ACC Geschäftsleitungskosten *pl*; ~ **agreement** *n* MGMNT Leitungsvereinbarung *f*; ~ **aid** *n* MGMNT Leitungsinstrument *nt*; ~ **audit** *n* ACC, HRM Leistungsbeurteilung *f* und -bewertung *f* von Führungskräften; ~ **board** *n* GEN COMM Vorstand *m*, HRM Vorstandsgremium *nt*, Leitungsgremium *nt*, Board *nt*; ~ **bonus** *n* HRM, MGMNT Tantieme *f*; ~ **buy-in** *n* (*MBI*) ECON, FIN, STOCK Management-Buy-In *nt*; ~ **buyout** *n* (*MBO*) ECON, FIN Management-Buy-Out *nt*; ~ **by crisis** *n* MGMNT Management *nt* nach dem Krisenprinzip; ~ **by exception** *n* MGMNT Management *nt* nach dem Ausnahmeprinzip, Management *nt* by Exception MGMNT management by exception; ~ **by objectives** *n* (*MBO*) ADMIN, MGMNT Management *nt* nach Zielvorgaben, Führung *f* durch

Zielvereinbarung, Management *nt* by objectives, zielge-steuerte Unternehmensführung *f*; **~ by walking around** *n* (*MBWA*) MGMNT Management *nt* durch Pflege persönlicher Kontakte; **~ chart** *n* MATH Management-grafik *f*, MGMNT Businessgrafik *f*, Leitungsschema *nt*; **~ committee** *n* ECON, GEN COMM *executive committee* geschäftsführender Ausschuß *m*, MGMNT Geschäfts-führungsausschuß *m*, geschäftsführender Ausschuß *m*, Führungsausschuß *m*, Verwaltungsausschuß *m*, POL geschäftsführender Ausschuß *m*; **~ company** *n* ECON flexibler Investmentfonds *m*, Verwaltungsgesellschaft *f*; **~ competence** *n* MGMNT Leitungsbefugnis *f*, Leitungs-kompetenz *f*; **~ consultancy** *n* MGMNT Unternehmensberatungsfirma *f*; **~ consultant** *n* COMP, MGMNT Unternehmensberater, in *m,f*

Management: **~ Consultants Association** *n BrE* (*MCA*) MGMNT Verband der Unternehmensberater

management: **~ consulting** *n* GEN COMM Betriebsbera-tung *f*, MGMNT Unternehmensberatung *f*; **~ contract** *n* MGMNT Managementvertrag *m*; **~ control** *n* ACC *auditing* Führungskontrolle *f*; **~ cycle** *n* MGMNT Managementzyklus *m*; **~ development** *n* HRM, MGMNT Entwicklung *f* des Managements, Weiterbildung *f* von Führungskräften; **~ expenses** *n* ACC Geschäftslei-tungskosten *pl*; **~ fee** *n* BANK Führungsprovision *f*, Provision *f* der Konsortialführung, Vermögensverwal-tungsgebühr *f*, Verwaltungsgebühr *f*, STOCK *managing portfolio* Konsortialgebühr *f*; **~ game** *n* MGMNT Plan-spiel *nt*; **~ guide** *n* MGMNT Managementhandbuch *nt*; **~ hierarchy** *n* HRM Hierarchie *f* des Führungsperso-nals; **~ information** *n* COMP, MGMNT Führungsinformation *f*, Managementinformation *f*; **~ information system** *n* (*MIS*) COMP, MGMNT Füh-rungsinformationssystem *nt*, Management-Informationssystem *nt* (*MIS*); **~ of inventories** *n* ACC Inventarverwaltung *f*; **~ method** *n* MGMNT Führungs-methode *f*, Leitungsmethode *f*; **~ operating system** *n* MGMNT Arbeitssystem *nt* des Managements, Opera-tionssystem *nt* des Managements; **~ operation** *n* MGMNT Leitungsprozeß *m*, Managementaktivität *f*; **~ organization** *n* HRM Management-Organisation *f*; **~ and personnel office** *n* (*MPO*) ADMIN Geschäfts-führungs- und Personalbüro *nt*; **~ potential** *n* GEN COMM Managementpotential *nt*, MGMNT Führungspo-tential *nt*, Leitungspotential *nt*; **~ practice** *n* MGMNT Managementpraxis *f*, Betriebsführungspraxis *f*, Lei-tungsgebaren *nt*, Leitungsmethode *f*; **~ prerogative** *n* HRM Vorrecht *nt* der Geschäftsleitung; **~ ratio** *n* HRM Verhältnis *nt* der leitenden Angestellten zur Beleg-schaft, MGMNT betriebswirtschaftliche Kennziffer *f*, Leitungsverhältnis *nt*, Verhältnis *nt* der leitenden Angestellten zur Belegschaft; **~ reshuffle** *n* MGMNT Leitungsumbildung *f*; **~ science** *n* MGMNT Führungs-lehre *f*, Wissenschaft *f* der Unternehmensführung; **~ service** *n* FIN, MGMNT Managementservice *m*; **~ skills** *n pl* MGMNT Führungsqualitäten *f pl*; **~ staff** *n* HRM Führungskräfte *f pl*, MGMNT Führungskräfte *f pl*, Führungspersonal *nt*; **~ structure** *n* MGMNT Führungs-struktur *f*, Leitungsaufbau *m*; **~ style** *n* MGMNT Führungsstil *m*; **~ succession planning** *n* MGMNT Planung *f* der Leitungsnachfolge; **~ support** *n* HRM Management-Unterstützung *f*; **~ system** *n* MGMNT Leitungssystem *nt*, Managementsystem *nt*, Verwal-tungssystem *nt*; **~ team** *n* HRM Führungsgruppe *f*, MGMNT Führungsgruppe *f*, Führungsmannschaft *f*,

Leitungskollektiv *nt*; **~ technique** *n* MGMNT Führungs-instrument *nt*, Leitungsmethode *f*, Managementtechnik *f*; **~ theory** *n* MGMNT Führungslehre *f*, Führungstheorie *f*; **~ training** *n* HRM Managementschulung *f*, Weiter-bildung *f* von Führungskräften, MGMNT Managementausbildung *f*, Weiterbildung *f* von Füh-rungskräften

manager *n* (*MGR*) GEN COMM Direktor, in *m,f*, Verwalter, in *m,f*, HRM Leiter, in *m,f*, Manager, in *m,f*, LAW Verwalter, in *m,f*, MGMNT Betriebsleiter, in *m,f*, Geschäftsführer, in *m,f*, Leiter, in *m,f*, Manager, in *m,f*, Verwalter, in *m,f*, POL Verwalter, in *m,f*

manageress *n* GEN COMM Direktorin *f*, Verwalterin *f*, HRM Leiterin *f*, Managerin *f*, LAW Verwalterin *f*, MGMNT Betriebsleiterin *f*, Geschäftsführerin *f*, Leiterin *f*, Managerin *f*, Verwalterin *f*, POL Verwalterin *f*

managerial *adj* MGMNT betrieblich, geschäftlich, leitend; **~ accounting** *n* ACC entscheidungsorientiertes Rech-nungswesen *nt*; **~ control** *n* MGMNT Leitungskontrolle *f*; **~ effectiveness** *n* MGMNT Führungseffektivität *f*, Lei-tungseffektivität *f*; **~ function** *n* MGMNT Führungsfunktion *f*, Managementfunktion *f*; **~ grid** *n* MGMNT *leadership behaviour* Verhaltensgitter *nt*; **~ model** *n* MGMNT *of firm* Führungsmodell *nt*; **~ position** *n* HRM, MGMNT Führungsposition *f*; **~ prerogative** *n* HRM Vorrecht *nt* der Unternehmens-leitung; **~ staff** *n pl* HRM, MGMNT Führungskräfte *f pl*; **~ structure** *n* HRM Leitungsstruktur *f*, MGMNT Füh-rungsstruktur *f*, Leitungsstruktur *f*; **~ style** *n* MGMNT Führungsstil *m*, Leitungsstil *m*; **~ utility function maximization** *n* MGMNT Maximierung *f* der Nutzen-funktion des Managements

manager: **~'s office** *n* ADMIN Büro *nt* des Geschäfts-führers

managers: **~ and workers** *n pl* HRM Manager und Arbeiter *m pl*

managing *adj* ADMIN geschäftsführend, leitend, GEN COMM verwaltend, HRM geschäftsführend, leitend, MGMNT, POL verwaltend; **~ agent** *n* MGMNT Geschäftsführer, in *m,f*; **~ director** *n* (*MD*) GEN COMM Geschäftsführer, in *m,f*, HRM Generaldirektor, in *m,f*, Vorsitzende(r) *mf* [decl. as adj] des Vorstandsgremiums, MGMNT Hauptgeschäftsführer, in *m,f*, geschäftsführen-der Direktor *m* (*GD*), geschäftsführende Direktorin *f* (*GD*), leitender Direktor *m*, leitende Direktorin *f*; **~ owner** *n* TRANSP *shipping* vom Eigner eingesetzter Schiffsführer *m*; **~ partner** *n* HRM geschäftsführender Gesellschafter *m*, geschäftsführende Gesellschafterin *f*

man: **the ~ at the top** *n infrml* HRM Mann *m* an der Spitze

Manchester: **~ Commodity Exchange** *n* STOCK Manche-ster Warenbörse *f*; **~ school** *n BrE* ECON Manchester-Liberalismus *m*, Manchester-Schule *f*

M&A *abbr* (*mergers and acquisitions*) ECON Fusionen und Akquisitionen *f pl*, Fusionen und Übernahmen *f pl*, STOCK Beteiligungs- und Fusionsberatungsservice *m*, Firmenfusionen und Übernahmen *f pl*, Fusionen und Akquisitionen *f pl*

mandant *n* ACC Auftraggeber, in *m,f*

mandarin *n* POL *government* Apparatschik *m* (*infrml*), Bonze *m* (*infrml*), entfremdeter Funktionär *m*, schlauer Bürokrat *m*

mandate *n* GEN COMM Vollmacht *f*, Geschäftsbesorgungsvertrag *m*, LAW Mandat *nt*, Vollmacht *f*, Auftrag *m*, Vollstreckungsbeschluß *m*

mandated: **~ program** *AmE*, **~ programme** *BrE n* MEDIA verordnetes Programm *nt*

mandatory 1. *adj* LAW obligatory zwingend, obligatorisch; **2.** *n* LAW Beauftragte(r) *mf* [decl. as adj]

mandatory: **~ copy** *n* S&M *advertising* Pflichtwerbetext *m*; **~ provision** *n* INS Mußvorschrift *f*, unabdingbare Bestimmung *f*; **~ quote period** *n* STOCK obligatorischer Notierungszeitraum *m*; **~ retirement** *n* *AmE* (*cf compulsory retirement BrE*) HRM Zwangspensionierung *f*

man: **~-hour** *n* MGMNT Arbeitsstunde *f*, Mannstunde *f*

manifest 1. *n* IMP/EXP Ladungsverzeichnis *nt*, Manifest *nt*, TRANSP Ladungsmanifest *nt*, Manifest *nt*; **2.** *vt* IMP/EXP im Ladungsverzeichnis anzeigen, im Ladungsverzeichnis aufführen, manifestieren, TRANSP manifestieren

manifest: **~ of cargo** *n* TRANSP Ladungsmanifest *nt*; **~ crisis** *n* POL deutliche Krise *f*, offensichtliche Krise *f*

manifold *n* GEN COMM Durchschlagpapier *nt*

man: **the ~ in the street** *phr* GEN COMM der kleine Mann *m*, der Mann *m* auf der Straße

manipulate *vt* GEN COMM manipulieren; ♦ **~ accounts** ACC die Bücher frisieren (*infrml*); **~ the market** STOCK Börsenkurse manipulieren

manipulation *n* GEN COMM, MGMNT Manipulation *f*

manipulator *n* GEN COMM, IND Manipulator, in *m,f*, STOCK *of the market* Kursbeeinflusser, in *m,f*

man: **~-machine system** *n* ADMIN Mann-Maschinen System *nt*; **~-made** *adj* IND künstlich, nachgemacht, synthetisch; **~-made fiber** *AmE*, **~-made fibre** *BrE n* ENVIR, IND Chemiefaser *f*; **~-made material** *n* ENVIR, IND Kunststoff *m*

manning *n* HRM Bemannung *f*, Besetzung *f*; **~ level** *n* HRM, MGMNT Personalbestand *m*, TRANSP Bemannung *f*

manpower *n* GEN COMM, HRM, MGMNT Mitarbeiter *m pl*, Personalbestand *m*; **~ aid** *n* HRM *for developing countries* Mitarbeiterunterstützung *f*; **~ analysis** *n* ECON Mitarbeiteranalyse *f*; **~ assignment** *n* ECON Personaleinsatz *m*; **~ audit** *n* ACC, HRM Beurteilung *f* von Personal, Prüfung *f* von Personal; **~ costs** *n pl* ACC Lohnkosten *pl*; **~ forecast** *n* HRM Personalbedarfsprognose *f*; **~ forecasting** *n* GEN COMM Beschäftigungsprognose *f*, HRM Personalbedarfsprognose *f*; **~ management** *n* HRM Personalverwaltung *f*, Personalwirtschaft *f*, MGMNT Arbeitskräfteeinsatz *m*, Arbeitskräftelenkung *f*; **~ planning** *n* HRM Personalplanung *f*, MGMNT Arbeitskräfteplanung *f*, Personalplanung *f*, Stellenplanung *f*; **~ policy** *n* HRM Beschäftigungspolitik *f*; **~ reserve** *n* IND Arbeitskräftereserven *f pl*

manual 1. *adj* GEN COMM, HRM manuell; **2.** *n* GEN COMM *reference* Handbuch *nt*

manual: **~ feed** *n* COMP manuelle Papierzuführung *f*, manueller Papiereinzug *m*; **~ labor** *AmE*, **~ labour** *BrE n* ECON, HRM ungelernte Arbeitskräfte *f pl*

manually *adv* GEN COMM manuell

manual: **~ skill** *n* HRM manuelle Fertigkeit *f*; **~ system** *n* (*MS*) TRANSP *shipping* Handsystem *m*, manuelles System *nt*; **~ union** *n* *BrE* HRM Arbeitergewerkschaft *f*; **~ work** *n* HRM körperliche Arbeit *f*; **~ worker** *n* HRM Arbeiter, in *m,f*

manufacture 1. *n* IND *product* Erzeugnis *nt*, Produkt *nt*,

production Erzeugung *f*, Fertigung *f*, Herstellung *f*; **2.** *vt* IND erzeugen, fabrizieren, herstellen, fertigen, produzieren, fabrikmäßig herstellen; ♦ **~ under licence** *BrE*, **~ under license** *AmE* IND unter Lizenz herstellen

manufactured *adj* (*mfd*) GEN COMM hergestellt, IND produziert (*prod.*); **~ goods** *n pl* ECON Industriegüter *nt pl*; **~ home** *n* PROP Fertighaus *nt*; **~ product** *n* ECON Fabrikat *nt*, Industrieerzeugnis *nt*

manufacturer *n* (*mfr*) GEN COMM Hersteller, in *m,f*, IND Erzeuger, in *m,f*, Fabrikant, in *m,f*, Herstellerfirma *f*, Industrielle(r) *mf* [decl. as adj], Produzent, in *m,f*, S&M Hersteller, in *m,f*; **~'s agent** *n* S&M Vertreter, in *m,f* der Herstellerfirma; **~'s brand** *n* S&M *marketing* Herstellermarke *f*

manufacturers': ~ and contractors' liability insurance *n* INS *company* Produkthaftpflichtversicherung *f* der Hersteller und Bauunternehmer

manufacturer: **~'s export agent** *n* IMP/EXP Exportvertreter, in *m,f*; **~'s output insurance** *n* INS *company* Produktionsausfallversicherung *f*; **~'s price** *n* S&M *sales* Herstellungspreis *m*, Erzeugerpreis *m*; **~'s recommended price** *n* (*MRP*) S&M *sales* Herstellerrichtpreis *m*

manufactures *n pl* ECON Industriegüter *nt pl*

manufacturing *n* IND Fabrikation *f*, fabrikmäßige Herstellung *f*, Herstellung *f*, Verarbeitung *f*; **~ activity** *n* IND Fabrikationstätigkeit *f*, Produktionstätigkeit *f*; **~ area** *n* GEN COMM Erzeugungsgebiet *f*; **~ base** *n* IND Produktionsbasis *f*; **~-based economy** *n* ECON industrialisierte Volkswirtschaft *f*, Industriegesellschaft *f*; **~ capacity** *n* IND Fabrikationskapazität *f*, Fertigungskapazität *f*, Produktion *f*, Produktionskapazität *f*; **~ control** *n* IND Betriebskontrolle *f*, Fertigungssteuerung *f*, Kontrolle *f* der Fertigung; **~ cost** *n* ACC *profit and loss account* Fertigungskosten *pl*, Produktionskosten *pl*; **~ costs** *n pl* ECON Fertigungskosten *pl*, IND Erzeugungskosten *pl*; **~ expenses** *n pl* ACC Herstellungskosten *pl*; **~ industry** *n* IND Erzeugerindustrie *f*, Fertigungsindustrie *f*, verarbeitende Industrie *f*; **~ inventory** *n* IND *production* Lagerbestand *m* im Fertigungsbereich; **~ method** *n* IND Fertigungsmethode *f* Bearbeitungsverfahren *nt*; **~ order** *n* IND Fertigungsauftrag *m*; **~ overheads** *n pl* ACC Herstellungskosten *pl*, ECON Fertigungsgemeinkosten *pl*, Fertigungskosten *pl*, Herstellungsgemeinkosten *pl*; **~ plant** *n* IND Produktionsanlage *f*, Fabrik *f*; **~ process** *n* IND Herstellungsprozess *m*; **~ rights** *n pl* LAW Herstellungsrechte *nt pl*; **~ sector** *n* ECON Fertigungsbereich *m*, Produktionszweig *m*, IND Produktionssektor *m*, Produktionszweig *m*; **~ supplies** *n* ECON Hilfs- und Betriebsstoffe *m pl*; **~ system** *n* IND Fertigungssystem *nt*, Herstellungssystem *nt*; **~ under licence** *BrE*, **~ under license** *AmE n* IND lizenzierte Herstellung *f*, Lizenzfertigung *f*, lizenzberechtigte Herstellung *f*; **~ workforce** *n* HRM Fertigungsarbeitskräfte *f pl*

many: ~-valued function *n* ECON mehrdeutige Funktion *f*

map *n* COMP Abbild *nt*, Abbildung *f*, Bildschirmformat *nt*, Map *f* (*jarg*)

mapping *n* MATH Abbildung *f*

MARAD *abbr* *AmE* (*Maritime Administration*) TRANSP Behörde *f* für Schiffahrtsangelegenheiten, Schiffahrtsministerium *nt*

margin n ACC Gewinnspanne f, Handelsspanne f, ADMIN Marge f, Spanne f, COMP *printed page* Seitenrand m, MEDIA *printed page* Papierrand m, Rand m, Satzrand m, Satzkante f, Seitenrand m, PATENTS *printed page* Rand m, S&M *printed page* Rand m, *difference* Handelsspanne f, Gewinnspanne f, Verdienstspanne f, STOCK *futures* Marge f, Einschußzahlung f; ◆ **on ~** FIN, STOCK kreditfinanziert

margin: **~ account** n STOCK Effektenkreditkonto nt, Einschußkonto nt

marginal adj GEN COMM marginal, Grenz-; **~ account** n BANK Einschußkonto nt; **~ accounts** n pl ECON schlechte Adressen f pl; **~ analysis** n ACC Grenzwertanalyse f, Marginalanalyse f, ECON Grenzwertanalyse f, FIN Grenzbetrachtung f, Marginalanalyse f; **~ areas** n pl S&M Randgebiete nt pl; **~ constituency** n BrE POL nur mit knapper Mehrheit gehaltener Wahlkreis, wackeliger Parlamentssitz m; **~ cost** n ECON Grenzkosten pl, marginale Kosten pl; **~ cost curve** n ECON Grenzkostenkurve f; **~ costing** n ACC Deckungsbeitragsrechnung f, Grenzkostenrechnung f, ECON Grenzplankostenrechnung f, FIN Grenzkostenrechnung f; **~ cost pricing** n ECON Grenzplankostenkalkulation f; **~ costs** n pl ACC, ECON, FIN Grenzkosten pl; **~ efficiency of capital** n ECON Grenzleistungsfähigkeit f des Kapitals; **~ efficiency of investment** n ECON Grenzleistungsfähigkeit f der Investition; **~ employment subsidy** n ECON marginaler Beschäftigungszuschuß m; **~ firm** n ECON Grenzbetrieb m, Grenzproduzent m; **~ groups** n pl POL Randgruppen f pl; **~ income tax rates** n pl TAX Einkommenssteuergrenzsatz m, marginale Einkommenssteuersätze m pl

marginalism n ECON Marginalanalyse f, Marginalismus m

marginalist n ECON Marginalist m

marginalize vt ECON marginalisieren

marginally adv GEN COMM marginal

marginal: **~ note** n ADMIN Randbemerkung f; **~ physical product** n (MPP) ECON physisches Grenzprodukt nt; **~ pricing** n ACC Grenzkostenrechnung f, marginale Preisfestsetzung f, ECON Grenzpreisbildung f, S&M kostendeckende Preisfestsetzung f; **~ principle of allocation** n (MPA) ECON Marginalprinzip nt der Allokation; **~ private cost** n ECON private Grenzkosten pl; **~ private damage** n (MPD) ECON privater Grenzschaden m; **~ producer** n ECON Grenzproduzent m; **~ product** n IND Grenzprodukt nt; **~ productivity** n ECON Grenzproduktivität f; **~ productivity theory** n ECON Grenzproduktivitätstheorie f; **~ product of labor** AmE, **~ product of labour** BrE n ECON Grenzprodukt nt der Arbeit; **~ profit** n ECON Grenzerlös m, Grenzumsatz m; **~ propensity to consume** n (MPC) ECON marginale Konsumquote f; **~ propensity to import** n (MPM) IMP/EXP marginale Importquote f; **~ propensity to invest** n ECON marginale Investitionsquote f; **~ propensity to save** n (MPS) ECON marginale Sparquote f; **~ property** n PROP Grundbesitz, der gerade so viel einbringt, daß die Betriebskosten damit beglichen werden können; **~ rate of substitution** n (MRS) ECON Grenzrate f der Substitution; **~ rate of transformation** n ECON Grenzrate f der Transformation; **~ reserve requirements** n ECON Zuwachsmindestreservesatz m; **~ return on capital** n FIN Grenzertrag m des investierten Kapitals; **~ revenue** n ECON Grenzerlös m;

~ revenue product n (MRP) ECON Grenzerlösprodukt nt, Grenzumsatzprodukt nt; **~ significance** n ECON marginale Signifikanz f; **~ social cost** n ECON soziale Grenzkosten pl; **~ social damage** n (MSD) ECON sozialer Grenzschaden m; **~ tax rate** n TAX Grenzsteuersatz m; **~ utility** n ECON Grenznutzen m; **~ worker** n HRM Arbeitnehmer, der nicht in einem festen, ununterbrochenen Beschäftigungsverhältnis mit nur einem Arbeitgeber steht

margin: **~ between the rates of interest** n ECON Zinsspanne f, Differenz f zwischen Zinssätzen; **~ call** n STOCK Nachschußforderung f; **~ department** n STOCK Abteilung f für Einschußzahlungen; **~ deposit** n STOCK *currency futures* Einschußeinzahlung f; **~ of error** n ACC Sicherheitsspanne f, Spielraum m, ADMIN Fehlergrenze f; **~ of fluctuation** n FIN Bandbreite f, Schwankungsbreite f; **~ leverage** n AmE STOCK *futures* Fremdkapitalanteil m beim Einschuß; **~ maintenance** n STOCK Deckungssumme f; **~ of profit** n ACC Gewinnspanne f; **~ requirement** n STOCK Einschußbedarf m, Einschußpflicht f, Mindesteinschußzahlung f; **~ requirements** n pl BANK Deckungserfordernisse nt pl, Einschußsätze m pl; **~ of safety** n FIN, HRM Sicherheitszuschlag m; **~ security** n STOCK Einschußsicherheit f; **~ shrinkage** n ACC Abnahme f der Gewinnspanne; **~ stop** n ADMIN Randauslösung f; **~ trading** n STOCK Effektendifferenzgeschäft nt, Wertpapierkauf m gegen Kredit

marine adj IMP/EXP, INS, TRANSP See-; **~ engineer** n HRM Schiffsingenieur, in m,f; **~ insurance** n INS Seeversicherung f; **~ insurance fraud** n INS Seeversicherungsbetrug m; **~ insurance policy** n (MIP) INS *marine* Seeversicherungspolice f; **~ insurance policy certificate** n INS Seeversicherungsschein m; **~ piracy** n TRANSP *shipping* Seeräuberei f

mariner n HRM Seemann m

marine: **~ risk analyst** n HRM, INS Seegefahranalytiker, in m,f; **~ superintendent** n HRM Seeaufsichtsbeamte(r) m [decl. as adj], Seeaufsichtsbeamtin f

Maritime: **~ Administration** n AmE (MARAD) TRANSP Behörde für Schiffahrtsangelegenheiten, Schiffahrtsministerium nt

maritime adj IMP/EXP, INS, TRANSP See-

maritime: **~ canal** n TRANSP *shipping* Seekanal m; **~ fraud** n TRANSP *shipping* Seebetrug m; **~ fraud prevention** n TRANSP *shipping* Verhinderung f von Seebetrug

Maritime: **~ Industrial Development Area** n (MIDA) IND Schiffbauindustriegebiet nt

maritime: **~ law** n LAW Seerecht nt; **~ lien** n LAW *shipping* Schiffspfandrecht nt, TRANSP *shipping* Seepfandrecht nt; **~ loan** n FIN Bodmereidarlehen nt; **~ peril** n INS Seegefahr f; **~ risk** n INS *marine* Seerisiko nt; **~ service** n TRANSP Seedienst m; **~ shipping** n TRANSP Seeschiffahrt f, Seeversand m; **~ terminal** n TRANSP *shipping* Hafenbahnhof m; **~ trade** n IMP/EXP Seehandel m

Maritime: **~ Transport Committee** n TRANSP OECD Seetransportkomitee nt

mark 1. n PATENTS Eigentumszeichen nt, Fabrikmarke f, Fabrikzeichen nt, Handelsmarke f, Handelszeichen nt, Marke f, Schutzmarke f, Schutzzeichen nt, Warenmarke f, Warenzeichen nt; ◆ **no ~** (n/m) TRANSP *shipping* keine

Markierung, ohne Markierung; **2.** *vt* GEN COMM bezeichnen; ◆ ~ **stock** ACC Lagerbestand kennzeichnen, *stocktaking* Inventur machen; ~ **to the market** STOCK Options- und Terminkontrakte täglich bewerten

mark down *vt* S&M *price* herabsetzen, reduzieren

mark up *vt* S&M *price* höher auszeichnen, heraufsetzen

mark: ~**-down** *n* S&M *price* Preisherabsetzung *f*, Preissenkung *f*

marked *adj* GEN COMM *decline, difference* stark; ~ **check** *AmE*, ~ **cheque** *BrE n* BANK, ECON bestätigter Scheck *m*; ~ **down** *adj* S&M reduziert; ~**-to-market** *adj* ECON, STOCK *futures* zum letzten Börsenkurs bewertet

market 1. *n* ECON, S&M Markt *m*, STOCK Börse *f*; ◆ **at** ~ STOCK *price* zum letzten Kurs; **at the** ~ **call** STOCK zur Börsenkursnotierung; **come onto the** ~ S&M auf den Markt kommen; **at the** ~ **price** FIN zu Marktpreisen, STOCK zum Börsenkurs; **on the** ~ PROP auf dem Markt; **2.** *vt* GEN COMM, S&M vertreiben

marketable *adj* GEN COMM verkäuflich, S&M marktfähig, STOCK *shares* börsenfähig; ~ **bond** *n* STOCK börsengängige Obligation *f*, börsengängige Schuldverschreibung *f*; ~ **equities** *n pl* STOCK börsengängige Dividendenwerte *m pl*; ~ **title** *n* PROP Eigentumsrecht *nt*, rechtsmängelfreier Grundbesitz *m*; ~ **value** *n* S&M Marktwert *m*

market: ~ **acceptance** *n* S&M Akzeptanz *f*; ~ **adjustment** *n* ECON Marktanpassung *f*; ~ **aggregation** *n* ECON Marktaggregation *f*; ~ **aim** *n* S&M Marktziel *nt*; ~ **analysis** *n* S&M *market research*, STOCK Marktanalyse *f*; ~ **analyst** *n* HRM, S&M, STOCK Marktanalyst *m*; ~ **anticipation** *n* S&M Markterwartung *f*; ~ **appraisal** *n* S&M Markteinschätzung *f*; ~ **area** *n* S&M Absatzgebiet *nt*, Marktbereich *m*; ~ **attrition** *n* S&M Marktzermürbung *f*; ~ **averages** *n pl* STOCK Durchschnittswerte *m pl*; ~ **awareness** *n* S&M Bekanntheit *f* auf dem Markt; ~ **balance of payments** *n* ECON Marktzahlungsbilanz *f*; ~ **base** *n* S&M Marktbasis *f*; ~ **basket** *n* ECON Warenkorb *m*; ~ **behavior** *AmE*, ~ **behaviour** *BrE n* S&M Marktverhalten *nt*; ~ **capitalization** *n* STOCK Börsenkapitalisierung *f*, Marktkapitalisierung *f*; ~ **clearing** *n* ECON Marktclearing *nt*; ~ **clearing price** *n* ECON Gleichgewichtspreis *m*; ~ **comparison approach** *n* PROP *real estate* Marktvergleich *m*; ~ **concentration** *n* ECON Marktkonzentration *f*; ~ **confidence** *n* S&M Vertrauen *nt* in den Markt; ~ **connection** *n* S&M Marktverbindung *f*; ~ **coverage** *n* S&M Absatzanteil *m*, Absatzbereich *m*; ~ **creation** *n* S&M Marktschaffung *f*; ~ **day** *n* STOCK Börsentag *m*; ~ **dealing** *n* FIN Börsenhandel *m*; ~ **demand** *n* ECON Gesamtnachfrage *f*, Marktnachfrage *f*; ~ **development** *n* S&M Marktentwicklung *f*; ~ **discrimination coefficient** *n* ECON Marktdiskriminierungskoeffizient *m*; ~ **distortion** *n* ECON Marktverzerrung *f*; ~ **domination** *n* S&M Marktbeherrschung *f*; ~**-dominant firm** *n* ECON marktbeherrschendes Unternehmen *nt*; ~**-driven** *adj* GEN COMM, S&M marktbestimmt; ~ **dynamics** *n pl* S&M Marktdynamik *f*; ~ **economy** *n* ECON Marktwirtschaft *f*, marktwirtschaftliche Ordnung *f*

marketeer *n* HRM, S&M Absatzexperte *m*, Absatzexpertin *f*, Absatzfachkraft *f*

market: ~ **entry** *n* S&M Marktzugang *m*, Markteinstieg *m*; ~ **entry guarantee scheme** *n* S&M Garantiekonzept *nt* für den Einstieg in einen Markt; ~ **entry option** *n*

IMP/EXP Marktzutrittsoption *f*; ~ **environment** *n* S&M Marktumfeld *nt*; ~ **equilibrium** *n* ECON Marktgleichgewicht *nt*; ~ **evaluation** *n* S&M Marktbewertung *f*; ~ **expansion** *n* S&M Marktexpansion *f*, Markterweiterung *f*; ~ **exploration** *n* S&M Markterkundung *f*; ~ **failure** *n* ECON Marktmängel *m pl*, Marktversagen *nt*; ~ **forces** *n pl* ECON, S&M Marktkräfte *f pl*; ~ **forecast** *n* GEN COMM, S&M Marktprognose *f*; ~ **form** *n* ECON Marktform *f*; ~ **fragmentation** *n* ECON, S&M Marktzersplitterung *f*; ~ **gap** *n* S&M Marktlücke *f*; ~ **gardener** *n BrE* (*cf truck farmer AmE*) ECON Gemüseanbauer *m*; ~ **gardening** *n BrE* (*cf truck farming AmE*) ECON *agriculture* Gartenbaubetrieb *m*, Gemüseanbau *m*, GEN COMM Erwerbsgartenbau *m*; ~ **holding** *n* STOCK *pricing strategy* Börsenbeteiligung *f*; ~ **index** *n* STOCK Börsenindex *m*

marketing *n* S&M Lehre *f* vom Warenabsatz, Marketing *nt*; ~ **agreement** *n* S&M Absatzvereinbarung *f*; ~ **appropriation** *n* S&M genehmigter Marketingfonds *m*; ~ **audit** *n* S&M Absatzprüfung *f*; ~ **authorization** *n* S&M *for pharmaceuticals* Marktzulassung *f*; ~ **board** *n* S&M Ausschuß *m* für Marketing; ~ **budget** *n* S&M Marketingbudget *nt*; ~ **chain** *n* S&M Absatzkette *f*; ~ **channel** *n* S&M Absatzkanal *m*; ~ **communications** *n pl* S&M Marketing-Kommunikation *f*; ~ **communications channel** *n* S&M Marketing-Kommunikationskanal *m*; ~ **communications manager** *n* S&M Marketing-Kommunikationsmanager, in *m,f*; ~ **communications mix** *n* S&M Marketing-Kommunikationsmix *m*; ~ **concept** *n* S&M Marketingkonzept *nt*; ~ **conference** *n* S&M Absatzkonferenz *f*; ~ **costs** *n pl* S&M Vertriebskosten *pl*; ~ **cost variance** *n* S&M Marketingkostenabweichung *f*; ~ **department** *n* S&M Vertriebsabteilung *f*; ~ **director** *n* HRM Marketingdirektor, in *m,f*, MGMNT Marketingdirektor, in *m,f*, Marketingleiter, in *m,f*, Leiter, in *m,f* der Abteilung Marketing; ~ **intelligence** *n* S&M Marktinformationen *f pl*; ~ **manager** *n* HRM Absatzleiter, in *m,f*, Marketingdirektor, in *m,f*, MGMNT Marketingdirektor, in *m,f*, Leiter, in *m,f* der Abteilung Marketing; ~ **mix** *n* S&M Marketingmix *m*; ~ **models** *n pl* S&M Absatzmodelle *nt pl*; ~ **objective** *n* S&M Absatzziel *nt*; ~ **officer** *n* HRM Marketing-Sachbearbeiter, in *m,f*; ~ **orientation** *n* S&M Absatzorientierung *f*; ~ **plan** *n* S&M Absatzplanung *f*; ~ **policy** *n* S&M Absatzpolitik *f*; ~ **profile** *n* S&M Marketingprofil *nt*; ~ **research** *n* S&M Marktforschung *f*, Absatzanalyse *f*; ~ **and sales plan** *n* S&M Vertriebs- und Umsatzplan *m*; ~ **services** *n pl* S&M Marketing-Dienstleistungen *f pl*; ~ **services manager** *n* S&M Marketing-Dienstleistungsmanager, in *m,f*; ~ **strategy** *n* S&M Absatzstrategie *f*; ~ **tools** *n pl* S&M Absatzwerkzeuge *nt pl*

market: ~ **intelligence** *n* S&M umfassende Marktinformationen *f pl*; ~ **leader** *n* GEN COMM, S&M Marktführer *m*; ~ **leadership** *n* S&M Marktführung *f*; ~ **letter** *n AmE* STOCK Börsenbrief *m*; ~ **maker** *n* STOCK Marktmacher *m*, Market Maker *m*, Primärhändler *m*, Wertpapierhändler, in *m,f*; ~ **management** *n* MGMNT Marktsteuerung *f*, S&M Absatzmanagement *nt*; ~ **mechanism** *n* ECON Marktmechanismus *m*; ~ **niche** *n* S&M Marktlücke *f*; ~ **objective** *n* S&M Marktzielsetzung *f*; ~ **opening** *n* S&M Marktöffnung *f*; ~ **operation** *n* STOCK Marktvorgang *m*; ~ **opportunity** *n* S&M Absatzmöglichkeit *f*; **~-oriented** *adj* ECON, S&M marktorientiert; **~ outperformer** *n* STOCK Marktführer *m*; **~ participant** *n* STOCK *futures* Marktteilnehmer, in *m,f*; **~ penetration** *n* S&M Marktdurchdringung *f*, Marktpenetration *f*

marketplace *n* GEN COMM Marktplatz *m*, S&M Markt *m*, Marktplatz *m*

market: **~ plan** *n* S&M Absatzplan *m*; **~ planning** *n* S&M Vertriebsplanung *f*; **~ plunge** *n* *AmE* STOCK Kurseinbruch *m*; **~ position** *n* STOCK *currency* Marktposition *f*; **~ potential** *n* S&M Marktpotential *nt*; **~ power** *n* ECON Marktmacht *f*; **~ presence** *n* S&M Marktpräsenz *f*; **~ price** *n* ECON, S&M Marktpreis *m*; **~ pricing** *n* FIN marktorientierte Preisfestsetzung *f*; **~ profile** *n* S&M Marktprofil *nt*; **~ prospects** *n pl* S&M Absatzerwartungen *f pl*; **~ prospects service** *n* S&M Absatzmarktberatungsdienst *m*; **~ rate** *n* STOCK Effektivverzinsung *f*, Effektivzins *m*; **~ rate of discount** *n* GEN COMM effektiver Diskontsatz *m*; **~ rate of interest** *n* ECON Marktzins *m*; **~ rating** *n* S&M Marktkurs *m*; **~ reach** *n* S&M Reichweite *f* des Marktes; **~ receptiveness** *n* STOCK Marktaufnahmefähigkeit *f*; **~ recognition** *n* S&M Markterkennung *f*; **~ rent** *n* ECON Marktmiete *f*; **~ report** *n* S&M Marktbericht *m*, STOCK Börsenbericht *m*; **~ research** *n* S&M Marktforschung *f*

Market: **~ Research Corporation of America** *n* (*MRCA*) S&M Marktforschungsgesellschaft von Amerika

market: **~ researcher** *n* S&M Marktforscher, in *m,f*; **~ resistance** *n* S&M Marktwiderstand *m*; **~ review** *n* FIN Marktüberblick *m*; **~ rigger** *n* STOCK Kurstreiber, in *m,f*; **~ rigging** *n* STOCK Kursmanipulation *f*; **~ risk premium** *n* STOCK Marktrisikoprämie *f*; **~ saturation** *n* GEN COMM, S&M Marktsättigung *f*; **~ sector** *n* S&M Marktsektor *m*; **~ segment** *n* S&M Marktsegment *nt*, Teilmarkt *m*; **~ segmentation** *n* S&M Marktsegmentierung *f*; **~ selection overseas** *n* ECON *international trade* Erschließung *f* von Überseemärkten; **~-sensitive** *adj* S&M marktempfindlich, STOCK marktreagibel; **~ sensitivity** *n* S&M Marktempfindlichkeit *f*; **~ share** *n* GEN COMM, S&M Marktanteil *m*; **~ situation** *n* GEN COMM Marktlage *f*; **~ skimming** *n* S&M *pricing strategy* Marktabschöpfung *f*; **~ slump** *n* STOCK Kurseinsturz *m*, Marktrückgang *m*; **~ socialism** *n* ECON Marktsozialismus *m*; **~ stabilization** *n* STOCK Kursstabilisierung *f*; **~ strength** *n* GEN COMM, S&M Marktstärke *f*; **~ structure** *n* ECON, GEN COMM, S&M Marktstruktur *f*; **~ study** *n* GEN COMM Marktuntersuchung *f*, S&M *market research* Marktstudie *f*; **~ support** *n* S&M Marktunterstützung *f*; **~ survey** *n* S&M *market research* Marktuntersuchung *f*; **~ system** *n* ECON Marktwirtschaft *f*; **~ target selection** *n* S&M Zielgruppenauswahl *f*; **~ test** *n* S&M Markterkundung *f*; **~ testing** *n* S&M Markttest *m*, Markterkundung *f*; **~ tone** *n* STOCK Börsenstimmung *f*, Marktklima *nt*; **~ transparency** *n* GEN COMM, S&M Markttransparenz *f*; **~ trend** *n* ECON Markttrend *m*, Preistendenz *f*, GEN COMM Markttrend *m*, S&M Markttendenz *f*, Markttrend *m*; **~ value** *n* ACC *balance sheets* Tageswert *m*, Zeitwert *m*, Marktwert *m*, FIN Verkehrswert *m*, Börsenwert *m*, Marktwert *m*, Tageswert *m*, Kurswert *m*, S&M Marktwert *m*, STOCK Börsenwert *m*, Kurswert *m*, Marktwert *m*; **~ value clause** *n* INS *property* Marktwertklausel *f*, Zeitwertklausel *f*; **~-value-weighted index** *n* STOCK gewichteter Preisindex *m*,

marktwertgewichteter Index *m*; **~ view** *n* STOCK Marktmeinung *f*; **~ weight** *n* S&M Marktgewicht *m*

mark: **~ with high reputation** *n* PATENTS hochangesehene Marke *f*

marking *n* FIN Kennzeichnung *f*, Kursfeststellung *f*, Kurskennzeichen *nt*, Notierung *f*, GEN COMM Beschriftung *f*; **~ down** *n* S&M Preisherabsetzung *f*, Preissenkung *f*, Reduzierung *f*, STOCK Preisanhebung *f*, Anheben *nt*

mark: **~-on** *n* ECON *price* Bruttoaufschlag *m*

Markov: **~ chain model** *n* MATH Markov-Kettenmodell *nt*

mark: **~-up** *n* FIN Preiserhöhung *f*, MEDIA *print* Manuskriptaufbereitung *f*, Notizen *f pl*, Satzvorbereitung *f*, Satzkorrekutur *f*, S&M *price* Preisaufschlag *m*, Aufschlag *m*, *sales*, *margin* Preisheraufsetzung *f*, Preiserhöhung *f*, STOCK Aufschlag *m*; **~-up inflation** *n* ECON Inflationsverstärkung *f* durch Gewinnspannenerhöhung; **~-up pricing** *n* ECON Vollkostenkalkulation *f*, S&M Aufschlagskalkulation *f*, Zuschlagskalkulation *f*

marriage: **~ allowance** *n* TAX Heiratszulage *f*, Ehegattenfreibetrag *m*; **~ deduction** *n* TAX Heiratsabzug *m*, Ehegattenabzug *m*; **~ penalty** *n* *AmE* TAX Zulage *f* bei Eheschließung

married *adj* LAW, TAX verheiratet; **~ couples' allowance** *n* *BrE* TAX Ehegattenfreibetrag *m*

marry: **~ up** *vt* S&M *sales, auction* einen schlecht verkäuflichen Gegenstand einem anderen beifügen

marshal *vi* TRANSP rangieren, ordnen

marshalling: **~ yard** *n* TRANSP Rangierbahnhof *m*

Marshall-Lerner: **~ condition** *n* ECON Marshall-Lerner-Bedingung *f*

Marshall: **~ Plan** *n* ECON Marshall-Plan *m*

mart *n* S&M *sales* Markt *m*, Handelszentrum *nt*

martingale *n* MATH Martingal *nt*

Marxian: **~ economics** *n* ECON Marxsche Ökonomie *f*

Marxism *n* POL Marxismus *m*

mask *vt* S&M *advertising* retuschieren

masked: **~ advertising** *n* ECON Schleichwerbung *f*

Maslow: **~'s hierarchy of needs** *n* MGMNT *motivation theory* Maslowsche Bedürfnispyramide *f*

mass *n* S&M Masse *f*

mass advertising *n* MEDIA, S&M Massenwerbung

mass-produce *vt* IND fabrikmäßig herstellen

massage *vt* ACC frisieren (*infrml*), FIN *figures* manipulieren

mass: **~ appeal** *n* S&M Massenanreiz *m*; **~ communication** *n* COMP Massenkommunikation *f*

massive *adj* GEN COMM groß

mass: **~ mailing** *n* MEDIA Massenkommunikation *f*; **~ market** *n* S&M Massenmarkt *m*; **~ marketing** *n* S&M Massenabsatz *m*; **~ media** *n* MEDIA Massenmedien *nt pl*; **~ memory** *n* COMP Massenspeicher *m*; **~ movement** *n* POL Massenbewegung *f*; **~-produced** *adj* IND in Großserie hergestellt, serienmäßig hergestellt; **~ production** *n* IND fabrikmäßige Herstellung *f*, Massenfertigung *f*, Massenproduktion *f*, Mengenfertigung *f*, Großserienanfertigung *f*, Serienproduktion *f*, serienmäßige Herstellung *f*; **~ rapid transit** *n* (*MRT*) TRANSP Massenschnelltransit *m*; **~ redundancy** *n* HRM Massenentlassung *f*; **~ risk** *n* INS Massenrisiko *nt*; **~ storage** *n* GEN COMM, TRANSP Massenspeicher *m*; **~ storage device** *n* COMP

Massenspeicher *m*; **~ transit railroad** *n AmE* (*MTR*) TRANSP Massentransitbahn *f*; **~ transit railway** *n BrE* (*MTR*) TRANSP Massentransitbahn *f*; **~ transit system** *n AmE* TRANSP Massentransitsystem *nt*; **~ unemployment** *n* ECON Massenarbeitslosigkeit *f*

master *n* HRM *shipping* Kapitän *m*, MEDIA *broadcast* Original *nt*, TRANSP *shipping* Kapitän *m*; **~ budget** *n* ACC Gesamtbudget *nt*

Master: **~ of Business Administration** *n* (*MBA*) HRM, MGMNT, WEL Magister *m* der Betriebswirtschaft

master: **~ card** *n* COMP Hauptkarte *f*; **~ change** *n* (*MC*) TRANSP *aviation* Änderung *f* der Originalvorlage, Änderung *f* des Bezugsteils

Master: **~ of Commerce** *n* (*MCom*) HRM Magister *m* der Betriebswirtschaft

master: **~ copy** *n* COMP Masterband *nt*, Systemurband *nt*, GEN COMM Originalkopie *f*; **~ document** *n* COMP Ursprungsbeleg *m*

Master: **~ of Economics** *n* (*MEcon*) HRM ≈ Diplomvolkswirt, in *m,f*, ≈ Diplomökonom, in *m,f*, Magister *m* der Wirtschaftswissenschaften

master: **~ file** *n* COMP Stammdatei *f*, GEN COMM Hauptdatei *f*; **~ lease** *n* PROP Hauptpacht *f*; **~ limited partnership** *n* GEN COMM Personengesellschaft *f*; **~ owner** *n* HRM Kapitäneigner *m*; **~ pallet** *n* TRANSP Hauptpalette *f*; **~ plan** *n* ECON, MGMNT Gesamtplan *m*, Rahmenplan *m*; **~ policy** *n AmE* INS Hauptpolice *f*; **~ production schedule** *n* ECON Primärprogramm *nt*; **~'s certificate** *n* TRANSP *shipping* Kapitänspatent *nt*

Master: **~ of Science** *n* (*MSc*) GEN COMM akademischer Grad der naturwissenschaftlichen Fakultät, Magister *m* der Naturwissenschaften

master: **~-servant rule** *n* LAW *commercial* Dienstverhältnis *nt*; **~ tradesman** *n* ECON Meister *m*

masthead *n* MEDIA *newspaper, magazine* Impressum *nt*

MAT *abbr* COMP (*machine-aided translation, machine-assisted translation*) maschinengestützte Übersetzung *f*, GEN COMM (*material*) Material *nt*, IND (*material*) Werkstoff *m*, MATH (*moving annual total*) *statistics* gleitende Jahressumme *f*

match *vt* GEN COMM *results of previous year* entsprechen, S&M *contend with* mithalten können mit

matched *adj* STOCK *securities* parallel; **~ book** *n* STOCK gedeckte Position *f*; **~ sample** *n* S&M abgestimmte Vergleichsstichprobe *f*

matching *adj* S&M zusammenpassend; **~ duty** *n* IMP/EXP Ausgleichszoll *m*; **~ grant** *n* FIN Ausgleichszuschuß *m*; **~ principle** *n AmE* ACC *costs with revenues* Grundsatz *m* der Periodenabgrenzung, Kongruenzprinzip *nt*

material **1.** *adj* GEN COMM *significant* materiell, LAW wesentlich; **2.** *n* (*MAT*) GEN COMM *information* Material *nt*, IND Werkstoff *m*

material: **~ alteration** *n* LAW *of contract* wesentliche Änderung *f* des Vertragsinhaltes; **~ balance** *n* ECON Materialbilanz *f*; **~ barrier** *n* ECON materielles Handelshemmnis *nt*, POL *EU* materielles Handelshemmnis *nt*, wesentliches Handelshemmnis *nt*; **~ circumstances** *n pl* INS, LAW *marine* rechtserhebliche Umstände *m pl*, wesentliche Umstände *m pl*; **~ fact** *n* GEN COMM Faktum *nt*; **~ good** *n* ECON materielles Gut *nt*; **~ interest** *n* ECON *in a company*, TAX wesentliche Beteiligung *f*

materialism *n* POL Materialismus *m*

materiality *n* ACC *accounting reports* Bilanzierungsgrund-

satz *m* der Wesentlichkeit, Erheblichkeit *f*, Wesentlichkeit *f*; **~ level** *n* ACC Gliederungstiefe *f*, Wesentlichkeit *f*

materialize *vi* GEN COMM verwirklichen

materially *adv* GEN COMM materiell

material: **~ representation** *n* INS *marine* Angabe *f* risikoerheblicher Tatbestände, vorvertragliche Anzeigepflicht *f*

materials: **~ accounting** *n* ACC Materialbuchführung *f*, Materialabrechnung *f*; **~ flow system** *n* ECON Materialflußsystem *nt*; **~ handling** *n* GEN COMM Materialtransport *m*; **~ management** *n* ECON Materialwirtschaft *f*, TRANSP Materialwirtschaft *f*, Steuerung *f* des Materialflusses; **~ transfer note** *n* GEN COMM Materialtransferbescheinigung *f*

material: **~ substance** *n* IND Stoff *m*

maternity: **~ allowance** *n* HRM Mutterschaftsgeld *nt*; **~ benefit** *n* HRM Mutterschaftsgeld *nt*; **~ leave** *n* HRM Mutterschaftsurlaub *m*, Karenzurlaub *m*; **~ pay** *n* HRM Mutterschaftsgeld *nt*; **~ protection** *n* INS Mutterschutz *m*

mate: **~'s receipt** *n* (*MR*) IMP/EXP, TRANSP *shipping* Bordempfangsschein *m*, Steuermannsquittung *f*, Verladebescheinigung *f*

mathematical: **~ economics** *n* ECON mathematische Ökonomie *f*; **~ programming** *n* MATH mathematische Programmierung *f*; **~ probability** *n* ECON, IND mathematische Wahrscheinlichkeit *f*

matinée *n* LEIS *theatre* Frühvorstellung *f*

matrix *n* COMP, GEN COMM, MATH, MGMNT, STOCK Matrix *f*; **~ analysis** *n* ECON Matrizenanalyse *f*; **~ management** *n* MATH, MGMNT Matrixmanagement *nt*, Matrixorganisation *f*; **~ of opportunity costs** *n* ECON Opportunitätskostenmatrix *f*; **~ organization** *n* MATH, MGMNT Matrixmanagement *nt*, Matrixorganisation *f*; **~ printer** *n* COMP Matrixdrucker *m*; **~ trading** *n* STOCK Matrixhandel *m*

matter *n* GEN COMM Angelegenheit *f*; ♦ **the ~ is sub judice** LAW die Angelegenheit ist rechtsabhängig

matter: *n* GEN COMM Ansichtssache *f*; **~ in dispute** *n* LAW Streitgegenstand *m*; **~ at hand** *n* GEN COMM vorliegende Sache *f*

matters: **~ to be followed up** *n pl* GEN COMM weiter zu verfolgende Angelegenheiten *f pl*

matter: **~ of urgency** *n* GEN COMM dringende Angelegenheit *f*

mature **1.** *adj* BANK, FIN abgelaufen, verfallen, GEN COMM *debt* fällig, *person* reif; **2.** *vi* BANK, FIN verfallen, *debt* fällig werden

matured *adj* STOCK fällig; **~ bonds** *n pl* STOCK fällige Obligationen *f pl*, fällige Schuldverschreibungen *f pl*; **~ endowment** *n* INS *personal* fällige Auszahlung *f*

mature: **~ economy** *n* ECON reife Volkswirtschaft *f*; **~ market** *n* S&M gesättigter Markt *m*

maturing *adj* BANK, FIN fällig werdend; **~ security** *n* STOCK Wertpapier *nt* mit kurzer Restlaufzeit; **~ value** *n* STOCK in Kürze fällig werdende Valuta

maturity *n* BANK Fälligkeit *f*, Verfall *m*, FIN Fristigkeit *f*, Laufzeit *f*, Fälligkeit *f*; ♦ **at ~** FIN bei Fälligkeit, STOCK bei Fälligkeit, zum Fälligkeitstermin; **on ~** FIN, STOCK bei Fälligkeit

maturity: **~ band** *n* ECON Laufzeit *f*; **~ mismatch** *n* BANK divergierende Laufzeiten *f pl*, Fristeninkongruenz *f*,

Laufzeiteninkongruenz *f*; **~ structure of debt** *n* ECON Fälligkeitsstruktur *f* der Schulden; **~ transformation** *n* FIN Fristentransformation *f*, Laufzeitentransformation *f*; **~ value** *n* BANK, ECON Fälligkeitswert *m*; **~ yield** *n* STOCK Rendite *f* einer langfristigen Anleihe, Rückzahlungsrendite *f*

max. *abbr* (*maximal, maximum*) GEN COMM, MATH max. (*maximal, maximum*)

maximal *adj* (*max.*) GEN COMM, MATH maximal (*max.*), maximum (*max.*)

maximin *n* ECON Maximin-Regel *f*, Minimax-Regel *f*

maximization *n* ACC, FIN, GEN COMM Maximierung *f*; **~ of annual withdrawals** *n* ECON Entnahmemaximierung *f*

maximize *vt* ACC, FIN, GEN COMM maximieren

maximum 1. *adj* (*max.*) GEN COMM, MATH höchstzulässig, maximal (*max.*), maximum (*max.*); **2.** *n* GEN COMM, MATH Maximum *nt*; ◆ **up to a ~ of** GEN COMM bis höchstens

maximum: **~ awareness** *n* S&M maximale Aufmerksamkeit *f*, maximale Sensibilisierung *f*, maximales Bewußtsein *nt*; **~ capacity** *n* IND *production* Höchstkapazität *f*; **~ capital gains mutual fund** *n* STOCK offener Investmentfonds *m* für maximale Kapitalgewinne; **~ coverage** *n* STOCK maximale Deckung *f*; **~ efficiency** *n* ECON Maximaleffizienz *f*; **~ likelihood estimator** *n* (*MLE*) MATH *statistics* Maximum-Likelihood-Schätzfunktion *f*; **~ load** *n* TRANSP Beladungsgrenze *f*, Höchstbelastung *f*, Maximalbelastung *f*; **~ output** *n* ECON Maximalertrag *m*; **~ permissible** *n* GEN COMM höchstzulässig; **~ permitted load** *n* TRANSP Nutzlast *f*; **~ practical capacity** *n* ECON Betriebsoptimum *nt*, praktisch realisierbare Höchstkapazität *f*; **~ price** *n* S&M Höchstpreis *m*; **~ price fluctuation** *n* STOCK maximale Preisfluktuation *f*; **~ rate** *n* BANK Höchstsatz *m*; **~ return** *n* STOCK *options* maximaler Ertrag *m*; **~ risk** *n* STOCK *options* Höchstrisiko *f*

Mb *abbr* (*megabyte*) COMP MB (*Megabyte*), MByte (*Megabyte*)

MBA *abbr* (*Master of Business Administration*) HRM, MGMNT, WEL Magister *m* der Betriebswirtschaft

MBE *abbr* BrE (*Member of the Order of the British Empire*) POL britischer Verdienstorden

MBI *abbr* (*management buy-in*) FIN, MGMNT MBI (*Management-Buy-In*)

MBIM *abbr* (*Member of the British Institute of Management*) MGMNT Mitglied des britischen Instituts für Unternehmensführung

MBO *abbr* ADMIN (*management by objectives*) Management *nt* nach Zielvorgaben, Management *nt* by Objectives, Führung *f* durch Zielvereinbarung, zielgesteuerte Unternehmensführung *f*, FIN (*management buy-out*) MBO (*Management Buy-Out*), MGMNT (*management by objectives*) Management *nt* nach Zielvorgaben, zielgesteuerte Unternehmensführung *f*, (*management buy-out*) MBO (*Management Buy-Out*), Management *nt* by Objectives, Führung *f* durch Zielvereinbarung

MBWA *abbr* (*management by walking around*) MGMNT Management *nt* durch Pflege persönlicher Kontakte

MCA *abbr* ECON (*Monetary Compensatory Amount*) EU WAB (*Währungsausgleichsbetrag*), Grenzausgleich *m*, Grenzausgleichzahlungen *f pl*, MGMNT (*Management Consultants Association*) Verband der Unternehmensberater

M-CATS *abbr* (*municipal certificate of accrual on tax-exempted securities*) STOCK Steuerfreies Kommunalzertifikat mit Zinsansammlung

mcht *abbr* (*merchant*) HRM Kfm. (*Kaufmann*), Kauffrau *f*

mchy *abbr* (*machinery*) ECON, IND Maschinen *f pl*

MCO *abbr* (*miscellaneous charges order*) TRANSP *aviation* Auftrag *m* mit verschiedenen Frachtraten

MCom *abbr* (*Master of Commerce*) HRM Magister *m* der Betriebswirtschaft

MCT *abbr* (*minimum connecting time*) TRANSP Mindestanschlußzeit *f*, Mindestverbindungszeit *f*

MD *abbr* HRM, MGMNT (*managing director*) GD (*Generaldirektor, geschäftsführender Direktor*), Vorsitzende(r) *mf* [decl. as adj] des Vorstandsgremiums, WEL (*doctor of Medicine*) Dr. med. (*Doktor der Medizin*)

MDW *abbr* (*measured daywork*) HRM gemessene Zeitlohnarbeit *f*, Tagesakkord *m*

meal: **~ allowance** *n* HRM Essenszuschuß *m*

meals: **~ on wheels** *n pl* BrE WEL Essen *nt* auf Rädern

mean *n* MATH *statistics* Mittelwert *m*; **~ audit date** *n* S&M mittleres Revisionsdatum *nt*; **~ cost** *n* ACC Durchschnittskosten *pl*; **~ deviation** *n* MATH *statistics* mittlere Abweichung *f*; **~ effective pressure** *n* (*mep*) IND mittlerer Arbeitsdruck *m* (*MEP*)

meaning *n* GEN COMM Bedeutung *f*

mean: **~ price** *n* ECON Mittelkurs *m*; **~ return** *n* STOCK *security analysis* Durchschnittsrendite *f*

means *n* ECON, GEN COMM Mittel *nt pl*; ◆ **live beyond one's ~** GEN COMM über seine Verhältnisse leben; **have the ~ to do sth** GEN COMM über die Mittel verfügen, etw zu tun

means: **~ of conveyance** *n* TRANSP Beförderungsmittel *nt*, Transportmittel *nt*; **~ of payment** *n* BANK Zahlungsmittel *nt*; **~ test** *n* WEL Bedürftigkeitsprüfung *f*; **~ of transport** *n* TRANSP Beförderungsmittel *nt pl*, Transportmittel *nt*

mean: **~ time** *n* (*MT*) GEN COMM mittlere Zeit *f*; **~ time between failures** *n* (*MTBF*) IND mittlerer Ausfallabstand *m*; **~ value** *n* MATH *statistics* Mittelwert *m*

measure 1. *n* ECON Messung *f*, GEN COMM *measuring* Messung *f*, Maß *nt*, *step* Maßnahme *f*, LAW Bemessungsgrundlage *f*, MATH Messung *f*, S&M Maß *nt*, Maßnahme *f*, TAX Bemessungsgrundlage *f*, TRANSP *instrument* Meßinstrument *nt*, Meßgerät *nt*, *standard unit* Maßeinheit *f*; **2.** *vt* ECON, GEN COMM, MATH messen; ◆ **~ sb's performance** HRM jds Leistung messen

measure: **~ of capacity** *n* TRANSP Raummaß *nt*; **~ of control** *n* ECON *prices* Kontrollmaßnahme *f*

measured: **~ daywork** *n* (*MDW*) HRM gemessene Zeitlohnarbeit *f*; Tagesakkord *m*

measure: **~ of economic welfare** *n* (*MEW*) ECON *econometrics* Maß *nt* des wirtschaftlichen Wohlstands, Messung *f* der ökonomischen Wohlfahrt; **~ of indemnity** *n* INS Maßstab *m* für Entschädigung, Umfang *m* der Entschädigung, Umfang *m* der Schadloshaltung

measurement *n* ECON, GEN COMM Messung *f*, Messen *nt*, MATH *measure* Maß *nt*, *measuring* Messung *f*, Messen *nt*, *unit* Maßeinheit *f*, *value* Meßwert *m*, TRANSP *nautical* Tonnengehalt *m*; **~ freight** *n* TRANSP Sperrgut *nt*; ~ **goods** *n pl* TRANSP Sperrgut *nt*; ~ **of ordinal utility** *n* ECON ordinale Nutzenmessung *f*

measure: ~ **of performance** *n* ECON Erfolgskriterium *nt*, Leistungskennzahl *f*

measures: ~ **of monetary policy** *n pl* ECON geldpolitische Maßnahmen *f pl*

measuring *n* ECON, GEN COMM, MATH Messung *f*; ~ **tape** *n* ADMIN, GEN COMM Maßband *nt*

meat: ~-**axe reduction** *n infrml* ECON pauschale Kürzung *f*; ~ **mountain** *n* ECON *EU* Fleischberg *m*

mechanic *n* GEN COMM Reparaturmechaniker, in *m,f*,HRM Monteur, in *m,f*

mechanical: ~ **bookbinding** *n* S&M mechanisches Buchbinden *nt*; ~ **data** *n pl* S&M maschinelle Daten *pl*; ~ **engineering** *n* IND Maschinenbau *m*; ~ **handling equipment** *n* (*MHE*) TRANSP *cargo handling equipment* mechanische Abfertigungsausrüstung *f*, mechanische Förderausrüstung *f*

mechanically *adv* IND maschinell, mechanisch

mechanical: ~ **sales talk** *n* S&M mechanisches Verkaufsgespräch *nt*

mechanism *n* GEN COMM *procedure* Mechanik *f*, Mechanismus *m*, IND Mechanik *f*, mechanischer Teil *m*, Mechanismus *m*

mechanization *n* GEN COMM Mechanisierung *f*, IND *production* Mechanisierung *f*, Umstellung *f* auf Maschinen, TRANSP Mechanisierung *f*

mechanize *vt* GEN COMM, IND, TRANSP mechanisieren, auf mechanischen Betrieb umstellen

mechanized *adj* GEN COMM mechanisiert, IND maschinell, mechanisch, mechanisiert, mit Kraftantrieb, TRANSP mechanisiert

MEcon *abbr* (*Master of Economics*) HRM Magister *m* der Wirtschaftswissenschaften

media *n pl* GEN COMM, MEDIA, S&M *mass media, collectively* Medien *nt pl*; ◆ **give ~ coverage** MEDIA in den Medien Bericht erstatten

media: ~ **analysis** *n* ECON, MEDIA Media-Analyse *f*, Werbeträgeranalyse *f*, S&M Medienanalyse *f*; ~ **analyst** *n* S&M Medienberater, in *m,f*; ~ **broker** *n* S&M Medienmakler, in *m,f*; ~ **budget** *n* MEDIA Medienbudget *nt*; ~ **buyer** *n* S&M *advertising* Streuplaner, in *m,f*; ~ **buying** *n* S&M *advertising* Medienwerbung *f*; ~ **commission** *n* S&M Medienkommission *f*; ~ **coverage** *n* MEDIA, S&M Berichterstattung *f* in den Medien, Medienberichterstattung *f*, Berichterstattung *f* durch die Werbeträger; ~ **evaluation** *n* MEDIA, S&M Bewertung *f* als Werbeträger; ~ **event** *n* MEDIA Medienereignis *nt*; ~ **fragmentation** *n* S&M Media-Fragmentierung *f*, *advertising* Zersplitterung *f* durch die Medien; ~-**independent** *adj* S&M medienunabhängig; ~ **mix** *n* S&M Medienmischung *f*, Medien-Mix *m*

median *n* MATH *statistics* Median *m*; ~ **income** *n* ECON mittleres Einkommen *nt*

media: ~ **option** *n* S&M *advertising* Mediaoption *f*; ~ **owners** *n pl* S&M Medienbesitzer *m pl*; ~ **plan** *n* S&M *advertising* Mediaplan *m*; ~ **planner** *n* S&M *advertising* Mediaplaner, in *m,f*; ~ **planning** *n* MEDIA, S&M *advertising* Medienplanung *f*; ~ **relations** *n pl* MEDIA, S&M Beziehungen *f pl* zu den Medien; ~ **research** *n* S&M Medienforschung *f*; ~ **schedule** *n* MEDIA Medienprogramm *nt*; ~ **selection** *n* MEDIA *advertising*,

S&M Medienauswahl *f*; ~ **strategy** *n* S&M Medienstrategie *f*

mediate *vi* HRM vermitteln; ◆ ~ **between** HRM vermitteln zwischen [+dat]

mediation *n* ECON Schlichtung *f*, HRM Vermittlung *f*; ~ **board** *n* HRM Vermittlungsstelle *f*; ~ **committee** *n* HRM Vermittlungsstelle *f*

mediator *n* HRM Vermittler, in *m,f*

media: ~ **weight** *n* S&M *advertising* Gesamtwerbeaufwand *m*

Medicaid *n AmE* GEN COMM *for poor people* staatlicher Gesundheitsdienst *m*

medical *adj* GEN COMM, WEL medizinisch, ärztlich; ~ **assistance** *n* GEN COMM, WEL medizinische Hilfe *f*; ~ **care to out-patients** *n* WEL *health* ambulante Versorgung *f*; ~ **costs** *n pl* GEN COMM, WEL medizinische Kosten *pl*; ~ **engineering** *n* IND medizinische Technik *f*; ~ **examination** *n* WEL ärztliche Untersuchung *f*; ~ **grounds** *n pl* HRM gesundheitliche Gründe *m pl*, medizinische Gründe *m pl*, WEL medizinische Gründe *m pl*; ~ **insurance** *n* HRM, INS, WEL Krankenversicherung *f*; ~ **insurance premium** *n* HRM, INS, WEL Krankenversicherungsprämie *f*; ~ **officer of health** *n* (*MOH*) HRM Amtsarzt *m*, Amtsärztin *f*

Medicare *n AmE* GEN COMM, WEL *for people over 65* staatlicher Gesundheitsdienst *m*

mediocre *adj* GEN COMM mittelmäßig

Mediterranean: ~ **basin** *n* GEN COMM Mittelmeerbecken *nt*; ~ **bloc** *n* GEN COMM Mittelmeerblock *m*

medium 1. *adj* GEN COMM mittelmäßig; ◆ **in the ~ term** GEN COMM mittelfristig; **2.** *n* GEN COMM *communication*, MEDIA, S&M *radio, television* Medium *nt*

medium: ~ **account** *n* ECON mittlerer Betrieb *m*; ~-**dated** *adj* STOCK mittelfristig; ~ **of exchange** *n* ECON Tauschmittel *m*, Valuta *f*; ~-**frequency radiotelephony** *n* TRANSP *shipping* drahtloses Mittelfrequenzfernsprechwesen *nt*, Mittelfrequenzsprechfunk *m*; ~ **of redemption** *n* ECON Rückzahlungsmittel *nt*, Tilgungsmittel *nt pl*

mediums *n pl* BANK, FIN, STOCK mittelfristige Schuldtitel *m pl*

medium: ~-**sized enterprise** *n* GEN COMM mittelständischer Betrieb *m*; ~-**term** *adj* FIN, GEN COMM mittelfristig; ~-**term bond** *n* STOCK mittelfristige Obligation *f*, mittelfristige Schuldverschreibung *f*; ~-**term Euronote** *n* STOCK *money market* mittelfristige Euronote *f*; ~-**term financial strategy** *n* (*MTFS*) ECON mittelfristige Finanzstrategie *f*; ~-**term instrument** *n* STOCK mittelfristiges Handelspapier *nt*; ~-**term loan** *n* (*MTL*) BANK mittelfristiger Kredit *m*, mittelfristiges Darlehen *nt*; ~-**term notes** *n pl* (*MTN*) BANK, FIN, STOCK mittelfristige Schuldtitel *m pl*

meet *vt* ECON befriedigen, FIN *costs* begleichen, GEN COMM treffen, *conditions* erfüllen, einhalten, *costs, targets* erreichen, bestreiten, *obligations* nachkommen, MGMNT *goal* erreichen; ◆ ~ **a deadline** GEN COMM einen Termin einhalten; ~ **costs** ACC für die Kosten aufkommen, GEN COMM die Kosten tragen, die Kosten bestreiten; ~ **demands** MGMNT Forderungen erfüllen; ~ **the needs of** GEN COMM den Bedarf an etw decken

meeting *n* GEN COMM Treffen *nt*, Zusammenkunft *f*, MGMNT Beratung *f*, Sitzung *f*, Versammlung *f*; ~ **of the minds** *n* LAW *commercial* Übereinstimmung *f*, Wil-

lenseinigung *f*; **~ place** *n* GEN COMM Treffpunkt *m*;
~ point *n* GEN COMM Treffpunkt *m*

mega- *pref* COMP, GEN COMM, IND Mega-

mega *adj* GEN COMM riesengroß

megabit *n* COMP Megabit *nt*

megabucks *n pl infrml* GEN COMM große Geldsumme

megabyte *n* (*Mb*) COMP Megabyte *nt* (*MB, MByte*)

megacorp *n* GEN COMM Megaunternehmen *nt*

mega: **~ electron volt** *n* (*MeV*) IND Megaelektronenvolt
nt (*MeV*)

megalomania *n* HRM Größenwahn *m*

megalomaniac *n* HRM Größenwahnsinnige(r) *mf* [decl.
as adj]

megawatt *n* (*MW*) IND Megawatt *nt*

member *n* HRM *of a union* Mitglied *nt*, *of company*
Aktionär, in *m,f*; **~ of** *n* HRM Angestellte(r) *mf* [decl. as
adj]; **~ bank** *n* AmE BANK dem Zentralbanksystem der
USA angeschlossene Bank; **~ of the board** *n* HRM,
MGMNT Board-Mitglied *nt*, Vorstandsmitglied *nt*; **~ of
the board of management** *n* MGMNT Board-Mitglied
nt, Mitglied *nt* des Verwaltungsrats

Member: **~ of the British Institute of Management** *n*
(*MBIM*) MGMNT Mitglied des Britischen Institutes für
Unternehmensführung

member: **~ of building society** *n* BrE (*cf member of
savings and loan association AmE*) FIN Bausparer, in *m,f*

Member: **~ of Congress** *n* AmE (*cf Member of Parliament BrE*) POL Kongreßabgeordnete(r) *mf* [decl. as adj],
Parlamentsmitglied *nt*

member: **~ corporation** *n* STOCK Börsenmitglied *nt*; **~ of
the crew** *n* TRANSP Mitglied *nt* des Fahrpersonals

Member: **~ of the European Parliament** *n* (*MEP*) POL
Abgeordnete(r) *mf* [decl. as adj] des Europaparlaments,
Mitglied *nt* des Europaparlaments (*MEP*)

member: **~ firm** *n* STOCK Brokerhaus, das Mitglied einer
Börse ist

Member: **~ of the Institute of Chartered Accountants** *n*
BrE (*MICA*) GEN COMM Mitglied des Instituts der
Wirtschaftsprüfer

member: **~ of the jury** *n* LAW Geschworene(r) *mf* [decl. as
adj]

Member: **~ of the Order of the British Empire** *n* (*MBE*)
POL britischer Verdienstorden; **~ of Parliament** *n* BrE
(*MP, cf Member of Congress AmE*) POL Abgeordnete(r)
mf [decl. as adj], (*Abg.*) Parlamentsmitglied *nt*

member: **~ of the public** *n* GEN COMM Mitglied *nt* der
Öffentlichkeit; **~ of savings and loan association** *n*
AmE (*cf member of building society BrE*) FIN
Bausparer, in *m,f*

membership *n* GEN COMM Mitgliedschaft *f*, Zugehörigkeit *f*; **~ card** *n* GEN COMM Mitgliedskarte *f*; **~ fee** *n*
GEN COMM Beitragssatz *m*, Mitgliedsbeitrag *m*

member: **~ short sale ratio** *n* STOCK
Mitgliederleerverkaufsverhältnis *nt*

members: **~ of the House** *n pl* FIN Börsenmitglieder *nt pl*

member: **~ state** *n* (*MS*) POL Mitgliedsstaat *m*; **~ of the
supervisory board** *n* HRM Board-Mitglied *nt*, Mitglied
nt des Aufsichtsrates; **~ of a syndicate** *n* FIN Syndikatsmitglied *nt*; **~ of a union** *n* HRM
Gewerkschaftsmitglied *nt*

memo *n* (*memorandum*) ADMIN kurzer Vermerk *m*,
Memo *nt* (*Memorandum*), GEN COMM Ausarbeitung *f*,
LAW Memo *nt* (*Memorandum*)

memoranda: **~ and articles** *n pl* LAW Satzung *f*; **~ and
articles of association** *n pl* BrE LAW Satzung *f*

memorandum *n* (*memo*) ADMIN kurzer Vermerk *m*,
Memorandum *nt* (*Memo*), GEN COMM Ausarbeitung *f*,
LAW Memorandum *nt* (*Memo*); **~ of association** *n* LAW
Gründungsvertrag *m*; **~ of insurance** *n* INS vorläufige
Deckungszusage *f*, vorläufige Versicherungspolice *f*;
~ of intent *n* GEN COMM Absichtserklärung *f*

memory *n* COMP Speicher *m*, GEN COMM Gedächtnis *nt*;
~ bank *n* COMP Speichermodul *nt*; **~ capacity** *n* COMP
Speicherkapazität *f*; **~ card** *n* COMP Speicherkarte *f*;
~ chip *n* COMP Speicherchip *m*; **~ dump** *n* COMP
Speicherauszug *m*; **~ expansion board** *n* COMP
Speichererweiterungskarte *f*; **~ extension** *n* COMP
Speichererweiterung *f*; **~-hungry** *adj infrml* COMP
speicherfressend; **~ lapse** *n* S&M Gedächtnisschwäche
f; **~ print-out** *n* COMP Speicherausdruck *m*; **~-resident**
adj COMP speicherresident; **~ typewriter** *n* ADMIN
Speicherschreibmaschine *f*, Schreibmaschine *f* mit
Speicher

menial *adj* HRM untergeordnet; **~ job** *n* HRM untergeordnete Tätigkeit *f*

men: **~'s department** *n* S&M Herrenabteilung *f*

mens rea: *n* LAW Schuldbewußtsein *nt*

mental: **~ reservation** *n* LAW *contract law* geheimer
Vorbehalt *m*

mention *vt* GEN COMM erwähnen, zur Sprache bringen

mentioned: **~ below** *adv* GEN COMM unten erwähnt

mention: **~ in leader column** *n* S&M Erwähnung *f* im
Leitartikel

menu *n* COMP, GEN COMM, LEIS Menü *nt*; **~ bar** *n* COMP
Menüleiste *f*; **~-driven** *adj* COMP menügesteuert

MEP *abbr* (*Member of the European Parliament*) POL
Abgeordnete(r) *mf* [decl. as adj] des Europaparlaments,
MEP (*Mitglied des Europaparlaments*)

mercantile *adj* ECON, GEN COMM merkantil; **~ affairs** *n pl*
GEN COMM geschäftliche Angelegenheiten *f pl*;
~ agency *n* S&M Auskunftei *f*; **~ bank** *n* BANK, ECON,
FIN Handelsbank *f*; **~ banker** *n* BANK, ECON, FIN
Handelsbanker *m*; **~ broker** *n* LAW Handelsmakler, in
m,f; **~ exchange** *n* STOCK Produktenbörse *f*; **~ law** *n*
LAW Handelsgesetz *nt*; **~ marine** *n* TRANSP Handelsmarine *f*; **~ open-stock burglary insurance** *n* INS
company Geschäftsversicherung *f* des Lagerbestands
gegen Diebstahl; **~ safe burglary insurance** *n* INS
company Geschäftstresor-Einbruchdiebstahlversicherung *f*

mercantilism *n* ECON, GEN COMM Merkantilismus *m*

merchandise *n* S&M Waren *f pl* (*Wa.*); **~ balance of
trade** *n* ECON, GEN COMM Handelsbilanz *f*; **~ broker** *n*
S&M Produktenmakler, in *m,f*; **~ control** *n* S&M
Warenkontrolle *f*; **~ inventory** *n* ACC *balance sheets*
Bestände *m pl* an Handelswaren; **~ movements** *n pl*
ECON Warenverkehr *m*

merchandiser *n* HRM *in supermarket* beratender Verkäufer *m*, beratende Verkäuferin *f*

merchandise: **~ samples** *n* ECON Warenproben *f pl*

merchandising *n* S&M Steuerung *f* von Vertrieb und
Verkauf; **~ director** *n* HRM Leiter, in *m,f* der
Verkaufsförderungsabteilung; **~ service** *n* S&M Ver-
triebs- und Verkauftätigkeit *f*

merchant *n* (*mcht*) HRM Kaufmann *m*, Kauffrau *f*

merchantable *adj* ECON, GEN COMM handelsfähig, S&M
lieferbar; **~ quality** *n* ECON handelsübliche Qualität *f*,

S&M *legal* marktgängige Ware *f*; ~ **title** *n* PROP Eigentumsrecht *nt*, rechtsmängelfreier Grundbesitz *m*

merchant: ~ **bank** *n* BANK auf das Großkundengeschäft ausgerichtete Bank *f*, *retail* auf das Emissions- und Akzeptgeschäft spezialisierte Bank *f*, Merchantbank *f*; ~ **banking** *n* BANK Merchant-Banking *nt*, Großkundengeschäft *nt* der Banken; ~ **capitalism** *n* ECON Handelskapitalismus *m*; ~ **haulage** *n* (*MH*) IMP/ EXP, TRANSP Handelstransport *m*; ~ **marine** *n* TRANSP Handelsmarine *f*; ~ **navy** *n* TRANSP Handelsmarine *f*

Merchant: ~ **Navy Establishment** *n* BrE (*MNE*) GEN COMM Niederlassung der Handelsmarine

merchant: ~ **service** *n* TRANSP Handelsschiffahrt *f*; ~ **ship** *n* TRANSP Handelsschiff *nt*; ~ **shipping** *n* TRANSP Handelsschiffahrt *f*

Merchant: ~ **Shipping Act** *n* (*MSA*) TRANSP Handelsschiffahrtsgesetz *nt*

merchant: ~ **trading** *n* ECON Transithandel *m*; ~ **vessel** *n* TRANSP Handelsschiff *nt*

Mercosur *n* ECON *international trade* Freihandelsabkommen zwischen Argentinien, Brasilien, Paraguay und Uruguay

merge 1. *n* COMP *document, computer file* Mischen *nt*; **2.** *vt* ADMIN *files* zusammenfügen, zusammenlegen, COMP mergen (*jarg*), ECON fusionieren, FIN fusionieren, verschmelzen, STOCK fusionieren; ♦ ~ **and purge** S&M *advertising* überschneidungsfreie Adressenliste herstellen; **3.** *vi* ECON fusionieren, FIN fusionieren, verschmelzen, STOCK fusionieren, sich zusammenschließen

merger *n* FIN Fusion *f*, Unternehmenszusammenschluß *m*, Verschmelzung *f*, STOCK Fusion *f*, Unternehmenszusammenschluß *m*; ~ **accounting** *n* BrE (*cf pooling of interests AmE*) ACC Fusionsbuchführung *f*, Konsolidierung *f*; ~ **arbitrage** *n* STOCK Fusionsarbitrage *f*; ~ **company** *n* FIN fusionierende Gesellschaft *f*

mergers: ~ **and acquisitions** *n pl* (*M&A*) ECON Fusionen und Akquisitionen *f pl*, Fusionen und Übernahmen *f pl*, STOCK Beteiligungs- und Fusionsberatungsservice *m*, Fusionen und Akquisitionen *f pl*, Firmenfusionen und Übernahmen *f pl*

merger: ~ **wave** *n* ECON Fusionswelle *f*

meridian *n* GEN COMM Meridian *m*

merit: ~ **bad** *n* ECON meritorisches Ungut *nt*; ~ **good** *n* ECON meritorisches Gut *nt*; ~ **increase** *n* (*cf merit raise AmE*) HRM *pay* leistungsbezogene Gehaltssteigerung *f*

meritocracy *n* HRM Leistungsgesellschaft *f*

merit: ~ **pay** *n* HRM Leistungslohn *m*; ~ **raise** *n* AmE (*cf merit increase*) HRM leistungsbezogene Gehaltssteigerung *f*; ~ **rating** *n* GEN COMM, HRM Leistungsbewertung *f*, Leistungsbeurteilung *f*; ~ **wants** *n pl* ECON meritorische Bedürfnisse *nt pl*

merits: on its ~ *phr* LAW *examination* materiellrechtlich

MES *abbr* (*minimum efficiency scale*) ECON minimale Produktivitätsskala *f*

mesoeconomy *n* ECON Mesoökonomik *f*

mesokurtic *n* MATH *statistics* mesokurtische Verteilungskurve *f*

message *n* COMMS, COMP Meldung *f*, GEN COMM Mitteilung *f*, S&M Botschaft *f*; ~ **feedback** *n* COMMS Meldung *f*, COMP Fehlerkontrolle *f* mit Rückwärtsübertragung; ~ **handling** *n* COMMS, COMP Nachrichtenbehandlung *f*; ~ **processing** *n* ADMIN Nachrichtenverarbeitung *f*; ~ **source** *n* S&M

Nachrichtenquelle *f*; ~ **switching** *n* COMMS, COMP Speichervermittlung *f*

messenger *n* COMMS *office*, GEN COMM Bote *m*, Botin *f*, Melder *m*; ~ **boy** *n* COMMS, GEN COMM Bote *m*, Botenjunge *m*; ~ **robbery insurance** *n* INS *company* Botenberaubungsversicherung *f*

metacentric: ~ **height** *n* GEN COMM metazentrische Höhe *f*

metal *n* GEN COMM Metall *nt*; ~ **can** *n* ENVIR, TRANSP Metalldose *f*; ~ **industry** *n* IND Metallindustrie *f*

metalliferous: ~ **ore** *n* ENVIR Metallerz *nt*

metallist *n* ECON Vertreter, in *m,f* des Metallismus

metallurgist *n* HRM Metallurg, in *m,f*

metal: ~ **market** *n* STOCK Metallmarkt *m*; ~ **packaging** *n* ENVIR, IND Metallverpackung *f*; ~ **trading** *n* ECON Metallhandel *m*

metalworker *n* HRM Metallarbeiter, in *m,f*

metamarketing *n* S&M Meta-Marketing *nt*

metastable: ~ **equilibrium** *n* ECON neutrales Gleichgewicht *nt*

meteoric *adj* GEN COMM rasant; ~ **rise** *n* HRM, MGMNT rasanter Aufstieg *m*

meter AmE *see* metre BrE

meterage *n* AmE (*cf meter rate*) GEN COMM Zählerpreis *m*

metered *adj* COMMS freigestempelt; ~ **mail** *n* COMMS freigestempelte Post *f*

meter: ~ **rate** *n* (*cf meterage AmE*) GEN COMM Zählerpreis *m*

metes: ~ **and bounds** *n pl* PROP *limits of property* natürliche Grenzlinien *f pl*

methetics *n* MATH Methetik *f*

method *n* GEN COMM Methode *f*, MGMNT Arbeitsweise *f*, Methode *f*, Verfahren *nt*, S&M Methode *f*; ~ **of calculation** *n* GEN COMM Berechnungsmethode *f*

methodology *n* MGMNT Methodenlehre *f*, Methodik *f*

method: ~ **of payment** *n* FIN Zahlungsmodus *m*, Zahlungsweise *f*; ~ **of preparation** *n* ACC *of accounts* Buchhaltungsmethode *f*

methods: ~ **of depreciation** *n* ECON Abschreibungsmethoden *f pl*, Abschreibungsarten *f pl*; ~ **engineering** *n* GEN COMM Methodentechnik *f*; ~ **study** *n* GEN COMM Methodenuntersuchung *f*; ~ **-time measurement** *n* (*MTM*) MGMNT Methods-Times-Measurement *nt* (*MTM*)

method: ~ **of valuation** *n* ACC Bewertungsmethode *f*

me: ~ **-too-product** *n* ECON Eigenentwicklung *f*

metre *n* BrE (*m*) GEN COMM Meter *m* (*m*)

metres: ~ **per second** *n pl* BrE GEN COMM Meter *m pl* pro Sekunde

metrication *n* GEN COMM metrische Messung *f*

metric: ~ **system** *n* GEN COMM metrisches System *nt*; ~ **tonne** *n* (*mton*) GEN COMM metrische Tonne *f*

metropolitan *adj* GEN COMM großstädtisch; ~ **area** *n* ECON Großstadtgebiet *nt*; ~ **town** *n* GEN COMM Großstadt *f*

MEW *abbr* (*measure of economic welfare*) ECON Maß *nt* des wirtschaftlichen Wohlstands, Wohlfahrtsmaß *nt*, Messung *f* der ökonomischen Wohlfahrt

mezzanine: ~ **bracket** *n* STOCK Zwischenstufe *f*; ~ **finance** *n* FIN Mischung *f* zwischen Fremd- und Eigenkapitalfinanzierung, ungesicherte Restfinanzie-

rung *f*; ~ **funding** *n* FIN Mezzanin-Finanzierung *f*;
~ **level** *n* FIN *venture capital* Mezzanin-Ebene *f*

MFA *abbr* ADMIN (*Ministry of Foreign Affairs*) Außenministerium *nt*, Ministerium *nt* für auswärtige
Angelegenheiten, ECON (*multi-fiber arrangement AmE*,
multi-fibre arrangement BrE) Multifaserabkommen *nt*,
Welttextilabkommen *nt*, POL (*Ministry of Foreign
Affairs*) ≈ Außenministerium *nt*, Ministerium *nt* für
auswärtige Angelegenheiten

mfd *abbr* (*manufactured*) GEN COMM hergestellt, prod.
(*produziert*)

MFN *abbr* ECON (*most favored nation AmE*, *most favoured
nation BrE*) Land *nt* mit Meistbegünstigungsstatus,
(*most favored nation treatment AmE*, *most favoured
nation treatment BrE*) Meistbegünstigung *f*

M-form *n* ECON M-Form *f*

mfr *abbr* (*manufacturer*) GEN COMM, IND, S&M *company*
Herst. (*Hersteller*)

mg *abbr* (*milligram, milligramme*) GEN COMM mg
(*Milligramm*)

MGR *abbr* (*manager*) HRM, MGMNT Leiter, in *m,f*,
Manager, in *m,f*

MH *abbr* (*merchant haulage*) IMP/EXP, TRANSP Handelstransport *m*, *by road* Handelstransport *m* per LKW, *by
sea* Handelsschiffahrt *f*

MHE *abbr* (*mechanical handling equipment*) TRANSP *cargo
handling* mechanische Abfertigungsausrüstung *f*,
mechanische Förderausrüstung *f*

MICA *abbr* BrE (*Member of the Institute of Chartered
Accountants*) ACC Mitglied des Instituts der Wirtschaftsprüfer

micro- *pref* GEN COMM Mikro-

microchip *n* COMP Mikrochip *m*, Mikroprozessor *m*

microcomputer *n* COMP Kleinrechner *m*, Mikrorechner
m

microdisk *n* COMP Mikrodiskette *f*

microeconomic *adj* ECON mikroökonomisch

microeconomics *n* ECON Mikroökonomie *f*,
Mikroökonomik *f*

microelectronic *adj* IND *production* mikroelektronisch

microelectronics *n* IND *production* Mikroelektronik *f*

microfiche *n* ADMIN Mikrofiche *m*

microfilm *n* ADMIN Mikrofilm *m*; ~ **reader** *n* ADMIN
Mikrofilmlesegerät *nt*

micromarketing *n* S&M Mikromarketing *nt*

microphone *n* COMMS Mikrofon *nt*

microprocessor *n* COMP Mikrochip *m*, Mikroprozessor
m

microproduction: ~ **function** *n* ECON
Mikroproduktionsfunktion *f*

microprogram *n* COMP Mikroprogramm *nt*

microsecond *n* GEN COMM Mikrosekunde *f*

Microsoft®: ~ **disk operating system** *n* (*MS-DOS*)
COMP Microsoft®-Plattenbetriebssystem *nt* (*MS-DOS*)

MIDA *abbr* (*Maritime Industrial Development Area*) IND
Schiffsbauindustriegebiet *nt*

Mid-America: ~ **Commodity Exchange** *n* STOCK Mittel-
amerikanische Warenbörse *f*

midcareer: ~ **plateau** *n* HRM mittleres Karriereplateau *nt*

middle *adj* GEN COMM mittlere; ~ **income bracket** *n*
ECON mittlere Einkommensteuergruppe *f*, mittlere
Einkommensteuerklasse *f*, mittlere Einkommensstufe

f; ~ **issue price** *n* STOCK *options* mittlerer Emissionskurs *m*; ~ **management** *n* HRM Management *nt* auf
mittlerer Führungsebene, Mittelmanagement *nt*, mittlere Führungsebene *f*, MGMNT mittlere Führungsebene
f; ~ **manager** *n* HRM, MGMNT mittlere Führungskraft *f*;
~ **market business** *n* ECON Mittelunternehmen *nt*;
~ **office** *n* FIN Vermittlungsbüro *nt*; ~ **price** *n* STOCK
Einheitskurs *m*; ~ **range of the market** *n* S&M mittlere
Marktposition *f*; ~ **rate** *n* ECON, FIN Devisenmittelkurs
m

Middle: ~ **Seven** *n* ACC die Nummern 7 bis 13 der größten
Wirtschaftsprüfungsgesellschaften

middle: ~ **strike price** *n* STOCK mittlerer Abschlußkurs
m, mittlerer Optionsbasispreis *m*

middling: ~ **quality** *n* ECON Mittelsorte *f*

midnight: ~ **deadline** *n* GEN COMM mitternächtlicher
Schlußtermin *m*

mid: ~ **price** *n* STOCK Mittelkurs *m*

midrange *n* COMP Mittelklasse *f*

Midwest: ~ **Stock Exchange** *n* AmE STOCK Midwest
Börse *f*

midyear *n* GEN COMM Jahresmitte *f*

MIGA *abbr* ECON, FIN (*multilateral investment guarantee
agency*) multilaterale Investitionsgarantieagentur *f*,
(*multilateral investment guarantee association*) multilaterale Vereinigung *f* für Investitionsgarantien

migrant: ~ **labor** *AmE*, ~ **labour** *BrE n* ECON, HRM
Wanderarbeiter *m*, Gastarbeiter *m pl*; ~ **worker** *n*
ECON, HRM ausländischer Arbeitnehmer *m*, ausländi-
sche Arbeitnehmerin *f*, *mobile within country*
Wanderarbeiter *m pl*

migration *n* COMP *data* Systemumstellung *f*, ECON, POL
Wanderung *f*; ~**-fed unemployment** *n* ECON migra-
tionsbedingte Arbeitslosigkeit *f*

migratory: ~ **worker** *n* ECON, HRM Wanderarbeiter *m*,
ausländischer Arbeitnehmer *m*, ausländische Arbeitnehmerin *f*

mileage: ~ **allowance** *n* TAX Kilometergeld *nt*

miles: ~ **per gallon** *n pl* (*mpg*) GEN COMM Meilen *f pl* je
Gallone; ~ **per hour** *n pl* (*mph*) GEN COMM Meilen *f pl*
pro Stunde

milestone: ~ **chart** *n* MATH Meilenstein-Diagramm *nt*

MILIC *abbr* (*moderately indebted low-income country*) FIN
mäßig verschuldetes Land *nt* mit niedrigem Einkommen

military: ~ **Keynesianism** *n* POL militärischer Keynesianismus *m*

milk *vt infrml* GEN COMM *opportunity* ausnehmen, melken
(*infrml*), S&M ausbeuten; ♦ ~ **profits** ECON *infrml*
Gewinne abschöpfen, Gewinne abziehen

milking: ~ **strategy** *n* S&M Ausbeutung *f*

milk: ~ **round** *n* BrE WEL jährliche Besuchsrunde von
Wirtschaftsunternehmen an britischen Universitäten und
Hochschulen zur Anwerbung neuer Mitarbeiter

mill *n* AmE TAX Tausendstel eines Dollars; ~ **cost of sales**
n ECON Herstellungskosten *pl*

milli- *pref* GEN COMM Milli-

milligram *see* milligramme

milligramme *n* (*mg*) GEN COMM Milligramm *nt* (*mg*)

milliliter *AmE see* millilitre *BrE*

millilitre *n BrE* (*ml*) GEN COMM Milliliter *m* (*ml*)

millimeter *AmE see* millimetre *BrE*

millimeters *AmE see* millimetres *BrE*

millimetre *n* BrE (*mm*) GEN COMM Millimeter *m* (*mm*)

millimetres: ~ **per second** *n pl* BrE (*mm/s*) GEN COMM Millimeter *m pl* pro Sekunde (*mm/s*)

million *n* BANK, GEN COMM, MATH Million *f* (*Mio.*, *Mill.*)

millionaire *n* GEN COMM Millionär, in *m,f*; ~ **on paper** *n* GEN COMM Wertpapiermillionär, in *m,f*

millionairess *n* GEN COMM Millionärin *f*

millisecond *n* GEN COMM Millisekunde *f*

MIMIC *abbr* (*moderately indebted middle-income country*) FIN mäßig verschuldetes Land *nt* mit mittlerem Einkommen

min. *abbr* (*minimum*) GEN COMM, MATH Min. (*Minimum*), minimal, Mindest-

min B/L *abbr* (*minimum bill of lading*) IMP/EXP, TRANSP Minimalkonnossement *nt*

mine *n* IND Zeche *f*

mineral: ~-**based economy** *n* ECON auf Bodenschätzen basierende Wirtschaft *f*; ~ **industry** *n* ENVIR Mineralindustrie *f*; ~ **oil product** *n* IND Mineralölprodukt *nt*; ~ **resources** *n pl* ENVIR Bodenschätze *m pl*; ~ **right** *n* LAW, PROP Abbaurecht *nt*

Mines: ~ **and Quarries Inspectorate** *n* BrE WEL Aufsichtsamt für Gruben und Tagebau

mini- *pref* GEN COMM Mini-

minicomputer *n* COMP Minicomputer *m*

mini: ~ **franchise** *n* S&M Abteilungsfranchise *f*

minimal *adj* GEN COMM, MATH minimal; ~ **cost flow** *n* ECON kostenminimaler Fluß *m*; ~ **state** *n* POL Minimalstaat *m*

minimax *n* ECON *games theory* Minimax-Regel *f*; ~ **principle** *n* MGMNT Minimaxprinzip *nt*; ~ **strategy** *n* ECON Minimax-Strategie *f*

minimization *n* ACC, FIN, GEN COMM Minimierung *f*

minimize *vt* ACC, FIN, GEN COMM minimieren

minimum 1. *adj* (*min.*) GEN COMM, MATH minimal, Mindest-; **2.** *n* (*min.*) GEN COMM, MATH Minimum *nt* (*Min.*)

minimum: ~ **acceptable rate of return** *n* FIN minimal zulässige Verzinsung *f*, erstrebte Mindestverzinsung *f*; ~ **balance** *n* BANK Mindestguthaben *nt*; ~ **bill of lading** *n* (*min B/L*) IMP/EXP, TRANSP Minimalkonnossement *nt*; ~ **bill of lading charge** *n* IMP/EXP, TRANSP Mindesfracht *f*, Minimalfracht *f*; ~ **charge** *n* TRANSP Mindestgebühr *f*; ~ **connecting time** *n* (*MCT*) TRANSP Mindestanschlußzeit *f*, Mindestverbindungszeit *f*; ~ **efficiency scale** *n* (*MES*) ECON minimale Produktivitätsskala *f*; ~ **freight** *n* IMP/EXP, TRANSP Mindesfracht *f*; ~ **grade** *n* HRM *required in exam* Mindestnote *m*; ~ **lease payments** *n pl* PROP *capital lease* Mindestpachtzahlung *f*; ~ **lending rate** *n* BrE (*MLR*) BANK Mindestzins *m*, Mindestzinssatz *m*, ECON, FIN Mindestzinssatz *m*; ~ **list heading** *n* BrE (*MLH*) GEN COMM Minimallistenüberschrift *f*; ~ **living wage** *n* HRM Existenzminimum *nt*; ~ **lot area** *n* AmE PROP Mindestgrundstücksgebiet *nt*; ~ **maintenance** *n* STOCK Mindestkontoführung *f*; ~ **margin** *n* STOCK *options* Mindesteinschuß *m*; ~ **pay** *n* GEN COMM Mindestgehalt *nt*; ~ **pension liability** *n* FIN Mindestpensionsverpflichtung *f*; ~ **price change** *n* STOCK Mindestpreisänderung *f*; ~ **price fluctuation** *n* STOCK minimale Preisfluktuation *f*; ~ **quality standard** *n* S&M Mindestqualitätsstandard *m*; ~ **quote size** *n* BrE (*MQS*) STOCK Mindestnotierungsgröße *f*, minimale

Notierungsgröße *f*; ~ **reserve deposit** *n* BANK mindestreserveähnliche Einlage *f*; ~ **reserve requirement** *n* (*MRR*) ECON Mindestreservesoll *nt*; ~ **state** *n* GEN COMM, POL Minimalzustand *m*; ~ **supply price of labor** *AmE*, ~ **supply price of labour** BrE *n* ECON Mindestangebotslohnsatz *m*, Mindestangebotspreis *m* für Arbeit; ~ **temperature** *n* (*MT*) GEN COMM, IND Minimumtemperatur *f*; ~ **transfer** *n* (*MT*) GEN COMM Mindestüberweisung *f*, Mindesttransfer *m*; ~ **wage** *n* ECON garantierter Mindestlohn *m*, HRM gesetzlicher Mindestlohn *m*, Mindestlohn *m*; ~ **yield** *n* ECON Mindestrendite *f*

mining *n* IND Bergbau *m*, Grubenbetrieb *m*; ~ **company** *n* IND bergrechtliche Gesellschaft *f*, Bergbaugesellschaft *f*, Bergbauunternehmen *nt*, Zechengesellschaft *f*, LAW bergrechtliche Gesellschaft *f*; ~ **industry** *n* IND Bergbau *m*, Montanindustrie *f*; ~ **right** *n* LAW, PROP Abbaurecht *nt*; ~ **shares** *n pl* BrE (*cf mining stocks AmE*) STOCK Bergbauaktien *f pl*; ~ **stocks** *n pl AmE* (*cf mining shares BrE*) STOCK Bergbauaktien *f pl*

minipage *n* S&M *advertising* Miniseite *f*

miniseries *n* MEDIA *broadcast* Miniserie *f*

minister *n* HRM *clergy* Pfarrer, Pastor *m*, POL Minister, in *m,f*

ministerial: ~ **order** *n* LAW, POL Ministerialerlaß *m*

minister: ~ **without portfolio** *n* POL Minister, in *m,f* ohne Geschäftsbereich, Minister, in *m,f* ohne Portefeuille

ministry *n* ECON, POL Ministerium *nt*

Ministry: ~ **of Agriculture, Fisheries and Food** *n* BrE (*MAFF*) POL Ministerium für Landwirtschaft, Fischerei und Nahrungsmittel; ~ **of Defence** *n* BrE (*MOD*) ADMIN, POL Verteidigungsministerium *nt*; ~ **of Education** *n* WEL Erziehungsministerium *nt*; ~ **of Finance** *n* BANK Finanzministerium *nt*; ~ **of Foreign Affairs** *n* (*MFA*) POL Außenministerium *nt*; ~ **of International Trade and Industry** *n* (*MITI*) ADMIN, IND, POL japanisches Ministerium für internationalen Handel und Industrie, ≈ Handelsministerium *nt*; ~ **of Overseas Development** *n* BrE ADMIN, ECON, POL Ministerium *nt* für Entwicklungshilfe; ~ **of Tourism** *n* ADMIN, POL Ministerium *nt* für Touristik; ~ **of Transport test** *n* BrE (*MOT*) TRANSP ≈ Technischer Überwachungs-Verein *m* (*TÜV*)

Minneapolis: ~ **Grain Exchange** *n* STOCK Getreidebörse *f* in Minneapolis

minor 1. *adj* GEN COMM gering; **2.** *n* LAW Minderjährige(r) *mf* [decl. as adj]

minor: ~ **defect** *n* LAW *contracts* geringfügiger Mangel *m*

minority *n* ACC, GEN COMM, STOCK Minderheit *f*; ~ **holding** *n* GEN COMM Minderheitsbeteiligung *f*; ~ **interest** *n* ACC Minderheitsbeteiligung *f*, GEN COMM Minderheitsanteil *m*, in Fremdbesitz *m*, Fremdbeteiligung *f*, STOCK Minderheitsbeteiligung *f*; ~ **interests in profit** *n* ACC Minderheitsbeteiligung *f* am Gewinn, Gewinnanteil *m* von Minderheitsbeteiligten, Gewinnanteil *m* Dritter mit Minderheitsbeteiligung; ~ **investment** *n* STOCK Minderheitsbeteiligung *f*; ~ **participation** *n* ACC Minderheitsbeteiligung *f*; ~ **shareholding** *n* STOCK Minderheitsbeteiligung *f*; ~ **stake** *n* STOCK Minderheitsbeteiligung *f*

mint 1. *n* ECON *coins* Münzamt *nt*, Münzanstalt *f*, Münze *f*; **2.** *vt* ECON ausprägen, *coins* prägen

mint: ~ **par** *n* ECON Münzparität *f*; ~ **par of exchange** *n* FIN Münzparität *f*

minus n MATH *symbol* Minus nt; **~ advantage** n GEN COMM negativer Vorteil m; **~ growth** n ECON negatives Wachstum nt, Minuswachstum nt; **~ sign** n MATH Minuszeichen nt

minute: **~ book** n ADMIN *of a company* Protokollbuch nt; **~ number** n FIN *Treasury board* Eintragungsnummer f

minutes n pl ADMIN *legal* Niederschrift f, Protokoll nt

minutiae n pl GEN COMM Einzelheiten f pl

MIP abbr (*marine insurance policy*) INS Seeversicherungspolice f

MIRAS abbr BrE (*Mortgage Income Relief at Source*) TAX Steuervergünstigung f für Hypothekentilgung an der Quelle

mirror: **~ contract** n ECON Gegengeschäft nt

MIS abbr (*management information system*) COMP, MGMNT MIS (*Management-Informationssystem*)

misaligned: **~ rate of exchange** n ECON ständig abweichender Wechselkurs m, falsch angesetztes Kursverhältnis nt

misallocation n ECON Fehlleitung f, Fehlallokation f

misapply vt LAW unzulässig verwenden

misapprehension n GEN COMM Mißverständnis nt

misappropriate vt FIN unterschlagen, veruntreuen, widerrechtlich verwenden

misappropriation n FIN Unterschlagung f, Veruntreuung f, Zweckentfremdung f, widerrechtliche Verwendung f, LAW widerrechtliche Aneignung f; **~ of funds** n GEN COMM widerrechtliche Verwendung f von Geldern; **~ of money** n ACC, LAW Unterschlagung f von Geldern

misc. abbr (*miscellaneous*) GEN COMM Versch. (*Verschiedenes*)

miscalculate vt GEN COMM falsch berechnen

miscalculation n GEN COMM Fehlberechnung f

miscarriage: **~ of justice** n LAW *false judgment* Fehlurteil nt, Rechtsbeugung f

miscellaneous adj (*misc.*) GEN COMM Verschiedenes nt (*Versch.*); **~ charges order** n (*MCO*) IMP/EXP Auftrag m mit verschiedenen Frachtraten

Miscellaneous: **~ Estimates Committee** n POL ständiger Haushaltsausschuß für sonstige Voranschläge

miscellaneous: **~ expenses** n pl ACC verschiedene Kosten pl

miscoding n COMP Fehlcodierung f

misconduct n HRM Verfehlung f

misconnection n LEIS falsche Verbindung f

misdeclaration n TAX *VAT* falsche Erklärung f

misdemeanor AmE *see* misdemeanour BrE

misdemeanour n LAW Vergehen nt

misery: **~ index** n ECON Elendsindex m

misfile vt GEN COMM falsch ablegen

mishandling n GEN COMM Fehlbearbeitung f, falsche Handhabung f

misjudgment n LAW Fehlurteil nt

mislead vt GEN COMM, LAW, PATENTS, S&M irreführen

misleading adj GEN COMM, LAW, PATENTS, S&M irreführend; **~ advertising** n GEN COMM, S&M irreführende Werbung f

mismanage vt MGMNT schlecht wirtschaften, schlecht verwalten

mismanagement n MGMNT Mißmanagement nt, Mißwirtschaft f, schlechte Verwaltung f

mismatched: **~ maturity** n BANK, ECON divergierende Laufzeiten f pl, Fristeninkongruenz f, Laufzeiteninkongruenz f

misperformance n LAW *contract law* Schlechterfüllung f

mispricing n FIN falsch auszeichnen, mit falschem Preis versehen

misprint n ADMIN Druckfehler m

misrepresent vt GEN COMM falsch darstellen

misrepresentation n LAW *transaction* falsche Angaben f pl; **~ intended to deceive** n LAW arglistige Täuschung f

miss vt GEN COMM *appointment* verpassen

missing: **~ bill of lading** n IMP/EXP (*mslb*), TRANSP (*msbl*) *shipping* fehlendes Konnossement nt; **~ cargo** n (*msca*) TRANSP Fehlfracht f, fehlende Fracht f; **~ flight** n TRANSP überfälliger Flug m; **~ market** n ECON fehlender Markt m; **~ person** n LAW Verschollene(r) mf [decl. as adj]; **~ vessel** n TRANSP verschollenes Schiff nt

mission n S&M Auftrag m, Ziel nt

missionary: **~ work** n HRM Missionarsarbeit f

mission: **~ budgets** n pl S&M aufgabenorientierte Budgets nt pl; **~ costing** n S&M aufgabenorientierte Kostenplanung f, aufgabenorientierte Kostenerfassung f; **~ statement** n MGMNT Auftragsbericht m

misstatement: **~ of age** n INS *personal* falsche Altersangabe f, unrichtige Altersangabe f

mistake n GEN COMM Fehler m, Irrtum m; **~ of law** n LAW Rechtsirrtum m

mistaken adj GEN COMM, INS irrtümlich

mistype vt ADMIN sich verschreiben

misunderstand vt GEN COMM mißverstehen

misunderstanding n GEN COMM Mißverständnis nt

misuse n ENVIR *chemicals* Mißbrauch m

misused: **~ funds** n ECON zweckentfremdete Mittel nt pl

MITI abbr (*Ministry of International Trade and Industry*) ADMIN, IND, POL japanisches Ministerium für internationalen Handel und Industrie, ≈ Handelsministerium nt

mitigating: **~ circumstances** n pl LAW mildernde Umstände m pl

mitigation: **~ of damages** n LAW Schadensminderung f

mix n GEN COMM Mix m, Zusammensetzung f, MEDIA *recording* Mischung f, S&M Gemischtwaren f pl, Mischung f

mixed adj ACC, ECON, FIN, IND, S&M gemischt, Misch-; **~ account** n STOCK Kundenkonto nt mit Plus- und Minuspositionen; **~-activity holding company** n ACC, BANK Holdinggesellschaft f mit verschiedenen Tätigkeitsbereichen, FIN gemischte Dachgesellschaft f, Holdinggesellschaft f mit verschiedenen Tätigkeitsbereichen, GEN COMM, STOCK Holdinggesellschaft f mit verschiedenen Tätigkeitsbereichen; **~ bundling** n S&M *sales* Mischbündelung f; **~ cargo** n TRANSP Stückgut nt; **~ carload** n AmE TRANSP *rail* Stückgut nt; **~ consignment** n TRANSP gemischte Ladung f, Sammelladung f; **~ cost** n ACC Mischkosten pl; **~ credit** n FIN Mischkredit m; **~ economic system** n ECON gemischte Wirtschaftsform f, gemischtwirtschaftliches System nt; **~ economy** n ECON Mischwirtschaft f; **~ farming** n ECON *agriculture* landwirtschaftlicher Mischbetrieb m; **~ good** n ECON Mischgut nt; **~ media** n S&M verschiedene Medien nt pl; **~ network** n COMP Verbundnetz nt; **~ perils** n pl AmE INS gemischtes Risiko nt; **~ policy** n INS kombinierte Police f, Zeit- und Reisepolice f; **~ results** n pl GEN COMM gemischte Ergebnisse *nt pl*; **~ signals** *n pl* GEN COMM unklare Signale *m pl*

mixture *n* GEN COMM Vermischung *f*

ml *abbr* (*milliliter AmE, millilitre BrE*) GEN COMM ml (*Milliliter*)

MLE *abbr* (*maximum likelihood estimator*) MATH *statistics* Maximum-Likelihood-Schätzfunktion *f*

MLH *abbr* (*minimum list heading*) GEN COMM Minimallistenüberschrift *f*

MLM *abbr* (*multilevel marketing*) S&M Marketing *nt* auf mehreren Ebenen, mehrschichtiges Marketing *nt*

MLR *abbr BrE* (*minimum lending rate*) BANK Mindestzins *m*, Mindestzinssatz *m*, ECON, FIN Mindestzinssatz *m*

MLS *abbr AmE* (*Multiple Listing Service*) PROP Maklerkartell

mm *abbr* (*millimeter AmE, millimetre BrE*) GEN COMM mm (*Millimeter*)

MMC *abbr BrE* ECON (*Monopolies and Mergers Commission*) Monopol- und Fusionskommission *f*, Kartellaufsicht *f*, FIN (*money market certificate*) Geldmarktzertifikat *nt*

MMDA *abbr AmE* (*money market deposit account*) FIN verzinsliches Einlagenkonto *nt*, Geldmarkteinlagenkonto *nt*

MMF *abbr AmE* (*money market fund*) STOCK Geldmarkt-Investmentfonds *m*

MMMF *abbr AmE* (*money market mutual fund*) FIN Geldmarktfonds *m*

mm/s *abbr* (*millimeters per second AmE, millimetres per second BrE*) GEN COMM mm/s (*Millimeter pro Sekunde*)

MNC *abbr* (*multinational corporation*) GEN COMM multinationales Unternehmen *nt*

MNE *abbr* GEN COMM (*Merchant Navy Establishment*) Niederlassung der Handelsmarine, (*multinational enterprise*) multinationale Gesellschaft *f*, multinationales Unternehmen *nt*

MO *abbr* GEN COMM (*modus operandi*) Vorgehensweise *f*, S&M (*mail order*) Postauftrag *m*

mobicentric: **~ manager** *n* MGMNT mobizentrischer Manager *m*, mobizentrische Managerin *f*

mobile 1. *adj* COMMS mobil, GEN COMM beweglich, mobil; **2.** *n* COMMS *telephone* Handy *nt* (*infrml*), bewegliches Telefon *nt*, mobiles Telefon *nt*, Mobiltelefon *nt*, schnurloses Telefon *nt*, tragbares Telefon *nt*

mobile: **~ crane** *n* (*MC*) TRANSP Mobilkran *m*; **~ home certificate** *n AmE* STOCK hypothekarisch gesichertes Wertpapier, das auf Basis von Hypotheken für Wohnmobile ausgegeben wird; **~ home park** *n* PROP Siedlung für transportable Wohnhäuser; **~ offshore drilling unit** *n* (*MODU*) IND Bohrinsel *f*, Bohrplattform *f*; **~ phone** *n* COMMS bewegliches Telefon *nt*, mobiles Telefon *nt*, Mobiltelefon *nt*, Handy *nt* (*infrml*), schnurloses Telefon *nt*, tragbares Telefon *nt*; **~ telephone** *n* COMMS bewegliches Telefon *nt*, mobiles Telefon *nt*, Mobiltelefon *nt*, Handy *nt* (*infrml*), schnurloses Telefon *nt*, tragbares Telefon *nt*; **~ worker** *n* HRM mobile Arbeiterin *f*, mobiler Arbeiter *m*

mobility *n* ECON Arbeitsmobilität *f*, HRM Arbeitsmobilität *f*, Mobilität *f*, S&M, WEL Mobilität *f*; **~ clause** *n BrE* HRM Mobilitätsklausel *f*; **~ of labor** *AmE*, **~ of labour** *BrE n* ECON, HRM Arbeitsmobilität *f*; **~ status** *n* ECON Mobilitätsstatus *m*; **~ trap** *n* ECON Mobilitätsfalle *f*

mobilize *vt* ECON flüssig machen, mobilisieren

MoC *abbr BrE* (*mother of chapel*) HRM *publishing, printing trade unions* Betriebsratsvorsitzende *f* [decl. as adj]

mock: **~-up** *n* S&M Anschauungsmodell *nt*, Verkaufsmodell *nt*

MOD *abbr BrE* (*Ministry of Defence*) ADMIN, POL Verteidigungsministerium *nt*

mode *n* COMP Betrieb *m*, Modus *m*, MATH *statistics* häufigster Wert *m*, Modus *m*; **~ of transport** *n pl* TRANSP Beförderungsmittel *nt pl*, Transportmittel *nt pl*

model *n* GEN COMM, MATH Modell *nt*; **~ articles of association** *n* ECON Mustersatzung *f*

modeling *AmE see* **modelling** *BrE*

modelling *n BrE* MATH Erstellung *f* eines Modells, Modellbildung *f*

model: **~ profile** *n* GEN COMM Modellprofil *nt*

modem *n* (*modulator-demodulator*) COMP, MATH Modem *nt* (*Modulator-Demodulator*); **~ link** *n* COMP Modemverbindung *f*

moderate: **~ income** *n* FIN bescheidenes Einkommen *nt*

moderately: **~ indebted low-income country** *n* (*MILIC*) FIN mäßig verschuldetes Land *nt* mit niedrigem Einkommen; **~ indebted middle-income country** *n* (*MIMIC*) FIN mäßig verschuldetes Land *nt* mit mittlerem Einkommen

modern *adj* ECON, GEN COMM, IND modern; **~ economics** *n* ECON moderne Volkswirtschaftslehre *f*; **~ economy** *n* ECON moderne Volkswirtschaft *f*, moderne Wirtschaft *f*

modernization *n* GEN COMM Modernisierung *f*

modernize *vt* GEN COMM modernisieren

modernizing: **~ and refitting older buildings** *n* GEN COMM Altbausanierung *f*

modest *adj* ECON gemäßigt, moderat, GEN COMM *increase* bescheiden; **~ cyclical recovery** *n* ECON schwache zyklische Erholung *f*

modestly *adv* GEN COMM *slightly* geringfügig

modification *n* ACC, ECON Modifizierung *f*, GEN COMM Modifizierung *f*, *data* Änderung *f*, MATH Modifizierung *f*, PROP *buildings* Änderung *f*, S&M Modifizierung *f*

modified: **~ absorption costing** *n* ECON modifizierte Vollkostenrechnung *f*; **~ accrual** *n* ACC modifizierte Abgrenzungsposten *m pl*; **~ life insurance** *n* INS *personal* abgeänderte Lebensversicherung *f*, flexible Lebensversicherung *f*; **~ mean** *n* MATH modifizierter Mittelwert *m*; **~ rebuy** *n* S&M *marketing* modifizierter Wiederkauf *m*; **~ union shop** *n AmE* HRM Betrieb *m* mit modifizierter Gewerkschaftsbindung

modify *vt* ACC, ECON modifizieren, GEN COMM anpassen, modifizieren, verändern, *product* abändern, MATH, S&M modifizieren

MODU *abbr* (*mobile offshore drilling unit*) IND Bohrinsel *f*, Bohrplattform *f*

modular *adj* IND erweiterbar; **~ concept** *n* IND Baukastenprinzip *nt*; **~ housing** *n AmE* PROP Errichten *nt* von Häusern in Modellbauweise, Errichten *nt* von Häusern nach dem Baukastensystem

modularity *n* GEN COMM Modularität *f*, MATH Baukastenprinzip *nt*

modular: **~ production** *n* IND bausteinartige Produktion *f*, erweiterbare Produktion *f*, Modularproduktion *f*, Produktion *f* nach dem Baukastensystem; **~ structure** *n* ECON Modulstruktur *f*

modulation *n* COMMS Modulation *f*

modulator: ~-**demodulator** *n* (*modem*) COMP Modulator-Demodulator *m* (*Modem*)

modulus: ~ **of precision** *n* ECON Präzisionsmaß *nt*

modus *n* LAW Auflage *f*; ~ **operandi** *n* (*MO*) GEN COMM Vorgehensweise *f*, Arbeitsweise *f*

MOH *abbr* (*medical officer of health*) HRM Amtsarzt *m*, Amtsärztin *f*

moisture: ~-**proof** *adj* TRANSP feuchtigkeitsfest

mold *AmE see* **mould** *BrE*

mole *n* TRANSP *shipping* Mole *f*

mom: ~-**and-pop store** *n* *AmE* (*cf corner shop BrE*) S&M Tante-Emma-Laden *m*, Nachbarschaftsladen *m*, Laden *m* an der Ecke, Geschäft *nt* mit Artikeln des täglichen Bedarfs

moment *n* GEN COMM Augenblick *m*, MATH *statistics* Moment *m*

momentum *n* ECON Momentum *nt*

monadic *adj* S&M einstellig, eingliedrig

M1 *abbr BrE* (*money 1*) ECON enggefaßte Geldmengendefinition, M1 (*Geldvolumen M1*)

monetarism *n* ECON, FIN, GEN COMM Monetarismus *m*

monetarist *n* ECON, FIN, GEN COMM *econometrics* Monetarist, in *m,f*; ~ **approach to the balance of payments** *n* ECON, FIN, GEN COMM monetaristischer Zahlungsbilanzansatz *m*, monetaristische Zahlungsbilanzauffassung *f*

monetarization *n* ECON Monetisierung *f*

monetary *adj* ECON, FIN, GEN COMM monetär; ~ **aggregate** *n BrE* ECON Geldmengenaggregat *nt*; ~ **approach to the balance of payments** *n* ECON monetaristische Zahlungsbilanzauffassung *f*, monetaristischer Zahlungsbilanzansatz *m*; ~ **assets** *n pl* ACC Geldvermögen *nt*; ~ **authorities** *n pl* BANK Währungsbehörden *f pl*; ~ **base** *n* ECON Zentralbankgeldmenge *f*; ~ **bloc** *n* ECON Währungsblock *m*; ~ **compensation** *n* FIN Währungsausgleich *m*; ~ **compensatory amount** *n* FIN *EU* Währungsausgleichsbetrag *m*

Monetary: ~ **Compensatory Amount** *n* (*MCA*) ECON *EU, agricultural* Grenzausgleich *m*, Grenzausgleichzahlungen *f pl*, Währungsausgleichsbetrag *m* (*WAB*)

monetary: ~ **course** *n* ECON monetäre Entwicklung *f*; ~ **economics** *n pl* ECON Geldtheorie *f* und -politik, Geldwirtschaft *f*; ~ **fine** *n* INS, LAW Bußgeld *nt*; ~ **inducement** *n* FIN Geldanreiz *m*; ~ **inflation** *n* ECON Geldinflation *f*; ~ **item** *n* ACC *balance sheets* Geldposten *m*; ~ **overhang** *n* ECON Geldüberhang *m*; ~ **policy** *n* ECON Geldpolitik *f*, Währungsfragen *f pl*, Währungspolitik *f*; ~ **reserves** *n pl* ECON Währungsreserven *f pl*; ~ **restriction** *n* ECON geldpolitische Restriktion *f*; ~ **standard** *n* ECON Währungsstandard *m*; ~ **stringency** *n* ECON restriktive Geldpolitik *f*; ~ **support** *n* ECON Währungsbeistand *m*; ~ **support operations** *n pl* FIN Aktionen *f pl* zur Unterstützung von Währungen; ~ **target** *n* ECON Geldmengenziel *nt*, FIN geldpolitisches Ziel *nt*; ~ **tightness** *n* ECON Geldknappheit *f*; ~ **transactions** *n pl* FIN Zahlungsverkehr *m*; ~ **union** *n* ECON Währungsunion *f*; ~ **unit** *n* FIN Geldeinheit *f*, Währungseinheit *f*; ~ **veil** *n* ECON Geldschleier *m*

money *n* ECON Geld *nt*, Geldsorte *f*, Münze *f*, *wealth* Vermögen *nt*, *amount* Geldbetrag *m*, FIN, GEN COMM Geld *nt*, Kohle *f* (*infrml*), Knete *f* (*infrml*), Mäuse *f pl* (*infrml*), Kies *m* (*infrml*); ◆ **at the** ~ FIN zum Preis,

STOCK Basispreis entspricht dem Marktpreis; **come into** ~ GEN COMM zu Geld kommen (*infrml*); ~ **is no object** GEN COMM Geld spielt keine Rolle

money: ~ **at call** *n* BANK, FIN Geld *nt* auf Abruf, Tagesgeld *nt*; ~ **broker** *n* BANK, FIN Finanzmakler, in *m,f*, Geldmakler, in *m,f*, Kreditmakler, in *m,f*; ~ **center bank** *AmE*, ~ **centre bank** *BrE n* BANK Geschäftsbank *f*; ~ **compensation** *n* FIN Abfindung *f*; ~ **dealing** *n* ECON Geldhandel *m*; ~ **desk** *n* BANK Geldhandelsabteilung *f*; ~ **GDP** *n* ECON nominales BIP; ~ **illusion** *n* ECON Geldillusion *f*; ~ **income** *n* ECON Geldeinkommen *nt*; ~ **laundering** *n* FIN Geldwäscherei *f*; ~ **lender** *n* FIN Geldgeber *m*; ~-**losing deal** *n* ECON Verlustgeschäft *nt*

moneymaker *n* GEN COMM Geldverdiener, in *m,f*

money: ~ **market** *n* BANK Geldmarkt *m*; ~ **market certificate** *n AmE* (*MMC*) FIN Geldmarktzertifikat *nt*; ~ **market deposit account** *n AmE* (*MMDA*) BANK Anlagekonto *nt* mit eingeschränkter Zahlungsverkehrsmöglichkeit, FIN verzinsliches Einlagenkonto *nt*, Geldmarkteinlagenkonto *nt*; ~ **market fund** *n* (*MMF*) STOCK Geldmarktkapital *nt*, Geldmarkt-Investmentfonds *m*; ~ **market instrument** *n* STOCK Geldmarktdokument *nt*, Geldmarkturkunde *f*; ~ **market mutual fund** *n AmE* (*MMMF*) FIN Geldmarktfonds *m*; ~ **market paper** *n* STOCK Geldmarktpapier *nt*; ~ **market rate** *n* STOCK Geldmarktsatz *m*; ~ **market returns** *n pl* STOCK Geldmarkterträge *m pl*; ~ **mart** *n* STOCK Geldmarkt *m*; ~ **matters** *n pl* GEN COMM Geldangelegenheiten *f pl*; ~ **measurement** *n* FIN monetäre Größe *f*; ~ **multiplier** *n* ECON Geldmultiplikator *m*; ~-**off pack** *n* S&M Sonderangebotspackung *f*; ~ **1** *n BrE* (*M1*) ECON enggefaßte Geldmengendefinition, Geldvolumen M1 (*M1*); ~ **order** *n AmE* BANK indossierbare Anweisung *f*; ~ **paid out** *n* FIN ausgezahlte Geldmittel *nt pl*; ~ **reserve** *n* BANK Geldreserve *f*; ~ **restraint** *n* ECON restriktive Geldpolitik *f*; ~-**spinner** *n infrml* GEN COMM Dukatenesel *m* (*infrml*), Gelddreher *m*, Kassenschlager *m* (*infrml*); ~ **squeeze** *n* ECON Geldverknappung *f*; ~ **supply** *n* ECON Geldangebot *nt*, Geldmenge *f*, GEN COMM Geldvorrat *m*; ~ **3** *n BrE* (*M3*) ECON weitgefaßte Geldmengendefinition, Geldvolumen *nt* M3 (*M3*); ~ **transactions** *n pl* FIN Zahlungsverkehr *m*; ~ **transfer order** *n* BANK Dauerauftrag *m*; ~ **transmission** *n* BANK Überweisung *f*, Umbuchung *f*; ~ **2** *n BrE* (*M2*) ECON Geldvolumen *nt* M2 (*M2*); ~ **up front** *n* GEN COMM Vorauszahlung *f*, Vorauskasse *f*, Vorausgebühren *f pl*, Vorabgebühren *f pl*

monies: ~ **in** *n pl* FIN Einzahlungen *f pl*, Geldeingänge *m pl*; ~ **paid in** *n* ACC Geldausgänge *m pl*, GEN COMM Einzahlungen *f pl*, Einschüsse *m pl*; ~ **received** *n pl* FIN Einzahlungen *f pl*, Geldeingänge *m pl*

monitor 1. *n* COMP Bildschirm *m*, Monitor *m*, GEN COMM Monitor *m*; **2.** *vt* COMP *security* überwachen, GEN COMM, HRM, MGMNT *performance* überwachen, S&M *market*, TRANSP *rates* überwachen

monitoring *n* FIN Überwachung *f*; ~ **costs** *n pl* ECON Kontrollkosten *pl*

Monnet: ~'**s law** *n* ECON Monnet-Gesetz *nt*

monochrome: ~ **screen** *n* COMP Schwarzweißbildschirm *m*

mono: ~-**economics** *n* ECON Monowirtschaft *f*

monogram *n* GEN COMM Monogramm *nt*

Monopolies: ~ **and Mergers Commission** *n* *BrE* (*MMC*) ECON Monopol- und Fusionskommission *f*, Kartellaufsicht *f*

monopolist *n* ECON Monopolist, in *m,f*

monopolistic: ~ **competition** *n* ECON monopolistische Konkurrenz *f*

monopoly *n* ECON Monopol *nt*, IND Alleinherstellungsrecht *nt*, ausschließliche Gewerbeberechtigung *f*, Monopol *nt*, Monopolstellung *f*; ~ **capitalism** *n* ECON Monopolkapitalismus *m*; ~ **power** *n* ECON Monopolmacht *f*; ~ **price** *n* ECON Monopolpreis *m*; ~ **profit** *n* ECON Monopolgewinn *m*; ~ **rent** *n* PROP Monopolgewinn *m*

monopsony *n* ECON Monopson *nt*, Nachfragemonopol *nt*

monorail *n* TRANSP Einschienenbahn *f*

montage *n* MEDIA Bildmontage *f*, Fotomontage *f*

Monte Carlo: ~ **method** *n* MATH *statistics* Monte-Carlo-Methode *f*

month *n* (*MTH*) GEN COMM Monat *m*; ♦ **a** ~ **in advance** GEN COMM einen Monat im voraus

monthly 1. *adj* GEN COMM monatlich; ♦ **in** ~ **instalments** *BrE* ACC in Monatsraten; **2.** *adv* GEN COMM monatlich

monthly: ~ **compounding of interest** *n* BANK monatliche Zinsberechnung *f*, monatliche Aufzinsung *f*; ~ **expenses** *n pl* GEN COMM monatliche Ausgaben *f pl*; ~ **installment** *AmE*, ~ **instalment** *BrE* FIN Monatsrate *f*, monatliche Teilzahlung *f*, monatliche Ratenzahlung *f*; ~ **investment plan** *n* STOCK monatlicher Investitionsplan *m*; ~ **prepayment notice** *n* TAX monatliche Voranmeldung *f*; ~ **rent** *n* PROP Monatsmiete *f*; ~ **return** *n* ACC *income* Monatsertrag *m*, *statement* Monatsübersicht *f*, Monatsauszug *m*, Monatsbericht *m*; ~ **sales** *n pl* S&M monatliche Verkäufe *m pl*; ~ **savings** *n* HRM *of an employee* monatliche Ersparnisse *f pl*; ~ **statement** *n* BANK Monatsauszug *m*, FIN *credit card* Monatsaufstellung *f*, Monatsbericht *m*

month: **this** ~'**s actuals** *n pl* ACC tatsächliche Einnahmen *f pl* des laufenden Monats

months: ~ **after date** *n pl* GEN COMM Monate *m pl* nach Datum, Monate *m pl* nach heute; ~ **after sight** *n pl* (*m/s*) BANK Monate *m pl* nach Sicht; ~ **traded** *n pl* STOCK gehandelte Monate *m pl*

month: ~**-to-month tenancy** *n* LAW monatlich sich verlängerndes Mietverhältnis *nt*, monatlich sich verlängerndes Pachtverhältnis *nt*, PROP monatliche Vermietung *f*, Vermietung *f* auf Monatsbasis, Vermietung *f* von Monat zu Monat

monument *n* *AmE* PROP Vermessungspunkt *m*

mood *n* STOCK Stimmung *f*; ~ **advertising** *n* S&M stimmungserzeugende Werbung *f*; ~ **conditioning** *n* S&M Stimmungsbeeinflussung *f*

Moody: ~'**s investment grade** *n* *AmE* FIN Moody's Anlagenbewertung *f*; ~'**s investor service** *n* *AmE* FIN Moody's Anlegerdienst *m*, Moody's Kapitalanlegerservice *m*

moonlight: ~ **economy** *n* ECON Schattenwirtschaft *f*

moonlighter *n* HRM Doppelverdiener, in *m,f*, Schwarzarbeiter, in *m,f*

moonlighting *n* *infrml* ECON Nebentätigkeit *f*, HRM Doppelverdienen *nt*, Nebentätigkeit *f*, Schwarzarbeit *f*

morale *n* HRM Arbeitsmoral *f*

moral: ~ **hazard** *n* INS Risiko *nt* unehrlichen Verhaltens, subjektives Risiko *nt*; ~ **law** *n* LAW Sittengesetz *nt*; ~ **obligation bond** *n* STOCK Anleihe *f* eines Bundesstaates; ~ **suasion** *n* BANK Einsatz *m* der moralischen Autorität, Seelenmassage *f* (*infrml*), Maßhalteappell *m*, Wirtschaftspolitik *f* des gütlichen Zuredens

moratorium *n* FIN Moratorium *nt*, Zahlungsaufschub *m*, GEN COMM Moratorium *nt*

Morgan: ~ **Stanley Capital International World Index** *n* STOCK Morgan Stanley Internationaler Welt-Kapital-Index *m*

morgue *n* *infrml* MEDIA Archiv *nt*

morning: **in the** ~ *phr* GEN COMM vormittags

morphological: ~ **analysis** *n* FIN, MATH morphologische Analyse *f*

mortality: ~ **table** *n* INS Sterbetabelle *f*, Sterblichkeitstafel *f*

mortg. *abbr* (*mortgage*) BANK, ECON, PROP Hyp. (*Hypothek*)

mortgage 1. *n* (*mortg.*) BANK, PROP Hypothek *f* (*Hyp.*); **2.** *vt* BANK, PROP hypothekarisch belasten, verpfänden

mortgage out *vt* BANK, FIN, PROP voll finanzieren

mortgage: ~ **account** *n* BANK Hypothekenkonto *nt*; ~ **assumption** *n* BANK Übernahme *f* einer Hypothek; ~**-backed certificate** *n* FIN hypothekengesicherter Anteilsschein *m*; ~**-backed security** *n* *AmE* FIN hypothekarisch gesichertes Wertpapier *nt*, hypothekengesicherter Pfandbrief *m*; ~ **bank** *n* BANK Hypothekenbank *f*; ~ **bond** *n* ACC, FIN, STOCK Pfandbrief *m*; ~ **bond creditor** *n* STOCK Pfandbriefgläubiger *m*, Pfandbriefinhaber, in *m,f*; ~ **bond debt** *n* STOCK Pfandbriefschuld *f*; ~ **bond redemption premium** *n* ACC Pfandbrieftilgungsprämie *f*; ~ **broker** *n* *AmE* FIN Hypothekenmakler, in *m,f*, Vermittler, in *m,f* von Hypothekenkrediten; ~ **ceiling** *n* PROP Beleihungsplafond *m*, Hypothekenobergrenze *f*; ~ **commitment** *n* FIN Hypothekenkreditzusage *f*; ~ **correspondent** *n* FIN Person, die ein Hypothekendarlehen abzahlt; ~ **credit association** *n* FIN Hypothekenkreditverband *m*

mortgaged *adj* PROP verpfändet

mortgage: ~ **debt** *n* BANK Hypothekenschuld *f*; ~ **discount** *n* FIN Hypothekennachlaß *m*

mortgagee *n* BANK Hypothekengläubiger, in *m,f*

Mortgage: ~ **Income Relief at Source** *n* (*MIRAS*) TAX Steuervergünstigung *f* für Hypothekentilgung an der Quelle

mortgage: ~ **insurance** *n* INS *personal* Hypothekenversicherung *f*; ~ **insurance policy** *n* INS *personal* Hypothekenversicherungspolice *f*; ~ **lender** *n* BANK Hypothekengeldgeber *m*; ~ **lendings** *n pl* FIN Aktivhypotheken *f pl*; ~ **lien** *n* LAW, PROP *property* Grundpfandrecht *nt*; ~ **life insurance** *n* *AmE* (*cf endowment policy BrE*) INS *personal* Hypothekentilgungsversicherung *f*; ~ **loan** *n* BANK Hypothekendarlehen *nt*; ~ **loan company** *n* BANK Hypothekenbank *f*, Hypothekengesellschaft *f*

mortgager *n* BANK Hypothekenschuldner, in *m,f*

mortgage: ~ **rate** *n* BANK Hypothekenkonditionen *f pl*, Hypothekenzins *m*; ~ **redemption** *n* BANK Hypothekentilgung *f*; ~ **repayment** *n* BANK Hypothekenrückzahlung *f*, Hypothekentilgung *f*; ~ **rescue scheme** *n* *BrE* PROP Hypothekensanierungsplan; ~ **servicing** *n* FIN Bedienung *f* von

Hypothekenkrediten, Zins- und Tilgungszahlungen *f pl* auf Hypothekenkredite

mortgaging *n* PROP Verpfändung *f*

most: ~ **active list** *n* STOCK Liste *f* der umsatzstärksten Aktien; ~ **favored nation** *AmE*, ~ **favoured nation** *BrE* *n* ECON Land *nt* mit Meistbegünstigungsstatus; ~ **favoured nation clause** *n BrE* ECON, LAW Meistbegünstigungsklausel *f*; ~ **favoured nation treatment** *n BrE* ECON Gewährung *f* der Meistbegünstigung

MOT *abbr BrE (Ministry of Transport test)* TRANSP *test certificate* ≈ TÜV *(Technischer Überwachungs-Verein)*

motherboard *n* COMP Grundplatine *f*, Mutterkarte *f*, Mutterplatte *f*, Hauptplatine *f*

mothercard *n* COMP Mutterkarte *f*

mother: ~ **ship** *n* TRANSP Mutterschiff *nt*, Zubringerschiff *nt*

motif *n* GEN COMM Firmenzeichen *nt*, *idea* Motiv *nt*, Leitidee *f*

motion: ~ **of censure** *n* POL Mißbilligungsantrag *m*, Tadelsantrag *m*; ~ **economy** *n* ECON Bewegungsökonomie *f*; ~ **of no confidence** *n* POL Mißtrauensantrag *m*; ~ **picture** *n AmE* LEIS, MEDIA Film *m*, Kinofilm *m*; ~ **picture advertising** *n AmE* S&M Filmwerbung *f*, Kinoreklame *f*, Kinowerbung *f*; ~ **picture industry** *n AmE* LEIS Filmbranche *f*, Filmindustrie *f*, MEDIA Filmindustrie *f*; ~ **study** *n* ECON, MATH, MGMNT Bewegungsstudie *f*

motivate *vt* GEN COMM, HRM, MGMNT, S&M motivieren

motivation *n* GEN COMM, HRM, MGMNT, S&M Motivation *f*, Motivierung *f*

motivational *adj* GEN COMM, HRM, MGMNT, S&M motivierend; ~ **analysis** *n* HRM Motivationsanalyse *f*; ~ **research** *n* S&M Motivforschung *f*

motivator *n* GEN COMM, HRM, MGMNT Motivator, in *m,f*

motive *n* GEN COMM Beweggrund *m*

motor *n* TRANSP Motor *m*; ~ **freight** *n* TRANSP Straßentransport *m*; ~ **industry** *n* IND Automobilindustrie *f*, Kraftfahrzeugindustrie *f*, TRANSP Kraftfahrzeugindustrie *f*; ~ **insurance** *n BrE (cf automobile insurance AmE)* INS Kraftfahrzeugversicherung *f*, Autoversicherung *f*; ~ **insurance premium** *n* INS Kraftfahrzeugprämie *f*

motorist: ~ **inclusive tour** *n* LEIS Autokomplettreise *f*, Autopauschalreise *f*

motor: ~ **merchant vessel** *n (M/V)* TRANSP Motorhandelsschiff *nt*; ~ **mileage allowance** *n BrE* TAX ≈ Kilometergeld *nt*

motors *n* ECON Automobilwerte *m pl*

motor: ~ **ship** *n (MS)* TRANSP Motorschiff *nt*; ~ **spirit** *n* TRANSP *fuel* Motorenbenzin *nt*, Ottokraftstoff *m*; ~ **tanker** *n* TRANSP Motortanker *m*; ~ **transport officer** *n (MTO)* HRM Motortransportbeamte(r) *m* [decl. as adj], Motortransportbeamtin *f*, MGMNT Fuhrparkleiter, in *m,f*; ~ **truck cargo insurance** *n AmE* INS *property* LKW-Ladungsversicherung *f*; ~ **vehicle insurance** *n* INS Kraftfahrzeugversicherung *f*; ~ **vehicle insurance agreement** *n* INS Kraftfahrzeugversicherungsvertrag *m*; ~ **vehicle tax** *n* TAX, TRANSP Kfz-Steuer *f*, Kraftfahrzeugsteuer *f*; ~ **vessel** *n (MV)* TRANSP Motorschiff *nt*

motorway *n BrE (cf expressway AmE, superhighway AmE)* TRANSP Autobahn *f*, Autostraße *f*, Kraftfahrstraße *f*; ~ **services** *n pl BrE* LEIS, TRANSP

Rasthaus *nt*, Raststätte *f*; ~ **service station** *n BrE* LEIS, TRANSP Rasthaus *nt*, Raststätte *f*

mould *vt BrE* MEDIA *public opinion* bilden, formen

mountain *n* ADMIN Berg *m*; ~ **of debt** *n* ECON Schuldenberg *m*; ~ **resort** *n* LEIS Gebirgsort *m*, Erholungsort *m* in den Bergen

mounting *adj* GEN COMM *increasing* steigend; ~ **competition** *n* ECON zunehmender Wettbewerb *m*

mouse *n* COMP Maus *f*; **--driven** *adj* COMP mausgesteuert; ~ **driver** *n* COMP Maustreiber *m*; ~ **mat** *n* COMP Mausunterlage *f*

move 1. *n* ECON *in currency* Schwankung *f*, GEN COMM *to new premises* Umzug *m*, *measure* Maßnahme *f*, TRANSP Umzug *m*; **2.** *vt* GEN COMM verschieben; ♦ ~ **house** GEN COMM umziehen; **3.** *vi* GEN COMM *to new premises* umziehen; ♦ ~ **in tandem** STOCK sich im Gleichschritt bewegen; ~ **into the money** STOCK *short calls, short puts* Gewinn erzielen; ~ **to larger premises** GEN COMM in größere Geschäftsgebäude umziehen ~ **out of** GEN COMM *premises* ausziehen aus; ~ **together** ECON *currencies* sich aufeinanderzubewegen

moveable *adj* GEN COMM beweglich; ~ **goods** *n pl* LAW bewegliche Güter *nt pl*; ~ **objects** *n pl* LAW bewegliche Gegenstände *m pl*; ~ **property** *n* LAW bewegliches Eigentum *nt*, bewegliches Vermögen *nt*, PROP bewegliches Vermögen *nt*

moveables *n* LAW bewegliche Sachen *f pl*

movement *n* GEN COMM *market*, POL Bewegung *f*; ~ **certificate** *n* IMP/EXP Warenverkehrsbescheinigung *f*; ~ **of deposits** *n* ECON Einlagenentwicklung *f*; ~ **of freight** *n* TRANSP Frachtverkehr *m*, Güterverkehr *m*; ~ **of labor** *AmE*, ~ **of labour** *BrE* *n* ECON Arbeiterbewegung *f*, Wahl *f* des Arbeitsplatzes; ~ **of operations** *n* ECON Betriebsverlegung *f*

movements: ~ **on shareholders' equity** *n pl* ACC Eigenkapitalentwicklung *f*

mover: ~ **and shaker** *n infrml* MGMNT bewegende Kraft *f*

movetime *n* TRANSP Transportzeit *f*

movie *n AmE* LEIS, MEDIA Kinofilm *m*; ~ **theater** *n AmE (cf cinema BrE)* LEIS Kino *nt*

moving *n* GEN COMM, TRANSP Umzug *m*; ~ **annual total** *n (MAT)* MATH *statistics* gleitende Jahressumme *f*; **--average method** *n* MATH Methode *f* der gleitenden Mittelwerte; **--average process** *n* MATH Prozeß *m* gleitender Durchschnittswerte; ~ **into surplus** *n* ECON *balance of payments*, IMP/EXP Aktivierung *f*; ~ **pavement** *n BrE* TRANSP Rollsteig *m*; ~ **projection** *n* ECON gleitende Prognose *f*; ~ **stairway** *n BrE* GEN COMM Rolltreppe *f*; ~ **up** *adj* STOCK anziehend

MP *abbr* GEN COMM *(multipurpose)* Mehrzweck-, Vielzweck-, POL *(Member of Parliament BrE)* Abg. *(Abgeordnete(r))*, Parlamentsmitglied *nt*

MPA *abbr (marginal principle of allocation)* ECON Marginalprinzip *nt* der Allokation

MPC *abbr (marginal propensity to consume)* ECON marginale Konsumquote *f*

MPD *abbr (marginal private damage)* ECON privater Grenzschaden *m*

mpg *abbr (miles per gallon)* GEN COMM Meilen *f pl* je Gallone

mph *abbr (miles per hour)* GEN COMM Meilen *f pl* pro Stunde

MPM *abbr* (*marginal propensity to import*) IMP/EXP marginale Importquote *f*

MPO *abbr* (*management and personnel office*) ADMIN Geschäftsführungs- und Personalbüro *nt*

MPP *abbr* (*marginal physical product*) ECON physisches Grenzprodukt *nt*

MPS *abbr* (*marginal propensity to save*) ECON marginale Sparquote *f*

MQS *abbr BrE* (*minimum quote size*) STOCK Mindestnotierungsgröße *f*, minimale Notierungsgröße *f*

MRA *abbr* (*multiple regression analysis*) ECON, FIN, MATH Mehrfachregressionsanalyse *f*

MRCA *abbr* (*Market Research Corporation of America*) S&M Marktforschungsgesellschaft von Amerika

MRO *abbr* (*maintenance, repair and overhaul*) TRANSP Wartung *f*, Reparatur *f* und Überholung *f*

MRP *abbr* ECON (*marginal revenue product*) Grenzerlösprodukt *nt*, Grenzumsatzprodukt *nt*, S&M (*manufacturer's recommended price*) Herstellerrichtpreis *m*

MRR *abbr* (*minimum reserve requirement*) ECON Mindestreservesoll *nt*

MRS *abbr* (*marginal rate of substitution*) ECON Grenzrate *f* der Substitution

MRT *abbr* (*mass rapid transit*) TRANSP Massenschnelltransit *m*

m/s *abbr* BANK (*months after sight*) Monate *m pl* nach Sicht, GEN COMM (*meters per second AmE, metres per second BrE*) Meter *m pl* pro Sekunde

MS *abbr* POL (*member state*) Mitgliedsstaat *m*, TRANSP (*motor ship*) *shipping* Motorschiff *nt*, (*machinery survey*) Maschinenprüfung *f*, (*manual system*) Handsystem *m*, manuelles System *nt*

MSA *abbr* ADMIN (*Mutual Security Agency*) Büro *nt* für gegenseitige Sicherheit, TRANSP (*Merchant Shipping Act*) Handelsschiffahrtsgesetz *nt*

msbl *abbr* (*missing bill of lading*) TRANSP fehlendes Konnossement *nt*

MSc *abbr* (*Master of Science*) HRM Magister *m* der Naturwissenschaften

msca *abbr* (*missing cargo*) TRANSP Fehlfracht *f*, fehlende Fracht *f*

MSD *abbr* (*marginal social damage*) ECON sozialer Grenzschaden *m*

MS-DOS® *abbr* (*Microsoft disk operating system*) COMP MS-DOS® (*Microsoft-Plattenbetriebssystem*)

MT *abbr* BANK, COMMS (*mail transfer*) briefliche Auszahlung *f*, Postüberweisung *f*, COMP (*machine translation*) MÜ (*Maschinenübersetzung*), GEN COMM (*minimum transfer*) Mindestüberweisung *f*, Mindesttransfer *m*, (*mean time*) mittlere Zeit *f*, (*minimum temperature*) Minimumtemperatur *f*, TAX (*mainstream tax*) Körperschaftssteuerabschlußzahlung *f*

MTBF *abbr* (*mean time between failures*) TRANSP mittlerer Ausfallabstand *m*

MTFS *abbr* (*medium-term financial strategy*) ECON mittelfristige Finanzstrategie *f*

mth *abbr* (*month*) GEN COMM Mt. (*Monat*)

M3 *abbr BrE* (*money 3*) ECON weitgefaßte Geldmengendefinition, M3 (*Geldvolumen M3*)

MTL *abbr* BANK (*medium-term loan*) mittelfristiger Kredit *m*, mittelfristiges Darlehen *nt*

MTM *abbr* (*methods-time measurement*) MGMNT MTM (*Methods-Times-Measurement*)

MTN *abbr* BANK (*medium-term notes*) mittelfristige Schuldtitel *m pl*, ECON (*multilateral trade negotiations*) *international trade* MHV (*multilaterale Handelsgespräche*), FIN (*medium-term notes*) mittelfristige Schuldtitel *m pl*

mton *abbr* (*metric ton, metric tonne*) GEN COMM metrische Tonne *f*

MTR *abbr* (*mass transit railway*) TRANSP Massentransitbahn *f*

M2 *abbr BrE* (*money 2*) ECON M2 (*Geldvolumen M2*)

M/U *abbr* (*making-up price*) GEN COMM letzter Abrechnungskurs *m*, letzter Kurs *m*

muckraker *n* GEN COMM Schnüffler *m*

multi- *pref* GEN COMM multi-

multiaccess *n* COMP, GEN COMM Mehrfachzugriff *m*

multi: **~-accident** *n* TRANSP Großunfall *m*

multibrand: **~ strategy** *n* S&M Mehrmarkenstrategie *f*

multi: **~-client survey** *n* S&M Kundenumfrage *f*

multicollinearity *n* ECON, MATH *statistics* Multikollinearität *f*

multicopy: **~ order** *n* ECON Sammelbestellung *f*

multi: **~-crew levels** *n pl* TRANSP *shipping* Mehrfach-Crew-Levels *m pl*

multicurrency: **~ loan** *n* BANK Mehrwährungsdarlehen *nt*, Mehrwährungsanleihe *f*; **~ rate** *n* ECON gespaltener Wechselkurs *m*, multiple Wechselkurse *m pl*

multi: **~-delivery** *n* TRANSP Sammellieferung *f*; **~-dimensional scaling** *n* S&M mehrdimensionale Gradeinteilung *f*; **~-employer bargaining** *n* HRM Tarifverhandlungen *f pl* auf Verbandsebene; **~-entry visa** *n* ADMIN Visum *nt* zur mehrmaligen Einreise; **~-family dwelling** *n* WEL Mehrfamilienhaus *nt*; **~-fiber arrangement** *AmE*, **~-fibre arrangement** *BrE n* (*MFA*) ECON Multifaserabkommen *nt*, Welttextilabkommen *nt*; **~-jurisdiction** *n* LAW vielstaatliche Gerichtsbarkeit *f*

multilateral: **~ agency** *n* ECON *development aid* multilaterale Behörde *f*; **~ agreement** *n* ECON *international trade* multilaterale Vereinbarung *f*, multilaterales Abkommen *nt*; **~ aid** *n* ECON multilaterale Hilfe *f*; **~ development bank** *n* FIN multilaterale Entwicklungsbank *f*; **~ disbursement** *n* ECON *development aid* multilaterale Auszahlung *f*; **~ donor** *n* ECON *development aid* multilaterale Geberorganisation *f*; **~ investment guarantee agency** *n* (*MIGA*) ECON multilaterale Investitionsgarantieagentur *f*; **~ investment guarantee association** *n* (*MIGA*) FIN multilaterale Behörde *f* für Investitionsgarantien

multilateralism *n* ECON *international trade* Multilateralismus *m*

multilateral: **~ permit** *n* TRANSP multilaterale Genehmigung *f*; **~ trade agreement** *n* ECON *international* multilaterales Handelsabkommen *nt*; **~ trade negotiations** *n* (*MTN*) ECON *international* multilaterale Handelsgespräche *nt pl* (*MHV*); **~ trade organization** *n* ECON *in place of GATT* multilaterale Handelsorganisation *f*

multilevel: **~ addressing** *n* ECON indirekte Adressierung *f*; **~ distributorship** *n* ECON Vertrieb *m* nach dem Schneeballsystem; **~ marketing** *n* (*MLM*) S&M Multilevel-Marketing *nt*, Marketing *nt* auf mehreren Ebenen, mehrschichtiges Marketing *nt*

multimedia: ~ **training** *n* HRM Multimediaschulung *f*

multimillion: ~ **pound deal** *n* FIN Millionen-Pfund-Geschäft *nt*

multimodal *adj* TRANSP kombiniert, multimodal; ~ **distribution** *n* MATH *statistics* mehrgipflige Verteilung *f*; ~ **frequency curve** *n* MATH *statistics* mehrgipflige Häufigkeitskurve *f*; ~ **transport** *n* TRANSP kombinierter Transport *m*, multimodaler Verkehr *m*, kombinierter Verkehr *m*; ~ **transport law** *n* LAW Gesetz *nt* zum kombinierten Verkehr; ~ **transport operator** *n* HRM, TRANSP Spediteur *m* im kombinierten Verkehr; ~ **transport service** *n* TRANSP kombinierter Verkehrsservice *m*, multimodaler Transportservice *m*

multinational *adj* BANK, GEN COMM, IMP/EXP, TRANSP multinational; ~ **bank** *n* BANK multinationale Bank *f*; ~ **company** *n* GEN COMM multinationales Unternehmen *nt*; ~ **corporation** *n* (*MNC*) GEN COMM multinationales Unternehmen *nt*; ~ **crew** *n* TRANSP *shipping* multinationale Besatzung *f*; ~ **enterprise** *n* (*MNE*) GEN COMM multinationale Gesellschaft *f*, multinationales Unternehmen *nt*; ~ **export credit** *n* IMP/EXP multinationaler Exportkredit *m*; ~ **trading** *n* IMP/EXP multinationaler Handelsverkehr *m*

multi: ~-**plant bargaining** *n* HRM Tarifverhandlungen *f pl* für mehrere Betriebe

multiple 1. *adj* GEN COMM mehrfach, Mehrfach-; **2.** *n* MATH Vielfache(s) *nt* [decl. as adj]

multiple: ~ **activity chart** *n* COMP Arbeitsplanungsbogen *m*; ~ **buyer** *n* S&M Mehrfachkäufer *m*; ~-**choice question** *n* S&M Frage *f* mit Mehrfachwahlmöglichkeit, Mehrfachauswahlfrage *f*, Multiple-Choice-Frage *f*; ~-**contract finance-projected line of credit** *n* FIN Mehrfachvertrag *m* mit einer Finanzschätzungskreditlinie; ~ **correlation** *n* MATH *statistics* Mehrfachkorrelation *f*, multiple Korrelation *f*; ~ **delivery contract** *n* LAW Sukzessivlieferungsvertrag *m*; ~ **exchange rate** *n* ECON multipler Wechselkurs *m*

Multiple: ~ **Listing Service** *n AmE* (*MLS*) PROP Maklerkartell

multiple: ~ **management** *n* MGMNT mehrgleisige Unternehmensführung *f*, mehrstufige Betriebsführung *f*; ~ **management plan** *n* HRM System *nt* der mehrstufigen Betriebsführung; ~ **peril insurance** *n* INS Versicherung *f* gegen mehrere Gefahren; ~ **protection insurance** *n* INS Vielschutzversicherung *f*; ~ **readership** *n* S&M Mehrfachleserschaft *f*; ~ **regression** *n* MATH multiple Regression *f*, *statistics* Mehrfachregression *f*; ~ **regression analysis** *n* (*MRA*) ECON, FIN, MATH Mehrfachregressionsanalyse *f*; ~ **retirement ages** *n pl* HRM unterschiedliches Pensionierungsalter *nt*; ~ **risk insurance** *n* INS kombinierte Versicherung *f*; ~ **supplier system** *n* COMP Mehrfachanbietersystem *nt*; ~ **unit pricing** *n* S&M Mehrstückpreis *m*

multiplication *n* MATH Vervielfältigung *f*

multiplier *n* ECON Multiplikator *m*; ~ **accelerator model** *n* ECON Multiplikator-Akzelerator-Modell *nt*; ~ **effect** *n* ECON *econometrics* Multikatoreffekt *m*; ~ **principle** *n* ECON *econometrics* Multiplikatorprinzip *nt*

multiply *vt* MATH vervielfachen, multiplizieren

multiprocessing *n* COMP Simultanverarbeitung *f*, Mehrprozessorbetrieb *m*

multiprocessor *n* COMP Mehrprozessorsystem *nt*

multiprogramming *n* COMP Mehrprogrammbetrieb *m*, Mehrprogramming *nt*, Programmverzahnung *f*

multipurpose *adj* (*MP*) GEN COMM Mehrzweck-, Vielzweck-; ~ **oil** *n* IND Mehrbereichsöl *nt*; ~ **vessel** *n* TRANSP Mehrzweckschiff *nt*

multi: ~-**quote** *n* TRANSP Mehrfach-Quote *f*; ~-**risk insurance** *n* INS kombinierte Versicherung *f*; ~-**segmented operation** *n* S&M mehrfach segmentierte Verfahren *nt pl*

multistage: ~ **sampling** *n* MATH *statistics* mehrstufiges Stichprobensystem *nt*; ~ **tax** *n* TAX Mehrphasensteuer *f*, Mehrphasenumsatzsteuer *f*

multi: ~-**stop** *adj* TRANSP *container movement* Mehrfachstopp *m*

multistorey 1. *adj BrE* PROP mehrgeschossig; **2.** *n BrE* PROP, WEL Hochhaus *nt*

multistorey: ~ **car park** *n* PROP, TRANSP Parkhaus *nt*

multistory *AmE see* multistorey *BrE*

multitasking *n* COMP Multitasking *nt*

multi: ~-**union bargaining** *n* HRM Tarifverhandlungen *f pl* mit mehreren Gewerkschaften

multiunionism *n* HRM Industriezweig, in dem mehrere Gewerkschaften vertreten sind

multi: ~-**union plant** *n* HRM Betrieb, der an mehrere Gewerkschaften gebunden ist; ~-**user** *adj* COMP Mehrbenutzer-; ~-**user document** *n* COMP Mehrbenutzerdokument *nt*; ~-**user route** *n* TRANSP Gemeinschaftsroute *f*; ~-**user system** *n* COMP Mehrbenutzersystem *nt*

multivariate: ~ **analysis** *n* MATH mehrdimensionale Analyse *f*, Multivariatenanalyse *f*

multi: ~-**year** *adj* FIN, GEN COMM mehrjährig; ~-**year operational plan** *n* (*MYOP*) FIN operativer Mehrjahresplan *m*; ~-**year rescheduling agreement** *n* (*MYRA*) FIN mehrjährige Umschuldungsvereinbarung *f*; ~-**year resource envelope** *n* FIN Mehrjahresressourcenplanung *f*; ~-**year restructuring agreement** *n* (*MYRA*) FIN mehrjährige Umschuldungsvereinbarung *f*; ~-**year spending envelope** *n* FIN Mehrjahresausgabenplanung *f*

Mundell-Fleming: ~ **model** *n* ECON Mundell-Fleming-Modell *nt*

muni *n AmE* STOCK Kommunalanleihe *f*

municipal *adj* GEN COMM kommunal, Kommunal-; ~ **administration** *n* ADMIN, POL Stadtverwaltung *f*; ~ **authority** *n* ADMIN Kommunalbehörde *f*; ~ **bond** *n* BANK Kommunalobligation *f*, STOCK Kommunalobligation *f*, Kommunalschuldverschreibung *f*; ~ **bond insurance** *n* INS Versicherung gegen kommunale Schuldverschreibungen; ~ **bond insurance association** *n* INS Versicherungsgesellschaft zur Deckung von Kommunalschuldverschreibungen; ~ **bond offering** *n* BANK Emission *f* von Kommunalobligationen, Emission *f* von Kommunalschuldverschreibungen; ~ **certificate of accrual on tax-exempted securities** *n* (*M-CATS*) STOCK Steuerfreies Kommunalzertifikat mit Zinsansammlung; ~ **corporation** *n BrE* (*cf municipal government AmE*) ADMIN, POL Kommunalregierung *f*, Kommunalverwaltung *f*, Stadtverwaltung *f*; ~ **government** *n AmE* (*cf municipal corporation BrE*) ADMIN, POL Kommunalregierung *f*, Kommunalverwaltung *f*, Stadtverwaltung *f*

municipality *n* ADMIN örtliche Gebietskörperschaft *f*, Kommunalverwaltung *f*, POL *area* Kommune *f*, Kreis *m*, *governing body* Kommunalverwaltung *f*, Magistrat *m*; ~ **borough** *n AmE* POL Stadtbezirk *m*

municipal: ~ **loan** *n AmE* FIN Kommunalanleihe *f*;
~ **notes** *n pl* BANK kommunale Schuldverschreibung *f*;
~ **securities rulemaking board** *n* STOCK aufsichts-
führende Börse *f* für Kommunalanleihen

muniments *n pl* LAW *of title* Grundeigentumsurkunden *f*
pl; ~ **of title** *n pl* LAW *property* Grundeigentumsurkunden *f pl*

Murphy: ~**'s law** *n* GEN COMM Murphys Gesetz *nt*

must: ~ **fit** *adj* LAW aufeinander abgestimmt; ~ **match** *adj*
LAW aufeinander abgestimmt

mutatis mutandis *phr* ECON, LAW analog, sinngemäß,
entsprechend, mit den nötigen Abänderungen, mutatis
mutandis (*m.m.*)

Muth-Mills: ~ **model** *n* ECON Muth-Mills-Modell *nt*

mutilated: ~ **note** *n* BANK beschädigter Geldschein *m*;
~ **security** *n* STOCK beschädigtes Wertpapier *nt*

mutual *adj* GEN COMM beiderseitig, wechselseitig, gemeinschaftlich; ◆ **by** ~ **agreement** GEN COMM, LAW in
gegenseitigem Einvernehmen, in gegenseitigem Einverständnis; **by** ~ **consent** GEN COMM *private*
agreement, LAW in gegenseitigem Einvernehmen

mutual: ~ **aid pact** *n* ECON *international trade* Beistandspakt *m*; ~ **association** *n* FIN Gegenseitigkeitsverband
m; ~ **benefit** *n* GEN COMM beiderseitiger Vorteil *m*;
~ **benefit society** *n* INS Versicherungsverein *m* auf
Gegenseitigkeit (*VVaG*); ~ **border** *n* IMP/EXP gemeinsame Grenze *f*; ~ **company** *n* FIN
Gegenseitigkeitsgesellschaft *f*; ~ **consent** *n* LAW Willenserklärung *f*; ~ **contract** *n* LAW gegenseitiger Vertrag
m; ~ **fund** *n AmE* FIN Investmentfonds *m*, offener
Investmentfonds *m*; ~ **fund custodian** *n* BANK
Treuhänder, in *m,f* eines offenen Investmentfonds;
~ **insurance** *n* INS Versicherung *f* auf Gegenseitigkeit;

~ **insurance company** *n* INS Versicherungsverein *m* auf
Gegenseitigkeit (*VVaG*), VVaG (*Versicherungsverein auf*
Gegenseitigkeit); ~ **insurance society** *n BrE* INS Ver-
sicherungsverein *m* auf Gegenseitigkeit (*VVaG*), VVaG
(*Versicherungsverein auf Gegenseitigkeit*); ~ **insurer** *n*
INS Versicherer *m* auf Gegenseitigkeit

mutuality *n* BANK Gegenseitigkeit *f*; ~ **agreement** *n* HRM
Gegenseitigkeitsabkommen *nt*; ~ **of contract** *n* LAW
Gegenseitigkeit *f* des Vertrags

mutually *adv* GEN COMM wechselseitig; ◆ ~ **exclusive**
GEN COMM beiderseitig ausgeschlossen, sich gegenseitig
ausschließend

Mutual: ~ **Offset System** *n* STOCK *Eurodollar futures*
gegenseitiges Verrechnungssystem *nt*

mutual: ~ **recognition** *n* LAW *of national laws and*
regulations within the EU gegenseitige Anerkennung *f*;
~ **savings bank** *n* BANK, ECON genossenschaftsähnliche
Bank *f*, genossenschaftsähnliche Sparkasse *f*

Mutual: ~ **Security Agency** *n AmE* (*MSA*) ADMIN
Sicherheitsagentur *f*

mutual: ~ **support policy** *n* POL Politik *f* gegenseitiger
Unterstützung

MV *abbr* (*motor vessel*) TRANSP *shipping* Motorschiff *nt*

M/V *abbr* (*motor merchant vessel*) TRANSP
Motorhandelsschiff *nt*

MW *abbr* (*megawatt*) GEN COMM MW (*Megawatt*)

MYOP *abbr* (*multi-year operational plan*) FIN operativer
Mehrjahresplan *m*

MYRA *abbr* (*multi-year restructuring agreement*) FIN
mehrjährige Umschuldungsvereinbarung *f*

mystery: ~ **shopper** *n jarg* S&M *advertising*
Scheinkäufer, in *m,f*

N

N *abbr* (*new*) GEN COMM neu

n/a *abbr* (*no account*) BANK kein Konto, keine Deckung

N/A *abbr* GEN COMM (*not applicable*), nicht zutreffend, (*no advice*) kein Avis, ohne Avis

nadir *n* GEN COMM, STOCK Tiefpunkt *m*

NAEGA *abbr* (*North American Export Grain Association*) GEN COMM nordamerikanische Getreideexportvereinigung

NAFA *abbr* (*net acquisition of financial assets*) FIN Nettoerwerb *m* finanzieller Vermögenswerte

NAFTA *abbr* (*North American Free Trade Area*) ECON Nordamerikanische Freihandelszone *f*

NAHB *abbr AmE* (*National Association of Home Builders*) PROP Bundesverband der Bauherren

NAIC *abbr AmE* (*National Association of Insurance Commissioners*) INS Bundesverband der Versicherungskommissare

naked: ~ **call option** *n* STOCK ungedeckte Kaufoption *f*; ~ **option** *n* STOCK Nacktoption *f*, ungedeckte Option *f*; ~ **position** *n* STOCK ungesicherte Long- oder Short-Position *f*; ~ **put** *n* STOCK *options* ungedeckte Verkaufsoption *f*; ~ **short option position** *n* STOCK ungedeckte Baisse-Optionsposition *f*; ~ **short puts** *n pl* STOCK *options* ungedeckte Baisse-Verkaufsoption *f*; ~ **writer** *n* STOCK ungedeckter Verkäufer *m* einer Option

NALGO *abbr BrE* (*National and Local Government Officers Association*) HRM Gewerkschaft nationaler und kommunaler Beamten

NAM *abbr AmE* (*National Association of Manufacturers*) IND nationaler Industriellenverband

Namas *abbr* (*National Measurement Accreditation Service*) GEN COMM nationaler Dienst zur Beglaubigung von Maßeinheiten

name *n* GEN COMM *company* Firma *f* (*Fa.*), Handelsname *m*, Name *m* (*N*); ~ **of an account** *n* ACC Kontobezeichnung *f*; ~ **and address** *n* COMMS Name *m* und Anschrift *f*; ~ **badge** *n* GEN COMM Namensschild *nt*; ~ **bond** *n* INS Personengarantieversicherung *f*; ~ **brand** *n* S&M Markenname *m*; ~ **of business** *n* GEN COMM Firmenname *m*, Firmenschild *nt*

named *adj* GEN COMM bezeichnet

name: ~ **day** *n* STOCK Abrechnungstag *m*, Aufgabetag *m*, Skantrierungstag *m*

named: ~ **peril policy** *n* INS Police zur Deckung genannter Gefahren

nameplate *n* ADMIN Türschild *nt*, GEN COMM Schild *nt*, Namensschild *nt*

name: ~ **position bond** *n* INS *company* Kautionsversicherung des Arbeitgebers gegen firmeninterne Veruntreuung

nanny: ~ **state** *n infrml* ECON Bevormundungsstaat *m*, Wohlfahrtsstaat *m*

NAR *abbr AmE* (*National Association of Realtors*) PROP Bundesverband der Immobilienmakler

narcodollars *n pl* ECON Drogengeld *nt*

narrow 1. *adj* STOCK begrenzt; **2.** *vt* STOCK *spread* begrenzen

narrow: ~ **band** *n* ECON *Exchange Rate Mechanism* enges Band *nt*; ~~**based taxes** *n pl AmE* ECON, TAX spezielle Steuern *f pl*

narrowing: ~ **inflation gap** *n* ECON schrumpfende inflatorische Lücke *f*

narrowly: ~ **defined money supply** *n* ECON eng definierte Geldmenge *f*, Geldmenge *f* in der engen Definition

narrow: ~ **margin** *n* ACC geringe Spanne *f*; ~ **market** *n* STOCK begrenzter Markt *m*, enger Markt *m*, flauer Markt *m*

NASA *abbr* TRANSP (*North Atlantic Shippers' Association*) Vereinigung der Nordatlantik-Seehafenspediteure, (*National Aeronautics and Space Administration AmE*) US Luft- und Raumfahrtbehörde

NASDAQ *abbr AmE* (*National Association of Securities Dealers Automated Quotations*) STOCK automatisiertes Kursnotierungssystem der Vereinigung der US-Wertpapierhändler

NASDIM *abbr AmE* (*National Association of Securities Dealers*) STOCK Vereinigung der US-Wertpapierhändler

Nash: ~ **bargaining** *n* ECON Nash-Verhandlungen *f pl*

nat. *abbr* (*national*) GEN COMM staatl. (*staatlich*), inländisch, Bundes-, *EU* einzelstaatlich

NATFHE *abbr BrE* (*National Association of Teachers in Further and Higher Education*) WEL nationale Lehrergewerkschaft

nation *n* POL Nation *f*, Volk *nt*

national 1. *adj* (*nat.*) GEN COMM staatlich (*staatl.*), inländisch, Bundes-, *EU* einzelstaatlich; **2.** *n* ADMIN Staatsbürger, in *m,f*

national: ~ **account** *n* S&M volkswirtschaftliche Gesamtrechnung *f*; ~ **accounting** *n* ACC, ECON volkswirtschaftliche Gesamtrechnung *f*; ~ **accounts manager** *n* HRM Großkundensachbearbeiter, in *m,f*

National: ~ **Aeronautics and Space Administration** *n AmE* (*NASA*) TRANSP US Luft- und Raumfahrtbehörde

national: ~ **agency** *n* ADMIN nationale Behörde *f*; ~ **airline** *n* LEIS, TRANSP Inlandsfluglinie *f*, nationale Fluggesellschaft *f*

National: ~ **Association of Home Builders** *n AmE* (*NAHB*) PROP Bundesverband der Bauherren; ~ **Association of Insurance Commissioners** *n AmE* (*NAIC*) INS nationale Vereinigung der Versicherungskommissare; ~ **Association of Manufacturers** *n AmE* (*NAM*) IND nationaler Industriellenverband; ~ **Association of Realtors** *n AmE* (*NAR*) PROP Bundesverband der Immobilienmakler; ~ **Association of Securities Dealers** *n AmE* (*NASDIM*) STOCK Vereinigung der US-Wertpapierhändler; ~ **Association of Securities Dealers Automated Quotations** *n AmE* (*NASDAQ*) STOCK automatisiertes Kursnotierungssystem der Vereinigung der US-Wertpapierhändler; ~ **Association of Teachers in Further and Higher Education** *n BrE* (*NATFHE*) WEL nationale Lehrergewerkschaft

national: ~ **average** *n* ECON nationaler Durchschnitt *m*; ~ **balance sheet** *n* ECON Volksvermögensrechnung *f*; ~ **bank** *n AmE* BANK retail von der Bundesregierung zugelassene Bank, Nationalbank *f*

National: ~ **Bank for Foreign Trade** *n* BANK Nationalbank für Außenhandel; **~ Banking Act** *n AmE* BANK *1863* Gesetz über Nationalbanken; **~ Board for Prices and Incomes** *n BrE* (*NBPI*) ECON staatliche Preis- und Einkommensüberwachungsstelle

national: **~ border** *n* GEN COMM Staatsgrenze *f*; **~ boundary** *n* IMP/EXP, POL Landesgrenze *f*, Staatsgrenze *f*; **~ branch network** *n* GEN COMM inländisches Filialnetz *nt*; **~ brand** *n* S&M überregionale Herstellermarke *f*

National: **~ Bureau of Economic Research** *n AmE* ECON nationales Büro für Wirtschaftsforschung; **~ Bureau of Standards** *n AmE* ADMIN nationales Institut für Normung; **~ Business Publications** *n AmE* MEDIA nationale Unternehmenspublikationen

national: **~ campaign** *n* S&M überregionale Kampagne *f*

National: **~ Carriers** *n* (*NC*) TRANSP nationale Beförderungsunternehmen; **~ Contingency Fund** *n* FIN staatlicher Rücklagenfonds; **~ Council on International Trade Documentation** *n* (*NCITD*) GEN COMM nationaler Rat für die Dokumentation des internationalen Handels; **~ Council of Voluntary Organizations** *n BrE* (*NCVO*) WEL Nationaler Rat der Wohltätigkeitsorganisationen

national: **~ currency** *n* ECON Landeswährung *f*

National: **~ Curriculum** *n BrE* WEL *for schools* nationaler Lehrplan; **~ Data Processing Service** *n BrE* (*NDPS*) GEN COMM *subsidiary of British Telecom* staatlicher Datenverarbeitungsservice

national: **~ debt** *n* ECON öffentliche Verschuldung *f*, Staatsschuld *f*

National: **~ Economic Development Council** *n BrE* (*NEDC, Neddy*) ECON nationaler Rat für wirtschaftliche Entwicklung, ≈ Bundeswirtschaftsrat *m*; **~ Economic Development Office** *n BrE* (*NEDO*) ECON nationales Amt für die Untersuchung der wirtschaftlichen Entwicklung

national: **~ economy** *n* ECON Gesamtwirtschaft *f*, Volkswirtschaft *f*

National: **~ Employment Agency** *n* HRM Nationales Arbeitsvermittlungsbüro, ≈ Arbeitsamt *nt*; **~ Executive Committee** *n BrE* (*NEC*) POL geschäftsführender Ausschuß *m*

national: **~ expenditure** *n* ECON Staatsausgaben *f pl*

National: **~ Farmers Union** *n BrE* (*NFU*) IND nationaler Bauernverband; **~ Federation of American Shipping** *n* (*NFAS*) TRANSP nationaler Verband der amerikanischen Schiffahrt; **~ Futures Association** *n AmE* (*NFA*) STOCK Aufsichtsorgan für den Terminhandel; **~ Grid** *n BrE* IND Verbundnetz *nt*; **~ Health Service** *n BrE* (*NHS*) POL, WEL staatlicher Gesundheitsdienst *m*

national: **~ identity card** *n* ADMIN, POL Personalausweis *m*; **~ income** *n* ECON *econometrics* Volkseinkommen *nt*

National: **~ Income and Product Accounts** *n* (*NIPA*) ECON *econometrics* Entstehungs- und Verteilungsrechnung *f*; **~ Industrial Recovery Act** *n AmE* IND Gesetz über den Wiederaufbau der Wirtschaft; **~ Institute for Economic and Social Research** *n BrE* (*NIESR*) ECON Nationales Institut für Wirtschafts- und Sozialforschung, Konjunkturinstitut; **~ Insurance** *n BrE* (*NI*) HRM Sozialversicherung *f*; **~ Insurance Contributions** *n pl BrE* (*NICs*) TAX Sozialversicherungsbeiträge *m pl*

national: **~ interest** *n* POL nationales Interesse *nt*

nationalism *n* POL Nationalismus *m*

nationality *n* POL Staatsangehörigkeit *f*

nationalization *n* ECON Vergesellschaftung *f*, Verstaatlichung *f*, POL, PROP Vergesellschaftung *f*

nationalize *vt* ECON vergesellschaften, in Gemeineigentum überführen, GEN COMM verstaatlichen, POL vergesellschaften, in Gemeineigentum überführen, PROP vergesellschaften

nationalized: **~ industry** *n* ECON, IND verstaatlichter Industriezweig *m*; **~ sector** *n* IND verstaatlichter Sektor *m*

National: **~ Joint Committee** *n BrE* (*NJC*) HRM nationales Arbeitgeber-Arbeitnehmergremium; **~ Joint Industrial Council** *n BrE* (*NJIC*) HRM nationales Arbeitgeber-Arbeitnehmergremium; **~ Labor Relations Board** *n AmE* (*NLRB*) IND Bundesamt zur Regelung der Beziehungen zwischen Arbeitgebern und Arbeitnehmern

national: **~ law** *n* LAW *in US, Germany* Bundesgesetz *nt*, *in EU* einzelstaatliches Gesetz *nt*; **~ legislation** *n* LAW nationale Gesetzgebung *f*, *in US, Germany* Bundesgesetzgebung *f*, *in EU* einzelstaatliche Rechtsvorschriften *f pl*, Bundesgesetz *nt*

National: **~ and Local Government Officers Association** *n BrE* (*NALGO*) HRM Gewerkschaft nationaler und kommunaler Beamten

national: **~ lottery** *n* FIN Staatslotterie *f*, staatliche Lotterie *f*

National: **~ Maritime Board** *n* (*NMB*) TRANSP *shipping* nationales Seeamt

national: **~ market advisory board** *n* STOCK Beratungsgremium *nt* des staatlichen Marktes

National: **~ Measurement Accreditation Service** *n* (*Namas*) GEN COMM nationaler Dienst zur Beglaubigung von Maßeinheiten; **~ Mediation Board** *n AmE* IND Bundesschlichtungsausschuß

national: **~ nature reserve** *n* ENVIR nationales Naturschutzgebiet *nt*; **~ newspaper** *n* GEN COMM überregionale Tageszeitung *f*, *in US, Germany* bundesweite Tageszeitung *f*; **~ noise standard** *n* ENVIR nationale Schallnorm *f*; **~ patent** *n* PATENTS Inlandspatent *nt*; **~ press** *n* MEDIA *print* überregionale Presse *f*; **~ product** *n* ECON Sozialprodukt *nt*; **~ quota** *n* ECON *international trade* nationale Quote *f*

National: **~ Savings** *n pl BrE* FIN, STOCK Schatzbriefe *m pl*; **~ Savings Bank** *n BrE* (*NSB*) BANK ≈ Postsparkasse *f*; **~ Savings Certificate** *n BrE* BANK staatlicher Sparbrief *m*; **~ Savings Income** *n BrE* BANK ≈ Postsparzinsen *m pl*; **~ Savings Investment Account** *n BrE* STOCK höher verzinsliches Postsparkassen-Einlagenkonto, ≈ Postsparkonto *nt*; **~ Shipping Authority** *n AmE* TRANSP nationale Schiffahrtsbehörde

national: **~ standard shipping note** *n* (*NSSN*) IMP/EXP, TRANSP Einheitswarenbegleitschein *m*, nationale Standardversandanzeige *f*, nationaler Standardladeschein *m*, nationaler standardmäßiger Ladeschein *m*, nationaler standardmäßiger Warenbegleitschein *m*; **~ subsidiary structure** *n* GEN COMM *company structure* inländische Filialstruktur *f*

National: **~ Trade Union Council** *n* (*NTUC*) HRM Dachverband der britischen Gewerkschaften

national: **~ trend** *n* ECON Inlandstrend *m*, Trend *m* im Inland

National: **~ Trust** *n BrE* ENVIR Verband zur Erhaltung kulturbedeutender Bauten

national: **~ union** *n AmE* HRM Gewerkschaftsverband *m*

National: **~ Union of Marine Aviation and Shipping Transport** *n BrE* (*NUMAST*) HRM nationale Marinegewerkschaft; **~ Union of Mineworkers** *n BrE*

(*NUM*) HRM nationale Gewerkschaft der Bergarbeiter; **~ Union of Public Employees** *n BrE* (*NUPE*) HRM nationale Gewerkschaft der Angestellten im öffentlichen Dienst; **~ Union of Seamen** *n BrE* (*NUS*) HRM nationale Seeleutegewerkschaft; **~ Water Resources Council** *n* ENVIR staatlicher Rat für Wasserressourcen

national: **~ wealth** *n* ECON Volksvermögen *nt*

nationhood *n* GEN COMM Zustand *m* nationaler Einheit

nationless *adj* ADMIN staatenlos

nationwide *adj* GEN COMM landesweit

native: **~ industry** *n* IND einheimische Industrie *f*

NATO *abbr* (*North Atlantic Treaty Organization*) POL NATO (*Nordatlantikpakt*)

natural: **~ break** *n* S&M natürliche Pause *f*; **~ business year** *n* GEN COMM normales Geschäftsjahr *nt*; **~ gas** *n* ENVIR Erdgas *nt*; **~ monopoly** *n* ECON natürliches Monopol *nt*; **~ number** *n* COMP natürliche Zahl *f*; **~ person** *n* PATENTS natürliche Person *f*; **~ population increase** *n* ECON natürliches Bevölkerungswachstum *nt*; **~ price** *n* ECON natürlicher Preis *m*; **~ rate of growth** *n* ECON natürliche Wachstumsrate *f*; **~ rate of interest** *n* ECON natürlicher Zins *m*; **~ rate of unemployment** *n* ECON natürliche Arbeitslosigkeit *f*; **~ resources** *n pl* ECON, ENVIR Bodenschätze *m pl*, natürliche Hilfsquellen *f pl*, natürliche Ressourcen *f pl*, Naturressourcen *f pl*, Naturschätze *m pl*; **~ rights** *n pl* LAW natürliche Rechte *nt pl*, naturrechtliche Ansprüche *m pl*; **~ wastage** *n* ECON natürlicher Schwund *m*, natürlicher Verschleiß *m*, ENVIR Naturverschwendung *f*, HRM natürlicher Arbeitskräfteabgang *m*, IND üblicher Abgang *m* an Arbeitskräften; **~ wear and tear** *n* ECON natürlicher Verschleiß *m*

nature *n* GEN COMM *character*, PATENTS Art *f*; **~ of the invention** *n* PATENTS Art *f* der Erfindung, Zweck *m* der Erfindung

nautical: **~ mile** *n* GEN COMM Seemeile *f*; **~ registration** *n* TRANSP Schiffseintragung *f*, Schiffszulassung *f*

NAV *abbr* (*net asset value*) ACC, FIN Inventarwert *m*, Liquidationswert *m*, Nettoinventarwert *m*, Substanzwert *m*

naval: **~ architect** *n* IND, TRANSP Schiffsbauer *m*, Schiffsbauingenieur *m*, Schiffsbaumeister *m*

navigation *n* TRANSP Navigation *f*; **~ laws** *n pl* LAW *commercial* Schiffahrtsgesetzgebung *f*

NAWFA *abbr* (*North Atlantic Westbound Freight Association*) TRANSP Nordatlantikvereinigung *f* für Westfracht

NB *abbr* GEN COMM (*nota bene*) bitte beachten, NB (*nota bene*)

NBCC *abbr* (*Netherlands-British Chamber of Commerce*) GEN COMM Niederländisch-Britische Handelskammer *f*

NBPI *abbr BrE* (*National Board for Prices and Incomes*) ECON staatliche Preis- und Einkommensüberwachungsstelle

N/C *abbr* (*new crop*) ECON *agricultural* neue Ernte *f*

NCAD *abbr* (*notice of cancellation at anniversary date*) INS Kündigung *f* zum Ausstellungsdatum der Police, Rücktritt *m* zum Ausstellungsdatum der Police

NCI *abbr* (*New Community Instrument*) ECON *EU* NGI (*Neues Gemeinschaftsinstrument*)

NCITD *abbr* (*National Council on International Trade Documentation*) GEN COMM nationaler Rat für die Dokumentation des internationalen Handels

NCR *abbr* (*net cash requirement*) FIN Nettobargeldbedarf *m*, Nettogeldbedarf *m*

NCS *abbr* (*noncallable securities*) STOCK nicht vorzeitig kündbare Wertpapiere

n.c.v. *abbr* GEN COMM (*no commercial value*) ohne Handelswert, IMP/EXP (*no customs value*) ohne Zollwert

NCVO *abbr BrE* (*National Council of Voluntary Organizations*) WEL nationaler Rat der Wohltätigkeitsorganisationen

ND *abbr* S&M (*no discount*) kein Nachlaß *m*, TRANSP (*new deck*) *shipping* neues Deck *nt*

NDPS *abbr BrE* (*National Data Processing Service*) GEN COMM staatlicher Datenverarbeitungsservice

NE *abbr* (*no effects*) GEN COMM keine Deckung

near: **~ bank** *n* ECON bankähnliches Institut *nt*, Near Bank *f*, Quasibank *f*

nearby: **~ contract** *n* STOCK Terminkontrakt *m* kurz vor Fälligkeit

near: **~ cash** *n* ECON kurzfristige Anlagen *f pl*, STOCK kurzfristige, hochliquide Anlagen *f pl*; **~ completion** *phr* GEN COMM fast fertig

nearest: **~ month** *n* STOCK nächste Monat *m*; **or ~ offer** *phr* (*ono*) S&M oder Angebot

near: **~ future** *n* GEN COMM nahe Zukunft *f*; **~ letter quality** *n* (*NLQ*) COMP NLQ-Druckmodus *m*, beinahe Schönschrift *f* (*obs*); **~-letter-quality printer** *n* COMP Schönschriftdrucker *m*; **~ money** *n* ECON Beinahgeld *nt*, geldähnliche Forderungen *f pl*, Geldsurrogat *nt*, leicht liquidierbare Einlagen *f pl*, Quasigeld *nt*, GEN COMM Beinahgeld *nt*; **or ~ offer** *phr* S&M oder Angebot

NEC *abbr BrE* (*National Executive Committee*) POL geschäftsführender Ausschuß *m*

necessary *adj* GEN COMM notwendig; **the ~ funds** *n pl* FIN die nötigen finanziellen Mittel *nt pl*; **~ labor** *AmE*, **~ labour** *BrE n* HRM erforderliche Arbeitskräfte *f pl*

necessitate *vt* GEN COMM erfordern

necessities *n pl* S&M *home comforts* lebensnotwendige Güter *nt pl*

NEDC *abbr BrE* (*National Economic Development Council*) ECON nationaler Rat für wirtschaftliche Entwicklung

Neddy *abbr infrml BrE* (*National Economic Development Council*) ECON nationaler Rat für wirtschaftliche Entwicklung

NEDO *abbr BrE* (*National Economic Development Office*) ECON nationales Amt für die Untersuchung der wirtschaftlichen Entwicklung

need 1. *n* GEN COMM *of client* Bedarf *m*, Bedürfnis *nt*; **2.** *vt* GEN COMM brauchen

need: **~ arousal** *n* S&M Wecken *nt* von Bedürfnissen

needle: **~ time** *n* MEDIA *broadcast* Nadelzeit *f*

needs: **~ analysis** *n* S&M Bedarfsanalyse *f*

need: **~ satisfaction** *n* MGMNT Bedürfnisbefriedigung *f*

needs: **~ economy** *n* ECON Bedarfswirtschaft *f*; **~ standard** *n* ECON Bedarfsstandard *m*; **~ of trade** *n* BANK Handelsanforderungen *pl*

need: **~-to-know basis** *n* MGMNT Muß-Wissen-Basis *f* (*jarg*)

needy: **the ~** *n pl* WEL die Bedürftigen *pl*

negative *adj* ACC, ECON, FIN, GEN COMM, TAX negativ; ♦ **go ~** *jarg* GEN COMM umkippen, POL einen negativen Wahlkampf führen, S&M eine negative Werbekampagne führen

negative: ~ **amortization** *n* FIN Negativamortisierung *f*; ~ **carry** *n* FIN Nettobestandhaltekosten *pl*; ~ **cash flow** *n* ACC, FIN negativer Cashflow *m*; ~ **correlation** *n* MATH negative Korrelation *f*; ~ **elasticity** *n* ECON negative Elastizität *f*; ~ **feedback** *n* COMP negative Rückkopplung *f*; ~ **file** *n* BANK Negativdatei *f*; ~ **income tax** *n* (*NIT*) TAX negative Einkommenssteuer *f*; ~ **interest** *n* BANK Negativzins *m*, Strafzins *m*; ~ **interest rate gap** *n* STOCK *futures* negatives Zinsgefälle *nt*; ~ **investment** *n* FIN Desinvestition *f*, Verkauf *m* von Anlagen; ~ **monetary compensatory amount** *n* FIN negativer geldwerter Ausgleichsbetrag *m*, negativer Währungsausgleichsbetrag *m*; ~ **net worth** *n* ECON negatives Eigenkapital *nt*; ~ **pledge** *n* BANK Negativerklärung *f*; ~ **pledge clause** *n* BANK Negativklausel *f*; ~ **prescription** *n* LAW Verjährung *f*; ~ **reserve** *n* ACC negative Rücklagen *f pl*; ~ **saving** *n* ECON Entsparen *nt*, negative Ersparnis *nt*, FIN Vermögensaufzehrung *f*; ~ **sum game** *n* ECON Negativsummenspiel *nt*; ~ **targeting** *n* POL, S&M negative Zielbildung *f*, negatives Abzielen *nt* (*jarg*); ~ **tax expenditure** *n* TAX negative Steueraufwendungen *f pl*; ~ **working capital** *n* ACC *balance sheets* negatives Betriebskapital *nt*; ~ **yield curve** *n* ECON negative Zinsstrukturkurve *f*

neglect *vt* LAW versäumen

neglect: ~ **clause** *n* INS Fahrlässigkeitsklausel *f*, Versäumnisklausel *f*

neglected *adj* GEN COMM verwahrlost

negligence *n* LAW Fahrlässigkeit *f*; ~ **clause** *n* INS *marine*, LAW, TRANSP *shipping* Fahrlässigkeitsklausel *f*

negligent *adj* LAW fahrlässig

negligible *adj* GEN COMM geringfügig, unbedeutend, zu vernachlässigen

negotiable *adj* BANK, FIN begebbar, negotiierbar, GEN COMM übertragbar, verhandelbar, STOCK bankfähig, begebbar, börsenfähig; **not** ~ *adj* BANK nicht übertragbar, nur zur Verrechnung; ~ **bill** *n* BANK durch Indossament übertragbarer Wechsel *m*; ~ **bill of lading** *n* TRANSP Orderkonnossement *nt*; ~ **instrument** *n* BANK übertragbares Wertpapier *nt*, ECON begebbares Instrument *nt*, LAW *transactions*, STOCK umlauffähiges Wertpapier *nt*; ~ **issue** *n* HRM aushandelbarer Punkt *m*, verhandlungsbedürftige Frage *f*; ~ **order of withdrawal** *n* AmE (*NOW*) BANK, FIN übertragbare Zahlungsanweisung *f*, übertragbarer Abhebungsauftrag *m*; ~ **order of withdrawal account** *n* AmE BANK, FIN NOW-Konto *nt*, verzinsliches Kontokorrentkonto *nt*, verzinstes Sparkonto *nt*; ~ **securities** *n pl* STOCK frei begebbare Wertpapiere *nt pl*

negotiate *vt* BANK *loan* aushandeln, begeben, FIN begeben, GEN COMM, HRM aushandeln, STOCK aushandeln, begeben; ♦ ~ **a loan** BANK ein Darlehen aushandeln; ~ **from strength** GEN COMM auf starker Ausgangsbasis verhandeln

negotiated: ~ **coordination** *n* ECON vereinbarte Koordination *f*; ~ **market price** *n* ECON ausgehandelter Marktpreis *m*; ~ **price** *n* ECON, S&M ausgehandelter Preis *m*; ~ **underwriting** *n* STOCK ausgehandelte Risikoübernahme *f*

negotiating: ~ **bank** *n* BANK einlösende Bank *f*, negoziierende Bank *f*; ~ **machinery** *n* HRM *industrial relations* Verhandlungsmaschinerie *f*; ~ **partner** *n* GEN COMM Verhandlungspartner, in *m,f*; ~ **procedure** *n* HRM Verhandlungsprozedur *f*; ~ **range** *n* HRM

Verhandlungsspielraum *m*; ~ **round** *n* HRM Tarifrunde *f*; ~ **table** *n* MGMNT Verhandlungstisch *m*

negotiation *n* GEN COMM Negoziierung *f*, Verhandlung *f*; ~ **credit** *n* ECON Negoziierungskredit *m*; ~ **fee** *n* BANK Konsortialprovision *f*; ~ **position** *n* GEN COMM Verhandlungsposition *f*

negotiations *n pl* GEN COMM Verhandlung *f*, MGMNT Gespräche *nt pl*; ~ **for collective agreement** *n pl* BrE (*cf union contract negotiations* AmE) ECON, HRM Tarifverhandlung *f*

negotiation: ~ **strategy** *n* GEN COMM Verhandlungsstrategie *f*

negotiator *n* MGMNT Unterhändler, in *m,f*

neighborhood AmE *see* neighbourhood BrE; ~ **store** *n* AmE (*cf corner shop* BrE) S&M Nachbarschaftsladen *m*, Laden *m* an der Ecke, Geschäft *nt* mit Artikeln des täglichen Bedarfs, Tante-Emma-Laden *m*

neighboring AmE *see* neighbouring BrE

neighbourhood *n* BrE GEN COMM Nachbarschaft *f*, Umgebung *f*; ~ **effect** *n* BrE ECON externe Effekte *m pl*, Externalität *f*, Nachbarschaftseffekt *m*

neighbouring *adj* BrE GEN COMM angrenzend, benachbart; ~ **country** *n* BrE GEN COMM Nachbarland *nt*, Nachbarstaat *m*

neo- *pref* GEN COMM Neo-

neoclassical: ~ **theory** *n* ECON Neoklassik *f*, neoklassische Theorie *f*

neocorporatism *n* ECON Neo-Korporatismus *m*

neo-: ~**Keynesian** *n* ECON Neo-Keynesianer, in *m,f*; ~**Malthusian** *n* ECON Neo-Malthusianer, in *m,f*; ~**Marxist** *n* ECON Neo-Marxist, in *m,f*

neomercantilism *n* ECON Neo-Merkantilismus *m*

neon: ~ **sign** *n* GEN COMM Neonschild *nt*, S&M Transparent *nt*

neo-: ~**Ricardian** ECON Neo-Ricardianer, in *m,f*; ~**Ricardian theory** *n* ECON neo-ricardianische Theorie *f*

NEP *abbr* (*New Economic Policy*) ECON NEP (*Neue Ökonomische Politik*)

nepotism *n* HRM Vetternwirtschaft *f*

nerve: ~ **center** AmE, ~ **centre** BrE *n* MGMNT Gehirn *nt*, Nervenzentrum *nt*

NES *abbr* (*not elsewhere specified*) GEN COMM nicht anderweitig spezifiziert

nest *vt* COMP verschachteln

nested *adj* COMP *data* verschachtelt

nest: ~ **egg** *n* ECON, GEN COMM Notgroschen *m*

nesting *n* COMP Schachtelung *f*, *data* Verschachtelung *f*, TRANSP *cargo handling* Schachtelung *f*; ~ **berth** *n* TRANSP *shipping* Gruppenliegeplatz *m*

net 1. *adj* GEN COMM per saldo, netto; ♦ ~ **of taxes** ACC, ECON, GEN COMM, TAX nach Steuern, versteuert; **2.** *vt* FIN netto erbringen, netto verdienen

net: ~ **acquisition of financial assets** *n* (*NAFA*) FIN Nettoerwerb *m* finanzieller Vermögenswerte; ~ **acquisitions** *n pl* ECON Nettoakquisitionen *f pl*; ~ **amount** *n* ECON Nettobetrag *m*; ~ **asset amount** *n* ACC Reinvermögenbetrag *m*; ~ **assets** *n pl* ACC Nettovermögen *nt*, Reinvermögen *nt*, ECON, FIN Reinvermögen *nt*; ~ **assets per share** *n pl* FIN Eigenkapital *nt* je Aktie; ~ **asset value** *n* (*NAV*) ACC, FIN Inventarwert *m*, Liquidationswert *m*, Nettoinventarwert *m*, Substanzwert *m*; ~ **audience** *n* MEDIA, S&M tatsächliche Zuhörerschaft *f*; ~ **barter**

terms of trade *n pl* IMP/EXP Nettotauschgeschäftsbedingungen *f pl*; ~ **book value** *n* FIN Buchwert *m* nach Abschreibungen, Nettobuchwert *m*; ~ **capital** *n* ACC, ECON, FIN, STOCK Nettokapital *nt*; ~ **capital expenditure** *n* ECON Nettoinvestitionsaufwand *m*, Nettoinvestitionsausgaben *f pl*, Nettokapitalaufwand *m*; ~ **capital gain** *n* ECON, FIN Nettokapitalgewinn *m*; ~ **capital loss** *n* ACC Nettokapitalverlust *m*; ~ **capital requirement** *n* STOCK Nettokapitalbedarf *m*; ~ **capital spending** *n* ECON Nettoinvestitionsaufwand *m*; ~ **cash** *n* ACC, GEN COMM Barzahlung *f* ohne Abzug; ~ **cash flow** *n* ACC Netto-Cashflow *m*; ~ **cash outflow** *n* FIN *in preinvestment analysis* Anschaffungswert *m*; ~ **cash requirement** *n* (*NCR*) FIN Nettobargeldbedarf *m*, Nettogeldbedarf *m*; ~ **commission income** *n* ACC Nettoprovisionseinkommen *nt*; ~ **contribution** *n* ACC Nettobeitrag *m*; ~ **cost** *n* ACC Nettokosten *pl*; ~ **credit** *n* STOCK *options* Nettokredit *m*; ~ **current assets** *n pl* ACC *balance sheets* Nettoumlaufvermögen *nt*, FIN Betriebskapital *nt*, Nettoumlaufvermögen *nt*; ~ **daily loss** *n* FIN *chartering* Tagesnettoverlust *m*; ~ **daily surplus** *n* FIN *chartering* Tagesnettogewinn *m*; ~ **debit** *n* STOCK *options* Nettosollsaldo *m*; ~ **disbursement** *n* ECON *development aid* Nettoauszahlung *f*; ~ **dividend** *n* ACC, STOCK Nettodividende *f*; ~ **domestic investment** *n* ACC Nettoinlandsinvestition *f*; ~ **earnings** *n pl* ACC Nettoverdienst *m*; ~ **equity** *n* ACC Nettoeigenkapital *nt*, ECON Nettoanteil *m*, FIN Nettovermögen *nt*; ~ **estate** *n* TAX Nettonachlaßvermögen *nt*; ~ **foreign assets** *n pl* BANK Nettoauslandsvermögen *nt*; ~ **foreign investment** *n* ACC Nettoauslandsinvestition *f*; ~ **gain** *n* ACC Nettogewinn *m*; ~ **gainer** *n* ECON Nettogewinner, in *m,f*

Netherlands-British: ~ **Chamber of Commerce** *n* (*NBCC*) GEN COMM Niederländisch-Britische Handelskammer *f*

net: ~ **income** *n* ACC Nettogewinn *m*, Reingewinn *m*, ECON, FIN Reingewinn *m*; ~ **income per share of common stock** *n* ACC Nettogewinn *m* je Stammaktie; ~ **income to net worth ratio** *n* ADMIN, GEN COMM Eigenkapitalrendite *f*, Verhältnis *nt* von Reingewinn zum Eigenkapital; ~ **interest income** *n* BANK Nettozinseinkommen *nt*; ~ **interest margin** *n* ACC Nettozinsspanne *f*; ~ **interest yield** *n* FIN *investment* Nettozinsertrag *m*; ~ **investment** *n* BANK, ECON Nettoinvestition *f*; ~ **investment in property, plant and equipment** *n* ACC Buchwert *m* des Anlagevermögens; ~ **investment position** *n* BANK Nettoinvestitionsposition *f*; ~ **leasable area** *n* PROP *floorspace* Nettomietfläche *f*, Nettopachtfläche *f*; ~ **lease** *n* AmE LAW *property* Nettomietvertrag *m*, Nettopachtvertrag *m*; ~ **lending** *n* BANK Nettoausleihung *f*; ~ **lending by the public sector** *n* ECON Nettoausleihungen *f pl* des Staates, Nettokreditvergabe *f* der öffentlichen Hand; ~ **line** *n* INS Höchstgrenze *f* des Selbstbehalts; ~ **liquid funds** *n pl* BANK Nettofonds *m*, Nettoliquidität *f*, FIN Nettobargeld *nt*; ~ **listing** *n* PROP Grundstücksmaklervertrag *m* mit Nettoangebot; ~ **loss** *n* ACC Nettoverlust *m*; ~ **margin** *n* ACC, ECON, FIN Nettogewinnspanne *f*, Reingewinn *m*; ~ **national income** *n* ECON Volkseinkommen *nt*, Nettosozialprodukt *nt* zu Faktorkosten; ~ **national product** *n* ECON Nettosozialprodukt *nt*; ~ **operating income** *n* ACC Nettobetriebseinkommen *nt*; ~ **operating loss** *n* ACC Nettobetriebsverlust *m*;

~ **operating profit** *n* ACC Nettobetriebsgewinn *m*, Reingewinn *m* vor Steuern; ~ **output** *n* ECON Nettoproduktionswert *m*; ~ **paid circulation** *n* S&M verkaufte Auflage *f*; ~ **pay** *n* HRM Nettoeinkommen *nt*; ~ **premium** *n* STOCK *options* Nettoprämie *f*; ~ **present value** *n* (*NPV*) ACC, ECON, FIN Barwert *m*, Kapitalwert *m*; ~ **price** *n* S&M Nettopreis *m*; ~ **proceeds** *n pl* (*np*) PROP Reinertrag *m*; ~ **profit** *n* ACC, ECON Reingewinn *m*, FIN Nettogewinn *m*, Reinerlös *m*, Reingewinn *m*; ~ **profit for the current year** *n* ACC Nettogewinn *m* für das laufende Jahr; ~ **profit for the year** *n* ACC Bilanzgewinn *m*, Jahresüberschuß *m*; ~ **profit margin** *n* ACC Nettoumsatzrendite *f*; ~ **property income from abroad** *n* PROP Nettoeinkünfte *pl* von Auslandsimmobilien; ~ **quick assets** *n pl* ACC Betriebskapital *nt*, Nettoumlaufvermögen *nt*; ~ **rate** *n* ACC *on a loan* Nettozinssatz *m*, INS Bedarfsprämie *f*, Nettorisikoprämie *f*; ~ **rate of return** *n* ACC Nettorendite *f*; ~ **rate of return after tax** *n* ACC, TAX Nettorendite *f* nach Steuern; ~ **reach** *n* S&M tatsächliche Reichweite *f*; ~ **realizable value** *n* (*NRV*) ACC Nettorealisationswert *m*, realisierbarer Nettowert *m*, FIN realisierbarer Verkaufserlös *m*, realisierbarer Verkaufswert *m*, S&M *advertising* realisierbarer Nettowert *m*; ~ **realized capital gains** *n pl* STOCK netto realisierte Kapitalgewinne *m pl*; ~ **receipts** *n pl* ACC Nettoeinnahmen *f pl*; ~ **receipts pool** *n* TRANSP Nettoeinnahmen-Pool *m*; ~ **recorded assets** *n pl* ACC Nettovermögen *nt*; ~ **registered tonnage** *n* GEN COMM Nettoregistertonnage *f*; ~ **register ton** *n* (*NRT*) GEN COMM Nettoregistertonne *f*; ~ **register tonnage** *n* GEN COMM Nettoregistertonnengehalt *m*; ~ **relevant earnings** *n pl* TAX *pensions* relevanter Nettoverdienst *m*; ~ **reserve adjustment amount** *n* ACC Nettoreserveanpassungsbetrag *m*; ~ **resource income** *n* ACC *of corporation* Anlagen-Umsatzrendite *f*; ~ **result** *n* ECON Endergebnis *nt*; ~ **sales** *n pl* ACC Nettoabsatz *m*, Nettoauftragseingang *m*; ~ **security gain** *n* ECON Nettoertrag *m* aus Wertpapieren; ~ **tangible assets per share** *n pl* STOCK Nettorealkapital *nt* pro Aktie; ~ **tare weight** *n* GEN COMM Nettotara *f*, reines Verpackungsgewicht *nt*; ~ **terms** *n pl* (*Nt*) IMP/EXP, TRANSP *shipping* Nettobedingungen *f pl*; ~ **tonnage** *n* GEN COMM Nettotonnage *f*; ~ **total assets** *n pl* ECON Eigenkapital *nt*; ~ **trading surplus** *n* ACC Nettobetriebsgewinn *m*; ~ **transaction** *n* STOCK Nettotransaktion *f*; ~ **value** *n* ACC Nettowert *m*; ~ **voting** *n* FIN Nettostimmenverrechnung *f*, Stimmverrechnung *f*; ~ **weight** *n* GEN COMM Nettogewicht *nt*

network 1. *n* COMP Netz *nt*, Netzwerk *nt*; **2.** *vt* COMP vernetzen

network: ~ **analysis** *n* COMP Netzanalyse *f*, MGMNT Netzwerkanalyse *f*; ~ **architecture** *n* COMP Netzarchitektur *f*; ~ **building** *n* GEN COMM Aufbau *m* eines Netzwerks

networker *n* COMP, ECON an ein Netzwerk angeschlossene Heimarbeiterin *f*, an ein Netzwerk angeschlossener Heimarbeiter *m*, Netzanwender, in *m,f*

networking *n* COMP Netzwerkbetrieb *m*, vernetztes Arbeiten *nt*, GEN COMM Nutzung *f* von Geschäftskontakten, MEDIA *broadcasting* Sendernetz *nt*

net: ~ **working capital** *n* ACC, ECON Nettobetriebskapital *nt*, Nettoumlaufvermögen *nt*, Working Capital *nt*

networking: ~ **economy** n ECON Netz-werkvolkswirtschaft f; ~ **software** n COMP Netzsoftware f, Netzwerksoftware f

network: ~ **marketing** n S&M Absatz m über Händ-lernetz; ~ **of sales outlets** n S&M Netz nt von Verkaufsstellen

net: ~ **worth** n ACC Eigenkapital nt, Nettowert m, Reinvermögen nt, ECON Eigenkapital nt, Reinvermögen nt, FIN Reinvermögen nt, STOCK Nettoanteil m, Nettowert m; ~ **worth assessment** n ACC Eigenkapitalbewertung f; ~ **worth at end of winding-up** n FIN Abwicklungsendvermögen nt; ~ **yield** n ACC of a share Nettorendite f, Reinertrag m

neutral adj GEN COMM neutral; ~ **budget** n ECON, POL ausgeglichenes Budget nt, neutraler Haushaltsplan m; ~ **covered long** n STOCK options neutrale gedeckte Hausseposition f; ~ **covered short** n STOCK options neutral gedeckte Baisseposition f

neutralism n GEN COMM Neutralismus m

neutrality n POL Neutralität f; ~ **of goals** n ECON Zielindifferenz f, Zielneutralität f; ~ **of money** n ECON Geldneutralität f

neutral: ~ **technical progress** n ECON neutraler tech-nischer Fortschritt m; ~ **to bearish** adj STOCK neutral bis Baisse, neutral bis fallend

new adj (N) GEN COMM neu; ◆ ~ **for old** INS neu für alt; ~ **money preferred** STOCK neues Geld bevorzugt; **be under ~ management** MGMNT eine neue Leitung haben

new: ~ **account report** n STOCK neuer Kontobericht m; ~ **business** n GEN COMM neues Geschäft nt; ~ **Cambridge economics** n BrE ECON neue Cambridge-Wirtschaftstheorie f; ~ **charter** n TRANSP shipping neue Charter f; ~ **classical economics** n ECON neue klassische Wirtschaftstheorie f

New: ~ **Commonwealth** n POL neues Commonwealth; ~ **Community Instrument** n (NCI) ECON EU Neues Gemeinschaftsinstrument nt (NGI)

new: ~ **crop** n (N/C) ECON agricultural neue Ernte f

New: ~ **Deal** n AmE POL New Deal m

new: ~ **deck** n (ND) TRANSP shipping neues Deck nt; ~ **democracies** n pl GEN COMM politics junge Demo-kratien f pl

New: ~ **Earnings Survey** n BrE ECON econometrics Einkommens- und Verbrauchsstichprobe f; ~ **Econom-ic Mechanism** n ECON neuer Wirtschaftsmechanismus m; ~ **Economic Policy** n (NEP) ECON neue Ökonomi-sche Politik f (NEP)

new: ~ **economics** n ECON moderne Wirtschaftswissen-schaft f; ~ **edition** n MEDIA print Neuauflage f; ~ **federalism** n AmE POL neuer Föderalismus m; ~ **international division of labor** AmE, ~ **international division of labour** BrE n ECON neue internationale Arbeitsteilung f

New: ~ **International Economic Order** n (NIEO) ECON neue Weltwirtschaftsordnung f

new: ~ **issue** n STOCK Neuemission f; ~ **Keynesian** n ECON Neo-Keynesianer, in m,f

New: ~ **Left** n ECON, POL Neue Linke f

newly: ~ **elected** adj GEN COMM neugewählt; ~ **indus-trialized country** n (NIC) ECON, IND Schwellenland nt; ~ **industrializing economies** n pl (NIEs) ECON auf-strebende Wirtschaftsnationen f pl; ~ **privatized** adj ECON frisch privatisiert, gerade privatisiert

new: ~ **microeconomics** n ECON neue Mikroökonomik f; ~ **orders** n pl ECON, GEN COMM Auftragseingang m

New Orleans: ~ **Commodity Exchange** n STOCK New Orleans Warenbörse

new: ~ **plant and equipment** n ECON Anlageinvestitionen f pl; ~ **product development** n S&M Entwicklung f eines neuen Produktes; ~ **protectionism** n ECON Neoprotektionismus m; ~ **realism** n BrE HRM neuer Realismus m

New: ~ **Right** n ECON, POL Neue Rechte f

news n GEN COMM, MEDIA Nachrichten f pl; ~ **advisory** n MEDIA public relations Ankündigung f von Neuigkeiten; ~ **agency** n BrE (cf wire service AmE) COMMS, GEN COMM, MEDIA Nachrichtenagentur f; ~ **blackout** n MEDIA Nachrichtensperre f; ~ **bulletin** n COMMS amtli-che Nachrichtenverlautbarung f, Bulletin nt

newscaster n MEDIA broadcast Nachrichtensprecher, in m,f

news: ~ **conference** n MEDIA Nachrichtenkonferenz f; ~ **coverage** n GEN COMM Berichterstattung f; ~ **editor** n MEDIA Nachrichtenredakteur, in m,f

newsflash n MEDIA Kurznachricht f

new: ~ **share** n STOCK Neuaktie f, junge Aktie f

news: ~ **headlines** n MEDIA print Kurznachrichten f pl; ~ **item** n MEDIA Pressemeldung f, Pressenotiz f

newsletter n GEN COMM, MEDIA Mitteilungsblatt nt

news: ~ **magazine** n MEDIA Nachrichtenmagazin nt

newspaper n COMMS Blatt nt, GEN COMM Zeitung f, MEDIA Blatt nt; ~ **advertising** n S&M Zeitungsanzeige f, Zeitungswerbung f; ~ **publisher** n MEDIA print Zei-tungsverleger m

Newspaper: ~ **Publishers' Association** n BrE (NPA) MEDIA Vereinigung der Zeitungsverleger

newspaper: ~ **syndicate** n MEDIA Pressezentrale f, Zeitungssyndikat nt

news: ~ **picture** n MEDIA Nachrichtenbild nt; ~ **release** n MEDIA Freigabe f von Nachrichten

newsroom n MEDIA print Nachrichtenredaktion f

news: ~ **round up** n MEDIA Nachrichtenübersicht f

new: ~ **technologies** n pl GEN COMM neue Technologien f pl, IND neue Technologien f pl, neue technologische Errungenschaften f pl; ~ **technology agreement** n BrE HRM Abkommen über neue technologische Entwicklungen; ~ **town** n ECON, PROP, WEL Trabantenstadt f; ~ **world order** n POL neue Weltordnung f

New York: ~ **Coffee, Sugar and Cocoa Exchange** n STOCK New Yorker Kaffee-, Zucker- und Kakaobörse; ~ **Cotton Exchange and Petroleum and Citrus Associates** n STOCK New Yorker Baumwollbörse; ~ **Curb Exchange** n STOCK New Yorker Freiverkehrsbörse; ~ **Futures Exchange** n (NYFE) STOCK New Yorker Terminbörse; ~ **Mercantile Exchange** n (NYMEX) STOCK New Yorker Rohstoff- und Warenterminbörse; ~ **prime loan rate** n (NYPLR) BANK New Yorker Kreditzins für erste Adressen; ~ **Shipping Association** n (NYSA) TRANSP New Yorker Versandsvereinigung; ~ **Stock Exchange** n (NYSE) STOCK New Yorker Wertpapierbörse; ~ **Stock Exchange Composite Index** n STOCK New Yorker Börsengesamtindex

next: ~-**day** adj TRANSP delivery am nächsten Tag; ~-**to-reading matter** n S&M textanschließende Anzeige f

NF abbr (no funds) GEN COMM keine Deckung, ohne Deckung

N/F *abbr* (*no funds*) GEN COMM keine Deckung, ohne Deckung

NFA *abbr AmE* (*National Futures Association*) STOCK Aufsichtsorgan für den Terminhandel

NFAS *abbr* (*National Federation of American Shipping*) TRANSP nationaler Verband der amerikanischen Schiffahrt

NFTZ *abbr* (*Non Free Trade Zone*) IMP/EXP Nichtfreihandelszone

NFU *abbr BrE* (*National Farmers' Union*) IND nationaler Bauernverband

NGO *abbr* (*nongovernmental organization*) GEN COMM NRO (*Nichtregierungsorganisation*)

NHP *abbr* (*nominal horsepower*) GEN COMM Nennpferdestärke *f*, nominelle Pferdestärke *f*

NHS *abbr BrE* (*National Health Service*) GEN COMM staatlicher Gesundheitsdienst *m*

NI *abbr BrE* (*National Insurance*) HRM SV (*Sozialversicherung*)

NIA *abbr* (*National Irrigation Administration*) ENVIR nationale Bewässerungsbehörde

NIB *abbr* (*Nordic Investment Bank*) BANK Nordische Investitionsbank *f*

NIC *abbr* (*newly industrialized country*) ECON Schwellenland *nt*

niche *n* HRM Niche *f*, S&M Marktlücke *f*, Nische *f*; ~ **bank** *n* BANK Nischenbank *f*; ~ **market** *n* S&M Nischenmarkt *m*, Marktlücke *f*; ~ **marketing** *n* S&M Marketing *nt* in Marktlücken; ~ **study** *n* S&M Marktlückenstudie *f*; ~ **trading** *n* GEN COMM Nischenhandel *m*

NICs *abbr BrE* (*National Insurance Contributions*) TAX Sozialversicherungsbeiträge *m pl*

NIDL *abbr* (*new international division of labor AmE*, *new international division of labour BrE*) ECON neue internationale Arbeitsteilung *f*

NIEO *abbr* (*New International Economic Order*) ECON neue Weltwirtschaftsordnung *f*

NIEs *abbr* (*newly industrializing economies*) ECON aufstrebende Wirtschaftsnationen *f pl*

NIESR *abbr BrE* (*National Institute for Economic and Social Research*) ECON Nationales Institut für Wirtschafts- und Sozialforschung, Konjunkturinstitut

night: ~ **depository** *n* BANK Nachtschalter *m*, Nachttresor *m*; ~ **differential** *n* ECON Nachtarbeitszuschlag *m*; ~ **letter** *n* AmE COMMS Brieftelegramm *nt*; ~ **safe** *n* BANK Nachtsafe *m*, Nachttresor *m*; ~ **shift** *n* HRM Nachtschicht *f*; ~ **trunk** *n* TRANSP Nachtverbindung *f*; ~ **watchman state** *n* ECON Nachtwächterstaat *m*; ~ **work** *n* HRM Nachtarbeit *f*

Nikkei: ~ **average** *n* ECON, FIN, STOCK Nikkei-Durchschnitt *m*; ~ **index** *n* ECON, FIN, STOCK Nikkei-Index *m*

Nikkeiren *n* STOCK Zusammenschluß von japanischen Arbeitgeberverbänden

nil *n* GEN COMM Null *f*; ~ **paid** *adj* STOCK Bezeichnung für nicht ausgeübte Bezugsrechte

nimble *adj* GEN COMM gewandt

NIMBY *abbr* (*not in my back yard*) ENVIR, POL nicht bei uns; ~ **principle** *n* ENVIR, POL Sankt-Florians-Prinzip *nt*

ninety: ~-**nine-year lease** *n* BANK Miete *f* auf neunundneunzig Jahre, Pacht *f* auf neunundneunzig Jahre, PROP Miete *f* auf neunundneunzig Jahre

NIPA *abbr* (*National Income and Product Accounts*) ECON *econometrics* Entstehungs- und Verteilungsrechnung *f*

NIT *abbr* (*negative income tax*) TAX negative Einkommenssteuer *f*

nixie: ~ **mail** *n* AmE COMMS Post *f* mit unleserlicher Adresse, unzustellbare Post *f*, nicht zustellbare Post *f*

NJC *abbr BrE* (*National Joint Committee*) HRM nationales Arbeitgeber-Arbeitnehmergremium

NJIC *abbr BrE* (*National Joint Industrial Council*) HRM nationales Arbeitgeber-Arbeitnehmergremium

NLQ *abbr* (*near letter quality*) COMP NLQ-Druckmodus *m*, beinahe Schönschrift *f* (*obs*)

NLRB *abbr AmE* (*National Labor Relations Board*) IND Bundesamt zur Regelung der Beziehungen zwischen Arbeitgebern und Arbeitnehmern

NMB *abbr* (*National Maritime Board*) TRANSP *shipping* nationales Seeamt

NMS *abbr* (*normal market size*) STOCK normale Marktgröße *f*

NNRF *abbr* (*non-negotiable report of findings*) GEN COMM endgültiger Untersuchungsbericht *m*, endgültiges Untersuchungsergebnis *nt*

no. *abbr* (*number*) GEN COMM, MATH Anz. (*Anzahl*), Nr. (*Nummer*)

no-account *adj* (*n/a*) BANK keine Deckung, kein Konto

Nobel: ~ **Prize for Economics** *n* ECON Nobelpreis *m* für Wirtschaftswissenschaften

no-claims: ~ **bonus** *n* BrE INS Schadenfreiheitsrabatt *m*

node *n* COMP Knoten *m*

no-fault: ~ **automobile insurance** *n* AmE (*cf no-fault motor insurance BrE*) INS *personal* Autoversicherung *f* für Personenschäden ohne Prüfung; ~ **motor insurance** *n* BrE (*cf no-fault automobile insurance AmE*) INS *personal* Autoversicherung *f* für Personenschäden ohne Prüfung

no-growth *adj* ECON statisch

noise *n* COMP Geräusch *nt*, Verzerrung *f*, ECON *econometrics* Verzerrung *f*; ~ **abatement** *n* ENVIR Lärmbekämpfung *f*, Lärmschutz *m*; ~ **emission** *n* ENVIR Lärmemission *f*, Schallabgabe *f*; ~ **insulation** *n* ENVIR Lärmisolierung *f*; ~ **level** *n* ENVIR Geräuschpegel *m*, Lärmpegel *m*

no-lien: ~ **affidavit** *n* LAW eidesstattliche Versicherung *f*

nolo contendere *phr* LAW Nicht-Bestreiten *nt*

nominal *adj* GEN COMM *minimal, negligible* unbedeutend, *theoretical* nominal, nominell, Nenn-; ~ **assets** *n pl* ACC Nominalvermögen *nt*; ~ **capital** *n* ACC Nominalkapital *nt*, FIN Stammkapital *nt*; ~ **cost** *n* FIN Nominalkosten *pl*; ~ **damages** *n pl* LAW nomineller Schaden *m*; ~ **GDP** *n* ECON nominales Bruttosozialprodukt *nt*; ~ **growth** *n* ECON Nominalwachstum *nt*; ~ **holdings** *n pl* FIN anonymer Aktienbesitz *m*; ~ **horsepower** *n* (*NHP*) GEN COMM Nennpferdestärke *f*, nominelle Pferdestärke *f*; ~ **ledger** *n* ACC nominales Hauptbuch *nt*; ~ **loan rate** *n* FIN Nominalkreditzins *m*

nominally *adj* GEN COMM *in name only* nur dem Namen nach

nominal: ~ **pay** *n* GEN COMM Nominalgehalt *nt*; ~ **price** *n* ACC nominaler Preis *m*; ~ **quotation** *n* STOCK Notierung *f* ohne Umsätze; ~ **scale** *n* GEN COMM nomineller Maßstab *m*; ~ **tax rate** *n* TAX Nominalsteuersatz *m*; ~ **value** *n* ACC Nennwert *m*; ~ **wage** *n* HRM Nominallohn *m*; ~ **yield** *n* FIN Nominalverzinsung *f*, Rendite *f*, Ertrag *f* aus der Normalverzinsung, STOCK *fixed-income security* Nominalverzinsung *f*

nominate *vt* GEN COMM nominieren, ernennen

nomination *n* GEN COMM Ernennung *f*, POL Kandidatur *f*

nominee *n* POL Kandidat, in *m,f*, STOCK Strohmann *m*; **~ account** *n* STOCK Strohmannkonto *nt*; **~ company** *n* STOCK Briefkastengesellschaft *f*, Strohmanngesellschaft *f*; **~ name** *n* STOCK Strohmannname *m*; **~ shareholder** *n* STOCK als Aktionär vorgeschobener Strohmann *m*

nonacceptance *n* GEN COMM Annahmeverweigerung *f*; **~ of delivery** *n* LAW *contracts* Annahmeverweigerung *f*

nonaccruing: ~ loan *n* BANK Kredit, auf den keine Zinszahlungen geleistet werden

nonagricultural: ~ use *n* PROP nichtlandwirtschaftliche Nutzung *f*

non-aligned *adj* POL neutral, ungebunden

no-name: ~ product *n* S&M markenfreies Produkt *nt*, No-name-Produkt *nt*

non-appealability *n* GEN COMM, LAW Unanfechtbarkeit *f*

nonappearance *n* LAW Nichterscheinen *nt*

nonapproved *adj* STOCK *options* nicht genehmigt; **~ pension scheme** *n* FIN nicht genehmigter Pensionsplan *m*

non-assignment: ~ clause *n* GEN COMM Abtretungsverbotsklausel *f*

nonbank: ~ bank *n* BANK Nichtbank-Bank *f*, Nonbank-Bank *f*; **~ banking** *n* BANK Nichtbank-Bankgeschäfte *nt pl*, Nonbank-Banking *nt*; **~ deposit** *n* FIN Nichtbankeneinlage *f*; **~ financial institution** *n* ECON, FIN intermediäres Finanzinstitut *nt*; **~ sector** *n* FIN bankfremder Sektor *m*, Nichtbankensektor *m*

nonbasic: ~ commodity *n* ECON Nichtrohstoffe *m pl*; **~ industry** *n* IND Nebenindustrie *f*

noncallable: ~ bond *n* ECON unkündbare Anleihe *f*, STOCK nicht vorzeitig kündbare Anleihe *f*; **~ securities** *n* (*NCS*) STOCK nicht vorzeitig kündbare Wertpapiere

noncall: ~ provision *n* ECON Nichtkündbarkeitsklausel *f*

noncash: ~ benefit *n* ECON Sachleistung *f*; **~ contribution** *n* ECON Sachleistung *f*; **~ payment** *n* BANK bargeldlose Zahlung *f*; **~ payment system** *n* BANK bargeldloser Zahlungsverkehr *m*; **~ rewards** *n pl* HRM bargeldlose Vergütungen *f pl*

noncommercial: ~ cargo *n* TRANSP nichtkommerzielle Fracht *f*

non-committed *adj* POL blockfrei, ungebunden

noncompeting: ~ group *n* HRM nicht konkurrierende Gruppe *f*

noncompetitive: ~ bid *n* STOCK *US Treasury Bills* nicht wettbewerbsfähiges Angebot *nt*

noncompliance: ~ with an order *n* LAW Nichteinhaltung *f* einer Anordnung

noncompulsory *adj* ECON, GEN COMM, INS freiwillig; **~ contribution** *n* INS freiwillige Leistung *f*; **~ expenditure** *n* ECON nichtobligatorische Ausgaben *f pl*

nonconcessional *adj* GEN COMM nicht konzessionierbar

nonconforming *adj* ECON, GEN COMM nicht vertragsgemäß, IND fehlerhaft; **~ goods** *n pl* ECON nicht vertragsmäßige Ware *f*; **~ use** *n* LAW, PROP nicht vorschriftsmäßige Benutzung *f*

nonconformity *n* LAW Abweichung *f*

nonconsolidated *adj* ACC nichtkonsolidiert

noncontestability: ~ clause *n* INS Nichtanfechtbarkeitsklausel *f*

noncontractual: ~ agreement *n* LAW *transactions* Gefälligkeitsvereinbarung *f*

noncontribution: ~ clause *n* INS Klausel *f* zur Beitragsbefreiung

noncontributory: ~ pension fund *n* HRM Pensionsplan *m* ohne Beitragsleistungen der Arbeitnehmer; **~ pension plan** *n* FIN beitragsfreie Betriebspension *f*, beitragsfreier Pensionsplan *m*, nicht beitragspflichtiger Rentenplan *m*; **~ pension scheme** *n* FIN beitragsfreie Betriebspension *f*, beitragsfreier Pensionsplan *m*, HRM Pensionsplan *m* ohne Beitragsleistungen der Arbeitnehmer, nicht beitragspflichtiger Rentenplan *m*

noncumulative: ~ preference share *n* BrE (*cf noncumulative preferred stock AmE*) STOCK Vorzugsaktie *f* ohne Nachbezugsrecht; **~ preferred stock** *n* AmE (*cf noncumulative preference share BrE*) STOCK nichtkumulative Vorzugsaktie *f*, Vorzugsaktie *f* ohne kumulativen Dividendenanspruch, Vorzugsaktie *f* ohne Nachbezugsrecht; **~ tax** *n* TAX gewöhnliche Steuer *f*, nichtkumulative Steuer *f*

noncurrent: ~ asset *n* ACC Anlagevermögen *nt*

nondebugged *adj* COMP nicht auf Programmfehler geprüft, unausgetestet

nondeductibility: ~ of employer contributions *n* HRM Nichtabzugsfähigkeit *f* der Arbeitgeberbeiträge

nondefaulting: ~ party *n* FIN, LAW *transactions* vertragstreue Partei *f*

nondemise: ~ charter party *n* TRANSP *shipping* nicht übertragbarer Befrachtungsvertrag *m*

nondestructive: ~ testing *n* IND zerstörungsfreie Prüfung *f*

nondisclosure *n* INS Unterlassen *nt* einer Mitteilung, Verschweigen *nt*

nondiscretionary: ~ trust *n* BrE (*cf fixed-investment trust AmE*) STOCK Investmentfonds *m* mit unveränderlichem Portefeuille, Kapitalanlagegesellschaft *f* mit festgelegten Anteilen

nondisturbance: ~ clause *n* LAW, PROP *mortgage contract, mineral rights* Nichtbeeinträchtigungsklausel *f*

nondurable: ~ goods *n pl* S&M kurzlebige Güter *nt pl*, kurzlebige Konsumgüter *nt pl*, kurzlebige Verbrauchsgüter *nt pl*

nondurables *n pl* S&M kurzlebige Güter *nt pl*, kurzlebige Konsumgüter *nt pl*, kurzlebige Verbrauchsgüter *nt pl*

nonemployment *n* HRM Beschäftigungslosigkeit *f*

non-EU: ~ national *n* GEN COMM Nicht-EU-Bürger, in *m,f*

nonexecution *n* LAW Nichtausführung *f*, Nichterfüllung *f*

non-executive *adj* HRM nicht an der Geschäftsführung beteiligt, nichtleitend; **~ director** *n* HRM, MGMNT Direktor, in *m,f* ohne Geschäftsbereich, nebenamtlicher Geschäftsführer *m*, nebenamtliche Geschäftsführerin *f*

nonexempt *adj* TAX nicht befreit

nonfactor: ~ income *n* ECON Transfereinkommen *nt*

nonfeasance *n* LAW *commercial* schuldhaftes Unterlassen *nt*

nonfinancial: ~ assets *n pl* ECON Sachvermögen *nt*; **~ corporation** *n* ECON Nichtbankunternehmen *nt*

nonforfeitable *adj* ECON, LAW nicht verfallbar

nonforfeiture *n* ECON, LAW Nichtverfallbarkeit *f*

Non: ~ Free Trade Zone *n* (*NFTZ*) IMP/EXP Nichtfreihandelszone *f*

nonfulfillment *AmE see nonfulfilment BrE*

nonfulfilment *n BrE* LAW Nichterfüllung *f*; **~ of contract** *n BrE* LAW Nichterfüllung *f* eines Vertrags

nonfungible: ~ **goods** *n pl* ACC nichtfungible Waren *f pl*, nichtvertretbare Waren *f pl*

nongoal: ~ **equilibrium** *n* ECON Nichtzielgleichgewicht *nt*

nongovernmental: ~ **organization** *n* (*NGO*) GEN COMM Nichtregierungsorganisation *f* (*NRO*)

non-interest-bearing: ~ **deposit** *n* BANK unverzinsliche Einlage *f*; ~ **securities** *n pl* STOCK nicht verzinsliche Wertpapiere *nt pl*, unverzinsliche Werte *m pl*

noninterest-earning *adj* BANK unverzinslich; ~ **deposit** *n* BANK unverzinsliche Einlage *f*

nonintervention *n* ECON Nichteinmischung *f*

non-key: ~ **jobs** *n pl* ECON sonstige Tätigkeiten *f pl*

nonleviable *adj* FIN unpfändbar

nonliability *n* INS, LAW Haftungsausschluß *m*

nonlife: ~ **insurance** *n* INS Nichtlebensversicherung *f*

nonlinear: ~ **pricing** *n* ECON Preisdiskriminierung *f* zweiten Grades; ~ **programming** *n* COMP, MATH nicht-lineare Programmierung *f*, nichtlineares Programmieren *nt*

nonluxury: ~ **item** *n* S&M Gebrauchsartikel *m*

nonmandatory *adj* LAW *guidelines* nicht obligatorisch

nonmanual: ~ **union** *n* HRM Angestelltengewerkschaft *f*

nonmarket: ~ **sector** *n* ECON Nichtmarkt-Sektor *m*

nonmember *n* ADMIN Nichtmitglied *nt*; ~ **bank** *n* AmE BANK *Federal Reserve* nicht dem Zentralbanksystem angeschlossene Bank

nonmembership *n* HRM *of a union* Nichtmitgliedschaft *f*

nonmerchantable: ~ **title** *n* AmE PROP Grundbesitz *m* mit beschränkten Rechten, nicht rechtsmängelfreies Liegenschaftsrecht *nt*

nonmetropolitan *adj* GEN COMM nicht großstädtisch

nonmonetary: ~ **capital** *n* ECON Sachkapital *nt*; ~ **compensation** *n* GEN COMM, HRM Sachbezug *m*; ~ **economy** *n* ECON Tauschwirtschaft *f*; ~ **investment** *n* HRM nichtmonetäre Investition *f*; ~ **reward** *n* GEN COMM, HRM Sachbezug *m*

non-negotiable *adj* GEN COMM nicht begebbar, nicht übertragbar; ~ **bill of lading** *n* IMP/EXP, TRANSP *shipping* Namenskonnossement *nt*, nicht übertragbares Konnossement *nt*; ~ **cheque** BANK Verrechnungsscheck *m*; ~ **instrument** *n* BANK nicht übertragbares Wertpapier *nt*; ~ **report of findings** *n* (*NNRF*) GEN COMM endgültiger Untersuchungsbericht *m*, endgültiges Untersuchungsergebnis *nt*

nonobservance: ~ **of conditions** *n* GEN COMM, LAW Mißachtung *f* von Bedingungen

nonobvious *adj* GEN COMM nicht offensichtlich

nonoccupying: ~ **owner** *n* PROP nicht im Eigentum wohnender Eigentümer

nonofficial: ~ **trade organization** *n* (*NOTO*) HRM inoffizielle Handelsorganisation

nonoil: ~ **balance** *n* ECON, ENVIR Nicht-Öl-Bilanz *f*; ~ **countries** *n pl* ECON, ENVIR Nicht-Ölländer *nt pl*

nonoperating: ~ **expense** *n* ACC betriebsfremder Aufwand *m*, neutrale Kosten *pl*, nichtbetriebliche Kosten *pl*; ~ **result** *n* ECON neutrales Ergebnis *nt*; ~ **revenue** *n* ACC neutrale Einnahmen *f pl*, nichtbetriebliche Einnahmen *f pl*

nonparametric: ~ **statistics** *n pl* MATH parameterfreie Statistik *f*, verteilungsfreie Statistik *f*

nonpar: ~ **share** *n* ECON nennwertlose Aktie *f*

nonparticipating: ~ **policy** *n* ECON nicht gewinnberechtigte Police *f*

nonpartisan: ~ **expert** *n* ECON unparteiische Gutachterin *f*, unparteiischer Gutachter *m*

nonpatrial *adj* BrE *obs* ADMIN ohne ständigen Wohnsitz

nonpayment *n* GEN COMM Nichtbezahlung *f*

nonpecuniary: ~ **returns** *n pl* HRM nichtmaterieller Lohn *m*, Sachbezüge *m pl*

nonperformance *n* LAW Nichterfüllung *f*

nonperforming: ~ **credit** *n* BANK notleidender Kredit *m*, notleidendes Darlehen *nt*

nonprice: ~ **competition** *n* ECON, S&M außerpreislicher Wettbewerb *m*

nonproductive *adj* IND, MGMNT unproduktiv; ~ **loan** *n* BANK *retail* unproduktives Darlehen *nt*

nonprofit: ~ **accounting** *n* ACC nicht gewinnorientierte Buchführung *f*; ~ **corporation** *n* AmE GEN COMM gemeinnützige Gesellschaft *f*; ~ **enterprise** *n* (*NPE*) ECON gemeinnütziges Unternehmen *nt*, nichterwerbswirtschaftlich ausgerichtetes Unternehmen *nt*

non-profit-making *adj* ACC, FIN, GEN COMM, TAX gemeinnützig; ~ **company** *n* GEN COMM gemeinnützige Gesellschaft *f*; ~ **organization** *n* ECON gemeinnützige Organisation *f*, Organisation *f* ohne Erwerbscharakter

nonprofit: ~ **organization** *n* AmE ECON gemeinnützige Organisation *f*, Organisation *f* ohne Erwerbscharakter

nonproject: ~ **aid** *n* ECON *development aid* nicht projektgebundene Hilfe *f*

nonproperty: ~ **owner** *n* ECON, LAW, PROP Besitzlose(r) *mf* [decl. as adj]

nonpublic: ~ **information** *n* AmE GEN COMM nicht für die Öffentlichkeit bestimmte Information

nonrandom: ~ **sample** *n* ECON nicht zufällige Stichprobe *f*

nonrecourse *adj* FIN regreßlos; ~ **export financing** *n* FIN Forfaitierung *f*, regreßlose Exportfinanzierung *f*; ~ **loan** *n* FIN projektgebundenes Darlehen *nt*

nonrecurrent: ~ **income** *n* ACC außerordentlicher Ertrag *m*, ECON einmalige Erträge *f pl*

nonrecurring: ~ **appropriation** *n* FIN einmalige Emission von Fondsanteilen; ~ **charge** *n* ACC *annual accounts*, FIN außerordentlicher Aufwand *m*; ~ **expenditure** *n* STOCK einmalige Aufwendungen *f pl*, einmalige Ausgabe *f*

nonrecyclable *adj* ENVIR nicht recyclefähig, nicht wiederverwertbar, GEN COMM nicht wiederverwertbar

nonrefundable *adj* TAX nicht erstattungsfähig; ~ **deposit** *n* S&M nicht erstattungsfähige Einlage *f*; ~ **fee** *n* S&M nicht erstattungsfähige Gebühr *f*; ~ **taxes** *n pl* TAX nicht erstattungsfähige Steuern *f pl*

nonrenewable: ~ **natural resources** *n pl* ENVIR nicht erneuerbare Bodenschätze *m pl*; ~ **resource** *n* ECON, ENVIR nicht erneuerbarer Rohstoff *m*, nicht nachwachsender Rohstoff *m*; ~ **resources** *n pl* ENVIR nicht erneuerbare Ressourcen *f pl*

nonresident *n* GEN COMM Devisenausländer, in *m,f*, LAW Gebietsfremde(r) *mf [decl. as adj]*; ~ **company** *n* LAW nichtansässige Gesellschaft *f*; ~ **deposit** *n* FIN Auslandseinlage *f*; ~ **deposits** *n pl* BANK Auslandsguthaben *nt pl*; ~ **issuer** *n* FIN ausländische Emittentin *f*, ausländischer Emittent *m*; ~'s **holding** *n* ECON Auslandsbesitz *m*

nonreturnable: ~ **packaging** *n* S&M Einwegverpackung *f*

nonreversible: ~ **laytime** *n* TRANSP *shipping* nicht umsteuerbare Liegezeit *f*

nonroutine: ~ **decision** *n* GEN COMM Ausnahmeentscheidung *f*, nicht-routinemäßige Entscheidung *f*

nonscheduled *adj* HRM außerplanmäßig

nonsmoking: ~ **lounge** *n* LEIS Nichtraucherraum *m*

nonstatutory *adj* LAW nicht satzungsgemäß

nonsterling: ~ **area** *n* (*NSA*) ECON Nicht-Sterling-Gebiet *nt*

nonstop: ~ **flight** *n* TRANSP Direktflug *m*, Non-Stop-Flug *m*

nonstore: ~ **retailing** *n* S&M Einzelhandel *m* ohne Ladengeschäft

nontariff: ~ **barrier** *n* (*NTB*) ECON *international trade*, GEN COMM, IMP/EXP zollfremdes Handelshemmnis *nt*, nichttarifäres Handelshemmnis *nt*; ~ **trade barrier** *n* ECON nichttarifäres Handelshemmnis *nt*

nontaxable: ~ **transactions** *n pl* FIN nicht steuerpflichtige Umsätze *m pl*

nontax: ~ **income** *n* TAX steuerfreies Einkommen *nt*

nonterminable *adj* LAW unkündbar

nontradeables *n pl* ECON nicht handelsfähige Güter *nt pl*

nontrading: ~ **partnership** *n* LAW Dienstleistungsgesellschaft *f*

nontransferable: ~ **debentures** *n pl* BANK nicht übertragbare Schuldtitel *m pl*; ~ **security** *n* FIN nicht übertragbares Wertpapier

nonunion *adj* HRM nichtorganisiert; ~ **firm** *n* HRM *industrial relations* gewerkschaftsfreies Unternehmen *nt*; ~ **labor** *AmE*, ~ **labour** *BrE n* HRM nichtorganisierte Arbeitskräfte *f pl*, nichtorganisierte Arbeiter *m pl*

nonutilized *adj* GEN COMM *line of credit* nicht in Anspruch genommen

nonvariable *adj* BANK fest, fix

nonverbal: ~ **communication** *n* GEN COMM, MGMNT nonverbale Kommunikation *f*

non-viable: ~ **enterprise** *n* GEN COMM nicht lebensfähiges Unternehmen *nt*

nonvoting: ~ **share** *n* STOCK stimmrechtslose Aktie *f*; ~ **stock** *n* STOCK stimmrechtslose Aktie *f*

nonwarranty: ~ **clause** *n* LAW Freizeichnungsklausel *f*

nonworking: ~ **spouse** *n* HRM nicht arbeitende Ehegattin *f*, nicht arbeitender Ehegatte *m*

non-zero-sum: ~ **game** *n* ECON Nichtnullsummenspiel *nt*

no-par: ~ **stock** *n* STOCK nennwertlose Aktie *f*, Quotenaktie *f*; ~ **value** *n* STOCK nennwertlos

no-par-value: ~ **share** *n* STOCK nennwertlose Aktie *f*

no-profit: ~ **competition** *n* ECON gewinnlose Konkurrenz *f*

Nordic: ~ **countries** *n pl* GEN COMM nordische Länder *nt pl*; ~ **Investment Bank** *n* (*NIB*) BANK Nordische Investitionsbank *f*

norm *n* GEN COMM Norm *f*

normal *adj* GEN COMM üblich, normal; ~ **capacity** *n* ECON Normalkapazität *f*

normalcy *n* *AmE* (*cf normality BrE*) GEN COMM Normalität *f*

normal: ~ **distribution** *n* MATH *statistics* Gaußsche Normalverteilung *f*, Normalverteilung *f*; ~ **good** *n* ECON Normalgut *nt*; ~ **investment practice** *n* FIN übliche Investitionspraxis *f*

normality *n* *BrE* (*cf normalcy AmE*) GEN COMM Normalität *f*

normal: ~ **laytime** *n* TRANSP *shipping* normale Liegezeit *f*; ~ **market size** *n* *BrE* (*NMS*) STOCK normale Marktgröße *f*; ~ **price** *n* ECON normaler Preis *m*; ~ **profit** *n* ECON Normalgewinn *m*; ~ **rate** *n* GEN COMM Normaltarif *m*, TAX Regelsteuersatz *m*; ~ **retirement** *n* HRM normale Pensionierung *f*; ~ **retirement age** *n* HRM normales Pensionsalter *nt*; ~ **standard cost** *n* ECON flexible Normalkosten *pl*; ~ **sustainable capacity** *n* ECON normale Kapazität *f*; ~ **wear and tear** *n* ACC *depreciation* gewöhnliche Abnutzung *f*

normative *n* MGMNT Normativ *nt*, Richtlinie *f*; ~ **economics** *n* ECON normative Wirtschaftswissenschaft *f*; ~ **forecasting** *n* GEN COMM normative Prognose *f*

norm: ~ **for competition** *n* GEN COMM Wettbewerbsnorm *f*

Norris-La Guardia: ~ **Act** *n* *AmE* HRM *1932* Norris-La Guardia-Gesetz *nt*

North: ~ **American Export Grain Association** *n* (*NAEGA*) GEN COMM nordamerikanische Getreideexportvereinigung; ~ **American Free Trade Area** *n* (*NAFTA*) ECON Nordamerikanische Freihandelszone *f*; ~ **Atlantic** *n* GEN COMM, POL, TRANSP Nordatlantik *m*; ~ **Atlantic rates** *n* TRANSP Nordatlantiktarife *m pl*; ~ **Atlantic Shippers' Association** *n* (*NASA*) TRANSP Vereinigung der Nordatlantik-Seehafenspediteure; ~ **Atlantic Treaty Organization** *n* (*NATO*) POL Nordatlantikpakt *m* (*NATO*); ~ **Atlantic Westbound Freight Association** *n* (*NAWFA*) TRANSP Nordatlantikvereinigung *f* für Westfracht; ~ **Sea** *n* GEN COMM, TRANSP Nordsee *f*; ~ **Sea gas** *n* ENVIR, IND Nordseegas *nt*

Norwegian: ~ **Chamber of Commerce** *n* (*NCC*) GEN COMM Norwegische Handelskammer *f*

nos. *abbr* (*numbers*) MATH Nummern *f pl*, Zahlen *f pl*

nosedive *n* ECON *of prices* Kursverfall *m*, Preissturz *m*

no-show *n* LEIS Nichterscheinen *nt*, nichterschienener Passagier *m*

no-smoking: ~ **area** *n* ENVIR *pollution* Nichtraucherzone *f*

no-strike: ~ **agreement** *n* GEN COMM, HRM, IND Streikverzichtabkommen *nt*; ~ **clause** *n* GEN COMM, HRM, IND *union* Streikverbotsklausel *f*

nota bene *phr* (*NB*) GEN COMM bitte beachten, nota bene (*NB*)

notarial *adj* LAW notariell; ~ **authentication** *n* LAW notarielle Beglaubigung *f*, notarielle Beurkundung *f*

notarize *vt* LAW notariell beglaubigen, notariell beurkunden

notarized *adj* LAW notariell beglaubigt, notariell beurkundet

notary: ~ **public** *n* LAW Notar, in *m,f*

note 1. *n* BANK, FIN *payable, receivable draft* Wechsel *m*, *BrE* (*cf bill AmE*) *money* Banknote *f*, Schein *m*, GEN COMM Aufzeichnung *f*, Vermerk *m*; **2.** *vt* GEN COMM aufzeichnen, *point* vermerken

notebook *n* COMP Notebook *nt*

note: ~ **disclosure** *n* GEN COMM Bekanntmachung *f* von Aufzeichnungen; ~ **issue** *n* BANK Emission *f* eines Schuldtitels, Notenausgabe *f*, ECON Banknotenausgabe *f*; ~ **purchased under resale agreement** *n* ACC *asset* gekaufter Wechsel *m* mit Wiederverkaufsvereinbarung;

~ receivable *n* ACC, FIN ausstehender Schuldschein *m*, Besitzwechsel *m*, Schuldscheinforderung *f*, Wechselforderung *f*

notes: **~ payable** *n pl* ACC, FIN Schuldscheinverbindlichkeiten *f pl*, Schuldwechsel *m pl*, Wechselverbindlichkeiten *f pl*; **~ receivable** *n pl AmE* (*cf bills receivable BrE*) ACC, FIN Besitzwechsel *m pl*, Schuldscheinforderungen *f pl*, Wechselforderungen *f pl*; **~ to the accounts** *n pl* ACC Anmerkungen *f pl*; **~ to the financial statements** *n pl* ACC Anhang *m* zur Bilanz; **~ under repurchase agreement** *n pl* ACC *liabilities* Wechsel *m* mit Rückkaufsvereinbarung

not-for-profit *adj* GEN COMM gemeinnützig

notice 1. *n* GEN COMM Avis *m or nt*, Benachrichtigung *f*, LAW *of accident* Unfallmeldung *f*; ♦ **at two days'** ~ GEN COMM mit einer Frist von zwei Tagen; **give sb his ~** HRM jdm kündigen; **give ~ of** GEN COMM benachrichtigen; **give ~ of sth** LAW *trade law* etw zur Kenntnis bringen, Kenntnis von etw geben; **give ~ to quit** PROP *landlord, tenant* kündigen; **2.** *vt* GEN COMM bemerken

notice: **~ of abandonment** *n* INS *marine* Abandonerklärung *f*, Abandonfrist *f*, Verlusterklärung *f*; **~ of appeal** *n* PATENTS Berufungseinlegung *f*; **~ of assignment** *n* ACC Abtretungsanzeige *f*; **~ board** *n BrE* COMMS Anschlagbrett *nt*, Anzeigenbrett *nt*, Nachrichtentafel *f*, HRM schwarzes Brett *nt*; **~ of cancellation at anniversary date** *n* (*NCAD*) INS Kündigung *f* zum Ausstellungsdatum der Police, Rücktritt *m* zum Ausstellungsdatum der Police; **~ of cancellation clause** *n* INS Klausel *f* über die Erklärung der Vertragsaufhebung; **~ of default** *n* FIN Anzeige *f* der Nichterfüllung, Inverzugsetzung *f*; **~ of defect** *n* LAW *contract law* Mängelrüge *f*; **~ of opposition** *n* PATENTS Einspruchseinlegung *f*; **~ period** *n* HRM Kündigungsfrist *f*; **~ of readiness** *n* TRANSP *shipping* Ladebereitschaftsmitteilung *f*; **~ of shipment** *n* TRANSP Erklärung *f* der Lieferbereitschaft; **~ to quit** *n* PROP Kündigung *f*, Pacht- und Mietkündigung *f*; **~ to treat** *n BrE* LAW, PROP *land compensation* Inanspruchnahme eines Grundstücks für öffentliche Zwecke

notification *n* GEN COMM Avis *m or nt*, LAW *transactions* Benachrichtigung *f*, Übermittlung *f*, PATENTS Anzeige *f*, Mitteilung *f*, Notifikation *f*; **~ of acceptance** *n* FIN Akzeptmeldung *f*; **~ by stock exchange authorities** *n* STOCK Bekanntmachung *f* der Börsenorgane; **~ of vacancies** *n* ECON *for internal competition* Submission *f* von Arbeitsplätzen

notifier *n* LAW Übermittler *m*

notify *vt* GEN COMM avisieren, informieren, in Kenntnis setzen, unterrichten, verständigen, PATENTS, POL mitteilen; ♦ **~ sb of a decision** LAW jdn über eine Entscheidung benachrichtigen; **~ sb of sth** GEN COMM jdm etw mitteilen

notify: **~ address** *n* TRANSP Benachrichtigungsadresse *f*; **~ party** *n* TRANSP Benachrichtigungsadresse *f*

noting: **~ score** *n* S&M *advertising* Prozentsatz der Leser, die eine Anzeige gesehen haben

notional *adj* FIN *saving, charge, profit, loan* fiktiv, imaginär, nominell, rechnerisch; **~ rent** *n* PROP fiktive Miete *f*

NOTO *abbr* (*nonofficial trade organization*) HRM inoffizielle Handelsorganisation

no-trade: **~ equilibrium** *n* ECON handelsfreies Gleichgewicht *nt*

notwithstanding *adv* GEN COMM ungeachtet

nought *n* GEN COMM Nichts *nt*

novation *n* LAW *commercial* Novation *f*

novelty *n* PATENTS Neuheit *f*; **~ value** *n* S&M Neuheitswert *m*

NOW *abbr AmE* (*negotiable order of withdrawal*) BANK, FIN übertragbare Zahlungsanweisung *f*, übertragbarer Abhebungsauftrag *m*; **~ account** *n AmE* BANK, FIN NOW-Konto *nt*, verzinsliches Kontokorrentkonto *nt*, verzinstes Sparkonto *nt*

noxious: **~ gas** *n* ENVIR schädliches Gas *nt*

np *abbr* (*net proceeds*) PROP Reinertrag *m*

NPA *abbr BrE* (*Newspaper Publishers' Association*) MEDIA Vereinigung der Zeitungsverleger

NPE *abbr* (*nonprofit enterprise*) ECON gemeinnütziges Unternehmen *nt*, nicht erwerbswirtschaftlich ausgerichtetes Unternehmen *nt*

NPV *abbr* (*net present value*) ACC, ECON, FIN Barwert *m*, Kapitalwert *m*

nr *abbr* (*no risk until confirmed*) INS kein Risiko bis zur Bestätigung

NR *abbr* (*nuclear reactor*) IND Atommeiler *m*, Kernreaktor *m*, Reaktor *m*

nrad *abbr* (*no risk after discharge*) INS kein Risiko nach Löschung

NRT *abbr* (*net register ton, net register tonne*) GEN COMM Nettoregistertonne *f*

NRV *abbr* (*net realizable value*) FIN realisierbarer Verkaufserlös *m*, realisierbarer Verkaufswert *m*

NSA *abbr* (*nonsterling area*) ECON Nicht-Sterling-Gebiet *nt*

NSB *abbr BrE* (*National Savings Bank*) BANK Postsparkasse *f*

NSC *abbr* (*nuclear science center AmE, nuclear science centre BrE*) IND Kernforschungszentrum *nt*, wissenschaftliches Zentrum *nt* für Kerntechnik

nsf *abbr* (*not sufficient funds*) GEN COMM keine ausreichende Deckung

nspf *abbr* (*not specially provided for*) GEN COMM nicht speziell vorgesehen

NSSN *abbr* (*national standard shipping note*) IMP/EXP, TRANSP Einheitswarenbegleitschein *m*, nationale Standardversandanzeige *f*, nationaler Standardladeschein *m*, nationaler standardmäßiger Ladeschein *m*, nationaler standardmäßiger Warenbegleitschein *m*

Nt *abbr* (*net terms*) IMP/EXP, TRANSP *shipping* Nettobedingungen *f pl*

NTB *abbr* (*nontariff barrier*) ECON, GEN COMM, IMP/EXP nichttarifäres Handelshemmnis *nt*, zollfremdes Handelshemmnis *nt*

NTUC *abbr BrE* (*National Trade Union Council*) HRM Dachverband der britischen Gewerkschaften

nuance *vt* GEN COMM nuancieren

nuclear *adj* ENVIR, IND Atom-, Kern-; **~-based industry** *n* IND Atomwirtschaft *f*; **~ energy** *n* ENVIR, IND Kernkraft *f*; **~ energy program** *AmE*, **~ energy programme** *BrE n* ECON Atomprogramm *nt*; **~ industry** *n* IND Nuklearindustrie *f*

Nuclear: **~ Installations Inspectorate** *n BrE* IND, WEL Aufsichtsamt für Nuklearanlagen

nuclear: **~ physicist** *n* HRM, IND Kernphysiker, in *m,f*; **~ plant** *n* IND Kernreaktoranlage *f*; **~ power** *n* ENVIR, IND Kernkraft *f*; **~ power station** *n* IND Atomkraftwerk *nt*, Kernkraftwerk *nt* (*KKW*), Kernreaktoranlage *f*; ~ **reactor** *n* (*NR*) IND Atommeiler *m*, Kernreaktor *m*, Reaktor *m*; ~ **risk insurance** *n* LAW Atomrisiko-Versicherung *f*; ~ **science center** *AmE*, ~ **science centre** *BrE n* (*NSC*) IND Kernforschungszentrum *nt*, wissenschaftliches Zentrum *nt* für Kerntechnik; ~ **waste** *n* ENVIR, IND Atommüll *m*

nudum pactum *n* GEN COMM unverbindlicher Vertrag *m*

nugatory: ~ **payment** *n* FIN, LAW rechtsunwirksame Zahlung *f*

nuisance *n* GEN COMM Ärgernis *nt*, LAW besitzstörende Tätigkeit *f*

null: ~ **hypothesis** *n* MATH *statistics* Nullhypothese *f*

nullification *n* LAW Aufhebung *f*

nullify *vt* LAW aufheben

nullity *n* LAW Ungültigkeit *f*; ~ **suit** *n* LAW Nichtigkeitsklage *f*

null: ~ **and void** *phr* LAW null und nichtig

NUM *abbr BrE* (*National Union of Mineworkers*) HRM nationale Gewerkschaft der Bergarbeiter

NUMAST *abbr BrE* (*National Union of Marine Aviation and Shipping Transport*) HRM nationale Marinegewerkschaft

number 1. *n* (*no.*) GEN COMM Anzahl *f*, *of magazine* Ausgabe *f*, MATH Nummer *f*, Anzahl *f*, Zahl *f*; **2.** *vt* GEN COMM numerieren; ◆ ~ **consecutively** MEDIA, PATENTS fortlaufend numerieren

number: ~ **cruncher** *n infrml* COMP Rechenkünstler, in *m,f*, Zahlenfresser *m* (*infrml*); ~ **crunching** *n infrml* ACC Zahlenverarbeitung *f*, COMP Zahlenfressen *nt* (*infrml*), ECON, FIN Zahlenverarbeitung *f*

numbered: ~ **account** *n* BANK Nummernkonto *nt*

number: ~ **of employees** *n* ACC *balance sheet* Anzahl *f* der Angestellten, ECON, GEN COMM Belegschaft *f*, Beschäftigtenanzahl *f*; ~ **one priority** *n* GEN COMM höchste Priorität *f*; ~ **of participants** *n* GEN COMM Teilnehmerzahl *f*; ~ **plate** *n BrE* (*cf license plate AmE*) TRANSP Nummernschild *nt*, polizeiliches Kennzeichen

nt; ~ **processing** *n* ACC, ECON, FIN Zahlenverarbeitung *f*

numbers *n pl* (*nos.*) MATH Nummern *f pl*, Zahlen *f pl*

number: ~ **of spectators** *n* LEIS, MEDIA Zuschauerzahl *f*; ~ **of subscribers** *n* COMMS Teilnehmerzahl *f*, Zahl *f* der Abonnenten, Anzahl *f* der Bezieher; ~ **of terms** *n* ECON, FIN Laufzeit *f* der Verzinsung, Zinsdauer *f*; ~ **of viewers** *n* LEIS, MEDIA Zuschauerzahl *f*

numeraire *n* ECON Bezugsgröße *f* des Währungssystems

numeric *adj* COMP numerisch

numerical: ~ **control** *n* FIN numerische Kontrolle *f*, MATH numerische Steuerung *f*; ~ **filing** *n* GEN COMM numerische Ablage *f*; ~ **flexibility** *n* HRM numerische Flexibilität *f*

numeric: ~ **alphabetic** *adj* MATH alphanumerisch; ~ **character** *n* MATH numerisches Zeichen *nt*; ~ **keypad** *n* COMP *keyboard* Zifferntastatur *f*

NUPE *abbr BrE* (*National Union of Public Employees*) HRM Gewerkschaft der Angestellten im öffentlichen Dienst

nuplex *n* IND Nuplex *m*

nurse: ~ **a business** *phr* ECON ein Unternehmen wieder hochbringen

nursery: ~ **finance** *n* FIN langfristige zinsgünstige Kredite für Unternehmensneugründungen; ~ **school** *n* WEL Kindergarten *m*

nursing: ~ **home daily rate** *n* WEL Pflegesatz *m*

NUS *abbr BrE* (*National Union of Seamen*) HRM britische Seeleutegewerkschaft

NVD *abbr* (*no value declared*) IMP/EXP ohne Wertangabe

NYFE *abbr* (*New York Futures Exchange*) STOCK New Yorker Terminbörse

NYPLR *abbr* (*New York prime loan rate*) BANK New Yorker Kreditzins für erste Adressen

NYSA *abbr* (*New York Shipping Association*) TRANSP New Yorker Versandsvereinigung

NYSE *abbr* (*New York Stock Exchange*) STOCK New Yorker Wertpapierbörse

O

oa *abbr* (*overall*) GEN COMM insg. (*insgesamt*), gesamt

o/a *abbr* (*on account*) BANK à Konto, GEN COMM gegen Kredit, per Kreditkonto *nt*

OA *abbr* (*office automation*) ADMIN, COMP, IND Büroautomation *f*, Büroautomatisierung *f*

O&M *abbr* (*organization and methods*) MGMNT O&M (*Organisation und Methoden*)

OAP *abbr* BrE (*old age pensioner*) HRM, WEL Pensionär, in *m,f*, Rentner, in *m,f*

OAS *abbr* (*Organization of American States*) POL OAS (*Organisation amerikanischer Staaten*)

oath *n* LAW Eid *m*; ◆ **under ~** LAW unter Eid

OAU *abbr* (*Organization of African Unity*) POL OAU (*Organisation der Afrikanischen Einheit*)

OBE *abbr* BrE (*Officer of the Order of the British Empire*) POL britischer Verdienstorden

obey *vt* LAW *ruling* befolgen, *summons* nachkommen [+dat]

obiter dictum *n* GEN COMM beiläufige Bemerkung *f*

object 1. *n* GEN COMM Objekt *nt*, *aim* Ziel *nt*; **2.** *vi* LAW *make objections* Einwände erheben; ◆ **~ to** GEN COMM *proposal* ablehnen, LAW einwenden gegen

objection *n* GEN COMM Einwand *m*, LAW Einspruch *m*, PATENTS Widerspruch *m*; ◆ **have no ~** GEN COMM keinen Einwand haben; **~ overruled** LAW dem Einspruch wird nicht stattgegeben; **~ sustained** LAW dem Einspruch wird stattgegeben

objective 1. *adj* GEN COMM objektiv, sachlich; **2.** *n* GEN COMM Ziel *nt*, Zielvorstellung *f*, Zweck *m*

objective: **~ function** *n* MATH Zielfunktion *f*; **~ indicators** *n pl* GEN COMM Zielindikatoren *m pl*; **~ selling** *n* S&M zielorientiertes Verkaufen *nt*; **~-setting** *n* MGMNT Zielsetzung *f*; **~ value** *n* ECON objektiver Wert *m*

obligate *vt* FIN *AmE* für einen bestimmten Zweck festlegen, GEN COMM verpflichten

obligated *adj* GEN COMM verpflichtet; **~ material** *n* AmE FIN auftragsgebundenes Material *nt*

obligation *n* GEN COMM Verpflichtung *f*, LAW *contract law* Pflicht *f*, Schuldverhältnis *nt*, Verbindlichkeit *f*; ◆ **no ~ to buy** S&M *in shop* ohne Kaufverpflichtung

obligation: **~ bond** *n* FIN *mortgage* Anleiheschuld *f*; **~ of performance** *n* LAW *contract law* primäre Leistungspflicht *f*; **~ to accept** *n* LAW *contract law* Annahmepflicht *f*; **~ to buy** *n* S&M Kaufverpflichtung *f*, Kaufzwang *m*; **~ to pay** *n* BANK, FIN Zahlungsverpflichtung *f*; **~ to supply unascertained goods** *n* LAW *contracts* Gattungsschuld *f*; **~ under a contract** *n* LAW Vertragspflicht *f*

obligatory *adj* GEN COMM verbindlich, verpflichtend

oblige *vt* GEN COMM *compel* verpflichten, zwingen; ◆ **~ sb to do sth** GEN COMM jdn verpflichten, etw zu tun

obliged *adj* GEN COMM *compelled* verpflichtet, *grateful* dankbar; ◆ **be ~ to** GEN COMM verpflichtet sein zu

obligee *n* LAW Gläubiger, in *m,f* (*Gl.*), Berechtigte(r) *mf* [decl. as adj]

obligor *n* LAW Schuldner, in *m,f*, Verpflichtete(r) *mf* [decl. as adj]

OBRA *abbr* (*Omnibus Budget Reconciliation Act*) FIN, TAX Gesamthaushaltsberichtigungsgesetz *nt*, umfassendes Haushaltsabstimmungsgesetz *nt*

observance *n* LAW *of rule, regulation* Einhaltung *f*; **~ of contract** *n* LAW Vertragseinhaltung *f*

observant: **~ party** *n* LAW *contract law* vertragstreue Partei *f*

observation *n* GEN COMM Beobachtung *f*; **~ list** *n* GEN COMM Beobachtungsliste *f*; **~ test** *n* ACC *auditing* Beobachtungstest *m*

observe *vt* GEN COMM *watch* beobachten, LAW *rules, regulations* einhalten

observer *n* GEN COMM Beobachter, in *m,f*

obsolescence *n* GEN COMM Veralterung *f*, Obsoleszenz *f*; **~ clause** *n* INS Veralterungsklausel *f*

obsolescent: **~ product** *n* S&M veraltetes Produkt *nt*

obsolete *adj* GEN COMM überaltert, veraltet

obstacle *n* GEN COMM Hindernis *nt*; **~ of performance** *n* ECON Erfüllungshinderniss *nt*

obstruct *vt* GEN COMM hindern, *growth* behindern, LAW vereiteln

obstruction *n* GEN COMM Hindernis *nt*, Behinderung *f*

obtain *vt* BANK *loan*, FIN *funds* aufnehmen, GEN COMM erzielen, erhalten, erlangen, LAW *permission*, PATENTS *consent* erhalten; ◆ **~ a loan** BANK ein Darlehen aufnehmen; **~ permission in writing** COMMS schriftliche Erlaubnis erhalten; **~ sth by fraud** LAW etw betrügerisch erlangen

obtainable *adj* GEN COMM erhältlich, erreichbar

obtained *adj* GEN COMM erlangt

obtainment *n* GEN COMM Erlangung *f*

obvious *adj* GEN COMM offensichtlich

o/c *abbr* (*overcharge*) GEN COMM Überteuerung *f*, S&M zuviel berechneter Betrag *m*

OC *abbr* ECON (*old crop*) *agricultural* letzte Ernte *f*, INS (*open cover*) laufende Police *f*

OCAS *abbr* (*Organization of Central American States*) POL Organisation *f* zentralamerikanischer Staaten

occasion *n* GEN COMM *point in time* Gelegenheit *f*, *circumstance* Fall *m*, *reason* Veranlassung *f*

occasional *adj* GEN COMM gelegentlich; **~ customer** *n* S&M gelegentlicher Kunde *m*, gelegentliche Kundin *f*; **~ worker** *n* HRM Gelegenheitsarbeiter, in *m,f*

occupancy *n* PROP Belegung *f*, Besitz *m*; **~ level** *n* PROP Belegungsstufe *f*; **~ rate** *n* PROP *hotel, hospital* Belegung *f*

occupant *n* HRM *of a position, post* Inhaber, in *m,f*, PROP Bewohner, in *m,f*

occupation *n* GEN COMM *employment* Beruf *m*, Tätigkeit *f*, HRM *union action* Besetzung *f*, LAW Besitz *m*, PROP Besetzung *f*

occupational: **~ accident** *n* HRM, INS, WEL Betriebsunfall *m*, Berufsunfall *m*; **~ analysis** *n* HRM Arbeitsplatzanalyse *f*; **~ disease** *n* WEL Berufskrankheit *f*; **~ hazard** *n* HRM, WEL Berufsrisiko *nt*,

Arbeitsplatzrisiko *nt*; ~ **health** *n* WEL Gesundheit *f* am Arbeitsplatz; ~ **illness** *n* WEL Berufskrankheit *f*; ~ **mobility** *n* HRM berufliche Mobilität *f*; ~ **outfit** *n* GEN COMM Berufsausrüstung *f*; ~ **pension** *n* FIN, HRM Berufsrente *f*; ~ **pension plan** *n* FIN, HRM Betriebsrentenkasse *f*, betriebliche Pensionskasse *f*, betriebliche Pensionsregelung *f*; ~ **pension scheme** *n BrE* FIN, HRM Betriebsrentenkasse *f* betriebliche Pensionskasse *f*, betriebliche Pensionsregelung *f*; ~ **retraining** *n* HRM Umschulung *f*; ~ **segregation** *n* ECON berufliche Trennung *f*; ~ **test** *n* HRM Eignungsprüfung *f*; ~ **union** *n BrE* HRM Berufsgewerkschaft *f*

occupation: ~ **tax** *n* ECON Gebühr *f* für Gewerbezulassung

occupied *adj* GEN COMM belegt

occupier *n* PROP Bewohner, in *m,f*

occupy *vt* GEN COMM *position, post* innehaben, *person* beschäftigen, PROP besitzen, bewohnen

OCD *abbr* (*other checkable deposits*) BANK, FIN sonstige Kontokorrenteinlagen *f pl*, sonstige Sichteinlagen *f pl*

ocean: ~ **bill of lading** *n* IMP/EXP, TRANSP Bordkonnossement *nt*, Seekonnossement *nt*, Seefrachtbrief *m*; ~ **carrier** *n* TRANSP Frachtunternehmen *nt*; ~ **freight** *n* TRANSP Seefracht *f*; ~-**going ship** *n* TRANSP Hochseeschiff *nt*; ~ **liner** *n* TRANSP Ozeanlinienschiff *nt*; ~ **marine protection and indemnity insurance** *n* INS Seeschadens- und Schutzversicherung *f*

OCIMF *abbr* (*Oil Companies International Marine Forum*) ENVIR Internationales Meeresforum der Ölgesellschaften

OCR *abbr* (*optical character recognition*) COMP OCR (*optische Zeichenerkennung*)

OCTs *abbr* (*overseas countries and territories*) POL *of European Union member states* überseeische Gebiete *nt pl*

O/D *abbr* ACC (*on demand*) bei Sicht, bei Vorlage, *at sight* gegen Vorlage, BANK (*overdraft*) Kontoüberziehung *f*, Überziehung *f*, (*overdrawn*) überzogen, GEN COMM (*on demand*) auf Verlangen

ODA *abbr* ECON (*official development assistance*) staatliche Entwicklungshilfe *f*, POL (*Overseas Development Administration BrE*) Behörde für Entwicklungshilfe

odd *adj* COMP, MATH *number* ungerade, restlich; ~ **change** *n* GEN COMM restliches Wechselgeld *nt*; ~ **job person** *n* HRM Gelegenheitsarbeiter, in *m,f*; ~ **jobs** *n pl* HRM Gelegenheitsarbeit *f*

oddment *n* S&M Rest *m*

odd: ~ **sizes** *n* IND ausgefallene Größen *f pl*, nicht gängige Größen *f pl*

odds: ~ **ratio** *n* ECON relatives Risiko *nt*

odd: ~ **value pricing** *n AmE* S&M Preisauszeichnung mit ungeraden Zahlen

ODI *abbr BrE* (*Overseas Development Institute*) ECON Institut für Entwicklungshilfe

OEC *abbr* (*overpaid entry certificate*) IMP/EXP überzahlte Einfuhrbescheinigung *f*

OECD *abbr* (*Organization for Economic Cooperation and Development*) ECON OECD (*Organisation für wirtschaftliche Zusammenarbeit und Entwicklung*)

OECF *abbr* (*Overseas Economic Cooperation Fund*) ECON Fonds für wirtschaftliche Zusammenarbeit in Übersee

OEEC *abbr obs* (*Organization for European Economic Cooperation*) ECON OEEC (*Organisation für europäische wirtschaftliche Zusammenarbeit*)

OEIC *abbr* (*open-end investment company, open-ended investment company*) FIN offene Investmentgesellschaft *f*

OEM *abbr* (*original equipment manufacturer*) COMP OEM (*Originalgerätehersteller*)

off *adv* COMP aus

off-balance *adj* ACC bilanzunwirksam, bilanzneutral, außerhalb der Bilanz; ~-**sheet** *adj* ACC ohne Belastung der Bilanzstruktur, bilanzunwirksam, ECON, FIN bilanzunwirksam; ~-**sheet commitments** *n pl* ACC bilanzunwirksame Verbindlichkeiten *f pl*; ~-**sheet finance** *n* ACC, FIN bilanzunwirksame Finanzierung *f*; ~-**sheet financing** *n* ACC, FIN bilanzunwirksame Finanzierung *f*

off-board: ~ **trading** *n* STOCK außerbörslicher Handel *m*, ungeregelter Freiverkehr *m*

offence *n BrE* LAW strafbare Handlung *f*, Vergehen *nt*, Verstoß *m*, PATENTS Verstoß *m*; ~ **against property** *n BrE* LAW Eigentumsdelikt *nt*

offend *vt* LAW verstoßen gegen

offend against *vt* LAW sich vergehen gegen

offense *AmE see* offence *BrE*

offer **1.** *n* GEN COMM Angebot *nt*, STOCK Angebot *nt*, *selling rate* Briefkurs *m*; ♦ **on** ~ S&M im Angebot; **under** ~ *BrE* PROP *house* im Angebot; ~ **and acceptance correspond** LAW *contract law* Angebot und Annahme stimmen überein; **2.** *vt* GEN COMM anbieten, *scope* bieten, HRM *job* anbieten; ♦ ~ **for subscription** FIN auflegen; ~ **one's services** GEN COMM seine Dienste anbieten

offer: ~ **and acceptance** *n* LAW *commercial* Angebot *nt* und Annahme *f*; ~ **of a contract** *n* LAW Vertragsangebot *nt*; ~ **document** *n* GEN COMM Angebotsunterlagen *f pl*

offeree *n* GEN COMM Angebotsempfänger, in *m,f*

offerer *n* GEN COMM Anbieter, in *m,f*

offering: ~ **date** *n* STOCK *new issue* Emissionsdatum *nt*; ~ **price** *n* STOCK Emissionskurs *m*, Zeichnungskurs *m*

offer: ~ **price** *n* GEN COMM Angebotspreis *m*, STOCK Brief *m*, Briefkurs *m*

off-exchange: ~ **instrument** *n* FIN, STOCK außerbörsliches Handelspapier *nt*

office *n* GEN COMM Büro *nt*, *public position* Amt *nt*, LAW Kanzlei *f*; ♦ **be in** ~ HRM *person* im Amt sein, POL an der Regierung sein; **for** ~ **use only** ADMIN nur zum Dienstgebrauch, nur für dienstliche Zwecke

office: ~ **accommodation** *n* PROP Büroräume *m pl*; ~ **aid** *n* GEN COMM Bürohilfe *f*; ~ **automation** *n* (*OA*) ADMIN, COMP, IND Büroautomation *f*, Büroautomatisierung *f*; ~ **block** *n* PROP Bürogebäude *nt*, Bürohaus *nt*; ~ **boy** *n* HRM Bürobote *m*; ~ **building** *n* PROP Bürogebäude *nt*; ~ **burglary and robbery insurance** *n* INS *property* Büroeinbruchdiebstahl- und Raubversicherung *f*; ~ **communication** *n* GEN COMM Bürokommunikation *f*; ~ **of the district attorney** *n AmE* LAW Staatsanwaltschaft *f*; ~ **equipment** *n* ADMIN Büroausstattung *f*, Büromaschinen *f pl*; ~ **expenses** *n pl* ACC Bürokosten *pl*

Office: ~ **of Fair Trading** *n BrE* (*OFT*) S&M Kartellbehörde *f*, Kartellamt *nt*; ~ **of Gas Supply** *n BrE* (*Ofgas*) ADMIN Aufsichtsbehörde für die Gasindustrie

office: ~ **hours** *n pl* GEN COMM Bürostunden *f pl*,

Geschäftszeiten *f pl*, Arbeitsstunden *f pl*, Parteienverkehr *m* (*Öst*)

Office: **~ of International Trade** *n* (*OIT*) GEN COMM Amt für internationalen Handel; **~ of Interstate Land Sales Registration** *n AmE* (*OILSR*) PROP Amt für zwischenstaatlichen Landverkauf

office: **~ job** *n* GEN COMM Bürotätigkeit *f*; **~ management** *n* MGMNT Büroleitung *f*, Büroorganisation *f*, Büroverwaltung *f*

Office: **~ of Management and Budget** *n AmE* (*OMB*) POL dem Präsidenten direkt unterstelltes Amt, das in enger Zusammenarbeit mit den Fachministern den Bundeshaushaltsplan für den Präsidenten zur späteren Vorlage im Kongreß erarbeitet, Amt *nt* für Management und Haushaltsplanung

office: **~ manager** *n* HRM, MGMNT Bürovorsteher, in *m,f*, Bürochef, in *m,f*, Büroleiter, in *m,f*; **~ planning** *n* MGMNT Büroplanung *f*

Office: **~ of Population Censuses and Surveys** *n BrE* (*OPCS*) WEL Amt für Volkszählungen und statistische Untersuchungen

office: **~ premises** *n pl* PROP Büroräume *m pl*, Geschäftsräume *m pl*

officer *n* HRM Funktionär, in *m,f*, Führungskraft *f*, *accountable* Sachbearbeiter, in *m,f*, Beamte(r) *m* [decl. as adj], Beamtin *f*

office: **~ for recordation of personal status** *AmE*, **~ for registration of personal status** *BrE n* ADMIN Standesamt *nt*; **~ requisites** *n pl* ADMIN Bürobedarf *m*

Officer: **~ of the Order of the British Empire** *n* (*OBE*) GEN COMM, POL britischer Verdienstorden

office: **~ routine** *n* GEN COMM Büroalltag *m*; **~ space** *n* PROP Büroräume *m pl*, Bürofläche *f*; **~ staff** *n* HRM Büropersonal *nt*; **~ stationery** *n* ADMIN Büromaterial *nt*, Bürobedarf *m*; **~ supplies** *n pl* ADMIN Bürobedarfsartikel *m pl*; **~ technology** *n* ADMIN Bürotechnik *f*; **~ of telecommunications** *n BrE* COMMS Fernmeldeamt *nt*; **~ work** *n* HRM Büroarbeit *f*; **~ worker** *n* HRM Bürokraft *f*, Büroangestellte(r) *mf* [decl. as adj]

official 1. *adj* GEN COMM amtlich, offiziell; ♦ **for ~ use only** GEN COMM nur für den Dienstgebrauch; **2.** *n* HRM Beamte(r) *m* [decl. as adj], Beamtin *f*, Funktionär, in *m,f*

official: **~ action** *n BrE* HRM organisierte Arbeitskampfmaßnahme *f*; **~ agency** *n* ADMIN Dienststelle *f*; **~ announcement** *n* LAW amtliche Bekanntmachung *f*; **~ approval** *n* LAW amtliche Genehmigung *f*; **~ broker** *n* STOCK amtlicher Kursmakler *m*, amtliche Kursmaklerin *f*; **~ call** *n* COMMS Dienstgespräch *nt*; **~ channels** *n pl* GEN COMM Dienstweg *m*; **~ depository** *n* MEDIA *print* offizieller Aufbewahrungsort *m*; **~ development assistance** *n* (*ODA*) ECON staatliche Entwicklungshilfe *f*; **~ document** *n* ADMIN behördliches Dokument *nt*

officialese *n infrml* ADMIN Behördendeutsch *nt* (*infrml*), Beamtenchinesisch *nt* (*infrml*), Beamtendeutsch *nt* (*infrml*)

official: **~ exchange rate** *n* ECON, FIN offizieller Wechselkurs *m*, amtlicher Wechselkurs *m*; **~ figures** *n pl* GEN COMM amtliche Zahlen *f pl*; **~ financing** *n* ECON Staatsverschuldung *f*; **~ foreign exchange quotation** *n* ECON, FIN amtlicher Devisenkurs *m*

Official: **~ Journal** *n* (*OJ*) ADMIN, POL Amtsblatt *nt* (*ABl.*), Amtsblatt *nt* der Europäischen Union (*ABl.*)

official: **~ log** *n* TRANSP offizielles Logbuch *nt*, offizielles Schiffstagebuch *nt*

officially *adv* GEN COMM offiziell, amtlich; ♦ **~ attested** LAW amtlich beglaubigt; **~ authenticated** *adj* LAW amtlich beglaubigt; **~ listed** STOCK amtlich zugelassen; **~ quoted** STOCK amtlich zugelassen

officially: **~-supported export credits** *n pl* FIN staatlich subventionierte Exportkredite *m pl*

official: **~ market** *n* ECON amtlicher Markt *m*; **~ notice of sale** *n* FIN offizielle Verkaufsankündigung *f*; **~ quotation** *n* STOCK amtliche Börsennotiz *f*; **~ rate** *n* BANK amtlicher Kurs *m*; **~ receiver** *n* LAW Konkursverwalter, in *m,f*, Zwangsverwalter, in *m,f*; **~ reserves** *n pl* ECON, FIN amtliche Währungsreserven *f pl*; **~ secret** *n* POL Dienstgeheimnis *nt*; **~ spread** *n* FIN Bandbreite *f*; **~ statement** *n* GEN COMM öffentliche Erklärung *f*; **~ strike** *n* HRM organisierter Streik *m*, offizieller Streik *m*; **~ valuer** *n* LAW amtlicher Schätzer *m*; **~ visit** *n* GEN COMM offizieller Besuch *m*

off-licence *n BrE* LAW, S&M *permit* Lizenz zum Verkauf von alkoholischen Getränken, die aber nicht an Ort und Stelle konsumiert werden dürfen, *shop* (*cf package store AmE*, *liquor store AmE*) Wein- und Spirituosengeschäft *nt*

off-limits: **~ area** *n* GEN COMM Bereich *m* der nicht betreten werden darf

off-line 1. *adj* COMP off-line, rechnerunabhängig, Offline-; **2.** *adv* COMP off-line, rechnerunabhängig

offload 1. *vt* GEN COMM *responsibility, work* abladen, IND, TRANSP *goods, cargo* abladen, ausladen, entladen; **2.** *vi* IND, TRANSP *goods, cargo* abladen

offloading *n* GEN COMM *of responsibility, work* Ablaben *nt*, IND, TRANSP Ausladen *nt*, Ausladung *f*, Entladen *nt*, *cargo* Abladen *nt*

off-peak 1. *adj* COMMS, TRANSP außerhalb der Hauptzeiten; **2.** *n* COMMS, TRANSP Talzeit *f*

off-peak: **~ charges** *n pl* COMMS, TRANSP Kosten *pl* außerhalb der Hauptzeiten; **~ day** *n* COMMS, TRANSP verkehrsarmer Tag *m*, Tag *m* mit verbilligtem Tarif; **~ ticket** *n* TRANSP Fahrkarte *f* außerhalb der Hauptzeiten

off-sale: **~ date** *n* MEDIA *broadcast* Zeitpunkt, an dem ein Kommissionsgeschäft endet

off-season 1. *adj* GEN COMM außerhalb der Hochsaison *f*, außerhalb der Saison; **2.** *n* GEN COMM Nebensaison *f*

offset 1. *adj* ACC, ECON, FIN *counterbalancing* aufgerechnet, ausgeglichen, verrechnet, *compensatory* kompensiert; **2.** *n* ACC, FIN *compensation* Ausgleich *f*, Kompensation *f*, *counterbalancing* Verrechnung *f*, Aufrechnung *f*, MEDIA *printing*, Offsetdruck *m*, STOCK Glattstellung *f*; **3.** *vt* ACC, FIN *counterbalance* verrechnen, aufrechnen, *compensate* ausgleichen, kompensieren

offset: **~ account** *n* ACC Verrechnungskonto *nt*, Wertberichtigungskonto *nt*; **~ agreement** *n* LAW *contract law* Kompensationsgegengeschäft *nt*

offsetting 1. *adj* ACC, FIN *counterbalancing* verrechnend, *compensatory* ausgleichend, kompensierend, aufrechnend; **2.** *n* ACC, FIN Aufrechnung *f*, Ausgleich *m*, Kompensation *f*, Verrechnung *f*

offsetting: **~ entry** *n* ACC Ausgleichsbuchung *f*, Gegenbuchung *f*; **~ error** *n* ACC ausgleichender Fehler *m*; **~ item** *n* ACC Ausgleichsposten *m*

offshore *adj* BANK *capital, investment* ausländisch, auswärtig, exterritorial, ENVIR *oil* küstennah, vor der Küste gelegen, FIN *capital, investment* ausländisch, auswärtig, exterritorial; **~ banking** *n* BANK Offshore-Banking *nt*, Offshore-Bankgeschäfte *nt pl*; **~ center** *AmE*, **~ centre** *BrE n* BANK Offshore-Zentrum *nt*; **~ dollars** *n pl* BANK Offshore-Dollars *m pl*; **~ funds** *n pl* FIN, TAX Investmentfonds mit Sitz in einer Steueroase, Offshore-Fonds *m*; **~ installation** *n* ENVIR, IND küstennahe Installation *f*, Offshore-Installation *f*; **~ investment** *n* BANK, FIN Offshore-Investition *f*; **~ oilfield** *n* ENVIR, IND küstennahes Ölfeld *nt*, Offshore-Ölfeld *nt*, in Küstennähe gelegenes Ölfeld; **~ place** *n* BANK Offshore-Bankplatz *m*, FIN ausländischer Bankplatz *m*; **~ protectionism** *n* TRANSP Offshore-Protektionismus *m*; **~ takeover** *n* FIN im Ausland getätigte Übernahme *f*; **~ technology** *n* IND Offshore-Technologie *f*; **~ trust** *n* LAW Auslandstrust *m*

off-site: **~ cost** *n* PROP *construction* Kosten *pl* außerhalb der Baustelle

off-the-board: **~ price** *n* STOCK außerbörslicher Kurs *m*

off-the-job: **~ training** *n BrE* HRM außerbetriebliche Weiterbildung *f*

off-the-peg *adj* GEN COMM von der Stange

off-the-record *adj* MEDIA, POL nicht amtlich, inoffiziell

off-the-shelf: **~ company** *n* GEN COMM Standardunternehmen *nt*

Ofgas *abbr BrE* (*Office of Gas Supply*) ADMIN Aufsichtsbehörde für die Gasindustrie

OFT *abbr BrE* (*Office of Fair Trading*) S&M Kartellamt *nt*, Kartellbehörde *f*

OGIL *abbr* (*open general import licence BrE, open general import license AmE*) IMP/EXP allgemeine Importgenehmigung *f*, allgemeine Rahmeneinfuhrgenehmigung *f*, allgemeine Rahmengenerallizenz *f*, Freiliste *f* für Importwaren

OHMS *abbr BrE* ADMIN, POL (*On Her Majesty's Service*) zu Diensten Ihrer Majestät

OID *abbr* (*original issue discount*) FIN, STOCK Abzinsungsbetrag *m*, Emissionsdisagio *nt*

oil 1. *n* ENVIR, IND Öl *nt*, Erdöl *nt*; **2.** *vt* ♦ **~ sb's palm** *infrml* GEN COMM jdn bestechen, jdn schmieren (*infrml*)

oil: **~ analyst** *n* IND Ölanalytiker, in *m,f*, Öluntersuchungschemiker, in *m,f*; **~-bearing** *adj* ENVIR, IND erdölführend, erdölhaltig; **~ carrier** *n* TRANSP *ship* Öltanker *m*, Öltransporter *m*

Oil: **~ Companies International Marine Forum** *n* (*OCIMF*) ENVIR Internationales Meeresforum der Ölgesellschaften

oil: **~ company** *n* ENVIR, IND Ölgesellschaft *f*; **~ deposit** *n* ENVIR Erdöllagerstätte *f*; **~ exploration licence** *BrE*, **~ exploration license** *AmE n* ENVIR, LAW Ölbohrkonzession *f*, Ölbohrlizenz *f*, Genehmigung *f* zur Erdölsuche; **~-exporting country** *n* ECON, ENVIR, IND ölexportierendes Land *nt*

oilfield *n* ENVIR, IND Ölfeld *nt*, Erdölfeld *nt*

oil: **~ gage** *AmE see oil gauge BrE*; **~ and gas lease** *n* LAW Öl- und Gas-Leasing *nt*; **~ and gas limited partnership** *n* ECON, ENVIR Öl- und Gasgesellschaft *f*; **~ gauge** *n BrE* IND *car, machine* Ölstandsanzeiger *m*; **~ glut** *n* ENVIR Ölschwemme *f*; **~ industry** *n* ENVIR, IND Erdölindustrie *f*; **~ pipeline** *n* IND Ölleitung *f*, Ölpipeline *f*; **~ platform** *n* IND Bohrinsel *f*, Bohrplattform *f*; **~ pollution** *n* ENVIR Ölverschmutzung *f*, Ölverseuchung *f*; **~ price increase** *n* ECON Ölpreisanstieg *m*, Anstieg *m* des Ölpreises; **~-producing country** *n* ECON, ENVIR, IND

erdölproduzierendes Land *nt*, Ölförderland *nt*, Ölproduzent *m*; **~ refinery** *n* ENVIR, IND Ölraffinerie *f*, Erdölraffinerie *f*; **~-rich** *adj* ECON *country* reich an Öl; **~ rig** *n* IND Bohrinsel *f*, Bohrplattform *f*, Bohrturm *m*

oils *n pl* STOCK Erdölwerte *m pl*

oil: **~ shock** *n* ECON Ölkrise *f*; **~ shortage** *n* ECON Ölknappheit *f*; **~ slick** *n* ENVIR Ölfleck *m*, Öllache *f*, Ölteppich *m*; **~ spill** *n* ENVIR Ölteppich *m*, Ölverschüttung *f*; **~ spillage** *n* ENVIR ausgeflossenes Öl *nt*

OILSR *abbr AmE* (*Office of Interstate Land Sales Registration*) PROP Amt für zwischenstaatlichen Landverkauf

oil: **~ tanker** *n* TRANSP Öltanker *m*; **~ tax** *n* TAX Mineralölsteuer *f*; **~ terminal** *n* IND, TRANSP Ölhafen *m*, Ölumschlagstelle *f*

oiltight *adj* IND, TRANSP öldicht

OIML *abbr* (*International Organization for Legal Metrology*) IND Internationale Organisation *f* für Eichung

OIT *abbr* (*Office of International Trade*) GEN COMM Amt für internationalen Handel

OJ *abbr* (*Official Journal*) ADMIN, POL ABl. (*Amtsblatt, Amtsblatt der Europäischen Union*)

old: **~-age allowance** *n BrE* TAX Altersfreibetrag *m*; **~-age insurance benefit** *n AmE* (*cf retirement benefit BrE*) HRM, WEL Rente *f*; **~-age pension** *n* HRM, WEL Altersrente *f*, Rente *f*; **~-age pensioner** *n BrE* (*OAP*) HRM, WEL Pensionär, in *m,f*, Rentner, in *m,f*; **~-age pension scheme** *n* FIN Altersrentensystem *nt*; **~ charter** *n* TRANSP alte Charter *f*, alte Konzession *f*; **~ crop** *n* (*OC*) ECON *agricultural* letzte Ernte *f*; **~-fashioned** *adj* GEN COMM altmodisch; **~-line industry** *n* ECON veralteter Wirtschaftszweig *m*; **~ share** *n* STOCK alte Aktie *f*

oligopolist *n* ECON Oligopolist *m*

oligopolistic *adj* ECON oligopolistisch

oligopoly *n* ECON Oligopol *nt*

oligopsony *n* ECON Oligopson *nt*

OM *abbr* (*options market*) STOCK Optionsmarkt *m*

OMA *abbr* (*orderly market agreement*) ECON Selbstbeschränkungsabkommen *nt*

OMB *abbr AmE* (*Office of Management and Budget*) POL dem Präsidenten direkt unterstelltes Amt, das in enger Zusammenarbeit mit den Fachministern den Bundeshaushaltsplan für den Präsidenten zur späteren Vorlage im Kongreß erarbeitet, Amt *nt* für Management und Haushaltsplanung

ombudsman *n* GEN COMM, POL Ombudsmann *m*, Ombudsfrau *f*

OMC *abbr AmE* (*Open Market Committee*) ECON Offenmarktausschuß *m*

omission *n* GEN COMM *omitting* Auslassen *nt*, *thing omitted* Auslassung *f*, LAW *lapse* Unterlassung *f*, Versäumnis *nt*

omit *vt* GEN COMM *leave out* auslassen, weglassen, LAW *lapse* versäumen; ♦ **~ to do** LAW unterlassen

omitted: **~ dividend** *n* ACC ausgefallene Dividende *f*

Omnibus: **~ Budget Reconciliation Act** *n* (*OBRA*) FIN, TAX Gesamthaushaltsberichtigungsgesetz *nt*, umfassendes Haushaltsabstimmungsgesetz *nt*

omnibus: **~ survey** *n* S&M *market research* Mehrthemenbefragung *f*

omnicarrier *n* TRANSP Allzweckfrachter *m*

on-board *adj* COMP eingebaut

on-carriage *n* TRANSP *freight* Vorlauf *m*

on-deck: **~ bill of lading** *n* IMP/EXP, TRANSP *shipping* Seekonnossement *nt*, Seefrachtbrief *m*, An-Deck-Konnossement *nt*

on-demand: **~ bond** *n* BANK *merchant* Bei-Sicht-Anleihe *f*, Sichtanleihe *f*

one: **~-bank holding company** *n* AmE ACC, BANK, FIN, GEN COMM, STOCK Holding mit eigener Bank als 100%-iger Tochter; **~-cent sale** *n* AmE S&M Verkauf von zwei Produkten zum Preis von einem plus einem zusätzlichen Cent; **~-crop economy** *n* ECON Monokultursystem *nt*; **~-family home** *n* PROP, TAX Einfamilienhaus *nt*; **~-house veto** *n* AmE POL Ein-Haus-Veto *nt*, von einem Haus eingelegtes Veto *nt*; **~-hundred-percent location** *n* S&M hundertprozentiger Standort *m*; **~-hundred-percent reserve banking** *n* BANK hundertprozentige Rücklagenbildung *f*; **any ~ location** (*AOLOC*) *phr* INS *marine* jeder Standort *m*; **~-man business** *n* GEN COMM Alleinbetrieb *m*, Einmannbetrieb *m*, Einzelunternehmen *nt*; **~-minute manager** *n* MGMNT oberflächlicher Leiter *m*, oberflächliche Leiterin *f*, oberflächlicher Manager *m*, oberflächliche Managerin *f*; **~ month's notice** *n* GEN COMM Monatsfrist *f*; **~-off** *adj* GEN COMM einzeln angefertigt; **~-off cash gift** *n* TAX einmaliges Geldgeschenk *nt*; **~-off issue** *n* STOCK Einmalemission *f*; **~-off payment** *n* FIN einmalige Zahlung *f*; **~-off production** *n* IND Einmalfertigung *f*; **~-price law** *n* ECON Einheitspreisgesetz *nt*, Einpreisgesetz *nt*

1Q *abbr* (*first quarter*) GEN COMM erstes Quartal *nt*

one: **~-shot deal** *n* GEN COMM einmaliges Geschäft *nt*; **~-sided** *adj* GEN COMM einseitig; **~-stop financing** *n* ECON, FIN Allfinanz *f*, Finanzierung *f* aus einer Hand; **~-stop shopping center** AmE, **~-stop shopping centre** BrE *n* S&M Supermarkt *m*, Warenhaus *nt*; **~-tailed test** *n* MATH *statistics* einseitiger Test *m*; **~-time buyer** *n* S&M Einmalkäufer *m*; **~-time rate** *n* S&M *advertising* Einmaltarif *m*; **~-trial learning** *n* WEL Erwerb einer Fähig- oder Fertigkeit in einem einzigen Lernschritt; **~-way fare** *n* TRANSP einfache Fahrkarte *f*, einfache Fahrt *f*, einfacher Fahrpreis *m*; **~-way lease** *n* PROP einfache Pacht *f*; **~ top and three copies** *phr* ADMIN ein Original und drei Kopien; **any ~ vessel** *n* (*AOV*) INS *marine* jedes Schiff *nt*

ongoing *adj* GEN COMM andauernd, im Gang befindlich, laufend, fortbestehend; **~ concern** *n* GEN COMM Daueranliegen *nt*, laufende Angelegenheit *f*; **~ management system** *n* MGMNT kontinuierliches Leitungssystem *nt*

on-lending *n* FIN Weiterleihen *nt*

on-line 1. *adj* COMP on-line, rechnerabhängig, On-line-; **2.** *adv* COMP on-line, rechnerabhängig

on-line: **~ database** *n* COMP On-line-Datenbank *f*; **~ data service** *n* COMP On-line-Datendienst *m*; **~ help** *n* COMP On-line-Hilfe *f*; **~ rate** *n* TRANSP *air freight* On-line-Tarif *m*; **~ system** *n* COMP rechnerabhängiges System *nt*

ono *abbr* (*or nearest offer*) S&M oder Angebot

on-pack *adj* S&M auf der Verpackung; **~ price reduction** *n* S&M auf der Verpackung aufgedruckter Preisnachlaß *m*

on-sale: **~ date** *n* AmE MEDIA *print* Zeitpunkt, zu dem ein Kommissionsgeschäft beginnt

onset *n* GEN COMM Beginn *m*

onshore: **~ terminal** *n* ENVIR Binnenumschlagplatz *m*, Festlandumschlagplatz *m*

on-the-job: **~ safety** *n* HRM Arbeitssicherheit *f*; **~ training** *n* HRM innerbetriebliche Weiterbildung *f*

on-the-spot: **~ reporter** *n* MEDIA Reporter, in *m,f* vor Ort

onward: **~ flight** *n* TRANSP Anschlußflug *m*, Weiterflug *m*

O/o *abbr* (*order of*) GEN COMM i.A. (*im Auftrag von*)

OOG *abbr* (*out of gage AmE, out of gauge BrE*) TRANSP das Lademaß überschreitend

op *abbr* (*out of print*) MEDIA vergr. (*vergriffen*)

OP *abbr* (*open cargo insurance policy*) INS Versicherungspolice *f* ohne Wertangabe der Fracht

OPCS *abbr* BrE (*Office of Population Censuses and Surveys*) WEL Amt für Volkszählungen und statistische Untersuchungen

OPEC *abbr* (*Organization of Petroleum-Exporting Countries*) ECON, ENVIR, POL OPEC (*Organisation erdölexportierender Länder*)

open 1. *adj* COMP *file, document*, GEN COMM offen; ◆ **~ all day** GEN COMM durchgehend geöffnet; **~ to debate** GEN COMM bereit zur Aussprache; **~ all hours** GEN COMM Tag und Nacht geöffnet; **~ for subscription** FIN aufgelegt; **2.** *vt* BANK *account* eröffnen, COMP *file* öffnen; ◆ **~ an account with** BANK *a particular bank* ein Konto eröffnen bei; **~ a business** GEN COMM ein Geschäft aufmachen

open up 1. *vt* GEN COMM *market* erschließen; ◆ **open the market up to competition** S&M den Markt dem Wettbewerb öffnen; **2.** *vi* GEN COMM *opportunities* sich öffnen

open: **~ account** *n* BANK Kontokorrent *nt*; **~ account business** *n* BANK Kontokorrentgeschäft *nt*; **~ admissions** *n pl* WEL uneingeschränkte Zulassung zum Studium; **~ bid** *n* MGMNT offenes Angebot *nt*; **~ cargo insurance policy** *n* (*OP*) INS Versicherungspolice *f* ohne Wertangabe der Fracht

opencast: **~ mining** *n* BrE (*cf strip mining AmE*) IND Abraumbau *m*, Tagebau *m*

open: **~ charter** *n* TRANSP offene Charter *f*; **~ check** AmE, **~ cheque** BrE *n* BANK, FIN Barscheck *m*; **~ competition** *n* ECON offener Wettbewerb *m*; **~ container** *n* TRANSP offener Container *m*; **~ cover** *n* (*OC*) INS laufende Police *f*; **~ credit** *n* BANK Kontokorrentkredit *m*, offener Kredit *m*; **~ dating** *n* AmE S&M Haltbarkeitsangabe *f*; **~ distribution** *n* TRANSP offene Verteilung *f*; **~ dock** *n* TRANSP offenes Dock *nt*; **~-door policy** *n* MGMNT, POL Politik *f* der offenen Tür; **~ economy** *n* ECON offene Volkswirtschaft *f*; **~-end contract** *n* LAW offener Vertrag *m*, Vertrag *m* auf unbestimmte Dauer; **~-ended** *adj* COMP ausbaufähig, offen, GEN COMM mit nicht begrenzter Zahl auszugebender Anteile, ohne feste Grenze; **~-ended agreement** *n* HRM Tarifvertrag *m* mit offener Laufzeit; **~-ended contract** *n* LAW offener Vertrag *m*; **~-ended flight reservation** *n* TRANSP unbefristete Flugreservierung *f*; **~-ended fund** *n* FIN offener Investmentfonds *m*; **~-ended investment company** *n* (*OEIC*) FIN offene Investmentgesellschaft *f*; **~-ended mortgage** *n* BANK, FIN offene Hypothek *f*, aufstockbare Hypothek *f*; **~-ended question** *n* S&M *market research* offener Fragetyp *m*, frei beantwortbare Frage *f*; **~-ended questionnaire** *n* S&M *market research* Fragebogen *m* mit offenen Fragen; **~-end fund** n FIN offener Investmentfonds m; **~-end investment company** n (*OEIC*) FIN offene Investmentgesellschaft f; **~-end management company** n FIN offene Verwaltungsgesellschaft f; **~-end mortgage** n BANK, FIN offene Hypothek f, aufstockbare Hypothek f; **~ general import licence** *BrE*, **~ general import license** *AmE* n (*OGIL*) IMP/EXP allgemeine Importgenehmigung f, allgemeine Rahmeneinfuhrgenehmigung f, allgemeine Rahmengenerallizenz f, Freiliste f für Importwaren, Rahmengeneraleinfuhrlizenz f; **~ housing** n *AmE* WEL freie Wohnungswahl ohne Diskriminierung; **~ individual licence** *BrE*, **~ individual license** *AmE* n IMP/EXP Rahmeneinzelgenehmigung f, Rahmeneinzellizenz f

opening n GEN COMM Eröffnung f, STOCK *of day's trading* Eröffnung f, Beginn m; ♦ **at the ~** *phr* STOCK bei Eröffnung f

opening: **~ balance** n ACC Anfangsbestand m, Eröffnungsbestand m, Eröffnungsbilanz f, BANK Eröffnungsbilanz f; **~ balance sheet** n ACC Anfangsbilanz f, LAW *company in liquidation* Abwicklungseröffnungsbilanz f; **~ bank** n BANK Akkreditivbank f, akkreditiveröffnende Bank f; **~ bid** n GEN COMM erstes Gebot nt, Eröffnungsangebot nt; **~ of a business** n GEN COMM, LAW, TAX Geschäftseröffnung f, Betriebseröffnung f; **~ hours** n pl ADMIN, GEN COMM Öffnungszeiten f pl, Parteienverkehr m (*Öst*); **~ inventory** n ACC Anfangsbestand m, Anfangsinventar f; **~ of tenders** n GEN COMM Ausschreibung f von Angeboten, Angebotseröffnung f

open: **~ list** n GEN COMM offene Preisliste f; **~ listing** n PROP offener Maklervertrag m; **~ market** n ECON freier Markt m, Freiverkehr m, offener Markt m, Offenmarkt m

Open: **~ Market Committee** n *AmE* (*OMC*) ECON Offenmarktausschuß m

open: **~-market operation** n ECON Offenmarktgeschäft nt, Transaktion f am offenen Markt; **~-market rate** n BANK Offenmarktsatz m; **~-market trading** n ECON *international trade* Offenmarkthandel m; **~ mortgage** n BANK, FIN offene Hypothek f, aufstockbare Hypothek f; **~ network** n COMP offenes Netz nt; **~-plan office** n ADMIN Großraumbüro nt; **~ policy** n INS laufende Police f; **~ population** n ECON offene Bevölkerung f; **~ port** n TRANSP offener Hafen m; **~ position** n STOCK offene Position f; **~ sea** n TRANSP Hochsee f; **~-shelf filing** n ADMIN Aktenablage f in offenen Regalen; **~ shop** n HRM nicht gewerkschaftspflichtiger Betrieb m; **~ space** n PROP *in a developed area* freie Fläche f, Freifläche f, unbebautes Gelände nt; **~ stock** n S&M ständig vorrätige Ware f; **~ storage** n TRANSP offene Lagerung f; **~ systems interconnection** n (*OSI*) COMP Kommunikation f offener Systeme (*OSI*), Open-Systems-Interconnection f (*OSI*); **~ tendering** n GEN COMM offene Ausschreibung f; **~ ticket** n LEIS offenes Ticket nt; **~-to-buy** n *AmE* S&M Einkaufsbudget für bestimmten Zeitraum; **~ union** n HRM Gewerkschaft, die jeden Arbeitnehmer als Mitglied aufnimmt; **~ university** n WEL Fernuniversität f

operand n COMP, MATH Operand m

operate 1. *vt* GEN COMM betreiben, LAW gelten; **2.** *vi* GEN COMM funktionieren; ♦ **~ in tandem** MGMNT im Tandembetrieb arbeiten; **~ in the red** BANK, GEN COMM rote Zahlen schreiben (*infrml*)

operating: **~ account** n BANK Betriebskonto nt, Erfolgskonto nt; **~ budget** n ACC Betriebsvoranschlag m, Betriebsbudget nt, operativer Rahmenplan m; **~ capacity** n ECON Betriebskapazität f, IND betriebliche Leistungsfähigkeit f; **~ capital** n ECON Betriebskapital nt; **~ capital requirements** n pl FIN betriebsnotwendiger Kapitalbedarf m; **~ costs** n pl ACC Betriebsaufwand m, Betriebskosten pl, betriebliche Aufwendungen f pl, betriebsbedingter Aufwand m; **~ cycle** n ACC Betriebszyklus m, betriebliche Durchlaufzeit f, Geschäftsumschlagperiode f; **~ efficiency** n ECON Gesamtrentabilität f, IND betriebliche Leistungsfähigkeit f; **~ expenditure** n ACC Betriebsaufwand m, betriebliche Aufwendungen f pl, betriebsbedingter Aufwand m; **~ expenditure vote** n ACC *government* Bewilligung f von betrieblichen Aufwendungen; **~ expenses** n pl ACC Betriebsaufwand m, Betriebskosten pl, betriebliche Aufwendungen f pl, betriebsbedingter Aufwand m; **~ grant** n ACC Betriebsbewilligung f, Betriebsgewährung f; **~ income** n ACC Betriebsertrag m, betriebliche Erträge m pl; **~ instructions** n pl IND Bedienungsanleitung f; **~ lease** n FIN kurzfristiger Leasingvertrag m; **~ leasing** n FIN Ausrüstungsvermietung f, Operating-Leasing nt; **~ leverage** n *AmE* ACC Umsatz-Leverage nt; **~ loss** n ACC *balance sheets* Betriebsverlust m, Geschäftsverlust m; **~ management** n HRM, IND, MGMNT Betriebsleitung f; **~ plan** n TRANSP Betriebsplan m; **~ plant** n IND Betriebsanlage f; **~ profit** n ACC Betriebsgewinn m; **~ rate** n IND Ausnutzungsgrad m, Auslastung f; **~ results** n pl ACC Betriebsergebnis nt; **~ revenue** n ACC betriebliche Erträge m pl; **~ schedule** n TRANSP Ablaufplan m, Arbeitsplan m; **~ statement** n ACC Betriebsergebnisrechnung f, Ergebnisrechnung f, Gewinn- und Verlustrechnung f; **~ strategy** n MGMNT Betriebsstrategie f; **~ subsidy** n FIN Betriebssubvention f, Betriebszuschuß m; **~ system** n (*OS*) COMP Betriebssystem nt; **~ year** n FIN *machine, plant* Betriebsjahr nt

operation n GEN COMM *process* Vorgang m, Arbeitsvorgang m, Betrieb m, *enterprise* Geschäftsbereich m, Konzernunternehmen nt, Operation f, Unternehmen nt, Unternehmensbereich m, Unternehmung f, Zweigwerk nt; ♦ **come into ~** LAW wirksam werden

operational *adj* GEN COMM betrieblich; **~ analysis** n ACC, HRM Betriebsanalyse f; **~ audit** n MGMNT Innenrevision f, Kontrolle f des Arbeitsablaufs, Prüfung f der Betriebsabläufe; **~ balances** n pl *BrE* BANK Guthaben bei der Bank von England; **~ budget** n FIN Produktionsbudget nt; **~ control** n MGMNT Innenrevision f; **~ data** n pl ACC, HRM Betriebsunterlagen f pl; **~ investment** n ACC *buildings, equipment* betriebsbezogene Investitionen f pl, betriebsinterne Investitionen f pl; **~ manager** n HRM, MGMNT Leiter, in m,f der Ablauforganisation, Betriebsleiter, in m,f; **~ plan framework** n MGMNT operativer Rahmenplan m, Rahmen m des operativen Plans; **~ planning** n MGMNT Ablaufplanung f, betriebliche Planung f, Betriebsplanung f; **~ research** n (*OR*) MGMNT, S&M Operations-Research nt (*OR*), Unternehmensforschung f; **~ sequence** n HRM Arbeitsablauf m; **~ staff** n HRM operatives Personal nt

operation: **~ cycle** n COMP Arbeitszyklus m; **~ flow chart** n IND Arbeitsflußdiagramm nt; **~ lease** n FIN Ausrüstungsvermietung f, TRANSP Betriebspachtvertrag m

operations n pl GEN COMM *business transactions* Geschäftsvorgänge m pl, Geschäfte nt pl, betriebliche Prozesse m pl; **~ analysis** n ACC, HRM Betriebsanalyse f;

~ audit *n* MGMNT Innenrevision *f*, Kontrolle *f* des Arbeitsablaufs, Prüfung *f* der Betriebsabläufe; **~ breakdown** *n* GEN COMM, IND *disruption* Betriebsstillstand *m*, Betriebszusammenbruch *m*, MGMNT *analysis of business* Betriebsanalyse *f*; **~ director** *n* MGMNT für den Betriebsablauf zuständiger Direktor *m*; **~ management** *n* MGMNT Betriebsleitung *f*, Unternehmensleitung *f*; **~ manager** *n* MGMNT Betriebsleiter, in *m,f*, Leiter, in *m,f* der Ablauforganisation; **~ research** *n* (*OR*) MGMNT, S&M Operations-Research *nt* (*OR*), Unternehmensforschung *f*

operation: **~ ticket** *n* GEN COMM, IND Arbeitsauftrag *m*; **~ time** *n* GEN COMM Laufzeit *f*

operative *n* HRM, MGMNT Bedienungskraft *f*

operator *n* COMP Operator, in *m,f*, GEN COMM *company* Unternehmer *m*, IND *of electrical equipment* Bediener *m*, *of machinery* Maschinenarbeiter, in *m,f*; **~ control panel** *n* COMP Bedienungsfeld *nt*

opinion *n* GEN COMM *judgment, belief* Meinung *f*, Ansicht *f*, *stance* Stellungnahme *f*, Gutachten *nt*, POL Anschauung *f*; ◆ **give an expert ~ on** GEN COMM begutachten

opinion: **~ leader** *n* S&M *market research* Meinungsführer *f*, Meinungsbildner *m*; **~ poll** *n* S&M *market research* Meinungsumfrage *f*; **~ polling** *n* S&M *market research* Durchführen *nt* von Meinungsumfragen; **~ shopping** *n* ACC *audit opinions* Meinungsumfrage *f*; **~ survey** *n* S&M *market research* Meinungsumfrage *f*

OPM *abbr* FIN (*other people's money*) Geld *nt* anderer Leute, STOCK (*option price model*) Optionspreismodell *nt*

opportunism *n* POL Opportunismus *m*

opportunist **1.** *adj* POL opportunistisch; **2.** POL Opportunist, in *m,f*

opportunities: **~ to hear** *n pl* (*OTH*) S&M *radio advertising* Wahrnehmungsmöglichkeiten *f pl*; **~ to see** *n pl* (*OTS*) S&M *television advertising* Wahrnehmungsmöglichkeiten *f pl*

opportunity *n* ACC Opportunität *f*, ECON, FIN, GEN COMM, POL Chance *f*, Gelegenheit *f*, Möglichkeit *f*, Opportunität *f*; ◆ **give sb the ~ to do sth** GEN COMM jdm Gelegenheit geben, etw zu tun; **have the ~ to do sth** GEN COMM die Gelegenheit haben, etw zu tun

opportunity: **~ cost** *n* ACC, ECON, FIN Opportunitätskosten *pl*; **~ costs** *n pl* ACC, ECON, FIN Alternativkosten *pl*, Opportunitätskosten *pl*, alternative Kosten *pl*

oppose *vt* GEN COMM ablehnen, Einspruch erheben gegen, sich widersetzen [+dat], LAW widersprechen

opposing: **~ votes** *n pl* POL Gegenstimmen *f pl*

opposite: **~ number** *n* HRM *in organization* Gegenspieler, in *m,f*; **~ transaction** *n* GEN COMM Gegengeschäft *nt*

opposition *n* GEN COMM *resistance* Widerstand *m*, Opposition *f*, LAW Anfechtung *f*, Widerspruch *m*, PATENTS Patentanfechtung *f*, Patenteinspruch *m*, POL Opposition *f*, Oppositionspartei *f*; **~ proceedings** *n pl* PATENTS Einspruchsverfahren *nt*

oppress *vt* POL unterdrücken

oppressed *adj* POL unterdrückt

oppression *n* LAW *contract law* Druckausübung *f*, POL Unterdrückung *f*

opt *vi* MGMNT optieren, sich entscheiden, wählen; ◆ **~ for** MGMNT optieren für, sich entscheiden für

opt out *vi* ECON aussteigen, GEN COMM auf sein Optionsrecht verzichten; ◆ **~ of** GEN COMM austreten aus

optical: **~ character recognition** *n* (*OCR*) COMP optische Zeichenerkennung *f* (*OCR*); **~ scanner** *n* COMP optischer Leser *m*, Scanner *m*; **~ wand** *n* COMP Lesestift *m*

optimal *adj* GEN COMM optimal, günstigst; **~ control** *n* ECON optimale Kontrolle *f*

optimality *n* ECON Optimalität *f*

optimal: **~ peg** *n* ECON optimale Kursstützung *f*; **~ rate of pollution** *n* ECON, ENVIR optimale Verschmutzungsrate *f*; **~ tariff** *n* ECON optimaler Zoll *m*; **~ taxation** *n* TAX optimale Besteuerung *f*; **~ work effort** *n* ECON optimale Arbeitsanstrengung *f*

optimism *n* GEN COMM Optimismus *m*

optimist *n* GEN COMM Optimist, in *m,f*

optimistic *adj* GEN COMM optimistisch

optimization *n* GEN COMM Optimierung *f*; **~ problem** *n* MATH Optimierungsproblem *nt*

optimize *vt* GEN COMM optimieren; ◆ **~ the objective function** GEN COMM die Zielfunktion optimieren

optimum *adj* GEN COMM optimal, günstigst; **~ allocation of resources** *n* ECON optimale Ressourcenallokation *f*; **~ capacity** *n* ECON Optimalkapazität *f*, IND Höchstaufnahmefähigkeit *f*, Höchstlast *f*, optimales Fassungsvermögen *nt*, optimales Leistungsvermögen *nt*; **~ city** *n* ECON optimale Stadt *f*; **~ combination of labor, equipment and materials** *AmE*, **~ combination of labour, equipment and materials** *BrE n* HRM Arbeitsgestaltung *f*; **~ currency area** *n* ECON optimaler Währungsraum *m*; **~ firm** *n* ECON Optimalbetrieb *m*; **~ population** *n* ECON Bevölkerungsoptimum *nt*

option *n* FIN Option *f*, GEN COMM *ability to choose* Entscheidungsfreiheit *f*, freie Wahl *f*, *alternative* Alternative *f*, Wahlmöglichkeit *f*, *right to buy* Vorkaufsrecht *nt*, STOCK Option *f*; **~ account** *n* FIN *credit card* Abrechnung *f* für Optionsgeschäfte

optional: **~ character** *n* COMP beliebiges Zeichen *nt*; **~ modes of settlement** *n pl* INS *life insurance* Regulierung *f* nach Wahl; **~ retirement** *n* HRM freiwillige Pensionierung *f*

option: **~ demand** *n* STOCK Optionsnachfrage *f*; **~ fee** *n* FIN *hire purchase* Optionsgebühr *f*; **~ forward** *n* STOCK Optionsgeschäft *nt* mit Termindevisen; **~ holder** *n* STOCK Optionsinhaber, in *m,f*; **~ on actuals** *n* STOCK Option *f* auf Kassakontrakte; **~ on futures** *n* STOCK Option *f* auf Terminkontrakte; **~ price model** *n* (*OPM*) STOCK Optionspreismodell *nt*

options: **~ market** *n* (*OM*) STOCK Optionsmarkt *m*

option: **~-trading** *n* STOCK Optionshandel *m*; **~ writer** *n* STOCK Optionsverkäufer, in *m,f*

opt-out: **~ clause** *n* LAW Ausweichklausel *f*, Rücktrittsklausel *f*

OR *abbr* (*operational research, operations research*) MGMNT, S&M OR (*Operations-Research*), Unternehmensforschung *f*

oral: **~ contract** *n* LAW mündliche Vereinbarung *f*; **~ note** *n* POL mündliche Nachricht *f*; **~ proceedings** *n pl* PATENTS mündliche Verhandlung *f*

orange: **~ goods** *n pl* S&M Produkte mit mittlerer Lebensdauer, orange Waren *f pl*

orchestrate *vt* ECON aufeinander abstimmen, koordinieren

ord. *abbr* (*order*) GEN COMM Auftrag *m*, Order *f*, *sequence*

Reihenfolge *f*, LAW Weisung *f*, *courts* Anordnung *f*, Verfügung *f*, Beschluß *m*, POL Weisung *f*, S&M *goods and services* Order *f*, Auftrag *m*, STOCK Auftrag *m*

order 1. *n* (*ord.*) GEN COMM Auftrag *m*, Order *f*, *sequence* Reihenfolge *f*, LAW Weisung *f*, *courts* Anordnung *f*, Verfügung *f*, Beschluß *m*, POL Weisung *f*, S&M *goods and services* Order *f*, Auftrag *m*, STOCK Auftrag *m*; ◆ **as per ~** GEN COMM auftragsgemäß; **on ~** S&M bestellt; **out of ~** GEN COMM außer Betrieb, nicht funktionstüchtig, *at meeting* außer der Reihe; **~ of** (*O/o*) GEN COMM im Auftrag von (*i.A.*); **to the ~ of** LAW, S&M an die Order von; **in ~ of importance** GEN COMM nach Bedeutung; **in ~ of priority** GEN COMM nach Priorität; **in the ~ specified** GEN COMM in der festgelegten Reihenfolge, in der festgesetzten Reihenfolge; **for orders** (*fo*) GEN COMM bei Aufträgen, für Aufträge; **2.** *vt* GEN COMM bestellen

order: **~ bill of lading** *n* IMP/EXP, TRANSP Orderfrachtbrief *m*, Orderkonnossement *nt*; **~ book** *n* GEN COMM Auftragsbuch *nt*; **~ by mail** *AmE*, **~ by post** *BrE* *n* COMMS, S&M Versandbestellung *f*; **~ card** *n* S&M Auftragskarte *f*; **~ control** *n* GEN COMM Auftragsüberwachung *f*; **~ entry** *n* S&M Auftragseingang *m*; **~ filling** *n* GEN COMM Auftragsabwicklung *f*; **~ flow pattern** *n* S&M *direct mail* Auftragszugangsmuster *nt*; **~ form** *n* S&M *direct marketing* Auftragsformular *nt*; **~ for payment of a debt** *n* LAW Zahlungsbefehl *m*; **~ for relief** *n* ECON Konkursbeschluß *m*, Vergleichsbeschluß *m*; **~ from abroad** *n* GEN COMM Auslandsauftrag *m*; **~ handling** *n* GEN COMM Auftragsabwicklung *f*, Auftragsbearbeitung *f*

ordering: **~ procedure** *n* S&M Bestellverfahren *nt*

order: **~ intake** *n* GEN COMM Auftragseingang *m*

orderly: **~ market agreement** *n* (*OMA*) ECON Selbstbeschränkungsabkommen *nt*

order: **~ of magnitude** *n* MATH Größenordnung *f*; **~ number** *n* S&M Auftragsnummer *f*; **~ paper** *n* BANK Orderpapier *nt*; **~ point system** *n* TRANSP Bestellpunktsystem *nt*; **~ of preference** *n* ECON Präferenzstruktur *f*, Bedarfsstruktur *f*; **~ processing** *n* GEN COMM Auftragsabwicklung *f*; **~ regulation** *n* GEN COMM Auftragsdurchführungsverordnung *f*

orders: **~ on hand** *n pl* GEN COMM Auftragsbestand *m*, vorliegende Aufträge *m pl*; **~ received** *n pl* GEN COMM Auftragseingang *m*

order: **~ to negotiate** *n* FIN Ankaufermächtigung *f*; **~ to pay** *n* ACC, FIN Zahlungsauftrag *m*, Zahlungsanweisung *f*

ordinalist: **~ revolution** *n* ECON ordinalistische Revolution *f*

ordinal: **~ scale** *n* MATH Ordinalskala *f*, Rangskala *f*; **~ utility** *n* ECON ordinaler Nutzen *m*

ordinance *n* LAW Verordnung *f*

ordinarily: **~ resident** *adj* LAW wohnhaft

ordinary: **~ account** *n* BANK niedrigverzinsliches Sparkonto *nt*; **~ care** *n* LAW verkehrsübliche Sorgfalt *f*; **~ cargo** *n* TRANSP Normalfracht *f*; **~ competitive price** *n* FIN üblicher Wettbewerbspreis *f*; **~ diligence** *n* LAW verkehrsübliche Sorgfalt *f*; **~ gain** *n* TAX ordentliches Einkommen *nt*; **~ income** *n* TAX ordentliches Einkommen *nt*; **~ interest** *n* FIN gewöhnlicher Zins *m*; **~ loss** *n* TAX alle Verluste außer Kapitalverlusten; **~ and necessary business expenses** *n pl* TAX gewöhnliche und notwendige Geschäftsausgaben *f pl*, normale und

notwendige Geschäftsausgaben *f pl*; **~ payroll exclusion endorsement** *n* INS Nachtrag *m* bei Ausscheiden aus der Firma; **~ profit before taxation** *n* ACC *annual accounts* ordentlicher Gewinn *m* vor Steuern; **~ return** *n* LEIS *travel ticket* normales Hin- und Rückflugticket *nt*; **~ seaman** *n* HRM Leichtmatrose *m*; **~ share** *n* *BrE* (*cf equity share AmE*) STOCK Stammaktie *f*; **~ single** *n* LEIS *travel ticket* normales Einfachticket *nt*; **~ ticket** *n* LEIS normale Fahrkarte *f*, *air travel* normaler Flugschein *m*

ore *n* ENVIR, IND Erz *nt*; **~ carrier** *n* TRANSP Erzfrachter *m*

ore/oil: **~ ship** *n* TRANSP Öl/Erzschiff *nt*

org. *abbr* (*organization*) GEN COMM *enterprise, arrangement* Org. (*Organisation*), *enterprise* Unternehmen *nt*

organic *adj* ECON *structure, growth* organisch, ENVIR organisch, biologisch, organischbiologisch, *meat* aus artengerechter Tierhaltung, *vegetables, groceries* aus biologischem Anbau, MGMNT *structure* organisch; **~ composition of capital** *n* ECON organische Zusammensetzung *f* des Kapitals; **~ farming** *n* ENVIR organischbiologische Landwirtschaft *f*; **~ foodstuffs** *n pl* ENVIR organischbiologische Lebensmittel *nt pl*; **~ growth** *n* ECON organisches Wachstum *nt*, immanentes Wachstum *nt*

organicity *n* MGMNT Grad der Arbeitnehmermitbestimmung bei der Entscheidungsfindung innerhalb einer Organisation

organic: **~ material** *n* ENVIR organisches Material *nt*; **~ premium** *n* ECON *agricultural* Prämie *f* für organisch-biologische Produkte

organization *n* (*org.*) GEN COMM *enterprise, arrangement* Organisation *f* (*Org.*), *enterprise* Unternehmen *nt*

Organization: **~ of African Unity** *n* (*OAU*) POL Organisation *f* der Afrikanischen Einheit

organizational: **~ behavior** *AmE*, **~ behaviour** *BrE* *n* MGMNT, S&M Organisationsverhalten *nt*; **~ change** *n* MGMNT organisatorische Veränderung *f*; **~ chart** *n* MGMNT Organigramm *nt*, Organisationsplan *m*, Geschäftsverteilungsplan *m*; **~ convenience** *n* GEN COMM organisationelle Praktikabilität *f*; **~ development** *n* MGMNT Organisationsentwicklung *f*, Organisationswirtschaftslehre *f*; **~ economics** *n* ECON Organisationstheorien *f pl*; **~ effectiveness** *n* MGMNT Effektivität *f* der Organisationsstruktur; **~ environment** *n* ECON Betriebsumfeld *nt*; **~ lines** *n pl* ECON betriebliche Instanzen *f pl*; **~ pathology** *n* HRM Organisationspathologie *f*; **~ politics** *n pl* POL Organisationspolitik *f*; **~ psychology** *n* MGMNT Arbeitspsychologie *f*, Organisationspsychologie *f*; **~ shape** *n* GEN COMM Organisationsform *f*; **~ size** *n* GEN COMM Organisationsumfang *m*; **~ skills** *n pl* MGMNT Organisationstalent *nt*; **~ symbol** *n* GEN COMM *logo* Firmenlogo *nt*; **~ unit** *n* ADMIN Organisationseinheit *f*, ECON Instanz *f*, Ressort *nt*

Organization: **~ of American States** *n* (*OAS*) POL Organisation *f* amerikanischer Staaten; **~ of Central American States** *n* (*OCAS*) POL Organisation *f* zentralamerikanischer Staaten

organization: **~ and methods** *f pl* (*O&M*) MGMNT Organisation und Methoden (*O&M*); **~ chart** *n* MGMNT Organigramm *nt*, Organisationsplan *m*, Geschäftsverteilungsplan *m*; **~ cost** *n* ACC, FIN Gründungsaufwand *m*, Gründungskosten *pl*, Organisationskosten *pl*; **~ culture** *n* MGMNT Organisationskultur *f*;

~ development *n* MGMNT Organisationsentwicklung *f*; **~ expense** *n* ACC, FIN Gründungsaufwand *m*, Gründungskosten *pl*, Organisationskosten *pl*

Organization: **~ for Economic Cooperation and Development** *n* (*OECD*) ECON Organisation *f* für wirtschaftliche Zusammenarbeit und Entwicklung (*OECD*); **~ for European Economic Cooperation** *n obs* (*OEEC*) ECON Organisation *f* für europäische wirtschaftliche Zusammenarbeit (*OEEC*); **~ for Trade Cooperation** *n* (*OTC*) ECON *international trade* Organisation *f* für Handelskooperation

organization: **~ meeting** *n* MGMNT Gründungsversammlung *f*

Organization: **~ of Petroleum-Exporting Countries** *n* (*OPEC*) ECON, ENVIR, POL Organisation *f* erdölexportierender Länder (*OPEC*)

organization: **~ planning** *n* MGMNT Planung *f* der Organisation, Organisationsplanung *f*; **~ structure** *n* MGMNT Organisationsstruktur *f*; **~ theory** *n* MGMNT Organisationslehre *f*, Organisationstheorie *f*

organize *vt* GEN COMM organisieren, veranstalten, einrichten

organized: **~ crime** *n* LAW organisiertes Verbrechen *nt*; **~ labor** *AmE*, **~ labour** *BrE* *n* HRM gewerkschaftlich organisierte Mitarbeiter *m pl*, organisierte Arbeitskräfte *f pl*; **~ market** *n* ECON organisierter Markt *m*; **~ stock market** *n* ECON geregelter Wertpapiermarkt *m*

organizer *n* GEN COMM *person* Organisator, in *m,f*, *diary, address book* Zeitplaner *m*, Terminplaner *m*, *electronic* elektronisches Notizbuch *nt*

orientation *n* GEN COMM Ausrichtung *f*, HRM *for newcomer* Arbeitsplatzeinweisung *f*, POL Orientierung *f*

original 1. *adj* GEN COMM *not copy* original; **2.** *n* ADMIN Erstausfertigung *f*, Original *nt*

original: **~ address** *n* COMMS originale Adresse *f*; **~ bid** *n* GEN COMM Originalangebot *nt*, Originalkostenvoranschlag *m*, Originalofferte *f*; **~ capital** *n* FIN Anfangskapital *nt*, Gründungskapital *nt*, Grundkapital *nt*; **~ cost** *n* ACC *public utilities accounting* Herstellungskosten *pl*, Anschaffungskosten *pl*, Gestehungskosten *pl*, Gründungsaufwand *m*; **~ custodian** *n* FIN Erstverwahrer, in *m,f*; **~ document** *n* ADMIN, LAW Originaldokument *nt*, Originalurkunde *f*; **~ entry** *n* ACC *book-keeping* Eingangsbuchung *f*, Grundbuchung *f*; **~ equipment manufacturer** *n* (*OEM*) COMP Originalgerätehersteller *m* (*OEM*), Wiederverkäufer *m*; **~ firm** *n* GEN COMM Stammhaus *nt*; **~ impossibility** *n* LAW anfängliche Unmöglichkeit *f*; **~ insurer** *n* INS Direktversicherer *m*, Erstversicherer *m*, Zedent *m*; **~ invoice** *n* GEN COMM Originalfaktura *f*, Originalrechnung *f*; **~ issue discount** *n* (*OID*) FIN, STOCK Abzinsungsbetrag *m*, Emissionsdisagio *nt*; **~ issue discount bond** *n* FIN, STOCK Abzinsungsobligation *f*; **~ margin** *n* STOCK Anfangseinschuß *m*; **~ maturity** *n* STOCK ursprüngliche Laufzeit *f*; **~ order** *n* S&M Erstauftrag *m*, ursprünglicher Auftrag *m*; **~ plan** *n* GEN COMM Originalplan *m*; **~ slip** *n* INS Originalbeleg *m*, Originalschein *m*; **~ subscriber** *n* STOCK Erstzeichner, in *m,f*

originate *vi* GEN COMM herstammen, seinen Ursprung haben; ◆ **~ in** GEN COMM stammen aus

originator *n* BANK Auftraggeber, in *m,f*

origin: **~ and destination study** *n* S&M *market research* Studie *f* über Herkunfts- und Bestimmungsort

o.s. *abbr* (*out of stock*) S&M ausverkauft, nicht auf Lager, nicht vorrätig

OS *abbr* (*operating system*) COMP Betriebssystem *nt*

OSA *abbr* (*overseas sterling area*) ECON überseeisches Sterlinggebiet *nt*

OSAS *abbr* (*Overseas Service Aid Scheme*) ECON Entwicklungshilfeprojekt *nt*

OSI *abbr* (*open systems interconnection*) COMP OSI (*Open-Systems-Interconnection*, *Kommunikation offener Systeme*)

ostensible: **~ company** *n* ECON Scheingesellschaft *f*

OT *abbr* (*overtime*) HRM *working hours* Überstunden *f pl*

OTAR *abbr* (*overseas tariff and regulations*) IMP/EXP Auslandtarife *m pl* und -bestimmungen *f pl*, Überseetarife *m pl* und -bestimmungen *f pl*

OTC *abbr* ECON (*Organization for Trade Cooperation*) *international trade* Organisation *f* für Handelskooperation, STOCK (*over-the-counter*) im Freiverkehr, nicht börsengehandelt, S&M (*over-the-counter*) offen, WEL (*over-the-counter*) *medication* rezeptfrei, freiverkäuflich, nicht rezeptpflichtig

OTCM *abbr* *AmE* (*over-the-counter market*) ECON, STOCK dritter Markt *m*, Freiverkehr *m*, Freiverkehrsbörse *f*

OTH *abbr* (*opportunities to hear*) S&M *radio advertising* Wahrnehmungsmöglichkeiten *f pl*

other: **~ assets** *n pl* FIN sonstige Aktiva *pl*; **any ~ business** *n* (*AOB*) GEN COMM *in meeting* Sonstiges *nt*; **~ checkable deposits** *n pl* (*OCD*) BANK, FIN sonstige Kontokorrenteinlagen *f pl*, sonstige Sichteinlagen *f pl*; **any ~ competent business** *n* (*AOCB*) GEN COMM *in meeting* sonstige Angelegenheiten *f pl*; **~ engagement** *n* GEN COMM anderweitige Verabredung *f*; **~ income** *n* ACC betriebsfremde Erträge *m pl*, neutrale Erträge *m pl*, sonstige Erträge *m pl*; **~ insurance clause** *n* INS Überschneidungsklausel *f*; **~ liabilities** *n pl* ACC sonstige Verbindlichkeiten *f pl*, sonstige Verpflichtungen *f pl*, andere Verpflichtungen *f pl*; **~ people's money** *n* (*OPM*) FIN Geld *nt* anderer Leute; **~ receivables** *n pl* ACC *assets* sonstige Forderungen *f pl*; **~ revenue** *n* ACC betriebsfremde Erträge *m pl*, neutrale Erträge *m pl*

otherwise: **not ~ provided** *phr* GEN COMM nichts Gegenteiliges vorgesehen; **not ~ specified** *phr* GEN COMM nicht anderweitig spezifiziert

OTS *abbr* *BrE* ECON (*Overseas Trade Statistics*) Außenhandelsstatistik *f*, S&M (*opportunities to see*) *television, advertising* Wahrnehmungsmöglichkeiten *f pl*

ounce *n* (*oz*) GEN COMM Unze *f*

oust *vt* GEN COMM verdrängen; ◆ **~ sb from their job** HRM jdn aus seiner Stellung verdrängen

out: **~ of** *adv* GEN COMM außerhalb; ◆ **be ~ of** *adv* GEN COMM nicht mehr vorrätig haben

outage: **~ time** *n* IND Ausfallzeit *f*

outbid *vt* S&M *auction* überbieten

outcome *n* GEN COMM Ausgang *m*, Ergebnis *nt*, Folge *f*, Resultat *nt*

outcompete *vt* ECON überflügeln

outcry *n* GEN COMM *auction* Auktion *f*; **~ market** *n* STOCK Auktionsmarkt *m*; **open ~** *n* STOCK *on the floor* offener Zuruf *m*

outdate *vt* GEN COMM überholen

outdated *adj* GEN COMM *idea, product* überaltert, überholt, veraltet

outdoor: ~ **advertising** n S&M Außenwerbung f, Plakatwerbung f

outer: ~ **pack** n S&M äußere Verpackung f; ~ **suburbs** n pl GEN COMM Außenbezirke m pl

outflow n ACC, ECON, FIN of funds Abfluß m, Kapitalabfluß m; ~ **of foreign exchange** n ECON Devisenabfluß m

outflows n pl FIN in pre-investment analysis Ausgaben f pl

outgoing: ~ **goods** n pl GEN COMM Warenausgang m; ~ **mail** n COMMS ausgehende Post f, Ausgangspost f

outgoings n pl FIN Ausgang m, Aufwendungen f pl, Ausgaben f pl (Ausg.)

outhouse n PROP Nebengebäude nt, Seitengebäude nt

outlaw vt LAW ächten, verbieten

outlay n ACC, FIN Ausgabe f (Ausg.), cash Ausgaben f pl, Auslagen f pl, Barausgaben f pl; ~ **creep** n FIN schleichender Ausgabenanstieg m; ~ **curve** n ECON Ausgabenkurve f

outlays n pl ACC, FIN Ausgaben f pl, Auslagen f pl

outlay: ~ **tax** n TAX indirekte Steuer f, Ausgabensteuer f

outlet n S&M Absatzgebiet nt, Absatzfeld nt, shop Verkaufsstelle f; ~ **store** n S&M Resteladen m, Werksverkaufsstelle f

outlier n MATH statistics Ausreißer m

outline 1. n GEN COMM summary Grundriß, Entwurf m, Übersicht f; **2.** vt GEN COMM umreißen, summarize grob umreißen, entwerfen

outline: ~ **process chart** n IND Arbeitsablaufschaubild nt

outlying: ~ **districts** n pl GEN COMM Außenbezirke m pl, Randgebiet nt

outmoded adj GEN COMM überholt, veraltet

out-of-court: ~ **settlement** n LAW außergerichtlicher Vergleich m

out-of-favor AmE see out-of-favour BrE

out-of-favour: ~ **industry** n BrE FIN currently unpopular with investors unbeliebte Industrie f; ~ **stock** n BrE FIN currently unpopular with investors unbeliebte Aktie f

out-of-pocket: ~ **expenses** n pl ACC Spesen pl

out-of-state: ~ **corporation** n LAW ausländische Gesellschaft f

out-of-stock: ~ **cost** n GEN COMM Fehlmengenkosten pl

out-of-the-money: ~ **call** n STOCK Call m aus dem Geld (jarg), Call m out of the money (jarg), Kaufoption m, Call m out of the money (jarg), Kaufoption, Abschlußpreis über dem Marktpreis des Wertpapiers liegt; ~ **option** n STOCK Option, deren Abschlußpreis bei einer Kaufoption über dem Marktpreis, bei einer Verkaufsoption unter dem Marktpreis liegt; ~ **put** n STOCK Put m aus dem Geld (jarg), Put m out of the money (jarg), Verkaufsoption, deren Abschlußpreis unter dem Marktpreis des Wertpapiers liegt

out-of-town adj S&M shop, restaurant außerhalb der Stadt; ~ **center** AmE, ~ **centre** BrE n S&M außerhalb der Stadt gelegenes Zentrum nt, Geschäftszentrum nt auf der grünen Wiese; ~ **food store** n S&M Lebensmittelgeschäft nt außerhalb der Stadt; ~ **shopping** n S&M Einkaufen nt außerhalb der Stadt; ~ **store** n S&M Laden m außerhalb der Stadt

outpace vt GEN COMM überholen

outpaced adj GEN COMM überholt

outpatients': ~ **clinic** n BrE WEL Poliklinik f; ~ **department** n WEL Ambulanz f

outperform vt ECON growth, trade volume, productivity übertreffen

outplacement n HRM Beratung f beim Positionswechsel, Outplacement nt; ~ **agency** n HRM Outplacement-Beratung f

output 1. n ACC amount Ertrag m, Output m, COMP data, text Ausgabe f (Ausg.), Output m, ECON quantity Ausstoß m, HRM work Arbeitsleistung f, IND process Produktion f, quantity Produktionsmenge f; **2.** vt COMP data, text ausgeben, IND produzieren

output: ~ **bonus** n HRM Produktionsprämie f; ~ **budget** n ACC, FIN Produktionsbudget nt; ~ **budgeting** n ACC, FIN Produktionsplanung f; ~ **data** n pl COMP Ausgabedaten pl; ~ **device** n COMP Ausgabegerät nt; ~ **file** n COMP Ausgabedatei f; ~ **per head** n IND Leistung f pro Kopf, Personenleistung f; ~ **per hour** n IND Leistung f pro Stunde, Stundenleistung f; ~ **tax** n TAX Bruttomehrwertsteuer f; ~ **variance** n MATH statistics Output-Varianz f; ~ **volume** n IND Produktionsvolumen nt

outright adj GEN COMM ownership direkt, bedingungslos, vollständig, ohne Vorbehalt; ~ **consolidation** n ECON Fusion f; ~ **forward purchase** n ECON international trade Outright-Terminkauf m; ~ **forward transaction** n STOCK einfaches Termingeschäft nt; ~ **gift** n TAX bedingungslose Zuwendung f

outset n GEN COMM Anfang m, Beginn m; ♦ **at the** ~ GEN COMM zu Anfang, zu Beginn

outshipment n IMP/EXP, TRANSP Ausfuhrsendung f

outside: ~ **broadcast** n MEDIA Sendung f außerhalb des Studios; ~ **capital** n BANK, ECON, FIN Fremdmittel nt pl, Fremdkapital nt, Fremdmittel nt pl; ~ **director** n HRM Mitglied des Firmenvorstands, das nicht gleichzeitig der Geschäftsleitung angehört, MGMNT Direktor, in m,f ohne Geschäftsbereich, nebenamtlicher Geschäftsführer m, nebenamtliche Geschäftsführerin f; ~ **facilities** n pl IND Außenanlagen f pl; ~ **finance** n ACC, FIN Außenfinanzierung f; ~ **lag** n POL äußere Verzögerung f; ~ **party** n GEN COMM Außenstehende(r) mf [decl. as adj]; ~ **person** n GEN COMM Außenstehende(r) mf [decl. as adj]; ~ **production** n ECON Fremdproduktion f

outsider n GEN COMM Außenseiter, in m,f, HRM Nichtmitglied nt, Außenstehende(r) mf [decl. as adj]

outsider: ~ **wage setting** n HRM außerbetriebliche Lohnfestsetzung f

outsourcing n IND Produktionsverlagerung f, MGMNT Produktionsverlagerung f, Outsourcing nt

outstanding 1. adj GEN COMM debt, amount, obligation ausstehend, unbeglichen, affairs unerledigt; **2.** n ACC Außenstände m pl

outstanding: ~ **advance** n ACC aufgenommenes Darlehen nt; ~ **amount** n GEN COMM ausstehender Betrag m; ~ **amounts** n pl ACC Buchforderungen f pl, ausstehende Beträge m pl; ~ **balance** n ACC ausstehende Restzahlung f; ~ **capital stock** n STOCK ausstehende Aktien f pl, ausgegebenes Aktienkapital nt, ausgegebenes Kapital nt, ausstehende Einlagen f pl; ~ **commitment** n ACC zugesagte, aber noch nicht ausgezahlte Finanzmittel; ~ **contributions** n pl ACC ausstehende Einlagen f pl; ~ **credits** n pl ACC Kreditvolumen nt; ~ **debts** n pl ACC Außenstände m pl; ~ **entry** n ACC ausstehende Buchung f; ~ **item** n ACC ausstehender Posten m; ~ **matter** n GEN COMM unerledigte Angelegenheit f; ~ **orders** n GEN COMM unerledigte Aufträge *m pl*; ~ **shares** *n pl* STOCK ausgegebene Aktien *f pl*

out-tray *n* ADMIN Ablagekorb *m* für abgehende Sendungen, Korb *m* für ausgehende Post, Postausgangskorb *m*

outvote *vt* MGMNT, POL überstimmen, durch Stimmenmehrheit besiegen; ♦ **be outvoted** MGMNT, POL überstimmt sein

outward: ~ **bill of lading** *n* IMP/EXP Exportkonnossement *nt*; ~ **cargo** *n* IMP/EXP ausgehende Ladung *f*, Ausreisefracht *f*, Hinfracht *f*; ~ **freight department** *n* IMP/EXP Ausfuhrabteilung *f*; ~ **leg** *n* LEIS *of journey* Hinreise *f*, erste Etappe *f*; ~-**looking** *adj* GEN COMM *approach* nach außen blickend; ~ **mission** *n* IMP/EXP Auswärtsmission *f*; ~ **payment** *n* FIN Auslandszahlung *f*; ~ **transit** *n* TRANSP Ausgangsversand *m*; ~ **voyage** *n* TRANSP Ausreise *f*

outweigh *vt* GEN COMM überwiegen

outwork *n* HRM Heimarbeit *f*

outworker *n* HRM Heimarbeiter, in *m,f*

over *n* FIN Kassenüberschuß *m*

overaccumulation *n* ECON Überansammlung *f*

over-achiever *n* WEL leistungsorientierte Person *f*

overage *n* GEN COMM *excess* Überschuß *m*, Bestandsüberschuß *m*, Mehrbetrag *m*

overaged: ~ **population** *n* ECON überalterte Gesellschaft *f*

overall 1. *adj* (*oa*) GEN COMM gesamt; **2.** *adv* (*oa*) GEN COMM insgesamt (*insg.*)

overall: ~ **company objectives** *n pl* GEN COMM Gesamtziele *nt pl* des Unternehmens; ~ **construction activity** *n* ECON Baukonjunktur *f*; ~ **development** *n* ECON Gesamtentwicklung *f*; ~ **economic plan** *n* ECON gesamtwirtschaftlicher Rahmenplan *m*; ~ **expenses method** *n* ACC Gesamtkostenmethode *f*; ~ **length** *n* (*LOA*) TRANSP Länge *f* über alles (*Lüa*); ~ **performance** *n* ECON Gesamtleistung *f*; ~ **rate of return** *n* ACC Unternehmensrentabilität *f*, Gesamtkapitalrentabilität *f*; ~ **width** *n* TRANSP Gesamtbreite *f*

overbid *vt* S&M überbieten

overbook 1. *vt* ADMIN, LEIS, TRANSP *flight, hotel* überbuchen; **2.** *vi* ADMIN, LEIS, TRANSP *flight, hotel* zu viele Buchungen vornehmen, zu viele Buchungen annehmen

overbooked *adj* ADMIN, LEIS, TRANSP *flight, hotel* überbucht

overbooking *n* ADMIN, LEIS, TRANSP *flight, hotel* Überbuchen *nt*, Überbuchung *f*, Overbooking *nt*

overburden *vt* HRM überlasten

overburdening *n* HRM Überlastung *f*

overcapacity *n* GEN COMM Überkapazität *f*

overcapitalization *n* FIN Überkapitalisierung *f*

overcapitalize *vt* FIN überkapitalisieren, GEN COMM, HRM überkompensieren

overcapitalized *adj* GEN COMM überkapitalisiert

overcharge 1. *n* (*o/c*) GEN COMM, S&M Überteuerung *f*, S&M zuviel berechneter Betrag *m*; **2.** *vt* S&M überhöhen

overcharged *adj* ECON überhöht

overcome *vt* GEN COMM *prejudice* überwinden

overcommitment *n* FIN zu starke Belastung *f*, zu starke Verpflichtung *f*

overcompensation *n* HRM Überkompensation *f*

overdependence *n* GEN COMM übermäßige Abhängigkeit *f*

overdraft *n* (*O/D*) BANK Kontoüberziehung *f*, Überziehung *f*; ~ **facility** *n* BANK Dispokredit *m*, Dispositionskredit *m*, Kreditlinie *f*, Überziehungskredit *m*, Überziehungsmöglichkeit *f*; ~ **rate** *n* BANK Überziehungskreditsatz *m*

overdraw 1. *vt* BANK überziehen; **2.** *vi* BANK Bankkonto überziehen

overdrawn *adj* (*O/D*) BANK überzogen

overdue *adj* ACC überfällig, ADMIN, FIN, GEN COMM rückständig; ~ **account** *n* FIN überfällige Forderung *f*; ~ **claim** *n* ACC überfällige Forderung; ~ **dividend** *n* STOCK rückständige Dividende *f*; ~ **payment** *n* FIN rückständige Zahlung *f*

overemployment *n* ECON Überbeschäftigung *f*

overestimate 1. *n* ACC, ECON, FIN Überbewertung *f*, zu hohe Schätzung *f*; **2.** *vt* ACC, ECON, FIN überschätzen, überbewerten

overestimated *adj* ACC, ECON, FIN überschätzt, überbewertet

overestimation *n* ACC, ECON, FIN Überschätzung *f*, Überbewertung *f*

overexploitation *n* ENVIR Raubbau *m*

overextend *vt* ECON überhöhen, überziehen

overextended *adj* ECON überhöht, überzogen; ~ **credit** *n* BANK ungenügend gedeckter Kredit *m*

overflow 1. *n* COMP Überlauf *m*; **2.** *vi* COMP überlaufen

overfund *vt* FIN überfinanzieren

overfunding *n* FIN Überfinanzierung *f*

overhang *n* STOCK Überhang *m*

overhaul 1. *n* GEN COMM Überholung *f*, MGMNT *of system* gründliche Überprüfung *f*, Revision *f*, TRANSP *of engine* Überholung *f*; **2.** *vt* MGMNT *system* überprüfen, revidieren, TRANSP *engine* überholen

overhead: ~ **capital** *n* ECON Infrastruktur *f*; ~ **charge** *n* ACC Gemeinkosten *pl*, indirekte Kosten *pl*, ECON, FIN indirekte Kosten *pl*; ~ **costs** *n pl* ACC Gemeinkosten *pl*; ~ **projector** *n* ADMIN Overheadprojektor *m*

overheads *n pl* ACC, FIN betriebliche Kosten *pl*, laufende Kosten *pl*, Gemeinkosten *pl*; ~ **recovery** *n* ACC, FIN Rückgewinnung *f* der Gemeinkosten, Gemeinkostendeckung *f*

overheat *vi* ECON sich überhitzen

overheated: ~ **economy** *n* ECON überhitzte Volkswirtschaft *f*

overheating *n* ECON Überhitzung *f*

overindebtedness *n* BANK, ECON Überschuldung *f*

overinsurance *n* INS Überversicherung *f*

overinsure *vt* INS überversichern

overinsured *adj* INS überversichert

overkill *n infrml* S&M *advertising* Overkill *m* (*infrml*)

overland: ~ **transport** *n* TRANSP Überlandtransport *m*

overlap 1. *n* COMP Überlappung *f*, GEN COMM, HRM *dates, holidays, responsibilities* Überschneidung *f*; **2.** *vi* COMP überlappen, GEN COMM, HRM *dates, holidays, responsibilities* sich überschneiden

overlapping: ~ **contract** *n* LAW übergreifender Vertrag *m*

overlay *n* COMP *guide* Überlagerung *f*

overlearning *n* WEL überflüssige Wiederholung einer Sequenz von Lernschritten

overload *vt* TRANSP überladen

overloading *n* TRANSP Überladen *nt*

overly: ~ **aged population** *n* ECON überalterte Gesellschaft *f*

overman *vt* HRM *department* überbesetzen

overmanned *adj* HRM überbesetzt

overmanning *n* HRM Überbesetzung *f*

overnight *adv* GEN COMM über Nacht; ~ **loan** *n* BANK, FIN Überlassung *f* von Tagesgeld, Tagesgeldausleihung *f*, Überbrückungskredit *m*; ~ **money** *n* BANK, FIN Tagesgeld *nt*; ~ **rate** *n* BANK, FIN Tagesgeldsatz *m*; ~ **travel** *n* LEIS Nachtreise *f*

overpaid *adj* HRM überbezahlt; ~ **entry certificate** *n* (*OEC*) IMP/EXP überzahlte Einfuhrbescheinigung *f*

overpay *vt* GEN COMM, HRM überbezahlen

overpayment *n* HRM Überbezahlung *f*

overplacing *n* BANK Überplazierung *f*

overprice *vt* S&M einen zu hohen Preis fordern für, den Preis zu hoch ansetzen für

overpriced *adj* S&M überteuert

overprint 1. *n* MEDIA Überdruck *m*; **2.** *vt* S&M überdrucken

overproduce *vi* IND zuviel produzieren

overproduction *n* ECON Überproduktion *f*

overprovision *n* ECON Überversorgung *f*

overrate *vt* ACC, ECON, FIN überbewerten, überschätzen

overrated *adj* ACC, ECON, FIN überbewertet, überschätzt

overrating *n* ACC, ECON, FIN Überbewertung *f*, Überschätzung *f*

overrepresent *vt* S&M *on the market* überrepräsentieren

overrepresentation *n* S&M *on the market* Überrepräsentation *f*

override *vt* GEN COMM, POL sich hinwegsetzen über [+acc], *decision* aufheben, LAW außer Kraft setzen

overriding *adj* GEN COMM *importance* überragend, *trend, factor, consideration* vorrangig, vordringlich, POL *importance* überragend; ~ **commission** *n* INS *underwriting* Abschlußprovision *f* des Generalvertreters, Superprovision *f*, LEIS *travel industry* übergeordnete Kommission *f*, STOCK Maklerprovision *f*

overrule *vt* GEN COMM, POL *decision* aufheben, *person* überstimmen

overrun 1. *n* ECON Überschreitung *f*, IND Überlauf *m*; **2.** *vt* ECON überschreiten, IND überlaufen

overseas *adj* GEN COMM ausländisch; ~ **agent** *n* GEN COMM Auslandsvertreter, in *m,f*; ~ **aid** *n* ECON Auslandshilfe *f*, Überseehilfe *f*; ~ **assets** *n pl* ECON Auslandsaktiva *pl*; ~ **body** *n* GEN COMM überseeische Einrichtung *f*; ~ **branch** *n* BANK, IMP/EXP *direct export trading* Auslandsniederlassung *f*, Überseefiliale *f*; ~ **company** *n* GEN COMM ausländisches Unternehmen *nt*, Auslandsunternehmen *nt*, überseeische Firma *f*; ~ **countries and territories** *n pl* (*OCTs*) POL *of European Union member states* überseeische Gebiete *nt pl*; ~ **customer** *n* S&M Überseekunde *m*

Overseas: ~ **Development Administration** *n BrE* (*ODA*) POL Behörde für Entwicklungshilfe; ~ **Development Institute** *n BrE* (*ODI*) ECON Institut für Entwicklungshilfe; ~ **Economic Cooperation Fund** *n* (*OECF*) ECON Fonds für wirtschaftliche Zusammenarbeit in Übersee

overseas: ~ **governments** *n pl* POL ausländische Regierungen *f pl*; ~ **investment cover** *n* INS Deckung *f* bei Auslandsinvestitionen; ~ **investor** *n* ECON ausländi-

scher Investor *m*; ~ **market** *n* ECON Überseemarkt *m*; ~ **portfolio diversification** *n* STOCK internationale Streuung *f* des Portefeuilles; ~ **postage** *n* COMMS Auslandsporto *nt*; ~ **project fund** *n* ECON *international trade* Fonds *m* für Überseeprojekte

Overseas: ~ **Service Aid Scheme** *n* (*OSAS*) ECON *international ODA* Entwicklungshilfeprojekt *nt*

overseas: ~ **status report** *n* IMP/EXP Auslandslagebericht *m*; ~ **sterling area** *n* (*OSA*) ECON überseeisches Sterlinggebiet *nt*; ~ **tariff regulation** *n* IMP/EXP Auslandstarifbestimmung *f*, Überseetarifbestimmung *f*; ~ **tariff and regulations** *n* (*OTAR*) IMP/EXP Auslandstarife *m pl* und -bestimmungen *f pl*, Überseetarife *m pl* und -bestimmungen *f pl*; ~ **tourism** *n* LEIS Auslandstourismus *m*; ~ **tourist** *n* LEIS Tourist, in *m,f* aus Übersee

Overseas: ~ **Trade Board** *n BrE* ECON Büro *nt* für Überseehandel; ~ **Trade Statistics** *n pl BrE* (*OTS*) ECON Außenhandelsstatistik *f*

overseas: ~ **visitor** *n* GEN COMM Besucher, in *m,f* aus Übersee

oversee *vt* GEN COMM, HRM, MGMNT beaufsichtigen

overseer *n* HRM, MGMNT Aufseher, in *m,f*, Vorarbeiter, in *m,f*

oversell *vi* S&M zu viel verkaufen

overselling *n* S&M übertriebene Verkaufspolitik *f*

overshoot *vt* GEN COMM hinausschießen über [+acc], übertreiben

overshooting: ~ **price** *n* ECON überschießender Preis *m*

overside: ~ **discharge** *n* TRANSP *shipping* Überbord-Entladung *f*; ~ **loading** *n* TRANSP *shipping* Überbord-Ladung *f*

overspend 1. *n* ACC, ECON, FIN Haushaltsüberschreitung *f*, Überschreitung *f* der Haushaltsansätze; **2.** *vt* ACC, ECON, FIN überschreiten; ♦ ~ **a target** FIN eine Ausgabengrenze überschreiten; **3.** *vi* ACC, ECON, FIN zuviel ausgeben

overspill: ~ **town** *n* ECON, PROP, WEL Satellitenstadt *f*, Trabantenstadt *f*

overstaff *vt* HRM überbesetzen

overstaffed *adj* HRM *department, firm* überbesetzt

overstaffing *n* HRM *of department, firm* Überbesetzung *f*

overstate *vt* ECON, FIN überbewerten

overstatement *n* ECON, FIN Überbewertung *f*

overstrain 1. *n* HRM Überlastung *f*; **2.** *vt* HRM überlasten

overstress *n* HRM Überlastung *f*

overstretch: ~ **oneself** *phr* FIN sich finanziell übernehmen

oversupply *n* ECON, GEN COMM Überangebot *nt*

over-the-counter *adj* (*OTC*) STOCK im Freiverkehr, nicht börsengehandelt, S&M offen, WEL *medication* nicht rezeptpflichtig, rezeptfrei, freiverkäuflich; ~ **derivative instrument** *n AmE* STOCK OTC-Derivat *nt*, derivatives OTC-Instrument *nt*, außerbörsliches sekundäres Handelspapier *nt*; ~ **market** *n AmE* (*OTCM*) ECON, STOCK dritter Markt *m*, OTC-Markt *m*, Freiverkehr *m*, Freiverkehrsbörse *f*; ~ **medicine** *n* WEL im freien Handel erhältliches Arzneimittel *nt pl*, freiverkäufliches Arzneimittel *nt*, nicht rezeptpflichtiges Arzneimittel *nt*; ~ **retailing** *n* S&M offenes Verkaufen *nt*; ~ **trading** *n* FIN Freiverkehrshandel *m*

overthrow 1. *n* POL *of government* Sturz *m*, Umsturz *m*; **2.** *vt* POL *government* stürzen, umstürzen

overtime n (*OT*) HRM *working hours* Überstunden f pl; **~ ban** n HRM Überstundenstopp m; **~ hours** n pl HRM *working hours* Überstunden f pl; **~ pay** n HRM Überstundenvergütung f; **~ premium** n HRM Überstundenzuschlag m

overtrade vi STOCK überspekulieren

overtrading n STOCK Überspekulation f, Spekulation f ohne Deckung

overurbanization n ECON Überurbanisierung f

overurbanize vt ECON überurbanisieren

overurbanized adj ECON überurbanisiert

overvaluation n ACC, ECON, FIN Überbewertung f, Überschätzung f

overvalue vt ACC, ECON, FIN überbewerten, überschätzen

overvalued adj ACC, ECON, FIN überbewertet, überschätzt; **~ currency** n ECON überbewertete Währung f

overview n GEN COMM Überblick m

overweight 1. adj TRANSP überladen; **2.** n TRANSP Übergewicht nt

overwork 1. n HRM Überarbeitung f; **2.** vt HRM überanstrengen; **3.** vi HRM sich überarbeiten

owe vt GEN COMM *under obligation* verdanken [+dat], *money* schulden, schuldig sein [+dat]

owing adj GEN COMM unbezahlt

own 1. adj GEN COMM eigen; **2.** vt GEN COMM besitzen

own: **~ account operator** n TRANSP Eigenbetreiber, in m,f; **~ account trading** n ECON Eigenhandel m; **~ brand** n S&M Eigenmarke f, Hausmarke f

owner n GEN COMM Besitzer, in m,f, Eigentümer, in m,f, *of enterprise* Inhaber, in m,f, PROP Bewohner, in m,f,

Eigentümer, in m,f, TRANSP *of ship* Eigner m; ♦ **at ~'s risk** INS auf Gefahr des Eigentümers

owner: **~ of a fractional share of property** n LAW Bruchteilseigentümer, in m,f; **~-manager** n MGMNT Eigentümer-Unternehmer m, Leiter, in m,f im eigenen Betrieb; **~-occupation** n PROP Eigennutzung f; **~-occupied apartment** n AmE (*cf owner-occupied flat BrE*) PROP selbstgenutzte Eigentumswohnung f; **~-occupied farmland** n PROP eigengenutzte landwirtschaftliche Fläche f; **~-occupied flat** n BrE (*cf owner-occupied apartment AmE*) PROP selbstgenutzte Eigentumswohnung f; **~-occupier** n PROP, TAX Eigenheimbesitzer, in m,f, Eigenheimbewohner m; **~-operator** n GEN COMM Eigenbetrieb m

owners': **~ and contractors' protective liability insurance** n AmE INS Bauherrenhaftpflichtversicherung f

ownership n GEN COMM Eigentum nt, Eigentumsrecht nt, Inhaberschaft f an Rechten, Besitz m; ♦ **under new ~** GEN COMM in neuer Eigentümerschaft, unter neuer Leitung

owners': **~, landlords' and tenants' liability policy** n INS, PROP Haus- und Grundbesitzerhaftpflichtpolice f

own: **~ funds** n pl FIN Eigenmittel nt pl; **~ label** n S&M eigene Marke f, Hausmarke f; **~ rate of interest** n ECON Eigenzinssatz m; **~-risk clause** n INS Selbstbehaltsklausel f; **~ shares** n pl BrE (*cf treasury stock AmE*) ACC, STOCK eigene Aktien f pl

oz abbr (*ounce*) GEN COMM Unze f

ozone n ENVIR, IND Ozon nt; **~ depletion** n ENVIR Ozonabbau m; **~ layer** n ENVIR Ozonschicht f

P

p *abbr* (*page*) COMP, GEN COMM S. (*Seite*)

p.a. *abbr* GEN COMM (*per annum*) p.a. (*per annum*), pro Jahr, INS (*particular average*) besondere Havarie *f*

PA *abbr* ADMIN (*personal assistant*) Chefsekretär, in *m,f*, Privatsekretär, in *m,f*, COMMS (*public address system*) Lautsprecheranlage *f*, HRM (*personal assistant*) Chefsekretär, in *m,f*, Privatsekretär, in *m,f* persönlicher Mitarbeiter *m*, persönliche Mitarbeiterin *f*, LAW (*power of attorney*) *administrative* Bevollmächtigung *f*, Vollmachtsurkunde *f*, Vollmacht *f*, schriftliche Vollmacht *f*, MGMNT (*personal assistant*) Chefsekretär, in *m,f*, persönlicher Mitarbeiter *m*, persönliche Mitarbeiterin *f*

Paasche: **~ index** *n* ECON *econometrics* Paasche-Index *m*

PABX *abbr BrE* (*private automatic branch exchange*) COMMS *telephone* Wahlnebenstellanlage *f*

pace *n* GEN COMM *of a trend* Tempo *nt*

pacesetter *n* GEN COMM *company* Schrittmacher *m*

Pacific: **~ Rim** *n* GEN COMM pazifische Randgebiete *nt pl*; **~ Stock Exchange** *n* STOCK Pazifische Börse

pacify *vt* GEN COMM, POL befrieden, beschwichtigen

pack 1. *n* COMMS, TRANSP Packung *f*; **2.** *vt* COMMS, COMP *data* packen, GEN COMM einpacken, verpacken, TRANSP packen

package *n* (*pkg., pkge*) COMMS Päckchen *nt*, Paket *nt*, Bündel *nt*, Packung *f*, COMP Kompaktbaugruppe *f*, FIN Paket *nt*, S&M *advertising, direct mail* Packstück *nt*, Bündel *nt*, TRANSP Päckchen *nt*, Paket *nt*, Packung *f*; **~ code** *n* S&M *market research* Verpackungscode *m*; **~ deal** *n* GEN COMM Gesamtvereinbarung, die mehrere Verhandlungspunkte regelt, HRM Verhandlungspaket *nt*, LAW Kopplungsgeschäft *nt*, LEIS Inklusivangebot *nt*, Pauschalangebot *nt*; **~ design** *n* S&M *market research* Verpackungsdesign *nt*

packaged: **~ goods** *n pl* S&M verpackte Ware *f*; **~ software** *n* COMP Programmpaket *nt*

package: **~ freight** *n AmE* TRANSP Stückgutfracht *f*; **~ holiday** *n* LEIS Pauschalurlaub *m*, Pauschalreise *f*; **~ mortgage** *n* FIN Hypothek, die sich auch auf Nebenleistungen erstreckt; **~ offer** *n* ECON Pauschalangebot *nt*; **~ pay** *n* ECON Lohn *m* mit Nebenleistungen; **~ store** *n AmE* (*cf off-licence BrE*) S&M Wein- und Spirituosengeschäft *nt*; **~ tour** *n* LEIS Pauschalreise *f*; **~ tour operator** *n BrE* LEIS Pauschalreiseunternehmen *nt*

packaging *n* IND Packmaterial *nt*, Verpackung *f*, TRANSP Emballagen *f pl*; **~ certificate** *n* TRANSP *containers* Verpackungszertifikat *nt*; **~ cost** *n* IND, S&M Verpackungskosten *pl*; **~ credit** *n* BANK Akkreditivbevorschussung *f*, Versandbereitstellungskredit *m*; **~ laws** *n pl* GEN COMM, LAW Verpackungsgesetze *nt pl*; **~ list** *n* IMP/EXP Packliste *f*, Versandliste *f*, TRANSP Packliste *f*; **~ material** *n* IND, S&M Verpackungsmaterial *nt*

packer *n* IND *machine* Packmaschine *f*, *person* Packer *m*, Verpacker *m*

packet *n* (*pkt.*) COMMS, TRANSP Päckchen *nt*, Paket *nt*

packing *n* GEN COMM Einpacken *nt*, Verpackung *f*; **~ credit** *n* BANK Versandbereitstellungskredit *m*; **~ density** *n* COMP *data* Zeichendichte *f*; **~ instruction** *n* IND, TRANSP Verpackungsanweisung *f*; **~ list** *n* IMP/EXP Packliste *f*, Versandliste *f*, TRANSP Packliste *f*

pack: **~ shot** *n* S&M *advertising* Endaufnahme *f*

Pac-Man: **~ defense** *n AmE* STOCK *corporate mergers and acquisitions* Verteidigung *f* gegen Übernahme

pact *n* GEN COMM *agreement* Pakt *m*, Vertrag *m*

pacta sunt servanda *phr* LAW *contracts* pacta sunt servanda, Verträge müssen eingehalten werden

pad *n* COMP, GEN COMM Block *m*, Notizblock *m*

padding *n* GEN COMM Füllmaterial *nt*

page 1. *n* (*p*) COMMS Blatt *nt*, COMP, GEN COMM Seite *f* (*S.*), MEDIA Blatt *nt*; **2.** *vt* COMMS *telecom* ausrufen

page: **~ break** *n* COMP Seitenumbruch *m*; **~ depth** *n* COMP Satzhöhe *f*; **~ length** *n* COMP Seitenlänge *f*; **~ number** *n* COMP Seitenzahl *f*; **~ proof** *n* MEDIA *print*, S&M Seitenabzug *m*; **~ rate** *n* S&M Anzeigenpreis *m* für eine Schwarzweißseite; **~ setting** *n* MEDIA *print* Setzen *nt* einer Seite; **~ traffic** *n* S&M *advertising* geschätzte Leserzahl *f* einer Publikation; **~-turner** *n* MEDIA *book* Schmöker *m* (*infrml*), spannendes Buch *nt*

paginate *vt* COMP, MEDIA *document, wordprocessing* paginieren, umbrechen

pagination *n* COMP, MEDIA Paginierung *f*

paging: **~ device** *n* COMP Seitenspeichergerät *nt*

PAI *abbr* (*performance appraisal interview*) HRM Leistungsbeurteilungsgespräch *nt*

paid *adj* BANK, FIN beglichen, GEN COMM beglichen, bezahlt; ◆ **~ in advance** GEN COMM im voraus bezahlt; **~ by agent** (*PBA*) TRANSP *shipping* vom Agenten bezahlt; **be ~ by the hour** HRM stundenweise bezahlt werden; **~ by the piece** HRM Bezahlung *f* pro Stück; **~ in cash** GEN COMM in bar bezahlt; **~ on delivery** (*POD*) TRANSP bezahlt bei Lieferung; **~ for** GEN COMM bezahlt; **~ piece rate** HRM nach Akkord bezahlt

paid: **~-in surplus** *n AmE* ACC *balance sheets* Agioerlös *m*, zusätzlich eingezahltes Kapital *nt*; **~ leave** *n BrE* (*cf paid vacation AmE*) HRM bezahlter Urlaub *m*; **~-up capital** *n* FIN eingezahltes Grundkapital *nt*, voll eingezahltes Kapital *nt*; **~-up member** *n BrE* HRM zahlendes Mitglied *nt*; **~ vacation** *n AmE* (*cf paid leave BrE*) HRM *bezahlter Urlaub m*

painstaking *adj* GEN COMM gewissenhaft

painstakingly *adv* GEN COMM gewissenhaft

paired: **~ comparison** *n pl* GEN COMM Paarvergleich *m*

PAL *abbr BrE* (*programme adjustment loan*) FIN Programmanpassungskredit *m*

pallet *n* IND, TRANSP Palette *f*; **~ fork** *n* IND, TRANSP *cargo handling* Palettengabel *f*

palletizable *adj* IND, TRANSP palletisierbar

palletization *n* IND, TRANSP Palletisieren *nt*, Pallettierung *f*

palletize *vt* IND, TRANSP auf Paletten packen, palletisieren, palletieren

palletized: **~ stowage** *n* IND, TRANSP palletiertes Verstauen *nt*

pallet: **~ net** *n* TRANSP Palettennetz *nt*; **~ track** *n* TRANSP Palettenspur *f*

palm off *vt infrml* GEN COMM andrehen; ♦ **palm sth off on sb** *infrml* GEN COMM jdm etw andrehen (*infrml*)

palm: ~ **oil** *n* IND Palmöl *nt*

pamphlet *n* GEN COMM, MEDIA Flugblatt *nt*, Prospekt *m*, S&M Prospekt *m*

P&I *abbr* (*protection and indemnity*) TRANSP P&I (*Reederhaftpflicht*); ~ **club** *n* TRANSP Reedervereinigung *f* für die Versicherung von Risiken

P&L *abbr* (*profit and loss*) ACC *annual accounts* Gewinn und Verlust *m* (*GuV*); ~ **account** *n* ACC GuV-Rechnung *f*

p&p *abbr* (*postage and packing*) COMMS Porto *nt* und Verpackung *f*

P&S *abbr* (*purchase and sale statement*) STOCK Schlußnote *f*, Schlußschein *m*

panel *n* GEN COMM, POL, S&M Panel *nt*; ~ **data** *n pl* S&M Paneldaten *pl*; ~ **envelope** *n* ADMIN Fensterbriefumschlag *m*; ~ **of experts** *n* MGMNT Expertengruppe *f*; ~ **testing** *n* S&M *market research* Panelerhebung *f*

pan-European *adj* POL paneuropäisch; ~ **company** *n* GEN COMM paneuropäisches Unternehmen *nt*

panic *n* FIN Börsenpanik *f*, Panik *f*, MEDIA Panik *f*, STOCK Börsenpanik *f*, Panik *f*; ~ **buying** *n* GEN COMM Angstkäufe *m pl*

paper *n* COMMS *newspaper* Blatt *nt*, FIN Wechsel *m*, Schuldtitel *m*, GEN COMM Ausarbeitung *f*, Papier *nt*, MEDIA Schrift *f*, *newspaper* Blatt *nt*

paperback *n* MEDIA Taschenbuch *nt*, Paperback *nt*, broschiertes Buch *nt*

paper: ~ **company** *n infrml* GEN COMM Scheinfirma *f*, Übungsfirma *f*; ~ **currency** *n* ECON Papierwährung *f*; ~ **eligible for discount** *n* BANK rediskont- und lombardfähiges Papier *nt*, bankfähiges Papier *nt*; ~ **feed** *n* COMP Papiereinzug *m*; ~ **gold** *n* BANK Papiergold *nt*; ~ **industry** *n* ENVIR Papierindustrie *f*

paperless: ~ **entry** *n* BANK beleglose Buchung *f*; ~ **trading** *n* COMP belegloser Handel *m*

paper: ~**-lined textile bag** *n* TRANSP Stoffsack *m* mit Papierfutter; ~ **loss** *n* STOCK nicht realisierter Kursverlust *m*; ~ **mill** *n* ENVIR Papierfabrik *f*; ~ **money** *n* BANK Banknoten *f pl*, FIN Banknoten *f pl*, Papiergeld *nt*; ~ **punch** *n* ADMIN Papierlocher *m*; ~ **qualifications** *n pl* WEL Befähigungsnachweis *m*; ~ **shredder** *n* ADMIN, COMP Reißwolf *m*; ~ **tape** *n* COMP, GEN COMM Lochstreifen *m*; ~ **throw** *n* COMP Papiervorschub *m*; ~ **track** *n* COMP Papierführung *f*

paperwork *n* ADMIN Schreibarbeit *f*

par *n* FIN, STOCK Parikurs *m*, Pariwert *m*; ♦ **at** ~ FIN, STOCK zu pari, zum Nennwert

paradox *n* GEN COMM Paradox *nt*; ~ **of thrift** *n* ECON Sparparadoxon *nt*, Paradox *nt* der Sparsamkeit; ~ **of value** *n* ECON Wertparadoxon *nt*; ~ **of voting** *n* ECON Wahlparadoxon *nt*

paragraph *n* ADMIN Absatz *m*, Abschnitt *m*, LAW *law* Paragraph *m*

paralegal *adj* LAW rechtskundig

parallel 1. *adj* FIN, GEN COMM, IND parallel; **2.** *n* GEN COMM Parallele *f*; ♦ **in** ~ GEN COMM parallel; **in** ~ **with** GEN COMM parallel zu

parallel: ~ **access** *n* COMP Parallelzugriff *m*; ~ **currency** *n* ECON Parallelwährung *f*; ~ **currency strategy** *n* ECON Parallelwährungsstrategie *f*; ~ **import** *n* IMP/EXP Parallelimport *m*; ~ **interface** *n* COMP Parallelschnittstelle *f*

parallelism *n* LAW *international private law* Parallelismus *m*

parallel: ~ **loan** *n* BANK, FIN Parallelanleihe *f*, Paralleldarlehen *nt*, Parallelkredit *m*; ~ **market economy** *n* ECON Schattenwirtschaft *f*; ~ **plants** *n* IND *production* parallele Produktionsstätten *f pl*; ~ **pricing** *n* ECON gleichgerichtete Preisgestaltung *f*; ~ **processing** *n* COMP *of tasks* Parallelverarbeitung *f*; ~ **standard** *n* GEN COMM Parallelwährung *f*; ~ **trading** *n* GEN COMM parallele Geschäfte *nt pl*

parameter *n* COMP, MATH *statistics* Parameter *m*; ~**-driven software** *n* COMP parametergesteuerte Software *f*

parametric: ~ **programming** *n* COMP parametrisches Programmieren *nt*, MATH parametrische Programmierung *f*; ~ **statistics** *n pl* MATH parametrische Statistik *f*

paramount *adj* GEN COMM, POL überragend, vorrangig

parasitic: ~ **city** *n* ECON parasitäre Stadt *f*

parcel *n* COMMS Bündel *nt*, *package sent through a common carrier* Päckchen *nt*, Paket *nt*, PROP *of land* Grundstück *nt*, Parzelle *f*, STOCK *of shares* Aktienpaket *nt*, TRANSP Päckchen *nt*; ~ **awaiting delivery** *n* GEN COMM zu lieferndes Paket *nt*; ~ **post** *n* COMMS Paketpost *f*, Paketsendung *f*; ~ **post insurance** *n* COMMS, INS *property* Paketpostversicherung *f*

parcels: ~ **market** *n* TRANSP Paketmarkt *m*; ~ **van** *n* TRANSP Paketwagen *m*

pare down *vt* GEN COMM beschneiden, kürzen

parent *n* COMP Ursprung *m*

parental: ~ **leave** *n* HRM Elternschaftsurlaub *m*

parent: ~ **company** *n* ACC, GEN COMM Dachgesellschaft *f*, Muttergesellschaft *f*, Stammhaus *nt*; ~ **company dividend** *n* ACC Dividende *f* einer Muttergesellschaft

parenthesis *n* COMP, MEDIA Klammer *f*, Parenthese *f*

parent: ~ **population** *n* POL Grundgesamtheit *f*; ~ **service** *n* TRANSP Grundservice *m*

Pareto: ~ **analysis** *n* ECON Pareto-Analyse *f*; ~ **efficiency** *n* ECON Pareto-Effizienz *f*; ~ **improvement** *n* ECON Pareto-Verbesserung *f*; ~**'s Law** *n* ECON *income distribution theory* Pareto-Gesetz *nt*, Gesetz *nt* von Pareto; ~ **optimality** *n* ECON Pareto-Optimalität *f*; ~ **optimum** *n* ECON Pareto-Optimum *nt*

paring: ~ **down** *n* GEN COMM Kürzung *f*, ECON Beschneidung *f*

pari passu *phr* GEN COMM gleichberechtigt, gleichrangig

Paris: ~ **Club** *n* ECON Pariser Club *m*; ~ **Financial Futures Exchange** *n* STOCK Pariser Finanzterminbörse *f*; ~ **Interbank Offered Rate** *n* (*PIBOR*) BANK Pariser Interbankenangebotssatz *m*; ~ **Stock Exchange** *n* STOCK Pariser Wertpapierbörse *f*; ~ **Trader Options Exchange** *n* STOCK Pariser Handelsoptionsbörse *f*

parity *n* COMP, ECON, INS, LAW Parität *f*; ~ **bit** *n* COMP Paritätsbit *nt*; ~ **check** *n* COMP Paritätskontrolle *f*; ~ **clause** *n* INS Paritätsklausel *f*; ~ **of exchange** *n* BANK Kursparität *f*, Wechselkursparität *f*; ~ **on rates** *n* TRANSP Gleichheit *f* bei den Raten; ~ **price** *n* ECON *for a commodity or service* Paritätskurs *m*; ~ **pricing** *n* ECON Paritätspreisbildung *f*; ~ **realignment** *n* ECON Realignment *nt*, Wechselkursanpassung *f*, Neufestsetzung *f* der Wechselkurse; ~ **money** *n* STOCK Gelder vorübergehend anlegen

parking: ~ **facilities** *n pl* TRANSP Parkmöglichkeit *f*; ~ **lot** *n AmE* (*cf car park BrE*) TRANSP Parkmöglichkeit *f*, Parkplatz *m*

Parkinson: ~'s **law** *n* HRM Parkinsonsches Gesetz *nt*

park: ~ **and ride** *n* TRANSP Park-und-Ride *nt* (*P&R*)

Parliament *n* POL Parlament *nt*

parliamentary *adj* POL parlamentarisch; ~ **appropriation** *n* ACC Mittelbewilligung *f* aus dem Nachtragshaushalt, FIN parlamentarische Haushaltsmittelbereitstellung *f*, POL Mittelbewilligung *f* aus dem Nachtragshaushalt; ~ **group** *n* POL Fraktion *f*; ~ **party** *n* POL Fraktion *f*; ~ **procedure** *n* POL parlamentarische Geschäftsordnung *f*; ~ **vote** *n* POL parlamentarische Stimme *f*

Parliament: ~ **of the Commonwealth** *n* POL Parlament *nt* des Commonwealth

part 1. *n* GEN COMM *portion, share* Teil *m*, IND *component, piece of equipment* Teil *nt*; **2.** *vi* ♦ ~ **with** LAW, PROP aufgeben

part: ~-**analysis training** *n* GEN COMM Teileanalyse-Ausbildung *f*; ~-**cancellation** *n* LAW, PATENTS *of a trade mark* Teillöschung *f*; ~ **exchange** *n* GEN COMM Kauf *m* unter Inzahlungnahme

partial *adj* GEN COMM teilweise; ~ **acceptance** *n* GEN COMM Teilakzept *nt*, teilweise Annahme *f*; ~ **basis** *n* FIN Teilbasis *f*; ~ **consideration** *n* ACC Teilentschädigung *f*; ~ **consignment** *n* GEN COMM Teillieferung *f*; ~ **delivery** *n* STOCK Teillieferung *f*; ~ **equilibrium** *n* ECON partielles Gleichgewicht *nt*; ~ **equilibrium analysis** *n* ECON *econometrics* partielle Gleichgewichtsanalyse *f*; ~ **eviction** *n* PROP Teilräumung *f*; ~ **invalidity** *n* LAW *trade contract* Teilunwirksamkeitsklausel *f*; ~ **loss** *n* (*PL*) INS Teilschaden *m*, Teilverlust *m*

partiality *n* GEN COMM Parteilichkeit *f*

partial: ~ **provision basis** *n* ACC *for calculating deferred taxation* Teilrückstellung *f*; ~ **regression** *n* ECON partielle Regression *f*; ~ **release** *n* LAW *property* Teilbelastung *f*, Teilfreigabe *f*, PROP Teilbelastung *f*; ~ **taking** *n* LAW *property* Teilfreistellung *f*; ~ **total loss** *n* (*PTL*) INS teilweiser Gesamtschaden *m*, teilweiser Totalschaden *m*, teilweiser Totalverlust *m*; ~ **unemployment** *n* HRM partielle Arbeitslosigkeit *f*; ~ **value** *n* ACC Teilwert *m*; ~ **withdrawal** *n* ECON *of investments* Teilliquidation *f*; ~ **write-off** *n* ACC Teilausbuchung *f*

participant *n* GEN COMM Teilnehmer, in *m,f*

participate *vi* GEN COMM teilnehmen

participating *adj* GEN COMM teilnehmend; ~ **carrier** *n* TRANSP teilnehmender Spediteur *m*, teilnehmendes Beförderungsunternehmen *m*; ~ **insurance** *n* INS *personal* Versicherung *f* mit Überschußbeteiligung; ~ **preference share** *n BrE* (*cf participating preferred stock AmE*) FIN, STOCK Vorzugsaktie *f* mit Gewinnbeteiligung; ~ **preferred stock** *n AmE* (*cf participating preference share BrE*) FIN, STOCK Vorzugsaktie *f* mit Gewinnbeteiligung; ~ **profit policy** *n* INS Police *f* mit Gewinnbeteiligung, Versicherungspolice *f* mit Gewinnbeteiligung

participation *n* ACC Beteiligung *f*; ~ **agreement** *n* LAW Beteiligungsvertrag *m*; ~ **loan** *n* BANK Konsortialkredit *m*, FIN Gemeinschaftsdarlehen *nt*; ~ **rate** *n* HRM Erwerbsquote *f*

participative: ~ **budgeting** *n* FIN, MGMNT partizipative Finanzplanung *f*; ~-**democratic** *adj* MGMNT *one of Likert's four leadership styles* partizipativ-demokra-

tisch; ~ **leadership** *n* MGMNT partizipativer Führungsstil *m*; ~ **management** *n* MGMNT partizipatives Management *nt*

particular 1. *adj* GEN COMM bestimmt; ♦ **with** ~ **average** (*WPA*) INS einschließlich besonderer Havarieschäden; **2.** *n* GEN COMM Einzelheit *f*

particular: ~ **average** *n* (*p.a.*) INS besondere Havarie *f*; ~ **charge** *n* INS Sonderzuschlag *m*

particulars *n pl* GEN COMM Angaben *f pl*, Einzelheiten *f pl*; ~ **of sale** *n pl* PROP Einzelheiten *f pl* zum Verkauf

parties: ~ **to a collective agreement** *n pl* HRM Tarifpartner *m pl*

partition 1. *n* ADMIN *in office* Aufteilung *f*, COMP Partition *f*, LAW *property* Grundstücksteilung *f*, S&M Aufteilung *f*; **2.** *vt* S&M aufteilen

part: ~-**load** *n* TRANSP Teilladung *f*, *Bahn* Stückgut *nt*

partly: ~ **finished goods** *n pl* ACC, ECON, GEN COMM Halbfabrikate *nt pl*, unfertige Erzeugnisse *nt pl*; ~ **responsible** *adj* LAW mitschuldig

part: ~ **method** *n* WEL Lernen *nt* in kleinen Einheiten

partner *n* GEN COMM, HRM Gesellschafter, in *m,f*, Partner, in *m,f*, Teilhaber, in *m,f*, *in a business* Beteiligte(r) *mf* [decl. as adj]

partnership *n* ECON Gesellschaftsvertrag *m*, GEN COMM Gesellschaft *f* bürgerlichen Rechts, offene Handelsgesellschaft *f*, Personengesellschaft *f*, Partnerschaft *f*, Teilhaberschaft *f*, POL Partnerschaft *f*; ~ **agreement** *n* ECON Gesellschaftsvertrag *m*; ~ **life and health insurance** *n* INS *company* Partnerlebens- und Unfallversicherung *f*; ~ **liquidation contract** *n* LAW Liquidationsvertrag *m*

part: ~ **owner** *n* BANK, LAW, PROP Miteigentümer, in *m,f*; ~ **ownership** *n* BANK, LAW, PROP Miteigentum *nt*; ~ **payment** *n* FIN Abschlagszahlung *f*, Ratenzahlung *f*, Teilzahlung *f*; ♦ **in** ~ **payment** HRM auf Abschlag

part: ~-**shipment** *n* GEN COMM Teillieferung *f*

parts: ~ **per million** *n pl* (*ppm*) GEN COMM partes per millionem (*ppm*)

part: ~-**time** *adj* HRM Teilzeit-; ~-**time employee** *n* HRM Teilzeitarbeiter, in *m,f*, Teilzeitarbeitskraft *f*, Teilzeitkraft *f*; ~-**time employment** *n* HRM Teilzeitbeschäftigung *f*; ~-**time job** *n* HRM Teilzeitarbeit *f*; ~-**timer** *n* HRM Teilzeitarbeiter, in *m,f*, Teilzeitarbeitskraft *f*, Teilzeitkraft *f*; ~-**time work** *n* HRM Teilzeitarbeit *f*; ~-**time worker** *n pl* HRM Teilzeitarbeiter, in *m,f*, Teilzeitarbeitskraft *f*, Teilzeitkraft *f*

party *n* LAW *in a contract* Partei *f*, Teil *m*, POL Partei *f*; ~ **autonomy** *n* LAW *contracts* Parteiautonomie *f*; ~ **in default** *n* LAW *contract law* in Verzug befindliche Partei *f*, säumige Partei *f*; ~ **liable under contract** *n* LAW vertraglich verpflichtete Partei *f*; ~ **line** *n* COMMS *telephone service* Gemeinschaftsanschluß *m*, POL *on policy* Parteilinie *f*; ~-**political** *adj* POL parteipolitisch; ~-**political scene** *n* POL Parteienlandschaft *f*; ~ **selling** *n* S&M Partyverkauf *m*; ~'s **intention** *n* LAW *contracts* Parteiwille *m*; ~ **ticket** *n* LEIS *for group* Gruppenreiseticket *nt*; ~ **to an agreement** *n* HRM Vertragspartei *f*; ~ **to a contract** *n* LAW Vertragspartei *f*; ~ **to an estate** *n* LAW am Grundstück Berechtigte(r) *mf* [decl. as adj]; ~ **to a negotiation** *n* GEN COMM Verhandlungspartner, in *m,f*; ~ **wall** *n* INS Brandmauer *f*, PROP Trennmauer *f*

par: ~ **value** *n* ACC Nennwert *m*, Wert *m* al pari; ~ **value**

of currency *n* STOCK Währungsparität *f*; ~ **value share** *n* STOCK Nennwertaktie *f*; **no ~ value share** *n* STOCK Quotenaktie *f*; ~ **value system** *n* ECON Paritätssystem *nt*

pass 1. *n* ADMIN *permit* Passierschein *m*; **2.** *vt* ECON *budget* beschließen, verabschieden, LAW *act* verabschieden, *a bill* annehmen, beschließen; ♦ ~ **a dividend** FIN eine Dividende ausfallen lassen; ~ **a resolution** LAW eine Resolution verabschieden; ~ **for press** MEDIA *print* das Imprimatur geben, für pressetauglich erklären; ~ **judgment** LAW Urteil erlassen; ~ **sentence on sb** LAW Strafe über jdn verhängen, Passierschein *m*; **3.** *vi* ♦ ~ **into the ownership of** LAW übergehen auf [+acc]

pass along *vt* ECON, FIN *costs* abwälzen, überwälzen

pass on *vt* ECON, FIN *costs* abwälzen, überwälzen, GEN COMM *information* weitergeben, weiterleiten; ♦ ~ **to** ECON, FIN *costs* abwälzen auf [+acc]

pass to *vi* LAW übergehen auf [+acc]

passage *n* LAW *enactment of bill into law* Annahme *f*, MEDIA Passage *f*, TRANSP Durchfahrt *f*, Durchreise *f*, *by sea* Überfahrt *f*, Schiffsreise *f*

pass: **~-along** *n* ECON Abwälzung *f*, Überwälzung *f*; **~-along readership** *n* S&M *advertising* Sekundärleserschaft *f*

passbook *n* BANK Sparbuch *nt*

passed *adj* GEN COMM mit Erfolg geprüft, LAW verabschiedet; ~ **dividend** *n* FIN nichtausgeschüttete Dividende *f*, rückständige Dividende *f*

passenger *n* LEIS, TRANSP Insasse *m*, Insassin *f*, Passagier *m*; ~ **aircraft** *n* TRANSP Passagierflugzeug *nt*; ~ **analysis** *n* LEIS Passagieranalyse *f*; ~ **car** *n* TRANSP Personenkraftwagen *m* (*PKW*); ~ **care** *n* LEIS Passagierbetreuung *f*; ~ **certificate** *n* BrE (*PC*) TRANSP Zulassung *f* für Personenbeförderung, Zulassungsschein *m* für Personenbeförderung; ~ **control** *n* LEIS Passagierkontrolle *f*; ~ **coupon** *n* LEIS Passagierkupon *m*; ~ **dues** *n* LEIS, TRANSP Passagiergebühren *f pl*; ~ **fare** *n* TRANSP Fahrpreis *m*, Personentarif *m*; ~ **ferry** *n* TRANSP Personenfähre *f*; ~ **lift** *n* TRANSP Passagierlift *m*; ~ **liner** *n* TRANSP Passagierlinienschiff *nt*, Passagierdampfer *m* (*obs*); ~ **list** *n* TRANSP Passagierliste *f*; ~ **lounge** *n* TRANSP Passagier-Lounge *f*; ~ **market** *n* TRANSP Passagiermarkt *m*; ~ **miles per vehicle hour** *phr* TRANSP Passagiermeilen pro Fahrzeugstunde; ~ **number certificate** *n* TRANSP Zertifikat *nt* bezüglich der Passagierzahl; **~-rated traffic** *n* TRANSP passagierklassifizierter Verkehr *m*; ~ **return** *n* TRANSP Passagierbericht *m*; ~ **safety certificate** *n* TRANSP Passagiersicherheitszertifikat *nt*; ~ **service** *n* TRANSP Personenverkehr *m*; ~ **ship** *n* TRANSP Fahrgastschiff *nt*, Passagierschiff *nt*; ~ **strategy** *n* TRANSP Passagierstrategie *f*; ~ **tariff** *n* TRANSP Personentarif *m*; ~ **terminal** *n* TRANSP Passagierterminal *m*; ~ **throughput**, ~ **thruput** *AmE* *n* TRANSP Passagierdurchsatz *m*; ~ **toll** *n* LEIS, TRANSP Passagiergebühr *f*; ~ **tonnage** *n* TRANSP Passagiertonnage *f*; ~ **train** *n* TRANSP Personenzug *m*; ~ **transport** *n* TRANSP Personenbeförderung *f*; ~ **vehicle** *n* TRANSP Personenkraftwagen *m* (*PKW*); ~ **vehicle ferry** *n* TRANSP Fähre *f* für Personenwagen, PKW-Fähre *f*

passer: **~-by** *n* GEN COMM, S&M *audience of poster advertising* Passant, in *m,f*

passing *n* GEN COMM Übergang *m*, LAW *of law* Verab-

schiedung *f*; **~-on** *n* ECON Überwälzung *f*, Weiterwälzung *f*, Weitergabe *f*; ~ **of risk** *n* INS Gefahrübergang *m*, Risikoabwälzung *f*

passionate *adj* GEN COMM *debate* leidenschaftlich

passive *adj* GEN COMM *advertising* passiv; ~ **activity** *n* TAX passive Tätigkeit *f*; ~ **income** *n* TAX Einkünfte *pl* aus Kapitalvermögen; ~ **investor** *n* FIN passiver Anleger *m*, passiver Investor *m*; ~ **loss** *n* TAX Verlust *m* aus Kapitalvermögen; ~ **trade** *n* ECON Einfuhrhandel *m*; ~ **transit trade** *n* ECON passiver Transithandel *m*

passport *n* ADMIN, LEIS, TRANSP Paß *m*, Reisepaß *m*; ~ **check** *n* ADMIN, LEIS, TRANSP Paßkontrolle *f*; **~-holder** *n* ADMIN, LEIS, TRANSP Paßinhaber, in *m,f*

pass: **~-through loan** *n* FIN Durchlaufdarlehen *nt*; **~-through security** *n* FIN Wertpapier *nt* mit laufender Zinszahlung

password *n* COMP Paßwort *nt*

paste *vt* COMP *word processed document* einkleben

pasteboard *n* IND *sheet lined board* kaschierte Pappe *f*, Klebekarton *m*, *type of fibreboard* zusammengeklebte Pappe *f*, geklebter Karton *m*, Schichtenpappe *f*

paste: **~-up** *n* MEDIA Bildmontage *f*, Schriftmontage *f*

past: ~ **service benefit** *n* AmE FIN *private pension plan* in der Vergangenheit liegender Leistungsanspruch *m*, Anwartschaft *f*; ~ **year** *n* GEN COMM vergangenes Jahr *nt*

pasting *n* COMP *word processed document* Einklebung *f*

pat. *abbr* (*patent*) PATENTS Pat. (*Patent*)

patent 1. *n* (*pat.*) LAW Patent *nt* (*Pat.*), PATENTS Freibrief *m*, Konzession *f*, Patent *nt* (*Pat.*); ♦ ~ **pending** (*pat. pend.*) PATENTS Patent angemeldet, Patentanmeldung läuft; **2.** *vt* PATENTS patentieren

patentability *n* LAW, PATENTS Patentfähigkeit *f*, Patentierbarkeit *f*

patentable *adj* LAW *intellectual property*, PATENTS patentfähig, patentierbar; ~ **invention** *n* PATENTS patentfähige Erfindung *f*

patent: ~ **agent** *n* PATENTS technische Patentanwältin *f*, technischer Patentanwalt *m*; ~ **application** *n* PATENTS Patentanmeldung *f*; ~ **application proceedings** *n pl* PATENTS Anmeldeverfahren *nt*; ~ **certificate** *n* PATENTS Patenturkunde *f*

Patent: ~ **Cooperation Treaty** *n* (*PCT*) LAW, PATENTS Patentkooperationsvertrag *m*, Vertrag *m* über die Zusammenarbeit im Patentwesen

patented *adj* PATENTS patentiert

patentee *n* PATENTS Patentinhaber, in *m,f*

Patent: ~ **Information Network** *n* BrE LAW, PATENTS *intellectual property* Patentinformationsnetz *nt*

patent: ~ **infringement** *n* LAW, PATENTS Patentverletzung *f*; ~ **of invention** *n* LAW Erfindungspatent *nt*; ~ **law** *n* LAW, PATENTS Patentrecht *nt*; ~ **life** *n* LAW Dauer *f* des Patentschutzes, Patentdauer *f*; ~ **proprietor** *n* PATENTS Patentinhaber, in *m,f*; ~ **protection** *n* LAW, PATENTS Patentschutz *m*; ~ **renewal fee** *n* LAW, PATENTS Patenterneuerungsgebühr *f*; ~ **right** *n* LAW, PATENTS Patentrecht *nt*; ~ **rights** *n pl* LAW, PATENTS Patentrechte *nt pl*; ~ **royalty** *n* FIN Patentgebühr *f*; ~ **specification** *n* LAW Patentschrift *f*, PATENTS *printed* Beschreibung *f*, Patentbeschreibung *f*, Patentschrift *f*; ~ **trading** *n* PATENTS Patenthandel *m*

paternalism *n* MGMNT Paternalismus *m*

paternity: ~ **leave** *n* HRM Vaterschaftsurlaub *m*, Karenzurlaub *m*

path *n* COMP Pfad *m*; ~**-goal theory** *n* MGMNT Weg-Ziel-Theorie *f*; ~ **of least resistance** *n* GEN COMM Weg *m* des geringsten Widerstands

pat.: ~ **pend.** *abbr* (*patent pending*) PATENTS Patent angemeldet, Patentanmeldung läuft

patrimonial: ~ **industry** *n* IND Patrimonialindustrie *f*

pattern *n* COMP Muster *nt*, GEN COMM Probe *f*, *of consumption* Muster *nt*, Musterkarte *f*, Modell *nt*, S&M Muster *nt*; ~ **bargaining** *n* HRM Branchentarifverhandlungen *f pl*; ~ **of economic activity** *n* ECON Muster *nt* der Wirtschaftsaktivität; ~ **settlement** *n* ECON Musterabschluß *m*

paucity: ~ **of information** *n* GEN COMM Informationsdefizit *nt*

pauper *n* GEN COMM Unterstützungsempfänger,in *m,f*, Bedürftige(r) *mf* [decl. as adj]

pause *n* GEN COMM Pause *f*

pave: ~ **the way for** *phr* GEN COMM den Weg bahnen für

pawn 1. *n* FIN Pfand *nt*, Pfandsache *f*; ♦ **in** ~ FIN verpfändet; **2.** *vt* LAW verpfänden

pawnage *n* FIN Pfändung *f*

pawnbroker *n* FIN Pfandleiher *m*

pawnbroking *n* FIN Pfandleihgeschäft *nt*

pawned *adj* FIN verpfändet

pawner *n* FIN Verpfänder, in *m,f*

pawning *n* FIN Verpfändung *f*

pawnshop *n* FIN Leihhaus *nt*, Pfandhaus *nt*, Pfandleihanstalt *f*

pawn: ~ **ticket** *n* FIN Pfandschein *m*

pay 1. *n* HRM Lohn *m*; ♦ ~ **as paid** GEN COMM Zug-um-Zug-Zahlung *f*; **2.** *vt* GEN COMM *invoice, debt* begleichen, bezahlen, *sum* zahlen, PATENTS *fee* begleichen, zahlen; ♦ ~ **the bill** GEN COMM die Rechnung zahlen; ~ **cash** GEN COMM bar zahlen; ~ **a dividend** FIN eine Dividende ausschütten; ~ **an installment** *AmE*, ~ **an instalment** *BrE* FIN eine Rate zahlen; ~ **interest on** BANK verzinsen; ~ **lip service to sth** GEN COMM für etw ein Lippenbekenntnis ablegen; ~ **tax** ACC, ECON, FIN, GEN COMM, TAX Steuern abführen, versteuern; **3.** *vi* GEN COMM *make financial settlement* zahlen; ♦ **it does not** ~ GEN COMM das rechnet sich nicht; ~ **as cargo** IMP/EXP, INS, TRANSP als Fracht zahlen, als Frachtgut zahlen; ~ **by giro** BANK per Überweisung zahlen; ~ **by the quarter** GEN COMM vierteljährlich entlohnen, vierteljährlich zahlen; ~ **by the year** GEN COMM jährlich entlohnen, jährlich zahlen; ~ **for** GEN COMM bezahlen; ~ **for cargo by measurement** TRANSP Fracht nach Abmessung bezahlen; ~ **for the expenses** GEN COMM die Kosten übernehmen; ~ **in cash** GEN COMM bar zahlen; ~ **in full** FIN restlos bezahlen; ~ **in kind** FIN in Sachwerten bezahlen; ~ **in settlement** GEN COMM abgelten; ~ **in specie** GEN COMM in barer Münze zahlen, in klingender Münze zahlen

pay back *vt* ACC *debt, mortgage* abtragen, zurückzahlen, BANK *debt, mortgage* tilgen, zurückzahlen, abtragen, FIN zurückzahlen

pay in 1. *vt* BANK einzahlen, **2.** *vi* BANK einzahlen

pay off *vt* ACC *debt, mortgage* abtragen, zurückzahlen, BANK *debt, mortgage* abtragen, tilgen, zurückzahlen, FIN abfinden, auszahlen, GEN COMM amortisieren, HRM auszahlen, LAW befriedigen; ♦ ~ **in installments** *AmE*,

~ **in instalments** *BrE* FIN abzahlen; ~ **one's debts** FIN Schulden zurückzahlen

pay out 1. *vt* GEN COMM *spend* ausgeben, *count out* auszahlen; **2.** *vi* GEN COMM bezahlen

payable *adj* BANK einlösbar, ECON, GEN COMM *due* fällig, zahlbar; ♦ **make** ~ **to** BANK ausstellen auf [+acc]; ~ **at sight** FIN, GEN COMM zahlbar bei Sicht; ~ **in advance** GEN COMM im voraus zahlbar; ~ **on** FIN *date* zahlbar am; ~ **on demand** GEN COMM zahlbar bei Sicht; ~ **three months after date** GEN COMM zahlbar drei Monate ab dato

payables *n pl AmE* (*cf creditors BrE*) ACC unbezahlte Verbindlichkeit *f*, Verbindlichkeiten *f pl*; ~ **at year-end** *n pl AmE* ACC Verbindlichkeiten *f pl* beim Jahresabschluß

pay: ~**-as-you-earn** *n* (*PAYE*) ACC *deductions at source*, HRM Quellenabzugsverfahren *nt*, TAX Abzüge *m pl* von Lohn oder Gehalt, Quellenabzugsverfahren *nt*; ~**-as-you-go** *n AmE* HRM Quellenbesteuerung *f*

payback *n* FIN Amortisation *f*, Auszahlung *f*, S&M *marketing* Amortisation *f*; ~ **method** *n* FIN Amortisationsrechnung *f*, Kapitalrückflußrechnung *f*; ~ **period** *n* HRM Amortisationszeit *f*; ~ **provision** *n* FIN Rückzahlungsmaßnahme *f*

pay: ~ **bill** *n AmE* (*cf payroll BrE*) ACC, HRM Gehaltsliste *f*, Lohnliste *f*; ~ **board** *n* HRM Lohnausschuß *m* (*obs*); ~ **check** *AmE*, ~ **cheque** *BrE n* BANK Gehaltsscheck *m*, Lohnscheck *m*, HRM Gehaltsscheck *m*; ~ **comparability** *n* HRM Vergleichbarkeit *f* der Bezahlung; ~ **and conditions** *n pl* HRM Arbeits- und Gehaltsbedingungen *f pl*

payday *n* HRM Zahltag *m*

pay: ~ **differentials** *n pl BrE* HRM Lohngefälle *nt*

PAYE *abbr* (*pay-as-you-earn*) ACC, HRM *deductions at source* Quellenabzugsverfahren *m*, TAX Abzüge *m pl* von Lohn oder Gehalt, Quellenabzugsverfahren *nt*; ~ **audit** *n BrE* TAX *specialist section of the Inland Revenue* Prüfung *f* des Quellenabzugs

payee *n* ACC Zahlungsempfänger, in *m,f*

PAYE: ~ **remittances** *n pl BrE* TAX Überweisungen *f pl* der einbehaltenen Beträge

pay: ~ **freeze** *n* ECON, HRM Lohnpause *f*, Lohnstopp *m*, Lohnstillstand *m*, Lohn- und Gehaltsstopp *m*, POL Lohnstopp *m*

paying: ~ **agent** *n* FIN Einlösungsstelle *f*, TAX Zahlstelle *f*; ~ **bank** *n* BANK beauftragte Bank *f*, einlösende Bank *f*, Zahlstellenbank *f*, auszahlende Bank *f*; ~ **guest** *n* (*PG*) LEIS Feriengast *m*, Pensionär, in *m,f*, Pensionsgast *m*, zahlender Gast *m*; ~**-in book** *n* BANK Einzahlungsbuch *nt*, Einzahlungsheft *nt*; ~**-in form** *n BrE* (*cf pay-in slip AmE*) BANK Einzahlungsbeleg *m*, Einzahlungsschein *m*

pay: ~**-in slip** *n AmE* (*cf paying-in form BrE*) BANK Einzahlungsbeleg *m*, Einzahlungsschein *m*; ~ **in lieu of notice** *n* HRM Zahlung *f* anstelle einer Kündigungsfrist

Paymaster: ~ **General** *n* (*PMG*) HRM Beamter an der Spitze einer Abteilung des Schatzamtes

payment *n* (*PYT*) FIN Abgeltung *f*, Entrichtung *f*, GEN COMM Auszahlung *f*, Bezahlung *f*, Entlohnung *f*, Zahlung *f*; ♦ ~ **in full on allotment** FIN vollständig zahlbar bei Zuteilung

payment: ~ **of annuity** *n* TAX Rentenzahlung *f*; ~ **before due date** *n* GEN COMM vorzeitige Zahlung *f*; ~ **bond** *n* LAW Zahlungsgarantie *f*; ~ **by installment** *AmE*, ~ **by instalment** *BrE n* ACC Zahlung *f* in Raten; ~ **by results**

n (*PBR*) HRM Leistungslohn *m*; ~ **by standing order** *n* BANK Abbuchung *f*; ~ **card** *n* BANK Zahlkarte *f*; ~ **clause** *n* LAW Zahlungsklausel *f*; ~ **of debts** *n* ECON, FIN, LAW Tilgung *f* von Verbindlichkeiten; ~ **due** *n* FIN fällige Zahlung *f*; ~ **guarantee** *n* ACC Zahlungsgarantie *f*; ~ **guaranty** *n* LAW Zahlungsgarantie *f*; ~ **in arrears** *n pl* ACC rückständige Zahlung *f*, Zahlungsrückstände *m pl*; ~ **in advance** *n* ACC Vorauszahlung *f*; ~ **in kind** *n* ECON Sachleistung *f*, GEN COMM Entlohnung *f* in Sachwerten, Naturalleistung *f*, Sachbezug *m*, Sachentlohnung *f*, Sachleistung *f*, HRM Deputat *nt*, Sachbezug *m*, INS Sachleistung *f*; ~-**in-kind bond** *n* (*PIK bond*) FIN Sachleistungsobligation *f*; ~ **of interest** *n* BANK Verzinsung *f*; ~ **method** *n* S&M Zahlungsmethode *f*; ~ **on account** *n* BANK Abschlagszahlung *f*, Akontozahlung *f*, Anzahlung *f*, Teilzahlung *f*; ~ **on behalf of others** *n* ACC Zahlung *f* im Namen Dritter; ~ **order** *n* (*p.o.*) ACC, BANK, FIN Zahlungsauftrag *m*; ~ **risk** *n* ECON Ausfallrisiko *nt*

payments *n pl* GEN COMM *cash or in kind* Zahlungen *f pl*

payment: ~ **system** *n* ECON Zahlungsverkehrssystem *nt*, Zahlungssystem *nt*; ~ **of tax** *n* ACC, ECON, GEN COMM, TAX Steuerzahlung *f*, Versteuerung *f*; ~ **transactions** *n* FIN Zahlungsverkehr *m*; ~ **transfer** *n* BANK Überweisung *f*, Umbuchung *f*; ~ **type** *n* S&M Zahlungsmethode *f*; ~ **under protest** *n* LAW Zahlung unter Protest *f*

payoff *n* ECON *payment* Auszahlung *f*, GEN COMM *bribe* Bestechung *f*, Bestechungsgeld *nt*, Schmiergeld *nt* (*infrml*), HRM Auszahlung *f*, Abfindung *f*

payola *n* AmE *infrml* S&M *advertising* Bestechungsgelder *nt pl*

payout *n* FIN, S&M *marketing* Amortisation *f*; ~ **rate** *n* FIN *dividend* Ausschüttungssatz *m*; ~ **ratio** *n* FIN Ausschüttungskennzahl *f*, Ausschüttungsquote *f*, S&M *marketing* Amortisationsverhältnis *nt*

pay: ~ **packet** *n* BrE HRM Lohntüte *f*; ~ **pause** *n* ECON, HRM Lohn- und Gehaltsstopp *m*, Lohnpause *f*, Lohnstillstand *m*, Lohnstopp *m*, POL Lohnstopp *m*; ~ **phone** *n* BrE (*cf pay station AmE*) COMMS Münztelefon *nt*; ~ **policy** *n* HRM Lohn- und Gehaltspolitik *f*; ~ **review** *n* HRM Lohn- und Gehaltsrevision *f*

payroll *n* BrE (*cf pay bill AmE*) ACC, HRM Lohnliste *f*, Gehaltsliste *f*; ♦ **off the ~** HRM arbeitslos; **on the ~** HRM zur Belegschaft gehörend, auf der Lohn- oder Gehaltsliste stehend

payroll: ~ **costs** *n pl* HRM Personalkosten *pl*; ~ **deduction** *n* HRM *from gross earnings* Gehaltsabzug *m pl*; ~ **deductions** *n pl* ACC Gehaltsabzüge *m pl*; ~ **deduction scheme** *n* TAX *for payments to charities* Abzüge *m pl* von Lohn oder Gehalt; ~ **tax** *n* TAX Sozialversicherungssteuer *f*

pay: ~ **round** *n* HRM Lohnrunde *f*, Tarifrunde *f*; ~ **sheet** *n* HRM Gehälterliste *f*; ~ **slip** *n* HRM Lohnstreifen *m*; ~ **station** *n* AmE (*cf pay phone BrE*) COMMS Münztelefon *nt*; ~ **talks** *n pl* HRM, MGMNT Lohnverhandlungen *f pl*; ~-**TV** *n* MEDIA Abonnentenfernsehen *nt*, Pay-TV *nt*; ~ **for work at time rates** *n* HRM Zeitlohn *m*, Arbeitsentgelt *nt* zum Zeitlohnsatz

PBA *abbr* (*paid by agent*) TRANSP *shipping* vom Agenten bezahlt

PBDS *abbr* BrE (*Publishers and Booksellers Delivery Service*) MEDIA Lieferservice der Verleger und Buchhändler

PBR *abbr* (*payment by results*) HRM Leistungslohn *m*

PBS *abbr* AmE (*Public Broadcasting Services*) MEDIA öffentliche Rundfunk- und Fernsehanstalten *f pl*

PBX *abbr* (*private branch exchange*) COMMS private Vermittlungsanlage *f*

pc *abbr* (*per cent*) GEN COMM p.c. (*percentum, Prozent, prozentig, prozentual*), v.H. (*vom Hundert*)

pc. *abbr* GEN COMM (*piece*) St. (*Stück*), FIN (*price current*) Preisbericht *m*, Preisliste *f*, Preisverzeichnis *nt*

PC *abbr* COMP (*personal computer*) PC (*Personalcomputer*), TRANSP (*passenger certificate BrE*) Zulassung *f* für Personenbeförderung, Zulassungsschein *m* für Personenbeförderung

P/C *abbr* FIN (*price current*) Preisbericht *m*, Preisliste *f*, Preisverzeichnis *nt*, GEN COMM (*per cent*) p.c. (*percentum, Prozent, prozentig, prozentual*), v.H. (*vom Hundert*)

PC: ~-**based** *adj* COMP *software, hardware, service* computergestützt, computerunterstützt, PC-unterstützt, PC-gestützt, rechnergestützt, rechnerunterstützt

PCC *abbr* ECON (*price consumption curve*) Preiskonsumkurve *f*

PC: ~-**compatibility** *n* COMP PC-Kompatibilität *f*

pcs *abbr* (*pieces*) GEN COMM St. (*Stück*)

PCT *abbr* (*Patent Cooperation Treaty*) LAW, PATENTS Patentkooperationsvertrag *m* Vertrag *m* über die Zusammenarbeit im Patentwesen

PD *abbr* COMMS (*postdated*) nachdatiert, GEN COMM vordatiert, IMP/EXP, TRANSP (*port dues*) Hafengebühren *f pl*

PDI *abbr* ECON (*personal disposable income*) persönliches verfügbares Einkommen *nt* nach Steuern, persönliches Nettoeinkommen *nt*, verfügbares Einkommen *nt*, TRANSP (*predelivery inspection*) Inspektion *f* vor Lieferung

PDM *abbr* (*physical distribution management*) MGMNT Vertriebsleitung *f*, TRANSP Management *nt* der physischen Verteilung, Verteilungsmanagement *nt* durch den Handel

p.e. *abbr* (*probable error*) MATH *statistics* wahrscheinliche Abweichung *f*, wahrscheinlicher Fehler *m*

peace: ~ **dividend** *n* POL Friedensdividende *f*

peaceful: ~ **picketing** *n* HRM *industrial action*, POL nicht aggressiv durchgeführtes Streikpostenstehen *nt*

peak 1. *n* ECON Höchststand *m*, Spitze *f*; **2.** *vi* ECON einen Höchststand erreichen

peak: ~ **hour** *n* MEDIA *broadcast* Hauptbelastungszeit *f*, Hauptsendezeit *f*; ~ **importing season** *n* IMP/EXP Haupteinfuhrzeiten *f pl*; ~-**load pricing** *n* ECON Preisbildung *f* bei Spitzenbelastung; ~ **period** *n* ENVIR, TRANSP Spitzenzeit *f*; ~ **rate** *n* GEN COMM Spitzentarif *m*, Hochtarif *m*; ~ **season** *n* ECON Hauptsaison *f*; ~ **time** *n* S&M *television viewing* Spitzenzeit *f*

peanuts *n pl infrml* GEN COMM Kleingeld *nt*

Pearson: ~ **Report** *n* ECON Pearson-Bericht *m*

peculate *vt* FIN, LAW veruntreuen

peculation *n* FIN, LAW *public money* Veruntreuung *f*

pecuniary *adj* GEN COMM finanziell, geldlich, FIN vermögensrechtlich; ~ **damage** *n* FIN Vermögensschaden *m*; ~ **economy of scale** *n* ECON pekuniäre Skalenerträge *m pl*; ~ **external economy** *n* ECON pekuniäre externe Ersparnisse *f pl*; ~ **peer** *n* ECON gleichrangige Mitarbeiterin *f*, gleichrangiger Mitarbeiter *m*; ~ **returns**

n ECON monetärer Ertrag *m*; **~ spillover** *n* ECON monetärer externer Effekt *m*

pedestrian *n* GEN COMM Fußgänger, in *m,f*

pedestrianization *n* S&M *of a shopping street* Umwandlung *f* in Fußgängerzone

pedlar *n* GEN COMM fliegender Händler *m*, Hausierer *m*, Straßenhändler, in *m,f*, Straßenverkäufer, in *m,f*

peer: ~ group *n* S&M Gruppe *f* von Gleichrangigen, Peer-Gruppe *f*

peg *vt* ECON *price of a currency*, GEN COMM stützen, fixieren

pegged *adj* ECON, GEN COMM fixiert, gestützt, fest; **~ exchange rate** *n* ECON fester Wechselkurs *m*; **~ price** *n* ECON *currency* gestützter Kurs *m*, *commodity* subventionierter Preis *m*, FIN gestützter Kurs *m*

pegging: ~ device *n* ECON Stützungsinstrument *nt*; **~ system** *n* ECON Interventionssystem *nt*, Stützsystem *nt*

peg: ~ point *n* ECON Interventionspunkt *m*

pen *n* COMP Eingabestift *m*

penalize *vt* LAW mit einer Strafe belegen

penalty *n* LAW Strafe *f*, *contracts* Vertragsstrafe *f*; **~ clause** *n* LAW *in contract* Konventionalstrafklausel *f*; **~ for breach of contract** *n* LAW Konventionalstrafe *f* wegen Vertragsbruch; **~ for late tax payment** *n* TAX Zuschlag *m* für verspätete Steuerzahlung; **~ for noncompliance** *n* LAW Konventionalstrafe *f*; **~ interest** *n* BANK Strafzins *m*; **~ notice** *n* LAW Bußgeldbescheid *m*; **~ rate** *n* BANK *tax* Strafzins *m*

pen: ~-based computer *n* COMP Pen-Computer *m*

pencil in *vt* GEN COMM vormerken

pending *adj* GEN COMM noch nicht entschieden, schwebend, LAW unentschieden, unerledigt; **~ business** *n* ECON, GEN COMM schwebende Geschäfte *nt pl*; **~ tray** *n* ADMIN Ablagekorb *m* für unerledigte Arbeiten

pendulum: ~ arbitration *n* HRM Pendelschiedsverfahren *nt*

penetrate *vt* GEN COMM eindringen in [+acc], S&M durchdringen; ◆ **~ a market** ECON, S&M in einen Markt eindringen, einen Markt erobern

penetration *n* S&M *advertising* Penetration *f*; **~ pricing** *n* GEN COMM Niedrigpreisstrategie *f*, S&M Penetrationspreispolitik *f*; **~ rate** *n* S&M Penetrationsrate *f*

penny: ~ shares *n pl BrE* (*cf penny stock AmE*) STOCK Aktien *f pl* mit sehr niedrigen Nennbeträgen und Kursen, Kleinaktien *f pl*; **~ stock** *n AmE* (*cf penny shares BrE*) STOCK Aktien *f pl* mit sehr niedrigen Nennbeträgen und Kursen, Kleinaktien *f pl*

pension *n* FIN, HRM, WEL Pension *f*, Ruhegehalt *nt*, Rente *f*

pension off *vt* HRM in den Ruhestand versetzen, pensionieren

pensionable *adj* FIN, HRM, INS, WEL pensionsberechtigt, pensionsfähig; **~ age** *n* HRM, WEL Pensionsalter *nt*, Rentenalter *nt*

pension: **~ charges** *n pl* ACC Rentenbeitrag *m*; **~ contributions** *n pl* TAX Beiträge *m pl* zur Altersversorgung; **~ costs** *n pl* ACC Rentenbeitrag *m*; **~ for occupational invalidity** *n* WEL Berufsunfähigkeitsrente *f*; **~ fund** *n* ACC, FIN, INS Pensionsfonds *m*, Pensionskasse *f*; **~-holder** *n* FIN Rentenempfänger, in *m,f*; **~ liability** *n* ACC Pensionsverbindlichkeit *f*; **~ payment** *n* TAX Pensionszahlung *f*; **~ plan funding** *n* FIN Betriebsrentenfinanzierung *f*, Pensionsplanfinanzierung *f*

penthouse *n* PROP Penthouse *nt*

pent: ~-up demand *n* ECON aufgestaute Nachfrage *f*, Nachholbedarf *m*; **~-up energy** *n* GEN COMM Nachholenergie *f*

people *n* POL Volk *nt*; **~-intensive** *adj* HRM personalintensiv; **~-mover** *n infrml* TRANSP öffentliches Verkehrsmittel *nt*

PEP *abbr BrE* (*Personal Equity Plan*) FIN, STOCK auf Aktien basierendes staatliches Vermögensbildungsprogramm

pep up *vt infrml* ECON *demand* ankurbeln

PER *abbr* (*price-earnings ratio*) FIN KGV (*Kurs-Gewinn-Verhältnis*)

per: ~ annum *phr* (*p.a.*) GEN COMM per annum (*p.a.*), pro Jahr

P/E: ~ ratio *n* (*price-earnings ratio*) FIN KGV (*Kurs-Gewinn-Verhältnis*)

per: **~ capita** *adj* GEN COMM pro Kopf; **~ capita debt** *n* ECON Verschuldung *f* pro Kopf der Bevölkerung; **~ capita GDP** *n* ECON Pro-Kopf-BIP *nt*; **~ capita income** *n* ECON Pro-Kopf-Einkommen *nt*

perceived: ~ benefit *n* GEN COMM wahrgenommener Nutzen *m*

per cent 1. *adv* (*pc, P/C*) GEN COMM vom Hundert (*v.H.*), percentum (*p.c.*), prozentig (*p.c.*), prozentual (*p.c.*); **2.** *n* (*pc, P/C*) GEN COMM Prozent *nt* (*p.c.*)

percentage *n* GEN COMM Prozent *nt* (*p.c.*), MATH Prozentsatz *m*; **~ analysis** *n* MATH *statistics* Prozentanalyse *f*; **~ of annual profits** *n* HRM *as bonus*, MGMNT Gewinnbeteiligung *f*, Tantieme *f*; **~ of capital held** *n* ACC *balance sheet* Anteil *m* des gehaltenen Kapitals; **~ change** *n* FIN prozentuale Änderung *f*; **~ of depreciation** *n* FIN Abschreibungssatz *m*, Prozentsatz *m* der Wertminderung, Prozentsatz *m* des Wertverlusts; **~ distribution** *n* MATH *statistics* Prozentverteilung *f*; **~ grant** *n* WEL anteiliger Bundeszuschuß *m*; **~ lease** *n* PROP *retail property* Umsatzpacht *f*; **~-of-completion basis** *n* ACC Prorata-temporis-Basis *f*; **~-of-completion method** *n* ACC Bewertung *f* nach Baufortschritt; **~-of-sales method** *n* S&M *advertising, advertising budgets* Umsatzprovisionsmethode *f*; **~ of product price spent on its promotion** *n* S&M *advertising* Prozentsatz des Produktpreises, der für Verkaufsförderung aufgewendet wird; **~ return on sales** *n* FIN Umsatzrendite *f*, Umsatzrentabilität *f*

percentagewise *adv* MATH prozentual

percentile *n* MATH Perzentil *nt*; **~ ranking** *n* MATH *statistics* Rangordnung *f* nach Perzentilen

perception *n* GEN COMM *of sth* Auffassung *f*, Wahrnehmung *f*

per: **~ contra item** *n* ACC Ausgleichsposten *m*; **~ day** *adv* GEN COMM *output* pro Tag; **~ diem** *adv* GEN COMM pro Tag; **~ diem allowance** *n* INS Tagegeld *nt*

perestroika *n* ECON, POL Perestroika *f*

perfect *adj* GEN COMM vollkommen; **~ competition** *n* ECON vollständige Konkurrenz *f*, vollständiger Wettbewerb *m*; ◆ **in ~ condition** GEN COMM makellos

perfected: ~ security interest *n* ECON registriertes Sicherungsrecht *nt*

perfect: **~ market** *n* ECON vollkommener Markt *m*; **~ monopoly** *n* ECON reines Monopol *nt*; **~ price**

discrimination *n* ECON vollkommene Preisdiskriminierung *f*; ~ substitute *n* ECON *thing* vollwertiger Ersatz *m*
perform *vt* GEN COMM erfüllen, Leistung erbringen, verrichten, darbieten, vorführen, TAX ausüben; ♦ ~ the office of PA HRM das Amt des PA ausüben

performance *n* ACC *of company* Leistung *f*, GEN COMM *of services* Vorführung *f*, Erfüllung *f*, Ausführung *f*, Durchführung *f*, Verrichtung *f*, Leistung *f*, LAW *of contractual duty* Erfüllung *f*, S&M Leistung *f*, STOCK *securities* Entwicklung *f*, Wertentwicklung *f*, Performance *f*, TAX Ausübung *f*; ~ against objectives *n* HRM Leistung *f* im Vergleich zur Zielsetzung, MGMNT *comparison* Plan-Ist-Vergleich *m*, Zielerreichungsgrad *m*; ~ analysis *n* ECON Ergebnisanalyse *f*; ~ appraisal *n* HRM, MGMNT Leistungsbewertung *f*, Leistungseinschätzung *f*, Leistungsbeurteilung *f*; ~ appraisal interview *n* (*PAI*) HRM *work* Leistungsbeurteilungsgespräch *nt*; ~ bond *n* BANK Gewährleistungsgarantie *f*, GEN COMM Erfüllungsgarantie *f*, Leistungsgarantie *f*; ~ bonus *n* FIN Leistungsbonus *m*, Leistungsprämie *f*; ~ budget *n* FIN Leistungsbudget *nt*; ~ budgeting *n* ACC zielorientierte Budgetierung *f*, zielorientierte Budgetplanung *f*, HRM ertragsorientiertes Budget erstellen; ~ by a third party *n* GEN COMM Leistung durch Dritte *f*; ~ characteristics *n pl* IND Arbeitskenngrößen *f pl*; ~ contract *n* GEN COMM Leistungsvertrag *m*; ~ of contract *n* LAW Vertragserfüllung *f*; ~ evaluation *n* HRM, MGMNT Leistungsbewertung *f*, Leistungsbeurteilung *f*; ~ guarantee *n* S&M Leistungsgarantie *f*; ~ indicator *n* GEN COMM Planerfüllungsindikator *m*, HRM Leistungsindikator *m*; ~ in kind *n* GEN COMM Sachlieferung *f*; ~ marketing *n* S&M Leistungsmarketing *nt*; ~ measurement *n* HRM, MGMNT Leistungsmessung *f*; ~ monitoring *n* (*PM*) GEN COMM, HRM Leistungsüberwachung *f*, IND Betriebskontrolle *f*, Fertigungsüberwachung *f*, Leistungsüberwachung *f*, MGMNT Leistungsüberwachung *f*, Leistungskontrolle *f*; ~ rating *n* FIN *investment* Leistungsbewertung *f*, Leistungseinstufung *f*, HRM, IND Leistungsgradschätzen *nt*; ~-related indicator *n* GEN COMM *rent review for commercial property* leistungsbezogener Indikator *m*; ~-related pay *n* (*PRP*) HRM gewinnbezogene Bezahlung *f*, gewinnbezogenes Arbeitsentgelt *nt*, leistungsbezogene Bezahlung *f*, Leistungslohn *m*; ~ review *n* ACC Leistungsüberprüfung *f*, GEN COMM Leistungsüberblick *m*, HRM Leistungsbewertung *f*, Leistungsbeurteilung *f*; ~ of services *n* GEN COMM Erbringung *f* von Dienstleistungen; ~ standard *n* ACC Leistungsstandard *m*, HRM Leistungsmaßstab *m*; ~ target *n* ECON Ertragsziel *nt*, MGMNT Leistungsziel *nt*, Vorgabe *f*; ~ testing *n* IND Funktionsprüfung *f*, *packaging term* Leistungsprüfung *f*, *staff psychology* Eignungsprüfung *f*; ~ upon counter-performance *n* LAW *contract* Zug-um-Zug-Abwicklung *f*

performer *n* ECON Umsatzträger, in *m,f*

performing: ~ rights *n pl* LAW Aufführungsrechte *nt pl*

peril *n* INS *marine, insurance* Gefahr *f*; ♦ all ~ INS alle Gefahren, jedes Risiko *nt*; at one's own ~ GEN COMM auf eigene Gefahr

peril: ~ point *n* IMP/EXP Mindestzoll *f*, Warngrenze *f*

period *n* ECON Dauer *f*, Zeitraum *m*, GEN COMM *of time* Frist *f*, Laufzeit *f*, Periode *f*, Zeitdauer *f*; MEDIA *AmE* (*cf full stop BrE*) Punkt *m*; ♦ for the ~ ACC für den Zeitraum; over the ~ of GEN COMM in der Zeit von;

over a ~ of time GEN COMM über eine Zeitdauer, über einen längeren Zeitraum

period: ~ cap *n* FIN periodische festgesetzte Obergrenze *f*; ~ cost *n* ACC wiederkehrende Aufwendungen *f pl*; ~ of digestion *n* STOCK Absatzphase *f*; ~ entry scheme *n* IMP/EXP periodisiertes Zolldeklarationssystem *nt*; ~ expense *n* ACC zeitabhängige Kosten *pl*; ~ of extension *n* TAX Stundungsfrist *f*; ~ of grace *n* FIN tilgungsfreie Zeit *f*, LAW Gnadenfrist *f*, PATENTS Aufschub *m*, Gnadenfrist *f*

periodic *adj* GEN COMM periodisch, regelmäßig wiederkehrend, S&M periodisch

periodical 1. *adj* GEN COMM periodisch; **2.** *n* MEDIA Zeitschrift *f*

periodically *adv* GEN COMM in regelmäßigen Abständen

periodical: ~ survey *n* TRANSP regelmäßige Prüfung *nt*

periodic: ~ inventory method *n* ACC Stichtagsinventurmethode *f*, periodische Bestandsaufnahme *f*; ~ payment plan *n* FIN laufender Zahlungsplan *m*

period: ~ of notice *n* HRM Kündigungsfrist *f*; ~ of payment *n* ECON Zahlungsfrist *f*, GEN COMM Zahlungsziel *nt*; ~ of redemption *n* FIN Laufzeit *f*, Tilgungsfrist *f*, Amortisationszeit *f*; ~ of service *n* HRM Dienstzeit *f*; ~ set aside for appeal *n* LAW Berufungsfrist *f*; ~ of time *n* GEN COMM Zeitspanne *f*; ~ of training *n* HRM Volontariat *nt*; ~ of transition *n* ECON Übergangszeit *f*; ~ under review *n* ECON, GEN COMM Berichtszeitraum *m*

peripheral *adj* COMP, ECON peripher, GEN COMM nebensächlich, IND peripher; ~ capitalism *n* ECON peripherer Kapitalismus *m*; ~ computer *n* COMP Peripheriecomputer *m*; ~ device *n* COMP, IND Peripheriegerät *nt*; ~ equipment *n* COMP, IND periphere Geräte *nt pl*, Peripherie *f*, Peripheriegerät *nt*; ~ firm *n* ECON peripheres Unternehmen *nt*; ~ matter *n* GEN COMM Nebensache *f*

peripherals *n pl* COMP, IND Peripherie *f*, periphere Geräte *nt pl*

peripheral: ~ worker *n* HRM Arbeitnehmer, der nicht in einem dauerhaften, festen, ganztägigen, ununterbrochenen Beschäftigungsverhältnis mit nur einem Arbeitgeber steht, geringfügig Beschäftigte(r) *mf* [decl. as adj]

periphery *n* S&M *public relations* Randgruppe *f*

perish *vi* GEN COMM verderben

perishable *adj* GEN COMM verderblich; ~ foodstuffs *n pl* GEN COMM leicht verderbliche Lebensmittel *nt pl*; ~ goods *n pl* ECON, GEN COMM leicht verderbliche Güter *nt pl*, leicht verderbliche Waren *f pl*

perishables *n pl* ECON, GEN COMM leicht verderbliche Waren *f pl*, S&M kurzlebige Konsumgüter *nt pl*, kurzlebige Verbrauchsgüter *nt pl*

perjury *n* LAW Meineid *m*

perk *n infrml* HRM Nebenleistung *f*, Vergünstigung *f*, MGMNT Vergünstigung *f*

per: ~-kilometer rate *AmE*, ~-kilometre rate *BrE n* TRANSP *taxis* Kilometergeld *nt*, Kilometersatz *nt*

perks: ~ of the job *n pl* HRM Nebeneinkünfte *pl* der Tätigkeit

PERL *abbr* (*public enterprise rehabilitation loan*) FIN Rationalisierungsanleihe *f* eines Staatsunternehmens

permanent *adj* GEN COMM beständig, fest, fortlaufend, dauerhaft, langfristig; ~ account *n* ACC Dauerkonto *nt*; ~ address *n* COMMS ständige Adresse *f*; ~ appointment *n* HRM Festanstellung *f*; ~ employment *n* HRM

Dauerbeschäftigung *f*; ~ **establishment abroad** *n* TAX ausländische Betriebsstätte *f*; ~ **financing** *n* FIN Dauerfinanzierung *f*, langfristige, festverzinsliche Hypothek *f*; ~ **income hypothesis** *n* ECON permanente Einkommenshypothese *f*; ~ **job** *n* HRM Dauerposten *m*; ~ **labor** *AmE*, ~ **labour** *BrE n* HRM feste Arbeitskräfte *f pl*; ~ **participation** *n* ACC *balance sheet* Dauerbeteiligung *f*, langfristige Beteiligung *f*; ~ **position** *n* HRM Dauerposten *m*; ~ **residence** *n* LAW ständiger Wohnsitz *m*; ~ **resident** *n* LAW Person *f* mit ständigem Wohnsitz; ~ **tenure** *n* HRM Anstellung *f* auf Lebenszeit

permanently *adv* GEN COMM fest

permissible *adj* LAW zulässig; ~ **error** *n* GEN COMM zulässiger Fehler *m*

permission *n* COMP Berechtigung *f*

permit 1. *n* LAW Erlaubnis *f*, Genehmigung *f*, Lizenz *f*; **2.** *vt* LAW erlauben, genehmigen

permit: ~**-free** *adj* GEN COMM, LAW genehmigungsfrei

permitted *adj* GEN COMM erlaubt, zulässig

permutation *n* MATH Permutation *f*

perpendicular: ~ **spread** *n* STOCK vertikaler Spread *m*

perpetual: ~ **inventory** *n* ACC *accounting*, FIN *balance sheets* Buchinventur *f*, laufende Inventur *f*, permanente Inventur *f*

perpetuity *n* FIN unbegrenzte Dauer *f*, STOCK ewige Rente *f*, lebenslängliche Rente *m*; ♦ **in** ~ GEN COMM fortwährend

per pro *prep* (*per procurationem*) GEN COMM per procura (*frml*) (*pp., ppa.*)

per procurationem *prep frml* (*pp, per pro*) GEN COMM per procura (*frml*) (*pp., ppa.*)

perquisite *n frml* HRM Nebenleistung *f*, Vergünstigung *f*, MGMNT Vergünstigung *f*

per se *adv* GEN COMM an sich, für sich allein, schlechthin, per se, LAW schlechthin

persistent *adj* GEN COMM hartnäckig, *permanent* ständig, *tenacious* beharrlich; ~ **demand** *n* S&M anhaltende Nachfrage *f*; ~ **inflation** *n* ECON Dauerinflation *f*

person *n* GEN COMM *administrative* Person *f*; ♦ **in** ~ GEN COMM persönlich

persona grata *n* LAW Persona grata *f*

personal *adj* GEN COMM persönlich; ~ **assistant** *n* (*PA*) ADMIN, HRM Chefsekretär, in *m,f*, Privatsekretär, in *m,f*,MGMNT Chefsekretär, in *m,f*, persönliche Mitarbeiterin *f*, persönlicher Mitarbeiter *m*; ~ **baggage** *n* IMP/EXP persönliches Gepäck *nt*, Privatgepäck *nt*; ~ **bank** *n* BANK Privatbank *f*; ~ **capital** *n* GEN COMM Eigenkapital *nt*; ~ **computer** *n* (*PC*) COMP Personalcomputer *m* (*PC*); ~ **credit line** *n* BANK Dispokredit *m*, Dispositionskredit *m*; ~ **data sheet** *n* ADMIN Personalbogen *m*, Bogen *m* mit Personalangaben, *curriculum vitae* tabellarischer Lebenslauf *m*; ~ **disposable income** *n* (*PDI*) ECON persönliches verfügbares Einkommen *nt* nach Steuern, persönliches Nettoeinkommen *nt*, persönliches verfügbares Einkommen *nt*; ~ **dossier** *n* GEN COMM Personalakte *f*; ~ **effects** *n pl* ADMIN persönliche Gegenstände *m pl*

Personal: ~ **Equity Plan** *n* (*PEP*) FIN, STOCK auf Aktien basierendes staatliches Vermögensbildungsprogramm

personal: ~ **estate** *n* LAW Mobiliarvermögen *nt*, PROP bewegliche Habe *f*, bewegliches Vermögen *nt*, Mobiliarvermögen *nt*; ~ **file** *n* ADMIN Personalakte *f*; ~ **financial**

planning software *n* COMP, FIN Software *f* für persönliche Finanzplanung; ~ **growth** *n* HRM Entfaltung *f* der Persönlichkeit; ~ **guarantee** *n* BANK *of a loan* persönliche Bürgschaft *f*; ~ **holding company** *n* AmE (*PHC*) TAX kleine Holding *f*; ~ **income** *n* ECON persönliches Einkommen *nt*; ~ **income distribution** *n* ECON persönliche Einkommensverteilung *f*; ~ **influence** *n* GEN COMM persönlicher Einfluß *m*; ~ **injury** *n* INS Körperschaden *m*, Körperverletzung *f*, Personenschaden *m*, LAW Körperschaden *m*, Körperverletzung *f*; ~ **interview** *n* S&M persönliches Gespräch *nt*

personality *n* MGMNT Persönlichkeit *f*; ~ **promotion** *n* BrE *jarg* S&M *advertising* Prominentenwerbung *f*

personalization *n* S&M *advertising* Personalisierung *f*

personalized: ~ **letter** *n* S&M persönlich adressierter Brief *m*

personally *adv* GEN COMM persönlich; ♦ ~ **liable** LAW persönlich haftbar; ~ **responsible** LAW persönlich haftbar

personal: ~ **money** *n* FIN Eigengeld *nt*, persönliches Kapital *nt*; ~ **particulars** *n pl* ADMIN Personalangaben *f pl*; ~ **pension scheme** *n* BrE FIN, WEL *tax* private Rentenversicherung *f*; ~ **property** *n* PROP bewegliches Privateigentum *nt*; ~ **property floater** *n* INS Abschreibepolice *f* über persönliches Eigentum/bewegliche Sachwerte; ~ **requirements** *n* ACC Eigenbedarf *m*; ~ **saving** *n* BANK Ersparnisbildung *f* der privaten Haushalte; ~ **secretary** *n* (*P/Sec, PS*) ADMIN, HRM Chefsekretär, in *m,f*, Privatsekretär, in *m,f*; ~ **sector** *n* ECON Haushaltssektor *m*; ~ **sector liquid assets** *n* FIN verfügbare Mittel *nt pl* des Haushaltssektors; ~ **selling** *n* S&M *marketing* Direktverkauf *m* durch Vertreter; ~ **share** *n* STOCK Namensaktie *f*

personalty *n* TAX bewegliches Vermögen *nt*

personal: ~ **wealth** *n* ECON persönlicher Wohlstand *m*

personam: **in** ~ *phr* LAW persönlich, schuldrechtlich

persona non grata *n* LAW Persona non grata *f*, unerwünschte Person *f*

person: ~ **entitled in expectancy** *n* LAW *contracts* Anwartschaftsberechtigte(r) *mf* [decl. as adj]; ~ **entitled under a life interest** *n* LAW Nießbrauchberechtigte(r) *mf* [decl. as adj] auf Lebenszeit; ~ **entitled under a limited interest** *n* LAW Nießbrauchberechtigte(r) *mf* [decl. as adj] auf Zeit; ~ **with full capacity to contract** *n* LAW Geschäftsfähige(r) *mf* [decl. as adj]; ~ **of independent means** *n* GEN COMM finanziell Unabhängige(r) *mf* [decl. as adj], Rentier *m*

personnel *n* GEN COMM Belegschaft *f*, HRM, MGMNT Personal *nt*; ~ **administration** *n* HRM Personalverwaltung *f*; ~ **department** *n* HRM Personalabteilung *f*; ~ **director** *n* HRM, MGMNT Leiter, in *m,f* der Personalabteilung, Personalchef, in *m,f*, Personaldirektor, in *m,f*, Personalleiter, in *m,f*; ~ **expenses** *n pl* HRM Personalkosten *pl*; ~ **growth** *n* HRM Personalwachstum *nt*; ~**-intensive** *adj* HRM industry personalintensiv; ~ **management** *n* HRM Personalleitung *f*, Personalverwaltung *f*, Personalwirtschaft *f*; ~ **manager** *n* HRM, MGMNT Personalchef, in *m,f*, Personalleiter, in *m,f*; ~ **overheads** *n pl* HRM Personalgemeinkosten *pl*; ~ **placement** *n* HRM Personaleinsatz *m*; ~ **policy** *n* HRM Personalpolitik *f*; ~ **psychology** *n* HRM, MGMNT Arbeitspsychologie *f*; ~ **rating** *n* HRM Leistungsbewertung *f*, Leistungsbeurteilung *f*; ~ **specification** *n* HRM Personalspezifikation *f*

person: ~ **on fixed income** *n* FIN, HRM Bezieher, in *m,f* eines festen Einkommens; ~ **receiving benefit** *n* BrE (*cf welfare recipient AmE*) HRM Wohlfahrtsempfänger, in *m,f*

persons: **the ~ concerned** *n pl* GEN COMM die betreffenden Personen *f pl*, die Betreffenden *pl* [decl. as adj]

person: ~ **serving a third party notice** *n* LAW Streitverkünder, in *m,f*

perspective *n* GEN COMM Ausblick *m*, Perspektive *f*

per: ~ **square foot** *adv* (*psf*) GEN COMM, PROP *rent* pro Quadratfuß; ~ **stirpes** *adv* LAW *distribution of an estate* nach Stämmen

persuade *vt* GEN COMM überreden, überzeugen

persuasion *n* GEN COMM *influence* Überredung *f*, Überzeugung *f*

persuasive *adj* GEN COMM überzeugend; ~ **communication** *n* S&M verführende Kommunikation *f*

PERT *abbr* (*program evaluation and review technique AmE, programme evaluation and review technique BrE*) MGMNT Methode zur Berechnung und Kontrolle des Arbeitsablaufs, Projektfortschrittsplanung *f* mit stochastischer Netzplantechnik

pertaining: ~ **to** *adj* GEN COMM *a document* betreffend

pertinence: ~ **tree** *n* MGMNT Pertinenzbaum *m*

pertinent *adj* GEN COMM, LAW sachdienlich, sachlich

per: ~**-unit tax** *n* TAX Stücksteuer *f*

perverse: ~ **price** *n* ECON perverser Preis *m*

PESC *abbr* (*Public Expenditure Survey Committee*) ECON Ausschuß *m* zur Untersuchung der Staatsausgaben

pessimism *n* ECON, STOCK Pessimismus *m*

pessimistic *adj* ECON, STOCK pessimistisch; ◆ **be ~** GEN COMM schwarz sehen

pesticide *n* ENVIR Pestizid *nt*

Peter: ~ **principle** *n* HRM Peterprinzip *nt*

petition *n* GEN COMM Eingabe *f*, Ersuchen *nt*, Gesuch *nt*, Bittschrift *f*, LAW Petition *f*, Verfahrensantrag *m*; ~ **for relief** *n* AmE (*cf petition in bankruptcy BrE*) FIN Konkursantrag *m*; ~ **in bankruptcy** BrE *n* (*cf petition for relief AmE*) FIN Konkursantrag *m*

petrochemicals: ~ **industry** *n* ENVIR, IND Petrochemie *f*

petrocurrency *n* BANK, ECON, IMP/EXP Petrowährung *f*

petrodollar *n* BANK, ECON Petrodollar *m*, IMP/EXP Öldollar *m*, Ölgeld *nt*, Petrodollar *m*

petrol *n* BrE (*cf gas AmE, gasoline AmE*) ENVIR, TRANSP Benzin *nt*

petroleum *n* ENVIR, IND Erdöl *nt*; ~ **company** *n* GEN COMM Ölgesellschaft *f*

Petroleum: ~ **Compensation Revolving Fund** *n* FIN revolvierender Fonds *m* für Erdölausgleichszahlung

petroleum: ~ **industry** *n* ENVIR, IND Erdölindustrie *f*; ~ **revenue tax** *n* (*PRT*) TAX Steuern *f pl* auf Einnahmen aus Erdölgewinnung

petroliferous *adj* ENVIR, IND erdölhaltig

PETs *abbr* BrE (*potentially exempt transfers*) TAX potentiell befreite Übertragungen *f pl*

petty *adj* ACC, FIN, GEN COMM klein; ~ **cash** *n* ACC *book-keeping* Handkasse *f*, kleine Kasse *f*, Nebenkasse *f*, Portokasse *f*, kleine Ausgaben *f pl*, Bagatellbeträge *m pl*; ~ **cash book** *n* ACC, ADMIN Kassenbuch *nt*; ~ **cash**

voucher *n* ACC *book-keeping* Barzahlungsbeleg *m*, Eingangsbeleg *m* der Handkasse; ~ **expenses** *n pl* ACC kleine Ausgaben *f pl*, FIN kleine Ausgaben *f pl*, kleine Spesen *f pl*; ~ **official** *n* HRM mittlere Beamtin *f*, mittlere(r) Beamte(r) *m* [decl. as adj]; ~ **regulations** *n pl* FIN engstirnige Bestimmungen *f pl*

Petty: ~**'s law** *n* ECON Petty-Gesetz *nt*

PEWP *abbr* BrE (*Public Expenditure White Paper*) ECON Weißbuch *nt* der Staatsausgaben

PFP *abbr* (*policy framework paper*) ECON, STOCK politischer Rahmenbericht *m*

PG *abbr* (*paying guest*) GEN COMM, LEIS Feriengast *m*, Pensionsgast *m*, zahlender Gast *m*

phantom: ~ **share option** *n* STOCK Scheinaktienoption *f*; ~ **stock plan** *n* STOCK Verfahren zur Berechnung von Mitarbeitergratifikationen

pharmaceutical *adj* IND pharmazeutisch; ~ **industry** *n* IND Arzneimittelindustrie *f*, Pharmaindustrie *f*, pharmazeutische Industrie *f*

pharmaceuticals *n pl* IND Pharmaprodukte *nt pl*, Arzneimittel *nt pl*, Pharmazeutika *nt pl*, STOCK Pharmatitel *m pl*

phase *n* GEN COMM *of project* Etappe *f*, Phase *f*, Stadium *nt*, Stufe *f*

phase in *vt* GEN COMM *technology, service, system* einlaufen lassen, schrittweise anheben, schrittweise einführen

phase out *vt* GEN COMM *technology, service, system* auslaufen lassen, schrittweise abbauen, schrittweise aufheben

phased: ~ **distribution** *n* S&M zonale Distribution *f*

phase: ~**-in period** *n* ECON Anlaufphase *f*; ~**-out** *n* GEN COMM *production* Auslaufen *nt*, IND, S&M Produktionseinstellung *f*; ~**-out period** *n* ECON Auslaufsphase *f*

phasing-out *n* GEN COMM allmähliche Abschaffung *f*, schrittweiser Abbau *m*

PHC *abbr* AmE (*personal holding company*) TAX kleine Holding *f*

PhD *abbr* (*Doctor of Philosophy*) HRM, WEL *person* Dr. Phil. (*Doktor der Philosophie*), *qualification* Doktorgrad *m*

Philadelphia: ~ **Stock Exchange** *n* AmE (*PHLX*) STOCK Philadelphia Wertpapierbörse *f*

Phillips: ~ **curve** *n* ECON, POL Phillips-Kurve *f*

PHLX *abbr* AmE (*Philadelphia Stock Exchange*) STOCK Philadelphia Wertpapierbörse *f*

phone 1. *n* COMMS, GEN COMM Telefon *nt*; **2.** *vt* COMMS, GEN COMM anrufen

phone: ~ **book** *n* COMMS Fernsprechteilnehmerverzeichnis *nt*, Telefonbuch *nt*; ~ **call** *n* COMMS Telefonanruf *m*, Telefongespräch *nt*; ~ **card** *n* COMMS Telefonkarte *f*; ~**-in poll** *n* COMMS, MEDIA, POL Abstimmung *f* per Telefon; ~**-in program** AmE, ~**-in programme** BrE *n* COMMS, MEDIA *radio, TV* Beteiligung von Zuschauern an einem Radio- oder Fernsehprogramm mittels Telefon; ~ **marketing** *n* S&M Telefon-Marketing *nt*; ~ **number** *n* COMMS Anschluß *m*, Anschlußnummer *f*, Telefonnummer *f*

phoning *n* COMMS Telefonieren *nt*

photo *n* MEDIA Foto *nt*

photocall *n* MEDIA, S&M Fototermin *m*

photocell *n* S&M Fotozelle *f*

photocopier *n* ADMIN Fotokopierautomat *m*

photocopy 1. *n* ADMIN Fotokopie *f*; **2.** *vt* ADMIN fotokopieren

photograph *n* MEDIA Foto *nt*; **~ session** *n* MEDIA, S&M Fototermin *m*

photogravure *n* S&M Fotogravur *f*

photosetter *n* AmE (*cf* **filmsetter** BrE) MEDIA *print* Fotosatzgerät *nt*

photosetting *n* AmE (*cf* **filmsetting** BrE) MEDIA *print* Fotosatz *m*

photostat *n* ADMIN Fotokopie *f*, GEN COMM *dated* Ablichtung *f*

physical *adj* GEN COMM materiell, Sach-; **~ asset** *n* GEN COMM Sachwert *m*; **~ assets** *n pl* ECON materielle Wirtschaftsgüter *nt pl*, Sachanlagegüter *nt pl*, Sachanlagevermögen *nt*; **~ collateral** *n* BANK physischer Sicherungsgegenstand *m*; **~ commodity** *n* STOCK Effektivware *f*; **~ depreciation** *n* ACC *annual accounts* Gebrauchsabschreibung *f*, kalkulatorische Abschreibung *f*, verbrauchsbedingte Wertminderung *f*; **~ deterioration** *n* ACC *annual accounts* verbrauchsbedingte Wertminderung *f*; **~ distribution** *n* S&M Verteilung *f* durch den Handel; **~ distribution management** *n* (*PDM*) MGMNT Vertriebsleitung *f*, TRANSP Management *nt* der physischen Verteilung, Verteilungsmanagement *nt* durch den Handel; **~ examination** *n* GEN COMM *of an object* körperliche Durchsuchung *f*, WEL ärztliche Untersuchung *f*; **~ impossibility of performance** *n* LAW *contracts* objektive Unmöglichkeit *f* der Leistung; **~ injury** *n* INS Personenschaden *m*; **~ inventory** *n* ACC effektive Bestandsaufnahme *f*, körperliche Inventur *f*

physically *adv* GEN COMM körperlich, materiell

physical: **~ quality of life index** *n* (*PQLI*) ECON *econometrics* Index *m* der physischen Lebensqualität

physiocrat *n* ECON Physiokrat *m*

PIBOR *abbr* (*Paris Interbank Offered Rate*) BANK Pariser Interbankenangebotssatz *m* (*PIBOR*)

pick up 1. *vt* TRANSP *cargo* abholen; ♦ **~ the tab** *infrml* GEN COMM die Rechnung bezahlen, die Zeche bezahlen; **2.** *vi* ECON *recover* sich erholen, GEN COMM *prices* aufholen

picked: **~ ports** *n pl* (*pp*) TRANSP *shipping* ausgesuchte Häfen *m pl*

picket 1. *n* GEN COMM, HRM, IND Streikposten *m*; **2.** *vt* GEN COMM, HRM, IND Streikposten aufstellen; ♦ **~ a factory** HRM vor einer Fabrik Streikposten aufstellen

pick: **~-up** *n* ECON *recovery* Erholung *f*, MEDIA Aufzeichnung *f*, Aufnahme *f*, im voraus aufgezeichnete Sendung *f*, TRANSP *collection* Abholung *f*; **~-up cost** *n* TRANSP Abholungskosten *pl*; **~-up service** *n* TRANSP Abholdienst *m*, Abholungsservice *m*; **~-your-own** *n* BrE S&M *farm produce* Selbstpflücken *nt*

pictogram *n* MATH *statistics* Piktogramm *nt*

pictorial: **~ material** *n* MEDIA Bildmaterial *f*; **~ presentation** *n* S&M illustrierte Präsentation *f*, zeichnerische Darstellung *f*

picture *n* GEN COMM *outlook, prospects* Bild *nt*, Erscheinungsbild *nt*, LEIS, MEDIA Kinofilm *m*; **~ caption** *n* MEDIA, S&M Bildtext *m*

piddling: **~ sum** *n* *infrml* ECON, FIN Bagatellbetrag *m*

piece *n* GEN COMM Stück *nt*, Teil *m*; ♦ **at ~ rate** HRM zum Stücklohnsatz

piece: **~ of advice** *n* MGMNT Ratschlag *m*; **~ of**

information *n* GEN COMM eine Information *f*; **~ of legislation** *n* LAW Teil *m* der Gesetzgebung; **~ of news** *n* MEDIA *print* Nachricht *f*, Neuigkeit *f*

pieces *n pl* (*pcs*) GEN COMM Stück *nt* (*St.*)

piece: **~ wage** *n* HRM Stücklohn *m*

piecework *n* GEN COMM, HRM Akkordarbeit *f*, INS Akkord *m*; **~ rate** *n* IND Akkordlohn *m*; **~ system** *n* HRM Akkordsystem *nt*; **~ wage** *n* IND Akkordlohn *m*

pie: **~ chart** *n* COMP Tortendiagramm *nt*, MATH Kreisdiagramm *nt*

pier *n* TRANSP *shipping* Pier *m*

pierage *n* IMP/EXP, TRANSP Kaigebühren *f pl*, Kaigeld *nt*

piercing: **~ the corporate veil** *n* LAW *commercial liability for corporate activity* Durchgriffshaftung *f* bei juristischen Personen, Haftungsdurchgriff *m*

pigeonhole 1. *n* ADMIN Sortierfach *nt*; **2.** *vt* GEN COMM *classify* einstufen

piggyback: **~ export scheme** *n* S&M Huckepackausfuhrsystem *nt*; **~ legislation** *n* LAW Huckepackgesetzgebung *f*; **~ loan** *n* FIN Huckepackanleihe *f*; **~ promotion** *n* S&M Huckepackverkaufsförderung *f*; **~ registration** *n* STOCK Huckepackregistrierung *f*; **~ selling** *n* S&M Huckepackverkauf *m*; **~ traffic** *n* AmE (*cf* **road-rail transport** BrE) TRANSP Huckepackverkehr *m*, Straße-Schiene-Transport *m*

Pigou: **~ effect** *n* ECON Pigou-Effekt *m*

Pigouvian: **~ subsidy** *n* ECON Pigou-Subvention *f*; **~ tax** *n* ECON Pigou-Steuer *f*

PIK: **~ bond** *n* (*payment-in-kind bond*) FIN Sachleistungsobligation *f*

pilot *n* HRM, TRANSP *shipping* Lotse *m*, *air* Pilot, in *m,f*, MEDIA Pilotfilm *m*, Pilotsendung *f*

pilotage *n* TRANSP *shipping* Lotsengeld *nt*

pilot: **~ boat** *n* TRANSP Lotsenboot *nt*; **~-in-command** *n* HRM, TRANSP *air* Flugkapitän *m*; **~ launch** *n* S&M *marketing* Testeinführung *f*; **~ order** *n* GEN COMM Erstauftrag *m*; **~ plant** *n* IND Pilotanlage *f*, Versuchsanlage *f*; **~ production** *n* GEN COMM Versuchsproduktion *f*, Vorserie *f*, IND Prototypproduktion *f*, Nullserie *f*, Vorserie *f*, MGMNT Nullserie *f*, Pilotproduktion *f*, Probebetrieb *m*; **~ project** *n* MGMNT Pilotprojekt *nt*; **~ run** *n* GEN COMM Probelauf *m*, Versuchslauf *m*; **~ scheme** *n* GEN COMM Pilotprogramm *nt*; **~ study** *n* GEN COMM Probebefragung *f*, Probeerhebung *f*, Probeuntersuchung *f*, Vorstudie *f*

pin *n* COMP *paper feeder* Stift *m*; ♦ **~ one's hopes on** GEN COMM seine Hoffnungen auf etw setzen

pinion *n* TRANSP Kleinrad *nt*, Ritzel *nt*

Pink: **~ Book** *n* BrE ECON britische Zahlungsbilanz

pink: **~ economy** *n* *jarg* ECON rosa Wirtschaft *f*; **~ paper** *n* BrE POL parlamentarische Notiz mit den Details aller dem Parlament vorgelegten oder auf Anordnung der Regierung gedruckten Papiere; **~ sheets** *n pl* AmE (*cf* **Stock Exchange Official List** BrE) STOCK Kursblatt *nt*; **~ slip** *n* AmE (*cf* **redundancy letter** BrE) ECON Entlassungsschreiben *nt*, HRM *notice in writing* Begleitnotiz *f*, Entlassungspapiere *nt pl*, MGMNT *notice in writing* Begleitnotiz *f*; **get the ~ slip** *phr* AmE *infrml* GEN COMM gekündigt werden

pin: **~ money** *n* GEN COMM geringfügige Entlohnung *f*, Taschengeld *nt*

pint *n* (*pt*) GEN COMM Pint *nt* (*pt*)

pioneer 1. *n* GEN COMM, IND Bahnbrecher, in *m,f*, Pionier *m*, Vorkämpfer, in *m,f*, Vorreiter, in *m,f*, Wegbereiter, in *m,f*; **2.** *vt* GEN COMM, IND bahnbrechend wirken, den Weg bereiten für

pioneering *adj* GEN COMM bahnbrechend, einführend; **~ advertising** *n* ECON, S&M Einführungswerbung *f*

pioneer: **~ product** *n* IND, S&M Pionierprodukt *nt*

pipe: **~-laying ship** *n* TRANSP Rohrlegerschiff *nt*

pipeline *n* COMMS Rohrleitung *f*, IND, TRANSP Hauptleitung *f*, Hauptrohrleitung *f*, Pipeline *f*, Rohrleitung *f*; ◆ **be in the ~** GEN COMM *orders* in Vorbereitung sein, *project* geplant sein, in Bearbeitung sein

piracy *n* COMP, IND, S&M Plagiat *nt*, ECON Raubkopieren *nt*, GEN COMM *book* Raubdruck *m*, unzulässiger Nachdruck *m*, *record* Raubpressung *f*, LAW unzulässiger Nachdruck *m*, MEDIA Raubkopieren *nt*

pirate 1. *vt* COMP, LAW, MEDIA illegal kopieren; **2.** *vi* IND Plagiat begehen

pirate: **~ copy** *n* COMP *software* Raubkopie *f*, illegale Kopie *f*, ECON Raubkopie *f*, GEN COMM Raubkopie *f*, illegale Kopie *f*, LAW, MEDIA Raubkopie *f*

pirated: **~ product** *n* S&M unerlaubt kopiertes Produkt *nt*

pirate: **~ radio** *n* MEDIA *broadcast* Piratensender *m*; **~ version** *n* ECON, MEDIA Raubkopie *f*

pirating *n* LAW geistiger Diebstahl *m*

pit *n* STOCK Bieterraum *m*, Maklerstand *m*, Ring *m*

pitch *n* COMP Abstand *m*, S&M Verkaufsgespräch *nt*; **~ rent** *n* MEDIA, S&M Platzmiete *f*

pitfall *n* GEN COMM Fallstrick *m*, Falle *f*

pit: **~ trader** *n* STOCK Makler *m* auf eigene Rechnung

pittance *n* GEN COMM Hungerlohn *m*

Pittsburgh: **~-plus** *n* AmE ECON Stahlpreise mit Frachtbasis Pittsburgh

pixel *n* COMP Bildelement *nt*, Pixel *nt*

pizazz *n* ECON Reklamerummel *m*

pkg. *abbr* (*package*) COMMS, TRANSP Bündel *nt*, Päckchen *nt*, Packung *f*, Paket *nt*

pkge *abbr* (*package*) COMMS, TRANSP Bündel *nt*, Päckchen *nt*, Packung *f*, Paket *nt*

pkt. *abbr* (*packet*) COMMS, TRANSP Päckchen *nt*, Paket *nt*

PL *abbr* (*partial loss*) INS Teilschaden *m*, Teilverlust *m*

PLA *abbr* (*Port of London Authority*) TRANSP Londoner Hafenbehörde *f*

placard *n* GEN COMM Anschlag *m*, S&M Plakat *nt*

place 1. *n* GEN COMM Ort *m*, Örtlichkeit *f*, Platz *m*; **2.** *vt* FIN unterbringen, GEN COMM vergeben, *order* erteilen, STOCK plazieren; ◆ **~ a ban on** LAW ein Verbot verhängen über; **~ a deposit** STOCK *Eurodollar time deposit* eine Einzahlung machen, einen Betrag hinterlegen; **~ emphasis on** GEN COMM betonen; **~ an issue** STOCK eine Emission unterbringen; **~ a question on the agenda** MGMNT eine Frage auf die Tagesordnung setzen; **~ on record** GEN COMM beurkunden; **~ in trust** LAW in Treuhandverwaltung geben; **~ under guardianship** WEL unter Vormundschaft stellen; **~ under sequestration** LAW der Zwangsverwaltung unterstellen

place: **~ of abode** *n* LAW Aufenthaltsort *m*; **~ of acceptance** *n* (*POA*) TRANSP Ort *m* der Abnahme

placed *adj* GEN COMM *order* erteilt

place: **~ of delivery** *n* (*POD*) TRANSP Erfüllungsort *m*, Lieferort *m*; **~ of destination** *n* GEN COMM Bestim-

mungsort *m*, Zielort *m*; **~ of discharge** *n* TRANSP Löschplatz *m*

placement *n* COMMS *job* Vermittlung *f*, HRM Volontärstelle *f*, STOCK *bonds* Plazierung *f*, Unterbringung *f*; **~ of employees** *n* HRM Arbeitsvermittlung *f*; **~ ratio** *n* FIN Plazierungskennziffer *f*; **~ test** *n* HRM Einstufungstest *m*

place: **~ of origin** *n* TRANSP Herkunftsland *nt*, Herkunftsort *m*; **~ of payment** *n* LAW *contract law* Zahlungsort *m*; **~ of performance** *n* LAW *contract law* Erfüllungsort *m*; **~ of residence** *n* LAW Aufenthaltsort *m*; **~ of transshipment** *n* GEN COMM Umschlagplatz *m*; **~ utility** *n* ECON räumlicher Nutzen *m* eines Gutes; **~ of work** *n* GEN COMM, HRM Arbeitsplatz *m*, Betrieb *m*, IND Arbeitsstätte *f*

placing *n* STOCK Plazierung *f*, Unterbringung *f*; **~ of orders** *n* GEN COMM Auftragsvergabe *f*; **~ price** *n* STOCK Plazierungskurs *m*

plain: **be ~** *phr* GEN COMM eine deutliche Sprache sprechen; **~ bond issue** *n* STOCK ungesicherte Anleihe *f*; **in ~ language** *phr* GEN COMM mit deutlichen Worten; **~-spoken** *adj* GEN COMM direkt, offen

plaintiff *n* LAW Kläger, in *m,f*

plain: **~ vanilla model** *n* infrml ECON Basismodell *nt*; **~ vanilla swap** *n* infrml FIN einfacher Zinsswap *m*

plan 1. *n* GEN COMM Konzept *nt*, Plan *m*, Programm *nt*, Projekt *nt*, Vorhaben *nt*, MGMNT Vorhaben *nt*; ◆ **the ~ does not hold water** infrml GEN COMM der Plan ist nicht wasserdicht (*infrml*), der Plan ist nicht hieb- und stichfest (*infrml*); **the ~ has no substance** GEN COMM der Plan hat weder Hand noch Fuß (*infrml*); **the ~ is not sound** GEN COMM der Plan ist nicht stichhaltig; **the ~ makes no sense** GEN COMM der Plan hat weder Hand noch Fuß (*infrml*); **2.** *vt* GEN COMM entwerfen, planen, vorhaben; **3.** *vi* GEN COMM planen; ◆ **~ ahead for sth** GEN COMM etw im voraus planen; **~ on sth** GEN COMM mit etw rechnen

plank *n* POL Pfeiler *m*, Stütze *f*, zentraler Aspekt *m* einer Politik, wesentlicher Programmpunkt *m* einer Agenda

planned: **~ capacity** *n* ECON geplante Kapazität *f*; **~ economy** *n* ECON, POL Planwirtschaft *f*, planwirtschaftliches System *nt*; **~ obsolescence** *n* ECON, S&M geplanter Verschleiß *m*, geplantes Veralten *nt*; **~ selling** *n* S&M geplanter Verkauf *m*, Planverkauf *m*; **~ unit development** *n* (*PUD*) PROP geplantes Grundstückserschließungsprojekt *nt*

planning *n* GEN COMM Einteilung *f*, Planung *f*; **~ approval** *n* PROP Baugenehmigung *f*; **~ authority** *n* ADMIN, ENVIR Baubehörde *f*, Planungsbehörde *f*; **~ commission** *n* ECON Planungskommission *f*; **~ committee** *n* GEN COMM Planungsausschuß *m*

Planning: **~ and Compensation Act** *n* BrE LAW Gesetz *nt* über Planung und Entschädigung

planning: **~ department** *n* ADMIN, MGMNT Betriebsbüro *nt*, Planungsabteilung *f*, Planungsbüro *nt*; **~ horizon** *n* ECON Planungshorizont *m*, Planungszeitraum *m*; **~ permission** *n* ADMIN, LAW, PROP Baugenehmigung *f*; **~ policy** *n* ADMIN, GEN COMM *regional development* regionale Entwicklungsplanung *f*; **~ of process layout** *n* IND, MGMNT Arbeitsvorbereitung *f*; **~ programming budget** *n* POL Programmbudget *nt*, outputorientiertes Budget *nt*; **~, programming and budgeting** *n* (*PPB*) ACC, ECON, FIN, MGMNT Planung, Programmierung und Budgetierung *f* (*PPB*); **~, programming and budgeting**

system *n* (*PPBS*) ACC, ECON, FIN, MGMNT Planungs-, Programmierungs- und Budgetierungssystem *nt* (*PPB-System*); **~ restrictions** *n pl* PROP Bauauflagen *f pl*; **~ total** *n* ECON Planungssumme *m*

plans: **~ board** *n* S&M Planungsstab *m*; **the ~ came unstuck** *phr infrml* GEN COMM die Pläne fielen ins Wasser (*infrml*)

plant *n* IND Anlage *f*, Betriebsanlage *f*, Einrichtung *f*, Fabrikgrundstück *nt*, Installation *f*; **~ agreement** *n* HRM Betriebsvereinbarung *f*

plantation *n* ECON *agricultural economics* Plantage *f*

plant: **~ bargaining** *n* GEN COMM, HRM betriebliches Tarifwesen *nt*; **~ capacity** *n* GEN COMM, IND *electrical* Betriebskapazität *f*, betriebliche Leistungsfähigkeit *f*; **~ closure** *n* IND Betriebsschließung *f*, Betriebsstillegung *f*; **~ hire** *n* GEN COMM Anlagenverpachtung *f*, IND Vermietung *f* ganzer Betriebsanlagen, Maschinenverleih *m*, Mobilienvermietung *f*; **~ incentive scheme** *n* HRM Anreizsystem *nt* auf Betriebsebene, betriebliches Anreizsystem *nt*; **~ interruption** *n* GEN COMM Anlagenunterbrechung *f*; **~ layout study** *n* GEN COMM Studie *f* zur Auslegung der Anlage, Studie *f* zur Werksplanung, IND Anlagenplanung *f*, Betriebsplanstudie *f*, Werksplanung *f*; **~ location** *n* GEN COMM Anlagenerhaltung *f*, Standort *m* der Anlage, IND Betriebsgelegenheit *f*, Fabriklage *f*; **~ and machinery** *n* IND technische Anlagen und Maschinen *f pl*; **~ maintenance** *n* GEN COMM Werkserhaltung *f*; **~ management** *n* IND, MGMNT Betriebsleitung *f*, Werksleitung *f*; **~ manager** *n* IND, MGMNT Betriebsführer, in *m,f*, Betriebsleiter, in *m,f*, Fabrikleiter, in *m,f*, Werksleiter, in *m,f*; **~ manufacturing** *n* IND Anlagenherstellung *f*, Anlagenproduktion *f*; **~ operator** *n* IND Bediener, in *m,f*; **~ utilization** *n* ECON Kapazitätsausnutzung *f*; **~ utilization rate** *n* IND Ausnutzungsgrad *m*; **~ varieties** *n pl* IND Anlagenauswahl *f*, Betriebsauswahl *f*; **~ welfare facilities** *n pl* HRM, WEL betriebliche Wohlfahrtseinrichtungen *f pl*

plastics *n pl* ENVIR, IND Kunststoffe *m pl*

plastic: **~ waste** *n* ENVIR, IND Kunststoffmüll *m*

plat 1. *n* PROP Katasterplan *m*; **2.** *vt* PROP Aufteilungsplan erstellen

plat: **~ book** *n* AmE (*cf land register BrE*) ADMIN, PROP Grundbuch *nt*, Kataster *m*

plate: **~ mark** *n* BANK Feingehaltsstempel *m*

platform *n* COMP *software, hardware* Plattform *f*, ENVIR Bohrinsel *f*, Bohrplattform *f*, IND Plattform *f*, MEDIA, POL Podium *nt*, TRANSP Plattform *f*; **~ crane** *n* (*Pc*) IND Plattformkran *m*; **~ vehicle** *n* TRANSP Plattformwagen *m*

PLATO *abbr* (*Pollution Liability Agreement Among Tanker Owners*) INS, LAW, TRANSP *shipping* Haftungsvereinbarung *f* zwischen Tankereignern in Bezug auf Umweltverschmutzung

platykurtic: **~ frequency distribution** *n* MATH *statistics* flachgipflige Verteilungskurve *f*, platykurtische Verteilungskurve *f*

platykurtosis *n* MATH *statistics* Flachgipfligkeit *f*, Platykurtosis *f*

play 1. *n* GEN COMM Spiel *nt*, STOCK Spekulation an der Börse *f*; ◆ **come into ~** GEN COMM *factor* ins Spiel kommen; **2.** *vt* STOCK *market* spekulieren; ◆ **~ a part in** GEN COMM eine Rolle spielen bei; **~ it by ear** *infrml* GEN COMM improvisieren; **~ sb off against** GEN COMM jdn ausspielen gegen; **3.** *vi* ◆ **~ safe** GEN COMM auf Nummer Sicher gehen, kein Risiko eingehen

playback *n* MEDIA, S&M Playback *nt*

play: **~ book** *n* AmE GEN COMM Betriebsunterlagen *f pl*; **~ down** *vt* GEN COMM, POL herunterschrauben, herunterspielen

plc *abbr BrE* (*public limited company*) ECON, GEN COMM, STOCK AG (*Aktiengesellschaft*), Kapitalgesellschaft *f*

PLC *abbr BrE* (*public limited company*) ECON, GEN COMM, STOCK AG (*Aktiengesellschaft*), Kapitalgesellschaft *f*

plea-bargain *vi* LAW über Schuldigerklärung absprechen, aushandeln

plea-bargaining *n* LAW Verhandlungen zwischen Anklage und Verteidigung, in denen der Angeklagte zustimmt, sich in einem weniger schwerwiegenden Anklagepunkt schuldig zu bekennen, wenn andere Anklagepunkte dafür fallengelassen werden

plead *vi* LAW plädieren; **~ for sb** *phr* GEN COMM für jdn plädieren; **~ guilty** *phr* LAW sich schuldig bekennen; **~ ignorance** *phr* LAW sich auf Unwissenheit berufen

pleading *n* LAW Plädieren *nt*

pleasant: **~ working environment** *n* HRM angenehmes Arbeitsumfeld *nt*

please *vt* GEN COMM zufriedenstellen

please: **~ note** *phr* GEN COMM bitte beachten, nota bene (*NB*); **~ turn over** *phr* (*pto*) COMMS bitte wenden (*b.w.*)

pleasure: **~ shopping** *n* S&M Vergnügungseinkauf *m*; **~ trip** *n* TRANSP Vergnügungsreise *f*

pledge *vt* LAW verpfänden

pledge: **in ~** *phr* FIN verpfändet

pledged *adj* LAW verpfändet

pledger *n* LAW Verpfänder, in *m,f*

pledging *n* LAW Verpfändung *f*

plenary: **~ chamber** *n* POL Plenarsaal *m*; **~ powers** *n pl* FIN unbeschränkte Vollmacht *f* des Geschäftsführers; **~ session** *n* POL Plenarsitzung *f*

plentifulness *n* GEN COMM Ergiebigkeit *f*

plinth *n* S&M Sockel *m*

plot 1. *n* GEN COMM Anschlag *m*, Gelände *nt*, Grundriß *m*, Grundstück *nt*, Intrige *f*, Verschwörung *f*, LAW Verschwörung *f*, PROP *of land* Baugrundstück *nt*, Grundstück *nt*, Parzelle *f*; **2.** *vt* MATH *graph* auftragen; **3.** *vi* GEN COMM, LAW sich verschwören

plot: **~ plan** *n* PROP Grundstücksplan *m*

plottage: **~ value** *n* PROP geschätzter Wert *m* von Grundstücken

plotter *n* COMP Kurvenzeichner *m*, Plotter *m*

plotting: **~ board** *n* COMP Zeichentisch *m*; **~ paper** *n* ADMIN Millimeterpapier *nt*; **~ pen** *n* COMP Zeichenstift *m*; **~ scale** *n* GEN COMM Zeichenmaßstab *m*; **~ table** *n* GEN COMM Zeichentisch *m*

plough back *vt BrE* FIN *profits* reinvestieren, GEN COMM *earnings* einbehalten, nicht ausschütten, thesaurieren, STOCK reinvestieren; ◆ **~ profits into a business** *BrE* FIN, STOCK reinvestieren

ploughback *n BrE* ACC einbehaltener Gewinn *nt*, reinvestierter Gewinn *m*

ploughed: **~-back profits** *n pl BrE* ACC thesaurierte Gewinne *m pl*

plow *AmE see plough BrE*

plowback *AmE see ploughback BrE*

Plowden: ~ **Committee** *n* ECON Plowden-Ausschuß *m*

plowed *AmE see ploughed BrE*

PLR *abbr (public lending right)* MEDIA gebührenpflichtiges Ausleihungsrecht *nt*

PLTC *abbr (port liner terms charge)* TAX, TRANSP *shipping* Hafenabgabe *f*, Hafengebühr *f*, Hafengeld *nt*, Hafenkosten *pl*, Terminabgabe *f*, Termingebühr *f*

plug 1. *n* COMP Stecker *m*, MEDIA, S&M *advertising* Gratiswerbesendung *f*, Schleichwerbung *f*; **2.** *vt* COMP einstecken; ♦ ~ **a gap** ECON eine Lücke schließen

plug in *vt* COMP einstecken

plug into *vt* COMP anschließen an [+acc]

plum: ~ **book** *n AmE* ADMIN Buch *nt* mit den begehrenswertesten Stellen

plunge 1. *n* FIN, STOCK Kurssturz *nt*, Reinfall *m*; **2.** *vi* GEN COMM plötzlich fallen

pluralism *n* HRM, POL *industrial relations* Pluralismus *m*

plus 1. *n* GEN COMM *symbol* Plus *nt*; **2.** *prep* GEN COMM, MATH plus

plus: ~-**minus conflict** *n* GEN COMM *business administration* Ambivalenzkonflikt *m*; ~ **sign** *n* MATH Pluszeichen *nt*; ~ **tick** *n* STOCK Mindestkursschwankung *f* aufwärts

plying: ~ **limit** *n* TRANSP *shipping* Verkehrsgrenze *f*

plywood *n* IND Sperrholz *nt*

p.m. *abbr (post meridiem)* GEN COMM nachmittags

PM *abbr* IND *(performance monitoring)* Betriebskontrolle *f*, Fertigungsüberwachung *f*, Leistungsüberwachung *f*, POL *(prime minister)* Premierminister, in *m,f*

PMG *abbr* HRM *(Paymaster General)* Beamter an der Spitze einer Abteilung des Schatzamtes, *(Postmaster General)* Postamtsvorsteher

PMSA *abbr AmE (primary metropolitan statistical area)* MATH primäres statistisches Großstadtgebiet *nt*

PMTS *abbr (predetermined motion time system)* ECON, FIN, MGMNT System *nt* vorgegebener Bewegungszeiten

PN *abbr (promissory note)* BANK, FIN Eigenwechsel *m*, Schuldanerkenntnis *f*, Schuldschein *m*, Solawechsel *m*, GEN COMM Schuldanerkenntnis *f*

P/N *abbr (promissory note)* BANK, FIN Eigenwechsel *m*, Schuldanerkenntnis *f*, Schuldschein *m*, Solawechsel *m*, GEN COMM Schuldanerkenntnis *f*

PNQ *abbr BrE (private notice question)* POL private Frage eines Parlamentsmitglieds

p.o. *abbr (payment order)* ACC Zahlungsauftrag *m*

PO *abbr* BANK *BrE (postal order)* Geldüberweisung *f* durch die Post, Postanweisung *f*, COMMS, GEN COMM *(post office)* Postamt *nt*, *BrE (postal order)* Geldüberweisung *f* durch die Post, Postanweisung *f*

POA *abbr (place of acceptance)* TRANSP Ort *m* der Abnahme

poach *vt* HRM *employees*, S&M *customers* abwerben

poaching *n* HRM Abwerbung *f*, *between trade unions* Mitgliederabwerbung *f* zwischen Gewerkschaften, S&M Abwerbung *f*

PO: ~ **box** *n (post office box)* COMMS Postfach *nt*

pocket *n* ECON *of the consumer* Geldbeutel *m*, GEN COMM Tasche *f*

pocketbook: ~ **issues** *n pl AmE infrml* POL politische Themen, die für die Wähler von wahrem Interesse sind, meist das ihnen zur Verfügung stehende Geld und dessen Kaufkraft betreffend

pocket: ~ **calculator** *n* COMP Taschenrechner *m*;

~ **money** *n* GEN COMM Taschengeld *nt*; ~ **out** *n* ECON tatsächliche Bezahlung *f*

POD *abbr* FIN *(proof of debt)* Forderungsnachweis *m*, TRANSP *(paid on delivery)* bezahlt bei Lieferung, *(proof of delivery)* Liefernachweis *m*, *(place of delivery)* Erfüllungsort *m*, Lieferort *m*

podium *n* GEN COMM, MEDIA Podium *nt*

point *n* FIN *commercial lending* ein Prozentpunkt *m*, 1 % des Nennwerts, GEN COMM *for discussion* Punkt *m*, *stance, position* Standpunkt *m*, *head of negotiating team* Leiter, in *m,f* eines Verhandlungsteams, leitender *m* Verhandlungspartner, leitende Verhandlungspartnerin *f*, POL Favorit *m*, STOCK Einheit *f* bei Kursschwankungen, Punkt *m*, 1 % des Nennwerts; ♦ **the ~ is still undecided** GEN COMM der Punkt ist noch offen, der Punkt ist noch unentschieden

point: ~ **of acceptance** *n* GEN COMM Annahmestelle *f*; ~ **of departure** *n* IMP/EXP, TRANSP Abfahrtsort *m*; ~ **elasticity** *n* ECON Punktelastizität *f*; ~ **of entry** *n* GEN COMM *into a country* Grenzübergangsstelle *f*, Zollhafen *m*, TRANSP Zollhafen *m*

pointer *n* COMP *indicator* Zeiger *m*, GEN COMM *hint* Hinweis *m*, Andeutung *f*, Tip *m*, Fingerzeig *m*, *presentation aid* Zeigestock *m*, *to a possible solution* Anzeichen *nt*, MGMNT Hinweis *m*

point: ~ **estimate** *n* MATH Punktschätzung *f*; ~ **of export** *n* IMP/EXP Exportort *m*; ~ **of law** *n* LAW Rechtsfrage *f*; ~-**of-sale** *n (POS)* S&M Ort *m* des Verkaufs, Point-of-Sale *m (POS)*, Verkaufsort *m*, Verkaufspunkt *m*, Verkaufsstelle *f*; ~-**of-sale advertising** *n* S&M Datenerfassungswerbung *f*, Werbung *f* am Verkaufsort, Werbung *f* am Verkaufspunkt; ~-**of-sale material** *n* S&M Material *nt* am Verkaufspunkt; ~-**of-sale promotion** *n* S&M Verkaufsförderung *f* am Verkaufsort, Werbung *f* am Verkaufspunkt; ~ **of origin** *n* TRANSP Herkunftsland *nt*, Herkunftsort *m*; ~ **price** *n* STOCK *options* Punktpreis *m*; ~ **of purchase** *n* S&M Verkaufsstelle *f*

points: ~ **rating** *n* HRM, INS, MGMNT Punktbewertung *f*; ~-**rating method** *n* HRM Punktbewertungsmethode *f*, INS Punktbewertungsmethode *f*, Stufenwertzahlverfahren *nt*, MGMNT Punktbewertungsmethode *f*; ~ **of suspension** *n pl* ADMIN vorläufige Einstellung *f*

point: ~ **of view** *n* GEN COMM Gesichtspunkt *m*, Standpunkt *m*, Meinung *f*

poison *n* ENVIR Gift *nt*; ~-**pen letter** *n* GEN COMM anonymer Brief *m*; ~ **pill** *n* ECON Anti-Übernahme-Strategie *f*, GEN COMM strategischer Schachzug einer von Übernahme bedrohten Firma, mit dem sie versucht, ihre Aktien weniger attraktiv für einen potentiellen Aufkäufer zu machen

poisonous *adj* ENVIR giftig

Poisson: ~ **distribution** *n* MATH *statistics* Poisson-Verteilung *f*

polar: ~ **angle** *n* MATH Abweichung *f*

polarization *n* COMMS, FIN Polarisation *f*, Polarisierung *f*

police *n* LAW Polizei *f*; ~ **force** *n* LAW Polizei *f*; ~ **intelligence** *n* LAW polizeilicher Nachrichtendienst *m*

policeman *n* POL Polizist *m*

police: ~ **power** *n* LAW *coercion* Polizeigewalt *f*; ~ **record** *n* LAW Strafregister *m*

policewoman *n* POL Polizistin *f*

policy *n* INS Police *f*, MGMNT Marschroute *f*, Methode *f*, Politik *f*, Verfahrensweise *f*, POL Politik *f*; ~ **of the big**

stick *n* *infrml* POL Politik *f* des großen Knüppels (*infrml*); **~ decision** *n* GEN COMM Grundsatzentscheidung *f*, MGMNT, POL Politikentscheidung *f*; **~ execution** *n* GEN COMM Ausführung *f* der Politik, POL Durchführung *f* einer politischen Maßnahme, Implementierung *f* einer bestimmten Politik, Umsetzung *f* einer bestimmten Politik; **~ and expenditure management system** *n* FIN geschäfts- und budgetpolitisches Managementsystem *nt*, Managementsystem *nt* für Geschäftspolitik und Ausgaben; **~ formulation** *n* GEN COMM, MGMNT politische Planung *f*, Zielformulierung *f*; **~ framework paper** *n* (*PFP*) ECON, STOCK politischer Rahmenbericht *m*; **~ harmonization** *n* ECON, POL politische Harmonisierung *f*; **~ lag** *n* POL zeitverzögerte Wirkung *f* einer bestimmten Politik; **~ loan** *n* INS *personal* Beleihung *f* einer Versicherungspolice, Policendarlehen *nt*; **~ of low interest rates** *n* S&M Niedrigzinspolitik *f*; **~ maker** *n* GEN COMM führende Persönlichkeit *f* des Wirtschaftslebens, POL Parteiideologe *m*, Parteiideologin *f*, Politikmacher, in *m,f*; **~ making** *n* MGMNT Politikgestaltung *f*, Politikmachen *nt*; **~ mix** *n* MGMNT Kombination *f* politischer Mittel, Methodenvielfalt *f*, POL Kombination *f* politischer Mittel; **~ of optimum** *n* ECON *cash holdings* Kassenhaltungspolitik *f*

Policy: **~ Planning Staff** *n* *AmE* (*PPS*) POL *Department of State* Abteilung für strategische Planung

policy: **~ statement** *n* GEN COMM Grundsatzerklärung *f*, Grundsatzprogramm *nt*, POL politische Willenserklärung *f*; **~ to bearer** *n* TAX Inhaberpolice *f*

Polish: **~ notation** *n* MATH polnische Schreibweise *f*

political *adj* POL politisch, staatspolitisch; **~ affairs** *n pl* POL Politik *f*, politische Angelegenheiten *f pl*, politische Beziehungen *f pl*; **~ business cycle** *n* ECON, POL Phillips-Kurve *f*; **~ change** *n* POL politischer Umschwung *m*; **~ climate** *n* POL politisches Klima *nt*; **~ cooperation** *n* POL politische Zusammenarbeit *f*; **~ donation** *n* POL parteipolitische Spende *f*; **~ economy** *n* ECON, POL Nationalökonomie *f*, politische Ökonomie *f*, POL Nationalökonomie *f*, Volkswirtschaft *f*; **~ fund** *n* HRM politischer Fonds *m*; **~ group** *n* POL politische Gruppe *f*, politische Gruppierung *f*, **~ institution** *n* POL politische Einrichtung *f*, politische Institution *f*; **~ issue** *n* POL politische Kernfrage *f*, politisches Problem *nt*; **~ levy** *n* POL parteipolitischer Beitrag *m*; **~ party** *n* POL politische Partei *f*; **~ practice** *n* POL politische Praxis *f*; **~ risk** *n* POL politisches Risiko *nt*; **~ situation** *n* POL politische Lage *f*, politische Situation *f*; **~ stability** *n* POL politische Stabilität *f*; **~ strike** *n* HRM politischer Streik *m*; **~ system** *n* POL politisches System *nt*; **~ thaw** *n* POL politisches Tauwetter *nt*; **~ thinking** *n* POL politisches Denken *nt*, politisches Bewußtsein *nt*; **~ union** *n* POL politische Vereinigung *f*, *European Union* politische Union *f*; **~ unity** *n* POL politische Einheit *f*

politician *n* POL Politiker, in *m,f*

politicize *vt* POL politisieren

politics *n* POL Politik *f*

poll *n* S&M Stichprobenerhebung *f*, Umfrage *f*

polling *n* COMP *network, modem* Polling *nt*, Sendeaufruf *m*, Umfragebetrieb *m*; **~ booth** *n* POL Wahlkabine *f*; **~ day** *n* POL Wahltag *m*; **~ station** *n* POL Wahllokal *nt*

poll: **~ tax** *n* *BrE* *obs* TAX, WEL Kopfsteuer *f*

pollutant *n* ENVIR Schadstoff *m*

pollute *vt* ENVIR belasten

polluted *adj* ENVIR belastet, verschmutzt; **~ air** *n* ENVIR verschmutzte Luft *f*

polluter *n* ENVIR Umweltverschmutzer *m*, Verschmutzer *m*; **~ pays principle** *n* ENVIR *international and EU legislation* Verursacherprinzip *nt*

pollution *n* ENVIR Belastung *f*, Umweltbelastung *f*, Verschmutzung *f*, Verunreinigung *f*, IND *of a product* Verunreinigung *f*; **~ charge** *n* ENVIR Verschmutzungsgebühr *f*; **~ control** *n* ENVIR, IND, POL *pollution* Reinhaltung *f*, Schadstoffbekämpfung *f*, Schadstoffkontrolle *f*, Umweltkontrolle *f*, Umweltschutz *m*

Pollution: **~ Liability Agreement Among Tanker Owners** *n* (*PLATO*) ENVIR, INS, LAW, TRANSP *shipping* Haftungsvereinbarung *f* zwischen Tankereignern in Bezug auf Umweltverschmutzung

pollution: **~ monitoring** *n* ENVIR, IND Umweltüberwachung *f*, Umweltverschmutzungsüberwachung *f*; **~ tax** *n* ENVIR, POL, TAX Umweltsteuer *f*

polycentrism *n* POL Polyzentrismus *m*

pony *n* *AmE* MEDIA Schlagzeilen *f pl* des Tages

pony up *vi* *infrml* GEN COMM zahlen

POO *abbr* (*Port Operations Officer*) HRM, TRANSP Hafenoperationsbeamte(r) *m* [decl. as adj], Hafenoperationsbeamtin *f*

pool 1. *n* ECON Kartell *nt* höherer Ordnung, FIN, GEN COMM gemeinsamer Fonds *m*, INS Pool *m*, Konsortium *nt*, Interessengemeinschaft *f*, STOCK Zusammenschluß *m* von Investoren zur Beeinflussung des Effekte; **2.** *vt* **~ resources** ECON Mittel vereinen, Mittel zusammenfassen

pool: **~ of costs** *n* GEN COMM Kostenblock *m*

pooling: **~ arrangements** *n pl* GEN COMM Gewinnpoolungsvertrag *m*; **~ of interests** *n* *AmE* (*cf merger accounting BrE*) ACC *balance sheets* Interessengemeinschaft *f*, Interessenvereinigung *f*; **~ system** *n* TRANSP Pooling-System *nt*

pools *n pl* LEIS *gambling on sports results* Toto *m or nt*

pool: **~ of vehicles** *n* TRANSP Fahrzeugpark *m*, Fuhrpark *m*, Wagenbestand *m*

poor 1. *adj* ECON *demand* schwach, *country, person* arm, mittellos, GEN COMM *quality* schlecht, HRM, WEL arm; **2. the ~** *n pl* WEL die Bedürftigen *pl*, die Armen *pl* (*obs*)

poor: **~ market** *n* ECON schleppender Absatz *m*; **~ person** *n* WEL Bedürftige(r) *mf* [decl. as adj]; **~ service** *n* S&M schlechter Service *m*

pop: **~-down menu** *n* COMP Balkenmenü *nt*

popular: **~ capitalism** *n* ECON, POL Volkskapitalismus *m*

popularist *n* POL Popularist *m*

popularity: **~ poll** *n* GEN COMM, MEDIA Meinungsumfrage *f* nach Beliebtheit bestimmter Personen; **~ rating** *n* MEDIA, POL Beliebtheitsgrad *m*, Popularität *f*; **~ ratings** *n pl* GEN COMM, MEDIA, POL Bewertung *f* bestimmter Personen nach deren Beliebtheit

popularize *vt* GEN COMM popularisieren

popular: **~ price** *n* S&M beliebter Preis *m*; **by ~ request** *phr* GEN COMM auf allgemeinen Wunsch

population *n* ECON Bevölkerung *f*, S&M *marketing* statistische Menge *f*; **~ census** *n* GEN COMM, MATH *statistics* Volkszählung *f*; **~ count** *n* ECON Bevölkerungszählung *f*; **~ density** *n* ECON Bevölkerungsdichte *f*; **~ explosion** *n* ECON

Bevölkerungsexplosion *f*; **~ policy** *n* ECON Bevölkerungspolitik *f*; **~ statistics** *n* *pl* ECON, MATH Bevölkerungsstatistik *f*; **~ structure** *n* ECON Bevölkerungsaufbau *m*

pop: **~-up** *n* S&M *advertising* hochklappbare Reklame *f*; **~-up menu** *n* COMP Balkenmenü *nt*

porcupine: **~ provisions** *n* *pl* FIN *takeovers* Übernahmeabwehr-Klausel *f*

pork *n* AmE *infrml* POL Gelder des Bundes für politisch interessante Personen oder Gegenden; **~ barrel** *n* AmE *infrml* POL Schweinetrog *m*; **~ barrel legislation** *n* AmE *infrml* LAW Gesetzgebung *f* im Interesse der örtlichen Wähler; **~ chop** *n* AmE *infrml* HRM Pöstchenjäger, in *m,f*

port *n* COMP Anschluß *m*, Port *m*, TRANSP Hafen *m*; ♦ **~ to port** (*P to P*) IMP/EXP, TRANSP Hafen-Hafen, von Hafen zu Hafen, Kai-Kai, von Kai zu Kai

portability *n* COMP Datenaustauschbarkeit *f*, Portabilität *f*, GEN COMM Tragbarkeit *f*

portable *adj* COMP *hardware, software* portabel, *software* portierbar, GEN COMM tragbar; **~ computer** *n* COMP tragbarer Rechner *m*, Aktentaschencomputer *m* (*obs*); **~ phone** *n* COMMS mobiles Telefon *nt*, tragbares Telefon *nt*, Mobiltelefon *nt*; **~ telephone** *n* COMMS mobiles Telefon *nt*, tragbares Telefon *nt*, Mobiltelefon *nt*

port: **~ access** *n* TRANSP Hafenzugang *m*; **~ agent** *n* TRANSP Hafenagent, in *m,f*

portal: **~-to-portal pay** *n* HRM Lohnvergütung *f* für den Anmarschweg zum Arbeitsplatz

port: **~ of arrival** *n* IMP/EXP, TRANSP Ankunftshafen *m*; **~ charges** *n* *pl* TAX, TRANSP Hafengebühren *f* *pl*; **~ control** *n* TRANSP Hafenkontrolle *f*; **~ of delivery** *n* TRANSP Löschplatz *m*; **~ of destination** *n* IMP/EXP, TRANSP Bestimmungshafen *m*; **~ director** *n* HRM, TRANSP Hafendirektor, in *m,f*; **~ disbursements** *n* *pl* TRANSP Hafenauslagen *f* *pl*; **~ of discharge** *n* TRANSP Entladehafen *m*; **~ dues** *n* *pl* (*PD*) IMP/EXP, TRANSP Hafengebühren *f* *pl*; **~ of entry** *n* IMP/EXP Einfahrtshafen *m*, Eingangshafen *m*, Zollabfertigungshafen *m*; **~ facilities** *n* *pl* TRANSP Hafenanlagen *f* *pl*, Hafeneinrichtungen *f* *pl*

portfolio *n* BANK, ECON Bestand an Wertpapieren *m*, Portefeuille *nt*, Wertpapierbestand *m*, FIN Bestand an Wertpapieren *m*, Portefeuille *nt*, Portfolio *nt*, Wertpapierbestand *m*, GEN COMM Aktenmappe *f*, Geschäftssystem *nt*, INS Bestand *m*, Portfolio *nt*, MGMNT Portefeuille *nt*, Portfolio *nt*, POL *of government activity* Geschäftsbereich *m*, Referat *nt*, Portefeuille *nt*, Ressort *nt*, S&M Portfolio *nt*, STOCK Portfolio *nt*, Bestand *m*; **~ analysis** *n* S&M Portfolio-Analyse *f*; **~ beta score** *n* STOCK *volatility of portfolio* Beta-Stand *m* des Portefeuilles; **~ income** *n* STOCK Portefeuille-Einkommen *nt*; **~ insurance** *n* INS Bestandsversicherung *f*, STOCK Absicherung *f* eines Wertpapierportefeuilles gegen Kursverlust; **~ investment** *n* FIN indirekte Investition *f*, Portfolio-Investition *f*, STOCK Direktinvestition *f* *pl*; **~ management** *n* BANK Vermögensverwaltung *f*, FIN Effektenverwaltung *f*, Portefeuille-Verwaltung *f*, Portfolio-Management *nt*, Vermögensverwaltung *f*, Wertpapierverwaltung *f*, MGMNT Effektenverwaltung *f*, Portefeuille-Verwaltung *f*, Wertpapierverwaltung *f*, STOCK Kauf *m* und Verkauf *m* von Effekten, Portfolio-Management *nt*, Vermögensverwaltung *f*; **~ management service** *n* BANK Vermögensverwal-

tungsservice *m*; **~ management theory** *n* FIN, STOCK *investment decision approach* Portfolio-Management-theorie *f*, Vermögensverwaltungstheorie *f*; **~ manager** *n* FIN, STOCK Effektenverwalter, in *m,f*, Portfolio-Manager, in *m,f*; **~ reinsurance** *n* INS Portfolio-Rückversicherung *f*, Rückversicherungsbestand *m*; **~ section** *n* FIN Portefeuille-Abschnitt *m*, STOCK Portfolio-Abteilung *f*; **~ selection** *n* FIN Anlagenauswahl *f*, optimales Depotmanagement *nt*, Portfolio-Selektion *f*; **~ split** *n* FIN Portefeuille-Aufteilung *f*; **~ theory** *n* FIN, STOCK *investment decision approach* Portfolio-Theorie *f*; **~ transfer** *n* INS Bestandsübertragung *f*, Portfolio-Übertragung *f*; **~ turnover** *n* FIN Portefeuille-Umschichtung *f*

port: **~ health authority** *n* TRANSP Hafengesundheitsbehörde *f*; **~ interchange** *n* TRANSP Hafenaustausch *m*

portion *n* GEN COMM Teil *m*

port: **~ layout** *n* TRANSP Hafenanordnung *f*; **~ liner terms charge** *n* (*PLTC*) TAX Hafenabgabe *f*, Hafengebühr *f*, Hafengeld *nt*, Hafenkosten *pl*, Hafenabgabe *f*, Hafengebühr *f*, Hafengeld *nt*, Hafenkosten *pl*, Terminabgabe *f*, Termingebühr *f*; **~ of loading** *n* TRANSP Verladehafen *m*

Port: **~ of London Authority** *n* (*PLA*) GEN COMM Londoner Hafenbehörde *f*

port: **~ management** *n* TRANSP Hafenverwaltung *f*; **~ manager** *n* HRM, TRANSP Hafenverwalter, in *m,f*; **~ of necessity** *n* TRANSP Nothafen *m*; **~ operation** *n* TRANSP Hafenbetrieb *m*

Port: **~ Operations Officer** *n* (*POO*) HRM, TRANSP Hafenoperationsbeamte(r) *m* [decl. as adj], Hafenoperationsbeamtin *f*

portrait *n* COMP *document layout*, MEDIA *page format* Hochformat *nt*, S&M *advertising, printing* Porträt *nt*

portray *vt* GEN COMM darstellen

port: **~ of registry** *n* TRANSP Heimathafen *m*; **~ of shipment** *n* TRANSP Verschiffungshafen *m*; **~ statistics** *n* *pl* TRANSP Hafenstatistik *f*; **~ surcharge** *n* TAX, TRANSP Hafenzuschlag *m*; **~ tariffs** *n* *pl* TAX, TRANSP Hafentarif *m*; **~ tax** *n* TAX, TRANSP Hafenabgabe *f*, Hafengebühr *f*, Hafensteuer *f*; **~ throughput**, **~ thruput** *AmE* *n* TRANSP Hafendurchsatzleistung *f*; **~ traffic** *n* TRANSP Hafenverkehr *m*; **~ traffic control** *n* TRANSP Hafenverkehrskontrolle *f*; **~ turnaround time** *AmE*, **~ turnround time** *BrE* *n* TRANSP Be- und Entladungszeit *f* im Hafen, Hafenumschlagszeit *f*, Liegezeit *f* im Hafen, Wendezeit *f*; **~ users' committee** *n* TRANSP Komitee *nt* der Hafenbenutzer

POS *abbr* (*point-of-sale*) GEN COMM, S&M Ort *m* des Verkaufs, POS (*Point-of-Sale*), Verkaufsstelle *f*, Verkaufsort *m*, Verkaufspunkt *m*; **~ advertising** *n* S&M Datenerfassungswerbung *f*, Werbung *f* am Verkaufsort, Werbung *f* am Verkaufspunkt

pose *vt* GEN COMM *question, problem* aufwerfen; ♦ **~ a threat** GEN COMM eine Bedrohung darstellen

position 1. *n* ACC Finanzlage *f*, ADMIN Stellung *f*, BANK Bestand *m*, FIN Position *f*, GEN COMM *point of view* Standpunkt *m*, *situation* Arbeitsplatz *m*, Lage *f*, HRM Position *f*, Stelle *f*, Stellung *f*, Amt *nt*, S&M Position *f*, STOCK Stellung *f*, Wertpapierposition *f*, Position *f*; ♦ **be in a ~ to** GEN COMM in der Lage sein zu:; 2. *vt* GEN COMM positionieren, STOCK auf eigene Rechnung kaufen, plazieren, eine Position eröffnen; ◆ ~ **a product** GEN COMM, S&M ein Produkt positionieren

position: ~ **account** *n* STOCK Positionskonto *nt*

positional: ~ **goods** *n pl* ECON Statusgüter *nt pl*

position: ~ **of authority** *n* HRM *work, hierarchy* verantwortungsvolle Stellung *f*; ~ **chart** *n* ECON Stellenplan *m*

positioning *n* FIN Positionierung *f*, S&M Plazierung *f*, Positionierung *f*, STOCK Positionierung *f*; ~ **of advertising** *n* S&M Anzeigenplazierung *f*; ~ **theory** *n* S&M Positionierungstheorie *f*

position: ~-**keeping** *n* STOCK Positionsführung *f*; ~ **limit** *n* STOCK Positionslimit *nt*; ~ **media** *n* S&M Positionsmedien *nt pl*; ~ **net credit** *n* STOCK *options* Nettokreditposition *f*; ~ **net delta** *n* STOCK *options* Netto-Delta-Position *f*; ~ **paper** *n* POL Grundsatzpapier *nt*, Positionsmeldung *nt*, richtungsweisende Stellungnahme *f*, Standortklärung *f*; ~ **schedule bond** *n* INS Kaution *f* zur Ausübung einer bestimmten Tätigkeit; ~ **squaring** *n* STOCK Positionsbereinigung *f*; ~ **trader** *n* STOCK Spekulant, in *m,f*

positive *adj* GEN COMM *favourable* konstruktiv, positiv; ◆ **be ~ about** GEN COMM überzeugt sein von

positive: ~ **cash flow** *n* ACC, FIN, TAX positiver Cashflow *m*; ~ **confirmation** *n* ACC *auditing* positive Bestätigung *f*, vorbehaltlose Bestätigung *f*; ~ **correlation** *n* MATH *between two variables* positive Korrelation *f*; ~ **discrimination** *n* BrE (*cf affirmative action AmE*) ADMIN, ECON, HRM, POL aktive Förderungsmaßnahmen *f pl*, positive Diskriminierung *f*; ~ **economics** *n* ECON *econometrics* positive Wirtschaftswissenschaften *f pl*; ~ **feedback** *n* ECON positive Rückmeldung *f*, positive Reaktion *f*, positives Echo *nt*; ~ **integer** *n* MATH positive ganze Zahl *f*

positively *adv* GEN COMM positiv

positive: ~ **monetary compensatory amount** *n* FIN positiver geldwerter Ausgleichsbetrag *m*; ~ **neutrality** *n* POL eindeutige Neutralität *f*, positive Neutralität *f*; ~ **response** *n* GEN COMM positive Antwort *f*; ~ **sum game** *n* ECON Positivsummenspiel *nt*; ~ **yield curve** *n* ECON positive Zinsertragskurve *f*

POS: ~ **machine** *n* S&M Datenerfassungskasse *f*; ~ **material** *n* S&M Material *nt* am Verkaufspunkt; ~ **promotion** *n* S&M Werbung *f* am Verkaufspunkt

possession *n* LAW *property* Besitz *m*

possessor *n* LAW Besitzer, in *m,f*

possessory: ~ **claim** *n* LAW Besitzanspruch *m*; ~ **lien** *n* ECON, LAW Rückbehaltungsrecht *nt*

possibilism *n* POL Possibilismus *m*, Strategie *f* des Möglichen

possibility *n* GEN COMM Möglichkeit *f*

possible *adj* GEN COMM möglich

post 1. *n* COMMS Post *f*, GEN COMM Arbeitsplatz *m*, HRM Posten *m*, Stelle *f*, Stellung *f*, STOCK Stand *m*; ◆ **by ~** COMMS auf dem Postweg; **by the same ~** GEN COMM mit gleicher Post; **2.** *vt* ACC ausweisen, buchen, eintragen, verbuchen, ADMIN anschlagen, GEN COMM aufgeben, abschicken, *through letterbox* einstecken, einwerfen, HRM aufstellen, STOCK *a margin deposit* eintragen; ◆ ~ **an entry** ACC einen Eintrag verbuchen, einen Posten einbuchen; ~ **margin** STOCK *in order to open a position by selling an option* Marge ankündigen; ~ **up an account** BANK ein Konto abschließen; **3.** *prep* GEN COMM nach; ◆ ~ **meridiem** (*p.m.*) GEN COMM nachmittags

postage *n* COMMS Frankierung *f*, Porto *nt*, Portospesen *pl*; ◆ ~ **and packing** (*p&p*) COMMS Porto *nt* und Verpackung *f*; ~ **paid** COMMS franko, Gebühr bezahlt, Porto bezahlt, portofrei, postfrei, gebührenfrei

postage: ~ **due** *n* COMMS Nachporto *nt*, Nachgebühr *f*; ~-**due stamp** *n* COMMS Nachgebührstempel *m*; ~-**free** *adj* COMMS, GEN COMM franko ~ **meter** *n* COMMS Frankiermaschine *f*, GEN COMM Freistempler *m*; ~-**paid impression** *n* (*PPI*) COMMS Postgebührenstempel *m*; ~ **rate** *n* COMMS Postgebühr *f*; ~ **stamp** *n* COMMS Briefmarke *f*

postal: ~ **address** *n* COMMS Postanschrift *f*, Postzustelladresse *f*; ~ **ballot** *n* HRM, POL Briefwahl *f*; ~ **checking account** *n* AmE BANK Postgirokonto *nt*; ~ **export** *n* IMP/EXP Export *m* per Post; ~ **money order** *n* AmE (*cf postal order BrE*) BANK, FIN, GEN COMM Geldüberweisung *f* durch die Post, Postanweisung *f*; ~ **order** *n* BrE (*PO, cf postal money order AmE*) BANK, FIN, GEN COMM Geldüberweisung *f* durch die Post, Postanweisung *f*; ~ **remittance** *n* ACC Postüberweisung *f*; ~ **service** *n* COMMS Postdienst *m*, Postverkehr *m*; ~ **vote** *n* POL Briefwahl *f*, Stimmabgabe *f* per Post; ~ **worker** *n* HRM Postarbeiter, in *m,f*; ~ **wrapper** *n* ADMIN Streifband *nt*; ~ **zone** *n* COMMS Postleitzone *f*, Postzustellbereich *m*

post: ~-**balance-sheet event** *n* ACC Ereignis *f* nach dem Bilanzstichtag

postbox *n* BrE (*cf mailbox AmE*) ADMIN, COMMS Briefeinwurf *m*, Briefkasten *m*

post: ~-**capitalize** *vt* ECON nachaktivieren

postclosing: ~ **trial balance** *n* ACC berichtigte Probebilanz *f*, Probebilanz *f* nach Bilanzstichtag

postcode *n* BrE (*cf zip code AmE*) COMMS, GEN COMM Postleitzahl *f* (*PLZ*)

post-Communist *adj* ECON, POL nachkommunistisch, postkommunistisch

postdate *vt* COMMS nachdatieren, später datieren, GEN COMM *cheque, document* vordatieren

postdated *adj* (*PD*) COMMS nachdatiert, GEN COMM vordatiert

posted *adj* ADMIN, HRM versetzt; ~ **price** *n* ECON, GEN COMM *of oil* Erdöllistenpreis *m*

post: ~-**entry** *n* IMP/EXP *shipping* Nachtrag *m*, Nachverzollung *f*, TRANSP *shipping* Nachverzollung *f*; ~-**entry discrimination** *n* ECON Diskriminierung *f* nach Einstellung, nachträgliche Diskriminierung *f*

poster *n* GEN COMM, S&M Werbeplakat *nt*, Anschlag *m*, Plakat *nt*; ~ **advertising** *n* S&M Plakatwerbung *f*; ~ **display** *n* S&M *advertising* Plakatwerbung *f*

poste restante 1. *adj* COMMS postlagernd; **2.** *n* COMMS Aufbewahrungsstelle *f* für postlagernde Sendungen

poste restante: ~ **letter** *n* COMMS postlagernder Brief *m*

poster: ~ **site** *n* S&M *advertising* Anschlagstelle *f*; ~ **site classification** *n* S&M Anschlagstellenklassifizierung *f*; ~ **size** *n* S&M Plakatgröße *f*

post-free 1. *adj* COMMS gebührenfrei; **2.** *adv* COMMS gebührenfrei

postgraduate *n* GEN COMM Hochschulabsolvent, in *m,f*, *PhD candidate* Doktorand, in *m,f*

posthedging: ~ **transaction** *n* ECON Sicherungsgeschäft *nt*

post: ~-**industrial society** *n* ECON nachindustrielle Gesellschaft *f*

posting n COMMS Posteinlieferung f, job Versetzung f, ACC Verbuchung f, GEN COMM, HRM Versetzung f, LAW Aufstellen nt, commercial Buchungsverfahren nt, Eintragungsverfahren nt, civil procedure öffentliche Bekanntmachung f; ~ **error** n ACC Fehlbuchung f

post-Keynesian adj ECON post-Keynesianisch

postman n BrE (cf mailman AmE) COMMS Briefträger m, Postbote m

postmark 1. n COMMS Datumsstempel m, Poststempel m, Tagesstempel m; **2.** vi COMMS letter stempeln

Postmaster: ~ **General** n (PMG) HRM Postamtsvorsteher, in m,f

post: ~ **office** n (PO) COMMS Post f, Postamt nt; ~ **office box** n (PO box) COMMS Postfach nt, Schließfach nt; ~ **office savings bank** n BrE BANK ≈ Postsparkasse f

postpaid adj (p.p.) COMMS im voraus bezahlt, Porto bezahlt, portofrei, postfrei

postpone vt GEN COMM aufschieben, verschieben, vertagen, zurückstellen; ♦ ~ **sth for a week** GEN COMM etw um eine Woche verschieben

postponement n GEN COMM Aufschub m, Verschiebung f, Vertagung f, Zurückstellung f

post: ~-**purchase advertising** n S&M Werbung f nach dem Verkauf; ~-**purchase remorse** n S&M Reue f nach dem Kauf; ~-**sales service** n S&M Kundendienst m

postscript n (ps., PS) COMMS Nachschrift f, Nachtrag m, Postscriptum nt (P.S.), GEN COMM Nachsatz m

PostScript®: ~ **printer** n COMP PostScript®-Drucker m

post: ~-**shipment inspection** n TRANSP Inspektion f nach Versand; ~ **stacker** n TRANSP Stapeleinrichtung f; ~ **test** n S&M Abschlußtest m

postulate vt GEN COMM postulieren

postwar: ~ **boom** n ECON Nachkriegsaufschwung m, Nachkriegsboom m; ~ **period** n ECON Nachkriegszeit f

potential 1. adj GEN COMM möglich, potentiell; **2.** n GEN COMM Hilfsquelle f, Leistungsvermögen nt, Möglichkeit f, Potential nt, capacity Kapazität f; ♦ **have ~** GEN COMM über Potential verfügen

potential: ~ **buyer** n S&M potentielle Käuferin f, potentieller Käufer m; ~ **commitment** n GEN COMM mögliche Verbindlichkeit f, mögliche Verpflichtung f; ~ **customer** n ECON Interessent, in m,f; ~ **income** n ECON potentielles Einkommen nt; ~ **investor** n STOCK potentielle Anlegerin f, potentieller Anleger m

potentially adv GEN COMM potentiell; ~ **exempt transfers** n pl BrE (PETs) TAX potentiell befreite Übertragungen f pl

potential: ~ **output** n ECON potentieller Ausstoß m einer Volkswirtschaft; ~ **profit** n STOCK potentieller Gewinn m; ~ **trouble spot** n GEN COMM Schwachstelle f; ~ **user** n S&M potentieller Nutzer m

pound n (lb) ECON pound sterling Pfund nt, GEN COMM Pfund nt (Pfd.); ♦ ~ **spot and forward** ECON Kassakurs und Terminkurs des Pfundes

pounds: ~ **per square inch** n pl (PSI) TRANSP Pfund nt pro Quadratzoll

pour autre vie phr LAW auf die Lebensdauer eines Dritten

pour: ~ **money into** phr ECON investieren in [+acc]

poverty n WEL Armut f, Not f; ~ **line** n WEL Armutsgrenze f; ~-**stricken** adj FIN verarmt; ~ **trap** n WEL Armutsfalle f

power 1. n COMP electricity Strom m, Spannung f, ENVIR Spannung f, GEN COMM Macht f, capability Vermögen nt, authority, authorization Befugnis f, Ermächtigung f, IND Energie f, Kraft f, Leistung f, electrical Netzstrom m, Starkstrom m, Spannung f; ♦ **give sb a ~ of attorney** LAW jdm eine Vollmacht erteilen; **in ~** POL government an der Macht; **2.** vt COMP, IND betreiben

power: ~ **of appointment** n GEN COMM Ernennungsrecht nt, LAW Ernennungsbefugnis f; ~ **of attorney** n (PA) LAW Bevollmächtigung f, schriftliche Vollmacht f, Vollmacht f, certificate Vollmachtsurkunde f; ~ **of disposal** n LAW Verfügungsgewalt f; ~ **of disposition** n LAW Verfügungsgewalt f; ~ **failure** n COMP Netzausfall m, Stromausfall m, Spannungsausfall m

powerful adj GEN COMM überzeugend, bedeutend, kraftvoll, leistungsstark, influential einflußreich

power: ~-**generating capacity** n IND Kraftwerksleistung f; ~ **generation** n IND Energieerzeugung f, Krafterzeugung f; ~ **industries** n pl IND Energiewirtschaft f; ~ **pack** n TRANSP Stromversorgungseinheit f; ~ **of persuasion** n GEN COMM Überredungskunst f; ~ **politics** n pl POL Machtpolitik f, Realpolitik f; ~ **of recourse** n LAW Regreßbefugnis f; ~ **of sale** n LAW property Veräußerungsbefugnis f; ~ **station** n IND Elektrizitätswerk nt (E-Werk), Kraftwerk nt; ~ **struggle** n POL Machtkampf m; ~ **surge** n COMP Spannungsstoß m; ~ **to sign** n ADMIN Zeichnungsberechtigung f; ~ **to weight ratio** n TRANSP spezifisches Leistungsgewicht nt

powering: ~ **up** n COMP Einschalten nt

pp abbr (per procurationem) GEN COMM pp. (per procura), ppa. (per procura)

p.p. abbr (postpaid) COMMS, GEN COMM im voraus bezahlt, Porto bezahlt, portofrei

PPB abbr (planning, programming and budgeting) ACC, ECON, FIN, MGMNT PPB (Planung, Programmierung und Budgetierung)

PPBS abbr (planning, programming and budgeting system) ACC, ECON, FIN, MGMNT PPB-System nt (Planungs-, Programmierungs- und Budgetierungssystem)

ppd abbr (prepaid) FIN, GEN COMM, S&M, TRANSP vorausbezahlt

PPF abbr ECON (production possibility frontier) Produktionsmöglichkeitenkurve f, FIN (Project Preparation Facility) Projektvorbereitungsfazilität f

PPI abbr COMMS (postage paid impression) Postgebührenstempel m, ECON (producer price index) econometrics Erzeugerpreisindex m

ppm abbr (parts per million) GEN COMM ppm (partes per millionem)

PPP abbr ECON (purchasing power parity) Kaufkraftparität f, MGMNT (profit and performance planning) Gewinn- und Leistungsplanung f, WEL (Private Patients Plan) privater Krankenversicherungsvertrag

PPS abbr AmE (Policy Planning Staff) POL Department of State Abteilung für strategische Planung

PQLI abbr (physical quality of life index) ECON econometrics Index m der physischen Lebensqualität

pr. abbr (price) GEN COMM Pr. (Preis)

PR abbr (public relations) HRM, S&M Öffentlichkeitsarbeit f, PR (Public Relations)

practical adj GEN COMM praktisch, Nutz-; ~ **application** n GEN COMM Nutzanwendung f; ~ **capacity** n ECON Betriebsoptimum nt, praktisch realisierbare Kapazität f; ~ **politics** n pl POL Politik f in Aktion, praktische

Politik *f*, Realpolitik *f*; ~ **use** *n* HRM *application of skills* praktischer Nutzen *m*

practically *adv* GEN COMM praktisch

practice 1. *n* LAW Praxis *f*; ◆ **in** ~ GEN COMM in der Praxis; **2.** *vt AmE see* practise *BrE*; **3.** *vi AmE see* practise *BrE*

practicing *AmE see* practising *BrE*

practise 1. *vt BrE* GEN COMM, LAW ausüben; ◆ ~ **a profession** *BrE* ECON einen freien Beruf ausüben; **2.** *vi BrE* GEN COMM *exercise* üben, LAW praktizieren; ◆ ~ **as** *BrE* LAW tätig sein als

practising *adj BrE* LAW praktizierend; ~ **lawyer** *n BrE* LAW Anwalt *m*, Anwältin *f*

PR: ~ **agency** *n* S&M PR-Agentur *f*, *advertising* Werbeagentur *f*

pragmatic *adj* GEN COMM, POL pragmatisch

praxeology *n* ECON Praxeologie *f*

PRD *abbr* (*public relations department*) HRM, S&M Abteilung *f* für Öffentlichkeitsarbeit

pre-acquisition: ~ **profits** *n pl* ACC Gewinn *m* vor Akquisition, vor der Übernahme erzielte Gewinne *m pl*

preamble *n* GEN COMM Einleitungsformeln *f pl*, *to agreement, contract* Vorrede *f*, MGMNT, LAW Präambel *f*, PATENTS Einleitung *f*, Vorbemerkung *f*

pre-approach *n* S&M Vertragsvorbereitung *f*

pre-arranged *adj* GEN COMM fixiert, im voraus vereinbart

prebill 1. *n* S&M Vorfakturierung *f*; **2.** *vt* S&M vorfakturieren

prebilling *n* S&M Vorfakturierung *f*

Prebisch-Singer: ~ **thesis** *n* ECON Prebisch-Singer-These *f*

pre-Budget *phr* ECON vor Verabschiedung des Haushalts

pre-campaign: ~ **exposure** *n* S&M Ausstellung *f* vor Beginn einer Werbekampagne

precautionary: ~ **demand for money** *n* ECON Vorsorgemotiv *nt* der Geldnachfrage; ~ **motive** *n* GEN COMM Vorsorgemotiv *nt*; ~ **saving** *n* ECON Vorsorgesparen *nt*

precede *vt* GEN COMM über etw stehen, vorangehen, vorausgehen

precedence: ~ **rating** *n* ECON Dringlichkeitsstufe *f*

precedent *n* LAW Präzedenzfall *m*

preceding *adj* GEN COMM vorangehend, vorhergehend; ~ **speaker** *n* GEN COMM Vorredner, in *m,f*; ~ **year** *n* GEN COMM Vorjahr *nt*

precharacterizing: ~ **portion** *n* PATENTS Vorkennzeichen *nt*, vorkennzeichnender Teil *m*, Vormerkmal *nt*

precious: ~ **metal** *n* GEN COMM Edelmetall *nt*; ~ **metal account** *n* BANK Edelmetallkonto *nt*; ~ **stones** *n pl* GEN COMM Edelsteine *m pl*

precise *adj* GEN COMM präzise, genau, pünktlich

precision: ~ **engineering** *n* IND Feinmechanik *f*, Feintechnik *f*, Präzisionstechnik *f*

preclude *vt* GEN COMM ausschließen; ◆ ~ **misunderstanding** GEN COMM Mißverständnisse ausschließen

preclusive: ~ **buying** *n* S&M Ausschlußkauf *m*

precoded *adj* S&M präkodiert

precompute *vt* FIN *interest in instalment loans* vorausberechnen

precondition *n* GEN COMM Vorbedingung *f*, Bedingung *f*

pre-currency: ~ **reform claims** *n pl* FIN Altlasten *f pl*

predate 1. *n* S&M vordatierte Ausgabe *f*; **2.** *vt* GEN COMM *document, cheque* rückdatieren, vorausgehen, zurückdatieren

predated *adj* GEN COMM rückdatiert

predating *n* GEN COMM Rückdatierung *f*

predator *n* GEN COMM raubgierige Geschäftsfrau *f*, raubgieriger Geschäftsmann *m*

predatory: ~ **competition** *n* GEN COMM rücksichtsloser Wettbewerb *m*, Verdrängungswettbewerb *m*; ~ **pricing policy** *n* ECON Verdrängungswettbewerb *m*

predecessor: ~ **in title** *n* PATENTS Rechtsvorgänger, in *m,f*, Voreigentümer, in *m,f*, vorherige Eigentümerin *f*, vorheriger Eigentümer *m*

predelivery: ~ **inspection** *n* (*PDI*) TRANSP Inspektion *f* vor Lieferung

predetermine *vt* GEN COMM, MGMNT, STOCK vorausbestimmen, vorher ermitteln, vorgeben

predetermined *adj* GEN COMM, MGMNT, STOCK vorausbestimmt, vorher ermittelt, vorgegeben; ~ **motion time system** *n* (*PMTS*) ECON, FIN, MGMNT System *nt* vorgegebener Bewegungszeiten; ~ **price** *n* STOCK festgesetzter Preis *m*

predict *vt* GEN COMM prognostizieren, vorausberechnen, vorhersagen, vorhersehen

predictable *adj* GEN COMM berechenbar, voraussagbar, vorhersehbar; ~ **life** *n* ACC *of business assets* vorhersehbare Laufzeit *f*

predicted *adj* GEN COMM prognostiziert, vorausberechnet, vorhergesagt, vorhergesehen; ~ **costs** *n pl* ECON, GEN COMM Plankosten *pl*, Sollkosten *pl*

prediction *n* GEN COMM Voraussage *f*, Vorausschau *f*, Vorhersage *f*, Prognose *f*

pre-eminent *adj* GEN COMM überragend, herausragend, hervorragend

pre-emptive: ~ **bid** *n* STOCK großzügiges Übernahmeangebot, das mögliche Mitbieter abschreckt; ~ **right** *n AmE* LAW *commercial* Vorkaufsrecht *nt*

pre-emptor *n AmE* LAW Erwerber, in *m,f* auf Grund eines Vorkaufsrechts

pre-empt: ~ **spot** *n* S&M durch Ausübung des Vorkaufsrechtes erworbener Werbespot *m*

pre-entry: ~ **closed shop** *n BrE* ECON Diskriminierung *f* vor der Einstellung; ~ **discrimination** *n* ECON Diskriminierung *f* vor der Einstellung

pre-existing: ~ **use** *n* PROP frühere Nutzung *f*

pref. *abbr* (*preference*) GEN COMM Bevorzugung *f*, Vorrang *m*, Vorzug *m*

prefab: ~ **house** *n* PROP Fertighaus *nt*

prefabricated *adj* PROP vorgefertigt; ~ **house** *n* PROP Fertighaus *nt*

prefer *vt* ACC, FIN, GEN COMM, S&M bevorzugen

preference *n* (*pref.*) GEN COMM Bevorzugung *f*, Vorrang *m*, Vorzug *m*, *inclination* Neigung *f*; ~ **dividend** *n BrE* (*cf preferred dividend AmE*) ACC Vorzugsdividende *f*; ~ **item** *n* GEN COMM Präferenzgut *nt*; ~ **offer** *n* ECON Vorzugsangebot *nt*; ~ **share** *n BrE* (*cf preferred stock AmE*) FIN, STOCK Vorzugsaktie *f*; ~ **system** *n* ECON Bedarfsstruktur *f*

preferential: ~ **form** *n* STOCK Sonderformular *nt*; ~ **hiring** *n AmE* GEN COMM bevorzugte Einstellung *f*; ~ **import** *n* IMP/EXP begünstigte Einfuhr *f*; ~ **interest rate** *n* BANK Vorzugszinssatz *m*, TRANSP Präferenzseefrachtrate *f*; ~ **interest rates** *n pl* BANK Vorzugszinsen *m pl*; ~ **price** *n* ECON Vorzugspreis *m*;

~ **rate** *n* GEN COMM Präferenzsatz *m*; ~ **rehiring** *n* LAW *Civil Rights Act* bevorzugte Wiedereinstellung *f*; ~ **right** *n* STOCK Vorrecht *nt*; ~ **shop** *n* HRM *industrial relations* Betrieb, der bevorzugt Gewerkschaftsmitglieder einstellt; ~ **terms** *n pl* GEN COMM Vorzugskonditionen *f pl*; ~ **treatment** *n* GEN COMM Bevorzugung *f*, Vorzugsbehandlung *f*

preferred *adj* ACC, FIN, GEN COMM, S&M bevorzugt; ~ **dividend** *n AmE (cf preference dividend BrE)* ACC Vorzugsdividende *f*; ~ **dividend coverage** *n* ACC bevorzugte Dividendendeckung *f*; ~ **habitat theory** *n* FIN Theorie *f* der bevorzugten Wohngebiete; ~ **position** *n* S&M bevorzugte Position *f*; ~ **risk** *n* INS bevorzugtes Risiko *nt*; ~ **stock** *n AmE (cf preference share BrE)* FIN, STOCK Vorzugsaktie *f*

prejudice 1. *n* GEN COMM *damage* Befangenheit *f*, Voreingenommenheit *f*, Vorurteil *nt*; **2.** *vt* LAW beeinflussen

prejudiced *adj* GEN COMM voreingenommen

prejudicial *adj* GEN COMM nachteilig, schädlich; ◆ **be ~ to** GEN COMM sich nachteilig auswirken auf

preliminary *n* GEN COMM vorbereitende Maßnahme *f*; ~ **agreement** *n* LAW *contract* Vorvertrag *m*; ~ **budget** *n* FIN Voranschlag *m*; ~ **calculation** *n* ACC Vorkalkulation *f*; ~ **costing** *n* ACC Vorkalkulation *f*; ~ **draft** *n* FIN Vorentwurf *m*; ~ **estimate** *n* GEN COMM Vorausschätzung *f*; ~ **examination** *n* PATENTS Vorprüfung *f*, Voruntersuchung *f*; ~ **expenses** *n pl* ACC Gründungskosten *pl*; ~ **investigation** *n* LAW vorläufige Untersuchung *f*; ~ **pages** MEDIA Vorbemerkungen *f pl*; ~ **prospectus** *n* STOCK vorläufiger Emissionsprospekt *m*; ~ **research** *n* PATENTS amtliche Vorprüfung *f*; ~ **statement** *n* LAW Vorbemerkung *f*; ~ **VAT return** *n BrE* TAX USt-Voranmeldung *f*

preloading: ~ **inspection** *n* TRANSP Inspektion *f* vor Verladung

premature *adj* GEN COMM verfrüht, voreilig, vorzeitig

premerger: ~ **notification duty** *n* LAW Anzeigepflicht *f* bei Fusionen

premiere *n* LEIS, MEDIA Premiere *f*

premise 1. *n* GEN COMM Voraussetzung *f*; ◆ **on the ~ that** GEN COMM unter der Voraussetzung, daß; **2.** *vt* GEN COMM postulieren

premises *n pl* IND Grund und Boden, Standort *m*, PROP Anwesen *nt*, Gelände *nt*, Grundstück *nt*, *building* Räumlichkeiten *f pl*

premium *n* FIN Agio *nt*, GEN COMM Aufschlag *m*, Bonifikation *f*, HRM Zulage *f*, INS Prämie *f*, S&M *advertising* Vorzugsangebot *nt*, STOCK Aufgeld *nt*; ◆ **at a ~** FIN, STOCK *shares* mit einem Agio

premium: ~ **adjustment** *n* INS Prämienberichtigung *f*; ~ **bond** *n* BANK, FIN Prämienanleihe *f*, STOCK Agioanleihe *f*, Prämienanleihe *f*; ~ **bonus** *n* HRM, STOCK Prämienlohn *m*; ~ **bonus scheme** *n* HRM Prämienlohnsystem *nt*; ~ **default** *n* FIN, INS Prämienverzug *m*; ~ **deferral** *n* INS Prämienstundung *f*; ~ **for the call** *n* GEN COMM, STOCK Vorprämie *f*; ~ **grade gasoline** *n AmE (cf four-star petrol BrE)* ENVIR Qualitätsbenzin *nt*, Superbenzin *nt*, Superkraftstoff *m*; ~ **grading** *n* GEN COMM Beitragsstaffelung *f*; ~ **holiday** *n* INS Prämienfreijahre *nt pl*; ~ **income** *n* INS Beitragseinzug *m*, Prämieneinnahme *f*; ~ **increase** *n* INS Prämienerhöhung *f*; ~ **loan** *n* BANK Beleihung *f* einer Versicherungspolice; ~ **maturity** *n* FIN Prämienfälligkeit

f; ~ **offer** *n* S&M *marketing* Sonderangebot *nt*; ~ **on exchange** *n* FIN Devisenaufgeld *nt*; ~ **over bond value** *n* STOCK Prämie *f* oberhalb des Anleihewertes; ~ **over conversion value** *n* STOCK Prämie *f* oberhalb des Umwandlungswertes; ~ **pay** *n* HRM Lohnzuschlag *m*; ~ **price** *n* S&M Höchstpreis *m*; ~ **pricing** *n* S&M Höchstpreisfestlegung *f*; ~ **quotations** *n* STOCK *Eurodollar options contract specifications* Prämiennotierung *f*; ~ **raid** *n* STOCK Höchstaufkäufe *m pl*; ~ **rate** *n* INS Prämiensatz *m*, Tarifbeitrag *m*, Bedarfsprämie *f*, STOCK Prämiensatz *m*; ~ **reserve** *n* FIN Deckungsrückstellung *f*, Prämienreserve *f*, INS Deckungskapital *nt*

Premium: ~ **Savings Bond** *n BrE* FIN Prämiensparbrief *m*, Sparprämienanleihe *f*

premium: ~ **statement** *n* FIN Beitragsabrechnung *f*, Prämienabrechnung *f*; ~ **transfer** *n* INS Beitragsübertrag *m*

prenuptial: ~ **agreement** *n* LAW Ehevertrag *m*, vorehelicher Vertrag *m*; ~ **contract** *n* LAW Ehevertrag *m*, vorehelicher Vertrag *m*

preoccupied *adj* GEN COMM *with one's problems* beschäftigt

pre-operating: ~ **expenses** *n pl* ACC, FIN Anlaufkosten *pl*

preowned *adj* GEN COMM *motor trade* aus zweiter Hand

prepackage *vt* S&M vorverpacken

prepackaged *adj* GEN COMM, S&M *goods* vorverpackt

prepackaging *n* S&M Vorverpackung *f*

prepaid *adj (ppd)* FIN, GEN COMM, S&M, TRANSP vorausbezahlt; ~ **charge** *n* TRANSP vorausbezahlte Gebühr *f*; ~ **charges** *n pl* TRANSP vorausbezahlte Kosten *pl*; ~ **costs** *n pl* S&M vorausbezahlte Kosten *pl*; ~ **expenses** *n pl* ACC transitorischer Posten *m pl*; ~ **interest** *n* FIN vorausbezahlte Zinsen *m pl*; ~ **ticket advice** *n (PTA)* TRANSP Mitteilung *f* bezüglich vorausbezahlter Fahrscheine

preparation *n* ACC Aufstellung *f*, GEN COMM Ausarbeitung *f*, Vorbereitung *f*, Aufstellung *f*, Erstellung *f*, MGMNT Erarbeitung *f*, Erstellung *f*, Vorbereitung *f*; ◆ **in ~** MEDIA in Vorbereitung sein

preparation: ~ **of a balance sheet** *n* ACC Bilanzaufstellung *f*

preparatory: ~ **work** *n* GEN COMM Vorarbeit *f*, vorbereitende Arbeiten *f pl*

prepare *vt* ACC aufstellen, GEN COMM aufstellen, erstellen, vorbereiten, ausarbeiten, erarbeiten; ◆ ~ **a budget** MGMNT ein Budget aufstellen; ~ **a schedule of assets** FIN die Vermögensaufstellung vorbereiten; ~ **the statement of net assets** FIN die Vermögensaufstellung vorbereiten

prepay *vt* ACC, BANK, FIN, TAX vorauszahlen

prepayment *n* ACC Vorauszahlung *f*, BANK Vorauszahlung *f*, Vorfälligkeit *f*, FIN Vorauszahlung *f*, GEN COMM Anzahlung *f*, TAX Vorauszahlung *f*, Vorauskasse *f*; ~ **clause** *n* FIN Klausel, die den Schuldner zur vorzeitigen Rückzahlung eines Darlehens berechtigt; ~ **penalty** *n* BANK Vorfälligkeitsentschädigung *f*; ~ **privilege** *n* FIN vorzeitiges Tilgungsprivileg *nt*

preplan *vt* GEN COMM vorausplanen

preplanned *adj* GEN COMM vorausgeplant

preplanning *n* GEN COMM Vorausplanung *f*

preproduction: ~ **cost** *n* ACC Vorlaufkosten *pl*

prerecorded *adj* LEIS, MEDIA im voraus aufgezeichnet,

vorher aufgezeichnet; **~ broadcast** n MEDIA Aufnahme f, Aufzeichnung f, im voraus aufgezeichnete Sendung f

prerequisite n GEN COMM Bedingung f, Erfordernis nt, Voraussetzung f, Vorbedingung f

preretirement: **~ pension** n FIN Vorruhestandsrente f, vorzeitige Rente f

prerogative n LAW Vorrecht nt

Pres. abbr (President) HRM, MGMNT, POL Präs. (Präsident)

presale n PROP Verkauf m vor Fertigstellung; **~ order** n STOCK Vorverkaufsauftrag m; **~ service** n S&M Dienst m am Kunden vor dem Verkauf, Vorverkaufskundendienst m

preschool: **~ center** AmE, **~ centre** BrE n WEL Kindergarten m, Vorschule f

prescribe vt LAW requirements vorschreiben

prescribed: **~ price** n GEN COMM vorgeschriebener Preis m, vorschriftsmäßiger Preis m; **~ time** n GEN COMM vorgesehene Frist f, vorgesehene Zeit f

prescription n PROP acquisition Ersitzung f, regulation Vorschrift f, WEL health Rezept nt

prescriptive: **~ right** n LAW, PROP ersessenes Recht nt

preselected: **~ campaign** n S&M im voraus gewählte Kampagne f

presence n GEN COMM Anwesenheit f

present 1. adj GEN COMM präsent, anwesend, current gegenwärtig, augenblicklich; ♦ **at the ~ time** GEN COMM im Moment; **be ~** GEN COMM anwesend sein, zugegen sein; **in the ~ state of affairs** GEN COMM bei derzeitiger Lage der Dinge; **2.** n MEDIA, S&M Präsent nt; **3.** vt BANK einreichen, bill MEDIA report, LAW evidence vorlegen, S&M vorführen; ♦ **~ a bill for acceptance** BANK einen Wechsel zur Annahme vorlegen; **~ a bill for discount** BANK einen Wechsel zur Diskontierung vorlegen; **~ a check for payment** AmE, **~ a cheque for payment** BrE BANK einen Scheck zur Einlösung vorlegen, einen Scheck zur Zahlung vorlegen; **~ a draft for acceptance** BANK, FIN, GEN COMM eine Tratte zur Annahme vorlegen; **~ in an easy format** GEN COMM leicht verständlich darlegen; **~ fairly** ACC auditing ordnungsgemäß darstellen, wirtschaftlich angemessen darstellen; **~ a report** GEN COMM Bericht vorlegen

presentation n BANK Einreichung f, GEN COMM Vorlage f, Vorlegung f, Vorstellung f, LAW Vorlegung f, MGMNT Darstellung f, Vorstellung f, S&M Präsentation f, Vorführung f; ♦ **on ~** ACC, FIN, GEN COMM, LAW bei Vorlage, gegen Vorlage

presentation: **~ copy** n MEDIA of book Freiexemplar nt; **~ of documents** n IMP/EXP Dokumentenvorlage f, Einreichung f der Dokumente; **~ of goods ready for inspection** n TRANSP Darlegung f; **~ of goods to be cleared** n TRANSP Darlegung f

presenter n MEDIA broadcast Moderator, in m,f

present: **~ value** n ACC Barwert m, FIN Barwert m, Gegenwartswert m; **~ value of an expectancy** n INS Barwertanwartschaft f; **~ value factor** n FIN Barwertfaktor m; **~ value method** n ACC Buchführung f mit Bewertung zum Zeitwert, ECON Kapitalwertmethode f, FIN Zeitwertmethode f

preservation n ENVIR of habitats Erhaltung f

preservatives n pl IND, S&M Konservierungsmittel nt pl; ♦ **no ~** IND, S&M ohne Konservierungsstoffe; **no ~ or additives** IND, S&M ohne Konservierungs- oder Zusatzstoffe

preserve vt ENVIR erhalten, GEN COMM aufrechterhalten, bewahren, haltbar machen, IND haltbar machen; ♦ **~ jobs** GEN COMM Arbeitsplätze erhalten

preserved adj GEN COMM eingemacht; **~ food** n IND, S&M haltbares Lebensmittel nt, Konserve f

preset adj COMP voreingestellt

preshipment: **~ inspection** n TRANSP Inspektion f vor Lieferung

preside vi GEN COMM at meeting den Vorsitz haben; ♦ **~ over** GEN COMM meeting, commission vorsitzen

presidency n MGMNT, POL Präsidentschaft f, Vorsitz m

president n HRM Präsident, in m,f, Vorsitzende(r) mf [decl. as adj], Vorstandsvorsitzende(r) mf [decl. as adj], MGMNT of business Generaldirektor, in m,f, Vorstandsvorsitzende(r) mf [decl. as adj]

President n (Pres.) GEN COMM, POL Präsident m (Präs.)

president: **~ of the group executive board** n AmE HRM Präsident, in m,f des Konzernvorstands

presidential: **~ election cycle theory** n ECON Präsidentschaftswahl-Konjunkturzyklustheorie f

President: **~ of the Treasury Board** n AmE FIN Präsident, in m,f des Schatzamtes

presidium n HRM Präsidium nt

press 1. n MEDIA, POL, S&M Presse f; ♦ **go to ~** MEDIA print in Druck gehen; **have a bad ~** GEN COMM eine schlechte Presse haben; **have a good ~** GEN COMM eine gute Presse haben; **2.** vt COMP drücken

press: **~ advertisement** n S&M Zeitungswerbung f; **~ advertising** n S&M Anzeigenwerbung f; **~ agency** n MEDIA print Presseagentur f; **~ campaign** n MEDIA print Pressekampagne f; **~ card** n MEDIA Presseausweis m; **~ clipping** n AmE (cf press cutting BrE) MEDIA print Zeitungsausschnitt m; **~ conference** n MEDIA print Pressekonferenz f; **~ copy** n MEDIA print Pressekopie f; **~ coverage** n MEDIA print Presseberichterstattung f; **~ cutting** n BrE (cf press clipping AmE) MEDIA print Zeitungsausschnitt m; **~ date** n MEDIA Redaktionsschluß m

pressing: **~ financial needs** n ECON dringender Kapitalbedarf nt

press: **~ kit** n MEDIA, S&M print Pressemappe f; **~ launch** n MEDIA print Pressevorstellung f; **~ mentions** n pl S&M Erwähnungen f pl in der Presse; **~ office** n MEDIA Presseamt nt, Pressestelle f, POL Presseamt nt; **~ officer** n HRM Pressereferent, in m,f, MEDIA Pressereferent, in m,f, Pressesprecher, in m,f, POL Pressesprecher, in m,f; **~ pack** n MEDIA, S&M Pressemappe f; **~ photographer** n MEDIA print Pressefotograf, in m,f; **~ reception** n S&M Aufnahme f in der Presse; **~ relations** n pl MEDIA Beziehungen f pl zur Presse; **~ release** n COMMS Presseverlautbarung f, MEDIA freigegebene Pressemitteilung f, freigegebene Presseverlautbarung f, freigegebenes Pressematerial nt; **~ report** n MEDIA Pressebericht m; **~ statement** n MEDIA Pressemitteilung f

pressure n GEN COMM Beanspruchung f, Belastung f, Druck m; ♦ **come under ~** GEN COMM to do sth unter Druck geraten

pressure: **~ group** n POL Interessengruppe f, Lobby f, Interessenverband m, Interessenvereinigung f, Interessenvertretung f; **~ selling** n S&M Verkauf m unter Druck

pressurize *vt* ECON, HRM *person* unter Druck setzen

prestige *n* GEN COMM Renommee *nt*, Prestige *nt*; ~ **advertising** *n* S&M Repräsentationswerbung *f*; ~ **pricing** *n* S&M Festsetzung *f* von Prestigepreisen

prestigious *adj* GEN COMM angesehen, repräsentativ, vornehm, renommiert, *influential* einflußreich

presumable *adj* GEN COMM voraussichtlich

presume *vt* GEN COMM annehmen, vermuten, unterstellen, voraussetzen, MEDIA annehmen, vermuten

presumption *n* GEN COMM Annahme *f*, Unterstellung *f*, Vermutung *f*, Voraussetzung *f*, LAW Vermutung *f*, PATENTS Annahme *f*; ~ **of ownership** *n* GEN COMM Eigentumsvermutung *f*

presumptive: ~ **tax** *n* TAX vermutete Steuer *f*

pre-tax *adj* TAX vor Abzug der Steuern, vor Steuern; ~ **earnings** *n pl* TAX Gewinn *m* vor Steuern; ~ **rate of return** *n* TAX Rendite *f* vor Steuern

pretence *n* LAW Vortäuschung *f*

pre-test *n* S&M *acceptance test* Pretest *m*, *advertising* Werbewertprüfung *f*, *interview* Probetest *m*, Probeinterview *nt*

pre-testing *n* S&M *interview* Probetest *m*, *advertising* Werbewertprüfung *f*; ~ **copy** *n* S&M Anzeigentext *m* für Probetest

pre-treat *vt* ENVIR, *waste* vorbehandeln

pre-treatment *n* ENVIR *of waste, wastewater* Vorbehandlung *f*

prevail *vi* GEN COMM vorherrschen; ♦ ~ **against** GEN COMM sich durchsetzen gegen

prevailing *adj* GEN COMM allgemein geltend, gängig, handelsüblich, herrschend, maßgeblich; ~ **party** *n* LAW obsiegende Partei *f*

prevent *vt* GEN COMM verhüten, verhindern, vermeiden, vorbeugen

prevention *n* GEN COMM Verhütung *f*, Verhinderung *f*, Vermeidung *f*, Vorbeugung *f*

Prevention: ~ **of Fraud Act** *n BrE* LAW Gesetz *nt* gegen Investitionsbetrug

preventive *adj* GEN COMM, MGMNT vorbeugend; ~ **inspection** *n* GEN COMM vorbeugende Prüfung *f*; ~ **maintenance** *n* ADMIN Vorsorgemaßnahmen *f pl* zur Instandhaltung, GEN COMM Vorsorgemaßnahmen *f pl* zur Werkserhaltung, MGMNT vorbeugende Instandhaltung *f*, vorbeugende Wartung *f*; ~ **measure** *n* GEN COMM vorbeugende Maßnahme *f*

preview 1. *n* MEDIA Pressevorstellung *f*, Programmvorschau *f*; 2. *vt* COMP *wordprocessed document* sichten

previous *adj* GEN COMM vorherig; ~ **application** *n* PATENTS Voranmeldung *f*; ~ **history** *n* HRM Vorgeschichte *f*; ~ **speaker** *n* GEN COMM Vorredner, in *m,f*; ~ **year** *n* GEN COMM vorhergehendes Jahr *nt*, Vorjahr *nt*

price 1. *n* (*pr.*) ECON, FIN Kurs *m* GEN COMM Kaufpreis *m*, Marktpreis *m*, Preis *m*, PROP Angebotspreis *m*, S&M Kaufpreis *m*, Marktpreis *m*, STOCK Briefkurs *m*, Kurs *m*; ~ **on application** GEN COMM Preis auf Anfrage *m*; ♦ **the** ~ **has declined to compensate for the fall in demand** GEN COMM der Preis ist gefallen, um den Nachfragerückgang auszugleichen; 2. *vt* FIN berechnen, GEN COMM, S&M auszeichnen; ♦ ~ **oneself out of the market** S&M *marketing* sich durch zu hohe Preise vom Markt ausschließen

price: ~ **advance** *n* FIN, S&M Preisanstieg *m*, STOCK Kurssteigerung *f*; ~ **auditing** *n* ACC, S&M Preisprüfung

f; ~ **behavior** *AmE*, ~ **behaviour** *BrE* *n* STOCK *of options* Preisverhalten *nt*; ~ **bid** *n* STOCK Geldkurs *m*, Preisangebot *nt*; ~ **booster** *n* ECON Preistreiber *m*; ~ **boosting** *n* ECON Preistreiberei *f*; ~ **ceiling** *n* ECON Höchstpreis *m*, STOCK Kurslimit *nt*; ~ **change** *n* STOCK *futures* Preisänderung *f*

Price: ~ **Commission** *n BrE* ECON Preiskommission *f*

price: ~ **competitiveness** *n* S&M preisliche Wettbewerbsfähigkeit *f*; ~~**consumption curve** *n* (*PCC*) ECON Preiskonsumkurve *f*; ~ **control** *n* ECON Preiskontrolle *f*; ~ **cue** *n* S&M Preishinweis *m*; ~ **current** *n* (*pc.*) FIN Preisbericht *m*, Preisliste *f*, Preisverzeichnis *nt*; ~ **cut** *n* ECON, FIN, S&M Preisreduzierung *f*, Preissenkung *f*; ~ **cutting** *n* ECON, GEN COMM, FIN, S&M Preissenkung *f*, Preisunterbietung *f*, *underselling* Preisdrückung *f*; ~ **of delivery** *n* GEN COMM Bezugspreis *m*; ~~**demand elasticity** *n* S&M Preisnachfrageelastizität *f*; ~~**demand function** *n* ECON Preisabsatzfunktion *f*; ~ **deregulation** *n* GEN COMM Preisderegulation *f*; ~ **deterioration** *n* ECON Preisverschlechterung *f*; ~ **determinant** *n* S&M Preisbildungsfaktor *m*; ~ **determination** *n* ECON, FIN, LAW, S&M Preisbestimmung *f*, Preisfestsetzung *f*, Kursfeststellung *f*; ~ **differential** *n* ECON, HRM Preisgefälle *nt*, Preisunterschied *m*, S&M Preisdifferenzierung *f*, STOCK Kursgefälle *nt*; ~ **discrimination** *n* S&M Preisdiskriminierung *f*; ~ **discrimination cartel** *n* ECON Preiskartell *nt*; ~~**earnings multiple** *n* ACC Kurs-Gewinn-Verhältnis *nt* (*KGV*); ~~**earnings ratio** *n* FIN (*P/E ratio, PER*) Kurs-Gewinn-Verhältnis *nt* (*KGV*); ~ **effect** *n* ECON Preiseffekt *m*; ~ **elasticity of demand** *n* ECON Preiselastizität *f* der Nachfrage; ~ **enquiry** *n* GEN COMM Preisanfrage *f*; ~ **escalation** *n* ECON nach oben, Gleiten *nt* des Preises, FIN, S&M Preisanstieg *m*; ~~**fixing** *n* FIN Preisabsprache *f*, Preisbindung *f*, Preisfestsetzung *f*, Preisvereinbarung *f*, LAW, S&M Preisabsprache *f*, Preisbindung *f*, Preisfestsetzung *f*, Preisvereinbarung *f*, *in dishonest way* illegale Preisabsprache *f*; ~ **flexibility** *n* ECON Preisflexibilität *f*; ~ **floor** *n* ECON niedrigster Preis *m*; ~ **formation** *n* ECON, S&M Preisbildung *f*; ~ **freeze** *n* ECON, GEN COMM, S&M Preisstopp *m*, Einfrieren *nt* der Preise; ~ **gap** *n* STOCK Preisschere *f*; ~ **guarantee** *n* S&M Preisgarantie *f*; ~ **incentive** *n* S&M Preisanreiz *m*; ~ **increase** *n* ECON Preissteigerung *f*, FIN, S&M Preisanstieg *m*, Preiserhöhung *f*, Preissteigerung *f*; ~ **index** *n* ACC, ECON, FIN, STOCK Preisindex *m*; ~ **index level** *n* ACC, ECON, FIN, STOCK Kursindexniveau *nt*, Preisindexniveau *nt*; ~ **inelasticity** *n* ECON Unelastizität *f* der Preise; ~ **inflation** *n* ECON Preisinflation *f*; ~ **label** *n* S&M Preisetikett *nt*, Preisschild *nt*; ~ **leader** *n* ECON, S&M *low-priced article* Lockvogel *m*, *firm* Preisführer *m*; ~ **leadership** *n* ECON, S&M Preisführerschaft *f*; ~ **level** *n* GEN COMM Kursniveau *nt*, ECON, S&M Preisniveau *nt*; ~ **level accounting** *n* ACC indizierte Abrechnung *f*; ~ **level change** *n* GEN COMM Veränderung *f* des Preisniveaus; ~ **limit** *n* STOCK Kurslimit *nt*; ~ **lining** *n* S&M Verkauf *m* von Produkten zum gleichen Preis; ~ **look-up procedure** *n* S&M Preisabrufverfahren *nt*; ~ **loss** *n* STOCK Kursverlust *m*; ~ **maintenance** *n* FIN, LAW, S&M Preisbindung *f*, Preisbindung *f* der zweiten Hand; ~ **maintenance scheme** *n* S&M Preisbindungsregelung *f*; ~ **maker** *n* ECON Preisfixierer *m*; ~ **margin** *n* S&M Preisspanne *f*; ~ **mark-down** *n* GEN COMM Preissenkung *f*; ~ **marker** *n* GEN COMM Preisangeber *m*; ~ **marking** *n* S&M Auszeichnung *f*; ~ **mechanism** *n*

ECON Marktpreismechanismus *m*; ~ **move** *n* STOCK Kursentwicklung *f*, Preisentwicklung *f*; ~ **offered** *n* STOCK Brief *m*, Briefkurs *m*; ~ **perception** *n* ECON Preiswahrnehmung *f*; ~**performance ratio** *n* GEN COMM Preis-Leistungsverhältnis *nt*; ~ **pressures** *n pl* ECON, S&M Preisdruck *m*; ~ **protection** *n* STOCK *futures price* Preisschutz *m*; ~**quality ratio** *n* S&M Preis-Qualitäts-Verhältnis *nt*

pricer *n* FIN *person* Preiskalkulator *m*

price: ~ **range** *n* ECON Preisbereich *m*, GEN COMM Preislage *f*, S&M Preisskala *f*, Preisbereich *m*, Preisspanne *f*, Preisspektrum *nt*; ~ **rate** *n* ECON Preisrate *f*; ~ **regulation** *n* ECON, S&M Preisregulierung *f*; ~ **rigidity** *n* ECON Preisstarrheit *f*; ~ **rise** *n* ECON, S&M Teuerung *f*

prices: ~ **can go down as well as up** *phr* ECON, FIN, STOCK Kurse können sowohl fallen als auch steigen

price: ~ **scanner** *n* S&M Preisscanner *m*; ~ **schedule** *n* S&M Preisliste *f*; ~**sensitive** *adj* ECON, S&M preisempfindlich; ~**sensitive information** *n* ECON, STOCK kursempfindliche Informationen *f pl*; ~ **sensitivity** *n* S&M Preisempfindlichkeit *f*

prices: **at ~ ranging from x to y** *phr* GEN COMM zu Preisen, die sich von x bis y bewegen, zu Preisen, die zwischen x und y schwanken; **at ruling ~** *phr* FIN, STOCK zu gegenwärtigen Börsenkursen, zu gegenwärtigen Preisen, zu geltenden Preisen, *at daily rates* zu Tagespreisen, zu Tageskursen; ~ **and incomes agreement** *n* HRM Preis- und Lohnabkommen *nt*; ~ **and incomes policy** *n* ECON Preis- und Einkommenspolitik *f*; ~ **have been marked down** *phr* STOCK die Preise sind herabgesetzt worden, Kurse sind niedriger notiert worden

price: ~ **spread** *n* S&M Preisspanne *f*

prices: ~ **receded** *phr* GEN COMM die Preise gaben nach

price: ~ **stability** *n* ECON, S&M Preisstabilität *f*; ~ **stabilization** *n* ECON, S&M Preisstabilisierung *f*; ~ **staggering** *n* ECON Preisstaffelung *f*; ~ **sticker** *n* S&M Preisschild *nt*; ~ **structure** *n* ECON, FIN, S&M Preisstruktur *f*; ~ **supervision** *n* ECON Preisüberwachung *f*; ~ **supervisor** *n* ECON Preisüberwacher, -in *m,f*; ~ **supplement** *n* GEN COMM Preisaufschlag *m*; ~ **support** *n* ECON Kursstützung *f*, FIN Kursstützung *f*, Preisstützung *f*; ~ **support level** *n* ECON, FIN Kursstützungsniveau *nt*; ~ **surge** *n* STOCK Kursauftrieb *m*; ~ **system** *n* ECON Preissystem *nt*; ~ **tag** *n* S&M Preismarke *f*; ~ **taker** *n* ECON Preisabnehmer, -in *m,f*; ~ **taking** *n* ECON Mengenanpassung *f*; ~ **tick** *n* STOCK *currency market* Mindestkursschwankung *f*; ~ **ticket** *n* S&M Preisetikett *nt*, Preisschild *nt*; ~ **trend** *n* FIN Kurstendenz *f*, Preistendenz *f*; ~ **twist** *n* ECON, POL Preis-Twist *m*; ~ **variance** *n* GEN COMM Preisabänderung *f*, Preisabweichung *f*; ~ **variation clause** *n* S&M Preisgleitklausel *f*; ~ **volatility** *n* STOCK *of shares* Kursvolatilität *f*, Kursvariabilität *f*; ~ **war** *n* ECON, S&M Preiskrieg *m*; ~**weighted index** *n* STOCK kursgewichteter Index *m*

pricey *adj infrml* GEN COMM happig (*infrml*), kostspielig, teuer

pricing *n* S&M Preisfestlegung *f*; ~ **arrangement** *n* ECON, S&M Preisbildungsvereinbarung *f*; ~ **down** *n* S&M Niedrigpreisfestsetzung *f*; ~ **of input factors** *n* ACC kalkulatorische Bewertung *f*; ~ **of an issue** *n* STOCK Kursfestsetzung *f*; ~ **margin** *n* ECON Kalkulationsspanne *f*; ~ **mix** *n* S&M Mischung *f* von Preis- und Rabattpolitik; ~ **policy** *n* ECON Preispolitik *f*, S&M Preispolitik *f*, Preisbildungspolitik *f*, Preisfestsetzungs-

politik *f*; ~ **pressure** *n* ECON, S&M Preisdruck *m*; ~ **review** *n* S&M Preisberichtigung *f*; ~ **strategy** *n* S&M Preisstrategie *f*; ~ **tactics** *n pl* S&M Preisbildungstaktiken *f pl*; ~ **up** *n* S&M Festsetzen *nt* eines hohen Preises

prima facie *phr* GEN COMM nach dem ersten Anschein

primarily *adv* GEN COMM hauptsächlich, in der Hauptsache, in erster Linie, primär, *above all* vor allem

primary *adj* GEN COMM hauptsächlich, primär, Primär-; ~ **action** *n* GEN COMM, HRM, IND Streik *m*; ~ **activities** *n pl* GEN COMM Kerngeschäft *nt*, Primärgeschäft *nt*; ~ **boycott** *n* HRM primärer Boykott *m*; ~ **capital** *n* ECON primäres Eigenkapital *nt*; ~ **commodity** *n* ECON Grundstoff *m*, Rohstoff *m*, STOCK Grundstoff *m*; ~ **commodity prices** *n pl* STOCK Preise *m pl* für unverarbeitete oder halbverarbeitete Rohstoffe; ~ **data** *n pl* S&M Primärdaten *pl*; ~ **dealer** *n* ECON Primärhändler *m*; ~ **deficit** *n* ECON primäres Defizit *nt*; ~ **earnings per share** *n* STOCK tatsächlicher Gewinn *m* je Aktie; ~ **goods** *n pl* GEN COMM Primärgüter *nt pl*; ~ **industry** *n* ECON Grundstoffindustrie *f*; ~ **input** *n* FIN Primäraufwand *m*; ~ **labor market** *AmE*, ~ **labour market** *BrE* *n* ECON Hauptarbeitsmarkt *m*, Primärarbeitsmarkt *m*, primärer Arbeitsmarkt *m*; ~ **liquidity** *n* BANK Primärliquidität *f*; ~ **market** *n* STOCK *future market* Markt *m* für Neuemissionen, Primärmarkt *m*; ~ **market area** *n* STOCK Primärmarktbereich *m*; ~ **market dealer** *n* STOCK Primärmarkthändler *m*; ~ **metropolitan statistical area** *n AmE* (*PMSA*) MATH primäres statistisches Großstadtgebiet *nt*; ~ **money** *n* ECON Primärgeld *nt*; ~ **movements** *n pl* ECON, STOCK primärer Warenverkehr *m*; ~ **objective** *n* FIN Primärziel *nt*; ~ **package** *n* GEN COMM Grundverpackung *f*; ~ **point** *n AmE* GEN COMM Hauptumschlageplatz für landwirtschaftliche Erzeugnisse, Zentrallagerstelle *f*; ~ **product** *n* ECON Grundstoff *m*, GEN COMM Grundstoff *m*, Vorprodukt *nt*; ~ **ratio** *n* ECON Primärrate *f*; ~ **readership** *n* S&M Primärleserschaft *f*, hauptsächlicher Leserstamm *m*; ~ **resource** *n* ENVIR Primärressource *f*; ~ **route** *n* COMP Direktweg *m*; ~ **sector** *n* ECON primärer Sektor *m*; ~ **standard** *n* ENVIR *air pollution* Emissionshöchstwert *m*

prime *adj* GEN COMM erste; ~ **age worker** *n* HRM Arbeiter *m* auf der Höhe seiner Schaffenskraft, Arbeiterin *f* auf der Höhe ihrer Schaffenskraft; ~ **bank** *n* BANK Primabank *f*; ~ **bill** *n* STOCK erstklassiger Wechsel *m*; ~ **contract** *n* LAW Hauptvertrag *m*, Vertrag *m* mit Generalunternehmen; ~ **contractor** *n* GEN COMM Hauptlieferant *m*; ~ **costs** *n pl* ECON Fertigungseinzelkosten *pl*, Gestehungskosten *pl*, GEN COMM Gestehungskosten *pl*; ~ **entry** *n* ACC Ersteintragung *f*, IMP/EXP Hauptzollanmeldung *f*; ~ **goal** *n* ECON Primärziel *nt*; ~ **investment** *n* FIN erste Anlage *f*; ~ **lending rate** *n* FIN Bankzinssatz *m* für erste Adressen, Leitzinssatz *m*; ~ **listening time** *n* MEDIA *for broadcasts* Haupteinschaltzeit *f*; ~ **location** *n* PROP bevorzugte Lage *f*; ~ **market** *n* ECON, GEN COMM Hauptabsatzmarkt *m*; ~ **minister** *n* (*PM*) POL Premierminister, -in *m,f*

Prime-1 *n AmE* BANK, STOCK *Moody's investor service* höchste Bonitätseinstufung eines Commercial Paper

prime: ~ **paper** *n* STOCK erstklassiges Handelspapier *nt*, Primapapier *nt*; ~ **position** *n* S&M *in market* Spitzenposition *f*; ~ **quality** *n* GEN COMM erste Wahl *f*; ~ **rate of interest** *n* BANK Kreditzins *m* für erste

Adressen, Prime-Rate *f*; ~ **site** *n* PROP Vorzugslage *f*; ~ **supplier** *n* GEN COMM Hauptlieferant *m*; ~ **time** *n* MEDIA Hauptsendezeit *f*, *broadcast* Haupteinschaltzeit *f*; ~ **underwriter** *n* BANK, FIN *organization* Konsortialführer, in *m,f*; ~ **unit** *n* PROP Vorzugseinheit *f*; ~ **viewing time** *n* MEDIA *broadcast* Hauptfernsehzeit *f*

primitive: ~ **economy** *n* ECON primitive Wirtschaft *f*

princely: ~ **salary** *n* ECON fürstliches Gehalt *nt*

principal 1. *adj* GEN COMM hauptsächlich; **2.** *n* ACC Auftraggeber, in *m,f*, BANK Erstverpflichtete(r) *mf* [decl. as adj], FIN Auftraggeber, in *m,f*

principal: ~ **accounting system** *n* ACC, FIN Hauptbuchführungssytem *nt*; ~ **assets** *n pl* ACC Hauptvermögen *nt*; ~ **bidder** *n* GEN COMM Hauptanbieter *m*; ~ **carrier** *n* TRANSP Hauptbeförderer *m*, Hauptspediteur *m*; ~ **customer** *n* GEN COMM Hauptkunde *m*, Hauptkundin *f*; ~ **debtor** *n* FIN, S&M Hauptschuldner, in *m,f*; ~ **establishment** *n* GEN COMM Hauptniederlassung *f*; ~ **executive committee** *n* BrE HRM *of union* Exekutivausschuß *m*

principally *adv* GEN COMM grundsätzlich, hauptsächlich

principal: ~ **place of business** *n* ACC, BANK Hauptsitz *m*, GEN COMM Hauptniederlassung *f*, Hauptsitz *m*, HRM, MGMNT Hauptsitz *m*; ~ **stockholder** *n* STOCK Großaktionär, in *m,f*, Hauptaktionär, in *m,f*; ~ **sum** *n* FIN *finance, insurance* Gesamtsumme *f*, Kapitalbetrag *m*; ~ **value** *n* STOCK Kapitalwert *m*, Nennwert *m*

principle *n* GEN COMM Grundsatz *m*, Leitsatz *m*, Prinzip *nt*; ♦ **in** ~ GEN COMM grundsätzlich; **on** ~ GEN COMM aus Prinzip, prinzipiell, grundsätzlich

principle: ~ **of accrual** *n* ACC Prinzip *nt* der Periodenabgrenzung; ~ **of caution** *n* ACC Vorsichtsprinzip *nt*; ~ **of conservatism** *n* ACC Vorsichtsprinzip *nt*; ~ **of equivalence** *n* INS Äquivalenzprinzip *nt*

print 1. *n* MEDIA Druck *m*; ♦ **out of** ~ (*op*) MEDIA vergriffen (*vergr.*); **2.** *vt* COMP, MEDIA drucken

print out *vt* COMP ausdrucken

print: ~ **column** *n* COMP, MEDIA Druckspalte *f*

printed: ~ **form** *n* GEN COMM Vordruck *m*, vorgedrucktes Formular *nt*; ~ **in bold type** *phr* MEDIA fettgedruckt; ~ **matter** *n* GEN COMM, MEDIA Drucksache *f*; ~ **paper rate** *n* BrE (*cf library rate AmE*) COMMS ermäßigtes Porto *nt* für Büchersendungen; ~ **return** *n* TAX vorgedruckte Steuererklärung *f*; **the** ~ **word** *n* COMMS das gedruckte Wort *nt*; ~ **writing paper** *n* COMMS bedrucktes Schreibpapier *nt*

printer *n* COMP *device* Drucker *m*, GEN COMM, MEDIA *person* Drucker, in *m,f*; ♦ **go to the printers** MEDIA in Druck gehen

printer: ~ **driver** *n* COMP Druckertreiber *m*; ~ **font** *n* COMP Druckerschrift *f*; ~ **port** *n* COMP Druckeranschluß *m*, Druckerport *m* (*jarg*), Druckerschnittstelle *f*

printing *n* COMP, MEDIA Druck *m*, Drucken *nt*; ~ **press** *n* MEDIA Druckmaschine *f*, Druckpresse *f*; ~ **speed** *n* COMP Druckgeschwindigkeit *f*; ~ **unit** *n* GEN COMM Druckaggregat *nt*, Druckgerät *f*; ~ **works** *n* MEDIA Druckerei *f*

print: ~ **line** *n* COMP Druckzeile *f*; ~ **media** *n* MEDIA Druckmedien *nt pl*

printout *n* ADMIN, COMP Ausdruck *m*

print: ~ **preview** *n* COMP Druckvorschau *f*; ~ **run** *n* ADMIN, MEDIA Auflage *f*, Druckauflage *f*

prior *adj* GEN COMM früher, vorherig, vorrangig; ♦ ~ **to** GEN COMM vor

prior: ~ **art** *n* PATENTS Stand *m* der Technik; ~ **consent** *n* GEN COMM vorherige Zusage *f*; ~ **debt** *n* FIN Altschulden *f pl*

prioritize *vt* ADMIN zur Priorität machen, GEN COMM bevorzugt behandeln

priority 1. *adj* GEN COMM vorrangig; **2.** *n* GEN COMM *goal, target* Hauptziel *nt*, Priorität *f*, *precedence* Vorrang *m*, Vorzug *m*, *order of preference* Rangfolge *f*, *urgency* Dringlichkeit *f*, PATENTS Vorrang *m*, Vorrecht *nt*; ♦ **give** ~ **to sth** GEN COMM etw Priorität verleihen

priority: ~ **allocation** *n* STOCK *of shares* Vorzugszuteilung *f*; ~ **date** *n* LAW, PATENTS *intellectual property* Prioritätsdatum *nt*; ~ **level** *n* ECON Dringlichkeitsstufe *f*; ~ **mail** *n* AmE (*cf express mail BrE*) COMMS Eilpost *f*, Expreßpost *f*; ~ **right** *n* LAW, PATENTS Vorzugsrecht *nt*; ~ **share** *n* FIN Prioritätsaktie *f*

prior: ~**-lien bond** *n* STOCK Erstpfandrechtsanleihe *f*; ~ **mortgage** *n* PROP vorrangige Hypothek *f*; ~ **patent** *n* PATENTS älteres Patent *nt*, Vorzugspatent *nt*; ~ **period** *n* ACC vorhergehender Zeitraum *m*; ~**-preferred stock** *n* STOCK erststellige Vorzugsaktien *f pl*, Sondervorzugsaktien *f pl*; ~ **tax** *n* TAX Vorsteuer *f*; ~ **use** *n* PATENTS Vorbenutzung *f*, Vorbenutzungsfall *m*; ~ **year adjustment** *n* ACC Vorjahresanpassung *f*

prisoner: ~**'s dilemma** *n* ECON Gefangenen-Dilemma *nt*

privacy: ~ **law** *n* LAW, MEDIA Gesetz *nt* zum Schutz des Persönlichkeitsrechts

private *adj* GEN COMM persönlich, privat, vertraulich; ♦ **by** ~ **contract** GEN COMM freihändig, unter der Hand, LAW durch privatschriftlichen Vertrag; ~ **and confidential** GEN COMM streng vertraulich, vertraulich; **go** ~ INS *medicine* sich privat versichern, STOCK Aktien vom Publikum zurückkaufen, Börsenzulassung aufgeben

private: ~ **account** *n* ACC privates Konto *nt*; ~ **agency** *n* GEN COMM privates Institut *nt*; ~ **arrangement** *n* GEN COMM gütliche Einigung *f*, LAW private Vereinbarung *f*, privates Abkommen *nt*; ~**-asset contribution** *n* FIN Privateinlage *f*; ~ **attorney** *n* LAW Beauftragte(r) *mf* [decl. as adj], Stellvertreter, in *m,f*; ~ **automatic branch exchange** *n* BrE (*PABX*) COMMS *telephone* Wahlnebenstellanlage *f*; ~ **bank** *n* BANK Privatbank *f*; ~ **branch exchange** *n* (*PBX*) COMMS private Vermittlungsanlage *f*; ~ **brand** *n* S&M Hausmarke *f*; ~ **call** *n* COMMS Privatgespräch *nt*; ~ **carrier** *n* S&M Gelegenheitsspediteur *m*, TRANSP Beförderungsunternehmen *nt*; ~ **company** *n* (*Pte*) GEN COMM personenbezogene Kapitalgesellschaft *f*, Privatunternehmen *nt*, LAW privatrechtliches Unternehmen *nt*; ~ **consumption** *n* ECON privater Konsum *m*, GEN COMM Eigenverbrauch *m*, Selbstverbrauch *m*; ~ **contract** *n* GEN COMM Privatabkommen *nt*, privater Vertrag *m*; ~ **contribution** *n* ECON *towards development assistance* privater Beitrag *m*; ~ **cost** *n* ECON individuelle Kosten *pl*, Privatausgaben *f pl*, private Kosten *pl*; ~ **enterprise** *n* ECON Privatbetrieb *m*, Privatwirtschaft *f*, *economic system* private Marktwirtschaft *f*, GEN COMM Privatunternehmen *nt*, *economic system* private Marktwirtschaft *f*; ~ **enterprise system** *n* ECON Privatwirtschaft *f*, privatwirtschaftliches System *nt*; ~ **good** *n* ECON Individualgut *nt*; ~ **health fund** *n* HRM, INS, WEL private Krankenkasse *f*; ~ **health insurance** *n* BrE HRM, INS, WEL Privatkrankenversicherung *f*, private Krankenversicherung *f*; ~ **health scheme** *n* BrE (*cf Blue Shield AmE*, *cf*

Blue Cross AmE) HRM, INS, WEL privater Krankenversicherungsplan *m*, privates Krankenversicherungssystem *nt*; ~ **hearing** *n* LAW *evidentiary hearing* Beweisaufnahme *f* unter Ausschluß der Öffentlichkeit; ~ **hospital treatment** *n* HRM, WEL private Krankenhausbehandlung *f*, private stationäre Behandlung *f*; ~ **household** *n* GEN COMM Privathaushalt *m*; ~ **individual** *n* GEN COMM Privatmann *m*, Privatperson *f*; ~ **institution** *n* PROP private Anstalt *f*, private Einrichtung *f*, private Institution *f*, privates Institut *nt*; ~ **investment** *n* FIN private Investition *f*; ~ **investment client** *n* BANK privater Kapitalanleger *m*; ~ **investor** *n* FIN, STOCK Privatanleger *m*, privater Anleger *m*; ~ **law** *n* LAW *civil law* Privatrecht *nt*; ~ **ledger** *n* ACC privates Register *nt*; ~ **limited company** *n* GEN COMM Gesellschaft *f* mit beschränkter Haftung (*GmbH, Ges.m.b.H.* Öst); ~ **limited partnership** *n* LAW, STOCK Kommanditgesellschaft *f* (*KG*)

privately *adv* GEN COMM privat; ~**-owned company** *n* ECON Privatunternehmen *nt*, Unternehmen *nt* in Privatbesitz

private: ~ **means** *n pl* FIN private Mittel *nt pl*; ~ **mortgage insurance** *n* INS Restschuldversicherung *f*; ~ **notice question** *n* BrE (*PNQ*) POL private Frage eines Parlamentsmitglieds; ~ **office** *n* ADMIN Privatbüro *nt*; ~ **ownership** *n* GEN COMM, PROP Privatbesitz *m*, Privateigentum *nt*; ~ **patient** *n* WEL Privatpatient, in *m,f*

Private: ~ **Patients Plan** *n* (*PPP*) WEL private Krankenversicherung

private: ~ **placement** *n* BANK, FIN Privatplazierung *f*; ~ **placing** *n* BANK, FIN Privatplazierung *f*; ~**-purpose bond** *n* STOCK Anleihe *f* für private Zwecke; ~ **rate of discount** *n* BANK Diskontsatz *m* der Geschäftsbanken; ~ **school** *n* WEL Privatschule *f*; ~ **secretary** *n* ADMIN, HRM Privatsekretär, in *m,f*; ~ **sector** *n* ECON privater Sektor *m*, Privatwirtschaft *f*; ~ **sector awards** *n pl* HRM privatwirtschaftliche Gehaltserhöhung *f*; ~ **sector company** *n* ECON, GEN COMM privates Unternehmen *nt*; ~ **sector enterprise** *n* ECON Privatwirtschaft *f*, GEN COMM privatwirtschaftliches Unternehmen *nt*; ~ **sector investment** *n* ECON Privatinvestitionen *f pl*; ~ **sector liquidity** *n* (*PSL*) ECON liquide Mittel *nt pl* des Privatsektors; ~ **siding** *n* BrE TRANSP Privatanschlußgleis *nt*; ~ **terms** *n pl* (*pt*) LAW privatrechtliche Bedingungen *f pl*; ~ **transport** *n* BrE (*cf private transportation AmE*) GEN COMM, TRANSP Individualverkehr *m*; ~ **transportation** *n* AmE (*cf private transport BrE*) GEN COMM, TRANSP Individualverkehr *m*; ~ **treaty** *n* PROP freihändiger Verkauf *m*; ~ **tuition** *n* WEL Einzelunterricht *m*, Nachhilfeunterricht *m*, Privatunterricht *m*

privatization *n* ECON, GEN COMM, POL Entstaatlichung *f*, Privatisierung *f*; ~ **proceeds** *n pl* ECON Privatisierungserlös *m*; ~ **program** AmE, ~ **programme** BrE *n* ECON Privatisierungsprogramm *nt*

privatize *vt* ECON entstaatlichen, privatisieren

privilege *n* GEN COMM Privileg *nt*, HRM, MGMNT Vergünstigung *f*, STOCK Option *f*, Vorrecht *nt*

privileged *adj* FIN, GEN COMM *in law* bevorrechtigt

privity *n* LAW unmittelbare Rechtsbeziehung *f*, zivilrechtliches Verhältnis *nt*

privy *n* LAW Beteiligte(r) *mf* [decl. as adj]

Privy: ~ **Council** *n* BrE LAW Geheimer Staatsrat *m*, Kronrat *m*

prize: ~ **bond** *n* BANK, FIN, STOCK Prämienanleihe *f*; ~ **broker** *n* STOCK Prämienhändler, in *m,f*; ~ **competition** *n* ECON Auslosung *f*

PRO *abbr* HRM, S&M public relations officer

pro 1. *n* (*professional*) GEN COMM Profi *m*; **2.** *prep* GEN COMM, LAW an Stelle von

proactive *adj* MGMNT proaktiv; ~ **strategy** *n* MGMNT proaktive Strategie *f*

pro-American *adj* POL proamerikanisch

probability *n* MATH *statistics* Wahrscheinlichkeit *f*; ~ **sample** *n* MATH *statistics* Wahrscheinlichkeitsstichprobe *f*; ~ **theory** *n* MATH, MGMNT Wahrscheinlichkeitstheorie *f*

probable *adj* GEN COMM glaubhaft, mutmaßlich, voraussichtlich, wahrscheinlich, MATH wahrscheinlich; ~ **error** *n* (*p.e.*) GEN COMM wahrscheinlicher Fehler *m*, MATH *statistics* wahrscheinliche Abweichung *f*, wahrscheinlicher Fehler *m*

probate: ~ **court** *n* LAW Nachlaßgericht *nt*; ~ **duty** *n* LAW Erbschaftssteuer *f*; ~ **price** *n* STOCK Erbschaftssteuerpreis *m*

probationary: ~ **employee** *n* HRM Mitarbeiter, in *m,f* auf Probe; ~ **period** *n* HRM Probezeit *f*

probation: ~ **period** *n* HRM Probezeit *f*

probe: ~ **a market** *phr* ECON einen Markt erproben

problem *n* GEN COMM Problem *nt*; ~ **analysis** *n* MATH, MGMNT Problemanalyse *f*; ~ **area** *n* GEN COMM Problembereich *m*, Problemgebiet *nt*; ~ **assessment** *n* MGMNT Problembeurteilung *f*, Problembewertung *f*, Problemeinschätzung *f*

problematic *adj* GEN COMM problematisch

problem: ~ **batch** *n* IND Problemgruppe *f*; ~ **customer** *n* S&M Problemkunde *m*; ~ **determination** *n* COMP Problembestimmung *f*; ~ **loan** *n* FIN Problemkredit *m*, Risikokredit *m*; ~ **solving** *n* GEN COMM Problemlösung *f*

procedural *adj* ADMIN, GEN COMM, LAW, MGMNT verfahrensrechtlich; ~ **agreement** *n* HRM Verfahrensvereinbarung *f*; ~ **delay** *n* MGMNT verfahrensrechtliche Verzögerung *f*; ~ **issue** *n* MGMNT verfahrensrechtliche Frage *f*, verfahrensrechtliches Problem *nt*; ~ **rules** *n pl* LAW Verfahrensregeln *f pl*

procedure *n* ADMIN Ablauf *m*, Arbeitsweise *f*, Verfahren *nt*, COMP Ablauf *m*, Prozedur *f*, Verfahren *nt*, GEN COMM, HRM Ablauf *m*, Verfahren *nt*, Vorgehen *nt*, Verfahrensweise *f*, POL Geschäftsordnung *f*; ~ **agreement** *n* HRM Verfahrensvereinbarung *f*

procedures *n pl* GEN COMM Verfahrensregeln *f pl*

proceed *vi* LAW *bring action* prozessieren; ♦ ~ **on the assumption** GEN COMM annehmen

proceeding: ~ **pending before a court** *n* LAW anhängiger Rechtsstreit *m*, lis pendens

proceedings *n pl* LAW Verfahren *nt*, Verhandlung *f*

proceeds *n pl* GEN COMM Erlös *m*; ~ **from resale** *n pl* GEN COMM Erlös *m* vom Wiederverkauf, Gewinn *m* vom Wiederverkauf; ~ **in cash** *n pl* GEN COMM Barerlös *m*; ~ **of an issue** *n pl* FIN Emissionserlös *m*; ~ **on disposal** *n pl* ECON Veräußerungserlös *m*; ~ **of sales** *n pl* GEN COMM Verkaufserlös *m*

process 1. *n* COMP Prozeß *m*, GEN COMM Verfahren *nt*, HRM Arbeitsablauf *m*, IND Prozeß *m*, Verarbeitung *f*,

Vorgang m, *method* Arbeitsweise f, Verfahren nt; ♦ **be in ~** GEN COMM in Arbeit sein, in der Herstellung sein; **2.** *vt* BANK bearbeiten, COMP *data* abarbeiten, abfertigen, verarbeiten, GEN COMM abfertigen, abwickeln, *incoming mail* bearbeiten, IND bearbeiten, *foodstuffs* haltbar machen, *production* aufbereiten, verarbeiten, PATENTS bearbeiten; ♦ **~ an export transaction** IMP/EXP ein Exportgeschäft abwickeln; **~ an order** ADMIN einen Auftrag bearbeiten

process: **~ of adjustment** n ECON, GEN COMM Anpassungsprozeß m; **~ analysis** n GEN COMM Verfahrensanalyse f; **~ chart** n COMP Ablaufdiagramm nt; **~ computer** n IND Prozeßcomputer m, Prozeßrechner m; **~ control** n GEN COMM Fertigungskontrolle f, IND *by computer* Prozeßleitsystem nt, Prozeßsteuerung f, Prozeßsteuersystem nt, *progress* Prozeßführung f, Prozeßleitung f, Prozeßlenkung f, *of quality* Arbeitskontrolle f, Fertigungskontrolle f, Qualitätskontrolle f; **~ costing** n ACC Divisionskalkulation f, IND Berechnung f der Produktionskosten, Kostenrechnung f für Serienfertigung

processable *adj* COMP verarbeitbar

processed: **~ foods** n pl IND Fertiglebensmittel nt pl, zubereitete Lebensmittel nt pl; **~ product** n IND Veredelungserzeugnis nt

process: **~ engineering** n IND Fertigungsplanung f, Verfahrenstechnik f; **~ industry** n IND Prozeßindustrie f

processing n BANK *of cheques* Bearbeitung f, COMP Verarbeitung f, GEN COMM Bearbeitung f, Abwicklung f, IND Zubereitung f, Bearbeitung f, Verarbeitung f, PATENTS *of application* Bearbeitung f, Weiterbearbeitung f; **~ industry** n IND verarbeitende Industrie f, weiterverarbeitende Industrie f; **~ plant** n IND Aufbereitungsanlage f, Verarbeitungsbetrieb m; **~ stage** n IND Fertigungsphase f, Verarbeitungsstufe f; **~ time** n ADMIN, COMP Bearbeitungszeit f, GEN COMM Abwicklungszeit f, IND Bearbeitungszeit f

processor n COMP Prozessor m, Zentraleinheit f

process: **~ planning** n IND, MGMNT Arbeitsvorbereitung f

procuration n STOCK Vollmacht f; **~ fee** n ADMIN Maklergebühr f

procuratory: **~ letter** n LAW Vollmachtsurkunde f

procure *vt* FIN *bill of exchange* anschaffen, GEN COMM beschaffen

procurement n FIN Anschaffung f, GEN COMM Beschaffung f, Bezug m, Vermittlung f, S&M Beschaffung f; **~ agent** n GEN COMM Beschaffungsvertreter, in m,f; **~ budgeting** n IND Bereitstellungsplanung f; **~ contract** n FIN Beschaffungsvertrag m; **~ costs** n pl GEN COMM Beschaffungskosten pl; **~ department** n GEN COMM Beschaffungsabteilung f; **~ manager** n GEN COMM Disponent, in m,f, Leiter, in m,f der Beschaffungsabteilung, HRM Einkäufer, in m,f, MGMNT Disponent, in m,f, Leiter, in m,f der Beschaffungsabteilung; **~ officer** n GEN COMM Beschaffungsbeamte(r) m [decl. as adj], Beschaffungsbeamtin f; **~ of outside capital** n FIN Fremdkapitalaufnahme f; **~ planning** n GEN COMM Beschaffungsplanung f

procuring: **~ cause** n LAW Hauptursache f

prodigality n GEN COMM Verschwendung f

produce 1. n ECON, GEN COMM landwirtschaftliche Produkte nt pl; **2.** *vt* ECON erzeugen, herstellen, *yield*

abwerfen, GEN COMM vorführen, IND produzieren, LAW *evidence* vorlegen

produced *adj* IND produziert; ♦ **~ in serial form** IND in Serie hergestellt

producer n ECON Erzeuger, in m,f, GEN COMM, IND, S&M Hersteller, in m,f; **~ advertising** n S&M Herstellerwerbung f; **~ buyer** n IND Herstellereinkäufer m; **~ cooperative** n ECON Produzentengenossenschaft f; **~ goods** n pl ECON Produktionsgüter nt pl; **~ price index** n (*PPI*) ECON *econometrics* Erzeugerpreisindex m; **~'s brand** n S&M Herstellermarke f; **~'s profits** n pl LEIS Gewinn m des Produzenten; **~'s risk** n ECON Lieferantenrisiko nt, Produzentenrisiko nt; **~'s surplus** n ECON Produzentenrente f; **~ subsidy equivalent** n ECON Erzeugerbeihilfe-Äquivalent nt

product n ECON Produkt nt, Ware f, GEN COMM, IND Artikel m, Fabrikat nt, Ware f, Erzeugnis nt, S&M Produkt nt; ♦ **broaden the ~ base** S&M die Produktbasis verbreitern; **this ~ is underpriced** S&M dieses Produkt wird zu billig gehandelt

product: **~ acceptance** n S&M Produktakzeptanz f; **~ adaptation** n S&M Produktanpassung f; **~ advertising** n S&M Produktwerbung f; **~ analysis** n S&M Produktanalyse f; **~ attribute** n GEN COMM, S&M Produkteigenschaft f; **~ awareness** n S&M Produktbekanntheit f; **~ benefit** n S&M Produktnutzen m, Produktvorteil m; **~ category** n S&M Produktgruppe f; **~ classification** n IND, S&M Produktklassifikation f; **~ clutter** n S&M Produktwirrwarr nt; **~ compatibility** n IND, S&M Produktkompatibilität f; **~ conception** n S&M Produktkonzept nt; **~ cost** n S&M Produktkosten pl; **~ costing** n ACC Produktkostenberechnung f, S&M Herstellungsaufwand m; **~ creation** n S&M Produktschaffung f; **~ cue** n S&M Produkthinweis m; **~ cycle** n S&M Produktzyklus m; **~ design** n S&M Produktgestaltung f; **~ development** n S&M Produktentwicklung f; **~ development cycle** n S&M Produktentwicklungszyklus m; **~ differentiation** n S&M Produktdifferenzierung f; **~ dynamics** n pl S&M Produktdynamik f; **~ engineer** n HRM, S&M Produktingenieur, in m,f; **~ engineering** n S&M Fertigungstechnik f; **~ evaluation** n S&M Produktbewertung f; **~ field** n S&M Produktfeld nt; **~ generation** n S&M Produktgeneration f; **~ group** n S&M Produktgruppe f; **~ image** n S&M Produktimage nt; **~ improvement** n S&M Produktverbesserung f; **~ initiation** n S&M Produkteinführung f; **~ introduction** n S&M Produkteinführung f

production n GEN COMM Erzeugung f, Vorlage f, Vorführung f, IND Erzeugung f, Fabrikation f, Fertigung f, Herstellung f, Produktion f, *extract, mine* Gewinnung f, *preparation* Zubereitung f, LAW Vorlegung f; **~ area** n GEN COMM Erzeugungsgebiet nt; **~ asymmetry** n ECON Produktionsasymmetrie f; **~ bonus** n IND Leistungsprämie f; **~ capacity** n IND Produktionskapazität f; **~ chain** n IND Produktionskette f; **~ changeover** n IND Produktionsumstellung f; **~ complex** n IND Produktionskomplex m; **~ control** n IND Arbeitskontrolle f, Fertigungskontrolle f, Fertigungsüberwachung f, Terminverfolgung f; **~ costs** n pl ACC Herstellungskosten pl, ECON Fertigungskosten pl, Produktionskosten pl, IND Erzeugungskosten pl, Fertigungsaufwand m, Herstellkosten pl, Produktionsaufwand m, Produktionskosten pl;

~ **cutback** *n* IND Produktionseinschränkung *f*, Produktionskürzung *f*; ~ **department** *n* IND Fertigungsabteilung *f*, Herstellungsabteilung *f*, Produktionsabteilung *f*; ~ **director** *n* HRM, IND, MGMNT Direktor, in *m,f* der Produktionsabteilung, Produktionsdirektor, in *m,f*, Produktionsleiter, in *m,f*; ~ **ecology** *n* ENVIR Produktionsökologie *f*; ~ **engineering** *n* IND, MGMNT Betriebstechnik *f*, Produktionstechnik *f*, Fertigungstechnik *f*; ~ **equipment** *n* IND Produktionszubehör *nt*; ~ **facility** *n* IND Produktionseinrichtung *f*; ~ **figures** *n pl* IND Produktionsziffern *f pl*; ~ **function** *n* ECON Ertragsfunktion *f*, Produktionsfunktion *f*; ~ **implement** *n* GEN COMM Produktionswerkzeug *nt*; ~ **incentive** *n* HRM Akkordprämie *f*; ~ **line** *n* IND Förderband *nt*; ~ **management** *n* IND, MGMNT Produktionssteuerung *f*; ~ **manager** *n* HRM, IND Fertigungsleiter, in *m,f*, Betriebsleiter, in *m,f*, Fabrikationsleiter, in *m,f*, Herstellungsleiter, in *m,f*, Produktionsleiter, in *m,f*, *of department* Direktor, in *m,f* der Produktionsabteilung, MEDIA *print*, MGMNT Produktionsleiter, in *m,f*; ~ **method** *n* IND Produktionsmethode *f*, Produktionsverfahren *nt*, Produktionsweise *f*; ~ **order** *n* IND Fabrikationsauftrag *m*; ~-**oriented organization** *n* GEN COMM produktionsorientierte Organisation *f*; ~ **planning** *n* IND, MGMNT Produktionsplanung *f*, Produktplanung *f*; ~ **planning and control** *n* IND, MGMNT Fertigungsplanung und -kontrolle *f*, Produktionsplanung und -steuerung *f*; ~ **plant** *n* IND Produktionsanlage *f*; ~ **possibility frontier** *n* (*PPF*) ECON Produktionsmöglichkeitenkurve *f*; ~ **process** *n* IND Produktionsgang *m*, Produktionsverfahren *nt*, *steel processing* Formgebungsverfahren *nt*; ~ **rate** *n* IND Produktionsleistung *f*, Produktionstempo *nt*; ~ **run** *n* IND Fortdruck *m*, Produktionsablauf *m*, Produktionsverlauf *m*; ~ **schedule** *n* IND, MGMNT Fertigungsplan *m*, Produktionsplan *m*, Produktionsprogramm *nt*, Terminplan *m*; ~ **scheduling** *n* IND, MGMNT Fertigungsplanung *f*, Fertigungsvorbereitung *f*, Produktionsplanung *f*, Produktionsprogrammierung *f*, Terminplanung *f*, *work* Arbeitsvorbereitung *f*; ~ **slump** *n* ECON, IND Produktionsabfall *m*; ~ **standard** *n* IND, MGMNT *of workers* Leistungsfähigkeit *f* der Arbeiter, Produktionsstandard *m*; ~ **target** *n* IND Produktionsziel *nt*; ~ **technology** *n* IND Fertigungstechnik *f*, Herstellungstechnik *f*; ~ **volume** *n* IND Produktionsstand *m*, Produktionsumfang *m*, Produktionsvolumen *nt*; ~ **worker** *n* HRM, IND Produktionsarbeiter, in *m,f*

productive *adj* ADMIN produktiv, ECON *profitable* gewinnbringend, GEN COMM ertragreich, HRM, IND *workforce* produktiv; ~ **capital** *n* ECON produktiv eingesetztes Kapital *nt*; ~ **maintenance** *n* ADMIN Produktionsinstandhaltung *f*, produktive Wartung *f*; ~ **potential** *n* ECON Produktionspotential *nt*

productivity *n* HRM, IND Produktivität *f*, Ergiebigkeit *f*, Ertragsfähigkeit *f*, Produktivität *f*; ~ **agreement** *n* HRM Produktivitätsvertrag *m*, IND Produktivitätsabkommen *nt*, Produktivitätsvereinbarung *f*, LAW Produktivitätsvereinbarung *f*; ~ **bargaining** *n* HRM Tarifvereinbarung *f* mit Produktivitätsbezug, Produktivitätsverhandlung *f*, am Produktivitätszuwachs orientierte Tarifvereinbarung *f*, IND produktivitätsorientierte Tarifvereinbarung *f*; ~ **campaign** *n* IND Ertragskampagne *f*, S&M Produktivitätskampagne *f*; ~ **drive** *n* IND Produktivitätsfeldzug *m*; ~ **gains** *n pl* IND Produktivi-

tätszuwachs *m*; ~ **incentive** *n* HRM Produktivitätsanreiz *m*; ~ **measurement** *n* IND Produktivitätsmessung *f*; ~ **peak** *n* ECON Produktivitätsspitze *f*; ~ **shock** *n* ECON Produktivitätsschock *m*

product: ~ **knowledge** *n* S&M Produktkenntnis *f*; ~ **launch** *n* S&M *marketing* Produkteinführung *f*; ~ **liability** *n* INS Produkthaftung *f*, S&M Produkthaftbarkeit *f*; ~ **life cycle** *n* S&M Lebenszyklus *m* eines Produktes, Entwicklungszyklus *m* eines Produktes; ~ **life expectancy** *n* S&M Lebenserwartung *f* eines Produktes; ~ **management** *n* HRM Produktmanagement *nt*, MGMNT, S&M Produktüberwachung *f*, Produktmanagement *nt*, *brand* Markenbetreuung *f*, Produktpflege *f*; ~ **manager** *n* HRM, MGMNT Markenbetreuer, in *m,f*, Produktleiter, in *m,f*, Produktmanager, in *m,f*; ~ **marketing** *n* S&M Produktmarketing *nt*; ~ **mix** *n* S&M Produktmix *nt*, gemischtes Produktionsprogramm *nt*; ~ **moment formula** *n* MATH *statistics* Produktmomentformel *f*; ~ **organization** *n* MGMNT produktbezogene Betriebsorganisation *f*; ~ **performance** *n* S&M Produktleistung *f*; ~ **planning** *n* S&M Marktreifgestaltung *f*; ~-**plus** *n* S&M Produktvorteil *m*; ~ **portfolio** *n* FIN Produktbestand *m*, S&M Produktinvestitionen *f pl*, STOCK Produktportfolio *nt*; ~ **positioning** *n* S&M Produktpositionierung *f*; ~ **profile** *n* S&M Produktprofil *nt*; ~ **profitability** *n* ACC, FIN, S&M Produktrentabilität *f*; ~ **quality differentiation** *n* S&M Produktqualitätsdifferenzierung *f*; ~ **range** *n* S&M Produktpalette *f*; ~ **reliability** *n* S&M Produktverläßlichkeit *f*; ~ **research** *n* S&M Produktforschung *f*; ~ **research and development** *n* IND Produktforschung und Entwicklung *f*

products: ~ **carrier** *n* TRANSP Produktentanker *m*, Produktentransporter *m*; ~ **and completed operations insurance** *n* INS Versicherung *f* von Fertigerzeugnissen und abgeschlossenen Dienstleistungen

product: ~ **standard** *n* LAW Warennorm *f*, Produktnorm *f*, S&M Produktstandard *m*; ~ **strategy** *n* S&M Produktstrategie *f*; ~ **tanker** *n* TRANSP Produktentanker *m*; ~ **testing** *n* IND, S&M Produkttest *m*

Prof. *abbr* (*Professor*) HRM Prof. (*Professor*)

profession *n* GEN COMM, HRM Beruf *m*

professional 1. *adj* GEN COMM beruflich, professionell, Fach-, LEIS professionell; **2.** *n* (*pro*) GEN COMM *sport* Professional *m*, Profi *m* (*infrml*)

professional: ~ **achievements** *n pl* GEN COMM *on CV* beruflicher Erfolg *m*; ~ **association** *n* ECON, GEN COMM Fachverband *m*, Berufsverband *m*; ~ **body** *n* GEN COMM Berufsverband *m*, Fachgremium *nt*; ~ **ethics** *n pl* GEN COMM Berufsethos *nt*; ~ **experience** *n* HRM Berufserfahrung *f*; ~ **fee** *n* ADMIN, GEN COMM Honorar *nt*; ~ **indemnity insurance** *n* INS Berufshaftpflichtversicherung *f*

professionalism *n* GEN COMM Professionalismus *m*, Fachwissen *nt*, Spezialistentum *nt*

professionalization *n* GEN COMM Professionalisierung *f*

professional: ~ **journal** *n* GEN COMM, MEDIA Fachblatt *nt*, Fachzeitschrift *f*; ~ **liability** *n* LAW Berufshaftung *f*; ~ **misconduct** *n* LAW standeswidriges Verhalten *nt*; ~ **qualifications** *n pl* HRM berufliche Qualifikationen *f pl*, fachliche Eignung *f*; ~ **secrecy** *n* GEN COMM Berufsgeheimnis *nt*; ~ **services** *n* GEN COMM freiberufliche Dienstleistungen *f pl*, berufliche

Dienstleistungen *f pl*; ~ **success** *n* GEN COMM beruflicher Erfolg *m*; ~ **trader** *n* ECON Berufshändler, in *m,f*
Professor *n* (*Prof.*) HRM Professor, in *m,f* (*Prof*)
proficiency: ~ **pay** *n* ECON Leistungszulage *f*
profile *n* GEN COMM Profil *nt*, Querschnitt *m*; ~ **risk** *n* FIN
Profilrisiko *nt*
profit 1. *n* GEN COMM Profit *m*; ♦ **at a ~ of** GEN COMM bei
einem Profit von; 2. *vi* GEN COMM profitieren
profitability *n* ACC, ECON, FIN Rentabilität *f*, Wirtschaftlichkeit *f*, Ertragslage *f*; ~ **analysis** *n* ACC, FIN
Rentabilitätsanalyse *f*; ~ **ratio** *n* FIN Erfolgskennzahl *f*,
Rentabilitätskennzahl *f*
profitable *adj* ACC gewinnbringend, rentabel, GEN COMM
nutzbringend; ♦ **be ~** GEN COMM sich bezahlt machen
profitable: ~ **firm** *n* ACC gewinnbringende Firma *f*
profit: ~ **before taxes** *n* ACC Gewinn *m* vor Steuern;
~ **carried forward** *n* ACC Gewinnvortrag *m*; ~ **ceiling** *n*
ECON Gewinnplafond *m*; ~ **center** *AmE*, ~ **centre** *BrE*
n ACC Profit-Center *nt*, ECON, FIN Ergebniseinheit *f*,
Profit-Center *nt*, MGMNT Erfolgsbereich *m*,
Ergebniseinheit *f*; ~ **centre accounting** *n BrE* ACC
Abteilungserfolgsrechnung *f*, Profit-Center-Abrech-
nung *f*, Profit-Center-Rechnungswesen *nt*, FIN
Buchhaltung *f* des Profitzentrums, Profit-Center-
Abrechnung *f*, Profit-Center-Rechnungswesen *nt*
profiteer *n* GEN COMM Geschäftemacher, in *m,f*,
Profitmacher, in *m,f*, Schieber, in *m,f* (*infrml*)
profit: ~ **factor analysis** *n* FIN Ertragsfaktoranalyse *f*,
Gewinnfaktoranalyse *f*; ~ **for the financial year** *n* ACC
Gewinn *m* im Geschäftsjahr; ~ **for the year after tax** *n*
TAX Jahresgewinn *m* nach Steuern; ~ **goal** *n* FIN
Gewinnziel *nt*; ~ **graph** *n* FIN Gewinndiagramm *nt*,
Gewinnschaubild *nt*; ~ **impact** *n* FIN
Gewinnauswirkungen *f pl*, Gewinneffekt *m*, GEN COMM
Einfluß *m* auf den Gewinn; ~ **implication** *n* FIN
Gewinnbegleiterscheinung *f*, Gewinnfolgen *f pl*, GEN
COMM Auswirkung *f* auf den Gewinn; ~ **improvement**
n FIN Gewinnverbesserung *f*, GEN COMM Gewinnsteige-
rung *f*, Gewinnverbesserung *f*; ~ **and loss** *phr* (*P&L*)
ACC Gewinn und Verlust *m*; ~ **and loss account** *n* ACC
Gewinn- und Verlustrechnung *f* (*GuV-Rechnung*);
~ **and loss statement** *n* ACC Gewinn- und Verlustrech-
nung *f*; ~**-making enterprise** *n* GEN COMM
gewinnbringendes Unternehmen *nt*; ~ **margin** *n* ECON,
FIN Gewinnmarge *f*, Gewinnspanne *f*, Umsatzrendite *f*,
Umsatzrentabilität *f*; ~ **maximization** *n* ECON, FIN, GEN
COMM Gewinnmaximierung *f*; ~ **motive** *n* ECON, FIN
Gewinnmotiv *nt*, Profitmotiv *nt*, GEN COMM
Gewinnmotiv *nt*; ~ **optimization** *n* ECON, FIN
Gewinnoptimierung *f*, Profitoptimierung *f*, GEN COMM
Gewinnoptimierung *f*; ~ **outlook** *n* FIN, GEN
COMM Gewinnaussichten *f pl*; ~ **performance** *n* FIN
Ergebnis *nt*, Unternehmenserfolg *m*, GEN COMM Unter-
nehmenserfolg *m*; ~ **and performance planning** *n*
(*PPP*) MGMNT Gewinn- und Leistungsplanung *f*;
~ **planning** *n* FIN, GEN COMM Erfolgsplanung *f*,
Gewinnplanung *f*, Ergebnisplanung *f*, MGMNT
Gewinnplanung *f*; ~ **potential** *n* STOCK
Gewinnpotential *nt*; ~ **profile** *n* STOCK *for a straddle*
Gewinnprofil *nt*; ~ **projection** *n* FIN Gewinnprognose *f*,
GEN COMM Gewinnprojektierung *f*; ~**-related pay** *n*
(*PRP*) HRM gewinnbezogenes Arbeitsentgelt *nt*,
gewinnbezogenes Entgelt *nt*, leistungsbezogene Bezah-
lung *f*, Leistungslohn *m*; ~ **retentions** *n pl* ACC
thesaurierte Gewinne *m pl*

profits: **with-~ endowment assurance** *n* INS Versicherung *f* mit Gewinnbeteiligung
profit: ~ **sensitivity analysis** *n* ACC *project assessment*
Gewinnempfindlichkeitsanalyse *f*; ~ **share** *n* FIN Beteiligung *f* am Gewinn; ~**-sharing** *n* ACC, ECON, HRM
Erfolgsbeteiligung *f*, Gewinnbeteiligung *f*; ~**-sharing**
bonus *n* HRM, MGMNT Tantieme *f*; ~**-sharing plan** *n*
AmE ~**-sharing scheme** *BrE n* ACC *employee benefits*
Gewinnbeteiligungsplan *m*, Gewinnbeteiligungssystem
nt, GEN COMM Erfolgsbeteiligungsplan *m*, TAX *employee*
benefits Gewinnbeteiligungsplan *m*; ~ **situation** *n* FIN
Ertragslage *f*
profits: ~ **policy** *n* INS Profitpolice *f*
profit: ~ **squeeze** *n* ECON Gewinndruck *m*
profits: ~ **surpassed forecasts in the first quarter** *phr*
FIN Gewinne übertrafen die Vorhersagen im ersten
Quartal; ~ **tax** *n* ACC, TAX Ertragssteuer *f*, Gewinnsteuer *f*
profit: ~ **strategy** *n* FIN, GEN COMM Erfolgsstrategie *f*,
Gewinnstrategie *f*; ~ **taking** *n* ECON Gewinnmitnahme
f, Gewinnrealisierung *f*; ~**-taking strategy** *n* MGMNT,
STOCK Gewinnmitnahmestrategie *f*, Gewinnrealisierungsstrategie *f*; ~ **target** *n* ACC Gewinnziel *nt*,
FIN Gewinnplanziel *nt*; ~ **test** *n* ACC Gewinnprüfung *f*;
~**-turnover ratio** *n* ACC, FIN Umsatzrendite *f*,
Umsatzrentabilität *f*; ~**-volume ratio** *n* (*P/V*) ACC
Gewinn-Volumen-Verhältnis *nt*; ~ **wedge** *n* ECON
Gewinnzone *f*
pro forma *adj* ADMIN, GEN COMM, IMP/EXP pro forma;
~ **balance sheet** *n* ACC Probebilanz *f*; ~ **invoice** *n*
ADMIN, ACC, GEN COMM, IMP/EXP, S&M Proformarechnung *f*, vorläufige Rechnung *f*, *in advance*
Vorausfaktura *f*
prognosis *n* GEN COMM Prognose *f*
prognosticate *vt* GEN COMM vorhersagen
prognostication *n* GEN COMM Vorhersage *f*, Vorschau *f*
program 1. *n* COMP Programm *nt*, GEN COMM *AmE see*
programme BrE; 2. *vt* COMP programmieren, GEN COMM
AmE see programme BrE
program: ~ **analyst** *n* COMP Systemanalytiker, in *m,f*;
~ **bug** *n* COMP Programmfehler *m*; ~ **deal** *n* COMP,
ECON, STOCK Programmhandel *m*; ~ **file** *n* COMP
Programmdatei *f*; ~ **flow** *n* COMP Programmablauf *m*;
~ **library** *n* COMP Programmbibliothek *f*
programmable: ~ **function** *n* COMP programmierbare
Funktion *f*
programmatic *adj* COMP programmatisch
programme 1. *n BrE* GEN COMM *plan* Plan *m*, Programm
nt, MEDIA *broadcast* Programm *nt*; 2. *vt BrE* GEN COMM
programmieren
programme: ~ **of action** *n BrE* ECON, GEN COMM
Aktionsprogramm *nt*, Handlungsprogramm *nt*;
~ **adjustment loan** *n BrE* (*PAL*) FIN
Programmanpassungskredit *m*; ~ **aid** *n BrE* ECON
development aid Entwicklungshilfe *f*, Programmhilfe *f*,
Projekthilfe *f*; ~ **deal** *n BrE* ECON Programmhandel *m*
programmed: ~ **instruction** *n* COMP programmierte
Unterweisung *f*; ~ **learning** *n* WEL programmierter
Unterricht *m*; ~ **management** *n* MGMNT programmge-
steuerte Betriebsführung *f*, programmiertes
Management *nt*
programme: ~ **evaluation plan** *n BrE* GEN COMM
Programmauswertungsplan *m*, Programmbe-
wertungsplan *m*, Programmevaluationsplan *m*;

~ evaluation and review technique *n* *BrE* (*PERT*) MGMNT Methode zur Berechnung und Kontrolle des Arbeitsablaufs, Projektfortschrittsplanung *f*, Netzplantechnik *f*; **~ forecast** *n* *BrE* GEN COMM Programmvoraussage *f*, Programmvorschau *f*; **~ structure** *n* *BrE* GEN COMM Programmstruktur *f*

programmer *n* COMP Programmierer, in *m,f*

programming *n* COMP Programmieren *nt*, Programmierung *f*, GEN COMM Programmierung *f*; **~ language** *n* COMP Programmiersprache *f*

program: **~ package** *n* COMP, FIN, MGMNT Programmpaket *nt*; **~ testing** *n* COMP Programmtest *m*; **~ trade** *n* COMP, ECON, STOCK Programmhandel *m*; **~ trading** *n* COMP computergestützte Wertpapiertransaktionen *f pl*, ECON, STOCK Programmhandel *m*

progress 1. *n* GEN COMM Fortschritt *m*; **2.** *vi* GEN COMM fortschreiten

progress: **~ of the arts** *n* PATENTS technischer Fortschritt *m*; **~ control** *n* GEN COMM Arbeitskontrolle *f*, Fertigungskontrolle *f*, IND Entwicklungskontrolle *f*, Fortschrittsüberwachung *f*, MGMNT Ablaufkontrolle *f*, Terminkontrolle *f*

progessive *adj* GEN COMM fortschreitend, progressiv

progressively *adv* GEN COMM progressiv, schrittweise

progress: **~ obsolescence** *n* S&M Fortschrittsveraltung *f*; **~ payments** *n pl* FIN Abschlagszahlungen *f pl*, Anzahlungen *f pl*; **~ report** *n* GEN COMM Arbeitsfortschrittsbericht *m*, Tätigkeitsbericht *m*

prohibit *vt* COMP verbieten, LAW gesetzlich verbieten, verbieten

prohibited: **~ goods** *n pl* IMP/EXP Konterware *f*, Schmuggelware *f*, verbotene Ware *f*; **~ risk** *n* INS unversicherbares Risiko *nt*

prohibition *n* GEN COMM Verbot *nt*; **~ notice** *n* HRM, WEL *health and safety* Beschäftigungsverbot *nt*; **~ right** *n* PATENTS Prohibitionsrecht *nt*, Verbotsrecht *nt*; **~ of a strike** *n* GEN COMM, HRM, IND Streikverbot *nt*

project 1. *n* COMP, ECON, FIN, GEN COMM, HRM, MGMNT, TRANSP Projekt *nt*; **2.** *vt* GEN COMM *forecast* vorhersagen

project: **~ aid** *n* ECON *development aid* POL, WEL Projekthilfe *f*; **~ analysis** *n* FIN, MGMNT Projektanalyse *f*, Projektauswertung *f*; **~ appraisal** *n* MGMNT Projektabschätzung *f*; **~ approval** *n* GEN COMM Projektbewilligung *f*, Projektgenehmigung *f*; **~ assessment** *n* FIN, MGMNT Projektbewertung *f*, Projekteinschätzung *f*

projected: **~ benefit application** *n* HRM beabsichtigte Leistungsverwendung *f*

project: **~ engineer** *n* HRM, IND, MGMNT Projektingenieur, in *m,f*; **~ finance** *n* FIN Finanzlage *f* des Projektes; **~ forwarding** *n* TRANSP Projektbeförderung *f*

projecting *n* GEN COMM Planung *f*

projection *n* GEN COMM Planung *f*, Prognose *f*, *prediction* Vorhersage *f*, *estimate* Schätzung *f*, Projektion *f*, LEIS Vorschau *f*

projective: **~ test** *n* S&M projektiver Test *m*

project: **~ leader** *n* HRM, MGMNT Projektleiter, in *m,f*; **~ link** *n* ECON Projektbindung *f*; **~ management** *n* HRM, MGMNT Projektleitung *f*, Projektmanagement *nt*; **~ manager** *n* HRM, MGMNT Projektleiter, in *m,f*, Projektmanager, in *m,f*; **~ participants insolvency cover** *n* INS Deckung *f* gegen Insolvenz der Projektteilnehmer, Versicherungsschutz *m* gegen Insolvenz

der Projektteilnehmer; **~ planning** *n* HRM, MGMNT Projektplanung *f*; **~ preparation facility** *n* (*PPF*) FIN Projektvorbereitungsfazilität *f*

project: **~ sponsor** *n* ECON Projektträger *m*; **~-typing** *n* ECON Projektbindung *f*

proletarian *adj* ECON, POL proletarisch

prolong *vt* GEN COMM prolongieren

prolongation: **~ of debt** *n* FIN Stundung *f* von Forderungen

prolonged *adj* GEN COMM gestundet, verlängert

prominent *adj* GEN COMM berühmt, prominent

promise 1. *n* GEN COMM Versprechen *nt*, LAW *contract* bindendes Versprechen *nt*; **2.** *vt* GEN COMM versprechen, zusagen, zusichern

promisee *n* LAW Berechtigte(r) *mf* [decl. as adj]

promise: **~ to deliver** *n* TRANSP Auslieferungsversprechen *nt*; **~ to pay** *n* FIN Wechsel *m*, Zahlungsversprechen *nt*, GEN COMM Zahlungszusicherung *f*; **~ to sell** *n* S&M Verkaufszusage *f*

promising *adj* GEN COMM *prospects* vielversprechend

promissory: **~ note** *n* (*P/N*, *PN*) BANK, FIN Eigenwechsel *m*, Schuldanerkenntnis *f*, Schuldschein *m*, Solawechsel *m*, GEN COMM Schuldanerkenntnis *f*

promo *abbr* *infrml* (*promotion*) S&M *of product, service* Reklame *f*, Verkaufsförderung *f*

promote *vt* GEN COMM fördern, unterstützen, begünstigen, HRM *employee* befördern, S&M Reklame machen für, werben für; ♦ **~ efficiency** GEN COMM die Wirksamkeit fördern

promoted: **be ~** *phr* HRM aufsteigen, befördert werden

promotion *n* ECON *employment, work* Arbeitsförderung *f*, GEN COMM Unterstützung *f*, HRM *personnel* Beförderung *f*, S&M (*promo*) *of product, service* Reklame *f*, Verkaufsförderung *f*, Förderung *f*

promotional *adj* GEN COMM fördernd, werbend, S&M fördernd, verkaufsfördernd; **~ allowance** *n* S&M *advertising* Verkaufsförderungsbonus *m*; **~ budget** *n* S&M *advertising* Verkaufsförderungsbudget *nt*; **~ exercise** *n* S&M Werbeaktion *f*; **~ mix** *n* S&M *advertising* Werbemix *nt*; **~ platform** *n* S&M verkaufsförderndes Programm *nt*; **~ policy** *n* GEN COMM Werbepolitik *f*, S&M Verkaufsförderungspolitik *f*, Werbepolitik *f*

promotion: **~ cost** *n* FIN *start-up costs* Gründungskosten *pl*, *product* Verkaufsförderungskosten *pl*, S&M *product* Verkaufsförderungskosten *pl*; **~ ladder** *n* HRM Karriereleiter *f*; **~ mix** *n* S&M *advertising* Verkaufsförderungsmix *m*, Werbemix *m*

prompt 1. *adj* GEN COMM prompt, unverzüglich; **2.** *n* COMP Prompt *nt* (*jarg*), Systemaufforderung *f*, Eingabeaufforderung *f*; **3.** *vt* GEN COMM veranlassen

promptly *adv* GEN COMM unverzüglich

prompt: **~ note** *n* ACC, FIN Mahnzettel *m*, Zahlungserinnerung *f*; **~ payment** *n* FIN prompte Zahlung *f*; **~ payment of invoices** *n* FIN pünktliche Rechnungsbezahlung *f*, sofortige Rechnungsbegleichung *f*

pronounce *vt* GEN COMM aussprechen

proof *n* LAW Beweis *m*, MEDIA *printing, photography* Kontrollabzug *m*, Korrekturbogen *m*, Probebild *nt*, Probeabzug *m*, Probeandruck *m*; ♦ **at ~ stage** MEDIA *publishing* in der Korrekturbogenphase, in der Probezugsphase, zum Zeitpunkt des Korrekturlesens; **under ~** GEN COMM, IMP/EXP *spirits* unter Normalstärke

proof: **~ of ability** *n* GEN COMM Befähigungsnachweis *m*;

~ **of debt** *n* (*POD*) FIN Forderungsnachweis *m*; ~ **of delivery** *n* (*POD*) TRANSP Liefernachweis *m*; ~ **of loss** *n* INS, LAW Schadenbeweis *m*, Schadennachweis *m*; ~ **of ownership** *n* STOCK *of registered shares* Eigentumsnachweis *m*, Eigentumsurkunde *f*

proofreading *n* MEDIA Korrekturlesen *nt*

proofs *n pl* MEDIA *print, photography* Druckfahnen *f pl*

proof: ~ **sheet** *n* MEDIA Probeabzug *m*, Probeandruck *m*, Probebild *nt*; ~ **sheets** *n pl* GEN COMM Andruckbögen *m pl*, MEDIA *print, photography* Andruckbögen *m pl*, Druckfahnen *f pl*; ~ **of title** *n* LAW Eigentumsnachweis *m*

prop up *vt* ECON *currency* stützen

propaganda *n* POL, S&M Propaganda *f* (*jarg*); ~ **campaign** *n* POL, S&M Propagandafeldzug *m* (*jarg*)

propellant: ~ **forces** *n pl* ECON Antriebskräfte *f pl*

propensity *n* ECON, GEN COMM Neigung *f*; ~ **to consume** *n* ECON Konsumbereitschaft *f*, Konsumneigung *f*; ~ **to invest** *n* ECON Investitionsneigung *f*; ~ **to save** *n* ECON Sparneigung *f*, Sparquote *f*; ~ **to work** *n* ECON, HRM, WEL Arbeitsbereitschaft *f*, Arbeitsfreude *f*

proper: ~ **law of the contract** *phr* LAW das auf den Vertrag anzuwendende Recht; **go through the** ~ **channels** GEN COMM *company* ordnungsgemäß vorgehen

propertied: ~ **class** *n* PROP begüterte Klasse *f*

property *n* ECON Vermögensgegenstand *m*, Immobilien *f pl*, GEN COMM Besitz *m*, PROP Eigentum *nt*, Objekt *nt*, Immobilien *f pl*, S&M *advertising, hot property* Anlageobjekt *nt*; ♦ ~ **situated at** LAW belegte Sache *f*

property: ~ **account** *n* ECON Anlagenkonto *nt*; ~ **acquired** *n* PROP erworbenes Eigentum *nt*; ~ **bonds** *n pl* PROP Immobilienfondszertifikat *nt*; ~ **and casualty policy insuring agreement** *n* INS Versicherungsvertrag *m* gegen Vermögensschaden und Unglücksfall; ~ **company** *n* GEN COMM, PROP Immobiliengesellschaft *f*; ~ **damage** *n* PROP Sachschaden *m*; ~ **depreciation insurance** *n* INS Versicherung *f* gegen Vermögensabwertung; ~ **developer** *n* PROP Bauträgerfirma *f*; ~ **development** *n* PROP Grundstückserschließung *f*; ~ **development project** *n* PROP Grundstückserschließungsprojekt *nt*; ~ **dividend** *n* FIN Sachdividende *f*; ~ **and entrepreneurship** *n* ACC, TAX Einkommen *nt* aus Unternehmenstätigkeit und Vermögen; ~ **held in joint names** *n* PROP gemeinsames Eigentum *nt*; ~ **insurer** *n* INS Sachversicherer *m*, Vermögensschadenversicherer *m*; ~ **line** *n* PROP Eigentumsgrenze *f*; ~ **management** *n* BANK, FIN Vermögensverwaltung *f*, PROP Grundstücksverwaltung *f*, STOCK Vermögensverwaltung *f*; ~ **market** *n* PROP Grundstücksmarkt *m*; ~ **owner** *n* PROP Immobilieneigentümer, in *m,f*; ~ **rights** *n pl* PROP Eigentumsrechte *nt pl*; ~ **speculator** *n* PROP Grundstücksspekulant, in *m,f*; ~ **tax** *n* ECON, FIN, TAX Vermögenssteuer *f*

proportion *n* MATH Anteil *m*, Verhältnis *nt*; ♦ **as a** ~ **of** GEN COMM als ein Anteil von, als ein Teil von; **in** ~ **to** MATH im Verhältnis zu

proportional *adj* GEN COMM proportional, verhältnismäßig; ~ **consolidation** *n* ACC anteilige Konsolidierung *f*, verhältnismäßige Konsolidierung *f*; ~ **income tax** *n* TAX Proportionaleinkommenssteuer *f*

proportionality *n* GEN COMM Verhältnismäßigkeit *f*

proportionally *adv* GEN COMM verhältnismäßig; ~**-spaced printing** *n* COMP, MEDIA Proportionalschrift *f*

proportional: ~ **rate** *n* FIN Proportionaltarif *m*; ~ **representation** *n* POL *politics* Verhältniswahl *f*

proportionate *adj* GEN COMM anteilig, im richtigen Verhältnis, verhältnismäßig, *appropriate* angemessen; ~ **grant** *n* ECON anteiliger Zuschuß *m*; ~ **share in loss** *n* ACC anteiliger Bilanzverlust *m*

proportionately *adv* GEN COMM verhältnismäßig

proposal *n* GEN COMM Angebot *nt*, Vorschlag *m*; ♦ **the** ~ **still stands** GEN COMM der Vorschlag gilt noch immer

proposal: ~ **drawings** *n pl* ECON Angebotszeichnungen *f pl*

propose *vt* GEN COMM planen, vorschlagen, MGMNT vorhaben, *meeting* vorschlagen, als Vorschlag unterbreiten; ♦ ~ **a motion** POL einen Antrag stellen; ~ **an amendment** LAW eine Abänderung einreichen, eine Abänderung vorlegen

proposed *adj* GEN COMM vorgeschlagen; ~ **amendment** *n* LAW, POL Abänderungsantrag *m*; ~ **revision** *n* LAW, POL Abänderungsantrag *m*

proposer *n* GEN COMM, INS Antragsteller, in *m,f*

proposition *n* GEN COMM Angebot *nt*, Vorhaben *nt*

proprietary *adj* GEN COMM urheberrechtlich geschützt; ~ **brand** *n* GEN COMM Handelsname *m*, Markenname *m*; ~ **company** *n* (*Pty*) GEN COMM Dachgesellschaft *f*, *Singapore, Australia* Gesellschaft mit beschränkter Haftung *f* (*GmbH, Ges.m.b.H. Öst*), Muttergesellschaft *f*; ~ **drug** *n* GEN COMM gesetzlich geschütztes Arzneimittel *nt*; ~ **goods** *n pl* GEN COMM Markenartikel *m pl*, Markenwaren *f pl*, S&M Markenartikel *m pl*; ~ **insurance** *n* INS Versicherung *f* auf Aktien; ~ **rights** *n pl* STOCK Eigentumsrechte *nt pl*; ~ **software** *n* COMP anwendereigene Software *f*

proprietor *n* GEN COMM *sole trader* Einzelunternehmer, in *m,f*, *of a business* Eigentümer, in *m,f*, Inhaber, in *m,f*, Besitzer, in *m,f*, LAW, PATENTS *intellectual property* Inhaber, in *m,f*

pro rata 1. *adj* GEN COMM, HRM anteilig, dem Anteil entsprechend, verhältnismäßig; **2.** *adv* GEN COMM verhältnismäßig

pro rata: ~ **financing** *n* FIN anteilige Finanzierung *f*; ~ **freight** *n* TRANSP Distanzfracht *f*; ~ **unearned premium reserve** *n* INS Deckungsrückstellung *f*

prorate *vt* GEN COMM anteilmäßig aufteilen, umlegen

prorated: ~ **cost** *n* ACC anteilige Kosten *pl*

proration *n* TRANSP anteilmäßige Verrechnung *f*, Prorationsverrechnung *f*; ~ **mileage** *n* *AmE* TRANSP anteilmäßige Aufteilung *f* auf der Grundlage der Kilometerzahl; ~ **rate** *n* TRANSP Aufteilungssatz *m*

pros: ~ **and cons** *n pl* GEN COMM Für *nt* und Wider *nt*, Vor- und Nachteile *m pl*

prosecutable *adj* LAW strafrechtlich verfolgbar, verhandelbar

prosecute *vt* LAW strafrechtlich verfolgen, verfolgen, PATENTS *application* durchführen; ♦ ~ **sb for forgery** LAW jdn wegen Urkundenfälschung belangen

prosecution *n* LAW Verfolgung *f*; **the** ~ *n* LAW die Staatsanwaltschaft *f*

prospect 1. *n* GEN COMM Aussicht *f*; **2.** *vi* IND nach Bodenschätzen suchen; ♦ ~ **for oil** IND nach Öl bohren

prospective *adj* GEN COMM voraussichtlich, S&M *customer* zukünftig; ~ **buyer** *n* S&M Kaufinteressent, in *m,f*; ~ **customer** *n* S&M, S&M *potential buyer* Interessent, in *m,f*, potentielle Verbraucherin *f*, potentieller Verbraucher *m*, voraussichtliche Kundin *f*, voraussichtlicher Kunde *m*; **~ rating** *n* INS prospektive Bewertung *f*, voraussichtliche Veranlagung *f*

prospectus *n* FIN, STOCK Emissionsprospekt *m*, Gründungsprospekt *m*

prosper *vt* GEN COMM reich werden

prosperity *n* ECON Reichtum *m*, Wohlstand *m*; **~ indicator** *n* ECON Wohlstandsindikator *m*

prosperous *adj* ECON reich, wohlhabend

pro tanto *adv* GEN COMM insofern, insoweit

protect *vt* LAW *interests* protegieren, schützen, POL protegieren; ◆ **~ goods** *tariff barriers* GEN COMM Waren durch Schutzzölle schützen; **~ oneself** GEN COMM sich schützen; **~ sb's interests** GEN COMM *country, producers, consumers* jds Interessen schützen, jds Interessen wahrnehmen

protected *adj* LAW protegiert, geschützt; ◆ **~ by copyright** LAW urheberrechtlich geschützt

protecting *adj* GEN COMM schützend

protection *n* ECON Protektion *f*, Schutz *m*, ENVIR Schutz *m*, GEN COMM Abwehr *f*, LAW *intellectual property* Schutz *m*; **~ against wrongful dismissal** *n* HRM, LAW Kündigungsschutz *m*; **~ by copyright** *n* ECON Urheberrechtsschutz *m*; **~ of the environment** *n* ENVIR, POL Umweltschutz *m*; **~ from litigation** *n* ACC *provisions*, LAW Rechtsschutz *m*; **~ and indemnity** *n* (*P&I*) TRANSP Reederhaftpflicht *f* (*P & I*)

Protection: ~ and Indemnity Association *n* INS *marine* Interessenverband der Schadensversicherer; **~ of Interest Act 1980** *phr* LAW *contract law* Gesetz zum Schutz britischer Interessen 1980

protectionism *n* ECON Protektionismus *m*, Schutzzollpolitik *f*, IMP/EXP Schutzzollpolitik *f*

protectionist: ~ policy *n* ECON protektionistische Politik *f*

protection: ~ of property *n* PROP, IND Objektschutz *m*

protective: ~ award *n* HRM Schutzschiedsspruch *m*; **~ covenant** *n* FIN Schutzbestimmung *f*; **~ duties** *n pl* ECON, IMP/EXP Schutzzoll *m*; **~ location** *n* TRANSP *oil tanker* Sicherheitsstandort *m*; **~ quota** *n* ECON Abwehrquote *f*; **~ safety screen** *n* GEN COMM Sicherheitsabschirmung *f*; **~ tariff** *n* ECON Abwehrzoll *m*, Schutzzoll *m*

protest 1. *n* GEN COMM Protest *m*, PATENTS Widerspruch *m*, TRANSP *shipping* Seeprotest *m*; **2.** *vt* GEN COMM *decision* protestieren; **3.** *vi* GEN COMM protestieren; ◆ **~ against** LAW widersprechen

protest: ~ charges *n pl* LAW Protestkosten *pl*; **~ for absence** *n* STOCK Abwesenheitsprotest *f*; **~ strike** *n* HRM Proteststreik *m*; **~ vote** *n* POL Proteststimme *f*

protocol *n* COMP Protokoll *nt*, GEN COMM Verhandlungsniederschrift *f*, POL Protokoll *nt*

prototype *n* S&M Prototyp *m*

prove *vt* GEN COMM belegen, Beweis erbringen, beweisen, LAW antreten, beweisen; ◆ **~ a debt** ACC eine Schuld nachweisen; **~ a market** S&M einen Markt erproben; **~ an assertion** GEN COMM eine Behauptung beweisen; **~ one's identity** LAW sich ausweisen

proven *adj* GEN COMM bewährt

provide *vt* FIN *cover* anschaffen, *funds* bereitstellen, GEN COMM *assistance* leisten, *goods and services* versorgen mit, bereitstellen, beschaffen, LAW vorschreiben; ◆

~ the base for sth BANK *market* die Grundlage für etw bilden, STOCK *shares* einen Markt schaffen

provide against *vt* GEN COMM Maßnahmen treffen gegen, verhindern; ◆ **~ a risk** INS für ein Risiko Vorsorge treffen

provided: not ~ for *phr* BANK keine ausreichende Deckung; **~ that** *phr* GEN COMM sofern, vorausgesetzt, daß, LAW vorbehaltlich

provident: ~ fund *n* FIN Sicherheitsfonds *m*, Unterstützungskasse *f*

provider *n* ECON Lieferant, in *m,f*, Lieferer *m*

provincial: ~ Crown corporation *n* BrE ADMIN provinzielles staatliches Unternehmen *nt*; **~ press** *n* MEDIA Provinzpresse *f*

provision *n* ACC Wertberichtigung *f*, Rückstellung *f*, BANK, FIN Rückstellung *f*, GEN COMM Bereitstellung *f*, Rückstellung *f*, LAW *of act* Bestimmung *f*, Vorschrift *f*, *contract* Vertragsbestimmung *f*, LEIS Versorgung *f*, TAX Rückstellung *f*

provisional *adj* GEN COMM, INS, PATENTS einstweilig, vorläufig, *temporary* übergehend; **~ acceptance** *n* GEN COMM *of goods, on delivery, before testing* einstweilige Annahme *f*, vorläufige Annahme *f*

Provisional: ~ Collection of Taxes Act *n* TAX Gesetz *nt* zur einstweiligen Steuereinziehung

provisional: **~ deposit** *n* ECON Bietungsgarantie *f*; **~ invoice** *n* GEN COMM, IMP/EXP vorläufige Rechnung *f*

provisionally *adv* GEN COMM vorläufig; ◆ **~ invalid** LAW schwebend unwirksam

provisional: **~ policy** *n* INS Interimspolice *f*, vorläufige Police *f*; **~ protection** *n* PATENTS vorläufiger Schutz *m*, zeitweiliger Schutz *m*

provision: **~ for bad debts** *n* ACC Wertberichtigung *f* auf uneinbringliche Forderungen; **~ for contingent losses** *n* ACC Delkredererückstellung *f*; **~ for depreciation** *n* ACC Rückstellung *f* für Abschreibungen; **~ for loan loss** *n* BANK Rückstellung *f* für Darlehensverlust; **~ of funds** *n* FIN Mittelzuweisung *f*, Ausstattung *f*, Dotierung *f*; **~ of land for building sites** *n* LAW Baulandbeschaffung *f*; **~ of services** *n* GEN COMM Bereitstellung *f* von Dienstleistungen

proviso: ~ clause *n* LAW Vorbehaltsklausel *f*; ◆ **with the ~ that** LAW vorbehaltlich

prox. *abbr* (*proximo*) COMMS n.M. (*nächsten Monats*)

proximo *adv* (*prox.*) COMMS nächsten Monats (*n. M.*)

proxy *n* GEN COMM Stellvertreter, in *m,f*, STOCK Vollmacht *f*; **~ battle** *n* AmE STOCK Kampf *m* um Stimmrechte

proxyholder *n* LAW *civil law* Stimmbevollmächtigte(r) *mf* [decl. as adj]

proxy: **~ statement** *n* LAW Vollmachtsanweisung *f*, *shareholders* Aktionärsinformation *f*; **~ vote** *n* POL durch einen Bevollmächtigten abgegebene Stimme *f*, Stellvertreterstimme *f*, Stimmabgabe im Auftrag *f*

PRP *abbr* (*profit-related pay*) HRM gewinnbezogenes Entgelt *nt*, gewinnbezogenes Arbeitsentgelt *nt*, leistungsbezogene Bezahlung *f*, Leistungslohn *m*

PRT *abbr* (*petroleum revenue tax*) TAX Steuern *f pl* auf Einnahmen aus Erdölgewinnung

prudent *adj* GEN COMM sorgfältig, umsichtig, vorsichtig

prudential *adj* AmE GEN COMM *local administration* beratend; **~ committee** *n* AmE GEN COMM Beirat *m*, Beratungsausschuß *m*, Verwaltungsausschuß *m*

prudently *adv* GEN COMM besonnen, haushälterisch

prudent: ~ **man rule** *n* GEN COMM Vorschrift über die Sorgfaltspflicht eines Treuhänders in Vermögensfragen

prune *vt* GEN COMM kürzen

pruning *n* GEN COMM Kürzung *f*, Reduzierung *f*, Zusammenstreichen *nt*

ps. *abbr* (*postscript*) COMMS Nachschrift *f*, Nachtrag *m*, P.S. (*Postscriptum*)

PS *abbr* ADMIN (*personal secretary*) Chefsekretär, in *m,f*, Privatsekretär, in *m,f*, COMMS (*postscript*) Nachschrift *f*, Nachtrag *m*, P.S. (*Postscriptum*), HRM (*personal secretary*) Chefsekretär, in *m,f*, Privatsekretär, in *m,f*

P/S *abbr* (*public sale*) ECON Versteigerung *f*, S&M Auktion *f*, Versteigerung *f*

PSBR *abbr BrE* (*public sector borrowing requirement*) ECON, FIN Fremdmittelbedarf *m* der öffentlichen Hand, Kreditbedarf *m* der öffentlichen Hand, Kreditbedarf *m* des öffentlichen Dienstes

PSDR *abbr BrE* (*public sector debt repayment*) ECON Tilgung *f* öffentlicher Schulden

PSE *abbr* (*public service employment*) HRM Beschäftigung *f* im öffentlichen Dienst

P/Sec *abbr* (*personal secretary*) ADMIN, HRM Chefsekretär, in *m,f*, Privatsekretär, in *m,f*

pseudo- *pref* GEN COMM Pseudo-; ~**problem** *n* ECON Scheinproblem *nt*; ~**production function** *n* ECON Pseudoproduktionsfunktion *f*; ~**product testing** *n* S&M Pseudoproduktest *m*

psf *abbr* (*per square foot*) GEN COMM pro Quadratfuß

PSI *abbr* (*pounds per square inch*) IND Pfund *nt* pro Quadratzoll

PSL *abbr* (*private sector liquidity*) ECON liquide Mittel *nt pl* des Privatsektors

PSV *abbr* (*public service vehicle*) TRANSP öffentliches Verkehrsmittel *nt*

psychographics *n pl* S&M *advertising* Psychographie *f*

psychological: ~ **breaking point** *n* ECON Höchstbelastungssatz *m*; ~ **hook** *n* S&M psychologischer Blickfang *m*; ~ **price** *n* S&M psychologischer Preis *m*; ~ **pricing** *n* S&M psychologische Preisfestsetzung *f*; ~ **test** *n* HRM psychologischer Test *m*

psychology *n* ECON Psychologie *f*; ~ **of selling** *n* S&M Verkaufspsychologie *f*

psychometrics *n pl* HRM Psychometrie *f*

psychometric: ~ **testing** *n* HRM, S&M psychometrischer Test *m*

pt *abbr* GEN COMM (*pint*) pt (*Pint*), LAW (*private terms*) privatrechtliche Bedingungen *f pl*

PTA *abbr* (*prepaid ticket advice*) TRANSP Mitteilung *f* bezüglich vorausbezahlter Fahrscheine

PTL *abbr* (*partial total loss*) INS teilweiser Gesamtschaden *m*, teilweiser Totalschaden *m*, teilweiser Totalverlust *m*

pto *abbr* (*please turn over*) COMMS b.w. (*bitte wenden*)

P to P *abbr* (*port to port*) IMP/EXP, TRANSP Hafen-Hafen, Kai-Kai, von Hafen zu Hafen, von Kai zu Kai

Pty *abbr* (*proprietary company*) GEN COMM *Singapore, Australia* GmbH (*Gesellschaft mit beschränkter Haftung*), Ges.m.b.H. (*Öst*) (*Gesellschaft mit beschränkter Haftung*)

public **1.** *adj* GEN COMM öffentlich; ♦ **be under** ~ **ownership** ECON, POL in öffentlichem Eigentum sein; **bring under** ~ **ownership** ECON, POL in Gemeineigentum überführen; **go** ~ FIN in eine Publikumsgesellschaft umwandeln; **2.** *n* GEN COMM Allgemeinheit *f*, Publikum *nt*, Öffentlichkeit *f*, LAW Allgemeinheit *f*

public: ~ **access** *n* ADMIN, LAW, POL *to information* öffentlicher Zugang *m*; ~ **address system** *n* (*PA*) COMMS Lautsprecheranlage *f*; ~ **administration** *n* ADMIN behördliche Verwaltung *f*; ~ **affairs** *n pl* POL öffentliche Angelegenheiten *f pl*; ~ **amenity** *n* WEL öffentliche Einrichtung *f*

publican: ~'s **licence** *n BrE* LAW Schankerlaubnis *f*

publication *n* MEDIA Herausgabe *f*, Publikation *f*, Schrift *f*, Veröffentlichung *f*; ~ **date** *n* MEDIA Erscheinungsdatum *nt*

public: ~ **at large** *n* GEN COMM breite Öffentlichkeit *f*, Allgemeinheit *f*, LAW Allgemeinheit *f*; ~ **auction** *n* GEN COMM öffentliche Versteigerung *f*; ~ **authorities** *n pl* ECON Behörden *f pl*; ~ **authority** *n* GEN COMM öffentliche Hand *f*, Behörde *f*, Staatsgewalt *f*; ~ **body** *n* ADMIN öffentlicher Rechtsträger *m*, Anstalt *f* des öffentlichen Rechts, GEN COMM öffentlicher Rechtsträger *m*, Anstalt *f* des öffentlichen Rechts, Körperschaft *f* des öffentlichen Rechts; ~ **bond** *n* AmE FIN Staatsschuldverschreibung *f*

Public: ~ **Broadcasting Services** *n pl AmE* (*PBS*) MEDIA öffentliche Rundfunk- und Fernsehanstalten *f pl*

public: ~ **choice theory** *n* ECON Public-Choice-Theorie *f*; ~ **company** *n* GEN COMM öffentliches Unternehmen *nt*, Publikumsgesellschaft *f*, Aktiengesellschaft *f*; ~ **consumption** *n* ECON öffentlicher Verbrauch *m*; ~ **contract** *n* GEN COMM *for engineering companies* öffentlicher Auftrag *m*, Staatsauftrag *m*, LAW Staatsauftrag *m*; ~ **corporation** *n* ADMIN Körperschaft *f* des öffentlichen Rechts, GEN COMM allgemeine Kapitalgesellschaft *f*; ~ **debt** *n* ECON öffentliche Schuld *f*, Schulden *f pl* der öffentlichen Hand, Verschuldung *f* der öffentlichen Hand, FIN Staatsverschuldung *f*; ~ **debt charges** *n pl* FIN Staatsverschuldungskosten *pl*; ~ **debt envelope** *n* FIN Staatsverschuldungspaket *nt*; ~ **debt service** *n* FIN öffentlicher Schuldendienst *m*; ~ **development** *n* ECON *of land* öffentliche Erschließung *f*, Erschließung *f* durch die öffentliche Hand; ~ **distribution of securities** *n* STOCK öffentliche Wertpapierausschüttung *f*; ~ **domain software** *n* COMP freibenutzbare Software *f*, Public-Domain-Software *f*; ~ **economics** *n* ECON Finanzwissenschaft *f*, Nationalökonomie *f*, Volkswirtschaftslehre *f*; ~ **enterprise** *n* ADMIN staatliches Unternehmen *nt*, ECON öffentliches Wirtschaftsunternehmen *nt*, Staatsbetrieb *m*, staatliches Unternehmen *nt*, FIN staatliches Unternehmen *nt*, GEN COMM öffentliches Wirtschaftsunternehmen *nt*, Staatsbetrieb *m*, staatliches Unternehmen *nt*; ~ **enterprise rationalization loan** *n* (*PERL*) FIN Rationalisierungsanleihe *f* eines Staatsunternehmens; ~ **enterprise reform loan** *n* (*PERL*) FIN Rationalisierungsanleihe *f* eines Staatsunternehmens; ~ **enterprise rehabilitation loan** *n* (*PERL*) FIN Rationalisierungsanleihe eines Staatsunternehmens; ~ **examination** *n* HRM, WEL staatliche Prüfung *f*; ~ **expenditure** *n* ECON Ausgaben *f pl* der öffentlichen Hand, Staatsausgaben *f pl*, FIN Ausgaben *f pl* der öffentlichen Hand; ~ **expenditure control** *n* ECON Haushaltskontrolle *f*, Kontrolle *f* der Staatsausgaben; ~ **expenditure survey** *n* ECON Untersuchung *f* der Staatsausgaben

Public: ~ **Expenditure Survey Committee** *n* (*PESC*) ECON Ausschuß *m* zur Untersuchung der Staatausgaben; ~ **Expenditure White Paper** *n BrE* (*PEWP*) ECON Weißbuch *nt* der Staatsausgaben

public: ~ **finance** *n* FIN Finanzwissenschaft *f*, öffentliches Finanzwesen *nt*; ~ **finances** *n pl* ECON öffentliche Finanzen *f pl*, Finanzwirtschaft *f*, Staatsfinanzen *f pl*; ~ **funds** *n pl* GEN COMM, POL öffentliche Mittel *nt pl*; ~ **good** *n* ECON öffentliches Gut *nt*; ~ **health** *n* WEL öffentliches Gesundheitswesen *nt*, Volksgesundheit *f*; ~ **holiday** *n* GEN COMM, HRM, LAW gesetzlicher Feiertag *m*; ~ **housing authority bond** *n* STOCK Anleihe *f* der öffentlichen Wohnungsbaubehörde; ~ **interest company** *n* ECON Unternehmen *nt* des öffentlichen Interesses; ~ **investor** *n* FIN staatlicher Investor *m*; ~ **invitation to bid** *n* GEN COMM öffentliche Angebotseinholung *f*, öffentliche Ausschreibung *f*

publicity *n* HRM Werbewesen *nt*, MEDIA Publizität *f*, S&M Werbewesen *nt*, Werbung *f*, Publizität *f*; ~ **department** *n* S&M Werbeabteilung *f*; ~ **expenses** *n pl* S&M Werbeausgaben *f pl*; ~ **man** *n* HRM Werbefachmann *m*; ~ **manager** *n* HRM, S&M Werbeleiter, in *m,f*; ~ **material** *n* S&M Werbematerial *nt*; ~ **stunt** *n* S&M Werbegag *m*

public: ~ **law** *n* LAW öffentliches Recht *nt*; ~ **lending right** *n* (*PLR*) MEDIA gebührenpflichtiges Ausleihungsrecht *nt*; ~ **limited company** *n BrE* ECON (*plc BrE*), GEN COMM (*PLC BrE*), STOCK (*cf corporation, plc BrE*) Aktiengesellschaft *f* (*AG*), Kapitalgesellschaft *f*; ~ **limited partnership** *n* LAW, STOCK Kommanditgesellschaft *f* (*KG*); ~ **loan** *n* FIN öffentlicher Kredit *m*, Staatsanleihe *f*

publicly: ~ **assisted housing** *n* WEL sozialer Wohnungsbau *m*; ~ **funded** *adj* GEN COMM öffentlich gefördert; ~ **held company** *n* GEN COMM allgemeine Kapitalgesellschaft *f*; ~ **listed company** *n* ECON Unternehmen *nt* der öffentlichen Hand, FIN amtlich notierte Firma *f*, GEN COMM Kapitalgesellschaft *f*; ~ **owned company** *n* ECON Staatsbetrieb *m*, GEN COMM Staatsbetrieb *m*, staatliche Gesellschaft *f*; ~ **traded company** *n* STOCK Aktiengesellschaft *f* (*AG*)

public: ~ **notice** *n* LAW Bekanntmachung *f*; ~ **offering** *n* STOCK öffentliches Zeichnungsangebot *nt*, zur öffentlichen Zeichnung aufgelegte Emission *f*; ~ **opinion** *n* GEN COMM öffentliche Meinung *f*

Public: ~ **Order Act** *n BrE* HRM *1986* Gesetz *nt* zur Aufrechterhaltung von Ruhe und Ordnung

public: ~ **ownership** *n* ECON, FIN, POL Staatseigentum *nt*, Gemeineigentum *nt*; ~ **pricing** *n* ECON administrierte Preisbildung *f*, staatliche Preisfestsetzung *f*; ~ **procurement** *n* ECON öffentliches Vergabewesen *nt*, öffentliches Auftragswesen *nt*; ~ **procurement contract** *n* GEN COMM öffentlicher Auftrag *m*; ~ **prosecutor** *n* LAW Staatsanwältin *f*, Staatsanwalt *m*; ~ **prosecutor's office** *n* LAW Staatsanwaltschaft *f*; ~ **purse** *n* ECON, POL Staatskasse *f*, Staatssäckel *m* (*infrml*); ~ **records** *n pl* ADMIN Staatsurkunden *f pl*; ~ **relations** *n* (*PR*) HRM, S&M Öffentlichkeitsarbeit *f*, Public Relations *pl* (*PR*); ~ **relations agency** *n* S&M *advertising* Werbeagentur *f*, PR-Agentur *f*; ~ **relations consultancy** *n* HRM, S&M PR-Beratung *f*; ~ **relations consultant** *n* HRM, S&M PR-Berater, in *m,f*, PR-Sachbearbeiter, in *m,f*; ~ **relations department** *n* (*PRD*) HRM, S&M PR-Abteilung *f*, Abteilung *f* für Öffentlichkeitsarbeit; ~ **relations executive** *n* HRM, S&M PR-Berater, in *m,f*, PR-Sachbearbeiter, in *m,f*; ~ **relations officer** *n* HRM, S&M PR-Berater, in *m,f*,

PR-Sachbearbeiter, in *m,f*; ~ **resources** *n pl* FIN öffentliche Mittel *nt pl*; ~ **sale** *n* (*P/S*) ECON Versteigerung *f*, S&M Auktion *f*, Versteigerung *f*; ~ **school** *n* WEL *AmE* öffentliche Schule *f*, staatliche Schule *f*, städtische Schule *f*, *BrE* Privatschule *f*; ~ **sector** *n* ECON öffentlicher Sektor *m*, staatlicher Sektor *m*; ~ **sector balance sheet** *n* ECON Bilanz *f* des öffentlichen Sektors; ~ **sector borrowing requirements** *n pl BrE* (*PSBR*) ECON, FIN Kreditbedarf *m* der öffentlichen Hand *m*; ~ **sector debt repayment** *n BrE* (*PSDR*) ECON Tilgung *f* öffentlicher Schulden; ~ **sector deficit** *n* ECON Defizit *nt* der öffentlichen Haushalte; ~ **sector pay** *n* ECON Bezahlung *f* im öffentlichen Dienst; ~ **service** *n* ADMIN Staatsdienst *m*, GEN COMM Verwaltungsdienst *m*; ~ **service advertising** *n* S&M Werbung *f* der öffentlichen Hand; ~ **service contract** *n* GEN COMM Vertrag *m* zur Bereitstellung von Versorgungsdiensten; ~ **service corporation** *n AmE* ADMIN kommunaler Eigenbetrieb *m*, Versorgungsunternehmen *nt*; ~ **service employment** *n* (*PSE*) HRM Beschäftigung *f* im öffentlichen Dienst; ~ **services** *n pl* HRM Dienstleistungssektor *m*; ~ **service vehicle** *n* (*PSV*) TRANSP öffentliches Verkehrsmittel *nt*; ~ **spending** *n* ECON öffentliche Ausgaben *f pl*, Staatsausgaben *f pl*; ~ **spending plans** *n pl* ECON Plan *m* der Staatsausgaben; ~ **spending ratio** *n* ECON Staatsquote *f*; ~ **transport** *n BrE* (*cf public transportation AmE*) TRANSP öffentliche Verkehrsmittel *nt pl*, öffentlicher Verkehr *m*, öffentliches Verkehrswesen *nt*; ~ **transportation** *n AmE* (*cf public transport BrE*) TRANSP öffentliche Verkehrsmittel *nt pl*, öffentlicher Verkehr *m*, öffentliches Verkehrswesen *nt*; ~ **transportation system** *n AmE* (*cf public transport system BrE*) TRANSP öffentliches Verkehrssystem *nt*; ~ **transport system** *BrE n* (*cf public transportation system AmE*) TRANSP öffentliches Verkehrssystem *nt*; ~ **use** *n* PATENTS Verwendung *f* im öffentlichen Interesse; ~ **utility** *n* ADMIN, ECON, GEN COMM öffentliches Versorgungsunternehmen *nt*, Versorgungsunternehmen *nt*; ~ **utility company** *n* ECON, GEN COMM öffentliches Versorgungsunternehmen *nt*; ~ **wants** *n pl* ECON öffentliche Bedürfnisse *f pl*; ~ **warning** *n* GEN COMM öffentliche Warnung *f*; ~ **welfare** *n* WEL öffentliche Wohlfahrt *f*, Sozialfürsorge *f*; ~ **works** *n pl* ECON, GEN COMM öffentliche Bauarbeiten *f pl*, staatliche Bauvorhaben *nt pl*

Public: ~ **Works Department** *n* (*PWD*) GEN COMM, WEL Amt *nt* für öffentliche Arbeiten

public: ~ **works program** *AmE*, ~ **works programme** *BrE n* GEN COMM, WEL Arbeitsbeschaffungsprogramm *nt*, Programm *nt* für öffentliche Arbeiten

publish *vt* GEN COMM bekanntgeben, herausgeben, publizieren, MEDIA herausgeben, publizieren, veröffentlichen, verlegen, PATENTS bekanntgeben, publizieren, veröffentlichen; ♦ ~ **in loose-leaf form** MEDIA als Loseblattsammlung herausgeben

published *adj* GEN COMM herausgegeben, publiziert, MEDIA herausgegeben, publiziert, veröffentlicht, PATENTS publiziert, veröffentlicht; ♦ ~ **monthly** MEDIA *print* erscheint monatlich

published: ~ **accounts** *n pl* ACC veröffentlichter Abschluß *m*; ~ **charge** *n* TRANSP veröffentlichte Gebühr *f*; ~ **fare** *n* TRANSP veröffentlichter Fahrpreis *m*; ~ **information** *n* GEN COMM veröffentlichte Information *f*; ~ **price** *n* GEN COMM, S&M Ladenpreis *m*; ~ **rate**

n TRANSP veröffentlichter Tarif *m*; ~ **research** *n* MATH *statistics* Forschungsberichte *m pl*

publisher *n* MEDIA *organization* Verlag *m*, *person* Herausgeber, in *m,f*, Verleger, in *m,f*

Publishers: ~ and Booksellers Delivery Service *n* BrE (*PBDS*) MEDIA Lieferservice der Verleger und Buchhändler

publisher: ~'s **statement** *n* S&M geprüfte Auflagenmeldung *f*

publishing: ~ **house** *n* MEDIA *print* Verlag *m*; ~ **trade** *n* MEDIA Verlagswesen *nt*

PUD *abbr* (*planned unit development*) PROP geplantes Grundstückserschließungsprojekt *nt*

PUF *abbr* (*purchase underwriting facility*) FIN Kaufübernahmefazilität *f*

puff *n* GEN COMM, S&M übertriebene Werbung *f*, überzogene Werbung *f*

pull 1. *n* MEDIA *print* Probeabzug *m*; **2.** *vt infrml* GEN COMM *deal* durchziehen (*infrml*); ♦ ~ **strings** BrE (*cf pull wires AmE*) GEN COMM Beziehungen spielen lassen, Einfluß geltend machen; ~ **wires** *AmE* (*cf pull strings BrE*) GEN COMM Beziehungen spielen lassen, Einfluß geltend machen

pull down *vt* FIN *profits* herunterdrücken, PROP abbrechen; ♦ **pull inflation down** ECON Inflation drücken

pull off *vt infrml* GEN COMM *succeed in* schaffen (*infrml*); ♦ ~ **a deal** GEN COMM einen Handel erfolgreich abschließen

pull in *vt infrml* GEN COMM *earn* kassieren (*infrml*); ♦ ~ **sales** S&M Umsatz bringen

pull together *vi* GEN COMM *cooperate* zusammenarbeiten

pull: ~-**down menu** *n* COMP Balkenmenü *nt*, Pull-down-Menü *nt*

pulp *vt* GEN COMM einstampfen

pulse *n* COMMS *telephone* Puls *m*, COMP Impuls *m*; ~ **dialing** *AmE*, ~ **dialling** *BrE n* COMMS Impulswahl *f*

pump: ~ **funds into sth** *phr* FIN in etw Kapital stecken

punch 1. *n* GEN COMM Locher *m*; **2.** *vt* COMP lochen; ♦ ~ **a hole in** IND einstanzen, lochen; ~ **the time clock** HRM, IND seine Karte stechen, seine Stechkarte in die Stechuhr stecken

punch: ~ **card** *n* COMP, GEN COMM Lochkarte *f*; ~ **code** *n* COMP, GEN COMM Lochkartencode *m*

punched: ~ **paper** *n* AmE LEIS *theatre* Freikarte *f*

punch: ~ **list** *n* COMP, GEN COMM Lochkartenliste *f*

punchy *adj* MEDIA publikumswirksam

punctual *adj* GEN COMM pünktlich

punctuality *n* TRANSP Pünktlichkeit *f*; ~ **analysis** *n* TRANSP Pünktlichkeitsanalyse *f*; ~ **performance** *n* TRANSP Pünktlichkeitsleistung *f*

puncturing *n* TRANSP Durchschlag *m*, Einstich *m*

punishable *adj* LAW strafbar

punitive: ~ **damages** *n pl* INS Entschädigung *f* mit Strafcharakter, *fine* Buße *f*, Bußgeld *nt*, LAW pönale Geldbuße *f*, pönalisierender Schadensersatz *m*, *fine* Buße *f*, Bußgeld *nt*

punter *n infrml* S&M *customer* Macker *m* (*infrml*), STOCK Börsenspekulant *m*

purchase 1. *n* ECON Erwerb *m*, GEN COMM Ankauf *m*, Kauf *m*; **2.** *vt* ACC anschaffen, GEN COMM anschaffen, kaufen; ♦ ~ **forward** STOCK auf Termin kaufen

purchase: ~ **acquisition** *n* FIN käuflicher Erwerb *m*; ~ **of assets** *n* GEN COMM Kauf *m* von Wirtschaftsgütern;

~ **book** *n* S&M Wareneingangsbuch *nt*; ~ **commitment** *n* LAW *contract law* Abnahmeverpflichtung *f*; ~ **cost** *n* ACC *of assets* Kaufkosten *pl*

purchased: ~ **company** *n* GEN COMM übernommene Gesellschaft *f*

purchase: ~ **decision** *n* GEN COMM Kaufentscheidung *f*; ~ **denominated in foreign currency** *n* ACC Kauf *m* in Fremdwährung; ~ **for settlement** *n* STOCK Kauf *m* zur Abrechnung; ~ **group agreement** *n* FIN Übernahmekonsortialvereinbarung *f*; ~ **invoice** *n* GEN COMM Eingangsrechnung *f*, Einkaufsrechnung *f*; ~ **method** *n* ACC *acquisition* Ankaufsmethode *f*; ~ **money mortgage** *n* PROP Restkaufhypothek *f*; ~ **order** *n* ACC Auftrag *m*, Bestellung *f*, GEN COMM Auftrag *m*; ~ **price** *n* ECON Einkaufspreis *m*, GEN COMM, S&M Kaufpreis *m*; ~ **price method** *n* STOCK *valuation for interest-bearing investments* Einkaufspreisbewertungsmethode *f*

purchaser *n* GEN COMM, S&M Aufkäufer, in *m,f*, Erwerber, in *m,f*, Käufer, in *m,f*

purchase: ~ **returns and allowances** *n pl* S&M Warenrücksendungen und Gutschriften *f pl*; ~ **and sale statement** *n* (*P&S*) STOCK Schlußnote *f*, Schlußschein *m*

purchases: ~ **journal** *n* ACC Einkaufskontenbuch *nt*

purchase: ~ **tax** *n* IMP/EXP, TAX Verbrauchssteuer *f*; ~ **underwriting facility** *n* (*PUF*) FIN Kaufübernahmefazilität *f*

purchasing *n* ACC Anschaffung *f*, GEN COMM Anschaffung *f*, Einkauf *m*, S&M *function in company* Einkauf *m*; ~ **company** *n* GEN COMM übernehmende Gesellschaft *f*; ~ **costs** *n pl* GEN COMM Beschaffungskosten *pl*, Bezugskosten *pl*; ~ **department** *n* GEN COMM Abteilung *f* für Einkauf, Einkaufsabteilung *f*; ~ **executive** *n* MGMNT Einkaufschef, in *m,f*, Einkäufer, in *m,f*; ~ **manager** *n* HRM, MGMNT Einkaufsleiter, in *m,f*; ~ **motivator** *n* S&M kaufmotivierender Faktor *m*; ~ **officer** *n* HRM Einkäufer, in *m,f*; ~ **pattern** *n* S&M Einkaufsverhalten *nt*; ~ **power** *n* ECON Kaufkraft *f*; ~ **power parity** *n* (*PPP*) ECON Kaufkraftparität *f*; ~ **time** *n* GEN COMM Beschaffungszeit *f*

pure: ~ **bundling** *n* ECON reine Bündelung *f*; ~ **burning cost** *n* INS technische Bedarfsprämie *f*; ~ **capitalism** *n* ECON reiner Kapitalismus *m*; ~ **competition** *n* ECON vollständige Konkurrenz *f*, vollständiger Wettbewerb *m*; ~ **credit economy** *n* ECON reine Kreditwirtschaft *f*; ~ **discretion** *n* ADMIN echter Ermessensspielraum *m*; ~ **economic rent** *n* ECON rein wirtschaftliche Miete *f*; ~ **holding company** *n* BANK reine Holdinggesellschaft *f*; ~ **inflation** *n* ECON reine Inflation *f*; ~ **interest rate** *n* ECON Nettozins *m*; ~ **loss cost** *n* INS technische Bedarfsprämie *f*; ~ **market economy** *n* ECON reine Marktwirtschaft *f*; ~ **monopoly** *n* ECON echtes Angebotsmonopol *nt*, reines Monopol *nt*; ~ **play** *n* STOCK reine Spekulation *f*; ~ **profit** *n* ACC Reingewinn *m*, ECON Reinertrag *m*, Unternehmerreingewinn *m*, Reingewinn *m*, FIN Reingewinn *m*

purge: ~ **date** *n* COMP Freigabedatum *nt*

purification *n* ENVIR Klärung *f*, Reinigung *f*

purify *vt* ENVIR reinigen

purpose *n* GEN COMM Zweck *m*; ~-**built** *adj* PROP, TRANSP speziell gebaut; ~-**built block** *n* PROP *of flats* Zweckbau *m*, zweckgebundener Wohnungsbau *m*; ~-**built tonnage** *n* TRANSP speziell gebaute Tonnage *f*; ~-**built vehicle** *n*

TRANSP Zweckfahrzeug *nt*; ~ **loan** *n* STOCK zweckgebundenes Darlehen *nt*

purposes: ~ **statement** *n* STOCK Absichtserklärung *f*

purse *n* FIN *resources, funds* Geldbörse *f*, Rücklage *f*

purser *n* HRM *shipping, air* Zahlmeister, in *m,f*

pursuant: ~ **to article** *phr* LAW gemäß Artikel

pursue *vt* GEN COMM verfolgen, WEL *studies* betreiben

pursuit *n* GEN COMM Verfolgung *f*

purveyor: ~ **of fine foods** *n* GEN COMM Lieferant *m* von Delikatessen; ~ **of services** *n* GEN COMM Anbieter *m* von Dienstleistungen; ~ **to the Royal Household** *n pl BrE* GEN COMM Hoflieferant *m*

pushback *n* TRANSP *aircraft* Zurückschieben *nt*, Zurückstoßen *nt*

push: ~ **button** *n* COMP *on device, peripheral* Druckknopf *m*, Schaltfläche *f*; **--button telephone** *n* COMMS Tastentelefon *nt*

pusher *n* infrml GEN COMM Ehrgeizling *m*

push: ~ **incentive** *n* S&M *advertising* Anreiz *m* für Verkaufsanstrengungen; ~ **money** *n* GEN COMM, HRM *redundancy* Abfindung *f*, S&M *sales bonus* Verkaufsprämie *f*; ~ **sb to the limit** *phr* GEN COMM jdn bis zum Äußersten treiben; ~ **up prices** *phr* S&M Preise hochschleusen

put 1. *n* STOCK Rückprämie *f*; **2.** *vt* ♦ ~ **a call through** ADMIN, GEN COMM ein Gespräch durchstellen; ~ **a cap on** *infrml* GEN COMM begrenzen; ~ **a check in the box** *AmE* (*cf put a tick in the box BrE*) GEN COMM abhaken; ~ **a damper on** *infrml* GEN COMM einen Dämpfer aufsetzen; ~ **forth a claim** LAW einen Anspruch geltend machen; ~ **a house on the market** PROP ein Haus auf den Markt bringen; ~ **a plan into action** GEN COMM einen Plan realisieren, einen Plan umsetzen; ~ **a suggestion before a committee** GEN COMM einem Komitee einen Vorschlag unterbreiten, einem Komitee einen Vorschlag vorlegen; ~ **a tick in the box** *BrE* (*cf put a check in the box AmE*) GEN COMM abhaken; ~ **a veto on** GEN COMM Einspruch erheben; ~ **in order** ADMIN, GEN COMM ordnen; ~ **in touch** GEN COMM miteinander in Kontakt bringen; ~ **into effect** GEN COMM *policies* realisieren; ~ **into execution** GEN COMM ausführen; ~ **into force** LAW *ruling, act* in Kraft setzen; ~ **into receivership** LAW der Zwangsverwaltung unterstellen; ~ **money down** FIN Geld investieren, Geld anlegen; ~ **on the back burner** *infrml* GEN COMM zurückstellen; ~ **one's affairs in order** GEN COMM seine Angelegenheiten in Ordnung bringen; ~ **one's seal to sth** GEN COMM einer Sache zustimmen; ~ **pressure on sb** GEN COMM auf jdn Druck ausüben; ~ **sb in for a job** HRM jdn für einen Arbeitsplatz empfehlen; ~ **sb in the picture** GEN COMM jdn ins Bild setzen; ~ **sb on short allowance** GEN COMM jdm wenig Spesen geben; ~ **sth in order** GEN COMM etw in Ordnung bringen; ~ **sth into production** IND etw in Produktion geben; ~ **sth on**

record GEN COMM etw offiziell erklären, etw in die Akten eintragen; ~ **sth on the agenda** ADMIN, MGMNT etw auf die Tagesordnung setzen; ~ **sth to the test** GEN COMM etw auf die Probe stellen, etw praktisch erproben; ~ **the final touch to sth** GEN COMM einer Sache den letzten Schliff geben; ~ **under seal** LAW amtlich versiegeln

put away *vt* BANK *money* sparen, zurücklegen

put down *vt* COMMS *telephone receiver* auflegen, GEN COMM *in writing* aufzeichnen

put forward *vt* BANK vorverlegen, MGMNT *suggestions* beantragen, einbringen, vorschlagen; ♦ ~ **proposals** MGMNT Vorschläge einbringen

put in *vt* GEN COMM *report* einfügen, einschieben; ♦ ~ **a claim** LAW einen Anspruch erheben; ~ **an application** HRM eine Bewerbung unterbreiten; ~ **a job application** HRM sich um eine Stellung bewerben; ~ **a plea** LAW eine Einrede vorbringen; ~ **a word for sb** GEN COMM für jdn ein Wort einlegen; ~ **for** HRM *job, promotion* sich bemühen um

put off *vt* GEN COMM *postpone* aufschieben; ♦ **put sth off** GEN COMM *idea* etw auf die lange Bank schieben, etw auf Eis legen

put out *vt* MEDIA *book* herausbringen; ♦ ~ **a statement** MEDIA eine Erklärung abgeben; ~ **for tender** GEN COMM, S&M, STOCK ausschreiben

put through *vt* COMMS *call* durchstellen, STOCK durchsetzen; ♦ ~ **under the control of** ECON unterstellen

put up *vt* FIN *capital* aufnehmen, *money* aufbringen, GEN COMM anschlagen

put: ~ **buying hedge** *n* STOCK Sicherungsgeschäft *nt* für den Kauf einer Verkaufsoption; ~ **and call** *n* STOCK Rück- und Vorprämiengeschäft *nt*, Stellage *f*; ~ **delta** *n* STOCK Verkaufsoptionsdelta *nt*; ~ **of more option** *n* STOCK Nochgeschäftsoption *f*; ~ **option** *n* STOCK Rückprämie *f*; ~ **premium** *n* STOCK Rückprämie *f*; ~ **strike** *n* STOCK *options* Basispreis *m* einer Verkaufsoption; ~ **writer** *n* STOCK *options on currency futures* Verkäufer, in *m,f* einer Verkaufsoption

P/V *abbr* (*profit-volume ratio*) ACC Gewinn-Volumen-Verhältnis *nt*

PWD *abbr* (*Public Works Department*) GEN COMM, WEL Amt *nt* für öffentliche Arbeiten

pyramidal *adj* GEN COMM pyramidenförmig

pyramid: ~ **hierarchy** *n* HRM Pyramidenhierarchie *f*

pyramiding *n* FIN Anhäufung *f* von Gewinnen durch Spekulation, STOCK mehrmaliger Erwerb *m* der gleichen Aktie bei steigendem Kurs

pyramid: ~ **selling** *n* ECON Vertrieb *m* nach dem Schneeballsystem, S&M Schneeballsystem *nt*

pyrometer *n* GEN COMM Pyrometer *nt*

PYT *abbr* (*payment*) GEN COMM Ausz. (*Auszahlung*), Bez. (*Bezahlung*), Entlohnung *f*, Z. (*Zahlung*)

Q

QC *abbr* GEN COMM, IND (*quality control*) Gütekontrolle *f*, Qualitätskontrolle *f*, Qualitätsüberwachung *f*, LAW (*Queen's Counsel BrE*), Anwalt *m* der Krone, Anwältin *f* der Krone, S&M (*quality control*) Gütekontrolle *f*, Qualitätskontrolle *f*, Qualitätsüberwachung *f*

QL *abbr* (*query language*) COMP Abfragesprache *f*, Datenbank-Abfragesprache *f*

qnty *abbr* (*quantity*) GEN COMM Menge *f*, Quant. (*Quantität*), MATH Anteil *m*, Quant. (*Quantität*)

QR *abbr* (*quantitative restrictions*) ECON Mengenbeschränkung *f*

qt *abbr* (*quart*) GEN COMM Quart *f*

qtr *abbr* (*quarter*) GEN COMM Quartal *nt*, Viertel *nt*

qty *abbr* (*quantity*) GEN COMM Menge *f*, Quant. (*Quantität*), MATH Anteil *m*, Quant. (*Quantität*)

quadriad *n AmE* ECON die vier für die amerikanische Wirtschaftspolitik Verantwortlichen

quadripartite: ~ **agreement** *n* GEN COMM, POL Viermächteabkommen *nt*

quadruple: ~ **stacker** *n* TRANSP Vierfachstapler *m*

quadruplicate: **in** ~ *phr* GEN COMM in vierfacher Ausfertigung, vierfach

qualification *n* ACC Einschränkung *f*, Vorbehalt *m*, GEN COMM *suitability* Qualifikation *f*, Eignung *f*, *academic* Qualifizierung *f*, HRM Befähigung *f*, Qualifikation *f*, WEL *act of qualifying* Abschluß *m*, Qualifizierung *f*, *certificate* Befähigungsnachweis *m*, *aptitude* Eignung *f*, Qualifikation *f*; ◆ **have the right qualifications for the job** HRM die richtigen Qualifikationen für die Arbeitsstelle haben

qualification: ~ **of opinion** *n* FIN Einschränkung *f* des Gutachtens; ~ **pattern** *n* ECON Qualifikationsstruktur *f*; ~ **period** *n* WEL Ausbildungszeitraum *m*, Einschränkung *f*, Vorbehalt *m*, Zulassungsfrist *f*; ~ **shares** *n pl* STOCK Pflichtaktien *f pl* der Mitglieder des Verwaltungsrates

qualified *adj* GEN COMM *suitable* geeignet, qualifiziert, POL, WEL qualifiziert; ◆ **be** ~ **to do sth** GEN COMM, HRM die Qualifikation für etw haben; ~ **accountant** *n* ACC amtlich geprüfte Buchhalterin *f*, amtlich geprüfter Buchhalter *m*; ~ **approval** *n* GEN COMM eingeschränkte Genehmigung *f*; ~ **auditor** *n* ACC amtlich geprüfte Buchprüferin *f*, amtlich geprüfter Buchprüfer *m*; ~ **endorsement** *n* BANK eingeschränktes Indossament *nt*, Indossament *nt* ohne Obligo; ~ **majority** *n* POL einfache Mehrheit *f*, eingeschränkte Mehrheit *f*, qualifizierte Mehrheit *f*; ~ **majority vote** *n* POL *particularly EU* qualifizierte Mehrheitsabstimmung *f*, qualifizierter Mehrheitsbeschluß *m*; ~ **opinion** *n* ACC eingeschränkter Bestätigungsvermerk *m*, GEN COMM qualifizierte Meinung *f*; ~ **report** *n* ACC eingeschränkter Bestätigungsvermerk *m*, *acceptance* Annahme *f* unter Vorbehalt

qualify 1. *vt* GEN COMM, HRM befähigen, qualifizieren; ◆ ~ **sb to do sth** HRM jdn befähigen, etw zu tun, jdn berechtigen, etw zu tun; **2.** *vi* GEN COMM sich qualifizieren; ◆ ~ **for holiday pay** HRM Anspruch auf Urlaubsgeld haben

qualifying: ~ **annuity** *n* FIN Rentenberechtigung *f*, Rentennachweis *m*; ~ **distribution** *n* ACC *made by a company* Dividendenzahlungen, auf die man vorzeitig Steuer bezahlen muß; ~ **holding** *n* FIN maßgeblicher Anteil *m*, maßgeblicher Wertpapierbestand *m*; ~ **shares** *n pl* STOCK nach den Statuten vorgeschriebener Aktienbesitz *m*, Pflichtaktien *f pl*; ~ **stock option** *n* STOCK Aktienoption *f*, die zur Wahrnehmung bestimmter Rechte berechtigt

qualitative *adj* GEN COMM der Güte nach, qualitativ, S&M qualitativ; ~ **analysis** *n* S&M *market research* qualitative Analyse *f*; ~ **characteristic** *n* IND Attribut *nt*; ~ **control** *n* BANK *lending directives* Qualitätskontrolle *f*

qualitatively *adv* GEN COMM der Güte nach, qualitativ

qualitative: ~ **methodology** *n* S&M *market research* qualitative Methode *f*; ~ **research** *n* S&M *market research* qualitative Forschung *f*

quality *n* ECON Qualität *f*, GEN COMM Ausführung *f*, Qualität *f*, Sorte *f*, IND, MGMNT Qualität *f*, S&M Güte *f*, Qualität *f*; ~ **assessment** *n* GEN COMM, IND, MGMNT, S&M Gütebestätigung *f*, Gütesicherung *f*, Qualitätsurteil *nt*; ~ **assurance** *n* GEN COMM, IND, MGMNT, S&M Qualitätssicherung *f*; ~ **certificate** *n* IMP/EXP Gütepaß *m*; ~ **circle** *n* HRM, IND, MGMNT *Japanese management system* Qualitätsgruppe *f*, Qualitätszirkel *m*, Werkstattkreis *m*; ~ **control** *n* (*QC*) GEN COMM, IND, S&M Gütekontrolle *f*, Qualitätsüberwachung *f*, Qualitätskontrolle *f*; ~ **of earnings** *n* FIN Qualität *f* der Gewinne; ~ **engineering** *n* MGMNT Qualitätskontrolltechnik *f*; ~ **of farm land** *n* ECON Bonität *f*; ~ **goods** *n pl* GEN COMM Qualitätsgüter *nt pl*, Qualitätswaren *f pl*; ~ **label** *n* GEN COMM Gütezeichen *nt*; ~ **of labor force** *AmE*, ~ **of labour force** *BrE n* ECON Qualität *f* der Arbeitskräfte; ~ **of life** *n* ECON, HRM Lebensqualität *f*; ~ **management** *n* IND Qualitätsmanagement *nt* (*QM*), Qualitätsleitung *f*, MGMNT Qualitätsüberwachung *f*; ~ **market** *n* S&M Qualitätsmarkt *m*; ~ **newspaper** *n* MEDIA *print* anspruchsvolle Zeitung *f*; ~-**price ratio** *n* GEN COMM Verhältnis *nt* Preis-Qualität; ~ **protection** *n* GEN COMM, IND, MGMNT, S&M Qualitätssicherung *f*; ~ **requirement** *n* IND Qualitätsanforderung *f*; ~ **specification** *n* IND Qualitätsvorschrift *f*; ~ **standard** *n* GEN COMM Qualitätsnorm *f*, Qualitätsstandard *m*, IND, MGMNT Qualitätsnormen *f pl*, Qualitätsstandard *m*; ~ **of working life** *n* (*QWL*) HRM Qualität *f* des Arbeitslebens

quango *n BrE* (*quasi-autonomous nongovernmental organization*) ADMIN quasi-autonome nichtstaatliche Organisation *f*

quantification *n* ADMIN, MATH Quantifikation *f*

quantify *vt* ADMIN, MATH quantifizieren

quantitative *adj* ECON quantitativ, GEN COMM mengenmäßig, quantitativ, IND, MATH, MGMNT, S&M quantitativ; ~ **analysis** *n* IND quantitative Analyse *f*, quantitative Bestimmung *f*, MATH quantitative Analyse *f*, MGMNT Mengenanalyse *f*, quantitative Analyse *f*, S&M *market research* quantitative Analyse *f*;

~ controls *n pl* BANK *on lending, deposits* Mengenbeschränkungen *f pl*; **~ methodology** *n* S&M *market research* quantitative Methode *f*; **~ research** *n* S&M *market research* quantitative Forschung *f*; **~ restrictions** *n pl* (*QR*) ECON Mengenbeschränkung *f*; **~ target** *n* ECON quantitative Zielvorgabe *f*

quantity *n* (*qnty, qty*) GEN COMM Menge *f*, Quantität *f* (*Quant.*), MATH Anteil *m*, Quantität *f* (*Quant.*); **~ buyer** *n* GEN COMM Großabnehmer *m*; **~ discount** *n* ACC, GEN COMM, S&M Mengenrabatt *m*; **~ effect** *n* ECON Mengeneffekt *m*; **~ permitted** *n* IMP/EXP zulässige Menge *f*; **~ supplied** *n* ECON gelieferte Menge *f*; **~ surveying** *n* IND, PROP Baukostenkalkulation *f*, Preiskalkulation *f*; **~ surveyor** *n* IND, PROP Bausachverständige(r) *mf* [decl. as adj], Preiskalkulator, in *m,f*; **~ theory of money** *n* ECON Quantitätstheorie *f*

quantum *n* GEN COMM Menge *f*, Quantum *nt*; **~ merit** *n* GEN COMM angemessene Vergütung *f*

quarantine *n* GEN COMM Isolierung *f*, Quarantäne *f*, Vierzigtagehausrecht *nt*, IMP/EXP Quarantäne *f*; **~ dues** *n pl* IMP/EXP Quarantänegebühren *f pl*

quart *n* (*qt*) GEN COMM Quart *f*

quarter 1. *n* (*qtr*) GEN COMM *of year* Quartal *nt*, Viertel *nt*; **2.** *vt* GEN COMM vierteln

quarter: **~-end accounts** *n pl* ACC Quartalsabschluß *m*

quartering *n* HRM *industrial relations* Vierteilen *nt*

quarterly 1. *adj* GEN COMM vierteljährlich, quartalsmäßig; **2.** *adv* GEN COMM quartalsweise, vierteljährlich; **3.** *n* GEN COMM, MEDIA *print* Vierteljahresschrift *f*

quarterly: **~ installment** *AmE*, **~ instalment** *BrE n* ACC Vierteljahresrate *f*

quarter: **~ page advertisement** *n* S&M Viertelseitenanzeige *f*; **~ up price** *n* STOCK um ein Viertel gestiegener Kurs *m*

quartile: **~ deviation** *n* ECON halber Quartilabstand *m*, mittlerer Quartilabstand *m*

quasi *adv* GEN COMM gewissermaßen, gleichsam, quasi, Quasi-; **~-autonomous nongovernmental organization** *n BrE* (*quango*) ADMIN quasi-autonome nichtstaatliche Organisation *f*; **~-contract** *n* LAW Quasikontrakt *m*; **~-independence** *n* GEN COMM Quasiunabhängigkeit *f*, Scheinunabhängigkeit *f*; **~-manufacturer** *n* IND *retail chain* aufeinander abgestimmte Hersteller *m pl*; **~-money** *n* ECON Beinahgeld *nt*, GEN COMM Beinahgeld *nt*, Quasigeld *nt*; **~-rent** *n* ECON Quasirente *f*; **~-statutory allocation** *n* LAW gesetzähnliche Bestimmung *f*

quay *n* IMP/EXP Kai *m*, TRANSP Kai *m*, Landungsbrücke *f*; ◆ **~ to quay** IMP/EXP, TRANSP Kai-Kai, von Kai zu Kai

quayage *n* IMP/EXP, TRANSP Kaigebühren *f pl*, Kaigeld *nt*

Queen: **~'s Award to Industry** *n BrE* S&M von der Königin verliehener Preis an die Industrie; **~'s Counsel** *n BrE* (*QC*) LAW Anwalt der Krone *m*, Anwältin der Krone *f*; **~'s enemies** *n pl BrE* LAW Staatsfeinde *m pl*

query 1. *n* COMP Abfrage *f*, GEN COMM Monitum *nt*, Rückfrage *f*; **2.** *vt* GEN COMM in Frage stellen

query: **~ language** *n* (*QL*) COMP Abfragesprache *f*, Datenbank-Abfragesprache *f*

question 1. *n* GEN COMM Frage *f*; ◆ **in ~** GEN COMM betreffend; **2.** *vt* GEN COMM befragen, *doubt* bezweifeln

questionable *adj* GEN COMM fraglich, fragwürdig

questionnaire *n* GEN COMM, S&M Fragebogen *m*

question: **~ time** *n* POL Pressefragestunde *f*, *parliament* Fragestunde *f*

queue 1. *n* COMP *of data*, GEN COMM *BrE* (*cf line AmE*) *of people* Warteschlange *f*; **2.** *vi BrE* (*cf wait in line AmE*) GEN COMM in Reihe und Glied warten, Schlange stehen, sich anstellen

queue up *vi BrE* (*cf wait in line AmE*) GEN COMM in Reihe und Glied warten, Schlange stehen, sich anstellen

queueing: **~ system** *n* ECON Warteschlangenmodell *nt*; **~ theory** *n* ECON, MATH Bedienungstheorie *f*, Warteschlangentheorie *f*

quick *adj* GEN COMM aktiv, gewandt, prompt, schnell; **~ assets** *n pl* ACC, FIN flüssige Mittel *nt pl* und Forderungen *f pl*; **~ assets ratio** *n* ACC, FIN Liquidität *f* ersten Grades; **~ fix** *n* GEN COMM Patentlösung *f*; **~-frozen** *adj* IND tiefgekühlt; **~ ratio** *n* ACC Liquidität *f* zweiten Grades; **~ returns** *n pl* FIN schneller Umsatz *m*; **~ sale** *n* GEN COMM schneller Verkauf *m*

quid pro quo *phr* GEN COMM, LAW Gegenleistung *f*

quiet *adj* GEN COMM *market, business* flau, ruhig; **~ enjoyment** *n* LAW, PROP ungestörter Besitz *m*; **~ possession** *n* LAW, PROP ungestörter Besitz *m*; **~ title suit** *n* LAW, PROP Eigentumsfeststellungsverfahren *nt*

quintal *n* GEN COMM Doppelzentner *m*

quit *vt* COMP beenden

quitclaim *n* LAW Anspruchsverzicht *m*; **~ deed** *n* PROP Überlassungsvertrag *m*

quiz *vt* GEN COMM ausfragen

quod vide *phr* (*q.v.*) GEN COMM siehe dies (*s.d.*)

quondam *adj* GEN COMM ehemalig, einstmalig

quorate: **be ~** *phr* MGMNT beschlußfähig sein

quorum *n* GEN COMM Beschlußfähigkeit *f*, Quorum *nt*; ◆ **have a ~** MGMNT beschlußfähig sein

quota *n* GEN COMM Kontingent *nt*, IMP/EXP Quote *f*, MGMNT Pensum *nt*, POL Quote *f*; **~ agreement** *n* ECON Produktionskartell *nt*

quotable *adj* STOCK notierbar

quota: **~ fixing** *n* GEN COMM Kontingentierung *f*; **~ sample** *n* S&M *market research* Quotenauswahl *f*, Quotenstichprobe *f*; **~ sampling** *n* GEN COMM, S&M Quotenauswahlverfahren *nt*; **~ system** *n* GEN COMM Kontingentierungssystem *nt*, Quotensystem *nt*, IMP/EXP Quotensystem *nt*

quotation *n* GEN COMM *offer* Angebot *nt*, *from book* Zitat *nt*, STOCK Notierung *f*; **~ department** *n* ADMIN Abteilung *f* für Börsenzulassung

quote 1. *n* GEN COMM Angebot *nt*; **2.** *vt* GEN COMM notieren, *from book* zitieren, STOCK notieren; ◆ **~ a reference number** COMMS ein Geschäftszeichen angeben; **~ in the official list** STOCK amtlich notieren

quoted: **~ company** *n* ECON, GEN COMM, STOCK börsennotierte Gesellschaft *f*, börsennotiertes Unternehmen *nt*; ◆ **~ on the stock exchange** ACC, STOCK an der Börse notiert, börsennotiert

quoted: **~ price** *n* ECON Angebotspreis *m*, Kursnotierung *f*, STOCK Kurs *m*, Kursnotierung *f*; **~ securities** *n pl* ECON, STOCK börsennotierte Wertpapiere *nt pl*; **~ share** *n* STOCK börsennotierte Aktie *f*

quotient *n* MATH Quotient *m*

quo warranto *phr* LAW *proceeding* Verfahren *nt* wegen Amtsanmaßung

q.v. *abbr* (*quod vide*) GEN COMM s.d. (*siehe dies*)

qwerty: ~ **keyboard** *n* COMP *English standard* QWERTY-Tastatur *f*

qwertz: ~ **keyboard** *n* COMP *German standard* QWERTZ-Tastatur *f*

QWL *abbr* (*quality of working life*) HRM Qualität *f* des Arbeitslebens

R

R *abbr* IND (*refrigerated*) kühl aufbewahrt, tiefgekühlt, Kühl-, (*refrigeration*) Kühlung *f*, TRANSP (*reduced class rate*) *air freight classification* ermäßigter Gruppenfrachttarif *m*, Tariflohnreduktion *f*

R/A *abbr* (*refer to acceptor*) GEN COMM an Akzeptant

race: **~ barrier** *n* HRM, POL Rassenschranke *f*; **~ discrimination** *n* HRM Rassendiskriminierung *f*

Race: **~ Relations Act** *n* *BrE* (*RRA*) LAW Rassendiskriminierungsverbotsgesetz *nt*

racial: **~ barrier** *n* HRM, POL Rassenschranke *f*; **~ discrimination** *n* HRM Rassendiskriminierung *f*

rack *n* COMP Gestell *nt*, Rahmen *m*; ♦ **go to ~ and ruin** *infrml* GEN COMM *economy* in Schutt und Asche fallen

racket *n* GEN COMM Bankbetrug, betrügerisches Unternehmen *nt*

racketeer *n* GEN COMM Schieber, in *m,f* (*infrml*)

racking *n* TRANSP Schrägverziehung *f*

rackrent *n* LAW Wuchermiete *f*

radar *n* TRANSP *shipping* Radar *nt*; **~ alert** *n* STOCK Radaralarm *m*

Radcliffe: **~ Report** *n* *BrE* ECON Radcliffe-Bericht *m*

radiation: **~ pollution** *n* ENVIR Strahlungsverseuchung *f*

radical *adj* GEN COMM einschneidend, radikal, POL radikal; **~ economics** *n* ECON Radikalökonomie *f*

radio *n* COMMS Funk *m*, Hörfunk *m*, Radio *nt*, Rundfunk *m*, *private* Privatfunk *m*, MEDIA Funk *m*

radioactive: **~ fallout** *n* ENVIR radioaktiver Niederschlag *m*

radio: **~ advertising** *n* MEDIA Radiowerbung *f*, Rundfunkwerbung *f*, S&M Radiowerbung *f*; **~ announcement** *n* MEDIA *broadcast* Radioansage *f*; **~ announcer** *n* MEDIA *broadcast* Rundfunksprecher, in *m,f*; **~ authority** *n* S&M Rundfunkbehörde *f*; **~ broadcast** *n* MEDIA Rundfunksendung *f*; **~ commercial** *n* MEDIA, S&M Werbesendung *f* im Radio, Werbespot *m* im Radio; **~ direction finder** *n* TRANSP *shipping* Funkpeiler *m*, Funkpeilgerät *nt*, Funkpeilanlage *f*

radiogram *n* COMMS Radiogramm *nt*

radio: **~ message** *n* COMMS Funkspruch *m*

radiophone *n* (*RP*) COMMS Sprechfunkgerät *nt*

radio: **~ program** *AmE*, **~ programme** *BrE* *n* MEDIA *broadcast* Radioprogramm *nt*, Rundfunkprogramm *nt*; **~ set** *n* MEDIA Radioapparat *m*; **~ station** *n* MEDIA Radiosender *m*

radiotelegram *n* COMMS Funktelegramm *nt*

radiotelephone *n* COMMS Funksprechgerät *nt*

radiotelephony *n* (*RT*) COMMS *shipping* drahtlose Telefonie *nt*, Funktelegraphie *m*, Sprechfunk *m*

radix *n* COMP Basis *f*

rag *n* *infrml* MEDIA *print* Käseblatt *nt* (*infrml*), Schundblatt *nt* (*infrml*)

raid *vt* GEN COMM ausnehmen, plündern; ♦ **~ a company** STOCK gezielt Aktien einer Unternehmung aufkaufen; **~ the market** STOCK den Kurs einer Aktie durch Verkäufe drücken

rail *n* TRANSP Bahn *f*, Eisenbahn *f*; **~-air link** *n* TRANSP Bahn-Flug-Verbindung *f*

railcar *n* TRANSP *railway* Eisenbahnwagen *m*

rail: **~ charges** *n pl* TRANSP Bahnfrachtkosten *pl*

Rail: **~ Europe Senior Card** *n* LEIS Europa Bahnseniorenkarte *f*

rail: **~ freight** *n* TRANSP Bahnfracht *f*; **~ freight traffic** *n* TRANSP Eisenbahngüterverkehr *m*; **~ guided tour** *n* LEIS Bahnreise *f* mit Führung

railhead *n* TRANSP *terminus station* Kopfbahnhof *m*, Schienenkopf *m*

rail: **~ link** *n* TRANSP Bahnverbindung *f*

railman *n* *AmE* (*cf railwayman BrE*) HRM Eisenbahner *m*

rail: **~ network** *n* TRANSP Bahnanlage *f*, Eisenbahnnetz *nt*

railroad *n* *AmE* (*cf railway BrE*) TRANSP Bahn *f*, Eisenbahn *f*, Eisenbahnwesen *f*; **~ bill of lading** *n* *AmE* (*cf railway bill of lading BrE*) FIN Eisenbahnfrachtbrief *m*; **~ car** *n* *AmE* (*cf railway coach BrE*) TRANSP Eisenbahnwagen *m*, Zugwagen *m*; **~ network** *n* *AmE* (*cf railway network BrE*) TRANSP Bahnanlage *f*, Eisenbahnnetz *nt*; **~ service** *n* *AmE* (*cf railway service BrE*) TRANSP Eisenbahnverbindung *f*; **~ station** *n* *AmE* (*cf railway station BrE*, *train station BrE*) TRANSP Bahnhof *m*, Bahnstation *f*; **~ system** *n* *AmE* (*cf railway system BrE*) TRANSP Eisenbahnnetz *nt*, Schienennetz *nt*, Streckennetz *nt*

Railrover *n* *BrE* LEIS Bahncard *f*

rail: **~ shares** *n pl* STOCK Eisenbahnaktien *f pl*; **~ shipment** *n* TRANSP Bahnversand *m*; **~ strike** *n* HRM Eisenbahnstreik *m*; **~ terminal** *n* TRANSP Eisenbahnterminal *m*; **~ tour** *n* LEIS Bahnreise *f*; **~ traffic** *n* TRANSP Schienenverkehr *m*; **~ transport** *n* TRANSP Bahnbeförderung *f*, Bahntransport *m*, Bahnfrachtgeschäft *nt*; **~ traveler** *AmE*, **~ traveller** *BrE* *n* TRANSP Bahnreisende(r) *mf* [decl. as adj], Zugpassagier *m*, Zugreisende(r) *mf* [decl. as adj]; **~ and water terminal** *n* GEN COMM Umschlagplatz *m*

railway *n* *BrE* (*rly, cf railroad AmE*) TRANSP Bahn *f*, Eisenbahn *f*, Eisenbahnwesen *f*; **~ bill** *n* *BrE* TRANSP Bahnfrachtbrief *m*; **~ bill of lading** *n* *BrE* (*cf railroad bill of lading AmE*) FIN Eisenbahnfrachtbrief *m*; **~ coach** *n* *BrE* (*cf railroad car AmE*) TRANSP Eisenbahnwagen *m*, Zugwagen *m*; **~ consignment note** *n* *BrE* TRANSP Bahnfrachtbrief *m*

railwayman *n* *BrE* (*cf railman AmE*) HRM Eisenbahner *m*

railway: **~ network** *n* *BrE* (*cf railroad network AmE*) TRANSP Eisenbahnnetz *nt*; **~ securities** *n pl* *BrE* STOCK Eisenbahnwertpapiere *nt pl*; **~ service** *n* *BrE* (*cf railroad service AmE*) TRANSP Eisenbahnverbindung *f*; **~ siding** *n* *BrE* TRANSP Seitengleis *nt*; **~ station** *n* *BrE* (*cf railroad station AmE*) TRANSP Bahnhof *m*, Bahnstation *f*; **~ system** *n* *BrE* (*cf railroad system AmE*) TRANSP Eisenbahnnetz *nt*, Schienennetz *nt*, Streckennetz *nt*

rainbow: **~ book** *n* *BrE* ADMIN Buch, das die Gehälter von Stadträten und anderen Beamten auflistet

rainforest *n* ENVIR Regenwald *m*

rain: **~ insurance** *n* INS Regenversicherung *f*

rainmaker *n AmE* LAW Rechtsanwalt, der seine politischen Verbindungen dazu nutzt, sich Arbeit zu verschaffen

raise 1. *n AmE (cf rise BrE)* HRM *in salary* Erhöhung *f,* Gehaltserhöhung *f,* Gehaltssteigerung *f;* **2.** *vt* ENVIR *awareness* steigern, FIN *money* aufbringen, beschaffen, *loan* aufnehmen, GEN COMM *value* aufheben, erhöhen, steigern, HRM *staff salary* aufbessern, STOCK *capital* beschaffen; ♦ **~ a check** *AmE,* **~ a cheque** *BrE* BANK einen Scheck ausstellen; **~ a loan** BANK ein Darlehen aufnehmen, FIN eine Anleihe aufnehmen; **~ a presumption** GEN COMM Anlaß zu einer Vermutung geben; **~ an objection** GEN COMM einen Einwand erheben; **~ external funds** GEN COMM Fremdkapital aufnehmen; **~ finance** FIN Finanzierung besorgen; **~ funds** FIN Geldmittel beschaffen; **~ money on a mortgage** GEN COMM Geld auf eine Hypothek aufnehmen; **~ money on sth** GEN COMM Geld auf etw aufnehmen; **~ the alarm** GEN COMM Alarm geben, Alarm schlagen; **~ up** GEN COMM hinaufsetzen

raised: ~ check *AmE,* **~ cheque** *BrE n* BANK durch Eintragung einer höheren Summe gefälschter Scheck *m*

raising *n* GEN COMM *prices* Anheben *nt;* ♦ **~ finance from the public** ECON Marktfinanzierung *f*

rake in *vt infrml* GEN COMM scheffeln *(infrml);* ♦ **~ profits** *infrml* GEN COMM Gewinne einheimsen *(infrml);* **rake it in** *infrml* GEN COMM Geld scheffeln *(infrml)*

rally 1. *vt* STOCK aufholen; **2.** *vi* STOCK anziehen, sich erholen; ♦ **~ strongly** STOCK *market* sich stark erholen

rallying *n* STOCK Erholung *f,* Preisaufschwung *m;* **~ point** *n* GEN COMM Sammelplatz *m,* Sammelpunkt *m*

RAM *abbr (random access memory)* COMP RAM *(Direktzugriffsspeicher)*

Rambouillet: ~ summit *n* ECON Rambouillet-Gipfel *m*

RAM: ~ disk *n* COMP RAM-Disk *f,* virtuelle Festplatte *f*

ramp *n* GEN COMM *swindle* Bankbetrug *m,* Betrug *m,* TRANSP Rampe *f;* **~ stillage** *n* TRANSP Rampenpalette *f*

Ramsey: ~ prices *n pl* ECON Ramsey-Preise *m pl;* **~ saving rule** *n* ECON Ramsey-Sparregel *f;* **~ savings model** *n* ECON Ramsey-Ersparnismodell *nt*

R&CC *abbr (riots and civil commotions)* WEL Ausschreitungen und politische Unruhen *f pl*

R&D *abbr (research and development)* IND F&E *(Forschung und Entwicklung)*

random: at ~ *phr* GEN COMM aufs Geratewohl, willkürlich, ziellos; **~ access** *n* COMP Direktzugriff *m;* **~ access memory** *n (RAM)* COMP Direktzugriffsspeicher *m (RAM);* **~ check** *n* MATH *statistics* Zufallsprüfung *f;* **~ error** *n* ADMIN, MATH *statistics* Zufallsfehler *m;* **~ factor** *n* ECON Zufallseinfluß *m,* Zufallsfaktor *m*

randomization *n* MATH *statistics* Randomisierung *f*

randomly *adv* GEN COMM aufs Geratewohl, willkürlich, ziellos

random: ~ number *n* COMP, MATH Zufallszahl *f;* **~ number generator** *n* MATH *statistics* Zufallszahlengenerator *m;* **~ observation method** *n* MATH, MGMNT Zufallsbeobachtungsmethode *f,* S&M Methode *f* der Zufallsauswahl; **~ sample** *n* ECON, MATH, S&M Zufallsstichprobe *f;* **~ sampling** *n* MATH *statistics* Zufallsstichprobenverfahren *nt,* S&M Stichproben *f pl;* **~ selection** *n* MATH Zufallsauswahl *f,* Zufallsstichprobenauswahl *f;* **~ test** *n* GEN COMM, S&M Stichprobe *f;* **~ variable** *n* MATH *statistics* stochastische Variable *f,* Zufallsvariable *f;* **~ variation** *n* ECON, MATH Zufallsab-

weichung *f;* **~ walk theory** *n* ECON, STOCK Irrfahrttheorie *f*

range *n* GEN COMM Bereich *m, of products* Serie *f,* STOCK *futures market* Schwankungsbreite *f;* ♦ **be out of ~** GEN COMM außer Reichweite sein; **~ of activity** *n* GEN COMM Tätigkeitsbereich *m;* **~ of goods** *n* GEN COMM Auswahl *f,* Sortiment *nt;* **~ of options** *n* GEN COMM verschiedene Möglichkeiten *f pl;* **~ of products** *n* S&M Produktpalette *f;* **~ of services** *n* ADMIN Dienstleistungspalette *f,* ECON Leistungspalette *f*

rank 1. *n* GEN COMM Stand *m,* STOCK Stellung *f;* **2.** *vi* ECON rangieren; ♦ **~ above** GEN COMM bedeutender sein als, einen höheren Rang einnehmen als; **~ after** STOCK im Rang nachgehen; **~ below** GEN COMM einen niedrigeren Rang einnehmen als, weniger bedeutend sein als

rank: ~-and-file *adj* POL einfach; **~-and-file** *n* GEN COMM Fußvolk *nt;* HRM *of company* Belegschaft *f, of trade union* einfache Mitglieder *nt pl;* **~ correlation** *n* MATH *statistics* Rangkorrelation *f*

ranking *n* GEN COMM *listing in order* Rangfolge *f,* Rang *m,* Rangordnung *f,* HRM Rangordnung *f;* **~ of commodities** *n* ECON rangmäßige Bewertung *f* von Gütern

rank: ~ order *n* MATH Rangordnung *f*

rapid *adj* GEN COMM rasant, schnell, stürmisch; **~ growth** *n* ECON starkes Wachstum *nt;* **~ premium decay** *n* STOCK *options* schneller Prämienverfall *m;* **~ sales** *n pl* S&M reißender Absatz *m;* **~ technological progress** *n* ECON rasanter technischer Fortschritt *m;* **~ transit system** *n* TRANSP Schnell-Transit-System *nt*

rapidly *adv* ECON, GEN COMM rapid

rapprochement *n* POL Rapprochement *nt,* Wiederannäherung *f*

raster *n* COMP Raster *m*

ratchet: ~ effect *n* ECON Sperrklinkeneffekt *m*

rate 1. *n* COMP Geschwindigkeit *f,* Rate *f,* ECON *speed* Geschwindigkeit *f,* Satz *m,* Tempo *nt,* FIN *of pay, tax* Satz *m,* GEN COMM Rate *f,* Tarif *m,* STOCK *currencies* Notierung *f,* Kurs *m;* **2.** *vt* GEN COMM tarifieren, taxieren

rateable *adj* ECON anteilig, GEN COMM bewertbar, schätzbar, TAX steuerpflichtig; **~ value** *n BrE obs* TAX, PROP Einheitswert *m*

rate: ~ below cost *n* TRANSP nicht kostendeckender Tarif *m,* Tarif *m* unter Kosten; **~ bill** *n BrE* TAX Gemeindesteuerbescheid *m;* **~ of capacity utilization** *n* IND Ausnutzungsgrad *m;* **~ card** *n* S&M Anzeigenpreisliste *f;* **~ ceiling** *n* ECON *interest rates* Zinsobergrenze *f;* **~ class** *n* TRANSP Tarifklasse *f;* **~ of contribution** *n* WEL Beitragssatz *m;* **~ cutting** *n* HRM einseitige Lohnkürzung *f,* TRANSP Frachtratenunterbietung *f*

rated: not ~ *adj* GEN COMM *securities rating services and mercantile agencies* nicht klassifiziert

rate: ~ of the day *n* BANK Tageskurs *m;* **~ of decay** *n* STOCK *options* Verfallsgeschwindigkeit *f;* **~ of depreciation** *n* ACC Abschreibungssatz *m;* **~ differential** *n* STOCK *interest rate futures* Konditionengefälle *nt,* Zinsgefälle *nt;* **~ dilution** *n* TRANSP Frachtsatzverringerung *f*

rate: ~ policy *n* INS Versicherung *f* zu erhöhter Prämie

rate: ~ of exchange *n* ECON Devisenkurs *m,* Umrechnungskurs *m,* Wechselkurs *m,* FIN Umrechnungskurs *m;* **~ of exploitation** *n* FIN Ausbeutungsgrad *m;* **~ fixing** *n*

FIN Tariffestsetzung *f*, HRM Festlegung *f* von Akkord-sätzen, TAX Tariffestsetzung *f*; ~ **flexibility** *n* GEN COMM Tarifflexibilität *f*; ~ **for the job** *n* GEN COMM, HRM herrschender Lohnsatz *m*; ~ **of increase** *n* ECON Expansionsrate *f*, Zuwachsrate *f*; ~ **of interest** *n* BANK, ECON, FIN, GEN COMM Zinsfuß *m*, Zinssatz *m*; ~ **of inventory turnover** *n* FIN Umschlagshäufigkeit *f* des Lagerbestands; ~ **list** *n* S&M Anzeigenpreisliste *f*; ~ **of new orders** *n* GEN COMM Auftragseingang *m*

ratepayer *n* TAX Grundsteuerzahler *m*

rate: ~ **of inflation** *n* ECON Inflationsrate *f*; ~ **of relief** *n* TAX Freibetragsatz *m*; ~ **of return** *n* ACC Kapitalverzinsung *f*, Rendite *f*, ECON, FIN Kapitalverzinsung *f*, TAX Rendite *f*; ~ **of return on capital employed** *n* (*RORCE*) ECON Rentabilität *f* des eingesetzten Kapitals

rates *n pl* ECON *for postage, advertising*, FIN, GEN COMM Gebühren *f pl*, Tarif *m*, TAX Gemeindegrundsteuern *f pl*, Gemeindesteuer *f* auf Grundbesitz; ~ **collector** *n* BrE ADMIN Gemeindesteuereinnehmer, in *m,f*; ~ **formulation** *n* GEN COMM Tarifformulierung *f*; ~ **review** *n* TRANSP Tarifüberprüfung *f*; ~ **strategy** *n* TRANSP Tarifstrategie *f*; ~ **structure** *n* TRANSP Tarifstruktur *f*

rate: ~ **support grant** *n* BrE (*RSG*) ECON Staatszuschuß an die Kommunen, kommunale Finanzausgleichszuweisung; ~ **of surplus value** *n* BANK Mehrwertrate *f*; ~ **of taxation** *n* TAX Steuersatz *m*; ~ **to be agreed** *n* (*RTBA*) TRANSP zu vereinbarender Satz *m*; ~ **trend** *n* TRANSP Tariftrend *m*; ~ **of turnover** *n* STOCK Umsatzgeschwindigkeit *f*; ~ **war** *n* TRANSP Preiskrieg *m*

ratification *n* GEN COMM *of treaty* Ratifizierung *f*

ratify *vt* GEN COMM *treaty* genehmigen, ratifizieren

rating *n* FIN *evaluation* Bewertung *f*, Klassifizierung *f* von Emittenten, Klassifizierung *f* von Schuldtiteln, Rating *nt*, *setting of rates* Tariffestsetzung *f*, S&M Klassifizierung *f*, TAX Tariffestsetzung *f*; ~ **agency** *n* FIN Kreditauskunftei *f*, STOCK Rating-Agentur *f*; ~ **scale** *n* GEN COMM Beurteilungsskala *f*, Bewertungsskala *f*, Einstufungsskala *f*

ratio *n* ACC Kennziffer *f*, Verhältnis *nt*, Verhältniszahl *f*; ~ **analysis** *n* ADMIN, MATH *statistics* Kennziffernanalyse *f*

ratio decidendi *n* GEN COMM Entscheidungsgrund *m*

ratio: ~ **of external debt to exports** *n* ECON Verhältnis *nt* von Auslandsverschuldung zu Exporten; ~ **of merchandise to receivables** *n* ECON Verhältnis *nt* Lagervorräte zu Forderungen

rational *adj* GEN COMM rational, vernünftig, zweckmäßig; ~ **decision** *n* GEN COMM *game theory* rationale Entscheidung *f*

rationale *n* GEN COMM Begründung *f*, Beweggrund *m*, Grund *m*, *principles* Grundsatzerklärung *f*

rational: ~~**economic** *adj* ECON rationalökonomisch; ~ **expectations** *n pl* (*RE*) ECON rationale Erwartungen *f pl*

rationality *n* GEN COMM Rationalität *f*

rationalization *n* ECON, FIN Rationalisierung *f*, IND Rationalisierung *f*, wirtschaftliche Vereinfachung *f*, Wirtschaftlichkeit *f*, MGMNT Rationalisierung *f*; ~ **investment** *n* FIN Anpassungsinvestition *f*; ~ **program** *AmE*, ~ **programme** *BrE* *n* ECON Rationalisierungsprogramm *nt*

rationalize *vt* ECON, FIN rationalisieren, GEN COMM

rationalisieren, zweckmäßiger gestalten, wirtschaftlich gestalten, IND, MGMNT rationalisieren

rationally *adv* GEN COMM vernünftig

rational: ~ **management** *n* MGMNT rationaler Führungsstil *m*, rationelles Management *nt*

rationing *n* ECON Rationierung *f*

ratio: ~ **scale** *n* MATH einfach-logarithmischer Maßstab *m*

rat: ~ **race** *n* *infrml* GEN COMM Konkurrenzkampf *m*, HRM Pöstchenjägerei *f*

ratten *vt* *AmE* HRM an der Arbeit hindern

raw *adj* COMP roh, unbearbeitet; ~ **data** *n pl* COMP Ausgangsdaten *pl*, Rohdaten *pl*, MATH *statistics* Rohdaten *pl*; ~ **land** *n* ECON unerschlossenes Grundstück *nt*, PROP unbebautes Land *nt*

Rawlsian: ~ **difference principle** *n* ECON Rawlsches Differenzprinzip *nt*; ~ **justice** *n* ECON Rawlsche Gerechtigkeit *f*

raw: ~ **material** *n* IND Ausgangsmaterial *nt*, Rohmaterial *nt*, Rohstoff *m*

RBT *abbr* (*rebuilt*) ECON, IND, GEN COMM wiederaufgebaut, wiederhergestellt

r/c *abbr* (*return cargo*) TRANSP Rückfracht *f*

RCC *abbr* BrE (*Rural Community Council*) POL ländliche Gemeindeverwaltung

RCC&S *abbr* (*riots, civil commotions and strikes*) WEL Ausschreitungen, politische Unruhen und Streiks *pl*

RCH *abbr* (*recognized clearing house*) BANK anerkannte Clearingstelle *f*

rcpt *abbr* (*receipt*) GEN COMM *of goods* Annahme *f*, Erhalt *m*, *for payment* Quittung *f*, S&M Annahme *f*

rd *abbr* (*running day*) TRANSP laufender Kalendertag *m*

Rd *abbr* (*road*) GEN COMM Str. (*Straße*), Weg *m*

RD *abbr* BANK (*refer to drawer*) zurück an Aussteller, ECON (*reserve deposits*) Reserveinlagen *f pl*

RDA *abbr* BrE (*Rural Development Area*) ECON ländliches Entwicklungsgebiet *nt*, ländliches Fördergebiet *nt*

RDB *abbr* (*relational database*) COMP relationale Datenbank *f*

RDC *abbr* (*running-down clause*) INS *marine* Kollisionsklausel *f*

RDS *abbr* AmE (*rural delivery service*) COMMS freie Zustellung *f* in ländlichen Gebieten

re *prep* COMMS *correspondence* betreffs

RE *abbr* ECON (*rational expectations*) rationale Erwartungen *f pl*, STOCK (*Royal Exchange BrE*) Londoner Börsengebäude

reach 1. *n* S&M Einflußbereich *m*, Reichweite *f*; **2.** *vt* GEN COMM, LAW *agreement* erzielen; ♦ ~ **the age limit** GEN COMM die Altersgrenze erreichen; ~ **an all-time high** STOCK einen historischen Höchststand erreichen; ~ **a deadlock** GEN COMM einen toten Punkt erreichen; ~ **a deal** GEN COMM einen Abschluß erreichen, einen Abschluß tätigen; ~ **an impasse** GEN COMM einen toten Punkt erreichen; ~ **a low** ECON, GEN COMM, STOCK einen Tiefstand erreichen; ~ **saturation point** GEN COMM den Sättigungspunkt erreichen; ~ **a stalemate** GEN COMM ein Patt erreichen; ~ **a total of** GEN COMM insgesamt ergeben

reach: ~ **and frequency** *n* S&M *market penetration* Reichweite *f* und Häufigkeit *f*

reachable: ~ **on arrival** *phr* TRANSP *shipping* bei Ankunft erreichbar

reachback *n* TAX Rückwirkung *f*

react: **~ well under stress** *phr* HRM gut auf Streß reagieren

reaction *n* GEN COMM, HRM, POL Reaktion *f*

reaction: **~ function** *n* ECON Reaktionsfunktion *f*; **~ time** *n* ADMIN Reaktionszeit *f*

reactivate *vt* COMP *software* reaktivieren

reactivated *adj* COMP reaktiviert

reactive: **~ response** *n* GEN COMM Gegenreaktion *f*; **~ strategy** *n* GEN COMM Gegenstrategie *f*

read 1. *n* COMP, MEDIA, S&M Lesen *nt*; **2.** *vt* COMP einlesen, lesen, MEDIA, S&M lesen; ♦ **~ the tape** STOCK den Börsenticker ablesen; **3.** *vi* ♦ **~ for a university degree** HRM studieren

reader *n* COMP *device* Leser *m*, MEDIA, S&M *person* Leser, in *m,f*, *advertisement* Textanzeige *f*; **~ involvement** *n* S&M Leserbeteiligung *f*; **~ service card** *n* S&M Leserdienstkarte *f*

readership *n* MEDIA *of newspaper, book* Leserschaft *f*; **~ profile** *n* S&M *market research* Leserprofil *nt*; **~ survey** *n* S&M *market research* Leserstudie *f*

read: **~ head** *n* COMP Lesekopf *m*

readiness: **~ to contract** *n* LAW Vertragsbereitschaft *f*

reading: **~ notice** *n* MEDIA redaktionell aufgemachte Textanzeige

Readme: **~ document** *n* COMP Liesmichdokument *nt*, Readme-Dokument *nt*; **~ file** *n* COMP Liesmichdatei *f*, Readme-Datei *f*

re-admission *n* GEN COMM, WEL Wiederaufnahme *f*

re-admit *vt* GEN COMM, WEL *patients* wiederaufnehmen

read: **~-only memory** *n* (*ROM*) COMP Festspeicher *m* (*ROM*); **~-write head** *n* COMP Schreiblesekopf *m*

ready *adj* GEN COMM präsent; ♦ **make ~** S&M vorbereiten; **make ~ for use** GEN COMM bereitstellen; **~ for shipment** TRANSP versandbereit; **~ to hand** GEN COMM bei der Hand, zur Hand; **~ to move into** PROP bezugsfertig; **~ to operate** IND betriebsfertig; **~, willing and able** GEN COMM *brokerage* handlungsbereit und verfügungsberechtigt

ready: **~ cash** *n* *BrE* GEN COMM Bargeld *nt*; **~-made meal** *n* S&M Fertiggericht *nt*; **~ market** *n* STOCK aufnahmefähiger Markt *m*; **~ money** *n* GEN COMM jederzeit verfügbares Geld *nt*; **~ reckoner** *n* GEN COMM Umrechnungstabelle *f*

reaffirm *vt* GEN COMM erneut bestätigen

reafforestation *n* ENVIR Wiederaufforstung *f*

Reaganomics *n* ECON Reaganomics *pl*

real: **~ address** *n* COMP reale Adresse *f*; **~ agreement** *n* LAW *contract* dinglicher Vertrag *m*, *real estate* Liegenschaftsvertrag *m*; **~ bills doctrine** *n* ECON Doktrin *f* der realen Wechsel; **~ capital** *n* ECON Sachkapital *nt*; **~ cost** *n* ACC Realkosten *pl*, tatsächliche Kosten *pl*; **~ earnings** *n pl* HRM Realeinkommen *nt*; **~ economy of scale** *n* ECON realer Größenvorteil *m*, realer Skaleneffekt *m*; **~ estate** *n* ECON, PROP Immobilien *f pl*; **~-estate agency** *n* *AmE* (*cf estate agency BrE*) PROP Immobilienbüro *nt*; **~-estate agent** *n* *AmE* (*cf estate agent BrE*) PROP Immobilienmakler, in *m,f*; **~-estate bureau** *n* *AmE* (*cf estate agency BrE*) PROP Immobilienbüro *nt*; **~ estate closing** *n* *AmE* LAW, PROP Unterzeichnung *f* des Grundstücksvertrages; **~-estate commission** *n* PROP Immobilienprovision *f*; **~-estate company** *n* GEN COMM, PROP Immobiliengesellschaft *f*;

~-estate fund *n* ACC, BANK, PROP Immobilienfonds *m*; **~-estate industry** *n* PROP Immobilienbranche *f*; **~-estate investment trust** *n* *AmE* (*REIT*) ACC, BANK Immobilienfonds *m*, FIN Immobilieninvestmentgesellschaft *f*; **~-estate market** *n* PROP Immobilienmarkt *m*; **~-estate office** *n* *AmE* (*cf estate agency BrE*) PROP Immobilienbüro *nt*; **~ exchange rate** *n* STOCK realer Wechselkurs *m*; **~ GDP growth** *n* ECON Realwachstum *nt* des Bruttoinlandsprodukts; **~ growth** *n* ECON reales Wachstum *nt*, Realwachstum *nt*; **~ income** *n* ACC Realeinkommen *nt*; **~ investment** *n* BANK *for hospitals, schools* Sachinvestition *f*

realism *n* GEN COMM, LAW, POL Realismus *m*

realistic *adj* GEN COMM realistisch, wirklichkeitsnah

realizable *adj* ACC realisierbar, FIN kapitalisierbar, realisierbar, verkäuflich, STOCK realisierbar; **~ assets** *n pl* ACC, FIN flüssige Mittel *nt pl* und Forderungen *f pl*

realization *n* GEN COMM Veräußerung *f*; **~ of assets** *n* ACC Veräußerung *f* von Vermögen

realize *vt* ACC *profit* realisieren, FIN *profit* kapitalisieren, verkaufen, GEN COMM *goal* verwirklichen, STOCK *profit* realisieren; ♦ **~ assets** STOCK Vermögenswerte flüssigmachen

realized: **~ cost of funds** *n* STOCK eingetretene Kapitalbeschaffungskosten *pl*, enstandene Refinanzierungskosten *pl*; **~ gains** *n pl* ACC, FIN realisierte Gewinne *m pl*; **~ losses** *n pl* FIN realisierte Verluste *m pl*; **~ minimum return** *n* STOCK *interest rate futures* realisierte Mindestrendite *f*, realisierter Minimalertrag *m*

reallocate *vt* ACC *funds* umschichten, *redistribute* neuverteilen

reallocation *n* ACC Umschichtung *f*, COMP Neuzuweisung *f*, FIN Neuverteilung *f*, Neuzuteilung *f*, GEN COMM Reallokation *f*

reallowance *n* STOCK Wiederverkäuferrabatt *f*

real: **~ money** *n* ECON realer Geldwert *m*; **~ net national product** *n* ECON reales Nettosozialprodukt *nt*; **~ number** *n* COMP reelle Zahl *f*; **~ pay** *n* HRM Nettoverdienst *m*; **~ price** *n* ECON Realpreis *m*; **~ property** *n* PROP unbewegliches Vermögen *nt*; **~ property tax** *n* TAX Grundsteuer *f*; **~ right of preemption** *n* LAW dingliches Vorkaufsrecht *nt*; **~ security** *n* LAW dingliche Sicherheit *f*; **~ storage** *n* COMP realer Speicher *m*; **in ~ terms** *phr* ECON real; **~ time** *n* ACC, COMP, ECON Echtzeit *f*, Realzeit *f*

realtor *n* *AmE* (*cf estate agent BrE*) PROP Immobilienmakler, in *m,f*

real: **~ volume** *n* IND *of production* Ist-Menge *f*, Ist-Volumen *nt*; **~ wage** *n* ACC, ECON, HRM Reallohn *m*; **~-wage hypothesis** *n* ECON Reallohnhypothese *f*

reap: **~ rewards** *phr* GEN COMM Belohnungen erhalten

reason *n* GEN COMM Begründung *f*, Beweggrund *m*, Motiv *nt*; ♦ **for any ~** GEN COMM aus beliebigem Grund; **for that ~** GEN COMM aus diesem Grund

reasonable *adj* ACC angemessen, GEN COMM angemessen, tragbar, vernünftig, HRM angemessen; **~ compensation** *n* GEN COMM angemessene Entschädigung *f*, angemessene Vergütung *f*; **~ expense** *n* GEN COMM angemessene Auslagen *f pl*, angemessene Kosten *pl*; **~ person** *n* GEN COMM besonnener Mensch *m*, vernünftiger Mensch *m*; **~ price** *n* GEN COMM angemessener Preis *m*, vernünftiger Preis *m*; **~ time** *n* ACC angemessene Frist *f*

reasonably *adv* GEN COMM vernünftig, vernünftigerweise, *fairly* ganz

reassign *vt* ADMIN umbesetzen, FIN zurückübertragen, GEN COMM, HRM umbesetzen

reassignment *n* ADMIN Umbesetzung *f*, COMP Neuzuordnung *f*, HRM Umbesetzung *f*

rebagging *n* TRANSP Neuverpackung *f*

rebate *n* FIN *discount* Rabatt *m*, Preisnachlaß *m*, Nachlaß *m*, *of money paid* Rückvergütung *f*, GEN COMM, STOCK Rabatt *m*

rebateable *adj* TRANSP nachlaßfähig

rebate: ~ **granted for repeat advertising** *n* S&M Wiederholungsrabatt *m*

reboot *vt* COMP neu booten (*jarg*), neu urladen

rebooting *n* COMP erneutes Booten *nt* (*jarg*), erneutes Urladen *nt*

rebuild *vt* COMP *hardware* rekonstruieren, ECON wiederaufbauen

rebuilding *n* ECON Wiederaufbau *m*

rebuilt *adj* (*RBT*) ECON, IND, GEN COMM wiederaufgebaut, wiederhergestellt

rebuttable *adj* LAW widerlegbar

rebuy *vt* S&M erneut kaufen

recalculate *vt* MATH neuberechnen

recall 1. *n* STOCK *of option* Rückruf *m*; **2.** *vt* STOCK *option* zurückrufen

recall: ~ **test** *n* GEN COMM Gedächtnistest *m*

recapitalization *n* ECON, FIN Kapitalumschichtung *f*, Sanierung *f*; ~ **balance sheet** *n* ECON Sanierungsbilanz *f*; ~ **gains** *n pl* ECON Sanierungsgewinne *m pl*

recapturable: ~ **depreciation** *n* ACC rückgängig zu machende Abschreibung *f*, widerrufbare Abschreibung *f*

recapture *vt* ECON *costs* hereinholen, wiedergewinnen

recargo *n* GEN COMM Aufschlag *m*

recast *vt* FIN *debt* neu kalkulieren

recd *abbr* (*received*) GEN COMM empfangen

receipt 1. *n* GEN COMM (*rcpt*, *recpt*) *of goods* Annahme *f*, Erhalt *m*, *for goods, payment* Bon *m*, Quittung *f*, Empfangsbescheinigung *f*, S&M (*rcpt*, *recpt*) Annahme *f*; ◆ **on** ~ **of** GEN COMM bei Erhalt von; **be in** ~ **of** GEN COMM *letter, payment* erhalten haben **2.** *vt* GEN COMM Empfang bestätigen, *payment* quittieren, *goods* den Empfang bescheinigen

receipt: ~ **book** *n* GEN COMM Einnahmebuch *nt*, Quittungsblock *m*; ~ **for documents** *n* PATENTS Empfangsbestätigung *f* für Dokumentation, Empfangsbestätigung *f* für Dokumente; ~ **for payment** *n* GEN COMM Quittung *f*; ~ **for shipment bill of lading** *n* TRANSP Übernahmekonnossement *nt*; ~ **of goods** *n* (*ROG*) TRANSP *cargo* Warenannahme *f*, Warenempfang *m*

receipts *n pl* STOCK *futures* Einnahmen *f pl*, Quittungen *f pl*; ~ **credited to the fund** *n pl* FIN dem Fonds gutgeschriebene Eingänge *m pl*; ~ **and payments account** *n* ACC Einnahmen-Ausgaben-Rechnung *f*

receipt: ~ **stamp** *n* COMMS Eingangsstempel *m*

receivables *n pl* ACC Forderungen *f pl*; ~ **turnover** *n* FIN Debitorenumschlag *m*, Forderungsumschlag *m*

receive *vt* GEN COMM empfangen, erhalten, *recognition* kassieren (*infrml*); ◆ ~ **be on welfare** *BrE* (*cf be on welfare AmE*) HRM Sozialhilfe beziehen; ~ **a pay rise** HRM eine Gehaltserhöhung bekommen; ~ **unemploy-**ment benefit (*cf be on welfare AmE*) HRM Arbeitslosenunterstützung empfangen, WEL Arbeitslosenunterstützung beziehen; ~ **unemployment compensation** *AmE* HRM Arbeitslosenunterstützung empfangen, WEL Arbeitslosenunterstützung beziehen; ~ **versus payment** FIN gegen Zahlung erhalten

received *adj* (*recd*) GEN COMM empfangen, *payment* bezahlt; ~ **for shipment bill of lading** *n* IMP/EXP für Seefrachtbrief übernommen

receiver *n* HRM Empfänger, in *m,f*, LAW *bankruptcy* Konkursverwalter, in *m,f*, Zwangsverwalter, in *m,f*; ~ **and manager** *n* LAW *bankruptcy* Vermögensverwalter, in *m,f* mit Geschäftsführungsbefugnis; ~**'s agent** *n* HRM Agent, in *m,f* des Vermögensverwalters; ~**'s certificate** *n* FIN Schuldschein *m* zugunsten des Konkursverwalters

receivership *n* ACC Konkursverwaltung *f*, FIN Zwangsverwaltung *f*; ◆ **go into** ~ LAW die Zwangsverwaltung veranlassen

receiver: ~ **of the wreck** *n* HRM, TRANSP *senior customs officer* Strandvogt *m*

receiving: ~ **carrier** *n* TRANSP Empfangsspediteur *m*, Empfangstransporter *m*; ~ **country** *n* ECON Aufnahmeland *nt*, Bestimmungsland *nt*; ~ **department** *n* GEN COMM Warenannahme *f*, Warenempfangsabteilung *f*; ~ **forwarding agent** *n* GEN COMM Adreßspediteur *m*; ~ **and loading of cargo** *n* TRANSP Erhalt *m* und Verladen *nt* von Fracht; ~ **office** *n* (*RO*) GEN COMM, PATENTS Anmeldeamt *nt*, Annahmestelle *f*; ~ **order** *n* (*RO*) TRANSP Konkurseinleitungsbeschluß *m*; ~ **station** *n* TRANSP *rail* Empfangsstelle *f* der Wareneingangsabteilung

recent: **in** ~ **years** *phr* GEN COMM in den letzten Jahren

reception *n* ADMIN, GEN COMM Empfang *m*, LEIS Empfang *m*, Rezeption *f*, TRANSP Empfang *m*; ~ **area** *n* ADMIN Empfangshalle *f*, GEN COMM Empfang *m*, Rezeption *f*, *goods* Warenannahmestelle *f*, LEIS Empfang *m*, Rezeption *f*; ~ **depot** *n* TRANSP Empfangsdepot *nt*

receptionist *n* FIN, GEN COMM Rezeptionist, in *m,f*, HRM *in hotel* Empfangschef, in *m,f*, *in office* Empfangssekretär, in *m,f*

reception: ~ **point** *n* LEIS Empfangsbereich *m*

recession *n* ECON Konjunkturrückgang *m*, Rezession *f*, GEN COMM Rezession *f*

recessionary *adj* ECON rezessiv; ~ **gap** *n* ECON Rezessionslücke *f*, Rezessionsloch *nt*; ~ **phase** *n* ECON Rezessionsphase *f*, rezessive Phase *f*

recession: ~~**proof industry** *n* ECON rezessionssichere Branche *f*

recipe *n* MGMNT Rezept *nt*

recipient: ~ **of an allowance** *n* HRM Empfänger *m* eines Zuschusses

reciprocal 1. *adj* GEN COMM gegenseitig, reziprok, wechselseitig; **2.** *n* MATH reziproker Wert *m*

reciprocal: ~ **agreement** *n* HRM Gegenseitigkeitsabkommen *nt*, LAW *intellectual property* gegenseitiger Vertrag *m*; ~ **buying** *n* S&M wechselseitige Lieferbeziehungen *f pl*

reciprocally *adv* GEN COMM gegenseitig, wechselseitig

reciprocal: ~ **principle** *n* ECON Reziprozitätsprinzip *nt*, GEN COMM Gegenseitigkeitsprinzip *nt*; ~ **ratio** *n* MATH reziprokes Verhältnis *nt*; ~ **trading** *n* ECON, GEN COMM

Handel *m* auf Gegenseitigkeitsbasis, *international trade* Handel *m* auf Reprozitätsbasis

reciprocity *n* BANK Gegenseitigkeit *f*

reckoning *n* ACC Abrechnung *f*, Rechnen *nt*

reclaim *vt* ENVIR *land* neu gewinnen, GEN COMM herausverlangen, zurückfordern

reclaim: ~ **area** *n* LEIS, TRANSP Gepäckausgabe *f*

reclaiming *n* TRANSP *of cargo* Frachtanforderung *f*, *of luggage* Gepäckanforderung *f*

recmd *abbr* (*recommissioned*) GEN COMM reaktiviert, wieder in Dienst gestellt

recognition *n* GEN COMM, LAW *of claim* Anerkennung *f*; ~ **lag** *n* ECON Erkennungsverzögerung *f*; ~ **of loss** *n* ACC Verlustanerkennung *f*; ~**-only clause** *n* HRM Anerkennungsklausel *f*; ~ **test** *n* S&M Wiedererkennungstest *m*

recognize *vt* ACC ausweisen, verbuchen, GEN COMM *acknowledge* anerkennen, *know again* wiedererkennen, HRM *union*, LAW *right*, POL *government* anerkennen

recognized *adj* GEN COMM anerkannt; ~ **clearing house** *n* (*RCH*) BANK anerkannte Clearingstelle *f*; ~ **gain** *n* TAX anerkannter Gewinn *m*; ~ **investment exchange** *n* (*RIE*) STOCK anerkannte Investmentbörse *f*; ~ **professional body** *n* (*RPB*) FIN anerkannter Berufsverband *m*; ~ **profit** *n* TAX ausgewiesener Gewinn *m*; ~ **third-world investment firms** *n* FIN anerkannte Beteiligungsfirmen *f pl* der Dritten Welt; ~ **trade union** *n* HRM anerkannte Gewerkschaft *f*

recommend *vt* GEN COMM empfehlen

recommendation *n* GEN COMM Empfehlung *f*

recommended: ~ **retail price** *n* (*RRP*) S&M Einzelhandelsrichtpreis *m*, Preisempfehlung *f*, Richtpreis *m* für den Einzelhandel, *not binding* unverbindliche Preisempfehlung *f*

recommission *vt* GEN COMM reaktivieren

recommissioned *adj* (*recmd*) GEN COMM reaktiviert, wieder in Dienst gestellt

recompile *vt* COMP neu kompilieren

reconcile *vt* ACC abstimmen, *account* ausgleichen, berichtigen, FIN *people* aussöhnen, versöhnen, GEN COMM *facts, figures* miteinander in Einklang bringen; ♦ ~ **an account** ACC, BANK, FIN ein Konto abstimmen

reconciled *adj* ACC abgestimmt, berichtigt

reconciliation *n* ACC *of statements* Abstimmung *f*, *account* Ausgleich *m*, BANK Berichtigung *f*, FIN Abstimmung *f*, Ausgleichung *f*, Berichtigung *f*, GEN COMM, LAW, PATENTS Berichtigung *f*; ~ **account** *n* BANK Abstimmungskonto *nt*, Berichtigungskonto *nt*, STOCK Kontenberichtigung *f*; ~ **bill** *n* AmE ECON Schlichtungsvereinbarung *f*; ~ **of cash** *n* ECON Kassenabstimmung *f*; ~ **statement** *n* ACC Abstimmungsübersicht *f*, Saldenanerkenntnis *nt*; ~ **table** *n* ACC Abstimmungsliste *f*, Berichtigungstabelle *f*

recondition *vt* GEN COMM aufarbeiten, überholen

reconditioned *adj* GEN COMM aufgearbeitet, überholt

reconditioning: ~ **property** *n* PROP Instandsetzung *f* von Eigentum

reconfiguration *n* COMP, GEN COMM Rekonfiguration *f*

reconfigure *vt* COMP, GEN COMM rekonfigurieren

reconsider *vt* GEN COMM neubedenken, nochmals erwägen

reconsign *vt* TRANSP umleiten

reconstruct *vt* ECON reorganisieren, umbauen, GEN COMM rekonstruieren

reconstruction *n* ECON Reorganisation *f*, Umbau *m*, *of company* Wiederaufbau *m*, GEN COMM Rekonstruktion *f*

reconversion *f* COMP Rückwandlung *f*

reconvert *vt* COMP rückwandeln, zurückkonvertieren

reconveyance *n* PROP Rückübereignung *f*

record 1. *n* ADMIN Niederschrift *f*, COMP Datensatz *m*, ECON Dividendenstichtag *m*, GEN COMM *written* Aufzeichnung *f*, Vorgang *m*, TAX *bookkeeping* Beleg *m*; ♦ **on** ~ GEN COMM registriert; **give** ~ **of** GEN COMM *expenses, deficit* protokollieren; 2. *vt* ACC aufzeichnen, *accounts, register* eintragen, ADMIN protokollieren, COMP aufzeichnen, GEN COMM erfassen, registrieren, *contract* beurkunden, *meeting* aufnehmen, aufzeichnen, MEDIA *music, programme* aufnehmen, aufzeichnen

record: ~ **of acknowledgement** *n* LAW Bestätigungsschein *m*; ~ **breaker** *n* HRM Rekordbrecher, in *mf*; ~ **date** *n* FIN Bezugsrechtsstichtag *m*, Stopptag *m*

recorded *adj* ADMIN eingetragen, GEN COMM erfaßt, eingetragen, INS eingetragen, LEIS aufgezeichnet, PATENTS eingetragen; ~ **by a notary** *adj* LAW notariell beglaubigt, notariell beurkundet; ~ **economy** *n* ECON offizielle Wirtschaft *f*; ~ **market information** *n* STOCK ausgewiesene Marktinformationen *f pl*

record: ~ **format** *n* COMP Datensatzformat *nt*; ~ **high** *n* ECON *profits, unemployment* historischer Höchststand *m*, Rekordhöhe *f*, Spitzenwert *m*, GEN COMM Rekordhöhe *f*

recording *n* ADMIN Registrierung *f*, COMP Aufzeichnung *f*; ~ **of business transactions** *n* ECON Erfassung *f* von Geschäftsvorfällen; ~ **fee** *n* GEN COMM Registrierungsgebühr *f*

record: ~ **in the register** *n* PATENTS Eintragung *f* im Register, Eintragung *f* in der Patentrolle; ~ **keeper** *n* ADMIN, HRM Archivar, in *m,f*, Dokumentar, in *m,f*; ~ **key** *n* COMP Datensatzschlüssel *m*; ~ **label** *n* MEDIA Plattenfirma *f*; ~ **locking** *n* COMP Datensatzsperre *f*; ~ **result** *n* GEN COMM Rekordergebnis *nt*

records *n pl* ACC, ADMIN Aufzeichnungen *f pl*, GEN COMM Unterlagen *f pl*

record: ~ **sales** *n pl* S&M Rekordabsatz *m*

records: ~ **management** *n* MGMNT Aktenverwaltung *f*

recoup *vt* GEN COMM *loss* ausgleichen, wettmachen

recourse *n* GEN COMM Rückgriff *m*, Regreß *m*, INS Rückgriff *m*; ♦ **with** ~ GEN COMM mit Rückgriff, INS *company* mit Rückgriff, mit Regreß; **without** ~ BANK ohne Gewähr, ohne Obligo, ohne Regreßmöglichkeit, FIN ohne Regreß, GEN COMM ohne Rückgriff *m*, INS *company* ohne Rückgriff *m*, ohne Regreß

recourse: ~ **loan** *n* FIN Darlehen *nt* mit Regreß

recover 1. *vt* COMP wiederherstellen, ECON eintreiben, wiedererlangen, zurückerhalten, ENVIR *for recycling* rückgewinnen, GEN COMM wiedergewinnen, *expenditure* wiedereinbringen, *debts* einholen, eintreiben, *assets* wiederhereinholen, LAW *damages* erhalten; 2. *vi* ECON sich erholen

recoverable: ~ **debt** *n* ACC beitreibbare Forderung *f*; ~ **input tax** *n* TAX anrechenbare Vorsteuer *f*; ~ **material** *n* ENVIR *recycling* rückgewinnbares Material *nt*; ~ **reserves** *n pl* ENVIR *of raw materials* abbauwürdige Vorräte *m pl*, förderwürdige Reserve *f*, nachgewiesene Vorräte *m pl*, sichere Reserven *f pl*

recovered: ~ **bad debt** *n* ACC eingetriebene Forderung *f*

recovery *n* COMP *of lost file, data* Wiederherstellung *f*, Rückgewinnung *f*, ECON Belebung *f*, ENVIR Rückgewinnung *f*, FIN Eintreibung *f*; ◆ **the ~ is under way** ECON der Aufschwung ist im Gang, die Erholung ist im Gang

recovery: **~ of basis** *n* TAX Rückgewinnung *f* der Basis; **~ of damage** *n* LAW *contracts* Schadensersatzerlangung *f*, Schadensersatzerwirkung *f*; **~ of losses** ACC Wiederausgleich *m* von Verlusten; **~ plan** *n* ECON Plan *m* zur Konjunkturbelebung, Wiederaufbauplan *m*; **~ program** *AmE*, **~ programme** *BrE n* GEN COMM Programm *nt* zur Belebung der Konjunktur, Wiederaufbauprogramm *nt*; **~ vehicle** *n* TRANSP Abschleppwagen *m*, Bergungsfahrzeug *nt*, Reparaturwagen *m*, Werkstattwagen *m*

recpt *abbr* (*receipt*) GEN COMM *of goods* Annahme *f*, Erhalt *m*, *for goods, payment* Quittung *f*, S&M Annahme *f*

recreational: **~ facilities** *n pl* LEIS Freizeiteinrichtungen *f pl*, Erholungseinrichtungen *f pl*

recruit *vt* HRM einstellen

recruiting: **~ office** *n* HRM Anwerbungsbüro *nt*; **~ officer** *n* HRM Einstellungssachbearbeiter, in *m,f*

recruitment *n* HRM Anwerbung *f*, Einstellung *f*, Personalbeschaffung *f*; **~ advertising** *n* S&M Stellenanzeigen *f pl*; **~ bonus** *n* HRM Anwerbungsprämie *f*; **~ consultant** *n* HRM Personalberater, in *m,f*; **~ country** *n* HRM Anwerbeland *nt*; **~ manager** *n* HRM Leiter, in *m,f* der Personalbeschaffung; **~ and selection** *n* HRM Anwerbung *f* und Auswahl

rectification *n* GEN COMM Behebung *f*, Berichtigung *f*, *amendment* Abänderung *f*, *situation* Richtigstellung *f*, Entzerrung *f*

rectified *adj* GEN COMM berichtigt

rectify *vt* GEN COMM beheben, berichtigen, *amend* abändern, *situation* entzerren, richtigstellen

recto *n* (*ro.*) MEDIA *front of page* Vorderseite *f*

recurrent: **~ disability** *n* HRM *work, illness* wiederkehrende Arbeitsunfähigkeit *f*; **~ spot contracting** *n* HRM tageweise Anstellung *f* von Arbeitskräften

recursive: **~ system** *n* ECON *econometrics* rekursives System *nt*

recyclable *adj* ENVIR recycelfähig, wiederverwertbar, GEN COMM wiederverwertbar; **~ material** *n* ENVIR rückgewinnbares Material *nt*

recycle *vt* ENVIR rückgewinnen, recyceln, *reuse* wiederverwenden, wiederverwerten, zurückführen, GEN COMM wiederverwenden, wiederverwerten, aufbereiten

recycled: **~ paper** *n* ENVIR Recyclingpapier *nt*, Umweltschutzpapier *nt*, GEN COMM aufbereitetes Papier *nt*, Recyclingpapier *nt*

recycling *n* ENVIR Wiederverwendung *f*, Rückgewinnung *f*, Recycling *nt*, *reuse* Wiederverwertung *f*, GEN COMM Wiederverwertung *f*, *reuse* Wiederverwendung *f*; **~ of waste** *n* ENVIR Abfallwiederaufbereitung *f*

red. *abbr* (*redeemable*) STOCK tilgbar

red: **in the ~** *phr* BANK, GEN COMM in den roten Zahlen, in den Roten (*infrml*)

Red: **~ Book** *n AmE infrml* FIN Rotbuch *nt*

red: **~ button** *n BrE* STOCK *settlement room clerk* mit der Abwicklung betraute(r) Angestellte(r) *mf* [decl. as adj]; **~ clause** *n* BANK *international trade* Red Clause *f*, rote

Klausel *f*; **~ clause credit** *n* TRANSP *shipping* Red Clause-Kredit *m*, Vorschußakkreditiv *nt*

redeem *vt* BANK, FIN, GEN COMM rückzahlen, STOCK rückzahlen, tilgen

redeemable *adj* (*red.*) BANK, FIN, GEN COMM rückzahlbar, STOCK tilgbar, rückzahlbar; **~ bonds** *n pl* ACC ablösbare Schuldverschreibungen *f pl*; **~ preference share** *n* STOCK rückzahlbare Vorzugsaktie *f*; **~ share** *n* STOCK rückzahlbare Aktie *f*

redeemed *adj* STOCK eingezogen; **~ share** *n* STOCK eingezogene Aktie *f*

redeliver *vt* GEN COMM rückliefern

redelivery *n* GEN COMM, TRANSP Rücklieferung *f*

redemption *n* ACC Tilgung *f*, BANK Auslösung *f*, FIN Tilgung *f*, GEN COMM *of token, pawned object* Einlösung *f*, STOCK Tilgung *f*; **~ amount** *n* STOCK Rückzahlungsbetrag *m*, Tilgungsbetrag *m*; **~ before due date** *n* FIN Tilgung *f* vor dem Fälligkeitstermin, vorzeitige Tilgung *f*; **~ bond** *n* STOCK Amortisationsanleihe *f*, Tilgungsanleihe *f*, Umschuldungsanleihe *f*; **~ commitments** *n pl* FIN Tilgungsverpflichtungen *f pl*; **~ date** *n* STOCK Einlösungstermin *m*, Rückzahlungstermin *m*, Tilgungstermin *m*; **~-free year** *n* FIN Freijahr *nt*, tilgungsfreies Jahr *nt*; **~ fund** *n* FIN Tilgungsfonds *m*; **~ funds** *n pl* ECON Tilgungsmittel *nt pl*; **~ installment** *AmE*, **~ instalment** *BrE n* FIN Tilgungsrate *f*; **~ of a loan** *n* FIN Tilgung *f* einer Anleihe; **~ mortgage** *n* FIN Tilgungshypothek *f*, Annuitätenhypothek *f*; **~ payment** *n* ECON Tilgungszahlung *f*; **~ period** *n* FIN Einlösungsfrist *f*; **~ premium** *n* ACC Rückkaufsprämie *f*, Rückzahlungsagio *nt*; **~ table** *n* FIN Tilgungsplan *m*; **~ yield** *n* BANK, GEN COMM, STOCK Effektivverzinsung *f*, Rückzahlungsrendite *f*

redeploy *vt* ADMIN versetzen, GEN COMM versetzen, *restructure* umgruppieren, HRM *transfer* versetzen

redeployment *n* ADMIN Versetzung *f*, GEN COMM Versetzung *f*, *of worker* Einsatz *m* an anderem Arbeitsplatz, *restructuring* Umgruppierung *f*, HRM *of workers* Versetzung *f*; **~ premium** *n* HRM Versetzungsprämie *f*

redevelop *vt* ECON, PROP sanieren

redevelopment *n* ECON, PROP Sanierung *f*

red: **~ goods** *n pl* S&M *advertising* rote Ware *f*; **~ and green system** *n* IMP/EXP *for customs declaration* Rot-Grün-System *nt*; **~ herring** *n* STOCK Vorankündigung *f* eines Emissionsprospektes; **~-herring prospectus** *n* STOCK Vorankündigung *f* einer Emission, vorläufiger Börseneinführungsprospekt *m*

redhibition *n* LAW *contracts* Gewährsmangel *m*

redhibitory: **~ defect** *n* LAW *contracts* Sachmangel *m*

rediscountable *adj* ACC, BANK, FIN rediskontfähig

rediscounter *n* ACC, BANK, FIN Rediskontierer, in *m,f*, Rediskontinstitut *nt*

rediscounting *n* ACC, BANK, FIN Rediskontierung *f*

rediscount *n* ACC, BANK, FIN Rediskont *m*; **~ rate** *n* ACC Rediskontsatz *m*

red: **~-line clause** *n* INS *in cargo policy* Ausschlußklausel *f*

redlining *n jarg* FIN willkürlicher Ausschluß *m* von Bankkunden, GEN COMM Ausschluß *m*

redraft 1. *n* ECON, POL Umformulierung; **2.** *vt* ADMIN umformulieren

redress 1. *n* LAW Abhilfe *f*, Entschädigung *f*, Wiedergutmachung *f*; **2.** *vt* GEN COMM *balance* wiederherstellen, *situation* bereinigen, ins Gleichgewicht bringen, LAW *grievance* abhelfen, beseitigen, *wrong* wiedergutmachen; ◆ **~ the balance** ACC das Gleichgewicht wiederherstellen

REDS *abbr* BrE (*registered excise dealers and shippers*) IMP/EXP eingetragene Händler und Spediteure für zu versteuernde Güter

red: **~ tape** *n* ADMIN, HRM Bürokratismus *m*

reduce *vt* ECON *prices, investment* verringern, herabsetzen, reduzieren, zurückführen, senken, GEN COMM ausdünnen, *expenses* reduzieren, *prices* nachlassen, abbauen, verkürzen, verringern, ermäßigen, verbilligen, *inflation rate* ermäßigen, LAW mindern, S&M abbauen; ◆ **~ in size** GEN COMM verkleinern

reduced *adj* ECON *price, price support* herabgesetzt, niedrig, reduziert, verringert, GEN COMM reduziert, verbilligt; **~ class rate** *n* (*R*) TRANSP *air freight classification* ermäßigter Gruppenfrachttarif *m*, Tariflohnreduktion *f*; **~ fare** *n* LEIS ermäßigter Fahrpreis *m*; **~ form equation** *n* ECON, MATH reduzierte Form *f*; **~ lead time** *n* IND reduzierte Vorlaufzeit *f*; **~ price** *n* S&M herabgesetzter Preis *m*; **~ rate** *n* GEN COMM, TAX *National Insurance contributions* ermäßigter Satz *m*; **~ tax** *n* TAX ermäßigte Steuer *f*; **~ weight** *n* (*RW*) TRANSP reduziertes Gewicht *nt*

reducing: **~ balance** *n* ACC, FIN degressive Abschreibung *f*; **~-balance method** *n* ACC *depreciation* degressive Abschreibung *f*; **~-installment system** *AmE*, **~-instalment system** *BrE n* ECON degressive Abschreibung *f*

reduction *n* ECON Herabsetzung *f*, Verringerung *f*, Reduzierung *f*, GEN COMM Ermäßigung *f*, Nachlaß *m*, Reduzierung *f*, Verkürzung *f*, Verringerung *f*, *discount* Rabatt *m*, LAW Minderung *f*; **~ for children** *n* LEIS Kinderermäßigung *f*; **~ in capital** *n* ACC, ADMIN Kapitalherabsetzung *f*, STOCK Verringerung *f* des Kapitals; **~ in force** *n* (*RIF*) HRM Personalabbau *m*; **~ in size** *n* GEN COMM Verkleinerung *f*, Verringerung *f*; **~ in working hours** *n* HRM Arbeitszeitverkürzung *f*; **~ of liability** *n* INS, LAW *contracts* Haftungsminderung *f*; **~ of premiums** *n* INS *marine* Prämienreduzierung *f*; **~ of price due to defects** *n* LAW *contracts* Minderung *f* des Kaufpreises wegen Mängeln; **~ of profit** *n* FIN Ertragsminderung *f*; **~ of sentence** *n* LAW Strafherabsetzung *f*

reductions: **~ in profit** *n pl* FIN Ertragseinbußen *f pl*

redundancy *n* COMP Redundanz *f*, HRM Entlassung *f*; **~ check** *n* COMP Redundanzprüfung *f*; **~ consultation** *n* HRM Entlassungsrücksprache *f*; **~ letter** *n* BrE (*cf pink slip AmE*) HRM, MGMNT *notice in writing* Kündigungsschreiben *nt*; **~ pay** *n* HRM Abfindungszahlung *f*; **~ payment** *n* GEN COMM Entlassungsabfindung *f*, HRM Abfindungszahlung *f*

Redundancy: **~ Payments Act** *n* BrE (*RPA*) HRM britisches Gesetz zur Regelung von Entlassungsabfindungen

redundancy: **~ procedure** *n* HRM Entlassungsverfahren *nt*, Verfahrensregeln *f pl* bei Entlassung; **~ severance pay** *n* HRM soziale Abfindung *f* im Kündigungsfall

redundant *adj* GEN COMM *unneeded* überflüssig; ◆ **be made** ~ HRM den Arbeitsplatz verlieren; **make ~** HRM entlassen

redundant: **~ farmland** *n* ENVIR überschüssige landwirtschaftliche Nutzfläche *f*

re-educate *vt* GEN COMM, HRM umerziehen, umschulen

re-education *n* GEN COMM, HRM Umerziehung *f*

reefer *n* TRANSP *container* Kühlschiff *nt*; **~ carrier** *n* TRANSP Kühlschiff *nt*; **~ ship** *n* TRANSP Kühlschiff *nt*

reel *n* COMP Band *nt*, Bandspule *f*

re-election *n* GEN COMM Wiederwahl *f*

re-emphasize *vt* GEN COMM neubetonen

re-employ *vt* GEN COMM, HRM wiedereinstellen

re-employment *n* GEN COMM, HRM Wiedereinstellung *f*

re-enactment *n* LAW Wiederinkraftsetzung *f*

re-endorsement *n* BANK Re-Indossament *nt*

re-engage *vt* GEN COMM, HRM wiedereinstellen

re-engagement *n* GEN COMM, HRM *of dismissed employee* Wiedereinstellung *f*

re-enter *vt* COMP *data, program* rückverzweigen

re-establish *vt* POL *diplomatic relations* wiederaufnehmen

re-establishment *n* GEN COMM Neugründung *f*, Wiedereinsetzung *f*, Wiederherstellung *f*, POL *of diplomatic relations* Wiederaufnahme *f*

re-examine *vt* GEN COMM erneut überprüfen

re-examination *n* GEN COMM Nachprüfung *f*, Wiederholungsprüfung *f*

re-exportation *n* IMP/EXP Reexport *m*, Wiederausfuhr *f*

re-exporter *n* IMP/EXP Reexporteur, in *m,f*, Wiederausfuhrhändler, in *m,f*

ref. *abbr* (*reference*) GEN COMM Aktenzeichen *nt*, Geschäftszeichen *nt*; ◆ **our ~** *abbr* (*our reference*) COMP unser Zeichen

refer *vt* GEN COMM sich beziehen auf, verweisen; ◆ **~ back to** GEN COMM, HRM *industrial relations* zurückverweisen an [+acc]; **~ sb to sth** GEN COMM jdn auf etw hinweisen; **~ to** GEN COMM verweisen, verweisen auf, *mention* sprechen von, erwähnen, *consult person* sich wenden an [+acc], *relate to* sich beziehen auf [+acc], betreffen, Bezug nehmen auf [+acc], LAW *case* verweisen, weiterleiten, PATENTS *previous, single claim* verweisen auf [+acc], Bezug nehmen auf [+acc]; **~ to acceptor** (*R/A*) GEN COMM an Akzeptant; **~ to drawer** (*RD*) GEN COMM zurück an Aussteller

referee *n* HRM *for job applicant* Referenz *f*, LAW Schiedsrichter, in *m,f*

reference *n* (*ref.*) COMMS *in document* Bezugnahme *f*, GEN COMM Verweis *m*, Aktenzeichen *nt*, Verweisung *f*, Geschäftszeichen *nt*, HRM *testimonial* Zeugnis *nt*, Referenz *f*, *referee* Referenz *f*, MEDIA Quellenangabe *f*; ◆ **~ to** PATENTS Bezugnahme auf; **our ~** *n* (*our ref.*) COMP unser Zeichen; **outside the ~ of** GEN COMM außerhalb der Bezugnahme auf; **with ~ to** COMMS bezugnehmend auf, GEN COMM in bezug auf, unter Bezugnahme auf; **with ~ to your enquiry** COMMS bezugnehmend auf Ihre Anfrage; **with ~ to your letter** COMMS bezugnehmend auf Ihr Schreiben

reference: **~ bank** *n* BANK Referenzbank *f*; **~ currency** *n* ECON Referenzwährung *f*; **~ cycle** *n* ECON Referenzzyklus *m*; **~ group** *n* GEN COMM Bezugsgruppe *f*, Interessengruppe *f*; **~ level** *n* FIN Bezugsniveau *nt*, Referenzniveau *nt*; **~ line** *n* PATENTS Bezugskategorie *f*, Bezugslinie *f*; **~ material** *n* ADMIN Referenzmaterial *nt*; **~ number** *n* GEN COMM Kennziffer *f*, HRM Chiffrenummer *f*; **~ point** *n* GEN COMM Bezugspunkt *m*; **~ sign** *n* PATENTS Bezugszeichen *nt*; **~ value** *n* ECON Bezugswert *m*

referendum *n* GEN COMM Referendum *nt*, Volksentscheid *m*

referral *n* GEN COMM Verweisung *f*

referring: ~ **to** *phr* GEN COMM bezugnehmend auf, sich beziehend auf, unter Bezugnahme auf

refinance *vt* FIN umschulden

refinance: ~ **credit** *n* BANK Refinanzierungskredit *m*

refinancing *n* FIN Refinanzierung *f*; ~ **line** *n* BANK, FIN Refinanzierungsplafond *m*

refine *vt* IND *sugar, cocoa butter, oil* raffinieren, veredeln, verfeinern, *substances* reinigen

refined *adj* IND fein, geläutert, verfeinert, *chemical substances* gereinigt, *sugar, cocoa butter, oil* raffiniert; ~ **metal** *n* ENVIR Raffinatmetall *nt*

refinement *n* IND Veredelung *f*, Verfeinerung *f*

refiner *n* IND Raffineriebetrieb *m*, Verarbeiter *m*

refinery *n* IND Raffinerie *f*

refining *n* IND Raffination *f*, Raffinieren *nt*

reflation *n* ECON Reflation *f*, GEN COMM, POL Ankurbelung *f*

reflationary: ~ **policy** *n* ECON Ankurbelungspolitik *f*

reflect *vt* GEN COMM *expression* widerspiegeln

reflected: **be ~ in** *phr* GEN COMM sich spiegeln in [+dat], sich widerspiegeln in [+dat]

refloat *vt* BANK umstrukturieren, ECON sanieren; ♦ ~ **a loan** BANK eine Anleihe neu auflegen

refloated *adj* BANK umstrukturiert

reflotation *n* BANK Umstrukturierung *f*

refocusing *n* GEN COMM erneute Fokussierung *f*, Umorientierung *f*, Wiedereinrichtung *f*

reform 1. *n* GEN COMM, POL, WEL Reform *f*; **2.** *vt* GEN COMM *improve* reformieren, *reshape* neu gestalten, POL, WEL reformieren

reformat *vt* COMP *disk* neu formatieren

reformatory *n obs* WEL Besserungsanstalt *f (obs)*

reform: ~ **package** *n* POL Bündel *nt* von Reformen, Reformpaket *nt*; ~ **program** *AmE*, ~ **programme** *BrE* *n* ECON Reformprogramm *nt*

reforwarding *n* TRANSP Weiterbeförderung *f*

refresh *vt* COMP *computer screen* auffrischen, *memory* neuanzeigen

refresher *n* LAW außerordentliche Anwaltsgebühr *f*; ~ **training** *n* COMP auffrischende Ausbildung *f*

refrigerate *vt* GEN COMM, TRANSP kühlen

refrigerated *adj (R)* IND kühl aufbewahrt, tiefgekühlt, Kühl-; ~ **box van** *n* TRANSP Kühlkastenwagen *m*; ~ **capacity** *n* IND *of container* Kühlleistung *f*; ~ **container** *n* TRANSP Kühlcontainer *m*; ~ **lorry** *n BrE* (*cf refrigerated truck AmE*) TRANSP Kühllastwagen *m*; ~ **ship** *n* TRANSP Kühlschiff *nt*; ~ **truck** *n AmE* (*cf refrigerated lorry BrE*) TRANSP Kühllastwagen *m*; ~ **vessel** *n* TRANSP Kühlschiff *nt*; ~ **warehouse** *n* IND Kühlhaus *nt*

refrigeration *n (R)* IND Kühlung *f*; ~ **engineering** *n* IND Kältetechnik *f*

refuel: ~ **inflation** *phr* ECON die Inflation anheizen

refueling *AmE see* **refuelling** *BrE*

refuelling *n BrE* TRANSP Auftanken *nt*

refugee *n* GEN COMM Aussiedler, in *m,f*, Emigrant, in *m,f*, Flüchtling *m*; ~ **capital** *n* FIN Fluchtkapital *nt*, heißes Geld *nt (jarg)*

refund 1. *n* BANK, ECON, FIN Rückerstattung *f*, GEN COMM Rückerstattung *f*, Rückzahlung *f*, Rückvergütung *f*, IMP/EXP Ausfuhrerstattung *f*, PATENTS Rückerstattung *f*, Rückvergütung *f*, TAX Rückerstattung *f*; **2.** *vt* BANK, FIN rückzahlen, GEN COMM *cost* erstatten, *money* zurückzahlen, rückzahlen, STOCK rückzahlen

refundable: ~ **expenses** *n pl* GEN COMM erstattungsfähige Kosten *pl*

refunding: ~ **loan** *n* FIN Ablösungsschuldverschreibung *f*, Refundierungsanleihe *f*

refund: ~ **of premium** *n* INS Beitragsrückerstattung *f*

refurbish *vt* GEN COMM verschönern, PROP renovieren, verschönern

refurbishment *n* GEN COMM, PROP Renovierung *f*, Verschönerung *f*

refusal *n* GEN COMM Ablehnung *f*, Absage *f*, Verweigerung *f*, *negative response* abschlägige Antwort *f*, PATENTS Ablehnung *f*; ~ **to accept** *n* LAW *contracts* Annahmeverweigerung *f*; ~ **to fulfill an obligation** *AmE*, ~ **to fulfil an obligation** *n BrE* LAW Erfüllungsverweigerung *f*, Leistungsverweigerung *f*

refuse 1. *n* ENVIR, GEN COMM Abfall *m*, Müll *m*; **2.** *vt* GEN COMM verweigern; ♦ ~ **acceptance of a draft** BANK die Annahme einer Tratte verweigern; ~ **sb bail** LAW einen Haftbefehl gegen Sicherheitsleistungen aussetzen

refuse: ~ **collection** *n* ENVIR, GEN COMM Müllabfuhr *f*

refused *adj* GEN COMM verweigert

refuse: ~ **disposal** *n* ENVIR, GEN COMM Entsorgung *f*, Müllbeseitigung *f*

refutable *adj* MATH anfechtbar; ~ **assertion** *n* MATH anfechtbare Behauptung *f*

regard: **have a high ~ for sb** *phr* GEN COMM jdn hoch schätzen; **with ~ to** *phr* GEN COMM in bezug auf

regarding *adv* COMMS betreffs, bezüglich, GEN COMM in bezug auf, betrifft

regd. *abbr (registered)* COMMS eingeschrieben, per Einschreiben

regime *n* POL Ordnung *f*, Regierungssystem *nt*, System *nt*

region *n* COMP Bereich *m*, ECON Region *f*, GEN COMM Bereich *m*, Gebiet *nt*, Region *f*; ♦ **in the ~ of** GEN COMM im Bereich von

regional *adj* GEN COMM räumlich begrenzt, regional, überörtlich, Regional-; ~ **agreement** *n* ECON *international trade* Regionalabkommen *nt*; ~ **bank** *n* BANK Landesbank *f*, Regionalbank *f*; ~ **banking pacts** *n* BANK Abkommen *nt pl* zwischen Regionalbanken; ~ **center** *AmE*, ~ **centre** *BrE n* GEN COMM Gebietszentrum *nt*, regionales Zentrum *nt*; ~ **development** *n* ECON regionale Entwicklung *f*, Regionalentwicklung *f*; ~ **economics** *n* ECON Regionalökonomik *f*; ~ **employment premium** *n (REP)* HRM regionale Arbeitsplatzprämie *f*; ~ **grouping** *n* ECON *North American Free Trade Agreement* regionaler Zusammenschluß *m*; ~ **manager** *n* MGMNT Gebietsleiter, in *m,f*; ~ **market** *n* S&M regionaler Markt *m*; ~ **multiplier** *n* ECON regionaler Multiplikator *m*; ~ **organization** *n* MGMNT Regionalorganisation *f*; ~ **patent** *n* PATENTS Lokalpatent *nt*, Regionalpatent *nt*; ~ **planning policy** *n* ECON Raumordnungspolitik *f*; ~ **policy** *n* ECON Regionalpolitik *f*; ~ **press** *n* S&M Regionalpresse *f*; ~ **quota** *n* ECON *international trade* regionale Quote *f*; ~ **representation** *n* S&M *of store chain* regionale Vertretung *f*; ~ **selective assistance** *n (RSA)* ECON selektive Regionalhilfe *f*; ~ **stock exchange** *n* STOCK Regionalbörse *f*; ~ **tax effect** *n* ACC regionale Steuerwirkung *f*; ~ **trend** *n* S&M regionaler Trend *m*; ~ **wage bargaining** *n* HRM regionale Tarifverhandlungen *f pl*

register 1. *n* ADMIN Register *nt*, Verzeichnis *nt*, COMP Liste *f*, Register *nt*, PATENTS Patentrolle *f*, Register *nt*, Verzeichnis *nt*; **2.** *vt* ADMIN *in book, file* eintragen, *fact, figure* registrieren, COMP registrieren, GEN COMM registrieren, beurkunden, *change of name* anmelden, eintragen lassen, LAW *business name* eintragen; ◆ ~ **a high** GEN COMM *on stock market* ein Hoch verzeichnen; **3.** *vi* GEN COMM *as student* sich einschreiben, *at hotel* sich anmelden, *on list, roll* sich eintragen; ◆ ~ **as unemployed** HRM sich arbeitslos melden

register: ~ **of bills payable** *n* ACC Akzeptebuch *nt*

Register: ~ **Book** *n* TRANSP *shipping* Schiffsregister *nt*

register: ~ **of companies** *n* ADMIN Firmenregister *nt*

registered *adj (regd.)* ADMIN eingetragen, COMMS eingeschrieben, per Einschreiben, GEN COMM registriert, eingetragen, INS, PATENTS eingetragen; ~ **address** *n* GEN COMM feststehende Adresse *f*, registrierte Adresse *f*; ~ **applicant** *n pl* GEN COMM *for work* registrierter Stellenbewerber *m*, registrierte Stellenbewerberin *f*; ~ **baggage** *n* TRANSP aufgegebenes Gepäck *nt*; ~ **check** *AmE*, ~ **cheque** *BrE n* BANK Bankscheck *m*; ~ **company** *n* ADMIN, LAW eingetragene Gesellschaft *f*; ~ **design** *n* LAW eingetragenes Gebrauchsmuster *nt*; ~ **equity market maker** *n* STOCK eingetragener Aktienmarktmacher *m*; ~ **excise dealers and shippers** *n BrE* (*REDS*) IMP/EXP eingetragene Händler und Spediteure für zu versteuernde Güter

Registered: ~ **International Exchange** *n* (*RIE BrE*) STOCK Internationale Börse in Großbritannien

registered: ~ **letter** *n* COMMS eingeschriebener Brief *m*, Einschreiben *nt*; ~ **luggage** *n* TRANSP aufgegebenes Gepäck *nt*; ~ **mail** *n AmE* (*cf registered post BrE*) COMMS Einschreiben *nt*; ~ **manager** *n* MGMNT Handlungsbevollmächtigte(r) *mf* [decl. as adj]; ~ **mark** *n* PATENTS eingetragenes Firmenzeichen *nt*, eingetragenes Warenzeichen *nt*; ~ **market maker** *n* STOCK eingetragener Marktmacher *m*; ~ **office** *n* ADMIN, LAW *of company* eingetragener Sitz *m*, eingetragener einer Gesellschaft *f*; ~ **options trader** *n* STOCK eingetragener Optionshändler *m*; ~ **parcel** *n* COMMS Wertpaket *nt*; ~ **post** *n BrE* (*cf registered mail AmE*) COMMS Einschreiben *nt*; **by** ~ **post** *phr* COMMS per Einschreiben; ~ **proprietor** *n* PROP eingetragener Eigentümer *m*, eingetragene Eigentümerin *f*; ~ **representative** *n* STOCK registrierter Vertreter *m*, registrierte Vertreterin *f*, registrierte(r) Bevollmächtigte(r) *mf* [decl. as adj]; ~ **retirement income fund** *n* (*RRIF*) INS eingetragene Pensionskasse *f*, eingetragener Alters-Versorgungsfonds *m*, eingetragener Pensionsfonds *m*; ~ **retirement savings plan** *n* (*RRSP*) INS eingetragener Pensionssparplan *m*, eingetragener Sparplan *m* für den Ruhestand; ~ **secondary offering** *n* STOCK registriertes Angebot *nt* von Wertpapieren im Sekundärmarkt; ~ **share** *n* ACC, STOCK Namensaktie *f*; ~ **shareholder** *n* STOCK eingetragener Aktionär *m*, eingetragene Aktionärin *f*; ~ **society** *n* GEN COMM, POL, STOCK eingetragener Verein *m*; ~ **stockholder** *n* STOCK eingetragener Aktionär *m*, eingetragene Aktionärin *f*; ~ **title** *n* ADMIN eingetragener Rechtsanspruch *m*; ~ **trademark** *n* GEN COMM, LAW eingetragenes Warenzeichen *nt*, PATENTS eingetragenes Firmenzeichen *nt*, eingetragenes Warenzeichen *nt*; ~ **trader** *n* STOCK eingetragener Wertpapierhändler *m*; ~ **unemployed** *adj* GEN COMM als arbeitslos gemeldet; ~ **unemployment** *n* HRM gemeldete Arbeitslosigkeit *f*; ~ **user** *n* PATENTS eingetragener Lizenznehmer

Register: ~ **of Members** *n* LAW *of corporation, public limited company* Aktienbuch *nt*, Aktionärsregister *m*

register: ~ **office** *n* ADMIN Standesamt *nt*; ~ **of shipping** *n* TRANSP Schiffahrtsregister *f*; ~ **ton** *n* TRANSP Registertonne *f*; ~ **tonnage** *n* TRANSP Registertonnage *f*

registrar: ~ **of companies** *n* ADMIN Amtsgericht *nt*, Führer, in *m,f* des Handelsregisters beim Amtsgericht, Registerführer, in *m,f*; ~ **of deeds** *n* LAW, PROP Registerführer, in *m,f* im Grundbuchamt

Registrar: ~ **General** *n BrE* ADMIN oberste(r) Standesbeamte(r) *m* [decl. as adj], oberste Standesbeamtin *f*

registrar: ~**'s department** *n* BANK *Bank of England* Abteilung *f* zur Registrierung von Staats- und anderen Anleihen; ~**'s office** *n* ADMIN Registratur *f*, Standesamt *nt*; ~ **of transfers** *n* FIN Umschreibungsbeamte(r) *m* [decl. as adj], Umschreibungsbeamtin *f*

registration *n* ADMIN, GEN COMM Eintragung *f*, Registrierung *f*, LAW *of car* Anmeldung *f*, Zulassung *f*, PATENTS Eintragung *f*, Registrierung *f*; ~ **fee** *n* GEN COMM Anmeldegebühr *f*, Registrierungsgebühr *f*; ~ **office** *n* ADMIN Anmeldestelle *f*, Einwohnermeldeamt *nt*; ~ **system** *n* PATENTS Anmeldesystem *nt*; ~ **threshold** *n* TAX *VAT* Anmeldungsschwelle *f*, Meldeschwelle *f*

registry *n* ADMIN *office* Registratur *f*, *place* Registrierungsort *m*; ~ **of deeds** *n* LAW, PROP Grundbuchamt *nt*; ~ **office** *n* ADMIN amtliches Register *nt*, *for marriages etc* Standesamt *nt*

regression *n* ECON, MATH *statistics* Regression *f*; ~ **analysis** *n* ECON, MATH *statistics* Regressionsanalyse *f*; ~ **curve** *n* MATH *statistics* Regressionskurve *f*

regressive: ~ **expectations** *n* MATH *statistics* regressive Erwartungen *f pl*; ~ **supply** *n* ECON regressives Angebot *nt*; ~ **tax** *n* TAX regressive Steuer *f*

regressivity *n* TAX Regressivität *f*

regret 1. *n* GEN COMM Bedauern *nt*; **2.** *vt* GEN COMM bedauern; ◆ **we** ~ **to inform you that** GEN COMM wir müssen Ihnen leider mitteilen, daß

regretfully *adv* GEN COMM mit Bedauern

regroup *vt* GEN COMM umgruppieren, umschichten

regrouping *n* GEN COMM Umgruppierung *f*

regular: ~ **accounting practices** *n pl* ECON übliche Rechnungslegungsverfahren *nt pl*; ~ **annual payment** *n* FIN Annuität *f*; ~ **expenditure** *n* FIN regelmäßige Ausgaben *f pl*; ~ **hours** *n pl* GEN COMM normale Zeiten *f pl*, HRM normale Arbeitszeiten *f pl*; ~ **income** *n* FIN regelmäßige Einnahmen *f pl*; ~ **meeting** *n* MGMNT ordentliche Sitzung *f*, reguläre Sitzung *f*; ~ **payment** *n* GEN COMM Geldrente *f*, regelmäßige Zahlung *f*; ~ **service** *n* LEIS regulärer Dienst *m*; ~ **statement** *n* GEN COMM regelmäßig erstellter Bericht *m*; ~ **Supplementary Estimates** *n pl* FIN regelmäßiger Nachtragshaushalt *m*; ~ **way delivery** *n* FIN Lieferung *f* am vierten Werktag, GEN COMM Lieferung *f* am vierten Werktag, normale und fristgerechte Lieferung *f*

regulate *vt* ECON, FIN *industry, market* lenken, ordnen, regeln, regulieren, LAW regulieren, STOCK regeln

regulated *adj* ECON, FIN reguliert; ~ **commodities** *n pl* STOCK Waren *f pl*, die den Marktbestimmungen unterliegen; ~ **firm** *n* ECON öffentlich gebundenes Unternehmen *nt*, reguliertes Unternehmen *nt*; ~ **invest-**

ment company n ECON steuerbegünstigte Investmentgesellschaft f, FIN regulierter Investmentfonds m, TAX steuerbegünstigte Investmentgesellschaft f; **~ market** n FIN regulierter Markt m

regulation n ECON Bestimmung f, *government* Maßnahme f der staatlichen Wirtschaftslenkung, *directive* Richtlinie f, Regulierung f, Regelung f, Vorschrift f, GEN COMM Ausführungsverordnung f, Durchführungsverordnung f, *rules* Regelung f, Verordnung f

Regulation: ~ School n ECON *French economic thinkers* Theorie f der Regulierung

regulation: ~ **Z** n AmE ECON Richtlinie f Z

regulator n TAX Regler m

regulatory adj LAW regelnd; **~ agency** n ECON Regulierungsbehörde f, GEN COMM Aufsichtsbehörde f; **~ authority** n GEN COMM, LAW Aufsichtsbehörde f; **~ body** n LAW Kontrollbehörde f; **~ capture** n ECON Versagen nt der Regulierungskommissionen; **~ committee** n POL Aufsichtsausschuß m, Ausschuß m der Aufsichtsbehörde; **~ system** n LAW Kontrollsystem nt; **~ theory** n GEN COMM Theorie f der Überwachung staatlicher Unternehmen

rehabilitate vt ENVIR *dumping site* restaurieren, sanieren, GEN COMM *reputation, company* rehabilitieren, LAW wiedereingliedern

rehabilitation n ECON Sanierung f, ENVIR *of dumping sites* Wiederherstellung f, Restaurierung f, Sanierung f, GEN COMM *of reputation, company* Rehabilitation f, LAW Wiedereingliederung f; **~ import credit** n (*RIC*) FIN Importsanierungskredit m; **~ import loan** n (*RIL*) FIN Importsanierungsanleihe f

rehypothecation n STOCK Weiterverpfändung f, zweite Lombardierung f

reign n GEN COMM Herrschaft f, Regierungszeit f

re-image vt S&M ein neues Image schaffen für

reimbursable adj BANK, FIN, GEN COMM, STOCK rückzahlbar

reimburse vt BANK, FIN rückzahlen, GEN COMM *expenses* erstatten, *person* entschädigen, rückzahlen, PATENTS abgelten, entschädigen, STOCK rückzahlen, TAX erstatten

reimbursement n GEN COMM *of expenses* Aufwandsentschädigung f, Auslagenersatz m, Erstattung f, *of sum* Rückzahlung f, Rückvergütung f, PATENTS Abgeltung f, Entschädigung f; **~ fund** n INS Deckungskapital nt, Rückstellung f für unverdiente Prämien; **~ of travel expenses** n GEN COMM Reisekostenerstattung f

reimpose vt GEN COMM neuauferlegen, neuaufzwingen

reinforce vt ECON stützen, GEN COMM *effect, impact* stützen, untermauern, verstärken; **~ capital** ECON Kapital erhöhen

reinforcement n GEN COMM Stärkung f, Verstärkung f

reinfusion n FIN erneuter Geldzufluß m

reinstate vt GEN COMM, HRM wiedereinstellen, LAW wiederherstellen

reinstatement n GEN COMM *of employee* Wiedereinsetzung f, Wiedereinstellung f, HRM Wiedereinstellung f, INS Weiterversicherung f, LAW Wiederherstellung f

reinsurance: ~ company n INS Rückversicherungsgesellschaft f

reintegration n LAW Wiedereingliederung f

reintermediation n BANK Mittelrückfluß m ins Banksystem

reinvent: ~ the wheel phr GEN COMM sich mit gelösten Problemen beschäftigen, das Rad neu erfinden

reinvest vt FIN, STOCK reinvestieren, wiederanlegen

reinvested: ~ earnings n ECON einbehaltene Gewinne m pl

reinvestment n ACC Ersatzinvestition f, reinvestierter Gewinn m, STOCK Reinvestition f; **~ privilege** n STOCK Wiederanlagevorrecht nt; **~ rate** n STOCK *interest rate futures* Reinvestitionsrate f

reinvigorate vt ECON, GEN COMM beleben

REIT abbr AmE (*real-estate investment trust*) BANK Immobilienfonds m

reiterate vi GEN COMM wiederholen

reiteration n GEN COMM Wiederholung f

reject vt GEN COMM verweigern, zurückweisen, LAW *contract* zurückweisen, PATENTS ablehnen, zurückweisen; ♦ **~ a claim** LAW einen Anspruch zurückweisen; **~ a request** GEN COMM einen Antrag ablehnen

rejected adj GEN COMM verweigert

rejection n GEN COMM Verweigerung f, Zurückweisung f, LAW *of contract* Zurückweisung f, PATENTS Ablehnung f, Zurückweisung f

rejects n pl IND Ausschuß m

related adj LAW verwandt; **~ company** n GEN COMM verbundenes Unternehmen nt; **~ events** n pl HRM aufeinander bezogene Ereignisse nt pl; **~ files** n LAW Beiakte f; ♦ **~ to national policy** GEN COMM staatspolitisch

relational: ~ database n (*RDB*) COMP relationale Datenbank f

relations n pl GEN COMM *between parties* Beziehungen f pl, Verbindungen f pl; **~ analysis** n HRM Beziehungsanalyse f

relationship n FIN Beziehung f, GEN COMM Beziehung f, Verhältnis nt, verwandtschaftliche Beziehung f

relative adj GEN COMM bezüglich, relativ, verhältnismäßig; ♦ **in ~ terms** GEN COMM relativ; **~ to** GEN COMM im Verhältnis zu

relative: **~ concentration** n MATH *statistics* relative Konzentration f; **~ error** n COMP relativer Fehler m; **~ income hypothesis** n ECON relative Einkommenshypothese f

relatively adv GEN COMM verhältnismäßig

relative: **~ market share** n S&M relativer Marktanteil m; **~ price** n ECON relativer Preis m; **~ price level** n ECON Relativpreisniveau nt; **~ surplus value** n ECON relativer Mehrwert m

relativism n POL Relativismus m

relativities n pl HRM jeweilige Umstände m pl

relaunch 1. n GEN COMM, S&M Wiedereinführung f; **2.** vt GEN COMM *programme, product* wiederauflegen, wiedereinführen, S&M erneut einführen, wiedereinführen

relax 1. vt GEN COMM, MGMNT *control, restrictions* lokkern, *efforts* nachlassen; **2.** vi LEIS sich entspannen

relaxation n GEN COMM *of rules*, MGMNT Lockerung f

release 1. n ACC Auflösung f, COMP *of software, product* Freigabe f, LAW Erlaß m; **2.** vt ACC auflösen, COMP *software, product* freigeben, FIN erlassen, GEN COMM *publish* freigeben; ♦ **~ sb on bail** LAW jdn gegen Kaution freilassen, jdn gegen Sicherheitsleistung aus der Haft entlassen; **~ a debt** ECON eine Forderung erlassen; **~ sb from a debt** LAW jdm eine Schuld erlassen *release*: ~ **date** *n* STOCK *for shares allocated to employees* Freigabedatum *nt*; ~ **of debt** *n* LAW Schulderlaß *m*; ~ **for shipment** *n* TRANSP Versandfreigabe *f*; ~ **from liability** *n* INS, LAW *contract* Haftungsfreistellung *f*; ~ **from obligations** *n* LAW Befreiung *f* von Verbindlichkeiten; ~ **note** *n* (*RN*) TRANSP *cargo* Freigabe *f*, Freigabemitteilung *f*, Freigabeschein *m*; ~ **of pay checks** *AmE*, ~ **of pay cheques** *BrE* *n* BANK Freigabe *f* von Gehaltsschecks, Freigabe *f* von Lohnschecks; ~ **principle** *n* LAW *Community contracts* Ausklinkprinzip *nt*; ~ **of recognizance** *n* LAW Entlassung *f* aus einer Verpflichtung vor Gericht

relevant: ~ **act** *n* LAW *trade unions* sachdienliches Gesetz *nt*; ~ **cost approach** *n* MGMNT Differenzkostenmethode *f*, Methode *f* der relevanten Kosten; ~ **documents** *n pl* ADMIN, LAW sachdienliche Unterlagen *f pl*; ~ **earnings** *n* FIN *for pension purposes* maßgebliche Einnahmen *f pl*

reliability *n* GEN COMM Zuverlässigkeit *f*, *financial* Kreditwürdigkeit *f*, Bonität *f*, *personal* Vertrauenswürdigkeit *f*; ~ **test** *n* GEN COMM Zuverlässigkeitsprüfung *f*

reliable *adj* GEN COMM verläßlich, *person* vertrauenswürdig, zuverlässig; ~ **news** *n* MEDIA zuverlässige Nachrichten *f pl*; ~ **source** *n* GEN COMM zuverlässige Quelle *f*

reliance *n* GEN COMM Vertrauen *nt*, Zutrauen *nt*

relief *n* TAX Entlastung *f*; ~ **goods** *n pl* IMP/EXP Hilfsgüter *nt pl*; ~ **on business assets** *n* ACC Sonderabschreibung *f* auf das Anlagevermögen; ~ **shift** *n* HRM zusätzliche Schicht *f*

relieve *vt* GEN COMM ablösen, befreien, LAW befreien, TAX entlasten

relieved: ~ **of** *phr* LAW befreit von

religious: ~ **discrimination** *n* HRM religiöse Diskriminierung *f*; ~ **monitoring** *n* HRM religiöse Überwachung *f*

relinquish *vt* GEN COMM *power, freedom*, LAW *renounce* verzichten auf [+acc], aufgeben, überlassen

relinquishment *n* GEN COMM Überlassung *f*, Verzicht *m*, LAW Preisgabe *f*, Überlassung *f*, Verzicht *m*

reload *vt* COMP *software* nachladen, neu laden, TRANSP umladen

reloading *n* TRANSP Umladung *f*

relocatable *adj* COMP *area of memory* relativierbar; ~ **address** *n* COMP relative Adresse *f*

relocate 1. *vt* ECON umsiedeln, GEN COMM *employee* versetzen, *company, headquarters* verlegen, umsiedeln, HRM versetzen, IND *company, headquarters* umsiedeln; **2.** *vi* GEN COMM umsiedeln, PROP, TRANSP umziehen

relocated *adj* ADMIN, HRM versetzt

relocation *n* ADMIN Versetzung *f*, COMP Verschiebung *f*, ECON Umsiedlung *f*, GEN COMM *of company, employee* Umsiedlung *f*, Umzug *m*, Verlagerung *f*, Versetzung *f*, *business* Verlegung *f*, HRM Versetzung *f*, TRANSP Umzug *m*; ~ **assistance** *n* HRM Umzugskostenbeihilfe *f*

rely: ~ **on** *phr* GEN COMM sich verlassen auf [+acc], *person* vertrauen, LAW vertrauen; ~ **on sth** *phr* GEN COMM mit etw rechnen

remainder *n* MATH Rest *m*

remainderman *n* FIN Anwartschaftsberechtigte(r) *mf* [decl. as adj], Bezugsberechtigte(r) *mf* [decl. as adj]

remaining *adj* GEN COMM restlich; ~ **stock** *n* GEN COMM Restposten *m*

remake *n* LEIS, MEDIA Neuverfilmung *f*

remand 1. *n* LAW Haftprüfung *f*; ♦ **be on** ~ LAW sich in Untersuchungshaft befinden; **2.** *vt* ♦ ~ **in custody** LAW in Untersuchungshaft behalten

remargining *n* FIN Nachschießen *nt*, Nachschuß *m*, STOCK Nachschießen *nt*, Nachschußforderung *f*

remark 1. *n* GEN COMM Bemerkung *f*; **2.** *vt* GEN COMM bemerken

remarkable *adj* GEN COMM bemerkenswert

remedy 1. *n* GEN COMM Remedium *nt*, *legal, financial* Rechtsmittel *nt*, Abhilfe *f*, LAW *contracts* Rechtsbehelf *m*; **2.** *vt* GEN COMM abhelfen; ♦ ~ **an abuse** GEN COMM einem Mißbrauch abhelfen

remind *vt* ACC, FIN, LAW mahnen

reminder *n* ACC, FIN Mahnung *f*, Anmahnung *f*, GEN COMM Erinnerung *f*, LAW Mahnbescheid *m*; ~ **advertising** *n* S&M Erinnerungswerbung *f*

remise *n* GEN COMM Aufgabe *f* eines Rechts

remission *n* ECON Rückerstattung *f*, LAW *of sentence* Erlaß *m*, TAX *refund* Rückerstattung *f*, Rückzahlung *f*; ~ **of charges** *n* TAX Gebührenerlaß *m*; ~ **of debt** *n* LAW Schulderlaß *m*; ~ **of a penalty** *n* LAW Straferlaß *m*

remit *vt* ECON überweisen, FIN anschaffen

remittal *n* LAW *of sentence, debt* Erlaß *m*

remittance *n* FIN Überweisung *f*, Überweisungsanzeige *f*; ~ **advice** *n* FIN Überweisungsanzeige *f*; ~ **for collection** *n* BANK Inkassoüberweisung *f*, Überweisung *f* zum Inkasso; ~ **order** *n* GEN COMM Überweisungsauftrag *m*; ~ **slip** *n* GEN COMM Überweisungsträger *m*

remnants *n pl* GEN COMM Reste *m pl*, Überreste *m pl*

remonstration: ~ **of an official** *n* LAW Dienstaufsichtsbeschwerde *f*

remote *adj* COMP rechnerfern, GEN COMM entfernt, fern; ~ **access** *n* COMP Fernzugriff *m*; ~ **batch processing** *n* COMP Stapelfernverarbeitung *f*; ~ **control** *n* COMMS Fernsteuerung *f*; ~-**controlled** *adj* COMP ferngesteuert; ~ **data processing** *n* ADMIN Datenfernverarbeitung *f*; ~ **maintenance** *n* COMP Fernwartung *f*; ~ **possibility** *n* GEN COMM entfernte Möglichkeit *f*; ~ **printing** *n* COMP rechnerfernes Drucken *nt*; ~ **processing** *n* COMP Fernverarbeitung *f*; ~ **support** *n* COMP Fernunterstützung *f*

removal *n* GEN COMM Behebung *f*, *of problem* Beseitigung *f*, *new home* Umzug *m*, *of attachment, cover, office* Entfernung *f*, *of tariff barriers, restrictions* Aufhebung *f*, TRANSP Umzug *m*; ~ **note** *n* IMP/EXP Auslagerungsvermerk *m*; ~ **of tax distortions** *n* TAX Beseitigung *f* von Steuerverzerrungen; ~ **van** *n* TRANSP Möbelwagen *m*

remove *vt* COMP entfernen, ECON abbauen, GEN COMM *obstacle, problem* beseitigen, *restrictions* aufheben, beheben

remuneration *n* ADMIN Honorar *nt*, GEN COMM Bezahlung *f*, Dienstbezüge *m pl*, Entlohnung *f*, Honorar *nt*, Vergütung *f*, HRM Arbeitsentgelt *nt*, Dienstbezüge *m pl*; ~ **package** *n* HRM Leistungspaket *nt*

rename *vt* COMP umbenennen

render *vt* GEN COMM *report* vorlegen; ♦ ~ **an accounting for sth** ACC Abrechnung verlegen; ~ **null and void** LAW null und nichtig machen

rendering: ~ **of services** *n* GEN COMM Erbringung *f* von Dienstleistungen

renegotiate *vt* GEN COMM erneut verhandeln, neuaushandeln

renegotiated: ~ **rate mortgage** n PROP neuverhandelte Hypothek f

renegotiation n GEN COMM erneute Verhandlung f, Neuverhandlung f

renew vt GEN COMM erneuern, prolongieren, verlängern

renewable: ~ **resource** n ECON erneuerbarer Rohstoff m, nachwachsender Rohstoff m, ENVIR nachwachsender Rohstoff m

renewal n GEN COMM Verlängerung f, PATENTS, WEL urban areas Erneuerung f; ~ **clause** n BANK Verlängerungsklausel f; ~ **coupon** n STOCK Talon m; ~ **fee** n PATENTS Erneuerungsgebühr f, Patentverlängerungsgebühr f; ~ **option** n PROP Option f auf Verlängerung; ~ **orders** n pl GEN COMM Anschlußaufträge m pl

renewed adj COMP, GEN COMM erneut

renounce vt GEN COMM aufgeben, ausschlagen, verzichten auf [+acc], LAW aufgeben; ♦ ~ **an inheritance** LAW eine Erbschaft ausschlagen

renounceable: ~ **document** n STOCK kündbare Urkunde f

renouncing n LAW Aufgeben nt

renovate vt PROP renovieren

renovated adj COMP, GEN COMM erneut

renovation n GEN COMM Erneuerung f, Renovierung f, PROP Renovierung f

renown n GEN COMM guter Leumund m, guter Name m, guter Ruf m

renowned adj GEN COMM angesehen, namhaft, renommiert

rent 1. n ECON Miete f, ökonomische Rente f, PROP, WEL Miete f; **2.** vt GEN COMM mieten, PROP mieten, verpachten; ♦ **for** ~ AmE (cf to let BrE) PROP zu vermieten

rent out vt AmE (cf let BrE) PROP vermieten

rentable: ~ **area** n PROP vermietbare Fläche f

Rent: ~-**a-Container** n (Rentcon) TRANSP Rent-a-Container

rental n IMP/EXP Miete f, PROP Mieteinnahme f, Pachteinnahme f, Miete f, TRANSP, WEL Miete f; ~ **agreement** n GEN COMM Mietvertrag m; ~ **car** n AmE (cf hire car BrE) LEIS Mietwagen m; ~ **equipment** n ECON Mietanlagen f pl; ~ **level** n PROP Mietstufe f

rent: ~ **allowance** n WEL Mietbeihilfe f, Mietzuschuß m

rental: ~ **rate** n PROP Mietpreis m; ~ **right** n LAW Erbbaurecht nt, Erbpacht f; ~ **term** n PROP Mietdauer f; ~-**turnover ratio** n ACC Mietsaufkommen-Umsatz-Verhältnis nt

rent: ~ **charge** n WEL Erbzins m, Grundrente f, Miete f; ~ **collector** n PROP Mieteinzieher, in m,f

rented: ~ **car** n AmE (cf hired car BrE) LEIS Mietwagen m

rent: ~-**free** adj HRM, PROP, WEL mietfrei; ~-**free period** n PROP mietfreie Zeit f; ~ **freeze** n PROP Mietpreisstopp m

rentier n PROP Rentier m

renting n PROP Verpachtung f

rent: ~ **pcm** n (rent per calendar month) PROP Miete f pro Kalendermonat; ~ **per calendar month** n (rent pcm) PROP Miete f pro Kalendermonat; ~ **rebate** n WEL Mietbeihilfe f, Mietnachlaß m, Mietzuschuß m; ~ **receipt** n PROP Mieteinnahme f, Mietquittung f; ~ **seeking** n PROP Verlangen nt von Miete; ~ **subsidy** n HRM, WEL Wohngeld nt; ~-**up period** n PROP Zeitspanne f vom Bau bis zur vollständigen Vermietung

renunciation n LAW Verzicht m

renvoi n LAW conflict of laws Renvoi nt

reopen vt LAW case, proceedings wiederaufnehmen

reopener: ~ **clause** n HRM Revisionsklausel f

reopening n LAW of case, proceedings Wiederaufnahme f

reorder vt GEN COMM nachbestellen; ~ **form** n GEN COMM Nachbestellungsformular nt, Nachbestellungsvordruck m; ~ **point** n ACC kritischer Lagerbestand m

reorganization n ADMIN Umbesetzung f, ECON Sanierung f, Umstrukturierung f, FIN Neugestaltung f, Umorganisation f, Umstrukturierung f, GEN COMM Umorganisation f, HRM Umbesetzung f, MGMNT Reorganisation f, Umgestaltung f, Umstrukturierung f, Umwandlung f

reorganize vt ADMIN umbesetzen, ECON, FIN umstrukturieren, GEN COMM umorganisieren, umbesetzen, MGMNT reorganisieren, umgestalten, umstrukturieren, umwandeln

reorganized adj FIN, MGMNT umorganisiert, umstrukturiert

rep. abbr (representative) GEN COMM Repräsentant, in m,f, Vertreter, in m,f, Bevollmächtigte(r) mf [decl. as adj], PATENTS Repräsentant, in m,f

rep n infrml (sales representative) HRM, S&M Handelsvertreter, in m,f, Reisende(r) mf [decl. as adj], Verkaufsvertreter, in m,f, Vertreter, in m,f

REP abbr (regional employment premium) HRM regionale Arbeitsplatzprämie f

Rep. n AmE (Representative) POL Abg. (Abgeordnete(r))

repackage vt IMP/EXP umpacken, S&M umpacken, in neuer Form anbieten

repackaging n IMP/EXP, S&M Umpacken nt, Wiederverpackung f

repackaging: ~ **of risks** n FIN Risikoumstrukturierung f, Risikoumbündelung f

repair n GEN COMM Wiederinstandsetzung f, office machinery Reparatur f; ~ **kit** n GEN COMM Flickzeug nt, Reparaturmaterial nt; ~ **shop** n GEN COMM Reparaturwerkstatt f; ~ **time** n ECON Instandsetzungszeit f

reparation: ~ **for damage** n INS Schadensersatz m, Schadensersatzzahlung f

repatriate vt ECON profits repatriieren

repatriation n ECON profits Rückführung f; ~ **of funds** n ECON Kapitalrückführung f; ~ **of overseas funds** n ECON Rückführung f ausländischen Kapitals; ~ **of profits** n ECON Gewinnrückführung f

repay vt ACC debt, mortgage abtragen, zurückzahlen, BANK debt, mortgage abtragen, tilgen, zurückzahlen, FIN abbauen, einlösen, zurückzahlen, rückzahlen, GEN COMM einlösen, zurückzahlen, rückzahlen, STOCK rückzahlen

repayable adj BANK rückzahlbar, tilgbar, FIN, GEN COMM rückzahlbar, STOCK rückzahlbar, tilgbar; ♦ ~ **on demand** BANK, FIN auf Verlangen rückzahlbar

repayment n ACC Tilgung f, BANK, FIN, GEN COMM Rückerstattung f, Rückzahlung f, Tilgung f, PATENTS Rückerstattung f; ~ **claim** n TAX Rückzahlungsanspruch m; ~ **date** n FIN Tilgungstermin m; ~ **of a debt** n FIN Rückzahlung f einer Schuld; ~ **over five years** n BANK, GEN COMM Rückzahlung f innerhalb von fünf Jahren; ~ **period** n FIN Tilgungsperiode *f*, Abzahlungsperiode *f*; ~ **term** *n* FIN Rückzahlungszeitraum *m*

repeal 1. *n* LAW Aufhebung *f*; **2.** *vt* LAW *regulations* aufheben; ◆ ~ **a law** LAW ein Gesetz abschaffen, ein Gesetz aufheben

repealed *adj* LAW aufgehoben

repeat 1. *n* MEDIA *TV, radio programme* Wiederholung *f*; **2.** *vt* GEN COMM, MEDIA wiederholen

repeat: ~ **business** *n* GEN COMM Wiederholungsgeschäft *nt*; ~ **buying** *n* S&M Wiederholungskäufe *m pl*

repeater: ~ **loan** *n* BANK Wiederholungsdarlehen *nt*

repeating: ~ **audit** *n* ECON periodische Prüfung *f*

repeat: ~ **order** *n* GEN COMM Nachbestellung *f*; ~ **purchase** *n* GEN COMM Nachkauf *m*; ~ **rate** *n* S&M Wiederholungsrate *f*; ~ **sales** *n pl* S&M Verkauf *m* aufgrund von Erinnerungswerbung

repercussion *n* GEN COMM Auswirkung *f*, Rückwirkung *f*

repertoire *n* COMP *instructions* Vorrat *m*

repetition *n* GEN COMM Wiederholung *f*

repetitive: ~ **strain injury** *n* (*RSI*) HRM Schäden *m pl* durch wiederholte Belastung

replace *vt* COMMS *telephone receiver* auflegen, GEN COMM *stolen or lost goods* ersetzen, *machine part* auswechseln, *exchange* austauschen, verdrängen, LAW wiederherstellen; ◆ ~ **sb** GEN COMM an die Stelle treten von

replaceable *adj* COMMS, ECON, GEN COMM austauschbar

replaced: ~ **asset** *n* TAX Ersatzinvestition *f*, ersetztes Wirtschaftsgut *nt*

replacement *n* GEN COMM Anlageerneuerung *f*, *purchase of substitute* Ersatzbeschaffung *f*, *repurchase* Wiederbeschaffung *f*, *delivery of substitute* Ersatzlieferung *f*, *person* Ersatzmann *m*, Nachfolger, in *m,f*, *substitute, substitution* Ersatz *m*, ECON Ersetzung *nt*, IND Austausch *m*, LAW Wiederherstellung *f*; ~ **capital** *n* FIN Ersatzinvestition *f*; ~ **clause** *n* INS Wiederbeschaffungsklausel *f*; ~ **cost accounting** *n* ACC Buchführung *f* zu Wiederbeschaffungskosten, Wiederbeschaffungskostenrechnung *f*; ~ **costing** *n* ACC Buchführung *f* zu Wiederbeschaffungskosten, Wiederbeschaffungskostenrechnung *f*; ~ **costs** *n pl* ACC Wiederbeschaffungskosten *pl*, Wiederherstellungskosten *pl*, Gestehungskosten *pl*, ECON Wiederbeschaffungskosten *pl*, INS Auswechslungskosten *pl*; ~ **engine** *n* GEN COMM Austauschmotor *m*; ~ **labor force** AmE, ~ **labour force** BrE *n* HRM Ersatzbelegschaft *f*; ~ **market** *n* GEN COMM Markt *m* für Ersatzbeschaffung; ~ **part** *n* GEN COMM Ersatzteil *nt*; ~ **period** *n* ECON Umschlagzeit *f*; ~ **planning** *n* FIN Wiederbeschaffungsplanung *f*; ~ **price** *n* S&M Wiederbeschaffungspreis *m*; ~ **ratio** *n* WEL Einkommensersatzrate *f*; ~ **value** *n* ACC Wiederbeschaffungswert *m*

replay *vt* COMP abspielen

replenish: ~ **one's stocks** *phr* GEN COMM seine Lagerbestände aufstocken

replenishment: ~ **of inventories** *n* MGMNT Auffüllung *f* von Lagerbeständen

replevin *n* LAW Herausgabeklage *f*

reply 1. *n* GEN COMM Beantwortung *f*, LAW Erwiderung *f*; ◆ **in** ~ **to your letter** COMMS in Beantwortung Ihres Schreibens (*frml*); **2.** *vi* GEN COMM antworten

reply: ~ **device** *n* S&M *mail order merchandising* Rückantwortträger *m*; ~ **paid** *n* COMMS bezahlte Rückantwort *f*; ~**-paid card** *n* COMMS Antwortpostkarte *f*;

~**-paid envelope** *n* ADMIN, COMMS Freiumschlag *m*; ~ **vehicle** *n* S&M *mail order merchandising* Rückantwortmedium *nt*

repo *abbr* FIN, GEN COMM (*repurchase agreement*) Wertpapierpensionsgeschäft *nt*, Rückkaufvereinbarung *f*, LAW, PROP (*repossession*) Wiederinbesitznahme *f*

repo: ~ **man** *n infrml* GEN COMM Inkassobeauftragte(r) *m* [decl. as adj]

répondez: ~ **s'il vous plaît** *phr* (*RSVP*) COMMS um Antwort wird gebeten (*u. A. w. g.*)

report 1. *n* ADMIN Rechenschaftsbericht *m*, COMP, GEN COMM Bericht *m*, Report *m*, MEDIA Erfahrungsbericht *m*; **2.** *vt* ACC ansetzen, ausweisen, GEN COMM *accident, crime* melden, MEDIA berichten; ◆ ~ **a loss** ACC einen Verlust ausweisen, einen Verlust melden; ~ **a profit** ACC einen Gewinn melden; ~ **one's conclusions** GEN COMM über seine Entscheidung berichten, über seine Schlußfolgerung berichten; ~ **one's findings** GEN COMM über seine Ergebnisse berichten; **3.** *vi* GEN COMM berichten, Bericht erstatten; ◆ ~ **to sb** GEN COMM *be answerable to* jdm unterstehen, *present oneself* sich melden bei jdm

report: ~ **card** *n* HRM Bewertung *f*, Leistungskarte *f*

reported *adj* GEN COMM ausgewiesen; ~ **earnings** *n pl* ACC ausgewiesener Gewinn *m*; ~ **equity** *n* ACC ausgewiesene eigene Mittel *nt pl*; ~ **equity capital** *n* ACC ausgewiesenes Eigenkapital *nt*; ~ **income** *n* ACC ausgewiesener Gewinn *m*

report: ~ **file** *n* COMP Berichtsdatei *f*; ~ **generation** *n* COMP Berichtserzeugung *f*, Reportgenerierung *f*

reporting *n* ACC *rendering an account* Rechenschaftslegung *f*, GEN COMM Berichtswesen *nt*, Berichterstattung *f*; ~ **company** *n* GEN COMM berichtende Gesellschaft *f*; ~ **corporation** *n* GEN COMM berichtende Gesellschaft *f*; ~ **currency** *n* FIN Rechnungslegungswährung *f*; ~ **date** *n* ACC Stichtag *m*, GEN COMM Berichtszeitpunkt *m*; ~ **day** *n* GEN COMM *shipping* Berichtszeitpunkt *m*; ~ **dealer** *n* STOCK berichterstattender Händler *m*, berichterstattende Händlerin *f*, Notifizierungshändler, in *m,f*; ~ **object** *n* GEN COMM Berichtsobjekt *nt*; ~ **period** *n* ECON, GEN COMM Berichtszeitraum *m*; ~ **policy** *n* FIN Versicherungspolice *f* mit periodischer Wertangabe; ~ **restrictions** *n pl* MEDIA Einschränkungen *f pl* bei der Berichterstattung; ~ **standards** *n pl* ACC Berichtsnormen *f pl*, GEN COMM Berichterstattungsnormen *f pl*; ~ **system** *n* FIN Berichtssystem *nt*

report: ~ **terminal** *n* COMP Berichtsterminal *m*, Reportterminal *m*

repositioning *n* S&M Neupositionierung *f*

repository *n* ADMIN Aufbewahrungsstelle *f*, Behälter *m*, Lager *nt*

repossession *n* (*repo*) FIN Rückkaufvereinbarung *f*, GEN COMM Rückkaufvereinbarung *f*, Wiederinbesitznahme *f*, LAW, PROP Wiederinbesitznahme *f*, STOCK Rückkaufvereinbarung *f*, Wiederinbesitznahme *f*

repo: ~ **woman** *n infrml* GEN COMM Inkassobeauftragte *f* [decl. as adj]

represent *vt* GEN COMM *depict* darstellen, *deputize for* vertreten

representation *n* GEN COMM Darstellung *f*, *statement* Repräsentation *f*, *by deputy* Stellvertretung *f*, *of a firm by an agent* Agentur *f*, Vertretung *f*, LAW Schilderung *f*; ~ **allowance** *n* GEN COMM Aufwandsentschädigung *f*

representative 1. *adj* GEN COMM repräsentativ; **2.** *n* (*rep.*)

GEN COMM Repräsentant, in *m,f*, Vertreter, in *m,f*, Beauftragte(r) *mf* [decl. as adj], Obfrau *f*, Obmann *m*, Bevollmächtigte(r) *mf* [decl. as adj], PATENTS Beauftragte(r) *mf* [decl. as adj], Repräsentant, in *m,f*, POL Obfrau *f*, Obmann *m*, S&M Vertreter, in *m,f*

Representative *n AmE* (*Rep.*) POL Abgeordnete(r) *mf* [decl. as adj]

representative: ~ **firm** *n* ECON Durchschnittsfirma *f*, repräsentatives Unternehmen *nt*; ~ **sample** *n* MATH *statistics* repräsentative Stichprobe *f*; ~ **selling agent** *n* S&M Agent *m*

repressive *adj* TAX repressiv; ~ **tax** *n* TAX repressive Steuer *f*, Steuer *f* mit negativen Leistungsanreizen

reprimand *n* HRM Verweis *m*

reprint *n* GEN COMM Abdruck *m*, MEDIA Neuauflage *f*

reprisal *n* GEN COMM Vergeltungsmaßnahme *f*

reprivatization *n* ECON Reprivatisierung *f*

reprivatize *vt* ECON reprivatisieren

reprivatized *adj* ECON reprivatisiert

reprocess *vt* ECON, IND weiterverarbeiten

reproduce *vt* GEN COMM reproduzieren, wiedergeben

reproduction *n* ECON Nachbildung *f*, Reproduktion *f*, Vervielfältigung *f*, GEN COMM Abdruck *m*; ~ **costs** *n pl* ACC Wiederherstellungskosten *pl*; ~ **rate** *n* ECON Reproduktionsrate *f*

reprogram *vt* COMP umprogrammieren

reprography *n* GEN COMM Reprographie *f*

repro: ~ **pull** *n* S&M Probeabzug *m*

Republican: ~ **Party** *n AmE* POL Republikaner *m pl*

republish *vt* MEDIA *print* neuveröffentlichen

repudiate *vt* GEN COMM zurückweisen, HRM *industrial action* ablehnen, LAW *claim* zurückweisen

repudiation *n* GEN COMM Zurückweisung *f*, HRM Ablehnung *f*, LAW Zurückweisung *f*

repurchase *vt* ECON *debt* zurückkaufen, zurücknehmen

repurchase: ~ **agreement** *n* (*RP, repo*) FIN, GEN COMM Wertpapierpensionsgeschäft *nt*, Rückkaufvereinbarung *f*; ~ **rate** *n* BANK, FIN Pensionssatz *m*, Rücknahmekurs *m*

reputation *n* GEN COMM Ansehen *nt*, guter Name *m*, Leumund *m*, Ruf *m*, *renown* Renommee *nt*

request 1. *n* COMMS, COMP Anforderung *f*, GEN COMM Anforderung *f*, Aufforderung *f*, Verlangen *nt*, *desire* Bitte *f*, Wunsch *m*, PATENTS Anfrage *f*, Antrag *m*; ♦ **at the** ~ **of** GEN COMM auf Bitte von; **2.** *vt* COMMS, COMP anfordern, GEN COMM anfordern, nachsuchen um, verlangen

request: ~ **for change** *n* (*RFC*) TRANSP Änderungsantrag *m*, Änderungsgesuch *nt*; ~ **for information** *n* LAW Auskunftsersuchen *nt*; ~ **for payment** *n* FIN, GEN COMM Zahlungsaufforderung *f*; ~ **for proposals** *n* FIN Aufforderung *f* zur Angebotsabgabe; ~ **for subsequent improvement** *n* LAW *contracts* Aufforderung *f* zur Nachbesserung; ~ **to offload** *n* TRANSP Entladeantrag *m*; ~ **to pay** *n* ECON Zahlungsaufforderung *f*

require *vt* GEN COMM Bedarf haben an, brauchen, erfordern, verlangen, *demand* fordern; ♦ ~ **sb to do sth** GEN COMM jdn auffordern, etw zu tun; ~ **sth of sb** GEN COMM etw von jdm verlangen

required: ~ **action** *n* GEN COMM erforderliches Handeln *nt*; ~ **freight rate** *n* (*RFR*) TRANSP Mindestfrachtrate *f*; ~ **rate of return** *n* FIN angestrebte Mindestverzinsung *f*;

~ **rental on capital** *n* ECON geforderte Kapitalverzinsung *f*; ~ **reserve ratio** *n* BANK Mindestreservesatz *m*; ~ **reserves** *n pl* BANK Mindestreserven *f pl*

requirement *n* GEN COMM Anforderung *f*, Bedürfnis *nt*, Bedarf *m*, *condition* Erfordernis *nt*, Forderung *f*, LAW Auflage *f*

reroute *vt* TRANSP umleiten

rerouting *n* TRANSP *route* Änderung *f* einer Transportstrecke, *ticket* Umleitung *f*, Umschreibung *f* eines Flugscheins, *way bill* Umschreibung *f* eines Frachtbriefs

rerun 1. *n* COMP Wiederholungslauf *m*, Wiederanlauf *m*, GEN COMM Wiederholung *f*; **2.** *vt* GEN COMM wiederholen

resale *n* GEN COMM, STOCK Weiterverkauf *m*, Wiederverkauf *m*; ~ **price** *n* S&M Wiederverkaufspreis *m*; ~ **price maintenance** *n* (*RPM*) FIN, LAW, S&M Preisbindung *f* der zweiten Hand, vertikale Preisbindung *f*; ~ **value** *n* S&M Wiederverkaufswert *m*

reschedule *vt* FIN *loan* umschulden

rescind *vt* LAW *dispute, claim* aufheben, annullieren, rückgängig machen, für ungültig erklären, wandeln, anfechten, widerrufen, PATENTS anfechten; ♦ ~ **a contract** LAW einen Vertrag aufheben

rescindable *adj* BANK, GEN COMM, LAW annullierbar

rescission *n* LAW Ungültigkeitserklärung *f*, Widerruf *m*, Rückgängigmachung *f*, Anfechtung *f*, *of contract* Rücktritt *m* vom Vertrag, Annullierung *f*, Aufhebung *f*; ~ **of contract for work and labor** *AmE*, ~ **of contract for work and labour** *BrE n* LAW Wandlung *f*; ~ **of sale** *n* LAW Wandlung *f*

res communis *phr* LAW, PROP öffentliches Eigentum *nt*, Gemeinschaftseigentum *nt*, Gemeinschaftsvermögen *nt*

rescription *n* STOCK *bills and money market paper* Reskription *f* (*Sch*)

rescue: ~ **company** *n* HRM Auffanggesellschaft *f*

research 1. *n* GEN COMM Forschung *f*; **2.** *vt* GEN COMM forschen

research: ~ **budget** *n* ACC Forschungsbudget *nt*; ~ **department** *n* IND Forschungsabteilung *f*, S&M Forschungsabteilung *f*, Versuchsabteilung *f*; ~ **and development** *n* (*R&D*) IND Forschung *f* und Entwicklung *f* (*F&E*); ~ **director** *n* HRM Forschungsdirektor, in *m,f*, MGMNT Leiter, in *m,f* der Forschungsabteilung; **~-intensive** *adj* IND forschungsintensiv; ~ **laboratory** *n* IND Entwicklungslabor *nt*, Forschungsanstalt *f*, Forschungslabor *nt*, Untersuchungslabor *nt*; ~ **objective** *n* GEN COMM Forschungsziel *nt*; **~-oriented** *adj* IND forschungsorientiert; ~ **program** *AmE*, ~ **programme** *BrE n* IND Forschungsprogramm *nt*; ~ **student** *n* WEL Forschungsstudent, in *m,f*; ~ **team** *n* S&M *market research* Forschungsteam *nt*

resell *vt* GEN COMM, STOCK wiederverkaufen

reseller *n* GEN COMM, STOCK Wiederverkäufer, in *m,f*; ~ **market** *n* S&M Wiederverkäufermarkt *m*

reservation *n* GEN COMM Reservierung *f*, Buchung *f*, *of company name* Vorbehaltsklausel *f*, Vorbehalt *m*, LEIS *booking* Vorbestellung *f*, Reservierung *f*; ♦ **off the** ~ *AmE jarg* (*cf without the whip BrE*) POL nicht mehr der Parteidisziplin unterworfen, parteiabtrünnig, parteiuntreu; **on the** ~ *AmE jarg* (*cf under the whip BrE*) POL der Parteidisziplin unterworfen, parteitreu

reservation: ~ **of cargo** *n* TRANSP Reservierung *f* der Fracht; ~ **counter** *n* GEN COMM Reservierungsschalter *m*; ~ **form** *n* LEIS Reservierungsformular *nt*; ~ **price** *n*

S&M *auction sales* Mindestverkaufspreis *m*; ~ **system** *n* LEIS Reservierungssystem *nt*; ~ **of title** *n* LAW *contracts* Eigentumsvorbehalt *m*; ~ **wage** *n* HRM Mindestlohn *m*

reserve 1. *n* ACC Wertberichtigung *f*, FIN Reserve *f*, Rücklage *f* S&M *auction sales* Reservierungspreis *m*; **2.** *vt* GEN COMM *room, seat* buchen, reservieren, sich vorbehalten, LEIS *room, seat* reservieren; ♦ ~ **judgment** LAW eine Urteilsverkündung vorbehalten

reserve: ~ **army of labor** *AmE*, ~ **army of labour** *BrE n* HRM industrielle Reservearmee *f*; ~ **assets** *n pl* BANK, ECON *reserve facilities* Reservemedien *nt pl*, Reserveinstrumente *nt pl*, Reserveguthaben *nt*; ~~**assets ratio** *n* FIN Mindestreservesatz *m*; ~ **balances** *n pl* ECON Währungsreserven *f pl*

Reserve: ~ **Bank of Australia** *n* BANK Australische Zentralbank *f*

reserve: ~ **base** *n* BANK Basisgeldreserven *f pl*; ~ **currency** *n* FIN, GEN COMM Reservewährung *f*; ~ **deposits** *n pl* (*RD*) ECON Reserveeinlagen *f pl*, Reservehaltung *f*

reserved *adj* GEN COMM, LEIS reserviert; ~ **material** *n* GEN COMM auftragsgebundenes Material *nt*

reserve: ~ **entry** *n* ACC Wertberichtigungsbuchung *f*; ~ **for doubtful accounts** *n* ECON Rückstellung *f* für zweifelhafte Forderungen; ~ **for statutory overruns** *n* ACC Rückstellung *f* für satzungsgemäße Kostenüberschreitung; ~ **of potential labor** *AmE*, ~ **of potential labour** *BrE n* ECON Beschäftigungsreserve *f*; ~ **price** *n* GEN COMM Preislimit *nt*, Vorbehaltspreis *m*; ~ **ratio** *n* BANK Deckungssatz *m*, Mindestreservesatz *m*; ~ **requirement** *n* BANK Mindestreserveanforderung *f*, Mindestreserve *f*

reserves *n pl* ACC Rücklagen *f pl*, Reserven *f pl*, INS Rücklagen *f pl*

reserve: ~~**stock control** *n* GEN COMM Lagerbestandskontrolle *f*, Lagerhaltungskontrolle *f*

reset 1. *n* COMP Rücksetzen *nt*, Wiederanlauf *m*; **2.** *vt* COMP *clock, counter, data* wiederanlaufen lassen, zurücksetzen

reset: ~ **button** *n* COMP Rücksetztaste *f*, Reset-Taste *f*

resettle *vt* ECON, GEN COMM umsiedeln, POL wiedereingliedern

resettlement *n* ECON Umsiedlung *f*, GEN COMM Neubesiedlung *f*, Umsiedlung *f*, Wiedereingliederung *f*, POL Wiedereingliederung *f*

res gestae *phr* LAW *facts of case* Sachverhalt *m*

reshape *vt* ECON, FIN, MGMNT umstrukturieren

reshuffle 1. *n* ECON, FIN, MGMNT Umstrukturierung *f*, POL *cabinet* Umbesetzung *f* des Kabinetts; **2.** *vt* ECON, FIN, MGMNT umstrukturieren

reside: ~ **and work** *phr* LAW wohnen und arbeiten

residence *n* GEN COMM Aufenthalt *m*; ~ **allowance** *n* HRM, WEL Wohngeld *nt*; ~ **for tax purposes** *n* TAX steuerlicher Wohnsitz *m*; ~ **permit** *n* ADMIN Aufenthaltsgenehmigung *f*; ~ **visa** *n* ADMIN Aufenthaltsvisum *nt*

resident *adj* COMP speicherresident, GEN COMM wohnhaft, gebietsansässig, ansässig; ~ **alien** *n* ADMIN Ausländer, in *m,f* mit Aufenthaltsgenehmigung; ~ **for tax purposes** *n* TAX Steuerinländer, in *m,f*

residential *adj* PROP Wohn-; ~ **accommodation** *n* GEN COMM Wohngebäude *nt*, Wohnraum *m*; ~ **amount** *n* HRM Ortszulage *f*; ~ **area** *n* PROP Wohngebiet *nt*; ~ **building** *n* PROP Wohnhaus *nt*; ~ **construction** *n* PROP

Wohnungsbau *m*; ~ **course** *n* HRM, MGMNT Seminar *nt* mit Übernachtung; ~ **energy credit** *n* ENVIR Freibetrag *m* für Haushaltsenergie; ~ **occupancy** *n* PROP Nutzung *f*, Wohnnutzung *f*, Wohnzwecke *m pl*; ~ **service contract** *n* INS, PROP Wartungsvertrag *m* für Wohnungsgebäude; ~ **suburb** *n* HRM Wohnvorort *m*

resident: ~ **manager** *n* PROP ansässiger Verwalter *m*, ansässige Verwalterin *f*; ~ **population** *n* ECON Wohnbevölkerung *f*; ~ **taxpayer** *n* TAX Steuerinländer, in *m,f*

residual: ~ **error** *n* ECON Restfehler *m*; ~ **family** *n* WEL Restfamilie *f*; ~ **value** *n* FIN Altwert *m*, Restwert *m*, Veräußerungswert *m*, Schrottwert *m*

residuary: ~ **estate** *n* LAW Nachlaß *m* nach Zahlung aller Verbindlichkeiten, Reinnachlaß *m*; ~ **legatee** *n* LAW Nachvermächtnisnehmer *m*

residue *n* ENVIR, IND *from industrial production* Rückstand *m*, Rest *m*

residuum *n* GEN COMM Rückstand *m*, Rest *m*, Residuum *nt*, LAW Reinnachlaß *m*

resign *vi* GEN COMM zurücktreten, HRM kündigen

resignation *n* ADMIN *action* Rücktritt *m*, HRM *action* Kündigung *f*, Rücktritt *m*, *letter* Rücktrittsgesuch *nt*

resilience *n* ECON Stärke *f*, Beweglichkeit *f*, Spannkraft *f*, Elastizität *f*

res integra *phr* LAW Fall, der bis dahin noch nicht vor Gericht anhängig war

res ipsa loquitur *phr* GEN COMM, LAW die Sache spricht für sich selbst, es spricht für sich selbst

resistance *n* GEN COMM Widerstand *m*; ~ **level** *n* STOCK Widerstandslinie *f*

resistant: ~ **to cold** *adj* GEN COMM kältebeständig

res judicata *phr* LAW rechtskräftig entschiedene Sache *f*

res nullius *phr* LAW, PROP herrenlose Sache *f*

resolution *n* COMP *computer screen* Auflösung *f*, GEN COMM Beschlußfassung *f*, Entschluß *m*, LAW Resolution *f*, MGMNT Beschluß *m*, Lösung *f*; ~ **of contract** *n* LAW Vertragsaufhebung *f*

Resolution: ~ **Trust Corporation** *n AmE* (*RTC*) ECON Liquidationsbehörde der US-Bundesregierung

resolve 1. *n* GEN COMM Entschluß *m*; **2.** *vt* GEN COMM *differences* beheben, beilegen, beseitigen, MGMNT lösen; ♦ ~ **to do sth** GEN COMM beschließen, etw zu tun

resource *n* ADMIN *office supplies* Lieferant *m*, Bezugsquelle *f*, GEN COMM, IND Rohstoff *m*, Betriebsmittel *nt*; ~ **aggregation** *n* GEN COMM Ressourcenaggregation *f*; ~ **allocation** *n* ACC Mittelbewilligung *f*, Mittelverteilung *f*, Mittelzuteilung *f*, COMP Betriebsmittelzuteilung *f*, ECON, FIN, MGMNT Mittelbewilligung *f*, Mittelverteilung *f*, Mittelzuteilung *f*, Mittelzuweisung *f*, Allokation *f* der Ressourcen; ~ **appraisal** *n* MGMNT Ressourcenbewertung *f*; ~ **availability** *n* FIN Mittelverfügbarkeit *f*; ~ **economics** *n* ECON Ressourcentheorie *f*; ~ **industry** *n* IND Betriebsmittelindustrie *f*; ~ **management** *n* GEN COMM, MGMNT Betriebsmittelverwaltung *f*, Ressourcenmanagement *nt*, Ressourcenbewirtschaftung *f*, Ressourcenverwaltung *f*; ~ **management policy** *n* GEN COMM, MGMNT auf Erhaltung der Bodenschätze ausgerichtete Politik *f*; ~ **market** *n* ECON Faktormarkt *m*; ~~**of-land policy** *n* GEN COMM Bodenvorratspolitik *f*; ~ **profile** *n* GEN COMM Ressourcenprofil *nt*

resources *n pl* ECON, FIN, HRM Mittel *nt pl*, Vermögenswerte *m pl*, Ressourcen *f pl*

resource: ~ **time** *n* GEN COMM Nutzungsdauer *f*

respect 1. *n* LAW Achtung *f*; ♦ **in ~ of** GEN COMM hinsichtlich; **in this ~** GEN COMM in dieser Hinsicht; **2.** *vt* GEN COMM *person, customs* achten, respektieren; ♦ **~ the law** LAW das Gesetz einhalten

respectively *adv* GEN COMM beziehungsweise, respektive (*resp*)

respects: in other ~ *phr* GEN COMM in sonstiger Hinsicht

respond *vi* GEN COMM antworten; ♦ **~ to** GEN COMM *invitation, advertisement* antworten auf

respondeat superior *n* GEN COMM Deliktshaftung *f*, Haftung *f* für den Erfüllungsgehilfen, Haftung *f* des Dienstherren für Gehilfen, Haftung *f* für den Erfüllungsgehilfen

respondent *n* S&M *market research* Befragte(r) *mf* [decl. as adj]; **~ bank** *n* BANK Korrespondenzbank *f*

response *n* ECON Reaktion *f*, GEN COMM Antwort *f*; ♦ **in ~ to** GEN COMM als Antwort auf

response: ~ **elasticity** *n* S&M Reaktionselastizität *f*; ~ **function** *n* S&M Reaktionsfunktion *f*; ~ **projection** *n* S&M *advertising* Rücklaufplanung *f*; ~ **rate** *n* S&M Rücklaufquote *f*

responsibility *n* GEN COMM Haftbarkeit *f*, Haftung *f*, Verantwortung *f*, Verantwortlichkeit *f*, LAW Haftbarkeit *f*, Haftpflicht *f*, Haftung *f*; **~ accounting** *n* ACC Verantwortungsrechnung *f*, FIN Kostenplanung *f* nach Verantwortungsbereichen, Verantwortungsrechnung *f*; ~ **budgeting** *n* ACC Budgetierung *f* nach Verantwortungsbereichen; ~ **center** *AmE*, ~ **centre** *BrE n* FIN, MGMNT Verantwortungszentrum *nt*; ~ **centre manager** *n BrE* ACC Manager, in *m,f* eines Verantwortungszentrums

responsible *adj* GEN COMM haftbar, verantwortlich, verantwortungsvoll, HRM zuständig, LAW haftbar; ♦ ~ **for** GEN COMM verantwortlich für; **be ~ for** LAW haften für, verschulden, INS haften für; **~ in law** LAW rechtsverantwortlich

responsible: ~ **officer** ACC rechenschaftspflichtige(r) Angestellte(r) *mf* [decl. as adj]

responsive *adj* ECON reagibel

rest: ~ **assured that** *phr* GEN COMM Seien Sie versichert, daß; ~ **heavily on** *phr* GEN COMM sich hauptsächlich auf etwas stützen; ~ **one's case** *phr* LAW erklären, daß die eigene Beweisführung abgeschlossen ist; ~ **of the world** *n* (*ROW*) ECON die übrige Welt, der Rest der Welt

restart 1. *n* COMP Neustart *m*, ECON *economic recovery* Wiederanlauf *m*, Wiederbelebung *f*, GEN COMM Wiederbelebung *f*; **2.** *vt* COMP *system, hardware* neustarten, ECON wiederanlaufen lassen, wiederbeleben, GEN COMM wiederbeleben

restart: ~ **program** *n* COMP Wiederanlaufprogramm *nt*

restaurant *n* GEN COMM Gaststätte *f*, Restaurant *nt*; ~ **car** *n* LEIS Speisewagen *m*; ~ **proprietor** *n* HRM Restaurantbesitzer, in *m,f*

restaurateur *n* HRM Gastwirt, in *m,f*, Restaurantbesitzer, in *m,f*

restitutio in integrum *n* LAW Wiederherstellung *f*; GEN COMM, LAW Wiedereinsetzung *f* in den vorigen Stand, Wiederherstellung *f*

restitution *n* LAW *of price* Rückerstattung *f*; ~ **compromise** *n* LAW *contracts*

Rückerstattungsvergleich *m*; ~ **order** *n* LAW *contracts* Rückerstattungsbeschluß *m*

restitutor *n* LAW Rückerstattungspflichtige(r) *mf* [decl. as adj]

restock *vt* ECON Lager auffüllen, S&M wieder auf Lager nehmen

restoration *n* GEN COMM Rehabilitation *f*

restore *vt* COMP *file, directory* wiederherstellen, GEN COMM rehabilitieren, *confidence* wiederherstellen, *reputation* rehabilitieren; ♦ ~ **law and order** LAW Recht und öffentliche Ordnung wiederherstellen

restrain *vt* GEN COMM zurückhalten

restraint *n* GEN COMM, POL Zurückhaltung *f*; ~ **of alienation** *n* LAW Veräußerungsbeschränkung *f*; ~ **on trade** *n* ECON Wettbewerbsbeschränkung *f*, wettbewerbsbeschränkendes Verhalten *nt*, LAW wettbewerbsbeschränkendes Verhalten *nt*

restrict *vt* ECON drosseln, GEN COMM begrenzen, beschränken, LAW *rights* beeinträchtigen, eingrenzen, einschränken

restricted *adj* GEN COMM begrenzt, eingeschränkt, *application* nur für den Dienstgebrauch, POL geheim, nicht für die Allgemeinheit bestimmt; ~ **area** *n* TRANSP Sperrgebiet *nt*, Stadtteil *m* mit Geschwindigkeitsbegrenzung, *aviation* Flugbeschränkungsgebiet *nt*; ~ **article** *n* TRANSP beschränkter Artikel *m*, zu deklarierender Artikel *m*; ~ **articles terminal system** *n* (*RATS*) TRANSP Terminalsystem *nt* für beschränkte Artikel; ~ **market** *n* ECON beschränkter Markt *m*; ~ **surplus** *n AmE* (*cf undistributable reserves BrE*) ACC nicht ausschüttungsfähiger Gewinn *m*; ~ **trading** *n* STOCK beschränkter Handel *m*

restriction *n* GEN COMM Begrenzung *f*, Beschränkung *f*, Einschränkung *f*, Eingrenzung *f*; ~ **of credit** *n* BANK, ECON, FIN Kreditverknappung *f*

restrictions: ~ **on capital movements** *n* ECON, IMP/EXP Beschränkung *f* des Kapitalverkehrs, Kapitalverkehrskontrollen *f pl*

restriction: ~ **to entry** *n* ECON, IMP/EXP Zugangsbeschränkung *f*, Eintrittssperre *f*

restrictive *adj* ECON, GEN COMM *policy* restriktiv, kontraktiv, beschränkend, einschränkend; ~ **monetary policy** *n* ECON restriktive Geldpolitik *f*; ~ **practices** *n pl* ECON Kartelle *nt pl*, wettbewerbsbeschränkende Praktiken *f pl*, Wettbewerbsbeschränkungen *f pl*, wettbewerbsbeschränkende Verhaltensweisen *f pl*, wettbewerbsbeschränkendes Verhalten *nt*, GEN COMM, LAW wettbewerbsbeschränkendes Verhalten *nt*

Restrictive: ~ **Practices Court** *n BrE* LAW Kartellgericht *nt*

restrictive: ~ **trade practices** *n pl* ECON, LAW wettbewerbsbeschränkendes Verhalten *nt*, wettbewerbsbeschränkende Praktiken *f pl*

rest: ~ **rooms** *n pl AmE* GEN COMM Aufenthaltsräume *m pl*, Waschräume *m pl*

restructure *vt* ECON *company* umstrukturieren, sanieren, FIN umstrukturieren, umschulden, sanieren, MGMNT reorganisieren, umstrukturieren

restructuring *n* ECON Restrukturierung *f*, Sanierung *f*, Umstrukturierung *f*, FIN Sanierung *f*, Umschuldung *f*, Umstrukturierung *f*, MGMNT Neuordnung *f*, Umstrukturierung *f*; ~ **of assets** *n* ECON Vermögensumstrukturierung *f*

result *n* GEN COMM Ausgang *m*, Ergebnis *nt*, Resultat *nt*;

♦ **as a** ~ GEN COMM als Ergebnis, als Resultat, infolgedessen; **with the** ~ **that** GEN COMM mit dem Ergebnis, daß, mit der Folge, daß
result in vt GEN COMM zur Folge haben
results n pl GEN COMM trading figures Ergebnisse nt pl; ♦ **get** ~ GEN COMM, HRM Ergebnisse erzielen
resume vt COMP start again, LAW proceedings, POL diplomatic relations wiederaufnehmen
résumé n ADMIN AmE (cf curriculum vitae, CV BrE) career outline Lebenslauf m, GEN COMM summary zusammengefaßte Darstellung f, HRM AmE (cf curriculum vitae, CV BrE) career outline Lebenslauf m
resumption n COMP, LAW, POL Wiederaufnahme f
resurgence: ~ **in prices** n GEN COMM Wiederanstieg m der Preise
resyndication: ~ **limited partnership** n AmE PROP Konsortial-Kommanditgesellschaft f
retail: ~ **audit** n S&M Handelspanel nt; ~ **bank** n BANK auf das Privatkundengeschäft spezialisierte Bank f; ~ **business** n ECON Einzelhandelsbetrieb m, S&M Einzelhandel m, Einzelhandelsunternehmen nt; ~ **center** AmE, ~ **centre** BrE n PROP Einkaufszentrum nt, Einzelhandelszentrum nt; ~ **cooperative** n S&M Einzelhandelsgenossenschaft f, Einkaufsgenossenschaft f des Einzelhandels; ~ **customer credit** n BANK Dispokredit m, Dispositionskredit m; ~ **deposit** n BANK Privatkundeneinlage f; ~ **display allowance** n S&M Displaynachlaß m im Einzelhandel
retailer n GEN COMM Wiederverkäufer, in m,f, S&M Einzelhändler, in m,f, STOCK Wiederverkäufer, in m,f
retailers': ~ **cooperative** n S&M Einzelhandelsgenossenschaft f
retail: ~ **floorspace** n S&M Verkaufsfläche f Ausstellungsfläche f für den Einzelhandel; ~ **food business** n S&M Lebensmitteleinzelhandelsgeschäft nt; ~ **house** n FIN Einzelhandelsmakler, in m,f
retailing n IND Einzelhandel m, S&M Einzelhandelsverkauf m, Detailverkauf m, Einzelhandelsunternehmen nt
retail: ~ **management** n IND, MGMNT Einzelhandelsleitung f, Einzelhandelsmanagement nt, S&M Einzelhandelsleitung f; ~ **margin** n S&M Einzelhandelsspanne f; ~ **marketing** n S&M Einzelhandelsmarketing nt, Einzelhandelsvertrieb m; ~ **network** n S&M Einzelhandelsnetz nt; ~ **offer** n STOCK Angebot nt an Privatkunden; ~ **park** n S&M Einkaufszentrum nt; ~ **personal deposit** n BANK Privatkundeneinlage f; ~ **price index** n (RPI) ECON, GEN COMM, S&M Einzelhandelspreisindex m; ~ **price maintenance** n (RPM) S&M Preisbindung f der zweiten Hand, Wiederverkaufspreisbindung f; ~ **property** n PROP Einzelhandelsbesitz m; ~ **sale** n S&M Ladenverkauf m; ~ **sales** n FIN Einzelhandelsumsätze m pl; ~ **sales analysis** n S&M Umsatzanalyse f im Einzelhandel; ~ **store** n S&M Einzelhandelsgeschäft nt; ~ **takeover** n FIN Einzelhandelsübernahme f; ~ **trade** n IND Einzelhandel m, Einzelhandelsgewerbe nt; ~ **trader** n S&M Einzelhändler, in m,f
retain vt STOCK shares, TAX einbehalten; ♦ ~ **sb's services** GEN COMM jds Dienste in Anspruch nehmen
retainage n PROP Zurückhaltung f
retained: ~ **earnings** n pl ACC einbehaltener Gewinn m, thesaurierte Gewinne m pl; ~ **income** n ACC nicht ausgeschüttete Gewinne m pl, Rücklagen f pl, INS

Rücklagen f pl; ~ **profits** n pl ACC einbehaltener Gewinn m, Rücklagen f pl, FIN einbehaltene Gewinne m pl, Gewinnvortrag m, nicht ausgeschüttete Gewinne m pl, INS Rücklagen f pl
retainer n LAW Honorarvorschuß m, Vorschuß m; ♦ **on a** ~ GEN COMM auf Vorschuß
retaliation n GEN COMM, LAW Vergeltung f; ♦ **in** ~ **for** LAW als Vergeltung für
retaliatory: ~ **eviction** n PROP Retorsionszwangsräumung f; ~ **measure** n GEN COMM Repressalie f, Vergeltungsmaßnahme f
retention n INS Selbstbehalt m, Zurückbehaltung f, STOCK Aufbewahrung f, TAX Einbehaltung f; ~ **bond** n ECON international trade Garantiezurückbehaltung f; ~ **date** n GEN COMM Retentionsdatum nt; ~ **money** n GEN COMM einbehaltene Garantiesumme f, Sicherheitssumme f, PROP einbehaltene Garantiesumme f; ~ **period** n STOCK for shares allocated to employees Aufbewahrungsfrist f, Einbehaltungszeitraum m; ~ **requirement** n TAX Einbehaltungserfordernis f; ~ **of wages** n HRM Lohneinbehaltung f
rethink vt GEN COMM überdenken
retire vi GEN COMM, HRM in den Ruhestand treten; ♦ ~ **from business** GEN COMM sich vom Geschäft zurückziehen, sich zur Ruhe setzen; ~ **on a pension** HRM sich pensionieren lassen
retired adj HRM ausgedient, pensioniert, INS pensioniert; ~ **asset** n TAX ausgeschiedenes Wirtschaftsgut nt; ~ **person** n BrE (cf retiree AmE) FIN, GEN COMM Pensionär, in m,f, Rentner, in m,f
retiree n AmE (cf retired person BrE) FIN, GEN COMM Pensionär, in m,f, Rentner, in m,f
retirement n ADMIN Rücktritt m, FIN, HRM, INS, WEL Pensionierung f, HRM Ausscheiden nt, Ruhestand m; ♦ **go into** ~ WEL in Pension gehen, in Rente gehen
retirement: ~ **age** n HRM Pensionierungsalter nt, Rentenalter nt; ~ **annuity policy** n FIN, TAX Rentenversicherungspolice f; ~ **benefit** n BrE (cf old-age insurance benefit AmE) WEL Rente f, Altersruhegeld nt; ~ **fund** n ACC, FIN, INS Pensionsfonds m, Rentenfonds m; ~ **income security act** n HRM Gesetzgebung f zur Sicherung des Renteneinkommens; ~ **pay** n FIN, WEL Ruhegehalt nt, Altersrente f, Pension f; ~ **payments** n pl FIN Rentenzahlungen f pl; ~ **pension** n FIN, WEL Altersrente f, Altersversorgung f, Pension f, Ruhegehalt nt, Rente f; ~ **pension rights** n pl FIN EU Altersversorgungsanwartschaften f pl; ~ **plan** n HRM Pensionssystem nt; ~ **relief** n BrE TAX Pensionsfreibetrag m; ~ **savings program** AmE, ~ **savings programme** BrE n FIN Rentenanparprogramm nt, Rentensparplan m; ~ **scheme** n FIN, HRM Pensionsplan m
retiring: ~ **age** n HRM, WEL pensionsfähiges Alter nt; ~ **allowance** n FIN, WEL Altersrente f, Altersversorgung f, Pension f, Ruhegehalt nt
retortion n LAW Vergeltung f
retouch vt S&M retuschieren
retracement n GEN COMM Zurückverfolgung f
retrain vt HRM umschulen
retraining n HRM Umschulung f; ~ **course** n HRM Umschulungslehrgang m
retransfer 1. n ACC Rückübertragung f, of reserves Auflösung f; 2. vt ACC rückübertragen, of reserves auflösen

retranslation *n* ECON *of foreign currency* Rücktausch *m*, Rückumtausch *m*

retribution *n* LAW Vergeltung *f*

retrieval: ~ **time** *n* COMP Abrufzeit *f*

retrieve *vt* COMP *data, file* abrufen, wiedergewinnen, ECON wiedererlangen

retroactive *adj* GEN COMM rückwirkend; ~ **adjustment** *n* ECON rückwirkende Anpassung *f*; ~ **classification** *n* POL rückwirkende Einstufung *f*; ~ **law** *n* LAW rückwirkendes Gesetz *nt*

retroactively *adv* GEN COMM rückwirkend

retroactivity *n* LAW Rückwirkung *f*

retrogress *vi* ECON sich verschlechtern, zurückgehen

retrogression *n* ECON Rückentwicklung *f*, Rückgang *m*

retrospective *adj* GEN COMM rückblickend, retrospektiv, rückwirkend; ~ **rebate** *n* TRANSP rückwirkender Nachlaß *m*

retrospectively *adv* GEN COMM rückwirkend

retrospectivity *n* LAW Rückwirkung *f*

return 1. *n* ACC Ertrag *m*, FIN Rendite *f*, GEN COMM Herausgabe *f*, *on investment* Rendite *f*, Rentabilität *f*, *arrival* Wiederkehr *f*, Rückkehr *f*, *giving back* Rückgabe *f*, *journey* Rückfahrt *f*, Rückreise *f*, *yield* Ertrag *m*, Verzinsung *f*, *report* Bericht *m*, STOCK Rentabilität *f*, *yield* Verzinsung *f*, Rendite *f*, Ertrag *m*, Gewinn *m*, TAX Steuererklärung *f*; ◆ **by** ~ **of post** COMMS postwendend; **in** ~ **for** LAW als Gegenleistung; **2.** *vt* COMMS *package* rückliefern, FIN *interest* abwerfen, GEN COMM *borrowed article* zurückgeben, zurückbringen, S&M *goods sold to supplier* zurücksenden; ◆ ~ **sb's call** COMMS *telephone* zurückrufen; ~ **to sender** COMMS zurück an Absender; ~ **to source** ACC auflösen; **3.** *vi* GEN COMM zurückkehren, zurückkommen

return: ~ **of amount overpaid** *n* GEN COMM *by tax-collection services* Rückerstattung *f* eines zuviel gezahlten Betrages

returnable: ~ **bottle** *n* ENVIR, S&M Pfandflasche *f*, Mehrwegflasche *f*; ~ **container** *n* ENVIR Mehrwegbehälter *m*; ~ **goods** *n pl* GEN COMM umtauschbare Waren *f pl*

return: ~ **address** *n* COMMS Adresse *f* des Absenders; ~ **cargo** *n* (r/c) TRANSP Rückfracht *f*; ~ **delivery** *n* GEN COMM, TRANSP Rücklieferung *f*

returned: ~ **book** *n* MEDIA zurückgegebenes Buch *nt*; ~ **goods** *n pl* GEN COMM Rückwaren *f pl*, Retouren *f pl*

return: ~ **fare** *n* BrE (*cf round-trip fare AmE*) TRANSP Fahrpreis *m* für Hin- und Rückfahrt, Reisepreis *m* für Hin- und Rückfahrt; ~ **flight** *n* LEIS Rückflug *m*; ~ **freight** *n* TRANSP Rückfracht *f*; ~ **of guarantee** *n* GEN COMM Garantierücksendung *f*, Rückerstattung *f* im Garantiefall; ~ **leg** *n* LEIS Rückreise *f*; ~ **load** *n* TRANSP Rückladung *f*; ~ **on assets** *n* (*ROA*) ACC Gesamtkapitalrentabilität *f*, FIN Anlagenrendite *f*, Gesamtkapitalrentabilität *f*; ~ **on capital** *n* (*ROC*) ACC, ECON, FIN Kapitalertrag *m*, Kapitalrendite *f*, Kapitalverzinsung *f*; ~ **on capital employed** *n* (*ROCE*) ACC, ECON, FIN Ertrag *m* aus Kapitalanlage, Kapitalrendite *f*, Kapitalverzinsung *f*, Rückfluß *m* auf das investierte Kapital, Rendite *f* des eingesetzten Kapitals, Rendite *f* des investierten Kapitals, Rentabilität *f* des Kapitaleinsatzes; ~ **on equity** *n* (*ROE*) ACC, ECON, FIN, STOCK Eigenkapitalrendite *f*, Eigenkapitalrentabilität *f*; ~ **on invested capital** *n* (*ROIC*) FIN Ertrag *m* des investierten Kapitals, Rentabilität *f* des investierten Kapitals; ~ **on**

investment *n* (*ROI*) ACC return on investment (*ROI*), Kapitalrendite *f*, ECON Kapitalrendite *f*, FIN Ertrag *m* des investierten Kapitals, Investitionsrentabilität *f*, Kapitalrendite *f*, Rendite *f* einer Kapitalanlage; ~ **on net assets** *n* ACC Eigenkapitalrendite *f*; ~ **on net assets employed** *n* ACC Eigenkapitalrendite *f*; ~ **on real estate** *n* PROP Ertrag *m* aus Immobilien; ~ **on sales** *n* ACC, FIN Umsatzrendite *f*, Umsatzrentabilität *f*, S&M Gewinnspanne *f*, *statistics* Verkaufsertrag *m*

returns *n pl* GEN COMM Rückwaren *f pl*; ~ **to scale** *n* ECON Niveaugrenzerträge *m pl*, Skalenerträge *m pl*

return: ~ **ticket** *n* BrE LEIS Rückfahrkarte *f*, *air* Rückflugschein *m*; ~ **to source** *n* ACC Auflösung *f*

retype *vt* COMP neu eingeben

reunification *n* GEN COMM *of Germany* Wiedervereinigung *f*, Vereinigung *f*

reusable *adj* ENVIR, GEN COMM wiederverwendbar, wiederverwertbar, Mehrweg-; ~ **packs** *n pl* S&M wiederverwendbare Packungen *f pl*, Mehrwegpackungen *f pl*

reuse 1. *n* ENVIR, GEN COMM Wiederverwendung *f*, Wiederverwertung *f*; **2.** *vt* ENVIR, GEN COMM wiederverwenden, wiederverwerten

REV *abbr* (*reversing*) GEN COMM Stornierung *f*, Rückbuchung *f*

revalorization *n* ECON Aufwertung *f*, Revalorisierung *f*, Rückbuchung *f*

revaluation *n* ACC Zuschreibung *f*, ECON, FIN *of currency* Aufwertung *f*, Neubewertung *f*, GEN COMM Aufwertung *f*; ~ **of assets** *n* ACC Neubewertung *f* des Vermögens, FIN Neubewertung *f* von Vermögenswerten; ~ **of exchange rate** *n* ECON Aufwertung *f* der Währung, ~ **rate** *n* ECON Aufwertungssatz *m*; ~ **reserves** *n* ACC Neubewertungsrücklage *f*, Neubewertungsreserve *f*

revalue *vt* ACC *assets*, ECON aufwerten, neubewerten

revamp 1. *n* FIN, GEN COMM Umorganisation *f*; **2.** *vt* GEN COMM *improve* auf Vordermann bringen (*jarg*), aufpolieren (*infrml*), *reorganize* umorganisieren, S&M *product image, shop design* aufpolieren (*infrml*)

revealed: ~ **preference** *n* ECON offenbarte Präferenz *f*, GEN COMM bekundete Präferenz *f*

revenue *n* ACC, ECON Einkünfte *pl*, Einkommen *nt*, Einnahme *f*, FIN Einnahmen *f pl*, GEN COMM Einkünfte *pl*, Einnahmen *f pl*, Erlös *m*, Umsatzerlös *m*, POL Staatseinnahme *f*; ~ **allocation** *n* TRANSP Einnahmenverteilung *f*; ~ **authority** *n* TAX Finanzbehörde *f*; ~ **budget** *n* ACC Einnahmebudget *nt*; ~ **center** *AmE*, ~ **centre** *BrE* *n* GEN COMM Ertragszentrum *nt*, Finanzzentrum *nt*; ~ **curve** *n* ECON Einnahmenkurve *f*; ~ **department** *n* TAX Fiskus *m*, Finanzverwaltung *f*; ~ **dependency** *n* FIN Abhängigkeit *f* von Einnahmen; ~ **dilution** *n* GEN COMM Ertragsverwässerung *f*; ~ **earner** *n* ECON Einnahmegenerator *m*; ~ **economy** *n* ECON Ertragswirtschaft *f*; ~ **and expenses** *n pl* ACC Aufwand *m* und Ertrag *m*, Einnahmen und Ausgaben *f pl*; ~ **from taxes** *n* FIN Aufkommen *nt* an Steuern, Steueraufkommen *nt*; ~ **loss** *n* TAX Steuerverlust *m*; ~ **maximization** *n* ECON Einnahmenmaximierung *f*, Erlösmaximierung *f*; ~**-neutral** *adj* TAX einnahmeneutral; ~ **office** *n* TAX Finanzamt *nt*; ~ **officer** *n* TAX Zollbeamte(r) *m* [decl. as adj], Zollbeamtin *f*, Angehörige(r) *mf* [decl. as adj] der Finanzverwaltung; ~ **production** *n* GEN COMM Ertragserwirtschaftung *f*; ~ **project** *n* GEN COMM Ertragsprojekt *nt*; ~ **ruling** *n* *AmE* TAX verbindliche

Auslegung eines steuerrechtlichen Tatbestandes durch die US-Bundessteuerbehörde; **~ sharing** _n AmE_ ECON Gewinnbeteiligung _f_, vertikaler Finanzausgleich _m_; **~ stamp** _n_ TAX Steuermarke _f_; **~ test** _n_ ACC Ertragstest _m_; **~ trust account** _n_ FIN Finanztreuhandkonto _nt_

reversal _n_ ACC _bookkeeping_ Rückbuchung _f_, Stornierung _f_, Auflösung _f_, LAW Aufhebung _f_, POL Umschwung _m_

reverse 1. _adj_ COMP invers, GEN COMM umgekehrt; **2.** _vt_ ACC stornieren, ECON umkehren, LAW aufheben; ♦ **~ course** ECON rückgängig machen; **~ a swap** STOCK ein gegengerichtetes Swapgeschäft abschließen; **~ a trend** GEN COMM eine Trendwende herbeiführen; **~ an entry** ACC eine Buchung stornieren; **~ the charges** _BrE_ (_cf_ _call collect AmE_) COMMS R-Gespräch anmelden

reverse: **~ annuity mortgage** _n_ BANK Hypothek, die eine private Rentenversicherung unterstützt; **~ causation hypothesis** _n_ ECON umgekehrte Kausalitätshypothese _f_; **~ channel** _n_ COMP Rückkanal _m_; **~ charge call** _n BrE_ (_cf_ _collect call AmE_) COMMS R-Gespräch _nt_; **~ conversion** _n_ STOCK dreiteiliges Wertpapiergeschäft _nt_; **~ discrimination** _n_ WEL Gegendiskriminierung _f_; **~ engineering** _n_ GEN COMM Nachahmung _f_ eines Produkts anhand des Originals, Rückwärtsentwicklung _f_, rückwärtige Konstruktion _f_; **~ entry** _n_ ACC Rückbuchung _f_; **~ gearing** _n BrE_ (_cf_ _reverse leverage AmE_) ACC negative Hebelwirkung _f_, umgekehrte Hebelwirkung _f_; **~ income tax** _n_ TAX negative Einkommensteuer _f_; **~ J-shaped frequency curve** _n_ ECON umgekehrte J-förmige Häufigkeitskurve _f_; **~ leverage** _n AmE_ (_cf reverse gearing BrE_) ACC negative Hebelwirkung _f_, umgekehrte Hebelwirkung _f_; **~ plate** _n_ S&M Negativklischee _nt_; **~ printing** _n_ COMP inverse Schrift _f_, Reverse Print _m_; **~ repurchase agreement** _n_ FIN Wertpapierpensionsgeschäft _nt_; **~ split** _n_ FIN Aktienzusammenlegung _f_; **~ takeover** _n_ ECON, FIN gegenläufige Fusion _f_; **~ triangular merger** _n_ GEN COMM gegenläufige Fusion _f_; **~ video** _n_ COMP Umkehranzeige _f_; **~ yield gap** _n_ STOCK inverses Renditengefälle _nt_

reversed _adj_ GEN COMM umgekehrt

reversible _adj_ GEN COMM reversibel; **~ lay days** _n pl_ TRANSP _shipping, charter party term_ Liegetage _m pl_ vor der Rückreise; **~ lay time** _n_ TRANSP _shipping, charter party term_ Liegezeit _f_ vor der Rückreise

reversing _n_ (_REV_) GEN COMM Stornierung _f_, Rückbuchung _f_; **~ entry** _n_ ACC Gegenbuchung _f_, Gegeneintrag _m_, Storno _m or nt_, Stornobuchung _f_

reversionary: **~ annuity** _n_ INS Rente _f_ auf den Überlebensfall, Überlebensrente _f_; **~ bonus** _n_ INS Summenzuwachs _m_; **~ factor** _n_ MATH _statistics_ reversionärer Faktor _m_; **~ interest** _n_ HRM Anwartschaftsrecht _nt_

review 1. _n_ GEN COMM Überprüfung _f_, _survey_ Überblick _m_, MEDIA _of play, film_ Besprechung _f_, Kritik _f_, Rezension _f_, MGMNT _examination_ Durchsicht _f_, Überprüfung _f_; **2.** _vt_ GEN COMM _examine_ überprüfen, durchsehen, _general account_ einen Überblick geben über, MEDIA _play, film_ besprechen, rezensieren, MGMNT _general account_ einen Überblick geben über, _examine_ durchsehen, überprüfen

review: **~ body** _n_ HRM Prüfungsausschuß _m_; **~ copy** _n_ MEDIA Besprechungsexemplar _nt_

reviewer _n_ MEDIA Rezensent, in _m,f_

revise _vt_ GEN COMM überarbeiten, verbessern, LAW _decision_ abändern, MEDIA überarbeiten; ♦ **~ downward** GEN COMM nach unten korrigieren, nach unten revidieren

revised _adj_ GEN COMM, MEDIA überarbeitet, verbessert; **~ edition** _n_ MEDIA _print_ überarbeitete Ausgabe _f_; **~ figures** _n pl_ GEN COMM bereinigte Zahlen _f pl_, berichtigte Zahlen _f pl_; **~ version** _n_ MEDIA _print_ überarbeitete Fassung _f_

revision _n_ ADMIN Überarbeitung _f_, GEN COMM _of guidelines_ Durchsicht _f_, Neuregelung _f_, Revision _f_, LAW, POL Abänderung _f_, MEDIA Überarbeitung _f_

revitalization _n_ ECON, GEN COMM Neubelebung _f_

revitalize _vt_ ECON, GEN COMM beleben, neu beleben

revival _n_ ECON, GEN COMM Regenerierung _f_, Wiederaufblühen _nt_, Wiederbelebung _f_, LAW Wiederinkraftsetzung _f_, LEIS _theatre_ Wiederaufführung _f_, Wiederaufnahme _f_; **~ of sales** _n_ ECON Absatzbelebung _f_

revive 1. _vt_ ECON, GEN COMM beleben, erneuern, regenerieren, wiederbeleben, LAW, LEIS wiederaufnehmen; **2.** _vi_ ECON sich beleben, wiederaufblühen, GEN COMM aufleben, sich beleben, wiederaufblühen, _recover_ sich erholen

revocability: **~ of declarations** _n_ LAW _contracts_ Widerruflichkeit _f_ von Erklärungen

revocable _adj_ GEN COMM widerruflich, zurücknehmbar; **~ trust** _n_ FIN widerrufbarer Trust _m_, widerrufbares Treuhandverhältnis _nt_

revocation _n_ FIN Widerruf _m_, PATENTS Widerruf _m_, Zurücknahme _f_

revoke _vt_ FIN aufheben, widerrufen, zurückziehen, PATENTS _licence_ widerrufen, zurücknehmen

revolt _n_ POL Aufruhr _m_

revolving _adj_ ECON, FIN revolvierend; **~ charge account** _n_ BANK revolvierende Teilzahlungsvereinbarung _f_; **~ fund** _n_ ACC _government_ rückzahlbare Staatssubvention _f_, FIN revolvierender Fonds _m_, rückzahlbare Staatssubvention _f_, Umlauffonds _m_; **~ line of credit** FIN revolvierende Kreditlinie _f_; **~ underwriting facility** _n_ (_RUF_) BANK Fazilität, die eine Liquiditätsbeschaffung über die revolvierende Plazierung von Schuldtiteln ermöglicht

reward _n_ GEN COMM, S&M Anerkennung _f_, Belohnung _f_; ♦ **as a ~ for** GEN COMM als Belohnung für, als Entgelt für

rewarding _adj_ GEN COMM _financially_ einträglich, HRM _job_ lohnend

rewind _vt_ COMP _tape_, MEDIA _cassette, tape_ zurückspulen

rework _vt_ MEDIA überarbeiten

rewrite _vt_ ADMIN neuabfassen, COMP _software_ neu schreiben, umschreiben, GEN COMM neufassen, MEDIA _print_ umschreiben

RFR _abbr_ (_required freight rate_) TRANSP Mindestfrachtrate _f_

RHA _abbr BrE_ (_Road Haulage Association_) TRANSP britischer Güterkraftverkehrsverband

Rhinelands: **~ hourglass** _n_ ECON Gürtel der wirtschaftlich starken EU-Städte

RHV _abbr_ (_road haulage vehicle_) TRANSP Fahrzeug _nt_ im Straßentransport

ribbon _n_ COMP _printer_ Farbband _nt_, MEDIA kleingedruckte Schlagzeile über der Hauptschlagzeile, _typewriter_

Farbband *nt*, *web printing* Strang *m*; ~ **cartridge** *n* COMP Farbbandkassette *f*

RIC *abbr* (*rehabilitation import credit*) FIN Importsanierungskredit *m*

rich: ~ **oil strike** *n* ENVIR reiches Ölvorkommen *nt*

ride: ~ **the clock** *phr AmE infrml* HRM die Stempeluhr umgehen

RIE *abbr* STOCK (*recognized investment exchange*) anerkannte Investmentbörse *f*, (*Registered International Exchange BrE*) internationale Börse in Großbritannien

RIF *abbr* (*reduction in force*) HRM Personalabbau *m*

rig *vt* STOCK *market* manipulieren

rigger *n* HRM Flugzeugmonteur *m*, TRANSP Flugzeugmonteur *m*, *shipping* Rigger *m*, Takler *m*

right 1. *adj* GEN COMM richtig; ♦ **be on the ~ track** GEN COMM auf der richtigen Fährte sein; **2.** *n* LAW Recht *nt*; ♦ **be in the ~** GEN COMM im Recht sein; **in its own ~** GEN COMM in eigenem Recht; **give sb the ~ to do sth** GEN COMM jdm das Recht erteilen, etw zu tun; **with no ~ of appeal** LAW ohne Rechtsmittel

right: ~ **of abandonment** *n* LAW Abandonrecht *nt*; ~ **of appeal** *n* LAW Rechtsmittel *nt*; ~ **of avoidance** *n* LAW Anfechtungsrecht *nt*; ~ **column** *n* ACC, FIN Habenseite *f*; ~ **combination** *n* LAW logische Schlußfolgerung *f*; ~ **of disposal** *n* LAW Verfügungsrecht *nt*; ~ **of distraint** *n* FIN, LAW Pfandrecht *nt*; ~ **of entry** *n* LAW Recht *nt* auf Inbesitznahme; ~ **of establishment** *n* LAW Niederlassungsrecht *nt*; ~ **of first refusal** *n* ECON, LAW Vorkaufsrecht *nt*

rightful *adj* GEN COMM, LAW berechtigt; ~ **claim** *n* LAW berechtigter Anspruch *m*; ~ **heir** *n* LAW berechtigter Erbe *m*; ~ **heiress** *n* LAW berechtigte Erbin *f*; ~ **owner** *n* LAW rechtmäßiger Besitzer *m*, rechtmäßige Besitzerin *f*, rechtmäßiger Eigentümer *m*, rechtmäßige Eigentümerin *f*, wirklicher Eigentümer *m*, wirkliche Eigentümerin *f*

right: ~-**hand column** *n* ACC Habenseite *f*, GEN COMM rechte Spalte *f*

Right: ~ **Honourable** *adj BrE* (*Rt Hon*) POL Sehr Ehrenwerte(r)

right: ~ **in course of acquisition** *n* LAW Anwartschaft *f*; ~ **in personam** *n* LAW obligatorisches Recht *nt*

rightism *n* POL *Communism* rechtsgerichtete politische Gesinnung *f*, rechtsorientierte Haltung *f*

right: ~-**justified** *adj* COMP rechts ausgerichtet, rechtsbündig; ~ **of lien** *n* FIN, LAW Pfandrecht *nt*; ~ **of ownership** *n* ECON Eigentumsrecht *nt*; ~ **of preemption** *n* STOCK Vorkaufsrecht *nt*; ~ **of protection from risks** *n* LAW *contracts* Recht *nt* zum Schutz vor Risiko, Sicherheitsrecht *nt*; ~ **of recourse** *n* FIN Regreßanspruch *m*; ~ **of recovery** *n* LAW Entschädigungsanspruch *m*; ~ **of redemption** *n* FIN Rückerwerbsrecht *nt* eines Schuldners, Rückzahlungsrecht *nt*; ~ **of redress** *n* LAW Recht *nt* auf Entschädigung, Recht *nt* auf Wiedergutmachung; ~ **of reply** *n* LAW Erwiderungsrecht *nt*; ~ **of resale** *n* S&M Wiederverkaufsrecht *nt*; ~ **of rescission** *n* LAW *contract* Aufhebungsrecht, Rücktrittsrecht *nt*; ~ **of residence** *n* ADMIN Aufenthaltsgenehmigung *f*; ~ **of resumption** *n* LAW Recht *nt* zur Wiederaufnahme; ~ **of retention** *n* LAW *contracts* Rückbehaltungsrecht *nt* Zurückbehaltungsrecht *nt*; ~ **of return** *n* GEN COMM Rückgaberecht *nt*

rights *n pl* LAW *intellectual property* Recht *nt* am geistigen Eigentum; ~ **and actions** *n pl* LAW *intellectual property* Rechte *nt pl* und Rechtsstreit *m*; ♦ ~ **afforded by** PATENTS Rechte gewährt durch; **all ~ reserved** LAW alle Rechte vorbehalten

right: ~ **of segregation** *n* LAW *bankruptcy* Aussonderungsrecht *nt*; ~ **shift key** *n* COMP rechte Umschalttaste *f*; ~ **of stoppage in transitu** *n* LAW *of unpaid goods* Verfolgungsrecht *nt*

rights: ~ **issue** *n* ACC, FIN, STOCK Bezugsrechtsausgabe *f*, Bezugsrechtsemission *f*

right: ~ **of survivorship** *n* LAW Anwachsungsrecht *nt* des Überlebenden; ~ **to associate** *n* POL Koalitionsrecht *nt*; ~ **to asylum** LAW, POL Asylrecht *nt*; ~ **to be heard** *n* LAW Anhörungsrecht *nt*; ~ **to capitalize** *n* ACC Aktivierungsrecht *nt*; ~ **to cost exemption** *n* LAW Armenrecht *f*; ~ **to delivery** *n* TRANSP Auslieferungsanspruch *m*; ~ **to dispose of** *n* LAW Verfügungsrecht *nt*; ~ **to dissociate** *n* HRM Recht *nt*, sich zu distanzieren; ~ **to information** *n* POL Auskunftsrecht *nt*; ~ **to know** *n* POL Anrecht *nt* auf Information, Auskunftsrecht *nt*, Recht *nt* auf Auskunft; ~ **to life insurance benefits** *n* INS Bezugsrecht *nt*; ~ **to manage** *n* HRM Leitungsrecht *nt*, Vorrecht *nt* der Unternehmensleitung; ~ **to organize** *n* HRM Recht *nt* zur gewerkschaftlichen Organisation; ~ **to a patent** *n* PATENTS Patentrecht *nt*; ~ **to seek asylum** *n* LAW, POL Asylrecht *nt*; ~ **to strike** *n* GEN COMM, HRM, IND Streikrecht *nt*; ~ **to a tax refund** *n* TAX Steuererstattungsanspruch *m*; ~ **to usufruct** *n* LAW Recht *nt* auf Nießbrauch; ~ **to vote** *n* FIN Stimmrecht *nt*, POL *in elections* Wahlrecht *nt*, STOCK Stimmrecht *nt*; ~ **to withdraw from performance** *n* LAW *contracts* Leistungsverweigerungsrecht *nt*; ~ **to work** *n* LAW *without trade union membership* Recht *nt* auf Arbeit; ~-**to-work state** *n AmE* LAW Staat, in dem das Recht auf Arbeit gilt; ~ **of way** *n* LAW Wegerecht *nt*, TRANSP *for vehicle* Vorfahrt *f*; ~-**wing** *adj* POL rechts, rechtsgerichtet, rechtsorientiert

RIL *abbr* (*rehabilitation import loan*) FIN Importsanierungsanleihe *f*

ring *vt* COMMS, GEN COMM anrufen; ~-**fence** *vt* ECON, FIN *money, subsidy* bestimmen, vorsehen, Zweckbindung *f* vornehmen

ringfencing *n* ECON, FIN *money, subsidy* Zweckbindung *f*

ringing: ~ **out** *n* STOCK *futures market* Erfüllung *f* von Warenterminkontrakten vor Fälligkeit

ring: ~ **road** *n* TRANSP Umgehungsstraße *f*

riots *n pl* POL Unruhen *f pl*; ~ **and civil commotions** *n pl* (*R&CC*) WEL Ausschreitungen und politische Unruhen *f pl*; ~, **civil commotions and strikes** *n pl* (*RCC&S*) WEL Ausschreitungen, politische Unruhen und Streiks *pl*

riparian: ~ **rights** *n pl* LAW Flußanliegerrechte *nt pl*

rip-off: ~ **merchant** *n infrml* S&M Nepper *m* (*infrml*)

ripper: ~ **bill** *n AmE* POL Gesetzentwurf mit der Absicht, die Opposition zu spalten

ripple: ~ **effect** *n* ECON Ansteckungseffekt *m*

rise 1. *n* ECON Hausse *f*, GEN COMM Anstieg *m*, Zunahme *f*, Aufwärtsbewegung *f*, *in prices* Steigen *nt*, Steigerung *f*, HRM *BrE* (*cf raise AmE*) *in salary* Erhöhung *f*, Gehaltserhöhung *f*, Gehaltssteigerung *f*, STOCK Aufwärtsbewegung *f*, *in shares* Hausse *f*; **2.** *vi* ECON ansteigen, FIN *income, earnings* anziehen, GEN COMM in Gang kommen, anziehen, steigen, *parliament* die Sitzung beenden, sich vertagen, HRM aufsteigen, POL *parliament* die Sitzung beenden; ♦ **give ~ to** GEN COMM *interest* erregen, *suspicions* Anlaß geben; **~ in line with inflation** ECON *price, benefit* mit der Inflation mitgehen, mit der Inflation steigen; **~ again** ECON wieder steigen

rise: **~ in prices** *n* ECON, S&M Teuerung *f*; **~ in wages** *n* HRM Lohnerhöhung *f*

rises: **~ and falls** *n pl BrE* (*cf gains and losses AmE*) ECON Gewinne und Verluste *m pl*

rising *adj* ECON anziehend, steigend, GEN COMM anziehend; **~ costs** *n* ECON steigende Kosten *pl*; **~ interest rate** *n* ECON steigender Zinssatz *m*; **~ unemployment** *n* ECON steigende Arbeitslosigkeit *f*

risk 1. *n* ECON Wagnis *nt*, INS, MATH *statistics* Risiko *nt*; ♦ **at buyer's ~** STOCK auf Risiko des Käufers; **at owner's ~** GEN COMM auf eigenes Risiko, zum Selbstbehalt, INS auf eigene Gefahr; **at receiver's ~** GEN COMM auf Gefahr des Empfängers, auf Risiko des Empfängers; **at ~** GEN COMM gefährdet, in Gefahr, STOCK auf Risiko; **no ~ after discharge** (*nrad*) INS kein Risiko nach Löschung; **~ passes with property** LAW *contractual principal* Risiko geht mit Eigentum über; **no ~ until confirmed** (*nr*) INS kein Risiko bis zur Bestätigung; **2.** *vt* GEN COMM wagen

risk: **~ of accidental destruction** *n* LAW *contracts* Risiko *nt* des zufälligen Untergangs der Sache; **~-adjusted discount rate** *n* FIN risikoangepaßter Diskontsatz *m*; **~ analysis** *n* FIN, INS Risikoanalyse *f*; **~ arbitrage** *n* STOCK Risikoarbitrage *f*; **~ assessment** *n* FIN, INS Risikobewertung *f*, MGMNT Risikobeurteilung *f*, Risikobewertung *f*, Risikoeinschätzung *f*; **~ asset system** *n* BANK System *nt* zur Beurteilung der Risiken im Aktivgeschäft; **~-averse** *adj* GEN COMM *game theory* risikoscheu; **~-avoiding** *adj* FIN risikomeidend; **~-avoiding capital** *n* FIN risikomeidendes Kapital *nt*; **~-based banking standards** *n pl* BANK risikoorientiertes Bankmanagement *nt*, Risikostandards *m pl* im Bankgeschäft; **~-based premium** *n* INS Prämie *f* auf Risikobasis, risikobezogene Prämie *f*; **~-bearing capital** *n* FIN risikotragendes Kapital *nt*, Spekulationskapital *nt*; **~ capital** *n* BANK, ECON, FIN Risikokapital *nt*, risikotragendes Kapital *nt*, Wagniskapital *nt*, GEN COMM Risikokapital *nt*; **~ cover** *n* ECON Risikoabdeckung *f*; **~ distribution** *n* INS, LAW Risikoverteilung *f*; **~ exposure** *n* ACC Kreditrisiko *nt*; **~ of financial reliability** *n* INS, LAW *contracts* Bonitätsrisiko *nt*; **~-free** *adj* STOCK risikolos; **~-free debt instrument** *n* STOCK *Treasury bills* risikolose Schuldurkunde *f*, risikoloser Schuldtitel *m*; **~-free transaction** *n* STOCK risikolose Transaktion *f*, risikoloser Geschäftsabschluß *m*; **~ in the goods** *n* INS, LAW, TRANSP Warenrisiko *nt*; **~ of liability** *n* INS, LAW *contracts* Haftungsrisiko *nt*; **~ management** *n* FIN Risikomanagement *nt*, wirksames Begrenzen *nt* von Risiken, MGMNT, STOCK Risikomanagement *nt*, Risikostreuung *f*; **~ manager** *n* INS Risikomanager *m*; **~-minimizing** *adj* STOCK risikominimierend; **~ monitoring** *n* MGMNT Risikoüberwachung *f*, Risikokontrolle *f*; **~-oriented** *adj* GEN COMM risikoorientiert; **~ package** *n* FIN Risikopaket *nt*; **~ pooling** *n* INS Risikopooling *f*, Risikoverteilung *f*; **~ position** *n* STOCK Risikoposition *f*; **~ profile** *n* INS Risikoprofil *nt*; **~ sharing** *n* INS Risikoteilung *f*; **~ of transportation** *n* LAW, TRANSP *contracts* Beförderungsrisiko *nt*; **~ weighting** *n* FIN *degrees of credit risk* Risikogewichtung *f*

risks: **all ~** *phr* (*A/R*) INS alle Gefahren, jedes Risiko *nt*

risky *adj* BANK risikobehaftet, ECON riskant, GEN COMM gewagt, risikofreudig, riskant; **~ asset** *n* BANK risikobehafteter Vermögenswert *m*

rival *n* GEN COMM Konkurrent, in *m,f*; **~ brand** *n* S&M Konkurrenzmarke *f*; **~ goods** *n* S&M Konkurrenzprodukt *nt*, Konkurrenzerzeugnis *nt*

river *n* GEN COMM Fluß *m*; **~ pollution** *n* ENVIR Flußverschmutzung *f*, Flußverunreinigung *f*; **~ tonnage dues** *n pl* TRANSP Flußtonnagengebühren *f pl*

rly *abbr BrE* (*railway*) TRANSP Bahn *f*, Eisenbahn *f*, Eisenbahnwesen *f*

RN *abbr* (*release note*) TRANSP *cargo* Freigabe *f*, Freigabemitteilung *f*, Freigabeschein *m*

ro. *abbr* (*recto*) MEDIA *front of page* Vorderseite *f*

RO *abbr* GEN COMM, PATENTS (*receiving office*) Anmeldeamt *nt*, Annahmestelle *f*, FIN (*receiving order*) Konkurseinleitungsbeschluß *m*

ROA *abbr* (*return on assets*) ACC Gesamtkapitalrentabilität *f*, FIN Anlagenrendite *f*, Gesamtkapitalrentabilität *f*

road *n* (*Rd*) GEN COMM Straße (*Str.*) *f*, Weg *m*; ♦ **be on the ~** GEN COMM geschäftlich unterwegs sein, TRANSP unterwegs sein

road: **~ building** *n* ECON Straßenbau *m*; **~ fatalities** *n pl* TRANSP Verkehrstote *m pl*; **~ haulage** *n* TRANSP Beförderung *f* im Straßenverkehr, Güterkraftverkehr *m*, Straßengüterverkehr *m*, Straßentransport *m*; **~ haulage company** *n BrE* TRANSP Fuhrunternehmen *nt*, Fuhrunternehmer *m*, Güterkraftverkehrsunternehmen *nt*

Road: **~ Haulage Association** *n BrE* (*RHA*) TRANSP britischer Güterkraftverkehrsverband

road: **~ haulage company** *n* TRANSP Fuhrunternehmen *nt*, Speditionsbetrieb *m*, Straßentransportunternehmen *nt*; **~ haulage contractor** *n* TRANSP Speditionsbetrieb *m*; **~ haulage vehicle** *n* (*RHV*) TRANSP Fahrzeug *nt* im Straßentransport; **~ network** *n* TRANSP Straßennetz *nt*; **~-rail transport** *n BrE* (*cf piggyback traffic AmE*) TRANSP Huckepackverkehr *m*, Straße-Schiene-Transport *m*; **~ safety** *n* TRANSP Sicherheit *f* im Straßenverkehr

roadshow *n* FIN, GEN COMM, S&M Roadshow *f*, LEIS *cinema* Wanderkino *nt*

roadside: **~ site** *n* S&M *for advertising poster* an der Straße gelegene Anschlagstelle *f*

road: **~ tax** *n BrE* TAX, TRANSP Kraftfahrzeugsteuer *f*, Kfz-Steuer; **~ toll** *n* ECON, GEN COMM Straßenbenutzungsgebühr *f*; **~ traffic** *n* TRANSP Straßenverkehr *m*; **~ transport** *n* TRANSP Straßengüterverkehr *m*, Straßentransport *m*; **~-use tax** *n* ECON, GEN COMM Straßenbenutzungsgebühr *f*

roadway *n* IND *mining* Strecke *f*, TRANSP Fahrbahn *f*

roadworks *n pl* TRANSP Straßenbaustelle *f*

Robertsonian: **~ lag** *n* ECON Robertsonsche Verzögerung *f*, Robertson-Lag *m*

robot *n* IND Roboter *m*

robotics *n* IND Robotertechnik *f*, Robotik *f*

robotize 1. *vt* IND automatisieren; **2.** *vi* IND Roboter einsetzen

robot: **~-like** *adj* IND roboterhaft; **~ salespeople** *n pl* S&M roboterhafte Verkäufer *m pl*

robust *adj* GEN COMM robust, widerstandsfähig

ROC *abbr* (*return on capital*) ACC, ECON, FIN Kapitalertrag *m*, Kapitalrendite *f*, Kapitalverzinsung *f*

ROCE *abbr* (*return on capital employed*) ACC, ECON, FIN Rendite *f* des investierten Kapitals, Ertrag *m* aus Kapitalanlage, Kapitalrendite *f*, Kapitalverzinsung *f*, Rendite *f* des eingesetzten Kapitals, Rentabilität *f* des Kapitaleinsatzes

rock: **~-bottom price** *n* ECON Tiefstpreis *m*, GEN COMM äußerster kalkulierter Preis *m*, bester Preis *m*, niedrigster Kurs *m*, Tiefstpreis *m pl*

rocket *vi infrml* GEN COMM *prices* emporschnellen, in die Höhe schießen; **~ scientist** *n* STOCK Börsenspezialist für schnell steigende Aktien

rocks: **be on the ~** *phr infrml* GEN COMM bankrott sein (*infrml*)

ROE *abbr* (*return on equity*) ACC, ECON, FIN, STOCK Eigenkapitalrendite *f*, Eigenkapitalrentabilität *f*

ROG *abbr* (*receipt of goods*) GEN COMM, TRANSP Warenannahme *f*, Warenempfang *m*

ROI *abbr* (*return on investment*) ACC, ECON, FIN Ertrag *m* des investierten Kapitals, Investitionsrentabilität *f*, Kapitalrendite *f*, Rendite *f* einer Kapitalanlage

ROIC *abbr* (*return on invested capital*) ACC, ECON, FIN Ertrag *m* des investierten Kapitals, Rentabilität *f* des investierten Kapitals

role *n* GEN COMM Rolle *f*; **~-playing** *n* MGMNT *training* Rollenspiel *nt*; **~ set** *n* MGMNT Rollenbesetzung *f*

roll down *vt* STOCK verlangsamen

roll out *vt* GEN COMM auswalzen, hinausrollen, IND produzieren

roll over *vt* BANK, FIN umschulden, *interest rates* den Zinssatz neu festsetzen

roll: **~-back** *n* ECON Preisherabsetzung *f*

rolled: **~-up income** *n* TAX angehäuftes Einkommen *nt*

roller: **~ swap** *n* FIN Rollswap *m*

rolling: **~ options position** *n* STOCK *on Eurodollar futures* rollende Optionsposition *f*; **~ plan** *n* GEN COMM rollender Plan *m*; **~ program** *AmE*, **~ programme** *BrE n* FIN, MGMNT Rollprogramm *nt*, variables Programm *nt*; **~-rate note** *n* FIN zinsvariabler Schuldtitel *m*; **~ settlement** *n* STOCK fortlaufende Abrechnung *f*

roll: **~-on container** *n* TRANSP Rollbehälter *m*, Rollcontainer *m*; **~-on-lift-off** *n* (*ro-lo*) TRANSP *cargo* Roll-on-Lift-off (*Ro-Lo*); **~-on-roll-off** *n* (*ro-ro*) TRANSP *cargo* Roll-on-Roll-off (*Ro-Ro*); **~-on-roll-off ship** *n* (*ro-ro-ship*) IMP/EXP Roll-on-Roll-off-Schiff *nt* (*Ro-Ro-Schiff*); **~-out** *n* TRANSP *vehicle* Ausrollen *nt*

rollover: **~ budget** *n* ECON Wiederholungsbudget *nt*; **~ date** *n* BANK Zinsanpassungskredit bei einem Rollover-Kredit; **~ loan** *n* BANK Rollover-Kredit *m*; **~ mortgage** *n* BANK Hypothekendarlehen *nt* mit regelmäßig neu ausgehandeltem Zinssatz; **~ ratio** *n* BANK Rollover-Quote *f*; **~ relief** *n* TAX Überrollungsentlastung *f*

ro-lo *abbr* (*roll-on-lift-off*) TRANSP *shipping* Ro-Lo (*Roll-on-Lift-off*)

ROM *abbr* (*read-only memory*) COMP ROM (*Festspeicher*)

Romalpa: **~ sale** *n* BANK Verkauf *m* unter Eigentumsvorbehalt

roof: **~ load** *n* TRANSP *containers* Dachlast *f*; **~ rail** *n* TRANSP *container* Dachrahmen *m*; **~ tax** *n* TAX Dachsteuer *f*

Rooker: **~ Wise Amendment** *n* FIN Rooker Wise Nachtrag *m*, Rooker Wise Novelle *f*

room *n* GEN COMM Raum *m*; ◆ **~ to negotiate** *n* HRM Verhandlungsspielraum *m*

root *n* COMP Wurzel *f*; **~ directory** *n* COMP Stammverzeichnis *nt*, Wurzelverzeichnis *nt*; **~ segment** *n* COMP Wurzelsegment *nt*

ROP *abbr* (*run of paper*) MEDIA *print run* Papierverlauf *m*, S&M *advertising* Anzeigenplazierung *f* nach Wahl des Verlegers

RORCE *abbr* (*rate of return on capital employed*) ACC, ECON, FIN Rentabilität *f* des eingesetzten Kapitals

ro-ro *abbr* (*roll-on-roll-off*) TRANSP Ro-Ro (*Roll-on-Roll-off*); **~-ship** *n* TRANSP Ro-Ro-Schiff *nt*

roster *n* GEN COMM, HRM *personnel duty* Dienstplan *m*

rostrum *n* MEDIA, POL Podium *nt*

rosy *adj* GEN COMM *prospects* rosig

rotating: **~ shift** *n* HRM Wechselschicht *f*

rotation: **in ~** *phr* GEN COMM im Rotationsverfahren; **~ clause** *n* BANK *underwriting* Rotationsklausel *f*

rotogravure *n* S&M Rotationstiefdruck *m*

rough: **~ draft** *n* LAW erster Entwurf *m*, Vorentwurf *m*; **~ estimate** *n* GEN COMM grobe Schätzung *f*; **~ guide** *n* GEN COMM Faustregel *f*

roughly: **~ equivalent** *phr* GEN COMM etwa gleichwertig

round 1. *adj* GEN COMM rund; ◆ **in ~ figures** GEN COMM in runden Zahlen; **2.** *n* ECON Runde *f*

round down *vt* MATH *number* abrunden

round off *vt* GEN COMM *meeting* abschließen, beschließen

round up *vt* MATH *number* aufrunden

roundabout *n* *BrE* (*cf traffic circle AmE*) TRANSP *roads* Kreisverkehr *m*; **~ production** *n* ECON Umwegproduktion *f*

round: **~ brackets** *n pl* COMP, MEDIA *typography* runde Klammern *f pl*; **~ charter party** *n* (*round C/P*) TRANSP Rundreise-Chartervertrag *m*, Rundreise-Frachtvertrag *m*; **~ C/P** *n* (*round charter party*) TRANSP Rundreise-Chartervertrag *m*, Rundreise-Frachtvertrag *m*

rounding: **~ error** *n* MATH Rundungsfehler *m*; **~-off buying** *n* GEN COMM Arrondierungskauf *m*

round: **~ lot** *n* ACC Mindestmenge *f*, STOCK *obligations at the face value of $ 1.000* volle hundert Aktien *f pl*, voller Börsenschluß *m*; **~ robin** *n* COMMS *letter* gemeinsame Petition *f*, gemeinsamer Antrag *m*

rounds: **do the ~** *phr infrml* POL abklappern (*infrml*)

round: **~ sum allowances** *n pl BrE* TAX Pauschalbeträge *m pl*; **~ table** *n* MGMNT Konferenztisch *m*, Verhandlungstisch *m*, Round Table *m*; **~-the-clock** *adj* GEN COMM den ganzen Tag dauernd, durchgehend, rund um die Uhr; **~-the-clock service** *n* GEN COMM Dienstbereitschaft *f* rund um die Uhr, Tag- und Nachtdienst *m*; **~-the-world service** *n* (*Rws*) TRANSP *shipping* Weltweit-Service *m*

roundtrip *vt* STOCK Aktienfluktuation mittragen

round: **~ trip** *n* STOCK Durchhandeln *nt*, TRANSP Hin- und Rückreise *f*; **~-trip cost** *n* TRANSP Hin- und Rückreisekosten *pl*; **~-trip fare** *n AmE* (*cf return fare BrE*) TRANSP Fahrpreis *m* für Hin- und Rückfahrt, Reisepreis *m* für Hin- und Rückfahrt; **~-trip rate** *n* TRANSP Hin- und Rückreisetarif *m*; **~-trip ticket** *n AmE* (*cf return ticket BrE*) LEIS Rückfahrkarte *f*; **~-trip time** *n* TRANSP Hin- und Rückreisezeit *f*; **~-trip trade** *n* STOCK Durchhandeln *nt*; **~ of wage negotiations** *n* HRM Tarifrunde *f*

route 1. *n* TRANSP Route *f*; **2.** *vt* TRANSP leiten *route*: ~ **analysis** *n* TRANSP Streckenanalyse *f*; ~ **capacity** *n* TRANSP Streckenkapazität *f*; ~ **diversion** *n* TRANSP Umleitung *f*; ~ **option** *n* TRANSP Streckenoption *f*; ~ **order** *n* TRANSP Streckenanweisung *f*, Streckenorder *f*; ~ **planning** *n* TRANSP Streckenplanung *f*; ~ **section** *n* TRANSP Streckenabschnitt *m*

routine 1. *adj* GEN COMM gewohnheitsmäßig, routinemäßig; **2.** *n* COMP Programmroutine *f*, Routine *f*, GEN COMM Formsache *f*, Gewohnheit *f*, Routine *f*; ◆ **as a matter of** ~ GEN COMM gewohnheitsmäßig, routinemäßig

routine: ~ **check** *n* GEN COMM laufende Kontrolle *f*; ~ **control** *n* TRANSP planmäßige Kontrolle *f*; ~ **duty** *n pl* GEN COMM laufende Pflichten *f pl*; ~ **maintenance** *n* GEN COMM laufende Wartung *f*; ~ **response behavior** *AmE*, ~ **response behaviour** *BrE* *n* S&M Käuferreaktion *f* in Routinesituationen, Kaufverhalten *nt* in Routinesituationen

routing *n* COMP *data* Leitweglenkung *f*, GEN COMM Leitweg *m*, TRANSP Festlegung *f* des Leitwegs, Festlegung *f* der Route, Streckenfestlegung *f*; ~ **certificate** *n* TRANSP Arbeitsplanzertifikat *nt*, Beförderungsbescheinigung *f*, Beförderungszertifikat *nt*, Routenbescheinigung *f*, Routenzertifikat *nt*; ~ **order** *n* TRANSP *cargo* Anordnung *f* eines Leitwegs, Anweisung *f* über den Transportweg; ~ **slip** *n* ADMIN Laufzettel *m*; ~ **symbol** *n* FIN Bankleitzahl *f*

row *n* GEN COMM *of figures* Reihe *f*, TRANSP *shipping* Blockreihe *f*, Reihe *f*

ROW *abbr* (*rest of the world*) ECON die übrige Welt *f*, der Rest *m* der Welt

row: ~ **house** *n* AmE (*cf terraced house BrE*) PROP Reihenhaus *nt*

Royal: ~ **Assent** *n* BrE LAW königliche Genehmigung *f*; ~ **Economic Society** *n* ECON Königlicher Ökonomieverband; ~ **Exchange** *n* (*RE BrE*) STOCK Londoner Börsengebäude; ~ **Mail** *n BrE* staatlicher britischer Postdienst, ≈ Deutsche Bundespost *f* (*obs*); ~ **Mint** *n BrE* ECON britische Münzanstalt, ≈ staatliche Münze *f*

royalty *n* ECON Abgabe *f*, GEN COMM *to author, composer* Lizenzgebühr *f*, *to landowner* Abgabe *f*, MEDIA *to author, composer* Tantieme *f*, *print* Gewinnanteil *m*, PATENTS Patentgebühr *f*, Tantieme *f*; ~ **trust** *n* ENVIR Lizenztrust *m*

RP *abbr* COMMS (*radiophone*) Sprechfunkgerät *nt*, FIN, GEN COMM, STOCK (*repurchase agreement*) Rückkaufvereinbarung *f*, Pensionsgeschäft *nt*, Wertpapierpensionsgeschäft *nt*

RPA *abbr BrE* (*Redundancy Payments Act*) HRM britisches Gesetz zur Regelung von Entlassungsabfindungen

RPB *abbr BrE* (*recognized professional body*) FIN anerkannter Berufsverband *m*

RPI *abbr* (*retail price index*) ECON, GEN COMM, S&M Einzelhandelspreisindex *m*

RPM *abbr* FIN, LAW, S&M (*resale price maintenance*) Preisbindung *f* der zweiten Hand, vertikale Preisbindung *f*, (*retail price maintenance*) Wiederverkaufspreisbindung *f*

RRA *abbr BrE* (*Race Relations Act*) HRM, LAW Rassendiskriminierungsverbotsgesetz *nt*

RRIF *abbr* (*registered retirement income fund*) INS ein-

getragene Pensionskasse *f*, eingetragener Altersversorgungsfonds *m*, eingetragener Pensionsfonds *m*

RRP *abbr* (*recommended retail price*) GEN COMM Preisempfehlung *f*, S&M Einzelhandelsrichtpreis *m*, Preisempfehlung *f*, Richtpreis *m* für den Einzelhandel, *not binding* unverbindliche Preisempfehlung *f*

RRR *abbr* (*real rate of return*) BANK, FIN effektive Rendite *f*

RRSP *abbr* (*registered retirement savings plan*) INS eingetragener Pensionssparplan *m*, eingetragener Sparplan *m* für den Ruhestand

RSA *abbr BrE* (*regional selective assistance*) ECON selektive Regionalhilfe *f*

RSG *abbr BrE* (*rate support grant*) ECON Staatszuschuß an die Kommunen, kommunale Finanzausgleichszuweisung

RSI *abbr* (*repetitive strain injury*) HRM, WEL Schäden *m pl* durch wiederholte Belastung

RSVP *abbr* (*répondez s'il vous plaît*) COMMS u.A.w.g. (*um Antwort wird gebeten*)

RT *abbr* (*radiotelephony*) COMMS drahtlose Telefonie *nt*, Funktelegraphie *m*, Sprechfunk *m*

RTBA *abbr* (*rate to be agreed*) TRANSP zu vereinbarender Satz *m*

RTC *abbr AmE* (*Resolution Trust Corporation*) ECON Liquidationsbehörde der US-Bundesregierung

Rt Hon *abbr BrE* (*Right Honourable*) POL Sehr Ehrenwerte(r)

rub: ~ **out** *vt* GEN COMM ausradieren

rubber *n* STOCK Gummi *m*; ~ **stamp** *n* GEN COMM Gummistempel *m*

rubbish *n BrE* (*cf garbage AmE, trash AmE*) ENVIR, GEN COMM Abfall *m*, Müll *m*; ~ **bin** *n BrE* (*cf trashcan AmE*) ENVIR Abfalleimer *m*, Tonne *f*

rubble *n* GEN COMM Schutt *m*

rudder *n* TRANSP *shipping* Ruder *nt*, Steuerruder *nt*

RUF *abbr* (*revolving underwriting facility*) BANK Fazilität, die eine Liquiditätsbeschaffung über die revolvierende Plazierung von Schuldtiteln ermöglicht

rule *n* MGMNT Norm *f*, Regel *f*, Vorschrift *f*, PATENTS Richtlinie *f*, Verfügung *f*, Vorschrift *f*; ◆ **under the** ~ *jarg* STOCK börsenmäßig

rule off *vi* ACC die Bücher abschließen, das Konto abschließen

rule out *vt* GEN COMM *exclude* ausschließen

rule: ~ **book** *n* GEN COMM Arbeitsordnung *f*, Kodex *m*

ruled: ~ **paper** *n* GEN COMM liniertes Papier *nt*

rule: ~ **of law** *n* LAW Rechtsstaatlichkeit *f*

ruler *n* GEN COMM *instrument* Lineal *nt*, POL *of state* Herrscher, in *m,f*

rules *n pl* LAW Statuten *nt pl*; ◆ ~ **versus discretion** ECON Regeln *f pl* versus Entscheidungsfreiheit *f*

rules: ~ **of competition** *n pl* ECON, GEN COMM, LAW Wettbewerbsregeln *f pl*; ~ **of court** *n pl* LAW Verfahrensordnung *f*; ~ **of fair practice** *n pl* STOCK Regeln *f pl* über anständiges Geschäftsgebaren; ~ **of practice** *n pl* LAW Verfahrensordnung *f*; ~ **of procedure** *n pl* LAW Verfahrensordnung *f*, Verfahrensregeln *f pl*; ~ **and regulations** *n pl* LAW Durchführungsbestimmungen *f pl*, Vorschriften *f pl*

rule: ~ **of thumb** *n* GEN COMM Faustregel *f*

ruling *n* LAW Entscheidung *f*; ◆ **give a** ~ **in favor of sb** *AmE*, **give a** ~ **in favour of sb** *BrE* GEN COMM eine

Entscheidung zugunsten von jdm fällen, zugunsten von jdm entscheiden

ruling: ~ **class** *n* GEN COMM herrschende Klasse *f*, privilegierte Klasse *f*; ~ **price** *n* S&M geltender Preis *m*, STOCK Tageskurs *m*, Tagespreis *m*

rummage: ~ **sale** *n AmE* (*cf jumble sale BrE*) S&M Ramschverkauf *m*

rumor *AmE see rumour BrE*

rumour *n BrE* GEN COMM Gerücht *nt*, Gerede *nt*

run 1. *n* IND Durchgang *m*, Durchlauf *m*; **2.** *vt* COMP *program* laufen lassen, GEN COMM *manage* betreiben; ♦ ~ **a business** GEN COMM ein Geschäft betreiben; ~ **a deficit** ECON einen Verlust erwirtschaften, Verlust machen; ~ **an errand** GEN COMM einen Botengang machen; ~ **the risk of** GEN COMM Gefahr laufen, das Risiko eingehen; ~ **a surplus** ECON Gewinn erwirtschaften, Gewinn machen; **3.** *vi* COMP *program* laufen; ♦ ~ **aground** TRANSP *ship* auf Grund laufen, auflaufen, stranden; ~ **ashore** TRANSP *ship* auf Grund laufen, auflaufen, stranden; ~ **into debt** BANK in Schulden *f pl* geraten, verschulden; ~ **empty** TRANSP *bus, train* leer fahren, ohne Passagiere fahren; ~ **short** GEN COMM knapp werden; ~ **with the land** LAW dinglich mit dem Grundstück verbunden sein; ~ **low** STOCK nachlassen; ~ **on time** TRANSP pünktlich verkehren

run back *vi* STOCK zurückgehen

run down *vi* ECON *liquid assets* abbauen, verringern

run on *vi* ACC, BANK, FIN, GEN COMM, STOCK auflaufen

run out *vi* FIN, GEN COMM zu Ende gehen, auslaufen

run up *vt* GEN COMM *incur* machen; ♦ ~ **a debt** BANK Schulden machen, in Schulden geraten, Schulden anhäufen; ~ **a deficit** FIN ein Defizit auflaufen lassen; ~ **an overdraft** BANK Konto überziehen

runaround *n* MEDIA ein Klischee umgebender Text *m*, umlaufender Text *m*

runaway: ~ **industry** *n* IND schnellen Veränderungen unterworfene Industrie *f*; ~ **inflation** *n* ECON galoppierende Inflation *f*; ~ **shop** *n* HRM Unternehmen, das sich durch Standortwechsel gewerkschaftlicher Präsenz entzieht

run: ~-**in** *n* TRANSP *shipping* Einlauf *m*

runner *n* COMMS Bote *m*, Botin, *f*, GEN COMM *messenger* Bote *m*, Botin *f*, *manager* Geschäftsführer, in *m,f*, *tout* Schlepper *m* (*infrml*), HRM Passagiermakler, in *m,f*

running: **be in the** ~ **for** *phr* GEN COMM *promotion* gut im Rennen liegen; **be out of the** ~ *phr* GEN COMM aus dem Rennen sein; ~ **broker** *n* STOCK führender Broker *m*; ~ **cost** *n* ECON *of Civil Service*, GEN COMM laufende Kosten *pl*; ~ **costs** *n pl* FIN Betriebskosten *pl*; ~ **day** *n* (*rd*) TRANSP laufender Kalendertag *m*; ~-**down clause** *n* (*RDC*) INS *marine* Kollisionsklausel *f*; ~ **expense** *n* ACC, FIN, GEN COMM Betriebskosten *pl*, laufende

Ausgaben *f pl*, laufende Kosten *pl*; ~ **hour** *n* TRANSP *shipping* laufende Stunde *f*; ~-**in period** *n* GEN COMM Einfahrzeit *f*, Einlaufzeit *f*; ~ **interest** *n* FIN Stückzinsen *m pl*; ~ **mate** *n* AmE POL Mitkandidat, in *m,f*; ~ **operations** *n pl* ECON laufender Geschäftsbetrieb *m*; **in** ~ **order** *adj* GEN COMM funktionstüchtig; ~ **time** *n* ECON Laufzeit *f*; ~ **total** *n* ACC laufende Summe *f*, GEN COMM laufende Summe *f*, laufender Betrag *m*; ~ **workday** *n AmE* (*cf running working day BrE*) TRANSP laufender Arbeitstag *m*; ~ **working day** *BrE* (*cf running workday AmE*) *n* TRANSP laufender Arbeitstag *m*; ~ **yield** *n* ECON Umlaufrendite *f*

run: ~-**off** *n* INS Auslauf *m*, Abwicklung *f*, POL Stichwahl *f*; ~-**off election** *n* POL Stichwahl *f*; ~-**off primary** *n AmE* POL endgültige Präsidentschaftsvorwahl *f*; ~-**of-the-mill** *adj* GEN COMM gewöhnlich, durchschnittlich, Routine-, Standard-; ~ **on a bank** *n* BANK Ansturm *m* auf eine Bank, Bankrun *m*; ~ **on the banks** *n* BANK Ansturm *m* auf die Banken, Run *m* auf die Banken; ~ **on the dollar** *n* GEN COMM starke Dollarnachfrage *f*; ~ **of paper** *n* (*ROP*) MEDIA *print run* Papierverlauf *m*, S&M *advertising* Ausgabe *f* einer Zeitung

runtime *n* COMP *program* Laufzeit *f*

run: ~-**up** *n* GEN COMM *elections* Vorfeld *nt*, STOCK Steigerung *f*; ♦ **in the** ~-**up to** GEN COMM *elections* im Vorfeld von

runway *n* TRANSP Ablaufbahn *f*, Landebahn *f*, Rollbahn *f*, Startbahn *f*

rural: ~ **area** *n* ECON ländlicher Raum *m*, ländliches Gebiet *nt*; ~ **community** *n* ECON Gemeinde *f* im ländlichen Raum, ländliche Gemeinde *f*

Rural: ~ **Community Council** *n BrE* (*RCC*) POL ländliche Gemeindeverwaltung

rural: ~ **delivery service** *n AmE* (*RDS*) COMMS freie Zustellung *f* in ländlichen Gebieten

Rural: ~ **Development Area** *n BrE* (*RDA*) ECON ländliches Entwicklungsgebiet *nt*, ländliches Fördergebiet *nt*

rural: ~ **sector** *n* IND landwirtschaftlicher Sektor *m*

rush 1. *n* S&M Andrang *m*; **2.** *vi* GEN COMM eilen

rush: ~ **hour** *n* GEN COMM Feierabendverkehr *m*; ~ **job** *n* GEN COMM Eilauftrag *m*, vordringlicher Auftrag *m*; ~ **on the dollar** *n* BANK lebhafte Dollarnachfrage *f*; ~ **order** *n* ECON, GEN COMM Eilauftrag *m*

rustbelt *n AmE* IND altes Industriegebiet *nt*, Rostgürtel *m*

rusty *adj* GEN COMM *person* aus der Übung

RW *abbr* GEN COMM (*reduced weight*) reduziertes Gewicht *nt*, IND (*riveted and welded*) genietet und geschweißt

Rws *abbr* (*round-the-world service*) TRANSP *shipping* Weltweit-Service *m*

Rybczynski: ~ **theorem** *n* ECON Rybczynski-Theorem *nt*

S

s/a *abbr* (*safe arrival*) TRANSP sichere Ankunft *f*

sack 1. *vt BrE infrml* HRM entlassen, rausschmeißen (*infrml*), feuern (*infrml*), hinauswerfen (*infrml*); **2.** *n BrE infrml* HRM Entlassung *f*, Rausschmiß *m* (*infrml*); ◆ **get the** ~ *BrE infrml* HRM gekündigt werden, rausgeschmissen werden (*infrml*); **give sb the** ~ *BrE infrml* HRM jdn entlassen, jdn rausschmeißen (*infrml*), jdn an die Luft setzen (*infrml*)

sacrifice 1. *n* INS Verzicht *m*; **2.** *vt* INS aufgeben, verzichten auf [+acc]

sacrifice: ~ **theory** *n* ECON Opfertheorie *f*

SAD *abbr* ADMIN, IMP/EXP, TRANSP (*single administrative document*) EU Einheitsformular *nt*, Einzelverwaltungsdokument *nt*

saddle: ~ **point** *n* ECON *game theory* Kreuzungspunkt *m*, Sattelpunkt *m*

s.a.e. *abbr BrE* (*stamped addressed envelope*) COMMS frankierter Rückumschlag *m*, freigemachter Rückumschlag *m*

SAEF *abbr BrE* (*SEAQ Automated Execution Facility*) STOCK Teil des elektronischen Börsenhandels- und Quotierungssystems der Londoner Börse

SAF *abbr* (*structural adjustment facility*) FIN Strukturanpassungsfazilität *f*

safe 1. *adj* BANK, ECON, FIN sicher; ◆ **be on the** ~ **side** GEN COMM auf Nummer Sicher gehen; **2.** *n* BANK Tresor *m*, Panzerschrank *m*, Safe *m or nt*

safe: ~ **arrival** *n* (*s/a*) TRANSP sichere Ankunft *f*; ~ **asset** *n* FIN sicherer Vermögenswert *m*; ~ **berth** *n* TRANSP *shipping* sicherer Liegeplatz *m*; ~ **custody department** *n* BANK Depotverwahrung *f*; ~-deposit box *n* BANK Schließfach *nt*; ~ **deposit fee** *n* BANK Safemiete *f*, FIN Aufbewahrungsgebühr *f*; ~ **deposit vault** *n* BANK Tresor *m*; ~ **estimate** *n* GEN COMM vorsichtige Schätzung *f*

safeguard 1. *n* LAW *clause* Schutzklausel *f*; **2.** *vt* GEN COMM *assets* sichern, *secret* schützen; **3.** *vi* ◆ ~ **against inflation** ECON gegen Inflation sichern

safeguarding *n* GEN COMM Sicherung *f*; ~ **of jobs** *n* HRM Arbeitsplatzsicherung *f*

safe: ~ **harbor rule** *AmE*, ~ **harbour rule** *BrE n* TAX gesetzliche Bestimmung, die entweder rechtlich zulässige Formen der Steuervermeidung oder einen Verkauf von Steuervergünstigungen vorsieht; ~ **hedge** *n* STOCK Absicherung *f*, Sicherungsgeschäft *nt*; ~ **investment** *n* BANK sichere Anlage *f*

safekeeper *n* BANK, LAW Verwahrer, in *m,f*

safekeeping *n* BANK, LAW Verwahrung *f*, Aufbewahrung *f*; ~ **of assets** *n* BANK Depotverwahrung *f* von Vermögenswerten

safe: ~ **port** *n* TRANSP sicherer Hafen *m*

safety *n* GEN COMM Sicherheit *f*; ~ **at work** *n* HRM Sicherheit *f* am Arbeitsplatz; ~ **belt** *n* TRANSP Sicherheitsgurt *m*; ~ **check** *n* GEN COMM Sicherheitsprüfung *f*; ~ **code** *n* GEN COMM Sicherheitskodex *m*, Sicherheitsvorschriften *f pl*

Safety: ~ **Commission** *n AmE* WEL *government sector* Arbeitsschutzkomitee *nt*, Sicherheitsausschuß *m*;

~ **Committee** *n AmE* WEL *private sector* Arbeitsschutzkomitee *nt*, Sicherheitsausschuß *m*

safety: ~ **deposit bank** *n* BANK Bank mit mietbaren Schließfächern; ~ **deposit box** *n* BANK Bankschließfach *nt*, Safe *m or nt*, Tresorfach *nt*; ~ **engineer** *n* GEN COMM Sicherheitsingenieur, in *m,f*, Sicherheitstechniker, in *m,f*; ~ **equipment** *n* GEN COMM Schutzausrüstung *f*; ~ **equipment certificate** *n* IND Sicherheitszertifikat *nt*; ~ **hazard** *n* GEN COMM Sicherheitsrisiko *nt*; ~ **management** *n* HRM, MGMNT Sicherheitsmanagement *nt*, Sicherheitsverwaltung *f*; ~ **margin** *n* ACC Differenz *f* zwischen Anleihenennwert und Beleihungswert, Sicherheitsspanne *f*, GEN COMM Sicherheitsgrenze *f*; ~ **measure** *n* GEN COMM Sicherheitsmaßnahme *f*; ~ **officer** *n* HRM Sicherheitsbeauftragte(r) *mf* [decl. as adj]; ~ **precaution** *n* GEN COMM Schutzmaßnahme *f*, Sicherheitsvorkehrung *f*; ~ **regulations** *n pl* GEN COMM Sicherheitsbestimmungen *f pl*, Sicherheitsvorschriften *f pl*; ~ **representative** *n* HRM Industrieschutzbeauftragte(r) *mf* [decl. as adj]; ~ **requirement** *n* IND *for products* sicherheitstechnische Anforderung *f*; ~ **standard** *n* GEN COMM, IND Sicherheitsstandard *m*, Sicherheitsnorm *f*; ~ **stock** *n* GEN COMM Sicherheitsbestand *m*, IND Mindestbestand *m*, Mindestlagerbestand *m*; ~ **vault** *n* BANK Stahlkammer *f*; ~ **violation** *n* LAW Verletzung *f* der Sicherheitsvorschriften

safe: ~ **working load** *n* IND Höchstlast *f*, zulässige Arbeitsbelastung *f*, zulässige Beanspruchung *f*

sag *vi* BANK, S&M, STOCK *prices, rates* abschwächen, nachgeben, sinken

sagging 1. *adj* BANK, S&M, STOCK *prices, rates* nachgebend; **2.** *n* BANK, S&M, STOCK *of prices, rates* Nachgeben *nt*

sailing *n* TRANSP Abfahrt *f*, Auslaufen *nt*; ~ **card** *n* TRANSP Segelwindrose *f*, Verladeanweisung *f*; ~ **date** *n* (*S/D*) TRANSP Abfahrtsdatum *nt*; ~ **schedule** *n* TRANSP Fahrplan *m*

sailor *n* HRM, TRANSP Seemann *m*

salable *AmE see* saleable *BrE*

salaried: ~ **agent** *n* HRM Handelsvertreter, in *m,f* mit Festgehalt; ~ **employee** *n* GEN COMM Angestellte(r) *mf* [decl. as adj], Gehaltsempfänger, in *m,f*; ~ **person** *n* HRM Gehaltsempfänger, in *m,f*; ~ **staff** *n* HRM Gehaltsempfänger *m pl*

salaries: ~ **and wages** *n pl* ECON, HRM *paid by employer* Löhne *m pl* und Gehälter *nt pl*; ~**, wages and fringe benefits** *n pl* ECON, HRM *paid by employer* Löhne *m pl*, Gehälter *nt pl* und Nebenleistungen *f pl*

salary *n* GEN COMM, HRM *monthly* Gehalt *nt*, *yearly* Jahresgehalt *nt*; ◆ ~ **to be negotiated** HRM Gehalt nach Vereinbarung

salary: ~ **adjustment** *n* HRM Gehaltsanpassung *f*; ~ **adjustment reserve allotment** *n* (*SARA*) ACC, HRM Rücklagenzuweisung *f* für Gehaltserhöhungen; ~ **advance** *n* HRM Gehaltsvorschuß *m*; ~ **base** *n* HRM Gehaltsgrundlage *f*; ~ **bracket** *n* HRM Gehaltsgruppe *f*; ~ **deduction** *n* ACC, HRM Gehaltsabzug *m*; ~ **demands** *n pl* HRM Gehaltsforderung *f*; ~ **earner** *n* HRM

Gehaltsempfänger, in *m,f*; ~ **grade** *n* HRM Gehaltsstufe *f*, Gehaltsklasse *f*, Besoldungsgruppe *f*; ~ **increase** *n* HRM Gehaltserhöhung *f*; ~ **payment** *n* HRM Gehaltszahlung *f*; ~ **progression curve** *n* HRM Gehaltsentwicklungskurve *f*; ~ **rate** *n* HRM Besoldungssatz *m*; ~ **reduction plan** *n* HRM Gehaltssenkungsplan *m*; ~ **review** *n* HRM Gehaltsüberprüfung *f*, Gehaltsrevision *f*; ~ **sacrifice scheme** *n* BrE TAX Gehaltsverzichtplan *m*; ~ **scale** *n* HRM Gehaltsskala *f*; ~ **scheme** *n* HRM Gehaltssystem *nt*; ~ **structure** *n* ECON, HRM Gehaltsstruktur *f*

sale *n* LAW, PROP *alienation* Veräußerung *f*, S&M *act of selling* Verkauf *m*, *transaction* Geschäft *nt*, Abschluß *m*, *at reduced prices* Ausverkauf *m*; ♦ **for** ~ S&M zu verkaufen; **not for** ~ S&M unverkäuflich; ~ **as is** GEN COMM Tel quel; **on** ~ **or return** S&M Kauf *m* mit Rückgaberecht; ~ **subject to safe arrival** S&M einwandfreier Erhalt als Voraussetzung für Verkauf; ~ **with all faults** GEN COMM Tel quel

saleable *adj* BrE LAW, PROP veräußerlich, S&M *fit for selling* verkäuflich, *marketable* marktfähig

sale: ~ **at auction** *n* ACC, S&M Auktion *f*; ~ **by auction** *n* S&M Verkauf *m* durch Versteigerung; ~ **by court order** *n* LAW Zwangsversteigerung *f*; ~ **by tender** *n* S&M Submissionsverkauf *m*; ~ **commission** *n* S&M Verkaufsprämie *f*, Verkaufsprovision *f*; ~ **for delivery** *n* STOCK Verkauf *m* zur Lieferung; ~ **of goods** *n* S&M Verkauf *m* von Waren; ~ **and leaseback** *n* GEN COMM Verkauf *m* mit anschließender Rückmiete; ~ **on approval** *n* S&M Kauf *m* auf Probe; ~ **on commission** *n* S&M Kommissionsgeschäft *nt*; ~ **or exchange** *n* S&M Verkauf *m* mit Umtauschrecht; ~ **or return** *n* S&M Kauf *m* mit Rückgaberecht; ~ **price** *n* S&M Ausverkaufspreis *m*; ~ **and purchase agreement** *n* STOCK Pensionsgeschäft *nt*

sales *n pl* S&M Absatz *m*, *turnover* Umsatz *m*; ~ **account** *n* S&M Verkaufskonto *nt*, Warenausgangskonto *nt*; ~ **activity** *n* S&M Absatzaktivität *f*, Verkauftätigkeit *f*; ~ **agency** *n* S&M Verkaufsagentur *f*, Verkaufsniederlassung *f*; ~ **agent** *n* HRM, S&M Handelsvertreter, in *m,f*, Verkaufsagent, in *m,f*; ~ **aid** *n* S&M Verkaufshilfe *f*; ~ **analysis** *n* S&M Verkaufsanalyse *f*; ~ **analyst** *n* S&M Absatzanalytiker *m*, Umsatzanalyst *m*; ~ **appeal** *n* S&M Kaufanreiz *m*; ~ **approach** *n* S&M Verkaufspolitik *f*; ~ **area** *n* S&M *in store* Verkaufsbereich *m*, *territory* Verkaufsgebiet *nt*; ~ **book** *n* S&M Warenverkaufsbuch *nt*; ~ **budget** *n* S&M Verkaufsetat *m*; ~ **call** *n* S&M Vertreterbesuch *m*; ~ **campaign** *n* S&M Verkaufsaktion *f*, Verkaufskampagne *f*; ~ **charge** *n* S&M Abschlußgebühr *f*, STOCK Abschlußgebühr *f*, Ankaufgebühren *f pl*; ~ **clerk** *n* AmE (*cf shop assistant BrE*) HRM, S&M Verkäufer, in *m,f*; ~ **conference** *n* S&M Absatzgremium *nt*; ~ **contest** *n* S&M Verkaufswettbewerb *m*; ~ **contract** *n* S&M Kaufvertrag *m*; ~ **control** *n* S&M Verkaufskontrolle *f*; ~ **costs** *n pl* S&M Vertriebskosten *pl*; ~ **coverage** *n* S&M Verkaufsreichweite *f*; ~ **department** *n* S&M Verkauf *m*, Verkaufsabteilung *f*; ~ **development costs** *n pl* ACC, INS, S&M Akquisitionskosten *pl*; ~ **director** *n* HRM, MGMNT, S&M Vertriebsdirektor, in *m,f*, Verkaufsleiter, in *m,f*, Verkaufschef, in *m,f*; ~ **discount** *n* S&M Kundenrabatt *m*; ~ **drive** *n* S&M Hochdruckverkauf *m*; ~ **effectiveness test** *n* S&M Verkaufswirksamkeitstest *m*; ~ **effort** *n* S&M Verkaufsanstrengungen *f pl*; ~ **engineer** *n* HRM Vertriebsingenieur *m*; ~ **enquiry** *n* S&M Verkaufs-

umfrage *f*; ~ **estimate** *n* S&M Umsatzschätzung *f*; ~ **executive** *n* HRM, MGMNT, S&M Führungskraft *f* im Verkauf, Verkaufsdirektor, in *m,f*, Vertriebsdirektor, in *m,f*, Verkaufsleiter, in *m,f*, Vertriebsleiter, in *m,f*; ~ **feature** *n* S&M Verkaufsmerkmal *nt*; ~ **figures** *n pl* S&M Absatzzahlen *f pl*; ~ **folder** *n* S&M Verkaufsordner *m*; ~ **force** *n* S&M Absatzorganisation *f*, Verkaufspersonal *nt*; ~ **forecast** *n* S&M Absatzprognose *f*, Verkaufsvoraussage *f*; ~ **goal** *n* S&M Absatzziel *nt*; ~ **goods** *n pl* S&M Verkaufsgüter *nt pl*

Sales: ~ **of Goods Act** *n* BrE 1979 LAW Gesetz über den Warenverkauf

sales: ~ **incentive** *n* S&M Kaufanreiz *m*; ~ **interview** *n* S&M Verkaufsinterview *nt*; ~ **invoice** *n* S&M Verkaufsrechnung *f*; ~ **journal** *n* S&M Warenausgangsbuch *nt*; ~ **kit** *n* S&M Verkaufsausrüstung *f*; ~ **lead** *n* S&M *competition* Verkaufsvorsprung *m*; ~ **leaflet** *n* S&M Werbeflugblatt *nt*; ~ **ledger** *n* ACC Verkaufskontenbuch *nt*, Debitorenbuch *nt*, Kundenbuch *nt*; ~ **letter** *n* S&M Werbeschreiben *nt*; ~ **literature** *n* S&M Verkaufsprospekt *m*, Werbematerial *nt*

salesman *n* GEN COMM Kaufmann *m*, HRM, S&M Verkäufer *m*, Vertreter *m*

sales: ~ **management** *n* S&M Absatzleitung *f*, Vertriebsleitung *f*, Verkaufsmanagement *nt*; ~ **manager** *n* HRM, MGMNT, S&M Verkaufsdirektor, in *m,f*, Verkaufsleiter, in *m,f*, Verkaufschef, in *m,f*, Vertriebsdirektor, in *m,f*, Vertriebsleiter, in *m,f*, Vertriebschef, in *m,f*

salesmanship *n* S&M Verkaufsgewandtheit *f*, Verkaufstalent *nt*

sales: ~ **manual** *n* S&M Verkaufshandbuch *nt*; ~ **maximization** *n* S&M Absatzmaximierung *f*; ~ **meeting** *n* S&M Vertretertagung *f*; ~ **mix** *n* S&M Absatzmix *m*, Absatzprogramm *nt*; ~ **network** *n* S&M Absatznetz *nt*; ~ **objective** *n* S&M Umsatzziel *nt*, Verkaufsziel *nt*; ~ **offensive** *n* S&M Verkaufsoffensive *f*; ~ **office** *n* S&M Verkaufsbüro *nt*; ~ **office manager** *n* S&M Verkaufsstellenleiter, in *m,f*; ~ **opportunity** *n* S&M Absatzmöglichkeit *f*; ~ **order** *n* GEN COMM Auftrag *m*; ~ **organization** *n* S&M Verkaufsorganisation *f*; ~ **orientation** *n* S&M Verkaufsorientierung *f*; ~ **outlet** *n* S&M Verkaufsstelle *f*; ~ **penetration** *n* S&M Marktdurchdringung *f*

salesperson *n* HRM, S&M Verkäufer, in *m,f*, Vertreter, in *m,f*

sales: ~ **personnel** *n* S&M Verkaufspersonal *nt*; ~ **pitch** *n* S&M Verkaufsargument *nt*; ~ **planning** *n* S&M Verkaufsplanung *f*; ~ **platform** *n* S&M Verkaufsprogramm *nt*; ~ **policy** *n* S&M Absatzpolitik *f*, Verkaufspolitik *f*, Vertriebspolitik *f*; ~ **portfolio** *n* S&M Salesportfolio *nt*, Verkaufsbestand *m*, Verkaufsportefeuille *nt*; ~ **potential** *n* S&M Verkaufspotential *nt*; ~ **presentation** *n* S&M Produktpräsentation *f*; ~ **projection** *n* S&M Absatzplan *m*; ~ **promotion** *n* S&M Verkaufsförderung *f*; ~ **prospects** *n pl* S&M Verkaufsaussichten *f pl*; ~ **push** *n* S&M Verkaufsanstrengungen *f pl*; ~ **quota** *n* S&M Verkaufskontingent *nt*; ~ **receipt** *n* S&M Verkaufserlös *m*; ~ **record** *n* S&M Kassenbeleg *m*, Verkaufserfolg *m*; ~ **rep** *n* infrml (*sales representative*) HRM, S&M Handelsvertreter, in *m,f*, Verkaufsvertreter, in *m,f*, Vertreter, in *m,f*; ~ **representative** *n* (*rep, sales rep*) HRM, S&M Handelsvertreter, in *m,f*, Verkaufsvertreter, in *m,f*, Vertreter, in *m,f*, Reisende(r) *mf* [decl. as adj]; ~ **research** *n* S&M Verkaufsforschung *f*; ~ **resistance** *n* S&M Kaufunlust *f*, Verkaufswiderstand *m*; ~ **returns** *n pl* S&M *unsold items* Retouren *f pl*, Rücksendungen *f pl*, Rückwaren *f pl*, *profits* Verkaufserlöse *m pl*; ~ **revenue** *n* ACC Umsatzertrag *m*, S&M Gesamtverkaufseinnahmen *f pl*, Umsatzerlös *m*; ~ **service** *n* S&M Kundendienst *m*; ~ **slip** *n* GEN COMM Kassenbon *m*, *cash register, receipt* Kassenzettel *m*; ~ **slump** *n* S&M rückläufige Verkaufsergebnisse *nt pl*; ~ **strategy** *n* S&M Verkaufsstrategie *f*; ~ **talk** *n* S&M Verkaufsgespräch *nt*; ~ **target** *n* S&M Absatzziel *nt*, Verkaufsziel *nt*; ~ **technique** *n* S&M Verkaufstechnik *f*; ~ **territory** *n* S&M Absatzgebiet *nt*; ~ **test** *n* S&M Testmarktaktion *f*, Werbetest *m*; ~ **tools** *n pl* S&M Verkaufsinstrumente *nt pl*; ~ **training** *n* S&M Verkaufsschulung *f*; ~ **turnover** *n* S&M Warenumsatz *m*; ~ **volume** *n* S&M Verkaufsvolumen *nt*

saleswoman *n* HRM, S&M Verkäuferin *f*, Vertreterin *f*

sale: ~ **under an execution** *n* LAW Zwangsversteigerung *f*; ~ **value** *n* S&M Verkaufswert *m*

Salt Lake City: ~ **Stock Exchange** *n* STOCK Salt Lake City Wertpapierbörse

salvage *n* TRANSP *shipping* Bergen *nt*, Bergung *f*; ~ **agreement** *n* TRANSP *shipping* Bergungsvertrag *m*; ~ **bond** *n* STOCK Restanleihe *f*; ~ **charges** *n pl* (*sc*) TRANSP *shipping* Bergungskosten *pl*; ~ **goods** *n pl* INS Strandgut *nt*; ~ **loss** *n* INS Bergungsverlust *m*; ~ **value** *n* ECON Restwert *m*, Schrottwert *m*, Veräußerungswert *m*

salvor *n* TRANSP *shipping* Berger *m*

same: ~~**day** *adj* IMP/EXP, TRANSP *postal, courier service* taggleich; ~~**day delivery** *n* COMMS, TRANSP Lieferung *f* am gleichen Tage, Sofortlieferung *f*; ~~**day service** *n* COMMS, TRANSP 24-Stunden-Service *m*; ~ **size** *n* S&M gleiche Größe *f*

sample *n* COMP Probe *f*, GEN COMM Muster *nt*, Musterkarte *f*, Handelsmuster *nt*, MATH *statistics* Sample *nt*, Stichprobe *f*; ~ **audit** *n* ACC Probebuchprüfung *f*, Proberevision *f*; ~ **card** *n* GEN COMM Musterkarte *f*, Probekarte *f*; ~ **case** *n* S&M Musterkoffer *m*; ~ **data** *n pl* COMP Probedaten *pl*; ~ **drawing** *n* MATH *statistics* Stichprobenentnahme *f*; ~ **licence** *BrE*, ~ **license** *AmE n* IMP/EXP Musterlizenz *f*, Zollpapiere *nt pl* für vorübergehende Ausfuhr; ~ **mailing** *n* COMMS Mustersendung *f*; ~ **mean** *n* MATH *statistics* Stichprobendurchschnitt *m*; ~ **rate** *n* COMMS Tarif *m* für Mustersendung; ~ **study** *n* S&M *market research* Teilerhebung *f*; ~ **survey** *n* S&M *market research* Teilerhebung *f*

sampling: ~ **by attributes** *n* IND Attributenkontrolle *f*; ~ **deviation** *n* MATH *statistics* Stichprobenabweichung *f*; ~ **error** *n* MATH *statistics* Stichprobenfehler *m*; ~ **frame** *n* MATH *statistics* Stichprobenrahmen *m*; ~ **grid** *n* MATH *statistics* Stichprobengitter *nt*; ~ **offer** *n* GEN COMM Musterangebot *nt*; ~ **point** *n* S&M Auswahleinheit *f* der ersten Stufe, Stichprobenpunkt *m*; ~ **variance** *n* MATH *statistics* Varianz *f* der Stichprobe

sanction 1. *n* ECON *measure taken* Sanktion *f*, GEN COMM *approval* Zustimmung *f*, Billigung *f*, LAW *measure taken* Sanktion *f*; **2.** *vt* GEN COMM *approve* sanktionieren

s&c *abbr* (*shipper and carrier*) IMP/EXP, TRANSP Befrachter und Beförderer *m*

S&FA *abbr* (*shipping and forwarding agent*) HRM, IMP/EXP, TRANSP Schiffsmakler und Spediteur *m*

S&H/exct *abbr* (*Sundays and holidays excepted*) GEN COMM außer an Sonn- und Feiertagen, Sonn- und Feiertage ausgenommen

S&L *abbr AmE* (*savings and loan association*) FIN Spar- und Darlehensverein, ≈ Bausparkasse *f*

sandwich: ~ **board** *n* S&M Brust- und Rückenplakat *nt*; ~ **lease** *n infrml* PROP Sandwich-Leasing *nt* (*infrml*)

sansserif 1. *adj* COMP, MEDIA *typography* serifenlos; **2.** *n* COMP, MEDIA *typeface* serifenlose Schrift *f*, *character* serifenloser Buchstabe *m*

SARA *abbr* (*salary adjustment reserve allotment*) HRM Rücklagenzuweisung *f* für Gehaltserhöhungen

s.a.s.e. *abbr* (*self-addressed stamped envelope*) COMMS frankierter Rückumschlag *m*, freigemachter Rückumschlag *m*

satellite *n* COMMS, COMP, MEDIA Satellit *m*; ~ **broadcasting** *n* MEDIA Satellitübertragung *f*; ~ **communication** *n* COMMS Satellitenverbindung *f*; ~ **communications** *n pl* COMMS Satellitenkommunikation *f*, Satellitenverkehr *m*; ~ **computer** *n* COMP Satellitenrechner *m*; ~ **television** *n* MEDIA Satellitenfernsehen *nt*; ~ **town** *n* ECON, PROP, WEL Satellitenstadt *f*, Trabantenstadt *f*

satisfaction *n* ACC Tilgung *f*, FIN *of debt* Tilgung *f*, Zahlung *f*, GEN COMM *contentedness* Befriedigung *f*, Nutzen *m*, Zufriedenheit *f*, Zufriedenstellung *f*; ◆ **in ~ of** ACC zur Erfüllung von

satisfaction: ~ **of a debt** *n* FIN Schuldentilgung *f*, Tilgung *f* einer Schuld; ~ **level** *n* ECON Nutzenniveau *nt*; ~ **of wants** *n* MGMNT Bedürfnisbefriedigung *f*

satisfactory *adj* GEN COMM befriedigend, zufriedenstellend

satisfied *adj* GEN COMM zufrieden

satisfy *vt* FIN *debt* tilgen; GEN COMM *requirement* zufriedenstellen, befriedigen, abgelten; ◆ ~ **the demand for sth** GEN COMM den Bedarf an etw decken

saturate *vt* ECON, S&M *market* sättigen

saturation *n* ECON, S&M *of market* Sättigung *f*; ~ **campaign** *n* S&M *advertising* Sättigungskampagne *f*; ~ **point** *n* ECON, S&M Sättigungspunkt *m*

save 1. *vt* COMP *data* sichern, GEN COMM *money* sparen, *materials, costs* einsparen; ◆ ~ **energy** ENVIR Energie sparen; **2.** *vi* GEN COMM sparen; ◆ ~ **as you earn** *BrE* (*SAYE*) ECON staatlich gefördertes Prämiensparsystem in Großbritannien; ~ **for a rainy day** GEN COMM etw auf die hohe Kante legen (*infrml*), einen Notgroschen zurücklegen

save up 1. *vt* GEN COMM sparen; **2.** *vi* GEN COMM sparen

saving *n* GEN COMM *of money* Sparen *nt*, *of materials, costs* Einsparung *f*, *amount saved* Ersparnis *nt*; ~ **clause** *n* LAW Vorbehaltsklausel *f*

savings *n pl* BANK Spareinlagen *f pl*; ~ **bank** *n* BANK Sparkasse *f*; ~ **bond** *n* *AmE* BANK Sparbrief *m*; ~ **certificate** *n* BANK Sparbrief *m*; ~ **deposit** *n* BANK Spareinlage *f*, Spargeld *nt*; ~ **function** *n* ECON Sparfunktion *f*; ~~**linked** *adj* GEN COMM mit Ersparnissen verbunden, mit Spareinlagen verbunden, Ersparnis-; ~ **and loan association** *n AmE* (*S&L*) FIN Spar- und Darlehensverein, ≈ Bausparkasse *f*; ~ **ratio** *n* ECON Sparquote *f*; ~~**to-income ratio** *n* ECON Sparquote *f*, FIN Verhältnis *nt* zwischen Ersparnissen und Einkommen

sawbuck *n AmE* GEN COMM Zehn-Dollar-Schein

SAYE *abbr BrE* (*save as you earn*) ECON staatlich gefördertes Prämiensparsystem in Großbritannien

Say: ~'s **law** *n* ECON Saysches Theorem *nt*

say: **have a ~ in sth** *phr infrml* GEN COMM bei etw Mitspracherecht haben, bei etw ein Wörtchen mitzureden haben; **that is to ~** *phr* GEN COMM das heißt (*d.h.*)

SB *abbr* (*short bill*) FIN kurzfristig fälliger Wechsel *m*

SBA *abbr AmE* (*small business administration*) GEN COMM US-Bundesbehörde für Mittelstandsbetriebe

SBDB *abbr* (*small business development bond*) GEN COMM Investitionskredit *m* für kleine und mittlere Betriebe

sc *abbr* (*salvage charges*) TRANSP *shipping* Bergungskosten *pl*

scab *n BrE infrml* GEN COMM, HRM, IND Streikbrecher, in *m,f*; ~ **union** *n BrE infrml* HRM *industrial relations* arbeitgeberfreundliche Gewerkschaft *f*

scalar: ~ **organization** *n* MGMNT Skalarorganisation *f*; ~ **principle** *n* HRM Skalarprinzip *nt*

scale 1. *n* GEN COMM Maßstab *m*, Skala *f*, Umfang *m*; **2.** *vt* ◆ ~ **the ladder** HRM die Leiter erklimmen; ~ **back expectations** GEN COMM die Erwartungen zurücknehmen

scale down *vt* GEN COMM maßstäblich verkleinern, verkleinern, verringern, STOCK repartieren, zuteilen

scale up *vt* GEN COMM aufstocken, maßstäblich vergrößern

scale: ~ **charge** *n* TAX tarifliche Abgabe *f*, Gebühr *f* nach Tarif; ~ **of charges** *n* GEN COMM Gebührenordnung *f*, Gebührentabelle *f*, Tarif *m*; ~ **of commission** *n* STOCK Provisionstabelle *f*; ~ **economies** *n pl* ECON Größenvorteile *m pl*; ~ **fee** *n* LAW Gebühr *f* nach Gebührenordnung; ~ **platform** *n* TRANSP Brückenwaage *f*

scaling: ~-**down** *n* GEN COMM, HRM, MGMNT *of workforce* Abbau *m*, Verkleinerung *f*, Verringerung *f*; ~-**up** *n* GEN COMM Aufstockung *f*

scalp *vi* STOCK *futures market* für kleine Kursgewinne handeln

scalper *n* STOCK *securities* Spekulant *m* in Terminkontrakten

scamp 1. *n* S&M *advertising* Designentwurf *m*; **2.** *vt* GEN COMM *work* schludrige Arbeit leisten (*infrml*), schludrig arbeiten (*infrml*)

scan *vt* COMP abtasten, scannen

scan: ~ **area** *n* COMP Abtastbereich *m*

scanner *n* COMP Abtastgerät *nt*, Scanner *m*, elektronischer Belegleser *m*

scanning *n* COMP Abtasten *nt*, Abtastung *f*, Scannen *nt*

scant: ~ **coverage** *n* MEDIA geringe Deckung *f*, knappe Deckung *f*

scarce *adj* ECON *resources* knapp; ◆ **in ~ supply** GEN COMM bei geringem Angebot

scarcity *n* ECON Knappheit *f*, Mangel *m*; ~ **index** *n* ECON Knappheitsindex *m*; ~ **value** *n* ECON Seltenheitswert *m*

scare: ~ **buying** *n* S&M Angstkäufe *m pl*

scaremongering *n* FIN, MEDIA, STOCK Panikmache *f* (*infrml*)

scare: ~ **tactics** *n pl* FIN, MEDIA, STOCK Panikmacherei *f*

scatter *n* MATH Streuung *f*; ~ **diagram** *n* MATH *statistics*, MGMNT Streudiagramm *nt*

scattergram *n* MATH *statistics*, MGMNT Streudiagramm *nt*

scavenger: ~ **sale** *n infrml* PROP Immobilie, die wegen Nichtzahlung von Miete zum Verkauf steht

SCC *abbr* (*single column centimeter AmE, single column centimetre BrE*) MEDIA Einzelspaltenzentimeter *m*

scenario *n* MEDIA *of film, play* Drehbuch *nt*, MGMNT *prediction of events* Szenario *nt*; ~-**writing** *n* MGMNT Verfassen *nt* eines Szenarios

sceptic *n BrE* GEN COMM Skeptiker, in *m,f*

sceptical *adj BrE* GEN COMM skeptisch

scepticism *n BrE* GEN COMM Skeptizismus *m*, zweifelnde Haltung *f*

schedular: ~ **tax** *n BrE* TAX Schedulensteuer *f*

schedule 1. *n* GEN COMM *programme of events* Plan *m*, Programm *nt*, Zeitplan *m*, *AmE list* Liste *f*, Verzeichnis *nt*, Aufstellung *f*, TRANSP *timetable* Fahrplan *m*; ◆ **on ~** GEN COMM planmäßig, termingerecht; **be on ~** GEN COMM im Plan liegen, im Zeitplan liegen; **2.** *vt* GEN COMM *programme* planen, festlegen, *AmE list* auflisten, tabellarisch zusammenstellen

schedule: ~ **of assets** *n AmE* ACC Vermögensaufstellung *f*

scheduled *adj* GEN COMM planmäßig, zeitlich geplant; ◆ **be ~ for** GEN COMM *meeting* anberaumt sein für

scheduled: ~ **arrival** *n* TRANSP planmäßige Ankunft *f*; ~ **departure** *n* TRANSP planmäßige Abfahrt *f*; ~ **flight** *n* LEIS, TRANSP Linienflug *m*; ~ **service** *n* LEIS, TRANSP Liniendienst *m*; ~ **start** *n* GEN COMM vorgesehener Beginn *m*

schedule: ~ **of job operations** *n* IND Arbeitsplan *m*

scheduling *n* GEN COMM *programming* Ablaufplanung *f*, Planung *f*, *AmE listing* Auflistung *f*, Terminierung *f*, Zeitplanung *f*

Schengen: ~ **Agreement** *n* POL *EU* Schengen-Abkommen *nt*

school: ~ **fees** *n pl* WEL Schulgeld *nt*

schooling *n* HRM Schulausbildung *f*, schulische Ausbildung *f*

school: ~ **leaver** *n BrE* HRM Schulabgänger, in *mf*

SCI *abbr* (*single column inch*) MEDIA Einzelspaltenzoll *m*

science: ~ **of business management** *n* MGMNT Betriebswirtschaft *f*, Betriebswirtschaftslehre *f*; ~ **park** *n* IND Technologiepark *m*

scientific *adj* GEN COMM wissenschaftlich; ~ **management** *n* GEN COMM, MGMNT Betriebswissenschaft *f*, wissenschaftliche Arbeitsorganisation *f*, wissenschaftliche Betriebsführung *f*, wissenschaftliches Management *nt*; ~ **programming** *n* COMP, MATH wissenschaftliches Programmieren *nt*; ~ **research expenditure** *n BrE* ACC, TAX *capital allowances* Aufwand *m* für wissenschaftliche Forschung, Forschungsaufwand *m*

scientist *n* HRM Wissenschaftler, in *m,f*

scion *n* LAW Nachkomme *m*

Scitovsky: ~ **reversal test** *n* ECON Scitovsky-Paradoxon *nt*

SCN *abbr* (*specification change notice*) TRANSP *aviation* Änderung *f* der Originalvorlage, Änderung *f* des Bezugsteils

scoop *n* MEDIA *print* Erstmeldung *f*, Exklusivmeldung *f*

scope *n* GEN COMM Spielraum *m*, PATENTS *of claims* Bereich *m*, Gültigkeitsbereich *m*, Umfang *m*; ~ **of agreement** *n* HRM vertraglicher Geltungsbereich *m*, Vertragsrahmen *m*; ~ **of application** *n* GEN COMM Anwendungsbereich *m*, Aufgabenkreis *m*, Geltungsbereich *m*, Wirkungskreis *m*; ~ **of bargaining** *n* HRM

Verhandlungsrahmen *m*; **~ of coverage** *n* GEN COMM Erfassungsbreite *f*, Erfassungsbereich *m*, INS Deckungsbereich *m*, Deckungsumfang *m*; **~ of employment** *n* HRM Aufgabenkreis *m*; **~ for advancement** *n* HRM Aufstiegschancen *f pl*; **~ for improvement** *n* GEN COMM Raum *m* für Verbesserungen; **~ of tender** *n* GEN COMM Ausführungsgrenzen *f pl*

score: **~ a hit** *phr* GEN COMM stark beeindrucken

scout out *vt* HRM ausfindig machen

SCP *abbr* BANK (*sterling commercial paper*) Sterling Commercial Paper *nt*, Sterling-Handelspapier *nt*, kurzfristiges Sterling-Geldmarktpapier *nt*, ECON (*structure conduct performance model*) Strukturführungsleistungsmodell *nt*, IMP/EXP (*simplified clearance procedure*) *customs* vereinfachtes Abfertigungsverfahren *nt*, STOCK Sterling Commercial Paper *nt*; **~ market** *n* (*Sterling Commercial Paper market*) STOCK Markt *m* für Sterling Commercial Paper, Markt *m* für Sterling-Geldmarktpapier

scrap 1. *n* IND Schrott *m*; **2.** *vt* GEN COMM *idea, project* fallenlassen, IND verschrotten

scrap: **~ and build regulations** *n pl* TRANSP *shipping* Verschrottungs- und Bauvorschriften *f pl*; **~ dealer** *n* GEN COMM Altwarenhändler, in *m,f*

scrape along *vi infrml* GEN COMM sich mühsam durchschlagen

scrape through *vi* GEN COMM durchrutschen

scrap: **~ of evidence** *n* GEN COMM Spur *f* eines Beweises; **~ metal** *n* IND Altmetall *nt*; **~ paper** *n* ENVIR, GEN COMM Altpapier *nt*

scrapping *n* IND Verschrottung *f*

scrap: **~ value** *n* ECON Restwert *m*; **~ yard** *n* IND Schrottlager *nt*, Schrottplatz *m*

scratch: **~ area** *n* COMP Arbeitsbereich *m*; **come up to ~** *phr infrml* GEN COMM den Erwartungen entsprechen; **~ disk** *n* COMP Arbeitsplatte *f*; **~ file** *n* COMP Arbeitsdatei *f*, ungeschützte Datei *f*; **~ pad** *n* COMP Arbeitspuffer *m*

screamer *n infrml* MEDIA *headline* riesige Sensationsschlagzeile *f*

screen 1. *n* COMP Bildschirm *m*, Raster *m*; **2.** *vt* GEN COMM *applicants* überprüfen, *protect* abschirmen, schützen; ♦ **~ sb for a job** HRM jdn einer gründlichen Prüfung unterziehen

screen out *vt* HRM aussieben

screen: **~ advertising** *n* S&M Bildschirmwerbung *f*; **~-based text system** *n* COMMS, COMP bildschirmorientiertes Textsystem *nt*; **~ capture** *n* COMP Speichern *nt* der Bildschirmdarstellung; **~ copy** *n* COMP Bildschirmauszug *m*; **~ driver** *n* COMP Bildschirmtreiber *m*; **~ dump** *n* COMP Bildschirmauszug *m*

screened *adj* GEN COMM *protected* abgeschirmt, geschützt

screen: **~ editor** *n* COMP Bildschirmeditor *m*

screening *n* GEN COMM Überprüfung *f*, HRM *of candidates for a job* Auswahl *f*; **~ board** *n* HRM Prüfungsausschuß *m*; **~ process** *n* HRM Prüfverfahren *nt*; **~ technique** *n* HRM Auswahltechnik *f*, Auswahlverfahren *nt*

screen: **~ printing machine** *n* MEDIA Rasterdrucker *m*; **~ test** *n* MEDIA Filmtest *m*, Probeaufnahme *f*; **~ trading system** *n* STOCK Computerbörse *f*

scrimp: **~ and save** *phr* GEN COMM geizen und sparen, knausern und sparen

scrip *n* FIN, STOCK Interimsschein *m*, vorläufiges Zertifikat *nt*; **~ dividend** *n* FIN, STOCK Schuldscheinausgabe *f* als Dividendenersatz, Zuteilung *f* von Gratisaktien anstelle einer Bardividende; **~ issue** *n* FIN, STOCK Emission *f* von Berichtigungsaktien

scripophily *n* STOCK Sammeln *nt* alter Aktien und Wertpapiere

scroll 1. *vt* COMP *image, text* blättern, rollen; **2.** *vi* COMP scrollen

scroll down 1. *vt* COMP abrollen, *text on screen* vorrollen, vorscrollen; **2.** *vi* COMP *on screen* vorrollen, vorscrollen

scroll up 1. *vt* COMP aufrollen, *text on screen* zurückrollen, zurückscrollen; **2.** *vi* COMP *on screen* zurückrollen, zurückscrollen

scroll: **~ arrow** *n* COMP Rollpfeil *m*; **~ bar** *n* COMP Rollbalken *m*

scrolling *n* COMP Bildverschiebung *f*

scrutiny: **come under ~** *phr* GEN COMM einer genauen Prüfung unterzogen werden

s/d *abbr* (*small damage*) INS geringer Schaden *m*, geringfügiger Schaden *m*

SD *abbr* COMP (*single density*) einfache Dichte *f*, einfache Speicherdichte *f*, IND (*standard design*) Standarddesign *nt*, Standardkonstruktion *f*, INS (*sea damage*) Havarie *f*, Seeschaden *m*, (*short delivery*) Minderlieferung *f*, unvollständige Lieferung *f*, TRANSP (*sea damage*) Havarie *f*, Seeschaden *m*

S/D *abbr* BANK (*sight draft*) Sichttratte *f*, Sichtwechsel *m*, TRANSP (*sailing date*) Abfahrtsdatum *nt*

SDA *abbr BrE* (*Sex Discrimination Act*) HRM, LAW Gesetz *nt* gegen geschlechtsbezogene Diskriminierung, Gesetz *nt* gegen sexuelle Diskriminierung

SDR *abbr* (*special drawing rights*) BANK SZR (*Sonderziehungsrechte*)

SEA *abbr* (*Single European Act*) LAW EEA (*Einheitliche Europäische Akte*)

seaborne *adj* TRANSP *freight* auf dem Seewege, auf See befindlich

sea: **~ carrier** *n* TRANSP Seeverfrachter *m*; **~ damage** *n* (*SD*) INS, TRANSP Havarie *f*, Seeschaden *m*; **~-damaged** *adj* TRANSP *shipping* auf See beschädigt

seafarming *n* ECON Hochseefischerei *f*

sea: **~ insurance** *n* INS Seeversicherung *f*

seal 1. *n* IMP/EXP, IND Plombe *f*; ♦ **under ~** COMMS, LAW verplombt, versiegelt; **2.** *vt* GEN COMM *deal* besiegeln, versiegeln, LAW versiegeln

sea: **~ law** *n* LAW Seerecht *nt*

sealed *adj* COMMS, LAW verplombt, versiegelt; ♦ **in a ~ envelope** GEN COMM in versiegeltem Umschlag

sealed: **~-bid tendering** *n* GEN COMM Submissionsangebot *nt* im verschlossenen Umschlag; **~ instrument of debt** *n* INS gesiegelte Schuldurkunde *f*; **~ tender** *n* GEN COMM versiegeltes Angebot *nt*

sea: **~ letter** *n* TRANSP Passierschein *m*, Schiffsbrief *m*, Schiffspaß *m*

sealing *n* IMP/EXP, IND Plombierung *f*, Siegelung *f*, Verplombung *f*; **~ wax** *n* GEN COMM Siegelwachs *nt*

seal: **~ of quality** *n* GEN COMM Qualitätssiegel *nt*

seaman *n* HRM Seemann *m*

sea: **~ port** *n* TRANSP Seehafen *m*

SEAQ *abbr* (*Stock Exchange Automated Quotations*)

STOCK elektronisches Börsenhandels- und Notierungssystem der Londoner Börse für britische Wertpapiere, elektronische Börseninformation *f*; **~ Automated Execution Facility** *n BrE* (*SAEF*) STOCK Teil des elektronischen Börsenhandels- und Notierungssystem der Londoner Börse

SEAQI *abbr BrE* (*Stock Exchange Automated Quotation International*) STOCK elektronisches Börsenhandels- und Notierungssystem für internationale Wertpapiere, internationale elektronische Börseninformation *f*

SEAQ: **~ International** *n BrE* (*Stock Exchange Automated Quotation International*) STOCK elektronisches Börsenhandels- und Notierungssystem für internationale Wertpapiere, internationale elektronische Börseninformation *f*

search 1. *n* COMP Suchen *nt*, GEN COMM Suche *f*, Suchen *nt*, *examination* Durchsuchung *f*, Überprüfung *f*, *research* Nachforschung *f*, Recherche *f*; ◆ **be in ~ of sth** GEN COMM auf der Suche nach etw sein; **2.** *vt* COMP *file, document* suchen, GEN COMM suchen, *examine* prüfen, durchsuchen, *research* forschen, recherchieren, PATENTS prüfen; ◆ **~ a file** COMP eine Akte überprüfen, eine Akte prüfen

search out *vt* HRM ausfindig machen

Search: **~ and Advisory Service** *n BrE* PATENTS *of the UK Patent Office* Prüfungs- und Beratungsdienst *m*

search: **~ key** *n* COMP Suchschlüssel *m*; **~ and replace** *n* COMP *on word processor* Suchen/Ersetzen *nt*; **~ report** *n* PATENTS Nachforschungsbericht *m*, Prüfbericht *m*; **~ result** *n* COMP Abfrageergebnis *nt*; **~ and seizure** *n* LAW unberechtigte Durchsuchung *f* und Beschlagnahme *f*; **~ warrant** *n* LAW Hausdurchsuchungsbefehl *m*

sea: **~ risks** *n pl* INS *marine insurance*, TRANSP Gefahren *f pl* des Meeres, Seegefahren *f pl*; **~ route** *n* TRANSP Seeschiffahrtsstraße *f*, Seeweg *m*

seasonal *adj* GEN COMM saisonal, saisonbedingt, Saison-; **~ adjustment** *n* ECON, FIN, GEN COMM, HRM Saisonbereinigung *f*; **~ concentration** *n* S&M saisonbedingte Konzentration *f*; **~ discount** *n* S&M Nachlaß *m* außerhalb der Saison; **~ factor** *n* ECON saisonaler Faktor *m*; **~ fluctuation** *n* ECON Saisonbewegung *f*, Saisonschwankung *f*

seasonality: **~ of demand** *n* ECON Saisonabhängigkeit *f* der Nachfrage

seasonal: **~ loan** *n* BANK Saisonkredit *m*

seasonally: **~ adjusted** *adj* ECON, FIN, GEN COMM, HRM saisonbereinigt; **~-adjusted figure** *n* FIN saisonal angeglichener Preis *m*, saisonbereinigter Preis *m*, saisonbereinigte Zahl *f*; **~-unadjusted employment figure** *n* ECON, HRM nicht saisonbereinigte Beschäftigungsziffer *f*

seasonal: **~ rate** *n* S&M Saisonsatz *m*; **~ swing** *n* GEN COMM jahreszeitlicher Wechsel *m*; **~ unemployment** *n* HRM saisonbedingte Arbeitslosigkeit *f*; **~ variation** *n* ECON Saisonschwankung *f*; **~ worker** *n* HRM Saisonarbeiter, in *m,f*

seasoned *adj* GEN COMM erfahren, erprobt; **~ CD** *n* STOCK am Markt eingeführtes Einlagenzertifikat *nt*

season: **~ ticket** *n* GEN COMM Dauerkarte *f*, TRANSP *BrE* (*cf commutation ticket AmE*) Abonnementsfahrkarte *f*, Zeitfahrkarte *f*, Zeitkarte *f*, *monthly* Monatsfahrkarte *f*, *rail* Eisenbahnabonnement *nt*; **~ ticket holder** *n* GEN COMM Dauerkarteninhaber, in *m,f*, TRANSP *BrE* (*cf commutation ticket holder AmE*), Zeitkarteninhaber, in *m,f*

seat *n* GEN COMM *principal place of business* Firmensitz *m*, Sitz *m*, LEIS Platz *m*, POL Amtssitz *m*, Regierungssitz *m*, *in Parliament* Sitz *m*

SEATAG *abbr* (*South East Asia Trade Advisory Group*) GEN COMM Beratungsgruppe für Handel mit Südostasien

sea: **~ trade** *n* GEN COMM Seehandel *m*; **~ transport** *n* TRANSP Seetransport *m*, Seeverkehr *m*

seat: **~ reservation system** *n* LEIS Platzreservierungssystem *nt*

sea: **~ waybill** *n* IMP/EXP, TRANSP Seefrachtbrief *m*

seaworthiness *n* TRANSP Seefähigkeit *f*, Seetüchtigkeit *f*

sec *abbr* GEN COMM (*second*) Sek. (*Sekunde*)

sec. *abbr* ADMIN (*secretary*) Sekretär, in *m,f*, GEN COMM (*second*) Sek. (*Sekunde*), HRM (*secretary*) Sekretär, in *m,f*

SEC *abbr AmE* (*Securities and Exchange Commission*) STOCK Börsenaufsichtsbehörde *f*

SECAL *abbr* (*sector adjustment loan*) FIN Bereichsanpassungsanleihe *f*

second 1. *n* (*sec, sec.*) GEN COMM Sekunde *f* (*Sek.*); **2.** *vt* HRM abstellen

secondary *adj* GEN COMM sekundär, zweitrangig, nebensächlich, subsidiär; **~ action** *n* HRM *unions* Kampfmaßnahmen gegen Betriebe, die nicht unmittelbar an dem betreffenden Arbeitskonflikt beteiligt sind; **~ activity** *n* GEN COMM Sekundärgeschäft *nt*; **~ bank** *n* BANK Finanzierungs- und Teilzahlungskreditinstitut *nt*; **~ banking crisis** *n* BANK Krise *f* im Finanzierungs- und Teilzahlungskreditgeschäft; **~ boycott** *n* HRM *unions* Boykott gegen einen nicht direkt am Arbeitskonflikt beteiligten Betrieb; **~ claim** *n* ACC Nebenforderung *f*; **~ data** *n pl* S&M Sekundärdaten *pl*; **~ distribution** *n* STOCK Wertpapierangebot *nt* im Sekundärmarkt; **~ education** *n* WEL höhere Schulbildung *f*; **~ employment** *n* HRM Nebenerwerb *m*, Zweitbeschäftigung *f*; **~ income** *n* FIN Sekundäreinkommen *nt*; **~ labor market** *AmE*, **~ labour market** *BrE n* HRM Sekundärarbeitsmarkt *m*, zweiter Arbeitsmarkt *m*; **~ legislation** *n* LAW sekundäre Gesetzgebung *f*; **~ meaning** *n* S&M Nebenbedeutung *f*; **~ need** *n* S&M sekundäres Bedürfnis *nt*; **~ offering** *n* STOCK Angebot *nt* von Wertpapieren im Sekundärmarkt; **~ product** *n* ECON Nebenprodukt *nt*; **~ protection** *n* IND Sekundärschutz *m*; **~ readership** *n* S&M Sekundärleserschaft *f*; **~ sector** *n* ECON Fertigungssektor *m*, Sekundärsektor *m*

second: **~ ballot** *n* POL Stichwahl *f*; **~-best** *adj* ECON *Pareto optimum* zweitbeste; **~-class** *adj* GEN COMM zweitklassig; **~-class citizen** *n* GEN COMM Staatsbürger, in *m,f* zweiter Klasse; **~-class mail** *n* COMMS langsamere und billigere Postzustellung; **~-class paper** *n* FIN zweitklassiges Geldmarktpapier *nt*; **~ debenture** *n* FIN zweite Obligation *f*; **~-degree price discrimination** *n* S&M Preisdiskriminierung *f* zweiten Grades; **~ domicile** *n* LAW Zweitwohnsitz *m*; **~ economy** *n* ECON Schattenwirtschaft *f*; **~ generation** *n* MEDIA zweite Generation *f*, zweite Vervielfältigung *f*; **~-generation computer** *n* COMP Computer *m* der zweiten Generation, Rechner *m* der zweiten Generation; **~-generation product** *n* S&M Produkt *nt* zweiter Generation; **~ half of the year** *n* GEN COMM zweite Hälfte *f* des Jahres, zweites Halbjahr *nt*; **~-hand** *adj* GEN COMM gebraucht, aus zweiter Hand; **~-hand market** *n* GEN COMM Gebrauchtwarenmarkt *m*, Trödelmarkt *m*; **~-hand shop** *n* GEN COMM Gebrauchtwarengeschäft *nt*; **~ home** *n* PROP Zweitwohnung *f*; **~ installment base** *AmE*, **~ instalment base** *BrE n* TAX Berechnungsgrundlage *f* für die zweite Rate; **~ job** *n* HRM Nebenbeschäftigung *f*; **~-largest** *adj* GEN COMM zweitgrößte; **~ market** *n* ECON Sekundärmarkt *m*

secondment *n* HRM Abstellung *f*

second: **~ mortgage** *n* BANK, FIN nachrangige Hypothek *f*, zweite Hypothek *f*; **~ mortgage lending** *n* FIN Geschäft *nt* mit nachrangigen Hypotheken, Zweithypothekengeschäft *nt*; **~ offence** *BrE*, **~ offense** *AmE n* LAW Rückfalltat *f*; **~ quarter** *n* (*2Q*) GEN COMM zweites Quartal *nt*; **~-rate** *adj* GEN COMM zweitklassig; **~ reading** *n* LAW *of bill, directive* zweite Lesung *f*; **~ residence** *n* LAW Zweitwohnsitz *m*; **~ tier company** *n* GEN COMM nachgeschaltete Gesellschaft *f*

Second: **~ World War** *n* (*WW2*) POL Zweiter Weltkrieg *m* (*WK II*)

secrecy *n* GEN COMM Geheimhaltung *f*

secret *adj* GEN COMM geheim

secretarial: **~ pool** *n* HRM Schreibzimmer *nt*; **~ staff** *n* HRM Sekretariatskräfte *f pl*

secretariat *n* ADMIN, HRM, POL *government* Sekretariat *nt*

secretary *n* (*sec.*) ADMIN, HRM Sekretär, in *m,f*; **~'s office** *n* ADMIN Sekretariat *nt*

Secretary: **~ of State** *n* POL *AmE* Außenminister, in *m,f*, *BrE* Kabinettsminister, in *m,f*; **~ of State for the Environment** *BrE n* ENVIR, POL Umweltminister, in *m,f*; **~ of State for Transport** *n BrE* TRANSP Verkehrsminister, in *m,f*; **~ of the Treasury** *n AmE* ECON, FIN Finanzminister, in *m,f*, Schatzkanzler, in *m,f*

secret: **~ ballot** *n* HRM *industrial action*, POL geheime Abstimmung *f*; **~ payment** *n* HRM geheime Zahlung *f*; **~ reserve** *n* ACC, FIN geheime Rücklage *f*, stille Rücklage *f*

section *n* GEN COMM Abschnitt *m*, *department* Abteilung *f*, LAW *of act* Artikel *m*, Kapitel *nt*, Paragraph *m*

sectional: **~ rate** *n* TRANSP *aviation* Teiltarif *m*

section: **~ head** *n* MGMNT Abteilungsleiter, in *m,f*

sector 1. *n* COMP *disk* Sektor *m*, ECON Branche *f*, Sektor *m*, GEN COMM Bereich *m*; **2.** *vt* COMP *disk* in Sektoren aufteilen

sector: **~ adjustment lending** *n* ECON, FIN Anpassungssubvention *f*; **~ adjustment loan** *n* (*SECAL*) FIN Bereichsanpassungsanleihe *f*

sectoral *adj* ECON, MGMNT *interests* sektoral; **~ accounting plan** *n* ACC sektoraler Wirtschaftsplan *m*; **~ strategy** *n* MGMNT Branchenstrategie *f*, sektorale Strategie *f*; **~ unemployment** *n* ECON, MGMNT sektorale Arbeitslosigkeit *f*

sector: **~ analysis** *n* FIN, GEN COMM Branchenanalyse *f*; **~ investment and maintenance loan** *n* (*SIM*) FIN Bereichsinvestitions- und Erhaltungsanleihe *f*; **~-specific** *adj* ECON branchenspezifisch; **~-specific aid** *n* ECON *development assistance* branchenspezifische Hilfe *f*

secular: **~ trend** *n* ECON säkularer Trend *m*

secure 1. *adj* BANK sicher, ECON *financially* gesichert, sicher, FIN sicher; **2.** *vt* BANK besichern, GEN COMM befestigen, STOCK *price in futures contract* absichern, besichern, sichern; ◆ **a debt by mortgage** BANK eine Verbindlichkeit hypothekarisch sichern; **~ new orders** GEN COMM Aufträge beschaffen, Aufträge hereinholen, neue Aufträge sichern

secured: **~ advance** *n* BANK besichertes Darlehen *nt*; **~ bonds** *n pl* ECON gesicherte Industrieobligationen *f pl*; **~ credit** *n* FIN abgesicherter Kredit *m*; **~ creditor** *n* ACC, ECON, FIN gesicherter Gläubiger *m*, gesicherte Gläubigerin *f*, bevorrechtigter Gläubiger *m*, bevorrechtigte Gläubigerin *f*; **~ debenture** *n* FIN gesicherte Schuldverschreibung *f*, besicherter Schuldschein *m*; **~ debt** *n* FIN gesicherte Verbindlichkeit *f*; **~ fixed-term loan** *n* BANK besicherter Kredit *m* mit fester Laufzeit; **~ party** *n* FIN Faktoringgesellschaft *f*, Sicherungsnehmer *m*; **~ personal loan** *n* BANK besicherter Personalkredit *m*

secure: **~ investment** *n* BANK sichere Kapitalanlage *f*; **~ job** *n* HRM gesicherter Arbeitsplatz *m*

securing *n* GEN COMM Befestigung *f*, Sicherung *f*

securities *n pl* STOCK Wertpapiere *nt pl*, Valoren *f pl*; ◆ **~ wanted** STOCK Wertpapiere gesucht

securities: **~ account** *n* BANK Depot *nt*, Depotkonto *nt*, STOCK Wertpapierkonto *nt*; **~ administration** *n AmE* FIN Wertpapierverwaltung *f*; **~ analysis** *n* FIN Wertpapieranalyse *f*

Securities: **~ and Exchange Commission** *n AmE* (*SEC*) STOCK Börsenaufsichtsbehörde *f*; **~ and Futures Authority** *n BrE* STOCK Behörde für Wertpapier- und Terminkontraktgeschäfte; **~ and Investment Board** *n BrE* (*SIB*) STOCK Aufsichtsbehörde für den britischen Finanz- und Wertpapierhandel

securities: **~ arbitrage** *n* STOCK Effektenarbitrage *f*

Securities: **~ Association** *n BrE* STOCK Selbstüberwachungsorganisation der Londoner City für den Wertpapierhandel

securities: **~ borrowing** *n* BANK Wertpapierkreditaufnahme *f*, Wertpapierlombardierung *f*; **~ business** *n* STOCK Wertpapiergeschäft *nt*

Securities: **~ Exchange Act** *n AmE* LAW *1934* Wertpapiergesetz

securities: **~ dealer** *n* STOCK Wertpapierhändler, in *m,f*; **~ department** *n* STOCK Wertpapierabteilung *f*; **~ deposited under wrapper** *n pl* FIN Streifbanddepot *nt*; **~ held in trust** *n pl* STOCK treuhänderisch verwaltete Wertpapiere *nt pl*; **~ holdings** *n pl* BANK, STOCK Wertpapierbestand *m*; **~ house** *n* STOCK Wertpapierhaus *nt*; **~ in portfolio** *n pl* STOCK Wertpapiere *nt pl* im Portefeuille; **~ loan** *n* STOCK Effektendarlehen *nt*, Lombardkredit *m*; **~ market** *n* FIN, STOCK Wertpapiermarkt *m*; **~ portfolio** *n* BANK, STOCK Wertpapierbestand *m*, Wertpapierportefeuille *nt*; **~ of short maturity date** *n pl* STOCK Kurzläufer *m pl* (*jarg*), Wertpapiere *nt pl* mit kurzer Laufzeit; **~ tax** *n* TAX Wertpapiersteuer *f*; **~ trade** *n* STOCK Effektenhandel *m*, Wertpapierhandel *m*

securitization *n* BANK, FIN, STOCK Substitution *f* von Bankkrediten durch handelbare Wertpapiere, Verbriefung *f* von Kredit- und Einlagepositionen, wertpapiermäßige Unterlegung *f* von Verbindlichkeiten

security *n* ADMIN *safety, protection* Sicherheit *f*, BANK Wertpapier *nt*, COMP *protection* Sicherheit *f*, FIN *share* Wertpapier *nt*, *pledge* Bürgschaft *f*, Garantie *f*, Sicherheit *f*, Kaution *f*, HRM *of job* Sicherheit *f*, STOCK *certificate, asset* Titel *m*, Wertpapier *nt*; **~ analyst** *n* STOCK Wertpapieranalytiker, in *m,f*; **~ backup** *n* COMP

Sicherungskopie *f*; ~ **balance** *n* FIN, STOCK Effektenbestandsguthaben *nt*; ~ **bond for down payment** *n* STOCK Anzahlungsgarantie *f*; ~ **borrowing** *n* FIN Wertpapierlombardierung *f*; ~ **copy** *n* COMP Sicherungskopie *f*; ~ **deposit subdivision** *n* ACC Unterdepot *nt*; ~ **of employment** *n* HRM Beschäftigungssicherheit *f*, Sicherheit *f* des Arbeitsplatzes; ~ **flotation** *n* STOCK Wertpapieremission *f*; ~ **holding** *n* FIN, STOCK Effektenbestand *m*; ~ **issue** *n* STOCK Wertpapieremission *f*; ~ **issued by a bank** *n* BANK Bankpapier *nt*; ~ **issue tax** *n* STOCK, TAX Emissionssteuer *f*; ~ **leak** *n* GEN COMM Sicherheitsleck *nt*; ~ **lending** *n* FIN Kreditbewilligung *f* gegen Sicherheiten, Lombardkredit *m*, Wertpapierleihe *f*; ~ **loan** *n* FIN Effektenkredit *m*; ~ **market line** *n* STOCK Wertpapiermarktlinie *f*; ~ **measure** *n* ADMIN Sicherheitsmaßnahme *f*; ~ **price** *n* STOCK Wertpapierkurs *m*; ~ **price structure** *n* STOCK Wertpapierkursgefüge *nt*; ~ **right** *n* LAW *contract* Sicherheitsrecht *nt*; ~ **risk** *n* INS Sicherheitsrisiko *nt*; ~ **service** *n* ADMIN Sicherheitsdienst *m*; ~ **of tenure** *n* PROP Mietschutz *m*

sedentary *adj* GEN COMM sitzend

SEDOL *abbr BrE* (*Stock Exchange Daily Official List*) STOCK amtliches Börsenkursblatt *nt*

seed: ~ **capital** *n* FIN Gründungskapital *nt*, Startkapital *nt*; ~ **money** *n* FIN Gründungskapital *nt*, Startkapital *nt*

seek *vt* GEN COMM fragen um, *approval, help* erbitten, suchen, *employment* sich bewerben um; ♦ ~ **advice** GEN COMM um Rat fragen; ~ **legal advice** LAW sich anwaltschaftlich beraten lassen; ~ **a market** STOCK einen Markt suchen; ~ **redress** LAW Wiedergutmachung verlangen; ~ **sb's approval** GEN COMM jds Genehmigung einholen

segment 1. *n* ACC, COMP, MATH, MGMNT Segment *nt*, S&M *of the market* Bereich *m*, Segment *nt*; **2.** *vt* ACC, COMP, MATH, MGMNT, S&M segmentieren; **3.** *vi* ACC, COMP, MATH, MGMNT, S&M sich teilen

segmental: ~ **reporting** *n* ACC detaillierte Berichterstattung *f*, segmentorientierte Berichterstattung *f*

segmentation *n* ACC, COMP, MATH, MGMNT, S&M Segmentierung *f*; ~ **strategy** *n* S&M Segmentierungsstrategie *f*

segmented: ~ **labor market theory** *AmE*, ~ **labour market theory** *BrE n* (*SLM*) ECON Theorie *f* des segmentierten Arbeitsmarkts

segment: ~ **information** *n* GEN COMM Teilinformationen *f pl*; ~ **margin** *n* ACC Segmentspanne *f*; ~ **profit** *n* ACC Marktsegmentgewinn *m*

segregate *vt* GEN COMM trennen, LAW aussondern

segregated *adj* GEN COMM getrennt

segregation *n* GEN COMM, POL Trennung *f*; ~ **of duties** *n* HRM, MGMNT Aufgabentrennung *f*

seigniorage *n* FIN Münzgewinn *m*

seize *vt* IMP/EXP beschlagnahmen

seizure *n* IMP/EXP Beschlagnahme *f*, Beschlagnahmung *f*; ~ **of property** *n* LAW Vermögenseinziehung *f*

select 1. *adj* GEN COMM *chosen* auserwählt, auserlesen, *exclusive* exklusiv; **2.** *vt* GEN COMM aussuchen, auswählen

select: ~ **committee** *n* POL Sonderausschuß *m*, Untersuchungsausschuß *m*

selected *adj* GEN COMM auserlesen, exklusiv; ~ **dealer agreement** *n* STOCK Exklusivhandelsvertrag *m*, Vereinbarung *f* für ausgewählte Händler

selection *n* GEN COMM *choosing* Auswahl *f*, Wahl *f*, Auslese *f*; ~ **bias** *n* MATH *statistics* verzerrte Auswahl *f*; ~ **board** *n* HRM Auswahlkommission *f*; ~ **of suppliers** *n* S&M Lieferantenauswahl *f*

selective *adj* GEN COMM selektiv; ~ **attention** *n* S&M selektive Aufmerksamkeit *f*; ~ **distribution** *n* S&M Selektivdistribution *f*, Vertrieb *m* durch ausgewählte Händler

Selective: ~ **Employment Tax** *n BrE* TAX selektive Beschäftigungssteuer *f*; ~ **Financial Assistance** *n BrE* ECON *regional development* selektive Finanzhilfe *f*

selective: ~ **perception** *n* S&M selektive Wahrnehmung *f*; ~ **positioning** *n* S&M selektive Positionierung *f*; ~ **selling** *n* S&M selektiver Verkauf *m*

self: **~-actualization** *n* HRM, MGMNT Selbstverwirklichung *f*; **~-addressed envelope** *n* COMMS Rückumschlag *m*; **~-addressed stamped envelope** *n* (*s.a.s.e.*) COMMS frankierter Rückumschlag *m*, freigemachter Rückumschlag *m*; **~-amortizing mortgage** *n* BANK kurzfristige unbesicherte Hypothek *f*; **~-appraisal** *n* HRM Eigenbeurteilung *f*; **~-catering** *n* LEIS Selbstverpflegung *f*; **~-contained** *adj* GEN COMM selbstgenügsam, separat, unabhängig; **~-control** *n* GEN COMM, POL Selbstbeherrschung *f*; **~-dealing** *n* FIN, LAW *contracts* Insichgeschäft *nt*, Selbstkontrahieren *nt*; **~-drive hire** *n* LEIS, TRANSP Autovermietung *f*; **~-educated person** *n* WEL Autodidakt, in *m,f*; **~-employed** *adj* HRM, TAX selbständig, freiberuflich; **~-employed person** *n* HRM Freiberufler, in *m,f*, Selbständige(r) *mf* [decl. as adj]; **~-employed worker** *n* HRM selbständig Erwerbstätige(r) *mf* [decl. as adj]; **~-employment** *n* HRM, TAX selbständige Tätigkeit *f*; **~-financing** *adj* ACC, FIN selbstfinanzierend; **~-financing** *n* ACC, FIN Eigenfinanzierung *f*, Selbstfinanzierung *f*; **~-financing ratio** *n* FIN, STOCK Eigenfinanzierungsquote *f*, Selbstfinanzierungsquote *f*; **~-fulfilling prophecy** *n* GEN COMM eine sich selbst bewahrheitende Voraussage; **~-generated** *adj* ACC, FIN *increase in capital and reserves* eigenerwirtschaftet; **~-generated funds** *n pl* ACC, FIN Eigenmittel *nt pl*; **~-generating** *adj* GEN COMM selbsterzeugend; **~-governing** *adj* POL autonom, selbständig, souverän; **~-governing nation** *n* POL selbständige Nation *f*, souveräner Staat *m*; **~-governing port** *n* TRANSP autonomer Hafen *m*; **~-government** *n* POL Selbstverwaltung *f*; **~-help** *n* GEN COMM, HRM Selbsthilfe *f*; **~-help passenger luggage trolley** *n* LEIS Selbstbedienungsgepäckwagen *m*; **~-image** *n* S&M Selbstbild *nt*; **~-insurance** *n* INS firmeneigene Versicherung *f*, Selbstversicherung *f*; **~-insurance fund** *n* INS Selbstversicherungsfonds *m*; **~-liquidating** *adj* FIN sich automatisch abdeckend, sich automatisch liquidierend; **~-liquidating credit** *n* FIN aus Warenerlös der finanzierten Ware automatisch zurückbezahlter Kredit; **~-loading** *adj* IND, TRANSP selbstladend; **~-loading trailer** *n* TRANSP selbstladender Anhänger *m*; **~-mailer** *n* S&M Versandprospekt *m* ohne Umschlag; **~-managed** *adj* HRM, MGMNT autonom; **~-management** *n* HRM, MGMNT Selbstmanagement *nt*, Selbstverwaltung *f*; **~-motivating** *adj* HRM, MGMNT aus eigenem Antrieb; **~-motivation** *n* HRM, MGMNT Selbstmotivation *f*; **~-regulating organization** *n* (*SRO*) GEN COMM Selbstverwaltungskörperschaft *f*; **~-regulation** *n* ECON freiwillige Selbstkontrolle *f*; **~-regulatory organization** *n* (*SRO*) GEN COMM Selbstverwaltungskörperschaft *f*;

~-reliant *adj* ECON, GEN COMM autark, selbstversorgend; **~-restraint** *n* GEN COMM Selbstbeschränkung *f*; **~-selection** *n* S&M Selbstbedienung *f*; **~-service** *n* S&M Selbstbedienung *f*; **~-service store** *n* S&M Selbstbedienungsgeschäft *nt*; **~-starter** *n* GEN COMM *car* automatischer Anlasser *m*, Selbstanlasser *m*, HRM ehrgeizige, selbstmotivierte Person *f*; **~-styled** *adj* GEN COMM selbsternannt; **~-sufficiency** *n* ECON, GEN COMM Autarkie *f*, Selbstversorgung *f*; **~-sufficient** *adj* ECON, GEN COMM autark, selbständig, selbstversorgend, *independent* unabhängig; **~-sufficient economy** *n* ECON autarke Wirtschaft *f*; **~-supply** *n* ECON Selbstversorgung *f*; **~-supporting** *adj* GEN COMM selbsttragend, sich selbst unterhaltend, sich selbst versorgend, wirtschaftlich unabhängig; **~-supporting debt** *n* FIN selbsttragende Schuld *f*; **~-taught person** *n* WEL Autodidakt, in *m,f*

sell 1. *vt* FIN begeben, GEN COMM verkaufen, *goods* absetzen, veräußern, *turn over* umsetzen, *deal in* vertreiben; ♦ **~ a bear** STOCK Leerverkäufe abschließen; **~ by** GEN COMM verwendbar bis; **~ by auction** GEN COMM öffentlich versteigern, verauktionieren (*infrml*); **~ for the account** STOCK auf Termin verkaufen; **~ for the delivery** STOCK auf Termin verkaufen; **~ for future delivery** GEN COMM auf Termin verkaufen; **~ for the settlement** STOCK zum Ausgleich verkaufen; **~ in bulk** S&M en gros verkaufen, im großen verkaufen; **~ on close** STOCK *futures market* zum Börsenschluß verkaufen; **~ on commission** S&M auf Kommissionsbasis verkaufen; **~ on credit** S&M auf Kredit verkaufen; **~ one's wares** GEN COMM seine Waren absetzen; **~ on trust** S&M auf Kredit verkaufen; **~ shares** STOCK Aktien verkaufen; **~ short** STOCK fixen, Leerverkäufe abschließen; **~ spot** STOCK per Kasse verkaufen, am Kassamarkt verkaufen; **~ sth by private treaty** GEN COMM freihändig verkaufen, etw unter der Hand verkaufen; **~ sth for scrap** GEN COMM etw zum Schrottwert verkaufen; **2.** *vi* GEN COMM *person* verkaufen, *product* sich verkaufen; ♦ **~ like hot cakes** *infrml* GEN COMM wie warme Semmeln weggehen (*infrml*)

sell back *vt* STOCK zurückverkaufen

sell forward *vt* STOCK auf Termin verkaufen

sell off *vt* GEN COMM abstoßen, verkaufen, STOCK abstoßen, glattstellen

sell out *vt* FIN, GEN COMM, S&M ausverkaufen, STOCK *futures market* glattstellen

sell up *vt* GEN COMM *house, business* verkaufen, S&M *jarg at high price* jdm etw andrehen (*infrml*), zu Geld machen

sell: **~ and report agreement** *n* S&M Verkaufs- und Berichterstattungsvereinbarung *f*; **~-by date** *n* S&M *food* Mindesthaltbarkeitsdatum *nt*

seller *n* GEN COMM Verkäufer, in *m,f*, Veräußerer *m*; **~'s market** *n* ECON, PROP, STOCK Verkäufermarkt *m*; **~'s option** *n* (*S.O.*) STOCK Verkäuferoption *f*; **~'s rate** *n* STOCK Verkaufskurs *m*, *shares* Briefkurs *m*

sellers: **~ over** *n pl* STOCK Angebotsüberhang *m*

selling *n* GEN COMM, S&M, STOCK Verkauf *m*; **~ climax** *n* STOCK Verkaufshöhepunkt *m*; **~ commission** *n* FIN, S&M Bonifikation *f*, Verkaufsprovision *f*; **~ concession** *n* STOCK Plazierungsprovision *f*, Verkaufsprovision *f*; **~ expenses** *n pl* ACC Vertriebsgemeinkosten *pl*, GEN COMM Verkaufskosten *pl*; **~ point** *n* GEN COMM unterer Interventionspunkt *m*, S&M Verkaufsargument *nt*, Ver-

kaufsstelle *f*; **~ policy** *n* S&M Verkaufspolitik *f*; **~ price** *n* S&M Verkaufspreis *m*; **~ proposition** *n* S&M Verkaufsvorschlag *m*; **~ short** *n* STOCK Leerverkauf *m*; **~ space** *n* S&M Verkaufsfläche *f*; **~ stop order** *n* STOCK Stop-Loss-Auftrag *m*

sell: **~-off** *n* STOCK Glattstellungsverkauf *m*

sellout *n* *infrml* GEN COMM Verkaufsschlager *m*, LEIS *theatre* ausverkauftes Haus *nt*

SEM *abbr* (*special employment measures*) ECON, HRM ABM (*Arbeitsbeschaffungsmaßnahmen*)

semantic: **~ differential** *n* S&M semantischer Unterschied *m*

semi-black: **~ market** *n* ECON grauer Markt *m*

semiconductor *n* COMP, IND Halbleiter *m*

semi-detached: **~ house** *n* *BrE* PROP Doppelhaushälfte *f*

semi-durable: **~ goods** *n pl* GEN COMM Konsumgüter mit einer Lebensdauer von 6 Monaten bis zu 3 Jahren

semi-finished: **~ goods** *n pl* IND Halbfabrikate *nt pl*, Halbfertigwaren *f pl*; **~ product** *n* IND Halberzeugnis *nt*, Halbfabrikat *nt*, Halbfertigprodukt *nt*

semi-fixed: **~ costs** *n pl* ACC, ECON, FIN teilvariable Kosten *pl*

semi-industrialized *adj* ECON *country* halbindustrialisiert

semi-interquartile: **~ range** *n* MATH *statistics* halber Quartilsabstand *m*

seminar *n* HRM, MGMNT Seminar *nt*

semi-private: **~ bank** *n* BANK gemischtwirtschaftliche Bank *f*, halbprivate Bank *f*

semi-processed: **~ product** *n* GEN COMM halbveredeltes Produkt *nt*

semi-skilled *adj* HRM angelernt; **~ labor** *AmE*, **~ labour** *BrE* *n* ECON, HRM angelernte Arbeitskraft *f*; **~ worker** *n* HRM angelernter Arbeiter *m*, angelernte Arbeiterin *f*

semi-structured *adj* GEN COMM halbstrukturiert

semi-trailer *n* TRANSP Sattelauflieger *m*

semi-variable: **~ costs** *n pl* ACC, ECON, FIN teilvariable Kosten *pl*; **~ expense** *n* ACC, ECON, FIN teilvariable Kosten *pl*

semi-wholesaler *n* S&M Demigrossist, in *m,f*, Halbgrossist, in *m,f*

senate *n* POL Senat *m*

Senate *n* *AmE* POL amerikanisches Oberhaus, ≈ Bundesrat *m*

senator *n* POL Senator *m*

Senator *n* *AmE* POL Mitglied des amerikanischen Oberhauses

send *vt* COMMS senden, schicken, übersenden, verschicken, *electronically* übermitteln, IMP/EXP, TRANSP verschicken; ♦ **~ by fax** COMMS per Fax übermitteln, faxen; **~ by post** COMMS per Post versenden; **~ sb for sth** GEN COMM jdn nach etw schicken; **~ sth by parcel post** COMMS etw per Paketpost versenden; **~ sth via an agent** GEN COMM etw durch einen Beauftragten schicken, etw durch einen Bevollmächtigten schicken; **~ under plain cover** COMMS in neutralem Umschlag versenden, in neutraler Verpackung versenden; **~ a written request** GEN COMM ein schriftliches Gesuch senden, einen schriftlichen Antrag senden

send in *vt* GEN COMM *order* einsenden, schicken, *request* einreichen

send out *vt* GEN COMM verschicken, versenden, *person* hinausschicken

sender *n* COMMS Absender, in *m,f*, Versender, in *m,f*

senior 1. *adj* (*Snr*) GEN COMM senior (*sen.*), *in rank* vorgesetzt, übergeordnet, *in age* älter, *leading* leitend, LAW übergeordnet, älter, senior (*sen.*); **2.** *n* GEN COMM Vorgesetzte(r) *mf* [decl. as adj]

senior: ~ **bond** *n* FIN erststellige Schuldverschreibung *f*; ~ **civil servant** *n* HRM höhere(r) Staatsbeamte(r) *m* [decl. as adj], höhere Staatsbeamtin *f*; ~ **clerk** *n* HRM, MGMNT Bürovorsteher, in *m,f*, Bürochef, in *m,f*, Büroleiter, in *m,f*, leitende(r) Büroangestellte(r) *mf* [decl. as adj]; ~ **creditor** *n* ECON, FIN bevorrechtigter Gläubiger *m*, bevorrechtigte Gläubigerin *f*; ~ **debt** *n* BANK vorrangige Verbindlichkeit *f*, vorrangiger Schuldtitel *m*; ~ **executive** *n* HRM, MGMNT leitende(r) Angestellte(r) *mf* [decl. as adj], gehobene Führungskraft *f*; ~ **export clerk** *n* HRM rangältester Exportsachbearbeiter *m*, rangälteste Exportsachbearbeiterin *f*, ranghöchste Exportsachbearbeiter *m*, ranghöchste Exportsachbearbeiterin *f*; ~ **import clerk** *n* HRM rangältester Importsachbearbeiter *m*, rangälteste Importsachbearbeiterin *f*, ranghöchster Importsachbearbeiter *m*, ranghöchste Importsachbearbeiterin *f*

Senior: ~ **Information Officer** *n* (*SIO*) HRM *civil service* ranghoher Dienstgrad im Nachrichtendienst

seniority *n* HRM *length of service* Dienstalter *nt*, *rank* Seniorität *f*; ~ **allowance** *n* HRM Dienstalterszulage *f*; ~ **bonus** *n* HRM Dienstalterszulage *f*; ~ **pay** *n* HRM Beförderungszulage *f*; ~ **premium** *n* HRM Dienstalterszulage *f*; ~ **principle** *n* HRM Dienstaltersprinzip *nt*; ~ **system** *n* HRM Dienstaltersplan *m*

senior: ~ **loan** *n* BANK erststelliges Darlehen *nt*, im Rang vorgehendes Darlehen *nt*, vorrangiges Darlehen *nt*; ~ **management** *n* HRM, MGMNT Führungskräfte *f pl*, obere Leitungsebene *f*, oberes Management *nt*, Unternehmensspitze *f*; ~ **manager** *n* HRM, MGMNT hochstehende(r) Angestellte(r) *mf* [decl. as adj], leitender Mitarbeiter *m* der Geschäftsführung, leitende Mitarbeiterin *f* der Geschäftsführung, leitender Mitarbeiter *m* der Unternehmensleitung, leitende Mitarbeiterin *f* der Unternehmensleitung, ranghoher Mitarbeiter *m* der Geschäftsführung, ranghohe Mitarbeiterin *f* der Geschäftsführung, ranghoher Mitarbeiter *m* der Unternehmensleitung, ranghohe Mitarbeiterin *f* der Unternehmensleitung; ~ **mortgage** *n* BANK, FIN, PROP erstrangige Hypothek *f*, erststellige Hypothek *f*, vorrangige Hypothek *f*; ~ **officer** *n* (*SO*) HRM höhere(r) Beamte(r) *m* [decl. as adj], höhere Beamtin *f*, leitende(r) Angestellte(r) *mf* [decl. as adj]; ~ **refunding** *n* STOCK bevorrechtigte Umfinanzierung *f*, vorrangige Umschuldung *f*; ~ **security** *n* FIN, STOCK mit Vorrechten ausgestattetes Wertpapier *nt*, vorrangiges Wertpapier *nt*; ~ **vice president** *n* MGMNT ranghöchster Stellvertreter *m* des Vorstandsvorsitzenden, ranghöchste Stellvertreterin *f* des Vorstandsvorsitzenden, ranghöchster stellvertretender Generaldirektor *m*, ranghöchste stellvertretende Generaldirektorin *f*, ranghöchster Vizepräsident *m*, ranghöchste Vizepräsidentin *f*

sense: ~ **of realism** *n* GEN COMM Wirklichkeitssinn *m*; ~ **of responsibility** *n* GEN COMM Verantwortungsgefühl *nt*

sensible *adj* GEN COMM vernünftig

sensibly *adv* GEN COMM vernünftig

sensitive *adj* STOCK *market* empfindlich, marktreagibel, sensibel; ~ **market** *n* STOCK empfindlich reagierende Börse *f*

sensitivity *n* GEN COMM Feingefühl *nt*, Sensibilität *f*,

Sensitivität *f*; ~ **analysis** *n* FIN, MATH *statistics* Sensitivitätsanalyse *f*; ~ **training** *n* GEN COMM, HRM, MGMNT Reaktionstraining *nt*, Sensitivitätstraining *nt*

sensitize *vt* GEN COMM, IND sensibilisieren

sensory: ~ **deprivation** *n* MGMNT Gefühlsverarmung *m*; ~ **overload** *n* MGMNT Überbeanspruchung *f* der Sinne

sentence 1. *n* LAW Strafurteil *nt*; **2.** *vt* LAW verurteilen

sentencing *n* LAW Verurteilung *f*

separable: ~ **costs** *n pl* ECON zurechenbare Kosten *pl*

separate 1. *adj* GEN COMM separat; ♦ **under ~ cover** COMMS mit getrennter Post; **2.** *vt* GEN COMM trennen

separate: ~ **customer** *n* STOCK separater Kunde *m*; ~ **tax return** *n* TAX getrennte Veranlagung *f*

separation *n* GEN COMM Abtrennung *f*, Teilung *f*, Trennung *f*

sequence *n* GEN COMM Aufeinanderfolge *f*, Reihenfolge *f*, Folge *f*; ~ **error** *n* COMP Folgefehler *m*; ~ **of movements** *n* IND Bewegungsablauf *m*; ~ **number** *n* COMP Folgenummer *f*, MATH Ordnungsziffer *f*; ~ **of operations** *n* HRM Arbeitsprozeß *m*, Betriebsablauf *m*, Arbeitsablauf *m*; ~ **orders** *n pl* GEN COMM Anschlußaufträge *m pl*

sequential *adj* COMP sequentiell, GEN COMM aufeinanderfolgend, der Reihe nach, in regelmäßiger Folge, MATH sequentiell; ~ **access** *n* COMP sequentieller Zugriff *m*, serieller Zugriff *m*; ~ **analysis** *n* FIN Sequenzanalyse *f*, Verlaufsanalyse *f*, MATH *statistics* Folgeprüfung *f*, S&M Folgeanalyse *f*; ~ **externality** *n* ECON sequentielle Externalität *f*; ~ **number** *n* MATH Folgenummer *f*, laufende Nummer *f*; ~ **sampling** *n* MATH *statistics* sequentielles Stichprobenverfahren *nt*

sequester *vt* LAW sequestrieren, konfiszieren, beschlagnahmen

sequestrate *vt* LAW sequestrieren, konfiszieren, beschlagnahmen

sequestration *n* LAW Sequestration *f*, Konfiszierung *f*, Beschlagnahme *f*, Beschlagnahmung *f*, Zwangsverwaltung *f*

sequestrator *n* LAW Zwangsverwalter, in *m,f*

serial *adj* COMP seriell; ~ **access** *n* COMP sequentieller Zugriff *m*, serieller Zugriff *m*; ~ **adaptor** *n* COMP serieller Adapter *m*; ~ **bond** *n* FIN Serienanleihe *f*; ~ **computer** *n* COMP serieller Rechner *m*; ~ **correlation** *n* MATH *statistics* Reihenkorrelation *f*

serialized *adj* IND in Serie hergestellt

serial: ~ **number** *n* GEN COMM laufende Nummer *f*, Fabrikationsnummer *f*, Seriennummer *f*; ~ **operation** *n* COMP serieller Betrieb *m*; ~**-parallel** *adj* COMP seriellparallel; ~ **port** *n* COMP serieller Anschluß *m*; ~ **printer** *n* COMP serieller Drucker *m*, Zeichendrucker *m*; ~ **processing** *n* COMP serielle Verarbeitung *f*; ~ **reader** *n* COMP serielles Abtastgerät *nt*

seriatim *adv* GEN COMM der Reihe nach

series *n pl* STOCK Reihe *f*; ~ **of options** STOCK Reihe *f* von Optionen; ~**-produced goods** *n pl* ECON in Serie *f* gefertigte Produkte, Serienprodukte *nt pl*

serious: ~ **misdeclaration penalty** *n* BrE TAX erhebliche Strafe *f* für Falschangaben

SERPS *abbr* BrE (*State Earnings-Related Pension Scheme*) ECON lohnbezogener Pensionsplan *m* des Staates, lohngekoppelte Staatspension *f*

serve *vt* GEN COMM *community* dienen, *customer* abfertigen, bedienen, LAW *order* zustellen, S&M *market*, *customer* bedienen; ◆ ~ **a counter-notice** LAW *land compensation* eine Gegenklage zustellen; ~ **a purpose** GEN COMM einem Anliegen dienen, einem Zweck dienen; ~ **sb with a warrant** LAW jdm einen Gerichtsbefehl zustellen

server *n* COMP Server *m*

service 1. *n* GEN COMM Dienst *m*, Dienstleistung *f*, Service *m*, Leistung *f*, Wartung *f*; ◆ ~ **not included** GEN COMM Service nicht eingeschlossen, Wartung nicht inbegriffen; ~ **of a writ** LAW Ladung *f*; **2.** *vt* GEN COMM *market* bedienen, pflegen; ◆ ~ **a loan** FIN ein Darlehen bedienen

service: ~ **abuse** *n* GEN COMM Leistungsmißbrauch *m*, Mißbrauch *m* von Dienstleistungen; ~ **agreement** *n* GEN COMM Dienstvereinbarung *f*, Dienstvertrag *m*, Dienstleistungsabkommen *nt*, Dienstleistungsvereinbarung *f*, Wartungsvertrag *m*; ~ **boat** *n* TRANSP Betriebsboot *nt*, Verkehrsschiff *nt*; ~ **bureau** *n* GEN COMM Serviceunternehmen *nt*; ~ **card** *n* COMP Kundenkarte *f*; ~ **charge** *n* ADMIN Bearbeitungsgebühr *f*, GEN COMM Bedienungsaufschlag *m*; ~ **company** *n* GEN COMM Dienstleistungsbetrieb *m*, Dienstleistungsunternehmen *nt*, Dienstleistungsgewerbe *nt*, *manufacturer* Wartungsfirma *f*; ~ **contract** *n* GEN COMM Dienstvertrag *m*, Dienstleistungsvertrag *m*, Wartungsvertrag *m*, Werkvertrag *m*; ~ **delivery** *n* GEN COMM Bereitstellung *f* von Dienstleistungen, Erbringung *f* von Dienstleistungen; ~ **department** *n* S&M Kundendienstabteilung *f*; ~ **economy** *n* ECON Dienstleistungsgesellschaft *f*; ~ **engineer** *n* HRM Kundendiensttechniker, in *m,f*; ~ **enterprise** *n* GEN COMM Dienstleistungsbetrieb *m*, Dienstleistungsunternehmen *nt*; ~ **fee** *n* GEN COMM Bearbeitungsgebühr *f*, Grundgebühr *f*; ~ **handbook** *n* GEN COMM Servicehandbuch *nt*; ~ **hours** *n pl* GEN COMM Kundendienststunden *f pl*, Servicestunden *f pl*; ~ **income** *n* ECON Arbeitseinkommen *nt*; ~ **industry** *n* ECON, IND Dienstleistungsgewerbe *nt*, Dienstleistungsindustrie *f*, Dienstleistungssektor *m*; ~ **job** *n* HRM Wartungsjob *m*; ~ **life** *n* ECON Nutzungsdauer *f*; ~ **manual** *n* GEN COMM Bedienungshandbuch *nt*; ~ **mark** *n* LAW Dienstleistungsmarke *f*, PATENTS Dienstleistungsmarke *f*, Gebrauchszeichen *nt*

services *n pl* GEN COMM Dienstleistungen *f pl*; ◆ **for ~ rendered** GEN COMM für erbrachte Leistungen

services: ~ **account** *n* ECON *balance of payments* Dienstleistungsbilanz *f*

service: ~ **sector** *n* ECON Dienstleistungssektor *m*; ~ **station** *n* TRANSP Tankstelle *f*; ~ **transactions** *n pl* ECON Dienstleistungsverkehr *m*

servicing *n* COMP Wartung *f*, FIN *of debt* Bedienung *f*, IND Wartung *f*

session *n* ADMIN Tagung *f*, COMP Arbeitssitzung *f*, Sitzung *f*, MGMNT Tagung *f*, POL *of parliament* Sitzung *f*, Sitzungsperiode *f*

set 1. *n* COMP *data, values* Set *nt*, FIN Reihe *f*, GEN COMM Satz *m*; **2.** *vt* ECON *value* festlegen, festsetzen, GEN COMM *record* setzen; ◆ ~ **a date** GEN COMM ein Datum festsetzen; ~ **the fashion** GEN COMM, S&M die Mode festlegen; ~ **limits on** GEN COMM begrenzen; ~ **in motion** GEN COMM in Bewegung setzen; ~ **a new high** ECON einen neuen Höchstwert festsetzen; ~ **objectives** GEN COMM, HRM Arbeitsziele festsetzen; ~ **the pace** GEN COMM das Tempo angeben, das Tempo festlegen; ~ **parameters** MATH Parameter festsetzen; ~ **a price-point** ECON einen Preispunkt bestimmen, einen Preispunkt festlegen; ~ **the standard** MGMNT einen Maßstab setzen, Richtlinien aufstellen; ~ **a trend** GEN COMM die Richtung geben, richtungsweisend sein

set against *vt* ACC, FIN aufrechnen, verrechnen

set aside *vt* LAW *a judgment* annullieren

set down *vt* GEN COMM *in writing* schriftlich niederlegen

set forth *vt* GEN COMM darlegen, vorbringen; ◆ ~ **the spending authority** ADMIN die Zahlungsvollmacht festlegen

set off *vt* ACC, FIN saldieren, verrechnen, GEN COMM *panic, reaction, dispute* auslösen, LAW aufrechnen; ◆ ~ **a debit against a credit** ACC eine Lastschrift mit einer Gutschrift verrechnen

set out *vt* GEN COMM *conditions* aufstellen, darlegen

set over *vt* INS, LAW abtreten

set up *vt* COMP einstellen, einrichten, GEN COMM errichten, geltend machen, *business* eröffnen, gründen, sich niederlassen; ◆ ~ **a claim** LAW eine Forderung stellen, einen Anspruch erheben; ~ **an interview** HRM ein Interview arrangieren; ~ **on one's own account** GEN COMM seine eigene Rechnung aufstellen

set: ~ **of accounts** *n* ACC Kontensatz *m*

setback *n* GEN COMM Rückschlag *m*, Verschlechterung *f*, STOCK Einbruch *m*

set: ~ **of bills** *n* FIN ein Satz *m* Wechsel; ~ **of chattels** *n* LAW bewegliche Sachen *f pl*, Mobiliar *nt*; ~ **of claims** *n* PATENTS Ansprüche *m pl*, Forderungen *f pl*; ~ **of machines** *n* IND Aggregat *nt*; ~ **of measures** *n* FIN Maßnahmenpaket *nt*, Reihe *f* von Maßnahmen; ~**-off** *n* ACC, FIN Verrechnung *f*, LAW Aufrechnung *f*; ~**-off difference** *n* ACC Aufrechnungsdifferenz *f*; ~ **of options** *n* STOCK Optionensatz *m*; ~ **of rules** *n* GEN COMM gesammelte Richtlinien *f pl*; ~ **rules** *n pl* GEN COMM festgelegte Regeln *f pl*, Vorschriften *f pl*

sets: in ~ of *phr* GEN COMM in Mengen von, in Sätzen von

setting *n* COMP Einstellung *f*, GEN COMM *of date, price* Festsetzung *f*; ~ **aside** *n* LAW Annullierung *f*, Aufhebung *f*; ~ **error** *n* MEDIA Setzfehler *m*; ~ **off with equivalent goods** *phr* IMP/EXP Äquivalenzverkehr *m*

settings *n pl* COMP Einstellungen *f pl*

setting: ~**-up costs** *n pl* ACC, FIN Gründungskosten *pl*

settle 1. *vt* ACC saldieren, BANK *account* begleichen, ausgleichen, *transactions* glattstellen, sich vergleichen mit, FIN abwickeln, *account* ausgleichen, GEN COMM begleichen, *dispute* schlichten, beilegen, *sum, figures* ausgleichen, *question* klären, bereinigen; ◆ ~ **an account** ACC, BANK, FIN ein Konto abschließen, ein Konto ausgleichen; ~ **a dispute** HRM Streitigkeiten schlichten; ~ **the figure** LAW *of compensation* den Betrag feststellen; ~ **old scores** GEN COMM alte Rechnungen begleichen; **2.** *vi* GEN COMM *in job, residence, country* sich niederlassen, *pay* bezahlen; ◆ ~ **amicably** HRM sich gütlich einigen; ~ **in cash** GEN COMM bar abrechnen

settled *adj* BANK, FIN begleichen, GEN COMM begleichen, bereinigt, *debt* bezahlt, *resident* seßhaft; ~ **claim** *n* INS regulierter Schaden *m*

settlement *n* GEN COMM *of dispute* Beilegung *f*, Ausgleich *m*, Zahlung *f*, Bereinigung *f*, HRM Abfertigung *f*; ◆ **in ~ of** BANK, FIN *debt* zur Tilgung von

settlement: ~ **account** *n* BANK Verrechnungskonto *nt*; ~ **of account** *n* BANK Kontoausgleich *m*; ~ **of balance** *n* BANK Saldenausgleich *m*; ~ **date** *n* FIN Begleichungstermin *m*, STOCK Abwicklungstermin *m*; ~ **day** *n* STOCK

Abrechnungstag *m*, Erfüllungstag *m*, Liquidationstermin *m*; **~ of debts** *n* BANK *with other banks or government* Begleichung *f* von Schulden; **~ discount** *n* FIN Diskont *m*, Skonto *m*; **~ of a dispute** *n* LAW Beilegung *f* eines Streitfalls; **~ per contra** *n* BANK Aufrechnung *f*; **~ period** *n* STOCK Abrechnungsperiode *f*; **~ price** *n* STOCK Abrechnungskurs *m*, Schlußwert *m*

settlements: **~ department** *n* BANK *merchant bank* Abrechnungsabteilung *f*, Back Office *nt*

settling: **~ of an annuity** *n* LAW Feststellung der Jahresrente *f*; **~ of inter-bank transactions** *n* BANK Bankenabrechnung *f*, Interbanken-Clearing *nt*

settlor *n* LAW Treugeber *m*

set: **~-up** *n* COMP Einstellung *f*

sever: **~ links with sb** *phr* GEN COMM Verbindungen mit jdm abbrechen

severance *n* LAW Abtrennung *f*, PROP *from land* Trennung *f*; **~ pay** *n* HRM Abfindungszahlung *f*, Entlassungsabfindung *f*; **~ payment** *n* HRM Abfindungszahlung *f*, Auslösung *f*; **~ wage** *n* HRM Entlassungsabfindung *f*

severe *adj* GEN COMM streng

severely *adv* GEN COMM streng; **~-disabled worker** *n* HRM schwerbehinderter Arbeitnehmer *m*, schwerbehinderte Arbeitnehmerin *f*; **~-indebted low-income country** *n* (*SILIC*) ECON, FIN stark verschuldetes Land *nt* mit niedrigem Einkommen; **~-indebted middle-income country** *n* (*SIMIC*) ECON, FIN stark verschuldetes Land *nt* mit mittlerem Einkommen

sewage: **~ disposal** *n* ENVIR Abwasserbeseitigung *f*; **~ levy** *n* ENVIR Abwasserabgabe *f*; **~ treatment works** *n* ENVIR Abwasserkläranlage *f*

sex: **~ discrimination** *n* HRM, LAW geschlechtsbezogene Diskriminierung *f*, sexuelle Diskriminierung *f*

Sex: **~ Discrimination Act** *n BrE* (*SDA*) HRM, LAW Gesetz *nt* gegen geschlechtsbezogene Diskriminierung, Gesetz *nt* gegen sexuelle Diskriminierung

sex: **~ stereotyping** *n* HRM sexuelles Klischeedenken *nt*

sexual: **~ discrimination** *n* LAW geschlechtsbezogene Diskriminierung *f*; **~ harassment** *n* HRM, LAW *at work* sexuelle Belästigung *f*

SFTC *abbr* (*standard freight trade classification*) TRANSP Standardfrachthandelklassifizierung *f*

SG *abbr* (*specific gravity*) IND spezifisches Gewicht *nt*

sgd *abbr* (*signed*) GEN COMM gez. (*gezeichnet*), unterschrieben

shading *n* COMP *illustration* Schattierung *f*, Schraffierung *f*

shadow *n* ECON, GEN COMM Schatten *m*, Spur *f*, POL Schatten *m*; **~ cabinet** *n BrE* POL Schattenkabinett *nt*; **~ chancellor** *n BrE* POL Schatzkanzler *m* im Schattenkabinett, Warteschleifenkanzler *m*; **~ economy** *n* ECON Schattenwirtschaft *f*; **~ price** *n* ACC Schattenpreis *m*

shady *adj infrml* GEN COMM zweifelhaft; **~ practices** *n pl infrml* LAW unsaubere Geschäftsmethoden *f pl*

shake off *vt* GEN COMM abschütteln, loswerden

shake out *vt* GEN COMM ausschütteln, herausschütteln

shake up *vt* GEN COMM umbesetzen, umorganisieren

shakedown *n AmE infrml* GEN COMM Angleichung *f*, Anpassung *f*, Umstrukturierung *f*

shake: **~-out** *n* GEN COMM, IND, STOCK Krise, in der die Schwächeren aus dem Markt gedrängt werden, Gesundschrumpfen *nt*, Gesundschrumpfung *f*, HRM

Personalabbau *m*; **~-up** *n* FIN, GEN COMM Umbesetzung *f*, Umorganisation *f*

shaky *adj infrml* GEN COMM wackelig (*infrml*)

shallow: **~ market** *n* STOCK flacher Markt *m*

sham: **~ dividend** *n* FIN fiktive Dividende *f*; **~ trading** *n* STOCK Scheinhandel *m*; **~ transaction** *n* FIN Scheingeschäft *nt*

shape *n* ECON *of economy* Zustand *m*, MATH *of curve* Form *f*

shape up *vi* GEN COMM sich entwickeln

shape: **the ~ of things to come** *n* GEN COMM die Gestalt *f* künftiger Dinge; **~ of the world economy** *n* ECON Zustand *m* der Weltwirtschaft

Shapley: **~ value** *n* ECON Shapley-Wert *m*

share 1. *n* (*cf stock AmE*) ACC Anteil *m*, Wertpapier *nt*, Aktie *f*, *of profits* Beteiligung *f*, FIN Wertpapier *nt*, Anteil *m*, Aktie *f*, GEN COMM *fraction* Anteil *m*, STOCK Aktie *f*, Anteil *m*, langfristige Verpflichtung *f*, Wertpapier *nt*; ◆ **have a ~ in a business** GEN COMM einen Geschäftsanteil an einem Unternehmen besitzen; **~ prices reached an all-time high** *BrE* STOCK die Aktienkurse erreichten einen Höchstand; **2.** *vt* COMP *software, peripherals* gemeinsam benutzen, GEN COMM teilen; ◆ **~ sth with sb** GEN COMM etw mit jdm teilen

share out *vt* GEN COMM *work, money* verteilen

share: **~ acquisition** *n* FIN, STOCK Aktienübernahme *f*; **~ allotment** *n* STOCK Aktienzuteilung *f*; **~ bonus** *n BrE* FIN Aktiensplit *m*; **~ buyback** *n* STOCK Aktienrückkauf *m*; **~ capital** *BrE* (*cf capital stock AmE*) *n* ECON Aktienkapital *nt*, Betriebskapital *nt*, Grundkapital *nt*, FIN Aktienkapital *nt*, Geschäftskapital *nt*, Stammkapital *nt*, STOCK Aktienkapital *nt*; **~ certificate** *n BrE* (*cf stock certificate AmE*) STOCK Aktienurkunde *f*, Aktienzertifikat *nt*, Anteilschein *m*; **~ consolidation** *n* FIN Aktienzusammenlegung *f*

sharecropper *n AmE* ECON *agricultural* Naturalpächter *m*

shared: **~ appreciation mortgage** *n* BANK, PROP Hypothek *f* mit Gewinnbeteiligung des Gläubigers; **~-cost program** *AmE*, **~-cost programme** *BrE n* ECON, POL Programm *nt* der öffentlichen Hand mit Kostenbeteiligung, Regierungsprogramm *nt* mit anteiliger Kostenübernahme; **~ database** *n* COMP gemeinsam genutzte Datenbank *f*, gemeinsame Datenbank *f*

share: **~ dealings** *n pl* ECON Aktiengeschäfte *nt pl*; **~ dividend** *n* STOCK Aktiendividende *f*

shared: **~ monopoly** *n* ECON Teilmonopol *nt*

share: **~ draft** *n* FIN Zahlungsanweisung eines Mitglieds einer Genossenschaftsbank zu Lasten der eigenen Einlage; **~ economy** *n* ECON Aktionärswirtschaft *f*; **~ fishing** *n* ECON *agricultural* Pachtfischerei *f*

shareholder *n* (*cf stockholder AmE*) HRM Aktionär, in *m,f*, Anteilseigner, in *m,f*, STOCK Aktieninhaber, in *m,f*; **~ commitment contract** *n* LAW *innominate contract* Aktionärsbindungsvertrag *m*; **~ employee** *n* STOCK *staff* Belegschaftsaktionär, in *m,f*; **~ group** *n* ECON Aktionärsgruppe *f*; **~ loan** *n* FIN Aktionärsdarlehen *nt*

shareholders': **~ annual meeting** *n* STOCK Hauptversammlung *f* (*HV*); **~ equity** *n AmE* STOCK Reinvermögen *nt*; **~ general meeting** *n* STOCK Aktionärshauptversammlung *f*; **~ meeting** *n* STOCK Aktionärsversammlung *f*

shareholding *n* STOCK Aktienbesitz *m*, Aktienbeteiligung *f* *share*: ~ **incentive scheme** *n* STOCK Aktienerwerb *m* durch leitende Angestellte; ~ **index** *n* STOCK Aktienindex *m*; ~ **of the inheritance** *n* LAW Erbanteil *m*; ~ **investments in other companies** *n pl* ACC *annual accounts* Beteiligungen *f pl* an anderen Gesellschaften; ~ **issue** *n* STOCK Aktienemission *f*; ~ **market** *n* STOCK Aktienmarkt *m*; ~ **of market** *n* S&M Marktanteil *m*; ~ **option right** *n* STOCK Aktienbezugsrecht *nt*; ~ **option scheme** *n* STOCK, TAX *employee benefits* Aktienbezugsrechtsplan *m*; ~ **participation scheme** *n* STOCK *for employees* Aktiengewinnbeteiligungsprogramm *nt*; ~ **portfolio** *n BrE (cf stock portfolio AmE)* STOCK Aktienbestand *m*, Aktienportefeuille *nt*; ~ **premium** *n (cf stock issue premium AmE)* ACC, FIN, STOCK Aktienprämie *f*, Aktienagio *nt*, Agio *nt* aus Aktienemission, Aktienemissionsagio *nt*; ~ **premium account** *n BrE* FIN Emissionsagiorücklage *f*, Kapitalrücklage *f*; ~ **premium reserve** *n BrE* ACC Agiorücklage *f*, Kapitalrücklage *f*; ~ **price index** *n* STOCK Aktienindex *m*, Aktienpreisindex *m*, Kursindex *m*; ~ **price performance** *n* FIN, STOCK Aktienkursentwicklung *f*; ~ **prices** *n pl BrE* STOCK Aktienkurse *m pl*; ~ **of production plan** *n* IND Produktionsplanbeteiligung *f*; ~ **purchase warrant** *n* STOCK Aktienbezugsrecht *nt*, Bezugsrecht *nt*; ~ **pushing** *n* STOCK Aktienschwindel *m*, betrügerischer Verkauf *m* wertloser Aktien; ~ **quotation** *n* STOCK Kursnotierung *f*; ~ **register** *n* STOCK Aktienregister *nt*, Aktionärsbuch *nt*; ~ **repurchase plan** *n* STOCK Aktienrückkaufplan *m*

shares: ~ **authorized** *n* STOCK autorisierte Aktien *f pl*

share: ~ **scheme** *n* STOCK *for company employees* Aktienbeteiligungsplan *m*

shares: ~ **held in treasury** *n pl* STOCK Vorratsaktien *f pl*; ~ **moved ahead** *n pl* STOCK Aktien *f pl* im Aufwärtstrend; ~ **outstanding** *n pl* STOCK im Umlauf befindliche Aktien *f pl*

share: ~ **split** *n* STOCK Aktiensplit *m*

shares: ~ **quoted officially** *n BrE (cf stock quoted officially AmE)* STOCK amtlich notierte Aktien *f pl*

share: ~ **support operation** *n* STOCK Aktienstützungsaktion *f*; ~ **transfer** *n* STOCK Aktienübertragung *f*

shareware *n* COMP Shareware *f*

shark *n infrml* S&M *sales representative* Nepper *m* (*infrml*)

sharp: ~ **drop** *n* ECON drastischer Rückgang *m*, STOCK Baisse *f*; ~ **protest** *n* GEN COMM scharfer Protest *m*; ~ **rally** *n* GEN COMM rapide Wiederbelebung *f*; ~ **rise** *n* ECON *in prices, rates* drastischer Anstieg *m*

shattered: ~ **finance** *n* ECON zerrüttete Finanzen *f pl*

shed *vt* GEN COMM abstoßen, entlassen; ♦ ~ **jobs** GEN COMM Arbeitsplätze einsparen; ~ **light on** GEN COMM Licht werfen auf

sheet *n* COMMS, MEDIA *of paper* Blatt *nt*, Bogen *m*, S&M *advertising* großformatige Anzeige *f*; ~ **feeder** *n* COMP Einzelblatteinzug *m*, Einzelblattzuführung *f*; ~ **feeding** *n* COMP Einzelblatteinzug *m*, Einzelblattzuführung *f*

shelf *n* GEN COMM, S&M Regal *nt*; ~ **display** *n* S&M *marketing* Regalauslage *f*; ~ **filler** *n* S&M Regalfüller *m*; ~ **labeling** *AmE*, ~ **labelling** *BrE n* S&M Regalauszeichnung *f*; ~ **life** *n* S&M Haltbarkeit *f*, Lagerbeständigkeit *f*; ~ **price** *n* S&M Regalauszeichnung *f*; ~ **registration** *n AmE* STOCK Vorausregistrierung *f*; ~ **space** *n* S&M Lagerfläche *f*,

Regalfläche *f*; ~ **talker** *n* S&M *advertising* Kleinplakat *nt* mit Werbung zum Aufstellen

shell: ~ **company** *n* GEN COMM Firmenmantel *m*, TAX Strohfirma *f*; ~ **corporation** *n* GEN COMM Firmenmantel *m*; ~ **operation** *n* STOCK Übernahme *f* eines Unternehmens

shelter *vt* TAX *from tax* schützen vor

sheltered: ~ **employment** *n* HRM Beschäftigung *f* in beschützenden Werkstätten; ~ **industries** *n pl* IND durch Einfuhrzölle geschützte Industriezweige

shelve *vt* GEN COMM aufschieben, zurückstellen; ♦ ~ **a decision** GEN COMM eine Entscheidung aufschieben

Sherman: ~ **Act** *n AmE* ECON Kartellgesetz von 1890

SHEX *abbr* (*Sundays and holidays excepted*) GEN COMM außer an Sonn- und Feiertagen, Sonn- und Feiertage ausgenommen

shield *vt* GEN COMM abschirmen, absichern, schützen vor [+dat]

shift 1. *n* COMP *on keyboard* Umschalten *nt*, HRM *working hours* Schicht *f*; **2.** *vt* FIN umschichten, GEN COMM *emphasis* verschieben, HRM *redeploy* umsetzen, TAX überwälzen; ♦ ~ **on to** GEN COMM *responsibility* abwälzen auf [+acc]; ~ **the emphasis** GEN COMM den Akzent verschieben

shift: ~ **differential** *n* HRM Schichtzuschlag *m*; ~ **in consumption** *n* S&M Konsumverlagerung *f*; ~ **in demand** *n* S&M Nachfrageverschiebung *f*; ~ **in demand curve** *n* ECON Verschiebung *f* der Nachfragekurve; ~ **in deposits** *n* FIN Einlagenumschichtung *f*

shifting *n* FIN Umschichtung *f*, GEN COMM Verlagerung *f*, TAX Steuerüberwälzung *f*, Überwälzung *f*; ~ **of target dates** *n* ECON Terminverlagerung *f*

shift: ~ **key** *n* COMP Umschalttaste *f*; ~ **rotation** *n* HRM Schichtwechsel *m*; ~ **in supply curve** *n* ECON Verschiebung *f* der Anbegotskurve

shiftwork *n* HRM Schichtarbeit *f*

shiftworker *n* HRM Schichtarbeiter, in *m,f*

SHINC *abbr* (*Sundays and holidays included*) GEN COMM einschließlich Sonn- und Feiertage, inklusive Sonn- und Feiertage, Sonn- und Feiertage eingeschlossen

ship 1. *n* TRANSP Schiff *nt*; **2.** *vt* COMMS befördern, übersenden, verschicken, IMP/EXP, TRANSP *freight* übersenden, verschicken, versenden; ♦ ~ **by rail** TRANSP mit der Bahn verschicken

shipbroker *n* IMP/EXP, INS, TRANSP Schiffsmakler, in *m,f*

shipbuilder *n* IND, TRANSP Schiffsbauer *m*

shipbuilding *n* IND, TRANSP Schiffsbau *m*

ship: ~ **conversion** *n* TRANSP Schiffsumbau *m*; ~ **management** *n* TRANSP Schiffsmanagement *nt*, Schiffsverwaltung *f*

shipment *n* COMMS, IMP/EXP, TRANSP Beförderung *f*, Übersendung *f*, Verladen *nt*, Verladung *f*, Versand *m*, Verschiffung *f*; ♦ **on ~** COMMS, IMP/EXP, TRANSP bei Versand

shipowner *n* IMP/EXP, TRANSP Reeder, in *m,f*, Schiffseigner, in *m,f*; ~**'s liability** *n* (*SOL*) INS, LAW, TRANSP Schiffseignerhaftung *f*

shipped *adj* COMMS, IMP/EXP, TRANSP verschifft; ♦ ~ **on board** IMP/EXP, TRANSP an Bord verschifft, an Bord gebracht

shipped: ~ **bill** *n* IMP/EXP, TRANSP Bordkonnossement *nt*, Verschiffungskonnossement *nt*; ~ **bill of lading** *n* IMP/EXP, TRANSP Bordkonnossement *nt*

shipper *n* COMMS Verlader *m*, IMP/EXP, TRANSP Befrachter *m*, Verlader *m*, Versender, in *m,f*; ~ **and carrier** *n* (*s&c*) IMP/EXP, TRANSP Befrachter *m* und Beförderer *m*; **'s letter of instruction** *n* IMP/EXP, TRANSP Befrachteranweisungen *f pl*; ~**'s load and count** *n* (*sl&c*) TRANSP Ladung *f* und Kontrolle *f* des Befrachters, Ladung *f* und Zählung *f* des Befrachters

shipping *n* COMMS, IMP/EXP, TRANSP Schiffahrt *f*, *transportation* Verladen *nt*, Verladung *f*, Versand *m*, Verschiffung *f*, Versendung *f*; ~ **address** *n* TRANSP Versandanschrift *f*; ~ **agency** *n* TRANSP Schiffsagentur *f*, Speditionsfirma *f*; ~ **agent** *n* TRANSP Schiffsmakler, in *m,f*, Seehafenspediteur *m*; ~ **bill** *n* IMP/EXP Konnossement *nt*, TRANSP Frachtbrief *m*, Konnossement *nt*; ~ **business** *n* GEN COMM Reederei *f*; ~ **clerk** *n* TRANSP Expedient *m*; ~ **documents** *n pl* GEN COMM Warenpapiere *nt pl*, IMP/EXP, TRANSP Transportpapiere *nt pl*, Versandpapiere *nt pl*, Verschiffungsdokumente *nt pl*; ~ **and forwarding agent** *n* (*S&FA*) HRM, IMP/EXP, TRANSP Schiffsmakler und Spediteur *m*; ~ **instructions** *n pl* TRANSP Versandanweisungen *f pl*, Versandvorschriften *f pl*; ~ **invoice** *n* GEN COMM, IMP/EXP Versandrechnung *f*; ~ **lane** *n* TRANSP Schiffahrtsroute *f*, Schiffahrtsweg *m*; ~ **line** *n* TRANSP Schiffahrtslinie *f*; ~ **note** *n* (*S/N*) IMP/EXP, TRANSP Ladeschein *m*, Schiffszettel *m*, Versandanzeige *f*; ~ **office** *n* IMP/EXP, TRANSP Reederei *f*; ~ **officer** *n* IMP/EXP, TRANSP Reeder, in *m,f*, Schiffsmakler, in *m,f*, Seehafenspediteur *m*; ~ **papers** *n pl* IMP/EXP, TRANSP Transportpapiere *nt pl*, Versandpapiere *nt pl*, Verschiffungsdokumente *nt pl*; ~ **port** *n* TRANSP Versandhafen *m*; ~ **register** *n* TRANSP Schiffahrtsregister *f*; ~ **trade** *n* IMP/EXP, TRANSP Seetransportgeschäft *nt*

ship: ~ **plan** *n* TRANSP Schiffsplan *m*; ~ **planning** *n* IND, TRANSP *design* Schiffskonstruktion *f*; ~**'s agent** *n* TRANSP Reedereivertreter, in *m,f*; ~**'s articles** *n pl* TRANSP Heuervertrag *m*, Seemannsordnung *f*; ~**'s delivery order** *n* IMP/EXP, TRANSP Schiffslieferschein *m*; ~**'s inward report** *n* IMP/EXP Schiffsankunftsmeldung *f*; ~**'s log** *n* TRANSP Logbuch *nt*, Schiffstagebuch *nt*; ~**'s papers** *n pl* LAW, TRANSP Schiffsdokumente *nt pl*, Schiffspapiere *nt pl*; ~ **specification** *n* TRANSP Schiffsspezifikation *f*; ~ **turnaround time** *AmE*, ~ **turnround time** *BrE n* TRANSP Liegezeit *f* im Hafen, Schiffumlaufzeit *f*

shipwreck *n* TRANSP Strandung *f*

shirk *vi infrml* HRM sich drücken

shirker *n infrml* HRM Drückeberger *m* (*infrml*)

shock: ~ **inflation** *n* ECON Schockinflation *f*; ~ **loss** *n* ECON unerwartet hoher Verlust *m*

shoot *n* MEDIA, S&M *advertising, film, photo session* Filmaufnahme *f*

shoot up *vi* GEN COMM scharf ansteigen, emporschnellen, in die Höhe schießen

shooting: ~ **script** *n* MEDIA, S&M Drehplan *m*

shop 1. *n* S&M *BrE* (*cf store AmE*) Laden *m*, *advertising agency* kleines Unternehmen *nt*; **2.** *vi* S&M einkaufen, Einkäufe machen

shop around *vi* S&M sich umsehen; ♦ ~ **for the best price** S&M sich nach dem besten Preis umsehen

shop: ~ **assistant** *n BrE* (*cf sales clerk AmE*) HRM, S&M Verkäufer, in *m,f*; ~ **audit** *n* S&M Händlerbefragung *f*; ~ **closing times** *n pl BrE* (*cf store closing times AmE*)

GEN COMM Ladenschlußzeiten *f pl*; ~ **floor** *n* GEN COMM Werkstatt *f*, IND *place* Produktion *f*, Werkstatt *f*, *staff* Belegschaft *f*, Fabrikarbeiter *m pl*, S&M Verkaufsfläche *f*; **on the ~ floor** *phr* HRM, IND im Betrieb, in der Werkstatt; ~**-floor agreement** *n BrE* HRM Betriebsvereinbarung *f*; ~**-floor bargaining** *n BrE* HRM Verhandlungen *f pl* auf Betriebsebene; ~**-floor participation** *n* HRM Arbeiterbeteiligung *f*; ~ **front** *n* S&M Ladenfront *f*, *display* Schaufenster *nt*, Auslage *f*

shopkeeper *n BrE* (*cf storekeeper AmE*) S&M Ladeninhaber, in *m,f*

shoplifting *n* S&M Ladendiebstahl *m*, Warenhausdiebstahl *m*

shopper *n* S&M Käufer, in *m,f*

shopping *n* GEN COMM *items purchased* Einkäufe *m pl*, *act* Einkaufen *nt*; ~ **arcade** *n* GEN COMM Einkaufspassage *f*; ~ **bag** *n* S&M Tragetüte *f*, Tragetasche *f*; ~ **basket** *n* GEN COMM Warenkorb *m*; ~ **center** *AmE*, ~ **centre** *BrE n* GEN COMM Einkaufszentrum *nt*, Geschäftszentrum *nt*; ~ **goods** *n pl* GEN COMM Ware *f* des nichttäglichen Bedarfs; ~ **mall** *n AmE* GEN COMM Einkaufszentrum *nt*, Geschäftszentrum *nt*; ~ **precinct** *n BrE* GEN COMM Einkaufszentrum *nt*

shop: ~**'s articles** *n pl* HRM Betriebsvereinbarungsbestimmungen *f pl*; ~ **steward** *n* HRM, IND, MGMNT gewerkschaftlicher Obmann *m*, gewerkschaftlicher Vertrauensmann *m*; ~ **talk** *n infrml* Fachsimpelei (*infrml*); ~ **traffic** *n* S&M Ladenverkehr *m*; ~ **unit** *n BrE* S&M Geschäftseinheit *f*; ~ **window** *n* S&M Schaufenster *nt*, Schaufensterscheibe *f*

short 1. *adj* GEN COMM kurz; ♦ **be ~ of** GEN COMM fehlen an [+dat]; **be in ~ supply** GEN COMM nur beschränkt lieferbar sein; **be on ~ time** HRM Kurzarbeit leisten; **2.** *n* STOCK Leerverkauf *m*, *futures market* Baisseposition *f*

short: ~ **account** *n* STOCK Kundenkonto eines Maklers zur Abwicklung von Leerverkäufen, Baisseengagement *nt*, Baisseposition *f*; ~ **against the box** *n* STOCK Leerverkauf *m* eines Haussiers

shortage *n* ECON Knappheit *f*, Mangel *m*, GEN COMM *cash, stock or missing entries in accounts* Defizit *nt*, Fehlbetrag *m*, Manko *nt* (*infrml*), HRM Arbeitsmangel *m*; ~ **economy** *n* ECON Mangelwirtschaft *f*; ~ **of manpower** *n* HRM Arbeitskräftemangel *m*, Personalmangel *m*

short: ~ **bill** *n* (*SB*) FIN kurzfristig fälliger Wechsel *m*; ~ **butterfly** *n* STOCK kurzfristige kombinierte Optionsposition *f*; ~ **call position** *n* STOCK Baisse-Kauf-Optionsposition *f*; ~**-change sb** *phr* GEN COMM jdm nicht genügend Wechselgeld herausgeben

short-circuit 1. *n* IND Kurzschluß *m*; **2.** *vt* IND kurzschließen

short: ~ **coupon** *n* STOCK Bond *m* mit kurzer Restlaufzeit; ~ **covering** *n* STOCK Deckung *f*, Deckungskauf *m* zum Ausgleich eines Leerverkaufs; ~ **credit** *n* FIN, STOCK kurzfristiger Kredit *m*; ~**-dated** *adj* STOCK kurzfristig; ~**-date financing rate** *n* STOCK *futures* kurzfristige Finanzierungsrate *f*; ~ **delivery** *n* (*SD*) INS Minderlieferung *f*, unvollständige Lieferung *f*

shorten *vt* GEN COMM verkürzen, INS abkürzen, STOCK kürzen, reduzieren, verkürzen

shortened *adj* STOCK reduziert

shortening *n* GEN COMM Verkürzung *f*, STOCK Kürzung *f*, Verkürzung *f*

shorter: **~-term option** n STOCK kürzerfristige Option f; **~ working hours** n pl HRM Arbeitszeitverkürzung f

shortfall n ACC goods Fehlmenge f, money Fehlbetrag m, GEN COMM Fehlmenge f, Fehlbetrag m, Deckungslücke f; **~ in earnings** n GEN COMM Gewinnausfall m, Gewinndefizit nt

short: **~ form** n IMP/EXP, TRANSP bill of lading auf kurze Zeit ausgestelltes Konnossement nt, Kurzkonnossement nt, detailliertes Formular nt, kurzfristiger Frachtbrief m; **~ form bill of lading** n IMP/EXP, TRANSP auf kurze Zeit ausgestelltes Konnossement nt, Kurzkonnossement nt; **~ futures position** n STOCK Verkaufsposition f am Terminkontraktmarkt

shorthand n ADMIN Kurzschrift f, Stenographie f, Steno f (infrml); **~ dictation** n ADMIN Diktat nt

short: **be ~-handed** phr HRM unter Personalmangel leiden; **~-handedness** n HRM Mangel m an Personal

shorthand: **~ and typing skills** n pl ADMIN, HRM Steno- und Schreibmaschinenkenntnisse f pl; **~ typist** n ADMIN, HRM Stenotypist, in m,f

short: **~ haul** n TRANSP Kurzstrecke f, Nahverkehr m; **~ hedge** n STOCK Verkaufssicherungsgeschäft nt; **~ interest** n BANK kurzfristiger Zins m, STOCK securities and futures trading Baisseengagement nt; **~ interest theory** n STOCK Baisseengagement-Theorie f, Baissepositions-Theorie f; **~ key** n COMP Kurzeingabe f, Kurztaste f, Tastenkürzel nt; **~-landed** adj TRANSP cargo unvollständig

shortlist 1. n GEN COMM Auswahlliste f, Vorauswahl f, HRM Auswahlliste f, Vorauswahl f, Kandidatenliste f; **2.** vt GEN COMM, HRM eine Vorauswahl treffen, in die engere Auswahl nehmen; ♦ **be shortlisted** GEN COMM, HRM in die engere Auswahl kommen

short: **~-lived** adj GEN COMM kurzlebig, von kurzem Bestand; **~ loan** n FIN, STOCK kurzfristiger Kredit m; **~ notice** n GEN COMM kurze Frist f; **~ option position** n STOCK Verkaufsposition f am Optionsmarkt; **~ position** n STOCK Baisseposition f, Baisseengagement nt, Leerverkaufsposition f; **~ position in a currency** n BANK Währungsleerposition f; **~ pull** n STOCK kurzfristiger Gewinn m; **~-range** adj GEN COMM kurzfristig; **~-range maturity date** n STOCK kurzfristiger Fälligkeitstermin m, kurzfristiges Fälligkeitsdatum nt; **~-range planning** n FIN, MGMNT Kurzzeitplanung f, kurzfristige Planung f; **~ run** n (SR) IND Kleinauflage f; **in the ~ run** phr GEN COMM kurzfristig

shorts n pl STOCK kurzfristige Staatspapiere nt pl, government stocks Kurzläufer m pl, Schuldtitel m pl mit kurzer Laufzeit

short: **~-sale rule** n STOCK Leerverkaufsregel f; **~ sea shipping** n TRANSP große Küstenfahrt f; **~ sea trade** n TRANSP großer Küstenhandel m; **~ seller** n STOCK Blankoverkäufer, in m,f; **~ selling** n STOCK Baissegeschäft nt; **~ shipment** n TRANSP Minderlieferung f; **~-shipped** adj TRANSP mindergeliefert, unvollständig geliefert; **~-sighted** adj GEN COMM policy, decision kurzsichtig; **be ~-staffed** phr HRM business, firm unter Personalmangel leiden, zu wenig Personal haben; **~ straddle** n STOCK options kurzfristige kombinierte Optionsposition f; **~ tail** n INS risk beschränktes Eigentumsrecht nt, beschränktes Erbrecht nt; **~-term** adj GEN COMM kurzfristig; **~ term** n STOCK kurzfristige Laufzeit f; **in the ~ term** phr GEN COMM kurzfristig; **~-term bond** n STOCK kurzfristige Schuldverschreibung f; **~-term contract** n HRM kurzfristiger

Vertrag m; **~-term debt** n BANK Kurzläufer m, kurzfristige Schuldtitel m pl, kurzfristige Verbindlichkeit f; **~-term deposit** n STOCK kurzfristige Einlage f; **~-term fluctuation** n ECON kurzfristige Fluktuation f; **~-term gain** n STOCK kurzfristiger Gewinn m; **~-term interest rate** n ECON Zinssatz m für kurzfristige Kredite; **~-term interest rate futures contract** n STOCK kurzfristiger Zinsterminkontrakt m; **~-term interest rate risk** n STOCK financial futures kurzfristiges Zinssatzrisiko nt; **~-term investment asset** n ACC, ADMIN kurzfristige Aktiva nt pl, kurzfristiges Investitionsgut nt; **~-term investment portfolio** n STOCK kurzfristiges Beteiligungsportefeuille nt, kurzfristiges Wertpapierportefeuille nt; **~-term liability** n ACC, STOCK kurzfristige Verbindlichkeit f; **~-term loss** n STOCK kurzfristiger Verlust m; **~-term market** n STOCK kurzfristiger Markt m; **~-term money market** n STOCK kurzfristiger Geldmarkt m; **~-term objective** n GEN COMM kurzfristiges Ziel nt; **~-term planning** n FIN, MGMNT Kurzfristplanung f, kurzfristige Planung f; **~-term prepayment** n ACC kurzfristige Vorauszahlung f; **~-term security** n STOCK kurzfristiges Wertpapier nt; **~-term vehicle park** n (STVP) TRANSP Kurzzeitfahrzeugpark m; **~-term worker** n HRM Hilfskraft f mit kurzfristigem Vertrag; **~-time working** n HRM Kurzarbeit f

shoulder vt GEN COMM burden übernehmen, tragen

shoulder: **~ period** n GEN COMM product Degenerationsphase f

show 1. n GEN COMM, S&M Ausstellung f; **2.** vt ACC ansetzen, GEN COMM bekunden, anzeigen, demonstrate zeigen; ♦ **~ a balance of sth** ACC einen Saldo von etw ausweisen; **~ a loss** ACC einen Verlust ausweisen; **~ on the books** ACC ausweisen; **~ one's hand** infrml GEN COMM seine Karten auf den Tisch legen; **~ a proven track record** HRM gute Leistungen vorzuweisen haben; **~ a surplus** ACC profit einen Überschuß aufweisen

show: **~ apartment** n AmE (cf show flat BrE) PROP Modellwohnung f; **~ business** n LEIS, MEDIA Show Business nt, Vergnügungsindustrie f, Unterhaltungsindustrie f; **~ card** n S&M Aufstellplakat nt, Musterkarte f, window display Werbeplakat nt

showcase n S&M display Schaukasten m, Vitrine f

showdown n infrml GEN COMM Kraftprobe f

show: **~ flat** n BrE (cf show apartment AmE) GEN COMM, PROP Modellwohnung f; **~ house** n PROP Modellhaus nt

showpiece n GEN COMM collection Ausstellungsstück nt, Glanzstück nt

shredder n ADMIN Dokumentenvernichter m, Papieraktenvernichter m, Aktenvernichter m, Reißwolf m

shrink vi ECON abnehmen, sinken, schwinden

shrinkage n ECON Rückgang m, Schwund m, S&M due to theft Ladendiebstahl m, Warenhausdiebstahl m

shrinking adj STOCK rückläufig; **~ market** n GEN COMM rückläufiger Aktienmarkt m, schrumpfender Markt m, STOCK rückläufiger Aktienmarkt m; **~ profits** n pl GEN COMM schrumpfende Gewinne m pl, zurückgehende Gewinne m pl

shrink: **~-packaging** n GEN COMM Schrumpfverpackung f; **~-wrapping** n GEN COMM Schrumpfverpackung f

shunt vt TRANSP rangieren; ♦ **~ to the sideline** ECON vom Markt verdrängen

shunter n BrE FIN, HRM, STOCK Arbitrageur m

shunting *n BrE* FIN, HRM, STOCK Arbitrage *f* zwischen zwei Parallelmärkten

shut down 1. *vt* GEN COMM *branch, company* schließen, zumachen *(infrml)*, IND *permanently* stillegen; **2.** *vi* GEN COMM *branch, company* schließen, zumachen *(infrml)*, IND *permanently* stillgelegt werden; **3.** *adj* GEN COMM stillgelegt

shut off *vt* GEN COMM abschalten, abstellen, ausschalten

shutdown *n* GEN COMM *factory* Betriebsschließung *f*, Schließung *f*, Stillegung *f*, Betriebsstillegung *f*

shut: **~-out** *n* TRANSP Ausschließung *f*; **~-out cargo** *n* TRANSP nicht verladene Fracht *f*

shutting: **~ off** *n* GEN COMM Abschalten *nt*

shuttle *n* TRANSP *flight, bus, train* Pendelverkehr *m*, Shuttle *m*; **~ service commuter traffic** *n* TRANSP Pendelverkehr *m*, Shuttleverkehr *m*

shut: **~ up shop** *phr* GEN COMM das Geschäft schließen

shyster *n infrml* LAW, POL Rechtsverdreher *m* *(infrml)*

SIB *abbr BrE* (*Securities and Investment Board*) STOCK Aufsichtsbehörde für den britischen Finanz- und Wertpapierhandel

SIBOR *abbr* (*Singapore Interbank Offered Rate*) BANK SIBOR (*Singapur Interbankenangebotssatz*)

SIC *abbr* (*standard industrial classification*) IND amtliche Branchenklassifikation *f*, amtliche Systematik *f* der Betriebsstätten

sick: be off ~ *phr* HRM aus Krankheitsgründen abwesend sein *(frml)*; **be on ~ leave** *phr* HRM krankgeschrieben sein; **~ building syndrome** *n* ADMIN Syndrom *nt* der ausbesserungsbedürftigen Gebäude

sickness *n* HRM, INS, WEL Krankheit *f*; **~ benefit** *n* HRM Krankengeld *nt*; **~ insurance** *n* HRM, INS, WEL Krankenversicherung *f*; **~ insurance premium** *n* HRM, INS, WEL Krankenversicherungsprämie *f*

sick: **~ pay** *n* HRM Krankengeld *nt*; **~ pay scheme** *n BrE* HRM Krankengeldregelung *f*

side: on the ~ *phr* GEN COMM nebenher; **~-by-side trading** *n* STOCK Handel mit einem Wertpapier und der Option auf dieses Wertpapier an derselben Börse; **~ deal** *n* ECON Nebenabsprache *f*; **~ effects** *n pl* GEN COMM Nebenwirkungen *f pl*; **~ issue** *n* GEN COMM Randproblem *nt*

sideline: **~ job** *n* HRM Nebenbeschäftigung *f*; **~ market** *n* S&M Nebenmarkt *m*; **~ point** *n* TRANSP *cargo tariff* Nebentarif *m*

sidetrack *n AmE* (*cf siding BrE*) TRANSP *rail* Abstellgleis *nt*, Anschlußgleis *nt*, Ausweichgleis *nt*, Nebengleis *nt*, Seitengleis *nt*, Überholungsgleis *nt*

sideways: **~ market** *n* STOCK uneinheitlich tendierender Markt *m*

siding *n BrE* (*cf sidetrack AmE*) TRANSP *rail* Abstellgleis *nt*, Anschlußgleis *nt*, Ausweichgleis *nt*, Nebengleis *nt*, Seitengleis *nt*, Überholungsgleis *nt*

siege: **~ economy** *n* ECON Belagerungswirtschaft *f*

siftproof: **~ packaging** *n* TRANSP dichte Verpackung *f*; **~ receptacle** *n* TRANSP dichter Behälter *m*

sight *n* FIN Sicht *f*; ◆ **at ~** (*a/s*) FIN bei Sicht, bei Vorlage, gegen Vorlage, bei Vorlegung

sight: **~ bill** *n* BANK, FIN Sichtwechsel *m*; **~ deposit** *n* BANK Sichteinlage *f*, Giroeinlage *f*; **~ draft** *n* (*S/D*) BANK Sichttratte *f*, Sichtwechsel *m*; **at ~ draft** *n* BANK Sichttratte *f*; **~ rate** *n* FIN Devisenkurs für kursfristige

Auslandszahlungsmittel, Sichtkurs *m*; **~-seeing tour** *n* LEIS Besichtigung *f*

sign 1. *n* GEN COMM *indication* Anzeichen *nt*, Spur *f*, *plate* Schild *nt*, MATH *symbol* Zeichen *nt*; **2.** *vt* GEN COMM zeichnen, *contract* unterschreiben, unterzeichnen; ◆ **~ a legal agreement** LAW eine rechtliche Vereinbarung unterschreiben; **~ on the dotted line** ADMIN *on form* auf der punktierten Linie unterschreiben, auf der gestrichelten Linie unterschreiben

sign in *vi* HRM registrieren

sign off *vi* HRM kündigen

sign on *vi* HRM *for unemployment benefit* sich als arbeitslos registrieren lassen

sign up 1. *vt* GEN COMM einstellen, verpflichten; **2.** *vi* GEN COMM sich verpflichten

signal *n* GEN COMM *indication* Signal *nt*, Zeichen *nt*

signaling *AmE see* **signalling** *BrE*

signal: **~ light** *n* COMP Signalleuchte *f*, Signallicht *nt*

signalling *n BrE* COMMS Übermittlung *f* von Signalen, Signalisierung *f*

signatory *n* LAW *of contract, treaty*, POL *of treaty* Unterzeichner, in *m,f*; ◆ **be a ~ to sth** LAW, POL *agreement, convention* Unterzeichner von etw sein

signature *n* ADMIN, COMMS, COMP, GEN COMM, LAW Unterschrift *f*, Unterzeichnung *f*, Zeichnung *f*; ◆ **for ~** ADMIN, GEN COMM zur Unterzeichnung

signature: **~ tune** *n* MEDIA *broadcast*, S&M Erkennungsmelodie *f*, Pausenzeichen *nt*, Sendermelodie *f*

signed *adj* (*sgd*) GEN COMM gezeichnet (*gez.*), unterschrieben; ◆ **~ and sealed** LAW *contract* unterschrieben und mit Siegel versehen

signed: **~ articles** *n pl* TRANSP *shipping, crew* Heuerbedingungen *f pl*, Heuervertrag *m*

significance *n* GEN COMM Bedeutung *f*, Belang *m*, Signifikanz *f*; **~ test** *n* MATH *statistics* Signifikanztest *m*

significant *adj* GEN COMM bedeutsam, wichtig, bedeutend

signify *vt* GEN COMM *indicate* bedeuten, erkennen lassen, mitteilen, zum Ausdruck bringen; ◆ **~ acceptance by conduct** LAW *contracts* Annahme durch Willenserklärung nach außen bekanntgeben

signing *n* GEN COMM Zeichnung *f*; **~ authority** *n* ECON Zeichnungsvollmacht *f*; **~ officer** *n* BANK Zeichnungsberechtigte(r) *mf* [*decl. as adj*]; **~ on** *n BrE* WEL Beantragung *f* von Arbeitslosenunterstützung; **~ slip** *n* FIN Zeichnungszettel *m*

signpost *n* TRANSP Wegweiser *m*

SIG *abbr* (*special interest group*) GEN COMM Gruppe *f* mit besonderen Interessen

SIL *abbr* FIN (*specific investment loan*) spezifische Investitionsanleihe *f*, spezifisches Investitionsdarlehen *nt*, IMP/EXP, TRANSP (*specific individual licence BrE*, *specific individual license AmE*) Sondereinzelgenehmigung *f*

silent: the ~ majority *n* POL die schweigende Mehrheit *f*; **~ partner** *n AmE* (*cf sleeping partner BrE*) ECON, FIN, GEN COMM, LAW stiller Gesellschafter *m*, stille Gesellschafterin *f*, stiller Teilhaber *m*, stille Teilhaberin *f*; **~ salesperson** *n* S&M stummer Verkäufer *m*

SILIC *abbr* (*severely indebted low-income country*) ECON, FIN stark verschuldetes Land *nt* mit niedrigem Einkommen

silicon: **~ chip** *n* COMP, IND Siliziumchip *m*

silly: **~ season** *n BrE* MEDIA Sauregurkenzeit *f* *(infrml)*

silk: **~ screening** *n* S&M Siebdruck *m*

silver: ~ **ore** *n* ENVIR, IND Silbererz *nt*; ~ **ring** *n jarg* FIN Silberring *m*; ~ **standard** *n* ECON Silberwährung *f*

SIM *abbr* (*sector investment and maintenance loan*) FIN Bereichsinvestitions- und Erhaltungsanleihe *f*

SIMIC *abbr* (*severely indebted middle-income country*) ECON, FIN stark verschuldetes Land *nt* mit mittlerem Einkommen

similar *adj* GEN COMM ähnlich, gleichartig; ♦ **of a ~ kind** GEN COMM ähnlicher Art; **on a ~ occasion** GEN COMM bei ähnlicher Gelegenheit

similarity *n* PATENTS Ähnlichkeit *f*, Gleichartigkeit *f*

simple *adj* GEN COMM einfach; ~ **contract** *n* LAW einfacher Vertrag *m*, alltäglicher Vertrag *m*; ~ **deferment** *n* FIN *accounts system* einfacher Aufschub *m*; ~ **fraction** *n* MATH einfacher Bruch *m*; ~ **interest** *n* BANK einfache Zinsen *m pl*, Kapitalzinsen *m pl*; ~ **linear regression** *n* ACC einfache lineare Regression *f*; ~ **majority** *n* POL einfache Mehrheit *f*, eingeschränkte Mehrheit *f*; ~ **task** *n* GEN COMM, IND einfache Arbeit *f*; ~ **yield** *n* STOCK einfache Rendite *f*, einfacher Ertrag *m*

simplification *n* GEN COMM Vereinfachung *f*

Simplification: ~ **of International Trade Procedures Board** *n BrE* ADMIN Behörde für die Vereinfachung von Verfahren im internationalen Handel

simplified *adj* GEN COMM vereinfacht; ~ **clearance procedure** *n* (*SCP*) IMP/EXP *customs* vereinfachtes Abfertigungsverfahren *nt*; ~ **employee pension plan** *n* HRM vereinfachte betriebliche Altersversorgung *f*

simplify *vt* GEN COMM vereinfachen

simulate *vt* GEN COMM *artificially recreate* simulieren, *feign* vorgeben, vortäuschen

simulated: ~ **sale** *n* ECON Scheinverkauf *m*

simulation *n* GEN COMM *recreation* Simulation *f*, *feigning* Vortäuschung *f*; ~ **model** *n* ECON Simulationsmodell *nt*; ~ **modeling** *AmE*, ~ **modelling** *BrE n* ECON Erstellung *f* eines Simulationsmodells, Simulationsmodell *nt*

simulcast *abbr* (*simultaneous broadcast*) MEDIA Simultansendung *f*

simultaneous *adj* GEN COMM gleichzeitig, simultan; ~ **broadcast** *n* (*simulcast*) MEDIA Simultansendung *f*; ~ **payments clause** *n* FIN, INS *reinsurance* sofortige Zahlungsklausel *f*; ~ **translation** *n* COMMS Simultanübersetzung *f*

sincere *adj* GEN COMM aufrichtig

Sincerely: ~ **yours** *phr* (*cf Yours sincerely*) COMMS *letter-closing* Hochachtungsvoll (*frml*), mit freundlichen Grüßen

sincerity *n* GEN COMM Aufrichtigkeit *f*

sinecure *n* HRM Sinekure *f*

sine die *phr* FIN, GEN COMM, LAW ohne festen Termin

Singapore: ~ **Interbank Offered Rate** *n* (*SIBOR*) BANK Singapur Interbankenangebotssatz

single 1. *adj* GEN COMM einzeln, einzige, LAW, TAX *unmarried* ledig, unverheiratet; **2.** *n* TRANSP Einzelfahrkarte *f*

single out *vt* GEN COMM auswählen

single: ~ **administrative document** *n* (*SAD*) EU ADMIN, IMP/EXP, TRANSP Einheitsformular *nt*, Einzelverwaltungsdokument *nt*; ~ **arbitrator** *n BrE* HRM einziger Schiedsrichter *m*; ~ **back** *n* TRANSP *road* Leerrückfahrt *f*; ~-**berth cabin** *n* TRANSP Einbettkabine *f*; ~ **capacity** *n BrE* STOCK strikte Trennung der Broker- und Jobberfunktion; ~-**capacity trading** *n BrE* STOCK Handel

mit getrennten Jobber- und Brokerfunktionen; ~ **column centimeter** *AmE*, ~ **column centimetre** *BrE n* (*SCC*) MEDIA Einzelspaltenzentimeter *m*, Zeilenzentimeter *m*; ~ **column inch** *n* (*SCI*) MEDIA Einzelspaltenzoll *m*; ~ **commission** *n* STOCK nur eine Kommissionszahlung beim Kauf einer Aktie; ~-**country data capture** *n* ADMIN Datenerfassung *f* für ein einzelnes Land; ~ **currency** *n* GEN COMM Einheitswährung *f*; ~-**decker** *n BrE* TRANSP *bus* einstöckiger Bus *m*; ~-**deck plane** *n* TRANSP *aircraft* Eindecker *m*; ~-**deck ship** *n* TRANSP Eindecker *m*; ~ **density** *n* (*SD*) COMP einfache Dichte *f*, einfache Speicherdichte *f*; ~-**digit** *adj* MATH einstellig; ~-**employer bargaining** *n BrE* HRM Verhandlungen über einen Haustarifvertrag; ~-**entry bookkeeping** *n* ACC einfache Buchführung *f*; ~-**entry visa** *n* ADMIN Visum *nt* zur einmaligen Einreise

Single: ~ **European Act** *n* (*SEA*) LAW Einheitliche Europäische Akte *f* (*EEA*)

single: ~ **European currency** *n* ECON einheitliche europäische Währung *f*; ~ **European market** *n* ECON einheitlicher Binnenmarkt *m*, europäischer Binnenmarkt *m*; ~ **factorial terms of trade** *n pl* ECON einfach faktorales Austauschverhältnis *nt*; ~-**family dwelling** *n* PROP, TAX Einfamilienhaus *nt*; ~-**family house** *n* PROP, TAX Einfamilienhaus *nt*; ~ **fare** *n* TRANSP einfacher Fahrpreis *m*, einfache Fahrkarte *f*, einfache Fahrt *f*, *rail* Einzelfahrt *f*; ~ **finance** *n* FIN einheitliche Finanzierung *f*, Finanzierung *f* aus einer Hand; ~ **labor market** *AmE*, ~ **labour market** *BrE n* HRM elementarer Arbeitsmarkt *m*; ~ **man** *n* LAW Junggeselle *m*, lediger Mann *m*; ~ **market** *n* ECON *EU* einheitlicher Binnenmarkt *m*, einheitlicher Markt *m*, Gemeinschaftsmarkt *m*; ~ **option** *n* STOCK einfache Option *f*; ~ **payment** *n* FIN Einmalzahlung *f*; ~-**person household** *n* S&M Einpersonenhaushalt *m*; ~ **precision** *n* COMP einfache Genauigkeit *f*; ~ **premium** *n* HRM Einmalprämie *f*; ~-**premium deferred annuity** *n* FIN, WEL private Rentenversicherung *f* mit einer Einmalprämie; ~-**premium life insurance** *n* INS Lebensversicherung *f* gegen Einmalprämie, Lebensversicherung *f* gegen Zahlung einer Einmalprämie; ~-**process production** *n* IND Einfachfertigung *f*; ~-**purpose association** *n* LAW ad hoc Verband *m* (*frml*), Augenblicksverband *m*; ~ **room** *n* LEIS Einzelzimmer *nt*; ~-**room supplement** *n* LEIS Einzelzimmerzuschlag *m*; ~ **sheet** *n* COMP Einzelblatt *nt*; ~-**sheet feeder** *n* COMP Einzelblatteinzug *m*, Einzelblattzuführung *f*; ~-**sided** *adj* COMP einseitig; ~-**sided disk** *n* (*SSD*) COMP einseitige Magnetplatte *f*; ~-**sided double-density** *adj* (*SSDD*) COMP einseitig mit doppelter Speicherdichte; ~-**sided single-density** *adj* (*SSSD*) COMP einseitig mit einfacher Speicherdichte; ~-**sourced** *adj* GEN COMM aus einer einzigen Bezugsquelle; ~ **sourcing** *n* GEN COMM Beziehen der Waren von einem einzigen Lieferanten; ~ **spacing** *n* COMP einzeiliger Abstand *m*; ~ **staffing** *n* TRANSP Einfachbesetzung *f*; ~-**state municipal bond fund** *n* FIN staatlicher Kommunalobligationsfonds *m*; ~-**table bargaining** *n BrE* HRM Tarifverhandlungen *f pl* für den gesamten Industriezweig; ~ **tax movement** *n obs* POL, TAX *historic* Einheitssteuerbewegung *f* (*obs*); ~ **ticket** *n* TRANSP einfache Fahrkarte *f*, Einzelfahrkarte *f*; ~ **track** *n* TRANSP eingleisige Strecke *f*; ~ **transport document** *n* ADMIN einfaches Transportdokument *nt*; ~-**union agreement** *n BrE* HRM Tarifvertrag *m* mit einer

Gewerkschaft; **~-union deal** *n BrE* HRM Tarifvertrag *m* mit einer Gewerkschaft; **~-union no-strike agreement** *n BrE* GEN COMM, HRM, IND Streikverzichtabkommen *nt* mit einer einzigen Gewerkschaft, einzelgewerkschaftliches Streikverbotsabkommen *nt*; **~-user port** *n* TRANSP Einplatzhafen *m*; **~ woman** *n* LAW Junggesellin *f*, ledige Frau *f*

singly *adv* GEN COMM einzeln, einzig

sink *vt* FIN *money, funds* anlegen, *mortgage* amortisieren, tilgen

sinking: **~ fund** *n* FIN Amortisationsfonds *m*, Tilgungsfonds *m*; **~-fund bond issue** *n* FIN Tilgungsanleihe *f*; **~-fund installment** *AmE*, **~-fund instalment** *BrE n* FIN Tilgungsrate *f*; **~-fund loan** *n* FIN Tilgungsanleihe *f*; **~-fund method** *n* FIN Rücklagentilgung *f*; **~-fund requirements** *n pl* FIN Rückzahlungsverpflichtung *f*, Tilgungsverpflichtungen *f pl*; **~-fund reserve** *n* FIN Tilgungsrücklage *f*

SIO *abbr* (*Senior Information Officer*) HRM *civil service* ranghoher Dienstgrad im Nachrichtendienst

siphon off *vt* GEN COMM *funds* abschöpfen

sister: **~ company** *n* ECON, GEN COMM Schwestergesellschaft *f*; **~ ship** *n* TRANSP Schwesterschiff *nt*

sit *vi* POL *parliament* tagen; ♦ **~ in judgment** LAW zu Gericht sitzen; **~ on the fence** GEN COMM das Ergebnis abwarten, neutral bleiben, sich neutral verhalten; **~ tight** GEN COMM bei seiner Meinung bleiben

sit. *abbr* (*situation*) GEN COMM *profile* Lage *f*, HRM *job* Stellung *f*

SIT *abbr* (*standard interchange facilities*) TRANSP Standardaustauscheinrichtungen *f pl*

SITC *abbr* (*standard international trade classification*) GEN COMM internationales Warenverzeichnis *nt* für den Außenhandel

sit: **~-down strike** *n* HRM Sitzstreik *m*

site *n* GEN COMM Platz *m*, Standort *m*, örtliche Lage *f*, *building work* Bau *m*, Bauplatz *m*, Baustelle *f*; **~ audit** *n* GEN COMM Standortprüfung *nt*; **~ development** *n* ENVIR, IND, PROP, WEL Erschließung *f* von Bauland; **~ engineer** *n* COMP technischer Anlagenbetreuer *m*, IND technischer Anlagenbetreuer *m*, Werkstechniker, in *m,f*; **~ foreman** *n* HRM Baustellenleiter *m*; **~ licence** *BrE*, **~ license** *AmE n* COMP Aufstellungsort *m*, Standortlizenz *f*; **~ manager** *n* IND Bauleiter, in *m,f*; **~ operation** *n* ENVIR *dumping* Betreiben *nt* einer Deponie, Deponiebetrieb *m*; **~ planning** *n* COMP Standortplanung *f*; **~ protection** *n* GEN COMM, IND Objektschutz *m*; **~ selection** *n* ENVIR *for dumping* Standortwahl *f*; **~ of special scientific interest** *n BrE* (*SSSI*) ENVIR Standort *m* von besonderem wissenschaftlichen Interesse

sit: **~-in** *n* HRM *industrial action* Sit-in *nt*

siting *n* IND Aufstellung *f*, Standortwahl *f*, Standortbestimmung *f*, Standortfestlegung *f*

sit: **~-in strike** *n* HRM Sitzstreik *m*

sitrep *n* (*situation report*) GEN COMM Lagebericht *m*

sits. vac. *abbr BrE* (*situations vacant*) HRM offene Stellen *f pl*

situate *vt* LAW belegen

situation *n* (*sit.*) GEN COMM *profile* Lage *f*, Situation *f*, HRM *job* Stellung *f*; **~ report** *n* (*sitrep*) GEN COMM Lagebericht *m*

situations: **~ vacant** *n pl BrE* (*sits. vac.*) HRM offene Stellen *f pl*

six: **~-monthly period** *n* GEN COMM Halbjahresfrist *f*, Halbjahresperiode *f*

size *n* COMP Format *nt*, Größe *f*, ECON *of economy, population* Größe *f*, Umfang *m*

size up *vt infrml* GEN COMM abschätzen, einschätzen; ♦ **~ the situation** GEN COMM die Lage prüfen

sizeable *adj* ECON beträchtlich, erheblich

size: **~ distribution** *n* MATH *statistics* Größenverteilung *f*

sizing: **~ up** *n infrml* GEN COMM Einschätzung

skeleton: **~ case** *n* TRANSP *method of cargo packing* Skelettbehälter *m*, Skelettcontainer *m*; **~ contract** *n* GEN COMM Rahmenvertrag *m*; **~ service** *n* TRANSP Notdienst *m*; **~ staff** *n* HRM Stammbelegschaft *f*

skeptic *AmE see* sceptic *BrE*

skeptical *AmE see* sceptical *BrE*

skepticism *AmE see* scepticism *BrE*

sketch 1. *n* GEN COMM Entwurf *m*, Skizze *f*; **2.** *vt* GEN COMM entwerfen, grob umreißen

sketched *adj* GEN COMM entworfen

skewed: **~ frequency curve** *n* MATH *statistics* schiefe Häufigkeitskurve *f*

skewness *n* MATH *of distribution* Schiefe *f*

skid *n* TRANSP *cargo handling* Gleitkufe *f*

skill *n* GEN COMM, HRM Fähigkeit *f*, Fertigkeit *f*, geistige Fähigkeit *f*, Geschicklichkeit *f*

skilled *adj* ECON, HRM gelernt, Fach-; **~ labor** *AmE*, **~ labour** *BrE n* ECON, HRM Facharbeiter, in *m,f*, gelernte Arbeitskräfte *f pl*; **~ union** *n BrE* HRM Fachgewerkschaft *f*; **~ worker** *n* HRM Facharbeiter, in *m,f*

skill: **~-intensive** *adj* HRM mit hohen Ansprüchen an handwerkliches Geschick

skills: **~ analysis** *n* HRM Fertigkeitenanalyse *f*

skimming *n* GEN COMM Abschöpfung *f*; **~ policy** *n* S&M Abschöpfungspolitik *f*

skimp *vt* GEN COMM *work in a careless way* nachlässig arbeiten, schludrig arbeiten (*infrml*), schludrige Arbeit leisten, *be sparing with* sparen an [+dat]

skint: **be ~** *phr infrml BrE* GEN COMM pleite sein (*infrml*), knapp bei Kasse sein

skip 1. *n* COMP Überspringen *nt*; **2.** *vt* COMP übergehen, überlesen, überspringen; ♦ **~ the details** GEN COMM die Einzelheiten übergehen, die Einzelheiten auslassen; **~ work** *infrml* HRM blaumachen (*infrml*)

skip: **~-payment privilege** *n* FIN Privileg *nt* der verzögerten Zahlung

skyrocket *vi* GEN COMM sprunghaft ansteigen, scharf ansteigen

SL *abbr* (*surveillance licence BrE, surveillance license AmE*) IMP/EXP Aufsichtsgenehmigung *f*, Kontrollgenehmigung *f*, Überwachungslizenz *f*

slack 1. *adj* ECON, GEN COMM *trade* flau, schwach; ♦ **be ~** HRM *neglect one's duties* nachlässig sein; **2.** *n* GEN COMM Nachlassen *nt*

slack off *vi* GEN COMM nachlassen

slacken 1. *vt* ECON nachlassen, STOCK abbröckeln; ♦ **~ the reins** ECON, MGMNT die Zügel lockern; **2.** *vi* ECON *economic recovery* abflauen, nachgeben, nachlassen

slacken off *vi* GEN COMM nachlassen

slackening *n* ECON Abflauen *nt*, Nachgeben *nt*, Nachlassen *nt*

slack: ~ **fill** *n* S&M *marketing* aufgeblähte Verpackung *f*; ~ **period** *n* GEN COMM Flaute *f*, stille Saison *f*; ~ **season** *n* GEN COMM Sauregurkenzeit *f* (*infrml*); ~ **water** *n* TRANSP *shipping* Stauwasser *nt*, Tidehochwasser *nt*

sl&c *abbr* (*shipper's load and count*) TRANSP Ladung *f* und Kontrolle *f* des Befrachters, Ladung *f* und Zählung *f* des Befrachters

slander 1. *n* LAW Beleidigung *f*, Verleumdung *f*; **2.** *vt* LAW *person* verleumden

slander: ~ **action** *n* LAW Verleumdungsverfahren *nt*

slanderous *adj* LAW beleidigend, verleumderisch

slapdash *adj* GEN COMM flüchtig, nachlässig, schludrig (*infrml*)

slash *n* COMP, MEDIA *typography* Schrägstrich *m*

slate *n* AmE POL Kandidatenliste *f*

slaughterhouse *n* GEN COMM Schlachthof *m*

S/LC *abbr* (*sue and labor clause AmE, sue and labour clause BrE*) INS, LAW Klausel *f* über Schadensabwendung und Schadensminderung, Beteiligungszusage *f* der Versicherung bei Klageerhebung

sleeper *n* HRM potentieller Verkaufsschlager *m*, TRANSP *railway carriage* Schlafwagen *m*

sleeping: ~ **beauty** *n* *infrml* STOCK potentielles Übernahmeobjekt *nt*; ~ **car** *n* TRANSP Schlafwagen *m*; ~ **economy** *n* ECON schlafende Wirtschaft *f*; ~ **partner** *n* BrE (*cf silent partner AmE*) ECON, FIN, GEN COMM, LAW stiller Gesellschafter *m*, stille Gesellschafterin *f*, stiller Teilhaber *m*, stille Teilhaberin *f*

sleeve *n* GEN COMM *of book, compact disc* Hülle *f*

slice: ~ **of the market** *n* S&M Marktanteil *m*

slide 1. *n* STOCK *in prices* Nachgeben *nt*; **2.** *vi* STOCK nachgeben

slide: ~ **projector** *n* MEDIA Diaprojektor *m*; ~ **rule** *n* GEN COMM Rechenschieber *m*

sliding: ~~**price clause** *n* LAW Preisgleitklausel *f*; ~ **scale** *n* FIN gleitende Skala *f*, bewegliche Skala *f*, bewegliche Preisskala *f*; ~~**scale tariff** *n* IMP/EXP Gleitzoll *m*; ~ **wage scale** *n* HRM gleitende Lohnskala *f*, gleitender Lohntarif *m*

slight *adj* GEN COMM geringfügig, leicht, unbedeutend

slightly *adv* GEN COMM leicht

slim *vt* HRM, MGMNT *workforce* abbauen

slim down *vt* HRM, MGMNT *workforce* verkleinern, abspecken (*jarg*)

slimline *adj* COMP *hardware design* flach

slip 1. *n* TAX Beleg *m*; **2.** *vi* STOCK fallen, zurückgehen

slip back *vi* GEN COMM fallen, STOCK sinken

slippage *n* GEN COMM Nachgeben *nt*, Rückstand *m*, IND Rückstand *m*

slip: ~ **of the tongue** *n* COMMS Sprechfehler *m*, Versprecher *m* (*infrml*)

slipshod *adj* *infrml* GEN COMM schludrig (*infrml*)

SLM *abbr* (*segmented labor market theory AmE, segmented labour market theory BrE*) ECON Theorie *f* des segmentierten Arbeitsmarkts

SLMA *abbr* AmE (*student loan marketing association*) FIN Marketingvereinigung *f* für Studentendarlehen

slog *n* HRM mühselige Arbeit *f*

slogan *n* S&M *advertising* Slogan *m*

slope *n* GEN COMM Gefälle *nt*, Richtungskoeffizient *m*, MATH Richtungskoeffizient *m*, TRANSP Neigung *f*

slot *n* COMP *for expansion card* Steckplatz *m*, Slot *m* (*jarg*), GEN COMM Platz *m*, time Zeitnische *f*, Schlitz *m*, Einschnitt *m*, MEDIA *copy desk* Innenseite des halbrunden Redaktionstischs, *television* Sendezeit *f*, TRANSP *shipping* enger Raum *m*

slot: ~ **machine** *n* GEN COMM Automat *m*, S&M Verkaufsautomat *m*

slow 1. *adj* ECON *economic recovery*, GEN COMM, STOCK, TRANSP langsam; ◆ **be ~ to respond** GEN COMM die Antwort hinausschieben, sich mit der Antwort Zeit lassen; **2.** *vt* ECON verlangsamen; **3.** *vi* ECON sich verlangsamen

slow down 1. *vt* ECON, GEN COMM verlangsamen, dämpfen; **2.** *vi* ECON, GEN COMM abflauen, sich abschwächen, sich verlangsamen

slow: ~ **decline** *n* STOCK *currency expectations* langsamer Rückgang *m*

slowdown *n* ECON *in economy* Abschwächung *f*, Konjunkturrückgang *m*, Verlangsamung *f*, HRM AmE (*cf go-slow BrE*) *industrial action* Bummelstreik *m*

slowly *adv* GEN COMM, STOCK, TRANSP langsam

slow: ~ **payer** *n* FIN säumiger Zahler *m*; ~ **rise** *n* STOCK *currency expectation* langsamer Anstieg *m*

sluicegate: ~ **price** *n* ECON EC Einschleusungspreis *m*

slump 1. *n* ECON, STOCK *in oil prices, world trade* Einbruch *m*, Rezession *f*; **2.** *vi* ECON, STOCK *market* stürzen

slumpflation *n* ECON Inflation *f* bei gleichzeitiger Rezession, Slumpflation *f* (*jarg*)

slump: ~ **in sales** *n* S&M Absatzeinbruch *m*, Absatzrückgang *m*

slush: ~ **fund** *n* FIN, POL Bestechungsfonds *m*, Geheimfonds *m*, Kasse *f* für Schmiergelder, Schmiergelderfonds *m*

Slutsky: ~ **effect** *n* ECON Slutsky-Effekt *m*; ~ **equation** *n* ECON Slutsky-Gleichung *f*

small *adj* GEN COMM *purchase, amount* gering, klein; ◆ **on a ~ scale** GEN COMM in geringem Maße

small: ~ **ad** *n* S&M Kleinanzeige *f*, Kleininserat *nt*; ~ **business** *n* GEN COMM Kleinbetrieb *m*, Kleinunternehmen *nt*, kleines Unternehmen *nt*, Kleinfirma *f*; ~ **business administration** *n* AmE (*SBA*) GEN COMM US-Bundesbehörde für Mittelstandsbetriebe; ~ **business bond** *n* GEN COMM Anleihe *f* für ein Kleinunternehmen; ~ **business development bond** *n* (*SBDB*) GEN COMM Investitionskredit *m* für kleine und mittlere Betriebe; ~ **change** *n* COMMS, GEN COMM *coins* Kleingeld *nt*, *unimportant matter* läppisches Gerede *nt*, Lappalie *f*; ~ **claims** *n pl* LAW *up to £500* kleinere Forderungen *f pl*; ~~**claims court** *n* LAW Amtsgericht *nt*; ~ **damage** *n* (*s/d*) INS geringer Schaden *m*, geringfügiger Schaden *m*; ~ **earnings** *n pl* BrE TAX niedrige Einkommen *nt pl*; ~ **employer** *n* HRM Kleinbetrieb *m*; ~ **enterprise** *n* GEN COMM Kleinbetrieb *m*, kleines Unternehmen *nt*, Kleinfirma *f*, Kleinunternehmen *nt*; ~ **firm** *n* GEN COMM Kleinbetrieb *m*, kleines Unternehmen *nt*, Kleinfirma *f*, Kleinunternehmen *nt*

smallholder *n* ECON *agricultural* Kleinbauer *m*

small: ~ **industry** *n* IND Kleinindustrie *f*; ~ **investor** *n* FIN Kleinanleger, in *m,f*; ~ **and medium-sized enterprises** *n pl* (*SME*) GEN COMM kleine und mittelständische

Unternehmen *nt pl* (*KMU*); ~ **parcel** *n* COMMS, TRANSP Päckchen *nt*; **in ~ print** *n* LAW *in contract* Kleingedrucktes *nt*; ~ **savings** *n pl* FIN geringe Ersparnisse *f pl*; ~~**scale technology** *n* ECON sanfte Technologie *f*, weiche Technologie *f*; ~ **speculator** *n* STOCK kleiner Spekulant *m*, kleine Spekulantin *f*; ~~**time crook** *n infrml* LAW Gauner *m* (*infrml*)

smart: ~ **card** *n* BANK, COMP Chipkarte *f*, Computerkarte *f*, intelligente Kreditkarte *f*, Smartcard *f*; ~ **money** *n* FIN rentable Anlage *f*; **the ~ set** *n* GEN COMM die Schickeria *f* (*infrml*); ~ **terminal** *n* COMP halbintelligentes Terminal *nt*

SME *abbr* (*small and medium-sized enterprises*) GEN COMM KMU *nt pl* (*kleine und mittelständische Unternehmen*)

smelt *vt* IND einschmelzen, flüssig machen, zusammenschmelzen

smelting: ~ **works** *n pl* IND Eisenhütte *f*, Erzhütte *f*, Hüttenwerk *nt*, Metallhütte *f*

smokestack *n* IND Kamin *m*, Schlot *m*, Schornstein *m*; ~ **industry** *n* GEN COMM, IND Schornsteinindustrie *f*, Altindustrie *f*

smoking: ~ **is not permitted** *phr* GEN COMM Rauchen ist nicht erlaubt, Rauchen ist nicht gestattet; ~ **prohibited** *phr* GEN COMM Rauchen verboten; ~ **room** *n* GEN COMM Rauchsalon *m*, Rauchzimmer *nt*

smooth *adj* GEN COMM *trouble-free* glatt, reibungslos, störungsfrei

smooth out *vt* ECON *fluctuations* ausgleichen, verstetigen, GEN COMM aus dem Weg räumen, ausräumen, glätten

Smoot: ~ **Hawley Tariff Act** *n* ECON amerikanisches Protektionismusgesetz von 1930

smoothly *adv* GEN COMM reibungslos

smooth: ~ **running** *n* GEN COMM reibungsloser Ablauf *m*

SMP *abbr* (*special multiperil insurance*) INS Sonderversicherung *f* gegen mehrfache Gefahren

SMSA *abbr* (*Standard Metropolitan Statistical Area*) MATH standardisierter statistischer Bereich *m* einer Großstadt

smuggle *vt* IMP/EXP, LAW schmuggeln; ◆ ~ **sth through customs** IMP/EXP, LAW etw durch die Zollkontrolle schmuggeln

smuggled: ~ **goods** *n pl* LAW Konterware *f*, Schmuggelware *f*, unter Ein- oder Ausfuhrverbot stehende Waren *f pl*

smuggler *n* IMP/EXP, LAW Schmuggler, in *m,f*

S/N *abbr* (*shipping note*) IMP/EXP, TRANSP Ladeschein *m*, Schiffszettel *m*, Versandanzeige *f*

SNA *abbr* (*System of National Accounts*) ACC VGR (*Volkswirtschaftliche Gesamtrechnung*), gesamtwirtschaftliches Rechnungswesen *nt*

snag *n infrml* GEN COMM Haken *m*, Schwierigkeit *f*

snake *n* ECON *jointly floated EC currencies* Schlange *f*

snakecheck *n jarg* POL Fettnäpfchencheck *nt* (*jarg*)

snap up *vt* GEN COMM wegschnappen

snap: ~ **strike** *n* HRM illegaler Streik *m*

snatch *vt* GEN COMM ergattern, greifen

sneak: ~ **preview** *n* MEDIA *cinema* Sneak Preview *f*, Vorpremiere *f*

SNIG *abbr* (*sustained non-inflationary growth*) ECON stetiges inflationsfreies Wachstum *nt*, stetiges nicht-inflationäres Wachstum *nt*

snip *n* S&M günstiger Kauf *m*, Schnäppchen *nt*

snipe *n AmE* POL an freien Flächen angebrachte politische Plakate

snowball *vi* GEN COMM lawinenartig anwachsen

snowbelt *n AmE* ECON, IND Schneegürtel *m*

Snr *abbr* (*senior*) GEN COMM sen. (*senior*), *in rank* vorgesetzt, übergeordnet, *in age* älter, *leading* leitend, LAW sen. (*senior*), übergeordnet, älter

SO *abbr* (*senior officer*) HRM höhere(r) Beamte(r) *m* [decl. as adj], höhere Beamtin *f*, leitende(r) Angestellte(r) *mf* [decl. as adj]

S.O. *abbr* BANK (*standing order*) Dauerauftrag *m*, STOCK (*seller's option*) Verkäuferoption *f*

soar *vi* GEN COMM *profits, prices* in die Höhe schnellen, emporschnellen, scharf ansteigen, sprunghaft ansteigen

soaring *adj* GEN COMM rasch aufsteigend, schnell zunehmend

so-called *adj* GEN COMM angeblich, sogenannt

social *adj* GEN COMM gesellschaftlich, sozial; ◆ **be on ~ security** HRM Sozialhilfe beziehen

social: ~ **accounting** *n* ACC Sozialberichterstattung *f*, Sozialkostenrechnung *f*; ~ **adjustment cost** *n* HRM Kosten *pl* der sozialen Anpassung; ~ **analysis** *n* S&M, WEL Gesellschaftsanalyse *f*, Sozialdiagnose *f*; ~ **capital** *n* ECON, FIN Sozialfonds *m*, Sozialkapital *nt*; ~ **capital investments** *n pl* ECON Sozialinvestitionen *f pl*; ~ **category** *n* S&M *market research* soziale Kategorie *f*

Social: ~ **Charter** *n* GEN COMM Sozialcharta *f*

social: ~ **choice theory** *n* ECON Social Choice-Theorie *f*, Theorie *f* der Wahlentscheidung; ~ **contract** *n* HRM Sozialvertrag *m*; ~ **conscience fund** *n* ECON Investmentfonds *m* des sozialen Gewissens; ~ **consciousness mutual fund** *n* FIN gegenseitiger Fonds *m* für soziales Bewußtsein

Social: ~ **Contract** *n BrE* HRM *mid-1970s* Sozialvereinbarung *f*

social: ~ **cost** *n* ECON, WEL gesellschaftliche Kosten *pl*, volkswirtschaftliche Kosten *pl*, soziale Kosten *pl*; ~ **cost of monopoly** *n* ECON volkswirtschaftliche Kosten *pl* des Monopols; ~ **cost of unemployment** *n* ECON, HRM soziale Kosten *pl* der Arbeitslosigkeit; ~ **credit** *n* GEN COMM Sozialkredit *m*; ~ **democracy** *n* POL Sozialdemokratie *f*

Social: ~ **Development Committee** *n* POL Regierungskommission *f* für soziale Entwicklung

social: ~ **dividend scheme** *n* ECON Plan *m* der sozialen Dividende, Sozialdividendenplan *m*; ~ **good** *n* ECON öffentliches Gut *nt*, Kollektivgut *nt*; ~ **grade** *n* GEN COMM soziale Gruppe *f*, soziale Klasse *f*; ~ **insurance** *n* HRM, WEL Sozialversicherung *f*

socialism *n* ECON, POL Sozialismus *m*

socialist 1. *adj* ECON, POL sozialistisch; **2.** *n* ECON, POL Sozialist, in *m,f*

socialist: ~ **economy** *n* ECON, POL sozialistische Wirtschaft *f*

socialization *n* HRM, WEL Sozialisation *f*

social: ~ **liberalism** *n* ECON Sozialliberalismus *m*

socially: ~ **necessary labor time** *AmE*, ~ **necessary labour time** *BrE n* HRM gesellschaftlich erforderliche Arbeitszeit *f*

social: ~ **market economy** *n* ECON soziale Marktwirtschaft *f*; ~ **opportunity cost of foreign exchange** *n* STOCK volkswirtschaftliche Opportunitätskosten *pl* von Devisen; ~ **organization** *n* POL gesellschaftliche

Organisation *f*, soziale Einrichtung *f*, soziale Organisation *f*; ~ **overhead capital** *n* ECON, FIN Sozialkapital *nt*; ~ **ownership** *n* HRM gemeinschaftliches Eigentum *nt*; ~ **policy** *n* WEL Gesellschaftspolitik *f*, Sozialpolitik *f*; ~ **product** *n* ECON Sozialprodukt *nt*; ~ **profit** *n* ECON gesellschaftlicher Gewinn *m*; ~ **rate of discount** *n* FIN soziale Zinsrate *f*, sozialer Diskontsatz *m*; ~ **security** *n* HRM, WEL Sozialversicherung *f*

Social: ~ **Security Act 1935** *n* LAW Sozialversicherungsgesetz von 1935; ~ **Security benefit** *n* HRM Sozialversicherungsleistung *f*

social: ~ **security contributions** *n pl* HRM, WEL Sozialversicherungsbeitrag *m*; ~ **security creditor** *n* ACC Sozialversicherungsgläubiger, in *m,f*; ~ **security recipient** *n* HRM, WEL Wohlfahrtsempfänger, in *m,f*; ~ **spending** *n* FIN Sozialausgaben *f pl*; ~ **standing** *n* WEL gesellschaftlicher Rang *m*, gesellschaftliches Ansehen *nt*; ~ **status** *n* WEL sozialer Status *m*; ~ **stratification** *n* WEL soziale Schichtung *f*; ~ **studies** *n pl* WEL Gesellschaftskunde *f*, Gesellschaftslehre *f* (*obs*), Sozialkunde *f*; ~ **system** *n* WEL Gesellschaftssystem *nt*; ~ **wage** *n BrE* HRM Soziallohn *m*; ~ **wants** *n pl* ECON, WEL Kollektivbedürfnissse *nt pl*; ~ **weight** *n* ECON Sozialgewicht *nt*; ~ **welfare** *n* WEL öffentliche Wohlfahrt *f*, soziales Wohl *nt*, Sozialfürsorge *f*, Sozialhilfe *f*; ~ **welfare function** *n* ECON gesellschaftliche Wohlfahrtsfunktion *f*; ~ **worker** *n* HRM, WEL Sozialarbeiter, in *m,f*

societal: ~ **marketing concept** *n* S&M soziales Marketingkonzept *nt*

society *n* GEN COMM *social community* Gesellschaft *f*, *company* Gesellschaft *f*, *organization* Verein *m*, Gesellschaft *f*

Society: ~ **for Worldwide Interbank Financial Telecommunications** *n* (*SWIFT*) BANK SWIFT, internationales Datenfernübertragungsnetz für Auslandszahlungen

sociocultural *adj* S&M soziokulturell

socioeconomic *adj* ECON, S&M, WEL sozioökonomisch; ~ **climate** *n* ECON sozialwirtschaftliches Klima *nt*; ~ **groups** *n pl* S&M sozioökonomische Gruppen *f pl*; ~ **status** *n* ECON sozioökonomischer Status *m*

sociometric *adj* MATH, S&M soziometrisch

sociopolitical *adj* POL, WEL sozialpolitisch

socio: ~-**technical system** *n* ADMIN sozialtechnisches System *nt*

SOFFEX *abbr* (*Swiss Options and Financial Futures Exchange*) STOCK Schweizer Börse für Optionen und Finanzterminkontrakte

soft: ~ **budget** *n* FIN großzügiger Haushaltsplan *m*; ~ **commodity** *n* STOCK Weichware *f*; ~ **copy** *n* COMP Bildschirmausgabe *f*, Softcopy *f* (*jarg*); ~ **cost** *n* GEN COMM weiche Kosten *pl*; ~-**cover book** *n* MEDIA Taschenbuch *nt*; ~ **currency** *n* ECON, GEN COMM weiche Währung *f*

soften up *vt* GEN COMM weichmachen (*infrml*)

soft: ~ **error** *n* COMP Fehler, der durch Neueinlesen des Bandes behoben werden kann; ~ **funding** *n* ADMIN, FIN entgegenkommende Schuldenkonsolidierung *f*; ~ **goods** *n pl* ECON kurzlebige Konsumgüter *nt pl*, kurzlebige Verbrauchsgüter *nt pl*; ~ **landing** *n* ECON weiche Landung *f* (*infrml*), sanfte Landung *f*; ~ **loan** *n* ECON, FIN zinsbegünstigte Anlage *f*, zinsgünstiger Kredit *m*; ~ **market** *n* ECON, STOCK rückläufiger

Aktienmarkt *m*; ~ **modeling** *AmE*, ~ **modelling** *BrE* *n* ECON Erstellung *f* eines flexiblen Modells; ~ **money** *n* FIN Papiergeld *nt*; ~ **offer** *n* GEN COMM weiches Angebot *nt*

soft-pedal 1. *vt* GEN COMM dämpfen, herunterschrauben, herunterspielen, mildern; **2.** *vi* GEN COMM einen Dämpfer aufsetzen, zurücksetzen

soft: ~ **sectoring** *n* COMP Softsektorierung *f*; ~ **sell** *n* S&M weiche Tour *f*; ~ **technology** *n* ECON, ENVIR sanfte Technologie *f*, weiche Technologie *f*

software *n* COMP Software *f*; ~ **application** *n* COMP Software-Anwendung *f*; ~ **company** *n* COMP Software-Haus *nt*, Software-Unternehmen *nt*, Software-Firma *f*; ~-**driven** *adj* COMP softwaregesteuert; ~ **engineer** *n* COMP Software-Ingenieur, in *m,f*, Systemanalytiker, in *m,f*; ~ **engineering** *n* COMP Software-Entwicklung *f*; ~ **house** *n* COMP Software-Haus *nt*, Software-Unternehmen *nt*, Software-Firma *f*; ~ **language** *n* COMP Software-Sprache *f*; ~ **package** *n* COMP Software-Paket *nt*; ~ **piracy** *n* COMP Raubkopieren *nt*; ~ **release** *n* COMP Software-Freigabe *f*, Software-Release *nt*; ~ **rot** *n* COMP Software-Verfall *m*

soil: ~ **bank** *n AmE* ECON *agricultural* US-Programm zur Förderung der Fruchtbarkeit des Bodens; ~ **degradation** *n* ENVIR Bodendegradierung *f*, Bodenverschlechterung *f*; ~ **erosion** *n* ENVIR Bodenabschwemmung *f*, Bodenabtrag *m*, Bodenauswaschung *f*

SOL *abbr* (*shipowner's liability*) INS, LAW, TRANSP Schiffseignerhaftung *f*

solar: ~ **power** *n* ENVIR Solarenergie *f*, Sonnenenergie *f*

sold: ~ **daybook** *n* GEN COMM Verkaufskladde *f*, S&M Verkaufsjournal *nt*; ~ **ledger** *n* S&M Verkaufsjournal *nt*, Verkaufsbuch *nt*; ~ **note** *n* STOCK Effektenverkaufsabrechnung *f*; ~ **out** *adj* GEN COMM ausverkauft, *book* vergriffen (*vergr.*); ~-**out market** *n* STOCK ausverkaufter Markt *m*

sole: ~ **agency** *n* ECON, S&M Alleinvertretung *f*; ~ **agent** *n* GEN COMM Alleinvertreter, in *m,f*; ~ **arbitrator** *n* INS Einzelschiedsrichter, in *m,f*; ~ **bargaining agent** *n BrE* HRM Alleinverhandlungspartner *m* für Tarifverhandlungen; ~ **bargaining rights** *n pl BrE* HRM Alleinverhandlungsrechte *nt pl*; ~ **buyer** *n* GEN COMM Alleinabnehmer *m*, Alleinabnehmerin *f*; ~ **concessionaire** *n* GEN COMM Alleinkonzessionär, in *m,f*; ~ **heir** *n* LAW Alleinerbe *m*, Alleinerbin *f*; ~ **inventor** *n* PATENTS Alleinerfinder, in *m,f*, alleiniger Erfinder *m*, alleinige Erfinderin *f*; ~ **legatee** *n* LAW Alleinerbe *m*, Alleinerbin *f*; ~ **with the** ~ **object of** *phr* GEN COMM mit dem alleinigen Ziel, daß; ~ **owner** *n* LAW Alleineigentümer, in *m,f*, PROP Alleinbesitzer, in *m,f*; ~ **ownership** *n* LAW alleiniges Eigentumsrecht *nt*; ~ **proprietor** *n* MGMNT alleiniger Eigentümer *m*, alleinige Eigentümerin *f*, Alleineigentümer, in *m,f*, Alleininhaber, in *m,f*; ~ **proprietorship** *n* GEN COMM *type of firm* Einzelfirma *f*, LAW *ownership* alleiniges Eigentumsrecht *nt*; ~ **right to a patent** *n* PATENTS alleiniges Patentrecht *nt*; ~ **selling right** *n* S&M alleiniges Vertriebsrecht *nt*; ~ **trader** *n* GEN COMM *person* Alleininhaber, in *m,f*, alleiniger Inhaber *m*, alleinige Inhaberin *f*, Einzelkaufmann *m*, *company* Einzelfirma *f*, Alleinbetrieb *m*

solicit *vt* GEN COMM erbitten, sich bemühen um, sich bewerben um; ♦ ~ **new business** GEN COMM Aufträge beschaffen, Aufträge hereinholen

solicitation: not a ~, for information only *phr* STOCK keine Auftragswerbung, sondern nur zur Information

solicitor *n* LAW Anwalt *m*, Anwältin *f*, Rechtsanwalt *m*, Rechtsanwältin *f*

solidarism *n* ECON Solidarismus *m*

solidarity: ~ action *n* HRM *industrial action* Solidaritätshandlung *f*

solid: on ~ ground *phr* GEN COMM auf solider Basis; **~ line** *n* MATH *on graph* durchgezogene Linie *f*; **~-state** *adj* GEN COMM in festem Zustand befindlich, Festkörper-

Solow: ~ residual *n* ECON Solow-Rest *m*

solus: ~ position *n* S&M alleinstehend

solution *n* GEN COMM *of problem* Behebung *f*, Lösung *f*

solve *vt* GEN COMM *problem* aufklären, lösen

solvency *n* ACC, BANK, FIN Solvenz *f*, Zahlungsfähigkeit *f*, Liquidität *f*; **~ margin** *n* FIN Liquiditätsmarge *f*; **~ ratio** *n* ACC, FIN *credit institution* Liquiditätskennzahl *f*, Liquiditätsgrad *m*

solvent *adj* ACC, BANK, FIN solvent, zahlungsfähig, liquid; **~ debtor** *n* BANK solventer Schuldner *m*, zahlungsfähiger Schuldner *m*

s.o.p. *abbr* (*standard operating procedure*) GEN COMM einheitliches Betriebsverfahren *nt*, Standardverfahren *nt*, standardisierte Fertigungsmethode *f*

SOP *abbr* (*standard operating procedure*) GEN COMM einheitliches Betriebsverfahren *nt*, Standardverfahren *nt*, standardisierte Fertigungsmethode *f*

sophisticated *adj* GEN COMM auf hohem Niveau stehend, hoch differenziert, hochentwickelt, hochintelligent, hochtechnisiert, hochtechnologisch, ausgeklügelt, technisch ausgereift; **~ market** *n* STOCK hochentwickelter Markt *m*

sophistication *n* GEN COMM Differenziertheit *f*, S&M *of market* Differenzierung *f*

sort 1. *n* COMP Sortierung *f*; **2.** *vt* COMP, GEN COMM sortieren

sort out *vt* GEN COMM aussortieren

sort: ~ code *n* BrE BANK Bankleitzahl *f* (*BLZ*)

sorter *n* COMP Sortiergerät *nt*, Sortierer *m*

sort: ~ file *n* COMP Sortierdatei *f*; **~ key** *n* COMP Sortierschlüssel *m*

sought: ~-after *adj* GEN COMM gefragt, gesucht

sound 1. *adj* BANK gesund, kreditfähig, solide, GEN COMM einwandfrei, fehlerfrei, unbeschädigt, unversehrt, *firm, customer* kreditwürdig, fundiert; ◆ **on a ~ footing** GEN COMM auf solider Grundlage; **2.** *n* COMMS Ton *m*, COMP, MEDIA Klang *m*, Ton *m*

sound out *vt* GEN COMM *person* ausfragen, *intentions* herausfinden

sound: ~ currency *n* GEN COMM gesunde Währung *f*; **~ effects** *n pl* MEDIA Geräusche *nt pl*, Klangeffekte *m pl*, Toneffekte *m pl*; **~ insulation** *n* COMMS, ENVIR Schalldämmung *f*, Schallschutz *m*

soundtrack *n* COMMS, MEDIA Soundtrack *m* (*jarg*), Tonspur *f*

source *n* COMP Quelle *f*, Ursprung *m*, FIN, GEN COMM *of funds, information* Herkunft *f*, Quelle *f*, Ursprung *m*; **~ address** *n* COMP Quellenadresse *f*; **~ and application of funds** *n* ACC, FIN Mittelherkunft und -verwendung *f*; **~ and application of funds statement** *n* ACC, FIN Bewegungsbilanz *f*; **~ and disposition of funds** *n* ACC, FIN Mittelherkunft und -verwendung *f*; **~ of capital** *n*

FIN Kapitalherkunft *f*; **~ code** *n* COMP Primärcode *m*, Quellcode *m*, Quellencode *m*; **~ computer** *n* COMP Source-Computer *m*; **~ credibility** *n* S&M Glaubwürdigkeit *f* der Informationsquelle; **~ data** *n pl* COMP Ursprungsdaten *pl*; **~ disk** *n* COMP Ursprungsdiskette *f*; **~ document** *n* FIN Herkunftsdokument *nt*; **~ file** *n* COMP Quelldatei *f*, Ursprungsdatei *f*; **~ of funds** *n* ACC, FIN Mittelherkunft *f*; **~ language** *n* COMMS *translation* Ausgangssprache *f*, COMP *programming* Quellensprache *f*, Ursprungssprache *f*, Quellsprache *f*; **~ program** *n* COMP Quellenprogramm *nt*, Ursprungsprogramm *nt*; **~ of revenue** *n* GEN COMM Einnahmequelle *f*

sourcing *n* S&M Akquisition *f*, Einkaufspolitik *f*; **~ expert** *n* S&M Einkaufsexperte *m*, Einkaufsexpertin *f*, Sourcing-Experte *m*, Sourcing-Expertin *f*

South: ~ East Asia Trade Advisory Group *n* (*SEATAG*) GEN COMM Beratungsgruppe für Handel mit Südostasien

South: ~ Pacific rates *n pl* TRANSP Südpazifiktarife *m pl*

sovereign *n* FIN *obs coin* britische Goldmünze, POL *person* Herrscher, in *m,f*, Souverän *m*; **~ loan** *n* FIN staatliche Anleihe *f*, staatliches Darlehen *nt*; **~ risk** *n* FIN Länderrisiko *nt*, staatliches Risiko *nt*

sovereignty *n* POL Hoheit *f*

Soviet: ~-type economy *n* ECON Zentralverwaltungswirtschaft *f*, staatssozialistische Volkswirtschaft *f* des sowjetischen Typs

SPA *abbr* (*subject to particular average*) INS der besonderen Schadenbeteiligung unterworfen, der besonderen Schadenbeteiligungsklausel unterworfen

space *n* COMP Leerzeichen *nt*, *in text* Abstand *m*; **~ arbitrage** *n* GEN COMM Belegungsarbitrage *f*; **~ bar** *n* COMP Leertaste *f*; **~ broker** *n* S&M *advertising* Werbungsmittler, in *m,f*; **~ buyer** *n* S&M *advertising* Anzeigenkäufer, in *m,f*; **~ buying** *n* S&M *advertising* Anzeigenkauf *m*

space: ~ rates *n pl* S&M *advertising* Anzeigentarife *m pl*; **~ shuttle** *n* TRANSP Raumfähre *f*, Space-Shuttle *nt*; **~ writer** *n* MEDIA *print* Autor, der nach dem Umfang seines Beitrags bezahlt wird

span: ~ of control *n* GEN COMM Kontrollspanne *f*

spanking: ~ new *adj* *infrml* GEN COMM funkelnagelneu (*infrml*)

SPAR *abbr* (*standard portfolio analysis of risk*) FIN Standard-Portfeuille-Risikoanalyse *f*

spare *n* IND Ersatzteil *nt*; **~ capacity** *n* ECON, IND, TRANSP freie Kapazität *f*, Reservekapazität *f*, Kapazitätsreserve *f*; **~ cash** *n* GEN COMM Bargeldreserve *f*; **~ part** *n* IND Ersatzteil *nt*, Verschleißteil *nt*; **~ time** *n* LEIS Freizeit *f*

spark off *vt* GEN COMM auslösen, entfachen, verursachen

sparsely: ~ populated *adj* ECON dünn besiedelt; **~ populated area** *n* ECON dünn besiedeltes Gebiet *nt*

spate *n* GEN COMM Flut *f*, Schwall *m*

spatial: ~ benefit limitation *n* ECON Begrenzung *f* des räumlichen Nutzens; **~ duopoly** *n* ECON räumliches Duopol *nt*; **~ equalization** *n* ECON räumlicher Ausgleich *m*; **~ monopoly** *n* ECON räumliches Monopol *nt*; **~ oligopoly** *n* ECON räumliches Oligopol *nt*

SPC *abbr* (*supplementary protection certificate*) GEN COMM, PATENTS Zusatzschutzurkunde *f*

speaker *n* GEN COMM *in meeting* Sprecher, in *m,f*, MEDIA, POL Referent, in *m,f*

spearhead *n* GEN COMM Angriffsspitze *f*, Spitze *f*

Spearman: ~'s **rank correlation formula** *n* MATH *statistics* Spearmansche Rangkorrelationsformel *f*

spec: **on** ~ *phr* (*on speculation*) GEN COMM auf Verdacht, auf die Vermutung hin, auf Spekulation, HRM *job application* spekulationsweise; ~ **house** *n* PROP Spekulationshaus *nt*

special: ~ **account** *n* ACC Sonderkonto *nt*; ~ **arbitrage account** *n* STOCK Sonderarbitragekonto *nt*; ~ **arrangement** *n* GEN COMM Sondervereinbarung *f*; ~ **bracket firm** *n* BANK Unternehmen *nt* einer besonderen Kategorie; ~ **case** *n* LAW Sachverhalt *m* für ein Zwischenurteil; ~ **circumstances** *n pl* GEN COMM besondere Umstände *m pl*; ~ **clearing** *n BrE* BANK Spezialclearing *nt*; ~ **commercial exchange rate** *n* ECON Sonderwechselkurs *m* für den Handel; ~ **commissioner** *n BrE* TAX *tax appeals* Sonderbeauftragte(r) *mf* [decl. as adj]; ~ **committee** *n* POL Sonderausschuß *m*; ~ **conditions** *n pl* ECON Sonderkonditionen *f pl*; ~ **contingency reserve** *n* INS Sonderrücklagen *f pl*; ~ **contract** *n* LAW gesiegelter Vertrag *m*; ~ **delivery** *n* COMMS Eilzustellungsdienst *m*; ~ **deposit** *n* BANK Hinterlegung *f* von Geld oder Wertpapieren, mindestreserveähnliche Einlage *f*; ~ **district bond** *n* STOCK Sonderbezirksanleihe *f*; ~ **dividend** *n* STOCK Sonderdividende *f*; ~ **drawing rights** *n pl* (*SDR*) BANK Sonderziehungsrechte *nt pl* (*SZR*)

Special: ~ **Economic Zone** *n* ECON *China* Sonderwirtschaftszone *f*

special: ~ **employment measures** *n pl* (*SEM*) ECON, HRM Arbeitsbeschaffungsmaßnahmen *f pl* (*ABM*); ~ **feature** *n* S&M Besonderheit *f*; ~ **interest group** *n* (*SIG*) GEN COMM Gruppe *f* mit besonderen Interessen; ~ **intermediate survey** *n* TRANSP Sonderzwischenprüfung *f*

specialist 1. *adj* GEN COMM fachmännisch; **2.** *n* GEN COMM Fachmann *m*, Kader *m*, STOCK amtlicher Kursmakler *m*, amtliche Kursmaklerin *f*

specialist: ~ **block purchase and sale** *n AmE* STOCK Kauf und Verkauf von Aktienpaketen durch Kursmakler; ~ **field** *n* GEN COMM Fachgebiet *nt*; ~ **information** *n* GEN COMM fachmännische Auskunft *f*; ~ **knowledge** *n* GEN COMM Fachkenntnisse *f pl*; ~ **shop** *n* STOCK Fachgeschäft *nt*; ~'s **short-sale ratio** *n* STOCK Leerverkaufsverhältnis *nt* des amtlichen Kursmaklers

speciality *n* GEN COMM *selling point* besonderes Merkmal *nt*, Spezialität *f*, Besonderheit *f*, *product* Spezialartikel *m*, *field* Spezialgebiet *nt*; ~ **advertising** *n* S&M Werbung *f* für Spezialerzeugnisse, Werbung *f* für Spezialartikel; ~ **goods** *n pl* S&M Spezialartikel *m pl*; ~ **retailer** *n* S&M Facheinzelhändler, in *m,f*, Spezialitäteneinzelhändler, in *m,f*; ~ **salesperson** *n* S&M Fachverkäufer, in *m,f*; ~ **selling** *n* S&M Verkauf *m* von Spezialartikeln; ~ **store** *n* STOCK Fachgeschäft *nt*

specialization *n* GEN COMM Fachgebiet *nt*, Spezialisierung *f*

specialize *vi* GEN COMM sich spezialisieren; ◆ ~ **in** GEN COMM sich spezialisieren auf [+acc]

specialized *adj* GEN COMM, IND spezialisiert

special: ~ **journal** *n* ACC Sonderjournal *nt*; ~ **jury** *n* LAW außerordentliches Geschworenengericht *nt*

specially *adv* GEN COMM speziell; ◆ **not** ~ **provided for** (*nspf*) GEN COMM nicht speziell vorgesehen

special: ~ **meeting** *n* MGMNT außerplanmäßige Sitzung *f*,

außerplanmäßige Tagung *f*, außerplanmäßige Versammlung *f*, außerplanmäßige Zusammenkunft *f*, außerplanmäßiges Treffen *nt*, Sondersitzung *f*; ~ **meeting of shareholders** *n* FIN, MGMNT außerordentliche Hauptversammlung *f*; ~ **multiperil insurance** *n* (*SMP*) INS Sonderversicherung *f* gegen mehrfache Gefahren; ~ **nonmarketable bond** *n* STOCK spezielle nichtbörsenfähige Anleihe *f*; ~ **offer** *n* S&M *advertising* Sonderangebot *nt*; ~ **partner** *n* LAW Sondergesellschafter, in *m,f*; ~ **partnership** *n* LAW Arbeitsgemeinschaft *f*; ~ **position** *n* S&M besondere Position *f*; ~ **provision** *n BrE* TAX *National Insurance contributions* Sonderbedingung *f*; ~ **purchase** *n* S&M *advertising* Sonderkauf *m*; ~-**purpose allotment** *n* GEN COMM Sonderzuteilung *f*, zweckgebundene Zuweisung *f*; ~-**purpose reserve** *n* ACC Sonderrücklagen *f pl*; ~ **reserve** *n* ACC besondere Rücklage *f*, Sonderreserve *f*; ~ **situation** *n* GEN COMM besondere Lage *f*; ~ **survey** *n* (*SS*) TRANSP Sonderprüfung *f*; ~ **tax bond** *n* STOCK, TAX spezielle Steueranleihe *f*; ~ **terms for the trade** *n pl* GEN COMM Sonderkonditionen *f pl* für den Handel; ~ **traffic notice** *n* (*STN*) TRANSP Verkehrssondermitteilung *f*

specialty *AmE see speciality*

special: ~ **type** *n* TRANSP Sonderausführung *f*, Spezialausführung *f*; ~ **warrant** *n* POL besondere Vollmacht *f*, spezielle Befugnis *f*

specie *n* GEN COMM Hartgeld *nt*; ◆ **in** ~ GEN COMM *payment* in bar

specie: ~ **flow mechanism** *n* BANK Hartgeldfluß-Mechanismus *m*; ~ **point** *n* GEN COMM Goldpunkt *m*

specific *adj* GEN COMM bestimmt, deutlich, fest umrissen, kennzeichnend, speziell, spezifisch

specifically *adv* GEN COMM speziell

specific: ~ **amount** *n* GEN COMM bestimmte Menge *f*, bestimmter Betrag *m*

specification *n* LAW Patentschrift *f*, MATH *statistics* Spezifikation *f*, PATENTS Patentschrift *f*; ~ **change notice** *n* (*SCN*) TRANSP *aviation* Änderung *f* der Originalvorlage, Änderung *f* des Bezugsteils; ~ **of goods** *n* PATENTS Warenverzeichnis *nt*; ~ **of services** *n* PATENTS Dienstleistungsverzeichnis *nt*

specific: ~ **commitment** *n* GEN COMM spezielle Verpflichtung *f*; ~ **commodity rate** *n* IMP/EXP *air freight* Tarif *m* für bestimmte Ware, Tarif *m* für konkrete Ware; ~ **duty** *n* IMP/EXP, TAX spezifischer Zoll *m*; ~ **egalitarianism** *n* ECON spezifischer Egalitarismus *m*; ~ **gravity** *n* (*SG*) IND spezifisches Gewicht *nt*; ~ **individual licence** *BrE*, ~ **individual license** *AmE n* (*SIL*) IMP/EXP, TRANSP Sondereinzelgenehmigung *f*; ~ **investment loan** *n* (*SIL*) FIN spezifische Investitionsanleihe *f*, spezifisches Investitionsdarlehen *nt*; ~ **obligation** *n* LAW spezifische Verpflichtung *f*; ~ **offer** *n* S&M spezielles Angebot *nt*; ~ **payment** *n* GEN COMM spezielle Zahlung *f*; ~ **performance** *n* LAW vertragsgemäße Erfüllung *f*; ~ **tax** *n* IMP/EXP, TAX spezifische Steuer *f*, Mengensteuer *f*; ~ **training** *n* HRM Spezialausbildung *f*

specified *adj* ACC spezifiziert, GEN COMM einzeln aufgeführt, mit genauen Angaben versehen, spezifiziert; ~-**purpose account** *n* ACC Konto *nt* für bestimmte Zwecke; ~ **rate** *n* TRANSP angegebener Tarif *m*, spezifizierter Tarif *m*

specify *vt* GEN COMM, PATENTS beschreiben, festsetzen

specimen: ~ **invoice** *n* GEN COMM Musterrechnung *f*; ~ **signature card** *n* BANK Unterschriftskarte *f*

spectacular *n* S&M Werbegroßanlage *f*

speculate *vi* GEN COMM, STOCK spekulieren; ♦ ~ **for a fall in prices** STOCK auf Baisse spekulieren

speculation *n* GEN COMM Spekulation *f*; ♦ **on** ~ (*on spec*) GEN COMM auf Verdacht, auf die Vermutung hin, auf Spekulation, HRM *job application* spekulationsweise

speculative *adj* GEN COMM spekulativ; ~ **buyer** *n* GEN COMM Aufkäufer, in *m,f*; ~ **demand for money** *n* ECON spekulative Geldnachfrage *f*; ~ **trading** *n* STOCK Spekulationshandel *m*

speech *n* POL Rede *f*; ~ **processing** *n* COMP Sprachverarbeitung *f*; ~ **recognition** *n* COMP Spracherkennung *f*; ~ **recognition software** *n* COMP Spracherkennungssoftware *f*; ~ **writer** *n* POL Redenschreiber *m*, Redenverfasser *m*

speed *n* GEN COMM Geschwindigkeit *f*

speed up 1. *vt* GEN COMM beschleunigen, *work, process* verantreiben; **2.** *vi* GEN COMM beschleunigen, sich beschleunigen, schneller werden

speedily *adv* GEN COMM schnell

speed: ~-**up** *n* GEN COMM, HRM Beschleunigung *f*, Steigerung *f*, Vorantreiben *nt*

speedy *adj* GEN COMM prompt, zügig

spell out *vt* GEN COMM darlegen, klarmachen, verdeutlichen

spellcheck *n* COMP Rechtschreibprüfung *f*, Rechtschreibhilfe *f*

spellchecker *n* COMP Rechtschreibprüfung *f*, Rechtschreibhilfe *f*

spend 1. *vt* GEN COMM ausgeben, verausgaben; ♦ ~ **on** GEN COMM anlegen für; **2.** *vi* GEN COMM Geld ausgeben

spending: ~ **authority** *n* FIN Ausgabeermächtigung *f*, POL Ausgabenbefugnis *f*; ~ **level** *n* GEN COMM Ausgabengrenze *f*, Ausgabenhöhe *f*; ~ **limitation** *n* BANK, ECON, HRM Ausgabenbegrenzung *f*; ~ **money** *n* GEN COMM Taschengeld *nt*; ~ **patterns** *n pl* GEN COMM Ausgabenmodelle *nt pl*, Ausgabenschema *nt*; ~ **power** *n* GEN COMM Ausgabenkompetenz *f*, Kaufkraft *f*; ~ **spree** *n infrml* GEN COMM Großeinkauf *m*; ~ **surge** *n* GEN COMM rascher Ausgabenanstieg *m*; ~ **target** *n* ECON Ausgabenziel *nt*, Ausgabengrenze *f*

spendthrift *n* GEN COMM Verschwender, in *m,f*

sphere *n* GEN COMM Bereich *m*; ~ **of action** *n* GEN COMM Tätigkeitsbereich *m*; ~ **of activity** *n* GEN COMM Aufgabenbereich *m*, Geschäftsbereich *m*, Wirkungskreis *m*

spiel *n infrml* GEN COMM Gequassel *nt* (*infrml*), Geschwätz *nt*

spike *vt jarg* MEDIA *reject for publication* in der Schublade verschwinden lassen

spill over *vi* GEN COMM überquellen, überschwappen, sich ausbreiten, *meeting* sich hinziehen

spillage *n* ENVIR treibendes Ölfeld *nt*

spill: ~-**off effect** *n* GEN COMM Auslaufeffekt *m*

spillover *n* ECON externe Wirkung *f*, Nebenwirkungen *f pl*; ~ **effect** *n* GEN COMM externer Effekt *m*, Überlaufeffekt *m*

spin-off *n* ECON, FIN, GEN COMM *separation* Ausgliederung *f*, Abspaltung *f*, *company* Ableger *m*, *product* Nebenprodukt *nt*, IND *development* Nebenentwicklung

f, *product* Nebenprodukt *nt*, S&M *product* Nebenprodukt *nt*

spin: ~ **red tape** *phr* ADMIN die Bürokratie auf Trab bringen

spine *n* MEDIA Rücken *m*

spir *n infrml* MEDIA Schieber, in *m,f*

spiral *n* ECON *prices* Spirale *f*

spiralling: ~ **inflation** *n* ECON schnellwachsende Inflation *f*

spirit: ~ **of enterprise** *n* GEN COMM Einstellung *f* des Unternehmens, Unternehmensgeist *f*

splash *n* MEDIA *print* Aufmacher *m*, große Aufmachung *f* in der Presse

splash out *vt infrml* GEN COMM *money* hinauswerfen (*infrml*)

splintered: ~ **authority** *n* MGMNT Splitterbehörde *f*

splinter: ~ **group** *n* POL Splittergruppe *f*; ~ **union** *n* HRM Splittergewerkschaft *f*

split 1. *n* BANK Aufteilung *f*; **2.** *vt* BANK aufspalten, aufteilen; ♦ ~ **the difference** GEN COMM sich auf einen Kompromiß einigen, sich auf halbem Wege entgegenkommen, sich in die Differenz teilen

split up 1. *vt* ADMIN, GEN COMM aufteilen, spalten, POL spalten; **2.** *vi* ADMIN, GEN COMM sich spalten

split: ~ **charter** *n* TRANSP *air freight* aufgeteilter Chartervertrag *m*; ~ **commission** *n* ECON *payment* geteilte Provision *f*, POL *committee* in zwei Lager gespaltenes Gremium *nt*, Teilausschuß *m*; ~ **dollar insurance** *n* AmE INS Arbeitnehmerversicherung *f* durch den Arbeitgeber; ~ **offering** *n* STOCK in zwei oder mehr Tranchen aufgelegte Emission *f*; ~ **rating** *n* FIN gespaltene Einstufung *f*; ~ **run** *n* S&M *advertising* Anzeigensplit *m*; ~ **screen** *n* COMP Bildschirmaufteilung *f*, unterteilter Bildschirm *m*; ~-**second timing** *n* GEN COMM sekundengenaue Abstimmung *f*; ~ **shift** *n* HRM unterbrochene Arbeitsschicht *f*; ~ **ticket** *n* AmE POL *presidential elections* die Möglichkeit, für zwei Kandidaten unterschiedlicher Parteizugehörigkeit zu stimmen

splitting *n* GEN COMM Teilung *f*; ~ **spreads** *n pl* STOCK *options on Eurodollar futures* Spread-Splitting *nt*, Teilung *f* von Margen

spoil *vt* GEN COMM beeinträchtigen, verderben

spoilage *n* GEN COMM Ausschuß *m*, Makulatur *f*, Verderb *m*, IND Ausschuß *m*

spoiled: ~ **ballot paper** *n* POL unbrauchbarer Stimmzettel *m*, ungültiger Stimmzettel *m*; ~ **voting paper** *n* POL unbrauchbarer Stimmzettel *m*, ungültiger Stimmzettel *m*

spoiler *n* AmE POL Spielverderber *m*

spoils: ~ **system** *n* AmE POL Futterkrippensystem *nt*

spoilt: ~ **ballot paper** *n* POL unbrauchbarer Stimmzettel *m*, ungültiger Stimmzettel *m*; ~ **voting paper** *n* POL unbrauchbarer Stimmzettel *m*, ungültiger Stimmzettel *m*

Spokane: ~ **Stock Exchange** *n* STOCK Spokane Wertpapierbörse

spokesman *n* MEDIA, POL Sprecher *m*, Pressesprecher *m*

spokesperson *n* MEDIA, POL Sprecher, in *m,f*, Pressesprecher, in *m,f*

spokeswoman *f* MEDIA, POL Sprecherin *f*, Pressesprecherin *f*

sponsor 1. *n* GEN COMM Förderer *m*, Förderin *f*, LEIS *of event* Schirmherr *m*, POL *of bill* Befürworter, in *m,f*, S&M

advertising Sponsor *m*, Geldgeber, in *m,f*; **2.** *vt* GEN COMM fördern, unterstützen, LEIS *event* die Schirmherrschaft übernehmen [+gen], POL *bill* befürworten, S&M *advertising* sponsern

sponsor: ~ **demand** *n* ECON Sponsor-Nachfrage *f*

sponsored: ~ **book** *n* S&M gefördertes Buch *nt*, gesponsertes Buch *nt*; ~ **events** *n pl* LEIS, S&M geförderte Ereignisse *nt pl*, gesponserte Veranstaltungen *f pl*; ~ **television** *n* MEDIA, S&M Sponsorenfernsehen *nt*

sponsorship *n* GEN COMM Förderung *f*, Unterstützung *f*, LEIS *of event* Schirmherrschaft *f*, POL *of bill* Befürwortung *f*, S&M *advertising* Sponsern *nt*, Sponsoring *nt*

spontaneity *n* GEN COMM Spontaneität *f*

spontaneous *adj* GEN COMM, S&M spontan; ~ **combustion** *n* IND Selbstentzündung *f*, Selbstverbrennung *f*; ~ **recall** *n* S&M spontane Erinnerung *f*

spool *n* COMP Bandspule *f*, Lochstreifenspule *f*, Magnetbandspule *f*; ~ **file** *n* COMP SPOOL-Datei *f*

spooling *n* COMP Spulen *nt*

spoon: ~ **feed** *phr* GEN COMM jdm übertriebene Hilfe geben, jdn gängeln

sporadic *adj* GEN COMM sporadisch, vereinzelt; ~ **maintenance** *n* GEN COMM unregelmäßige Wartung *f*; ~ **service** *n* TRANSP sporadisches Verkehrsangebot *nt*

sport *n* LEIS Sport *m*

sporting: ~ **event** *n* GEN COMM, LEIS Sportveranstaltung *f*

spot *n* MEDIA, S&M *advertising, of airtime* Werbespot *m*; ♦ **on the** ~ GEN COMM an Ort und Stelle, sofort

spot: ~ **business** *n* GEN COMM Lokogeschäft *nt*; ~ **charter** *n* TRANSP Spot-Chartervertrag *m*; ~ **check** *n* GEN COMM Prüfung *f* an Ort und Stelle, Stichprobe *f*; ~ **commodity** *n* STOCK Effektivware *f*, Kassaware *f*; ~ **cotton** *n* IND, STOCK lieferfertige Baumwolle *f*; ~ **coverage** *n* MEDIA Berichterstattung *f* an Ort und Stelle; ~ **credit** *n* BANK Sofortkredit *m*, FIN Kassakredit *m*; ~ **currency market** *n* ECON Devisenkassamarkt *m*; ~ **delivery** *n* STOCK *currency futures* Lieferung *f* zwei Tage nach Geschäftsabschluß; ~ **delivery month** *n* STOCK sofortiger Lieferungsmonat *m*; ~ **exchange rate** *n* ECON, STOCK Devisenkassakurs *m*; ~ **market** *n* STOCK Kassamarkt *m*; ~ **market transaction** *n* STOCK Effektivgeschäft *nt*; ~ **month** *n* STOCK Kassamonat *m*; ~ **position** *n* STOCK Kassaposition *f*; ~ **quotation** *n* STOCK Kassanotierung *f*; ~ **recall** *n* S&M Erinnerung *f* an einen Werbespot; ~ **transaction** *n* STOCK Kassageschäft *nt*; ~ **zoning** *n* PROP Bauausnahmegenehmigung *f* für die Errichtung von Geschäftshäusern

spousal ira *n* BANK Pensionskonto für Ehegatten

spouse: ~ **fare** *n* LEIS ermäßigter Fahrpreis *m* für Ehepartner

spread 1. *n* ECON Bandbreite *f*, Marge *m*, S&M *of stores in particular area* Streuung *f*, STOCK Stellage *f*, STOCK Spread *m*; **2.** *vt* ACC *costs* verteilen, COMMS verbreiten, ECON verteilen, GEN COMM ausbreiten; ♦ ~ **repayments** FIN Rückzahlungen verteilen; ~ **the risk** INS das Risiko verteilen; ~ **risks** INS Risiken mischen, Risiken streuen, Risiken verteilen

spread: ~ **effect** *n* ECON Ausbreitungseffekt *m*, Verteilungseffekt *m*

spreading *n* STOCK Spreading *nt*; ~ **agreement** *n* STOCK Spreading-Vereinbarung *f*

spreadover *n* HRM *industrial relations* Arbeitsstundenanpassung *f*; ~ **working** *n* HRM Arbeitsstundenanpassung *f* durch Gleitzeit oder Wechselschicht

spreadsheet *n* ACC, ADMIN, COMP, FIN, STOCK Abschlußblatt *nt*, Tabellenkalkulation *f*, Arbeitsblatt *nt*, Spreadsheet *nt*, Kalkulationstabelle *f*, Gliederungsbogen *m*; ~ **program** *n* COMP Tabellenkalkulationsprogramm *nt*

spread: ~ **trading** *n* STOCK *currency market* Arbitrage *f*, Spreading *nt*, gleichzeitige Eröffnung *f* von Kauf- und Verkaufspositionen

spring: ~ **multi-year operational plan** *n* AmE (*spring MYOP*) POL Frühjahrsplan für mehrjährige Betriebsplanung; ~ **multi-year operational plan submission** *n* AmE POL Einreichung des Frühjahrsplans für mehrjährige Betriebsplanung; ~ **MYOP** *n* AmE (*spring multi-year operational plan*) POL Frühjahrsplan für mehrjährige Betriebsplanung; ~ **tide** *n* TRANSP *shipping* Springflut *f*

spur 1. *n* GEN COMM *incentive* Anreiz *m*; **2.** *vt* GEN COMM *urge on* treiben, vorantreiben

sq *abbr* (*square*) GEN COMM q (*Quadrat*)

SQC *abbr* (*statistical quality control*) MATH SQC (*statistische Qualitätskontrolle*)

squander *vt* GEN COMM *time, money* vergeuden, *resources* verschwenden

squandering *n* GEN COMM Vergeudung *f*, Verschwendung *f*

square 1. *adj* (*sq*) GEN COMM Quadrat *nt* (*q*); **2.** *vt* ACC abstimmen, GEN COMM *an account* begleichen, STOCK glattstellen

square: ~ **brackets** *n pl* COMP, MEDIA *typography* eckige Klammern *f pl*; ~ **foot** *n* GEN COMM, PROP Quadratfuß *m*; ~ **footage** *n* PROP *of a building* Quadratfußzahl *f*; ~ **kilometer** *AmE*, ~ **kilometre** *BrE n* GEN COMM Quadratkilometer *m*; ~ **measure** *n* GEN COMM Flächenmaß *nt*; ~ **meter** *AmE*, ~ **metre** *BrE n* GEN COMM Quadratmeter *m*; ~ **mile** *n* GEN COMM Quadratmeile *f*

Square: ~ **Mile** *n* BANK, FIN *in London* das Banken- und Börsenviertel der City

squaring *n* GEN COMM Ausgleich *m*

squatter: ~**'s rights** *n pl* LAW, PROP Ersitzungsrecht *nt*

squeegee: ~ **agreement** *n jarg* STOCK Abmachung, in der jemand sich verpflichtet, ein Wertpapier für eine gewisse Zeit mit einem Verlust zu unterstützen

squeeze *vt* ECON *prices* unter Druck setzen; ♦ ~ **the bears** STOCK die Baissiers unter Druck setzen; ~ **dry** GEN COMM auspressen (*infrml*); ~ **the shorts** STOCK die Baissiers zu Deckungskäufen zwingen

SR *abbr* (*short run*) IND Kleinauflage *f*

SR&CC *abbr* (*strikes, riots and civil commotions*) LAW, POL Streik *m*, Aufruhr *m* und innere Unruhen *f pl*

SRO *abbr* (*self-regulating organization, self-regulatory organization*) GEN COMM Selbstverwaltungskörperschaft *f*

SSA *abbr* (*standard spending assessment*) ECON, FIN Standardausgabenbewertung *f*

SSAP *abbr BrE* (*Statement of Standard Accounting Practice*) ACC allgemein anerkannte Grundsätze *m pl* der Rechnungslegung, GoB (*Grundsätze ordnungsgemäßer Buchführung*)

SSD *abbr* (*single-sided disk*) COMP einseitige Magnetplatte *f*

SSDD *abbr* (*single-sided double-density*) COMP einseitig mit doppelter Speicherdichte

SSP *abbr* INS (*statutory sick pay*) gesetzlich festgesetztes Krankengeld *nt*, gesetzliches Krankengeld *nt*

SSSD *abbr* (*single-sided single-density*) COMP einseitig mit einfacher Speicherdichte

SSSI *abbr* BrE (*site of special scientific interest*) ENVIR Standort *m* von besonderem wissenschaftlichen Interesse

SST *abbr* (*supplementary service tariff*) TRANSP zusätzlicher Dienstleistungstarif *m*

stabex: ~ **system** *n* ECON *agricultural* STABEX-System *nt* zur Stabilisierung der Agrarexporterlöse

stability *n* GEN COMM Stabilität *f*; ~ **zone** *n* HRM, WEL *stress-free* Stabilitätszone *f*

stabilization *n* ECON *of exchange rates* Stabilisierung *f*; ~ **policy** *n* ECON Stabilitätspolitik *f*, Stabilisierungspolitik *f*

stabilize 1. *vt* ECON festigen, stabil halten, stabilisieren; 2. *vi* ECON sich stabilisieren

stabilized: ~ **currency** *n* FIN stabilisierter Wechselkurs *m*; ~ **price** *n* ECON stabilisierter Preis *m*

stabilizer *n* ECON Stabilisator *m*

stable 1. *adj* ECON stabil, GEN COMM *constant* beständig, *permanent, durable* dauerhaft, fest, *tenable* haltbar, stabil, S&M, TRANSP stabil; 2. *n* LEIS Stall *m*

stable: ~ **equilibrium** *n* ECON stabiles Gleichgewicht *nt*; ~ **market** *n* ECON, FIN stabiler Markt *m*; ~ **rate** *n* TRANSP stabile Rate *f*; ~**rate funds** *n pl* BANK Festzinsmittel *nt pl*

stack *n* COMP *data* Puffer *m*, Stack *m*, GEN COMM, MEDIA Stapel *m*, Packen *m* (*infrml*)

Stackelberg: ~ **duopoly model** *n* ECON Stackelbergsches Duopolmodell *nt*

stacker *n* TRANSP *container securing* Stapeleinrichtung *f*, Stapelförderer *m*

stacking *n* TRANSP *cargo handling* Stapelung *f*; ~ **of cargo** *n* TRANSP Stapelung von Fracht *f*; ~ **fitting** *n* TRANSP *container handling* Stapelausrüstung *f*

staff 1. *n* GEN COMM, HRM, MGMNT *workforce* Belegschaft *f*, Mitarbeiter *m pl*, Personal *nt*, Stab *m*; 2. *vt* GEN COMM, HRM, MGMNT *office* mit Personal besetzen

staff up *vi* GEN COMM, HRM, MGMNT den Personalbestand erhöhen

staff: ~ **appraisal** *n* HRM, MGMNT Mitarbeiterbeurteilung *f*, Personalbeurteilung *f*; ~ **assistant** *n* HRM Bürogehilfe *m*, Bürogehilfin *f*; ~ **association** *n* HRM Personalvertretung *f*; ~ **audit** *n* HRM, MGMNT innerbetriebliche Prüfung *f*, Personalbeurteilung *f*; ~ **canteen** *n* HRM Betriebskantine *f*; ~ **captain** *n* HRM *shipping* Staff Captain *m*; ~ **commitment** *n* HRM Engagement *nt* des Personals; ~ **cost** *n* FIN, HRM Personalaufwand *m*; ~ **council** *n* ADMIN, HRM, MGMNT Personalrat *m*; ~ **cutback** *n* HRM Personalabbau *m*; ~ **development** *n* HRM, MGMNT Personalentwicklung *f*, Mitarbeiterförderung *f*, Weiterbildung *f* der Mitarbeiter, Weiterbildung *f* des Personals

staffed *adj* GEN COMM, HRM, MGMNT mit Personal besetzt

staff: ~ **forecasting** *n* HRM, MGMNT Personalprognosen

f pl; ~ **incentives** *n pl* HRM, MGMNT Anreizsystem *nt* für Mitarbeiter

staffing *n* GEN COMM, HRM, MGMNT Personalbeschaffung *f*, Personalführung *f*, Stellenbesetzung *f*; ~ **level** *n* HRM Personalbelegung *f*, Personalbestand *m*; ~ **levels** *n pl* HRM Besetzungsebenen *f pl*; ~ **policy** *n* GEN COMM, HRM, MGMNT Personalpolitik *f*

staff: ~ **inspection** *n* HRM Personalinspektion *f*; ~ **lawyer** *n* LAW Syndikusanwalt *m*, Syndikusanwältin *f*; ~ **management** *n* HRM Personalleitung *f*, Personalverwaltung *f*, Personalwirtschaft *f*; ~ **manager** *n* HRM, MGMNT Personalchef, in *m,f*, Personalleiter, in *m,f*, Stabsleiter, in *m,f*; ~ **mobility** *n* HRM Personalmobilität *f*; ~ **organization** *n* HRM, MGMNT Personalorganisation *f*, Stablinienorganisation *f*; ~ **planning** *n* HRM, MGMNT Stellenplanung *m*, Personalplanung *f*; ~ **provident fund** *n* HRM Unterstützungsfonds *m* für die Belegschaft; ~ **relations** *n pl* HRM, MGMNT Betriebsklima *nt*; ~ **representation** *n* HRM, MGMNT Personalvertretung *f*; ~ **representative** *n* HRM, MGMNT Personalvertreter, in *m,f*; ~ **resourcing** *n* HRM, MGMNT Personalbeschaffung *f*; ~**shortage** *n* HRM, MGMNT Mangel *m* an Personal; ~ **status** *n* HRM, MGMNT Angestelltenstatus *m*; ~ **strategy** *n* HRM, MGMNT Personalstrategie *f*; ~ **training** *n* HRM, MGMNT Mitarbeiterschulung *f*, Personalschulung *f*, Weiterbildung *f* der Mitarbeiter, Weiterbildung *f* des Personals; ~ **transfer** *n* HRM, MGMNT Personaltransfer *m*; ~ **turnover** *n* ECON, GEN COMM, HRM Arbeitskräftefluktuation *f*, Fluktuationsrate *f*, Personalwechsel *m*; ~ **welfare fund** *n* HRM, MGMNT, WEL Unterstützungsfonds *m* für die Belegschaft

stag *n* FIN Spekulant, in *m,f*, STOCK Konzertzeichner, in *m,f*

stage 1. *n* GEN COMM *of a project* Etappe *f*, Stufe *f*, *state* Stand *m*, Stadium *nt*, Phase *f*, MEDIA, POL Podium *nt*; ◆ **at an early** ~ GEN COMM zu einem frühen Zeitpunkt; 2. *vt* MGMNT *conference*, S&M *publicity event* veranstalten; ◆ ~ **a go-slow** BrE (*cf stage a slowdown AmE*) HRM einen Bummelstreik machen; ~ **a slowdown** AmE (*cf stage a go-slow BrE*) HRM einen Bummelstreik machen; ~ **a strike** GEN COMM, HRM, IND einen Streik organisieren; ~ **a walkout** HRM eine Arbeitsniederlegung organisieren

staged: ~ **agreement** *n* BrE HRM Stufenvertrag *m*

stage: ~ **payment** *n* FIN Etappenzahlung *f*, Zahlung *f* in Etappen

stages: **by** ~ *phr* GEN COMM in Stufen, stufenweise; **in** ~ *phr* GEN COMM in Stufen, phasenweise

stage: ~ **of transition** *n* ECON *towards Western-style market economies*, Transformationsstadium *nt*, GEN COMM Übergangsstadium *nt*

stagflation *n* ECON Stagflation *f*

stagger 1. *n* GEN COMM *grading*, HRM, STOCK Staffelung *f*; 2. *vt* GEN COMM *costs* staffeln

staggered *adj* FIN gestaffelt, GEN COMM erschüttert, gestaffelt, versetzt angeordnet, HRM, STOCK gestaffelt; ~ **board of directors** *n* HRM Verwaltungsrat *m*; ~ **election** *n* GEN COMM zeitlich gestaffelte Wahl der Vorstandsmitglieder einer öffentlich-rechtlichen Gesellschaft, mit dem Ziel, etwaige Übernahmeversuche zu verzögern; ~ **holidays** *n pl* BrE (*cf staggered vacations BrE*) HRM Staffelung *f* der Urlaubszeiten, Urlaubsaufteilung *f*; ~ **vacations** *n pl* AmE (*cf staggered holidays BrE*)

Staffelung *f* der Urlaubszeiten, Urlaubsaufteilung *f*; **~ working hours** *n pl* HRM Gleichzeit *f*, gestaffelte Arbeitszeit *f*

staggering 1. *adj infrml* GEN COMM *prices* schwindelerregend, erschütternd; **2.** *n* GEN COMM *action* Staffelung *f*

staggering: **~ budget deficit** *n* FIN erschütterndes Haushaltsdefizit *nt*; **~of holidays** *n pl BrE* (*cf staggering of vacations AmE*) HRM Staffelung *f* der Urlaubszeiten, Urlaubsaufteilung *f*; **~ maturities** *n pl* STOCK gestaffelte Fälligkeiten *f pl*; **~ of vacations** *n AmE* (*cf staggering of holidays BrE*) HRM Staffelung *f* der Urlaubszeiten, Urlaubsaufteilung *f*

stagnant *adj* ECON stagnierend, stockend

stagnate *vi* ECON stagnieren, stocken

stagnation *n* ECON Stagnation *f*, Stillstand *m*

stainless: **~ steel** *n* IND Edelstahl *m*, rostfreier Stahl *m*

stake *n* FIN *in company* Einsatz *m*, Kapitalanlage *f*, GEN COMM *in company* Beteilung *f*, Einsatz *m*, *financial interest* Anteil *m*, STOCK Beteiligung *f*

stakeholders *n pl* GEN COMM Interessengruppe *f*

stake: **~ in a bank** *n* BANK Beteiligung an einer Bank *f*

stakes: **the ~ are high** *phr* GEN COMM der Einsatz ist hoch

stale: **~ bill of lading** *n* IMP/EXP verfallenes Konnossement *nt*, verjährtes Konnossement *nt*, TRANSP ungültiger Frachtbrief *m*; **~ market** *n* ECON, GEN COMM flauer Markt *m*, lustloser Markt *m*

stalemate *n* GEN COMM, POL Flaute *f*, Sackgasse *f*

stalemated *adj* GEN COMM, POL *talks* festgefahren

stall *vt* GEN COMM hinauszögern, hinhalten, *motor* abwürgen

stalls *n pl* LEIS *theatre* Parkett *nt*

stamp 1. *n* COMMS Briefmarke *f*, Postwertzeichen *nt* (*frml*), GEN COMM Stempel *m*, S&M *of seal* Abdruck *m*; **2.** *vt* COMMS stempeln, GEN COMM abstempeln; ♦ **~ the date** ADMIN *on form* das Datum auf ein Formular stempeln

stamp out *vt* ECON *inflation* beseitigen, unterdrücken, GEN COMM ausmerzen, niederschlagen, IND ausstanzen, POL *opposition* unterdrücken, *crime* ausrotten, WEL *disease* ausrotten

Stamp: **~ Act** *n BrE* LAW Stempelsteuergesetz *nt*

stamped: **~ addressed envelope** *n BrE* (*s.a.e.*) COMMS frankierter Rückumschlag *m*, freigemachter Rückumschlag *m*

stampede *n* GEN COMM Massenansturm *m*, Massenbewegung *f*, wilde Flucht *f*

stamping: **~ machine** *n* COMMS Frankiermaschine *f*, Stempelmaschine *f*

stamp: **~ pad** *n* GEN COMM Stempelkissen *nt*

stance *n* GEN COMM *on issue* Einstellung *f*, Haltung *f*, Standpunkt *m*, MGMNT, POL Haltung *f*; ♦ **what is your ~ on this issue?** GEN COMM welche Einstellung haben Sie zu dieser Frage?

stand 1. *n* S&M *advertising poster* Plakatanschlagfläche *f*, *at exhibition* Stand *m*, STOCK Stand *m*; **2.** *vt* ♦ **~ a good chance of** GEN COMM eine gute Chance haben für; **~ a loss** FIN einen Verlust tragen; **~ one's ground** GEN COMM, MGMNT seine Position halten, seinen Mann stehen, sich behaupten, sich durchsetzen; **~ security for** BANK Sicherheit leisten für; **~ surety for sb** BANK Bürgschaft für jdn leisten; **~ the test of competition** GEN COMM, S&M den Konkurrenztest bestehen; **3.** *vi* ♦

~ at GEN COMM *offer, price, bid* sich belaufen auf [+acc], liegen bei, stehen bei; **~ as guarantor for sb** FIN als Bürge für jdn agieren; **~ for election** POL kandidieren; **~ for the committee** GEN COMM für das Komitee kandidieren, für das Komitee eintreten; **~ in line** *AmE* (*cf queue BrE*) GEN COMM Schlange stehen, sich anstellen; **~ firm** GEN COMM fest bleiben; **~ firm in the belief that** GEN COMM fest daran glauben, daß; **~ up to wear** GEN COMM, IND haltbar sein, strapazierfähig sein

stand down *vi* HRM, POL zurücktreten; ♦ **~ in favor of the other candidate** *AmE*, **~ in favour of the other candidate** *BrE* POL *in election* zugunsten des anderen Kandidaten auf die eigene Kandidatur verzichten

stand for *vt* GEN COMM *initials* bedeuten, stehen für, POL *be candidate for* kandidieren für

stand in *vi* HRM einspringen; ♦ **~ for sb** HRM für jdn einspringen

stand off *vi* HRM Abstand halten

standage: **~ area** *n* TRANSP Stellbereich *m*

stand: **~~alone** *adj* COMP *computer, system* autonom, selbständig; **~~alone cost** *n* ACC Zusatzkosten *pl*; **~~alone system** *n* COMP autonomes System *nt*, Einzelsystem *nt*

standard 1. *adj* GEN COMM einheitlich, regulär, normal, üblich; ♦ **it is ~ practice to do so** GEN COMM es entspricht der üblichen Praxis, so zu handeln; **of ~ size** COMP normalgroß; **2.** *n* (*Std*) BANK Feingehalt *m*, GEN COMM Standard *m*, Norm *f*

standard: **~ agreement** *n* GEN COMM, LAW *contract* Einheitsvertrag *m*, Standardvertrag *m*; **~ allotment** *n* POL Standardration *f*, Standardzuweisung *f*; **~ banking** *n* BANK reguläres Bankgeschäft *nt*; **~ code** *n* GEN COMM allgemeine Regeln *f pl*; **~ commodity** *n* STOCK Standardware *f*; **~ conditions** *n pl* LAW *contracts* Einheitsbedingungen *f pl*; **~ contract** *n* GEN COMM, LAW Standardvertrag *m*, Einheitsvertrag *m*; **~ cost** *n* ACC Plankosten *pl*, Richtkosten *pl*; **~ cost accounting** *n* ACC Plankostenrechnung *f*, Normalkostenrechnung *f*; **~ costing** *n* ACC Plankostenrechnung *f*, Normalkostenrechnung *f*; **~ costs** *n pl* ACC, FIN Standardkosten *pl*, Normalkosten *pl*, Standardherstellungskosten *pl*; **~ cost system** *n* ACC, FIN Plankostenrechnung *f*, Standardkostensystem *nt*; **~ design** *n* (*SD*) GEN COMM, IND, TRANSP *of vessel* Standarddesign *nt*, Standardkonstruktion *f*; **~ deviation** *n* FIN Standardabweichung *f*, MATH *statistics* mittlere quadratische Abweichung *f*, Standardabweichung *f*; **~ directory of advertisers** *n* S&M Standardverzeichnis *nt* von Werbeagenturen; **~ earnings** *n pl* ECON, HRM Normaleinkommen *nt*; **~ of equalization** *n* GEN COMM Ausgleichsstandard *m*; **~ error** *n* MATH *statistics* Standardfehler *m*; **~ error of estimate** *n* MATH *statistics* Standardschätzfehler *m*; **~ error of the mean** *n* MATH *statistics* Standardfehler *m* des arithmetischen Mittels; **~ export levy** *n* IMP/EXP Standardausfuhrabschöpfung *f*, Standardexportabgabe *f*; **~ fire policy** *n* INS Einheitspolice *f* der Feuerversicherung; **~~form contract** *n* LAW Standardvertrag *m*, Einheitsvertrag *m*; **~ freight classification** *n* (*SFTC*) TRANSP Standardfrachthandelsklassifizierung *f*; **~ grade** *n* GEN COMM Einheitssorte *f*, Standard *m*, standardisierte Qualität *f*; **~ of hygiene** *n* WEL Hygienestandard *m*; **~ industrial classification** *n* (*SIC*) IND amtliche Branchenklassifikation *f*, amtliche Systematik *f* der Betriebsstätten; **~ interchange facilities** *n pl* (*SIT*)

TRANSP Standardaustauscheinrichtungen *f pl*; **~ inter-national trade classification** *n* (*SITC*) GEN COMM internationales Warenverzeichnis *nt* für den Außenhandel; **be up to ~** HRM den Anforderungen genügen

standardization *n* ACC, GEN COMM, IND, LAW, S&M Standardisierung *f*, Vereinheitlichung *f*; **~ agreement** *n* GEN COMM, LAW Standardisierungsabkommen *nt*

standardize *vt* ACC standardisieren, typisieren, vereinheitlichen, BANK regulieren, GEN COMM, LAW, S&M standardisieren, typisieren, vereinheitlichen, normen

standardized *adj* ACC genormt, standardisiert, vereinheitlicht, BANK reguliert, GEN COMM, LAW, S&M genormt, standardisiert, vereinheitlicht, typisiert; **~ production** *n* IND Fließfertigung *f*, vereinheitlichte Herstellung *f*; **~ sales presentation** *n* S&M standardisierte Verkaufspräsentation *f*

standard: **~ letter** *n* GEN COMM, S&M Standardbrief *m*; **~ of living** *n* ECON, WEL Lebensstandard *m*; **~ measure** *n* ENVIR Urmaß *nt*

Standard: **~ Metropolitan Statistical Area** *n AmE* (*SMSA*) MATH *statistics* standardisierter statistischer Bereich *m* einer Großstadt

standard: **~ object** *n* ECON, POL Standardobjekt *nt*, Standardposten *m*; **~ object code** *n* COMP Standardmaschinencode *m*, Standardobjektcode *m*; **~ object of expenditure** *n* ECON, POL Standardausgabenobjekt *nt*, Standardausgabenposten *m*; **~ object of revenue** *n* ECON, POL Standardeinnahmeobjekt *nt*; **~ operating procedure** *n* (*s.o.p., SOP*) GEN COMM einheitliches Betriebsverfahren *nt*, Standardverfahren *nt*, standardisierte Fertigungsmethode *f*; **~ performance** *n* GEN COMM, HRM Normalleistung *f*, Standardleistung *f*; **~ portfolio analysis of risk** *n* (*SPAR*) FIN Standard-Portfeuille-Risikoanalyse *f*; **~ practice** *n* GEN COMM übliche Praxis *f*, LAW *contracts* Gepflogenheiten *f pl*; **~ price** *n* FIN Einheitspreis *m*, fester Verrechnungspreis *m*, S&M Standardpreis *m*; **~ rate** *n* TAX Proportionalsatz *m*, Standardsteuersatz *m*, Einheitssteuersatz *m*, Normalsatz *m*, *National Insurance contributions* Einheitssatz *m*, Regelsteuersatz *m*; **~-rated** *adj* TAX zum Einheitssatz, zum Einheitssteuersatz, zum Normalsatz; **~-rate tax** *n* TAX proportionale Steuer *f*; **~ shipping note** *n* IMP/EXP, TRANSP Standardschiffszettel *m*, Standardversandanzeige *f*; **~ slip** *n* GEN COMM, TRANSP *shipping* Standardbeleg *m*; **~ specimen signature card** *n* BANK Standardunterschriftskarte *f*; **~ spending assessment** *n* (*SSA*) ECON, FIN Standardausgabenbewertung *f*

standards: **~ and practices** *n pl* GEN COMM Normen *f pl* und Praktiken, LAW Standard- und Verhaltensnormen *f pl*

standard: **~ terms and conditions** *n pl* HRM, LAW allgemeine Geschäftsbedingungen *f pl*; **~ time** *n* GEN COMM Einheitszeit *f*, Normalzeit *f*, Vorgabezeit *f*, HRM Normalarbeitszeit *f*; **~ of valuation** *n* ACC Bewertungsgrundsatz *m*; **~ of value** *n* LAW, TAX Bewertungsgrundsatz *m*; ♦ **~ at a discount** STOCK mit einem Disagio notiert werden, unter dem Nennwert notiert werden; **~ at a premium** STOCK über dem Nennwert notiert werden, mit einem Agio notiert werden

standby *adj* COMP, FIN Bereitschafts-, HRM Stellvertreter, in *m,f*, Standby-; **~ agreement** *n* BANK Vereinbarung *f* einer Bankgarantie, FIN Bereitschafts-

kreditabkommen *nt*, GEN COMM, LAW Stillhaltevereinbarung *f*, Unterstützungsabkommen *nt*; **~ charges** *n pl* BANK Gebühren *f pl* für Bereitschaftskredit; **~ credit** *n* BANK, FIN Beistandskredit *m*, Bereitschaftskredit *m*, Stützungskredit *m*, Standby-Kredit *m*; **~ facility** *n* FIN Standby-Fazilität *f*, Verfügungsmöglichkeit *f* über Bereitstellungskredit, Beistandskredit *m*; **~ fees** *n pl* FIN Bereitstellungsgebühren *f pl*, **~ loan** *n* FIN Bereitschaftsdarlehen *nt*, Bereitstellungsdarlehen *nt*; **~ power plant** *n* IND Ersatzanlage *f*, Reservekraftwerk *nt*; **~ rate** *n* HRM Arbeitsentgelt *nt* für Bereitschaftsdienst; **~ ticket** *n* TRANSP *last-minute departures* Standby-Ticket *nt*; **~ underwriter** *n* FIN *securities, lending* Übernahmekonsortium für nicht abgesetzte Bezugsrechte

standfirst *n* MEDIA *print* einführender Bericht *m*

stand: **~-in** *n* HRM Stellvertreter, in *m,f*

standing 1. *adj* BANK laufend, GEN COMM beständig; 2. *n* GEN COMM *reputation* Ansehen *nt*, Ruf *m*, Bonität *f*, STOCK Stellung *f*

standing: **~ advance** *n* BANK laufender Kredit *m*; **~ authorization** *n* IMP/EXP Dauergenehmigung *f*; **~ committee** *n* POL *European Parliament* ständiger Ausschuß *m*

Standing: **~ Committee on Miscellaneous Estimates** *n* POL ständiger Haushaltsausschuß für sonstige Voranschläge; **~ Committee on Public Accounts** *n* POL Rechnungsprüfungsausschuß *m*

standing: **~ deposit** *n* IMP/EXP Dauereinlage *f*; **~ expenses** *n pl* FIN feste Kosten *pl*; **~ order** *n* (*S.O.*) BANK Dauerauftrag *m*; **~ procedure** *n* GEN COMM feststehendes Verfahren *nt*; **~ travel advance** *n* GEN COMM Dauerreisekostenvorschuß *m*

standoff *n* HRM *negotiations*, POL verfahrene Situation *f*

standstill *n* ECON, GEN COMM Stillstand *m*; ♦ **come to a ~** GEN COMM zum Stillstand kommen, IND zum Erliegen kommen; **~ agreement** *n* GEN COMM Moratorium *nt*, Stillhalteabkommen *nt*, Stillhaltevereinbarung *f*

staple: **~ commodities** *n* GEN COMM Stapelwaren *f pl*; **~ commodity** *n* ECON Hauptartikel *m*, Massenartikel *m*; **~ export** *n* IMP/EXP Stapelexport *m*; **~ goods** *n pl* GEN COMM Stapelwaren *f pl*; **~ product** *n* S&M Hauptprodukt *nt*, Massenerzeugnis *nt*

staples *n* GEN COMM Stapelwaren *f pl*

starboard *n* TRANSP *shipping* Steuerbord *nt*; **~ side** *n* TRANSP Steuerbordseite *f*

Star: **~ Chamber** *n BrE* ECON Regierungsausschuß für den Haushaltsentwurf

star: **~ network** *n* COMP Sternnetz *nt*; **~ product** *n* S&M wachstumsstarkes Produkt *nt* mit großem Marktanteil

start 1. *n* COMP *machine, peripheral* Start *m*, GEN COMM *commencement* Anfang *m*, Beginn *m*, TRANSP Abfahrt *f*; ♦ **get off to a flying ~** GEN COMM *business, project* vielversprechend beginnen; 2. *vt* COMP *file* starten, GEN COMM *firm, company* aufmachen *(infrml)*, beginnen, gründen; 3. *vi* GEN COMM anfangen; ♦ **~ from scratch** GEN COMM ganz neu beginnen; **~ in business** GEN COMM ein Geschäft aufmachen, sich selbständig machen

start up *vt* ECON gründen, GEN COMM *business* anfangen, aufnehmen, eröffnen, IND in Betrieb nehmen

start: **~ bit** *n* COMP Startbit *nt*; **~ of building work** *n* PROP Baubeginn *m*

starter: **~ home** *n* PROP erstes Haus *nt*

starting: ~ **from Monday** *phr* GEN COMM ab Montag; **~-load costs** *n pl* ACC, FIN Anlaufkosten *pl*; ~ **point** *n* GEN COMM Ansatzpunkt *m*, Ausgangspunkt *m*; ~ **price** *n* STOCK Einsatzpreis *m*; ~ **salary** *n* HRM Anfangsgehalt *nt*; ~ **wage** *n* HRM Anfangslohn *m*

start-up 1. *n* ECON Inbetriebnahme *f*, *business* Neugründung *f*, GEN COMM Anfang *m*, Anlauf *m*, Inbetriebnahme *f*; **2.** *adj* GEN COMM anfänglich

start-up: ~ **capital** *n* FIN Gründungskapital *nt*, Anfangskapital *nt*, Startkapital *nt*; ~ **costs** *n pl* ACC, FIN Anlaufkosten *pl*, Startkosten *pl*; ~ **phase** *n* GEN COMM Anlaufphase *f*

starvation: ~ **wage** *n* HRM, WEL Hungerlohn *m*

state 1. *n* COMP *condition* Status *m*, Zustand *m*, GEN COMM Status *m*, POL Staat *m*; ♦ **in a ~ of neglect** GEN COMM in verwahrlostem Zustand; **2.** *vt* ACC ansetzen, GEN COMM angeben, bekunden, *account* nennen; ♦ ~ **categorically** GEN COMM kategorisch erklären; ~ **the obvious** GEN COMM nichts Neues bringen; ~ **one's opinions** GEN COMM seine Ansichten äußern

state: ~ **of affairs** *n* GEN COMM Stand *m* der Dinge; **~-aided** *adj* ECON, POL mit staatlicher Hilfe; ~ **of the art** *n* GEN COMM neuester Entwicklungsstand *m*, Stand *m* der Technik, gegenwärtiger Stand *m* der Technik; ~ **bond** *n* FIN Staatsschuldverschreibung *f*, STOCK Anleihe *f* eines Bundesstaates; ~ **budget** *n* ECON, POL Staatshaushalt *m*; ~ **capitalism** *n* ECON, POL Staatskapitalismus *m*; ~ **coffers** *n pl* POL Staatssäckel *m* (*infrml*); ~ **control** *n* ECON staatliche Kontrolle *f*; ~ **where the judgment was rendered** LAW Urteilsstaat *m*

stated *adj* ACC angegeben, GEN COMM ausgewiesen, erwähnt; ~ **capital** *n* ACC ausgewiesenes Kapital *nt*, Grundkapital *nt*

stated: ~ **value** *n* ACC angegebener Wert *m*, ausgewiesener Wert *m*

State: ~ **Department** *n* AmE POL Außenministerium *nt*; ~ **Earnings-Related Pension Scheme** *n* BrE (*SERPS*) ECON lohnbezogener Pensionsplan *m* des Staates, lohngekoppelte Staatspension *f*

state: ~ **of the economy** *n* ECON, POL Konjunkturlage *f*, Zustand *m* der Volkswirtschaft; ~ **enterprise** *n* ADMIN, ECON, FIN, GEN COMM staatliches Unternehmen *nt*; ~ **examination** *n* HRM, WEL Staatsprüfung *f*; ~ **government tribunal** *n* LAW, POL Landesgericht *nt*; ~ **help** *n* WEL staatliche Hilfe *f*; ~ **intervention** *n* ECON, GEN COMM, POL Eingreifen *nt* des Staates, staatliche Intervention *f*

stateless *adj* ECON, POL staatenlos; ~ **currency** *n* ECON staatenlose Währung *f*

State: ~ **Medical Board of Registration** *n* AmE (*cf General Medical Council BrE*) GEN COMM Staatliche medizinische Registrierungsbehörde, ≈ Ärztekammer *f*

statement *n* ACC Bilanz *f*, BANK Kontoauszug *m*, COMP Anweisung *f*, GEN COMM Angabe *f*, *written* Aussage *f*, Erklärung *f*, HRM Angabe *f*, LAW *claim* Behauptung *f*, Protokoll *f*, MEDIA, POL Erklärung *f*, *to the press* Presseerklärung *f*; ♦ **as per ~** BANK laut Kontoauszug

statement: ~ **of account** *n* ACC Rechnungsauszug *m*, BANK Auszug *m*; ~ **of affairs** *n* BANK *in bankruptcy* Konkursbilanz *f*, Vermögensaufstellung *f* des Konkursschuldners, LAW Vermögensaufstellung *f*, *of case facts* Sachverhalt *m*, *of affairs* Vergleichsbilanz *f*; ~ **analysis** *n* ACC Bilanzanalyse *f*; ~ **of assets and liabilities** *n* ACC

Aufstellung *f* der Aktiven und Passiven, Bilanzstatus *m*; ~ **of average** *n* INS Dispache *f*; ~ **of claim** *n* LAW Klagebegründung *f*; ~ **of condition** *n* BANK, FIN Finanzstatus *m*, Bilanzaufstellung *f*; ~ **of earnings** *n* ACC Gewinn- und Verlustrechnung *f*; ~ **of financial position** *n* ACC Bilanz *f*, Finanzbericht *m*; ~ **for the press** *n* MEDIA Presseerklärung *f*; ~ **of income** *n* ACC Gewinn- und Verlustrechnung *f*; ~ **in lieu of prospectus** *n* BrE STOCK Vorgründungsbericht an das Handelsregister, Prospektersatzerklärung *f*; ~ **of instruments issued** *n* BANK Ausweis *m* der ausgegebenen Instrumente; ~ **of net assets** *n* ACC Nettovermögensaufstellung *f*; ~ **of objectives** *n* GEN COMM, MGMNT Zielformulierung *f*; ~ **of prosecution** *n* LAW Aussage *f* der Staatsanwaltschaft; ~ **of revenue and expense** *n* ACC Einnahmen-Ausgaben-Rechnung *f*

Statement: ~ **of Standard Accounting Practice** *n* BrE (*SSAP*) ACC allgemein anerkannte Grundsätze *m pl* der Rechnungslegung, Grundsätze *m pl* ordnungsgemäßer Buchführung (*GoB*)

statement: ~ **of terms and conditions** *n* HRM Geschäftsbedingungen *f pl*, Angabe *f* der Bedingungen; ~ **of witness** *n* LAW Zeugenaussage *f*

state: **~-owned enterprise** *n* ADMIN staatliches Unternehmen *nt*, ECON Staatsbetrieb *m*, Staatsunternehmen *nt*, staatliches Unternehmen *nt*, FIN staatliches Unternehmen *nt*, GEN COMM Staatsbetrieb *m*, staatliches Unternehmen *nt*; ~ **ownership** *n* ECON, FIN Staatseigentum *nt*; ~ **pension** *n* FIN, WEL Pension *f*, Rente *f*, Ruhegehalt *nt*; ~ **of registry** *n* TRANSP Staat *m* der Registrierung; **~-run enterprise** *n* ADMIN, ECON, FIN, GEN COMM staatliches Unternehmen *nt*; ~ **school** *n* BrE GEN COMM öffentliche Schule *f*, staatliche Schule *f*; ~ **subsidy** *n* ECON staatliche Subvention *f*; ~ **tax** *n* AmE TAX Steuer *f* der Einzelstaaten; ~ **theory** *n* ECON Staatstheorie *f*; ~ **trading organization** *n* GEN COMM Staatshandelsorganisation *f*

static *adj* ECON *output, prices* statisch; ~ **discounting method** *n* ACC statische Abzinsung *f*; ~ **model** *n* ECON statisches Modell *nt*; ~ **risk** *n* INS, MATH *statistics* statisches Risiko *nt*

statics *n* IND Statik *f*

station *n* (*stn*) COMP Station *f*, TRANSP *railway* Bahnhof *m*, *stop* Station *f*

stationary: ~ **economy** *n* ECON stationäre Volkswirtschaft *f*; ~ **equilibrium** *n* ECON stationäres Gleichgewicht *nt*; ~ **state** *n* ECON stationärer Zustand *m*; ~ **state economy** *n* ECON stationäre Volkswirtschaft *f*

station: ~ **break** *n* AmE COMMS, S&M *radio advertising* Sendeunterbrechung *f* für Werbedurchsagen, Sendeunterbrechung *f* für Werbung

stationer *n* ADMIN Papierwarenhändler, in *m,f*, Schreibwarenhändler, in *m,f*

stationery *n* GEN COMM Büromaterial *nt*, Schreibwaren *f pl*

stationmaster *n* TRANSP Bahnhofsvorsteher *m*

station: ~ **time** *n* AmE MEDIA *broadcast* Ortszeit *f*, Sendezeit *f*; ~ **wagon** *n* AmE (*cf estate car BrE*) TRANSP Kombiwagen *m*, Kombi *m* (*infrml*)

statistical *adj* ECON, GEN COMM, MATH statistisch; ~ **control** *n* MATH statistische Kontrolle *f*; ~ **inference** *n* MATH statistische Inferenz *f*

statistically: ~ **significant** *adj* MATH statistisch signifikant

statistical: ~ **modeling** *AmE*, ~ **modelling** *BrE n* MATH statistische Modellbildung *f*, Erstellung *f* eines statistischen Modells; ~ **population** *n* MATH statistische Grundgesamtheit *f*, statistische Population *f*; ~ **process control** *n* MATH statistische Fertigungskontrolle *f*; ~ **quality control** *n* (*SQC*) MATH statistische Qualitätskontrolle *f* (*SQC*)

Statistical: ~ **Return** *n BrE* TAX *VAT* Statistik *f*, statistischer Bericht *m*

statistical: ~ **returns** *n pl* MATH Statistiken *f pl*; ~ **sampling** *n* MATH mathematisches Stichprobenverfahren *nt*, S&M Markt- und Meinungsforschung *f*; ~ **significance** *n* MATH statistische Signifikanz *f*; ~ **software** *n* COMP, MATH *computer program* Statistik-Software *f*; ~ **spread** *n* MATH statistische Streuung *f*

statistician *n* MATH Statistiker, in *m,f*

statistics *n* MATH Statistik *f*

status *n* ACC Status *m*, Finanzlage *f*, ADMIN Stellung *f*, COMP Status *m*, Zustand *m*, GEN COMM Lage *f*, Status *m*, Zustand *m*, STOCK Stellung *f*; ~ **bar** *n* COMP Statuszeile *f*; ~ **information** *n* COMP Status-Anzeige *f*, GEN COMM Angabe *f* des Familienstandes, Lageinformation *f*; ~ **inquiry** *n* S&M Statusprüfung *f*, Vermögensauskunft *f*; ~ **line** *n* COMP Statuszeile *f*; ~ **message** *n* COMP Statusmeldung *f*; ~ **offender** *n AmE* LAW heranwachsender Straftäter *m*; ~ **of possession** *n* LAW Besitzstand *m*; ~ **quo** *n* HRM, LAW Status quo *m*; ~ **quo clause** *n* HRM Status-quo-Klausel *f*; ~ **report** *n* GEN COMM, MGMNT Bericht *m* einer Auskunftei, Informationen *f pl* über die Geschäftslage, Lagebericht *m*, Zustandsbericht *m*; ~ **seeker** *n* GEN COMM, HRM Geltungssüchtige(r) *mf* [decl. as adj]; ~ **symbol** *n* GEN COMM Statussymbol *nt*

statute *n* LAW Gesetz *nt*, Satzung *f*, Statut *nt*; ♦ **by** ~ LAW durch Gesetz, gesetzlich, satzungsgemäß, statutarisch; ~~**barred** *adj* LAW verjährt; ~ **book** *n BrE* LAW Gesetzbuch *nt*; ~ **law** *n* LAW, PATENTS kodifiziertes Recht *nt*; ~ **of limitations** *n* LAW gesetzliche Verjährungsvorschriften *f pl*, Verjährung *f*, Verjährungsfrist *f*

statutes: ~ **of limitation of action** *n pl* LAW gesetzliche Vorschriften *f pl* über die Klageausschlußfrist, gesetzliche Klageausschlußfristvorschriften *f pl*

statutory *adj* GEN COMM, INS, LAW gesetzlich, POL gesetzlich, rechtskräftig; ♦ **have** ~ **effect** LAW Gesetzeskraft haben; ~ **accounts** *n pl* ACC gesetzlicher Jahresabschluß *m*; ~ **allocation** *n* POL gesetzlich vorgeschriebene Zuweisung *f*, gesetzliche Zuweisung *f*; ~ **appropriation** *n* ACC satzungsmäßige Rücklage *f*, satzungsmäßige Gewinnverteilung *f*, LAW gesetzlicher Eigentumserwerb *m*, gesetzliche Bereitstellung *f*; ~ **audit** *n* ACC Pflichtprüfung *f*, vorgeschriebene Abschlußprüfung *f*, gesetzliche Buchprüfung *f*; ~ **authority** *n* POL gesetzliche Vollmacht *f*, gesetzliche Ermächtigung *f*, rechtskräftige Vollmacht *f*; ~ **basis** *n* LAW Gesetzesgrundlage *f*; ~ **body** *n* LAW öffentlich-rechtliche Anstalt *f*; ~ **books** *n pl* LAW gesetzlich vorgeschriebene Bücher und Verzeichnisse *nt pl*; ~ **company** *n* GEN COMM durch besonderes Parlamentsgesetz begründetes Versorgungsunternehmen; ~ **exclusion** *n* INS *marine* Ausschluß *m* laut Satzung oder Gesetz; ~ **exemption** *n* LAW gesetzliche Ausnahme *f*; ~ **expenditure** *n* GEN COMM satzungsmäßige Ausgabe *f*, POL gesetzlich festgelegte Ausgaben *f pl*, gesetzlich

vorgeschriebene Aufwendungen *f pl*; ~ **foreclosure** *n* LAW gesetzliches Hindernis *nt*, gesetzlich zugelassener Pfandverkauf *m*; ~ **forms** *n pl* LAW *contracts* gesetzliche Formvorschriften *f pl*; ~ **grounds for dissolution** *n pl* LAW Auflösungsgründe *m pl*; ~ **holiday** *n AmE* (*cf bank holiday BrE*) GEN COMM, HRM, LAW gesetzlicher Feiertag *m*, Bankfeiertag *m*, allgemeiner Feiertag *m*; ~ **immunities** *n pl* HRM, LAW *trade union* gesetzliche Privilegien *nt pl*, Gewerkschaftsprivilegien *nt pl*; ~ **immunity** *n* LAW gesetzliche Immunität *f*; ~ **incidence** *n* TAX gesetzliche Inzidenz *f*; ~ **instrument** *n* LAW Rechtsverordnung *f*, gesetzliche Verfügung *f*; ~ **investment** *n* FIN gesetzlich vorgeschriebene Investition *f*; ~ **item** *n* POL gesetzlich festgelegter Posten *m*, gesetzlich vorgeschriebener Haushaltsposten *m*; ~ **meeting** *n* LAW *corporation* gesetzlich vorgeschriebene Gründungsversammlung *f*; ~ **merger** *n* LAW gesetzliche Fusion *f*; ~ **notice** *n* LAW gesetzliche Kündigungsfrist *f*; ~ **obligation** *n* LAW gesetzliche Verpflichtung *f*; ~ **policy** *n BrE* HRM staatliche Intervention *f*; ~ **program** *AmE*, ~ **programme** *BrE n* POL Gesetzesprogramm *nt*, gesetzlich vorgeschriebenes Programm *nt*; ~ **report** *n* GEN COMM Gründungsbericht *m*; ~ **requirement** *n* POL gesetzliche Vorschrift *f*, gesetzliche Voraussetzungen *f pl*; ~ **right** *n BrE* LAW Gesetzesrecht *nt*; ~ **sick pay** *n BrE* (*SSP*) INS gesetzlich festgesetztes Krankengeld *nt*, gesetzliches Krankengeld *nt*; ~ **voting** *n* LAW gesetzesgemäße Stimmenabgabe *f*

stave off *vt* GEN COMM abwehren, abwenden, *defer* hinhalten

stay *n* GEN COMM Aufenthalt *m*

staying: ~ **power** *n* FIN Standfestigkeit *f*, MGMNT Durchstehvermögen *nt*

stay: ~~**in strike** *n* HRM Sitzstreik *m*

Std *abbr* (*standard*) GEN COMM Standard *m*

STD *abbr BrE* (*subscriber trunk dialling*) COMMS Selbstwählferndienst *m*, Selbstfernwahl *f*, Teilnehmerfernwahl *f*

steadily *adv* GEN COMM fest, stetig

steady *adj* ECON beständig, GEN COMM fest, stetig; ~ **growth method** *n* GEN COMM *subscription source evaluation technique* Methode *f* des gleichgewichtigen Wachstums, Methode *f* des stetigen Wachstums

steadying: ~ **factor** *n* ECON stabilisierender Faktor *m*

steady: ~~**state growth** *n* ECON Wachstumsgleichgewicht *nt*; ~~**state inflation** *n* ECON antizipierte Inflation *f*

steam *n* IND, TRANSP Dampf *m*

steamroller *n* IND Dampfwalze *f* (*obs*)

steel *n* IND, TRANSP Stahl *m*; ~~**collar worker** *n* HRM Stahlarbeiter *m*; ~ **covers** *n pl* TRANSP Stahlabdeckung *f*, Stahldeckel *m*; ~ **industry** *n* IND Stahlindustrie *f*; ~~**intensive** *adj* IND stahlintensiv

steels *n pl* STOCK Stahlaktien *f pl*, Stahlwerte *m pl*

steel: ~ **securities** *n pl* STOCK Stahlaktien *f pl*, Stahlwerte *m pl*; ~ **shares** *n pl BrE* (*cf steel stocks AmE*) STOCK Stahlaktien *f pl*, Stahlwerte *m pl*; ~ **stocks** *n pl AmE* (*cf steel shares BrE*) STOCK Stahlaktien *f pl*, Stahlwerte *m pl*

steelworker *n* IND Stahlarbeiter *m*, Stahlwerker *m*

steelworks *n pl* IND Stahlhütte *f*, Stahlwerk *nt*

steep *adj* ECON, GEN COMM gepfeffert (*infrml*), steil, happig (*infrml*)

steepen *vi* MATH *curve* steiler werden

steeply *adv* ECON, GEN COMM steil

steer *vt* LAW lenken

steering *n* LAW, PROP Lenkung *f*; **~ committee** *n* BANK, FIN Lenkungsausschuß *m*, Organisationsausschuß *m*; **~ system** *n* TRANSP Lenksystem *nt*

stem 1. *n* GEN COMM Stiel *m*, Stamm *m*; **2.** *vt* GEN COMM eindämmen, Einhalt gebieten

stem from *vt* GEN COMM herrühren von, stammen aus

stencil *n* ADMIN Matrize *f*

stenographer *n* ADMIN, Stenograf, in *m,f*

stenography *n* ADMIN Kurzschrift *f*

step 1. *n* GEN COMM *action taken* Schritt *m*, Maßnahme *f*, Stufe *f*; ♦ **~ by step** GEN COMM schrittweise

step in *vi* GEN COMM *intervene* eingreifen, einschreiten, sich einschalten

step up *vt* GEN COMM *increase* erhöhen

step: **~ back** *n* GEN COMM Rückschritt *m*; **~ cost** *n* ACC Sprungkosten *pl*, FIN gestaffelte Kosten *pl*

stepped: **~ bond** *n* STOCK gestaffelte Anleihe *f*, gestaffelte Schuldverschreibung *f*; **~-up basis** *n* TAX erhöhte Grundlage *f*

steps: **~ method** *n* COMP Schrittmethode *f*

step: **~-up lease** *n* FIN Mietvertrag *m* mit stufenweiser Mieterhöhung; **~-variable cost** *n* ACC Sprungkosten *pl*

sterling *n* BANK, FIN, STOCK Sterling *m*; **~ area** *n* GEN COMM Sterlinggebiet *nt*; **~ balance** *n* FIN Sterlingguthaben *nt*, Sterlingsaldo *m*; **~ commercial paper** *n* (*SCP*) BANK, STOCK kurzfristiges Sterling-Geldmarktpapier *nt*, Sterling Commercial Paper *nt*

Sterling: **~ Commercial Paper market** *n* BrE (*SCP market*) STOCK Markt *m* für Sterling Commercial Paper, Markt *m* für Sterling-Handelspapiere

sterling: **~ M3** *n* ECON Sterling-Geldvolumen *nt* M3, Geldmenge *f* M3 für Sterling; **~ warrant into gilt-edged stock** *n* BrE (*SWING*) STOCK Sterling-Bezugsrechtsschein *m* für Staatsanleihen

stevedore *n* (*stvdr*) HRM Schauermann , *m*, TRANSP Schauermann *m*, Schiffsbelader *m*, Stauer *m*

stevedoring: **~ department** *n* TRANSP Verladeabteilung *f*

stick: **~ no bills** *phr* S&M *advertising* Zettelankleben verboten

sticker *n* COMMS, GEN COMM, S&M *label* Aufkleber *m*

sticking: **~ point** *n* GEN COMM kritischer Punkt *m*, Knackpunkt *m* (*infrml*), gewisse Grenze *f*

stick: **~-on label** *n* COMMS, S&M Aufkleber *m*

sticky *adj* GEN COMM *prices* stabil, *situation, person* heikel, schwierig; **~ deal** *n* STOCK unbewegliche Wertpapieremission *f*; **~ price** *n* ECON starrer Preis *m*

stiff: **~ competition** *n* ECON, GEN COMM scharfer Wettbewerb *m*

stiffen *vt* GEN COMM *regulations* enger fassen, verschärfen

stillage *n* IND Palette *f*, TRANSP Gestell *nt*, Palette *f*

stimulate *vt* ECON beleben, stimulieren, wiederankurbeln, GEN COMM *demand* ankurbeln, anregen, beleben, stimulieren, HRM stimulieren

stimulated *adj* ECON belebt

stimulating *adj* ECON, HRM *experience* stimulierend; **~ forces** *n pl* ECON Antriebskräfte *f pl*

stimulation *n* ECON Anreiz *m*, Antrieb *m*

stimulative *adj* ECON, HRM stimulierend; **~ measure** *n* ECON stimulierende Maßnahme *f*

stimulus *n* GEN COMM Anreiz *m*, Ansporn *m*, Anstoß *m*, Impuls *m*; ♦ **be a ~ for exports** IMP/EXP exportstimulierend wirken

stint: **do one's ~** *phr* HRM sein Pensum bewältigen

stipulate *vt* GEN COMM sich ausbedingen, vereinbaren, festsetzen, vertraglich festlegen, zur Bedingung machen, LAW sich ausbedingen

stipulation *n* GEN COMM Vereinbarung *f*, Festsetzung *f*, LAW *contract law* Bedingung *f*, Bestimmung *f*, Vertragsbestimmung *f*, Vertragsklausel *f*; ♦ **by ~** LAW *contract law* einverständlich; **on the ~ that** GEN COMM mit der Auflage, daß, unter der Bedingung, daß; **with the ~ that** GEN COMM mit der Auflage, daß, unter der Bedingung, daß; **~ as to venue** *n* LAW *contracts* Gerichtsstandsvereinbarung *f*; **~ going to the root of the contract** *n* LAW wesentliche Vertragsbedingung *f*

stk exch *abbr* (*stock exchange*) ECON, FIN, STOCK Aktienbörse *f*, Effektenbörse *f*, Wertpapierbörse *f*

stn *abbr* (*station*) COMP Station *f*, TRANSP *railway* Bahnhof *m*, *stop* Station *f*

STN *abbr* (*special traffic notice*) TRANSP Verkehrssondermitteilung *f*

stochastic: **~ process** *n* GEN COMM stochastischer Prozeß *m*; **~ simulation** *n* MGMNT stochastische Modellierung *f*, stochastische Simulation *f*; **~ term** *n* MATH *statistics* stochastischer Term *m*

stock *n* (*cf share BrE*) ACC, FIN Aktie *f*, Anteil *m*, Wertpapier *nt*, Aktienkapital *nt*, Schuldverschreibung *f*, GEN COMM Vorrat *m*, Lager *nt* (*Lag.*), S&M *in shop* Bestand *m*, STOCK Aktie *f*, Anteil *m*, Schuldverschreibung *f*, lanfristige Verplichtung *f*, Wertpapier *nt*; ♦ **in ~** (*i.s.*) ECON, GEN COMM, S&M vorrätig; **out of ~** (*o.s.*) ECON, GEN COMM, S&M ausverkauft, nicht auf Lager, nicht vorrätig; **~ prices reached an all time high** *phr* STOCK die Aktienkurse erreichten einen historischen Höchststand

stock: **~ adjustment principle** *n* STOCK Aktienanpassungsprinzip *nt*; **~ allotment** *n* STOCK Aktienzuteilung *f*; **~ arbitrage** *n* STOCK Effektenarbitrage *f*; **~ borrowing** *n* STOCK Effektenleihe *f*, Lombardierung *f* von Wertpapieren

stockbreeder *n* GEN COMM Viehzüchter *m*

stockbroker *n* FIN, STOCK Aktienmakler, in *m,f*, Börsenmakler, in *m,f*, Effektenmakler, in *m,f*, Wertpapierhändler, in *m,f*

stockbroking *n* FIN, STOCK Aktienhandel *m*

stockbuilding *n* MGMNT Auffüllung *f* von Lagerbeständen

stock: **~ of bullion** *n* GEN COMM Edelmetallvorräte *m pl*; **~ certificate** *n* AmE (*cf share certificate BrE*) STOCK Aktienurkunde *f*, Aktienzertifikat *nt*, Aktiensammelurkunde *f*; **~ check** AmE, **~ cheque** BrE *n* BANK Aktienscheck *m*; **~ control** *n* ACC Bestandsführung *f*, Bestandsverwaltung *f*, Lagerkontrolle *f*, Lagerwirtschaft *f*, ECON Bestandsüberwachung *f*, Lagerkontrolle *f*, Lagerwirtschaft *f*; **~ controller** *n* HRM Lagerkontrolleur *m*, MGMNT Lagerverwalter, in *m,f*; **~ corporation** *n* GEN COMM Aktiengesellschaft *f* (*AG*); **~ corporation law** *n* LAW Aktienrecht *nt*, Gesellschaftsrecht *nt*; **~ dividend** *n* AmE (*cf free issue of new shares BrE*) ACC Stockdividende *f*; **~ exchange** *n* (*stk exch*) ECON, FIN, STOCK Aktienbörse *f*, Effektenbörse *f*, Wertpapierbörse *f*; **~ exchange admission fee** *n* STOCK Börseneinführungskosten *pl*

Stock: **~ Exchange Automated Quotation International**

n BrE (*SEAQI, SEAQ International*) STOCK elektronisches Börsenhandels- und Notierungssystem für internationale Wertpapiere, internationale elektronische Börseninformation *f*; **~ Exchange Automated Quotations** *n* (*SEAQ*) STOCK elektronisches Börsenhandels- und Notierungssystem der Londoner Börse für britische Wertpapiere, elektronische Börseninformation *f*; **~ Exchange Daily Official List** *n BrE* (*SEDOL*) STOCK amtliches Börsenkursblatt *nt*

stock: **~ exchange dealings** *n pl* STOCK Börsenhandel *m*

Stock: **~ Exchange Official List** *n BrE* (*cf pink sheets AmE*) STOCK Kursblatt *nt*, Kurszettel *m*

stock: **~ exchange price** *n* STOCK Börsenkurs *m*; **~ exchange price index** *n* STOCK Börsenkursindex *m*; **~ exchange quotation** *n* STOCK Börsenkurs *m*; **~ exchange report** *n* STOCK Börsenbericht *m*; **~ exchange securities** *n pl* STOCK Effekten *pl*; **~ exchange speculator** *n* STOCK Börsenspekulant, in *m,f*; **~ exchange trader** *n* STOCK Börsenhändler, in *m,f*; **~ exchange transaction** *n* STOCK Börsengeschäft *nt*; **~ exchange transfer tax** *n* TAX Börsenumsatzsteuer *f*

stockholder *n* HRM Aktionär, in *m,f*, Anteilseigner, in *m,f*, MGMNT Anteilseigner, in *m,f*, STOCK Aktieninhaber, in *m,f*; **~ diffusion** *n* STOCK Aktionärsausschüttung *f*

stockholders': **~ equity** *n* ACC, STOCK Eigenkapital *nt*, Aktienkapital *nt*, Stammanteile *m pl*

stockholding *n* ECON Lagerhaltung *f*, FIN Aktienbestand *m*, Aktienbeteiligung *f*

Stockholm: **~ School** *n* ECON Stockholmer Schule *f*

stock: **~ index** *n* STOCK Aktienindex *m*, Börsenindex *m*; **~ index arbitrage** *n* STOCK Aktienindex-Arbitrage *f*; **~ indexes and averages** *n pl* STOCK Aktien- und Kursindizes *m pl*; **~ index futures market** *n* STOCK Markt *m* für Terminkontrakte auf Börsenindizes; **~ in hand** *n* GEN COMM verfügbare Ware *f*, Vorratslager *nt*, Vorratsvermögen *nt*, Warenbestand *m*; **~ inventory** *n* ACC, GEN COMM, S&M Bestandsaufnahme *f*; **~ issue** *n* GEN COMM, IND Materialausgabe *f*, STOCK Aktienemission *f*; **~ issue bonus** *n* ACC *balance sheet* Aktienemissionsaufgeld *nt*; **~ issue premium** *n AmE* (*cf share premium BrE*) STOCK Aktienemissionsagio *nt*

stockist *n BrE* GEN COMM einschlägiges Geschäft *nt*, Fachgeschäft *nt*, Fachhändler, in *m,f*; **~ agent** *n* HRM Fachhandelsagent, in *m,f*, Fachhändler, in *m,f*

stockjobber *n BrE obs* STOCK Eigenhändler, in *m,f* in Aktien

stockkeeping: **~ unit** *n* GEN COMM Lagerbestandseinheit *f*, Warenbestandseinheit *f*, Artikelposition *f*

stock: **~ line** *n* S&M Lagererzeugnis *nt*; **~ list** *n* GEN COMM Bestandsliste *f*, Inventar *nt*, STOCK Kursblatt *nt*, Verzeichnis *nt* der zum Börsenhandel zugelassenen Wertpapiere; **~ long pull** *n* TAX langfristiger Gewinn *m*

stockman *n AmE* GEN COMM *livestock breeder* Viehzüchter *m*, *storeman* Lagerverwalter *m*, Lagerist *m*, Lagerarbeiter *m*, Lagerhalter *m*

stock: **~ management** *n* S&M Lagerverwaltung *f*; **~ market** *n* ECON, FIN, STOCK Aktienbörse *f*, Börse *f*; **~ market listing** *n* STOCK Börsenkursnotierung *f*; **~ market price index** *n* STOCK Börsenpreisindex *m*; **~ market prices** *n pl* STOCK Aktienkurse *m pl*, Effektennotierung *f*, Börsenpreise *m pl*; **~ market slump** *n* STOCK Baisse *f*; **~ market supervisory authority** *n* STOCK Börsenaufsichtsbehörde *f*; **~ option**

n STOCK Aktienoption *f*; **~ option plan** *n* STOCK Aktienoptionsplan *m*; **~ option right** *n* STOCK Aktienbezugsrecht *nt*

stockout: **~ cost** *n* GEN COMM Fehlmengenkosten *pl*, Kosten *pl* durch Fehlbestand

stock: **~ output ratio** *n* GEN COMM Verhältnis *nt* Vorräte zur Gesamtproduktion

stockpile *n* GEN COMM Lager *nt* (*Lag.*), Vorrat *m*

stockpiling *n* GEN COMM Anlegen *nt* von Vorräten, Bevorratung *f*, Vorratshaltung *f*, Vorratswirtschaft *f*; **~ loan** *n* FIN Einlagerungskredit *m*

stock: **~ portfolio** *n* (*cf share portfolio BrE*) FIN, STOCK Aktienbestand *m*, Aktienportefeuille *nt*; **~ power** *n* STOCK Vollmacht *f* zum Verkauf von Aktien, Effektenvollmacht *f*; **~ prices** *n pl* STOCK Aktienkurse *m pl*; **~ purchase plan** *n* STOCK Aktienbezugsplan *m*, Aktienoptionsplan *m*; **~ purchase warrant** *n* STOCK Aktienbezugsrecht *nt*, Bezugsrecht *nt*; **~ quotation** *n* STOCK Aktiennotierung *f*; **~ quoted officially** *n BrE* (*cf shares quoted officially AmE*) GEN COMM amtlich notierte Aktien *f pl*; **~ ratio** *n* ACC Aktienverhältnis *nt*; **~ receipt** *n* GEN COMM Wareneingang *m*, STOCK Aktienquittung *f*; **~ record** *n* STOCK Aktienregister *nt*, Aktionärsverzeichnis *nt*; **~ register** *n* GEN COMM Inventarbuch *nt*, Lagerbuch *nt*, STOCK Aktienbuch *nt*, Aktienverzeichnis *nt*; **~ rotation** *n* S&M Lagerumschlag *m*, Lagerbestandswechsel *m*

stocks *n pl* ACC Vorräte *m pl*, Lagerbestände *m pl*; ◆ **while ~ last** S&M solange vorrätig; **~ and bonds** *n pl* FIN, STOCK Effekten *pl*

stock: **~ sheet** *n* GEN COMM Bestandsliste *f*, Lagerliste *f*; **~ shortage** *n* GEN COMM ungenügende Vorräte *m pl*; **~ split** *n AmE* ACC Aktiensplit *m*, STOCK Aktienaufteilung *f*, Aktiensplit *m*; **~ splitdown** *n* GEN COMM Aktienzusammenlegung *f*; **~ takeover** *n* FIN, STOCK Aktienübernahme *f*

stocktaking *n* ECON, GEN COMM Bestandsaufnahme *f*, Inventur *f*; **~ sale** *n* GEN COMM Inventurausverkauf *m*, Ausverkauf *m* anläßlich der Inventur; **~ value** *n* ACC Inventurwert *m*

stock: **~ tips** *n pl* STOCK Börsentips *m pl*; **~ trading** *n* FIN Effektenhandel *m*, STOCK Aktienhandel *m*; **~ transfer agent** *n* STOCK Aktienübertragungs-Broker *m*; **~ transfer form** *n* STOCK Aktienübertragungsformular *nt*; **~ turn** *n* GEN COMM Warenumschlag *m*; **~ turnover** *n* ACC, ECON Lagerumsatz *m*, Lagerumschlag *m*, GEN COMM Lagerumschlag *m*, IND Lagerumsatz *m*, Lagerumschlag *m*; **~ valuation** *n* ACC Bewertung *f* von Aktien, GEN COMM Lagerbestandsbewertung *f*, Vorratsbewertung *f*

stockwoman *n AmE* GEN COMM Lagerarbeiterin *f*, Lagerverwalterin *f*, Lageristin *f*

stockyard *n* GEN COMM Viehhof *m*

stock: **~ yield** *n* STOCK Aktienrendite *f*

Stolper: **~ Samuelson theorem** *n* ECON Stolper-Samuelson-Theorem *nt*

stop *vt* LAW *bankruptcy proceedings* einstellen; ◆ **~ bidding** GEN COMM *at auction sale* das Gebot beenden; **~ sb's allowance** GEN COMM jds finanzielle Unterstützung einstellen, jds Zuschuß sperren; **~ a stock** STOCK Aktie sperren

stop: **~ bit** *n* COMP Stop-Bit *nt*; **~-go cycle of inflation** *n* ECON Stop-and-go-Inflationszyklus *m*; **~-go policy** *n BrE* ECON Stop-and-go-Politik *f*, Zickzackpolitik *f*;

~ **limit order** n STOCK Stop-Limit-Order f; ~ **loss** n STOCK Stop-Loss m; ~ **loss insurance** n INS Gesamtschaden-Exzedenten-Rückversicherung f, Jahresüberschadensrückversicherung f; ~ **loss order** n STOCK *futures market* Stop-Loss-Order f; ~ **motion** n S&M Zeitraffer m; ~ **order** n FIN Schecksperre f, STOCK Sperre f einer Aktienemission, Stop-Order f; **~-out price** n AmE STOCK Kursuntergrenze f, Niedrigstkurs m

stopover n LEIS, TRANSP Reiseunterbrechung f, Zwischenlandung f, Zwischenstation f

stoppage n GEN COMM Einstellung f, HRM Stillstandszeit f, TRANSP Anhalten nt; ~ **of trade** n GEN COMM Einstellung des Handels f, Handelssperre f; ~ **of work** n BrE HRM Arbeitsniederlegung f

stop: **~-payment order** n BANK Auszahlungssperre f

stopped: ~ **bonds** n pl FIN gesperrte Anleihen f pl, gesperrte Schuldverschreibungen f pl; ~ **stock** n STOCK gesperrte Aktien f pl

stopper n S&M *advertising* Blickfang m

stopping: ~ **of a cheque** n BrE FIN Schecksperre f; ~ **train** n TRANSP Bummelzug m

stop: ~ **signal** n COMP, TRANSP Stoppsignal nt; ~ **time** n COMP Stoppzeit f

stopwatch: ~ **studies** n pl MGMNT Zeitnahme f, Arbeitszeitstudien f pl

storage n COMP *place* Speicher m, *action* Speichern nt, Speicherung f, GEN COMM, IND, TRANSP *action* Lagerung f, Einlagerung f, *place* Lager nt (*Lag.*); ~ **allocation** n COMP Speicherzuweisung f; ~ **area** n COMP Speicherbereich m, GEN COMM Lagerfläche f; ~ **capacity** n GEN COMM Lagerkapazität f, Speicherkapazität f; ~ **charges** n pl GEN COMM, TRANSP Lagerspesen pl, Lagergebühren f pl, Lagergeld nt; ~ **device** n COMP Speichergerät nt; ~ **dump** n COMP Speicherauszug m; ~ **map** n COMP Speicherbelegung f; ~ **medium** n COMP Speichermedium nt; ~ **requirements** n pl COMP Speicherplatzbedarf m

store 1. n AmE (cf shop BrE) S&M Laden m; **2.** vt COMP archivieren, *data* speichern, GEN COMM, IND, TRANSP *goods* lagern

store: ~ **accounting** n ACC Lagerbuchhaltung f; ~ **audit** n ACC Lagerprüfung f; ~ **brand** n S&M Eigenmarke f; ~ **closing times** n pl GEN COMM Ladenschlußzeiten f pl; ~ **demonstration** n S&M Ladenvorführung f; ~ **group** n S&M Einzelhandelskette f, Einzelhandelskonzern m

storehouse n GEN COMM Depot nt (*Dep.*), Lager nt (*Lag.*), Lagergebäude nt, Lagerhaus nt, Speicher m, IMP/EXP Speicher m, TRANSP Depot nt (*Dep.*), Speicher m

storekeeper n GEN COMM Lagerhalter, in m,f, Lagerverwalter, in m,f, Lagerist, in m,f, S&M AmE (cf shopkeeper BrE) Ladeninhaber, in m,f; **~'s liability insurance** n INS Lagerhalterhaftpflichtversicherung f, Lagerverwalterhaftpflichtversicherung f

storeman n GEN COMM Lagerarbeiter m, Lagerhalter m, Lagerverwalter m, Lagerist m

store: ~ **promotion** n S&M Verkaufsförderung f im Laden

storeroom n GEN COMM, IMP/EXP, TRANSP Speicher m, Lager nt, *food* Vorratskammer f, Vorratsraum m

store: ~ **traffic** n S&M Ladenverkehr m; ~ **of value** n ECON *money* Wertaufbewahrungsmittel nt

storewoman n GEN COMM Lagerarbeiterin f, Lagerhalterin f, Lagerverwalterin f, Lageristin f

storyboard n S&M *advertising* Entwurfsskizze f einer Werbesendung

stow vt TRANSP *cargo* stauen

stowage n TRANSP Beladen nt, Stauen nt, *fee* Staugebühr f, Staugeld nt; ~ **area** n TRANSP Ladebereich m; ~ **factor** n GEN COMM Staufaktor m; ~ **order** n TRANSP *shipping* Stauanordnung f; ~ **plan** n TRANSP *shipping* Stauplan m

St Petersburg: ~ **paradox** n ECON St.-Petersburg-Paradox nt

straddle n STOCK Straddle m, kombinierte Baisseoptionsposition f, Stellage f; ~ **combination** n STOCK Straddlekombination f

straight: ~ **bill of lading** n IMP/EXP, TRANSP *shipping* auf den Namen ausgestelltes Konnossement nt, Namenskonnossement nt, nicht übertragbares Konnossement nt, Rektakonnossement nt; ~ **bond** n FIN konventionelle Anleihe f, STOCK Festsatzbond m, Festzinsanleihe f; ~ **credit** n FIN Akkreditiv nt bei einer definierten Bank

straight: ~ **investment** n BANK klassische Anlage f; ~ **lease** n FIN Mietvertrag m mit gleichbleibendem Zinssatz, Mietvertrag m mit konstantem Zins; **~-life insurance** n AmE INS Todesfallversicherung f; **~-life insurance policy** n AmE INS Todesfallversicherungspolice f; ~ **lift** n TRANSP *cargo handling equipment* gerader Lift m; **~-line depreciation** n ACC lineare Abschreibung f; **~-line method** n ACC *depreciation* gleichbleibende Abschreibungsmethode f; ~ **loan** n BANK ungesichertes Darlehen nt, FIN Festzinskredit m, ungesichertes Darlehen nt; ~ **market** n FIN Festzinsanleihenmarkt m, Festzinsbondsmarkt m

strained adj GEN COMM gekünstelt, gespannt, *relations, conversation* gezwungen

strait n TRANSP Meeresstraße f, Meerenge f

Straits: ~ **Times Industrial index** n STOCK Hauptindex der Singapur Börse

stranded: ~ **goods** n pl INS Strandgut nt

stranglehold: **have a ~ on the market** phr ECON den Markt fest im Griff haben

strap: ~ **option** n STOCK Strap-Option f

strategic adj ECON, GEN COMM, MGMNT strategisch; ~ **alliance** n MGMNT strategisches Bündnis nt; ~ **business unit** n MGMNT strategische Geschäftseinheit f, strategische Unternehmenseinheit f, strategischer Unternehmensbereich m; ~ **innovation** n S&M strategische Innovation f; ~ **interdependence** n MGMNT strategische Interdependenz f, strategische Verflechtung f; ~ **issue** n MGMNT strategische Frage f; ~ **overview** n POL strategische Übersicht, Planungsübersicht f; ~ **plan** n GEN COMM, MGMNT strategischer Plan m, langfristiger Geschäftsplan m; ~ **planning** n GEN COMM, MGMNT strategische Planung f; ~ **pricing** n S&M strategische Preispolitik f; ~ **tax planning** n TAX strategische Steuerplanung f

strategy n ECON, GEN COMM Strategie f; ~ **formulation** n ECON Strategiebestimmung f, GEN COMM, MGMNT Ausarbeitung f einer Strategie, Entwicklung f einer Strategie; ~ **implementation** n GEN COMM, MGMNT Durchsetzung f einer Strategie, Realisierung f einer Strategie, Verwirklichung f einer Strategie

stratification n S&M Schichtung f

stratified: ~ **random sampling** n MATH *statistics* geschichtetes Zufallsstichprobenverfahren nt; ~ **sampling** n MATH *statistics* geschichtetes Stichprobenverfahren nt

stratifying: ~ **the market** *n* S&M Aufteilung *f* des Marktes in Schichten

strawboard *n* IND Strohpappe *f*, Strohzellstoffpappe *f*

straw: ~ **poll** *n* S&M *market research* Probeabstimmung *f*; ~ **vote** *n* S&M *market research* Probeabstimmung *f*

stray: ~ **from sth** *phr* GEN COMM von etw abweichen

stream: **come on** ~ *phr* IND in Betrieb gehen; **be on** ~ *phr* IND go into operation in Betrieb sein; **go against the** ~ *phr* GEN COMM gegen den Strom schwimmen

streamer *n* COMP Bandlaufwerk *nt*, MEDIA *print* Balkenschlagzeile *f*, Überschrift *f* über volle Seitenbreite

streamline *vt* ECON rationalisieren, *company* straffen, IND, MGMNT modernisieren, rationalisieren

streamlined *adj* ECON, IND, MGMNT modernisiert, rationalisiert

streamlining *n* ECON Rationalisierung *f*, *company* Straffung *f*, Vereinfachung *f*, IND, MGMNT Modernisierung *f*, organisatorische Straffung *f*, Rationalisierung *f*

street *n* (*St*) GEN COMM Straße *f* (*Str.*); ~ **dealings** *n pl* STOCK Nachbörse *f*; ~ **money** *n AmE* POL Entgelt für Wahlhelfer, die von Haus zu Haus gehen; ~ **name** *n* GEN COMM Scheinfirma *f*; ~ **price** *n* STOCK Notierung *f* im Telefonverkehr, nachbörsliche Kurse *m pl*; ~ **trader** *n BrE* (*cf street vendor AmE*) GEN COMM fliegender Händler *m*, fliegende Händlerin *f*, Straßenhändler, in *m,f*, Straßenverkäufer, in *m,f*, S&M Straßenhändler, in *m,f*; ~ **vendor** *n AmE* (*cf street trader BrE*) GEN COMM fliegender Händler *m*, fligende Händlerin *f*, Straßenhändler, in *m,f*, Straßenverkäufer, in *m,f*, S&M Straßenhändler, in *m,f*

strength *n* STOCK *of currency* Stärke *f*; ♦ **on the** ~ **of** GEN COMM aufgrund von

strengthen *vt* GEN COMM *relations* festigen, *material, building*, verstärken, *efforts* steigern

strengthened *adj* GEN COMM gefestigt

strengthening *n* ECON *of currency* Stärkung *f*, GEN COMM Festigung *f*, Verstärkung *f*

strength: ~ **of materials** *n* IND Materialfestigkeit *f*, Werkstoffestigkeit *f*

strengths: ~, **weaknesses, opportunities and threats analysis** *n* (*SWOT*) S&M Analyse *f* von Stärken, Schwächen, Chancen und Risiken

stress 1. *n* GEN COMM *emphasis* Hervorhebung *f*, HRM *strain* Streß *m*; **2.** *vt* GEN COMM hervorheben

stress: ~ **interview** *n* HRM Streß-Interview *nt*

strict *adj* GEN COMM streng; ~ **adherence to the contract** *n* LAW strikte Vertragseinhaltung *f*, genaues Einhalten *nt* des Vertrags; ~ **cost price** *n* ACC reiner Anschaffungspreis *m*, reiner Herstellungspreis *m*; ~ **foreclosure** *n* LAW Anordnung *f* des endgültigen Pfandverkaufs

strictly *adv* GEN COMM streng; ♦ ~ **confidential** GEN COMM streng vertraulich

strict: ~ **time limit** *n* GEN COMM fester Fristablauf *m*, fester Schlußtermin *m*

strife: ~-**ridden period** *n* HRM von Arbeitskonflikten geprägter Zeitraum *m*

strike 1. *n* GEN COMM, HRM, IND Streik *m*, Ausstand *m*; ♦ **on** ~ GEN COMM, HRM, IND im Streik; **go on** ~ GEN COMM, HRM, IND *industrial relations* streiken; **go on** ~ **against** HRM *industrial relations* bestreiken; **2.** *vt* GEN COMM *agreement* sich einigen auf [+acc]; ♦ ~ **a balance** GEN COMM die Bilanz ziehen; ~ **a bargain** GEN COMM

ein Geschäft abschließen, LAW *contract law* handelseinig werden; ~ **a deal** GEN COMM ein Geschäft abschließen; ~ **off the list** GEN COMM aus der Liste streichen; ~ **it rich** *infrml* GEN COMM das große Geld machen (*infrml*), eine Goldgrube entdecken (*infrml*), groß abkassieren (*infrml*); ~ **a jury** LAW die Geschworenen auswählen; **3.** *vi* GEN COMM, HRM, IND streiken

strike down *vt* LAW aufheben

strike: ~ **action** *n* HRM Streik *m*; ~ **ballot** *n* GEN COMM, HRM, IND Streikabstimmung *f*, Urabstimmung *f*; ~ **benefits** *n pl* GEN COMM, HRM, IND Streikzahlungen *f pl*, Streikgeld *nt*

strikebound *adj* HRM bestreikt

strikebreaker *n* GEN COMM, HRM, IND Streikbrecher, in *m,f*

strikebreaking *n* GEN COMM, HRM, IND Streikbruch *m*

strike: ~ **call** *n* GEN COMM, HRM, IND Streikausruf *m*; ~ **clause** *n* GEN COMM, HRM, IND Streikklausel *f*; ~ **committee** *n* GEN COMM, HRM, IND Streikausschuß *m*; ~-**free agreement** *n BrE* HRM Abkommen *nt* über Nichtbeteiligung an Streiks; ~ **fund** *n* GEN COMM, HRM, IND Streikfonds *m*, Streikkasse *f*

strikeover *n* COMP *on wordprocessor* Überschreiben *nt*

strike: ~ **pay** *n* GEN COMM, HRM, IND Streikzahlungen *f pl*, Streikgeldzahlung *f*; ~ **price** *n* STOCK Basispreis *m*, Ausübungspreis *m*, *options on Eurodollar futures* Abrechnungskurse *m pl*; ~ **price intervals** *n pl* STOCK *options* Abrechnungskurszeiträume *m pl*

striker *n* GEN COMM, HRM, IND Streikende(r) *mf* [decl. as adj]

strike: ~ **rate** *n* S&M Trefferquote *f* (*jarg*)

strikes: ~, **riots and civil commotions** *phr* (*SR&CC*) LAW Streik *m*, Aufruhr *m* und innere Unruhen *f pl*

strike: ~ **threat** *n* GEN COMM, HRM, IND Streikdrohung *f*; ~ **vote** *n* HRM Urabstimmung *f*

striking: ~ **down** LAW Aufhebung *f*; ~ **price** *n* STOCK Basispreis *m*, Ausübungspreis *m*

string *n* COMP Kette *f*, Zeichenfolge *f*, String *m* (*jarg*)

stringent *adj* GEN COMM *measures, programme* streng, zwingend

stringently *adv* GEN COMM streng, zwingend

stringent: ~ **money market** *n* FIN angespannter Geldmarkt *m*

stringer *n* MEDIA *part-time journalist* Korrespondent, in *m,f*, Lokalreporter, in *m,f*

strings: **no** ~ **attached** *phr* GEN COMM ohne Klauseln, ohne Nebenklauseln, ohne Bedingungen

strip: ~ **development** *n* GEN COMM streifenweise Grundstückserschließung *f*; ~ **mining** *n AmE* (*cf opencast mining BrE*) IND Tagebau *m*

stripped: ~ **security** *n* STOCK leeres Wertpapier *nt*

strong *adj* GEN COMM *indication* stark, *reputation* gut; ♦ **be a** ~ **supporter of** POL ein starker Anhänger sein von, sich engagiert einsetzen für; **with a** ~ **appeal** S&M publikumswirksam; ~ **bearish play** *n* STOCK *options* starke Baissespekulation *f*; ~ **bullish play** *n* STOCK *options* starke Haussespekulation *f*

Strong-Campbell: ~ **Interest Inventory** *n* HRM Strong-Campbell-Berufsinteresse-Formular *nt*

strong: ~ **competition** *n* S&M starke Konkurrenz *f*; ~ **equilibrium** *n* ECON stabiles Gleichgewicht *nt*

strongly *adv* GEN COMM stark

strongroom *n* BANK Tresor *m*

Strong: ~ **Vocational Interest Blank** *n* HRM Strong-Berufsinteresse-Fragebogen *m*

structural: ~ **adjustment** *n* MGMNT Strukturangleichung *f*, Strukturanpassung *f*, strukturelle Bereinigung *f*; ~ **adjustment facility** *n* (*SAF*) FIN Strukturanpassungs-fazilität *f*; ~ **adjustment loan** *n* ECON Strukturanpassungskredit *m*; ~ **adjustment policy** *n* ECON Strukturanpassungspolitik *f*; ~ **change** *n* MGMNT Strukturveränderung *f*, Strukturwandel *m*; ~ **crisis** *n* ADMIN Strukturkrise *f*; ~ **deficit** *n* ECON strukturelles Defizit *nt*, Strukturdefizit *nt*; ~ **engineering** *n* IND Bautechnik *f*, Bauwesen *nt*; ~ **funds** *n pl* ECON *EU* Strukturfonds *m*; ~ **inflation** *n* ECON strukturelle Inflation *f*; ~ **model** *n* ECON Strukturmodell *nt*; ~ **transformation** *n* ECON, FIN, MGMNT Umstrukturierung *f*; ~ **unemployment** *n* ECON, HRM strukturelle Arbeitslosigkeit *f*

structure 1. *n* FIN Ausstattung *f*, GEN COMM Aufbau *m*, Struktur *f*, *arrangement* Gliederung *f*, *of company* Gefüge *nt*, Zusammenstellung *f*, Anordnung *f*, IND, PROP Bauwerk *nt*; **2.** *vt* GEN COMM gliedern, strukturieren, zusammenstellen

structure: ~ **conduct performance model** *n* (*SCP*) ECON Strukturführungsleistungsmodell *nt*

structured *adj* GEN COMM gegliedert, strukturiert, zusammengestellt; ~ **interview** *n* HRM strukturiertes Vorstellungsgespräch *nt*; ~ **programming** *n* COMP strukturierte Programmierung *f*

structure: ~ **extending over a boundary** *n* LAW Überbau *m*

structuring *n* GEN COMM Anordnung *f*, Strukturierung *f*, Zusammenstellung *f*

stub: ~ **equity** *n* STOCK Restkapitallaufzeit *f*

student *n* HRM, WEL Student, in *m,f*; ~ **loan marketing association** *n* *AmE* (*SLMA*) FIN Marketingvereinigung *f* für Studentendarlehen

studio *n* GEN COMM Atelier *nt*, Studio *nt*

study 1. *n* GEN COMM, HRM Studie *f*, Studium *nt*, Untersuchung *f*, WEL Studie *f*; **2.** *vt* GEN COMM studieren, untersuchen, HRM studieren; ◆ ~ **for a university degree** HRM studieren

study: ~ **day** *n* WEL Studienfahrt *f*, Studientag *m*; ~ **group** *n* GEN COMM Arbeitsausschuß *m*, Arbeitsgemeinschaft *f*, Arbeitsgruppe *f*, Studiengruppe *f*, POL Arbeitsgruppe *f*; ~ **trip** *n* WEL Studienreise *f*

stuffer *n* S&M Werbebeilage *f*

stuffing *n* IND Packen *nt*, TRANSP Füllmaterial *nt*, Packen *nt*; ~ **and stripping** *n* IND, TRANSP Packen *nt* und Auspacken

stumbling: ~ **block** *n* GEN COMM Stolperstein *m*

stump up 1. *vt BrE infrml* GEN COMM *money* berappen (*infrml*), aufbringen; **2.** *vi BrE infrml* GEN COMM *pay* berappen (*infrml*), zahlen

stunt: ~ **advertising** *n* S&M Reklamemätzchen *nt pl* (*infrml*)

stvdr *abbr* (*stevedore*) HRM, TRANSP Schauermann *m*

STVP *abbr* (*short-term vehicle park*) TRANSP Kurzzeitfahrzeugpark *m*

style *n* COMP Schriftstil *m*, IND *of clothes* Machart *f*, MGMNT *of management* Führungsstil *m*, Stil *m*; ~ **of account** *n* ECON Kontobezeichnung *f*, Kontenart *f*

stylist *n* GEN COMM Formgestalter, in *m,f*, Modedesigner, in *m,f*, Stilist, in *m,f*, MEDIA Stilist, in *m,f* Haarstilist, in *m,f*

stylize *vt* GEN COMM einem Stil angleichen, stilisieren

stylized: ~ **fact** *n* ECON stilisiertes Faktum *nt*

stylus *n* COMP *pen-based device* Eingabestift *m*, *video* Stift *m*

stymie *vt* GEN COMM *opponent* matt setzen, verhindern

sub *abbr* GEN COMM (*subscription*) Abo *nt* (*infrml*) (*Abonnement*), HRM (*subsistence allowance*) Unterhaltszuschuß *m*, MEDIA, STOCK (*subscription*) Abo *nt* (*infrml*) (*Abonnement*), WEL (*subsistence allowance*) Unterhaltszuschuß *m*

subaccount *n* ACC Unterkonto *nt*

subactivity *n* ECON, GEN COMM Subaktivität *f*

subagent *n* GEN COMM Spezialvertreter, in *m,f* Substitut, in *m,f*, Unteragent, in *m,f*, Untervertreter, in *m,f*, Zwischenspediteur *m*

subagreement *n* LAW Nebenabrede *f*

suballotment *n* FIN, GEN COMM partielle Zuteilung *f*, Teilzuweisung *f*

sub-branch *n* GEN COMM Zweigstelle *f*

subchapter *n* MEDIA, TAX Unterkapitel *nt*

subcharter *vt* TRANSP einen Unterfrachtvertrag abschließen für

subclassification *n* GEN COMM Aufschlüsselung *f*

subclassify *vt* GEN COMM aufschlüsseln

subcompact *adj* GEN COMM subkompakt

subcontract 1. *n* GEN COMM, HRM, IND, LAW Nebenabrede *f*, Nebenvertrag *m*, Subkontrakt *m*, Untervertrag *m*, Zulieferauftrag *m*, Unterauftrag *m*, Zulieferungsvertrag *m*; **2.** *vt* GEN COMM, HRM, IND, LAW einen Untervertrag abschließen für, einen Unterauftrag vergeben für, *order* untervergeben, Unteraufträge vergeben für, an einen Subunternehmer vergeben, Unteraufträge vergeben für; **3.** *vi* GEN COMM, HRM, IND, LAW Unteraufträge vergeben

subcontracting *n* ECON Auswärtsvergabe *f*, Untervergabe *f*, GEN COMM Abschluß *m* von Nebenverträgen, Untervergabe *f*, Vergabe *f* von Zulieferungsverträgen, HRM Übernahme *f* von Arbeiten als Zulieferant

subcontractor *n* HRM Subunternehmer, in *m, f*, Unterlieferant, in *m, f*

subdirectory *n* COMP Unterverzeichnis *nt*

subdivide *vt* GEN COMM aufschlüsseln, untergliedern, unterteilen, MGMNT untergliedern, unterteilen

subdivided *adj* GEN COMM, MGMNT untergliedert, unterteilt

subdivision *n* FIN Gebietskörperschaft *f*, GEN COMM Aufschlüsselung *f*, MGMNT Aufteilung *f*, Einteilung *f*, Unterabteilung *f*, Untergliederung *f*, Unterteilung *f*

subentry *n* COMP Untereintrag *m*

subfile *n* ADMIN Beiakte *f*, COMP Subdatei *f*

subgroup *n* GEN COMM Untergruppe *f*

subhead *n* S&M Untertitel *m*

subject *n* GEN COMM *of agreement, of speech* Gegenstand *m*, Thema *nt*; ◆ ~ **unsold** GEN COMM Gegenstand nicht verkauft; ~ **area** *n* GEN COMM Sachgebiet *nt*, Themenbereich *m*, Materie *f*; ~ **of discussion** *n* GEN COMM Beratungsgegenstand *m*; ~ **filing** *n* GEN COMM Ablage *f* nach Sachgebieten; ~ **index** *n* ADMIN Sachregister *nt*

subjective *adj* GEN COMM, S&M einseitig, subjektiv; **~ perception** *n* S&M subjektive Wahrnehmung *f*

subject: **~ matter** *n* GEN COMM behandelter Gegenstand *m*, Inhalt *m*, Stoff *m*, Thema *nt*, PATENTS behandelter Gegenstand *m*, Gegenstand *m* der Erfindung, Stoff *m*; **~ matter of the action** *n* LAW Streitgegenstand *m*; **~ matter of contract** *n* LAW Vertragsgegenstand *m*

subject: **~ to** *prep* GEN COMM, INS, LAW vorbehaltlich; ◆ **be ~ to** LAW unterliegen; **~ to approval** GEN COMM, S&M genehmigungspflichtig; **~ to breakage** INS vorbehaltlich Bruchschaden; **~ to change** GEN COMM variabel; **~ to change without notice** GEN COMM Änderungen vorbehalten; **~ to collection** BANK Eingang vorbehalten; **~ to confirmation** GEN COMM freibleibend, ohne Gewähr, unverbindlich; **~ to limited tax liability** LAW, TAX beschränkt steuerpflichtig; **~ to mortgage** BANK, PROP hypothekengebunden; **~ to particular average** (*SPA*) INS der besonderen Schadenbeteiligung unterworfen, der besonderen Schadenbeteiligungsklausel unterworfen; **~ to pay tax** TAX abgabenpflichtig; **~ to price controls** ECON, IND *products* der Preiskontrolle unterworfen; **~ to quota** GEN COMM quotenabhängig; **~ to taxation** TAX steuerpflichtig

subjoined: **~ copy of letter** *n* COMMS beigefügte Kopie *f* des Schreibens, Kopie des Schreibens als Anlage beigefügt

sublease *n* GEN COMM Untermiete *f*, Unterpacht *f*, Untervermietung *f*, Unterverpachtung *f*

sublicence *n* BrE GEN COMM, PATENTS Nebenlizenz *f*, Unterlizenz *f*

sublicense *AmE see* sublicence *BrE*

subliminal: **~ advertising** *n* S&M unterschwellige Werbung *f*

submission *n* ECON Einreichung *f*, Unterbreitung *f*, Unterwerfung *f*, GEN COMM Unterbreitung *f*, Vorlage *f*, LAW, PATENTS Einreichung *f*, Vorlegung *f*, POL Einreichung *f*, Unterwerfung *f*; **~ of bids** *n* GEN COMM, MGMNT Abgabe *f* von Angeboten, Angebotsabgabe *f*

submit *vt* GEN COMM *bid* unterbreiten, abgeben, LAW *claim, application* stellen, einreichen, erheben, vorlegen, vorbringen, MGMNT *proposal* unterbreiten, einbringen, PATENTS einreichen, vorlegen; ◆ **~ a certificate** ECON eine Bescheinigung beibringen; **~ a dispute to arbitration** LAW einen Streitfall schiedsgerichtlich beilegen; **~ for approval** GEN COMM zur Bestätigung einreichen, zur Bestätigung vorlegen; **~ a proposal** MGMNT einen Vorschlag unterbreiten; **~ a report** GEN COMM einen Bericht vorlegen; **~ a statement of one's affairs** FIN einen Bericht über seine Vermögenslage vorlegen; ◆ **please ~ your quotations** *phr* GEN COMM unterbreiten Sie bitte Ihre Angebote

submortgage *n* BANK nachrangige Hypothek *f*, Unterverpfändung *f*

suboffice *n* GEN COMM Filiale *f*, Nebenstelle *f*, Zweigbüro *nt*, Zweigstelle *f*

suboptimization *n* ECON, FIN, GEN COMM Suboptimierung *f*, Unteroptimierung *f*

suboptimize *vt* ECON, GEN COMM suboptimieren, unteroptimieren

subordinate **1.** *adj* GEN COMM untergeordnet, STOCK nachgeordnet; **2.** *vt* GEN COMM nachstellen, unterordnen, unterstellen

subordinated: **~ assets** *n pl* ACC nachrangiges Vermögen *nt*; **~ bond** *n* STOCK nachrangige Schuldverschreibung *f*;

~ bond issue *n* STOCK nachgeordnete Schuldverschreibungsemission *f*; **~ convertible bond issue** *n* STOCK nachgeordnete Wandelschuldverschreibungsemission *f*; **~ debenture** *n* STOCK nachrangige Schuldverschreibung *f*

subordinate: **~ debt** *n* FIN, GEN COMM, IND nachrangige Verbindlichkeiten *f pl*, nachrangiger Schuldtitel *m*

subordinated: **~ interest** *n* BANK nachrangiges Eigentumsrecht *nt*, FIN nachrangiger Zins *m*; **~ liabilities** *n pl* ACC nachrangige Verbindlichkeiten *f pl*; **~ loan** *n* FIN nachrangiges Darlehen *nt*; **~ warrant issue** *n* STOCK nachgeordnete Optionsscheinemission *f*

subordinates *n pl* HRM Untergebene *pl* [decl. as adj]

subordination *n* ECON, POL Unterordnung *f*; **~ agreement** *n* ADMIN Unterordnungsvereinbarung *f*

subparagraph *n* ADMIN Unterparagraph *m*

subpoena *n* LAW Zwangsvorladung *f*

sub-post: **~ office** *n* COMMS Zweigpostamt *nt*, Postfiliale *f*

subprogram *n* COMP Teilprogramm *nt*, Unterprogramm *nt*

sub-representative *n* GEN COMM Substitut, in *m,f*

subrogation: **~ clause** *n* LAW Rechtsnachfolgeklausel *f*

subroutine *n* COMP, GEN COMM Subroutine *f*, Unterprogramm *nt*

subscribe *vi* STOCK *for shares* zeichnen; ◆ **~ for a loan** BANK Anleihe zeichnen; **~ for shares** STOCK Aktien zeichnen; **~ to** GEN COMM subskribieren, *magazine, service* abonnieren; **~ to an issue** FIN eine Emission zeichnen

subscribed: **~ capital** *n* GEN COMM ausgegebenes Kapital *nt*, gezeichnetes Kapital *nt*; **~ circulation** *n* S&M abonnierte Auflage *f*

subscriber *n* COMMS, COMP Teilnehmer, in *m,f*, GEN COMM Abonnent, in *m,f*, MEDIA Abonnent, in *m,f*, Bezieher, in *m,f*, S&M Abonnent, in *m,f*, STOCK Zeichner, in *m,f*; **~ trunk dialling** *BrE* *n* (*STD*) (*cf direct distance dialing AmE*) COMMS Selbstwählferndienst *m*, Selbstfernwahl *f*, Teilnehmerfernwahl *f*

subscript *n* COMP Subskript *nt*

subscription *n* (*sub*) ACC *of shares* Zeichnung *f*, COMP Subskription *f*, FIN Beitrag *m*, Subskription *f*, GEN COMM Abonnement *nt* (*Abo infml*), Mitgliedsbeitrag *m*, Subskription *f*, Bezug *m*, MEDIA *print* Vorbestellung *f*, Abonnement *nt* (*Abo infml*), STOCK Abonnement *nt* (*Abo infml*), Bezug *m*

subscription: **~ charges** *n pl* BANK Zeichnungsgebühr *f*; **~ day** *n* FIN Zeichnungstermin *m*; **~ for shares** STOCK Aktienzeichnung *f*; **~ money** *n* FIN Zeichnungsbetrag *m*; **~ offer** *n* STOCK Zeichnungsangebot *nt*; **~ price** *n* FIN Emissionskurs *m*, Zeichnungskurs *m*, Bezugspreis *m*, GEN COMM Abonnementspreis *m*, Subskriptionspreis *m*; **~ privilege** *n* STOCK Zeichnungsprivileg *nt*, Zeichnungsvorrecht *nt*; **~ ratio** *n* STOCK Bezugsverhältnis *nt*; **~ right** *n* STOCK Bezugsrecht *nt*, Zeichnungsrecht *nt*

subscriptions: **~ receivable** *n pl* ACC Forderungen *f pl* aus Anleihezeichnungen

subscript: **~ list** *n* COMP Indexliste *f*

subsequent *adj* GEN COMM folgend, nachfolgend, nachträglich, *in time* anschließend; ◆ **at a ~ date** GEN COMM zu einem späteren Termin; **~ event** *n* ACC nachfolgendes Ereignis *nt*; ~ **impossibility of performance** *n* LAW *contracts* nachträgliche Unmöglichkeit *f* der Leistung

subsequently *adv* GEN COMM anschließend; ◆ ~ **to** GEN COMM im Anschluß an

subset *n* GEN COMM Teilmenge *f*

subshare *n* STOCK Aktienbruchteil *m*

subsidence: ~ **damage** *n* IND Bergschäden *m pl*

subsidiarity *n* ECON, GEN COMM Subsidiarität *f*

subsidiary 1. *adj* GEN COMM subsidiär, Tochter-, Hilfs-, HRM subsidiär, untergeordnet, STOCK subsidiär; **2.** *n* ADMIN, FIN, GEN COMM Tochtergesellschaft *f*

subsidiary: ~ **account** *n* ACC Nebenkonto *nt*, Unterkonto *nt*; ~ **accounting record** *n* ACC Hilfsbücher *nt pl*; ~ **accounting system** *n* ACC Nebenkontensystem *nt*; ~ **company** *n* BrE (*cf subsidiary corporation AmE*) GEN COMM Tochtergesellschaft *f*; ~ **corporation** *n* AmE (*cf subsidiary company BrE*) GEN COMM Tochtergesellschaft *f*; ~ **dividends** *n pl* ACC, FIN, STOCK Dividenden *f pl* einer Tochtergesellschaft; ~ **firm** *n* GEN COMM Tochterfirma *f*, Tochterunternehmen *nt*; ~ **ledger** *n* ACC Nebenkontenbuch *nt*

subsidization *n* ECON Subventionierung *f*, GEN COMM Unterstützung *f*

subsidize *vt* ECON subventionieren, GEN COMM unterstützen

subsidized *adj* ECON *prices* subventioniert; ~ **export** *n* ECON subventionierter Export *m*; ~ **housing** *n* WEL subventionierter Wohnungsbau *m*, Sozialwohnungen *f pl*; ~ **price** *n* GEN COMM gestützter Preis *m*, künstlich gehaltener Preis *m*, subventionierter Preis *m*; ~ **travel** *n* LEIS bezuschußte Reise *f*

subsidizing *n* GEN COMM Bezuschussung *f*

subsidy *n* FIN, GEN COMM Subvention *f*, Zuschuß *m*

subsistence *n* WEL Lebensunterhalt *m*, Subsistenz *f*; ~ **allowance** *n* (*sub*) HRM, WEL Unterhaltszuschuß *m*; ~ **crops** *n pl* ECON *agricultural* Ernte *f* zur Eigenbedarfsdeckung; ~ **farming** *n* ECON *agricultural* Kleinbauernhof *m*, Subsistenzwirtschaft *f*; ~ **theory of wages** *n* ECON Existenzminimumtheorie *f* des Lohnes

substance *n* ECON *intrinsic value* Substanz *f*, IND Masse *f*, Materie *f*; ◆ ~ **over form** ACC *accounting principles* Inhalt vor Form

substandard *adj* GEN COMM, IND *work, goods, quality, knowledge* minderwertig, unterdurchschnittlich, unter der Norm liegend, unzulänglich

substantial *adj* GEN COMM beträchtlich, erheblich, *amount of money* namhaft, *financial standing* kapitalkräftig, solide, wesentlich, STOCK erheblich; ~ **investment** *n* ECON, TAX wesentliche Beteiligung *f*; ~ **rights** *n pl* GEN COMM materielle Rechte *nt pl*; ~ **risk** *n* FIN, STOCK erhebliches Risiko *nt*

substantially *adv* GEN COMM beträchtlich, im wesentlichen, in hohem Maße

substantiate: ~ **a claim** *phr* LAW eine Klage begründen, einen Anspruch begründen

substantiation *n* GEN COMM Begründung *f*, LAW Bekräftigung *f*

substantive: ~ **agreement** *n* HRM substantieller Vertrag *m*; ~ **law** *n* LAW materiell rechtliches Gesetz *nt*

substitute 1. *n* ECON Ersatzstoff *m*, *person* Vertreter, in *m,f*, LAW, S&M Ersatz *m*; **2.** *vt* ECON substituieren

substitute: ~ **delivery** *n* LAW *contracts* Ersatzlieferung *f*

substituted: ~ **expenses** *n pl* INS Ersatzkosten *pl*;

~ **mode of performance** *n* LAW Annahme *f* einer nicht geschuldeten Leistung

substitute: ~ **goods** *n pl* ECON Substitutionsgut *nt*, Substitut *nt*, S&M Ersatzgüter *nt pl*

substitution *n* ECON Ersetzung *f*, Substituierung *f*, Substitution *f*; ~ **coefficient** *n* ECON Substitutionskoeffizient *m*; ~ **effect** *n* ECON Substitutionseffekt *m*; ~ **principle** HRM *of job* Ersetzungsprinzip *nt*

substructure *n* GEN COMM Grundlage *f*, Infrastruktur *f*

subtenant *n* PROP Untermieter, in *m,f*

subtitle *n* MEDIA, S&M Untertitel *m*

subtotal *n* MATH Zwischensumme *f*

subtract *vt* MATH subtrahieren

suburb *n* GEN COMM, PROP Vorort *m*, Vorstadt *f*

suburbs *n pl* GEN COMM Peripherie *f*, Umgebung *f*, Vororte *m pl*, Vorstädte *f pl*

subversion *n* POL Umsturz *m*

subvert *vt* POL umstürzen

subway *n* AmE (*cf underground BrE*) TRANSP U-Bahn *f*, Untergrundbahn *f*, *for pedestrians* Unterführung *f*

succeed 1. *vt* GEN COMM *follow* folgen [+dat], folgen auf [+acc], nachfolgen [+dat]; **2.** *vi* GEN COMM *achieve success* erfolgreich sein, Erfolg haben, gelingen, LAW erben

succeeding *adj* GEN COMM folgend, nachfolgend; ~ **account** *n* FIN Folgekonto *nt*, Nachfolgekonto *nt*

success *n* GEN COMM Erfolg *m*

successful *adj* GEN COMM, S&M erfolgreich, gelungen; ~ **outcome** *n* GEN COMM *to negotiations* erfolgreiches Ergebnis *nt*; ~ **venture** *n* ECON erfolgreiches Unternehmen *nt*

succession *n* GEN COMM Reihenfolge *f*, LAW Erbfolge *f*; ~ **law** *n* LAW Erbrecht *nt*

successive *adj* GEN COMM aufeinanderfolgend, sukzessiv; ~ **calls** *n pl* FIN aufeinanderfolgende Einzahlungsaufforderungen *f pl*

successively *adv* GEN COMM der Reihe nach

successor *n* GEN COMM Nachfolger, in *m,f*

successors: ~ **in title** *n pl* PATENTS Rechtsnachfolger *m pl*

success: ~ **story** *n* S&M *advertising, public relations* Erfolgsgeschichte *f*

sue 1. *vt* LAW belangen, verklagen; ◆ ~ **sb for infringement of patent** PATENTS jdn wegen Patentverletzung verklagen; ~ **sb for libel** LAW jdn wegen übler Nachrede verklagen; **2.** *vi* LAW klagen, prozessieren

sue: ~ **and labor** AmE, ~ **and labour** BrE *n* INS Schadensabwendung *f* und Schadensminderung *f*; ~ **and labour charges** *n pl* BrE INS Kosten *pl* für Schadensminderung und Schadensabwendung, Schadenminderungskosten *pl*; ~ **and labour clause** *n* BrE (*S/LC*) INS, LAW Klausel *f* über Schadensabwendung und Schadensminderung, Beteiligungszusage *f* der Versicherung bei Klageerhebung

suffer *vt* ECON, GEN COMM erleiden, leiden, PATENTS erleiden; ◆ ~ **the consequences** GEN COMM die Folgen tragen; ~ **damage** ECON *business* Schaden erleiden, Schaden nehmen; ~ **loss** LAW einen Verlust erleiden; ~ **a loss** GEN COMM eine Einbuße erleiden; ~ **a setback** GEN COMM einen Fehlschlag erleiden, einen Rückschlag erleiden

sufferance: ~ **wharf** *n* TRANSP Freihafenniederlage *f*

sufficient *adj* GEN COMM auskömmlich, ausreichend,

genügend, genug, hinreichend; ♦ **not ~ funds** (*nsf*) GEN COMM keine ausreichende Deckung

sufficient: **not ~ funds check** *AmE*, **not ~ funds cheque** *BrE* n BANK nicht ausreichend gedeckter Scheck *m*, Scheck *m* ohne ausreichende Deckung

suffrage *n* POL Wahlrecht *nt*, Stimmrecht *nt*

suggest *vt* GEN COMM vorschlagen

suggestion *n* GEN COMM Vorschlag *m*; ♦ **there is no ~ of corruption** LAW es gibt keinen Vortrag wegen Korruption; **~ box** *n* GEN COMM Kasten *m* für Verbesserungsvorschläge; **~ scheme** *n* GEN COMM, HRM betriebliches Vorschlagswesen *nt*, MGMNT Vorschlagswesen *nt*; **~ selling** *n* S&M Kundenbeeinflussung *f*

suit *n* LAW Klage *f*, Verfahren *nt*

suitability: **~ rules** *n pl* FIN Eignungsregeln *f pl*

suitable *adj* GEN COMM geeignet, passend, sachdienlich, zweckmäßig; **~ person for the job** *n* HRM geeignete Person *f* für die Stelle

suitcase *n* LEIS, TRANSP Koffer *m*

sulfur *AmE see* **sulphur** *BrE*

sulphur *n BrE* ENVIR Schwefel *m*; **~ dioxide** *n BrE* ENVIR *acid rain* Schwefeldioxid *nt*; **~ emission** *n BrE* ENVIR Schwefelausstoß *m*

sum *n* GEN COMM Summe *f*; ♦ **this ~ does not appear in the accounts** ACC dieser Betrag erscheint nicht in den Büchern

sum up 1. *vt* ACC, MATH *add up* zusammenzählen, summieren, GEN COMM *summarize* zusammenfassen; **2.** *vi* GEN COMM, LAW *give summary* zusammenfassen, resümieren

sum: **~ advanced** *n* GEN COMM Vorschußsumme *f*; **~ assured** *n* INS Versicherungsbetrag *m*, Versicherungssumme *f*; **~ insured** *n* GEN COMM Versicherungssumme *f*

summarize *vt* GEN COMM kurz zusammenfassen, resümieren

summarized *adj* GEN COMM zusammengefaßt

summary 1. *adj* GEN COMM kurz; **2.** *n* GEN COMM Abriß *m*, Kurzbericht *m*, kurze Übersicht *f*, Kurzfassung *f*, Zusammenfassung *f*, zusammengefaßte Darstellung *f*, Resümee *nt*, Übersicht *f*

summary: **~ dismissal** *n* HRM fristlose Entlassung *f*; **~ of input factors** *n* ECON Faktorbündel *nt* list Einsatzfaktorenübersicht *f*; **~ judgment** *n* GEN COMM abgekürztes Verfahren *nt*; **~ possession** *n* LAW Besitzübersicht *f*; **~ proceedings** *n pl* GEN COMM abgekürztes Verfahren *nt*, Schnellverfahren *nt*, LAW abgekürztes Verfahren *nt*; **~ report** *n* GEN COMM Kurzbericht *m*; **~ statement** *n* GEN COMM zusammenfassende Darstellung *f*

summation *n* GEN COMM Addition *f*

summer: **~ recess** *n BrE* POL *Parliament* Sommerpause *f*; **~ sale** *n* S&M Sommerschlußverkauf *m*; **~ time** *n* GEN COMM Sommerzeit *f*

summing: **~ up** *n* LAW Plädoyer *nt*, Resümee *nt*

summit *n* POL Gipfel *m*; **~ conference** *n* GEN COMM, POL Gipfelkonferenz *f*, Gipfeltreffen *nt*; **~ meeting** *n* GEN COMM *international*, POL Gipfeltreffen *nt*

summon *vt* LAW vorladen

summoning *n* POL Einberufung *f*

summons *n* LAW Ladung *f*, Vorladung *f*

sum: **~-of-the-year's digit method of depreciation** *n*

ACC arithmetische degressive Abschreibung *f*, digitale Abschreibung *f*

sumptuary: **~ laws** *n pl* LAW Gesetze *nt pl* zur privaten Ausgabenbegrenzung, verbrauchsbeschränkende Gesetze *nt pl*

sunbelt *n AmE* IND Sonnengürtel *m*

Sundays: **~ and holidays excepted** *phr* GEN COMM (*S&H/exct, SHEX*) außer an Sonn- und Feiertagen, Sonn- und Feiertage ausgenommen; **~ and holidays included** *phr* (*SHINC*) GEN COMM, TRANSP einschließlich Sonn- und Feiertage, inklusive Sonn- und Feiertage, Sonn- und Feiertage eingeschlossen

sundries *n pl* ACC Verschiedenes *pl* (*Versch.*)

sundry: **~ accounts** *n pl* ACC, GEN COMM Sonstige Kontengruppe *f*; **~ articles** *n pl* GEN COMM diverse Artikel *m pl*; **~ expenses** *n pl* ACC sonstige Aufwendungen *f pl*

sunk: **~ cost fallacy** *n* FIN einmaliger Produktionskostentrugschluß *m*, Sunk Cost-Irrtum *m*; **~ costs** *n pl* ACC gefallene Kosten *pl*, Vergangenheitskosten *pl*, versunkene Kosten *pl*, Sunk Costs *pl*

sunrise: **~ industry** *n* IND Anfangsindustrie *f*, aufstrebende Industrie *f*, Hochtechnologieindustrie *f*

sunset: **~ act** *n AmE* POL Gesetz *nt* mit begrenzter Geltungsdauer, Gesetz *nt* mit zeitlich begrenzter Gültigkeit; **~ industry** *n* IND Altindustrie *f*, veraltete Industrie *f*; **~ law** *n AmE* LAW Gesetz *nt* mit begrenzter Geltungsdauer; **~ provision** *n* LAW Bestimmung über die Nullstellung laufender Bewilligungen bis zum Ende des Finanzjahres; **~ report** *n* POL Bericht *m* mit begrenzter Geltungsdauer, Bericht *m* mit zeitlich begrenzter Aktualität

sunshine: **~ law** *n AmE* LAW Gesetz, das die Öffentlichkeit von Behördensitzungen vorschreibt

superabundant *adj* GEN COMM überreichlich

superannuated *adj* FIN, HRM, INS, WEL pensioniert

superannuation *n* FIN, HRM, INS, WEL Pension *f*, Ruhegehalt *nt*; **~ account** *n* INS Pensionskonto *nt*, Ruhegehaltskonto *nt*; **~ contribution** *n* HRM Altersversicherungsbeitrag *m*; **~ fund** *n* FIN Pensionsfonds *m*, HRM Pensionskasse *f*; **~ of the population** *n* ECON Überalterung *f* der Bevölkerung

supercomputer *n* COMP Großrechner *m*, Supercomputer *m*

superdividend *n* FIN außerordentliche Dividende *f*, Superdividende *f*

superficial: **~ loss** *n* GEN COMM leichter Verlust *m*

superfund *n AmE* FIN Pensionsfonds *m*, Pensionskasse *f*

superhighway *n AmE* (*cf motorway BrE*) TRANSP Autobahn *f*, Autostraße *f*, Kraftfahrstraße *f*

superintendence *n* GEN COMM Betriebsleitung *f*, Oberaufsicht *f*

superintendent: **~ of bankruptcy** *n* LAW *commercial* Konkursgericht *nt*, Konkursrichter *m*

Superintendent: **~ of Insurance** *n* INS Versicherungsaufsicht *f*

superior 1. *adj* GEN COMM überlegen; **2.** *n* HRM Vorgesetzte(r) *mf* [*decl. as adj*], *manager* Chef, in *m,f*

superior: **~ knowledge** *n* GEN COMM Informationsvorsprung *m*

supermarket *n* S&M Supermarkt *m*

super: **~ multiplier** *n* ECON Supermultiplikator *m*

superneutrality *n* ECON *policies* Superneutralität *f*

super: **~ NOW account** *n* AmE BANK höherverzinsliches Kontokorrentkonto *nt*

supernumerary *n* HRM Aushilfskraft *f*, Hilfsarbeiter, in *m,f*

superpower *n* POL Supermacht *f*

superscript 1. *adj* COMP, MEDIA *typography* hochgestellt; **2.** *n* COMP, MEDIA *typography* hochgestelltes Zeichen *nt*

supersede *vt* GEN COMM ablösen, abschaffen, einstellen, ersetzen, verdrängen, LAW aufheben, an die Stelle treten von

supersedence *n* LAW Aufhebung *f*

super: **~ site** *n* S&M Superstandort *m*

superstore *n* S&M großer Verbrauchermarkt *m*

supertanker *n* TRANSP Supertanker *m*

super: **~ video graphics adapter** *n* (*SVGA*) COMP Super-Videografikadapter *m* (*Super-VGA*); **~ video graphics array** *n* (*SVGA*) COMP Super-Videografikanordnung *f* (*Super-VGA*)

supervise *vt* GEN COMM, HRM, MGMNT beaufsichtigen, überwachen, kontrollieren

supervision *n* GEN COMM, HRM, MGMNT Aufsicht *f*, Beaufsichtigung *f*, Kontrolle *f*, Überwachung *f*; **~ of credit institutions** *n* FIN Bankenaufsicht *f*, Beaufsichtigung *f* der Kreditinstitute

supervisor *n* COMP Supervisor *m*, HRM, MGMNT, S&M Aufseher, in *m,f*, Kontrolleur, in *m,f*, Vorarbeiter, in *m,f*, BrE (*cf checker* AmE) Aufsichtsbeamte(r) *m* [decl. as adj], Aufsichtsbeamtin *f*

supervisory *adj* COMP, GEN COMM, HRM, MGMNT überwachend, beaufsichtigend; **~ board** *n* ACC, GEN COMM, HRM, MGMNT Aufsichtsrat *m*, Kontrollausschuß *m*; **~ management** *n* HRM, MGMNT Aufsichtsverwaltung *f*, Führungspersonal *nt* mit Aufsichtsfunktionen; **~ office** *n* LAW Aufsichtsamt *f*, Aufsichtsbüro *nt*; **~ personnel** *n* HRM Aufsichtspersonal *n*

supplement 1. *n* GEN COMM Ergänzung *f*, Supplement *nt*, LAW *to contract* Vertragsergänzung *f*, S&M Beilage *f*; **2.** *vt* GEN COMM ergänzen, vervollständigen, LAW ergänzen, S&M beilegen

supplemental: **~ agreement** *n* GEN COMM Zusatzabkommen *nt*, Zusatzvereinbarung *f*, Zusatzvertrag *m*; **~ budget** *n* FIN Nachtragshaushalt *m*; **~ technology** *n* GEN COMM Zusatztechnologie *f*

supplementaries *n pl* FIN Nachtragsetat *m*, Ergänzendes *nt*, Zusätzliches *nt*, Nachträge *m pl*

supplementary *adj* GEN COMM ergänzend, nachträglich, zusätzlich; **~ accounting system** *n* ACC ergänzendes Buchhaltungssystem *nt*; **~ agreement** *n* LAW Nebenabrede *f*; **~ benefit** *n* BrE WEL Sozialhilfe *f*; **~ company pension scheme** *n* FIN Betriebszusatzrente *f*, Betriebsrentensystem *nt*, betriebliche Zusatzrente *f*; **~ cost** *n* ACC, FIN Zusatzkosten *pl*, direkte und indirekte Gemeinkosten *pl*; **~ entry** *n* ACC Nachbuchung *f*

Supplementary: **~ Estimates** *n pl* BrE FIN Haushaltsnachtrag *m*, Nachträge *m pl*, Nachtragsetat *m*, POL Haushaltsnachtrag *m*, Nachtragsetat *m*; **~ Financing Facility** *n* FIN zusätzliche Finanzierungsfazilität *f*

supplementary: **~ intercompany pension scheme** *n* FIN überbetriebliche Zusatzrente *f*; **~ pension scheme** *n* FIN Zusatzrente *f*; **~ period** *n* TAX Nachtragszeitraum *m*; **~ protection certificate** *n* (*SPC*) GEN COMM, PATENTS Zusatzschutzurkunde *f*; **~ service tariff** *n*

(*SST*) TRANSP zusätzlicher Dienstleistungstarif *m*; **~ special deposits scheme** *n* BANK ergänzendes Sondereinlageprogramm *nt*, FIN zusätzlicher Spezialeinlagenplan *m*; **~ stocks guarantee** *n* IMP/EXP zusätzliche Warengarantie *f*; **~ tax** *n* FIN, TAX Nachsteuer *f*, Zusatzsteuer *f*

supplemented *adj* GEN COMM vervollständigt, ergänzt

supplier *n* ECON, GEN COMM Lieferant, in *m,f*, Lieferer *m*, Anbieter, in *m,f*; **~ credit** *n* IMP/EXP Lieferkredit *m*, Lieferantenkredit *m*

supplies *n pl* ECON, GEN COMM Bestände *m pl*, Lieferungen *f pl*, Betriebsstoffe *m pl*

supply 1. *n* COMP *power, mains* Versorgung *f*, ECON Angebot *nt*, GEN COMM Bereitstellung *f*, POL *of money to meet government expenses* Mittelbereitstellung *f*, bewilligter Etat *m*; **2.** *vt* GEN COMM *information* bereitstellen, liefern, beliefern, versorgen mit; ♦ **~ goods on trust** GEN COMM Waren auf Kredit liefern; **~ security for** FIN besichern

supply: **~ bill** *n* ECON *budgeted amount* Bereitstellungsantrag *m*, Vorlage *f* für den Nachtragshaushalt, POL *budget* Vorlage *f* für den Nachtragshaushalt, Bereitstellungsantrag *m* für das Ausgabenbudget, Bereitstellungsantrag *m*; **~ and demand** *n* ECON, GEN COMM Angebot *nt* und Nachfrage *f*; **~ committee** *n* POL Haushalts-Bewilligungsausschuß *m*; **~ control** *n* ECON Angebotskontrolle *f*, Steuerung *f* des Angebots; **~ curve** *n* ECON Angebotskurve *f*; **~ of electric current** *n* IND Stromlieferung *f*; **~ function** *n* ECON Angebotsfunktion *f*; **~ of goods** *n* ECON Güterangebot *nt*; **~-induced recession** *n* ECON angebotsinduzierte Rezession *f*; **~ industry** *n* GEN COMM Zulieferindustrie *f*, Ausrüstungsindustrie *f*; **~ of jobs** *n* ECON Arbeitsplatzangebot *nt*; **~ network** *n* AmE (*cf mains* BrE) COMP Lichtnetz *nt*, Netz *nt*, Stromversorgungsnetz *nt*; **~-oriented economic policy** *n* ECON angebotsorientierte Wirtschaftspolitik *f*; **~ price** *n* ECON Angebotspreis *m*, Lieferpreis *m*; **~ revolving fund** *n* ECON revolvierender Beschaffungsfonds *m*; **~ of services** *n* ECON Dienstleistungsangebot *nt*, Erbringung *f* von Dienstleistungen; **~ shock** *n* ECON Angebotsschock *m*; **~-side economics** *n* ECON angebotsorientierte Wirtschaftspolitik *f*; **~-side shock** *n* ECON Angebotsschock *m*; **~ source** *n* GEN COMM Bezugsquelle *f*

support 1. *n* COMP, ECON Unterstützung *f*, GEN COMM *financial, moral* Beistand *m*, Stützung *f*, LAW Unterhalt *m*, MGMNT Unterstützung *f*; **2.** *vt* COMP unterstützen, ECON *currency* stützen, GEN COMM begünstigen, *currency* unterstützen, verfechten, stützen, LAW unterhalten, MGMNT *currency* stützen, unterstützen

support: **~ activities** *n pl* COMP Betreuungsmaßnahmen *f pl*, GEN COMM Unterstützungsaktivitäten *f pl*; **~ activity** *n* GEN COMM Stützungsgeschäft *nt*, MGMNT Stützungsmaßnahme *f*, Unterstützungsmaßnahme *f*; **~ buying** *n pl* FIN Stützungskäufe *m pl*

supported: **~ price** *n* GEN COMM Stützungspreis *m*, gestützter Preis *m*, künstlich gehaltener Preis *m*, subventionierter Preis *m*

supporter *n* GEN COMM Anhänger, in *m,f*, Befürworter, in *m,f*, Verfechter, in *m,f*

support: **~ hotline** *n* COMP Hotline *f*

supporting: **~ book entry** *n* ACC Buchungsbeleg *m*; **~ credit** *n* BANK, FIN Stützungskredit *m*; **~ data** *n pl*

MATH Belege *m pl*; **~ documents** *n pl* ADMIN sachdienliche Unterlagen *f pl*, GEN COMM Unterlagen *f pl*, LAW Belegdokumente *nt pl*, sachdienliche Unterlagen *f pl*; **~ receipt** *n* GEN COMM Quittungsbeleg *m*

support: **~ operations** *n pl* FIN Stützungskäufe *m pl*; **~ points** *n* FIN Interventionspunkte *m pl*; **~ service** *n* GEN COMM, WEL Unterstützungsleistung *f*

suppose *vt* GEN COMM annehmen, voraussetzen

supposition *n* GEN COMM Voraussetzung *f*

suppress *vt* COMP *remove* unterdrücken

suppressed *adj* COMP, ECON unterdrückt; **~ inflation** *n* ECON zurückgestaute Inflation *f*

suppression *n* ECON, POL Unterdrückung *f*

supranational *adj* ECON, GEN COMM, POL übernational, überstaatlich, supranational

Supreme: **~ Court** *n* LAW Oberster Gerichtshof *m*

surcharge *n* GEN COMM Aufschlag *m*, Ergänzungsabgabe *f*, Sonderabgabe *f*, Zuschlag *m*, Aufgeld *nt*; **~ value** *n* TRANSP Aufschlagswert *m*, Zuschlagswert *m*

surety *n* FIN Bürgschaftsleistung *f*, Sicherheit *f*; **~ in cash** *n* LAW Bürgschaftsleistung *f* in bar; **~ liability** *n* BANK Bürgenhaftung *f*

suretyship *n* LAW Bürgschaft *f*

surface: **~ area** *n* ECON Fläche *f*; **~ transport** *n* TRANSP Bodentransport *m*

surge: **~ of export orders** *n* IMP/EXP, S&M Exportwelle *f*

surpass *vt* GEN COMM übertreffen

surplus **1.** *adj* GEN COMM überschüssig; **2.** *n* GEN COMM Überhang *m*, Überschuß *m*, Mehrbetrag *m*, *profit* Gewinn *m*; ♦ **in ~** ECON im Überschuß

surplus: **~ approach** *n* ECON Mehrwerttheorie *f*; **~ of assets over liabilities** *n* ACC Überschuß *m* des Vermögens über die Schulden; **~ capacity** *n* ECON, IND Überschußkapazität *f*, ungenutzte Kapazität *f*; **~ on current account** *n* ECON, IMP/EXP *international trade* Leistungsbilanzüberschuß *m*, aktive Leistungsbilanz *f*; **~ dividend** *n* FIN außerordentliche Dividende *f*, Dividendenzuschlag *m*, Superdividende *f*; **~ labor** *AmE*, **~ labour** *BrE* *n* HRM Überschuß *m* an Arbeitskräften; **~ offers** *n pl* ECON Angebotsüberschuß *m*; **~ reserve** *n* ACC Gewinnrücklage *f*; **~ reserves** *n pl* FIN Gewinnrücklagen *f pl*, Gewinnrückstellung *f*, zweckgebundene offene Rücklagen *f pl*; **~ of selling orders** *n* STOCK Angebotsüberhang *m*; **~ value** *n* FIN Mehrwert *m*

surrender: **on ~ of the bill of lading** *phr* IMP/EXP, TRANSP bei Frachtbriefvorlage; **~ charge** *n* INS Stornoabschlag *m*, Stornoabzug *m*, Abzug *m* vom Rückkaufswert

surrendered *adj* GEN COMM übergeben

surrender: **~ of a patent** *n* LAW, PATENTS Patentverzicht *m*; **~ value** *n* ACC *insurance policy* Rückkaufwert *m*, *shares* Rückgabewert *m*

surrogate *n* POL Stellvertreter, in *m,f* eines Kandidaten

surrounded *adj* GEN COMM *encumbered* behaftet, umgeben

surrounding: **~ area** *n* GEN COMM *of town* Umgebung *f*

surveillance *n* LAW *electronic surveillance* Überwachung *f*; **~ department of exchanges** *n* STOCK Devisenaufsichtsabteilung *f*; **~ licence** *BrE*, **~ license** *AmE* *n* IMP/EXP Aufsichtsgenehmigung *f*, Kontrollgenehmigung *f*, Überwachungslizenz *f*

survey **1.** *n* GEN COMM *investigation* Untersuchung *f*, *expert opinion* Gutachten *nt*, Prüfung *f*, *questionnaire* Umfrage *f*, Erhebung *f*, *overview* Übersicht *f*, *of land*

Vermessung *f*, Überblick *m*, PROP Vermessung *f*, S&M Erhebung *f*; **2.** *vt* GEN COMM erheben, *examine* begutachten, *investigate* prüfen, untersuchen, *question* befragen, *monitor* überwachen, PROP *land* vermessen

survey: **~ certificate** *n* GEN COMM Besichtigungsschein *m*; **~ fee** *n* FIN *finance houses* Erhebungsgebühr *f*, Untersuchungsgebühr *f*, GEN COMM Gutachtergebühr *f*, Vermessungsgebühr *f*, Prüfungsgebühr *f*, Besichtigungsgebühr *f*, PROP Vermessungsgebühr *f*

surveyor *n* HRM *marine engineer* amtlich bestellter Schiffssachverständiger *m* [decl. as adj], amtlich bestellte Schiffssachverständige *f* [decl. as adj], MGMNT Gutachter, in *m,f*, PROP Landvermesser, in *m,f*, Vermesser, in *m,f*

survey: **~ report** *n* INS Besichtigungsbericht *m*, Expertise *f*; **~ research** *n* S&M *market purposes* Marktuntersuchung *f*, Erhebungsforschung *f*

survival: **~ process** *n* ECON *firms* Überlebensprozeß *m*; **~ strategy** *n* ECON, GEN COMM Überlebensstrategie *f*

survive *vi* GEN COMM überleben, überstehen

survivor: **~ policy** *n* INS Hinterbliebenenversicherungspolice *f*, Überlebensversicherungsklausel *f*

survivorship *n* LAW *property* Überlebensfall *m*; **~ account** *n* BANK Hinterbliebenenkonto *nt*; **~ annuity** *n* FIN einseitige Hinterbliebenenrente *f*, PROP Überlebensrente *f*; **~ clause** *n* *AmE* INS Hinterbliebenenversicherungsklausel *f*, Überlebensversicherungsklausel *f*; **~ insurance** *n* INS Hinterbliebenenversicherung *f*, Überlebensversicherung *f*

susceptible *adj* GEN COMM beeinflußbar; **~ to industrial application** *phr* PATENTS industriell anwendbar, industrieller Anwendung unterliegend, gewerblich verwendbar

suspect: **~ bill of health** *n* WEL Gesundheitspaß *m* mit dem Vermerk ansteckungsverdächtig

suspend *vt* BANK *halt* einstellen, GEN COMM aussetzen, unterbrechen, *trading, authorization* zeitweilig aufheben, suspendieren, HRM *from job* suspendieren, LAW zeitweilig aussetzen, aussetzen, STOCK *quotation of shares*, TAX aussetzen; ♦ **~ payments** FIN, GEN COMM Zahlungen einstellen; **~ trading** STOCK den Handel aussetzen

suspended: **be ~** *phr* GEN COMM ruhen; **~ sentence** *n* LAW ausgesetzte Strafe *f*; **~ solid** *n* IND Schwebstoff *m*; **~ tax assessment** *n* TAX ausgesetzte Steuerfestsetzung *f*; **~ trading** *n* STOCK ausgesetzter Handel *m*

suspense: **in ~** *phr* GEN COMM in der Schwebe, in Ungewißheit, schwebend; **~ account** *n* ACC, BANK Übergangskonto *nt*, Zwischenkonto *nt*; **~ collator** *n* GEN COMM Suspenskollator *m*; **~ entry** *n* ACC transitorische Buchung *f*, Zwischeneintrag *m*

suspension *n* BANK Einstellung *f*, GEN COMM zeitweilige Aufhebung *f*, Aussetzung *f*, Suspension *f*, Unterbrechung *f*, HRM Suspension *f*, LAW zeitweilige Aussetzung *f*, STOCK, TAX Aussetzung *f*; **~ from office** *n* HRM Beurlaubung *f*; **~ of payments** *n* BANK, GEN COMM Zahlungseinstellung *f*

suspensive: **~ condition** *n* *BrE* LAW auflösende Bedingung *f*, aufschiebende Bedingung *f*, aufschiebende Voraussetzung *f*

sustain *vt* ACC *loss* erleiden, ECON *economic growth* aufrechterhalten, GEN COMM stattgeben, *confidence* bewahren, LAW *loss, injury* ertragen; ♦ **~ a loss** ACC einen Verlust erleiden; **~ one's claim** LAW seinen Anspruch aufrechterhalten

sustainability *n* ECON, ENVIR Nachhaltigkeit *f*

sustainable *adj* ECON, ENVIR, GEN COMM, MEDIA nachhaltig; **~ development** *n* ECON nachhaltige Entwicklung *f*; **~ economic growth rate** *n* ECON nachhaltige Wachstumsrate *f*; **~ growth** *n* ECON nachhaltiges Wachstum *nt*, stetiges Wachstum *nt*

sustained: ~ non inflationary growth *n* (*SNIG*) ECON stetiges inflationsfreies Wachstum *nt*, stetiges nichtinflationäres Wachstum *nt*; **~ rally** *n* STOCK anhaltende Kurserholung *f*; **~ resurgence** *n* ECON *of growth* dauerhafte Wiederkehr *f*

sustaining: ~ grant *n* GEN COMM, POL Grundzuschuß *m*, Zuschuß *m* zum Lebensunterhalt

SVGA *abbr* COMP (*super video graphics adapter*) Super-VGA (*Super-Videografikadapter*), (*super video graphics array*) Super-VGA (*Super-Videografikanordnung*)

swatch *n* GEN COMM Musterkollektion *f*, Swatch *f*

sway *vt* GEN COMM *outcome* schwanken, schwingen, beeinflussen

swear 1. *vt* LAW schwören; ◆ **~ an affidavit that** LAW eine eidesstattliche Erklärung abgeben, daß; **~ on affidavit that** LAW eine schriftliche Aussage beschwören; **~ sb to secrecy** GEN COMM jdn auf Geheimhaltung einschwören; **2.** *vi* LAW schwören

sweated: ~ goods *n pl* GEN COMM für Hungerlöhne hergestellte Waren; **~ trade** *n* GEN COMM mühsames Geschäft *nt*

sweatshop *n* HRM Ausbeutungsbetrieb *m*; **~ labor** *AmE*, **~ labour** *BrE n* HRM *workforce* ausgebeutete Arbeiter *m pl*, *work carried out* unterbezahlte Schwerarbeit *f*

Swedish: ~ School *n* ECON Schwedische Schule *f*, Stockholmer Schule *f*

sweeping *adj* GEN COMM, POL *changes* drastisch, grundlegend, radikal

sweetener *n* *infrml* FIN *bribe* Bestechungsgeld *nt*, Schmiergeld *nt* (*infrml*)

swell *vi* BANK wachsen

SWIFT *abbr* (*Society for Worldwide Interbank Financial Telecommunications*) BANK SWIFT, internationales Datenfernübertragungsnetz für Auslandszahlungen

swimming: ~ market *n* GEN COMM glattes Geschäft *nt*

swindle 1. *n* GEN COMM Betrug *m*, Schwindel *m*, Schwindelgeschäft *nt*; **2.** *vt* GEN COMM beschwindeln, betrügen

swindler *n* GEN COMM Betrüger, in *m,f* (*infrml*), Gauner, in *m,f* (*infrml*)

swing 1. *n* BANK Swing *m*, ECON Fluktuation *f*, GEN COMM *of market* Bewegung *f*, Schwankung *f*, POL Umschwung *m*; **2.** *vt* **~ the deal** *phr* GEN COMM das Geschäft perfekt machen, das Geschäft unter Dach und Fach bringen

SWING *abbr BrE* (*sterling warrant into gilt-edged stock*) STOCK Sterling-Bezugsrechtsschein *m* für Staatsanleihen

swing: ~ credit margin *n* BANK Swing-Grenze *f*; **~ line** *n* FIN Bedarfs-Kreditlinie *f*; **~ loan** *n* BANK zinsloser Überziehungskredit *m*; **~ overdraft** *n* BANK Swing-Überschreitung *f*; **~ shift** *n* HRM zusätzliche Schicht *f*; **~ to the left** *n* POL Linksruck *m*; **~ to the right** *n* POL Rechtsruck *m*; **~ voter** *n* POL Wechselwähler *m*

Swiss: ~ National Bank *n* ECON Schweizerische Natio-

nalbank *f*; **~ Options and Financial Futures Exchange** *n* (*SOFFEX*) STOCK Schweizer Börse für Optionen und Finanzterminkontrakte

switch 1. *n* COMP *program* Programmschalter *m*, *device* Schalter *m*, ECON Kompensationsgegengeschäft *nt*, Switch-Geschäft *nt*, GEN COMM Umstellung *f*, *exchange* Tausch *m*, POL *in policy* Änderung *f*; **2.** *vt* FIN einwechseln, umschichten, GEN COMM umstellen, tauschen, POL ändern; ◆ **~ off** GEN COMM ausschalten; **~ on** GEN COMM einschalten, anschalten; **~ production** IND die Produktion umschalten; **3.** *vi* ◆ **~ over to** GEN COMM sich umstellen auf [+acc], wechseln an

switchboard *n* COMP Schalttafel *f*, GEN COMM *telephone exchange* Vermittlung *f*, *in firm* Zentrale *f*; **~ operator** *n* COMMS, HRM Telefonist, in *m,f*

switched: ~ off *adj* GEN COMM ausgeschaltet; **~ on** *adj* GEN COMM angeschaltet, eingeschaltet

switcher *n* GEN COMM Weichensteller *m*, POL Wechselwähler *m*

switching *n* COMP Schalten *nt*, FIN Umschichtung *f*, GEN COMM Tausch *m*, Umstellung *f*; **~-in rate** *n* GEN COMM Einwechselrate *f*; **~-out rate** *n* GEN COMM Auswechselrate *f*

switchover *n* GEN COMM plötzlicher Wandel *m*, Umstellung *f*, völliger Wechsel *m*; ◆ **~ to** GEN COMM Umstellung *f* auf

switch: ~ selling *n* S&M, STOCK Switch-Verkauf *m*; **~ trading** *n* GEN COMM devisenfreier Außenhandel *m*, Switch-Handel *m*, STOCK Switch-Handel *m*

swop 1. *n* GEN COMM Tausch *m*, ECON Tauschgeschäft *nt*, STOCK Swap *m*, Swapgeschäft *nt*; **2.** *vt* GEN COMM tauschen

swop: ~ contract *n* LAW *international* Devisentauschgeschäft *nt*, Devisentauschvertrag *m*; **~ line** *n* FIN Swaplinie *f*; **~ market** *n* STOCK Swapmarkt *m*; **~ network** *n* STOCK Netz gegenseitiger Kreditlinien im Devisengeschäft

swoprate *n* ECON Swapsatz *m*

swoption *n* FIN Optionsswap *m*, Swaption *f* (*jarg*)

SWOT *abbr* (*strengths, weaknesses, opportunities and threats analysis*) S&M Analyse *f* von Stärken, Schwächen, Chancen und Risiken

Sy *abbr* (*synchronous system*) IND Synchronsystem *nt*

Sydney: ~ Futures Exchange *n* STOCK Terminbörse in Sidney

symbiotic: ~ marketing *n* S&M symbiotisches Marketing *nt*

symbol *n* COMP, GEN COMM, PATENTS, S&M Kennzeichen *nt*, Symbol *nt*

symbolic *adj* COMP, GEN COMM, POL, S&M symbolisch; **~ association** *n* S&M symbolische Assoziation *f*

symmetric *adj* MATH, STOCK symmetrisch

symmetrical: ~ frequency curve *n* MATH *statistics* symmetrische Häufigkeitskurve *f*

symmetry *n* MATH, STOCK Symmetrie *f*

sympathetic: ~ action *n* HRM *industrial relations* Sympathieaktion *f*, Sympathiemaßnahme *f*; **~ damage** *n* TRANSP Nebenschaden *m*; **~ strike** *n* HRM Sympathiestreik *m*

sympathizer *n* POL Sympathisant, in *m,f*

sympathy: ~ action *n* HRM Sympathieaktion *f*; **~ strike** *n* HRM Sympathiestreik *m*

symposium *n* GEN COMM Symposium *nt*, wissenschaftlicher Meinungsaustausch *m*

sync *abbr* (*synchronization*) GEN COMM Gleichlauf *m*, Synchronisation *f*, zeitliche Übereinstimmung *f*; ♦ **out of ~** ECON nicht synchron

synchronization *n* (*sync*) GEN COMM Gleichlauf *m*, Synchronisation *f*, zeitliche Übereinstimmung *f*

synchronize *vt* GEN COMM gleichlaufen, synchronisieren, zeitlich übereinstimmen, S&M synchronisieren

synchronized *adj* GEN COMM aufeinander abgestimmt, gleichmäßig, synchronisiert

synchronous *adj* COMP synchron; **~ assembly-line production** *n* IND Bandfertigung *f*, Bandproduktion *f*; **~ system** *n* (*Sy*) IND Synchronsystem *nt*

syncro: **~ marketing** *n* S&M synchrones Marketing *nt*

syndicalism *n* HRM Syndikalismus *m*

syndicate *n* BANK Bankenkonsortium *nt*, Konsortium *nt*, FIN Konsortium *nt*, Syndikat *nt*, GEN COMM Finanzgruppe *f*, Versicherungsgruppe *f*, Interessengemeinschaft *f*, Konsortium *nt*, Syndikat *nt*, HRM, LAW, PROP, STOCK Konsortium *nt*; **~ agreement** *n* STOCK Konsortialvertrag *m*

syndicated: **~ column** *n* MEDIA *print* in mehreren Zeitungen gleichzeitig erscheinende Spalte; **~ loan** *n* BANK Konsortialkredit *m*, FIN Gemeinschaftskredit *m*, Konsortialkredit *m*, syndizierte Anleihe *f*; **~ swap** *n* FIN syndizierter Swap *m*

syndicate: **~ of investors** *n* STOCK Kapitalanlegerkonsortium *nt*; **~ leader** *n* GEN COMM Konsortialführer, in *m,f*

syndication: **~ capacity** *n* ADMIN Konsortialkapazität *f*; **~ official** *n* BANK Konsortialbeamte(r) *m* [decl. as adj], Konsortialbeamtin *f*

synergism *n* ECON, GEN COMM Synergie *f*, Synergismus *m*

synergy *n* ECON, GEN COMM Synergie *f*, Zusammenwirken *nt*

synopsis *n* GEN COMM *as regards content*, MEDIA, S&M Abriß *m*, Übersicht *f*, Synopse *f*, Zusammenfassung *f*

syntax *n* COMP Syntax *f*; **~ error** *n* COMP Syntaxfehler *m*; **~ error message** *n* COMP Satzaufbaufehlermeldung *f*, Syntaxfehlermeldung *f*

synthesis *n* GEN COMM Synthese *f*

synthetic *adj* COMP, GEN COMM, IND synthetisch; **~ bond** *n* STOCK synthetische Anleihe *f*; **~ incentive** *n* ECON *socialist economies* synthetischer Anreiz *m*; **~ material** *n* ENVIR, IND Kunstoff *m*

system *n* ADMIN, COMP System *nt*, GEN COMM System *nt*, Methode *f*, *hi-fi* Anlage *f*; **~ of accounts** *n* ACC Kontensystem *nt*; **~ administrator** *n* COMP Systemverwalter, in *m,f*

systematic *adj* GEN COMM planmäßig, systematisch; **~ cost basis** *n* ACC systematische Kostenbasis *f*; **~ risk** *n* STOCK systematisches Risiko *nt*, Systemrisiko *nt*, unvermeidbares Wertpapierrisiko *nt*; **~ sampling** *n* MATH *statistics* systematische Auswahl *f*

systematize *vt* GEN COMM systematisieren

system: **~-based audit** *n* ACC systemorientierte Buchprüfung *f*; **~ crash** *n* COMP Absturz *m*; **~ design** *n* COMP Systementwurf *m*; **~ development** *n* COMP Systementwicklung *f*; **~ disk** *n* COMP Systemdiskette *f*; **~ failure** *n* COMP Systemversagen *nt*; **~ file** *n* COMP Systemdatei *f*; **~ of financial administration** *n* FIN Finanzverwaltungssystem *nt*; **~-managed company** *n* GEN COMM, MGMNT systemgeleitetes Unternehmen *nt*

System: **~ of National Accounts** *n* (*SNA*) ACC Volkswirtschaftliche Gesamtrechnung *f* (*VGR*), gesamtwirtschaftliches Rechnungswesen *nt*

system: **~-provider** *n* COMP, COMP Systemanbieter *m*, Provider (*jarg*), Systemversorger *m*; **~ requirement** *n* COMP Systemanforderung *f*

systems: **~ analyst** *n* COMP Systemanalytiker, in *m,f*; **~ analysis** *n* COMP Systemanalyse *f*; **~ approach** *n* COMP Systemansatz *m*; **~-based auditing** *n* ACC systemorientierte Buchprüfung *f*; **~ design** *n* COMP Systementwurf *m*; **~ engineer** *n* COMP Systemanalytiker, in *m,f*; **~ engineering** *n* COMP Systementwicklung *f*; **~ management** *n* COMP Systemverwaltung *f*, MGMNT Systemmanagement *nt*

system: **~ software** *n* COMP Systemsoftware *f*

systems: **~ planning** *n* COMP, GEN COMM Systemplanung *f*; **~ and procedures** *n pl* COMP Systeme und Verfahren *nt pl*, GEN COMM Methoden und Verfahrensregeln *f pl*; **~ programmer** *n* COMP Systemprogrammierer, in *m,f*; **~ programming** *n* COMP Systemprogrammierung *f*; **~ theory** *n* MGMNT Systemtheorie *f*

system: **~ of taxation** *n* ECON Steuersystem *nt*

T

t *abbr* (*ton, tonne*) GEN COMM t (*Tonne*)

t. *abbr* (*tare*) IND, TRANSP Tara *f*

ta *abbr* TRANSP (*tank*) Behälter *m*, Tank *m*, (*tanktainer*) Tanktainer *m*

TA *abbr* COMMS (*telegraphic address*) telegrafische Adresse *f*, FIN, GEN COMM (*transactional analysis*) Analyse der Geschäftsabschlüsse *f*, Transaktionsanalyse *f*, HRM (*technical assistant*) technischer Assistent *m*, technische Assistentin *f*, (*Training Agency*) Schulungsbehörde *f*, Schulungsagentur *f*, MGMNT (*transactional analysis*) Transaktionsanalyse *f*, Analyse der Geschäftsabschlüsse *f*

TAA *abbr* (*transferable account area*) ACC übertragbarer Abrechnungsbereich *m*

tab 1. *n* COMP *word processing* Tabulator *m*; **2.** *vi* COMP eine Tabulatorstelle weiterspringen

TAB *abbr* AmE (*tax anticipation bill*) TAX Steuergutschein *m*

table 1. *n* COMP Tabelle *f*, GEN COMM, MATH, MEDIA *printing* Tabelle *f*; **2.** *vt* GEN COMM *proposal*, POL *draft bill* BrE vorlegen, AmE auf die lange Bank schieben (*infrml*), zurückstellen; ♦ **~ an amendment** BrE LAW eine Abänderung einreichen, eine Abänderung vorlegen; **~ a motion** BrE *frml* POL einen Antrag einbringen (*frml*)

table: **~ of contents** *n* GEN COMM, MEDIA Inhaltsverzeichnis *nt*, Register *nt*; **~ of par values** *n* STOCK Tabelle *f* von Nominalwerten; **~ top** *n* S&M *advertising* Stilllebensaufnahme eines Produkts ohne Personen im Bild

tabloid *n* MEDIA Boulevardzeitung *f*; **~ press** *n* MEDIA Boulevardpresse *f*, Regenbogenpresse *f*

tab: **~ setting** *n* COMP Tabulatoreinstellung *f*; **~ stop** *n* COMP Tabulatorstelle *f*

tabular *adj* COMP, MATH tabellarisch; ♦ **in ~ form** COMP, MATH tabellarisch

tabular: **~ bookkeeping** *n* ACC amerikanische Buchführung *f*; **~ premium** *n* INS Tarifprämie *f*; **~ report** *n* ADMIN tabellarischer Bericht *m*

tabulate *vt* COMP, MATH, MEDIA tabellarisieren, tabellarisch anordnen

tabulated: **in ~ form** *phr* COMP, MATH, MEDIA tabellarisch angeordnet

tabulating: **~ department** *n* ADMIN Tabellierungsabteilung *f*; **~ machine** *n* ADMIN Tabelliermaschine *f*

tabulation *n* COMP Aufstellung *f*, tabellarische Anordnung *f*, Tabellierung *f*, GEN COMM Auftabellierung *f*, MATH, MEDIA tabellarische Anordnung *f*, Tabellierung *f*

T-account *n* ACC *book-keeping* T-Konto *nt*

tachograph *n* TRANSP Fahrtenschreiber *m*, Tachograph *m*

tacit *adj* LAW *acceptance* stillschweigend; **~ agreement** *n* LAW stillschweigendes Übereinkommen *nt*; **by ~ agreement** *phr* LAW nach stillschweigender Vereinbarung; **~ knowledge** *n* ECON, LAW, POL nicht übertragbares Wissen *nt*; **~ renewal** *n* GEN COMM stillschweigende Verlängerung *f*

tackle *vt* GEN COMM *treat* behandeln, MGMNT *problem* anpacken, in Angriff nehmen

TACs *abbr* (*total allowable catches*) ENVIR *fishing quotas* zulässige Fangquote *f*

tactical: **~ plan** *n* GEN COMM taktischer Plan *m*; **~ planning** *n* GEN COMM taktische Planung *f*; **~ pricing** *n* S&M taktische Preispolitik *f*

tactile: **~ keyboard** *n* COMP Tastatur *f* für Sehgeschädigte

Taft-Hartley: **~ Act** *n* AmE ECON *1947* Bundesgesetz, das der Unternehmerseite in gewerkschaftlich organisierten Industrien einen Teil der Verhandlungsstärke zurückgab, die sie durch gewerkschaftliche Gesetzgebung vor dem Zweiten Weltkrieg verloren hatte

tag *n* COMP, S&M, TRANSP *for identification of cargo* Anhänger *m*, Etikett *nt*, Kennzeichen *nt*

tagboard *n* AmE GEN COMM Anschlagtafel *f*

tagline *n* MEDIA, S&M *advertisements* Schlußwort *nt*

tag: **~ reader** *n* COMP Kleinlochstreifenleser *m*

tail *n* GEN COMM *of list* Ende *nt*, Schluß *m*, STOCK *insurance, treasury auctions, underwriting* Kursdifferenz *f*

tail away *vi* GEN COMM *demand* abflauen, abnehmen, sich abschwächen

tail: **~ end of the season** *n* GEN COMM Saisonabschluß *m*

tailor: **~ to** *vt* GEN COMM abstimmen mit, ausrichten auf [+acc], zuschneiden auf [+acc], *clothes* schneidern

tailorable *adj* GEN COMM anpassungsfähig

tailored *adj* GEN COMM, S&M zugeschnitten, ausgerichtet, *clothes* maßgeschneidert

tailoring *n* GEN COMM Ausrichtung *f*, Zuschnitt *m*, *profession* Schneiderei *f*

tailor: **~-made** *adj* GEN COMM *package* maßgeschneidert, zugeschnitten, *clothes* nach Maß gefertigt, S&M *advertising* kundenspezifisch, zugeschnitten; **~-made service contract** *n* LAW maßgeschneiderter Dienstvertrag *m*

take 1. *n* ♦ **be on the ~** *infrml* GEN COMM auf Beute aus sein (*infrml*), auf Fang gehen (*infrml*); **2.** *vt* GEN COMM abnehmen, einnehmen, STOCK *profit* mitnehmen; ♦ **~ aboard** IMP/EXP, TRANSP *cargo, passengers* an Bord nehmen; **~ an accommodation credit** FIN *loan* einen Überbrückungskredit aufnehmen; **~ account of** GEN COMM berücksichtigen, einkalkulieren, in Betracht ziehen; **~ account of the stress factor** HRM den Streßfaktor in Betracht ziehen; **~ action** GEN COMM, MGMNT Maßnahmen ergreifen, Schritte unternehmen, tätig werden; **~ action against** GEN COMM Maßnahmen ergreifen gegen, Maßnahmen treffen gegen; **~ administrative control of a company** GEN COMM die Leitung einer Firma übernehmen; **~ advantage of** GEN COMM *situation, person* ausnutzen, sich zunutze machen; **~ advantage of an opportunity to do sth** GEN COMM eine Chance ergreifen, etw zu tun, eine Gelegenheit wahrnehmen, etw zu tun; **~ an appeal to court** LAW Beschwerde führen; **~ an average** MATH den Durchschnitt nehmen, den Mittelwert nehmen; **~ a bath** *jarg* STOCK *speculation* baden gehen (*infrml*); **~ a break** GEN COMM Pause machen; **~ bribes** GEN COMM, POL sich bestechen lassen; **~ a cleaning** *infrml* FIN einen hohen finanziellen Verlust erleiden; ~ **control** GEN COMM die Kontrolle übernehmen; ~ **delivery of sth** GEN COMM eine Lieferung von etw abnehmen; ~ **a deposit** STOCK *Eurodollar time deposit* eine Bankeinlage hinterlegen; ~ **a different view** GEN COMM anderer Meinung sein, eine andere Meinung vertreten; ~ **drastic action** MGMNT, POL eisern durchgreifen; ~ **early retirement** GEN COMM, HRM sich vorzeitig pensionieren lassen; ~ **effect** GEN COMM *date* wirksam werden, LAW *enter into force* in Kraft treten, *date* wirksam werden; ~ **effect from** GEN COMM, LAW, POL wirksam werden ab; ~ **an equity stake in** STOCK eine Kapitalbeteiligung erwerben in; ~ **expert advice** GEN COMM einen Fachmann zu Rate ziehen, sich fachlich beraten lassen; ~ **an extra day off** HRM einen Tag Sonderurlaub nehmen; ~ **a flier** STOCK spekulieren; ~ **French leave** GEN COMM ohne Abschied weggehen, sich auf französisch verabschieden (*infrml*), sich unerlaubt entfernen; ~ **a gloomy view of the situation** GEN COMM die Lage pessimistisch betrachten; ~ **a holiday** *BrE* (*cf take a vacation AmE*) GEN COMM, HRM, LEIS Ferien machen, in die Ferien gehen, Urlaub nehmen; ~ **industrial action** GEN COMM, HRM, IND Arbeitskampfmaßnahmen ergreifen, in den Streik treten, streiken; ~ **the initiative** MGMNT die Initiative ergreifen, vorangehen; ~ **into account** GEN COMM anrechnen, in Betracht ziehen, einkalkulieren, in die Rechnung einbeziehen, berücksichtigen; ~ **into consideration** BANK *problems* berücksichtigen, GEN COMM berücksichtigen, in Betracht ziehen, in Erwägung ziehen; ~ **into custody** LAW verhaften; ~ **inventory** ACC Inventur machen, Bestände aufnehmen; ~ **a job** HRM Arbeit aufnehmen; ~ **the lead** GEN COMM *innovation* die Führung übernehmen, vorangehen; ~ **leave** GEN COMM, HRM in die Ferien gehen, Urlaub nehmen; ~ **legal action** LAW Klage im ordentlichen Zivilprozeß erheben; ~ **legal advice** GEN COMM, LAW Rechtsberatung in Anspruch nehmen; ~ **a loss** STOCK einen Verlust in Kauf nehmen; ~ **measures** GEN COMM, LAW Maßnahmen ergreifen; ~ **measures against** GEN COMM, LAW Maßnahmen ergreifen gegen, Maßnahmen treffen gegen; ~ **the minutes of** GEN COMM *a meeting* protokollieren; ~ **the offensive** GEN COMM in die Offensive gehen; ~ **one's pick** *infrml* GEN COMM seine Auswahl treffen, wählen; ~ **orders** GEN COMM Bestellungen annehmen; ~ **part in sth** GEN COMM an etw teilnehmen, sich an etw beteiligen; ~ **a partner** GEN COMM einen Partner aufnehmen, einen Teilhaber aufnehmen; ~ **place** GEN COMM stattfinden; ~ **a position** GEN COMM Stellung übernehmen, *point of view* Standpunkt beziehen, STOCK eine Wertpapierposition übernehmen; ~ **possession of** PROP Besitz ergreifen von; ~ **priority over** GEN COMM Vorrang haben vor; ~ **the rate** STOCK den angegebenen Börsenkurs akzeptieren; ~ **a reading** GEN COMM, IND *from equipment* ablesen; ~ **responsibility for sth** GEN COMM die Verantwortung für etw übernehmen, LAW die Haftung für etw übernehmen; ~ **a risk** GEN COMM ein Risiko eingehen; ~ **the risk of** GEN COMM wagen; ~ **a sample** MATH *statistics* eine Stichprobe entnehmen; ~ **sb to court** LAW gegen jdn prozessieren; ~ **sb's word for it** GEN COMM jdm glauben; ~ **shape** GEN COMM *idea* Gestalt annehmen, sich herauskristallisieren, Fortschritte machen; ~ **a share in sth** GEN COMM sich an etw beteiligen, zu etw beitragen; ~ **sides with** GEN COMM Partei ergreifen für; ~ **steps** GEN COMM Schritte ergreifen, Schritte unternehmen, MGMNT Schritte unternehmen; ~ **stock**

ACC Bestände aufnehmen, GEN COMM den Bestand aufnehmen, inventarisieren, Inventur machen; ~ **a straddle position** STOCK eine Straddle-Position erwerben; ~ **such steps as are considered necessary** LAW die als notwendig erachteten Schritte einleiten; ~ **a turn** GEN COMM *for the better, worse* eine Wendung nehmen; ~ **a vacation** *AmE* (*cf take a holiday BrE*) GEN COMM, HRM, LEIS Ferien machen, in die Ferien gehen, Urlaub nehmen; ~ **at face value** GEN COMM für bare Münze nehmen

take apart *vt* GEN COMM auseinandernehmen

take away *vt* GEN COMM *licence, passport* wegnehmen, abnehmen

take back *vt* GEN COMM *former employee* wiedereinstellen, *returned goods* zurücknehmen, HRM *former employee* wiedereinstellen

take down *vt* GEN COMM *in writing* aufzeichnen, notieren; ♦ ~ **in shorthand** ADMIN in Kurzschrift aufnehmen, stenographieren

take in *vt* *infrml* GEN COMM *work* übernehmen, *car* in Zahlung nehmen; ♦ ~ **extra work** HRM zusätzliche Arbeit annehmen; ~ **stock** GEN COMM Lager aufstocken, STOCK Aktien hereinnehmen

take off *vi* TRANSP *aircraft* starten; ♦ ~ **the market** GEN COMM, S&M vom Markt nehmen

take on *vt* GEN COMM *responsibility* übernehmen, HRM *staff* einstellen; ♦ ~ **additional staff** HRM zusätzliches Personal einstellen; ~ **hands** HRM zusätzliche Fabrikarbeiter einstellen; ~ **sb's job** GEN COMM jds Stelle einnehmen

take out *vt* BANK abschließen, *loan* aufnehmen, INS abschließen; ♦ ~ **an insurance policy** INS eine Versicherung abschließen, sich versichern lassen; ~ **a patent on sth** PATENTS *invention* ein Patent anmelden, ein Patent erwirken, etw patentieren lassen; ~ **a subscription** GEN COMM, MEDIA abonnieren

take over 1. *vt* GEN COMM *buy* aufkaufen, *company, business, stock* übernehmen; ♦ ~ **an issue** STOCK eine Emission übernehmen; ~ **liabilities** ACC Verbindlichkeiten übernehmen; ~ **sb's debts** GEN COMM jds Schulden übernehmen; **2.** *vi* GEN COMM *take control* die Leitung übernehmen; ♦ ~ **from sb** GEN COMM jdn ablösen

take up *vt* BANK *loan* aufnehmen, GEN COMM *challenge* annehmen, *stance* beziehen, einnehmen, *offer* Gebrauch machen von, WEL, *money, benefit* aufnehmen; ♦ ~ **legal residence** ADMIN, GEN COMM *person* Wohnsitz nehmen, *corporate domicile* Gesellschaftssitz nehmen, sich ordnungsgemäß niederlassen; ~ **sb's references** HRM jds Referenzen nachprüfen; ~ **a loan** FIN eine Anleihe aufnehmen; ~ **an option** STOCK eine Option übernehmen; ~ **a permanent place of residence** GEN COMM einen ständigen Wohnsitz nehmen, seßhaft werden; ~ **a position** GEN COMM einen Standpunkt vertreten; ~ **residence in a place** GEN COMM sich an einem Ort niederlassen; ~ **the slack** *infrml* ECON *organization* straffen; ~ **stocks** STOCK Aktien übernehmen

takeback: ~ **bargaining** *n* HRM Tarifverhandlungen, bei denen Rückzieher gemacht werden

take: ~-**home pay** *n* GEN COMM, HRM, TAX Nettolohn *m*

taken: **not to be** ~ **away** *phr* GEN COMM nicht mitzunehmen; **be** ~ **in** *phr* GEN COMM getäuscht werden, hereinfallen

takeoff *n* ECON Anstieg *m*, Aufstieg *m*, GEN COMM wirtschaftlicher Aufschwung *m*, TRANSP *of aircraft* Start *m*

takeout: ~ **price** *n* STOCK Ausstiegskurs *m*

takeover *n* ECON, GEN COMM Geschäftsübernahme *f*, Übernahme *f*, Aufkauf *m*, MGMNT, STOCK Übernahme *f*; ~ **bid** *n* (*TOB*) ACC, FIN, STOCK Übernahmeangebot *nt*

taker: ~ **for a put and call** *n* STOCK Optionsgeber *m* für eine Verkaufs- und Kaufoption

take: ~**-up** *n* FIN *of Treasury bills,* STOCK *of new issue* Aufnahme *f*, WEL *social work* Inanspruchnahme *f*; ~**-up rate** *n* FIN Zeichnungsrate *f*, STOCK Übernahmesatz *m*, WEL Anteil der Sozialhilfeberechtigten, der seine Ansprüche tatsächlich geltend macht

taking: ~ **all factors into account** *phr* GEN COMM unter Einbezug aller Faktoren; ~ **delivery** *n* STOCK *of commodities, securities* Abnahme *f*

TAL *abbr* (*technical assistance loan*) FIN Darlehen *nt* für technische Hilfe

talk: ~ **business** *phr* GEN COMM über das Geschäft reden, *get to the point* zur Sache kommen; ~ **sb into sth** *phr infrml* GEN COMM jdm etw aufschwatzen (*infrml*); ~ **shop** *phr* GEN COMM fachsimpeln

talking: ~ **head** *n* MEDIA *jarg television* Gesprächsleiter, in *m,f*

talks *n pl* GEN COMM, POL Gespräche *nt pl*

tally up *vt* GEN COMM zusammenrechnen, zusammen-zählen

tally: ~ **clerk** *n* HRM *shipping* Frachtkontrolleur, in *m,f*, Kontrolleur, in *m,f*, Tallymann *m*

tallyman *n* S&M Ladungskontrolleur *m*, TRANSP Ladungs-kontrolleur *m*, Staugutkontrolleur *m*

tally: ~ **register** *n* GEN COMM Kontrolliste *f*, Warenliste *f*; ~ **roll** *n* GEN COMM Kontrollstreifen *m*; ~ **sheet** *n* HRM Kontrolliste *f*, Strichliste *f*, TRANSP Zählblatt *nt*; ~ **trade** *n* BrE GEN COMM Abzahlungsgeschäft *nt*, Teilzahlungsgeschäft *nt*

talon *n* STOCK Erneuerungsschein *m*, Talon *m*

tamper: ~**-proof** *adj* GEN COMM, IND *machinery* fäl-schungssicher

TAN *abbr* AmE (*tax anticipation note*) TAX Steuergutschein *m*

tandem: ~ **account** *n* BANK Gemeinschaftskonto *nt*

tangible *adj* ACC materiell, greifbar, ECON greifbar, GEN COMM Sach-; ~ **asset** *n* GEN COMM Sachwert *m*; ~ **assets** *n pl* ACC Sachanlagen *f pl*, ECON materielles Vermögen *nt*; ~ **capital property** *n* ACC Sachanlagever-mögen *nt*, materieller Vermögenswert *m*; ~ **fixed assets** *n pl* ACC, FIN Sachanlagevermögen *nt*, Sachanlagen *f pl*, materielles Anlagevermögen *nt*; ~ **net worth** *n* ACC materielles Unternehmensvermögen *nt*, Betriebsvermö-gen *nt* abzüglich immaterieller Anlagewerte, Eigenkapital *nt* minus Firmenwert; ~ **personal property** *n* PROP persönliches Sachanlagevermögen *nt*; ~ **wealth** *n* ACC, GEN COMM Sachvermögen *nt*

tank *n* (*ta*) TRANSP Behälter *m*, Tank *m*; ~ **container** *n* TRANSP Tank-Container *m*

tanker *n* TRANSP Tanker *m*; ~ **broker** *n* HRM Tankschiff-broker *m*; ~ **lorry** *n* BrE (*cf tank truck AmE*) TRANSP Tankfahrzeug *nt*, Tankwagen *m*, Tanklastwagen *m*; ~ **motor vessel** *n* TRANSP Tankmotorschiff *nt*; ~ **own-ers' voluntary agreement concerning liability for oil**

pollution *n* (*TOVALOP*) ENVIR, INS, TRANSP freiwillige Übereinkunft der Eigentümer von Tankern bezüglich der Haftung bei Ölverschmutzung

tank: ~ **farm** *n* TRANSP Tankanlage *f*, Tanklager *nt*; ~ **pressure** *n* TRANSP Behälterdruck *m*

tanktainer *n* (*ta*) TRANSP Tanktainer *m*

tank: ~ **truck** *n* AmE (*cf tanker lorry BrE*) TRANSP Tankfahrzeug *nt*, Tankwagen *m*, Tanklastwagen *m*

tantième *n* HRM, MGMNT *share of profits* Tantieme *f*

tap 1. *n* BANK, STOCK Daueremission *f*; **2.** *vt* COMMS *telephone line* abhören, mithören, ENVIR *resources* ausbeuten, *oil resources* anzapfen, GEN COMM *resources* ausbeuten, erschließen, anzapfen, *market* erschließen, anzapfen (*infrml*); ♦ ~ **the market for** S&M den Markt erschließen für [+acc]

tap into *vt* COMMS *telephone line* abhören, mithören

tap: ~ **bill** *n* STOCK laufend emittierter Schatzwechsel *m*

tape 1. *n* COMMS, COMP, MEDIA Band *nt*; ♦ **the meeting is on** ~ GEN COMM die Sitzung wurde mitgeschnitten; **on** ~ MEDIA auf Band; **2.** *vt* ADMIN verkleben, COMMS, GEN COMM zukleben, MEDIA auf Band aufnehmen

tape: ~ **cartridge** *n* COMP Bandkassette *f*; ~ **drive** *n* COMP Bandlaufwerk *nt*; ~ **feed** *n* COMP Streifendurchlauf *m*; ~ **file** *n* COMP Banddatei *f*; ~ **library** *n* COMP, GEN COMM Bandarchiv *nt*; ~ **measure** *n* GEN COMM Bandmaß *nt*, Maßband *nt*; ~ **punch** *n* COMP Lochstreifenlocher *m*, Perforator *m*, GEN COMM Lochstreifenlocher *m*

taper *vi* TAX *tax relief* auslaufen

taper off *vi* ECON auslaufen, zu Ende gehen

tape: ~ **recording** *n* GEN COMM *of meeting*, MEDIA Magnetbandaufzeichnung *f*, Tonbandaufnahme *f*, Magnetbandaufnahme *f*

tapering *n* GEN COMM *form* Verjüngung *f*, HRM Abbau *m* des Lohngefälles

tape: ~ **unit** *n* MEDIA Tonbandanlage *f*

tap: ~ **issue** *n* BANK, STOCK Daueremission *f*, Tap-Emission *f*; ~ **stock** *n* BANK Regierungsanleihe *f*

tapping *n* ENVIR *oil resources*, GEN COMM *resources* Anzapfen *nt*, *telephone* Mithören *nt*

tare 1. *n* (*t.*) IND, TRANSP *packaging* Tara *f*; **2.** *vt* IND, TRANSP tarieren

tare: ~ **weight** *n* GEN COMM Verpackungsgewicht *nt*, TRANSP Eigengewicht *nt*, Leergewicht *nt*, Tara *f*

target 1. *n* COMP Ziel *nt*, GEN COMM Sollvorgabe *f*, Ziel *nt*, S&M Ziel *nt*, *customers* Zielgruppe *f*; **2.** *vt* GEN COMM *customer* abzielen auf, als Zielgruppe haben, *goal* zum Ziel bestimmen, anpeilen, anvisieren, S&M anstreben; ♦ ~ **at** GEN COMM, S&M abzielen auf [+acc]

target: ~ **audience** *n* GEN COMM Interessentenkreis *m*, Zielkundenkreis *m*, Zielpublikum *nt*, MEDIA, S&M *radio, music* Zielhörerschaft *f*, *books, newspapers* Zielleserschaft *f*, *television, films* Zielzuschauerschaft *f*; ~ **buyer** *n* GEN COMM, S&M Zielkäufer, in *m,f*; ~ **company** *n* GEN COMM, STOCK *takeover bid* Zielfirma *f*; ~ **computer** *n* COMP Zielcomputer *m*; ~ **cost** *n* ACC, ADMIN Sollkosten *pl*, Vorgabekosten *pl*; ~ **date** *n* GEN COMM angestrebter Termin *m*, Endtermin *m*, Fertigstellungstermin *m*, Zieltermin *m*, Stichtag *m*

targeted *adj* S&M *consumer base* gezielt; ~ **campaign** *n* S&M gezielte Kampagne *f*

target: ~ **field** *n* COMP Zielfeld *nt*; ~ **group index** *n* S&M Zielgruppenindex *m*

targeting *n* ECON gezielter Einsatz *m*, GEN COMM Zielbestimmung *f*, S&M Abzielen *nt*

target: ~ **language** *n* COMP *computing, linguistics*, GEN COMM Zielsprache *f*; ~ **market** *n* GEN COMM, S&M Zielmarkt *m*; ~ **marketing** *n* S&M zielorientiertes Marketing *nt*; ~ **price** *n* ECON Richtpreis *m*, Übernahmepreis *m*, Vertragspreis *m*, GEN COMM, S&M angestrebter Preis *m*, Orientierungspreis *m*, Richtpreis *m*, Zielpreis *m*; ~ **pricing** *n* GEN COMM Zielpreisbildung *f*, Zielpreisfestsetzung *f*; ~ **range** *n* ECON Zielkorridor *m*; ~ **rate** *n* STOCK *interest rate futures* angestrebter Zinssatz *m*; ~ **rate of return** *n* FIN Rentabilitätsziel *nt*, angestrebte Kapitalverzinsung *f*; ~ **risk** *n* INS attraktives Risiko *nt*; ~ **segment** *n* S&M *marketing* Zielsegment *nt*, Teilziel *nt*; ~ **setting** *n* GEN COMM Zielstellung *f*, S&M Zielsetzung *f*; ~ **variable** *n* ECON Zielvariable *f*, Zwischenzielvariable *f*; ~ **zone** *n* ECON *exchange rates* Zielbereich *m*, Zielzone *f*

tariff *n* ECON Preisliste *f*, Preisverzeichnis *nt*, *customs* Zolltarif *m*, GEN COMM Tarif *m*, *price list* Preisliste *f*, IMP/EXP Zolltarif *m*, Zolltarifsatz *m*, Zollgebühr *f*, TAX Zoll *m*

Tariff: ~ **Act** *n* BrE IMP/EXP Zollgesetz *nt*

tariff: ~ **barrier** *n* ECON, IMP/EXP Zollschranke *f*; ~ **expenditure** *n* ACC Tarifausgaben *f pl*; ~-**free** *adj* IMP/EXP zollfrei

tariffication *n* FIN, TAX *EU* Tariffestsetzung *f*, Tarifierung *f*

tariff: ~ **law** *n* IMP/EXP Zollgesetz *nt*; ~ **legislation** *n* LAW Zollgesetzgebung *f*; ~ **level** *n* TAX Tarifniveau *nt*; ~ **protection** *n* ECON, IMP/EXP Schutz *m* durch Zölle, Zollschutz *m*; ~ **quota** *n* ECON, GEN COMM, IMP/EXP Zollkontingent *nt*; ~ **rate** *n* IMP/EXP Tarifsatz *m*, Zollsatz *m*; ~ **schedule** *n* GEN COMM Gebührentabelle *f*, IMP/EXP Zolltarif *m*; ~ **wall** *n* GEN COMM Zollschranke *f*, IMP/EXP Zollmauer *f*, Zollschranke *f*; ~ **war** *n* GEN COMM Tarifkampf *m*, Zollkrieg *m*

taring *n* IND, TRANSP Tarierung *f*

task 1. *n* COMP Aufgabe *f*, GEN COMM Arbeit *f*, Aufgabe *f*, Auftrag *m*, HRM Aufgabe *f*; **2.** ~ **sb with sth** ECON, GEN COMM, POL jdn mit etw betrauen, jdn zu etw heranziehen

task: ~ **closure** *n* GEN COMM ein Geschäft zum Abschluß führen; ~ **flexibility** *n* HRM Einsatzflexibilität *f*; ~ **force** *n* HRM *industry* im Akkord arbeitende Belegschaft *f*; ~ **initiation** *n* COMP Aufgabeninitiierung *f*; ~ **management** *n* COMP, GEN COMM, MGMNT Aufgabenmanagement *nt*, Aufgabenverwaltung *f*; ~ **scheduling** *n* COMP, GEN COMM, MGMNT Arbeitsablaufplanung *f*, Arbeitsplanung *f*; ~ **setting** *n* GEN COMM Aufgabenerteilung *f*, Aufgabenstellung *f*; ~ **work** *n* GEN COMM Akkordarbeit *f*, Arbeitspensum *nt*

taste *n* ECON Bedürfnis *nt*, Bedarf *m*, S&M *customer preferences* Geschmack *m*

TAT *abbr* (*transitional automated ticket*) TRANSP automatisiertes Übergangsticket *nt*, Übergangsautomatenschein *m*

TAURUS *abbr* BrE *obs* (*Transfer & Automated Registration of Uncertified Stock*) STOCK TAURUS

TAWB *abbr* (*through air waybill*) IMP/EXP, TRANSP Durchluftfrachtbrief *m*, Transitluftfrachtbrief *m*

tax *n* ECON, TAX Abgabe *f*, Staatssteuer *f*, Steuer *f*, *fee* Taxe *f*, *contribution* Beitrag *m*, Gebühr *f*; ~ **abatement** *n* TAX Steuernachlaß *m*

taxable *adj* LAW, TAX abgabenpflichtig, steuerpflichtig; ~ **base** *n* TAX Bemessungsgrundlage *f*; ~ **capacity** *n* ECON, TAX Steuerkraft *f*, *taxation principle* steuerliche Leistungsfähigkeit *f*, steuerliche Belastungsgrenze *f*; ~ **event** *n* LAW, TAX Steuertatbestand *m*, Besteuerungsgegenstand *m*; ~ **income** *n* ACC, ECON, GEN COMM, TAX steuerpflichtiges Einkommen *nt*, zu versteuerndes Einkommen *nt*; ~ **municipal bond** *n* TAX steuerpflichtige Anleihe eines Bundesstaates oder einer Gemeinde; ~ **net gain** *n* ACC Nettosteuergewinn *m*; ~ **profit** *n* ACC steuerpflichtiger Gewinn *m*; ~ **quota** *n* TAX steuerpflichtige Quote *f*; ~ **social security benefit** *n* TAX steuerpflichtige Sozialversicherungsleistung *f*; ~ **value** *n* TAX Steuerwert *m*

tax: ~ **adjustment** *n* TAX Steuerbereinigung *f*, Steuerberichtigung *f*; ~ **administration** *n* ADMIN Steuerverwaltung *f*; ~ **anticipation bill** *n* AmE (*TAB*) (*cf tax credit certificate BrE*) TAX Steuergutschein *m*; ~ **anticipation note** *n* AmE (*TAN*) TAX Steuergutschein *m*; ~ **appeal** *n* TAX Einspruch *m* gegen einen Steuerbescheid; ~ **arrears** *n pl* TAX Steuerrückstände *m pl*; ~ **assessment** *n* TAX Steuerveranlagung *f*

taxation *n* ECON, TAX Besteuerung *f*; ~ **creditor** *n* ACC Steuergläubiger, in *m,f*; ~ **office** *n* TAX Finanzamt *nt*; ~ **policy** *n* TAX Steuerpolitik *f*

tax: ~ **authority** *n* TAX Finanzbehörde *f*, Steuerbehörde *f*; ~ **avoidance** *n* ECON, GEN COMM, TAX Steuerausweichung *f*, Steuerumgehung *f*, Steuervermeidung *f*; ~-**based incomes policy** *n* (*TIP*) ECON, POL steuerorientierte Einkommenspolitik *f*; ~ **basis** *n* ECON, TAX Steuerbemessungsgrundlage *f*; ~ **bond** *n* TAX Steuerbürgschaft *f*; ~-**bracket creep** *n* ECON heimliche Steuererhöhung *f*, schleichende Steuererhöhung *f*; ~ **burden** *n* TAX Steuerbelastung *f*, Steuerlast *f*; ~ **capitalization** *n* ECON, TAX Steueramortisation *f*, Steuertilgung *f*; ~ **category** *n* TAX Steuerklasse *f*; ~ **charge** *n* TAX Steuerlast *f*; ~ **collector** *n* GEN COMM, TAX *person* Steuerbeamte(r) *m* [decl. as adj], Steuerbeamtin *f*, *authority* Finanzamt *nt*, Steuerbehörde *f*; ~ **concession** *n* TAX steuerliche Vergünstigung *f*, Steuererleichterung *f*, Steuervergünstigung *f*; ~ **consultant** *n* TAX Steuerberater, in *m,f*; ~ **consultant's bureau** *n* TAX Steuerberaterbüro *nt*; ~ **court** *n* TAX Finanzgericht *nt*; ~ **credit** *n* ECON Steueranrechnung *f*, Steuergutschrift *f*, TAX Steueranrechnung *f*, Steuergutschrift *f*, Anrechnung *f* der Körperschaftsteuer; ~ **credit certificate** *n* BrE (*cf tax credit anticipation bill AmE*) TAX Steuergutschein *m*; ~ **declaration** *n* TAX Steuererklärung *f*; ~-**deductible** *adj* ACC, TAX abzugsfähig, steuerlich abzugsfähig; ~-**deductible expenditure** *n* AmE, ~-**deductible expenses** *n pl* BrE TAX steuerlich abzugsfähige Ausgaben *f pl*; ~ **deduction** *n* TAX Steuerabzug *m*, steuerliche Absetzung *f*; ~ **disc** BrE, ~ **disk** AmE TAX *in vehicle* Steuermarke *f*; ~ **district** *n* BrE TAX Steuerbezirk *m*; ~ **dodger** *n infrml* TAX Steuerumgeher *m*; ~ **dodging** *n infrml* TAX Steuerumgehung *f*; ~ **domicile** *n* TAX steuerlicher Wohnsitz *m*

taxed: ~ **at source** *adj* ACC, FIN, TAX quellenbesteuert

tax: ~-**efficient** *adj* TAX steuerlich wirksam; ~-**efficient investment** *n* TAX steuerwirksame Investition *f*; ~ **elasticity** *n* TAX Steuerelastizität *f*; ~ **equalization account** *n* TAX Steuerausgleichskonto *nt*; ~ **equalization scheme** *n* TAX *maintained by foreign employers* Steuerausgleichsplan *m*

Tax: ~ **Equity and Fiscal Responsibilty Act** *n AmE* (*TEFRA*) TAX Gesetz über Steuerausgleich und fiskalische Verantwortung

tax: ~ **erosion** *n* TAX Aushöhlung *f* der Steuerbasis

taxes: ~ **actually paid** *n pl* ACC, TAX wirklich bezahlte Steuern *f pl*; ~ **due** *n pl* ACC fällige Steuern *f pl*; ~ **from income and property** *n pl* FIN, TAX Besitzsteuern *f pl*; ~ **withheld** *n pl* ACC, TAX einbehaltene Steuern *f pl*

tax: ~ **evasion** *n* TAX Steuerhinterziehung *f*; ~~**exempt** *adj* TAX steuerfrei; ~ **exemption** *n* TAX Befreiung *f*, Freibetrag *m*, Steuerbefreiung *f*, Steuerfreiheit *f*; ~~**exempt security** *n* TAX steuerfreies Wertpapier *nt*

Tax: ~ **Exempt Special Savings Account** *n BrE* (*TESSA*) BANK, TAX steuerfreies Sparkonto *nt*

tax: ~ **exile** *n* TAX Steuerexil *nt*; ~ **expenditure** *n* ECON Steueraufwendung *f*, TAX Steueraufwand *m*, Steueraufwendung *f*

taxflation *n jarg* ECON, TAX Steuerinflation *f*

tax: ~ **foreclosure** *n* TAX Steuerpfändung *f*; ~~**free** *adj* (*cf duty-free BrE*) IMP/EXP *goods* nicht zollpflichtig, zollfrei, TAX steuerfrei; ~~**free allowance** *n* TAX steuerfreier Betrag *m*; ~~**free amount** *n* TAX Freibetrag *m*, Steuerfreibetrag *m*; ~~**free income** *n* TAX steuerfreies Einkommen *nt*; ~~**free shop** *n AmE* (*cf duty-free shop BrE*) IMP/EXP Geschäft *nt* für zollfreie Waren, Zollfreiladen *m*, LEIS Duty-Free-Laden *m*, Duty-Free-Shop *m*, Geschäft *nt* für zollfreie Waren, Laden *m* für zollfreie Waren; ~ **guidelines** *n pl* TAX Steuerrichtlinien *f pl*; ~ **harmonization** *n* ECON, TAX Steuerharmonisierung *f*; ~ **haven** *n* ECON, TAX Steueroase *f*; ~ **holiday** *n* TAX Steuerfreijahre *nt pl*

taxi *n BrE* (*cf cab AmE*) TRANSP Taxi *nt*; ~ **charge** *BrE* (*cf cab charge AmE*) *n* TRANSP Taxigebühr *f*

tax: ~ **immunity** *n* ECON, TAX Steuerimmunität *f*; ~ **incentive** *n* ECON, TAX steuerlicher Anreiz *m*, Steueranreiz *m*; ~ **incidence** *n* ECON, TAX Steuerinzidenz *f*; ~ **inflation** *n* ECON Steuerinflation *f*; ~ **influence** *n* ACC Steuerwirkung *f*; ~ **installment** *AmE*, ~ **instalment** *BrE n* TAX Steuerrate *f*

taxi: ~ **rank** *n BrE* (*cf cab stand AmE*) TRANSP Taxistand *m*; ~ **stand** *n BrE* (*cf cab stand AmE*) TRANSP Taxistand *m*

tax: ~ **lien** *n* TAX Pfandrecht *nt* der Steuerbehörde, Steuerpfandrecht *nt*; ~ **load** *n* TAX Steuerbelastung *f*, Steuerlast *f*; ~ **and loan account** *n* BANK Konto der US-Regierung bei den Geschäftsbanken; ~ **loophole** *n* TAX Steuerlücke *f*, Steuerschlupfloch *nt*; ~ **loss carryback** *n* ACC, TAX steuerlicher Verlustrücktrag *m*; ~ **loss carryforward** *n* TAX steuerlicher Verlustvortrag *m*

taxman *n* TAX Finanzamt *nt*, Steuerbehörde *f*

tax: ~ **offset** *n* TAX Steueraufrechnung *f*; ~ **on speculative profits** *n* TAX Spekulationssteuer *f*; ~ **paid** *phr* ACC, ECON, GEN COMM, TAX versteuert

taxpayer *n* ACC, GEN COMM, TAX Steuerzahler *m*; ~'**s reference number** *n* TAX Steuernummer *f*

tax: ~ **planning** *n* TAX Steuerplanung *f*; ~ **position** *n* TAX Steuerposition *f*; ~ **preference item** *n* TAX Wareneinheit *f* mit Steuerpräferenz; ~ **pressure** *n* TAX steuerlicher Druck *m*; ~ **privilege** *n* TAX Steuervergünstigung *f*; ~~**privileged** *adj* TAX steuerbegünstigt; ~ **proposal** *n* TAX geplante Steuermaßnahme *f*, Steuervorschlag *m*; ~ **provision** *n* ACC, TAX Steuerrückstellung *f*; ~ **purpose** *n* ACC Steuerzweck *f*; ~ **rate** *n* TAX Steuersatz *m*; ~ **receipt** *n* TAX

Steueraufkommen *nt*, Steuereinnahmen *f pl*; ~ **reform** *n* ECON, POL, TAX Steuerreform *f*; ~ **reform act** *n* TAX Steuerreformgesetz *nt*; ~ **refund** *n* TAX Steuerrückzahlung *f*; ~ **relief** *n* TAX Steuererleichterung *f*, Steuernachlaß *m*, Steuervergünstigung *f*, Freibetrag *m*, Steuerfreibetrag *m*; ~ **relief at source** *n* TAX Steuererleichterung *f* an der Quelle; ~ **relief for business cars** *n* TAX Steuererleichterung *f* für Firmenwagen; ~ **remission** *n* TAX Steuererlaß *m*; ~~**reserve certificate** *n* TAX Steuergutschein *m*; ~ **restriction** *n* TAX steuerliche Beschränkung *f*; ~ **return** *n* TAX Steuererklärung *f*; ~ **return depreciation** *n* ACC, TAX steuerliche Abschreibung *f*; ~ **roll** *n* TAX Steuerliste *f*, Steuerrolle *f*; ~ **sale** *n* TAX *property* Zwangsversteigerung *f* zur Deckung von Steuerschulden; ~ **schedule** *n* TAX Steuertarif *m*; ~ **selling** *n* TAX steuerlich motivierter Absatz *m* von Wertpapieren; ~~**sheltered** *adj* TAX steuerbegünstigt; ~~**sheltered account** *n* BANK, TAX steuerbegünstigtes Anlagekonto *nt*; ~ **software** *n* COMP, TAX Steuersoftware *f*; ~ **stamp** *n* TAX Steuermarke *f*; ~ **stimuli** *n pl* TAX Steueranreize *m pl*; ~ **strategy** *n* ECON, TAX Steuerstrategie *f*; ~ **structure** *n* ECON, TAX Steuerstruktur *f*; ~ **take** *n* TAX Steueraufkommen *nt*; ~ **threshold** *n* TAX Steuereingangsstufe *f*, Steuergrundfreibetrag *m*; ~ **transparency** *n* TAX Steuertransparenz *f*; ~ **umbrella** *n* TAX Nichtbesteuerung *f*; ~ **unit** *n* ECON, TAX Besteuerungseinheit *f*; ~ **voucher** *n* STOCK, TAX Steuergutschein *m*, Steuergutschrift *f*, Steuerbeleg *m*; ~ **wedge** *n* ECON Steuerkeil *m*; ~ **write-off** *n* ACC, TAX steuerliche Abschreibung *f*; ~ **year** *n* ACC, FIN, GEN COMM, TAX Haushaltsjahr *nt*, Steuerjahr *nt*, Veranlagungszeitraum *m* (*Vz.*) (*frml*), Wirtschaftsjahr *nt*; ~ **yield** *n* TAX Steueraufkommen *nt*

T-bill *n AmE* (*Treasury bill*) FIN Schatzwechsel *m*, Schatzwechsel *m* mit 3-monatiger Laufzeit

TBN *abbr* (*total base number*) IND TBN (*Gesamtbasenzahl*)

TC *abbr* (*till canceled AmE, till cancelled BrE*) S&M *advertising* b. a. W. (*bis auf Widerruf*), bis zur Stornierung

T/C *abbr* GEN COMM (*till countermanded*) b.a.W. (*bis auf Widerruf*), bis zur Stornierung, TRANSP (*time charter*) Zeitcharter *f*

TCDC *abbr* (*technical cooperation among developing countries*) ECON United Nations initiative technische Zusammenarbeit *f* zwischen den Entwicklungsländern

TDA *abbr* (*transport distribution analysis*) TRANSP Transportverteilungsanalyse *f*

TDED *abbr* (*Trade Data Elements Directory*) ECON Branchenverzeichnis *nt*

TDI *abbr* (*Trade Data Interchange*) ECON Austausch *m* von Handelsdaten

TDP *abbr* (*tradeable discharge permit*) ECON handelbares Emissionszertifikat *nt*

teaching: ~ **company** *n* WEL Ausbildungsstätte *f*; ~ **machine** *n* HRM, IND, WEL Lehrmaschine *f*

team *n* HRM, MGMNT Team *nt*, Mannschaft *f*, TRANSP Mannschaft *f*; ~ **briefing** *n* MGMNT Gruppenbesprechung *f*, Gruppeneinweisung *f*, Teambesprechung *f*; ~ **building** *n* COMP Zusammenstellung *f* einer oder mehrerer Arbeitsgruppen, HRM, MGMNT Teambildung *f*; ~ **leader** *n* HRM, MGMNT Teamleiter, in *m,f*, Gruppenleiter, in *m,f*,

Mannschaftsführer, in *m,f*; ~ **player** *n* HRM, MGMNT Teamplayer *m*; ~ **spirit** *n* HRM Gemeinschaftssinn *m*

Teamsters: **the** ~ *n pl* HRM *union* amerikanische Gewerkschaft für Fern- und LKW-Fahrer

team: ~ **theory** *n* ECON Gruppentheorie *f*

teamwork *n* HRM, MGMNT Teamarbeit *f*

tear: **~-off calendar** *n* GEN COMM Abreißkalender *m*; **~-off coupon** *n* GEN COMM Abreißkupon *m*; **~-proof** *adj* IND reißfest; ~ **strip** *n* GEN COMM Belegstreifen *m*

teaser: ~ **ad** *n* S&M Rätselreklame *f*; ~ **campaign** *n* S&M *advertising* Neugier erregende Kampagne *f*; ~ **rate** *n* FIN Anreizrate *f*

TEC *abbr* (*Training and Enterprise Council*) HRM *in England and Wales* britische Behörde zur Förderung von Ausbildung und Unternehmensgeist

technical *adj* GEN COMM fachlich, fachmännisch, fachspezifisch, technisch; ~ **analysis** *n* STOCK technische Aktienanalyse *f*; ~ **analyst** *n* STOCK Wertpapieranalytiker, in *m,f*; ~ **assistance** *n* COMP, IND technische Hilfe *f*; ~ **assistance loan** *n* (*TAL*) FIN Darlehen *nt* für technische Hilfe; ~ **assistant** *n* (*TA*) HRM technischer Assistent *m*, technische Assistentin *f*; ~ **barrier** *n* POL *to trade in European Community* technische Handelsschranke *f*, technisches Handelshemmnis *nt*; ~ **barrier to trade** *n* ECON, IMP/EXP technisches Handelshemmnis *nt*; ~ **college** *n* BrE WEL Fachhochschule *f*; ~ **cooperation** *n* IND *overseas development* technische Zusammenarbeit *f*; ~ **cooperation among developing countries** *n* (*TCDC*) ECON *United Nations* technische Zusammenarbeit *f* zwischen den Entwicklungsländern; ~ **data** *n pl* GEN COMM technische Daten *pl*, IND technische Unterlagen *f pl*; ~ **director** *n* HRM, MGMNT Direktor, in *m,f* der technischen Abteilung, technischer Direktor *m*, technische Direktorin *f*; ~ **education institution** *n* WEL Fachschule *f*; ~ **efficiency** *n* ECON physischer Wirkungsgrad *m*, IND Produktivität *f*; ~ **field** *n* PATENTS technischer Bereich *m*; ~ **help to exporters** *n* (*THE*) IMP/EXP technische Hilfe *f* für Exportfirmen; ~ **hitch** *n* GEN COMM, IND technische Schwierigkeit *f*, technische Störung *f*

technicality *n* GEN COMM, IND fachliches Detail *nt*, technische Einzelheit *f*, *formality* Formsache *f*

technical: ~ **knowledge** *n* GEN COMM, HRM Fachkenntnisse *f pl*; ~ **language** *n* GEN COMM Fachsprache *f*

technically *adv* GEN COMM technisch, fachlich

technical: ~ **manager** *n* HRM, MGMNT technischer Direktor *m*, technische Direktorin *f*, technischer Leiter *m*, technische Leiterin *f*; ~ **mastery** *n* GEN COMM fachliches Können *nt*, fachliche Perfektion *f*; ~ **point** *n* LAW technische Frage *f*; ~ **press** *n* S&M Fachpresse *f*; ~ **profile** *n* GEN COMM technisches Profil *nt*; ~ **salesman** *n* HRM technischer Verkäufer *m*, technischer Vertreter *m*; ~ **salesperson** *n* HRM technischer Verkäufer *m*, technische Verkäuferin *f*, technischer Vertreter *m*, technische Verteterin *f*; ~ **saleswoman** *n* HRM technische Verkäuferin *f*, technische Vertreterin *f*; ~ **support** *n* COMP, IND technische Betreuung *f*, *for developing countries* technische Hilfeleistung *f*, technische Unterstützung *f*; ~ **university** *n* WEL Technische Hochschule *f* (*TH*)

technics *n* IND *production* Technologie *f*

technique *n* IND Methode *f*, Verfahren *nt*

technocratic *adj* GEN COMM technokratisch

technological *adj* IND technologisch; ~ **advance** *n* IND technischer Fortschritt *m*, technologischer Fortschritt *m*; ~ **change** *n* IND Änderung *f* der Technologie, technologischer Wandel *m*; ~ **cooperation** *n* IND technologische Zusammenarbeit *f*; ~ **edge** *n* IND technologischer Vorsprung *m*; ~ **forecast** *n* IND technologische Prognose *f*; ~ **forecasting** *n* IND technologische Prognose *f*; ~ **gap** *n* IND technische Lücke *f*, technischer Rückstand *m*; ~ **innovation** *n* IND technische Neuerung *f*, technologische Innovation *f*, technologische Verbesserung *f*

technologically *adv* IND technologisch; ~ **advanced** *adj* ECON, IND mit hochentwickelter Technologie, mit modernster Technologie, technisch fortgeschritten, technologisch hochentwickelt

technological: ~ **obsolescence** *n* IND *product* technische Veralterung *f*, entwicklungsbedingtes Überholtsein *nt*; ~ **progress** *n* IND technischer Fortschritt *m*; ~ **rent** *n* ECON technologische Rente *f*

technology *n* IND Technik *f*, Technologie *f*; ~ **and market interface** *n* GEN COMM Verhältnis *nt* von Technologie und Markt; **~-based industry** *n* IND Hochtechnologie-Industrie *f*; ~ **cooperation** *n* GEN COMM technologische Zusammenarbeit *f*; ~ **park** *n* IND Technologiepark *m*, Technologiezentrum *nt*; ~ **transfer** *n* (*TT*) ECON, IND Technologietransfer *m*

TEFRA *abbr* AmE (*Tax Equity and Fiscal Responsibilty Act*) TAX Gesetz über Steuerausgleich und fiskalische Verantwortung

tel. *abbr* (*telephone*) COMMS, GEN COMM Tel. (*Telefon*); ~ **add.** *abbr* (*telephone address*) COMMS Fernsprechadresse *f*

telcon *n* AmE *infrml* (*telephone conversation*) COMMS Telefongespräch *nt*

tele- *pref* COMMS, COMP, ECON Tele-

telebanking *n* BANK Telebanking *nt*

telecast *n* AmE MEDIA TV Fernsehsendung *f*

telecommunicate *vt* COMMS fernmündlich mitteilen

telecommunication *n* COMMS Telekommunikation *f*, Datenfernübertragung *f* (*DFÜ*); ~ **network** *n* COMMS Fernmeldenetz *nt*

telecommunications *n pl* COMMS Telekommunikation *f*, Fernmeldetechnik *f*, Fernmeldewesen *nt*; ~ **satellite** *n* COMMS Fernmeldesatellit *m*, Nachrichtensatellit *m*

telecommunication: ~ **technology** *n* COMMS Fernmeldetechnik *f*

telecommuting *n* COMP, HRM Telearbeit *f*

teleconference *n* COMMS, COMP, S&M Telekonferenz *f*, Fernsprechkonferenz *f*

telegram *n* COMMS Telegramm *nt*

telegraph *n* COMMS Telegraf *m*

telegraphic *adj* COMMS telegrafisch; ~ **address** *n* (*TA*) COMMS telegrafische Adresse *f*, Telegrammadresse *f*; ~ **money order** *n* (*TMO*) BANK, FIN telegrafische Geldanweisung *f*, telegrafische Geldüberweisung *f*; ~ **transfer** *n* (*TT*) BANK, FIN telegrafische Auszahlung *f*, telegrafische Überweisung *f*

telemarket *n* COMMS, S&M Telemarkt *m*

telemarketing *n* COMMS, FIN, S&M Telemarketing *nt*

telematics *n* COMMS, COMP Telekommunikation *f* und Automatik *f* (*Telematik*)

telemessage *n* (*TMESS*) COMMS Telegramm *nt*, telegraphische Mitteilung *f*

teleordering *n* COMP, S&M elektronische Bestellung *f*

telephone 1. *n* (*tel.*) COMMS, GEN COMM Fernsprecher *m* (*frml*), Telefon *nt* (*Tel.*); ♦ **by ~** COMMS telefonisch; **over the ~** COMMS *talk, negotiate* am Telefon, per Telefon, telefonisch; **2.** *vt* COMMS, GEN COMM anrufen

telephone: **~ address** *n* (*tel. add.*) COMMS Fernsprechadresse *f*; **~ answering service** *n* COMMS, S&M Anrufbeantwortungsdienst *m*; **~ bill** *n* COMMS Telefonrechnung *f*; **~ book** *n* COMMS Fernsprechteilnehmerverzeichnis *nt*, Telefonbuch *nt*; **~ booking** *n* LEIS *theatre* telefonische Reservierung *f*; **~ booth** *n* COMMS Telefonzelle *f*; **~ box** *n* COMMS Telefonzelle *f*; **~ charges** *n pl* COMMS Fernsprechgebühren *f pl*; **~ conversation** *n* (*telcon AmE*) COMMS Telefongespräch *nt*; **~ dealing** *n* STOCK Telefonhandel *m*; **~ directory** *n* COMMS Fernsprechteilnehmerverzeichnis *nt*, Telefonbuch *nt*, Telefonverzeichnis *nt*; **~ exchange** *n* COMMS Fernmeldeamt *nt*, Fernsprechvermittlung *f*; **~ extension** *n* (*X*) COMMS Nebenanschluß *m*, Nebenstelle *f*; **~ interviewing** *n* S&M *market research* telefonische Befragung *f*; **~ message** *n* COMMS telefonische Nachricht *f*; **~ number** *n* (*tel. no.*) COMMS, GEN COMM Anschlußnummer *f*, Telefonnummer *f* (*Tel. Nr.*); **~ operator** *n* COMMS Auskunft *f*, Telefonist, in *m,f*, HRM Telefonist, in *m,f*; **~ rates** *n pl AmE* COMMS Fernsprechgebühren *f pl*; **~ receiver** *n* COMMS Telefonhörer *m*; **~ sales** *n pl* S&M Telefonverkauf *m*; **~ selling** *n* S&M Telefonverkauf *m*; **~ subscriber** *n* COMMS Anschlußteilnehmer, in *m,f*, Fernsprechteilnehmer, in *m,f*; **~ tapping** *n* COMMS, COMP, GEN COMM Abhören *nt*, Anzapfen *nt* der Telefonleitung; **~ traffic** *n* COMMS, STOCK Telefonverkehr *m*

telephonic *adj* COMMS telefonisch

telephony *n* COMMS Fernsprechwesen *nt*

teleprinter *n BrE* (*cf teletypewriter AmE*) ADMIN, COMMS Fernschreiber *m*, Fernschreibgerät *nt*; **~ message** *n BrE* (*cf teletype message AmE*) ADMIN, COMMS Fernschreiben *nt*, Telex *nt*

teleprocessing *n* ADMIN Datenfernverarbeitung *f*, COMP Fernverarbeitung *f*

telesales *n* COMMS, FIN *division* Televerkauf *m*, S&M *division* Televerkauf *m*, *transactions* Telefonverkauf *m*; **~ person** *n* COMMS, FIN, S&M Televerkaufsperson *f*

teleshopping *n* FIN Teleshopping *nt*

teletex *n* COMP, MEDIA *broadcast* nicht dialogfähiges Videotextsystem *nt*, Teletext® *m*, Bildschirmtext *m* (*Btx*), Videotext *m*

Teletex: **~ Output of Price Information by Computer** *n BrE* (*TOPIC*) STOCK elektronisches Börseninformationssystem der Londoner Börse

Teletext® *n* COMP, MEDIA *broadcast* nicht dialogfähiges Videotextsystem *nt*, Teletext® *m*, Bildschirmtext *m* (*Btx*), Videotext *m*

teletype: **~ message** *n AmE* (*cf teleprinter message BrE*) ADMIN, COMMS Fernschreiben *nt*, Telex *nt*; **~ operator** *n AmE* ADMIN, COMMS Fernschreiber, in *m,f*

teletyper *n AmE* ADMIN, COMMS *machine* Fernschreiber *m*, Fernschreibgerät *nt*, *person* Fernschreiber, in *m,f*

teletypewriter *n AmE* (*cf teleprinter BrE*) ADMIN, COMMS Fernschreiber *m*, Fernschreibgerät *nt*

teletypist *n AmE* ADMIN, COMMS Fernschreiber, in *m,f*

television *n* (*TV*) MEDIA Fernsehen *nt* (*FS*), Television *f* (*TV*); **~ advertising** *n* MEDIA, S&M Fernsehwerbung *f*; **~ commercial** *n* MEDIA, S&M Werbesendung *f* im Fernsehen; **~ consumer audit** *n* S&M *market research* Überprüfung *f* der Fernsehkonsumenten; **~ network** *n* MEDIA Fernsehnetz *nt*; **~ rating** *n* (*TVR*) MEDIA, S&M Bewertung *f* von Fernsehsendungen durch Zuschauer; **~ screen** *n* COMMS, GEN COMM Fernsehbildschirm *m*, Fernsehschirm *m*; **~ support** *n* S&M *advertising* Fernsehunterstützung *f*

televisual: **~ audience data** *n pl* MEDIA, S&M Fernsehzuschauerdaten *nt pl*, Informationen *f pl* über Fernsehzuschauerschaft, TV-Media-Daten *nt pl*

telework *n* COMP, HRM Telearbeit *f*

teleworker *n* COMP, HRM Telearbeiter, in *m,f*

telewriter *n* ADMIN, COMMS *machine* Fernschreiber *m*, Fernschreibgerät *nt*

telex *n* (*tx.*) ADMIN, COMMS *machine* Telex *nt*, Fernschreiber *m*, *message* Fernschreiben *nt*; **~ operator** *n* ADMIN, COMMS Fernschreiber, in *m,f*

tel.: **~ no.** *abbr* (*telephone number*) COMMS, GEN COMM Anschlußnummer *f*, Tel. Nr. (*Telefonnummer*)

tel: **~ quel** *phr* GEN COMM tel quel; **~ quel rate** *n* STOCK Tel-quel-Kurs *m*

teller *n* BANK Kassierer, in *m,f*

temp 1. *n* GEN COMM, HRM Aushilfskraft *f*, Zeitarbeitskraft *f*, *secretary* Aushilfssekretär, in *m,f*; **2.** *vi* GEN COMM, HRM Zeitarbeit machen, *as secretary* als Aushilfssekretär arbeiten

temperature: **~-controlled transport** *n* TRANSP isothermischer Kühltransport *m*

temping: **~ agency** *n* GEN COMM, HRM Stellenvermittlung *f* für Aushilfskräfte

template *n* COMP Schablone *f*, GEN COMM Muster *nt*, Schablone *f*, IND *design* Modell *nt*, Schablone *f*

temporal *adj* GEN COMM zeitlich; **~ method** *n* ACC Temporalmethode *f*, *of currency translation for consolidated accounts* Methode zur Umrechnung von Fremdwährungspositionen in der konsolidierten Bilanz

temporarily *adv* GEN COMM provisorisch, zeitweilig

temporary *adj* GEN COMM behelfsmäßig, einstweilig, temporär, vorübergehend, vorläufig, zeitweilig, provisorisch; **~ difference** *n* ACC *deferred tax* vorläufige Differenz *f*; **~ employment** *n* GEN COMM, HRM Aushilfsarbeit *f*; **~ equilibrium** *n* ECON temporäres Gleichgewicht *nt*; **~ importation** *n* IMP/EXP vorübergehende Einfuhr *f*; **~ injunction** *n* LAW gerichtliche einstweilige Verfügung *f*; **~ measure** *n* GEN COMM Provisorium *nt*; **~ residence** *n* LAW *permit* vorübergehende Aufenthaltsgenehmigung *m*; **~ residence permit** *n* WEL zeitlich beschränkte Aufenthaltsgenehmigung *f*; **~ residence visa** *n* WEL zeitlich beschränktes Aufenthaltsvisum *nt*; **~ resident** *n* WEL nur vorübergehend Ansässige(r) *mf* [decl. as adj]; **~ secretary** *n* HRM Aushilfssekretär, in *m,f*; **~ status** *n* LAW vorläufiger Status *m*; **~ transfer** *n* HRM Abstellung *f*; **~ unemployment** *n* HRM vorübergehende Arbeitslosigkeit *f*; **~ work** *n* GEN COMM, HRM Aushilfsarbeit *f*; **~ worker** *n* GEN COMM, HRM Aushilfe *f*, Aushilfskraft *f*, Zeitarbeitskraft *f*, Aushilfsarbeiter, in *m,f*

tenancy *n* LAW, PROP *of house, flat* Mietverhältnis *nt*, *of farm, shop* Pachtverhältnis *nt*; **~ at will** *n* LAW, PROP jederzeit fristlos kündbares Mietverhältnis *nt*, jederzeit fristlos kündbares Pachtverhältnis *nt*; **~ by the entirety** *n* LAW, PROP Gütergemeinschaft *f*; **~ for years** *n* FIN,

PROP zeitlich begrenzter Pachtbesitz *m*; **~ in common** *n* LAW, PROP Immobilie *f* als Bruchteileigentum, Miteigentum *nt* in Bruchteilen

tenant *n* LAW, PROP *of farm, shop* Pächter, in *m,f, of house, flat* Mieter, in *m,f*; **~'s repairs** *n pl* WEL Mieterreparaturen *f pl*; **~ right** *n* BrE LAW, PROP *compensation for land* Erstattungsanspruch *m* für Aufwendungen während der Mietzeit, Erstattungsanspruch *m* für Aufwendungen während der Pachtzeit, Mieterrecht *nt*, Pächterrecht *nt* Erstattungsanspruch *m* für Aufwendungen während der Pachtzeit; **~ in severalty** *n* LAW, PROP alleinberechtigter Mieter *m*, alleinberechtigte Mieterin *f*, alleinberechtigter Pächter *m*, alleinberechtigte Pächterin *f*

tend *vi* FIN, STOCK *in certain direction* tendieren; ♦ **~ to do sth** GEN COMM dazu neigen, etw zu tun, dazu tendieren, etw zu tun; **~ toward** GEN COMM *figure, level* tendieren zu

tendency *n* GEN COMM, S&M Trend *m, direction of trend* Entwicklungsrichtung *f*, Entwicklungstendenz *f*, *general trend* allgemeine Richtung *f*, *inclination* Tendenz *f*, Neigung *f*

tendentious *adj* GEN COMM, POL tendenziös

tender 1. *n* FIN Ausschreibungsverfahren *nt*, GEN COMM Angebot *nt*, Offerte *f*, Tender *m, buying* Lieferangebot *nt*, Submissionsangebot *nt*, STOCK *of exercise notice* Tender *m*, Zeichnungsangebot *nt*, Vorlegung *f*; ♦ **by ~** ADMIN, S&M durch Ausschreibung, auf dem Submissionsweg; **2.** *vt* GEN COMM anbieten, bieten, HRM einreichen, STOCK einreichen, vorlegen; ♦ **~ money in discharge of debt** LAW Zahlung zum Begleichen einer Schuld anbieten; **~ notice** STOCK ausüben; **3.** *vi* GEN COMM ein Angebot unterbreiten, sich an einer Ausschreibung beteiligen, MGMNT *for contract* ein Angebot abgeben, sich bewerben; ♦ **~ for** GEN COMM *project* sich bewerben um

tender: **~ bond** *n* BANK *international banking* Bietungsgarantie *f*; **~ by private contract** *n* S&M freihändige Angebotsabgabe *f*; **~ documents** *n pl* BANK Angebotsunterlagen *f pl*

tenderer *n* GEN COMM Anbieter, in *m,f*

tendering *n* GEN COMM Angebotsabgabe *f*; **~ procedure** *n* GEN COMM Ausschreibungsverfahren *nt*

tender: **~ offer** *n* ACC, FIN, GEN COMM, STOCK Übernahmeangebot *nt*; **~ panel** *n* FIN Tender-Gruppe *f*; **~ price** *n* GEN COMM Angebotspreis *m*; **~ rate** *n* FIN Emissionssatz *m*; **~ system** *n* STOCK Tenderverfahren *nt*; **~ to contract** *n* (*TTC*) GEN COMM Ausschreibung *f*, LAW Auftragsangebot *nt*, Vertragsangebot *nt*; **~ to contract cover** *n* INS *company* Versicherungsangebot zur Deckung in Fremdwährung *nt*

tenement *n* PROP Mietshaus *nt*, Mietskaserne *f*

Ten-Forty *n* AmE ECON amerikanisches Formular für die Einkommenssteuererklärung

10K: **~ report** *n* STOCK von der US-Wertpapier- und Börsenaufsichtsbehörde verlangter Geschäftsbericht von Emittenten und bestimmten Gesellschaften

tenor *n* FIN, STOCK, TRANSP Laufzeit *f*; ♦ **at the specified ~** GEN COMM gemäß spezifiziertem Inhalt

tenor: **~ bill** *n* TRANSP Laufzeitwechsel *m*

ten: **~ percent guideline** *n* TAX Zehn-Prozent-Richtlinie

tentative: **~ agenda** *n* GEN COMM vorläufige Tagesordnung *f*; **~ agreement** *n* LAW Vorvertrag *m*; **~ estimate** *n* GEN COMM vorläufige Schätzung *f*,

vorsichtige Schätzung *f*; **~ plan** *n* GEN COMM vorläufiger Plan *m*

ten: **~ times** *adv* MATH zehnfach

tenure *n* GEN COMM Besitz *m*, HRM, POL *of office* Amtszeit *f*

tenured: **~ post** *n* HRM Lebensstellung *f*; **~ staff** *n* HRM Personal *nt* in Lebensstellung

tenure: **~ in land** *n* PROP Landpacht *f*

term *n* BANK Laufzeit *f*, GEN COMM Begriff *m*, Bezeichnung *f*, Wort *nt*, POL *of government, office* Amtsperiode *f, of treaty* Dauer *f*; **~ account** *n* FIN Festgeldkonto *nt*; **~ annuity** *n* INS Zeitrente *f*; **~ bill** *n* FIN Nachsichtwechsel *m*; **~-certain annuity** *n* FIN Rentenversicherung *f* mit festgelegter Laufzeit; **~ credit** *n* FIN Nachsichtakkreditiv *nt*; **~ day** *n* GEN COMM festgesetzter Tag *m*; **~ deposit** *n* BANK Festgeld *nt*, Termineinlage *f*; **~ draft** *n* BANK Nachsichtwechsel *m*, Zeitsichtwechsel *m*, Zieltratte *f*

terminable *adj* LAW befristet, kündbar

terminal *n* COMP Terminal *nt*, GEN COMM Umschlagplatz *m*, Zielhafen *m*, TRANSP Terminal *nt*, Verladestation *f*; **~ bonus** *n* INS Schlußdividende *f*; **~ charges** *n pl* TRANSP Terminalgebühren *f pl*; **~ computer** *n* COMP Datenstationsrechner *m*; **~ loss** *n* ACC Abschlußverlust *m*; **~ manager** *n* TRANSP Terminalmanager, in *m,f*; **~ operator** *n* COMP *person* Bildschirmoperator, in *m,f*; **~ payment** *n* FIN letzte Ratenzahlung *f*; **~ screen** *n* COMP Bildschirm *m*; **~ throughput, ~ thruput** AmE *n* TRANSP Terminaldurchsatz *m*; **~ traffic** *n* TRANSP Terminalverkehr *m*; **~ value** *n* FIN Restwert *m*

terminate *vt* COMP beenden, GEN COMM *meeting* beenden, *contract, lease* lösen, kündigen, LAW aufheben, beenden, kündigen; ♦ **~ a fund** FIN einen Investmentfonds kündigen; **~ sb's employment** HRM jds Arbeitsvertrag auflösen

terminated *adj* COMP beendet, GEN COMM aufgehoben, gelöst, beendet, HRM aufgelöst, *employment* beendet, LAW *contract* beendet, aufgehoben

termination *n* COMP Beenden *nt*, Beendigung *f*, GEN COMM *of appointment* Kündigung *f*, Lösung *f*, Beenden *nt*, Beendigung *f*, HRM Auflösung *f*, *of employment* Beendigung *f*, LAW *of contract* Beenden *nt*, Aufhebung *f*, Beendigung *f*, Kündigung *f*, Vertragsbeendigung *f*, PROP *of lease* Mietkündigung *f*, Pachtkündigung *f*; **~ benefits** *n pl* HRM Entlassungsabfindung *f*; **~ clause** *n* LAW *in contract* Bestimmung *f* über die Vertragsdauer; **~ papers** *n pl* HRM *dismissal* Entlassungspapiere *f pl*; **~ pay** *n* HRM Abfindungszahlung *f*; **~ payment** *n* HRM Auslösung *f*; **~ payments** *n pl* TAX *received on retirement* Abfindung *f*

terminology *n* GEN COMM Fachsprache *f*, Terminologie *f*

term: **~ insurance** *n* INS abgekürzte Todesfallversicherung *f*, kurzfristige Todesfallversicherung *f*, Risikolebensversicherung *f*

terminus: **~ station** *n* TRANSP Kopfbahnhof *m, bus, rail* Endstation *f*

term: **~ life insurance** *n* INS abgekürzte Todesfallversicherung *f*, Risikolebensversicherung *f* mit Umtauschrecht; **~ of limitation** *n* GEN COMM, LAW Ausschlußfrist *f*, Verjährungsfrist *f*; **~ loan** *n* FIN mittelfristiger Kredit *m*; **~ of a loan** *n* FIN Anleihelaufzeit *f*; **~ of office** *n* GEN COMM, HRM, POL Amtsperiode *f*, Amtszeit *f*, Dienstzeit *f*; **~ of patent** *n* PATENTS Patentdauer *f*, Schutzdauer *f* eines Patents,

Schutzfrist *f*; ~ **of payment** *n* BANK Zahlungsziel *nt*; ~ **policy** *n* INS Lebensversicherung *f* ohne Rückkaufswert, Terminversicherung *f*, Seeversicherungspolice *f*; ~ **premium** *n* ECON Laufzeitprämie *f*; ~ **purchase** *n* GEN COMM Terminkauf *m*

terms *n pl* BANK Bedingungen *f pl*, Konditionen *f pl*, *provisos* Modalitäten *f pl*, *of loan* Ausstattung *f*, FIN Konditionen *f pl*, GEN COMM, LAW *of agreement* Wortlaut *m*, *contract* Bedingungen *f pl*; ♦ **come to** ~ GEN COMM sich einigen; **come to ~ with sb** LAW *contract law* mit jdm handelseinig werden, sich mit jdm einigen; **in ~ of** GEN COMM in Form von, als, im Sinne, ausgedrückt in, hinsichtlich; **not on any ~** GEN COMM unter gar keinen Umständen; **on the same ~** GEN COMM zu den gleichen Bedingungen; **under the ~ of the contract** LAW gemäß den vertraglichen Bedingungen, gemäß den vertraglichen Bestimmungen

terms: ~ **of acceptance** *n pl* FIN Annahmebedingungen *f pl*; ~ **and conditions** *n pl* GEN COMM Verkaufs- und Lieferbedingungen *f pl*, INS Versicherungsbedingungen *f pl*; ~ **and conditions of employment** *n pl* HRM Anstellungsbedingungen *f pl*; ~ **and conditions of an issue** *n pl* STOCK Verkaufs- und Lieferbedingungen *f pl* einer Emission; ~ **of contract** *n pl* LAW Vertragsbedingungen *f pl*, vertragliche Bestimmungen *f pl*; ~ **of credit** *n pl* BANK Kreditbedingungen *f pl*, Kreditkonditionen *f pl*; ~ **of export sale** *n pl* IMP/EXP, S&M Exportverkaufsbedingungen *f pl*, Modalitäten *f pl* des Auslandsabsatzes; ~ **of issue** *n pl* FIN Emissionskonditionen *f pl*, Ausstattung *f*; ~ **of payment** *n pl* BANK Zahlungsbedingungen *f pl*, Zahlungsmodalitäten *f pl*; ~ **of redemption** *n pl* FIN Tilgungsmodalitäten *f pl*; ~ **of reference** *n pl* GEN COMM *of committee* Zuständigkeitsbereich *m*, Aufgabenbereich *m*, Aufgabenstellung *f*; ~ **of sale** *n pl* IMP/EXP, S&M Absatzmodalitäten *f pl*, Verkaufsbedingungen *f pl*; ~ **of shipment** *n pl* IMP/EXP Transportkonditionen *f pl*, Versandbedingungen *f pl*; ~ **of tender** *n pl* GEN COMM Ausschreibungsbedingungen *f pl*; ~ **of trade** *n pl* ECON reales Austauschverhältnis *nt*, Terms of Trade *pl* (*ToT*)

term: ~ **structure** *n* FIN Laufzeitstruktur *f*; ~ **structure of interest rates** *n* ECON Fristigkeitsstruktur *f* der Zinssätze, Zinsstruktur *f*; ~ **to maturity** *n* STOCK Restlaufzeit *f*

terotechnology *n* ECON *theories* Terotechnologie *f*

terraced: ~ **house** *n* BrE (*cf row house* AmE) PROP Reihenhaus *nt*

terrestrial *adj* GEN COMM, MEDIA *broadcasting technology* erdgebunden, terrestrisch

territorial: ~ **waters** *n pl* LAW Hoheitsgewässer *nt pl*

territory *n* GEN COMM *of agent* Bezirk *m*, *of state* Hoheitsgebiet *nt*, Territorium *nt*, Gebiet *nt*, HRM, MGMNT Bezirk *m*, Gebiet *nt*; ~ **manager** *n* HRM Bezirksleiter, in *m,f*, MGMNT Gebietsleiter, in *m,f*

terrorem: **in ~** *phr* GEN COMM als Abschreckung

terrorism *n* POL Terrorismus *m*

tertiary: ~ **activities** *n pl* GEN COMM Tertiärgeschäft *nt*; ~ **education** *n* GEN COMM, WEL Hochschulbildung *f*, tertiäres Bildungswesen *nt*; ~ **product** *n* ECON Dienstleistung *f*, tertiäres Produkt *nt*; ~ **sector** *n* ECON Dienstleistungssektor *m*, tertiärer Sektor *m*

TESSA *abbr* BrE (*Tax Exempt Special Savings Account*) BANK steuerfreies Sparkonto *nt*

test 1. *n* COMP, GEN COMM, S&M Erprobung *f*, Prüfung *f*,

Test *m*, Probe *f*; **2.** *vt* GEN COMM probieren, ausprobieren, austesten, versuchen

testamentary: ~ **gift** *n* LAW Vermächtnis *nt*; ~ **trust** *n* LAW testamentarisch errichtete Stiftung *f*

test: ~ **area** *n* S&M *marketing* Testgebiet *nt*; ~ **audit** *n* GEN COMM Testprüfung *f*

test: ~ **bed** *n* GEN COMM, IND Prüfstand *m*, Versuchsstand *m*; ~ **bench** *n* IND Prüfstand *m*; ~ **drilling** *n* ENVIR, IND Probebohrung *f*; ~ **drive** *n* TRANSP Probefahrt *f*

testee *n* GEN COMM Prüfling *m*, Testperson *f*

test: ~ **equipment** *n* COMP, IND Meßgerät *nt*, Prüfeinrichtung *f*, Prüfgerät *nt*, Testgerät *nt*; ~ **flight** *n* TRANSP Probeflug *m*

testify *vi* LAW bekunden, bezeugen

testimonial: ~ **advertisement** *n* S&M Testimonial-Anzeige *f*

testimony *n* LAW Zeugenaussage *f*

testing *n* IND *for products* Prüfung *f*; ~ **equipment** *n* IND Prüfmaschine *f*; ~ **plant** *n* IND Prüfanlage *f*, Prüfstand *m*; ~ **procedure** *n* IND Prüfverfahren *nt*, Prüfung *f*

test: ~ **mailing** *n* S&M *advertising* Testmailing *nt*, Versuchspostversand *m*; ~ **marketing** *n* S&M Durchführung *f* eines Markttests; ~ **print** *n* GEN COMM, MEDIA Andruck *m*; ~ **problem** *n* GEN COMM Testaufgabe *f*; ~ **run** *n* GEN COMM *system, machine* Probelauf *m*; ~ **shot** *n* MEDIA *film* Probeaufnahme *f*; ~ **statistic** *n* ECON Prüfgröße *f*, Prüfmaß *nt*, MATH Prüfgröße *f*; ~ **town** *n* GEN COMM Versuchsstadt *f*; ~ **transit** *n* TRANSP *distribution* Testtransport *m*

text *n* COMP, GEN COMM, S&M Text *m*

textbook: ~ **case** *n* GEN COMM Musterbeispiel *nt*, Paradefall *m*; ~ **operation** *n* GEN COMM Musterbetrieb *m*

text: ~ **editing** *n* COMP Textbearbeitung *f*; ~ **editor** *n* COMP *software* Texteditor *m*

textile: ~ **industry** *n* IND Textilindustrie *f*

textiles *n pl* IND Textilien *pl*

text: ~ **in full** *n* GEN COMM voller Wortlaut *m*, Volltext *m*, vollständiger Text *m*; ~ **mode** *n* COMP Textmodus *m*; ~ **processing** *n* COMP Textverarbeitung *f*

TF *abbr* (*till forbid*) S&M *advertising* b. a. W. (*bis auf Widerruf*), bis zur Stornierung

T-form *n* IMP/EXP *customs* T-Formular *nt*

tfr *abbr* (*transfer*) ACC Umbuchung *f*, ADMIN Versetzung *f*, BANK Überweisung *f*, COMP, ECON, FIN Transfer *m*, GEN COMM *of responsibilities, liabilities* Übertragung *f*, Versetzung *f*, HRM Umsetzung *f*, Versetzung *f*, Transfer *m*, INS Abtretung *f*, LAW Abtretung *f*, Übereignung *f*, Veräußerung *f*, PATENTS Übertragung *f*, Zession *f*, Abtretung *f*, Überschreibung *f*, PROP *of property* Übertragung *f*, STOCK Umschreibung *f*, Übertragung *f*, TAX *of money* Abführung *f*, TRANSP Transfer *m*, Umsteigung *f*

T-group: ~ **training** *n* HRM T-Gruppen-Schulung *f*

TGWU *abbr* BrE (*Transport and General Workers' Union*) IND Transportarbeitergewerkschaft

thanking: ~ **you in advance** *phr* COMMS vielen Dank im voraus; ~ **you in anticipation** *phr* COMMS vielen Dank im voraus

thank: ~ **you for your letter** *phr* COMMS vielen Dank für Ihr Schreiben; ~~**you letter** *n* GEN COMM Dankschreiben *nt* thanks: we should like to express our ~ *phr* COMMS wir bedanken uns sehr

Thatcherism *n BrE* ECON, POL Thatcherismus *m*

THE *abbr* (*technical help to exporters*) IMP/EXP technische Hilfe *f* für Exportfirmen

theft *n* GEN COMM, INS, TRANSP Diebstahl *m*; ~ risk *n* INS Diebstahlrisiko *nt*

theme: ~ advertising *n* S&M thematische Werbung *f*; ~ park *n* LEIS Themenpark *m*; ~ tune *n* MEDIA, S&M *broadcast* Erkennungsmelodie *f*

theonomy *n* ECON Theonomie *f*

theorem *n* GEN COMM Theorem *nt*

theoretical *adj* GEN COMM theoretisch

theoretically *adv* GEN COMM theoretisch

theoretical: ~ maximum plant capacity *n* GEN COMM theoretische Maximalkapazität *f*

theory *n* GEN COMM Theorie *f*; ♦ in ~ GEN COMM theoretisch

theory: ~ of clubs *n* ECON Klubtheorie *f*; ~ of comparative costs *n* ECON Theorie *f* der komparativen Kosten; ~ of economic stages *n* ECON ökonomische Stufentheorie *f*; ~ of property rights *n* ECON Theorie *f* der Eigentumsrechte; ~ of secular stagnation *n* ECON säkulare Stagnationstheorie *f*

thermal: ~ container *n* TRANSP Thermalcontainer *m*; ~ energy *n* ENVIR, IND thermische Energie *f*; ~ power *n* ENVIR, IND Wärme *f*; ~ power station *n* IND Wärmekraftwerk *nt*

thermostatic: ~ fan *n* IND Warmluftventilator *m*

Thiebout: ~ hypothesis *n* ECON Thiebout-Hypothese *f*

thin *adj* STOCK begrenzt; ~ capitalization *n* ACC Kapitalausstattung *f* mit geringem Eigenkapitalanteil, GEN COMM kurze Kapitaldecke *f* (*infrml*)

thinking *n* GEN COMM *attitude* Gesinnung *f*, *opinion* Meinung *f*, *reasoning* Gedankengang *m*, Denken *nt*

think: ~-tank *n infrml* GEN COMM Denkfabrik *f* (*infrml*)

thin: ~ market *n* STOCK enger Markt *m*, begrenzter Markt *m*

third *adj* GEN COMM dritte; ~ age *n* ECON dritter Lebensabschnitt *m*; ~ carrier *n* TRANSP *air distribution* dritter Frachtführer *m*; ~-class *adj* TRANSP *accommodation* drittklassig; ~-class mail *n AmE* COMMS Drucksache *f*; ~-class matter *n AmE* COMMS drittklassige Sache *f*, Postsendung *f* dritter Klasse; ~ country *n* ECON *international trade* Drittland *nt*; ~-country cooperation *n* ECON *international trade* Einbeziehung *f* von Drittländern, Zusammenarbeit *f* mit Drittländern; ~-country trade *n* ECON Transithandel *m*; ~ currency *n* GEN COMM Drittwährung *f*; ~-degree price discrimination *n* ECON unfaire Preisunterbietung *f*; ~-flag carrier *n* TRANSP Befrachter unter fremder Flagge

thirdly *adv* GEN COMM drittens

third: ~ market *n* ECON, FIN, STOCK außerbörslicher Handel *m* mit börsennotierten Aktien, Börsendrittmarkt *m*, ungeregelter Freiverkehr *m*

Third: ~ Market *n BrE* ECON dritter Markt *m*

third: ~ party *n* INS, LAW, PATENTS Dritte(r) *mf* [decl. as adj], dritte Person *f*; ~-party account *n* FIN Anderkonto *nt*; ~-party beneficiary *n* FIN, LAW Drittbegünstigte(r) *mf* [decl. as adj]; ~-party check *AmE*, ~ party cheque *BrE n* BANK Scheck *m* zugunsten Dritter; ~-party claim *n* LAW Anspruch *m* eines Dritten; ~-party currency *n*

IMP/EXP Drittwährung *f*; ~-party damage *n* LAW *contracts* Drittschaden *m*; ~-party endorsement *n* S&M Genehmigung *f* durch Dritte; ~-party, fire and theft *n* INS Haftpflicht, Feuer und Diebstahl, Teilkaskoversicherung *f*; ~-party insurance cover *n* INS Haftpflichtdeckung *f*, Haftpflichtversicherungsschutz *m*; ~-party insurance policy *n* INS Haftpflichtversicherungspolice *f*; ~-party intervention *n* HRM Intervention *f* durch Dritte; ~-party liability *n* LAW *insurance* gesetzliche Haftpflicht; ~-party motor vehicle insurance *n* INS, TRANSP Kfz-Haftpflichtversicherung *f*, Kraftfahrzeughaftpflichtversicherung *f*; ~-party notice *n* LAW Streitverkündigung *f*; ~-party risk *n* INS Haftpflichtrisiko *nt*, Drittschadenhaftpflichtrisiko *nt*; ~-party sale *n* S&M Verkauf *m* durch Dritte; ~ person *n* GEN COMM Dritte(r) *mf* [decl. as adj]; ~ quarter *n* (*3Q*) GEN COMM drittes Quartal *nt*; ~-rate *adj* GEN COMM drittklassig, drittrangig, minderwertig; ~-rate goods *n pl* GEN COMM minderwertige Waren *f pl*; ~ way *n* ECON dritter Weg *m*

Third: ~ World *n* GEN COMM Dritte Welt *f*; ~ World country *n* ECON Dritte-Welt-Land *nt*, Entwicklungsland *nt*

thirty: ~-day wash rule *n AmE* TAX Dreißig-Tage-Richtlinie

Thirty: ~ Share Index *n* STOCK Aktienkursindex der Financial Times aus dreißig Werten

Thomson: ~ Report *n* ECON Thomson-Bericht *m*

thousand *n* (*k*) GEN COMM Tausend *nt*

thrash out *vt infrml* GEN COMM *problem* ausdiskutieren

threat: ~ effect *n* ECON Droheffekt *m*

three: ~-course rotation *n* ECON *agriculture* Dreifelderwirtschaft *f*; ~-digit *adj* GEN COMM dreistellig; ~-digit industry *n* ECON dreistellige Branchengliederung *f*; ~-line whip *n BrE* POL Fraktionszwang *m*; ~-month add-on yield *n* STOCK dreimonatige Zusatzrendite *f*; ~-month call *n* STOCK *money repayable* dreimonatige Kündigungsfrist *f*; ~-month discount yield *n* STOCK dreimonatige Abzinsungsrendite *f*; ~-month Eurodollar time deposits *n pl* STOCK Dreimonats-Eurodollar-Festgelder *nt pl*; ~-month funds *n pl* FIN Dreimonatsgeld *nt*; ~-month maturities *n pl* FIN Dreimonatspapiere *nt pl*; ~-month rate *n* FIN Dreimonatsrate *f*; ~-month US Treasury bills *n pl* STOCK Dreimonats-US-Schatzwechsel *m pl*; ~-ply organization *n jarg* GEN COMM dreiteilige Organisation *f*

3Q *abbr* (*third quarter*) GEN COMM drittes Quartal *nt*

three: ~-stage least squares method *n* ECON dreistufige Methode *f* der kleinsten Quadrate; ~-way call *n AmE* COMMS Konferenzschaltung *f*; ~-way split *n* GEN COMM Dreifachsplitting *nt*; ~-way switch deal *n* IMP/EXP Dreiecksgeschäft *nt*

threshold *n* GEN COMM Schwelle *f*; ~ agreement *n* HRM Schwellenvereinbarung *f*, Lohnindexierung *f*; ~ of divergence *n* FIN *European Monetary System* Abweichungsschwelle *f*; ~ level *n* GEN COMM Schwellenwert *m*, *reporting* Meldeschwelle *f*; ~ point *n* STOCK Schwellenpunkt *m*; ~ population *n* ECON Schwellenpopulation *f*; ~ price *n* GEN COMM Eingangspreis *m*, Schwellenpreis *m*, HRM Schwellenpreis *m*; ~ rate *n* HRM Schwellentarif *m*; ~ value *n* COMP Schwellenwert *m*; ~ worker *n AmE* ECON Auszubildende(r) *mf* [decl. as adj] (*Azubi*), HRM

Auszubildende(r) *mf* [decl. as adj] (*Azubi*), Praktikant, in *m,f,* Anlernling *m*

thrift *n AmE* BANK Sparkasse *f;* ~ **account** *n AmE* FIN Sparkonto *nt;* ~ **bank** *n AmE* BANK Sparkasse *f;* ~ **price** *n AmE* IMP/EXP Niedrigpreis *m*

Thrifts: the ~ *n pl AmE infrml* BANK die Sparkassen *f pl*

thrift: ~ **shop** *n AmE* (*cf second-hand shop BrE*) GEN COMM Gebrauchtwarengeschäft *nt*

thrive *vi* GEN COMM florieren, gedeihen, sich gut entwickeln

thriving *adj* ECON, GEN COMM blühend, florierend, flott gehend, gut gehend

through: ~ **air waybill** *n* (*TAWB*) IMP/EXP, TRANSP Durchluftfrachtbrief *m,* Transitluftfrachtbrief *m;* ~ **bill of lading** *n* IMP/EXP, TRANSP *shipping* Durchfrachtkonnossement *nt,* Durchkonnossement *nt;* ~ **charge** *n* IMP/EXP Durchgangskosten *pl,* Frachtkosten *pl* für durchgehende Ladungen, TRANSP Durchgangsgebühr *f;* ~ **coach** *n* TRANSP *road transport* direkte Busverbindung *f,* direkter Bus *m, rail transport* Kurswagen *m;* ~ **fare** *n* TRANSP Durchgangsfahrpreis *m;* ~ **flight** *n* TRANSP Direktflug *m;* ~ **freight** *n* TRANSP Durchfracht *f*

throughput *n* COMP *processing capacity* Durchsatz *m,* FIN Durchlauf *m,* Durchsatz *m,* IND Durchsatz *m;* ~ **rate** *n* IND Durchsatzleistung *f,* Mengenleistung *f*

through: ~ **rate** *n* GEN COMM Durchfracht *f,* Durchgangstarif *m,* IMP/EXP Durchgangsfrachtsatz *m,* Frachtsatz *m* für Ladungen unter einem Zentner, TRANSP Durchgangstarif *m;* ~ **route** *n* TRANSP Direktroute *f;* ~ **shipment** *n* TRANSP Durchgangsladung *f;* ~ **train** *n* TRANSP direkte Zugverbindung *f,* Direktverbindung *f,* durchgehender Zug *m;* ~ **transport operator** *n* TRANSP Haus-zu-Haus-Betreiber *m;* ~ **transport system** *n* TRANSP Haus-zu-Haus-System *nt*

throw: ~ **light on** *phr* GEN COMM klarmachen, Licht werfen auf; ~ **the rule book at sb** *phr* GEN COMM jdm die Regeln vor Augen halten; ~ **a spanner in the works** *phr* ECON, GEN COMM Sand ins Getriebe streuen

throwaway: ~ **society** *n* ECON, ENVIR, GEN COMM Wegwerfgesellschaft *f*

thruput *AmE see throughput*

thrust: ~ **block** *n* TRANSP *shipping* Schubblock *m*

thumb: ~ **index** *n* GEN COMM Daumenindex *m*

TIBOR *abbr* (*Tokyo Interbank Offered Rate*) BANK Tokioter Interbankenangebotssatz *m*

tick 1. *n* GEN COMM *BrE* (*cf check AmE*) mark Haken *m,* Häkchen *nt,* Kontrollzeichen *nt,* Kontrollvermerk *m,* STOCK *rate deviation* Mindestkursschwankung *f;* **2.** *vt BrE* (*cf check AmE*) GEN COMM *mark* abhaken; ◆ ~ **the box** *BrE* (*cf check the box AmE*) GEN COMM das Kästchen ankreuzen

tick off *vt BrE* (*cf check off AmE*) GEN COMM *on list* abhaken

tick: ~ **box** *BrE* (*cf check box AmE*) *n* COMP, GEN COMM Auswahlfeld *nt*

ticker *n* STOCK Kursanzeiger der amerikanischen Börsen, Börsenticker *m;* ~ **symbol** *n* STOCK Börsentickersymbol *nt;* ~ **tape** *n* STOCK Lochstreifen *m,* Papierstreifen *m*

ticket *n* GEN COMM, LEIS Eintrittskarte *f,* Karte *f, travel* Fahrkarte *f,* POL Kandidatenliste *f,* TRANSP Fahrschein *m,* Karte *f,* Fahrkarte *f, air* Flugticket *nt,* Ticket *nt,* Schein *m,* Flugschein *m;* ~ **agency** *n* GEN COMM, LEIS Kartenverkaufsstelle *f, for advance tickets*

Kartenvorverkaufsstelle *f,* TRANSP *air travel* Flugkartenverkaufsstelle *f,* Kartenverkaufsstelle *f,* Fahrkartenverkaufsstelle *f;* ~ **analysis** *n* TRANSP Ticket-Analyse *f;* ~ **collector** *n* GEN COMM, TRANSP Fahrkartenkontrolleur, in *m,f;* ~ **day** *n BrE* STOCK Aufgabetag *m,* Skontrierungstag *m;* ~ **holder** *n* LEIS Kartenbesitzer, in *m,f,* TRANSP Fahrscheininhaber, in *m,f,* Kartenbesitzer, in *m,f;* ~ **office** *n* LEIS Kartenverkaufsstelle *f,* Kasse *f,* TRANSP Fahrkartenausgabe *f,* Fahrkartenschalter *m,* Kartenverkaufsstelle *f;* ~ **policy** *n* INS Blockpolice *f;* ~ **tout** *n* LEIS Kartenschwarzhändler, in *m,f*

tickler: ~ **file** *n* BANK Terminablage *f*

tick: ~ **mark** *n BrE* (*cf check mark AmE*) GEN COMM Haken *m,* Häkchen *nt,* Kontrollzeichen *nt,* Kontrollvermerk *m;* ~ **size** *n* STOCK Umfang *m* der Mindestkursschwankung

tidal: ~ **dock** *n* TRANSP Tidebecken *nt;* ~ **power** *n* ENVIR Gezeitenenergie *f*

tide over *vt* GEN COMM überbrücken

tie *n* GEN COMM *bond* Band *nt*

tie up *vt* FIN *funds* festlegen, binden

tiebreaking: ~ **vote** *n* HRM ausschlaggebende Stimme *f*

tied: ~ **aid** *n* ECON gebundene Entwicklungshilfe *f;* ~ **cottage** *n* ECON, WEL mietrechtlich gebundene Werkswohnung *f;* ~ **house** *n* GEN COMM *rented by brewery to employee* gebundene Gaststätte *f*

tie: ~**-down** *n* TRANSP *shipping* Containerbefestigungsvorrichtung *f*

tied: **be** ~ **to** *phr* GEN COMM gebunden sein an; ~ **up** *adj* FIN fest angelegt, GEN COMM, MGMNT, STOCK festgelegt; ~**-up capital** *n* ACC festgelegtes Kapital *nt*

tie: ~**-in** *n* FIN Kopplung *f;* ~**-in advertising** *n* S&M Verbundwerbung *f;* ~**-in display** *n* S&M *advertising* Verbundwerbeschau *f;* ~**-in promotion** *n* S&M *manufacturer and retailer* aufeinander abgestimmte Werbung *f,* gemeinsame Werbung *f* von Hersteller und Einzelhändler, *two products at once* Kombinationsverkaufsförderung *f;* ~**-in sale** *n* S&M Kopplungsgeschäft *nt,* Kopplungsverkauf *m;* ~**-on label** *n* GEN COMM Anhänger *m,* Anhängezettel *m*

tier *n* TRANSP Etagengestell *nt*

Tier: ~ **One assets** *n pl BrE* STOCK *sterling assets* erstklassige Vermögenswerte *m pl*

tiger: ~ **team** *n AmE jarg* POL Eliteteam für Kniffliges

tight *adj* ECON *monetary policy* restriktiv, STOCK *market* begrenzt; ◆ **be on a** ~ **budget** FIN über ein knappes Budget verfügen; **be in a** ~ **spot** *infrml* GEN COMM in der Klemme sitzen (*infrml*)

tight: ~ **control** *n* LAW strenge Kontrolle *f*

tighten *vt* ECON, GEN COMM *credit controls* verschärfen, straffen; ◆ ~ **one's belt** ECON, GEN COMM den Gürtel enger schnallen; ~ **the monetary reins** ECON die Zügel der Geldpolitik straffen

tighten up *vt* GEN COMM *security* verschärfen

tightening *n* ECON, GEN COMM *of credit controls* Verschärfung *f,* Straffung *f;* ~**-up** *n* GEN COMM *of rules etc.* Verschärfung *f*

tight: ~ **fiscal policy** *n* ECON, TAX restriktive Finanzpolitik *f,* straffe Fiskalpolitik *f;* ~ **labor market** *AmE,* ~ **labour market** *BrE n* ECON angespannter Arbeitsmarkt *m;* ~ **liquidity position** *n* FIN angespannte Liquiditätslage *f;* ~ **market** *n* STOCK enger Markt *m,* begrenzter Markt *m*; ~ **monetary policy** *n* ECON kontraktive Geldpolitik *f*, Politik *f* des teuren Geldes; ~ **money** *n* FIN Geldknappheit *f*; ~ **money policy** *n* ECON kontraktive Geldpolitik *f*, Politik *f* des teuren Geldes; ~ **ship** *n* infrml MGMNT straffe Betriebsführung *f*

till 1. *n* GEN COMM, S&M Ladenkasse *f*, Kasse *f*; **2.** *prep* ♦ ~ **canceled** *AmE*, ~ **cancelled** *BrE* (*TC*) S&M *advertising* bis auf Widerruf (*b. a. W.*), bis zur Stornierung; ~ **countermanded** (*T/C*) GEN COMM bis auf Widerruf (*b. a. W.*), bis zur Stornierung; ~ **forbid** (*TF*) S&M *advertising* bis auf Widerruf (*b. a. W.*), bis zur Stornierung

till: ~ **money** *n* ECON Kassenhaltung *f*, Mindestsatz *m* an Barmitteln; ~ **receipt** *n* BANK Kassenstreifen *m*

tilt 1. *n* TRANSP Wagendecke *f*; **2.** *vt* ♦ ~ **the balance** GEN COMM den Ausschlag geben, die Bilanz kippen

tilt: ~ **trailer** *n* TRANSP *road* Kippanhänger *m*

timber *n* *BrE* (*cf lumber AmE*) IND Bauholz *nt*, Nutzholz *nt*; ~ **industry** *n* IND Holzindustrie *f*

time *n* GEN COMM Zeit *f*; ♦ **at a certain** ~ GEN COMM zu einem bestimmten Zeitpunkt; **for the** ~ **being** GEN COMM vorläufig; **this** ~ **last year** GEN COMM zu dieser Zeit im letzten Jahr; **this** ~ **next week** GEN COMM um diese Zeit nächste Woche; ~ **is of the essence** LAW Fristeinhaltung ist Vertragsgrundlage; **with** ~ **to spare** GEN COMM früher als geplant, vor der Zeit

time: ~ **agreement** *n* GEN COMM Zeitvertrag *m*; ~ **and methods study** *n* GEN COMM, MGMNT Zeit- und Methodenstudie *f*; ~ **and motion study** *n* ECON, GEN COMM, IND, MATH, MGMNT *efficiency in workplace* Arbeitsplatzstudie *f*, Bewegungs-Zeit-Studie *f*, Rationalisierungsstudie *f*, Zeit- und Bewegungsstudie *f*; ~ **arbitrage** *n* GEN COMM Zeitarbitrage *f*; ~ **band** *n* TRANSP Zeitraum *m*; ~ **bar** *n* LAW *in contract* Ausschlußfrist *f*; ~ **bargain** *n* STOCK Fixgeschäft *nt*; ~**barred** *adj* LAW verjährt; ~ **bill** *n* *BrE* (*cf time draft AmE*) BANK Nachsichtwechsel *m*, Zielwechsel *m*; ~ **book** *n* HRM Arbeitsbuch *nt*; ~ **budget** *n* ECON, MGMNT Zeitbudget *nt*, verfügbare Zeit *f*, Zeitplan *m*; ~ **budget survey** *n* ECON, MGMNT Zeitverwendungsumfrage *f*; ~ **buyer** *n* MEDIA, S&M *advertising, radio, TV* Sachbearbeiter, in *m,f* für Funkwerbung; ~ **card** *n* HRM, IND Stechkarte *f*; ~ **charter** *n* (*T/C*) TRANSP Zeitcharter *f*; ~ **charter party** *n* (*time C/ P*) TRANSP *shipping* Zeitchartervertrag *m*; ~ **of circulation** *n* GEN COMM, TRANSP Umlaufzeit *f*; ~ **clock** *n* HRM, IND Kontrolluhr *f*, Stechuhr *f*, Stempeluhr *f*; ~ **component** *n* GEN COMM Zeitkomponente *f*; ~ **constraint** *n* GEN COMM, HRM, IND Zeitzwang *m*; ~**consuming** *adj* GEN COMM zeitaufwendig, zeitraubend, MGMNT zeitaufwendig; ~ **C/P** *n* (*time charter party*) TRANSP *shipping* Zeitchartervertrag *m*

timed: ~ **backup** *n* COMP zeitlich festgelegte Sicherung *f*, zeitlich festgelegtes Backup *nt* (*jarg*)

time: ~ **deposit** *n* *AmE* (*cf fixed deposit BrE*) BANK Festgeld *nt*, Termineinlage *f*, ECON befristete Einlage *f*; ~ **deposit account** *n* *AmE* (*cf fixed deposit account BrE*) BANK Festgeldkonto *nt*; ~ **discount** *n* S&M *advertising* Funkwerbungsmengenrabatt *m*; ~ **draft** *n* *AmE* (*cf time bill BrE*) BANK Nachsichtwechsel *m*, Zielwechsel *m*

timed: ~ **sequence** *n* IND Takt *m*

time: ~ **frame** *n* GEN COMM verfügbare Zeit *f*, zeitlicher Rahmen *m*, Zeitrahmen *m*; ~ **freight** *n* TRANSP Zeitfracht *f*; ~ **of going to press** *n* MEDIA Redaktionsschluß *m*; ~ **horizon** *n* MGMNT Zeithorizont *m*

timekeeper *n* ADMIN Arbeitszeitkontrolleur, in *m,f*

time: ~ **lag** *n* ECON Verzögerung *f*, Wirkungsverzögerung *f*, TAX Wirkungsverzögerung *f*, zeitliche Verzögerung *f*; ~ **limit** *n* GEN COMM Frist *f*, Gültigkeitsdauer *f*, Termin *m*, Zeitlimit *nt*, LAW Ausschlußfrist *f*, Zeitraum *m*

timely *adj* GEN COMM fristgemäß, rechtzeitig, zeitgemäß; ~ **objection** *n* LAW *contracts* fristgemäßer Widerspruch *m*

time: ~ **management** *n* MGMNT Zeitplanung *f*; ~ **off** *n* HRM, LEIS Freizeit *f*; ~ **off work** *n* HRM, LEIS *holiday* Freizeit *f*; ~ **on risk** *n* INS Dauer *f* der provisorischen Deckung; ~ **out** *n* COMP Zeitüberschreibung *f*, Zeitsperre *f*; ~ **policy** *n* INS befristete Police *f*, Zeitversicherungspolice *f*; ~ **pressure** *n* GEN COMM, MGMNT Termindruck *m*, Zeitdruck *m*

timer *n* COMP Timer *m*, Zeitgeber *m*

time: ~ **rate** *n* ECON Zeitlohn *m*; ~ **risk** *n* INS Zeitrisiko *nt*; ~**saving** *adj* COMP, GEN COMM zeitsparend

timescale *n* ECON, FIN, GEN COMM, MGMNT Zeitmaßstab *m*, Zeitplan *m*, zeitlicher Rahmen *m*

time: ~ **segment** *n* S&M *advertising* Zeitsegment *nt*; ~ **series** *n* ECON, MATH *statistics* Zeitreihe *f*; ~ **series analysis** *n* ECON Zeitreihenanalyse *f*

timeshare *n* ECON, PROP Zeitteilung *f*; ~ **developer** *n* PROP Timeshare-Bauunternehmer, in *m,f*; ~ **property** *n* PROP Timeshare-Eigentum *nt*; ~ **sale contract** *n* LAW, PROP zeitanteiliger Ferienwohnungs-Kaufvertrag *m*

time: ~~**sharing** *n* COMP gleichzeitige Benutzung eines Computers von zwei Benutzern, Gemeinschaftsbetrieb *m*, Timesharing *nt*, HRM, PROP Timesharing *nt*; ♦ **on a** ~~**sharing basis** PROP auf Timesharing-Basis; ~~**sharing company** *n* PROP Timesharing-Betrieb *m*; ~ **sheet** *n* HRM Arbeitszeinachweis *m*; ~ **slot** *n* GEN COMM gewohnte Sendezeit; ~ **span** *n* ECON *of worker* Entscheidungshorizont *m*, *of plan, project* Zeitspanne *f*, GEN COMM Frist *f*, Zeitraum *m*, Zeitspanne *f*; ~ **span of discretion** *n* GEN COMM Ermessenszeitraum *m*; ~ **study** *n* GEN COMM Arbeitszeitstudie *f*, IND, MATH *statistics* Zeitstudie *f*

times: ~ **uncovered** *n pl* FIN ungedeckte Zeitspanne *f*

timetable *n* LEIS *of airline* Flugplan *m*, *of bus, boat, train service* Kursbuch *nt*, Fahrplan *m*, MGMNT *for project* Programm *nt*, Zeitplan *m*, TRANSP *of airline* Flugplan *m*, *of bus, boat, train service* Kursbuch *nt*, Fahrplan *m*; ~ **analysis** *n* MGMNT Terminplananalyse *f*; ~ **planning** *n* MGMNT *for project* Zeitplanungsgestaltung *f*, TRANSP Fahrplangestaltung *f*

time: ~ **value** *n* STOCK *options* Aufgeld *nt*, Zeitwert *m*; ~ **value rate of decay** *n* STOCK *options* Verfallgeschwindigkeit *f* des Zeitwertes; ~ **work** *n* HRM Zeitlohnarbeit *f*; ~ **zone** *n* GEN COMM Zeitzone *f*

timewise *adv* GEN COMM zeitlich

timing *n* COMP Zeitberechnung *f*, zeitliche Abstimmung *f*, GEN COMM Timing *nt* (*jarg*) *of project* Zeitnahme *f*, *of repayments* Bestimmung *f* des richtigen Zeitpunktes; ~ **differences** *n pl* ACC *deferred tax* zeitliche Abgrenzungen *f pl*

tin *n* IND Zinn *nt*

TINA *abbr* (*there is no alternative*) GEN COMM es gibt keine Alternative *tin*: ~ **ore** *n* ENVIR, IND Zinnerz *nt*; ~ **plate** *n* IND Weißblech *nt*; ~ **price** *n* STOCK Zinnpreis *m*; ~ **shares** *n pl* STOCK Zinnaktien *f pl*

tinware *n* IND Blechwaren *f pl*

tip 1. *n* GEN COMM *advice* Tip *m*, *gratuity* Trinkgeld *nt*; **2.** *vt* ♦ ~ **the scales** GEN COMM den Ausschlag geben

TIP *abbr* (*tax-based incomes policy*) ECON, TAX steuer-orientierte Einkommenspolitik *f*

tip: ~~**in** *n* MEDIA *printing* Einklebung *f*; ~~**off** *n* GEN COMM gezielter Hinweis *m*, Tip *m*, Wink *m*

tipper *n* ENVIR, TRANSP Selbstentlader *m*

tipping *n* ENVIR, TRANSP Umkippen *nt*

TIPS *abbr* (*Treasury Inflation Protection Securities*) ECON, STOCK durch Indexierung inflationsgeschützte US-Staats-anleihen, TIPS

tips: ~ **and gratuities** *n pl* ACC, GEN COMM Bedienungs-gelder *nt pl*

TIR: ~ **carnet** *n* IMP/EXP Carnet TIR *nt*, Zollbegleitscheinheft *nt*

title *n* GEN COMM *to goods* Anspruch *m*, LAW Rechtsan-spruch *m*, Titel *m*, MEDIA *magazines* Überschrift *f*, Titel *m*; ~ **of an account** *n* ACC Kontobezeichnung *f*; ~ **deed** *n* LAW, PROP Besitzurkunde *f*, Eigentumsurkunde *f*, Grundstücksurkunde *f*; ~ **insurance** *n* INS Versicherung *f* der Eigentumsrechte, Versicherung *f* gegen Rechts-mängel bei Grundstückserwerb; ~ **of the invention** *n* PATENTS Erfinderrecht *nt*; ~ **page** *n* MEDIA *publications* Titelblatt *nt*, Titelseite *f*; ~ **protection insurance** *n* INS Rechtstitelschutzversicherung *f*, Titelschutzversiche-rung *f*; ~ **under a right** *n* LAW Anspruch *m* aus einem Recht

titular: ~ **head of an organization** *n* HRM, MGMNT Galionsfigur *f*

T/L *abbr* (*total loss*) INS Gesamtschaden *m*, Totalschaden *m*, Totalverlust *m*

TLC *abbr* (*transferable loan certificates*) FIN übertragbare Kreditzertifikate *nt pl*

TLI *abbr* (*transferable loan instruments*) FIN übertragbare Kreditinstrumente *nt pl*

TLO *abbr* (*total loss only*) INS nur bei Totalverlust, nur gegen Totalverlust versichert

TMESS *abbr* (*telemessage*) COMMS Telegramm *nt*, tele-graphische Mitteilung *f*

TMO *abbr* (*telegraphic money order*) BANK, FIN telegra-fische Geldüberweisung *f*

TNC *abbr* (*transnational corporation*) ECON transnationa-le Gesellschaft *f*

TOA *abbr* BrE (*total obligational authority*) FIN Ausgabeermächtigung *f*

TOB *abbr* (*takeover bid*) ACC, FIN, STOCK Übernahmeangebot *nt*

tobacco: ~ **products** *n pl* S&M, TAX Tabakerzeugnisse *nt pl*, Tabakprodukte *nt pl*, Tabakwaren *f pl*

Tobin: ~ **tax** *n* ECON, TAX Tobin-Steuer *f*

Tobit: ~ **model** *n* ECON Tobit-Modell *nt*

today: ~'s **rate** *n* BANK *of exchange*, FIN Tageskurs *m*

toe: **get a** ~ **in the market** *phr* GEN COMM auf dem Markt Fuß fassen; ~ **toes up** *infrml* GEN COMM bankrott gehen, bankrott machen

toggle 1. *n* COMP Kippschalter *m*; **2.** *vi* COMP umschalten

toggle: ~ **switch** *n* COMP Kippschalter *m*

toil *vi* HRM schwer arbeiten

token *n* COMP Zeichen *nt*, GEN COMM Münze *f*; ~ **coin** *n* BANK Scheidemünze *f*

tokenism *n* LAW Anwendung der Quotenregelung

token: ~ **money** *n* FIN Ersatzgeld *nt*, Geldersatz *m*, Geldsurrogat *nt*, Notgeld *nt*; ~ **payment** *n* BANK Draufgeld *nt*, symbolische Bezahlung *f*, GEN COMM symbolische Bezahlung *f*, Teilzahlung *f* als Anerken-nung einer Zahlungsverpflichtung; ~ **stoppage** *n* HRM Warnstreik *m*; ~ **strike** *n* HRM Warnstreik *m*

Tokyo: ~ **Interbank Offered Rate** *n* (*TIBOR*) BANK Tokioter Interbankenangebotssatz *m*; ~ **Round** *n* ECON Tokio-Runde *f*

told: **all** ~ *phr* GEN COMM alles angegeben, insgesamt

tolerance *n* GEN COMM Remedium *nt*, Toleranz *f*, IND Toleranz *f*; ~ **level** *n* FIN Toleranzniveau *nt*

toll *n* TRANSP Maut *f*, *for bridge* Brückengeld *nt*, *for road* Straßenbenutzungsgebühr *f*

tollbooth *n* TRANSP Mautstation *f*

tollbridge *n* TRANSP gebührenpflichtige Brücke *f*, Mautbrücke *f*

toll: ~ **call** *n* AmE COMMS Ferngespräch *nt*

toll-free 1. *adj* COMMS AmE (*cf Freefone BrE*) gebühren-frei, TRANSP gebührenfrei, mautfrei; **2.** *adv* COMMS AmE gebührenfrei, TRANSP gebührenfrei, mautfrei

toll-free: ~ **call** *n* AmE (*cf Freefone*® *BrE*) COMMS, S&M kostenloser Anruf *m*; ~ **number** *n* AmE (*cf Freefone number BrE*) COMMS, S&M gebührenfreie Rufnummer *f*, Rufnummer *f* zum Nulltarif

toll: ~ **model** *n* ECON Gebührenmodell *nt*; ~ **motorway** *n* BrE (*cf turnpike AmE*) TRANSP gebührenpflichtige Autobahn *f*; ~ **road** *n* BrE (*cf turnpike AmE*) TRANSP Mautstraße *f*

tombstone *n* ECON Finanzanzeige *f*; ~ **ad** *n* FIN Anzeige in Finanzblättern über plazierte Anleiheemission, Emissions-anzeige *f*

tomorrow *adv* GEN COMM morgen; ♦ ~ **week** GEN COMM morgen in einer Woche

ton *n* (*t*) GEN COMM Tonne *f* (*t*); ~ **kilometer** *AmE*, ~ **kilometre** *BrE n* TRANSP Tonnenkilometer *m*; ~ **miles per vehicle hour** *n pl* TRANSP Tonnenmeilen *f pl* pro Fahrzeugstunde

tone *n* STOCK Stimmung *f*

toner *n* COMP *for fax machine, photocopier* Toner *m*

tongs *n pl* TRANSP *cargo lifting equipment* Zange *f*

tonnage *n* IND, TRANSP *shipping* Tonnage *f*; ~ **calculation** *n* TRANSP *shipping, chartering* Tonnagenberechnung *f*; ~ **dues** *n pl* TRANSP Frachtraumgebühren *f pl*; ~ **dues slip** *n* IMP/EXP, TRANSP *shipping* Beleg *m* über Fracht-raumgebühren, Tonnagenbeleg *m*; ~ **mark** *n* TRANSP *shipping* Tonnenmarke *f*; ~ **measurement** *n* TRANSP Tonnengehalt *m*

tonne *see* ton

tons: ~ **deadweight** *n pl* TRANSP Tragfähigkeit *f*

tool *n* COMP Tool *nt* (*jarg*), Werkzeug *nt*, GEN COMM, IND Instrument *nt*, Werkzeug *nt*, MEDIA *of reference* Mittel *nt*

tool up *vt* IND bestücken, mit Werkzeugen ausstatten

tool: ~ **bar** *n* COMP Werkzeugleiste *f*

toolmaker *n* IND Werkzeugmacher *m*

toolroom *n* IND Werkzeugmacherei *f*

tools: ~ **of the trade** *n pl* GEN COMM Berufsausrüstung *f*, Handwerkszeug *nt*

top 1. *n* GEN COMM Spitze *f*; ♦ ~ **down** GEN COMM,

MGMNT *planning* retrograd, von oben nach unten, Top-Down-; **at the ~ end** GEN COMM *of a scale* am oberen Ende; **at the ~ rate** TAX zum Spitzensteuersatz; **be on ~ of one's job** HRM die Arbeit im Griff haben; **be ~ of the league** GEN COMM Spitzenreiter sein, Tabellenführer sein; **~ wages paid** HRM *job offers, recruitments* wir zahlen Spitzenlöhne; **2.** *vt* GEN COMM *surpass* übertreffen; ◆ **~ the list** GEN COMM an erster Stelle stehen, ganz oben auf der Liste stehen

top out *vi* GEN COMM *rate, price, cost* einen Höchststand erreichen

top up *vt* GEN COMM *savings* abschließen, aufstocken

top: **~ copy** *n* GEN COMM Original *nt*; **~-down approach to investing** *n* FIN Top-Down-Untersuchung *f* der Bedingungen einer Investition; **~-down linkage model** *n* ECON Top-Down-Modell *nt*; **~ end of the market** *n* S&M *marketing* Markt *m* für Qualitätsprodukte, oberer Marktbereich *m*; **~ end of the range** *n* S&M *marketing* oberer Bereich *m* der Skala; **~ executive** *n* MGMNT Aufsichtratmitglied *nt*, HRM oberste Führungskraft *f*; **~-flight** *adj* GEN COMM erstklassig, führend, hochkarätig (*infrml*); **~-grade securities** *n pl* STOCK erstklassige Wertpapiere *nt pl*; **~ hand** *n* AmE GEN COMM, HRM Spitzenkraft *f*, Spitzenmann *m* (*infrml*); **~-hat pension** *n infrml* FIN, HRM Vorstandspension *f*; **~-hat scheme** *n infrml* FIN, HRM Vorstandspension *f*; **~-heavy** *adj* ADMIN *organization* kopflastig, FIN überkapitalisiert, GEN COMM *structure, organization, price* überbewertet, überkapitalisiert, TRANSP oberlastig

topic *n* GEN COMM Thema *nt*

TOPIC *abbr BrE* (*Teletex Output of Price Information by Computer*) STOCK elektronisches Börseninformationssystem der Londoner Börse

top: **~-level efficiency** *n* ECON, MGMNT Spitzeneffizienz *f*; **~-level talks** *n pl* MGMNT Gespräche *nt pl* auf höchster Ebene, Spitzengespräch *nt*; **~ of the line** *n* GEN COMM Markenführer *m*, Spitzenmarke *f*; **~-loader container** *n* TRANSP Toplader-Container *m*; **~ management** *n* MGMNT oberste Betriebsführung *f*, oberste Leitungsebene *f*, Spitzenmanagement *nt*, Top-Management *nt*, Unternehmensspitze *f*; **~ management approach** *n* MGMNT Top-Management-Lösung *f*

topper *n* GEN COMM *entertainment industry* Geschäftsführer, in *m,f*

topping: **~ out** *n* (*jarg*) STOCK Erreichung *f* des Höchststandes; **~-up clause** *n BrE* BANK Aufstockungsklausel *f*

topple *vt* POL *government* stürzen

top: **~ price** *n* GEN COMM, STOCK Spitzenpreis *m*, Höchstkurs *m*, Höchstpreis *m*; **~ quality** *n* GEN COMM beste Qualität *f*, erste Wahl *f*, Spitzenqualität *f*; **~ of the range** *n* GEN COMM führende Position *f*, Spitzenstellung *f*; **~-ranking** *adj* GEN COMM hochgestellt, hochrangig; **~-ranking official** *n* ADMIN höchste(r) Beamte(r) *m* [decl. as adj], höchste Beamtin *f*, Spitzenbeamte(r) *m* [decl. as adj], Spitzenbeamtin *f*; **~-rank product** *n* GEN COMM, S&M erstklassiges Erzeugnis *nt*, Spitzenprodukt *nt*; **~ rate of tax** *n* TAX Spitzensteuersatz *m*; **~ salaries review body** *n BrE* HRM, MGMNT Prüfungsgremium *nt* für Spitzengehälter; **~-secret** *adj* GEN COMM, POL streng geheim; **~-selling article** *n* S&M Verkaufsschlager *m*; **~-sided federalism** *n* ECON, POL Föderalismus *m* mit bundesstaatlichem Übergewicht; **~ of the tree** *n infrml* GEN COMM, HRM, MGMNT Spitze *f*

Toronto: **~ Composite** *n* STOCK Toronto-Gesamtindex *m*; **~ Stock Exchange** *n* STOCK Wertpapierbörse *f* in Toronto

tort *n* LAW *England and Wales* Delikt *nt*; **~ feasor** *n* LAW Gesetzesübertreter, in *m,f*, Missetäter, in *m,f*, Schadensstifter, in *m,f*; **~ liability** *n* LAW *civil law* Haftung *f* aus unerlaubter Handlung

tot up *vt BrE infrml* GEN COMM zusammenzählen, addieren

total 1. *adj* GEN COMM total; **2.** *n* ECON Summe *f*, FIN Gesamtbetrag *m*, Summe *f*, GEN COMM Summe *f*

total: **~ allowable catches** *n pl* (*TACs*) ENVIR *fishing* quotas zulässige Fangquote *f*; **~ amount loaned** *n* FIN Ausleihungen *f pl*; **~ assets** *n pl* ACC Gesamtvermögen *nt*; **~ audience package** *n* S&M *music, radio* Werbespot *m* für die gesamte Zuhörerschaft, *television, films* Werbespot *m* für die gesamte Zuschauerschaft; **~ base number** *n* (*TBN*) IND Gesamtbasenzahl *f* (*TBN*); **~ budget** *n* FIN Gesamtbudget *nt*; **~ capitalization** *n* FIN Gesamtkapitalisierung *f*; **~ cost of the credit to the consumer** *n* FIN *including interest and other charges* Gesamtkreditkosten *pl* für den Verbraucher; **~ costs** *n pl* ECON, GEN COMM Gesamtkosten *pl*; **~ domestic expenditure** *n* ECON Absorption *f*; **~ effective exposure** *n* S&M *advertising* Gesamtzahl *f* der Werbeträger; **~ estimates** *n pl* FIN Gesamtausgabenansätze *m pl*; **~ fertility rate** *n* (*TRF*) ECON Gesamtfertilitätsrate *f*; **~ funds applied** *n pl* FIN eingesetzte Mittel *nt pl* insgesamt; **~ funds provided** *n pl* FIN gesamte zur Verfügung gestellte Mittel *nt pl*, Mittelbereitstellung *f* insgesamt

totalizator *n* GEN COMM Summenzählwerk *nt*

totalize *vt* GEN COMM zusammenfassen, zusammenzählen

total: **~ liabilities** *n pl* ACC, INS Summe *f* der Verbindlichkeiten; **~ loss** *n* (*T/L*) GEN COMM, INS Gesamtschaden *m*, Totalschaden *m*, Totalverlust *m*; **~ loss only** *phr* (*TLO*) GEN COMM, INS nur bei Totalverlust, nur gegen Totalverlust versichert; **~ net flow** *n* ECON gesamter Nettofluß *m*; **~ net redemptions** *n pl* BANK *investment banking* Nettotilgungsvolumen *nt*; **~ non-budget** *adj* FIN nichtbudgetiert insgesamt; **~ number of man-hours worked** *n* ECON Arbeitsvolumen *nt*, HRM Mannstunden *f pl* insgesamt; **~ obligational authority** *n* (*TOA*) FIN Ausgabeermächtigung *f*; **~ plant maintenance** *n* GEN COMM, IND Gesamtanlagenwartung *f*; **~ production cost** *n* ACC, IND Selbstkosten *pl*; **~ public debt** *n* ECON, POL gesamte Staatsverschuldung *f*, Gesamtverschuldung *f* des Staates, öffentliche Verschuldung *f*; **~ public spending** *n* ECON, POL Gesamtbetrag *m* der Staatsausgaben, gesamte öffentliche Ausgaben *f pl*; **~ quality control** *n* (*TQC*) IND, MGMNT Gesamtqualitätskontrolle *f*; **~ quality management** *n* (*TQM*) MGMNT Gesamtqualitätsleitung *f*, Gesamtqualitätsüberwachung *f*, Gesamtqualitätssicherung *f*, Total Quality Management *nt* (*TQM*); **~ revenue** *n* ECON Gesamteinnahmen *f pl*, Gesamtsteueraufkommen *nt*, TAX Gesamtsteueraufkommen *nt*; **~ social charges** *n pl* ACC *yearly* gesamte Soziallasten *f pl*; **~ standard spending** *n* ECON Summe *f* der Standardausgaben; **~ to date** *n* FIN aktueller Gesamtbetrag *m*; **~ votes cast** *n pl* GEN COMM, POL *in ballot, election* Zahl *f* der abgegebenen Stimmen; **~ wages and salaries** *n pl* ACC, HRM gesamte Löhne *m* und Gehälter *nt pl*, Lohn- und Gehaltssumme *f*; **~ yield** *n* ECON, IND, S&M Gesamtrendite *f*

tote: ~ **bin** *n* TRANSP Transportbehälter *m*

touch: ~-**activated** *adj* COMP mit Sensoreingabe, sensoraktiviert; ~-**and-go** *adj* ECON gefährlich, riskant, GEN COMM riskant

touched: ~ **bill of health** *n* GEN COMM nicht ganz einwandfreier Gesundheitsspaß *m*

touch: ~ **key** *n* COMP Sensortaste *f*; ~-**sensitive screen** *n* COMP Sensorbildschirm *m*; ~-**tone phone** *n* COMMS Tastentelefon *nt*

touch-type *vi* ADMIN, COMP blind tippen, blindschreiben

touch-typing *n* ADMIN, COMP Blindschreiben *nt*

tough *adj* GEN COMM *conditions* hart, schwierig; ~ **competition** *n* GEN COMM harter Konkurrenzkampf *m*, harter Wettbewerb *m*, scharfe Konkurrenz *f*; ~ **competitor** *n* GEN COMM harter Konkurrent *m*; ~ **stance** *n* GEN COMM feste Haltung *f*

tour *n* GEN COMM, LEIS Exkursion *f*, Reise *f*, Rundreise *f*, Besichtigung *f*

touring: ~ **company** *n* LEIS *theatre group* Gastspielensemble *nt*

tourism *n* LEIS Fremdenverkehr *m*, Tourismus *m*

tourist *n* LEIS Tourist, in *m,f*; ~ **attraction** *n* LEIS Touristenattraktion *f*

Tourist: ~ **Board** *n* BrE LEIS Verkehrsamt *nt*, Verkehrsverein *m*

tourist: ~ **class** *n* LEIS, TRANSP *air travel* Touristenklasse *f*; ~ **exchange rate** *n* ECON *formerly in Russia* Wechselkurs *m* für Touristen, Touristenkurs *m* (*infrml*); ~ **information bureau** *n* LEIS Fremdenverkehrsbüro *nt*, Touristeninformation *f*; ~ **information office** *n* LEIS Fremdenverkehrsbüro *nt*, Touristeninformation *f*; ~ **office** *n* LEIS Verkehrsamt *nt*, Verkehrsverein *m*; ~ **season** *n* LEIS Touristensaison *f*; ~ **tax** *n* TAX Touristenabgabe *f*; ~ **trade** *n* LEIS Fremdenverkehrsgewerbe *nt*, Tourismusgeschäft *nt*,˙ Touristikbranche *f*, Fremdenverkehr *m*; ~ **visa** *n* ADMIN Touristenvisum *nt*

tour: ~ **operator** *n* LEIS Reiseunternehmen *nt*; ~ **organization** *n* LEIS Reiseorganisation *f*, Tourorganisation *f*; ~ **organizer** *n* LEIS Reiseveranstalter, in *m,f*, Tourorganisator *m*

tout **1.** *n* GEN COMM, LEIS Kundenfänger, in *m,f*, Schwarzhändler, in *m,f*; **2.** *vt* LEIS *tickets* anbieten; **3.** *vi* ♦ ~ **for business** *infrml* GEN COMM Käufer anreißen (*infrml*); ~ **for custom** GEN COMM auf Kundenfang sein; ~ **for customers** *infrml* GEN COMM Kunden anreißen (*infrml*)

TOVALOP *abbr* (*tanker owners' voluntary agreement concerning liability for oil pollution*) ENVIR, INS, TRANSP freiwillige Übereinkunft der Eigentümer von Tankern bezüglich der Haftung bei Ölverschmutzung

tow **1.** *n* TRANSP Schleppzug *m*, Schubverband *m*; **2.** *vt* TRANSP *car* abschleppen, *trailer, boat* schleppen

towage: ~ **charges** *n pl* TRANSP *shipping* Bugsiergebühr *f*, Schleppgebühr *f*; ~ **contractor** *n* TRANSP *shipping* Schleppunternehmer *m*; ~ **dues** *n pl* TRANSP *shipping* Bugsiergebühr *f*, Schleppgebühr *f*

towaway: ~ **zone** *n* AmE TRANSP Abschleppzone *f*

towboat *n* TRANSP Bugsierschiff *nt*, Bugsierschlepper *m*, Schlepper *m*

tow: ~ **cloth** *n* TRANSP Packleinwand *f*, Sackleinwand *f*

tower: ~ **block** *n* PROP, WEL Hochhaus *nt*

tow: ~ **hook** *n* TRANSP *trailer* Anhängerzughaken *m*

towing *n* TRANSP Abschleppen *nt*, Schleppen *nt*; ~ **ambulance** *n* TRANSP Abschleppwagen *m*; ~ **boat** *n* TRANSP Bugsierschiff *nt*, Bugsierschlepper *m*, Schlepper *m*; ~ **dolly** *n* TRANSP Schlepprollbock *m*; ~ **gear** *n* TRANSP Schleppeinrichtung *f*; ~ **hawser** *n* TRANSP Schlepptau *nt*, Schlepptrosse *f*

towline *n* TRANSP *ship* Leine *f*, Schlepptau *nt*

town: ~ **administration** *n* ADMIN, POL Stadtverwaltung *f*; ~ **bill** *n* BANK Platzwechsel *m*; ~ **center** *AmE*, ~ **centre** *BrE n* GEN COMM Stadtmitte *f*, Stadtzentrum *nt*; ~ **clearing** *n* BANK *banking* Platzgiroverkehr *m*; ~ **council** *n* ADMIN, POL Stadtrat *m*; ~ **councillor** *n* ADMIN, GEN COMM, POL Stadtverordnete(r) *mf* [decl. as adj], Stadtrat *m*, Stadträtin *f*

Town: ~ **and Country Planning Act** *n* BrE LAW Regionalplanungsgesetz *nt*

town: ~ **hall** *n* ADMIN, GEN COMM, POL Rathaus *nt*; ~ **house** *n* PROP Stadthaus *nt*; ~ **planner** *n* ADMIN, GEN COMM, POL, PROP Stadtplaner, in *m,f*; ~ **planning** *n* (*TP*) ADMIN, POL, PROP Städtebau *m*, städtebauliche Planung *f*, Stadtplanung *f*

towpath *n* TRANSP *ship* Leinpfad *m*

towrope *n* TRANSP Abschleppseil *nt*

tow: ~ **truck** *n* AmE (*cf breakdown van BrE*) TRANSP Abschleppwagen *m*, Bergungsfahrzeug *nt*, Werkstattwagen *m*

toxic *adj* ENVIR giftig, toxisch; ~, **explosive, corrosive, hazardous cargo** *n* (*TECH cargo*) TRANSP explosive, korrodierende, gefährliche Fracht *f*

toxicity *n* ENVIR Giftigkeit *f*, Toxizität *f*

toxicological *adj* ENVIR toxikologisch

toxic: ~ **waste** *n* ENVIR Giftmüll *m*

toxin *n* ENVIR Gift *nt*, Toxin *nt*

TP *abbr* (*town planning*) ADMIN, POL, PROP Städtebau *m*, städtebauliche Planung *f*, Stadtplanung *f*

TPC *abbr* (*tonnes per centimeter AmE, tonnes per centimetre BrE*) GEN COMM Tonnen *f pl* pro Zentimeter

TPI *abbr* (*Tropical Products Institute*) ECON Institut *nt* für Tropenprodukte

TQC *abbr* (*total quality control*) MGMNT Gesamtqualitätskontrolle *f*

TQM *abbr* (*total quality management*) MGMNT Gesamtqualitätsleitung *f*, Gesamtqualitätsüberwachung *f*, Gesamtqualitätssicherung *f*, TQM (*Total Quality Management*)

tr. *abbr* (*transfer*) ACC Umbuchung *f*, ADMIN Versetzung *f*, BANK *of funds* Überweisung *f*, Umbuchung *f*, COMP, ECON, FIN Transfer *m*, GEN COMM *of responsibilities, liabilities* Übertragung *f*, Versetzung *f*, HRM Umsetzung *f*, Versetzung *f*, Transfer *m*, INS Abtretung *f*, LAW Abtretung *f*, Übereignung *f*, Veräußerung *f*, PATENTS Übertragung *f*, Zession *f*, Abtretung *f*, Überschreibung *f*, PROP *of property* Übertragung *f*, STOCK Umschreibung *f*, Übertragung *f*, TAX *of money* Abführung *f*, TRANSP Transfer *m*, Umsteigung *f*

TR *abbr AmE* (*triple reduction*) GEN COMM dreifache Senkung *f*

trace *vt* GEN COMM lokalisieren, *follow trail of* nachfolgen [+dat], TRANSP verfolgen; ♦ ~ **a call** COMMS einen Anruf verfolgen; ~ **a payment** BANK eine Zahlung zurückverfolgen

trace back *vt* GEN COMM zurückverfolgen

tracer *n* GEN COMM Laufzettel *m*, Suchzettel *m*

tracing *n* GEN COMM, IND, MEDIA Pause *f*
track 1. *n* TRANSP *rail* Gleis *nt*, *railway* Strecke *f*; ◆ **on ~** GEN COMM auf der richtigen Spur, TRANSP *rail* auf Achse; **2.** *vt* GEN COMM *spending* kontrollieren, verfolgen
trackball *n* COMP *pointer device* Trackball *m*
track: **~ connection** *n* TRANSP *rail* Gleisverbindung *f*
tracking *n* GEN COMM *sales, costs, expenses* Kontrolle *f*; **~ study** *n* MEDIA, S&M *market research* Wiederholungsbefragung *f*; **~ system** *n* GEN COMM Kontrollsystem *nt*, Überwachungssystem *nt*
track: **~ record** *n* GEN COMM bisherig gezeigte Leistungen *f pl*, HRM nachweisbarer Berufsverlauf *m*, S&M Verkaufserfolg *m*; **~ scales** *n pl* TRANSP *rail* Gleiswaage *f*, Waggonwaage *f*; **~ storage charge** *n* TRANSP Wagenstandsgeld *nt*
tractive: **~ machine** *n* TRANSP Zugmaschine *f*
tractor: **~-fed** *adj* COMP mit Friktionsantrieb; **~ feed** *n* COMP Friktionsantrieb *m*, Traktorzuführung *f*
trade 1. *adj* GEN COMM gewerblich; **2.** *n* ECON, GEN COMM *sector of economy* Wirtschaftszweig *m*, Branche *f*, *commerce* Handel *m*, Handelsverkehr *m*, Geschäft *m*, *exchange* Güteraustausch *m*, HRM *job, profession* Beruf *m*; **3.** *vt* ECON, GEN COMM *deal in* handeln mit, *exchange* austauschen; ◆ **~ raw materials for manufactured goods** GEN COMM Rohstoffe gegen Fertigerzeugnisse handeln; **4.** *vi* ECON, GEN COMM Handel treiben, handeln; ◆ **~ as** GEN COMM ein Gewerbe betreiben als, ein Gewerbe treiben als, tätig sein als; **~ at** STOCK handeln an, *shares* einen Kurs haben von, liegen bei; **~ down** GEN COMM mit Billigerzeugnissen handeln; **~ for one's account** STOCK auf eigene Rechnung handeln; **~ in stocks and bonds** STOCK Aktien und Anleihen kaufen und verkaufen; **~ under the name of Smith** GEN COMM den Geschäftsnamen Smith führen
trade in *vt* GEN COMM, STOCK eintauschen, in Zahlung geben
trade off *vt* ECON ausgleichen, eintauschen; ◆ **~ market share against profit margins** ECON Marktanteile gegen Gewinnmargen eintauschen
tradeability *n* ECON, GEN COMM Handelsfähigkeit *f*, Negoziierbarkeit *f*
tradeable *adj* ECON, GEN COMM gängig, handelbar; **~ discharge permit** *n* (*TDP*) ECON handelbares Emissionszertifikat *nt*; **~ emission permit** *n* ECON, ENVIR handelbares Emissionszertifikat *nt*
trade: **~ acceptance** *n* GEN COMM, IMP/EXP Handelsakzept *nt*, Handelswechsel *m*, Warenwechsel *m*, Außenhandelsakzept *nt*; **~ account** *n* GEN COMM Kundenkonto *nt*; **~ account receivables** *n pl AmE* ACC Forderungen *f pl* aus Lieferungen und Leistungen; **~ accounts payable** *n pl AmE* ACC Verbindlichkeiten *f pl* aus Lieferungen und Leistungen; **~ accounts receivable** *n pl* ACC Warenforderungen *f pl*; **~ advertising** *n* S&M Händlerwerbung *f*; **~ agreement** *n* ECON, LAW Handelsabkommen *nt*, Handelsvereinbarung *f*; **~ allowance** *n* GEN COMM Großhandelsrabatt *m*, Rabatt *m* für Wiederverkäufer; **~ and industry** *n* ECON gewerbliche Wirtschaft *f*; **~ association** *n* ECON, GEN COMM Fachverband *m*, Berufsgenossenschaft *f*, Berufsvereinigung *f*, Gewerbeverband *m*, Handelsverband *m*, Unternehmerverband *m*, Wirtschaftsverband *m*; **~ balance** *n* ECON, GEN COMM Handelsbilanz *f*; **~ barrier** *n* ECON, GEN COMM, IMP/EXP Handelsschranke

f, Handelshemmnis *nt*; **~ bill** *n* BANK Handelswechsel *m*, Warenwechsel *m*, STOCK Handelswechsel *m*; **~ brief** *n* ECON *international trade* Handelsbulletin *nt*; **~ car** *n* TRANSP Handelswagen *m*; **~ chamber** *n* ECON, GEN COMM, LAW Handelskammer *f* (*HK*); **~ channel** *n* GEN COMM Absatzkanal *m*, Absatzweg *m*, Beschaffungsweg *m*; **~ counter** *n* S&M *in shop* Theke *f*, Verkaufstheke *f*, Verkaufstisch *m*, Verkaufsschalter *m*; **~ creation** *n* ECON handelsschaffende Wirkungen *f pl*; **~ credit** *n* ACC Handelskredit *m*, BANK Warenkredit *m*; **~ creditor** *n* ACC, GEN COMM Handelsgläubiger, in *m,f*, Gläubiger, in *m,f* aus Lieferungen und Leistungen, Lieferantengläubiger, in *m,f*, Lieferantenkreditgeber, in *m,f*, Warengläubiger, in *m,f*; **~ custom** *n* GEN COMM Handelsbrauch *m*; **~ cycle** *n* ECON Konjunkturphase *f*, Konjunkturzyklus *m*; **~ cycle policy** *n* ECON, POL Konjunkturpolitik *f*
Trade: **~ Data Elements Directory** *n* (*TDED*) ECON Branchenverzeichnis *nt*; **~ Data Interchange** *n* (*TDI*) ECON Austausch *m* von Handelsdaten
trade: **~ debtor** *n* ACC Handelsschuldner *m*; **~ debtors** *n pl* ACC Forderungen *f pl* aus Lieferungen und Leistungen; **~ deficit** *n* ECON, IMP/EXP, POL Außenhandelsbilanzdefizit *nt*, Außenhandelsdefizit *nt*, Handelsdefizit *nt*, passive Handelsbilanz *f*; **~ description** *n* S&M *advertising* Warenbeschreibung *f*
Trade: **~ Descriptions Act** *n BrE* LAW, S&M *advertising* Gesetz über wahrheitsgemäße Angaben auf Waren und Verpackung
trade: **~ directory** *n* GEN COMM Branchenverzeichnis *nt*, Firmenverzeichnis *nt*, Handelsadreßbuch *nt*; **~ discount** *n* ACC, GEN COMM, S&M Nachlaß *m*, Skonto *m or nt*; **~ dispute** *n* HRM Auseinandersetzung *f* mit der Gewerkschaft; **~ distortion** *n* ECON Handelsverzerrung *f*; **~ diversion** *n* ECON Handelsablenkung *f*, IMP/EXP Handelsverlagerung *f*
traded: **~ option** *n* STOCK handelbare Option *f*
trade: **~ entrance** *n* GEN COMM Lieferanteneingang *m*; **~ exhibition** *n* S&M *for professionals* Fachausstellung *f*; **~ facilitation** *n* ECON *international trade* Handelserleichterung *f*; **~ fair** *n* GEN COMM Messe *f*, S&M *advertising* Gewerbeausstellung *f*, *professionals only* Fachmesse *f*; **~ fair insurance** *n* INS Ausstellungsversicherung *f*; **~ figures** *n pl* ECON, GEN COMM, POL Außenwirtschaftszahlen *f pl*, Handelsziffern *f pl*; **~ fixtures** *n pl* PROP gewerbliche Einbauten *m pl*; **~ flow** *n* ECON Handelsstrom *m*; **~ gap** *n* ECON, IMP/EXP, POL Außenhandelsbilanzdefizit *nt*, Außenhandelsdefizit *nt*, Handelsbilanzdefizit *nt*; **~-in allowance** *n* GEN COMM Inzahlungnahme *f* einer gebrauchten Sache; **~ in industrial goods** *n* GEN COMM Handel *m* mit Industriewaren; **~ investments** *n pl* ECON Beteiligung *f*, Finanzanlageinvestition *f*; **~ journal** *n* GEN COMM, MEDIA Fachblatt *nt*, Fachorgan *nt*, Fachzeitschrift *f*, Verbandszeitung *f*; **~ liberalization** *n* ECON, GEN COMM, LAW Handelsliberalisierung *f*, Liberalisierung *f* des Handels; **~ magazine** *n* GEN COMM Fachblatt *nt*, Fachzeitschrift *f*, MEDIA Fachzeitschrift *f*
trademark *n* ACC, GEN COMM Handelszeichen *nt*, Schutzmarke *f*, Warenzeichen *nt*, LAW *intellectual property* Warenzeichen *nt*, PATENTS, S&M Warenzeichen *nt*, Schutzmarke *f*, Markenzeichen *nt*, Handelsmarke *f*; **~ agent** *n* LAW Warenzeichenvertreter, in *m,f*
trade: **~ mart** *n* GEN COMM, S&M Handelszentrum *nt*;

~ name *n* GEN COMM, S&M Firmenname *m*, *of product* Handelsbezeichnung *f*, Markenname *m*; **~ number** *n* FIN Auftragsnummer *f*; **~-off** *n* ECON Austauschbeziehung *f*, Trade-off *m*, *between growth and profitability* Ausgleich *m*, *unemployment, inflation* Abstimmung *f*, Kompromiß *m*; **~ organization** *n* GEN COMM Fachorganisation *f*, Handelsorganisation *f*; **~ park** *n* AmE PROP Gewerbegebiet *nt*, Gewerbepark *m*, Gewerbefläche *f*; **~ and payment agreement** *n* LAW Handels- und Zahlungsabkommen *nt*; **~ policy** *n* ECON, IMP/EXP Außenhandelspolitik *f*, Handelspolitik *f*; **~ practice** *n* GEN COMM Handelspraktik *f*; **~ practice rules** *n pl* ECON, GEN COMM, LAW Wettbewerbsregeln *f pl*; **~ practices** *n pl* GEN COMM Handelspraktiken *f pl*; **~ press** *n* MEDIA *print* Fachpresse *f*; **~ promotion** *n* S&M *advertising* Handelsförderung *f*; **~ protectionism** *n* ECON, IMP/EXP *international trade* Handelsprotektionismus *m*, Schutzzollsystem *nt* im Handel

trader *n* GEN COMM, S&M Händler, in *m,f*, Wertpapierhändler, in *m,f*, Unternehmer, in *m,f*, Geschäftsmann *m*, Geschäftsfrau *f*

trade: **~ receivables** *n pl* ACC Forderungen *f pl* aus Warenlieferungen; **~ regime** *n* ECON, IMP/EXP, POL Außenhandelspolitik *f*; **~ register** *n* GEN COMM, S&M Handelsregister *nt*; **~-related** *adj* ECON auf den Handel bezogen; **~ restriction** *n* ECON *international trade*, GEN COMM *imposed by government*, IMP/EXP *quotas* Handelsbeschränkung *f*, Handelsrestriktion *f*; **~ returns** *n pl* GEN COMM Handelsstatistik *f*; **~ route** *n* ECON, IMP/EXP, TRANSP Handelsroute *f*, Handelsweg *m*; **~ sanctions** *n pl* ECON, POL Wirtschaftssanktionen *f pl*; **~ secret** *n* GEN COMM Berufsgeheimnis *nt*, Geschäftsgeheimnis *nt*; **~ show** *n* S&M Fachausstellung *f*, Fachmesse *f*, *film show* geschlossene Filmvorstellung *f*; **~ sign** *n* GEN COMM Firmenzeichen *nt*, Gewerbezeichen *nt*

tradesman: **~'s entrance** *n* GEN COMM Lieferanteneingang *m*, Nebeneingang *m*; **~'s lien** *n* PROP gesetzliches Handwerkerpfandrecht *nt*

tradespeople *n pl* GEN COMM Geschäftsleute *pl*, Gewerbetreibende *pl* [decl. as adj], Handelsleute *pl*

trade: **~ strategy** *n* ECON, GEN COMM Handelsstrategie *f*

Trades: **~ Union Congress** *n* BrE (*TUC*) HRM Dachorganisation der britischen Gewerkschaften, ≈ Deutscher Gewerkschaftsbund *m* (*DGB*)

trade: **~ surplus** *n* ECON, IMP/EXP, POL Außenhandelsüberschuß *m*, Handelsbilanzüberschuß *m*; **~ talks** *n pl* ECON Handelsgespräche *nt pl*; **~ terms** *n pl* GEN COMM, LAW *trade agreements* Handelsbedingungen *f pl*, handelsübliche Vertragsformeln *f pl*; **~ union** *n* BrE (*TU, cf labor union AmE*) GEN COMM, HRM, POL Gewerkschaft *f* (*Gew.*)

Trade: **~ Union Act 1984** *n* BrE (*TUA*) ECON, LAW britisches Gewerkschaftsgesetz über interne Wahlen und Koalitionsfreiheit

trade: **~ union contributions** *n pl* BrE HRM Gewerkschaftsbeiträge *m pl*; **~ union dues** *n pl* BrE HRM Gewerkschaftsbeiträge *m pl*; **~ unionism** *n* BrE HRM Gewerkschaftsbewegung *f*; **~ unionist** *n* BrE HRM Gewerkschafter, in *m,f*

Trade: **~ Union and Labour Relations Act 1976** *n* BrE (*TULRA*) ECON, HRM, LAW britisches Gewerkschaftsgesetz zur Konsolidierung des Verhältnisses zwischen Arbeitgebern und Arbeitnehmern

trade: **~ union recognition** *n* BrE HRM Anerkennung *f* einer Gewerkschaft; **~ union subscription** *n* BrE HRM Gewerkschaftsbeitrag *m*; **~ volume** *n* ECON, GEN COMM Handelsvolumen *nt*; **~ war** *n* ECON Handelskrieg *m*; **~ week** *n* S&M Handelswoche *f*; **~-weighted exchange rate** *n* ECON gewogener Außenwert *m* einer Währung, GEN COMM nach Handelsvolumen gewichteter Umrechnungskurs *m*; **~-weighted external value** *n* ECON *of currency* gewogener Außenwert *m*; **~ within the EU** *n* ECON, GEN COMM, POL, S&M Binnenhandel *m*, EU-Handel *m*

trading *n* STOCK Verkehr *m*; **~ account** *n* ACC, BANK Erfolgskonto *nt*, Verkaufskonto *nt*; **~ area** *n* ECON Absatzgebiet *nt*, Handelszone *f*, S&M *shop* Verkaufszone *f*, *territory* Verkaufsgebiet *nt*; **~ authorization** *n* GEN COMM Gewerbeerlaubnis *f*, Handelserlaubnis *f*; **~ bloc** *n* ECON Handelsblock *m*; **~ book** *n* FIN *of institution* Börsenhandelsbuch *nt*, Trading Book *nt* (*jarg*); **~ company** *n* GEN COMM, IMP/EXP gewerbliches Unternehmen *nt*, Handelsgesellschaft *f*, kaufmännisches Unternehmen *nt*; **~ debts** *n pl* FIN Geschäftsschulden *f pl*; **~ dividend** *n* STOCK Handelsdividende *f*; **~ down** *n* S&M Handel mit Billigerzeugnissen zwecks Umsatzsteigerung; **~ estate** *n* IND Industriegebiet *nt*, Industriegelände *nt*, Industriezone *f*, PROP Gewerbegebiet *nt*, Gewerbepark *m*, Industriepark *m*, Industriegebiet *nt*; **~ floor** *n* STOCK Parkett *nt*; **~ halt** *n* STOCK Aussetzen *nt* der Notierung; **~ income** *n* FIN Handelseinkommen *nt*; **~ life** *n* STOCK *currency futures* Handelslaufzeit *f*; **~ limit** *n* STOCK Kurslimit *nt*, *futures* maximale Preisfluktuation *f*, TRANSP *shipping* Handelsgrenze *f*; **~ links** *n pl* GEN COMM, IMP/EXP, POL Handelsbeziehungen *f pl*; **~ losses** *n pl* ACC Betriebsverlust *m*, FIN Geschäftsverluste *m pl*; **~ member** *n* STOCK *of exchange* Händler, in *m,f*, Marktteilnehmer, in *m,f*; **~ name** *n* GEN COMM, LAW, PATENTS Handelsname *m*; **~ on the equity** *n* ECON *company capital structure* Fremdfinanzierung *f*, Variation *f* der Finanzierungsquoten; **~ operation** *n* BANK Handelsgeschäft *nt*; **~ partner** *n* ECON, POL Handelspartner *m*; **~ party** *n* STOCK *money market* Teilnehmer, in *m,f* am Handel; **~ pattern** *n* STOCK Handelsmuster *nt*; **~ pit** *n* STOCK Handelsmaklerstand *m*; **~ port** *n* TRANSP Handelshafen *m*; **~ portfolio** *n* BANK *investment banking* Handelsbestand *m*; **~ program** *AmE*, **~ programme** *BrE n* FIN, GEN COMM Börsenhandelsprogramm *nt*, Geschäftsprogramm *nt*, Handelsprogramm *nt*; **~ range** *n* STOCK *commodities, securities* Kursspanne *f*; **~ results** *n pl* ACC, FIN, GEN COMM Betriebsergebnis *nt*, Handelsergebnis *nt*; **~ rules** *n pl* STOCK Bestimmungen *f pl* für den Aktienhandel; **~ stamp** *n* COMMS, PATENTS Rabattmarke *f*; **~ standards** *n pl* GEN COMM Handelsnormen *f pl*

Trading: **~ Standards Office** *n* AmE ECON Gewerbeaufsichtsamt *nt*

trading: **~ unit** *n* STOCK *Eurodollar options contract specifications* Börsenschlußeinheit *f*, Kontraktgröße *f*; **~ up** *n* S&M Handel mit Waren höherer Preislage und Gewinnspanne; **~ variation** *n* STOCK Abschlußspanne *f*; **~ vessel** *n* TRANSP Handelsschiff *nt*; **~ volume** *n* GEN COMM Handelsumfang *m*; **~ year** *n* ACC, GEN COMM Berichtsjahr *nt*, Geschäftsjahr *nt*

tradition *n* GEN COMM Tradition *f*

traditional *adj* GEN COMM herkömmlich, traditionell

traffic 1. *n* GEN COMM *trade* Handel *m*, Handelsverkehr *m*, TRANSP Verkehr *m*; **2.** *vi* GEN COMM handeln; ~ **in** GEN COMM handeln mit

traffic: ~ **analysis** *n* TRANSP Verkehrsanalyse *f*; ~ **circle** *n* AmE (*cf roundabout BrE*) TRANSP Kreisverkehr *m*; ~ **congestion** *n* TRANSP Verkehrsstau *m*; ~ **control** *n* TRANSP Verkehrskontrolle *f*; ~ **control tower** *n* TRANSP *airport, seaport* Kontrollturm *m*, Verkehrskontrollturm *m*; ~ **count** *n* ENVIR *pollution*, TRANSP Verkehrszählung *f*; ~ **density** *n* TRANSP Verkehrsdichte *f*; ~ **department** *n* S&M *advertising* Terminüberwachung *f*, *department store* Zustellabteilung *f*, TRANSP Versandabteilung *f*; ~ **flow** *n* ENVIR, TRANSP Verkehrsfluß *m*; ~ **forecast** *n* TRANSP Verkehrshinweis *m*; ~ **jam** *n* TRANSP Stau *m*, Stauung *f*, Verkehrsstau *m*, Verstopfung *f*

trafficker *n* GEN COMM Dealer, in *m,f*, Schieber, in *m,f* (*infrml*), Schwarzhändler, in *m,f*

traffic: ~ **lane** *n* TRANSP Fahrbahn *f*, Fahrspur *f*; ~ **manager** MGMNT Leiter, in *m,f* des Wareneingangs; ~ **mixture** *n* TRANSP Verkehrsgemisch *nt*; ~ **planning** *n* TRANSP *advertising* Verkehrsplanung *f*; ~ **potential** *n* TRANSP Verkehrspotential *nt*; ~ **rights** *n pl* TRANSP Verkehrsrechte *nt pl*; ~ **separation scheme** *n* TRANSP Verkehrslenkungsprogramm *nt*; ~ **sign** *n* TRANSP Verkehrszeichen *nt*; ~ **superintendent** *n* (*TS*) HRM Fahrdienstleiter, in *m,f*; ~ **trend** *n* TRANSP Verkehrstrend *m*

trail *vt* MEDIA *broadcast* ankündigen

trailblazing *adj* GEN COMM, IND, MEDIA *campaign* bahnbrechend

trailer *n* LEIS Vorfilm *m*, MEDIA *for film, TV programme* Vorschau *f*, Vorspann *m*, Programmvorschau *f*, TRANSP Anhänger *m*, Hänger *m*; ~ **on flat car** *n* AmE (*cf trailer on flat wagon BrE*) TRANSP *rail* Flachwagenanhänger *m*, Huckepackverkehr *m*; ~ **on flat wagon** *n* BrE (*cf trailer on flat car AmE*) TRANSP *rail* Flachwagenanhänger *m*, Huckepackverkehr *m*; ~ **park** *n* TRANSP Platz *m* für Wohnwagen; ~ **unladen weight** *n* GEN COMM Anhängerleergewicht *nt*; ~ **utilization** *n* TRANSP Anhängerausnutzung *f*, Anhängernutzung *f*

train *vi* HRM *as chemist, nurse* sich ausbilden lassen

trainee *n* HRM Auszubildende(r) *mf* [decl. as adj] (*Azubi*), Praktikant, in *m,f*, Anlernling *m*; ~ **manager** *n* HRM, MGMNT Manager, in *m,f* in Ausbildung

traineeship *n* HRM Praktikum *nt*, Volontariat *nt*

trainee: ~ **turnover** *n* HRM Praktikantenfluktuation *f*; ~ **typist** *n* ADMIN Schreibkraft *f* in Ausbildung

trainer *n* GEN COMM, HRM, MGMNT Ausbilder, in *m,f*

train: ~ **fare** *n* TRANSP Eisenbahntarif *m*; ~ **ferry** *n* TRANSP Eisenbahnfährschiff *nt*, Eisenbahnfähre *f*; ~ **ferry deck** *n* TRANSP *shipping* Zugfährendeck *nt*

training *n* GEN COMM, HRM Ausbildung *f*, Einarbeitung *f*, Schulung *f*, Berufsvorbereitung *f*

Training: ~ **Agency** *n* BrE (*TA*) HRM Schulungsagentur *f*, Schulungsbehörde *f*

training: ~ **allowance** *n* HRM Ausbildungsbeihilfe *f*; ~ **center** AmE, ~ **centre** BrE *n* HRM Ausbildungsstätte *f*, Schulungszentrum *nt*; ~ **course** *n* HRM Ausbildungslehrgang *m*; ~ **and education system** *n* HRM Bildungswesen *nt*

Training: ~ **and Enterprise Council** *n* (*TEC*) HRM *in England and Wales* britische Behörde zur Förderung von Ausbildung und Unternehmensgeist

training: ~ **manager** *n* GEN COMM, HRM, MGMNT Ausbildungsleiter, in *m,f*, Direktor, in *m,f* für Aus-

und Weiterbildung, Schulungsleiter, in *m,f*; ~ **needs** *n pl* GEN COMM, HRM, S&M Ausbildungsbedarf *m*, Ausbildungsmängel *m pl*; ~ **needs analysis** *n* GEN COMM Analyse *f* des Ausbildungsbedarfs, HRM Analyse *f* der Anforderungen an das Ausbildungsprogramm, S&M Ausbildungsbedarfsanalyse *f*; ~ **officer** *n* GEN COMM, HRM, MGMNT Ausbildungsleiter, in *m,f*, Ausbildende(r) *mf* [decl. as adj]; ~ **pack** *n* HRM, MGMNT Ausbildungspaket *nt*; ~ **package** *n* HRM, IND, MGMNT Ausbildungsprogramm *nt*, Schulungsprogramm *nt*, Weiterbildungsprogramm *nt*; ~ **program** *AmE*, ~ **programme** *BrE n* HRM Entwicklungsprogramm *nt*, Fortbildungsprogramm *nt*, Ausbildungsprogramm *nt*, Schulungsprogramm *nt*; ~ **scheme** *n* BrE HRM Ausbildungsprogramm *nt*; ~ **of trainers** *n* HRM Ausbildung *f* der Ausbilder; ~ **within industry** *n* (*TWI*) HRM, IND Fachausbildung *f*, innerbetriebliche Weiterbildung *f*, Weiterbildung *f* für Mitarbeiter

train: ~ **number** *n* TRANSP Zugnummer *f*; ~ **station** *n* BrE (*cf railroad station AmE*) TRANSP Bahnhof *m*, Bahnstation *f*

transact *vt* ACC abschließen, GEN COMM *business* abschließen, durchführen, handeln, umsetzen, vorgehen, S&M tätigen

transaction *n* ACC Abschluß *m*, GEN COMM Handel *m*, Transaktion *f*, Umsatz *m*, Vorgang *m*, Durchführung *f*, Abschluß *m*

transactional: ~ **analysis** *n* (*TA*) FIN, MGMNT Analyse *f* der Geschäftsabschlüsse, Transaktionsanalyse *f*

transaction: ~ **balance report** *n* ACC Bilanzbericht *m* über Abschlüsse, Transaktionsbilanz *f*; ~ **charge** *n* FIN Buchungsgebühr *f*; ~ **contrary to public policy** *n* LAW sittenwidriges Rechtsgeschäft *nt*; ~ **cost economics** *n* ECON Transaktionskostenökonomie *f*; ~ **exposure** *n* STOCK Abschlußrisiko *nt*, Transaktionsrisiko *nt*, Umrechnungsrisiko *nt*; ~ **file** *n* COMP Bewegungsdatei *f*; ~ **management** *n* FIN, MGMNT Transaktionsmanagement *nt*; ~ **management software** *n* COMP Transaktionsmanagement-Software *f*; ~ **processing** *n* COMP, FIN Transaktionsverarbeitung *f*; ~ **risk** *n* STOCK Abschlußrisiko *nt*, Transaktionsrisiko *nt*, Umrechnungsrisiko *nt*

transactions: ~ **balance** *n* ECON Transaktionskasse *f*; ~ **costs** *n pl* ECON Transaktionskosten *pl*; ~ **holdings** *n pl* ECON Transaktionskasse *f*

transaction: ~ **slip** *n* STOCK Abschlußbestätigung *f*; ~ **status** *n* GEN COMM, IND, S&M Geschäftslage *f*

transactions: ~ **tax** *n* STOCK Umsatzsteuer *f* (*USt*)

transcode *vt* COMMS umwandeln

transcoder *n* COMMS Codeumwandler *m*

transcribe *vt* COMP transkribieren, umschreiben, GEN COMM *copy* abschreiben, *from shorthand* übertragen, *speech* mitschreiben, *meeting* aufzeichnen

transcriber *n* COMP, COMMS Umschreiber *m*

transcript *n* LAW Protokoll *nt*

transcription *n* COMP Umschreibung *f*, Transkription *f*, GEN COMM *of meeting* Aufzeichnung *f*, *from shorthand* Übertragung *f*, *copy* Abschreibung *f*, *of speech* Mitschreibung *f*

transducer *n* COMP Umwandler *m*, Wandler *m*

transeuropean *adj* POL transeuropäisch; ~ **network** *n* COMMS, TRANSP Transeuropanetz *nt*

transfer 1. *n* (*tr.*, *tfr*) ACC Umbuchung *f*, ADMIN Versetzung *f*, BANK *of funds* Überweisung *f*, Umbuchung *f*, COMP, FIN Transfer *m*, GEN COMM *of responsibilities, liabilities* Übertragung *f*, Versetzung *f*, HRM Umsetzung *f*, Versetzung *f*, Transfer *m*, INS Abtretung *f*, LAW Abtretung *f*, Übereignung *f*, Veräußerung *f*, PATENTS Übertragung *f*, Zession *f*, Abtretung *f*, Überschreibung *f*, PROP *of property* Übertragung *f*, STOCK Umschreibung *f*, Übertragung *f*, TAX *of money* Abführung *f*, TRANSP Transfer *m*, Umsteigung *f*; **2.** *vt* ACC umbuchen, ADMIN versetzen, BANK überweisen, umbuchen, ECON, FIN, *funds* übertragen, überweisen, GEN COMM übertragen, versetzen, HRM *person* versetzen, umsetzen, INS abtreten, zedieren, LAW abtreten, veräußern, übereignen, überschreiben, PATENTS übertragen, abtreten, überschreiben, PROP übertragen, STOCK umschreiben, übertragen, TAX abführen, TRANSP *change train, bus* umsteigen; ♦ **~ by endorsement** BANK durch Indossament übertragen; **~ the charges** COMMS die Gebühren überweisen; **~ a debt** ACC eine Schuld übertragen; **~ ownership of sth** LAW etw übereignen, PROP das Eigentum einer Sache übertragen; **3.** *vi* TRANSP *from one train to another* umsteigen

transferability *n* STOCK *of registered shares* Abtretbarkeit *f*, Transferierbarkeit *f*, Übertragbarkeit *f*

transferable *adj* STOCK abtretbar, *options* übertragbar; **~ account area** *n* (*TAA*) ACC übertragbarer Abrechnungsbereich *m*; **~ loan certificates** *n pl* (*TLC*) FIN übertragbare Kreditzertifikate *nt pl*; **~ loan instruments** *n pl* (*TLI*) FIN übertragbare Kreditinstrumente *nt pl*; **~ security** *n* FIN, STOCK frei transferierbares Wertpapier *nt*, umschreibbares Wertpapier *nt*, *in companies* übertragbares Wertpapier *f*

transfer: **~ account** *n* BANK Girokonto *nt*; **~ address** *n* COMP Übertragungsadresse *f*

Transfer: **~ & Automated Registration of Uncertified Stock** *n BrE obs* (*TAURUS*) STOCK TAURUS

transfer: **~ of assets** *n* ACC Übertragung *f* von Vermögen; **~ of development rights** *n* PROP Übertragung *f* von Erschließungsrechten

transferee *n* BANK Erwerber, in *m,f*, Übertragungsempfänger, in *m,f*, Zessionar *m*, INS Zessionar *m*, LAW Abtretungsempfänger, in *m,f*, Zessionar *m*; **~ company** *n* FIN, GEN COMM übernehmende Gesellschaft *f*; **~ gains** *n pl* FIN Umrechnungsgewinn *m*, Währungsgewinne *m pl*

transferees *n pl* BANK Rechtsnachfolger *m pl*

transfer: **~ of engagement** *n BrE* HRM *unions* Transfer *m* an eine andere Gewerkschaft; **~ fees** *n pl* LAW *banking* Übertragungsgebühren *f pl*; **~ form** *n* LAW *trade law* Übertragungsformular *nt*; **~ of funds voucher** *n* BANK Überweisungsbeleg *m*; **~ income** *n* ECON Transfereinkommen *nt*; **~ manifest** *n* TRANSP Transfermanifest *nt*

transferrer *n* BANK Übergeber *m*, INS Abtretende(r) *mf* [decl. as adj], LAW Abtretende(r) *mf* [decl. as adj], Übertragende(r) *mf* [decl. as adj], Treugeber *m*, Veräußerer *m*, Zedent, in *m,f*, TAX *inheritance tax* Zedent, in *m,f*; **~ company** *n* GEN COMM übertragende Gesellschaft *f*

transfer: **~ order** *n* FIN Überweisungsauftrag *m*; **~ payment** *n* ECON Transferzahlung *f*; **~ price** *n* GEN COMM Verrechnungspreis *m*; **~ pricing** *n* ACC Übernahmepreissetzung *f*, ECON pretiale Lenkung *f*, FIN Übernahmekursfestsetzung *f*, GEN COMM Festsetzung *f* des Verrechnungspreises, S&M *multinational companies* Übernahmekursfestsetzung *f*; **~ problem** *n*

ECON Transferproblem *nt*; **~ of property inter vivos** *n* LAW, TAX Schenkung *f* unter Lebenden, Schenkung *f* zu Lebzeiten

transferral *n* HRM Umsetzung *f*

transfer: **~ rate** *n* COMP Transferrate *f*

transferred *adj* ADMIN, HRM versetzt

transferor *see transferrer*

transfers: **~ to business** *n pl* GEN COMM Geschäftszuweisung *f*

transfer: **~ of stock** *n* GEN COMM Bestandsübertragung *f*; **~ of technology** *n* ECON, IND Technologietransfer *m*; **~ of technology method** *n* ECON Methode *f* des Technologietransfers; **~ of voting rights** *n* FIN Stimmrechtsübertragung *f*

transform *vt* GEN COMM *economy* transformieren, umgestalten, umwandeln, INS umformen, MATH abbilden, transformieren

transformable *adj* COMMS, FIN, GEN COMM, LAW, MGMNT, STOCK umwandelbar

transformation *n* COMP Umwandlung *f*, ECON Transformation *f*, GEN COMM Übergang *m*, Umgestaltung *f*, Umwandlung *f*, INS Umformung *f*, MATH Abbildung *f*, Transformation *f*; **~ curve** *n* ECON Kapazitätslinie *f*, Transformationskurve *f*; **~ industries** *n pl* IND *in transition* Transformationsindustrien *f pl*, Umformungsindustrien *f pl*, Umspannungsindustrien *f pl*; **~ of legal form of business organization** *n* LAW Änderung *f* der Rechtsform des Unternehmens; **~ problem** *n* ECON Transformationsproblem *nt*

transfrontier *adj* GEN COMM, IMP/EXP, S&M grenzüberschreitend

transient *adj* GEN COMM kurzlebig, vorübergehend; **~ medium** *n* S&M Zwischenmedium *nt*; **~ worker** *n* HRM Aushilfe *f*

transit *n* IMP/EXP, LEIS, TRANSP Transit *m*, Transport *m*; ♦ **in ~** BANK unterwegs, TRANSP auf Transport befindlich

transit: **~ bond note** *n* IMP/EXP Transitvermerk *m*, Versandschein *m*; **~ card** *n* LEIS *airline travel*, TRANSP Transitkarte *f*; **~ clause** *n* INS *cargo policy* Transitklausel *f*; **~ credit** *n* BANK Transitkredit *m*; **~ document** *n* IMP/EXP, TRANSP Transitdokument *nt*, Transitpapier *nt*

transition *n* GEN COMM Übergang *m*

transitional *adj* GEN COMM übergangsweise; **~ automated ticket** *n* (*TAT*) TRANSP automatisiertes Übergangsticket *nt*, Übergangsautomatenschein *m*; **~ economy** *n* ECON *central and eastern Europe* Transformationswirtschaft *f*, Übergangswirtschaft *f*; **~ period** *n* GEN COMM Übergangszeit *f*, Übergangsperiode *f*; **~ provisions** *n pl* TAX Übergangsbestimmungen *f pl*; **~ stage** *n* ECON Übergangsstadium *nt*

transition: **~ period** *n* GEN COMM Übergangsperiode *f*, Übergangszeit *f*

transit: **~ lounge** *n* LEIS, TRANSP Transitraum *m*; **~ market** *n* FIN Transitmarkt *m*; **~ number** *n* FIN Bankleitzahl *f*

transitory: **~ income** *n* ACC, ECON durchlaufende Einnahmen *f pl*, transitorische Einnahmen *f pl*

transit: **~ passenger** *n* LEIS, TRANSP Transitreisende(r) *mf* [decl. as adj]; **~ rights** *n pl* TRANSP Transitrechte *nt pl*; **~ shed** *n* IMP/EXP Transitlager *nt*, Zolldurchgangsschuppen *m*; **~ store** *n* IMP/EXP Transitlager *nt*; **~ time** *n* IMP/EXP, TRANSP

Transportzeit *f*; ~ **trade** *n* ECON Zwischenhandel *m*, IMP/EXP, TRANSP Transithandel *m*; ~ **traffic** *n* TRANSP Transitverkehr *m*; ~ **visa** *n* ADMIN Durchreisevisum *nt*

translate *vt* COMMS übersetzen, ECON *currency* umrechnen

translating *n* COMMS Übersetzen *nt*; ECON *currency* Umrechnung *f*

translation *n* COMMS Übersetzung *f*, ECON *currency* Umrechnung *f*; ~ **difference** *n* ACC *from consolidation of foreign subsidiaries* Umrechnungsdifferenz *f*; ~ **differential** *n* ECON, FIN Umrechnungsdifferenz *f*; ~ **loss** *n* ECON, FIN *international trade* Umrechnungsverlust *m*; ~ **profit** *n* ECON, FIN *international trade* Umrechnungsgewinn *m*; ~ **risk** *n* ECON, FIN Verlustrisiko *nt* aus Währungsumrechnungen, Währungsrisiko *nt*

translator *n* GEN COMM *person* Übersetzer, in *m,f*, COMP, *program* Übersetzungsprogramm *nt*, GEN COMM Übersetzer, in *m,f*

transmission *n* COMMS *broadcast* Sendung *f*, *process* Übertragung *f*, Übermittlung *f*, COMP *data* Übertragung *f*, GEN COMM Weiterleitung *f*; ~ **expenses** *n pl* ACC *profit and loss account* Übertragungskosten *pl*; ~ **mechanism** *n* ECON Transmissionsmechanismus *m*

transmit *vt* COMMS *broadcast, signal* senden, *information* übermitteln, COMP übertragen, GEN COMM überliefern, übermitteln, übertragen, weiterleiten

transmitted: ~ **credit** *n* FIN Durchlaufkredit *m*

transmitter *n* COMMS Übermittler *m*, Sender *m*

transmitting *adj* COMMS, COMP übertragend, Sende-

transnational *adj* BANK, GEN COMM, IMP/EXP, TRANSP grenzüberschreitend, multinational, transnational; ~ **corporation** *n* (*TNC*) ECON, GEN COMM transnationale Gesellschaft *f*, multinationales Unternehmen *nt*

transnationally *adv* GEN COMM multinational

transparency *n* ADMIN Transparent *nt*

transponder *n* COMMS Transponder *m*

transport 1. *n* TRANSP Beförderung *f*, Transport *m*, Verkehr *m*, Transportwesen *nt*; **2.** *vt* GEN COMM, TRANSP befördern, transportieren; ♦ ~ **by air** TRANSP per Flugzeug transportieren

transportable *adj* TRANSP transportabel, transportfähig, transportierbar, versandfähig

Transport: ~ **Act** *n* BrE LAW, TRANSP Verkehrsgesetz *nt*

transport: ~ **advertising** *n* S&M, TRANSP Verkehrsmittelwerbung *f*; ~ **agent** *n* IMP/EXP, TRANSP Spediteur *m*

transportation *n* TRANSP Beförderung *f*, Transport *m*, Transportwesen *nt*, Verkehr *m*; ~ **advertising** *n* S&M, TRANSP Verkehrsmittelwerbung *f*; ~ **car** *n* TRANSP Transportfahrzeug *nt*; ~ **contract** *n* LAW Beförderungsvertrag *m*; ~ **document** *n* IMP/EXP, TRANSP Transportdokument *nt*; ~ **equipment** *n* TRANSP Transporteinrichtungen *f pl*; ~ **expenses** *n pl* TRANSP Transportkosten *pl*; ~ **system** *n* TRANSP Transportsystem *nt*

transport: ~ **company** *n* IMP/EXP Speditionsunternehmen *nt*, TRANSP Beförderungsunternehmen *nt*, Speditionsunternehmen *nt*; ~ **controller** *n* HRM, TRANSP Versandleiter, in *m,f*; ~ **distribution analysis** *n* (*TDA*) TRANSP Transportverteilungsanalyse *f*; ~ **document** *n* IMP/EXP, TRANSP *shipping* Transportdokument *nt*; ~ **emergency card** *n* (*trem card*) TRANSP *road transport scheme* Transport-Notkarte *f*; ~ **expenses** *n pl* TRANSP Beförderungskosten *pl*; ~ **facilitation** *n* TRANSP Ver-

kehrseinrichtung *f*; ~ **facilities** *n pl* GEN COMM, TRANSP Beförderungsmittel *nt pl*, TRANSP Transportmöglichkeiten *f pl*, TRANSP Verkehrseinrichtungen *f pl*

Transport: ~ **and General Workers' Union** *n* BrE (*TGWU*) IND Transportarbeitergewerkschaft

transport: ~ **instruction** *n* TRANSP Transportanweisung *f*; ~ **instruction form** *n* TRANSP Transportanweisung *f*; ~ **insurance** *n* INS Transportversicherung *f*

Transport: ~ **International Routier carnet** *n* IMP/EXP Carnet TIR *nt*, Zollbegleitscheinheft *nt*

transport: ~ **link** *n* TRANSP Verkehrsanbindung *f*, Verkehrsverbindung *f*; ~ **mode** *n* TRANSP Transportart *f*; ~ **quota** *n* TRANSP Transportkontingent *nt*, Transportquote *f*; ~ **system** *n* TRANSP Transportsystem *nt*, Verkehrswesen *nt*; ~ **unit** *n* TRANSP Beförderungseinheit *f*

transposal *n* LAW *EU* Umstellung *f*

transposition: ~ **error** *n* COMP Vertauschungsfehler *m*, GEN COMM Umstellungsfehler *m*

transship *vt* TRANSP umladen, umschlagen

transshipment *n* TRANSP Umladung *f*, Umschlag *m*; ~ **bill of lading** *n* IMP/EXP, TRANSP Umladekonnossement *nt*; ~ **bond** *n* IMP/EXP, TRANSP Umladeschein *m*, Zolldurchfuhrschein *m*, Umladeurkunde *f*; ~ **delivery order** *n* IMP/EXP, TRANSP Umladelieferschein *m*; ~ **entry** *n* IMP/EXP, TRANSP Umladeerklärung *f*; ~ **freight** *n* IMP/EXP, TRANSP Umladefracht *f*

transshipped *adj* TRANSP umgeladen, umgeschlagen

trash *n* AmE (*cf rubbish BrE*) ENVIR, GEN COMM Abfall *m*

trashcan *n* AmE ENVIR (*cf litter bin BrE, rubbish bin BrE*) Abfalleimer *m*, Tonne *f*

trashy: ~ **goods** *n pl* AmE *infrml* GEN COMM Kitsch *m*, minderwertige Waren *f pl*, Schund *m*

travel: ~ **advance** *n* ECON, GEN COMM Reisekostenvorschuß *m*; ~ **agency** *n* LEIS Reiseagentur *f*, Reisebüro *nt*; ~ **agent** *n* LEIS *person* Reisebürokaufmann *m*, Reisebürokauffrau *f*, Reisebüroangestellte(r) *mf* [*decl. as adj*], *agency* Reiseagentur *f*, Reisebüro *nt*; ~ **allowance** *n* GEN COMM Reisekostenzuschuß *m*, Reisespesen *pl*

travelator *n* GEN COMM rollender Fußsteig *m*, Rollsteig *m*

travel: ~ **bureau** *n* LEIS Reisebüro *nt*; ~ **claim** *n* GEN COMM Antrag *m* auf Reisekostenerstattung; ~ **document** *n* LEIS Reisedokument *nt*, Reisepapier *m*

traveler *AmE see* **traveller** *BrE*

travel: ~ **expense claim** *n* GEN COMM, TAX Antrag auf Reisekostenerstattung *m*; ~ **expenses** *n pl* ACC, GEN COMM, TAX, TRANSP Reisekosten *pl*; ~ **incentive** *n* BrE GEN COMM, HRM Reiseanreiz *m*, S&M *advertising* Anreiz *m* für den Reiseverkehr

traveling *AmE see* **travelling** *BrE*

traveller *n* BrE LEIS Reisende(r) *mf* [*decl. as adj*]; ~**'s cheque** *n* BrE BANK Reisescheck *m*

travelling: ~ **allowance** *n* BrE GEN COMM Reisekostenzuschuß *m*, Reisespesen *f pl*; ~ **exhibition** *n* BrE S&M Wanderausstellung *f*; ~ **fair** *n* BrE S&M Wanderausstellung *f*; ~ **salesman** *n* BrE HRM Geschäftsreisende(r) *m* [*decl. as adj*], Handelsreisende(r) *m* [*decl. as adj*]; ~ **saleswoman** *n* BrE HRM Handelsreisende *f* [*decl. as adj*]

travel: ~ **restrictions** *n pl* TRANSP Reisebeschränkungen *f* pl; **~ services** n pl ECON balance of trade in services Reiseverkehr m; **~ voucher** n TRANSP Reisebeleg m

traversable adj LAW bestreitbar

traverse n LAW Bestreiten nt

trawler n TRANSP Trawler m

treasure n GEN COMM Schatz m

treasurer n FIN, HRM, MGMNT Finanzdirektor, in m,f; **~ check** AmE, **~ cheque** BrE n BANK Bankscheck m; **~'s report** n FIN Bericht m des Finanzdirektors

treasury n BANK Fiskus m, ECON Staatskasse f, FIN, POL Schatzamt nt

Treasury n ECON Schatzamt nt, Finanzministerium nt; **~ bill** n AmE (T-bill) FIN Schatzwechsel m, Schatzwechsel m mit drei-monatiger Laufzeit; **~ Board contingencies vote** n ECON, POL Geldbewilligung f der Finanzbehörde für unvorhergesehene Ausgaben, Bewilligung f des Feuerwehrfonds; **~ Board Secretariat** n ECON, POL Sekretariat nt der Finanzbehörde, Sekretariat nt des Finanzministeriums; **~ bond** n AmE FIN Schatzobligation f; **~ Inflation Protection Securities** n pl (TIPS) ECON, STOCK durch Indexierung inflationsgeschützte US-Staatsanleihen, TIPS; **~ model** n ECON Konjunkturprognosemodell des britischen Finanzministeriums

treasury: **~ note** n AmE (cf Exchequer bond BrE) FIN, STOCK Schatzanweisung f; **~ stock** n AmE (cf own shares BrE) ACC eigene Aktien f pl, STOCK Vorratsaktien f pl

Treasury: **~ stock** n BrE STOCK langfristige Staatspapiere nt pl

treat vt ENVIR sewage, waste behandeln, GEN COMM behandeln, abhandeln, IND behandeln, bearbeiten; ♦ **~ information confidentially** LAW Information vertraulich behandeln; **~ unfavorably** AmE, **~ unfavourably** BrE LAW diskriminieren

treat: **~ effect** n ECON Spendiereffekt m

treating n ENVIR Behandlung f, IND material Bearbeitung f, Behandlung f

treaty n GEN COMM, POL Staatsvertrag m, völkerrechtliches Abkommen nt, Vertrag m; **~ port** n TRANSP Vertragshafen m; **~ reinsurance** n INS Vertragsrückversicherung f

Treaty: **~ of Rome** n ECON, POL EEC Römische Verträge m pl

treble adj GEN COMM dreifach

tree: **~ structure** n COMP Baumstruktur f

trem: **~ card** n (transport emergency card) TRANSP road transport scheme Transport-Notkarte f

trend n GEN COMM Trend m, Tendenz f; **~ analysis** n ECON Trendanalyse f; **~ of events** n GEN COMM Lauf m der Dinge; **~ of profits** n FIN Ertragsentwicklung f; **~ reversal** n GEN COMM Trendwende f

trendsetter n GEN COMM Schrittmacher m, Trendsetter m

trendsetting adj GEN COMM richtungsweisend

trendy adj GEN COMM, S&M in Mode, hochmodisch

trespasser n LAW Besitzstörer, in m,f

trespassers: **~ will be prosecuted** phr LAW Besitzstörer werden gerichtlich verfolgt

trespassing: **no ~** phr LAW Betreten verboten; **~ on private property** n LAW widerrechtliches Betreten nt von Privateigentum

TRF abbr (total fertility rate) ECON Gesamtfertilitätsrate f

trial n GEN COMM testing Probe f, Versuch m, LAW Prozeß m; ♦ **on a ~ basis** GEN COMM probeweise

trial: **~ attorney** n AmE LAW Prozeßanwalt m, Prozeßanwältin f; **~ balance** n ACC Probebilanz f, Rohbilanz f; **~ close** n S&M of new product Ende nt der Versuchsperiode; **~ and error method** n ECON systematisches Probieren nt, Versuch-und-Irrtum-Methode f; **~ examiner** n LAW mit Rechtshilfevernehmung beauftragter Beamter m, mit Rechtshilfevernehmung beauftragte Beamtin f; **the ~ jury** n pl LAW die Geschworenen pl; **~ lawyer** n AmE LAW Prozeßanwalt m, Prozeßanwältin f; **~ offer** n GEN COMM, S&M Probeangebot nt; **~ order** n GEN COMM, S&M Probeauftrag m, Probebestellung f; **~ period** n GEN COMM, HRM Probezeit f; **~ purchase** n S&M Probekauf m; **~ run** n GEN COMM Probefahrt f, Probelauf m; **~ of strength** n GEN COMM Kraftprobe f; **~ subscriber** n S&M, MEDIA Probeabonnent, in m,f; **~ subscription** n (TS) S&M, MEDIA Probeabonnement nt (Probeabo infrml)

triangle n GEN COMM, MATH Dreieck nt; **~ service** n TRANSP Dreiecksverkehr m

triangular adj GEN COMM, MATH dreieckig; **~ compensation** n ECON with financial switch Dreieckskompensation f; **~ merger** n GEN COMM Dreiecksfusion f; **~ operation** n ECON Dreiecksgeschäft nt

triangulation n IMP/EXP Dreieckshandel m

tribunal n LAW Tribunal nt; **~ of enquiry** n LAW parlamentarische Untersuchungskommission f; **~ entitled to adjudicate** n LAW urteilsbefugte Tribunale nt pl

trickle: **~-down theory** n ECON Theorie f des Sikkereffekts

trickle in vi GEN COMM in kleinen Gruppen kommen, langsam kommen

tricks: **~ of the trade** n pl infrml GEN COMM Branchenkenntnisse f pl, Handelskniffe m pl

tricky adj GEN COMM heikel; **~ situation** n GEN COMM kniffliges Problem nt, schwierige Situation f

tried: **~ and tested** adj GEN COMM bewährt

trifle n ECON, FIN small sum of money Bagatellbetrag m

trifling 1. adj GEN COMM belanglos, geringfügig; **2.** n FIN, LAW Bagatelle f

trifling: **~ amount** n ECON, FIN Bagatellbetrag m

trigger vt GEN COMM cost increases verursachen, panic, reaction, dispute auslösen; ♦ **~ off a strike** GEN COMM, HRM, IND einen Streik auslösen

trigger: **~ mechanism** n GEN COMM Auslösemechanismus m; **~ price** n IMP/EXP Schwellenpreis m; **~ pricing** n GEN COMM Mindestpreissystem nt

trim 1. n TRANSP of ship Gleichgewichtslage f, Schwimmlage f; **2.** vt ♦ **~ the investment program** AmE, **~ the investment programme** BrE FIN das Investitionsprogramm kürzen; **~ the workforce** HRM das Personal abbauen

trimmings n pl GEN COMM Besatzartikel m pl, Zubehör nt; Extras nt pl; ♦ **with no ~** GEN COMM ohne Extras, ohne Zubehör

trip n GEN COMM, TRANSP Fahrt f

tripack n GEN COMM Dreierpack m

trip: **~ advance** n GEN COMM Reisekostenvorschuß m; **~ analysis** n TRANSP Reiseanalyse f

tripartism n HRM, POL Dreiseitigkeit f

trip: ~ **charter** n TRANSP *shipping* Fahrcharter f, Fahrtchartervertrag m

triple 1. *adj* GEN COMM dreifach; **2.** *vt* GEN COMM verdreifachen

triple-A *adj* FIN, GEN COMM, STOCK höchstklassifiziert; ~ **bond** n (*AAA bond*) STOCK höchstklassifizierte Schuldverschreibung; ~ **rating** n STOCK Einstufung in die höchste Klasse

triple: ~ **reduction** n *AmE* (*TR*) GEN COMM dreifache Senkung f; ~ **tax exempt** n *AmE* TAX Befreiung von allen Steuern und Ausgaben, die durch Bund, Staaten oder Kommunen erhoben werden können

triplicate 1. *adj* GEN COMM dreifach; **2.** *n* ♦ **in** ~ GEN COMM dreifach

TRK *abbr* (*trunk*) TRANSP Überseekoffer m, Schrankkoffer m

troika n *AmE* POL Troika f

Tropical: ~ **Products Institute** n (*TPI*) ECON Institut nt für Tropenprodukte

tropical: ~ **rainforest** n ENVIR tropischer Regenwald m

trouble: **get out of** ~ *phr* GEN COMM Schwierigkeiten loswerden; **go to a lot of** ~ GEN COMM sich viel Mühe geben

trouble: ~-**free** *adj* GEN COMM *machine* problemlos

troubleshooter n COMP, GEN COMM Fehlersucher m, Krisenmanager m, Schlichter m

troubleshooting n COMP *debugging* Störungssuche f, GEN COMM Fehlersuche f

trouble: ~ **spot** n GEN COMM, POL Gefahrenherd m, Krisenzentrum nt, Unruheherd m

trough 1. n ECON Talsohle f, *of graph, curve* Konjunkturtief nt, Tief nt, Tiefpunkt nt; **2.** vi FIN *interest rate* einen Tiefstand erreichen

troy: ~ **ounce** n FIN *of gold* Troy-Unze f; ~ **weight** n GEN COMM Edelmetallgewicht nt, Troygewicht nt

truck 1. n *AmE* (*cf lorry BrE*) TRANSP *road vehicle* Lastkraftwagen m (*LKW*), Lastwagen m, *rail* Güterwagen m; **2.** vt TRANSP *goods* per LKW transportieren

truckage n IMP/EXP Spedition f, TRANSP Spedition f, Transport m, *by rail* Eisenbahntransport m, *charges* Frachtkosten pl

truck: ~ **driver** n *AmE* (*cf lorry driver BrE*) TRANSP Lastkraftwagenfahrer, in m,f, Lastwagenfahrer, in m,f, LKW-Fahrer, in m,f

trucker n *AmE* (*cf lorry driver BrE*) TRANSP Lastkraftwagenfahrer, in m,f, Lastwagenfahrer, in m,f, LKW-Fahrer, in m,f

truck: ~ **farmer** n *AmE* (*cf market gardener BrE*) ECON Gemüseanbauer m; ~ **farming** n *AmE* (*cf market gardening BrE*) ECON Gartenbaubetrieb m, Gemüseanbau m, Erwerbsgartenbau m

trucking n *AmE* TRANSP Lastwagenservice m, Lastwagentransport m; ~ **bill of lading** n *AmE* TRANSP Frachtbrief m, Güterkraftverkehrkonnossement nt; ~ **charges** n pl *AmE* TRANSP Beförderungskosten pl, Rollgeld nt; ~ **company** n *AmE* TRANSP Güterkraftverkehrsunternehmen nt; ~ **contractor** n *AmE* TRANSP Fuhrunternehmen m, Fuhrunternehmer m, Unternehmer m im Güterkraftverkehr

truck: ~-**mounted crane** n *AmE* (*cf lorry-mounted crane BrE*) TRANSP Automobilkran m; ~ **reception area** n *AmE* (*cf lorry reception area BrE*) TRANSP LKW-Annahmebereich m; ~ **service** n *AmE* (*cf lorry service BrE*) TRANSP Lastwagenservice m, Lastwagentransport m

true: ~ **and fair** *adj* ACC *audit, view* den tatsächlichen Verhältnissen entsprechend; ~ **and fair view** n *BrE* (*cf fair presentation AmE*) ACC Rechnungswesen im Sinne der Grundsätze ordnungsgemäßer Buchführung, eine den tatsächlichen Verhältnissen entsprechende Bilanz; ~ **lease** n FIN, TAX steuerbegünstigtes Leasing nt; ~ **owner** n LAW rechtmäßiger Eigentümer m, rechtmäßige Eigentümerin f, rechtmäßiger Besitzer m, rechtmäßige Besitzerin f, wirklicher Eigentümer m, wirkliche Eigentümerin f; ~ **rate of return** n BANK effektive Rendite f, Effektivverzinsung f, Effektivzins m

trump n GEN COMM Trumpf m; ~ **card** n GEN COMM Trumpfkarte f

truncate vt COMP abbrechen, abschneiden, GEN COMM beschneiden, kürzen

truncation n BANK *cheque* belegloses Verfahren nt, COMP Abbruch m, GEN COMM Beschneidung f, Kürzung f

trunk n TRANSP (*TRK*) Überseekoffer m, Schrankkoffer m, *AmE* (*cf boot BrE*) *of car* Kofferraum m; ~ **call** n *BrE* COMMS *obs* Ferngespräch nt; ~ **exchange** n *AmE* COMMS Fernmeldeamt nt

trunking n TRANSP *containers* Containerverkehr m

trunk: ~ **line** n COMMS Fernleitung f, TRANSP *rail* Fernstrecke f, Hauptlinie f, Hauptstrecke f; ~ **road** n *BrE* (*cf highway AmE*) TRANSP ≈ Bundesstraße f, Fernstraße f

trust 1. n BANK Treuhand f, ECON Treuhandvermögen nt, LAW Treuhand f, Treuhandverwaltung f, Trust m; **2.** vt GEN COMM, LAW vertrauen

trust: ~ **agreement** n LAW Treuhandabkommen nt, Treuhandvereinbarung f, Treuhandvertrag m; ~ **bank** n BANK Treuhandbank f; ~ **banking** n BANK Treuhandbankgeschäft nt

trustbusting n *AmE infrml* GEN COMM Entflechtung f

trustee n BANK, FIN Vermögensverwalter, in m,f, LAW Treuhänder, in m,f, STOCK Vermögensverwalter, in m,f; ~ **in bankruptcy** n BANK Konkursverwalter, in m,f

trusteeship n LAW Treuhandschaft f

trustee: ~ **status** n STOCK Treuhandstatus m

trust: ~ **fund** n ECON treuhänderisch verwaltetes Vermögen nt, Treuhandfonds m

trustify vt LAW in einem Trust zusammenfassen

trust: ~ **instrument** n LAW *act or testament* Treuhandurkunde f; ~ **mortgage** n BANK Sicherungshypothek f

trustor n *AmE* LAW Treugeber m

trust: ~ **receipt** n ACC Treuhandquittung f, GEN COMM Depotbescheinigung f, Hinterlegungsschein m; ~ **share** n MGMNT Geschäftsanteil m

trustworthiness n GEN COMM Glaubwürdigkeit f, Vertrauenswürdigkeit f

trustworthy *adj* GEN COMM glaubwürdig, vertrauenswürdig

truth: ~ **in lending** n *AmE* BANK wahrheitsgemäße Kreditkostenangaben; ~ **in lending act** n BANK, LAW *1968* Gesetz zur wahrheitsgemäßen Kreditkostenangabe

try vt GEN COMM probieren, versuchen

try out vt GEN COMM probieren, ausprobieren, testen

tryout n COMP Erprobung f, GEN COMM Erprobung f, Probe f, S&M Erprobung f

TS *abbr* HRM (*traffic superintendent*) Fahrdienstleiter, in *m,f*, MEDIA (*trial subscription*) Probeabo *nt* (*infrml*) (*Probeabonnement*)

TT *abbr* BANK, FIN (*telegraphic transfer*) telegrafische Auszahlung *f*, telegrafische Überweisung *f*, ECON, IND (*technology transfer*) Technologietransfer *m*

TTC *abbr* (*tender to contract*) GEN COMM Ausschreibung *f*, LAW Auftragsangebot *nt*, Vertragsangebot *nt*

TTC/FES: ~ **cover** *abbr* (*tender to contract and forward exchange supplement cover*) GEN COMM Kurssicherung *f* zwischen Angebotsabgabe und Vertragsabschluß

T-test *n* MATH *statistics* T-Test *m*

TU *abbr* BrE (*trade union*) GEN COMM, HRM, POL Gew. (*Gewerkschaft*)

TUA *abbr* BrE (*Trade Union Act 1984*) ECON, LAW britisches Gewerkschaftsgesetz über interne Wahlen und Koalitionsfreiheit

tube *n* BrE (*cf subway AmE*) TRANSP U-Bahn *f*, Untergrundbahn *f*

TUC *abbr* BrE (*Trades Union Congress*) HRM Dachorganisation der britischen Gewerkschaften, ≈ DGB (*Deutscher Gewerkschaftbund*)

tug 1. *n* (*T*) TRANSP Schleppboot *nt*; **2.** *vt* TRANSP schleppen

tugboat *n* TRANSP Schleppboot *nt*, Schlepper *m*, Schleppschiff *nt*

tugmaster *n* TRANSP *shipping, port* Schlepperführer *m*

tug: ~**-of-war** *n* GEN COMM Tauziehen *nt*

tuition: ~ **fee** *n* WEL Studiengebühr *f*; ~ **fees** *n pl* WEL Schulgeld *nt*

TULRA *abbr* BrE (*Trade Union and Labour Relations Act 1976*) ECON, HRM , LAW britisches Gewerkschaftsgesetz zur Konsolidierung des Verhältnisses zwischen Arbeitgebern und Arbeitnehmern

tumble *vi* ECON *prices* stürzen, GEN COMM *prices, rate* plötzlich fallen, stark fallen, STOCK *prices* stürzen

tumult *n* POL Aufruhr *m*

tuning *n* GEN COMM Abstimmung *f*

tunnel *n* GEN COMM Tunnel *m*; ~ **toll** *n* TRANSP *tariffs* Tunnelgebühr *f*

turbine: ~ **steamship** *n* TRANSP Turbinendampfer *m*

turbo: ~**-electric** *adj* IND turboelektrisch

turf: ~ **accountant** *n frml* LEIS *sport* Buchmacher *m*

turmoil *n* POL Aufruhr *m*

turn 1. *n* STOCK Provision *f* eines Wertpapierhändlers; ◆ **in ~** GEN COMM der Reihe nach; **2.** *vt* ◆ ~ **one's attention to** GEN COMM seine Aufmerksamkeit richten auf

turn around *vt* FIN wenden, IND *goods* fertigstellen

turn away *vt* GEN COMM *business* ablehnen, zurückweisen, PATENTS zurückweisen

turn off *vt* COMMS, COMP, IND abschalten, ausschalten

turn on *vt* COMMS, COMP, IND einschalten

turn over *vt* GEN COMM, S&M umsetzen, TRANSP umschlagen

turn round *vt* FIN wenden

turn out *vi* GEN COMM ausrücken; ◆ ~ **on strike** GEN COMM, HRM, IND *industrial relations* streiken; ~ **to vote** POL zur Wahl gehen

turnabout *n* FIN Tendenzwende *f*, *financing established* Umschwung *m*, GEN COMM Kurswechsel *m*, Wende *f*

turnaround *AmE see* turnround *BrE*

turning: ~ **basin** *n* TRANSP *shipping, port* Wendebecken *nt*; ~ **circle** *n* TRANSP Wendekreis *m*; ~**-off** *n* COMMS, COMP Abschalten *nt*, GEN COMM Abschalten *nt*, Ausschalten *nt*; ~**-on** *n* COMMS, COMP, GEN COMM Einschalten *nt*; ~ **point** *n* GEN COMM Wendepunkt *m*

turnkey *adj* GEN COMM *system, project* bezugsfertig, schlüsselfertig, ECON schlüsselfertig, IMP/EXP betriebsfertig, schlüsselfertig, PROP bezugsfertig; ~ **contract** *n* ECON Bauvertrag *m* mit schlüsselfertiger Übergabe, LAW pauschaler Werkvertrag *m* bis zur schlüsselfertigen Übergabe

turnout *n* GEN COMM Teilnehmerzahl *f*, IMP/EXP Inspektion *f*, POL *in election* Beteiligung *f*

turnover *n* ACC *inventory* Lagerumschlag *m*, GEN COMM Umsatz *m*, Volumen *nt*, HRM *of staff* Fluktuation *f*, STOCK Volumen *nt*, Umsatz *m*; ~ **equalization tax** *n* TAX Ausgleichssteuer *f*; ~ **rate** *n* GEN COMM Umsatzhäufigkeit *f*, Umsatzquote *f*, STOCK Umsatzgeschwindigkeit *f*; ~ **ratio** *n* HRM Personalwechselrate *f*; ~ **tax** *n* TAX Umsatzsteuer *f* (*USt*)

turnpike *n* AmE TRANSP (*cf toll road BrE*) Mautstraße *f*, (*cf toll motorway BrE*) *expressway* gebührenpflichtige Autobahn *f*; ~ **theorem** *n* ECON Schlagbaumtheorem *nt*

turnround *n* BrE FIN Tendenzwende *f*, Umschwung *m*, GEN COMM *of company* Umschwung *m*, Wende *f*, Turnaround *m*, POL *on issue* Wende *f*, TRANSP Liegezeit *f*, Wendezeit *f*, Umschlag *m*; ~ **time** *n* BrE ECON Umschlagszeit *f*, GEN COMM Postlaufzeit *f*, Umlaufzeit *f*, Umschlagszeit *f*, IND, TRANSP *loading and unloading time* Umschlagszeit *f*, Umlaufzeit *f*, Verweildauer *f*, Verweilzeit *f*

turn: ~ **time** *n* TRANSP *shipping, port* Törnzeit *f*

TV *abbr* (*television*) MEDIA FS (*Fernsehen*), TV (*Television*); ~ **network** *n* MEDIA Fernsehnetz *nt*, TV-Netz *nt*

TVR *abbr* (*television rating*) MEDIA, S&M Bewertung *f* von Fernsehsendungen durch Zuschauer

twenty: ~**-foot equivalent unit** *n* (*TEU*) TRANSP *containers* Maßeinheit, die zwanzig Fuß entspricht; ~**-four-hour** *adj* GEN COMM rund um die Uhr; ~**-four-hour service** *n* GEN COMM Tag- und Nachtdienst *m*, Service *m* rund um die Uhr; ~**-four-hour trading** *n* STOCK Handel *m* rund um die Uhr, Rund-um-die-Uhr-Handel *m*

TWI *abbr* (*training within industry*) HRM, IND Fachausbildung *f*, innerbetriebliche Weiterbildung *f*, Weiterbildung *f* für Mitarbeiter

twilight: ~ **shift** *n* BrE HRM Abendschicht *f*

twin: ~**-bedded room** *n* LEIS Zweibettzimmer *nt*; ~ **room** *n* LEIS Zweibettzimmer *nt*

twist *vt* FIN strudeln, wirbeln

twisting *n* FIN Gaunerei *f*

two: ~**-axle vehicle** *n* TRANSP zweiachsiges Fahrzeug *nt*; ~**-berth cabin** *n* TRANSP Kabine *f* mit zwei Schlafkojen; ~**-bit** *adj* AmE *infrml* GEN COMM billig, wertlos; ~**-bits** *pl* AmE *infrml* FIN 25-Cent-Stück; ~**-class vessel** *n* TRANSP Zweiklassenschiff *nt*; ~**-color** *AmE*, ~**-colour** *BrE adj* S&M zweifarbig; ~**-digit inflation** *n* ECON, FIN zweistellige Inflationsrate *f*; ~**-dollar broker** *n* AmE STOCK unabhängiger Makler *m*, unabhängige Maklerin *f*; ~**-gap development model** *n* ECON Entwicklungsmodell *nt*, das zwei Lücken berücksichtigt; ~**-lane deck**

n TRANSP *shipping* zweispuriges Deck *nt*; **~-part tariff** *n* ECON kombinierter Tarif *m*

2Q *abbr* (*second quarter*) GEN COMM zweites Quartal *nt*

two: **~-rate system** *n* TAX gespaltenes Steuersystem *nt*, System *nt* mit gespaltenem Steuersatz, Zwei-Steuersatz-System *nt*; **~-sided** *adj* COMP doppelseitig, zweiseitig; **~-sided market** *n* STOCK *interbank money market* Markt *m* mit Geld und Brief; **~-stage least squares method** *n* ECON zweifache Methode *f* der kleinsten Quadrate; **~-tailed test** *n* MATH *statistics* zweiseitiger Test *m*; **~-tier bargaining** *n* HRM zweistufige Tarifverhandlungen *f pl*; **~-tier system** *n* GEN COMM zweischichtiges System *nt*, Zweistufensystem *nt*; **~-tier wage structure** *n* HRM gespaltene Lohnstruktur *f*; **~-way analysis of variance** *n* MATH *statistics* zweiseitige Varianzanalyse *f*; **~-way scheme** *n* TRANSP *shipping, port* Zweiwegeverkehr *m*; **~-way split** *n* GEN COMM Zweiteilung *f*

tx. *abbr* (*telex*) ADMIN, COMMS *machine* Telex *nt*, Fernschreiber *m*, *message* Fernschreiben *nt*

tycoon *n* GEN COMM, HRM Großindustrielle(r) *mf* [decl. as adj], Tycoon *m*, Magnat *m*

tying: **~ arrangement** *n* ECON Kopplungsvertrag *m*; **~ contract** *n* ECON Kopplungsvertrag *m*

type 1. *n* COMP *typography* Type *f*, GEN COMM *typology* Art *f*, MEDIA *typography* Type *f*; **2.** *vt* ADMIN, COMP mit der Maschine schreiben, tippen (*infrml*); **3.** *vi* ADMIN, COMP maschinenschreiben, tippen (*infrml*)

type in *vt* COMP eingeben, eintasten

type: **~ area** *n* S&M Satzspiegel *m*

typebar *n* COMP Typenhebel *m*

type: **~ of costs** *n* FIN Kostenart *f*

typed *adj* ADMIN, GEN COMM, maschinengeschrieben

typeface *n* COMP, MEDIA Schriftart *f*

typefont *n* COMP, MEDIA Schrift *f*, Schriftart *f*

type-II: **~ error** *n* MATH *statistics* Beta-Fehler *m*

typesetter *n* COMP, MEDIA, S&M Setzer, in *m,f* (*obs*)

typesetting *n* COMP Satz *m*, Schriftsatz *m*, Schriftsetzen *nt*, Setzen *nt*, GEN COMM Satztechnik *f*, Setzen *nt*

types: **~ of shares** *n pl* STOCK Aktienarten *f pl*

typewrite 1. *vt* ADMIN, GEN COMM mit der Maschine schreiben, tippen (*infrml*); **2.** *vi* ADMIN, GEN COMM maschinenschreiben, tippen (*infrml*)

typewriter *n* ADMIN, GEN COMM Schreibmaschine *f*; **~ ball** *n* ADMIN, GEN COMM Schreibmaschinenkugelkopf *m*

typewriting *n* GEN COMM Maschinenschreiben *nt*

typewritten *adj* ADMIN, GEN COMM, maschinegenschrieben, getippt (*infrml*)

typical *adj* GEN COMM bezeichnend, typisch

typically *adv* GEN COMM bezeichnend, typisch

typify *vt* GEN COMM typisieren

typing: **~ error** *n* GEN COMM Druckfehler *m*, Schreibfehler *m*, Tippfehler *m*, MEDIA *misprint* Druckfehler *m*, Schreibfehler *m*, *print* Setzfehler *m* (*jarg*); **~ pool** *n* HRM Schreibzimmer *nt*; **~ speed** *n* ADMIN, COMP Tippgeschwindigkeit *f*

typist *n* ADMIN Schreibkraft *f*, Typist, in *m,f*, GEN COMM Schreibkraft *f*

typo *n* (*typographical error*) ADMIN, COMP, GEN COMM, MEDIA *misprint* Druckfehler *m*, Schreibfehler *m*, Tippfehler *m*, *print* Setzfehler *m* (*jarg*)

typographer *n* COMP, MEDIA, S&M Schriftsetzer, in *m,f*, Typograph, in *m,f*

typographical: **~ error** *n* (*typo*) ADMIN, COMP, GEN COMM, MEDIA *misprint* Druckfehler *m*, Schreibfehler *m*, Tippfehler *m*, *print* Setzfehler *m* (*jarg*)

typological: **~ analysis** *n* S&M typologische Analyse *f*

typology *n* S&M Typologie *f*

U

U *abbr* TRANSP (*universal container*) Universal-Container *m*, (*unit load*) *distribution* Containerstapel *m*, Einheitsladung *f*

U/a *abbr* (*underwriting account*) INS Versicherungskonto *nt*, Verwaltungskonto *nt*

UAW *abbr* AmE (*United Automobile Workers*) HRM amerikanische Autoarbeitergewerkschaft

UAWB *abbr* (*universal air waybill*) IMP/EXP, TRANSP Einheitsluftfrachtbrief *m*, Universal-Luftfrachtbrief *m*

uberrimae fidei *n* GEN COMM uberrimae fidei, LAW *insurances* höchste Gutgläubigkeit *f* und Redlichkeit *f*

ubi remedium ibi jus *phr* GEN COMM wo ein Mittel ist, ist ein Recht, ubi remedium ibi ius

UBR *abbr* (*Uniform Business Rate*) FIN von der Regierung festgelegte, einheitliche Grundsteuer für Betriebe

UC&P *abbr* (*Uniform Customs and Practice for Documentary Credits*) ECON *international trade* ERA (*Einheitliche Richtlinien und Praktiken für Dokumenten-Akkreditive*)

UCITS *abbr* (*undertakings for collective investment in transferable securities*) FIN Unternehmen *nt* für gemeinschaftliche Investition in übertragbaren Wertpapieren

U-form *n* ECON U-Form *f*

U-hypothesis *n* ECON U-Hypothese *f*

UKAEA *abbr* (*United Kingdom Atomic Energy Authority*) ENVIR, IND britische Atomenergiebehörde

UKASTA *abbr* (*United Kingdom Agricultural Supply Trade Association*) IND Wirtschaftsvereinigung für landwirtschaftliche Bedarfsdeckung

UK: **~ economic forecasting** *n* ECON Wirtschaftsprognose *f* für das VK; **~ gilt-edged stocks** *n pl* STOCK britische Staatsanleihepapiere *nt pl*; **~ gilts market** *n* STOCK Markt *m* für britische Staatsanleihepapiere; **~ government stocks** *n pl* STOCK britische Staatsanleihen *f pl*; **~-incorporated** *adj* LAW *institution* eingetragen in Großbritannien oder Nordirland

UKOOA *abbr* (*United Kingdom Offshore Operators' Association*) IND Verband britischer Offshore-Unternehmer

UK: **~ Patent Office** *n* PATENTS britisches Patentamt *nt*

UKREP *abbr* (*United Kingdom Permanent Representative to the European Economic Community*) ECON, POL Ständiger Vertreter *m* Großbritanniens bei der Europäischen Gemeinschaft

UK: **~ resident trust** *n* LAW britische Steuerinländertreuhand *f*; **~ stock exchanges** *n pl* STOCK britische Wertpapierbörsen *f pl*

UKTA *abbr* (*United Kingdom Trade Agency*) ECON *development agency* Britisches Handelsamt

UKTOTC *abbr* (*United Kingdom tariff and overseas trade classification*) ECON *international trade* Britische Klassifikation *f* für Zoll und Überseehandel

ULD *abbr* (*unit load device*) TRANSP *aviation* Ladeeinheit *f*

ullage *n* TRANSP *shipping* Leerraum *m*, Schwund *m*

ult. *abbr* (*ultimo*) GEN COMM des letzten Monats (*obs*)

ultimate: **~ consumer** *n* GEN COMM, S&M Endverbraucher *m*

ultimatum: **give sb an ~** *phr* GEN COMM jdm ein Ultimatum stellen

ultimo *adv* (*ult.*) GEN COMM des letzten Monats (*obs*)

ultra: **~-large crude carrier** *n* TRANSP sehr großer Rohöltanker *m*

ultra vires *phr* LAW in Überschreitung der satzungsgemäßen Befugnisse, vollmachtsüberschreitend; **~ activities** *n pl* LAW *of corporation* Handlungen *f pl* in Überschreitung der satzungsmäßigen Befugnisse; **~ borrowing** *n* BANK satzungsmäßig nicht gestattete Kreditaufnahme *f*

u/m *abbr* (*undermentioned*) GEN COMM unten erwähnt

UMA *abbr* (*union membership agreement*) HRM Tarifausschlußklausel *f*

umbrella: **under the ~ of** *phr* GEN COMM unter dem Schutz von; **~ agent** *n* TRANSP Hauptagent *m*; **~ brand name** *n* PATENTS Dachmarke *f*; **~ committee** *n* GEN COMM Dachkomitee *nt*; **~ fund** *n* FIN zentraler Dachfonds *m*; **~ group** *n* FIN Dachkonzern *f*; **~ liability insurance** *n* INS Pauschalhaftpflichtversicherung *f*; **~ policy** *n* INS Dachpolice *f*; **~ project** *n* GEN COMM Rahmenprojekt *nt*

UN *abbr* (*United Nations*) POL VN (*Vereinte Nationen*), UN (*United Nations*)

unable *adj* GEN COMM, HRM, LAW unfähig; ♦ **~ to do sth** GEN COMM unfähig, etw zu tun; **~ to pay** ACC zahlungsunfähig

unabridged *adj* GEN COMM, MEDIA ungekürzt

unaccepted *adj* BANK, GEN COMM *bill* nicht akzeptiert

unaccompanied: **~ baggage** *n* LEIS, TRANSP unbegleitetes Gepäck *nt*

unaccounted: **~ for** *adj* GEN COMM nicht ausgewiesen, ungeklärt; ♦ **be ~ for in the balance sheet** ACC *amount, item* in der Bilanz ungeklärt geblieben sein

unacknowledged *adj* GEN COMM nicht anerkannt, unbestätigt, *letter* unbeantwortet

unadjusted *adj* MATH *statistics* unbereinigt; ♦ **in ~ figures** GEN COMM in nicht bereinigten Zahlen, in unbereinigten Zahlen

unadvertised *adj* GEN COMM nicht angekündigt, nicht ausgeschrieben, ohne Werbung; **~ job** *n* GEN COMM nicht ausgeschriebene Stelle *f*

unadvisable *adj* GEN COMM nicht empfehlenswert

unaffiliated *adj* ECON selbständig, unabhängig, GEN COMM nicht eingegliedert, selbständig, unabhängig; **~ union** *n* HRM unabhängige Gewerkschaft *f*

unallocated *adj* COMP nicht zugeteilt, nicht zugewiesen

unallotted *adj* STOCK *shares* nicht zugeteilt

unaltered *adj* GEN COMM, STOCK *share prices* unverändert

unamortized *adj* ACC nicht abgeschrieben; **~ bond discount** *n* STOCK nicht abgeschriebenes Disagio *nt*; **~ discount on Treasury bills** *n* STOCK nicht abgeschriebenes Disagio *nt* von Schatzwechseln; **~ portion of actuarial deficiencies** *n* FIN Disagioanteil *m* versicherungstechnischer Verlängerungen; **~ premiums on investments** *n pl* STOCK nicht abgeschriebenes Agio *nt* auf Investitionen

unanimity *n* GEN COMM, POL Einmütigkeit *f*, Einstimmigkeit *f*

unanimous *adj* GEN COMM, POL *decision* einstimmig

unanimously *adv* GEN COMM, POL einstimmig; ◆ **~ accepted** GEN COMM einstimmig angenommen

unanimous: **~ resolution** *n* GEN COMM einstimmiger Beschluß *m*

unanticipated *adj* GEN COMM unerwartet, unvorhergesehen

unappealable *adj* LAW unanfechtbar, rechtskräftig

unappropriated: **~ profit** *n* ACC nicht zweckgebundener Gewinn *m*, freie Rücklage *f*; **~ retained earnings** *n pl* ACC Bilanzgewinn *m*, FIN nicht zweckgebundene, einbehaltene Erträge *m pl*; **~ surplus** *n* GEN COMM allgemeine Rücklage *f*, Bilanzgewinn *m*, nicht verteilter Gewinn *m*

unapproved: **~ funds** *n pl* FIN nicht genehmigte finanzielle Mittel *nt pl*

unassailable *adj* GEN COMM unanfechtbar, unbestreitbar

unassessed *adj* GEN COMM unbewertet, TAX nicht veranlagt

unassignable *adj* LAW nicht übertragbar

unassured *adj* INS nicht versichert, unversichert

unattainable *adj* COMMS, GEN COMM *objective* unerreichbar

unattended: **~ machinery spaces** *n pl* IND unbesetzte Stellen *f pl* an einer Maschine

unaudited *adj* ACC nicht geprüft, nicht testiert

unauthenticated *adj* LAW unverbürgt, unbeglaubigt; **~ signature** *n* LAW unbeglaubigte Unterschrift *f*

unauthorized *adj* GEN COMM unbefugt, LAW unberechtigt; **~ shares** *n pl* STOCK nicht genehmigte Aktien *f pl*; **~ strike** *n* HRM wilder Streik *m*

unavailability *n* GEN COMM Nichtverfügbarkeit *f*

unavailable *adj* GEN COMM nicht erhältlich, nicht erreichbar, nicht verfügbar, nicht vorhanden, *person* nicht zu erreichen, nicht zu sprechen

unavoidable *adj* GEN COMM unumgänglich, unvermeidlich

unbalanced: **~ growth** *n* ECON ungleichgewichtiges Wachstum *nt*; **~ trade** *n* ECON *international trade* unausgeglichener Handel *m*

unbankable *adj* BANK nicht bankfähig, nicht diskontfähig; **~ paper** *n* BANK nicht diskontfähiger Wechsel *m*

unbiased *adj* GEN COMM unparteiisch, unvoreingenommen; **~ estimator** *n* ECON erwartungsfreie Schätzfunktion *f*

unblock *vt* FIN entsperren, freigeben

unbounded: **~ risk** *n* STOCK *of futures* schrankenloses Risiko *nt*

unbranded: **~ goods** *n pl* GEN COMM markenfreie Waren *f pl*, Waren *f pl* ohne Markenzeichen

unbudgeted: **~ expenditure** *n* GEN COMM außerplanmäßige Ausgaben *f pl*

unbundle *vt* BANK zerlegen, GEN COMM entflechten

unbundling *n* BANK Zerlegung *f*, GEN COMM Entflechtung *f*

uncallable *adj* FIN unkündbar

uncalled: **~ capital** *n* FIN nicht eingefordertes Kapital *nt*

UNCED *abbr* (*United Nations Conference on Environment and Development*) GEN COMM Konferenz *f* der Vereinten Nationen für Umwelt und Entwicklung

uncertain *adj* ECON unsicher, GEN COMM ungewiß, LAW unklar

uncertainty *n* ECON, GEN COMM Unbestimmtheit *f*, Ungewißheit *f*, Unsicherheit *f*

uncertified *adj* LAW unbeglaubigt

unchanged *adj* GEN COMM *forecast* unverändert

unchecked *adj* GEN COMM *figures* nicht überprüft, unkontrolliert; **~ baggage** *n* TRANSP Handgepäck *nt*; **~ inflationary economy** *n* ECON unkontrollierte inflationäre Wirtschaft *f*

UNCITRAL *abbr* (*United Nations Commission on International Trade Law*) LAW Kommission *f* der Vereinten Nationen für Internationales Handelsrecht

unclaimed: **~ letter** *n* COMMS nicht abgeholter Brief *m*; **~ right** *n* LAW nicht beanspruchtes Recht *nt*

unclear *adj* GEN COMM undeutlich, LAW unklar

uncollectable *adj* TAX *revenue, claim* uneinbringlich; **~ account** *n* ACC uneinbringliche Forderung *f*

uncollected: **~ funds** *n pl* BANK nicht eingezogene Gelder *nt pl*; **~ receivables** *n pl* ACC Außenstände *m pl*

uncommitted: **~ funds** *n pl* FIN nicht gebundene finanzielle Mittel *nt pl*

uncompromising *adj* GEN COMM kompromißlos, unnachgiebig

unconditional *adj* COMP bedingungslos, unbedingt, FIN bedingungslos, GEN COMM unbedingt, uneingeschränkt, LAW bedingungslos; **~ acceptance** *n* GEN COMM bedingungslose Annahme *f*, uneingeschränktes Akzept *nt*; **~ grant** *n* FIN uneingeschränkte Beihilfe *f*; **~ remission** *n* FIN *of debt* uneingeschränkter Erlaß *m*

unconfirmed *adj* GEN COMM unbestätigt

unconscionable *adj* GEN COMM *use of funds, demand* sittenwidrig; **~ contract** *n* LAW sittenwidriger Vertrag *m*

unconsolidated: **on an ~ basis** *phr* ACC, FIN auf nicht konsolidierter Basis, nicht konsolidiert, *debts* unfundiert

unconstitutional *adj* LAW, POL verfassungswidrig; **~ strike** *n* HRM verfassungswidriger Streik *m*

uncontainerable: **~ goods** *n pl* TRANSP nicht containerfähige Güter *nt pl*

uncontrollable *adj* ECON, FIN, GEN COMM *inflation, costs, increase* nicht beeinflußbar, unkontrollierbar; **~ expenditures** *n pl* FIN nicht kontrollierbare Ausgaben *f pl*

uncontrolled *adj* GEN COMM unkontrolliert

unconverted *adj* BANK nicht gewandelt

unconvincing *adj* GEN COMM nicht überzeugend

uncorrected *adj* GEN COMM, MEDIA nicht berichtigt, nicht korrigiert

uncovered *adj* FIN ungedeckt; **~ advance** *n* BANK nicht gedeckter Kredit *m*, ungedeckter Vorschuß *m*, STOCK Blankodarlehen *nt*; **~ balance** *n* FIN ungedeckter Saldo *m*; **~ call** *n* STOCK ungesicherte Kaufoption *f*; **~ call option** *n* STOCK ungedeckte Kaufoption *f*; **~ call writer** *n* STOCK Verkäufer, in *m,f* einer ungedeckten Kaufoption; **~ check** *AmE*, **~ cheque** *BrE* *n* BANK Scheck *m* ohne Deckung, ungedeckter Scheck *m*; **~ hedge loss** *n* STOCK ungedeckter Sicherungsverlust *m*; **~ option** *n* STOCK ungedecktes Optionsgeschäft *nt*; **~ put** *n* STOCK ungedeckte Verkaufsoption *f*; **~ writer** *n* STOCK Verkäufer, in *m,f* einer ungedeckten Option

UNCTAD *abbr* (*United Nations Conference on Trade and Development*) ECON UNCTAD (*Welthandels- und*

Entwicklungskonferenz der Vereinten Nationen); **~ MMO** *abbr* (*UNCTAD multimodal transport convention*) ECON *international trade* UNCTAD-Konvention *f* über kombinierten Verkehr; **~ multimodal transport convention** *n* (*UNCTAD MMO*) ECON *international trade* UNCTAD-Konvention *f* über kombinierten Verkehr

uncurbed *adj* GEN COMM *competition* zügellos

uncurtailed *adj* GEN COMM *competition, rights* uneingeschränkt

uncustomed *adj* IMP/EXP zollfrei

undamaged *adj* GEN COMM unbeschädigt, unversehrt *reputation* makellos

undamped *adj* ECON *demand* ungebremst, ungedämpft, unvermindert

undated *adj* GEN COMM undatiert

undecided *adj* GEN COMM unentschieden, unentschlossen

undeliverable *adj* COMMS unzustellbar; **~ check** *AmE*, **~ cheque** *BrE n* BANK unzustellbarer Scheck *m*

undelivered: **if ~ please return to sender** *phr* COMMS falls unzustellbar, an Absender zurück

undepletable: **~ externality** *n* ENVIR unerschöpfliche externe Effekte *m pl*

undepreciated *adj* ACC nicht abgeschrieben; **~ cost** *n* ACC nicht abgeschriebene Kosten *pl*

undepressed *adj* STOCK nicht rückläufig, nicht stagnierend

underabsorb *vt* ACC *costs* nicht voll übernehmen, nicht voll tragen

underabsorption *n* ACC *of costs* Kostenmehranfall *m*, Kostenunterdeckung *f*, Unterdeckung *f*

underapplied: **~ overhead** *n* ACC Gemeinkostenunterdeckung *f*

underassess *vt* TAX steuerlich unterbewerten

underassessment *n* TAX Unterveranlagung *f*, zu niedrige Veranlagung *f*

underbid sb *vt* GEN COMM ein günstigeres Angebot machen als jd, unterbieten

undercapacity *n* GEN COMM Kapazitätsmangel *m*, Unterkapazität *f*, IND nicht ausreichende Kapazität *f*, zu niedrige Kapazität *f*

undercapitalized *adj* GEN COMM unterkapitalisiert, IND nicht genügend kapitalisiert, unterkapitalisiert

undercharged: **~ account** *n* BANK gering belastetes Konto *nt*

underclass *n* ECON Unterklasse *f*, Unterschicht *f*

under-cost: **~ freight rate** *n* TRANSP *distribution* Frachttarif *m* unter Kosten

undercover: **~ audit** *n* ACC geheime Bilanzprüfung *f*; **~ payment** *n* GEN COMM heimliche Zahlung *f*

undercut *vt* ECON *competitor* unterbieten, GEN COMM *competitor* unterbieten, unterschreiten, S&M *goods* unter Preis verkaufen

undercutting 1. *adj* S&M preisunterschreitend; **2.** *n* GEN COMM Unterbieten *nt*, Unterschreitung *f*

underdeveloped: **~ country** *n* ECON, GEN COMM, POL unterentwickeltes Land *nt*, unterentwickelter Staat *m*

underdevelopment *n* ECON, GEN COMM Unterentwicklung *f*

underemployed *adj* HRM *person* unterbeschäftigt

underemployment *n* ECON, HRM Unterbeschäftigung *f*

underestimate *vt* GEN COMM unterbewerten, unterschätzen

underestimated *adj* GEN COMM unterbewertet

underestimation *n* GEN COMM Unterbewertung *f*, Unterschätzung *f*

underfunded *adj* FIN unterkapitalisiert

undergo *vt* GEN COMM durchmachen, erleben

undergraduate *n* WEL Student, in *m,f* im Grundstudium

underground *n* *BrE* (*cf subway AmE*) TRANSP U-Bahn *f*, Untergrundbahn *f*; **~ economy** *n* ECON Schattenwirtschaft *f*, Untergrundwirtschaft *f*; **~ mining** *n* IND Untertagearbeit *f*; **~ working** *n* IND Untertagearbeit *f*

underinvestment *n* BANK zu geringe Investition *f*

underlessee *n* PROP Untermieter, in *m,f*, Unterpächter, in *m,f*

underline 1. *n* COMP *text* Unterstreichung *f*; **2.** *vt* COMP *text*, MEDIA unterstreichen

underlying: **~ assets** *n pl* FIN zugrundeliegende Vermögen *nt pl*, STOCK Basiswerte *m pl*, Basisobjekte *nt pl*; **~ company** *n* *AmE infrml* FIN, GEN COMM vollständig abhängige Tochtergesellschaft, die nur wegen nicht übertragbarer Rechte oder Konzessionen fortbesteht; **~ debt** *n* FIN, PROP, STOCK *real estate, securities* Grundschuld *f*; **~ futures** *n pl* STOCK zugrundeliegende Termingeschäfte *nt pl*, zugrundeliegende Terminkontrakte *m pl*; **~ futures contract** *n* STOCK zugrundeliegender Terminkontrakt *m*; **~ inflation** *n* ECON Grundinflation *f*; **~ inflation rate** *n* ECON Inflationssockel *m*, Grundinflationsrate *f*; **~ instrument** *n* FIN Basiswert *m*; **~ net assets** *n pl* FIN zugrundeliegende Nettovermögen *nt pl*; **~ rate** *n* ECON *cost, inflation* Trendrate *f*, grundlegende Rate *f*; **~ security** *n* FIN von der Tochterfirma emittierte Schuldverschreibung, deren Rückzahlung von der Muttergesellschaft garantiert wird, STOCK zugrundeliegendes Wertpapier *nt*, Basiswert *m*, Basisprodukt *nt*; **~ tendency** *n* ECON, GEN COMM Grundtendenz *f*; **~ trend** *n* ECON, GEN COMM zugrundeliegender Trend *m*

undermanned *adj* HRM, TRANSP *shipping* unterbesetzt

undermanning *n* HRM Unterbesetzung *f*

undermentioned *adj* (*u/m*) GEN COMM unten erwähnt

undermine *vt* GEN COMM *influence, power* schwächen, untergraben

underpay *vt* GEN COMM, HRM schlecht entlohnen, unterbezahlen

underperform *vi* ECON sich unterdurchschnittlich entwickeln, GEN COMM das Ziel nicht erreichen, hinter den Erwartungen zurückbleiben, HRM weniger leisten als möglich

underpin *vt* ECON *currency*, GEN COMM stützen

underpopulated *adj* GEN COMM unterbevölkert

underprice *vt* ECON *competitor* unterbieten, S&M unter Preis anbieten, STOCK unterbewerten

underpriced *adj* S&M unter Preis angeboten, STOCK unterbewertet

underpricing *n* STOCK Unterbewertung *f*

underprivileged *adj* GEN COMM benachteiligt, unterprivilegiert

underproduce *vt* IND nicht genügend produzieren, unterproduzieren

underproduction *n* IND ungenügende Erzeugung *f*, ungenügende Produktion *f*

under-proportionately *adv* MATH unterproportional

underqualified *adj* GEN COMM, HRM unterqualifiziert

underquote *vt* GEN COMM unterbieten

underrate *vt* GEN COMM unterschätzen

underrecovery: ~ **of overhead costs** *n* ACC Gemein-kostenunterdeckung *f*, nicht volle Wiedereinholung *f* von Gemeinkosten

underreport *vt* GEN COMM zu niedrig ausweisen

underreporting *n* GEN COMM zu niedriges Ausweisen *nt*

underrepresent *vt* GEN COMM unterrepräsentieren, zu wenig vertreten

underscore 1. *n* COMP Unterstreichung *f*; **2.** *vt* COMP *text* unterstreichen, GEN COMM hervorheben, MEDIA unter-streichen

underscoring *n* GEN COMM Hervorhebung *f*

undersecretary: ~ **of state** *n* HRM, POL Staatssekretär, in *m,f*

undersell: ~ **oneself** *phr* GEN COMM sich unter Wert verkaufen

underselling *n* S&M *prices* Preisunterbietung *f*   .

undershoot *vt* ECON unterschreiten

undershooting *n* ECON Unterschreitung *f*

undersign *vt* GEN COMM unterschreiben, unterzeichnen

underspend 1. *n* ♦ **there was an ~ on new equipment** FIN es wurde zu wenig in neue Geräte investiert; **2.** *vt* ECON, FIN, POL zu wenig ausgeben; ♦ ~ **the budget** ACC das Budget nicht voll ausschöpfen; **3.** *vi* ECON, GEN COMM nicht voll ausgeben, zu wenig ausgeben

underspending *n* ECON Zurückhaltung *f* bei Ausgaben

understaffed *adj* HRM ungenügend bemannt, unterbe-setzt

understaffing *n* HRM Unterbesetzung *f*

understand 1. *vt* GEN COMM *language* verstehen, *concept, difficulty* begreifen; **2.** *vi* GEN COMM verstehen

understanding *n* GEN COMM Übereinkommen *nt*, LAW Verständigung *f*; ♦ **come to an** ~ GEN COMM sich einigen, zu einem Einvernehmen kommen, LAW sich verständigen; **come to an** ~ **with sb** GEN COMM sich mit jdm einigen, mit jdm übereinkommen; **have an** ~ **with sb** S&M eine Vereinbarung mit jdm haben; **on the** ~ **that** GEN COMM unter der Voraussetzung, daß

understate *vt* ACC unterbewerten

understated *adj* ACC unterbewertet

understatement *n* ACC, ECON Unterbewertung *f*

undersubscribed *adj* FIN nicht vollständig gezeichnet

undertake *vt* ECON unternehmen, GEN COMM *risk* ein-gehen, *promise* versprechen, *task, responsibility* übernehmen; ♦ ~ **to do sth** GEN COMM sich verpflich-ten, etw zu tun

undertaking *n* GEN COMM Projekt *nt*, Unterfangen *nt*, Betrieb *m*, *promise* Versprechen *nt*, *venture* Unter-nehmen *nt*, Ausführung *f*, LAW Verpflichtung *f*, Zusicherung *f*

undertakings: ~ **for collective investment in transfer-able securities** *n pl* (*UCITS*) FIN Unternehmen *nt* für gemeinschaftliche Investition in übertragbaren Wert-papieren

undertax *vt* TAX zu niedrig besteuern

under-the-counter: ~ **sale** *n* (*infrml*) S&M Verkauf *m* unter dem Ladentisch (*infrml*)

underuse *vt* GEN COMM nicht auslasten

underutilize *vt* GEN COMM *resources* zu wenig nutzen

undervaluation *n* ACC, ECON *exchange rate*, FIN Unterbewertung *f*, GEN COMM Unterbewertung *f*, Unterschätzung *f*

undervalue *vt* ACC, FIN unterbewerten, GEN COMM unterbewerten, unterschätzen, zu niedrig bewerten

undervalued *adj* ACC, FIN unterbewertet; ~ **currency** *n* ECON, FIN unterbewertete Währung *f*

underwrite *vt* INS versichern, zeichnen

underwriter *n* (*U/W*) FIN Konsortialmitglied *nt*, INS Versicherer *m*, Versicherungsgeber, in *m,f*, Zeichner, in *m,f*

underwriting *n* INS Zeichnung *f*, Risikoübernahme *f*; ~ **account** *n* (*U/a*) INS Versicherungskonto *nt*, Verwal-tungskonto *nt*; ~ **agreement** *n* STOCK Konsortialvertrag *m*, Übernahmevertrag *m*; ~ **business** *n* FIN, STOCK Effektenemissionsgeschäft *nt*; ~ **commission** *n* FIN Provision *f* aus einer Kon-sortialbeteiligung, Übernahmeprovision *f*; ~ **fee** *n* BANK Übernahmeprovision *f*, FIN Übernahmespesen *f pl*; ~ **house** *n* FIN Emissionsfirma *f*; ~ **profit** *n* FIN Emissionsgewinn *m*; ~ **prospectus** *n* FIN Emissions-prospekt *m*; ~ **spread** *n* STOCK Konsortialspanne *f*; ~ **syndicate** *n* FIN Emissionsübernahmekonsortium *nt*, Emissionskonsortium *nt*, Übernahmekonsortium *nt*, INS Garantiekonsortium *nt*

undesirable *adj* GEN COMM unerwünscht

undetermined *adj* GEN COMM unbestimmt

undeveloped *adj* PROP unerschlossen; ~ **land** *n* BrE (*cf vacant lot* AmE) ECON unerschlossenes Grundstück *nt*, PROP unbebautes Grundstück *nt*

undifferentiated *adj* GEN COMM undifferenziert; ~ **marketing** *n* S&M undifferenziertes Marketing *nt*; ~ **products** *n pl* S&M undifferenzierte Produkte *nt pl*

undischarged *adj* FIN, GEN COMM *debt* nicht beglichen, nicht ausgeglichen, TRANSP *cargo* nicht entladen; ~ **commitment** *n* ACC unbezahlte Verpflichtung *f*

undisclosed *adj* GEN COMM ungenannt; ~ **sum** *n* FIN, GEN COMM nicht offengelegter Betrag *m*

undisposed: ~ **of** *phr* GEN COMM *stock* nicht verteilt, unverkauft

undistributable: ~ **capital** *n* FIN einbehaltenes Kapital *nt*, nicht ausschüttbares Kapital *nt*; ~ **reserves** *n pl* (*cf restricted surplus* AmE) ACC unverteilbare Rücklage *f*

undistributed: ~ **allotment** *n* GEN COMM unverteilte Zuteilung *f*; ~ **income** *n* ACC einbehaltener Gewinn *m*, unverteilter Gewinn *m*; ~ **profit** *n* ACC unverteilter Gewinn *m*, FIN Gewinnvortrag *m*, nicht ausgeschütteter Gewinn *m*, thesaurierter Gewinn *m*

undisturbed *adj* GEN COMM ungestört; ~ **growth** *n* ECON störungsfreies Wachstum *nt*

undivided *adj* GEN COMM *profits* ungeteilt; ~ **interest** *n* FIN Nutznießung *f* zur gesamten Hand; ~ **profit** *n* ACC unverteilter Gewinn *m*; ~ **property** *n* PROP ungeteilter Besitz *m*

undocumented: ~ **workers** *n pl* LAW Arbeitskräfte *f pl* ohne Papiere

UNDP *abbr* (*United Nations Development Programme*) ECON UNDP (*Entwicklungsprogramm der Vereinten Nationen*)

UNDRO *abbr* (*United Nations Disaster and Relief Organization*) ECON Katastrophenhilfswerk *nt* der Ver-einten Nationen

undue: ~ **influence** *n* GEN COMM unzulässige Beein-flussung *f*

unduly *adv* GEN COMM *excessively* übermäßig, *unjustifiably* ungerechterweise

unearned *adj* ACC, GEN COMM, TAX unverdient; **~ income** *n* ACC, FIN, TAX Besitzeinkommen *nt*, Einkommen *nt* aus Vermögen, Kapitaleinkommen *nt*, fundiertes Einkommen *nt*, ohne Arbeit erzieltes Einkommen *nt*; **~ increment** *n* FIN, PROP unverdienter Wertzuwachs *m*; **~ increment of land** *n* PROP leistungslose Bodenwertsteigerung *f*; **~ premium** *n* FIN, LAW noch nicht verdiente Prämie *f*; **~ premium reserve** *n* INS Deckungskapital *nt*, Deckungsrückstellung *f*

uneconomic *adj* ECON, GEN COMM unrentabel, unwirtschaftlich, unökonomisch

uneconomical *adj* GEN COMM unökonomisch, unrentabel, unwirtschaftlich

unemployability *n* HRM Beschäftigungsunfähigkeit *f*

unemployable *adj* HRM beschäftigungsunfähig

unemployed *adj* ECON, HRM, WEL arbeitslos; **the ~** *n pl* ECON, HRM, WEL die Arbeitslosen *pl*; **~ labor force** *AmE*, **~ labour force** *BrE n* ECON, HRM, WEL arbeitslose Arbeitskräfte *f pl*; **~ person** *n* ECON, HRM, WEL Arbeitslose(r) *mf* [decl. as adj]

unemployment *n* ECON, HRM, WEL Arbeitslosigkeit *f*; **~ benefit** *n BrE* (*cf unemployment compensation AmE*) ECON, HRM, WEL Arbeitslosengeld *nt*, Arbeitslosenunterstützung *f*; **~ benefit office** *n BrE obs* WEL Amt für Arbeitslosenunterstützung; **~ compensation** *n AmE* (*cf unemployment benefit BrE*) ECON, HRM, WEL Arbeitslosengeld *nt*, Arbeitslosenunterstützung *f*; **~ figures** *n pl* ECON, HRM Arbeitslosenzahlen *f pl*; **~ insurance** *n* ECON, HRM, INS Arbeitslosenversicherung *f*; **~ insurance account** *n* ECON, HRM, INS Arbeitslosenversicherungskonto *nt*; **~ pay** *n* ECON, HRM, WEL Arbeitslosenunterstützung *f*; **~ rate** *n* ECON, HRM Arbeitslosenquote *f*, Arbeitslosigkeit *f*, Arbeitslosenzahl *f*; **~ statistics** *n pl* ECON, HRM Arbeitslosenstatistik *f*; **~ trap** *n* ECON, HRM, WEL Arbeitslosigkeitsfalle *f*

unencumbered *adj* PROP unbelastet; **~ estate** *n* PROP unbelastete Immobilie *f*; **~ property** *n* PROP schuldenfreies Eigentum *nt*

unenforceable *adj* LAW nicht klagbar; **~ contract** *n* LAW nicht einklagbarer Vertrag *m*, nicht erzwingbarer Vertrag *m*, nicht klagbarer Vertrag *m*

unequaled *AmE see unequalled BrE*

unequal: **~ exchange** *n* GEN COMM ungleicher Tausch *m*

unequalled *adj BrE* GEN COMM unerreicht

uneven *adj* GEN COMM *trend* ungleichmäßig; **~ lot** *n* GEN COMM unausgewogener Posten *m*

unexchangeable *adj* GEN COMM nicht austauschbar

unexcused: **~ absence from work** *n* HRM Blaumachen *nt infrml*

unexpected: **~ loss** *n* ECON unerwarteter Verlust *m*; **~ profit** *n* ECON, GEN COMM unerwarteter Gewinn *m*

unexpended *adj* FIN nicht ausgegeben; **~ balance** *n* FIN *of an appropriation* nicht verbrauchter Saldo *m*, nicht verbrauchtes Guthaben *nt*

unexpired: **~ cost** *n* ECON nicht erfolgswirksame Kosten *pl*

unexploited *adj* ECON unerschlossen

unfailing *adj* GEN COMM unerschöpflich

unfair *adj* GEN COMM ungerecht; **~ dismissal** *n* HRM grundlose Entlassung *f*, ungerechtfertigte Entlassung

f; **~ labor practice** *AmE*, **~ labour practice** *BrE n* HRM unfaire Praktiken *f pl* im Arbeitsleben; **~ shop** *n* HRM lohnschwacher Betrieb *m*; **~ trade** *n* GEN COMM unlauteres Geschäft *nt*; **~ trading practices** *n pl* GEN COMM unlauterer Wettbewerb *m*, unlauteres Geschäftsgebaren *nt*

unfavorable *AmE see unfavourable BrE*

unfavourable *adj BrE* GEN COMM *price, conditions* ungünstig, unvorteilhaft; **~ balance of trade** *n BrE* ECON, IMP/EXP, POL passive Handelsbilanz *f*; **~ exchange** *n BrE* FIN ungünstiger Wechselkurs *m*; **~ rate of exchange** *n BrE* FIN ungünstiger Wechselkurs *m*; **~ treatment** *n BrE* LAW Benachteiligung *f*

unfeasible *adj* GEN COMM undurchführbar

unfilled: **~ orders** *n pl* GEN COMM Arbeitsvorrat *m*, Auftragsbestand *m*, Auftragsrückstand *m*, unerledigte Aufträge *m pl*; **~ vacancy** *n* HRM freie Stelle *f*

unfinished *adj* IND unbearbeitet

unfit *adj* HRM untauglich; ◆ **~ for consumption** GEN COMM nicht zum Verzehr geeignet; **~ to do sth** GEN COMM unfähig, etw zu tun

unfledged *adj* GEN COMM *organization, person* unerfahren, HRM unreif

unforeseeable *adj* GEN COMM unabsehbar, unvorhersehbar; **~ expenditure** *n* ACC unvorhergesehene Ausgaben *f pl*

unforeseen *adj* GEN COMM unerwartet, unvorhergesehen; **~ circumstances** *n pl* GEN COMM unvorhergesehene Umstände *m pl*

unformatted *adj* COMP *disk, storage* unformatiert

unfounded *adj* GEN COMM *rumour, allegation* leer, unbegründet

unfriendly: **~ takeover attempt** *n* FIN, GEN COMM feindliche Übernahmeofferte *f*

unfulfilled *adj* GEN COMM *condition, promise* unerfüllt

unfunded: **~ debt** *n* FIN nicht konsolidierte Schuld *f*, schwebende Schuld *f*

ungeared: **~ balance sheet** *n* ACC unangepaßte Bilanz *f*

ungraded *adj* GEN COMM nicht abgestuft, unsortiert

UNHCR *abbr* (*United Nations High Commission for Refugees*) ECON UNHCR (*Hochkommissariat der Vereinten Nationen für Flüchtlinge*)

unhedged *adj* STOCK ungesichert

unhesitating *adj* GEN COMM bedenkenlos

unidentified *adj* GEN COMM unerkannt

UNIDO *abbr* (*United Nations Industrial Development Organization*) ECON UNIDO (*Organisation der Vereinten Nationen für industrielle Entwicklung*)

unification *n* GEN COMM Vereinheitlichung *f*, *of Germany* Wiedervereinigung *f*, Vereinigung *f*

unified *adj* GEN COMM vereinheitlicht, *Germany* wiedervereinigt, vereinigt; **~ credit** *n* TAX Nachlaßsteuerfreibetrag *m*

uniform *adj* GEN COMM einheitlich, konstant; **~ accounting** *n* ACC einheitliche Buchführung *f*

Uniform: **~ Business Rate** *n* (*UBR*) FIN von der Regierung festgelegte, einheitliche Grundsteuer für Betriebe; **~ Commercial Code** *n AmE* LAW einheitliches Handelsrecht *nt*; **~ Customs and Practice for Documentary Credits** *n* (*UC&P*) ECON *international trade* einheitliche Richtlinien *f pl* und Praktiken *f pl* für Dokumenten-Akkreditive (*ERA*)

uniformity *n* GEN COMM Einheitlichkeit *f*; **~ assumption** *n* ECON Gleichmäßigkeitsannahme *f*

uniform: **~ practice code** *n* AmE STOCK einheitliche Richtlinien der Vereinigung der US-Wertpapierhändlerfirmen; **~ price** *n* FIN Einheitspreis *m*; **~ rules for collections** *n pl* BANK einheitliche Inkassorichtlinien *f pl*, einheitliche Richtlinien *f pl* für Inkassi

unify *vt* GEN COMM einigen, vereinheitlichen

unilateral *adj* ECON, HRM, POL einseitig; **~ agreement** *n* ECON einseitig bindendes Abkommen *nt*, einseitiges Abkommen *nt*, unilaterales Abkommen *nt*

unilaterally *adv* GEN COMM einseitig

unilateral: **~ measure** *n* ENVIR, POL einseitige Maßnahme *f*; **~ reference** *n* HRM einseitige Referenz *f*; **~ regulation** *n* HRM einseitig verpflichtende Vorschrift *f*

unimodal: **~ distribution** *n* MATH *statistics* eingipflige Verteilung *f*

unimpeachable *adj* GEN COMM *contract, evidence* unanfechtbar

unimpressive *adj* GEN COMM nicht überzeugend, wenig beeindruckend

unimproved *adj* GEN COMM *raw material* unveredelt, *situation, work* nicht verbessert

unincorporated: **~ company** *n* LAW Unternehmen *nt* ohne eigene Rechtspersönlichkeit, nicht rechtsfähiges Unternehmen *nt*

uninhabited *adj* PROP unbewohnt

uninsurable *adj* INS nicht versicherungsfähig, unversicherbar; **~ title** *n* INS nicht versicherungsfähiger Titel *m*, unversicherbarer Titel *m*

uninsured *adj* INS nicht versichert, unversichert

unintended *adj* GEN COMM unbeabsichtigt; **~ investment** *n* BANK Fehlinvestition *f* aufgrund falscher Umsatzprognosen

unintentional *adj* GEN COMM unabsichtlich, unbeabsichtigt

uninterruptible: **~ power supply** *n* (*UPS*) COMP unterbrechungsfreie Stromversorgung *f*

uninvested *adj* BANK nicht investiert

union *n* GEN COMM, HRM *workers* Gewerkschaft *f*, POL *workers* Gewerkschaft *f*, Union *f*, Vereinigung *f*; ◆ **belong to a ~** HRM einer Gewerkschaft angehören

union: **~ affiliation** *n* HRM Gewerkschaftszugehörigkeit *f*; **~ agreement** *n* AmE HRM Tarifvertrag *m*; **~ bashing** *n* BrE *infrml* HRM Einprügeln *nt* auf die Gewerkschaften (*infrml*); **~ certification** *n* HRM Ausstellung *f* des Unabhängigkeitszertifikats für eine Gewerkschaft; **~ contract** *n* AmE HRM Tarifvertrag *m*; **~ contract negotiations** *n pl* AmE (*cf negotiations for collective agreement BrE*) ECON, HRM Tarifverhandlung *f*; **~ density** *n* HRM Dichte *f* der Gewerkschaftsangehörigkeit; **~ fees** *n pl* HRM Gewerkschaftsbeiträge *m pl*; **~ government** *n* HRM Gewerkschaftsverwaltung *f*; **~ immunities** *n pl* HRM, LAW Gewerkschaftsprivilegien *nt pl*, Gewerkschaftsrechte *nt pl*

unionization *n* HRM gewerkschaftliche Zusammenfassung *f*

unionized *adj* HRM gewerkschaftlich organisiert

union: **~ label** *n* HRM Gewerkschaftsetikett *nt*; **~ leader** *n* HRM Gewerkschaftsführer *m*; **~ leave** *n* HRM Gewerkschaftspflichten; **~ liability** *n* HRM Gewerkschaftspflichten *f pl*; **~ membership** *n* HRM Gewerkschaftsmitgliedschaft *f*; **~ membership**

agreement *n* (*UMA*) HRM Tarifausschlußklausel *f*; **~ movement** *n* HRM Gewerkschaftsbewegung *f*; **~ officer** *n* HRM Gewerkschaftsfunktionär, in *m,f*; **~ official** *n* HRM Gewerkschaftsfunktionär, in *m,f*; **~-only practice** *n* BrE HRM Praxis *f* der Gewerkschaftszugehörigkeitspflicht; **~ rate** *n* HRM Mindestlohnsatz *m*, Tariflohn *m*; **~ recruitment** *n* HRM Gewerkschaftsanwerbung *f*; **~ representative** *n* HRM Gewerkschaftsvertreter, in *m,f*; **~ rights** *n pl* HRM Gewerkschaftsrechte *nt pl*; **~ rule book** *n* HRM anerkanntes Gewerkschaftsstatut *nt*; **~ rules** *n pl* HRM gewerkschaftliche Vorschriften *f pl*; **~ safety officer** *n* HRM Untersuchungsbeauftragte(r) *mf* [decl. as adj] einer Gewerkschaft; **~ shop** *n* HRM Betrieb, der nur gewerkschaftlich organisierte Arbeitnehmer beschäftigt

Union: **~ of Shop, Distributive & Allied Workers** *n* BrE (*USDAW*) HRM Gewerkschaft der im Handel, Vertrieb und verwandten Gebieten beschäftigten Arbeiter

unions: **~ and management** *n pl* HRM Gewerkschaften *f pl* und Unternehmensleitung *f*, Tarifpartner *m pl*

union: **~ structure** *n* HRM Gewerkschaftsstruktur *f*; **~ wage effect** *n* FIN, HRM Tariflohneffekt *m*; **~ wage policy** *n* HRM gewerkschaftliche Tarifpolitik *f*

unique *adj* GEN COMM außergewöhnlich, einmalig, einzigartig, unvergleichlich; **~ impairment** *n* INS einmalige Beeinträchtigung *f*, einmalige Schädigung *f*; **~ opportunity** *n* S&M einmalige Gelegenheit *f*; **~ position** *n* PATENTS Alleinstellung *f*; **~ reference number** *n* (*URN*) ADMIN besondere Kennziffer *f*; **~ selling point** *n* (*USP*) S&M einmaliges Verkaufsargument *nt*; **~ selling proposition** *n* (*USP*) S&M einmaliges Verkaufsargument *nt*

unissued: **~ capital** *n* STOCK nicht gezeichnetes Kapital *nt*; **~ capital stock** *n* STOCK nicht ausgegebenes Aktienkapital *nt*; **~ shares** *n* BrE (*cf union stock AmE*) STOCK zur Ausgabe genehmigte, aber noch nicht emittierte Aktien; **~ stock** *n* AmE (*cf union shares BrE*) STOCK zur Ausgabe genehmigte, aber noch nicht emittierte Aktien

unit *n* GEN COMM Stück *nt*; **~ of account** *n* ACC Rechnungseinheit *f*

UNITAR *abbr* (*United Nations Institute for Training and Research*) HRM UNITAR (*Institut der Vereinten Nationen für Ausbildung und Forschung*)

unitary: **~ approach** *n* WEL ganzheitliche Betrachtungsweise *f*; **~ model** *n* WEL *social work* ganzheitliches Modell *nt*

Unitas: **~ all share index** *n* STOCK Unitas Gesamtaktienindex *m*

unit: **~ banking** *n* BANK Einzelbankensystem *nt*; **~ of a collective investment undertaking** *n* FIN Fondsanteil *m* einer Unternehmung für gemeinsame Kapitalanlagen; **~ cost** *n* ACC Stückkosten *pl*

unite 1. *vt* GEN COMM zusammenschließen, zusammenfassen; **2.** *vi* GEN COMM sich zusammenschließen; ◆ **~ with** GEN COMM sich verbinden mit, sich vereinigen mit

united *adj* GEN COMM vereinigt

United: **~ Automobile Workers** *n* AmE (*UAW*) HRM amerikanische Autoarbeitergewerkschaft *f*; **~ Kingdom Agricultural Supply Trade Association** *n* (*UKASTA*) IND britische Wirtschaftsvereinigung für landwirtschaftliche Bedarfsdeckung; **~ Kingdom Atomic Energy Authority** *n* (*UKAEA*) ENVIR, IND britische Atomenergiebehörde; **~ Kingdom Offshore Operators' Association** *n*

(*UKOOA*) IND Verband britischer Offshore-Unternehmer, Verband britischer Offshore-Arbeiter; ~ **Kingdom Permanent Representative to the European Economic Community** n (*UKREP*) ECON, POL Ständiger Vertreter m Großbritanniens bei der Europäischen Gemeinschaft; ~ **Kingdom tariff and overseas trade classification** n (*UKTOTC*) ECON *international trade* britische Klassifikation f für Zoll und Überseehandel; ~ **Kingdom Trade Agency** n (*UKTA*) ECON *development agency* britisches Handelsamt; ~ **Nations** n (*UN*) POL Vereinte Nationen f pl (*VN*), United Nations f pl (*UN*); ~ **Nations Commission on International Trade Law** n (*UNCITRAL*) LAW Kommission f der Vereinten Nationen für Internationales Handelsrecht; ~ **Nations Conference on Environment and Development** n (*UNCED*) ENVIR Konferenz f der Vereinten Nationen für Umwelt und Entwicklung; ~ **Nations Conference on Trade and Development** n (*UNCTAD*) ECON Welthandels- und Entwicklungskonferenz f der Vereinten Nationen (*UNCTAD*); ~ **Nations Development Programme** (*UNDP*) ECON Entwicklungsprogramm nt der Vereinten Nationen (*UNDP*); ~ **Nations Disaster and Relief Organization** n (*UNDRO*) ECON Katastrophenhilfswerk nt der Vereinten Nationen; ~ **Nations High Commission for Refugees** n (*UNHCR*) ECON Hochkommissariat nt der Vereinten Nationen für Flüchtlinge (*UNHCR*); ~ **Nations Industrial Development Organization** n (*UNIDO*) ECON Organisation f der Vereinten Nationen für industrielle Entwicklung; ~ **Nations Institute for Training and Research** n (*UNITAR*) HRM Institut nt der Vereinten Nationen für Ausbildung und Forschung (*UNITAR*); ~ **Nations Organization** n (*UNO*) POL Vereinten Nationen f pl (*VN*), United Nations f pl (*UN*); ~ **Nations Research Institute for Social Development** n (*UNRISD*) WEL Forschungsinstitut nt der Vereinten Nationen für soziale Entwicklung; ~ **States East Coast** n (*USEC*) GEN COMM Ostküste f der Vereinigten Staaten; ~ **States Environmental Protection Agency** n ENVIR Umweltschutzbehörde f der Vereinigten Staaten; ~ **States Maritime Commission** n (*USMC*) TRANSP Schiffahrtskommission f der Vereinigten Staaten; ~ **States Mint** n (*USM*) BANK Münze f der Vereinigten Staaten; ~ **States West Coast** n (*USWC*) GEN COMM Westküste f der Vereinigten Staaten

unitization n ECON Aufteilung f von Immobilien in handelsfähige Einheiten

unit: ~ **labor cost** AmE, ~ **labour cost** BrE n ECON Arbeitsaufwand m je Produkteinheit; ~ **labour costs** n pl BrE ACC, ECON, HRM Lohnstückkosten pl; **~-linked assurance** n BrE INS fondsgebundene Lebensversicherung f; ~ **load** n (*U*) TRANSP *distribution* Containerstapel m, Einheitsladung f; ~ **load device** n (*ULD*) TRANSP *aviation* Ladeeinheit f; ~ **of measure** n GEN COMM Maßeinheit f; ~ **pack** n S&M Einzelpackung f; ~ **price** n GEN COMM Stückpreis m, S&M Einzelpreis m, Preis m pro Einheit; ~ **tax** n TAX Einzelsteuer f; ~ **of trading** n STOCK Handelsgröße f, Schlußeinheit f; ~ **trust** n FIN, STOCK Investmentgesellschaft f; ~ **trust management** n BrE FIN, STOCK Verwaltung f eines offenen Investmentfonds; ~ **value** n GEN COMM Einheitswert m, Wert m pro Einheit; ~ **value index** n (*UVI*) ECON Einheitswertindex m

unity n PATENTS Einheit f, Übereinstimmung f; ~ **of European patent** n PATENTS Einheit f des europäischen Patents, Übereinstimmung f des europäischen Patents; ~ **of invention** n PATENTS Einheit f der Erfindung, Einheitlichkeit f der Erfindung, Erfindungsübereinstimmung f

universal adj FIN universal; ~ **agent** n GEN COMM, LAW Generalvertreter, in m,f; ~ **air waybill** n (*UAWB*) IMP/EXP, TRANSP Einheitsluftfrachtbrief m, Universal-Luftfrachtbrief m; ~ **bank** n BANK Universalbank f; ~ **container** n (*U*) TRANSP Universal-Container m

universalism n GEN COMM Universalismus m

universal: ~ **suffrage** n POL allgemeines Wahlrecht nt; ~ **time** n (*UT*) GEN COMM abgestimmte Weltzeit f; ~ **time coordinated** n (*UTC*) GEN COMM abgestimmte Weltzeit f

universe n MATH, S&M Grundgesamtheit f (*obs*)

university n HRM Universität f; ~ **degree** n HRM Hochschulabschluß m, Univertätsabschluß m

unjust adj GEN COMM unbillig, ungerecht

unjustified adj COMP im Flattersatz, nicht ausgerichtet, LAW unberechtigt, ungerechtfertigt; ~ **threat** n LAW ungerechtfertigte Drohung f

unknown adj GEN COMM unbekannt; ♦ ~ **at this address** COMMS Adressat unbekannt; **of ~ origin** n GEN COMM unbekannten Ursprungs

unladen: ~ **weight** n GEN COMM Leergewicht nt, TRANSP Eigengewicht nt, Leergewicht nt

unlawful adj LAW gesetzwidrig, rechtswidrig, unrechtmäßig; ~ **act** n LAW Delikt nt, unerlaubte Handlung f; ~ **picketing** n HRM unerlaubtes Streikpostenstehen nt; ~ **trespass** n LAW rechtswidriges Betreten nt

unleaded adj ENVIR, TRANSP bleifrei; ~ **gas** AmE, ~ **petrol** n BrE ENVIR bleifreies Benzin nt

unless: ~ **caused by** phr INS *marine* sofern nicht verursacht durch; ~ **general** phr INS vorbehaltlich großer Havarie; ~ **otherwise agreed** phr GEN COMM, LAW sofern nicht anders vereinbart; ~ **otherwise specified** phr GEN COMM, LAW sofern nicht anders angegeben

unleveraged: ~ **program** AmE, ~ **programme** BrE n FIN Programm nt ohne Verschuldung, Programm nt ohne Fremdkapitalaufnahme

unlicensed: ~ **broker** n STOCK nicht zugelassener Broker m

unlimited n GEN COMM unbefristet, unbegrenzt, unbeschränkt, STOCK unlimitiert; ~ **accounts** n pl BANK Unternehmen, denen Kredite in beliebiger Höhe eingeräumt werden; ~ **company** n GEN COMM Kapitalgesellschaft f mit unbeschränkter Haftung; ~ **fine** n LAW unbegrenzte Geldstrafe f; ~ **letter of credit** n BANK unbeschränktes Akkreditiv nt; ~ **liability** n GEN COMM, LAW unbegrenzte Haftung f, unbeschränkte Haftung f; ~ **mileage** n TRANSP *car hire* unbegrenzte Kilometerzahl f; ~ **on the upside** adj STOCK *options* nach oben keine Begrenzung, nach oben unbegrenzt; ~ **securities** n pl STOCK unlimitierte Wertpapiere nt pl; ~ **tax bond** n AmE STOCK Kommunalschuldverschreibung, die durch die Steuereinnahmen der emittierenden Gebietskörperschaft gedeckt ist, unbegrenzte Steuerbürgschaft f

unliquidated: ~ **damages** n pl LAW vertraglich nicht festgesetzter Schadensersatzanspruch

unlisted adj AmE (*cf ex-directory* BrE) COMMS nicht im Telefonverzeichnis aufgeführt; ~ **company** n ECON, GEN COMM nicht börsennotierte Gesellschaft f, STOCK nicht zugelassene Firma f, nicht börsennotierte Gesellschaft f; ~ **market** n STOCK Freiverkehr m

Unlisted: ~ **Securities Market** n BrE (USM) STOCK Freiverkehrsbörse f, geregelter Freiverkehr m, geregelter Markt m

unlisted: ~ **security** n FIN amtlich nicht notierter Wert m, STOCK amtlich nicht notierter Wert m, Freiverkehrswert m; ~ **share** n STOCK nicht zur amtlichen Notierung zugelassene Aktie f; ~ **trading** n STOCK Handel m in Freiverkehrswerten

unload vt FIN abstoßen, GEN COMM, IND abladen, ausladen, TRANSP abladen, ausladen, auspacken, entladen, löschen; ♦ ~ **stocks on the market** STOCK Aktien auf dem Markt abstoßen

unloader: ~ **crane** n TRANSP Entladekran m

unloading n GEN COMM, IND Ausladen nt, Ausladung f, Abladen nt, STOCK Abstoßen nt, TRANSP Abladen nt, Ausladen nt, Entladen nt, Entladung f, Löschung f; ~ **risk** n GEN COMM, INS, TRANSP Löschrisiko nt

unlock vt COMP keyboard entsperren, FIN auflösen; ♦ ~ **funds** FIN Kapital auflösen

unmanageable adj GEN COMM object schwer zu handhaben, situation unkontrollierbar

unmanifested: ~ **cargo** n TRANSP nicht manifestierte Fracht f

unmanned: ~ **machinery spaces** n pl IND unbesetzte Stellen f pl an einer Maschine

unmanufactured: ~ **material** n IND Rohmaterial nt

unmarketable adj GEN COMM nicht marktfähig; ~ **title** n PROP nicht rechtsmängelfreies Liegenschaftsrecht nt

unmatched adj STOCK konkurrenzlos

unmatured: ~ **debt** n STOCK noch nicht fällige Schuld f

unmortgaged adj BANK nicht hypothekarisch belastet, PROP nicht hypothekarisch belastet, nicht verpfändet

unnamed adj COMP disk, file unbenannt

unnegotiable adj BANK nur zur Verrechnung, GEN COMM nicht begebbar, nicht übertragbar

unnoticed: **go** ~ phr GEN COMM unbemerkt bleiben

UNO abbr (United Nations Organization) POL VN (Vereinte Nationen), UN (United Nations)

unobtainable adj GEN COMM goods nicht erreichbar

unoccupied adj PROP unbewohnt

unofficial adj ADMIN, GEN COMM, POL inoffiziell; ~ **industrial action** n HRM gewerkschaftlich nicht genehmigte Arbeitskampfmaßnahmen f pl; ♦ **in an** ~ **capacity** GEN COMM in nichtoffizieller Eigenschaft

unofficial: ~ **leader** n HRM inoffizielle Leiterin f, inoffizieller Leiter m; ~ **strike** n HRM nicht genehmigter Streik m

unpack vt GEN COMM auspacken

unpacked adj GEN COMM lose, unverpackt

unpaid adj ACC, FIN, GEN COMM bill, debt unbeglichen, unbezahlt; ~ **call on capital** n BrE ACC ausstehende Einlagen f pl; ~ **dividend** n FIN ausgeschüttete, aber noch nicht ausgezahlte Dividende f; ~ **trainee** n HRM Volontär, in m,f

unpalatable adj GEN COMM ungenießbar

unparalleled adj GEN COMM beispiellos, unvergleichlich

unpatented adj PATENTS nicht patentiert

unplug vt GEN COMM den Stecker herausziehen von

unpopular adj GEN COMM unbeliebt, unpopulär

unpracticable adj GEN COMM undurchführbar

unprecedented adj GEN COMM beispiellos, noch nicht abgelaufen, noch nie dagewesen

unpredictable adj GEN COMM unabsehbar, unberechenbar, unvorhersehbar

unprejudiced adj GEN COMM unparteiisch, unvoreingenommen

unpresented: ~ **check** AmE, ~ **cheque** BrE n BANK nicht eingereichter Scheck m, nicht zur Zahlung vorgelegter Scheck m

unpriced adj GEN COMM nicht ausgepreist, ohne Preisangabe

unprocessable adj COMP data nicht verarbeitbar

unprocessed adj COMP data, GEN COMM unverarbeitet

unproductive adj IND, MGMNT unproduktiv, STOCK nicht ertragreich, unergiebig; ~ **labor** AmE, ~ **labour** BrE n HRM nicht produktive Arbeitskräfte f pl, unproduktive Arbeitskräfte f pl

unprofessional: ~ **behavior** AmE, ~ **behaviour** BrE n HRM nicht berufsmäßiges Verhalten nt; ~ **conduct** n GEN COMM berufsstandswidriges Verhalten nt, Verstoß m gegen die Standesregeln

unprofitable adj ECON, FIN unrentabel, GEN COMM unergiebig, unrentabel; ~ **investment** n BANK Fehlinvestition f

unprompted: ~ **response** n S&M spontane Reaktion f

unprotected adj PATENTS ungeschützt

unprotested adj BANK nicht protestiert, FIN nicht protestiert, ohne Widerspruch

unproven adj GEN COMM unbewiesen

unpublished adj GEN COMM, MEDIA unveröffentlicht

unqualified adj GEN COMM agreement, approval uneingeschränkt, HRM worker unqualifiziert; ~ **acceptance** n FIN unbeschränktes Akzept nt, uneingeschränkte Annahme f; ~ **opinion** n ACC uneingeschränkte Erklärung f

unquestionable adj GEN COMM unbestreitbar, unzweifelhaft

unquoted: ~ **shares** n pl STOCK amtlich nicht notierte Aktien f pl; ~ **trading company** n ECON Unternehmen, dessen Aktien im Freiverkehr gehandelt werden

unrealistic adj GEN COMM unrealistisch

unrealized: ~ **gains** n pl FIN, TAX nicht realisierte Gewinne m pl; ~ **loss** n ACC nicht realisierter Verlust m; ~ **profit** n FIN, TAX nicht realisierte Gewinne m pl

unreasonable adj GEN COMM demand, price, behaviour unangebracht, unangemessen, ungerechtfertigt, unpassend

unreceipted adj GEN COMM invoice ohne Quittung, unquittiert

unrecognized adj GEN COMM nicht anerkannt, unerkannt

unrecorded adj GEN COMM nicht eingetragen, nicht erfaßt; ~ **deed** n GEN COMM, LAW, PROP nicht amtlich eingetragene Urkunde f; ~ **employment** n HRM Schwarzarbeit f

unrecoverable adj COMP data, file nicht wiederherstellbar, FIN, GEN COMM debt nicht eintreibbar, uneinbringlich

unregistered adj LAW auf den Inhaber lautend, nicht angemeldet; ~ **labor** AmE, ~ **labour** BrE n HRM nicht registrierte Arbeitskräfte f pl; ~ **mark** n PATENTS nicht eingetragenes Firmenzeichen nt, nicht eingetragenes Warenzeichen nt; ~ **stock** n STOCK Inhaberaktie f; ~ **trademark** n GEN COMM nicht eingetragenes Warenzeichen nt

unreliable *adj* GEN COMM, HRM *information, estimate* unzuverlässig

unremunerative *adj* GEN COMM nicht einträglich, unrentabel

unrepealed *adj* LAW nicht aufgehoben

unrequired: **~ dividend** *n* ACC nicht beanspruchte Dividende *f*, nicht verlangte Dividende *f*

unresolved *adj* MGMNT *problem, question* ungeklärt, ungelöst

unresponsive *adj* GEN COMM *market* gleichgültig, nicht reagierend

unrest *n* POL Unruhen *f pl*

unrestricted *adj* GEN COMM unbeschränkt, uneingeschränkt; **~ access** *n* GEN COMM uneingeschränkter Zugang *m*; **~ quota** *n* GEN COMM unbeschränktes Kontingent *nt*

unrewarding *adj* GEN COMM nicht lohnend

UNRISD *abbr* (*United Nations Research Institute for Social Development*) WEL Forschungsinstitut *nt* der Vereinten Nationen für soziale Entwicklung

unrivaled *see* unrivalled *BrE*

unrivalled *BrE adj* GEN COMM konkurrenzlos, unerreicht, unübertroffen

unsafe *adj* IND unsicher; **~ paper** *n* FIN dubioses Papier *nt*

unsalable *AmE see* unsaleable *BrE*

unsaleable *adj BrE* S&M nicht marktfähig

unsatisfactory *adj* GEN COMM unbefriedigend, ungenügend, unzureichend

unscheduled *adj* GEN COMM außerplanmäßig

unschooled *adj* HRM, WEL ungeschult

unscramble *vt* GEN COMM entflechten, entschlüsseln

unscreened *adj* GEN COMM *unchecked* nicht überprüft, *unprotected* nicht abgeschirmt, ungeschützt

unscrupulous *adj* GEN COMM bedenkenlos, gewissenlos, skrupellos

unseasonable *adj* GEN COMM nicht der Jahreszeit entsprechend

unseat: **~ the board** *phr* MGMNT den Vorstand absetzen

unsecured *adj* BANK *credit* ungedeckt, STOCK ungesichert; **~ advance** *n* BANK unbesichertes Darlehen *nt*; **~ bond issue** *n* STOCK ungesicherte Anleihe *f*; **~ creditor** *n* ACC nicht gesicherte Gläubigerin *f*, nicht gesicherter Gläubiger *m*; **~ debt** *n* FIN unbesicherte Forderung *f*, nicht bevorrechtigte Konkursforderung *f*; **~ fixed-term loan** *n* BANK Blankokredit *m* mit fester Laufzeit, unbesicherter Kredit *m* mit fester Laufzeit; **~ loan** *n* ACC nicht gesichertes Darlehen *nt*; **~ overdraft** *n* BANK Blanküberziehungskredit *m*

unserviceable *adj* (*U/S*) GEN COMM unbrauchbar

unsettle *vt* GEN COMM beunruhigen

unsettled *adj* FIN, GEN COMM *bill, debt* unbeglichen, unbezahlt

unshipment *n* TRANSP Ausladung *f*, Entladung *f*

unsigned *adj* GEN COMM nicht unterschrieben, ohne Unterschrift

unskilled *adj* HRM, WEL unausgebildet, ungelernt; **~ labor** *AmE*, **~ labour** *BrE n* ECON ungelernte Arbeitskräfte *f pl*, HRM ungelernte Arbeitskräfte *f pl*, ungelernte Hilfskräfte *f pl*; **~ worker** *n* HRM Hilfsarbeiter, in *m,f*; **~ workers** *n pl* ECON, HRM ungelernte Arbeitskräfte *f pl*, ungelernte Hilfskräfte *f pl*

unsocial: **~ hours** *n pl* HRM außerhalb der normalen Arbeitszeiten

unsold *adj* GEN COMM unverkauft; **~ goods** *n pl* S&M unverkaufte Ware *f*

unsolicited *adj* GEN COMM freiwillig, unaufgefordert; **~ application** *n* HRM unaufgeforderte Bewerbung *f*; **~ goods and services** *n pl* S&M unverlangte Güter *nt pl* und Dienstleistungen *f pl*; **~ testimonial** *n* LAW unaufgeforderte Aussage *f*

unsorted *adj* (*u/s*) GEN COMM unsortiert

unsound *adj* GEN COMM ungesund; **~ risk** *n* GEN COMM, INS ungesundes Risiko *nt*

unspent *adj* FIN nicht verbraucht; **~ budget balances** *n pl* ECON Ausgabenreste *m pl*; **~ cash balance** *n* ACC *governmental accounting* nicht verausgabter Saldo *m*, nicht verausgabtes Guthaben *nt*

unstable *adj* GEN COMM unbeständig; **~ government** *n* POL instabile Regierung *f*

unstamped: **~ debentures** *n pl* STOCK ungestempelte gesicherte Schuldverschreibungen *f pl*

unsteady *adj* GEN COMM schwankend, unbeständig, unstet

unstocked *adj* GEN COMM geräumt

unstructured *adj* GEN COMM unstrukturiert; **~ interview** *n* HRM unstrukturiertes Interview *nt*

unsubsidized *adj* GEN COMM nicht subventioniert, unsubventioniert

unsubstantiated *adj* GEN COMM aus der Luft gegriffen (*infrml*), unbegründet

unsuccessful *adj* GEN COMM erfolglos; **~ job application** *n* HRM erfolglose Bewerbung *f*

unsuitable *adj* GEN COMM unangemessen, ungeeignet, unzulässig, unzweckmäßig, zweckwidrig, HRM untauglich

unsuited *adj* GEN COMM ungeeignet

unsystematic: **~ risk** *n* FIN vermeidbares Risiko *nt*

untapped *adj* GEN COMM *resources, market* unerschlossen, ungenutzt

untargeted *adj* S&M *consumer base* ungezielt

untested *adj* GEN COMM unerprobt, ungeprüft

untied *adj* ECON *development aid* ungebunden

until *prep* GEN COMM bis; ◆ **~ further notice** GEN COMM bis auf weitere Nachricht, bis auf weiteres

untimely *adj* GEN COMM unpassend, unzeitgemäß, vorzeitig

untitled *adj* COMP *disk, file* unbenannt, LAW ohne Rechtsanspruch *m*

untrained *adj* HRM, WEL unausgebildet, ungelernt, ungeschult

untransferable *adj* STOCK nicht übertragbar

untreated *adj* IND unbearbeitet

untried *adj* GEN COMM unerprobt, ungeprüft

untrustworthy *adj* GEN COMM, HRM unseriös

unused *adj* GEN COMM brachliegend, nicht beansprucht, ungenutzt, *new* unbenutzt; **~ relief** *n* TAX nicht in Anspruch genommene Entlastung *f*

unusual *adj* GEN COMM ungewöhnlich; **~ item** *n* GEN COMM, S&M ungewöhnlicher Artikel *m*; **~ quality** *n* GEN COMM, S&M Besonderheit *f*

unusually *adv* GEN COMM ungewöhnlich

unvalued: ~ **policy** n INS Pauschalpolice f, Police f ohne Wertangabe

unveil vt GEN COMM proposals, plans enthüllen

unverified adj GEN COMM unbestätigt, unbewiesen

unvouched: ~ **for** phr GEN COMM unbestätigt, unverbürgt

unwanted adj GEN COMM unerwünscht

unwarranted adj GEN COMM ohne Gewähr, ungerechtfertigt, unverbürgt

unweighted adj GEN COMM index, figures ungewogen

unworkable adj GEN COMM nicht funktionsfähig, undurchführbar

unworked adj IND unbearbeitet

unwrap vt GEN COMM auspacken, TRANSP auspacken, auswickeln

unwritten: ~ **agreement** n GEN COMM mündliche Abmachung f, mündliche Vereinbarung f

up 1. vt GEN COMM bid, offer hinaufsetzen; **2.** prep ♦ ~ **front** GEN COMM in advance im voraus

up-and-coming adj GEN COMM aufstrebend, vielversprechend

upbeat adj GEN COMM optimistisch

upcoming: ~ **fiscal year** n TAX bevorstehendes Steuerjahr nt; ~ **year** n TAX kommendes Jahr nt

update 1. n COMP software Update nt (jarg), action Aktualisierung f, GEN COMM letzte Information f, neueste Information f; **2.** vt COMP auf den neuesten Stand bringen, updaten (jarg), GEN COMM aktualisieren, auf den neuesten Stand bringen, modernisieren

updating n ACC, COMP Fortschreibung f, GEN COMM Aktualisierung f, Modernisierung f

up-front: ~ **cost** n GEN COMM Investitionskosten pl, Anschaffungskosten pl

upgradable adj GEN COMM anhebbar, mit Aufstiegschancen, verbesserungsfähig

upgrade 1. n COMP Ausbau m, Erweiterung f; **2.** vt COMP memory verbessern, ausbauen, erweitern, GEN COMM in quality aufwerten, LEIS Angebot verbessern; ♦ ~ **a post** HRM eine Stelle höher einstufen

upgradeable adj COMP ausbaubar, erweiterungsfähig

upgraded adj COMP verbessert, erweitert, S&M product, shop angepaßt; ♦ **be** ~ HRM befördert werden

upgrading n COMP Ausbau m, Erweiterung f, GEN COMM, HRM Beförderung f, of post Höherstufung f

upheaval n GEN COMM Umbruch m, Umwälzung f

uphold vt LAW aufrechterhalten

upload vt COMP data übermitteln

up-market adj S&M clientele anspruchsvoll, product exklusiv; ~ **product** n S&M Produkt nt des gehobenen Marktes; ~ **segment** n GEN COMM gehobene Preisklasse f, oberes Marktsegment nt; ~ **service** n S&M Dienstleistungen f pl der gehobenen Preisklasse

upon: ~ **application** phr GEN COMM auf Antrag; ~ **further consideration** phr GEN COMM bei weiterer Betrachtung, bei weiterer Überlegung; ~ **the initiative** phr LAW auf Antrag; ~ **request** phr GEN COMM auf Antrag

upper: ~ **cap** n BrE TAX on basic rate of relief obere Grenze; ~ **case** n COMP, MEDIA typography Großbuchstaben m pl, Versal m; ~-**case letter** n COMP, MEDIA typography Großbuchstabe m; ~-**case letters** n pl COMP, MEDIA typography Großbuchstaben m pl, Versal m; ~ **house** n POL Oberhaus nt; ~ **limit** n GEN COMM Höchstgrenze f, GEN COMM, STOCK on value of

shares allocated to an employee Obergrenze f; ~ **quartile** n MATH statistics oberes Quartil nt

upright adj TRANSP aufrecht, senkrecht, stehend

uprising n POL Aufruhr m

UPS abbr COMP (uninterruptible power supply) unterbrechungsfreie Stromversorgung f

upscale: ~ **product** n AmE (cf high-quality product BrE) GEN COMM hochwertiges Produkt nt

upset: ~ **price** n GEN COMM auction sale Mindestpreis m

upside: ~ **break even** n STOCK options höchster Break-Even-Punkt m; ~ **break even point** n STOCK oberer Break-Even-Punkt m; ~ **potential** n FIN Kursspielraum m nach oben; ~ **profit potential** n STOCK options Gewinnpotential nt nach oben; ~ **risk** n STOCK options Risiko nt nach oben; ~ **trend** n ECON Aufwärtsbewegung f, Aufwärtstrend m, Aufwärtsentwicklung f

upskilling n HRM Verbesserung f der Fertigkeiten, Verbesserung f der Kenntnisse

upstream 1. adj ECON, GEN COMM vorgeordnet, vorgelagert; **2.** adv GEN COMM vorgelagert

upstream: ~ **loan** n FIN Darlehen nt der Tochtergesellschaft an die Muttergesellschaft

upsurge n GEN COMM in activity Hinaufschnellen nt; ~ **in equities** n FIN, STOCK Aktienhausse f

upswing n ECON Aufschwung m

uptick n STOCK Aktie f mit leicht steigender Tendenz, höherer Aktienkurs m als vorher notiert

up-to-date adj GEN COMM aktuell, auf dem laufenden, modern, zeitgemäß; ♦ **be** ~ **on** GEN COMM auf dem laufenden sein mit

up-to-date: ~ **information** n GEN COMM aktuelle Information f

up-to-the-minute adj GEN COMM information aktuell

up-to-sample adj GEN COMM mustergemäß, mustergetreu

uptrend n ECON Aufwärtsbewegung f, Aufwärtsentwicklung f, Aufwärtstrend m

upturn n ECON Aufschwung f, Belebung f, Besserung f, GEN COMM Aufschwung m, Aufwärtsbewegung f

upvaluation n GEN COMM Aufwertung f, Höherbewertung f

upward 1. adj COMP aufwärts; **2.** adv GEN COMM move aufwärts

upward: ~ **compatibility** n COMP Aufwärtskompatibilität f

upwardly: ~ **mobile** phr GEN COMM aufstrebend, HRM sozial aufsteigend

upward: ~ **movement** n GEN COMM Aufwärtsbewegung f; ~ **pressure** n ECON on budget Aufwertungsdruck m; ~ **revaluation** n GEN COMM Aufwertung f; ~ **revision** n GEN COMM prices Anpassung f nach oben, Pluskorrektur f

upwards adv GEN COMM move aufwärts

upward: ~ **spiral** n GEN COMM in wages, prices Aufwärtsspirale f

urban: ~ **area** n ADMIN Stadtgebiet nt, GEN COMM geschlossene Ortschaft f, POL Stadtgebiet nt; ~ **development** n ADMIN, POL, PROP Städtebau m, städtebauliche Planung f, Stadtplanung f

Urban: ~ **Development Corporation** n BrE ECON Gesellschaft f für Stadtentwicklung

urban: ~ **economics** *n* ECON Stadtökonomie *f*, Urbanistik *f*

urbanization *n* ECON Urbanisierung *f*, Verstädterung *f*, GEN COMM Urbanisierung *f*

urbanize *vt* ECON urbanisieren, verstädtern, GEN COMM urbanisieren

urbanized *adj* ECON, GEN COMM urbanisiert

urban: ~ **planner** *n* ADMIN, GEN COMM, POL, PROP Stadtplaner, in *m,f*

Urban: ~ **Programme Area** *n* ADMIN Stadtentwicklungsgebiet *nt*, GEN COMM Stadtsanierungsgebiet *nt*, POL Stadtentwicklungsgebiet *nt*

urban: ~ **renewal** *n* ADMIN Stadterneuerung *f*, ECON, GEN COMM Stadtsanierung *f*, POL Stadterneuerung *f*

urge: ~ **sb to do sth** *phr* GEN COMM jdn dringend bitten, etw zu tun, jdn ersuchen, etw zu tun

urgent *adj* GEN COMM akut, dringend; ♦ **be in ~ need of** GEN COMM dringend brauchen, dringend nötig haben

urgently *adv* GEN COMM dringend

urgent: ~ **order** *n* GEN COMM Eilauftrag *m*, Eilbestellung *f*

URN *abbr* (*unique reference number*) ADMIN besondere Kennziffer *f*

Uruguay: ~ **Round** *n* ECON *1993* Uruguay-Runde *f*

u/s *abbr* (*unsorted*) GEN COMM unsortiert

U/S *abbr* (*unserviceable*) GEN COMM unbrauchbar

usable *adj* GEN COMM verwendbar

usance *n* BANK, TRANSP Usance *f*; ♦ **at thirty days' ~** FIN zu einer Laufzeit von dreißig Tagen, zu einer Wechselfrist von dreißig Tagen

usance: ~ **bill** *n* BANK Usancewechsel *m*, Usowechsel *m*, FIN Wechselfrist *f*; ~ **credit** *n* BANK Usancekredit *m*

USDAW *abbr* BrE (*Union of Shop, Distributive & Allied Workers*) HRM Gewerkschaft der in Vertrieb, Handel und verwandten Gebieten beschäftigten Arbeiter

use 1. *n* GEN COMM Benutzung *f*, PATENTS Gebrauch *m*, Nutzung *f*; ♦ **have the ~ of sth** GEN COMM den Nutzen von etw haben; **2.** *vt* ENVIR *natural resources* verbrauchen, GEN COMM benutzen, verwenden; ♦ **a window of opportunity** GEN COMM eine Gelegenheit nutzen; ~ **strong-arm tactics** GEN COMM gewaltsam eingreifen; ~ **to capacity** GEN COMM auslasten

use up *vt* GEN COMM aufbrauchen

useable *adj* GEN COMM verwendbar; ~ **floor space** *n* PROP Nutzfläche *f*

use: ~-**by date** *n* GEN COMM, S&M Haltbarkeitsdatum *nt*

USEC *abbr* (*United States East Coast*) GEN COMM Ostküste *f* der Vereinigten Staaten

used: ~ **assets** *n pl* TAX gebrauchte Vermögenswerte *m pl*; ~ **car** *n* TRANSP Gebrauchtwagen *m*

useful *adj* GEN COMM nützlich, zweckmäßig; ♦ **be ~ to sb** GEN COMM jdm nützlich sein, jdm von Nutzen sein

useful: ~ **economic life** *n* ACC, ECON wirtschaftliche Nutzungsdauer *f*; ~ **life** *n* ACC *of asset*, ECON, GEN COMM *of machine* Nutzungsdauer *f*

usefulness *n* PATENTS Brauchbarkeit *f*

use: ~ **of funds** *n* ACC Verwendung *f* von Geldern, Verwendung *f* von Mitteln; ~ **of the quota system** *n* GEN COMM Anwendung *f* der Quotenregelung

user *n* COMP Auftraggeber, in *m,f*, Benutzer, in *m,f*, User *m*, GEN COMM Benutzer, in *m,f*, Nutzer, in *m,f*, Anwender, in *m,f*; ~ **attitude** *n* S&M Benutzerverhalten

nt; ~ **charge** *n* ACC Benutzungsgebühr *f*; ~ **class** *n* COMP Benutzerklasse *f*; ~ **cost** *n* FIN, GEN COMM Benutzungskosten *pl*; ~-**friendliness** *n* COMP, S&M Benutzerfreundlichkeit *f*; ~-**friendly** *adj* COMP, S&M anwenderfreundlich, benutzerfreundlich; ~ **group** *n* COMP Anwendergruppe *f*, Benutzergruppe *f*; ~ **interface** *n* COMP Benutzerschnittstelle *f*; ~ **manual** *n* COMP Benutzerhandbuch *nt*; ~-**oriented** *adj* COMP anwenderorientiert, benutzerorientiert, S&M benutzerorientiert; ~ **profile** *n* S&M *marketing* Benutzerprofil *nt*; ~ **strategy** *n* GEN COMM Nutzerstrategie *f*, S&M Benutzerstrategie *f*; ~-**unfriendly** *adj* COMP, S&M anwenderfeindlich, anwenderunfreundlich, benutzerfeindlich, benutzerunfreundlich

use: ~ **value** *n* ECON Gebrauchswert *m*

US: ~ **federal finance** *n* FIN US-bundesstaatliches Finanzwesen; ~ **federal government paper** *n* STOCK US-Bundesstaatspapier

USM *abbr* BANK (*United States Mint*) Münze *f* der Vereinigten Staaten, STOCK (*Unlisted Securities Market*) Freiverkehrsbörse *f*, geregelter Freiverkehr *m*, geregelter Markt *m*

USMC *abbr* (*United States Maritime Commission*) TRANSP Schiffahrtskommission der Vereinigten Staaten

USP *abbr* (*unique selling proposition*) S&M einmaliges Verkaufsargument *nt*

US: ~-**style variable tender** *n* FIN amerikanischer Zinstender *m*; ~ **Trade Representative** *n* HRM Handelsvertretung *f* der Vereinigten Staaten; ~ **Treasury bond** *n* STOCK US-Schatzanleihe *f*; ~ **Treasury bond market** *n* STOCK US-Schatzanleihe-Markt *m*; ~ **Treasury market** *n* FIN Markt *m* in US-Schatzpapieren

usual *adj* GEN COMM üblich; ♦ **with the ~ proviso** LAW unter dem üblichen Vorbehalt; **on ~ terms** GEN COMM zu den üblichen Bedingungen

usufruct *n* LAW *right to utilize* Nießbrauch *m*

usufructuary *n* LAW *person entitled to utilization* Nießbraucher, in *m,f*

usurer *n* FIN Wucherer *m*

usurious *adj* BANK, FIN wucherisch; ~ **interest** *n* BANK, FIN Wucherzinsen *m pl*; ~ **moneylending** *n* BANK, FIN Wucher *m*

usury *n* BANK, FIN Wucher *m*

USWC *abbr* (*United States West Coast*) GEN COMM Westküste *f* der Vereinigten Staaten

UT *abbr* (*universal time*) GEN COMM abgestimmte Weltzeit *f*

UTC *abbr* (*universal time coordinated*) GEN COMM abgestimmte Weltzeit *f*

util *n* ECON Nutzeneinheit *f*

utilitarianism *n* ECON Nützlichkeitslehre *f*, Utilitarismus *m*

utilities *n pl* STOCK Energiewerte *m pl*; ~ **sector** *n* IND Versorgungsbereich *m*

utility *n* COMP Dienstprogramm *nt*, ECON Nützlichkeit *f*, Nutzen *m*, IND Versorgungsbetrieb *m*

utility: ~ **certificate** *n* PATENTS Gebrauchsbescheinigung *f*, Gebrauchszertifikat *nt*; ~ **function** *n* ECON Nutzenfunktion *f*; ~ **maximization** *n* ECON Nutzenmaximierung *f*; ~ **model** *n* PATENTS Gebrauchsmodell *nt*; ~ **possibility frontier** *n* ECON Nutzenmöglichkeitskurve *f*; ~ **program** *n* COMP

Dienstprogramm *nt*, Hilfsprogramm *nt*; ~ **revenue bond** *n* FIN Versorgungswert *m*

utilization *n* ENVIR *of natural resources* Nutzung *f*, GEN COMM *of natural resources* Nutzung *f*, Verwendung *f*, Einsatz *m*, PATENTS Verwendung *f*; ~ **percent** *n* GEN COMM Ausnutzungsgrad *m*

utilize *vt* ENVIR einsetzen, nutzen, verwerten, GEN COMM ausnutzen, einsetzen, nutzen, verwenden, verwerten, *opportunity* wahrnehmen, IND verwerten, nutzen, einsetzen, PATENTS verwerten

utilized *adj* FIN, GEN COMM, IND, PATENTS verwertet; ~ **capacity** *n* IND benutzte Kapazität *f*, verwertete Kapazität *f*

utmost: ~ **good faith** *n* INS höchste Gutgläubigkeit *f*, höchste Redlichkeit, unbedingte Beachtung *f* von Treu und Glauben, LAW höchste Gutgläubigkeit *f*

UVI *abbr* (*unit value index*) ECON Einheitswertindex *m*

U/W *abbr* (*underwriter*) INS Versicherer *m*, Versicherungsgeber, in *m,f*

V

v *abbr* (*versus*) GEN COMM geg. (*gegen*), vs. (*versus*)

VA *abbr* (*value analysis*) FIN, S&M Wertanalyse *f*

vacancy *n* HRM freie Stelle *f*

vacant *adj* PROP unbewohnt; ~ **land** *n* PROP unbebautes Land *nt*; ~ **lot** *n* AmE (*cf undeveloped land BrE*) PROP unbebautes Grundstück *nt*; ~ **possession** *n* LAW aufgegebener Besitz *m*

vacate *vt* PROP verlassen

vacation *n* AmE (*cf holiday BrE*) GEN COMM, HRM, LEIS Ferien *pl*, Urlaub *m*; ◆ **on** ~ AmE (*cf on holiday BrE*) LEIS im Urlaub, auf Urlaub; **go on** ~ (*cf go on holiday BrE*) GEN COMM, HRM, LEIS Ferien machen, in die Ferien gehen, in Urlaub gehen

vacation: ~ **allowance** *n* AmE (*cf holiday allowance BrE*) HRM Urlaubsgeld *nt*; ~ **bonus** *n* AmE (*cf holiday bonus BrE*) HRM Urlaubsgeld *nt*

vacationer *n* AmE (*cf holiday-maker BrE*) LEIS Urlauber, in *m,f*

vacation: ~ **guest** *n* AmE (*cf holiday guest BrE*) LEIS Feriengast *m*

vacationist *n* AmE (*cf holiday-maker BrE*) LEIS Urlauber, in *m,f*

vacation: ~ **pay** *n* AmE (*cf holiday pay BrE*) HRM Urlaubsgeld *nt*; ~ **period** *n* AmE (*cf holiday period BrE*) LEIS Urlaubszeit *f*

vaccination *n* WEL Impfung *f*, Schutzimpfung *f*

vacuum *n* IND Vakuum *nt*; ~ **packaging** *n* IND Vakuumverpackung *f*

Valdez: ~ **principles** *n pl* ENVIR Valdez-Prinzipien *nt pl*

valid *adj* ADMIN *passport* gültig, GEN COMM *argument, excuse* stichhaltig

validate *vt* COMP validieren, GEN COMM *document, claim* bestätigen, für gültig erklären

validation *n* COMP Gültigkeitsprüfung *f*, GEN COMM *document, claim* Bestätigung *f*

valid: ~ **claim** *n* LAW berechtigter Anspruch *m*; ~ **invoice** *n* GEN COMM gültige Rechnung *f*

validity *n* GEN COMM Geltung *f*, *of claim* Berechtigung *f*, PATENTS Gültigkeit *f*, Gültigkeitsdauer *f*, Rechtswirksamkeit *f*; ~ **period** *n* GEN COMM Gültigkeitsdauer *f*

valid: ~ **passport** *n* ADMIN gültiger Reisepaß *m*; ~ **reason** *n* GEN COMM triftiger Grund *m*

valise *n* GEN COMM kleiner Handkoffer *m*, Reisetasche *f*

valorization *n* ECON Valorisation *f*, Preisregelung *f*, Valorisierung *f*, FIN Valorisation *f*, Valorisierung *f*, GEN COMM Aufwertung *f*, S&M Preisregelung *f*

valorize *vt* ECON valorisieren, GEN COMM aufwerten, valorisieren

valuable *adj* GEN COMM wertvoll, kostbar, nützlich, wert; ~ **consideration** *n* GEN COMM geldwerte Gegenleistung *f*; ~ **papers insurance** *n* INS Versicherung *f* wichtiger Urkunden

valuables *n pl* GEN COMM Valoren *f pl*, Wertgegenstände *m pl*, Wertsachen *f pl*

valuation *n* GEN COMM Bewertung *f*, Begutachtung *f*, Taxe *f*, PROP *of property* Schätzung *f*; ~ **account** *n* ACC Wertberichtigungskonto *nt*; ~ **adjustment** *n* ACC Wertanpassung *f*, *correction* Wertberichtigung *f*; ~ **allowance** *n* ACC *bonds* Wertberichtigung *f*; ~ **basis** *n* GEN COMM Bewertungsgrundlagen *f pl*; ~ **charge** *n* TRANSP Wertzuschlag *m*; ~ **clause** *n* (*VC*) INS *marine* Bewertungsklausel *f*; ~ **criteria** *n pl* ACC Bewertungskriterien *nt pl*, Bewertungsgrundlagen *f pl*; ~ **data** *n pl* GEN COMM Bewertungsunterlagen *f pl*; ~ **of inventory** *n* ACC Wertbestimmung *f* des Lagerbestands; ~ **principles** *n pl* ACC Bewertungsgrundlagen *f pl*; ~ **report** *n* GEN COMM Gutachten *nt*; ~ **restrictions** *n pl* ECON *of currency* Bewertungsbeschränkungen *f pl*; ~ **of stocks** *n* ACC Wertbestimmung *f* des Lagerbestands

value 1. *n* BANK Valuta *f*, GEN COMM Wert *m*, *usefulness* Nutzen *m*; ◆ **no** ~ **declared** (*NVD*) IMP/EXP ohne Wertangabe; **get good** ~ **for money** ECON etw für sein Geld bekommen; ~ **as in original policy** (*VOP*) INS Wert wie in Ursprungspolice; **2.** *vt* GEN COMM schätzen, *estimate value* bewerten, taxieren, bestimmen; ◆ ~ **sth for probate** LAW etw zur Testamentsvollstreckung bewerten

value: ~ **added** *n* ECON Wertschöpfung *f*; ~**-added** *adj* COMP, ECON *corporate economics*, FIN, TAX Mehrwert-; ~**-added network** *n* (*VAN*) COMP Netz mit erweiterten Übertragungsmöglichkeiten, Mehrwertnetz *nt*; ~**-added services** *n pl* ECON Mehrwertdienste *m pl*; ~**-added reseller** *n* (*VAR*) COMP Mehrwertdienstleister *m*, Wiederverkäufer *m* mit Mehrwertleistungen; ~**-added statements** *n pl* ACC Mehrwertaufstellung *f*, Mehrwertbericht *m*, Mehrwerterklärung *f*, Wertschöpfungsrechnung *f*; ~**-added tax** *n BrE* (*VAT*) GEN COMM, TAX Mehrwertsteuer *f* (*MwSt.*); ~**-added tax paid** *n* TAX abgeführte Mehrwertsteuer *f*; ~ **analysis** *n* (*VA*) FIN, S&M *marketing* Wertanalyse *f*; ~ **as marine policy** *n* (*VMP*) INS Wert *m* als Seepolice; ~ **at cost** *n* ACC Herstellungswert *m*; ~ **of a balance sheet item** *n* ACC Bilanzwert *m*; ~ **chain** *n* FIN Wertkette *f*; ~ **concept** *n* FIN Wertkonzept *nt*; ~ **of the contract** *n* STOCK *futures* Vertragswert *m*

valued: **be** ~ **at** *phr* STOCK bewertet sein mit

value: ~ **date** *n* BANK Valuta *f*; ~**-discrepancy hypothesis** *n* ECON Hypothese *f* der Wertdiskrepanz

valued: ~ **policy** *n* INS Police *f* mit vereinbarter Wertangabe, taxierte Police *f*, Versicherung *f* nach Taxe

value: ~ **engineering** *n* ACC Wertanalyse *f*, FIN Konzeptwertanalyse *f*, Wertanalyse *f* im Entstehungsstadium; ~ **of an enterprise as a whole** *n* HRM Arbitriumwert *m*; ~ **for collection** *n* ACC Inkassowert *m*; ~ **for money** *n* GEN COMM Geldwert *m*, Preis-Leistungsverhältnis *nt*; ~ **in exchange** *n* ECON Tauschwert *m*; ~ **in use** *n* ECON Gebrauchswert *m*; ~ **judgment** *n* GEN COMM Werturteil *nt*

valueless *adj* GEN COMM nutzlos, wertlos

Value: ~ **Line Composite Index** *n* AmE STOCK Gesamtwertindex *m*

value: ~ **line investment survey** *n* FIN Investitionsuntersuchung *f* zur Wertlinie; ~ **of money** *n* ECON Geldwert *m*, Kaufkraft *f* des Geldes; ~ **of one point** *n* STOCK Wert *m* eines Punktes; ~ **proposal** *n* ACC, FIN Wertvorschlag *m*

valuer *n* GEN COMM, PROP Schätzer *m*

value: ~ **share** *n* STOCK Aktienverkehrswert *m*; ~ **subtractor** *n* ECON wertminderndes Unternehmen *nt*; ~ **surcharge** *n* TRANSP Wertzuschlag *m*; ~ **to weight ratio** *n* TRANSP *of conveyed goods* Verhältnis *nt* Wert zu Gewicht

VAN *abbr* (*value-added network*) COMP Netz mit erweiterten Übertragungsmöglichkeiten, Mehrwertnetz *nt*

vandalism: ~ **and malicious mischief insurance** *n* INS Versicherung *f* gegen Vandalismus und böswilligen Schaden, Versicherung *f* gegen Vandalismus und vorsätzliche Beschädigung

vanguard: **in the** ~ **of progress** *phr* GEN COMM an der Spitze des Fortschritts

VAR *abbr* COMP (*value-added reseller*) Mehrwertdienstleister *m*, Wiederverkäufer *m* mit Mehrwertleistungen, MATH (*vector autoregression*) *statistics* Vektorautoregression *f*

variability *n* ECON, GEN COMM, MATH Schwankung *f*, Variabilität *f*

variable 1. *adj* GEN COMM variabel; **2.** *n* COMP, GEN COMM, MATH Variable *f*

variable: ~ **budget** *n* ECON flexibles Budget *nt*; ~ **capital** *n* FIN variables Kapital *nt*; ~ **charge** *n* (*VC*) GEN COMM variable Gebühr *f*; ~ **costs** *n pl* ACC, ECON, FIN variable Ausgaben *f pl*, variable Kosten *pl*, TRANSP variable Ausgaben *f pl*; ~ **expenses** *n pl* ACC, ECON, FIN variable Ausgaben *f pl*, variable Kosten *pl*, TRANSP variable Ausgaben *f pl*; ~ **gross margin** *n* ACC Deckungsbeitrag *m*; ~ **lending rate** *n* (*VLR*) FIN schwankender Zinssatz *m* für Ausleihungen, variabler Zinssatz *m* für Ausleihungen; ~ **overhead cost** *n* FIN variable Gemeinkosten *pl*; ~**-rate** *adj* FIN variabel verzinslich; ~ **rate** *n* BANK, ECON variabler Zins *m*, FIN variabler Kurs *m*, variabler Zins *m*; ~**-rate demand note** *n* BANK variabel verzinslicher Schuldschein *m*; ~**-rate mortgage** *n* BANK, PROP variabel verzinsliche Hypothek *f*; ~ **rates of interest** *n pl* BANK, ECON, FIN variable Zinsen *m pl*; ~**-size font** *n* COMP *typography*, MEDIA Schriftart *f* mit variabler Schriftgröße

variables: ~ **sampling** *n* MATH *statistics* Variablenauswahl *f*

variance *n* ACC *disagreement* Abweichung *f*, Uneinigkeit *f*, FIN *discrepancy* Abweichung *f*, Unvereinbarkeit *f*, GEN COMM Abweichung *f*, Veränderung *f*, LAW *discordance* Unvereinbarkeit *f*, MATH *statistics* Varianz *f*; ◆ **be at** ~ **with sb about sth** GEN COMM mit jdm über etw streiten, mit jdm über etw uneins sein, zu jdm wegen etw im Widerspruch stehen

variance: ~ **analysis** *n* ACC Uneinigkeitsanalyse *f*

variation *n* ECON *revenue, expenditure* Schwankung *f*, GEN COMM Abweichung *f*, Variation *f*, Veränderung *f*; ~ **margin** *n* STOCK *term* Nachschußzahlung *f*, variabler Einschuß *m*

variety: ~ **reduction** *n* ECON, GEN COMM Sortimentsbeschränkung *f*, Sortimentseinschränkung *f*, Sortimentsverkleinerung *f*

variometer *n* IND Feinhöhenmesser *m*, Variometer *nt*

vary 1. *vt* GEN COMM ändern, variieren; ◆ ~ **the terms of a contract** LAW die vertraglichen Bestimmungen ändern; **2.** *vi* GEN COMM variieren, wechseln, *change* sich ändern

varying *adj* GEN COMM unterschiedlich; ◆ **with** ~ **degrees** GEN COMM in unterschiedlichem Maße

VAT *abbr BrE* (*value-added tax*) GEN COMM, TAX MwSt. (*Mehrwertsteuer*); ~ **paid** *n BrE* TAX abgeführte Mehrwertsteuer *f*; ~ **payment** *n BrE* TAX MwSt.-Zahlung *f*; ~**-registered trader** *n BrE* TAX MwSt.-eingetragener Wertpapierhändler *m*, MwSt.-eingetragene Wertpapierhändlerin *f*; ~ **registration number** *n BrE* TAX MwSt.-Kennummer *f*; ~ **return** *n BrE* TAX MwSt.-Erklärung *f*

vault: ~ **cash** *n* BANK Barreserve *f*, Bargeld *nt* einer Bank für den täglichen Bedarf, im Tresor liegende Gelder *nt pl*; ~ **reserve** *n AmE* BANK Barreserve *f*, Bargeld *nt* einer Bank für den täglichen Bedarf, im Tresor liegende Gelder *nt pl*

VC *abbr* GEN COMM (*variable charge*) variable Gebühr *f*, IMP/EXP (*ventilated container*) *agricultural goods* belüfteter Container *m*, INS (*valuation clause*) *marine* Bewertungsklausel *f*, TRANSP (*ventilated container*) *agricultural goods* belüfteter Container *m*

VCR *abbr* (*video cassette recorder*) COMMS, COMP, MEDIA, S&M Videorekorder *m*

VDT *abbr AmE* (*visual display terminal, cf VDU BrE*) COMP Bildschirmgerät *nt*, DSG (*Datensichtgerät*)

VDU *abbr BrE* (*visual display unit, cf VDT AmE*) COMP Bildschirmgerät *nt*, DSG (*Datensichtgerät*)

Veblen: ~ **good** *n* ECON Veblen-Gut *nt*

vector *n* MATH Vektor *m*; ~ **autoregression** *n* (*VAR*) MATH *statistics* Vektorautoregression *f*

veep *n AmE infrml* HRM, MGMNT, POL VP (*Vizepräsident*)

veer *vi* FIN *from financial plan*, GEN COMM sich plötzlich ändern, umschwenken

vegetative: ~ **control** *n* ECON vegetative Steuerung *f*

vehicle *n* GEN COMM Fahrzeug *nt*, Kraftfahrzeug *nt* (*Kfz*), TRANSP Fahrzeug *nt*; ~ **leasing** *n* TRANSP Fahrzeug-Leasing *nt*; ~ **transshipment** *n* IMP/EXP, TRANSP Fahrzeugumladung *f*; ~ **turnaround time** *AmE*, ~ **turnround time** *BrE n* TRANSP Fahrzeugumlaufzeit *f*, Fahrzeugwendezeit *f*; ~ **unladen weight** *n* TRANSP Fahrzeug-Eigengewicht *nt*

vehicular: ~ **ferry** *n* TRANSP Fahrzeugfähre *f*

velocity *n* GEN COMM Geschwindigkeit *f*, Tempo *nt*; ~ **of circulation** *n* FIN Umschlagsgeschwindigkeit *f*, Umlaufgeschwindigkeit *f*; ~ **of circulation of money** *n* ECON Geldumlaufgeschwindigkeit *f*, Umlaufgeschwindigkeit *f* des Geldes

vendee *n AmE* GEN COMM Erwerber, in *m,f*

vendible *adj* GEN COMM gängig, verkäuflich

vending *n* GEN COMM, S&M Verkauf *m*; ~ **machine** *n* GEN COMM Automat *m*, S&M Verkaufsautomat *m*

vendor *n* COMP Händler, in *m,f*, GEN COMM, HRM, LAW Verkäufer, in *m,f*, PROP Veräußerer *m*, S&M Verkäufer, in *m,f*; ~ **company** *n* GEN COMM einbringende Gesellschaft *f*, veräußernde Gesellschaft *f*; ~ **finance** *n* FIN Verkäuferfinanzierung *f*

vent: ~ **for surplus** *n* ECON Überschußtheorie *f*

ventilate *vt* IND *factory, workplace* ventilieren

ventilation: ~ **industry** *n* IND lufttechnische Industrie *f*

venture 1. *n* ECON Risiko *nt*, Unternehmung *f*, Wagnis *nt*, INS *shipping* risikoreiches Unternehmen *nt*; **2.** *vt* GEN COMM wagen, riskieren

venture on *vt* GEN COMM *project* sich einlassen auf [+acc], sich wagen an [+acc]

venture: ~ **capital** *n* BANK, ECON, FIN, GEN COMM Risikokapital *nt*, Spekulationskapital *nt*, Wagniskapital *nt*, Beteiligungskapital *nt*; ~ **capital**

company *n* BANK, ECON, FIN, GEN COMM
Wagniskapitalgesellschaft *f*; **~ capitalism** *n* BANK,
ECON, FIN, GEN COMM Wagniskapitalismus *m*;
~ capitalist *n* BANK, ECON, FIN, GEN COMM
Risikokapitalgeber *m*, Risikounternehmer *m*,
Spekulant, in *m,f*; **~ capital limited partnership** *n*
BANK, ECON, FIN, GEN COMM
Wagniskapitalkommanditgesellschaft *f*; **~ manage-
ment** *n* MGMNT Unternehmensleitung *f*; **~ team** *n* S&M
Unternehmensgruppe *f*

venue *n* GEN COMM *for meeting, conference* Treffpunkt *m*

VER *abbr* (*voluntary export restraint*) IMP/EXP freiwillige
Ausfuhrbeschränkung *f*, freiwillige Exportbeschränkung *f*

verbal *adj* GEN COMM *offer, promise* mündlich;
~ agreement *n* GEN COMM mündliche Absprache *f*,
mündliche Vereinbarung *f*; **~ communication** *n* GEN
COMM, HRM, MGMNT mündliche Mitteilung *f*; **~ offer** *n*
GEN COMM mündliches Angebot *nt*; **~ warning** *n* HRM,
MGMNT *disciplinary procedure* mündliche Warnung *f*

verbatim: **~ account** *n* GEN COMM wortgetreuer Bericht
m

verdict *n* LAW *jury trial* Strafurteil *nt*

Verdoorn: **~'s law** *n* LAW Verdoorn-Gesetz *nt*

verge: **on the ~ of bankruptcy** *phr* GEN COMM am Rande
des Bankrotts (*infrml*), am Rande des Konkurses

verifiable *adj* ACC, GEN COMM nachprüfbar, nachweisbar

verification *n* ACC, GEN COMM Beurkundung *f*, Bestätigung *f*, Prüfung *f*, Verifizierung *f*, LAW Beglaubigung *f*;
~ of accounts *n* ACC Bestätigung *f* der Richtigkeit der
Buchführung; **~ phase** *n* GEN COMM Prüfungsphase *f*

verified: **if ~** *phr* GEN COMM nach Richtigbefund

verify *vt* ACC, GEN COMM auf Richtigkeit prüfen,
beglaubigen, bestätigen, beurkunden, verifizieren

versatility *n* COMP *hardware, system*, GEN COMM, S&M *of
product* Vielseitigkeit *f*

versed: **~ in the law** *phr* GEN COMM, LAW rechtskundig

version *n* COMP Version *f*, GEN COMM Fassung *f*, Variante
f, Version *f*

verso *n* (*vo.*) MEDIA *back of page* Rückseite *f*

versus *prep* (*v, vs*) GEN COMM gegen (*geg.*), versus (*vs.*)

vertical *adj* GEN COMM vertikal; **~ access** *n* TRANSP
shipping Vertikalzugriff *m*; **~ amalgamation** *n* ECON,
GEN COMM vertikale Fusion *f*, vertikaler Zusammenschluß *m*; **~ analysis** *n* ACC vertikale Analyse *f*;
~ balance sheet *n* ACC vertikale Bilanz *f*; **~ business
combination** *n* ECON, GEN COMM vertikaler Unternehmenszusammenschluß *m*; **~ combination** *n* ECON
Vertikalkonzern *m*; **~ communication** *n* GEN COMM
vertikale Kommunikation *f*; **~ discrimination** *n* ECON
vertikale Diskriminierung *f*; **~ expansion** *n* GEN COMM
vertikale Expansion *f*; **~ formation** *n* GEN COMM
vertikale Gründung *f*; **~ integration** *n* ECON, GEN
COMM vertikale Integration *f*

verticalized: **~ cargo space** *n* TRANSP *shipping* vertika-
lisierter Frachtraum *m*

vertical: **~ line charting** *n* STOCK Chart erstellt durch
Verbinden der senkrechten Linienpunkte; **~ merger** *n*
ECON, GEN COMM vertikale Fusion *f*; **~ mobility** *n*
HRM vertikale Mobilität *f*; **~ organization** *n* GEN COMM,
MGMNT vertikaler Aufbau *m*; **~ planning** *n* GEN COMM,
MGMNT vertikale Planung *f*; **~ profit and loss account
format** *n* ACC Gewinn- und Verlustrechnung *f* in
Staffelform; **~ promotion** *n* HRM Beförderung *f*;

~ specialization *n* GEN COMM vertikale Spezialisierung
f

very: **~ high frequency** *n* (*VHF*) COMMS, MEDIA Ultrakurzwelle *f* (*UKW*)

vessel *n* GEN COMM *container, receptacle* Gefäß *nt*,
TRANSP Schiff *nt*; **~ broker** *n* IMP/EXP, TRANSP
Schiffsmakler, in *m,f*; **~ crossing** *n* TRANSP Schiffs-
überfahrt *f*; **~ traffic management system** *n* TRANSP
Schiffverkehrsmanagement *nt*; **~ traffic services** *n pl*
TRANSP Schiffverkehrsangebot *nt*

vest *vt* GEN COMM übergeben, LAW verleihen; ♦ **~ sb with
authority** LAW jdm eine Vollmacht erteilen; **~ sth in sb**
GEN COMM, LAW etw auf jdn übertragen; **~ with** GEN
COMM, POL ausstatten mit

vested: **have a ~ interest in sth** *phr* GEN COMM ein
begründetes Anrecht auf etw besitzen, ein persönliches
Interesse an etw haben; **~ benefits** *n pl* INS verbriefte
Leistungen *f pl*, verbriefte Versicherungsleistungen *f pl*;
~ interest *n* GEN COMM gesichertes Recht *nt*; **~ rights** *n
pl* GEN COMM Besitzstand *m*

vestibule: **~ period** *n* GEN COMM Einarbeitungszeit *f*

vet *vt* GEN COMM auf Herz und Nieren prüfen, genauestens überprüfen, POL *for security clearance* überprüfen

Veterans: **~ Administration mortgage** *n* AmE BANK
Hypothek der Versorgungsverwaltung für ehemalige Kriegs-
teilnehmer

veterinary: **~ certificate** *n* IMP/EXP Veterinärzeugnis *nt*;
~ control *n* IMP/EXP Veterinäraufsicht *f*,
Veterinärkontrolle *f*

veto *n* GEN COMM, POL Veto *nt*

vetting *n* GEN COMM, POL Sicherheitsüberprüfung *f*

vexed *adj* GEN COMM *question* schwierig, ärgerlich, *person*
verärgert

VGA *abbr* COMP (*video graphics adapter*) VGA (*Videografikadapter*), (*video graphics array*) Video-
Grafikanordnung *f*; **~ card** *n* COMP VGA-Karte *f*

VHF *abbr* (*very high frequency*) COMMS, MEDIA UKW
(*Ultrakurzwelle*); **~ radiotelephony** *n* COMMS, TRANSP
UKW-Sprechfunk *m*

via *prep* COMMS per, via

viability *n* FIN finanzielle Leistungsfähigkeit *f*, Rentabilität *f*, GEN COMM Erfolgsaussicht *f*, Lebensfähigkeit *f*,
Realisierbarkeit *f*, *of project* Durchführbarkeit *f*, MATH
statistics Realisierbarkeit *f*; **~ study** *n* GEN COMM
Rentabilitätsstudie *f*

viable *adj* FIN, GEN COMM entwicklungsfähig, lebensfähig,
realisierbar, rentabel, MATH realisierbar

VIC *abbr* (*very important cargo*) TRANSP sehr wichtige
Fracht *f*

vicarious: **give ~ authority to sb** *phr* LAW jdm stellvertretende Vollmacht erteilen; **~ liability** *n* LAW Haftung *f*
für Dritte

vice: **~-chairman** *n* HRM, MGMNT stellvertretende(r)
Vorsitzende(r) *mf* [decl. as adj], stellvertretender
Tagungsleiter *m*, stellvertretende Tagungsleiterin *f*,
stellvertretender Versammlungsleiter *m*, stellvertretende
Versammlungsleiterin *f*; **~ president** *n* (*VP, veep* AmE)
HRM, MGMNT stellvertretende(r) Vorsitzende(r) *mf* [decl.
as adj], Stellvertreter, in *m,f* des Vorstandsvorsitzenden, stellvertretende(r) Vorstandsvorsitzende(r) *mf*
[decl. as adj], stellvertretender Generaldirektor *m*,
stellvertretende Generaldirektorin *f*, Vizepräsident, in
m,f (*VP*), POL Vizepräsident, in *m,f* (*VP*); **~ president
engineering** *n* AmE HRM, MGMNT technischer Direktor

m, technische Direktorin *f*; ~ **president finance** *n AmE* HRM Finanzvorstand *m*

vicious: ~ **circle** *n* ECON Teufelskreis *m*; ~ **cycle** *n* ECON Teufelskreis *m*

victimization *n* HRM unfaire Maßregelung *f*, ungerechte Behandlung *f*

video *n* COMMS, MEDIA Video *nt*; ~ **camera** *n* COMMS, MEDIA Videokamera *f*; ~ **card** *n* COMP Videokarte *f*; ~ **cassette** *n* COMMS, MEDIA Videokassette *f*; ~ **cassette recorder** *n* (*VCR*) COMMS, MEDIA Videorekorder *m*; ~ **cassette recording** *n* COMMS, MEDIA Videoaufnahme *f*; ~ **conference** *n* COMMS, COMP, S&M Videokonferenz *f*; ~ **conferencing** *n* COMMS, COMP, S&M Videokonferenz *f*; ~ **disk** *n* COMP optische Platte *f*, Videoplatte *f*; ~ **display** *n* COMMS, COMP, MEDIA, S&M Bildschirmgerät *nt*, Videobildschirm *m*; ~ **graphics adapter** *n* (*VGA*) COMP Videografikadapter *m* (*VGA*); ~ **graphics array** *n* (*VGA*) COMP Videografikanordnung *f*; ~ **monitor** *n* COMMS, COMP, MEDIA Videomonitor *m*; ~ **piracy** *n* LAW, MEDIA Videokopierdiebstahl *m*; ~ **shopping** *n* S&M Videoeinkauf *m*

videotape 1. *n* COMMS, MEDIA Videoband *nt*; **2.** *vt* COMMS, MEDIA auf Videoband aufzeichnen

videotape: ~ **recorder** *n* (*VTR*) COMMS, COMP, MEDIA, S&M Videorekorder *m*; ~ **recording** *n* (*VTR*) COMMS, COMP, MEDIA, S&M Videoaufnahme *f*

video: ~ **terminal** *n* COMMS, COMP, MEDIA Bildschirmgerät *nt*

Videotex® *n* COMMS, COMP Bildschirmtext *m*, Videotext *m*

videotext *n* COMMS, COMP Bildschirmtextsystem *nt*, bildschirmorientiertes Textsystem *nt*; ~ **system** *n* COMMS, COMP Bildschirmtextsystem *nt*

vie *vi* GEN COMM konkurrieren; ♦ ~ **with** GEN COMM wetteifern mit

Viennese: ~ **Stock Exchange** *n* STOCK Wiener Börsenkammer *f*

view 1. *n* GEN COMM Anschauung *f*, *opinion* Ansicht *f*, Meinung *f*; ♦ **in ~ of the circumstances** GEN COMM unter Berücksichtigung der Umstände; **with this in ~** GEN COMM, LAW im Hinblick darauf, daß; **with a ~ to** GEN COMM im Hinblick auf; **with a ~ to doing sth** GEN COMM in der Absicht, etw zu tun, mit dem Ziel, etw zu tun; **2.** *vt* COMP *word processed document* lesen

Viewdata® *n* COMMS, COMP Bildschirmtext *m*, Bildschirmtextsystem *nt*

viewing *n* PROP *of house, business premises* Besichtigung *f*; ~ **by appointment only** *phr* PROP Besichtigung nur nach Voranmeldung; ~ **habits** *n pl* MEDIA Sehgewohnheiten *f pl*; ~ **room** *n* MEDIA Vorführraum *m*; ~ **time** *n* MEDIA *of broadcast* Einschaltzeit *f*

viewpoint *n* GEN COMM *opinion* Sicht *f*, Standpunkt *m*

view: ~ **screen** *n* COMP Anzeigebildschirm *m*

vignette *n* S&M *advertising*, TRANSP Vignette *f*

vigorous *adj* GEN COMM energisch, kraftvoll, *defence* nachdrücklich

village: ~ **school** *n* GEN COMM Gemeindeschule *f*

vindicate *vt* GEN COMM *person* rehabilitieren, *opinion, action* rechtfertigen, verteidigen, *right* bestätigen, LAW verteidigen

vindication *n* GEN COMM *of person* Rehabilitation *f*, *of*

opinion, action Rechtfertigung *f*, Verteidigung *f*, *of right* Bestätigung *f*, LAW Verteidigung *f*

vineyard *n* GEN COMM Weinberg *m*

vintage *n* GEN COMM *harvest* Weinernte *f*, Weinertrag *m*, *year* Jahrgang

vintner *n* GEN COMM Weinhändler, in *m,f*, Winzer, in *m,f*

VIO *abbr* (*very important object*) TRANSP sehr wichtiges Objekt *nt*

violate *vt* LAW *law, regulations* verletzen, verstoßen gegen, *contract, law* brechen, PATENTS verletzen, verstoßen gegen

violation *n* LAW Bruch *m*, Verletzung *f*, Verstoß *m*, PATENTS Verletzung *f*, Verstoß *m*; ♦ **in ~ of** GEN COMM in Verletzung von

violation: ~ **of contract** *n* LAW Vertragsverletzung *f*; ~ **of the law** *n* LAW Gesetzesübertretung *f*; ~ **of a treaty** *n* LAW Vertragsbruch *m*

violator *n* LAW Verletzer *m*

VIP *abbr* (*very important person*) GEN COMM VIP (*bedeutende Persönlichkeit, sehr wichtige Person, hohes Tier*)

virtual *adj* COMP virtuell

virtute officii *phr* GEN COMM kraft seines Amtes

virus *n* COMP Virus *m or nt*; **~-free** *adj* COMP nicht infiziert, virenfrei

visa *n* ADMIN Visum *nt*

vis-à-vis *prep* GEN COMM gegenüber

Visby: ~ **Rules** *n pl* TRANSP Visby-Regeln *f pl*

viscosity *n* GEN COMM Viskosität *f*, Zähflüssigkeit *f*

visible *adj* FIN, GEN COMM, IMP/EXP sichtbar; ~ **balance** *n* ECON, GEN COMM Handelsbilanz *f*; ~ **export** *n* ECON, IMP/EXP sichtbarer Export *m*, Warenausfuhr *f*; ~ **hand** *n* ECON sichtbare Hand *f*; ~ **import** *n* ECON, IMP/EXP sichtbarer Import *m*, Wareneinfuhr *f*

visibles *n pl* ECON sichtbare Ein- und Ausfuhren *f pl*, sichtbare Posten *m pl*

visible: ~ **trade balance** *n* ECON Bilanz *f* des Warenhandels, Warenhandelsbilanz *f*

vision *n* GEN COMM, MGMNT Vision *f*, Vorstellung *f*

visit 1. *n* GEN COMM Besuch *m*; **2.** *vt* GEN COMM besuchen

visitation *n* GEN COMM offizieller Besuch *m*, Visitation *f*

visiting: ~ **card** *n* GEN COMM Visitenkarte *f*; ~ **professor** *n* HRM *at university* Gastprofessor *m*, außerordentlicher Professor *m*

visitor *n* GEN COMM Besucher, in *m,f*, *in hotel* Gast *m*

visual *n* MEDIA, S&M Fototermin *m*; ~ **aid** *n* MEDIA, S&M Anschauungsmaterial *nt*; ~ **arts** *n pl* MEDIA bildende Künste *f pl*; ~ **demonstration material** *n* S&M Anschauungsmaterial *nt*; ~ **display terminal** *n AmE* (*VDT*) COMP Bildschirmgerät *nt*, Datensichtgerät *nt* (*DSG*); ~ **display unit** *n BrE* (*VDU*) COMP Bildschirmgerät *nt*, Datensichtgerät *nt* (*DSG*); ~ **impact** *n* GEN COMM sichtbare Auswirkung *f*

visualizer *n* S&M grafischer Ideengestalter *m*, grafische Ideengestalterin *f*

visual: ~ **material** *n* MEDIA, S&M Bildmaterial *f*

visuals *n pl* GEN COMM, S&M *for presentation* Anschauungsmaterial *nt*

visual: ~ **telephone** *n* COMMS Bildtelefon *nt*

vital: ~ **interest** *n* LAW berechtigtes Interesse *nt*; ~ **records management** *n* MGMNT Verwaltung *f* wichtiger Akten

VLR *abbr* (*variable lending rate*) FIN schwankender Zinssatz *m* für Ausleihungen, variabler Zinssatz *m* für Ausleihungen

VMP *abbr* (*value as marine policy*) INS Wert *m* als Seepolice

vo. *abbr* (*verso*) MEDIA *back of page* Rückseite *f*

vocation *n* GEN COMM, HRM Beruf *m*

vocational: **~ counseling** *AmE*, **~ counselling** *BrE* *n* HRM, WEL Berufsberatung *f*; **~ counsellor** *BrE*, **~ counselor** *AmE* *n* HRM, WEL Berufsberater, in *m,f*; **~ experience** *n* HRM Berufserfahrung *f*; **~ guidance** *n* HRM Berufsberatung *f*; **~ guide** *n* HRM Berufsberater, in *m,f*; **~ qualifications** *n pl* HRM berufliche Qualifikationen *f pl*; **~ rehabilitation** *n* HRM berufliche Rehabilitation *f*; **~ retraining** *n* HRM Umschulung *f*; **~ school** *n* WEL Berufsschule *f*, berufsbildende Schule *f*; **~ training** *n* HRM, WEL Berufsausbildung *f*, berufsbezogene Ausbildung *f*, berufliche Bildung *f*; **~ training grant** *n* FIN, HRM Berufsausbildungszuschuß *m*

voice: **~-activated** *adj* COMP sprachaktiviert; **~-actuated** *adj* COMP sprachgesteuert; **~ mail** *n* COMP Sprachpost *f*; **~ recognition** *n* COMP Spracherkennung *f*

void *adj* GEN COMM ungültig; ◆ **make ~** GEN COMM aufheben

voidable *adj* BANK, GEN COMM, INS, LAW anfechtbar, annullierbar; **~ policy** *n* INS anfechtbare Police *f*; **~ transaction** *n* LAW anfechtbare Rechtshandlung *f*

voidance *n* GEN COMM Nichtigkeit *f*

void: **~ policy** *n* INS rechtsunwirksame Police *f*, ungültige Police *f*

vol. *abbr* (*volume*) ACC, ECON, GEN COMM, STOCK Vol. (*Volumen*)

volatile *adj* COMP flüchtig, ECON schwankend, unstetig, POL *situation* brisant, STOCK *prices* volatil

Volcoa *abbr* (*volume contract of affreightment*) TRANSP Volumenfrachtvertrag *m*

voltage *n* ENVIR, IND Spannung *f*; **~ regulator** *n* ENVIR Spannungsregler *m*

volume *n* (*vol.*) ACC Umsatzvolumen *nt*, Volumen *nt* (*Vol.*), COMP *sound* Lautstärke *f*, ECON Volumen *nt* (*Vol.*), GEN COMM *of trade* Umsatz *m*, Volumen *nt* (*Vol.*), *extent* Umfang *m*, MEDIA *book* Band *m*, STOCK Volumen *nt* (*Vol.*); **~ charge** *n* TRANSP *tariff* Volumengebühr *f*; **~ contract of affreightment** *n* (*Volcoa*) TRANSP Volumenfrachtvertrag *m*; **~ deleted** *n* STOCK gelöschte Börsenumsätze *m pl*; **~ of deposits** *n* BANK Einlagenbestand *m*; **~ discount** *n* GEN COMM Mengenrabatt *m*; **~ of exports** *n* ECON, IMP/EXP Exportvolumen *nt*, Ausfuhrvolumen *nt*; **~ of foreign trade** *n* ECON, IMP/EXP Außenhandelsvolumen *nt*; **~ index** *n* GEN COMM Mengenindex *m*; **~ of loans granted** *n* FIN Auszahlungsvolumen *nt*; **~ of notes and coins in circulation** *n* ECON Bargeldvolumen *nt*; **~ of orders** *n* GEN COMM Auftragsumfang *m*; **~ ratio** *n* ECON Volumenverhältnis *nt*; **~ rebate** *n* TRANSP *cargo* Mengenrabatt *m*; **~ of retail sales** *n BrE* ECON Umfang *m* des Einzelhandelsgeschäfts; **~ shipping** *n* IMP/EXP, TRANSP Großverladung *f*, Massenverladung *f*, Mengenversand *m*; **~ of trade** *n* ECON, STOCK Umsatz *m*; **~ of trading** *n* ECON Handelsvolumen *nt*, GEN COMM Geschäftsumfang *m*, Handelsvolumen *nt*; **~ of traffic** *n* TRANSP Verkehrsaufkommen *nt*

voluntarism *n* HRM Freiwilligkeitsprinzip *nt*

voluntary *adj* GEN COMM, WEL freiwillig; ◆ **go into ~ liquidation** GEN COMM freiwillig in Liquidation gehen

voluntary: **~ accumulation plan** *n* FIN freiwilliger Kapitalansammlungsplan *m*; **~ agency** *n* WEL private Einrichtung *f*, private Organisation *f*; **~ arbitration** *n* HRM frei vereinbarte Schiedsgerichtsbarkeit *f*; **~ bankruptcy** *n* FIN Konkurs *m* auf Antrag des Gemeinschuldners, selbst beantragte Konkurserklärung *f*, freiwilliger Konkurs *m*, freiwillige Konkurserklärung *f*; **~ body** *n* WEL freiwillige Körperschaft *f*; **~ chain** *n* GEN COMM freiwillige Großhandelskette *f*, freiwillige Handelskette *f*, freiwillige Ladenkette *f*; **~ contribution** *n* TAX, WEL Spende *f*; **~ contributions** *n pl BrE* TAX *National Insurance* freiwillige Beiträge *m pl*; **~ controls** *n pl* S&M freiwillige Kontrollen *f pl*; **~ export restraint** *n* (*VER*) IMP/EXP freiwillige Ausfuhrbeschränkung *f*, freiwillige Exportbeschränkung *f*; **~ group** *n* S&M Einkaufsvereinigung *f*; **~ insurance** *n* INS freiwillige Versicherung *f*; **~ liquidation** *n* FIN freiwillige Liquidation *f*; **~ policy** *n* HRM Selbstbeschränkung *f* bei Lohnforderungen; **~ redundancy** *n BrE* HRM freiwillige Entlassung *f*; **~ settlement** *n* LAW außergerichtlicher Vergleich *m*; **~ winding up** *n* GEN COMM, FIN *of company* freiwillige Abwicklung *f*, freiwillige Liquidation *f*; **~ work** *n* HRM ehrenamtliche Tätigkeit *f*

volunteer 1. *n* HRM Freiwillige(r) *mf* [decl. as adj], Volontär, in *m,f*; **2.** *vt* GEN COMM *information* freiwillig geben; **3.** *vi* GEN COMM sich anbieten, sich freiwillig melden, sich melden; ◆ **~ for sth** GEN COMM sich freiwillig für etw zur Verfügung stellen, sich bereit erklären, etw zu tun

volunteer: **~ development worker** *n* GEN COMM Entwicklungshelfer, in *m,f*

VOP *abbr* (*value as in original policy*) INS Wert wie in Ursprungspolice

vote 1. *n* HRM, POL Stimme *f*, *act of voting* Wahl *f*, Abstimmung *f*, Votum *nt*, Bewilligung *f* durch Abstimmung, *result* Wahlergebnis *nt*; **2.** *vt* HRM, POL wählen; ◆ **~ full supply** POL volle Bereitstellung von Mitteln beschließen; **~ interim supply** POL vorübergehende Bereitstellung von Mitteln beschließen; **~ out of office** POL abwählen; **3.** *vi* HRM, POL abstimmen, *elections* wählen; ◆ **~ against** HRM, POL stimmen gegen; **~ for** HRM, POL stimmen für, wählen

vote: **~ by show of hands** *n* HRM, POL Abstimmung *f* durch Handaufheben; **~ netting** *n* FIN Nettostimmenverrechnung *f*, Stimmverrechnung *f*; **~-netting revenue** *n* FIN Stimmverrechnungsertrag *m*

voter *n* POL Wähler, in *m,f*; **~ turnout** *n* POL Wahlbeteiligung *f*

vote: **~ structure** *n* POL *government accounting* Stimmenaufgliederung *f*, Struktur *f* des Votums, Struktur *f* des Wahlergebnisses

voting *n* HRM, MGMNT *at board meetings* Abstimmung *f*, Beschlußfassung *f*, Stimmabgabe *f*, POL Wahl *f*; **~ booth** *n* POL Wahlkabine *f*; **~ capital** *n* STOCK stimmberechtigtes Kapital; **~ paper** *n* HRM *in union ballot* Stimmzettel *m*; **~ power** *n* FIN, STOCK Stimmrecht *nt*; **~ procedures** *n pl* HRM, POL Wahlverfahren *nt*; **~ proxy** *n* HRM Stimmrechtsvollmacht *f*; **~ right** *n* HRM, POL Stimmrecht *nt*; **~ share** *n* FIN, STOCK stimmberechtigte Aktie *f*; **~ stock** *n* FIN, STOCK stimmberechtigte Aktie *f*; **~ trust certificate** *n* STOCK stimmberechtigtes Treuhandzertifikat *nt*

voucher *n* ACC Buchungsbeleg *m*, BANK Verrechnungsscheck *m*, GEN COMM *coupon* Beleg *m*, Bon *m*,
Gutschein *m*, S&M *advertising, voucher copy* Belegkopie
f, Durchführungsbeleg *m*; ~ **system** *n* ACC Belegsystem
nt, Belegbuchhaltung *f*

vouch: ~ **mark** *n* ACC Buchungsbeleg *m*

voy *abbr* (*voyage*) TRANSP Reise *f*, *by sea* Seereise *f*

voyage *n* (*voy*) LEIS, TRANSP Reise *f*, *by sea* Seereise *f*;
~ **account report** *n* TRANSP Reisekostenbericht *m*;
~ **charter** *n* TRANSP Reisecharter *f*; ~ **charter party** *n*
(*voyage C/P*) TRANSP Reisechartervertrag *m*; ~ **C/P** *n*
(*voyage charter party*) TRANSP Reisechartervertrag *m*;
~ **estimate** *n* TRANSP Reiseschätzung *f*; ~ **expenses** *n*
pl ACC, GEN COMM, TAX, TRANSP Reisekosten *pl*;
~ **fixture** *n* TRANSP Reisefestlegung *f*; ~ **policy** *n* INS

Einzelpolice *f*, Reisepolice *f*; ~ **report** *n* TRANSP
Reisebericht *m*

VP *abbr* (*vice president*) HRM, MGMNT, POL VP (*Vizepräsident*)

vs *abbr* (*versus*) GEN COMM geg. (*gegen*), vs. (*versus*)

VTR *abbr* COMMS, COMP, MEDIA, S&M (*videotape recorder*)
Videorekorder *m*, (*videotape recording*) Videoaufnahme
f

vulgarize *vt* GEN COMM *debase* herabwürdigen, *popularize*
der Masse zugänglich machen

vulnerable *adj* ECON wehrlos, GEN COMM verletzlich, HRM
ungeschützt, anfällig

vulture: ~ **fund** *n* *infrml* FIN Fonds *m* für Investitionen in
abgewirtschaftete Unternehmen

W

w *abbr* (*wood*) IND Holz *nt*

W.A. *abbr* (*with average*) INS *maritime* einschließlich Havarie

WACCC *abbr* (*Worldwide Air Cargo Commodity Classification*) TRANSP weltweite Luftfrachtgüter-Klassifizierung *f*

wad *n* BANK *of notes* Banknotenbündel *nt*, GEN COMM Packen *m* (*infrml*)

wage 1. *n* ECON Arbeitslohn *m*, GEN COMM, HRM Lohn *m*, TRANSP *shipping* Heuer *f*; **2.** *vt* ♦ **~ a campaign** POL eine Kampagne führen; **~ a price war** GEN COMM, S&M einen Preiskrieg führen

wage: **~ adjustment** *n* HRM Lohnanpassung *f*, Lohnangleichung *f*, Tarifangleichung *f*; **~ agreement** *n* HRM Lohnvereinbarung *f*; **~ and price guidelines** *n pl* HRM Lohn- und Preisleitlinien *f pl*; **~ arbitration** *n* HRM Schlichtung *f* von Lohnstreitigkeiten; **~ assignment** *n* GEN COMM, HRM Lohnabtretung *f*; **~ bargaining round** *n* HRM Tarifrunde *f*; **~ bonus** *n* HRM Prämienlohn *m*; **~ bracket** *n* HRM Lohnstufe *f*; **~ ceiling** *n* HRM Höchstlohn *m*; **~ claim** *n* HRM Lohnforderung *f*; **~ control** *n* ECON staatliche Lohnkontrolle *f*; **~ differentials** *n pl* ECON, HRM Lohngefälle *nt*; **~ diffusion** *n* ECON Lohndiffusion *f*; **~ drift** *n* ECON, HRM Lohndrift *f*; **~ explosion** *n* ECON, HRM Lohnexplosion *f*; **~ flexibility** *n* ECON, HRM Lohnflexibilität *f*; **~ floor** *n* HRM Grundlohn *m*; **~ freeze** *n* HRM Lohn- und Gehaltsstopp *m*, Lohnpause *f*, Lohnstillstand *m*, Lohnstopp *m*; **~ gap** *n* HRM Lohndrift *f*; **~ incentive** *n* HRM gewinnbezogene Bezahlung *f*, gewinnbezogenes Arbeitsentgelt *nt*, leistungsbezogene Bezahlung *f*, Leistungslohn *m*; **~ increase** *n* HRM Lohnerhöhung *f*; **~ indexation** *n* HRM Lohnindexbindung *f*; **~ inflation** *n* ECON Lohninflation *f*; **~ level** *n* ECON, HRM Lohnniveau *nt*; **~ negotiations** *n pl* HRM, MGMNT Lohnverhandlungen *f pl*; **~ per hour** *n* HRM Stundenlohn *m*; **~ policy** *n* HRM Lohnpolitik *f*; **~ price-indexation** *n* ECON Lohn-Preis-Indexierung *f*; **~-price inflation spiral** *n* ECON Lohn-Preis-Inflationsspirale *f*; **~-price spiral** *n* ECON Lohn-Preis-Spirale *f*; **~ push inflation** *n* ECON Lohndruckinflation *f*

wager 1. *vt* LEIS wetten; **2.** *vi* LEIS wetten

wage: **~ rate** *n* ECON Lohnsatz *m*, Arbeitslohn *m*; **~-rental ratio** *n* ECON Lohn-Miet-Verhältnis *nt*; **~ restraint** *n* ECON, HRM, POL Selbstbeschränkung *f* bei Lohnforderungen; **~ rigidity** *n* ECON Starrheit *f* der Löhne; **~ round** *n* ECON Lohnrunde *f*

wages *n pl* ECON, HRM Arbeitslöhne *m pl*, Lohn *m*, Löhne *m pl*; **~ act** *n* LAW Lohnfortzahlungsgesetz *nt*

wage: **~ and salary administration** *n* HRM Lohn- und Gehaltsabrechnung *f*; **~ and salary survey** *n* HRM Lohn- und Gehaltsrevision *f*; **~ scale** *n* HRM Lohntarif *m*, Lohnskala *f*

Wages: **~ Council** *n* BrE HRM Lohnausschuß *m* (*obs*), Tarifkommission *f*

wage: **~ settlement** *n* HRM Lohnabschluß *m*, Tarifabschluß *m*

wages: **~ fund theory** *n* ECON Lohnfondstheorie *f*

Wages: **~ Inspectorate** *n* BrE IND Lohnaufsichtsamt

wages: **~ policy** *n* HRM Lohnpolitik *f*

wage: **~ spread** *n* HRM Lohnspanne *f*; **~ stabilization** *n* HRM Lohnstabilisierung *f*; **~ stop** *n* HRM Lohnstopp *m*; **~ structure** *n* HRM Lohngefüge *f*; **~ subsidy** *n* ECON Lohnsubvention *f*; **~ system** *n* HRM Lohnsystem *nt*; **~ talks** *n pl* HRM, MGMNT Lohnverhandlungen *f pl*; **~-tax spiral** *n* ECON, TAX Lohn-Steuer-Spirale *f*; **~ theory** *n* ECON Lohntheorie *f*; **~ withholding** *n* HRM Lohneinbehaltung *f*; **~ worker** *n* AmE HRM Lohnempfänger *m*

Wagner: **~'s law** *n* ECON Wagnersches Gesetz *nt*

wagonload: **~ rate** *n* TRANSP *rail* Wagenladungstarif *m*

wait: **~-and-see policy** *n* ECON abwartende Haltung *f*, Politik *f* des Abwartens

waiter *n* BrE STOCK Börsendiener *m*

wait: **~ for the other shoe to drop** *phr* GEN COMM auf ein Ereignis warten, das im unmittelbaren Zusammenhang mit einem vorhergehenden Ereignis steht

waiting: **~ line theory** *n* GEN COMM Warteschlangentheorie *f*; **~ list** *n* GEN COMM Vormerkliste *f*, Warteliste *f*, LEIS *aviation*, TRANSP *cargo, passengers* Warteliste *f*; **~ period** *n* STOCK Sperrfrist *f*; **~ time** *n* GEN COMM Wartezeit *f*

wait: **~ in line** *phr* AmE (*cf queue up BrE*) GEN COMM anstehen, in Reihe und Glied warten, Schlange stehen

waive *vt* FIN erlassen, LAW, PATENTS, TAX aufgeben, verzichten auf [+acc]

waiver: **~ clause** *n* INS *in contract* Verzichtserklärungsklausel *f*; **~ of premium** *n* INS Beitragsbefreiung *f*

waiving *n* FIN Erlassung *f*, LAW, PATENTS, TAX Aufgeben *nt*, Verzicht *m*; **~ of a debt** *n* FIN Erlassung *f* einer Schuld

walk out *vi* HRM, IND in den Streik treten, streiken

walkie: **~-talkie** *n* COMMS tragbares Funkgerät *nt*, Walkie-talkie *nt*

walking: **~-around money** *n* AmE POL Entgelt für Wahlhelfer

walkout *n infrml* GEN COMM, HRM, IND Arbeitsniederlegung *f*, Ausstand *m*, Streik *m*

walkover *n infrml* GEN COMM Kinderspiel *nt* (*infrml*)

walk: **~-up** *n* AmE *infrml* PROP mehrstöckiges Mietshaus ohne Lift

wall: **go to the ~** *phr infrml* BANK, ECON Pleite machen (*infrml*), GEN COMM *person* Pleite machen (*infrml*), *company* in Konkurs gehen, Konkurs machen, STOCK Pleite machen (*infrml*)

wall out *vt* AmE GEN COMM ausschließen; ♦ **~ car imports** AmE IMP/EXP keine Autoimporte zulassen

wallflower *n jarg* STOCK nicht gängige Aktie *f*

Wall: **~ Street** *n* FIN, STOCK amerikanischer Geld- und Kapitalmarkt, New Yorker Finanzzentrum; **~ Street Crash** *n* FIN, STOCK Wall Street-Börsenkrach; **~-Streeter** *n* FIN, STOCK Händler an der Wall Street

Walrasian: **~ stability** *n* ECON Walrassche Stabilität *f*

Walras: **~'s law** *n* ECON Walrassches Gesetz *nt*

wampum *n* *AmE* *infrml* ECON, FIN Geld *nt*, GEN COMM Geld *nt*, Kohle *f* (*infrml*), Knete *f* (*infrml*), Mäuse *f pl* (*infrml*), Kies *m* (*infrml*)

WAN *abbr* (*wide-area network*) COMMS, COMP WAN (*großflächiges Netz, Weitverkehrsnetz*)

wane *vi* GEN COMM nachlassen

want *n* GEN COMM *requirement* Bedürfnis *nt*; **~-satisfying ability** *n* ECON Bedürfnisbefriedigungsfähigkeit *f*, wirtschaftlicher Wert *m*

war *n* INS, POL Krieg *m*; ~ **babies** *n pl jarg* STOCK Aktien *f pl* von Rüstungsunternehmen; ~ **chest** *n* *AmE* FIN Kriegskasse *f*; ~ **clause** *n* INS *marine insurance* Kriegsklausel *f*

ward *n* LAW *under a guardian* Mündel *nt*

warehouse **1.** *n* (*whse*) GEN COMM, IMP/EXP, TRANSP, S&M Depot *nt* (*Dep.*), Lager *nt* (*Lag.*), Lagergebäude *nt*, Lagerhaus *nt*, Magazin *nt* (*Mag.*), Speicher *m*, Warenlager *nt*, Zollgutlager *nt*; **2.** *vt* GEN COMM, IMP/EXP, TRANSP lagern, speichern

warehouse: ~ **book** *n* (*WB*) IMP/EXP, TRANSP *stock control* Bestandbuch *nt*, Lagerbuch *nt*; ~ **charges** *n pl* IMP/EXP Lagergeld *nt*, Lagerspesen *f pl*, Speichergebühren *f pl*, TRANSP Lagerungsgebühren *f pl*, Speicherkosten *pl*; ~ **entry** *n* IMP/EXP *customs* Deklaration *f* zur Einlagerung unter Zollverschluß, TRANSP *customs* Lagerhauseintrag *m*; ~ **keeper** *n* GEN COMM *stock control* Lagerhalter, in *m,f*, Lagerverwalter, in *m,f*, Magazinhalter, in *m,f*, Magazinverwalter, in *m,f*, Spediteur *m*, Speicherverwalter, in *m,f*, IMP/EXP Zollbeamte(r) *m* [decl. as adj] in Zollgutlager, Zollbeamtin *f* in Zollgutlager

warehouseman *n* GEN COMM Lagerhalter *m*, Lagerverwalter *m*, Lagerist *m*

warehouse: ~ **officer** *n* GEN COMM *stock control* Lagerhalter, in *m,f*, Lagerverwalter, in *m,f*, Magazinhalter, in *m,f*, Spediteur *m*, Speicherverwalter, in *m,f*, gewerbliche Lagerhalterin *f*, gewerblicher Lagerhalter *m*, IMP/EXP Lagerist, in *m,f*, Zollbeamte(r) *m* [decl.as adj] in Zollgutlager, Zollbeamtin *f* in Zollgutlager; ~ **receipt** *n* (*WR*) IMP/EXP, IND, LAW, TRANSP Einlagerungsschein *m*, Lagerschein *m*; ~ **supervisor** *n* GEN COMM, IMP/EXP, TRANSP Lageraufseher, in *m,f*; ~ **warrant** *n* (*WW*) LAW *commercial* Lagerschein *m*, Orderlagerschein *m*, S&M Lagerschein *m*

warehousewoman *n* GEN COMM Lagerverwalterin *f*, Lagerhalterin *f*, Lageristin *f*

warehousing *n* GEN COMM, IMP/EXP *storekeeping* Lagerhaltung *f*, Magazinverwaltung *f*, IND, TRANSP *storage* Einlagerung *f*, Lagerhaltung *f*, Lagerung *f*

war: ~ **loan** *n* *BrE* FIN Kriegsanleihe *f*

warm: ~ **restart** *n* COMP Warmstart *m*; **~-up session** *n* MGMNT Vorbereitungssitzung *f*

warn *vt* GEN COMM warnen; ♦ ~ **sb against sth** GEN COMM jdn vor etw warnen

warning *n* HRM *prior to disciplinary action* Warnung *f*; ~ **device** *n* GEN COMM Warnanlage *f*, Warngerät *nt*; ~ **indicator** *n* GEN COMM Warnanzeige *f*, Warngerät *nt*; ~ **limit** *n* IMP/EXP Warngrenze *f*; ~ **sign** *n* GEN COMM *notice* Warnschild *nt*, *threat* ernstes Anzeichen *nt*

warrant **1.** *n* FIN Garant *m*, *certificate* Optionsschein *m*, INS Berechtigung *f*, LAW Gerichtsbefehl *m*, *for arrest* Haftbefehl *m*, POL *authority* Berechtigung *f*, Befugnis *f*, *mandate* Vollmacht *f*, STOCK Optionsschein *m*; **2.** *vt* GEN COMM zusichern

warrant: ~ **of attorney** *n* LAW unwiderrufliche Prozeßvollmacht *f*; ~ **bond** *n* BANK Optionsanleihe *f*; ~ **discounting** *n* FIN Optionsscheindiskontierung *f*

warranted *adj* (*W/d*) INS garantiert, gerechtfertigt, zugesichert; ~ **rate** **of** **growth** *n* ECON Gleichgewichtswachstumsrate *f*

warrantee *n* GEN COMM, LAW Garantieinhaber, in *m,f*, Sicherheitsempfänger, in *m,f*

warranter *n* GEN COMM, LAW Zusichernde(r) *mf* [decl. as adj]

warrant: ~ **issue** *n* FIN Emission *f* von Bezugsrechtsscheinen, Optionsanleihe *f*

warrantless: ~ **investigation** *n* POL nicht autorisierte Untersuchung *f*

warranty *n* GEN COMM Garantie *f*, INS Gewährleistung *f*, LAW Zusicherung *f*; ~ **card** *n* BANK Garantiekarte *f*; ~ **of merchantability** *n* GEN COMM Gewährleistung *f* der Durchschnittsqualität, Zusicherung *f* der Mindestqualität; ~ **obligation** *n* GEN COMM Gewährleistungspflicht *f*; ~ **of quality** *n* LAW Sachmängelhaftung *f*; ~ **of title** *n* GEN COMM Rechtsmängelgewähr *f*

war: ~ **risk** *n* INS Kriegsgefahrrisiko *nt*, Kriegsrisiko *nt*; ~ **risk only** *phr* (*wro*) INS nur gegen Kriegsrisiko versichert

Warsaw: ~ **Convention** *n* TRANSP *air transport* Warschauer Abkommen *nt*

wash: ~ **sale** *n* STOCK *securities* Scheingeschäft *nt*

wastage *n* GEN COMM Ausschuß *m*, Vergeudung *f*, Verlust *m*

waste **1.** *n* ENVIR, GEN COMM Abfall *m*, Müll *m*; **2.** *vt* GEN COMM *time, money* vergeuden, *resources* verschwenden

waste: ~ **bin** *n* ENVIR Abfalleimer *m*; ~ **circulation** *n* S&M *advertising* Fehlstreuung *f*; ~ **disposal** *n* ENVIR, GEN COMM Abfallbeseitigung *f*, Abfallentsorgung *f*, Müllentsorgung *f*; ~ **disposal industry** *n* ENVIR, GEN COMM Abfallwirtschaft *f*; ~ **dumping** *n* ENVIR Lagerung *f* von Abfall

wasteful: ~ **expenditure** *n* FIN, GEN COMM verschwenderische Ausgaben *f pl*; ~ **spending** *n* FIN, GEN COMM Verschwendung *f* von Geld

wasteland *n* PROP Ödland *nt*

waste: ~ **management** *n* ENVIR Abfallwirtschaft *f*; ~ **oils** *n pl* ENVIR Altöl *nt*

wastepaper *n* ENVIR, GEN COMM Altpapier *nt*

waste: ~ **prevention** *n* ENVIR Abfallvermeidung *f*; ~ **product** *n* ENVIR *recyclage* Abfallprodukt *nt*; ~ **recycling** *n* ENVIR Abfallaufbereitung *f*, Abfallrecycling *nt*; **the ~ society** *n* GEN COMM die Wegwerfgesellschaft *f*; ~ **treatment** *n* ENVIR, GEN COMM Müllbehandlung *f*

wastewater *n* ENVIR Abwasser *nt*; ~ **disposal** *n* ENVIR Abwasserbeseitigung *f*; ~ **treatment** *n* ENVIR Abwasseraufbereitung *f*, Abwasserbehandlung *f*

wasting: ~ **asset** *n* ACC, ECON kurzlebiger Vermögenswert *m*, kurzlebiges Wirtschaftsgut *nt*, Vermögen *nt* mit begrenzter Nutzungsdauer, Wirtschaftsgut *nt* mit begrenzter Nutzungsdauer

watch *vt* FIN *markets*, GEN COMM *performance*, STOCK *value* beobachten

watchdog *n* GEN COMM *consumer interests*

Überwachungsorganisation *f*, Aufpasser *m*, Aufsichts-behörde *f*; ~ **committee** *n* GEN COMM Aufpasser-Komitee *nt*, POL Aufsichtsausschuß *m*, Ausschuß *m* der Aufsichtsbehörde, Überwachungsausschuß *m*

watchman *n* HRM Wachmann *m*

watch: ~ **trade** *n* IND Uhrmachergewerbe *nt*

watchword *n* GEN COMM, S&M Kennwort *nt*, Parole *f*

waterborne: ~ **agreement** *n* INS Kriegsrisikodeckung *f* unter der Bedingung schwimmender Fracht

water down *vt* GEN COMM *idea, politics, statement* abschwächen, verwässern, *wine, milk* panschen

water: ~ **damage** *n* GEN COMM, INS Wasserschaden *m*

watered: ~ **capital** *n* FIN verwässertes Kapital *nt*; ~ **shares** *n pl* STOCK verwässerte Aktien *f pl*

Waterguard: ~ **Service** *n* *BrE* IMP/EXP, TRANSP Hafenzollwache *f*

watermark *n* ECON *on banknote* Wasserzeichen *nt*

watermarked *adj* ECON *banknote* mit Wasserzeichen versehen

water: ~ **pipe** *n* ENVIR, IND, TRANSP Wasserleitung *f*; ~ **pollution** *n* ENVIR, IND Gewässerverschmutzung *f*, Gewässerverunreinigung *f*; ~ **pollution control levy** *n* ENVIR, LAW Abwasserabgabengesetz *nt*

waterproof *adj* GEN COMM, IND, TRANSP wasserdicht; ~ **paper** *n* COMMS, IND bituminiertes Papier *nt*, Teerpapier *nt*, Unterlagspapier *nt*, wasserdichtes Papier *nt*

water: ~ **purification** *n* ENVIR, IND Wasserreinigung *f*; ~ **supply** *n* ENVIR, IND Wasserversorgung *f*; ~ **system** *n* ENVIR, IND Wasserversorgung *f*

watertight *adj* GEN COMM *plan, excuse* einwandfrei, wasserdicht, unanfechtbar, hieb- und stichfest

water: ~ **transportation** *n* TRANSP Wassertransport *m*; ~ **treatment** *n* ENVIR Wasseraufbereitung *f*

waterway *n* TRANSP Wasserstraße *f*

waterworks *n* IND Wasserwerk *nt*

wavelength: **be on the same ~ as** *phr infrml* GEN COMM konform gehen mit, die gleiche Wellenlänge haben wie (*infrml*)

wave: ~ **power** *n* ENVIR, IND *electricity generation* Wellenenergie *f*

way: **be under ~** *phr* GEN COMM im Gang sein, schon angefangen haben

waybill *n* IMP/EXP, TRANSP *detailing route, cost* Frachtbrief *m*

way: ~ **of life** *n* GEN COMM Lebensart *f*, Lebensgewohnheit *f*

ways: ~ **and means** *n pl* ECON Mittel *nt pl* und Wege *m pl*

Ways: ~ **and Means Committee** *n* *AmE* FIN Geldbeschaffungsausschuß *m*, POL Steuerbewilligungsausschuß *m*

WB *abbr* (*warehouse book*) TRANSP Bestandsbuch *nt*, Lagerbuch *nt*

w.c. *abbr* (*without charge*) GEN COMM gebührenfrei, kostenlos, wertfrei

wccon *abbr* (*whether cleared customs or not*) IMP/EXP mit oder ohne Zollabfertigung

W/d *abbr* (*warranted*) INS garantiert, gerechtfertigt, zugesichert

WDA *abbr* (*Welsh Development Agency*) ECON Behörde für die wirtschaftliche Entwicklung von Wales

weak *adj* ECON, LAW *protection* schwach

weaken *vt* ECON *currency value*, GEN COMM abschwächen, schwächen

weakest: ~ **link theory** *n* GEN COMM Theorie *f* des schwächsten Glieds

weak: ~ **market** *n* STOCK *general declining trend in prices* Marktschwäche *f*, schwacher Markt *m*

weakness: ~ **investigation** *n* ACC Schwächenanalyse *f*

wealth *n* ECON Reichtum *m*, Wohlstand *m*; ~ **distribution** *n* ECON Verteilung *f* des Wohlstands; ~ **effect** *n* ECON Realkasseneffekt *m*

Wealth: ~ **of Nations** *n* ECON Wohlstand *m* der Nationen

wealth: ~ **of opportunities** *n* GEN COMM, HRM Fülle *f* von Möglichkeiten; ~ **tax** *n* ECON, FIN, TAX Vermögensteuer *f*

wealthy 1. *adj* ECON reich, wohlhabend, GEN COMM wohlhabend; **2. the ~** *n pl* GEN COMM die Reichen *pl*, die Wohlhabenden *pl*

wearout: ~ **factor** *n* S&M *advertising* Abnutzungsfaktor *m*

wear: ~ **and tear** *n* ECON *depreciation* Abschreibung *f* durch Wertminderung, GEN COMM Abnutzung *f*, Abnutzung *f* durch Gebrauch, Verschleiß *m*, *depreciation* Abschreibung *f* durch Wertminderung

weather 1. *n* GEN COMM Wetter *nt*; ♦ ~ **permitting** (*WP*) GEN COMM, TRANSP bei günstigem Wetter; **2.** *vt* ECON *recession* überstehen

weather: ~ **deck** *n* TRANSP *shipping* Wetterdeck *nt*; ~ **report** *n* GEN COMM Wetterbericht *m*; ~ **working day** *n* (*wwd*) TRANSP *charter party, unloading* nach Wetterlage möglicher Arbeitstag *m*

weaving: ~ **loom** *n* IND Webstuhl *m*; ~ **mill** *n* IND Weberei *f*; ~ **trade** *n* IND Weberhandwerk *nt*

web: ~ **offset** *n* S&M Rotationsdruck *m*

wedge *n* TRANSP Keil *m*

weed out *vt* GEN COMM auskämmen, aussondern

week *n* (*wk.*) GEN COMM Woche *f* (*W*); ♦ **a ~ in advance** GEN COMM eine Woche im voraus

weekdays: **on ~** *phr* GEN COMM an Werktagen

weekend: ~ **freight tariff** *n* TRANSP Wochenend-Frachttarif *m*; ~ **return** *n* TRANSP *tariff* Wochenendrückfahrt *f*; ~ **travel home allowance** *n* GEN COMM Wochenendheimfahrtenvergütung *f*

weekly: ~ **pay** *n* HRM wöchentliche Bezahlung *f*; ~ **pay packet** *n* HRM wöchentliche Lohntüte *f* (*obs*); ~ **rent** *n* PROP Wochenmiete *f*; ~ **return** *n* BANK Wochenausweis *m*; ~ **wage** *n* HRM Wochenlohn *m*; ~ **wage packet** *n* HRM wöchentliche Lohntüte *f* (*obs*)

wef *abbr* (*with effect from*) GEN COMM m. W. v. (*mit Wirkung von*)

weigh *vt* GEN COMM *idea, proposal* abwägen, *object* wiegen; ♦ ~ **the pros and cons** GEN COMM die Vor- und Nachteile abwägen

weigh up *vt* GEN COMM *idea, proposal* abwägen

weighbridge *n* TRANSP Brückenwaage *f*, Plattformwaage *f*

weight 1. *n* GEN COMM (*wgt, wt*), MATH (*wgt, wt*), TRANSP (*wgt, wt*) Gewicht *nt* (*Gw.*); **2.** *vt* STOCK *option positions* gewichten

weight: ~ **allowed free** *n* GEN COMM Reingewicht *nt*; ~ **ascertained** *n* GEN COMM festgestelltes Gewicht *nt*; ~ **of cargo** *n* TRANSP Frachtgewicht *nt*, Gewicht *nt* der Fracht; ~ **charge** *n* TRANSP *tariff* Gewichtskosten *pl*

weighted *adj* ECON, MATH gewogen, TAX gewichtet; ~ **average** *n* ECON gewogener Mittelwert *m*, GEN COMM

Bewertungsdurchschnitt *m*, gewogenes Mittel *nt*, MATH gewichtetes Mittel *nt*, gewogenes Mittel *nt*; ~ **average cost** *n* ACC gewogene Durchschnittskosten *pl*; ~ **index** *n* GEN COMM gewichteter Index *m*, gewogener Index *m*

weighting *n* FIN Abwägen *nt*, Gewichtung *f*, S&M *marketing* Gewichtung *f*

weight: ~ **limit** *n* GEN COMM, TRANSP Gewichtsgrenze *f*

weight/measurement *n* TRANSP *tariff* Gewicht/Maß *nt*

weight: ~ **note** *n* GEN COMM Wiegeschein *m*

weights: ~ **and measures** *n pl* GEN COMM Maße und Gewichte *nt pl*

weight: ~ **ton** *n* GEN COMM Gewichtstonne *f*; ~ **when empty** *n* GEN COMM Leergewicht *nt*

welcome 1. *n* GEN COMM Begrüßung *f*; **2.** *vt* GEN COMM begrüßen, willkommen heißen

welcome: ~ **message** *n* COMP *in software package* Begrüßung *f*, Begrüßungsmeldung *f*

welcoming: ~ **party** *n* GEN COMM *celebration* Begrüßungsfeier *f*, *group* Empfangskomitee *nt*

welfare *n* HRM *of employee* Wohl *nt*, Wohlfahrt *f*, WEL *assistance* Sozialhilfe *f*, Wohlfahrt *f*; ◆ **be on** ~ AmE HRM, WEL Arbeitslosenunterstützung empfangen, Sozialhilfe beziehen

welfare: ~ **agency** *n* HRM, WEL Sozialamt *nt*, Wohlfahrtsbehörde *f*; ~ **benefits** *n pl* WEL Sozialhilfe *f*; ~ **department** *n* HRM, WEL Sozialabteilung *f*; ~ **economics** *n* ECON Wohlfahrtsökonomik *f*, Wohlfahrtstheorie *f*; ~ **legislation** *n* HRM, POL, WEL Wohlfahrtsgesetzgebung *f*; ~ **payments** *n pl* HRM, WEL Wohlfahrtsunterstützung *f*; ~ **recipient** *n* AmE (*cf person receiving benefit* BrE) HRM, WEL Wohlfahrtsempfänger, in *m,f*; ~ **services** *n pl* HRM, WEL Wohlfahrtsdienste *m pl*; ~ **state** *n* ECON, POL, WEL Bevormundungsstaat *m*, Wohlfahrtsstaat *m*; ~ **trap** *n* WEL Sozialfürsorgeteufelskreis *m*, Wohlfahrtsfalle *f*; ~ **worker** *n* HRM, WEL Fürsorger, in *m,f*

welfarist *adj* POL, WEL wohlfahrtsstaatlich

well *adv* GEN COMM gut; ◆ **be ~ advised** GEN COMM gut beraten sein, richtig beraten sein; **be ~ placed** GEN COMM gut im Rennen liegen

well: ~-**balanced** *adj* GEN COMM gut ausgewogen; ~-**educated** *adj* GEN COMM gut ausgebildet; ~-**established** *adj* GEN COMM *business* fundiert, gut eingeführt; ~-**grounded** *adj* GEN COMM *justified* wohlbegründet, HRM *trained* gut ausgebildet, mit einer guten Vorbildung, LAW wohlbegründet

wellhead: ~ **cost** *n* FIN, IND *oil industry* Bohrlochkosten *pl*; ~ **prices** *n pl* GEN COMM Quellenpreis *m*

well: ~-**informed** *adj* GEN COMM, POL kenntnisreich, gut informiert, gut unterrichtet; ~-**known** *adj* GEN COMM, S&M bekannt; ~-**known mark** *n* PATENTS, S&M vertrautes Markenzeichen *nt*, vertrautes Warenzeichen *nt*, wohlbekanntes Markenzeichen *nt*, wohlbekanntes Warenzeichen *nt*; ~-**meaning** *adj* GEN COMM, WEL wohlmeinend; ~-**motivated** *adj* HRM gut motiviert; ~-**off** *adj* GEN COMM gut situiert, gut versorgt, reich, wohlhabend; ~-**packaged** *adj* S&M gut präsentiert, TRANSP gut verpackt; ~-**paid** *adj* HRM gut dotiert; ~-**placed** *adj* GEN COMM in guter Position; ~-**positioned** *adj* GEN COMM am rechten Platz; ~-**situated for business** *phr* GEN COMM in guter Geschäftslage; ~-**stocked** *adj* GEN COMM gutbestückt, mit reichhaltigem Sortiment; ~-**to-do** *adj* GEN COMM wohlhabend; ~-**tried** *adj* GEN COMM bewährt, erprobt

Welsh: ~ **Development Agency** *n* (*WDA*) ECON Behörde für die wirtschaftliche Entwicklung von Wales

Werner: ~ **Report** *n* ECON Werner-Bericht *m*

WESA *abbr* (*West Europe Airports Association*) TRANSP Westeuropäischer Flughafenverband *m*

westbound *adj* TRANSP nach Westen fahrend, nach Westen laufend

West: ~ **End** *n* BrE LEIS Londoner Theaterviertel

Western: ~ **Europe** *n* GEN COMM Westeuropa *nt*; ~ **European Union** *n* (*WEU*) ADMIN, POL *defence* Westeuropäische Union *f* (*WEU*); ~ **industrialized nations** *n pl* ECON westliche Industriestaaten *m pl*

western: ~-**style** *adj* ECON westlich, westlichen Typs

West: ~ **Europe Airports Association** *n* (*WESA*) TRANSP Westeuropäischer Flughafenverband *m*

wet: **he's still ~ behind the ears** *phr infrml* HRM er ist noch nicht trocken hinter den Ohren (*infrml*)

wetback *n* AmE *infrml* GEN COMM illegaler mexikanischer Einwanderer in die USA

wet: ~ **bulk cargo** *n* TRANSP flüssige Massengutladung *f*; ~ **dock** *n* GEN COMM Schleusenhafen *m*, TRANSP *port* Dockhafen *m*, Schwimmdock *nt*; ~ **goods** *n pl* STOCK flüssige Ware *f*; ~ **sell** *n infrml* S&M im Wirtshaus getätigtes Geschäft *nt*; ~ **stock** *n* GEN COMM nasse Ware *f* (*infrml*); ~ **textile waste** *n* ENVIR, TRANSP *dangerous cargo* Naßtextilabfall *m*

WEU *abbr* (*Western European Union*) ADMIN, POL *defence* WEU (*Westeuropäische Union*)

WFP *abbr* (*World Food Programme*) ECON WFP (*Welthungerhilfeprogramm*)

WFSE *abbr* (*World Federation of Stock Exchanges*) STOCK Börsenweltverband *m*

WFTU *abbr* (*World Federation of Trade Unions*) HRM IGB (*Internationaler Gewerkschaftsbund*), Weltgewerkschaftsbund *m*

WFUNA *abbr* (*World Federation of United Nations Associations*) ADMIN Weltweite Organisation *f* der UN-Verbände

wgt *abbr* (*weight*) GEN COMM, MATH, TRANSP Gw. (*Gewicht*)

WH *abbr* (*workable hatch*) TRANSP Arbeitsluke *f*

wharf *n* IMP/EXP, TRANSP *port* Kai *m*, Pier *m*

wharfage *n* IMP/EXP, TRANSP *tariff* Kaigebühren *f pl*, Kaigeld *nt*

wharfowner: ~'s **liability** *n* (*WOL*) LAW Haftung *f* des Kaibesitzers

Wharton: ~ **model** *n* ECON Wharton-Modell *nt*

what: ~-**if games** *n pl* GEN COMM Wenn-dann-Spiele *nt pl*; ~ **you see is what you get** *phr* (*WYSIWYG*) COMP wirklichkeitsgetreue Darstellung auf dem Bildschirm (*WYSIWYG*)

wheel *n* IND, TRANSP Rad *nt*; ◆ **the ~ has come full circle** GEN COMM der Kreis hat sich geschlossen

wheeler: ~-**dealer** *n infrml* GEN COMM gerissener Geschäftemacher *m* (*infrml*), Geschäftemacher *m* (*infrml*), Schlitzohr *nt* (*jarg*)

wheelhouse *n* TRANSP *of ship* Ruderhaus *nt*

wheeling: ~ **and dealing** *n infrml* GEN COMM intensives Verhandeln *nt*, STOCK intensive Verhandlung *f*

wheels: **the ~ of government** *n pl* POL die Mühlen *f pl* der Regierung, die Regierungsmaschinerie *f*; ~ **within wheels** *n pl* GEN COMM gewisse Verbindungen *f pl*

wherefore: the ~ clauses *n pl* GEN COMM die Gründe *m pl*

whether: ~ cleared customs or not *phr* (*wccon*) IMP/EXP mit oder ohne Zollabfertigung; **~ in berth or not** *phr* TRANSP am Liegeplatz oder nicht

whichever: ~ is later *phr* GEN COMM was auch immer später eintritt; **~ is sooner** *phr* GEN COMM was auch immer eher eintritt

whip *n BrE* POL *call* Anordnung *f* des Fraktionsführers, *person* Fraktionseinpeitscher *m*, Fraktionsführer *m*; ♦ **under the ~** *BrE jarg* (*cf on the reservation AmE*) POL der Parteidisziplin unterworfen, parteitreu

whip up *vt* GEN COMM, S&M *interest* anheizen, antreiben

whipsaw 1. *n AmE* HRM, POL Politiker, der von beiden Seiten kassiert, aber nur einer Seite liefert; **2.** *vt AmE* STOCK den Markt so zu manipulieren, daß der Konkurrent gezwungen wird, hoch zu kaufen und niedrig zu verkaufen

whipsawed: be ~ *phr AmE* STOCK doppelten Verlust erleiden

whiskey: ~ seat *n AmE infrml* LEIS *theatre* Platz *m* am Gang

whistle: ~-blower *n infrml* GEN COMM Denunziant, in *m,f*

whistle-stop *vi* (*jarg*) POL abklappern (*infrml*), Stippvisite *f* (*jarg*)

whistle-stop: ~ campaign *n* POL Wahlkampagne mit möglichst vielen Stippvisiten in kürzester Zeit

white: ~ coal *n* ENVIR Wasserkraft *f*; **~ coat rule** *n* S&M *advertising* Regel, die es verbietet, in der Werbung Ärzte oder als Ärzte gekleidete Schauspieler einzusetzen; **~-collar** *adj* HRM angestellt, Angestellten-; **~-collar crime** *n* LAW Wirtschaftsverbrechen *nt*; **~-collar job** *n* HRM Bürotätigkeit *f*; **~-collar union** *n* HRM Angestelltengewerkschaft *f*; **~-collar worker** *n* HRM Angestellte(r) *mf* [decl. as adj]; **~ goods** *n pl* GEN COMM, S&M *large domestic appliances* Haushaltsgeräte' *nt pl*, weiße Ware *f*

Whitehouse: ~ factor *n jarg* POL Moralökonomiefaktor *m*, Moralwächterfaktor *m*

white: ~ knight *n infrml* FIN *takeovers* Retter *m* in der Not (*infrml*); **~ land** *n* PROP Außenbereich *m*; **~ market** *n* ECON weißer Markt *m*; **~ noise** *n* MATH *statistics* weißes Rauschen *nt*

White: ~ Paper *n BrE* LAW Gesetzesvorlage *f*

white: ~ revolution *n* ECON *agricultural* weiße Revolution *f*

whitewash *vt infrml* GEN COMM rehabilitieren, reinwaschen, schönfärben, wieder zahlungsfähig erklären, MEDIA, POL reinwaschen

whitewashing *n infrml* GEN COMM Rehabilitation *f*

whittle down *vt* GEN COMM *costs, commissions* beschneiden, kürzen

whittling: ~ down *n* GEN COMM Beschneidung *f*, Kürzung *f*

whiz: ~ kid *n infrml* GEN COMM Genie *nt*, kluger Kopf *m* (*infrml*), Wunderkind *nt*, MGMNT Senkrechtstarter *m* (*infrml*)

WHO *abbr* (*World Health Organization*) ECON, WEL WHO (*Weltgesundheitsorganisation*)

whole *adj* GEN COMM ganz, gesamt; **~-cargo charter** *n* TRANSP Gesamtfrachtcharter *f*; **~-life assurance** *n BrE* (*cf insurance payable at death AmE, whole-life insurance AmE*) INS Lebensversicherung *f* auf den Todesfall, Todesfallversicherung *f*; **~-life assurance policy** *n BrE*

(*cf whole-life insurance policy AmE*) INS Todesfallversicherungspolice *f*; **~-life insurance** *n AmE* (*cf assurance payable at death BrE, whole-life assurance BrE*) INS Lebensversicherung *f* auf den Todesfall, Todesfallversicherung *f*; **~-life insurance policy** *n AmE* (*cf whole-life assurance policy BrE*) INS Todesfallversicherungspolice *f*; **~ loan** *n* FIN *property* Gesamtdarlehen *nt*

wholesale *n* GEN COMM Großhandel *m*; ♦ **by ~** GEN COMM im Großhandel, zum Großhandelspreis

wholesale: ~ bank *n* BANK auf das Großkundengeschäft ausgerichtete Bank *f*; **~ business** *n* GEN COMM Engrosverkauf *m*, Großhandel *m*, Großhandelsgeschäft *nt*; **~ dealer** *n* ECON, GEN COMM, S&M *firm* Großhandelsbetrieb, *person* Großhändler, in *m,f*, Großhandelskauffrau *f*, Großhandelskaufmann *m*, Großhandelsperson *f*, Grossist, in *m,f*; **~ delivery** *n* GEN COMM, S&M Großhandelslieferung *f*; **~ deposits** *n pl* BANK, FIN Geldanlage *f* im Interbankgeschäft, Geldmarktanlagen *f pl*; **~ goods** *n pl* ECON, GEN COMM, IND Großhandelsartikel *m pl*, Großhandelserzeugnisse *nt pl*; **~ manufacture** *n* ECON, GEN COMM, IND fabrikmäßige Herstellung *f*, Massenfabrikation *f*, Serienfabrikation *f*; **~ market** *n* GEN COMM Großmarkt *m*, Großhandelsmarkt *m*; **~ merchant** *n* ECON, S&M *firm* Großhandelsbetrieb, *person* Großhändler, in *m,f*, Großhandelskauffrau *f*, Großhandelskaufmann *m*, Großhandelsperson *f*, Grossist, in *m,f*; **~ money market** *n* FIN Interbankengeldmarkt *m*; **~ price** *n* GEN COMM, S&M Großhandelspreis *m*; **~ price index** *n* MATH *statistics* Großhandelspreisindex *m*; **~ price inflation** *n* ECON Großhandelspreisinflation *f*; **~ purchasing** *n* S&M Großhandelskauf *m*

wholesaler *n* ECON, S&M *firm* Großhandelsbetrieb, *person* Großhändler, in *m,f*, Großhandelskauffrau *f*, Großhandelskaufmann *m*, Großhandelsperson *f*, Grossist, in *m,f*

wholesale: ~ trade *n* ECON, S&M Großhandel *m*; **~ trader** *n* ECON, S&M *firm* Großhandelsbetrieb, *person* Großhändler, in *m,f*, Großhandelskaufmann *m*, Großhandelskauffrau *f*, Großhandelsperson *f*, Grossist, in *m,f*

wholesaling *n* ECON, S&M Großhandelsgewerbe *nt*

wholly: ~ and exclusively *phr* LAW vollständig und ausschließlich

whse *abbr* (*warehouse*) GEN COMM, IMP/EXP, S&M, TRANSP Dep. (*Depot*), Lag. (*Lager*), Lagergebäude *nt*, Lagerhaus *nt*, Mag. (*Magazin*), Speicher *m*, Warenlager *nt*, Zollgutlager *nt*

wide *adj* GEN COMM breit; ♦ **~ of the mark** *infrml* GEN COMM ganz unzutreffend

wide: ~-area network *n* (*WAN*) COMMS, COMP, MGMNT großflächiges Netz *nt* (*WAN*), Weitverkehrsnetz *nt* (*WAN*); **~-body aircraft** *n* TRANSP Großraumflugzeug *nt*; **~-cut gasoline** *n AmE* TRANSP *aircraft* Flugkraftstoff *m*

widely *adv* GEN COMM breit; **~ recognized** *phr* GEN COMM allgemein anerkannt

widen 1. *vt* GEN COMM ausdehnen, erweitern, vertiefen, TAX *tax base* erweitern; **2.** *vi* GEN COMM *gap* vertiefen

widened *adj* GEN COMM ausgedehnt, erweitert, vertieft, TAX erweitert

widening *n* GEN COMM Ausdehnung *f*, Erweiterung *f*, Vertiefung *f*, TAX Erweiterung *f*

wide: ~ range *n* GEN COMM, S&M *of goods, products*

breites Sortiment *nt*; **~-ranging** *adj* GEN COMM, POL *legislation* weitreichend

wider: ~ **share ownership** *n* ECON breit gestreuter Aktienbesitz

widespread *adj* GEN COMM üblich, weitverbreitet

widow: **~-and-orphan stock** *n* STOCK sichere Aktien mit hoher Dividende, mündelsichere Wertpapiere *nt pl*; **~'s bereavement allowance** *n* TAX Witwenfreibetrag *m*

wild: ~ **card** *n* COMP Globalzeichen *nt*, Joker *m*

wildcat: ~ **drilling** *n* ENVIR Versuchsbohrung *f* nach Erdöl; ~ **strike** *n* HRM wilder Streik *m*; ~ **venture** *n* GEN COMM gewagte Sache *f*, riskante Sache *f*, Schwindelunternehmen *nt*

wilfully: ~ **misrepresent the facts** *phr* LAW *contract* absichtlich falsche Angaben machen

will *n* LAW Testament *nt*

Williams: ~ **act** *n* LAW Williams-Gesetz *nt*

win *vt* GEN COMM, S&M *customers* werben; ♦ ~ **one's spurs** GEN COMM sich die Sporen verdienen; ~ **sb's favor** *AmE*, ~ **sb's favour** *BrE* GEN COMM jdn für sich gewinnen, jds Gunst erringen

win over *vt* GEN COMM überreden, herumkriegen (*jarg*), für sich gewinnen; ♦ **win sb over to one's way of thinking** GEN COMM jdn zur eigenen Denkungsart bekehren

Winchester: ~ **disk** *n* COMP *obs hardware* Winchesterplatte *f* (*obs*)

wind down *vt* GEN COMM *activities* reduzieren, *production* zurückfahren

wind up *vt* ACC abwickeln, GEN COMM *meeting* auslaufen lassen, *company, firm* zu Ende bringen, liquidieren, MGMNT *meeting* beenden

windfall: ~ **gain** *n* ECON, GEN COMM Zufallsgewinn *m*; ~ **loss** *n* ECON unerwarteter Verlust *m*; ~ **profit** *n* ECON, GEN COMM Zufallsgewinn *m*, unerwarteter Gewinn *m*; ~ **profits tax** *n* TAX Zusatzbesteuerung *f*; ~ **tax** *n* TAX Spekulationssteuer *f*

winding: ~ **down** *n* GEN COMM Reduzierung *f*; ~ **up** *n* GEN COMM *of company*, LAW Abwicklung *f*, Auflösung *f*, Liquidation *f*, MGMNT *of company* Abwicklung *f*, Liquidation *f*, *of meeting* Beenden *nt*; **~-up arrangements** *n pl* LAW *company law* Liquidationsvereinbarung *f*; **~-up order** *n* LAW gerichtlicher Liquidationsbeschluß *m*; **~-up period** *n* LAW Abwicklungszeitraum *m*; **~-up procedure** *n* LAW Abwicklungsverfahren *nt*; **~-up sale** *n* GEN COMM Ausverkauf *m* wegen Geschäftsaufgabe; **~-up value** *n* ACC *final value* Abschlußwert *m*, *liquidation* Liquidationswert *m*

window *n* COMP Fenster *nt*, GEN COMM *for tickets* Schalter *m*, *in shop* Fenster *nt*, Schaufenster *nt*, *opportunity* Gelegenheit *f*; ~ **bill** *n* GEN COMM Schaufensterplakat *nt*; ~ **display** *n* GEN COMM, S&M Auslage *f*, Schaufensterauslage *f*; **~-dressing** *n* ACC *annual accounts* Bilanzfrisur *f*, Frisieren *nt* der Bilanz, Window-Dressing *nt*, Bilanzkosmetik *f*, GEN COMM, S&M *shop display* Auslagendekoration *f*, Schaufensterdekoration *f*; ~ **envelope** *n* ADMIN Fensterbriefumschlag *m*, S&M Umschlag *m* mit Sichtfenster; **~-shopping** *n* GEN COMM Schaufensterbummel *m*; ~ **sticker** *n* GEN COMM Fensteraufkleber *m*

wind: ~ **power** *n* ENVIR Windenergie *f*

winds: ~ **of change** *n pl* GEN COMM, POL Umbruchstimmung *f*

wine: **~-bottling** *n* IND Weinabfüllung *f*; ~ **grower** *n* ECON *agriculture* Weinbauer, in *m,f*, Winzer, in *m,f*; ~ **growing** *n* ECON *agriculture* Weinanbau *m*; **~-growing district** *n* ECON Weinanbaugebiet *nt*, Weinbaugebiet *nt*; ~ **harvest** *n* ECON Weinernte *f*, Weinlese *f*; ~ **industry** *n* IND Weinindustrie *f*; ~ **list** *n* LEIS Weinkarte *f*; ~ **merchant** *n* GEN COMM Weinhändler, in *m,f*; **~-producing area** *n* ECON Weinanbaugebiet *nt*, Weinbaugebiet *nt*

winery *n* GEN COMM Weingut *nt*, Weinkellerei *f*

wine: ~ **trade** *n* GEN COMM Weinhandel *m*; ~ **waiter** *n* HRM, LEIS Weinkellner *m*; ~ **warehouse** *n* IMP/EXP *stock control* Weinlager *nt*

wing *n* TRANSP Flügel *m*

winged: ~ **pallet** *n* TRANSP Flügelpalette *f*

wing: ~ **tank** *n* TRANSP *shipping* Flügeltank *m*

winning *adj* GEN COMM siegreich

winter: ~ **sales** *n pl* S&M Winterschlußverkauf *m*

WIP *abbr* (*work in process AmE, work in progress BrE*) ACC, ECON, GEN COMM laufende Arbeit *f*, noch nicht abgeschlossene Arbeit *f*, unfertige Erzeugnisse *nt pl*

wipe off *vt* FIN *debt* zurückzahlen

wipe out *vt* GEN COMM ausradieren, ausrotten

WIPO *abbr* (*World Intellectual Property Organization*) LAW Weltorganisation *f* für geistiges Eigentum

wireless: ~ **certificate** *n* TRANSP Funk-Zertifikat *nt*; ~ **log book** *n* TRANSP Funk-Logbuch *nt*

wire: ~ **service** *n* *AmE* (*cf news agency BrE*) COMMS *press*, GEN COMM, MEDIA Nachrichtenagentur *f*

wiretapping *n* COMMS Abhören *nt* (*jarg*), Anzapfen *nt* von Leitungen

withdraw 1. *vt* ACC auflösen, BANK abheben, streichen, ECON, FIN, GEN COMM abheben, *offer* entziehen, zurückziehen, INS, LAW austreten; ♦ ~ **from circulation** GEN COMM, FIN aus dem Umlauf ziehen; ~ **a sum from a bank account** BANK einen Betrag von einem Bankkonto abheben; **2.** *vi* GEN COMM sich zurückziehen; ♦ ~ **from** GEN COMM austreten aus, *contract* zurücktreten von

withdrawal *n* ACC Auflösung *f*, BANK Abhebung *f*, Streichung *f*, ECON, FIN, GEN COMM Abhebung *f*, Entziehung *f*, Rückzug *m*, Ausscheiden *nt*, Zurückziehung *f*, INS, LAW Austritt *m*; ~ **of capital** *n* BANK Kapitalentnahme *f*; ~ **from stocks** *n* ACC, ADMIN Lagerentnahme *f*, GEN COMM Reserveentnahme *f*; ~ **plan** *n* STOCK Entnahmeplan *m*; ~ **warrant** *n* BANK Auszahlungsermächtigung *f*

withhold *vt* GEN COMM einbehalten, zurückhalten; ♦ ~ **information** LAW Information zurückhalten

withholding *n* STOCK *securities, taxes* Abzug *m*, Einbehaltung *f*; ~ **tax** *n* TAX Abzugssteuer *f*, Quellensteuer *f*, *on capital invested* einbehaltene Kapitalertragssteuer *f*

within *prep* GEN COMM innerhalb; ♦ ~ **the allotted time frame** GEN COMM im zeitlichen Rahmen; ~ **the bounds of possibility** GEN COMM im Bereich des Möglichen; ~ **the framework of** GEN COMM im Rahmen von; ~ **a period of** GEN COMM innerhalb einer Frist von; ~ **prescribed limits** LAW innerhalb vorgeschriebener Grenzen; ~ **the prescribed time** GEN COMM innerhalb der vorgeschriebenen Zeit; ~ **reach** GEN COMM in Reichweite

without *prep* GEN COMM exklusive, ohne; ♦ ~ **any liability on our part** GEN COMM, LAW ohne jegliche Haftung unsererseits, ohne jegliche Verpflichtung unsererseits; ~ **authorization** GEN COMM unbefugt; ~ **charge** (*w.c.*) GEN COMM gebührenfrei, kostenlos, wertfrei; ~ **delay** GEN COMM unverzüglich; ~ **engagement** GEN COMM freibleibend, ohne Gewähr, unverbindlich; ~ **fault** GEN COMM fehlerfrei; ~ **a hitch** GEN COMM reibungslos; ~ **just cause** LAW unbegründet; ~ **notice** GEN COMM fristlos; ~ **obligation** GEN COMM unverbindlich, S&M ohne Verpflichtung; ~ **permanent residence** LAW ohne festen Wohnsitz; ~ **prejudice** (*wp*) GEN COMM ohne Verbindlichkeit, *unprejudiced* unvoreingenommen, INS ohne Rechtsnachteil; ~ **previous warning** GEN COMM ohne Vorwarnung; ~ **privilege** (*x pri*) GEN COMM ohne Vorrecht; ~ **qualification** ACC *auditing* bedingungslos, ohne Vorbehalt *m*, vorbehaltslos, LAW *contracts* bedingungslos; ~ **respite** COMMS *from work* ohne Aufschub; ~ **stipulation** LAW *contracts* bedingungslos; ~ **warning** GEN COMM unerwartet; ~ **the whip** *BrE jarg* (*cf off the reservation AmE*) POL nicht mehr der Parteidisziplin unterworfen, parteiabtrünnig, parteiuntreu

witness 1. *n* GEN COMM, LAW Zeuge *m*, Zeugin *f*; **2.** *vt* GEN COMM *signature* bestätigen; ♦ ~ **sth** LAW *observe* Zeuge von etw sein

witness: ~ **for the defence** *BrE*, ~ **for the defense** *AmE* *n* LAW Verteidigungszeuge *m*, Verteidigungszeugin *f*, Zeuge *m* der Verteidigung, Zeugin *f* der Verteidigung; ~ **for the prosecution** *n* LAW Belastungszeuge *m*, Belastungszeugin *f*, Zeuge *m* der Anklage, Zeugin *f* der Anklage, Zeuge *m* der Staatsanwaltschaft, Zeugin *f* der Staatsanwaltschaft

wizard *n* COMP Computergenie *nt*

wk. *abbr* (*week*) GEN COMM W (*Woche*)

WMO *abbr* (*World Meteorological Organization*) ENVIR Weltorganisation *f* für Meteorologie

WOL *abbr* (*wharfowner's liability*) LAW *commercial* Haftung *f* des Kaibesitzers

wolf *n jarg* STOCK gerissener Börsianer

won: ~ **invoice** *n* GEN COMM gewonnene Rechnung *f*

wood *n* (*w*) IND Holz *nt*; ~ **cover** *n* IND Holzbelag *m*

wooden: ~ **pallet** *n* TRANSP *distribution* Holzpalette *f*

woodlands *n pl* ENVIR, GEN COMM Waldgebiet *nt*, Waldland *nt*

wood: ~**-processing industry** *n* IND holzverarbeitende Gewerbe *nt pl*

woods: **be out of the** ~ *phr* GEN COMM über den Berg sein

wool *n* GEN COMM Wolle *f*; ~ **industry** *n* IND Wollindustrie *f*

woollen: ~ **manufacturer** *n* IND Hersteller *m* von Wollwaren

wool: ~ **merchant** *n* GEN COMM Wollhändler, in *m,f*; ~ **trade** *n* GEN COMM Wollhandel *m*

word *n* GEN COMM Wort *nt*; ~ **of advice** *n* GEN COMM, MGMNT Hinweis *m*, Rat *m*, Ratschlag *m*; ~ **count** *n* COMP, MEDIA Wörterzählung *f*; ~ **and device mark** *n* PATENTS Wort- und Bildzeichen *nt*; ~ **engineering** *n* POL Manipulation *f* des Wortlauts, staatlich gefilterte Information *f*, verbale Fügung *f*; ~ **of honour** *n* LAW Ehrenwort *nt*

wording *n* GEN COMM, LAW *of contract* Formulierung *f*, Wortlaut *m*, POL Kommentierung *f*; ~ **of a vote** *n* GEN COMM Wortlaut *m* einer Abstimmung

word: ~ **length** *n* COMP Wortlänge *f*; ~**-of-mouth**

advertising *n* S&M Mund-zu-Mund Werbung *f*; ~**-of-mouth marketing** *n* S&M Mund-zu-Mund Werbung *f*; ~**-perfect** *adj AmE* ADMIN textsicher, sicher in Textbeherrschung; ~ **processing** *n* COMP Textverarbeitung *f*; ~ **processing center** *AmE*, ~ **processing centre** *BrE n* COMP Textverarbeitungsabteilung *f*, Textverarbeitungsarbeitsplatz *m*, Textverarbeitungszentrum *nt*; ~ **processing software** *n* COMP Textverarbeitungssoftware *f*; ~ **processing system** *n* COMP Textverarbeitungssystem *nt*; ~ **processor** *n* (*WP*) COMP Textverarbeitungssystem *nt*

words: ~ **per minute** *n pl* (*wpm*) ADMIN Wörter *nt pl* pro Minute

word: ~ **of warning** *n* GEN COMM mahnendes Wort *nt*, Warnung *f*; ~ **wrap** *n* COMP Zeilenumbruch *m*

work 1. *n* GEN COMM Arbeit *f*; ♦ **be at** ~ GEN COMM *machine in use* im Betrieb sein, im Gang sein, *person* arbeiten; **get down to** ~ GEN COMM sich an die Arbeit machen; **be out of** ~ HRM arbeitslos sein; **be up to one's neck in** ~ *infrml* HRM mit Arbeit eingedeckt sein **2.** *vt* PATENTS ausnutzen, auswerten, praktisch verwerten; **3.** *vi* GEN COMM *machine* funktionieren, *person* arbeiten; ♦ ~ **alongside** HRM zusammenarbeiten mit; ~ **alternate weekends** GEN COMM jedes zweite Wochenende arbeiten; ~ **as part of a team** HRM im Team arbeiten; ~ **as a temp** GEN COMM, HRM als Aushilfssekretär arbeiten; ~ **closely with sb** GEN COMM eng mit jdm zusammenarbeiten; ~ **flat out** *infrml* GEN COMM auf Hochtouren arbeiten (*infrml*), sich voll verausgaben; ~ **for abeyance** GEN COMM, HRM für eine unbesetzte Stelle arbeiten; ~ **for a living** HRM, WEL seinen Lebensunterhalt verdienen; ~ **full-time** HRM, WEL ganzzeitlich arbeiten; ~ **half-time** GEN COMM halbtags arbeiten; ~ **in partnership with** GEN COMM, MGMNT sich assoziieren mit, zusammenarbeiten mit; ~ **in shifts** HRM Schichtarbeit machen; ~ **in tandem with** GEN COMM gemeinsam arbeiten mit; ~ **overtime** HRM Überstunden machen; ~ **together** GEN COMM zusammenarbeiten; ~ **to a very tight schedule** GEN COMM ein volles Programm haben, nach knapp bemessenem Zeitplan arbeiten

work down *vt* GEN COMM *inventories* abarbeiten, verringern

work off *vt* FIN *debts* abarbeiten, GEN COMM abarbeiten, abbauen; ♦ ~ **a debt** FIN eine Schuld abarbeiten

work out *vt* GEN COMM *settlement* herbeiführen, *terms, details* festlegen, *total, interest* berechnen, ausrechnen, HRM *one's notice* ausarbeiten; ♦ ~ **at** GEN COMM *amount* to betragen

work through *vt* HRM durcharbeiten

workable *adj* GEN COMM funktionsfähig; ~ **competition** *n* ECON effektiver Wettbewerb *m*, funktionsfähiger Wettbewerb *m*; ~ **hatch** *n* (*WH*) TRANSP *charter party* Arbeitsluke *f*

workaholic *n* HRM Arbeitsbesessene(r) *mf* [decl. as adj], Workaholic *m*

work: ~ **area** *n* GEN COMM Arbeitsbereich *m*, Arbeitsplatz *m*; ~ **assignment** *n* HRM Arbeitsanweisung *f*; ~ **attitude** *n* HRM Arbeitsmoral *f*; ~ **backlog** *n* GEN COMM, IND Angebotsüberhang *m*, Rückstand *m*, unerledigte Aufträge *m pl*; ~ **by contract** *n* HRM Vertragsarbeit *f*; ~ **center** *AmE*, ~ **centre** *BrE n* GEN COMM Arbeitsplatz *m*; ~ **classification** *n* HRM Berufszugehörigkeit *f*; ~ **content** *n* GEN COMM Arbeitsinhalt *m*, Arbeitsvolumen *nt*; ~ **cycle** *n* GEN COMM Arbeitstakt *m*, HRM Arbeitsgang *m*, IND Produktionszyklus *m*

workday *n AmE* (*cf working day BrE*) GEN COMM, HRM, IND Arbeitstag *m*

work: ~ **design** *n* GEN COMM Arbeitsgestaltung *f*

worker *n* HRM Arbeiter, in *m,f*, Arbeitskraft *f*; ~ **buyout** *n* FIN, HRM Aufkauf *m* durch die Belegschaft, Betriebsübernahme *f* durch Arbeitnehmer, Buy-out *nt* von Arbeitskräften; ~ **compensation insurance** *n* HRM, INS Berufsunfall- und Krankenversicherung *f*, Unfallversicherung *f*; ~ **control** *n* HRM Arbeiterselbstbestimmung *f*; ~ **director** *n* HRM, MGMNT Arbeitsdirektor, in *m,f*; ~ **involvement** *n* HRM Arbeitspartizipation *f*, Arbeiterbeteiligung *f*; ~ **participation** *n* HRM Arbeitspartizipation *f*

workers': ~ **collective** *n* HRM Arbeiterkollektiv *nt*; ~ **compensation** *n* HRM Unfallentschädigung *f*; ~ **compensation act** *n* HRM Gesetzgebung zur Betriebshaftpflicht; ~ **compensation and employers' liability insuring agreement** *n* INS Berufsunfallpflichtversicherung *f*, Haftpflichtversicherung *f* des Arbeitgebers für Arbeitsunfälle, obligatorische Arbeitsunfallversicherung *f*; ~ **control** *n* HRM Arbeiterselbstbestimmung *f*; ~ **cooperative** *n* ECON, HRM Arbeitergenossenschaft *f*

work: ~ **ethic** *n* HRM, MGMNT Arbeitsethos *nt*; ~ **experience** *n* GEN COMM, HRM, MGMNT Arbeitserfahrung *f*

workfare *n* ECON Sozialleistungen *f pl* mit Gegenleistung

work: ~ **file** *n* ADMIN Arbeitsdatei *f*; ~ **flow** *n* GEN COMM Arbeitsablauf *m*; ~ **flow planning** *n* GEN COMM, MGMNT Arbeitsablaufplanung *f*

workforce *n* GEN COMM, HRM, IND *staff* Arbeiterschaft *f*, Belegschaft *f*, Beschäftigte *pl*, Personalbestand *m*, MGMNT Personalbestand *m*

work: ~ **history** *n* HRM beruflicher Werdegang *m*; ~**-in** *n* HRM *in EC regulations* Work-in *nt*

working 1. *adj* GEN COMM arbeitend; ♦ **have a** ~ **knowledge of sth** GEN COMM, HRM Grundkenntnisse von etw haben; **in** ~ **order** GEN COMM, IND *equipment* funktionstüchtig; ~ **time saved** TRANSP *charter party* eingesparte Arbeitszeit *f*; **all** ~ **time saved** TRANSP *charter party* eingesparte Gesamtarbeitszeit *f*; **2.** *n* GEN COMM Arbeiten *nt*, *utilization of resources* Verwertung *f*, IND, PATENTS Auswertung *f*, Patentauswertung *f*, Verwertung *f*

working: ~ **account** *n* BANK Erfolgskonto *nt*; ~ **area** *n* HRM *in office* Arbeitsbereich *m*, Arbeitsplatz *m*, Arbeitsraum *m*; ~ **atmosphere** *n* HRM, POL Arbeitsklima *nt*; ~ **breakfast** *n* GEN COMM Arbeitsfrühstück *nt*; ~ **capital** *n* FIN, GEN COMM Betriebskapital *nt*, Betriebsmittel *nt*; ~ **capital advance** *n* FIN, GEN COMM Betriebskapitalvorschuß *m*, Betriebsmittelvorschuß *m*; ~ **class** *n* HRM Arbeiterklasse *f*; ~ **conditions** *n pl* HRM Arbeitsbedingungen *f pl*; ~ **day** *n BrE* (*cf workday AmE*) GEN COMM, HRM, IND Arbeitstag *m*; ~ **dinner** *n* GEN COMM Arbeitsessen *nt*; ~ **environment** *n* HRM Arbeitsumfeld *nt*, Arbeitsumwelt *f*; ~ **group** *n* GEN COMM, POL Arbeitsgruppe *f*; ~ **holiday** *n* GEN COMM Arbeitsurlaub *m*; ~ **hours** *n pl* GEN COMM, HRM Arbeitszeit *f*; ~ **hypothesis** *n* GEN COMM Arbeitshypothese *f*; ~ **interest** *n* FIN arbeitender Zins *m*; ~ **life** *n* HRM Berufsleben *nt*; ~ **lunch** *n* GEN COMM Arbeitsessen *nt*; ~ **man** *n* HRM Arbeiter *m*, berufstätiger Mann *m*;

~ **meeting** *n* ACC Arbeitssitzung *f*; ~ **paper** *n* ACC Arbeitsdokument *nt*, ADMIN, POL Arbeitspapier *nt*, Arbeitsunterlage *f*; ~ **party** *n* (*WIP*) GEN COMM, HRM, POL Arbeitsgruppe *f*, Arbeitsausschuß *m*; ~ **patterns** *n pl* HRM Arbeitsrhythmus *m*; ~ **poor** *n pl* HRM Arbeitnehmer, deren Einkommen unter dem Existenzminimum liegt; ~ **population** *n* HRM Erwerbsbevölkerung *f*; ~ **practice** *n* GEN COMM Arbeitspraxis *f*; ~ **pressure** *n* (*WP*) IND Arbeitsdruck *m*, Betriebsdruck *m*; ~ **program** *n* COMP Arbeitsprogramm *nt*, GEN COMM *AmE see working programme BrE*; ~ **programme** *n BrE* GEN COMM Arbeitsplan *m*; ~ **session** *n* GEN COMM Arbeitssitzung *f*; ~ **storage** *n* COMP Arbeitsspeicher *m*; ~ **time** *n* GEN COMM, HRM Arbeitszeit *f*; ~ **timetable** *n* GEN COMM Arbeitszeitplan *m*; ~ **visa** *n* ADMIN Arbeitserlaubnis *f*; ~ **week** *n BrE* (*cf workweek AmE*) HRM Arbeitswoche *f*; ~ **woman** *n* HRM Arbeiterin *f*, berufstätige Frau *f*; ~ **year** *n* GEN COMM Betriebsjahr *nt*

work: ~ **in process** *n AmE* (*WIP, cf work in progress BrE*) ACC, ECON, GEN COMM laufende Arbeit *f*, noch nicht abgeschlossene Arbeit *f*, unfertige Erzeugnisse *nt pl*; ~**-in-process document** *n AmE* (*cf work-in-progress document BrE*) GEN COMM Arbeitsdokument *nt*; ~**-in-progress** *n BrE* (*WIP, cf work-in-process AmE*) ACC, ECON, GEN COMM laufende Arbeit *f*, noch nicht abgeschlossene Arbeit *f*, unfertige Erzeugnisse *nt pl*; ~**-in-progress document** *n BrE* (*cf work-in-process document AmE*); GEN COMM Arbeitsdokument *nt*

workless *adj* ECON, HRM, WEL arbeitslos

workload *n* GEN COMM, HRM, IND, MGMNT Arbeitsbelastung *f*, Arbeitspensum *nt*, Arbeitsvorrat *m*

work: ~ **location** *n* HRM Arbeitsplatz *m*

workman *n* HRM Arbeiter *m*

work: ~ **management** *n* HRM, MGMNT Arbeitseinteilung *f*

workmanship *n* GEN COMM Arbeit *f*, Arbeitsqualität *f*

workmate *n* GEN COMM Arbeitskamerad, in *m,f*, Arbeitskollege *m*, Arbeitskollegin *f*

work: ~ **order** *n* GEN COMM Arbeitsauftrag *m*, HRM Arbeitsanweisung *f*, IND Arbeitsauftrag *m*; ~ **organization** *n* GEN COMM Arbeitsorganisation *f*; ~ **permit** *n* HRM Arbeitserlaubnis *f*

workplace *n* ADMIN, GEN COMM, HRM Arbeitsplatz *m*, Betrieb *m*; ~ **bargaining** *n* HRM Tarifverhandlungen *f pl* auf Betriebsbasis; ~ **layout** *n* HRM Arbeitsplatzgestaltung *f*

work: ~ **prospects** *n pl* HRM Berufsaussichten *f pl*

works *n* IND Arbeitsplatz *m*, Betrieb *m*, Werk *nt*

works: ~ **canteen** *n* HRM Betriebskantine *f*

work: ~ **schedule** *n* ADMIN, GEN COMM, MGMNT Arbeitsplan *m*, Arbeitsprogramm *nt*, Arbeitszeiteinteilung *f*; ~ **scheduling** *n* IND Arbeitsplanung *f*, Arbeitsvorbereitung *f*, MGMNT Arbeitsvorbereitung *f*

works: ~ **committee** *n BrE* HRM Betriebsrat *m*; ~ **contract** *n* GEN COMM, LAW Werkvertrag *m*; ~ **council** *n BrE* HRM Betriebsrat *m*

work: ~**-sharing** *n* HRM Arbeitsteilung *f*; ~ **sheet** *n* ACC, COMP Arbeitsblatt *nt*, Abschlußblatt *nt*

workshop *n* GEN COMM *for training* Werkstatt *f*, IND kleiner Betrieb *m*, Werkstatt *f*; ~ **bargaining** *n* HRM Tarifverhandlungen *f pl* auf Betriebsbasis

work: ~ **simplification** *n* HRM, MGMNT Arbeitsvereinfachung *f*

works: ~ **manager** *n* HRM, IND Betriebsleiter, in *m,f*, Werkleiter, in *m,f*

work: ~ **space** n HRM Arbeitsraum m, IND Arbeitsbereich m

works: ~ **regulations** n pl HRM, WEL Betriebsordnung f

work: ~ **station** n ADMIN Dienstort m, COMP Datenstation f, Workstation f (jarg), GEN COMM Arbeitsplatz m, Workstation f (jarg), HRM Datenstation f; ~ **stoppage** n HRM Arbeitsunterbrechung f; ~ **stress** n HRM, MGMNT Arbeitsstreß m; ~ **structuring** n GEN COMM, HRM Arbeitsgestaltung f; ~ **study** n GEN COMM, HRM, MGMNT Arbeitsstudie f; ~ **time study** n GEN COMM, HRM, IND, MGMNT Arbeitszeiteinteilung f, Arbeitszeitermittlung f, Arbeitszeitstudie f, Zeitstudie f

workweek n AmE (cf working week BrE) HRM Arbeitswoche f

World: ~ **Bank** n BANK Weltbank f; ~ **Bank classification of countries** n ECON Länderklassifikation f der Weltbank

world n GEN COMM Welt f; ◆ **all over the** ~ GEN COMM in der ganzen Welt, weltweit

World: ~ **Federation of Stock Exchanges** n (WFSE) STOCK Börsenweltverband m; ~ **Federation of Trade Unions** n (WFTU) HRM Internationaler Gewerkschaftsbund m (IGB), Weltgewerkschaftsbund m; ~ **Federation of United Nations Associations** n (WFUNA) ADMIN Weltweite Organisation f der UN-Verbände

world: ~ **class** n GEN COMM Weltklasse f, Weltrang m; ~ **confederation** n ECON Weltverband m; ~ **consumption** n ECON, ENVIR Weltverbrauch m; ~ **debt problem** n ECON Problem nt der Weltverschuldung, weltweites Schuldenproblem nt; ~ **economic groupings** n pl ECON Weltwirtschaftsgruppierungen f pl; ~ **economic summit** n ECON, POL Weltwirtschaftsgipfel m; ~ **economy** n ECON Weltwirtschaft f; ~ **exports** n pl IMP/EXP Weltexporte m pl; ~ **of finance** n FIN Finanzwelt f

World: ~ **Food Programme** n (WFP) ECON, WEL Welthungerhilfeprogramm nt (WFP); ~ **Health Organization** n (WHO) ECON, WEL Weltgesundheitsorganisation f (WHO)

world: ~ **inflation** n ECON weltweite Inflation f

World: ~ **Intellectual Property Organization** n (WIPO) LAW, PATENTS Weltorganisation f für geistiges Eigentum

world: ~ **leader** n GEN COMM, IND, S&M weltweit führendes Unternehmen nt; ~ **market** n ECON Weltmarkt m

World: ~ **Meteorological Organization** n (WMO) ENVIR Weltorganisation f für Meteorologie

world: ~ **monetary reserve assets** n pl FIN Weltwährungsreservevermögen nt; ~ **monetary system** n FIN Weltwährungssystem nt

World: ~ **Power Conference** n ENVIR, POL Weltenergiekonferenz f

world: ~ **price** n ECON Weltpreis m; ~ **systems perspective** n ECON Weltsystemperspektive f; ~ **trade** n ECON Welthandel m; ~ **trade center** AmE, ~ **trade centre** BrE n (WTC) ECON, S&M Welthandelszentrum nt; ~ **trade route** n TRANSP shipping Welthandelsroute f

World: ~ **University Service** n (WUS) WEL weltweiter Universitätsdienst m; ~ **War I** n POL Erster Weltkrieg m; ~ **War II** n POL Zweiter Weltkrieg m (WK II)

world: ~ **welfare** n ECON, WEL weltweiter Wohlstand m

worldwide 1. adj GEN COMM global, weltumspannend, weltweit; ◆ **on a** ~ **scale** GEN COMM weltweit reichend; **2.** adv GEN COMM weltweit

Worldwide: ~ **Air Cargo Commodity Classification** n (WACCC) TRANSP weltweite Luftfrachtgüter-Klassifizierung f

World: ~ **Wide Fund for Nature** n (WWF) ENVIR Weltverband m zum Schutz wildlebender Tiere (WWF)

worn: ~ **out** adj GEN COMM ausgedient, HRM person erschöpft

worried adj GEN COMM beunruhigt

worry vt GEN COMM beunruhigen

worsen vi GEN COMM sich verschlechtern

worsening n GEN COMM Verschlechterung f; ~ **in the balance of payments** n FIN Zahlungsbilanzverschlechterung f

worse: ~ **off** adj GEN COMM schlechtergestellt

worst: ~-**case projection** n ECON, GEN COMM Projektion f des ungünstigsten Falles; ~-**case scenario** n ECON, GEN COMM Szenario nt für den ungünstigsten Fall

worth 1. adj ◆ **be** ~ STOCK wert sein; **2.** n GEN COMM Wert m

worthless adj GEN COMM wertlos

worthwhile adj GEN COMM der Mühe wert, lohnend

wound: ~ **down** adj GEN COMM reduziert

wove: ~ **paper** n ADMIN ungeripptes Papier nt

wp abbr (without prejudice) INS ohne Rechtsnachteil

WP abbr COMP (word processor) Textverarbeitungssystem nt, IND (working pressure) Arbeitsdruck m, Betriebsdruck m

W/P abbr (working party) GEN COMM, POL Arbeitsgruppe f

WPA abbr (with particular average) INS einschließlich besonderer Havarieschäden

wpm abbr (words per minute) ADMIN WpM(Wörter pro Minute)

WR abbr (warehouse receipt) IMP/EXP, LAW, TRANSP Lagerschein m

wrap vt GEN COMM verpacken

wrap up vt GEN COMM meeting, discussion zu Ende bringen, package einwickeln

wraparound n COMP memory zyklische Adreßfolge f, text Zeilenumbruch m; ~ **annuity** n FIN Zusatzannuität f; ~ **mortgage** n BANK Zusatzhypothek f

wrapped adj GEN COMM eingeschlagen, eingewickelt

wrapper n GEN COMM, S&M Schutzumschlag m, Verpackung f

wrapping n GEN COMM Verpackung f, IND Umhüllung f, S&M Verpackung f

wrap: ~-**up** n AmE POL Abschlußrede f, Schlußformulierung f einer Rede

wreck n TRANSP Wrack nt

wreckage n TRANSP Strandgut nt

writ n LAW Verfügung f; ~ **of attachment** n LAW Arrestbefehl m; ~ **of summons** n LAW Ladung f

write 1. vt COMP to disk, memory, GEN COMM schreiben; ◆ ~ **against sth** STOCK gegen etw verkaufen; ~ **business** INS Versicherungsverträge abschließen; ~ **a fair copy** GEN COMM, MEDIA, S&M advertisement eine Reinschrift anfertigen; ~ **an option against another option** STOCK eine Option gegen eine andere Option verkaufen; ~ **a stock option** STOCK eine Aktienoption verkaufen

write back 1. *vt* ACC auflösen, zurückbuchen; **2.** *vi* COMMS schriftlich antworten, zurückschreiben

write down *vt* ACC abschreiben, GEN COMM *make note of* aufschreiben, STOCK im Wert verringern

write off *vt* ACC abbuchen, ausbuchen, FIN abschreiben, GEN COMM, INS abschreiben, ausbuchen; ◆ **~ over ten years** ACC über zehn Jahre abschreiben lassen; **~ the debts incurred by a country** BANK die von einem Land aufgenommenen Kredite abschreiben

write out *vt* ADMIN ausführlich beschreiben, GEN COMM *cheque, receipt* ausstellen, LAW ausfertigen

write up *vt* ACC *as an asset* zuschreiben

write-in: **~ candidate** *n AmE* POL auf einem Stimmzettel selbst einzutragender Kandidat; **~ vote** *n AmE* POL Stimme für den auf der freien Zeile des Stimmzettels eingetragenen Kandidat

write-off *n* ACC, FIN Ausbuchung *f*, GEN COMM Abschreibung *f*, *event* Reinfall *m*, INS *vehicle* Totalschaden *m*; ◆ **be a ~** *infrml* GEN COMM vollständig abgeschrieben sein

write-protect *vt* COMP mit Schreibschutz versehen

write-protected *adj* COMP schreibgeschützt

writ: **~ of error** *n* LAW Revisionszulassungsbeschluß *m*

write-up *n* ACC Zuschreibung *f*, GEN COMM Höherbewertung *f*, MEDIA *in press* Bericht *m*, Pressebericht *m*, *of play, film* Kritik *f*

writing *n* COMMS, GEN COMM Schrift *f*; ◆ **in ~** COMMS, GEN COMM in Schriftform, schriftlich

writing: **~ back** *n* ACC Rückbuchung *f*, Zurückbuchung *f*, Auflösung *f*; **~-down allowance** *n* TAX Abschreibungsbetrag *m*; **~ naked** *n* STOCK ungedeckter Verkauf *m*; **~-off** *n* ACC Abschreibung *f*; **~ pad** *n* GEN COMM Schreibpapier *nt*

writ: **~ of sequestration** *n* LAW gerichtliche Einsetzung *f* eines Zwangsverwalters; **~ of subpoena** *n* LAW Ladung *f* unter Strafandrohung

written *adj* COMMS, GEN COMM schriftlich; **~ agreement** *n* GEN COMM, LAW schriftliche Vereinbarung *f*; **~ call** *n* STOCK verkaufte Kaufoption *f*; **~ declaration** *n* GEN COMM, LAW schriftliche Erklärung *f*; **~-down value** *n* ACC Restwert *m*, GEN COMM Buchwert *m*; **~ evidence** *n* LAW schriftlicher Beweis *m*; **~ line** *n* INS akzeptierter Anteil *m*; **~ off** *adj* ACC abgeschrieben, INS ausgebucht;

~ offer *n* GEN COMM schriftliches Angebot *nt*; **~-off receivables** *n pl* FIN abgeschriebene Forderungen *f pl*; **~ option** *n* STOCK verkaufte Option *f*; **~ order to pay** *n* ACC schriftlicher Zahlungsbefehl *m*; **~ put** *n* STOCK verkaufte Verkaufsoption *f*; **~ warning** *n* HRM schriftliche Warnung *f*

wro *abbr* (*war risk only*) INS nur gegen Kriegsrisiko versichert

wrong 1. *adj* GEN COMM *answer* falsch, unrichtig; ◆ **be in the ~ job** HRM im falschen Job sein; **be on the ~ track** GEN COMM auf der falschen Fährte sein, auf der falschen Spur sein; **2.** *n* LAW Unrecht *nt*; ◆ **be in the ~** GEN COMM Unrecht haben

wrong: **~ connection** *n* COMMS *telephone* falsche Verbindung *f*

wrongdoing *n* LAW Missetat *f*

wronged: **~ party** *n* LAW Geschädigte(r) *mf* [decl. as adj], Verletzte(r) *mf* [decl. as adj]

wrongful *adj* LAW unrechtmäßig; **~ dismissal** *n* HRM, LAW grundlose Entlassung *f*, ungerechtfertigte Entlassung *f*

wrongly *adv* GEN COMM fälschlicherweise, zu Unrecht, falsch

wt *abbr* (*weight*) GEN COMM, MATH, TRANSP Gw. (*Gewicht*)

WTC *abbr* ECON, S&M (*world trade center AmE, world trade centre BrE*) Welthandelszentrum *nt*

wunderkind *n* COMP, GEN COMM, MATH Wunderkind *nt*

WUS *abbr* (*World University Service*) WEL weltweiter Universitätsdienst *m*

WW *abbr* (*warehouse warrant*) LAW, S&M Lagerschein *m*

wwd *abbr* (*weather working day*) TRANSP *shipping* nach Wetterlage möglicher Arbeitstag *m*

WWF *abbr* (*World Wide Fund for Nature*) ENVIR WWF (*Weltverband zum Schutz wildlebender Tiere*)

WW2 *abbr* (*Second World War, World War Two*) POL WK II (*Zweiter Weltkrieg*)

WYSIWYG *abbr* (*what you see is what you get*) COMP WYSIWYG (*wirklichkeitsgetreue Darstellung auf dem Bildschirm*)

X

X *abbr* (*telephone extension*) COMMS Nebenanschluß *m*, Nebenstelle *f*

x-c. *abbr* (*ex-coupon*) GEN COMM, STOCK ex Gratisaktien, ex Kupon, ohne Kupon

x-d. *abbr* (*ex-dividend*) FIN ex Dividende

X-efficiency *n* ECON X-Effizienz *f*

xerographic *adj* ADMIN xerographisch

Xerox® **1.** *n* ADMIN Fotokopie *f*, Xerokopie® *f*; **2.** *vt* ADMIN fotokopieren, xerokopieren®

X-form *n* ECON X-Form *f*

x-interest *n* FIN x-Zinssatz *m*, Zinssatz-x *m*

xl & ul *abbr* (*exclusive of loading and unloading*) IMP/EXP, TRANSP ausschließlich Laden und Löschen, ausschließlich Be- und Entladung

x-pri *abbr* (*without privilege*) GEN COMM ohne Vorrecht

x-quay *abbr* (*ex quay*) IMP/EXP, TRANSP x-Kai (*ab Kai*), frei Kai, frei Dock, x-Pier (*ab Pier*)

x-ship *abbr* (*ex ship*) IMP/EXP, TRANSP ab Schiff, frei Schiff, x-Schiff (*ex Schiff*)

x-warehouse *abbr* (*ex warehouse*) IMP/EXP, TRANSP *Incoterms* ab Lager

x-wharf *abbr* (*ex wharf*) IMP/EXP, TRANSP *Incoterms* frei Kai, frei Löschplatz, frei Dock, frei Landeplatz, x-Kai (*ab Kai*)

X-Y: **~ plotter** *n* ADMIN XY-Plotter *m*, COMP Kurvenschreiber *m*

Y

yacht: ~ broker *n* HRM Jachtmakler, in *m,f*

Yankee: ~ bond *n AmE* STOCK Anleihemarkt *m* für ausländische Emittenten; ~ bond market *n AmE* STOCK Anleihemarkt *m* für ausländische Emittenten

Yankees *n pl jarg* STOCK amerikanische Wertpapiere *nt pl*

YAR *abbr* (*York Antwerp Rules*) INS York-Antwerp Regeln über Große Havarie

yard *n* (*yd*) GEN COMM Yard *nt*

yardage *n* GEN COMM Bezahlung *f* für Platznutzung

yardstick *n* GEN COMM *to measure performance* Kriterium *nt*, Maßstab *m*; ♦ these figures are a ~ of the economy's progress GEN COMM an diesen Zahlen läßt sich der wirtschaftliche Fortschritt messen

yd *abbr* (*yard*) GEN COMM Yard *nt*

year *n* (*yr*) GEN COMM Jahr *nt* (*J.*); ~ of acquisition *n* ACC Zugangsjahr *nt*; ~ of assessment *n* ACC Veranlagungsjahr *nt*

yearbook *n* MEDIA Jahrbuch *nt*

year: ~-end *n* ACC Jahresende *nt*, Jahresultimo *m*; ~-end adjustment *n* ACC Jahresendberichtigung *f*; ~-end adjustments for accrued expenses *n pl* FIN Ultimoausgleich *m* für antizipatorische Passiva; ~-end audit *n* ACC Jahresabschlußprüfung *f*; ~-end closing *n* ACC Jahresbericht *m*; ~-end dividend *n* ACC Jahresabschlußdividende *f*; ~ ended *n* ACC Jahresende *nt*; ~-end procedures *n pl* ACC Jahresabschlußarbeiten *f pl*; ~ estimates *n pl* FIN Jahresschätzungen *f pl*; ~ of grace *n* FIN, TRANSP Freijahr *nt*; ~ of grace survey *n* (*YGS*) TRANSP *shipping* Freijahrbesichtigung *f*, Freijahrinspektion *f*; ~ of issue *n* STOCK *bonds* Emissionsjahr *nt*

yearling *n BrE* ECON Jährling *m*

yearly 1. *adj* GEN COMM jährlich; 2. *adv* GEN COMM jährlich

yearly: ~ payment *n* GEN COMM Jahreszahlung *f*; ~ salary *n* GEN COMM, HRM Jahresgehalt *nt*; ~ settlement *n* ACC Jahresabrechnung *f*

year: ~ under review *n* ACC Berichtsjahr *nt*; ~-on-year *adj* ACC, MGMNT *decline* im Jahresvergleich; ~-to-year *adj* GEN COMM jährlich

yellow: ~-dog democrat *n AmE* (*cf dyed-in-the-wool democrat BrE*) POL eingefleischter Demokrat *m*, eingefleischte Demokratin *f*; ~ metal *n* IND Gelbguß *m*

Yellow: ~ Pages® *n pl* COMMS *telephone directory* Gelbe Seiten® *f pl*

YGS *abbr* (*year of grace survey*) TRANSP *shipping* Freijahrbesichtigung *f*, Freijahrinspektion *f*

yield 1. *n* ECON *agriculture* Ernte *f*, Ertrag *m*, FIN Rendite *f*, GEN COMM Ertrag *m*, STOCK Rendite *f*; 2. *vt* ECON ertragen, FIN *income* einbringen, GEN COMM abwerfen, STOCK *loss* abwerfen; ♦ ~ interest BANK sich verzinsen, FIN Zinsen abwerfen, Zinsen bringen

yield: ~ adjustment *n* ACC Ertragsanpassung *f*; ~ comparison *n* STOCK *Treasury bills and Eurodollar contracts* Zinsertragsvergleich *m*; ~ curve *n* BANK Ertragskurve *f*; ~ gap *n* ECON Renditegefälle *nt*; ~ load *n* TRANSP Fließdruck *m*; ~ per acre *n* ECON *agricultural* Hektarertrag *m*; ~ to average life *n* STOCK Rendite *f* auf durchschnittliche Laufzeit; ~ GEN COMM Rendite *f* einer kündbaren Anleihe; ~ to maturity *n* (*YTM*) BANK, STOCK Rückzahlungsrendite *f*, Rendite *f* auf die Endfälligkeit; ~ variance *n* GEN COMM Ertragsabweichung *f*

York: ~ Antwerp Rules *n pl* (*YAR*) INS York-Antwerp Regeln über Große Havarie

young: ~ entrepreneur *n* GEN COMM Jungunternehmer, in *m,f*; ~ upwardly mobile professional *n* (*yumpie AmE, yuppie BrE*) GEN COMM, S&M Yumpie *m*, Yuppie *m*; ~ worker *n* HRM Jungarbeiter, in *m,f*

Yours: ~ faithfully *phr* COMMS *letter closing* Hochachtungsvoll (*frml*), Mit freundlichen Grüßen; ~ sincerely *phr* COMMS *letter closing* Hochachtungsvoll (*frml*), Mit freundlichen Grüßen; ~ truly *phr* COMMS *letter closing* Hochachtungsvoll (*frml*), Mit freundlichen Grüßen

youth: ~ training *n BrE* (*YT*) HRM Jugendausbildungsprogramm *nt*; ~ training scheme *n BrE obs* (*YTS*) HRM Jugendausbildungsprogramm *nt*

yo-yo *vi infrml* GEN COMM *prices* schwanken

yo-yo: ~ stock *n infrml* STOCK stark schwankende Aktien *f pl*

yr *abbr* (*year*) GEN COMM J. (*Jahr*)

YT *abbr BrE* (*youth training*) HRM Jugendausbildungsprogramm *nt*

YTM *abbr* (*yield to maturity*) BANK, STOCK Rückzahlungsrendite *f*, Rendite *f* auf die Endfälligkeit

YTS *abbr BrE obs* (*youth training scheme*) HRM Jugendausbildungsprogramm *nt*

yumpie *n AmE infrml* (*young upwardly mobile professional*) GEN COMM, S&M Yumpie *m*, Yuppie *m*

yuppie *n BrE infrml* (*young upwardly mobile professional*) GEN COMM, S&M Yumpie *m*, Yuppie *m*

Z

ZBB *abbr* (*zero-base budgeting*) ACC, FIN Nullbasis-Budgetierung *f*, Budgetierung *f* auf Nullbasis, Etatisierung *f* vom Ausgangspunkt, Zero-Base-Budgeting *nt*

Z: ~ **chart** *n* MATH Z-Diagramm *nt*

zero 1. *n* GEN COMM Null *f*; **2.** *vt* COMP auf Null setzen

zero: ~**-base budget** *n* ACC Nullbasis-Budget *nt*, FIN Etatisierung *f* vom Ausgangspunkt; ~**-base budgeting** *n* (*ZBB*) ACC, FIN Nullbasis-Budgetierung *f*, Budgetierung *f* auf Nullbasis, Etatisierung *f* vom Ausgangspunkt; Zero-Base-Budgeting *nt*; ~**-coupon bond** *n* STOCK Nullkuponanleihe *f*, Zero-Bond *m*; ~**-coupon convertible security** *n* STOCK wandelbares Wertpapier *nt* mit Nullkupon; ~**-coupon security** *n* STOCK Nullkuponwertpapier *nt*; ~ **defects** *n pl* ACC null Fehler *m pl*, FIN Nullmängel *m pl*; ~ **growth** *n* ECON Nullwachstum *nt*; ~ **lot line** *n* PROP Grundstücksnullgrenze *f*; ~ **option** *n* POL Nullösung *f*; ~ **population growth** *n* (*ZPG*) ECON Nullbevölkerungswachstum *nt*; ~**-priced** *adj* GEN COMM ohne Preis; ~ **profit** *n* FIN Nullgewinn *m*; ~ **rate** *n* TAX Mehrwertsteuerbefreiung *f*; ~**-rated** *adj* TAX *for sales* mehrwertsteuerfrei, von der Mehrwertsteuer befreit, nicht mit Umsatzsteuer veranschlagt; ~**-rated goods** *n pl* TAX von der Mehrwertsteuer befreite Ware *f*; ~**-rated supplies** *n pl* TAX von der Mehrwertsteuer befreite Betriebsstoffe *m pl*; ~**-rate taxation** *n* TAX Mehrwertsteuerbefreiung *f*; ~**-rating** *n* TAX *for sales* Befreiung *f* von der Mehrwertsteuer, Mehrwertsteuerbefreiung *f*; ~ **real interest** *n* FIN Zero-Realzins *m*; ~ **state** *n* COMP Nullage *f*, Nullzustand *m*; ~ **sum** *n* ECON Nullsumme *f*; ~**-sum game** *n* ECON, GEN COMM, MGMNT, POL Nullsummenspiel *nt*

zip *abbr* AmE (*zone improvement plan*) COMMS Postleitzahlensystem; ~ **code** *n* AmE (*cf postcode BrE*) COMMS Postleitzahl *f* (*PLZ*)

zonal: ~ **distribution** *n* S&M zonale Distribution *f*

zone *n* COMP *screen* Zone *f*, GEN COMM Bereich *m*, Zone *f*

Zone: ~ **A** *n* FIN Zone A *f*; ~ **A credit institution** *n* FIN Zone-A-Kreditinstitut *nt*; ~ **B** *n* FIN Zone B *f*; ~ **B credit institution** *n* FIN Zone-B-Kreditinstitut *nt*

zoned: ~ **advertising** *n* S&M in Gebiete aufgeteilte Werbung *f*; ~ **campaign** *n* S&M *advertising* in Gebiete aufgeteilte Kampagne *f*; ~ **decimal format** *n* COMP gezontes Dezimalformat *nt*

zone: ~ **of employment** *n* HRM, INS Unfallversicherungsbereich *m*; ~ **of freedom** *n* TRANSP Freiheitszone *f*; ~ **improvement plan** *n* AmE (*zip*) COMMS Postleitzahlensystem; ~ **pricing** *n* S&M Preisfestsetzung *f* nach Zonen

zoning *n* PROP Flächenaufteilung *f*; ~ **ordinance** *n* PROP Bebauungsplan *m*

zoom *n* COMP, MEDIA Gummilinse *f*, Zoomobjektiv *nt*

zoom in *vi* COMP, MEDIA zoomen; ♦ ~ **on** COMP, MEDIA heranholen, vergrößern

zoom out *vi* COMP, MEDIA aufziehen, verkleinern

zooming *n* COMP, MEDIA Zoomen *nt*

zoo: ~ **plane** *n* AmE *infrml* POL Flugzeug für die Gefolgschaft des Kandidaten während des Wahlkampfes

ZPG *abbr* (*zero population growth*) ECON Nullbevölkerungswachstum *nt*

Z: ~ **score** *n* MATH *statistics* Z-Punkt *m*

Zürich: ~ **Stock Exchange** *n* STOCK Züricher Wertpapierbörse *f*

English–German appendix/
Anhang Englisch–Deutsch

Contents/Inhalt

Business correspondence and documents/ Geschäftsbriefe und -dokumente

Job application/Stellenbewerbung

Dear Mrs Jones,

Application for the position of technical translator

I am writing in response to your advertisement in the August issue of the *ITI Bulletin* for the post of Technical Translator with German.

I am an English native speaker and I am fluent in both German and French. I took my degree in Modern Languages and European Studies at the University of the West of England in 1992 and have been working in various jobs since. At present I am working as a translator in British Telecom's sales and export department, which requires a good command of business and technical German.

While working as an editorial assistant and clerical assistant I have gained general administrative skills, in addition to the organizational skills needed to work as a translator. The use of IT systems was an integral part of my work, and I am also familiar with technical and scientific dictionaries as tools for translation.

I hope my application will be of interest to you and I would appreciate the chance to discuss it further.

I look forward to hearing from you.

Yours sincerely,

Anne Drummond

Curriculum vitae/Lebenslauf

NAME:	**Anne Drummond**
ADDRESS:	10 Keswick Road London SW10 3BA
TELEPHONE:	0171 772 2890
NATIONALITY:	British
DATE OF BIRTH:	12th September, 1969

EDUCATION

1993–1994	**University of Westminster** Postgraduate diploma in Technical and Specialized Translation (part-time course) in French and German
1992–1993	**INSEAD (European Institute of Business Administration), Fontainbleau, France** MBA course in French and German
1988–1992	**University of the West of England** BA (Hons) MODERN LANGUAGES AND EUROPEAN STUDIES (French, German and Spanish)
1982–1987	**South Hampstead High School, London** 9 'O' levels: English Language, English Literature, Mathematics, French, German, Biology, Physics, Geography, Home Economics 3 'A' levels: English, French, German

WORK EXPERIENCE

May 1995–present	**British Telecom, London** Translator from German into English. Duties include coordinating and supervising the work of other translators and undertaking technical and commercial translations for the sales and exports department
January 1995– May 1995	**European Parliament, Strasbourg, France** Translator and ad hoc interpreter for the Department of the Environment
February 1994– November 1994	**Routledge Publishers, London** Editorial Assistant on the Language and Linguistics book list

August 1993 –   **Johnathan Allbright's Ltd, London**
December 1993   Clerical Assistant in Managing Director's
                        office. Duties included general office administration and
                        organizing hotels and travel for Managing Director

1987–1988   **Thomson Holidays**
                        Tour representative on the Costa del Sol, Spain. The
                        position involved greeting guests at the airport and
                        directing them to their respective hotels, offering support
                        and advice during their stay and coordinating excursions

OTHER SKILLS: Word processing experience (WordPerfect 5.1, 6.1 & Word
                        for Windows 6.0)
                        Lotus 123, Microsoft Excel 5.0
                        Database experience including Foxpro
                        Full, clean British driving licence

HOBBIES: I enjoy travelling, skiing, aerobics, reading, singing and
                        going to the cinema, the theatre and art exhibitions

REFERENCES: available on request

Offer of employment/Stellenangebot

Dear Ms Drummond,

I have pleasure in formally offering you the position of Technical Translator. The position is based at our offices in central London.

Salary
Your salary will be at the rate of £25,000 per annum, and your appointment will be subject to a probationary period which will not exceed twenty-four weeks. You will be informed by your head of department when your probationary period has ended. Luncheon vouchers are paid at the rate of £52.50 per month.

Hours of work
Your hours of work will be 9am to 5pm Monday to Friday, with one hour for lunch.

Holidays
The holiday year runs with the calendar year, and holiday entitlement is calculated on the basis of 22 working days in the first calendar year after joining, with one extra day per full year of service up to a maximum of 28 days. Holidays for the actual year of joining are calculated pro rata of 22 days. Holiday dates must be agreed with your line manager two weeks prior to the start of the leave period.

Notice Period
The period of notice of termination of employment will be one month on either side.

I would like you to take up your appointment on 15 August 1997. If there are any aspects of this contract you would like to discuss with me, please do not hesitate to telephone.

Will you please be good enough to let me have your acceptance of the appointment on the terms and conditions set out above by signing the attached copy of this letter and returning this to me as soon as possible.

Yours sincerely,

P Jones
Personnel Manager

I accept the above position in accordance with the terms and conditions set out above.

Signed .... Date ....

Invitation to supply further information/
Anforderung weiterer Unterlagen

Dear Ms Spencer,

Pre-qualification enquiry for Cleaning Contract

We are in receipt of your response to our advertisement for applications from Contractors wishing to be considered to tender the provision of cleaning services at Castle-Fergusson Ltd. As our advertisement explained, applicants will be required to satisfactorily complete pre-qualification documentation. On no account should this letter be construed or interpreted as your Company's automatic inclusion on our list of selected contractors.

We should therefore be pleased if you would provide us with complete and specific information on your organization in the sequence identified. The use of our reply boxes where possible will help facilitate an expeditious evaluation.

Your response should, where applicable, be supported by any relevant company documentation, e.g. policies, manuals, sales literature, procedures etc. Specific reference(s) should be made to page, paragraph or clause as appropriate. Please provide a completed dossier of information and do not refer to information you may have passed us earlier.

It is important that your response be endorsed and dated by an Officer of the Company.

It is essential that you treat this letter and its contents as strictly confidential. On no account should you divulge any of this information to a third party without our specific authorization. Please arrange for two copies of all documentation to arrive at our address by 24 October 1996, marked 'Private and Confidential' and addressed to the Contracts Manager.

Please acknowledge receipt of this letter and attachments by return, confirming your intention to submit the required information by the date specified herein. Please also supply the name of someone in your organization to whom any further queries may be addressed.

We will write on 6 January 1997 to notify you whether your company has been successful in being invited to tender. We will not enter into any correspondence or respond to telephone enquiries on this contract letting procedure.

Yours faithfully,

Mr D Hammer
Contracts Manager

Invitation to tender for a contract/Angebotsaufforderung

Dear Ms Spencer,

Contract for the Provision of Cleaning Services

I am pleased to inform you that your company is invited to tender for the above contract.

Please find enclosed a hard copy of the tender document and a copy of the document on disk (Microsoft Word 6.0).

The tendering programme will be as follows:

1. Issue invitations to tender 14 February 1997

2. Tenderers' visit to site 21 February 1997

   a) 10.00am   arrive, coffee
   b) 10.30am   presentation and briefing in Conference Room
   c) 10.45am   site tour
   d) 11.30am   debrief and questions in Conference Room

   Note:
   i) A maximum of three (3) representatives from each company will attend.
   ii) Verbal questions and discussions held during the site visit will not form any part of the Contract.

3. Written questions pertinent to the Contract, are to be received by the end of business on Tuesday 25 February 1997. Faxes are acceptable but are to be followed by hard copy. Please address questions to the Operations Director.

4. Answers to questions received will be sent to Tenderers on 3 March 1997.

5. Tender bids are to be received at this address by 12 noon on 14 March 1997.

   Requests for extension of time will not be entertained.

6. Tenderers should return three (3) copies of the documents issued completed as directed. Bids should not be bound except in ring binders.

7. To facilitate the work of the evaluation team and aid acceptance of its bid, the Tenderer should return its bid by completing the form as supplied. Any supplementary information should be supplied under separate cover in triplicate.

8. Award of the contract should be announced on 27 March 1997 with commencement on 13 May 1997.

Yours sincerely,

N Jackson
Operations Director

Balance sheet/Jahresbilanz

	(millions of £)	
December 31	1996	1995
Assets		
Current assets:		
Cash and short-term investments, at cost which approximates market	37.2	50.1
Receivable from sale of property	46.7	-
Accounts receivable	91.9	84.4
Inventories	35.0	31.3
Prepaid expenses and other current assets	32.7	34.6
	243.5	200.4
Property	160.3	155.8
Equipment	76.2	72.8
Goodwill	196.9	156.5
Other assets	34.0	34.7
	710.9	620.2
Liabilities and shareholders' equity		
Current liabilities:		
Short-term indebtedness	1.6	22.4
Accounts payable	136.3	119.8
Deferred revenue	65.1	63.1
Current portion of long-term debt	7.7	2.6
Finance leases	11.0	0.5
	221.7	208.4
Long-term debt	281.6	317.4
Finance leases	31.5	36.2
Other liabilities	46.1	42.9
Deferred income taxes	38.8	34.3
	398.0	430.8
Shareholders' equity:		
Share capital	97.8	85.8
Cumulative translation adjustment	(27.4)	(35.4)
Retained earnings	242.5	139.0
	312.9	189.4
	710.9	620.2

Approved by the Board

Ken Knight, *Director*   Barry Brown, *Director*

Job titles used in commerce/
Berufsbezeichnungen in der Wirtschaft

in the UK and US *in Großbritannien und in den Vereinigten Staaten*	in Germany *in Deutschland*
account executive	*PR, advertising* Kontakter,in *m,f,* Sachbearbeiter,in *m,f* eines Werbeetats, *commerce,finance* Kontakter,in *m,f,* Sachbearbeiter,in *m,f*
account manager	Kundenbetreuer,in *m,f*
administration officer	*commerce* Verwaltungsangestellte(r) *mf* [decl. as adj], *public sector* Verwaltungsbeamte(r) *m* [decl. as adj], Verwaltungsbeamtin *f*
administrator	Verwaltungsfachmann *m,* Verwaltungsfachfrau *f,* Verwalter,in *m,f,* Verwaltungsleiter,in *m,f, estate,* *inheritance* Nachlaßverwalter,in *m,f, software* Systemverwalter,in *m,f*
advertising director	Direktor,in *m,f* der Werbeabteilung
advertising manager	Werbeleiter,in *m,f*
after-sales manager	Kundendienstleiter,in *m,f*
agency representative	Agenturvertreter,in *m,f*
area manager	Bereichsleiter,in *m,f,* Gebietsleiter,in *m,f*
art manager	Atelierleiter,in *m,f*
asset manager	Anlagenverwalter,in *m,f,* Vermögensverwalter,in *m,f*
assistant controller	Assistent,in *m,f* im Rechnungswesen
assistant director	stellvertretender Direktor *m,* stellvertretende Direktorin *f*
assistant director general	stellvertretender Generaldirektor *m,* stellvertretende Generaldirektorin *f*
assistant general manager	stellvertretender Generaldirektor *m,* stellvertretende Generaldirektorin *f*
assistant head of section *BrE*	stellvertretender Abteilungsleiter *m,* stellvertretende Abteilungsleiterin *f*
assistant manager	stellvertretender Direktor *m,* stellvertretende Direktorin *f, shop* stellvertretender Geschäftsführer *m,* stellver- tretende Geschäftsführerin *f, department* stellvertre- tender Abteilungsleiter *m,* stellvertretende Abteilungs- leiterin *f*
assistant section head *BrE*	stellvertretender Abteilungsleiter *m,* stellvertretende Abteilungsleiterin *f*
brand manager	Markenbetreuer,in *m,f,* Produktmanager,in *m,f*
cash manager	Kassenführer,in *m,f*
chair	Gesprächsleiter,in *m,f,* Vorsitzende(r) *mf* [decl. as adj]
chairman	Vorsitzende(r) *mf* [decl. as adj], Tagungsleiter,in *m,f,* Versammlungsleiter,in *m,f*
chairman and chief executive *AmE*	Vorstandsvorsitzende(r) *mf* [decl. as adj]
chairman and general manager	Vorsitzender und Generaldirektor *m,* Vorsitzende und Generaldirektorin *f,* Vorsitzender und Hauptge- schäftsführer *m,* Vorsitzende und Hauptgeschäftsfüh- rerin *f*

in the UK and US *in Großbritannien und in den Vereinigten Staaten*	in Germany *in Deutschland*
chairman and managing director *BrE*	Vorsitzender und geschäftsführender Direktor *m*, Vorsitzende und geschäftsführende Direktorin *f*, Vorstandsvorsitzende(r) *mf* [decl. as adj]
chairman of the administrative board	Verwaltungsratsvorsitzende(r) *mf* [decl. as adj]
chairman of the board	Aufsichtsratsvorsitzende(r) *mf* [decl. as adj]
chairman of the board of directors	Verwaltungsratsvorsitzende(r) *mf* [decl. as adj], Vorstand *m* der Geschäftsleitung
chairman of the board of management	Verwaltungsratsvorsitzende(r) *mf* [decl. as adj], Vorstand *m* der Geschäftsleitung
chairman of the executive committee	Vorstandsvorsitzende(r) *mf* [decl. as adj]
chairman of the supervisory board	Aufsichtsratsvorsitzende(r) *mf* [decl. as adj]
chairperson	Vorsitzende(r) *mf* [decl. as adj], Tagungsleiter,in *m,f*, Versammlungsleiter,in *m,f*
chairwoman	Vorsitzende *f*, Tagungsleiterin *f*, Versammlungsleiterin *f*
charge hand	*construction industry* Vorarbeiter,in *m,f*
chief accountant	Hauptbuchhalter,in *m,f*
chief buyer	Haupteinkäufer,in *m,f*, Einkaufschef,in *m,f*
chief clerk	Bürochef,in *m,f*, Büroleiter,in *m,f*, leitende(r) Büroangestellte(r) *mf* [decl. as adj]
chief designer	Chefkonstrukteur,in *m,f*, Leiter,in *m,f* Abteilung Design
chief executive	Hauptgeschäftsführer,in *m,f*, Generaldirektor,in *m,f*, leitender Direktor *m*, leitende Direktorin *f*, Gemeindedirektor,in *m,f*, oberste(r) Verwaltungsbeamte(r) *m* [decl. as adj], oberste Verwaltungsbeamtin *f*
chief executive officer *AmE*	Hauptgeschäftsführer,in *m,f*
chief financial officer	Finanzleiter,in *m,f*, Finanzchef,in *m,f*
chief immigration officer	Leiter,in *m,f* der Informationsbehörde
chief information officer	Leiter,in *m,f* der Informationsbehörde
chief inspector	leitender Inspektor *m*, leitende Inspektorin *f*
chief operating officer	Chef,in Management *m,f*, Hauptgeschäftsführer,in *m,f*, Betriebsleiter,in *m,f*
circulation manager	Vertriebsleiter,in *m,f*
claims inspector	Schadensbeauftragte(r) *mf* [decl. as adj]
claims manager	Leiter,in *m,f* der Schadenabteilung
co-director	Mitdirektor,in *m,f*, Kodirektor,in *m,f*
co-manager	Mitdirektor,in *m,f*, Kodirektor,in *m,f*
commercial and development manager	Leiter,in *m,f* Vertrieb und Entwicklung
commercial director	kaufmännischer Direktor *m*, kaufmännische Direktorin *f*
commercial manager	kaufmännischer Leiter *m*, kaufmännische Leiterin *f*
comptroller	Chef,in *m,f* des Rechnungswesens
confidential secretary	Privatsekretär,in *m,f*
consumer relations manager	Kundendienstleiter,in *m,f*
consultant	Berater,in *m,f*
contracts manager	Vertragsleiter,in *m,f*
contracts officer	Vertragsbearbeiter,in *m,f*
controller	Chef,in *m,f* des Rechnungswesens
co-owner	Miteigentümer,in *m,f*
credit controller	Finanzbuchhalter,in *m,f*, Kreditsachbearbeiter,in *m,f*
customer relations manager	Kundendienstleiter,in *m,f*
customer service manager	Kundendienstleiter,in *m,f*
department head	Abteilungsleiter,in *m,f*
departmental manager	Abteilungsleiter,in *m,f*
deputy chairman	stellvertretende(r) Vorsitzende(r) *mf* [decl. as adj]
deputy chairman of the board of management	stellvertretende(r) Verwaltungsratsvorsitzende(r) *mf* [decl. as adj], stellvertretender Vorstand *m* der Geschäftsleitung

in the UK and US *in Großbritannien und in den Vereinigten Staaten*	in Germany *in Deutschland*
deputy chairman of the supervisory board	stellvertretende(r) Vorsitzende(r) des Aufsichtsrats *mf* [decl. as adj]
deputy chief executive	stellvertretender Hauptgeschäftsführer *m*, stellvertretende Hauptgeschäftsführerin *f*, stellvertretender Generaldirektor *m*, stellvertretende Generaldirektorin *f*, *public sector* stellvertretender Gemeindedirektor *m*, stellvertretende Gemeindedirektorin *f*
deputy director	stellvertretender Direktor *m*, stellvertretende Direktorin *f*, stellvertretender Leiter *m*, stellvertretende Leiterin *f*
deputy head of department	stellvertretender Abteilungsleiter *m*, stellvertretende Abteilungsleiterin *f*
deputy manager	stellvertretender Direktor *m*, stellvertretende Direktorin *f*, stellvertretender Leiter *m*, stellvertretende Leiterin *f*
deputy managing director	stellvertretender Hauptgeschäftsführer *m*, stellvertretende Hauptgeschäftsführerin *f*, stellvertretender Generaldirektor *m*, stellvertretende Generaldirektorin *f*
deputy member of the board of management	stellvertretendes Mitglied *nt* des Verwaltungsrats
development director	Leiter,in *m,f* der Entwicklungsabteilung
development manager	Leiter,in *m,f* der Entwicklungsabteilung
director	Direktor,in *m,f*, Geschäftsführer,in *m,f*, Leiter,in *m,f*, Vorstandsmitglied *nt*
director general	Generaldirektor,in *m,f*
director of labor relations *AmE*	Koordinator,in *m,f* Arbeitgeber-Arbeitnehmer-Interessen
director of labour relations *BrE*	Koordinator,in *m,f* Arbeitgeber-Arbeitnehmer-Interessen
director of public relations	PR-Direktor,in *m,f*, Leiter,in *m,f* für Öffentlichkeitsarbeit
distribution manager	Vertriebsleiter,in *m,f*
division head	Abteilungsleiter,in *m,f*, Bereichsleiter,in *m,f*, Sparten-manager, in *m,f*
division manager	Abteilungsleiter,in *m,f*, Bereichsleiter,in *m,f*, Sparten-manager,in *m,f*
divisional director	Bereichsleiter,in *m,f*
engineering manager	Leiter,in *m,f* der technischen Abteilung
executive	Sachbearbeiter,in *m,f*, leitende(r) Angestellte(r) *mf* [decl. as adj], Führungskraft *f*
executive director	geschäftsführender Direktor *m*, geschäftsführende Direktorin *f*, hauptamtlicher Geschäftsführer *m*, hauptamtliche Geschäftsführerin *f*
executive manager	Führungskraft *f*, leitende(r) Angestellte(r) *mf* [decl. as adj]
executive officer	Führungskraft *f*, leitende(r) Angestellte(r) *mf* [decl. as adj]
executive vice-president	geschäftsführender Vizepräsident *m*, geschäftsführende Vizepräsidentin *f*
export coordinator	Exportsachbearbeiter,in *m,f*, Koordinator,in *m,f* Export
export director	Exportdirektor,in *m,f*, Direktor,in *m,f* Export
export manager	Exportleiter,in *m,f*, Leiter,in *m,f* Export
export marketing manager	Leiter,in *m,f* Marketing Export
field sales manager	Außendienstleiter,in *m,f*
finance director *BrE*	Finanzdirektor,in *m,f*
financial director	Finanzvorstand *m*
financial executive	Finanzvorstand *m*
financial manager	Finanzleiter,in *m,f*
first vice-president	erster Vizepräsident *m*, erste Vizepräsidentin *f*
first-line supervisor	unmittelbare(r) Vorgesetzte(r) *mf* [decl. as adj]
fleet manager	Fuhrparkleiter,in *m,f*

in the UK and US *in Großbritannien und in den Vereinigten Staaten*	in Germany *in Deutschland*
foreman	Meister,in *m,f*, Vorarbeiter,in *m,f*
general counsel *AmE*	Leiter,in *m,f* der Rechtsabteilung, Syndikus *m*
general executive manager	Generaldirektor,in *m,f*
general manager *BrE*	*insurance* Generaldirektor,in *m,f*, Hauptgeschäftsführer,in *m,f* *commercial* leitende(r) Angestellte(r) *mf* [decl. as adj], leitender Direktor *m*, leitende Direktorin *f*
general partner	*in limited partnership* Komplementär,in *m,f*, persönlich haftender Gesellschafter *m*, persönlich haftende Gesellschafterin *f*
group leader	Kolonnenführer,in *m,f*
head buyer	Haupteinkäufer,in *m,f*, Einkaufsleiter,in *m,f*
head clerk	Bürochef,in *m,f*, Büroleiter,in *m,f*, leitende(r) Büroangestellte(r) *mf* [decl. as adj]
head foreman	leitender Vorarbeiter *m*, leitende Vorarbeiterin *f*
head of legal department *BrE*	Leiter,in *m,f* der Rechtsabteilung, Syndikus *m* einer Unternehmung
head of personnel	Leiter,in *m,f* der Personalabteilung, Personalleiter,in *m,f*, Personalchef,in *m,f*
honorary chairman	Ehrenvorsitzende(r) *mf* [decl. as adj]
honorary chairman of the board of directors	Ehrenvorsitzende(r) *mf* des Verwaltungsrats [decl. as adj], Ehrenvorstand *m* der Geschäftsleitung
honorary president *BrE*	ehrenamtlicher Präsident *m*, ehrenamtliche Präsidentin *f*, Ehrenpräsident,in *m,f*
import director	Importdirektor,in *m,f*
import documentation supervisor	Sachbearbeiter,in *m,f* für Einfuhrpapiere
import manager	Importleiter,in *m,f*
import sales executive	Importverkaufsleiter,in *m,f*
indoor sales manager	Innendienst-Verkaufsleiter,in *m,f*, Sachbearbeiter,in *m,f* im Importverkauf
industrial relations director	Koordinator,in *m,f* Arbeitgeber-Arbeitnehmer-Interessen
industrial relations manager	Koordinator,in *m,f* Arbeitgeber-Arbeitnehmer-Interessen
information officer	*public sector* Referent,in *m,f* für Öffentlichkeitsarbeit
inspector	Inspektor,in *m,f*
investigation officer	Ermittlungsbeamte(r) *m* [decl. as adj], Ermittlungsbeamtin *f*
joint director	Mitdirektor,in *m,f*
joint manager	Mitdirektor,in *m,f*
junior manager	nachrückende Führungskraft *f*
limited partner	beschränkt haftender Gesellschafter *m*, beschränkt haftende Gesellschafterin *f*, Kommanditist,in *m,f*, Teilhafter *m*
line executive	Führungskraft *f* mit Linienfunktion, Linienmanager,in *m,f*
line manager	Linienmanager,in *m,f*, Produktionsleiter,in *m,f*
line supervisor	Vorarbeiter,in *m,f* der Produktion
manager	Leiter,in *m,f*, Manager,in *m,f*, Betriebsleiter,in *m,f*, Direktor,in *m,f*, *of shop* Geschäftsführer,in *m,f*, *of department* Abteilungsleiter,in *m,f*
managing director *BrE*	Generaldirektor,in *m,f*, leitender Direktor *m*, leitende Direktorin *f*, Hauptgeschäftsführer,in *m,f*
managing partner	geschäftsführender Gesellschafter *m*, geschäftsführende Gesellschafterin *f*
marketing director	Marketingdirektor,in *m,f*, Leiter,in *m,f* der Abteilung Marketing

in the UK and US *in Großbritannien und in den Vereinigten Staaten*	in Germany *in Deutschland*
marketing manager	Marketingdirektor,in *m,f*, Leiter,in *m,f* der Abteilung Marketing
marketing officer	Marketing-Sachbearbeiter,in *m,f*
member of the board of management	Mitglied *nt* des Verwaltungsrats
member of the supervisory board	Mitglied *nt* des Aufsichtsrats
merchandising director	Leiter,in *m,f* der Verkaufsförderungsabteilung
merchandising manager	Leiter,in *m,f* der Verkaufsförderungsabteilung
middle manager	mittlere Führungskraft *f*
motor transport officer	Fuhrparkleiter,in *m,f*
national accounts manager	Großkunden-Betreuer,in *m,f*
non-executive director	Direktor,in *m,f* ohne Geschäftsbereich, nebenamtlicher Geschäftsführer *m*, nebenamtliche Geschäftsführerin *f*
office manager	Büroleiter,in *m,f*, Bürochef,in *m,f*
operational manager	Leiter,in *m,f* der Ablauforganisation, Betriebsleiter,in *m,f*
operations manager	Leiter,in *m,f* der Ablauforganisation, Betriebsleiter,in *m,f*
outside director	Direktor,in *m,f* ohne Geschäftsbereich, nebenamtlicher Geschäftsführer *m*, nebenamtliche Geschäftsführerin *f*
overseer	Vorarbeiter,in *m,f*
owner-manager	Eigentümer-Unternehmer,in *m,f*, Leiter,in *m,f* im eigenen Betrieb
partner	Gesellschafter,in *m,f*, Teilhaber,in *m,f*
personal assistant	Chefsekretär,in *m,f*
personal secretary	Chefsekretär,in *m,f*, Privatsekretär,in *m,f*
personnel director	Personaldirektor,in *m,f*, Leiter,in *m,f* der Personalabteilung, Personalchef,in *m,f*, Personalleiter,in *m,f*
plant manager	Betriebsführer,in *m,f*, Betriebsleiter,in *m,f*, Fabrikleiter,in *m,f*, Werksleiter,in *m,f*
personnel officer	Personalreferent,in *m,f*, Personalleiter,in *m,f*
president	Präsident,in *m,f*, Generaldirektor,in *m,f*, Vorsitzende(r) *mf* [decl. as adj]
press officer	Pressereferent,in *m,f*, Pressesprecher,in *m,f*
private secretary	Privatsekretär,in *m,f*
procurement manager	Disponent *m*, Leiter,in *m,f* der Beschaffungsabteilung, Einkäufer,in *m,f*
product manager	Markenbetreuer,in *m,f*, Produktleiter,in *m,f*, Produktmanager,in *m,f*
production director	Direktor,in *m,f* der Produktionsabteilung, Produktionsdirektor,in *m,f*, Produktionsleiter,in *m,f*
production manager	Fertigungsleiter,in *m,f*, Produktionsleiter,in *m,f*, Betriebsleiter,in *m,f*, Fabrikationsleiter,in *m,f*, Direktor,in *m,f* der Produktionsabteilung, Herstellungsleiter,in *m,f*
production worker	Produktionsarbeiter,in *m,f*
project leader	Projektleiter,in *m,f*
project manager	Projektleiter,in *m,f*, Projektmanager,in *m,f*
public relations executive	PR-Berater,in *m,f*, PR-Sachbearbeiter,in *m,f*
public relations officer	PR-Berater,in *m,f*, PR-Sachbearbeiter,in *m,f*
publicity manager	Werbeleiter,in *m,f*
purchasing executive	Einkäufer,in *m,f*
purchasing manager	Einkaufsleiter,in *m,f*
purchasing officer	Einkäufer,in *m,f*
recruitment consultant	Personalbeschaffung *f*
regional manager	Gebietsleiter,in *m,f*
registered manager	Handlungsbevollmächtigte(r) *mf* [decl. as adj], Prokurist,in *m,f*

in the UK and US *in Großbritannien und in den Vereinigten Staaten*	in Germany *in Deutschland*
research director	Forschungsdirektor,in *m,f*, Leiter,in *m,f* der Forschungs- abteilung
sales director	Vertriebsdirektor,in *m,f*, Verkaufsleiter,in *m,f*, Verkaufs- chef,in *m,f*
sales executive	Sachbearbeiter,in *m,f* im Verkauf
sales manager	Vertriebsdirektor,in *m,f*, Verkaufsdirektor,in *m,f*, Ver- kaufsleiter, in *m,f*, Vertriebsleiter,in *m,f*, Verkaufs- chef,in *m,f*, Vertriebschef,in *m,f*
section head	Abteilungsleiter,in *m,f*
senior civil servant	höhere(r) Staatsbeamte(r) *m* [decl. as adj], höhere Staatsbeamtin *f*
senior clerk	Bürochef,in *m,f*, Büroleiter,in *m,f*, leitende(r) Büro- angestellte(r) *mf* [decl. as adj]
senior executive	leitende(r) Angestellte(r) *mf* [decl. as adj], gehobene Führungskraft *f*
senior export clerk	ranghöchster Exportsachbearbeiter *m*, ranghöchste Exportsachbearbeiterin *f*
senior import clerk	ranghöchster Importsachbearbeiter *m*, ranghöchste Importsachbearbeiterin *f*
senior manager	leitender Mitarbeiter *m* der Geschäftsführung, leitende Mitarbeiterin *f* der Geschäftsführung
senior officer	*public sector* höhere(r) Beamte(r) *m* [decl. as adj], höhere Beamtin *f*
senior vice-president *AmE*	ranghöchster Stellvertreter *m* des Vorstandsvorsitzenden, ranghöchste Stellvertreterin *f* des Vorstandsvorsitzen- den, ranghöchster stellvertretender Generaldirektor *m*, ranghöchste stellvertretende Generaldirektorin *f*, ranghöchster Vizepräsident *m*, ranghöchste Vizeprä- .sidentin *f*
shareholder *BrE*	Aktionär,in *m,f*, Anteilseigner,in *m,f*, Aktieninhaber,in *m,f*
site foreman	Baustellenleiter,in *m,f*
staff manager	Personalchef,in *m,f*, Personalleiter,in *m,f*
stock controller	Lagerkontrolleur,in *m,f*, Lagerverwalter,in *m,f*
stockholder *AmE*	Aktionär,in *m,f*, Anteilseigner,in *m,f*, Aktieninhaber,in *m,f*
supervisor	Aufseher,in *m,f*, Kontrolleur,in *m,f*, Vorarbeiter,in *m,f*, *public sector* Aufsichtsbeamte(r) *m* [decl. as adj], Aufsichtsbeamtin *f*
team leader	Gruppenleiter,in *m,f*, Teamleiter,in *m,f*
technical director	Direktor,in *m,f* der technischen Abteilung, technischer Direktor *m*, technische Direktorin *f*
technical manager	technischer Leiter *m*, technische Leiterin *f*
territory manager	Gebietsleiter,in *m,f*
top executive	oberste Führungskraft *f*, Aufsichtsratmitglied *nt*
traffic executive	Versandleitung *f*
traffic manager	Versandleiter,in *m,f*, Leiter,in *m,f* des Wareneingangs, Terminüberwacher,in *m,f*
traffic superintendent	Fahrdienstleiter,in *m,f*
trainee manager	Manager,in *m,f* in Ausbildung
training officer	Ausbildungsleiter,in *m,f*, Ausbildende(r) *mf* [decl. as adj]
transport controller	Versandleiter,in *m,f*
treasurer *AmE*	Finanzdirektor,in *m,f*
undersecretary of state	Staatssekretär,in *m,f*
veep *AmE*	Vizepräsident,in *m,f*

in the UK and US *in Großbritannien und in den Vereinigten Staaten*	in Germany *in Deutschland*
vice-chairman	stellvertretende(r) Vorsitzende(r) *mf* [decl. as adj], stell- vertretender Tagungsleiter *m*, stellvertretende Tagungsleiterin *f*, stellvertretender Versammlungs- leiter *m*, stellvertretende Versammlungsleiterin *f*
vice-president *AmE*	stellvertretende(r) Vorsitzende(r) *mf* [decl. as adj], Vize- präsident,in *m,f*, stellvertretender Generaldirektor *m*, stellvertretende Generaldirektorin *f*
vice-president finance *AmE*	Finanzvorstand *m*
works manager	Betriebsleiter,in *m,f*, Werksleiter,in *m,f*

Stock exchanges/Börsenplätze

English name / *Englischer Name*	Country, city / *Land, Stadt*	German name / *Deutscher Name*
	UK / ***Großbritannien***	
Baltic Futures Exchange	London	Baltische Terminbörse
Belfast Stock Exchange	Belfast	Belfaster Börse
Birmingham Stock Exchange	Birmingham	Börse in Birmingham
Glasgow Stock Exchange	Glasgow	Glasgower Börse
International Stock Exchange (*also* London Stock Exchange)	London	Internationale Börse (in London), Londoner Börse
Liverpool Commodity Exchange	Liverpool	Warenbörse in Liverpool
Liverpool Stock Exchange	Liverpool	Börse in Liverpool
London Commodity Exchange	London	Londoner Warenbörse
London Futures and Options Exchange	London	Londoner Termin- und Optionsbörse
London International Financial Futures Exchange	London	Londoner Internationale Finanztermin-börse
London Metal Exchange	London	Londoner Metallbörse
London Trader Options Exchange	London	Londoner Handelsoptionsbörse
Manchester Commodity Exchange	Manchester	Manchester Warenbörse
Royal Exchange	London	Londoner Börsengebäude
Unlisted Securities Market	London	Freiverkehrsbörse, geregelter Freiverkehr, geregelter Markt
	USA / ***Vereinigte Staaten***	
American Stock Exchange	New York	amerikanische Börse
Amex Commodity Exchange	New York	Amex Warenbörse
Boston Stock Exchange	Boston	Bostoner Börse
Chicago Mercantile Exchange	Chicago	Chicago Produktenbörse
Chicago Board Options Exchange	Chicago	Chicago Optionsbörse
Chicago Stock Exchange (Midwest Stock Exchange)	Chicago	Börse in Chicago
Cincinnati Stock Exchange	Cincinnati	Cincinnati Börse
Mid-America Commodity Exchange	Chicago	Mittelamerikanische Warenbörse
Minneapolis Grain Exchange	Minneapolis	Minneapolis Getreidebörse
New Orleans Commodity Exchange	New Orleans	New Orleans Warenbörse
New York Coffee, Sugar and Cocoa Exchange	New York	New Yorker Kaffee-, Zucker- und Kakaobörse
New York Cotton Exchange and Petroleum and Citrus Associates	New York	New Yorker Baumwollbörse
New York Curb Exchange	New York	New Yorker Freiverkehrsbörse
New York Mercantile Exchange	New York	New Yorker Rohstoff- und Waren-terminbörse
New York Stock Exchange	New York	New Yorker Börse
Pacific Stock Exchange (*also* Los Angeles Stock Exchange *or* San Francisco Stock Exchange)	Los Angeles & San Francisco	Pazifische Börse
Philadelphia Stock Exchange	Philadelphia	Philadelphia Börse
Salt Lake City Stock Exchange	Salt Lake City	Salt Lake City Börse
Spokane Stock Exchange	Spokane	Spokane Börse

English name *Englischer Name*	Country, city *Land, Stadt*	German name *Deutscher Name*
	Canada ***Kanada***	
Toronto Stock Exchange	Toronto	Börse in Toronto
	France ***Frankreich***	
Paris Financial Futures Exchange	Paris	Pariser Finanzterminbörse
Paris Stock Exchange	Paris	Pariser Börse
Paris Trader Options Exchange	Paris	Pariser Handelsoptionsbörse

Financial and economic indexes/
Finanz- und Wirtschaftsindizes

English name *Englischer Name*	German name *Deutscher Name*
General coverage	
adjusted index	bereinigter Index *m*
balance of trade	Handelsbilanz *f*
bond index	Rentenindex *m*
commodities price index	Rohstoffpreisindex *m*
composite index	zusammengesetzter Index *m*
composite leading index	zusammengesetzter Index *m* der Frühindikatoren
construction cost index	Baukostenindex *m*
consumer price index	Verbraucherpreisindex *m*
cost-of-living index	Lebenshaltungsindex *m*, Lebenshaltungskostenindex *m*, Preisindex *m* für die Lebenshaltung
diffusion index	Diffusionsindex *m*
discomfort index	Elendsindex *m*, Problemindex *m*
employment index	Beschäftigungsindex *m*, Anspannungsindex *m*
gross national income	Bruttovolkseinkommen *nt*
gross national product	Bruttosozialprodukt *nt*
growth index	Wachstumsindex *m*
Herfindahl-Hirschman index	Herfindahl-Hirschman-Index *m*
implied price index	impliziter Preisindex *m*
income per capita	Pro-Kopf-Einkommen *nt*
index of lagging indicators	Index *m* der Spätindikatoren
index of leading indicators	Index *m* der Frühindikatoren
index fund	Indexfonds *m*
index linkage	Indexbindung *f*, Indexverbindung *f*, Indexkoppelung *f*
index linking	Indexbindung *f*, Indexverbindung *f*, Indexkoppelung *f*
index number	Indexzahl *f*
index option	Indexoption *f*
index point	Indexpunkt *m*
index price	Indexpreis *m*
market index	Börsenindex *m*
market value-weighted index	kursgewichteter Börsenindex *m*
misery index	Elendsindex *m*
Laspeyre's index	Laspeyres-Index *m*
Lerner index	Lerner-Index *m*
national expenditure	Staatsausgaben *f pl*
net national product	Nettosozialprodukt *nt*
Paasche index	Paasche-Index *m*
price index	Preisindex *m*
price index level	Preisindexniveau *m*
price-weighted index	gewichteter Preisindex *m*
producer price index	Erzeugerpreisindex *m*
rate of inflation	Inflationsrate *f*
retail price index	Einzelhandelspreisindex *m*
salary grade	Gehaltsstufe *f*, Gehaltsklasse *f*, Besoldungsgruppe *f*
share index	Aktienindex *m*

English name *Englischer Name*	German name *Deutscher Name*
share price index	Aktienpreisindex *m*, Kursindex *m*
stock exchange price index	Börsenkursindex *m*
stock index	Aktienindex *m*
stock market index	Börsenindex *m*
stock market price index	Börsenpreisindex *m*
stock price index	Aktienpreisindex *m*, Kursindex *m*
unemployment rate	Arbeitslosenzahl *f*, Arbeitslosenziffer *f*
volume index	Mengenindex *m*
weighted index	gewogener Index *m*, gewichteter Index *m*
wholesale price index	Großhandelspreisindex *m*
Asia	
SET index	Wertpapierbörsenindex *m* von Thailand
Straits Times Industrial Index	Haupt-Preis-Anzeiger *m* der Singapur Börse
Australia	
All Ordinaries Index	Stammaktienindex *m*
Europe	
Eurodollar Index	Eurodollar-Index *m*
FT-SE Eurotrack 100 Index	gewichteter Index *m* von 100 Aktien in Europa
FT-SE Eurotrack 200 Index	gewichteter Index *m* von 200 Aktien in Europa
Finland	
Unitas All Share Index	Unitas Gesamtaktienindex *m*
Germany	
German shares index	Deutscher Aktienindex *m* (DAX)
Hong Kong	
Hang Seng Index	Hang Seng Index *m*
International	
Divisia money Index	Divisia-Geldindex *m*
Italy	
Morgan Stanley Capital International World Index	Morgan Stanley internationaler Welt-Kapital-Index *m*
Comit index	Comit-Index *m*
Netherlands	
CBS Tendency Index	CBS-Tendenzindex *m*
New Zealand	
Barclays Index	Barclays Index *m*
Switzerland	
Credit suisse index	Schweizer Kreditindex *m*
UK	
Financial Times Actuaries All Share Index, All Share Index	Industrieaktienindex *m* der Financial Times
Financial Times Index (FT Index)	Financial Times Index *m*
Financial Times Industrial Ordinary Share Index	Industrieaktienindex *m* der Financial Times
Financial Times Stock Exchange index, FT-SE 100 Share Index	Börsenindex *m* der Financial Times
Index of Industrial Production	Index *m* der industriellen Produktion
Thirty-Share Index	Industrieaktienindex *m* der Financial Times
US	
Dow-Jones index	Dow-Jones Index *m*
New York Stock Exchange Composite Index	New Yorker Börsengesamtindex *m*

Countries/Länder

Country *Land*	Capital *Hauptstadt*	Inhabitant *Einwohner*	Official language(s) *Offizielle Sprache(n)*	Currency *Währung*
Afghanistan	Kabul	Afghan	Pushtu, Dari	afghani
Afghanistan nt	*Kabul nt*	*Afghane m, Afghanin f*	*Paschtu, Dari*	*Afghani m*
Albania	Tirana	Albanian	Albanian	lek
Albanien nt	*Tirana nt*	*Albaner, in m, f*	*Albanisch/Toskisch*	*Lek m*
Algeria	Algiers	Algerian	Arabic, French	dinar
Algerien nt	*Algier nt*	*Algerier, in m, f*	*Arabisch, Französisch*	*Algerischer Dinar m*
Andorra	Andorra la Vella	Andorran	Catalan, French, Spanish	French franc, peseta
Andorra nt	*Andorra la Vella nt*	*Andorraner, in m, f*	*Katalanisch, Französisch, Spanisch*	*Französischer Franc m, Spanische Peseta f*
Angola	Luanda	Angolan	Portuguese	New kwanza
Angola nt	*Luanda nt*	*Angolaner, in m, f*	*Portugiesisch*	*Neuer Kwanza m*
Antigua and Barbuda	St. John's	Antiguan, Barbudian	English	East Caribbean dollar
Antigua und Barbuda pl	*St. Johns nt*	*Antiguaner, in m, f, Barbudianer, in m, f*	*Englisch*	*Ostkaribischer Dollar m*
Argentina	Buenos Aires	Argentinian/Argentine	Spanish	peso
Argentinien nt	*Buenos Aires nt*	*Argentinier, in m, f*	*Spanisch*	*Peso m*
Armenia	Yerevan	Armenian	Armenian	dram
Armenien nt	*Jerewan nt*	*Armenier, in m, f*	*Armenisch*	*Dram m*
Australia	Canberra	Australian	English	Australian dollar
Australien nt	*Canberra nt*	*Australier, in m, f*	*Englisch*	*Australischer Dollar m*
Austria	Vienna	Austrian	German	schilling
Österreich nt	*Wien nt*	*Österreicher, in m, f*	*Deutsch*	*Österreichischer Schilling m*
Azerbaijan	Baku	Azeri/Azerbaijani	Azeri, Russian, Turkish	manat
Aserbaidshan/ Aserbeidshan nt	*Baku nt*	*Aserbaidschaner, in m, f/ Aserbeidscha- ner, in m, f*	*Aseri, Russisch, Türkisch*	*Manat m*
Bahamas	Nassau	Bahamian	English	Bahamian dollar
die Bahamas pl	*Nassau nt*	*Bahamer, in m, f/ Bahamaner, in m, f*	*Englisch*	*Bahama-Dollar m*
Bahrain/Bahrein	Manama	Bahraini	Arabic	dinar
Bahrain nt	*Manama nt*	*Bahrainer, in m, f*	*Arabisch*	*Bahrain-Dinar m*
Bangladesh	Dhaka	Bangladeshi	Bengali	taka
Bangladesch nt	*Dacca nt*	*Bangladeshi mf*	*Bengali*	*Taka m*
Barbados	Bridgetown	Barbadian	English	Barbados dollar
Barbados nt	*Bridgetown nt*	*Barbadier, in m, f*	*Englisch*	*Barbados-Dollar m*
Belarus	Minsk	Belarussian	Belarussian	Belarussian rouble
Weißrußland nt	*Minsk nt*	*Weißrusse m, Weißrussin f*	*Weißrussisch*	*Weißrussischer Rubel m*
Belgium	Brussels	Belgian	French, Flemish, German	Belgian franc
Belgien nt	*Brüssel nt*	*Belgier, in m, f*	*Französisch, Flämisch, Deutsch*	*Belgischer Franc m*
Belize	Belmopan	Belizean	English, Spanish, Creole	Belize dollar
Belize nt	*Belmopan nt*	*Belizer, in m, f*	*Englisch, Spanisch, Kreolisch*	*Belize-Dollar m*

| Country | Capital | Inhabitant | Official language(s) | Currency |
Land	*Hauptstadt*	*Einwohner*	*Offizielle Sprache(n)*	*Währung*
Benin	Porto Novo	Beninese	French	C.F.A. franc
Benin nt	*Porto Novo nt*	*Beniner, in m,f*	*Französisch*	*CFA-Franc m*
Bermuda	Hamilton	Bermudan/Bermudian	English	US dollar
die Bermudas/	*Hamilton nt*	*von den Bermudas*	*Englisch*	*US-Dollar m*
Bermudainseln pl				
Bhutan	Thamphu	Bhutanese/Bhutani	Dzongka	ngultrum, Indian rupee
Bhutan nt	*Thimphu nt*	*Bhutaner, in m,f*	*Dzonga*	*Ngultrum m, indische Rupie f*
Bolivia	La Paz	Bolivian	Spanish, Indian languages	Boliviano
Bolivien nt	*La Paz nt*	*Bolivianer, in m,f*	*Spanisch, indianische Sprachen*	*Boliviano m*
Bosnia-Herzegovina	Sarajevo	Bosnian	Serbo-Croat	dinar
Bosnien-Herzegovina nt	*Sarajevo nt*	*Bosnier, in m,f*	*Serbokroatisch*	*Dinar m*
Botswana	Gaborone	Botswanan	English, Setswana	pula
Botswana nt	*Gaborone nt*	*Botswaner, in m,f*	*Englisch, Setswana*	*Pula m*
Brazil	Brasilia	Brazilian	Portuguese	cruzeiro real
Brazilien nt	*Brasilia nt*	*Brazilianer, in m,f*	*Portugiesisch*	*Cruzeiro Real m*
Brunei	Bandar Seri Begawan	Brunei/Bruneian	Malay, English	Brunei dollar
Brunei nt	*Bandar Seri Begawan nt*	*Bruneier, in m,f*	*Malaiisch, Englisch*	*Brunei-Dollar m*
Bulgaria	Sofia	Bulgarian	Bulgarian	lev
Bulgarien nt	*Sofia nt*	*Bulgare m, Bulgarin f*	*Bulgarisch*	*Lew m*
Burkina Faso	Ouagadougou	Burkinabe	French, Mossi	C.F.A. franc
Burkina Faso nt	*Ouagadougou nt*	*Burkiner, in m,f*	*Französisch, Mossi*	*CFA-Franc m*
Burundi	Bujumbura	Burundian	Kirundi, French	Burundi franc
Burundi nt	*Bujumbura nt*	*Burundier, in m,f*	*Ki-Rundi, Französisch*	*Burundi-Franc m*
Cambodia	Phnom Penh	Cambodian	Khmer	riel
Kambodscha nt	*Phnom Penh nt*	*Kambodschaner, in m,f*	*Khmer*	*Riel m*
Cameroon	Yaoundé	Cameroonian	French, English	C.F.A. franc
Kamerun nt	*Yaoundé nt*	*Kameruner, in m,f*	*Französisch, Englisch*	*CFA-Franc m*
Canada	Ottawa	Canadian	English, French	Canadian dollar
Kanada nt	*Ottawa nt*	*Kanadier, in m,f*	*Englisch, Französisch*	*Kanadischer Dollar m*
Cape Verde Islands	Praia	Cape Verdean	Portuguese	Cape Verde escudo
die Kapverden/ Kapverdische Inseln pl	*Praia nt*	*Kapverdier, in m,f*	*Portugiesisch*	*Kap-Verde-Escudo m*
Central African Republic	Bangui	from the Central African Republic	French, Sango	C.F.A. franc
die Zentralafrikanische Republik f	*Bangui nt*	*aus der Zentralafrikanischen Republik*	*Französisch, Sango*	*CFA-Franc m*
Chad	N'Djamena	Chadian	Arabic, French	C.F.A. franc
der Tschad m	*N'Djamena nt*	*Tschader, in m,f*	*Arabisch, Französisch*	*CFA-Franc m*
Chile	Santiago	Chilean	Spanish	peso
Chile nt	*Santiago nt*	*Chilene m, Chilenin f*	*Spanisch*	*Chilenischer Peso m*
China	Beijing/Peking	Chinese	Mandarin, Chinese languages	Renminbi yuan
China nt	*Peking nt*	*Chinese m, Chinesin f*	*Mandarin, chinesische Sprachen*	*Renminbi Yuan m*

Country	Capital	Inhabitant	Official language(s)	Currency
Land	*Hauptstadt*	*Einwohner*	*Offizielle Sprache(n)*	*Währung*
Colombia	Bogotá	Colombian	Spanish	Columbian peso
Kolumbien nt	*Bogota nt*	*Kolumbianer,in m,f*	*Spanisch*	*Kolumbianischer Peso m*
Comoros	Moroni	Comorian/Comoran	French, Arabic	Comorian franc
die Komoren pl	*Moroni nt*	*Komorer,in m,f*	*Französisch, Arabisch*	*Komoren-Franc m*
Congo	Brazzaville	Congolese	French	C.F.A. franc
Kongo m	*Brazzaville nt*	*Kongolese m, Kongolesin f*	*Französisch*	*CFA-Franc m*
Costa Rica	San José	Costa Rican	Spanish	colón
Costa Rica nt	*San José nt*	*Costaricaner,in m,f*	*Spanisch*	*Costa-Rica-Colón m*
Croatia	Zagreb	Croat/Croatian	Serbo-Croat	kuna
Kroatien nt	*Zagreb nt*	*Kroate m, Kroatin f*	*Serbokroatisch*	*Kuna m*
Cuba	Havana	Cuban	Spanish	Cuban peso
Kuba nt	*Havanna nt*	*Kubaner,in m,f*	*Spanisch*	*Kubanischer Peso m*
Cyprus	Nicosia	Cypriot	Greek, Turkish	Cyprus pound
Zypern nt	*Nikosia nt*	*Zypriot,in m,f*	*Griechisch, Türkisch*	*Zypern-Pfund nt*
Czech Republic	Prague	Czech	Czech	Czech koruna
die Tschechische Republik f	*Prag nt*	*Tscheche m, Tschechin f*	*Tschechisch*	*Tschechische Krone f*
Denmark	Copenhagen	Dane	Danish	Danish krone
Dänemark nt	*Kopenhagen nt*	*Däne m, Dänin f*	*Dänisch*	*Dänische Krone f*
Djibouti	Djibouti	Djibuti/Djibutian	Arabic, French	Djibouti franc
Djibouti/ Dschibuti nt	*Djibouti/ Dschibuti nt*	*aus Djibouti*	*Arabisch, Französisch*	*Franc m de Djibouti*
Dominica	Roseau	Dominican	English	East Caribbean dollar
Dominica nt	*Roseau nt*	*aus Dominica*	*Englisch*	*Ostkaribischer Dollar m*
Dominican Republic	Santo Domingo	Dominican	Spanish	Dominican peso
die Dominika- nische Republik f	*Santo Domingo nt*	*Dominikaner,in m,f*	*Spanisch*	*Dominikanischer Peso m*
Ecuador	Quito	Ecuadorian/Ecuadoran	Spanish	sucre
Ecuador/ Ekuador nt	*Quito nt*	*Ecuadorianer,in m,f/ Ekuadorianer,in m,f*	*Spanisch*	*Sucre m*
Egypt	Cairo	Egyptian	Arabic	Egyptian pound
Ägypten nt	*Kairo nt*	*Ägypter,in m,f*	*Arabisch*	*Ägyptisches Pfund nt*
El Salvador	San Salvador	Salvadoran/Salvadorean	Spanish	colón
El Salvador nt	*San Salvador nt*	*Salvadorianer,in m,f*	*Spanisch*	*El-Salvador-Colón m*
England	London	Englishman, Englishwoman	English	Sterling pound
England nt	*London nt*	*Engländer,in m,f*	*Englisch*	*Pfund Sterling nt*
Equatorial Guinea	Malabo	Equatorial Guinean	Spanish	C.F.A. franc
Äquatorial- Guinea/Äqua- torialguinea nt	*Malabo nt*	*aus Äquatorial-Guinea*	*Spanisch*	*CFA-Franc m*
Eritrea	Asmara	Eritrean	Arabic, English	birr
Eritrea nt	*Asmara nt*	*Eritreer,in m,f*	*Arabisch, Englisch*	*Birr m*
Estonia	Tallinn	Estonian	Estonian	kroon
Estland nt	*Tallinn nt*	*Este m, Estin f*	*Estnisch*	*Estnische Krone f*
Ethiopia	Addis Ababa	Ethiopian	Amharic	birr
Äthiopien nt	*Addis Abeba nt*	*Äthiopier,in m,f*	*Amharisch*	*Birr m*

Country	Capital	Inhabitant	Official language(s)	Currency
Land	*Hauptstadt*	*Einwohner*	*Offizielle Sprache(n)*	*Währung*
Fiji	Suva	Fijian	English	Fiji dollar
die Fidschiinseln pl	*Suva nt*	*Fidschianer,in m,f*	*Englisch*	*Fidschi-Dollar m*
Finland	Helsinki	Finn	Finnish, Swedish	markka
Finnland nt	*Helsinki nt*	*Finne m, Finnin f*	*Finnisch, Schwedisch*	*Finnmark f*
France	Paris	Frenchman, Frenchwoman	French	French franc
Frankreich nt	*Paris nt*	*Franzose m, Französin f*	*Französisch*	*Französischer Franc m*
Gabon	Libreville	Gabonese	French	C.F.A. franc
Gabun nt	*Libreville nt*	*Gabuner,in m,f*	*Französisch*	*CFA-Franc m*
Gambia	Banjul	Gambian	English	dalasi
Gambia nt	*Banjul nt*	*Gambier,in m,f*	*Englisch*	*Dalasi m*
Georgia	Tbilisi	Georgian	Georgian	kupon
Georgien nt	*Tiflis nt*	*Georgier,in m,f*	*Georgisch*	*Kupon m*
Germany	Berlin	German	German	German Mark
Deutschland nt	*Berlin nt*	*Deutsche(r) mf [decl. as adj]*	*Deutsch*	*Deutsche Mark f*
Ghana	Accra	Ghanaian	English	cedi
Ghana nt	*Accra nt*	*Ghanaer,in m,f*	*Englisch*	*Cedi m*
Greece	Athens	Greek	Greek	drachma
Griechenland nt	*Athen nt*	*Grieche m, Griechin f*	*Griechisch*	*Drachme f*
Grenada	St. George's	Grenadian	English	East Caribbean dollar
Grenada nt	*St. George's nt*	*von Grenada*	*Englisch*	*Ostkaribischer Dollar m*
Guatemala	Guatemala City	Guatemalan	Spanish	quetzal
Guatemala nt	*Guatemala-Stadt nt*	*Guatemalteke m, Guatemaltekin f*	*Spanisch*	*Quetzal m*
Guinea	Conakry	Guinean	French	Guinean franc
Guinea nt	*Conakry nt*	*Guineer,in m,f*	*Französisch*	*Guinea-Franc m*
Guinea-Bissau	Bissau	from Guinea-Bissau	Portuguese	Guinea-Bissau peso
Guinea-Bissau nt	*Bissau nt*	*aus Guinea-Bissau*	*Portugiesisch*	*Guinea-Bissau Peso m*
Guyana	Georgetown	Guyanese/Guyanan	English	Guyana dollar
Guyana nt	*Georgetown nt*	*Guyaner,in m,f*	*Englisch*	*Guyana-Dollar m*
Haiti	Port-au-Prince	Haitian	French	gourde
Haiti nt	*Port-au-Prince nt*	*Haitianer,in m,f*	*Französisch*	*Gourde m*
Honduras	Tegucigalpa	Honduran	Spanish	lempira
Honduras nt	*Tegucigalpa nt*	*Honduraner,in m,f*	*Spanisch*	*Lempira m*
Hong Kong	Victoria	from Hong Kong	English	Hong Kong dollar
Hong Kong nt	*Victoria nt*	*aus Hong Kong*	*Englisch*	*Hong-Kong-Dollar m*
Hungary	Budapest	Hungarian	Hungarian	forint
Ungarn nt	*Budapest nt*	*Ungar,in m,f*	*Ungarisch*	*Forint m*
Iceland	Reykjavik	Icelander	Icelandic	Icelandic krona
Island nt	*Reykjavik nt*	*Isländer,in m,f*	*Isländisch*	*Isländische Krone f*
India	New Delhi	Indian	Hindi, English	Indian rupee
Indien nt	*Neu-Delhi nt*	*Inder,in m,f*	*Hindi, Englisch*	*Indische Rupie f*
Indonesia	Jakarta	Indonesian	Bahasa Indonesia	Indonesian rupiah
Indonesien nt	*Jakarta nt*	*Indonesier,in m,f*	*Bahasa Indonesisch*	*Rupiah f*
Iran	Tehran/Teheran	Iranian	Iranian	rial
der Iran m	*Teheran nt*	*Iraner,in m,f*	*Iranisch*	*Rial m*
Iraq/Irak	Baghdad	Iraqi/Iraki	Arabic	Iraqi dinar/Iraki dinar
der Irak m	*Bagdad nt*	*Iraker,in m,f*	*Arabisch*	*Irak-Dinar m*

Country	Capital	Inhabitant	Official language(s)	Currency
Land	*Hauptstadt*	*Einwohner*	*Offizielle Sprache(n)*	*Währung*
Ireland	Dublin	Irishman, Irishwoman	Irish Gaelic, English	Irish pound/punt
Irland nt	*Dublin nt*	*Ire m, Irin f / Irländer,in m,f*	*Gälisch, Englisch*	*Irisches Pfund nt*
Israel	Jerusalem	Israeli	Hebrew, Arabic	New shekel
Israel nt	*Jerusalem nt*	*Israeli mf*	*Hebräisch, Arabisch*	*Neuer Israel Schekel m*
Italy	Rome	Italian	Italian	lira
Italien nt	*Rom nt*	*Italiener,in m,f*	*Italienisch*	*Italienische Lira f*
Ivory Coast	Yamoussoukro	Ivorian	French	C.F.A. franc
die Elfenbein-küste/Côte-d'Ivoire f	*Yamoussoukro nt*	*von der Elfenbeinküste*	*Französisch*	*CFA-Franc m*
Jamaica	Kingston	Jamaican	English	Jamaica dollar
Jamaika nt	*Kingston nt*	*Jamaikaner,in m,f*	*Englisch*	*Jamaika-Dollar m*
Japan	Tokyo	Japanese	Japanese	yen
Japan nt	*Tokio nt*	*Japaner,in m,f*	*Japanisch*	*Yen m*
Jordan	Amman	Jordanian	Arabic	Jordan dinar
Jordanien nt	*Amman nt*	*Jordaner,in m,f*	*Arabisch*	*Jordanischer Dinar m*
Kazakhstan	Alma-Ata	Kazakh/Kazak	Kazakh	Tenge
Kasachstan nt	*Almaty nt*	*Kasache m, Kasachin f*	*Kasachisch*	*Tenge m*
Kenya	Nairobi	Kenyan	Swahili, English	shilling
Kenia nt	*Nairobi nt*	*Kenianer,in m,f*	*Swahili, Englisch*	*Kenia-Schilling m*
Kiribati	Bairiki	from Kiribati	English, Gilbertese	Australian dollar
Kiribati nt	*Bairiki*	*aus Kiribati*	*Englisch, Gilbertesisch*	*Australischer Dollar m*
Kuwait	Kuwait City	Kuwaiti	Arabic	Kuwaiti dinar
Kuwait nt	*Kuwait-Stadt nt*	*Kuwaiter,in m,f*	*Arabisch*	*Kuwait-Dinar m*
Kyrgyzstan	Bishkek	Kyrgyz	Kyrgyz	som
Kirgistan nt	*Bischkek nt*	*Kirgise m, Kirgisin f*	*Kirgisisch*	*Kirgistan-Som m*
Laos	Vientiane	Laotian	Lao	kip
Laos nt	*Vientiane nt*	*Laote m, Laotin f*	*Lao*	*Kip m*
Latvia	Riga	Latvian	Latvian	lat
Lettland nt	*Riga nt*	*Lette m, Lettin f*	*Lettisch*	*Lat m*
Lebanon	Beirut	Lebanese	Arabic	Lebanese pound
Libanon nt	*Beirut nt*	*Libanese m, Libanesin f*	*Arabisch*	*Libanesisches Pfund nt*
Lesotho	Maseru	Mosotho/Basotho	Sotho, English	loti
Lesotho nt	*Maseru nt*	*Lesother,in m,f*	*Sotho, Englisch*	*Loti m*
Liberia	Monrovia	Liberian	English	Liberian dollar
Liberien nt	*Monrovia nt*	*Liberianer,in m,f / Liberier,in m,f*	*Englisch*	*Liberianischer Dollar m*
Libya	Tripoli	Libyan	Arabic	Libyan dinar
Libyen nt	*Tripolis nt*	*Libyer,in m,f*	*Arabisch*	*Libyscher Dinar m*
Liechtenstein	Vaduz	Liechtensteiner	German	Swiss franc
Liechtenstein nt	*Vaduz nt*	*Liechtensteiner,in m,f*	*Deutsch*	*Schweizer Franken m*
Lithuania	Vilnius	Lithuanian	Lithuanian	litas
Litauen nt	*Vilnius/Wilna nt*	*Litauer,in m,f*	*Litauisch*	*Litas m*
Luxembourg	Luxembourg	Luxemburger	French, German	Luxembourg franc
Luxemburg nt	*Luxemburg nt*	*Luxemburger,in m,f*	*Französisch, Deutsch*	*Luxemburgischer Franc m*
Macedonia	Skopje	Macedonian	Macedonian	dinar
Makedonien/ Mazedonien nt	*Skopje nt*	*Makedonier,in m,f / Mazedonier,in m,f*	*Makedonisch/ Mazedonisch*	*Makedonischer Dinar m*

Country	Capital	Inhabitant	Official language(s)	Currency
Land	*Hauptstadt*	*Einwohner*	*Offizielle Sprache(n)*	*Währung*
Madagascar	Antananarivo	Madagascan	Malagasy, French	Malagasy franc
Madagaskar nt	*Antananarivo nt*	*Madegasse m, Madegassin f*	*Malagassy, Französisch*	*Madagaskar-Franc m*
Malawi	Lilongwe	Malawian	English	kwacha
Malawi nt	*Lilongwe nt*	*Malawier,in m,f*	*Englisch*	*Malawi-Kwacha m*
Malaysia	Kuala Lumpur	Malaysian/Malay	Malay	Malaysian ringgit
Malaysia nt	*Kuala Lumpur nt*	*Malaysier,in m,f*	*Malaiisch*	*Ringgit m*
Maldives	Malé	Maldivian	Divehi	Maldivian rupee
die Malediven pl	*Malé nt*	*Maledive m, Maledivin f*	*Divehi*	*Rufiyaa f*
Mali	Bamako	Malian	French	C.F.A. franc
Mali nt	*Bamako nt*	*Malier,in m,f*	*Französisch*	*CFA-Franc m*
Malta	Valletta	Maltese	Maltese, English	Maltese lira
Malta nt	*Valletta nt*	*Malteser,in m,f*	*Maltesisch, Englisch*	*Maltesische Lira f*
Marshall Islands	Dalap-Uliga-Darrit	from the Marshall Islands	Marshallese/Kahjin-Majol	US dollar
die Marshall-Inseln pl	*Dalap-Uliga-Darrit nt*	*von den Marshall-Inseln*	*Kajin-Majol*	*US-Dollar m*
Mauritania	Nouakchott	Mauritanian	Arabic, French	ouguiya
Mauretanien nt	*Nouakchott nt*	*Mauretanier,in m,f*	*Arabisch, Französisch*	*Ouguiya nt*
Mauritius	Port Louis	Mauritian	English, French	Mauritian rupee
Mauritius nt	*Port Louis nt*	*Mauritier,in m,f*	*Englisch, Französisch*	*Mauritius-Rupie f*
Mexico	Mexico City	Mexican	Spanish	Mexican new peso
Mexiko nt	*Mexiko-Stadt nt*	*Mexikaner,in m,f*	*Spanisch*	*Neuer Mexikanischer Peso m*
Micronesia	Kolonia	from Micronesia	English	US dollar
Mikronesien nt	*Kolonia nt*	*aus Mikronesien*	*Englisch*	*US-Dollar m*
Moldova	Kishinyev	Moldovan	Romanian/Rumanian	Moldovan leu
Moldawien nt	*Kischinew nt*	*Moldawier,in m,f*	*Rumänisch*	*Lei m*
Monaco	Monaco	Monegasque	French	French franc
Monaco nt	*Monaco-Ville nt*	*Monegasse m, Monegassin f*	*Französisch*	*Französischer Franc m*
Mongolia	Ulaanbaatar/Ulan Bator	Mongolian	Khalkha/Mongol	tugrik
die Mongolei f	*Ulan Bator nt*	*Mongole m, Mongolin f*	*Mongolisch*	*Tugrik m*
Montenegro	Podgorica	Montenegrin	Serbo-Croat	dinar
Montenegro nt	*Podgorica nt*	*Montenegriner,in m,f*	*Serbokroatisch*	*Dinar m*
Morocco	Rabat	Moroccan	Arabic, French	dirham
Marokko nt	*Rabat nt*	*Marokkaner,in m,f*	*Arabisch, Französisch*	*Dirham m*
Mozambique	Maputo	Mozambican	Portuguese	metical
Mozambique/Mosambik nt	*Maputo nt*	*aus Mozambique*	*Portugiesisch*	*Metical m*
Myanmar/Burma	Yangon/Rangoon	Burmese	Burmese	kyat
Myanmar/Burma nt	*Yangon/Rangun nt*	*Burmese m, Burmesin f/Birmane m, Birmanin f*	*Burmesisch/Birmanisch*	*Kyat m*
Namibia	Windhoek	Namibian	English, Afrikaans	Namibian dollar
Namibia nt	*Windhuk nt*	*Namibier,in m,f*	*Englisch, Afrikaans*	*Namibischer Dollar m*
Nauru	Yaren District	from Nauru	English, Naurian	Australian dollar
Nauru nt	*Yaren nt*	*Nauruer,in m,f*	*Englisch, Nauruisch*	*Australischer Dollar m*
Nepal	Kathmandu	Nepalese/Nepali	Nepali	Nepali rupee
Nepal nt	*Katmandu nt*	*Nepalese m, Nepalesin f*	*Nepalesisch/Nepali*	*Nepalesische Rupie f*

Country	Capital	Inhabitant	Official language(s)	Currency
Land	*Hauptstadt*	*Einwohner*	*Offizielle Sprache(n)*	*Währung*
the Netherlands/ Holland	Amsterdam	Netherlander/ Dutchman, Dutchwoman	Dutch	guilder
die Niederlande pl/Holland nt	*Amsterdam*	*Niederländer,in m,fl Holländer,in m,f*	*Niederländisch*	*Gulden m*
New Zealand	Wellington	New Zealander	English, Maori	New Zealand dollar
Neuseeland nt	*Wellington nt*	*Neuseeländer,in m,f*	*Englisch, Maori*	*Neuseeland-Dollar m*
Nicaragua	Managua	Nicaraguan	Spanish	cordoba
Nicaragua nt	*Managua nt*	*Nicaraguaner,in m,f*	*Spanisch*	*Córdoba m*
Niger	Niamey	from Niger	French	C.F.A. franc
Niger nt	*Niamey nt*	*Nigrer,in m,f*	*Französisch*	*CFA-Franc m*
Nigeria	Abuja	Nigerian	English	naira
Nigeria nt	*Abuja nt*	*Nigerianer,in m,f*	*Englisch*	*Naira m*
North Korea	Pyongyang	North Korean	Korean	won
Nordkorea nt	*Pjöngyang nt*	*Nordkoreaner,in m,f*	*Koreanisch*	*Won m*
Northern Ireland	Belfast	Irishman, Irishwoman	Irish Gaelic, English	Sterling pound
Nordirland nt	*Belfast nt*	*Irländer,in m,fl Ire m, Irin f*	*Gälisch, Englisch*	*Pfund Sterling nt*
Norway	Oslo	Norse (*pl* only)	Norwegian	Norwegian krone
Norwegen nt	*Oslo nt*	*Norweger,in m,f*	*Norwegisch*	*Norwegische Krone f*
Oman	Muscat	Omani	Arabic	Omani rial
Oman nt	*Maskat nt*	*Omaner,in m,f*	*Arabisch*	*Rial Omani m*
Pakistan	Islamabad	Pakistani	Urdu, English	Pakistan rupee
Pakistan nt	*Islamabad nt*	*Pakistani mfl Pakistaner,in m,f*	*Urdu, Englisch*	*Pakistanische Rupie f*
Panama	Panama City	Panamanian	Spanish	balboa
Panama nt	*Panama-Stadt nt*	*Panamaer,in m,fl Panamese m, Panamesin f*	*Spanisch*	*Balboa m*
Papua New Guinea	Port Moresby	from Papua New Guinea, Papuan	English	kina
Papua-Neuguinea nt	*Port Moresby nt*	*Papua mf*	*Englisch*	*Kina m*
Paraguay	Asunción	Paraguayan	Spanish	guarani
Paraguay nt	*Asunción nt*	*Paraguayer,in m,f*	*Spanisch*	*Guarani m*
Peru	Lima	Peruvian	Spanish, Quechua	nuevo sol
Peru nt	*Lima nt*	*Peruaner,in m,f*	*Spanisch, Ketschua*	*Nuevo Sol m*
Philippines	Manila	Philippine/Filipino	Filipino, English	Philippine peso
die Philippinen pl	*Manila nt*	*Filipino mfl Philippine m, Philippinin f*	*Filipino, Englisch*	*Philippinischer Peso m*
Poland	Warsaw	Pole	Polish	zloty
Polen nt	*Warschau nt*	*Pole m, Polin f*	*Polnisch*	*Zloty m*
Portugal	Lisbon	Portuguese	Portuguese	escudo
Portugal nt	*Lissabon nt*	*Portugiese m, Portugiesin f*	*Portugiesisch*	*Escudo m*
Puerto Rico	San Juan	Puerto Rican	Spanish, English	U.S. dollar
Puerto Rico nt	*San Juan nt*	*Puertoricaner,in m,f*	*Spanisch, Englisch*	*US-Dollar m*
Qatar	Doha	Qatari	Arabic	Qatar riyal
Katar nt	*Dauha nt*	*aus Katar*	*Arabisch*	*Katar-Riyal m*
Romania/ Rumania	Bucharest	Romanian/Rumanian	Romanian/Rumanian	Romanian leu
Rumänien nt	*Bukarest nt*	*Rumäne m, Rumänin f*	*Rumänisch*	*Lei m*
Russia	Moscow	Russian	Russian	rouble
Rußland nt	*Moskau nt*	*Russe m, Russin f*	*Russisch*	*Rubel m*

Country *Land*	Capital *Hauptstadt*	Inhabitant *Einwohner*	Official language(s) *Offizielle Sprache(n)*	Currency *Während*
Rwanda *Ruanda/Rwanda* *nt*	Kigali *Kigali nt*	Rwandan, Rwandese *Ruander,in m,fl* *Rwander,in m,f*	French, Kinyarwanda *Französisch,* *Kinyarwanda*	Rwanda franc *Rwanda-Franc m*
Saint Kitts and Nevis *Saint Kitts und* *Nevis pl*	Basseterre *Basseterre nt*	from Saint Kitts and Nevis *von Saint Kitts und Nevis*	English *Englisch*	East Caribbean dollar *Ostkaribischer Dollar* *m*
Saint Lucia *Saint Lucia nt*	Castries *Castries nt*	Saint Lucian *von Saint Lucia*	English *Englisch*	East Caribbean dollar *Ostkaribischer Dollar* *m*
Saint Vincent and the Grenadines *Saint Vincent nt* *und die* *Grenadinen pl*	Kingstown *Kingstown nt*	Vincentian *von Saint Vincent und* *den Grenadinen*	English *Englisch*	East Caribbean dollar *Ostkaribischer Dollar* *m*
San Marino *San Marino nt*	San Marino *San Marino nt*	San Marinese *Sanmarinese m,* *Sanmarinesin f*	Italian *Italienisch*	Italian lira *Italienische Lira f*
São Tomé and Principe *São Tomé und* *Principe nt*	São Tomé *São Tomé nt*	from São Tomé *von São Tomé*	Portuguese *Portugiesisch*	dobra *Dobra f*
Saudi Arabia *Saudi-Arabien nt*	Riyadh *Riad nt*	Saudi/Saudi Arabian *Saudi mfl* *Saudiaraber,in m,f*	Arabic *Arabisch*	riyal *Saudi-Riyal m*
Scotland *Schottland nt*	Edinburgh *Edinburg nt*	Scot/Scotsman, Scotswoman *Schotte m, Schottin f*	English *Englisch*	Sterling pound *Pfund Sterling nt*
Senegal *Senegal nt*	Dakar *Dakar nt*	Senegalese *Senegalese m,* *Senegalesin f*	French *Französisch*	C.F.A. franc *CFA-Franc m*
Serbia *Serbien nt*	Belgrade *Belgrad nt*	Serb *Serbe m, Serbin f*	Serbo-Croat *Serbokroatisch*	dinar *Dinar m*
Seychelles *die Seychellen pl*	Victoria *Victoria nt*	Seychellois/Seselwa *von den Seychellen*	English, French, Creole *Englisch, Französisch,* *Kreolisch*	Seychelles rupee *Seychellen-Rupie f*
Sierra Leone *Sierra Leone f*	Freetown *Freetown nt*	Sierra Leonean *Sierraleoner,in m,f*	English *Englisch*	leone *Leone m*
Singapore *Singapur nt*	Singapore *Singapur nt*	Singaporean *Singapurer,in m,f*	English, Malay, Chinese languages, Tamil *Englisch, Malaiisch,* *chinesische Sprachen,* *Tamil*	Singapore dollar *Singapur-Dollar m*
Slovakia *die Slowakei f*	Bratislava *Bratislava/* *Preßburg nt*	Slovak *Slowake m, Slowakin f*	Slovak *Slowakisch*	Slovak koruna *Slowakische Krone f*
Slovenia *Slowenien nt*	Ljubljana *Ljubljana/Laibach* *nt*	Slovenian/Slovene *Slowenier,in m,fl/Slowene* *m, Slowenin f*	Slovene *Slowenisch*	tolar *Tolar m*
Solomon Islands *die Salomonen pl*	Honiara *Honiara nt*	from the Solomon Is- lands *von den Salomonen*	English *Englisch*	Solomon Islands dollar *Salomonen-Dollar m*

Country	Capital	Inhabitant	Official language(s)	Currency
Land	*Hauptstadt*	*Einwohner*	*Offizielle Sprache(n)*	*Währung*
Somalia	Mogadishu	Somali	Somali, Arabic	Somali shilling
Somalia nt	*Mogadishu nt*	*Somali mfl Somalier, in m,f*	*Somali, Arabisch*	*Somalia-Schilling m*
South Africa	Pretoria	South African	Afrikaans, English	rand
Südafrika nt	*Pretoria nt*	*Südafrikaner, in m,f*	*Afrikaans, Englisch*	*Rand m*
South Korea	Seoul	South Korean	Korean	won
Südkorea nt	*Seoul nt*	*Südkoreaner, in m,f*	*Koreanisch*	*Won m*
Spain	Madrid	Spaniard	Spanish	peseta
Spanien nt	*Madrid nt*	*Spanier, in m,f*	*Spanisch*	*Peseta f*
Sri Lanka	Colombo	Sri Lankan	Singhalese, Tamil, English	Sri Lanka rupee
Sri Lanka nt	*Colombo nt*	*Srilanker, in m,f*	*Singhalesisch, Tamil, Englisch*	*Sri-Lanka-Rupie f*
Sudan	Khartoum	Sudanese	Arabic	Sudanese pound
Sudan nt	*Khartum nt*	*Sudaner, in m,fl Sudanese m, Sudanesin f*	*Arabisch*	*Sudanesisches Pfund nt*
Surinam	Paramaribo	Surinamese	Dutch, English	Surinam guilder
Surinam nt	*Paramaribo nt*	*Surinamer, in m,f*	*Niederländisch, Englisch*	*Surinam-Gulden m*
Swaziland	Mbabane	Swazi	Swazi, English	lilangeni
Swasiland nt	*Mbabane nt*	*Swasi mf*	*Si-Suati, Englisch*	*Lilangeni m*
Sweden	Stockholm	Swede	Swedish	Swedish krona
Schweden nt	*Stockholm nt*	*Schwede m, Schwedin f*	*Schwedisch*	*Schwedische Krone f*
Switzerland	Bern	Swiss	French, German, Italian	Swiss franc
die Schweiz f	*Bern nt*	*Schweizer, in m,f*	*Französisch, Deutsch, Italienisch*	*Schweizer Franken m*
Syria	Damascus	Syrian	Arabic	Syrian pound
Syrien nt	*Damaskus nt*	*Syrier, in m,fl Syrer, in m,f*	*Arabisch*	*Syrisches Pfund nt*
Taiwan	Taipei	Taiwanese	Mandarin, Chinese languages	Taiwan dollar
Taiwan nt	*Taipeh nt*	*Taiwaner, in m,f*	*Mandarin, chinesische Sprachen*	*Taiwan-Dollar m*
Tajikistan	Dushanbe	Tajik	Tajik	rouble
Tadschikistan nt	*Duschanbe nt*	*Tadschike m, Tadschikin f*	*Tadschikisch*	*Rubel m*
Tanzania	Dodoma	Tanzanian	Swahili, English	Tanzanian shilling
Tansania nt	*Dodoma nt*	*Tansanier, in m,f*	*Swahili, Englisch*	*Tanzania-Schilling m*
Thailand	Bangkok	Thai	Thai	baht
Thailand nt	*Bangkok nt*	*Thailänder, in m,fl Thai mf*	*Thai*	*Baht m*
Togo	Lomé	Togolese	French	C.F.A. franc
Togo nt	*Lomé nt*	*Togoer, in m,f*	*Französisch*	*CFA-Franc m*
Tonga	Nuku'alofa	Tongan	English, Tongan	pa'anga
Tonga nt	*Nuku'alofa nt*	*Tongaer, in m,f*	*Englisch, Tonga*	*La'anga m*
Trinidad and Tobago	Port of Spain	Trinidadian/Tobagoan/ Tobagodian	English	Trinidad and Tobago dollar
Trinidad und Tobago nt	*Port of Spain nt*	*von Trinidad und Tobago*	*Englisch*	*Trinidad-und-Tobago-Dollar m*
Tunisia	Tunis	Tunisian	Arabic	dinar
Tunesien nt	*Tunis nt*	*Tunesier, in m,f*	*Arabisch*	*Tunesischer Dinar m*
Turkey	Ankara	Turk	Turkish	Turkish lira
die Türkei f	*Ankara nt*	*Türke m, Türkin f*	*Türkisch*	*Türkische Lira f*
Turkmenistan	Ashkhabad	Turkmen	Turkmen	Turkmenian manat
Turkmenistan nt	*Aschchabad nt*	*Turkmene m, Turkmenin f*	*Turkmenisch*	*Manat m*

Country	Capital	Inhabitant	Official language(s)	Currency
Land	*Hauptstadt*	*Einwohner*	*Offizielle Sprache(n)*	*Währung*
Tuvalu	Funafuti	from Tuvalu	English	Australian dollar
Tuvalu ntl	*Funafuti nt*	*Tuvaluer,in m,f*	*Englisch*	*Australischer Dollar*
Ellice-Inseln pl				*m*
Uganda	Kampala	Ugandan	Swahili, English	Uganda shilling
Uganda nt	*Kampala nt*	*Ugander,in m,f*	*Swahili, Englisch*	*Uganda-Schilling m*
Ukraine	Kiev	Ukrainian	Ukrainian	karbovanet
die Ukraine f	*Kiew nt*	*Ukrainer,in m,f*	*Ukrainisch*	*Karbowanez m*
United Arab	Abu Dhabi	from the United Arab	Arabic	dirham
Emirates		Emirates		
die Vereinigten	*Abu Dhabi nt*	*aus den Vereinigten*	*Arabisch*	*Dirham m*
Arabischen		*Arabischen Emiraten*		
Emirate pl				
United Kingdom/	London	Briton	English	Sterling pound
Great Britain				
Vereinigtes	*London nt*	*Brite m, Britin f*	*Englisch*	*Pfund Sterling nt*
Königreich/				
Großbritannien nt				
United States of	Washington, D.C.	American	English	dollar
America				
die Vereinigten	*Washington, D.C.*	*Amerikaner,in m,f*	*Englisch*	*US-Dollar m*
Staaten pl von	*nt*			
Amerika				
Uruguay	Montevideo	Uruguayan	Spanish	peso
Uruguay nt	*Montevideo nt*	*Uruguayer,in m,f*	*Spanisch*	*Peso Uruguayo m*
Uzbekistan	Tashkent	Uzbek	Uzbek	som
Usbekistan nt	*Taschkent m*	*Usbeke m, Usbekin f*	*Usbekisch*	*Usbekistan-Sum m*
Vanuatu	Port Vila	from Vanuatu	English, French, Bislama	vatu
Vanuatu ntl/Neue	*Vila nt*	*aus Vanuatu*	*Englisch, Französisch,*	*Vatu m*
Hebriden pl			*Bislama*	
Venezuela	Caracas	Venezuelan	Spanish	bolivar
Venezuela nt	*Caracas nt*	*Venezolaner,in m,f*	*Spanisch*	*Bolivar m*
Vietnam	Hanoi	Vietnamese	Vietnamese	dong
Vietnam nt	*Hanoi nt*	*Vietnamese m,*	*Vietnamesisch*	*Dong m*
		Vietnamesin f		
Wales	Cardiff	Welshman, Welshwoman	English, Welsh	Sterling pound
Wales nt	*Cardiff nt*	*Waliser,in m,f*	*Englisch, Walisisch*	*Pfund Sterling nt*
Western Samoa	Apia	from Western Samoa	English, Samoan	tala
Westsamoa nt	*Apia nt*	*aus Westsamoa*	*Englisch, Samoanisch*	*Tala m*
Yemen	San'a	Yemeni	Arabic	Yemeni dinar
der Jemen m	*Sana nt*	*Jemenit,in m,f*	*Arabisch*	*Jemen-Rial m*
Zaïre	Kinshasha	Zaïrese/Zairean	French	New zaïre
Zaire/Zaïre nt	*Kinshasa nt*	*Zairer,in m,f*	*Französisch*	*Neuer Zaïre m*
Zambia	Lusaka	Zambian	English	kwacha
Sambia nt	*Lusaka nt*	*Sambesi mf*	*Englisch*	*Kwacha m*
Zimbabwe	Harare	Zimbabwean	English	Zimbabwe dollar
Zimbabwel	*Harare nt*	*Zimbabwer,in m,fl*	*Englisch*	*Zimbabwe-Dollar m*
Simbabwe nt		*Simbabwer,in m,f*		

All languages listed in this table are neuter/Alle Sprachen in dieser Tabelle sind neutrum

Cardinal and ordinal numbers/
Kardinal- und Ordinalzahlen

Cardinal Kardinalzahlen	English Englisch	German Deutsch	Ordinal Ordinalzahlen	English Englisch	German Deutsch
1	one	eins	1st	first	erste
2	two	zwei	2nd	second	zweite
3	three	drei	3rd	third	dritte
4	four	vier	4th	fourth	vierte
5	five	fünf	5th	fifth	fünfte
6	six	sechs	6th	sixth	sechste
7	seven	sieben	7th	seventh	siebte
8	eight	acht	8th	eighth	achte
9	nine	neun	9th	ninth	neunte
10	ten	zehn	10th	tenth	zehnte
11	eleven	elf	11th	eleventh	elfte
12	twelve	zwölf	12th	twelfth	zwölfte
13	thirteen	dreizehn	13th	thirteenth	dreizehnte
14	fourteen	vierzehn	14th	fourteenth	vierzehnte
15	fifteen	fünfzehn	15th	fifteenth	fünfzehnte
16	sixteen	sechzehn	16th	sixteenth	sechzehnte
17	seventeen	siebzehn	17th	seventeenth	siebzehnte
18	eighteen	achtzehn	18th	eighteenth	achtzehnte
19	nineteen	neunzehn	19th	nineteenth	neunzehnte
20	twenty	zwanzig	20th	twentieth	zwanzigste
21	twenty-one	einundzwanzig	21st	twenty-first	einundzwanzigste
22	twenty-two	zweiundzwanzig	22nd	twenty-second	zweiundzwanzigste
23	twenty-three	dreiundzwanzig	23rd	twenty-third	dreiundzwanzigste
24	twenty-four	vierundzwanzig	24th	twenty-fourth	vierundzwanzigste
25	twenty-five	fünfundzwanzig	25th	twenty-fifth	fünfundzwanzigste
30	thirty	dreißig	30th	thirtieth	dreißigste
40	forty	vierzig	40th	fortieth	vierzigste
50	fifty	fünfzig	50th	fiftieth	fünfzigste
60	sixty	sechzig	60th	sixtieth	sechzigste
70	seventy	siebzig	70th	seventieth	siebzigste
80	eighty	achtzig	80th	eightieth	achtzigste
90	ninety	neunzig	90th	ninetieth	neunzigste
100	hundred	(ein)hundert	100th	one hundredth	(ein)hundertste
101	one hundred and one	(ein)hundert(und)eins	101st	one hundred and first	(ein)hundert-(und)erste
156	one hundred and fifty-six	(ein)hundert-sechsundfünfzig	156th	one hundred and fifty-sixth	(ein)hundertsechs-undfünfzigste
200	two hundred	zweihundert	200th	two hundredth	zweihundertste
300	three hundred	dreihundert	300th	three hundredth	dreihundertste
400	four hundred	vierhundert	400th	four hundredth	vierhundertste
1 000	one thousand	(ein)tausend	1 000th	one thousandth	(ein)tausendste

| Cardinal | English | German | Ordinal | English | German |
Kardinalzahlen	Englisch	Deutsch	Ordinalzahlen	Englisch	Deutsch
1 001	one thousand and one	(ein)tausend(und)eins	1 001st	one thousand and first	(ein)tausend (und)erste
1 247	one thousand, two hundred and forty-seven	eintausend zweihundert(und)- siebenundvierzig	1 247th	one thousand, two hundred and forty- seventh	(ein)tausendzwei- hundert(und)- siebenundvierzigste
2 000	two thousand	zweitausend	2 000th	two thousandth	zweitausendste
3 000	three thousand	dreitausend	3 000th	three thousandth	dreitausendste
10 000	ten thousand	zehntausend	10 000th	ten thousandth	zehntausendste
20 000	twenty thousand	zwanzigtausend	20 000th	twenty thousandth	zwanzigtausendste
100 000	one hundred thousand	(ein)hunderttausend	100 000th	one hundred thousandth	(ein)-hundert- tausendste
200 000	two hundred thousand	zweihunderttausend	200 000th	two hundred thousandth	zweihundert- tausendste
1 000 000	one million	eine Million	1 000 000th	one millionth	(ein)millionste
10 000 000	ten million(s)	zehn Millionen			
100 000 000	one hundred million(s)	(ein)hundert Millionen			
1 000 000 000	one thousand million(s) (*BrE*) (one billion *AmE*)	eine Milliarde			
1 000 000 000 000	one billion (*BrE*) (one trillion *AmE*)	eine Billion